THE INTERNATIONAL
AUTHORS AND WRITERS WHO'S WHO
1976

THE INTERNATIONAL AUTHORS AND WRITERS WHO'S WHO

EDITORIAL DIRECTOR:
ERNEST KAY

Consultant Editor:
Peter Townend

Editorial Manager:
Judy Boothroyd

Head of Research:
Bernadette Lalonde

All communications to: IAWWW, International Biographical Centre,
Cambridge CB2 3QP, England

THE
INTERNATIONAL
AUTHORS AND WRITERS
WHO'S WHO

SEVENTH EDITION
1976

Editor
ERNEST KAY

MELROSE PRESS
Cambridge England

First published 1934
Second Edition 1935
Third Edition 1948
Fourth Edition 1960
Fifth Edition 1963
Sixth Edition 1972
Reprinted 1972
Seventh Edition 1976

I-SBN 0 900332 34 4

Typesetting by Herts Typesetting Services Ltd, Hertford.
Printed by The Camelot Press Ltd, Southampton
and bound by The Dorstel Press Ltd, Harlow, England

CONTENTS

FORWORD BY THE EDITORIAL DIRECTOR

Nearly five years ago, Melrose Press Ltd., of Cambridge, England, began to research into the possibilities of producing a new international biographical reference book for authors. We made two false starts — *County Authors Today* of which nine volumes were actually published, covering the whole of Scotland, the whole of Wales, and fifteen English Counties as they were at that time; and *American Authors Today* which it was hoped would be published in fifty volumes, one for each State. *County Authors Today* had to be discontinued because of economics and the fact that some counties were reconstructed under the new Local Government Act; and *American Authors Today* never saw the light of day as it proved to be a far too ambitious project. We next sought to acquire existing books dealing with authors but we were unsuccessful so we decided in 1973 to launch an entirely new title, *The World Who's Who of Authors.*

Beginning in February 1974, authors throughout the world began to receive questionnaires from us for the new *World Who's Who of Authors,* incorporating, as we stated, *County Authors Today* and *American Authors Today.* Many authors' organizations, particularly in the United States, co-operated closely and supplied us with the names of their members. Authors' agents and book publishers of many nations were also helpful.

In the middle of the mailing of questionnaires we were successful in acquiring *The Authors and Writers Who's Who* which had been published under the imprint of Burke's Peerage Ltd. since 1934. We were able to overprint the remaining questionnaires stating that *The World Who's Who of Authors* would also incorporate *The Authors and Writers Who's Who.* The result of this somewhat complicated series of events is this present volume which is published as *The International Authors and Writers Who's Who* and will continue to be so titled for future editions.

This issue contains some ten thousand biographical entries. All commercial advertising has been omitted, in accordance with the long-standing policy of Melrose Press, and the typesetting, printing and production have all been greatly improved. This book has taken twenty months to produce.

Recording the activities of authors has been a most congenial task for me. As the author of five hard-bound books myself and the editor of another thirty, it has been pleasant to read through so many questionnaires from fellow-authors. A considerable number of authors of the one-off book, pamphleteers and highly technical or specialised writers have been omitted. Every included author has received a typescript of his or her entry for correction before publication in the interests of accuracy. Should there be any errors, even after the most meticulous checking, my apologies in advance.

It cannot be too strongly emphasized that there is no charge or fee of any kind for biographical inclusion nor is there any obligation to purchase.

International Biographical Centre,
Cambridge CB2 3QP,
England.
July, 1975

TABLE OF ABBREVIATIONS

A.A.—Associate of Arts
AAAS—American Association for the Advancement of Science
AAUP—American Association of University Professors
AAUW—American Association of University Women
A.B.—Bachelor of Arts
ABC—American Broadcasting Corporation
Acad.—Academy, Academic
Acct.—Accountant
Acctcy.—Accountancy
Acctng.—Accounting
A.C.P.—American College of Physicians
A.C.S.—American College of Surgeons
A.C.T.—Australian Capital Territory
Adj.—Adjunct
Admin.—Administration
Admnstr.—Administrator
Admnstv.—Administrative
Adv.—Advance, Advanced
Advsr.—Advisor
Advsry.—Advisory
Advt.—Advertisement, Advertising
AFB—Air Force Base
A.F.D.—Doctor of Fine Arts
Agcy.—Agency
Agric.—Agriculture
Agricl.—Agricultural
Agt.—Agent
A.I.A.—American Institute of Architects
A.I.M.—American Institute of Management
Ala.—Alabama
ALA—American Library Association
Alta.—Alberta
Am.—American, America
A.M.—Master of Arts
AMA—American Medical Association
Amb.—Ambassador
Appt.—Appointment
Apr.—April
Apt.—Apartment
Arch.—Architecture
Archt.—Architect
Archtl.—Architectural
Ariz.—Arizona
Ark.—Arkansas
Arts.D.—Doctor of Arts
ASCAP—American Society of Composers, Authors & Publishers
Assn.—Association
Assoc.—Associate, Associated
Asst.—Assistant
Astron.—Astronomy
Attng.—Attending
Atty.—Attorney
Aug.—August
AUS—Army of the United States
Aust.—Australia, Australian
Auth.—Authority
Aux.—Auxiliary
Ave.—Avenue

b.—born
B.A.—Bachelor of Arts
Bach.—Bachelor
B.Agric.—Bachelor of Agriculture
Balt.—Baltimore
Bapt.—Baptist
B.Arch.—Bachelor of Architecture

B.A.S.—Bachelor of Agricultural Science
B.B.A.—Bachelor of Business Administration
BBC—British Broadcasting Corporation
B.C.—British Columbia
B.C.E.—Bachelor of Civil Engineering
B.Chir.—Bachelor of Surgery
B.C.L.—Bachelor of Civil Law
B.C.S.—Bachelor of Commercial Science
Bd.—Board
B.D.—Bachelor of Divinity
B.E.—Bachelor of Education
Beds.—Bedfordshire
B.E.E.—Bachelor of Electrical Engineering
Berks.—Berkshire
B.F.A.—Bachelor of Fine Arts
Bibliog.—Bibliography
Biog.—Biography, Biographical
B.J.—Bachelor of Journalism
Bklyn.—Brooklyn
B.L.—Bachelor of Letters
Bldg.—Building
B.L.S.—Bachelor of Library Science
Blvd.—Boulevard
B.Mus.—Bachelor of Music
B.Mus.Ed.—Bachelor of Music Education
Bot.—Botany
Botan.—Botanical, Botanist
Br.—Branch
Brig. Gen.—Brigadier General
Brit.—Britain, British
B.S.—Bachelor of Science
B.S.A.—Bachelor of Agricultural Science
B.Sc.—Bachelor of Science
B.S.T.—Bachelor of Sacred Theology
B.Th.—Bachelor of Theology
Bucks.—Buckinghamshire
Bur.—Bureau
Bus.—Business

Calif.—California
Cambs.—Cambridgeshire
Can.—Canada, Canadian
Cand.—Candidate
Cantab.—Cantabrigian (Cambridge University degrees)
Capt.—Captain
Cath.—Catholic
C.B.—Companion of the Bath
CBC—Canadian Broadcasting Corporation
C.B.E.—Commander, Order of the British Empire
CBS—Colombia Broadcasting System
CCNY—City College of New York
Cert.—Certificate, Certified
Ch.—Church
Chap.—Chaplain
Chapt.—Chapter
Ch.D.—Doctor of Chemistry
Chem.—Chemist, Chemistry, Chemical
Chgo.—Chicago
Chmbr. of Comm.—Chamber of Commerce
Chmn.—Chairman
CIA—Central Intelligence Agency
Cinn.—Cincinnati
Civ.—Civil, Civilian
Clin.—Clinic, Clinical
C.M.—Master in Surgery
Cmdng.—Commanding
Cmdr.—Commander
Cmdt.—Commandant

Cnslr.—Counsellor
Co.—County, Company
C.O.—Commanding Officer
C. of E.—Church of England
Col.—Colonel
Coll.—College
Collect.—Collection
Colo.—Colorado
Comm.—Committee
Commn.—Commission
Commng.—Commissioning
Commnr.—Commissioner
Comp.—Comparative
Conf.—Conference
Confedn.—Confederation
Congl.—Congregational
Conn.—Connecticut
Cons.—Consultant, Consulting
Conserv.—Conservative, Conservation
Const.—Constitution
Constl.—Constitutional
Constrn.—Construction
Contbn.—Contribution
Contbng.—Contributing
Contbr.—Contributor
Conven.—Convention
Coop.—Cooperative, Cooperation
Coord.—Coordinator, Coordinating
Corp.—Corporation
Corres.—Correspondent, Corresponding
Coun.—Council
C.P.A.—Certified Public Accountant
Cres.—Crescent
Ct.—Court
Ctr.—Centre, Center
Ctrl.—Central
CUNY—City University of New York
Curric.—Curriculum
C'wlth.—Commonwealth
Czech.—Czechoslovakia

d.—Died
D.Agric.—Doctor of Agriculture
DAR—Daughters of the American
  Revolution
D.B.E.—Dame Commander, Order of the
  British Empire
D.C.—District of Columbia
D.C.L.—Doctor of Civil Law
D.C.M.—Distinguished Conduct Medal
D.C.S.—Doctor of Commercial Science
D.D.—Doctor of Divinity
D.D.S.—Doctor of Dental Surgery
Dec.—December
dec.—Deceased
Def.—Defence, Defense
Del.—Delaware
Deleg.—Delegate
Dem.—Democratic, Democrat
D.Eng.—Doctor of Engineering
Dept.—Department
Derbys.—Derbyshire
Dev.—Development
D.F.C.—Distinguished Flying Cross
D.F.M.—Distinguished Flying Medal
D.H.L.—Doctor of Humane Letters
Dip.—Diploma
Dipl.—Diplomat(e)
Dir.—Director
Dist.—District
Distbn.—Distribution
Distbr.—Distributor

Disting.—Distinguished
Div.—Division
div.—Divorced
D.Lit.—Doctor of Letters
D.Litt.—Doctor of Literature
D.M.D.—Doctor of Dental Medicine
D.M.S.—Doctor of Medical Science
D.Mus.—Doctor of Music
Doct.—Doctorate, Doctoral
D.Ph.—Doctor of Philosophy
Dpty.—Deputy
Dr.—Doctor, Drive
Dr.P.H.—Doctor of Public Health, Doctor of
  Public Hygiene
D.Sc.—Doctor of Science
D.S.C.—Distinguished Service Cross
D.S.M.—Distinguished Service Medal
D.S.O.—Distinguished Service Order
D.S.T.—Doctor of Sacred Theology
D.Th.—Doctor of Theology
D.V.M.—Doctor of Veterinary Medicine
D.V.S.—Doctor of Veterinary Science

E.—East
Econ(s).—Economic(s)
Ed.—Editor, Editorial
ed.—Edition
E.D.—Doctor of Engineering
Ed.B.—Bachelor of Education
Ed.D.—Doctor of Education
Ed.M.—Master of Education
Educ.—Education
Educl.—Educational
EEC—European Economic Community
Elec.—Electric, Electrical
Electn.—Electrician
Elem.—Elementary
Ency.—Encyclopedia
Engl.—English
Engr.—Engineer
Engrng.—Engineering
ENT—Ear, Nose & Throat
Episc.—Episcopal, Episcopalian
esp.—Especially
Estab.—Established, Establishment
E. Sussex—East Sussex
etc.—Et cetera
Exam.—Examination
Exec.—Executive
Exhib.—Exhibit, Exhibition
Exhibnr.—Exhibitioner
Exped.—Expedition
Expmtl.—Experimental
Ext.—Extension

Fac.—Faculty
FAO—Food and Agriculture Organisation
F.C.A.—Fellow, Institute of Chartered
  Accountants
F.C.I.I.—Fellow, Chartered Insurance
  Institute
F.C.I.S.—Fellow, Chartered Institute of
  Secretaries
Feb.—February
Fed.—Federal
Fedn.—Federation
F.G.S.—Fellow, Geological Society
F.I.B.—Fellow, Institute of Bankers
Fin.—Finance, Financial
Fla.—Florida
Fndng.—Founding
Fndn.—Foundation

Fndr.—Founder
For.—Foreign
F.P.S.—Fellow, Pharmaceutical Society
F.R.A.M.—Fellow, Royal Academy of Music
F.R.C.P.—Fellow, Royal College of
   Physicians
F.R.C.S.—Fellow, Royal College of Surgeons
F.R.G.S.—Fellow, Royal Geographical
   Society
F.R.I.B.A.—Fellow, Royal Institute of
   British Architects
F.R.I.C.—Fellow, Royal Institute of
   Chemistry
F.R.I.C.S.—Fellow, Royal Institute of
   Chartered Surveyors
F.R.S.—Fellow, Royal Society
F.R.S.A.—Fellow, Royal Society of Arts
F.R.S.L.—Fellow, Royal Society of
   Literature
F.S.A.—Fellow, Society of Antiquaries,
   Society of Arts
F.S.E.—Fellow, Society of Engineers
Ft.—Fort
F.Z.S.—Fellow, Zoological Society

Ga.—Georgia
Gall.—Gallery
GB—Great Britain
G.B.E.—Knight (or Dame), Grand Cross
   Order of the British Empire
G.C.—George Cross
G.C.B.—Knight, Grand Cross of the Bath
Gdns.—Gardens
Gen.—General
Geog.—Geography, Geographer
Geogl.—Geographical
Geo. Wash. Univ.—George Washington
   University
Glos.—Gloucestershire
GM.—George Medal
Gov.—Governor
Govng.—Governing
Govt.—Government
Govtl.—Governmental
Grad.—Graduate
Grp.—Group
Gt.—Great
Gtr.—Greater
Gtr. Manc.—Greater Manchester

Hants.—Hampshire
Hd.—Head
Hereford & Worcs.—Hereford &
   Worcester
Herts.—Hertfordshire
HEW—Department of Health, Education
   and Welfare
H.H.D.—Doctor of Humanities
Hist.—History
Histl.—Historical
Histn.—Historian
Hlth.—Health
Hon.—Honorary, Honour
Ho. of Dels.—House of Delegates
Ho. of Reps.—House of Representatives
Hort.—Horticulture, Horticultural
Hosp.—Hospital
HQ—Headquarters
HS—High School
Hwy.—Highway

IBA—Independent Broadcasting Authority
ibid.—in the same place
I.B.M.—International Business Machines
   Corporation
i/c—in charge
ICA—Institute of Contemporary Arts
IEEE—Institute of Electrical and
   Electronics Engineers
Ill.—Illinois
ILO—International Labour Organisation
Inc.—Incorporated
Incl.—Include
Inclng.—Including
Ind.—Indiana, Industry
Indep.—Independent
Indl.—Industrial
Indpls.—Indianapolis
Info.—Information
Ins.—Insurance
Insp.—Inspector, Inspection
Inst.—Institute
Instn.—Institution
Instr.—Instructor
Instrn.—Instruction
Int.—International

Jan.—January
J.B.—Jurum Baccalaureus
J.D.—Doctor of Jurisprudence
J.P.—Justice of the Peace
Jr.—Junior
Jrnl.—Journal
Jrnlsm.—Journalism
Jrnlst.—Journalist
J.S.D.—Doctor of Juristic Science
Jt.—Joint

Kan.—Kansas
K.B.E.—Knight Commander, Order of the
   British Empire
K.C.B.—Knight Commander of the Bath
Kt.—Knight
Ky.—Kentucky

La.—Louisiana
Lab.—Laboratory
Lancs.—Lancashire
Lang.—Language
Ldr.—Leader
Lectr.—Lecturer
Legis.—Legislation, Legislative
Leics.—Leicestershire
L.H.D.—Doctor of Humane Letters
L.I.—Long Island
Lib.—Library
Libn.—Librarian
Lic.—License, Licentiate
Lincs.—Lincolnshire
Lit.—Literature, Literary
Litt.B.—Bachelor of Letters
Litt.D.—Doctor of Letters
LL.B.—Bachelor of Laws
LL.D.—Doctor of Laws
LL.M.—Master of Laws
Lt.—Lieutenant
Ltd.—Limited
Luth.—Lutheran

m.—Married
M.A.—Master of Arts
Mag.—Magazine
M.Agric.—Master of Agriculture

Maj.—Major
Man.—Manitoba
Mar.—March
M.Arch.—Master of Architecture
Mass.—Massachusetts
M.A.T.—Master of Arts in Teaching
Math.—Mathematical
Mathn.—Mathmatician
Maths.—Mathematics
M.B.—Bachelor of Medicine
M.B.A.—Master of Business Administration
M.B.E.—Member, Order of the British
 Empire
Mbr.—Member
Mbrship.—Membership
M.C.E.—Master of Civil Engineering
M.C.S.—Master of Commercial Science
Md.—Maryland
M.D.—Doctor of Medicine
Mech.—Mechanics, Mechanical
Med.—Medicine, Medical
M.Ed.—Master of Education
M.E.E.—Master of Electrical Engineering
Mem.—Memorial
Metall.—Metallurgy, Metallurgical
Meth.—Methodist
Metrop.—Metropolitan
M.F.A.—Master of Fine Arts
Mfg.—Manufacturing
Mfr.—Manufacturer
Mgmt.—Management
Mgr.—Manager
Mich.—Michigan
Mid Glam.—Mid Glamorgan
Mil.—Military
Min.—Minister, Ministry
Minn.—Minnesota
Misc.—Miscellaneous
Miss.—Mississippi
MIT—Massachusetts Institute of Technology
Mkt.—Market
Mktng.—Marketing
M.L.—Master of Laws
MLA—Modern Language Association
M.Lit.—Master of Literature
M.Litt.—Master of Letters
M.L.S.—Master of Library Science
M.M.—Military Medal
M.M.E.—Master of Mechanical Engineering
M.Mus.—Master of Music
Mng.—Managing
Mo.—Missouri
Mod.—Modern
Mont.—Montana
MP—Member of Parliament
Mpls.—Minneapolis
M.S.—Manuscript, Master of Science
M.Sc.—Master of Science
MSS—Manuscripts
M.S.T.—Master of Sacred Theology
Mt.—Mount
Mtn.—Mountain
Mus.—Museum
Mus.B.—Bachelor of Music
Mus.D.—Doctor of Music
Mus.M.—Master of Music

N.—North
NAACP—National Association for the
 Advancement of Colored People
Nat.—National

NATO—North Atlantic Treaty
 Organisation
N.B.—New Brunswick
NBC—National Broadcasting Corporation
N.C.—North Carolina
N.D.—North Dakota
NEA—National Education Association
Neb.—Nebraska
Nev.—Nevada
Nfld.—Newfoundland
N.H.—New Hampshire
N.J.—New Jersey
N.M.—New Mexico
Northants.—Northamptonshire
Notts.—Nottinghamshire
Nov.—November
N.S.—Nova Scotia
NSC—National Security Council
NSF—National Science Foundation
N.S.W.—New South Wales
N.T.—Northern Territory
Num.—Numerous
N.Y.—New York
NYC—New York City
N. Yorks.—North Yorkshire
N.Y. Univ.—New York University
NZ—New Zealand

OBE—Officer, Order of the British Empire
Observ.—Observatory
Obst.—Obstetrics
Obstrn.—Obstetrician
Oct.—October
OECD—Organisation of European
 Cooperation and Development
OEEC—Organisation of European
 Economic Cooperation
Off.—Officer, Office
Okla.—Oklahoma
O.M.—Order of Merit
Ont.—Ontario
Op.—Operation
Orch.—Orchestra
Orchl.—Orchestral
Ore.—Oregon
Org.—Organisation
Oxon.—Oxfordshire

Pa.—Pennsylvania
Parl.—Parliament
Parly.—Parliamentary
P.C.—Privy Councillor
P.E.I.—Prince Edward Island
PEN—Poets, Playwrights, Editors, Essayists
 and Novelists
Perf.—Performer
Pharm.—Pharmacy, Pharmaceutical
Pharm.D.—Doctor of Pharmacy
Pharm.M.—Master of Pharmacy
Ph.B.—Bachelor of Philosophy
Ph.D.—Doctor of Philosophy
Phil.—Philharmonic
Phila.—Philadelphia
Philos.—Philosophy, Philosopher
Philosl.—Philosophical
Phys.—Physical, Physics
Physn.—Physician
Pitts.—Pittsburgh
Pk.—Park
Pkg.—Packaging
Pkwy.—Parkway
Pl.—Place

Pol.—Politics, Political
Postgrad.—Postgraduate
P.Q.—Quebec Province
PR—Public Relations
Prac.—Practice
Pres.—President
Presby.—Presbyterian
Prin.—Principal
Prod.—Producer, Production
Prof.—Professor
Profl.—Professional
Profn.—Profession
Prog.—Program, Programme
Psych.—Psychiatrist, Psychiatric, Psychiatry
PTA—Parent-Teacher Association
Ptnr.—Partner
Pt.-time—Part-time
Pub.—Public
Publng.—Publishing
Publr.—Publisher
Publs.—Publications
Pvte.—Private

Q.C.—Queen's Counsel
Qld.—Queensland
QM—Quartermaster
QMG—Quartermaster General

RAAF—Royal Australian Air Force
RAF—Royal Air Force
RC—Roman Catholic
RCAF—Royal Canadian Air Force
RCN—Royal Canadian Navy
Rd.—Road
Rdr.—Reader
Recip.—Recipient
Ref.—Reference
Reg.—Region, Regional
Regt.—Regiment
Rehab.—Rehabilitation
Relig.—Religion, Religious
Rels.—Relations
Rep.—Representative
Repub.—Republic, Republican
Res.—Resident, Residence
Ret'd.—Retired
Rev.—Reverend
R.I.—Rhode Island
RN—Royal Navy
Rsch.—Research
Rte.—Route
Rt. Hon.—Right Honourable
Rt. Rev.—Right Reverend

S.—South
s.—Son
S.A.—Société Anonyme, South Australia
San Fran.—San Francisco
SAR—Sons of the American Revolution
Sask.—Saskatchewan
S.B.—Bachelor of Science
S.C.—South Carolina
Sc.B.—Bachelor of Science
S.C.D.—Doctor of Commercial Science
Schl.—School
Schlr.—Scholar
Schlrship.—Scholarship
Sci.—Science, Scientific, Scientist
S.D.—South Dakota
SEATO—Southeast Asia Treaty Organisation
Sec.—Secretary

Second.—Secondary
Sect.—Section
Sem.—Seminary
Sen.—Senator
Sept.—September
Serv.—Service
Sev.—Several
S.Glam.—South Glamorgan
Sgt.—Sergeant
SHAEF—Supreme Headquarters, Allied Expeditionary Forces
SHAPE—Supreme Headquarters, Allied Powers in Europe
S.J.D.—Doctor of Juristic Science
S.M.—Master of Science
Soc.—Society
Sr.—Senior
St.—Street
Staffs.—Staffordshire
Statn.—Statistician
Stats.—Statistics
S.T.B.—Bachelor of Sacred Theology
S.T.D.—Doctor of Sacred Theology
S.T.M.—Master of Sacred Theology
Stn.—Station
Sub.—Subsidiary
SUNY—State University of New York
Supt.—Superintendent
Suptng.—Superintending
Supvsr.—Supervisor
Surg.—Surgeon, Surgical, Surgery
Switz.—Switzerland
Symph.—Symphony
S. Yorks.—South Yorkshire

Tas.—Tasmania
Tchr.—Teacher
Tchng.—Teaching
T.D.—Teachers Training Diploma
Tech.—Technical
Techn.—Technician
Tenn.—Tennessee
Tex.—Texas
Th.D.—Doctor of Theology
Th.M.—Master of Theology
T.P.N.G.—Territory of Papua & New Guinea
Transl.—Translation, Translator
Transl'd.—Translated
Transp.—Transport, Transportation
Treas.—Treasurer
Trng.—Training
T.T.D.—Teachers Training Diploma
TV—Television
TVA—Tennessee Valley Authority
Ty.—Territory

UAR—United Arab Republic
UCLA—University of California at Los Angeles
UK—United Kingdom
UN—United Nations
Undergrad.—Undergraduate
UNESCO—United Nations Educational, Scientific and Cultural Organisation
UNICEF—United Nations International Children's Emergency Fund
Univ.—University
USA—United States of America
USAAF—United States Army Air Force
USAF—United States Air Force

USDA—United States Department of
   Agriculture
USN—United States Navy
USNR—United States Naval Reserve
USSR—Union of Soviet Socialist Republics

Va.—Virginia
VA—Veterans' Administration
Var.—Various
Vet.—Veterinary
VFW—Veterans of Foreign Wars
Vic.—Victoria
Vis.—Visiting, Visitor
Voc.—Vocational
Vol.—Volunteer, Voluntary, Volume
VP—Vice President
Vt.—Vermont

W.—West
w.—with
W.A.—Western Australia
Warwicks.—Warwickshire

Wash.—Washington
Wash. DC—Washington D.C.
W. Glam.—West Glamorgan
WHO—World Health Organisation
Wilts.—Wiltshire
Wis.—Wisconsin
Wk.—Week
Wm. & Mary Coll.—William and Mary
   College
W. Midlands—West Midlands
W. Sussex—West Sussex
W.Va.—West Virginia
WWI—World War I
WWII—World War II
Wyo.—Wyoming
W. Yorks.—West Yorkshire

YMCA—Young Men's Christian Association
Yr.—Year
YWCA—Young Women's Christian
   Association

INTERNATIONAL AUTHORS AND WRITERS WHO'S WHO

AALTONEN, (Ilta) Annikki (Tyyne), pen name MARUNA, Annikki, b. 21 May 1911, Pori, Finland. Author. Educ: Univ. studies, 4 yrs. Publs: A Senseless Caprise (novel), 1946; A Storm (novel), 1948; Human Beings in a Critical Period (short stories), 1951; The Hands (play), 1960; The Death of Klaus Fleming (play), 1963; Restless Young People & a Testament (play), 1970. Mbrships: Union of Finnish Authors; Union of Finnish Dramatists. Recip., 3rd prize, histl. drama competition, 1963. Address: Ohjaajantie 3 A 3, 00400 Helsinki 40, Finland.

AARONOVITCH, Sam, b. 27 Dec. 1919, London, UK. Lecturer in Economics. Educ: D.Phil., Univ. of Oxford. Publs: Crisis in Kenya, 1947; Monopoly, 1955; The Ruling Class, 1961; Economics for Trade Unionists, 1964; Big Business, 1975. Address: 19 Bromwich Ave., London N6 6QH, UK.

ABBAN, Frank Adams, b. 13 June 1925, Sekondi, Ghana, W. Africa. Specialist Medical Practitioner; Author. Educ: Bradford Univ., UK; Vienna Univ., Austria. Publs: Obesity & Diabetes, 1963; Zur Frage die Sichelzellanaemie, 1968; Some Clinical Aspects of Sickle-Cell Disease in Africa, & Management with Special Reference to Ghana, 1972. Contbr. to: Vienna Med. Wkly. Address: St. Francis Research Clinic, P.O. Box 6041, Accra N., Ghana, W. Africa.

ABBAS, Khwaja Ahmad, b. 7 June 1914, Panipat, India. Journalist; Film Director; Author. Educ: B.A., LL.B., Aligarh Muslim Univ. Publs. incl: Outside India (travelogue), 1940; Inqilab (novel), 1955; Face to Face with Khruschchov (biog.), 1960; Return of the Red Rose (biog., Indira Gandhi), 1966; That Woman — Indira Gandhi's Years in Power, 1973; over 60 books in Engl., Urdu, Hindi, w. num. transls., other Indian & for. langs. Contbr. to: Asia Mag., N.Y., USA; Life & Letters Today, London, UK; Illustrated Wkly. of India; Blitz Newsmag., Bombay. Recip., var.' nat., state & profl. hons. Address: Philomena Lodge, Church Rd., Juhu, Bombay-400 054, India.

ABBASI, Najmuddin, pen name ABBASI, Najam, b. 18 Oct. 1927, Khanwahan, Sindh, Pakistan. Medical Doctor; Writer in the Sindhi Language. Educ: M.B.B.S. Publs: Toofan-ji-Tammana (short stories), 1968; Pathar-te-leeko (short stories), 1973; Garho Lalteen (drama). Contbr. to: Mahran; Nai Zindagi; Suhni; Koonj; Tahreek; Insan; Rooh-Rehan; Sojhro (all Sindhi mags.). Mbr., Bd. of Dirs., Sindhi Writers Coop. Soc. Ltd. Recip., Lit. Awards from Sindh Univ. & Pakistan Writers Guild, for Toofan-ji-Tammana, 1969. Address: Gadi Khato, Hyderabad, Sindh, Pakistan.

ABBOTT, May Laura, b. 1916, London, UK. Author; Journalist; Broadcaster; Crossword Compiler. Publs: Working with Animals, 1962, latest ed., 1967; Me & the Bee, 1965; Careers in Art & Design, 1969; Daily Telegraph 50 Years of Crosswords, forthcoming. Contbr. to: Daily Telegraph; Sunday Telegraph; BBC; etc. Mbrships: Nat. Union Jrnlsts.; London Press Club; Wig & Pen Club; Nat. Trust. Address: 48 Berwyn Rd., Richmond, Surrey, UK.

ABBOTT, R(obert) Tucker, b. 28 Sept. 1919, Watertown, Mass., USA. Malacologist; Editor; Writer. Educ: B.S., Harvard Coll., 1942; M.S., 1949, Ph.D., 1955, George Washington Univ., D.C. Publs: American Seashells, 1954 (second ed. 1974); Sea Shells of the World, 1962; Seashells of North America, 1968; The Shell (w. H. Stix), 1968; Kingdom of the Seashell, 1972; Shells in Colour, 1973; Ed., The Nautilus, 1959—; Indo-Pacific Mollusca, 1959—; Swainson's Exotic Conchology, 1971; Ed.-in-Chief, American Malacologists. Contbr. to: Quarterly Review Biology; Natural Hist. Mag., N.Y.; Sci. Digest; Sci.; Ency. Britannica; Ency. Americana; & 30 other jrnls. Mbrships. incl: Life, Fellow, AAAS; Am. Malacol. Union (Life mbr., Pres., 1959); Co-Fndr., Life mbr., Phila. Shell Club; Soc. Systematic Zool. (Sec., 1956-59); & num. other malacol.

socs. Hons: Cert. Award, Smithsonian Instn., 1953; Award of Excellence, Books, Comm. Arts Mag., 1967; Cert. Award, Delaware Valley Graphic Arts Exhib., 1968. Address: Delaware Museum of Natural History, P.O. Box 3937, Greenville, DE 19807, USA.

ABBOTT, Rowland Aubrey Samuel, b. 17 Nov. 1909, Oxford, UK. Electrical Engineer (Retired). Publs: The Fairlie Locomotive, 1970; Crane Locomotives, 1974. Contbr. to: Engr.; Engrng.; Locomotive; Country Life; Model Engr.; Model Railway News; Transactions of Caernarvonshire Histl. Soc.; Jrnl. of S. Elec. Bd. Mbrships: Newcomen Soc., Sci. Mus., London; Talyllyn Railway Preservation Soc. Address: 8 Springfield R., Old Botley, Oxford OX2 9HJ, UK.

ABDEL-RHAMAN, Aisha, pen name EL-SHATI, Bint. University Professor; Writer. Educ: Cairo Univ. Publs. incl: Rissalet el Ghorfam by Abul Ala'a, 1950; New Values in Arabic Literature, 1961; The Koran: Literary Interpretation, 1962; Ibn Seeda's Arabic Dictionary, 1962; Contemporary Arab Women Poets, 1963; 6 books on illustrious women of Islam; 2 novels; 4 books of short stories. Mbr., Higher Coun. of Arts & Letters. Hons incl: Acad. of Arabic Lang. Awards, for Textual Studies, 1950, & Short Story, 1954. Address: 13 Agam St., Heliopolis, Cairo, Egypt.

ABE, Kobo, b. 7 Mar. 1924, Tokyo, Japan. Novelist; Playwright. Educ: Grad., Tokyo Univ. Publs. incl: (in Japanese) Red Cocoon, 1949; The Wall, 1951; Hunger Union, 1954; Here is a Ghost, 1959; The Woman in the Dunes, 1962; The Face of Another, 1964; The Friends, 1967; The Ruined Map, 1969; Premeditated Act of Uncertain Consequences, 1971; Love's Spectacles are Colored Glass, 1973; The Box Man, 1973; Green Stocking, 1974; Wee, 1975; (in English) Inter Ice Age 4, 1970. Contbr. to: Shincho; Gunzo; Sekai; etc. Hons: Akutagawa Prize, 1951; Kishida Drama Prize, 1958; Yomiuri Lit. Prize, 1962; Tanizaki Prize, 1967; Prize, Art Festival of Japan, 1967. Address: 1-22-10 Wakaba-cho, Chofu City, Tokyo, Japan.

ABERCROMBIE, Nigel James, b. 5 Aug. 1908, Satara, India. Writer. Educ: B.A., 1929, D.Phil., 1933, M.A., 1934, Oriel Coll., Oxford. Publs: Origins of Jansenism, 1936; St. Augustine & French Classical Thought, 1938; Life & Work of Edmund Bishop, 1959; The Arts in the South-East, 1974. Contbr. to: Dublin Review (Ed., 1953-55); French Studies; Month. Mbrships: Authors' Soc.; V.P., S.-E. Arts Assn., 1974-; Sec.-Gen., Arts Coun. of GB, 1963-68, Chief Regional Advsr., 1968-73. Hons: Paget Toynbee Prize, Oxford Univ., 1934. Address: 32 Springett Avenue, Ringmer, Lewes, Sussex BN8 5HE, UK.

ABETTI, Giorgio, b. 5 Oct. 1882, Padua, Italy. Astronomer; University Professor. Educ: Ph.D., Univ. of Padua; Univ. of Rome. Publs: Scienzia d'Oggi, 1945; Amici di Galileo, 1945; Storia dell'Astronomia, 1949, 1963, Engl. ed. 1954, Spanish ed. 1956; Il Sole, 1952, Engl. ed. 1955; Le Nebulose e gli Universi- Isole, 1959; L'Unita del Cosmo, 1964, Spanish ed. 1965. Contbr. to: Memorie della Spedizione F. De Filippi, Osservazioni e Memorie dell' Osservatorio di Arcetri, Firenze; La Stampa. Mbrships: Int. Astron. Union (former VP); Italian Astron. Soc. (Pres.). Hons. incl: Silver Medal, Royal Italian Geogl. Soc., 1917; Gold Medals, Min. Pub. Instruction, 1957, Italian Astron. Soc., 1964, City of Florence, 1972. Address: Inst. of Optics, Largo Enrico Fermi, 7 — Florence, Italy.

ABLEMAN, Paul, b. 13 June 1927, Leeds, Yorks., UK. Writer. Educ: King's Coll., London. Publs: (novels) I Hear Voices, 1958; As Near As I Can Get, 1962; Vac, 1968; The Twilight of the Vilp, 1969; (plays) Green Julia, 1966; Tests, 1966; Blue Comedy: Madly in Love, Hawk's Night, 1968; Bits: Some Prose Poems, 1969; The Mouth & Oral Sex, 1969. Contbr. to: Transatlantic Review; Men Only. Address: Flat 37, Duncan House, Fellows Rd., London NW3, UK.

ABODY, Béla, b. 14 June 1931, Budapest, Hungary. Author; Critic; Director, Vidám Szinpad Theatre, Budapest. Educ: Eötvös Loránd Univ., Budapest. Publs: Indulatos utazás (essays), 1957; Párbeszéd a szenttel (short stories), 1960; Mindent bele! (short stories & plays), 1970; Nyomozás (collected plays & autobiog.), 1970; Félidö (collected essays), 1973; Gyere velem operába (collected essays & music criticism), 1973. Contbr. to: Élet és Irodalom; Kritika; Muzsika; etc. Mbrships. incl: PEN; Assn. Hungarian Writers. Recip., József Attila Prize, 1973. Address: Kökörcsin u. 14, 1113 Budapest, Hungary.

ABRAHAM, Claude Kurt, b. 13 Dec. 1931, Lorsch, Germany. Professor of French. Educ: A.B., Univ. of Cinn., 1953; M.A., ibid, 1956; Ph.D., Ind. Univ., 1959. Publs. incl: Molière: Le Bourgeois gentilhomme (ed.), 1966; Enfin Malherbe, 1971; Pierre Corneille, 1972; Theatre complet de Tristan l'Hermite (critical ed., w. others), 1974. Contbr. to: French Review; Studies in Philol.; Baroque; etc. Mbrships. incl: MLA (Chmn., French 3, 1974); SAMLA (Chmn., French 1, 1969). Recip., SAMLA Studies Award, 1970. Address: Dept. of Romance Languages, University of Florida, Gainesville, FL 32611, USA.

ABRAHAM, Edward Penley, b. 10 June 1913, Southampton, UK. Professor of Chemical Pathology. Educ: Queen's Coll., Oxford. Publs: Biochemistry of some Peptide & Steroid Antibiotics, 1957, Biosynthesis & Enzymic Hydrolysis of Penicillins & Cephalosporns, 1974. Contrb. of articles to var. sci. jrnls. Mbrships: FRS; The Athenaeum. Hons: C.B.E., 1973; Royal Medallist, Royal Soc., 1973. Address: Badgers Wood, Bedwell Heath, Boars Hill, Oxford, UK.

ABRAHAMI, Izzy, b. 18 Apr. 1930, Sofia, Bulgaria. Writer. Publs: The Game, 1973, Argentinian, Dutch, French, Italian, Israeli & German eds., 1974. Contbr. to: Algemeen Handelsblad, Netherlands; Aftenposten, Norway; Der Tagesspiegel, Berlin, Germany; Helsingin Sanomat, Finland. Mbr., Authors' Guild of Am. Address: 301 E. 22nd St., Apt. 9E, N.Y., NY 10010, USA.

ABRAHAMS, Peter, b. 1919, Johannesburg, S. Africa. Journalist; Broadcaster. Publs: Mineboy; Song of the City; Dark Testament; Path of Thunder; Wild Conquest, 1949; Tell Freedom, 1950; Return to Goli, 1951; Wreath for Udomo, 1953; A Night of Their Own, 1965; This Island Now, 1967; Jamaican Island Mosaic, 1956. Contbr. to: Jamaican Radio; ed., West Indian Economist. Mbrships: PEN; Authors' League; Jamaican Press. Assn. Address: Red Hills, P.O., St. Andrews, Jamaica, West Indies.

ABRAHAMS, Roger D., b. 12 June 1933, Phila., Pa., USA. Professor. Educ: B.A., Swarthmore Coll., 1955; M.A., Columbia Univ., 1959; Ph.D., Univ. of Pa., 1961. Publs. incl: Deep Down in the Jungle — Negro Narrative Folklore from the Streets of Philadelphia, 1964, revised ed., 1970; Anglo-American Folksong Style (w. Geo. Foss, Jr.), 1968; Jump Rope Rhymes — A Dictionary, 1969; Positively Black, 1970; A Singer & Her Songs, 1970; Deep the Water, Shallow the Shore, in press; Counting Out Rhymes — A Dictionary (w. Lois Rankin), in press. Contbr. of chapts. to books & articles to jrnls. Mbr. & Fellow, Am. Folklore Soc. Address: Rt. 10, Box 123, Austin, TX, USA.

ABRAM, Theresa Williams, b. Magnolia, Ark., USA. Teacher. Educ: B.S., Langston Univ.; Workshops, Union Theol. Sem., NYC. Publs: Abram's Treasures, 1970; Rhythm & Animals, 1972; Freedom Herod What Price to Pay, 1974. Contbr. to newspapers & US, for. poetry anthols. Hons: State Prize, Best Humorous Poem, 1968; State Prize, Best Poem about Poet Laureate, 1969. Address: 2333 NE 22, Okla. City, OK 73111, USA.

ABRAMOW, Jaroslaw, b. 17 May 1933, Warsaw, Poland. Playwright. Educ: Polish Philol. studies, Warsaw Univ. Publs: (plays) Remanent, 1962; Aniol na Dworcu, 1965; Derby w Pazacu, 1966; Ucieczka z Wielkich Bulwarow, 1969; Wyciag do Nieba, 1972; Klik-Klak, 1972; Darz Bor, 1974. Contbr. to: Dialog (Warsaw). Mbrships: Polish Writers' Union; PEN; Sec., Polish Dramatic Writers' Club; Presidium Mbr., Polish Sect., Int. Theatre Ctr. Hons: Stanislaw Pietak Lit. Award, Warsaw, 1965; Koscielskis' Award, Geneva, 1967. Address: Filtrowa 81, Apt. 21, Warsaw 02-032, Poland.

ABRAMS, Mark, b. 27 Apr. 1906, London, UK. Sociologist. Educ: B.Sc., Ph.D., Univ. of London; Eastman Fellowship, Brookings Instn., Wash. D.C., USA. Publs: The Condition of the British People, 1911-1946, 1946; Social Surveys & Social Action, 1951. Contbr. to: Ecounter; Fin. Times; Pol. Quarterly; sev. other jrnls. Mbrships. incl: Past Chmn., Brit. Market Rsch. Soc.; Past Pres., World Assn. for Pub. Opinion Rsch.; Vice-Chmn., Pol. & Econ. Planning. Address: 12 Pelham Sq., Brighton, Sussex, UK.

ABRAMS, Sybil Nash, b. 22 Feb. 1900, Gurdon, Ark., USA. Poet. Publs: Laurel Branches (co-author), 1969; We Are What We Think All the Day, 1970; Months of the Year, 1973. Contbr. to num. Ark. newspapers & profl. jrnls. Mbrships: Authors, Composers & Artists Soc. of Ark.; Poets Roundtable of Ark.; State, Nat. Fedn. of Poetry Socs.; DAR. Hons: Sybil Nash Abrams Award estab. 1969; Special Award, Nat. Poetry Day, from Ercil Francis Brown; Poet Laureate of Ark., 1970; Silver Jubilee Award, Nat. Poetry Day, 1972; Num. poetry prizes. Address: 2908 Lee Ave., Little Rock, AR 72205, USA.

ABRAMSON, Martin, b. 25 Jan. 1921, Brooklyn, N.Y., USA. Writer. Educ: B.A., City Coll. of N.Y.; Univ. of Calif. Publs: The Real Al Jolson, 1957; The Barney Ross Story, 1959; Hollywood Surgeon, 1965; The Padre of Guadalcanal Story, 1967; Forgotten Fortunes, 1973; The Trial of Chaplain Jensen, 1974. Contbr. to: Esquire; Playboy; Good Housekeeping; Reader's Digest; True; Cosmopolitan; Holiday; & sev. newspapers. Mbrships: Soc. of mag. Writers; Overseas Press Club. Recip., US Defense Dept. Citation as combat corres., WWII. Address: 827 Peninsula Blvd., Woodmere, N.Y. 11598, USA.

ABRECHT, Viktor Johan Ernst, pen name JEVAN, Viktor, b. 23 Sept. 1941, Lengnau, Switz. Danish Playwright. Plays incl: War Start; Fiol-teatret as Guestplay; Paracelsus (Copenhagen, Zurich, TV); Do it; The Theatre of Secret Service; Don Ranudo (Copenhagen); etc. Contbr. to: Ekstra Bladet; Notat; Politisk Revy; Information; radio & TV progs.; etc. Mbrships: Danish Drama Union; Danish Writer's Union; Feigenberg Agency. Address: Frederik VII'sgade 25, 2200 Copenhagen, Denmark.

ABSALOM, Roger Neil Lewis, b. 28 Oct. 1929, Bebington, Cheshire, UK. Head, Modern Languages Dept. Educ: B.A. (French & Russian); Fellow, Inst. of Linguistics (Italian). Publs: Passages for Translation from Italian, 1967; Mussolini & the Rise of Italian Fascism, 1969; France 1968: The May Events, 1970; Advanced Italian (w. Potestà), 1970. Mbrships. incl: Soc. for Italian Studies; Società di Linguistica Italiana. Address: 5 The Mill, Edale, Derbys., UK.

ABSE, Dannie, b. 22 Sept. 1923, Cardiff, Wales, UK. Poet. Publs: Ash on a Young Man's Sleeve, 1954; Tenants of the House, 1957; Poems, Golden Green, 1962; A Small Desperation, 1968; Selected Poems, 1970; Funland & Other Poems, 1973; A Poet in the Family, 1974. Contbr. to: New Statesman; Sunday Times; Encounter; BBC. Hons: Charles Henry Foyle Award, 1960; Jewish Chronicle Book of the Yr., 1970; Welsh Arts Coun. Lit. Prize, 1970. Address: 85, Hodford Rd., London NW11, UK.

ABSE, David Wilfred, b. 15 Mar. 1915, Cardiff, UK. Professor of Psychiatry. Educ: B.Sc., 1935, M.D., 1948, Univ. of Wales; M.B., B.Ch., 1938, Welsh Nat. Schl. Med.; Dip. Psychol. Med., London Univ., 1940. Publs: The Diagnosis of Hysteria, 1950; Marriage Counselling in Medical Practice, 1964; Hysteria & Related Mental Disorders, 1966; Speech & Reason: Language Disorder in Mental Disease, 1971; Marital & Sexual Counselling in Medical Practice, 2nd ed., 1974. Contbr. to num. med. publs. Mbrships. incl: F.R.S. Med.; Fellow Am. Psych. Assn.; Am. Med. Assn.; Int. Psychoanalytic Assn. Hons: Fellow, Brit. Psychol. Soc.; Fellow, Royal Coll. Psychs. Address: Dept. of Psych., Box 203, Univ. of Va. Schl. Med., Charlottesville, VA, USA.

ABU ZAYD, Abdu-r-Rahman, b. 1 Jan. 1938, Merwi, Sudan. University Lecturer. Educ: B.A., M.A., Islamic Studies. Publs: Al-Ghazali On Divine Predicates & Their Properties, 1970. Contbr. to: Jrnl. Asiatic & African Studies; Islamic Rsch. Mbrships. incl: Am. Oriental Soc.; Middle East Studies Assn. of N. Am.; Muslim League, Mecca. Recip., Awards from Rotary Int. Fndn. & Ford Fndn. Address: Dept. of Religious Studies & Philosophy, Makerere Univ., Kampala, P.O. Box 7062, Kampala, Uganda.

ACHARD, Marcel, b. 5 July 1899. Playwright. Publs. incl: La Messe est dite, 1923; La femme silencieuse, 1925; Jean de la Lune, 1929; Domino, 1931; Mlle. de Panama, 1942; Nous irons à Valparaiso, 1949; Le Moulin de la

Galette, 1951; Les Compagnons de la Marjolaine, 1953; Le Mal d'amour, 1955; Patate, 1957; Noix de coco, L'Idiote, La Polka des Lampions, Turlututu, Eugene le Mysterieux, Machin-Chouette, La Petaudiere (play), 1968; Gugusse (play), 1968. Mbr., Acad. Française, 1959-. Hons: Cmdr., Legion of Hon.; Ordre de la Couronne, Belgium. Address: 8 rue de Courty, Paris 7ᵉ, France.

ACHEBE, Chinua, b. 16 Nov. 1930, Ogidi, E. Nigeria. Writer; Editor. Educ: Govt. Coll., Umuahia; Univ. Coll., Ibadan; B.A.(London). Publs: Things Fall Apart, 1958; No Longer at Ease, 1960; Arrow of God, 1964; A Man of the People, 1966; Chike & the River, 1966; Beware Soul Brother, 1971; Girls at War, 1972; Christmas in Biafra, 1972; How the Leopard Got His Claws (co-author), 1972; Morning Yet on Creation Day, 1975. Contbr. to: Okike (Ed., 1971-); Atlantic Monthly; N.Y. Review of Books; etc. Mbr., MLA (Hon. Fellow). Hons. incl: Nigerian Nat. Trophy, 1960; C'wlth. Poetry Prize, 1972; var. docts., UK & USA. Address: Heinemann Educl. Books, 48 Charles St., London W1X 8AH, UK.

ACHTERNBUSCH, Herbert, b. 23 Nov. 1938, Munich, Bayern, Germany. Writer; Film-maker. Educ: Akademie der bildenden Künste. Publs: Die Alexanderschlacht, 1971; Der Tag wird kommen, 1973; Die Stunde des Todes, 1975; (film) Das Andechser Gefühl, 1974. Address: Schrimpfstr.7 (BRD), 8035 Gauting, W. Germany.

ACKAH, Christian Abraham, b. 2nd June 1908, Cape Coast, Ghana. Educationist. Educ: B.A., M.A., Ph.D., London Schl. of Econs., UK. Publs: West Africa — A General Certificate Geography, 1959; Akan Ethics, forthcoming. Contbr. to: Brit. Jrnl. Sociol.; Proceedings, Ghana Acad. Arts & Scis.; Ghana Jrnl. Sociol. Mbrships: Royal Geogl. Soc.; Brit. Sociol. Assn.; Royal Inst. Philos.; Ghana Acad. Arts & Scis. Address: Baffoa Lodge, P.O. Box 264, Cape Coast, Ghana.

ACKLAND, Rodney. Playwright. Publs: Improper People; Strange Orchestra; Ballerina (adapt., Lady Eleanor Smith's novel); The Old Ladies (adapt., Hugh Walpole's novel); After October; The Dark River; Crime & Punishment (adapt., Dostoevsky); Diary of a Scoundrel (adapt., Ostrovsky); Before the Party (adapt., Somerset Maugham's novel); The Pink Room; A Dead Secret. Address: c/o Eric Glass, 28 Berkeley Sq., London W1, UK.

ACOSTA MONTORO, José, b. 23 July 1932, Ciudad Real, Spain. Journalist; Author. Educ: Degrees in Law & Jrnlsm., Univ. of Madrid. Publs: incl: Relatos de la Tierra Ardiente, 1962; Esa Niebla que No Levanta, 1963; Peregrino de la Ira, 1967; Periodismo y literatura, 1973; Cinco periodistas escritores, 1974; also essays. Contbr. to: El Diario Vasco; Hoja del Lunes. Dir., Kirolak mag. Mbrships: Past Pres., Press Assn., San Sebastian; Fellow, Juan March Fndn.; Madrid Hons: Premio Union Artesana for Short Stories; Ciudad de Irun Prize for Essays; Juan March Fndn. Grant. Address: Villa Coro, Miraconcha, San Sebastian, Spain.

ACQUARONI, José Luis, b. 22 Sept. 1920, Madrid, Spain. Editor. Educ: studies in Philos. & Letters. Publs. incl: (novels) El cuclillo de la madrugada, 1955; El turbión, 1967; (essay) La Corrida de Toros, 1957; (travel stories) Andalucía, 1964; (short stories) La rueda Catalina; Nuevas de este lugar, 1965. Contbr. to: ABC (Madrid newsmagazine); El Universal (Venezuela); Mundo Hispánico; Cuadernos Hispanoamericanos; Ed., Spanish Rdrs. Digest. Hons: Platero Mag. Prize, 1954; Insula Mag. Prize, 1955; Ateneo Mag. Prize, 1955; Costa del Sol Prize, 1966; Vicente Blasco Ibáñez Prize, 1967; Hucha de Oro Prize, 1967. Address: Calle Pradillo 19, 4°C, Madrid 2, Spain.

ACTON, Harold Mario, b. 1904. Author; former Lecturer in English Literature. Educ: B.A., Christ Church, Oxford Univ. Publs: Aquarium, 1923; An Indian Ass, 1925; Five Saints & an Appendix, 1927; Humdrum, 1928; This Chaos, 1930; The Last Medici, 1932; Chinese Poetry, 1936; (co-author) Peonies & Ponies, 1941; Memoirs of an Aesthete, 1948; Prince Isidore, 1950; The Bourbons of Naples, 1956; The Last Bourbons of Naples, 1961; Old Lamps for New, 1965; More Memoirs of an Aesthete, 1970; (co-author) Famous Chinese Plays, 1937. Hons: C.B.E.; F.R.S.L. Address: La Pietra, Florence, Italy.

ADAIR, Ian Hugh, b. 1942, Kilmarnock, Scotland, UK. Author; Lecturer; Scriptwriter; Magical Inventer. Publs: Conjuring as a Craft; Party Planning & Entertainment;

Magic Step by Step; Encyclopaedia of Dove Magic, vols. 1-3; Oceans of Notions; TV Puppet Magic; Magical Menu; TV Dove Magic; TV Card Manipulations; A La Zombie; Ideen. Contbr. to: Magigram; Pentagram; Abracadabra; Linking Ring; Genii; Magic Wand; Magical Digest. Mbrships incl: Int. Brotherhood Magicians; Magic Circle. Address: 1 Rockmount Terrace, Pitt Lane, Bideford, Devon, UK.

ADAIR, John, b. 1934, Luton, UK. Historian. Educ: M.A., Univ. of Cambridge; B.Litt., Univ. of Oxford; Ph.D., Univ. of London. Publs: Hastings to Culloden, (w. P. Young), 1964; Training for Leadership, 1968; Roundhead General, 1969; Training for Decisions, 1971; Training for Communication, 1973; Action Centred Leadership, 1973; Cheriton 1644, 1973; Management & Morality, 1974. Mbrship: Fellow, Royal Histl. Soc. Address: 1 Crockford Pk. Rd., Addlestone, Weybridge, Surrey, UK.

ADAMEC, Ludwig, W., b. 10 Mar. 1924, Vienna, Austria. Professor of Oriental Studies; Writer. Educ: B.A., M.A., & Ph.D. (1966), UCLA, Calif. Publs. incl: Afghanistan 1900-23 — A Diplomatic History, 1967; Political & Historical Gazetteer of Afghanistan, 6 vols., 1972—; Afghanistan's Foreign Affairs to the Mid-Twentieth Century — Relations with the USSR, Germany, & Britain, 1974; Historical and Political Who's Who of Afghanistan, 1974. Contbr. to jrnls. in field incing: Afghanistan Jrnl. (Ed. for USA); Oriens; The Middle E. Jrnl. Hons. incl: Outstanding Jrnlsm. Grad., UCLA, 1960; many rsch. grants. Address: 5601 E. Hawthorne, Tucson, AZ 85711, USA.

ADAMS, Cindy, b. NYC, USA. Journalist; Radio Comentator. Publs: Sukarno: An Autobiography, as told to Cindy Adams, 1965; My Friend the Dictator, 1967. Contbr. to nat. mags. incing: Esquire, Family Weekly, Parade, TV Guide, Pageant. Address: 1050 5th Ave., N.Y., NY 10028, USA.

ADAMS, Hazard Simeon, pen name PANDARUS, b. 15 Feb. 1926, Cleveland, Ohio, USA. Professor. Educ: B.A., Princeton Univ.; M.A., Ph.D., Univ. of Wash. Publs: incl: Lady Gregory, 1973; The Truth About Dragons: An Antiromance, 1971; The Interests of Criticism, 1969; The Horses of Instruction: A Novel, 1968; Poetry: An Introductory Anthology, 1968; The Contexts of Poetry, 1963; Blake & Yeats: The Contrary Vision, 1955. Contbr. to lit. jrnls. incing: Mod. Fiction Studs.; Criticism; New Lit. Hist.; Poetry; etc. Mbr., Am. Soc. for Aesthetics; etc. Hons: Fulbright Fellow, 1962-63; Guggenheim Fellow, 1974-75. Address: 1121 Oxford Lane, Newport Beach, CA 92660, USA.

ADAMS, Kenneth Menzies, b. 28 Oct. 1922, Melbourne, Australia. Teacher. Educ: B.A., B.Ed., Univ. of Melbourne. Publs: Seeing History, Vol. 1, The First Australians, 1968; Seeing History, Vol. 2, Australia: Gaol to Colony, 1968; Seeing History, Vol. 3, Australia: Colonies to Commonwealth, 1971; Seeing History, Vol. 4, Twentieth Century Australia, 1972. Mbrships: Royal Victorian Histl. Soc. (Life Mbr.); N.E. Histl. Soc. (Fndn. Pres. & Life Mbr.); Melbourne Univ. Grads. Union. Address: 20 Leoni Ave., Heathmont, Victoria, Australia.

ADAMS, Lillian Loyce, b. 10 Jan. 1912, Cadiz, Tex., USA. Professor; Writer; Poet. Educ: B.B.A., Tex. A&I Univ., 1931; M.B.A., 1935, Ph.D., 1959, Univ. of Tex. Publs: Guaging Leaves, 1940; Three Wishes, 1947; The Three T's — Teach, Travel & Tell, 1960; Managerial Psychology, 1965. Contbr. to bus. publs. & poetry mags., anthols. Mbrships: Am. Bus. Writing Assn. (Am. Bus. Communication Assn.), Past Chmn., SW Region. Hons: Southern Fellowship Grants., 1956-58; Var. poetry prizes; Order of Gregg Artists, Gold Seal. Address: 216 Elmwood, Huntsville, TX 77340, USA.

ADAMS, Michael Evelyn, b. 1920, Addis Ababa, Ethiopia. Author. Educ: M.A., Christ Church, Oxford. Publs: Suez & After, 1958; Umbria, 1964; Chaos or Rebirth, 1968; Voluntary Service Overseas, 1968. Contbr. to: Times; Spectator; Sunday Times; Encounter; Guardian; Pol. Quarterly; BBC; Ed., Middle East Int., 1972—. Address: 105 Grand Buildings, Trafalgar Square, London WC2, UK.

ADAMS, Richard, b. 1922, Berks., UK. Retired Civil Servant, Department of the Environment. Educ: Bradfield Schl.; Univ. of Oxford. Publs: Watership Down, 1973; Shardik. Hons: Carnegie Medal & Guardian Children's Writer Award, 1973, for Watership Down.

ADAMS, Sylvia Mary, pen names DON, Stella, S. M. A., b. 26 Feb. 1919, Devizes, Wilts., UK. Journalist. Contbr. to: NZ Newspapers Ltd.; Suburban Newspapers; Christchurch Press; NZ Woman's Weekly; NZ Woman; NZ Farmer; Blackies Annuals; NZ Broadcasting Co. Mbrships: NZ Women Writers' Soc., Inc.; Sec., Writers' Fellowship, 2 yrs.; Pres., 1967; Pres., S. Island Writers' Assn., Inc., 1968; NZ Book Coun. Hons: L. F. de Berry Mem. Award for Short Story, 1968; Penwomen's Club Speer Cup for Radio Story, 1969; Donovan Cup for Poem, NZ Women Writers' Soc., 1970. Address: 25 Athelstan St., Christchurch 2, NZ.

ADAMS, Theodore Floyd, b. 26 Sept. 1898, Palmyra, N.Y., USA. Baptist Clergyman; Professor of Preaching. Educ: B.A. & D.D., Denison Univ., Granville, Ohio; B.D., Rochester Theol. Sem.; D.D., Univ. of Richmond, Va.; D.D., Wm. & Mary Coll.; D.D., Baylor Univ.; L.H.D., Hampden-Sydney Coll.; D.D., McMaster Univ.; LL.D., Keuka Coll.; D.D., Wake Forest Univ. Publs: Making Your Marriage Succeed, 1953; Making the Most of What Life Brings, 1957; Tell Me How, 1964; Baptists Around the World, 1967. Contbr. to sev. books inclng: The Living Christ in the Life of Today; Best Sermons of 1944; Best Sermons of 1945; Christian Faith in Action. Num. mbrships. incl: V.P., Bapt. Young Peoples Union of Am.; Bd. of Dirs., Rockefeller Fund for Theol. Educ. Recip., sev. hons. Address: 5100 Monument Ave., Richmond, VA 23230, USA.

ADAM SMITH, Patsy, b. 1926, Melbourne, Australia. Manuscripts Field Officer. Publs: Hear the Train Blow, 1964; Moonbird People, 1965; There was a Ship, 1966; Tiger Country, 1967; Hobart Sketchbook, 1968; Folklore of Australia's Railwaymen, 1969; The Rails Go Westward. Mbrships: AJA; FAW. Address: Flat 35, 98 Nicholson St., Fitzroy, Victoria 3065, Australia.

ADAMSON, Donald, b. 1939, Culcheth, Cheshire, UK. Teacher. Educ: Magdalen Coll., Oxford; Univ. of Paris, Sorbonne, France; B.Litt.; M.A.; D.Phil. Publs: The Genesis of "Le Cousin Pons", 1966; The Black Sheep (transl. of Balzac's La Rabouilleuse), 1970; Dusty Heritage: a National Policy for Museums & Libraries, 1971; Ed., T. S. Eliot: a Memoir, by the Late Robert Sencourt, 1971; The House of Nell Gwyn: the Fortunes of the Beauclerk Family, 1670-1974 (w. P. Beauclerk Dewar), 1974; Transl., Balzac's Ursule Mirouët, 1975. Contbr. to: Times; Daily Telegraph; Crossbow; French Studies; Mod. Lang. Review; Symposium; etc. Mbrships: Royal Automobile Club; Carlton Club. Address: Dodmore House, The Street, Meopham, Kent DA13 0AJ, UK.

ADAMSON, Joy F. V., b. 20 Jan. 1910, Troppau, Austria. Author; Painter. Educ: Piano, Dip., Dress Making, Gremium, Staatsprüfung, Vienna; Sculpting, Metalwork, Kunstgewerbe Schule. Grad. course, Med. Publs: Born Free, 1965; Living Free, 1961; Elsa, 1961; Forever Free, 1962; Elsa & Her Cubs, 1965; The Story of Elsa, 1966; The Peoples of Kenya, 1967; The Spotted Sphinx, 1969; Pippa & Her Cubs, 1970; Joy Adamson's Africa, 1972; Pippa's Challenge, 1972. Contbr. to var. natural hist., geog., popular jrnls. etc. Fndr., Elsa Wild Animal Appeals, UK, Kenya, USA, Can. Address: "Elsamere", Box 254, Naivasha, Kenya.

ADCOCK, Almey St. John, pen name MARCH, Hilary, b. Neasden, London, UK. Journalist. Publs: The Man Who Lived Alone, 1923; This Above All, 1924; Winter Wheat, 1926; Master Where He Will, 1926; The Judas Tree, 1928; Poacher's Moon, 1929; The Street Paved With Water, 1930; Up Hill, 1932; The Woman at Iron Crag, 1934; Tin Town, 1939; The Warped Mirror, 1948; also 3 novels under name Hilary March. Contbr. to: BBC Radio. Mbr., PEN. Address: 20 Ebrington Rd., West Malvern, Malvern, Worcs. WR14 4NL, UK.

ADCOCK, Fleur, b. 1934, Papakura, NZ. Assistant Librarian, Foreign & Commonwealth Office since 1963. Educ: Wellington Girls' Coll.; Victoria Univ., Wellington. Publs: (poetry) The Eye of the Hurricane, 1964; Tigers, 1967; High Tide in the Garden, 1971; The Scenic Route, 1974. Contbr. to: Ambit; Encounter; Listener; London Mag.; New Statesman; Times Lit. Supplement. Mbr., Poetry Soc. Address: 14 Lincoln Rd., London N2 9DL, UK.

ADDINGTON, Arthur Charles, b. 25 May 1939, St. Albans, Herts., UK. Genealogist. Publs: The Royal House of Stuart — The Descendants of King James VI of Scotland, James I of England, 3 Vols., 1969, 71, 75. Contbr. to var. Brit. & continental geneal. jrnls. Mbrships: Soc. of Authors;

Soc. of Geneals.; Royal Stuart Soc. Address: 6 Fairfield Close, Harpenden, Herts., UK.

ADDISON, Herbert, b. 1889, Crowle, Lincs., UK. Professor of Hydraulic Machines. Educ: M.Sc., Univ. of Leeds. Publs: A Treatise on Applied Hydraulics; Hydraulic Measurements; Centrifugal & other Rotodynamic Pumps; Land, Water & Food; Sun & Shadow at Aswan. Contbr. to: Publs. of Inst. of Civ. Engrs., Inst. of Mech. Engrs.; etc. Mbrships: Fellow, Inst. of Civ. Engrs., Inst. of Mech. Engrs. Address: 9a Denbigh Gdns., Richmond, Surrey, UK.

ADDLESHAW, (The Very Rev.) George William Outram, b. 1 Dec. 1906, Gorefield, Wisbech, Cambs., UK. Priest of the Church of England, Dean of Chester. Educ: B.A., 1929, M.A., 1932, B.D., 1935; Trinity Coll., Oxford Univ., Cuddesdon Coll., Oxford. Publs: The High Church Tradition; The Architectural Setting of Anglican Worship (w. Frederick Etchells), 1948. Contbr. to: Church Quarterly Review; Jrnl. Ecclesiastical Hist. Mbrships: F.S.A.; Fellow Royal Histl. Soc.; Athenaeum Club; Yorks. Club (York); Grosvenor Club, Chester. Address: Deanery, Chester, UK.

ADDO, Joyce Na Adole, b. 4 May 1932, Sekondi, Ghana. Broadcaster; TV Producer/Director. Educ: Trng. w. CBC in TV Prod. Publs: Avenue A (60 One-Hour TV Plays in English on Ghanaian family life, shown on Ghana TV), 1974-75; Ghost Town (series), forthcoming. Contbr. to: Presence Africaine, 1971; URTNA Review; (anthols.) Voices of Ghana, 1957; Ghanaian Writing (Germany), 1973; etc. Mbrships: Critical Quarterly Soc., London, UK; Ghana Soc. of Writers; Ghana Film Ind. Corp. (Bd. of Dirs., 1972-74). Recip., TV Drama Awards, 1971 & 1974. Address: House no. G 106, Dansoman Estate, Accra-North, Ghana.

ADDO, Nelson Otu, b. 4 Nov. 1933, Kukurantumi, Ghana. Sociologist; Demographer. Educ: B.Sc.(Sociol.); M.Sc., Ph.D., London Univ., UK. Publs: Ed., Population & Economic Change in West Africa (w. Caldwell & others), 1974; 4 monographs; Ed., 6 monographs. Contbr. to: Ghana Sociol. Jrnl.; Econ. Bulletin of Ghana; Ghana Population Studies; over 45 acad. & profl. articles on migration, urbanization, population policies & manpower in Ghana & Africa. Mbrships: Int. Union for Sci. Study of Population; Ghana Sociol. Assn. (Sec.); Population Assn. of Africa (Coun.). Address: Univ. of Ghana, Legon, Ghana.

ADKINS, Arthur William Hope, b. 17 Oct. 1929, Leicester, UK. Professor of Greek. Educ: M.A., D.Phil., Univ. of Oxford. Publs: Merit & Responsibility: A Study in Greek Values, 1960; Greek Religion in Historia Religionum, 1969; From the Many to the One: A Study of Personality & Views of Human Nature in the Context of Ancient Greek Society, Values & Beliefs, 1970; Moral Values & Political Behaviour in Ancient Greece, 1972. Contbr. to: Classical Quarterly; Classical Review; Classical Philol.; Jrnl. of Hellenic Studies; Gnomon; Didaskalos; Antichthon; Times Higher Educl. Supplement. Mbrships: Hellenic Soc.; Am. Philol. Assn.; Classical Assn.; Prehistoric Soc. Address: Dept. of Classics, Univ. of Chgo., Chgo., IL 60637, USA.

ADKINS, Bernard, b. 26 Dec. 1903, Sulgrave, Northants., UK. Chartered Electrical Engineer. Educ: M.A., D.Sc., Clare Coll., Cambridge Univ.; Grad. apprentice, B.T.H. Co., Rugby. Publs: Polyphase Commutator Machines; The General Theory of Electrical Machines; The General Theory of Alternating Current Machines. Contbr. to: Proceedings, Instn. Elec. Engrs. (20 papers). Fellow, Instn. Elec. Engrs. Hons: 6 Premiums for papers publd. in Proceedings Instn. Elec. Engrs. Address: 7 Harcourt Dr., Earley, Reading RG6 2TL, UK.

ADLARD, Mark, b. 19 June 1932, Seaton Carew, UK. Steel Industry Manager. Educ: M.A., Trinity Coll., Cambridge; Dept. of Educ., Oxford; B.Sc.(Econ.), Univ. of London. Publs: Interface, 1971; Volteface, 1972. Contbr. to: Penthouse; Mayfair. Agent: John Farquharson Ltd. Address: "Fourways", 22 Ham Lane, Lenham, Near Maidstone, Kent, UK.

ADLER-KARLSSON, Gunnar, b. 6 Mar. 1933, Karlshamn, Sweden. University Professor. Educ: LL.D., 1962; Ph.D. (econs.), 1968, Univ. of Roskilde, Denmark. Publs: Western Economic Warfare, 1947-67, 1968; Functional Socialism: a Swedish Theory for Democratic Socialization, 1967 (10 eds. in 7 langs. by 1974); Kuba-Rapport, Sieg oder Niederlage?, 1973. Contbr. to var.

Swedish & int. jrnls. Mbr., var. econ. assns. Address: RUC, Box 260, DK-4000 Roskilde, Denmark.

ADOBOE, John Yao, b. 19 July 1934, Ve Deme, Volta Region, Ghana. Cinematographer. Educ: Studied TV & Film Prod. Technique, Can., 1964. Films: Tema, The Harbour City, 1961; Physical Education in Ghana, 1961; num. TV films, 1965-72; The Ordinary Man, 1973. Contbr. to: Visnews Ltd., London, UK (stringer); NBC News, N.Y., USA (stringer). Hons: Award for News Film, 1961; Award for TV film, The Child from the North, 1972. Address: P.O. Box 6871, Accra-North, Ghana.

ADOUT, Jacques, b. 22 Sept. 1914, Lausanne, Switz. Radio Producer. Educ: Lic. és Lettres, Lausanne Univ. Publs: L'Homme et Le Chien, 1945; Venise, Album d'Artiste, 1945; Images dans le Ciel (w. René Creux), 1962; On Cause, On Cause . . . , 1971. Contbr. to: Swiss Radio & TV. Mbrships: PEN; French Soc. of Men of Letters. Address: Liaudoz 73, 1012 — Lausanne, Switz.

ADRIAANSE, Paul Alexander, b. 1 July 1943, Winschoten, Netherlands. Film Director & Producer. Educ: Univ. of Amsterdam; R.I.T.C.S., State Higher Tech. Inst. for Theatre & Mass Media; Dip., Film Dir. Film: HEE!; Ansfred; BM-EU 420; Belgium UnLtd; Toys; Paras; Cerebel & Collicul; Hoffmann's Erzählunger, (co-writer); Rolande or The Chronicle of a Passion (co-adaptor); Once in the Snow. Mbrships: Union of Belgian Film & TV Authors; Union of Belgian Prods. Hons: Film HEE!, selected by Belgian Film Bd. to represent Belgium in Nat. Film Weeks Abroad, 1969-1974. Address: Rue de la Cambre, 336, 1150 - Brussels, Belgium.

af GEIJERSTAM, Brita Hedvig Elizabeth, b. 20 Mar. 1902, Klippan, Sweden. Publs. incl: Mia Pia, 1958; Mia Pia och Masse, 1960; Mia Pia i 3:an, 1961; På riktigt och på låtsas (poetry for children), 1962; Filippas dagbok, 1965; transls. into Swedish of works by A. A. Milne. Contbr. of stories & verse to var. newspapers. Mbrships: Swedish Authors' Assn.; Swedish Translators' Assn. Recip., Stockholm City Culture Award, 1973. Address: Örnbogatan 41, 161 39 Bromma, Sweden.

af GEIJERSTAM, Carl-Erik, b. 11 Feb. 1914, Skövde, Sweden. Teacher; Writer. Educ: Fil.Lic., Uppsala Univ. Publs: Väktare Vid Spannet, 1936; Bortom Ordens Skyar, 1941; Bindemedel, 1950; Det Personliga Experimentet, 1963; Uppenbar Hemlighet, 1967; Genomfärd, 1972; Varseblivet, 1975. Contbr. to: Bonniers Litterära Magasin (BLM); Nya Argus. Mbrships: Sveriges Författarförbund; Pen. Address: Gropgränd 2A, S 752 35 Uppsala, Sweden.

AFGHANI, Ali-Mohammad, b. 1926, Kermanshah, Iran. Businessman; Author. Educ: Mil. Coll. Publs: Shohare Ahou Khanom (Ahu Kahnum's Husband), 1961; Shadkamane Darrehe Gharassou (The Joyful People of Gharasu Valley), 1963. Hons: Award for best book of yr., Anjomane Ketab (Soc. of Books), 1961; Royal Prize, King of Iran, 1962. Address: No. 39, Chehrazi St., Ave. Pahlavi, P.O. Box 2354, Teheran, Iran.

af KLINTBERG, Bengt, b. 25 Dec. 1938, Stockholm, Sweden. Author; Lecturer on Folklore. Educ: Fil.kand., 1962. Publs: (poetry) Paths, 1959; The Crown of the Snake-King, 1961; The Stockholm Game, 1966; (Ed., anthols.) Swedish Magic Spells, 1965; Swedish Folk Poetry, 1971; Swedish Folk Legends, 1972; (play) Seven Voices on Almqvist, 1966. Contbr. to folklore & poetry progs., Swedish Radio, 1964—. Mbrships: Fluxus Grp.; Swedish Union of Authors. Recip., Best Pvte. Theatre Play of Yr. Award, for Lidner, 1965. Address: Vendevägen 13, 18131 Lidingö, Sweden.

AĞAOĞLU, Adalet, b. 23 Oct. 1929, Nallihan, Ankara, Turkey. Writer. Educ: Univ. of Ankara. Publs: (plays) Marriage Game, 1964; Crack on the Roof, 1969; On the Frontiers, 1969; Lotto, 1969; Uc Oyun (three plays), 1974; (novel) Olmeye Yatmak, 1973; (short stories) High Tension, 1974. Mbr., Turkish Writers' Assn. Hons: Theater Award, Inst. of Turkish Lang., 1974. Address: Ataturk Bul Ilbank Apt. A/72, Kavaklidere, Ankara, Turkey.

AGAR, Herbert Sebastian, b. 29 Sept. 1897. Writer; Journalist. Educ: Columbia & Princeton Univs.; A.B.; A.M.; Ph.D.; Litt.D.; LL.D. Publs. incl: The People's Choice, 1933; Land of the Free, 1935; Pursuit of Happiness, 1938; A Time for Greatness, 1943; The Price of Union, 1950; Declaration of Faith, 1952; Abraham Lincoln, 1952; The Price of Power (UK title, The Unquiet Years), 1957; The

Saving Remnant, 1960; The Perils of Democracy, 1965; Britain Alone, 1972. Recip., Pulitzer Prize for Am. Hist., 1933. Address: Beechwood, Petworth, Sussex, UK.

AGARWAL, Chandra Prakash, b. 14 Dec. 1915, Farrukhabad, India. Lecturer in Hindi; Author. Educ: LL.B., 1942; M.A.(Hindi), 1959, Agra Univ.; Ph.D.(Hindi), 1967. Publs: In the Name of Justice, 1955; A Dream, 1957; Duty, 1958; A Ray, 1960. Contbr. to: Kanpur Univ. Mag.; Sri Venkateshwar Univ. Oriental Jrnl. Mbrships: Indian Br., PEN; Fellow, Royal Asiatic Soc. Address: Kedarnath St. (Senapat), Farrukhabad, U.P., India.

AGBODEKA, Francis, b. 31 Dec. 1931, Anloga, Ghana. University Professor of History. Educ: B.A., London, 1956; Ph.D., Univ. of Ghana, 1968. Publs: The Rise of the Nation States, 1965; African Politics & British Policy in the Gold Coast 1868-1900, 1971; Ghana in the Twentieth Century, 1972. Contbr. to: Transactions of Histl. Soc. Ghana; Jrnl. of Univ. of Cape Coast; Organ of African Studies Assn., USA; Ghana Tchrs'. Jrnl. Mbrships. incl: Hon. Keeper W. African Histl. Mus., Cape Coast. Recip., acad. hons. Address: Dept. of Hist., Univ. of Cape Coast, Cape Coast, Ghana.

AGELASTO, Charlotte Priestley, b. 1904, Leeds, UK. Writer. Educ: M.A., D.Th.P.T., Durham Univ. Publs: Fabulae Aesopi, 1965; The Growth of Rome, 1967; Selections from Ovid's Metamorphoses (w. A. C. Reynell), 1968; Riding with BP, 1970. Contbr. to: Pneu Mag.; Lib. Review; Horse & Hound; Riding; Country Gentleman's Mag.; Greek Gazette. Mbrships: Authors' Soc.; S.W.W.J.; Nat. Book League. Address: Greenacre, Copperkins Lane, Amersham, Bucks., UK.

AGER, Derek Victor, b. 21 Apr. 1923, Harrow, UK. University Professor; Writer. Educ: B.Sc., 1951, Ph.D., 1954, London Univ.; D.Sc., 1968. Publs: Introducing Geology, 1961; Principles of Paleoecology, 1963; The Nature of the Stratigraphical Record, 1973. Contbr. of papers & articles to sci. publs. Recip. of sev. profl. awards. Address: Dept. of Geol. & Oceanog., Univ. Coll. of Swansea, Singleton Park, Swansea SA2 8PP, UK.

AGERHOLM, Margaret, b. 27 Nov. 1917, Vancouver, Can. Physician. Educ: M.A., B.M., B.Ch., Somerville Coll., Oxford. Publs: Handbook on Poliomyelitis, 1955; Equipment for the Disabled, 1951, revised ed., 1966. Contbr. to: Lancet; Rehab.; Physiotherapy. Mbrships: Royal Soc. of Med.; Brit. Med. Assn.; Int. Soc. of Paraplegia; Int. Continence Soc.; Nat. Exec. Comm., Disablement Income Grp.; Trustee, Cheshire Fndn. Homes for the Sick. Address: 3 Downside Ct., Downs Lane, Leatherhead, UK.

AGOSTI, Luis, b. 30 Aug. 1909, Santander, Spain. Physician; Author. Educ: B.A., M.D., D.A., F.F.A.R.C.S., Madrid & London, UK. Publs: Gimnasia Educativa, 1948, 3rd ed., 1974; Nuevas Técnicas y Conceptos en Anestesiología y Reanimación, 1956; Fieras, Selvas y Salvajes, 1968; chapt. contbns., anesthesiol., blood grps., etc. to sev. books. Contbr. to: Trofeo (Madrid); Revista Espanola de Anestesiología y Reanimación; Revista Italiana de Anestesiología; Der Anaesthetist (Germany). Address: Padre Damian 46, Madrid 16, Spain.

AGRO, Ghulam Rabbani, b. 5 Nov. 1933, Agra, Sindh, Pakistan. Chief Executive Officer, Sindhi Adabi Board (for the promotion of Sindhi Language & Literature). Educ: B.A. (Pol. Sci. & Eng. Lit.). Publs: Collection of Short Stories (in Sindhi); Transl., Selected American Short Stories. Contbr. to all Sindhi lang. mags. Recip., 1st Prize for the Best Sindhi Short Story, Sindhi Adabi Sangat, Karachi. Address: Secretary, Sindhi Adabi Board, Hyderabad, Sindh, Pakistan.

AGUILAR, Luis Enrique, b. 16 June 1926, Manzanillo, Cuba. Professor; Writer; Lawyer. Educ: LL.B., Havana Univ., 1949; D.S.Sc., Madrid Univ., 1950; Ph.D., Am. Univ., Wash. D.C., USA, 1963. Publs: Pasado y Ambiente en el Proceso Cubano, 1952; Marxism in Latin America, 1968; Cuba 1933, Prologue to Revolution, 1972; Cuba, Conciencia y Revolucion, 1973. Contbr. to: Problems of Communism; Hispanic Am. Histl. Review; New Ldr.; Reporter; Cuadernos Americanos; Revista da Ciencias Sociales (Chile). Address: 6836 Tulip Hill Ter., Bethesda, MD 20016, USA.

AHLFORS, Bengt (Gunnar Richard), b. 28 Dec. 1937, Helsinki, Finland. Theatre Director. Educ: M.A., Univ. of

Helsinki. Author, Sånger & dikter (poems), 1971. Also num. plays, theatre & TV. Mbrships: Finlands svenska författareförening; Finlands Dramatikerförbund; Sveriges Dramatikerförbund. Recip., Award for Best TV Film Script, Marta Larsson 65, Prague Festival, 1971. Address: Stora Robertsgatan 16 A, SF-00120 Helsinki, Finland.

AHLO, Börje Walter, b. 19 Nov. 1932, Jakobstad, Finland. Writer. Publs: i debutdiktantologin Tre, 1968; I skuggen av ditt leende, 1972. Contbr. to: Horizon; Hembygden; Capital News; Jakobstad's News; etc. Hons: Jakobstad Culture Comm. Grants, 1969, 1971, 1973; Swedish Culture Fund, Author Grants, 1970, 1973; Min. of Educ., Lib. Grant, 1973. Address: Lindskogsgatan 26, 68620 Jakobstad 2, Finland.

AHMAD, Razia Fasih, b. 1 Sept. 1934, Moradabad, India. Writer. Educ: B.A., M.A. Publs: Seemeen, 1964; Abla Paa, 1964; Sair-E-Pakistan, 1965; Intizar-E-Mosam-E-Gul, 1965; Ek Jahan Aur Bhi Hai, 1966; Do Patan Ke Beech, 1966; Mata-E-Dard, 1969; Tapti Chhaun, 1969; Azar-E-Ishq, 1971. Contbr. to: Naqush; Seep; Pakistan Quarterly; Scintilla; Fanoon; Naya Daur; Afkar; Mah-E-Nau. Mbr., Pakistan Writers Guild. Hons: Writers Guild Prize for Best Short Story, 1961; Taraqui-E-Urdu Board Prize for Best Book for Children, 1965; Adamji Prize for Lit., Best Fiction of Yr., 1964-65. Address: 19/g Block 6, Pakistan Employees Co. Housing Soc., Karachi 29, Pakistan.

AHN, Soo-gil, pen name NAM SUK, b. 3 Nov. 1911, Heung-Nam, Korea. Novelist. Educ: Tchrs. Coll., Waseda Univ. Publs. incl: (short story collects.) North Plain, 1943; The Third Man Type, 1954; First Love, 1955; Windmill, 1963; Rice Sheaves, 1964; (novels) Hyangsu (Nostalgia), 1954; Flower Wreath, 1955; Second Youth, 1958; Floating Bridge, 1960, 1972; Thinking Reed, 1962, 1973; White Night, 1964; North Chentau, 1967 (transl'd into Engl.) Passage, 1969; The Sung Chun River, 1974. Contbr. to: Hyundai Moonhak; Thought & Lit.; Shin-Dong-A; maj. newspapers. Mbrships: PEN (V.P., Korea, 1970-72); Korean Assn. of Writers (Bd. of Dirs.). Hons: Freedom Lit. Award, 1955; Seoul City Cultural Award, 1968; Samil Cultural Award, 1973. Address: 123-71 Chong Am Dong, Sungbooku, Seoul, Korea.

AHONEN, Erkki Paavali, b. 8 Jan. 1932, Kiuruvesi, Finland. Author. Educ: Hum.kand. Publs: (poetry) Hyppy, 1960; (novels) Tänään ei paljon tapahdu, 1961; Kyyditys, 1962; Kiviä vuoret, 1965; Paperihanskat, 1967; Kuumatka, 1969; Kylmä paikka, 1970; (sci. fiction) Paikka nimeltä Plaston, 1968; Tietokonelapsi, 1972. Contbr. to: Parnasso; Aika. Mbr., Finnish Soc. of Authors. Address: 03710 Uusitalo, Finland.

AICHINGER, Ilse, b. 1 Nov. 1921. Writer. Educ: Vienna Univ. Publs: Die Grössere Hoffnung (novel), 1948; Knöpfe (radio play), 1952; Der Gefesselte (short stories), 1953; Zu keiner Stunde (dialogues), 1957; Besuch im Pfarrhaus (radio play), 1961; Wo ich wohne (stories, dialogues, poems), 1963; Eliza, Eliza (stories), 1965; Nachricht von Tag (stories), 1970. Hons. incl: Literaturpreis der Bayerischen Akademie, 1961; Nelly-Sachs-Preis, Dortmund, 1971. Address: Postfach 27, 8232 Bayerisch Gmain, W. Germany.

AICKMAN, Robert Fordyce, b. London, UK. Author. Publs: We Are For the Dark (w. Elizabeth J. Howard), 1951; Know Your Waterways, 1954; The Story of Our Inland Waterways, 1955; The Late Breakfasters, 1964; Dark Entries, 1964; The Attempted Rescue (autobiog.), 1966; Powers of Darkness, 1966; Sub Rosa, 1968; Cold Hand in Mine, forthcoming; Ed., the Eight Fontana Books of Great Ghost Stories. Contbr. to: The Third Ghost Book (ed. Lady Cynthia Asquith); The Fourth Ghost Book; 19th Century & After; Country Life; Field; Tatler; Illustrated London News; Fortnightly Review; etc. Address: 530 Willoughby House, Barbican, London EC2, UK.

AIKEN, Conrad (Potter), b. 5 Aug. 1889, Savannah, Ga., USA. Writer. Educ: A.B., Harvard Univ., 1912. Publs. incl: Blue Voyage (novel), 1927; Great Circle (novel), 1933; The Collected Short Stories of Conrad Aiken, 1960; (verse) The Morning Song of Lord Zero: Poems Old & New, 1963; A Seizure of Limericks, 1964; The Clerk's Journal: An Undergraduate Poem, Together with a Brief Memoir of Dean LeBaron Russell Briggs, T. S. Eliot, & Harvard, in 1911, 1971; Collected Poems 1916-70, 1971. Mbr., Am. Acad. of Arts & Letters, 1957. Hons: Gold Medal for Poetry, Nat. Inst. of Arts & Letters, 1958; Nat. Medal for

Lit., 1969. Address: Forty-One Doors, Stony Brook Rd., Brewster, MA 02631, USA.

AIKEN, Joan Delano, b. 4 Sept. 1924, Rye, Sussex, UK. Writer. Publs. incl: The Wolves of Willoughby Chase, 1962; Night Fall, 1969; Smoke from Cromwell's Time, 1970; The Cuckoo Tree, 1971; The Kingdom Under the Sea, 1971; A Harp of Fishbones, 1972; Died on a Rainy Sunday, 1972; Midnight is a Place, 1974; Arabel's Raven, 1974; Not What You Expected, 1974; Voices in an Empty House, 1975; (plays) Winterthing, 1972; The Mooncusser's Daughter, 1973. Contbr. to var. mags. Mbrships. incl: Soc of Authors; Crime Writers Assn.; Mystery Writers Am. Recip., Guardian Award for Children's Fiction, 1969. Address: White Hart House, High St., Petworth, Sussex, UK.

AIRD, Alisdair, pen name FAIRLEY, Alisdair, b. 10 Aug. 1940, Edinburgh, UK. Editorial Consultant. Educ: B.A., Univ. of Oxford. Publs: The Automotive Nightmare, 1972; Ed., Motoring Which, 1969-74; Ed., Holiday Which, 1973-74; Mng. Ed., Which, 1971-73. Contbr. to: Listener. Agent: A. D. Peters. Address: 18 E Heath Rd., London, NW3, UK.

AITKEN, Jonathan William Patrick, b. 30 Aug. 1942, Dublin, Repub. of Ireland. Member of Parliament. Educ: M.A., Oxford Univ., UK. Publs: A Short Walk on the Campus, 1967; The Young Meteors, 1968; Land of Fortune: A Study of the New Australia, 1970; Officially Secret, 1971. Contbr. to: Evening Standard, London; Sunday Telegraph; Daily Mail; Spectator; Harpers; num. other Brit. newspapers & mags. Address: House of Commons, London SW1A 0AA, UK.

AITMATOV, Chingiz, b. 1928, Sherker, USSR. Author. Educ: Lit. Inst., Moscow. Publs: Dzamilya, 1958; First Teacher, 1960; To Have & Not to Have, 1960; Motler's Field, 1963; Farewell, Gulsary, 1966; The White Steamer, 1969. Hons: Lenin Prize, 1963; State Prize, 1967. Address: Flat 1, 43 Dzerzhinsky, Frunze, Kirgiz SSR, USSR.

AJAYI, Jacob Festus Ade, b. 26 May 1929, Ikole-Ekiti, Nigeria. Historian; Vice-Chancellor, University of Lagos. Educ: B.A., Univ. Coll., Ibadan, 1951; B.A., Univ. Coll., Leicester, UK, 1955; Ph.D., Univ. of London, 1958. Publs: Milestones in Nigerian History, 1962; Yoruba Warfare in the 19th Century (w. R. S. Smith), 1964; Christian Missions in Nigeria, 1841-91, 1965; Ed., A Thousand Years of West African History (w. I. Espie), 1966; Ed., A History of West Africa (w. M. Crowder), 2 vols., 1971-74; Ed., The University of Ibadan, 1948-73: A History of the 1st Twenty-Five Years (w. T. N. Tamuno). Contbr. to: Jrnl. of African Hist.; Jrnl. of the Histl. Soc. of Nigeria; Jrnl. of Negro Educ.; Daedalus; Nigeria Mag.; sev. encys. Mbrships. incl: Pres., Histl. Soc. of Nigeria; Fellow, Ghana Histl. Soc.; Gen. Ed., Ibadan Hist. Series, 1966-. Address: Univ. of Lagos, Lagos, Nigeria.

ÅKESSON, Sonja, b. 19 Apr. 1926, Buttle, Sweden. Writer. Publs. incl: Situationer, 1957; Glasveranda, 1959; Skvallerspegel, 1960; Leva livet, 1961; Efter balen, 1962; Husfrid, 1963; Ute skiner solen, 1965; Jag bor i Sverige, 1966; Man får vara glad och tacka Gud, 1967; Pris, 1968; Ljuva sextiotal, 1970; Mamman och pappan som gjorde aebetsbyte, 1970; Dödens ungar, 1973; Sagan om Siv, 1974; (w. Jarl Hammarberg-Åkesson) Strålande dikter/nej så fan heller, 1967; Kändis, 1969; Hå vi är väg, 1972. Mbr., Swedish Authors' Union. Hons: Ferlinpriset, 1970; De nios stora pris, 1974. Address: Hertig Knutsgatan 43 C, 302 50 Halmstad, Sweden.

AKILANDAM, Perungalur Vaithialingam, pen name AKILON, b. 27 June 1922, Perungalur, India. Writer. Educ: Maharaja's Coll., Pudukkottai. Publs. (all in Tamil lang.) incl: Nenjin Alaigai (novel), 1953; Pavai Vilakku (novel), 1958; Vengaiyin Maindan (novel), 1961; Sahodarar Andro? (stories), 1963; Ponmalar (novel), 1964; Kayalvizhi (novel), 1967; Chittirap Paavai (novel), 1967; Nellore Arisi (stories), 1967; Erimalai (stories), 1971. Mbrships. incl: Tamil Writers' Assn. Hons. incl: Tamilnadu Govt. Awards, 1968 & 1973. Address: 171 Lloyds Rd., Madras 14, India.

AKRILL, Caroline, b. 24 Dec. 1943, Burton-upon-Trent, Staffs., UK. Writer; Equine Journalist. Publs: I'd Rather Not Gallop, 1975. Contbr. to: Light Horse; Pony Mag.; Riding; Horse & Pony; The Field. Mbr., Horse & Pony Breeding & Benefit Fund (Comm.). Address: The Sword in Hand, Westmill, nr. Puckeridge, Herts., UK.

ALANDER, Rainer, b. 2 June 1937, Turku, Finland. Naval Officer (Merchant Service). Publs: Ansiktet, 1963; Sandkornet, 1964; Personerna, 1969; Lastmärket, 1972; En sorts frihet, 1974. Address: Furuvägen 13, 20540 Abo 54, Finland.

AL-AZM, Sadik, J., b. 7 Nov. 1934, Damascus, Syria. Editor; University Teacher; Writer. Educ: B.A., Am. Univ. of Beirut, 1957; M.A., 1959, Ph.D., 1961, Yale Univ. Grad. Schl., New Haven, Conn., USA. Publs. incl: Critique of Religious Thought (in Arabic), 1969, 3rd ed., 1970; Leftist Studies about the Palestine Problem (in Arabic), 1970; The Origins of Kant's Arguments in the Antinomies (in Engl.), 1972; A Critical Study of the Palestinian Resistance Movement (in Arabic), 1973. Contbr. to Engl. & Arabic acad. jrnls., Ed., Arabic Studies Review. Address: c/o Cultural Studies Prog., Am. Univ. of Beirut, Beirut, Lebanon.

ALBEE, Edward Franklin, b. 12 Mar. 1928. Playwright. Educ: Columbia Univ. Plays incl: The Death of Bessie Smith; The American Dream; The Sand Box, 1961; The Zoo Story, 1961; Who's Afraid of Virginia Woolf, 1962; Tiny Alice, 1964; A Delicate Balance, 1966; Everything in the Garden (after play by Giles Cooper), 1967; Box & Quotations from Chairman Mao (2 one-act plays), 1968; All Over, 1971; also stage adaptations of novels. Recip., Pulitzer Prize, 1967. Address: c/o The Wm. Morris Agcy., 1350 Ave. of the Ams., N.Y., NY 10019, USA.

ALBERTSON, Dean, b. 22 Aug. 1920, Denver, Colo., USA. Historian. Educ: B.A., Hist., 1942, M.A., 1947, Univ. of Calif., Berkeley; Ph.D., Columbia Univ., 1955. Publs: Roosevelt's Farmer, 1961; Eisenhower as President, 1963; Main Problems in American History, (w. Howard H. Quint & Milton Cantor), 1964, revised 1968 & 72; American History Visually, 1969; The American Counterculture, 1974. Recip. of grants from Am. Coun. of Learned Socs., Soc. Sci. Rsch. Coun. & Am. Philosophical Soc., 1962-64. Address: Dept. of Hist., Univ. of Mass., Amherst, MA 01002, USA.

ALBERY, Peter James, b. 8 Dec. 1912, London, UK. Theatre Impresario. Educ: B.A., French & German, Oxford Univ.; B.A., Engl., London Univ. Publs: (plays) Anne Boleyn (published in Plays of the Year), 1954; Another Man's Daughter; No Instructions?, 1970. Contbr. to: Am. Sci. Monitor. Mbrships: Vincents Club, Oxford Univ.; Fndr. & Chmn., Theatre Roundabout. Recip., Brit. Arts Coun. Award, for Another Man's Daughter. Address: 859 Finchley Rd., London NW11, UK.

ALBRAND, Martha, pen names LAMBERT, Christine; HOLLAND, Katrin, b. 1912, Rostock, Germany. Educ: Univ. of Zürich, Switz. Publs: Man Spricht über Jacqueline; Carlotta Torresani; Das Frauen-Haus; Without Glory; No Surrender; Endure No Longer; The Other Side of the Moon; The Obsession of Emmet Booth; After Midnight; Les Morts ne Parient Plus; Meet Me Tonight; A Door Fell Shut; Rhine Replica; Manhattan North; Zurich AZ 900. Contbr. to: Saturday Evening Post; John Bull; Town & Country; Ladies' Home Jrnl. Mbr., PEN. Hons: Ph.D., Colo. State Christian Coll.; Grand Prix de Romans Literature Policiers (for Les Morts ne parient plus). Agents: A. P. Watt & Son; in USA, Robert Lautz.

ALDERMAN, Clifford Lindsey, b. Springfield, Mass., USA. Writer. Educ: B.S., US Naval Acad., Annapolis, Md. Publs. incl: Liberty, Equality, Fraternity, 1966; Story of the Thirteen Colonies, 1967; The Devil's Shadow, 1967; Death to the King, 1968; Blood Red the Roses, 1971; Wearing of the Green, 1972; The Golden Century, 1972; The War We Could Have Lost, 1974; The Connecticut Colony, 1975; Colonists for Sale, 1975. Contbr. to: Saturday Evening Post; Atlantic Monthly; Argosy; Toronto Star Weekly. Mbrships: Authors Guild; Friends of N.Y. Pub. Lib.; Naval Acad. Assn. of N.Y. Address: 5461 Lemon Tree Lane, Pinellas Park, FL 33565, USA.

ALDING, Peter, b. 1926, London, UK. Barrister-at-Law. Educ: Dept. of Navigation, Univ. of Southampton. Publs: 7 books inclng. The Murder Line. Mbrships: Paternosters Club; Crime Writers' Assn. Agent: John Long Ltd. Address: Bourne Farm, Aldington Frith, Near Ashford, Kent, UK.

ALDISS, Brian Wilson, pen name SHACKLETON, C. C., b. 18 Aug. 1925, Dereham Norfolk, UK. Writer; Critic. Publs: (fiction) Non-Stop, 1958; Hothouse, 1962; Greybeard, 1964; Report on Probability A, 1968; Barefoot in the Head, 1969; The Hand-Reared Boy, 1970; A Soldier Erect, 1971; The Moment of Eclipse, 1971; Frankenstein Unbound, 1973; The Eighty-Minute Hour, 1974; (non-fiction) Cities & Stones, 1966; The Shape of Further Things, 1970; Billion Year Spree, 1973. Contbr. to: New Statesman; New Review; Punch; etc. Hons. incl: Ditmar Award, World's Best Contemporary Sci. Fiction Author, 1970; Brit. Sci. Fiction Assn. Fantasy Award, 1972. Address: Heath House, Southmoor, Near Abingdon; Oxon. OX13 5BG, UK.

ALDOUS, Tony, b. 20 Dec. 1935, London, UK. Journalist. Educ: LL.B., Bristol Univ., 1963. Publs: Battle for the Environment, 1972; Goodbye, Britain? 1975. Contbr. to: The Times; Archts'. Jrnl.; Building; Country Life; Illustrated London News; New Soc.; New Scientist. Mbrships: Arch. Club; Land Use Soc; Reform Club. Address: 12 Eliot Hill, London SE13 7EB.

ALDRED, Margaret Gertrude, b. 24 Apr. 1914, Norfolk, UK. Author. Publs: 4 children's books. Contbr. to: Times Educl. Supplement; World Digest; Eastern Daily Press; Illustrated London News; Coins & Medals; Richmond & Twickenham Times. Grand Duchy of Luxemburg Paper; Mags. in India, Malta, Brit. W. Indies, Gibraltar, S. Africa, Ceylon, USA, Can.; etc. F.R.S.A. Address: Knowle Cottage, Little Knowle, Budleigh Salterton, Devon, UK.

ALDRIDGE, A. Owen, b. 16 Dec. 1915, Buffalo, N.Y., USA. Professor; Editor. Educ: B.S., Ind. Univ., 1937; M.A., Univ. of Ga., 1938; Ph.D., Duke Univ., 1942; D.U.P., Univ. of Paris (Sorbonne), 1955. Publs: Franklin & His French Contemporaries, 1957; Man of Reason — Life of Thomas Paine, 1959; Jonathan Edwards, 1964; Benjamin Franklin — Philosopher & Man, 1965; Benjamin Franklin & Nature's God, 1967; Comparative Literature: Matter & Method, 1969; The Ibero-American Enlightenment, 1971. Contbr. to profl, jrnls. Address: Univ. of Ill., Dept. of Comparative Lit., 2070 For. Lang. Bldg., Urbana, IL 61801, USA.

ALDRIDGE, James. Publs: A Captive in the Land; The Diplomat; The Last Exile; Cairo. Address: c/o Curtis Brown, 13 King St., London WC2, UK.

ALDRIDGE, John Watson, b. 26 Sept. 1922, Sioux City, Iowa, USA. Author; Professor, University of Michigan. Educ: Univ. of Chattanooga, 1940-43; Fellow, Breadloaf Schl. of Engl., 1942; B.A., Univ. of Calif., Berkeley, 1947. Publs: After the Lost Generation, 1951; Critiques & Essays on Modern Fiction, 1952; In Search of Heresy, 1956; The Party at Cranton, 1960; Time to Murder & Create, 1966; In the Country of the Young, 1970; The Devil in the Fire, 1972. Contbr. to Saturday Review; N.Y. Times Book Review; etc. Mbrships: Authors League of Am.; PEN. Address: 1050 Wall St., No. 4-c, Ann Arbor, MI 48105, USA.

ALDRIDGE, Richard Boughton, b. 12 Nov. 1930, NYC, USA. Poet; Teacher. Educ: B.A., Amherst Coll.; M.A., Worcester Coll. Oxford Univ., UK. Publs: (poetry) The Fantasy Poets No. 32, 1956; An Apology Both Ways, 1957; Down Through the Clouds, the Sea, 1963; The Wild White Rose, 1974; Ed., Maine Lines: 101 Contemporary Poems About Maine, 1970; Poetry Amherst: A Sesquicentennial Anthology of Poems by Alumin of Amherst College, 1972. Contbr. to: Oxford Poetry, 1956; New Poems by Am. Poets No. 2, 1957; Poems for Seasons & Celebrations, 1961; In Other Words: Amherst in Prose & Verse, 1964; The N.Y. Times Book of Verse, 1970; num. periodicals. Hons: Collin Armstrong Poetry Prize, Amherst Coll., 1952; 2 Fulbright Schlrships, Oxford Univ. 1955-57. Address: Star Route Box 127, Sebasco Estates P.O., ME 04565, USA.

ALEGRIA, Fernando, b. 26 Sept. 1918, Santiago, Chile. Writer; Professor. Educ: Ph.D., Univ. of Calif., Berkeley, USA. Publs: Walt Whitman in Hispanoamerica, 1954; Caballo de Copas, (trans. into Engl., French, Romanian, Russian, etc.), 1957; Historia de la Novela Hispanoamericana, 1959, 5th ed., 1974; Los dias contados, 1968; Amerika, Amerikka, Amerikkka, 1970. Contbr. to: Revista Iberoamericana; Ramparts; Saturday Review; etc. Mbr., Instituto Internacional de Literatura Iberoamericana. Hons: Latin Am. Lit. Prize, Pan Am. Union, 1943; Premio Municipal Chile, 1958; Premio Atenea, Univ. of Concepcion, 1958. Address: Dept. of Spanish & Portuguese, Stanford Univ., Stanford, CA 94305, USA.

ALEIXANDRE, Vicente, b. 26 Apr. 1898, Seville, Spain. Writer. Educ: Lic., Univ. of Madrid. Publs incl: Ambito, 1928; Espadas como labios, 1932; La destruccion o el amor, 1935; Sombra del Paraiso, 1944; Mundo a solas, 1950; Historia del corazon, 1954; Los encuentros, 1958; En Un Vasto Dominio, 1962; Obras completas, 1968; Poemas de la consumacion, 1968; Dialogos del conocimiento, 1974. Mbrships: Royal Spanish Acad.; Hispanic Soc. of Am.; Monde Latin Acad., Paris, France; Fellow, Profs. of Spanish Assn., USA; Corres. Mbr., Scis. & Arts Acad., Puerto Rico; Arts Acad., Malaga, Spain; Hispano-Americana Acad., Bogotá, Colombia. Hons: Nat. Prize of Lit., 1933. Address: Velintonia 3, Madrid 3, Spain.

ALEXANDER, Boyd, pen name LACEY, John, b. 1913, Cranbrook, Kent, UK. Past Curator of Beckford Papers; Lecturer. Educ: B.A., Magdalen Coll., Oxford. Publs: Ed., Journal of W. Beckford in Portugal & Spain, 1954; Life at Fonthill, 1957; England's Wealthiest Son, A Study of W. Beckford, 1962; Ed., Beckford's Recollections of an Excursion to the Monasteries of Alcobaca & Batalha, 1972. Contbr. to: Country Life; Hist. Today; Quarterly Review; Cornhill; Apollo; Ency Britannica; Cairo Studies in Engl.; Yale Univ. Gazette; Yale Univ. Lib. Centenary Exhib. Catalogue of Beckford; Underdogs (book), 1961; Mendelssohn Studien, Berlin, 1972, 1975; Burns Chronicle; etc. Mbrships: Soc. of Authors; PEN. Address: Prospect House, Upton, Didcot OX11 9HU, UK.

ALEXANDER, Colin James, pen name, JAY, Simon, b. 10 Apr. 1920, Bennington, UK. Medical Practitioner; Author. Educ: M.D., Ch.B., Univ. of Otago, NZ. Publs: Death of a Skindiver, 1964; Sleepers Can Kill, 1968. Address: 49 Richard Farrell Ave., Remuera, Auckland 5, NZ.

ALEXANDER, Eugenie Mary, b. 2 Sept. 1919, Wallasey, Cheshire, UK. Writer & Artist. Educ: N.D.D.; A.T.D.; Chelsea Schl. of Art; Goldsmiths' Coll. of Art; St. Anne's Coll., Sanderstead (Demonstration Schl. for Froebel Educl. Inst.). Publs: Art for Young People, 1958; Fabric Pictures, 1959; Museums & How to Use Them, 1974. Contbr. to: Observer Colour Supplement; Daily Telegraph; Guardian; House & Garden; She; Art & Craft Educ.; The Tchr.; Woman's Own; Woman's Realm (features, art exhib. & book reviews); also 5 one-man exhibs. of fabric collages. Mbr., Hurlingham Club. Address: 56 King George St., Greenwich, London SE10 8QD, UK.

ALEXANDER, Henry (Heinz) Gustav, b. 31 Mar. 1914, Berlin, Germany. Foreign Correspondent. Educ: Dr. Juris, Prague German Univ.; Univs. of Hamburg, Edinburgh, Prague. Publs: Zwischen Bonn und London, 1958. Contbr. to: Der Spiegel; Die Tat; St. Galler Tagblatt. Mbrships: VP, For. Press Assn., London (Pres., 1969-71); PEN; Inst. of Strategic Studies; Int. Schutzverband Deutscher Schriftsteller, Zuerich; Assn. of European Jrnlsts. Address: 5 Salisbury House, Somerset Rd., London SW19 5HY, UK.

ALEXANDER, Ione (Miss), b. 7 May 1892, Jarrell, Tex., USA. Businesswoman; Instructor. Pvte. educ. Contbr. to num. newspapers, mags. & poetry jrnls. Mbrships: Mbr.-at-Large (Advsr.), Exec. Bd., Nat. League of Am. Pen Women, 1974-76; Pres., 7 terms, Kansas City Quill Club; Pres., Kansas City Chapt., Mo. State Writers Guild. Hons. incl: Citation for Cultural Contbn. to Life of State of Mo., Nat. League of Am. Pen Women, 1971; Mo. State Writers Guild Award, for serious poetry, 1968; Num. poetry, prose awards. Address: 507 E. 75th St., Kansas City, MO 64131, USA.

ALEXANDER, (Mrs.) Janet, pen name McNEILL, Janet, b. 14 Sept. 1907, Dublin, Repub. of Ireland. Educ: M.A., St. Andrew's Univ., UK. Novels incl: A Child in the House, 1955; As Strangers Here, 1960; The Maiden Dinosaur, 1964; Talk to Me, 1965; Children's Books incl: My Friend Specs McCann, 1955; This Happy Morning, 1959; The Battle of St. George Without, 1966; The Prisoner in the Park, 1971; The Other People, 1972; We, Three Kings, 1974. Contbr. to: Punch; Homes & Gardens; The Horn Book, etc. Recip., Hon. Book Award for The Battle of St. George Without, Book World Children's Spring Festival, 1968. Address: 3 Grove Park, Redland, Bristol BS6 6PP, UK.

ALEXANDER, John Aleck, b. 21 Nov. 1912, Coumani, Elis, Greece. Professor of History. Educ: A.B., 1934; M.A., 1935, Emory Univ.; Grad. Fellow, Wash. Univ.; Ph.D., Johns Hopkins Univ., 1939. Publs: Potidaea, Its History & Remains, 1963. Contbr. to histl. jrnls., abstracts & symposia; Princeton Dictionary of Classical Archaeology. Address: 1284 Citadel Dr., NE, Atlanta, GA 30324, USA.

ALEXANDER, Peter, b. 1922, Munich, Germany. Professor of Radiobiology; Author. Educ: Univ. Coll. Schl., London, UK; Imperial Coll. of Sci.; D.Sc., Ph.D. Publs: Wool — Its Chemistry & Physics; Fundamentals of Radiobiology; Atomic Radiations & Life. Contbr. to: Sci. Am.; New Sci.; Sunday Times; var. sci. jrnls.; Ed., Biochem. Pharmacol. Address: Old Denshott, Leigh, Reigate, Surrey, UK.

ALEXANDER, Theron, b. 31 Aug. 1913, Springfield, Tenn., USA. Psychologist; Writer. Educ: B.A., M.A., Ph.D., Univ. of Chgo. Publs: Psychotherapy in Our Society, 1963; Children & Adolescents: A Biocultural Approach to Psychological Development, 1969; Human Development in an Urban Age, 1973. Contbr. to: Intellect (Assoc. Ed. for Psychol.); Child Dev. Monographs; Behavioral Sci.; Jrnl. of Genetic Psychol. Mbrships: Fellow, Am. Psychol. Assn.; Soc. for Rsch. in Child Dev.; Sigma Xi; Eastern Psychol. Assn. Address: Temple University, Ritter Hall, Philadelphia, PA 19122, USA.

ALEXANDER, (Lord) William Picken, b. 13 Dec. 1905, Paisley, UK. Educational Administrator. Educ: Ph.D., M.Ed., M.A., B.Sc., Glasgow Univ. Publs: Intelligence Concrete & Abstract; The Educational Needs of Democracy; A Performance Scale for the Measurement of Technical Ability; A Parents' Guide to the Education Act, 1944; Education in England; Towards a New Education Act, 1969; Councils & Education Press Ltd. Contbr. to: Educ.; etc. Mbrships: Sec., Assn. of Educ. Comms., 1945-; Local Authorities Panel of Burnham Comms., 1947-73; Fellow, Coll. of Preceptors, Brit. Psychol. Soc. Hons: Life Peerage, 1974; Kt., 1961; L.H.D., Columbia Univ., 1954. Address: Woodley, 11 Pembroke Rd., Moor Park, Herts. HA6 2HP, UK.

ALEXANDROWICZ, Charles Henry, b. 13 Oct. 1902, Lemberg, Austria. Fellow, Centre of International Studies, Cambridge, UK. Educ: Scottish Coll., Vienna; Dr.Jur., Jagellonian Univ., Cracow, Poland; LL.D., Sydney Univ., Aust.; Barrister-at-Law, Lincoln's Inn, UK. Publs: International Economic Organisations, 1952; Constitutional Developments in India, 1957; World Economic Agencies — Law & Practice, 1962; History of the Law of Nations in the East Indies, 1967; The Law of Global Communications, 1971; The European-African Confrontation, 1973; The Law Making Functions of the Specialised Agencies of the UN, 1974. Contbr. to var. profl. jrnls. Address: 8 Rochester Gdns., Croydon, Surrey, UK.

ALGREN, Nelson, b. 28 Mar. 1909, Detroit, Mich., USA. Writer. Educ: Univ. of Ill., Urbana, 1927-31. Publs. incl: (novels) Somebody in Boots, 1935; Never Come Morning, 1942; The Man with the Golden Arm, 1949; A Walk on the Wild Side, 1955; The Neon Wilderness (short stories), 1946; Chicago: City on the Make, 1951; Conversations with Nelson Algren, 1963; Notes from a Sea-Diary: Hemingway All the Way, 1965; Ed., Nelson Algren's Own Book of Lonesome Monsters, 1960. Contbr. to var. mags, newspapers, etc. Hons: Grant, Nat. Inst. of Arts & Letters, 1947; Newberry Lib. Fellowship, 1947; Nat. Book Award, 1950. Address: 1958 West Evergreen, Chgo., IL 60622, USA.

AL-HIMYARI, Basim Mohammed, b. 30 Sept. 1944, Baghdad, Iraq. Management Consultant. Educ: Higher Nat. Dip. in Bus. Studies, Bournemouth Coll. of Technol., UK, 1968. Contbr. to: Commerce (Baghdad Chmbr. of Comm.); Al-Sinai (Iraqi Fed. of Inds.). Mbrships: Assoc., Brit. Inst. of Mgmt.; Assn. of Iraqi Mgrs. Address: 534-1-20 Adal Quarter, Baghdad, Iraq.

ALI, Ahmed, b. 1 July 1910, Delhi, India. Writer; Teacher; Diplomat. Educ: M.A. Publs. incl: Twilight in Delhi, 1940; Flaming Earth, 1949; Purple Gold Mountain, 1960; Ocean of Night, 1964; Short Stories in Urdu (5 vols.) 1934-44; Ghalib: Selected Poems, 1969; The Golden Tradition, 1973. Contbr. to: New Writing; Penguin New Writing; Atlantic Monthly; Jrnl. S. Asian Lit.; Eastern Horizon; Illustrated Weekly of India; New Directions. Mbrships: Indian Progressive Writers Movement (co-founder). Address: 21-A Faran, Hyder Ali Road, Karachi — 5, Pakistan.

ALISKY, Marvin Michael Howard, b. 12 Mar. 1923, Kansas City, Mo., USA. University Professor; Writer. Educ: B.A., 1946, M.A., 1947, Ph.D., Latin Am. Politics, Univ. of Tex., 1953; Cert., Instituto Tecnologico de Monterrey, Mexico, 1951. Publs. incl: Latin American Journalism Bibliography, Mexico, 1958, reprinted USA 1972; The

Foreign Press, 1964, 2nd ed. 1970; Who's Who in Mexican Government, 1969; Uruguay: A Comtemporary Survey, USA & UK, 1970; Govt. of Mex. State of Sonora, Govt. of Mex. State of Nuevo Leon, 1971; Peruvian Political Perpsective, 1972. Contbr. num. articles to mags., 1950—. Mbrships. incl: Pres. Ariz., Sigma Delta Chi Soc. of Profl. Jrnlsts., 1958; Schlrship. Chmn., Inter-Am. Press Assn. Hons: Fulbright Prof., Nat. Univ. of Nicaragua & Cath. Univ., Lima, Peru. Address: Dept. of Pol. Sci., Ariz. State Univ., Tempe, AZ 85281, USA.

ALLAN, Elkan, b. London, UK. Reporter; Feature Writer; Interviewer; Script Writer; Freelance Film Director; Columnist. Publs: Ed., Living Opinion, 1947; Good Listening, 1948; Off You Go, 1968; Love in Our Time, 1969; The Sunday Times Guide to Movies on Television, 1973. Contbr. to: Daily Express; Odhams; BBC; Rediffusion; Sunday Times. Mbrships: NUJ; S.F.T.A. Address: c/o Sunday Times, 200 Gray's Inn Rd., London WC1, UK.

ALLAN, Mabel Esther, pen names ESTORIL, Jean; PILGRIM, Anne; HAGON, Priscilla; b. 11 Feb. 1915, Wallasey, Cheshire, UK. Author. Publs. incl: The May Day Mystery, 1971; Time to Go Back, 1972; An Island in a Green Sea, 1972 & 73; The Wood Street Helpers, 1973; The Secret Players, 1974; Ship of Danger, 1974; The Night Wind, 1974; Bridge of Friendship, 1975. Mbrships: English Speaking Union; Crime Writers' Assn.; Mystery Writers of Am. Hons: Best Children's Book of Year, France, 1960; Scroll Mystery Writers of Am., 1972; Honor Book in Boston Globe Horn awards, 1973. Agents: John Farquharson, Ltd., London, UK; Julian Bach Agency, Inc., N.Y., USA. Address: Glengarth, 11 Oldfield Way, Heswall, Wirral, Merseyside L60 6RQ, UK.

ALLAN, Mea, b. 23 June 1909, Bearsden, Dunbartonshire, UK. Writer. Educ: Ctrl. Schl. of Speech Trng. & Dramatic Art, London. Publs. incl: Base Rumour, 1962; The Tradescants: their Plants, Gardens & Museum (1570-1662), 1964; The Hookers of Kew, 1967; Fisons Guide to Gardens, 1970; Tom's Weeds, the Story of Rochford's & their House Plants, 1970; Palgrave of Arabia, 1972; E.A. Bowles & his Garden at Myddelton House, 1973; Plants that Changed our Gardens, 1974. Contbr. to var. mags. & jrnls. Mbrships: Royal Hort. Soc.; Soc. of Authors. Address: West Wood, Walberswick, Southwold, Suffolk, UK.

ALLAUN, Frank, b. 27 Feb. 1913, Manchester, UK. Member of Parliament; Writer. Educ: B.Comm. (External), Univ. of London. Publs: Heartbreak Housing; No Place Like Home; Stop the H-Bomb Race. Contbr. to: Tribune; Guardian; Labour Weekly; New Statesman. Address: 1 South Drive, Manchester 21, UK.

ALLBEURY Theo Edward le Bouthillier, pen names FINCH, Oliver; BUTLER, Richard, b. 24 Oct. 1917, Stockport, UK. Marketing & Public Relations Consultant. Publs: A Choice of Enemies, 1973; Snowball, 1974; Palomino Blonde, 1975; Where All the Girls are Sweeter, 1975; The Special Collection, 1975. Contbr. to: Punch; Fin. Times; Computer Wkly.; Mgmt. Today; Photography. Agent: Curtis Brown. Address: Cheriton House, Furnace Lane, Lamberhurst, Tunbridge Wells, Kent, UK.

ALLEGRO, John Marco, b. 17 Feb. 1923, London, UK. Author. Educ: B.A.(Hons.), M.A., Manchester Univ.; Oxford Univ. Publs: The Dead Sea Scrolls, 1956, 2nd ed., 1964; The People of the Dead Sea Scrolls, 1958; The Treasure of the Copper Scroll, 1960, 2nd ed., 1964; Search in the Desert, 1964; The Shapira Affair, 1964; Discoveries in the Deserts of Judah: Qumran Cave 4, 1968; The Sacred Mushroom & the Cross, 1970; The End of a Road, 1970; The Chosen People, 1971; Lost Languages, 1975. Contbr. to var. acad. jrnls. on Semitic philol. & lit. Hons. incl: Leverhulme Rsch. Award, 1958. Address: Craigmore, Ballasalla, Isle of Man, UK.

ALLEN, Alfred John, pen name HELLINGS, David, b. 20 Mar. 1930, London, UK. Political, Economic & Social Research Consultant; Parliamentary Adviser. Educ: B.Sc., Univ. Coll., London. Publs: The English Voter, 1964; Management & Men, 1967; The Woman Director — Women in Top Jobs, 1971. Contbr. to: Economist; Guardian; Birmingham Post; Parliamentary Affairs; Pol. Studies; Times Higher Educ. Supplement; New Outlook; Director; Pol. & Econ. Planning Bulletins; Insight — The Facts in Pols.; etc. Mbrships: Soc. of Authors; Pol. Studies Assn.;

Royal Statistical Soc. Address: 194-5 Palace Chambers, Bridge St., London SW1A 2JT, UK.

ALLEN, Charles Edmund, b. 6 May 1915, Nottingham, UK. Manufacturer's Agent; Specialist on Motorcycle History. Publs: First Vintage Motorcycle Roadtest Journal, 1973; Second Vintage Motorcycle Roadtest Journal, 1974. Contbr. to Motorcycle Sport. Fndr., Vintage Motorcycle Club. Recip., British Empire Medal. Address: 10 Woodsend Close, Burton Joyce, Nottingham, UK.

ALLEN, Clifford Edward, b. 23 Oct. 1902, Gravesend, UK. Retired Consultant Psychiatrist. Educ: M.B.B.S., M.D., Univ. of London; M.R.C.S.; M.R.C.P. Publs: Modern Discoveries in Medical Psychology, 1937, 3rd ed., 1965; The Sexual Perversions & Abnormalities, 1940; Homosexuality, 1958; A Textbook of Psychosexual Disorders, 1962; Passing Examinations; Passing School Examinations; Planning a Career; (novels) The Palm Grove; The Shorn Lamb; The Underlings; The Untroubled Wolves; Trampled Pastures; The Dark Places. Contbr. to: Ency. Britannica; Nature; Lancet; Brit. Med. Jrnl.; Int. Jrnl. of Sexol.; etc. Mbrships. incl: Fndr., F.R.C. Psych.; Fellow, Royal Soc. of Med.; Brit. Med. Assn. Address: The Lodge, Llwyn Offa, Mold, Clwyd, N. Wales, UK.

ALLEN, David Elliston, b. 17 Jan. 1932, Southport, Lancs., UK. Scientific Administrator. Educ: M.A., Univ. of Cambridge; London Schl. of Econs. Publs: British Tastes, 1968; The Victorian Fern Craze, 1969. Contbr. to: Country Life; Var. learned jrnls. Mbrships: Past Hon. Gen. Sec., Botan. Soc. of the Brit. Isles; Mkt. Rsch. Soc.; Royal Statistical Soc.; Econ. Hist. Soc. Agent: Murray Pollinger. Address: Lesney Cottage, Middle Rd., Winchester, Hants., UK.

ALLEN, Donald Emerson, b. 9 June 1917, Columbus, Ohio, USA. Professor of Sociology, Oklahoma State University. Educ: Ohio State Univ.; Univ. of Mo.; B.A.; M.A.; Ph.D. Publs: (4 chapts. in) Social Behavior, 1965, Portuguese ed., O Comportamento Social, 1970; From Man to Society: Introduction to Sociology (w. G. Acuff & L. Taylor), 1973; Conversation Analysis: Sociology of Talk with R. Guy, 1974. Contbr. to: Am. Jrnl. of Sociol.; Soc. Forces; Int. Jrnl. of Sociol. of the Family; Int. Jrnl. of Comparative Sociol.; Can. Sociol. Review. Mbrships. incl: Am. Sociol. Assn.; Int. Sociol. Assn.; Cons., VISTA; Cons., Headstart. Address: 1012 W. Eskridge Ave., Stillwater, OK 74074, USA.

ALLEN, Eric, pen name BUSBY, Jonathan, b. 30 Sept. 1916, Roland, Okla., USA. Writer. Educ: jrnlsm. courses, Northeastern State Coll., Tahlequah, Okla. Publs., 18 novels inclng: Hangtree Country, 1958, 2nd ed., 1965; Shadow of Quantrill's Flag, 1960; Like Wild, 1962; God Walks the Dark Hills, 1966, in 6th ed.; Voices in the Wind, 1967, in 6th ed.; Tales & Legends of the Ozarks, 1974; Crossfire in the Cooksons, 1974. Contbr. short stories & articles to num. mags. Mbrships: Western Writers of Am.; Okla. Press Assn. Recip., var. hons. Address: P.O. Box 621, Ft. Smith, AK, USA.

ALLEN, Gay Wilson, b. 1903, Lake Junaluska, N.C., USA. Professor of English. Educ: Duke Univ.; Univ. of Wis.; A.B.; M.A.; Ph.D. Publs. incl: American Prosody; Walt Whitman Handbook; Co-Ed., Masters of American Literature; The Solitary Singer; Ed., Walt Whitman Abroad; Co-Ed., Walt Whitman's Poems; William James: A Biography, 1967; Herman Melville & His World, 1970; A Reader's Guide to Walt Whitman, 1970. The New Walt Whitman Handbook, 1975. Contbr. to: Saturday Review; N.Y. Times Book Review; N.Y. Herald Tribune Books; New Repub.; Am. Lit.; Ency. Britannica; other encys. Mbr., PEN, N.Y. Address: 454 Grove St., Oradell, NJ 07649, USA.

ALLEN, Geoffrey Francis, b. 25 Aug. 1902, Mobberley, UK. Retired Anglican Bishop. Educ: B.A., 1925, M.A., 1928, Ribon Hall, Univ. Coll., Oxford. Publs: Tell John (w. Rev. Canon John McKay), 1932; He that Cometh, 1932; Christ the Victorious, 1935; The Courage to be Real, 1938; Law with Liberty, 1942. Contbr. to: The Churches & Christian Unity, 1963; The Mod. Churchman; Ch. Quarterly Review, etc. Mbrships: Athenaeum Club; Engl. Speaking Union. Hons: D.D., Lambeth, 1947; Hon. Fellow, Lincoln Coll., Oxford, 1959. Address: The Knowle, Deddington, Oxford OX5 4TB, UK.

ALLEN, George Cyril, b. 1900, Kenilworth, Warwicks., UK. Professor of Political Economy. Educ: M.Com., Ph.D.,

Univ. of Birmingham. Publs. incl: British Industries & their Organisation; A Short Economic History of Modern Japan; Japan; The Hungry Guest; Japan's Economic Expansion; Western Enterprise in Far Eastern Economic Development; Western Enterprise in Indonesia & Malaya; The Structure of Industry in Britain; Japan As a Market & Source of Supply; Monopoly & Restrictive Practices. Contbr. to: Econ. Jrnl.; Economica; Kyklos; Spectator; etc. Mbrships: F.B.A.; Reform Club. Hons: C.B.E.; Order of the Rising Sun, 3rd Class. Address: Quinces, Beech Close, Cobham, Surrey, UK.

ALLEN, Harry Cranbrook, b. 23 Mar. 1917, Watford, UK. Professor of American Studies. Educ: M.A., Univ. of Oxford, 1938. Publs. incl: Great Britain & the United States: A History of Anglo-American Relations, 1783-1952, 1954; Bush & Backwoods: A Comparison of the Frontier in Australia & the United States, 1959; The Anglo-American Predicament: The British Commonwealth, The United States & European Unity, 1960; A Concise History of the United States, 1970. Mbrships: Fndr. Mbr., & Comm., Brit. Assn. for Am. Studies, Chmn., 1974—; Fellow, Royal Histl. Soc. Address: 13 Riverside Close, Lower Hellesdon, Norwich, Norfolk NR6 5AU, UK.

ALLEN, Jerry, b. 1911, Benton, Wis., USA. Author; Journalist. Educ: B.A., Univ. of Wis.; M.S., Columbia Univ. Publs: Hearth in the Snow, 1952; The Adventures of Mark Twain, 1954; The Thunder & the Sunshine, 1958; The Sea Years of Joseph Conrad, 1965; Ed., Great Short Works of Joseph Conrad; Great Short Works of Herman Melville; Moby Dick; The Picture of Dorian Gray, 1966. Contbr. to: Ency. Britannica; Columbia Univ. Forum; Rdrs. Digest; Nat. Geogl. Mag.; Paris Herald; Brit. & C'wlth. newspapers; etc. Mbrships. incl: Authors' Guild; Authors' League; Women in Communications. Hons. incl: Nat. Inst. Arts & Letters Award, 1969; Academie de Marine, France, Silver Medal, 1969; Chancellor's Award, Univ. of Wis., 1971. Agent: McIntosh & Otis Inc. Address: 240 Central Park South, N.Y., NY 10019, USA.

ALLEN, John Bryan Lorton, b. 1921, Leicester, UK. Headmaster. Educ: Selwyn Coll., Cambridge; Univs. of Lille, London & Reading; M.A.; M.Ed.; Lic.ès Lettres; Ph.D. Publs: Desk Book of Plain English (w. A. W. Rowe), 1965; Headship in the 70's, 1969; The French Oral Examinations, 1969; Print Collecting, 1970; Italian Oral Exam, 1973; English for the Commerce Student, 1974. Contbr. to: Am. Art Quarterly; Antique Dealers' & Collectors' Guide; Educ.; Times Educl. Supplement. Mbr., Headmasters' Assn. Address: 8 Charminster, Craneswater Park, Southsea, Hants., UK.

ALLEN, John Eldridge, b. 11 Sept. 1911, Morehead City, N.C., USA. Researcher; Writer; Editor. Educ: B.B.A., Univ. of Miami, Coral Gables, Fla., 1934; M.A., Geo. Wash. Univ., Wash. D.C., 1937. Contbr. to: U.S. Congressional Records & Hearings Record Books of Congressional sub-comms. (Var. monographs); monthly Bulletins, DC Soc. SAR (Ed., 1952-53); D.C. Histl. Soc. Annual Reports (1949-52); Ed. & Indexer, Allen Personal Papers and Jrnls., 1973—. Mbrships. incl: D.C. Histl. Soc. (VP, 1953-54); Lincoln Histl. Grp., D.C. (Pres., 1951-52); Renaissance Soc. of Am. (Fndr. Mbr.). Hons. incl: Abraham Lincoln Medallion, 1960. Address: 7339 S.W. 82nd St., South Miami, FL 33143, USA.

ALLEN, John Elliston, pen names DANFORTH, Paul M; AQUARIUS; BISONIUS, b. 7 Feb. 1921, London, UK. Specialist in Aeronautics. Educ: Northants Engrng. Coll.; Univ. of London; B.Sc.; D.N.E.C. Publs: Aerodynamics — A Space-Age Survey, 1963; Future of Aeronautics, 1970; Transport Control UK, 1970; Transportation, 1970; Space Flight Technology, 1960. Contbr. to: Fin. Times; Times; Energy & Humanity; Futures; Flight Int.; etc. Mbrships. incl: F.R.S.A.; Royal Aeronautical Soc.; Hons. incl: J.E. Hodgson Prize, 1959; Manchester Assn. of Engrs., Constantine Medal, 1966. Address: 2 Cradhurst, Westcott, Dorking, Surrey RH4 3NU, UK.

ALLEN, Kenneth S., pen names CARTER, Avis Murton; SCOTT, Alastair, b. 1913, Southend-on-Sea, UK. Author. Publs. incl: Story of London Town; Exploring the Cinema; World's Greatest Sea Disasters; The Wild West; Fighting Men & Their Uniforms. The Story of Gunpowder; The Wars of the Roses; The Battle of the Atlantic; Transporting People; Transporting Goods; Ships of Long Ago; Knights & Castles; Pirates & Buccaneers; Fighting Ships; The Vikings; Earthquakes & Volcanoes; One Day in Rome; Look In Book of Ships; Look In Book of Railways;

That Bounty Bastard! Address: 74 Eastbury Rd., Northwood, Middx., UK.

ALLEN, Kevin John, b. 25 Nov. 1941, Warrington, UK. University Lecturer. Educ: B.A., Univ. of Nottingham; Univ. of Newcastle. Publs: Regional Policy in EFTA: An Examination of the Growth Centre Idea (w. T. Hermansen), 1968; Nationalised Industries (w. G. L. Reid), 1970; Regional Problems & Policies in Italy & France (w. M. C. Maclennan), 1971; Nationalised Industries: The Fuel Sector (w. G. L. Reid & D. J. Harris), 1973; An Introduction to the Italian Economy (w. A. A. Stevenson), 1974. Mbr., Royal C'wlth. Soc. Address: 38 Mitre Rd., Glasgow G14 9LE, UK.

ALLEN, Richard C., b. 24 Jan. 1926, Swampscott, Mass., USA. Professor of Law; Chairman, Dept. of Forensic Sciences; Author. Educ: A.B., Wash. Univ., St. Louis, Mo., 1948; J.D., Schl. of Law, ibid., 1950; LL.M., Univ. of Mich. Law Schl., 1963. Publs: Mental Impairment & Legal Incompetency (co-author), 1968; Readings in Law & Psychiatry (co-author), 1968, 2nd ed., 1975; Legal Rights of the Disabled & Disadvantaged, 1969. Contbr. to: Ed.-in-Chief, M.H. (quarterly jrnl. of Nat. Assn. Mental Hlth.); Menninger Quarterly; Am. Jrnl. Orthopsych.; Fed. Probation; var. law jrnls. & periodicals. Recip., Rosemary F. Dybwad Int. Award for rsch. & writing, mental retardation & law. Address: Geo. Wash. Univ., Wash DC 20052, USA.

ALLEN, Robert Joseph, b. 1902, Indpls., Ind., USA. Professor of English. Educ: Eastern Ill. Normal Schl.; Univs. of Ill. & Harvard; A.B.; M.A.; Ph.D. Publs: The Clubs of Augustan London; Life in 18th Century England; Addison & Steele. Contbr. to books & jrnls., inclng: Review of Engl. Studies; Philol. Quarterly; Harvard Studies & Notes; Pope & His Contemporaries. Mbrships: AAUP; Williams Fac. Club; Williams Club. Address: Cluett Dr., Williamstown, MA, USA.

ALLEN, Steve, occasional pen name, STEVENS, Christopher, b. 26 Dec. 1921, NYC, USA. Entertainer. Publs: Bop Fables, 1955; 14 For Tonight, 1955; The Funny Men, 1956; Wry on the Rocks, 1956; The Girls on the 10th Floor, 1958; The Question Man, 1959; Mark It & Strike It, 1960; Not All of Your Laughter, Not All of Your Tears, 1962; Letter To A Conservative, 1965; The Ground Is Our Table, 1966; Bigger Than A Breadbox, 1967; A Flash of Swallows (under pseudonym), 1969, 2nd ed., 1972; The Wake, 1972; Curses! Or . . . How Never to Be Foiled Again, 1973; Princess Snip Snip & The Puppy Kittens, 1973. Contbr. to num. jrnls. Address: 15201 Burbank Blvd., Van Nuys, CA 91401, USA.

ALLEN, Velta Myrle, b. 9 Feb. 1898, Holmesville, Neb., USA. Poet; Artist; Teacher. Publs. of Poems: Random Treasure, 1947; Within Adobe Walls, 1948; Me & My Shadows, 1948; Poems, 1950; Towards the Horizon, 1952; No Narrow Grooves, 1954; Men . . . Not Angels (epic poem), 1964; Meditation On a Hill Top, 1966. Also a book in prose, w. 28 art pages, Paleography & Scroll Painting, 1964. Contbr. to: Oakland Tribune; Sunshine Mag.; Valley Forge Family Album; K.C. Poetry Mag.; San Fernando Daily Times; Mind Digest; etc. Hons. incl: Award for Meritorious Serv. to Poets & Poetry, 1954; var. poetry, lit., art prizes & awards. Address: 846 Termino Ave., Long Beach, CA 90804, USA.

ALLEN, Victor Thomas, b. 1898, Dubuque, Iowa, USA. Professor of Geology. Educ: Univ. of Minn., Mpls.; Univ. of Calif.; A.B.; M.S.; Ph.D. Publs: This Earth of Ours; Ione Formation of California; Contbr. to var. sci. jrnls. inclng: ECO; Geology; Am. Jrnl. of Sci.; Am. Mineralogist. Address: 94 Roxbury St., Santa Clara, CA 95050, USA.

ALLEN, Walter Ernest, b. 1911, Birmingham, UK. Author. Educ: B.A., Birmingham Univ. Publs: Innocence is Drowned, 1938; Blind Man's Ditch, 1939; Living Space, 1940; Rogue Elephant, 1946; The Black Country, 1946; Arnold Bennet, 1948; Writers on Writing, 1948; Dead Man over All, 1950; The English Novel, 1954; Six Great Novelists, 1955; All in a Lifetime, 1959. Contbr. to: New Statesman; Times Lit. Supplement; Listener; Daily Telegraph; N.Y. Times Book Review. Mbr., Soc. of Authors. Address: 6 Canonbury Sq., London N1, UK.

ALLEN, William Stannard, b. 23 Feb. 1913, Southampton, UK. Writer; Lecturer. Educ: B.A., London Univ. Publs: Living English Structure, 1947, 5th rev. ed., 1974; ditto for Schools, 1958; Living English Speech & Tapes, 1954, 2nd rev. ed., 1964; Living English for the

Arab World, & ditto secondary course (8 yr. course in constant revision, now an audio-visual course, Progressive Living English for the Arab World); (music) Yugoslav Folkdances; BBC Progs., Keep up your English, 1962; Advsr., Walter & Connie, TV series. Contbr. to var. profl. jrnls. Mbrships: Soc. of Authors; Musicians' Union. Address: 4 Tollgate, Merrow, Guildford, Surrey, UK.

ALLENBY, (Rt. Rev.) David Howard Nicholas, b. 28 Jan. 1909, London, UK. Anglican Bishop. Educ: M.A.; House of the Sacred Mission, Kelham, Ordained 1934. Publs: Pray with the Church (w. A. G. Hebert), 1937; Ed., Southwell Review, 1950-57. Contbr. to: Daily Telegraph; Birmingham Post; sev. other jrnls. & newspapers. Mbrships: Royal C'wlth. Soc.; Royal Overseas League. Address: St. Oswald's, The Tything, Worcester WR1 1HR, UK.

ALLOWAY, David Nelson, b. 26 Sept. 1927, Emmaus., Pa., USA. Professor of Sociology. Educ: A.B., Muhlenberg Coll., 1950; M.A., Columbia Univ., 1955; Ph.D., N.Y. Univ., 1965. Publs: A Goodly Heritage, 1964; Economic History of the U.S., 1966; Agony of the Cities, 1970; Minorities & the American City, 1971; The German Community in America, 1975. Contbr. to Ency. Britannica (1964 ed.); Reviewer, Choice mag., Co-ed., special issue on Poverty, Jrnl. of Human Relations. Hons: Best Sr. Thesis, Muhlenberg Coll., 1950. Address: 1303-B Troy Towers, Bloomfield, NJ 07003, USA.

ALLSOPP, Bruce, b. 1912, Oxford, UK. University Reader; Publisher. Educ: B.Arch., Univ. of Liverpool; Dip. C.D. Publs. incl: Possessed; The Naked Flame; Style in the Visual Arts; The Future of the Arts; A General History of Architecture; A History of Renaissance Architecture; Ecological Morality, Towards a Humane Architecture; Return of the Pagan. Contbr. to: R.I.B.A. Jrnl.; etc. Mbrships. incl: F.R.I.B.A.; F.S.A.; Soc. of Arch. Histns. of GB (Chmn., 1959-65); Art Workers Guild (Master, 1970). Address: Woodburn, Batt House Rd., Stocksfield, Northumberland NE43 7QZ, UK.

ALLUM, Nancy Patricia Eaton (Mrs. Draper), b. Chiswick, London, UK. Author; Journalist; Reviewer. Publs: Monica Joins the WRAC, 1961; A Commission in the Women's Royal Army Corps, 1961; Monica Takes A Commission, 1965; Spina Bifida, 1975. Contbr. to: The Times; Autocar; SHE; BBC; Books & Bookmen; Ctrl. Off. of Info. Mbrships: Press Club, London; Int. Assn. of Women & Home Page Jrnlsts.; Int. PEN. Address: 24 Gordon Mansions, Huntley St., London WC1, UK.

ALLWARD, Maurice Frank, pen name COMMEN-TATOR, b. 1923, London, UK. Technical Publications Executive. Publs: Wings for Tomorrow (w. J. W. R. Taylor); Spitfire (w. J. W. R. Taylor); Encyclopedia of Space; Combat Aircraft of the World; Triumphs of Flight; Safety in the Air; A Source Book of Aircraft; Lore of Flight; Daily Mirror Book of Space; The Story of Flight; Italian Fighting Aircraft 1939-45; Hurricane Special. Contbr. to: Flight; Spaceflight; Ian Allen Aerospace Annual; Sunday Times Mag.; Air Pictorial; Jane's All the World's Aircraft. Address: Satellite Two, 107 Byng Dr., Potters Bar, Herts., UK.

ALLWOOD, Martin Samuel, b. 13 Apr. 1916, Jönköping, Sweden. Author; Translator; Professor. Educ: B.A., Cambridge Univ., UK, 1938; M.A., Columbia Univ., USA, 1949; Dr.rer.pol., Univ. of Darmstadt, W. Germany, 1953. Publs. incl: Middlevillage, 1943; The Cemetery of the Cathedrals, 1945; 20th Century Scandinavian Poetry, 1950; Bombed City, Europe, 1954; Toward A New Sociology, 1964; American & British, 1964; Collected English Poems, 1965; Poems in March & Other Months, 1971; augusti-mönster, 1972; Lillans Dagbok, 1972; Way Out Of My Mind, 1973. Contbr. to: Horisont. Mbr., Swedish Soc. of Authors. Recip., Lifetime Grant, Sveriges Författarfond. Address: Marston Hill, 560 41 Mullsjö, Sweden.

ALMANSA, Jose Manuel, b. 7 Apr. 1938, Malaga, Spain. University Professor & Administrator; Author. Educ: Dr. Law. Publs: La Participacion del Trabajador en la Administracion de la Empresa, 1965; La Relacion Laboral del Capitan de la Marina Mercante, 1967; El Despido Nulo, 1968; Derecho de la Seguridad Social, 1973. Contbr. to: Revista de Politica Social; Revista Iberoamericana de Seguridad Social; Revista de Trabajo. Address: Calle Alemania No. 6, Valencia 10, Spain.

ALNAES, Finn, b. 20 Jan. 1932, Baerum, Oslo, Norway. Author. Educ: Ctrl. Schl. of Speech Trng. & Dramatic Art & Webber Douglas Schl. of Singing &

Dramatic Art, London, UK; Nat. Theatre, Oslo, Norway. Publs: Koloss (novel), 1963; Gemini (novel), 1968; Festningen Faller (novel), 1971; On the Rack of Freedom (essays), 1972. Contbr. to: Vinduet; Samtiden; also sev. newspapers. Mbrships: PEN, Norwegian Ctr.; Norwegian Assn. Writers; Norwegian Alliance of Conservation of Nature. Hons: 1st Prize, Norwegian Novel Competition, 1963; Prize, Norwegian Coun. of Culture, 1968; Prize, Assn. of Norwegian Lit. Critics, 1968; Prize, Norwegian Booksellers, 1969. Address: Vangen, 2372 Bröttum, Norway.

ALONSO, Dámaso, b. 1898, Madrid, Spain. University Professor; Writer. Educ: Ph.D, Madrid Univ. Publs. incl: Góngora y el Polifemo (criticism), 1960, 3rd ed., 1967; Dos españoles del Siglo de Oro, 1960; Primavera temprana de la literatura europea, 1961; Cuatro poetas españoles, 1962; Del Siglo de Oro a este Siglo de siglas, 1962, 2nd ed., 1968; Poemas escogidos (poetry), 1969; En Torno a Lope (criticism), 1972; Obras Completas I-III (poetry), 1971-74; transls. of James Joyce, G. M. Hopkins & von Wartburg. Mbrships. incl: Dir., Royal Spanish Acad. Recip., num. hon. degrees. Address: Avenida A. Alcocer 23, Madrid 16, Spain.

ALONSO OLEA, Manuel, b. 19 June 1924, Melilla, Spain. Professor of Law. Educ: Licenciado en Derecho, 1946; Dr. en Derecho, 1952. Publs: Introduccion al Derecho del Trabajo, 1962, 3rd ed., 1974; Derecho del Trabajo, 1971, 3rd ed., 1974; Derecho Processal del Trabajo, 1969, 1972; Instituciones de Seguridad Social, 1959, 5th ed. 1974. Contbr. to all maj. Spanish & Latin Am. periodicals on Labor Law & Social Security. Mbrships: Exec. Comm., Int. Assn. for Labor Law & Social Security; Int. Assn. of Admstv. Scis.; Pres., Assn. Española de Derecho del Trabajo. Address: Fernando el Catolica 77, Madrid (15), Spain.

ALÓS, Concha, b. 22 May 1922, Valencia, Spain. Educ: Tchrs. Cert. Publs: Los enanos, 1963; Los cien pájaros, 1964; Las hogueras, 1965; El caballo rojo, 1967; La madama, 1969; Rey de gatos, 1972. Contbr. to: La Vanguardia (Barcelona newspaper); Destino mag. Mbr., Soc. of Authors of Spain. Hons: Spanish Readers Digest Prize for Los Enanos, 1964; Planeta Prize for Las hogueras,1964. Address: Calle Martinez de la Rosa 44, sobreático 2, Barcelona 12, Spain.

ALPERS, Antony, b. 10 Sept. 1919, Christchurch, NZ. University Professor. Publs: Katherine Mansfield, 1953; Dolphins, 1960; Maori Myths, 1964; Legends of the South Seas, 1970. Address: Dept. of English, Queen's Univ., Kingston, Ont., Can.

ALPORT, (Rt. Hon. Lord) Cuthbert James McCall, b. 22 Mar. 1912, Johannesburg, S. Africa. Banker. Educ: Pembroke Coll., Cambridge, UK. Publs: Kingdoms in Partnership, 1937; Hope in Africa, 1952; The Sudden Assignment, 1965. Contbr. to: Spectator; Sunday Times; 19th Century; BBC. Barrister-at-Law, Middle Temple. Hons: Privy Counsellor; Pro Chancellor, City Univ. Address: Cross House, Layer de la Haye, Colchester, Essex, UK.

AL-SAMARIE, Saeid, b. 6 Apr. 1930, Samarra, Iraq. Research Economist. Educ: B.Sc., Econs., Coll. of Arts & Sci. Publs: Means of Industrialization in Iraq; Iraq & Sterling Area; Monetary & Banking System in Iraq; Public Sector in Iraq; Economic History of Iraq; European Common Market & Its Effect on the Economics of Iraq & Other Arab Countries. Contbr. to: Econ. Review, Iraq News Agcy., Baghdad. Mbr., Iraqi Economists Assn. Address: Al-Mansour City, House No. 13/6/20, Baghdad, Iraq.

AL-SIFOU, Walid Ismail, b. 1 July 1945, Mosul, Iraq. Lecturer. Educ: B.Sc. (Econs. & Pol.). Contbr. to: The Univ., The Socialist, (Mosul Univ.); The Economist (Iraqi Soc. of Econs.); Baghdad Commercial Mag.; Mosul Commercial Mag. Mbr., Iraqi Soc. of Econs. Address: Dept. of Agricl. Economics & Extension Coll. of Agric. & Forestry, Mosul Univ., Hammam-Al-Alil, Mosul, Iraq.

ALSOP, Joseph Wright, b. 11 Oct. 1910, Avon, Conn., USA. Journalist; Author. Educ: B.A., Harvard Univ. Publs: The 168 Days (w. Turner Catledge); Men Around the President (w. Robert Kintner), 1938; The American White Paper (w. Kintner), 1940; We Accuse (w. Stewart Alsop), 1955; The Reporter's Trade (w. Stewart Alsop), 1958; From the Silent Earth, 1964. Hons: Legion of Merit; Order of Cloud Banner, China. Address: 2720 Dumbarton Ave. N.W., Wash. DC 10007, USA.

ALSPACH, Russell K, b. 22 Feb. 1901, Phila., Pa., USA. Retired US Army Officer; University Professor Emeritus of English. Educ: B.A., M.A., Ph.D., Univ. of Pa., Phila. Publs: Irish Poetry from the English Invasion to 1798, 1943, rev. ed., 1964; Variorum Edition of the Poetry of W. B. Yeats (w. P. Allt), 1957; Variorum Edition of the Plays of W. B. Yeats, 1965. Contbr. to: Mod. Lang. Notes; Jrnl. of Am. Folklore; Shakespeare Assn. Bulletin; sev. other profl. jrnls. Mbrships. incl: MLA; AAUP; Am. Folklore Soc. Address: 324 Pomeroy Lane, Amherst, MA 01002, USA.

ALSTON, (Arthur) Rex, b. 1901. Broadcaster; Journalist. Educ: Univ. of Cambridge. Publs: Taking the Air, 1950; Over to Rex Alston, 1953; Test Commentary, 1956; Watching Cricket, 1962. Mbr., M.C.C. Address: Ryders, Oakwood Hill, Dorking, Surrey RH5 5NB, UK.

ALTHOFF, Phillip Stanley, b. 30 Aug. 1941, Centralia, Ill., USA. University Professor. Educ: B.A., Ill. State Univ., 1963; M.A., 1966, Ph.D., 1970, Univ. of Iowa. Publs: An Introduction to Political Sociology (co-author), 1971; Preventing Nuclear Theft: Guidelines for Industry & Government (co-ed.), 1972. Contbr. to: Jrnl. of Pol.; Environment & Behavior; Jrnlsm. Quarterly; Rocky Mtn. Social Sci. Jrnl.; Am. Pol. Quarterly; Nat. Civic Review; Social Sci. Quarterly; Int. Jrnl.; Papers of Mich. Acad. of Sci., Arts & Letters; Midwest Jrnl. of Pol. Sci. Address: Dept. of Political Science, Kansas State University, Manhattan, KS 66506, USA.

ALTMAN, Wilfred, b. 13 Oct. 1927. Journalist; Author; Business Consultant; Chairman, Coordinated Marketing Services Ltd. Educ: Polytechnic, London; City Lit. Inst., London. Publs: Industrial & Economic Tracts for Professional Institutes. Contbr. to: Times; Fin. Times; Daily Mail; Advt. Quarterly; Adweek Campaign, Manchester Evening News; Super Marketing; Investors' Chronicle. Mbr., Soc. of Authors. Address: 21 Gt. Portland St., London W1N 5DB, UK.

ALUKO, Timothy Mofolorunso, b. 14 June 1918, Ilesha, Nigeria. Civil Engineer. Educ: Higher Coll., Yaba, Lagos; London Univ.; B.Sc.(Eng.) 1948; Dip., Town Planning, 1950; M.Sc.(Eng.), Univ. of Newcastle-upon-Tyne, 1969. Publs: One Man, One Wife, 1959; One Man, One Matchet, 1964; Kinsman & Foreman, 1966; Chief the Honourable Minister, 1970; His Worshipful Majesty, 1973. Contbr. to profl. jrnls. Hons: O.B.E., 1963. Address: 1 Igbobi Coll. Access, Igbobi, Lagos, Nigeria.

ALVAREZ, Alfred, b. 1929, London, UK. Poet, Novelist & Critic. Educ: M.A., Corpus Christi Coll., Oxford. Publs: The Shaping Spirit, 1958; Stewards of Excellence, (USA); The School of Donne, 1961; The New Poetry, 1962; Under Pressure, 1965; Beyond all this Fiddle, 1968; Lost, 1968; Penguin Modern Poets 18, 1970; The Savage God, 1971; Apparition, 1971; Beckett, 1973; Hers, 1974; (film script) The Anarchist. Contbr. to: Observer; etc. Recip., Vachel Lindsay Prize for Poetry, 1961. Address: c/o The Observer, London EC4, UK.

ALVIN, Juliette Louise, b. Versailles, France. Musician; Broadcaster; Lecturer. Educ: Conservatoire National de Musique, Paris. Soloist with principal philharmonic orchestras. Publs. incl: Rudiments of Music & Instrumental Technique; Cello Tutor for Beginners, Book I, 1955, Book II, 1958; Music for the Handicapped Child, 1965; Research Project on Music Therapy with Subnormal Boys, 1970; Music Therapy, 1975. Contbr. to: Special Educ.; World's Sci. Review; Am. Jrnl. of Mental Deficiency; BBC; Enfance; Froebel Bulletin; etc. Mbrships: Brit. Soc. for Music Therapy, Chmn. & Fndr; Amer. Nat. Assn. for Music Therapy. Address: 48 Lancaster Rd., Highgate, London N6, UK.

ALY, Bower, b. 1903, Crystal City, Mo., USA. Professor of Speech (retired). Educ: B.S., A.M., Ph.D.; S.E. Mo. State Coll.; Columbia, Mo., Calif., Univs. Publs: The Rhetoric of Alexander Hamilton, 1941; Alexander Hamilton: Selections Representing His Life, His Thought & His Style, 1957; The Fundamentals of Speaking (co-author), 1951; Speeches in English (co-author), 1968; A Rhetoric of Public Speaking (co-author), 1973. Contbr. to: Quarterly Jrnl. Speech; Discussion & Debate Manual. Mbrships: Comm. Discussion & Debate Materials from 1934 (Exec. Sec.); Speech Assn. Am., 1944 (Pres.). Address: 1138 E. 22nd Ave., Eugene, OR, USA.

AMABILE, George, b. 29 May 1936, Jersey City, N.J., USA. Associate Professor of English. Educ: A.B., Amherst

Coll., 1957; M.A., Univ. of Minn., Mpls., 1961; Ph.D., Univ. of Conn., Storrs, 1969. Publs: Blood Ties, 1972. Contbr. to: Best Poems of 1964, 1965; The New Yorker Book of Poems, 1969; Made In Canada, New Poems of the '70s, 1970; num. lit. jrnls. Mbrships: League of Can. Poets; CPPA; Poets & Writers; Western Can. Publrs. Assn. Address: No. 608-77 University Crescent, Winnipeg, Man. R3T 2N5, Canada.

AMADO, Jorge, b. 10 Aug. 1912, Bahia, Ferradas, Brazil. Writer. Educ: LL.D., Brazil Law Univ., Rio de Janeiro. Publs: (Engl. transls. of novels in Portuguese) The Violent Land; Gabriela, Clove & Cinnamon; Shepherds of the Night; Quincas Wateryell; Dona Flor & Her Two Husbands; Tent of Miracles; & 13 other novels transl'd. into 36 langs. Mbrships. incl: Brazilian Acad. Letters; num. int. writers' socs. Hons. incl: Stalin Int. Peace Prize; sev. lit. prizes Brazil, France, Italy, etc. Address: rua Alagoinhas 33, Rio Vermelho Salvador, Bahia 40000, Brazil.

AMANKWAH, Harrison Alexander, b. 19 Apr. 1939, Kadjebi-Akan, Ghana. Lecturer. Educ: B.A.; LL.B.; LL.M. Contbr. to: Cornell Int. Law Jrnl.; Univ. of Ghana Law Jrnl.; Daily Graphic; W. Africa Market Review; Focus Mag. Mbr., Ghana Bar Assn. Recip., Rothstein Int. Affairs Prize, Schl. of Law, Cornell Univ., Ithaca, N.Y., USA, 1968. Address: Fac. of Soc. Scis., Univ. of Sic. & Technol., Kumasi, Ashanti, Ghana.

AMANN, Victor Francis, b. 29 Aug. 1927, Richardton, N.D., USA. Agricultural Economist. Educ: B.S., 1956, Ph.D., 1962, Univ. of Minn. Publs: Co-Ed., Nutrition & Food in An African Economy (2 vols.), 1972; Ed., Agricultural Policy Issues in East Africa, 1973; Ed., Agricultural Employment & Labour Migration in East Africa, 1974; Co-Ed., Project Appraisal & Evaluation in Agriculture, 1974. Contbr. to: E. Africa Jrnl. of Rural Dev. (Ed., 1970-); E. African Geogl. Review; etc. Mbrships: Am. Agric. Econs. Assn.; E. Africa Agric. Econs. Soc.; Int. Agric. Econs. Soc. Address: Office of Int. Programs, W.Va. Univ., Morgantown, WV 25606, USA.

AMBATSIS, Jannis, b. 2 Jan. 1926, Athens, Greece. Immigration & Naturalization Official; Author. Educ: Univ. of Stockholm. Publs. incl: Grekisk Mat, 1963; Grekland, 1964; Grekland i Fickan (phrasebook), 1965; Levande Grekland, 1966; Citronträdets dotter, 1964; Nygrekiska Sägner och Legender, 1967; Grekiska Folkvisor, 1968; Nygrekisk Litteratur, 1970, Grekiska Folksagor, 1975; Invandrar-folklor, 1975. Contbr. to var. works. Mbrships: Swedish Soc. of Authors; Minerva; Swedish Soc. of Translators; PEN. Recip., Swedish Authors: Fund Prize. Address: Bollhusgränd 6[1], 11131 Stockholm, Sweden.

AMBLER, Eric, b. 1909, London, UK. Author of Novels & Screenplays. Educ: London Univ. Novels incl: The Dark Frontier; Uncommon Danger; Epitaph for a Spy; Cause for Alarm; The Mask of Dimitrios; Journey into Fear; Judgement on Deltchev; The Schirmer Inheritance; The Night-Comers; Passage of Arms; The Light of Day; The Ability to Kill; A Kind of Anger, Dirty Story; The Intercom Conspiracy. Screenplays incl: The Way Ahead; The October Man; The Passionate Friends; Highly Dangerous; The Magic Box; Encore; The Card; The Purple Plain; A Night to Remember; Rough Shoot; The Cruel Sea; Lease of Life; Yangtse Incident; Wreck of the Mary Deare. Contbr. to Holiday Mag. Mbr. Garrick & Savile Clubs. Address: c/o Peter Janson-Smith Ltd., 42 Gt. Russell St., London WC1, UK.

AMBLER, Mary Cary, b. 22 Feb. 1945, NYC, N.Y., USA. Writer. Educ: B.A., Sweet Briar Coll., Va., 1967; M.F.A., Columbia Univ., 1970. Publs: The Second Crow Tree, 1975; & var. publs. for the State of N.Y. incl: Distinctive Sites Along the Hudson River Valley; The Tourway Guide for the Hudson River Valley; Town Plan for the Town of Irvington. Contbr. to: Mademoiselle; N.Y. mag.; The Va. Psychiatric Review; Graphics; Assoc. Press Educl. Features; etc. Mbrships. incl: MLA; National Trust, GB; Chmn., Community Services Comm. for the Elderly, N.Y.; Assn. Residence for Women, 1971-74. Hons. incl: First Prize Ed. Award, US Students' Press Assn., 1967. Address: Apt. 5G, 344 W. 72 St., NYC, N.Y. 10023, USA.

AMBRIÈRE, Francis, b. 27 Sept. 1907. Writer; Journalist. Educ: Univs. of Dijon & Paris. Publs: La Vie Secrète des Grands Magasins, 1932, revised ed., 1938; Le Favori de François Ier, 1936; Les Grandes Vacances, 1946; Le Solitaire de La Cervara, 1947; La Galerie Dramatique, 1949; Le Maroc, 1952. Mbr., VP of Jury, Prix

Albert-Londres, 1972-. Hons: Off., Legion of Hon. & Order of Cedar (Lebanon); Cmdr., Arts & Letters; Order Polonia Restituta; Prix Goncourt, 1946. Address: 15 rue Sainte Geneviève Bonvillers, 60 Cauvigny, France.

AMBROSE, Stephen Edward, b. 10 Jan. 1936, Decatur, Ill., USA. Writer; Teacher. Educ: B.S., Univ. of Wis., 1956; M.A., La. State Univ., 1957; Ph.D., Univ. of Wis., 1963. Publs: Halleck — Lincoln's Chief of Staff, 1957; Upton & the Army, 1960; Duty, Honor, Country: A History of West Point, 1964; Eisenhower & Berlin: The Decision to Stop at the Elbe, 1966; The Papers of Dwight David Eisenhower, 5 vols. (assoc. ed.), 1968; The Supreme Commander: The War Years of Dwight D. Eisenhower, 1970; Rise to Globalism: American Foreign Policy, 1938-1968, 1972. Contbr. to var. newspapers. Mbrships: Am. Histl. Assn.; Bd. of Trustees, Am. Mil. Inst. Address: 1623 Mirabeau Ave., New Orleans, LA 70122, USA.

AMBROZ, Oton, b. 3 Sept. 1905, Kronberg, Slovenia, Yugoslavia. Journalist; Columnist; Magazine Writer; Rome and Paris Foreign Correspondent, Research Analyst, Comparative Communism. Educ: M.A., 1934, Dr.Iuris, 1935, Zagreb Univ.; Schl. of Mod. Langs., 1935-38. Publs: Realignment of World Power: The Russo-Chinese Schism Under the Impact of Mao Tse-Tung's Last Revolution, vols. I & II, 1972. Contbr. to: East Europe Mag. (Assoc. Ed.), N.Y. Mbrships: Liberal Int. Exile Group, London; Assembly of Captive European Nations, N.Y.; Am. Newspaper Guild, N.Y. Recip., acad. hons. Address: 925 West End Ave. N.Y., NY 10025, USA.

AMERY, (The Rt. Hon.) Harold Julian, b. 1919, UK. Member of Parliament; Former Minister of State, Foreign & Commonwealth Office. Educ: Univ. of Oxford. Publs: Sons of the Eagle, a Study in Guerrilla War, 1950; The Life of Joseph Chamberlain, vol. IV, 1950, vols. V & VI, 1969; Approach March: A Venture in Autobiography, 1973. Address: 112 Eaton Sq., London SW1, UK.

AMES, Winslow, b. 3 July 1907, Victoria, Maullín, Chile. Art Historian; Author. Educ: B.A., Columbia Univ., N.Y., 1929; M.A., Harvard Univ., 1932. Publs: Italian Drawings (vol. I of Great Master Drawings of All Time), 1962; Prince Albert & Victorian Taste, 1967. Contbr. to: Art Quarterly; Antiques; Jrnl. of Soc. of Archtl. Histns.; Gazette des Beaux-Arts; Art Jrnl.; Master Drawings; var. vols. of essays. Mbrships: Authors' Guild; Soc. of Archtl. Histns. Address: 80 Ferry Road, Saunderstown, RI 02874, USA.

AMEY, Leonard, b. 28 Sept. 1909, Cambridge, UK. Agricultural Correspondent. Contbr. to: Anglian Daily Times; The Times; & num. agricl. jrnls. in UK, Scandinavia, Germany, France, Switz., Ireland, USA, S.Am., Aust. & NZ. Mbrships: Sr. Fellow, Past Chmn., & Past Pres., Guild of Agricl. Jrnlsts.; Exec. Comm., Int. Fedn. of Agricl. Jrnlsts. Address: 303 Cherryhinton Rd., Cambridge CB1 4DB, UK.

AMIEL, Denys, b. 5 Oct. 1884, Aude, France. Author; Dramatist. Educ: Sorbonne; Licencie es-lettres. Publs: 40 plays performed in France & abroad, on radio & TV; 4 plays performed by la Comedie Française; 12 vols. of plays published. Contbr. to: L'Illustration; var. mags. Mbrships: Societe des Auteurs (former VP); Int. Confedn. of Authors (former Gen. Sec.). Hons: Officer, Legion d'Honneur; Commandeur de la Couronne d.Italie; Paul Hervieu Prize; Grand Prix du Theatre. Address: Domaine de la Condamine, 06610 La Gaude, France.

AMIN, Khalidah Adibah, pen names DELIMA, Sri; AIDA, KALMIN, Aida, b. 19 Feb. 1936, Johore Baru, Malaysia. Journalist; Author. Educ: B.A.(Hons.), Univ. of Malaya, Singapore; Dip.Ed., Univ. of Malaya, Kuala Lumpur. Publs: Puteri Asli, 1950; Gadis Sipu, 1951; Bangsawan Tulin, 1952; Seraja Masih Di Kalam, 1966; Kukenegara, 1970; No Harvest But A Thorn (Engl. translation of Ranjau Sepanjang Jalan, by Shahron Ahmad), 1971; Sharpen Up Your Bahasa Malaysia (guide to Malaysian nat. lang.). Contbr. to: New Straits Times; Hiburan; Mastika; Dewan Masyarakat. Mbrships: Nat. Writers' Assn. of Malaysia; Nat. Union of Jrnlsts.; Malaysian Women Jrnlsts. Assn. Recip., Book Prize, Univ. of Malaya, 1956. Address: New Straits Times, Jalan Riang, Kuala Lumpur, Malaysia.

AMIS, Kingsley William, b. 1922, London, UK. Author; former Professor of English. Educ: M.A., St. John's Coll., Oxford. Publs: A Frame of Mind, 1953; Lucky Jim, 1954,

filmed 1957; That Uncertain Feeling, 1955, filmed as Only Two Can Play, 1962; A Case of Samples, 1956; I Like it Here, 1958; Take a Girl Like You, 1960; New Maps of Hell, 1960; My Enemy's Enemy, 1962; One Fat Englishman, 1963; The James Bond Dossier, 1965; The Egyptologists (w. R. Conquest), 1965; The Anti-Death League, 1966; A Look Round the Estate, 1967; Colonel Sun (as Robert Markham), 1968; I Want it Now, 1968; The Green Man, 1968; What Became of Jane Austen? 1970; Girl 20, 1971; On Drink, 1972; The Riverside Villas Murder, 1973; Ending Up, 1974. Contbr. to: Spectator; Observer; etc. Agent: A. D. Peters. Address: Lemmons, Hadley Common, Barnet, Herts., UK.

AMIS, Martin Louis, b. 25 Aug. 1949, Oxford, UK. Novelist; Journalist. Educ: B.A., Oxford Univ. Publs: The Rachel Papers, 1974; Dead Babies, forthcoming. Mbr., Nat. Union Jrnlsts. Recip., The Somerset Maugham Award, 1974. Agent: A. D. Peters, Lit. Agents. Address: c/o 10 Buckingham St., London WC2N 6BU, UK.

AMMERMAN, Gale Richard, b. 6 Mar. 1923, Sullivan, Ind., USA. Professor of Food Technology. Educ: B.S., 1950, M.S., 1953, Ph.D., 1957, Purdue Univ., Lafayette, Ind. Publs: Sweet Potatoes, Production, Processing & Marketing (w. J. B. Edmond), 1971; Your Future in Food Technology, 1974. Contbr. to: Food Processing; Miss. Farm Rsch.; Catfish Farmer; The Canner & Freezer; Food Technol.; Jrnl. of Food Sci.; sev. other sci. jrnls. Mbrships. incl: Inst. of Food Technols.; Am. Soc. for Hort. Sci. Address: Dept. of Hort., P.O. Drawer T, Miss. State Univ., MS 39762, USA.

ANAND, Mulk Raj, pen name MUNI, Narad, b. 12 Dec. 1905, Peshawar, India. Broadcaster; Script Writer; Magazine Editor. Educ: B.A., Punjab Univ.; Cambridge Univ., UK; Ph.D., London Univ. Publs. incl: Seven Summers; The Big Heart; Coolie; Untouchable; The Barbers' Trade Union & Other Stories; Lines Written to an Indian Air; Apology for Heroism; Morning Face; Hindu View of Art; Persian Painting. Contbr. to var. mags. in Europe & India. Mbrships. incl: Fellow, Lalit Kala Akademi; Sahitya Akademi; Nat. Book Trust. Hons. incl: Tagore Prof., Univ. of Punjab, 1963-66, 1973; Sahitya Akademi Lit. Award, 1972. Address: 25 Cuffe Parade, Bombay 400005, India.

ANANIAN, Vakhtang Stepanovich, b. 1905, Armenia. Writer. Publs. incl: A Chrestomathy of Hunters Stories, 7 vols., 1948-71; At the Shore of Lake Sevan, 1950; The Childhood in Mountains, 1954; Steep Paths, 1955; The Prisoners of Leopard's Valley, 1956; Animal World of Armenia, vol. I, 1961, vol. II, 1961, vol. III, 1965, vol. IV, 1967; Fatherland Mountains, 1963; Complete Works, (6 vols.), 1968-71. Hons: Orders of Red Banner & of Labour; Badge of Hon. Address: Erevan 15, Paronian St. I, Floor 12, Armenian S.S.R., USSR.

ANASTASI, Anne, b. 19 Dec. 1908, NYC, USA. Professor of Psychology. Educ: A.B., Barnard Coll., 1928; Ph.D., Columbia Univ., 1930. Publs: Differential Psychology, 1937, 3rd ed. 1958; Psychological Testing, 1954, 4th ed. 1975; Fields of Applied Psychology, 1964; Ed., Individual Differences, 1965; Ed., Testing Problems in Perspective, 1966. Contbr. to: Annual Review Psychol.; Psychol. Review; Psychol. Bulletin; Am. Psychologist; Am. Jrnl. Psychol.; Jrnl. Gen. Psychol., etc. Mbrships: Am. Psychol. Assn. (Pres., 1971-72); other profl. assns. Hons. incl: Litt.D., Windsor, Can., 1967; Paed. D., Villanova, 1971; Sc.D., Cedar Crest, 1971. Address: Fordham Univ., Bronx, NY 10458, USA.

ANATOLI, A. (formerly known as KUZNETSOV, Anatoli), b. 18 Aug. 1929, Kiev, Ukraine. Author. Educ: Gorki Inst. of Lit., Moscow. Publs: Sequel of a Legend (novel), 1957; At Home (novel), 1964; Babi Yar (novel/documentary), 1966; Firex (novel), 1969; We, Two Men (film scenario); Encounter at Dawn (film scenario); 4 vols. of short stories. Recip. of prizes at 3 lit. competitions, Ukraine & Moscow. Address: c/o David Floyd Esq., The Daily Telegraph, 135 Fleet St., London EC4, UK.

ANDERBERG, Bengt Niklas, b. 17 Apr. 1920, Gothenburg, Sweden. Author. Educ: Coll.; Mil. Schl. Publs: En kvall om varen, 1945; Fanny, 1946; Faglar, 1946; Kain, 1948; Niklas, 1950; Sagospel, 1954; Pittoresk album, 1958; I flykten, 1968. Contbr. to: Expressen, Sweden. Mbr., Swedish Soc. of Authors. Hons: Svenska Dagbladets Lit. Prize, 1947; Bonnier's Prize for Children's Books, 1950. Address: DK 3751 Oster-Marie, Denmark.

ANDERS, Edith Mary, pen name ENGLAND, E. M., b. 1 July 1899, Townsville, Qld., Australia. Writer. Publs: (novels) The Sealed Temple; Where the Turtles Dance; Road Going North (co-author); The House of Bondage; Queensland Days; Where the Old Road Ran; Tornado (short stories); Happy Monarch (verse). Contbr. to: Sydney Bulletin; Melbourne Australasian; Hoofs & Horns; Expression Mag.; Triad; Christian Sci. Monitor; London Evening News; etc. Hons. incl: Fellowship, Aust. Writers of Brisbane. Assoc., Trinity Coll. Music, London, UK; Play Award, Aust. Broadcasting Comm., 1942; Warana Festival Poem Awards, Brisbane, 1964, 1967. Address: 22 Lowanna Street, Kenmore, Brisbane, Australia 4069.

ANDERSCH, Alfred, b. 4 Feb. 1914. Broadcaster; Writer. Publs. incl: San Gaetano (narrative), 1957; Geister und Leute (stories), 1958; Die Rote (novel), 1960; Wanderungen im Norden, 1962; Ein Liebhaber des Halbschattens (stories), 1963; Aus einem römanischen Winter, 1966; Efraim (novel), 1967; Hohe Breitengrade, 1969; Mein Verschwinden in Providence (stories), 1971; Norden Süden rechts und links (essays), 1972; many radio scripts. Mbr., Grp. 47. Hons. incl: Nelly Sachs Preis & Prix Charles Veillon, 1968. Address: Berzona (Valle Onsernone), Ticcino, Switz.

ANDERSON, Bernhard Word, b. 25 Sept. 1916, Dover, Mo., USA. Teacher; Author. Educ: B.A., Coll. of Pacific, 1936; M.A., 1938, B.D., 1939, D.D., 1960; Pacific Schl. Relig.; Ph.D., Yale, 1945; D.D., Colgate Univ., 1965; S.T.D., Univ. of Pacific, 1961. Publs: Rediscovering the Bible, 1951; Understanding the Old Testament, 1957, 3rd ed., 1975; The Old Testament & Christian Faith, 1963; Creation versus Chaos, 1967; Out of the Depths, 1974; Co-Ed., Israel's Prophetic Heritage, 1962; Transl., Contbr., A History of Pentateuchal Traditions, 1970. Contbr. to num. acad. & theol. jrnls., etc. Mbrships. incl: Am. Theol. Soc.; Soc. Biblical Lit.; Am. Acad. Relig. Recip., acad. hons. Address: 89 Mercer St., Princeton, NJ 08540, USA.

ANDERSON, Hans, b. 14 May 1934, Stockholm, Sweden. Author & Illustrator. Publs: För a vårens skull, 1968; Höstdagar, 1969; Till Labrador, 1970; Minns Du sommaren, 1971. Contbr. to var. mags. Mbrships: Swedish Union of Authors; Swedish Union of Illustrators; Swedish Mus. Assn. Hons. incl: Statens Konstnärsstipendium, 1970; Längmanska Kulturfondens Stipendium, 1970; Statligt Författarstipendium, 1970, 72, & 73. Address: Fack 52, S-960 40 Jokkmokk, Sweden.

ANDERSON, J., b. 1939, Rusape, S. Rhodesia. Senior Lecturer, University of New England. Educ: Univs. of Queensland & New England; B.A.; M.Ed.; Ph.D. Publs: Study Methods, 1969; Efficient Reading, 1969; Thesis & Assignment Writing, 1970; Psycholinguistic Experiments in Foreign Language Testing. Contbr. to: Jrnl. of Reading; Brit. Jrnl. Math. Stat. Psych.; Aust. Jrnl. of Psych.; Educational Rsch.; Papua & New Guinea Jrnl. of Educ; etc. Mbrships: Aust. Psych. Soc.; Aust. & New Zealand Assn. for Advancement of Sci. Address: Fac. of Educ., Univ. of New England, Armidale, NSW 2351, Australia.

ANDERSON, (Rev.) John Edward, b. 1903, Bordighera, Italy. Chaplain; Translator. Educ: B.A., Univ. Coll., Oxford Univ., UK. Publs: Outline Sermons for Country Churches, 2 vols., 1951, 1961; Transl., Alain, Propos; Transl. from French & German of 18 books on Theol., Hist., Belles-Lettres, Biog., Econs., Gen. Sci., & Essays. Mbr., I.A.A.M. Address: Kingsfold, Chepbourne Rd., Bexhill-on-Sea, Sussex, UK.

ANDERSON, John Richard Lane, b. Georgetown, 1911. Journalist; Author. Publs: The Lost Traveller, 1964; Vinland Voyage, 1967; East of Suez, 1969; The Ulysses Factor, 1970; The Upper Thames, 1970; Reckoning in Ice, 1971; Death on the Rocks, 1972; Death in the Thames, 1974; The Discovery of America, 1973; The Vikings, 1974. Address: Wick Cottage, Charney Bassett, Wantage OX12 0EN, UK.

ANDERSON, Joy Mary, b. 15 Aug. 1938, Northampton, UK. Administrator. Publs: Quicksilver (w. R. C. Anderson), 1973. Address: The Mount, Hook Cross, Bickington, Near Newton Abbot, Devon, UK.

ANDERSON, Marjorie Ogilvie, b. 9 Feb. 1909, St. Andrews, Scotland, UK. Historian. Educ: B.A., Univ. of Oxford. Publs: Co-Ed., Chronicle of Melrose, 1936; Ed., Chronicle of Holyrood, 1938; Ed. & Transl. (w. A. O. Anderson), Adomnan's Life of Columba, 1961; Kings &

Kingship in Early Scotland, 1973; chapt. in The Scottish Tradition, 1974. Contbr. to: Scottish Histl. Review; Histl. Studies. Mbrships: Fellow, Soc. of Antiquaries of Scotland. Hons: D.Litt., Univ. of St. Andrews, 1973; Agnes Mure Mackenzie Prize, Saltire Soc., 1974. Address: W. View Cottage, Lade Braes Lane, St. Andrews, Fife KY16 9EP, UK.

ANDERSON, Mary, b. 20 Jan. 1939, Manhattan, NYC, USA. Author of Children's Books. Educ: Hunter Coll., New Schl. Social Rsch. Publs: There's a Pizza Back in Cleveland (w. Hope Campbell), 1972; Matilda Investigates, 1973; Emma's Search For Something, 1973; I'm Nobody! Who are You?, 1974; Just the Two of Them, 1974. Mbr.: Authors' Guild. Address: 270 Riverside Dr., N.Y., NY 10025, USA.

ANDERSON, Matthew Smith, b. 1922, Perth, UK. Professor. Educ: M.A., Ph.D., Univ. of Edinburgh. Publs: Britain's Discovery of Russia 1553-1815, 1958; Europe in the Eighteenth Century 1713-1783, 1961; The Eastern Question, 1774-1923, 1966; The Ascendancy of Europe 1815-1914, 1972. Contbr. to: Engl. Histl. Review; Slavonic & E. European Review; Am. Slavic & E. European Review; etc. Address: 45 Cholmeley Cres., London N6 5EX, UK.

ANDERSON, Mona, b. 11 Mar. 1910, Christchurch, NZ. Author. Publs: A River Rules my Life, 1963; The Good Logs of Algidus, 1965; Over the River, 1966; The Wonderful World at my Doorstep, 1968; A Letter from James, 1971; also author of scripts for N.Z.B.C. Address: McMillan Street, Darfield, Canterbury, NZ.

ANDERSON, Olive, b. 1926, Edinburgh, UK. Reader in History, University of London. Educ: M.A. & B.Litt., Univ. of Oxford. Author, A Liberal State at War, 1967. Contbr. to: Engl. Histl. Review; Econ. Hist. Review; Histl. Jrnl.; etc. Fellow, Royal Histl. Soc. Address: 45 Cholmeley Crescent, London N6, UK.

ANDERSON, Patrick, b. 4 Aug. 1915, Ashtead, Surrey, UK. Poet; Author; Principal Lecturer; Visiting Professor. Educ: B.A., M.A., Worcester Coll., Oxford; A.M.; Columbia Univ., USA. Publs. incl: The White Centre, 1946; The Colour as Naked, 1953; Snake Wine, 1955; Search Me, 1957; Dolphin Days, 1963; The Character Ball, 1963; The Smile of Apollo, 1964; Over the Alps, 1969; Foxed! Or Life in the Country, 1971. Contbr. to: Observer; Sunday Telegraph; Spectator; Fin. Times; London Mag.; Can. Forum; Montreal Star. etc. Hons: Harriet Monroe Lyric Prize, 1945; Fellowship Prize, Poetry Chgo., 1947. Address: Field House, Gosfield Lake, Halstead, Essex, UK.

ANDERSON, Robert Woodruff, b. 28 Apr. 1917, NYC, USA. Playwright; Screenwriter; Novelist. Educ: A.B.(magna cum laude), 1939, M.A., 1940, Harvard Univ. Publs: (plays) Tea & Sympathy, 1953; All Summer Long, 1954; Silent Night, Lonely Night, 1959; The Days Between, 1965; You Know I Can't Hear When the Water's Running, 1967; I Never Sang for My Father, 1968; Solitaire/Double Solitaire, 1971; (novel) After, 1973; (screenplays) The Nun's Story, 1959; The Sand Pebbles, 1966; etc. Mbrships: Dramatists Guild (Pres., 1971-73); Authors League Coun.; Writers Guild of Am., W.; Am. Playwrights Theatre (Bd. of Trustees). Recip., Awards for I Never Sang for My Father, Writers Guild, 1970, UCLA, 1973. Address: Bridgewater, Conn., USA.

ANDERSON, Roy Claude, b. 23 Dec. 1931, Cleethorpes, S. Humberside, UK. Manager, Coach & Travel Organisation. Publs: History of Tramways of Bournemouth & Poole; History of Tramways of East Anglia; History of Royal Blue Express Services (w. G. Frankis); Quicksilver: A Hundred Years of Coaching 1750-1850 (w. J. M. Anderson); History of Llandudno & Colwyn Bay Electric Railway (booklet); History of Great Orme Railway (booklet). Contbr. to: Modern Tramway; Motor Transport; Tramway Review. Fellow, Chartered Inst. of Transport. Address: The Mount, Hook Cross, Bickington, Nr. Newton Abbot, Devon, UK.

ANDERSON-IMBERT, Enrique, b. 12 Feb. 1910, Cordoba, Argentina. Professor of Hispanic Literature. Educ: M.A., Harvard Univ.; Ph.D., Univ. of Buenos Aires. Publs. incl: Historia de la literatura hispanoamericana, 1954, 7th ed., 1974; El Grimotio, 1961; Genio y figura de Sarmiento, 1967; Métodos de crítica literatia, 1969; La sandia y otros cuentos, 1969; La locura juega al ajedrez, 1971; La flecha en el aire, 1972; Los domingos del profesor, 1972; Estudios sobre letras hispanicas, 1974; La

Botella de Klein, 1974; Mbrships. incl: Am. Acad. of Arts & Scis.; Hispanic Soc. of Am. Recip., Lit. Award, 1934, Buenos Aires Municipal Govt. Address: 20 Elizabeth Rd., Belmont, MA 02178, USA.

ANDREEV, Georgy, pen name ANDREEV, Vesselin, b. 16 Feb. 1918, Pirdop, Bulgaria. Writer. Publs. (in Bulgarian): Partisan Tales, 1963; Youth Stays with Us, 1963; Moments in Egypt, 1963; They Died Immortal, 1973; Meditations, 1973; I can't do without you, 1973. Contbr. to: September; Plamak; Literatouren Front. Mbrships: Union of Bulgarian Writers; PEN. Recip., Prize, Union of Bulgarian Writers, 1973. Address: Sofia-4, ul. Dimitur Polyanov 13, Bulgaria.

ANDRÉN-RASMUSON, Margareta, b. 31 July 1913, Stockholm, Sweden. Writer; Housewife. Publs: Solen skiner ocn det regnar, 1936; Barnen I Villervallan, 1940; Misstänkt, 1944; Kata ocn fallet Rockstorp, 1960; Dit stigen bär, 1963; Ett husmed torn på, 1965. Mbr., Sveriges Författarförbund (Swedish Authors' Union). Address: Kampementsgatan 28, 11538 Stockholm, Sweden.

ANDREO, Lorenzo, b. 3 July 1926, Alhama de Murcia, Spain. Pharmacist. Educ: B.Sc., Univ. of Madrid. Publs: El valle de los caracas, 1968, 3rd ed. 1973; Los brazos del pulpo, 1972; El emigrante a Ultramar, ese desconocido, 1973. Contbr. to: Estafeta Literaria; var. newspapers. Mbrships. incl: Assn. of Spanish Writers & Artists. Hons. incl: Aguilas Novel Prize, 1968. Address: González Cebrian 10, Murcia, Spain.

ANDRESCO, Victor, pen name, de GUETARIA, Vicente María, b. 3 Nov. 1919, San Sebastian, Guipúzoa, Spain. Writer; Journalist; Translator. Publs: 5 Cuentos Infantiles; Historia del ballet ruso; Antología de cuentos rusos; (biog.) Juan de la Cosa; M.K. Gandhi; José Planes; (short stories) El cartero rural. Contbr. to: Semana; Chicas. Dígame; Fotogramas; Garbo; El Ruedo; Cine Mundo; Estilo; Esfera Automovilística; Vidrio y Cerámica; Oriental (Peru), etc. Mbrships: past Officer, Junta Directiva, Círculo de Escritores cinematográficos; Assn. of Spanish Artists & Writers; Mutualidad de Escritores de Libros. Recip., Medal, Premio Anual de Periodismo. Address: Ronda de Valencia 9, Madrid 5, Spain.

ANDRESKI, Stanislav Leonard, b. 18 May 1919, Czestochowa, Poland. Author; University Teacher. Educ: Studies in Econs. & Jurisprudence, Univ. of Poznan, 1938-39; L.S.E., UK., 1942-43. Publs. incl: Elements of Comparative Sociology, 1964; Parasitism & Subversion, 1966; The African Predicament: a Study in Pathology of Modernisation, 1968; Social Sciences as Sorcery, 1972; Prospects of a Revolution in the USA, 1973; Mental Pollution & Other Aspects of the Decadence of Industrial Civilisation, forthcoming. Mbr., Brit. Assn., Philos. of Sci. Recip., Alfred Jurzykowski Fndn. Award, 1974. Address: Sociology Dept., Reading Univ., Reading, UK.

ANDREW, (Sister) Mary (Mulcahy), b. 16 Aug. 1897, NYC, USA. Professor of the Fine Arts. Educ: B.A., 1927, M.A., 1929, Coll. of Mt. St. Vincent, N.Y.; Postgrad. study at var. univs. Articles: The Modern Methods of Manuscript Illumination, 1948; Co-author, Masterpiece & Rembrandt Editions of the Catholic Bible, 1964; 24 Fine Arts Books Reviews, 1946-48. Contbr. to: The Catholic Ency. for Home & School. Mbr., The Metropolitan Mus. of Art; Citizens for Decent Lit.; Founder & 1st Pres., Catholic Fine Arts Soc. Address: New York Foundling Hospital, 1175 Third Ave., N.Y., NY 10021, USA.

ANDREWS, Dorothy Westlake, b. 22 Jan. 1916, Pitts., Pa., USA. Authoress; Lecturer. Educ: B.S., Univ. of Pitts., Pa.; Grad. work, Occidental Coll. Publs: God's World & Johnny, 1945; Davie Decides, 1946; Holiday for Helpers, 1947; Sammy Moves to Brookdale, 1950; The Secret Suitcase, 1954; Flaco, 1957; He Hath Done Marvellous Things, 1965; When I Think of Jesus, 1965; David, a Boy With a Song, 1965; 250 original stories, Hoffman Reading Program, 1969-72; Encore, 3 vols., 1972. Contbr. to: Christian Herald; Presby. Life; Walt Disney Prods. Mbrships: Pres., Calif. Writers' Guild; PEN. Address: 2385 Sherwood Rd., San Marino, CA 91108, USA.

ANDREWS, John Williams, b. 10 Nov. 1898, Bryn Mawr, Pa., USA. Writer; Lawyer. Educ: A.B., Yale, 1920; J.D., 1929. Publs. incl: Georgia Transport (verse play for radio), 1938; First Flight, the Story of the Wright Brothers at Kitty Hawk, N.C.; Hill Country North, a Vermont Cycle, 1965; A.D. Twenty-One Hundred, A Narrative of Space,

Legends of Flight, Triptych for the Atomic Age. Ed.-in-Chief, Poet Lore; Ed., St. Lawrence Sea Way Fact Sheet, 1958-61. Contbr. of articles & poems to var. publs. Co-recip., Robert Frost Narration Poetry Award, 1963. Mbrships. incl: Poetry Soc. of Am.; Cath. Poetry Soc. of Am. Address: 52 Cranbury Rd., Westport, CT 06830, USA.

ANDREWS, Lyman, b. 1938, Denver, Colo., USA. Poet; Lecturer; Poetry Critic; Editor. Educ: B.A., Brandeis Univ.; King's Coll., London, UK; Univ. of Calif., Berkeley, USA. Publs: (poetry) Ash Flowers, 1958; Fugitive Visions, 1962; The Death of Mayakovsky, 1968; Kaleidoscope, 1973. Contbr. to: Encounter; Partisan Review; Evergreen Review; Transatlantic Review; Stand; Les Lettres Nouvelles; Poetry Review. Mbrships: PEN; Nat. Poetry Ctr. Hons: Fulbright Schlrship., 1960-61; Phelan Fellowship in Lit., Univ. of Calif., Berkeley, 1963-64. Address: c/o Dept. of English, The University, Leicester LE1 7RH, UK.

ANDREWS, Wayne, pen name, O'REILLY, Montagu, b. 5 Sept. 1913, Kenilworth, Ill., USA. Author; Educator; Photographer. Publs. incl: Who Has Been Tampering With These Pianos? (under pseudonym), 1948; Architecture, Ambition & Americans, 1955; Architecture in America, 1960; Germaine — A Portrait of Madame de Staël, 1963; Architecture in Chicago & Mid-America, 1968; Architecture in New York, 1969; Siegfried's Curse — The German Journey from Nietzsche to Hesse, 1972. Contbr. to: Harper's Bazaar; N.Y. Times Book Review; N.Y. Herald Tribune Book Review; Saturday Review, etc. Address: 521 Neff Rd., Grosse Pointe, MI 48230, USA.

ANDRIC, Ivo, b. 1892. Author. Publs: Bosnian Story, 1958; The Bridge on the Drina, 1959; The Vizier's Elephant, 1962; Devil's Yard, 1962; Bosnian Chronicle, 1963; The Woman from Sarajevo; The Pasha's Concubine & Other Tales, 1965-68. Recip., Nobel Prize, 1961. Address: Proleterskih brigada 2 a, Beograd, Yugoslavia.

ANDRIESSE, Peter, b. 5 July 1941, Arnheim, Netherlands. Author. Educ: M. Phil. (Psychol.), Univ. of Amsterdam, 1964. Publs: Verboten te jodelen! (short stories), 1969; Beweren en bewijzen zijn twee (essays), 1971; Zuster Belinda en het geheime leven van dokter Dushkind (novel), 1971; De roep van de tokeh (short stories), 1972. Contbr. to: Propria Cures; Hollands Maandblad; etc. Mbr., Vereniging van Letterkundigen. Recip., Mention by Reina Prinsen-Geerligsprijs, 1965. Address: Singel 80', Amsterdam, Netherlands.

ANDRUSS, Harvey Adolphus, b. 1902, Ft. Worth, Tex., USA. President Emeritus, Bloomsburg State College. Educ: Univ. of Okla., Norman; N.-Western Univ., Ill.; Pa. State Univ.; A.B.; M.B.A.; Ed.D. Publs: Ways to Teach Book-keeping & Accounting, 1937, 2nd ed. 1942; Better Business Education, 1942; Burgess Business Law, revised ed., 1952. Contbr. to: Jrnl. of Acctcy.; Pa. Schl. Jrnl.; Balance Sheet; Jrnl. of Bus. Educ.; Bus. Educ. World. Address: Country Club Dr., Bloomsburg, PA 17815, USA.

ANDRZEJEWSKI, Jerzy, b. 19 Aug. 1909, Warsaw, Poland. Writer. Educ: Warsaw Univ. Publs. incl: Harmony of the Heart, 1938; (play) Winkelried's Day (co-author), 1945; Ashes & Diamonds, 1948; Darkness Covers the Earth, 1957; The Gates of Paradise, 1961; He Cometh Leaping Upon the Mountains, 1963; The Appeal, 1967; (play) Prometheus, 1972; also a book of reminiscence & sev. short stories. Contbr. to: Cultural Review (Ed.-in-Chief, 1952-54); Lit. Weekly. Mbrships: PEN; Polish Writers Assn., VP, 1949-53; & Br. Pres., var. periods. Hons. incl: Odrodzenie Award, 1948; Zloty Klos Award, 1965; Order of Banner of Labour, 1st Class. Address: Swierczewskiego 53/4, 03-402 Warsaw, Poland.

ANGELI, Siro, b. 27 Sept. 1913, Udine, Italy. TV Director & Executive. Educ: Degree in lit. & philos. Publs. incl: (plays) La Casa, 1937; Dentro di noi, 1939; Assurdo, 1942; Male di Vivere, 1951; Odore di Terra, 1957; (verse) Il Fiume va, 1937; L'Ultima Libertà, 1962; Il Grillo della Suburra, 1975. Contbr. to: Studi Romani; Letteratura; La Fiera Letteraria; Ency. dello Spettacolo; etc. Mbrships. incl: Italian Soc. Dramatic Authors (exec. coun.); Italian Soc. Authors & Publrs. Hons. incl: Pro Civitate Christiana Prize (theatre), Assisi, 1957; Vann'Anto Prize (poetry), Messina, 1965; Botte di Frascati Prize, 1971. Address: Via Cavour 211, Rome, Italy.

ANGELOV, Dimitar, b. 27 Sept. 1904, Blateshtnitsa, Bulgaria. Writer. Publs: (in Bulgarian) Life or Death, 1953; The Brave Choung, 1953; The Earth Faces Destruction,

1956. Contbr. to: September; Literatouren Front. Mbr., Union of Bulgarian Writers. Hons: Dimitrov Laureate Prize, 1959; Honoured Worker in Culture, 1970. Address: Sofia, bul. Skobelev, 44, Bulgaria.

ANGLESEY (Marquess of), George Charles Henry Victor Paget, b. 8 Oct. 1922, London, UK. Peer of the Realm. Publs: The Capel Letters 1814-1817, 1955; One-Leg, 1961; Sergeant Pearman's Memoirs, 1968; Little Hodge, 1971; A History of the British Cavalry 1816-1919, vol. I, 1973, vol. II, 1975. Contbr. of reviews to Sunday Telegraph. Mbrships: F.S.A.; F.R.S.L. Address: Plas Newydd, Anglesey, N. Wales, UK.

ANGOFF, Charles, b. 22 Apr. 1902, Minsk, Russia. Author; Editor; Professor of English. Educ: A.B., Harvard Coll., 1923; Litt.D., Fairleigh Dickinson Univ., 1966. Publs. incl: The Tone of the Twenties (essays). 1966; Memoranda for Tomorrow (poems), 1968; Season of Mists (novel), 1972; Mid-Century (novel), 1974. Contbr. to num. publs. in UK, Sweden, France, Italy, Israel, Spain & S. Africa; Ed., Lit. Review, 1957—; Chief Ed., Fairleigh Dickinson Univ. Press, 1967—. Mbrships. incl: Pres., Poetry Soc. of Am., 1969-73; Fellow, Jewish Acad. Arts & Scis. of Am. Hons: Daroff Fiction Awards, 1954, 1969; NN.J. Assn. of Tchrs. of Engl. Awards, 1970, 1971, 1973. Address: 140 W. 86th St. 14B, N.Y., NY 10024, USA.

ANGUS-BUTTERWORTH, Lionel Milner, b. 29 June, 1900, Altrincham, Cheshire, UK. Author. Retired Company Director. Educ: Univs. of Manchester, Sheffield & Toulouse (France); M.A., F.R.G.S.; F.S.A.Scot.; F.C.I.S.; C.Eng.; F.I.Mech.E. Publs: The Manufacture of Glass, 1948; British Table & Ornamental Glass, 1956; Ten Master Historians, 1961; Pottery & Porcelain, 1964; The Chinese Kitchen (Tales of the Occult & Macabre), 1967; Robert Burns & Scottish Vernacular Poetry, 1969; Scottish Folk-Song, 1971; Poems, 1973. Contbr. to num. jrnls. Mbrships: Pres., Lancs. Authors' Assn.; Past Pres., Manchester Lit. Club. Address: Ashton New Hall, Aston-on-Mersey, via Sale, Cheshire, UK.

ANING, Ben Akosa, b. 4 Dec. 1926, Dampong, Ghana. Teacher. Educ: Presby. Tchrs. Trng. Coll., Akropong, 1943-46; L.R.S.M., Coll. of Arts, Sci. & Technol., Kumasi, 1952-54; Dip. in African Music, Univ. of Ghana, Legon, 1964; Special studies, Columbia Univ. & Univ. of Calif., USA, 1964-66; M.A., Univ. of Ghana, 1969. Publs: An Annotated Bibliography of Music & Dance in English Speaking Africa, 1967. Contbr. to: Jrnl., Int. Folk Music Coun.; Papers in African Studies, Legon; Ghana Jrnl. of Educ. Mbr., var. nat. & int. music assns. Address: Institute of African Studies, University of Ghana, Legon, Ghana.

ANKENBRUCK, John, b. 10 Oct. 1925, Fort Wayne, Ind., USA. Journalist. Educ: B.S., Univ. of Notre Dame; Univ. of Geneva, Switz. Publs: Five Forts: Historical Account of Old Northwest, 1972; Voice of the Turtle: Biography of Miami Chief Little Turtle, 1974. Mbrships: Nat. Conf. of Ed. Writers; VP, Fortnightly Lit. Club; Mayor's Advsry. Bd., U.S. Bicentennial 1776-1976; VP, Allen Co. Councilman, 1963-68. Named Newsman of the Yr., Fort Wayne Press Club, 1968. Address: 4415 Karen Ave., Fort Wayne, IN 46805, USA.

ANNAND, Archibald McKenzie, b. 24 Feb. 1905, Tientsin, China., Estate Agent (retired); Army Officer (retired). Publs: Ed., Cavalry Surgeon, Reminiscences of Surgeon-General John Henry Sylvester, Bombay Army, 1971. Contbr. to: Jrnl. of Soc. for Army Histl. Rsch. Mbrships. incl: Scottish Hist. Soc.; Soc. for Army Histl. Rsch.; Mil. Histl. Soc.; 1745 Assn. & Nat. Hist. Soc.; Royal United Servs. Inst. Recip., T.D. Address: Magdalen, High Street, Findon, Worthing, Sussex BN14 0TA.

ANNESS, Milford Edwin, b. 14 Feb. 1918, Metamora, Ind., USA. Lawyer. Educ: A.B., 1940, J.D., 1957, Ind. Univ. Publs: Song of Metamoris, 1964; Forever the Song, 1967; Stars Above America, 1968; Sing a New Song of Glory (songs), 1973. Contbr. to newspapers. Address: P.O. Box 623, Columbus, IN 47201, USA.

ANNIGONI, Pietro, b. 7 June 1910, Milan, Italy. Painter. Educ: Acad. of Fine Arts, Florence. Publs: Spanish Sketchbook (w. A Sterling), 1957; Nudi e un Saggio Sul Disegno, 1964; Frammenti d. Diario, 1966; Diario, 1971. Mbrships: Accademia Arti del Disegno, Florence; Accademia di San Luca, Rome. Address: Borgo Albizi 8, Florence, Italy.

ANOUILH, Jean, b. 1910, Bordeaux, France. Playwright. Educ: Sorbonne, Paris. Publs: L'Ermine (The Ermine); La Sauvage (Restless Heart); Voyageur Sans Bagages (Traveller Without Luggage); Eurydice (Point of Departure); Antigone; Romeo & Jeannette; Médée (Medea); Le Bal des Voleurs (Thieves' Carnival); Le Rendezvous de Senlis (Dinner with the Family); Léocadia (Time Remembered); L'Invitation au Château (Ring Around the Moon); La Répétition (The Rehearsal); L'Alouette (The Lark); Colombe; Ardèle; La Valse des Toréadors (The Waltz of the Toreadors); Cécile (School for Fathers); L'hurluberlu (The Fighting Cock); Poor Bitos; Dear Antoine; Becket; The Director of the Opera; Ne Réveillez-Pas Madame; Tu Etais si Gentil; L'Arrestation; Calman Levy & La Table Ronde. Address: c/o Dr. Jan van Loewen Ltd., Int. Copyright Agcy., 81/83 Shaftesbury Ave., London W1, UK.

ANSEL, Walter, b. 25 Aug. 1897, Elgin, III., USA. Retired Rear Admiral; Author & Farmer. Educ: US Naval Acad.; Naval War Coll.; US Marine Corps Field Offs. Course; Univs. of Freiburg, W. Germany, & N.C. & Md., USA. Publs: Hitler Confronts England, 1960; Hitler & the Middle Sea, 1971. Contbr. to US Naval Inst. Mbrships. incl: Army & Navy Club, Manila. Hons: Fellow, Naval Hist., US Naval Acad., 1951-52. Address: Gavea RFD 2, Box 279, Annapolis, MD, USA.

ANSON, Luis Maria, b. 8 Feb. 1935, Madrid, Spain. Journalist. Educ: Ph.D., Univ. of Madrid. Publs: La Monarquia Hoy, 1956; El Gengis Khan Rojo, 1960; Sobre la Creacion Postica, 1962; La Justa Distribucion de la Riqueza Mundial, 1963; El Grito de Oriente, 1966; La Negritud, 1971. Mbrships: Asociacion de la Prensa; Asociacion de Corres. de Prensa Ibero-Am; I.E.R.I.; Assn. of Writers & Artists; Vice Dir., ABC, Madrid. Hons: Nat. Prize for Lit., 1965; Miguel de Unamuno Prize, 1965; Mariano de Cavia Prize, 1964; Luca de Tena Prize, 1960. Poligono Prize, 1972; Legazpi Prize, 1966; Juan Palomo Prize, 1970. Address: Garcia Morato 135, Madrid, Spain.

ANSON, Peter Frederick, b. 1889, Portsmouth, UK. Publs. incl: The Pilgrim's Guide to Franciscan Italy, 1927; Fishermen & Fishing Ways, 1931; The Quest of Solitude, 1932; Mariners of Brittany, 1932; The Catholic Church in Modern Scotland, 1937; The Benedictines of Caldey, 1940; British Sea Fishermen, 1944; The Church & the Sailor, 1949; Abbot Extraordinary, 1958; Fashions in Church Furnishings 1840-1940, 1959; Call of the Desert, 1964; Bishops at Large, 1964; Fisher Folklore, 1965; Life on Low Shore, 1969; Underground Catholicism in Scotland, 1970; Building up the Waste Places, 1973. Contbr. to fishing & relig. jrnls. Address: Caldey Island, Tenby, Dyfed SA70 7UH, UK.

ANSORGE, (Sir) Eric Cecil, b. 6 Mar. 1887, London, UK. Retired. Educ: M.A., Oxford. Publs: Silk in India (w. late Prof. Maxwell Lefroy); The Macrolepidoptera of Buckinghamshire; Supplement to the Macrolepidoptera of Buckinghamshire. Contbr. to var. entomol. mags. Mbrships: Fellow, Royal Entomol. Soc.; Fellow, Ancient Monuments Soc.; Brit. Entomol. Soc. Address: Timbers, Welders Lane, Chalfont St. Peter, Bucks., UK.

ANSTEY, Edgar, b. 1917, Bombay, India. Civil Service Administrator; Author. Educ: M.A., Ph.D., King's Coll., Cambridge. Publs: Interviewing for the Selection of Staff, 1956; Staff Reporting & Staff Development, 1961; Committees, How They Work & How to Work Them, 1962; Psychological Tests, 1966. Address: 27 Cumberland Drive, Esher, Surrey KT10 0BG, UK.

ANSTRUTHER, Godfrey, b. 5 Mar. 1903, London, UK. Dominican Friar. Educ: Hawkesyard Priory, Rugeley, Staffs.; B.ès Sc.Hist., Univ. of Louvain, Belgium. Publs: Foundations of Thomistic Philosophy (transl.), 1931; St. Thomas Aquinas & his Work (transl.), 1933; Vaux of Harrowden, 1953; A Hundred Homeless Years, 1958; The Seminary Priests, I, 1969, II, 1975. Contbr. to: Archivum Ordinis Praedicatorum, Rome; Tablet; Blackfriars; Recusant Hist. Address: c/o St. Dominic's Priory, London NW5, UK.

ANTHONY, Barbara, pen name BARBER, Antonia, b. 10 Dec. 1932, London, UK. Writer. Educ: B.A., Univ. of London. Publs: The Affair of the Rockerbye Baby, 1966; The Ghosts, 1969, filmed as The Amazing Mr. Blunden, 1972. Agent: A. M. Heath & Co. Ltd. Address: Hornes Place Oast, Appledore, Ashford, Kent, UK.

ANTHONY, Evelyn, b. 1928, London, UK. Writer. Publs: Imperial Highness; Curse Not the King; Far Fly the

Plamak; September; Savremennik; Literatouren Front. Mbr., Union of Bulgarian Writers. Recip., People's Worker in Culture & Art Award. Address: Sofia, ul Venelin, 40, Bulgaria.

ARGOW, Sylvia, b. NYC, USA. Executive Secretary; Poet. Educ: N.Y. Univ.; CUNY; Community Coll. Publs: Poems in num. anthols. inclng: Lyrics of Love, Outstanding Contemporary Poetry, Premier Poets, Shore Poetry Anthol.; Creator of new poetry form, "the Argonelle". Contbr. to num. poetry jrnls., USA, Italy, India, UK. Mbrships. incl: Histn., N.Y. Poetry Forum, Inc.; Life Mbr., Int. Clover Poetry Assn.; Centro Studi E. Scambi Int., Rome; Fndn. Fellow-designate, Int. Poetry Soc.; Am. Poetry Fellowship. Soc.; World. Poetry Soc. Int.; Maj. Poets Chapt., Pierson Mettler Assoc.; Women's Press Club of NYC; Poetry Soc. Inc., London; Mark Twain Assn., NY. Hons. incl: num. prizes & certs. of merit. Address: 2075 Grand Concourse, Bronx, NY 10453, USA.

ARIES, Philippe, b. 21 July 1914, Blois, France. Information Officer; Historian. Educ: Sorbonne Univ., Paris. Publs: Les traditions dans les pays de France, 1943; Histoire des populations françaises & de leurs attitudes devant la vie, 1948, 1971; Le temps de l'histoire, 1954; L'enfant & la vie familiale sous l'ancien regime, 1960, 1973; Centuries of Childhood, 1962; Padri e figli nell'Europa medievale e moderna, 1968; Western Attitudes towards Death, 1974. Address: 94 rue Jean Mermoz, Maisons Lafitte 78, Yvelines, France.

ARIT, Aydin, b. 19 Feb. 1928, Istanbul, Turkey. Playwright. Educ: B.A., Robert Coll., Istanbul. Publs: Sapiklar, 1959; Bal Sinegi, 1965; Aya Bir Yolcu, 1967; Uçamayan Kuşlar Tutulur, 1974; Masal Masal Matitas, 1974. Contbr. to: Ellery Queen Mag., USA; var. Turkish mags. Mbr., Turkish Playwrights' Soc. Hons. incl: 50th Anniversary of Turkish Repub. Prize for Theatre, 1973; Best Playwright of Yr., 1974. Address: Beyaz Karanfil Sokak 3, Levent, Istanbul, Turkey.

ARKIN, Marcus, b. 13 May 1926, Cape Town, S. Africa. Director-General, South African Zionist Federation; Former Economics Professor. Educ: B.A., B.Comm., 1947, Ph.D., 1959, Univ. of Cape Town. Publs: John Company at the Cape, 1972; Supplies for Napoleon's Gaolers, 1964; Agency & Island, 1965; South African Economic Development: An Outline Survey, 1966; Economists & Economic Historians, 1968; Introducing Economics, the Science of Scarcity, 1971; The Economist at the Breakfast Table, 1972; Storm in a Teacup, 1973. Contbr. to var. econ. jrnls. Mbr., Royal Econ. Soc. Address: 16 Sussex Rd., Parkwood, Johannesburg, S. Africa.

ARLAND, Marcel, b. 5 July 1899. Novelist; Essayist. Publs. incl: La Prose française: Anthologie, histoire et critique d'un art (essays), 1951; La Consolation du Voyageur, 1952; L'Eau de le Feu, 1956; A perdre Haleine, 1960; Je vous ecris . . . (essays), 1960; La Nuit et les Sources (essays), 1962; Le Grand Pardon, 1965; Carnets de Gilbert (essays), 1967; La Musique des Anges (essays), 1967; Attendez l'aube (essays) 1970; Proche du Silence (essays), 1973. Mbr., Acad. Française. Hons. incl: Grand Prix Nat. du Lettres, 1960. Address: 5 rue Sébastien-Bottin, Paris 7e, France.

ARLANDSON, Leone Ryland, pen names, RYLAND, Lee; ARLANDSON, Lee, b. 30 Oct. 1917, Baker, Ore., USA. Author; Editor. Educ: Grad., bus. coll. Publs: Mr. Puffer-Bill, Train Engineer, 1965; Gordon & the Glockenspiel, 1966; The Whistle-Bell Train, 1967; Know About the Appaloosa Horse, 1973. Contbr. to juvenile & adult mags. inclng: Jack & Jill; Horseman; True West. Mbrships. incl: Western Writers of Am.; Rogue Valley Authors Guild. Hons. incl: Award for Juvenile Non-fiction, Pacific N.W. Writers Conf., 1970. Address: 2170 Milford Dr., Medford, OR 97501, USA.

ARLETT, Vera Isabel, b. 18 Aug. 1896, Penn, Wolverhampton, Staffs., UK. Author; Lecturer. Publs. incl: Poems, 1927; Permanence, 1929; The Road to Assisi; England, 1940; Saint Alban; Six London Plays, (w. H. F. Rubinstein); Keeper of the Keys; The Gardener; Midnight Melodrama; The Lonely Place. Former contbr. to: Western Morning News; Sunday Times; Observer; Time & Tide; Sussex Co. Mag.; Homes & Gdns.; Poetry Review; etc. Mbrships: Fellow, PEN; Life Fellow, Int. Inst. of Arts & Letters. Recip., Medal for Lyric Poetry, Univ. of Liverpool, 1931. Address: 92 Lavington Rd., Worthing, Sussex, UK.

ARLEY, Catherine, b. 30 Dec. 1932, Paris, France. Writer. Publs: 13 books, most in for. transls., inclng. La Femme de Paille (Woman of Straw); Le Talion (Ready Revenge); La Baie des Trespassés (Dead Man's Bay); Duel au Premier Sang; Le Pique-Feu; Le Fait du Prince; Mourir sans Toi. Contbr. to: Mystery Mag.; Lui; L'illustré Suisse. Mbr., Soc. des gens de lettres. Recip., Suspense Prize, 1968. Address: 3 Rue Jean Sicard, Paris 750015, France.

ARLOTT, John, b. 25 Feb. 1914, Basingstoke, UK. Writer; Broadcaster. Publs: Landmarks (w. G. R. Hamilton), 1943; Of Period & Place, 1944; Clausentum, 1945; First Time in America, 1949; Concerning Cricket, 1949; How to Watch Cricket, 1949; English Cheeses of the South & West; Vintage Summer, 1967; Fred: Portrait of a Fast Bowler, 1971; The Ashes, 1972. Contbr. to: The Guardian (cricket corres.; wine corres.); Hampshire County Mag.; The Cricketer. Hons: O.B.E., M.A., Univ. of Southampton. Address: The Old Sun, Alresford, Hants., UK.

ARMAH, Ayi Kwei, b. 1939, Takoradi, Ghana. Writer. Educ: A.B., Harvard Univ., USA; Columbia Univ., N.Y. Publs: (novels) The Beautiful Ones Are Not Yet Born, 1968; Fragments, 1970. Contbr. to: Transl., Revolution Africaine Mag., Algiers; Scriptwriter, Ghana TV; Ed., Jeune Afrique Mag., Paris, 1967-68. Address: c/o Houghton Mifflin Co., 2 Park St., Boston, MA 02107, USA.

ARMFELT, Nicholas, b. 1935, Exeter, Devon, UK. Teacher. Educ: M.A., King's Coll., Cambridge Univ. Publs: Catching Up, 1971; Smudge, 1975. Contbr. to: Musical Times. Address: c/o Agent: A. D. Peters & Co., 10 Buckingham St., London WC2N 6BU, UK.

ARMITAGE, Angus, b. 1902, Holmesfield, Sheffield, UK. University Reader in History & Philosophy of Science; Author. Educ: M.Sc., Ph.D., Univ. Coll., London. Publs: Copernicus, the Founder of Modern Astronomy, 1938, 2nd ed., 1957; Sun Stand Thou Still, 1947, 2nd ed., 1948; A Century of Astronomy, 1950; William Herschel, 1962; Edmond Halley, 1966; John Kepler, 1966. Contbr. to: Lynchnos; Annals of Sci.; Endeavour; Sci. Progress; Popular Astron.; Notes & Records of the Royal Soc.; Memoirs of the Brit. Astron. Assn.; Discovery. Address: 52 Parkhill Rd., Hampstead, London NW3, UK.

ARMOUR, Richard, b. 15 July 1906, San Pedro, Calif., USA. Writer; Lecturer; Former University Professor. Educ: B.A., Pomona Coll., Claremont, Calif.; M.A., Ph.D., Harvard Univ. Publs: Over 50 books inclng. Coleridge the Talker, 1940; Light Armour, 1954; The Classics Reclassified, 1960; American Lit Relit, 1964; My Life with Women, 1968; A Short History of Sex, 1970; Writing Light Verse & Prose Humor, 1971; Out of My Mind, 1971; It All Started with Freshman English, 1973; Going Like Sixty, 1974; Sea Full of Whales, 1974; The Academic Bestiary, 1974. Contbr. to ca. 200 jrnls. Mbrships. incl: PEN; Calif. Writers' Guild. Hons. incl: Litt.D.; L.H.D.; LL.D.; Author-of-the-Yr., Univ. of Calif., 1966. Address: 460 Blaisdell Dr., Claremont, CA 91711, USA.

ARMSTRONG, Alice Catt, b. Ft. Scott, Kan., USA. Former Actress & Teacher, Dramatic Arts; Author; Editor; Publisher. Publs. incl: Who's Who in Los Angeles County, 1950, 3rd ed., 1954; Who's Who in California, 1954 (10 eds. to date); Who's Who — Dining & Lodging on the North American Continent, 1958; Who's Who Executives in California, 1963; Short stories; Children's stories; Poetry; Stage skits; Radio dialogues; Travelogues. Contbr. to num. newspapers & mags. Num. hons. incl: 6 Univ. doctorates; 5 Grand Dame awards. Address: 1331 Cordell Pl., "Cordell Views", Doheny Hills, L.A., CA 90069, USA.

ARMSTRONG, Andrew, b. 1934, Chadwell Heath, UK. Technical Writer. Educ: Scotland, England & Sweden. Mbrships: Soc. of Authors, London; Inst. of Linguists, London. Address: 118 Red Barn Rd., Brightlingsea, Colchester, Essex CO7 0SN, UK.

ARMSTRONG, Arthur Hilary, b. 1909, Hove, Sussex, UK. University Professor. Educ: M.A., Jesus Coll., Cambridge. Publs: The Architecture of the Intelligible Universe in the Philosophy of Plotinus; An Introduction to Ancient Philosophy; Plotinus; Christian Faith & Greek Philosophy (w. R. A. Markus); The Cambridge History of Later Greek & Early Mediaeval Philosophy. Contbr. to: Ency. Britannica; Classical Quarterly; Classical Review; Phronesis; Jrnl. Theol. Studies; Heythrop Jrnl.; Downside Review; etc. Fellow, Brit. Acad. Address: The Hollins, Whitton, Ludlow, Salop SY8 3AE, UK.

ARMSTRONG (Rev.), Claude Blakeley, b. 31 Oct. 1889, Dublin, Repub. of Ireland. Canon Emeritus of Worcester; Author. Educ: M.A., B.D., Trinity Coll., Dublin Univ. Publs: Transl., The Persae of Aeschylus; Ed., Roman Society in Gaul; Foundations Unshaken; Outline of Western Philosophy; Creeds & Credibility. Contbr. to: Ch. Quarterly Review; Hibbert Jrnl.; Punch; Jrnl. of Theol. Studies; Ed., Veritas. Address: 12A College Green, Worcester WR1 2LH, UK.

ARMSTRONG, David Malet, b. 1926, Melbourne, Australia. Professor of Philosophy. Educ: Univ. of Sydney; Univ. of Oxford, UK; B.A.; B.Phil.; Ph.D. Publs: Berkeley's Theory of Vision, 1960; Perception & the Physical World, 1961; Bodily Sensations, 1962; A Materialist Theory of the Mind, 1968; Belief, Truth & Knowledge, 1973. Contbr. to profl. jrnls. Address: 125 Windsor St., Paddington, N.S.W., Australia, 2021.

ARMSTRONG, Douglas Albert, pen names WINDSOR, Rex; DOUGLAS, Albert, b. 1920, Windsor, Berks., UK. Journalist. Contbr. to: Ed., Automobile Yr.; London Ed., S.A. Motor, Die Motor, (S. Africa); London Motoring Corres., The Herald, Melbourne, Aust.; etc. Mbrships: Chmn., Guild of Motoring Writers, 1961; Comm.; Wig & Pen Club; Brit. Racing Drivers' Club. Address: North Lodge, Shurlock Row, Berks., UK.

ARMSTRONG (The Rev.), Edward Allworthy, b. 1900, Belfast, UK. Retired Clergyman. Educ: B.A., Queen's Univ., Belfast; M.A., Univ. of Leeds; Ridley Hall, Cambridge. Publs. incl: Birds of the Grey Wind; Bird Display & Behaviour; The Folklore of Birds; Shakespeare's Imagination; The Gospel Parables, 1967; A Study of Bird Song, 1973; St. Francis: Nature Mystic, 1973; Discovering Bird Song, 1975; The Bird: Life, History & Magic, 1975. Contbr. to: New Dict. of Birds, 1964; A.A. & Rdrs. Digest Bird Book, 1969; Man, Myth & Magic, 1970; Folklore; sev. other books, jrnls., & encys. Hons. incl: Union Medal, Brit. Ornithols. Union; Stamford Raffles Award, Zool. Soc.; M.A., Univ. of Cambridge. Address: 23 Leys Rd., Cambridge, CB4 2AP, UK.

ARMSTRONG, John Alexander, b. 4 May 1922, St. Augustine, Fla., USA. University Professor. Educ: Ph.D., M.A., Univ. of Chgo.; Univ. of Frankfurt; Ph.D., Columbia Univ. Publs. incl: The Soviet Bureaucratic Elite: A Case Study of the Ukrainian Apparatus, 1959, 1966; The Politics of Totalitarianism, 1961; Ideology, Politics, & Government in the Soviet Union, 1962, 3rd ed., 1974; The European Administrative Elite, 1973. Contbr. to var. profl. jrnls. Mbrships: Pres., Am. Assn. for the Advancement of Slavic Studies, 1965-67; Bd. of Dirs., Conf. on European Problems, 1971-. Address: 2118 Chamberlain Ave., Madison, WI 53705, USA.

ARMSTRONG, Martin Donisthorpe, b. 1882, Newcastle upon Tyne, UK. Author; former Literary Editor. Educ: B.A., Pembroke Coll., Cambridge. Publs. incl: Exodus, & Other Poems, 1912; The Buzzards, 1921; The Stepson, 1927; Adrian Glynde, 1930; Lover's Leap, 1932; General Buntop's Miracle, 1934; (ed.) The Major Pleasures of Life, 1934; A Case of Conscience, 1937; The Snake in the Grass, 1938; Simplicity Jones, 1940; The Butterfly, 1941; Said the Cat to the Dog, 1945; Said the Dog to the Cat, 1948; George Borrow, 1950; Selected Stories, 1951. Contbr. to: Spectator (Lit. Ed., 1922-24). Address: Sutton, Nr. Pulborough, Sussex, UK.

ARMSTRONG, Naomi Young, b. 17 Oct. 1918, Dermott, Ark., USA. Teacher; Actress; Poet. Educ: A.A., Woodrow Wilson Jr. Coll., 1957; B.S., Northwestern Univ., 1961; Chgo. Tchrs. Coll.; John Marshall Law Schl. Publs: A Child's Easter, 1971; Expression I, 1973. Contbr. to poetry jrnls. Mbrships: Co.-chmn., Poetry Comm., Int. Platform Assn.; World Poets Resource Ctr. & Poetry Soc. of London; United Poets Laureate Int.; Centro Studi E. Scambi Int. Hons: Awards, 2nd World Congress of Poets; 3rd Hon. Mention, Poetry Contest, Int. Platform Assn., 1973; H.L.D., l'Université Libre (Asie), 1974. Address: 9257 S. Burnside Ave., Chgo., IL 60619, USA.

ARMSTRONG, Robert, b. 22 Apr. 1901, Islington, London, UK. Poet; Author. Educ: London Schl. of Econs., London Univ., 1924-26. Publs. incl: Seventeen Poems, 1950; Entr'acte, 1955; Collected Lyrics, 1957; Ghosts of Highgate Hill, 1966; The Poetic Vision, 1973; Finnish Christmas Song Cycle, 1973. Contbr to jrnls. inclng: The Times; Poetry Review; New Statesman; Brit. Weekly; Books & Bookmen. Mbrships: VP, Poetry Soc., 1967-; Pres., Order

of Bards & Druids, 1968-, & York Poetry Soc., 1967-; For. Mbr., Am. Poetry Soc. Hons. incl: Lit. Prize, Wihuri Fndn., Finland, 1974. Address: 16 Harford Walk, Hampstead Gdn. Suburb, London N2, UK.

ARMSTRONG, Thomas, b. 3 Sept. 1899, Airedale, Yorks., UK. Author. Educ: Royal Naval Coll., Keyham. Publs: The Crowthers of Bankdam (filmed as Master of Bankdam); Dover Harbour; King Cotton; Adam Brunskill; Pilling Always Pays; A Ring Has No End; Sue Crowther's Marriage; The Face of a Madonna; Our London Office. Address: Lawn House, Low Row, Swaledale, N. Yorks., UK.

ARNADÓTTIR (Arnsson), Thorbjörg Dýrleif, b. 8 Feb. 1898, Skútustadir, Mývatnsveit, Iceland. Public Health Nurse. Educ: Grad., Commercial Schl. of Iceland, 1916; Grad. Nursing Schl., Bispebjerg Hosp., Copenhagen, Denmark, 1923; B.S., 1941, M.N., 1945, Univ. of Wash., Seattle. Publs: Sveitin Okkar, 1949; Mother & Child, 1950; Draumur Dalastulkunnar (Valley Girl), (play), 1951; Pilagrimsför & Ferdathaettir, 1959; (novels) Signý, 1964; Leynigöngin (Secret Passage), 1966; Öldurót (Turbulent Waves), 1969; (radio play) Hvítar Rósir, 1962. Contbr. to: Icelandic Jrnl. of Nursing (Ed., 5 yrs.); num. mags. & newspapers. Mbr., Icelandic Writers' Assn. Recip., Lit. Prize, Althing, 1951. Address: Lynghagi 1, Reykjavik, Iceland.

ARNDT, Ernst H. D., b. 27 May 1899, Bloemfontein, Orange Free State, S. Africa. Retired Banker. Educ: B.A., Grey Univ. Coll.; A.M., Ph.D., Columbia Univ. Publs: Banking & Currency Development in South Africa, 1652-1927, 1928; An Analysis of the Investment Policies of Life Insurance Companies in the Union of South Africa, 1937; The South African Mints, 1939; People's Banks in South Africa, 1941; Insuring Our Insurance, 1941. Contbr. to: S. African Jrnl. of Econs.; S. African Banker. Mbr., sev. profl. orgs. Address: 292 Orient St., Arcadia, Pretoria 0002, S. Africa.

ARNDT, Ruth S., b. 2 June 1890, Toronto, Ont., Can. Educationist. Educ: B.A., Univ. of Toronto; Ph.D., Columbia Univ. Publs: Prohibition in Canada, 1919; Education as Growth, 1925; John Dewey, 1929. Mbr., Nursery School Assn. of S. Africa. Address: 292 Orient St., Arcadia, Pretoria 0002, S. Africa.

ARNE, Sigrid, b. 9 May 1900, NYC, USA. News Reporter. Educ: B.A., Univ. of Mich. Publs: The United Nations Primer, 1954, rev. ed., 1948. Mbr., Am. Newspaper Women's Club, Wash. D.C. Address: 17701 Riverway, Lakewood, OH 44107, USA.

ARNHEIM, Rudolf, b. 15 July 1904, Berlin, Germany. University Professor. Educ: Ph.D., Berlin, 1928. Publs: Art & Visual Perception, 1954; 2nd ed., 1974; Film as Art, 1957; Genesis of a Painting (Picasso's Guernica), 1962; Towards a Psychology of Art, 1966; Visual Thinking, 1969; Entropy & Art, 1971. Contbr. to: Psychol. Review; Jrnl. of Aesthetics & Art Criticism; Leonardo. Mbrships: Am. Psychol. Assn.; Am. Soc. Aesthetics; Coll. Art Assn. Recip., J.S. Guggenheim Fellowship, 1941-42. Address: 1050 Wall St., Apt. 6c, Ann Arbor, MI 48105, USA.

ARNOLD, Denis Midgley, b. 15 Dec. 1926, Sheffield, UK. Professor of Music. Educ: B.A., 1947; B.Mus., 1948; A.R.C.M., 1948; M.A. by thesis, 1950. Publs: Monteverdi, 1963; Marenzio, 1965; Giovanni Gabrieli, 1974; Ed., Giovanni Gabrieli: Opera Omnia, 6 vols., 1957-74; Ed., The Monteverdi Companion (w. N. Fortune), 1968; Ed., The Beethoven Companion (w. N. Fortune), 1971. Contbr. to: Musical Quarterly; Music & Letters; Monthly Musical Record; Musica Disciplina; The Musical Times. Rivista Musicale Italiana; The Listener; The Gramophone; Early Music. Mbrships: Royal Musical Assn.; Int. Musicol. Soc.; Gesellschaft für Musikforschung; Italian Musicol. Soc.; Hon. mbr., R.A.M. Address: c/o Faculty of Music, Univ. of Oxford, Oxford, UK.

ARNOLD, Harry John Philip, b. 1932, Portsmouth, Hants., UK. Company Director; Former Journalist & P.R.O. Educ: M.A., Wadham Coll., Oxford Univ. Publs: Aid for Developing Countries, 1962; Aid for Development, 1966; Photographer of the World, 1969; Another World, 1975. Contbr. to: Financial Times (staff mbr., 1956-60); Daily Telegraph Mag. Address: 30 Fifth Ave., Denvilles, Havant, Hants., UK.

ARNOT, Robin Page, pen name CADE, Jack, b. 1890, Greenock, UK. Author; Editor. Educ: M.A., Dr.Econ.Sci., Glasgow Univ. Publs. incl: Trade Unionism on the Railways (w. G. D. H. Cole), 1917; Ed., Labour Year Book of 1916; Facts from the Coal Commission, 1919; The Politics of Oil, 1924; Russia & Her Neighbours, 1927; William Morris: A Vindication, 1934; A History of the Miners' Federation of Great Britain (3 vols.), 1939, 1953, 1961; A History of the Scottish Miners, 1955; William Morris: The Man & The Myth, 1964; South Wales Miners, 1967. Contbr. to: Labour Monthly (Co-Fndr., 1921, Assoc. Ed., 1921-74); Communist Int.; Daily Worker; etc. Mbr., Soc. of Authors. Address: 46 Byne Road, London SE26 5JE, UK.

ARNOTHY, Christine, b. 1930, Budapest, Hungary. Writer. Publs: I am Fifteen & I do not Want to Die, 1956; Those Who Wait, 1957; It is Not so Easy to Live, 1958; The Charlatan 1959; Women of Japan, 1959; The Serpent's Bite, 1961; La Peau de Singe, 1961; The Captive Cardinal, 1964; The Black Garden, 1968; Jouer a l'Ete, 1967; Shalom Aviva!, 1970; Chiche, 1970; Un Type Merveilleux, 1972, 2nd ed., 1974; Lettre ouverte aux rois nus, 1974. Address: 168 Avenue Victor Hugo, Paris XVI, France.

ARNOW, Harriette Louisa Simpson, b. 7 July 1907, Coopersville, Ky., USA. Writer. Educ: A.B., Univ. of Louisville. Publs: Mountain Path, 1936; Hunter's Horn, 1949; The Dollmaker, 1954; Seedtime on the Cumberland (soc. hist.), 1960; Flowering of the Cumberland (soc. hist.), 1963; The Weedkiller's Daughter, 1970; The Kentucky Trace, 1974. Contbr. book reviews to: N.Y. Times Book Mag.; Sat. Review; Nation. Mbrships: PEN Am. Ctr.; Authors Guild. Hons. incl: Award of Merit, Am. Assn. for State & Local Hist., 1961. Address: 3220 Nixon, Rte. 6, Ann Arbor, MI 48105, USA.

ARON, Raymond Claude Ferdinand, b. 1905, Paris, France. University Professor. Educ: Agrégé de Philos. & Dr. ès lettres, Ecole Normale Superieure & Sorbonne. Publs: La sociologie allemande contemproaine (Contemporary German Sociology); Introduction à la philosophie de l'histoire (Introduction to the Philosophy of History); Les guerres en chaine (Century of Total War); L'Opium des intellectuels (The Opium of the Intellectuals); On War; Main Currents of Sociological Thought; Paix et Guerre; Progress & Disillusion: Republique Impériale (Imperial Republic). Contbr. to jrnls. Address: 87 Bd. Saint Michel, Paris 5, France.

ARONPURO, Kari Kalervo, b. 30 June 1940, Tampere, Finland. Librarian. Educ: Qualified Libn. Publs: (poems): Peltiset Enkelit (Plate Angels) 1964; Lokomonyliopisto (Locomo-University), 1970; Kiinan ja Rääkkylän Runot (China & Rääkkylä Poems), 1972; Moskovan Ikävä (Longing for Moscow), 1973; (collage) Aperitiff — Avoin Kaupunki (Aperitiff — Open City), 1965. Mbr., Finnish Soc. of Authors (SKL). Address: Kauppakatu 18 A 19, 94100 Kemi 10, Finland.

ARONSON, Theo, b. 13 Nov. 1930, Kirkwood, S. Africa. Writer. Educ: B.A., Univ. of Cape Town. Publs: The Golden Bees, 1965; Royal Vendetta, 1966; The Coburgs of Belgium, 1969; The Fall of the Third Napoleon, 1970; The Kaisers, 1971; Queen Victoria & the Bonapartes, 1972; Grandmama of Europe, 1973. Contbr. to num. mags. Address: Gum Tree Cottage, Teubes Rd., Kommetjie 7976, S. Africa.

ARPINO, Giovanni, b. 27 Jan. 1927. Writer. Educ: Univ. degli Studi, Turin, Italy. Publs: Sei stato felice (novel), 1952; Barbaresco (poems), 1954; Il prezzo dell'oro (poems), 1955; Gli anni del Giudizio (novel), 1958; La suora giovane (novel), 1959; Rafé e Micropiede (for children), 1960; Mille e una Italia for children, 1961; Una Nuvola d'ira (novel), 1962; L'ombra delle colline (novel), 1964; Un'anima persa (novel), 1966. Contbr. to num. jrnls. Hons: Bancarellino Prize, 1960; Strega Prize, 1964. Address: Via Leopardi 15, Milan, Italy.

ARTHUR, Donald Ramsay, b. 1 May 1917, Ammanford, S. Wales, UK. University Professor, King's College, University of London; Writer. Educ: Univ. of Wales, Aberystwyth. Publs: Ticks — A monograph of Ixodoidea Pt. V, 1960; Ticks & Disease, 1962; British Ticks, 1962; Ticks of the Genus Ixodes in Africa, 1965; Survival — Man & His Environment, 1969; Oil Pollution & Littoral Organisms (Ed. w. J. D. Carthy), 1968. Contbr. to var. acad. jrnls. Mbrships: Ed. Beds., Parasitol., Int. Jrnl. of Environmental Studies, & Biol. Scis.; Advsry. Bd., Zero

Population Inc. Address: 57 Rushgrove Ave., Colindale, London NW9 6RG, UK.

ARTHUR, Frank, b. 1902, London, UK. Writer. Publs: Who Killed Netta Maul? (republished as: The Suva Harbour Mystery); Another Mystery in Suva; Murder in the Tropic Night; The Throbbing Dark; The Abandoned Woman, the Story of Lucy Walter; Confession to Murder; Plays by French, Evans, Miller etc. Contbr. to: sev. papers & mags. in London & NZ. Mbrships: Crime Writers Assn.; Civil Service Club. Address: 106 Southborough Rd., Bromley, Kent, UK.

ARTHUR, Ruth M., b. 1905, Glasgow, UK. Former Froebel Teacher; Writer. Educ: Pvte. Schl. Publs: My Daughter Nicola, 1965; A Candle in Her Room, 1966; Requiem for a Princess, 1967; Portrait of Margarita, 1968; The Whistling Boy, 1969; The Saracen Lamp, 1970; The Little Dark Thorn, 1971; The Autumn People, 1973; After Candlemas, 1974; On the Wasteland, 1975. (all publd. UK & USA). Mbrships: Nat. Book League; Soc. of Authors; Engl. Speaking Union; PEN (Scottish Ctr.); Nat. Trust. Address: 46 Victoria Ave., Swanage, Dorset, UK.

ARTISS, Percy Harold, b. 14 Jan. 1903, London, UK. Nurseryman. Publs: Market Gardening, 1948. Address: Hill Rise Nursery, 295 Bath Rd., Slough SL1 5PR, UK.

ASBELL, Bernard, b. 8 May 1923, Bklyn., USA. Author; Former University Teacher of Non-Fiction Writing. Publs: When F.D.R. Died, 1961; The New Improved American, 1965; What Lawyers Really Do, 1970; Careers in Urban Affairs, 1970; The F.D.R. Memoirs, 1973; (as Nicholas Max) President McGovern's First Term. Contbr. to sev. nat. mags., 1956-. Mbr., Soc. of Mag. Writers (Pres., 1963). Hons: Schl. Bell Award, NEA, 1965; Educl. Writers Assn., 1st Prize mag. coverage, 1965 & Special Citation, 1966. Address: 326 Colonial Rd., Guildford, CT 06437, USA.

ASCHER-NASH, Franzi, b. 28 Nov. 1910, Vienna, Austria. Writer. Educ: Matura cum laude, Humanistisches Maedchengymnasium; Musik-Akademie, Vienna. Publs: Bilderbuch aus der Fremde, 1948; Gedichte eines Lebens — Poems of a Lifetime, 1975. Contbr. to: Decision; The German Quarterly; Austro-Am. Tribune (1945-49); Inspiré, Switz. (1949-52); Neues Oesterreich, Austria (1948-50); classical record jackets; The Story of the Art Song (radio prog., 1962-64); Aufbau, N.Y. (poetry); Lyrica Germanica (poetry); Opera News; etc. Mbr., Verband deutschsprachiger Autoren in Amerika. Recip., lit. awards. Address: 40-25 Hampton St., Elmhurst, NY 11373, USA.

ASH, Douglas, b. 22 Dec. 1914, London, UK. Author; Lecturer. Publs: How to Identify English Drinking Glasses & Decanters 1680-1830, 1962; English Silver Drinking Vessels 600-1830, 1964; Dutch Silver, 1965; Dictionary of English Antique Furniture, 1970; Dictionary of British Antique Silver, 1972. Contbr. to: Connoisseur; Antique Collector; Collectors Guide; etc. Mbrships: Fellow, Soc. of Antiquaries; F.R.S.A. Meyrick Soc.; Glass Circle. Recip., Citation for Gallantry, WWII. Address: 51 Great College St., Brighton, Sussex BN2 1HJ, UK.

ASHBY, Gwynneth Margaret, b. 1922, Birmingham, UK. Writer; Lecturer. Publs: Mystery of Coveside House, 1946; The Secret Ring, 1948; The Cruise of the Silver Spray, 1951; The Land & People of Sweden, 1951; The Land & People of Belgium, 1955; Let's Look at Austria, 1966; Looking at Norway, 1967; Looking at Japan, 1969. Contbr. to: Lady; Autocar; Animals; Guide; Christian Sci. Monitor; children's TV plays; schls. radio scripts. Mbrships: Soc. of Authors; R.G.S. Address: 13 Greenfield, Edenbridge, Kent, UK.

ASHE, Geoffrey Thomas, b. 29 Mar. 1923, London, UK. Writer; Lecturer. Educ: B.A., Univ. of B.C., Can.; B.A., Trinity Coll., Cambridge, UK. Publs. incl: The Tale of the Tub, 1950; King Arthur's Avalon, 1957; From Caesar to Arthur, 1960; Land to the West, 1962; The Land & the Book, 1965; Gandhi, 1968; The Quest for Arthur's Britain, 1968; All About King Arthur, 1969; Camelot & the Vision of Albion, 1971; The Art of Writing Made Simple, 1972; The Finger & the Moon, 1973; Do What You Will, 1974. Contbr. to var. lit. publs. Mbrships: F.R.S.L.; Co-Fndr. & Sec., Camelot Rsch. Comm.; Int. Arthurian Soc. Address: c/o A. D. Peters & Co., 10 Buckingham St., London WC2N 6BU, UK.

ASHFORD, Frederick Charles, b. 22 Apr. 1909, Wimbledon, UK. Design Consultant. Publs: Designing for

Industry, 1955; The Aesthetics of Engineering Design, 1969. Contbr. to: Design Mag.; Engrng. Design & Materials; Chartered Engr. Fellow, Soc. of Indl. Artists & Designers. Address: 22 South St., Gargrave, Skipton, Yorks., UK.

ASHFORD, Jeffrey, b. 1926, London, UK. Barrister; Author. Educ: Dept. of Navigation, Univ. of Southampton; The Bar. Publs: Counsel for the Defence, 1960; Investigations are Proceeding, 1961; The Burden of Proof, 1962; Will Anyone Who Saw the Accident, 1963; Enquiries are Continuing; 1964; The Hands of Innocence, 1965; Consider the Evidence, 1966; Forget What You Saw, 1967; Prisoner at the Bar, 1969; To Protect the Guilty, 1970; Bent Copper, 1971; A Man Will be Kidnapped Tomorrow, 1972; The Double Run, 1973; The Colour of Violence, 1974; Three Layers of Guilt, 1975. Mbrships: Paternosters Club; Crime Writers Assn. Address: Bourne Farm, Aldington Frith, Near Ashford, Kent, UK.

ASHLEY, Joseph D., pen name Joe, b. 20 Sept. 1912, Ilion, N.Y., USA. Retired Newspaper Retail Advertising Manager; Writer. Educ: Ithaca Coll. Contbr. to: The Sportsman's Handbook; Campfire Chatter; Shots & Casts (wkly. column); SummerScope. Mbrships: Outdoor Writers Assn. of Am.; New England Outdoor Writers Assn.; Nat. Rifle Assn.; Trout Unlimited; Nat. Wild Turkey Fedn.; Deer Sportsman of Am.; num. other orgs. concerned w. conserv. Address: The Transcript, 124 American Legion Drive, N. Adams, MA 01247, USA.

ASHLEY, Leonard R(aymond) N(elligan), b. 5 Dec. 1928, Miami, Fla., USA. Professor of English; Writer; Editor. Educ: B.A., 1949, M.A., 1950, McGill Univ.; A.M., 1953, Ph.D., 1956, Princeton Univ. Publs. incl: Colley Cibber, 1965; 19th Century British Drama, 1968; Other People's Lives: 34 Stories, 1970; Mirrors for Man: 26 Plays of the World Drama, 1974; Ed., var. educl. books. Contbr. to: History of the Theatre, 1968; Educl. Theatre Jrnl.; Names; etc. Mbrships. incl: MLA; Int. Soc. Gen. Semantics; Coll. Engl. Assn.; etc. Shakespeare Gold Medal, 1949. Address: 1901 Ave. H, Bklyn., NY 11230, USA.

ASHLEY, Maurice Percy, b. London, UK. Author. Educ: B.A., D.Phil., New Coll., Oxford. Publs. incl: England in the Seventeenth Century; The Greatness of Oliver Cromwell, 1957; Churchill as Historian, 1968; The Golden Century 1598-1715; 1969; Charles II: The Man & the Statesman, 1971. Contbr. to: Listener (Ed., 1958-67); Times Lit. Supplement; Encounter; Hist. Today; etc. Mbrships: Pres., Cromwell Assn.; Soc. of Authors; Reform Club. Address: 34 Wood Lane, Ruislip, Middlesex HA4 6EX, UK.

ASHMORE, Owen, b. 1920, Disley, Cheshire, UK. Acting Director, University Extra-Mural Department. Publs: Development of Power in Britain, 1967; Industrial Archaeology of Lancashire, 1969. Contbr. to: Local Histn.; Transactions of Historic Soc. of Lancs. & Cheshire; Transactions of Lancs. & Cheshire Antiquarian Soc. Address: 5 Flowery Field, Woodsmoor, Stockport, Cheshire, UK.

ASHTON-WARNER, Sylvia (Constance), b. 17 Dec. 1908, Stratford, NZ. Professor of Education. Educ: Wairarapa Coll., Masterton; Tchrs. Coll., Auckland, 1928-29. Publs: (novels) Spinster, 1958; Incense to Idols, 1960; Teacher, 1963; Bell Call, 1964; Greenstone, 1966; Three, 1970; (other) Myself, 1967. Contbr. to: NZ Listener; Here & Now; NZ Monthly Review. Address: Aspen Community School, Box 1939, Aspen, CO 81611, USA.

ASIMOV, Isaac, b. 1920, Petrovichi, USSR. Professor of Biochemistry. Educ: B.S., M.A., Ph.D., Columbia Univ. Publs. incl: The Words of Science; The Realm of Numbers; The Living River; Inside the Atom; Building Blocks of the Universe; The Naked Sun; Nine Tomorrows; XXI, Robot; Contbr. to: Astounding Sci. Fiction; Galaxy; Science World; etc. Mbr., Authors' League of Am. Address: 45 Greenough St., West Newton 65, Mass., USA.

ASK-UPMARK, Karl Erik Fritz, b. 4 Oct. 1901, Lund, Sweden. Professor of Medicine; Physician. Educ: Final Med. Educ., 1928; Assoc. Prof. of Med., Lund, 1935; Prof. of Med., Uppsala, 1946. Publs. incl: Cartoid Sinus & Cerebral Circulation, 1935; Applied Anatomy, 1950; Acute Medicine, 1959-69; Bedside Medicine, 1963; Nervous System & Internal Disorders, 1963; High Blood Pressure, 1967; Medical Masqueraders, 1969; Voyage Through the Years, 1969; Headache, 1970. Contbr. to Acta Med. Scand.

& var. med. periodicals throughout Europe. Mbrships: Swedish Med. Soc.; Soc. of Scis., Uppsala; Lund Med. Soc.; N.Y. Acad. of Scis.; Med. Acad., Argent. Address: Svartbäcksgatan 37A, 753 32 Uppsala, Sweden.

ASMODI, Herbert Christian Ernst, b. 30 Mar. 1923. Playwright. Educ: Ruprecht-Karl Univ., Heidelberg, Germany. Publs. (all comedies): Pardon wird nicht gegeben; Nachsaison; Die Menschenfresser; Mohrenwäsche; Dichtung und Wahrheit oder der Pestalozzi-Preis; Stirb & Werde (2 episodes from the German recovery); Nasarin oder Die Kunst zu Träumen; Marie von Brinvillers; Geld. Mbr., PEN. Hons: Gerhart Hauptmann Preis der Freien Volksbühne Berlin, 1954; Tukan Prize, Munich, 1971. Address: Occamstr. 3, Munich 40, W. Germany.

ASTBURY, Norman Frederick, b. 1 Dec. 1908, Normacot, Staffs., UK. Physicist. Educ: B.A., 1929, M.A. 1933, St. John's Coll., Cambridge; Sc.D., 1954. Publs: Industrial Magnetic Testing, 1952; Introduction to Electrical Applied Physics, 1957. Contbr. to profl. jrnls. inclng: Royal Soc.; Phys. Soc.; Ceramic Soc.; Elec. Engrs. Mbrships. incl: Fellow, Inst. of Phys.; FIEE. Recip., C.B.E., 1968. Address: 13 Allerton Rd., Trentham, Stoke-on-Trent ST4 8PB, UK.

ASTLEY, Thea (Beatrice May), b. 25 Aug. 1925, Brisbane, Qld., Australia. University Senior Tutor in English. Educ: B.A., Univ. of Qld., Brisbane, 1947. Publs: (novels) Girl with a Monkey, 1959; A Descant for Gossips, 1960; The Well-Dressed Explorer, 1962; The Slow Natives, 1965; A Boat Load of Home Folk, 1968; Ed., Coast to Coast, 1969-1970, 1971. Contbr. to: Coast to Coast; Southerly. Hons: C'wlth. Lit. Fund Fellowship, 1961, 1964; Miles Franklin Award, 1962, 1965; Moomba Award, 1965. Address: Dept. of English, Macquarie University, North Ryde, Sydney, N.S.W., Australia.

ÅSTRÖM, Paul, F. K., b. 15 Jan. 1929, Sundsvall, Sweden. Professor of Classical Archaeology. Educ: Ph.D., Lund Univ., 1958. Publs: The Middle Cypriote Bronze Age, 1957; Excavations at Kalopsidha & Ayios Iakovos in Cyprus, 1966; The Thread of Ariadne, 1970; Who's Who in Cypriote Archaeology, 1972; The Swedish Cyprus Expedition, vol. IV — 1B, 1C, 1D, 1972. Contbr. to archaeol. jrnls. Mbrships. incl: Soc. of Letters, Lund; German Archaeol. Inst., Royal Soc. of Letters, Gothenburg. Recip. of Faxe Prize for Best Dissertation, 1958. Address: Södra Vägen 61, S-41254 Göteborg, Sweden.

ATANASOV, Gercho, b. 12 Sept. 1931, Shoumen, Bulgaria. Editor. Publs: (in Bulgarian) A Town Sky, 1961; Intimate, 1963; The Naive Man, 1965; While We are Waiting, 1972; As it is in Life, 1974; By the Side of the Highway, 1974. Contbr. to: Plamak; September; Literatouren Front. Mbrships: Union of Bulgarian Writers; Union of Bulgarian Jrnlsts. Address: Sofia-4, ul. Boycho Voyvoda, 4, Bulgaria.

ATHAS, Daphne, b. 1923, Cambridge, Mass., USA. University Professor. Educ: Univ. of N.C.; Harvard Schl. of Educ.; McDowell Fellowship, 1961, 1962. Publs: Weather of the Heart, 1947; The Fourth World, 1956; (play) Ding-Dong Bell (co-author), 1958; Greece by Prejudice, 1963; Entering Ephesus, 1972. Contbr. to: Transatlantic Review; Envoi; New World Writing; Beloit Poetry Jrnl.; etc. Mbrships. incl: N.C. Lit. & Hist. Soc.; Authors League. Hons. incl: Nat. Fndn. Arts & Humanities Award, 1969; Sir Walter Raleigh Fiction Award, 1972; Fulbright Award, 1973-74; Nat. Endowment of Arts Award, 1974-75. Address: Box 224, Chapel Hill, NC 27514, USA.

ATKIN, Ronald Harry, b. 2 Jan. 1926, Martin Dales, Lincs., UK. Mathematician. Educ: B.A., M.A., Emmanuel Coll., Cambridge Univ.; B.Sc., M.Sc., London Univ. Publs: Mathematics & Wave Mechanics, 1956; Classical Dynamics, 1959; Theoretical Electromagnetism, 1962; Urban Structure Research Reports, I-IV, 1972-74; Mathematical Structure in Human Affairs, 1974; Multi-Dimensional Man, 1975. Contbr. to: Economist (reviews); Int. Jrnl. Man-Machine Studies; Environment & Planning. Mbrships: London Math. Soc.; Cambridge Philosl. Soc. Address: 57 Victoria Rd., Colchester, Essex, UK.

ATKINS, John Alfred, b. 26 May 1916, Carshalton, UK. University Teacher. Educ: B.A.(Hons.), Bristol Univ. publs: Cat on Hot Bricks, 1948; The Art of Ernest Hemingway, 1952; Rain & the River, 1952; George Orwell, 1954; Land Fit for Eros (w. J. B. Pick), 1954; Arthur

Koestler, 1955; Tomorrow Revealed, 1955; Aldous Huxley, 1956; Graham Greene, 1957; Sex in Literature, Vols. I & II, 1970, 1973. Contbr. to: Penguin New Writing; Times Educl. Supplement; Books & Bookmen; Tribune. Mbrships: Writers' Guild; Writers' Action Grp.; PEN; Soc. of Authors. Recip., Arts Coun. Award, 1970. Agent: David Higham Assocs. Ltd. Address: Braeside Cottage, Birch Green, Colchester CO2 0NH, UK.

ATKINSON, Carroll, Sr., b. 24 Oct. 1896, Fairbury, Neb., USA. Retired College Professor; Writer. Educ: A.B., Lawrence Coll., 1920; M.A., Univ. of S. Calif., 1929; Ph.D., George Peabody Coll., 1938. Publs. incl: The Confessions of a Ph.D., 1939; I Knew the Voice of Experience, 1943; Intellectual Tramp, 1955; The Story of Education, 2nd ed., 1965. Contbr. to num. jrnls.; Past Ed., Am. Educator; Assoc. Ed., Mod. Lang. Jrnl. & Dictionary of Education. Address: 3021 N. Oleander, Daytona Beach, FL 32018, USA.

ATKINSON, Frank, b. 9 Feb. 1925, Hessle, Yorks., UK. Librarian. Educ: F.L.A., Polytech. of N. London. Publs: The English Newspaper Since 1900: a Bibliography, 1960; The Computer in Education: a Bibliography, 1968; The Public Library, 1970; Yesterday's Money (w. John Fines), 1971; Librarianship: an Introduction to the Profession, 1974; Illustrated Teach Yourself Coins (w. John Matthews), 1975. Contbr. to numismatic & lib. jrnls. Mbr., Lib. Assn. Address: Corner Cottage, Broad Oak, Heathfield, Sussex, UK.

ATKINSON, James, b. 1914, Tynemouth, Northumberland, UK. Professor of Biblical Studies. Educ: Univ. of Durham, UK; Univ. of Muenster, Germany; M.A.; M.Litt.; Dr.Theol. Publs: Library of Christian Classics, vol. XVI, 1962; Rome & Reformation, 1966; Luther's Works, vol. 44, 1966; Luther & the Birth of Protestantism, 1968; Paternoster Church History, vol. 4, Luther & the Reformation, 1968; The Trial of Luther, 1971. Contbr. to var. schlrly. jrnls. Mbr., Soc. for Study of Theol. Address: Leach House, Hathersage, Sheffield S30 1BA, UK.

ATKINSON, Justin Brooks, b. 28 Nov. 1894, Melrose, Mass., USA. Journalist; Author. Educ: B.A., Harvard Univ. Publs. incl: Skyline Promenades, 1925; Henry Thoreau, the Cosmic Yankee, 1927; East of the Hudson, 1931; Once Around the Sun, 1951; Tuesdays & Fridays, 1963; Brief Chronicles, 1966; Broadway, 1970; This Bright Land, 1972; (ed.) Sean O'Casey Reader, 1968. Contbr. to: Boston Evening Transcript, 1919-22; N.Y. Times, 1922-65. Hons: Pulitzer Prize for Journalism, 1947; LL.D.; L.H.D.

ATKINSON, Nancy, pen name BENKO, Nancy, b. 9 Mar. 1910, Melbourne, Vic., Australia. Microbiologist; Author. Educ: B.Sc., M.Sc., Univ. of Melbourne; D.Sc., Univ. of Adelaide. Publs: Art & Artists of South Australia, 1969; The Art of David Boyd, 1973; Chapt., "Salmonellosis in Australia" in World Problem of Salmonellosis (Ed., van Oye). Contbr. of num. rsch. papers on antibiotics & salmonellosis to: Aust. Jrnl. of Expmtl. Biol. Med. Sci.; etc. Mbrships. incl: Aust. Soc. for Microbiol.; Aust. Inst. of Food Sci. & Technol.; lay mbr., Royal S. Aust. Soc. of Art. Recip., O.B.E., 1951. Address: 64 Strangways Terr., Nth. Adelaide, S. Australia 5006.

ATLAS, Helena, b. 27 Feb. 1909, Cracow, Poland. Translator. Educ: Absolutorium of Philos. Publs: Transl. of over 80 books into Polish inclng. Hichens, Bradley, Marshall, King, Parke, Parrot, Queen, Thomas, from Engl.; Maurois, Mauriac, Benoit, Morand, from French; Goll, Gaugenwald, Mauer, Kaus, Thomas, from German; var. short stories from Italian. Contbr. to: Ilustrowany Kurier Codizienny; As; Around the World; Detective; New Daily (Nowy Dziennik). Mbrships: PEN; Polski Zwiazek Literatow; Zaiks. Address: 340 W. 87th St., N.Y., NY 10024, USA.

ATREYA, Bhikhan Lal, b. 24 Sept. 1897, Judah, Dst. Saharanpur, U.P., India. Teacher. Educ: B.A., 1921, M.A., 1923, Banaras Hindu Univ.; D.Litt., 1930; Coll. of Sci., Calcutta Univ., 1937. Publs. incl: The Philosophy of Yogavasistha, 1936; An Introduction to Parapsychology, 1952; The Spirit of Indian Culture, 1952; A History of Indian Ethics, 1964; A Plea for Human Fellowship, 1967. Contbr. to var. profl. & lit. jrnls. Mbrships: Gen. Pres., Indian Philos. Congress, 1957; Pres., Psychol. & Educl. Sci. Sect., Indian Sci. Congress Assn., 1942. Hons: Prize, Illustrated Weekly of India Essay Competition, 1948; U.P.

Govt. Prize; Kt. Cmdr., Italy, 1948; Padmabhushan, India, 1954. Address: P.O. Hindu Univ., Varanasi-5, U.P., India.

ATTENBOROUGH, Bernard George, pen name RAND, James S., b. Moseley, Birmingham, UK. Company Director; Fleet St. Correspondent; Big Game Hunter-Angler. Publs: The Stake, 1959; Run for the Trees, 1967; Viva Ramirez, 1970; The Great Sky & the Silence. Contbr. to: News Chronicle; Sunday Times; Daily Mirror; var. mags., UK & USA. Mbrships: Big Game Fishing Assn., USA; Shark Club. Address: Green Meadows, Heads of Ayr, Scotland, UK.

ATTERBURY, Stella, b. 14 Aug. 1899, Hampstead, London, UK. Housewife. Publs: Never Too Late, 1963; Leave It To Cook, 1968; Cook Ahead, 1970; Waste Not, Want Not, 1972. Address: Hamewith, Beacon Rd. W., Crowborough, Sussex, UK.

ATTHILL, Robin, b. 1912, Netherhampton, UK. Schoolmaster. Educ: Univ. of Oxford. Publs: (poems) If Pity Departs, 1947; The Curious Past, 1955; Old Mendip, 1964; The Somerset & Dorset Railway, 1967, 2nd ed., 1970; The Picture History of the Somerset & Dorset Railway, 1970. Contbr. to: Engl.; Country Life; BBC. Address: Stoneleigh Cottage, Oakhill, Bath, Somerset, UK.

ATWOOD, Margaret, b. 18 Nov. 1939, Ottawa, Ont., Can. Writer; Former University Teacher. Educ: Univ. of Toronto; Radcliffe; Harvard Univ.; B.A.; A.M.; D.Litt. Publs: (poetry) The Circle Game, 1966, 1967; The Animals in that Country, 1968; The Journals of Susanna Moodie, 1970; Procedures for Underground, 1970; Power Politics, 1971; You Are Happy, 1974; (fiction) The Edible Woman, 1969; Surfacing, 1972; Survival: a Thematic Guide to Canadian Literature, 1972. Contbr. to: Tamarack Review; Atlantic Monthly; New Yorker; Can. Forum; num. lit. mags. Mbr., Writers' Union of Can. Hons. incl: 1st Prize, Centennial Commn. Poetry Competition, 1967; Prizes from Poetry (Chgo.), 1969, 1974; LL.D., Queens, 1974. Agent: Phoebe Larmore. Address: c/o Oxford Univ. Press, 70 Wynford Dr., Don Mills, Ont., Can.

AUCHINCLOSS, Louis Stanton, pen name LEE, Andrew, b. 27 Sept., 1917, Lawrence, N.Y., USA. Attorney. Educ: LL.B., Univ. of Va., Charlottesville, 1941. Publs: 24 books inclng. The Indifferent Children, 1947; Sybil, 1952; The Romantic Egoists, 1954; Venus in Sparta, 1958; The House of Five Talents, 1960; Reflections of a Jacobite, 1961; Powers of Attorney, 1963; The Embezzler, 1966; Tales of Manhattan, 1967; A World of Profit, 1968; Motiveless Malignity, 1969; Second Chance, 1970; Edith Wharton, 1971; I Come as a Thief, 1972; Richeloeu, 1972; The Partners, 1974; A Writer's Capital, 1974. Mbrships. incl: Nat. Inst. of Arts & Letters; Century Assn. Hons. incl: Gold Medal, Nat. Arts Club; D.Litt., N.Y. Univ., 1974. Address: 1111 Park Ave., N.Y., NY 10028, USA.

AUDRY, Colette, b. 6 July 1906. Writer. Educ: Ecole Normale Supérieure, Sèvres. Publs: On joue perdant; Aux yeux du souvenir; Léon Blum ou la politique du Juste; Connaissance de Sartre; Sartre ou la Realité humaine, 1966; L'Autre planete, 1972; Les Malheurs de Sophie (screen-play); La Bataille du rail (screen-play); Olivia (screen-play); Absence (screen-play); Liberté Surveillée (screen-play); Derrière la Baignoire (screen-play); Fruits amers (screen-play); Soledad (play). Contbr. to: Les Tempes Modernes, 1945-55. Recip., Prix Medicis, 1962. Address: Résidence du Val (3b), 91-Palaiseau, France.

AUDUS, Leslie John, b. 9 Dec. 1911, Isleham, Cambs., UK. Professor of Botany. Educ: M.A., Ph.D., Sc.D., Downing Coll., Cambridge Univ. Publs: Plant Growth Substances, 1953, 3rd ed. vol. 1, 1972; Ed., Physiology & Biochemistry of Herbicides, 1964; Ed., Herbicides: Biochemistry, Ecology & Physiology, forthcoming. Contbr. to: Nature; New Biol.; Endeavour; major int. jrnls. (sci. papers on plant physiol.); Jrnl. Expmtl. Biol. (Ed., 1965-74). Mbrships incl: Soc. Expmtl. Biol.; Linnean Soc. of London (VP, 1959-60); other profl. assns. Address: Botany Dept., Bedford Coll., Regent's Park, London NW1, UK.

AUERBACH, Arnold, b. 11 Apr. 1898, Liverpool, UK. Sculptor; Painter; Etcher; Former Visiting Art Lecturer. Publs: Sculpture, 1952; Modelled Sculpture & Plaster Casting, 1961. Former Mbr., Soc. of Authors. Address: 152 Holland Rd., Kensington, London W14, UK.

AUGER, H. A., b. 1917, London, UK. Managing Director. Publs: West African Vade Mecum; Trade Fairs &

Exhibitions. Contbr. to: Mktng.; Advt.; Just Ahead; Indian & African newspapers; Ed., All Informed. Mbrships: F.I.P.A.; M.I.P.R.; M.Inst.M.S.M.; F.R.S.A. Address: 90 Ashworth Mansions, Elgin Ave., Maida Vale, London W9, UK.

AUGER, Pierre Victor, b. 14 May 1899, Paris, France. University Professor. Educ: Agrégé des Scis., 1922, Doct. ès Sc., 1926, Ecole Normale Supérieure. Publs: What Are Cosmic Rays, 1941; Les Rayons Cosmiques; L'Homme Microscopique, 1951, 1965; Current Trends in Scientific Research, 1961. Contbr. to: Diogène; Impact; Revue des Deux Mondes; Revue Philos.; French Radio; Les Rencontres de Genève. Mbrships incl: F.R.S.A. (Hon. Sec., France); Fellow, Am. Phys. Soc.; Assn. des Ecrivains Scientifiques; Int. Acad. of Astronautics. Hons: Grand Off., Légion d'Honneur, 1961; Feltrinelli Int. Prize, 1961; Kalingh Prize for Sci. Writing. Address: 12 rue Emile Faguet, 75014 Paris, France.

AUMANN, Francis Robert, b. 21 Jan. 1901, Delaware, Ohio, USA. Professor of Political Science. Educ: B.A., Ohio Wesleyan Univ., 1928; M.A., Ohio State Univ., 1925; Ph.D., Univ. of Iowa, 1928. Publs: Municipal Administration of Justice in Iowa, 1929; The Changing American Legal System, 1940; History of the State of Ohio (w. others), 1941; The Instrumentalities of Justice, 1956; The Government & Administration of Ohio (w. H. Walker), 1956; State Constitutional Revision (w. others), 1960. Contbr. to num. scholarly, legal & popular jrnls. Mbrships incl: Am. Pol. Sci. Assn.; Ohio Histl. Soc. Address: 112 E. Como Av., Columbus, OH 43202, USA.

AUSTIN, Cedric Ronald Jonah, b. 30 Apr. 1912, London, UK. Author. Educ: Guildhall Schl. of Music, London; B.A., M.A., Univ. of London. Publs: Read to Write, 1954; Reading Today, 1956; Enjoy These Stories, 1962; Reason for Reading, 1965; The Science of Wine, 1968; Whys & Wherefores of Winemaking, 1970; The Good Wines of Europe, 1973; The Wine Answer Book, 1974. Mbrships: Soc. of Authors. Fndr. Mbr., Amateur Winemakers' Nat. Guild of Judges; Chmn., Assn. of Informed Drinkers. Address: 38 Mandeville Rd., Hertford, UK.

AUSTIN, Josephine Agnes Dorothy, b. 15 Mar. 1934, Richmond, Yorks., UK. Poet; Lecturer; Broadcaster. Educ: Dip., Spoken Engl., London Guildhall; Open Univ. Publs: In Focus, 1966; Further into Focus, 1968; Space Between, 1971; The Pisces Collection of Poems, 1974. Contbr. to: Tantrum; BBC Second Selection; Daily Telegraph; Women; Womens Own; Sussex Life; Indian Mag.; Norman Hiddews Dorkshop Press. Fndr. & Chmn., New Poetry Soc., Hastings, Eastbourne, Sussex & Kent Area. Address: Austins, 3 Lyndhurst Ave., Hastings, Sussex, UK.

AUSTIN, Muriel Howard, b. Lichfield, UK. Educationalist; Author. Publs: Counting Time; Reading & Making; My Little Writing Books; Plays for Infants; The Way to Number; Stories read in BBC Children's Hour. Contbr. to Child Educ. Address: Gaia Lane, Lichfield, Staffs, UK.

AUSTIN, Richard Joseph Byron, b. 1926, Castleconnell, Repub. of Ireland. Television Industrialist; Company Director. Publs: (novels) Watchman, What of the Night? 1973; The Hour Before Twilight, 1974; (poetry) Night Bird, 1971; Carnival, 1973; Nocturnes, 1973; (criticism) The Ballerina, 1974; Images of the Dance, 1975; (radio plays) Monday Night, 1969; Chanticleer, 1970; Dinner with Jane, 1970; October, 1970; Noontide, 1972. Contbr. to: Punch; Evening News; Mayfair; Ballet Today; Int. Storyteller; Tempo; Adam Int. Review; Writers' Review; Commonweal; Flair; num. poetry mags. Mbrships: PEN; Soc. of Authors; Radiowriters' Assn.; Writers' Guild. Address: 65 Chatsworth Court, Pembroke Rd., London W8, UK.

AUTIO, Orvokki Lea Miriam, b. 27 July 1941, Kurikka, Finland. Author. Educ: Univs. of Turku & Tampere. Publs: Kaukana Soi Haitapi (poems), 1969; Timanttihäät (novel), 1970; Puimakone bulevardills (novel), 1971; Sininen Kaappi (short stories), 1972. Mbrships: Finnish Soc. of Authors; Finnish Soc. of Cultural Wkrs. Hons: State Artists Prize; 2 Literary Prizes, City of Tampere; Literary Prize, Välinö Linna Fund. Address: Papinkatu 8A9, 33200 Tampere, 20 Finland.

AUTTON, (Rev.) Norman, b. 1920, Neath, UK. Hospital Chaplain. Educ: Selwyn Coll., Cambridge; St.

Michael's Theological Coll., Llandaff; M.A.; D.Litt. Publs: The Pastoral Care of the Mentally III, 1962; The Pastoral Care of the Dying, 1965; The Pastoral Care of the Bereaved, 1966; Pastoral Care in Hospitals, 1968; A Manual of Prayers & Readings with the Sick, 1970; (ed.) From Fear to Faith, 1970; Christianity & Change, 1971; When Sickness Comes, 1973; Visiting Ours, 1975. Contbr. to: A Guide to Oncological Nursing, 1974. Address: 77 Rhydhelig Av., The Heath, Cardiff CF4 4DB, UK.

AVALLONE, Michael (Angelo) Jr., pen names DALTON, Priscilla; DANE, Mark; MICHAELS, Steve; NILE, Dorothea; NOONE, Edwina; CONWAY, Troy; STUART, Sidney; HIGHLAND, Dora; DePRE, J. A.; STANTON, Vance, b. 27 Oct. 1924, NYC, USA. Writer. Publs. incl: Meanwhile back at the Morgue, 1960; The Living Bomb, 1963; There is Something about a Dame, 1963; The Brutal Kook, 1964; The Fat Death, 1966; The February Doll Murders, 1966; Assassins Don't Die in Bed, 1966; Darkening Windows, 1966; Felicie, 1964; Vampire Cameo, 1968; Daughter of Darkness, 1967; Seacliffe, 1968; The Beast with Red Hands, 1972; The Girls in Television, 1974; Beneath the Planet of the Apes, 1974; The Satan Sleuth Series, 1975. Hons: NN.J. Assn. of Tchrs. of Engl., 1969; Newark Schl. of Engrng., 1974. Address: 80 Hilltop Blvd., East Brunswick, NJ, USA.

AVELINE, Claude, b. 1901, Paris, France. Author. Publs. incl: Madame Maillart, 1932; Le temps mort, 1945; The Double Death of Frederic Belot, 1949; L'execution de Marineche, 1949; Prisoner Born, 1950; The Fountain of Marlieux, 1954; De Quoi Encore?, 1955; Le Bestaire inattendu, 1960; The Bird that Flew into the Sea, 1961; True — But Don't Believe It, 1961; Coach Seven, Seat Fifteen, 1962. Mbrships: Hon. Pres., Anatole France Soc.; Pres., Jean Vigo Prize jury. Hons: Grand Prix, Soc. de Gens de Lettres, 1952; Int. Italia Prize, 1955; Soc. of European Culture; PEN. Address: 31 rue de Veneuil, Paris VII, France.

AVERY, Peter William, b. 15 May 1923, Derby, UK. University Teaching Officer. Educ: B.A., London, 1949; M.A., Cambridge, 1958. Publs: Poems from Hafiz (w. John Heath-Stubbs), 1952; Modern Iran, 1965; Ruba'iyat of Omar Khayyam (w. John Heath-Stubbs). Contbr. to: Times Literary Supplement; Brit. Jrnl. of Middle E. Studies; Middle E. Jrnl. of Am.; Ency. Britannica; etc. Mbrships: Fellow, Royal Asiatic Soc.; Royal Ctrl. Asian Soc.; Royal Inst. of Int. Affairs; Am. Assn. of Middle E. Studies; Coun., Brit. Assn. of Middle E. Studies. Address: King's College, Cambridge CB2 1ST, UK.

AVILÉS FABILA, René, b. 15 Nov. 1940, México, D.F., México. Writer. Educ: Lic. in Int. Rels., Nat. Univ. of Mexico. Publs: Los Juegos, 1967; Hacia el Fin del Mundo, 1969; La Lluvia no Mata a las Flores, 1971; El Gran Solitario de Palacio, 1972; Nueva Utopía (y los Guerrilleros), 1973; La Desaparición de Hollywood, 1973. Contbr. to: Mundo Neuvo; Casa de las Américas; Hispamérica; Mexican & Argentine anthols. Hons: Fellowship, Mexican Writers Ctr., 1965-66; Citation Casa de las Américas, Havana, Cuba, 1972. Address: Reembolsos 76, México 13, D.F., México.

AWDRY, Wilbert Vere, b. 15 June 1911, Ampfield, Romsey, Hants., UK. Clergyman; Author. Educ: M.A., St. Peter's Coll., Oxford; Dip.Theol., Wycliffe Hall, Oxford. Publs: Three Railway Engines; Thomas the Tank Engine; James the Red Engine, & 23 other titles in this children's series; Industrial Archaeology in Gloucestershire, 1974. Mbrships: Soc. of Authors; Nat. Book League; Nat. Liberal Club. Address: Sodor, 30 Rodborough Avenue, Stroud, Glos. GL5 3RS, UK.

AXBERGER, Gunnar, b. 30 Sept. 1902, Västeras, Sweden. Professor of Literature. Educ: Ph.D., Univ. of Stockholm, 1936. Publs: (in Swedish) The Young Atterbom, 1936; (books about Swedish authors) Fredrika Bremer, 1951; Verner von Heidenstam, 1959; Hjalmar Bergman, 1960; Birger Sjöberg, 1960; Literary Fantasy & Fire: A Literary Study Incorporating Comparisons with Material from the Field of Forensic Psychiatry, 1967; Studies on problem of arson & fiction, Psychiatry, 1973; Annales Médico — Psychologiques, 1973. Mbrships. incl: PEN; Birger Sjöberg-sällskapet. Hons: Warburg Prize, 1938; Birger Sjöberg Prize, 1960; Övralid Prize, 1961; Prize of Swedish Acad., 1968. Address: Lokevägen 11, 182-61 Djursholm, Sweden.

AXELSON, Sture Fridolf Harald, b. 12 July 1913, Linköping, Sweden. Senior Latin, Greek & Italian Master. Educ: Ph.D., 1944. Publs. incl: (novel) Claudianus; (lyrical poetry) Blåsten Bläddrar I Bladen, 1964; Vuxenutbildning, 1972; Nyheter Från Norrköping, 1974; Transls. of Ancient Roman prose & poetry, mod. Italian poetry. Mbr., Soc. of Swedish Authors. Hons: Culture Prize, Town of Norrköping, 1962, Co. of Östergötland, 1971; Prize for Lyrical Poetry, Swedish Radio, 1974. Address: Timmermansgatan 66, 60359 Norrköping, Sweden.

AYCKBOURN, Alan, b. 1939, London, UK. Theatre Director; Playwright; Writer. Publs: (plays) Mr. Whatnot, 1963; Relatively Speaking, 1965; How the Other Half Loves, 1969; Time and Time Again, 1971; Absurd Person Singular, 1972; The Norman Conquests (Trilogy), 1973; Service Not Included (TV play), 1974. Contbr. to BBC Leeds (Radio Drama Prod., 1965-70). Agent: Margaret Ramsay Ltd. Address: 14a Goodwins Court, St. Martin's Lane, London WC2, UK.

AYGUESPARSE, Albert, b. 1 Apr. 1900, Brussels, Belgium. Writer. Publs. incl: Machinisme et Culture, 1931; Magie du Capitalisme, 1934; L'Heure de la Vérité, 1947; Notre Ombre nous précède, 1952; Le Mauvais Age, 1959; Selon toute vraisemblance, 1961; Ecrire la pierre, 1970; Le Partage des Jours, 1972; Les Armes de la guérison, 1973; Poèmes 1923-60. Contbr. to: Marginales (Dir.); Jrnl. des Poètes; La Revue Générale. Mbrships. incl: Royal Acad. of French Lang. & Lit.; Comm., PEN; Assn. for Belgian Writers. Hons. incl: Grand Off. Order of Leopald, Order of the Crown; Victor Rossel Prize, 1952; Camille Engelmann Prize, 1957; Chatrian Prize, 1967. Address: 118 rue Marconi, B-1180 Brussels, Belgium.

AYLEN, Leo William, b. 15 Feb. 1935, Vryheid, Natal, S. Africa. Poet; Writer; Film Director. Educ: B.A., New Coll., Oxford; Ph.D., Bristol Univ. Publs: Greek Tragedy & the Modern World, 1964; Discontinued Design, 1969; I, Odysseus, 1971; Greece for Everyone, 1975. Contbr. to: approx. 20 Engl. & European anthols.; Classical Drama & its Influence. Mbrships. incl: Writers Guild of Great Brit.; Soc. of Film & TV Arts; Assn. of Cinema & TV Technicians. Recip., nomination for Brit. TV awards for The Drinking Party, 1966. Address: 71 Chelsham Rd., London SW4, UK.

AYLING, Stanley Edward, b. 1909, London, UK. Educ: M.A., Emmanuel Coll., Cambridge. Publs: (biography) Portraits of Power, 1961, 5th ed., 1971; The Georgian Century, 1714-1837, 1966; Nineteenth Century Gallery, 1970; George the Third, 1972. Address: The Beeches, Middle Winterslow, Salisbury, Wilts., UK.

AYLMER, (Sir) Felix Edward Aylmer Jones, b. 1889, Corsham, Wilts., UK. President, Actors' Equity Union, 1949-69. Educ: B.A., Exeter Coll., Oxford. Publs: Dickens Incognito; The Drood Case. Address: 6 Painshill House, Cobham, Surrey, UK.

AYMAR, Gordon Christian, b. 24 July 1893, East Orange, N.J., USA. Portrait Painter; Author. Educ: B.A., Yale Univ., 1914; Schl. of the Museum of F.A., Boston, USA, 1917. Publs. incl: An Introduction to Advertising Illustration, 1929; Bird Flight, 1935; Start 'Em Sailing, 1941; A Treasury of Sea Stories, 1949; The Art of Portrait Painting, 1967. Contbr. to: Society. Mbrships. incl: 1st VP, Am. Water Color Soc.; Pres., N.Y. Art Dirs. Club; Pres. Nat. Soc. of Art Dirs. Hons. incl: Award of Merit, Am. Water Color Soc.; 1962; Prizes for Paintings, Conn. Classic Arts, 1962, 1974. Address: South Kent, CT 06785, USA.

AYNES (Major), Edith Annette, pen name PAT, b. 2 Apr. 1909, Atwood, Kan., USA. Administrator, Home for (Well) Aged; Retired Army Nurse. Educ: B.S., Nursing Educ., Univ. of Calif., Berkeley, 1950. M.A., Educ., Kean Coll., Union, N.J., 1963. Publs: From Nightengale to Eagle, 1973; Living the Later Years, forthcoming. Contbr. to: McCalls; Modern Hospital; Nursing Outlook; Hospitals; Am. Jrnl. of Nursing. Mbrships. incl: ASCAP; Nat. Writers Club; Int. Platform Assn.; var. nursing & Army assns. Recip., Legion of Merit, 1951. Address: 1125 Grand Concourse, Bronx, NY 10452, USA.

B

BABAEVSKY, Semyon Petrovich, b. 29 May 1909, Ukraine. Writer. Educ: Moscow Lit. Inst. Publs: Cavalier of the Golden Star; Geese Island, 1947; Light over the Earth, 1949; Well-Spring Grove, 1956; White Mosque; Sukhaya Buivola, 1958; Along Paths & Roads, 1959; Son's Mutiny, 1961; Native Land, 1965; The Whole World, 1969. Mbrships: Communist Pty of Soviet Union, 1939-; Bd., USSR Union of Writers. Hons: State Prizes, 1948, 1949, 1950; Order, Red Banner of Labour, 1959. Address: USSR Union of Writers, 52 Ulitsa Vorovskogo, Moscow, USSR.

BABB, Sanora, b. 21 Apr., 1907, Leavenworth, Kan., USA. Writer. Educ: A.A.; Garden City Jr. Coll., 1 yr.; Kan. Univ., 1 yr. Publs: The Lost Traveller, 1958; An Owl on Every Post, USA, 1970, UK, 1972; Whose Names Are Unknown, forthcoming. Contbr. to: Saturday Evening Post; Redbook. Outdoor World; Seventeen; Scholastics; Southern Review; Southwest Review; num. other jrnls.; Best Am. Short Stories; U.S. Stories; CrossSection; Borestone Mountain Poetry Awards Vol. 1967; other anthols. Mbr., Authors Guild. Recip., Nat. Five Arts Award (short story). Address: 1562 Queens Rd., Hollywood, CA 90069, USA.

BABCOCK, Frederic, b. 1896, Ord, Neb., USA. Editor. Publs: Hang up the Fiddle; Blood of the Lamb; Ed., The Real Nixon. Contbr. to: Thou Shalt Not Kill — Maybe; Denver Post (Drama Ed.); Chgo Tribune (Ed., Mag. of Books); Nation; Christian Century; Saturday Review; N.Y. Times Book Review. Mbrships. incl: Authors League of Am.; Chgo. Press Club; Soc. of Midland Authors; Thoreau Soc. Hons: Chgo. Fndn. of Lit. Award; Frederic Babcock Coll. in Boston Univ. Lib.; Judge, Pulitzer Prize for Fiction. Address: 1231 Via Estrella, Winter Park, FL 32789, USA.

BABINGTON, Anthony Patrick, b. 4 Apr. 1920, Cork, Repub. of Ireland. Circuit Judge. Educ: Barrister-at-Law. Publs: No Memorial, 1954; The Power to Silence, 1968; A House in Bow Street, 1969; The English Bastille, 1971; The Only Liberty, 1975. Address: 3 Gledhow Gardens, Kensington, London SW5 0BL, UK.

BABINGTON SMITH, Constance, b. 15 Oct. 1912, Puttenham, Surrey, UK. Writer. Publs: Evidence in Camera, 1958, 3rd ed., 1974; Air Spy, 1957; Testing Time, 1961; Ed., Letters to a Friend by Rose Macaulay, 1961, 2nd ed., 1968; Ed., Last Letters to a Friend by Rose Macaulay, 1962; Ed., Letters to a Sister by Rose Macaulay, 1964; Ed., Pleasure of Ruins by Rose Macaulay & Roloff Beny, 1964; Amy Johnson, 1967; Rose Macaulay: A Biography, 1972. Contbr. to: Aeroplane; Sunday Times; Sunday Telegraph; etc. Mbrships: F.R.S.L.; Nat. Book League. Hons. incl: M.B.E. (Mil.), 1945; Legion of Merit, USA, 1945. Agent: A. D. Peters. Address: c/o Agent, 10 Buckingham St., London WC2, UK.

BABRIS, Peter J., b. 31 Jan. 1917, Atasiene, Rezekne, Latvia. Educator. Educ: Univ. of Latvia; M.A., Univ. of S.D.; N. III. Univ.; Ph.D., Walden Univ. Publs: Baltic Youth under Communism, 1967; Persecution of Religion in the Baltic States, transl.; ed., Sardze pret Austrumiem; Genocide in the Soviet Empire, forthcoming; Siberia — Land of Punishment, forthcoming. Contbr. to Latvian Reviews. Address: 108 S. Patton, Arlington Heights, IL 60005, USA.

BABSON, Marian, b. Salem, Mass., USA. Writer. Publs: Cover-Up Story, 1971; Murder on Show, 1972; Pretty Lady, 1973; The Stalking Lamb, 1974; Unfair Exchange, 1974; Murder Sails at Midnight, 1975. Mbr., Crime Writers Assn. Address: c/o Collins Crime Club, Wm. Collins & Sons Ltd., 14 St. James Pl., London SW1, UK.

BACCARI, Antonio, pen names TOBA; L'EMIGRANTE, b. 7 July 1943, Paolisi, Benevento, Italy. Teacher. Educ: Book-keeping Dip.; Translator's credential; B.Ed., Univ. of Calgary. Publs: You Make My Sunshine, 1973. Contbr. poems & articles to var. jrnls. incing: Gauntlet; Il Secolo; Il Borghese; Il Gazzettino Di Benevento; Il Mormorantore (fndr.). Mbr., var. orgs. Recip., Howar Dip., 1973. Address: P.O. Box 394, Calgary, Alta., Can.

BACCHELLI, Riccardo, b. 19 Apr. 1891, Bologna, Italy. Publs. incl: Leopardi e Manzoni, 1960; Viaggi all'estro e vagabondaggi di fantasia, 1966; Giorno per giorno 1912-1922, 1966; America in confidenza, 1966; Rapporto segreto, 1967; Giorno per Giorno 1932-66, 1968; L'Afrodite, 1969; Africa tra Storia e Fantasia, 1969; La

Stella del Mattino, 1971; Bellezza e Umanita, 1972; Giorni di Vita e Temo di Poesia, 1973. Mbr., sev. cultural orgs. Hons: Grand Off., Italian Repub., 1953; hon. degrees, Univs. of Bologna & Milan. Address: Borgonuovo 20, 20121 Milan, Italy.

BACH, Richard. Writer; Pilot. Publs: Stranger to the Ground; Biplane; Nothing by Chance; Jonathan Livingstone Seagull (photographs by Russel Munson), 1970. Contbr. of articles & stories to aviation & gen. mags. Address: c/o The Macmillan Co., 866 Third Ave., N.Y., NY 10022, USA.

BACHCHAN, Harbans Rai, b. 27 Nov. 1907, Allahabad, India. Teacher; Writer; Former University Lecturer. Educ: M.A., Allahabad Univ.; Ph.D., Cambridge Univ., UK. Publs: ca. 60 works in poetry, prose & translations inclng. Madhushala, 1935, Eng. trans. The House of Wine, 1950; Mishanimantrau, 1938; Do Chattanen, 1964; W. B. Yeats & Occultism, 1965; (autobiog.) Kya Bhulun Kya Yad Karan, 1969. Prod. All India Radio, 1955. Hons. incl: Sabilya Akademy Award, 1969; Lotus Award (Afro-Asian Writers' Conf.), 1970. Address: c/o A. Bachchan, 20 Praiduny Society, North-South Road — 7, Jahu Park, Bombay 56, India.

BACKMAN, Jules, b. 3 May 1910, NYC, USA. Research Professor of Economics. Educ: B.C.S., 1931; A.M.; 1932; M.B.A., 1933; D.C.S., 1935, N.Y. Univ. Publs. incl: Price Practices & Price Policies, 1953; Business Problems of the Seventies, 1973; Labor, Technology & Productivity, 1974; Multinational Corporations, Trade & the Dollar, 1974. Contbr. to: N.Y. Times (Ed., 1943-48); Jrnl. of Pol. Econ.; Quarterly Jrnl. of Econs.; Nat. Tax Jrnl.; Labor Law Jrnl; etc. Mbrships. incl: Am. Econ. Assn.; Hon. Fellow, Am. Statistical Assn. Hons. incl: acad. hons., N.Y. Univ.; Am.—Judaism Award, 1970. Address: 59 Crane Rd., Scarsdale, NY 10583, USA.

BÄCKSTRÖM, Lars David, b. 18 Feb. 1925, Lulea, Sweden. Writer. Educ: Fil.lic., Univ. of Uppsala. Publs: Under välfärdens yta (criticism), 1959; Världen omkring oss (poetry), 1962; Erik Lindegren (criticism), 1962; Klippbok (criticism), 1965; Öppen stad (poetry), 1967; Litteratur-politik (criticism), 1970; Deb som flyr det privata kan inte förstå det allmänna (Collected poems 1957-67), 1971; Minnen från den nya klassen (autobiog.), 1972. Contbr. to: Ord & Bild; Författarförlagets Tidskrift; Uppsala Nya Tidning. Mbrships: Ed., Advsry. Bd. Mbr., Writers' Coop., 1970-73; Writers' Ctr.; Swedish Union of Authors. Address: Österplan 15B, S-75331, Uppsala, Sweden.

BACKUS, Jean, pen name MONTROSS, David, b. 1914, Pasadena, Calif., USA. Author. Educ: Univ. of Calif. Publs: Traitor's Wife, 1962; Troika, 1963; Fellow Traveller, 1964; Dusha, 1971. Mbrships: VP, Northern Calif. Chapt., Mystery Writers of Am., 1974-75. Address: 265 Purdue Avenue, Kensington, CA 94708, USA.

BACON, Edmund Norwood, b. 2 May 1910, Phila., Pa., USA. City Planner. Educ: B.Arch., Cornell Univ., 1932. Publs: Design of Cities, 1967, revised ed., 1974. Contbr. chapt. "New World Cities" to American Civilization (Daniel J. Boorstin, ed.), 1972. Mbrships: Fellow, Am. Inst. of Archts.; Am. Inst. of Planners. Address: 2117 Locust St., Phila., PA 19103, USA.

BACON, Lenice Ingram, b. 28 Jan. 1895, Rockwood, Tenn., USA. Writer; Lecturer. Educ: Curry Schl. of Expression, Boston, Mass., 1914-15. Publs: American Patchwork Quilts, 1973. Contbr. to: Christian Sci. Monitor; Telephone Topics; Yankee Mag. Mbrships. incl: Nat. League of Am. Pen Women; Boston Authors' Club; VP, Boston Browning Soc., 1969-; Trustee of Curry Coll., 1943-53, 1966-71, Hon. Trustee, 1971-; Bd. of Boston Ctr. for Adult Educ., 1953-57, 1959-65; Int. Platform Assn.; Women's City Club of Boston (Pres., 1953-56). Hons. incl: Outstanding Alumnus of Yr., 1968; Litt.D., 1974, Curry Coll. Address: 20 Chapel Street, Brookline, MA 02146, USA.

BACQUE, James Watson, b. 19 May 1929, Toronto, Can. Author; Publisher. Educ: B.A., Trinity Coll., Univ. of Toronto. Publs: The Lonely Ones, 1969, paperback reprint (re-titled Big Lonely), 1971; A Man of Talent, 1973. Contbr. to: Saturday Night Mag.; Can. Forum; Can. Dimension. Mbrships. incl: Writers' Union of Can.; Sec. Treas., Independent Publrs.' Assn. Recip., Can. Coun. Arts Bursaries, 1969 & 1970. Address: 422 Heath St., E. Toronto, Ont., Can.

BADDILEY, James, b. 1918, Manchester, UK. Research Laboratory Director; Head, School of Chemistry. Educ: Ph.D., D.Sc., Univ. of Manchester. Publs: Microbiology & Biochemistry. Contbr. of num. original papers & review articles to Brit., Am. & int. sci. jrnls. & text-books. Mbrships: F.R.S.; Hon. Mbr., Am. Soc. of Biol. Chems. Hons: Meldola Medal, Royal Inst. Chem.; Corday-Morgan Medal & Tilden Lectureship, Chem. Soc.; Davy Medal, Royal Soc., 1974. Address: Microbiological Chemistry Research Laboratory, Univ. of Newcastle upon Tyne, NE1 7RU, UK.

BADGER, Alfred Bowen, b. 1901, Llanelli, UK. Industrial Relations Adviser. Educ: M.A., Univ. Coll., London; Ph.D., Univ. of Hamburg, Germany; Inst. of Educ., London. Publs: Public Schools & the Nation; Man in Employment. Contbr. to var. mags. & jrnls., GB & Germany. Mbr., Soc. of Authors. Address: 10 Parkside, 14 Court Downs Rd., Beckenham, Kent, UK.

BADGER, John Darcy, b. 18 July 1917, London, UK. Publisher; Writer. Publs: The Arthuriad, 1972. Contbr. to: The Can. Sci.; NEW; Info. Sci. Address: 1624 Water's Edge Rd., Mississauga, Ont., Can.

BADHAM, Leslie, b. 27 Dec. 1908, Pembs., UK. Clergyman; Chaplain to H.M. The Queen. Educ: B.A. (Engl.), St. David's Univ. Coll., Lampeter, 1931; B.A. (Theol.), 1932, M.A., 1935, Jesus Coll., Oxford. Publs: These Greatest Things, 1942; Verdict on Jesus, 1950, 2nd ed. 1971; Love Speaks from the Cross, 1956. Contbr. to: The Times; & Ch. Mags. Mbrships: Pres., Maidenhead Windsor Fedn. CEMS, 1966-70; Chaplain, RAFA Windsor; Chaplain, Royal Warrant Holders. Address: 4 Cheynies Court, Arundel Way, Highcliffe, Christchurch, Hants., UK.

BADIAN, E., b. 8 Aug. 1925, Vienna, Austria. Professor of history; Author. Educ: B.A., 1944, M.A., 1945, Univ. of NZ; B.A., 1950, D.Phil., 1956, Oxford Univ., UK; Lit.D., Vic., NZ, 1962. Publs: Foreign Clientelae, 264-70 B.C., 1958; Studies in Greek & Roman History, 1964; Roman Imperialism in the Late Republic, 1967; Publicans & Sinners, 1972. Contbr. to: var. encys., classical & & histl. jrnls. Mbrships. incl: Soc. for Promotion of Hellenic Studies; Soc. for Promotion of Roman Studies; Classical Assn. of Can.; Am. Philol. Assn. Hons: Fellow, British Acad., 1965; Fellow, Am. Acad. Arts & Scis., 1974. Address: Dept. of History, Harvard University, Cambridge, MA 02138, USA.

BAER, Edith Ruth, b. 29 Apr. 1920, Mannheim, Germany. Executive Producer, BBC. Educ: B.A., Univ. of London, UK. Publs: (co-author) German for Beginners, 1962; Spanish for Beginners, 1963; Es geht weiter, 1965; Der arme Millionär, 1967; Reisebüro Atlas, 1968; Wiedersehen in Ausburg, 1970. Contbr. to num. BBC Radio progs. Mbrships: Fellow, Inst. of Linguists. Address: 42 Woodlands, London NW11, UK.

BAERT, Adriaan Gilles Coenraad, pen name GILLES, b. 28 July 1915, The Hague, Netherlands. Consultant for organization of international congresses; Author. Educ: LL.B., Univ. of Utrecht. Publs: Geographical Dictionary of the Netherlands, 1967; Grote Nederlandse Larousse Encyclopedie Section: Geography of the Netherlands (w. Dr. F. Ferrari), 1971—. Contbr. to: Netherlands Press Agcy.; var. mags., newspapers, periodicals, nat. & for. Address: 5 i Statenlaan, The Hague, Netherlands.

BAEZ, Joan, b. 9 Jan. 1941, NYC, USA. Singer. Educ: studied at Boston Univ. Fine Arts Schl., 1958. Publs: The Joan Baez Songbook, 1964; Daybreak, 1968. Contbr. to: Esquire; Playboy; Atlantic Monthly. Address: c/o Folklore Prods., 1671 Appian Way, Santa Monica, CA 90401, USA.

BAGBY, Wesley M. III, b. 15 June 1922, Albany, Ga., USA. Professor of History. Educ: A.B., 1943; M.A., 1945, Univ. of N.C.; Ph.D., Columbia Univ., 1953. Publs: The Presidential Campaign & Election of 1920, 1962; Chapter: The Harding Election: Wilson Repudiated, in History of the First World War, ed. by Peter Young, 1971. Contbr. to: Am. Histl. Review; The Historian; Mississippi Valley Histl. Review; etc. Mbrships: Am. Histl. Assn.; AAUP. Address: 770 Mountain View Pl., Morgantown, WV 26505, USA.

BAGLEY, Desmond, b. 1923, Kendal, Westmorland. Novelist. Publs: The Golden Keel, 1963; High Citadel, 1965; Wyatt's Hurricane, 1966; Landslide, 1967; The Vivero Letter, 1968; The Spoilers, 1969; Running Blind, 1970; The Snow Tiger, 1975. Contbr. to var. mags. &

newspapers. Mbrships: Authors Club; Authors Guild, USA; Mystery Writers of Am.; Soc. of Authors; Crime Writers Assn. Address: Hay Hill, Totnes, Devon, UK.

BAGLEY, John Joseph, b. 1908, St. Helens, Lancs., UK. Reader in History. Educ: M.A., Univ. of Liverpool. Publs. incl: History of Lancashire, 1956; Life in Medieval England, 1960; Henry VIII & his Times, 1962; Historical Interpretation, 2 vols., 1965 & 1971; Poor Law (w. A. J. Bagley), 1966; Lancashire Diarists, 1975. Contbr. to: Hist. Soc. of Lancs. & Cheshire; Lancs. Life. Mbrships: Assn. of Univ. Tchrs.; Tutors' Assn.; Fellow, Royal Histl. Soc. Address: 10 Beach Priory Gdns., Southport PR8 1RT, Merseyside, UK.

BAGNOLD, Enid (Lady Jones), 1889. Author. Publs. incl: A Diary Without Dates; (poems) Sailing Ships, 1917; (novels) The Happy Foreigner, 1920; Serena Blandish, 1924; National Velvet, 1935; The Loved & Envied, 1951; The Girl's Journey, 1956; (plays) Lottie Dundass, 1943; Poor Judas, 1951; The Chalk Garden, 1956; The Last Joke, 1960; The Chinese Prime Minister, 1964; Four Plays, 1970; (transl.) Alexander of Asia by Marthe Bibesco, 1955; Enid Bagnold's Autobiography, 1969. Hons: Arts Theatre Prize, 1951; Award of Merit, Am. Acad. of Arts & Sci., 1956. Address: North End House, Rottingdean, Sussex BN2 7HA, UK.

BAGSHAWE, Thomas Wyatt, b. 18 Apr. 1901, Norwood, Surrey, UK. Retired Engineer & Ironfounder. Educ: Gonville & Caius Coll., Cambridge. Publs: Notes on the Habits of the Gentoo & Ringed or Antarctic Penguins, 1938; Two Men in the Antarctic, 1939; Pompey was a Penguin, 1940. Contbr. to: Antiquaries Jrnl.; Jrnl. Brit. Archaeol. Assn.; Beds. Mag.; Folklore; Apollo; Antique Collector. Mbrships: F.S.A.; Fellow, Royal Histl. Soc.; Fellow, Museums Assn.; Fellow, Royal Anthropol. Inst. (VP, 1952-55); Liveryman, Curriers' Co.; Past Master; Pres., Antarctic Club, 1938. Hons: Name Given to Bagshawe Glacier, Danco Coast, Antarctica, 1958. Address: Bedford Charter House, Kimbolton Rd., Bedford MK40 2PU, UK.

BAHM, Archie J(ohn), b. 21 Aug. 1907, Imlay City, Mich., USA. Professor of Philosophy; Author. Educ: A.B., Albion Coll.; M.A., Ph.D., Univ. of Mich. Publs. incl: Philosophy, An Introduction, 1953; Philosophy of the Buddha, 1958, 3rd ed., 1969; Directory of American Philosophers, Vols. I-VII, 1962-74; The World's Living Religions, 1964, 2nd ed., 1971; Polarity, Dialectic, & Organicity, 1970; Metaphysics, An Introduction, 1974; Ethics as a Behavioral Science, 1974. Contbr. to var. profl. jrnls. Address: 1915 Las Lomas Rd., N.E., Albuquerque, NM 87106, USA.

BĂIEŞU, Ion, b. 2 Jan. 1933, Aldeni, Buzău, Romania. Writer. Educ: Bucharest Univ Publs: They Were Suffering Together, 1965; Humour, 1970; Theatre, 1970; Blue Grass, 1973; Who Digs a Pit for Others, 1974; (plays) Forgiveness, 1968; The Trainer, 1970; The Guilty, 1971; The Door Mat, 1972; Chiţimia, 1974. Contbr. to: Scînteia tineretului; Magazin; Informaţia Bucureştiului. Mbr., Romanian Union of Writers. Hons: Romanian Union of Writers Prizes, 1968, 1973; Romanian Acad. Prize, 1971. Address: Str. C.A. Rosetti 43A, Sect. II, Bucharest, Romania.

BAIL, Grace Monroe Shattuck, pen names BAIL, G. S., INGRAHAM, Grace, MONROE, Grace, b. 17 Jan. 1898, Cherry Creek, N.Y., USA. Music Teacher. Educ: Darlington Sem.; Meadville Coll. of Music; Dana Schl. of Music; Music Degree, Piano, Theory, 1919. Publs. incl: Arethusa, 1945; Singing Heart, 1947; Daily Bread, 1952; Phantasy, 1954; Whispering Leaves, 1957; For the Dreamer, 1965; Heartstrings, 1968; Golden Days, 1970; Cantabile, 1974; Num. musical compositions. Contbr. to num. jrnls., anthols.; Fndr., Poetry Columnist, Record-Gazette, Banning, Calif. Mbrships. incl: Calif. Fedn. of Chaparral Poets; Am. Poetry League; Past Nat. Dir., Composers, Authors & Artists of Am. Hons. incl: Bronze Medal, Centro Studi E Scambi, Int., 1965; Gold Medal, Int. Poets Shrine, 1969. Address: 873½ Beaumont Ave., Beaumont, CA 92223, USA.

BAILEY, Bernadine Freeman, b. Mattoon, Ill., USA. Writer. Educ: B.A., Wellesley Coll.; M.A., Univ. of Chgo.; Cert. of Studies, Sorbonne, Paris. Publs: 98 books, inclng: Abe Lincoln's Other Mother, 1941; Juan Ponce de Leon, 1958; Paris, I Love You, 1968; Famous Modern Explorers, 1963; Greenland, 1973; Rhodesia, 1974. Contbr. to num. newspapers, jrnls. Mbrships. incl: Press Club, London; Chgo. Press Club; Soc. of Midland Authors, Chgo.; Past

Pres., Ill. Women's Press Assn.; Past Regional VP, Mystery Writers of Am. Hons: Dip. de Medaille, Soc. des Arts, Scis. & Lettres, Paris. Address: 1516 Wabash Ave., Mattoon, IL 61938, USA.

BAILEY, David Charles, b. 19 May 1930, Battle Creek, Mich., USA. Professor of History. Educ: B.A., W. Mich. Univ., M.A., Univ. Notre Dame; Ph.D., Mich. State Univ. Publs: Viva Cristo Rey₁ The Cristero Rebellion & the Church-State Conflict in Mexico, 1974; Mexican Revolution: The Constitutionalist Years (co-author), 1972. Contbr. to: Hispanic Am. Histl. Review: The Americas; The French Review. Mbrships: Am. Histl. Assn.; Conf. on Latin Am. Hist.; Am. Cath. Histl. Assn. Address: 331 Carpenter Drive, Battle Creek, MI 49017, USA.

BAILEY, David Roy Shackleton, b. 10 Dec. 1917, Lancaster, UK. University Professor. Educ: B.A., M.A., Litt.D., Gonville & Caius Coll., Cambridge. Publs: The Satapancasatka of Matrceta, 1950; Propertiana, 1951; Towards a text of Cicero, Ad Atticum, 1960; Ciceronis Epistulae ad Atticum, IX-XVI, 1961; Cicero's Letters to Atticus, 7 vols., 1964-70; Cicero, 1970. Contbr. to var. orientalist & classical jrnls. Fellow of Brit. Acad. Address: Department of Classics, 319 Boylston Hall, Harvard University, Cambridge, MA 02138, USA.

BAILEY, (The Rev.) Derrick Sherwin, b. 1910, Alcester, UK. Retired Canon Residentiary & Precentor, Wells Cathedral. Educ: Ph.D., D.Litt., Univ. of Edinburgh. Publs: The Mystery of Love & Marriage; Sponsors at Baptism & Confirmation; Thomas Becon & the Reformation of the Church in England; Homosexuality & the Western Christian Tradition; Sexual Offenders & Social Punishment; The Man-Woman Relation in Christian Thought; Common Sense About Sexual Ethics; Ed., Wells Cathedral Chapter Act Book 1666-1683. Contbr. to: Theol.; Ch. Quarterly Review; The Churchman; Scottish Jrnl. of Theol.; Jrnl. of Ecclesiastical Hist.; etc. Mbr., A.C.I.I. Address: 23 Kippax Ave., Wells, Somerset, BA5 2TT, UK.

BAILEY, Norman Thomas John, b. 27 May 1923, Merton, UK. Statistician. Educ: M.A., Univ. of Cambridge; D.Sc., Univ. of Oxford. Publs: The Mathematical Theory of Epidemics, 1957; Statistical Methods in Biology, 1959; The Mathematical Theory of Genetic Linkage, 1961; The Elements of Stochastic Processes, 1964; The Mathematical Approach to Biology & Medicine, 1967; The Mathematical Theory of Infectious Diseases & its Applications, 1975. Contbr. to: Jrnl. of the Royal Statistical Soc.; Heredity; Biometrika; other profl. jrnls. Address: 4 Chemin sous l'Eglise, 1222 Vesenaz, Geneva, Switz.

BAILEY, Paul, b. 1937, London, UK. former Actor; Author. Publs: At the Jerusalem, 1967; Trespasses, 1970. Contbr. to: Observer; Listener; New Statesman; London Mag.; Weekend Telegraph; Sunday Times Mag.; Nova. Address: 32 St. Stephen's Gdns., London W2, UK.

BAILEY, Richard, b. Biddulph, Staffs., UK. Economics Consultant. Educ: B.Sc.(Econ.), London Univ. Publs: Problems of the World Economy; Managing the British Economy; Promoting Commonwealth Development; The European Community in the World. Contbr. to: Ency. Britannica; Financial Times; Times; Spectator; Director. Mbrships: Royal Inst. Int. Affairs; Overseas Dev. Inst. (Coun.). Address: 72 Ashley Gdns., Westminster, London SW1, UK.

BAILEY, Stella Winn Brown, b. 12 Mar. 1902, Elsberry, Mo., USA. Educator. Publs: History of Education in Tulare County, California, 1861-1910, 1962; Teacher Associations in American Education, 1966; Var. educl. handbooks. Contbr. to jrnls. Address: Stella W. Bailey, 474 N. Cherry St., Tulare, CA 93274, USA.

BAILY, Leslie, b. 1906, St. Albans, UK. Historian; Radio Scriptwriter & Producer. Publs: The BBC Scrapbooks, 1937; Travellers' Tales, 1945; The Gilbert & Sullivan Book, 1952; Scrapbook 1900-1914, 1957; Scrapbook for the Twenties, 1959; Craftsman & Quaker, 1959; Leslie Baily's BBC Scrapbook, 2 vols., 1966-68; Gilbert & Sullivan & Their World, 1973; (radio, TV, & film scripts) BBC Scrapbooks; Trial of William Penn; The Schubert Discoveries; Rise of the Labour Party; South with Shackleton; Lives of Gilbert & Sullivan; etc. Contbr. to num. jrnls. Mbrships: Fellow, Royal Histl. Soc.; Soc. of Authors. Address: 29 Saxon Way, Saffron Walden, Essex CB11 4EQ, UK.

BAIN, Cyril William Curtis, b. Heaton Mersey, Manchester, UK. Physician. Educ: M.A., D.M., Christ Church, Oxford; St. Thomas' Hospital; F.R.C.P. Publs: Recent Advances in Cardiology (w. Dr. Terence East), 5th ed., 1959. Contbr. to: Brit. Heart Jrnl.; Lancet; Brit. Med. Jrnl.; Practitioner. Recip. Mil. Cross. Address: Red Willows, The Belyars, St. Ives, Cornwall, UK.

BAINBRIDGE, Beryl Margaret, b. 21 Jan. 1934, Liverpool, UK. Writer. Educ: Arts Educl. Schls. Publs: Weekend with Claude, 1967; Another Part of the Wood, 1968; Harriet Said, 1972; The Dressmaker, 1973; The Bottle Factory Outing, 1974. Contbr. to: Listener. Hons: Short Listed, Booker Prize, 1973, 1974; Guardian Prize, 1974. Address: 42 Albert St., Camden Town, London NW1, UK.

BAINES, Anthony, b. 1912, London, UK. Bassoonist; Conductor of Ballet; Lecturer; Curator. Educ: M.A., Christ Church Coll., Oxford. Publs: Woodwind Instruments & their History, 1957; Bagpipes, 1960; Musical Instruments Through the Ages, 1961; European & American Musical Instruments, 1966; Catalogue of the Musical Instruments, II, Victoria & Albert Museum, 1967. Contbr. to: Galpin Soc. Jrnl.; Groves Dictionary of Music, 5th ed.; Etc. Address: 23 St. Margaret's Rd., Oxford, UK.

BAINTON, Roland Herbert, b. 30 Mar. 1894, Ilkeston, Derbys., UK. Teacher; Writer. Educ: B.A., Whitman Coll., Walla Walla, Wash., 1914; B.D., 1917, Ph.D., 1921, Yale Univ. Publs: over 30 books on hist. of Christianity, transl. into 12 langs., inclng. Here I Stand, a life of Martin Luther, 1950; The Reformation of the Sixteenth Century, 1952; The Horizon History of Christianity, 1964; Christendom, 2 vols., 1964-66; Erasmus of Christendom, 1968; Women of the Reformation in Germany & Italy, 1971, & in France & England, 1973 (2 vols.); Behold the Christ (Christ in art), 1974. Address: 363 St. Ronan St., New Haven, CT 06511, USA.

BAIRD, Alexander John, b. 28 Sept. 1925, Liverpool, UK. University Lecturer. Educ: M.A., Emmanuel Coll., Cambridge, 1953; Edinburgh Univ., 1953; Liverpool Univ., 1963; Ph.D., Univ. Coll., London, 1970. Publs: The Micky-Hunters, 1957; The Unique Sensation, 1959; Poems, 1963. Contbr. to: Encounter; London Mag.; Times Lit. Supplement. Mbr., PEN. Hons: Poetry Book Soc. Summer Choice, 1963. Address: c/o Dept. of English, Univ. of Exeter, Exeter, UK.

BAJOMI, Lázár Endre, pen name (in France) LAZAR, André, b. 19 Aug. 1914, Biharnagybajom, Hungary. Writer; Journalist; Translator; Publisher's Reader. Educ: Dip. Alliance Française, Paris. Publs: The Comet, Biography of Saint-Just, 1957; Rabelais, 1959; Panorama of Today's French Literature, 1962; (Parisian trilogy) Montmartre, 1967; Montparnasse, 1969; Quartier Latin, 1971; (anthol.) Surrealism, 1968; The World of Anatole France, 1973; The Red Virgin, a biography of Louise Michel, 1975; (autobiog.) Paris Don't Yet Lose Me. Contbr. to num. Hungarian dailies, mags., reviews; radio & TV. Mbrships incl: PEN; Union Hungarian Writers; Soc. Anatole France. Address: H-1133 Budapest, Karpat u.7., Hungary.

BAKELESS, John Edwin, b. 30 Dec. 1894, Carlisle Barracks, Pa., USA. Author; Editor. Educ: A.B., Williams Coll., 1918; M.A., 1920, Ph.D., 1936, Harvard. Publs: incl: Magazine Making, 1931; Christopher Marlowe, the Man in his Time, 1937; Daniel Boone, Master of the Wilderness, 1939; The Tragicall History of Christopher Marlowe, 1942; Eyes of Discovery, 1950; Background to Glory, 1957; Turncoats Traitors & Heroes, 1959; Spies of the Confederacy, 1970; var. juveniles. Contbr. to jrnls. Profl. Mbrships: Authors' League; PEN. Hons: Bowdoin Prize, Harvard, 1922 & 1923; Guggenheim Fellowships, 1936 & 1947; Huntington Fellow, 1968. Address: Elbowroom Farm, Great Hill, Seymour, CT 06483, USA.

BAKELESS, Katherine Little, b. 5 Dec. 1895, Bloomsburg, Pa., USA. Author; Piano Teacher. Educ: Musical Cert., 1916; Peabody Conservatory, Baltimore, 1917-20; piano instruction under var. teachers. Publs: Story Lives of Great Composers, 1940; Story Lives of American Composers, 1941; Birth of a Nation's Song, 1942; Glory Hallelujah, 1944; In the Big Time, 1955; & var. books in collab. w. John Bakeless. Contbr. to Plays Mag. Mbrships: Authors' League; Soc. of the Mayflower. Address: Elbowroom Farm, Great Hill, Seymour, Conn. 06483, USA.

BAKER, Arthur Lemprière Lancey, b. 1905, Exeter, UK. Emeritus Professor of Concrete Structures & Technology. Educ: Manchester Univ.; D.Sc.(Eng.), Hon. D. Tech., F.I.C.E., F.I.Struct.E., Hon. A.C.G.I.. Publs: Raft Foundations; The Ultimate Load Theory Applied to the Design of Reinforced & Prestressed Concrete Frames; The Inelastic Space Frame; Limit State Design of Reinforced Concrete. Address: Dept. of Civil Engineering, Imperial College of Science & Technology, London SW7 2BU, UK.

BAKER, Cyril Clarence Thomas, b. 1907, Newbridge, Mon., UK. Lecturer; Teacher. Educ: B.Sc., Univ. Coll. of Wales. Publs: Examples in Practical Mathematics, 1950; Practical Mathematics, 2 vols., 1954-55; 'O' Level Tests in Arithmetic, 1956; 'O' Level Tests in Alternative B Mathematics, 1959, revised 1970; Mathematics Dictionary, 1961; Introduction to Calculus, 1964; 'A' Level Tests in Mathematics, 1965; Introduction to Mathematics, 1966; Introduction to Trigonometry, 1967; O.N.C. Mathematics, 1970. Address: 41 Craneswater Park, Norwood Green, Middlesex, UK.

BAKER, Elliott, b. 15 Dec. 1922, Buffalo, N.Y., USA. Writer. Educ: B.S., Ind. Univ., Bloomington, 1944. Publs: (novels) A Fine Madness, 1964; The Penny Wars, 1968; Pocock & Pitt, 1971; The Penny Wars (play), 1969. Recip., Putnam Award, 1964. Address: 52 Park Close, London W14, UK.

BAKER, Frank, b. 15 Apr. 1910, Hull, UK. Professor, English Church History. Educ: B.A., Univ. Coll. of Hull, 1931; B.D., Univ. of Manchester, 1934; Ph.D., Univ. of Nottingham, 1952. Publs: A charge to Keep: An Introduction to the People called Methodists, 1947; The Story of Cleethorpes, 1953; Representative Verse of Charles Wesley, 1962; William Grimshaw, 1708-63; John Wesley & The Church of England, 1970. Contbr. to: London Quarterly Review; Ency. Britannica; Chambers' Ency.; & var. Ch. jrnls. Mbr., The Histl. Assn.; etc. Recip., Eayrs Essay Prize, 1936, 1941, 1942, 1947, & 1948. Address: 1505 Pinecrest Road, Durham, NC 27705, USA.

BAKER, Hendrik Maurice Ruitenga, b. 1910, Cardiff, UK. Stage Manager, Director & Designer; Author. Publs: Adaptations from S. G. Hulme Beaman, etc.; The Cruise of the Toytown Belle, 1953; Tea For Two, 1960; The Toytown Mystery, 1960; Larry the Plumber, 1961; The Toytown Treasure, The Arkville Dragon, The Tale of the Magician, The Showing Up of Larry the Lamb, The Mayor's Sea Voyage, all 1966; Stage Management & Theatrecraft, 1968; Stage Management, 1968; Adaptor & Dir., series of 26 TV films, Larry the Lamb in Toytown, 1970-74. Contbr. to: Arts Theatre. Mbrships: Soc. of Authors; Assn. of Brit. Theatre Technicians; Arts Theatre Club. Address: 7 Elder Court, Magpie Hall Rd., Bushey Heath, Herts. WD2 1NT, UK.

BAKER, Houston Alfred Jr., b. 22 Mar. 1943, Louisville, Ky., USA. Professor of English & Director of Afro-American Studies. Educ: B.A., Howard Univ., 1965; M.A., 1966, Ph.D., 1968, Univ. Calif. Publs: Ed., Black Literature in America, 1971; Ed., Twentieth Century Interpretations of Native Son, 1972; Long Black Song: Singers of Daybreak: Studies in Black American Literature, 1974. Contbr. to: Yale Review: Va. Quarterly Review; Jrnl. Popular Culture; Am. Lit.; Liberator; Black World; Negro Am. Lit. Forum; etc. Mbrships. incl: Modern Lang. Assn. Am. (Prog. Comm. & Deleg. Assembly). Hons. incl: Alfred Longueil Poetry Award, 1966. Address: 4828 Larchwood Ave., Phila., PA 19143, USA.

BAKER, John Randal, b. 1900, Woodbridge, UK. Reader Emeritus in Cytology. Educ: M.A.; D.Phil.; D.Sc., New Coll., Oxford. Publs: Sex in Man & Animals; Man & Animals in the New Hebrides; Cytological Technique; The Scientific Life; Science & the Planned State; Abraham Trembley of Geneva; Principles of Biological Microtechnique; Race. Address: The Mill, 26 Mill End, Kidlington, Oxford OX5 2EG, UK.

BAKER, Margaret, b. 1890, Langley Green, Birmingham, UK. Author. Publs: The Little Girl who Curtsied to the Owl; The Lost Merbaby; Patsy & the Leprechaun; The Roaming Doll, etc.; Tell-Them-Again Tales; The Wishing-Well, etc.; Here's Health to You! (N.B.W.T.A.U.); The Wide-Awakes' Own; Juby, 1970; Ed., The Land Where I Belong, etc., by Aubrey Seymour. Address: Tarver's Orchard, Sutton-under-Brailes, Banbury, Oxon., UK.

BAKER, Margaret Joyce, b. 21 May 1918, Reading, Berks., UK. Author. Educ: King's Coll., London Univ. Publs. incl: Nonsense, Said the Tortoise; Homer Sees the Queen; The Bright High Flyer; Lions in the Potting Shed; A Castle & Sixpence; The Family that Grew & Grew; Away Went Galloper; Castaway Christmas; Porterhouse Major; The Last Straw; The Shoe Shop Bears; Hannibal & the Bears; Bears Back in Business; Hi-Jinks Joins the Bears; Teabag & the Bears; Boots & the Ginger Bears; several books transl'd.; var. paperback eds. Mbrships incl: Soc. of Authors. Agent: Curtis Brown Ltd. Address: Prickets, Church Close, Old Cleeve, Minehead, Somerset, UK.

BAKER, Nelson Blaisdell, b. 24 Dec. 1905, Manchester, Mass., USA. Theological Seminary Professor; Author. Educ: B.S., Tufts Univ., Mass., 1927; B.D., 1931, M.Th., 1932, Eastern Bapt. Theol. Sem.; D.Th., 1933; Ph.D., Univ. of Southern Calif., 1951. Publs: What Is the World Coming To?, 1965; You Can Understand the Bible, By Its Unifying Themes, 1973. Contbr. to: Review & Expositor; Bulletin of Evangelical Theol. Soc.; Fndns.; Interpretation; Christian Review. Mbrships: Soc. of Biblical Lit.; Am. Acad. of Relig. Address: 62 Locust St., Apt. 225, Falmouth, MA 02540, USA.

BAKER, Reginald Owen, b. 22 Jan. 1909, Farnham, Surrey, UK. Journalist. Publs: Query Book for Hotelmen & Caterers, 1947; Second Query Book for Hotelmen & Caterers, 1949; Hotel & Restaurant Year Book, annually, 1948-65. Contbr. to: Caterer & Hotel Keeper (Ed, 1938-74); IPC hotel & catering jrnls (Cons. Ed., 1974-); Ency. Britannica Book of Yr. Mbr., Reunion des Gastronomes, 1961-. Address: 73 Bridgefield, Farnham, Surrey GU9 8AW, UK.

BAKER, Simeon, b. 29 July 1928, Lida, Poland (Naturalized American citizen, 1957). Journalist; Writer. Educ: Higher Educ. in Jrnlsm. & Pol. Sci. Author, num. essays & articles on travel. Contbr., newspaper reviews; syndicated columnist. Mbrships: For. Press Assn.; UN Correspondents' Assn.; Am. Acad. Pol. & Social Sci.; Am. Acad. of Pol. Sci. Address: 1071 E. 17th St., Brooklyn, NY 11230, USA.

BAKER, Stephen, b. 17 Apr. 1924, Vienna, Austria. Advertising Executive; Writer. Educ: B.A., William Jewell Coll.; M.A., N.Y. Univ.; Art Students League. Publs. incl: Advertising Layout & Art Direction, 1957, 1975; Visual Persuasion, 1959; How to Play Golf in the Low 120's, 1962; How to Look like Somebody in Business without being Anybody, 1963; How to Live with A Neurotic Wife, 1970; How to Live with a Neurotic Husband, 1971; How to be Psychoanalyzed by a Neurotic Psychoanalyst; The Making of a Television Commercial, 1975; Systematic Approach to Advertising Creativity, 1975; Man's Best Friend Should be His Wife, 1975. Contbr. to Ad Age. Recip., profl. awards. Address: 5 Tudor City Place, N.Y., NY 10017, USA.

BAKER, William Avery, b. 21 Oct. 1911, New Britain, Conn., USA. Naval Architect. Publs. incl: The New Mayflower: Her Design & Construction, 1958; Colonial Vessels, 1962; Sloops & Shallops, 1966; History of the Boston Marine Society, 1968; From Paddle-Wheeler to Nuclear Ship, 1968; C. J. A. Wilson's Ships, 1971; New England & the Sea (w. R. G. Albion & B. W. Labaree), 1972; A Maritime History of Bath, Maine, 1973; also chapts. in The Lore of Ships, 1963. Contbr. to var. marine jrnls. Address: 10 Rice Rd., P.O. Box 122, Hingham, MA 02043, USA.

BAKER, Wilson, b. 1900, Runcorn, UK. Emeritus Professor. Educ: M.A., Univ. of Oxford; D.Sc., Univ. of Manchester. Publs: Sidgwick's Organic Chemistry of Nitrogen. Contbr. to: Jrnl. of the Chem. Soc.; & other profl. jrnls. Mbrships: F.R.S. Address: Lane's End, Church Rd., Winscombe, Avon, UK.

BAKER WHITE, John, b. 12 Aug. 1902, W. Malling, Kent, UK. Journalist. Publs: Red Russia Arms; Dover-Nuremburg Return; The Red Network; Nationalisation; Chaos or Cure; The Soviet Spy System; The Big Lie; Pattern for Conquest; Sabotage is Suspected; True Blue. Contbr. to: Kentish Gazette; Ctrl. Press (features) Signature. Mbrships incl: Canterbury Soc.; Royal Utd. Service Instn. Hons: Justice of the Peace; Territorial Decoration. Address: Street End Place, Street End, Near Canterbury, Kent, UK.

BAKEWELL, Kenneth Graham Bartlett, b. 1931, Dudley, Worcs., UK. Lecturer. Educ: M.A., Queen's Univ. of Belfast; F.L.A.; A.M.B.I.M. Publs: How to Find Out: Management & Productivity, 2nd ed., 1970; Industrial Libraries Throughout the World, 1969; A Manual of Cataloguing Practice, 1972; Ed., Classification for Information Retrieval, 1968; Ed., Library & Information Services for Management, 1968. Contbr. to: Lib. Assn. Record; Int. Lib. Review; Five Years' Work in Librarianship; etc. Mbrships: Lib. Assn.; Aslib; Soc. of Indexers; Brit. Inst. of Mgmt. Address: 9 Greenacre Rd., Liverpool L25 0LD, UK.

BAKKER, Johan, pen name ROOTH, George, b. 26 Oct. 1919, Amsterdam, Netherlands. Author. Publs: In ieder geval actief blijven (novel), 1967; De hond van Baskervil, Asylium, Intiem journaal, Mare Tranquillitatis, De Orfiese miete, Kolderadatsj. (edited plays); Het wijfje Josien (novel); Een douche van Vuur (novel), forthcoming. Contbr. to: Mensa Berichten; Upi. Mbrships: Vereniging van Letterkundigen; Arti et Amicitiae; Mensa Select Nederland. Hons: Herman van Kuilenburg prize, 1966; Prijs van toneel groep Sater en literairblad Sigma. Address: Suze Groenewegstraat 193, Flat de Wilgenhoek 10 BW, Purmerend, Netherlands.

BAKSI, Mahmut, b. 16 Sept. 1944, Batman, Kurdistan. Writer. Publs: Mezra Botan, 1968; Sadi Alkilic Davasi, 1969; Vatandas Hakki, 1970; Kürt Sorunu, 1971; Kürt Tarihi, 1972. Contbr. to Dagens Nyheter, Folket I Bild. Mbr., Sveriges Forfattar Forbundet (Swedish Authors' Assn.). Address: Vidangsvagen 9/1207, 161 33 Bromma-Stockholm, Sweden.

BALBONTIN, José Antonio, b. 8 Oct. 1893, Madrid, Spain. Barrister; Writer; Former High Court Judge, Spain; Minister Counsellor, Spanish Republican Government in Exile, London, UK. Educ: D.L., Univ. of Madrid. Publs: Albores (poems), 1910; Inquietudes (poems), 1925; El Suicidio del Principe Ariel, 1929; La España de mi Experiencia, 1952; Three Spanish Poets, 1961; Dónde está la Verdad?, 1967; A la Busca del Dios perdido, 1969; Reflexiones sobre la no violencia, 1973. Mbrships: Madrid Atheaeum; Spanish Acad. of Jurisprudence. Recip., Nat. Poetry Prize, Madrid, 1925. Address: Miguel Angel 17-19, Madrid 10, Spain.

BALCHIN, William George Victor, b. 20 June 1916, Aldershot, Hants., UK. Academic Geographer. Educ: St. Catharine's Coll., Cambridge 1934-39; B.A., Cantab., 1937; M.A., 1941; Ph.D., London, 1951. Publs: Geography & Man (ed.), 1947, 2nd ed., 1955; Climate & Weather Exercises (w. A. W. Richards), 1949; Practical & Experimental Geography (w. A. W. Richards), 1952; Cornwall, The Making of the Landscape, 1954; Cornwall, Landscape through Maps, 1967; Geography for the Intending Student (ed.), 1970; Swansea & Its Region (ed.), 1971. Contbr. to num. acad. jrnls. Address: "Hillcrest", 189 Mayals Rd., Swansea SA3 5HQ, UK.

BALDWIN, Dorothy Anne Clare, b. 1 July 1934, London, UK. Educ: The Training Coll., Southampton. Publs: The End of the Beginning, 1968; Understanding Your Baby, 1975. Mbrships: Soc. Authors; PEN. Address: 3 Marlborough Court, Pembroke Rd., Kensington, London W8, UK.

BALDWIN, Edward R., b. 30 Apr. 1935, Concord, N.H., USA. Architect. Educ: B.A., 1957, M.Arch., 1961, Yale Univ. Publs: The Cross-Country Skiing Handbook, 1972; The Beginner's Guide to Cross-Country Skiing, 1974. Mbrships: Royal Archtl. Inst. of Can.; Am. Inst. Archts.; Ont. Assn. of Archts. Recip., AIA Award for Design, 1972. Address: 47 Colborne Street, Toronto, Ontario, Canada.

BALDWIN, James (Arthur), b. 2 Aug. 1924, NYC, USA. Writer. Publs. incl: (novels) Go Tell It on the Mountain, 1953; Giovanni's Room, 1955; Another Country, 1962; Tell Me How Long the Train's Been Gone, 1968; Going to Meet the Man (short stories), 1965; (plays) The Amen Corner, 1965; Blues for Mister Charley, 1964; (other) Notes of a Native Son, 1955. Contbr. to Partisan Review. Mbrships: Actors Studio, N.Y.; Nat. Advsry. Bd., Congress on Racial Equality; Nat. Comm. for a Sane Nuclear Policy; Nat. Inst. of Arts & Letters, 1964. Hons: For. Drama Critics Award, 1964; D.Litt., Univ. of B.C., Vancouver, 1964. Address: 137 West 71st St., N.Y., NY 10023, USA.

BALDWIN, Leland Dewitt, b. 23 Nov. 1897, Fairchance, Pa., USA. University Professor of History.

Educ: Ph.D., Univ. of Mich. Publs. incl: Whiskey Rebels, 1938; God's Englishman, 1943; Keelboat Age on Western Waters, 1941; Delectable Country, 1939; Best Hope of Earth; A Grammar of Democracy, 1948; Stream of American History, 1952; The American Quest, 1972; Reframing the Constitution: An Imperative for Modern America, 1973. Address: 1150 Coast Village Road – 302, Santa Barbara, CA 93108, USA.

BALDWIN, William Lee, b. 12 Apr. 1928, NYC, USA. Economist; Author. Educ: B.A., Duke Univ., 1951; M.A., 1953, Ph.D., 1958, Princeton Univ. Publs: The Structure of the Defense Market, 1955-64, 1967; Antitrust & the Changing Corporation, 1961. Contbr., var. profl. jrnls., encys., & dictionaries. Mbr., AAUP. Address: Dept. of Economics, Dartmouth College, Hanover, NH 03755, USA.

BALFOUR, William Raymond John Evelyn, pen name RUSSELL, Raymond, b. 1923, Worcester, UK. Freelance Photojournalist, 1965–. Contbr. to var. jrnls. inclng: Motoring; Ford Times; High Rd.; Everybody's (Aust.). Mbrships: Soc. of Authors; Inst. Inc. Photographers; Bur. Freelance Photographers. Address: c/o National Westminster Bank, Ltd., Belgravia Branch, 1 Grosvenor Gdns., London SW1W 0BG, UK.

BALL, Frederick Cyril, b. 1905, Hastings, UK. Author. Educ: WEA, Oxford. Publs: Poems, Radio Plays, 1964, 1967, 1969; (biography):Tressell of Mugsborough, 1951; A Breath of Fresh Air, 1961; A Grotto for Miss Maynier, 1965; BBC Entry, Radio Italia, 1965. Contbr. to Books & Bookmen, etc. Mbr., Soc. of Authors, London. Address: 4A Cotswold Close, Hastings, Sussex, UK.

BALL, John Dudley Jr., b. 8 July 1911, Schenectady, N.Y., USA. Author. Educ: B.A., Carroll Coll., Waukesha, Wis., USA., 1934. Publs. incl: Edwards: USAF Flight Test Center, 1962; Judo Boy, 1964; Arctic Showdown, 1966; In the Heat of the Night, 1965; Rescue Mission, 1966; The Cool Cottontail, 1966; Mis 1000 Spring Blossoms, 1968; Johnny Get Your Gun, 1969; Dragon Hotel, 1969; Last Plane Out, 1970; The First Team, 1971; Five Pieces of Jade, 1972; The Fourteenth Point, 1973; Mark One – The Dummy, 1974; The Winds of Mitamara, 1975; The Eyes of Buddha, forthcoming. Contbr. to var. publs. Mbrships. incl: Mystery Writers Am.; Brit. Crime Writers' Assn. Hons. incl: Brit. Crime Writers Golden Dagger Award, 1968. Address: 16401 Otsego St., Encino, CA 19436, USA.

BALLANTYNE, David Watt, b. 1924, Auckland, NZ. Journalist; Author. Publs: The Cunninghams, 1948; The Last Pioneer, 1963; And the Glory, 1963; A Friend of the Family, 1966; Sydney Bridge Upside Down, 1968. Contbr to: Auckland Star; London Evening News; London Evening Standard; Kenyon Review; Meanjin; Landfall; TV; etc. Mbrships: Aust. Soc. of Authors; PEN. Address: Ed. Dept., Auckland Star, P.O. Box 3697, Auckland, NZ.

BALLANTYNE, John Chalmers, b. 26 Sept. 1917, Nottingham, UK. Consultant Otolaryngologist. Educ: St. Mary's Hosp. Med. Schl., Univ. of London. Publs: Synopsis of Otolaryngology (co-author), 2nd ed., 1967; Deafness, 2nd. ed., 1970; Sr. Ed., Scott-Brown's Diseases of Ear, Nose & Throat, 3rd ed., 1971. Contbr. to med. jrnls. Mbrships. incl: VP, Sect. of Otol., Royal Soc. of Med.; Hon. Sec., Brit. Assn. of Otolaryngols.; Collegium Otorhinolaryngologicum Amicitiae Sacrum. Hons: James Yearsley Mem. Lect., 1970; Harrison Prize in Otol., Royal Soc. of Med., 1971; Guest Lectr., Rsch. Study Club, L.A., USA, 1972. Address: 61 Harley St., London W1N 1DD, UK.

BALLARD, J.G., b. 1930, Shanghai, China. Writer. Educ: King's Coll., Cambridge Univ. Publs: The Drowned World, 1963; The 4-Dimensional Nightmare, 1963; The Terminal Beach, 1964; The Drought, 1965; The Crystal World, 1966; The Disaster Area, 1967; The Atrocity Exhibition, 1970; Crash, 1973; Vermillion Sands, 1973; Concrete Island, 1974. Contbr. to: Ambit; Encounter; New Worlds; Playboy; Transatlantic Review; etc. Agent: John Wolfers. Address: 36 Charlton Rd., Shepperton, Middx., UK.

BALLINGER, William Sanborn (Bill S.), b. 13 Mar. 1912, Oskaloosa, Iowa, USA. Novelist; Dramatist. Educ: B.A., Univ. of Wis.; LL.D., Northern Colls. of Philippines. Publs: (27 novels in 28 countries & 13 transls.) Body in the Bed, 1948; The Tooth & the Nail, 1955; Not I, Said the Vixen, 1964; The Heir Hunters, 1966; 49 Days of Death, 1970; The Corsican, 1974; over 150 TV shows & films.

Contbr. to: Hollywood Radio Theatre; True Mag. (Contbng. Ed., 1975); etc. Mbrships: Past Exec. VP, Mystery Writers of Am.; Mbr., Bd. of Dirs., Writers Guild of Am. W.C.U. Hons: Prix Roman Policier, 1953; Edgar Allan Poe Award, 1961; Carnegie Fund Fellowship, 1968; Boucheron II, Masters, 1971. Address: P.O. Box 4034, N. Hollywood, CA 91607, USA.

BALLON, Robert Jean, b. 28 Apr. 1919, Laeken, Belgium. University Professor of Economics & International Business. Educ: B.A., 1941, M.A., 1947. Univ. of Louvain; M.A., Cath. Univ. of Am., Wash., 1957. Publs: Ed., Doing Business in Japan, 1967; Ed., Joint Ventures and Japan, 1967; Ed., The Japanese Employee, 1969; Ed., Japan's Market and Foreign Business, 1971; Co-Ed., Foreign Investment and Japan, 1972; Ed., Marketing in Japan, 1973; Corporate Financial Reporting in Japan (co-author), forthcoming. Contbr. to: Monthly Labor Review; Bus. Horizons; Far Eastern Econ. Review; etc. Mbrships incl: Japan Indl. Rels. Rsch. Assn.; Japan Mgmt. Rsch. Assn. Recip., US Civ. Serv. Commn. Merit Citation, 1962. Address: Sophia Univ., 7 Kioicho, Chiyoda-Ku, Tokyo 102, Japan.

BALOGH, László, b. 24 May 1919, Debrecen, Hungary. Head Producer of Hungarian Radio. Educ: Ph.D. Publs: Károly Szász's English Literary Connections, 1942; History of Hungarian Literature 1919-1945, 1955; Hungarian Literary Textbook, 1958; Attila József, 1969; István Asztalos, 1969; Literature & Communication, forthcoming; Seed Under Snow, (Endre Ady) forthcoming. Mbrships: Assn. Hungarian Writers; PEN. Address: 1800 Budapest, Brody S.u. 5-7, Hungary.

BALOGH, Penelope, pen name FOX, Petronella, b. 16 June 1916, Ipswich, Suffolk, UK. Psychotherapist. Educ: Dip. Psych., Oxford Univ. Publs: I'm Glad I Was Analysed; Up with the Joneses; Freud. Contbr. to: Guardian; Mother & Baby; Mbrships. incl: Royal Brit. Psych. Soc.; Assn. Psychotherapists. Address: 29 St. Mark's Cres., London NW1, UK.

BALOGH, Thomas (Lord Balogh), b. 2 Nov. 1905, Budapest, Hungary. Economist; Minister of State for Energy, UK; (Adviser to: British Cabinet, 1964-67, Prime Minister, 1968). Educ: Doct. rerum pol., Univ. of Budapest; Univs. of Berlin, Germany, & Harvard, USA. Publs: Studies in Financial Organisation, 1946; Dollar Crisis, 1949; Unequal Partners, 1962; Economics of Poverty, 1966; Labour & Inflation, 1970; Essay in International Monetary Reform, 1974. Contbr. to: Econ. Jrnl.; Quarterly Jrnl. of Econs.; Bulletin, Oxford Univ. Inst. of Stats.; Mbrships: Fabian Soc. (Chmn., 1970); Labour Party Financial & Exec. Office. Recip., Life Peerage, UK. Agent: Curtis Brown. Address: Old Bank House, 14 High St., Hampstead, London NW3, UK.

BALOTĂ, Nicholae, b. 26 Jan. 1925, Cluj, Rumania. Professor. Educ: Dr.Philol., Cluj Univ. Publs: Euphorion, 1969; Urmuz, 1970; Labirint (Labyrinth, essays), 1970; Lupta cu absurdul (The Struggle with the Absurd), 1971; Despre pasiuni (On Passions), 1971; Umanități (Humanities), 1973; Iakob Burkhardt, 1974; Introducere in opera lui Philippide (Introduction to Philippide's Work), 1974; De la Ion la Ioanide (From Ion to Ioanide, Rumanian Prose Writers of the XXth century), 1974. Contbr. to profl. jrnls. Mbrships. incl: Writers' Union, Rumania. Hons. incl: Prize of Rumanian Acad., 1973. Address: Str. Daniel Barcenu 26, Bucharest IV, Rumania.

BAMZAI, Kashi Nath, b. 1 July 1915, Srinagar, India. Civil Servant, Ministry of Information. Educ: B.A.; LL.B. Publs: Press in India (annual Publ.), 1967, 1968, 1969, 1970, 1971, & 1972. Mbrships: Press Club of India; Indian Coun. of World Affairs; India Int. Ctr. Address: 91 Lodi Estate, New Delhi – 110003, India.

BANAŠEVIĆ, Nikola, b. 15 Feb. 1895, Zavala, Yugoslavia. University Professor; Author. Educ: B.A., Univ. of Belgrade; Ph.D., Univ. of Paris, France. Publs: Jean Bastier de la Péruse, 1529-1554, 1923, 1970; Ciklus Marka Kraljevića i odjeci francusko-talijanske viteške književnosti, 1935; Letopis Popa Dukljanina i narodna predanja, 1971; P.P. Njegoš, Gorski Vijenac, w. commentary, 1973; Etudes d'histoire littéraire & de littérature comparée, 1975. Contbr. to: Revue des Etudes Slaves; Revue de Lit. Comparée; Le Français Mod., etc. VP, Int. Comp. Lit. Assn., 1964-70. Hons: Dr. honoris causa, Univ. of Bordeaux, 1961, Univ. of Clermont-Ferrand, 1965; Off.,

Légion d'Honneur, 1963. Address: 54 Ognjena Prize, 11000 Belgrade, Yugoslavia.

BANCROFT, Peter, 5 May 1916, Tucson, Ariz., USA. Educational Administrator. B.A., Univ. of Calif., Santa Barbara; M.S., Univ. of Southern Calif.; D.Ed., N. Colorado Univ. Publ: The World's Finest Minerals & Crystals, 1973. Contbr. to: Lapidary Jrnl.; Rock & Gem; etc. Mbr. Livermore, Calif., Chmbr. of Commerce, VP, Address: 3538 Oak Cliff Dr., Fallbrook, CA 92028, USA.

BANCROFT, Vivian Starck, b. 7 June 1913, Kenosha, Wis., USA. Teacher. Educ: B.A., M.H.E.E., Univ. of Ariz. Publs: It's So, Sew Easy, 1962, 2nd ed., 1970. Contbr. to Jrnl. of Home Economics. Address: 5305 N. Via Alcalde, Tucson, AZ 85718, USA.

BANDIĆ, M. I., b. 6 June 1930, Priština, Yugoslavia. Literary Critic; University Professor. Educ: Ph.D. (Lit.), 1963. Publs. incl: Vreme romana (The Time of the Novel), 1958; Ivo Andrić: Zagonetka vedrine (The Riddle of Brightness), 1963; Mihailo Lalić: Povest o ljudskoj hrabrosti (The Story of Human Courage), 1965; Savremena proza (Contemporary Prose), 1965, 1973. Contbr. to Newspapers & jrnls. inclng: Letopis Matice srpske; Politika; Književne novine; also to TV. Mbrships: incl: Assn. of Yugoslav Writers; M.L.A.; PEN. Recip., Lit. Prize for Criticism, 1963. Address: F. Rozmana 11, 11080 Zemun, SFR Yugoslavia.

BANK JENSEN, Thea, b. 30 Dec. 1913, Budapest, Hungary. Writer; Nurseryschool Teacher. Educ: Dip. Nursery Tchr.; Psychol. studies, Ericastiftelsen, Stockholm, Sweden. Publs. incl: Fra kravlegård til skolebaenk, 1966; Småt legetøj, stort legetøj, godt legetøj, 1967; Det levende i mennesket, 1968; Fisk, 1972; Glas, 1973; Mens Du sover, 1974; Bageren, 1974; Borgens forlag, 1974; Play with Paper (transl. into 7 langs.); Trine kan . . . (transl. into 5 langs.). Contbr. to: Helse; Bo bedre. Mbrships: Danish Authors' Soc.; working comm., Idr., toy exhib., OMEP; Working Comm., Int. Coun. for Children's Play. Address: Langemosegård, Lunden, Fagerkaersvej 9, 36 30 Jaegerspris, Denmark.

BANKS, Francis Richard, b. 1912, London, UK. Writer. Educ: Heaton Grammar Schl. & Rutherford Tech. Coll., Newcastle upon Tyne. Asst. Ed., The Blue Guides, 1949-54; Ed., Penguin Guides, 1954-. Publs. incl: Scottish Border Country; English Villages & Old English Towns; Blue Guides to England: Northern England, 5th & 6th eds.; Wales, 4th ed.; Sweden & Denmark, Penguin Guides to Kent, Surrey, Sussex, London, & Warwickshire; Discovering Britain; Letts' Motor Tour Guides to the Lake District, the Highlands, & others; The Peak District, 1975. Contbr. to: Times; Observer; Country Life; Countryman; etc. Address: 79 Empress Rd., Derby, UK.

BANNARD, Edward Yorke, b. 1919, Towcester, UK. Barrister-at-Law; Assistant Secretary, Department of Trade; Playwright. Educ: M.A., Queen's Coll., Oxford. Publs: (TV plays) A Small Crisis, 1961; Conflict in the Sun, 1961; The Night of the Reckoning, 1963; The Bastow Affair, 1964; The Mandarins, 1969; The Second Interview, 1970. Agent: David Higham Assocs. Address: 12 Great Spilmans, Dulwich, London SE22, UK.

BANNER, (Major) Edgar Harold Walter, b. 24 Nov. 1897, Kings Norton, Birmingham, UK. Chartered Electrical Engineer. Educ: Univ. of Birmingham, 1919; B.Sc., Elec. Engrng., 1923; M.Sc., 1924. Publs: Electronic Measuring Instruments, 1954, 1957; Electrical Measuring Instrument Practice, 1954; Electrical Measurements (Turner & Banner), 1935. Ed. & Contbr., Newnes Modern Electrical Engineer, 5th Ed., 1955; Ed., Gallipolian. Contbr. to var. profl. publs. Mbrships: Fellow, Instn. of Elec. Engrs., Instn. of Mech. Engrs., Inst. of Phys.; Fndr., Chmn., Hon. Sec., Gallipoli Assn. Recip., Territorial Decoration, 1950. Address: Delphi, Maresfield Park, Uckfield, Sussex TN22 2HB, UK.

BANNERMAN, David Armitage, b. 1886, Pendleton, Lancs. Ornithologist & Writer. Educ: Wellington & Pembroke Coll., Cambridge; M.A.; Sc.D.(Cantab.): LL.D. (Glas.) Publs. incl: The Birds of the Canary Islands: Birds of Tropical West Africa I-VIII; The Birds of the British Isles, Vol. I-XII; The Birds of Cyprus (w. Mary Bannerman); Birds of the Atlantic Islands Vol. I-IV; Handbook of the Birds of Cyprus & Migrants of the Middle East (w. Jane Bannerman) 1971. Mbrships: VP, Royal Soc. Protection of Birds; Hon. Pres., Scottish Ornithols. Club; Coun., Soc. Promotion Nature Reserves & Royal Geog. Soc.; Hon. Mbr., French, Spanish, Cyprus & Gambia Ornithol. Socs.; Hon.

Fellow, Am. Ornithol. Union; Hon. Assoc., Brit. Museum (Nat. Hist.), 1950; Hon. Curator, Royal Scottish Museum; Scientific Fellow, Zool. Soc. London; F.R.S.E. Awards: M.B.E., 1918; Gold Medallist, Brit. Ornithol. Union, 1958; O.B.E., 1960. Contbr. to newspapers & sci. publs. Address: Bailiff's House, Slindon, Arundel, Sussex, UK.

BANNERMAN, Kay, b. 11 Oct. 1919, Hove, Sussex, UK. Actress; Dramatic Author. Educ: Royal Acad. of Dramatic Art. Publs: see BROOKE, Harold for details. Address: Babergh Hall, Gt. Waldingfield, Sudbury, Suffolk, UK.

BANNISTER, Sybil Louise, b. 29 May 1910, Uckfield, UK. Publs: I Lived Under Hitler, 1957. Mbr., Soc. of Authors. Address: Riverswood, Hempstead Lane, Uckfield, E. Sussex, TN22 1DZ, UK.

BANTOCK, Gavin Marcus August, b. 4 July 1939, Barnt Green, UK. University Lecturer in English. Educ: M.A., Dip.Ed., New Coll., Oxford. Publs: Christ (epic poem), 1965; A New Thing Breathing, 1969; Poems & Anglo-Saxon Translations, 1970; Eirenikon (long poem), 1972; Poems, 1972; Modern Poetry, 1972; Land of the Setting Sun, 1973; Disunited Kingdom, 1974. Contbr. to: Poetry Review; Orbis; New Measure; Spectator. Mbr., Soc. of Authors. Hons: Richard Hillary Award, 1964; Alice Hunt-Bartlett Poetry Prize, 1966; Eric Gregory Award, 1969. Address: Reitaku University, Kashiwa-Shi, Chiba-Ken, Japan.

BANTON, Michael Parker, b. 1926, Birmingham, UK. Professor of Sociology. Educ: Univ. of Glasgow; London Schl. of Econs.; B.Sc.(Econ.); Ph.D.; D.Sc. Publs: The Coloured Quarter; West African City; White & Coloured; The Policeman in the Community; Roles; Race Relations; Racial Minorities; Police-Community Relations; The Race Concept. Address: 9 Canynge Rd., Bristol BS8 3JZ, UK.

BAQUERO, Arcadio, pen name Professor ARGOS, b. 27 July 1925, Gijon, Spain. Journalist; Chief Editor; Theatre Critic. Educ: Dipl. Jrnlism, Schl. of Jrnlism., Madrid, 1950; Lic., Info. Scis.; Dipl., Graphopsychol., Complutense Univ., Madrid, 1972; Dipl., Sci. Graphol., Higher Inst. of Humanities, Buenos Aires, 1972. Publs: Don Juan y su evolución dramática, 2 vols., 1966; El teatro de humor en España (in collab.), 1966. Contbr. to: La Estafeta Literaria; Nuestro Tiempo, etc.; Chief Ed., La Actualidad española. Mbrships: Advsr., Coun. on Theatre, Min. of Info. & Tourism; Graphol. Soc., Paris; Int. Inst. of Theatre, UNESCO. Hons: Nat. Theatre Prize, 1959-60; March Prize for Lit., 1962. Address: Calle Cavanilles 17, 7º-3ª, Madrid 7, Spain.

BARABAS, Steven, b. 7 Aug. 1904, Passaic, N.J., USA. College Professor of Theology. Educ: A.B., Princeton Univ., 1937; B.D., 1940; Th.D., 1948, Princeton Theol. Seminary. Publs: So Great Salvation: The History & Message of the Keswick Convention, 1952; Zondervan Pictorial Bible Dictionary (assoc. ed), 1963; Zondervan Pictorial Encyclopedia of the Bible, 5 vols. (assoc. Ed.), Contbr. to: Christianity Today; Eternity. Mbrships: Evangelical Theol. Soc. Address: 922 Scott St., Wheaton, IL 60187 USA.

BARABÁS, Tibor, b. 27 Aug. 1911, Pécel, Hungary. Writer. Publs: Stakes in Florence, 1940; Hungarian Pioneers of European Spirit, 1942; Educators of a People, 1946; Beethoven, 1955; Mozart's Journey to Paris, 1957; Memories of an Address-writer, 1957; Life of Chopin, 1960; Night-Patrol, 1969; Michelangelo, 1970; Uriel, 1973; By Order of the Emperor, forthcoming; The Lieutenant of Rakoczi, forthcoming. Contbr. to major Hungarian jrnls. Mbrships: Hungarian Writers' Assn.; PEN; Bd. Dirs., Artists' Club, Fészek. Hons incl: Jozsef Attilla Prize, Kossuth Prize, Order of Merit. Address: 1055 Budapest, V. Kossuth Lajos tér 18, Hungary.

BARACK, Nathan A., b. 2 July 1913, Ukraine, Russia. Rabbi. Educ: B.A., Lewis Inst., Chgo., USA; Rabbi, Hebrew Theol. Coll.; Dr. Heb. Lit., Jewish Theol. Sem., N.Y. Publs: The Tale of A Wonderful Ladder, 1943; Faith for Fallibles, 1952; Mount Moriah View, 1956; History of the Sabbath, 1965; The Jewish Way to Life, 1974. Contbr. to: Reconstructionist Mag.; Jewish Spectator; Conservative Judiasm; Jewish Digest. Mbrships: Rabbinical Assembly Am.; Relig. Zionists; Bd., Mental Hlth. Assn.; Bd., Assn. for Retarded; Bd., Human Rights Assn. Address: 2623 N. 10th St., Sheboygan, WI, USA.

BÁRÁNY, Tamás, b. 21 Mar. 1922, Budapest, Hungary. Literary & Art Historian. Educ: Ph.D. Publs. incl: (novels) And the Hills Move Off, 1947; Twenty Years, 1954; Fatherless Generation, 1960; Everything Begins With Us, 1969; (short stories) Summer at the Seaside, 1966; Bottle Mail, 1968; (plays) The Second Crowing, 1958; Even the Parents Are Human Beings, 1971. Contbr. to: Kortárs; Uj Irás; Élet és Irodalom. Mbrships. incl: Comm., Hungarian Writers' Union; Writers' Safeguarding Comm. (Chmn.). Hons: Attila József Prize, 1954, 1969; Andor Gábor Prize, 1972.

BARAT, Endre, pen name Carát, b. 24 Apr. 1907, Nagykáta, Hungary. Writer. Publs. incl: novels: Slaves, 1945; Honour, 1948; Paganini, 1964; Nightmare, 1968; Woman's Confession, 1974; Memnon (travel diary), 1962; plays; short stories. Contbr. to Magyarnemzet. Mbrships: Hungarian Writers' Soc.; PEN. Recip., States Medal, 1968. Address: 1068 Budapest, Szondy-Mtca 93, Hungary.

BARBER, Willard Foster, b. 21 Mar. 1909, Mitchell, S.D., USA. University Lecturer; Diplomat; Author. Educ: A.B., 1928, M.A., 1929, Stanford Univ., Calif. Publs: American Government (w. W. B. Guthrie), 1934; Internal Security & Military Power. Counterinsurgency & Civic Action in Latin America (w. C. N. Ronning), 1966. Contbr. to: Survey; Orbis; Saturday Review; Jrnl. Int. Affairs; etc. Address: 3718 University Ave., N.W., Wash. DC 20016, USA.

BARBOSA, Miguel, b. 22 Nov. 1925, Lisbon, Portugal. Writer; Painter. Educ: Degree Econ. & Fin., Lisbon Univ. Publs: (short stories) Retalhos de Vida, 1955; Manta de Trapos, 1962; (plays) O Palheiro, 1963; Os Carnivoros, 1964; O Piquenique, 1964; O Insecticida, 1965; A Mulher Parni a Franca, 1971; Los profetas do la Paja, 1973; (romance) Trineu do Morro, 1972; (novel) Mulher Macumba, 1973. Contbr. to: Yorick; Teatro en Movimento. Mbrships: Portuguese Soc. of Writers; Portuguese Soc. of Authors. Recip., 1st Prize, Maria Jereza Alves Viana, 1st Theatre Serv., Sao Paulo. Address: Av. yóao Crisostomo 91, 2° Lisbon, Portugal.

BARCELÓ, José Luis, b. 30 Mar. 1922, Madrid, Spain. Journalist; Author; Economist; Editor. Publs. incl: La Economia Internacional del Futuro, 1946; Inmobiliarias, 1948; Historia Economica de Espana, 1952; Contra la Guerra Atomica, 1953; La Conquista del Espacio, 1959; Animales Desaparecidos Sobre la Tierra, 1967; La Antartida, Pasado, Presente y Futuro, 1968; Astronautica y Filatelia, 1970. Contbr. to: ABC; Madrid; Portavoz; El Economista; Iberica; Campo; Ceres; Fndr. & Gen. Ed., El Mundo Financiero. Recip., Hon. Comendador de la Orden de la Medahuia; & profl. prizes. Address: P.O. Box 6119, Madrid, Spain.

BARCLAY, Alexander, b. 25 July 1896, London, UK. Former Keeper, Department of Chemistry & Photography, Science Museum. Educ: A.R.C.S., Royal Coll. of Sci. Publs: Descriptive Catalogues of Pure & Industrial Chemistry Collections, Science Museum. Contbr. to var. jrnls. on chem. & photography. Mbrships: Fellow, Royal Inst. Chem.; Royal Photographic Soc. (Hon. mbr.). Recip., C.B.E., 1957. Address: Towers End, Walberswick, Southwold, Suffolk, UK.

BARCLAY, (Brigadier) Cyril Nelson, b. 1896, Dartford, Kent. Retired Army Officer; Author; Publs: History of the Cameronians (Scottish Rifles) 1933-46; var. other regtl. hists.; The New Warfare; Against Great Odds; Part-Time Farmer; Battle 1066; Armistice 1918. Contbr. to Ency. Britannica (Mil. Advsr., 1958-); Army Quarterly & Defence Jrnl. (Ed., 1950-66); Brassey's Annual — Armed Forces Yr. Book (Asst. Ed., 1950-69); Chambers Ency.; N.Y. Times Mag.; Army (USA); Mil. Review (USA); Ency. Americana; etc. Hons: Bertrand Stewart Essay Prize, 1939; C.B.E.; D.S.O. Address: 44 Painters Field, St. Cross, Winchester, Hants. SO23 9RQ, UK.

BARCLAY, John Bruce, b. 30 Nov. 1909, Edinburgh, Scotland, UK. Deputy Director of Educational Studies (Extra-Mural), University of Edinburgh. Educ: M.A. & Ph.D., Univ. of Edinburgh; Moray House Coll. of Educ.; Univ. of Oxford. Publs: Edinburgh (from earliest times), 1965; The Tounis Scule, 1974. Contbr. of rsch. reports & publs. to field, also to var. jrnls. inclng: Times Educl. Supplement; Scottish Educl. Jrnl.; Scottish Jrnl. of Adult Educ. (Hon. Ed.); Scottish Adult Educ. Address: 25 Gardiner Rd., Edinburgh EH4 3RP, UK.

BARCLAY, Vera, b. Hertford Heath, Herts., UK. Writer. Publs: Books for Children (fiction & natural hist.); Books for Scouts & Scout Leaders; var. others inclng. biog., educl., relig. (RC). Address: 3 Old Salterns Gate, Seaview, Isle of Wight, UK.

BARCYNSKI, Leon, pen name PHILLIPS, Osborne, b. 23 May 1949, London, UK. Writer. Educ: Studies in Theravada Buddhism & Western Esotericism. Publs: Co-Author, The Magical Philosophy (vol. 1, Robe & Ring, 1974. vol. 2, the Apparel of High Magick, vol. 3, The Sword & the Serpent, vol. 4, The Triumph of Light, vol. 5, Mysteria Magica, all 1975). Mbrships: The Aurum Solis (Admnstr.-Gen., 1974-); The Ghost Club; R.I.L.K.O. Address: BM-Sacriverb, London WC1V 6XX, UK.

BARD, William E., pen name BARD, W. E., b. 8 June 1892, Knightstown, Ind., USA. Poet. Publs: A Little Flame Blown, 1934; Feather in the Sun, 1959; This Land This People, 1966; Burning Embers, 1970; As a Wild Bird Returning, 1973. Contbr. to jrnls., newspapers. Mbrships. incl: Poetry Soc. of Am.; Charter Mbr., Tex. Inst. of Letters; VP, Am., United Poets Laureate Int.; Past Pres., Poetry Soc. of Tex.; Fndr., Acad. of Am. Poets; Advsry. Bd., Poet Lore. Address: 11132 Pinocchio Dr., Dallas, TX 75229, USA.

BARDEN, Leonard William, b. 20 Aug. 1929, Croydon, UK. Journalist. Educ: B.A., Balliol Coll., Oxford. Publs: A Guide to Chess Openings, 1957; How Good is your Chess?, 1957; Modern Chess Miniatures, 1960; Ruy Lopez, 1963; Guardian Chess Book, 1967; Kings Indian Defence, 1969; How to Play the Endgame in Chess, 1975. Contbr. to: Guardian; Fin. Times; Evening Standard; Field; Hindu. Mbr., London Chess Club (Chmn.) Recip., Brit. Chess Championship, 1954. Address: 89 Tennison Rd., S. Norwood, London SE25, UK.

BARDENS, Dennis Conrad, b. 1911, Midhurst, Sussex, UK. Reporter; Author; Editor. Appts. incl: Reporter, Feature Writer, var. newspapers, until 1940; PR Off. to exiled Czech. Govt., 1943-45; Ed., Focus, BBC documentary radio series, 1949-52; Ed., Panorama, BBC TV mag. prog., 1953-54; Staff Writer, Soldier mag., War Off., 1960-62. Publs. incl: Training for Democracy, 1945; A Press in Chains — a Survey of the Soviet Press, 1953; Famous Cases of Norman Birkett K.C., 1963; Mysterious Worlds, 1970; (biographies): Portrait of a Statesman — biog. of Sir Anthony Eden, 1956; Princess Margaret, 1964; Churchill in Parliament, 1967. Contbr. to UK & overseas press. Mbr., Press & Reform Clubs. Address: 3 Horbury Mews, London W11 3NL, UK.

BARDIS, Panos D., b. 24 Sept. 1924, Lefcohorion, Arcadia, Greece. University Professor; Writer. Educ: B.A., Bethany Coll., W.Va., USA; M.A., Notre Dame Univ., Ind.; Ph.D., Purdue Univ., Ind. Publs: Ivan & Artemis, 1957; The Family in Changing Civilizations, 1967, 2nd ed., 1969; Encyclopedia of Campus Unrest, 1971. Contbr. to: Sociol. & Social Rsch.; Am. Jrnl. Phys.; Sci.; Jrnl. Educl. Sociol. & num. other profl. jrnls. Mbrships: Life Fellow, Int. Inst. Arts & Letters, Geneva, Switz.; Fellow, AAAS; AAUP; Fellow, Am. Sociol. Assn.; num. other nat. & int. profl. assns. Hons. incl: Museo de Historia, 1967. Address: 2533 Orkney, Ottawa Hills, Toledo, OH 43606, USA.

BÁRDOS, Pál, b. 30 Mar. 1936, Mako, Hungary. Script Editor. Educ: József Attila Univ.; M.S.; Ph.D. Publs: (in Hungarian) Eight Girls & the Dragon, 1959; Chaos, 1962; From Evening to Morning, 1966; Special Mark: Fear, 1967; Four Hundred Forints, 1971; The Unsolved Affair, 1974; (play) Manor Court, 1972. Contbr. to: Kortars; Uj Iras; Elet es Irodalom; Nepszabadsag. Mbrships: Union of Hungarian Writers; PEN. Address: Budapest 1071, Lovolde ter 2., fsz. 3., Hungary.

BAREHAM, John Derek, b. 5 July 1928, Sudbury, Suffolk, UK. Senior History Lecturer; History Consultant. Educ: Tchrs. Cert., Borough Rd. Trng. Coll. Middx.; External Student, Univ. of London; B.A., 1950; B.A. Hons. Hist., 1952. Publs. incl: History Course for Malaysian Primary Schools (co-author), 1962-66; Ed. & Co-author, Awake to History series for primary schls., 1964-66; Changing World History, for secondary schls., 1969-75; Cons., Picture Reference Books, 11 vols., 1968-75; Privilege & Poverty (6th form text), 1975. Contbr. to profl. jrnls.; Textbook reviewer, Schoolmaster, 1964-66; Specialist Hist. Question-setter, BBC Mastermind Quiz Prog., 1972—. Mbrships: Soc. of Authors; Educl. Writers Grp. Address: 427 Pinhoe Rd., Whipton, Exeter EX4 8EN, Devon, UK.

BARFIELD, Arthur Owen, pen name BURGEON, G. A. L., b. 9 Nov. 1898, London, UK. Solicitor (Retired). Educ.; B.C.L., M.A., B.Litt., Oxford Univ. Publs: History in English Words, 1926, 1954; Poetic Diction, 1928, 3rd ed., 1973; This Ever Diverse Pair, 1950; Saving the Appearances, 1957; Worlds Apart, 1963; Unancestral Voice, 1965; Speakers Meaning, 1967. Contbr. to: Contemporary Review; Saturday Evening Post; Encounter; Denver Quarterly. Mbr., Athenaeum. Address: Westfield, Hartley, Near Dartford, Kent, UK.

BARGELLINI, Piero, b. 5 Aug. 1897. Writer. Publs. incl: Pian dei Giullari, 12 vols., 1950; Nostalgico di Sandro Botticelli, 1951; Chiodi solari, 1952; Santa Chiara, 1952; Canto alle rondini, 1953; Sant'Antonio da Firenze, 1954; Tivurzi, 1955; Ghirlanda per Firenze, 1956; In Lizza per l'arte, 1957; Santi come uomini, 1957; Belvedere: arte Greca, arte etrusca, 2 vols., 1957-59; I santi del giorno, 1958; Il Natale nella storia, nella leggenda e nell'arte, 1959; Assisi città santa, 1960. Contbr. to num. newspapers & mags. Address: Via della Pinzochere 3, Florence, Italy.

BARKAS, Janet, b. 16 Dec. 1948, Manhattan, N.Y., USA. Author. Educ: B.A., Hofstra Univ., 1970. Publs: The Vegetable Passion; A History of the Vegetarian State of Mind, 1975; Meatless Cooking: Celebrity Style, 1975. Contbr. to: McCall's; N.Y. Times; Harper's; Family Hlth.; Contemp. Review; Times of India; Penthouse Forum; Backstage. Mbrships: Authors Guild, Inc.; Authors League of Am. Inc.; Soc. of Mag. Writers. Address: P.O. Box 31, Cooper Stn., NY 10003, USA.

BARKER, A. L., b. 13 Apr. 1918, Kent, UK. Journalist. Publs: Innocents, 1947; Novelette, 1951; A Case Examined, 1965; Femina Real, 1971; A Source of Embarrassment, 1974. Contbr. to: New Statesman; La Table Ronde; Bonnier's Lit. Mag.; Nova; Good Housekeeping; Atlantic Monthly; Argosy; Listener. Mbrships: F.R.S.A.; Writers' Guild of GB; Writers' Action Grp. Hons: Atlantic Award in Lit., 1946; Somerset Maugham Award, 1947; Cheltenham Festival of Lit. Award, 1962. Address: 103 Harrow Road, Carshalton, Surrey, UK.

BARKER, Arthur James, b. 20 Sept. 1918, Hull, UK. Former Army Officer; Technologist. Educ: Royal Mil. Coll. of Sci., Shrivenham, UK. Publs: March on Delhi, 1964; Suez: The 7 Day War, 1965; Eritrea 1941, 1966; The Bastard War: Mesopotamia 1914-18, 1967; Townshend of Kut, 1968; The Civilizing Mission, 1968; Behind Barbed Wire, 1974; Fortune Favours the Brave, 1974; (children's book) Weapons & Armour, 1973. Contbr. to: Battle; Army Quarterly; Int. Hist. Mag.; etc. Mbrships: PEN; F.R.S.A.; Authors' Guild; R.U.S.I.; Soc. for Army Histl. Rsch.; Recip., Knighthood of Mark Twain, 1967. Address: 53 Beechwood Ct., Queens Rd., Harrogate, Yorks., UK.

BARKER, Charles Edward, b. 1908, Leeds, Yorks., UK. Psychotherapist. Educ: Hartley Victoria Coll., Manchester, 1928-31. Publs: Nerves & their Cure, 1960; Psychology's Impact on the Christian Faith, 1964; The Church's Neurosis, 1975. Contbr. to: Psychol. Mag.; Bulletin, Brit. Assn. of Psychotherapists. Mbr., Brit. Assn. of Psychotherapists. Address: 2 Baltimore Ct., 74 The Drive, Hove, Sussex BN3 3PR, UK.

BARKER, Dennis, b. 21 June 1929, Lowestoft, UK. Journalist; Novelist. Publs: (novels) Candidate of Promise, 1969; The Scandalisers, 1974. Contbr. to: Guardian; BBC; Punch. Mbrships: Sec., Suffolk Br., Nat. Union of Jrnlsts. 1953-58; Chmn., 1958; Chmn., Home Cos. Dist. Coun., 1956-57; Life, Newspaper Press Fund; Writers' Guild of GB. Address: c/o The Guardian, 192 Grays Inn Rd., London WC1, UK.

BARKER, Dudley, b. 25 Mar. 1910, London, UK. Writer. Educ: B.A., Oriel Coll., Oxford. Publs. incl: The Man of Principle: A View of John Galsworthy (biog.), 1963; Writer by Trade: A View of Arnold Bennett (biog.), 1966; The Ladder, 1968; Outbreak, 1968; Prominent Edwardians (biog.), 1969; A Pillar of Rest, 1970; G. K. Chesterton (biog.), 1973; Also writer of crime works as Lionel Black (pen name). Contbr. to var. mags. & newspapers, GB & USA. Mbr., Writers Guild of GB. Address: 12 Wharfedale St., London SW10 9AL, UK.

BARKER, Elliott Speer, b. 25 Dec. 1886, Moran, Tex., USA. Wildlife Administrator; Forester; Rancher; Conservationist; Author. Publs: When the Dogs Bark 'Treed', 1946; Beatty's Cabin, 1953; Western Life &

Adventure 1889-1970, 1970, revised ed., 1974; (poetry) A Medley of Wilderness & Other Poems, 1962; Outdoors, Faith, Fun & Other Poems, 1968. Contbr. to: Outdoor Life; Field & Stream; Am. Forests; Empire; Colo. Mag.; Ford Times; etc. Mbrships. incl: Western Writers of Am.; Nat. Wildlife Fedn.; N.M. Wildlife Fedn-, 1915–, (Exec. Sec., 1959-66). Hons. incl: State Conservationist 1964, Nat. Wildlife Fedn.; Gold Spur Award for Best Non-Fiction book 1971, Western Writers of Am.; num. others. Address: 343 Palace Ave., Santa Fe, NM 87501, USA.

BARKER, Eric Leslie, b. 1912, Thornton Heath, UK. Author; Actor; Broadcaster. Publs: The Watch Hunt; Sea Breezes; Day Gone By; Steady Barker; Golden Gimmick. Address: Hillside Cottage, Stalisfield, Faversham, Kent, UK.

BARKER, George Granville, b. 1913, Loughton, UK. Poet; Professor of English. Educ: Regent St., Polytechnic, London. Publs: Poems, 1935; Calamiterror, 1936; Lament & Triumph, 1940; Eros in Dogma, 1950; The True Confessions of George Barker, 1950; A Vision of Beasts & Gods, 1950; Collected Poems, 1957; Essays, 1970; Runes & Rimes & Tunes & Chimes, 1970; To Aylsham Fair, 1970. Mbrships: Soc. of Authors; Royal. Soc. for the Preservation of Ancient Buildings. Address: c/o Faber & Faber, 24 Russell Sq., London WC1, UK.

BARKER, Nicolas John, b. 1932, Cambridge, UK. Production Manager. Educ: M.A., New Coll., Oxford. Publs: Publications of the Roxburghe Club, 1962; The Printer & the Poet, 1970; Stanley Morison (biog.), 1972. Contbr. to: Ed., Book Collector; The Library; Etoniana; Times Lit. Supplement. Mbr., Garrick Club. Address: 22 Clarendon Rd., London W11, UK.

BARKER, Ralph Hammond, b. 1917, Feltham, Middx., UK. Flight Lt., RAF (Retired). Educ: Hounslow Coll. Publs: Down in the Drink; The Ship Busters; The Last Blue Mountain; Strike Hard, Strike Sure; Ten Great Innings; The Thousand Plan; Great Mysteries of the Air; Aviator Extraordinary; Verdict on a Lost Flyer; Test Cricket, England v. Australia. Contbr. to: Sunday Express; The Cricketer. Address: Old Timbers, 16 Aldercombe Lane, Caterham, Surrey, UK.

BARKER, Ronald Ernest, pen name RONALD, E. B., b. 1920, London, UK. Publs: Books for All, 1956; Tendency to Corrupt, 1957; The Days are Long, 1959; (as E. B. Ronald) Cat & Fiddle Murders, 1954; Death by Proxy, 1956; A Sort of Madness, 1958. Contbr. to Bookseller. Mbrships: Crime Writers' Assn.; Soc. of Bookmen. Address: 111 Conisborough Crescent, London SE6, UK.

BARKER, Theodore Cardwell, b. 1923, Manchester, UK. Professor of Economic & Social History. Educ: M.A., Jesus Coll., Oxford; Ph.D., Manchester Univ. Publs. incl: A Merseyside Town in the Industrial Revolution (w. J. R. Harris), 1954; A History of London Transport (w. R. M. Robbins), Vol. I, 1963; Vol. II, 1974; A History of British Pewter (w. John Hatcher), 1974. Mbrships. incl: Hon. Treas., Brit. Nat. Comm., Int. Congress of Hist. Scis., 1973–; Hon. Sec., Econ. Hist. Soc., 1960-. Address: Minsen Dane, Faversham, Kent, UK.

BARKLEY, Mary Starr, b. 26 May 1906, Austin, Tex., USA. Educ: Univ. of Tex. Publs: The History of Travis County & Austin, 1963; A History of Central Texas, 1970. Contbr. to: state, nat. mags., 20 yrs. Hons: Cert. of Achievement, Essay Contest, Broadcast Music Inc.; Writer of Year, Altrusa Club, Austin, 1963. Address: 2203 Scenic Dr., Austin, TX 78703, USA.

BARKLEY, Sara Joyce Lowen, b. 8 Nov. 1913, Dalmeny, Sask., Can. Photo-Journalist; Women's Editor; Writer. Educ: Univ. of Ore., Eugene, 2 yrs.; Lewiston Normal Schl., Idaho, 1 yr. Mbrships. incl: Calif. Press Photog.'s Assn.; Chico Bus. & Profl. Women's Luncheon Club. Recip., 1st Place, Nat. Competition, Am. Laundry, Mfrs. Assn., 1959. Address: 1538 Sunset Ave., Chico, CA 95926, USA.

BARLOW, Derrick, b. 29 Apr. 1921, Stoke-on-Trent, UK. Fellow, Jesus College, Oxford. Educ: B.Litt., M.A., The Queen's Coll., Oxford Univ. Publs: T. Fontane, Die Poggenpuhls, 1957; F. Hebbel, Selected Essays, 1962; C. Zuckmayer, Three Stories, 1963; C. Zuckmayer, Die Fastnachtsbeichte, 1966; C. Sternheim, Bürger Schippel, 1969. Contbr. to: German Life & Letters; Mod. Lang. Review; Times Educl. Supplement. Mbrships incl: English

Goethe Soc.; Mod. Humanities Rsch. Assn.; Inst. of Germanic Studies. Address: 77 Mill St., Kidlington, Oxford, UK.

BARLOW, Frank, b. 1911, Wolstanton, UK. Professor of History. Educ: M.A., D.Phil., St. John's Coll., Oxford. Publs: An Edition of the Letters of Arnulf of Lisieux, 1939; Durham Annals & Documents of the Thirteenth Century, 1945; Durham Jurisdictional Peculiars, 1950; The Feudal Kingdom of England, 1955; The Life of King Edward Who Rests at Westminster, 1962; The English Church 1000-1066, 1963; William I & the Norman Conquest, 1965; Edward the Confessor, 1970. Mbrships: F.R.S.L.; F.B.A. Address: Middle Court Hall, Kenton, Exeter, Devon, UK.

BARLOW, Wilfred, b. 1915, Ashton, UK. Clinic Director. Educ: Trinity Coll., Oxford Univ.; St. Thomas's Hosp., London; M.A.; B.M., B.Ch. Publs: Knowing How to Stop, 1946; Posture & the Body Schema; The Alexander Principle. Contbr. to: The Lancet; Med. Press; Annals of Phys. Med.; Mod. Trends in Psychosomatic Med.; Therapeutic Exercise; Nature of Stress Disorder. Mbrships. incl: PEN; Royal Soc. of Med.; Soc. of Psychosomatic Rsch. Address: 3 Albert Ct., London SW7, UK.

BARNARD, Christian Johan, pen name BARNARD, Chris, b. 15 July 1939, Nelspruit, S. Africa. Journalist. Educ: B.A., Univ. of Pretoria. Publs: Bekende Onrus, 1961; Dwaal, 1964; Pa Maak Vir My 'n Vlieër Pa, 1964; Duiwel-in-die-Bos, 1968; Mahala, 1971; Die Rebellie van Lafras Verwey, 1971. Contbr. to: Standpunte; Die Huisgenoot. Mbrships: S. African Acad. of Arts & Sci.; Chmn., Afrikaans Writers' Guild of S. Africa. Hons. incl: SABC Prize for Radio Plays, 1971; Hertzog Prize for Lit., 1971. Address: 262 Acacia Rd., Blackheath, Johannesburg, S. Africa.

BARNARD, (Rev.) Leslie William, b. 22 Jan. 1924, Bromley, Kent, UK. Senior Lecturer in Theology, University of Leeds. Educ: M.A., St. Catherine's Coll., Oxford Univ.; Ph.D., Southampton Univ. Publs: A History of the Early Church, 1966; Studies in the Apostolic Fathers, 1966; Justin Martyr: His Life & Thought, 1967; C. B. Moss: Defender of the Faith, 1967; Athenagoras, 1972; The Graeco-Roman & Oriental Background of the Iconoclastic Controversy, 1974. Contbr. to: Jrnl. Theol. Studies; Vigiliae Christianae; Revue Benedictine; New Testament Studies; other theol. jrnls. Mbrships: Int. Conf. on Patristic Studies; Eccles. Hist. Soc. Recip., Leverhulme Rsch. Schlrship, 1957-58. Address: 3 Carlton Rd., Harrogate HG2 8DD, N. Yorks., UK.

BARNES, Cyril Charles, b. 1913, Manchester, UK. Consultant, author & lecturer in Electrical Engineering. Educ: Old Trafford Tech. Coll.; Southall Tech. Coll.; F.I.E.E.; F.I.E.E.(USA); A.B.I.M. Publs: Electric Cables, 1964; Power Cables, Their Design & Installation, 2nd edn. 1966; Power System Economics, 1969; & over 80 papers & pamphlets about Cable Engineering. Contbr. to: Elec. Review; Elec. Times; Machinery Lloyd; Power & Works Engrng.; Elec. Light & Power (USA); WIRE (Germany); Elec. Communication. Mbrships: Soc. of Authors. Address: 24 Mead Crescent, Sutton, Surrey SM1 3QS, UK.

BARNES, Djuna, b. 1892, Cornwall-on-Hudson, N.Y., USA. Author; Artist. Publs: A Book, 1923; Ryder, 1928; A Night Among the Horses, 1929; Nightwood, 1936; (play) The Antiphon, 1958; Selected Works Farrar, 1962; (short stories) Spillway, 1962. Mbrships: Nat. Inst. of Arts & Letters, N.Y.; Trustee, Dag Hammarskjold Fndn.; League of Dramatists, UK; Authors' Guild, N.Y. Address: 5 Patchin Pl. NYC, NY 10011, USA.

BARNES, Harold, b. Keighley, UK. Oceanographer & Marine Biologist. Educ: M.A., B.Sc., D.Sc., Univ. of Oxford; B.Sc., Ph.D., D.Sc., Univ. of London. Publs: Oceanography & Marine Biology: a Book of Techniques; Apparatus & Methods of Oceanography, I. Chemical; Some Contemporary Studies in Marine Science; Oceanography & Marine Biology, Annual Review; Ed., The Journal of Experimental Biology & Ecology. Contbr. to sev. sci. jrnls. Mbrships: F.R.I.C.; F.I.B.; F.R.S.(Edinburgh). Address: The Dunstaffnage Marine Rsch. Lab., Oban, Argyll, Scotland, UK.

BARNES, John A. G., b. 29 Dec. 1909, Arnside, Cumbria, UK. Author, Editor. Educ: M.A., Queen's Coll., Oxford. Publs: Ed., Birds of the British Isles & their Eggs, 1969; Natural History of the Lake District, 1970; The Titmice of the British Isles, forthcoming. Contbr. to: Brit. Birds; Bird Study; Countryside. Mbrships: Soc. of Authors; Brit. Ornithols.' Union. Recip., Bernard Tucker Medal, Brit. Trust for Ornithol., 1958. Address: Holly Wood, Arnside, Carnforth LA5 0AE, UK.

BARNES, John Arundel, b. 9 Sept. 1918, Reading, UK. Sociologist. Educ: B.A., St. John's Coll., Cambridge, 1939; D.Phil., Balliol Coll., Oxford, 1951. Publs: Marriage in a Changing Society, 1951; Politics in a Changing Society, 1954; Inquest on the Murngin, 1967; Three Styles in the Study of Kinship, 1971. Mbrships: Acad. of Soc. Scis., Aust.; Brit. Sociol. Assn.; Royal Anthropol. Inst.; Assn. of Soc. Anthropols.; Sociol. Assn. of Aust. & NZ. Address: Churchill Coll., Cambridge CB3 0DS, UK.

BARNES, (Dame) Josephine, b. 18 Aug. 1912, Sheringham, UK. Medical Practitioner; Consultant Gynaecologist. Educ: B.A., 1934, M.A., B.M., & B.Ch., 1937, D.M., 1941, Univ. of Oxford; M.R.C.P. & F.R.C.S., 1939, Univ. Coll. Hosp., Univ. of London; M.R.C.O.G., 1941; F.R.C.O.G., 1952; F.R.C.P., 1967. Publs: Gynaecological Histology, 1948; The Care of the Expectant Mother, 1954; Lecture Notes on Gynaecology, 1966, 3rd ed., 1975; Scientific Foundations of Obstetrics & Gynaecology, 1970. Contbr. to med. jrnls. Mbrships. incl: Pres., Med. Women's Fedn., 1966-67; Pres., Obst. Sect., Royal Soc. of Med., 1972-73; Sr. VP, Royal Coll. of Obst. & Gynaecol., 1974. Recip., D.B.E., 1974. Address: 7 Wimpole St., London W1M 7AB, UK.

BARNES, Kenneth Charles, b. 17 Sept. 1903, London, UK. Retired Headmaster. Educ: B.Sc., Univ. of London; M.R.S.T. Publs: Sex, Friendship & Marriage (w. F. Barnes), 1936; He & She, 1958, 2nd ed., 1962; The Creative Imagination, 1960; The Involved Man, 1969; Making Judgements & Decisions, 1971; A Vast Bundle of Opportunities, 1975. Contbr. to: What I Believe (symposium), 1966; Who are the Progressives Now? (symposium), 1969; The Friend; Quaker Monthly; Listener. Mbrships: Pres., Friends' Guild of Tchrs. Address: Ingsway, Bolton Percy, York YO5 7BA, UK.

BARNES, Peter, b. 10 Jan. 1931, London, UK. Dramatist. Publs: (plays) Sclerosis, 1965 (produced only); The Ruling Class, 1969; Leonardo's Last Supper, & Noonday Demons, 1970; Lulu, 1971; The Bewitched, 1974. Hons: John Whiting Award, 1968; Evening Standard Award, 1969. Agent: Margaret Ramsay Ltd. Address: 7 Archery Close, Connaught St., London W2, UK.

BARNETSON, (Sir) William Denholm, b. 1917, Edinburgh, UK. Company Chairman & Director. Educ: M.A., Edinburgh Univ. Mbrships: Chmn., United Newspapers, Reuters, Sheffield Newspapers, Bradbury Agnew, Farming Press; Dir., Drayton Consolidated Trust, Argus Press, Yorks. Post Newspapers, Brit. Elec. Traction Co., Earls Ct. & Olympia; Chmn., C'wlth. Press Union; Pres., Periodical Publrs. Assn., Press Club; Chmn., Scottish Int. Info. Comm., Mktng. Advsry. Comm., Open Univ.; Coun.; Trustee, Visnews, Times Trust, Newsvendors Benevolent Instn., Catherine Pakenham Award. Address: Broom, Chillies Lane, Crowborough, Sussex, UK.

BARNETT, Correlli Douglas, b. 1927, Norbury, Surrey, UK. Freelance Military Historian. Educ: Trinity Schl., Croydon; M.A., Exeter Coll., Oxford. Publs: The Hump Organisation, 1957; The Desert Generals, 1960 (also in USA); The Swordbearers, 1963 (also in USA); The Great War (BBC TV series, 1964); The Lost Peace 1918-1933 (BBC TV series, 1965); Britain & Her Army 1509-1970, 1970; The Collapse of British Power, 1972; The Commanders (BBC TV series, 1973); Marlborough, 1974. Contbr. to: Promise of Greatness; Governing Elites. Fellow, Royal Soc. of Lit. Address: Catbridge House, East Carleton, Norwich, Norfolk, UK.

BARNETT, Leonard P., b. 1919, Crewe, Cheshire, UK. Methodist Minister. Educ: Hartley Vic. Coll., Manchester; B.D., London Univ.; L.H.D., Pfeiffer, N.C., USA. Publs. incl: Adventure with Youth, 1953; For Christian Beginners, 1955; A Boy's Prayer Diary, 1961; Star Quality, 1964; Getting It Over, 1966; This is Methodism, 1967; Sex & Teenagers in Love, 1967; This I Can Believe, 1968; The Way to the Stars, 1970; A New Prayer Diary, 1975; Good Times with God, 1975; Homosexuality: Time to Tell the Truth, 1975. Contbr. to: Sunday Companion; Meth. Recorder; Brit. Wkly.; TV & Radio progs. Mbrships: Int. Bible Reading Assn.; Brit. Lessons Coun. Address: 26 Cromwell Avenue, Bromley, Kent BR2 9AQ, UK.

BARNETT, Samuel Anthony, b. 1915, Middx., UK. Professor of Zoology. Educ: M.A., Oxford Univ. Publs: A Century of Darwin (Ed.), 1958; 'Instinct' & 'Intelligence', 1967; The Human Species, 5th ed., 1971; Ethnology & Development (Ed.), 1973; The Rat: A Study in Behavior, 2nd ed. 1975. Contbr. to: New Statesman; New Society; Wash. Post; etc. Address: Zoology Dept., Australian National University, PO Box 4, Canberra, A.C.T. 2600, Australia.

BARNEY, William Lesko, b. 2 Feb. 1943, Kingston, Pa., USA. Historian; Professor. Educ: B.A., Cornell Univ.; M.A., Ph.D., Columbia Univ., N.Y. Publs: Road to Secession: A New Perspective on the Old South, 1972; The Secessionist Impulse: Alabama & Mississippi in 1860, 1974; Flawed Victory: A New Perspective on the Civil War, 1975. Contbr. to Hist. Tchr. as book reviewer. Mbrships: Assn. Am. Histns.; Org. Am. Histns.; Southern Histl. Assn. Hons: The Secessionist Impulse entered for Pulitzer Prize in category Letters, Drama & Music by Princeton Univ. Press. Address: 559 Bustleton Pike, Richboro, PA 18954, USA.

BARON, Alexander, b. 4 Dec. 1917. Author; former Editor. Publs: From the City, From the Plough, 1948; There's No Home, 1950; Rosie Hogarth, 1951; With Hope, Farewell, 1952; The Human Kind, 1953; The Golden Princess, 1954; Queen of the East, 1956; Seeing Life, 1958; The Lowlife, 1963; Strip Jack Naked, 1966; King Dido, 1969; The In-Between Times, 1971; & film scripts & TV plays. Contbr. to: Tribune, (asst. Ed., 1938-39); Ed., New Theatre, 1946-49. Mbr., PEN. Address: 30 Cranbourne Gdns., London NW11, UK.

BARON, Denis Neville, b. 3 Oct. 1924, London, UK. Chemical Pathologist. Educ: Middlesex Hosp. Med. Schl.; M.D.; D.Sc.; F.R.C.P.; F.R.C. Path. Publs: Essentials of Chemical Pathology; Recent Advances in Medicine (Co-Ed.), 16th ed. 1973; A Short Textbook of Chemical Pathology, 3rd ed. 1973. Contbr. to num. med. & sci. jrnls. Mbr., num. med. & sci. assns. Address: 47 Holne Chase, London N2 0QG, UK.

BARONAS, Aloyzas, b. 12 Dec. 1917, Vabalninkas, Lithuania. Editor. Educ: Kaunas Univ., Lithuania; J. W. Goethe Univ., Frankfurt, Germany. Publs: Novels, short stories, in Lithuanian & Latvian. Engl. eds. incl: Lithuanian Quartet (short stories); Footbridges & Abysses, 1965, Third Woman, 1968 (novels). Contbr. to Lithuanian mags.; Ed., Lithuanian Cath. Press Soc., Chgo., Ill. Mbr., Lithuanian Writers Assn. Hons: Daily Draugas Awards, 1961, 1973; Giedra Award, 1966. Address: 4545 W. 63rd St., Chicago, IL 60629, USA.

BAROUH, Victor Sabat, b. 2 June 1921, Sofia, Bulgaria. Writer. Publs: (in Bulgarian) Bridal Candles, 1968; Outside the Law, 1960; Children of the City, 1973. Contbr. to: Plamak; Literatouren Front; September. Mbr., Union of Bulgarian Writers. Recip., Sofia Prize, 1965. Address: Sofia, bil. Traycho Kostov, 39, Bulgaria.

BARQUERO PEÑA, Jose Enrique, pen name BARPE, b. 16 Feb. 1930, Las Nieves, La Coruña, Spain. Teacher. Educ: B.A. Publs: Rio de Asfalto, 1966; Generacion 66, 1968. Contbr. to jrnls. Mbr., Gen. Soc. of Spanish Writers. Address: Bda. Montserrat 15, Igualada, Barcelona, Spain.

BARR, Densil. Radio Dramatist. Publs: The Man with Only One Head, 1955, 1962; (broadcast plays) The Clapham Lamp-Post Saga, 1967, 1968, 1969; Gladys on the Wardrobe, 1970, 1971, 1972; But Petrovsky goes on Forever, 1971, 1972, 1974; The Last Tramp, 1972, 1973; The Square at Bastogne, 1973, 1974; The Battle of Brighton Beach, 1974. Contbr. to: Transatlantic Review; Int. Storyteller; Kolokon. Mbr., PEN. Address: 15 Churchfields, Broxbourne, Herts., UK.

BARR, Patricia Miriam, b. 1934, Norwich, UK. Writer. Educ: Univ. of Birmingham; Univ. of London; B.A., M.A. Publs: The Coming of the Barbarians, 1967; The Deer Cry Pavilion, 1968; A Curious Life for a Lady, 1970; To China with Love, 1972. Contbr. to: Spectator; New Soc.; Times; Guardian; Nova. Mbrships: Royal C'wlth. Soc.; Writers' Action Grp. Agent: Richard Simon. Address: 25 Montpelier Row, Blackheath, London SE3, UK.

BARRELL, Geoffrey Richard, b. 1917, Norwich, UK. Headmaster. Educ: B.Sc., St. Luke's Coll., Exeter; F.C.P.; Dip. Theol. Publs: Through the Church Gate; (1) The Church in England, 1965; (2) The Christian Year, 1965; (3) The Prayer Book & Human Life, 1966; Legal Cases for

Teachers, 1970; Teachers & The Law (4th ed.), 1975. Contbr. to: Congregational Quarterly; Times Educl. Supplement; Education; Scouter; Educ. Today; Head Teacher's Review; London Head Teacher. Mbrships: F.R.S.A.; Royal Commonwealth Soc.; M.R.S.T. Address: 59 Wellfields, Loughton, Essex 1G10 1PA, UK.

BARRENO, Maria Isabel, b. 10 July 1939, Lisbon, Portugal. Sociologist; Writer. Educ: Dip. in Hist. & Philos., Univ. of Lisbon. Publs: De Noite as Árvores São Negras, 1968; Os Outros Legitimos Superiores, 1970; Novas Cartas Portuguesas, 1972. Contbr. to: Expresso; Sempre-Fixe. Address: Rua Presidente Wilson, 4 – 4 ⁰ – D, Lisbon 1, Portugal.

BARRETT, Charles Kingsley, b. 4 May 1917, Salford, Lancs., UK. University Professor. Educ: B.A., 1938, M.A., 1942, B.D., 1948, D.D., 1956, Cambridge Univ. Publs. incl: The Holy Spirit & the Gospel Tradition, 1947; The New Testament Background, 1956; The Pastoral Epistles, 1963; The First Epistle to the Corinthians, 1968; The Signs of an Apostle, 1970; Das Johannesevangelium & das Judentum, 1970; New Testament Essays, 1972; The Second Epistle to the Corinthians, 1973. Contbr. to: Jrnl. Theol. Studies; N.T. Studies; Expository Times; num. symposia. Mbrships. incl: Fellow, Brit. Acad. Hons. incl: Burkitt Medal, 1966; var. docts. Address: 8 Prince's St., Durham DH1 4RP, UK.

BARRETT, Guy Crossland, b. 1925, Horsforth, Leeds, UK. Managing Director. Educ: Bradford Tech. Coll., C. Eng., F.I.Struct.E. Publs: Racing Pigeons. Contbr. to: sev. mags., pigeon racing. Fellow, Inst. of Structural Engrs. Address: Fence End, Calverley Lane, Horsforth, Leeds, UK.

BARRETT, Hugh Gilchrist, pen name BELLMAN, Walter, b. 8 Aug. 1917, Colchester, UK. Overseas Rural Developer. Publs: Early to Rise, 1967. Contbr. to: Proceedings of London Zool. Soc.; Int. Educl. Broadcasting. Mbrships: Fellow, Linnean Soc.; Nat. Guild of Agricl. Jrnlsts.; Authors Soc. Address: Moat Farm, Wetheringsett, Stowmarket, Suffolk, UK.

BARRETT, Laurence Irwin, b. 2 Sept. 1935, NYC, USA. Journalist; Editor. Educ: B.A., N.Y. Univ., 1956; M.S., Columbia Univ. Grad. Schl. of Jrnlsm., 1957. Author, The Mayor of New York, 1965. Contbr. to: Time Mag.; Columbia Journalism Review; The Nation; N.Y. Herald Tribune. Address: 28 Tenamy Rd., Tenamy, NJ 07670, USA.

BARRETT, Max, b. 17 Dec. 1930, Sydney, Australia. Writer. Educ: Christian Brothers Coll., E. Melbourne, Aust. Publs: A Woman of Character, 1965; Threat of Love, 1967; The Changing Wind, 1970; The Thorn in the Rose, 1972; Wild is the River, forthcoming. Mbr., Romantic Novelists Assn. Address: 26A Hugh St., London SW1, UK.

BARRETT, William Edmund, b. 1900, NYC, USA. Author & Book Reviewer. Educ: Manhattan Coll. Publs. (biog.): Women on Horseback, 1938; (fiction): Flight From Youth, 1940; The Evil Heart, 1945; The Number of my Days, 1946; To the Last Man, 1947; The Left Hand of God, 1952; The Shadows of the Images, 1954; The Sudden Strangers, 1957; The Empty Shrine, 1959; The Edge of Things, 1961; Lillies of the Field, 1962. Contbr. to: Saturday Evening Post; Redbook Mag; Cosmopolitan; McCalls; Colliers; Boston Transcript; Boston Post. Mbrships: Nat. Press Club; Denver Press Club; Authors Club; PEN. Hons: FIAL; Litt.D. Address: 1282 Detroit St., Denver, CO 80206, USA.

BARRIE, Alexander, b. 1923, Barnsley, UK. Writer. Educ: A.A. Schl. of Arch. Publs: War Underground; The Jonathan Kane Series: Fly for Three Lives, Operation Midnight, Let Them All Starve. Contbr. to: Daily Telegraph Mag.; Rdr's. Digest; etc. Address: 33 Manor Way, Blackheath, London SE3 9XG, UK.

BARRIE, Derek Stiven Maxwelton, b. 8 Aug. 1907, Newport, Mon., UK. Railway Official (Retired); Company Director; Journalist. Publs: numerous books & monographs on locomotives & railway history. Contbr. to: Rotary in the Ridings (Ed., 1973-75); Times; Yorks. Post; Railway Gazette; other transp. & tech. jrnls.; radio talks. Mbrships: Fellow, Chartered Inst. of Transp.; Inst. of Jrnlsts.; Railway Club, London; Brit. Rep., Railway & Locomotive Histl. Soc. of USA. Hons: M.B.E. (Mil.), 1945; Bronze Star of USA, 1945; Order of St. John, 1968; O.B.E.(Civil), 1969. Address: 20 Westgate, Old Malton, N. Yorks. Y017 OHE, UK.

BARROW, Lyn Norman, b. 1918, N.S.W., Australia. Writer & Columnist; Former Teacher & Psychologist. Educ: Tchrs.' Coll., Sydney; Sydney Univ.; Univ. of Qld.; B.A., Ph.D. Publs: Lands of Our Fathers, 1959; School Projects & How to Do Them (co-author), 1962; Teenagers & Drugs (w. Haydn Sargent), 1967; Child Psychology in Outline series, 7 titles, 1968-69; Preparing Your Child for School, 1969, revised ed., 1973; Compulsion, 1970; Children in Danger, 1970; Encouraging Creativity, 1971; Loneliness, 1975. Contbr. to var. jrnls. Mbr., Aust. Soc. of Authors. Address: 27 Keats St., Carlingford, N.S.W., Australia 2118.

BARRY, Clive, b. 1922, Sydney, Aust. UN Expert on Somalia & Congo. Publs: The Speargrinner, 1963; Crumb Bone, 1966; Fly Jamskoni, 1969. Mbr., Mensa. Address: Icao B.P.7248, Kinshasa, Congo.

BARRY, Donald Rex, b. 7 Sept. 1910, Easingwold, Yorks., UK. Writer; Journalist. Educ: Rusking Coll., Oxford. Contbr. to: Writers' Parade; Kangaroo Books; Convoy; Progress Publishing; Saturday Saga; Acorn Press; Story; Fore Publs.; New Advance; Seven Mag.; New Theatre; Theatre Newsletter; Poetry; Stage; Our Time; Campaign; IPC Mags.; BBC; Radio Bern; Radio Italiana. Mbrships: Soc. of Authors; Radio-writers' Assn.; Writers' Guild of GB. Address: 10 Arlington House, Arlington Way, London EC1R 1XB, UK.

BARRY, James P., b. 23 Oct. 1918, Alton, Ill., USA. Writer; Editor; Photographer; US Army Colonel, Ret'd. Educ: B.A., Ohio State Univ., 1940. Publs: Georgian Bay: The Sixth Great Lake, 1968; The Battle of Lake Erie, 1970; The Noble Experiment, 1972; Bloody Kansas, 1972; The Fate of the Lakes, 1972; The Louisiana Purchase, 1973; Henry Ford & Mass Production, 1973; Ships of the Great Lakes: 300 Years of Navigation, 1973; The Berlin Olympics, 1936, 1975. Contbr. to num. mags. & jrnls. Mbrships: Phi Beta Kappa; Royal Can. Yacht Club; Gt. Lakes Histl. Soc.; Marine Histl. Soc. Recip., Award for Ships of the Great Lakes, Am. Soc. for State & Local Hist., 1974. Address: 353 Fairway Blvd., Columbus, OH 43213, USA.

BARRY, Jane, b. 25 July, 1925, New Baltimore, N.Y., USA. Writer. Publs: The Long March, 1955; The Carolinians, 1959; A Time in the Sun, 1962; A Shadow of Eagles, 1964; Maximillian's Gold, 1966; Grass Roots, 1969; Ed., Centennial ed., Coxsackie Union News, 1952. Contbr. to: Empire State Iris Soc. Bulletin. Mbr., Am. Iris Soc. Address: Lotus Point, RD 3, Catskill, NY 12414, USA.

BARRY, Richard Hugh, b. 9 Nov. 1908, London, UK. Translator; Army Officer (retired). Educ: Royal Mil. Coll., Sandhurst, 1927-28; Staff Coll., Camberley, 1938; Imperial Defence Coll., 1957. Publs. (Translations): Inside Hitler's Headquarters, 1964; Stategy Series, 1965-67; Stauffenberg, 1967; The Order of the Death's Head, 1969; Twice through the Lines, 1972. contbr. to: Encounter. Mbr., Translators' Assn. Hons: Schlegel-Tieck Prize (German Translation), 1968 & 1972; Scott-Moncrieff Prize (French Translation), 1970. Address: Well Cottage, Shalden, Alton, Hants., GU34 4DX, UK.

BARSTOW, Stan, b. 28 June 1928, Horbury, Yorks., UK. Writer. Publs: A Kind of Loving, 1960; The Desperadoes, 1961; Ask Me Tomorrow, 1962; Joby, 1964; The Watchers on the Shore, 1966; Ed., Through the Green Woods, 1968; A Raging Calm, 1968; A Season with Eros, 1971; Plays (w. Alfred Bradley): Ask Me Tomorrow, 1966; A Kind of Loving, 1970; Stringer's Last Stand, 1972. TV Dramatizations: A Raging Calm (7 episodes), 1974; South Riding (from Winifred Holtby's novel; 13 episodes), 1974. Mbrships: Writers' Guild of G.B.; The Soc. of Authors; The Writers' Action Grp.; PEN (Engl. Ctr.). Address: Goring House, Goring Park Avenue, Ossett, W. Yorks., WF5 0HX, UK.

BART, Benjamin F., b. 21 Dec. 1917, Chgo., Ill., USA. Professor; Director, Comparitive Literature Program. Educ: A.B., 1938, M.A., 1946, Harvard Univ.; Ph.D., 1947. Publs: Flaubert's Landscape Descriptions, 1956; Madame Bovary & the Critics, 1966; Flaubert, 1967. Contbr. to var. lit. jrnls. Mbrships: sometime Sec. or Chmn., 19th Century Grp. & Romance Sect., MLA of Am.; Am. Assn. Tchrs. of French. Recip., var. scholastic grants & fellowships. Address: Dept. of French, Univ. of Pitts., Pitts., PA 15260, USA.

BARTALOS, Mihaly, b. 27 May 1935, Pozsony, Czechoslovakia. Physician. Educ: Univ. of Med. Scis.,

Budapest, Hungary; M.D., Fac. of Med., Univ. of Heidelberg, W. Germany, 1960; Schl. of Med., Johns Hopkins Univ., USA. Publs: Medical Cytogenetics, 1967; Genetics in Medical Practice, 1968. Address: 1 Eastwoods Lane, Scarsdale, NY 10583, USA.

BARTELS, Charles Kwamina, b. 16 June 1927, Onitsha, Nigeria. Journalist; Author; Public Relations Practitioner. Educ: Regent St. Polytechnic, London, UK; Dip., Jrnlsm., B.Sc., Columbia Univ., N.Y., USA. Publs: Ghana "Who's Who", 72-73 ed., 1973. Contbr. to: Jeune Afrique, Paris, France; Times of Zambia; Daily Graphic, Ghana; The Echo, Ghana. Mbrships: Ghana Assn. of Writers; Nat. Union of Jrnlsts., UK. Recip., D.F.C. Address: 44 Sobukwe Rd., P.O. Box 4446, Accra S.4., Ghana.

BARTELSKI, Leslaw, b. 8 Sept. 1920, Warsaw, Poland. Writer. Educ: LL.M., Warsaw Univ. Publs: (novels) Ludzie zza rzeki, 1951; Pejzaż dwukrotny, 1958; Wodorosty, 1964; Dialog z cieniem, 1968; Niedziela bez dzwonów, 1973; (essays) Genealogia ocalonych, 1963; Jeździec z Madary, 1963; Powstanie warszawskie, 1965; Warszawa walczaca, 1968; Mokotów 1944, 1971; Z glowa na karabinie, 1974. Mbrships: Pres., Writers' Union in Warsaw, 1972-; PEN. Hons: State Prize, 1951; Prize of Min. of State Defense, 1969; Warsaw Prize, 1969; Pietrzaks Prize, 1969. Address: Ul. Joliot Curie 17 M.1, 02-646 Warsaw, Poland.

BARTER, Arthur Reginald, b. 6 Nov. 1900, Birmingham, UK. Regular Army Officer (Retired); Modern Language Tutor (Retired). Educ: Royal Mil. Acad., Woolwich; Staff Coll., Camberley; B.A.(External), Univ. of London, 1949. Publs: Learning Languages — The Comparative Method, 1970; Portugal through her Literature, 1972; Word for Word — Comparatively Speaking, 1973. Contbr. to: Times Educl. Supplement; var. Mil. jrnls. Mbr., Philol. Soc. Address: Flat 2, 10 Downfield Rd., Clifton, Bristol BS8 2TH, UK.

BARTH, Alan, b. 21 Oct. 1906, NYC, USA. Journalist; Author. Educ: Ph.B., Yale Coll. Publs: The Loyalty of Free Men, 1951; Government by Investigation, 1955; The Price of Liberty, 1961; Prophets with Honor, 1974. Contbr. to: Harper's; N.Y. Times Mag.; Nat.; New Repub.; Rdr's. Digest; Esquire; Pub. Opinion Quarterly; etc. Mbrships: Nat. Press Club; Wash. Press Club. Hons: Sigma Delta Chi Award, 1947; Am. Newspaper Guild Special Citation, 1948; Sidney Hillman Award, 1952; Oliver Wendell Holmes Bill of Rights Award, 1964; Florina Lasker Civil Liberties Award, 1967. Address: 3520 Rodman St. N.W., Washington, DC 20008, USA.

BARTH, John Simmons, b. 1930, Cambridge, Md., USA. Author; Professor of English. Educ: B.A., M.A., Johns Hopkins Univ. Publs: The Floating Opera, 1956; The End of the Road, 1958; The Sot-Weed Factor, 1960. Address: P.O. Box, Pine Grove Mills, Pa., USA.

BARTHEL, Max, b. 17 Nov. 1893, Dresden, Germany. Writer. Publs. incl: Überfluss des Herzens (verse); An den Mond (verse); Morgenblau und Nachtmusik (verse); Sachen zum Lachen (children's songs); Wir spielen Zirkus (children's musical play); Frühling am Bodensee (song cycle); Das Lied vom Leben (cantata); Das Land auf den Bergen (novel); Kein Bedart an Welgeschichte (autobiog.); Das vergitterte Land 13 Indianer (stories); Deutschland, Erde unter den Füsen (report); Es Kommt der Star (poems for children). Address: 5207 Litterscheid 29, W. Germany.

BARTHELME, Donald, b. 7 Apr. 1931, Phila., Pa., USA. Writer. Publs: Snow White (novel), 1967; (short stories) Come back, Dr. Caligari, 1964; Unspeakable Practices, Unnatural Acts, 1968; City Life, 1971. Recip., Guggenheim Fellowship, 1966. Address: c/o The New Yorker, 25 West 43rd St., N.Y., NY 10036, USA.

BARTHOLOMAY, Julia Louise Adams, b. 19 Oct. 1923, Chgo., Ill., USA. Housewife; Teacher. Educ: B.A. with Tchng. Cert., Vassar Coll., N.Y.; 1944; B.A. (Engl.), Lake Forest Coll., Ill., 1970. Publs: The Shield of Perseus: The Vision & Imagination of Howard Nemerev, 1972. Mbrships: incl: Past Pres., Schlrship. & Guidance Assn.; Trustee, Mod. Poetry Assn.; Hon. Dir., Winnetka Public Schl. Nursery Bd.; Past Dir., Bd. of Trustees, North Shore Country Day Schl., Phi Beta Kappa, 1969. Recip., acad. hons. Address: 745 Locust St., Winnetka, IL 60093, USA.

BARTLETT, Vernon, b. 30 Apr. 1894, Westbury, Wilts., UK. Journalist. Publs: Journey's End (novel, w. R. C. Sheriff), 1930; Tuscan Retreat, 1964; Tuscan Harvest,

1964; Introduction to Italy, 1967; The Colour of their Skin, 1969; Central Italy, 1972; Northern Italy, 1973; 22 other titles. Mbrships: Garrick, Beefsteak, & Special Forces Clubs, London. Hons: Ennisfield Wolf Award, 1963; Hist. Book of Month Club Award, 1963. Address: Casa Bartlett, San Ginese di Compito, 55060 Lucca, Italy.

BARTLEY, Samuel Howard, b. 19 June 1901, Pitts., Pa., USA. University Professor of Psychology Emeritus. Educ: B.S., Greenville Coll.; M.A., Ph.D., Univ. of Kan. Publs. incl: Vision: A Study of Its Basis, 1941, 1963; Fatique & Impairment in Man (co-author), 1947, 1969; Beginning Experimental Psychology, 1950; Principles of Perception, 1958, 2nd ed., 1969; The Human Organism as a Person, 1967; Perception in Everyday Life, 1972. Contbr. of over 200 articles to profl. jrnls.; Assoc. Ed., Perceptual & Motor Skills, Psychological Record (jrnls.); Mbr., Ed. coun., Am. Jrnl. of Optometry. Address: 1960 N. Parkway, Apt. 801, Memphis, TN 38112, USA.

BARTLEY, William Warren, III, b. 2 Oct. 1934, Pitts., Pa., USA. Professor of Philosophy. Educ: A.B., 1956, A.M., 1958, Harvard; Ph.D., London, 1962. Publs: The Retreat to Commitment, 1962, 1964; Flucht ins Engagement, 1964; Morality & Religion, 1971; Wittgenstein, 1973, 1974. Contbr. to num. jrnls. inclng: Encounter; Harper's; Commentary; New Statesman; The Scientific Am.; Times Lit. Supplement; N.Y. Review of Books; Antaeus; The New Repub. Address: c/o Dept. of Philos., Calif. State Univ., Hayward, CA 94542, USA.

BARTON, Alan, b. 1913, Mevagissey, UK. Teacher of Mathematics. Educ: M.A., Trinity Coll., Cambridge.; F.I.M.A. Publs: An Introduction to Co-ordinate Geometry; Probability & Hypothesis Testing (co-author). Contbr. to: Mathematical Gazette. Head, Maths. Dept., Cheltenham Coll., 1946-73. Address: 9 Christ Church Rd., Cheltenham, Glos., UK.

BARTON, Arthur Henry, pen name BARTON, Harry, b. 13 Jan. 1916, Belfast, N. Ireland, UK. Writer; Broadcaster. Publs: With a Flag & a Bucket & a Gun, 1959; Yours Till Ireland Explodes, Mr. Mooney, 1973; Yours Again, Mr. Mooney, 1974; A Borderline Case (play), 1974. Contbr. to: BBC; Punch. Mbrships: Chmn., Londonderry Br., UN Assn.; Chmn., Bd. of Visitors, H.M. Prison, Magilligan; Chmn., Limavady Drama Club. Address: Hill House, Ballymaglin, Limavady, Co. Derry BT49 0HY, N. Ireland, UK.

BARTON, Eda, b. 8 Mar. 1908, Manchester, UK. Part-time Lecturer in German. Publs: German Once a Week (Books 1 & 2), 1963. Mbrships: Assn. Med. Secs.; Bolton Quest Club; Ladies' Hon. Sec., Bolton Bridge Club; Hon. Sec., Bolton Anglo-German Circle. Address: 52 Melbourne Road, Bolton, Lancs., UK.

BARTON, Otis, b. 5 June 1899, NYC, USA. Explorer; Undersea Filmmaker; Naturalist. Educ: A.B., Harvard Univ., 1922; M.A., Columbia Univ., 1928. Publs: The World Beneath the Sea, 1953. Contbr. to: Scientific American, Natural History, Atlantic mags., Copeia, Novitates Smithsonian papers. Address: Little River Rd., Cotuit, MA 02635, USA.

BARTOS-HÖPPNER, Barbara, b. 1923, Silesia. Writer. Publs: The Cossacks, 1962; Save the Khan, 1963; Avalanche Dog, 1966; Storm over the Caucasus, 1968; Hunters of Siberia, 1969. Mbrships: Verband Deutscher Schriftsteller; Int. PEN, London. Address: 2152 Nottensdorf, Am Walde 20, Haus im Bärenwinkel, W. Germany.

BARZELAY, Walter Moshe, b. 1 Dec. 1924, Vienna, Austria. Poet; Translator of Poetry. Educ: Dips., Cambridge Univ., Tel-Aviv Schl. of Jrnlism., & Tel-Aviv High Schl. of Painting. Publs: Guillen's Selected Verse (transl. into Hebrew), 1962; A Tinge of Purple, 1967; Variations On A Theme, 1970; Semantics of the Heart, 1971; From Past Nights' Shores, 1973; Sandra Fowler's In The Shape of Sun (ed.), 1973. Contbr. to anthols. & poetry mags. Mbr., Poetry Soc., London. Hons. incl: World Poetry Transl. Laureate & Bronze Medalist, World Acad. of Langs. & Lit. Address: P.O. Box 26464, Tel-Aviv, Israel.

BARZMAN, Ben, b. 1912, Toronto, Can. Screen-writer. Educ: B.A., Reed Coll., Portland, Ore., USA. Publs: Out of this World. Mbrships: Writer's Guild West, USA; Brit. Screen Writers Guild; Soc. des Auteurs des Films. Address: 30 rue des Perchamps, Paris 75016, France.

BASS, Clara May, pen name OVERY, Claire May, b. 10 May 1910, Grimsby, Lincs., UK. Poet. Educ: Certs. in Piano & Singing. Publs: Dreams of a Singer, 1963; Living Poetry, 1968; Major & Minor, 1970; Trio, 1973; Quintet, 1974. Contbr. to jrnls. & anthols. inclng: Orbis; Breakthru; Parnassus; Expression One; Village Review; Headland; Poetry of City & Machine Age, 1968. Mbrships. incl: Soc. of Authors; Fndr. Fellow, Int. Poetry Soc. Recip., Long Serv. Medal, Grimsby Amateur Operatic Soc. Address: 68 L'Estrange St., Cleethorpes, S. Humberside DN35 7HL, UK.

BASS, Flora Gardner, b. 25 June 1916, Manila, Philippines. Writer. Educ: Philippine Coll. of Commerce. Publs: Philippine Women & Dolls, 1955. For. Contbr. to Philippines Free Press, until 1969; Contbr. to newspapers & mags. Hons: Nine Awards, Top For. Contbr., Philippines Free Press, 1950-69. Address: P.O. Box 803, Laguna Beach, CA 92652, USA.

BASSANI, Giorgio, b. 1916. Writer. Educ: Univ. of Bologna. Publs: Cinque storie ferraresi, 1956; Gli occhiali d'oro (novel), 1958; Il giardino dei Finzi-Contini (novel), 1962; L'alba ai vetri (poems), 1963; Dietro la porta (novel), 1964; Le parole preparate (essays), 1966; L'airone (novel), 1968; Heron, 1970. Contbr. to jrnls. & TV. Hons: Strega Prize, 1956; Viareggio Prize, 1962; Campiello Prize, 1969; Nelly Sachs Prize, 1969. Address: Via G. B. De Rossi 33, Rome, Italy.

BASSEGODA NONELL, Juan, b. 9 Feb. 1930, Barcelona, Spain. University Professor; Architect. Publs: Atlas de Historia del Arte, 1968; Los Maestros de Obras de Barcelona, 1972; La Catedral de Barcelona, 1972; El Círculo del Liceo, 1973; El Templo Romano de Barcelona, 1974. Contbr. to: Arquitectura; Hogar y Arquitectura; Cuadernos de Arquitectura; La Vanguardia. Mbrships: Real Acad. de Bellas Artes de San Jorge, Barcelona (Sec.); Colegio Oficial de Arquitectos de Cataluña & Baleares; Real Acad. de Bellas Artes de San Fernando, Madrid (Corres.). Hons. incl: "Puig i Cadafalch" Prize, 1968; Crítico de arte, La Prensa, Barcelona, 1969. Address: Consejo de Ciento 314, Barcelona — 7, Spain.

BASSETT, Michael Edward Rainton, b. 28 Aug. 1938, Auckland, NZ. Member of Parliament (Labour). Educ: M.A., Univ. of Auckland, 1961; Ph.D., Duke Univ., USA, 1963. Publs: The Depression of the Thirties, 1967; Confrontation '51: The 1951 Waterfront Dispute, 1972. Contbr. to: Mid Am.; Aust. Jrnl. Pol & Hist.; Pol. Sci. (Wellington); NZ Listener. Mbrships: Aust.—NZ Am. Studies Assn.; Am. Histl. Assn.; Org. of Am. Histns. Hons: James B. Duke Fellowship, 1961-63; Am. Studies Fellowship, Am. Coun. Learned Socs., 1967-68. Address: c/o Parliament Bldgs., Wellington, NZ.

BASSETT, Ronald, pen name CLIVE, William, b. 1924, London, UK. Film Scriptwriter; Public Relations Consultant. Publs: The Carthaginian, 1963; The Pompeians, 1965; Witchfinder General, 1966; Amorous Trooper, 1968; Rebecca's Brat, 1969; Kill the Stuart, 1970; Dando on Delhi Ridge, 1971; Dando & the Summer Palace, 1972; The Tune that they Play, 1973; Dando & The Mad Emperor, 1974; Blood of an Englishman, 1975; & num. filmscripts. Contbr. to: Med. News; Nursing Mirror; Daily Telegraph Mag.; Film User. Mbr., Naval & Mil., Wig & Pen. Agent: A. M. Heath. Address: 9 Sidlaws Rd., Farnborough, Hants., UK.

BASTIN, John Sturgus, b. 1927, Melbourne, Australia. Historian; University Reader in Modern History of Southeast Asia. Educ: Univ. of Melbourne; Univ. of Leiden, Netherlands; Univ. of Oxford, UK; M.A.; D.Litt.; D.Phil. Publs: Raffles' Ideas on the Land Rent System in Java, 1954; The Native Policies of Sir Stamford Raffles, 1957; Essays on Malayan & Indonesian History, 1960; A History of Modern Southeast Asia (w. H. J. Benda), 1968. Contbr. to: Jrnl. of Malaysian Br., Royal Asiatic Soc.; Bijd. Taal-Land en Volkenkunde; Bulletin of the Schl. of Oriental & African Studies; Histl. Studies Aust. & NZ. Mbr., Royal Asiatic Soc. Address: Dept. of Hist., Schl. of Oriental & African Studies, Univ. of London, Malet St., London WC1E 7HP, UK.

BATA, Imre, b. 26 Aug. 1930, Egerlövö, Hungary. Scientific Librarian. Educ: Bachelor's Degree; Arts.D., Hungarian Lit., Univ. of Debrecen. Publs: Ivelö Pályák, 1964; Képek és Vonulatok, 1973. Contbr. to: Kortárs; Ujyrás; Kritika; Valóság; Iroda-Iomtörténet; Tiszatáj; Jelenkor; Napjaink; Forrás; Alföld; Élet és Irodalom; Új

Aurora. Mbr., Soc. of Hungarian Writers. Address: 1121 Budapest, XII, Budakeszi út 46/A, Hungary.

BATE, Sam, b. 1909, Warrington, UK. Actor; Freelance Journalist; Playwright. Publs: 60 plays inclng. Motive for Murder, 1962; End of the Honeymoon, 1964; These Ghoulish Things, 1970; Raising the Roof, 1973; Rumour, 1974; Playback, 1974; Date with Destiny, 1974; num. performances. Mbrships: Soc. of Authors; League of Dramatists; Richard III Soc.; Wildlife Preservation. Address: 16 Bridge Road, Illogan, Redruth, Cornwall, UK.

BATEMAN, Frederick, b. 1909, Woodford Green, Essex, UK. Retired Civil Servant. Educ: M.Sc., Queen Mary Coll., London Univ. Publs: Modern Experiments in Telepathy (w. S. G. Soal), Contbr. to: Handbook of Brit. Astronom. Assn.; Jrnl., Soc. for Psychical Rsch.; Jrnl. of Parapsychol. Address: Trenant, Polstrong, Cambourne, Cornwall, UK.

BATES, Alan, b. 6 Sept. 1929, Kensworth, Beds., UK. Editor, ABC Shipping Guide. Publs: Directory of Stage Coach Services 1836, 1969. Contbr. to: London Evening News. Mbrships: Omnibus Soc.; PSV Circle. Address: ABC Travel Guides Ltd., Oldhill, Dunstable, Beds. LU6 3EB, UK.

BATES, David Robert, b. 18 Nov. 1916, Omagh, N. Ireland, UK. University Teacher. Educ: Royal Belfast Acad. Instn.; M.Sc., Queen's Univ., Belfast; D.Sc., Univ. Coll., London. Publs. incl: Ed., The Planet Earth, 1957; Quantum Theory, 1961; Ed.-in-Chief, Planetary & Space Science, 1962-; Co-Ed., Advances in Atomic & Molecular Physics, 1965-. Contbr. to var. sci. jrnls. Mbrships-incl: F.R.S.; Hon. For. Mbr., Mbr., Am. Acad. of Arts & Scis.; Royal Irish Acad. Hons. incl: Hughes Medal, Royal Soc.; Chree Medal, Inst. Phys. Address: 6 Deramore Pk., Belfast BT9 5JT, UK.

BATES, Herbert Ernest, b. 1905. Journalist; Novelist. Publs. incl: The Two Sisters; A House of Women, 1936; Fair Stood the Wind for France, 1944; The Purple Plain, 1947; Dear Life, 1950; The Scarlet Sword, 1951; Colonel Julian, 1951; Love for Lydia, 1952; The Nature of Love, 1953; The Feast of July, 1954; The Sleepless Moon, 1956; Death of a Huntsman, 1957; Sugar for the Horse, 1957; The Darling Buds of May, 1958; An Aspidistra in Babylon; Now Sleeps the Crimson Petal; The Golden Oriole; Charlotte's Row; The Fallow Lane. Address: The Granary, Little Chart, Kent, UK.

BATES, James Arthur, b. 4 Aug. 1926, Ilkeston, UK. University Professor. Educ: B.A., 1951, Ph.D., 1955, Univ. of Nottingham. Publs: Business Economics (w. J. R. Parkinson), 1963, 2nd ed., 1969; The Financing of Small Business, 1964, 2nd ed., 1970; The Management of Northern Ireland Industry (w. M. Bell), 1971; Small Manufacturing Business in Northern Ireland (w. M. Bell), 1973. Contbr. to: Bankers' Mag.; Accountants' Mag.; The Banker; Jrnl. of Ind. Econs.; Brit. Jrnl. of Ind. Rels.; etc. Address: 10, Shrewbury Dr., Belfast, N. Ireland, UK.

BATES, Peter Watson, b. 25 June 1920, New Plymouth, NZ. Editor. Publs: Supply Company, 1955; The Red Mountain, 1966; Man Out of Mind, 1968; Old Men are Fools, 1970; A Kind of Treason, 1973. Contbr. to: Church & People (Managing Ed., 1958-68); Hutt News (Ed., 1968-). Mbrships. incl: PEN. Address: 43 Raukawa St., Stokes Valley, Lower Hutt, NZ.

BATES, Ronald Gordon Nudell, b. 3 Apr. 1924, Regina, Sask., Can. University Professor. Educ: B.A., Victoria Coll., Univ. of Toronto, Ont.; M.A., Ph.D., Univ. of Toronto. Publs: The Wandering World, 1959; The Unimaginable Circus, Theatre & Zoo, 1965; Changes, 1968. Contbr. to: New Directions Anthol., 1969; Tamarack Review; Prism; Mosaic; Maclean's Mag.; Dalhousie Review; James Joyce Quarterly; Can. Forum; Lit. Review; Contemporary Lit. in Transl. Mbrships: League of Can. Poets; PEN; Assn. Can. Tchrs. of Engl. Address: Dept. of English, Univ. of Western Ont., London, Ont., Can.

BATESON, Frederick Wilse, b. 1901, Styal, Cheshire, UK. University Lecturer (Retired). Educ: M.A., B.Litt., Trinity Coll., Oxford Univ.; Harvard Grad. Schl., USA. Publs: English Poetry & the English Language; Mixed Farming & Muddled Thinking; English Poetry: a Critical Introduction; Ed., Pope's Epistles to Several Persons; Wordsworth: a Re-interpretation; Ed., Selected Poems of William Blake; The Scholar Critic; Essays in Critical Dissent; Ed., Cambridge Bibliog. of Eng. Lit.; Essays in Criticism.

Contbr. to: Observer; New Statesman; Review of Engl. Studies. Hons: Fellow, Corpus Christi Coll., Oxford. Address: Brill, Aylesbury, Bucks., UK.

BATHO, Edith Clara, b. 1895, London, UK. Former Reader in English Literature; Former Principal of Royal Holloway College. Educ: M.A.; D.Lit., Univ. Coll., London. Publs: The Ettrick Shepherd, 1927; The Later Wordsworth, 1934; The Victorians & After (w. Bonamy Debree), 1938; Chronicles of Scotland by Hector Boece, Vol. I (co-ed., w. W. W. Seton & R. W. Chambers), 1936, Vol. II (co-ed., w. H. W. Husbands), 1941; A Wordsworth Selection, 1962. Contbr. to: Mod. Lang. Review; Review of Engl. Studies. Address: 130 Wood St., Barnet, Herts., UK.

BATHURST, Maurice Edward, b. 2 Dec. 1913, London, UK. Barrister-at-Law (Queen's Counsel). Educ: LL.B., LL.D., Univ. of London; Ph.D., Cambridge Univ.; LL.M., Columbia Univ., USA. Publs: Germany & the North Atlantic Community (co-author), 1956; Co-Ed., Legal Problems of an Enlarged European Community, 1972. Contbr. to: Europe & the Law, 1968; Whose Sea¯1974; Brit. Yr. Book Int. Law (Mbr., Ed. Comm.) Int. & Comp. Law Quarterly; Conveyancer & Real Property Lawyer, etc. Mbrships. incl: Gray's Inn (Master of the Bench); Brit. Ins. Law Assn. (Pres.). Hons. incl: D.C.L., 1946; C.B.E., 1947; C.M.G., 1953; Fellow, King's Coll., London, 1968. Address: Airlie, The Highlands, E. Horsley, Leatherhead, Surrey KT24 5BG, UK.

BATTEN, Lindsey Willett, b. 1889, London, UK. Physician. Educ: Cambridge Univ.; St. Bart's Hospital; B.A.; M.B.; B.Ch.; F.R.C.P. Publs: The Single-handed Mother, 1939; Health for the Young, 1942. Contbr. to: Lancet; Brit. Med. Jrnl.; Health Horizon; Parents; Nursing Mirror; Chapt. in Med. Ethics, 1957; etc. Address: Grange Cottage, Crockham Hill, Edenbridge, Kent, UK.

BATTEN Thomas Reginald, b. 30 Nov. 1904, Wimbledon, Surrey, UK. Community Development Consultant. Educ: B.A., 1926, Dip. Ed., 1927, M.A., 1937, St. John's Coll., Oxford Univ.; Ph.D., Univ. of London, 1962. Publs. incl: Teachers' History & Geography Handbook, 1933; Tropical Africa in World History, 4 vols., 1939-40; Problems of African Development, 2 vols., 1947-48; Communities & their Development, 1957; Training for Community Development, 1962; The Human Factor in Community Work, 1965; The Non-Directive Approach in Group & Community Work, 1967; The Human Factor in Youth Work, 1970. Contbr. to: Community Dev. Jrnl. (Chmn., Ed. Advsry. Comm.). Mbr., Soc. of Authors. Address: Tawh Cottage, Windyridge Close, Wimbledon Common, London SW19 5HB, UK.

BATTISCOMBE, Georgina, b. 21 Nov. 1905, London, UK. Educ: B.A., Lady Margaret Hall, Oxford. Publs: Charlotte Mary Yonge, 1943; Two on Safari, 1946; English Picnics, 1949; Mrs. Gladstone, 1956; John Keble, 1963; Queen Alexandra, 1969; Shaftesbury, 1974. Contbr. to: Times; Times Lit. Supplement; Country Life; Economist; Hist. Today; Theology. F.R.S.L. Recip., James Tait Black Prize for best biog. of yr., 1963. Agent: A.M. Heath. Address: 3 Queen's Acre, King's Rd., Windsor, Berks., UK.

BATTLE, Allen Overton, b. 19 Nov. 1927, Memphis, Tenn., USA. Clinical Psychologist; Writer. Educ: B.S., Siena Coll., Memphis, 1949; M.A., 1953, Ph.D., 1961, Cath. Univ. of Am., Wash., D.C.; Dipl., Clin. Psychol., Am. Bd. Profl. Psychol., N.Y., 1971. Publs: The Research Process as Applied to Nursing, 1967; The Psychology of Patient Care: A Humanistic Approach, 1975. Contbr. to: Disease of the Nervous System; Jrnl. of Am. Acad. of Gen. Prac.; num. other profl. jrnls. Mbrships. incl: Am. Psychol. Assn.; Am. Anthropol. Assn.; AAAS; N.Y. Acad. Sci.; Brit. Soc. Projective Psychol. Hons. incl: Sigma Xi, 1955; Disting. Serv. Award, Tenn. Mental Hlth. Assn., 1971. Address: 2220 Washington Ave., Memphis, TN 38104, USA.

BATTS, John Stuart, b. 8 Mar. 1938, Hereford, UK. Professor, University of Ottawa. Educ: B.A., Univ. of Wales; Dip.Ed., Univ. of London; M.A., Carleton Univ., Ont., Can.; Ph.D., Univ. of Ottawa. Author, British Manuscript Diaries of the Nineteenth Century, 1975. Mbrships: Engl. Assn.; MLA of Am.; Royal Coll. of Organists. Address: Dept. of Engl.; Univ. of Ottawa, Ottawa, Ont., K1N 6N5, Can.

BATTY, Charles David, b. 8 July 1932, Tynemouth, Northumberland, UK. Professor of Information Science. Educ: B.A., Univ. of Durham, 1954; Assoc., 1960, Fellow,

1963, Lib. Assn. Publs: An Introduction to the Dewey Decimal Classification, 1965; An Introduction to Colon Classification, 1966; Ed., The Library & the Machine, 1966; Ed., Libraries & Machines Today, 1967; An Introduction to the Dewey Decimal Classification (17th ed.), 1967. Contbr. to: Jrnl. Documentation; Lib. Assn. Record; Am. Documentation; etc. Mbrships: Lib. Assn.; Am. Soc. Info. Sci. (Coun., 1974-77); other profl. assns. Address: 247 du Dauphine, St. Lambert, P.Q., Can.

BATTY, Joseph, b. 29 Dec. 1929, Sheffield, UK. Company Director; Writer & Lecturer; Visiting Professor. Educ: B.Comm., M.Comm., Univ. of Durham; D.Comm., Univ. of Potchefstroom, S. Africa. Publs: Ed., Developments in Management Accountancy, 1968; Cost & Management Accountancy for Students, 1968; Management Accountancy, 4th ed., 1975; Industrial Administration & Management, 3rd ed., 1974; Standard Costing, 4th ed., 1975; Corporate Planning & Budgetary Control, 1970; Managerial Standard Costing, 1970; Accountancy for Managers, 1970; Understanding Old English Game, 1973; Advanced Cost Accountancy, 1974. Contbr. to profl. jrnls. Mbrships: Soc. of Authors; var. profl. orgs. Address: Woodlands Manor, Hill Brow, Liss, Hants.

BAUCOM, Margaret Dean, b. 25 Sept. 1909, Charlotte, N.C., USA. Writer; Poet. Publs: Mood Magic (poetry), 1974. Contbr. to num. US, for. jrnls. & anthols. Mbrships. incl: Nat. League of Am. Pen Women; World Poetry Soc. Intercontinental; Nat. Fedn. of Press Women; Am. Fellowship of Poets; Int. Poetry Soc., London; Centro Studi E. Scambi Int., Rome; United Poets Laureate Int. Hons: Etta Caldwell Harris Poetry Award, 1962; 1st Prize, Ill. State Poetry Soc. Address: 710 S. Hayne St., Monroe, NC 28110, USA.

BAUDISCH, Paul, b. 19 June 1899, Vienna, Austria. Author. Publs: Passion (Play), 1920; Die Pharisäer (Play), 1920; Schlumpf (Novel), 1920; Fragmente (Essays), 1920; Familie Mächtig (Play), 1922; Catilina (Play), 1922; Der Mann mit der schwarzen Warze (Novel), 1922; Thamar (Play), 1924; Babusch (Play), 1924; Die treue Maria (Play), 1955; Alice und Ali (Play), 1955; also num. transls. from Engl. & French. Mbr., German PEN; Verband deutscher Schriftsteller. Address: Grafikvägen 15, S-12143 Johanneshov, Sweden.

BAUER, Peter Thomas, b. 1915, Budapest, Hungary. Professor of Economics. Educ: M.A., Gonville & Caius Coll., Cambridge. Publs: The Rubber Industry, 1948; West African Trade, 1954; The Economics of Underdeveloped Countries (co-author), 1957; Economic Analysis & Policy in Underdeveloped Countries, 1958; Indian Economic Development & Policy; Markets, Market Control & Marketing Reform, 1968; Dissent on Development, 1972. Contbr. to: Econ. Jrnl.; etc. Address: L.S.E., Haughton St., London WC2, UK.

BAUGHAN, Peter Edward, b. 1934, Richmond, Surrey, UK. Local Government Officer; Writer. Publs: North of Leeds, 1966; The Railways of Wharfedale, 1969; The Chester & Holyhead Railway, vol. 1, 1972, vol. 2 in preparation. Contbr. to: Railway Mag.; The Leeds & Selby Railway; The Clayton W. Branch; Buxton Centenary; Railways of the Spen Valley; Arches for Britannia. Mbr., The Railway Club. Address: 97 Royal George Rd., Burgess Hill, Sussex, UK.

BAWDEN, Harry Reginald (Rex), b. 29 July 1921, Birkenhead, Cheshire, UK. BBC Local Radio Station Manager, Radio Merseyside. Contbr. (as jrnlst.) to: Birkenhead Advertiser; Evening Express, Liverpool; Evening Chronicle, Manchester; Manchester Evening News; Evening Chronicle, Newcastle-upon-Tyne; Evening Express, Aberdeen; Sunday Times; Liverpool Echo. Mbr., Nat. Union of Jrnlsts. Address: 14 Kingsmead Rd. South, Oxton, Birkenhead, Merseyside L43 6TA, UK.

BAWDEN, Nina, b. 1925, London, UK. Author. Educ: M.A., Somerville Coll., Oxford. Publs. incl: Who Calls the Tune, 1953; Change Here For Babylon, 1955; The Solitary Child, 1956; Devil by the Sea, 1958; Just Like a Lady, 1960; Tortoise by Candlelight, 1963; A Woman of my Age, 1967; The Grain of Truth, 1969; The Birds on the Trees, 1970; Anna Apparent, 1972; George Beneath a Paper Moon, 1974; (for children) The Secret Passage; The Witch's Daughter; A Handful of Thieves; The Runaway Summer; Squib; Carrie's War, 1973; The Peppermint Pig, 1975. Contbr. to Daily Telegraph (fiction reviews). Mbrships. incl:

PEN; Soc. of Authors; F.R.S.L. Agent: Curtis Brown Ltd. Address: 30 Hanger Hill, Weybridge, Surrey, UK.

BAX, Percy William Frederick, b. 1903, London, UK. Journalist. Educ: Christ's Hospital. Ed., Produce Markets Review, 1924-25; Ed., The Ironmonger Assistants' Journal, 1935-53; Ed.-in-chief, Ironmonger & Hardware Merchandiser, 1953-68; Pres., National Institute of Hardware, 1970. Address: 111 Carnarvon Ave., Enfield, Middx., UK.

BAXTER, Alexander Duncan, b. 17 June 1908, Liverpool, UK. Consultant Engineer. Educ: B.Eng., M.Eng., Univ. of Liverpool. Publs: Princeton Series on High Speed Aerodynamics & Jet Propulsion; Manual on Rocket Engines. Contbr. to: Engr.; Engrng.; Aircraft Engrng.; New Sci.; Nature; Var. tech. jrnls.; Times; Fin. Times; Sunday Times; etc. Mbrships: Fellow, Instn. of Mech. Engrs., Royal Aeronautical Soc.; Pres., 1966-67; Fellow, Inst. of Petroleum, Brit. Interplanetary Soc. Address: Court Farm, Pucklechurch, Avon, BS17 3RD, UK.

BAXTER, Brian, b. London, UK. Lecturer in Naval Architecture. Educ: King's Coll., Newcastle; Univ. of Durham; B.Sc.; M.Sc.; Ph.D.; F.R.I.N.A. Publs: Teach Yourself Naval Architecture; Naval Architecture; Examples & Theory; Know Your Own Ship. Address: Dunelm, Kilmacolm, Renfrewshire, UK.

BAXTER, Elmar, b. 30 Aug. 1924, L.A., Calif., USA. Writer; Photographer; Editor; Author; Director of Public Relations. Educ: Grad., US Merchant Marine Acad., Kings Pt., N.Y. Publs: The Baja Book-Map—Guide to Today's Baja California, 1974. Contbr. to: Sea; Salt Water Sportsman; Sports Southern Calif., Yachting News; Ed., The Skier; Travel & Outdoor Ed., L.A. Herald-Examiner, 1952-68. Mbrships. incl: Soc. of Am. Travel Writers; Outdoor Writers' Assn. of Am.; US Ski Writers' Assn., Pres., S.Calif. Chapt.; L.A. Press Club; Propeller Club. Hons: Hons: Outstanding Travel Writer, 1960, 63, & 65, Outstanding Outdoor Columnist, 1961 & 64, L.A. Press Club. Address: 5121 Blackpool Rd., Westminster, CA 92683, USA.

BAXTER, Eric Peter, b. 29 Oct. 1913, Lowestoft, Suffolk, UK. Schoolmaster. Educ: Goldsmith's Coll., London. Publs: Study Book of: Coal, 1959; Water Supply, 1959; Oil, 1960; Gas, 1961; Ships, 1963; Railways, 1964; Safety at Sea, 1969. Mbr., Metrop. Exec., Coll. of Preceptors. Address: 137 Brighton Rd., Purley, Surrey, CR2 4HE.

BAXTER, Walter, b. 1915. Author. Educ: Trinity Hall, Cambridge. Publs: Look Down in Mercy, 1951; The Image & the Search, 1953. Agent: David Higham Assocs. Address: c/o Agent, 119 Old Brompton Rd., London SW7, UK.

BAYLEN, Joseph O., b. 12 Feb. 1920, Chgo., Ill., USA. Regents' Professor of History; Author. Educ: B.Ed.(Hons.), Northern Ill. Univ., 1941; M.A., Emory Univ., 1947; Ph.D., Univ. of N.M., 1949. Publs. incl: Mme. Juliette Adam, Gambetta, & the Idea of a Franco-Russian Alliance, 1960; Lord Kitchener & the Viceroyalty of India, 1910, 1965; Soldier-Surgeon: The Crimean War Letters of Dr. Douglas A. Reid, 1855-56, 1968; East European & Russian Studies in the American South, (co-ed. w. O. Pidhainy), 1972; contbns., var. lit. & histl. vols. Contbr. to: The Histn., 19th Century Fiction, Am. Lit., Notes & Queries, Am. Quarterly, etc. Address: 916 Barton Woods Rd. N.E., Atlanta, GA 30307, USA.

BAYLEY, Barrington John, b. 9 Apr. 1937, Birmingham, UK. Author. Publs: The Star Virus, 1970; Annihilation Factor, 1972; Empire of Two Worlds, 1972, 1973; Collision Course, 1973; The Fall of Chronopolis, 1974; The Soul of the Robot, 1974. Contbr. to: New Worlds. Agent: Janet Freer Lit. Agcy; Scott Meredith Lit. Agcy., USA. Address: 48 Turreff Ave., Donnington, Telford TF2 8HE, Shropshire, UK.

BAYLOR, Robert Arthur, b. 7 Dec. 1925, Danville, Pa., USA. Teacher. Educ: B.S., Pa. State Coll., Bloomsburg; A.M., Columbia Univ., NYC. Publs: To Sting the Child, 1964; Detail & Pattern, 1969, revised ed., 1972; In the Presence of the Continent, 1971; Fine Frenzy, 1972. Address: 246 E. Arrow Highway, Claremont, CA 91711, USA.

BAYNES, Ken, b. 10 Apr. 1934, Eynsford, UK. Writer; Designer; Educator. Educ: Royal Coll. of Art. Publs: Industrial Design & the Community, 1967; Attitudes in

Design Education (Ed.), 1969; Evaluating New Hospital Buildings (Ed.), 1969; Art & Society Series: War, 1970, Work, 1970, Worship, 1971, Sex, 1972; Scoop Scandal & Strife (Ed.), 1971; Hospital Research & Briefing Problems (Ed.), 1971. Contbr. to: Times Lit. Supplement; Archtl. Review; Guardian; Design. Assoc., Soc. Indl. Artists & Designers. Rsch. Fellow, Royal Coll. of Art, 1974-. Address: Greystones, The Plain, Whiteshill, Stroud, Glos., UK.

BEACHCROFT, Thomas Owen, b. 3 Sept. 1902, Bristol, UK. Former Chief Publicity Officer with BBC Overseas Service. Educ: B.A., Balliol Coll., Oxford. Publs. incl: A Young Man in a Hurry, 1934; You Must Break Out Sometimes, 1936; The Parents Left Alone, 1940; Collected Stories, 1946; Malice Bites Back, 1948; Good-Bye Aunt Heather, 1955; The Modest Art — A Survey of the Short Story in English, 1968; Asking for Trouble; A Thorn in the Heart; Just Cats (co-author). Contbr. to: Criterion; BBC; var. lit. mags. & jrnls., UK & abroad. Mbrships: Authors' Soc.; PEN. Address: c/o Curtis Brown, 1 Craven Hill, London W2 3EW, UK.

BEACHER, Lester Lawrence, b. 18 Aug. 1905, Czerne, Czech. Optometrist; Author; Lecturer; Research Scientist. Educ: O.D., Pa. Coll. of Optometry, 1927; Ph.D., Phila. Coll. & Infirmary Osteopathy, 1945; M.D., McCormick Med. Coll., 1948; A.M., 1959, Ph.D., 1962 Philathea Theol. Sem. Publs. incl: Ocular Refraction & Diagnosis, 1931; Practical Optometry, 1934; Contact Lens Technique, 1941, 5th ed., 1974; Corneal Contact Lenses, 1955. Over 100 sci. treatises. Mbrships: Hon. Mbr., Mark Twain Soc., Eugene Field Soc. Hons: Lit. Award, N.J. Jrnl. of Optometry, 1966; Ed.D.; Sc.D.; Litt.D.; LL.D. Address: 41 Park Ave. at 36th St., N.Y., NY 10016, USA.

BEAL, Anthony Ridley, b. 28 Feb. 1925, Edgware, UK. Publisher. Educ: M.A.(Hons.), Downing Coll., Cambridge. Publs: D.H. Lawrence: Selected Literary Criticism, 1956; D. H. Lawrence, 1961. Contbr. to: Books & Bookmen; var. symposia on D. H. Lawrence. Address: 24 Loom Lane, Radlett, Herts., UK.

BEALEY, Frank William, b. 31 Aug. 1922, Bilston, Staffs., UK. University Teacher, Author. Educ: B.Sc., London Schl. of Econs. Publs: Labour & Politics (w. Henry Pelling), 1958; Constituency Politics (w. J. Blondel & W. P. McCann), 1965; The Social & Political Thought of the British Labour Party, 1970. Mbr., Assn. of Univ. Tchrs. Address: 355 Clifton Rd., Aberdeen, UK.

BEALS, Carleton, b. 1893, Medicine Lodge, Kan., USA. Author; Lecturer. Educ: Univ. of Calif.; Columbia Univ.; B.A.; M.A. Publs: Mexico: An Interpretation; Rome or Death: The Story of Fascism; Banana Cold; Mexican Maze; Porfirio Diaz; Brimston & Chili; Destroying Victor; Black River; Great Guerrilla Warriors; Stories told by the Aztecs; The Nature of Revolution. Mbrships: Authors' Guild; Dramatists' Guild; PEN; Latin Am. Inst. (Late Pres.). Address: Firetower Rd., Killingworth, Deep River, CT 06417, USA.

BEAN, Keith Fenwick, b. 1910, Geelong, Australia. Journalist. Educ: Melbourne Univ. Publs: Eternal Footman; History of the Green Howards; Famous Waterways of the World. Contbr. to: Int. Wine & Food; Dict. of Gastronomy; Good Housekeeping; Japan Times; Japan. Mbrships: Pres., Aust. Jrnlsts. Assn., London, UK, 1944-46; Sec. Gen., Int. Org. of Jrnlsts., 1946-47; Circle of Wine Writers. Address: 32 Woodstock Rd., Chiswick, London W4, UK.

BEANLAND, Arthur de Millichamp, b. 1909, Swansea, Wales, UK. Former College Master. Educ: M.Sc., Univ. of Wales. Publs: A Fortnight Motoring Abroad, 1959; A Fortnight on the Coasts of S.W. France, 1961; A Fortnight Camping Abroad, 1962; Camping Holidays in France, 1964; Camping Holidays in Europe, 1972. Contbr. to: Guardian; Times; Camping. Address: The College, Worksop, Notts., UK.

BEARDSLEY, Charles, pen names ELLIOTT, Owen; RADCLIFFE, Jocelyn, b. 18 Aug. 1914, Palo Alto, Calif., USA. Writer. Publs. incl: The Naked Hills, 1959; A Raging Wind, 1961; Past & Present, 1964; Baksheesh & Roses, 1968; The Motel, 1969; The Resort, 1971; The Convention; The Center; The Apartments; Saturday Night in San Francisco; Saturday Night in Los Angeles. Contbr. to: San Fran. Chronicle & Peninsula Living Mag (Book Reviewer). Mbr., Am. Soc. Tech. Writers. Address: Kingscote Gdns., Stanford, CA 94305, USA.

BEARDSWORTH, Millicent Monica, b. 10 Mar. 1915, Liverpool, UK. Teacher. Educ: L.R.A.M., L.G.S.M., Penrhos Coll., Colwyn Bay. Publs: King's Servant, 1966; King's Friend, 1968, 2nd ed., 1971; King's Endeavour, 1969; King's Adversary, 1972; King's Contest, 1975. Mbrships: Royal Stuart Soc. (Coun. Mbr.); Nat. Book League. Address: 214 Conway Road, Colwyn Bay, Clwyd, LL29 7LU, UK.

BEARE, Francis Wright, b. 16 Aug. 1902, Toronto, Can. University Professor; Anglican Priest; Author. Educ: B.A., Univ. of Toronto; Ph.D., Univ. of Chgo., USA. Publs: Commentary on the Epistle to the Philippians, 1929, 2nd ed., 1969; The First Epistle of Peter Blackwell, 1948, 3rd revised ed., 1970; The Earliest Records of Jesus, 1962; St. Paul & His Letters, 1962, 2nd ed., 1970. Contbr. to: Jrnl. Biblical Lit.; Anglican Theol. Review; Can. Jrnl. Theol.; Interpreter's Bible, etc. Mbrships. incl: Soc. Biblical Lit. (Pres., 1969); Can. Soc. Biblical Studies (Pres., 1940). Recip., McCaul Gold Medal, Univ. Coll., Toronto, 1925. Address: 122 Roxborough Dr., Toronto, Ont., M4W 1X4, Can.

BEARNSON, Margaret Sherrod, b. 1 Feb. 1896, Riverton, Ala., USA. School Teacher; Writer. Educ: B.S., 1930, M.S., 1931, Univ. of Utah; Grad. study, Univ. of Va., Univ. of Utah. Publs: The History of the Klu Klux Klan, 1931; Helping Children Live & Learn; Helping Children Grow Guidebook, 1952; It Must Be Magic, 1973. Contbr. to num. jrnls., mags. Hons: Role of Hon., O'Brien's Best Am. Short Stories, 1936, 1937; Montalvo Creative Writing Schlrship., Saratoga, Calif., 1962; Award, Juvenile Book, Utah State Inst. of Fine Arts, 1972 & 1974; 1st Place, Juvenile Story, 2nd Place, Narrative Verse, Penwomen Contest, 1974. Address: 1363 Ramona Ave., Salt Lake City, UT 84105, USA.

BEASLEY-MURRAY, George Raymond, b. 10 Oct. 1916, London, UK. Professor of New Testament Interpretation. Educ: Spurgeon's Coll., London; London Univ.; Cambridge Univ.; M.A.; B.D.; M.Th.; Ph.D.; D.D. Publs: Christ is Alive; Jesus & the Future; Preaching the Gospel from the Gospels; Commentary on Mark Thirteen; Baptism in the New Testament, 1960; Baptism Today & Tomorrow, 1966; Commentary on 2 Corinthians, 1971; Commentary on The Book of Revelation, 1974. Contbr. to Bapt. Times; Expository Times; etc. Mbrships: Studiorum Novi Testamenti Soc.; Engl. Speaking Union. Address: Southern Bapt. Theol. Sem., 2825 Lexington Rd., Louisville, KY 40206, USA.

BEATTIE, Jessie Louise, b. 1896, Blair, Ont., Can. Community Welfare Worker; Librarian; Schoolteacher. Educ: Univ. of Buffalo, USA; Univ. of Toronto, Can.; Drama Schl., Hart House. Publs: Hilltop, 1935; Three Measures, 1939; Blown Leaves; Shifting Sails (poetry); White Wings Around the World, 1953; Along the Road, 1954; John Christie Holland, 1956; Black Moses, 1958; The Split in the Sky, 1960; Hasten the Day, 1961; Strength for the Bridge, 1966; A Season Past, 1968; The Log Line, 1972; A Walk through Yesterday (autobiog.), forthcoming. Mbrships: Can. Women's Press Club; Can. Authors Assn. Address: 30 Roanoke Rd., Hamilton, Ont., Can.

BEATY, Betty, pen names CAMPBELL, Karen; ROSS, Catherine, b. 16 July 1922, Farsley, UK. Publs: (as BB) Maiden Flight; (as CR) From This Day Forward, 1959; The Colours of the Night, 1962; The Trysting Tower, 1964; (as KC) Suddenly in the Air, 1969; Thunder On Sunday, 1972; Wheel Fortune, 1973. Contbr. to: Woman's Weekly; Woman; Woman's Own; Woman & Home; BBC's Book at Bedtime. Mbrships: Authors' Soc.; Crime Writers' Assn. Address: Woodside, Hever, Edenbridge, Kent, UK.

BEATY, David, pen name STANTON, Paul, b. 28 Mar. 1919, Hatton, Ceylon. Author. Educ: M.A., Merton Coll., Oxford; Univ. Coll., London. Publs: The Takeoff, 1949; The Heart of the Storm, 1953; The Proving Flight, 1956; Cone of Silence, 1959; Call Me Captain, 1959; The Gun Garden, 1962; The Wind Off The Sea, 1962; The Siren Song, 1962; Sword of Honour, 1964; The Human Factor in Aircraft Accidents, 1969; The Temple Tree, 1971. Mbrships: Soc. of Authors; Royal Aeronautical Soc.; Brit. Air Line Pilots' Assn.

BEAUMAN, Eric Bentley, b. London, UK. Editor; Writer; Wing Commander (ret'd.). Educ: Geneva Univ., Switz. Publs: (Ed.) Winged Words; Book Soc. Choice; The Airmen Speak; We Speak from the Air (w. C. Day Lewis); Over to You; Living Dangerously (co-author); The Boys'

Country Book (co-author); Travellers' Tales. Contbr. to: Times; Field; BBC; Geogl. Mag. & Jrnl.; Dictionary of Nat. Biog.; Ency. Britannica; Cheshire Life; Listener; Nat. Review. RAF & Air Min., 1914-51. Address: 59 Chester Row, London SW1, UK.

BEAUMAN, Katharine Burgoyne Bentley (née Miller Jones), b. Leeds, UK. Author. Educ: M.A., Lady Margaret Hall, Oxford Univ. Publs: Wings on Her Shoulders; Short History of St. Michael's, Chester Square, C. of E. Secondary School; Partners in Blue; The Story of Women's Service with the RAF. Contbr. to: BBC; Yorks. Post (Former Woman Ed.); W.R.A.F. Officers Gazette (Ed.); Yorks. Evening Post; News Chronicle; R.A.F. Quarterly; W.V.S. Bulletin. Mbrships. incl: Coun., L.M.H. Settlement (VP & former Chmn.). Address: 59 Chester Row, London SW1, UK.

BEAUMONT, Albert, b. 1901, Sheffield, UK. Plant Pathologist. Educ: M.A., Univ. of Cambridge. Publs: Diseases of Garden Plants; Diseases of Farm Crops. Address: 10 Elm Ct., Truro, Cornwall, UK.

BEAUMONT, Cyril William, b. 1891. Writer on Theatre & Dance; Translator; Editor. Publs. incl: A Manual of the Theory & Practice of Theatrical Dancing (w. S. Idzikowski), 1922; A History of Ballet in Russia 1613-1881, 1930; The Complete Book of Ballets, 1937; Puppets & the Puppet Stage, 1938; The Diaghilev Ballet in London, 1940; Supplement to the Complete Book of Ballets, 1942; Ballet Design Past & Present, 1944; Ballets of Today, 1954; Ballets Past & Present, 1955; Bookseller at the Ballet, 1975. Contbr. to: Sunday Times (Ballet Critic, 1950-59); Dance Jrnl. (Ed., 1924-65). Mbrships. incl: F.R.S.L.; F.R.S.A.; Critics' Circle (Pres., 1957). Hons. incl: O.B.E.; var. foreign orders. Address: 68 Bedford Ct. Mansions, Bedford Ave., London WC1, UK.

BEAUVOIR, Simone de, b. 9 Jan. 1908, Paris, France. Author; Teacher. Educ: Univ. of Paris: Publs. incl: L'Invitee, 1943; Le Sang des Autres, 1944; Le Deuxieme Sexe, 1949; Les Mandarins, 1954; La Longue marche, 1957; Memoires d'une jeune fille rangee, 1958; La Force des choses, 1963; La Force de L'Age, 1960; Brigitte Bardot, 1960; Une mort tres douce, 1964; Les Belles Images, 1966; La Femme Rompue, 1968; La Vieillesse, 1970; Tout Compte fait, 1972; sev. publs. transl. into Engl. Recip., Prix Goncourt, for Les Mandarins, 1954. Address: 11 bis rue Schoelcher, Paris 14e, France.

BEAVER, (Rev.) Robert Pierce, b. 26 May 1906, Hamilton, Ohio, USA. Clergyman; Educator. Educ: A.B., M.A., Oberlin Coll.; Ph.D., Cornell Univ.; Yale & Columbia Univs.; Coll. Chinese Studies, Peking; Union Theol. Sem., N.Y. Publs. incl: Ecumenical Beginnings in Protestant World Mission, 1962; Envoys of Peace, 1964; Church, State & the American Indians, 1966; Pioneers in Mission, 1966; To Advance the Gospel, 1967; All Loves Excelling, 1968; The Missionary Between the Times, 1968; Ed., The Gospel & Frontier Peoples, 1973; Ed., Christian World Mission Books. Contbr. to: Ch. Hist.; Religion in Geschichte und Gegenwart; etc. Recip., Festschrift: The Future of the Christian World Mission: Studies in Honor of R. Pierce Beaver, 1971; D.D., Concordia Sem., St. Louis, 1972. Address: 12 A S. Sacramento Ave., Ventnor, NJ 08406, USA.

BECHER, Ulrich, b. 2 Jan. 1910, Berlin, Germany. Novelist & Playwright. Educ: studied law, Geneva, Switz. & Friedrich-Wilhelms-Univ., Berlin; studied drawing w. George Grosz, Berlin. Publs. incl: Manner Machen Fehler, 1932 (burned by Nazis in 1933); Die Eroberer, Geschichten aus Europa, 1936 (confiscated by Gestapo in 1938); Kurz Nach 4, Hamburg 1957, Paris 1960, Italy 1962, Poland 1966, Kiev 1969, Moscow 1971, Jugoslavia 1972; Murmeljagd, Hamburg 1959, Paris 1972, Jugoslavia 1972, Poland 1973, Budapest 1975, New York (Marmot-Hunt), 1975; Das Profil, Hamburg 1973, Paris 1975; New Yorker Novellen, Berlin 1969, Zurich 1974; 6 plays inclng. Biene Gib Mir Honig (comedy), 1974. Hons. incl: "William's Ex Casino" elected Book of the Month by Deutsche Akademie für Sprache & Dichtung, 1974. Address: Spalenring 95, Basle, Switz.

BECK, Béatrix Marie, b. 30 July 1914. Writer. Educ: Univ. of Grenoble. Publs: Barny; Une Mort irrégulière; Leon Morin, prêtre; Des accommodements avec le ciel; Le Premier Mai; Abram Krol; Le Muet; Cou coupé court toujours. Contbr. to newspapers & mags. Mbr., jury, Prix Fémina. Hons: Prix Goncourt; Prix Félix Fénéon. Address: c/o MM. Cailler (Editeurs), Geneva, Switz.

BECK, Earl Ray, b. 8 Sept. 1916, Junction City, Ohio, USA. University Professor of history. Educ: A.B., Capital Univ., 1937; M.A., 1939, Ph.D., Ohio State Univ.; Army Special Trng., Stanford Univ., 1944. Publs: Verdict on Schacht: A Study in the Problem of Political 'Guilt', 1955; The Death of the Prussian Republic, 1959; On Teaching History in Colleges & Universities, 1966; Germany Rediscovers America, 1968. Address: 2514 Killarney Way, Tallahassee, FL 32303, USA.

BECK, Warren, b. Richmond, Ind., USA. Professor of English. Educ: B.A., M.A., D.Litt., Columbia Univ. Publs: Final Score; Pause under the sky; Into Thin Air; Man in Motion: Faulkner's Trilogy, 1961; Joyce's Dubliners: Substance, Vision & Art, 1969; (short stories) The Blue Sash; The First Fish; The Far Whistle; The Rest is Silence, 1963. Contbr: Yale Review; Va. Quarterly; Poetry; Antioch Review; Kenyon Review; etc. Mbrships: Fellow, Am. Coun. of Learned Socs. Address: 207 N. Park Ave., Appleton, WI, USA.

BECKELHYMER, Paul Hunter, b. 23 Nov. 1919, Trenton, Mo., USA. Professor of Homiletics; Author; Editor. Educ: B.A., Park Coll., Kan. City, Mo., 1941; B.D., Univ. of Chgo. Divinity Schl., 1944. Publs: Meeting Live on Higher Levels, 1956; Questions God Asks, 1961; Hocking Valley Iron Man, 1962; Dear Connie, 1967; Ed., The Vital Pulpit of the Christian Church, 1969; Ed., The Word We Preach, 1970. Contbr. to: Christian; Disciple; Encounter; Pulpit; Christian Century; Relig. in Life; Preaching Today. Address: 5725 Whitman Ave., Fort Worth, TX 76133, USA.

BECKER, Jillian (née Friedman), b. 2 June 1932, Johannesburg, S. Africa. Author. Educ: B.A., Univ. of the Witwatersrand. Publs: The Keep, 1967, paperback ed., 1971; The Union, 1971. Contbr. to: South African Writing Today, 1967; Four Hemispheres, 1971; Times Saturday Review; Transatlantic Review. Mbrships: Soc. of Authors; PEN. Recip., Nat. Essay Prize, S. African Inst. of Race Rels., 1946. Agent: A. M. Heath & Co. Ltd. Address: 144 Hemingford Rd., London N1 1DE, UK.

BECKER, Jürgen, b. 10 July 1932, Cologne, Germany. Writer. Educ: Univ. of Cologne. Publs: Phasen (text & typography w. Wolf Vostell), 1960; Felder (prose), 1964; Ränder (prose), 1968; Bilder, Häuser (radio play), 1969; Happenings (documentary, Ed. w. Wolf Vostell), 1965. Contbr. to var. jrnls & to radio. Hons. incl: Förderpries des Landes Niedersachsen, 1964; Grp. 47 Prize, 1967; Lit. Prize of Cologne, 1968. Address: c/o Suhrkamp-Verlag, 6 Frankfurt/M, W. Germany.

BECKER, Peter, b. 27 Mar. 1921, Rivonia, S. Africa. Director; Consultant. Publs: Eureka, 1953; Sandy Tracks to the Kraals, 1956; The Peoples of South Africa, 3 vols., 1958; Path of Blood, 1962; Rule of Fear, 1964; Dingane King of the Zulu, 1966; Hill of Destiny, 1969; L'Attila Noir, 1969; Peoples of Southern Africa, 1971; Tribe to Township, 1973; Trails & Tribes in Southern Africa, 1974; Mauritius 1962, 1974. Mbr., S. African Authors PEN. Address: P.O. Box 2983, Johannesburg, S. Africa.

BECKER, Stephen (David), b. 31 Mar. 1927, Mt. Vernon, N.Y., USA. Novelist; Translator. Educ: B.A., Harvard Coll. 1947; Yenching Univ., Peking, China, 1948. Publs: The Season of the Stranger, 1951; Shanghai Incident, 1955; Juice, 1959; A Covenant with Death, 1965; The Outcasts, 1967; When the War is over, 1969; Dog Tags, 1973; The Chinese Bandit, 1975; Comic Art in America, 1959; Marshall Field III, 1964; sev. French translations. Contbr. to: Harper's; Atlantic; sev. short story anthologies. Hons: Paul Harris Fndn. Fellowship, 1947; Guggenheim Fellowship, 1954. Address: RFD, Conway, MA 01341, USA.

BECKERMAN, Bernard, b. 24 Sept. 1921, NYC, USA. Professor of Dramatic Arts & Dean, School of the Arts. Educ: B.S.S., CCNY, 1942; M.F.A., Yale Univ. Schl. of Drama, 1943; Ph.D., Columbia Univ., 1956. Publs: Shakespeare at the Globe, 1962; Dynamics of Drama, 1970. Contbr. to: Ency. Americana; Ency. Britannica. Mbrships: Chmn., Am. Soc. for Theatre Rsch., 1973-76; Bd. of Trustees, Nat. Theatre Conf., 1972-75; Fellow, Am. Theatre Assn. Address: 27 West 67 St., N.Y., NY 10023, USA.

BECKERS, Walter, b. 18 Jan. 1929, Antwerp, Belgium. Publisher; Author. Educ: Commercial schl. degree. Publs: Anno Atlantae, 1966; De Twaalf Jaagatijden van Banana, 1972; Boek 'A' — Science Fiction, 1972; Witboek — Het Boek dat Niet Bestaat, 1973; Moon Cigarettes, 1974; Opera Divabolica in Black, 1974; Ed., Banana Press; Ed., Beckers Art Promotion; Chief Ed., Beckers Club Books. Hons:

Grand Prix, Assn. Européenne de la Litt, Parallèle, 1967; Grand Prix of Diano Marina, Italy for progressive book-object design, 1972. Address: 10 Rozenlaan, 2080 Kapellen (bos), Belgium.

BECKETT, Arnold Heyworth, b. 12 Feb. 1920, Blackpool, UK. Professor of Pharmaceutical Chemistry. Educ: F.P.S., 1942, B.Sc., 1947, Univ. of London; Ph.D., 1950; D.Sc., 1959; F.R.I.C., 1951. Publs: Practical Pharmaceutical Chemistry, Parts 1 & 2 (w. J. B. Stenlake). Contbr. of over 300 papers to field & articles to num. jrnls. inclng: Jrnl. of Chem. Soc.; Jrnl. of Med. Pharm. Chem.; Progress in Med. Chem.; Jrnl. of Biochem. Pharm.; Brit. Med. Jrnl. Address: Dept. of Pharm., Chelsea Coll., Univ. of London; Manresa Rd., London SW3 6LX, UK.

BECKETT, Samuel, b. 1906, Dublin, Repub. of Ireland. Author. Educ: M.A., Trinity Coll., Dublin; T.C.D. Publs: (novels) Murphy; Molloy; Malone Dies; The Unnamable; Watt; (plays) Waiting for Godot; All That Fall; Endgame; Krapp's Last Tape; Embers; Happy Days; (poems) Whoroscope; Echo's Bones; Poems in English; (criticism) Proust; (transl.) Mexican Anthology. Address: c/o Editions de Minuit, 7 Rue Bernard Palissy, Paris, France.

BECKINSALE, Robert Percy, b. 23 July 1908, Stanford-in-Vale, Berks., UK. Lecturer; Author. Educ: B.A., M.A., London Univ.; M.A., D.Phil., Oxford Univ.; Dip. Ed. Publs: Spain & Portugal, 4 vols., 1941-45; Companion into Gloucestershire, 1948; Companion into Berkshire, 1951; History of the Study of Landforms, 1964; Land, Air & Ocean, 1966; Urbanisation & its Problems, 1968; Companion into Gloucestershire & the Cotswolds, 1973; History of the Study of Landforms, vol. 2, 1973; Southern Europe, 1974. Contbr. to: Chambers Ency.; Ency. Britannica; Ency. Americana; Nature; etc. Mbrships. incl: Soc. of Authors; F.R.G.S. Address: 194 Iffley Rd., Oxford, UK.

BECKLES WILLSON, Robina Elizabeth, b. 1930, London, UK. Teacher. Educ: M.A.; Dip. Ed., Liverpool Univ. Publs: Leopards on the Loire, 1961; A Time to Dance, 1962; A Seraph in a Box, 1963; Pineapple Palace, 1964; Anchor's Wharf, 1965; A Reflection of Rachel, 1967; The Leader of the Band, 1968; Pendulum Quest, 1969; Roundabout Ride, 1969; Musical Instruments, 1964; The Last Harper, 1972; What a Noise, 1974. Agent: A. M. Heath. Address: 44 Popes Ave., Twickenham, Middx., UK.

BECKMAN, Erik, b. 23 Apr. 1935, Vänersborg, Sweden. Writer. Educ: Studies at Univs. of Uppsala & Lund, 1955-61; Fil.mag., 1961. Publs: Farstu (poetry) 1963; Någon något (novel), 1964; Hertigens kartonger (novel), 1965; Varifrån dom observeras (poetry), 1966; Inlandsbanan (novel), 1967; Kyss er! (poetry), 1969; Kameler dricker vatten (novel), 1971; Sakernas tillstånd (mixed text), 1973; Tumme (poetry), 1974; also 4 plays for radio & TV. Mbr., Swedish Authors' Union. Hons: Aftonbladets Lit. Prize, 1966; BLM-Prize, Bonnier's Publng. House, 1970; Dobloug Prize, Swedish Acad., 1972. Address: Prästmon 2319, 870 52 Nyland, Sweden.

BECKMAN, Gail McKnight, b. 8 Apr. 1938, NYC, USA. Educator. Law. Educ: B.A., Bryn Mawr Coll.; M.A., Univ. of Pa.; J.D., Yale Univ.; Fulbright Dip., studies at Universität Tübingen, Germany. Publs: Law for Business & Management, 1975; Statutes at Large of Pennsylvania, 1680-1700, 1976; Estate Planning Considerations for US Citizens Abroad (monograph), 1974. Contbr. to num. law jrnls. Address: Ga. State Univ., Univ. Plaza, Atlanta, GA 30303, USA.

BECKWITH, John Gordon, b. 2 Dec. 1918, Southend-on-Sea, Essex, UK. Museum Curator; Author. Educ: Ampleforth Coll., York; Exeter Coll., Oxford; B.A., M.A. Publs: Art of Constantinople, 1961; Coptic Sculpture, 1963; Early Medieval Art, 1964; Early Christian & Byzantine Art, 1970; Ivory Carvings in Early Medieval England, 1972. Contbr. to: Art Bulletin; Burlington Mag.; Apollo; Connoisseur; Times Lit. Supplement; Etc. Mbrships: F.S.A.; Fellow, Brit. Acad. Address: Flat 12, 77 Ladbroke Grove, London W11, UK.

BECKWITH, Lillian, b. 25 Apr. 1916, Ellesmere Port, UK. Writer. Publs: The Hills is Lonely, 1959; The Sea for Breakfast, 1961; The Loud Halo, 1964; Green Hand, 1967; A Rope in Case, 1968; About My Father's Business, 1971; Lightly Poached, 1973; The Spuddy, 1974. Mbrships. incl: Soc. of Authors; Soc. of Women Writers & Jrnlsts. Address:

c/o The Hutchinson Publng. Co., 3 Fitzroy Square, London, W1P 6JD, UK.

BECSI, Kurt, b. 30 May 1920, Vienna, Austria. Head, Institute of Austrian Dramatic Arts. Educ: Ph.D., Univ. of Vienna, 1948. Publs. incl: Integrale Trilogie (plays), 1968; Dionysische Trilogie (plays), 1969; Theater der dreifachen Revolution (essay), 1970; Faust und der Mensch der Zunkunft (essay), 1971; Aufmarsch zur Apokalypse, 1971; Kosmische Trilogie (plays), 1972; 57 Thesen eines neuen kosmischen Theaters (essays), 1972; Das Indische Zeitalter, 1973. Contbr. to sev. series in field. Mbr., num. lit. orgs. Recip., var. awards. Address: Daringergasse 12 b/27/4, A-1190 Vienna, Austria.

BEDFORD, (Mrs.) Sybille, b. 1911, Charlottenburg, Germany. Author. Publs: The Sudden View, UK, 1953, USA, 1954; A Legacy, UK, 1956, USA, 1957; The Best We Can Do, the trial of Dr. Adams, UK, 1958, USA, 1959; The Faces of Justice, 1961; A Favourite of the Gods, 1963; A Compass Error, 1968; Aldous Huxley: A Biography, Vol. 1, UK, 1973, Vol. 2, 1974, both vols., USA, 1974. Contbr. to: Spectator; Observer; Life Mag.; Venture; N.Y. Review of Books; Horizon; Harper's Bazaar; Esquire Mag., etc. Mbrships: F.R.S.L.; PEN; Soc. of Authors. Agent: Evelyn Gendel, N.Y., USA. Address: c/o Coutts & Co., 440 Strand, London WC2, UK.

BEDWORTH, Albert Ernest, b. 2 Nov. 1924, Utica, N.Y., USA. Health Educator. Educ: B.S., 1950; M.S., 1957; SUNY, Cortland; advanced study, Cornell & Syracuse Univs. Publs: Basics of Drug Education, 1973; Exec. Ed., Jrnl. of Drug Educ. Mbrships: Am. Pub. & Am. Schl. Hlth. Assns.; N.Y. State Fedn. of Profl. Hlth. Educs.; Am. Alliance for Hlth., P.E. & Recreation. Address: R.D. No. 2, Hillsdale, NY 12529, USA.

BEECHER, (Most Rev.) Leonard James, b. 21 May 1906, London, UK. Minister of the Anglican Church (Retired). Educ: B.Sc., M.A., Dip.Ed., Univ. of London. Publs: Kikuyu-English Dictionary (co-author); Kikuyu & Swahili Bible (co-ed.); Report on Education of Africans in Kenya. Contbr. to: Kenya Ch. Review (Ed., 1944-51); var. jrnls. Hons: C.M.G., 1961; Wellcome Medal for Disting. Serv., Royal African Soc., 1971; D.D.(h.c.). Address: "Mascalls", P.O. Box 21066, 8 Naivasha Road, Dagoretti Corner, Nairobi, Kenya.

BEELEY, Harold, b. 15 Feb. 1909, London, UK. Diplomat (Retired). Educ: M.A., Queen's Coll., Oxford. Publs: Disraeli, 1936; The History Makers (contbng. author), 1973. Contbr. to: Int. Affairs; Middle E. Int. Chmn., Reform Club, 1971-73. Address: 2 Ormond Rd., Richmond, Surrey, UK.

BEER, Ethel Sophia, b. 14 May 1897, NYC, USA. Writer. Educ: N.Y. Univ.; Columbia Univ.; New Schl. for Soc. Rsch. Publs: Working Mothers & the Day Nursery (transl'd into French & Greek); The Greek Odyssey of an American Nurse; Marvelous Greece. Contbr. to: child care & family rels. jrnls. Mbrships. incl: Pen & Brush; Near E. Fndn.; Woman's Press Club; etc. Recip., Pen & Brush Award. Address: 41 Fifth Ave., N.Y., NY 10002, USA.

BEER, Gretel, b. Marchegg, Austria. Writer. Publs: Ice Cream Dish — How to make them, 1952; Sandwiches for Parties & Picnics, 1953; Austrian Cooking, 1954; The Diabetic Gourmet, 1974. Contbr. to: Daily Telegraph; Vogue; House & Garden; Evening News; Scotsman, etc. Mbrships: Inst. of Jrnlsts.; Press Club; Inst. of Dirs. Hons: Award, Frankfurt Book Fair, 1961; Gold Medal for Servs. to Austrian Tourism, 1972. Address: 3 South Square, Gray's Inn, London WC1, UK.

BEER, Otto F., b. 8 Sept. 1910, Vienna, Austria. Author; Theatre Critic. Educ: Dr.Phil., Univ. of Vienna, 1932. Publs: (novels) Ich-Rodolfo-Magier, 1965; Christin-Theres, 1967; (comedies) Man ist nur zweimal jung, 1965; Christin-Theres, 1967; (non-fiction) Bummel durch Wien, 1971; Der Fenstergucker, 1974. Contbr. to: Suddeutsche Zeitung, Munich; Zeit, Hamburg; Rheinischer Merkur, Cologne. Mbrships: PEN; Concordia Press Club. Hons: Professorship, 1964. Address: Lederergasse 27, A-1080 Vienna, Austria.

BEESON, (Rev.) Trevor Randall, b. 2 Mar. 1926, Darley Dale, Derbys., UK. Clergyman; Author. Educ: A.K.C., King's Coll., London; St. Boniface Coll., Warminster. Publs: New Area Mission, 1963; Worship in a United Church (co-author), 1964; Ed., Partnership in Ministry, 1964; An

Eye for an Ear, 1972; The Church of England in Crisis, 1973; Discretion & Valour, 1974. Contbr. to: Christian Century; Guardian. Mbrships: Chap., Guild of St. Bride, Fleet St. Address: St. Mary's Vicarage, Ware, Herts., SG12 0PT, UK.

BEFFEL, Eulalie C., b. 8 Apr. 1905, Milwaukee, Wis., USA. Teacher. Educ: B.A., Univ. of Wis.; M.A., Middlebury Coll. Publs: The Hero of Antietam, 1943; This Is My Tender Clown, 1948; Bitter Weather (poetry), 1974. Contbr. to poetry jrnls., pop. mags. Address: 306 Kensington Dr., Madison, WI 53704, USA.

BEGG, Neil Colquhoun, b. 13 Apr. 1915, Dunedin, NZ. Physician. Educ: M.B., Ch.B.; F.R.C.P.(E); M.R.C.P.; D.C.H. Publs: The New Zealand Child & His Family, 1970, 3rd ed., 1974; (w. A. C. Begg) Dusky Bay, 1966, 1968; James Cook & New Zealand, 1969, 1970; Port Preservation, 1973. Contbr. to: NZ Heritage; var. med. jrnls. Mbrships: Pres. elect, NZ Med. Assn., 1974; NZ Hist. Places Trust, 1974; Hon. Cons., Int. Childbirth Educ. Assn. Hons: Hubert Church Award, 1966; O.B.E., 1972; J.M. Sherrard Award, 1974. Address: 86 Newington Ave., Dunedin, NZ.

BEHREND, George Henry Sandham, b. 1922, London, UK. Travel Writer. Educ: M.A., Hertford Coll., Oxford. Publs. incl: Grand European Expresses, 1962; Railway Holiday in France, 1963; Railway Holiday in Switzerland, 1965; Stanley Spencer at Burghclere, 1965; Jersey Airlines, 1968; Gone With Regret, Recollections of the Great Western Railway, 1922-1947, 3rd ed., 1969; Yatakli-Vagon: Turkish Steam Travel (w. Vincent Kelly), 1969; Channel Silver Wings (w. Ian Scott-Hill); Hof Steam; Steam Over Switzerland, 1974. Contbr. to var. jrnls. & newspapers. Mbrships: F.R.G.S.; Assoc., C. Inst. T.; Guild of Travel Writers. Address: Villa Mon Contour, Fliquet, Jersey, Channel Islands.

BEICHMAN, Arnold, b. 1913, NYC, USA. University Associate Professor. Educ: Columbia Coll., N.Y.; Columbia Univ., N.Y.; B.A.; M.A.; Ph.D. Publs: The Other State Department, 1969; Nine Lies About America, 1972. Contbr. to: Int. Herald Tribune; Art Int.; Christian Sci. Monitor; Jrnl. of Brit. Studies; Encounter. Mbr., Am. Pol. Sci. Assn. Address: Univ. of Mass., Boston, MA 02125, USA.

BEIRNE, Bryan Patrick, b. 1918, Rosslare, Wexford, Repub. of Ireland. Pestologist; University Professor. Educ: M.A., M.Sc., Ph.D., Trinity Coll., Dublin. Publs: The Origin & History of the British Fauna; British Pyralid & Plume Moths; Pest Management. Contbr. to var. sci. jrnls. Address: Simon Fraser Univ., Burnaby, B.C., Can.

BEK, Alexandr Alfredovich, b. 3 Jan. 1903, Saratov, Russia. Writer. Educ: Moscow Univ. Publs. incl: Volokolamskoe shosse (novel), 1943, 1944; Domenshchiki (stories), 1946; Timofei — Otkrytoe Serdtse (1947); Molodye Lyudi (w. Nataliya Loiko), 1954; Zhizn Berezhkova, 1956; Stchastlivaya Ruka, 1959; Neskolko Dnei (sequel to Volokolamskoe schosse), 1960; Rezerv Generala Panfilova, 1961; Moi geroi, 1967. Contbr. to Pravda & mags. Mbr., Writer's Union. Address: USSR Union of Writers, 52 Ulitsa Vorovskogo, Moscow, USSR.

BELBEN, Rosalind, b. 1 Feb. 1941, Broadstone, Dorset, UK. Writer. Publs: Bogies, 1972; Reuben, Little Hero, 1973; The Limit, 1974; (radio plays) Metamorphoses, 1973, Damage, 1973. Mbrships: Writers' Guild of GB; Writers Action Grp. Recip., Arts Coun. Award, 1974. Agent: Anthony Sheil Assocs. Address: 12 Panorama Court, Shepherds Hill, London N6 5RP, UK.

BELFIELD, Eversley Michael Gallimore, b. 10 Sept. 1918, London, UK. University Lecturer. Educ: B.A., M.A., Pembroke Coll., Oxford. Publs: Unarmed into Battle (w. H. J. Parlham), 1956; Annals of the Addington Family, 1959; Battle from Normandy (w. H. Essame), 1965; Sieges, 1967; Oudenarde, 1972; Concise History of the Boer War, 1975. Mbr., Histl. Assn. (Mbr., Nat. Coun.). Address: Extra Mural Dept., Southampton Univ., Southampton, Hants., UK.

BELFRAGE, Cedric, b. 1904, London, UK. Journalist; Writer. Educ: Corpus Christi Coll., Cambridge Univ. Publs: Away From It All; Promised Land; Let My People Go; They All Hold Swords; Abide With Me; The Frightened Giant; Seeds of Destruction; My Master Columbus; Man at the Door with the Gun; American Inquisition. Mbr., Nat. Union Jrnlsts. Recip., Guggenheim Fellowship, 1946-47. Address: Apdo. 630, Cuernavaca, Mor, Mexico.

BELGION, Montgomery, b. 1892, Paris, France. Journalist; Editor. Publs: Our Present Philosophy of Life; The Human Parrot; News of the French; Reading for Profit; Epitaph on Nuremburg; Victors' Justice; H. G. Wells; David Hume; The Worship of Quantity: A Study of Megalopolitics; Armistice 1918 in Promise of Greatness; A. Malraux in the Politics of 20th Century Novelists. Contbr. to: Daily Mail; N.Y. World; N.Y. Herald, European Ed., (ed.-in-chief), 1915; Quarterly Review; Contemporary Review; Times Lit. Supplement; Listener; etc. Mbr., Athenaeum. Address: Titchmarsh, Kettering, Northants., UK.

BELIA, György, b. 2 December 1923, Nagyszeben, Transylvania. Literary Historian; Critic; Translator. Educ: Univ. Publs: Ady Endre válogatott levelei, 1956; Babits — Juhász — Kosztolányi levelezése, 1959; Essays & several translations from Rumanian, French, Russian & German. Contbr. to: Irodalomtörténeti Közlemények; Irodalomtörténet; Nagyvilág. Mbrships: Union of Hungarian Writers; Soc. of Lit. Hist. (Hungary). Address: H-1013 Budapest, Feszty Árpád utca 4, Hungary.

BELJON, Joop, pen name MAJORICK, Bernard, b. 11 Jan. 1922, Haarlem, Netherlands. Environmental Designer. Educ: Trng. in Sculpture & Typographic Design. Publs: Ontwerpen en Verwerpen, 1959; The Clocks of Chagall, 1960; Wonen, Gisteren en Vandaas, 1961; Bouwmeesters van Morgen, 1965; Waar Je Kijkt-Erotiek, 1967; Twelve Environments, 1975. Contbr. to: Int. Interior; Leonardo; Quadrat Prints; Aujourd'hui. Mbr., PEN. Address: Westvoorstr. 7, Oud Beÿerland, Netherlands.

BELL, Adrian Hanbury, b. 4 Oct. 1901. Author; Compiler of Times Crossword since 1930. Publs. incl: Corduroy, 1930; Silver Ley, 1931; The Cherry Tree, 1932; Folly Field, 1933; The Balcony, 1934; Poems, 1935; By-Road, 1937; Shepherd's Farm; 1939; Men & the Fields, 1939; Apple Acre, 1942; Sunrise to Sunset, 1944; The Budding Morrow, 1947; The Black Donkey, 1949; The Flower & the Wheel, 1949; The Path by the Window, 1952; Music in the Morning, 1954; A Young Man's Fancy, 1955; A Suffolk Harvest, 1956; The Mill House, 1958; My Own Master, 1961; A Street in Suffolk, 1964. (ed.) The Open Air, 1936.

BELL, Agnes Paton, b. 1891, Dalserf, Scotland, UK. Teacher. Educ: Tchr's Cert.; B.A., M.A., Melbourne Univ., Aust. Publs: Early Caulfield, 1957; Melbourne: John Batman's Village, 1965. Contbr. to: Jrnl. of Philos.; Jrnl., Royal Hist. Soc. of Vic. Mbrships: Aust. Assn. of Philos.; Soc. of Aust. Authors; Brighton Hist. Soc., Vic. Address: c/o 3/8 Spring Rd., Malvern 3144, Australia.

BELL, Albert Edward, b. Belfast, UK. Head of Mechanical & Production Engineering, Bolton Institute of Technology. Educ: B.Sc., M.Sc., Queen's Univ. of Belfast. Publs: Engineering Workshop Exercises, 1957, 2nd ed., 1962; Mechanical Engineering Science, 1970. Mbrships: I.Mech.E.; I.Prod.E.; I.Mar.E. Address: 5 Baldrine Park, Baldrine, Isle of Man, UK.

BELL, Colin Alexander, pen name BELL, Colin Kane, b. 20 Oct. 1919, Gisborne, NZ. University Teacher; Lecturer. Educ: M.A.; Dip.Ed.(NZ); Adv. Dip. Tchng. Publs: Why Birds Don't Cry, 1960; Po-Ling, the Cook from Ti-Tree Point, 1963; Co-Ed., Rotorua & Waikato Water Weeds, 1967; Why Pigs Have Curly Tails, 1971. Contbr. to: Workers' Educ. Assn. Review; Educ.; The Aust. Author. Mbrships: Soc. of Authors; Aust. Soc. of Authors; PEN (Life Mbr.). Address: NZ Police Coll., Private Bag, Trentham, NZ.

BELL, Colin John, b. 1 Apr. 1938, London UK. Writer. Educ: M.A., King's Coll., Cambridge. Publs: City Fathers, 1972; Bless General Wade, 1975; National Government 1931, 1975. Contbr. to: Sunday Times; Sunday Telegraph; New Statesman; Scotsman; Daily Telegraph; Daily Mirror; etc. Address: c/o Deborah Rogers Ltd., 29 Goodge St., London W1, UK.

BELL, Geoffrey F., b. 1896, Burton-on-Trent, UK. Headmaster. Educ: M.A., Balliol Coll., Oxford. Publs: Establishing a Fruit Garden, 1963; Seven Old Testament Figures, 1968; Bishop of London's Lent Book. Address: Widford, Weydown Rd., Haslemere, Surrey, UK.

BELL, George Howard, b. 1905, Ayr, UK. Professor of Physiology. Educ: B.Sc., M.D., Univ. of Glasgow. Publs: Textbook of Physiology & Biochemistry, (co-author), 8th ed., 1972; Biochemistry & Physiology of Bone (contbng. author w. A. Ascenzi), 2nd ed., 1972. Mbrships: F.R.C.P.G.; F.R.S.E.; Physiol. Soc. Address: 80 Grove Rd., Broughty Ferry, Dundee DD5 1LB, UK.

BELL, Harry, b. 1899, Aberdeen, UK. Rector (Retired). Educ: Univs. of Aberdeen & Cambridge; M.A., Publs: Ed., English for Air Cadets; Ed., Thirteen Short Stories; Gen. Ed., Oxford Comprehensive Course; Planned Interpretation (part author); Ed., Story of English Literature. Contbr. to: Brit. Jrnl. of Educl. Psychol.; Scottish Educ. Jrnl.; Times Educl. Supplement (Scotland); etc. Address: 31 Lawhead Rd. East, St. Andrews, Fife, UK.

BELL, Margaret Elizabeth, b. 29 Dec. 1898, Thorne Bay, Alaska, USA. Writer. Educ: Annie Wright Sem., Tacoma, Wash.; Univ. of Wash., Seattle. Publs: Watch for a Tall White Sail, 1948; The Totem Casts a Shadow, 1949; Ride Out the Storm, 1951; Kit Carson, Mountain Man (biog.), 1952; Love is Forever, 1954; Daughter of Wolf House, 1957; Touched With Fire (biog.), 1961; Flight from Love, 1968; To Peril Strait, 1971. Hons: Thomas Alva Edison Fndn. Award, 1961; D.Litt., Univ. of Alaska, 1970. Address: Route 1, Box 814, Ketchikan, AK 99901, USA.

BELL, Philip Michael Hett, b. 28 May 1930, Sheffield, UK. Senior Lecturer in History. Educ: B.A., Wadham Coll., Oxford; B.Litt., St. Antony's Coll., Oxford. Publs: Disestablishment in Ireland & Wales, 1969; A Certain Eventuality: Britain & the Fall of France 1940, 1975. Contbr. to Revue d'Histoire de la Deuxième Guerre Mondiale. Mbrships: F.R.Histl.Soc. Address: 20 Mere Farm Rd., Oxton, Birkenhead, Merseyside, UK.

BELL, (Rev.) Vicars Walker, b. 1904, Redhill, UK. Vicar. Educ: Goldsmiths' Coll.; King's Coll., London Univ. Publs: On Learning the English Tongue; Little Gaddesden; To Meet Mr. Ellis; The Dodo; This Way Home; Death & the Night Watches; Death Darkens Council; Two by Day & One by Night; Death has two Doors; Death Under the Stars; Death Walks by the River; Orlando & Rosalind; Steep Ways & Narrow; (nativity play) That Night; (Ed.) Prayers for Every Day. Contbr. to: Listener; Church Times; Use of Engl.; Moral Fndns. of Citizenship; Froebel Bull; etc. Recip., M.B.E. Address: Clawton Vicarage, Holsworthy, Devon, UK.

BELLAIRS, Angus d'Albini, b. 1918, Bournemouth, UK. Herpetologist; Professor of Verterbrate Morphology. Educ: Univ. of Cambridge; Univ. Coll. Hosp., Univ. of London; M.A., D.Sc., M.R.C.S., L.R.C.P., F.I.Biol. Publs: Reptiles, 1957, 2nd ed., 1968; The World of Reptiles (w. R. Carrington), 1966; The Life of Reptiles, 2 vols., 1969. Contbr. to sci. jrnls. inclng: Jrnl. of Anatomy; Jrnl. of Zool.; Jrnl. of Linnean Soc. Mbrships: Anatom. Linnean, & Zool. Socs. Address: 7 Champion Grove, London S.E.5, UK, & Vicarage Cottage, Ramsbury, Marlborough, Wilts., UK.

BELLAIRS, George, b. 19 Apr. 1902, Heywood, Lancs., UK. Author. Educ: B.Sc., London Univ.; M.A., Manchester Univ. Publs. incl: Dead March for Penelope Blow; Half Mast for the Deemster; Corpse at the Carnival; Death in High Provence; The Tormentors; Pomeroy Deceased; Devious Murder; Fear Round About. Contbr. to: The Guardian; Wine & Food; Cheshire Life; Manx Life. Mbrships: Isle of Man Arts Coun., Soc. of Authors; Manchester Club. Recip., M.A. (Honoris Causa), Manchester Univ. Address: Gat-y-Whing, Colby, Isle of Man, UK.

BELLAMY, Joe David, b. 29 Dec. 1941, Cinn., Ohio, USA. College Professor; Editor; Critic. Educ: B.A., Antioch Coll., Ohio, 1964; M.F.A., Univ. of Iowa, 1969. Publs: Apocalypse: Dominant Contemporary Forms, 1972; The New Fiction: Interviews with Innovative American Writers, 1974; Droll & Murderous Visions: American Fiction in Our Time, 1975. Contbr. to num. lit. reviews. Mbrships. incl: N.E. Mod. Lang. Assn. (Chmn., Contemp. Lit. Sect., 1971); Coord. Coun. Lit. Mags. Hons. incl: Bridgman Award, Middlebury Coll., 1973. Address: Dept. of Engl., St. Lawrence Univ., Canton, NY 13617, USA.

BELLERBY, John Rotherford, b. 1896, York, UK. University Professor. Educ: M.A.; B.Com.; Leeds Univ.; Harvard Univ., USA. Publs: Control of Credit as a Remedy for Unemployment; Stabilization of Employment in the United States; Monetary Stability; Coalmining; A European Remedy; A Contributive Society; The Conflict of Values; (Ed.) Factory Farming. Contbr. to: Econ. Reconstruction; Agriculture & Industry: Relative Income; Agricultural

Econ. Theory & the Indian Economy; Farm Animal Welfare & World Food. Hons: Mil. Cross. Address: 19, Norham Rd., Oxford, UK.

BELLHOUSE, Alan Robert, b. 28 June 1914, Sydney, Australia. Musician; Author. Educ: B.A., Dip.Ed., Sydney Univ.; Mus.D., Indep. Universal Acad.; M.A.C.E.; F.I.B.A. Publs. incl: An Introduction to the Appreciation of Music, 1937; Classroom Discipline & Teaching, 1960; The Theory of Music for Beginners, 1967; The Symphony Orchestra for Beginners, 1967; Opera for Beginners, 1968; A History of Music for Beginners (w. D. Holland), 1970; Musical Biographies for Beginners, 1973; Ballet Music for Beginners, 1974. Mbr., Australia Soc. of Authors. Address: 67 Kameruka Rd., Northbridge 2063, NSW, Australia.

BELLOW, Saul, b. 10 June 1915, Lachine, P.Q., Can. Professor, Committee on Social Thought. Educ: Univ. of Chgo., 1933-35; B.S., Northwestern Univ., 1937; Univ. of Wis., 1937. Publs. incl: (novels) The Victim, 1945; Henderson the Rain King, 1959; Herzog, 1964; Mr. Sammler's Planet, 1970; Mosby's Memoirs & Other Stories, 1969; The Wen (play), 1967; The Future of the Moon, 1970. Mbrships: Fellow, Acad. for Policy Study, 1966; Nat. Inst. of Arts & Letters. Hons: Nat. Book Award, 1954, 1965, 1971; D.Litt., Northwestern Univ., 1962, Bard Coll., 1963. Address: Committee on Social Thought, University of Chicago, 1126 East 59th St., Chgo., IL 60637, USA.

BELOFF, Max, b. 1913, London, UK. College Principal; Fellow. Educ: Corpus Christi & Magdalen Colls., Oxford; M.A. Publs. incl: Europe & the Europeans, 1957; The Great Powers, 1959; American Federal Government, 1959; New Dimensions in Foreign Policy, 1961; The United States & the Unity of Europe, 1963; The Balance of Power, 1968; The Future of British Foreign Policy, 1969; Imperial Sunset, Vol. 1, 1969; The Intellectual in Politics, 1970. Contbr. to var. jrnls. & newspapers. Mbrships: F.B.A.; Fellow, Royal Histl. Soc.; F.R.S.A. Hons: LL.D.; D.Litt.; D.C.L. Address: University College at Buckingham, Buckingham, UK.

BELOOF, Robert Lawrence, b. 30 Dec. 1923, Wichita, Kan., USA. Professor. Educ: B.A., Friends Univ., 1946; M.A., Middlebury Coll. (Breadloaf Schl. of Engl.), 1948; M.A., 1948, Ph.D., 1954, Northwestern Univ. Publs: The One-Eyed Gunner (poems), 1957; The Performing Voice in Literature, 1966; The Oral Study of Literature (co-author), 1966; Good Poems, 1973; The Children of Venus & Mars, 1974; 2 vol. LP album, Historical Anthology of American Poetry (ed. & reader). Contbr. to var. lit. jrnls. Recip., var. scholastic & arts grants. Address: Dept. of Rhetoric, Univ. of Calif., Berkeley, CA 94720, USA.

BELTING, Natalia Maree, b. 11 July 1915, Oskaloosa, Iowa, USA. Associate Professor of History. Educ: B.S., 1936, M.A., 1937, Ph.D., 1940, Univ. Ill. Publs. incl: Kaskaskia Under the French Regime, 1948, 2nd ed., 1975; The Modern High School Curriculum, 1942; History of Caps & Gowns, 1958; The Beginnings, Champaign in the 1850s & 1860s, 1960; How Many Miles to Babylon, 1970; (children's stories) The Moon is a Crystal Ball, 1952; The Long-Tailed Bear, 1961; Winter's Eve, 1969; Whirlwind is a Ghost Dancing, 1974. Contbr. to num. histl. & acad. publs., book reviews. Mbr., Authors' Guild. Hons. incl: Nomination of Whirlwind is a Ghost Dancing for 1974 Caldecott & Newberry Awards. Address: 309 Gregory Hall, Univ. Ill., Urbana, IL, 61801, USA.

BEMBERG, George, b. 30 Sept. 1915, Buenos Aires, Argentina. Author. Educ: B.A., Paris Univ., 1934; M.A., Harvard Univ., 1941. Publs: La Vie Absente, 1948; L'Innocence Americaine, 1948; Fils du Pays, 1948; Quatre Mains, 1953; The American Abel & His Brother Cain, 1966; New York, 1973. Contbr. to US, French jrnls. Address: 20 rue du Dragon, Paris 75006, France.

BENAWA, Abdul Raouf, b. 1913. Writer; Administrator. Publs. incl: Women in Afghanistan; Pusthu Songs: De Ghanamo Wazhai; A Survey of Pushtoonistan; Rahman Baba; Pir mohammad-Kakar; Khosh-hal Khan se Wai; Pushtoo Killi, vol. 4; Kazim Khan-e-Shaida; I-Zoor gonhgar (play); Ishtebah (play); Kari bar asal (play); Aashyanae aqab (play); Zarang (play); Chaoki der khater (play); Hakoomat baidar (play); num. transls. Contbr. to mags. & radio. Address: Afghan Embassy, Cairo, Egypt.

BENCHLEY, Peter B(radford), b. 8 May 1940, NYC, USA. Writer; Journalist. Educ: Phillips Exeter Acad., 1953-57; A.B. (cum laude), Harvard Univ., 1961. Publs:

Time & a Ticket, 1964; (jvnle.) Jonathan Visits the White House, 1964. Contbr. to: Holiday; New Yorker; Diplomat; Moderator; Vogue; N.Y. Herald-Tribune. Agent: Ashley Famous Agency, Inc. Address: 1 West 67th St., N.Y., NY 10023, USA.

BENDINER, Robert, b. 15 Dec. 1909, Pitts., Pa., USA. Writer. Educ: CUNY. Publs: The Riddle of the State Department, 1942; White House Fever, 1960; Obstacle Course on Capitol Hill, 1964; Just around the Corner, 1967; The Politics of Schools, 1969; The Strenuous Decade (Ed., w. Daniel Aaron), 1970. Contbr. to: N.Y. Times Mag.; Harper's; Horizon Et Al; etc. Mbrships: Pres., Soc. of Mag. Writers, 1964; Coffee House Club. Hons: Benjamin Franklin Mag. Award, 1955; Salzburg Lectr. Seminar in Am. Studies, 1956; Guggenheim Fellowship, 1962. Mbr., Editorial Bd., N.Y. Times. Address: 45 Central Pkwy., Huntington, NY 11743, USA.

BENEDETTA, Mary, b. 1 Feb. 1909, Leeds, Yorks., UK. Journalist. Publs: The Street Markets of London, 1936; A Girl in Print, 1937; Marriage Bureau, 1938. Contbr. to: Woman & Home; Woman's Weekly; Homes & Gardens; film scripts for BBC TV. Mbr., Inst. of Jrnlsts. Hon: Book chosen for Paris Exhibition, 1936. Address: 14 Pelham Place, London SW7 2NH.

BENEDETTI, Mario, b. 14 Sept. 1920, Paso de los Toros, Tacuarembo. Writer. Educ: Colegio Aleman. Publs. incl: Ida y Vuelta (play), 1958; La Tregua (fiction), 1963; Literatura uruguaya siglo XX (essays), 1963; Gracias por el Fuego (fiction), 1965; Poemas del Hoyporhoy, 1965; Inventario (poems), 1965; Contra los puentes levadizos (poems), 1966; A ras de sueño (poems), 1967; La muerte y otras sorpresas (fiction), 1968; Sobre artes y oficios (essays), 1968. Contbr. to var. newspapers & jrnls. Address: Velsen 4543, Montevideo, Uruguay.

BENEDICT, Stewart Hurd, b. 27 Dec. 1924. Mineola, N.Y., USA. Writer; Editor. Educ: A.B., Drew Univ.; M.A., Johns Hopkins Univ.; N.Y. Univ. Publs. incl: A Teacher's Guide to Modern Drama, 1967; A Teacher's Guide to Poetry, 1969; One Day in the Life of Ivy Dennison (play), 1969; A Teacher's Guide to Jonathon Livingston Seagull (booklet), 1973; Ed., Tales of Terror & Suspense, 1963, The Crime-Solvers, 1966; Ed., Revision of Harper's English Grammar. Contbr. to profl. jrnls. & textbooks; Author, over 250 book reviews for Publishers Weekly; Reviewer, theatre & books, The Jersey Jrnl. newspaper, 1964-70. Address: Apt. 4-A, 27 Washington Square, N.Y., NY 10011, USA.

BENEDICTUS, David Henry, b. 1938, London, UK. Writer. Educ: Balliol Coll., Oxford; Iowa State Univ., USA; B.A. Publs: The Fourth of June, 1962; You're a Big Boy Now, 1963; This Animal is Mischievous, 1965; Hump or Bone by Bone Alive, 1967; The Guru & the Golf Club, 1969. Contbr. to: Daily Express; Today; Vogue; Town; Sunday Telegraph; Observer; Plays & Players; Spectator; Queen Mag. Mbrships: PEN; New Arts Theatre Club. Address: Flat 5, 14 The Paragon, London SE3, UK.

BENEDIKT, Michael, b. 26 May 1937, NYC, USA. Writer. Educ: B.A., N.Y. Univ., 1957; M.A., Columbia Univ., 1961. Publs: The Body, 1968; Sky, 1970; Mole Notes, 1971; Ed., Theatre Experiment, 1967; Ed. & Transl., Modern French Theatre, 1964; Post-War German Theatre, 1967; Ring Around the World: Selected Poems of Jean L'Anselme, 1967; Modern Spanish Theatre, 1968; 22 Poems of Robert Desnos, 1971; Surrealism: Poetry, 1974. Contbr. to num. poetry jrnls. Mbrships: MLA; Wordsworth Circle. Hons: Guggenheim Fellowship for Poetry, 1969; Bess Hokin Award, 1969; Nat. Endowment for the Arts, 1969. Address: 315 West 98th Street, N.Y., NY 10025, USA.

BENFIELD, Derek, b. 11 Mar. 1926, Bradford, Yorks., UK. Actor; Writer. Educ: Royal Acad. of Dramatic Art, London. Publs: (plays) The Young in Heart, 1953; Champagne for Breakfast, 1954; The Way the Wind Blows, 1954; Wild Goose Chase, 1956; Running Riot, 1958; Out of Thin Air, 1961; Fish out of Water, 1963; Down to Brass Tacks, 1964; Third Party Risk, 1964; The Party, 1964; Post Horn Gallop, 1965; Murder for the Asking, 1967; Off the Hook, 1970; A Bird in the Hand, 1973. Mbr., Exec. Comm., League of Dramatists. Address: 4 Berkeley Rd., Barnes, London, S.W. 13, UK.

BENGTSSON, Gun Klara Maria, pen name GRB, b. 10 Dec. 1929, Linneryd, Sweden. Literary Critic; Translator;

Secondary Education Teacher. Educ: M.A. Publs: over 120 transls. of novels & plays from Engl., French, German, Danish & Norwegian (w. N. A. Bingtsson), 1954—. Contbr. to: Sydvenska Dagbladet. Mbrships: Sweden Union of Authors; Fédération Internationale des Traducteurs. Hons: Swedish Authors' Fund Award for Lit. merit, 1965; Malmö County Council, Cultural Award, 1968. Address: Box 21, 240 12, Torna Hällestad, Sweden.

BENITEZ DE CASTRO, Cecilio, pen names, TRIMALCIÓN, Fidelio; GRABB, Cesar, b. 24 June 1917, Ramales de la Victoria, Santander, Spain. Author; Editor of El Economista, Buenos Aires; Journalist; Lawyer. Educ: Licentiate Law, Univ. Barcelona, Spain; Univ. La Plata, Argentina. Publs. incl: Huracán sobre Asia, 1940; Los Días estan Contados, 1944; Historia de una Noche de Nieve, 1950; La Ciudad Sagrada (Sociologia de la Historia), 1954; La Iluminada, 1958; Sexy Bar, 1970; El Valle del Cuerno de Oro, 1974; also 10 films & 3 stage adaptations from own works. Contbr. to: The Economist; Vie Française; etc. Mbrships. incl: Auto Club, Argentina. Hons. incl: Losada Int. Novel Prize, 1958. Address: Suipacha 858 1ºD, Buenos Aires, Argentina.

BENIUC, Mihai, b. 20 Nov. 1907, Sebish, Arad, Romania. Writer; Professor of Psychology. Educ: Ph.D., Univ. of Cluj. Publs. incl: (verse) Songs of Desolation, 1938; New Songs, 1940; Poems, 1943; Colours of the Autumn, 1962; (prose) On the Edge of the Knife, 1959; Stopped Explosion, 1971; (criticism) Our Poetry, 1956; Mason Manole, 1959; The Road of Poetry, 1972; (Science) Learning & Intelligence, 1934; Animal Intelligence, 1970. Contbr. to: Igaz Szo; Utunk; etc. Mbrships. incl: Writers' Union (Chmn., 1962-65). Acad. of Romania. Hons: State Prizes, 1951, 1954; Order of Hero of Socialist Labour, 1971. Address: Strada Gradina Bordei 51, Bucharest, Romania.

BENJAMIN, Hiram B., b. 4 July 1901, Kolomia, Austria-Hungary. Surgeon; Professor. Educ: B.S., Univ. of Buffalo, N.Y., 1925; M.D., 1930, M.S., 1949, Marquette Univ., Milwaukee, Wis. Contbr. of about 212 papers to sci. jrnls. inclng: Am. Jrnl. of Surg.; Revue Canadienne de Biol.; Mil. Surg.; Annals of Surg.; Am. Jrnl. Gastroenterol.; Geriatrics; Am. Jrnl. Proctol. Mbrships. incl: Am. Med. Writers Assn.; Fellow, Am. Coll. of Chest Physns. Recip., sev. hons. Address: 6168 Washington Circle, Wauwatosa, WI, USA.

BENNETT, Alan, b. 9 May 1934, Leeds, UK. Author. Educ: Exeter Coll., Oxford. Publs: Beyond the Fringe (co-author), 1963; Forty Years On, 1969; Getting On, 1972; Habeas Corpus, 1973. Mbr. & Pres., Settle & Dist. Civic Soc. Hons: Evening Standard Awards, 1962, 1969, 1972. Address: c/o Michael Linnit, 113-117 Wardour Street, London W1, UK.

BENNETT, Charles Edward, b. 2 Dec. 1910, Canton, N.Y., USA. Member of United States House of Representatives. Educ: B.A., Dr. Juris, Univ. Fla., USA, 1934. Publs: Laudonniere & Fort Caroline, 1964; Settlement of Florida, 1968; Southernmost Battlefields of the Revolution, 1970; Congress & Conscience, 1970; Three Voyages, 1974. Contbr. to: Ency. Americana; Saturday Evening Post; Fla. Histl. Quarterly. Mbrships. incl: Am. Bar Assn. Hons. incl: H.H.D., Univ. Tampa, Fla., 1951; LL.D., Jacksonville Univ., 1972. Address: 2113 Rayburn Building, Wash. DC, USA.

BENNETT, Charles Moon, b. 1899, Canterbury, Kent. Author. Publs: Hereward the Wake; Pedro of the Black Death; Mutiny Island; A Buccaneer's Log; With Morgan on the Main; Tim Kane's Treasure; Red Pete the Ruthless; Rivals of Camperdown School; Camperdown Captains; Easy Mathematics; Civic English; Spell, Speak & Write; Happy English; Read & Make; Masters & Masterpieces; You & Your World; P.T.O. English Series; Captain Shrimp; Meet the Magnets; Find the Treasure; A Most Amazing Property-Box; Real Life English; Call of the Pipe. Address: 106 Clay Hill, Enfield, Middlesex, UK.

BENNETT, Donald Clifford Tyndall, b. 1910, Toowoomba, Australia. Managing Director, British South American Airways; Air Vice Marshal, R.A.F.(retired); A.O.C. Pathfinder Force, R.A.F. Bomber Command, 1939-45. Publs: Complete Air Navigator, 1935, 7th ed., 1968; Air Mariner, 1937, 2nd ed., 1943; Freedom from War, 1945; Pathfinder, 1958; Let's Try Democracy. Mbrships: F.R.A.S.; Royal Aero Club; UN Assn. GB

(Chmn.). Hons: C.B.; C.B.E.; D.S.O. Address: c/o Royal Aero Club, 30 Pall Mall, London SW1, UK.

BENNETT, Ethel Mary Granger, b. 11 Nov. 1891, Shroton, Dorset, UK. Writer; University Teacher; Housewife. Educ: B.A., Victoria Coll., Univ. of Toronto, Can.; Ph.D., Univ. of Wis., USA. Publs: Land for Their Inheritance, 1955; A Straw in the Wind, 1958; Short of the Glory, 1960 (all novels). Contbr. to: Dictionary of Can. Biog., Vol. I, 1966; The Clear Spirit, 1967; var. children's mags. Mbrships: Can. Authors' Assn.; Toronto Heliconian Club. Recip., Ryerson Fiction Award, 1960. Address: 27 Thorncliffe Park Dr., Apt. 504, Toronto, Can. M4H 1J2.

BENNETT, Geoffrey Martin, pen name (for fiction) SEA-LION, b. 7 June 1909, London, UK. Retired Naval Officer. Educ: Royal Naval Coll., Dartmouth. Publs. incl: Coronel & the Falklands, 1962; Cowan's War, 1963; The Battle of Jutland, 1964; 'Charlie B' (biog.), 1968; Naval Battles of the First World War, 1968; Battle of the River Plate, 1972; Loss of the 'Prince of Wales' & 'Repulse', 1973; (as Sea-Lion) 16 naval thrillers inclng. the Desmond Drake series, 1946-62. Contbr. to: Hist. of RN; Hist. Today; Int. Hist. Mag.; Hist. of Ships; other naval jrnls. Mbrships incl: Fellow, Royal Histl. Soc. Recip., D.S.C., 1944. Agent: Curtis Brown Ltd. Address: Stage Coach Cottage, 57 Broad St., Ludlow, Salop, UK.

BENNETT, Jack Arthur Walter, b. 1911, Auckland, NZ. University Professor of English. Educ: Auckland Univ. Coll.; Oxford Univ.; M.A.; D.Phil.(Oxon.); M.A.(Cantab.). Publs: The Parlement of Foules, 1957; Chaucer's Book of Fame, 1968; Gower, 1968; Piers Plowman, 1972; Chaucer at Oxford & Cambridge, 1974. Ed., Medium Aevum. Contbr. to: Times Lit. Supplement; Review of Engl. Studies; etc. Mbr., Coun., Early Engl. Text Soc. Address: 10 Adams Rd., Cambridge, UK.

BENNETT, John Godolphin, b. 1897, London, UK. Director & Consultant, Institute for Comparative Study History, Philosophy & the Sciences; Principal, International Academy for Continuous Education, Educ: Royal Mil. Acad., Woolwich; Schl. of Mil. Engrng., Chatham; Schl. of Oriental Studies, London Univ. Publs: The Crisis in Human Affairs, 1948; What are we Living For?, 1949; Dramatic Universe, vols. I-IV, 1957-63; Concerning Subud, 1958; Christian Mysticism & Subud, 1961; Witness, 1962; Gurdjieff: A Very Great Enigma, 1963; A Spiritual Psychology, 1962; Gurdjieff: Making a New World, 1973; Is There Life on the Earth?, 1974. Contbr. to: Jrnl. Inst. of Fuel; Broken Coal; Proceedings Royal Soc.; Unified Field Theory. Agent: Turnstone Books Ltd. Address: Sherborne House, Sherborne, Glos., UK.

BENNETT, Josephine Waters, b. 15 Jan. 1899, Lakeside, Ohio, USA. Teacher & Researcher; Writer. Educ: B.A., 1924, M.A., 1925, Ph.D., 1936, Ohio State Univ. Publs: The Evolution of The Faerie Queene, 1942, 1960; The Rediscovery of Sir John Mandeville, 1954; Measure for Measure as Royal Entertainment, 1966. Contbr. to: Studies in Philol.; Speculum; Mod. Philol.; Jrnl. of Engl. & Germanic Philol.; Shakespeare Quarterly; Mod. Lang. Quarterly; Mod. Lang. Notes, etc. Mbrships: Renaissance Soc. of Am. (Fndg. Comm., 1st Exec. Sec., Pres.); MLA (Chmn., sev. grps. & sects.); Mediaeval Acad.; AAUW, etc. Recip., acad. schlrships. & fellowships. Address: 509 Dayton St., Sandwich, IL 60548, USA.

BENNETT, William Robert, b. 11 July 1921, Durban, Natal, S. Africa. Author. Publs. incl: Suicide Sortie, 1963; War Wings, 1963; High Conflict, 1965; Fighter Pilot, 1965; Bandits Above, 1965; Night/Fighter, 1965; Angels Zero, 1965; Top Cover, 1965; The Proud Eagles, 1965; Wings Over Malta, 1965; Fighter/Bomber, 1965; Skybolt, 1966; The Devil's Angels, 1966; Flak Alley, 1966; Flames in the Sky, 1967; High Fury, 1967; The Man from Checkmate, 1971; Dossier on a Mantis, 1972. Contbr. to Aust. mags. & newspapers. Mbrships: United Serv. Club; Aust. Soc. of Authors. Address: 94 Solar St., Coorparoo, Brisbane, Qld., Australia 4151.

BENNETT-ENGLAND, Rodney Charles, b. 16 Dec. 1936, Romford, UK. Writer & Journalist. Publs: Dress Optional — The Revolution in Menswear, 1967; As Young as you Look, 1970; Ed., Inside Journalism, 1967. Contbr. to: Faith in Fleet Street, 1967; Sunday Express; Evening Standard; Life; Penthouse; Club Int.; Men Only; etc. Mbrships: V.P., Inst. of Jrnlsts., 1967-70, Chmn., London Dist., 1964-67; Chmn., Nat. Coun. for the Trng. of Jrnlsts., 1968-69; Soc. of Authors. Hons: I.C.I. Trophy for First

Fashion Writer of the Yr., Clothing Inst., 1967; Hon. mbr., Pi Delta Epsilon, USA; Freeman, City of London. Address: 3 Oakley St., Chelsea, London SW3 5NN, UK.

BENNING, (Barbara) Lee Edwards, b. 13 July 1934, Chgo., Ill., USA. President & Owner, Bird Mail Advertising Services Co. Educ: B.Sc., Coll. of Home Econs., Pa. State Univ. Publs: How to Bring Up a Child Without Spending a Fortune, 1975; What Every Mother Should Know About Allergies, forthcoming. Mbrships. incl: Corres. Sec., Phila. Chapt., Nat. Home Fashions League; Phila. Chapt., Fashion League. Address: Wingover Farm, Bethlehem Pike, R.D. No. 1, Ambler, PA 19002, USA.

BENOIT, Emile, b. 14 July 1909, NYC, USA. Professor; Author. Educ: B.A., 1932, M.A., 1933, Harvard Univ.; Ph.D., 1938. Publs: Europe at Sixes & Sevens, 1961; Disarmament & the Economy, 1962; Disarmament & World Economic Interdependence, 1966; Defense & Economic Growth in Developing Countries, 1973. Contbr. to: Am. Econ. Review; Int. Dev. Review; Am. Sociol. Review; Jrnl. of Int. Affairs; Jrnl. of World Bus.; N.Y. Times Mag. Sect.; etc. Mbrships: Ed. Advsry. Bds., Jrnl. of Conflict Resolution & Arms Control & Nat. Security. Address: Elka Park Rd., Elka Park, Greene Country, N.Y., NY 12427, USA.

BENOIT, Maurice Pierre, b. 3 Aug. 1906, Nancy, France. Roman Catholic Priest; Professor of New Testament & of Topography of Jerusalem. Educ: B.Sc. & B.Phil., Dominican Coll., Tournai, Belgium; Th.M., 1958. Publs: Epîtres de la Captivité, 1949, 3rd ed. 1959; Evangile selon Saint Matthieu, 1950, 4th ed. 1972; Bible de Jérusalem, 1956, 2nd ed. 1973; Exégèse & Théologie, 3 vols., 1961-68; Passion & Résurrection du Seigneur, 1966. Contbr. to: La Somme Théologique, 1947; Revue Biblique. Mbrships. incl: Pontifical Biblical Commn.; Past Pres., Studiorum Novi Testamenti Soc.; Soc. of Biblical Lit.; Cath. Biblical Assn. Hons. incl: D.D., Theol. Fac., Munich, W. Germany, 1972; Burkitt Medal for Biblical Studies. Address: French Biblical & Archaeol. Schl., Nablus Rd. 6, P.O. Box 19053, 91019 Jerusalem, Israel.

BENSON, Constantine Walter, b. 2 Feb. 1909, Trull, Taunton, Somerset, UK. Ornithologist. Educ: M.A., Magdalene Coll., Cambridge. Publs: A Check List of the Birds of Nyasaland, 1953; The Birds of Zambia (w. R. K. Brooke, R. J. Dowsett & M. P. Stuart Irwin), 1971. Contbr. to num. ornithol. jrnls. Mbrships: British Ornithologists' Union (VP, 1966-69); British Ornithologists' Club (Ed., Bull., 1969-74). Hons: British Ornithologists' Union Medal, 1960; O.B.E., 1964. Address: Dept. of Zoology, Downing St., Cambridge, UK.

BENSON, David, b. 25 July 1929, Johannesburg, S. Africa. Journalist; Ghost Writer. Educ: King Edward VII Schl., Johannesburg, S. Africa. Author, sev. books ghosted for leading personalities. Contbr. to: John Bull; Today; Woman; Sunday Times Colour Mag. Motoring Ed., Daily Express. Mbrships: Guild of Motoring Writers; Sportswriters Assn. Address: 42 Clarges Mews, Off Curzon St., Mayfair, London, W.1, UK.

BENSON, (Dorothy) Mary, b. 9 Dec. 1919, Pretoria, S. Africa. Author (biog., hist., novels, radio plays). Publs: Tshekedi Khama, 1960; The African Patriots, 1963; South Africa: The Struggle for a Birthright, 1966; At the Still Point, 1969. Contbr. to: London Mag.; Yale Theatre; New Statesman; Spectator. Mbr., Writers' Guild. Address: 34 Langford Court, London NW8, UK.

BENSON, Frank Atkinson, b. 1921, Grange-over-Sands, UK. Professor of Electronic & Electrical Engineering; Pro-Vice-Chancellor, University of Sheffield. Educ: B.Eng.; M.Eng., Univ. of Liverpool; Ph.D.; D.Eng., Univ. of Sheffield. Publs: Voltage Stabilizers; Voltage Stabilized Supplies. Electrical Engineering Problems with Solutions; Problems in Electronics with Solutions. Contbr. to: Electronic & Radio Engr.; Proceedings Inst. of Elec. Engrs.; Electronic Engrng.; Jrnl. of Sci. Instruments; Transaction of Illuminating Engrng. Soc.; etc. Address: 64 Grove Rd., Sheffield S7 2GZ, UK.

BENSON, Martin, b. 10 Aug. 1918, London, UK. Film Writer; Film Director; Actor. Mbrships: Soc. of Film & Television Arts; Savage Club. Hons: Merit Award, Rome Festival, 1966; Bronze Award, N.Y. Festival, 1970; Gold Award, Milan Festival, 1970; Silver Award, N.Y. Festival, 1971; 2 Silver Awards, N.Y. Festival, 1973; Bronze Award, N.Y. Festival, 1974. Address: Sebright House, Markyate, Herts., UK.

BENSON, Stephana Vere, b. 10 Feb. 1909, Bromley, Kent, UK. Writer; Ornithologist; Illustrator. Publs: Observer's Book of Birds, 1937; The Greatest of These, 1939; The Child's Own Book of Prayers & Hymns, 1940; Birds at Sight, 1943; Spotting British Birds, 1951; Birds of Lebanon & the Jordan Area, 1970. Mbrships. incl: Fndr. & Hon. Sec., Bird Lovers League; Brit. Ornithol. Union; Brit. Ornithol. Club; Brit. Trust for Ornithol.; Fellow, Royal Soc. for Protection of Birds; Patron, Int. Coun. for Bird Preservation; Wild Fowl Trust. Address: Fairbourne, 9 Great Austins, Farnham, Surrey, UK.

BENSTOCK, Bernard, b. 23 Mar. 1930, NYC, USA. Professor of English; Author. Publs: Joyce-again's Wake: An Analysis of Finnegans Wake, 1965; Sean O'Casey, 1970; Approaches to Ulysses: Ten Essays (co-ed.), 1970. Contbr. to: James Joyce Quarterly; Southern Review; Dublin Mag.; Forum; Contemporary Lit., etc. Mbrships. incl: James Joyce Fndn. Ltd.; Bd. of Trustees, ibid, 1967—, Pres., 1971-75; MLA of Am.; Midwest MLA; Sect. Chmn., ibid, 1969; Am. Comm. Irish Studies. Hon. Fulbright Lectr. in Am. Lit., Univ. of Tabriz, Iran, 1961-62. Address: Dept. of English, University of Illinois, Urbana, IL 61801, USA.

BENTLEY, James William Benedict, pen names NOSTALGIA; CLAUGHTON-JAMES, James, b. 1914, Hadley Wood, Herts., UK. Author. Publs. (as Nostalgia): The Years of the Locust; Lord of the Fens; The Undone Years; Lost Hearts; The Children of the Sun; The Vineyards of Engedi; Indian Summer; The Kingdoms; (as James Claughton-James): Mr. Tremayne's Statement. Contbr. to: Poetry Review; Living Church; Breakthru. Poem (in German), Weltkrieg und Vaterland, housed in archives of Bibliothek für Zeitgeschichte, Weltkriegsbücherei, Stuttgart. Mbrships: Royal Asiatic Soc.; Royal Soc. Antiquaries of Ireland; Soc. of Antiquaries of Scotland; Soc. of Authors; Japan Soc. Address: 151 Firhill Rd., Bellingham, London SE6, UK.

BENTLEY, Nicolas Clerihew, b. 14 June 1907, London, UK. Author; Publisher; Artist. Educ: Heatherley Schl. of Art. Publs. incl: The Tongue-Tied Canary; The Floating Dutchman; Third Party Risk; Ballet-Hoo; How Can You Bear to be a Human; A choice of Ornaments; A Version of the Truth; The Victorian Scene; Golden Sovereigns; Tales from Shakespeare; The Events of that Week. Mbrships: F.S.I.A. Address: 7 Hobury St., London SW10, UK.

BENTLEY, Phyllis Eleanor, b. 1894, Halifax, UK. Author. Educ: B.A. Publs: Inheritance; Sleep in Peace; The Rise of Henry Morcar; Quorum; Noble in Reason; Crescendo; A Man of His Time; Ring in the New; Panorama; Love & Money; (biography) O Dreams O Destinations; The Brontës; The Art of Narrative; The Pennine Weaver; The Brontës & Their World. Contbr. to: Yorks. Post; Homes & Gardens; Listener; BBC. Mbrships: Authors' Soc.; PEN; Nat. Book League; Engl. Speaking Union. Hons: O.B.E.; F.R.S.L.; Litt.D. Address: 8 The Grange, Warley, Halifax, Yorks., UK.

BENTON, Kenneth Carter, b. 4 Mar. 1909, Sutton Coldfield, UK. Retired Diplomat; Writer. Educ: B.A., London Univ.; Univs. of Vienna & Florence. Publs: Twenty-fourth Level, 1969; Sole Agent, 1970; Spy in Chancery, 1972; Craig & the Jaguar, 1973; Death on the Appian Way, 1974; Craig & the Tunisian Tangle, 1974; Craig & the Midas Touch, 1975. Contbr. to: Peru's Revolution from Above, 1969; Conflict Studies; Winter's Crimes, 1974. Mbrships. incl: Chmn., Crime Writers Assn. 1974-75; Soc. of Authors; Travellers' Club; Nat. Book League. Recip., C.M.G., 1966. Address: Vine House, Appledore, Kent, UK.

BENTON, Peggie, b. Valetta, Malta. Writer. Educ: Dip., Neuchâtel & Madrid Univs. Publs: Finnish Food, 1960; Cooking with Pomiane, 1961; Meat at Any Price (co-author), 1963; Chicken & Game (co-author), 1964; Fish for All Seasons, 1966; Peterman (under pen name), 1966; Eggs, Milk & Cheese, 1971; One Man Against the Drylands (under pen name), 1972. Contbr. to: Forum World Features; Ideal Home Mag. Mbr., Crime Writers Assn. Hons: Bronze Medal, Darmstadt, 1963; Bronze Medal, Frankfurt Book Fair, 1966. Address: Vine House, Appledore, Ashford, Kent TN26 2BU, UK.

BENTOV, Shmuel Paul, pen names BEN, P., AWI-DAFNA, S. P., RON, Paul A., b. 17 June 1929, Vienna, Austria. Journalist. Author, 144 Hours of Fate (poems of the 6-day war), 1972. Contbr. to Al Hamishmar, Israel. Address: 94 Weitzmann Str., P.O. Box 244, Nahariya 22-100, Israel.

BENY, Roloff, b. 7 Jan. 1924, Medicine Hat, Alta., Can. Photographer; Author. Educ: B.A., Trinity Coll., Toronto; M.A., M.F.A., State Univ. of Iowa, USA; M.A., Columbia Univ. & N.Y. Univ. Publs. incl: The Thrones of Earth & Heaven, 1958; A Time of Gods, 1962; Pleasure of Ruins, 1964; To Everything there is a Season, 1967; Japan in Colour, 1967; India, 1969; Island: Ceylon, 1970; In Italy, 1974; Persia: Bridge of Turquoise, forthcoming. Contbr. to: Status; Realities; Vogue; etc. Mbrships. incl: Authors' Guilds, UK & USA; Assoc., Royal Can. Acad. of Arts. Hons. incl: LL.D., Univ. of Lethbridge, 1972. Address: Lungotevere Ripa 3B, Rome, Italy.

BENZO-MESTRE, Miguel, b. 6 July 1922, Madrid, Spain. Priest; University Professor. Educ: D.Theol., Gregorian Univ., Rome. Publs: La pura naturaleza humana en la teología de Suárez, 1955; Teología para universitarios, 1961; Los sacramentos de la Eucaristís, Orden y Penitencia, 1965; Pastoral y laicado a la luz del Vaticano II, 1966; Moral para universitarios, 1967; Sobre el sentido de la vida, 1971. Contbr. to: Ya (newspaper); Vida Nueva (mag.). Address: Calle Sta. Cruz de Marcenado 13, Madrid 8, Spain.

BERCK, Martin G., b. 5 Feb. 1928, NYC, USA. Journalist. Educ: B.A., N.Y. Univ.; M.S., Cert., Grad. Studies in Jrnlsm. & Behavioral Scis., Columbia Univ. Contbr. to: Newsday (Nat. & U.N. Corres.); N.Y. Herald Tribune (former Nat. Ed. & Corres.); N.B.C. News (former writer-editor-producer); Reporter Mag.; M.D. Mag.; L.I. Mag.; Book Ed. Mbrships: Overseas Press Club; UN Corres. Assn.; Columbia Univ. & N.Y. Univ. Fac. Clubs. Hons. incl: Russell Sage Fellow. Address: 604 Ramapo Rd., Teaneck, NJ 07666, USA.

BERCOVITCH, Sacvan, b. 4 Oct. 1933, Montreal, Can. Professor of English & American Literature. Educ: B.A., Sir George Williams Coll., 1961; Ph.D., Claremont Grad. Schl., 1965. Publs: Horologicals to Chronometricals, 1970; Typology & American Literature, 1972; The Puritan Origins of the American Self, 1974; The American Puritan Imagination, 1974. Contbr. to: Jrnl. of Hist. of Ideas; Am. Lit.; Am. Quarterly; New England Quarterly; num. other profl. jrnls. Mbrships. incl: Nat. Endowment for Humanities (Nat. Bd.); Inst. Early Am. Hist. & Culture (Exec. Coun.); MLA. Hons. incl: Guggenheim Fellowship, 1969-70; Am. Coun. Learned Socs. Fellowship, 1971-72. Address: 415 Hamilton Hall, Columbia Univ., N.Y., NY, USA.

BERCZELI, A. Károly, b. 7 July 1904, Szeged, Hungary. Writer. Educ: Dr.Phil. Publs. incl: (poems) Mise, 1926; Ádám bukása, 1931; Julius, 1938; Höskor, 1942; Nyári éj, 1971; (novels) Mindenkiért, 1928; Mária próféta, 1936; Két pásztor, 1947; Kék ég alatt, 1958; Hullámsir, 1974; (plays) Fiatalok, 1933; Tigrisek, 1933; Sámson és Delila, 1935; Fekete Mária, 1937; Uram irgalmazz! , 1938; also var. transls. into Hungarian lang. Mbr., Hungarian Writers' Assn. Address: Margareta 11, 1126 Budapest, Hungary.

BERE, Rennie Montague, b. 1907, Bere Regis, Dorset, UK. Director & Chief Warden, Uganda National Parks (Retired); C.M.G. Educ: M.A., Selwyn Coll., Cambridge. Publs: The African Elephant; The Way to the Mountains of the Moon; Antelopes; Animals in an African National Park; The Life of Antelopes; Wild Mammals of Uganda; Birds in an African National Park; Crocodile's Eggs for Supper; Wildlife In Cornwall; Mammals of East & Central Africa. Contbr. to: Oryx; Alpine Jrnl.; Times Supplements. Mbr., Alpine Club. Agent: David Highams Assocs. Address: West Cottage, Bude Haven, Bude, Cornwall EX23 8LH, UK.

BEREDAY, George Z. F., 15 July 1920, Warsaw, Poland. Professor of Comparative Education, Columbia Univ. Educ: B.Sc., London Univ., 1944; B.A., M.A., Oxford Univ., UK, 1953; Ph.D., Harvard Univ., 1953. Publs. incl: Liberal Traditions in Education, 1958; Politics of Soviet Education, 1960; American Education Through Japanese Eyes, 1973; The Universities for All, 1973. Ed. Comp. Educ. Review; World Year Book of Educ.; Columbia Comp. Educ. Studies; Contbr. to sev. jrnls. Mbr: Schl. of Int. Affairs; Dir., Centre for Educ. in Indl. Nationa, Columbia Univ. Hons: Am. Heritage Award; Winifred Fisher Adult Educ. Award. Address: 106 Morningside Dr., N.Y., NY 10027, USA.

BÉRES, Attila, b. 6 May 1946, Budapest, Hungary. Librarian. Educ: Coll. of Libnship., Budapest; Aesthetics studies, Univ. of Marxism-Leninism, Budapest, 1975. Publs: (poetry) To be Hunted into the Garden of Eden, 1970; There's Tomorrow Already, 1974; short stories; novel, forthcoming. Contbr. to: Life & Lit.; New Writing; etc. Mbr., Hungarian Writers Assn. Address: 1144 Budapest, Füredi ùt 5/A, Hungary.

BERG, Eva Elisabet, b. 5 July 1904, Stockholm, Sweden. Author. Educ: B.A., Univ. of Stockholm. Publs: sev. novels & short stories, 1932—. Mbr., Union of Swedish Authors; Swedish Pen Club. Recip. of Novel Prize, 1939. Address: Skeppargatan 75, 11530 Stockholm, Sweden.

BERG, Irwin August, b. 9 Oct. 1913, Chicago, Ill., USA. Dean, College of Arts & Sciences; University Professor of Psychology. Educ: B.A., 1936, M.A., 1940, Ph.D., 1942, Univ. Mich. Publs: An Introduction to Clinical Psychology, 2nd ed., 1954; Developments in Objective Personality Assessment, 1959; Conformity & Deviation (w. B. M. Bass), 1961; An Introduction to Clinical Psychology, 3rd ed., 1967; Response Set in Personality Assessment, 1967. Contbr. to: Jrnl. Consulting Psychol.; Jrnl. Clinical Psychol.; Jrnl. Applied Psychol. Mbr., Am. Psychol. Assn. Address: Coll. of Arts & Sciences, Louisiana State Univ., Baton Rouge, LA 70803, USA.

BERG, Jean Horton Lietz, b. 30 May 1913, Clairton, Pa., USA. Author of Children's Books. Educ: B.S., M.A., Univ. of Pa. Publs. incl: Three Mice & a Cat, 1950; It's Fun to Peek, 1955; The Little Red Hen, 1963; Miss Tessie Tate, 1967; Next Best, 1973; Green Lady, 1973; Daniel In the Lion's Den, 1973; Saturday's Friends, 1973; All Because of Snow, 1973; The Phantom Hunter, 1974; The Tugboat Ranger, 1974; The Novaks, 1974; The Accidental Detective, 1974. Contbr. to: Ranger Rich; Jack & Jill; Humpty-Dumpty; etc. Mbrships. incl: Nat. League of Am. Pen Women; Authors' League; Authors' Guild. Hons. incl: Jr. Lit. Guild Award, 1967; Alumni Award of Merit, Univ. of Pa., 1969. Address: 207 Walnut Ave., Wayne, PA 19087, USA.

BERG, Leila, b. 1917, Salford, UK. Publs. incl: Look at Kids; Risinghill; The Train Back (w. Pat Chapman); Children's Rights (section of); Ed., Nippers; Ed., Little Nippers; (children's books) Folk Tales; My Dog Sunday; Little Pete; Adventures of Chunky; The Little Car; A Box for Benny; Fire Engine by Mistake. Address: 25 Streatham Common South, London SW16, UK.

BERG, Viola Jacobson, b. 29 Sept. 1918, Franksville, Wis., USA. Secretary; Writer; Poet. Publs. incl: The Heart of Things, 1969; Wings of Good Tidings, 1969; Harvest of the Heart, 1970; Move That Mountain, 1970; For Kindred Hearts, 1975. Contbr. to var. newspapers, anthols., etc. Mbr., Island Writers, L.I. Recip., lit. awards. Address: 5 Roosevelt Ave., Malverne, NY 11565, USA.

BERGEL, Franz, b. 13 Feb. 1900, Vienna, Austria. Emeritus Professor; Freelance Writer & Consultant. Educ: Vienna Univ.; D.Phil. Nat., Freiburg Univ. Germany; Edinburgh Univ., UK; Ph.D., D.Sc., London Univ. Publs: Experiments for Chemistry Course for Medical & Dental Students, 1931; Chemistry of Enzymes in Cancer, 1961; All about Drugs, 1970, 1971. Contbr. to num. sci. jrnls. inclng: Nature; Biochem. Jrnl.; New Sci.; etc. Mbrships. incl: F.R.S., London; F.R.S.A.; Fellow, Inst. of Biol.; F.R.I.C.; Fellow, Royal Soc. of Med.; Fellow, Chem. Soc. Hons: Lectr., Dept. of Pharmacol., Univ. Coll., London, 1946-74. Address: Magnolia Cottage, Bel Royal, Jersey, Channel Islands.

BERGER, Andrew John, b. 30 Aug. 1915, Warren, Ohio, USA. University Professor. Educ: A.B., Oberlin Coll., Ohio, 1939; M.A., 1947, Ph.D., 1950, Univ. of Mich., Ann Arbor. Publs: Fundamentals of Ornithology (w. J. Van Tyne), 1959; Bird Study, 1961; Elementary Human Anatomy, 1964; Avian Myology (w. J. C. George), 1966; Hawaiian Birdlife, 1972. Contbr. of about 100 papers to sci. jrnls. & chapts. in books. Mbrships. incl: AAAS; First VP, Wilson Ornithol. Soc., 1973-75; Fellow, Am. Ornithols. Union; VP, Hawaii Audubon Soc., 1966-68; Am. Soc. of Zools.; Int. Comm. for Avian Anatomical Nomenclature. Address: Dept. of Zool., Univ. of Hawaii, Honolulu, HI 96822, USA.

BERGER, John (Peter), b. 5 Nov. 1926, Stoke Newington, London, UK. Writer. Educ: Ctrl. Schl. of Art, Chelsea Schl. of Art, London. Publs. incl: (novels) A Painter of Our Time, 1958; The Foot of Clive, 1962; Corker's Freedom, 1964; G, 1972; (other) Permanent Red: Essays in Seeing, 1960; The Success & Failure of Picasso, 1965; A Fortunate Man: The Story of a Country Doctor, 1967; Art & Revolution: Ernst Neizvestny & the Role of the Artist in the USSR, 1969; The Moment of Cubism & Other Essays, 1969; The Look of Things (essays), 1971. Address: c/o Weidenfeld & Nicolson, 5 Winsley St., London W1, UK.

BERGER, Thomas (Louis), b. 20 July 1924, Cinn., Ohio, USA. Writer. Educ: B.A., Univ. of Cinn., 1948; Columbia Univ., N.Y., 1950-51. Publs: (novels) Crazy in Berlin, 1958; Reinhart in Love, 1962; Little Big Man, 1964; Killing Time, 1967; Vital Parts, 1970; Other People (play), 1970. Contbr. to: Playboy; Saturday Evening Post. Hons: Dial Fellowship, 1962; Western Heritage Award, 1965; Rosenthal Award, 1965. Address: c/o Harold Matson Co., 22 East 40th St., N.Y., NY 10016, USA.

BERGMAN SUCKSDORFF, Astrid, b. 17 Jan. 1927, Solna, Sweden. Author; Photographer. Publs: Micki, The Fox Cub, 1953; Chendru, The Boy & The Tiger, 1957; Ödetor pet, 1964; Tiger in Sight, 1965; The Roe Deer, 1967; Tooni, The Elephant Boy, 1970; Cranes at Lake Hornborga, 1971. Contbr. to var. hunting mags., etc. Mbr., The Swedish Union of Authors. Address: Dämman, S-54017 Lerdala, Sweden.

BERGONZI, Bernard, b. 1929, London, UK. University Professor. Educ: S.E. London Tech. Coll.; M.A., B.Litt., Wadham Coll., Oxford Univ. Publs: Descartes & the Animals, 1954; The Early H. G. Wells, 1961; Heroes' Twilight, 1965; The Situation of the Novel, 1970; T. S. Eliot, 1972; The Turn of a Century, 1973. Contbr. to: Observer; Hudson Review; New Society; Times Lit. Supplement. Agent: A. D. Peters & Co. Address: 6 Emscote Rd., Warwick, UK.

BERGSTEN, Gunilla Ulander, b. 11 Apr. 1933, Norrköping, Sweden. University Lecturer. Educ: Fil.dr., Univ. of Uppsala. Publs: Thomas Mann's Doktor Faustus. Untersuchungen zu den Quellen und zur Struktur des Romans, 1963, revised ed., 1974, Engl. ed. (Thomas Mann's "Doctor Faustus". The Sources & Structure of the Novel), 1969. Contbr. to: Världslitteraturens historia, 1973-74; Upsala Nya Tidning. Mbr., PEN, Stockholm. Address: Malma Ringväg 8, S — 752 45 Uppsala, Sweden.

BERGSTEN, Staffan, b. 12 Nov. 1932, Örebro, Sweden. University Lecturer. Educ: Fil.dr., Univ. of Uppsala. Publs: Time & Eternity. A Study in the Structure & Symbolism of T. S. Eliot's Four Quartets, 1960; Erotikern Stagnelius, 1966; Jaget och världen. Kosmiska analogier i svensk 1900-talslyrik, 1971; Östen Sjöstrand (in Engl.), 1974. Contbr. to: Världslitteraturens historia, 1973; Swedish Broadcasting Corp. Mbr., PEN, Stockholm. Address: Malma Ringväg 8, S — 752 45 Uppsala, Sweden.

BERGSTRÖM, Berit (Eva Maria), b. 11 Apr. 1942, Sölvesborg, Sweden. Writer; Psychotherapist. Educ: B.A. Publs: Dimensioner, Dissektioner (poetry), 1967; Exekutionen (novel), 1968; En Svensk Drom (novel), 1970; Brodet oct Stenarna (novel), 1973. Mbr., Swedish Authors' Union. Hons: Litteraturfrämjandet Prize, 1968; Authors' Union Prize, 1968; City of Stockholm Prize, 1968. Address: Hälsingegatan 6, 11323 Stockholm, Sweden.

BERK, Lotte, b. 1913, Cologne, Germany. Ballet Dancer. Educ: Mod. Ballet Wigman Schl. Publ: The Lotte Berk Book of Exercises, 1969. Address: 72 The Grampians, London W6, UK.

BERLYNE, Daniel Ellis, b. 25 Apr. 1924, Salford, UK. Professor of Psychology. Educ: B.A., 1947, M.A., 1949, Cambridge Univ.; Ph.D., Yale Univ., 1953. Publs: Conflict, Arousal & Curiosity, 1960; Structure & Direction in Thinking, 1965; Aesthetics & Psychobiology, 1971; Ed., Studies in the New Experimental Aesthetics, 1974. Contbr. to: reference manuals & psychol. jrnls. Mbrships. incl: Pres., Can. Psychol. Assn., 1972-73; Brit. Psychol. Soc.; Fellow, Royal Soc. of Can., 1973—; Fellow, Ctr. for Advanced Study of Behavioral Scis., 1956-57. Address: Psychol. Dept., Univ. of Toronto, Toronto M5S 1A1, Can.

BERMAN, Bruce David, b. 27 Sept. 1944, Boston, Mass., USA. Publisher. Educ: Northeastern Univ., Boston, Mass. Publs: Encyclopedia of American Shipwrecks, 1972. Contbr. to: Sightings; Sea Rsch. Soc. Jrnl.; Skin Diver Mag. Mbr., Sea Rsch. Soc. Recip., 1974 Aiga Pkg. Award of Excellence. Address: The Mariners Press Inc., Post Office Box 540, Boston, MA 02117, USA.

BERMAN, Morton, b. 21 Mar. 1924, Syracuse, NY, USA. Professor of English. Educ: A.B., Univ. of Ill., 1948;

A.M., 1950; Ph.D., 1957, Harvard Univ. Publs. incl: The Study of Literature, 1960; The Genius of the English Theater, 1962; A Dictionary of Literary, Dramatic, & Cinematic Terms, 1971; Nine Modern Classics: An Anthology of Short Novels, 1973; An Introduction to Literature, 5th ed., 1974. Mbrships: Mod. Lang. Assn. of Am.; AAUP. Hons: Ruskin Prize, 1954; Dexter Travelling Fellowship, 1954. Address: Dept. of English, Boston Univ., 236 Bay State Rd., Boston, MA 02215, USA.

BERMANT, Chaim, b. 1929, Breslev, Poland. Writer. Educ: Glasgow Univ., UK; London Schl. of Econs.; M.A., M.Sc., M.Litt. Publs: Jericho Sleep Alone, 1964; Berl Make Tea, 1965; Ben Preserve Us, 1965; Diary of an Old Man, 1966; Swinging in the Rain, 1967; Israel, 1967; Here Endeth the Lesson, 1969; Troubled Eden, 1969; Now Dowager, 1970; The Cousinhood, 1971; Roses are Blooming in Picardy, 1972; The Last Supper, 1973; The Walled Garden, 1975; Point of Arrival, 1975. Address: 18 Hill Rise, London NW11, UK.

BERNARD, Louis A., b. 3 July 1940, Granby, P.Q., Can. Agrologist; Consulting Editor. Educ: B.Sc.A., McGill Univ.; Mgmt. Dip., A. Hamilton Inst.; Jrnlsm. & Drama, Univ. du Québec. Publs: Initiatives, 1967-74; L'Agriculteur Progressif, 1970-74; Good Farming, 1970-73; Canadian Farm Equipment Dealer, 1970-73; Southam Business Publs., 1970-73. Contbr. to: La Terre de Chez Nous; Québec en Bref; Toastmasters Mag. Mbrships. incl: Assn. des Rédactuers Agricoles de Québec; Can. Farm Writers Fedn. Address: 4010 Maricourt St., Douville, St. Hyacinthe, P.Q. J2S 3S3, Can.

BERNARD, Oliver Owen, b. 1925, Chalfont St. Peter, Bucks., UK. English & Drama Teacher. Educ: Goldsmith's Coll. Publs: Country Matters (poems), 1962; Ed. & Transl., Rimbaud, 1962; Transl. (in verse), Apollinaire, Selected Poems. Contbr. to: Encounter; Poetry, Chgo.; Botteghe Oscure; Listener; Times Lit. Supplement. Mbr., Nat. Assn. Drama Advsrs. Address: The Walnut Tree, Banham, Norwich NR16 2HB, UK.

BERNFELD, Bella R. (Mrs. Myer Bernfeld), b. 16 July 1917, Nemeerov, USSR. Teacher; Writer. Educ: B.A., M.Ed., D.Ph., Univ. of Pitts.; Grad., Conservatorio Municipal de Música, Cuba. Publs: Development of a Culturally Enriched Curriculum for Second Year High School Spanish (dissertation), 1973; The Immigrant (radio play). Mbrships: NEA; Pa. State Educ. Assn.; Franklin Reg. Educ. Assn. of Westmoreland Co.; MLA; Am. Assn. Tchrs. of Slavic & E. European Langs.; Doct. Assn. Educators at Univ. of Pitts.; Sigma Kappa Phi, Nat. Hon. Lang. Fraternity; Pi Lambda Theta; Phi Delta Gamma. Address: 2038 Wightman St., Pittsburgh, PA 15217, USA.

BERNHARD, Carl Johan, b. 14 Aug. 1939, Stockholm, Sweden. Author. Publs: The Man with the Iron Feet (novelettes from London), 1963; The Tickertape Parade (novelettes from New York), 1964; The Stone Saw (documentation), 1968; The Horn (Weather-Treasures, Part 1), 1973. Mbr., Sveriges Författarförbund. Address: Garvaregränd 2, 150 30 Mariefred, Sweden.

BERRIDGE, Elizabeth Eileen, b. 3 Dec. 1921, London, UK. Novelist; Critic. Publs: House of Defence, 1945; Be Clean Be Tidy, 1949; Selected Stories, 1949; Rose Under Glass, 1962; Across the Common, 1964; Sing Me Who You Are, 1967; Ed., The Barretts at Hope End, 1974. Contbr. to: Country Life; Cornhill; London Mag.; Punch; Harper's Bazaar; John O'London's Weekly; Life & Letters Today; The Windmill; Daily Telegraph; Components of the Scene; Pick of Today's Short Stories; Triad One; Springtime Three; & others. Mbrships: Nat. Book League; Soc. of Authors; Browning Soc. Recip., Best Novel of the Yr. Award, Yorkshire Post, 1964. Address: 19 Broad Lane, Hampton, Middx., UK.

BERRIDGE, Percy Stuart Attwood, b. 10 June 1901, S. Croydon, Surrey, UK. Bridge Engineer. Educ: Dip. Civil Engrng., Royal Tech. Coll., Glasgow. Publs: The Girder Bridge, after Brunel & Others, 1969; Couplings to the Khyber, 1969; Electric Arc Welding as Applied to Bridges & Allied Structures (w. W. T. Everall); Notes on the Half Through Type Plate Girder Railway Bridge (w. F. M. Easton). Contbr. to: Engrng.; The Engr.; Railway Mag.; Int. Railway Gazette; Country Life; Countryman; Austin Mag. Mbrships incl: Fellow, Instn. Civil Engrs.; Fellow, Welding Inst. Hons. incl: M.B.E., 1945; Webb Prize, Instn. Civil Engrs., 1963-64. Address: 26 Higher Holcombe Rd., Teignmouth, Devon TQ14 8RJ, UK.

BERRY, Brewton, b. 1901, Orangeburg, S.C., USA. University Professor of Sociology & Anthropology; Author. Educ: A.B.; B.D.; Ph.D.; Yale Univ.; Univ. of Edinburgh. Publs: You & Your Superstitions; Almost White; Fundamentals of Sociology; Race Relations; Archaeological Investigations in Boone County; Archaeology of Wayne County; The Education of American Indians; The Blending of Races. Contbr. to: Am. Jrnl. Sociol.; Am. Antiquity; Social Forces; Social Sci.; S. Atlantic Quarterly; Collier's Ency., etc. Mbr., Ohio Valley Sociol. Soc. (Pres., 1955-56). Address: 2221 Brixton Rd., Columbus 21, OH, USA.

BERRY, David, b. 12 Apr. 1942, Bury St. Edmunds, UK. Snr. Lecturer in Sociology. Educ: B.A., 1964; M.A., 1967, Univ. of Liverpool. Publs: The Sociology of Grass Roots Politics, 1970; Central Ideas in Sociology, 1974. Contbr. to: Pol. Studies; Sociol.; Sociol. Review; Times Higher Educ. Supplement. Address: Dept. of Sociology, Univ. Coll., P.O. Box 78, Cardiff CF1 1XL, UK.

BERRY, Francis, b. 23 Mar. 1915, Ipoh, Malaya. Professor of English. Educ: B.A., Univ. of London; M.A., Exeter Univ. Publs: The Galloping Centaur, 1952, reprinted, 1970; Poets' Grammar, 1958, reprinted, 1974; Morant Bay & other Poems, 1961; Poetry & the Physical Voice, 1962; The Shakespeare Inset, 1965, reprinted, 1975; Ghosts of Greenland, 1966; Thoughts on Poetic Time, 1972; Ed., An Anthology of Medieval Verse (Penguin). Contbr. to: Times Lit. Supplement; Listener; New Statesman; Essays in Criticism; Critical Quarterly; other lit. jrnls. Mbrships: F.R.S.L. Address: 51 Willson Rd., Egham, Surrey TW20 0QB, UK.

BERRY, John, b. 5 Aug. 1907, Edinburgh, Scotland, UK. Biologist; Conservation Adviser; Consultant. Educ: M.A., Trinity Coll., Cambridge; Ph.D., St. Andrews Univ.; LL.D., Univ. of Dundee. Publs: The Status & Distribution of Wild Geese & Wild Duck in Scotland, 1939. Mbrships. incl: F.R.S. (Edinburgh). Address: Tayfield, Newport-on-Tay, Fife DD6 8HA, UK.

BERRY, Paul, b. 25 Dec. 1919, Weston-by-Welland, Market Harborough, Leics., UK. Lecturer; Author; Literary Executor for Winifred Holtby & Vera Brittain. Publs: Daughters of Cain (w. Renée Hussett), 1956, 3rd ed., 1972; By Royal Appointment — A Biography of Mary Anne Clarke, 1970. Contbr. to var. mags. Address: Bridgefoot Cottage, Stedham, Midhurst, Sussex, UK.

BERRY, Thomas Edwin, b. 19 Sept. 1930, Carbondale, Ill., USA. University Professor; Writer. Educ: B.S., Southern Ill. Univ.; Dip., Syracuse Univ. Russian Inst.; M.A., Univ. of Ill.; Indic Studies, Univ. of Chgo.; Ph.D., Univ. of Tex. Publs: The Seasons Through Russian Literature, 1969; A. K. Tolstoy; Russian Humorist, 1971. Mbrships: Gtr. Wash. ATSEEL Assn. (Pres., 1972-74); Am. Assn. for Advancement Slavic Studies. Address: Russian Dept., Univ. of Maryland, College Park, MD 20740, USA.

BERRY, Thomas William, b. 9 Nov. 1914, Greensboro, N.C., USA. Educator. Educ: Ph.D., Hist., Cath. Univ. of Am. Publs: Historical Theory of Giambattista Vico, 1949; Buddhism, 1967; Religions of India, 1971. Contbr. to profl. jrnls. Address: 5801 Palisade Ave., Bronx, NY 10471, USA.

BERTHELIUS, Jenny Elisabeth, b. 23 Sept. 1929, Stockholm, Sweden. Writer. Publs: Mördarens Ansikte, 1968; ... kom, ljuva Krusmynta, 1968; Den heta sommaren, 1969; Mannen med lien, 1970; Leksakspistolen, 1971; Offret, 1972; Sällskapslek, 1973; Skräckens ABC, 1974; num. Children's books. Mbr., Sveriges Författatförbund; Skånes Författarsällskap; Skånska Deckarsällskapet. Recip. of "Sherlock" statuette for best Swedish detective novel, 1969. Address: Ostra Bernadottegatan 116, 216 17 Malmö, Sweden.

BERTIN, Eddy Charly, pen names BRENDALL, Edith; GREYSUN, Doriac, b. 26 Dec. 1944, Hamburg-Altona, Germany (Belgian nationality). Bank Clerk; Science Fiction Writer. Educ: Commerce, Handels-en Talen Inst., Ghent, Belgium. Publs. incl: (in Dutch) The Eight-Yearly God, 1971; Something Small, Something Hungry, 1972; The Eye of the Vampire, 1973; Ed., The Innocent Monster, (anthol.), forthcoming. Contbr. to var. mags. in fields of sci. fiction, fantasy & horror; Fndr.-Ed., SF-GIDS. Mbrships: Brit. Sci. Fiction Assn.; Belgian, Dutch & Brit. Sci. Fiction Socs. Hons. incl: Europa Sci. Fiction Special , 1972. Address: Res. Murillo, Dr. Van Bockxstaelstr 80, B-9218 Ledeberg, Belgium.

BERTIN, Leonard, b. 20 Aug. 1918, London, UK. Editor; Author. Educ: Degree, Mod. & Medieval Langs., Selwyn Coll., Cambridge, UK. Publs: Atom Harvest; Boys' Book of Modern Scientific Wonders & Inventions; Boys' Book of Modern Engineering Wonders; Target 2067 — Canada's 2nd Century. Contbr. to: New Sci.; Rsch.; Discovery; Jet Propulsion; Saturday Review; Can. Electronic Engrng.; Mod. Power; Jrnl. of Atomic Scis.; Chatelaine; Readers' Digest; etc. Address: c/o University News Bureau, Univ. of Toronto, Toronto 5, Ont., Can.

BERTRAM, George Colin Lawder, b. 1911, Worcester, UK. Zoologist; Chairman, Sirenia Group, I.U.C.N. Survival Service Commission. Educ: M.A., Ph.D., Univ. of Cambridge. Publs: Arctic & Antarctic; Antarctica Today & Tomorrow; Adam's Brood; In Search of Mermaids. Contbr. to: Polar Records; Eugenics Review; Oryx; Geogl. Jrnl.; Arctic. Mbrships: Gen. Sec., Eugenics Soc., 1957-64; Hon. Sec., Royal Geogl. Soc., 1972–; Past Pres., Arctic Club; Past Pres., Antarctic Club; Coun., Fauna Soc.; Zool. Soc. Address: Linton House, Linton, Cambridge, UK, & St. John's Coll., Cambridge, UK.

BESSEMER, Auriel Alexsandor, b. 27 Feb. 1909, Nunica, Mich., USA. Artist; Illustrator; Poet. Educ: Western Reserve Acad., Hudson, Ohio, 1924-27; Columbia Coll., N.Y., 1927-30. Publs: (books illustrated) Light From Heavenly Lanterns, by El Morya; Climb the Highest Mountain, by Mark & Elizabeth Prophet. Contbr. to: Contemp. Am. Men Poets (anthol.); Aesthetics Mag.; Arte; Beacon; Flame; Cyclo-Flame; Wash. Post; etc. Mbrships. incl: Int. Poetry Inst., Inc.; World Poetry Soc. Intercontinental; Avalon World Arts Acad.; Centro Studi e Scambi Int., Italy. Hons. incl: Silver Medal, 1970, Gold Medal, 1972, Tomasso Campanella Acad., Italy. Address: c/o The Summit Lighthouse, First & Broadmoor, Colo. Springs, CO 80906, USA.

BEST, Carol Anne, pen names ASHE, Susan; WAYNE, Marcia; MARTIN, Ann; DARLINGTON, Con, b. Birmingham, UK. Publs: 80 paperback romantic thrillers. Agent: K. Routledge. Address: 11 Victoria Ave., Winton, Bournemouth, Hants., UK.

BEST, Charles Herbert, b. 27 Feb. 1899, West Pembroke, Maine, USA. Professor of Physiology & Medical Research. Educ: B.A., 1921, M.A., 1922, M.D., 1925, Univ. of Toronto; D.Sc., Univ. of London, UK, 1928. Publs. incl: Selected Papers of Charles H. Best, 1963; The Living Body, 5th ed., 1970; The Physiological Basis of Medical Practice (w. N. B. Taylor), 9th ed., 1973. Contbr. to var. profl. jrnls. Mbr. num. profl. socs. in Am. & Europe inclng: Can. Physiol. Soc. (past Pres.); F.R.S. Can.; F.R.S. London; F.R.C.P., London. Recip. over 40 civ., mil., acad. & sci. hons. inclng: C.B.E., 1944; Legion of Merit, US Govt., 1947; Companion, Order of Can., 1967; Companion of Hon., H.M. Queen Elizabeth II, 1971; num. hon. degrees. Address: 105 Woodlawn Ave. W., Toronto, Ont. M4V 1G6, Can.

BEST, Rayleigh Breton Amis, pen name AMIS, Breton, b. 1905, Leigh-on-Sea, UK. Journalist. Educ: Fleet St., 1924-38. Publs: Tomorrow will be Sunday, 1947; Park Royal, 1949; Hive of Glass, 1950; The House Called Yarrow, 1959; A Touch of Scarlet, 1960; The Honest Rogue, 1961; Daughters of the Bride, 1961; With Pink Trumpets, 1962; Pilot's Height, 1963; High Tide, 1964; Idle Rainbow, 1966; Broken Glass, 1967; Green Wood, 1967; The Selfish Ones, 1968; Dark Gold, 1969; The Tender Charge, 1970. Mbr. Soc. of Authors. Agent: K. Routledge. Address: 11 Victoria Ave., Winton, Bournemouth, Hants., UK.

BETHELL, (Lord) Nicholas William, b. 1938, London, UK. Freelance Writer. Educ: M.A., Pembroke Coll., Cambridge Univ. Publs: Slawomir Mrozek, Six Plays & Tango (transl.), 1966; Solzhenitsyn, Cancer Ward (co-transl.), 1968; Solzhenitsyn, The Love Girl & the Innocent (co-transl.), 1969; Gomulka, 1969; The War Hitler Won, 1972; Solzhenitsyn, Nobel Peace Prize Lecture (transl.), 1973; The Last Secret, 1974. Contbr. to: Times; Sunday Times; N.Y. Times; Harpers (N.Y.); New Statesman; Observer. Mbr., Soc. of Authors. Recip., Pilsudski Inst. Mem. Prize, 1973. Address: 73 Sussex Square, London W2, UK.

BETJEMAN, (Sir) John, b. 1906. Author; Poet Laureate. Educ: Magdalen Coll., Oxford. Publs: Mount Zion; Ghastly Good Taste; Continual Dew; An Oxford University Chest; Antiquarian Prejudice; Old Lights for New Chancels;

Selected Poems, 1948; First & Last Loves, 1952; A Few Late Chrysanthemums, 1954; The English Town in the Last Hundred Years, 1956; Shell Guides to Cornwall & Devon & (w. John Piper) Shropshire & Buckinghamshire. Recip., C.B.E. Address: The Mead, Wantage, Berks., UK.

BETTS, Carolyn McIlvaine Welch, b. 28 Dec. 1915, Phila., Pa., USA. Educator; Author. Educ: B.S., Beaver Coll., 1937; M.S., Pa. State Univ. Publs: Betts Basic Readers (Pre-school through Sixth Grade), 1948, 1958, 1963, 1965; Betts New Reading-Study Program, Beginning Reading, 1970; Teachers Guide to Alec Majors, to Cowboys & Cattle Trails of American Adventure Series, var. eds.; Author, co-author, over 300 books. Contbr. to Third Mental Measurements Yearbook. Address: 12255 SW 73rd Avenue, Miami, FL 33156, USA.

BETTS, Raymond Frederick, b. 23 Dec. 1925, Bloomfield, N.J., USA. Professor of History; Writer. Educ: A.B., Rutgers Univ.; M.A. & Ph.D., Columbia Univ.; Dr. of Univ., Univ. of Grenoble; Cert. in African Studies, Inst. of Pol. Studies, Univ. of Paris. Publs: Assimilation & Association in French Colonial Theory, 1890-1914, 1961, reprinted 1969; The Scramble for Africa (ed.), 1966, 2nd ed., 1972; Europe Overseas — Phases of Imperialism, 1968; The Ideology of Blackness (ed.), 1972; The False Dawn — European Imperialism in the Nineteenth Century, scheduled for 1975. Contbr. to: French Histl. Studies (on ed. staff). Address: 311 Mariemont Dr., Lexington, KY 40505, USA.

BEVAN, Bryan (Henry), b. 14 Mar. 1913, London, UK. Author; Historian. Educ: Jesus Coll., Cambridge Univ. Publs: The Real Francis Bacon, 1960; Trial of the Earl of Essex (play), 1962; I Was James the Second's Queen, 1963; King James the Third of England, 1967; Nell Gwyn, 1969; The Great Seamen of Elizabeth I, 1971. Charles II's French Mistress, 1972; James, Duke of Monmouth, 1973; Marlborough the Man, a biography of John, First Duke of Marlborough, 1975. Contbr. to: Contemporary Review; Country Life; etc. Mbrships. incl: Authors club (Comm.); Poetry Soc. Address: 7 Bonser Rd., Twickenham, Middlesex, UK.

BEVERIDGE, William Ian Beardmore, b. 1908, Junee, Australia. University Professor of Animal Pathology, Cambridge Univ., 1947-. Educ: D.V.Sc., Univ. of Sydney. Sc.D., Cambridge Univ. Publs: The Art of Scientific Investigations, 1950; Frontiers of Comparative Medicine, 1972. Contbr. to var. sci. jrnls. Mbrships: Fellow, Jesus Coll., Cambridge Univ.; Chmn., Permanent Comm., World Vet. Assn., 1959-. Address: Jesus Coll., Cambridge, UK.

BEYER, Werner William, b. 22 Mar. 1911, Laporte, Ind., USA. University Professor. Educ: A.B., 1934; M.A., 1936; Ph.D., 1945, Columbia Univ. Publs: The Prestige of C. M. Wieland in England, 1936; Keats & the Daemon King, 1947, 2nd ed. 1969; The Enchanted Forest, 1963; Bibliog. for The World in Literature, 1967. Contbr. to: Review of Engl. Studies; Mod. Philology; Encounter; Jrnl. of Engl. & Germanic Philology; etc. Mbrships: Mod. Lang. Assn. of Am. (Sec., Chmn., Comp. Lit. VI, 1960-62); Coll. Engl. Assn. Recip., 3 acad. hons. Address: Butler Univ., Indianapolis, IN 46203, USA.

BEYNON, D(aniel) Islwyn, b. 12 June 1920, Pontyates, Llanelli, Wales, UK. Baptist Minister; Writer. Educ: Presby. Coll., Carmarthen; Dip. in Theol., Univ. of Wales. Publs: Cyrchu At Y Sêr, 1963; Llwybrau'r Gorlan, 1964; Gwersi'r Gorlan, 1967; Hen Bentrefwyr, 1968; Meysydd Y Gorlan, 1969; Talcen Caled, 1971; Eseia Williams, Aberteifi, 1973; Mewn Trwbwl O Hyd, 1974; Pedol Yn Y Lludw, 1974. Contbr. to: Seren Cymru; Antur; Welsh Bapt. Year Book (ed., 1974). Address: "Maesgwyn", Carmel, Llanelli SA14 7TL, UK.

BEYNON, Huw, b. 10 Dec. 1942, Ebbw Vale, Wales, UK. Sociologist (Former University Lecturer; Research Fellow, 1973-75). Educ: B.A., Univ. Coll. of Wales, 1964; Univ. of Liverpool. Publs: Working for Ford, 1973. Contbr. to: Times Higher Educ. Supplement; Race; Sociol.; New Soc.; Address: 14 Rutland Ave., Liverpool 17, UK.

BHARATI, Agehananda, b. 20 Apr. 1923, Vienna, Austria. University Professor of Anthropology; Department Chairman. Educ: B.A. (Lic.), Univ. of Vienna, 1948; Acharya (D.Phil.), Samnyasa Mahavidyalaya, Varanasi, India, 1951. Publs: The Ochre Robe, 1963, 1970; A Functional Analysis of Indian Thought & Its Social Margins, 1964; The Tantric Tradition, 1969, 1970; The

Asians in East Africa: Jayhind & Uhuru, 1972. Ed., The Tibet Soc. Bulletin, USA; Corres. Ed., Universitas, Germany, Folia Humanistica, Spain. Contbr. to num. profl. jrnls. in Europe, Am., Aust., Asia. Mbr., var. profl. assns. Address: 500 University Pl., Syracuse, NY 13210, USA.

BHATIA, Jamunadevi, pen name RANA, J.; BHATIA, June; FORRESTER, Helen, b. 6 June 1919, Hoylake, Cheshire, UK. Novelist. Publs: Alien There is None (as J. Rana), 1959; The Latchkey Kid (as June Bhatia), 1970; Twopence to Cross the Mersey (non-fiction; as Helen Forrester), 1974. Contbr. to: Heritage Mag., Alta.; Can. Author & Bookman. Mbr., Can. Authors' Assn. Recip., Hudson's Bay Beaver Award for The Moneylenders of Shahpur (novel), 1970. Address: 8734- 117 Street, Edmonton, Alta. T6G 1R5, Canada.

BHATNAGAR, Joti, b. 4 Dec. 1935, Morabad, India. University Professor; Writer. Educ: B.Sc., 1955, LL.B., 1957, Agra Univ., India; P.G.C.E., 1962, M.A., 1964, Ph.D., 1969, London Univ., UK. Publs: Immigrants at School, 1970; Ed., Current Perspectives in Social Psychology of Education, 1971; A Social Psychology of Education (in preparation). Contbr. to: Educl. Studies; Psychol. Studies; Race; Race Today; Voc. Aspects of Educ. Mbrships: Int. Assn. Applied Psychol.; Can. Psychol. Assn.; Am. Educl. Rsch. Assn. Can. Soc. for Study of Educ.; Can. Assn. Deans & Dirs. of Educ. Address: 12425 Richer Blvd., Pierrefonds, P.Q., H8Z 1K7 Can.

BHATTACHARYA, Bhabani, b. 10 Nov. 1906, Bhagalpur, India. Visiting Professor. Educ: B.A., Patna Univ., 1927; B.A., 1931, Ph.D., 1934, Univ. of London, UK. Publs. incl: (novels) So Many Hungers! , 1947; Music for Mohini, 1952; He Who Rides a Tiger, 1954; A Goddess Named Gold, 1960; Shadow from Ladakh, 1966; (other) Steel Hawk & Other Stories, 1968; Some Memorable Yesterdays, 1940; Indian Cavalcade, 1944; Gandhi the Writer, 1969. Mbr., Advsry. Bd., Indian Nat. Acad. of Letters. Hons: Prestige Award, Univs. of NZ, 1962; Award, Indian Nat. Acad. of Letters, 1967; Ford Grant, 1968, 1969. Address: Hono Hale Towers, Apartment A-105, 827 Kahuna Lane, Honolulu, HI 96814, USA.

BHATTACHARYYA, Birendra Kumar, b. 16 Mar. 1924, Suffry Sigbsagar, Assam, India. Writer; Journalist. Educ: Cotton Coll., Gauhati; Calcutta & Gauhati Univs. Publs: Iyaruingam (novel); Rajpathe Ringiai (novel); Mother (novel); Sataghai (novel); Mrityunjay (novel); Pratipad (novel); Kolongajioboi (stories); Satsari (stories). Contbr. to: Ramdhenu (Ed., 1951-61); Sadiniya Navayung (Ed., 1963-67). Mbr., Exec., Sanjukta Socialist Pty., Assam. Recip., Sahitya Akademi Award for Assamese Lit., 1961. Address: Kharghuli Dev. Area, Gauhati I, Assam, India.

BHATTI, Rasheed, b. 20 Aug. 1933, Sukkur, Sind, Pakistan. Advocate; Author. Educ: B.A., LL.B. Publs: Great Short-stories of the World (Sindhi transl.), 1958; Idealist (short stories), 1962; Every Moment Is an Injury (short stories), 1964; State & Freedom (essays), 1966; Aadi Dhal ma Dhar (compiler & ed., epic Sindhi poetry), 1966; Aashique Zahar Pivak (play), 1968. Contbr. to: Hilal-e-Pakistan, Karachi; Sojhro, Karachi; Tahrik; Agtay; Qadam; Naeen Zindagi; Rooh Rehan; Mehran. Mbrships: Exec. Comm., W. Pakistan Writers' Guild, 1964-70; Sec., Sindhi Region, Pakistan Writers' Guild, 1964-70; Sec. Gen., All Sind Sindhi Adabi Sangat. Recip., Pakistan Writers' Guild Award, Best Sindhi Prose Writer, 1964. Address: Jagirani Muhallo, Barrage Rd., Sukkur, Sind, Pakistan.

BIANCO, Pamela Ruby, b. 31 Dec. 1906, London, UK. Artist; Author. Publs: Sing a Song of Journeys, 1937; also illustrated by author: The Starlit Journey, 1933; Beginning with A, 1947; Playtime in Cherry Street, 1948; Joy & The Christmas Angel, 1949; Paradise Square, 1950; Little Houses Far Away, 1951; The Look-Inside Easter Egg, 1952; The Doll in the Window, 1953; The Valentine Party, 1954; Toy Rose, 1957; Articles in: Writing & Criticism. A Book for Margery Bianco, 1951; Horn Book Reflections, 1969. Address: 428 Lafayette St., N.Y., NY 10003, USA.

BIBBY, Cyril, b. 1 May 1914, Liverpool, UK. College Principal. Educ: Liverpool Collegiate Schl.; M.A., Queens' Coll., Cambridge; M.Sc., Univ. of Liverpool; Ph.D., Univ. of London; Dip.Ed. Publs. incl: Experimental Human Biology,

1942; Sex Education, 1944; Healthy & Happy, 1948; Health Education, 1951; Race, Prejudice & Education, 1959; T. H. Huxley, 1959; Scientist Extraordinary, 1972. Contbr. of papers to var. sci., health, educl., pol., sociol. & gen. jrnls. Hons: Fellow, Linnean Soc., 1942; F.R.S.A., 1954 (Silver Medal, 1956); vis. lecturer, sev. US univs.; del. to num. int. congresses. Address: 246 Cottingham Rd., Hull, Humberside, UK.

BIDDISS, Michael Denis, b. 1942, Farnborough, Kent, UK. Lecturer in History. Educ: M.A., Ph.D., Queens' Coll., Cambridge. Publs: Ed., Gobineau: Selected Political Writings, 1970; Father of Racist Ideology, 1970; Disease & History (w. F. F. Cartwright), 1972. Contbr. to: Justice First, 1969; Wiener Lib. Bulletin; Études Gobiniennes; Univ. of Birmingham Review; Histl. Jrnl.; Hist. Today; Horizon; French Studies; Hist. Mbrships: Fellow, Royal Histl. Soc., 1974; Inst. Race Rels. Agent: Curtis Brown. Address: Dept. of Hist., The University, Leicester, UK.

BIEGEL, Paul, b. 25 Mar. 1925, Bussum, Netherlands. Writer. Publs. incl: Het Sleutelkruid, 1964, (Engl. transl. as The King of the Copper Mountains, 1969); De tuinen van Dorr, 1969 (Engl. transl. as The Gardens of Dorr, 1975); De kleine kapitein in het land van Waan en Wijs, 1974 (Engl. transl., 1974); De vloek Van Woestewolf (TV series), 1974. Contbr. to var. mags. Mbr., Dutch Authors' Soc. Hons. incl: Best Children's Bk. of the Yr. (for King of the Copper Mountains), 1965; Nienke van Hichtum Prize (for The Twelve Robbers), 1973; State Prize, 1974. Address: Keizersgracht 227, Amsterdam, Netherlands.

BIELAWSKI, Joseph Gerald, b. 28 Nov. 1925, Dickson City, Pa., USA. Editor; Author. Educ: B.S.; M.A. Publs: My Country, U.S.A., 1967; We Need Each Other, Phonics, 1970-71; Guide to Educational Technology: Preschool Years, 1973; Reading Games Make Reading Fun, 1974; Educational Technology: Elementary Years, 1974. Contbr. to Merry-Go-Round. Nat. Mbr., Smithsonian Instn. Address: 865 Jerome Ave., Bristol, CT 06010, USA.

BIELAWSKI, Walter Leonard, b. 6 Nov. 1926, Harvey, Ill., USA. Business Executive; Editor-Publisher. Educ: A.A., Thornton Jr. Coll.; B.S., M.B.A., Loyola Univ. Ed.-Publr., Harvey News-Bee, 1953-66; Columnist, The News, Lansing, Ill., 1966—; Contbr. to Ozark Mountaineer, Branson, Mo., 1972—. Address: 253 E. 159th St., Harvey, IL 60426, USA.

BIEN, Peter A., b. 28 May 1930, NYC, USA. Professor of English. Educ: B.A., Haverford Coll., 1952; M.A., 1957, Ph.D., 1961, Columbia Univ.; Bristol Univ., UK; Woodbrooke Coll., UK; Harvard Coll. Publs. incl: transls. of 3 Nikos Kazantzakis works into Engl.; L. P. Hartley, 1963; Constantine Cavafy, 1964; Nikos Kazantzakis, 1972; Kazantzakis & the Linguistic Revolution in Greek Literature, 1972; Demotic Greek (w. J. Rassias & C. Bien), 1972. Contbr. to: Asst. Ed., Byzantine & Mod. Greek Studies; Books Abroad. Mbr., MLA. Recip., E. Harris Harbison Award for Disting. Tchng., Danforth Fndn., 1968. Address: Dept. of Engl., Dartmouth Coll., Hanover, NH 03755, USA.

BIERMAN, James Henry, b. 10 July 1942, NYC, USA. University Professor. Educ: B.A., Princeton Univ.; Ph.D., Stanford Univ. Publs: transl. & introduction of Caesar Antichrist, by Alfred Jarry, 1971. Contbr. to Comparative Drama. Mbr., Am. Theatre Assn. Hons: Fulbright Scholar, 1966-67; Danforth Fndn. Assoc., 1970-; Sacramento State Coll. Nat. Playwriting Award, 1970. Address: Cowell Coll., Univ. of Calif., Santa Cruz, CA 95064, USA.

BIGELOW, Faye Scoggins, pen name SCOGGINS, Faye, b. 23 Mar. 1898, Carthage, Mo., USA. Teacher. Educ: B.A., M.A., W. Tex. State Univ.; Ariz. State Univ. Publs: Topping the Heights (poetry), 1969. Contbr. to jrnls. & anthols. Mbrships: Ariz. State Poetry Soc.; World Poetry Soc. Address: 2823 W. Rancho Dr., Phoenix, AZ 85017, USA.

BIGELOW, Robert Sidney, b. 26 Apr. 1918, Canning, Nova Scotia, Can. University Lecturer & Reader. Educ: B.Sc., Ph.D.; McGill Univ.; Oxford Univ., UK. Publs: Grasshoppers of New Zealand, 1967; The Dawn Warriors; Man's Evolution Toward Peace, 1969. Contbr. to: Can. Entomol.; Can. Jrnl. Zool.; Evolution; Systematic Zool.; Aust. Jrnl. Zool.; Aust. Jrnl. Sci.; Int. Social Scis. Jrnl.; World Anthropol.; etc. Mbrships: Soc. for Study of Evolution; Soc. of Systematic Zool.; Am. Soc. Naturalists;

Aust. & NZ Soc. Adv. of Sci.; Royal Soc. NZ.; NZ Ecol. & Entomol. Socs. Address: 14 Head Street, Christchurch 8, New Zealand.

BIHALJI-MERIN, Oto, pen names MERIN, Peter; THOENE, Peter, b. 3 Jan. 1904, Zemun, Yugoslavia. Critic; Essayist; Novelist. Educ: Belgrade & Berlin Acads. of Fine Art. Publs. incl: Au Revoir in October (novel), 1947; The Invisible Door (play), 1956; Thousands of Years of Art in Yugoslavia (Ed.), 1969; The End of Art in the Age of Science? , 1969; The Douanier Rousseau (co-author), 1970; Time-Light-Movement (essay), 1970; Modern Primitives (in Engl.), 1971; Marij Pregelj (monograph), 1971; Masters of Native Art, 1971, 1972; Bridges of the World (Ed.), 1971. Recip., sev. decorations. Address: Nemanjina ul. 3, Belgrade, Yugoslavia.

BIHARI, Klara, b. 8 Dec. 1917, Nagyszalonta, Hungary. Writer. Publs. incl: novels: Tomorrow, 1967; Solitaries, 1969; Why? , 1970; Selfdenial, 1971; Mene Tekel, 1972; The Seducer (short stories), 1971. Mbrships: PEN; Hungarian Writers' Soc. Recip., Jozsef Attila Literatura Medal. Address: 1068 Budapest, Szondy-St. 93, Hungary.

BILASH, Borislaw Nicholas, b. 9 May 1929, Winnipeg, Can. Educator; Writer. Educ: B.A., 1956, B.Ed., 1957, M.Ed., 1960, Univ. of Man.; Ph.D., 1965, Dr. Habilitatus, Ukrainische Freie Univ., Munich, Germany. Publs: Ukrainian with Ease, 1961, 5th ed., 1972; Ukrainska Mova: Ochyma Dytyny, 1972; Bilingual Public Schools in Manitoba, 1897-1916, 1974; Co-Author, Ukrainska Rozmova: Pochatkovey Kurs, 1972; Co-Author, Ukrainska Rozmova I, 1974. Contbr. to: Man. Mod. Lang. Bulletin (Fndr., Ed., 1966-); Ukrainian by the Audio-Visual Method (Chmn., Ed. Bd.) Mbrships: Advsry. Bd. to Min. of Educ., Province of Man., 1962-64; Man. Tchrs. Soc.; Man. MLA; num. other profl. assns. Address: 209 Scotia St., Winnipeg, Man., R2W 3X2, Can.

BILL, Valentine T., b. 4 Jan. 1909, Pavlovsk, Russia. Educator; Writer. Educ: Ph.D., Univ. of Berlin, Germany, 1936. Publs: The Forgotten Class — the Russian Bourgeoises, 1959; The Russian People: a Reader on their History & Culture, 3rd. ed., 1974. Contbr. to: Russian Review. Mbr., Assn. Russian-Am. Schlrs. in USA. Address: 26 Alexander St., Princeton, N.J. 08540, USA.

BILLETDOUX, François-Paul, b. 7 Sept. 1927. Writer; Actor; Director; Producer. Educ: Ecole d'Art Dramatique Charles Dulin; Inst. des Hautes Etudes Cinématographiques. Publs. incl: L'Animal (novel), 1955; Brouillon d'un bourgeois, 1961; Comment va le monde, Mòssieu? , Il tourne, Mòssieu! (play), 1964; Je n'étais pas chez moi (play), 1968; Famine chez les rats (TV script), 1970; Ai-je dit que je suis bossu? (radio script), 1971; Les veuves (play), 1972. Recip., num. prizes. Address: 31 square de Montsouris, Paris 14e, France.

BILLINGTON, Lillian Emily, b. Ashland, Wis., USA. Professor of Education: Textbook Author. Educ: B.A., San Jose State Univ., 1931; M.A., 1934, Ed.D., 1946, Stanford Univ.; Ph.D., Colo. Christian Coll., 1972. Publs: 108 books inclng: New Laurel Handwriting Series, 8 books, 1937; Towards Better Handwriting, 1962; Using Words, 8 books & tchrs. guides, 1943; Spelling & Using Words, 1958, 8 books & guides, rev. eds., 1962; Play & Learn Trade Books, 4 books, 1950; Word Power Through Spelling, 8 books & guides, 1950. Mbr., Nat. Writers Club, Denver, Colo. & Eugene Field Lit. Soc. Address: Kingscote Gardens No. 28, 586 Lomita, Stanford, CA 94305, USA.

BILLINGTON, Ray Allen, b. 28 Sept. 1903, Bay City, Mich., USA. Author. Educ: Ph.B., 1926, M.A., 1927, Univ. of Wis.; Ph.D., Harvard Univ., 1933; M.A., Oxford Univ., UK, 1953. Publs. incl: The Protestant Crusade, 1938; The United States, 1947; Westward Expansion, 1949; The Far Western Frontier, 1956; Frontier & Section, 1961; America's Frontier Heritage, 1966; Genesis of Frontier Thesis, 1971; Frederick Jackson Turner, 1973. Contbr. to: Am. Histl. Review; Am. Heritage; Jrnl. Negro Hist.; var. state & local histl. jrnls. Hons. incl: Cons. Lib. of Congress, 1974-; Bancroft Prize Winner, 1974; 7 hon. degrees. Address: 2375 Lombardy Road, San Marino, CA 91108, USA.

BING, Jon, pen name CATAMARAN, b. 30 Apr. 1944. Tønsberg, Norway. Author; Assistant Professor in Law & Computers. Educ: Cand.jur., 1969. Publs: Komplex, 1969; Det Myke landskapet, 1970; Scenario, 1972; Knuteskrift, 1974; Rundt solen i ning (w. Tor Åge Bringsvaerd), 1967; A

miste et romskip, 1969; Sesam 71, 1971. Contbr. to: Vinduet, Norway; Gyldendals mag., Denmark; Ambit, UK; Attenposten; Dagbladet. Mbrships: Bd., Norwegian Soc. of Authors, 1970-72; Legal Advsr., 1973–; Norwegian Soc. of Dramatists. Recip., Alvar, Swedish Sci. Fiction Acad. Yearly Prize, 1970. Address: Halvorsens vei 12a, N 1310 Blommenholm, Norway.

BINGHAM, Caroline (née Worsdell), b. 7 Feb. 1938, Hampstead, London, UK. Author. Educ: B.A., Bristol Univ. Publs: (biogs.) The Making of a King: The Early Years of James VI & I, UK, 1968, USA, 1969; James V, King of Scots, 1971; The Life & Times of Edward II, 1973; The Stewart Kingdom of Scotland, 1371-1603, 1974 (& USA, 1974). Contbr. to: The Scottish Nation, 1972; Jrnl. of Interdisciplinary Hist.; Scottish Field; In Brit. Agent: Int. Famous Agcy. Ltd. Address: 19 Farmer St., London W8, UK.

BINGLEY, Clive Hamilton, b. 2 Apr. 1936, Johannesburg, S. Africa. Publisher. Educ: M.A., Oxford, UK. Publs: Book Publishing Practice, 1966; The Business of Book Publishing, 1972. Contbr. to: The Bookseller; Ed., New Lib. World, 1971–. Mbr., M.C.C. Address: 16 Pembridge Rd., London W11, UK.

BINGLEY, David Ernest, pen names CHESHAM, Henry; HORSLEY, David; & 28 others, b. 16 Apr. 1920, Hunslet, Leeds, UK. Author; Teacher. Educ: Shenstone Training Coll., Worcs., 1947-48. Publs: 121 books, Crime, Westerns & War genres, incl: Naples, or Die!, 1964; also jvnls., incl: The Study Book of Bridges, 1969. Contbr. to var. mags. Mbr., Writers' Summer School, Derbys. (Comm. Mbr.). Address: 9 Mill Fields Road, Hythe, Kent, UK.

BINKLEY, Luther John, b. 7 Oct. 1925, Wernersville, Pa., USA. Professor. Educ: A.B., Franklin & Marshall Coll., 1945; B.D., Lancaster Theol. Sem. of the United Ch. of Christ, 1947; Ph.D., Harvard, 1950. Publs: The Mercersburg Theology, 1953; Contemporary Ethical Theories, 1961; Conflict of Ideals: Changing Values in Western Society, 1969. Mbr., Am. Philosl. Assn.; etc. Hons: Potomac Synod Fellowship for Grad. Study, 1948-49; Vis. Fellow, Cambridge Univ., 1959-60. Address: 445 N. President Ave., Lancaster, PA 17603, USA.

BINNEMANS, Charles-Louis, b. 2 Apr. 1922, Brussels, Belgium. Journalist. Educ: Lic. Philos. & Letters. Publs: L'Université belge du pari au défi; Henri Simonet ou le goût de pouvoir (pol. biog.); Robert Henrion, un escrimeur aux Finances (pol. biog.). Mbrships: Hon. Pres., Brussels Press; VP, Tourism Jrnlsts.' Assn.; Mbr., Assn. of French-speaking Jrnlsts. Address: Clos du Mouron, 5-1150 Bruxelles, Belgium.

BINNER, Ethel Ina, pen name BINNER, Ina, b. 24 July 1915, Darlington, UK. Author; Former Hairstylist, Manicurist & Beautician. Publs: Prince of the Blood Royal, 1970; Royal Pardon (play), 1971; King Without a Throne, 1973; Prince of Adversity, 1974; Two Royal Brothers, 1975; Monarch of Two Kingdoms, forthcoming. Contbr. to: Townswoman; N. Ridings Mag.; Country Life; Tail Wagger. Mbr., Yorks. Authors' & Writers' Assn. Address: "St. Chad's", 43 Green Lane, Acomb, Yorks. YO2, UK.

BINSTED, Raymond Horatio, b. 12 Mar. 1912, London, UK. Food Technologist; Editor; Author. Publs: Soup Manufacture & Canning, 1940, 3rd ed., 1970; Pickle & Sauce Making, 1939, 3rd ed., 1971; Tomato Paste & Other Tomato Products (co-author), 1964, 2nd ed., 1973; Hygiene in Food Manufacturing & Handling (co-author), 1964, 2nd ed., 1973; Quick Frozen Foods, 1972; Food Processing Hygiene (co-author), 1975. Contbr. of over 400 articles on food mfg. subjects to var. jrnls.; Ed., Food Trade Review, 1931–. Address: "Little Pleasaunce", Woodlands Close, Bickley BR1 2BD, UK.

BIÖRCK, Carl Gunnar Wilhelm, b. 4 Apr. 1916, Göteborg, Sweden. Professor; Physician. Educ: M.D., Stockholm, 1942. Publs: Vårt folk och vår framtid, 1940; Om hjärtat krånglar, 1953; Medicin för politiker, 1953; Sjukvårdens framtidsproblem, 1955; Människans möjligheter, 1956; Sjukvårdens villkor, 1966; Själ och hjärta, 1967; Journal 67, 1967; Läkaren i det moderna samhället, 1968; På andra sidan korridoren, 1970; Uppriktigt sagt, 1972; Till Serafimerlasarettets försvar, 1974; Enhet och mångfald, 1974; Den medicinska beslutsprocessen, 1974; Med stetoskop och värja, 1974. Contbr. to Svenska Dagbladet. Mbrships: F.R.C.P., London;

F.A.C.P., USA; The Swedish Publicist Club. Address: Bravallavägen 14, Djursholm, Sweden.

BIRCH, Anthony Harold, b. 17 Feb. 1924, Ventnor, UK. Professor of Political Science, University of Exeter. Educ: Univ. Coll., Nottingham; London Schl. of Econs.; B.Sc.(Econ.), 1945; Ph.D., 1951. Publs: Federalism, Finance & Social Legislation, 1955; Small-Town Politics, 1959; Representative & Responsible Government, 1964; The British System of Government, 1967, revised ed., 1973; Representation, 1971. Contbr. to publ. & sociol. jrnls. Address: c/o Dept. of Politics, Univ. of Exeter, Exeter, Devon, UK.

BIRCH, Charles Allan, b. 1903, Wigan, Lancs., UK. Physician; Author. Educ: M.D., Univ. of Liverpool. Publs: Common Symptoms Described for Nurses, 1953; Emergencies in Medical Practice, 10th ed., 1975; The House Physician's Handbook, 4th ed., 1975. Contbr. to: Lancet; Brit. Med. Jrnl.; Practitioner; etc. Address: Salter's Corner, High St., Hastings, Sussex, UK.

BIRCH, Dorothy, b. Morecambe, Lancs., UK. Author. Educ: Trinity Coll. of Music; Royal Acad. of Music; Tchrs. Trng. Course Cert. Publs: The Art of Good Speech, 1948; Training for the Stage, 1952; (novels) Dear Paradise, 1971; A Nightingale Sang, 1972; A Question of Caring, 1973. Contbr. to: Poetry Review; Poetry Quarterly; Spring Anthol., 1970, 1971, 1972 & 1973. Mbrships. incl: Soc. of Authors; Soc. of Women Writers & Jrnlsts.; Romantic Novelists' Assn. Address: 5 Elliott Terrace, The Hoe, Plymouth PL1 2PL, Devon, UK.

BIRCH, Leo Bedrich, b. 7 Feb. 1902, Prague, Czech. Poet; Educator (retired). Educ: B.A., Prague Univ., 1920; Univs. of Vienna, Austria; Heidelberg, Germany; Paris, France. Publs: The Old & the New Adam (verse), 1969; Poems & Translations: Mallarmé, Valéry, Péguy, 1971; 72 Fables translated from La Fontaine, 1974. Contbr. to: Poet Intercontinental; Poets' Guild of Idaho; Cyclo-Flame, Tex.; Orbis. Mbrships: World Poetry Soc. Intercontinental; Int. Poetry Soc., UK; Avalon World Arts Acad., Tex. Address: 1487 Teller Ave., Bronx, NY 10457, USA.

BIRCHAM, Deric Neale, b. 16 Dec. 1934, Wellington, NZ. Professional Photographer. Educ: F.N.Z.P.P.A.; F.I.I.P.; Hon. F.I.I.P.P.; F.R.P.S.; F.R.S.A. Publs: Seeing New Zealand, 1971, 3rd ed., 1974; Waitomo Tourist Caves, 1974. Address: 202 Nevay Rd., Miramar, Wellington, NZ.

BIRD, Dennis Leslie, pen name NOEL, John, b. 1930, Eastbourne, Sussex, UK. Administrative Civil Servant, Home Office; Writer. Publs: Figure Skating for Beginners, 1964. Contbr. to: The Times; Skating World; Ice & Roller Skate; Skating; US Olympic Book. Mbrships: Nat. Skating Assn. of GB; Tennyson Soc. Address: 37 The Avenue, Shoreham-by-Sea, Sussex BN4 5GJ, UK.

BIRD, William Richard, b. 11 May 1891, E. Mapleton, Cumberland Co., N.S., Can. Writer. Educ: Amherst Acad. Publs. incl: And We Go On, 1930; Thirteen Years After, 1932; Maid of the Marshes, 1935; Yorkshire, 1945; Sunrise for Peter, 1946; The Passionate Pilgrim, 1949; The Two Jacks, 1954; Off-Trail in Nova Scotia, 1956; Atlantic Anthology, 1959; So Much to Record, 1961; Ghosts Have Warm Hands, 1968; Angel Cove, 1972; & over 550 short stories in Can., Am. & British mags. Contbr. to: Can. Home Jrnl.; Nat. Home Weekly; Collier's, etc. Life Mbr., Can. Authors' Assn. Recip., Nat. Award in Letters, Univ. of Alta., 1965. Address: 963 Marlborough Ave., Halifax, Nova Scotia, Can.

BIRENBAUM, Halina, b. 15 Sept. 1929, Warsaw, Poland (Citizen of Israel, 1947-). Writer; Housewife. Publs: Nadzieja Umiera Ostatnia (autobiog. novel), 1967; Engl. transl. by Prof. D. Welsh, w. foreword by Prof. Ludwik Krzyzanowski, as Hope is the Last to Die, 1971, 3rd ed., 1973; other works in progress; books describe author's experiences as prisoner in Auschwitz during WWII. Address: 4 Givat Hatachmoset St., Herzlia B, Israel.

BIRKÁS, Endre, b. 5 Aug. 1913, Budapest, Hungary. Librarian & Head of Department, National Library. Educ: LL.D., Dr. Pol.Sci. Publs: Kelepce, 1942; Elfelejtett emberek, 1960; Kö és homok, 1961; Vakvágány, 1963; Ólmos eso, 1969; Mondd még meddig kell élni?, 1971; Álmatlan nappalok, 1972. Mbrships: Hungarian Writers' Assn.; Hungarian PEN. Address: Gellerthegy u.31, 1016 Budapest, Hungary.

BIRKBY, Carel, b. 31 July 1910, Johannesburg, S. Africa. Journalist. Educ: Univ. of Cape Town. Publs: Thirstland Treks, 1934; Zulu Journey, 1935; Airman Lost in Africa, 1936; Limpopo Journey, 1939; Springbok Victory, 1941; It's A Long Way to Addis, 1941; Close to the Sun, 1944; The Pagel Story, 1949; Saga of the Transvaal Scottish, 1951; In the Sun I'm Rich, 1953; Overload, 1971; The Black Box, 1972. Contbr. to var. jrnls. Recip., Schlesinger Prize for Reporting, 1941. Address: The Sunday Times, Johannesburg, S. Africa.

BIRKENHEAD, Elijah, pen name BIRKENHEAD, Edward, b. 3 June 1903, Garston, Liverpool, UK. Retired Electrician; Author (fiction). Contbr. to: City Mags., Ltd., UK; var. Scandinavian jrnls. Mbrships. incl: Soc. of Authors; Lancs. Authors' Assn. Recip., Short Story Awards, 1962, 1963, 1965, 1968, 1972. Address: 32 Jubilee House, Runcorn, Cheshire, UK.

BIRKENMAYER, Sigmund Stanley, b. 5 June 1923, Warsaw, Poland. University Professor of Slavic languages & literatures. Educ: B.A., 1948, M.A.(English), 1949, M.A.(Russian), 1957, Ph.D.(Slavic langs. & lit.), 1961, Univ. of Wis., USA. Publs: N. A. Nekrasov: His Life & Poetic Art, 1968; An Accented Dictionary of Place Names in the Soviet Union, 1968, Supplement, 1970; A Modern Polish Reader (w. J. Krzyzanowski), 1970. Contbr. to US, for. jrnls. Hons: Head, E. European Lit. Sect., Annual Int. Bibliog. of Mod. Lang. Assn. of Am. Address: N-438 Burrowes, Univ. Park, PA 16802, USA.

BIRKIN, Charles Lloyd (Bart), pen name LLOYD, Charles, b. 24 Sept. 1907, Nottingham, UK. Writer. Publs: Devil's Spawn, 1936; The Kiss of Death, 1964; The Smell of Evil, 1965; Where Terror Stalked, 1966; My Name Is Death, 1966; Dark Menace, 1968; So Pale, So Cold, So Fair, 1970; Spawn of Satan, 1970. Contbr. to anthols. & mags. inclng: John Creasy's Mystery Bedside Book, 1972; Fantasy & Science Fiction Mag.; Argosy Mag. Recip., 2nd Prize, Crime Writers Short Story Competition, 1972. Address: P.O. Box 105, Kyrenia, Cyprus.

BIRLEY, Anthony Richard, b. 8 Oct. 1937. Chesterholm, UK. Professor of Ancient History. Educ: B.A., 1960, M.A., 1963, Univ. of Oxford; D.Phil., 1966. Publs: Life in Roman Britain, 1964; Marcus Aurelius, 1966; Septimius Severus the African Emperor, 1971. Contbr. to: Historia; Jrnl. of Roman Studies; Britannia; Sev. other profl. jrnls. Fellow, Soc. of Antiquaries of London. Address: Dept. of History, Univ. of Manchester, Manchester M13 9PL, UK.

BIRNEY, Earle, b. 13 May 1904, Calgary, Alta., Can. Freelance Writer & Lecturer; University Professor (retired). Educ: B.A., Univ. B.C., 1926; M.A., 1927, Ph.D., 1936, Univ. Toronto; Univs. Calif., London. Publs. incl: (poetry) David, 1942; Now is Time, 1945; Strait of Anian, 1948; Near False Creek Mouth, 1964; Rag & Bone Shop, 1971; Bear on the Delhi Road, 1973; What's so big about Green?, 1973; Collected Poems, 1974; (novel) Turvey, 1952; (verse drama) Trial of a City, 1949. Contbr. to many jrnls. in UK, USA, Can., TV & radio talks, plays, & poetry reading tours of UK, Asia, Aust., NZ, Latin Am., etc. Hons. incl: LL.D., Univ. Alta., 1965. Address: c/o McClelland & Stewart Ltd., Publrs., 25 Hollinger Rd., Toronto, Ont. M4G 3B2, Can.

BIRO, Val B.S., b. 6)ct. 1921, Budapest, Hungary. Book Illustrator. Educ: Ctrl. Schl. of Arts & Crafts, London, UK. Publs: The Gumdrop series for children (7 books, 1967—); The Honest Thief. Contbr. to: Radio Times; The Field; Daily Telegraph; Sunday Express; Sie und Er; Homes & Gardens. Mbrships. incl: Fellow, Soc. Indl. Artists & Designers; Soc. of Authors; Vintage Sports Car Club. Address: 95 High St., Amersham, Bucks., UK.

BIRRELL, Mary Jo, b. 6 Oct. 1930, Tulsa, Okla., USA. Editor/Publisher. Educ: A.A., Jrnlsm., Northern Okla. Jr. Coll., 1949; B.A., Univ. of Okla., 1951. Contbr. to: Can. Rides (Ed./Publr.); Horseman; Western Riders' Yrbook. Mbr., Var. ch. & civic orgs. Hons. incl: Southam Press Award for 1st Place in Non-Fiction Competition, 1970. Address: Box 118, Bragg Creek, Alta. TOL 0K0, Can.

BIRT, Catherine, b. 1917, Smarden, Kent, UK. Author. Publs: Royal Sisters, Vol. I; H.R.H. Princess Margaret; Princess Margaret's 19th Birthday Book; H.M. Queen Elizabeth. Contbr. to: Toronto Star, Can.; num. mags. & newspapers in UK & overseas. Address: 16 Royal Chase, Tunbridge Wells, Kent TN4 8AY, UK.

BIRTILL, George Arthur, pen name PENDLE, Nicholas, b. 1 Feb. 1912, Leyland, Lancs., UK. Newspaper Editor. Publs: Enchanted Hills; Heather in My Hat; Follow Any Stream; Green Pastures; Over the Five-Barred Gate; Towpath Trek. Mbrships: Guild of Brit. Newspaper Eds.; Nat. Union Jrnlsts. Hons: O.B.E.; J.P. Address: 72 Carrington Road, Chorley, Lancs., UK.

BISCH, Edith, pen name de BORN, Edith, b. Vienna, Austria. Writer. Educ: Vienna Univ. Publs: 17 novels. Mbrships: PEN; Soc. of Authors. Address: 77 Rue du Marteau, 1040 Brussels, Belgium.

BISHOP, (Rev.) Eric Francis Fox, b. 1891, Clifton, Bristol, UK. Retired Missionary (Near East); Retired University Lecturer. Educ: M.A., Clare Coll., Ridley Hall, Cambridge. Publs: Jesus of Palestine; Apostles of Palestine; The Light of Inspiration & Secret of Interpretation (w. Mohamed Kaddah); Prophets of Palestine; Our Feet Shall Stand Within Thy Gates; Job the Transjordanian. Contbr. to: Int. Review of Missions; Muslim World Quarterly; Glasgow Univ. Oriental Soc.; Expository Times; The Bible Translator; Ch. Quarterly; Hibbert Jrnl. Address: Thabor, Redstone Hill, Redhill, Surrey RH1 4BG, UK.

BISHOP, Ian Benjamin, b. 18 Apr. 1927, Gillingham, Kent, UK. University Teacher. Educ: M.A., B.Litt., Queen's Coll., Oxford Univ. Publs: "Pearl" in its Setting: A Critical Study of the Structure & Meaning of the Middle English Poem, 1968. Contbr. to: Ency. Britannica; Medium Aevum; Review of Engl. Studies. Address: Univ. of Bristol, Dept. of English, 40 Berkeley Sq., Bristol BS8 1HY, UK.

BISHOP, Richard E. D., b. 1 Jan. 1925, London, UK. University Professor. Educ: D.Sc.(Engrng), University Coll., London; M.S., Ph.D., Stanford Univ., Calif., USA; M.A., Sc.D., Cambridge Univ., UK. Publs: Mechanics of Vibration (w. D. C. Johnson), 1960; Vibration, 1964; Matrix Analysis of Vibration (co-author), 1964; Probabilistic Theory of Ship Dynamics (w. W. G. Price), 1974. Contbr. to: Proceedings of Royal Soc.; Philos. Transactions of Royal Soc.; Jrnl. of Mech. Engrng. Sci.; Proceedings of Inst. Mech. Engrs.; Aero Quarterly. Mbr., var. profl. assns. Hons. incl: Hawksley Gold Medal, 1965; Krizik Gold Medal, 1969; Rayleigh Gold Medal, 1973; Clayton Prize, 1973. Address: Univ. Coll., Gower St., London WC1, UK.

BISK, Anatole, pen name BOSQUET, Alain, b. 28 Mar. 1919, Odessa, Russia. Writer; Critic. Educ: Free Univ. of Brussels; Univ. of Paris (Sorbonne). Publs. incl: Verbe et Vertige (on contemp. poetry), 1961; La Confession mexicaine (novel), 1965; Entretiens avec Salvador Dali, 1967; Dorothea Tanning, Le Middle West, 1967; Les Tigres de papier (novel), 1968; Les Américains sont-ils Adultes?, 1969; Notes pour un amour (poetry), 1972. Contbr. to var. jrnls. Hons. incl: Grand Prix de Poésie de l'Académie Française, 1967. Address: 32 rue de Laborde, Paris 8e, France.

BISZTRAY, Adam, b. 5 Nov. 1935, Bucharest, Romania. Librarian. Educ: Agricl. Univ., Gödöllö; Fac. of Arts, Eötvös Lorand Univ., Budapest, Hungary. Publs: Költok egymas közt (anthol.), 1969; Erdontuli taj (poems), 1972; Elfelejtett tel, farkasokkal (prose), 1974. Contbr. to: Kortars; Alföld; Jelenkor; Magyar Hirlap; Magyar Nemzet. Mbrships. incl: Union of Hungarian Writers; lit. sect., Hungart; Hungarian Soc. of Agricl. Scis.; Hungarian Econ. Assn.; Hungarian Folklore Soc. Address: 1158 Budapest XV, Frankovics M.u. 71, 7/23, Hungary.

BITTERWOLF, Alfons, b. 3 Mar. 1929, Illingen, Germany. Author; Publisher. Educ: D.Hist., Univ. of Freiburg im Breisgau, German Fed. Repub. Publs: Der weise Blitz, 1957; Das schuldlose Blut (play), 1962; Adolf Hitler vor dem Jungsten Gericht (histl. drama); Der Mitlaufer (novel); Das Schlachthaus (novel); Mitautor: Generalstab Gottes, 1962; Demokratie, Justiz, Verbrechen in Deutschland, 1975. Contbr. to: Blitz Illustrierte (Ed.-in-Chief); Deutsches Mannequin Jrnl. (Ed.-in-Chief). Mbr., Soc. of German Speaking Authors. Recip., ECON Publishing Prize. Address: Neuestrasse 32, 7551 Illingen, Germany.

BIVIN, Virginia Norwood Pritchett, b. 21 July 1922, Nashville, Tenn., USA. Former Journalist & Drama Critic. Educ: B.A., Vanderbilt Univ., 1943. Publs: author of 3 chapts. in: Footprints of Allen Dobson in the Sands of Time. Former contbr. to: Tenn. Conservationist; Nashville Banner (as columnist, drama critic & feature writer). Mbrships. incl: Nat. League Am. PEN Women (Nashville

br.); Woman's Club of Nashville (Life mbr.); Mortar Board, Vanderbilt Univ. (past Pres.). Recip., var. lit. hons. Address: 3611 Rainbow Place, Nashville, TN 37204, USA.

BIYIDI-AWALA, Alexandre, pen name BETI, Mongo, b. 30 June 1932, Mbalmayo, Cameroon. Literature Teacher. Educ: Univ. of Aix-Marseille, France; Sorbonne, Paris; B.Litt. Publs: Le Pauvre Christ de Bomba, 1956; Mission Terminée, 1957; Le roi miraculé, 1958; Main basse sur le Cameroun, 1972; Remember Ruben, 1974; Perpétue & l'habitude du malheur, 1974. Recip., Sainte-Beuve Prize, for Mission Terminee, 1958. Address: 6 Rue d'Harcourt, 76000 Rouen, France.

BIZZAH, Rodgers Cox Tapera, b. 13 July 1944, Maronda-Mashanu, Rhodesia. Labour Supervisor. Educ: Univ. Publs: Chaitemura Chava Kuseva, 1971. Address: 7 Rwenya Rd., New Mabvuku, P.O. Mabvuku, Salisbury, Rhodesia.

BJORKEGREN, Hans R., b. 26 Jan. 1933, Visby, Sweden. Foreign Editor, Swedish News Agency. Educ: B.A., M.A. Publs. incl: Den bla lyktgubben (short stories), 1950; Mistral (poetry), 1955; Manniskor i Sovjet (essays), 1967; Alexander Solzhenitsyn (biog. & documents), 1971, 1972, Norwegian, Dutch, US & UK eds.; Introducer, Transl., Solzhenitsyn, Yevtushenko, Okudzhava, Aksionov, Baklanov & Edgar Snow. Mbrships: Int. Press Inst.; Union of Swedish Writers; PEN; Swedish Inst. of Int. Affairs; Publicists' Club. Hons: Num. prizes for transls., inclng. Swedish Acad. of Sci. Prize, De Nio's Prize, Swedish Writers Fund. Address: Tidningarnas Telegrambyra, Sveavagen 17, Stockholm, Sweden.

BJÖRKMAN, Lars, b. 8 Aug. 1930, Stockholm, Sweden. Playwright. Publs. (plays): The Smiling Consumer, 1966; The Scandal, 1971; The Bigwig, 1972; The Summit-meeting, 1973; Waiting for Bardot, 1974. Mbr., Pres., Swedish Union of Playwriters. Address: Åsögatan 129, 116 24 Stockholm, Sweden.

BJÖRNSSON, Jón, b. 12 Mar. 1907, Holt in Síða, Skaftafellssýsla, Iceland. Librarian. Publs: The Earth's Power, 1942; Family Honor, 1944; The King's Friend, 1946; The Buddha Idol, 1948; Beauteous Day Brightens the Whole World, 1950; Valtýr in the Green Coat, 1951; The Fiery Test, 1952; Bergljot, 1954; All These Things Will I Give Thee, 1955; The Virgin Thordis, 1964. Contbr. of short stories & criticism to var. mags. Mbrships. incl: Writer's Assn. of Iceland. Hons. incl: Lit. Prize, Icelandic Writers Fndn., 1970. Address: Kárástígur 9, Reykjavík, Iceland.

BJÖRNSSON, Vigfus, pen names HANNSON, Gestur; HLYNUR, Hreggvidur; KARLSSON, Kári, b. 20 Jan. 1927, Ásar í Skaftártungu, V. Skaft., Iceland. Master Book-Binder. Publs: Strákur á kúskinnsskóm, 1958; Strákur í stríði, 1959; Vort strákablód, 1960; Strákar og heljarmenni, 1962; Imbúlimbimm, 1963; Pær fóru nordur, 1963; 2 tröfaldir & 4 einfaldir, 1967. Contbr. to: Jörd (Erth); Heime er bezt; etc. Mbr., Icelandic Authors Assn. Address: Ásabyggd 10, Akureyri, Iceland.

BLACK, Clinton Vane DeBrosse, b. 26 Aug. 1918, Kingston, Jamaica. Archivist. Educ: Archive Admin., University Coll., London, UK. Publs: Historic Port Royal (co—author), 1952; Report on Archives of British Guiana, 1955; Report on Archives of Trinidad & Tobago (co-author), 1958; The History of Jamaica, 1958; Spanish Town: The Old Capital, 1960; Our Archives, 1962; The Story of Jamaica, 1965; Tales of Old Jamaica, 1966; Port Royal, a History & Guide, 1970; A New History of Jamaica, 1973; Jamaica Guide, 1973. Contbr. to var. Jamaican & overseas mags. Mbrships incl: F.S.A., London; Soc. of Archivists; British Records Assn.; Jamaican Historical Soc.; Poetry League of Jamaica; Int. PEN (exec. comm., Jamaica Ctr., twice Pres.). Address: 5 Avesbury Ave., Kingston 6, Jamaica.

BLACK, Edward Loring, b. 3 May 1915, Sutton Coldfield, UK. Principal, College of Education. Educ: B.A., 1936, M.A., 1944, Univ. of Cambridge; M.Ed., Univ. of Manchester, 1954. Publs: Precis & Comprehension Practice (w. A. H. Lawley); Sporting Scenes; Youth on the Prow (w. J. P. Parry); Aspects of the Short Story; Starting Work; 1st, 2nd, 3rd, 4th & 5th Year English (w. E. R. Wood); Nine Modern Poets, 1966; Schooldays; 1914-18 in Poetry, 1970; Passport to Poetry. Contbr. to: Brit. Jrnl. of Educl. Psychol.; Use of Engl.; Engl. Address: Coll. of Educ., Middleton St. George, Darlington, Co. Durham, UK.

BLACK, Harold Stephen, b. 14 Apr. 1898, Leominster, Mass., USA. Electrical Engineer; Inventor; Consultant. Educ: B.S., Worcester Polytechnic Inst., 1921; D.Eng., 1955. Publs: Feedback Amplifiers, 1936; Modulation Theory, 1953; Holder, 347 patents in 35 countries. Contbr. of 25 articles to encys., num. articles to profl. jrnls. Num. hons. incl: Nat. Best Paper Prize in Theory & Rsch., Am. Inst. of Elec. Engrs., 1934. Address: 120 Winchip Rd., Countryside, Summit, NJ 07901, USA.

BLACK, Ian Stuart, b. 21 Mar. 1915, London, UK. Author; Scriptwriter. Educ: B.A., Manchester Univ. Publs: In the Wake of a Stranger, 1953; The Passionate City, 1958; The Yellow Flag, 1959; Love in Four Countries, 1961; The High Bright Sun, 1962; The Man on the Bridge; (play) We Must Kill Toni. Contbr. to: The Guardian. Mbr., Writers' Guild of GB. Address: Burwood, Rotherfield, Sussex, UK.

BLACK, Margaret Katherine, pen names HOWARD, Katherine; HOWORTH, Margaret, b. 22 Sept. 1921, London, UK. Publisher's Editor; Writer. Educ: Sorbonne Univ., Paris, France; B.A., Witwatersrand Univ., S. Africa. Publs. incl: The City Built on Gold, 1957; A South African Holiday, 1958; No Room for Tourists, 1960; Design for Living, 1968; Cooking for One, 1975. Contbr. to: House & Gdn.; Lady; Illustrated London News; Christian Sci. Monitor; Wine & Food; BBC Radio; etc. Mbrships. incl: Soc. of Authors; PEN; Royal Inst. of Int. Affairs. Recip., Short Story Award, Soc. of Women Jrnlsts., 1958. Agent: Hope Leresche & Steele. Address: 34 Shepherds Hill, London N6 5AH, UK.

BLACK, (Sir) Misha, b. 1910, Baku, Russia. Design Consultant. Publs: The Practice of Design (co-author); Exhibition Design; Public Interiors. Contbr. to archtl. & design press. Mbrships: Royal Designer for Ind.; Fellow, Soc. of Indl. Artists; Pres., 1954-56; Pres., Int. Coun., Socs. of Indl. Design, 1959-61; Inst. of Registered Archts.; Arch. Assn. Address: 160 Gloucester Rd., London SW7, UK.

BLACK, Percy, b. 6 Jan. 1922, Montreal, Can. University Professor of Psychology. Educ: B.Sc., Sir George Williams Coll., Montreal, 1944; M.Sc., McGill Univ., ibid. 1946; A.M., 1947, Ph.D., 1953, Harvard Univ., USA. Publs: The Mystique of Modern Monarchy, 1953. Contbr. to: Socs. Around the World, 1956; Mind; Sci.; Jrnl. of Psychol.; Human Rels.; Jrnl. of Comparative & Physiol Psychol.; Psychol. Bulletin. Mbrships: Am. Psychol. Assn.; Fellow, AAAS. Address: 29 Cross Hill Ave., Yonkers, NY 10703, USA.

BLACKBURN, Evelyn Barbara, pen name CASTLE, Frances, b. July 1898, Hereford, UK. Novelist; Playwright. Publs. incl: (novels) Return to Bondage, 1926; Good Times, 1935; Georgina Goes Home, 1951; Star Spangled Heavens, 1953; The Buds of May, 1955; Green for Lovers, 1958; Story of Alix, 1959; The Little Cousin, 1960; Doctor & Debutante, 1961; Learn her by Heart, 1962; City of Forever, 1963; Come Back my Love, 1963; (as Frances Castle) Tara's Daughter, 1970; The Thread of Gold, 1971; (play) Poor Man's Castle (w. Mundy Whitehouse), 1949. Address: Anchor Cottage, Latchingdon, Chelmsford, Essex, UK.

BLACKBURN, Geoffrey Herbert, b. 7 Nov. 1914, Melbourne, Australia. Minister of Religion, Syndal Baptist Church, Melbourne; Former Editor-in-Chief, Australian Baptist Board of Christian Education. Educ: Univ. of Melbourne; Bapt. Theol. Coll. of Victoria; Melbourne Coll. of Divinity; M.A.; B.D.; B.Ed.; Ph.D. Publs: Methods of Biblical Study in the Early Christian Church, 1968; Planner's Manual, 1971. Contbr. to: The Australian Baptist; Victorian Baptist Witness. Address: 10 Shirley Ave., Glen Waverly, Victoria, Australia 3150.

BLACKETT, Veronica Heath Stuart (née Tegner), pen name HEATH, Veronica, b. 20 Oct. 1927,London, UK. Writer; Housewife. Publs. incl: Your Pony; Susan's Riding School; Come Riding With Me; Come Show-Jumping With Me; Ponies in the Heath; Ponies; Ponies & Pony Management; Come Pony-Trekking With Me; So You Want to be a Showjumper, The Family Dog; Beginner's Guide to Riding. Contbr. to: Times; Horse & Hound; Country Life; Scottish Field; Shooting Times; etc. Address: W. House, Whalton, Morpeth, Northumberland, NE61 3UZ, UK.

BLACKHAM, Harold John, b. 1903, Birmingham, UK. Chairman, Social Morality Council. Educ: B.A., Univ. of Birmingham. Publs: Six Existentialist Thinkers, 1951; The Human Tradition, 1952; Political Discipline in a Free Society, 1961; Religion in a Modern Society, 1966; Humanism, 1968. Contbr. to: Objections to Humanism; Reality, Man & Experience; Ideas of Human Nature. Mbrships: Soc. of Authors; Nat. Book League. Agent: Shaw Maclean. Address: 22 The Avenue, Twickenham, Middlesex, UK.

BLACKMAN, Edwin Cyril, b. 1908, Portsmouth, UK. University Professor. Educ: Univ. of Cambridge; Univ. of Oxford; Univ. of Marburg; M.A.; B.D.; D.D. Publs: Marcion & His Influence; The Faith We Preach; The Epistle of James. Contbr. to: Can. Jrnl. Theol.; Jrnl. Biblical Lit.; Abingdon Bible Commentary; Interpreters Dict. of the Bible. Address: 6 Rathmore Rd., Cambridge CB1 4AD, UK.

BLACKSTONE, Geoffrey Vaughan, b. 9 May, 1910. Easton, Northants, UK. Retired Chief Fire Officer. Publs: Caroline Matilda, 1955; A History of the British Fire Service, 1957. Contbr. to: Times; Guardian. Hons: G.M., 1941; Off., Order of St. John, 1948; Queen's Fire Service Medal, 1964; C.B.E., 1956. Address: Dassels Bury, Ware, Herts., UK.

BLACKSTONE, Tessa, b. 27 Sept. 1942, London, UK. Lecturer in Social Administration. Educ: B.Sc., 1964; Ph.D., 1969. Publs: Students in Conflict, L.S.E. in 1967 (w. K. Gales, R. Hadley, & W. Lewis), 1970; A Fair Start: The Provision of Pre-school Education, 1971; The Academic Labour Market: Economic & Social Aspects of a Profession (w. G. Williams & D. Metcalf), 1974. Contbr. to: Brit. Jrnl. of Sociol.; Higher Educ.; Trends in Educ.; New Soc. Address: 11 Grazebrook Rd., London N16, UK.

BLADES, James, b. Peterborough, UK. Orchestral Timpanist; Tutor; Lecturer; Author. Publs: Orchestral Percussion Technique, 1961; Percussion Instruments & Their History, 1970. Contbr. to: Ency. Britannica; Music Teacher; Saturday Book, 1969; Musical Instruments Through the Ages. Hons: OBE; RAM. Address: 191 Sandy Lane, Cheam, Surrey, UK.

BLAIKIE, (Rev.) Robert Jackson, b. 8 Oct. 1923, Kijabe, Kenya, d. 8 Feb., 1975, NZ. Minister of Religion. Educ: M.A., Edinburgh Univ., UK; B.D., St. Andrews Univ. Publs: 'Secular Christianity' & God Who Acts, 1970. Contbr. to: Scottish Jrnl. of Theol.; Colloquium (Aust. & NZ).

BLAINEY, Geoffrey, b. 11 Mar. 1930, Melbourne, Australia. Professor of Economic History. Educ: Univ. of Melbourne. Publs. incl: Mines in the Spinifex, 1960; The Rush that never Ended, 1963; History of Camberwell, 1964; The Tyranny of Distance, 1966; Ed., If I Remember Rightly, 1967; Across a Red World, 1968; The Rise of Broken Hill, 1968; The Steel Master, 1971; The Causes of War, 1973. Contbr. to histl. & lit. jrnls. Mbrships: Bd., C'wlth Lit. Fund, 1967-73; Chmn., Lit. Bd., Aust. Coun. for the Arts, 1973-74. Hons. incl: Gold Medal, Aust. Lit. Soc., 1963; Capt. Cook Sesqui-centenary Prize (biog.), 1970. Address: 262 The Boulevard, E. Ivanhoe, Vic., Australia.

BLAIR, Alan, b. 25 May 1915, Melbourne, Australia. Translator. Publs: Over 30 transls. of Swedish & Finnish authors inclng. Stig Dagerman, Pär Lagerkvist, Göran Schildt, Olof Lagercrantz, Sjöwall-Wahlöö, Per Olov Enquist, K. M. Wallenius, Mika Waltari, Mauri Sariola, F. E. Sillanpää, Toivo Pekkanen. Mbrships: Soc. of Authors, London, UK; Swedish Authors' Union, Stockholm. Recip., Transl. Prize, Swedish Acad., 1971. Address: Konstgjutarvägen 55, S-121 44 Johanneshov, Sweden.

BLAIR, Arthur, b. Dunoon, UK. Editor. Educ: Univ. Coll., Univ. of London. Publs: World of Stamps & Stamp Collecting; Stamp Compendium; Stamps; Coins. Contbr. to: Ed., Coins & Medals; Cons. Ed., Stamp Mag.; Gen. Ed., Batsford Studies in Philately. Mbrships: Royal Philatelic Soc.; Royal Numismatic Soc. Address: 10/12 South Cres., Store St., London WC1E 7BG, UK.

BLAIR, Claude, b. 30 Nov. 1922, Manchester, UK. Keeper of Metalwork, Victoria & Albert Museum, London. Educ: B.A., M.A., Manchester Univ. Publs: European Armour, 1958; European & American Arms, 1962; Pistols of the World, 1968; The Silvered Armour of Henry VIII in the Tower of London, 1965; Catalogue of the James de Rothschild Collection, Waddesdon Manor: Arms, Armour & Miscellaneous Metalwork, 1974. Contbr. to: Ency. Britannica; Metropolitan Mus. Jrnl.; Jrnl. of the Arms & Armour Soc.; Archaeol. Jrnl.; & others. Mbrships. incl:

Royal Archaeol. Inst.; Soc. of Genealogists; Arms & Armour Soc.; Soc. of Antiquaries of London. Address: 90 Links Road, Ashtead, Surrey, UK.

BLAIR, Clay Drewry, Jr., b. 1 May 1925. Writer; Editor. Educ: Tulane & Columbia Univs. Publs: The Atomic Submarine & Admiral Rickover, 1954; The Hydrogen Bomb (co-author), 1954; Beyond Courage, 1955; Valley of the Shadow, 1955; Nautilus 90; North (co-author), 1959; Diving for Pleasure & Treasure, 1960; Always Another Dawn (co-author), 1960. Contbr. to: Time; Life; Sat. Evening Post. Address: Copper Beech Rd., Greenwich, CT, USA.

BLAIR, John George, b. 3 Dec. 1934, NYC, USA. University Professor of American Literature & Civilization. Educ: A.B., Brown Univ., 1956; M.A., Columbia Univ., 1957; Ph.D., Brown Univ., 1962. Publs: The Poetic Art of W. H. Auden, 1965. Contbr. to: Am. Quarterly; Am. Transcendental Quarterly; Shenandoah; Bulletin of Fac. of Letters, Strasbourg, France. Mbrships: Swiss Assn. of Univ. Tchrs. of Engl.; Am. Studies Assns. of Europe & USA; MLA of Am. Address: Faculty of Letters, Univ. of Geneva, 1204 Geneva, Switz.

BLAIR, Richard Lawrence, pen name HORTON, David, b. 31 May 1942, Middleboro, Mass., USA. Journalist. Educ: B.A., UCLA. Publs: Marketing Practices in Japan, 1973. Contbr. to: Sydney Morning Herald; Melbourne Age; London Sun; Nat. Enquirer. Mbr., For. Correspondents' Club of Japan. Address: 12 Suga Cho, Shinjuku, Tokyo, Japan.

BLAIR, Ruth Van Ness (Ruth Virginia), Mrs. Glenn M., b. 9 June 1912, St. Michael, Alaska. Writer; Former School Teacher. Publs: Puddle Duck, 1966; A Bear Can Hibernate — Why Can't I?, 1972; Willa-Willa, The Wishful Witch, 1972; Mary's Monster, 1975. Poetry contbr. to: Athene Mag.; Music Jrnl.: Christian Living. Gen. lit. contbns., Ency. Britannica Educ. Corp. Hons: Short Story Contest Winner, 1963, Essay Contest Double Winner, 1965, Writers' Digest. Address: 305 W. Delaware, Urbana, IL 61801, USA.

BLAIS, Marie-Claire, b. 5 Oct. 1939, Quebec City, P.Q., Can. Writer. Publs: La Belle Bête, 1959; Tête blanche, 1960; Le jour est noir, 1962; Une saison dans la vie d'Emmanuel, 1965; L'Insoumise, 1966; Les voyageurs sacres, 1969; Manuscrits de Pauline Archange, 1970; Pays Voiles (poems); Existences (poems). Hons. incl: Prix de la langue française, 1961; Prix France-Quebec, 1964; Prix Médicis, 1966. Address: c/o Les Editions du Jour, 1651 St. Denis, Montreal, P.Q., Can.

BLAKE, Nelson Manfred, b. 1908, Island Pond, Vt., USA. Former University Professor of History; Author. Educ: A.B.; M.A.; Ph.D.; Brown Univ.; Clark Univ. Publs: A History of American Life & Thought; Water for the Cities; Novelists' America: Fiction as History; The Road to Reno; A History of Divorce in the United States; Since 1900: A History of the United States in Our Times (co-author). Contbr. to: Am. Hist. Review; Miss. Valley Hist. Review; Am. Heritage. Mbrships: Am. Hist. Assn.; AAUP; Org. Am. Histns. Address: 400 S.E. 10th St., Apt. 218A, Deerfield Beach, FL, USA.

BLAKE, (Baron) Robert Norman William, of Braydeston, b. 1916, Brundall, UK. Provost of The Queen's College, Oxford. Educ: M.A., Magdalen Coll., Oxford. Publs.: (Ed.) The Private Papers of Douglas Haig, 1952; The Unknown Prime Minister: the Life & Times of Andrew Bonar Law 1858-1923, 1955; Disraeli, 1966; The Conservative Party from Peel to Churchill, 1971. Contbr. to: Sunday Times; Spectator; Etc. Mbrships: Fellow, Brit. Acad.; Royal Histl. Soc. Recip., Life Peer, 1971. Address: The Provost's Lodgings, Queen's Coll., Oxford, UK.

BLAKE, Sally, pen name SARA, b. 11 June 1925, Boston, Mass., USA. Writer. Educ: B.S., Boston Univ, 1945; M.A., San Fran. State Coll., 1964. Publs: Where Mist Clothes Dream & Song Runs Naked (novel), 1965, 3rd ed., 1974; A House Divided (novella & collect. of short stories), 1968. Contbr. to: My Name Aloud — A Jewish Anthol.; var. mags. & newspapers. Recip., O. Henry Award, 1964. Address: 200 Julia Ave., Mill Valley, CA 94941, USA.

BLAKISTON, Hugh Noel, b. 8 Dec. 1905, Horncastle, Lincs., UK. Civil Servant (Retired). Educ: B.A., Magdalene Coll., Cambridge. Publs. Canon James, 1951; Men of Letters, 1955; The Lecture, 1961; That Thoughtful Boy, 1965; The Roman Question, Despatches of Odo Russell

from Rome 1858-70, 1962; Inglesi e Italiani nel Risorgimento, 1972. Contbr. to: Burlington Mag.; Cornhill; La Cultura; Engl. Hist. Review; etc.; Catalogue of Archives of Eton Coll. Mbrships: Hon. Mbr., Istituto per la storia del Risorgimento italiano; Chmn., Chelsea Soc., 1967-. Hons: O.B.E., 1955; Hon. Fellow, Eton Coll., 1974. Address: 6 Markham Square, London SW3, UK.

BLAMIRES, Harry, b. 6 Nov. 1916, Bradford, Yorks., UK. College Dean & Lecturer. Educ: M.A., Univ. Coll., Oxford. Publs: (novels) The Devil's Hunting-Grounds, 1954; Cold War in Hell, 1955; Blessing Unbounded, 1955; (theol.) The Faith & Modern Error, 1956; The Kirkbride Conversations, 1958; The Christian Mind, 1963; A Defence of Dogmatism, 1965; (lit. criticism) The Bloomsday Book, 1966; Word Unheard, 1969; Milton's Creation, 1971; A Short History of English Literature, 1974; books on educ. & other theol. works. Mbr., Soc. of Authors. Address: 11 Worthy Lane, Winchester, Hants. SO23 7AB, UK.

BLANCH, Lesley, b. 1907, London, UK. Author. Publs: The Wilder Shores of Love, 1954; The Game of Hearts, 1955; Round the World in Eighty Dishes, 1956; The Sabres of Paradise, 1960; (travel) Under a Lilac—Bleeding Star, 1963; (fiction) The Nine Tiger man, 1965; (autobiography) Journey into the Mind's Eye, 1968. Address: Roquebrune Village, Cap Martin, Alpes Maritimes, France.

BLANCPAIN, Marc, b. 29 Sept. 1909. Writer. Educ: Colls. of Hirson & Laon; Univs. of Nancy & Paris (Sorbonne); Ecole Normale supérieure, Saint-Cloud. Publs. incl Vincennes Neuilly (stories), 1963; Grandes Heures d'un Village de la Frontière, 1964; Les Truffes du Voyage, 1965; Aujourd'hui, l'Amérique latine, 1966; Ulla des Antipodes (novel), 1967; Les Lumières de la France (essay), 1967; La Saga des Amants Séparés, vol. I, 1969, vol. II, 1970, vol. III, 1972. Mbrships. incl: PEN. Recip., num. awards & decorations. Address: 12 boulevard Jean Mermoz, 92 Neuilly-sur-Seine, France.

BLANDFORD, Percy William, b. 1912, Bristol, UK. Technical Author. Educ: M.CC.Ed.; Assoc., Royal Inst. Naval Archts. Publs: Netmaking; Rope Splicing; Wood Carving; Wood Turning; Boat Building; Metal Turning; Canoeing; Scouting on the Water; Build Your Own Boat; Canoes & Canoeing, USA; Practical Boatman, 1971; Sailing Dinghies of the World, 1972; Country Craft Tools, 1974; An Illustrated History of Small Boats, 1974; Boat Repairs Made Easy, USA, 1975. Contbr. to: Small Boat; Practical Boat Owner; Popular Camping. Address: Quinton House, Newbold-on-Stour, Stratford-on-Avon, Warwicks. CV37 8UA, UK.

BLANKENSHIP, A. B., b. 21 Aug. 1914, Lancaster, Pa., USA. Professor of Marketing; Author. Educ: A.B., Franklin & Marshall Coll.; A.M., Univ. of Ore.; Ph.D., Columbia Univ. Publs: Consumer & Opinion Research, 1943; Ed., How to Conduct Consumer & Opinion Research, 1946; Marketing: an Introduction (w. M. S. Heidingsfield), 1948, 3rd ed., 1974; Market & Marketing Research (w. M. S. Heidingsfield), 1963; Marketing Research Management (w. J. B. Doyle), 1965. Contbr. to: Jrnl. of Mktng.; Jrnl. of Mktng. Rsch.; Jrnl. of Advt. Rsch. Address: 504 Hillcrest Dr., Bowling Green, OH 43402, USA.

BLANKFORT, Michael Seymour, b. 10 Dec. 1907, NYC, USA. Writer. Educ: B.A., Univ. of Pa.; M.A., Princeton Univ. Publs: I Met a Man, 1937; The Brave & the Blind, 1940; A Time to Live, 1943; The Widow Makers, 1946; The Big Yankee, a biography of General Evans Carlson, USMC, 1947; The Juggler, 1952; The Strong Hand, 1956; Goodbye, I Guess, 1962; Behold the Fire, 1965; I Didn't Know I Would Live So Long, 1973. Mbrships: Nat. Chmn., Writers' Guild of Am.; Authors' League; Dramatists' Guild; PEN. Hons: Samuel Daroff Prize for The Juggler; C'wlth. Club Gold Medal for Best Novel by Californian, Behold the Fire; Writers' Guild 1st Prize, Broken Arrow. Address: 1636 Comstock Ave. L.A., CA 90024, USA.

BLANZAT, Jean, b. 1905. Writer. Educ: Coll. of Bellac; Ecole normale d'instituterus de Versailles. Publs: Enfance, 1930; A moi-même ennemi, 1933; Septembre, 1936; L'Orage du matin, 1942; La Gartempe, 1957; Le Faussaire, 1965; L'Idoine, 1966. Hons: Grand Prix du roman de l'Academie française, 1942; Prix Femina, 1965. Address: 7 rue de Navarre, Paris 5e, France.

BLATHWAYT, Jean, b. 1918, Melbury Osmond, Dorset, UK. Writer. Publs: 7 Children's books, 1957-60; The Mushroom Girl, 1960; On the Run for Home, 1965;

House of Shadows, 1967; Lucy's Brownie Road, 1970; River in the Hills, 1971; Lucy's Last Brownie Challenge, 1972. Contbr. to Girl Guide jrnls. Agent: Lloyd-George & Coward. Address: Sunbank, 9 E. Terrace, Budleigh Salterton, Devon, UK.

BLATTY, William Peter, b. USA. Screenwriter; Novelist. Educ: Georgetown Univ. Publs. incl: Which Way to Mecca, Jack? ; John Goldfarb, Please Come Home! ; I, Billy Shakespeare; Twinkle, Twinkle, 'Killer' Kane; The Exorcist (also Author-Prod. of screenplay); I'll Tell Them I Remember You; (screenplays) A Shot in the Dark; What Did You Do in the War, Daddy? ; Gunn; One Flew over the Cuckoo's Nest, from novel by Ken Kesey (forthcoming); Twinkle, Twinkle, 'Killer' Kane, (forthcoming). Hons: Blue Ribbon, Am. Film Festival; Gabriel Award, Nat. Catholic Broadcasters Assn.; Silver Medal for Lit., Commonwealth Club of Calif., for The Exorcist. Address: c/o Warner Bros.. Burbank, Calif., USA; & c/o Corgi Books, Transworld Publishers Ltd., Cavendish House, 57-59 Uxbridge Rd., London W5, UK.

BLAUSTEIN, Albert Paul, b. 12 Oct. 1921, NYC, USA. Legal Educator. Educ: A.B., Univ. of Mich., 1941; J.D., Columbia, 1948. Publs: over 20 books inclng: The American Lawyer (co-author), 1954, 1974; Desegregation & the Law (co-author), 1957, 1962; Civil Rights & the American Negro, 1968, title changed to Civil Rights & the Black American, 1968 & 1970; Intellectual Property: Cases & Materials (co-author), 1971 & 1973; Constitutions of the Countries of the World (co-author), 14 vols., 1971—; Housing Discrimination in New Jersey, 1972; Human Rights & the Bangladesh Trials, 1973; A Bibliography on the Common Law in French (co-author), 1974. Co-fndr., 1st Ed.-in-Chief, Columbia Law Schl. News, 1947; contbr. to var. legal jrnls. Address: Rutgers Univ., School of Law, Camden, NJ 08012, USA.

BLAUSTEIN, Esther, b. Newark, N.J., USA. Writer; Newspaper Editor. Educ: B.A., Fairleigh Dickinson Univ., Rutherford, N.J. Publs: When Mamma Was the Landlord, 1972. Contbr. to: N.Y. Times; Good Housekeeping; Wall St. Jrnl. Hons. incl: Awards for Ed. of Best Newspaper of Intermediate Cities, Coun. of Jewish Fedns. & Welfare Funds, 1972, '73, & '74. Address: 860 Ray Ave., Union, NJ 07083, USA.

BLAUTH-MUSZKOWSKI, Peter Christopher, pen name BLAUTH, Christopher, b. 1919, Warsaw, Poland. Educ: Grenoble Univ. France. Publs: Transl., Life in Both Hands — Maria Glinter. Contbr. to: Polish Wkly News. Mbrships: Transls. Sect., Soc. of Authors; Special Forces Club; City of London Club. Address: 45 Meadvale Rd., London W5, UK.

BLAXLAND, (William) Gregory, b. 1918, Norwich, UK. Writer. Educ: Sandhurst Mil. Coll. Publs: J. H. Thomas: A Life for Unity, 1964; Objective: Egypt, 1966; The Farewell Years: The Buffs, 1948-67, 1967; Amiens 1918, 1968; The Regiments Depart, 1971; The Buffs, 1972; Golden Miller, 1972; Destination Dunkirk, 1973. Mbrships: Fellow, Royal Histl. Soc.; United Serv. Club. Agent: A. M. Heath. Address: Lower Heppington, Street End, Canterbury, UK.

BLAZER, John Allison, b. 18 Apr. 1930, Nashville, Tenn., USA. Clinical Psychologist. Educ: B.A., Andrew Jackson Univ., 1954; LL.B., Blackstone Schl. of Law, 1955; A.A., Cumberland Univ., 1958; Univ. of Tenn.; B.S., 1959, M.S., 1960, Coll. of Wm. & Mary; M.A., Burton Coll., 1960; Vanderbilt, Miami Univs.; Ph.D. Free Protestant Epsic. Univ., 1962; Univ. of London; Sorbonne, Paris. Contbr. to profl. jrnls. Address: 308 Kensington Dr., Savannah, GA 31405, USA.

BLECHMAN, Burt, b. 2 Mar. 1927, NYC, USA. Writer. Educ: B.A., Univ. Vt.; M.S., Columbia Univ. Publs: How Much? , 1961; The War of Camp Omongo, 1963; Stations, 1964; The Octopus Papers, 1966; Maybe, 1967. Recip., Ingram Merill Fndn. Award, 1965. Address: 200 Waverly Pl., N.Y., NY 10014, USA.

BLEEKER, C. Jouco, b. 12 Sept. 1898, Beneden Knype, Netherlands. Former Minister, Dutch Reformed Church; Professor of the History of Religions. Educ: Univs. of Leyden, Netherlands, & Berlin, Germany. Publs: Die Geburt eines Gottes, eine Studie über den Ägyptischen Gott Min und sein Fest, 1956; The Sacred Bridge, Researches into the Nature & Structure of Religion, 1963; Hathor & Thoth, Two Key Figures of the Ancient Egyptian Religion, 1973. Contbr. to Numen & supplements; Ed.-in-Chief, & past Sec.-Gen., Int. Assn. for the Hist. of

Relig. Recip., Hon. Doct., Univ. of Strasbourg. Address: Churchill-laan, 290 1, Amsterdam, Netherlands.

BLENKIN, Hugh Linton, b. 1916, St. Albans, UK. Principal College Lecturer in Religious Studies. Educ: M.A., Univ. of Cambridge; S.Th. Publs: Church, Children & Holy Week, 1959; Immortal Sacrifice, 1964. Contbr. to: Theol.; View Review; Ch. Times. Address: Hill Brow, The Green, Pitton, Salisbury, Wilts., UK.

BLICKER, Seymour, b. 12 Feb. 1940, Montreal, Can. Writer. Educ: B.A., Loyola Coll. of Montreal, 1962. Publs: Blues Chased a Rabbit (novel), 1969; Shmucks (novel), 1972. Mbrships: PEN (Can. Ctr.); Can. Authors' Assn.; Writers' Guild of Am. Recip., Sr. Arts Grant, Can. Coun., 1974. Address: 8 Gayton Rd., Montreal H3X 1K7, P.Q., Can.

BLISH, James (Benjamin), pen name (for 2 books) ATHELING, William, Jr., b. 23 May 1921, Orange, N.J., USA. Author. Educ: B.Sc., Rutgers Univ., 1942; Columbia Univ. Publs. incl: Earthman, Come Home, 1955; The Seedling Stars, 1956; Galactic Cluster, 1959; A Life for the Stars, 1962; Doctor Mirabilis, 1963; Best SF Stories of James Blish, 1965, revised ed., 1973; Black Easter, 1968; Cities in Flight, 1970; The Day After Judgement, 1971; Midsummer Century, 1972; The Quincunx of Time, 1973; (as W. Atheling) The Issue at Hand, 1964; More Issues at Hand, 1970; also film & TV scripts. Contbr. to: Sewanee Review; Hopkins Review; Poetry; etc. Mbr., Sci. Fiction Writers of Am. Recip., Hugo Award for Best Sci. Fiction Novel, 1958. Agent: Robert P. Mills, Ltd. Address: Treetops, Woodlands Rd., Harpsden, Henley, Oxon., UK.

BLIVEN, Bruce, b. Emmetsburg, Iowa, USA. Journalist; University Lecturer. Educ: A.B., Stanford Univ. Publs: The Men Who Make the Future; Preview for Tomorrow; The World Changers; Five Million Words Later (autobiog.); A Mirror for Greatness; Ed., What the Informed Citizen Needs to Know; Twentieth Century Unlimited. Contbr. to: Manchester Guardian (N.Y. Corres., 1927-47); Saturday Evening Post; Ladies' Home Jrnl.; Reader's Digest; Harper's; Redbook; etc. Address: 21 Kingscote Gdns., Stanford, CA 94305, USA.

BLOCH, Marie Halun, b. 1 Dec. 1910, Komarno, Ukraine. Writer. Educ: Ph.B., Univ. of Chgo., 1935. Publs. incl: Tunnels, 1954; Tony of the Ghost Towns, 1956; Mountains on the Move, 1960; Aunt America, 1963; Bern, Son of Mikula, 1972; (transls.) Ukrainian Folk Tales, 1964; Ivanko & the Dragon, 1969. Contbr. to: Wash. Post, 1935-41; Denver Post (children's bk. reviews, 1950-60). Mbrships. incl: Ukrainian Acad., Arts & Scis. in USA; Soc. of Children's Book Writers. Hons. incl: Honor Book, N.Y. Herald Tribune, 1956; Notable Books, Am. Lib. Assn., 1963; Best Books of Yr., Christian Sci. Monitor, 1972. Address: 654 Emerson St., Denver, CO 80218, USA.

BLOCH, Raymond, b. 4 May 1914, Paris, France. Archaeologist; Professor, School of Applied Higher Studies, Paris. Publs: The Etruscans, 1958; The Origins of Rome, 1960; Recherches archéologiques en territoire volsinien, 1972. Sci. Ed., Les Grandes Civilisations series, 14 vols., 1960-. Contbr. to Sci. Am. Mbrships. incl: Pres., Nat. Soc. of Antiquaries of France; Comm. of Histl. & Sci. Works. Hons. incl: Albert Dumont Medal; Catenacci Prize, 1970. Address: 12 Rue Emile Faguet, 75014 Paris, France.

BLOCH, Robert, pen name FISKE, Tarleton, b. 5 Apr. 1917, Chgo., Ill., USA. Author. Publs. incl: The Opener of the Way, 1945; Psycho, 1959; Pleasant Dreams, 1960; Nightmares, 1961; Yours Truly, Jack the Ripper, 1962; Terror, 1962; The Skull of the Marquis de Sade, 1965; Chamber of Horrors, 1966; The Star Stalker, 1968; Bloch & Bradbury, 1969; It's all in your Mind, 1971; Sneak Preview, 1972; Fear Today, Gone Tomorrow, 1972; Night World, 1972; American Gothic, 1974. Contbr. to: Penthouse; Playboy; Cosmopolitan; etc.; also to films & TV. Mbrships. incl: Mystery Writers of Am.; Sci. Fiction Writers of Am.; Writers' Guild of Am. Hons. incl: World Sci. Fiction Hugo Award, 1959; Edgar Allan Poe Special Award, Mystery Writers of Am., 1960. Address: 2111 Sunset Crest Drive, L.A., CA 90046, USA.

BLOCKSIDGE, Kathleen Mary, b. 8 Apr. 1904, Hither Green, London, UK. Lecturer in Music. Publs: Making Musical Apparatus & Instruments for use in Nursery & Infant Schools. Contbr. to: Musical Educ. of Under-Twelves Bulletin. Mbrships: Hon. Sec., Musical Educ. of

Under-Twelves Assn.; Inc. Soc. of Musicians; Pipers' Guild. Address: 55 Farm Close, Seaford, Sussex BN25 3RY, UK.

BLOFELD, John Eaton Calthorpe, b. 2 Apr. 1913, London, UK. Writer. Educ: M.A., Downing Coll., Cambridge. Publs. incl: The Jewel in the Lotus, 1948; Red China in Perspective, 1951; The Wheel of Life, 1959, 2nd ed., 1972; People of the Sun, 1960; The Zen Teaching of Hui Hai, 1962; transl., the I-Ching, or Book of Change, 1965; The Way of Power, 1970; King Maha Mongkut of Siam, 1972; The Secret & Sublime, 1973; Beyond the Gods, 1974. Address: 80 Soi Sansabai, Rama IV Rd., Prakanong, Bangkok, Thailand.

BLOM, Karl Arne, b. 22 Jan. 1946, Nassjo, Sweden. Author. Educ: B.A. Publs: (in Swedish) Somebody Ought to Mourn, 1971; Somebody is Guilty, 1972; Somebody Hit Back, 1973; The Moment of Truth, 1974; An Old Murder, 1974. Contbr. to var. mags. Mbr. & Chmn., Soc. of Detective Story Writers, Skane. Address: Smaskolevagen 22, S-223 67 Lund, Sweden.

BLOMQUIST, Clarence D. D., b. 16 July 1925, Grand Rapids, Mich., USA. Psychiatrist; Assistant Professor of Medical Ethics; Author. Educ: M.D., Ph.D. Publs: The Ethics of Euthanasia, 1964; The Ethics of Therapeutic Abortions, 1966; The Art of Being a Doctor, 1966; Psychiatry, 1969, 3rd ed., 1974; Medical Ethics, 1971, 2nd ed., 1974; Soul & Mind (essays), 1974. Contbr. to Scandinavian & int. med. & psych. jrnls. Mbr., sev. Swedish & int. lit & psych. orgs. Recip., Lit. Prize., Fndn. for Swedish Authors, 1972. Address: Ryttmästarvägen 24, S-162 24 Vällingby, Sweden.

BLÖNDAL, Björn J., b. 9 Sept. 1902, Stafholtsey, Borgarfjarðarsysla, Iceland. Farmer; Teacher. Educ: Grad., Hvanneyri Agricl. Coll., 1923. Publs: Hamingjudagar, 1950; Að kvöldi dags, 1952; Vinafundir, 1953; Vatnaniður, 1956; Örlagadbraeðir, 1958; Lundrurin helgi, 1962; Daggardropar, 1967; Á heljarsóð, 1970; Vötnin ströng, 1972. Contbr. to: Veiðimaðurinn (The Angler). Mbrships: Assn. of Icelandic Authors; Fedn. of Icelandic Authors. Recip., sev. awards. Address: Laugarholt, Andakílshreppur, Borg., Iceland.

BLONDIN, Antoine, b. 11 Apr. 1922, Paris, France. Writer. Educ: Lic. ès Lettres, Univ. of Paris. Publs: L'Europe Buissonniére; Les Enfants du Bon Dieu; L'Humeur Vagabonde; Un Signe en Hiver; Un Garcon d'honneur; film scenarios. Contbr. to var. jrnls. inclng: Paris-Presse; Arts; La Parisienne. Hons: Prix des Deux-Magots, 1949; Prix Interallié, 1959. Address: 72 rue Mazarine, Paris 7e, France.

BLOOM, Alan Herbert Vawser, b. 19 Nov. 1906, Over, Cambs., UK. Nurseryman; Nurseries Director. Publs. incl: Bickers Broad (novel), 1975; Prelude to Bressingham, 1975. Mbrships: Soc. of Authors; E. Anglian Writers Assn. Recip., Vic. Medal of Hon., Royal Hort. Soc., 1971. Address: Bressingham Hall, Diss, Norfolk, UK.

BLOOM, Ursula, b. Chelmsford, Essex, UK. Writer. First book publ. privately at age of seven. Publs: Novels; Biographies; Plays; etc., over 400 books under sev. names. Address: 191, Cranmer Court, London SW3, UK.

BLOOMAN, Percival A., pen name P. A. B., b. 4 Jan. 1906, Southend, Essex, UK. Investment Company Director; Freelance Journalist. Educ: B.Com., Univ. of Leeds. Contbr. to: Bus. Blue Books of S. Africa; Bus. Systems & Equipment; Factory Systems & Equipment; Advt. & Press Annual of Africa; Nat. Trade Index of S. Africa; Former Ed., Nat. Publng. Co.; num. other trade, legal & fin. jrnls. Mbrships: Royal Econ. Soc.; Econ. Soc. of S. Africa. Address: P.O. Box 3631, Cape Town, 8000 S. Africa.

BLOSSOM, Thomas, b. 15 Feb. 1912, Dedham, Mass., USA. Professor of History; Author. Educ: A.B., Amherst Coll., 1934; M.A., Columbia Univ., 1935; Ph.D., Duke Univ., 1956. Publs: The Americas (co-author), 1964; Nations Around the Globe (co-author), 1966; Antonio Narino, Hero of Colombian Independence, 1967. Contbr. to: Am. Histl. Review; Hist.; Perspective; Ency. of World Biog., 1974. Address: 1417 Rust Drive, Virginia Beach, VA 23455, USA.

BLUE, Rose, b. NYC, USA. Author. Educ: B.A., Bklyn. Coll.; Grad. studies, Bank St. Coll. Publs: A Quiet Place, 1969; How Many Blocks is the World?, 1970; I am Here (Yo Estoy Aqui), 1971; A Month of Sundays, 1972; Grandma Didn't Wave Back, 1972; Nikki 108, 1973; also

num. song lyrics recorded & publ'd. Contbr. to: Tchr. Mag. Mbrships: Authors' Guild of Am.; Authors' League of Am.; Int. Platform Assn.; Broadcast Music Inc.; Profl. Women's Caucus; Mensa. Address: 1320 51st St., Bklyn., NY11219, USA.

BLUM, Virgil Clarence, b. 27 Mar. 1913, Defiance, Iowa, USA. Professor of Political Science. Educ: A.B., 1938, M.A., 1944, Ph.D., 1954, St. Louis Univ. Publs: Freedom of Choice in Education, 1958; Freedom in Education, 1965; Education: Freedom & Competition, 1967; Catholic Education: Survival or Demise, 1969; Catholic Education: Survival or Demise, 1969; Catholic Parents — Political Eunuchs, 1971. Contbr. to: Univ. of Chgo. & Notre Dame Law Reviews; Georgetown Law Jrnl.; Jrnl. of Higher Educ. Recip., Marquette Univ. Award for Tchng. Excellence, 1966. Address: 1404 West Wisconsin Avenue, Milwaukee, WI 53233, USA.

BLUMBERG, Nathan (Bernard), b. 8 Apr. 1922, Denver, Colo., USA. Educator; Journalist. Educ: B.A., M.A., Univ. of Colo.; D.Phil., Oxford Univ., UK. Publs: One-Party Press? , 1954. Contbr. to var. mags., jrnls. & reviews. Address: University of Montana, Missoula, MT 59801, USA.

BLUMENTHAL, Henry, b. 21 Oct. 1911, Graudenz, Germany. Historian. Educ: A.B., Univ. of Berlin, 1933; M.A., 1943, Ph.D., 1949, Univ. of Calif., Berkeley, USA. Publs: A Reappraisal of Franco-American Relations, 1830-71, 1959; France & the United States — their Diplomatic Relations, 1789-1914, 1970 & 1972. Contbr. to: New England Qrly.; Soc. Sci. Qrly.; Jrnl. of Negro History; Pacific Histl. Review; etc. Mbr., Am. Histl. Soc.; Org. of Am. Histns. Hons: Selman A. Wakeman Fellow in France, 1954-55. Address; 171 Vose Ave., South Orange, NJ 07079, USA.

BLUNT, (Sir) Anthony Frederick, b. 1907, Bournemouth, UK. Adviser for the Queen's Paintings & Drawings; Emeritus Professor of the History of Art; Former Director, Courtauld Institute. Educ: M.A., Ph.D., Trinity Coll., Cambridge Univ. Publs. incl: Artistic Theory in Italy; French Drawings at Windsor Castle; The Art of William Blake; Picasso, the Formative Years (w. P. Pool), 1962; Nicolas Poussin, 3 vols., 1967; Baroque Architecture in Sicily, 1968; Picasso's 'Guernica', 1969; Catalogues of Italian & French Drawings at Windsor, 1945-71. Contbr. to: Burlington Mag.; Jrnl. of Warburg & Courtauld Insts. Hons: K.C.V.O.; F.R.I.B.A.; num. hon. degrees. Address: 45 Portsea Hall, Portsea Pl., London W2, UK.

BLUNT, Wilfrid Jasper Walter, b. 1901, Ham, Surrey, UK. Gallery Curator. Educ: Assoc., Royal Coll. of Art. Publs: Desert Hawk; Black Sunrise; Lady Muriel; The Art of Botanical Illustration; Tulipomania; Sweet Roman Hand; Pietro's Pilgrimage; Sebastiano; A Persian Spring; The Dream King; The Complete Naturalist; The Golden Road to Samarkand; On Wings of Song: a Biography of Mendelssohn; Of Flowers & a Village, 1963; Cockerell, 1964; Omar, 1966; Isfahan, 1966; John Christie of Glyndebourne, 1968; England's Michelangelo: a Biography of G. F. Watts, 1975. Contbr. to num. periodicals. Mbrships: F.L.S. Agent: Curtis Brown. Address: The Watts Gallery, Compton, Guildford, Surrey, UK.

BLYTH, Chay, pen name CHAY, b. 1940, Hawick, UK. Company Director; Writer. Educ: Parachute Regiment, 1958-67. Publs: A Fighting Chance (w. John Ridgway), 1966; Innocent Aboard (w. M. Blyth), 1969; The Impossible Voyage, 1971; Theirs is the Glory, 1974. Hons: C.B.E.; B.E.M. Agent: Terry Bond. Address: 5 Brookhill, Kingswear, Dartmouth, Devon, UK.

BLYTH, Henry Edward, b. 1910, London, UK. Author; Screen & TV Writer. Educ: M.A., Univ. of Oxford. Publs. incl: Cinema Cavalcade, 2 vols., 1938-39; The Pocket Venus, 1966; Old Q, 1968; Hall & Hazard, 1969; High Tide of Pleasure, 1970; Skittles, 1970; Caro — The Fatal Passion, 1973; Madeleine Smith, 1975; original film stories (co-author), Bulldog Breed, 1960; V.I.P., 1961; Seven Keys, 1962; Crooks Anonymous, 1962; Fast Lady, 1962; A Stitch in Time, 1965; Father Came Too, 1965. Contbr. to var. newspapers & jrnls. Address: Southerndown, Rottingdean, Sussex, UK.

BLYTH, Jeffrey, b. 20 Mar. 1926, Chester-le-Street, Co. Durham, UK. Journalist; Foreign Correspondent. Contbr. to: Atlas World Review; Radio Times; Listener; Gen. Practitioner; UK Press Gazette; Ed. & Publr.; Drive;

Cinema/TV Today; & var. other publs. in UK & USA. Mbrships: For. Press Assn. of Am. (Pres., 1967-68); Press Club, London; Overseas Press Club, N.Y. Address: 90 Riverside Drive, N.Y., NY 10024, USA.

BLYTH, Myrna, b. NYC, USA. Writer; Editor. Educ: B.A., Bennington Coll. Publs: Cousin Suzanne, 1974. Contbr. to: For Girls Only (anthol.), 1967; McCall's Mag.; Redbook; New Yorker; Family Circle; Women's Day; Rdr.'s Digest; MS; & var. mags. in UK, S. Africa, Aust., Italy, Denmark & Sweden. Address: 90 Riverside Drive, N.Y., NY 10024, USA.

BLYTHE, Ronald George, b. 1922, Acton, Suffolk, UK. Freelance Writer; Critic. Publs: A Treasonable Growth, 1960; Immediate Possession, 1961; The Age of Illusion, 1963; Akenfield: Portrait of an English Village, 1969; Ed., Components of the Scene, 1966; Jane Austen, Emma, 1966; William Hazlitt: Selected Writings, 1970; Aldeburgh Anthology, 1972; Thomas Hardy: A Pair of Blue Eyes, 1975; (films) John Nash, BBC; John Constable, BBC; Akenfield. Mbrships: F.R.S.L.; Fndr., Colchester Lit. Soc., 1949. Hons: Heinemann Award, 1969; Travel Schlrship., Soc. of Authors, 1971. Agent: Deborah Rogers. Address: French's Folly, Debach, Woodbridge, Suffolk, UK.

BOALCH, Donald Howard, b. 1914, London, UK. Librarian; College Fellow. Educ: M.A., Corpus Christi Coll., Cambridge Univ. Publs: Twopart Canzonets of Thomas Morley, 1950; The Manor of Rothamsted, 1953; Catalogue of Serial Publication in the Rothamsted Library, 1954; Makers of the Harpsichord & Clavichord 1440-1840, 1956, 2nd ed., 1974; Prints & Paintings of British Farm Livestock 1780-1810, 1958; World Directory of Agricultural Libraries, 1960. Fellow, Soc. Antiquaries. Address: 4 Hill Top Rd., Oxford, UK.

BOARDMAN, Gwenn R., b. 16 Nov. 1924, London, UK. Professor of English & Japanese Literature; Writer-Photographer. Educ: B.A., Univ. of Calif., Berkeley, 1957; M.A., 1961, Ph.D., 1963, Claremont Grad. Schl., Calif. Publs: Carrying Cargo, 1968; Living in Tokyo, 1970; Living in Singapore, 1971; Graham Greene: The Aesthetics of Exploration, 1971. Contbr. to: Critique; Jrnl. Mod. Lit.; Mod. Fiction Studies; Renascence; The Review (Oxford); Kobe Coll. Studies; Mademoiselle; RN; Today's Health; Accent on Youth; Young World; num. other jrnls. Mbrships: MLA; Authors' Guild; Soc. Children's Book Writers. Address: 182 Stanyan St. (Apt. 3), San Fran., CA 94118, USA.

BOASE, Alan Martin, b. 23 June 1902, St. Andrews, UK. University Professor of French Language & Literature; Author. Educ: M.A.; Ph.D.; New Coll., Oxford; Trinity Coll., Cambridge. Publs: The Fortunes of Montaigne, 1935; Twentieth Century Literature; Les Poemes Français de Jean de Sponde, 1949; Jean de Sponde, Meditations sur les Psaumes (Ed.), 1954; The Poetry of France: an Anthology, vol. I, 1964, vol. III, 1967, vol. IV, 1969, vol. II, 1600-1800, 1973. Contbr. to: Mod. Lang. Review; French Studies, etc. Mbrships: PEN; Univ. Ct.; Assn. Hds. of French Depts. (former Pres.). Hons: Vis. Prof., Univ. of Calif. (Berkeley), 1962; Monash Univ., Melbourne, 1969; Collège de France, Paris, 1974. Address: 39 Inverleith Place, Edinburgh 3, UK.

BOBB, Bernard Earl, b. 21 Oct. 1917, Mitchell, S.D., USA. Professor of History. Educ: Ph.D., Univ. of Calif. Publs: The Viceregency of Antonio Maria Bucareli in New Spain, 1771-79, 1962. Contbr. to: Hispanic Am. Histl. Review; Pacific Histl. Review; Historia Mexicana; The Americas. Mbr: Pacific Coast Coun. on Latin Am. Studies. Address: S.E. 405 Grant St., Pullman, WA 99163, USA.

BOCHEŃSKI, Jacek, b. 29 July 1926, Lwów, Poland. Novelist; Essayist. Educ: Theatre Schl.; Univ. Lublin. Publs: (novels) Pożegnanie z Panna Syngilu (Goodbye to Mrs. Syngilu), 1960; Tabu (Taboo), 1965; Nazo Poeta (Naso the Poet), 1969; (essay) Boski Juliusz (The Divine Caesar), 1967. Mbr., PEN. Recip., Award for Artist-in-Residence, Berlin 1972/73. Address: 02-586 Warsaw, ul. Jarosłana Dąbrowskiego 69a 90, Poland.

BODE, Carl, b. 1911, Milwaukee, Wis., USA. University Professor; Author. Educ: Ph.B., Univ. of Chgo.; M.A., Ph.D., Northwestern Univ. Publs. incl: (cultural hist.) The American Lyceum; Antebellum Culture; The Half-World of American Culture; (poems) The Sacred Seasons; The Man behind You; (biog.) Mencken; (newspaper essays) Highly Irregular. Mbrships. incl: Am. Studies Assn. (Pres.);

Thoreau Soc. (Pres.); Popular Culture Assn. of Am. (VP); Soc. Am. Studies (VP); F.R.S.L. Address: Univ. of Maryland, College Park, MD 20742, USA.

BODECKER, N(iels) M(ogens), b. 13 Jan. 1922, Copenhagen, Denmark. Writer; Illustrator. Educ: Studies in Arch., Applied Arts & Commerce. Publs: Digtervandring (poetry), 1943; Graa Fugle, (poetry), 1946; Miss Jasters Garden (also illustrator), 1972; It's Raining said John Twaining (also illustrator), 1973; The Mushroom Centre Disaster, 1974; Let's Marry said the Cherry (also illustrator), 1974; Our House (also illustrator), 1975; Illustrator, num. other books. Contbr. to: Samleren; Nationaltidene; Politikens Magasinet; B.T., etc.; (as illustrator), num. Am. mags. Recip., Christopher Award, 1973. Address: Hancock, NH 03449, USA.

BODELSEN, Merete, b. 1907, London. Writer; Editor. Educ: Univ. of Copenhagen. Publs: Foreign Artists in Denmark, 1957; Gauguin Ceramics in Danish Collections, 1960; Gauguin's Ceramics: A Study in the Development of his Art, 1964; Toulouse Lautrec's Posters: Catalogue & Comments, 1964; Gauguin og Impressionisterne, 1968; Sèvres-Copenhagen Crystal Glazes & Stoneware at the Turn of the Century, 1975. Contbr. to: Gazette des Beaux Arts; Burlington Mag.; Ed., Nat. Biog. of Danish Artists I-III 1947-52 (Weilbachs Kunstnerleksikon); Danish Commnr., Coun. of Europe's Exhibition, Les Sources du XX Siecle. Address: 16 Travervaenget, 2920 Charlottenlund, Denmark.

BODINGTON, Nancy Hermione, pen name SMITH, Shelley, b. Richmond, Surrey, UK. Author. Publs: Come & Be Killed, 1946; He Died of Murder, 1947; The Woman in the Sea, 1948; How Many Miles to Babylon, 1950; Man With a Calico Face, 1951; Man Alone, 1952; Party At No. 5, 1954; An Afternoon To Kill, 1953; The Lord Have Mercy, 1956; Rachel Weeping, 1957; Ballad of the Running Man, 1961; A Grave Affair, 1971; (film) Tiger Bay, 1958. Mbr., Soc. of Authors. Agents: McIntosh & Otis Inc., N.Y.; A. M. Heath & Co. Address: Old Orchard, Steyning, W. Sussex, UK.

BODSWORTH, Charles Fred(erick), b. 1918, Port Burwell, Ont., Can. Reporter; Editor; Novelist. Publs: Last of the Curlews, 1954; The Strange One, 1960; The Atonement of Ashley Morden, 1964; The Sparrow's Fall, 1967; Illustrated Natural History of the Pacific Coast, 1969; num. transls. Contbr. to sev. mags. Mbrships: Fedn. of Ont. Naturalists; Toronto Men's Press; Can. Authors' Assn. Address: 294 Beech Ave., Toronto 260, Can.

BODY, Geoffrey, b. 12 Feb. 1929, Waddington, Lincs., UK. Director & General Manager, Pickford's Tank Haulage Ltd. Publs: British Paddle Steamers, 1971; Railway & Steam Enthusiasts' Handbook (bi-annual); Ed. & Publr. of var. booklets, inclng. annual Guide to Light Railways, Steamers & Historic Transport. Contbr. to County mags. Mbrships: MCIT; MIM; AMITA. Address: 9 Poplar Avenue, Westbury-on-Trym, Bristol BS9 2BE, UK.

BOGDAN, Cella, pen name SERGHI, Cella, b. 4 Nov. 1907, Constanta, Bucharest, Romania. Writer. Educ: Univ. Degree in Law. Publs: (novels) Pinza de Paianjen (Cobweb), 1938, sev. later eds.; Nirona (The Walls Came Tumbling Down), 1950, sev. later eds.; Gentiane (Gentian), 1970; Tubiri Paralele (Parallel Loves), 1974. Contbr. to var. lit. reviews & mags. Mbr., Romanian Writers' Soc. Address: Str. Sf. Constantin 24, Bucharest 7, Romania.

BOGDANOV, Lozan Ivanov, pen name STRELKOV, Lozan, b. 7 July 1912, Skomlya, Bulgaria. Writer. Publs: (in Bulgarian) Reconnaissance, 1950; Unforgettable Days, 1959; A Journey to the Truth, 1972; Not Subject of Appeal, 1972; (plays) There aren't a Hundred Truths, 1970; The Man from the Dossier, 1970; The Glowing Ember, 1970. Contbr. to: Plamak; September; Literatouren Front. Mbrships: Union of Bulgarian Writers; Union of Bulgarian Jrnlsts.; PEN. Hons: Dimitrov Prize, 1950; Prizes, Union of Bulgarian Writers, 1959, 1972; People's Worker in Culture, 1971; Hero of Socialist Labour, 1972. Address: Sofia, bul. Patriarh Evtimiy 26, Bulgaria.

BOGIE, David James, b. 1905, Kirkcaldy, Fife UK. Former Lecturer. Educ: B.Com., Ph.D., Edinburgh Univ. Publs: Group Accounts; Introduction to Group Accounts; Bogie on Group Accounts, 1973. Contbr. to Accts. Mag. Former Mbr., Gen. Exam. Bd., Inst. of Chartered Accts. of Scotland. Address: 14 Gamekeepers Rd., Edinburgh EH4 6LU, UK.

BOGZA, Nicolae, pen name TUDORAN, Radu, b. 8 Mar. 1910, Blejoi-Prahova, Romania. Novelist. Educ: Mil. Schl. Publs: A Harbour in the East, 1941; Seasons, 1943; The Flames, 1945; The Wasteful Son, 1947; All Sails Up! , 1954; The Over Flowed Danube, 1962; The Third Pole of the World, 1971; Mary & the Sea, 1973; etc. Contbr. to: (newspapers) Romanian World; Time; Tide; Event; Free Romania; Spark; (lit. mags.) Morning Star; Lit. Flow; Romanian Life; Lit. Gazette; Lit. Romania. Mbr., Union of Romanian Writers. Hons: Award, Min. of Culture, 1958; Acad. Prize, 1962 (for The Over Flowed Danube). Address: Sipotul Fîntînilor 5, Bucharest 45, Romania.

BOHRER, Karl Heinz, b. 26 Sept. 1932, Cologne, Germany. Literary Critic; Journalist. Educ: Univs. of Göttingen & Heidelberg; Ph.D. Publs: Die Gefährdete Phantasie oder Surrealismus und Terror, 1970; Der Lauf des Freitag: Die Lädierte Utopie & die Dichter, 1973. Contbr. to: Frankfurter Allgemeine Zeitung (Lit. Ed. & Cultural London Corres.); Merkur: Zeitschrift für Europäisches Denken; Neue Rundschau. Mbr: PEN. Recip: Drexel Prize, 1968. Address: 8 Bracknell Gdns., London NW3, UK.

BOLAND, Bertram John, b. 12 Feb. 1913, Birmingham, UK. Author; Playwright. Publs. incl: Short Story Technique, 1973; The League of Gentlemen; 35 Crime, Sci. Fiction novels, sev. hundred short stories & 2 plays for children. Mbrships: Writers' Summer Schl. (Chmn., 1958-60, 1973-75); Inst. Jrnlsts. (Chmn., Freelance Sect., 1959); Crime Writers' Assn. (Chmn., 1963); Writers' Guild GB (Chmn., Radio Comm., 1967-70); Mystery Writers Am. Recip., Writers' Guild GB, Zita Award for Best Drama Script Broadcast BBC, 1968. Address: The Red House, Mardens Hill, Crowborough, Sussex TN6 1XN, UK.

BOLAND, Bridget Mary, b. 13 Mar. 1913, London, UK. Author; Playwright. Educ: B.A., Oxford Univ., 1935. Publs: (novels) The Wild Geese, 1938; Portrait of a Lady in Love, 1942; (plays) Cockpit; The Prisoner; Temple Folly; Gordon; Zodiac in the Establishment; (films) Gaslight; The Prisoner; War & Peace; Anne of the Thousand Days. Address: Bolands, Hewshott Lane, Liphook, Hants., UK.

BOLAY, Karl H., pen names da BYOLA, Ugo, SVENSSON, Sven, b. 23 Nov. 1914, Saarbrücken, W. Germany. Author; Literary Critic; Chief Librarian. Educ: Socionom, 1955, Libn., 1955, Coll. of Social Scis., Helsinki, Finland. Publs. incl: (novel) Der Fall René Merlin, 1964; (poetry) Fanifestationer, 1971; The Square Moon, 1973; (non-fiction) AV i biblioteken, 1973. Ed., Nordisk Kulturtidskrift. Contbr. to num. profl. & lit. publs., Sweden, Finland, UK, Germany. Mbrships: Chmn., Int. Author's Progressiv; Sec., Author's Soc. of N.W. Scania. Hons: Sev. Awards, Swedish Author's Fndn.; Cultural Prize, Town of Tyresö, 1968. Address: Pilvägen 15, 260 40 Viken, Sweden.

BOLD, Alan, b. 20 Apr. 1943, Edinburgh, UK. Writer; Artist. Educ: Edinburgh Univ. Publs: Society Inebrious, 1965; The Voyage, 1966; To Find the New, 1967; A Perpetual Motion Machine, 1969; The State of the Nation, 1969; Penguin Modern Poets 15, 1969; The Penguin Book of Socialist Verse, 1970; A Pint of Bitter, 1971; A Century of People, 1971; The Auld Symie, 1971; He Will Be Greatly Missed, 1971; Hammer & Thistle, 1974. Contbr. to: Tribune; Times; Times Educl. & Lit. Supplements. Recip., Writer's Bursary, Scottish Arts Coun., 1967. Address: 19 Gayfield Square, Edinburgh EH1 3NX, UK.

BOLDIZSÁR, Iván, b. 30 Oct. 1912, Budapest, Hungary. Writer; Journalist. Educ: Budapest Univ. Publs. incl: Magyarország Utikönyv; Szuletésnap; Az éjszaka végén; Rokonok és idegenek; Zsiráffal Angliában (Doing England with a Giraffe), 1969; Királyalma; Tulélök (play); Az angyal lába; New York Percrol percre; A filozófus oroszlán; Haláliaim. Contbr. to var. jrnls. inclng. The New Hungarian Quarterly. Mbr., Pres., Hungarian PEN, 1964-. Hons: Doct., Union Coll., Schenectady, N.Y., USA, 1971; Labour Order of Merit Golden Degree. Address: Balogh Adám-utca 29, Budapest II, Hungary.

BOLGER, (Mrs.) Mary E. V., b. 19 Mar. 1918, Medicine Hat, Alta., Can. Writer; Journalist. Educ: Studies in Jrnlsm., Fiction Writing & Verse. Contbr. to: local newspaper (reporter-Ed. & co-mgr., until 1974); Royal Publng. Co., Tex.; Allstar, Tex.; The Calendar, Ont.; Sunday Vis., Ind.; Indep. Publng. Co., Ohio; Crown Recording, N.Y.; Poetry House, N.Y.; Crown Publrs., N.Y.; Young Publs., Va.; Liberty, Ont.; sev. anthols., etc. Address: 110 6th St. S.E., Medicine Hat, Alta., TIA IG8, Can.

BÖLL, Heinrich Theodor, b. 21 Dec. 1917, Cologne, Germany. Author. Educ: Cologne Univ. Publs. incl: (in German) The Train Was on Time, 1949; Wo warst du, Adam? , 1951; Acquainted with the Night, 1953; The Unguarded House, 1954; Irisches Tagebuch, 1957; (play) Ein Schluck Erde, 1962; End of a Mission, 1966; Gruppenbild mit Dame, 1971; Gedichte, 1973; num. radio plays, transls, etc. Mbrships. incl: German Acad. for Lang. & Poetry; Chmn., PEN; Union of German Transls. Recip. of num. prizes & awards incl. Nobel Prize, 1972. Address: Belvederestrasse 35, Köln-Müngersdorf, Fed. Repub. of Germany.

BOLL, Theophilus E. M., pen name BOLL, Ernest, b. 6 Jan. 1902, NYC, USA. University Teacher. Educ: A.B., A.M., Ph.D., Univ. of Pa. Publs: The Works of Edwin Pugh (1874-1930): A Chapter in the Novel of Humble London Life, 1934; Miss May Sinclair: Novelist, 1973; Biog. Note & Critical Essay on Stephen Hudson, in Richard, Myrtle & I, ed., Violet Schiff, 1962. Contbr. to num. profl. jrnls. Mbrships. incl: Dickens Fellowship, The Philibiblon Club. Address: 314 Bennett Hall, Univ. of Pa., Phila., PA 19104, USA.

BOLLES, Blair, b. 26 Feb. 1911, St. Louis, Mo., USA. Corporation Officer. Educ: Yale Coll. Publs: America's Chance of Peace, 1939; Tyrant From Illinois, 1951; How to Get Rich in Washington, 1952; Who Makes American Foreign Policy, 1952; Big Change in Europe, 1975; Men of Good Intentions, 1961; Corruption in Washington, 1961. Contbr. to var. mags. inclng: Harper's; Nation; New Repub.; Reader's Digest; N.Y. Times Book Review. Mbrships. incl: AAAS. Recip., Royal Order of St. Olav, Norway, 1950. Address: 4831 Linnean Ave., Wash. DC 20008, USA.

BOLLES, Richard Nelson, b. 19 Mar. 1927, Milwaukee, Wis., USA. Director, National Career Development Project, United Ministries in Higher Education; Writer. Educ: Alumnus, MIT, 1946-48; Bachelor's Degree, Harvard Univ., 1950; Master's Degree, Gen. Theol. Sem., 1957. Publs: What Color is Your Parachute? A Practical Manual for Job-Hunters & Career Changers, 1972, revised 1974; Where Do I Go from Here with my Life? A practical life/work planning manual (co-author), 1974. Mbrships: Mensa; Am. Personnel & Guidance Assn. Address: 627 Taylor St. No. 22, San Francisco, CA 94102, USA.

BOLSTER, (Sister) M. Angela, pen name BOLSTER, Evelyn, b. 1925, Mallow, Co. Cork, Repub. of Ireland. Teacher; Lecturer. Educ: M.A., Ph.D., H.Dip. in Ed., Bilingual Dip., Univ. Coll., Cork. Publs: The Sisters of Mercy in the Crimean War, 1965; A History of Mallow, 1971; The Lough Parish and its Historic Associations, 1971; A History of the Diocese of Cork, Vol. I, 1972. Contbr. to: Jrnl. Cork Histl. & Archaeol. Soc.; Jrnl. Kerry Archaeol. & Histl. Soc.; Archivium Hibernicum (Cath. Record Soc. of Ireland, Maynooth); Collectanea Hibernica (Sources for Irish Hist.). Hons. incl: Student of Yr. Award, Univ. Coll., Cork, 1950. Address: Convent of Our Lady of Mercy, St. Maries of the Isle, Cork, Republic of Ireland.

BOLT, David, b. 1927, Harrow, UK. Author. Publs: The Albatross, 1954; A Cry Ascending, 1955; Adam, 1960 (USA, 1961); The Man Who Did, 1963 (USA, 1964); Of Heaven & Hope, 1965; Gurkhas, 1967 (USA (1969); The Moon Princess, 1970. Address: 1 Draycott Place, London SW3, UK.

BOLT, Robert Oxton, b. 15 Aug. 1924, Sale, Cheshire, UK. Writer (Theatre & Films). Educ: Manchester Grammar Schl.; Univs. of Manchester & Exeter; B.A. Publs: (plays) Flowering Cherry, produced Haymarket, 1958; A Man for All Seasons, prod. Globe, 1960 (filmed 1967); The Tiger & the Horse, prod. Queen's, 1960; Gentle Jack, prod. Queen's, 1963; Vivat! Vivat! Regina! , prod. Piccadilly, 1969; (screenplays) Lawrence of Arabia (Brit. Film Acad. Award, 1962); Dr. Zhivago, 1965; Ryan's Daughter, 1970; Lady Caroline Lamb, 1972 (also Dir.); Prod., sev. radio plays. Mbrships: Chmn., Freelance Shop, Assn. of Cinematograph & TV Technicians. Recip., C.B.E., 1972. Address: c/o Margaret Ramsay Ltd., 14a Goodwin's Court, St. Martin's Lane, London WC2, UK.

BOLTON, Guy, b. 23 Nov. 1884, Broxbourne, Herts., UK. Playwright. Educ: Ecole des Beaux Arts. Publs. incl: (plays & musicals) Kissing-Time; Anything Goes; Who's Who; Hold on to Your Hats; Music at Midnight; Anastasia; Guardian Angel; Fireworks in the Sun; (films) The Love Parade; Words & Music; 'Til the Clouds Roll By; (autobiography) Bring on the Girls (w. P. G. Wodehouse),

1954; (novels) The Olympians, 1961; Gracious Living, 1965; A Man & His Wife, 1970; Jeeves (w. P. G. Wodehouse); Anya; The Enchantress. Address: Remsenburg, Long Island, N.Y., USA.

BOND, Christopher Geoffrey Dalgleish, b. 18 Mar. 1920, Yeadon, Yorks., UK. TV Drama Script Editor; Playwright. Publs: (plays) The Food of Love, 1954; A Policeman's Lot, 1957; (TV Series) The Newcomers, 1967-70; A. P. Herbert's Misleading Cases (co-author), 1968, 1970, 1971; The Doctors, 1970-71; It's Awfully Bad for Your Eyes, Darling (co-author), 1971; Owen M.D., 1972; General Hospital, 1972, 1973, 1974; The Terracotta Horse, 1973; Marked Personal, 1974. Contbr. to: World Med.; Radio Times. Mbrships: F.R.S.A.; Writers' Guild; Savage Club. Address: 43 Riverview Gardens, Barnes, London SW13, UK.

BOND, Derek William Douglas, b. 1920, Glasgow, Scotland, UK. Playwright. Publs: (plays) Akin to Death, 1962; Unscheduled Stop, 1968; Double String, 1969; Packdrill, 1970; Riverdale Dam, 1973; Sentence Deferred, 1973. Mbr., Writers' Guild of GB. Agent: Eric Glass Ltd. Address: 61 High St., Thames Ditton, Surrey, UK.

BOND, Edward, b. 1934, London, UK. Playwright. Publs: (plays) The Pope's Wedding, 1962; Saved, 1965; Early Morning, 1968; Narrow Road to the Deep North, 1968; Black Mass (one-act), 1970; Lear, 1971; Passion (one-act), 1971; The Sea, 1973; Bingo, 1974; (transl.) The Three Sisters (Chekov); Spring Awakening (Wedekind). Contbr. to: Sunday Times; Guardian. Agent: Margaret Ramsay. Address: c/o Margaret Ramsay, 14a Goodwins Court, St. Martin's Lane, London WC2, UK.

BOND, Geoffrey, b. 1924, Holt, Norfolk. Teacher-Headmaster. Educ: Leicester Univ. Publs: Echoes from Blakeney, 1948; Ed., Life & Adventure Series, 1948; Portrait of Cromer, 1949; Ed., Wayfarer Series, 1958; Ed., One World Series, 1968. Contbr. to: Times Educl. Supplement. Address: 51 The Avenues, Norwich, Norfolk, UK.

BOND, Michael, b. 1926, Newbury, UK. Writer. Publs: Paddington Bear Series (11 titles, transl'd into 14 langs.); Paddington Picture Book Series (6 titles); Thursday Series; The Tales of Olga da Polga; Olga Meets her Match; Parsley Series; The Day the Animals went on Strike; Windmill; Michael Bond's Book of Bears; Michael Bond's Book of Mice; (TV series) The Herbs (13 episodes); The Adventures of Parsley (32 episodes). Contbr. to: Guardian; London Opinion; Men Only; BBC. Agent: Harvey Unna. Address: Fairacre, Farnham Lane, Haslemere, Surrey, UK.

BONHAM, John B., b. 1907, Whitehaven, UK. Writer; Editor. Educ: B.Sc., Ph.D., Univ. of London; B.Sc.Econ., Ph.D., London Schl. Econs. Publs: The Middle Class Vote, 1954; Ed., The Financial Times International Business Yearbook, 1974; Ed., The Financial Times Who's Who in World Banking, 1975. Contbr. to Financial Times overseas serv. Mbrships: Brit. Sociol. Assn.; Senate & Standing Comm. of Convocation, Univ. of London; Authors' Soc.; Fabian Soc.; London Schl. Econs. Soc. Address: 30 Torrington Square, London WC1E 7JL, UK.

BONHAM-CARTER, Victor, b. 13 Dec. 1913, Bearsted, Kent, UK. Author. Educ: M.A., Cantab. Publs: Dartington Hall, 1970; In a Liberal Tradition, 1960; Soldier True, 1965; Surgeon in the Crimea, 1969; The Survival of the English Countryside, 1971. Contbr. to: Daily Telegraph; Times Lit. Supplement; The Countryman; etc.; also much radio broadcasting for BBC, 1947—. Mbrships: Jt. Sec., Soc. of Authors; Sec., Royal Lit. Fund; Mbr., Authors' Club. Address: Broomhall, East Anstey, Tiverton, Devon, UK.

BONINGTON, Christian, b. 1934, London, UK. Mountaineer; Writer; Photographer. Publs: I Chose to Climb (autobiog.), 1966; Annapurna South Face, 1971; Next Horizon (autobiog.), 1973; Everest South West Face, 1973; Contbr. to: Daily Telegraph Mag.; Observer Mag.; Geog. Jrnl.; Drive Mag.; Mtn. Mag.; Alpine Jrnl. Mbrships: F.R.G.S.; Int. Comm., Brit. Mountaineering Coun.; Alpine Club; Alpine Climbing Grp.; Climbers Club. Recip., Fndrs. Medal, Royal Geog. Soc. Agent: John Farquharson Ltd. Address: Badger Hill, Nether Row, Hesket Newmarket, Wigton, Cumberland, UK.

BONJOUR, Edgar Conrad, b. 21 Aug. 1898, Berne, Switz. University Professor. Educ: Univs. of Berne, Geneva, Paris & Berlin; Ph.D.; Doct. ès Lettres. Publs: Swiss

Neutrality, its History & Meaning, 1946; A Short History of Switzerland, (co-author), 1952; Johannes von Müller, 1953; Die Schweiz & Europa, 4 vols., 1958-75; Die Universität Basel, 1960, 2nd ed. 1971; Geschichtschreibung des Schweiz, 2 vols., 1962; Geschichte der Schweizerischen Neutralität, 8 vols., 1970-75. Contbr. to: Schweizerische Zeitschrift für Geschichte; Historische Zeitschrift, Munich; var. newspapers. Mbr., var. histl. assns. Hons. incl: Albrecht Haller-Medal, Berne, 1933; Doct. ès Lettres, Univ. de Neuchâtel; Ida Somazzi Prize, 1965. Address: Benkenstr. 56, 4054 Basel, Switz.

BONNEFOY, Yves, b. 1923, Tours, France. Writer; Lecturer; Editor. Publs: (poetry) Du Mouvement et de L'immobilité de Douve, 1953; Hier Régnant Désert, 1958; Anti-Platon, 1965; Piérre Ecrite, 1965; Dans le Leurre du Seuil, 1970; Selected Poems, 1968; (essays) L'Improbable, 1959; Un rêve fait a Mautoue, 1967; Arthur Rimbaud, 1961; Rome, 1630: l'horizon du premier baroque, 1970; sev. transl. from Shakespeare, Hamlet; King Lear; Winter's Tale; etc. Contbr. to: Mercure de France; Critique; Preuves Poetry; etc. Mbr., Soc. de Anglicistes. Address: 63 Rue Lepic, Paris 18, France.

BONNEKAMP, Sonja Maria, pen name BIASSEN, Sal, b. 6 July 1930, Amsterdam, Netherlands. Literary & Scientific Translator; Journalist; Linguistic Consultant. Educ: F.I.L.(Med. Sci. & Lit.). Publs: Amrita (transl. into Dutch of To Whom She Will), 1958. Contbr. of poetry & articles to var. jrnls. & mags., & colleges to exhibs. Mbrships: Soc. of Authors, Playwrights & Composers; Transls.' Guild, UK; Nederlands Genootschap van Vertalers; Am. Transl. Assn. Address: 47 Firs Close, Muswell Hill, London N10, UK.

BONTOFT de ST. QUENTIN, Reginald Arthur, b. 30 Jan. 1901, Nottingham, Notts., UK. Clerk in Holy Orders. Educ: M.A., Christ's Coll., Cambridge, 1925; Wycliffe Hall, Oxford. Author, Cyrenaica, 1944. Contbr. to var. mags. F.R.G.S. Address: 10 The Crescent, Frinton, Essex, UK.

BOOKER, Frank, b. 1909, Shoreham, Kent, UK. Journalist. Publs: Industrial Archaeology of the Tamar Valley, 1967; Wreck of the Torrey Canyon, 1968; History of Morwellham, 1970. Contbr. to: Jrnl. Indl. Archaeol.; Western Morning News (News Ed.); var. other newspapers. Address: 27 Widey Lane, Crownhill, Plymouth, UK.

BOOKSPAN, Martin, b. 30 July 1926, Boston, Mass., USA. Broadcaster; Administrator; Writer. Educ: B.S., Harvard Coll., 1947. Author, 101 Masterpieces of Music & Their Composers, 1968, revised ed., 1973. Contbr. to: N.Y. Times; & specialist jrnls. Address: c/o ASCAP, 1 Lincoln Plaza, N.Y., NY 10023, USA.

BOON, Violet Mary, pen name WILLIAMS, Violet M., b. Manchester, UK. Writer & Illustrator of Children's Books. Educ: Manchester Schl. of Art. Publs: var. children's books; Embroidery Books & Things to Make Books w. photographed illustrations. Contbr. of children's illustrated stories & embroidery features to var. mags. Mbrships: Soc. of Authors (Children's Writers' Grp.); Soc. of Women Writers & Jrnlsts. Address: 73 Castle Bank, Stafford, UK.

BOONE, Colin Campbell, b. 4 Apr. 1930, London, UK. University Lecturer in English; Writer; Translator. Educ: M.A., Trinity Coll., Cambridge; D.Phil., Sussex Univ. Publs: 3 English readers for German Schools, 1956-60; 2-vol. transl.: Portraits from German Cultural Life, Portraits from German Economic Life, 1966, 1968; Interpretation: englische Prosa, 1971. Mbr., Soc. of Authors. Address: Fairhaven, North Way, Seaford, Sussex, UK.

BOORE, Walter Hugh, b. 8 Nov. 1904, Cardiff, Wales, UK. Author. Publs: Winter Seas (verse), 1953; Eternity is Swift (verse), 1958; The Valley & the Shadow (novel), 1963; Flower After Rain (novel), 1964; A Window in High Terrace (novel), 1966; The Old Hand (novel), 1966; Cry on the Wind (novel), 1967; Riot of Riches (novel), 1968; Ship to Shore (novel), 1969; First Light — A Study in Belief (philos.), 1973. Contbr. to num. jrnls. & mags. Mbrships: PEN; Soc. of Authors; Yr Academi Gymreig; Pres., Birmingham Writers' Grp.; V.P., Swansea, Cardiff & Port Talbot Writers' Circles. Address: 12, Francis St., New Quay, Dyfed SA45 9QL, Wales, UK.

BOORMAN, Henry Roy Pratt, b. 21 Sept. 1900, Maidstone, UK. Newspaper Proprietor. Educ: M.A., Queens' Coll., Cambridge. Publs: incl: Kent Messenger Centenary, 1959; Newspaper Society's 125 Years of

Progress, 1961; Kent — A Royal County, 1966; Your Family Newspaper, 1968; Spirit of Kent — Lord Cornwallis, 1968. Contbr. to: Kent Life; Kent Messenger; War Corres., 1940, 1944. Mbrships: Chmn., Coun., Assn. of Men of Kent & Kentish Men, 1949-51; V.P., 1950; Pres., Newspaper Soc., 1960; Pres., Home & Southern Cos. Newspaper Proprietors' Fedn., 1968. Hons: Sir Edward Hardy Gold Medal, 1964; C.B.E., 1966; D.L., 1968. Address: St. Augustine's Priory, Bilsington, Ashford, Kent TN25 7AU, UK.

BOOST, Rolf, b. 5 Oct. 1939, Ansterdam, Netherlands. Journalist. Educ: hbs-b; NOIB. Publs: Groetjes van Radio Noordzee, 1973; Dr. O., Levenslang vergiftigd, 1973; Kruidendokter Van de Moosdijk, koopman in ijdele hoop, 1973. Contbr. to var. mags.; radio & TV. Mbr., Dutch Soc. of Jrnlsts. Hons: Press Prize, Nederlandse Vereniging van Naturisten. Address: Radboud 21, Landsmeer, Netherlands.

BOOTH, Andrew Donald, pen name GAMMA, b. 11 Feb. 1918, E. Molesey, Surrey, UK. Physicist; Educational Administrator; Author. Educ: B.Sc., London, UK; Ph.D., Birmingham; D.Sc., London. Publs. incl: Fourier Technique, 1948; Automatic Digital Calculators, 1953, 3rd ed., 1966; Mechanical Resolution of Linguistic Problems, 1955; Numerical Methods, 1955, 3rd ed., 1966; Progress in automation, 1960; Digital Computers in Action, 1965; Automation & Computing, 1966. Contbr. to: Philosl. Mag.; Nature; New Sci.; Sci. Lit. Ed., Saskatoon Star-Phoenix & Thunder Bay Chronicle-Jrnl. Hon. Fellow, Inst. of Linguists, 1958. Address: Lakehead University, Thunder Bay, Ont., Canada.

BOOTH, Daniel Rintoul, b. 14 May 1932, Northampton, Western Aust. Animal Sculptor; Writer. Publs: The Farming Handbook to End All Farming Handbooks, 1970; Livestock Farming, 1970; The Machine Age Farm, 1970; The Life of the Farm, 1970; Crops of the Farm, 1970; The Horseman's Handbook to End All Horseman's Handbooks, 1975. Contbr. to: East Anglian Book, 1971; Agric. Ed., E. Anglian Daily Times, 1958-69; BBC Farming Today; Fin. Times; Farm & Country; etc. Mbrships. incl: Fed. of Brit. Artists; Zool. Soc., London; Guild of Agric. Jrnlsts. Address: Chapel House, Aldham, Hadleigh nr. Ipswich, Suffolk, UK.

BOOTH, Harry John, pen names BARRETT, Paul; ELLIS, John; CASHEL, John, b. 1923, Hyde, Cheshire, UK. Chartered Engineer; Journalist. Educ: A.M.C.T.; A.R.T.C.S.; M.I.E.E.; M.I.Mech.E., M.J.I., Coll. of Tech., Manchester; Royal Tech. Coll., Salford. Publs: The Mining Electrical & Mechanical Engineer, (Asst. Ed., 1946-47, Ed., 1957-69). Contbr. to indl. & commercial jrnls. Address: Overdale, Woodford Road, Poynton, Cheshire, UK.

BOOTH, Rosemary Frances, pen name MURRAY, Frances. Teacher of History. Educ: M.A., Dip.Ed., Univ. of St. Andrews, 1961-66. Publs: Ponies on the Heather (juvenile), 1966, 2nd ed., 1973; The Dear Colleague, 1972; The Burning Lamp, 1973; The Heroine's Sister, 1975; Ponies & Parachutes (juvenile), in press. Contbr. scripts for hist. & geog. progs. to BBC Schls. Radio. Hons. incl: Major Award, Romantic Novelists Assn., Mary Elgin Award (Hodders), & Daughter of Mark Twain, all 1974. Address: The Lodge, Inchmunin, by Balmaha, Stirlingshire, UK.

BOOTHROYD, Geoffrey, b. 22 Jan. 1925, Preston, UK. Post, Imperial Chemical Industries Ltd. Publs: Gun Collecting, 1961; Guns Through the Ages, 1962; The Rifle & Rifle Shooting, 1965; The Handgun, 1970. Contbr. to: The Shooting Times; The Am. Rifleman; Deutsches Waffen Jrnl.; The Gun Report; Guns Review. Mbrships: Arms & Armour Soc.; Fellow, Soc. of Antiquaries of Scotland. Agent: Peter Janson-Smith Ltd. Address: 26 Darnley Rd., Pollokshields, Glasgow G41 4NB, UK.

BOOTHROYD, (John) Basil, b. 1910, Worksop, Notts., UK. Writer; Broadcaster. Publs: Home Guard Goings-on; Adastral Bodies; Are Sergeants Human? ; Are Officers Necessary? ; Lost; A Double Fronted Shop; The House about a Man; Motor if you Must; To my Embarrassment; You Can't Be Serious; The Whole Thing's Laughable; Let's Stay Married; Boothroyd at Bay; Life of the Duke of Edinburgh, forthcoming. Contbr. to: Punch (Asst. Ed., 1952, Mbr. of Punch Table); Homes & Gardens; Inst. of Bankers Jrnl.; New Law Jrnl.; Times; Ctrl. Off. of Info.; Radio & TV; etc. Hons: Freeman, City of London; Kt. of Mark Twain, USA. Address: Green Ridges, Cuckfield, Haywards Heath, Sussex, UK.

BOOTON, Harold William, b. 7 Nov. 1932, Stockton-on-Tees, Durham, UK. Architect; Landscape Architect; Author. Educ: Durham Univ.; Edinburgh Coll. of Art.; Heriot Watt Univ.; B.Arch., Dipl. LA, Dipl. TP., etc. Publs: Architecture of Spain, 1966; Great Tradition of Western Architecture (w. Bruce Allsopp & Ursula Clarke), 1967; Renaissance Architecture & Ornament in Spain (revision of Andrew N. Prentice's original publ., 1893), 1970. Contbr. to: Archts. Jrnl.; RIBA Jrnl. Mbr., Soc. of Archtl. Histns. (Gt. Britain). Address: White Cross House, 34 Main Street, Bishopthorpe, York, UK.

BORDEN, Morton, b. 23 Nov. 1925, Newark, N.J., USA. Professor of History. Educ: B.A., CCNY, 1948; M.A., N.Y. Univ., 1949; Ph.D., Columbia Univ., 1953. Publs: The Federalism of James A. Bayard, 1955; The Antifederalist Papers, 1965; Parties & Politics in the Early Republic, 1967; George Washington, 1969; America's Eleven Greatest Presidents, 1971; The American Tory, 1972; Portrait of a Nation, 1973. Contbr. to profl. jrnls. inclng: Wm. & Mary Quarterly; Jrnl. of Southern Hist.; Jrnl. of Am. Hist. Address: 1018 Monte Dr., Santa Barbara, CA 93110, USA.

BORER, Mary Cathcart, b. 3 Feb. 1906, London, UK. Scriptwriters; Author. Educ: B.Sc., Univ. Coll., London. Publs: Covent Garden; England's Markets; Britain: 20th Century; Africa; What Became of the Namelukes; Famous Rogues; Tabitha (play, w. Arnold Ridley), 1956; Two Villages, 1973; var. radio & TV scripts. Address: Robin Hill, Station Rd., Tring, Herts. HP23 5NG, UK.

BORGESE, Elisabeth Mann, b. 24 Apr. 1918, Munich, Germany. Writer; Senior Fellow, Center for the Study of Democratic Institutions. Educ: Conserv. of Zürich, 1936. Publs: To Whom It May Concern (short stories), 1961; Ascent of Woman, 1963; The Language Barrier, 1965; The Ocean Regime, 1968; Pacem in Maribus (ed.), 1972; The Drama of the Oceans, 1975. Contbr. to num. jrnls. Mbrships: Chmn., Planning Coun., Int. Ocean Inst., Malta; Acad. of Pol. Scis.; Authors Guild; Am. Assn., Int. Law. Address: San Domenico, Florence, Italy.

BORNEMAN, Ernest, pen name McCABE, Cameron, b. 12 Apr. 1915, Berlin, Germany. Author. Educ: Univ. level, London, Cambridge, Edinburgh, UK, N.Y. & Evanston, Ill., USA. Novels: The Face of the Cutting Room Floor (pen name), 1937, reprint, 1974; A Love Story, 1941; Tremolo, 1948; Tomorrow Is Now, 1959; Something Wrong, 1961; The Compromisers, 1962; The Man Who Loved Women, 1968. Sci. publs. incl: Lexikon der Liebe, 2 vols., 1968, 3rd ed., 1971; Sex im Volksmund, 1971, 2nd ed., 1974; Studien zur Befreiung des Kindes, 5 vols., 1973-76; Psychoanalyse des Geldes, 1973; Das Patriarchat, 1975. Mbrships: Writers' Guild of Gt. Britain; Verband Deutscher Schriftsteller. Recip., Book of Month Award, Darmstadt, for Sex im Volksmund. Address: A 4612 Scharten, Austria.

BORRIE, John, b. 22 Jan 1915, Port Chalmers, NZ. Cardio-thoracic Surgeon; Author. Publs. incl: Management of Emergencies in Thoracic Surgery, 1958, 2nd ed., 1972; Lung Cancer, Surgery & Survival, 1964; Olveston-Theomin Gallery, 1968, 8th ed., 1974; Hints to Graduates studying abroad for NZ PG Med. Fed. (16 eds.), 1974. Contbr. to var. med. jrnls. Hons. incl: M.B.E., 1946. Address: 37 Newington Ave., Dunedin, NZ.

BORRIE, Peter Forbes, b. 26 Mar. 1918, Basra, Iraq. Physician. Educ: M.A., M.D., Clare Coll., Cambridge; F.R.C.P. Publs: Common Skin Diseases, 14 eds.; Modern Trends in Dermatology. Contbr. to var. med. jrnls. Address: 115A Harley St., London W1, UK.

BOSCH, Andrés, b. 8 Oct. 1926, Palma, Majorca, Spain. Writer. Educ: Lic. Law. Publs: (novels) La noche, 1959; Homenaje privado, 1961; La revuelta, 1963; La estafa, 1965; Ritos profanos (collect. of short novels), 1967; El mago y la llama, 1970; El realismo y los realismos (lit. essay, w. M. García Viñó), 1973; El cazador de piedras, 1974. Hons: Premio Planeta, 1959; Premio Ciudad de Barcelona, 1961; Premio Olimpia, 1970. Address: Calle Burdeos 1 y 3, 6º, 2ª, Barcelona 15, Spain.

BOSCH, Juan, b. 1909. Writer; Politician. Publs: Camino Real (stories); Indios; La Mañosa (novel); Mujeres en la Vida de Hostos; Hostos — El Sembrador; Dos Pesos de Agua; Och Cuentos; La Muchacha de la Guaira; Cuba, la Isla Fascinante; Cuentos de Navidad; Life of Bolivar; Cuentos escritos en el Exilio; Trujillo: Causas de una tirania sin Ejemplo; The Unfinished Experiment: Democracy in the Dominican Republic, 1965; David, 1966; Pentagonism,

1969. Mbr., Fndr., Las Cuevas (lit. grp.). Address: c/o Dominican Revolutionary Pty., Benidorm, Spain.

BOSLEY, Harold Augustus, b. 19 Feb. 1907, Burchard, Neb., USA. United Methodist Clergyman; Author. Educ: A.B., Neb. Wesleyan Univ., 1930; B.D., 1932, Ph.D., 1933, Univ. of Chgo. Publs. incl: The Quest for Religious Certainty, 1939; On Final Ground, 1946; The Church Militant, 1952; Sermons on the Psalms, 1956; Sermons On Genesis, 1958; The Mind of Christ, 1966; The Character of Christ, 1967; The Deeds of Christ, 1969; Men Who Build Churches, 1972. Contbr. to: Christian Century; Relig. in Life; Christian Advocate; Rdrs.' Digest; etc. Hons: Award, Book of Month Club; 3 Awards, Pulpit Book of Month Club; 7 hon. degrees. Address: 137 Old Whaling Ln., Beach Haven Ter., NJ 08008, USA.

BOSS, Judy, b. 26 Nov. 1935, Mpls., Minn., USA. Author; Lecturer. Educ: B.S., Univ. of Minn.; Profl. Degree, Inst. of Psychorientol. Inc. Publs: In Silence They Return, 1972; A Garden of Joy, 1974. Mbrships: Acad. of Parapsychol. & Med.; Spiritual Frontiers Fellowship. Address: 1510 Edgcumbe Road, St. Paul, MN 55116, USA.

BOST, Pierre, b. 5 Sept. 1901. Writer. Educ: Lic. de Philosophie, Univ. of Paris (Sorbonne). Publs. incl: Hercule et Mademoiselle; Un An dans un Trou; Monsieur L'Amiral va bientôt mourir; La Haute Fourche; Dieu a besoin des hommes; L'Imbécile (play); Deux paires d'amis (play); many film scripts. Contbr. to jrnls. Address: 12 rue de L'Abbaye, Paris 6e, France.

BOSTICCO, Mary, b. Birmingham, UK. Editor; Writer; Press Officer, Bracknell Development Corp., UK. Educ: N.Y. Univ., USA. Publs: Modern Personnel Management, 1964; Personal Letters for Businessmen, 1965; Etiquette for the Businessman at Home & Abroad, 1967; Instant Business Letters, 1968; Top Secretary, 1970; Creative Techniques for Management, 1971; The Businessman's Wife, 1972. Contbr. to: Times; Fin. Times; Bus. Mgmt. Address: The Oasis, 7a Telston Close, Bourne End, Bucks., UK.

BOSTOCK, Donald Ivan, b. 1924, Macclesfield, UK. Musician; Writer. Publs: Choirmastery, 1966; Theory for Musicians, forthcoming. Contbr. to: Choir & Musical Jrnl.; Music Ministry; Choir Herald; Magic Wand. Address: Kerridge, Gorse Hill Lane, Virginia Water, Surrey, UK.

BOSTOCK, John, b. 20 Jan. 1892, Glasgow, Scotland, UK. Psychiatrist. Educ: London Hosp., Univ. of London; M.B., B.S., London; L.R.C.P., London; M.R.C.S., England; D.P.M., England. Publs. incl: The Nursing of Nervous Patients, 1942; The Pre-School Child & Society (w. Edna Hill), 1946; The Dawn of Australian Psychiatry (1788-1850), 1968. Contbr. to: Jrnl. of Mental Sci.; Med. Jrnl. of Aust.; Lancet; etc. Mbrships: Pres., Australasian Assn. of Psychs., Royal Soc. of Qld.; Fellow, Royal Coll. of Psychs., Aust. & N.Z. Coll. of Psychs., Royal Australasian Coll. of Physns.; Aust. Soc. of Authors. Address: 106 Bonney Ave., Clayfield, Brisbane, Qld., Australia 4011.

BOSTON, Lucy Maria, b. 10 Dec. 1892, Southport, Lancs., UK. Writer. Publs: Yew Hall, 1954; The Children of Green Knowe, 1954; The Chimneys of Green Knowe, 1957; The River at Green Knowe, 1959; A Stranger at Green Knowe, 1961; An Enemy at Green Knowe, 1964; The Sea Egg, 1967; The House that Grew, 1969; The Castle of Yew, 1969; Persephone, 1969; The Horned Man, 1970; Nothing Said, 1971; Memory in a House, 1973; The Guardians of the House, 1974. Recip., Carnegie Medal, 1961. Address: The Manor, Hemingford Grey, Huntingdon, UK.

BOSTON, Orlan William, b. 1891, Nashville, Mich., USA. Engineering Consultant. Educ: B.M.E., M.S.E., Mech. Engrng., Univ. of Mich. Publs: Bibliography on Cutting of Metals, 3 parts, 1932, 1935, 1945; Engineering Shop Practice, 2 vols., 1933, 1935; Materials of Aircraft Construction, 1935; Metal Processing, 1941, 2nd ed. 1951; A.S.M.E. Manual on the Cutting of Metals, 1952; over 300 papers publd. by var. tech. socs. Contbr. to: Marks' Mech. Engrs.' Handbook; A.S.M. Metals Handbook; Ency. Britannica; var. other handbooks & encys. Mbr., num. profl. assns. Address: 60 Lochmoor Blvd., Grosse Point Shores, MI 48236, USA.

BOTELLA-LLUSIA José, pen name PEPE, b. 18 Mar. 1912, Madrid, Spain. Doctor of Medicine; University Professor & Chairman of Gynaecology & Obstetrics. Educ: M.D., Madrid, 1936; Prof., Zaragoza, 1946, Madrid, 1948.

Publs: Endocrinologia de la Mujer, 1942, 4th ed. 1966; Endocrinology of Woman, 1973; Obstetrical Endocrinology, 1961; Tratado de Ginecologia, 3 vols., 10th ed., 1974. Contbr. to: Am. Jrnl. of Obst. & Gynecol.; Int. Jrnl. Fertility; Int. Jrnl. Ob. & Gynecol.; Acta Europaea Fertilitatis (Fndr.); Acta Gynaecologica (Fndr.); ABC, Madrid. Mbr., var. profl. assns. Address: Calle de Velázquez 83, Madrid (6), Spain.

BOTT, George, b. 1920, Ashbourne, Derbys., UK. Senior English Master & Librarian, Cockermouth Grammar School. Author. Educ: B.A., Leeds Univ. Publs: George Orwell: Selected Writings; Shakespeare, Man & Boy; Read & Relate; Sponsored Talk. Contbr. to: Times Educl. Supplement; Schl. Libn.; Books & Bookmen; Country Life; John O'London's Wkly.; Chambers Jrnl.; Writing Today; Jrnl. of Educ.; Cumberland Evening News; etc. Mbrships: Pres., Cumbrian Lit. Grp.; Pres., Keswick Lect. Soc. Address: 16 Penrith Rd., Keswick, Cumbria CA12 4HF, UK.

BOTTEL, Helen A., b. 13 Mar. 1914, Beaumont, Calif., USA. Columnist; Author. Educ: A.A., Riverside Coll., Calif.; S. Ore. Coll.; Ore. State Univ. Publs: To Teens With Love, 1969; Helen Help Us, 1972; Parent Survival Kit, 1975. Contbr. to num. mags. & publs.; Author of daily columns, Helen Help Us, & Generation Rap, King Features Syndicate, N.Y. Mbrships: Soc. of Mag. Writers, NYC; Calif. Writers' Club, Sacramento. Hons: 1st Prize for To Teens With Love, Calif. Press Women; 5 Awards for newspaper feature articles, 1955-58. Address: 2060 — 56th Ave., Sacramento, CA, USA.

BOTTRALL, (Francis James) Ronald, b. 1906, Camborne, Cornwall, UK. Former British Council Representative; Former FAO Executive. Writer; Poet. Educ: M.A.; Pembroke Coll., Cambridge; Princeton Univ., N.J., USA. Publs: The Loosening, 1931; Festivals of Fire, 1934; The Turning Path, 1939; Farewell & Welcome, 1945; Selected Poems, 1946; The Palisades of Fear, 1949; Adam Unparadised, 1954; Collected Poems, 1961; Rome, 1968; Day & Night, 1974; Poems 1955-73, 1974. Contbr. to mags. & jrnls. Mbrships: F.R.S.L.; PEN. Hons: O.B.E.; K.St.J.; Grand Off. of O. of M. of Repub. of Italy. Address: Via IV Fontane 16, Int. 6, 00184 Rome, Italy.

BOULANGER, Margo, pen name MARGO, b. 7 June 1920, Bucyrus, Kan., USA. Radio Announcer; Freelance Writer. Educ: Kan. State Coll., Pitts.; Kan. Univ., Lawrence; Kan. State Univ., Manhattan. Contbr. to: Okla. Ranch & Farm World; 'Round The Clock' column (by Troy Gordon), Tulsa World; Wkly. Sedan Times-Star; Coffeyville Jrnl.; Sedan Centennial celebrations, 1973 ("Saga of Sedan", audio-visual tape). Mbrships. incl: Kan. & Nat. Press Women; Kan. Authors. Hons. incl: 1st Prizes in sev. categories, Kan. Press Women contests, 1973 & 1974. Address: 317 N. Chautauqua, Sedan, KS 67361, USA.

BOULT, (Sir) Adrian Cedric, b. 1889, Chester, UK. Orchestral Conductor; Former Director of Music, BBC. Educ: D.Mus., Mus.Doc.; Christ Ch. Coll., Oxford; Leipzig Konservatorium, Germany. Publs: Thoughts on Conducting, 1963; Handbook on the Technique of Conducting, 1968; My Own Trumpet (autobiog.), 1973. Mbr., Athenaeum Club. Address: 38 Wigmore Street, London W1, UK.

BOULTON, Marjorie, b. 7 May 1924, Teddington, UK. Writer. Educ: M.A., B.Litt., reading for D.Phil., Somerville Coll., Oxford. Publs: The Anatomy of Poetry, 1953; The Anatomy of Prose, 1954; Kontralte (in Esperanto), 1955; The Anatomy of Drama, 1960; Saying What We Mean, 1959; Eroj (in Esperanto), 1959; Zamenhof, 1960, Esperanto ed., 1962; Words in Real Life, 1965; Okuloj (in Esperanto), 1967; Reading for Real Life, 1971; The Anatomy of the Novel, forthcoming. Contbr. to: Brit. Esperantist & other Esperanto mags. Mbr., Soc. of Authors. Recip., Esperanto Author of Yr. award, 1958. Address: 36 Stockmore St., Oxford OX4 1JT, UK.

BOUMAN, Jan Cornelis, b. 6 May 1912, Rotterdam, Netherlands. Psychoanalyst; Consulting Psychologist; Author. Educ: M.A.(Econs.), Univ. of Rotterdam; Ph.D.(Psychol.), Univ. of Stockholm, Sweden. Publs: Introduction to the Psychology of Neurosis, 1966; The Erotical Majorities, 1968; The Figure-Ground Phenomenon in Experimental & Phenomenological Psychology, 1968; An Alternative Theory of Neurosis, 1970; Female-Male, 1971; The School-Class-Society (Relations Between Teachers, Pupils & Parents), 1972; What does Neurosis Mean? , 1974;

var. sci. articles & monographs. Contbr. to var. mags. Hons. incl: Guest Prof., Duquesne Univ., USA, Summer 1971. Address: Stureparken 11, 114 26 Stockholm, Sweden.

BOUNDY, Wyndham Sydney, b. 30 Oct. 1892, Bishop's Nympton, Devon, UK. Historian; Retired Headmaster; Official Lecturer for W.E.A. (History & Music). Publs: Bushell & Harman of Lundy; "Here & There" by a Historian, 1975. Contbr. to: BBC (Advsry. Comm. on Hist. progs. for 10 yrs.); also articles on numismatics to var. jrnls. & newspapers. Address: Hawkerland Rd., Colaton Raleigh, Sidmouth, Devon EX10 0HL, UK.

BOUQUET, Michael Rome, b. 1915, St. Giles, Dorset, UK. Writer. Educ: M.A., Queens' Coll., Cambridge Univ. Publs: No Gallant Ship; Westcountry Sail, 1971; South Eastern Sail, 1972. Contbr. to: Country Life; Western Morning News. Address: Higher Lodfin, Bampton, Devon, UK.

BOURDEAUX, Michael Alan, b. 19 Mar. 1934, Praze, Cornwall, UK. Director of Centre for the Study of Religion & Communism (Keston College). Educ: Hons. degrees, Russian, French & Theol., St. Edmund Hall, Oxford, 1954-59; Moscow State Univ., USSR, 1959-60. Publs: Opium of the People, 1965; Religious Ferment in Russia, 1968; Patriarch & Prophets, 1969; Faith on Trial in Russia, 1971; Aida of Leningrad, 1972. Contbr. to the Ch. Times. Mbr., Rsch. Staff, Royal Inst. of Int. Affairs, 1971-73. Address: 34 Lubbock Rd., Chislehurst, Kent BR7 5JJ, UK.

BOURJAILY, Vance, b. 1922, Cleveland, USA. Critic; Editor; Professor of American Literature. Educ: B.A., Bowdoin Coll., USA. Publs: The End of My Life, 1947; The Hound of Earth, 1952; The Violated, 1958; Confessions of a Spent Youth, 1960; The Unnatural Enemy, 1963; Expedition, 1964. Contbr. to: Village Voice; Ed., Discovery; New Yorker; Esquire. Address: N. Liberty, Iowa, USA.

BOURKE, Vernon J(oseph), b. 17 Feb. 1907, North Bay, Ont., Can. Professor of Philosophy; Author. Educ: B.A.(Hons.), 1928, M.A., 1929, Univ. of Toronto; Ph.D., 1927. Publs: Augustine's Quest of Wisdom, 1945; St. Thomas & the Greek Moralists, 1947; Ethnics, 1950; The Pocket Aquinas, 1960; Will in Western Thought, 1964; Aquinas' Search for Wisdom, 1965; Ethics in Crisis, 1966; History of Ethics, 1968, French ed., 1970, Italian ed., 1972; The Essential Augustine, 1974. Contbr. to: The Monist; Commonweal; etc. Hons. incl: Aquinas Medal, Wash., 1963; Litt.D., Bellarmine Coll., 1974. Address: St. Louis University, St. Louis, MO 63103, USA.

BOURNE, Frank Card, b. 17 July 1914, Wells, Maine, USA. Professor. Educ: A.B., M.A., Ph.D., Princeton Univ. Publs: The Public Works of the Julio-Claudians & Flavians, 1946; A History of the Romans, 1966; co-author, Ancient Roman Statutes, 1961; Ed., Edward Gibbon, Decline & Fall, 1963. Contbr. to: Am. Jrnl. of Philology; Transactions of Am. Phil. Assoc.; Classical Jrnl. Mbrships. incl: Am. Philol. Assoc.; Classical Assn. of Atlantic States. Hons: Kennedy Professor of Latin Langs. & Lit., Princeton Univ., 1971–. Address: 103 East Pyne Bldg., Princeton, N.J., USA.

BOURNE, Ursula, b. 31 May 1921, Liverpool, UK. Educ: England, France & Switz. Publs: Portuguese Cookery, 1973; Spanish Cookery, 1974. Mbr., Brit. Puppet & Model Theatre Guild. Address: Shrublands, W. Bergholt, Colchester, Essex CO6 3JQ, UK.

BOVA, Ben(jamin) W., b. 8 Nov. 1932, Phila., Pa., USA. Writer; Editor. Educ: B.S., Temple Univ., 1954. Sci. Fiction publs. incl: The Star Conquerors, 1959; Star Watchman, 1964; Out of the Sun, 1968; Exiled from Earth, 1971; Forward in Time, 1973; Gremlins, Go Home!, 1974. Non-fiction publs. incl: The Uses of Space, 1965; In Quest of Quasars, 1970; The Amazing Lasar, 1972; Starflight & Other Improbabilities, 1973; Workshops in Space, 1974. Contbr. to: Smithsonian Mag.; IEEE Spectrum; Schl. Lib. Jrnl.; & num. sci. fiction mags.; Ed., Analog Sci. Fiction-Sci. Fact mag. Hons. incl: Sci. Fiction Achievement Award, 1973; E. E. Smith Mem. Award, New England Sci. Fiction Soc., 1974. Address: Analog Mag., 350 Madison Ave., N.Y., NY 10017, USA.

BOVERI, Margret Antonie, b. 14 Aug. 1900, Würzburg, Germany. Writer; Journalist. Educ: Univs. of Würzburg, Munich, & Berlin; D.Phil., 1932. Publs: Sir Edward Grey und das Foreign Office, 1933; Das Weltgeschehen am Mittelmeer, 1936; Vom Minarett zum Bohrturm, 1938; Ein Auto, Wüsten, blaue Perlen, 1939; Amerikafibel für erwachsene Deutsche, 1946; Der Diplomat vor Gericht, 1948; 16 Fenster und 8 Türen, 1953; Der Verrat im XX Jahrhundert, 4 vols., 1956-60; Indisches Kaleidoskop, 1961; Wir lügen alle — Eine Hauptstadtzeitung unter Hitler, 1965; Tage des Überlebens, Berlin 1945, 1968; Die Deutschen und der status quo, 1974. Mbrships: German Press Assn.; German Writers' Union; PEN. Hons: Joseph Drexel Prize, 1961; German Critics' Award, 1968. Address: Im Schwarzen Grund 16, D 1 Berlin 33, W. Germany.

BOWART, Walter H., pen names KALID RAH, A.; STONE MOUNTAIN; KARUS, Ike; CAHONES, Carolyn, b. 14 May 1939, Omaha, Neb., USA. Author; Editor; Publisher. Educ: Univ. of Okla.; New Schl. for Social Rsch. Publs: Pot Art, 1970; Women's Lip, 1973; Extra-Terrestrial Tourist Guide (anthols.), 1974; The High Way, 1974. Contbr. to: E. Village Other; Art Voices; Cavalier Mag.; Image Mag.; Writer's Yrbook.; The Underground Press. Recip., Schlrship. awards. Address: c/o Omen Communications, 7007 E. River Rd., Tucson, AZ 85715, USA.

BOWDEN, Jean, pen names DELL, Belinda; BLAND, Jennifer; CURRY, Avon, b. Edinburgh, UK. Former Civil Servant. Publs. incl: Grey Touched with Scarlet, 1959; Call an Ambulance, 1962; In a Winged World, 1964; You're Welcome, 1965; (as B. Dell) City of Strangers; Flowers for the Festival; Lake of Silver; (as A. Curry) A Place of Execution; Shack-Up; Hunt for Danger; (as J. Bland) Accomplice. Mbrships: Soc. of Authors; Soc. Women Writers & Jrnlsts.; Crimewriters' Assn. Agent: Laurence Pollinger Ltd. Address: Laurel Cottage, 138 Himley Rd., London SW17, UK.

BOWDEN, Roland Heywood, b. 1916, Lincoln, UK. Former Teacher of Art & English Lieterature. Educ: B.Arch., Liverpool Univ. Publs: Poems from Italy, 1970; The Last Analysis of Wilhelm Reich (2-Act Play), 1974. Contbr. to: Arts Review; Alchemist, Edinburgh; Kolokon; Oxymoron; World Quarterly; Poetry Quarterly. Address: 2 Roughmere Cottage, Lavant, Chichester, Sussex, UK.

BOWEN, Desmond, b. 1921, Ottawa, Ont., Can. Priest, Anglican Church of Canada; University Professor. Educ: Carleton Univ., Ottawa; Queen's Univ., Kingston; London Univ. UK; Ripon Hall, Oxford Univ.; Hon. B.A.; M.A.; Ph.D. Publs: Idea of the Victorian Church, 1968; Souperism: Myth or Reality, 1971. Contbr. to: Irish TV (in Thomas Davis Lectures, 1973); Prism; Christian Outlook; Can. Jrnl. Theol.; Voice of Theol.; etc. Mbrship: Fellow, Royal Soc. Antiquaries of Ireland. Agent: Gill & Macmillan. Address: 28 Melgund Ave., Ottawa, Ont. K1S 2S2, Can.

BOWEN, Elizabeth Dorothea Cole. Publs: The Hotel, 1927; The Last September, 1929; Friends & Relations, 1931; To the North, 1932; The House in Paris, 1935; The Death of the Heart, 1938; Bowen's Court, 1942; Seven Winters, 1943; The Heat of the Day, 1949; (essays) Collected Impressions, 1950; The Shelbourne, 1951; A World of Love, 1955; The Cat Jumps; Look at all those Roses; The Demon Lover. Address: Bowen's Court, Co. Cork, Repub. of Ireland.

BOWEN, Emrys George, b. 28 Dec. 1900, Carmarthen, Wales, UK. Emeritus Professor of Geography & Anthropology. Educ: B.A., M.A., 1926, D.Litt., 1972, Univ. Coll. of Wales, Aberystwyth. Publs: Wales: A Study in Geography & History, 1940; The Settlements of the Celtic Saints in Wales, 1954; Saints, Seaways & Settlements in the Celtic Lands, 1969; Britain & the Western Sea Ways, 1972; David Samwell, 1751-98, Surgeon of the "Discovery", 1974. Contbr. to profl. jrnls. Mbrships: Fellow, Soc. of Antiquaries of London; F.R.G.S.; Past Pres., Inst. of British Geographers; Past Pres., Geograph. Assn. of G.B. Address: Bryntywi, Brynglas Rd., Llanbadarn Fawr, Aberystwyth SY23 3DA, UK.

BOWEN, John Griffith, b. 5 Nov. 1924, Calcutta, India. Playwright; Author. Educ: M.A., Pembroke & St. Anthony's Colls., Oxford. Publs: The Truth Will Not Help Us; After the Rain; The Centre of the Green; Pegasus; The Mermaid & the Boy; The Essay Prize; The Bird-cage; Story-board; A World Elsewhere; (plays) I Love You, Mr. Patterson, 1965; After the Rain, 1967; Fall & Redemption, 1968; Little Boxes; 1968; The Disorderly Women, 1969; The Corsican Brothers, 1970; The Waiting Room, 1971. Robin Redbreast, 1974. Contbr. to: N.Y. Times Book Review; Sunday Times; London Mag.; The Sketch (Asst.

Ed., 1954-56); ATV (Script Advsr., Drama, 1961-65). Mbr., PEN. Address: Old Lodge Farm, Sugarswell Lane, Edgehill, Banbury, Oxon., UK.

BOWEN, Robert O., b. 7 May 1920, Bridgeport, Conn., USA. Employment Agency Proprietor. Educ: B.A., 1948, M.A., 1950, Univ. of Ala.; Univ. Coll. of N. Wales, UK, 1952-53. Publs: (novels) The Weight of the Cross, 1951; Bamboo, 1953; Sidestreet, 1954; Marlow the Master & Other Stories, 1963; The Christmas Child (opera libretto), 1960; The Truth about Communism, 1962; College Style Manual, 1963; An Alaskan Dictionary, 1965; Ed., Practical Prose Studies; A Critical Anthology of Contemporary American Prose Readings for the College Freshman, 1956; Ed., The New Professors, 1960; Alaska Literary Directory (Ed. w. Robert A. Charles), 1964. Address: P.O. Box 1862, Anchorage, AK 99501, USA.

BOWER, William Clayton, b. 6 Feb. 1878, Ind., USA. University Professor. Educ: incl: LL.D., Transylvania Univ.; D.D., Meadville Seminary. Publs: incl: A Survey of Religious Education in the Local Church, 1919; Character Through Creative Expression, 1930; Protestantism Faces its Educational Task Together, 1949; Through the Years: Personal Memoirs, 1957. Contbr. to num. Christian jrnls. Recip., Kentucky Citation for Disting. Service, 1950. Address: 658 N. Broadway, Lexington, KY 40508, USA.

BOWERING, George, b. 1 Dec. 1934, Kelowna, B.C., Can. Professor of English. Educ: M.A., Univ. of B.C. Publs: Mirror On the Floor (novel), 1967; Rocky Mountain Foot (poems), 1969; Touch: Selected Poems 1961-70, 1971; In the Flesh (poems), 1974; Flycatcher (stories), 1974. Contbr. to: Atlantic Monthly; London Mag.; Poetry; Tamarack Review; Open Letter; MacLean's. Hons: Gov.-Gen.'s Poetry Award, 1969; Sr. Award, Can. Coun., 1971. Address: 2499 West 37th Avenue, Vancouver, B.C. V6M 1P4, Canada.

BOWERS, Faubion, b. 29 Jan. 1917, Miami, Okla., USA. Writer. Educ: Columbia Univ.; Univ. of Poitiers, France; Juilliard Grad. Schl. of Music, N.Y., USA. Publs: Japanese Theatre, 1952; Theatre in the East, 1956; Scriabin, 1969; New Scriabin, 1972. Contbr. to: N.Y. Times; Village Voice; Wash. Post; Esquire; Saturday Review; Atlantic Monthly; Lectr. on theater. music & writing at var. colls.; & appearances in cultural progs. on CBS-TV. Address: 205 E. 94th St., N.Y., NY 10028, USA.

BOWETT, Derek William, B. 1927, Manchester, UK. Lecturer; College President. Educ: M.A., LL.B., Ph.D., Downing Coll., Cambridge Univ. Publs: Self-Defence in International Law; 1958; Law of International Institutions, 1964; United Nations Forces, 1964; The Law of the Sea, 1968; The Search for Peace, 1972. Contbr. to var. legal periodicals. Address: Queens' College, Cambridge, UK.

BOWLBY, John, b. 26 Feb. 1907, London, UK. Psychiatrist. Educ: Royal Naval Coll., Dartmouth; Trinity Coll., Cambridge; Univ. Coll. Hosp., London; M.A., M.D., F.R.C.P., F.R.C.Psych. Publs: Personal Aggressiveness & War (w. E. F. M. Durbin), 1939; Forty-four Juvenile Thieves, 1946; Maternal Care & Mental Health, 1951; Child Care & the Growth of Love, 1953; Attachment & Loss, vol. 1, Attachment, 1969, vol. 2, Separation, 1973. Mbrships. incl: Fellow, Brit. Psychol. Assn.; Int. Assn. for Child Psychiatry (Pres.) 1962-66); Brit. Psycho-analytical Soc. (Dpty. Pres., 1957-61). Hons. incl: D.Litt., 1971; C.B.E.; 1972; James Spence Medal, 1974. Address: Tavistock Centre, Belsize Lane, London NW3, UK.

BOWLE, John Edward, b. 19 Dec. 1905, Salisbury, Wilts., UK. Historian. Educ: M.A., Balliol Coll., Oxford. Publs: Western Political Thought, 1947; The Unity of European History, 1948, 2nd expanded ed., 1970; Hobbes & His Critics, 1951; Politics & Opinion in the 19th-Century, 1954; Viscount Samuel, 1957; Man Through the Ages, 1962; Henry VIII, 1964; England, a Portrait, 1966; The English Experience, 1971; Napoleon, 1974; The Imperial Achievement, 1974. Contbr. to: Times Lit. Supplement; The Listener; The Spectator; Punch. Recip., Arts Coun. Prize, 1966. Address: 24 Woodstock Close, Oxford, UK.

BOWLES, Jane, b. 1917, NYC, N.Y., USA. Author. Publs: Two Serious Ladies, 1943; Plain Pleasures, 1966; (play) In the Summer House, 1954. Contbr. to: Vogue; Harper's Bazaar; Mademoiselle. Address: 2117, Tanger Socco, Tangier, Morocco.

BOWLES, Paul Frederick, b. 1911, NYC, USA. Writer. Educ: Univ. of Va. Publs. incl: The Sheltering Sky; The Hours After Noon; Yallah; Their Heads Are Green & Their Hands Are Blue; Up Above the World; A Life Full of Holes (from the Arabic of Charhadi); Pages from Cold Point; The Time of Friendship; The Thicket of Spring; The Delicate Prey; Let It Come Down; The Spider's House; Transl., Choukri, For Bread Alone; Transl., Choukri, Jean Genet in Tangier; Without Stopping (autobiog.); (from the Arabic of M. Mrabet) Love with a Few Hairs; The Lemon; M'Hashish; The Boy Who Set the Fire. Contbr. to: Antaeus (Fndr. & Cons. Ed.); Am. Mercury; Esquire; Harper's Mag.; Harper's Bazaar; Mademoiselle; other lit. & popular mags. Agents: William Morris Agcy. Address: 2117 Tanger Socco, Tangier, Morocco.

BOWLEY, Marian E. A., b. 1911, Reading, Berks, UK. Professor Emeritus of Political Economy. Educ: London Schl. Econs., London Univ.; Univ. of Frankfurt, Germany; B.Sc.(Econ.); Ph.D. Publs: Nassau Senior & Classical Economics, 1937; Housing & the State 1919-44, 1945; Innovations in Building Materials: An Economic Study, 1960; The British Building Industry, 1966; Studies in the History of Economic Theory Before 1870, 1973. Contbr. to: Economica; Review of Econ. Studies; Pol. Quarterly; Jrnl. Royal Statistical Soc. Address: Brook Orchard, Graffham, Petworth, Sussex, UK.

BOWLEY, Rex Lyon, b. 27 July 1925, Exeter, UK. Schoolmaster. Educ: M.A., Trinity Coll., Dublin Univ.; H.Dip.Educ. Publs: Teaching Without Tears: A Guide to Teaching Technique, 1961, 4th ed., 1973; The Fortunate Islands: A History of the Isles of Scilly, 6th ed., 1968; The Standard Guidebook to Tresco, Isles of Scilly, 1970; The Isles of Scilly Standard Guidebook, 5th ed., 1975. Mbrships: Soc. of Authors; Histl. Assn.; I.A.A.M. Address: 16 Linden Cres., Woodford Green, Essex, UK.

BOWLT, John Ellis, b. 6 Dec. 1943, London, UK. University Lecturer. Educ: B.A., 1965; M.A., 1966; Ph.D., 1972. Publs: The Russian Avant-Garde: Theory & Criticism, 1902-34, 1975. Contbr. to: Studio Int.; Art Jrnl.; Art in Am.; Slavonic & E. European Review; Leonardo; Art News; The Burlington Mag.; Apollo; Russian Review; Soviet Studies; 20th Century Studies; Slavic Review; Forum. Mbr., var. profl. assns. Recip., Schlrship. to Moscow Univ., Brit. Coun., 1966-68. Address: Dept. of Slavic Langs. & Lits., Univ. of Texas, Austin, TX 78712, USA.

BOWMAN, Herbert Eugene, b. 8 Feb. 1917, Harrisburg, Pa., USA. University Professor; Writer. Educ: A.B., Univ. of Pa., 1938; M.A., 1941, Ph.D., 1950, Harvard Univ. Publs: Vissarion Belinski: A Study in the Origins of Social Criticism in Russia, 1954, 1969. Contbr. to: Slavic Review; Slavic & E. European Jrnl.; Survey. Mbrships: MLA (Conf. Chmn., 1966); Am. Assn. for Advancement of Slavic Studies (a VP, 1961). Hons: Phi Beta Kappa, 1938; Am. Coun. Learned Socs. Fellowship, 1959; Can. Coun. Sr. Fellowship, 1967. Address: Dept. of Slavic Languages & Literatures, Univ. of Toronto, 21 Sussex Ave., Toronto, Can.

BOWMAN, William Ernest, b. 1911, Scarborough, UK. Structural & Civil Engineer. Publs: The Ascent of Rum Doodle, 1956; The Cruise of the Talking Fish, 1957. Contbr. to: Studio; Structural Engr. Mbr., Soc. of Authors. Address: 56 Stoke Fields, Guildford, Surrey, UK.

BOWSKILL, Derek, pen names EDWARDES, Pauline; CLEWES, Jeremy, b. 1928, Scunthorpe, UK. Writer; Dramatist; Former Drama Adviser & Director of Research. Educ: Sheffield Univ.; Coll. of St. Peter, Birmingham; Rose Bruford Coll. of Speech & Drama. Publs: Acting & Stagecraft Made Simple, 1973; Person to Person, 1973; A Hard Sell & 6 other plays, 1973; Drama & The Teacher, 1974; Blind Man's Buff (TV play), 1974. Contbr. to: Higher Educ. Jrnl.; Engl. in Educ.; Young Drama; Forum; Opinion (Aust.); BBC Drama Workshop; etc. Agent: Hope, Leresche & Steele. Address: c/o Agents, 11 Jubilee Place, London SW3 3TE, UK.

BOWYER, Laura Ruth, b. 1907, Brechin, UK. Senior Lecturer in Social Psychology (retired). Educ: M.A., M.Ed., Univ. of Glasgow; B.Sc.(Econ.), Univ. of London. Publs: Mental Testing; The Lowenfeld World Technique. Contbr. to: Special Schls. Jrnl.; Spastics Quarterly; Brit. Jrnl. of Educl. Psychol.; Ed., Brit. Jrnl. of Projective Psychol., 1974. Address: 34 Morven Rd., Glasgow G61 3BX, UK.

BOX, Muriel Violette (Lady GARDINER), b. 1905, New Malden, Surrey, UK. Screenwriter; Feature Director; Playwright. Publs: Vigil, 1939; Forbidden Cargo, 1957; The Big Switch, 1964; The Trial of Marie Stopes, 1967; Odd Woman Out, 1974; (plays) Ladies Only; Petticoat Plays, 1934-35; Seventh Veil (w. Sidney Box), 1951; Stranger In My Bed, 1965; Odd Woman Out, 1974. Mbrships: Engl. Speaking Union; Arts Theatre Club; F.R.S.A. Recip., Oscar Award. Address: Mote End, Nan Clark's Lane, Mill Hill, London NW7, UK.

BOXER, Emily Hahn, b. 14 Jan. 1905, St. Louis, Mo., USA. Writer. Educ: B.Sc.; Univs. of Wis., Columbia, N.Y., USA & Oxford, UK. Publs: Diamond; Chiang Kai-Shek; Raffles of Singapore; Miss Jill; With Naked Foot; Mary Queen of Scots; Once Upon a Pedestal. Contbr. to: The New Yorker; N.Y. Times; Times Lit. Supplement; etc. Mbrships: Nat. Union of Jrnlsts.; Cosmopolitan Club. Recip., APA Media Award, 1969. Address: Ringshall End, Little Gaddesden, Berkhamsted, Herts., UK.

BOYCE, Gray Cowan, b. 19 Feb. 1899, San Fran., Calif., USA. Retired University Professor & Administrator; Author. Publs: The English-German Nation in the University of Paris during the Middle Ages, 1927; L. J. Paetow's Guide to the Study of Medieval History (w. Dana C. Munro), 2nd ed., 1931; The University of Prague (w. W. H. Dawson), 1937; The American Historical Association's Guide to Historical Literature (ed. — contbr.), 1961; Liber Receptorum Nationis Anglicanae (Alemanniae) in Universitate Parisiensis (w. A. L. Gabriel), 1964. Contbr. to: Speculum; Am. Histl. Review; Saturday Review; Annals of Am. Acad. of Pol. & Social Sci.; etc. Address: 3201 Bayo Vista Ave., Alameda, CA 94501, USA.

BOYD, Elizabeth Orr, pen name MACCALL, Isobel, b. 1912, Largs, UK. Author. Educ: Ardrossan Acad.; Glasgow Univ. Publs: Cross-Country Walks in the West Highlands, 1952. Contbr. to: Glasgow Herald; Scottish Field; Lady; Scots Mag. Mbr., Soc. of Authors. Address: Eddlyburn, Innellan, Argyll PA23 7SE, UK.

BOYD, Malcolm, b. 1923, Buffalo, N.Y., USA. Episcopal Priest; Educator; Author. Educ: B.A.; B.D.; S.T.M.; Univ. of Ariz.; Ch. Divinity Schl. of the Pacific; Union Theol. Sem. Publs: Are You Running With Me, Jesus, 1965; Free to Live, Free to Die, 1967; As I Live & Breathe, 1970; My Fellow Americans, 1970; Human Like Me, Jesus, 1971; The Lover, 1972; The Alleluia Affair, 1975; Christian, 1975. Contbr. to: Christian Century; N.Y. Times; Wash. Post; etc. Mbrships: Assoc. Fellow, Yale Univ.; NAACP; Clergy & Laity Concerned (Nat. Bd.); PEN; Am. Ctr. & Authors Guild. Address: 1334 Orkney St., Ann Arbor, MI 48103, USA.

BOYD, Margaret, b. 17 Jan. 1913, Strasburg, Germany (now France). Teacher. Educ: Bedford Coll. of Phys. Educ., UK; Inst. of Ray Therapy, London. Author. Lacrosse — Playing & Coaching, 1959, revised ed., 1969. Recip., O.B.E. Address: Pitkindie, Crossways, Berkhamsted, Herts., UK.

BOYD, Martin à Beckett, b. 1893, Lucerne, Switz. Publs. incl: Lucinda Brayford, 1946; Such Pleasure, 1948; The Cardboard Crown, 1952; A Difficult Young Man, 1955; Outbreak of Love, 1957; Much Else in Italy, 1958; When Blackbirds Sing, 1953. Contbr. to: Times Lit. Supplement. Address: c/o Aust. & NZ Bank, 71 Cornhill, London EC3, UK.

BOYER, Gwen Roberts, b. 7 Nov. 1910, E. Chgo., USA. Public Librarian, retired. Educ: Ind. Univ. Contbr. to 44 mags. & newspapers; 29 poetry anthols.; Poetry Ed., WCAE-TV Jrnl. Mbrships: United Poets Laureate Int.; Pres., Lake Co. (Ind.) Poetry Club. Hons: Poet Laureate, Ind. State Poets, 1957; Hon. H.L.D., l'Universite Libre d'Asien (Karachi, Pakistan), 1969. Address: 418 Keilman St., P.O. Box 128, Dyer, Ind., USA.

BOYES, Megan, b. 7 July 1923, Cardiff, Wales, UK. Author. Publs: Auntie Blodwen & the Pageant, 1967. Contbr. to: Radio Nottingham; Radio Derby; Manchester Evening News; Derby Evening Telegraph; Lady; Country Quest; Elizabethan; Look & Learn; The Townswoman; Christian Herald; My Weekly; Platford; Countryman. Mbrships: Soc. of Authors; Byron Soc.; Friends Nat. Lib. of Wales; Friends Derby Mus.; Derby Writers' Guild. Address: The Glade, 49 Evans Ave., Allestree, Derby DE3 2EP, UK.

BOYKIN, Lorraine Stith, b. 1 Feb. 1931, Crewe, Va., USA. University Professor of Nutrition. Educ: B.S., M.S.,

M.A., M.S., Profl. Dip., Nutrition, Ed.D., Nutrition. Publs: Nutrition in Nursing: Outline Series, 1974. Contbr. of articles & reviews to profl. jrnls. Mbr., Am. Medical Writers Assn. Address: 200 Montauk St., Valley Stream, NY 11580, USA.

BOYLE, Andrew Philip More, b. 19 May 1919, Dundee, Scotland, UK. Journalist; Broadcaster; Author. Educ: Sorbonne, Paris, France. Publs: No Passing Glory: The Biography of Group Captain Leonard Cheshire, V.C., 1955; Heroes of Humanity (co-auth.), 1960; Trenchard, Man of Vision, 1962; Montagu Norman, 1967; Only the Wind Will Listen: Reith of the BBC, 1971; "Poor, Dear Brendan": The Quest for Brendan Brackey, 1974; (co-auth.) The God I Want, 1970; The Future of Catholic Christianity, 1970; (in preparation) The Life of Erskine Childers. Contbr. to: New Statesman; New Soc.; Sunday Times; Sunday Telegraph. Mbr., Soc. of Authors, London. Address: 16 Deodar Rd., Putney, London, S.W.15, UK.

BOYLE, John Andrew, b. 10 Mar. 1916, Worcester Park, Surrey, UK. Professor, Persian Studies. Educ: B.A., Univ. of Birmingham, 1936; Ph.D., Univ. of London, 1947. Publs: A Practical Dictionary of the Persian Language, 1949; transl., Juvaini: History of the World-Conqueror, 1958; Modern Persian Grammar, 1960; Ed. & contbr., Cambridge History of Iran, vol. V, 1968; Rashid al-Din Commemoration Volume (1318-1968) (w. K. Jahn), 1970; transl., Rashid al-Din: Successors of Genghis Khan, 1971. Contbr. to: Times Lit. Supplement; History Today; & num. others. Mbr., Soc. of Authors. Address: 266 Rye Bank Rd., Manchester M21 1LY, UK.

BOYLE, Kay, b. 19 Feb. 1903, St. Paul, Minn., USA. Professor of English. Educ: Cinn. Conservatory of Music; Ohio Mech. Inst., 1917-19. Publs. incl: (novels) The Seagull on the Step, 1955; Generation Without Farewell, 1960; (short stories) Three Short Novels, 1958; Nothing Ever Breaks Except the Heart, 1966; (verse) Collected Poems, 1962; Testament for My Students, 1970; (other) The Long Walk at San Francisco State & Other Essays, 1970. Mbr., Nat. Inst. of Arts & Letters. Hons: Guggenheim Fellowship, 1934, 1961; O. Henry Award, 1935, 1941; D.Litt., Columbia Coll., Chgo., 1971. Address: c/o A. Watkins Inc., 77 Park Ave., N.Y., NY 10016, USA.

BOYLE, Wilfred, pen name BETA, b. Leeds, UK. Actor & Singer. Educ: Leeds Coll. of Music & Drama. Publs: (plays) Christmas Crackers; Look What Santa Claus Brought; num. sketches. Contbr. to: Theatre World; The Permanent Light; Yorks. Illustrated; Glasgow Citizen; Yorks. Post; Aust. Nat. Jrnl.; London Evening News; Christian Sci. Monitor; Daily Mail; Daily Express; Birmingham Post; Manchester Evening News; Yorks. Evening Post. Mbr., Brit. Actors Equity Assn. Address: Flat 5, 1 South Hill Rd., Bromley, Kent BR2 0RA, UK.

BOYNE, Donald Arthur Colin Aydon, b. 15 Feb. 1921, Farway, Devon, UK. Journalist; Editorial Director, Architectural Press. Educ: Archtl. Assn. Schl. of Arch., London. Publs: Architects' Working Details, Vols. 1-15, 1953 & vols. publd. at intervals since. Contbr. to: Archtl. Review; Archts'. Jrnl. Hon. F.R.I.B.A. Address: 9 Queen Anne's Gate, London SW1H 9BY, UK.

BRACE, Arthur William, b. 24 May 1923, Bristol, UK. Director of Companies. Educ: B.Sc., London Schl. of Econs. Publs: Magnesium Casting Technology (w. F. A. Allen); Technology of Anodising; Non-Ferrous Metals — A Survey of their Production & Potential in the Developing Countries (w. Tsvetinformatsaya, Moscow). Mbrships: Inst. of Corrosion Technol.; Inst. of Metals; Instn. of Metallurgists; Inst. of Metal Finishing. Address: 'Rose Lawn', 22 Ebley Rd., Stonehouse, Glos. GL10 2LQ, UK.

BRACEGIRDLE, Brian, b. 31 May 1933, Macclesfield, Cheshire, UK. Science Lecturer; Author. Educ: B.Sc., F.R.P.S., F.I.I.P., M.I.Biol., A.I.M.B.I., Dip.R.M.S., etc. Publs: An atlas of embryology (w. W. H. Freeman), 1963; An atlas of histology, 1966; Photography for books & reports, 1970; An atlas of invertebrate structure, 1971; An atlas of plant structure (w. Patricia H. Miles), vol. 1, 1971, vol. 2, 1973; Thomas Telford, 1972; The Darbys & the Ironbridge Gorge, 1973; The archaeology of the industrial revolution, 1973; An advanced atlas of histology, 1975. Contbr. to var. sci. jrnls. Address: 157 Shooters Hill, London, SE18 3HS, UK.

BRACEGIRDLE, Cyril, b. 1920, Manchester, UK. Writer. Publs: A First Book of Antiques, 1970; Zoos Are

News, 1972; The Dark River, 1972. Contbr. to: Antique Dealer & Collectors Guide; Lady; Country Life; She; Spinning Wheel, USA. Mbr., Soc. of Authors. Address: 40 Blue Bell Ave., Moston, Manchester M10 9PR, UK.

BRACHER, Karl Dietrich, b. 13 Mar. 1922, Stuttgart, Germany. University Professor; Author. Educ: Dr.phil., Univ. of Tübingen, 1948; postdoct. studies, Harvard Univ., USA, 1949-50. Publs: (in German) The Dissolution of the Weimar Republic, 1955; The Nazi Seizure of Power, 1960; Germany Between Democracy & Dictatorship, 1964; The German Dictatorship (in Engl.), 1970; The German Dilemma, 1971. Co-ed. & contbr. to sev. jrnls. & books in W. Germany, UK & USA. Mbr., PEN, W. German Ctr. Hons. incl: L.H.D., Fla. State Univ., USA, 1973; Premio Acqui Storia, Italy, 1973. Address: Stationsweg 17, Bonn, W. Germany.

BRACKEN, Dorothy Kendall, b. 16 May 1910, Dallas, Tex., USA. Professor; Writer. Educ: A.B., Daniel Baker Coll.; M.A., S. Meth. Univ.; Doctoral study, Univ. of Chgo., Columbia Univ. Num. publs. incl: Tactics in Reading, 2 books, 1961; English Textbooks, 8 books, 1961; Social Studies Textbooks, 4 books, 1968; Listening Program (12 grades), 1969; Reader Textbooks, 9 books, 1973. Contbr. to conf. proceedings; Contbr. & Ed., World Congress Proceedings, Int. Reading Assn., & to IRA Jrnl. Hons: Disting. Serv. Award, IRA, 1970; Pi Lambda Theta Award for best educl. book, 4th World Congress, IRA, 1973. Address: 3230 Daniel Ave., Dallas, TX 73205, USA.

BRACKENBURY, Rosalind Mary Hamilton, b. 14 May 1942, London, UK. Writer. Educ: Sherborne Schl. for Girls, Dorset; M.A., Girton Coll., Cambridge. Publs: A Day to Remember to Forget, 1971; A Virtual Image, 1971; Into Egypt, 1973. Contbr. to: The Cornhill Mag. Address: White House Farm, Barkby, Leics., UK.

BRACKFIELD, Peter, b. 26 Sept. 1922, Vienna, Austria. Banker. Educ: M.A., Trinity Coll., Cambridge, UK. Contbr. to Liverpool Daily Post; Yorks. Post; Glasgow Herald; Irish Press; Banker; Int. Investment; Stock Exchange Gazette. Mbrships: Fellow, Inst. of Bankers; Overseas Bankers' Club; Lombard Assn. Address: Flat 6, 58 Rutland Gate, London SW7, UK.

BRADBROOK, Muriel Clara, b. 27 Apr. 1909, Wallasey, Cheshire, UK. Professor of English & Mistress of Girton College, Cambridge University. Educ: M.A., Ph.D., Litt.D., Girton Coll., Cambridge. Publs. incl: Themes & Conventions of Elizabethan Tragedy, 1934; The School of Night, 1936; T. S. Eliot, 1950; Shakespeare & Elizabethan Poetry, 1951; Shakespeare the Craftsman, 1969; Malcolm Lowry, 1974. Contbr. to: Shakespeare Survey; Times Lit. Supplement; etc. Mbrships. incl: Trustee, Shakespeare's Birthplace; F.R.S.A.; F.R.S.L.; Renaissance Soc. of Am.; Mod. Lang. Assn. of Am. Hons: Litt.D., Univs. of Liverpool, 1964, Sussex, 1972, London, 1973; LL.D., Smith Coll., USA, 1965. Address: Girton Coll., Cambridge CB3 0JG, UK.

BRADBURY, Frederick Parnell, pen names (drama) DERMOTT, Stephen; (novels) BELL, H. D., b. 19 Jan. 1904, London, UK. Author; Playwright; Former Doctor of Osteopathy. Publs. incl: Calling All Kings, 1944; The Tree Was Quiet, 1947; Healing By Hand, 1957; Adventures in Healing, 1969; (plays) The China City, 1966; Talons, 1970; Blue Armour, 1970; The Hired Man, 1973; (novels) The Lemmings, 1973; Gods Flesh, 1974. Contbr. to var. profl. jrnls., radio & TV. Mbrships: PEN; Soc. of Authors; Co-Fndr., John Paterson Trust for Indep. Rsch. Agents: (plays) Eric Glass; (novels) Anne Powis-Lyybe. Address: Coxford Cottage, St. Genny's, Bude, Cornwall, UK.

BRADBURY, Malcolm Stanley, b. 1932, Sheffield, UK. Professor of American Studies. Educ: M.A., London Univ.; Ph.D., Manchester Univ.; Ind. Univ., USA. Publs. incl: (novels) Eating People is Wrong; Stepping Westward; (humour) How to Have Class in a Classless Society; All Dressed Up & Nowhere to Go; (poetry) Two Poets; (criticism) Evelyn Waugh; What Is a Novel? ; The Social Context of Modern English Literature; Possibilities: Essays on the State of the Novel. Contbr. to Radio, TV, Stage jrnls., newspapers, etc. Mbrships: Soc. of Authors; Comm.. PEN. Agent: Curtis Brown Ltd. Address: School of English & American Studies, University of East Anglia, University Plain, Norwich, UK.

BRADBURY, Ray Douglas, b. 1920, Waukegan Ill., USA. Writer. Publs. incl: Dark Carnival; The Martian Chronicles; The Illustrated Man, Farenheit 451; The Golden Apples of the Sun; Dandelion Wine; Something Wicked This Way Comes; (play) The Anthem Sprinters; (children's book) Switch on the Night; (Screenplay) Moby Dick. Contbr. to: Harper's; Gourmet; Nat. Bus.; Nation; Saturday Evening Post; Good Housekeeping; Cosmopolitan; Mag. of Fantasy & Sci. Fiction; Astounding Stories; etc. Mbrships: Bd., Screen Writers' Guild of Am.; Pres., Sci-Fantasy Writers of Am., 1951-53. Address: 10265 Cheviot Dr., L.A. 64, Calif., USA.

BRADDOCK, Joseph Edward, b. 1902, Streatham, UK. Poet; Author; Lecturer. Educ: M.A., St. John's Coll., Cambridge. Publs: Haunted Houses, 1956; The Bridal Bed, 1960; The Girl With a Leaf in her Mouth, 1963; Some Greek Islands, 1967; Sappho's Island, 1970; The Greek Phoenix, 1972; No Stronger than a Flower: Poems 1935-1960, 1960. Contbr. to: Fortnightly Review; Contemporary Review; Poetry Review; Outposts; Observer; Listener; Spectator; etc. Mbrships: Poetry Soc., London; Byron Soc. Address: Wyck Cottage, Wadhurst, Sussex, UK.

BRADDON, Russell Reading, b. 25 Jan. 1921, Sydney, Australia. Author; Lecturer; Broadcaster. Educ: B.A., Univ. of Sydney. Publs: 23 books inclng. The Naked Island, 1952; Nancy Wake, 1956; Joan Sutherland, 1962; Roy Thomson of Fleet Street, 1964; Committal Chamber, 1966; The Inseparables, 1967; When the Enemy is Tired, 1967; The Siege, 1969; Suez: Splitting of a Nation, 1973; 100 Days of Darien, 1974. Contbr. to num. jrnls. inclng: Daily Telegraph; Sunday Times; Daily Express. Agent: John Farquharson Ltd.

BRADDY, Haldeen, b. Fairlie, Tex., USA. University Professor. Educ: A.B., E. Tex. State Univ., 1928; A.M., Univ. of Tex., Austin, 1929; Ph.D., N.Y. Univ., NYC, 1934. Publs: Chaucer & the French Poet Graunson, 1947, 2nd ed., 1968; Chaucer's Parliament of Fowls, 1932, 2nd ed., 1969; Glorious Incense, Fulfillment of Edgar A. Poe, 1953, 2nd ed., 1968; Cock of the Walk, Legend of Panco Villa, 1955, 2nd ed., 1970; Hamlet's Wounded Name, 1964, 2nd ed., 1974; Pershing's Mission in Mexico, 1966, 2nd ed., 1972; Three Dimensional Poe, 1973. Mbrships: Shakespeare Assn. of Am.; MLA of Am. Address: 2109 Arizona Ave., El Paso, TX 79930, USA.

BRADE-BIRKS, (Rev. Canon) Stanley Graham, b. 2 Nov. 1887, Burnage, UK. Clergyman; Hon. Canon of Canterbury Cathedral. Educ: M.Sc., Univ. of Manchester; D.Sc., Univ. of London. Publs: Good Soil; Teach Yourself Archaeology; Ed., Concise Encyclopaedia of General Knowledge. Contbr. to: Ency. Britannica; Chamber's Ency. Mbrships. incl: F.S.A.; F.Z.S.; Hon. F.L.S. Address: The Vicarage, Godmersham, Canterbury, Kent, CT4 7DS, UK.

BRADFORD, Leland Powers, b. 12 July 1905, Chgo., Ill., USA. Behavioral Scientist; Educator. Educ: A.B., 1930, A.M., 1935, Ph.D., 1939, Univ. of Ill. Publs: History of the National Training Laboratories, 1974; T-Group Theory & Laboratory Method (w. others), 1968; The Laboratory Method of Learning & Changing (w. others), 1974. Contbr. of monographs & articles to profl. jrnls., chapts. to books. Address: Box 548, Pinehurst, NC 28374, USA.

BRADLEY, Gladys Lilian, b. Earlestown, Lancs., UK. Retired Headmistress. Educ: B.A. Hons. (Engl.), Univ. of Manchester. Publs: Punctuation Hints & Exercises, 1934; The Secret of Youth (lectures). Contbr. to: Guide Mag.; etc. Mbrships incl: Girl Guides' Assn.; var. educl. orgs. Address: 6 Belvedere Ct., Mooragh Promenade, Ramsey, Isle of Man, UK.

BRADLEY, (Sir) Kenneth Granville, b. 1904, Dehra Dun, India. Former Member of Colonial Administrative Service; Former Director, Commonwealth Institute. Educ: B.A., Univ. Coll., Oxford. Publs: Africa Notwithstanding; Hawks Alighting; Lusaka; Native Courts & Authorities in Northern Rhodesia; Story of Northern Rhodesia; Diary of a District Officer; Copper Venture; The Overseas Service as a Career; Britain's Purpose in Africa; Ed., The Living Commonwealth; Once a District Officer. Contbr. to var. C'wlth. newspapers. Mbrships: VP, Royal African Soc.; Royal C'wlth. Soc. Hons: Kt., 1963; C.M.G. Address: 10 Benson Place, Norham Road, Oxford, UK.

BRADLEY, Samuel McKee, pen name BRADLEY, Sam, b. 6 Feb. 1917, Huntingdon, W.Va., USA. Educator. Educ: B.A., Morehead State Univ., Ky.; M.A., Univ. of Wash., Seattle. Publs: Man — In Good Measure, 1966; Alexander and One World, 1967; Three New Soviet Poets:

Evtushenko, Martynov, Vinokurov (w. M. Bogojavlensky), 1968; Manspell/Godspell, 1973; Ed., Approach, 1957-67; Ed., Compass. Contbr. to: Antioch Review; Chelsea Review; Lit. Review; The Nation; N.Y. Times; West Coast Review & many others. Mbrships: African Studies Assn.; Phila. Lit. Fellowship. Hons. incl: Borestone Mt. Poetry Award, 1962, 1967, 1972; Ariz. Quarterly Award, 1972. Address: RD 1, Box 584, Honeybrook, PA 19344, USA.

BRAGG, Melvyn, b. 6 Oct. 1939, Carlisle, Cumberland, UK. Writer. Educ: M.A., Wadham Coll., Oxford. Publs: For Want of a Nail, 1965; Without a City Wall, 1968; The Hired Man, 1970; Josh Lawton, 1973; The Silken Net, 1974. Contbr. to: New Review; Listener. Mbrships: PEN; F.R.S.L.; Garrick Club. Hons: John Llewellyn Rhys Award, 1968; Northern Arts Assn. Prose Award, 1970; PEN Fiction Award, 1970. Address: 9 Gayton Road, London NW3 1TX, UK.

BRAHAM, Randolph L., b. 20 Dec. 1922, Bucharest, Romania. Professor of Political Science. Educ: M.S., CCNY, 1949; Ph.D., New Schl. for Soc. Rsch., NYC, 1952. Publs. incl: The Destruction of Hungarian Jewry. A Documentary Account, 2 vols., 1963; Education in the Romanian People's Republic, 1964; Soviet Politics & Government. A Reader, 1965; Hungarian-Jewish Studies, 3 vols., 1966-73; Education in the Hungarian People's Republic, 1970; Education in Romania. A Decade of Change, 1972. Contbr. to sev. pol. jrnls. Address: Dept. of Pol. Sci., City Coll., City Univ. of N.Y., N.Y., NY 10031, USA.

BRAHMS, Caryl, b. Surrey, UK. Critic; Novelist; Scriptwriter. Educ: Royal Acad. of Music. Publs. incl: The Moon on my Left, 1930; Footnotes to the Ballet, 1936; Casino for Sale, 1938; The Elephant is White, 1939; Envoybon Excursion, 1940; Don't Mr Disraeli, 1940; No Bed for Bacon, 1941; Titania has a Mother, 1944; Six Curtains for Stroganova, 1945; Rappel 1910, 1964; Benbow was his name, 1966; (film script) Girl/stroke/Boy, 1971; (play) Paying the Piper (adapt. from Feydeau), 1972. Hons: Ivor Novello Award, (shared), 1966; Evening Standard Book of the Year Award, 1940. Address: 3 Cambridge Gate, Regent's Park, London NW1, UK.

BRAINE, John Gerard, b. 1922, Bradford, UK. Author. Educ: Leeds Schl. of Librarianship. Publs: Room at the Top, 1957; The Vodi, 1959; Life at the Top, 1962; The Jealous God, 1964; The Crying Game, 1968; Stay with me Till Morning, 1970. Contbr. to: Books & Bookmen; Atlantic Monthly; Daily Express; Encounter; New Statesman; Spectator; Sunday Times; Twentieth Century. Mbrships: PEN; Authors' Club. Address: The Holt, Pyrford Heath, Woking, Surrey, UK.

BRAITHWAITE, Althea, pen name ALTHEA, b. 20 June 1940, Middx., UK. Publisher; Author; Illustrator. Educ: Felixstowe Coll. Publs: Althea's First Country Book; Althea's Second Country Book; (Children's paperbacks): National Trust Children's Series; Althea Series. Mbr., Soc. of Authors. Address: Beechcroft, Fen End, Over, Cambs., UK.

BRAMBLEBY, Ailsa, pen name CRAIG, Jennifer, b. 1915, Campbeltown, Argyl., UK. Teacher. Educ: Clapham & Streatham Hill Trng. Coll. Publs: The Brownie Pack, 1956; Dozens of Games for Brownies, 1960; Ten Tales for Brownies, 1960; The Brownie Book, 1961; More Tales for Brownies, 1963; Three for Trouble, 1963; Three for Pack Holiday, 1964; The Commonwealth Pack Story Book, 1965; Brownie Guide Handbook, 1968; Handbook for Guiders, 1968; Games with a Point, 1974. Contbr. to: Guider; Brownie; P.N.E.U. Jrnl.; Froebel Jrnl.; Brownie Annual. Mbrships: Soc. of Authors; Assn. of Asst. Mistresses; Guide Club; Girl Guides Assn. Address: Flat 2, 35 Bassett Cres. East, Southampton, Hants., UK.

BRAMHAM, Kenneth, b. 23 Nov. 1924, Bradford, UK. Writer. Publs: Handyman Afloat, 1970; Computer & Electronics Equipment Instruction Manuals, 1963-74; French-Engl. transls. Contbr. to: Autocar; Boating; Electronics World; Radio Electronics; Prac. Boat Owner; Yachting. Mbrships: IEEE; Soc. of Authors. Address: 11 rue Léon Bloy, 92260 Fontenay-aux-Roses, France.

BRAND, Millen, b. 19 Jan. 1906, Jersey City, N.J., USA. Writer. Educ: B.A., B.Lit., Columbia Univ., 1929. Publs: The Outward Room, 1937; The Heroes, 1939; Albert Sears, 1947; Some Love, Some Hunger, 1955; Dry Summer in Provence (poetry), 1966; Savage Sleep, 1968; Fields of Peace (non fiction), 1970; Local Lives (poetry), 1975. Contbr. to: Poetry Mag.; New Yorker; Am. Poetry Review; New Am. Review; The Nation; Harper's Bazaar; etc. Mbrships: Authors League; PEN; Soc. of Am. Histns. Address: 242 E. 77th St., N.Y., NY 10021, USA.

BRANDEN, Nathaniel, b. 9 Apr. 1930, Brampton, Ont., Can. Author; Psychologist. Educ: B.A., 1954, M.A., 1956, N.Y. Univ., USA; Ph.D., Calif. Grad. Inst., LA, 1972. Publs: Who Is Ayn Rand, 1962; The Psychology of Self-Esteem, 1969; Breaking Free, 1970; The Disowned Self, 1971. Mbrships. incl: Am. Psychol. Assn.; Am. Grp. Psychotherapy Assn.; AAAS. Address: 9255 Sunset Blvd., L.A., CA 90069, USA.

BRANDENBERG, Aliki, pen name ALIKI, b. Wildwood Crest, N.J., USA. Writer & Illustrator (children's books). Educ: Grad., Phila. Mus. Coll. of Art. Publs: A Weed Is a Flower: The Life of George Washington Carver, 1965; Three Gold Pieces, 1967; Keep Your Mouth Closed, Dear, 1966; Hush Little Baby, 1968; Diogenes, 1969; The Eggs, 1969; My Visit to the Dinosaurs, 1969; June 7, 1972; Fossils Tell of Long Ago, 1972; Go Tell Aunt Rhody, 1974. Recip., Jr. Book Award, Boys' Club of Am., 1968.

BRANDER, Michael William, b. 8 May 1924, Edinburgh, UK. Author. Publs. incl: The Roughshooter's Dog, 1957, revised ed. 1972; A Dictionary of Sporting Terms, 1968; À History of the 10th Royal Hussars, 1969; A Complete Guide to Horsemanship, 1971; Hunting & Shooting, 1971; The Highlanders & their Regiments, 1971; An International Encyclopaedia of Shooting (ed.), 1972; The Georgian Gentleman, 1973; The Life & Sport of the Inn, 1973; Scottish Crafts & Craftsmen, 1974; The Original Scotch, 1974; forthcoming: Scottish & Border Battles & Ballads; A Guide to Scotch Whisky; The Victorian Gentleman; The Country Divine. Address: c/o Agent, Peter Janson-Smith Ltd., 31 Newington Green, London N16 9PU, UK.

BRANDES, Rhoda, pen name RAMSAY, Diana, b. NYC, USA. Writer. Educ: B.A., Barnard Coll., N.Y. Publs: A Little Murder Music, 1972; Deadly Discretion, 1973; No Cause to Kill, 1974; Descent into the Dark (publd. as The Dark Descends, USA), 1975. Address: 37 Nevern Square, London SW5, UK.

BRANDI, Cesare, b. 8 Apr. 1906. Author; Art Critic. Educ: Univs. of Siena, Pisa & Florence. Publs. incl: Mostra della pittura riminese del'300, 1935; Giotto, 1938; Carmine o della pittura con due saggi su Duccio e Picasso, 1947; Morandi, 1942; Giovanni di Paolo, 1947; Quattrocentisti senesi, 1949; La fine dell'avanguardia, 1950; La fine dell'avanguardia e l'arte di oggi, 1952; Duccio, 1951; Celso o della poesia, 1957. Recip., Commendatore dell'Ordine al Merito della Repubblica, 1954. Address: Piazza S. Francesco di Paola 7, Rome, Italy.

BRANDON, Robert Benjamin, b. 1903, Strasbourg, France. Advertising Agent; Exhibition Promoter; Journalist; Author. Educ: London & Paris. Publs: As Hitler Sowed, 1943; Four Years of War, 1944; The Truth About Advertising, 1948; Costing for Advertising, 1955. Contbr. to: Advertising; Printing & Business Mags. in Britain, France & USA. Address: 16 Oslo Ct., Prince Albert Rd., London NW8, UK.

BRÄNDSTRÖM, Maud (Sara Gabriella), b. 2 Apr. 1928, Gothenburg, Sweden. Editor; Author. Educ: M.A., Univ. of Stockholm, 1968. Publs: Man vänjer sig (short stories), 1963; Sommarresan (children's book), 1965; Andra kinden (short stories), 1966; Vintern kommer — vintern går (children's book), 1967; Den riktiga julen (children's book), 1969. Mbrships: Swedish Union of Authors; Publishing-house of Authors; Authors' Centre. Hons: Litteraturfrämjandet, 1967; Pub. Schlrship. of Artists, 1969-70. Address: Brantingsgatan 36, 115 35 Stockholm, Sweden.

BRANDSTRUP, Ole John Christian, b. 4 Dec. 1917, Copenhagen, Denmark. Writer; Stage Director. Educ: Mag. art. Litt., Copenhagen Univ., 1945. Publs: Frokost I Det Grønne (essays), 1972; Laer At Behage (essays), 1973. Contbr. to: Berlingske Papers, 1946-71. Mbrships: Assn. of Danish Jrnlsts.; Assn. of Danish Dramatists; Assn. of Danish Stage Dirs. Recip., Frederik Schybergs Legat, 1967. Address: Elmevaenget 35, 2880 Bagsvaerd, Denmark.

BRANDYS, Kazimierz, b. 27 Oct. 1916, Lodz, Poland. Writer. Educ: LL.D., Univ. of Warsaw. Publs: The Invincible City, 1946; The Wooden Horse, 1946; Between The Two Wars, 1950; The Citizens, 1954; The Red Cap, 1956; Defence of Granada, 1956; The Mother of Kings, 1957; Letters to Mrs. Z., 1958-61; Romanticism, 1960; The Way to Be, 1964; Joker, 1966; The Market Place, 1968; A Little Book, 1970; Postal Variations, 1972; The Concept,

1974. Contbr. to: Les Temps Modernes, Paris; Tworczosc, Warsaw. Mbrships: PEN; Polish Writers' Union. Hons: Warsaw Lit. Prize, 1948; State Lit. Prize, 1955; Elba Prize, Italy, 1964. Address: Nowomiejzka 5, 00-271 Warsaw, Poland.

BRANFIELD, John Charles, b. 1931, Burrow Bridge, Somerset, UK. English Teacher. Educ: M.A., M.Ed.; Queen's Coll., Cambridge; Exeter Univ. Publs: A Flag in the Map, 1960; Look the Other Way, 1963; In the Country, 1966; Nancekuke, 1972; Sugar Mouse, 1973 (in USA as The Poison Factory, 1972; Why Me? , 1973). Agent: A. P. Watt & Son. Address: Mingoose Villa, Mingoose, Mount Hawke, Truro, Cornwall, UK.

BRANLEY, Franklyn M., b. 1915, USA. Astronomer & Chairman Emeritus, American Museum. Educ: N.Y. Univ.; Columbia Univ.; B.S.; M.A.; Ed.D. Publs: The Nine Planets; The Moon; Lodestar; Experiments with Microscope; Solar Energy; End of the World. Contbr. to: The Grade Tchr.; N.Y. Times; Sci. Tchr; Ed., Let's Read & Find out. Mbrships: Authors' Guild; Am. Astronomical Soc.; Royal Astronomical Soc. Address: American Museum, 81st St. & C.P.W., N.Y., NY 10024, USA.

BRANNON, William T, pen names TIBBETTS, William; HAMILTON, Jack; HAMILTON, William S.; PETERS, S. T.; McGLINN, Dwight; OBERHOLTZER, Peter; LEBERT, Randy; SMITH, Weldon S.; BRONSTON, William; BOWDOIN, William; SWANSTROM, Nils, b. 3 Mar. 1906, Meridian, Miss., USA. Author. Educ: Litt.D., Colo. State Christian Coll. Publs: Yellow Kid Weil, 1948; The Lady Killers, 1951; Life in Twelve Minutes, 1952; Con Man, 1957; The Crooked Cops, 1962; The Con Game & Yellow Kid Weil, 1974. Contbr. to num. anthols. & num. mags. Mbrships. incl: Fndr. Mbr., Mystery Writers of Am., 1st Reg. V.P., Midwest Chapt., 1946, Reg. V.P., Midwest Chapt., 1951, Bd. of Dirs., 1946-48, 1950-52, 1954-56, 1958-60 & 1962-64, Reg. Treas., 1952-63; Overseas Press Club of Am.; Fndg. mbr., Nat. Histl. Soc. Recip., Special Edgar Allan Poe Awards, Mystery Writers of Am., 1950 & 1951. Address: P.O. Box 10901, St. Petersburg, FL 33733, USA.

BRASCH, (Rabbi) Rudolph, b. 1912, Berlin, Germany. Rabbi; Author. Educ: Ph.D.; D.D.; Univs. of Berlin & Würzburg. Publs: The Star of David, 1955; The Eternal Flame, 1958; How Did It Begin? , 1965, var. eds., inclng. Japanese & German transls.; Mexico: a Country of Contrasts, 1967; The Unknown Sanctuary, 1969; The Judaic Heritage, 1969; How Did Sports Begin? , 1970; How Did Sex Begin? , 1973, 1974. Mbrships: Govng. Body, World Union Prog., Judaism; Life VP, Aust. & NZ Union for Prog. Judaism. Hons: O.B.E.; J.P. Address: 14 Derby St., Vaucluse, Australia 2030.

BRASHER, Christopher William, b. 21 Aug. 1928, Georgetown, Guyana. Journalist & Television Reporter. Educ: B.A., St. John's Coll., Cambridge. Publs: The Red Snows (w. Sir John Hunt), 1960; Sportsmen of our Time, 1962; Tokyo 1964 – a diary of the 18th Olympiad; Mexico 1968; Munich 72. Contbr. to: The Observer; Sports Illustrated. Hons: Sportswriter of the Year, 1968. Address: The Navigator's House, River Lane, Richmond TW10 7AG, Surrey, UK.

BRASHER, Norman Henry, b. 1922, Cheltenham, Glos., UK. Schoolmaster; Author. Educ: M.A., Jesus Coll., Cambridge. Publs: Studies in British Government, 1965, 2nd ed., 1971; Britain in the 20th Century 1900-64 (w. E. E. Reynolds), 1966; Arguments in History – Britain in the 19th Century, 1968;The Young Historian, 1970. Address: 79 Goddington Lane, Orpington, Kent BR6 9DT, UK.

BRASIER, Virginia, b. 31 July 1910, Toronto, Ont., Can. Poet. Publs: The Reflective Rib, 1955; Survival of the Unicorn, 1961; The Sandwatcher, 1974. Contbr. to: Ladies Home Jrnl.; Saturday Evening Post; Saturday Review of Lit.; Christian Sci. Monitor; Westways, LA; Chgo. Tribune; New Yorker. Mbrships: Acad. of Am. Poets; Calif. Writers' Guild. Hons: Poetry Prize, Redland's Univ., 1927; Annual Poetry Award, Yankee Mag., 1970; 1st Prize, Poetry, 2nd Prize, Light Verse, INA Coolbrith Golden Circle, 1971. Address: 7133 Perris Hill Rd., San Bernardino, CA 92404, USA.

BRATHWAITE, Errol Freeman, b. 1924, Hawkes Bay, NZ. Author; Former Soldier. Publs: Fear in the Night, 1959; An Affair of Men, 1961; Long Way Home, 1963; The Flying Fish, 1963; The Needle's Eye, 1965; The Evil Day, 1967; Companion Guide to the North Island of New

Zealand, 1970. Address: 12 Fulton Ave., Merivale, Christchurch, NZ.

BRATT, Bengt Arne, b. 2 May 1937, Boda, Sweden. Playwright. Publs: Plays & serials for TV & theatre. Mbrships: Swedish Union of Authors; Swedish Union of Playwrights. Hons: Nordiska TV-Teaterpriset, 1970; Prix Italia, 1973. Address: Södra Vägen 24, 412 54 Goteborg, Sweden.

BRAULT, Gerard Joseph, b. 7 Nov. 1929, Chicopee Falls, Mass., USA. Professor of French. Educ: A.B., Assumption Coll., Worcester, Mass., 1950; A.M., Laval Univ., Quebec City, Can., 1952; Ph.D., Univ. of Pennsylvania, Philadelphia, 1958. Publs: Cours de langue française destiné aux jeunes Franco-Américains, 1965; Celestine. A Critical Edition of the First French Translation (1527) of the Spanish Classic La Celestina, 1963; Early Blazon, 1972; Eight Thirteenth-Century Rolls of Arms in French & Anglo-Norman Blazon, 1973. Contbr. to: Mod. Lang. Jrnl.; PMLA; etc. Mbrships: VP, Société Rencesvals pour l'étude des épopées romanes; Fellow, Soc. of Antiquaries, London; & others. Hons: var. scholastic grants & Fellowships. Address: 705 Westerly Parkway, State Coll., PA 16801, USA.

BRAUN, Richard Emil, b. 22 Nov. 1934, Detroit, Mich., USA. Associate Professor of Classics. Educ: A.B., 1956, A.M., 1957, Univ. of Mich.; Ph.D., Univ. of Tex., 1969. Publs: Children Passing (poems), 1962; Bad Land (poems), 1971; The Foreclosure (poems), 1972; Sophocles' Antigone (transl. w. introduction & notes), 1973. Contbr. to: Accent; Arion; Mod. Poetry Studies; N.Y. Times; Saturday Review; Norton Anthol. of Mod. Poetry. Hons. incl: Robert Frost Fellowship, Bread Loaf, 1968; Can. Coun. Arts Bursary, 1969. Address: c/o Dept. of Classics, Univ. of Alta., Edmonton, Alta. T6G 2E6, Can.

BRAUNHOLTZ, Mary Antonie Beatrice (née Herford), b. 27 Sept. 1889, Aberystwyth, Wales, UK. Lecturer in Classics & Classical Archaeology. Educ: M.A., Manchester Univ.; Archaeol. studies, Somerville Coll., Oxford Univ., & Brit. Schl. Archaeol., Athens, Greece. Publs: A Handbook of Greek Vase-Painting, 1919. Contbr. to: Jrnl. Hellenic Studies; Classical Review; other profl. jrnls. Address: 78 Old Rd., Headington, Oxford, UK.

BRAUNTHAL, Gerard, b. 27 Dec. 1923, Gera, Germany. Professor of Political Science. Educ: B.A., Queens Coll., N.Y., 1947; M.A., Univ. of Mich., 1948; Ph.D., Columbia Univ., 1953. Publs: The Federation of German Industry in Politics, 1965; The West German Legislative Process: A Case Study of Two Transportation Bills, 1972. Contbr. to: Ency. Americana; Pol. Sci. Qrly.; The Western Pol. Qrly.; Europe-Archiv; The Mass. Review; The Jrnl. of Politics; etc. Mbr., Am. Pol. Sci. Assn. Address: Pol. Sci. Dept., Thompson Tower, Univ. of Mass., Amherst, MA 01002, USA.

BRAUTIGAN, Richard, b. 30 Jan. 1933, Tacoma, Wash., USA. Writer. Publs: (novels) In Watermelon Sugar, 1964; A Confederate General from Big Sur, 1965; Trout Fishing in America, 1966; The Abortion: An Historical Romance, 1971; Revenge of the Lawn (short stories), 1971; (verse) The Return of the Rivers, 1957; The Galilee Hitch-Hiker, 1958; The Octopus Frontier, 1960; The Pill Versus the Springhill Mine Disaster (Poems 1957-1968), 1968; Rommel Drives on Deep into Egypt, 1970. Recip., Grant, Nat. Endowment for the Arts, 1968. Address: c/o Simon & Schuster Inc., 630 Fifth Ave., N.Y., NY 10020, USA.

BRAV, Stanley R., pen name BARKTON, S. Rush, b. 22 Nov. 1908, Phila., Pa., USA. Rabbi. Educ: B.A., M.A., Univ. of Cinn.; Ph.D., Webster Univ.; B.H., Rabbi, D.D., Hebrew Union Coll. Publs: Jewish Family Solidarity, 1940; Marriage & the Jewish Tradition, 1951; Since Eve: A Sex-Ethic for Today, 1959; Telling Tales Out of School, 1965; Dawn of Reckoning: Self-Portrait of a Liberal Rabbi, 1971. Contbr. to num. jrnls., newspapers, books. Address: 5575 Gulf Blvd., St. Petersburg Beach, FL 33706, USA.

BRAYBROOKE, Neville Patrick Bellairs, b. 1928, London, UK. Writer & Editor. Publs: This is London, 1953; London Green: The Story of Kensington Gardens, Hyde Park, Green Park & St. James' Park, 1959; London in Colour, 1961; The Idler, 1961; The Delicate Investigation (play), 1969; Ed., T. S. Eliot: a Symposium for his 70th Birthday, 1958, 3rd ed., 1970; A Partridge in a Pear Tree, a Christmas Anthology, 1960; Pilgrim of the Future, Teilhard de Chardin Symposium, 1965, 2nd ed., 1966; Letters of J. R. Ackerley, 1975. Contbr. to num. jrnls. inclng: Guardian; Sunday Telegraph; The Times; Times Lit. Supplement; Saturday Review. Address: 10 Gardnor Rd., London NW3, UK.

BRAZIER, G. W., b. 1921, Wolverhampton, UK. Principal Lecturer. Educ: Loughborough Coll. Publs: Woodwork, 1957; Educational Filmstrips, 1957-68. Contbr. to: Practical Educ. Mbrships: Inst. of Craft Educ.; Assn. of Tchrs. in Depts. & Colls. of Educ. Address: 4 Sunningdale Rd., Sedgley, UK.

BRECHIN, Carlyse Bliss, pen name BLISS, Carlyse, b. Pensacola, Fla., USA. Poet. Educ: Univ. of Grenoble, France. Publs: Campus Caviar, 1941. Contbr. to Poet Lore, & The Church School. Mbrships: Councillor, Past Pres., Beaumont Chapt., Poetry Soc. of Tex.; Deleg., Poetry Soc. of Tex. to Nat. Conven., Nat. Fedn. of State Poetry Socs., 1971, 1972, 1973. Hons: Francis E. Abernathy Award, 1970, Lyndon Baines Johnson Mem. Award, 1973, Poetry Soc. of Tex.; Evans Spencer Wall Mem. Award, 1969, Golden Anniversary Award, 1971, Nat. Fedn. of State Poetry Socs.; Keeling-Huff Award, Poetry Soc. of Tex., 1973; K. Spalding Mem. Award, Nat. Fedn. of State Poetry Socs., 1974. Address: P.O. Box 7163, Beaumont, TX 77706, USA.

BREDSDORFF, Elias Lunn, b. 15 Jan. 1912, Roskilde, Denmark. University Reader in Scandinavian Studies; Author. Educ: Cand.mag., M.A., D.Phil., Univ. of Copenhagen. Publs. incl: D. H. Lawrence, 1937; John Steinbeck, 1943; H. C. Andersen & England, 1954; Hans Christian Andersen & Charles Dickens, 1956; Danish Grammar & Reader, 1956; Kinas vej, 1957; Bag Ibsens maske, 1962; Henrik Pontoppiean og Georg Brandes I-II, 1964; Kommer det os ved? , 1971; Den store Nordiske Krig om Seksualmoralen, 1973; Hans Christian Andersen, 1975. Contbr. to: Chamber's Ency.; Cassell's Ency. of Lit.; Ency. Britannica; Penguin Companions to Lit.; Scandinavica (Ed.). Address: 35 Millington Rd., Cambridge, UK.

BREDSDORFF, Jan, b. 19 Jan. 1942, Vordingborg, Denmark. Novelist; Playwright. Publs: Et kys på Væggen, 1964; Ash, 1966; Støv, 1967; Kinabilledbog, 1969; Mao Tse-tungs Tænkning, 1969; Udsigt fra de Hvide Skyers Bjerg, 1969; Kina, 1972. Contbr. to var. Danish & Int. publs. Mbrships: Union Danish Authors; Union Danish Playwrights. Address: Bodenhoffs Plads 2, 1430 Copenhagen K, Denmark.

BREEDEN, Stanley, b. 2 May 1938, Soest, Netherlands. Naturalist; Author; Photographer. Publs (w. Kay Breedon): Life of the Kangaroo, 1966; Tropical Queensland, 1970; Australia's Southeast, 1972; Wildlife of Eastern Australia, 1973; also 3 minor works. Contbr. to: Nat. Geographic Mag.; Readers Digest; Int. Wildlife; Audubon. Mbr., Aust. Soc. of Authors. Co-recip., 2nd Prize, Capt. Cook Bicentenary Lit. Competition, 1970.

BREEM, Wallace Wilfred Swinburne, b. 1926, Surbiton, Surrey, UK. Librarian. Publs: Eagle in the Snow, 1970; Cambridge Bibliography of English Literature, vol. 1 & 2 (co-author), 1971-74; The Legate's Daughter, 1974. Contbr. to: The Law Lib. Jrnl., USA; Law Libn.; Int. Jrnl. of Law Libs.; Times Lit. Supplement. Mbrships: Hon. Sec., Brit. & Irish Assn. of Law Libns.; Brit. Film Inst.; Brit. Museum Soc.; Soc. of Authors. Agent: Lloyd-George & Coward. Address: c/o Inner Temple Library; Inner Temple, London EC4, UK.

BREESE, Gerald (William), b. 4 June 1912, Horseheads, N.Y., USA. Professor of Sociology; Licensed Professional Planner; Author. Publs: The Daytime Population of the Central Business District of Chicago, 1949; Regional Analysis: Trenton-Camden Areas, 1954; Industrial Site Selection, 1954; Impact of Large Installations on Nearby Areas, 1966; Urbanization in Newly Developing Countries, 1966. Ed. & Contbr: The City in Newly Developing Countries, 1969; Urban Southeast Asia, 1973. Contbr. to: Econ. Dev. & Cultural Change; Am. Sociol. Review, etc. Address: Dept. of Sociology, Princeton University, NJ 08540, USA.

BREGSTEIN, Philo, b. 1 June 1932, Amsterdam, Netherlands. Film Director; Writer. Educ: Law Degree, Univ. Amsterdam; Degree Film Directing, Rome. Publs: (novels) Om de tijd te doden (To Kill Time), 1967; Persoons-bewijs (Identity Card), 1973; (films) The Compromise (90 min. feature), 1968; The Past that Lives,

1970; Otto Klemperer's Journey Through His Times, 1974. Contbr. to: Tirade; Hollands Maanblad; Revisor; Skoop. Mbr., PEN. Hons: Golden Dove Award, best 1st film, 1968 Venice (for The Compromise) & Volkshochschuljury Prize (for The Past That Lives), Mannheim Filmweek 1970. Address: Brouwersgracht 220, Amsterdam, Netherlands.

BREHM, Edythe Jackson (Mrs. Harold E.), b. 4 Sept. 1904, Jefferson, Iowa, USA. High School Teacher, Retired. Educ: B.A., Univ. of Tex.; Grad. study in Child Psychol. Publs: Heartwrought Filigree, 1943; Heritage of Song, 1945. Contbr. to poetry jrnls. & newspapers. Hons: Book Prize, Wildfire Mag., 1946; 3rd Place, Ed.'s Prize, Prairie Wings, 1947. Address: 400 Quince Circle, McAllen, TX 78501, USA.

BREIGHNER, Harry Daniel, b. 27 Feb. 1909, Bronaugh, Mo., USA. Writer. Educ: USN H.C.T.S., Hotel-Motel Mgr. Schl., Radio. Publs: Memories, 1967; Lincoln Country, 1968; Mini-History of Clinton, Illinois, 1969; Along Lincoln's Trail, 1972; Great Moments in Vacationland U.S.A., 1974; America Is Christmas, 1974. Contbr. to jrnls. & num. poetry anthols. Hons: Outstanding Achievement Award, Hon. Award, Laurel Int. Poetry Symposium, 1973. Address: 2627 E. La Palma 138, Anaheim, CA 92806, USA.

BREITBACH, Joseph, pen name SALECK, Jean Charlot, b. 20 Sept. 1903, Koblenz/Rhine, Germany (French citizen). Writer. Publs: (all in French & German) Rot gegen Rot (stories), 1928; Die Wandlung der Susanne Dasseldorf (novel), 1932; Bericht über Bruno (novel), 1962, also transl'd into 5 other langs.; Die Jubilarin (comedy), 1968; Genosse Veygond (comedy), 1970; Collected Plays, 1972; Die Rabenschlacht (stories), 1973; plays performed num. times. Mbrships: Deutsche Akad. für Sprache und Dichtung, Darmstadt (French Corres.); Bavarian Acad. of Fine Arts (French Corres.). Hons. incl: Prix Combat, Paris, 1965; Grosses Bundesverdienstkreuz, W. Germany, 1969. Address: 1 Place du Pantheon, F-75005 Paris, France.

BRELAND, Osmond Philip, b. 17 Sept. 1910, Decatur, Miss., USA. University Professor. Educ: B.S., Miss. State Univ., 1931; Ph.D., Ind. Univ., 1936. Publs: Manual Comparative Anatomy, 1943, revised ed., 1953; Animal Facts & Fallacies, 1948; Animal Friends & Foes, 1957; Laboratory Studies in Biology, 1962, revised ed., 1972; Animal Life & Lore, 1963, revised ed., 1972; Biology in the Laboratory, 1965. Contbr. to: Boy's Life; Natural Hist.; Entomol. News; & num. others. Address: Dept. of Zoology, University of Texas, Austin, TX 78712, USA.

BRELVI, Ebadat, b. 14 Aug. 1920, Bareilly, India. Professor of Urdu. Educ: B.A., M.A., Ph.D., Univ. of Lucknow, India. Publs: Tanqidi Zavie, 1947; Urdu Tanqid Ka Irtiqa (Development of Urdu Criticism), 1950; Ghazal Aur Mutzaz-I-Ghazal (Study of Ghazal), 1955; Revayat Ki Ahmiat (The Importance of Tradition), 1955; Jadid Shaeri (Modern Poetry), 1961; Momin, 1962; Ghalib, 1969. Contbr. to: Jrnl. of Rsch., Univ. of the Punjab; Ed., & Chmn., Ed. Bd., Oriental Coll. Mag.; Lahore; Urdu; Adabe Latif 5. Mbrships: Fellow, Royal Asiatic Soc., London, Uk; Bd. for Advancement of Lit., Pakistan. Recip., Sev. acad. prizes. Address: Principal, Univ. Oriental Coll., Lahore, Pakistan.

BRENDON, Piers George Rundle, b. 21 Dec. 1940, Stratton, Cornwall, UK. College Lecturer. Educ: M.A., Ph.D., Magdalene College, Cambridge. Publs: Hurrell Froude & the Oxford Movement, 1974; Hawker of Morwenstow: Portrait of a Victorian Eccentric, 1975; (anthols.) Reading They've Liked, 1967; Reading Matters, 1969; By What Authority, 1972 (all w. William Shaw). Contbr. to: New Statesman; Books & Bookmen. Agent: Curtis Brown Ltd. Address: 19 Chedworth St., Cambridge, UK.

BRENNAN, John N. H., pen name WELCOME, John, b. 1914, Wexford, Ireland. Editor & Author. Educ: Sedbergh & Oxford; B.A., Oxon. Publs: On the Stretch; sev. other thrillers; Ed., many of Fabers Best Story collections; (biography): Fred Archer, 1967; Neck or Nothing: The Story of Bob Sievier, 1970. Contbr. to: Blackwoods; Irish Times; Irish Field; Irish Horseman; etc. Address: Hermitage, Drinagh, Wexford, Repub. of Ireland.

BRENNAN, Niall, b. 3 Feb. 1918, Melbourne, Australia. Writer; Historian; Lecturer. Educ: Christian Brothers;

Melbourne Univ. Publs. incl: The Ballad of a Government Man, 1943; Ode to an Asiatic, 1946; Thirteen Verses, 1948; The Making of a Moron, 1953; A Hoax Called Jones, 1962; Dr. Mannix, 1964; John Wren Gambler, 1971; Men & War, 1972; A History of Nunawading, 1972; Chronicles of Dandenong, 1973; The Politics of Catholics, 1973; Village School, 1974. Contbr. to: BBC; Aust. Broadcasting Commn.; Integrity; Walkabout; Radio Aust.; The Age; etc. Fellow, Royal Geogl. Soc. Address: Kingajanik, Gladysdale, Vic., Australia 3797.

BRENT, Jim, b. 1898, Belfast, N. Ireland, UK. Author. Publs: At the Balance. Contbr. to: The Times. Address: 100 Gillsman's Hill, St. Leonard's-on-Sea, Sussex TN38 0SL, UK.

BRERETON, Geoffrey, b. 1906, Liverpool, UK. Writer. Educ: B.A., Oxford Univ.; D.-es-L., Paris Univ., France. Publs: A Short History of French Literature; An Introduction to the French Poets; French Tragic Drama in the 16th & 17th Centuries; Jean Racine, a Critical Biography; Principles of Tragedy; Ed., The Penguin Book of French Verse, Part 2, Transls. of Adamov, Claudel, Froissart, Perrault, Romains. Contbr. to: BBC; Cassell's Ency. of World Lit.; Times Educl. Supplement; Times Lit. Supplement; New Statesman; Guardian; Mod. Langs.; etc. Mbrships: F.R.S.L. Address: Cork House, Fairlight, Hastings, Sussex, UK.

BRETON-SMITH, Clare, pen names VERNON, Claire; WILDE, Hilary; CALDWELL, Elinor, b. 1 Sept. 1906, London, UK. Novelist. Publs: Over 70 novels, 1950-; Coronary Jane (non-fiction); num. short stories & articles. Mbrships: PEN; London Writers Circle; Women Writers & Jrnlsts. Address: P.O. Box 546, Manzini, Swaziland.

BRETT-JAMES, (Eliot) Antony, b. 4 Apr. 1920, London, UK. Head of War Studies, R.M.A. Sandhurst; Author. Educ: Cert. & Dip., Brit. Inst., Paris, France; M.A., Sidney Sussex Coll., Cambridge. Publs. incl: Report my Signals, 1948; Ball of Fire, 1951; General Graham, Lord Lynedoch, 1959; Wellington at War, 1794-1815, 1961; Imphal (co-author), 1962; The Hundred Days, 1964; 1812, 1966; Europe Against Napoleon, 1970; Life in Wellington's Army, 1972. Contbr. to: Times Lit. Supplement; Hist. Today; Purnell's Hist. of the 1st & 2nd World Wars. Fellow, Royal Histl. Soc. Address: 18 Station Rd., Petersfield, Hants., UK.

BRETT-SMITH, Richard Nigel, b. 1 Jan. 1923, Oxford, UK. Journalist. Educ: M.A., Christ Church, Oxford, 1949. Publs: Berlin '45: The Grey City, 1966, 1967; The Eleventh Hussars, 1969. Contbr. to: Daily Telegraph (For. Corres., 1959-59, 1963-64); Defence Corres., 1959-63); Sunday Telegraph; Spectator; Army Quarterly; Time & Tide; Wash. Star; Interavia, etc. Mbrships: Inst. of Jrnlsts.; Press Club, Salisbury, Rhodesia. Address: c/o Cavalry Club, 127 Piccadilly, London W1, UK.

BREUER, Marcel Lajos, b. 22 May 1902, Pecs, Hungary. Architect. Educ: Master's Degree, Weimar, Germany, 1924. Publs: Sun & Shadow: The Philosophy of an Architect (co-author), 1956; Buildings & Projects 1921-61, 1962; New Buildings & Projects, 1970. Mbrships. incl: Fellow, Am. Inst. of Archts.; Nat. Inst., Arts & Letters (VP, 1968); L'Ordre des Architectes; Fellow, Am. Acad., Arts & Scis. Hons. incl: La Rinascente's Compasso d'Oro Prize, 1957; Gold Medal, Am. Inst. of Archts., 1968; Univ. of Va. Thomas Jefferson Fndn. Medal, 1968. Address: Marcel Breuer & Assocs., 635 Madison Ave., N.Y., NY 10022, USA.

BREWER, Derek Stanley, b. 1923, Cardiff, UK. Lecturer in English, & Fellow of Emmanuel College, Cambridge; Publisher. Educ: M.A., Ph.D., Magdalen Coll., Oxford Univ. Publs: Chaucer, 1953, 3rd enlarged ed. 1973; Proteus, 1958; Chaucer in his Time, 1963, 1973; Ed., Parliament of Foulys, 1960, 1971; Ed., Chaucer & Chaucerians, 1966; Ed., Malory, The Morte d'Arthur, parts 7 & 8, 1968; Ed., Troilus & Criseyde (abridged), 1969; Ed., Chaucer (Writers & their Background series), 1974. Address: Emmanuel College, Cambridge, UK.

BREWER, Wilmon, b. 1 Apr. 1895, Hingham, Mass., USA. Author. Educ: A.B., 1917, A.M., 1920, Ph.D., 1925, Harvard Univ.; D.Sc., O Curry Coll., 1959. Publs. incl: Shakespeare's Influence on Sir Walter Scott, 1925; Ovid's Metamorphoses in European Culture, 3 vols., 1933-57; About Poetry & Other Matters, 1943; Adventures in Verse, 1945, 2nd ed., 1963; Life of Maurice Parker, 1954;

Adventures Further, 1958; Still More Adventures, 1966. Contbr. to US, for. jrnls., anthols. Mbrships: Past Pres., Am. Poetry Assn.; Past Pres., Boston Authors Club; London Authors Club; New England Poetry Club; Boston Manuscript Club. Hons: Rhyme & Rhythm Award, 1947; Double recording of poems for Woodbury Poetry Room, Harvard, 1964. Address: Great Hill, Hingham, MA 02043, USA.

BREWSTER, Dorothy, b. 1883, St. Louis, Mo., USA. Former Associate Professor of English. Educ: A.B., A.M., Ph.D., Columbia Univ. Publs: Aaron Hill; Modern Fiction (co-author); Modern World Fiction; Modern Short Stories; Ed., Contemporary Short Stories; East-West Passage; Virginia Woolf's London; Virginia Woolf; William Brewster of the Mayflower. Mbrships: Engl.-Speaking Union; MLA of Am. Address: 25 Mulberry Street, Rhinebeck, NY 12572, USA.

BRICE, Marshall Moore, b. 30 Aug. 1898, White Oak, S.C., USA. Professor of English, Retired. Educ: B.S., Clemson Coll.; M.A., Univ. of Wis.; Ed.D., Univ. of Va. Publs: Conquest of a Valley, 1965; The Stonewall Brigade Band, 1967; Daughter of the Stars, 1973. Contbr. to profl. jrnls. Address: P.O. Box 276, Staunton, VA 24401, USA.

BRICKHILL, Paul Chester Jerome, b. 20 Dec. 1916, Melbourne, Australia. Author. Educ: Sydney Univ. Publs: Escape to Danger (w. Conrad Norton), 1946; The Great Escape, 1951; The Dam Busters, 1951; Escape—or Die, 1952; Reach for the Sky, 1954; The Deadline, 1962. Recip., lit. awards. Agent: John Farquharson Ltd. Address: c/o Agent, 15 Red Lion Square, London WC1, UK.

BRICKNER, Richard P., b. 14 May 1933, NYC, USA. Writer. Educ: B.A., Columbia Univ., 1957 Publs: The Broken Year, 1962; Bringing Down the House, 1972. Contbr. to: N.Y. Times Book Review; New Leader; Life; Time; Monocle; Fiction; Am. Review; Sat. Review; etc. Mbr., PEN. Address: 245 E. 72nd St., N.Y., NY 10021, USA.

BRIDGES, John Gourlay, b. 1901, Glasgow, UK. Director-General of Tourist Association (Retired). Educ: Glasgow & W. of Scotland Commercial Coll. Publs: International Travel Statistics. Contbr. to travel mags. Mbrships: F.R.G.S.; F.R.S.A.; Assoc., Chartered Inst. of Transp.; Inst. of Travel Agents; Int. Assn. of Experts in Tourism, Berne; Overseas League; Transp. Users Consultative Comm. for Scotland; Scottish Tourist Consultative Coun.; Exec. Comm., Scottish Coun. (Dev. & Ind.). Recip., O.B.E. Address: 35A Cluny Drive, Edinburgh EH10 6DT, UK.

BRIERLEY, Marjorie Flowers, b. 1893, London, UK. Retired Psychoanalyst. Educ: B.Sc., M.B., B.S., Univ. of London. Publs: Trends in Psychoanalysis, 1951. Contbr. to: Int. Jrnl. of Psychoanalysis (Hon. Asst. Ed.); Brit. Jrnl. of Med. Psychol. Mbrships: Bd. of Forum, L.A.; Fellow, Brit. Psychol. Soc.; I.P.A.; B.P.S.; Former Coun. & Trng. Comm. mbr., Inst. of Psychoanalysis. Address: Rowling End, Newlands, Keswick, Cumbria, UK.

BRIFFAULT, Herma Hoyt, b. May 1898, Reedville, Ohio, USA. Ghost Writer; Editor; Translator. Educ: Tchrs. Dip., Normal Schl. Publs: (as ghost writer under names Marie Ritz, David Stanley Livingston, Richard Harrington, etc.); Cesar Ritz, Host to the World, 1938; Full & By, 1936; The Face of the Arctic, 1954; Translator of 50 books, inclng. The Illusionist, by Francoise Mallet, 1952; The Joker, by Jean Malaquais, 1954; The Sea Wall, by Marguerite Duras, 1952; The Pure & the Impure, by Colette, 1967. Mbrships: PEN; Lucy Stone League. Address: 137 W. 12th St., N.Y., NY 10011, USA.

BRIGGS, Asa, b. 7 May 1921, Keighley, Yorks., UK. Professor of History; Vice-Chancellor. Educ: History Tripos, Sidney Sussex Coll., Cambridge Univ., 1940, 1941, B.Sc.(Econ.), London Univ., 1941. Publs: Victorian People, 1954; Age of Improvement, 1959; History of Broadcasting in the United Kingdom, 3 vols., 1961, 1965, 1970; Victorian Cities, 1963; William Cobbett, 1967; How They Lived 1700-1815, 1969; Ed., The 19th Century, 1970; Ed., Publishing & Society, 1974. Contbr. to: Times Lit. Supplement; Guardian; New Society; New Statesman; The Economist; etc. Mbrships. incl: Gov., Brit. Film Inst.; Trustee, Int. Broadcast Inst. Recip., num. acad. hons. Address: Ashcombe House, Lewes, Sussex BN7 3JR, UK.

BRIGGS, George McSpadden, b. 21 Feb. 1919, Grantsburg, Wis., USA. Nutritionist. Educ: B.S., 1940, M.S., 1941, Ph.D., 1944, Univ. of Wis. Publs: Nutrition & Physical Fitness (w. L. J. Bogert & D. H. Calloway), 9th ed., 1973. Contbr. to: Exec. Ed., Jrnl. of Nutrition Educ., 1968-; Ency. Britannica; var. profl. jrnls. Mbrships. incl: Pres., Am. Inst. of Nutrition, 1967-68, Soc. for Nutrition Educ., 1968-69; Fellow, Am. Pub. Hlth. Assn. Hons. incl: Borden Award, 1958. Address: 9 Morgan Hall, Dept. of Nutritional Scis., Univ. of Calif., Berkeley, CA 94720, USA.

BRIGGS, Gilbert Arthur, b. 29 Dec. 1890, Clayton, Yorks., UK. Loudspeaker Builder; Author. Num. publs. incl: Loudspeakers, 1948, revised ed., 1958; Pianos, Pianists & Sonics, 1951; Stereo Handbook, 1959; Cabinet Handbook, 1962; More About Loudspeakers, 1963; Aerial Handbook, 1964, 1968; Musical Instruments & Audio, 1965; About Your Hearing, 1967. Contbr. of hi-fi articles to US & UK jrnls. Address: Woodville, Easby Dr., Ilkley, Yorks., UK.

BRIGGS, Katharine Mary, b. 1898, Hampstead, London, UK. Author; Folklorist. Educ: M.A., D.Phil., D.Litt., Lady Margaret Hall, Oxford Univ. Publs: The Anatomy of Puck, 1959; Pale Hecate's Team, 1962; The Fairies in Tradition & Literature, 1967; The Personnel of Fairyland, reprinted 1969; Hobberdy Dick, 1969, paperback 1972; A Dictionary of British Folktales in the English Language, 1970; The Last of the Astrologers, 1974; Cotswold Folklore, 1974; also The Witch Figure, Festschrift for 75th Birthday of K. M. Briggs, 1973. Contbr. to: Folklore; Man, Myth & Magic; Jrnl. Am. Folklore Soc.; Can. Med. Assn. Jrnl. Mbrships: Folklore Soc.; Bibliographical Soc. Agent: A. P. Watt & Son. Address: The Barn House, Burford, Oxford, UK.

BRIGGS, Victor William, b. 1935, Oldham, Lancs., UK. Journalist; Author. Publs: A Time & a Place, 1969; The Chairman, 1971; Never Make Love to a Woman with Big Hands, 1971; The Song & Dance Man, 1972; The Apollo Story, 1973; The Village, 1974; Churchill Centenary, 1974; The Sacred Ground (Part I of tril., A Way Ahead), 1975. Contbr. to var. mags. Address: 2 Maycroft Cottages, Stone Gate, Mayfield, Sussex, UK.

BRILEY, John Richard, b. 25 June 1925, Kalamazoo, Mich., USA. Screenwriter. Educ: A.B., M.A., Univ. of Mich.; Ph.D., Shakespeare Inst., Univ. of Birmingham, UK. Publs: The Traitors (UK title: How Sleep the Brave), 1969. Contbr. to: Shakespeare Quarterly; Shakespeare Survey; BBC talks. Mbrships: Writers Guild of Great Brit.; Writers Guild of Am., W.; Authors Guild, Inc., USA. Address: Trevone, 24 Highland Rd., Amersham, Bucks., UK.

BRIM, Orville Gilbert, Jr., b. 7 Apr. 1923, Elmira, N.Y., USA. Sociologist. Educ: B.A., 1947, M.A., 1949, Ph.D., 1951, Yale Univ. Publs: Sociology & the Field of Education, 1958; Education for Child Rearing, 1959; Personality & Decision Processes: Studies in the Social Psychology of Thinking, 1962; Socialization after Childhood: Two Essays, 1966; Intelligence: Perspectives, 1965, 1966; American Beliefs & Attitudes about Intelligence, 1969; The Dying Patient, 1970. Address: 172 Shore Rd., Old Greenwich, CT 06870, USA.

BRINES, Russell Dean, b. 13 Mar. 1911, Denver, Colo., USA. Travelling Journalist; Foreign Correspondent; War Correspondent; Lecturer on international affairs; Founder & First Editor, The Copley News Service, 1955. Educ: Pomona Coll.; Claremont Colls. Grad. Schl.; B.A., Pol. Sci. Publs: Until They Eat Stones, 1944; MacArthur's Japan, 1948; With MacArthur in Japan (w. Ambassador William Sebald), 1965; The Indo-Pakistani Conflict, 1968. Contbr. to: Coronet; Reporter Mags. Mbrships: Nat. Press Club, Wash. D.C.; Tokyo Correspondents' Club. Nominated, Pulitzer Prize, int. reporting, 1945. Address: 4518 North Glebe Rd., Arlington, VA 22207, USA.

BRINGSVAERD, Tor Åge, b. 16 Nov. 1939, Skien, Norway. Writer; Playwright. Educ: Cand. mag., 1968. Publs: Probok, 1968; Bazar, 1970; Bløtkakemannen & Apache-pikene, 1972; Karavane, 1974; Den som har begge beina på jorda står stille, 1974. Contbr. to: Ambit. Mbrships: Norwegian Authors Assn.; Bd., Assn. of Dramatists; PEN; Norwegian Acad. of Comics. Address: Stordamveien, Oslo 6, Norway.

BRINITZER, Carl, b. 30 Jan. 1907, Riga, Russia. Educ: L.D.; Univs. of Geneva, Switz.; Hamburg; Berlin; Munich; Kiel, Germany. Publs. incl: Strafrechtliche Massnahmen zur

Bekämpfung der Prostitution, 1933; Lichtenberg: Die Geschichte eines gescheiten Mannes, 1956; Heinrich Heine: Roman seines Lebens, 1960; Schiller's politisches Vermächtnis, 1962; Deutsche Dichter führen nach Italien, 1965; Liebeskunst ganz prosaisch: Variationen über ein Thema von Ovid, 1966; Hier spricht London, 1969; Bacchus, Gambrinus & Co., 1972; Immer Ärger mit den Frauen, 1973; Die Geschichte des Daniel Chadowiecki, 1973. Contbr. to Radio; var. jrnls. Address: Taurus, The Avenue, Kingston, nr. Lewes, Sussex, BN7 3LL, UK.

BRINK, André Philippus, b. 29 May 1935, Vrede, S. Africa. Lecturer. Educ: M.A. (Engl.), 1958, M.A. (Afrikaans), 1959, Potchefstroom Univ.; D.Litt., Rhodes Univ., 1975; Rsch., Sorbonne Univ., France, 1959-61. Publs: Lobola vir die Lewe, 1962; Die Ambassadeur, 1963; Looking on Darkness, 1974; also ca. 60 transls. into Afrikaans from Engl., French, Spanish & German. Contbr. to: Books Abroad, Okla., USA; sev. S. African lit. mags. Mbr., Maatschappij der Nederlandse Letterkunde, Netherlands, Hons: Reina Geerlings Prize, Netherlands, 1964; C.N.A. Lit. Award, 1964; S. African Acad. Award for Prose Transl., 1970. Address: Rhodes Univ., Grahamstown, S. Africa.

BRINK, Carol Ryrie, b. 1895, Moscow, Idaho, USA. Author. Educ: B.A.; Univ. of Idaho; Univ. of Calif. at Berkeley. Publs. incl: (novels) Buffalo Coat; Stopover; The Headland; Strangers in the Forest; Chateau St. Barnabé; Snow in the River; (non-fiction) The Twin Cities; (biog.) Harps in the Wind; (children's books) Caddie Woodlawn; Baby Island; All Over Town; The Pink Motel; Magical Melons; Family Grandstand; The Bad Times of Baumlein; Louly. Contbr. to: Child Life; Story Parade, etc. Mbr., Nat. League Am. Pen Women. Recip., John Newbery Medal, for Caddie Woodlawn. Address: 2404 Loring St., Pacific Beach, CA T.274-4110, USA.

BRION, Marcel, b. 1895, Marseilles, France. Writer. Educ: Coll. Champittet, Lansanne; Faculte de Droit, Aix en Provence, France. Publs. incl: Rose de Cire; La Chanson de l'Oiseau Etranger; Les Miroirs et les Gouffres; L'Ombre d'un Arbre Mort; L'Enchanteur; La Ville de Sable; La Peinture Romantique; Rembrandt; Michel Ange; L'Art Romantique; L'Art Fantastique; L'Art Abstrait; Dürer; Titien; Goethe; Frederick II de Hohenstaufen; Charles le Temeraire; Les Borgia. Contbr. to: num. periodicals. Mbrships: Acad. Française; PEN. Address: 32 Rue du Bac, Paris VII, France.

BRITEN, Paul William Peter, b. 24 Sept. 1942, Oxford, Uk. Deputy Headmaster. Educ: Borough Rd. Tchrs.' Trng. Coll.; Dip. Ed., London Univ. Publs: Dial for Discovery, 1970; Mathematics through Action, Books 3A & 3B, 1971. Address: 66 Gordon Rd., Shepperton, Middlesex TW17 8JX, UK.

BRITTAIN, Juliet Carrick, b. 14 May 1935, London, UK. Journalist. Editor, Time & Tide. Publs: short stories. Address: 14 Byron Court, Mecklenburgh Square, London WC1, UK.

BRITTON, Dorothea Sprague, b. 30 Oct. 1922, Cleveland, Ohio, USA. Hospital Director of Volunteers. Educ: A.B., M.A., Univ. of Mich. Publs: An Op-Art Easter Bazaar, 1969; Dot Britton's Christmas Book, 1970; Dot Britton's Christmas & Easter Bazaar Book, 1971; The Complete Book of Bazaars, 1973. Contbr. to: Family Circle Mag.; Ladies Home Jrnl.; Vol. Ldr. Mbrships. incl: Am. & N.Y. Assns. of Dirs. of Vol. Servs. Address: 4 Rock Hill Lane, Scarsdale, NY 10583, USA.

BROAD, Harold Peter, b. 1 Oct. 1909, Byfleet, Surrey, UK. Business Executive; Former RAF Officer. Educ: Lancing; RAF Coll., Cranwell. Publs: Death on the Beach, 1959. Contbr. to Flyfishers' Jrnl. Mbrships: Crime Writers' Assn.; Vincent's Club; Flyfishers' Club. Hons: D.F.C., 1940; M.A.(Oxon.), 1942; Legion of Merit, USA, 1945; C.B.E., 1946. Address: 28 Fishpool Street, St. Albans, Herts., UK.

BROADBENT, Donald Eric, b. 1926, Birmingham, UK. Psychologist. Educ: M.A., Sc.D., Univ. of Cambridge. Publs: Perception & Communication, 1958; Behaviour, 1961; Decision & Stress, 1971; In Defence of Empirical Psychology, 1973. Contbr. to: Jrnl. of Expmtl. Psychol.; Brit. Jrnl. of Psychol.; Quarterly Jrnl. of Expmtl. Psychol.; Ergonomics. Mbrships: Fellow, Brit. Psychol. Soc.; F.R.S.; Acoustical Soc. of Am. Hons: C.B.E.; D.Sc., Univ. of Southampton. Address: 1 S. Parks Rd., Oxford OX1 3PS, UK.

BROADHURST, (Brigadier) Ronald Joseph Callender, b. 25 Dec. 1906, Sidcup, Kent, UK. Army & Colonial Police Officer. Educ: King's Coll., Cambridge. Author, The Travels of Ibn Jubayr, 1951. Contbr. to var. jrnls. Mbrships: Brit. Assn. of Orientalists; Mil. Hist. Soc. of Ireland. N. Ireland Legis. Assembly (Deputy Speaker). Address: Belvedere, Ballyaughlis, Co. Down, N. Ireland, UK.

BROADSTON, Elizabeth Jeannette Herrnstein, b. 7 June 1908, Chillicothe, Ohio, USA. Writer, Lecturer on Nutrition. Educ: B.S., Univ. of Cinn.; Univ. of S. Calif., Calif. State Univ., Univ. of Calif. Contbr. to: Let's Live mag., 1953—; Health Food Age mag.; Modern Nutrition mag.; Lectr., churches, schls., clubs; Own radio prog., 34 weeks, KPFK-FM & KPFA-FM, Calif.; Guest apps., TV. Address: 19111 Sprague St., Tarzana, CA 91356, USA.

BROCHER, Tobias Heinz, pen name, BOE, Pieter, b. 21 Apr. 1917, Danzig, Germany. Psychiatrist; Psychoanalyst. Educ: A.B., Paulsen, Berlin, 1935; M.D., Berlin, 1942. Publs: The Ego in Family & Society (in Spanish, Italian & German), 1967; Adult Education & Group Dynamics (in German, Dutch & Swedish), 1968; Rebellion Against Tradition (in German), 1970; Are We Crazy? (in German), 1972. Contbr. to var. mags. & German TV. Mbrships. incl: PEN. Hons. incl: Book of the Month selection, Germany, 1973. Address: Box 829, The Menninger Fndn., Topeka, KS 66601, USA.

BROCKER, Hildegard Luise Hubertine, pen names RIEOL, Bernarda; FERRE, Sybille, b. 10 Dec. 1920, Cologne, Germany. Secretary. Contbr. of lays & poems to Feierabend-Anthologien, Vols. I-VII. Mbr., Soc. of German Speaking Authors, 1967-. Recip., Prize for poems published in Feierabend-Anthologien, 1967. Address: Ruckertstrasse 3, Berlin 4, Germany.

BROCKINGTON, Colin Fraser, b. 8 Jan. 1903, Worcester, UK. Professor Emeritus of Social & Preventive Medicine. Educ: M.A., M.D., Dip. Pub. Hlth., B.Ch., Cambridge Univ.; M.R.C.P., London Univ.; Barrister-at-Law, Middle Temple. Publs: Principles of Nutrition, 1953; The Health of the Community, 1954, 3rd ed. 1965; A Short History of Public Health, 1956, 2nd ed. 1966; World Health, 1958 (paperback), 3rd ed. 1975; Public Health in the Nineteenth Century, 1965. Contbr. to: Lancet; Pub. Hlth.; Brit. Med. Jrnl.; Med. Off.; Med. World; Med. Press; Can. Jrnl. Pub. Hlth. Recip., Hon. M.Sc., Manchester Univ. Address: Ballasalla, Isle of Man, UK.

BROCKINGTON, Raymond Bernard, b. 1937, Sutton Coldfield, UK. University Lecturer; Writer. Educ: B.Com., B.Sc.(Econ.), Univs. of Birmingham & London. Publs: Statistics for Accountants, 1965; Accounting: A First Year Course, 1969. Contbr. to: Birmingham Post; Acct.; Acctcy. Fellow, Inst. Chartered Accts. Address: School of Management, Univ. of Bath, Claverton Down, Bath BA2 7AY, UK.

BROCKLEHURST, Keith George, b. 1923, Stretford, UK. Biologist. Educ: M.A., Univ. of Cambridge. Publs: General School Biology; Introduction to Science, 2 vols.; A New Biology, Biology for Modern Courses. Mbr., Inst. of Biol. Address: 22 Park Rd., Leamington, Warwicks., UK.

BROCKWAY, (Lord) (Archibald) Fenner, b. 1888, Calcutta, India. Politician; Fromer Member of Parliament; Writer. Publs. incl: English Prisons Today (w. S. Hobhouse); Inside the Left; Socialism Over Sixty Years; Bermondsey Story; Hungry England; Bloody Traffic; Death Pays a Dividend; Red Liner; Outside the Right; The Colonial Revolution. Contbr. to: Tribune; New Statesman; Indian News & Features Alliance; Ed., Labour Ldr., 1911-15; Ed., New Ldr., 1932-46. Mbrships. incl: Gen. Sec., Indep. Labour Party, 1924-32; Liberation. Agent: David Higham Assoc. Address: 67 Southway, London N20, UK.

BROCKWAY, James Thomas, b. 21 Oct. 1916, Birmingham, UK. Literary Journalist; Translator. Educ: London Univ.; M.O.(A) degree, Netherlands. Publs: No Summer Song (poems), 1949; Adventure in Holland, 1950, 18th ed. 1973; Waar Zijn De Avro Young Men Gebleven?, 1965; (transls.) Christopher Isherwood's A Single Man, 1966; A Day at the Beach, 1967; Barbara Hepworth, 1968; The Abyss, 1973; Magritte, 1974, etc. Contbr. to num. Dutch & Engl. reviews. Mbrships: Soc. of Authors; Transls. Assn.; Writers Action Grp.; Writers Guild. Hons: Belgian Govt. Transl. Award, 1965; Dutch Martinus Nijhoff Transl. Prize, 1966. Address: Riouwstraat 58, The Hague, Netherlands.

BRODERICK, John, b. 30 July 1927, Athlone, Repub. of Ireland. Novelist; Critic. Publs: The Pilgrimage, 1961; The Fugitives, 1962; Don Juaneen, 1963; The Waking of Willie Ryan, 1965; An Apology for Roses, 1973; Cité Pleine de Rêves (in French), 1974. Contbr. to: Irish Times; Hibernia; Figaro. Mbr., Irish Acad. of Letters, 1968. Address: The Moorings, Athlone, Repub. of Ireland.

BRODEUR, Paul (Adrian Jr.), b. 16 May 1931, Boston, Mass., USA. Magazine Staff Writer; Lecturer. Educ: B.A., Harvard Univ., 1953. Publs: (novels) The Sick Fox, 1963; The Stunt Man, 1970; Downstream (short stories), 1972; Asbestos & Enzymes, 1972. Contbr. to: Staff Writer, New Yorker, 1958-. Address: c/o The New Yorker, 25 West 43rd St., N.Y., NY 10036, USA.

BRODRIBB, Gerald, b. 21 May 1915, Sussex, UK. Schoolmaster. Educ: M.A., Dip.Ed., Univ. Coll., Oxford. Publs. incl: The English Game, 1948; Book of Cricket Verse, 1953; Hastings & Men of Letters, 1954; Stamped Tiles of the Classis Britannica, 1969; The Croucher (biog. of Gilbert Jessop), 1974. Contbr. to: Daily Telegraph; Field; Cricketer; Spectator; Times Educl. Supp.; Sussex Archaeol. Collects. Mbrships. incl: F.S.A.; I.A.P.S.; M.C.C. Address: Stubbles, Ewhurst Green, Robertsbridge, Sussex, UK.

BRØGGER, Waldemar Christofer, b. 5 Dec. 1911, Stavanger, Norway. Author; Editor. Publs: Tre ganger dronning (novel), 1948, German ed., 1951; Mannen med de syv liv (novel), 1950, French ed., 1953; CAP Encyclopaedia (ed.), 1955; COMBI Encyclopaedia (ed.), 6 vols., 1968-70; Refleks Encyclopaedia (ed.), 4 vols., 1972; Ed., school book series, in geog., hist., & social subjects. Mbr., Norwegian Authors' Assn. Hons: Scandinavian Novel Prizes for Tre ganger dronning, & Mannen med de syv liv. Address: c/o J. W. Cappelens forlag, Kirkeg 15, Oslo 1, Norway.

BROME, Vincent, b. London, UK. Journalist; Editor. Publs. incl: Anthology, 1936; Clement Attlee, 1947; H. G Wells, 1951; Aneurin Bevan, 1953; The Last Surrender, 1954; Six Studies in Quarrelling, 1958; Sometimes at Night, 1959; Acquaintance with Grief, 1961; We Have Come a Long Way, 1962; The Problem of Progress, 1963; Love in Our Time, 1964; Four Realist Novelists, 1964; The World of Luke Jympson, 1966; Freud & the Early Circle, 1967; The Surgeon, 1967; The Revolution, 1968; Ah Me, Confessions of a Writer, 1970; The Brain Operators, 1971; Private Prosecutions, 1971. Mbr., PEN. Address: 45 Great Ormond St., London WC1, UK.

BROMIGE, Iris Amy Edna, b. 1910, London, UK. Writer. Publs: Fair Prisoner, 1960; Alex & the Raynhams, 1961; Rosevean, 1962; Come Love, Come Hope, 1962; The Family Web, 1963; The Young Romantic, 1964; A House Without Love, 1965; The Challenge of Spring, 1965; The Lydian Inheritance, 1966; The Stepdaughter, 1966; The Quiet Hills, 1967; An April Girl, 1967; Only Our Love, 1968; The Master of Heransbridge, 1969; The Tangled Wood, 1969; The Sheltering Tree, 1970. Contbr. to: Woman's Weekly; Woman & Home. Address: c/o Hodder & Stoughton, St. Paul's House, Warwick Lane, London EC4P 4AH, UK.

BROMILEY, (Rev.) Geoffrey William, b. 1915, Bromley Cross, Lancs., UK. Professor of Theology; Author. Educ: M.A.; Ph.D.; D.Litt.; Univs. of Cambridge & Edinburgh. Publs. incl: Baptism & the Anglican Reformers, 1953; Thomas Cranmer, Theologian, 1956; The Sacramental Teaching of the Reformation Churches, 1957; The Unity & Disunity of the Church, 1958; Christian Ministry, 1959; H. Thielicke's Evangelical Faith (Ed., Engl. transl.), 1974; J. Ellul's Ethics of Freedom (Ed., Engl. transl.), 1975. Contbr. to theol. jrnls., etc. Mbr., Comm., Am. Assn. Ch. Hist. Recip., Hon. D.D., Univ. of Edinburgh, 1961. Address: 2261 Queensberry Rd., Pasadena, CA, USA.

BROMKE, Adam, b. 11 July 1928, Warsaw, Poland. University Professor. Educ: M.A., Univ. of St. Andrews, 1950; Ph.D. (Slavic studies), Univ. of Montreal, 1953; Ph.D. (pol. Sci.), McGill Univ., 1964. Publs: The Communist States at the Crossroads (ed.), 1965; Poland's Politics, 1967; The Communist States & the West (co-ed.), 1967; The Communist States in Disarray (co-ed.), 1972; Gierek's Poland (co-ed.), 1973. Contbr. to num. histl. & pol. jrnls. Mng. Ed., Canadian Slavonic Papers, 1963-66. Address: 165 Little John Rd., Sherwood Park, Dundas, Ont. 19H 4G7, Can.

BRONKEN, Per Kain, b. 13 Mar. 1935, Tromsø Norway. Stage Director. Educ: Artium, 1953; Norwegian

State Theatre Acad., 1954-57; London Acad. of Music & Dramatic Art, 1960-61. Publs: Kom Drikk Også Mitt Blod, 1955; Dikt Før Daggry, 1956; Naken Som De Andre, 1958; Dypest På Bunnen Av Havet, 1960; Avbrutt Karneval, 1961. Contbr. to: Vinduet, Norway; Plamen, Czech.; Poezia Nordică Modernă, Rumania; Literary Review, USA; Bcecbit, Ukraine; Norwegian anthols. Address: Incognitogate 15B, Oslo 2, Norway.

BRONOWSKI, Jacob, b. 18 Jan. 1908, Poland, d. 1974. Philosopher of Science; Mathematician; Intellectual Historian. Educ: M.A., 1930, Ph.D., 1933, Jesus Coll., Cambridge, UK. Publs. incl: The Poet's Defence, 1939, 2nd ed., 1966; Spain, 1939; The Common Sense of Science, 1951; The Face of Violence, 1954, 2nd ed., 1967; Selections from William Blake, 1958, 2nd ed., 1973; Insight, 1964; William Blake & the Age of Revolution, 1944, 2nd ed., 1965; The Identity of Man, 1965, 2nd ed., 1972; Nature & Knowledge, 1969; The Ascent of Man, 1973. Contbr. to: Nature; Sci. American; The Listener; etc. Mbrships: F.R.S.L.; Fellow, World Acad. of Art & Sci. Hons. incl: Hon. mbr., Am. Acad. Arts & Scis.; Mellon lecturer, Nat. Gallery of Art, Wash. D.C., 1969; & num. other acad. hons.

BROOK, George Leslie, b. 6 Mar. 1910, Shepley, Huddersfield, Yorks., UK. University Professor. Educ: B.A., Univ. of Leeds, 1931; Ph.D., 1935; M.A., Univ. of Manchester, 1949. Publs: Ed., The Harley Lyrics, 1948; Introduction to Old English, 1955; History of the English Language, 1958; English Dialects, 1963; Ed., Layamon's Brut, 1963; The Modern University, 1965; The Language of Dickens, 1970; Varieties of English, 1973. Mbrships: MLA; Lancs. Dialect Soc.; Bibliog. Soc., London; Manchester Bibliog. Soc. Address: 26 Chandos Rd. South, Chorlton-cum-Hardy, Manchester M21 1TF, UK.

BROOKE, Bryan Nicholas, b. 21 Feb. 1915, Croydon, UK. Professor of Surgery. Educ: B.A., 1936, M.B. & B.Chir., 1940, M.Chir., 1944, Univ. of Cambridge; M.D., Univ. of Birmingham, 1954; M.R.C.S. & L.R.C.P., 1939; F.R.C.S., 1942. Publs. incl: Ulcerative Colitis & its Surgical Treatment, 1954; You & Your Operation, 1955; (Co-Ed.) Recent Advances in Gastroenterology, 1965, 2nd ed., 1972; Metabolic Derangements in Gastrointestinal Surgery (co-author), 1967; Understanding Cancer, 1971; Ed., Clinics in Gastroenterology: Crohn's Disease, 1972. Hons. incl: Hunterian Prof., Royal Coll. of Surgs., 1951; Copeman Medal for Sci. Rsch., Corpus Christi Coll., Cambridge, 1960. Address: Professorial Surg. Unit, St. George's Hosp., Blackshaw Rd., London, SW17 0QT, UK.

BROOKE, Christopher Nugent Lawrence, b. 1927, Cambridge, UK. University Professor of History. Educ: M.A., D.Litt., Gonville & Caius Coll., Cambridge. Publs. incl: From Alfred to Henry III, 1961; The Saxon & Norman Kings, 1963; Europe in the Central Middle Ages, 1964; Time the Archsatirist, 1968; The 12th Century Renaissance, 1970; The Structure of Medieval Society, 1971; Medieval Society & Church, 1971; The Heads of Religious Houses, England & Wales, 940-1216 (w. D. Knowles & V. London), 1972; The Monastic World, 1000-1300 (w. W. Swann), 1974; London 800-1200: The Shaping of a City (w. G. Keir), 1975. Contbr. to num. books & histl. jrnls. Mbrships: Fellow, Brit. Acad.; F.S.A.; Fellow, Royal Histl. Soc. Address: Dept. of Hist., Westfield Coll., Kidderpore Ave., London NW3 7ST, UK.

BROOKE, Dinah Josephine, b. 26 May 1936, Scunthorpe, Lincs., UK. Writer. Educ: B.A., London Univ. (external). Publs: Love Life of a Cheltenham Lady, 1971, USA 1972, also paperback ed.; Lord Jim at Home, 1973; The Miserable Child & Her Father in the Desert, 1974. Contbr. to: New Yorker; New Am. Review; Body Politic. Hons: New Fiction Book Soc. Choice, Arts Coun., Oct. 1974. Agent: Ann McDiarmid of David Highams.

BROOKE, Harold, b. 14 Sept. 1910, London, UK. Playwright. Educ: Marlborough Coll.; Clare Coll., Cambridge. Publs. (w. wife Kay Bannerman): (plays) Fit for Heroes, 1945; The Nest Egg, 1952; All For Mary, 1954; The Call of the Dodo, 1955 (also presented as Love & Marriage, 1957); There's a Yank Close Behind Me, 1963; Let's Be Frank, 1963; Once a Rake, 1957; Love at Law, 1958 (How Say You?, 1959); Handful of Tansy (Don't Tell Father), 1959; Death & All That Jazz, 1961; The Snowman, 1965; Let Sleeping Wives Lie, 1967; It Shouldn't Happen to a Dog, 1970; She Was Only an Admiral's Daughter, 1972; Take Zero, 1973; Amo, Amas, Amat,

1974; Flash Harry, 1974; (filmscripts) The Iron Maiden; No, My Darling Daughter; plays performed with success in Paris, Berlin, etc. Address: Babergh Hall, Gt. Waldingfield, Sudbury, Suffolk, UK.

BROOKE, John, b. 1920, Batley, Yorks., UK. Editor. Educ: B.A., Univ. of Manchester. Publs: The Chatham Administration, 1956; The History of Parliament: The House of Commons 1754-1790 (w. Sir Lewis Namier), 1964; Charles Townshend (w. Sir Lewis Namier), 1964; The Prime Minister's Papers, 1968; W. E. Gladstone, Autobiographical Memoranda 1832-1845, 1972; King George III, with a Foreword by H.R.H. The Prince of Wales, 1972. Fellow, Royal Histl. Soc. Address: 63 Hurst Ave., London E4 8DL, UK.

BROOKE-LITTLE, John Philip, b. 1927, London, UK. Richmond Herald of Arms. Educ: M.A., New Coll., Oxford. Publs: Royal London, 1953; Pictorial History of Oxford, 1954; Boutell's Heraldry (ed. w. C. W. Scott-Giles); Knights of the Middle Ages, 1966; The Prince of Wales, the Title & Its Holders, 1969; Ed., Fox-Davies' Complete Guide to Heraldry, 1969; Kings & Queens of Great Britain (w. D. Pottinger & Anne Tauté), 1970; An Heraldic Alphabet, 1973; St. Paul's (w. B. Barber & J. George), 1974; Beasts in Heraldry (w. M. Angel), 1974. Contbr. to var. mags., learned jrnls. etc. Mbrships: F.S.A.; F.S.G.; F.H.S. Recip., M.V.O. (4th Class). Agent: Curtis Brown. Address: Heyford House, Lower Heyford, Oxford, UK.

BROOKE-ROSE, Christine, b. Geneva, Switz. University Teacher. Educ: B.A., M.A., Somerville Coll., Oxford Univ. UK; B.A., Ph.D., London Univ. Publs. incl: The Languages of Love, 1957; A Grammar of Metaphor, 1958; Out, 1964; Such, 1966; Between, 1968; Go When You See the Green Man Walking (short stories), 1969; A ZBC of Ezra Pound, 1971; Thru, 1975. Contbr. to: (1965-68) Times Lit. Supplement; Observer; Sunday Times; Spectator; New Statesman; London Mag.; Review of Engl. Lit.; etc. Mbr., MLA (Hon.). Hons: Travelling Prize, Soc. of Authors, 1965; James Tait Black Prize, 1966; Transl. Prize, Arts Coun., 1969; Address: c/o Hamish Hamilton, 90 Great Russell St., London WC1, UK.

BROOKES, Edgar Harry, b. 4 Feb. 1897, Smethwick, UK. Clergyman. Educ: M.A., D.Litt., Univ. of S. Africa. Publs: The Colour Problems of South Africa, 1933; South Africa in a Changing World, 1953; The City of God & the Politics of Crisis, 1960; A History of Natal (w. C. de B. Webb), 1965; Apartheid: A Documentary Study of South African Politics, 1968; White Rule in South Africa 1830-1910, 1974. Contbr. to: Reality. Mbr., S. African Inst. of Race Rels. (3 times Pres.). Hons: Wellcome Medal, Royal Africa Soc.; hon. degrees. Address: 15 Elgarth, St. Patricks Rd., Pietermaritzburg 3201, S. Africa.

BROOKES, Kenneth Joseph Alban, b. 1928, London, UK. Technical Journalist; Author; Consultant. Educ: B.Sc.(Eng.) Met., London Univ. Publs: World Directory & Handbook of the Hardmetals Industry; Guide to Sintered Carbides; sev. books on lubrication, diesel engines, etc., & num. works on metallurgical subjects. Contbr. to: Metalworking Production; Engrs. Digest; Inco Nickel; Hist. of Aviation; Rivistalli Meccanica; Design Engrng.; Far E. Engrng.; Ingenieur Digest; etc. Mbrships: Fellow, Coun. Mbr., Educ. Comm. Mbr., Chmn., Freelance Div., Inst. of Jrnlsts; M.I.P.R.; F.S.M.A.E. Address: 33 Oakhurst Avenue, East Barnet, Herts. EN4 8DN, UK.

BROOKES, Murray, b. 1926, Salford, UK. University Lecturer; Reader in Anatomy & Human Morphology. Educ: M.A., D.M., Oxford Univ.; Guy's Hosp., London. Publs: Blood Supply of Bone, 1971. Contbr. to Recent Advances in Orthopaedic Surgery. Mbrships: Anatomy Soc. of GB; Brit. Soc. Dev. Biol. Address: Dept. of Anatomy, Guy's Hospital Medical School, London SE1, UK.

BROOKES, Reuben Solomon, b. 8 July 1914, Buenos Aires, Argentina. Minister of Religion; Director of Education. Educ: Dip. Theol., Univ. of Birmingham; B.Th., Th.D., Geneva Theol. Coll. Publs: Guide to Jewish Knowledge (co-author), 1956; Dictionary of Judaism, 1959; Guide to Jewish Names (co-author), 1967. Contbr. to: Jewish mags. & jrnls. Mbrships. incl: F.R.S.A.; F.R.S.L.; Fellow, Philos. Soc. of England. Recip., Waley Cohen Travelling Schlrship. to USA, 1968. Address: B2 Calthorpe Mansions, Fiveways, Birmingham B15 1QS, UK.

BROOKES, Vincent Joseph, b. 20 Sept. 1906, Paterson, N.J., USA. Retired State Police Officer; Physical Educator.

Educ: Silver Bay Coll.; Safety Engrs. Schl., Rutgers Univ.; War Schls., Princeton Univ., Columbia Univ., & Amherst Coll. Publs: Poisons, Their Chemical Identification & Emergency Treatments, 1946; The Starter's Gun, 1950; Plant Security, 1959; (wartime publs.) Air Raid Precautions: State of N.J.; Training Procedures on Emergency Work; Effects of Blast; Survival Swimming; etc. Contbr. to: 1st Aid Jrnl. Mbrships: Int. Mark Twain Soc.; Swimming Officials' Assn.; Nat. Rifle Assn. Hons: Man of the Month, The Medical Way, 1946; Red Cross Nat. Medal. Address: 47 Weston Ave., Trenton, N.J., USA.

BROOKS, Albert Ellison, b. 16 Aug. 1908, Melbourne, Australia. Retired Technical School Principal; Writer. Educ: B.Sc., Dips. in Educ., Mech. Engrng. & Electrical Engrng., Univ. of Melbourne. Publs: Australian Native Plants for Home Gardens, 1959, 5th ed., 1973; Tree Wonders of Australia, 1964, 2nd ed., 1969; Australia in the Making, 1970. Contbr. to: Walkabout Mag.; The Victorian Naturalist. Mbr., Aust. Soc. of Authors. Address: 42 Harold St., Sandringham, Vic., Australia 3191.

BROOKS, Edwin, b. 1929, Barry, UK. Member of Parliament, 1966-70; Senior Lecturer in Geography. Educ: M.A., Ph.D., Univ. of Cambridge. Publs: This Crowded Kingdom, 1973; Tribes of the Amazon Basin in Brazil 1972 (co-author), 1973. Contbr. to: Geogl. Mag.; Jrnl. of Biosocial Scis.; Jrnl. of Reproduction & Fertility; New Internationalist; Environmental Studies; Trans. Inst. Brit. Geogs.; Patterns of Prejudice; The Parliamentarian. Mbrships: Fellow, Royal Geogl. Soc. Address: 39 Waterpark Rd., Prenton, Birkenhead, Merseyside L42 8PN, UK.

BROOKS, Jeremy, b. 17 Dec. 1926, Southampton, UK. Writer. Educ: Magdalen Coll., Oxford; Camberwell Schl. of Art, London. Publs: incl: (novels) The Water Carnival, 1957; Jampot Smith, 1960; Henry's War, 1962; Smith as Hero, 1965; (English stage adaptations) The Government Inspector, 1967; Enemies, 1972; The Lower Depths, 1974; (screenplays) Our Mother's House; Work . . . is a Four-letter Word; On the High Road. Contbr. to: New Statesman; Spectator; PEN Poetry Anthols.; Guinness Book of Poetry; Theatre Quarterly; var. poetry mags. & newspapers. Mbrships. incl: Soc. of Authors; Writers' Guild of GB; Inst. Contemporary Arts; Royal Shakespeare Co. (Lit. Mgr., 1962-69, Script Advsr, 1969–). Address: 12 Bartholomew Rd., London NW5 2AJ, UK.

BROOKS, John, b. Hull Yorks., UK. Author. Educ: M.A., Emmanuel Coll., Cambridge Univ. Publs: Hat, 1971; The Expert, 1973. Contbr. to: Aeroplane; Blackwood's Mag.; She; Lady; Punch; Mfg. Chemist; Flying Tales from Blackwood's, 1967; Mbrships: Soc. Authors; W. Country Writers' Assn. (Dpty. Chmn.). Recip., Poetry Prize, Cheltenham Festival Lit., 1968. Address: 7 Clifton Close, Bristol BS8 3LR, UK.

BROOKS, Keith (NMI), b. 14 May 1923, Tigerton, Wis., USA. Professor of Communication & Department Chairman. Educ: B.S., M.S., Univ. of Wis.; Ph.D., Ohio State Univ. Publs: Practical Speaking for the Technical Man (w. J. Deitrich), 1958; The Communicative Arts & Sciences of Speech, 1967; The Communicative Act of Oral Interpretation (co-author), 1967; Literature for Listening (co-author), 1968. Contbr. to profl. jrnls. Address: 3732 Romnay Rd., Columbus, OH 43220, USA.

BROOKS, Peter Wright, b. 1920, Teddington, UK. Manager, International Collaboration, British Aircraft Corporation Ltd. Educ: B.Sc., Univ. of London. Publs: The World's Airliners; The Modern Airliner; Cierva's Autogiros; Aeronautics in History of Technology; The World's Sailplanes; Passengers by Air; Historic Airships; Flight Through the Ages. Contbr. to num. aeronautical jrnls. inclng: Flight; The Aeroplane; Aeronautics; Jrnl. of the Royal Aeronautical Soc.; Jrnl. of Transp. Hist.; World Helicopter. Mbrships: Fellow, Royal Aeronautical Soc.; A.C.G.I.; United Servs. & Royal Aeronautical Club. Address: The Pightle, Ford, Aylesbury, Bucks., UK.

BROOKS, Richard, b. 18 May 1912. Film Writer; Film Director. Educ: Temple Univ. Publs: Boiling Point (novel); The Producer (novel). Film scripts incl: The Brothers Karamazov; Cat on a Hot Tin Roof; Elmer Gantry; Lord Jim; In Cold Blood; The Professionals; Last Time I Saw Paris (co-author); Blackboard Jungle (co-author); Brute Force. Recip., Acad. Award for Screenplay, 1961. Address: c/o Metro-Goldwyn-Mayer, 10202 Washington Blvd., Culver City, CA 90230, USA.

BROOKS, Virginia Feild Walton, pen name SAFARI SCRIBE, b. 6 Aug. 1904, Jonesboro, Ark., USA. Author; Explorer; Genealogist; Estate Executive. Educ: Lindewood Jr. Coll., St. Charles, Mo., 1922-24. Publs: incl: "Laps I've Sat In" (Diary of a Pomeranian Puppy), 1933; Little Mike of Mexico, 1940; Screed of Safari Scribe, 1947; Spate of Safari Scribe, 1949; "Virginiana" (fam. geneaol.), 1955; Splendrous Oriental Flight, 1956. Contbr. to num. newspapers & jrnls. Mbrships. incl: (Fndr.) Tenn. Geneaol. Soc.; Tenn. Women's Press & Authors' Club. Recip., Hon. Ph.D.; etc. Address: Home Estate, Epping Forest Manor, 3661 James Rd., Memphis, TN 38128, USA.

BROOK-SHEPHERD, Gordon, b. 1918, Nottingham, UK. Newspaper Correspondent & Assistant Editor. Educ: Cambridge. Publs: Russia's Danubian Empire, 1954; The Austrian Odyssey, 1957; There the Lion Trod, 1960; Dollfuss, 1961; The Anschluss, 1963; Eagle & Unicorn, 1966; The Last Hapsburg, 1968; Between Two Flags, 1972; Uncle of Europe, 1975. Contbr. to: Sunday Telegraph; Daily Telegraph; var. UK & US mags. Mbrships: PEN; Travellers' Club. Address: 5 South Terrace, London SW7, UK.

BROOMFIELD, (Rev. Canon) Gerald Webb, b. 1895, London, UK. Former General Secretary, Universities Mission to Central Africa. Educ: M.A., D.D.; Oxford Univ.; Cuddesdon Theol. Coll. Publs: John, Peter & the Fourth Gospel; Revelation & Reunion; Colour Conflict; The Chosen People, or the Bible, Christianity & Race; Towards Freedom; many pamphlets & a number of books in the Swahili language. Contbr. to: Towards a United Church; Mission of the Anglican Communion. Hons: O.B.E. Address: 89 Mount Nod Road, London SW16, UK.

BROPHY, Brigid Antonia, b. 1929, London, UK. Author. Educ: St. Hugh's Coll., Oxford. Publs: Hackenfeller's Ape, 1953; The King of a Rainy Country, 1956; Flesh, 1962; The Finishing Touch, 1963; The Snow Ball, 1964; In Transit, 1969; The Adventures of God in his Search for the Black Girl, 1973; (plays) The Waste Disposal Unit; The Burglar; (non-fiction) Black Ship to Hell, 1962; Mozart the Dramatist, 1964; Don't Never Forget, 1966; 50 Works of English Literature We Could Do Without (w. M. Levey & C. Osborne), 1967; Black & White, a Portrait of Aubrey Beardsley, 1968; Prancing Novelist, 1973. Contbr. to: Listener; N.Y. Times; New Statesman. Address: Flat 3, 185 Old Brompton Rd., London SW5, UK.

BROSSARD, Chandler, pen name HARPER, Daniel, b. 18 July 1922, Idaho Falls, Idaho, USA. Writer. Publs: (novels) Who Walk in Darkness, 1952; The Bold Saboteurs, 1953; The Wrong Turn, 1954; All Passion Spent, 1954; The Double View, 1961; Wake Up. We're Almost There, 1971; (plays) Harry the Magician, 1961; Some Dreams Aren't Real, 1962; The Man with Ideas, 1962; (other) The Insane World of Adolf Hitler, 1967; The Spanish Scene, 1968; Ed., The Scene Before You: A New Approach to American Culture, 1955. Contbr. to: Reporter, Wash. Post, 1940-42; Writer, New Yorker, 1942-43; Sr. Ed., Time, 1944; Exec. Ed., Am. Mercury, 1950-51; Sr. Ed., Look, 1956-67. Address: 251 West 89th St., N.Y., NY 10024, USA.

BROSSMANN, Leopold Robert, b. 26 Nov. 1923, Frankfurt/Oder, Germany. Editor. Educ: Studied Forestry, Soil Science & Geography at Univ. Contbr. to: Allgemeine Forstzeitschrift (General Forestry Jrnl.), Munich. Mbr., Int. Union of Agric. Jrnlsts. Address: 7 Stuttgart-Heumaden, Mannspergerstr. 70, W. Germany.

BROSTER, Eric James, occasional pen name STATIST, b. 6 June 1904, Wolstanton, Staffs., UK. Author; Financial Journalist. Educ: Birmingham Univ.; L.S.E. Publs: Cost, Demand & Net Revenue Analysis, 1938; Appraising Capital Works, 1968; Planning Profit Strategies, 1971; Management Statistics, 1972; Glossary of Management Statistics, 1974. Contbr. to: Bankers Mag.; Acct.; Jrnl. Am. Statist. Assn.; Profl. Admin.; etc. Mbrships: Brit. Inst. of Mgmt.; Royal Econ. Soc. Address: Hawthorns, The Rampings, Longdon, Tewkesbury, Glos. GL20 6AL, UK.

BROUGH, John, b. 31 Aug. 1917, Dundee, Scotland, UK. Professor of Sanskrit, University of Cambridge. Educ: M.A., 1939, D.Litt., 1945, Univ. of Edinburgh; B.A., 1941, M.A., 1945, Univ. of Cambridge. Publs: Selections from Classical Sanskrit Literature, 1951; The Early Brahmanical System of Gotra & Pravara, 1953; The Gandhari Dharmapada, 1962; Poems from the Sanskrit, 1968. Contbr. to: Bulletin of the Schl. of Oriental & African

Studies; Jrnl. of the Royal Asiatic Soc.; Asia Major; Chambers' Ency.; Ency. Britannica. Mbrships: VP, The Philological Soc., 1969—; The Royal Asiatic Soc.; The Asiatic Soc., Calcutta; The Linguistic Soc. of India. Hons: F.B.A., 1961; Fellow, St. John's Coll., Cambridge, 1967—; S. C. Chakravarty Medal, The Asiatic Soc., Calcutta, 1969. Address: 5 Thorn Grove, Bishop's Stortford, Herts. CM23 5LB, UK.

BROUGHTON, Geoffrey, b. 1927, Navenby, Lincs., UK. Lecturer in Education. Educ: Univ. of Hull; London Univ.; B.A.; M.Phil.; Ph.D.; Assoc., Coll. of Preceptors. Publs: Ed., Bandoola, 1959; Climbing Everest, 1960; The Splendid Tasks, 1961; Gen. Ed., Pattern Readers, Secondary Level, 1964-66; New Nation English Course (co-author), 1964; A First Technical Reader, 1965; Peter & Molly, 1965; Success with English, 1968-70; Lets Go, 1973-74; Go, 1974. Contbr. to: Engl. Lang. Tchng.; Overseas Quarterly; Tchng. Engl. Mbrships. incl: F.R.S.A.; Soc. of Authors; B.A.A.L. Address: 3 The Avenue, Beckenham, Kent, UK.

BROUGHTON, James, b. 10 Nov. 1913, Calif., USA. Poet; Film Writer & Director; Playwright. Educ: B.A., Stanford Univ., Calif., 1936. Publs. incl: (poetry) The Playground, 1949; Look In Look Out, 1968; High Kukus, 1968; A Long Undressing, 1971; (films) Mother's Day, 1948; This is It, 1971; Dreamwood, 1972; Testament, 1974; (anthols.) Mark in Time, 1971; (Play) Bedlam, 1969. Hons. incl: James D. Phelan Award in Lit., 1948; Prix du fantaisie poetique, Cannes, 1954; Grand Prize, Bellevue Festival, 1970. Address: P.O. Box 183, Mill Valley, CA 94941, USA.

BROWDER, Olin L. Jr., b. 19 Dec. 1913, Urbana, Ill., USA. Law Professor. Educ: A.B., 1935; LL.B., 1937, Univ. of Ill.; S.J.D., Univ. of Mich., 1941. Publs: American Law of Property (w. others), 1952; Basic Property Law (w. R. A. Cunningham & J. R. Julin), 2nd ed. 1973; Family Property Settlements (w. L. W. Waggoner & R. V. Wellman), 2nd ed. 1973. Contbr. to var. Am. legal jrnls. Mbrships: Am. Bar Assn.; AAUP. Address: 1520 Edinborough Rd., Ann Arbor, MI 48104, USA.

BROWER, Daniel Roberts, b. 9 Jan. 1936, Evanston, Ill., USA. Professor. Educ: B.A., Carleton Coll., USA, 1957; Inst. Pol. Studies, Paris, 1956; Columbia Univ., M.A., 1959, Ph.D., 1963. Publs: The New Jacobins: The French Communist Party and the Popular Front, 1968; (Ed.) The Soviet Experience: Success or Failure? , 1971; Training the Nihilists: Education and Radicalism in Tsarist Russia, 1975. Contbr. to: Am. Histl. Review; Hist. of Educ. Quarterly. Mbrships: Am. Histl. Assn.; Am. Assn. for the Advancement of Slavic Studies. Address: 1215 Fordham Drive, Davis, CA 95616, USA.

BROWN, Clement, b. 1928, Sydney, Australia. Editor. Educ: B.Sc., Univ. of Southampton. Publs: Sound Recording, 1963; Q & A on Transistors, 1966; Q & A on Electronics, 1966; Q & A on Computers, 1969; Q & A on Hi-Fi, 1975. Contbr. to: Ed., Hi-Fi Sound; Fin. Times; Yorks. Post; Handelsblat; John O'Londons; Musical America; High Fidelity; Data Processing; Electronic & Elec. Trader; Elect. & Radio Trading; Records & Recording; Popular Mechanics. Address: c/o Haymarket Publishing Ltd., Regent House, 54-62 Regent St., London W1, UK.

BROWN, David Alexander, b. 8 Feb. 1916, Glasgow, UK. Professor of Geology; Author. Educ: M.Sc.(NZ); Ph.D.(London). Publs: The Tertiary Cheilostomatous Polyzoa of New Zealand, 1952; The Geological Evolution of Australia & New Zealand (w. K. S. W. Campbell & K. A. W. Crook), 1968; The Geochemistry of the Lovozero Alkaline Massif (translation from Russian), 2 vols., 1968; The Facies of Metamorphism (translation from Russian), 3 vols., 1972-73. Contbr. to: Palaeontology; Am. Jrnl. of Sci.; Ed., Geol. Soc. of Aust., 1965-69. Address: Dept. of Geology, Aust. National University, Canberra, A.C.T., Australia 2600.

BROWN, Ellen Mabel (Mabel E.), b. 19 Jan. 1914. Journalist; Editor; Publisher. Educ: Var. courses, Creative Writing, Western Hist., others. Publs: '— and then there was one', 1962; Jubilee Memories, 1965; Bits & Pieces, 9 vols., 1964-74. Contbr. to newspapers, mags. & poetry jrnls.; Ed., Writer, Publisher, Bits & Pieces for 10 yrs. Mbrships. incl: Wyo. Press Women; Assoc., Nat. Fedn. of Press Women. Hons. incl: Annual awards, 1961—, Wyo. Histl. Soc.; Annual Awards, 1962—, Wyo. Press Women; 2nd Place, Nat. Communications Award, 1974. Address: Box 746, Newcastle, WY 82701, USA.

BROWN, George Mackay, b. 1921, Stromness, Orkney, UK. Writer. Educ: M.A., Univ. of Edinburgh. Publs: (poetry) Loaves & Fishes, 1965; The Year of the Whale, 1965; Fishermen with Ploughs, 1971; Poems New & Selected, 1971; (short stories) A Calendar of Love, 1967; A Time to Keep, 1969; Hawkfall, 1974; The Two Fiddlers, 1974; (essays) Orkney Tapestry, 1969; (play) A Spell for Green Corn, 1970; (novels) Greenvoe, 1972; Magnus, 1973. Contbr. to: Atlantic; Harper's Bazaar; Glasgow Herald; Scotsman; New Statesman; Cornhill. Recip., O.B.E. Address: 3 Mayburn Court, Stromness, Orkney KW16 3DH, UK.

BROWN, Helen Gurley, b. 18 Feb. 1922, Ark., USA. Author; Editor; Television Personality. Publs: Sex & the Single Girl, 1962; Sex & the Office, 1965; Outrageous Opinions, 1966; Single Girl's Cookbook, 1969; Sex & the New Single Girl, 1970. Contbr. to: Cosmopolitan; Harper's; N.Y. Times; Playboy; etc. Mbrships: Am. Soc. of Mag. Eds.; Author's Guild, USA; Am. Fedn. of Radio & TV Artists. Hons: Francis Holmes Advt. Awards, 1956-59; Univ. of S. Calif. Disting. Achievement Award, 1971; Am. Newspaper Woman's Club Special Award, 1972; Jrnlsm. Schls Admnstrs. Award, 1972. Address: Hearst Corp.; 959 8th Ave., N.Y., NY 10019, USA.

BROWN, Hugh James Robert, b. 25 Apr. 1932, Thames, NZ. Teacher. Educ: M.A. Publs: Our Library, 1968; Let's Look at Books, 1972. Mbrships: Chmn., Auckland Regional Comm., NZ Historic Places Trust; Exec., Auckland Fest. Soc. Address: 20 Gilliam St., New Lynn, Auckland 7, NZ.

BROWN, Ivor John Carnegie, b. 1891, Penang, Malaya. Writer; Critic; Editor. Educ: Balliol Coll., Oxford. Publs. incl: Shakespeare; Way of My World; Summer in Scotland; Winter in London; Balmoral; Dark Ladies; Master Sanguine; Chosen Words; Shakespeare in His Time; A Rhapsody of Words; & over 50 other books. Contbr. to: N.Y. Times; Toronto Globe & Mail; Ed., Observer, 1942-48; Ed., Drama, since 1957. Mbrships: Chmn., Brit. Drama League, since 1955. Hons: C.B.E.; LL.D. Address: 20 Christchurch Hill, London NW3, UK.

BROWN, John, b. 1887, Grimsby, Lincs., UK. Author. Educ: B.A., Sidney Sussex Coll., Cambridge. Publs: Winning Tricks, 1947; Winning Defence, 1952; Bidding Craft; Bridge With Dora, 1965. Contbr. to: Bridge World (USA); Contract Bridge Jrnl. (renamed Brit. Bridge World); Bridge Mag. Mbrships: Lincs. Artists' Soc. Address: Bargate House, 34 Bargate, Grimsby, Lincs., UK.

BROWN, Leslie Hilton, b. 25 Aug. 1917, Coonoor, India. Author. Educ: B.Sc., 1938, D.Sc., 1972, St. Andrews Univ.; A.I.C.T.A., Trinidad, 1940. Publs. incl: Birds & I, 1946; Eagles, 1955; The Mystery of the Flamingoes, 1960; Ethiopian Episode, 1965; Africa, a Natural History, 1965; Eagles, Hawks & Falcons of the World (w. Dean Amaon), 1969; African Birds of Prey, 1970; Eagles, 1970; Life on the African Plains, 1971; East African Mountains & Lakes, 1971; Contbr. to: Ibis Ostrich; Jrnl. E. African Wildlife Soc.; Field, Blackwoods; etc.; Ency. Britannica; Times; etc. Mbrships. incl: Brit. Ornithol. Union; S. African Ornithol. Soc.; E. African Wildlife Soc.; Conservation Soc.; Soc. of Authors; Recip., O.B.E., for services to agriculture, 1963. Address: Box 24916, Karen, Kenya.

BROWN, Marion Marsh, b. 22 July, 1908, Brownville, Neb., USA. Author; Professor. Educ: A.B., Peru State Coll., Neb.; M.A., Univ. of Neb., Lincoln. Publs: Young Nathan, 1949; Swamp Fox, 1950; Frontier Beacon, 1953, reissued as Stuart's Landing, 1967; Broad Stripes & Bright Stars, 1955; Prairie Teacher, 1957; Learning Words in Context, 1961, revised ed. 1974; Silent Storm, (w. Ruth Crone), 1963; Nurse Abroad, 1963; Willa Cather, The Woman & Her Works (w. Ruth Crone), 1970; Marnie, 1971; The Pauper Prince, 1973; The Brownville Story 1854-1974, Portrait of a Phoenix, 1974. Mbr., Neb. Writers' Guild. Hons: Jr. Lit. Guild selections, 1949 & 1963; Boys' Clubs of Am., Bk. of the Yr., 1950; 1st place award, "Bks. for Boys and Girls", Nat. Press Women, 1963. Address: 2615 North 52nd St., Omaha, NB 68104, USA.

BROWN, Maurice John Edwin, b. 1906, London, UK. Author. Educ: B.Sc., B.Mus., London Univ. Publs: Schubert's Variations; Schubert: A Critical Biography; Chopin: A Thematic Catalogue. Contbr. to: Music & Letters; Music Review; Musical Quarterly; Musical Times; Österreichische Musikzeitschrift; Monthly Musical Record; Listener; Grove's Dict., etc. Address: 40 London Rd., Marlborough, Wilts., UK.

BROWN, Raymond Lamont, b. 20 Sept. 1939, Horsforth, Yorks., UK. Author; Broadcaster. Educ: M.A. Publs. incl: History of St. Mark's Church, Dewsbury, 1965; A Book of Epitaphs, 1967; Clarinda, 1968; Sir Walter Scott's Letters on Demonology & Witchcraft, 1969; Robert Burns's Commonplace Book, 1970; A Book of Witchcraft, 1971; Robert Burns's Tour of the Borders,1972; Phantoms, Legends, Customs & Superstitions of the Sea, 1973; A New Book of Epitaphs, 1973; Casebook of Military Mystery, 1974; The Magic Oracles of Japan, 1974. Contbr. to: Readers Digest; Writer; Archtl. Design, etc. Mbrships. incl: Scottish Comm., Soc. of Authors; PEN. Address: 25 Ladywell Rd., Tweedmouth, Berwick-upon-Tweed TD15 2AF, Northumberland, UK.

BROWN, Re Mona, b. 31 Oct. 1917, Menomonie, Wis., USA. Teacher; Writer. Educ: B.E., Superior State Univ., Wis., 1941. Publs: Kindergarten Calendar, 1970; Kindergarten Bulletin Board Ideas, 1971; Third Grade Bulletin Board Ideas, 1973; The 3 R's in the Kindergarten Calendar, 1974. Mbrships: Delta Kappa Gamma, Eta Chapt.; NEA; Wis. Educ. Assn. Address: 1020 Green Valley Drive, Waukesha, WI, USA.

BROWN, Royston, b. 1934, Romford, Essex, UK. Country Librarian. Publs: School Libraries: Theory & Practice (w. C. Dyer), 1970. Contbr. to: E. Anglian Mag.; Cambs., Hunts., & Peterborough Life; etc. Mbrships: Lib. Assn.; Brit. Inst. of Management. Address: 14 Priors Rd., Hemingford Grey, Hunts., UK.

BROWN, Sanborn C., b. 19 Jan. 1913, Beirut, Lebanon. Professor of Physics. Educ: A.B., 1935, M.A., 1937, Dartmouth Coll.; Ph.D., MIT, 1944. Publs. incl: Basic Data of Plasma Physics, 1959, revised ed., 1967; Count Rumford, Physicist Extraordinary, 1962; Introduction to Electrical Discharge in Gases, 1966; Count Rumford on the Nature of Heat, 1967; Collected Works of Count Rumford, 5 vols. (ed.), 1968-70; Natural Philosophy at Dartmouth, 1974. Contbr. to num. sci. jrnls. Mbrships. incl: Am. Physical Soc.; Am. Acad. of Arts & Scis.; Royal Instn. of G.B. Recip., var. scholastic awards. Address: 37 Maple Street, Lexington, MA 02173, USA.

BROWN, Sonia, b. 10 Dec. 1898, Russia. Writer. Educ: A.B. Publs: Strategy of Murder; Bufano, an Intimate Biography, 1972. Address: 10801 Chalon Rd., L.A., CA 90024, USA.

BROWN, Vinson, b. 7 Dec. 1912, Reno, Nev., USA. Writer-Naturalist. Educ: A.B., Univ. of Calif., Berkeley, 1939; M.A., Stanford Univ., Calif., 1946. Publs., 25 books inclng: Great Upon the Mountain, Crazy Horse of America, 1970; Backyard Birds of the East & Middle West, 1971; Rocks & Minerals of California (co-authors), 1972; Knowing the Outdoors in the Dark, 1973; Handbook of California Birds (co-author), 1973; Voices of Earth & Sky, The Vision Search of the Native Americans, 1974. Address: P.O. Box 1045, Happy Camp, CA 96039, USA.

BROWN, (Lord) Wilfred Banks Duncan, b. 1908, Greenock, UK. Industrial Executive; Former Minister of State, Board of Trade. Publs: Management, Men & Morale (co-author), 1947; Exploration in Management, 1960; Piecework Abandoned, 1962; Product Analysis Pricing (co-author), 1964; Glacier Project Papers (co-author), 1971; Organization, 1971; The Earnings Conflict, 1973. Contbr. to: Harvard Bus. Review; Calif. Mgmt. Review; Mgmt. Int.; Mgr.; Organizational Dynamics. Mbrships: Fellow, BIM & Int. Acad. of Mgmt.; Reform Club. Hons: P.C.; M.B.E.; D.Tech.; D.L.; D.Sc. Address: 23 Prince Albert Road, London NW1 7ST, UK.

BROWNE, Anna Maria, b. 27 Oct. 1938, London, UK. Computer Programmer. Educ: B.A., London Univ., 1966. Publs: Whom the Gods Love, 1959; Ed., Patrick Carnegy, 1974. Contbr. to: Christianity Revalued; The Times. Address: 54 Margravine Gdns., London W6, UK.

BROWNE, Courtney, b. 1915, Shanghai. Scriptwriter & Producer of Documentary Programmes, Thames Television; Former Foreign Correspondent in Far East. Publs: Taipan & the Pillow Book, 1956; The Ancient Pond, 1967; Tojo: The Last Banzai, 1968; The Tomorrow Jade, 1969. Mbrships: Soc. of Authors; Authors League of Am. Address: c/o Laurence Pollinger Ltd., 18 Maddox St., London W1, UK.

BROWNE, E. Martin, b. 29 Jan. 1900, Zeals, Wilts., UK. Theatre Director; Actor; Lecturer. Educ: B.A., 1923, M.A.,

1926, Christ Church, Oxford. Publs: The Making of T. S. Eliot's Plays, 1969. Contbr. to: 60th & 70th Birthday Symposia for T.S.E.; Tate, T. S. Eliot, the Man & his Work, 1966. Mbrships: F.R.S.L.; Garrick Club. Hons: C.B.E., 1952; D.Litt. (Lambeth), 1971. Agent: David Higham. Address: 20 Lancaster Grove, London NW3 4PB, UK.

BROWNE, Harry, b. 1918, Birmingham, UK. College Head of Faculty. Educ: M.A., Emmanuel Coll., Cambridge Univ. Publs: The Second World War, 1968; Struggle in the Deserts, 1968; Ed., Koestler, Darkness at Noon, 1968; Hitler & the Rise of Nazism, 1969; Suez & Sinai, 1971; World History, 2 vols., 1974; Joseph Chamberlain, Radical & Imperialist, 1974. Mbr., Royal C'wlth. Soc. Agent: Curtis Brown Ltd. Address: 4 Kentings, Comberton, Cambridge CB3 7DT, UK.

BROWNE, Laurence Edward, b. 17 Apr. 1887, Northampton, UK. Church of England Clergyman; University Professor. Educ: D.D., Univ. of Cambridge. Publs: Early Judaism, 1920; Eclipse of Christianity in Asia, 1933; The Quickening Word, 1955. Contbr. to: Peake's Bible Commentary, 1962. Address: 71 Maisemore Gardens, Emsworth, Hants., PD10 7JX, UK.

BROWNE, Martha Steffy, b. 12 Dec. 1898, Vienna, Austria. Professor of Economics. Educ: Univs. of Freiburg & Vienna; Ph.D., Univ. of Vienna; Grad. study, Columbia Univ., N.Y. Publs: Theorie der Staatlichen Wirschaftspolitik, 1929; The Place of Foreign Trade in the Japanese Economy (co-author), 1946. Contbr. to US & European profl. jrnls. Address: 510 E. 23rd St., Apt. 14F, N.Y., NY 10010, USA.

BROWNE, Roland Andrew, b. 18 Sept. 1910, Coppercliff, Ont., Can. University Professor; Author. Educ: B.A., 1933, M.A., 1934, Queen's Univ., Kingston, Ont.; postgrad. studies, Univs. of Paris & Grenoble (France), Heidelberg (W. Germany), Cinn. (USA). Publs: For Better Gardens, 1964; The Intelligent Dog's Guide to People-Owning, 1967; The Commonsense Guide to Flower Gardening, 1968; The Rose-Lover's Guide, 1974; The Holy Jerusalem Voyage of Ogier d'Anglure, 1975. Contbr. to: Collier's Educl. Forum; Educl. Record; Queen's Quarterly; Queen's Review; Tower; Woman's Day; gardening & other jrnls. Mbrships: Phi Delta Kappa; Philomathic Club (past Pres.) Recip., awards. Address: 256 Spartan Dr., Maitland, FL 32751, USA.

BROWNING, (Rev.) Wilfrid Robert Francis, b. 1918, London, UK. Canon of Christ Church, Oxford. Educ: M.A., B.D.; Christ Ch., Oxford; Cuddesdon Theol. Coll. Publs: Commentary on St. Luke's Gospel, 3rd edn., 1972; Meet the New Testament; Jt.- Transl. from French of Vocabulary of the Bible, 1965; Ed., The Anglican Synthesis, 1965. Contbr. to: Bulletin Anglican Écuménique (Ed.); Theol.; Ch. Quarterly Review; Verbum Caro. Address: Canon's Lodge, 1a Observatory Street, Oxford OX2 6EW, UK.

BROWNJOHN, Alan Charles, b. 1931, London, UK. Teacher & Lecturer. Educ: Merton Coll., Oxford Univ. Publs: (poems) The Railings, 1961; The Lions' Mouths, 1967; Sandgrains on a Tray, 1969; Brownjohn's Beasts (poems for children), 1970; Warrior's Career, 1972; Ed., First I Say This (anthol.), 1969; (as John Berrington) To Clear the River (children's novel), 1964, paperback 1966. Contbr. to: New Statesman; London Mag.; Ambit. Mbr., A.T.C.D.E. Address: 2 Belsize Park, London NW3, UK.

BROWNJOHN, John Nevil Maxwell, b. 1929, Rickmansworth, UK. Literary Translator. Educ: M.A., Lincoln Coll., Oxford. Publs: The Living Past, 1957; Power & Folly, 1958; Night of the Generals, 1962; Memories of Teilhard de Chardin, 1964; Klemperer Recollections, 1964; Brothers in Arms, 1965; Goya, 1965; Rodin, 1967; The Interpreter, 1967; Alexander the Great, 1968; The Poisoned Stream, 1969; The Human Animal, 1971; Here in the Tower, 1972; Strength through Joy, 1973; Madam Kitty, 1973; A Time for Truth, 1974; U-Boat, 1974; A Direct Flight to Allah, 1975. Mbr., Exec. Comm., Transls. Assn. Address: Orchard House, Marnhull, Dorset, UK.

BROWNLOW, Kevin, b. 2 June 1938, Crowborough, Sussex, UK. Film Director; Historian. Publs: The Parade's Gone By, 1968; How It Happened Here, 1968; Ed., Karl Brown, Adventures with D. W. Griffith, 1972. Address: 13 Queens Gate Pl., London SW7, UK.

BRUCE, Frederick Fyvie, b. 1910, Elgin, Morayshire, UK. Rylands Professor of Biblical Criticism & Exegesis.

Educ: M.A., D.D., F.B.A.; Univs. of Aberdeen & Cambridge; Univ. of Vienna, Austria. Publs. incl: The Spreading Flame; This is That; Tradition Old & New; The Message of the New Testament; The Epistles of John; The Hittites & the Old Testament; Are the New Testament Documents Reliable? ; The Epistle to the Hebrews; Paul & His Converts; New Testament History; The Letters to the Corinthians; Jesus & Christian Origins Outside The New Testament. Contbr. to: Evangelical Quarterly (Ed.); Ency. Britannica; Jrnls. of Semitic & Theol. Studies; Heythrop Jrnl.; etc. Address: The Crossways, Temple Road, Buxton, Derbyshire, UK.

BRUCE, George, b. Bedford, UK. Journalist; Author. Publs: A Family Called Field (biog.), 1959; Flightdeck (co-author), 1960; Retreat from Kabul, 1964; The Stranglers, 1968; Six Battles for India, 1969; Eva Peron (biog.), 1970; Dictionary of Battles (co-author), 1971; The Warsaw Uprising 1944, 1973; The Burmese Wars, 1973; The Nazis, 1974; Sea Battles of the 20th Century, 1975. Contbr. to: Sunday Times; Daily Telegraph; Telegraph Mag.; Fin. Times; Spectator; Wash. Star. Mbr., Nat. Union Jrnlsts. (Authors' Sub-Comm.) Agent: Richard Scott Simon Ltd. Address: The Red House, Elvendon Rd., Goring, Reading RG8 0DT, UK.

BRUCE, Robert, b. 20 Dec. 1927, Darlington, Co. Durham, UK. Medical Practitioner. Educ: Med. Schl., Durham Univ.; M.D., M.R.C.G.P., M.B.B.S. Publs: Cheaper Tackle, 1960; Fly Fishing — a Practical Introduction, 1963. Contbr. to: nat. press; Pulse; Dr.; On Call; Newcastle Med. Jrnl.; Brit. Jrnl. of Clin. Prac.; Brit. Med. Jrnl.; local press; BBC Radio; Indep. TV; Hlth.; RAMC Med. Jrnl.; G.P.A. Newsletter. Mbrships: Chmn., Gen. Practitioners' Assn.; Family Practitioners' Comm.; Area Hlth. Authority Comm. Address: "Torrish", Newcastle Rd., Chester-le-Street, Co. Durham, UK.

BRUCE LOCKHART, Robin, b. 1920, London, UK. Former Newspaper Executive; Member, London Stock Exchange; Company Director; Lecturer; Broadcaster. Educ: Univ. of Cambridge. Publs: Ace of Spies, 1967. Contbr. to: Fin. Times; Sunday Express; Daily Express; Evening Standard. Agent: Peter Janson-Smith Ltd. Address: Brookside, Ditchling, Hassocks, Sussex, UK.

BRÜEL, Per Vilhelm, b. 6 Mar. 1915, Copenhagen, Denmark. Company Director. Educ: M.Sc., 1939; D.Sc., 1945, Univ. of Technol., Copenhagen. Publs: Sound Insulation & Room Acoustics, 1948. Contbr. to B. & K. Tech. Review, 1954-. Mbrships: Fellow, Acoustical Soc. of Am.; Fellow, Swedish Acoustical Soc. Hons: La Medaille d'Argent de la Ville de Paris, 1965; Lord Rayleigh Gold Medal, 1974. Address: Fuglevangsvej 5, DK-2960 Rungsted Kyst, Denmark.

BRUFORD, Rose Elizabeth, b. 22 June 1904, London, UK. Principal of Drama School. Educ: Hons. Dip., Ctrl. Schl. of Speech Trng. & Dramatic Art, 1924; Hons. Cert., Tchrs. & Performers Inst. of Mime, 1930. Publs: Speech & Drama, 1948; Teaching Mime, 1958. Contbr. of articles to var. profl. jrnls.; also radio lectrs. Mbrships. incl: Fndr. Mbr. & Hon., Soc. of Tchrs. of Speech Drama; Fndr. Mbr. & Hon., Guild of Drama Adjudicators; Fndr. Mbr., The Drama Bd.; Soc. of Authors. Hons: Fellow, Inst. of Mime, 1931; Hon. Mbr., Royal Acad. of Music, 1944. Address: Old Kennels House, Otford, Nr. Sevenoaks, Kent, UK.

BRUHLMANN, Sepp, b. 5 July 1947, Appenzell, Switz. Businessman; Writer. Publs: Mitternacht; Angela. Mbr., Swiss Writers' Union. Address: Messikohmerstr. 39, 8620 Wetzikon ZH, Switzerland.

BRUINEMAN, Joan, b. 9 Nov. 1914, Amsterdam, Netherlands. Journalist; Author. Publs. incl: Dorp met de Groene Spieghel (hist.), 1966; Schimmen in het Muiderslot (hist.), 1972; 1970-74; Isabel's Ontdekkingen; Isabel Van der Witte Wimpel; Isabel danst de Czardas; Isabel in de Storm; (juvenile) Een Liedje voor Katrijne; Heb't goed Katrijne; Wat doe ju nu, Katrijne; Veel geluk, Katrijne; Het geheim van de Knotwilgen, 1975; Een blad in de Wind (A Leaf in the Wind) (hist.), 1975; De Kachina's dansen (hist.), 1975. Contbr. to: Spektator; Tijdschrift voor Neerlandistiek, Gem. Univ. Amsterdam; Tijdschrift Babel, KRO. Mbr., Vereniging van Letterlundigen; Bds., num. cultural orgs. Hons. incl: Music Advsr., Nederlandse Händelvereniging. Address: Huurmanlaan 10, Bussum, Netherlands.

BRUMM, Dieter Johann Gabriel, b. 22 June 1929, Wentorf bei Hamburg, Germany. Author. Educ: Philos. &

Art Hist., Univs. of Hamburg, Kiel, & Freiburg. Publs: (chapters in) Hauptschulserie Mit dem Latein am Ende, 1970; Wir leben in der Weltrevolution: Gespräche mit Sozialisten, 1971; Gesellschaftliche Kommunikation und Information, 2 vols., 1973. Contbr. to: Der Spiegel (Ed. bd., 1968-72); N. German Radio; Lectures on theory of mass media. Mbrships: German Authors' Union (VS), Printing & Paper Union; German Union of Jrnlsts., Printing & Paper Union. Address: 2000 Hamburg 13, Innocentiastr. 78, W. Germany.

BRUNDAGE, James A., b. 5 Feb. 1929, Lincoln, Neb., USA. Historian. Educ: B.A., 1950, M.A., 1951, Univ. of Neb.; Ph.D., Fordham Univ., 1955. Publs: The Chronicle of Henry of Livonia, 1961; The Crusades: A Documentary Survey, 1962; Medieval Canon Law & the Crusader, 1969; Richard Lion Heart: A Biography, 1974. Contbr. to: America; Am. Histl. Review; Balkan Studies; Cath. Histl. Review; Ch. Hist.; Classical Jrnl.; Erasmus; Jurist; Manuscripta; Mod. Langs. Review; Speculum; Studia Gratiana; Traditio; Jrnl. of Medieval Hist.; Jrnl. of Baltic Studies, etc. Mbrships. incl: Medieval Acad. of Am.; Am. Histl. Assn.; Chapt. Pres., AAUP, 1961-62; Pres., Midwest Medieval Conf., 1971-72. Address: Dept. of Hist., Univ. of Wis.-Milwaukee, Milwaukee, WI 53201, USA.

BRUNE, John Anatole, b. 21 Apr. 1926, Vienna, Austria. Interpreter & Translator. Educ: Vienna & Edinburgh, UK. Publs: The Foursome Reel, 1955; The Roving Songster, 1965; In the Life of a Romany Gypsy (compiler & ed.), 1973; Songs of the Travelling People, 1975; Resonant Rubbish: Musical Instruments from Waste, 1975. Contbr. to: Brit. Book News; Engl. Dance & Song. Address: 6 Vale Lodge, Perry Vale, London SE23 2LG, UK.

BRUNN, Harry O., Jr., b. 1919, Buffalo, N.Y., USA. Public Relations Manager; Programme Presentations Coordinator; Jazz Trombonist; Photographer; Freelance Writer; Lecturer. Publs: The Story of the Original Dixieland Jazz Band, 1960. Address: 39 Getzville Rd., Snyder, NY 14226, USA.

BRUNNER, John Kilian Houston, b. 24 Sept. 1934, Preston Crowmarsh, Oxon., UK. Writer. Publs. incl: (sci. fiction) Stand on Zanzibar, 1968; The Jagged Orbit, 1969; The Sheep Look Up, 1972; The Shockwave Rider, 1975; (adult fantasy) The Traveler in Black, 1971; (contemporary fiction) The Devil's Work, 1970; (story collects.) Entry to Elsewhen, 1972; From This Day Forward, 1972; (poetry) Life in an Explosive Forming Press, 1970; Trip, 1971; A Hastily Thrown-Together Bit of Zork, 1974. Contbr. to var. jrnls. Mbrships. incl: SF Writers of Am.; Br. Sci. Fiction Assn. (Chmn.). Hons. incl: Hugo Award; Br. Sci. Fiction Award (twice); Prix Apollo. Agent: (USA) Paul R. Reynolds Inc. Address: c/o Agent. (UK), John Farquharson Ltd., 15 Red Lion Sq., London WC1R 4QW, UK.

BRUNNER, Lillian Sholtis, b. Freeland, Pa., USA. Nurse; Author. Educ: B.S., Univ. of Pa., Phila; M.S., Case-Western Reserve Univ., Cleveland, Ohio. Publs: (co-author) Surgical Nursing, 10th ed., 1955; Eliason's Surgical Nursing, 1959; Art of Clinical Instruction, 1969; Textbook of Medical & Surgical Nursing, 1964, 3rd ed., 1975; Manual of Operating Room Technology, 1966; Lippincott Manual of Nursing Practice, 1974. Contbr. to: Nursing World (ed. staff); Am. Jrnl. Nursing; Operating Room Supvsr.; AORN Jrnl.; Nursing Clins. of N. Am. (Guest ed.); RN; Nursing '73. Mbrships. incl: Am. Med. Writers' Assn.; Nat. League of Am. Pen Women. Address: 1247 Berwyn-Paoli Rd., Berwyn, PA 19312, USA.

BRUNS, Henry Prentice, pen name HANK, b. 13 Aug. 1904, NYC, USA. Manufacturers Representative (Sporting Goods). Publs: Stories, 1964; Angling Books of the Americas, 1975. Contbr. to: Int. Fly Fishing Ency., 1975 (bibliog.); Sporting Goods Dealer Mag. (Fishing Tackle Ed.); Sports Age (Merchandise Ed.); Outdoor Life; Sports Afield; Field & Stream; Hunting & Fishing. Mbrships. incl: Outdoor Writers of Am.; Mus. of Am. Fly Fishing (Bibliog. Comm., Lib. & Trustee); Smithsonian Inst.; Audubon Soc. Hon: Mbr., Int. Fishing Hall of Fame. Address: 2450 W. Wesley Rd., N.W., Atlanta, GA 30327, USA.

BRUNTON, Paul, b. 1898, London, UK. Freelance Journalist (retired). Educ: Central Foundation Schl., London; McKinley-Roosevelt Coll., Chicago, Ill. Publs: A Search in Secret India, 1934; The Secret Path, 1934; A Search in Secret Egypt, 1935; A Hermit in the Himalayas; The Quest of the Overself, 1937; The Inner Reality, 1939;

The Hidden Teaching; Beyond Yoga, 1941; The Wisdom of the Overself, 1953; The Spiritual Crisis of Man, 1952. Address: c/o Rider & Co., 3 Fitzroy Square, London W1, UK.

BRUUN, Bertel, b. 13 Nov. 1937, Skelskor, Denmark. Neurologist. Educ: M.D., Univ. of Copenhagen, 1964; Neurol. Res., Columbia-Presby. Med. Ctr., USA, 1967-70. Publs. incl: Ducks, Geese, & Swans, 1964; Birds of North America, A Guide to Field Identification, 1966; British & European Birds in Color, 1969; Birds of North America, 1973; The Dell Encyclopedia of Birds, 1974; Contbr. of chapts. to Where the Fun Is Abroad, 1967, Animals of the World: North America, 1970. Contbr. to ornithol., med. jrnls. Address: 52 E. 73rd St., N.Y., NY 10021, USA.

BRUUN-RASMUSSEN, Knud, b. 21 July 1898, Hilleröd, Denmark. Poet; Novelist; Essayist. Publs: Digte, 1920; Kentaur, 1926; Novemberstorm, 1927; En Herre viser sig, 1929; Gaden og Mennesket, 1930; Dette ene Liv, 1932; Morgendrömme, 1933; Ansigtet i Spejlet, 1947; Hvordan skal jeg undervise?, 1953; Grundbog for talere, 1954; Bedömmelse af Mennesker, 1954; Kvinde og Mand i dagens lys, 1955; Talerkunst, 1963; Mundtlig Fremstilling, 1969; Mödeteknik, 1970; Indgang til Venezia, 1972. Address: Strandallien IC, 3000 Helsingor, Denmark.

BRYAN, Edwin H(orace), Jr., b. 13 Apr. 1898, Phila, Pa., USA. Museum Scientist & Biogeographer; Manager, Pacific Scientific Information Center. Educ: B.S., 1920, M.S., 1924, Univ. of Hawaii, Honolulu; Ph.B., Yale Univ., 1921. Publs. incl: Hawaiian Nature Notes, 1933; Ancient Hawaiian Life, 1938; American Polynesia, 1941, revised ed., American Polynesia & the Hawaiian Chain, 1942; Geography of the Pacific, 1944; Land in Micronesia & its Resources: an annotated bibliography, 1971; Guide to Place Names in the Trust Territory of the Pacific Islands, 1971; Life in the Marshall Islands, 1972; Panala'au Memoirs, 1974. Contbr. to newspapers & sci. jrnls. Mbrships. incl: Pres., Hawaiian Acad. of Sci., 1934; AAAS. Address: 2721 Ferdinand Ave., Honolulu, HI 96822, USA.

BRYAN, Jack Yeaman, b. 24 Sep. 1907, Peoria, Ill., USA. Author-Photographer; Former Diplomat. Educ: B.A., Univ. of Ariz., 1932, M.A., 1933; Fellow, Philos., Duke Univ., 1933-35; Ph.D., Univ. of Iowa, 1939. Publs: Come to the Bower (novel), 1963. Contbr. to num. mags., newspapers, US, Can., India, Brazil, Pakistan, & to pictorial books, Mexico, & Rivers of the West; Anthols. of short stories. Mbr., Tex. Inst. of Letters. Hons: Annual Prize for Best Fiction, Tex. Inst. of Letters & Summerfield Roberts Award, 1964. Address: 3594 Ramona Dr., Riverside, CA 92506, USA.

BRYAN, Leslie Aulls, b. Feb. 1900, Bath, N.Y., USA. Consultant. Educ: B.S., M.S., J.D., Syracuse Univ.; Ph.D., Am. Univ.; Sc.D.(Hon.), Southwestern Coll. Publs. incl: Aerial Transportation, 1925; Principles of Water Transportation, 1939; Air Transportation (w. G. L. Wilson), 1949; Fundamentals of Aviation & Space Technology (w. others), 1959, 5th ed., 1968; Aulls-Bryan & Allied Families, 1966; The Aulls Genealogy, 1974. Contbr. to num. Am. encys. & jrnls. Mbr., Aviation/Space Writers Assn. Address: 43 Fields E., Champaign, IL 61820, USA.

BRYANS, Robert Harbinson, pen name BRYANS, Robin; HARBINSON, Robert; CAMERON, Donald, b. 24 Apr. 1928, Belfast, N. Ireland, UK. Author. Publs: Gateway to the Khyber, 1959; Madeira, 1959; Summer Saga, 1960; No Surrender, 1960; Song of Erne, 1960; Up Spake the Cabin Boy, 1961; Danish Episode, 1961; Fanfare for Brazil, 1962; Tattoo Lily, 1962; The Azores, 1963; The Protege, 1963; The Far World, 1963; Ulster, 1964; Lucio, 1964; Morocco, 1965; Malta, 1966; The Field of Sighing, 1966; Trinidad, 1967; Best True Adventure Stories, 1967; Sons of El Dorado, 1968; Crete, 1969; Songs out of Oriel, 1973. Contbr. to newspapers. Address: Welkin Cottage, 39 Falmer Rd., Rottingdean, Brighton BN2 7DA, UK.

BRYANT, Edward Winslow Jr., pen name TALBOT, Lawrence, b. 27 Aug. 1945, White Plains, N.Y., USA. Writer. Educ: B.A., 1967, M.A., 1968, Univ. Wyo. Publs: Among the Dead, 1973; Phoenix Without Ashes, 1975; Cinnabar, 1975; Lynx, 1975. Contbr. to: The Nat. Lampoon; Mag. Fantasy & Sci. Fiction; Orbit; L.A. Free Press; New Dimensions; Rolling Stone; Cthulhu Calls; Universe. Mbr., Sci Fiction Writers Am. Hons: Gen. Motors Scholar, 1963-67; Ford Foundation Fellowship, 1967-68; New Am. Lib. Fiction Competition Winner, 1972; Nebula Award Finalist, 1974. Address: P.O. Box 18162, Denver, CO 80218, USA.

BRYANT, Margaret M., b. 3 Dec. 1900, Trenton, S.C., USA. Professor of English (Linguistics). Educ: A.B., Winthrop Coll., Rock Hill, S.C., 1921; A.M., 1925, Ph.D., 1931, Columbia Univ., N.Y. Publs: English in the Law Courts, 1930, 2nd ed., 1962; Psychology of English (w. J. R. Aiken), 1940, 2nd ed., 1962; A Functional English Grammar, 1945; Modern English & its Heritage, 1948, 2nd ed., 1962; Current American English, 1962. Contbr. to num. linguistic & educl. jrnls. Num. mbrships. incl: Pres., Am. Name Soc., 1958-59; Pres., Int. Linguistic Assn., 1973-74; Am. Dialect Soc.; MLA; Dir., Nat. Coun. of Engl., 1946-60; Ed., bds., sev. jrnls. Hons. incl: D.Litt., Cedar Crest Coll., Allentown, PA., 1966; L.H.D., Winthrop Coll., 1968. Address: 222 Hicks St., Bklyn., NY 11201, USA.

BRYCE-ECHENIQUE, Alfredo, b. 19 Feb. 1939, Lima, Peru. Writer; Teacher of Latin American Literature, Universities of Vincennes & la Sorbonne. Educ: M.A., San Marcos Univ., Lima; Dips. of Classic & Contemp. French lit., Sorbonne, Paris, France. Publs: (short stories) Huerto Cerrado, 1968; La Felicidad Ja Ja, 1974; (novel) Un Mundo Para Julius, 1971. Hons. incl: Guggenheim Fellowship, 1975; Nat. Prize for Lit., for novel, Peru, 1971. Address: 8 bis rue Amyot, 75005 – Paris, France.

BRYHER, Annie Winifred Ellerman, b. 1894, Margate, Kent, UK. Writer. Publs. incl: (novels) Civilians, 1927; The Lighthearted Student (w. Trude Weiss), 1930; The Fourteenth of October, 1952; The Player's Boy, 1953; Roman Wall, 1954; Beowulf, 1956; Gate to the Sea, 1958; Ruan, 1960; The Coin of Carthage, 1963; Visa for Avalon, 1965; This January Tale, 1966; The Colors of Vaud, 1969; Arrow Music (verse w. others), 1922; (other) West, 1925; Film Problems of Soviet Russia, 1929; Cinema Survey (w. others), 1937; The Heart to Artemis: A Writer's Memoirs, 1962; The Days of Mars: A Memoir, 1940-1946, 1972. Address: Kenwin, Burier, Vaud, Switz.

BRYL, Ivan Antonovich, b. 4 Aug. 1917, Odessa, Russia. Writer. Publs: Dark-Browed Girl, 1949; Maria, 1950; The Righteous & the Wicked, 1950; Downing in Zabologye, 1950; Galya, 1953; Inscription on a Wooden House, 1956; The Heart of a Communist, 1957; Confusion, 1959; My Native Land, 1959; Collected Works, 2 vols., 1960; House of Orphans, 1961; Conversation is Continued, 1962; Birds & Nests, 1967; Talks of Camp Fire, 1966. Mbr., Sec. of Bd., Union of Writers of Byelorussian SSR. Recip., many prizes & decorations. Address: Union of Writers of Byelorussian SSR, Minsk, USSR.

BRZOSTOWSKA, Janina, b. 9 July 1902, Wadowice, Poland. Poetess. Educ: Ph.B., Jagiellonian Univ., Cracow. Publs: Szczescie w cudzym miescie, 1925; O ziemi, 1925; Erotyki, 1926; Najpiekniejsza z przygod, 1929; Naszyjnik wiecznosci, 1939; Zywiol i spiew, 1939; Plomien w cierniach, 1947; Giordano Bruno, 1953; Wiersze, 1957; Zanim noc, 1961; Czas nienazwany, 1964; Obrona swiatla, 1968; Szczescia szukamy, 1974; Poezje wybrane, 1974. Contbr. to: Poezja; Tworczosc; Miesiecznik Literacki. Mbrships: PEN; Polish Writers' Union; ZAIKS. Recip., Polonia Restituta Cross, 1967. Address: Dabrowskiego 75 m. 113, 02-586 Warsaw, Poland.

BUBE, Richard Howard, b. 10 Aug. 1927, Providence, R.I., USA. Professor of Materials Science & Electrical Engineering; Author. Educ: Sc.B., Brown Univ., 1946; M.A., 1948, Ph.D., 1950, Princeton Univ. Publs: A Textbook of Christian Doctrine, 1955; Photoconductivity of Solids, 1960; The Encounter Between Christianity & Science, 1968; The Human Quest: A New Look at Science & Christian Faith, 1971; Electronic Properties of Crystalline Solids, 1974. Contbr. to: Eternity; Ch. Herald; Reformed Jrnl.; Ed., Jrnl. of Am. Sci. Affiliation; etc. Address: Dept. of Materials Sci. & Engrng., Stanford Univ., Stanford, CA 94305, USA.

BUBENNOV, Mikhail Semenovich, b. 20 Nov. 1909, Polomoshnovo, Altai Territory, Russia. Publs: The Thundering Year, 1932; At Flood Time (stories), 1940; Immortality, 1941; The Silver Birch Tree, 1947; Orlinaya Steppe, 1959; Immortality (stories), 1969. Mbr., Communist Pty., 1951-. Hons: State Prize, 1947; Order of Red Banner of Labour, 1959; Order of Red Star. Address: USSR Union of Writers, 52 Ulitsa Vorovskogo, Moscow, USSR.

BUCH, Hans Christoph, b. 13 Apr. 1944, Wetzlar, Germany. Writer. Educ: Ph.D., Technische Univ., Berlin; German & Russian studies, univs. of Bonn & Berlin. Publs: Unerhörte Begebenheiten (stories), 1966; Kritische Wälder (essays), 1972; Ut pictura poesis (criticism), 1972; Ed., anthol., Parteilichkeit der Literatur, 1972; Ed., Lu Hsün, Essays on Literature & Revolution in China, 1973. Contbr. to: Der Spiegel; Pardon; Konkret; Ed., Literaturmagazin. Mbrships: PEN, German Ctr.; Writers' Union; Literarisches Colloquium, Berlin. Recip., Fellowship, Int. Writers' Workshop, Univ. of Iowa, USA, 1967-68. Address: 1 Berlin 41, Dickhardtstr. 48, W. Germany.

BUCHAN, Thomas Buchanan, b. 19 June 1931, Glasgow, UK. Writer. Educ: M.A., Univ. of Glasgow, 1953. Publs: Ikons, 1957; Dolphins at Cochin, 1969; Exorcism, 1972; Poems 1969-72, 1972; (Plays produced) Tell Charlie Thanks for the Truss, 1972; The Great Northern Welly Boot Show, 1972; Knox & Mary, 1972. Contbr. to: Glasgow Herald; Scotsman; New Statesman; Listener; Scottish Int.; Lines Review. Mbrships: Writers' Guild; Writers' Action Grp.; Amnesty Int. Recip., Scottish Arts Coun. Publs. Award, 1969. Address: 10 Pittville St., Edinburgh EH15 2BY, UK.

BUCHANAN, Cynthia, b. 23 Oct. 1942, Des Moines, Iowa, USA. Novelist; Playwright; Journalist. Educ: B.A., Ariz. State Univ., 1964; M.A., Univ. of the Americas, 1966. Publs: (essay) The Indignant Years, 1972; (novels) Maiden, 1972; Cock Walk in Exile, forthcoming. Contbr. to: N.Y. Times; N.Y. Times Book Review; The Wash. Post; Playboy; OUI; Newsweek; Transatlantic Review; N. Am. Review; Trace; Mexico Quarterly Review; Harvard Advocate. Mbrships. incl: PEN; Authors' Guild. Hons. incl: Fulbright Scholar, 1968-70; Outstanding Young Women of Am., 1972; MacDowell Colony Fellow, 1970; Mademoiselle 10 Super Women 1972. Address: 1160 Third Ave., Apt. 8A, N.Y., NY 10021, USA.

BUCHANAN, George Henry Perrott, b. 9 Jan. 1904, Kilwaughter, Co. Antrim, N. Ireland, UK. Writer. Educ: Belfast Univ. Publs: A London Story; Entanglement; Passage through the Present; Words for Tonight; Rose Forbes; A Place to Live; Bodily Responses; Green Seacoast; Conversation with Strangers; Morning Papers; Naked Reason; Annotations: Minute-Book of a City; (plays) A Trip to the Castle; Tresper Revolution; War Song. Contbr. to: Times Lit. Supplement; The Times (Ed. Staff, 1930-35); News Chronicle (Ed. Staff, 1935-38). Mbrships: Writers Guild; Soc. Européenne de Culture. Address: 27 Ashléy Gdns., Westminster, London SW1, UK.

BUCHDAHL, Gerd, b. 1914, Mainz, Germany. University Reader. Educ: Brixton Coll. Bldg. & Technol., London, UK; Univ. of Melbourne, Aust.; M.A. Publs: The Image of Newton & Locke in the Age of Reason, 1961; Metaphysics & the Philosophy of Science, 1969. Contbr. to: Studies in Hist. & Philos. of Sci. (jt. Ed., 1970-); Mind; Brit. Jrnl. Philos. of Sci.; Philosl. & Phenomenol. Rsch.; Ratio; Hist. of Sci.; num. other collects. & philosl. encys., dicts. & jrnls. Mbr., var. profl. assns. Address: 11 Brookside, Cambridge CB2 1JE, UK.

BUCHMAN, Dian Dincin (Mrs.), b. 3 Sept. 1922, Manhattan, NY, USA. Writer; Herbalist; Lecturer on Preventive Medicine Techniques. Educ: B.S., N.Y. Univ. Publs: Trips for New York City Classes; The Sherlock Holmes of Medicine; The Complete Herbal Guide to Natural Health & Beauty, 1973; Feed Your Face, 1973; Feel Good, Look Great (forthcoming); The Stay Healthy Book (forthcoming); Producer-Interviewer, radio show, Tomorrow's People. Contbr. to: Show Mag.; McCalls; Harper's Bazaar; New York Mag.; Nutritional Update; documentary & educl. films; etc. Recip., Laudation Award, Soc. Mag. Writers. Address: 640 West End Ave., N.Y., NY 10024, USA.

BUCHWALD, Arthur, b. 20 Oct. 1925, Mt. Vernon, N.Y., USA. Journalist; Author; Lecturer. Educ: Univ. of S. Calif. Publs. incl: Paris After Dark, 1950; Art Buchwald's Paris, 1954; The Brave Coward, 1957; I Chose Caviar, 1957; More Caviar, 1958; A Gift From The Boys, 1958; Don't Forget to Write, 1960; Is It Safe to Drink the Water?, 1962; . . . and Then I told the President, 1965; Have I Ever Lied to You?, 1968; Oh, to be a Swinger, 1970; Getting High in Government Circles, 1971; I Never Dances at the White House, 1973. Contbr. to: N.Y. Herald Tribune; & num. newspapers & journals worldwide. Address: 1750 Pennsylvania Ave., NW, Washington, DC 20006, USA.

BUCK, Margaret Waring, b. 3 June 1910, Brooklyn, N.Y., USA. Writer; Artist. Publs. (all illustrated by author): In Woods & Fields, 1950; In Yards & Gardens, 1952; In Ponds & Streams, 1955; Pets from the Pond, 1958; Small Pets from Woods & Fields, 1960; Along the Seashore, 1964; Where They Go in Winter, 1968; How They Grow, 1972. Address: Mystic, CT 06355, USA.

BUCKERIDGE, Anthony, b. 20 June 1912, London, UK. Author. Educ: Univ. Coll. London. Publs: "Jennings" books: 23 titles, 1950-; "Rex Milligan" books: 4 titles, 1954-; A Funny Thing Happened, 1953; Stories for Boys (Ed.), 1964; Stories for Boys 2 (Ed.), 1966; In & Out of School (Ed.), 1965. Mbrships: Soc. of Authors; Writers' Guild of GB; Brit. Actors' Equity Assn. Address: East Crink, Barcombe, Lewes, Sussex, UK.

BUCKINGHAM, Christopher, b. 20 June 1937, Canterbury, UK. Antiquarian Bookseller. Educ: B.A. Hist., Univ. of Exeter. Publs: Lydden, a Parish History, 1966; Catholic Dover, 1968; Pages from a Nova Scotia Journal, 1967. Contbr. to var. jrnls.; Fndr., 1st Ed., Cantium, 1969. Address: 13 Harbour St., Whitstable, Kent, UK.

BUCKLE, Christopher Richard Sandford, b. 1916. Journalist; Ballet Critic. Educ: Balliol Coll., Oxford. Publs: John Innocent at Oxford, 1939; The Adventures of a Ballet Critic, 1953; In Search of Diaghilev, 1955; Modern Ballet Design, 1955; The Prettiest Girl in England, 1958; Harewood: a guidebook, 1959; Dancing with Diaghilev (w. Lydia Sokolova), 1960; (plays) Gossip Column, 1953; Family Tree, 1956. Contbr. to: Observer, Ballet Critic, 1948-55; Fndr., Ballet; Ballet Critic, Sunday Times since 1959; Dir., Epstein Mem. Exhibition, 1961. Address: 34 Henrietta St., London WC2, UK.

BUCKLER, Ernest, b. 1908, Dalhousie, N.S., Can. Writer. Educ: B.A.; M.A.; Univ. of Dalhousie; Univ. of Toronto. Publs: The Mountain & the Valley, 1952; The Cruelest Month, 1963; Oxbells & Fireflies, 1968. Contbr. to num. mags. Address: Bridgetown, N.S., Can.

BUCKLEY, William Frank Jr., b. 24 Nov. 1925, NYC, USA. Magazine Editor-in-Chief. Educ: B.A., Yale Univ., 1950. Publs: God & Man at Yale, 1951; McCarthy & His Enemies (w. L. Brent Bozell), 1954; Up From Liberalism, 1959; Rumbles Left & Right, 1963; The Unmaking of a Mayor, 1966; The Jeweler's Eye, 1968; The Governor Listeth, 1970; Cruising Speed, 1971; Inveighing We Will Go, 1972; Four Reforms, 1973. Contbr. to var. lit. publs. Mbrships: Nat. Press Club; Overseas Press Club. Recip., Disting. Achievement Award in Jrnlsm., Univ. of S. Calif., 1968. Address: 150 East 35 St., N.Y., NY 10016, USA.

BUCKMAN, Peter Michael Amiel, b. 1941, Amersham, Bucks., UK. Publisher; Writer. Educ: M.A., Balliol Coll., Oxford Univ. European Ed., McGraw Hill Inc., 1966-68. Publs: The Limits of Protest, 1970; Playground (novel), 1971; Ed., Education without Schools, 1973; Lafayette (biog.) (forthcoming); var. TV plays. Contbr. to: Sunday Times; Times; New Statesman; Oz; Listener; Punch. Agent: Deborah Rogers. Address: Ryman's Cottage, Little Tew, Oxon., UK.

BUCKMASTER, Henrietta, b. Cleveland, Ohio, USA. Writer. Publs: Let My People Go, 1944; Bread From Heaven, 1950; And Walk in Love, 1956; All The Living, 1963; The Lion in the Stone, 1968; Wait until Evening, 1974. Contbr. to: N.Y. Times; Saturday Review of Lit.; N. Am. Review. Recip., Guggenheim Fellowship. Address: 40 Clearway St., Boston, MA 02115, USA.

BUCZKOWSKI, Marian, pen name Ruth, b. 28 May 1910, Nakwasza, Poland. Writer. Educ: M.A. Publs: Tragic Generation, 1936; Chances & History, 1954-56; Anthology of Polish Jokes. Mbrships: Union of Polish Writers; PEN. Address: Warszawa, ul. Myslowicka 13, Poland.

BUDAY, George, b. 7 Apr. 1907, Kolozsvar, Transylvania. Artist; Writer. Educ: Doct., Szeged Univ. Hungary, 1934. Publs. incl: The Dances of Hungary, 1948; The Story of the Christmas Card, 1951; The History of the Christmas Card, 1954, 2nd ed., 1964; (George Buday's Little Books, I-XII, 1943-68) Christmas Keepsake; The Hearth; Proverbs Illustrated; Old Charms & Superstitions; The Language of Flowers; Cries of London, Ancient & Modern; The Rules of Etiquette; Proverbial Cats & Kittens; etc. Contbr. to: Geograph. Mag.; Penrose Annual; The Lib.; Gutenberg Jahrbuch. Hons. incl: Offs. Cross, Hungarian Order of Merit, 1947. Address: Downs House, Netherne, P.O. Box 150, Coulsdon, Surrey CR3 1YE, UK.

BUDDEE, Paul Edgar, b. 12 Mar. 1913, Perth, Australia. Headmaster; Author, Children's Books. Educ: M.A.C.E.

Publs: Osca & Olga trilogy, 1943-47; Stand Two & Other War Poems, 1943; The Mystery of Moma Island, 1969; The Escape of the Fenians, 1971; The Escape of John O'Reilly, 1973; Author, 28 children's books; Scriptwriter, Nat., Commercial TV, Australia. Contbr. to num. lit., educl. jrnls. Mbrships: Past Pres., WA Sect., Fellowship of Writers; Australia Soc. of Authors. Address: 161 Lockhart St., Como, WA 6152, Australia.

BUDDEN, Laura Madeline, b. 19 Aug. 1894, Surbiton, Surrey, UK. Teacher; Writer. Educ: B.A., Univ. of London. Publs: Pictorial & Practical Geography Books, 1, 2, 3, 4, 1953. Contbr. to: Times Educl. Supplement; Geogl. Mag., etc. Mbrships. incl: F.R.G.S.; Life, Geogl. Soc., Sheffield; Hon. Sec. & Treas., Tchrs'. Benevolent & Orphan Fund; Nat. Union Tchrs., Surbiton & Kingston Dist., 1922-30. Address: 2 Carroll Ave., Merrow, Guildford, Surrey, UK.

BUECHNER, (Rev.) Frederick, b. 11 July 1926, NYC, USA. Minister; Writer. Educ: A.B., Princeton Univ., 1947; B.D., Union Theol. Sem., 1958. Publs: A Long Day's Dying, 1950; The Seasons' Difference, 1952; The Return of Ansel Gibbs, 1958; The Final Beast, 1965; The Magnificent Defeat, 1966; The Hungering Dark, 1969; The Alphabet of Grace, 1970; The Entrance to Porlock, 1970; Lion Country, 1971; Open Heart, 1972; Wishful Thinking: A Theological ABC, 1973; Love Feast, 1974; The Faces of Jesus, 1974. Mbrships: PEN; Century Assn. Hons. incl: O. Henry Prize, 1955; Richard & Hinda Rosenthal Award, 1958. Address: c/o Atheneum Publrs., 122 E. 42 St., N.Y., NY 10021, USA.

BUEHLER, Carl James, b. 2 Aug. 1937, Chgo., Ill., USA. Editor. Educ: Kalamazoo Coll., Mich., 1955-58; B.A., Western Mich. Univ., 1961; Grad. studies, ibid, 1961, & Univ. of Maine, 1968. Publs: Ed., Objectives for Instructional Programs, 1973; Ed., Models for Teaching, 4 vols., 1973. Mbrships. incl: Nat. Schl. PR Assn.; Assn. for Supervision & Curriculum Dev.; Am. Soc. for Trng. & Dev.; Am. Assn. Schl. Admnstrs. Address: 604 Woodridge Circle, Rt. 8, Gales Ferry, CT 06335, USA.

BUERO-VALLEJO, Antonio, b. 29 Sept. 1916, Guadalajara, Spain. Playwright. Educ: B.F.A. Publs: Story of a Stairway, 1949; In the Burning Darkness, 1950; Today's a Holiday, 1956; The Cards Face Down, 1957; A Dreamer For a People, 1958; The Ladies-in-Waiting, 1960; The Concert at Saint Ovide, 1962; The Basement Window, 1967; The Double Case History of Doctor Valmy, 1968; The Sleep of Reason, 1970; The Foundation, 1974. Contbr. to: Revista de Occidente; Primer Acto; Yorick. Mbrships. incl: Hispanic Soc. of Am.; Soc. Gen. de Autores de Espana. Hons. incl: El Espectador y La Critica Prize, 1967, 1970; Leopoldo Cano Prize, 1967-68, 1971-72. Address: Calle Hermanos Miralles 36, Madrid 1, Spain.

BUITENHUIS, Peter, b. 8 Dec. 1925, London, UK. Professor of English; Author. Educ: B.A., 1948, M.A., 1953, Oxford Univ., UK; Ph.D., Yale Univ., USA, 1955. Publs: Selected Poems of E. J. Pratt (ed.), 1968; 20th Century Interpretations of Henry James's "The Portrait of a Lady", 1968; High MacLennan, 1969; The Grasping Imagination: the American Writings of Henry James, 1970, paperback ed., 1974. Contbr. to: Harper's Mag.; N.Y. Times Book Reviews; Toronto Globe & Mail; Can. Forum. Hons. incl: Fellowship, Am. Coun. of Learned Socs., 1972-73. Address: Dept. of English, McGill University, Montreal, Can.

BULATOVIC, Miodrag, b. 1930, Okladi, Bijelo Polje (Montenegro). Publs: Devils are Coming; Roman-Poem: The Wolf & the Bell, 1958; The Red Cockerel, 1962; & transl. into sev. langs. Address: Ravanicka 28, Beograd, Yugoslavia.

BULL, Geoffrey Taylor, b. 24 June 1921, Eltham, London, UK. Former Missionary; Author; Bible Teacher. Publs: When Iron Gates Yield, 1955; God Holds the Key, 1959; Coral in the Sand, 1962; The Sky is Red, 1965; Tibetan Tales, 1966; A New Pilgrim's Progress, 1969; The City & the Sign, 1970; Love Song in Harvest, 1972; Tell-Tale Books, 1972; Prisoner from Beyond the River, 1974; Hide & Seek Books, 1974. Address: 57 Drumlin Dr., Milngavie, Glasgow G62 6NF, UK.

BULL, (Rev.) Norman John, b. 1916, Portsmouth, UK. Clerk in Holy Orders; College Lecturer. Educ: M.A., Oxford Univ.; Ph.D., Reading Univ. Publs. incl: A Book of School Worship, 1954; Religious Education in the Primary School, 1958; Children of the Bible, 1961; My Catechism Book,

1963; The Rise of the Church, 1967; Moral Judgement from Childhood to Adolescence, 1969; Moral Education, 1969; 100 Great Lives, 1972; Colours, 1973; num. series of relig. readers, 1957-. Contbr. to: Schlmaster; Child Educ.; Ch. of England Newspaper; Times Educl. Supplement. Mbr., Soc. of Authors. Address: 21 Wonford Rd., Exeter EX4 2LH, Devon, UK.

BULL, Peter Cecil, b. 1912, London, UK. Actor. Educ: Winchester Coll.; Tours Univ., France. Publs: To Sea In A Sieve; Bulls in the Meadows; I Know The Face But . . . ; Not On Your Telly; I Say Look Here; It isn't All Greek to Me; Bear With Me, 1969; Life is a Cucumber, 1973. Contbr. to: Punch; N.Y. Sunday Times; Harper's Bazaar; My Family & Other Animals (screenplay). Hons: D.S.C. Address: Zodiac, the Astrological Emporium, 3 Kensington Mall, London W8, UK.

BULL, Sverre Hagerup, b. 17 Aug. 1892, Oslo, Norway. Retired Bank Director. Educ: Law Degree, Oslo Univ., 1916; Postgrad. study, Sorbonne & Univ. of Montpellier, France. Publs: Music & Musicians, Vols. I-II, 1930-32; Chief Ed., original Norwegian Musikkens Verden, 1951, Danish ed., 1954; New Musikkens Verden, 1963. Contbr. to: Robin Hood (musical comedy libretto, w. Ludvig I Jensen), 1945; approx. 200 radio broadcasts on music. Mbrships. incl: Bd., Norwegian Composers Soc.; Norwegian Authors Assn.; Past Chmn., Theatre & Music Critics Soc.; Music Cons., Norwegian Broadcasting Corp., 1946-53. Address: Kringsjåveien 6, Jar 1342, Norway.

BULLEN, Keith Edward, b. 29 June 1906, Auckland, NZ. Emeritus Professor of Applied Mathematics, University of Sydney. Educ: B.Sc., M.A., Univ. of NZ; M.A., Univ. of Melbourne; Ph.D., Sc.D., Univ. of Cambridge. Publs: Theory of Seismology, 1947, 3rd ed., 1965; Theory of Dynamics, 1948; Theory of Mechanics, 1949, 8th ed., 1971; Seismology, 1954; The Earth's Density, forthcoming. Contbr. to num. sci. jrnls. & over 20 books on maths. & sci. Mbrships. incl: ERS; Am. Acad. of Arts & Scis.; U.S. Nat. Acad. of Scis. Recip., num. acad. awards inclng. D.Sc., Univ. of Auckland. Address: c/o Dept. of Applied Maths., Univ. of Sydney, N.S.W., Australia 2006.

BULLER, F. H. E., b. 1926, London, UK. Gunmaker. Publs: Rigs & Tackles, 1967; Pike, 1970, paperback 1973; Falkus & Buller's Freshwater Fishing, 1975. Contbr. to: Creel; Angling; Angling Times. Mbrships: Gun Trade Assn. (Chmn., 1967); Gunmakers' Co.; Salmon & Trout Assn.; Freshwater Biol. Assn. Address: Hollytree, Wood Lane, South Heath, Great Missenden, Bucks., UK.

BULLER, Herman, b. 30 Apr. 1923, Montreal, P.Q., Can. Writer. Educ: B.A., Sir Geo. Williams Univ., 1943; B.C.L., McGill Univ., 1946; B.Ed., Univ. of Toronto, 1970. Publs: One Man Alone, 1963; Quebec in Revolt, 1965; Days of Rage, 1974. Contbr. to: Canadian Outlook; Le Digeste Québécois. Mbr., Can. Authors Assn. Recip., Canadiana Award for One Man Alone, 1963. Address: 9 Kingsbridge Ct., Apt. 401, Willowdale, Ont., Can.

BULLINS, Ed, b. 1935, Phila., Pa., USA. Playwright; Author. Publs: Five Plays by Ed Bullins, 1968; New Plays from the Black Theatre (Ed., play), 1969; The Duplex (play), 1971; The Hungered One (stories), 1971; Four Dynamite Plays, 1972; The Theme is Blackness (play), 1973; The Reluctant Rapist (novel), 1973; The New Lafayette Theatre Presents (Ed., play), 1974. Mbrships: Dramatist Guild; PEN; Writers' Guild of Am. Agent: Audrey Wood. Address: 932 E. 212th St., Bronx, NY 10469, USA.

BULLOCK, (Rev. Canon) Frederick William Bagshawe, b. 1903, Hastings, UK, d. 28 Nov. 1974. Former Canon Emeritus; Author. Educ: Ph.D., D.D., Cambridge; B.D., Manchester, Publs. incl: The History of Ridley Hall, Cambridge, 2 vols.; A History of the Parish Church of St. Mary, Truro, Cornwall; A History of the Parish Church of St. Helen, Ore, Sussex; A History of Training for the Ministry of the Church of England, 2 vols.; Evangelical Conversion in Great Britain, 2 vols.; Voluntary Religious Societies, 1520-1799. Address: c/o D. Ashton Bullock, Le Feugeral House, 14 Feugeral Estate, La Moye, Jersey, Channel Isles, UK.

BULLOCK, Michael Hale, b. 19 Apr. 1918, London, UK. University Associate Professor; Poet; Author. Publs: (poetry) Transmutations, 1938; Sunday Is a Day of Incest, 1960; World Without Beginning, Amen, 1963, 2nd ed.,

1973; Zwei Stimmen in meinem Mund, 1967; A Savage Darkness, 1969; (prose fiction) Sixteen Stories as They Happened, 1969; Green Beginning Black Ending, 1971; Randolph Cranstone & the Pursuing River, 1975. Contbr. to: Encounter; London Mag.; Can. Fiction Mag.; etc. Mbrships: Engl. Ctr., Pen (Past Exec. Comm. mbr.); Soc. of Authors; Transls.' Assn. (Past Chmn.). Recip., Schlegel-Tieck German Transl. Prize, 1966. Address: 3836 W. 18th Ave., Vancouver, B.C. V6S 1B5, Can.

BULLOCK, Roger, b. 15 Jan. 1943, Birmingham, UK. Sociologist. Educ: B.A., Leicester Univ.; M.A., Essex Univ. Publs: A Manual to the Sociology of the School (co-author), 1970; A Chance of A Lifetime? (co-author), 1975; After.Grace — Teeth (co-author), 1975. Contbr. to: Knowledge, Education & Cultural Change (ed. R. K. Brown), 1973; Varieties of Residential Experience (ed. Clarke, Sinclair & Tizard), 1975; var. sociol. & educl. jrnls. Mbr., Brit. Sociol. Assn. Address: 6 Lansdowne Park, Totnes, Devon, UK.

BULLOCK, Wilfred Arthur Charles, b. 11 June 1915, Lewisham, London, UK. Schoolmaster; Inspector of Schools. Educ: B.Sc., King's Coll., London, 1936. Publs: The Man Who Discovered Penicillin, 1962. Mbrships: Nat. Assn. of Insps. & Educ. Offs.; Assn. for Sci. Educ. Address: 13 West Way, Shirley, Croydon CR0 8RQ, UK.

BULLOUGH, Donald Auberon, b. 1928, Stoke-on-Trent, Staffs., UK. University Professor of Medieval History; Director of Publishing Company; Writer. Educ: M.A., St. John's Coll., Oxford. Publs: The Age of Charlemagne, 1965, 2nd ed. 1974; The Dark Ages, 1965; Italy & Her Invaders, 1968; The Study of Medieval Records, 1971; Tenth-Century Studies, 1975. Contbr. to: Engl. Hist. Review; Hist.; Jrnl. Ecclesiastic Hist.; Medium Aevum; Le Moyen Age; Deutsches Archiv.; Proceedings of Congresses, Italy & UK, 1961-74; Times Lit. Supplement; Saltire Review, etc. Mbrships: F.S.A.; Fellow, Royal Histl. Soc.; F.S.A. Scotland; Savage Club; Scottish Arts Club. Address: 23 South St., St. Andrews, Fife, UK.

BULLOUGH, Geoffrey, b. 27 Jan. 1901, Prestwich, Lancs., UK. University Professor (retired). Educ: B.A., M.A., D.Litt., Manchester Univ. Publs: Poems of Henry More, 1931; Poems & Dramas of Fulke Greville (2 vols.), 1939; The Trend of Modern Poetry, 1934, 2nd ed.; 1949; The Oxford Book of 17th-Century Verse (w. Sir H. J. C. Grierson), 1934; Milton's Dramatic Poems (w. D. M. Bullough), 1961; Mirror of Minds, 1962; Narrative & Dramatic Sources of Shakespeare (8 vols.), 1957-75. Contbr. to: Mod. Lang. Review; Engl. Studied; etc. Hon. Mbr., MLA of Am. Recip., num. acad. awards. Address: 182 Mayfield Rd., Edinburgh, EH9 3AX, UK.

BULLOUGH, William Sydney, b. 1914, London, UK. Professor of Zoology. Educ: Ph.D., D.Sc., Univ. of Leeds. Publs: Practical Invertebrate Anatomy; Vertebrate Sexual Cycles; The Evolution of Differentiation; (co-author) Introducing Animals; Introducing Animals with Backbones; Introducing Man. Contbr. to var. sci. jrnls; TV; etc. Mbr., Sorby Fellow, Royal Soc. Address: New Cottage, Uplands Rd., Kenley, Surrey, UK.

BULMAN, Joan Carroll Boone, b. 23 Dec. 1904, London, UK. Translator. Educ: M.A., Newnham Coll., Cambridge; Munich Univ., Germany; Stockholm Univ., Sweden. Publs: Strindberg & Shakespeare, 1933; Jenny Lind, 1956; (transl.) Wennerström the Spy, by H. K. Rönblom, 1966; The Princess, by Gunnar Mattsson, 1966; Danish Prehistoric Monuments, by P. V. Glob, 1971; The Mound People, by P. V. Glob, 1974; etc. Contbr. to: Britannica Bk. of the Yr., 1963-68; Purnell's New Engl. Ency., 1968. Mbrships: Soc. of Authors; Transls.' Assn. (Exec. Comm., 1968-70). Address: 5 King St., Bishop's Stortford, Herts. CM23 2NB, UK.

BULMER, Henry Kenneth, pen names HARDY, Adam; FRAZIER, Arthur; CORLEY, Ernest; JOHNS, Kenneth, b. London, UK. Author. Publs: incl: City Under the Sea, 1957; White-Out, 1960; Beyond the Silver Sky, 1961; The Demons, 1965; To Outrun Doomsday, 1967; The Doomsday Men, 1968; Keys to the Dimension series, 1967-72; The Ulcer Culture, 1970; On the Symb-Socket Circuit, 1972; The Fox series, 1972–; Ed., New Writings in SF, 1973–. Mbrships: V.P., Sci. Fiction Fndn.; Sci. Fiction Writers Am.; Hon. Life, Brit. Sci. Fiction Assn. Ltd.; Brit. Fantasy Soc.; Airship Assn. Address: 19 Orchard Way, Horsmonden, Tonbridge, Kent TN12 8LA, UK.

BULMER-THOMAS, Ivor, b. 1905, Cwmbran, Mon., UK. Former Journalist & Member of Parliament. Educ: M.A.; St. John's & Magdalen Colls., Oxford. Publs: Coal in the New Era; Selections Illustrating the History of Greek Mathematics, 1939-42; The Growth of the British Party System, 1965. Contbr. to: News Chronicle (Chief Ldr. Writer, 1937-39); Daily Telegraph (Ldr. Writer & Acting Dpty. Ed., 1952-56); Ency. Britannica; Dict. of Sci. Biog. Mbrships: F.S.A.; Athenaeum, Vincent's (Oxford) Clubs. Address: 12 Edwardes Square, London W8 6HG, UK.

BUNG, Klaus, b. 1935, Berlin, Germany. Lecturer. Educ: London Univ.; Ph.D., Cambridge Univ. Publs: Programmed Learning & the Language Laboratory, 2 vols., 1967, 1968; Arbeiten zum Programmierten Sprachunterricht, 2 vols., 1970; Towards a Theory of Programmed Language Instruction, 1973; The Specification of Objectives in a Language Learning System for Adults, 1973; A Theoretical Model for Programmed Language Instruction, 1975; 3 typing courses for children from 4-6, 6-10 & 10-14 respectively, forthcoming. Contbr. to: num. profl. jrnls. Mbrships incl: Assn. for Programmed Learning & Educl. Technol., (Coun., 1966-); Soc. of Authors; Brit. Assn. of Applied Linguistics. Address: 13 Wisteria Rd., London SE13 5HW, UK.

BUNTING, Josiah III, b. 8 Nov. 1939, Phila., Pa., USA. College President. Educ: B.A., Va. Mil. Inst., Lexington, 1963; Univ. of Oxford, UK; Columbia Univ., N.Y., USA. Publs: The Lionheads, 1972; The Advent of Frederick Giles, 1974. Contbr. to: Atlantic; N.Y. Times; Village Voice; World-view. Mbrships. incl: Coun. on Relig. & Int. Affairs; Coun. on For. Rels.; Assn. of Am. Rhodes Schlrs.; Mark Twain Soc. Hons. incl: Rhodes Schlr., Univ. of Oxford, UK, 1966; Burgess Fellow, Columbia Univ., USA, 1970-73. Address: 320 Elm Rd., Briarcliff Manor, NY 10510, USA.

BUÑUEL, Miguel, b. 5 July 1925, Castellote, Spain. Editor. Educ: Tech. Agronomic Engr.; Lic., Jrnlism; Lic., Cinema. Publs: El niño, la golondrina y el gato, 1960; Un lugar para vivir, 1962; Un mundo para todos, 1962; Rocinante de la Mancha, 1963; Las tres de la madrugada, 1967. Contbr. to: Índice; Alcalá; La Hora. Mbrships: Soc. of Authors of Spain; Spanish Unionist Assn. of Cinema Dirs. & Prods.; Circle of Cinema Writers. Hons: Gerper Prize, Valladolid Atheneum, 1958; Lazarillo Prize, 1959; Andersen Int. Picture of Hon. Prize, 1962; Spanish Language Readers Digest Prize, 1962. Address: Calle Suero de Quiñones 10, 3°D, Madrid 2, Spain.

BURANELLI, Agnes Wallace, pen name GILLESPIE, Nan, b. 3 Jan. 1917, Motherwell, UK. Writer; Translator. Educ: M.A., Glasgow Univ., Scotland; Sorbonne Univ.; Univ. Munich. Publs: A Time for Learning, 1968; The Nile (w. Vincent Buranelli), forthcoming; (transl.) The Art & Thought of Michelangelo, 1964, by Charles de Tolnay. Contbr. to: NY Times; Rotarian; Retirement Living; Relax Mag.; Revu. Drama; etc. Mbrships: Writers Am.; Nat. Geogl. Soc.; Glasgow Grads. Soc.; Histl. Soc. Princeton; Princeton French Circle; English Speaking Union; Guild of Profl. Translators. Address: 282 Mt. Lucas Rd., Princeton, NJ 08540, USA.

BURANELLI, Vincent John, b. 16 Jan. 1919, NYC, USA. Freelance Writer; Editor. Educ: B.A., 1947, M.A., 1948, Nat. Univ. Ireland; Ph.D., Cambridge Univ., UK, 1951. Publs: The Trial of Peter Zenger, 1957; Edgar Allan Poe, 1961; The King & the Quaker; A Study of William Penn & James II, 1962; Josiah Royce, 1964; Louis XIV, 1966; The Nile (w. Nan Buranelli), forthcoming. Contbr. to: Jrnl. Hist. Ideas; Ethics; etc. Mbrships. incl: Authors' Guild; Dutch Treat Club; Princeton Histl. Soc. Hons: Kaltenborn Fellow Jrnlism., 1952-53; N.J. Tchrs. Award Best Biog., 1964 by N.J. Author for Josiah Royce. Address: 282 Mt. Lucas Rd., Princeton, NJ 08540, USA.

BURDEN, Jean P., pen name AMES, Felicia, b. 1 Sept. 1914, Waukegan, Ill., USA. Free-lance Writer; Editor; Lecturer. Educ: B.A., Univ. of Chgo. Publs: Naked As the Glass, 1963; Journey Toward Poetry, 1966; A Celebration of Cats, 1974; 4 manuals of pet care. Contbr. to: Poetry; Saturday Review; Salmagundi; Beloit Poetry Jrnl.; N.Y. Times; Critic; Choice; Atlantic Monthly; Prairie Schooner; Mademoiselle; Woman's Day; Better Homes & Gdns.; Family Weekly; Good Housekeeping; Parents; Am. Home; Yankee; Author & Jrnlst.; House Beautiful; etc. Recip., 1st Prize, Borestone Mtn. Poetry Awards, 1962. Address: 1129 Beverly Way, Altadena, CA 91001, USA.

BURÉN, Märtha, b. 19 May 1910, Umeå, Sweden. Author. Publs: Garrison in the North, 1948; Today & Tomorrow, 1950; Camilla, 1955; A Need to Love, 1959; Where is Sylvia?, 1963; Books translated in 9 countries. Mbr., Swedish Authors' Soc. Address: Slipgatan 14, 11739 Stockholm, Sweden.

BURG, David (pen name of DOLBERG, Alexander), b. 1933, Moscow, USSR. Freelance Writer & Translator. Educ: Grad., Moscow State Univ., 1956; Cambridge Univ., UK; Harvard Univ., USA. Publs: Opposition Trends among Soviet Youth after the Thaw, 1960; Unpersoned: The Fall of Nikita Khrushchev, 1966; Co-transl., Solzhenitsyn, Cancer Ward, & The Love Girld & the Innocent, 1969; Co-transl., Y. Daniel, Prison Poems, 1971; A. Solzhenitsyn: A Biography, 1972. Contbr. to: var. scholarly books & jrnls. on Russia; Sunday Times; Times; N.Y. Times; etc; travel writer. Mbrships: Inst. Linguists; Nat. Union Jrnlsts; Soc. Authors. Agent: Deborah Rogers Ltd. Address: 63 Drayton Gdns., London SW10, UK.

BURG, Marie, b. Prague, Czechoslovakia. Schoolmistress. Educ: Univs. of Prague, Lausanne & Grenoble. Publs. incl: Modern German Unseens; Modern French Unseens; A Modern German Reader; Ferien am Bodensee; Stratford-on-Avon; Three Famous Englishmen of the 17th Century; The Young Traveller in Czechoslovakia; (adaptations) Chaponniere, Le Trésor de Pierrefeu; Kaestner, Die Konferenz der Tiere; Kusenberg, Mal Was Andres; (transls.) H. Smahelova, Youth on the Wing; Tales from Czechoslovakia. Contbr. to: Guardian; Times Educl. Supplement; BBC; etc. Mbrships. incl: Soc. of Authors. Address: The Cottage, 29A Chestnut Walk, Worcester WR1 1PR, UK.

BURGER, Henry G., b. 27 June 1923, NYC, USA. Cultural Anthropologist; Writer. Educ: A.B., 1947, M.A., 1965, Ph.D., 1967, Columbia Univ. Publs: Telesis: Facilitating directed cultural change by strategically designing chain reactions, 1967; American Indians & Educational Laboratories (co-author), 1967; Ethno-pedagogy, 2 eds., 1968; Ethnics on Education, 1969; Ethnic Live-in, 1970; Ethno-Strategy, 1972. Contbr. to num. schlrly. jrnls. & gen. mags. inclng: Am. Anthropol.; Current Anthropol.; Gen. Systems; Human Org. Mbrships: Fellow, Coun. on Anthropol. & Educ.; Fellow, Am. Anthropol. Assn.; Fellow, Soc. for Applied Anthropol.; Fellow, AAAS; Life Fellow, Royal Anthropl. Inst.; num. other profl. & acad. orgs. Recip., sev. acad. awards & grants. Address: 7306 Brittany, Shawnee Mission, KS 66203, USA.

BURGESS, Anthony, pen names KELL, Joseph; WILSON, John Burgess, b. 25 Feb. 1917, Manchester, UK. Writer; Former Teacher, Lecturer & Education Officer. Educ: Xaverian Coll., Manchester; B.A., Univ. of Manchester. Publs. incl: The Enemy in the Blanket, 1958; The Right to an Answer, 1960; Devil of a State (Book Soc. Choice), 1961; A Clockwork Orange, 1960 (filmed 1971); Nothing Like the Sun, 1964; Shakespeare, 1970; Joysprick, 1973; (as Joseph Kell) One Hand Clapping, 1961; (as John Burgess Wilson) English Literature — A Survey for Students, 1958. Contbr. to: Observer; Listener; Times Lit. Supplement; etc. Hons: Vis. Fellow, Princeton Univ., 1970-71; Disting. Prof., City Coll., N.Y., 1972; 1973. Address: c/o Wm. Heinemann Ltd., 14 Queen St., London W1, UK.

BURGESS, Christopher Victor, b. 1921, Dublin, Repub. of Ireland. Writer. Educ: Wesley Coll., Dublin; Alsager Tchrs. Trng. Coll., Cheshire. Publs. incl: Short Plays for Large Classes; More Plays for Large Classes; The Burgess Books; Talking of the Taylors; Careers Plays for Boys; Verse in Action; The Burgess Plays; It's Your Money; Classroom Playhouse; By Sword & Spell; Burgess Composition; Teach Yourself Speech Training; Arthur; Scope. Contbr. to: Tchr.; Tchr.'s World; Educl. Dev. Address: 92 Pitts Lane, Woodley, Reading, Berks., UK.

BURGESS, Eric, b. 1920, Stockport, UK. Communications Consultant. Educ: Coll. of Tech., Manchester, UK; Univ. of Calif., L.A.; F.B.I.S.; A.F.A.I.A.A. Publs. incl: Rocket Propulsion; Frontier to Space; Introduction to Rockets & Spaceflight; Guided Weapons; Satellites & Spaceflight; Rocket Encyclopaedia (co-author); Long Range Ballistic Missiles; Assault on the Moon; (ed.) On-Line Computing Systems; Journey to the Planets; The Next Billion Years. Contbr. to: New Scientist; London Mag.; Christian Sci. Monitor, 1969-72. Mbrships: F.R.A.S.; Chmn., Brit. Interplanetary Soc.; Am. Rocket

Soc. Address: 10960 Beckford Ave., Northridge, Calif., USA.

BURGESS, Moira (Mrs. A. M. Stirling), b. 1936, Campbeltown, Argyll, UK. Librarian; Writer. Educ: M.A., Univ. of Strathclyde. Publs: The Exiled (play), 1959; The Day Before Tomorrow (novel), 1971; The Glasgow Novel (bibliog.), 1972. Contbr. to: Scottish Libs. review (Ed., 1966-72); Glasgow Herald; Scotsman; Argosy; Scottish Field; Times; Guardian. Mbr., Soc. of Authors. Address: 2 Liddesdale Ave., Foxbar, Paisley PA2 0UF, UK.

BURGETT, Donald Robert, b. 5 Apr. 1925, Detroit, Mich., USA. Home Modernization & Building Contractor. Publs: Currahee! , 1967; Seven Roads to Hell, forthcoming. Contbr. to: Reader's Digest; Outdoor Life; Hunting & Fishing. Mbrships. incl: Am. VFW. Recip., endorsement by Gen. Dwight Eisenhower for "Currahee!" Address: 4848 Vines Rd., Howell, MI 48843, USA.

BURGHARDT, Andrew Frank, b. 5 Apr. 1924, NYC, USA. Professor of Geography; Author. Educ: B.A., Harvard Univ., 1949; M.S., 1951, Ph.D., 1958, Univ. of Wis., Madison. Publs: The Political Geography of Burgenland, 1958; Borderland, 1962. Contbr. to: Annals of Assn. Am. Geogs.; Geogl. Review; Can. Geog.; Jrnl. of Geog. Review Ed., Can. Geog., 1965-73. Address: 10 Parkside Ave., Dundas, Ont. L9H 2S6, Can.

BURKE, David, b. 1927, Melbourne, Australia. Radio Scriptwriter; Journalist; Public Relations; Independent Representative & Freelance Writer since 1962. Publs: Railways of Australia (w. C. C. Singleton), 1963; Monday at McMurdo, 1967. Contbr. to: Melbourne Herald; Sun-Pictorial; Sydney Morning Herald; Sun Herald; Aust. Fin. Review; etc. Mbrships: Am. Nat. Club; Aust. Soc. Authors; Aust. Jrnlsts. Assn.; Railway Histl. Soc. Address: 66 Moruben Rd., Mosman, N.S.W., Australia.

BURKE, James, b. 16 Sept. 1917, Toronto, Can. Novelist. Publs: Flee Seven Ways, 1963, 3rd ed., 1965; The Firefly Hunt, 1969. Address: 1 Falcon Ln., W. Hill, Ont. M1C 1N7, Can.

BURKE, James, b. 22 Dec. 1936, Londonderry, N. Ireland. Television Journalist. Educ: M.A., Oxford. Publs: Tomorrow's World, Vol. I, 1970, Vol. II, 1971. Contbr. to Punch. Recip., Royal Television Society Silver Medal for 'Creative Workshop', 1972. Address: c/o BBC TV, London, UK.

BURKE, John Frederick, pen names BURKE, Jonathan; JONES, Joanna; ESMOND, Harriet; GEORGE, Jonathan; SANDS, Martin, b. 1922, Sussex, UK. Freelance Writer. Publs. incl: Swift Summer, 1949; Echo of Barbara, 1959; Deadly Downbeat, 1962; Suffolk, 1971; Expo 80, 1972; Illustrated History of England, 1974; The Crew, 1974; Darsham's Folly, 1974; Ed., Tales of Unease, & More Tales of Unease; Film Novelizations of Look Back in Anger, & The Angry Silence. Contbr. to: New Frontiers; New Worlds; Sci. Fantasy; etc. Mbrships: E. Anglian Writers (Coun.); Soc. of Authors; Crime Writers' Assn. Recip., Atlantic Award in Lit., Rockefeller Fndn. Agent: David Higham Assoc. Address: 8 North Parade, Southwold, Suffolk, UK.

BURKE, Kenneth Duva, b. 1897, Pitts., Pa., USA. Professor of English; Music Critic. Educ: Ohio State Univ.; Columbia Univ. Publs: The White Oxen & Other Stories; Counter-Statement; Towards a Better Life; Permanence & Change; Attitudes Towards History; Philosophy of Literary Form; A Grammar of Motives; A Rhetoric of Motives; Book of Moments, Poems 1915-54; Rhetoric of Religion. Contbr. to: Dial, Music Critic, 1927-39; Nation, Music Critic, 1934-36; Sewanee; Kenyon; Hudson; Daedalus; etc. Mbr., Centre for Adv. Study in the Behavioural Sci, (fellow, 1957-58). Address: Andover, N.J., USA.

BURKE, Ulick Peter, b. 16 Aug. 1937, Stanmore, Middlesex, UK. University Teacher. Educ: M.A., St. John's Coll., Oxford Univ.; St. Antony's Coll., Oxford Univ. Publs: The Renaissance Sense of the Past, 1969; Culture & Society in Renaissance Italy, 1972, 2nd ed. as: Tradition & Innovation in Renaissance Italy, 1974; Venice & Amsterdam, 1974. Contbr. to: Times Lit. Supplement; var. other jrnls. Address: 15 Lower Market St., Hove, Sussex BN3 1AT, UK.

BURKHART, James Austin, b. 7 July 1914, Renova, Pa., USA. Professor; Author; Lecturer. Educ: B.A. & M.A., Univ. of Tex. Publs. incl: American Government: The Clash of Issues (co-author), 1960, 4th ed., 1972; Systems Approach to the Teaching of American Government (co-author), 1972; The New Politics (co-author), 1972; Strategies for Political Participation (co-author), 1972, 2nd ed., 1974; Graphic Guide to American Government, 1974. Contbr. to jrnls. Mbr., profl. orgs. Recip., var grants. Address: P.O. Box 2084, Stephens Coll., Columbia, MO 65201, USA.

BÜRKI, Roland, b. 10 Apr. 1906, Detligen, Bern, Switz. Teacher; Author. Educ: Teachers' Training Coll.; Univs. of Munich & Berlin. Publs. incl: Kinder erleben die Welt, 1936; Kinder im Wirbel der Zeit, 1941; Aus meiner Bubenzeit, 1942; Kleine Freunde (new ed. of Kinder erleben die Welt), 1951; (novel) Durch die Kraft des Herzens, 1953; Das grosse Finden, Tagebuch, 1956; Christoph und Elfriede, 1968; Inselkameraden, 1970; Brigittes seltsames Abenteuer, 1974. Mbrships. incl: Swiss Writers Assn.; Bern Writers Assn.; Swiss Teachers Union; Swiss Parapsychol. Assn. Address: Weingartstr. 19, 3014 Bern, Switz.

BURLAND, Brian, b. 23 Apr. 1931, Paget, Bermuda. Novelist. Educ: Univ. of Western Ont., London, Can. Publs: St. Nicholas & the Tub (children's book), 1964, 2nd ed., 1975; A Fall from Aloft, 1968, 4th ed., 1971; A Few Flowers for St. George, 1969; Undertow, 1971; The Sailor & the Fox, 1973, 4th ed., 1975; Surprise, 3 eds., 1975; Stephen Decatur, The Devil & The Endymion, 1975; The Foundering of the Phoenix, forthcoming. Contbr. to: Vogue; Good Housekeeping; BBC Radio; N.Y. Educl. Radio; other US educl. TV & radio networks. Mbrships: Authors Guild Inc.; Authors League of Am. Address: c/o Georges Borchardt Inc., 145 E. 52nd St., New York, NY 10022, USA.

BURLAND, Cottie Arthur, b. 17 Sept. 1905, London, UK. Ethnographer; Writer. Publs. incl: The Gods of Mexico, 1967; The Arts of the Alchemists, 1967; North American Indian Mythology, 1968; Montezuma Lord of the Aztecs, 1973; Gods & Demons in Primitive Art, 1973. Contbr. to: The Studio; Imago Mundi; Ethnog; Arts Review. Mbrships. incl: Fellow, Royal Anthropol. Inst.; Folklore Soc.; Société des Américanistes. Address: 246 Molesey Ave., W. Molesey, E. Molesey, Surrey, KT5 0ET, UK.

BURLEY, William John, b. 1 Aug. 1914, Falmouth, Cornwall, UK. Writer. Educ: M.A., Balliol Coll., Oxford Univ. Publs:(UK & USA, & in transl. in Germany, Italy, Denmark & Holland) A Taste of Power, 1966; Three Toed Pussy, 1968; Death in Willow Pattern, 1969; To Kill a Cat, 1970; Guilt Edged, 1971; Death in a Salubrious Place, 1973; Death in Stanley Street, 1974; Wycliffe and the Pea-Green Boat, 1975. Mbr., Crime Writers' Assn. Address: St. Patrick's, Holywell, Newquay, Cornwall, UK.

BURLINGHAM, Dorothy Tiffany, b. 11 Oct. 1891, NYC, USA. Psychoanalyst. Educ: Columbia Univ., N.Y. Publs: Young Children in War Time: Infants without Families (w. A. Freud), 1943; Twins: A Study of Three Pairs of Identical Twins, 1952; Psycho-analytic Studies of the Seeing & the Blind, 1972. Contbr. to psychol. jrnls. Mbrships: Brit. Psychoanalytical Soc.; Assn. for Child Psychoanalysis; Trustee, Hampstead Child Therapy Course & Clin., London, UK; Organizer, Hampstead Nurseries. Address: 20 Maresfield Gdns., London NW3 5SX, UK.

BURMAN, Ben Lucien, b. 1896, Covington, Ky., USA. Journalist; Author. Educ: A.B., Harvard Coll. Publs. incl: Steamboat round the Bend; Everywhere I Roam; The Four Lives of Mundy Tolliver; It's a Big Country; Seven Stars for Catfish Bend; The Street of the Laughing Camel; The Owl Hoots Twice at Catfish Bend; The Generals Wear Cork Hats; Look Down That Winding River. Contbr. to: Reader's Digest; Saturday Review. Mbrships incl: Authors League of Am. (former Dir.); PEN (former Dir.); Overseas Press Club. Hons. incl. French Legion of Honour; Gold Medal for Lit., Dutch Treat Club. Address: c/o Taplinger Publishing Co., Zoo Park Ave. S., N.Y., NY 10003, USA.

BURMAN, Jose Lionel, b. 10 Apr. 1917, Jagersfontein, O.F.S., S. Africa. Solicitor. Educ: B.A., LL.B., Univ. of S. Africa. Publs. incl: Safe to the Sea, 1962; A Peak to Climb, 1966; Great Shipwrecks of the Coast of South Africa, 1967; Who Really Discovered South Africa, 1969; Disaster Struck South Africa, 1971; 1652 & So Forth, 1973; The Saldanhe Story, 1974. Contbr. to Ency. of Southern Africa, Dictionary of S. African Biography. Mbr., PEN Club. Address: 11 Abingdon Rd., Kenilworth, Cape, S. Africa.

BURMEISTER, Magdalene, b. 7 Mar. 1902, Barton Co., Kan., USA. Writer. Educ: MacMurray Coll., Jacksonville, Ill.; Univ. of Ariz., Tucson. Publs: At the Sign of the Zodiac, 1950; Against the Shifting Sands. Contbr. to: Kan. Mag.; Poetry of Today; Mid-W. Chaparral; Writer's Voice; Christian Sci. Monitor; Univ. of Kan. Quarterly; Univ. of Kan. City Review; etc. Mbrships: Kan. Authors Club; Mid-W. Fedn. of Chaparral Poets; Nat. League of Am. Pen Women. Address: 2515 Russell Parkway, Gt. Bend, KS 67530, USA.

BURN, Andrew Robert, b. 1902, Kynnersley, Salop., UK. Historian. Educ: M.A., Christ Church, Oxford. Publs: Minoans, Philistines & Greeks, 1930; The Romans in Britain, 1932; The World of Hesiod, 1936; This Scepter'd Isle, 1940; The Modern Greeks, 1942; Alexander the Great, 1947; Pericles & Athens, 1948; Agricola & Roman Britain, 1953; The Lyric Age of Greece, 1960; Persia & the Greeks, 1962; A Traveller's History of Greece, 1965, paperback ed. as Pelican History of Greece, 1966; The Warring States of Greece, 1968; Greece & Rome, 1970. Contbr. to var. encys., jrnls., etc. Recip., Silver Cross of the Phoenix, Greece. Address: Apple Tree Cottage, Middle Barton, OX5 4BH, UK.

BURN, Joshua Harold, b. 6 Mar. 1892, Barnard Castle, Co. Durham, UK. Researcher & Teacher in Pharmacology. Educ: B.A., M.A., Emmanuel Coll., Cambridge Univ.; M.B., M.D., Guy's Hosp., London. Publs. incl: Background of Therapeutics, 1952; Functions of Autonomic Transmitters, 1956; Drugs, Medicine & Man (transl'd. into 8 langs.), 1961; The Autonomic Nervous System, 1965. Contbr. to: Jrnl. of Physiol.; Brit. Jrnl. Pharmacol.; Brit. Med. Jrnl.; other med. jrnls. (about 232 papers). Mbrships. incl: F.R.S.; Deutsche Akad. der Naturforscher, Leopoldina. Hons. incl: Gairdner Int. Award, Toronto, 1959; Schmeideberg Plakette, German Pharmacol. Soc., 1967; Hon. Degrees, Yale, Mainz, Paris, Bradford. Address: 3 Squitchey Lane, Oxford, UK.

BURNET, (Sir) (Frank) Macfarlane, b. 3 Sept. 1899, Traralgon, Vic., Australia. Medical Scientist; Emeritus Professor of Experimental Medicine. Educ: M.D., Ph.D., Univ. of Melbourne. Publs: Viruses & Man, 1955; Natural History of Infectious Diseases, 1962, 4th ed., 1972; Integrity of the Body, 1962; Biology & the Appreciation of Life, 1968; Changing Patterns: An Atypical Autobiography, 1968; Dominant Mammal, 1970; Genes, Dreams & Realities, 1971; Intrinsic Mutagenesis, 1974. Mbrships: F.R.S.; Pres., Aust. Acad. of Sci., 1965-69. Hons: O.M.; K.B.E. Address: Ormond Coll., Parkville, Vic., Australia 3052.

BURNETT, David Cecil Charles, b. 21 Sept. 1940, Melita, Man., Can. Publisher; Author. Educ: Jrnlsm.; Major, Maths. Contbr. to: The Deaf Can. Mag. Mbrships: Can. Assn. of the Deaf (Dir.); Western Can. Assn. of the Deaf (Pres.); Alta. Assn. of the Deaf (Pres. & Exec. Dir.); Calgary Assn. of the Deaf (Pres.); Alta. Coun. for the Hearing Handicapped (VP). Address: 1507-609-8th St. S.W., Calgary, Alta., T2P 2J3, Can.

BURNETT, Wanda M., b. Salt Lake City, Utah, USA. Writer; Editor. Educ: Univ. of Ill., Chgo.; Columbia Univ., N.Y. Publs: Guide to Medical Writing; Ed., med. books inclng. Initiation of Labor; Sudden Death in Infants; Neonatal Respiratory Adaptation; Communicating by Language — The Reading Process; Horizons in Perinatal Research. Contbr. to: Best Short Stories of Am.; Story Mag.; Story Anthol.; Parents' Mag.; Parents' Ency.; Tomorrow; Sci. Digest; Mag. Digest; Time; Newsweek; Your Life; Household; Nat. Geog. Mag.; etc. Mbr., Am. Med. Writers' Assn., Bd. of Dirs., 1967-69. Address: 5800 Anniston Rd., Bethesda, MD 20037, USA.

BURNIAUX, Constant, b. 1 Aug. 1892, Brussels, Belgium. Author. Educ: Tchrs. Trng. Coll., Brussels; Univ. course in Romance Langs. Publs. incl: (novels) La Bétise, 1925; Crânes tondus, 1930; Les Temps Inquiets, 5 vols., 1944-52; La Fille du Ciel, 1963; L'Odeur du Matin, 1967; (Stories) d'Humour & d'Amour, 1968; Kalloo, le Village Imaginé, 1972; (verse) Poésies (1922-63), 1965; 3 books for children. Contbr. to lit. jrnls. Mbrships. incl: Royal Acad. of French Lang. & Lit.; French PEN, Belgium (VP). Hons. incl: Prix L. Malpertuis, Belgian Acad., 1944; Grand. Lit. Prize, Belgian Govt., 1949; num. decorations. Address: 61 Ave. Commandant Lothaire, 1040 Brussels, Belgium.

BURNIAUX, Jeanne, pen name TAILLIEU, Jeanne, b. 21 Dec. 1898, Brussels, Belgium. Honorary Director of the

Bischoffsheim Technical Institute, Brussels; Author. Educ: B.Sc.(Educ.), Free Univ. of Brussels. Publs: La Vie Profonde de l'Enfance, 1944; Comprenons nos Enfants, Vol. I, L'Enfant de la Naissance à 6 Ans, Vol. II, L'Enfant de 6 à 12 Ans, 1961; L'Education des Filles, 1965; Crises, Chimères & Révoltes de l'Adolescence, 1967; La Réussite Scolaire, 1968; Sev. books for children. Contbr. to: L'Enfant; sev. jrnls. of psychol. & educ. Mbrships: V.P., Tchrs. Assqu.; Belgian PEN; Assn. of Belgian Writers. Hons: Off., Order of Leopols II; Kt., Order of Leopold. Address: 61 Avenue Commandant Lothaire, 1040 Brussels, Belgium.

BURNS, Alan, b. 1929, London, UK. Barrister-at-Law. Educ: Middle Temple, London. Publs: Buster, 1961; Europe After the Rain, 1965; Celebrations, 1967; Babel, 1969; (playscript) Palach. Contbr. to: Tribune; Running Man; New Worlds; Vogue; Kenyon Review; Surrealist Transformation. Mbr., I.C.A. Address: 26 Ladbroke Gardens, London W11, UK.

BURNS, Alan Cuthbert, b. 9 Nov. 1887, St. Kitts, W. Indies. Former Colonial Civil Servant. Publs: History of Nigeria, 1929-73; Colonial Civil Servant, 1949; History of British West Indies, 1954; In Defence of Colonies, 1957. Contbr. to: Times Lit. Supplement. Mbr., Athenaeum Club. Address: Flat 6, 16 Pall Mall, London SW1, UK.

BURNS, Arthur Edward, b. 3 Sept. 1908, Oakland, Calif., USA. University Professor; Administrator; Consultant; Writer. Educ: A.B., 1931, M.A., 1933, Univ. of Calif.; Ph.D., George Wash. Univ., 1935. Publs: Government Spending & Economic Expansion (co-author), 1940; Modern Economics (co-author), 1948, revised 1953; Sev. Monographs. Contbr. to: Am. Econ. Review; Revista Brasileira de Econ.; Univ. of Chgo. Jrnl. of Law & Econs.; Bell Jrnl. of Econs. & Mgmt. Sci., etc. Mbrships: Am. Econ. Assn.; Fellow, AAAS. Address: 4000 Massachusetts Ave. N.W., Wash., DC 20016, USA.

BURNS, Arthur F., b. 27 Apr. 1904, Stanislau, Austria. Economist. Educ: A.B., A.M., 1925, Ph.D., 1934, Columbia Univ., USA. Publs: incl: Production Trends in the United States since 1870, 1934; Economic Research & the Keynesian Thinking of our Times, 1946; Measuring Business Cycles (w. C. Mitchell), 1946; Frontiers of Economic Knowledge, 1954; The Management of Prosperity, 1966; Full Employment, Guideposts, & Economic Stability (w. P.A. Samuelson), 1967; The Defense Sector & the American Economy (co-author), 1968; The Business Cycle in a Changing World, 1969. Mbr., num. profl., acad. & bus. orgs. Recip., num. acad. hons. Address: Watergate East, 2510 Virginia Ave. N.W., Wash. DC 20037, USA.

BURNS, Eedson Louis Millard, b. 17 May 1897, Montreal, Can. Army Officer (ret'd); Foreign Service Officer (ret'd.); Author. Educ: Royal Mil. Coll.; Staff Coll., Quetta, India; Imperial Defence Coll., London, UK, 1939. Publs: Manpower in the Canadian Army, 1939-45, 1955; Between Arab & Israeli, 1962; Megamurder, 1966; General Mud, 1970; A Seat at the Table, 1972. Address: R.R.1, P.O. Box 132, Manotick, Ontario K0A 2NO, Can.

BURNS, Richard Dean, b. 16 June 1929, Des Moines, Iowa, USA. Professor of History. Educ: B.S., 1957, M.A., 1958, Ph.D., 1960, Univ. of Ill. Publs: Armament & Disarmament: A Continuing Dispute (co-ed.), 1964; Disarmament in Historical Prospective, 1919-1941 (co-author), 4 vols., 1969; Diplomats in Crisis: US-Chinese—Japanese Relations, 1919-1941 (co-ed.), 1974; The Vietnam Conflict — A Comprehensive Bibliography (co-compiler), 1973; Series Ed., War/Peace Bibliography Series, 1973—. Contbr. to US & for. jrnls.; Ed. Bd., Peace & Change: A Jrnl. of Peace Rsch. Hons: Larson Merit Schlrship. for M.A. thesis, 1958. Address: Dept. of Hist., Calif. State Univ., L.A., CA 90032, USA.

BURNS, Robert Whitehall, b. 20 Jan. 1904, Merchantville, N.J., USA. Clergyman; Pastoral Counselor. Educ: B.A., Wash. Univ., St. Louis, 1928; B.D., Eden Theol. Sem., 1930; D.D., Oglethorpe Univ., 1936. Publs: The Christian Life, 1930; The Art of Staying Happily Married, 1963. Contbr. to Ch. jrnls. Address: 1730 Barnesdale Way NE, Atlanta, GA 30309, USA.

BURNS, Vincent Godfrey, pen names BURNS, Bobby; POET OF THE AIR; RADIO, b. 17 Oct. 1893. Author; Poet; Lecturer. Educ: B.S., Pa. State Univ., 1916; A.M., Harvard, 1917; B.D., Union Theol. Sem., 1922. Publs: America I Love You!; I am a Fugitive from a Chain Gang;

Female Convict and 25 others. Contbr. to Christian Herald; Am. Opinion; Ideals. Mbrships. incl: Pres., Composers Authors & Artists Am.; Mil. Order of the WWs. Hons: Top Award, Freedoms Fndn.; Poet Laureate of Md., 1962; Poet Laureate Am., 4 times. Address: 304 Epping Way, Annapolis, MD 21401, USA.

BURNSHAW, Stanley (Alfred), b. 20 June 1906, NYC, USA. Writer. Educ: B.A., Univ. of Pittsburgh, 1925; M.A., Cornell Univ., 1933. Publs: André Spire & His Poetry, 1933; The Iron Land, 1936; The Sunless Sea, 1948; Early & Late Testament, 1952; The Poem Itself, 1960; Caged in an Animal's Mind, 1963; Modern Hebrew Poem Itself, 1965; The Seamless Web, 1970; In the Terrified Radiance, 1972. Contbr. to: The Sewanee Review; The N.Y. Times Book Review; The Saturday Review; Poetry; etc. Mbr., PEN (Am. Ctr.); Authors' League (N.Y.). Recip., Nat. Inst. of Arts & Letters Award (USA) for Creative Work in Lit., 1971. Address: Martha's Vineyard, MA, USA.

BURROUGHS, William Seward, b. 5 Feb. 1914, St. Louis, Mo., USA. Novelist. Educ: B.A., Harvard Univ. Publs: Junkie, 1953; Naked Lunch, 1959; The Soft Machine, 1961; The Ticket that Exploded, 1962; Dead Fingers Talk, 1963; Nova Express, 1964; The Wild Boys, 1971; Exterminator! , 1973; The Last Words of Dutch Schultz, 1975. Contbr. to: Harper's; Esquire; Atlantic; Playboy. Address: P.O. Box 842, Canal St. Station, N.Y., NY, USA.

BURROW, John Anthony, b. 1932, Loughton, Essex, UK. University Tutor in English Literature. Educ: M.A., Christ Ch., Oxford Univ. Publs: A Reading of Sir Gawain & the Green Knight, 1965, Am. ed., 1966; Ed., Geoffrey Chaucer, 1969; Ricardian Poetry, 1971; Ed., Sir Gawain & the Green Knight, 1972. Contbr. to: Isis; Paris Review; Essays in Criticism; Theatre Notebook; Review of Engl. Studies; Mod. Philol.; Notes & Queries; Medium Aevum; Chaucer Review; Neophilologus; Anglia; etc. Address: Jesus College, Oxford, UK.

BURROWAY, Janet Gay, b. 21 Sept. 1936, Tucson, Ariz., USA. Writer; Teacher. Educ: A.B., Barnard Coll., Columbia Univ., 1958; A.B., 1960, M.A., 1965, Cambridge Univ., UK; Yale Schl. of Drama, 1960-61. Publs: Descend Again (novel), 1960; But To The Season (poetry), 1961; The Dancer From The Dance (novel), 1965, 2nd ed., 1967; Eyes (novel), 1966, 2nd ed., 1966; The Buzzards (novel), 1969, 2nd ed., 1970; The Truck on the Track (for children), 1970, 3rd ed., 1972; The Giant Jam Sandwich (for children), 1972, 2nd ed., 1973. Contbr. to var. lit. jrnls. Recip., sev. awards, fellowships & schlrships. Address: 1514 Mabry St., Tallahassee, FL 32304, USA.

BURROWES, Mike, b. 1937, Guyana, S. Am. Author. Publs: North of Paola, 1965; Chinook, 1965; Action at Las Animas, 1966; Blood Trail, 1966; Deadly Justice, 1967; Requiem for a Gunfighter, 1967; Wolf-Creek Pass, 1968; Echoes of Shiloh, 1968; Hell in San Pedro, 1971. Address: Flat 1, 29 Norton Road, Hove BN3 2BF, Sussex, UK.

BURROWS, Leonard Ranson b. 1921, Sheffield, UK. Associate Professor of English; Writer. Educ: M.A., Univ. of Sheffield. Publs: Browning, An Introductory Essay, 1952; Charitable Malice, 1956; Browning the Poet, 1969. William Noble Fellow, Univ. of Liverpool. Address: 72 Bay View Terrace, Claremont, W.A., Australia 6010.

BURROWS, Miles James Edwin, b. 18 Feb. 1936, Leicester, UK. Lecturer, Cambridgeshire College of Arts & Technology; General Practitioner in Medicine. Educ: Charterhouse Schl.; Wadham Coll., Oxford; Univ. Coll. Hosp. Med. Schl.; M.A.; B.M.; B.Ch.; DPM. Author, A Vulture's Egg, 1966. Contbr. to: New Statesman (Reviewer); Poems printed in Listener, Times Literary Supplement, Ambit, Transatlantic Review; BBC Broadcast 'Poetry Now'. Address: 79 Broadway, Grantchester, Cambs., UK.

BURROWS, Millar, b. 26 Oct. 1889, Wyo., Ohio, USA. Clergyman; Educator; Author. Educ: B.A., Cornell Univ., 1912; B.D., Union Theol. Sem., N.Y., 1915; Ph.D., Yale Univ., 1925. Publs: Founders of Great Religions, 1931; What Mean These Stones?, 1941; Outline of Biblical Theology, 1946; The Dead Sea Scrolls, 1955; More Light on the Dead Sea Scrolls, 1958; Diligently Compared, 1964. Contbr. to Jrnl. of Biblical Lit., & other profl. jrnls. Mbrships: Soc. of Biblical Lit., Pres., 1954; Am. Acad. of Relig.; Am. Oriental Soc.; Fellow (Emeritus), Am. Acad.

Arts & Scis. Address: 1670 Woodland Ave., Winter Park, FL 32789, USA.

BURT, Olive Woolley, b. 26 May 1894, Ann Arbor, Mich., USA. Writer; Journalist. Educ: A.B., Univ. of Utah, 1918; Grad. studies, ibid & Columbia Univ. Publs. incl: Luther Burbank, Boy Wizard, 1948; Brigham Young, 1956; The Ringling Brothers, 1958; I Challenge the Dark Sea, 1960; First Book of Copper, 1966; Negroes in the Early West, 1968; Physician to the World, 1973; Black Women of Valor, 1974; The Horse in America, 1975. Contbr. to: Poetry Digest; etc. Mbrships. incl: Nat. Letters Chmn., Nat. League of Am. Pen Women; Fndr. & Pres., League of Utah Writers. Hons. incl: Edgar, Mystery Writers of Am., 1959; Nat. Woman of Achievement, Nat. Fedn. of Press Women, 1964. Address: 777 East South Temple 12D, Salt Lake City, UT 84102, USA.

BURTIS, Charles Edward, pen name BINTER, C. Edward, b. 18 June 1907, NYC, USA. Writer. Educ: Schl. of Life Scis. Publs: The Real American Tragedy, 1960; The Fountain of Youth, 1964; Nature's Miracle Medicine Chest, 1971. Contbr. to: Answer. Address: 1410 White Oak Circle, Ojai, CA 93023, USA.

BURTON, Annie Grace Oakes, pen name BURTON, Grace Oakes, b. 28 June 1902, Whitmell, Va., USA. Teacher, Retired. Educ: Longwood Coll.; Univ. of Va.; B.S., M.A.; Corres. courses, Univ. of N.C. Publs: Songs of My Heart, 1950; Sonnets & Songs of My Heart, 1956; Windows of Heaven, 1966 (all poetry). Contbr. to profl. jrnls. & poetry anthols. Mbrships: Poetry Soc. of Va.; Asst. Ed., The Colonade, lit. jrnl., Longwood Coll., 1950. Hons. incl: Winner, poetry contest, Longwood Coll., 1950; Blue Ribbon for State of Va., lit. contest, Va. Fedn. of Women's Clubs, 1961, 1966; Num. other awards for both serious & light verse. Address: 1648 Franklin Tpke., Danville, VA 24541, USA.

BURTON, (Rev.) Brian Keith, b. 1931, Parramatta, NSW, Australia. Ordained Presbyterian Minister; Parish Minister, Chatswood, 1972–. Educ: B.A., Univ. of Sydney; St. Andrew's Theological Coll. Publs: Teach Them No More, 1967; Flow Gently Past, 1973. Mbr., Aust. Soc. of Authors. Address: The Manse, 37 Anderson St., Chatswood, NSW 2067, Australia.

BURTON, Ernest James, b. 13 Oct. 1908, Crayford, Kent, UK. Educationist; Priest. Educ: B.A., 1928, M.A., 1930, Univ. Coll., London. Publs. incl: Teaching English Through Self Expression, 1949, 8th ed., 1967; Drama in Schools, 1954, revised ed., forthcoming; The British Theatre: Its Repertory & Practice, 1960; Students Guide to World Theatre, 1962, 1964; Students Guide to British Theatre, 1963; Communication of Religious Experience, 1968; A Faith of Your Own, 1969; poems publd. pvtely. Contbr. to var. profl. & theol. publs. Mbrships: F.R.S.A.; Sec., Soc. of Tchrs. of Speech & Drama, 1967-74; Coun., Engl. Speaking Bd.; Coun., Nat. Coun. of Theatre for Young People. Address: Roseries, Monks Horton, Sellindge, Ashford, Kent TN25 6EA, UK.

BURTON, Harry McGuire (Philip), b. 1898, London, UK. Former Assistant Director of Education, Wiltshire & Norfolk County Councils. Educ: M.A., Fitzwilliam Hall, Cambridge. Publs: The Education of the Countryman, 1943; There Was a Young Man, 1958; Shakespeare, 1958; Stamps & Stamp Collecting, 1959; Dickens, 1970; various educational works. Contbr. to: BBC; var. educl. jrnls. Mbr., Soc. of Authors. Address: 47 Maid's Causeway, Cambridge, UK.

BURTON, Ivor Flower, b. 2 Mar. 1923, Derby, UK. University Teacher. Educ; B.A., Queen's Univ., Belfast; Ph.D., Univ. of London, 1961. Publs: The Captain General — The Career of John Churchill, Duke of Marlborough, 1702-11, 1969. Contbr. to: Engl. Histl. Review; Parliamentary Affairs; Histl. Jrnl.; Bulleting of the Inst. of Histl. Rsch. Address: Bedford Coll., Regent's Park, London NW1 4NS, UK.

BURTON, John, b. Bath, UK. Ombudsman, World Health Organization. Educ: M.A., Trinity Coll., Cambridge. Contbr. to: Hlth. Educ. Jrnl. (Ed., 1951-58); WHO Dialogue OMS (Ed., 1971-74); var. med. & hlth. jrnls.; var. med. books. Mbrships: M.R.C.S.; L.R.C.P.; D.P.H. Address: WHO, Avenue Appia, Geneva, Switzerland.

BURTON, Maurice, b. 1898, London, UK. Author; Editor; Wild Life Observer. Educ: D.Sc., King's Coll.,

London Univ. Publs. incl: Purnell's Encyclopaedia of Animal Life (w. Robert Burton); Natural History; Story of Animal Life; Animal Courtship; Infancy in Animals; Phoenix Re-born; Living Fossils; Margins of the Sea; Animal Legends; More Animal Legends; Curiosities of Animal Life; Animals & Their Behaviour; Animal Families; Animal Senses; Systematic Dictionary of Mammals; Sixth Sense of Animals. Mbrships: F.R.S.A.; Fellow, Zool. Soc. Address: Weston House, Albury, Guildford, Surrey, UK.

BURTON, Robert Wellesley, b. 1941, Sherborne, Dorset, UK. Zoologist. Educ: M.A., Downing Coll., Cambridge Univ. Publs: Gen. Ed., Purnell's Encyclopedia of Animal Life; Animal Senses, 1970; Animals of the Antarctic, 1970; The Life & Death of Whales, 1973. Contbr. to: Animals; Sea Frontiers. Fellow, Zool. Soc. Agent: Murray Pollinger. Address: Kirrin Lodge, Eredine, Dalmally, Argyll, UK.

BURTSCHI, Mary Pauline, b. 22 Feb. 1911, Vandalia, Ill., USA. Writer; Lecturer; Historian. Educ: B.A., St. Louis Univ., Mo.; M.A., Univ. of Ill., Urbana. Publs. incl: Vandalia, Wilderness Capital of Lincoln's Land, 1963, reprinted, 1972. Contbr. to: Outdoor; DAR Nat. Mag.; Outdoor Ill.; Hobbies; Jrnl. of the Ill. State Histl. Soc. Mbrships. incl: Pres., 1962-65, Rsch. Histn., 1966–, VP, 1972–, Vandalia Histl. Soc.; Dir., 1965-68, VP, 1968–, Ill. State Histl. Soc. Hons. incl: Book Award, Ill. State Histl. Soc., 1965; Bronze Medallion (for A Port Folio for James Hall), Ill. Sesquicentennial Commn., 1968. Address: 307 N. 6th St., Vandalia, IL 62471, USA.

BURTT, Edwin Arthur, b. 11 Oct. 1892, Groton, Mass., USA. Teacher. Educ: B.A., Yale Univ., 1915; B.D., 1920, S.T.M., 1922, Union Theol. Sem.; Ph.D., Columbia Univ., 1925; L.H.D., Univ. of Chgo., 1951. Publs: Metaphysical Foundations of Modern Physical Science, 1925; The English Philosophers from Bacon to Hill, 1939; The Teachings of the Compassionate Buddha (ed.), 1955; Man Seeks the Divine, 1957; In Search of Philosophic Understanding, 1966. Contbr. to: Mind; The Jrnl. of Philos.; The Philos. Review; Philos. E. & W. Address: 277 Willard Way, Ithaca, NY 14850, USA.

BURTT, Everett Johnson, Jr., b. 6 Aug. 1914, Jackson, Mich., USA. University Professor; Writer. Educ: A.B., Berea Coll., Ky., 1935; M.A., 1937, Ph.D., 1950, Duke Univ., N.C. Publs: Labor Markets, Unions & Government Policies, 1963; Plant Relocation & the Core City Worker, 1967; Social Perspectives in the History of Economic Theory, 1972. Contbr. to: Monthly Labor Review; Rivista int. di sci. econ. & commeriali; Boston Univ. Jrnl., etc. Mbrships: Am. Econ. Assn.; Indl. Rels. Rsch. Assn.; Hist. of Econs. Soc.; AAUP. Recip., Shell Award, Boston Univ. Fac. Publs. Merit Award Comm., 1974. Address: 399 Clapboardtree St., Westwood, MA 02090, USA.

BURY, John Patrick Tuer, b. 30 July 1908, Trumpington, Cambridge, UK. Historian; Editor; Author. Educ: M.A., Litt.D., Corpus Christi Coll., Cambridge. Publs: Gambetta & the National Defence, 1936; France 1814-1940, 1949; The College of Corpus Christi B.V.M. 1822-1952, 1952; Ed., New Cambridge Modern History, Vol. X, 1960; Napoleon III & the Second Empire 1964; Ed., Romilly's Cambridge Diary 1832-42, 1967; France: The Insecure Peace, 1972; Gambetta & the Making of the Third Republic, 1973. Contbr. to: Theol.; Revue Historique; Annales A Normandie; French Histl. Studies; Histl. Jrnl.; Engl. Histl. Review. Fellow, Royal Histl. Soc. Address: 71 Grange Rd., Cambridge, UK.

BUSCH, Briton Cooper, b. 5 Sept. 1936, L.A., Calif., USA. Professor of History; Author. Educ: A.B., Stanford Univ.; M.A., Ph.D., Univ. of Calif., Berkeley. Publs: Britain & The Persian Gulf, 1894-1914, 1967; Britain, India & The Arabs, 1914-1921, 1971. Contbr. to: Am. Histl. Review; Middle E. Jrnl.; The Histn.; etc. Address: Dept. of History, Colgate University, Hamilton, NY 13346, USA.

BUSCH, Harald, b. 5 Aug. 1904, Godesberg, Germany. Author; Art Historian; Photographer. Educ: Ph.D., Marburg Univ., 1930. Publs: Inselsommer, 1939; Alt-Hamburg I, 1939; Meister des Nordens, 1941; U-Boot auf Feindfahrt, 1942; Jagd im Atlantik, 1943; So war der U-Boot-Krieg, 1952; Alt-Hamburg II, 1956; Germania Romanica, 1963; Deutsche Gotik, 1967; Das Chilehaus in Hamburg, 1974. Contbr. to about 50 works on Art. Mbr., A.H.V., Fridericiana-Marburg. Address: 623 Frankurt a/Main 80 (-Griesheim), Taläckerstr. 1, W. Germany.

BUSH, Eric Wheler, b. 12 Aug. 1899, Simla, India. Officer, Royal Navy. Educ: Royal Naval Colls., Osborne & Dartmouth. Publs: How to Become a Naval Officer (Special Entry), 1926; Bless Our Ship, 1958; The Flowers of the Sea, 1962; How to Become a Naval Officer (Dartmouth Entry), 1963; Salute the Soldier, 1966; Gallipoli, 1975. Mbr., United Services Club. Hons: D.S.C., 1915; D.S.O. & 2 Bars, 1940, 1942, 1944. Address: Hunters, Langton Green, Kent, UK.

BUSH, John Nash Douglas, b. 21 Mar. 1896, Morrisburg, Ont., Can. University Professor of English Literature. Educ: B.A., 1920, M.A., 1921, Univ. of Toronto; Ph.D., Harvard Univ., USA, 1923. Publs. incl: Mythology & the Renaissance Tradition in English Poetry, 1932, 2nd ed., 1963; English Literature in the Earlier 17th Century, 1945, 2nd ed., 1962; Ed., Keats: Selections, 1959; Ed., Milton: Complete Poetical Works, 1965; John Keats, 1966; Variorum Commentary on the Poetry of Milton, vol. I: Latin & Greek Poems (Ed.), 1970, vol. II: Minor English Poems (Co-Ed.), 1972; Jane Austen, 1975. Mbrships: Am. Philos. Soc.; Corres. Fellow, Brit. Acad. Recip., 11 hon. degrees. Address: 3 Clement Circle, Cambridge, MA 02138, USA.

BUSHNELL, Geoffrey Hext Sutherland, b. 1903, Hayling Island, Hants., UK. Archaeologist. Educ: M.A., Ph.D., Cambridge Univ. Publs: Archaeology of the Santa Elena Peninsula in South West Ecuador; Peru, Ancient Peoples & Places; Ancient American Pottery (w. A. Digby); Ancient Arts of the Americas; The First Americans. Contbr. to: Antiquity; Man; Nature; etc. Mbrships: F.B.A.; V.P., Soc. of Antiquaries of London, 1961-65. Address: 4 Wordsworth Grove, Cambridge, UK.

BUTCHER, H. John, b. 6 Sept., 1920, Southampton, UK. University Professor. Educ: B.A., St. John's Coll., Cambridge; Ph.D., Manchester. Publs: Human Intelligence, 1968; The Prediction of Achievement & Creativity (w. R. B. Cattell), 1968; Contemporary Problems in Higher Education (w. E. Rudd), 1972. Contbr. to: Brit. Jrnl. of Psychol.; Brit. Jrnl. of Educl. Psychol., etc. Fellow, Brit. Psychol. Soc. Address: Schl. of Cultural & Community Studies, Univ. of Sussex, Falmer, Brighton, Sussex BN1 9QN, UK.

BUTLER, Bill, pen names HASSAN i SABBAH; DEAST, Basil, b. 3 Nov. 1934, Spokane, Wash., USA. Poet; Author; Publisher. Publs: In Progress; Alder Gulch & Other Poems, 1961; Byrne's Atlas, 1969; Leaves of Grass, 1971; The Definitive Tarot, 1975. Contbr. to: The Guardian; The Scotsman; Friends; International Times; Time Out; Attila. Recip., Young Writers' Grant, Nat. Fndn. for the Arts, USA. Address: Nant Gwilw, Llanfynydd, Carmarthenshire, Wales, UK.

BUTLER, David Edgeworth, b. 17 Nov. 1924, London, UK. Fellow, in Political Studies. Educ: M.A., D.Phil., Oxford Univ. Publs: The Electoral System in Britain since 1918, 2nd ed. 1963; Political Change in Britain, 2nd ed. 1975; The Canberra Model; British Political Fact 1900-1975, 1975; works on each gen. election, 1951-. Address: Nuffield College, Oxford, UK.

BUTLER, Guy, b. 21 Jan. 1918, Cradock, S. Africa. Professor of English. Educ: M.A., Rhodes Univ.; M.A., Brasenose Coll., Oxford Univ., UK; D.Litt., Natal Univ. Publs: The Dam (play), 1953; The Dove Returns (play), 1956; Ed., A Book of South African Verse, 1959; Stranger to Europe (poems), 1960; South of the Zambesi (poems), 1966; Cape Charade (play), 1968; Ed., When Boys were Men, 1969; Take Root or Die (play), 1970; Ed., The 1820 Settlers, 1974. Contbr. to: New Coin Poetry Quarterly (Co-Ed.). Mbr., S. African English Acad. (Coun.). Address: High Corner, Somerset St., Grahamstown, 6140, S. Africa.

BUTLER, Gwendoline (née Williams), pen name MELVILLE, Jennie, b. London, UK. Educ: Lady Margaret Hall, Oxford Univ. Publs. incl: Receipt for Murder, 1956; Nell Alone, 1968; Coffins Dark Number, 1969; A Coffin from the Past, 1970; Coffin for Pandora, 1973; Nun's Castle, 1974. Mbrships: Crime Writers Assn.; Detection Club. Agent: John Farquarson. Address: The Principal's House, The Royal Holloway College, University of London, Egham, Surrey, UK.

BUTLER, Ivan, b. 1909, Heswall, Cheshire, UK. Actor & theatre director; Freelance Editor & Film Critic. Educ: Ctrl. Schl. Speech Trng. & Dramatic Art. Publs. incl: Horror in the Cinema, 1967, 2nd ed., 1970; Religion in the Cinema, 1969; Big Bad Mouse (co-author, play), 1969; The Cinema of Roman Polanski, 1970; A History of the British Film Institute, 1971; 100 Best Plays for Amateurs, 1972; Murderers' London, 1973; Cinema in Britain, 1973; Murderers' England, 1973; The War Film, 1974. Contbr. to: Amateur Stage; What's On; etc. Mbrships. incl: Soc. Indexers; Critics' Circle. Address: 9 Foxdell, Dene Road, Northwood, Middlesex HA6 2HU, UK.

BUTLER, Patrick Trevor, b. 1929, London, UK. Judo Coach; Sub. Postmaster. Educ: London Univ. Publs: Popular Judo; Advanced Judo & Self-Defence, 1960; Self-Defence Complete, 1961; Judo Complete, 1962; Your Book of Judo; Your Book of Self-Defence; Judo for Juniors; Judo & Self-Defence for Women & Girls; Introducing Course Fishing; Modern Judo & Self-Defence. Contbr. to var. jrnls. & mags. Mbrships. incl: Soc. of Authors. Address: 43 Downing Drive, Leicester LE5 6LL, UK.

BUTLER, Margaret Gwendoline, b. Nottingham, UK. Needlework Teacher in Schools & Training Colleges. Publs: Clothes — Their Choosing, Making & Care; Fabric Furnishings (w. B. S. Graves). Address: 83 Holland Rd., Clacton-on-Sea, Essex, CO15 6EU, UK.

BUTLER, Reginald, b. 1922, London, UK. Journalist. Educ: London Univ. Publs: At Large in the Sun. Contbr. to num. mags., trade jrnls., provincial newspapers, etc., specialising in holiday, travel & tobacco trade subjects. Mbr., Press Club. Address: Whin Cottage, Frieth, nr. Henley-on-Thames, Oxford., UK.

BUTLER, Richard, b. 29 Apr. 1925, Liverpool, UK. Author. Educ: Chester Coll., 1950. Publs: Fingernail Beach, 1964; South of Hell's Gates, 1967 (in USA as More Dangerous than the Moon, 1968); Sharkbait, 1970; The Buffalo Hook, 1974; The Men that God Forgot, 1975; The Doll (TV play), 1970. Mbr., Comm., Fellowship of Aust. Writers. Address: c/o Hutchinson Grp. (Aust.) Pty. Ltd., 32 Cremorne St., Richmond, Vic. 3121, Australia.

BUTLIN, Martin Richard Fletcher, b. 7 June 1929, Birmingham, UK. Keeper, British Collection, Tate Gallery; Author. Educ: M.A.,Trinity Coll., Cambridge; 1st Class Degree, Courtauld Inst., London Univ. Publs: Catalogue of the Works of William Blake in the Tate Gallery, 1957, 2nd ed., 1971; Turner Watercolours, 1962; Samuel Palmer's 1824 Sketchbook, 1962; Turner (co-author), 1963; Watercolours from the Turner Bequest, 1819-1845, 1968; The Blake-Varley Sketchbook of 1824, 1969; Turner 1775-1851 (W. A. Wilton & J. Gage), 1974. Contbr. to: Burlington Mag.; Connoisseur; Blake Newsletter. Address: The Tate Gallery, Millbank, London SW1, UK.

BUTLIN, S. J., b. 1910, Ryde, N.S.W., Australia. University Professor of Economic History; Writer. Educ: B.Ec.; M.A.; Litt.D.; Univs. of Sydney, Cambridge (UK), Freiburg (Germany). Publs: Australian Monetary System, 1953; War Economy 1939-42, 1955; Australia & New Zealand Bank, 1961. Contbr. to: Econ. Record; Aust. Econ. Hist. Review; Aust. Quarterly. Fellow, Acad. of Social Scis. in Aust. Address: 16 Carnarvon Rd., Roseville, N.S.W., Australia.

BUTOR, Michel Marie François, b. 14 Sept. 1926, Mons en Baroeul, France. Teacher. Educ: Dr. ès Lettres, Sorbonne, Paris. Publs: Passage de Milan, 1954; L'Emploi du Temps, 1956; La Modification, 1957; Le Génie du Lieu, 1958; Degrés, 1960; Répertoire, I-IV, 1960-74; Histoire Extraordinaire, 1961; Mobile, 1962; Réseau Aérien, 1963; Description de San Marco, 1964; Illustrations, I-III, 1964-73; 6810,000 Litres d'Eau par Seconde, 1965; Essais sur les Essais, 1968; Portrait de l'Artiste en Jeune Singe, 1967; La Rose des Vents, 1970; Dialogue avec 32 Variations, 1971; Intervalle, 1973. Contbr. to: Critique, Cahiers du Chemin; N.R.F. Address: Aux Antipodes, Chemin de Terra Amata, 23 blvd. Carnot, 06300 Nice, France.

BUTTER, Peter Herbert, b. 7 Apr. 1921, Coldstream, Scotland, UK. University Teacher. Educ: M.A., Balliol Coll., Oxford Univ. Publs: Shelley's Idols of the Cave, 1954; Francis Thompson, 1961; Edwin Muir, 1962; Edwin Muir; Man & Poet, 1966; Ed., Shelley's Alastor & other Poems, 1970; Ed., Selected Letters of Edwin Muir, 1974. Contbr. to: Review of Engl. Studies; Mod. Lang. Review; Review of Engl. Lit. Mbr., PEN. Address: Ashfield, Bridge of Weir, Renfrewshire, Scotland, UK.

BUTTERFIELD, (Sir) Herbert, b. 7 Oct. 1900, Oxenhope, Yorks., UK. Historian; Former University

Professor. Educ: Peterhouse, Cambridge, 1919-23. Publs. incl: Napoleon, (Great Lives), 1939; The Statecraft of Machiavelli, 1940; The Englishman & his History, 1944; George III, Lord North & the People, 1949; The Origins of Modern Science, 1949; Christianity, Diplomacy & War, 1953; Man on his Past, 1955; George III & the Historians, 1957. Contbr. to: Historical Jrnl., Cambridge; History; Times Lit. Supplement; etc. Mbrships: Hon. Fellow, Brit. Acad., 1965–; VP, Royal Histl. Soc. Hons: Knighted, 1968; Hon. D.Litt., Hong Kong, Harvard, Columbia, Bonn, Univ. Coll. Dublin & sev. UK univs.; Hon. Mbr., Am. Acad. Arts & Sci., Royal Irish Acad. & Am. Histl. Soc. Address: 28 High St., Sawston, Cambridge CB2 4BG, UK.

BUTTERWORTH, W(illiam) E(dmund) (III), b. 10 Nov. 1929, Newark, N.J., USA. Writer. Publs. incl: Comfort Me With Love, 1959; Hot Seat, 1960; Heartbreak Ridge, 1962; Hell On Wheels, 1963; Once More With Passion, 1964; The Wonders of Rockets & Missiles, 1965; Warrior's Way, 1965; Road Racer, 1967; Grand Prix Racing, 1968; Stars & Planets, 1969; Yankee Boy, 1970; Flying Army, 1971; The Sex Traveller, 1971; The Race Driver, 1972; Sky Jacked, 1972; Race Car Team, 1973; Yankee Driver, 1974; The 12-Cylinder Screamer, 1974; Stop Thief, 1975; Black Gold, 1975; M*A*S*H Goes to Paris (co-author of this & other titles in series), 1975. Address: c/o Paul R. Reynolds Inc., 12 E. 41st St., N.Y., NY 10017, USA.

BUTTON, Margaret Helen (Mrs. W. A. Button), pen name LEONA, b. 1906, London, UK. Solo Stage Performer; Lecturer; Drama Adviser; Teacher; Writer. Publs: (Transl.) The Man Who Killed Time, 1964, 1966; Don Quixote de la Mancha; The Song of Roland (play). Contbr. to: Speech of Our Time; Townswomen Mag.; Unity Theatre Mag. Mbrships: Arts Theatre; Soc. of Authors; B.C.T.A. Adjudicators Guild; Unicorn Theatre; Engl. Speaking Union (Comm.), etc. Address: 5 Garrick Close, Richmond Green, Surrey, UK.

BUTTREY, Douglas Norton, b. 1918, Harrogate, UK. Plastics Technician. Educ: M.Sc., Salford Univ. Publs: Cellulose Plastics, 1947; Plasticizers, 1950, 2nd ed., 1960; Plastics in the Furniture Industry, 1964; Ed., Plastics in Furniture, 1975. Contbr. to: Soc. Chem. Ind. (UK); Plastics & Polymers; Forest Soc. Jrnl.; Times Review of Ind.; Pack (Sweden); Financial Times. Mbrships: Fellow, Royal Inst. of Chem.; Fellow, Plastics Inst. (UK); PEN. Address: 15 Churchfields, Broxbourne, Herts., UK.

BUTTRICK, Goerge Arthur, b. 23 Mar. 1892, Seaham Harbour, Durham, UK. Minister of Religion; Lecturer. Educ: Manchester & Vic. Univs. Publs. incl: The Parables of Jesus, 1928; Jesus Came Preaching, 1931; Prayer, 1942; Christ & Man's Dilemma, 1946; So We Believe, So We Pray, 1951; Faith & Education, 1952; Sermons Preached in a University Church, 1959; Christ & History, 1963; God, Pain & Evil, 1966; The Beatitudes, 1968; The Power of Prayer Today, 1970; Gen. Ed., The Interpreter's Bible (12 vols.); Interpreter's Dictionary of the Bible. Fellow, Am. Acad. Arts & Scis., 1957-. Recip., num. hon. degrees. Address: Memorial Church, Harvard Univ., Cambridge, Mass., USA.

BUTTS, Dennis, b. 3 Aug. 1932, Bewdley, Worcs., UK. Lecturer in English. Educ: M.A., St. Catherine's, Oxford. Publs: Robert Louis Stevenson, 1966; Living Words, 1969; Contbr., Faber Book of Great Legends, 1973. Contbr. to: Use of English; Stand Mag., etc. Mbrships: N.A.T.E.; S.T.E. Address: 219 Church Rd., Earley, Reading, Berks., UK.

BUTZER, Karl W., b. 19 Aug. 1934, Mülheim-Ruhr, Germany. Professor of Anthropology & Geography. Educ: B.Sc., 1954, M.A., 1955, McGill Univ.; Dr. rer. nat., Univ. of Bonn, Germany, 1957. Publs: Environment & Archeology, 1964, 2nd ed. 1971; Desert & River in Nubia, 1968; Recent History of an Ethiopian Delta, 1971; Ed., Prehistoric Archaeology & Ecology. Mbr., Assn. of Am. Geogs. Hons: Meritorious Award, Assn. of Am. Geogs., 1968. Address: The Univ. of Chicago, 5828 S. Univ. Ave., Chgo., IL 60637, USA.

BUXBAUM, Martin, b. 27 June 1912, Richmond, Va., USA. Editor; Writer. Educ: M.A., Jrnlsm., Cranston Univ.; Newman Sudduth Schl. of Art; Columbia Tech. Publs: (poetry) Rivers of Thought, 1958; The Underside of Heaven, 1960; The Unsung, Vol. I, 1964, Vol. II, 1965; Whispers in the Wind, 1967; Once Upon a Dream, 1969; The Warm World of Martin Buxbaum, 1974; (fiction) Around Our House, 1963; Table Talk, 1972; Sing a Song of Sixpence, 1974. Contbr. to num. mags.; Own monthly publ., Table Talk, 21 yrs. Mbr., Md. Poetry Soc. Hons: Poet of Year, State of Md., 1967; Geo. Wash. Medal of Hon., Freedoms Fndn., for patriotic writings, 1967, 1970, 1971, 1972, 1973. Address: 7819 Custer Rd., Bethesda, MD 20014, USA.

BUXBAUM, Melvin H., b. 6 May 1934, Chgo., Ill., USA. Teacher. Educ: B.A., 1957; M.A., 1960, Roosevelt Univ.; Ph.D., Univ. of Chgo., 1968. Publs: Benjamin Franklin & the Zealous Presbyterians, 1974. Contbr. to: Wm. & Mary Quarterly; The Nation; Enlightenment Essays; Jrnl. of Presby. Hist.; Histl. Mag.; Protestant Episc. Ch. Mbrships: Enlightenment Essays (Assoc. Ed.); Mod. Lang. Assn: Am. Lit. Grp. & Early Am. Lit. Grp.; Histl. Soc. of Pa. Recip., Nat. Endowment for the Humanities, 1969. Address: 218 West End Ave., Freeport, NY 11520, USA.

BUXTON, David Roden, b. 1910, London, UK. Writer. Educ: M.A., Trinity Coll., Cambridge. Publs: Russian Mediaeval Architecture; Travels in Ethiopia; Transl., Early Churches of Rome, by Emile Male; The Abyssinians. Contbr. to: Jrnl., E. Africa & Uganda Nat. Hist. Soc.; Blackwood's; Antiquity; Archaeologia; Geogl. Jrnl.; Rassegna di Studi Etiopici (Rome). Fellow, Soc. of Antiquaries. Address: Old Ellwoods, Bridleway, Grantchester, Cambridge, UK.

BUXTON, (Edward) John (Mawby), b. 1912, Bramhall, UK. Reader in English Literature. Educ: M.A., New Coll., Oxford. Publs: Such Liberty, 1944; Atropos & other Poems, 1946; A Marriage Song for the Princess Elizabeth, 1947; The Redstart, 1950; Island of Skomer (w. R. M. Lockley), 1950; Sir Philip Sidney & the English Renaissance, 1954; Elizabethan Taste, 1963; A Tradition of Poetry, 1967; Byron & Shelley, 1968; Ed., Poems of Michael Drayton, 1953; Poems of Charles Cotton, 1958; Gen. Ed., Oxford History of English Literature. Contbr. to lit. & ornithol. jrnls. Mbrships: F.S.A.; Chmn., Malone Soc., 1970–. Hons: Atlantic Award in Engl. Lit., 1946; Warton Lectr., Brit Acad., 1970; Fellow, New Coll., Oxford. Address: Cole Pk., Malmesbury, Wilts., UK.

BUXTON, John, b. 16 Dec. 1912, Bramhall, UK. Reader in English Literature, Univ. of Oxford. Educ: M.A., New College, Oxford. Publs: Poems of Michael Drayton, 1953; Sir Philip Sidney & the English Renaissance, 1954; Poems of Charles Cotton, 1958; Elizabethan Taste, 1963; A Tradition of Poetry, 1967; Byron & Shelley, 1968. Contbr. to: Times Lit. Supplement; Mod. Lang. Review; Engl. Lit. Renaissance; etc. Mbrships: Fellow, Soc. of Antiquaries; Chmn., Malone Soc. (1970–). Recip., Atlantic Award in Engl. Lit., 1946. Address: New College, Oxford, UK.

BUZURA, Augustin, b. 22 Sept. 1938, Berintza, Maramures, Romania. Writer. Educ: M.A., Inst. Med., Cluj-Napoca, Romania. Publs: (short stories) Capul Bunei Sperante (The Cape of Good Hope), 1963; De ce zboară vulturul? (Why Does the Eagle Fly?), 1966; (novel) Absenţii (The Outsiders), 1970; Feţele tăcerii (The Faces of Silence), 1974. Contbr. to: Romania literară; Luceafărul; Tribuna; Steaua; etc. Mbr., Writers' Union Romania (Mgmt. Bd.). Recip., Writers' Union Prize 1970 for Best Novel Absenţii. Address: Cluj-Napoca, Str. Unirii 3, Apt. 26, Romania.

BYATT, A(ntonia) S(usan), b. 24 Aug. 1936, Sheffield, Yorks., UK. University Extra-Mural Lecturer. Educ: B.A., Newnham Coll., Cambridge, 1957; Bryn Mawr Coll., Pa., USA, 1957-58; Somerville Coll., Oxford, UK, 1958-59. Publs: (novels) Shadow of a Sun, 1964; The Game, 1967; (other) Degrees of Freedom: The Novels of Iris Murdoch, 1965; Wordsworth & Coleridge in Their Time, 1970. Hons: Fellowship, Engl. Speaking Union, 1957-58; Arts Coun. Grant, 1968. Address: 17 Earlsfield Rd., London SW18, UK.

BYDE, Alan Wallace, b. 6 July, 1928, Darlington, Co. Durham, UK. Teacher. Educ: T.D., Newcastle upon Tyne Trng. Coll. Publs: Living Canoeing, 1969; A Beginner's Guide to Canoeing, 1973; Canoe Building in GRP., 1974; Canoe Design & Construction, forthcoming. Contbr. to: Canoeing in Brit.; Canoeing. Mbrships: Brit. Canoe Union (senior coach, 1961); Soc. of Authors; Assn. for Outdoor Educ. Address: Old Post Office, Llanmaes, Llantwit, Glam. CF6 9XR, UK.

BYFORD-JONES, (Lt.-Col.) Wilfred. Author. Publs. incl: The Greek Trilogy; Adventure with Two Passports; Berlin Twilight; Both Sides of Severn; Oil on Troubled

Water; Forbidden Frontiers; Grivas & the Story of E.O.K.A.; Quest in the Holy Land; Uncensored Eyewitness; Journey out of Darkness; Four Faces of Peru; The Lightning War. Address: Badger Lodge, Artists' Valley, Eglwys Fach, Machynlleth, Powys, Wales, UK.

BYLES, (Rev.) Alfred Thomas Plested, b. 1902, Winchester, UK. Deputy Priest Vicar, Exeter Cathedral. Educ: King's Coll., London; Westcott House, Cambridge; M.A.; Ph.D.; A.K.C. Publs: Ordre of Chyvalry by William Caxton (ed.), 1928; Chivalry (contbr.), 1929; Fayttes of Armes by William Caxton (ed.), 1933. Contbr. to: The Lib. Address: The Chaplain's House, 9 Livery Dole, Exeter, Devon, UK.

BYLES, Marie Beuzeville, b. 8 Apr. 1900, Ashton-on-Mersey near Manchester, UK. Solicitor. Educ: Univ. of Sydney. Publs: By Cargo Boat & Mountain, 1931; Footprints of Gautama the Buddha, 1957; Journey Into Burmese Silence, 1962; The Lotus & the Spinning Wheel, 1963; Paths to Inner Calm, 1965. Contbr. to: Gandhi Marg; The Mountain Path; The Middle Way; World Buddhism; etc. Address: Ahimsa, Day Rd., Cheltenham, N.S.W., Australia 2119.

BYROM, James G. Bramwell, b. 1911, Edinburgh, UK. Author; Lecturer. Educ: B.A., Balliol Coll., Oxford. Publs: The Unfinished Man, 1957; Or Be He Dead, 1958; Take Only as Directed, 1959; Thou Shouldst Be Living, 1964. Address: Mas Castaly, Cante Perdrix, St. Jacques de Grasse, Provence, France.

BYRT, Edwin Andrew, b. 18 Nov. 1932, Melbourne, Vic., Australia. College Lecturer. Educ: B.Sc., Dip.Ed., Melbourne Univ. Publs: Contemporary Mathematics III, 1969; Contemporary Mathematics II, 1970; Contemporary Mathematics IV, 1971; Contemporary Mathematics I, 1972. Mbr., Math. Assn., UK. Address: 13 Westley St., Ferntree Gully, Victoria, Australia 3156.

BYSTRZYCKI, Przemysław Michael, pen names STANKIEWICZS, Michał; Przem.; P.B.; M.S., b. 23 May 1923, Przemyśl, Poland. Writer. Educ: Master of Pol. Economy, 1950, M.A., 1951, Univ. of Poznań. Publs: (short stories) Warkocze, 1955; Śmierć nad Agfar-wadi, 1960, 3rd ed., 1972; Szkockie pożegnania, 1963; Strumień, 1966; Anujka, 1969; (novels) Operacjka Milczacy Most, 1957, 4th ed., 1970; Wyspa Mauricius, 1963; Wronie uroczysko, 1964. Contbr. to var. lit. jrnls. Mbrships: Polish Writers' Union; PEN; Societas Scientiarum ac Litterarum Premisliensis; Adam Mickiewicz Assn. Address: ul. Wyspiańskiege 12 m. 11, 60-750 Poznań, Poland.

C

CABALLERO CALDERÓN, Eduardo, b. 6 Mar. 1910. Diplomatist; Writer. Educ: Univ. Externado de Colombia. Publs. incl: Tipacoque (stories), 1939; Americanos y Europeos, 1949; Cartas Colombianas, 1951; La Penultima Hora (novel), 1953; Siervo sin Tierra (novel), 1954; Memorias Infantiles (novel), 1964; Manuel Pacho (novel), 1965; El Buen Salvaje (novel), 1965; Cain (novel), 1965. Contbr. to jrnls. Mbrships. incl: Corres., Royal Spanish Acad. Recip., Eugenio Nadal Prize, 1965. Address: Calle 37, No. 19-07, Bogotá, Colombia.

CABANIS, José, b. 24 Mar. 1922. Writer. Educ: Univ. of Toulouse. Publs. incl: un essai sur Marcel Jouhandeau, 1960; le Bonheur du jour, 1961; les Cartes du temps, 1962; Plaisir et lectures, 1964, vol. II, 1968; les Jeux de la Nuit, 1964; la Bataille de Toulouse, 1966; Des Jardins en Espagne (criticism), 1969; Le Sacre de Napoleon (criticism), 1970; Charles X roi ultra (criticism), 1972. Hons. incl: Kt., Arts & Letters & Legion of Hon.; Prix Théophraste Renaudot, 1966; Prix des Ambassadeurs, 1972. Address: 5 rue Darquié, 31 Toulouse (Haute-Garonne), France.

CABLE, James, b. 1920, London, UK. Assistant Under-Secretary of State, Foreign & Commonwealth Office. Educ: Ph.D., Univ. of Cambridge. Publs: Gunboat Diplomacy, 1971. Mbr., Int. Inst. for Strategic Studies. Recip., C.M.G. Address: 18 Park Lawn Rd., Weybridge, Surrey KT13 9EU, UK.

CACCIATORE, Vera, b. Rome, Italy. Writer; Curator, Keats-Shelley Memorial House, Rome. Educ: Ph.D., Univ. of Rome. Publs: La Vendita all'asta, 1953; The Swing, 1959; La Palestra, 1961; Shelley & Byron in Pisa, 1961; La Forza Motrice, 1968; A Room in Rome, 1970. Hon. Mbr., Poetry Soc. of Am. Recip., M.B.E., UK. Address: Piazza di Spagna 26, Rome, Italy.

CADLE, Dean, b. 16 Jan. 1920, Middlesboro, Ky., USA. Librarian-Educator. Educ: B.A., Berea Coll., 1947; Columbia Univ., Stanford Univ., Univ. of Kan., Univ. of Tenn.; M.A., Univ. of Iowa, 1950; M.S. in Lib. Sci., Univ. of Ky., 1957. Contbr., fiction & criticism, num. mags. inclng. Yale Review, Southwest Review, Tomorrow, Philippine Free Press; Short stories in annuals & anthols.; Ed., The High Cost of Writing, by Rebecca Caudill; Ed. Bd., Western Review; Advsry. & Contbng. Ed., Appalachian Heritage; Hons: Winner, nat. short story contest, Tomorrow mag. & Creative Age Press, 1947; Wallace Stegner Creative Writing Fellowship, Stanford Univ., 1947-48; Stories listed in Honor Rolls of "The Best American Short Stories" (ed., M. Foley). Address: 30 Valle Vista Dr., Asheville, NC, USA.

CADY, Elwyn Loomis, Jr., b. 21 Feb. 1926, Ames, Iowa, USA. Medico-legal Consultant. Educ: Wash., Univ.; Univ. of Kan. City; J.D., Tulane Univ. Coll. of Law; B.S.Med., Schl. of Med., Univ. of Mo. Publs: Law & Contemporary Nursing, 1961, 1963; Chapts. in var. books inclng: The Medico-Legal Reader, 1956; Jensen's History & Trends of Professional Nursing, 1959, 1965; Volz' Federal Practice Methods, 1960, 1970. Contbr. to num. legal, med. jrnls. Mbrships: Past Pres., Mo. Writers Guild. Scribes; Sports Columnist & Ed. Writer, Paseo Press, 1942-43. Hons: 1st Prize, Am. Legion Essay Contest, 1939. Address: 1919 Drumm Ave., Independence, MO 64055, USA.

CAESAR, R. Dick, b. 1905, Maidstone, UK. Former Technical Press Officer, Bristol Siddeley Engines Ltd. Educ: B.A., Univ. of Cambridge. Publs: The Gobbling Billy (w. W. Mayne), 1959, 2nd ed., 1969. Contbr. to num. jrnls. & newspapers. Mbrships: Vintage Sports Car Club; Cambridge Univ. Automobile Club. Agent: David Higham Assoc. Ltd. Address: Lime Ridge, Cadbury Camp Lane, Clapton-in-Gordano, Bristol BS20 9SB, UK.

CAFFREY, Kate, (Mrs. TOLLER), b. Preston, Lancs., UK. Lecturer; Writer. Educ: B.A., London Univ.; M.A., Coll. of Wm. & Mary, Va., USA. Publs: The British to Southern Africa, Great Emigrations Series No. 3, 1973; Out In the Midday Sun: Singapore 1941-45, USA,1973, UK 1974; The Mayflower, USA 1974, UK 1975. Mbrships: F.R.S.A.; Assn. of Tchrs. in Colls. & Depts. of Educ. (Hon. Treas., Engl. Sect.); Brit. Assn. for Am. Studies. Address: 82 Castleton Ave., Wembley, Middlesex HA9 7QF, UK.

CAGNEY, Peter, b. 1918, Edgbaston, Birmingham, UK. Founder, Script Service Firm; Freelance Writer. Publs: A Grave for Madam, 1961; Non Sei Piu Niente, 1965;

Treasury of Wit & Humour, 1965; Second Treasury of Wit & Humour, 1967; Holiday Joke Book, 1975. Contbr. to: Courier; Stage; Observer; Spotlight, S. Africa; Radio; etc. Agent: Hope Leresche & Steele. Address: c/o P. C. Associates, 2nd Floor, 17 Second Ave., Hove, Sussex BN3 2LL, UK.

CAILLOIS, Roger, b. 3 Mar. 1913, Rheims, France. Writer; Editor. Educ: Agrégé de l'Univ., Sorbonne; Ecole Normale Supérieure. Publs: incl: Bellons ou la Pente de la Guerre, 1963; Instincts et société, 1964; Au Coeur du Fantastique, 1965; Pierres, 1966; Images, images . ., 1966; Obliques, 1967; L'Ecriture des Pierres, 1970; Cases d'un Echiquier, 1970; La Pieuvre, 1973; La Dissymétrie, 1973. Ed. &/or Dir., var. lit. reviews & anthols. Mbr., Acad. Française, 1971—. Recip., sev. decorations. Address: 34 ave. Charles Floquet, Paris 7e, France.

CAIN, James M(allahan), b. 1 July 1892, Annapolis, Md., USA. Writer. Educ: A.B., 1910, A.M., 1917, Wash. Coll., Chestertown, Md. Publs: incl: (novels) Past All Dishonor, 1946; The Butterfly, 1947; The Sinful Woman, 1947; The Moth, 1948; Jealous Woman, 1950; The Root of His Evil, 1951; Galatea, 1953; Mignon, 1962; The Magician's Wife, 1965; The Postman Always Rings Twice (play), 1936; (other) Our Government, 1930; Ed., For Men Only: A Collection of Short Stories, 1944. Contbr. to var. mags. Recip., Grand Masters Award, Mystery Writers of Am., 1970. Address: 6707 44th Ave., University Park, Hyattsville, MD 20782, USA.

CAIN, Maureen Elizabeth, b. 10 Mar. 1938, Ipswich, UK. University Lecturer. Educ: B.A., 1959, Ph.D., 1969, London Schl. of Econs. Publs: Society & the Policeman's Role, 1973. Contbr. to: Brit. Jrnl. Sociol.; Brit. Jrnl. Criminol.; Anglo-Am. Law Review; Brit. Jrnl. of Law & Society; other profl. jrnls. Mbrships: Int. Sociological Assn.; Brit. Sociological Assn.; Brit. Soc. Criminol. Address: Dept. of Sociology, Brunel Univ., Uxbridge, Middx., UK.

CAIRD, George Bradford, b. 1917, London, UK. College Principal; Author. Educ: Oxford & Cambridge Univs.; D. Phil., D.D. Publs: The Truth of the Gospel; The Shorter Oxford Bible; Our Dialogue with Rome; Introduction & Exegesis of I & II Samuel in Interpreter's Bible, Vol. II; The Apostolic Age; Principalities & Powers; The Gospel according to St. Luke; The Revelation of St. John the Divine. Contbr. to: Interpreters' Dict. of the Bible; Hastings' One Vol. Dict. of the Bible; Can. Jrnl. of Theol. Expository Times; Jrnl. of Theol. Studies; New Testament Studies. Mbrships: Fellow, Brit. Acad. Address: Mansfield College, Oxford, UK.

CAIRD (née KIRKWOOD), Janet Hinshaw, b. 24 Apr. 1913, Livingstonia, Malawi. Teacher; Writer. Educ: M.A.(Hons.), Edinburgh Univ., UK, 1935; Stevenson Schlr., Univ. of Grenoble, France, & Sorbonne, Paris, 1935-36. Publs: Angus the Tartan Partan (children's book); Murder Reflected, 1965; Perturbing Spirit, 1966; Murder Scholastic, 1966; The Loch, 1968; Murder Remote, 1973; poems, var. jrnls. Contbr. to: Scottish Short Stories, 1974. Mbr., Soc. of Authors. Address: 1 Drummond Cres., Inverness, Scotland, UK.

CAIRNCROSS, (Sir) Alexander Kirkland, b. 1911, Lesmahagow, Scotland. The Master, St. Peter's College, Oxford University. Educ: M.A., Glasgow Univ.; Ph.D., Cambridge Univ. Publs: Introduction to Economics; Home & Foreign Investment, 1870-1913; Factors in Economic Development; Essays in Economic Management; Control of Long-term International Capital Movements. Hons: K.C.M.G.; F.B.A. Address: Master's Lodgings, St. Peter's Coll., Oxford, UK.

CAIRNS, David, b. 1904, Ayton, UK. Former Professor of Practical Theology & Reader in Systematic Theology. Educ: Univs. of Oxford & Aberdeen, UK; Univ. of Zurich, Switz.; Univ. of Monpellier, France; M.A.; D.D. Publs: The Image of God in Man, 1953; A Gospel without Myth? 1960; In Remembrance of Me — Aspects of the Lord's Supper, 1967; "God Up There?" — A Study in Divine Transcendence. Transl. of num. theol. works from German. Contbr. to: Scottish Jrnl. of Theol. Mbr., Faith & Order Commn., 1958-68. Address: 1 St. Swithin St., Aberdeen AB1 6XH, UK.

CAJADE REY, Ramon, b. 19 July 1914, Santiago de Compostela, Spain. Law Court Official; Author. Educ: Law Degree. Publs: The Triumph of the Defeated, 1959; That Is Life, 1961; The Destiny Leads, 1962; The Lonely, 1963;

Life Is Sad. Contbr. to var. mags. Mbr., Soc. of Spanish Authors. Address: Juzgado Municipal 2, Corunna, Spain.

CALAFERTE, Louis, b. 14 July 1928, Turin, Italy. Author; Playwright. Publs. incl: Requiem des Innocents, 1952; Septentrion (novel), 1963; Rosa Mystica (novel), 1968; Portrait de L'Enfant, 1969; Hinterland, 1971; Limitrophe, 1972; Rag-Time (poems), 1972; Paraphe, 1974; La Vie Parallele, 1974; plays: Clotilde du Nord, 1955; Chez les Titch, 1973; Megaphonie, 1974. Contbr. to newspapers, radio & TV. Hons: Laureat de la Bourse Del Duca, 1953; Bourse Nationale des Lettres, 1956. Address: 9 bis, rue Roux-Soignat, 69003 Lyon, France.

CALDER, Angus, b. 5 Feb. 1942, Sutton, Surrey, UK. Author. Educ: M.A., King's Coll., Cambridge Univ.; Ph.D., Univ. of Sussex. Publs: The Peoples War: Britain 1939-45, 1969; Russia Discovered: In Nineteenth Century Fiction, 1975. Mbr., Soc. of Authors. Hons: Eric Gregory Award for Poetry, 1967; John Llewellyn Rhys Mem. Prize, 1970. Agent: A. D. Peters & Co. Address: c/o above, 10 Buckingham St., London WC2, UK.

CALDER, Joan Muriel Drury, pen name DRURY CALDER, Joan, b. 22 Apr. 1922, Frant, Kent, UK. Company Director & Accountant. Educ: Victoria Univ., Wellington, N.Z. Author of plays inclng. Still Grows the Tawny Weed. Contbr. to: N.Z. mags. & radio. Australian mags. & Am. mags. Mbrships: N.Z. Playwrights Assn.; N.Z. Women Writers Assn. Hons: 3rd Prize, N.Z. Br., Brit. Drama League One Act Playwriting Competition, 1963; 2nd Prize, 1964, 1966; 1st Prize, Christchurch Elmwood Players Playwriting Competition, 1970; 1st Prize, Playwriting, N.Z. Women Writers Soc., 1970; Highly Commended, Katherine Mansfield Mem. Lit. Award, 1973. Address: 121 Thorp St., Motueka, N.Z.

CALDER, Nigel David Ritchie, b. 2 Dec. 1931, London, UK. Science Writer. Educ: M.A., Sidney Sussex Coll., Cambridge Univ. Publs. incl: Electricity Grows Up, 1957; Ed., Unless Peace Comes, 1968; Violent Universe, 1969; Technopolis, 1969; Living Tomorrow, 1970; The Mind of Man, 1970; Restless Earth, 1972; Ed., Nature in the Round, 1973; The Life Game, 1973; The Weather Machine, 1974; num. TV documentaries, 1966—. Contbr. to: New Scientist (Ed., 1962-66); New Statesman (Sci. Corres., 1959-71); num. other jrnls., etc. Mbr., Assn. Brit. Sci. Writers (Chmn., 1962-64). Recip., UNESCO Kalinga Prize, 1972. Agent: Rena Feld. Address: 8 The Chase, Furnace Green, Crawley, Sussex, UK.

CALDER, Peter Ritchie (Lord Ritchie-Calder of Balmashamar), b. 1906, Forfar, Scotland, UK. Educ: M.A., Forfar Acad. Science Writer & Editor; Special Adviser, UN Agencies; Former University Professor of International Relations. Publs. incl: Conquest of Suffering; Start Planning Britain Now; Profile of Science; Science Makes Sense; Men Against Ignorance; Man & the Cosmos; Evolution of the Machine; How Long Have We Got? ; The Pollution of the Mediterranean. Contbr. to var. jrnls. Mbrships. incl: Sr. Fellow, Ctr. for Study of Democratic Instns., USA; Fndr.-Mbr., Assn. Brit. Sci. Writers; F.R.S.A. Hons. incl: C.B.E.; WHO Med. Soc. Medal, 1974. Address: 1 Randolph Place, Edinburgh, UK.

CALDER-MARSHALL, Arthur, b. 1908, London, UK. Writer. Educ: B.A., Hertford Coll., Oxford Univ. Publs. incl: Two of a Kind; Pie in the Sky; The Way to Santiago; A Man Reprieved; Occasion of Glory; The Magic of My Youth (autobiog.); The Scarlet Boy; (travel) Glory Dead; The Watershed; (biog.) No Earthly Command; Havelock Ellis; The Enthusiast; (juvenile) The Fair to Middling; Lone Wolf; Life of Jack London; (criticism) Prepare to Shed Them Now; The Ballads of George R. Sims; The Georgian Lady (forthcoming). Contbr. to: Sunday Telegraph; Evening Standard. Fellow, Royal Soc. Lit. Agent: Elaine Greene Ltd.

CALDWELL, Dennis, b. 24 Dec. 1919, London, UK. Chemist. Educ: B.Sc., London Univ. Publs: The Chemistry of Drugs (w. N. Evers), 1959. Mbrships: Fellow, Royal Soc. of Chem.; Inst. of Info. Scis. Address: Flat 8 Crastock Ct., 7 Queens Gdns., London W2 3BG, UK.

CALDWELL, Erskine, b. 17 Dec. 1903, Moreland, Ga., USA. Author. Educ: Univ. Va. Publs: 52 fiction & non-fiction books. Mbrships: Nat. Inst. Arts & Letters, N.Y.; San Fran. Press Club; Phoenix (Ariz.) Press Club. Address: P.O. Box 820, Dunedin, FL 33528, USA.

CALISHER, Hortense, b. 20 Dec. 1911, NYC, USA. Writer. Educ: A.B., Barnard Coll.; Columbia Univ. Publs: (novels) False Entry, 1961; Textures of Life, 1963; Journal from Ellipsis, 1965; The New Yorkers, 1969; Queenie, 1971; Standard Dreaming, 1972; Eagle Eye, 1973; (stories) In the Absence of Angels, 1951; (novella & stories) Tale for the Mirror, 1962; Extreme Magic, 1964; (two novellas) The Railway Police & The Last Trolleyride; (autobiog. memoir) Herself, 1972. Contbr. to: Harper's; New Yorker; anthols.; etc. Mbr., PEN. Hons. incl: Nat. Coun. Arts Award, 1967; Inst. Arts & Letters Award, 1967. Agent: Candida Donadio. Address: 11 W 57th St., NYC, NY 10019, USA.

CALKIN, Homer Leonard, b. 5 May 1912, Clearfield, Iowa, USA. Historian. Educ: B.A., 1935, M.A., 1936, Ph.D., 1939, Univ. Iowa. Publs: Castings from the Foundry Mold, 1968; Those Incredible Methodists, 1972 (contbr.); Documents on Germany, 1944-71 Co-Ed., 1971. Contbr. to: Pa. Mag. Hist. & Biog.; Le Sabretache; Irish Sword; Pub. Admin. Review; Civil War Hist.; Palimpsest; Schl. Review; Social Educ.; Meth. Hist.; etc. Mbrships: Am. Histl. Assn.; Cosmos Club; Org. Am. Histns.; Mil. Hist. Soc. Ireland; Southern Histl. Soc.; State Histl. Soc. Iowa. Address: 3830 Columbia Pike, Arlington, VA 22204, USA.

CALLAGHAN, Morley (Edward), b. 22 Sept. 1903, Toronto, Ont., Can. Writer. Educ: B.A., St. Michael's Coll., Univ. of Toronto, 1925; LL.B., Osgoode Hall Law Schl., 1928. Publs. incl: (novels) They Shall Inherit the Earth, 1935; More Joy in Heaven, 1937; Varsity Story, 1948; The Loved & the Lost, 1951; The Many Colored Coat, 1960; A Passion in Rome, 1961; (short stories) Now That April's Here, 1936; Stories, 2 vols., 1959, 1967; Turn Again George (play), 1940; (other) That Summer in Paris: Memories of Tangled Friendships with Hemingway, Fitzgerald & Some Others, 1963. Hons: Can. Coun. Medal, 1966; Moslon Award, 1969. Address: 20 Dale Ave., Toronto, Ont., Can.

CALLAHAN, North, b. 8 July 1908, Sweetwater, Tenn., USA. Author; Professor. Educ: A.B., Univ. of Tenn., Chattanooga; A.M., Columbia Univ.; Ph.D., N.Y. Univ. Publs: Smoky Mountain Country, 1952; Henry Knox — General Washington's General, 1958; Daniel Morgan — Ranger of the Revolution, 1961; Royal Raiders, vol. 1, The Tories of the American Revolution, 1963, vol. 2, Flight from the Republic, 1968; Carl Sandburg — Lincoln of Our Literature, 1970; George Washington — Soldier & Man, 1972. Contbr. to acad. jrnls., encys. & newspapers. Recip., award for best biog. of Am. Revolution, 1958. Address: 25 S. Germantown Rd., Chattanooga, TN 37411, USA.

CALLARD, Thomas Henry, pen name ROSS, Sutherland, b. 1912, Plymouth, UK. Schoolmaster. Educ: Peterborough Trng. Coll. Publs: Three Steps to Tyburn; Masque of Traitors, 1954; Freedom is the Prize, 1955; Vagabond Treasure; Lazy Salmon Mystery; The English Civil War, 1962. Address: 4 Round Berry Drive, Salcombe, Devon, UK.

CALLEJA GUIJARRO, Tomás, b. 31 Dec. 1922, Navares de Ayuso, Spain. Teacher. Inventor. Educ: Tchrs. Dip., Sociol. Publs. incl: La arqueología, la historia y la leyenda en torno a Las Vegas de Pedraza, 1965; Dramatizaciones, 2 vols., 1966; El mundo que ves, 2 vols., 1966 & 1967; Didática de "El mundo que ves", 1968; i Era el Arcipreste de Hita segoviano?, 1970. Contbr. to: Vida Escolar; Educadores; El Adelantado de Segovia; etc. Mbr., Assn. of Writers & Artists of Spain. Hons: Poetry Prize, Segovia, 1963; Min. Commn. planning pedagogy of Gen. Basic Educ. Address: Calle Melilla 12, 6° B, Madrid 5, Spain.

CALLOW, Philip Kenneth, b. 26 Oct. 1924, Birmingham, UK. Writer. Educ: Coventry Tech. Coll.; St. Luke's Coll., Exeter. Publs. incl: The Hosanna Man, 1956; Native Ground, 1959; Turning Point (poetry), 1961; Clipped Wings, 1963; The Real Life (poetry), 1964; In My Own Land, 1965; Going to the Moon, 1968; The Bliss Body, 1969; Flesh of Morning, 1971; Bare Wires (poetry), 1972; Yours, 1972; Son & Lover (biog.), 1975. Contbr. to: New Statesman; Spectator; Books & Bookmen; etc. Hons. incl: Arts Coun. Bursaries, 1966, 1970, 1973; C. Day Lewis Fellowship, 1973-74; Travelling Schlrship, Soc. of Authors, 1973. Address: Little Thatch, Haselbury, nr. Crewkerne, Somerset, UK.

CALLWOOD, June, b. 1924, Chatham, Can. Magazine Writer. Publs: A Woman Doctor Looks at Life & Love, 1957; Love, Hate, Fear & Anger, 1964; Mayo: The Story of my Family & Career, 1968; Sociological History of Canada in the 1890s, 1969; How to Talk to Practically Anybody about Practically Anything, 1970; We Mainline Dreams, 1973; Canadian Women & the Law, 1973. Contbr. to: Brantford Expositor; Globe & Mail (Reporter, 1941-45). Mbrships. incl: Can. Civil Liberties Assn. (Women's Hostels, Inc. (Pres.); num. civic orgs.; Writers' Union of Canada; Yorkville Digger House (Assoc. Fndr.). Hons: B'nai B'rith Woman of Yr., 1969; Medal of Merit, City of Toronto, 1974. Address: 21 Hillcroft Dr., Islington, Ont., Can.

CALMAN, Montague, b. 1917, London, UK. Freelance Journalist; Editorial Consultant; Scriptwriter; Critic. Publs: Letters to my Mother; Thesis of Eighteenth Century Culture — Age of Paradox; The London Drama Scene; (syndicated series) Montague Calman's Show Topics; Documentary film scripts (w. other writers); TV scripts. Contbr. to: Evening Standard; L.A. Times; Boston Globe; Epworth Press; Nat. Press Agcy.; Times Review of Ind.; Cambridge Daily News; Ballet Today; Med. Bulletin; United Empire; Brit. Weekly; Music & Musicians. Mbrships. incl: F.R.S.A.; Inst. of Jrnlsts; Royal C'wlth. Soc. Address: 1E Carlisle Pl., Westminster, London SW1P 1NP, UK.

CALVER, Gordon Anthony, b. 1921, Bromley, Kent, UK. Banker. Publs: The Banker's Guide to the Marine Insurance of Goods (w. Victor Dover), 1960; Iran Economic Review, 1968. Contbr. to: Times. Fellow, Inst. of Bankers. Address: c/o The British Bank of the Middle East, 20 Abchurch Lane, London EC4, UK.

CALVERT, James Michael, b. 6 Mar. 1913, Rohtak, India. Author & Editor; Former Army Officer & Civil Engineer. Educ: M.A., St. John's Coll., Cambridge Univ.; Hallsworth Rsch. Fellow, Manchester Univ. Publs: Prisoners of Hope, 1951; Fighting Mad, 1963; Slim, 1973; Chindits, 1973. Contbr. to: R.U.S.I. Jrnl.; Army Quarterly; Times; Spectator; Practitioner; ORBIS Hist. of WWII; Listener; R. E. Jrnl. Mbrships. incl: Instn. Civil Engrs.; Fellow, Royal Histl. Soc.; Royal United Servs. Inst.; Mil. Commentators Circle; Soc. of Authors; PEN. Hons: D.S.O. & Bar; num. for. mil. decorations. Address: 6A Gregory Pl., Holland St., London W8 4NG, UK.

CALVERT, Peter Anthony Richard, b. 19 Nov. 1936, Islandmagee, Co. Antrim, UK. Senior Lecturer in Politics. Educ: B.A., Cantab., 1960; A.M., Michigan, USA, 1961; M.A., Ph.D., Cantab., 1964. Publs: The Mexican Revolution 1910-14, 1968; The Diplomacy of Anglo-American Conflict, 1968; Latin America: Internal Conflict & International Peace, 1969; Revolution (Key Concepts in Political Science), 1970; A Study of Revolution, 1970; Mexico, 1973; The Mexicans — How They Live & Work, 1975. Contbr. to var. pol. jrnls. Mbrships. incl: Fellow, Royal Histl. Soc.; Pol. Studies Assn.; Soc. for Latin Am. Studies. Address: Dept. of Politics, Univ. of Southampton, Highfield, Southampton, SO9 5NH, UK.

CALVINO, Italo, b. 15 Oct. 1923, San Remo, Italy. Writer; Editor. Publs: Il Sentiero dei Nidi di Ragno, 1947; Ultimo visne il Corvo, 1949; Il Visconte dimezzato, 1952; L'Entrata in Guerra, 1954; Fiabe Italiane, 1956; Il Barone Rampante, 1957; I Racconti, 1958; Il Cavaliere Inesistente, 1959; La Giornata di uno Scrutatore, 1963; Le Cosmicomiche, 1966; Ti con zero, 1967; Le Città Invisibili, 1973; Il Castello dei Destini Incrociati, 1974. Address: c/o Giulio Einaudi Editore, Via Umberato Biancamano I, Turin, Italy.

CALVOCORESSI, Peter John Ambrose, b. 17 Nov. 1912, Karachi, Pakistan. Publisher. Educ: B.A., Oxford Univ., UK. Publs: Nuremberg: The Facts, the Law & the Consequences, 1947; Surveys of International Affairs, Vols. I—V, 1950-54; Middle East Crisis (w. G. Wint), 1957; South Africa & World Opinion, 1961; World Order & New States, 1962; World Politics Since 1945, 1968; Total War, 1974. Address: Guide House, Aspley Guise, Bletchley, Bucks., UK.

CAMBANELLIS, Iakovos. Writer; Film Director. Publs. incl: Dance of the Sheaves (play), 1950; The Seventh Day of Creation (play), 1956; The Courtyard of Miracles (play), 1957; Story Without a Title (play), 1959; Neighbourhood of Angels (play), 1963; Stella (film script); The River (film script); Snowdrop (film script). Contbr. to: Greek radio; Eleftheria. Address: Dervenion 19, Athens, Greece.

CAMERON, Alexander Durand, b. 4 Jan. 1924, Selkirk, Scotland, UK. Former History Teacher; Author. Educ: M.A., Univ. of Edinburgh; Lip.Ed. Publs: History for

Young Scots, 2 vols., 1963-64; Living in Scotland (1760-1820), 1969; The Caledonian Canal, 1972. Mbrships. incl: Fellow, Soc. of Antiquaries of Scotland; Scottish Hist. Soc. Address: 14 Esplanade Terrace, Edinburgh EH15 2ES, UK.

CAMERON, Allan Gillies, b. 1930, Kuala Lumpur. Head of Department. Educ: B.Sc., St. Andrew's Univ. Publs: A Chemical Approach to Food & Nutrition (w. B. A. Fox), 1961; Food Science: A Chemical Approach, 1970; Food Science (w. G. G. Birch & M. Spencer), 1971; Food-Facts & Fallacies, 1971; The Science of Food & Cooking, 3rd ed., 1973. Mbr., F.I.F.S.T. Address: Dept. of Applied Sci. & Food Technol., Coll. of Food & Domestic Arts, Summer Row, Birmingham B3 1JB, UK.

CAMERON, James, b. 17 June 1911, London, UK. Journalist; Author. Publs: Touch of the Sun, 1950; Mandarin Red, 1959; 1914, 1959; The African Revolution, 1961; 1916, 1962; Witness in Vietnam, 1966; Vicky: a Memoir, 1967; Point of Departure, 1967; What a Way to Run a Tribe, 1968; An Indian Summer, 1974. Contbr. to num. periodicals, UK & USA. Mbrships: NUJ; Soc. of Authors; Savile Club. Hons: Granada Journalist of the Year, 1965; Granada Foreign Correspondent of the Decade, 1966; Doct. of Lit., Lancaster, 1970; Italia Prize for 'The Pump' radio play, 1973. Address: 16 Binden Rd., London W12 9RJ, UK.

CAMERON, Kenneth, b. 21 May 1922, Burnley, Lancs., UK. University Teacher. Educ: B.A., Univ. of Leeds; Ph.D., Univ. of Sheffield. Publs: The Place-Names of Derbyshire (3 vols.), 1959; English Place Names, 1961; Scandinavian Settlement in the Territory of the Five Boroughs: The Place-Names Evidence, 1965. Contbr. to: Nottingham Medieval Studies; Medieval Scandinavia. Mbrships: Fellow, Royal Histl. Soc.; Pres., Viking Soc., 1972-4; Hon. Dir. & Sec., Eng. Place-Name Soc. Recip: Sir Israel Gollancz Mem. Prize, Brit. Acad., 1969. Address: 292 Queens Road, Beeston, Nottingham NG9 1JA, UK.

CAMERON, Roderick, b. 1913, NYC, USA. MI5 Official. Educ: UK & Switz.; Univ. of W. Germany; Courtauld Inst., London, UK. Off. of Strategic Servs., Wash. (USA) & London. Publs: My Travels History, 1950; Equator Farm, 1955; Shadows from India: An Architectural Album, 1958; Time of the Mango Flowers, 1958; Shells, 1961; The Golden Haze, 1964; The Viceroyalties of the West, 1968; Australia: History & Horizons, 1971; The Golden Riviera, 1974; all books also publd. in Braille. Contbr. to: Horizon; Hist. Today; Cornhill; Harper's Bazaar; Go; Archtl. Review; Vogue; Connaissance du Monde; etc. Hons: Book Soc. Recommendation (for Equator Farm), 1955; Readers' Union Double Choice, 1965. Address: c/o Clos Fiorentina, St Jean Cap Ferrat, 06 France.

CAMERON, William Frederick John, b. 20 Mar. 1905, Chipping Campden, Glos., UK. Translator; Author. Publs. incl: Common People (novel), 1938; The Day is Coming (novel), 1944; Everyday Britain for Scandinavians, 1949-61; (Engl. dialogues for for. students) I Went to Britain, 1952; I Toured Britain, 1954; London Schoolboy (elem. Engl. reading for Swedish jr. schls.), 1955; A Tangram Tale (children's book), 1972; (transls.) Nomads of the North (Anna Riwkin-Brick & Elly Jannes); Masterpieces of the Swedish National Museum (Sixten Strömbom), 1951. Address: High Street, Great Rollright, Chipping Norton, Oxon OX7 5RH, UK.

CAMERON, William Macdonald, b. 25 Feb. 1923, London, UK. College of Education Lecturer. Educ: Central Fndn. Schl., London; Goldsmiths Coll., London; Carnegie Coll., Leeds. Publs: Education in Movement – Gymnastics, 1963; Education in Movement in the Infant School, 1970; The Primary School Games Lesson, 1975. Mbrships. incl: Br. Assn. of Organisers & lectrs. in P.E.; N.U.T. Address: 8½ Great Oaks, Hutton, Brentwood, Essex, UK.

CAMP, John Michael Francis, b. 31 July 1915, London, UK. Writer; Author. Publs: Oxfordshire & Buckinghamshire Pubs, 1965; Discovering London Railway Stations, 1966; Discovering Bellringing, 1968; Portrait of Buckinghamshire, 1972; Bellringing, 1974; Magic, Myth & Medicine, 1974; Holloway Prison, 1975; The Folklore of Sex, 1975. Contbr. to: Rdrs'. Digest; Sunday Times; Guardian; Good Housekeeping; World Med., etc. Mbrships: Magistrates' Assn.; Soc. of Authors; Soc. for the Hist. of Pharmacy. Address: Thurston House, Wingrave, Aylesbury, Bucks. HP22 4QE, UK.

CAMP, William Newton Alexander, b. 12 May 1926, Nazareth, Palestine. Communications Consultant. Educ: M.A, Oriel Coll., Oxford, UK. Publs: (novels) Prospects of Love, 1957; Idle on Parade, 1958; The Ruling Passion, 1959; A Man's World, 1962; Two Schools of Thought, 1964; Flavour of Decay, 1967; The Father Figures, 1970; (biog.) The Glittering Prizes; F. E. Smith. Contbr. to: New Statesman; Tribune; Spectator. Address: 61 Gloucester Cres., London NW1, UK.

CAMPBELL, Alistair Te Ariki, b. 25 June 1925. Rarotonga, Cook Islands. Editor; Author; Poet. Educ: B.A., Vic. Univ. of Wellington, NZ. Publs: Mine Eyes Dazzle (verse), 1950; The Happy Summer (children's fiction), 1961; Wild Honey (verse), 1964; When the Bough Breaks (play), 1970; Kapiti: Selected Poems, 1947-71, 1972. Contbr. to: Landfall (NZ); The NZ Listener; Poetry Aust.; Islands (NZ). Address: 4 Rawhiti Rd., Pukerua Bay, NZ.

CAMPBELL, E., b. 1932, Launceston, Tas., Australia. Barrister & Solicitor; University Professor of Law; Writer. Educ: LL.B.; B.Ec.; Ph.D.; Univ. of Tas.; Duke Univ. Publs: Parliamentary Privilege in Australia, 1966; Freedom in Australia (co-author), 1966, 2nd revised ed., 1973; Legal Research (co-author), 1967. Contbr. to: Aust. Law Jrnl.; Sydney Law Review; Western Aust. Law Review; Tas. Univ. Law Review; Univ. of Qld. Law Review; Pub. Law. Address: Faculty of Law, Monash Univ., Clayton, Vic., Australia 3168.

CAMPBELL, Eugene Miller, b. 1922, Glasgow, UK. Press & Publications Officer, manufacturing company. Contbr. to: Merchandising Vision – mag. of Brit. Cellophane Ltd. (Ed., 1955–); Sunday Times; Guardian; Weekend; etc. Address: Applegarth, Milton Avenue, Chalfont St. Peter, Gerrards Cross, Bucks., UK.

CAMPBELL, Ian, b. 25 Aug. 1942, Lausanne, Switz. University Lecturer. Educ: M.A., Univ. of Aberdeen, 1964, Ph.D., Univ. of Edinburgh, 1970. Publs: incl: McLellan's Jamie the Saxt (co-ed.), 1970; Duke-Edinburgh ed., letters of Thomas & Jane Welsh Carlyle, 7 vols. (co-ed.), 1970-c, 76; Thomas Carlyle, 1974. Contbr. to: The Bibliothek; Criticism; Engl. Lang. Notes; Scottish Lit. Jrnl.; etc. Mbrships. incl: Fellow, Soc. of Antiquaries of Scotland; Coun., Assn. of Scottish Lit. Studies; VP, Carlyle Soc. Address: Dept. of Engl. Lit., Univ. of Edinburgh, David Hume Tower, George Sq., Edinburgh EH8 9JX, UK.

CAMPBELL, Ian Barclay, b. 1916, Christchurch, NZ. Director of Safety, Accident Compensation Commission; Secretary, Workers' Compensation Board. Educ: B.Com., Victoria Univ. of Wellington. Publs: Handbook to Workers Compensation Act 1956, 1958; Workers' Compensation Law in N.Z., 1964. Contbr. to: Safety News; etc. Mbrships: F.C.I.S.; A.C.A.; A.A.I.I. Address: 28 Burma Rd., Khandallah, Wellington 4, NZ.

CAMPBELL, James Joseph, b. Belfast, UK. Director of Institute of Education; Editor; University Senator. Educ: M.A., H.Dip.E., Queen's Univ., Belfast. Publs: Legends of Ireland; Sch. Ed. of Pro Lege Manilla & Pro Archia. Contbr. to: Irish Bookman (Ed.); BBC (short stories, talks, etc.); var. jrnls. Hons: J.P. Address: 3 Cross Avenue, Marlborough Park, Belfast BT9 6HQ, UK.

CAMPBELL, (John) Ramsey, b. 4 Jan. 1946. Author. Publs: The Inhabitant of the Lake, 1964; Demons by Daylight, 1973; The Height of the Scream, 1975; Ed., Super Horror, 1975. Contbr. to: New Writings in SF; Year's Best Horror Stories; num. anthols., ed., Lin Carter, Richard Davis, August Derleth, Michel Parry, David Sutton, Film Critic, BBC Radio Merseyside, 1960–. Mbrships: Sci. Fiction Writers Am.; Brit. Film Inst.; Pres., Brit. Fantasy Soc., 1972-74. Address: 54 Buckingham Rd., Liverpool L13 8A2, UK.

CAMPBELL, Michael Mussen, b. 1924, Dublin, Ireland. Novelist; Reporter. Educ: Trinity Coll., Dublin; BA; BL. Publs. (novels): Peter Perry; Oh, Mary, This London; Across the Water. Contbr. to: Punch; Spectator; Books & Bookmen; The Irish Times. Address: 39 Kendal Street, London W2, UK.

CAMPBELL, Patrick Gordon, Baron Glenavy, b. 1916. Author; Columnist. Educ: Pembroke Coll., Oxford. Publs. incl: A Long Drink of Cold Water, 1950; A Short Trot with a Cultured Mind, 1952; Life in Thin Slices, 1954; Patrick Campbell's Omnibus, 1956; Come Here Till I Tell You, 1960; How to Become a Scratch Golfer, 1963; Brewing Up in the Basement, 1963; My Life & Easy Times, 1967; The Coarse of Events, 1968; The High Speed Gasworks, 1970; Fat Tuesday Tails, 1972. Contbr. to: Sunday Times; Sunday Dispatch, 1947-59; writer & broadcaster on TV & Radio; etc. Address: 65/66 Eccleston Sq., London SW1, UK.

CAMPBELL, Peter Walter, b. 17 June 1926, Poole, UK. University Professor of Politics; Writer. Educ: B.A., 1947, M.A., 1951, New Coll., Oxford; Nuffield Coll., Oxford. Publs: Encyclopaedia of World Politics (w. W. Theimer), 1950; French Electoral Systems & Elections 1789-1957, 1958; The Constitution of the Fifth Republic (w. B. Chapman), 1958. Contbr. to: Parly. Affairs; Pol. Studies (Ed., 1964-69); Int. Affairs; Times Lit. Supplement; Revue Française de Sci. Pol., etc. Mbrships: Pol. Studies Assn. of UK (Hon. Sec.-Treas., 1955-58); Hansard Soc. (Cnslr., 1962–). Address: Dept. of Politics, The University, Reading, UK.

CAMPBELL, Robert Wellington, b. 4 Feb. 1926, Wichita, Kan., USA. Professor of Economics. Educ: A.B., 1948, M.A., 1950, Univ. of Kan., M.A., (Soviet Studies), 1952, Ph.D.(Econs.), 1956, Harvard. Publs: Soviet Economic Power, 1960, 3rd ed. 1973; Accounting in Soviet Planning & Management, 1963; The Economics of Soviet Oil & Gas, 1968. Address: 919 E. Hunter, Bloomington, IN 47401, USA.

CAMPION, Sidney Ronald, pen name SWAYNE, Geoffrey, b. 30 June 1891, Leicester, UK. Journalist; Author. Educ: Tchng. Dip., Chester Coll.; Barrister-at-Law, Gray's Inn; Wimbledon & St. Martin's Schls. of Art. Publs: Sunlight on the Foothills, 1941; Towards the Mountains, 1943; Reaching High Heaven, 1945; Only the Stars Remain, 1947; Post Office, 1961; The World of Colin Wilson, 1962; Press Gallery, 1964. Contbr. to: Sunday Times; Daily Telegraph; Yorkshire Post; Liverpool Daily Post; etc. Mbrships. incl: F.R.S.A.; Fellow, Inst. Jrnlsts.; Nat. Union Jrnlsts.; Francis Bacon Soc.; Recip., O.B.E. Address: 13 Argyle Court, Argyle Road, Southport PR9 9LQ, Merseyside, UK.

CAMPLING, (Rev. Canon) Christopher Russell, b. 4 July 1927, Brisbane, Australia. Clerk in Holy Orders. Educ: M.A., St. Edmund Hall, Oxford Univ.; Cuddesdon Theol. Coll. Publs: The Way, the Truth & the Life, 6 vols., 1964-65; Words for Worship, 1969; Ed., The Fourth Lesson for Daily Office, Book 1, 1973, Book 2, 1974. Contbr. to: Guide to Divinity Teaching; Theol.; Learning for Living; Guardian; A.R.E. Mbr., Soc. of Authors. Hon. Canon, Worcester Cathedral, 1974. Address: Pershore Vicarage, Worcs. WR10 1DT, UK.

CAMPOY, Antonio Manuel, b. 16 Nov. 1924, Cuevas de Almanzora, Spain. Lecturer in Art. Educ: Lic., Philos. Publs. incl: Viaje por España (Como nos ven los extranjeros), 1963; Museo del Prado, 1970; Diccionario Crítico del Arte Español Compemporáneo, 1973; 16 other books, 50 monographies on art, etc. Contbr. to ABC, Madrid; Fine Arts Review, Madrid; Goya Review, Madrid; Prog. III Nat. Radio of Spain. Mbrships: Int. Assn. of Art Critics, Paris; Acad. of Fine Arts of Isabel of Hungary, Seville; Bd. of Trustees, Spanish Mus. of Contemporary Art. Hons: Nat. Radio & TV Prize, 1963; Silver Medal for Culture, Italy, 1965; Nat. Prize for Art Criticism, 1972; Cross of Alfonso X el Sabio, 1966, 1974. Address: Prof. Waksman 4, Madrid 16, Spain.

CAMPTON, David, b. 1924, Leicester, UK. Freelance Writer; Actor; Theatre Director. Publs: The Lunatic View, 1960; The Laboratory, 1955; Soldier From the Wars Returning, 1963; On Stage, 1965; Little Brother; Little Sister; Out of the Flying Pan, 1966; The Cactus Garden, 1967; Ladies Night, 1967; On Stage Again, 1969; Laughter & Fear, 1969; The Life & Death of Almost Everybody, 1971; Jonah, 1972; Three Gothic Plays, 1973; Timesneeze, 1974. Contbr. to: Drama; Amateur Stage; Scottish Theatre. Mbrships. incl: Soc. of Authors; Writers' Guild of GB. Agent: ACTAC (Theatrical & Cinematic) Ltd. Address: 35 Liberty Road, Glenfield, Leicester LE3 8JF, UK.

CANAWAY, William Hamilton, b. 12 June 1925, Altrincham, Cheshire, UK. Author. Educ: B.A., Dip.Ed., M.A., Univ. of Wales. Publs: A Creel of Willow, 1957; The Ring-Givers, 1958; A Snowdon Stream, 1958; The Seal, 1959; Sammy Going South, 1961; The Hunter & the Horns, 1962; My Feet Upon A Rock, 1963; Crows in a Green Tree, 1965; The Grey Seas of Jutland, 1966; The Mules of Borgo San Marco, 1967; A Moral Obligation, 1969; A Declaration

of Independence, 1971; Harry Doing Good, 1973; Glory of the Sea, 1974. Mbrships. incl: PEN; Writers' Guild, GB; Brontë Soc. Hons: Royal Film Perf. of Sammy Going South; Box Off. Blue Ribbon Award for same film (as A Boy Ten Feet Tall), 1963. Address: c/o Agent, Curtis Brown & Spokesmen, 1 Craven Hill, London W2 3EW, UK.

CANDLIN, E. Frank, b. 29 May 1911, Brighton, UK. Technical College Principal. Writer. Educ: B.A., Dip. in Educ., King's Coll., Univ. of London. Publs: Teach Yourself Journalism, 1950; English for Professional Students, 1951; Teach Yourself Freelance Writing, 1952; Present Day English for Foreign Students, 1960-68; New Present Day English for Foreign Students, 1970-74. Contbr. to num. educl. jrnls. Mbrships: Int. Assn. of Tchrs. of Engl. as For. Lang.; Engl. Speaking Union. Address: 386 Woodstock Rd., Oxford, UK.

CANGEMI, Joseph Peter, b. 26 June 1936, Syracuse, N.Y., USA. Associate Professor of Psychology; Business Consultant for several major organizations. Educ: B.S., State Univ. N.Y., 1959; M.Sc., & Grad. work, Syracuse Univ., 1959-64; Ed.D. Indiana Univ., 1973; Univs. Wis. & Western Ky. Publs: Over 100 articles in mainly academic & business periodicals & books. Contbr. to: Jrnl. Negro Educ.; Education; Personnel Jrnl.; Daily Jrnl. (Venezuela); Rehab. Review; Coll. Student Jrnl. (Ed. Bd., 1973-75); TV & films. Mbrships. incl: Am. Personnel & Guidance Assn. (Life Mbr.); Int. Coun. Psychols.; Am. Assn. Schl. Admnstrs. (Life Mbr.) Hons. incl: Cert. US Army. Address: 1305 Woodhurst Dr., Bowling Green, KY 42101, USA.

CANNAN, Denis, b. 14 May 1919, Oxford, UK. Playwright. Publs: Max, 1949; Captain Carvallo, 1950. Colombe (transl'd. from Anouilh), 1951; Misery Me!, 1955; You & Your Wife, 1955; The Power & The Glory (adapted from Graham Greene), 1956; Who's Your Father?, 1958,US ed., (co-author), 1966; Ghosts (new version of Ibsen's play), 1967; One at Night, 1971; The IK (co-author), 1975; sev. feature films. Agent: P.L.R. Address: Godley's, Rudgwick, Horsham, W. Sussex RH12 3AJ, UK.

CANNING, Victor, b. 1911. Author. Publs. incl: Golden Salamander, 1948; Venetian Bird, 1951; Castle Minerva, 1954; His Bones are Coral, 1955; Manasco Road, 1957; The Dragon Tree, 1958; The Buring Eye, 1960; Black Flamingo, 1962; Mr Finchley Discovers his England; Mr Finchley Goes to Paris; Polycarp's Progress; Fly Away Paul; Matthew Silverman; Fountain Inn; Everyman's England; Green Battlefield; The Chasm; A Forest of Eyes; The Scorpio Letters; Doubled in Diamonds; The Python Project; Queen's Prawn & other works. Agent, Curtis Brown Ltd. Address: Riverside House, Alswear, S. Molton, N. Devon, UK.

CANNON, Garland, b. 5 Dec. 1924, Ft. Worth, Tex., USA. Professor. Educ: B.A., Univ. of Tex., M.A., Stanford Univ., Ph.D., Univ. of Tex. Publs: Sir William Jones, Orientalist, 1952; Oriental Jones: A Biography, 1964; Ed., The Letters of Sir William Jones, 1970; A History of the English Language, 1972. Contbr. to: Journalism Qrtly.; Mod. Lang. Jrnl.; Mod. Philol.; Publs: of the MLA; Philol. Qrtly; etc. Mbr., MLA. Recip., London Sunday Telegraph Book of Yr. Award for Letters of Sir William Jones, 1971. Address: Dept. of English, Texas A & M Univ., College Station, TX 77843, USA.

CANSDALE, George Soper, b. 1909, Brentwood, Essex, UK. Writer. Educ: B.A., B.Sc., Edmund Hall, Oxford Univ. Publs: Animals of West Africa; Animals & Man; Reptiles of West Africa; West African Snakes; George Cansdale's Zoo Book; George Cansdale's Pets Book; Animals of Bible Lands. Mbrships: Royal C'wlth. Soc.; Fellow, Linnean Soc. Address: Dove Cottage, Gt. Chesterford, Essex, CB10 1PL, UK.

CANTENS, Agustin, J., b. 15 Jan. 1937, Havana, Cuba. Accountant. Educ: B.B.A., La Salle Univ., Havana, 1961. Publs: Postal History of Cuba, in preparation. Contbr. to: Ed., SPA Jrnl.; Cuban Philatelist. Mbrships: Fndr. & currently Pres., Cuban Philatelic Soc. of Am.; Am. Philatelic Soc.; Soc. of Philatelic Ams.; Regional Dir., Soc. of Philaticians. Recip., 1st Prize, APS Lit. Competition, 1972. Address: P.O. Box 4500 55, Miami, FL 33145, USA.

CANTONI, Louis Joseph, b. 22 May 1919, Detroit, Mich., USA. University Professor. Educ: A.B., Univ. of Calif. at Berkeley, 1946; M. Soc. Work, 1949, Ph.D., 1953, Univ. of Mich. Publs: Ed., Placement of the Handicapped in Competitive Employment, 1957;

Counselling Your Friends (w. L. Cantoni), 1961; With Joy I Called to You (poetry), 1969; Poetry Ed., Cathedral Digest. Contbr. to num. profl. & lit. books & jrnls. Mbrships. incl: World Poetry Soc. Intercontinental; Fndr., Acad. of Am. Poets; South & West (poetry); Poetry Soc. of Mich.; Fndrs. Soc., Detroit Inst. of Arts; F.A.A.A.S.; Am. Philos. Assn.; Am. Psychol. Assn.; Am. Personnel & Guidance Assn.; Nat. Rehabilitation Assn. Address: 2591 Woodstock Dr., Detroit, MI 48203. USA.

CANTOR, Arthur, b. 12 Mar. 1920, Boston, Mass., USA. Theatrical Producer. Educ: A.B., Harvard Coll., Cambridge, Mass., 1940. Publs: The Playmakers (w. Stuart Little), 1970. Contbr. to: N.Y. Mag. Address: 1 W 72nd St., N.Y., USA.

CANTWELL, Robert Lloyd Emmett, b. 31 Jan. 1908, Little Falls, Wash., USA. Author. Educ: Univ. of Wash., Seattle. Publs: Laugh & Lie Down, 1931; The Land of Plenty, 1934; Nathaniel Hawthorne, the American Years, 1947; American Men of Letters, 1956; Alexander Wilson, Naturalist & Pioneer, 1960; The Real McCoy, the Life & Times of Norman Selby, 1971; The Hidden Northwest, 1972. Contbr. to: Fortune; Time; New Am. Writing. Ga. Review; New Repub.; Vanity Fair; Symposium; Hound & Horn; etc. Mbrships. incl: N.Y. Geol. & Biog. Soc.; Sigma Delta Chi. Address: 520 W. 114th St., N.Y., NY 10025, USA.

CAPDEVILA, Arturo, b. 18 Mar. 1889. Lawyer; Writer. Educ: Docts. in Laws & Soc. Sci., Univ. of Cordoba. Publs. incl: E Poema del Nenúfar; La Sulamita (play); Las Visperas de Caseros (hist.); Las Invasiones Inglesas (hist.); Babel y el Castellano; El gitano y su leyenda; Loores Platenses; Tierra Mía; Abraces; Maestro de amor; Adveniemiento; El gran Reidor Segovia; treatises on med. Recip., Spanish & Argentine awards. Address: Juncal 3575, Buenos Aires, Argentina.

CAPE, Peter, b. 17 Jan. 1929, Helensville, NZ. Writer; Commentator; Photographer. Educ: B.A., Auckland Univ.; B.A., Canterbury Univ.; L.Th., Selwyn Coll., Dunedin. Publs: Bear & Cindy; The Mine in the Hills; People At Work (series of 11); Artists & Craftsmen in New Zealand, 1969; Prints & Printmakers in New Zealand, 1974. Contbr. to: Landfall; N.Z. Listener; Nat. Bus. Review; Pub. Serv. Jrnl.; N.Z. Broadcasting Corp. Mbrships. incl: PEN Int.; TV Writers, Dirs. & Prods. Guild. Hons: Imperial Rels. Trust Bursary, 1962; Queen Elizabeth II Arts Coun. Rsch. Grant, 1974. Address: 385 Hill St., Richmond, Nelson, NZ.

CAPEK, Milic, b. 26 Jan. 1909, Trebechovice, Czech. Professor of Philosophy. Educ: M.A. & Ph.D., 1935, M.Sc., 1936, King Charles Univ. of Prague; Sorbonne; Univ. of Chgo. Publs: The Philosophical Impact of Contemporary Physics, 1961 (Spanish ed., 1965); Bergson & Modern Physics, 1971. Contbr. to: Philos. Review; Review of Metaphys.; Phil. & Phenomenol. Rsch.; Jrnl. of the Hist. of Ideas; Jrnl. of Philos.; Philos. Forum; Scientia; Diogenes; Boston Studies in the Philos. of Sci.; etc. Mbrships: Am. Philos. Assn.; Peirce Soc.; Metaphys. Soc. of Am.; Czech. Soc. of Arts & Scis. in USA. Address: 143 Hobart St., Hingham, MA 02043, USA.

CAPLAN, Gerald, b. 6 Mar. 1917, Liverpool, UK. Educator; Psychiatrist. Educ: B.Sc., Univ. of Manchester, 1937; D.P.M., Royal Coll. of Physns. & Surgs., London, 1942; M.B. & Ch.B., 1940; M.D., Univ. of Manchester, 1945. Publs. incl: An Approach to Community Mental Health, 1961; Adolescence — Psychosocial Perspectives, 1969; Theory & Practice of Mental Health Consultation, 1970; Support Systems & Community Mental Health, 1974. Mbrships: Fellow, Royal Coll. of Psychs., UK, 1971. Recip., Hon. M.A., Harvard Univ., 1970. Address: Lab. of Community Psych., 58 Fenwood Rd., Boston, MA 02115, USA.

CAPON, (Rev.) Anthony, b. 1926, Chislehurst, UK. Executive of Scripture Union of Canada; Writer. Educ: M.A.; B.D.; Trinity Coll., Cambridge; Oak Hill Coll., London; Wycliffe Coll., Toronto, Can.; Ordained, C. of E., 1953. Publs: The Church & the Child (w. E. Capon), 1967. Contbr. to: Eternity; Moody Monthly. Address: 114 Pricefield Rd., Toronto, Ont. M4W 1Z9, Can.

CAPONIGRI, A. Robert, b. 16 Nov. 1915, Chgo., Ill., USA. Professor of Philosophy; Writer. Educ: A.B., 1935; M.A., 1936, Loyola Univ., Chgo.; Ph.D., Univ. of Chgo., 1942. Publs. incl: Time & Idea: the Theory of History in Giambattista Vico, 1953; Modern Catholic Thinkers, 1960;

Transl. w. introduction, The Prince, by Machiavelli, 1963; A History of Western Philosophy, 5 vols., 1964-70; num. philosl. papers. Contbr. to: Humanitas (Genoa); Les Etudes Philosophiques (Paris); Modern Schlman. (USA); etc. Mbrships. incl: Exec. Comm., Am. Cath. Philosl. Assn.; Metaphys. Soc. of Am. Recip., num. acad. awards. Address: 1120 Memorial Library, Notre Dame, IN, USA.

CAPOTE, Truman, b. 1924, New Orleans, USA. Author; Journalist; Publs: Other Voices, Other Rooms; A Tree of Might; Local Color; The Grass Harp; The Muses are Heard; Breakfast at Tiffany's. Contbr. to: New Yorker; Atlantic Monthly; Harper's Bazaar; Botteghe Obscure; etc. Address: c/o Random House, 457 Madison Ave., N.Y., NY, USA.

CARADON, (Lord), (Hugh Mackintosh Foot), b. 8 Oct. 1907, Plymouth, UK. Colonial Administrator. Educ: B.A. St. John's Coll., Cambridge, 1929. Publs: A Start in Freedom, 1964. Hons: P.C.; G.C.M.G.; M.C.V.O.; O.B.E. Address: Trematon Castle, Saltash, Cornwall, UK.

CARAS, Roger Andrew, b. 24 May 1928, Methuen, Mass., USA. Naturalist; Author. Educ: A.B., Univ. of Southern Calif., L.A., 1954. Publs. incl: Death as a Way of Life, 1971; Vanishing Wildlife, 1971; Animal Children, 1971; Animal Architects, 1971; Birds & Flight, 1971; Protective Coloration, 1972; Animal Courtship, 1972; Boundary: Land & Sea, 1972; Creatures of the Night, 1972; Going to the Zoo with Roger Caras, 1973; Venomous Animals of the World, 1974; Roger Caras' Nature Quiz Books 1 & 2, 1974; Plum Gut, 1974; The Private Lives of Animals, 1974. Contbr. to num. mags. & jrnls. Many radio & TV appearances. Mbrships. incl: Fellow, Royal Soc. Arts, London; Assoc. Curator Rare Books, Cleveland Mus. of Nat. Hist.; V.P.; Humane Soc. U.S. Agent: Int. Famous Agcy. Address: c/o Int. Famous Agcy., 1301 Ave. of the Ams,. N.Y., NY 10019, USA.

CARBONELL-BASSET, Delfin, b. 28 Sept. 1938, Murcia Spain. Teacher. Educ: B.A., Duquesne Univ., USA; M.A., Univ. of Pitts.; Lic. Filos., Ph.D., Univ. of Madrid, Spain. Publs. incl: Hombres solitarios, 1963; Dictionary of English Idioms, 1971; Los Ahorcados, 1971; The Conquest of English, 1974. Contbr. to Spanish, US jrnls. Address: c. Maria Panes 4, Madrid 3, Spain.

CARDENA, Clement, pen name DELAUBE, b. 1914, Barcelona, Spain. Poet; Playwright; Lecturer. Educ: Univ. of Barcelona; M.A.; Ph.D. Publs. (Poetry): Oceans Animics, 1935; Gotims de raim, 1935; Somnis al vent, 1938; Alas, 1935; Fièvre, 1946; (Plays): Surmounting, 1944; Eclipse. Contbr. to poetry & lit. mags. Mbrships: Acad. de Langue d'Oc; Brit. League of Dramatists; Author's Club. Address: 10 Place de la Navigation, Geneva, Switzerland.

CÁRDENAS, Nancy, b. 29 May 1934, Parras, Coahuila, Mexico. Theatre Director; Journalist. Educ: Ph.D., Univ. Nacional Autónoma de Mexico; Yale Univ. Drama Schl., USA, 1960-61; Inst. for For. Students, Lódz, Poland. Publs. incl: El cántaro seco (play), 1960; El cine polaco (essay), 1962; Vuelo acordado (poems), 1971; var. transls. of plays. Contbr. to var. lit. jrnls. Mbrships: Sec., Awards Jury, PECIME; Pres., Fndr., Cons. Coun., CCCCM. Hons: Best Dir. of Yr., 1970; Heraldo, for Best Dir. of Yr., 1972; Best Dir., Monterrey Festival, 1973. Address: Felipe Villanueva 90-402, Mexico 20, D.F., Mexico.

CARDOSO-PIRES, Jose, b. 2 Oct. 1925, Peso, Portugal. Writer. Educ: Maths. studies, Univ. of Lisbon. Publs: Caminheiros & Outros Contos (short stories), 1949; Historias de Amor (short stories), 1952; O Anjo Ancorado (novel), 1959; O Render dos Herois (play); O Hospede de Job (novel); O Delfim (novel), 1972; Dinossauro Excelentissimo, 1974. Contbr. to: Esprit; Die Zeit; Index; etc. Mbrships: PEN; Associacao Portuguesa de Escritores. Recip., 1st Prize, Camilo Castelo Branco Award, 1963. Address: Rua Sao Joao de Brito, 7-, Lisbon 5, Portugal.

CARDWELL, Guy Adams, b. 14 Nov. 1905, Savannah, Ga., USA. Professor. Educ: A.B., Univ. of N.C., 1926; A.M., Harvard, 1932; Ph.D., Univ. of N.C., 1936. Publs: The Uncollected Poems of Henry Timrod, 1942; Readings from the Americas, 1947; Der Amerikanische Roman, 1850-1951, 1953; Twins of Genius, 1953; Discussions of Mark Twain, 1963. Contbr. to: Poetry; Saturday Review of Lit.; Yale Review; Sewanee Review; New Engl. Quarterly; Va. Quarterly Review. Hons: Story reprinted w. award in The Am. Lit. Anthol., III, 1970; Story reprinted w. 2nd prize in Prize Stories, 1971. Address: 984 Memorial Drive, Cambridge, MA 02138, USA.

CARÊME, Maurice, b. 12 May 1899, Wavre, Belgium. Poet; Writer. Publs. incl: (poetry) Mère, 1935; Femme, 1946; Petites Légendes, 1949; La Voix de Silence, 1951; Images Perdues, 1954; Pigeon Vole, 1958; Bruges, 1963; Brabant, 1967; Entre Deux Mondes, 1970; Poète de la Joie, 1971; Le Moulin de Papier, 1973; De Feu et de Cendre, 1974; Mains, 1974; (novels & tales) La Passagère Invisible, 1950; Un Trou dans la Tête, 1964; Du Temps où les Bêtes parlaient, 1966. Mbrships: PEN; Assn. of Belgian Writers. Hons. incl: Int. Grand Prix for Poetry, 1968; L'élu Prince des Poêts à Paris, 1972. Address: Ave. Nellie Melba 14, 1070 Brussels, Belgium.

CARETTE, Louis-Albert, pen name MARCEAU, Félicien, b. 1913, Cortenberg, Belgium. Author. Educ: Coll. de la Trinité, Louvain; Univ. of Louvain. Publs. incl: (fiction) Chasseneuil, 1947; Chair & Cuir, 1951; L'homme du Roi, 1952; Les Elans du Coeur, 1955; Creezy, 1969; (essays) Balzac & son Monde, 1955; (short stories) Secrètes Noces, 1954; (plays) Caterina, 1954; L'Oeuf, 1956; La Preuve Par Quatre, 1964; Un jour, j'ai rencontré la Verité, 1967; L'Homme En Question, 1973; & sev. publs. transl. into Engl. Contbr. to: Lavinia; Tableau de la Lit. Francaise; Now French Writing. Address: c/o Eds. Gallimard, 5 rue Sebastien-Bottin, Paris 7e, France.

CAREW, Jan Rynveld, b. 24 Sept. 1925, Agricola, Repub. of Guyana. Author; University Professor. Educ: Howard Univ., Wash. D.C., USA, 1945-46; Univ. of W. Reserve, Cleveland, Ohio, 1946-48; Dip., Adv. Sci. Rsch., Charles Univ., Prague, Czech., 1949-50; Sorbonne Univ., Paris, France, 1950-52. Publs incl: The Last Barbarian, 1959; Moscow Is Not My Mecca, 1964; The Third Gift, 1974; Rape the Sun, 1974; The Origins of Racism & Resistance in the Americas, 1974. Contbr. to: N.Y. Times Sunday Book Review; N.Y. Times; var. lit. publs. Mbrships: Am. Soc. of Authors; PEN; AAUP. Hons: Can. Arts Coun. Fellowship, 1969; Ill. Arts Coun. Award, 1974. Address: Northwestern Univ., Evanston, IL 60201, USA.

CARGAS, Harry James, b. 18 June 1932, Hamtramck, Mich., USA. Teacher; Author. Educ: B.A., 1957, M.A., 1958, Univ. of Mich.; Ph.D., St. Louis Univ., 1968. Publs. incl: Graham Greene, 1969; Death & Hope, 1971; The Continuous Flame: Teilhard in the Great Traditions, 1970; English as a Second Language, 1970; Daniel Berrigan & Contemporary Protest Poetry, 1972. Contbr. to num. lit. publs. Ed., Webster Review; Contbng. Ed., Focus Midwest, St. Louis Jrnlsm. Review. Mbrships: PEN; Nat. Assn. for Humanities Educ.; MLA. Address: Webster College, Webster Groves, MO 63119, USA.

CARLISLE, Lilian Baker, b. 1 Jan. 1912, Meridian, Miss., USA. Author; Lecturer. Educ: Dickinson Coll., Carlisle, Pa., 1929-30; Legal Secretarial Degree, Peirce Coll. of Bus. Admnstrn., Phila., Pa. Publs. incl: Carriages at Shelburne Museum, 1956; Pieced Work & Applique Quilts at Shelburne Museum, 1957; Hat Boxes & Bandboxes at Shelburne Museum, 1960; Inaugural Selection of 18th & 19th Century American Art, 1960; Vermont Clock & Watchmakers, Silversmiths & Jewellers, 1778-1878, 1970; ed., 6 "Look Around" books on Vt. towns. Contbr. to num. jrnls. on antiques & Am. hist. Mbrships: Past Pres., League of Vt. Writers; Am. Pen Women. Address: 117 Lakeview Terr., Burlington, VT, USA.

CARLSON, Dale Bick, b. 24 May 1935, NYC, USA. Writer. Educ: B.A., Wellesley Coll. Publs. incl: Perkins the Brain, 1964; Miss Maloo, 1966; Frankenstein, 1968; Dracula, 1969; Arithmetic, I, II, III, 1969; Warlord of the Genji, 1970; The Mountain of Truth, 1972; Good Morning Danny, 1973; Girls Are Equal Too, 1974; Baby Needs Shoes, 1974. Hons: Hon. Book, Spring Book Festival, for Mountain of Truth, 1972. Address: 116 E. 63rd St., N.Y., NY 10021, USA.

CARLSON, Natalie Savage, b. 1906, Winchester, Va., USA. Newspaper Reporter; Author. Publs: 25 jvnle. books inclng. The Talking Cat & Other Stories of French Canada; Alphonse, That Bearded One; The Family Under the Bridge; The Empty Schoolhouse. Mbr., Authors' Guild. Hons: N.Y. Herald Tribune Children's Spring Book Festival Awards, 1952 & 1954; Newbery Hon. Book Award, 1959; Child Study Assn. of Am. Award, 1965. Address: Doral Mobile Home Villas, 17 Clearwater, FL 33515, USA.

CARLSON, Ruth Kearney, b 2 June 1911, Ramona, Calif., USA. Professor, Cal-State University, Hayward, California. Educ: A.B., Univ. of Calif., 1932; M.A., ibid, 1944; Ed.D., 1959. Publs. incl: Emerging Humanity —

Multi-ethnic Literature for Children & Adolescents, 1972; Writing Aids through the Grades, 1970; Poetry for Today's Child, 1968; Sparkling Words — Two Hundred Practical & Creative Writing Ideas, 1965, revised, 1973. Contbr. to: Engl. Jrnl., etc. Mbr., Calif. Authors Club. Hons. incl: Cert. of Merit, Ctrl. Calif. Coun. of Tchrs. of Engl., 1970. Address: 1718 LeRoy Ave., Berkeley, CA, USA.

CARLTON, David, b. 16 July 1938, Bradford, UK. Senior Lecturer in Diplomatic History. Educ: London Schl. of Econs. & Pol. Sci.; King's Coll., London; B.A., 1960; Ph.D., 1966. Publs: MacDonald versus Henderson: The Foreign Policy of the Second Labour Government, 1970; Ed., The Dynamics of the Arms Race, 1975. Contbr. to: Histl. Jrnl.; Pol. Sci. Quarterly; Royal United Serv. Instn. Jrnl.; Jrnl. of Brit. Studies; Int. Affairs; Disarmament & Arms Control; Jrnl. of Contemporary Hist.; etc. Mbrships: Int. Inst. for Strategic Studies; Royal Inst. of Int. Affairs; Reform Club. Address: 28 Westminster Mansions, Great Smith St., London SW1P 3BP, UK.

CARLTON, Lessie, b. 4 Aug. 1903, Nacogdoches Co., Tex., USA. Professor of Education Emerita; Visiting Director, Reading Centre. Educ: B.S., M.S., N. Tex. Univ.; Ed.D., Univ. of Houston, Tex. Publs: Reading, Self-Directive Dramatization, & Self-Concept (w. R. H. Moore). Contbr. to num. profl. jrnls. & books in USA & abroad. Hons. incl: Invited Advsr., W. German Inst. for Early Childhood Educ.; Visiting Tchr., Cumberland Coll., Ky., 1972—; Award, Rsch. Projects — 190, US Ed. Office. Address: Melrose Acres, Rt. 1, Sand Flat Rd., Alto, TX 75925, USA.

CARMAN, William Young, b. 1909, Ottawa, Ont., Can. Deputy Director, National Army Museum, 1965-74. Publs. incl: A History of Firearms, 1955; British Military Uniforms from Contemporary Pictures, 1957; Indian Army Uniform (Cavalry), 1961; British Military Uniform, 1962; Sabretasches of the British Army, 1969; Headdress of the British Army (Cavalry), 1968; Headdress of the British Army (Yeomanry), 1970; Ed., Military Uniforms of the World, 1968; Dress Regulations of the Army 1900, 1969; Model Soldiers, 1972; Royal Artillery, 1973; Badges & Insignia of the Armed Forces (w. Commander May), 1974. Contbr. to: Soc. for Army Hist. Rsch.; Mil. Hist. Soc.; Ency. Britannica; etc. Mbrships: F.S.A.; Fellow, Royal Histl. Soc. Address: 94 Mulgrave Rd., Sutton, Surrey, UK.

CARNE, Peter Horwill, b. 9 June 1924, Bentley, Hants, UK. Newspaper Advertisement Sales Manager. Publs: See the South By Car, 1965; See More of the South By Car, 1966; Discovering Wessex, 1974. Ed., Deer. Contbr. to: Country Life; Countryman; Field; Gamekeeper & Countryside; Hampshire; Shooting Times & Country Mag.; Southern Evening Echo; etc. Address: Highland Water, The Drove, West End, Southampton SO3 3EF, UK.

CARNEGIE, James Alexander, b. 6 Apr. 1938, Kingston, Jamaica, W. Indies. Teacher. Educ: B.A., 1960, M.A., 1969, Univ. of W. Indies. Publs: Some Aspects of Jamaica's Politics 1918-1938, 1973; Herb McKenley, Olympic Star (co-author), 1974; George Headley (co-author), 1971; The People Who Came, Book 2 (co-author), 1970. Contbr. to: New World Quarterly; Tapia; Jamaica Jrnl.; Sportslife Mag.; Pub. Opinion Annual. Mbrships: Board Dirs. Jamaica School Music (Chmn.); Nat. Sports Ltd.; PEN. Recip., Silver Medal, 1st Olympic Press Games, Mexico City, 1969. Address: 46 Palmoral Ave., Kingston 6, Jamaica, W. Indies.

CARNER, Mosco, b. 1904, Vienna, Austria. Conductor of Orchestra; Music Advisor; Writer. Educ: Ph.D., Univ. of Vienna. Publs: A Study of 20th-Century Harmony; Of Men & Music; The Waltz; Puccini: A Critical Biography; Music Between World Wars I & II; Alban Berg, the Man & the Work. Contbr. to: BBC (Advsry. Panel, 1944-) The Times (Music Critic, 1961-69); Pelican Books; The Listener; Music & Letters; Musical Times. Address: 14 Elsworthy Rd., London NW3, UK.

CARNICER, Ramón, b. 24 Dec. 1912, Villafranca de Bierzo, Spain. Writer. Educ: Ph.D., Univ. of Barcelona. Publs: Cuentos de ayer y de hoy, 1961; Los árboles de oro, 1962; Vida y obra de Pablo Piferrer, 1963; Donde las Hurdes se llaman Cabrera, 1964; Sobre el lenguaje de hoy, 1969; Entre la Ciencia y la Magia. Mariano Cubí, 1969; Nueva York. Nivel de vida, nivel de muerte, 1970; También murió Manceñido, 1972; Nuevas reflexiones sobre el lenguaje, 1972; Las personas y las cosas, 1973. Contbr. to: var. jrnls. Mbrships: Mutualidad de Escritores de Libros;

Ateneo Barcelonés. Hons. incl: Premio Leopoldo Alas, 1961; Premio Menéndez Pelayo, 1961; Cruz de Alfonso X el Sabio, 1971. Address: Roca y Batlle 6, Barcelona 6, Spain.

CAROE, (Sir) Olaf Kirkpatrick, b. 15 Nov. 1892, Chelsea, London, UK. Former Indian Civil Servant, & Governor, N.W. Frontier Province. Educ: M.A., D.Litt., Magdalen Coll., Oxford Univ. Publs: Wells of Power, 1951; Soviet Empire, 1953; The Pathans, 1958; Poems of Khushhal. Contbr. to: Round Table (Coun. mbr.); Asian Affairs; Geogl. Jrnl.; Times; Spectator; Time & Tide; Foreign Affairs (N.Y.). Mbrships. incl: Royal Soc. Asian Affairs (Coun.); Tibet Soc. of UK. Hons: K.C.I.E., 1944; K.C.S.I., 1946; F.R.S.L. Lawrence of Arabia Medal, Royal Soc. Asian Affairs, 1973. Address: Newham House, Steyning, Sussex, UK.

CAROL, Joseph, b. 24 Dec. 1929, Martorell, Spain. Novelist. Educ: Univ. of Barcelona. Publs: The State Hotel, 1959; The Flood, 1966; Confessions of An Addict, 1971; Between the Sword & the Wall, 1974. Contbr. to: La Vanguardia Espanola; La Estafeta Literaria. Mbr., Nat. Assn. of Spanish Writers & Artists. Hons: Cafe Gijou Prize of Madrid, 1959; Planeta Prize Finalist, 1965. Address: Avda. Infanta Carlota 155 5 , 1 , Barcelona 15, Spain.

CARPENTER, Allan, b. 11 May 1917, Waterloo, Iowa, USA. Publisher; Author. Educ: B.A., Univ. of Northern Iowa. Publs. incl: 129 books, 52 in the series Enchantment of America, 42 in the series Enchantment of Africa & 20 in the series Enchantment of Latin America. Contbr. to: major periodicals. Mbr., Arts Club of Chgo. Address: Suite 4602, 175 E. Delaware Pl., Chgo., IL 60611, USA.

CARPENTIER Y VALMONT, Alejo, b. 26 Dec. 1904. Writer. Educ: Univ. of Havana. Publs: Ecue-Yambo-O (novel), 1933; A History of Cuban Music; El Reino de Este Mundo (novel), 1949; Los Pasos Perdidos (novel), 1953; El Acoso (novel), 1956; Guerra de Tiempo (stories), 1958; El Siglo de las Luces (novel), 1963. Contbr. to var. jrnls. Recip., Prix du Meilleur Livre Etranger, 1956. Address: Apartado 6153, Havana, Cuba.

CARR, Francis, b. 10 Apr. 1924, Warwick, UK. Impressario. Educ: Schl. of Slavonic Studies, London Univ. Publs: European Erotic Art, 1972; A History of Russia, 1975. Contbr. to: Army Quarterly; Everybody's; Birmingham Post; Contact. Address: 34 Hillgate Pl., London W8, UK.

CARR, John Dickson. Writer. Publs. incl: The Wax Works Murder; The Eight Swords; The Arabian Nights Murder; To Wake the Dead; The Burning Court; The Blind Barber; the Problem of the Wire Cage; The Emperor's Snuff Box; Till Death Do Us Part; The Sleeping Sphinx; The Crooked Hinge; Death Watch; The Bride of Newgate; The Devil In Velvet; The Case of the Constant Suicides; The Man who Could Not Shudder; The Lost Gallows; Captain Cut-Throat; Patrick Butler for the Defence; Fire Burn; & many other novels. Address: c/o Hamish Hamilton, 90 Great Russell St., London WC1, UK.

CARR, Ray de la Montayne, b. 26 Apr. 1902, Spartanburg, S.C., USA. Freelance Writer & Lecturer; Presbyterian Minister; Advertising Executive. Educ: A.B., Davidson Coll., N.C., B.D., U.T.S. Richmond, Va.; Th.M.; Cert. N.C. State Tchr.'s Coll. Contbr. to: Am. Bard.; Am. Courier; Am. Poetry Mag.; Anthol. 1 & 2; Boston Post; Charleston News & Courier; Christian Herald; Poetry Digest; Poet's Log Book; New Review; Reflections; Westminster Mag.; Ldr. Observer; N.Y. Times; New Poetry Digest; N.E. Courier, etc. Mbrships: Poetry Soc. of Am.; World Poetry Soc. Intercontinental; Bklyn. Poetry Soc.; Greenwich Village Poetry Soc. Address: 530 E. 23rd St., N.Y., NY 10010, USA.

CARRASCO MARTÍNEZ, Cástulo, pen names K'Rasco & Dr. Irónicus, b. 26 Mar. 1910, Terrinches, Spain. Essayist; Dramatist; Novelist. Publs. incl: (essays) Tres españolas, y algunos más, 1949; Por los blancos caminos del margen, 1952; Correspondencia con Alcaide Sánchez, 1955; El teatro de Miguel de Unamuno, 1960; El delirante mundo de Stringberg, 1968; (theatre) Película de aventuras, 1955; (novel) ¿ y el último crimen? 1957; A bordo de un teléfono, 1958; Los Nebrija en Brozas, 1971; (reference) Diccionario de Medecina, 1974. Contbr. to num. newspapers, inclng. column as Dr. Irónicus in Profesión Médica. Recip., sev. 1st prizes. Address: Calle Martínez Izquierdo 14, Madrid 28, Spain.

CARRINGTON, Charles Edmund, pen name EDMONDS, Charles, b. 1897, W. Bromwich, UK. Writer. Educ: M.A., Christ Ch., Oxford Univ.; M.A., Cantab. Publs. incl: A Subaltern's War, 1929; History of England (w. J. Hampden Jackson), 1932; T. E. Lawrence, 1935; An Exposition of Empire, 1947; The British Overseas, 1950; Life of J. R. Godley, 1951; Life of Rudyard Kipling, 1955; Cambridge History of the British Empire III (jt. author), 1959. Contbr. to: African Survey, 1957; Survey of International Affairs, 1957-58, 1959-60. Address: 56 Canonbury Pk. S., London N1, UK.

CARRINGTON, Noel Lewis, b. 1894, Hereford, UK. Publisher. Educ: B.A., Christ Ch., Oxford. Publs: Colour in Interior Decoration; Design in Civilisation; Popular Art; Village Life; This Man's Father; Face of the Land; Letters of Mark Gertler. Recip., O.B.E. Address: Long Acre Farm, Lambourn, Berks., UK.

CARRION, Alejandro, pen name JUAN SIN CIELO, b. 11 Mar. 1915, Loja, Ecuador. Writer; Journalist. Educ: Ph.B., Mejía Nat. Inst., Quito; M. Soc. Scis., Nat. Univ. of Loja. Publs. incl: (poetry) Luz del Nuevo Paisaje, 1937; Poesia del arbol y la sangre, 1954; La Sangre sobre la Tierra, 1957; Nunca! Nunca! , 1960; Poeta y Peregrino, 1968; (stories) La Manzana dañada, 1964; Muerte en su Isla, 1969; (novel) La Espina; La llave perdida, 1970. Contbr. to: Letras del Ecuador; num. other hispano-am. jrnls. Mbrships. incl: Soc. Juridica & Literaria, Quito; other lit. orgs. Hons. incl: South Am. Poetry Prize, 1937; Nat. Lit. Prize, Ecuador, 1958; Moors Cabot Prize, 1958; XIV Leopoldo Alas Prize, Barcelona, 1967. Doct., Columbia Univ., USA. Address: 715 College Pkwy., Rockville, MD 20850, USA.

CARROLL, Nicholas, b. 5 May 1916, London, UK. Journalist. Contbr. to: Sunday Times (Dpty. For. Ed. & Diplomatic Corres.); Daily Despatch, Manchester (Former London Ed. & Asst. Ed.); Kemsley Newspapers (For. Corres., 1946-48); BBC world & home servs. Mbrships. incl: Nat. Union Jrnlsts. Recip., O.B.E., 1944. Address: 29 Teignmouth Rd., London NW2.

CARSON, Edward Arthur, b. 20 Feb. 1911, Toronto, Can. Librarian & Archivist. Educ: B.A., M.A. Publs: The Ancient & Rightful Customs, 1972; The Records of the Bahamas (w. D. G. Saunders), .1973. Contbr. to: Jrnl. of Soc. of Archivists; Maritime Hist.; Mariners Mirror; Portsmouth Papers; New Lib. World. Mbrships: Fellow, Inst. of Linguists; Chmn., London Reg. Soc., Inst of Linguists; Soc. of Archivists; Chmn., Soc. of Archivists, S.E. Reg. (1973). Address: 66 Church St., Reigate, Surrey RH2 0SP, UK.

CARSWELL, John Patrick, b. 1918, London, UK. Secretary of University Grants Committee; Author. Educ: M.A., St. John's Coll., Oxford. Publs: The Adventures of Baron Munchausen (Ed.) 1947; The Prospector, 1950; The Old Cause, 1954; The South Sea Bubble, 1960; Lying Awake; The Political Journal of George Bubb Dodington (Ed. w. L. A. Dralle), 1965; The Civil Servant & His World, 1966; The Descent on England, 1969; From Revolution to Revolution 1688-1776, 1973; etc. Contbr. to: Times Lit. Supplement; Guardian; Hist. Today; Spectator; New Statesman; etc. Address: 32 Park Village E., London NW1, UK.

CARTER, Cedric Oswald, b. 26 Sept. 1917, Port Said, Egypt. Medical Geneticist. Educ: B.A., 1939, M.A., Queen's Coll., Oxford; B.M., B.Ch., 1942, D.M., St. Thomas' Hospital, London. Publs: Human Heredity, 1961; An ABC of Medical Genetics, 1969; The Genetics of Locomotive Disorders, 1974. Contbr. of articles to sev. med. jrnls. Mbrships: Pres., Engenics Soc.; Pres., Chem. Genetics Soc.; Fellow, Royal Coll. Physicians. Address: 42 Forest Drive, Keston, Kent, UK.

CARTER, Charles Frederick, b. 15 Aug. 1919, Rugby, UK. Vice-Chancellor, University of Lancaster. Educ: Rugby Schl.; M.A., St. John's Coll., Cambridge. Publs. incl: (w. G. L. S. Shackle & others) Uncertainty & Business Decisions, 1954; Investment in Innovation, 1958; The Science of Wealth, 1960, 3rd ed. 1973; The Northern Ireland Problem, 1962, 2nd ed. 1972; On Having a Sense of all Conditions, 1971; (w. J. L. Ford & others) Uncertainty & Expectation in Economics, 1972. Contbr. to: The Econ. Jrnl. Mbrships. incl: Sec.-Gen., Royal Econ. Soc.; Chmn., Ctr. for Studies in Social Policy. Hons: F.B.A., 1970; Mbr., Royal Irish Acad.; D.Econ.Sc., Nat. Univ. of Ireland. Address: Univ. House, Bailrigg, The Univ., Lancaster LA1 4YW, UK.

CARTER, Frances Tunnell, b. 22 May 1922, Pontotoc, Miss., USA. Teacher. Educ: A.A., Wood Jr. Coll., Miss., 1942; B.S., Univ. of Southern Miss., 1946; M.S., Univ. of Tenn., 1946; Ed.D., Univ. of Ill., 1954. Publs: Sammy in the Country, 1960; 'Tween-age Ambassadors, 1970; Sharing Times Seven, 1971. Contbr. to: Birmingham News; Ala. Schl. Jrnl.; var. sorority mags. & relig. periodicals. Mbrships. incl: Quill Club; Nat. League Am. Pen Women; Ala. Soc. Poetry; Nat. 1st V.P.; Kappa Delta Epsilon. Hons. incl: 1st prize, poetry, Author/Poet Publs,. 1970; 1st prize, patriotic story, Ala. Writer's Conclave, 1972; 1st prize, juvenile story, Quill Club, 1974. Address: 2561 Rocky Ridge Rd., Birmingham, AL 35243, USA.

CARTER, Francis William, b. 4 July, 1938, Staffs., UK. University Lecturer. Educ: B.A., Sheffield Univ.; Dip.Ed., Cambridge; M.A., London Univ.; D.Nat.Sc., Charles Univ., Prague, Czech. Publs: Dubrovnik (Ragusa): a Classic City State, 1972; Ed., An Historical Geography of the Balkans, 1975. Contbr. to: Jrnl. of Croatian Studies; L'information Geographique; Österreichische Osthefte; Transp. Hist.; Econ. Hist. Revue; etc. Mbrships: Inst. of Brit. Geogs.; PEN; F.R.G.S.; Royal Asiatic Soc. Recip., Award, Croatian-Acad. of Am., 1969. Address: Dept. of Geog., Univ. Coll., London WC1, UK.

CARTER, Gerald Emmett, b. 1 Mar. 1912, Montreal, P.Q., Can. Roman Catholic Bishop of London, Ont., Can. Educ: B.Th., Grand Sem. Montreal; B.A., 1933, M.A., 1940, Ph.D. & L.Th., 1947, Univ. of Montreal. Publs: The Catholic Public Schools of Quebec, 1957; Psychology & the Cross, 1959; The Modern Challenge to Religious Education, 1961. Mbrships. incl: Can. Cath. Histl. Assn. Hons. incl: LL.D., Univ. of Western Ont., 1966; D.H.L., Duquesne Univ., Pitts., Pa., 1962; Book of the Month, Thos. More Assn. Address: 1070 Waterloo St., London, Ont. N6A 3Y2, Can.

CARTER, Jeff, b. 1928, Melbourne, Australia. Freelance Journalist/Photographer; Author. Publs: People of the Inland, 1966; Life & Land of Central Australia, 1967; Outback in Focus, 1968; Stout Hearts & Leathery Hands, 1968; In the Tracks of the Cattle, 1968; Surf Beaches of Australia's East Coast, 1968; Four-Wheel Drive Swagman, 1969; In the Steps of the Explorers, 1969; The New Frontier, 1970; Wild Country, 1971; Wild Animal Farm, 1972; Guide to Central Australia, 1972; Home & Away, 1975. Contbr. to: Nat. Geog. Mag.; Life; Paris Match; Esquire; var. Aust. nat. mags. Address: Glenrock Farm, Foxground 2534, N.S.W., Australia.

CARTLAND, Barbara. Lecturer; President, National Association of Health. Publs. incl: Sweet Punishment; Not Love Alone; A Beggar Wished; First Class Lady?; Dangerous Experiment; The Forgotten City; Bitter Winds; But Never Free; Broken Barriers; The Gods Forget; The Leaping Flame; Stolen Halo; Again This Rapture; The Unpredictable Bride; Love Me Forever; The Captive Heart; Love is an Eagle; Love is the Enemy; Stars in My Heart; Sweet Adventure; Life & Sex; Vitamins for Vitality; (autobiography) We Danced All Night, 1919-29; The Isthmus Years, 1919-30; The Years of Opportunity, 1939-45; I Search for Rainbows, 1946-69. Contbr. to: Radio & TV. Address: Camfield Pl., Hatfield, Herts., UK.

CARUBA, Alan, b. 9 Oct. 1937, Newark, N.J., USA. Editorial Consultant; Director of Publications; Columnist. Educ: B.A., Univ. of Miami, 1959. Publs: People Touch, 1972; 1776 Revisited, 1973; Angelface, 1975; Nat. syndicated column, Bookviews, in newspapers. Contbr. to jrnls. & newspapers. Mbrships: Authors Guild of Am.; Soc. of Mag. Writers; N.J. Communicators; Am. Fedn. of Radio & TV Artists. Hons: Authors Award, N.J. Assn. of Tchrs. of Engl., 1972, Newark Coll. of Engrng., 1973, 1974; Andy Award, Advt. Club of N.Y., 1972. Address: P.O. Box 157, Maplewood, NJ 07040, USA.

CARUS-WILSON, Eleanora Mary, b. 1897, Montreal, Can. Professor of Economic History. Educ: M.A., LL.D., Univ. of London. Publs: The Overseas Trade of Bristol in the Later Middle Ages; The Woollen Industry (Cambridge Econ. Hist. of Europe, Vol. II); Medieval Merchant Venturers; England's Export Trade, 1275-1547. Contbr. to: Econ. Hist. Review; Revue du Nord; Medieval Archaeol. Hons: Fellow, Brit. Acad. Address: 14 Lansdowne Rd., London W11 3LW, UK.

CARVER, (Field Marshal Sir) Michael, b. 1915, Bletchingley, Surrey, UK. Chief Defence Staff. Educ: Royal Mil. Coll., Sandhurst. Publs: Second to None (hist. of Royal

Scots Greys), 1950; El Alamein, 1962; Tobruk, 1964. Contbr. to: R.U.S.I. Jrnl.; Royal Armoured Corps Jrnl.; Tank; Armour. Address: Shackleford Old Rectory, Godalming, Surrey GU8 6AE, UK.

CARVIC, Heron, b. London, UK. Dancer; Actor; Designer; Builder & Decorator; Market Gardener; Writer. Publs: Picture Miss Seeton, 1968, also USA & Germany; Miss Seeton Draws the Line, 1969, 1970; Witch Miss Seeton, 1971; Miss Seeton Sings, 1973, 1974; Odds on Miss Seeton, 1975. Mbrships: Crime Writers' Assn.; Writers Guild of GB. Address: c/o Curtis Brown Ltd., 1 Craven Hill, London W2 3EW, UK.

CARY, Robert William Lewis, b. 31 Aug. 1920, Plymouth, UK. Director; General Manager. Educ: Malvern Coll. & St. John's Coll., Oxford; M.A., 1946. Publs: A Time to Die, 1968; Charter Royal, 1970; Goodbye Tomorrow, 1971; Countess Billie, 1973; The Story of "Reps", 1975. Res. Book Critic, Rhodesia TV, 1962-67. Mbr., Chartered Inst. of Transp. Recip., Mil. Cross, 1943. Address: 'Denga Charakupa', 10 Boscobel Drive East, Highlands, Salisbury, Rhodesia.

CARY, William Lucius, b. 27 Nov. 1910, Columbus, Ohio, USA. Professor of Law. Publs. incl: Effects of Taxation on Corporate Mergers (co-author), 1951; Politics & the Regulatory Agencies, 1967; The Law & the Lore of Endowment Funds (co-author), 1969; Cases & Materials on Corporation, 4th ed., 1969. Contbr. to: Yale Law Jrnl.; Columbia Law Jrnl.; Harvard Law Review; Harvard Bus. Review. Mbrships. incl: Am. Acad. of Arts & Scis.; Coun. on For. Rels.; Chmn., SEC, 1961-64. Address: Columbia Univ. Schl. of Law, N.Y., NY 10027, USA.

CASEMENT, Christina, pen name MACLEAN, Christina, b. 1933, Wickham, Hants., UK. Writer. Publs: The Bunpenny, 1965; Wandering Robinson, 1969; Ringing Robinson, 1971; Robinson & Slyboots, 1974. Contbr. to: Woman's Own; Woman's Weekly; other mags. Address: Dene Cottage, W. Harting, Petersfield, Hants., UK.

CASEY, Juanita, b. 1925, Herefordshire, UK. Circus Horse Manager. Publs: Hath the Rain a Father?, 1965; Horse by the River, 1966; The Horse of Selene, 1971; The Circus, 1974. Contbr. to: Irish Times; Irish Press; Ireland of the Welcomes; Western Mail; Jrnl. of Irish Lit.; Cornhill Mag. Mbrships: Appaloosa Soc. of Am.; Irish Donkey Soc. Address: Cruachan, Gloragh, Sneem, Killarney, Co. Kerry, Repub. of Ireland.

CASH, Grace, occasional pen name CASH, Grady, b. 13 Apr. 1915, Hall Co., Ga., USA. Secretary. Educ: Tenn. Temple Coll., Morehead Coll.; Okla. Univ.; B.A., Brenau Coll. Publs: Highway's Edge, 1965, Promise Unto Death, 1966 (novels); 380 poems in mags. & anthols.; Over 400 short stories. Hons: Hon. Life Mbr., Mark Twain Soc. Address: Rte. 2, c/o Mrs. Rufus S. Cash, Flowery Branch, GA 30542, USA.

CASH, Joseph Harper, b. 3 Jan. 1927, Mitchell, S.D., USA. Professor of History. Educ: B.A., 1949, M.A., 1959, Univ. of S.D.; Ph.D., Univ. of Iowa, 1965. Publs: To Be an Indian (w. Herbert Hoover), 1971; The Sioux People, 1971; Working the Homestake, 1973; The Mandan, Arikara & Hidatsa People (w. G. Wolff), 1974; The Practice of Oral History, 1975. Contbr. to: Jrnl. of Am. Hist.; Western Histl. Quarterly; S.D. Hist.; S.D. Histl. Collects. Mbrships: Org. of Am. Histns.; Western Hist. Assn.; State Histl. Soc., S.D. (Exec. Bd.); Oral Hist. Assn. Recip., Disting. Serv. Citation, Univ. of S.D. Address: 609 Catalina Dr., Vermillion, SD 57069, USA.

CASKEY, John Langdon, b. 7 Dec. 1908, Boston, Mass., USA. Professor of Classical & Preclassical Archaeology; Field Director of Excavations in Greece. Educ: B.A., Yale Univ., 1931; Ph.D., Univ. of Cinn., 1939. Publs: Troy (w. Carl W. Blegen & others), vols. I-IV, 1950-58; chapts. on Early & Middle Bronze Age, Cambridge Ancient History, vols. I & II, 3rd ed. Contbr. to: Hesperia; Am. Jrnl. of Archaeol.; Jrnl. of Hellenic Studies; Archaiologikon Deltion; Kadmos. Mbr., many profl. socs. Address: Dept. of Classics, Univ. of Cinn., Cinn., OH 45221, USA.

CASPARY, Vera, b. Chgo., Ill., USA. Writer. Publs. incl: (novels & screenplays) Les Girls; Letter to Three Wives; Claudia & David; I Can Get It For You Wholesale; Wedding in Paris (musical comedy); The Husband; Thelma; The Weeping & the Laughter; Stranger than Truth; Bedelia;

Laura; The White Girl; Thicker than Water; Evvie; A Chosen Sparrow; The Man Who Loved His Wife; The Rosecrest Cell; Final Portrait; The Dreamers. Agent: Curtis Brown Ltd. Address: c/o W. H. Allen & Co., 43 Essex St., London WC2, UK.

CASS, Emily Elizabeth, b. 21 Aug. 1905, Beam, UK. Ophthalmic Surgeon. Educ: M.R.C.S. & L.R.C.P., London, 1927; M.B. & B.S., Univ. of London, 1928. Publs: Six Cases of Squint, 1934; Spanish Cooking, 1958, 3rd ed. 1973; Myopia in the Northwest Territories, 1974. Contbr. to: Brit. Jrnl. of Ophthalmol.; Sev. other profl. jrnls. Num. sci. papers read at int. congresses & other profl. confs. & meetings. Mbrships. incl: Fellow, Royal Soc. of Med.; Int. Soc. of Ophthalmol.; Pres., Int. Soc. of Geogl. Ophthalmol. Hons. incl: Order of Can., 1970; Spanish Order of Merit, 1972. Address: Box 688, Fort Smith, N.W.T., XOE OPO, Can.

CASS, Joan Evelyn, b. Southfleet, UK. Nursery School Headmistress; Lecturer, University Institute of Education; Social Worker. Num. publs. incl: Literature & the Young Child, 1957; The Cat Thief, 1961; The Cat Show, 1962; Blossom Finds a Home, 1963; The Canal Trip, 1966; The Cats Go To Market, 1968; An Anthology — The Patchwork Quilt, 1968; Aloysious the Redundant Engine, 1970; The Dragon Who was Too Hot, 1970; Chang & the Robbers, 1971; The Cats & the Car Thieves, 1971; The Significance of Children's Play, 1971; The Dragon Who Grew, 1973; Hubert Hippo, 1974; Milly Mouse, 1974. Contbr. to lit. & educl. jrnls. Mbrships. incl: Soc. of Authors; VP, Fedn. of Children's Books; Brit. Assn. for Early Childhood Educ. Address: 9 Walcot Gdns., London SE11, UK.

CASS, Thomas, b. 1931, York, UK. Senior Lecturer in Management. Educ: B.Sc., St. John's Coll., York. Publs: Statistical Methods in Management, 1969. Contbr. to: Jrnl. Inst. Work Study; Jrnl. Inst. Marketing. Address: 21 Neville Cres., Bromham, Beds., UK.

CASSIE, (William) Fisher, b. 1905, Montifieth, Angus, UK. University Professor. Educ: Univ. of St. Andrews; Univ. of Ill., USA; LL.D.; Ph.D.; M.S. Publs: Structural Analysis; Mechanics of Engineering Soils (w. P. L. Capper); Structure in Building (w. J. H. Napper); Fundamental Foundations; Statics, Structure & Stress. Contbr. to var. profl. jrnls. Mbrships: F.R.S.E.; F.I.C.E.; F.I.Struct.E.; P.P.I.H.E.; Past Chmn., Northern Cos. Assn., Inst. of Civ. Engrs.; Fndr. Chmn., Northern Cos. Br., Inst. of Structural Engrs.; Past Pres., Inst. of Hwy. Engrs. Address: Morwick House, Beal Bank, Warkworth, Northumberland NE65 0TB, UK.

CASSILL, R(onald) V(erlin), b. 17 May 1919, Cedar Falls, Iowa, USA. Writer; Professor of English. Educ: B.A., M.A., Univ. of Iowa; grad. study, Sorbonne, Paris, France. Publs: (novels) Clem Anderson, 1961; Pretty Leslie, 1963; The President, 1964; La Vie Passionée of Rodney Buckthorne, 1968; Doctor Cobb's Game, 1970; The Goss Women, 1974; (short stories) The Father, 1965; The Happy Marriage, 1967. Contbr. to: Esquire; Atlantic; Saturday Evening Post; N.Y. Times; Wash. Post. Mbrships: Authors' Guild; PEN. Hons: Rockefeller Grant in Creative Writing, 1954; Guggenheim Grant, 1968. Address: 22 Boylston Avenue, Providence, RI 02906, USA.

CASSOLA, Albert Maria, b. 1915, Valletta, Malta, d. 23 June 1974. Writer; Broadcaster. Educ: Univs. of Foreigners in Milan, Rome, Perugia, Siena, Italy. Publs. incl: Ghadu Kemm Jibda, 1947; Gabra ta Gawhar, 1948; Il Penitente, 1950; Vagiti, 1950; Gogo Rummiena, 1954, last ed., 1972; Whisky e Pastasciutta, 1960; Maltese in Easy Stages, 1962, last ed., 1969; Space Adventure, 1964; Il Micio nello Stivale, 1962; San Gregorio Magno, 1968; Novelli u Essays bil-Malti, 1971; Tliet Nisa u Ragel, 1972; Nina, 1973; It-Tfajla bil-Fjur fuq Sidirha, 1975. Contbr. to: Writer, Amateur Stage, Linguists' Review (all UK); Apollo; Selva; La Nazione; Il Malti; etc. Mbr. of var. acad. & lit. orgs. Hons. incl: Cav. Uff., Italian Repub. Address: "Greenmantle", St. Andrew's Drive, St. Andrew's, Malta.

CASSOLA, Carlo, b. 1917, Rome, Italy. Professor of History & Philosophy. Educ: Univ. of Rome. Publs: La Visita, 1942; Fausto e Anna, 1952; Il Taglio del Bosco, 1959; La Ragazza di Bube, 1960; Un Cuore Arido, 1961; Bebo's Girl, 1962. Address: Via Michelangelo 12, Grosseto, Italy.

CASSON, John, b. 28 Oct. 1909, London, UK. Former Stage Producer; Former Personnel Administrator; Communication Consultant. Publs: Using Words, 1968;

Lewis & Sybil, 1972. Contbr. to: Scottish Field; The Age; Rydges; & other jrnls. Mbrships. incl: Int. Soc. for Gen. Semantics. Recip., O.B.E.(Mil.), 1946. Address: 15 Lawrence St., London SW3 5NF, UK.

CASSOU, Jean, b. 9 July 1897. Writer. Educ: Lic. ès Lettres, Univ. of Paris (Sorbonne). Publs. incl: Les Harmonies Viennoises (novel), 1925; Grandeur et Infamie du Tolstoi (essays), 1932; Les Massacres de Paris (novel), 1936; Picasso (criticism), 1939; Trente-tois sonnets composés au secret, 1944; Ingres (criticism) 1947; Situation de l'Art Moderne, 1951; Le Voisinage des Cavernes (novel), 1971; La Creation des Mondes (art criticism), 1971. Mbr., Acad. Royale de langue et littérature françaises de Belgique. Recip., var. decorations. Address: 4 rue du Cardinal-Lemoine, Paris 5e, France.

CASTELLANETA, Carlo, b. 1930, Milan, Italy. Novelist. Publs: Viaggio col padre, 1958; Una lunga rabbia, 1961; Villa di delizia, 1965; Gli incantesimi, 1968; La dolce compagna, 1970; La Paloma, 1972; Tante Storie, 1973; Notti e nebbie, 1975; (transls.) A Journey with Father, 1962; Until the Next Enchantment, 1970; This Gentle Companion, 1971. Contbr. to: Storia Illustrata. Address: Via Muratori 29, Milan, Italy.

CASTEX, Pierre-Georges, b. 20 June 1915, Toulouse, France. Vice-President, University of Paris, Sorbonne; Professor. Educ: D. ès L. Publs. incl: Le Conte fantastique en France, 1951; Alfred de Vigny, 1952; Baudelaire critique d'art, 1969; Histoire de la littérature française, 1974; critical works on Balzac, Stendhal & others. Contbr. to: Revue d'histoire littéraire de la France (Comm.); L'Information littéraire (Comm.); etc. Mbrships: Acad. of Moral & Pol. Scis.; Conseil Supérieur de Lettres. Hons: Grand Prix de la Critique littéraire, 1957; Chev., Legion of Honour, 1964; Off., Order of Arts & Letters. Address: 2 rue Albert Malet, 75012 Paris, France.

CASTILLO, Othon, b. 30 June 1912, Portoviejo, Ecuador. Journalist; Writer. Educ: B.Philos. & Letters, Olmedo Coll., Portoviejo. Publs: Nuestro Suelo, 1942; Sed en el Puerto, 1962, 1965; Y la Trompeta de Gringo Lloraba, 1971; La Cruel Naturaleza, 1973. Contbr. to: Vistazo; Revista de la Casa de la Cultura Ecuatorianaj Norte; La Estafeta Literaria; newspapers in Mexico, Central & S. Am. Mbrships. incl: Fndng. Sec., Casa de la Cultura Ecuatorianaj; Fndng. Mbr., Union Nacional de Periodistas of Guayaquil. Hons. incl: Gold Medal & Scroll, Minicipal Coun, Portoviejo, 1971; Winner, Nat. Novelist Contest of El Eniverso, Guayaquil, 1972; Juan Montalvo Award, Asociacion de Periodistas Guayaquil, 1972. Address: P.O. Box 5579 Metropolitan Stn., L.A., CA 90055, USA.

CASTLE, Harold George, b. 1 Mar. 1907, Wembley, Middlesex, UK. Publisher (retired); Author; Journalist. Educ: Ardingly Coll. Publs: Children's Book of the Circus, 1948; Britain's Motor Industry, 1950; Boy's Book of Motor Racing, 1953, latest ed., 1955; Boy's Book of the Air, 1953, latest ed., 1955; Wonder Book of the Army, 1954; Case for the Prosecution, 1956. Contbr. to var. mags., newspapers & BBC. Address: 12 Hereford Ct., Worcester Rd., Sutton, Surrey SM2 6QN, UK.

CASTRESANA, Luis, b. 7 May 1925, Bilbao, Spain. Writer; Painter. Educ: Athénée Royal, Forest, Brussels, Belgium; Univ. of Amsterdam, Netherlands. Publs: El Otro Arbol de Guernica (novel), 1967; Adiós (novel), 1970; Retrato de Una Bruja (novel), 1972; Dostoievsky (biog.); Iparraguirre (biog.). Contbr. to: ABC; Blanco & Negro; La Gaceta del Norte; also var. newspapers, S. Am., inclng. Universal, Caracas, Venezuela, El Mercurio, Santiago de Chile, El Tiempo, Bogota, Colombia. Mbr., Asociacion Nacional de Escritores y Artistes Españoles, Madrid. Hons: Nat. Prize of Lit., 1967; Fastenrath Prize of Spanish Royal Acad. Address: Avenida Zumalacarregui 123, Bilbao 7, Spain.

ĆASULE, Kole, b. 2 Mar. 1921, Prilep, Jugoslavia. Writer; Politician; Jugoslav Ambassador to Peru. Publs. incl: (short stories) The First Days, 1950; Dramas: A Branch on the Wind, The City Clock, Darknesses, The Whirlpool, 1967; Prose: 1945-1967, 1968; (drama) Game or Socialist Eva, 1969; (novel) Standing Tall, 1970; (drama) Partiture of a Miron, 1970; (drama) As You Like It: Boredom at the Peak of Power, or Abdication of a Caribbean Minister of Internal Affairs, 1975. Contbr. to: Forum; Communist; Razgledi; New Macedonia; Politika; num. other jrnls. & newspapers. Mbrships. incl: PEN; Writers' Assn. of Jugoslavia; Jrnlsts. Assn. of Jugoslavia. Hons: 11th of

October Prize, for book, Dramas; Nat. Theatre Prize, for Darknesses; Yugoslav Nat. Award 4th of July. Address: ul. Dimitrije Tucović br. 12, 91000 Skopje, Jugoslavia.

CATE, Curtis Wilson, b. 22 May 1924, Paris, France. Writer. Educ: B.A., Harvard Univ., USA, 1947; Dip. in Russian Lang., Ecole des Langues Orientales, Paris, France, 1949; postgrad. studies, Magdalen Coll., Oxford, UK. Publs: Antoine de Saint-Exupéry, 1970; George Sand, 1975. Contbr. to: Horizon; Nat. Review (USA). Hons: Grand Prix Littéraire de l'Aéro-Club de France, for Antoine de Saint-Exupéry, 1974. Address: c/o A. D. Peters, 10 Buckingham Street, London WC2, UK.

CATER, Donald Brian, b. 14 Sept. 1908, Oundle, UK. Experimental Pathologist, ret'd.; Writer. Educ: M.A., M.D., Sc.D., Cambridge; F.R.C.S. Charing Cross Hosp. Med. Schl. Publs: Basic Pathology & Morbid Anatomy, 1953. Contbr. to: Ency. Britannica, 1957; Progress in Biophys., vol. 10, 1960; Reference Electrodes, 1961; over 100 contbns. to sci. lit. in pathol., physiol., biochem., radiobiol., & cancer rsch. Mbrships: Pathol. Soc. of GB & Ireland; Expmtl. Pathol. Club; Assn. Radiation Rsch. Recip., acad. hons. Address: 90 Gilbert Rd., Cambridge CB4 3PD, UK.

CATER, Douglass, b. 24 Aug. 1923, Montgomery, Ala., USA. Writer; Editor; Government Official. Educ: Harvard Univ. Publs: Ethics in a Business Society (w. Marquis Childs), 1953; The Fourth Branch of Government, 1959; Power in Washington, 1963; Dan, The Irrelevant Man, 1970. Address: 770 Welch Rd., Palo Alto, CA, USA.

CATHERALL, Arthur, b. 6 Feb. 1906, Bolton, Lancs., UK. Author of Novels and Short Stories. Publs: over 100 books in UK inclng. Vibrant Brass; Tomorrow's Hunter; Step in My Shoes (play, w. David Read); Vanishing Lapland; Ten Fathoms Deep, 1954; Tenderfoot Trapper, 1958; Strange Invader, 1964; Lapland Outlaw, 1960; Prisoners in the Snow, 1967; Kidnapped by Accident, 1968; Duel in the High Hills, 1969; 154 eds. in Norway, Sweden, Finland, Germany, Holland, France, Switz., Austria, Spain, Portugal, S. Africa, Brazil, USA; over 1000 short stories. Contbr. to: TOP, Belgian educl. mag.; educl. works in UK, Sweden, Aust. & USA. Mbrships: Chmn., N. Branch, Soc. of Authors. Recip., Lit. Guild Award, USA, 5 times. Address: 31 Parkgate Drive, Bolton BL1 8SD, Lancs., UK.

CATLING, Darrel Charles, b. 1909, London, UK. Film Director & Writer. Publs: The Independent Frame, 1948; Worse Verse (contbng. author), 1971. Contbr. to: Sight & Sound; Brit. Jrnl. of Photography; Photographic Jrnl.; Int. Photographer, USA; Amateur Photographer; Sunday Times. Mbrships: Fellow, Royal Photographic Soc.; Assn. of Cinematography, TV & Allied Technicians; Brit. Film Inst. Address: Travellers Rest, Church St., Old Hatfield, Herts., UK.

CATTELL, Raymond Bernard, b. 1905, Staffs., UK. Director, Institute for Research on Morality & Adjustment; Writer. Educ: M.A., Ph.D., D.Sc., London Univ. Publs: incl: Description & Measurement of Personality, 1946; Factor Analysis, 1952; Personality & Motivation Structure & Measurement, 1957; Personality & Social Psychology, 1965; Handbook of Multivariate Experimental Psychology, 1966; Abilities, Their Structural Growth & Action, 1971; A New Morality from Science & Beyondism, 1972. Contbr. to: var. jrnls. on psychol., UK, USA, France, Italy, etc. Mbrships: Eugenics Soc.; N.Y. Acad. Scis., etc. Address: 615 Kirby Ave., Champaign, IL, USA.

CATTON, Bruce, b. 9 Oct. 1899. Editor; Historian. Educ: Oberlin Coll., USA. Publs. incl: The Warlords of Washington, 1948; Mr. Lincoln's Army, 1951; Glory Road, 1952; A Stillness at Appomattox, 1953; Banners at Shenandoah, 1955; This Hallowed Ground, 1956; America Goes to War, 1958; The Coming Fury, 1961; Terrible Swift Sword, 1963; Never Call Retreat, 1965; Grant Takes Command, 1969; Waiting for the Morning Train, 1972. Contbr. to: Am. Heritage Mag., Senior Ed., since 1959. Mbr., Am. Acad. of Arts & Letters. Hons. incl: Pulitzer Prize for History, 1954; Nat. Book Award, 1954; Litt.D.; LL.D. Address: 551 Fifth Ave., NYC, NY 10017, USA.

CAU, Jean, b. 8 July 1925. Writer; Journalist. Educ: Lic.Phil., Univ. of Paris. Publs. incl: Le cour de barre; Les Paroissiens; La Pitié de Dieu; Mon village (stories); Les oreilles et la queue (chronicle); Les Parachutists (play); Le Mâitre Monde (play); Dans un Nuage de Poussiere (play), 1967; Les Yeux Creves, 1968; Numance; L'Agonie de la

Vieille; Tropicanas, 1970. Contbr. to jrnls. inclng: l'Express; le Figaro littéraire; Candide. Recip., Prix Goncourt, 1961. Address: 13 rue de Seine, Paris 6e, France.

CAUSLEY, Charles, b. 1917, Launceston, Cornwall, UK. Poet; Teacher; Broadcaster. Educ: Peterborough Trng. Coll. Publs. incl: (poetry) Union Street, 1957; Johnny Alleluia, 1961; Underneath the Water, 1968; Figure of 8, 1969; Figgie Hobbin, 1971; The Tail of the Trinosaur, 1973; As I went down Zig Zag, 1974; Collected Poems, 1975; The Animals' Carol, 1975. Co-Author, Penguin Modern Poets 3, 1962; (prose) Hands to Dance, 1951; Three Heads made of Gold, 1975; sev. anthols. Ed., The Puffin Book of Magic Verse, 1974. Contbr. to num newspapers & mags. Mbrships: F.R.S.L.; Arts Coun. Lit. Panel, 1962-66. Recip., sev. acad. & lit. awards. Agent: David Higham Assoc. Ltd. Address: 2 Cyprus Well, Launceston, Cornwall, UK.

CAUTE, (John) David, b. 1936, Alexandria, Egypt. Author; Playwright; Former University Reader. Educ: M.A., D.Phil., Univ. of Oxford, UK. Publs. incl: Communism & the French Intellectuals, 1964; The Decline of the West, 1966; The Essential Writings of Karl Marx, 1967; Fanon, 1970; The Occupation, 1971; The Illusion, 1971; The Fellow-Travellers, 1973; Collisions, 1974; Cuba, Yes?, 1974; (plays) The Demonstration, 1969; The Fourth World, 1973. Recip., Author's Club Award & John Llewelyn Rhys Prize, 1960. Agents: (UK) Elaine Greene Ltd.; (USA) Georges Borchardt Inc. Address: c/o Elaine Greene Ltd., 31 Newington Green, London N16 9PU, UK.

CAVALIERO, Glen Tilburn, b. 1927, Eastbourne, UK. Writer; Church of England Minister, 1952-65. Educ: Magdalen Coll., Oxford; St. Catharine's Coll., Cambridge; M.A.; Ph.D. Publs: The Ancient People (poetry), 1973; John Cowper Powys: Novelist (criticism), 1973. Contbr. to: Cambridge Review; Theol.; Outposts; New Yorker; Delta; Stand. Address: 29 Portugal Place, Cambridge CB5 8AF, UK.

CAVALLIN, Bertil Ivan Pontus, b. 20 Feb. 1934, Helsingborg, Sweden. High School Teacher. Educ: M.A., Univ. of Lund, 1959. Publs. incl: Hellenika I-III (w. Ingmar Niklasson), 1965; Tacitus — The Annals I-VI (transl.), 1966; Tacitus — The Annals XI-XVI (transl.), 1968; Urbi et Orbi I-III (Ingmar Niklasson), 1968; Lucretius, On the Nature of Things (transl.), 1972; Demosthenes, On the Crown, Cicero, Against Verres V & for Marcellus (transl.), 1973. Contbr. to: Swedish daily papers & radio broadcasts. Address: Backen, Lundsberg, 680 80 Storfors, Sweden.

CAVALLO, Agatha, b. 19 May 1903, St. Louis, Mo., USA. Educator; Lecturer; Author. Educ: Ph.B., M.A., grad. studies, Univ. of Chgo.; grad. studies, Univ. of Madrid, Spain & var. US univs. & insts. Publs: Co-ed., Zaragueta, 1933; Experimental College Classroom & Laboratory Methodology, 1955, 1957, 1960, 1961. Contbr. of poetry, articles, book & film reviews to var. jrnls. & newspapers; TV panelist. Mbrships. incl: Life, var. offs., Am. Assn. of Tchrs. of Spanish & Portuguese; Life, NEA, MLA, Int. New Thought Assn.; Metaphys. Soc. of Am.; Soc. of Biblical Lit.; AAUP; AAUW; Int. Soc. Gen. Semantics; Fndn. for Integrative Learning; var. hon. fraternities. Awarded Lazo de Dama, Orden del Merito Civil, Spain, 1964. Address: 457 Boca Ciega Point Blvd. N., St. Petersburg, FL 33708, USA.

CAVANAGH, Helen M., b. 1 July 1904, Homer, Mich., USA. Distinguished Professor of History. Educ: B.A., Randolph-Macon Coll., 1925; A.M., 1931, Ph.D., 1938, Univ. of Chgo. Publs: Antislavery Sentiment & Politics in Old Northwest, 1844-60, 1938; Seed, Soil & Science: Story of Eugene D. Funk, Sr., 1959; Funk of Funk's Grove: Farmer, Legislator, Cattle King of Old Northwest, 1797-1865, 1952. Contbr. of book reviews to profl. jrnls. Hons: Jameson Fellow, Manuscripts Div., Lib. of Congress, 1937-38; D.H.L., Towson Coll. Address: Apt. 301, 401 E. Washington, Bloomington, IL 61701, USA.

CAVANAH, Frances, b. 26 Sept. 1899, Princeton, Ind., USA. Author; Former Editor. Educ: A.B., DePauw Univ., Greencastle, Ind., 1920. Publs: Our Country's Story, 1945, 1961; They Lived in the White House, 1949, 1961; Holiday Roundup, 1951, 1961; We Came to America, 1954; Abe Lincoln Gets his Chance, 1959; Meet the Presidents, 1962, 1965; Jenny Laid & Her Listening Cat, 1961; The Secret of Madame Doll, 1965; Freedom Ency: American Liberties in the Making, 1968; When Americans came to New Orleans, 1970; Jenny Lind's America, 1970; We Wanted to be Free,

1971; Marta & the Nazis, 1974; The Real Uncle Tom, 1975. Contbr. to anthols. & schl. rdrs. Mbrships. incl: Authors League Am.; Soc. of Midland Authors; Childrens Book Guild. Recip., var. hons. Address: Apt. 1421, 2501 E. 104th Ave., Denver, CO 80233, USA.

CAVANNA, Betty, b. 1909, Camden, N.J., USA. Writer. Educ: B.Litt., Douglas Coll., New Brunswick, N.J. Publs. incl: Stars in her Eyes, 1958; The Scarlet Sail, 1959; Accent on April, 1960; Fancy Free, 1961; A Time for Tenderness, 1962; Almost Like Sisters, 1963; Jenny Kimura, 1964; Mystery at Love's Creek, 1965; A Breath of Fresh Air, 1966; The Country Cousin, 1967; Mystery in Marrakech, 1968; Spice Island Mystery, 1969; Mystery on Safari, 1970; The Ghost of Ballyhooly, 1971; Mystery in the Museum, 1972; Petey, 1973; Joyride, 1974; Ruffles & Drums, 1975. Contbr. to var. mags. Mbrships: Cosmopolitan Club, NYC; Phila. Art Alliance; Author's Guild, Boston Women's Travel Club. Address: 170 Barnes Hill Rd., Concord, Mass., USA.

CAVENAGH, Winifred Elizabeth, b. Prestwich, Lancs., UK. Professor of Social Administration & Criminology; Justice of the Peace. Educ: B.Sc., Ph.D., Univ. London; Univ. Birmingham. Publs: Juvenile Courts, The Child & the Law; Four Decades of Students in Social Work. Contbr. to: Brit. Jrnl. Criminol.; Pub. Admin. Jrnl.; etc. Mbr., Wages Coun. & Indl. Tribunal. Agent: Curtis Brown. Address: Fac. Commerce & Social Sci., Univ. Birmingham, UK.

CAWS, Mary Ann, b. 10 Sept. 1933, Wilmington, N.C., USA. Professor; Critic. Educ: B.A., Bryn Mawr Coll., 1954; M.A., Yale, 1956; Univ. of Kan., 1962. Publs: Surrealism & The Literary Imagination, 1966; The Poetry of Dada & Surrealism, 1970; André Breton, 1971; The Inner Theatre of Recent French Poetry, 1972; Approximate Man & Other Writings of Tristan Tzara (tr. & ed.), 1973; About French Poetry from Dada to Tel Quel: Theory & Text, 1974; Ed., Dada/Surrealism; Director, Le Siècle éclaté; Asst. Ed., French Review. Contbr. to: Books Abroad; Contemp. Lit.; Symposium; French Review. Mbr., Assn. for the Study of Dada & Surrealism. Hons: Guggenheim Fellowship, 1972-73; Nat. Endowment for Humanities, 1974. Address: 140 E. 81, N.Y., NY 10028, USA.

CAYLEY, Michael Forde, b. 26 Feb. 1950, London, UK. Civil Servant; Writer. Educ: B.A., St. John's Coll. Oxford. Publs: (poems) Moorings, 1971; The Spider's Touch, 1973; Ed., Selected Poems of Richard Crashaw, 1972. Contbr. to: Outposts; Southern Arts Review; Tribune; Poetry Nation. Address: 44 Earl's Court Square, London SW5 9DQ, UK.

CECIL, Lord Edward Christian David Gascoyne, b. 1902, London, UK. Professor of English Literature. Educ: M.A., Christ Church Coll., Oxford. Publs: The Stricken Deer, 1929; Early Victorian Novelists, 1934; The Young Melbourne, 1939; Hardy the Novelist, 1943; Two Quiet Lives, 1948; Poets & Story-tellers, 1949; Lord M, 1954; The Fine Art of Reading, 1957. Hons: Litt.D; LL.D. Address: 7 Linton Rd., Oxford, UK.

CELA, Camilo José, b. 11 May 1916. Writer. Educ: Univ. of Madrid. Publs. incl: Pisando la dudosa luz del día (poems), 1945; Mrs. Caldwell habla con su hijo, 1953; La Catira, 1955; Judíos, moros y cristianos, 1956; El molino de viento (stories), 1956; Nuevo retablo de don Cristobita, 1957; Viaje al Pirineo de Lerida, 1965; Diccionario Secreto I, 1968, II, 1971; San Camilo 1936, 1969; Maria Sabina, 1970; A vueltas con España (essays), 1973; Oficio de tinieblas 5, 1973. Recip., Primio de la critica, 1955. Address: La Bonanova, Palma de Mallorca, Spain.

CERDAN TATO, Enrique, b. 1 Aug. 1930, Alicante, Spain. Writer; Journalist. Educ: Air Acad.; Bus. Schl.; Naval Schl.; Tchr. Trng.; var. univ. courses. Publs: Un Agujero en la Luz; La primavera piedra; El tiempo prometido; El lugar mas lejano; Cazar ballenas en los charcos bajo la luz cenital; Esquema de la Literatura Soviética; Todos los enanos del mundo. Contbr. to: Cuadernos Hispanoamericanos; Estafeta Literaria; ABC; Cuadernos para el Dialogo. Mbrships: Soc. of Authors of Spain; Fndr. Mbr., Past Pres., Club of Friends of UNESCO; etc. Hons. incl: Gupuzcoa Int. Novel Prize, 1966; Ciudad de Badalona Story Prize, 1967. Address: Calle Manuel Anton 11, 7, Alicante, Spain.

CEREA, Doris, b. 20 Mar. 1929, Vertemate, Como, Italy. Journalist. Educ: Dip., Elem. Tchng.; Study of langs. Publs: short stories in maj. mags. Contbr. to num. Italian newspapers: For. Corres., 1953—. Mbrship: Albo dei Giornalisti, Milan;. Address: 822½ N. Seward St., L.A., CA 90038, USA.

ČERKEZ, Vladimir, pen name ČEZ, b. 26 Nov. 1923, Sarajevo, Bosnia, Yugoslavia. Writer; Councillor in Assembly of SR Bosnia & Hercegovina, Sarajevo. Publs. incl: (poems) On the Fields, 1948; Flags of Krajina, 1951; Flowers, 1952; Spies, 1954; Blood & Desire, 1958; Space, 1971; Suncana zemlja, 1975; (stories) Dream & Life, 1971; (novels) A Sun in Smoke, 1958; Arena, 1961; Time of Growing Ripe, 1965; Birch Among Trenches, 1971; A Brave Soldier, 1973. Contbr. to num. Yugoslav Mags. & reviews. Mbrships. incl: PEN, Union of Writers of Yugoslavia (mng. bd.). Hons. incl: Prize Union of Writers Bosnia & Hercegovina for novel A Sun in Smoke, 1959. Address: Djure Djakovića 1, 71000 Sarajevo, Yugoslavia.

CERNEY, James V., b. 27 Jan. 1914, Detroit, Mich., USA. Podiatrist; Mechanotherapist; Author; Lecturer. Educ: A.B., Miami Univ., 1939; D.P.M., Ohio Coll. of Podiatric Med., 1943; D.M., Ctrl. States Coll. of Psychiatrics, 1948. Publs: incl: Athletic Injuries, 1963; Confidence & Power for Successful Living, 1966; 13 Steps to New Personal Power, 1969; Acupuncture without Needles, 1974; Modern Magic of Natural Healing with Water Therapy, 1975. Contbr. to mags., jrnls., books. Mbr., Author's Guild. Address: Orchard Springs Med., Bldg., 5952 N. Main St., Dayton, OH 45415, USA.

CERUTTY, Percy Wells, b. 10 Jan. 1895, Melbourne, Australia. Writer; Electrical Engineer; Teacher. Publs: Athletics; How to Become a Champion; Middle Distance Running; Schoolboy Athletics; Success in Sport & Life; Sport is My Life; Be Fit, or be Damned. Contbr. to num. jrnls. Hons: M.B.E.; Hon.Ph.D., M.S., Olympic Coach Gold Medal, Tokyo Olympic Games. Address: "Ceres" Int. Health, Fitness & Athletic Ctr., 323-29 Hotham Rd., Portsea, 3944 Vic., Australia.

CEVASCO, George Anthony, b. 22 Sept. 1924, Brooklyn, N.Y., USA. Professor. Educ: B.A., St. John's Univ., 1948; M.A., Columbia Univ., 1949; D.Litt., London, UK, 1973. Publs: J-K. Huysmans in England & America, 1962; Grammar Self-Taught, 1963, 4th ed., 1967; Wordcraft, (w. J. Fee), 1964, 3rd ed., 1967; Functional English, (w. R. Dircks & J. Franzetti), 1959; Salvador Dali: Master of Surrealism & Modern Art, 1971; Oscar Wilde: British Author, Poet & Wit, 1972; The Population Problem, 1973; Poetry in Quartet & anthologized in var. vols. Contbr. to var. lit. jrnls. Mbr., Société Huysmans (Paris); Byron Soc.; Am. Soc. for Aesthetics; Shakespeare Soc. of Am. Address: 1 Maldon St., Malverne, NY 11565, USA.

CHADWICK, John, b. 21 May 1920, London, UK. University Teacher. Educ: B.A., 1939, M.A., 1949, Corpus Christi Coll., Cambridge; Litt.D., 1974. Publs: The Medical Works of Hippocrates (w. W. N. Mann), 1950; Documents in Mycenaean Greek (w. M. Ventris), 1956, 2nd ed., 1973; The Decipherment of Linear B, 1958, 2nd ed., 1970; The Mycenae Tablets III, 1962; The Knossos Tablets, 3rd ed. (w. J. T. Killen), 1964, 4th ed. (w. J. T. Killen & J. P. Olivier), 1971. Mbr., acad. orgs. Recip. num. acad. hons. Address: Downing Coll., Cambridge CB2 1DQ, UK.

CHADWICK, Owen, b. 20 May 1916, Bromley, Kent, UK. Historian. Educ: St. John's Coll., Cambridge. Publs: John Cassian, 1950, 2nd ed., 1968; From Bossuet to Neuman, 1957; Western Ascetisim, 1958; Mackenzie's Grave, 1959; The Mind of the Oxford Movement, 1960; Victorian Miniatures, 1960; The Reformation, 1964, 8th ed., 1974; The Victorian Church, 2 vols., 1966 & 1970, 3rd ed., vol. 1 & 2nd ed., vol. 2, 1972. Contbr. to: Sunday Times; Times Lit. Supplement; The Economist; Observer; & acad. jrnls. Address: Selwyn Coll., Cambridge, UK.

CHAFFIN, Lillie D., pen name DAY, Lila, CHAFFIN, Randall, b. Varney, Ky., USA. Author; Editor; Teacher. Educ: Akron Univ., B.S., Pikeville Coll., Morehead State Univ., M.A., Eastern Ky. State Univ. Publs. incl: A Garden Is Good, 1963; Lines & Points, 1965; A Stone for Sisyphus, 1967; I Have a Tree, 1969; Bear Weather, 1969; First Notes, 1969; America's First Ladies, 2 vols., 1969; A World of Books, 1970; John Henry McCoy, 1971; Freeman, 1972; Coal: Energy & Crisis, 1974. Contbr. to num. jrnls., mags., newspapers. Mbr., Ky. State Poetry Soc. Hons. incl: Best Book Award, Child Study Assn. of Am., 1971; Int. Poetry Prize, 1967; Best Picture Book Award, League of Am. Pen Women, 1963, 1969; Poet Laureate, Ky., 1974. Address: Box 42 Meta Stn., Pikeville, KY 41501, USA.

CHAFULUMIRA, William, pen name NAMKUNGWI, b. 25 June 1908, Chapananga Village, P.O. Chikwawa, Malawi. Retired Teacher & Tutor; Broadcaster. Publs. incl: Banja Lathu (Our Family), 1942; Unyamata (Youth), 1958; Mtendere (Happiness), 1953; Wopambana Ndani (Who is More Important?), 1957; Mkazi Wabwino (Good Wife), 1951; Mbiri Ya Amang'anja (History of Mang'anja Tribe); Kantini (Tea room), 1954; Gwaza (School Reader), 1960. Contbr. to: Moni Mag. Mbrships. incl: Review Comm. Bible Transl.; Farmers Club (Chmn.). Hons. incl: Cert. Hon. from Queen Elizabeth II, 1960; Best Teacher, Dept. Educ., 1948. Address: Kadikira Parish, P/A Chikowa, Chileka, Malawi.

CHAGALL, David, b. 20 Nov. 1930, Phila., Pa., USA. Author; Writer; Research Consultant. Educ: B.A., Pa. State Univ.; Sorbonne Univ. Publs: Diary of a Deaf Mute, 1960, latest ed., 1972; The Century God Slept, 1962, 4th ed., 1967; The Spieler For The Holy Spirit, 1973; The Pushbutton People (forthcoming). Contbr. to: Adam Int. Review (London); Wis. Review; Forum, Ball State Univ.; Spectrum, Univ. of Mass.; Zahir, Univ. N.H.; Realist, San Fran.; Progressive, Madison, Wis. Hons. incl: Carnegie Trust Grant, 1964; Univ. Wis. Poetry Prize, 1971; Nomination Nat. Book Award Fiction, 1972 for Diary of a Deaf Mute; Nomination Pulitzer Prize Letters, 1973 for The Spieler For the Holy Spirit. Address: P.O. Box 85, Agoura, CA 91301, USA.

CHAILLIE, Jean Humphrey, b. 23 Jan. 1925, Liberty, Mo., USA. Poet; Playwright. Publs. in anthols. incl: Melodies From a Jade Harp, 1968; Ballet on the Wind, 1969; Spring Anthology, 1970; Sing, Naked Spirit, 1970; From Sea to Sea in Song, 1972; The Anthology of New American Verse, 1974. Contbr. to: Poet; Poet Lore; Poet's Reed, etc. Mnrships. incl: Ariz. State Poetry Soc. (Pres., 1972-73); Nat. Fedn. State Poetry Socs. Inc. (Bd. Mbr., 1972-73); Phoenix Poetry Soc. (Pres., 1974). Recip., num. hon. mentions & awards, var. state & nat. poetry contests. Address: 4549 E. Montecito Ave., Phoenix, AZ 85018, USA.

CHAKOVSKY, Alexander Borisovick, b. 26 Aug. 1913, St. Petersburg, Russia. Writer. Educ: Maxim Gorky Inst. for Lit., Moscow. Publs: (tril.) It Was in Leningrad, 1944, Lyda, 1945, Peaceful Days, 1947; It is Already Morning with Us, 1950; Khvan Cher is on Guard, 1957; A Year of One Life, 1956; The Roads We Take, 1960; The Light of a Distant Star, 1962; Blockade, 4 vols., 1963-73; The Fiancée, 1966. Contbr. to: Literaturnaya Gazeta (Ed.-in-Chief); Znamya; Oktyavr; Zvezda; Soviet Literature. Mbrships: Union of Writers of USSR (Sec. of Bd., 1963-). Recip., USSR State Prize, 1950. Address: Editorial Office, Literaturnaya Gazeta, 30 Tsvetnoi Bulvar, Moscow, USSR.

CHALKE, Herbert Davis, pen name BLACKER, Hereth, b. 15 June 1897, Porth, Glam., Wales, UK. Physician; Author. Educ: M.A., St. John's Coll., Cambridge; St. Bartholomew's Hosp., London Univ.; Royal Inst. of Pub. Hlth. & Hygiene; M.R.C.S.; L.R.C.P.; M.R.C.P.; D.P.H.; F.F.C.M.; F.R.S.H. Publs. incl: Radiation & Health (Jt. Ed. & Contbr.), 1962; Hygiene & Public Health, 1962, 3rd ed., 1965; Families with Problems, (co-author), 1968; Alcohol & the Family (co-author), 1971. Contbr. to num. profl. publs. Ed., Jrnl. of Alcoholism. Mbrships: Former Pres. & Chmn. of Coun., Soc. of Med. Offs. of Hlth.; Former mbr., num. nat. comms. on health subjects; Fellow, Soc. of Authors. Address: 32 Severn Rd., Porthcawl, Glam. CF36 3LN, UK.

CHALMERS, Eric Brownlie, b. 1929, Glasgow, UK. Business Economist; Economic Adviser. Educ: M.A.(Hons.), Univ. of Edinburgh. Publs: The Gilt-Edged Market, 1967; Economics for Managers, 1967; UK Monetary Policy, 1968; Monetary Policy in the Sixties, UK, USA & W. Germany, 1968; Economics for Executives, 1971; International Interest Rate War, 1972; The Money World, 1974; Ed., Readings in the Eurodollar, 1969; Forward Exchange Intervention, 1971. Contbr. to: Banker; Bankers' Mag. Mbr., Soc. of Authors. Address: 2 Hambledon Vale, Woodcote Green, Epsom, Surrey, UK.

CHALMERS, Randolph Carleton, b. 31 Jan. 1908, Bathurst, N.B., Can. Professor of Theology. Educ: B.A., B.D.; Th.D. Publs: See The Christ Stand, 1945; The Pure Celestial Fire, 1948; The Protestant Spirit, 1953; A Gospel to Proclaim, 1958; Our Living Faith, 1949. Contbr. to: United Ch. Observer; United Churchman; Encyclopedia on Human Ideas Concerning Ultimate Reality & Meaning (in preparation). Mbr., var. Ch. orgs. Hons. incl: 3 Hon. D.D.

degrees; LL.D., Mt. Allison Univ., 1972. Address: 535 Duke St., Bathurst, N.B., Can.

CHAMBERLAND, Emile-L., b. 20 May 1929, Armagh (Bellechasse), P.Q., Can. Agronome; Professional Agrologist. Educ: Dip. in Agric., 1948; B.Sc. Agric., 1962; M.Sc.(Soils), 1969; Ph.D. studies, McGill Univ., 1969-71. Publs: La Culture du Lotier, 1965; L'Acériculture au Québec, 1967. Contbr. to: Communications in Soil Sci. Plant Analysis; Can. Jrnl. of Plant Sci.; Can. Jrnl. of Soil Sci.; Info. Technique, M.A. Québec. Mbr., var. profl. assns. Address: 3335 Rue Montpetit, Apt. 2, Sainte-Foy, P.Q., Can.

CHAMBERLIN, Eric Russell, b. 1926, Kingston, Jamaica. Historical Writer. Publs: The Count of Virtue, UK 1965, USA 1966; Everyday Life in Renaissance Times, UK & USA, 1966; Life in Medieval France, UK & USA, 1967; Cesare Borgia, 1969; The Bad Popes, USA 1969, UK 1970; Guildford, 1970; Life in Wartime Britain, UK, 1972; Marguerite of Navarre, USA, 1974; Fall of the House of Borgia, USA & UK, 1974; Antichrist & the Millennium, USA, 1975; var. hists. for children. Contbr. to: Hist. Today; Times; Archtl. Review; Guardian. Mbr., Soc. of Authors; NUJ. Address: 3 Harvey Gdns., Addison Rd., Guildford, Surrey, UK.

CHAMBERS, Aidan, pen name BLACKLIN, Malcolm, b. 1934, Chester-le-Street, Co. Durham, UK. Writer. Publs: Marle & Cycle Smash, 1967-68; (plays) Johnny Salter; The Car; The Chicken Run, 1965-67; Co-Ed., Topliner Ghosts, 1969; The Vase, 1968; The Reluctant Reader, 1969; Introducing Books to Children, 1973; Gen. Ed., Macmillan Topliner & Club 75 Series. Contbr. to: Times Educl. Supplement; The Times; Guardian; Books & Bookmen; Tchrs'. World; Children's Book News; The Horn Book. Mbr., Soc. of Authors. Address: Weaver's Cottage, Gydynap, Amberley, Glos. GL5 5BA, UK.

CHAMBERS, Jim Bernard, b. 18 Feb. 1919, Napier, NZ. Congregational Minister. Educ: Univs. of Auckland & Otago; M.A., Univ. of NZ; Trinity Meth. Theol. Coll. Publs: Karori Congregational Church 1842-1956, 1956; Hands Can Heal, 1958; Is Any Sick Among You, 1962, 5th ed., 1974; To God Be The Glory, 1965; Cambridge Terrace Congregational Church 1877-1967, 1967. Contbr. to profl. jrnls. Address: 28 Wright St., Wellington 2 NZ.

CHAMBERS, Margaret Ada Eastwood, pen name CHAMBERS, Peggy, b. 13 Aug. 1911, Long Eaton, Derbys., UK. Publs: Women & the World Today, 1954; Great Company, 1954; They Fought for Children, 1956; A Doctor Alone, 1956; Six Great Christians, 1958; The Governess (novel), 1960. Contbr. to: Children's Book of Famous Lives; Colyer's Ency. Agent: David Higham Assocs. Ltd. Address: 316 Derby Rd., Nottingham NG7 2DN, UK.

CHAMBERS, Merritt Madison, b. 26 Jan. 1899, Mt. Vernon, Ohio, USA. University Professor. Educ: B.A., 1922; Ohio Wesleyan Univ., M.A., 1922, Ph.D., 1931, Ohio State Univ. Num. publs. incl: The College & the Courts, 1st of 8 vols., 1936; Charters of Philanthropies, 1948; The Campus & the People, 1961; Higher Education: Who Pays? Who Gains?, 1968; Higher Education & State Government, 1974. Contbr., over 350 articles to profl. jrnls. & to encys. Address: Dept. of Ednl. Admin., Ill. State Univ., Normal, IL 61761, USA.

CHAMPION, Larry Stephen, b. 27 Apr. 1932, Shelby, N.C., USA. Professor of English; Author. Educ: A.B., Davidson Coll., N.C., 1954; M.A., Univ. of Va., Charlottesville, 1955; Ph.D., Univ. of N.C., Chapel Hill, 1961. Publs: Ben Jonson's "Dotages": A Reconsideration of the Late Plays, 1967; The Evolution of Shakespeare's Comedy, 1970, paperback ed., 1973; Quick Springs of Sense: Studies in the 18th Century (ed.), 1973; Shakespeare's Tragic Perspective: The Development of His Dramatic Technique, 1974. Contbr. to: Shakespeare Quarterly; Studies in Philol.; Mod. Lang. Quarterly; Forum, etc. Mbrships. incl: Mod. Lang. Assn. of Am.; Renaissance Soc. of Am.; Shakespeare Assn. Am. Address: 2010 Myron Dr., Raleigh, NC 27607, USA.

CHAMSON, Andre Jules Louis, b. 6 June 1900, Nimes, France. Author; Museum Keeper; Director General of Archives. Educ: Schl. of Palaeography, Paris. Publs. incl: Roux le Bandit, 1925; Les Hommes de la Route, 1928; Le Crime des Justes, 1929; Les Quatres Elements, 1935; Le Dernier Village, 1946; Le Puits des Miracles, 1946; L'Homme Qui Marchait devant Moi, 1952; La Superbe,

1967; La Tour de Constance, 1970; Les Taillons, ou La Terreur Blanche, 1974; La Reconquête, 1975. Contbr. to: Nouvelle Revue Francaise; Revue des Deux Mondes; Harper's Bazaar; etc. Mbrships: Acad. Francaise; PEN (Int. Pres., 1955-57, VP, 1958-). Hons. incl: Doct., Univ. Laval, Can.; Mbr., German Acad., Darmstad. Address: 35 rue Mirabeau, 75016 Paris, France.

CHANCELLOR, Valerie Edith, b. 22 Dec. 1936, Birmingham, UK. Senior Lecturer in History & Education. Educ: M.A., St. Hugh's Coll., Oxford Univ., 1958; M.Ed., Birmingham Univ., 1967. Publs: Medieval & Tudor Britain: Penguin Secondary History II, 1967; Master & Artisan in Victorian England, 1969; History for their Masters, 1970; Wemyss Reid's Life of W. E. Forster, Introduction, 1970. Contbr. to: Dictionary of World History, 1973. Address: 37 Hawkswell Gdns., Oxford OX2 7EX, UK.

CHANDLER, Arthur Bertram, pen names DUNSTAN, Andrew; WHITLEY, George, b. 28 Mar. 1912, Aldershot, UK. Writer; Sea Captain. Educ: Nautical Academies. Publs. incl: The Rim of Space, 1961; The Hamelin Plague, 1963; Glory Planet, 1964; Mayflower-Dell, 1967; The Rim Gods, 1968; Catch the Star Winds, 1969; The Sea Beasts, 1971; To Prime the Pump, 1971; Alternate Orbits, 1971; The Gateway to Never, 1972; The Inheritors, 1972; The Hard Way Up, 1972; The Bitter Pill, 1974; The Broken Cycle, 1975; The Big Black Mark, 1975. Contbr. to num. sci. fiction mags. Mbrships. incl: Merchant Serv. Guild Aust.; Sci. Fiction Writers of Am.; Aust. Soc. of authors. Address: Cell 7, Tara St., Woollahra, N.S.W. 2025, Australia; (bus.) Flat 23 Kanimbla Hall, 19 Tusculum St., Potts Point, N.S.W. 2011, Australia.

CHANDLER, David Geoffrey, b. 15 Jan. 1934, Withernsea, UK. Deputy-Head, Department of War Studies, Royal Mil. Acad., Sandhurst. Educ: B.A., 1955, Cert. Educ., 1956, M.A., 1960, Keble Coll., Oxford Univ. Publs: Travellers' Guide to the Battlefields of Europe, 2 vols., 1965; The Campaigns of Napoleon, USA 1966, UK 1967, Italy 1968; Two Soldiers of Marlborough's Wars, 1968; Marlborough as Military Commander, USA, 1973, UK 1973; The Art of Warfare on Land, 1974; Napoleon, 1974. Contbr. to: Hist. Today; Fin. Times; RUSI Jrnl.; Brit. Army Review; Purnell Hists. of WWI & WWII; Brit. Hist. Illus. Mbr., var. profl. assns. Address: Hindford, Monteagle Lane, Yateley, Camberley, Surrey GU17 7LT, UK.

CHANDLER, Geoffrey, b. 15 Nov. 1922, London, UK. Oil Company Executive; Writer. Educ: M.A., Trinity Coll., Cambridge. Publs: The Divided Land: an Anglo-Greek Tragedy, 1959; The State of the Nation: Trinidad & Tobago in the Later 1960s, 1969. Contbr. to: Fin. Times (Features Ed., 1952-56); Int. Affairs; Guardian; Petroleum Review; Hist. Today; Geogl. Mag.; etc. Mbrships: Overseas Dev. Inst. (Coun. & Exec. Comm.); Pres., Inst. of Petroleum, 1973-74; Hawks (Cambridge); Athenaeum. Address: 57 Blackheath Park, London SE3 9SQ, UK.

CHANDLER, George, b. 2 July 1915, Birmingham, UK. Librarian. Educ: Leeds Coll. of Commerce; M.A., Ph.D., Univ. of London. Publs. incl: Liverpool, 1207-1957, 1957; William Roscoe 1753-1831, 1953; How to Find Out, 1963, 4th ed., 1974; Libraries in the Modern World, 1965; Victorian & Edwardian Manchester, 1974; Liverpool & Literature, 1974. Contbr. to: Times Educl. Supplement; BBC; Lib. World; Liverpool Echo; etc. Mbrships. incl: F.L.A.; Fellow, Royal Histl. Soc.; Hon. Libn., Hist. Soc., Lancs. & Cheshire. Address: c/o Nat. Lib. of Aust., Canberra, Australia.

CHANDLER, Stanley Bernard, b. 31 May 1921, Canterbury, UK. University Professor; Writer. Educ: B.A., 1947, Ph.D., 1953, Univ. of London. Publs: The World of Dante: Six Essays in Language & Thought (co-ed. w. J. A. Molinaro), 1966, reprint 1968; Alessandro Manzoni, 1974. Contbr. to: Italica; La Bibliofilia; Giornale storico della Letteratura italiana; Philological Quarterly; Mosaic; etc. Mbrships. incl: Associazione internazionale per gli studi di lingua e letteratura italiana; V.P., ibid, 1973-76; MLA. Address: 9 Heathbridge Park Rd., Toronto, Ont. M4G 2Y6, Can.

CHANDLER, Tony John, b. 7 Nov. 1928, Leicester, UK. Professor of Geography. Educ: B.Sc., A.K.C., Univ. of London, 1949; Tchr.'s Dip., ibid, 1950; M.Sc., 1955; Ph.D., 1964. Publs: The Climate of London, 1965; The Air Around Us, 1968; Modern Meteorology & Climatology, 1972. Contbr. to most leading meterol. & geog. jrnls., also

Times Lit. Supplement & THES. Address: 7 Dorset Rd., Altrincham, Cheshire WA14 4QN, UK.

CHANEY, Jill, b. 5 June 1932, Radlett, Herts., UK. Writer. Publs: On Primrose Hill; Half a Candle; A Penny for the Guy; Mottram Park; Christopher's Dig; Return to Mottram Park, 1974; Christopher's Find, 1974; Taking the Woffle to Pebblecomb-on-Sea, 1974. Address: White Cottage, Berks Hill, Chorleywood, Herts., UK.

CHANG, Byoung-Hye, pen names, ILRAN; YOUNG, Peggy, b. 6 Dec. 1932, Seoul, Korea. Assistant Professor. Educ: B.A., Grove City Coll., Pa., USA; M.Litt., Univ. of Pitts., Pa.; Ph.D. Cand., Univ. of Hawaii; Tokyo Univ. Publs: Learn Korean Pattern Approach, vols. I-IV (co-author), 1962-64; Learn Korean College Text, vols. I-II (co-author), 1970-72; Evergreen Soul for Freedom (On Chang Taick-Sang, the late Prime Minister), 1973. Contbr. articles & book reviews to var. jrnls. Mbrships. incl: Int. PEN. Address: 1018 Waieli St., Honolulu, HI 96821, USA.

CHANG, Isabelle C., b. 20 Feb. 1924, Boston, Mass., USA. Librarian; Media Specialist; Teacher. Educ: B.S.C.S., Simmons Coll., A.M., Clark Univ. Publs: What's Cooking at Changs', 1959, revised, 1971; Chinese Fairy Tales, 1965; Tales from Old China, 1969; Gourmet on the Go, 1971. Contbr. to: Mass. Tchrs. Recip., John Chandler Greene Award, 1965. Address: 15 Fiske St., Shrewsbury, Mass., USA.

CHANG-RODRIGUEZ, Eugenio, b. 15 Nov. 1926, Trujillo, Peru. University Professor; Author. Educ: Ph.B., Univ. of San Marcos, Peru, 1946; B.A., William Penn Coll., USA, 1949; M.A., Univ. of Ariz., 1950; M.A., 1953, Ph.D., 1956, Univ. of Wash. Publs. incl: Continuing Spanish, 5 vols., (co-author), 1967; The Lingering Crisis: A Case Study of the Dominican Republic (co-ed.), 1969; Collins Spanish Dictionary (w. C. Smith & M. Bermejo), 1971. Contbr. to: Hispania; Hispanic Review; For. Langs. Annals; etc. Mbrships. incl: N. Am. Acad. Spanish Lang.; Instituto International de Literatura Iberoamericana; Conf. Chmn., Int. Linguistic Assn., 1966, 1969, 1973, 1974 (Pres., 1969-72). Address: 65-30 Kissena Blvd., Flushing, NY 11367, USA.

CHANNAH. Zeenat, pen name SHABNAM, b. 4 Jan. 1919, Sehwan, Sind, Pakistan. Housewife. Educ: Grad., Sindhi Lang.; Dip.Ed. Ed., monthly/weekly mag. for women of Sind in Sindhi Lang., 1956–. Contbr. to all maj. mags. in Sindhi lang. & radio progs. Mbrships: VP, All Pakistan Women's Assn.; Sind; Ladies' Club, Hyderabad, Sind; Jail Comm.; Pakistan Writers' Guild. Recip., Prize, Sindhi Debate, 1948. Address: Zeenat House, Doctor's Colony, Hyderabad (Sind), Pakistan.

CHANNING-RENTON (Capt.), Ernest Matthews, pen names BOHEMIAN; CHANNING, b. 30 July 1895, Plymouth, UK. Regular Army Officer, Retired; late British Vice-Consul; Author; Artist. Educ: Army Schls.; Med. Schls.; Jesus Coll., Cambridge Univ.; Plymouth Schl. of Art. Publs. incl: A Subaltern in the Field, 1920; Jesus College, Cambridge, in Black & White, 1921; History of the 1st Batt. D.C.L.I., 1914, 1923; Letters from Bohemian, 1939; Early Days, 1970; Between the Wars, 1971; Later Years, 1972; Gypsy Girl, 1972; From an Artist's Portfolio, 1973; At Random, 1974; En Passant, 1974. Contbr. to var. jrnls. & Rhodesian newspapers. Hons. incl: Palmes d'Officer d'Academie; Officier de l'Instruction Publique (France). Address: Channings, P.O. Sanyatwe, via Rusape, Rhodesia.

CHANOVER, Pierre, b. 10 Dec. 1932, Paris, France. Professor; Author. Educ: B.A., Brooklyn Coll., USA, 1957; M.A., Univ. of Kan., 1959; Ph.D., N.Y. Univ., 1974. Publs. incl: Chez les Francais, 1969; Ce Monde des Francais, 1970; Clapotis d'Outre-Mer (poems), 1971; The Marquis de Sade: A Bibliography, 1972. Contbr. of articles, poems, to num. US, French mags. Mbr., Am. Acad. of Poets & World Poetry Soc. Address: 6 Seton St., Huntingdon Stn., NY 11746, USA.

CHANTLER, David T., b. 24 May 1925, Pitts., Pa., USA. Writer. Educ: B.A., Northwestern Univ., Chgo. Publs: Fellow Creature, 1970; The Man who followed in Front, 1974. Mbrships: Writers Guild of Am.; Writers Guild of GB; Nat. Acad. of TV Arts & Sciences, USA. Address: Santa Monica Bay Club, Apt. 209, 2210 Third St., Santa Monica, CA 90405, USA.

CHAO, Yuen Ren, b. 3 Nov. 1892, Tientsin, China. Teacher; Writer; Translator. Educ: A.B., Cornell Univ., 1914; Ph.D., Harvard Univ., 1918. Publs: New Book of

(Chinese) Rhymes, 1922; Studies in the Modern Wu Dialects, 1928; Survey of Hupeh Dialects (co-author), 1938; Cantonese Primer, 1946; Mandarin Primer, 1947; A Grammar of Spoken Chinese, 1968; Language & Symbolic Systems, 1968. Translations into Chinese: Alice's Adventures in Wonderland, 1922; Autobiography of a Chinese Woman, 1947; Through the Looking Glass & What Alice Found There, 1968. Contbr. to: Science (Chinese) Language; Jrnl. of Am. Oriental Soc., etc. Hons. incl: Litt.D., Princeton Univ., 1946; LL.D., Univ. of Calif., 1962. Address: 1059 Cragmont Ave., Berkeley, CA 94708, USA.

CHAPIN, F. Stuart, Jr., b. 1 Apr. 1916, Northampton, Mass., USA. University Professor in City & Regional Planning. Educ: A.B., Univ. of Minn., 1937; B.Arch. in C.P., MIT, 1939; M.C.P., ibid, 1940. Publs: Urban Growth Dynamics (co-ed.), 1962; Urban Land Use Planning, 1965; Across the City Line — A White Community in Transition (co-author), 1974; Human Activity Patterns in the City — What People Do in Time & Space, 1974. Contbr. to: Jrnl. of the Am. Inst. of Planners; etc. Address: Dept. of City & Regional Planning, Univ. of N.C., Chapel Hill, NC 27514, USA.

CHAPLIN, Joyce Eva, b. 13 Nov. 1923, Chelmsford, Essex, UK. Freelance Consultant for Christian Publishers in UK, Africa & India. Educ: M.A., St. Anne's Coll., Oxford Univ., 1944. Publs: Adventure with a Pen, 1966; Make Known His Deeds, 1968; Fiction Writing, 1972; Have You Read This? , 1972. Contbr. to: Practical Anthropol. (USA); Spectrum (UK); Ministry (Africa); Read (S. Pacific); Write! (co-ed.). Mbrships: Africa Christian Press (UK Publicity Agent); Shoebox Lib. Club (Fndr.); UK Christian Writers' Club (Fndr.-Mbr.). Address: Ballachrink, Grove Mt., Ramsey, Isle of Man, UK.

CHAPLIN, Sidney, b. 1916, Shildon, Co. Durham, UK. Author. Educ: Fircroft Coll. For Working Men. Publs: The Leaping Lad, 1947; My Fate Cries Out, 1949; The Thin Seam, 1950; Lakes to Tyneside, 1951; The Big Room, 1960; The Day of the Sardine, 1961; The Watchers & the Watched, 1962; Sam in the Morning, 1965; Us Northerners (w. Arthur Wise), 1970. Contbr. to: Guardian; Sunday Times; etc. Mbrships: Lit. & Philosophical Soc., Newcastle upon Tyne; Soc. of Authors. Address: 11 Kimberley Gdns., Newcastle upon Tyne NE2 1HJ, UK.

CHAPMAN, Brian, b. 6 Apr. 1923, UK. Professor of Government. Educ: Magdalen & Nuffield Colls., Oxford, M.A., D.Phil. Publs: French Local Government (transl'd into French & Spanish), 1953; The Prefects & Provincial France (transl'd into Spanish), 1954; The Life & Times of Baron Hausman (co-author), 1956; The Profession of Government (transl'd into Turkish & Japanese), 1959; The Fifth Constitution (w. P. Campbell 1959; British Government Observed, 1963; The Police State (transl'd into German), 1970. Contbr. to int. acad. jrnls., newspapers & reviews. Address: Dept. of Government, Univ. of Manchester, Manchester M13 9PL, UK.

CHAPMAN, John, b. 27 May 1927, London, UK. Playwright. Educ: Royal Acad. of Dramatic Art. Publs: (plays) Dry Rot, 1956; Simple Spymen, 1960; The Brides of March, 1961; Diplomatic Baggage, 1966; Oh, Clarence, 1969; My Giddy Aunt (co-author), 1970; Not Now Darling, 1970; Move Over Mrs. Markham (co-author), 1972; There Goes the Bride (co-author), 1974; (TV Series) Hugh & I; Blandings Castle; The Liver Birds (Script Ed., 1972-74); Happy Ever After (w. E. Merriman), 1974. Mbr., The Dramatists Club. Agent: Laurence Fitch. Address: 48 Wildwood Rd., London NW11, UK.

CHAPMAN, Raymond, pen name NASH, Simon, b. 10 Jan. 1924, Cardiff, UK. University Teacher. Educ: B.A., 1945, M.A., 1959, Jesus Coll., Oxford; M.A., King's Coll., London Univ., 1947. Publs. incl: A Short Way to Better English, 1956; The Ruined Tower, 1961; Killed By Scandal, 1962; The Loneliness of Man, 1963; Unhallowed Murder, 1966; The Victorian Debate, 1968; Faith & Revolt, 1970; Linguistics & Literature, 1973; Letters to an Actress (co-author), 1974. Contbr. to: Mod. Lang. Review; Review of Engl. Studies; Engl.; Poetica; Notes & Queries; Theol.; Higher Educ. Jrnl. Mbrships: Engl. Assn.; Assn. Univ. Tchrs.; Sion Coll. Address: 6 Kitson Road, Barnes, London SW13, UK.

CHAPMAN, Richard Arnold, b. 15 Aug. 1937, Bexleyheath, Kent, UK. University Reader. Educ: B.A., Ph.D., Leicester Univ., M.A., Carleton Univ., A.M.B.I.M. Publs: Decision Making, 1968; The Higher Civil Service in

Britain, 1970. Style in Administration, (co-ed. w. A. Dunsire), 1971; The Role of Commissions in Policy Making, 1973; Teaching Public Administration, 1973. Contbr. to: Pub. Admin.; Admin.; Review of Pols.; Jrnl. of Admin. Overseas; Int. Review of Hist. & Pol. Sci., etc. Hons: Hon. Treas., Pol. Studies Assn., UK, 1964-67; Hon. Ed., PAC Bulletin, 1968-71. Address: Dept. of Pols., Univ. of Durham, 23-26 Old Elvet, Durham DH1 3HY, UK.

CHAPMAN, Samuel Greeley, b. 29 Sept. 1929, Atlanta, Ga., USA. Professor (Political Science). Educ: A.B., 1951, M.A., 1959, Univ. of Calif., Berkeley. Publs: Dogs in Police Work, 1960; The Police Heritage in England & America, 1962; Police Patrol Readings, 1964, rev. 1970; A Forward Step: Educational Backgrounds for Police, 1966. Contbr. to: Am. Pol. Sci. Review; The Int. Criminal Police Review (Paris, France); The Criminologist (London, UK); etc. Mbr., Int. Assn. of Chiefs of Police. Hons: City Councilman, Norman, Okla., 1972—; Mayor, 1974—. Address: 2421 Hollywood St., Norman, OK 73069, USA.

CHAPMAN, Stanley David, b. 31 Jan. 1935, Nottingham, UK. University Reader. Educ: B.Sc., 1956, Ph.D., 1968, Univ. of London; M.A., Univ. of Nottingham, 1960. Publs: The Early Factory Masters, 1967; The Beginnings of Industrial Britain (w. J. D. Chambers), 1970; Ed., History of Working Class Housing, 1971; The Cotton Industry in the Industrial Revolution, 1972; Jesse Boot of Boots the Chemists, 1974. Contbr. to: Econ. Hist. Review; Bus. Hist.; Bus. Hist. Review; Textile Hist.; Transactions of the Thoroton Soc. Address: 35 Park Lane, Sutton Bonington, Loughborough, Leics., UK.

CHAPMAN, Valentine Jackson, b. 1910, Alcester, Warwicks., UK. University Professor of Botany. Educ: M.A., Ph.D., Cambridge Univ. Publs: Introduction to the Study of Algae; Seaweeds & Their Uses; Salt Marshes & Salt Deserts; Salt Marshes & Mangrove Swamps of the Auckland Isthmus; The Algae; Coastal Vegetation. Contbr. to var. sci. jrnls. Hon: O.B.E. Address: 5 Coronation Road, Epsom, Auckland SE3, New Zealand.

CHAPP, Petronella Helen, b. 20 Apr. 1904, Westville, Ill., USA. Retired Teacher; Poet. Educ: Charleston (Ill.) Univ.; Normal (Ill.) Univ.; Southern Ill. Univ. (formerly Tchrs. Colls.). Contbr. to jrnls. & anthols. inclng. The Muse of 1942; United Poets Quarterly; Westville Centennial, 1973. Mbrships: Ill. State Poetry Soc.; Am. Poets' Fellowship Soc.; Egypt Br., Nat. League of Am. Pen Women. Address: 213 W. Short St., Westville, IL 61883, USA.

CHAPPELL, Fred, b. 1936, Canton, N.C., USA. University Professor; Writer. Educ: B.A., M.A., Duke Univ. Publs: It Is Time, Lord, N.Y., 1963, London & Paris, 1965; The Inkling, N.Y., 1965, London & Paris, 1967; Dagon, 1968; The World Between the Eyes, 1972; The Gaudy Place, 1973; River, 1975. Contbr. to: Holiday; Paris Review; Saturday Evening Post; Fly By Night; etc. Agent: Peter Watson, N.Y. Address: Dept. of Engl., Univ. of N.C. at Greensboro, Greensboro, NC 27412, USA.

CHAPPELOW, Allan (Gordon), b. Copenhagen, Denmark. Sociologist; Writer; Photographer; Sculptor. Educ: Oundle Schl., Northants.; Univ. of London; Slade Schl. of Fine Art; M.A., Cambridge Univ., 1948. Publs: Russian Holiday, 1955; Shaw the Villager, & Human Being, 1961 (US ed. 1962); Shaw — "The Chucker-Out", 1969 (US ed. 1971). Contbr. to: Times Lit. Supplement; Daily Mail; Guardian; Listener; Educ. Today; Jrnl. of Hellenic Studies; etc. Mbrships. incl: Grad. Mbr., Brit. Psychol. Soc.; F.R.S.A. Recip., Outstanding Acad. Books of the Year Selection, for Shaw — "The Chucker-Out", Choice Mag. (USA), 1973. Address: The Manor House, 9 Downshire Hill, London NW3, UK.

CHAPPLE, Eliot Dismore, b. 1909, Salem, Mass., USA. Director of Rehabilitation Centre; Author. Educ: A.B., Ph.D., Harvard Univ. Publs: Principles of Anthropology, 1942; The Measure of Management, 1961; Culture & Biological Man, 1970; Toward a Mathematical Model of Interaction: Preliminary Considerations; Explorations in Mathematical Anthropology; Ed., Cambridge. Contbr. to: Nat. Acad. of Scis.; Am. Jrnl. Psych.; Am. Anthropol.; Human Org.; AMA; Archives of Gen. Psych. Address: Research Facility, Rockland Psychiatric Ctr., Orangeburg, NY 10962, USA.

CHARD, Judy, b. 8 May 1916, Tuffley, Glos., UK. Author; Housewife. Publs: Through the Green Woods,

1974. Contbr. to: BBC Morning Story, Woman's Hour, Home This Afternoon, etc; Woman's Realm; The Lady; My Weekly; Woman's Story; Western Morning News; Devon Life. Mbrships: Romantic Novelists Assn.; Westcountry Writers Assn.; Soc. of Women Writers & Jrnlsts.; Crime Writers' Assn. Address: Morley, Morley Rd., Newton Abbot, Devon, UK.

CHARLES, Gerda, b. Liverpool, UK. Novelist; Critic. Publs: The True Voice, 1959; The Crossing Point, 1960; A Slanting Light, 1963; Modern Jewish Stories (ed.), 1963; A Logical Girl, 1967; The Destiny Waltz, 1971. Contbr. to: New Statesman; Daily Telegraph; N.Y. Times; Jewish Chronicle. Mbr., Engl. Exec., PEN; Soc. of Authors. Hons: James Tait Black Mem. Award for best novel of 1963; Whitbread £1,000 Fiction Award for best novel of 1971. Address: c/o Eyre Methuen Ltd., 11 New Fetter Lane, London EC4P 4EE, UK.

CHARLES, Gordon H., b. 23 Aug. 1920, Salisbury, N.C., USA. Outdoor & Travel Writer. Educ: Grad., Newspaper Inst. of Am., 1947. Publs: Pocket Field Guide to Nature, 1959; South Dakota's Game Birds & Animals, 1963-64; Guide to Sleeping Bear Dunes National Lakeshore, 1975. Contbr. to: num. Mich. newspapers; Former Ed., S.D. Conservation Digest, & Mich. Out-of-Doors; Mich. Ed., Gt. Lakes Sportsman mag. Mbrships: Pres., Mich. Outdoor Writers' Assn., 1960-61; Outdoor Writers' of Am. Assn.; Midwest Travel Writers' Assn. Recip., 3 Awards for Best Contbn. to Conservation through Writings, Mich. Outdoor Writers' Assn., 1971, 72, & 73; Mich. Winner, Safari Club Int. Outdoor Writing Award, 1974. Address: 1171 N. Pioneer Rd., P.O. Box 295, Honor, MI 49640, USA.

CHARLES-EDWARDS,   Thomas,   pen   name MUMPSIMUS, b. 6 Apr. 1902, Coventry, UK. Schoolmaster. Educ: M.A., Keble Coll., Oxford. Publs: Age of the Tudors & Stuarts, 1949; They Saw It Happen (w. B. Richardson), 1958. Contbr. to: Hist. Today; Tablet; Christian Order; Ampleforth Jrnl.; G.K.'s Weekly; Efrydiau Catholig; Yddraig Goch. Mbr., Honourable Soc. of Cymmrodorion. Address: Mowbray House, Ampleforth College, York, UK.

CHARLES-ROUX, Edmonde, b. 1922. Writer. Publs: Oublier Palerme, 1966. Contbr. to: Elle; French ed., Vogue (Features Ed. — Ed.-in-Chief, 1947-66). Recip., Prix Goncourt, 1966. Address: Editions Grasset, 61 rue des Saints-Pères, Paris 6e, France.

CHARLTON, Robert Foster, b. 1911, W. Stanley, Co. Durham, UK. Former Schoolmaster. Educ: Bede Coll., Durham; L.C.P. Publs: Revision Speed Tests in Arithmetic; Keep Fit Exercises in Mental Arithmetic; Adventure Mathematics (co-author); English in Action; Target Practice in Mental Mathematics. Address: Highfield, 19 Moorview Way, Skipton, Yorks, UK.

CHARLWOOD, Donald Ernest Cameron, b. 6 Sept. 1915, Melbourne, Australia. Air traffic Control Supervisor. Publs: No Moon Tonight, 1956; All the Green Year, 1965; An Afternoon of Time, 1966; Takeoff to Touchdown: the Story of Air Traffic Control, 1967; The Wreck of the Lock Ard: End of a Ship, End of an Era, 1971. Contbr. to: Blackwoods Mag.; var. anthols. Mbrships: Aust. Soc. of Authors; Fellowship, Aust. Writers; PEN. Address: Qualicum, Mount View Rd., Templestone, Vic. 3106, Australia.

CHARNOCK, Joan Paget, maiden name THOMSON, Joan, b. 12 Mar. 1903, Cambridge, UK. Writer; Social Worker. Publs: The Making of Russia, 1943; Russia, the Old & the New, 1948; Russia, the Land & the People, 1960; The Russian Twins, 1963; David & Carol as Cooks, 1964; The Land & People of Poland, 1967; Red Revolutionary. The Life of Lenin, 1968. Contbr. to The Times. Mbrships. incl: Engl. Speaking Union; Cambridge Women's Reading Circle. Agent: Winant, Towers Ltd. Address: 6 Adams Rd., Cambridge CB3 9AD, UK.

CHARQUES, Dorothy, b. 1899, Alcester, Warwicks., UK. Writer. Educ: M.A., B.Sc., Sheffield Univ. Publs: The Tramp & His Woman, 1937; Between Sleeping & Waking, 1938; Time's Harvest, 1940; The Returning Heart, 1943; Between the Twilights, 1947; Men Like Shadows, 1952; The Valley, 1954; The Dark Stranger, 1956; The Nunnery, 1959. Address: 143 Loxley Rd., Stratford-upon-Avon, UK.

CHARTERIS, Leslie, b. 12 May 1907, Singapore. Writer. Educ: King's Coll., Cambridge Univ. Publs: The Saint Meets the Tiger (original title, Meet the Tiger), & 49 other titles in The Saint series, 1928-75. Contbr. to: Saint Mag. (Ed., 1953-67); Gourmet (USA); major fiction mags.; many newspapers. Mbrships: MENSA; WAG; Savage Club. Address: B-12 St. James's Court, Serpentine Avenue, Dublin 4, Repub. of Ireland.

CHARVET, Patrice Edouard, b. 1903, Cowes, UK. Retired University Lecturer in French. Educ: M.A., Univ. of Cambridge. Publs: Ed., Vie de Madame Curie, by Eve Curie; Ed. (w. Introduction), La Reforme Intellectuelle & Morale, by Renan, 1968; Words with the Yewburys (w. Prof. Harmer); France; A Literary History of France, 19th Century; A Literary History of France, 19th & 20th Century; Transl. (w. Introduction & Notes). Baudelaire: Selected Writings on Art & Artists, 1972. Address: Cotswold House, Painswick, Stroud, Glos., UK.

CHARYN, Jerome, b. 13 May 1937, NYC, USA. Writer. Educ: B.A., Columbia Coll., 1959. Publs: Once Upon a Droshky, 1964; On the Darkening Green, 1965; The Man Who Grew Younger, 1967; Going to Jerusalem, 1967; American Scrapbook, 1969; Eisenhower, My Eisenhower, 1971; The Tar Baby, 1973; Blue Eyes, 1975. Contbr. to: N.Y. Times; Book Review; Commentary; The Paris Review; Fiction; Saturday Review; Mademoiselle. Mbr., Am. PEN. Address: Dept. of English, Herbert Lehman College, Bedford Park Blvd. W., Bronx, NY 10468, USA.

CHASE, Alice Elizabeth, b. 13 Apr. 1906, Ware, Mass., USA. Retired Teacher; Author. Educ: A.B., Radcliffe Coll., Cambridge, Mass., 1927; M.A., Yale Univ., 1943. Publs: Famous Paintings, 1951, 2nd ed., 1962; Famous Artists of the Past, 1964; Looking at Art, 1966. Address: 18 Pleasant St., Ware, MA 01082, USA.

CHASE, James Hadley, b. 1906, London, UK. Writer; former Editor RAF Journal. Publs: No Orchids for Miss Blandish; & 53 other books of suspense. Address: Villa Helias, Fonatanivent, Vaud, Switz.

CHATFIELD, Herbert Walter, b. 9 Mar. 1910, Croydon, Surrey, UK. Consulting Scientist. Educ: B.Sc., Ph.D., Univ. of London; F.R.I.C., M.I.Chem.E., C.Eng., F.P.I., F.I.A.L. Publs: Varnish Constituents; Varnish Manufacture & Plant; Varnished Cloths for Electrical Insulation; Chatfield's European Directory of Paints & Allied Products; God's Kingly Rule; Scientist in Search of God; Prisons under Sentence; Glossary of Terms used in the Paint, Varnish & Allied Trades. Mbrships: Chem. Soc.; Soc. of Chem. Ind. Address: St. Christopher's, 23 Woodcote Park Avenue, Purley, Surrey, UK.

CHATFIELD, Keith Trevor, b. 6 Dec. 1934, Worcester Park, UK. School Teacher. Educ: B.A., Bristol Univ., 1957; Dip., Sorbonne. Publs: Hatty Town Tales, series of 8 vols., 1968-73; Issi Noho, 1974; Issi Pandemonium, 1975. Address: 9 Sedgmoor Rd., Flackwell Heath, High Wycombe, Bucks., UK.

CHATTERJEE (CHATTOPADHYAYA), Partha, b. 2 Aug. 1939, Gobardanga, W. Bengal, India. Newspaper Reporter. Educ: B.A.(Hons.), M.A., Ph.D., Calcutta Univ. Publs. incl: (novels) The Far Sky, 1962; Another World, 1963; The Counter Hero, 1965; This is good That is good, 1967; (belles-lettres) Seen & Unseen, 1960; Date Line Dacca, 1973; (juvenile books) The Mystery of Cairo, 1964; A Cat from Kabul, 1974. Contbr. to: Ultarath; Prasad Cinema Jagat; Desh; etc. Mbrships: Exec. Comm., Bengal Lit. Coun.; Calcutta Press Club. Hons: C'wlth. Press Union Fellowship, 1960; Jefferson Fellowship, 1974. Address: Block H, Flat 56, CIT Buildings, Christopher Road, Calcutta 700014, India.

CHATTOPADHYAYA, Harindranath, b. 1898. Poet; Dramatist; Musician; Actor. Educ: studied under Stanislavsky & Meyerholdt. Publs. incl: Grey Clouds & White Showers; Poems & Plays; Five Plays in Verse; Five Plays in Prose; Dark Well; The Divine Vagabond; Horizon — Ends, Edgeways & the Saint; Crossroads; Life & Myself (vol. I of autobiog.); Hunter of Kalahasti (play); Treasury of Poems; Land of the New Man; The Toy-Maker of Kondapalli (play); Legend of Gautam Buddha (film script). Address: 3 Krishna Iyer St., Nungumbakam, Madras, India.

CHAUDHURI, Amitabha, b. 16 July 1928, Sylhet, India. Journalist. Educ: M.A., Calcutta Univ.; Dip. in Jrnlsm., Ind. Univ., Bloomington, USA. Publs: Anya Nagar

Darshan (Visit to Other Cities), 1962; Ikri Mikri (nonsense verse for children), 1971; Rabindranather Paralokcharcha (Tagore & the Other World), 1973; 12 others, all in Bengali. Contbr. to: Anandabazar Patrika (Bengali daily paper; News Ed.); Desh (Bengali lit. wkly.). Mbr., Exec. Coun. & Court, Vhisvabharati Univ. Address: 131 Regent Park, Block 19 Flat 6, Calcutta 40, India.

CHAUDHURI, Haridas, b. May 1913, Calcutta, India. Professor of Philosophy; President, California Institute of Asian Studies; President, Cultural Integration Fellowship, Inc. Educ: M.A., 1936, Ph.D., 1947, Univ. of Calcutta. Publs. incl: Integral Yoga: The Concept of Harmonious & Creative Living, 1965, 1970; The Philosophy of Integralism, 1967; Sri Aurobindo: Prophet of Life Divine, 1951, 1972; Philosophy of Meditation, 1965; Mahatma Gandhi: His Message for Mankind (co-ed. w. L. R. Frank), 1969; Being, Evolution & Immortality, 1974. Contbr. to num. US & Indian jrnls. Hons: Gold Medal for record marks in philos. M.A., Silver Medal for record marks, philos. of relig., Univ. of Calcutta, 1936. Address: 360 Cumberland St., San Fran., CA 94114, USA.

CHAUDHURI, Nirad Chandra, b. 23 Nov. 1897, Kishorganj, Bengal, India. Author. Educ: B.A., Calcutta Univ. Publs: The Autobiography of an Unknown Indian, 1951; A Passage to England, 1959; The Continent of Circe, 1965; The Intellectual in India, 1967; Woman in Bengali Life, 1968; To Live or not to Live, 1970; Scholar Extraordinary: A Biography of Max Müller, forthcoming. Contbr. to: Mod. Review; Prabasi; Statesman; Illustrated Weekly of India; Times; Daily Telegraph; Encounter; Atlantic Monthly; Pacific Affairs; N.Y. Review of Books; etc. Recip., Duff Cooper Mem. Prize, 1966. Address: P. & O. Buildings, Nicholson Rd., Delhi 6, India.

CHAYEFSKY, Paddy, b. 29 Jan. 1923, Bronx, N.Y., USA. Writer. Publs: Television Play, 1955; The Goddess, 1958; Middle of the Night, 1959; The Tenth Man, 1960; Gideon, 1961; The Passion of Josef D, 1964; The Latent Heterosexual, 1967. Contbr. to TV & film. Mbrships. incl: Dramatists' Guild; Screenwriters' Guild. Address: 850 7th Ave., N.Y., NY 10019, USA.

CHEETHAM, James Harold, pen name CHEETHAM, Hal, b. 30 Dec. 1921, Warrington, Lancs., UK. Architect. Publs: Shall I Be an Architect?, 1967; Shell Guide to Wiltshire, 1968; Portrait of Oxford, 1972; Gen. Ed., Redland Guide to the Building Industry, 1968–; Essence Books in Building, 1972–. Contbr. to: Blackwoods Mag.; House & Gdn.; Archts'. Jrnl. Assoc., Royal Inst. of Brit. Archts. Address: Kirkennan, Castle Douglas, Kirkcudbrightshire DG7 1PE, UK.

CHEETHAM, Robert Clifford, b. 12 June 1909, Bolton, UK. Research Chemist. Educ: A.M.C.T., Manchester Coll. of Sci. & Technol. Publs: Dyeing Fibre Blends, 1966. Contbr. to: Reports Progress of Applied Chem., Vols. LII, 1967; LIV, 1969; LVI, 1971; LVII, 1973. Mbrships: F.R.I.C.; F.S.D.C. Recip., Silver Medal, Soc. of Dyers & Colourists. Address: Rowlands, Hardcragg Way, Grange-over-Sands, Cumberland LA11 6BH, UK.

CHEEVER, John, b. 27 May 1912, Quincy, Mass., USA. Writer. Educ: Thayer Acad. Publs: (novels) The Wapshot Chronicle, 1957; The Wapshot Scandal, 1964; Bullet Park, 1969; (short stories) The Way Some People Live: A Book of Stories, 1943; The Enormous Radio & Other Stories, 1953; Stories (w. others), 1956; The Housebreaker of Shady Hill & Other Stories, 1958; Some People, Places & Things That Will Not Appear in My Next Novel, 1961; The Brigadier & the Golf Widow, 1964. Mbr., Nat. Inst. of Arts & Letters Hons: O. Henry Award, 1956, 1964; Nat. Book Award, 1958; Howells Medal, 1965. Address: Cedar Lane, Ossining, NY 10562, USA.

CHEN, Peng-j'en, b. 2 Dec. 1930, Tainan Shien, Taiwan, Republic of China. Writer. Educ: B.A., M.A., Meiji Univ., Tokyo; M.A., Seton Hall Univ., USA; Tokyo & Columbia Univs. Publs: New York, Tokyo & Taipei, 1972; Dr. Sun Yat-sen & the Japanese Friends, 1973; The Realm of Thought in Japan after World War II, 1974. Contbr. to: Newsdom, Hong Kong; Pol. Review, Taipei; Central Daily News, Taipei. Mbr., Japanese Critics' Assn. Address: 1-8-5 Higashi Azabu, Minatoku, Tokyo, Japan.

CHENEVIÈRE, Jacques, b. 17 Apr. 1886. Writer. Educ: Lic. ès Lettres, Paris Univ. Publs: Les Beaux Jours; La Chambre et le Jardin (poems); l'Ile déserte; Jouvence ou la Chimère; Les Messagers inutiles; La Jeune fille de neige; Innocences; Les Aveux Complets; Connais ton Cour; Valet, dames, roi; Les Captives; Le Bouquet de la Mariée; La Comtesse de Ségur, née Rostopchine (biog.); Campagne Genevoise; Retours et images. Hons. incl: Grand Prix du Rayonnement de la Langue Française, 1968. Address: 1293 Bellevue, nr. Geneva, Switz.

CHENEY, Christopher Robert, b. 1906, Banbury, UK. Emeritus Professor of Medieval History. Educ: M.A., Wadham Coll., Oxford Univ. Publs: English Synodalia of the 13th Century; English Bishops' Chanceries; From Becket to Langton; Selected Letters of Innocent III (w. W. H. Semple); Hubert Walter; The Letters of Pope Innocent III Concerning England & Wales (w. M. G. Cheney); Notaries Public in England; Medieval Texts & Studies; Councils & Synods of the English Church 1205-1313, 2 vols. (w. F. M. Powicke). Contbr. to schlrly. jrnls. Fellow, Brit. Acad. Recip., D.Litt., Glasgow. Address: 236 Hills Rd., Cambridge, UK.

CHENEY, L. Stanley, b. 12 Apr. 1928, Yuma, Ariz., USA. Writer; Poet; Photographer; Artist; Historian. Educ: Ctrl. Jr. Coll.; E.N.M. Univ.; Long Beach City Coll. Publs: Of Time . . . And Conquerors, 1962; Footsteps Across the Page, 1963; Nijo Castle, 1965; Walk With Me, 1966; How Soon the Night, 1968. Contbr: Over 1,000 poems, sev. hundred articles & drawings in 150 mags., USA, Europe, Japan, Canada. Mbrships: Pres., Avalon Acad. of World Arts; World Poetry Soc.; Ariz. State Poetry Soc. Num. hons. incl: Lilith Lorraine Award, for best poem of yr., 1966; Cinquain Poet of Yr., Swordsman Review, 1970; Disting. Citation, World Poetry Soc., 1970; Citation for contbrs. to lit., Ariz. State Univ., 1970. Address: P.O. Box 9053, San Diego, CA 92109, USA.

CHENEY, Sheldon (Warren), b. 29 June 1886, Berkeley, Calif., USA. Writer. Educ: A.B., Univ. of Calif., Berkeley, 1908; Study of art, San Fran., Berkeley; Postgrad. study, Harvard Univ. Publs. incl: The Theatre, 1929, latest rev. ed., 1972; A New World History of Art, 1937; Men Who Have Walked with God, 1945; Sculpture of the World: A History, 1968. Contbr. to mags., jnrls., Fndr., 1st Ed., Theatre Arts Mag. Mbrships: Authors League of Am.; Am. Fedn. of Arts. Hons: Benjamin Franklin Fellow, Royal Soc. of Arts, London. Address: 12 Stony Hill Road, New Hope, PA 18938, USA.

CHENG, Bin, b. 21 Jan. 1921, Peking, China. Professor of Air & Space Law. Educ: Friburg Univ., Switz.; Lic.-en-droit, Geneva Univ., Switz., 1944; Ph.D., 1955; LL.D., 1966, London Univ., UK. Publs: General Principles of Law as Applied by International Courts & Tribunals, 1953; The Law of International Air Transport, 1962. Contbr. to: Aeronaut. Jrnl; Ency. Britannica; Int. Affairs; Jrnl. du droit international; New Society; Nobel Symposium 7; etc. Mbrships. incl: Chmn., Air Law Comm., Int. Law, Assn., 1965-; Inst., Aeronaut. & Interplanetary Law, Buenos Aires. Address: Faculty of Laws, Univ. Coll., London WC1H 0EG, UK.

CHENG, Thomas Clement, b. 5 Nov. 1930, Nanking, China. University Professor & Administrator; Author. Educ: B.A., Wayne State Univ., Detroit, Mich., 1952; M.S., 1956, Ph.D., 1958, Univ. of Va., Charlottesville. Publs: The Biology of Animal Parasites, 1964; Marine Molluscs as Hosts for Symbioses, vol. 5 of Advances in Marine Biology, 1967; Symbiosis: Organisms Living Together, 1970; General Parasitology, 1973; Medical & Economic Malacology, 1974. Contbr. to: Jrnl. of Parasitol.; Parasitol.; Biol. Bulletin; Jrnl. of Invertebrate Pathol.; Quarterly Review of Biol.; etc. Recip., 20th Phila. Book Show Award, 1965. Address: 1805 Arlington St., Bethlehem, PA 18017, USA.

CHENNAULT, Anna C., b. 23 June 1925, Peiping, China. Vice-President, International Affairs, The Flying Tiger Line, Inc. Educ: B.A., Ling Nan Univ. Publs: A Thousand Springs, 1962; Chennault & The Flying Tigers, 1963; Dictionary of New Simplified Chinese Characters, 1963; Telegraphic Code Chinese-English Dictionary, 1963; 15 Books in Chinese, incl: Song of Yesterday, 1961; MEE, The Orient Book Store, 1963; My Two Worlds, 1965; The Other Half, 1966; Letters from USA, 1967. Contbr. to maj. mags. in Taiwan. Recip., sev. hon. degrees. Address: The Flying Tiger Line, Inc., 1020 Investment Building, 1511 K Street N.W., Wash. DC 20005, USA.

CHERNOFF, Arnold Marcus, b. 30 Sept. 1933, Chgo., Ill., USA. Antique Firearms Dealer & Consultant; Writer. Educ: Coll. grad. Contbr. to: Guns & Ammo Mag. (Antique

Arms Ed.); Gun Report Mag.(Antique Gun of the Month Ed.); Arms Gazette Mag. (Antique Colt Ed.); num. other mags. Mbrships: Fellow, Ancient Arms Armour Arts & Scis.; Life, Ohio Gun Collectors Assn.; Tex., Ill., Tenn., Wabash Valley, Wis. Gun Collectors Assns.; Potomac, Ga. Arms Collectors Assns.; Dir., Pen-Mar-Va Gun Collectors Assn.; Life, N.R.A. Address: 29 Londonderry Lane, Lincolnshire, Deerfield, IL 60015, USA.

CHERRETT, John Malcolm, b. 1935, Bishop Auckland, UK. University Senior Lecturer in Applied Zoology. Educ: Univ. of Durham; Inst. of Educ., Univ. of London; B.Sc.; Ph.D.; P.G.C.E. Publs: At Home in the World, 1968; The Control of Injurious Animals (w. J. B. Ford, J. B. Herbert & A. J. Probert). Contbr. to: Jrnl. of Animal Ecol.; Bulletin of Entomol. Rsch.; Tropical Agric. Mbrships: Brit. Ecol. Soc.; Fellow, Royal Entomol. Soc.; Assn. of Applied Biols. Address: The Shiel, Cae'r Gelach, Llandegfan, Menai Bridge, Anglesey, UK.

CHERRINGTON, Ernest (Hurst, Jr.), b. 1909, Westerville, Ohio, USA. Astronomer; College Professor. Educ: Ohio Wesleyan Univ., Delaware; Univ. of Calif., Berkeley; A.B.; M.S.; Ph.D. Publs: Exploring the Moon Through Binoculars, 1969. Contbr. to: Astrophys. Jrnl.; Astron. Jrnl.; Publs. of the Astron. Soc. of the Pacific; Sky & Telescope; This Week; N.Y. Times; Sci. Digest; Christian Advocate. Mbrships. incl: Am. Astron. Soc.; Royal Astron. Soc. of Can.; Astron. Soc. of the Pacific. Address: Jefferson Blvd., Braddock Heights, MD 21714, USA.

CHESNEY, Kathleen, b. 26 Apr. 1899, High Legh, Knutsford, UK. College Principal; University Teacher (retired). Educ: M.A., 1926, D.Phil., 1929, D.Litt., 1960, Oxon. Publs: Oeuvres poétiques de Guillaume Crétin, 1932; Fleurs de Rhétorique from Villon to Marot, 1950; More Poèmes de Transition, 1956. Contbr. to: Medium, Aexam; Mod. Lang. Review; French Studies; etc. Mbrships: Soc. for the Study of Medieval Langs. & Lit.; Univ. Women's Club. Address: Barber's Cross, Watlington, Oxford, UK.

CHESTER, (Sir) Daniel Norman, b. 1907, Manchester, UK. Educator; Writer. Educ: M.A., Manchester Univ. Publs: Public Control of Road Passenger Transport; Central & Local Government; Financial & Administrative Relations; The Nationalised Industries; The Organisation of British Central Government; Questions in Parliament (w. Nora Bowring); The Nationalisation of British Industry, 1945-51, 1975; Ed., Lesson of the British War Economy. Contbr. to: Ed., Pub. Admin.; other profl. jrnls. Recip., C.B.E. Address: 136 Woodstock Rd., Oxford, UK.

CHETHAM-STRODE, Warren, b. 1897, Pinner. UK. Writer. Publs: Mice & Management; Three men & a Girl; Top Of the Milk; The Years of Alison; (plays) Sometimes Even Now; The Day is Gone; Man Proposes; Heart's Content; Young Mrs Barrington; The Guinea-Pig; The Gleam; Background; The Pet Shop; The Stepmother; (films) Odette; The Lady with the Lamp; The Guinea-Pig; Background; The Blue Falcon; (radio play) The Barlowes of Beddington. Address: The Oast House, Playden, nr. Rye, Sussex, UK.

CHEVALIER, Elizabeth Pickett, b. 1896, Chicago, Ill., USA. Author; Film Scenarist. Educ: Wellesley Coll., Mass. AB; Litt.D. Publs: Official History of American Red Cross; Nursing Service, 1921; The American National Red Cross: Its Origin, Purposes & Service, 1922; Redskin, 1928; Drivin' Woman, 1942. Mbrships: PEN; Cosmo, NY; Pen & Brush, NY. Address: 401 N. Bowling Green, Los Angeles, CA 90049, USA.

CHHIBBER, Vishwa Nath, b. 14 Jan. 1930, Varanasi, India. Writer; Editor. Educ: M.Sc., M.A., Ph.D., Dip. Jrnlism. Publs: Jawaharlal Nehru: A Man of Letters, 1970; Rabindranath Tagore: A Man of Letters, 1974. Contbr. to Indian newspapers & periodicals. Mbrships: PEN; Indian Acad. of Letters. Address: Publications & Information Directorate, Hillside Rd., New Delhi 12, India.

CHIAPPELLI, Fredi, b. 24 Jan. 1921, Florence, Italy. Professor, Director of the UCLA Center for Medieval & Renaissance Studies. Educ: D.Litt., Univ. of Florence, Italy. Publs: Langagé traditionnel et Langage personnel dans la poésie italienne, 1951; Studi sul Linguaggio del Machiavelli, 1952; Studi sul Linguaggio del Tasso epico, 1957; Nuovi Studi sul Linguaggio del Machiavelli, 1969; Studi sul Linguaggio del Petrarca, 1972; Machiavelli e la Lingua Fiorentina, 1974. Contbr. to var. jrnls. Mbr., Medieval Acad. of Am.; Renaissance Soc. of Am.;

Accademia della Crusca (Florence); etc. Hons: Premio Tasso, 1964; Gold Medal for Culture (Italy), 1969; Guggenheim Fellowship (USA), 1974. Address: 600 N. Kenter Ave., L.A., CA 90049, USA.

CHIARI, Joseph, b. 12 Jan. 1911, Poggio-di-Nazza, Corsica, France. French Diplomat; Poet; Writer. Educ Lic.-és-Lettres; Dip. d'Etudes Supérieures; Dr.-ès-Lettres. Publs: Mary Stuart (verse play), 1955; Symbolisme, from Poe to Mallarmé, 1956; Realism & Imagination, 1960; Religion & Modern Society, 1964; The Aesthetics of Modernism, 1970; The Necessity of Being, 1973; Twentieth Century French Thought, 1975; The Time of the Rising Sea (poems), 1975. Contbr. to: TImes Lit. Supplement; New Engl. Review; Orion; Spectator; Guardian; Scottish Fields. Mbr., Soc. of Authors. Recip., 1st Prize of Dramatic Art, Biennale Azuréenne, 1970. Address: 15A Westleigh Ave., London SW15 6RF, UK.

CHIGWE, Charles Francisco Bradley, b. 9 Apr. 1948, Nkhotakota, Malaŵi. Agricultural Research Officer. Educ: Dip. in Photog., Pretoria; Dip. in Agric., Malaŵi; B.Sc. (Agric.), Malaŵi. Publs: Plant Breeding Practices, 1972; Cotton Breeding in Malaŵi, 1973. Mbr., Assn. for Advancement of Sci. of Malaŵi. Hons: Distinction Shield, 1970; Cash Prize for Essay, Nat. Fauna Preservation Soc. of Malaŵi, 1973. Address: Univ. of Malaŵi, Bunda Coll. of Agric., P.O. Box 219, Lilongwe, Malaŵi.

CHILDS, David Haslam, b. 25 Sept. 1933, Bolton, UK. University Lecturer; Writer. Educ: Wigan & Dist. Mining & Tech. Coll.; B.Sc. & Ph.D., London Univ., Hamburg Univ. Publs: From Schumacher to Brandt: The Story of German Socialism, 1966; East Germany, 1969; Germany Since 1918, 1971; Marx & the Marxist, 1973. Contbr. to jrnls. inclng: Flight; German Life & Letters; Guardian; Socialist Commentary; Times Educl. Supplement; World Today. Address: Dept. of Politics, Univ. of Nottingham, Univ. Park, Nottingham, UK.

CHILIPAINE, Francis Aliponse, b. 18 Feb. 1945, Likoma Island, Nkhata Bay, Malaŵi. Lecturer in French. Educ: B.A., Univ. of Malaŵi; Dip. de Culture Française Contemporaine, Cert. Supérieur d'enseignement de français a l'étranger, Lic.-es.-lettres, & Maîtrise en Linguistique Française, Sorbonne Nouvelle, Paris, France. Publs: Le sentiment de l'injustice tel qu'il apparaît dans Climbie et Afrique Debout, 1969; Etude contrastive du système verbal Francais/Chicheŵa (l'expression du Passé), 1974. Address: French Dept., Univ. of Malaŵi, P.O. Box 280, Zomba, Malaŵi.

CHILMAN, Eric, b. 28 June 1893, Beverley, E. Yorks., UK. Journalist. Educ: Tech. Coll., Hull. Publs: Sixty Lyrics & One, 1945; The Book of English Verse (selector w. M. G. Edgar), 1926. Contbr. to: Spectator; Observer; Sunday Times; Daily Telegraph; Country Life; Field; Countryman; Wine & Food; Tablet; Tatler. Mbrships: Inst. of Jnrlsts.; Chem. Club. Address: 7 Claigmar Gdns., Church End, London N3 2HR, UK.

CHIMET, Iordan, b. 18 Nov. 1924, Galatzi, Romania. Freelance Writer. Educ: B.A., Univ. of Bucharest, 1949; LL.B., Bucharest Fac. of Law, 1957. Publs: Lamento for Little Balthazar, the Fish, 1968; Close Your Eyes & You Will See the City, 1970; Heroes, Ghosts, Little Mice, 1970; An Anthology of Innocence, 1972; Collected Poems, 1971. Contbr. to: Romanian-Am. Review; Contemporanul; Romanian Lit. Mag.; Romanian RadioTV. Mbrships: Writers' Union of Romania; Nat. Cinematography Assn. of Romania. Hons. incl: Book Award, Nat. Youth Assn., 1968; Fiction Prize, Writers' Union, 1970; Award, L.A. Nat. Book Fair, 1973. Address: 18 Blvd. Leontin Salajan, Bl. B3bis, Sc. 2, apt. 58, Bucharest, Romania.

CHING-CHUN, Ho, pen name WUENG, Tuen, b. Nov. 1903, Chiang-Se, China. Lecturer. Publs: A New Interpretation of Lao Tzu, 1959; Anthology of Poems & Lyrics by Tuen Wueng, 1960; A Collection of Short Essays on Poetry by I Chieh Yen, 1962; Explanation of Cheang Tzu, 1965; Introduction to Lyric & Melody, 1975. Mbrships: Chinese Univ. of Hong Kong; Chu Hai Coll., Hong Kong; Hong Kong Bapt. Coll.; PEN. Address: 111 Broadway, 7th Floor, Flat C, Mei Foo Sun Chuen, Kowloon, Hong Kong.

CHIPPERFIELD, Joseph Eugene, occasional pen name CRAIG, John Eland, b. 20 Apr. 1912, St. Austell, Cornwall, UK. Author; Journalist. Publs: incl: Dog of Castle Crag (as John Eland Craig), 1952; Seokoo of the Black

Wind; Grey Dog of Galtymore; A Dog Against Darkness (in USA as A Dog to Trust); The Two Fugitives; Storm of Dancerwood; Banner, The Pacing White Stallion, 1972; Lobo, Wolf of the Wind River Range, 1974; (forthcoming) Night Train from Inverness; Hunter of Harter Fell. Contbr. to: Irish Monthly; Evening Standard; Indep.; Dog World; etc. Screenwriter, Screen Art Productions & Independent Documentary Films etc. Address: Innisfree, 26 Raheen Pk., Bray, Co. Wicklow, Repub. of Ireland; & c/o Hutchinson & Co. Ltd., 3 Fitzroy Sq., London W1, UK.

CHISHOLM, Leslie Lee, b. 6 Dec. 1900, Cairo, Ill., USA. University Professor. Educ: A.B., S. Ill. Univ., 1929; A.M., Univ. of Chgo., 1933; Ph.D., Columbia Univ., 1936. Publs. incl: The Economic Ability of the States to Finance Public Schools, 1936; The Shifting of Federal Taxes & Its Implications for the Public Schools, 1939; Guiding Youth in the Modern Secondary School, 1945, 1950; The Work of the Modern High School, 1953. Contbr. to num. profl. jrnls., studies, monographs, reports. Hons: Annual Award for Outstanding Rsch., Am. Educ. Rsch. Assn.; Author, one of 60 Best Books of Yr., 1945. Address: 14501 Winter Dr., Lutz, FL 33549, USA.

CHISSELL, Joan Olive, b. 22 May 1919, Cromer, UK. Music Critic. Educ: Assoc., Royal Coll. of Music; Grad., Royal Schl. of Music. Publs: Schumann, 1948; Chopin, 1965; Schumann's Piano Music, 1972; Chapts. in Benjamin Britten (a Symposium), 1952, The Concerto, 1952 & Chamber Music, 1957. Contbr. to: The Times (Asst. Music Critic); Music & Letters; Musical Times. Musical Opinion; Radio Times. Ency. Britannica; & sev. other jrnls. & dicts. Address: 7D Abbey Rd., London NW8, UK.

CHITTOCK, John Dudley, b. 29 May 1928, London, UK. Film Critic; Writer; Publisher; Chairman, British Federation of Film Societies. Educ: S.-W. Essex Tech. Coll. Publs. incl: Film & Effect, 1965; Ed., Focal Ency. of Photography, 1958; Ed., Industrial Screen, 1963; Exec. Ed., World Directory of Stockshot Libraries, 1969; Ed., Screen Digest, 1971-74; Ed., Video & Film Communication, 1974-. Contbr. to: Fin. Times (Film & Video Column, 1963-); World's Press News; New Educ.; Jrnl. of Soc. of Film & TV Arts; Observer; etc. Mbrships: Fellow, Royal Photographic Soc. of GB; Royal TV Soc.; etc. Recip., Hood Medal, Royal Photographic Soc. of GB. Address: 37 Gower St., London WC1E 6HH, UK.

CHITTY, Arthur Ben, b. 15 June 1914, Jacksonville, Fla., USA. Educational Administrator. Educ: B.A., Univ. of the South; M.A., Tulane Univ.; L.H.D., Canaan Coll.; LL.D., Cuttington Coll., Liberia. Publs: Reconstruction at Sewanee, 1954; Co-ed., Ely, Too Black, Too White, 1969, 1970. Contbr. to histl., relig. jrnls. Address: Assn. of Episc. Colls., Sewanee, TN 37375, USA.

CHITTY (Lady), Susan, b. 1929, London, UK. Member, Magazine Editorial Staff. Educ: Univ. of Oxford. Publs: Diary of a Fashion Model; White Huntress; &, Intelligent Woman's Guide to Good Taste; My Life & Horses; The Woman who Wrote Black Beauty; The Beast & the Monk. Contbr. to: Vogue (Ed. staff); Punch; Daily Telegraph; Sunday Telegraph. Address: c/o Curtis Brown, 1 Craven Hill, London W2, UK.

CHITTY, Thomas Willes, pen name HINDE, Thomas, b. 2 Mar. 1926, Felixstowe, UK. Writer. Educ: B.A., Univ. of Oxford. Publs: Mr. Nicholas, 1952; The Day the Call Came, 1964; The Village 1966; High, 1968; Bird, 1970; Generally a Virgin, 1972; Agent, 1974. Contbr. to: Sunday Times; Times Lit. Supplement; Observer; London Mag.; Spectator; New Review. Mbrships: Authors Soc.; Exec. Comm., PEN. Recip., Granada Arts Fellowship, 1964. Address: Bow Cottage, W. Hoathly, E. Grinstead, W. Sussex, UK.

CHOPRA, Jagat Narain, b. 31 May 1899, Lyallpur, Pakistan. Journalist; former Minister in Punjab Cabinet. Educ: B.A. Leader Writer; Daily Hind Samachar; Daily Punjab Kesari. Address: c/o Daily Hind Samachar, Jullundur, Punjab, India.

CHOPRA, Romesh Chander, b. 24 Dec. 1926, Lyallpur, Pakistan. Journalist. Educ: B.Sc., Lahore Univ. Contbr. to: Ed., Hind Samachar (in Urdu); &, Punjab Kesari (in Hindi); others mags. Mbrships: Exec., Indian & Eastern Newspaper Soc.; Exec., all India Newspapers Ed's Conf.; Local Advsry. Comm., D.A.V. Educl. Instns., Jullundur. Address: c/o Daily Hind, Samachar, Civil Lines, Jullundur 1, Punjab, India.

CHORAFAS, Dimitris N., b. 25 Mar. 1926, Athens, Greece. Management Consultant; University Professor. Educ: M.E., E.E., Nat. Tech. Univ., Athens; M.S.E., UCLA, USA; Dr.Maths., Sorbonne, Paris, France; P.E. Publs. incl: Developing the International Executive, 1967; The Knowledge Revolution, 1968; How to Manage Computers for Results, 1969; The Communication Barrier in International Management, 1970; Management Development, 1971; Information Systems Design, 1972; Computers in Medicine, 1972; Warehousing, 1973; Management Planning, 1973; Die Kranke Gesellschaft, 1974. Address: 11 rue Arc de Triomphe, Paris, France; & Domaine Vodmer, OL360 Saint Laurent d'Eze, France.

CHOU, Eric, pen name (for Chinese works) SUNG CHIAO, b. 21 Oct. 1915, Mukden, Manchuria, China. Journalist. Educ: B.A., Peking Normal Univ., 1938. Publs: Over 12 books in Chinese, inclng. Memoirs of an Aide-de-Camp, 1951-66; A Man Must Choose, UK & USA, 1963; The Dragon & the Phoenix, UK & USA, 1971; Tales of the Forbidden Palace, UK, 1974; A Chinese Boyhood, 1975. Contbr. to: Forum World Features, London, UK (syndicated thru'out. world). Mbrships: PEN, Engl. Ctr.; Wig & Pen Club. Recip., Fellowship, Chinese Acad., Repub. of China, Taiwan, 1968. Address: 34 Gunnersbury Ave., Ealing Common, London W5 3QL, UK.

CHOW, Chung-Cheng, b. 1908, China. Writer; Lecturer. Educ: D.Litt.; Nankai Univ., China; Ecole Libre des Sciences Politiques, Paris, France; Sorbonne, Paris. Publs: Kleine Sampan; (w. transls. into French as J'ai Dechiré la Soie, Italian as Piccolo Sampan, & Engl. as The Lotus Pool); Zehn Jahre des Glucks; König des Baumes; Die Kleinen Bunten Fische; Aber ein Vogel gehört zum Himmel und ein Fisch gehört zum Wasser; Sklavin Goldblume. Mbrships: U.S. & Gedok. Address: Hausdorffstrasse 250, Bonn, German Federal Republic.

CHOW, Yick-fu, b. 25 Sept. 1907, Fai-chow, Kwangtung, China. University Professor. Educ: B.A., China Univ., Peking; postgrad. rsch. work, London, UK. Publs: Christianity & China, 1965; Summary of Chinese Historical Books, 1965; Confucian Thought & Life, 1968; An Introduction to Chinese Literature, 1971; Biography of Canon Lee Shiu Keung, 1974. Contbr. to: Ching Feng (Ed.); Chmn., Soc. for Study of Relig. & Culture. Mbr., PEN. Address: 33 Man King Building, 8/F Jordan Road, Kowloon, Hong Kong.

CHOWDHARY, Savitri Devi, b. 5 Sept. 1907, Multan, India (now Pakistan). Housewife; Writer. Publs: Indian Cooking, 1954; I Made My Home In England, 1961. Contbr. to: Times; Vogue; Women's mags. Address: 174 Clay Hill Rd., Basildon, Essex S16 5AB, UK.

CHRIMES, Stanley Bertram, b. 1907, Sidcup, Kent, UK. University Professor; Writer. Educ: M.A., Ph.D., Litt.D., King's Coll., London & Trinity Coll., Cambridge. Publs: English Constitutional Ideas in XVth Century; English Constitutional History; An Introduction to the Administrative History of Medieval England; Ed. (w. A. L. Brown), Select Documents of English Constitutional History 1307-1405; Lancastrians, Yorkists & Henry VII; Henry VII. Contbr. to: Holdsworth's Hist. of Engl. Law, Vol. I (Ed.); Engl. Hist. Review; Law Quarterly Review; Hist. Address: Univ. Coll., Cardiff, UK.

CHRIST, Henry I., b. 1 Oct. 1915, Brooklyn, N.Y., USA. Teacher; Supervisor. Educ: B.A., 1936, M.S., 1938, CCNY. Publs: Winning Words, 1948, 3rd ed., 1967; Myths & Folklore, 1952, 1968; Modern English in Action, 1968; Adventures for Today, 1968; Modern World Biographies, 1970; Language & Literature, 1972; Short World Biographies, 1973. Contbr. to profl. jrnls. Address: 834 SE Edgewood Dr., Palm Bay, FL 32905, USA.

CHRISTENSEN, Christian Arthur Richardt, b. 17 Dec. 1906. Journalist; Author. Educ: Oslo Univ. Publs: Det hendte igdr, 1933; Verden igdr og idag, 3 vols., 1935-36, 2nd ed., 5 vols., 1953-54; last vol., History of the World (Grimberg), 1958; last 2 vols., Vårt folks historie, 1961; Norge under okkupasjonen, 1964; A History of the Norwegian Life Insurance Companies' Association; Dåd (on heroes of resistance in Norway), 1965; Life of Fridtjof Nansen, 1966. Contbr. to var. jrnls. Address: Hagan terrasse 5, Oslo 3, Norway.

CHRISTESEN, Clement Byrne, b. 1911, Townsville, Qld., Australia. Editor; Publisher; Lockie Fellow, University of Melbourne. Educ: King's Coll., Univ. of Qld. Publs: The

Hand of Memory, 1971. Ed., Australian Heritage, 1949; Coast to Coast, 1954; On Native Grounds, 1968; The Gallery on Eastern Hill, 1970. Contbr. to: Meanjin Quarterly (Ed., Publr. & Fndr.) Mbrships: Fellowship of Aust. Writers; Aust. Soc. of Authors. Hons: O.B.E.; Gold Medal, Aust. Lit. Soc.; Britannica Aust. Award for Humanities. Address: "Stanhope", Eltham, Victoria, Australia 3059.

CHRISTIAN, Carol Cathay (Tuttle), b. 15 Nov. 1923, Peking, China. Writer; Editor. Educ: B.A., Smith Coll., Northampton, Mass., USA. Publs: Into Strange Country, 1958; God & One Redhead: Mary Slessor of Calabar (w. G. Plummer), 1970; Sev. readers for English as a Foreign Language, 1972-75. Contbr. to: Woman's Realm; BBC. Mbr., Soc. of Authors. Address: 22 Pitfold Ave., Shottermill, Haslemere, Surrey, UK.

CHRISTIAN, John Wyrill, b. 9 Apr. 1926, Scarborough, Yorks., UK. University Professor; Author. Educ: B.A., 1946, M.A., D.Phil., 1949, Queen's Coll., Oxford. Publs: Metallurgical Equilibrium Diagrams (co-author), 1952; Theory of Transformations in Metals & Alloys, 1965, 2nd ed. in 2 vols., 1975. Contbr. to var. sci. jrnls. Address: Dept. of Metallurgy & Materials Science, Oxford Univ., Parks Rd., Oxford, UK.

CHRISTIAN, Reginald Frank, b. 9 Aug. 1924, Liverpool, UK. University Professor. Educ: M.A., Oxon. Publs: Korolenko's Siberia, 1954; Russian Syntax, 1959, 2nd ed., 1971; Tolstoy's War & Peace — A Study, 1962; Russian Prose Composition, 1964, 2nd ed., 1974; Tolstoy — A Critical Introduction, 1969. Contbr. to: Times Lit. Supplement; var. UK & USA profl. jrnls. Address: The Roundel, St. Andrews, Fife, UK.

CHRISTIANSEN, Rex Samuel, b. 22 Jan. 1930, Wallasey, Cheshire, UK. Author. Publs: The Cambrian Railways (co-author) Vol. 1, 1851-1888, 1967, Vol. 2, 1889-1968, 1968; The North Staffordshire Railway (co-author), 1970; Regional History of Railways: Vol. 7, The West Midlands, 1973; Forgotten Railways of North & Mid Wales, forthcoming. Mbrships: Histl. Model Railway Soc.; Railway & Canal Histl. Soc.; Br. Line Soc.; Wirral Railway Circle; Indl. Railway Soc.; Stephenson Locomotive Soc.; Railway Correspondence & Travel Soc. Address: 17 Rochford Avenue, Whitefield, Manchester M25 7PQ, UK.

CHRISTIANSSON, Hans (Johannes), b. 24 Sept. 1916, Nyköping, Sweden. University Lecturer; Author. Educ: Fil.kand., 1947; Fil.lic(Nordic Archaeol.), 1952; Fil.lic.(Art Hist. & Theory), 1956; Fil.dr.(Nordic Archaeol), 1959. Publs: Dunkers socken, 1945; Jellingestenens bildvarld, 1952; The Scelettal Remains from Russekeila, Vest Spitzbergen (w. others), 1969. Contbr. to: Svenska Dagbladet; Eskilstuna-Kuriren; Södermanlands-Nyheter; Västerbottens-Kuriren; Fornvännen; TOR (Uppsala); Västerbotten (Umeå); Kuml (Århus); etc. Mbr., Swedish Authors' Assn.; var. acad. assns. Hons: Vegastipendiet, 1960; Skellefteå Stads Cultural Award, 1965. Address: Slåttervägen 29 A, 752 46 Uppsala, Sweden.

CHRISTIE, Ian Ralph, b. 1919. Professor of Modern British History, University College, London. Educ: M.A., Magdalen Coll., Oxford Univ. Publs: The End of North's Ministry, 1780-1782, 1958; Wilkes, Wyvill & Reform, 1962; Crisis of Empire; Great Britain & the American Colonies, 1754-1783, 1966; Essays in Modern History selected from the Transactions of the Royal Historical Society (ed.), 1968; Myth & Reality in late eighteenth-century British Politics, 1970; The Correspondence of Jeremy Bentham, vol. 3 (ed.), 1973. Contbr. to profl. jrnls. Address: 10 Green Lane, Croxley Green, Herts., UK.

CHRISTIE-MURRAY, David, pen names CHRISTIE, Hugh; ARTHUR, Hugh, b. 12 July 1913, London, UK. Retired Schoolmaster; Author. Educ: Dip.Jrnlsm., London Univ.; M.A., St. Peter's Hall, Oxford Univ.; Wycliffe Hall, Oxford. Publs: Heraldry in the Churches of Beckenham, 1956; (series) School Heraldic Folders, 1956-66; Hamlyn's Children's Bible, 1974; A History of Heresy (forthcoming); Astrology (forthcoming). Contbr. to: Times Lit. & Educl. Supplements; Country Life; She; Heiress; Photography; Armorial; Coat of Arms; Bible Today etc. Address: Imber Court Cottage, Orchard Lane, East Molesey, Surrey KT8 0BN, UK.

CHRISTOPH, James Bernard, b. 1928, Waukesha, Wis., USA. University Professor of Political Science, & Director of West European Studies. Educ: Univ. of Wis., Madison;

Harvard Univ.; Univ. of Minn., Mpls.; Univ. of London, UK; B.A.. M.A.; Ph.D. Publs: Capital Punishment & British Politics, 1962; Cases in Comparative Politics, 1965, 3rd ed., 1975; Britain at the Crossroads, 1967. Contbr. to: Am. Pol. Sci. Review; Pol. Studies; Pol. Quarterly; Pol. Sci. Quarterly; Western Pol. Quarterly. Address: c/o Dept. of Pol. Sci., Ind. Univ., Bloomington, IN 47401, USA.

CHRISTOPHERSEN, Paul Hans, b. 1911, Copenhagen, Denmark. Professor of English, New University of Ulster. Educ: M.A., D.Phil., Univ. of Copenhagen; Ph.D., Corpus Christi Coll., Cambridge, UK. Publs. incl: The Articles; Bilingualism; The Ballad of Sir Aldinger; An English Phonetics Course; Second Language Learning; An Advanced English Grammar. Contbr. to: Engl. Studies; Engl. Lang. Tchng; Twentieth Century; Transactions of Philol. Soc.; etc. Mbr., Philological Soc. Agent: A.P. Watt & Son. Address: Hazelbank, 70 Mullaghinch Rd., Aghadowey, Coleraine, Co. Londonderry, N. Ireland.

CHRISTOWE, Stoyan, b. 1898, Macedonia. Author. Educ: Valparaiso Univ., 1918-22. Publs: Heroes & Assassins; Mara; This is My Country; The Lion of Yanina; My American Pilgrimage; Many Lives. Contbr. to: Atlantic Monthly; Harper's; Story; Sat. Review of Lit.; N.Y. Times Sun. Book Review; etc.; special corres. in Balkans, Chgo. Daily News, 1927-28. Mbrships. incl: Vt. Senate, 1965-72; Commnr., Educ. Commn. of the States, 1966-72. Address: West Dover, UT 05356, USA.

CHUBAK, Sadeq, b. 1918, Shiraz, Iran. Author. Educ: Am. Coll., Tehran. Publs. incl: The Puppet Show; The Dancing Monkey whose Juggler was Dead; Why the Sea Teared Stormy; The Last Lamp; transl. into num. foreign langs. Address: c/o Iranian Embassy, 11 Princes Gate, London SW7, UK.

CHUBB, Mary Alford, b. 1903, London, UK. Archaeological Expedition Field Assistant, UAR, Iraq. Publs: Nefertiti Lived Here, 1954; City in the Sand, 1957; An Alphabet of Ancient Egypt, 1966; An Alphabet of Ancient Greece (Early Days), 1967; An Alphabet of Ancient Greece (The Golden Years), 1968; An Alphabet of Assyria & Babylonia, 1969; An Alphabet of Ancient Rome, 1971; An Alphabet of The Holy Land, 1973. Contbr. to: Punch; ladies mags.; BBC. Mbrships: Soc. of Authors; Soc. of Hellenic Travel; Radio Writers Assn. Address: Greens, Weston Patrick, Basingstoke, Hants., UK.

CHUKS-ADOPHY (Chief), Victor, pen name CHUKS, b. 12 Mar. 1920, Lagos, Nigeria. Senior Civil Servant; Writer. Educ: King's Coll., Lagos; Fac. of Law, Univ. of London, UK. Publs: Marriage: An International Problem. Contbr. to: W. African Review, 1944-50; World Digest; W. African Pilot; Comet; Eastern Nigerian Guardian. Mbrships: Life Fellow, Int. Inst. Arts & Letters; Inst. of Jrnlsts., London & Overseas (Nigeria). Address: 39E Cameron Rd., Ikoyi, Lagos, Nigeria.

CHURCHILL, Rhona, b. London, UK. Journalist. Publs: White Man's God, 1962. Reporter, War Corres., Feature Writer, Foreign Corres., Daily Mail, 1938-71. Address: Sandy Lodge, Sandy Lane, Kingswood, Surrey, UK.

CHUTE, Marchette, b. 1909, Hazelwood, Wayzata, Minn., USA. Educ: B.A., Univ. of Minn., Mpls. Publs: Geoffrey Chaucer of England; Shakespeare of London; Ben Jonson of Westminster; Two Gentle Men, The Lives of George Herbert & Robert Herrick; The Search for God; The End of the Search; The First Liberty; Stories from Shakespeare; Jesus of Israel; etc. Contbr. to: Saturday Review; Holiday; Va. Quarterly; N.Y. Times. Mbrships. incl: Am. Acad. of Arts & Letters; PEN; Royal Soc. of Arts; Renaissance Soc. Recip., Hon. Litt.D. Address: 450 E. 63rd St., NYC, N.Y., USA.

CIABATTARI, Jane Dotson, b. 27 Mar. 1946, Emporia, Kan., USA. Writer; Editor. Educ: B.A., Stanford Univ., 1968. Contbr. to: (mng. Ed.) Calif. Living; Sunday Mag., San Fran. Examiner & Chronicle; (Former Supsvng. Ed.) Odyssey Press; (Assoc. Ed.) Redbook Mag.; (Columnist) Emporia Gazette; Mont. Standard; & contbr. to var. lit. jrnls. Mbrships: Press Chairwoman, Mont. Govs. Status of Women Comm., 1971-72; Nat. Org. for Women; AAUW; Women in Communications; Nat. Fedn. of Press Women; Media Women, N.Y., 1969-71; Newspaper Guild. Recip., Nat. Merit Schlrship., 1964-68. Address: 1784 Filbert St., San Fran., CA 94123, USA.

CICELLIS, Kay, b. 1926, Marseilles, France. Author. Publs: The Easy Way, 1950; No Name in the Street, 1952; Death of a Town, 1954; Ten Seconds From Now, 1956; The Way to Colonos, 1958. Contbr. to: Encounter; London Mag.; Vogue; Harper's Bazaar; Paris Review; Mademoiselle; Botteghe Obscure. Address: P.O. Box 2438, Lagos, Nigeria, West Africa.

CILENTO, Ruth Yolanda, b. 30 July 1925, Adelaide, Australia. Medical Practitioner. Educ: M.B., B.S., Qld. Univ., 1949. Publs: Moreton Bay Adventure, 1961. Mbr., Royal Qld. Art Soc. Address: P.O. Box 92, Strathpine, Queensland, Australia 4500.

CILLIERS, Andries Charl, b. 21 Nov. 1933, Stellenbosch, S. Africa. University Professor (Dean, Univ. of Port Elizabeth, S. Africa, 1969-72, 1974-75); Writer. Educ: B.A., 1953, LL.B., 1955, Univ. of Stellenbosch; B.A., 1958, M.A., 1962, Oxford, UK (Rhodes Schlr.); Doct. exam., Univ. of S. Africa, 1973. Publs: Herbstein & Van Winsen's The Civil Practice of the Superior Courts in South Africa (co-author, 2nd revised ed.), 1966, 1973; Law of Costs, 1972. Contbr. to: Jrnl. of Contemporary Roman-Dutch Law (Ed. Bd., 1968-). Mbrships: Law Revision Comm.; Bd. for Recognition of Exams. in Law; Advocate, Supreme Ct. of S. Africa. Apptd. Patron, Nat. Inst. for Prevention of Crime & Rehab. of Offenders, 1973. Address: 50 Louis Botha Crescent, Summerstrand, Port Elizabeth, 6001 S. Africa.

CIOFFARI, Vincenzo, b. 24 Feb. 1905, Calitri, Italy. Professor of Romance Languages; Author. Publs: Italian Review Grammar & Composition, 1937, 3rd ed., 1968; Fortune & Fate from Democritus to St. Thomas Aquinas, 1937; Spoken Italian, 1944; Spanish Review Grammar (w. Gonzalez), 1957, 3rd ed., 1972; Beginning Italian Grammar, 1958, 2nd ed., 1965; Guido da Pisa's Commentary on Dante's Inferno, 1974. Contbr. to: Dante Studies; Italica; Speculum; Hispania; Mod. Lang. Jrnl.; etc. Mbrships. incl: MLA; Dante Soc. of Am. (Pres., 1967-73); Hon. Life Mbr., Soc. Dantesca Italiana, Dante Alighieri Soc. of Boston. Address: 45 Amherst Rd., Waban, MA, USA.

CIPOLLA, Carlo M., b. 15 Aug. 1922, Pavia, Italy. University Professor; Author. Educ: Laureate, Univ. of Pavia, 1944. Publs: Studi di Storia della Moneta, 1948; Money, Prices & Civilization in the Mediterranean World, 1956; Le Avventure della Lira, 1958; The Economic History of World Population, 1962; Guns & Sails in the Early Phase of European Expansion, 1965; Clocks & Culture, 1967; Literacy & Development in the West, 1969; Cristofano & the Plague — A Study in the History of Public Health, 1973. Contbr. to: Econ. Hist. Review; Jrnl. of European Econ. Hist.; etc. Address: 271 Colgate Ave., Kensington, CA 94708, USA, via Montebello Battaglia 4, Pavia, Italy.

CITOVICH, Enid, pen name, BALDRY, Enid, b. 1902, London, UK. Writer. Educ: M.A., Edinburgh Univ. Publs: Swim Better; Dive Better, 1935; Swimming, 1964; Diving, 1964; The Music Badges (Guides), 1965. Contbr. of review to Musical Times. Mbrships: The Guide Club; Royal Overseas League. Agent: J. F. Gibson. Address: 18 Manor Terr., Felixtowe, Suffolk, UK.

CLAPHAM, John, b. 31 July 1908, Letchworth, U.K. Musicologist; University Reader; Author. Educ: Royal Acad. Music; Univ. of London; D.Mus., 1946. Publs: Antonin Dvorak: Musician & Craftsman, 1966; Smetana (Master Musicians Series), 1972. Contbr. to: Musical Quarterly; Music & Letters; Music Review; Listener; Musical Times; Musica; Proceedings of Royal Musical Assn.; Musikforschung; Hudebni veda; Grove's Dict. of Music & Musicians, 6th ed.; Die Musik in Geschichte und Gegenwart. Mbrships: F.R.A.M.; Soc. of Authors. Address: 26 Fernbank Rd., Bristol BS6 6PU, UK.

CLARIMON, Carlos, b. 4 Nov. 1920, Saragossa, Spain. Advertiser. Publs: detective novels, novels & tales, incing. Hombre a solas, 1961. Contbr. to: Índice; Juventud; Insula; Agora. Recip., Juventud Story Prize, 1955. Address: Plaza del Conde del Valle de Suchil 20, Madrid 15, Spain.

CLARK, Ann Nolan, b. 5 Dec. 1896, Las Vegas, N.M., USA. Writer. Educ: 3 yrs. of coll. studies. Publs: Hoof Print on the Wind; Circle of Seasons; Medicine Man's Daughter; Journey to the People; Santiago; Secret of the Andes; In My Mother's House; Summer Is for Growing. Mbrships: Soc. of SW Authors; Nat. Fedn. of Press Women. Hons.

incl: Newbery Medal; Regina Medal; BIA Disting. Serv. Medal. Address: P.O. Box 164, Cortaro, AZ 85230, USA.

CLARK, Anne, b. 4 Feb. 1933, London, UK. Local Government Officer. Educ: B.A., Birkbeck Coll., London Univ. Publs: Beasts & Bawdy, 1975. Contbr. to: Jabberwocky (Ed.). Mbr. & Sec., Lewis Carroll Soc. (founded 1969). Address: 2 Brinkburn Close, Edgeware, Middx., UK.

CLARK, David R., b. 1920, Seymour, Conn., USA. University Professor; Writer. Educ: B.A., M.A., Ph.D., Wesleyan Univ., Yale Univ. Publs. incl: Co-author, A Curious Quire, 1962; Author, W. B. Yeats & the Theatre of Desolate Reality, 1965; Co-Ed., Irish Renaissance, 1965; Author, Day Tree, 1966; Co-Ed., Reading Poetry, 1968; A Tower of Polished Black Stones, 1971; Druid Craft: The Writing of The Shadowy Waters, 1971, 1972; Author, Lyric Resonance, 1972. Contbr. to num. lit. jrnls. Mbrships. incl: MLA: Am. Comm. Irish Studies; Int. Soc. Advancement Irish Lit.; Can. Assn. Irish Studies. Address: Engl. Dept., Univ. of Mass., Amherst, MA 01002, USA.

CLARK, Eleanor, b. 6 July 1913, L.A., Calif., USA. Writer. Educ: B.A., Vassar Coll., Poughkeepsie, N.Y., 1934. Publs: (novels) The Bitter Box, 1946; Baldur's Gate, 1970; (other) Rome & a Villa, 1952; Song of Roland (juvenile), 1960; The Oysters of Locmariaquer, 1964; Transl., Dark Wedding by Ramón José Sender, 1943. Mbr., Nat. Inst. of Arts & Letters. Hons: Grant, Nat. Inst. of Arts & Letters, 1947; Guggenheim Fellowship, 1947, 1949; Nat. Book Award, for non-fiction, 1965. Address: 2495 Redding Rd., Fairfield, CT 06430, USA.

CLARK, Eric E., b. 29 July 1937, Birmingham, UK. Author; Journalist. Publs: Everybody's Guide to Survival, 1969; Corps Diplomatique, 1973, Am. publs. as Diplomat — The World of International Diplomacy, 1974; Sources of Conflict in British Industry (co-author), 1973. Contbr. to: The Observer; Sunday Times; Daily Telegraph Mag.; New Statesman; New Society; Reader's Digest. Mbrships: Soc. of Authors; Nat. Union of Jrnlsts. Address: c/o Child & Co., 1 Fleet St., London EC4, UK.

CLARK (Sir), George Norman, b. 27 Feb. 1890, Halifax, Yorks., UK. University Professor & Administrator; Author. Educ: M.A., D.Litt., Balliol Coll., Oxford; M.A., Cambridge. Publs: The 17th Century, 1929; The Later Stuarts, 1934; Early Modern Europe, 1954; History of the Royal College of Physicians, vols. I—II, 1964-66. Contbr. to: Engl. Histl. Review (Ed., 1920-26, Jt. Ed., 1937-39). Hons. incl: Cmdr., Order of Orange-Nassau, Netherlands, 1950; Kt.Bach., 1953; 8 hon. degrees. Address: 7 Ethelred Court, Headington, Oxford, UK.

CLARK, Gladys Pearl, b. 27 Feb. 1909, Beardstown, Ill., USA. Business-woman; Author; Artist. Educ: W. Ill. Univ., Pvte. study, Poetry Technique. Publs: Singing Silhouettes, 1970; Christmas Poems, 1973. Contbr. to maj. mags., reviews. Mbrships: Calif. Fedn. of Chaparral Poets; Centro Studi E. Scambi Int. Hons. incl: 3 Artistic Dips., ibid, 1969, 1970, 1971; 1st, 2nd Prizes, Camelia Poets Christmas Contest, 1967, 1963. Address: 6435 Orange Ave. No. 26A, Sacramento, CA 95823, USA.

CLARK, John Grahame Douglas, b. 1907, Beckenham, Kent, UK. University Professor of Archaeology, 1952-74; Master of Peterhouse, Cambridge Univ. Educ: M.A., Ph.D., Sc.D., Peterhouse, Cambridge. Publs. incl: Archaeology & Society, 1939, 3rd ed., 1957; Prehistoric England, 1940, 5th ed., 1962; From Savagery to Civilization, 1946; Prehistoric Europe: the economic basis, 1952; Excavations at Star Carr, 1954; World Prehistory: an Outline, 1961; World Prehistory: a New Outline, 1969; Aspects of Prehistory, 1970; The Early Stone Age Settlement of Scandinavia, 1974. Contbr. to: Antiquity; Antiquaries' Jrnl.; etc. Mbrships. incl: Ancient Monuments Bd.; F.B.A. Hons. incl: C.B.E.; Cmdr., Order of the Danebrog. Address: 19 Wilberforce Road, Cambridge, UK.

CLARK, John Howard, b. 6 June 1929, Hendon, Middlesex, UK. Senior Lecturer in Psychology. Educ: M.A., M.B., Cambridge Univ.; Westminster Hosp. Med. Schl., London; Dip. Psychol. Med. Publs: What are the Rules of the Bead-game? , 1970. Contbr. to: Information Processing '68, 1969; Survey of Cybernetics, 1969; Six Approaches to the Person, 1972; England Swings S.F. Address: Dept. of Psychology, Manchester Univ., Manchester M13 9PL, UK.

CLARK, Kenneth Edward, b. 1924, Tottenham, London, UK. Director, Textile Trade Publications Ltd.; Mng. Ed., Brit. Clothing Mfr. Mbr., Coun., Clothing Inst. Address: 51 Hillcrest Rd., Purley, Surrey, UK.

CLARK, Laurence, b. 1914, Maidstone, Kent, UK. Writer. Educ: M.A., Peterhouse, Cambridge Univ. Publs: Thirty Nine Preludes, 1953; Kingdom Come, 1958; More than Moon, 1961; Murder of the Prime Minister, 1965; A Father of the Nation, 1968; Democracy Has Three Dimensions, 1975. Contbr. to jrnls. inclng: The Economist; Poetry, London; Twentieth Century. Mbr., Soc. of Authors. Address: 6 Temple Gdns., Moor Park, Rickmansworth, Herts., UK.

CLARK, Leonard, b. 1905, St. Peter Port, Guernsey. Writer. Educ: Normal Coll., Bangor. Publs., num. books inclng: A Fool in the Forest (autobiog.); Grateful Caliban (autobiog); Sark Discovered; Good Company (poems for the young); The Broad Atlantic (poems for the young); Secret as Toads (poems); Walking with Trees (poems); The Hearing Heart (poems); Tribute to Walter de la Mare; Stories of Robert Andrew; Mr. Pettigrew's Harvest; Mr. Pettigrew's Train; Alfred Williams: Life & Work (biog.); Four Seasons. Contbr. to num. periodicals. Mbr., num. orgs. Hons. incl: O.B.E. Address: 50 Cholmeley Cres., Highgate, London N6, UK.

CLARK, Margaret Goff, b. 7 Mar. 1913, Okla. City, Okla., USA. Freelance Writer; Lecturer. Educ: B.S. Educ., State Univ. Coll., Buffalo, N.Y. Publs. incl: Mystery of Seneca Hill, 1961; Mystery of the Buried Indian Mask, 1962; Mystery at Star Lake, 1965; Mystery of the Missing Stamps, 1967; Freedom Crossing, 1969; Mystery Horse, 1972; John Muir, 1974; Death at their Heels, 1975. Contbr. to: Am. Girl Mag.; (poetry) N.Y. Times; etc. Mbrships. incl: Nat. League Am. Pen Women; Mystery Writers Am. Inc.; Assn. Profl. Women Writers. Hons. incl: Adoption by Seneca Indians, 1962. Address: 5621 Lockport Rd., Niagara Falls, NY 14305, USA.

CLARK, Marie Catherine Audrey, pen name CURLING, Audrey, b. London, UK. Writer. Publs: (novels) The Running Tide, 1963; Sparrow's Yard, 1964; (histl. novels) The Echoing Silence, 1967; Caste for Comedy, 1970; The Sapphire & the Pearl, 1970; Cry of the Heart, 1971; A Quarter of the Moon, 1972; Shadows on the Grass, 1973; (biog.) The Young Thackeray, 1966. Contbr. to: Homes & Gardens; Women's Jrnl.; Woman; Woman's Own; Lady; Woman's Realm. Mbrships: Soc. of Authors; Inst. Jrnlsts.; Romantic Novelists' Assn. (Comm. Mbr.). Hons: Finalist, Romantic Novelists' Major Award, 1972 & 1973. Address: 11 Milnthorpe Rd., Chiswick W4 3DX, UK.

CLARK, Marjorie, pen name RIVERS, Georgia, b. Melbourne, Aust. Writer. Publs: Jacqueline; Dantalego; The Difficult Art; She Dresses for Dinner; short stories. Contbr. to: Herald; Sun; Bulletin; Woman's Mirror; most Aust. newspapers. Mbrships: PEN; Vic. Fellowship of Aust. Writers. Recip., 2 short story prizes. Address: Flat 5, 8 Hepburn St., Hawthorn 3122, Vic., Australia.

CLARK, Robert, b. 1911, Darjeeling, India. Solicitor. Educ: LL.B., Univ. of Adelaide, Australia. Publs: (poetry) The Dogman, 1962; Segments of the Bowl, 1968; Ed., A Window at Night Poems of Max Harris, 1967; Co-Ed., Verse in Australia for 1958, 1959, 1960 & 1961. Contbr. to: Meanjin; Sydney Bulletin; Overland; Southerly; Quadrant; Sydney Morning Herald; Westerly; Aust. Letters; Poetry Aust.; sev. anthols. Mbr., Aust. Soc. of Authors. Hons: Short Story Prize, Aust. Broadcasting Comm., 1944; Poetry Prize, Sydney Morning Herald, 1956. Address: Hill Rd., Montacute, S.A., Australia.

CLARK, Ronald Harry, b. 1904, Norwich, UK. Draughtsman & Designer. Educ: Finsbury Tech. Coll., London. Publs: Development of the English Steam Wagon; Development of the English Traction Engine; Chronicles of a Country Works; Steam Engine Builders of Norfolk; Steam Engine Builders of Suffolk, Essex & Cambridgeshire; Steam Engine Builders of Lincolnshire; Savages Ltd., 1850-1964; The Development of Power; Brough Superior — The Rolls Royce of Motor Cycles; A Short History of the Midland & Great Northern Joint Railway; A Traction Engine Miscellany; Some Adventures of Samson Cogg. Contbr. to: Engr.; Engrng.; Model Engrng; etc. Address: Diamond Cottage, Shotesham All Saints, Norwich, Norfolk, UK.

CLARK, Russell John, pen name CARR, Michael, b. 2 Feb. 1931, Grays, Essex, UK. Journalist. Publs: Num.

histories of Brit. Cooperative Socs., 1953-63; Gen. Ed., Water (official jrnl., Nat. Water Coun.); Ed., N.W.C. Bulletin; Ed., London Rotarian. Contbr. to: Nat. & Int. Congresses of Water Supply Orgs.; nat. & tech. jrnls. Mbrships. incl: Brit. Inst. Mgmt.; Inst. of Jrnlsts.; Inst. of PR; Brit. Assn. Indl. Eds.; Int. Water Supply Assn. (Chmn., Int. Standing Comm. on PR). Address: 25 Ingrebourne Gdns., Upminster, Essex RM14 1BQ, UK.

CLARK, Sydney Aylmer, b. 18 Aug. 1890, Auburndale, Mass., USA. Travel Author. Educ: B.A., Dartmouth Coll. Publs: The Fifty Dollar Series; Old Glamors of New Austria; Many Colored Belgium; Cathedral France; "All the Best" series of travel books inclng. 20 vols. on Europe, The Orient, S. Pacific & Latin America. Contbr. to: Nat. Geog. Mag.; Holiday; Century Mag.; Rotarian; Travel Mag.; N.Y. Times; Coronet; Christian Sci. Monitor; etc. Mbrships: Soc. of Am. Travel Writers; Nat. Travel Club; N.Y. Travel Writers' Assn. Recip., var. citations & medals from European countries. Address: Sagamore Beach, MA 02562, USA.

CLARK, Ursula Mary, b. 24 Feb. 1940, Gosforth, Northumberland, UK. Freelance Photographer. Publs. w. Bruce Allsopp: Architecture of France, 1963; Architecture of Italy, 1964; Architecture of England, 1964; Photography for Tourists, 1966; The Great Tradition of Western Architecture (w. B. Allsopp & Harold W. Booton), 1966; Historic Architecture of Northumberland (w. B. Allsopp), 1969; Historic Architecture of County Durham (w. Neville Whittaker), 1971. Address: 48 Baroness Drive, Newcastle-upon-Tyne NE15 7AU, UK.

CLARK, William Donaldson, b. 1916, Northumberland, UK. Journalist. Educ: M.A., Oxford Univ.; Univ. of Chgo., USA. Publs: Less than Kin, a Study of Anglo-American Relations, 1957; What is the Commonwealth?, 1958; Number 10, 1966 (play version, w. Ronald Millar, 1967); Special Relationship, 1968. Contbr. to: Observer (Ed., Wk. Feature, 1958-60). Address: 3407 Rodman St., N.W. Wash. DC 20008, USA.

CLARKE, Amy Key, b. 21 Dec. 1892, London, UK. Teacher. Educ: St. Paul's Schl., London; Newnham Coll., Cambridge; M.A. Publs: (poetry) Persephone: A Masque, 1924; (prose) The Universal Character of Christianity, 1950. Contbr. to Oxford Book of English Mystical Verse (poem). Mbrships: Roman Soc.; Classical Assn.; Soc. of Authors. Address: St. Ninian's, 13 Victoria St., Cambridge CB1 1JP, UK.

CLARKE, Anna, b. 28 Apr. 1919, Cape Town, S. Africa. Author. Educ: B.Sc.(Econ.), Univ. of London, UK. 1945; B.A., Open Univ., 1971-74; Univ. of Sussex, Falmer. Publs: The Darkened Room, 1968; A Mind to Murder, 1971; The End of a Shadow, 1972; Plot Counter-Plot, 1974; My Search for Ruth, 1975. Mbr., Crime Writers Assn. Address: 12 Franklin Road, Brighton, Sussex, UK.

CLARKE, Arthur Charles, b. 16 Dec. 1917, Minehead, UK. Author. Educ: B.Sc., Univ. of London. Publs: ca. 50 books inclng. (non-fiction) The Promise of Space; Profiles of the Future; The Treasure of the Great Reef; (fiction) Childhoods End; Earthlight; A Fall of Moondust; The Lost Worlds of 2001; The Wind from the Sun; Rendezvous with Rama; 2001: A Space Odyssey (w. S. Kubrick). Contbr. to num. jrnls. Mbrships. incl: Soc. of Authors; Sci. Fiction Writers of Am.; Assn. of Brit. Sci. Writers; Int. Sci. Writers' Assn.; AAAS; Fellow & Past Chmn., Brit. Interplanetary Soc.; Fellow, Royal Astron. Soc. Recip., num. medals & other awards. Agent: David Higham Assocs. Address: 25 Barnes Pl., Colombo 7, Sri Lanka.

CLARKE, Austin Ardinel Chesterfield, b. 26 July 1934, Speightonstown, Barbados, WI. Novelist. Educ: Harrison Coll., Barbados; Trinity Coll., Univ. of Toronto, Canada. Publs. incl: Survivors of the Crossing, 1964; Amongst Thistles & Thorns, 1965; The Meeting Point, 1967; When He Was Free & Young & He Used To Wear Silks, 1971; Storm of Fortune, 1972; To Name the Bigger Light, 1975. Contbr. to US, for. jrnls. Hons: Belmont-Saturday Night Mag., 1st Prize (short story), 1965. Address: 432 Brunswick Ave., Toronto M5R 2Z4, Ont., Can.

CLARKE, (Rev.) Basil Fulford Lowther, b. 1908, Harlton, Cambs.. UK. Clergyman; Author. Educ: M.A.; St. John's Coll., Durham; Cuddesdon Theol. Coll. Publs: Church Builders of the Nineteenth Century; Lesson Notes on the Prayer Book; My Parish Church; Clement Joins the Church; Anglican Cathedrals Outside the British Isles; The

Building of the 18th Century Church; Parish Churches of London; English Churches (w. Sir John Betjeman). Contbr. to: Berks. Archaeol. Soc. Transactions; Collins' Pocket Guide to Engl. Parish Chs.; Concerning Arch. Address: 220 Henley Rd., Caversham, Reading, UK.

CLARKE, Brenda Margaret Lilian, pen name, HONEYMAN, Brenda, b. 30 July 1926, Bristol, UK. Writer. Publs: Richard By Grace of God, 1968; The Kingmaker, 1969; Richmond & Elizabeth, 1970; Harry the King, 1971; Brother Bedford, 1972; Good Duke Humphrey, 1973; The King's Minions, 1974; The Queen & Mortimer, 1974. Mbr., Wessex Writers' Assn. Address: 25 Torridge Rd., Keynsham, Bristol BS18 1QQ, UK.

CLARKE, Clorinda, b. 4 Mar. 1917, Utica, N.Y. USA. Journal Editor. Educ: B.A., Manhattanville Coll., Purchase, N.Y., 1938, Oxford Univ. 1939; M.A., Columbia Univ., 1943. Publs: American Revolution 1775-1783, 1964; American Revolution, A British View, 1967; The Young American Republic, 1970. Contbr. to: Ed., Nylic Review; Cath. World; Sign. Mbr., N.Y. Histl. Soc. Address: 38 Gramercy Pk., N.Y., NY 10010, USA.

CLARKE, David Waldo, b. 1907, Swansea, UK. Head of College Department of English; Author. Educ: B.A., Univ. Coll., Swansea; M.A., Jesus Coll., Oxford. Publs: Modern English Writers, 1947; William Shakespeare, 1950; The Man from Thunder River, 1951; Warbonnet, 1952; Ride on, Stranger, 1953; The Long Riders, 1957; Modern English Practice, 1957; Lariat, 1958; Ride the High Hills, 1961; Beat the Drum Slowly, 1962; No Man Rides Alone, 1965; Once in the Saddle, 1969; A History of English Literature, 1975. Agent: Rupert Crew Ltd. Address: 10 East Cliff, Southgate, Swansea SA3 2AS, UK.

CLARKE, Desmond, b. 2 July 1907, Castlebar, Co. Mayo, Repub. of Ireland. Librarian/Secretary, Ret'd.; Author. Educ: M.A.; F.L.A.I.; F.I.A.L. Publs: Thomas Prior, 1681-1751, 1951; Arthur Dobbs Esq.,- 1958; The Ingenious Mr. Edgeworth, 1966; The Unfortunate Countryman, 1966; Three Stories, 1973; Dublin Today & Yesterday, 1975, etc. Contbr. to: Dublin Mag.; The Bell; Chambers Mag.; Prairie Schooner; Studies; Irish Times; Irish Press, etc. Mbrships: Hon. Life, Royal Dublin Soc.; Fellow, Lib. Assn. of Ireland; Arts Club; Sci. Club of Ireland; Nat. Lib. of Ireland Society; Irish PEN. Address: St. Maur, 22 Palmerston Rd., Dublin 6, Repub. of Ireland.

CLARKE, Dorothy Madeline, b. Wynberg, S. Africa. Freelance Journalist. Publs: 1000 Curiosities of the World, 1939; No Time to Weep, 1942. Contbr. to var. mags. & periodicals in UK & USA. Mbr., Service Women's Club. Agent: A.M. Heath & Co. Address: Glovers, 1 Testers Close, Oxted, Surrey RH8 0HW.

CLARKE, Hugh Vincent, b. 1919, Brisbane, Australia. Director of Information & Public Relations Department of Aboriginal Affairs; Author; Journalist; Publs: The Tub, 1963; Corgi, 1965; Breakout, 1965; To Sydney by Stealth, 1966; The Long Arm, 1974. Contbr. to: Australia Writes; Australia at Arms. Mbrships: A.J.A.; A.S.A.; Servs. Club; Canberra Club. Address: 14 Chermside Street, Deakin, Canberra, A.C.T., Australia.

CLARKE, Margaret Archibald, b. 11 Oct. 1901, Kilmacolm, Scotland, UK. Writer; Researcher. Educ: B.A., 1921, M.A., 1922, Univ. of Sydney, Aust.; Dr., Univ. of Paris, France, 1927. Publs: Heine et la Monarchie de Juillet, 1927; Rimbaud et Quinet, 1945; The Archaic Principle in Education, 1962; Transl. (w. notes) The Essential Comte, 1974. Contbr. to: Art in Aust.; Aust. Broadcasting Commn. Weekly; Cath. Weekly, Sydney; 20th Century, Melbourne; Mod. Lang. Review; Listener; Revie de Littérature Comparée; Cath. Herald; Dublin Review. Mbrships: Soc. of Authors; Transls. Assn. Hons: Jones Medal for Tchng., 1922; Rsch. Fellowship, Univ. of Sydney, 1947. Address: 1 Stedham Chambers, Coptic St., London WC1, UK.

CLARKE, Martin Lowther, b. 1909, Cavendish, Suffolk, UK. Emeritus Professor of Latin. Educ: M.A., King's Coll., Cambridge Univ. Publs: Richard Porson; Greek Studies in England 1700-1830; Rhetoric at Rome; The Roman Mind; Classical Education in Britain, 1500-1900; George Grote; Paley; Higher Education in the Ancient World. Address: Lollingdon House, Cholsey, Wallingford OX10 9LS, UK.

CLARKE, Mary, b. 23 Aug. 1923, London, UK. Editor. Publs: The Sadler's Wells Ballet: A History & an Appreciation, 1955; Six Great Dancers, 1957; Dancers of Mercury: The Story of Ballet Rambert, 1962; Ballet: An Illustrated History (w. Clement Crisp), 1973; Making a Ballet (w. Clement Crisp), 1975. Contbr. to: Ency. Britannica; Guardian; Dance Mag., N.Y.; Dance News, N.Y.; Observer; Sunday Times; Ed., Dancing Times. Mbr., Gauthier Club. Recip., 2nd Prize, Cafe Royal Lit. Prize for best book on Theatre, 1955. Address: 11 Danbury St., London N1, UK.

CLARKE, Mary Gavin, b. 1881, Aberdeen, UK. Teacher & Lecturer. Educ: Aberdeen Univ.; Girton Coll., Cambridge Univ.; M.A., Cantab. & T.C.D.; LLD. Publs: Girton College Studies, No. 3; Sidelights on Teutonic History during the Migration Period; The Headmistress Speaks (jt. author); A Short Life of 90 Years (pvte. ed.), 1973. Contbr. articles to var. jrnls. inclng: Times Educl. Supplement; Manchester Guardian. Address: 3 Gordon Rd., Corstorphine, Edinburgh, UK.

CLARKE, Pauline, pen name CLARE, Helen, b. Notts., UK. Educ: M.A., Somerville Coll., Oxford. Publs: The Pekinese Princess, 1948; The White Elephant, 1952, 2nd ed., 1966; Five Dolls in a House, 1953; Smith's Hoard, 1955, 2nd ed., 1967; The Boy with the Erpingham Hood, 1956; James the Policeman, 1957; Torolv the Fatherless, 1959; The Robin Hooders, 1960; Keep the Pot Boiling, 1961; The Twelve & the Genii, 1962; Merlin's Magic, 1953, 2nd ed., 1963; The Two Faces of Silenus, 1972. Mbr., Soc. of Authors. Hons: Carnegie Medal, 1962; Deutsche Jugendbuch Prize, 1968. Agent: Curtis Brown Ltd. Address: 62 Highsett, Hills Rd., Cambridge, UK.

CLARKE, Peter Hugh, b. 18 Mar. 1933, London, UK. Author. Educ: B.A., Univ. of London. Publs: Mikhail Tal's Best Games of Chess, 1961; 100 Soviet Chess Miniatures, 1964; Petrosian's Best Games of Chess 1946-63, 1964; Chess, 1967. Contbr. to: Sunday Times (Chess Corres., 1974-); Chess; Brit. Chess Mag.; The Times; BBC; Brit. Book News. Mbrships: Soc. of Authors; Brit. Chess Fedn. Address: Oakdale, New Rd., Bush, Bude, Cornwall EX23 9LE, UK.

CLARKE, Robin Harwood, b. 19 Oct. 1937, Bedford, UK. Writer; Editor. Educ: B.A., Pembroke Coll., Cambridge Univ. Publs: The Diversity of Man, 1964; We All Fall Down, 1968; The Science of War & Peace; The Challenge of the Primitives (w. G. Hindley), 1975; Ed., Notes for the Future (anthol.), 1975; Technological Self-Sufficiency, 1975; Ed., World of Science Library (Thames & Hudson). Contbr. to: Sci. Jrnl. (Ed., 1964-69); Discovery (Asst. Ed., 1961-63, Ed., 1963-64); New Scientist; BBC; Listener; Daily Telegraph Mag. Mbr., Assn. Brit. Sci. Writers. Address: Criftin House, Wentnor, Near Bishops Castle, Shropshire, UK.

CLARKE, Thomas Ernest Bennett, b. 1907, Watford, UK. Journalist, 1927-43; Screenwriter from 1943. Educ: Clare Coll., Cambridge. Publs. incl: Go South — Go West; Jeremy's England; Two & Two Make Five; Cartwright was a Cad; Mr. Spirket Reforms; What's Yours? ; The World was Mine; The Wide Open Door; The Trail of the Serpent; (Screenplays) Passport to Pimlico; The Blue Lamp; The Magnet; The Lavender Hill Mob; The Titfield Thunderbolt; Gideon's Day; The Horse Without a Head; The Rainbow Jacket; Who Done It? , Sons & Lovers; A Tale of Two Cities, & var. TV Scripts. Recip., Academy Award for The Lavender Hill Mob. Address: Tanner's Mead, Oxted, Surrey, UK.

CLARKE, Tom, b. 7 Nov. 1918, Loughton, Essex, UK. Screen Writer. Educ: Barrister-at-Law, Gray's Inn, 1951. Publs. incl: num. TV screenplays; Mad Jack, 1971; Stocker's Copper, 1972. Mbrships: Writers' Guild; Soc. of Authors. Hons: Grand Prize, Monte Carlo, 1971; SFTA Award, 1971; UNRRA Silver Dove, 1971; Prague Festival Award, 1972; SFTA Award, 1972; Writers' Guild Award, 1972. Address: c/o Margaret Ramsay, 14a Goodwins Ct., London WC2N 4LL, UK.

CLARK of HERRIOTSHALL, Arthur Melville, b. 1895, Edinburgh, UK. Emeritus Reader in English. Educ: M.A., D.Litt., Edinburgh Univ.; D.Phil., Oriel Coll., Oxford. Publs: The Realistic Revolt in Modern Poetry; Thomas Heywood, Playwright & Miscellanist; Autobiography, Its Genesis & Phases; Spoken English; Studies in Literary Modes; Sonnets from the French, & other Verses; Sir Walter Scott; The Formative Years. Contbr. to encys., jrnls. etc. inclng: Cambridge Bibliography of Engl. Lit.; Lib. of Philos. Mbr., var. orgs. Address: 3 Woodburn Terr., Edinburgh, UK.

CLARK-KENNEDY, Archibald Edmund, b. 1893, Savernake, Wilts., UK. Physician; Writer. Educ: Corpus Christi Coll., Cambridge. Publs: Stephen Hales, 1929; London Hospital, 1963; Edith Cavell, 1965; Man, Medicine & Morality, 1969. Mbrships: Fellow, Corpus Christi Coll., Cambridge; Soc. of Authors. Address: 8 Grange Rd., Cambridge, UK.

CLARKSON, Anthony, pen name S.S., b. 1905, Dunsfold, Surrey, UK. Former Editor of Country Sportsman & of The Gamekeeper & Countryside. Contbr. to: Big Farm Management; Field; Times; etc. Occasional broadcasts on var. subjects connected w. countryside. Mbr., Kennel Club. Address: Flint's Orchard, West Burton, Pulborough, Sussex, UK.

CLARKSON, E. Margaret, b. 8 June 1915, Melville, Sask., Can. Public School Teacher; Author. Educ: Toronto Tchrs. Coll.; Univ. of Toronto. Publs: Let's Listen to Music, 1944; The Creative Classroom, 1958; Susie's Babies, 1969; Our Father, 1961; Clear Shining After Rain (poems), 1962; Growing Up, 1962; The Wondrous Cross, 1966; Rivers Among the Rocks (poems), 1967; God's Hedge, 1968; Grace Grows Best in Winter, 1972; var. songs, hymns, articles, etc. Contbr. to: His Mag.; Eternity; Christianity Today; var. relig. & educl. jrnls. Address: 72 Gwendolen Cres., Willowdale, Ont. M2N 2L7, Can.

CLARKSON, Stephen. Film & TV Writer, Director, Producer. Publs: (films) The Young Athlete; The Green Stars; Your Life Involved; Preparing for Sarah; Films written & directed for Min. of Def., Ctrl. Off. Info., United Steel, etc. on subjects incing. helicopters, Middle E. cultural life, def. procedures, steel manufacture, chems., rd. bldg., engrng., childbirth, infant feeding; Dir., Armchair Theatre series; Co-author, The Closing Net, etc. Mbr., A.C.T.T. Recip., Gold Medal & other film awards. Address: Peckhams North Lane, West Hoathly, East Grinstead, Sussex, UK.

CLASING, Henry Kurt, Jr., b. 9 Oct. 1938, Jersey City, N.J., USA. Investment Adviser. Educ: B.S. Chem. Engrng., Lehigh Univ., Bethlehem, Pa.; M.S. Ops. Rsch., Newark Coll. of Engrng., N.J.; M.B.A., N.Y. Univ. Publs: The Dow Jones—Irwin Guide to Put & Call Options, 1975. Mbrships: N.Y. Soc. of Security Analysts; Am. Inst. Chem. Engrs. Address: 230 S. Tryon St., Charlotte, NC 28202, USA.

CLAUDE, Richard Pierre, b. 20 May 1934, St. Paul, Minn., USA. Professor; Writer; Lecturer. Educ: B.A., Coll. of St. Thomas, 1956; M.S., Fla. State Univ., 1960; Ph.D., Univ. of Va., 1964. Publs: The Supreme Court & the Electoral Process, 1970; Guide to Political Science Research in Washington, D.C., 3rd ed., 1972; Comparative Human Rights, 1975. Contbr. to: Issues of Electoral Reform; Am. City Mag.; Jrnl. of Negro Hist.; Harvard Jrnl. on Legis.; Georgetown Law Jrnl.; Am. Pol. Sci. Review; Policy Studies Jrnl.; Pub. Opinion Quarterly; etc. Address: 5107 Moorland Ln., Bethesda, MD 20014, USA.

CLAUDEL, Calvin Andre, b. 7 July 1909, Goudeau, La., USA. Professor of French & Spanish. Educ: B.A., 1931, M.A., 1932, Tulane Univ.; Ph.D., Univ. of N.C. at Chapel Hill, 1947; Dip., Sorbonne, 1962. Contbrs. incl: Buying the Wind — Regional Folklore in U.S., ed., Richard Dorson, 1964; The Study of Foreign Languages, ed., Joseph Roucek, 1968; var. anthols.; French Review; PMLA; etc. Mbrships. incl: Past Pres. & Sec., La. State Poetry Soc.; Past Chancellor, Nat. Fedn. of State Poetry Socs.; Guest Ed., New Laurel Review, 1972. Hons. incl: Acad. Palms, France, 1965. Address: P.O. Box 353, Onley, VA 23418, USA.

CLAVEL, Bernard, b. 29 May 1923, Lons-le-Saunier, France. Novelist; Art Critic; Journalist; Radio & TV Writer. Publs. incl: L'Ouvrier de la nuit, 1956; Qui m'emporte, 1958; L'Espagnol, 1959; Malataverne, 1960; La Maison des autres, 1962; Celui qui voulait voir la mer, 1963; Le Coeur des vivants, 1964; Léonard de Vinci, 1967; Les Fruits de l'hiver, 1968; Le Tambour du bief, 1970; Le Massacre des innocents, 1970; Le Seigneur du fleuve, 1972; Bonlieu ou le silence des nymphes, 1973; Le Silence des armes, 1974; Radio & TV scripts. Contbr. to sev. jrnls. Num. hons. incl: Eugene Le Roy Prize, 1959; Grand Prize for Lit., City of Paris, 1968; Election to Goncourt Acad., 1971. Agent: Robert Laffont. Address: c/o Robert Laffont, 6 place St-Sulpice, Paris 6e, France.

CLAWSON, Mary Montgomery, b. 29 Dec. 1910, Suisun, Calif., USA. University Professor. Educ: Univ. of Calif., Berkeley; Mills Coll., Oakland; Am. Univ., Wash.

D.C., etc. A.B., M.A., Ph.D. Publs: Letters from Jerusalem (w. intro. by Eleanor Roosevelt), 1957; History of Legislation & Policy Formation of the Central Valley Project, California, 1946. Contbr. to: Hadassah Newsletter; Am.-Israel Bull.; Middle Eastern Affairs; Yosemite — Nature Notes; Davar, Israel. Mbrships: Phi Beta Kappa; Bd. Dirs., Temple Sinai, Was. D.C., 1967-69. Address: University Coll., Univ. of Md., College Park, Md., USA.

CLAY, Floyd Martin, pen name CLEE, F. M., b. 30 Dec. 1927, Lake Charles, La., USA. Author-Historian. Educ: B.A., McNeese State Coll., Lake Charles, La., 1960; M.A., La. State Univ., Baton Rouge, 1962; Ph.D., Univ. of Miss., Oxford, 1972. Publs: The Arkansas: Renaissance of a River, 4th ed., 1972; History of the Little Rock District, U.S. Corps of Engineers, 1971; Coozan Dudley J. LeBlanc: From Huey Long to Hadacol, 1974; A Century on the Mississippi: The U.S. Engineers at Memphis, 1975. Contbr. to num. newspapers & acad. jrnls. Mbrships. incl: Southern Histl. Assn.; Red River Valley Histl. Assn. Recip., Kt. of Mark Twain, 1974. Address: Box 34, Hist. Dept., Ark. State Univ. at Jonesboro, State Univ., AR 72467, USA.

CLAYRE, Alasdair, b. 9 Oct. 1935, UK. Writer; TV Producer; Song-writer. Educ: M.A., Oxford; Prize Fellow, All Souls Coll., Oxford. Publs: The Window; A Hundred Folksongs & New Songs; A Fire by the Sea & Other Poems; The Impact of Broadcasting (or) Mrs. Buckle's Wall is Singing; Adam & the Beasts & Other Songs; Work & Play: Ideas & Experience of Work & Leisure. Contbr. to: London Mag.; Observer; Guardian; Times Lit. Supplement; New Statesman; Listener; etc. Mbrships: Soc. of Authors; Poetry Soc. Co-recip., Richard Hillary Award, 1963. Address: BBC TV Open University, Alexandra Palace, London N22 4AZ, UK.

CLAYTON, Richard Henry Michael, pen name HAGGARD, William, b. 11 Aug. 1907. Writer. Educ: Christ Church, Oxford, Oxford Univ. Publs. incl: Slow Burner, The Telemann Touch, 1958; Venetian Blind, 1959; Closed Circuit, 1960; The Arena, 1961; The Unquiet Sleep, 1962; The High Wire, 1963; The Antagonists, 1964; The Hard Sell, 1965; The Power House, 1966; The Conspirators, 1967; A Cool Day for Killing, 1968; The Doubtful Disciple, 1969; The Hardliners, 1970; The Bitter Harvest, 1971; The Protectors, 1972; The Little Rug Book, 1972; The Old Masters, 1973. Address: Yew Tree Cottage, Farnborough St., Farnborough, Hants., UK.

CLAYTON, Sylvia Ruth, b. Cheltenham, Glos., UK. Novelist; Television Critic. Educ: M.A., Lady Margaret Hall, Oxford. Publs: The Crystal Gazers, 1961; The Peninsula, 1964; Top C, 1968; Sabbatical, 1972; Friends & Romans, forthcoming. Contbr. to: Daily Telegraph (TV Critic, 1966—). Mbrships: Critics' Circle; Soc. of Authors. Address: 54 Taylor Ave., Kew, Richmond, Surrey, UK.

CLEALL, Charles, b. 1927, Heston, Middlesex, UK. H.M. Inspector of Schools, Scottish Education Department, since 1972; Conductor, Aldeburgh Festival Choir, 1957-60. Educ: M.A., Univ. Wales; B.Mus., Univ. London; Jordanhill Coll., Glasgow. Publs. incl: John Merbecke's Music for the Congregation at Holy Communion, 1963; Music & Holiness, 1964; Plainsong for Pleasure, 1969; Voice Production in Choral Technique, revised & enlarged ed., 1970. Contbr. to: Musical Times; Promoting Church Music; Life of Faith; etc. Mbrships. incl: F.R.C.O. (Chmn.); A.D.C.M.; G.T.C.L.; L.R.A.M. Hons. incl: T.S.C. Address: 29 Colthill Circle, Milltimber, Aberdeenshire, UK.

CLEARY, Frances Alice, b. 3 Mar. 1914, Whangarei, NZ. Freelance Writer. Publs: This Mrs. Kingi, 1971; A Pocketful of Years, 1975. Contbr. to: var. NZ mags. for 30 yrs. Mbrships: NZ Women Writers' Soc.; NZ Penwomen's Club; Whangarei Lit. Grp. Hons: 1st Prize, Rothman Novel Competition, 1968; John Court Cup for Poetry, 1971. Address: 81 Fourth Ave., Whangarei, NZ.

CLEARY, Jon, b. 22 Nov. 1917, Sydney, Australia. Novelist. Publs: You Can't See Round Corners, 1947; The Sundowners, 1952; Climate of Courage, 1953; A Flight of Chariots, 1964; The High Commissioner, 1966; Mask of the Andes, 1971; 19 other novels & one book of short stories. Mbrships: Aust. Authors' Soc.; Aust. Writers' Guild. Hons: Co-winner, Aust. Broadcasting Nat. Radio Play Competition, 1945; 2nd Prize, Sydney Morning Herald Novel Competition, 1946; Aust. Lit. Soc. Gold Medal, 1951. Address: c/o John Farquharson Ltd., 15 Red Lion Sq., London WC1, UK.

CLEAVES, Freeman, b. 13 Oct. 1901, Buxton, Maine, USA. Editor; Author. Educ: B.A., Univ. of N.H., Durham; Harvard Univ.; N.Y. Univ. Publs: Old Tippecanoe, 1939; Rock of Chickanauga, 1948; Meade of Gettysburg, 1960. Contbr. to: Saturday Review of Lit.; New Yorker; N.Y. Times Book Review; Fin. World. Mbr. & Past Treas., N.Y. Soc. of Fin. Writers. Address: 22 Edgewood Terrace, Millburn, NJ 07041, USA.

CLEEVE, Brian Talbot, b. 22 Nov. 1921, Thorpe Bay, Essex, UK. Author. Educ: B.A., Univ. of S. Africa; Ph.D., Nat. Univ. of Ireland. Publs: Biographical Dictionary of Irish Writers, 3 vols., 1967-72; Cry of Morning, 1971; Tread Softly in this Place, 1972; The Dark Side of the Sun, 1973; A Question of Inheritance, 1974. Contbr. to: Sat. Evening Post; Argosy. Mbrships: Soc. of Authors; Br. Auditor, Nat. Union of Jrnlsts.; Royal Irish Automobile Club. Address: 60 Heytesbury Lane, Ballsbridge, Dublin 4, Repub. of Ireland.

CLEGG, John, b. 1909, Ormskirk, UK. Museum Curator. Publs: Freshwater Life of the British Isles; Insects; Observer's Book of Pond Life. Contbr. to: Country Life; Water Life; etc. Address: Haverbrack, Kentsford Road, Grange-over-Sands, Cumbria LA11 7AP, UK.

CLEGG, William Paul, pen name VALE, Keith, b. 27 July 1936, Nelson, UK. Shipping Agent. Educ: Ellesmere Coll., Salop. Publs: Steamers of British Railways, 1962; British Nationalised Shipping, 1969; European Ferry Fleets, 1974. Contbr. to: Humber Ind.; Lloyd's List; Sea Breezes. Mbrships; World Ship Soc.; Coastal Cruising Assn. Address: 11 Ashley Gdns., Bangor, Co. Down, UK.

CLELAND (née FARQUHAR), Marie Immaculee, b. 6 June 1905, Awatuna, Kaponga, Taranaki, NZ. Registered Nurse; Writer & Poet. Publs: It Just Goes To Show, 1970; Dear Cousin — Cheerio, Fred; Blank Cheque to Life (in preparation). Contbr. of verse to: Poems by NZ Women Writers, anthol., 1953; Wellington Evening Post, WWII. Mbr., NZ Women Writers Soc., 1946—, Comm. Mbr., 1953; Recip., var. awards, NZ Women Writers Soc. Address: 67 Creswick Terr., Northland, Wellington 5, NZ.

CLEMENCE, Richard Vernon, b. 13 Oct. 1910, Greenville, R.I., USA. Economist. Educ: Ph.B., 1934, A.M., 1937, Brown Univ., M.A., 1940, Ph.D., 1948, Harvard Univ. Publs: The Schumpeterian System, 1950; Income Analysis, 1951; The Economics of Defense, 1953; Economic Change in America, 1954; The Ruth Stout No-Work Garden Book, 1971. Contbr. to econo., hortl. jrnls. Hon. Mbr., Int. Mark Twain Soc. Hons: 1st Prize & Plaque, Essay Contest, Organic Gardening & Farming, 1959. Address: 61 Beverly Rd., Wellesley, MA 02181, USA.

CLEMENS, Brian Horace, pen name O'GRADY, Tony, b. 1931, Croydon, UK. Playwright; Script Editor; Producer. Films: Station Six-Sahara; Peking Medallion; The Major; And Soon the Darkness. TV Plays: Scene of the Crime; num. others; Script Ed., Danger Man; Writer/Producer, The Avengers. Mbrships: ACTT; Writers' Guild. Recip., Edgar Allan Poe Award for best TV Thriller of 1962. Address: c/o E.M.I., Elstree Studios, Boreham Wood, Herts., UK.

CLEMENTE, Josep Carles, b. 17 Dec. 1935, Barcelona, Spain. Journalist; Writer. Educ: Lic., Philos. & Letters; Tchng. & Bus. studies; Jrnlsm. studies. Publs: La Otra Cara de Cataluña, 1968; Hablando en Madrid, 1969; Cataluña Hoy, 1960; Los 90 Ministros de Franco, 1970; Conversaciones con las corrientes políticas de España, 1971; Conversaciones sobre el presente y el futuro político de España, 1972; Una cultura en crisis, 1973. Contbr. to: El Correo Catalán; La Actualidad Española; Diario de Barcelona; Esfuerzo Comun. Mbrships: Barcelona Press Assn.; Lib. of Cataluña. Recip., Kt. of Order of Civ. Merit. Address: Avda. San Antonio Maria Claret 50-62, Escalera derecha, Atico 2°, Barcelona 13, Spain.

CLEMENTS, Arthur L., b. 15 Apr. 1932, Brooklyn, N.Y., USA. University Educator. Educ: A.B., Princeton; M.A., Univ. of Conn.; Ph.D., Syracuse Univ. Publs: John Donne's Poetry, 1966; The Mystical Poetry of Thomas Traherne, 1969. Contbr. to: Engl. Lit. Renaissance; Criticism; Studies in Philol.; Studies in Engl. Lit.; Thoth.; Mod. Lang. Notes; Explicator; Lib. Chronicle; Poem Co.; Two Feet of Poetry. Mbrships: Phi Kappa Phi; MLA; AAUP. Hons. incl: Rsch. Fndn., SUNY Summer Fellowship, 1965, 1966, 1968, 1969, 1973, 1974; Nat. Endowment for Humanities Fellowship, 1967-68. Address: Box 27, Brown Rd., Friendsville Stage, Binghamton, NY 13903, USA.

CLEMENTS, Jonathan, b. 10 Feb. 1938, W. Looe, Cornwall, UK. Author. Educ: Kingston Coll. of Art, Surrey. Publs: New Readers Begin Elsewhere, 1968; Keep it Kinky, 1969; Sock it To Me Alice, 1969; Dearest Mummy, 1970; Jokes & Riddles, 1974; Crazy — But True, 1974; Kid's Stuff, 1974. Contbr. to: Punch; Spectator; In; New Statesman; Penthouse, Woman's Own; Men Only; Knave; 19; Forum; Pan; Rogue; Response; She; Club Int. Mbrships: Vice-Chmn., Charlton Lit. & Debating Soc. Address: Willowdene, Charlton St. Peter, Pewsey, Wilts., UK.

CLEMENTS, Julia (Lady Seton of Abercorn), b. 10 Apr. 1916, Kent, UK. Writer. Publs. incl: Fun with Flowers, 1952; Fun without Flowers; Party Pieces; Gift Book of Flower Arrangements; Flower Arrangements Month by Month; Flowers in Stately Homes; Show Pieces. Recip., Victoria Medal of Honour, Royal Horticultural Soc. Address: 122 Swan Court, London SW3 5RU, UK.

CLEMENTS, Ronald Ernest, b. 27 May 1929, London, UK. University Lecturer; Writer. Educ: B.D., London; M.A., B.D., Cambridge; Ph.D., Sheffield. Publs: God & Temple, 1965; Prophecy & Covenant, 1965; Abraham & David, 1968; Exodus, 1972; Prophecy & Tradition, 1975. Contbr. to: Vetus Testamentum; Theologisches Wörterbuch zum Alten Testament. Mbrships: Soc. for Old Testament Study (Hon. For. Sec., 1974-). Address: 8 Brookfield Rd., Coton, Cambridge CB3 7PT, UK.

CLEMO, Reginald John (Jack), b. 11 Mar. 1916, Goonamarris, St. Austell, Cornwall, UK. Writer. Publs: Wilding Graft (fiction), 1948; Confession of a Rebel (autobiog.), 1949; The Invading Gospel (theol.), 1958; The Map of Clay (poetry), 1961; Cactus on Carmel, 1967; The Echoing Tip, 1971; Broad Autumn, 1975. Contbr. to: London Mag.; Transatlantic Review; Twentieth Century. Hon. Mbr., W. Country Writers' Assn. Hons: Atlantic Award in Lit., 1948; Arts Coun. Festival Poetry Prize, 1951. Address: Goonamarris, St. Stephen's, St. Austell, Cornwall PL26 7QX, UK.

CLENDENIN, William Ritchie, Sr., b. 23 July 1917, Sparta, Ill., USA. Professor of Musicology. Educ: B.Mus., Univ. of Ill., 1940; S.M.M., Union Theol. Sem., 1942; Ph.D., Univ. of Iowa, 1952. Publs: Music: History & Theory, 1965; Visual Aids in Western Music, 3rd ed., 1967; History of Music, 1974. Contbr. to profl. jrnls. & The Dict. of Plainsong. Address: 4703 Harrison Ave., Boulder, CO 80303, USA.

CLEOBURY, (Rev.) Frank Harold, b. 1892, London, UK. Former Foreign Office & Commonwealth Relations Official; Clergyman. Educ: B.A., Ph.D., London Univ. Publs: God, Man & the Absolute, 1947; The Armour of Saul, 1957; Christian Rationalism & Philosophical Analysis, 1959; Liberal Christian Orthodoxy, 1963; A Return to National Theology, 1967; A Study in Christian Apologetic, 1972. Contbr. to: Mind; Philosl. Quarterly; Mod. Churchman. Address: 3 Conesford Drive, Norwich NR1 2BB, UK.

CLEWES, Howard Charles Vivian, b. 1916, York, UK. Writer. Publs: Sailor Come Home; Dead Ground; The Unforgiven; The Mask of Wisdow; The Long Memory; The Libertines. Mbrships: Authors' Soc.; PEN; Screenwriter's Guild. Address: Wildwood, North End, London NW3, UK.

CLIFFE, J. T., b. 1931, Halifax, UK. Civil Servant. Educ: B.A., Ph.D., Queen Mary Coll., London Univ. Publs: The Yorkshire Gentry: from the Reformation to the Civil War, 1969; Military Technology & The European Balance, 1972. Mbrships: Fellow, Royal Histl. Soc.; Royal C'wlth Soc. Address: 263 Staines Rd., Twickenham, Middx., UK.

CLIFFORD, Derek Plint, b. 1 Sept. 1915, Gillingham, Kent, UK. Author. Educ: M.A., King's Coll., Cambridge. Publs: Mad Pelynt & the Bullet, 1939; The Perracotts, 1948; Geraniums, 1953; Pelargoniums, 1958, revised 1970; A History of Garden Design, 1962, revised 1966; Watercolours of the Norwich School, 1965; John Crome (co-author), 1968; Art & Understanding, 1968; The Paintings of Philip de Lazlo, 1969; Collecting English Watercolours, 1970, revised 1975. Contbr. to Ency. Britannica. Mbr., Athenaeum. Agent: Bolt & Watson. Address: Hartlip Place, Sittingbourne, Kent, UK.

CLIFFORD, Francis, b. 1 Dec. 1917, Bristol, UK. Writer. Publs: Honour the Shrine; The Trembling Earth; Overdue; Something to Love; Act of Mercy; A Battle is Fought to be Won; Time is am Ambush; The Green Fields of Eden; The Hunting Ground; The Third Side of the Coin; The Naked Runner; All Men Are Lonely Now; Another Way of Dying; The Blind Side; A Wild Justice; Amigo, Amigo; The Grosvenor Square Goodbye. Contbr. to: Cosmopolitan; Playboy; Redbook; Sunday Telegraph; Evening Standard; Evening News; Irish Times; Argosy; etc. Agent: David Higham Assocs. Address: Grove Cottage, Grove Lodge, Old Ave., Weybridge, Surrey, UK.

CLIFFORD, Henry Dalton, b. 1911, Blackheath, London, UK. Architect. Publs: New Homes from Old Buildings (w. R. E. Enthoven); Home Decoration; New Houses for Moderate Means; Houses for Today; Designer, Herb & Spice Charts, BART Prints. Contbr. to: Country Life; Homes & Gdns., Furnishing Ed., 1952-54. Mbrships: Assoc., Royal Inst. of Brit. Archts.; M.Int.R.A. Address: The Abbey, Penzance, Cornwall, UK.

CLIFFORD, James Lowry, b. 24 Feb. 1901, Evansville, Ind., USA. Professor of English; Author. Educ: A.B., Wabash Coll., 1923; B.S., M.A., 1925; Ph.D., Columbia Univ., 1941. Publs: Hester Lynch Piozzi (Mrs. Thrale), 1941; Ed., Dr. Campbell's diary, 1947; Young Samuel Johnson, 1955; From Puzzles to Portraits, 1970. Contbr. to: N.Y. Times; var. acad. jrnls. Mbrships: PEN; MLA; Am. Soc. of 18th Century Studies (Pres., 1972-73); Engl. Inst.; Lichfield Johnson Soc. (Pres., 1958); F.R.S.L.; F.R.S.A. Recip., 4 hon. degrees. Address: 25 Claremont Ave., N.Y., NY 10027, USA.

CLIFTON, Harold Dennis, b. 3 Sept. 1927, Leeds, UK. Lecturer in Data Processing. Educ: B.Sc., Univ. of Leeds. Publs: Data Processing Systems Design, 1971; Systems Analysis for Business Data Processing, 1972, 2nd ed., 1974; Accounting & Computer Systems (co-author), 1973; Choosing & Using Computers, 1975. Mbr., Brit. Computer Soc. Address: 25 The Flashes, Gnosall, Stafford ST20 0HL, UK.

CLINE, Ruth (Eleanor) Harwood, b. 31 Oct. 1946, Middletown, Conn., USA. Literary Translator, French. Educ: A.B., Smith Coll., Northampton, Mass., 1968; M.A., Rutgers Univ., N.J., 1969. Publs: Engl. verse transl., Yvain, or The Knight with the Lion, by Chrétien de Troyes, 1975. Address: 5902 Devonshire Dr., Wash. DC 20016, USA.

CLISSOLD, John Stephen Hallett, b. 1913, Hazlemere, Bucks., UK. Author. Educ: M.A., Oxford Univ. Publs. incl: Whirlwind, 1948; Chilean Scrapbook, 1952; Conquistador — the Life of Pedro Sarmiento de Gamboa, 1954; Denmark, 1955; The Seven Cities of Cibola, 1961; Latin America — a Cultural Outline, 1965; In Search of the Cid, 1965; Ed., Yugoslavia — A Short History, 1966; Bernardo O'Higgins & the Independence of Chile, 1968; Spain, 1969; Ed., Soviet Relations with Latin America, 1970; Latin America — New World, Third World, 1972; The Saints of South America, 1972. Mbr., Royal Inst. for Int. Affairs. Agent: Antony Sheil. Address: 7 Cleveland Gdns., London W2, UK.

CLIVE, Mary Pakenham, b. 1907, London, UK. Journalist. Publs: Caroline Clive, 1949; Christmas with the Savages, 1955; The Day of Reckoning, 1964; Jack & the Doctor, a life of John Donne, 1966; This Sun of York, a life of Edward IV, 1973. Address: c/o Messrs. Child & Co., 1 Fleet St., London EC4, UK.

CLOETE, Edward Fairlie Stuart Graham, b. 1897, Paris, France. Former Rancher, 1925-35; Writer. Publs: Turning Wheels; Watch for the Dawn; Congo Song; Hill of the Doves; The Curve & the Tusk; Mamba; The Fiercest Heart; African Portraits; African Giant; Gazella; The Soldiers' Peaches; West with the Sun; The Silver Trumpet; The Mask. Contbr. to: Saturday Evening Post; Collier's; Vogue; Argosy; Esquire; Red Book; Ladies' Home Jrnl. Mbrships: Explorer's Club; Nat. Arts; Overseas Press, NYC. Address: c/o Guards Club, 16 Charles St., London W1, UK.

CLOSE, Reginald Arthur, b. 3 Feb. 1909, Wimbledon, London, UK. Former British Council Official; Author; Publishers' Adviser. Educ: Dip.Ed., B.A., King's Coll., London Univ.; M.Litt., Cath. Univ. of Santiago. Publs: The English We Use, 1961, 2nd ed., 1971; English as a Foreign Language, 1962; The New English Grammar, Vol. 1, 1964, Vol. 2, 1968; The English We Use for Science, 1965; Reference Grammar for Students of English, 1975. Contbr. to: Times; Guardian; Listener; Engl. Lang. Tchng.; etc.

Mbrships. incl: Soc. of Authors; Brit. Assn. Applied Linguistics; Linguistics Assn. of GB. Hons: O.B.E., 1950; C.B.E., 1967. Address: 8 Highgate Close, London N6 4SD, UK.

CLOSS, August, b. 9 Aug. 1898, Neumarkt, Austria. University Professor Emeritus; Author. Educ: M.A., Bristol Univ., UK; D.Phil., Graz, Austria. Publs: Medieval Exempla, 1934; The Genius of the German Lyric, 1938, paperback ed., 1965; Tristan & Isolt, 1944, 3rd ed., 1974; Medusa's Mirror, 1957; Reality & Creative Vision, 1963; 20th Century German Literature, 2nd ed., 1971. Contbr. to: Mod. Lang. Review; Times Higher Educ. Supplement; Germanistik; Universitas; & var. acad. jrnls. in Europe & USA. Mbrships: F.R.S.L.; PEN. Hons: Austrian Cross of Hon. in Sci. & Arts, 1st Class; Grand Cross for the W. German Order of Merit. Address: 40 Stoke Hill, Bristol 9, UK.

CLOUDSLEY-THOMPSON, John Leonard, b. 23 May 1921, Muree, India. Professor of Zoology. Educ: M.A., Ph.D., D.Sc., Pembroke Coll., Cambridge, UK. Publs. incl: Spiders, Scorpions, Centipedes & Mites, 1958; Animal Behaviour, 1960; Rhythmic Activity in Animal Physiology & Behaviour, 1961; Animal Conflict & Adaptation, 1965; Animal Twilight, 1967; The Zoology of Tropical Africa, 1969; The Temperature & Water Relations of Reptiles, 1971; Desert Life, 1974; Terrestrial Environments, 1975; The Water & Temperature Relations of Woodlice (Isopoda: Oniscoidea), 1975. Contbr. to var. profl. jrnls. Mbrships: Fellow, Inst. of Biol., Royal Entomol. Soc., Linnean Soc. of London; Sci. Fellow, Zool. Soc. of London; World Acad. Arts & Sci. Recip. Medal, Royal African Soc., 1969. Address: Birkbeck College, Malet St., London WC1E 7HX, UK.

CLOUGH, Shepard B., b. 1901, Bloomington, Ind., USA. Historian. Educ: Colgate Univ.; Sorbonne; Heidelberg & Columbia Univs.; A.B.; Ph.D. Publs: A History of the Flemish Movement; France 1789-1939; Making Fascists; An Economic History of Europe; The Rise & Fall of Civilization; Basic Values in Western Civilization; The European Past (w. others), 2nd ed., 1970); Economic History of Italy, 2nd ed., 1973; History of Italy; European Economic History, 2nd ed., 1974; A History of the Western World, 1974; Storia Dell'economia Italiana dal 1861 ad oggi, 1974. Contbr. to: var. reviews. Mbrships: Pres., French Histl. Soc., 1965; Pres., Soc. for Italian Histl. Studies, 1972-73; Ed. Bd., Jrnl. of European Econ. Hist., Rome, Italy. Address: 419 Independence Rd., W. Palm Beach, FL 33405, USA; & East Hill, East Peacham, VT 05862, USA.

CLOW, Archie, b. 1909, Aberdeen, UK. Senior Radio Consultant; Writer. Educ: M.A., Ph.D.; D.Sc.; F.R.S.E., Aberdeen Univ.; King's Coll.; Univ. of London. Publs: Hermann Boerhaave & Scottish Chemistry in An Eighteenth Century Lectureship in Chemistry, 1950; The Chemical Revolution (w. Nan. L. Clow), 1952; The Chemical Industry & the Industrial Revolution; In a History of Technology, vol. IV, 1958. Contbr. to: BBC (Prod., Sci. Survey, & Ed., Sci. Talks, 1947-70); Penguin Sci. News (Jt. Ed., 1956-59); num. histl. & sci. mags. Mbrships: F.R.I.C.; Brit. Sci. Writers Assn.; sev. acad. orgs. Recip., acad. hons. Address: The Open University, BBC, Alexandra Palace, Wood Green, London N22, UK.

CLUBBE, John Louis Edwin, b. NYC, USA. Professor of English. Educ: A.B., A.M., Ph.D., Columbia Univ. Publs: Victorian Forerunners: The Later Career of Thomas Hood, 1968; Selected Poems of Thomas Hood (ed.), 1970. The Letters of Thomas & Jane Welsh Carlyle, 1812-1828 (asst. ed.), 1970; Two Reminiscences of Thomas Carlyle (ed.), 1974. Contbr. to profl. jrnls. Mbr., var. profl. assns. incl: The Byron Soc. Address: English Dept., Duke Univ., Durham, NC 27708, USA.

CLUNE, Henry W., b. 6 Feb. 1890, Rochester, N.Y., USA. Newspaper Reporter & Columnist. Publs: The Good Die Poor, 1937; Monkey on a Stick, 1940; Main Street Beat, 1947; By His Own Hand, 1952; The big Fella, 1956; 6 o'clock Casual, 1960; The Genesee, 1963; O'Shaughnessy's Cafe, 1969; The Rochester I know, 1972. Contbr. to: Seen & Heard, 1933 & 35; The N. Am. Review; etc. Recip., Annual Lit. Award, Rochester Pub. Lib., 1965. Address: Scottsville, NY 14546, USA.

CLURMAN, Harold, b. 18 Sept. 1901, NYC, USA. Stage Director & Critic. Educ: Columbia Univ.; Dip., Univ. of Paris, France. Publs: The Fervent Years, 1945; Lies Like

Truth, 1958; The Naked Image, 1966; On Directing, 1972; The Divine Pastime, 1974; All People Are Famous, 1974. Contbr. to: Nation; Partisan Review; Observer; N.Y. Times Mag.; Harper's Mag. Mbr., Am. Acad. Arts & Scis. Hons: Legion of Hon., France, 1956; George Jean Nathan Awards for Dramatic Criticism, 1958, 1959; Sang Award for Dramatic Criticism, Knox Coll., 1965. Address: 205 West 57th Street, NYC, N.Y., USA.

CLUTE, Robert Eugene, b. 12 July 1924, Earlville, Iowa, USA. Professor of Political Science. Educ: B.A., Univ. of Ala., 1947; M.A., Geo. Wash. Univ., 1954; Ph.D., Duke Univ., 1958. Publs: The International Legal States of Austria, 1938-55, 1962; The International Law Standard & Commonwealth Developments, 1966. Contbr. to: Am. Jrnl. of Comp. Law; Am. Jrnl. of Int. Law; Background of World Pols.; Ga. Jrnl. of Int. & Comp. Law; Jrnl. of Asian & African Studies; Proceedings of Am. Soc. Int. Law. Mbr., var. legal & pol. sci. assns. Hons. incl: Danforth Assoc.; C'wlth. Fellowship; Fulbright Fellowship. Address: Hd., Dept. of Pol. Sci., Univ. of Ga., Athens, GA 30601, USA.

CLUTTERBUCK, Richard, b. 22 Nov. 1917, London, UK. University Lecturer in Politics. Educ: M.A., Cambridge Univ.; Ph.D., London Univ. Publs: Across the River, 1957; The Long Long War, 1966 (USA), 1967 (UK); Protest & the Urban Guerrilla, 1973 (UK), 1974 (USA); Riot & Revolution in Singapore & Malaya, 1973; Living with Terrorism, 1975. Mbrships: Fellow, Inst. Civ. Engrs.; Fellow Royal C'wlth. Soc.; Smeatonian Soc. Hons: O.B.E., 1958; C.B., 1972. Address: Dept. of Politics, The Univ., Exeter, UK.

CLUVER, Eustace Henry, b. 1894, Robertson, S. Africa. Emeritus Professor; Former Director of Medical Research; Writer. Educ: F.R.S.H.; M.A.; M.D.; B.Ch.; D.P.H.; Hertford & Magdalen Colls., Oxford, UK; King's Coll., London. Publs: Public Health in South Africa, 6th ed., 1959; Medical & Health Legislation in the Union of South Africa, 2nd ed., 1961; Recent Health Legislation; Social Medicine; Birthright. Contbr. to var. med. & sci. jrnls. Hons: K.St.J.; E.D. Address: Mornhill Farm, Wakerville, Transvaal, S. Africa.

CLYNE, Douglas George Wilson, b. 1912, Consultant Obstetrician. Educ: M.B., B.Ch., & M.A., Magdalen Coll., Oxford; Charing Cross Hosp. Med. Schl.; L.R.C.P.; F.R.C.S.; F.R.C.O.G.; Barrister-at-law. Publs. incl: Ladies in Emergency; Anchorage on the Costa Brava; Your Guide to the Costa Brava, to the Costa del Sol, & to Portugal; Handbook of Obstetrics & Gynaecology for Nurses; Concise Textbook for Midwives; Final Examination Questions for Nurses for the Final Examination in England & Wales; Gynaecology & Obstetrics. Address: Blue Waters, Porthpean, St. Austell, Cornwall, UK.

COATES, Austin, b. 16 Apr. 1922, London, UK. Author. Publs: Invitation to an Eastern Feast, 1953; Personal & Oriental, 1957; The Road, 1959; Basutoland, 1966; Prelude to Hongkong, 1966; City of Broken Promises, 1967; Rizal, Philippine Nationalist & Martyr, 1968; Myself a Mandarin, 1968; Western Pacific Islands, 1970; China, India & the Ruins of Washington, 1972; Islands of the South, 1974; Numerology, 1974. Address: 2-B The Peak, Cheung Chau Island, Hongkong.

COATES, Doreen Frances, b. 5 July 1912, Plymouth, UK. Teacher. Publs: Yellow Door Stories for Children, 1965; Red & Blue Door Stories, 1969; Number Cards, 1969; Number Stories, 1973; Extra-Methuen Number Cards Extended, 1974. Contbr. to var. tchrs.' jrnls. Mbr., Authors, London. Address: 42 Deanhill Ct., London SW14 7DL, UK.

COATES, Ken, b. 16 Sept. 1930, Leek, UK. University Teacher. Educ: B.A., Univ. of Nottingham. Publs. incl: Poverty, Deprivation & Morale (w. R. L. Silburn), 1967; The Morale of the Poor, 1968; Industrial Democracy in Great Britain (w. A. J. Topham), 1968; Poverty, the Forgotten Englishmen (w. R. L. Silburn), 1970; The Crisis of British Socialism, 1971; Essays in Industrial Democracy, 1972; The New Unionism (w. A. J. Topham), 1972; Ed., Socialism & the Environment, 1972; The Partial View (w. R. L. Silburn); Ed., Spokesman. Contbr. to: Tribune; Guardian; Bulletin of I.W.C. Dir., Bertrand Russell Peace Fndn. Address: 5 Trentside, W. Bridgford, Nottingham, UK.

COATES, Robert Myron, b. 1897, New Haven, Conn., USA. Art Critic; Author. Educ: B.A., Yale Univ. Publs: The Eater of Darkness; The Outlaw Years; Yesterday's Burdens;

All the Year Round; Bitter Seasons; Wisteria Cottage; The Hour After Westerly; The Farther Shore; The View From Here; Beyond the Alps; South of Rome. Contbr. to: New Yorker, Art Critic; etc. Mbrships: PEN; Nat. Inst. of Arts & Letters. Address: Old Chatham, NYC, N.Y., USA.

COATS, Alice M., b. 1905, Birmingham, UK. Artist; Writer. Educ: Birmingham Coll. of Arts; Slade Schl., Univ. Coll., London. Publs: Flowers & their Histories, 1956; 2nd ed., 1968; Garden Shrubs & Their Histories, 1963; The Quest for Plants, 1969; The Book of Flowers, 1973. Contbr. to jrnls. inclng: Gardener's Chronicle; Popular Gardening; Country Life; House & Garden; Jrnl. of the Royal Horticultural Soc. Address: 32 Radnor Rd., Handsworth, Birmingham 20, UK.

COATSWORTH, Elizabeth (Mrs. Henry Beston), b. 1893, Buffalo, N.Y., USA. Freelance writer; Poet; Novelist. Educ: B.A., M.A. Publs. incl: (poetry) Atlas & Beyond, 1923; Fox Footprints, 1927; Compass Rose, 1929; Down Half the World; about 100 books for children inclng. The Cat Who Went to Heaven, & the Sally Books series (5 vols.). Contbr. to: New Repub.; Harper's; Atlantic; Dial. Hons: Am. Runner-Up for Hans C. Anderson Award, 1968. Agent: Mark Paterson. Address: c/o Mark Paterson, 42 Canonbury Square, London N1 2AW, UK.

COBB, Winifred Mary Davis Bradley, b. 27 Aug. 1906. Monkstown, Tex., USA. Educator. Educ: B.A., Tex. Tech. Univ., M.A., E. New Mexico Univ. Publs: The Greening Branch, 1964; Spin the Golden Thread, 1966; Let the Mountains Stand, 1971 (poetry); Brook Haven (juvenile), 1964. Contbr. to Bouquets of Poems, 1974. Mbr., Poetry Soc. of Tex. Address: 1717 E. 21st St., Clovis, NM 88101, USA.

COBBINAH-ESSEM, Peter Kenneth, b. 23 Nov. 1937, Asankrangwa, Ghana. Journalist. Educ: Grad., Schl. of Jrnlsm., Columbia Univ., N.Y., USA. Publs: The Lebanese in Ghana: Study of an Enigma, 1975; A Fetch in the River at Dawn, 1975; Their Greedy Eyes on Gold, 1975. Contbr. to: Encore; Ghansporta; Ghanaian Times; Entwicklung und Zusammenarbeit; Deutsche Welle; Assoc. Press; Quincy Patriot Ledger, Mass.; Peoria Jrnl.-Star, Ill. Mbrships: World Press Soc.; Ghana Jrnlsts. Assn. Recip., 2 Engl. Essay Prizes, Govt. Secretarial Schls., Kumasi & Sekondi, 1957 & 1958. Address: P.O. Box M 363, Accra, Ghana.

COBBLE, Hubert Dann, pen name WOODSTOCK, Danny, b. 31 Dec. 1936, Copperhill, Tenn., USA. Writer; Cinematographer. Educ: Reinhardt Coll., Waleska, Ga.; Mercer Univ., Macon, Ga. Publs: (Writer/Cinematographer, 2 Documentary Films). The 202nd: History of a Military Unit; The Atlanta Pop Festival; also Biography, forthcoming. Contbr. of over 200 articles & short stories to: The Macon Telegraph; The Albany Jrnl.; United Press Int.; The Assoc. Press; CBS News Worldwide Sports; etc. Mbrships. incl: Outdoor Writers. Assn. of Am.; Ga. Outdoor Writers. Assn.; S.E. Outdoor Writers' Assn. Recip., Assoc. Press Award for Outstanding Gen. News Coverage, 1965. Address: P.O. Box 185, Morgan, GA 31766, USA.

COBURN, (Charles) Oliver (Louis), b. 16 Dec. 1917, London, UK. Author; Translator. Educ: B.A., M.A., Wadham Coll., Oxford. Publs: Youth Hostel Story, 1950; Flavius Josephus, 1972. Mbrships: Soc. of Authors; Transls. Assn. Address: 26a North Rd., Berkhamsted, Herts., UK.

COCCIOLI, Carlo, b. 15 May 1920, Leghorn, Italy. Writer. Educ: D.Sc.; Univs. of Naples & Rome. Publs. incl: The Valley of God, 1948; Heaven & Earth, 1950; The Daughter of the Town; The Eye & the Heart; Le Tourment de Dieu; & over 20 essays, documentaries etc. Contbr. to: Corriere della Sera, Italy; Il Giorno, Italy; Siempre mag., Mexico City. Recip., Prix Charles Veillon, 1950. Address: Apartado Postal 27-529, Mexico 7 D.F.

COCHRAN, Hamilton, b. 1898, Philadelphia, Pa., USA. Former Publishing Executive; Consultant. Educ: AB, Univ. of Mich. Publs: These are the Virgin Islands; Buccaneer Islands; Windward Passage; Captain Ebony; Silver Shoals; Rogue's Holiday; Blockade Runners of the Confederacy; Pirates of the Spanish Main; Noted American Duels; Freebooters of the Red Sea. Contbr. to: Saturday Evening Post; Esquire; Am. Legion; etc. Address: 4 Kershaw Rd., Wallingford, PA 19086, USA.

COCKCROFT, John, b. 8 Feb. 1919, Townsville, Qld., Australia. Author; Broadcaster; Company Director. Publs: Isles of the South Pacific, 1968; The Philippines, 1969;

Melanesian Isles, 1969; Polynesian Isles, 1970; Indonesia, 1971; Singapore-Malaysia, 1972; Plays, documentaries for TV, radio. Contbr. to periodicals. Mbrships: Royal Soc. for Lit.; Aust. Corres., Asian Mass Communication & Info. Ctr., Singapore. Hons: Logie Award, for best TV documentary, Australian Broadcasting Comm. Address: P.O. Box 533, Gosford, NSW 2250, Australia.

COCKERELL, Hugh Anthony Lewis, b. 16 May 1909, London, UK. Senior Research Fellow in Insurance Studies, City University, London. Educ: B.A., King's Coll., Univ. of London; Barrister, Middle Temple; Fellow, Chartered Ins. Inst. Publs: Sixty Years of The Chartered Insurance Institute, 1957; Insurance, 1957, 2nd ed., 1970. Contbr. to: Post Mag.; Policy; Jrnls. of Chartered Ins. Inst., Ins. Inst. of London; Jrnl. of Bus. Law. Mbrships: VP, Brit. Ins. Law Assn., Brit. Assn. for Commercial & Indl. Educ.; Chartered Ins. Inst.; Reform Club. Hons: O.B.E.; Cuthbert Heath Centenary Award, 1974. Address: 22 Mapesbury Road, London NW2 4JD, UK.

COCKETT, Mary, b. 1915, Yorks., UK. Editor; Author. Publs: (Fiction) Reading With Mother series (6 books); Rolling On; Mary Ann Goes to Hospital; Cottage by the Lock; Benny's Bazaar; The Birthday Ride; The Wild Place; Another Home Another Country; Rosanna the Goat; Boat Girl; the Joppy Books; Pelican Park; The Marvellous Stick; An Armful of Sparrows; Magic & Gold; Sunflower Giant; Bouncing Ball; Treasure; The Rainbow Walk; As Big as the Ark; Tower Raven; Look at the Little One; Snake in the Camp; Backyard Bird Hospital; He Cannot Really Read; The Magician; Mattie & the Monster; (non-fiction) Bridges; Roads & Travelling; Towns; Walls; Bells in our Lives; Dolls & Puppets; Story of Cars. Contbr. to: BBC; Teachers World; Child Educ.; Guardian; TLS. Address: 24 Benville Avenue, Bristol BS9 2RX, UK.

CODRINGTON, Kenneth De Burgh, b. 1899, Muree, India. University Professor. Educ: Corpus Christi Coll., Cambridge, UK; Wadham Coll., Oxford; M.A. Publs. incl: The Wood of the Image; Cricket in the Grass. Contbr. to: Man; Indian Antiquary; Criterion. Mbr., Athenaeum, 1936-66. Address: Rose Cottage, Appledore, Kent, UK.

COE, Arthur, b. 1897, Halifax, Yorks., UK. Gas Engineer; Principal & Founder, College of Fuel Technology; Director, Combustion Engineering Association. Educ: Halifax Tech. Coll. Publs: Science & Practice of Gas Supply, 3 vols., 1932-39; Economics for Everyman, 1948. Mbrships: Fellow, Inst. of Fuel; Royal Soc. for the Promotion of Health; PEN. Address: 90 Talbot Rd., Highgate, London N6, UK; & Thoral Cottage, Thoralby, Nr. Leyburn, N. Yorks., UK.

COE, Miriam, b. 1 July 1902, Liverpool, UK. Writer; Librarian. Educ: Hons. Dip., Union of Lancs. & Cheshire Insts.; Dip., Skerry's Civil Serv. Coll., Liverpool Univ., Univ. of Rochester, N.Y., USA; Columbia Univ., L.I. Univ.; Geo. Peabody Coll. for Tchrs.; Utah, Fla.,La. State Univs. Publs. incl: Children of Other Lands; Animal Stories; Fruit & Vegetables, 1938; Librarianship As A Career; Anthology of World Literature; Psychology of Music; Poems for the Young; Miscellaneous Poems; Haiku, Eastern & Western, Poems & Pictures; Irish Fairy Tales; Development of Education in England. Mbrships: Poetry Soc. of S. & S.W.; Acad. of Am. Poets. Address: P.O. Box 18184, La. State Univ., Baton Rouge, LA 70803, USA.

COE, Richard Nelson, b. 27 Oct. 1923, Rustington, Sussex, UK. Professor of French Literature; Author. Educ: B.A., M.A., Oriel Coll., Oxford, 1949; Sorbonne, Paris, France, 1949-50; Ph.D., Leeds, UK, 1954. Publs: Morelly: Ein Rationalist auf dem Wege aum Sozialismus, 1961; Ionesco, 1961; Beckett, 1964; The Vision of Jean Genet, 1968; The Theatre of Jean Genet, 1971. Editions & Translations: Life of Rossini (Stendhal), 1956; Rome, Naples & Florence (Stendhal), 1959; Crocodile (Chukovsky), & other children's poems, 1963; Haydn, Mozart & Metastasio (Stendhal), 1972. Contbr. to: Revue d'Histoire Littéraire de la France: Stendhal Club; Mod. Langs. Review; etc. Address: 27 Newbold Street, Leamington Spa, Coventry CV32 4HN, UK.

COEKELBERGHS, Amand Joseph Richard, pen name CAMAND, Richard, b. 3 Apr. 1922, Anderlecht, Belgium. Accountant; Author. Educ: Brevet of Candidate Accountant. Publs: (novels) Guirlande de Femmes, 1970; Le Bouton, 1970; La Verte et le Bleu, 1972; Par le Doit et l'Avoir, 1973. Other publs: Le Réverbère; Le Bal des Comptables; L'Agent ne Craint pas le Verglas;

Métamorphoses pour Christine. Contbr. to: L'Arche; La Dryade; Marginales; Les Feuillets du Spantole; La Revue Nationale; etc. Mbr., Association des Ecrivains Belges. Address: Rue Jean Van Lierde 76, 1070 Brussels, Belgium.

COERANT, Albert, b. 30 July 1928, Amsterdam, Netherlands. Journalist. Educ: LL.B. Contbr. to Vara, Kro, VPRO & Nos Radio/TV, Holland; Radio Holland Int.; BRT Radio/TV, Belgium; (newspapers) PAROOL, Amsterdam; Gelderlander Pers, Holland. GPD-Press, Holland; Net Vrye Volk, Rotterdam; Standaard, Brussels. Belgium. Mbrships: Int. Fedn. of Jrnlsts.; Nederlandse Journalisten Vereniging; For. Press Assn. of Greece. Address: Stilponos 31, Athens 502, Greece.

COFFEY, J. I., b. 13 Feb. 1916, St. Louis, Mo., USA. Professor of Public & International Affairs. Educ: US Mil. Acad., West Point, B.S., 1939; Columbia Coll., 1945; Ph.D., Georgetown Univ., USA, 1953. Publs: Forging a New Sword: A Study of Defence Organization, 1958; The Presidential Staff (co-author), 1961; Strategic Power & National Security, 1971; Deterrence in the 1970's, 1971. Contbr. to sev. jrnls. (esp. Military affairs). Mbrships: Am. Acad. of Political and Social Sci.; Coun. on Foreign Relations; Int. Inst. for Strategic Studies; Int. Studies Assn. Address: Univ. of Pitts.. 905 Bruce Hall, Pitts., PA 15260, USA.

COFFIN, Tristram, b. 25 July 1912, Hood River, Ore., USA. Writer; Editor. Educ: A.B., DePauw Univ., Greencastle, Ind. Publs: Missouri Compromise, 1947; Your Washington, 1972; Not to the Swift, 1961; The Passion of the Hawks (in paperback as The Armed Society), 1964; Mine Eyes Have Seen the Glory, 1964; The Sex Kick, 1966; Senator Fulbright, 1966; Ed., Wash. Watch Newsletter, 1968-74; The Wash. Spectator, 1975—. Contbr. to: Holiday; Bulletin of Atomic Scis.; Rdrs. Digest; Nation; New Repub. Mbr., PEN. Address: 5601 Warwick Pl., Chevy Chase, MD 20015, USA.

COGGAN, (The Most Rev.) Frederick Donald, b. 9 Oct. 1909, London, UK. The Lord Archbishop of Canterbury; Archbishop of York, 1961-74. Educ: M.A., D.D., HH.D., S.T.D.; St. John's Coll., Univ. of Cambridge; Wycliffe Hall, Oxford. Publs: A People's Heritage, 1944; The Ministry of the Word, 1945; The Glory of God, 1950; Stewards of Grace, 1958; Five Makers of the New Testament, 1962; Christian Priorities, 1963; The Prayers of the New Testament, 1967; Sinews of Faith, 1969; Word & World, 1971. Contbr. to: Theology; etc. Mbr., Athenaeum Club. Hons. incl: D.D., Univs. Toronto, Leeds, Cambridge, Hull, Tokyo, Huron, Manchester; D.Litt., Lancaster Univ.; LL.D., Liverpool Univ. Address: Lambeth Palace, London SE1 7JV, UK.

COGSWELL, Frederick William, pen name COGSWELL, Fred, b. 1917, E. Centreville, N.B., Can. Educator; Writer. Educ: B.A., M.A., Ph.D; Univ. of N.B.; Edinburgh Univ., UK. Publs: The Stunted Strong, 1954; The Haloed Tree, 1956; The Testament of Cresseid, 1957; Descent from Eden, 1959; Lost Dimension, 1960; Co-Ed., Arts in New Brunswick, 1967; The Enchanted Land, 1967; Star People, 1968; Immortal Plowman, 1969; In Praise of Chastity, 1970; The Chains of Liliput, 1971; The House Without a Door, 1973; Light Bird of Life, 1974; Transl., books of poetry; Ed., A Canadian Anthol. & other publs. Mbrships: League of Can. Poets; Can. Authors' Assn. Address: 769 Regent St., Fredericton, N.B., Can.

COGSWELL, (Brig.-Gen.) Theodore R., pen names ELLISON, Harlan; REYNOLDS, Mack, b. 10 Mar. 1918, Coatesville, Pa., USA. Professor of Digital Enumeration. Educ: B.A., Univ. of Colo., 1947; M.A., Univ. of Denver, 1948. Publs: The Wall Around the World, 1962. 2nd ed. 1974; Foot Care of the Modern Fighting Man, 1964; The Third Eye, 1968; Foot Soldier, 1969; Foot Bath Ballads, 1974. Contbr. to: Window; Dodo; Saturday Review; Analog Sci. Fact & Fiction; Galaxy; etc. Mbrships. incl: Inst. for 21st Century Studies (Gov.-Gen.); Sci. Fiction Writers of Am. (Sec. & Dir. Publs.). Hons. incl: Selection for Sci. Fiction Hall of Fame. Address: The Citadel, Chinchilla, PA 18410, USA.

COHEN, David, b. 20 Dec. 1930, Melbourne, Australia. Educator. Educ: B.Sc., B.Ed., Melbourne; Ph.D., Mich. State Univ., USA. Publs: Science Through Activity, Books 1 & 2, 1962, 1966; Science Activity Topics (Books 1-6, co-author), 1967-69; Destination Debatable: On Educational Objectives (co-author), 1974; Ed., Aust. Sci. Tchrs. Jrnl. (1968-72); Ed., Newsletter of Int. Coun. of Assns. of Sci. Educ. Contbr. to: The Australian; Nat. Times;

var. profl. jrnls. Mbrships: Chmn., Nat. Advsry. Comm., Ashton — Scholastic, Publrs.; Ed. Bd., Nat. Sci. Curric. Materials Project; Aust. Soc. of Authors; var. educl. orgs. Recip., educl. awards. Address: 32 Denman St., Turramurra, N.S.W., Australia 2074.

COHEN, Elie Aron, b. 16 July 1909, Groningen, Netherlands. Psychotherapist; Author. Educ: Doctorate, 1952. Publs: Human Behavior in Concentration Camps, 1953; The Abyss, 1973. Contbr. to: The Post-Concentration Syndrome; Med. Weekly of the Netherlands; Med. Monthly; etc. Recip., Royal Award, Officier orde Oranje Nassau, 1974. Address: Wagnerlaan 67, Arnhem, Netherlands.

COHEN, Florence Chanock, b. 14 Feb. 1927, Pitts., Pa., USA. Writer. Publs: Portrait of Deborah, 1962; Freedom Next Time, 1972; My Name Aloud (An Anthology of Short Stories), 1971; Isaac & Ishmael: Congregations of the Just, 1975. Contbr. short stories & articles to var. publs. inclng: Epoch; Prairie Schooner; Yankee; New Outlook; Society. Mbrships: PEN Engl. Ctr., London; Soc. of Midland Authors. Hons: cited 3 times in Best. Am. Short Stories. Address: 125 Laurel Ave., Wilmette, IL 60091, USA.

COHEN, John, b. Tredegar, Wales, UK. University Professor. Educ: M.A., Ph.D., Univ. Coll., London. Publs. incl: Human Nature, War & Society; Humanistic Psychology; Behaviour in Uncertainty; Human Robots in Myth & Science; Psychological Probability; Causes & Prevention of Road Accidents (co-author); Information & Choice (co-author); Psychological Time in Health & Disease; Elements of Child Psychology; Chance, Skill & Luck; Everyman's Psychology; Risk & Gambling (co-author); Readings in Psychology (ed.); Advances in Psychology (ed.). Contbr. to: Nature; New Sci.; Scientific Am.; Brit. Jrnl. Psychol.; Brit. Med. Jrnl.; Hist. Today; Times Lit. Supplement; Guardian; etc. Agent: Shaw Maclean. Address: Dept. of Psychology, The University, Manchester M13 9PL, UK.

COHEN, John Michael, b. 1903, London, UK. Writer; Translator. Educ: B.A., Queen's Coll., Cambridge. Publs. incl: (transls.) Don Quixote; Rousseau's Confessions; Rabelais; The Life of St. Teresa; Montaigne's Essays; Bernal Diaz, Conquest of New Spain; Zarate, Discovery & Conquest of Peru; The Four Voyages of Christopher Columbus; (other publs.) Robert Browning; History of Western Literature; Poetry of this Age; Comic & Curious Verse; More Comic & Curious Verse; Selected Poems of Boris Pasternak; Robert Graves; English Translators & Translations. Address: Knapswood, Upper Basildon, Reading, Berks., UK.

COHEN, Laurence Jonathan, b. 1923, London, UK. Fellow & Praelector. Educ: M.A., Balliol Coll., Oxford. Publs: The Principles of World Citizenship, 1954; The Diversity of Meaning, 1962, 2nd ed., 1966; The Implications of Induction, 1970. Contbr. to: Mind; Arist. Soc. Proceedings; Philos. Analysis; Philos. Quarterly; Am. Philos. Quarterly; Jrnl. Symbolic Log.; Synthese; Review of Int. Philos.; Jrnl. of Philos.; etc. Mbrships: Fellow, Brit. Acad. Address: Queen's College, Oxford, UK.

COHEN, Leonard (Norman), b. 21 Sept. 1934, Montreal, P.Q., Can. Writer; Composer; Singer. Educ: B.A., McGill Univ., Montreal, 1955; Columbia Univ., N.Y., USA. Publs: (novels) The Favorite Game, 1963; Beautiful Losers, 1966; (verse) Let Us Compare Mythologies, 1956; The Spice-Box of Earth, 1961; Flowers for Hitler, 1964; Parasites of Heaven, 1966; Selected Poems, 1956-1968, 1968; Leonard Cohen's Song Book, 1969. Hons: Lit. Award, McGill Univ., 1956; Can. Coun. Award, 1960; P.Q. Lit. Award, 1964; D.L., Dalhousie Univ., Halifax, N.S., 1971. Address: c/o Machat & Kronfeld, 1501 Broadway, 30th Floor, N.Y., NY 10036, USA.

COHEN, Morton Norton, b. 1921, Calgary, Alta., Can. University Professor. Educ: B.A., Tufts Univ.; M.A., Ph.D., Columbia Univ. Publs: Rider Haggard: His Life & Works, 1960, 2nd ed., 1968; Rudyard Kipling to Rider Haggard: The Record of a Friendship, 1965; 2nd ed., 1968; Punky: Mouse for a Day, 1962, 2nd ed., 1963; A retelling for children of Prokofiev's The Love for Three Oranges, 1966. Contbr. to: Bulletin of N.Y. Pub. Lib.; N.Y. Times Book Review; Times; Daily Telegraph; Kipling Jrnl.; etc. Mbrships. incl: PEN; MLA; Kipling Soc.; Tennyson Soc.; Housman Soc.; Lewis Carroll Soc. Agent: A.P. Watt & Son. Address: 72 Barrow St., Apt. 3-N, N.Y., NY 10014, USA.

COHEN, Percy, b. 1891, London, UK. Former Department Head, Central Office & Joint Director, Conservative Research Department. Publs: British System of Social Insurance, 1932; Unemployment Insurance & Assistance in Britain, 1938; Ed., Conservative Election Handbook, 1945; Campaign Guides, 1950, 1951, 1955, 1959. Contbr. to: Notes on Current Politics (Ed., 1942-59). Mbr., Constitutional Club. Address: 115 Grove Hall Court, London NW8, UK.

COHEN, Selma Jeanne. Magazine Editor; Educator. Educ: Ph.D., Univ. of Chgo. Publs: The Modern Dance: Seven Statements of Belief, 1966; Doris Humphrey: An Artist First, 1972; Dance as a Theatre Art: Sourse Readings in Dance History, 1974. Contbr. to: The Dance Has Many Faces, 1966; Aesthetic Inquiry, 1966; Aesthetics & the Arts, 1868; Mng. Ed., 1959-65, Ed., 1954, Dance Perspectives; var. encys. & dance jrnls. Mbrships. incl: Bd. of Trustees, Am. Soc. for Aesthetics, 1963-65, 1973—; Exec. Comm., Am. Soc. for Theatre Rsch., 1967-70, 1973—. Address: Dance Perspectives, 29 E. 9th St., N.Y., NY 10003, USA.

COHEN, Stanley, b. 23 Feb. 1942, Johannesburg, S. Africa. University Professor of Sociology. Educ: Univ. of Witwatersrand, Johannesburg; London Schl. of Econs., Univ. of London, UK; B.A.; Ph.D. Publs: Ed., Images of Deviance, 1971; Folk Devils & Moral Panics, 1972; Psychological Survival: The Experience of Long Term Imprisonment (w. L. Taylor), 1972; The Manufacture of News (w. J. Young), 1973. Contbr. to: New Soc.; Times Higher Educ. Supplement; Guardian; Brit. Jrnl. of Sociol.; Brit. Jrnl. of Criminol. Mbrships: Brit. Soc. of Crimonol.; Brit. Sociol. Assn. Address: Dept. of Sociology, Univ. of Essex, Wivenhoe Park, Colchester, Essex, UK.

COHEN of BIRKENHEAD, (Lord) (Henry Cohen) b. 1900, Birkenhead, UK. Former Professor of Medicine, University of Liverpool; Chancellor, University of Hull. Educ: Univ. of Liverpool; C.H.; M.D.; Sc.D.; F.R.C.P.; F.R.C.P.I.; F.R.C.P.E.; F.R.C.S.; F.R.C.O.G. Publs: Sherrington: Physiologist, Philosopher, Poet; New Pathways in Medicine; The Evolution of Modern Medicine; Ed., British Encyclopaedia of Medical Practice. Contbr. to: Medical Ethics; Lloyd Luke Text Book of Rheumatism; Early Diagnosis. Mbrships. incl: Pres., Gen. Med. Cncl.; Royal Soc. Med.; Royal Soc. of Hlth.; Nat. Soc. for Clean Air; Chmn., Standing Med. Advsry. Comm., & Ctrl. Hlth. Servs. Coun., Min. of Hlth. Hons. incl: D.C.L.; LL.D.; F.S.A.; F.P.S.; J.P.; D.L.; Master of Bench, Inner Temple; Fellow, Jesus Coll., Cambridge. Address: 31 Rodney St., Liverpool 1, UK.

COHN, Norman, b. 1915, London, UK. University Professor. Educ: Christ Ch., Oxford. M.A., Oxford; D.Litt., Glasgow. Publs: Gold Khan & other Siberian Legends, 1946; The Pursuit of the Millennium, 1957, 3rd ed., 1970; Warrant for Genocide, 1967, 2nd ed. 1970; Europe's Inner Demons, 1975. Contbr. to: Millennial Dreams in Action; Caste & Race; Witchcraft Confessions & Accusations; Horizon; Twentieth Century; Commentary; Encounter; Horizon, USA; etc. Fellow, Royal Histl. Soc. Recip., Anisfield-Wolf Award in Race Rels., USA, 1967. Agent: A. D. Peters. Address: 61 New End, London NW3, UK.

COINTREAU, Edouard, b. 28 Feb. 1947, Paris, France. President, Stamps Information Associates Inc. Educ: Ecole Supérieure de Commerce, Paris; Sloan Schl.; M.I.T., USA. Publs: Privacy & Computers, 1971; Report on Stamp Investing, 1971; Guide to Catalogues, 1972. Contbr. to Stamp Wholesaler. Mbrships: Assn. Int. des Journalistes Philatéliques; Philatelic Traders Soc. of GB; Am. Stamp Dealer Assn. Address: 675 Massachusetts Ave., Cambridge, MA 02139, USA.

COLAKOVIC, Rodoljub, pen name BOSANAC, R., b. 7 June 1900, Bijeljina, Bosnia, Yugoslavia. Journalist. Publs: Kuca Oplakana, 1941; Zapisi iz oslobodilackog rata, I-V, 1946-54; Kazivanje o jednom pokoljenju, I-III, 1967-72. Mbr., Union of Writers of Yugoslavia. Recip., Prize of Avnoj. Address: Drajzerov Prolaz Br.2, Belgrade, Yugoslavia.

COLBECK, Maurice, b. 1925, Batley, Yorks., UK. Journalist; Editor; Author. Publs: White God's Fury; Four Against Crime; Jungle Rivals; Mosquitoes; Sister Kenny of the Outback; How to be a Family Man (w. William Geldart); Yorkshire (in preparation). Ed., Yorks. Life; Asst. Ed., E. J. Arnold & Son Ltd.; Reporter & Sub-Ed., var. Yorks. newspapers. Address: 164 Soothill Lane, Batley, Yorks., UK.

COLDHAM, James Desmond Bowden, b. 8 Jan. 1924, Stoke Fleming, Dartmouth, Devon, UK. Publs: Northamptonshire Cricket: A History, 1959; William Brockwell: His Triumph & Tragedy, 1970. Contbr. to: The Cricketer; Irish Cricket; Devon Co. Cricket Club Tr. Book; Ed., Jrnl. of The Cricket Soc.; etc. Mbrships. incl: Arts & Lib. Comm., MCC; Chmn., Lit. Award Comm., The Cricket Soc.; Cricket Writers' Club. Address: "Anmer", Lytton Rd., Woking, Surrey GU22 7BH, UK.

COLE, Barry, b. 13 Nov. 1936, Woking, Surrey, UK. Writer; Civil Servant. Publs: Moonsearch, 1968; A Run Across the Island, 1968; The Search for Rita, 1970; Joseph Winter's Patronage, 1969; The Visitors, 1970; The Giver, 1972; Pathetic Fallacies, 1973. Contbr. to: New Statesman; Spectator; Tribune; Atlantic Monthly; Transatlantic Review; London Mag.; Times Educl. Supplement; Brit. Book News; Tchr.; Child Educ.; etc. Hons: Fellow in Lit., Univ. of Newcastle-upon-Tune & Durham, 1970-72; Arts Coun. Grant, 1969, 1972. Address: 18 Great Percy St., London WC1, UK.

COLE, Eugene Roger, b. 14 Nov. 1930, Cleveland, Ohio, USA. Writer; Critic. Educ: B.A., St. Edward's Coll., 1954; M.Div., Sulpician Sem. of N.W., 1958; A.B., Ctrl. Wash. State Coll., 1960; M.A., Seattle Univ., 1970. Publs: April Is The Cruelest Month, 1970; Ed., Grand Slam: 13 Great Bridge Stories, 1975; Selected Poems, 1975. Contbr. to num. anthols., mags. & newspapers; Acting Ed., Experiment: An International Review. Hons: Dragonfly Award, 1974. Address: 26301 Shirley Ave., Euclid, OH 44132, USA.

COLE, (Lt.-Col.) Howard Norman, b. 1911, London, UK. Soldier. Educ: Royal Savoy Schl. Publs: The Story of Aldershot; Heraldry in War — Formation Badges 1939-45; Badges on Battledress; Coronation & Commemorative Medals 1887-1953; The Story of Bisley; On Wings of Healing (The Story of the Airborne Medical Services 1940-60); Ed., Defence, The Territorial Mag., 1937-39. Contbr. to: The Citizen Soldier; Hampshire & N.W. Surrey Group of Newspapers & Service & Military Histl. Jrnls. Mbrships: F.R.S.A.; F.R.Hist.S. Hons: O.B.E.; T.D.; O.St.J.; D.L. Address: 4 Summer Cottages, Guildford Rd., Ash, Aldershot, Hants., UK.

COLE, John Alfred, b. 21 Apr. 1905, Abbey Wood, Kent, UK. Writer. Educ: Dip. in Social Studies, London Univ. Publs: Come Dungeon Dark, 1935; This Happy Breed, 1937; A Stranger Myself, 1938; Just Back from Germany, 1938; To Make Us Glad, 1941; My Host Michel, 1955; Nobody Got into Trouble, 1962; Lord Haw-Haw — and William Joyce, 1964; Press Power: A Study of Axel Springer (transl. & ed.), 1969. Contbr. to: Calligraphy & Palaeography (essays, ed., A. S. Osley), 1965; talks & features, BBC German Lang. Serv. Address: 4 Crane Court, Fleet St., London EC4A 2EJ, UK.

COLE, (Dame) Margaret Isabel, b. 1893, Cambridge, UK. Political Writer. Educ: Girton Coll., Cambridge. Publs. incl: Beatrice Webb; Growing up into Revolution; Robert Owen of New Lanark; Marriage; Past & Present; Makers of the Labour Movement; Servant of the Country; Story of Fabian Socialism; (Ed.) Our Partnership; Beatrice Webb's Diaries; & about 30 detective novels (w. G. D. H. Cole). Contbr. to: New Statesman; Listener; Tribune; Plebs; Highway; Guardian; etc. Hons: O.B.E., 1965; D.B.E., 1970. Address: 74 Addison Way, London NW11, UK.

COLE, Marion, b. 1901, Reading, UK. Teacher; Producer & Speech Therapist; Appeal Organiser & Speaker. Publs: Fogie (Life of Elsie Fogerty), 1967. Address: Helena Club, Lower Sloane St., London SW1W 8BS, UK.

COLEBURT, James Russell, b. 1920, Wimbledon, UK. Schoolmaster. Educ: M.A., Exeter Coll., Oxford. Publs: An Introduction to Western Philosophy; The Search for Values; Christian Evolution. Contbr. to: Downside Review. Address: Worth School, Crawley, Sussex, UK.

COLEGATE, Isabel, b. 10 Sept. 1931, London, UK. Novelist. Publs: The Blackmailer, 1958; A Man of Power, 1960; The Great Occasion, 1962; Statues in a Garden, 1965; Orlando King, 1968; Orlando at the Brazen Threshold, 1971; Agatha, 1974. Contbr. to var. lit. jrnls. Address: Midford Castle, Bath, UK.

COLEMAN, (Charles) John Danent Blake, b. 13 May 1928, London, UK. Schoolmaster. Educ: M.A., Oxford; M.A., London. Publs: Coleman's Drive, 1962; Childscourt,

1967; Your Book of Vintage Cars, 1968; Your Book of Veteran & Edwardian Cars; Your Book of Racing & Sports Cars. Mbrships: Nat. Union of Tchrs.; Soc. of Authors; Sound Money League; Assn. for Therapeutic Educ. Address: The Nook, Hook Village, Warsash, Near Southampton, UK.

COLEMAN, James Andrew, b. 1921, Niagara Falls, N.Y., USA. Professor. Educ: B.A., M.A., Columbia Univ. Publs: Relativity for the Layman, 1959; Relativity for the Layman, revised ed., 1969; Modern Theories of the Universe, 1963; Early Theories of the Universe, 1967. Address: American International Coll., Springfield, MA 01109, USA.

COLEMAN, James Covington, b. 19 Oct. 1914, Salem, N.H., USA. University Professor; Author. Educ: B.A., 1938, Ph.D., 1942, Univ. of Calif. Publs: Abnormal Psychology & Modern Life, 1950, 5th ed., forthcoming; Contemporary Psychology & Effective Behaviour, 1960, 3rd ed., 1974; Deep Sea Adventure Series, 1959, 3rd ed., 1967. Contbr. to: Contemporary Psychol.; etc. Mbrships. incl: Fellow, Am. Psychol. Assn.; N.Y. Acad. Sci.; Nat. Acad. Pol. Sci.; Dipl., Am. Bd. Profl. Examiners (in Psychol.). Hons. incl: The Christopher Fndn. (Pres.); Fellow, Royal Soc. of Health. Address: 20178 Rockport Way, Malibu, CA 90265, USA.

COLEMAN, Terry, b. 13 Feb. 1931, Bournemouth, UK. Journalist; Historian. Educ: LL.B., London Univ. Publs: A Girl for the Afternoon (novel), 1965; The Railway Navvies (hist.), 1965; The Only True History (Collected Journalism), 1969; Passage to America (hist.), 1972; The Liner She's a Lady, 1975; Providence & Mr. Hardy (biog., co-author), 1966; The Pantheretti: Collected Poems, 1973. Contbr. to: Guardian (former Chief Feature Writer); Sunday Times; N.Y. Times; Sat. Evening Post; etc. Hons: Yorks. Post Prize for Best First Book of 1965; Commended Descriptive Writer of the Yr., I.P.C. Awards, London, 1972. Address: The Daily Mail, London EC4, UK.

COLEMAN-COOKE, John, pen name FORD, Langridge, b. 1914, Burton-on-Trent, UK. Publs: Discovery II in the Antarctic, 1963; The Harvest that Kills, 1967; Ed., The Exmoor National Park Guide, 1970; Soldier Don't Shoot, 1975. Contbr. to: Radio & TV Critic, Western Morning News, 1948-54; Scriptwriter, Ed., var. BBC series, 1955-59; The Field; Country Life; Drive Mag. Mbr., Soc. of Authors. Agent: John Farquharson Ltd. Address: Crow Beach House, Braunton, N. Devon, UK.

COLES, J. M., b. 1930, Woodstock, Ont., Can. University Lecturer. Educ: Univs. of Toronto, Cambridge & Edinburgh. Publs: Studies in Ancient Europe (Ed. w. D. Simpson), 1968; The Archaeology of Early Man (w. E. S. Higgs), 1969; The Awakening of Man (Ed.), 1970; Field Archaeology in Britain, 1972; Archaeology by Experiment, 1973. Contbr. to schlrly. jrnls. inclng: Proceedings of Prehist. Soc.; Antiquaries Jrnl.; Antiquity. Fellow, Soc. of Antiquaries. Address: Dept. of Archaeol., Cambridge, UK.

COLES, K. Adlard, b. 1 Sept. 1901, London, UK. Author. Former Publisher. Educ: M.A., Clare Coll., Cambridge; F.C.A. Publs: Creeks & Harbours of the Solent, 1933; Shell Pilot to the South Coast Harbours, 1937; Channel Harbours & Anchorages, 1956; North Biscay Pilot, 1959; North Brittany Pilot, 1965; Heavy Weather Sailing, 1967 (transld. into 8 langs.). Contbr. to yachting mags. Address: Ailsa Croft, Poles Lane, Lymington, Hants., UK.

COLES, Robert, b. 12 Oct. 1929, Boston, Mass., USA. Child Psychiatrist. Educ: A.B., Harvard Coll.; M.D., Columbia Univ. Coll. of Physns. & Surgs. Publs: Children of the Crisis (3 vols: A Study of Courage & Fear, 1967; Migrants Sharecroppers Mountaineers, 1972; The South Goes North, 1972); The Image is You, 1969; Wages of Neglect, 1969; Still Hungry in America, 1969; Erik H. Erikson, 1970; Geography of Faith, 1971; The Middle Americans, 1971; Farewell to the South, 1972; A Spectacle Unto the World, 1973; The Old Ones of New Mexico, 1973. Contbr. to profl. & lit. publs. Hons. incl: Weatherford Prize, Berea Coll. & Coun. of the Southern Mts., 1973; Lillian Smith Award, Southern Regional Coun., 1973; Pulitzer Prize 1973. Address: Harvard Univ. Hlth. Servs., 75 Mt. Auburn St., Cambridge, MA 02138, USA.

COLEY, Rex, pen name RAGGED STAFF, b. 1898, Birmingham, UK. Journalist; Lecturer. Publs: Cycling is Such Fun, 1948; Cycling, 1952; Joyous Cycling, 1953; Laughter on Two Wheels, 1963. Contbr. to: Cycling

(Touring Ed., 1967-); Bicycle (Features Ed., 1942-47, Ed., 1948-51); Am. Bicyclist; Aust. Cyclist; Cycle-Touring; var. outdoor jrnls. Mbrships: Cyclists' Touring Club; Midland Cycling & Athletic Club. Address: Dormy House, Brancaster, Norfolk PE31 8AT, UK.

COLLBERG, Sven Axel Sigurd, b. 10 Sept. 1919, Karlskrona, Sweden. Schoolmaster; Translator. Educ: M.A., Univ. of Göteborg, 1943. Publs. incl: Sassoon's Sherston trilogy (transl.), 1949, 1952, 1955; Parken (The Park), 1950; Lejonet och enhörningen (The Lion & The Unicorn), 1954; Baudelaire selection (transl.), 1957; Emblem, 1966. Mbr., Swedish Union of Authors. Hons: Transls. Prize, Authors of Sweden Fund, 1972; Cultural Prize, City of Lund, Sweden, 1973. Address: Svaneg. 5, 222 24 Lund, Sweden.

COLLERTON, Jeffrey Alban, b. 3 Oct. 1946, Masterton, NZ. Magazine Editor. Publs: Motorcycle Racing Pictorial, 1972; Australian Bike, 1973; Speedway World, 1974; Naturally Free (film script), 1974. Contbr. to: Motor Cycle (London); Motor Cycle Weekly (USA); Revs (Ed.). Address: Edinburgh Rd., Marrickville, N.S.W., Australia.

COLLIE, Michael John, b. 8 Aug. 1929, Eastbourne, UK. Professor of English Literature. Educ: B.A., 1942, M.A., 1956, Cantab. Publs: Poems, 1959; Skirmish with Fact, 1960; Laforgue, 1964; Jules Laforgue: Derniers Vers, 1965; The House, 1967; Kerdruc Notebook, 1972; New Brunswick, 1974; George Meredith: A Bibliography, 1974; A Bibliography of the Writings of George Gissing, 1974. Mbrships. incl: Mod. Humanities Rsch. Assn.; Soc. of Authors; FRSA. Address: Corner Cottage, Shepreth, Herts., UK.

COLLIER, Henry Oswald Jackson, b. Natal, Brazil. Director of Research; Writer. Educ: Trinity Hall, Cambridge, UK; B.A., PhD., Sc.D., F.I. Biol. Publs: Chemotherapy of Infections; sev. BBC Feature Progs. Contbr. to: New Biol.; New Sci.; Sci. News; Discovery; Observer; Nature; Lancet; Brit. Jrnl. of Pharmacol., etc. Address: 23 Campden Hill Rd., London W8 7DX, UK.

COLLIER, John, b. 3 May 1901, London, UK. Writer. Publs: (novels) His Monkey Wife; or, Married to a Chimp, 1930; Full Circle: A Tale, 1933; Defy the Foul Fiend; or, The Misadventures of a Heart, 1934; (short stories) No Traveller Returns, 1931; Epistle to a Friend, 1931; Green Thoughts, 1932; The Devil & All, 1934; Variation on a Theme, 1935; Presenting Moonshine: Stories, 1941; A Touch of Nutmet & More Unlikely Stories, 1943; Fancies & Goodnights, 1951; Pictures in the Fire, 1958; Gemini: Poems, 1931; Wet Saturday (play); Just the Other Day: An Informal History of Britain since the War (w. Iain Lang, 1932. Address: c/o A. D. Peters & Co., 10 Buckingham St., London WC2, UK.

COLLIER, (John) Basil, b. 1908, Westcliff-on-Sea, UK. Military Historian. Publs: Jam Tomorrow; Local Thunder; To Meet the Spring; Catalan France; The Defence of the United Kingdom; Leader of the Few; The Quiet Places; Heavenly Adventurer; Brasshat; The Battle of Britain; The Battle of the V-Weapons, 1944-45; Barren Victories; A Short History of the Second World War; The War in the Far East, 1941-1945; The Lion & the Eagle; Battle of Britain; Dunkirk; The Desert War. Address: The Burnt House, Newick, Lewes, E. Sussex, UK.

COLLIER, Kenneth Gerald, b. 24 Mar. 1910, E. Sheen, Surrey, UK. College Administrator; Author. Educ: B.A., 1931, M.A., 1935, St. John's Coll., Cambridge; Dip.Ed., Oxford Univ., 1945. Publs: Science of Humanity, 1949; Social Purposes of Education, 1959; New Dimensions in Higher Education, 1968; Ed., Innovation in Higher Education, 1974; Values & Moral Development in Higher Education (co-ed.), forthcoming. Contbr. to: Univs. Quarterly; Times Educl. & Higher Educ. Supplements; British Jrnl. of Educl. Technol.; Jrnl. of Curriculum Studies; Jrnl. of Moral Educ. Address: Principal's House, Bede College, Durham DH1 1TB, UK.

COLLIER, (Sir) Laurence, b. 13 June 1890, London, UK. Retired Diplomat; Writer. Educ: 1st class Hons., Mod. Hist., Balliol Coll., Oxford. Publ: Flight from Conflict, 1944. Contbr. to: Geogl. Jrnl.; Geogl. Mag; Blackwoods; Times Lit. Supplement; Homes & Gdns., etc. Mbr., Royal Geogl. Soc. Recip., K.C.M.G., 1944. Address: Monkswell Gate, 37 Granville Rd., Limpsfield, Surrey, UK.

COLLIER, Richard Hughesdon, b. 8 Mar. 1924, London, UK. Author. Publs: Captain of the Queens (co-author), 1956; Ten Thousand Eyes, 1958; The City That Wouldn't Die, 1959; A House Called Memory, 1960; The Sands of Dunkirk, 1961; The Great Indian Mutiny, 1963; The General Next to God, 1965; Eagle Day, 1966; The River that God Forgot, 1968; Duce! , 1971; The Plague of the Spanish Lady, 1974; also num. for. eds. Contbr. to: Rdr's. Digest; Holiday; The Times; etc. Mbrships: Author's Club; Brit. Film Inst.; Royal Hort. Soc. Recip., Kt. of Mark Twain, 1972. Agent: Curtis Brown Ltd. Address: c/o Agent, 1 Craven Hill, London W2, UK.

COLLINGE, John Gregory, b. 10 May 1939, Hastings, NZ. Solicitor; Author. Educ: LL.B., Univ. of Auckland; B.Litt., Univ. Coll., Oxford, UK. Publs: Restrictive Trade Practices & Monopolies in New Zealand, 1969; Tutorials in Contract, 1970; The Law of Marketing in Australia & New Zealand, 1971. Contbr: Australian Law Jrnl. Address: c/o Nicholson, Gribbin & Co., Solicitors, P.O. Box 160, Auckland, NZ.

COLLINGS, Edwin Geoffrey, pen name, BLACKWELL, John, b. 13 July 1913, Devonport, UK. Retired Civil Servant. Publs: Security Risk (novel), 1955. Mbr., Soc. of Authors. Address: 38 Upper E. Hayes, Bath, UK.

COLLINGWOOD, Frances, b. 21 June 1895, London, UK. Freelance Journalist. Contbr. to about 200 jrnls. Mbr., PEN. Address: 65 Harrington Gdns., London SW7, UK.

COLLINS, Bernard John, b. 3 July 1909, London, UK. Chartered Surveyor; Town Planner; Writer. Educ: Coll. of Estate Mgmt.; F.R.I.C.S.; F.R.I.P.I. Publs: Mind your own Middlesex, 1950; Development Plans Explained, 1951; Middlesex Survey & Development Plan, 1952; Greater London Report of Studies & Development Plan, 1969. Contbr. to: The Chartered Surveyor; Jrnl. of Royal Town Planning Inst.; Economist; Town Planning Review. Mbrships. incl: Controller, Planning & Transp., Gtr. London Coun., 1964-74; Pres., Royal Instn. Chartered Surveyors, 1974-75. Recip., C.B.E., 1960. Address: Foxella, Matfield, Tonbridge TN12 7ET, UK.

COLLINS, David, b. 2 Feb. 1926, London, UK. Teacher; Writer; Staff, Cantab College, Toronto; Staff, York University; Creative Writers' Workshop, 1970-73; Teacher, Ryerson Polytechnical Institute; Freelance Writer since 1968. Educ: UK & S. Africa. Publs: Gold in the Cariboo, 1969; Wings of Progress, forthcoming. Contbr. to: Illustrated London News; Toronto Globe & Mail; CBC; etc. Mbrships: Aviation Space Writers' Assn.; Aviation. Address: Apt. 504, 130 Rosedale Valley Rd., Toronto M4W 1P9, Ont., Can.

COLLINS, Freda, b. 15 May 1904, Richmond, Surrey, UK. Writer. Publs. incl: Pow-wow Stories (for Brownies), 1948, reproduced as paperback 1974; Children in the Market Place, 1942; Acting Games, rev. 1968; Put on the Armour of Light (drama textbooks); The 40th Man (one-act play); Yes God; & num. children's books, textbooks, plays. Contrb. to var. periodicals; broadcasting, BBC Radio Medway. Mbr., Authors' Soc.; Relig. Drama Soc. Hons. incl: 1st Prize, Playwrights' Club, 1937. Address: 9 Pembridge Villas, London W11 3EW, UK.

COLLINS, Geoffrey Morison, b. 1923, Parramatta, N.S.W., Australia. Psychiatrist. Educ: B.A., M.B., B.S., Univ. of Sydney. Publs: The Secure Child, 1968. Contbr. to: Mental Hlth. in Aust. (Ed., 1965-); Mbrships: F.A.N.Z.C.P.; D.P.M.; Aust. Med. Assn.; Mental Hlth. Assn. of N.S.W.; Aust. Soc. of Authors. Address: 31 Ross Crescent, Blaxland, NSW, Australia 2774.

COLLINS, (Rev. Canon) Lewis John, b. 23 Mar. 1905, Hawkhurst, Kent, UK. Canon & Treasurer, St. Paul's Cathedral. Educ: 1st class Theol. Tripos, Cambridge Univ. Publs: The New Testament Problem, 1937; A Theology of Christian Action, 1949; (autobiog.) Faith Under Fire, 1965. Contbr. to: The Priest as Student, 1939; This War & Christian Ethics, 1940; Three Views of Christianity, 1962. Mbrships: Wig & Pen; Christian Action, & Int. Def. & Aid Fund. Recip., Order of Grand Companion of Freedom, 3rd Div. Address: 2 Amen Court, London EC4M 7BX, UK.

COLLINS, Mary, b. 1895, Edinburgh, UK. University Reader in Psychology (retired). Educ: M.A., M.Ed., Ph.D., Univ. Edinburgh; F.R.S.E. Publs. incl: Colour Blindness; Psychology & Practical Life (co-author); A First Laboratory Guide in Psychology; Performance Tests of Intelligence (co-author); etc. Contbr. to: Brit. Jrnl. Psychol.; etc. Mbr., Ladies' Caledonian Club. Address: 90 Oxgangs Rd., Edinburgh 10, UK.

COLLINS, Norman Richard, b. 3 Oct. 1907, Beaconsfield, Bucks., UK. Company Director; Author. Publs: The Facts of Fiction, 1932; Penang Appointment, 1934; The Three Friends, 1935; Trinity Town, 1936; Flames Coming Out of the Top, 1937; Love in Our Time, 1938; I Shall Not Want, 1940; Anna, 1942; London Belongs To Me, 1945; Black Ivory, 1947; Children of the Archbishop, 1951; The Bat That Flits, 1952; The Bond Street Story, 1958; The Governor's Lady, 1968. Address: 1 Radlett Place, London NW8, UK.

COLLINS, Peter Blumfeld, pen name ROKEBY, John, b. 24 Nov. 1909, Corfe Castle, Dorset, UK. Journalist; Consultant. Educ: B.Sc., Royal Coll. of Sci. (Imperial Coll.); A.R.C.S. Publs: Household Pests, 1936; Millions Still Go Hungry, 1957; Trees of Britain, 1959; A Mandate for Refugees, 1970; also brochures, tech. reports, etc. for UN Agencies. Contbr. to num. jrnls. inclng: Sunday Times; The Guardian; Nature; New Sci.; Dev. Forum; World Crops. Mbrships. incl: Inst. of Biol.; Assn. of Brit. Sci. Writers. Address: 5 Umbria St. London SW15 5DP, UK.

COLLINS, Philip Arthur William, b. 28 May 1923, London, UK. University Professor of English. Educ: M.A., Emanuel Coll., Cambridge. Publs. incl: James Boswell, 1956; A Dickens Bibliography, 1970; Ed., Dickens: the Critical Heritage, 1971; Ed., A Christmas Carol: The Public Reading Version, 1971; Reading Aloud: a Victorian Metier, 1972; Ed., Dickens's Public Readings, 1975. Mbrships: Sec., Leicester Theatre Trust Ltd., 1963; Arts Coun. Drama Panel, Policy & Fin. Comm., Reg. Comm., 1970. Hons: Annual Lectureship, Byron, Nottingham Univ., 1969, Annie Talbot Cole, Bowdoin Coll., 1972, Tennyson Soc., Lincoln, 1972. Address: Dept. of English, The University, Leicester LE1 7RH, UK.

COLLINSON, Kenton, b. 31 May 1916, Winfield, Kan., USA. Businessman. Educ: B.S.S., S.O.S., Northwestern Univ., Ill. Contbr. to: Kan. City Star; Topeka Jrnl.; Wichita Eagle; Bavarian Observer, W. Germany. Mbrships: Kan. Authors' Club; Grad., Newspaper Inst., Am. Address: 909 E. 10th Ave., Winfield, KS, USA.

COLLINSON, Laurence Henry, b. 1925, Leeds, Yorks., UK. Freelance Journalist; Sub-Editor; Author. Educ: Univ. of Qld., Aust. Publs: (poetry) The Moods of Love, 1957; Who is Wheeling Grandma? 1967; (novel) Cupid's Crescent, 1973. Contbr. to: Overland; Meanjin; Bulletin; The Australian; Sydney Morning Herald; Age; Tribune; Outposts; PEN Anthol.; etc. Asst. Ed., Publs. Br., Victorian Educ. Dept., 1961-64; Sub-Ed., Int. Publng. Corp., 1965-73. Mbrships: PEN; Soc. of Authors; Writers Guild of GB; Nat. Union Jrnlsts. Recip., Writing Grant, Aust. Coun. for Arts, 1974-75. Agent: Margery Vosper. Address: 97 Edgwarebury Lane, Middx. HA8 8NA, UK.

COLLINSON, Patrick, b. 1929, Ipswich, UK. Professor of History, University of Sydney. Educ: Univ. of Cambridge; Univ. of London; M.A.; Ph.D. Author, The Elizabethan Puritan Movement, 1967. Contbr. to: Times Lit. Supplement; Spectator; Engl. Histl. Review; Econ. Hist. Review; Hist.; Jrnl. of Ecclesiastical Hist.; Theol. Fellow, Royal Histl. Soc. Address: Dept. of Hist., Univ. of Sydney, Sydney, N.S.W., Australia 2006.

COLLINS PERSSE, Michael Dudley de Burgh, b. 10 May 1931, Toowoomba, Qld., Australia. Schoolmaster. Educ: M.A., Balliol Coll., Oxford, UK, 1955; Oxford Univ.; Westcott House, Cambridge, 1958. Publs: Their Succeeding Race, 1958, 1960; The Education of a Civilised Man (ed.), 1962, 1963; William Charles Wentworth, 1972, 1973. Ed., The Corian: The Geelong Grammar Schl. Quarterly, 1966—. Contbr. to: Aust. Dictionary of Biog. Mbrships: Aust. Coll. of Educ.; Aust. Soc. of Authors; Vic. Fellowship of Aust. Writers. Address: Geelong Church of England Grammar School, Corio, Vic., Australia.

COLLIS, John Stewart, b. 1900, Co. Dublin, Repub. of Ireland. Author; Journalist. Educ: B.A., Balliol Coll., Oxford. Publs: Shaw, 1925; Forward to Nature, 1927; Farewell to Argument, 1935; The Sounding Cataract, 1936; an Irishman's England, 1937; While Following the Plough, 1946; Down to Earth, 1947; The Triumph of the Tree, 1950; The Moving Waters, 1955; Paths of Light, 1959; An Artist of Life, 1959; Marriage of Genius for Spring, 1963; Leo Tolstoy, 1969. Mbrships: Soc. of Authors; F.R.S.L. Address: 54 West St., Ewell, Surrey, UK.

COLLIS, Louise, b. 25 Jan. 1925, Burma. Author. Educ: B.A., Reading Univ. Publs: (novels) Without a Voice, 1951; A Year Passed, 1952; After the Holiday, 1954; The Angel's Name, 1955; The Great Flood, 1966; (non-fiction) Seven in the Tower (histl. essays), 1958; The Apprentice Saint (Biog.), 1964; Soldier in Paradise (biog.), 1965; A Private View of Stanley Spencer (biog.), 1972. Contbr. to: Arts Review; Jrnl. of Royal Ctrl. Asiatic Soc. Mbrships: Soc. of Authors; Int. Assn. Art Critics. Address: 65 Cornwall Gardens, London SW7, UK.

COLLISON, Peter, b. 1925, London, UK. University Professor. Educ: Birmingham Univ.; Nuffield Coll., Oxford; M.A.; Ph.D. Publs: The Cutteslowe Walls, 1963. Contbr. to: Am. Jrnl. of Sociol.; Brit. Jrnl. of Sociol.; Sociol.; New Soc. Address: Dept. of Social Studies, The University, Newcastle upon Tyne NE1 7RU, UK.

COLLISS, Gertrude Florence Mary, b. Ruabon, N. Wales, UK. Retired teacher. Educ: Tchrs. Trng. Coll., Brighton, Sussex. Publ: Family of Forty, 1956. Former contbr. to: Child Educ. Address: Mulberry Cottage, St. Mary's Close, Littlehampton, Sussex, UK.

COLLOMS, Brenda, pen name HUGHES, Brenda, b. 14 Jan. 1919, London, UK. Writer; Lecturer. Educ: B.A., London Univ.; M.A., Liverpool Univ. Publs: The Film Hamlet, 1948; Film Star Diary, 1948-63; New Guinea Folk Tales, 1959; Chilean Folk Tales, 1962; Human Geography text series, 1964-66; Certificate History, Books 1-4, 1966-70; Israel, 1971; Mayflower Pilgrims, 1973; Charles Kingsley, 1975. Contbr. to: Working Men's Coll. Jrnl. Mbrships. incl: Soc. of Authors; London Freelance Br., Nat. Union of Jrnlsts. Address: 123 Gloucester Avenue, London NW1 8LB, UK.

COLONY, Horatio, b. 22 Sept. 1900, Keene, N.H., USA. Retired Executive. Educ: B.A., Harvard Coll. Publs. incl: Free Forester (novel); Verse — A Brook of Leaves, 1935; Bacchus & Krishna, 1952; Young Malatesta, 1957; The Early Land, 1962; Demon in Love, 1968; Flower Myth, 1970; The Amazon's Hero, 1973. Contbr. to num. periodicals. Mbrships: Boston Authors Club; Poetry Soc. of Am.; Cath. Poetry Soc.; N.H. Poetry Soc. Address: 199 Main St., Keene, NH 13431, USA.

COLQUHOUN, (Rev. Canon) Frank, b. 1909, Ventnor, Isle of Wight. Canon Residentiary, Norwich Cathedral. Educ: M.A., Univ. of Durham; Tyndale Hall, Bristol. Publs: The Living Church in the Parish; The Fellowship of the Gospel; Harringay Story; Your Child's Baptism; Christ's Ambassadors; The Gospels; Total Christianity; Parish Prayers; Preaching Through the Christian Year; Preaching at the Parish Communion; New Every Morning (Ed.), 1973; Contemporary Parish Prayers. Ed., The Churchman, 1946-51; Evangelical Christendom, 1951-54; Crusade, 1955-59. Address: 27 The Close, Norwich NR1 4DZ, UK.

COLQUHOUN, Keith, b. 1927, London, UK. Publs: The Money Tree; Point of Stress; The Sugar Coating; St. Petersburg Rainbow. Address: 16 King's Walk, Shoreham Beach, Sussex, UK.

COLSON, Elizabeth Florence, b. 15 June 1917, Hewitt, Minn., USA. Anthropologist. Educ: B.A., 1938, M.A., 1940, Univ. of Minn.; M.A., 1941, Ph.D., 1945, Radcliffe Coll. Publs: The Makah, 1953; Marriage & the Family Among the Plateau Tonga, 1958; Social Organization of the Gwembe Tonga, 1960; The Plateau Tonga, 1962; The Social Consequences of Resettlement, 1971; Tradition & Contract, 1974; Autobiographies of Three Pomo Women, 1974. Contbr. to: Africa; Current Anthropol.; Southwestern Jrnl. of Anthropol.; etc. Mbrships. incl: Royal Anthropol. Inst.; Am. Ethnol. Soc.; Am. Anthrop. Assn.; Am. Assn. African Studies. Hons. incl: Fellow, Ctr. for Adv. Study in Behavioral Scis., 1967-68. Address: Dept. of Anthropology, Univ. of California, Berkeley, CA, USA.

COLSON, John Henry Charles, b. 1918, Bury St. Edmunds, UK. Director of Rehabilitation, Fieldhead Hospital, Wakefield. Publs: Occupational Therapy; Remedial Gymnastics; Postural & Relaxetion Training; Progressive Exercise Therapy; Sports Injuries & their Treatment. Contbr. to: Physiotherapy; World Med.; Hlth. & Soc. Serv. Jrnl. Mbrships: F.C.S.P.; M.B.A.O.T.; F.S.R.G. Address: 18 The Russets, Sandal, Wakefield, W. Yorks., UK.

COLVIN, Brenda, b. 8 June 1897, Simla, India. Landscape Architect. Publs: Land & Landscape; Trees for

Town & Country. Contbr. to: Inst. of Landscape Archts. Jrnl.; Landscape Design; Archtl. Review; Master Builder; Times Lit. Supplement; Country Life; Observer. Mbrships: Fndr. Mbr., Inst. of Landscape Archts. (Pres., 1951-53); Int. Fedn. of Landscape Archts.; Women's Farm & Garden Assn.; Engl. Speaking Union. Recip., C.B.E. Address: Filkins, Lechlade, Glos., UK.

COLŸN, Marianne Margaretha, b. 11 May 1912, Sumatra, Indonesia. Speech & Voice Therapist. Educ: Inst. for Logopaedy & Phoniatry, Amsterdam. Publs: Te vuur en te zwaard, 1957; Spin in de morgen, 1960; Nacht zonder ontmoeting, 1963; Tekens van leven, 1969; De klap van de boemerang, 1973. Mbrships. incl: PEN Int.; Netherlands Lit. Assn.; Lit. Soc.; Die Kogge (writers' soc.). Hons: Prize, Belgian & Netherlands Radio, 1966; Prize, Netherlands Dept. of Culture & Sci., 1973. Address: Hazelaarlaan 49, Hilversum, Netherlands.

COMBS, Joseph Franklin, early pen name UNCLE GILLIS, b. 23 Nov. 1892, Center, Tex., USA. Writer; Columnist. Educ: B.S. Equivalent, Tex. A. & M. Univ., 1917. Publs: Growing Pastures in the South, 1936; Farm Corner, Nature Stories, 1963; Legends of the Pineys, 1965; Gunsmoke in the Redlands, 1968; Kudjo Quatterman, 1972. Contbr. to farm jrnls. & newspapers. Hons: 1st Prize, Tex. Ext. Agts. News Writing Contest, 1932. Address: 5635 Duff Ave., Beaumont, TX 77706, USA.

COMFORT, Alexander, b. 1920, London, UK. Surgeon; Physician. Educ: M.A., M.B., Trinity Coll., Cambridge; London Hospital; Ph.D.; M.R.C.S.; L.R.C.P.; D.C.H. Publs. incl: (novels) No Such Liberty; The Almond Tree; On This Side Nothing; Come out to play; (short stories) Letters from an Outpost; (verse) A Wreath for the Living; The Song of Lazarus; The Signal to Engage; (essays) The Anxiety Makers; (other publs.) Art & Social Responsibility; The Novel & Our Time; Barbarism & Sexual Freedom; Sexual Behaviour in Society; The Biology of Senescence; The Pattern of the Future; Darwin & the Naked Lady. Contbr. to num. jrnls. Address: 44 The Avenue, Loughton, Essex, UK.

COMMAGER, Henry Steele, b. 25 Oct. 1902. Professor of History. Educ: B.A., 1923, M.A., 1924, Ph.D., 1928, Univ. of Chgo.; Univ. of Copenhagen. Publs. incl: Theodore Parker, 1936; Story of the Second World War, 1945; The American Mind, 1950; Living Ideas in America, 1951; Freedom, Loyalty, Dissent, 1954; History: Nature & Purpose, 1965; Search for a Usable Past, 1967; The American Character, 1970; The Use & Abuse of History, 1972; (Editor) The Struggle for Racial Equality; Why the Confederacy Lost the Civil War; etc. Contbr. to num. jrnls. Mbr., Am. Acad. of Arts & Letters. Num. hons. incl: Knight of the Order of Dannebrog (Denmark); LL.D.; Hillman Fndn. Award; US Army Special Citation; etc.

CONAN, Arthur Robert, b. 1910, Co. Dublin, Ireland. Economist. Educ: Trinity Coll., Dublin; London Schl. of Econs. Publs: The Sterling Area, 1952; Capital Imports into Sterling Countries, 1960; The Rationale of the Sterling Area, 1961; The Problem of Sterling, 1966. Contbr. to: The Times; Banker; Westminster Bank Review; Banker's Mag.; Round Table; New C'wlth.; etc. Address: c/o Nat. Westminster Bank Ltd., Cromwell Pl., London SW7 2LB, UK.

CONCHON, Georges, b. 1925, Saint-Avit, France. Journalist; Civil Servant. Educ: Sorbonne Univ., Paris. Publs: Les Grandes Lessives, 1953; Les Chemins Ecartés, 1954; Tous Comptes Faits, 1957; La Corrida de la Victoire, 1960; The Hollow Victory, 1962; L'Esbroufe, 1961; L'Etat Sauvage, 1964; L'Apprenti Gaucher, 1967. Contbr. to: France-Soir; La Table Ronde; Arts. Recip., Prix Goncourt, 1964. Address: 159 rue de Rome, Paris 17, France.

CONDE ABELLÁN, Carmen, pen names DEL MAR, Florentina; NOGUERA, Magdalena, b. 15 Aug. 1907, Cartagena, Spain. Writer; Professor of Present Day Literature. Educ: Tchr. Trng.; Univ. Studies. Publs. incl: (poetry) Brocal, 1929; Obra Poética (1929-66), 1967; Canciones de la enamorada, 1971; (prose) Vidas contra su espejo (novel), 1944; Acompañando a Francisca Sánchez (Memories of Ruben Dario), 1964; Poesia femenina española viviente, 1955; Don Juan de Austria (jvnle.), 1943; Helen (Drama, w. Matilde Salvador), 1953. Contbr. to var. lit. jrnls.; Spanish radio & TV. Mbr. & VP, Ateneo of Madrid. Hons. incl: Doncel Children's Theatre Prize, 1965;

Nat. Poetry Prize, 1967; Nat. Lit. Prize, 1967. Address: Calle Ferroz 69, Buzón Postal 33, Madrid 8, Spain.

CONDIT, Carl Wilbur, b. 29 Sept. 1914, Cinn., Ohio, USA. University Professor. Educ: B.S., Purdue Univ., 1936; M.A., 1939, Ph.D., 1941, Univ. of Cinn. Publs. incl: The Rise of the Skyscraper, 1952; American Building Art: The 19th-Century, 1960; American Building Art: The 20th-Century, 1961; The Chicago School of Architecture, 1964; Chicago, 1910-29: Building, Planning, & Urban Technology, 1973; Chicago, 1930-70: Building, Planning, & Urban Technology, 1974. Contbr. to var. technol. jrnls. Mbr., var. technol. & histl. socs. Recip., sev. awards for technol. Address: 9300 Linder Ave., Morton Grove, IL 60053, USA.

CONDON, Richard, b. 18 Mar. 1915, NYC, USA. Novelist. Publs: The Oldest Confession, 1958; The Manchurian Candidate, 1959; Some Angry Angel, 1960; A Talent for Loving, 1961; An Infinity of Mirrors, 1964; Any God Will Do, 1966; The Ecstasy Business, 1967; Mile High, 1969; The Vertical Smile, 1971; Arigato, 1972; The Mexican Stove (w. Wendy Bennett), 1973; And Then We Moved to Rossenarra, 1973; Winter Kills, 1974; The Star Spangled Crunch, 1974; Money Is Love, 1975. Agent: Harold Matson, 22 East 40th St., N.Y., NY 10016, USA. Address: Rossenarra House, Kilmoganny, Co. Kilkenny, N. Ireland, UK.

CONE, Molly (Lamken), b. 3 Oct. 1918, Tacoma, Wash., USA. Author of Children's Books. Educ: Univ. of Wash., 1936-39. Publs. incl: Crazy Mary, 1966; Hurry Henrietta, 1966; Purim, 1967; The Other Side of the Fence, 1967; The House in the Tree, 1968; The Green Green Sea, 1968; Mishmash & Uncle Looey, 1968; Annie Annie, 1968; Leonard Bernstein, 1970; Simon, 1970; The Ringling Brothers, 1971; You Can't Make Me If I Don't Want To, 1971; Hear O Israel Story Books, 1971, 1972; Number Four, 1972; Dance Around the Fire, 1974. Mbrships. incl: Authors League Am.; Bd., Pacific N.W. Writers Conf., 1970, 1971, 1972; Wash. State Press Women. Hons. incl: 1st place award, Wash. Press Women, 1969, 1970; 1st place award, Nat. Fedn. Press Women, 1971. Address: 6500 50th Ave., N.E., Seattle, WA 98115, USA.

CONIL, Jean Marie Joseph, b. 28 Aug. 1917, Fontenay-le-Conte, Vendée, France. Master Chef; Food Technologist; Catering Consultant. Educ: B.Sc.; Adv. Dip., London Inst.; Dip. Ed. Publs. incl: Haute Cuisine, 1950; French Cookery, 1952; Gastronomic Tour of France, 1958; Epicurean Book, 1959. Contbr. to: Sunday Times; Woman's Own; Hotel Keeper; Food Review. Mbrships: Pres., Int. Culinary Inst.; Fellow, Hotel & Catering Inst.; Corres., Acad. Culinaire de Paris. Hons: Gold Medal, Culinary Competition, Bernes; Les Fourchettes d'Or, Comité de l'Excellence Européenne. Address: 282 Dollis Hill Lane, London NW2, UK.

CONLEY, Enid Mary Cooper, b. 30 Jan. 1917, Coffs Harbor, N.S.W., Australia. Writer. Educ: Cert. Shorthand Tchr. (Pitmans). Publs: The Dangerous Bombora, 1968; The Gully, 1975. Contbr. to: Aust. Women's Weekly; Woman's Day; The Australian. Mbrships: PEN; Pres., Soc. of Women Writers, 1974; A.S.A.; F.A.W.; Writers Guild; Tchr.'s Club. Address: 148 Cammeray Rd., Cammeray, Australia 2062.

CONLON, Kathleen Annie, b. 4 Jan. 1943, Southport, Lancs., UK. Writer. Educ: King's Coll., Durham. Publs: Apollo's Summer Look, 1968; Tomorrow's Fortune, 1971; My Father's House, 1972; A Twisted Skein, 1975. Mbr., Soc. of Authors. Address: 26A Brighton Rd., Birkdale, Southport, Merseyside, UK.

CONNELL, Brian Reginald, b. 12 Apr. 1916, London, UK. Author; Journalist; Broadcaster. Educ: Univs. of Madrid, Spain; Berlin, Germany. Publs. incl: Manifest Destiny; Portrait of a Whig Peer; The Plains of Abraham; Return of the Tiger; Regina v Palmerston: The Correspondence between Queen Victoria & Her Minister, 1837-65; Hitler: The Missing Years, 1922-34 (w. Hanfstaengl); A Silver Plated Spoon (w. the Duke of Bedford); The Grand Design (w. Franz Joseph Strauss); Ed. & Trans., Von Papen: Memoirs; The Bombard Story; Ed., Napier, The War in the Peninsula; Ed., Knox, Journal of the Campaigns in North America. Contbr. to: World Review; Economist; Fndr. Ed., European Review. Mbrships. incl: Exec. Comm., The Pilgrims; Inst. of Journlsts. Address: Rose Hall, Bungay, Suffolk, UK.

CONNELL, Evan Shelby Jr., b. 1924, Kansas City, Mo., USA. Writer. Educ: B.A.; Dartmouth Coll.; Univ. of Kan.; Stanford Univ.; Columbia Univ.; San. Fran. State Coll. Publs: The Anatomy Lesson & Other Stories; Mrs. Bridge; The Patriot. Contbr. to: Esquire; Am. Mercury; Western Review; Paris Review; New World Writing; & var. anthols. of short stories. Address: 2215 Drury Lane, Kansas City, Mo., USA.

CONNELL, William Fraser, b. 1916, Lockhart, N.S.W., Australia. University Reader & Professor of Education. Educ: Univs. of Melbourne, London & Illinois. Publs: The Educational Thought & Influence of Matthew Arnold, 1950; Growing Up in an Australian City, 1959; The Foundations of Secondary Education, 1961; (Ed.) The Foundations of Education, 1963; (co-author) Social Science for Secondary Schools, 1969; (co-author) China at School, 1974; (co-author) Twelve to Twenty: Studies of City Youth, 1975. Contbr. to: Year Book of Educ.; Aust. Jrnl. of Educ. (Ed., 1957-). Mbrships. incl: Social Sci. Rsch. Coun. of Aust.; Comp. Educ. Soc. of Europe. Hons: Vis. Fellow, Wolfson Coll., Univ. of Cambridge, UK, 1974. Address: 84 Bay St., Beauty Point, N.S.W., Australia.

CONNELLY, Marcus Cook, b. 13 Dec. 1890. Dramatist. Publs: The Green Pastures; The Wisdom Tooth; A Souvenir from Qam, 1965; Voices Off Stage, 1968; Beggar on Horseback (co-author); Dulcy (co-author); Merton of the Movies (co-author); To the Ladies (co-author); The Farmer Takes a Wife (co-author); Hunter's Moon (co-author); Helen of Troy N.Y. (musical comedy). Mbrships: Authors' League of Am.; Nat. Inst. of Arts & Letters. Hons: Pulitzer Prize; O. Henry Award, 1930; Litt.D, Bowdoin Coll. Address: 25 Ctrl. Pk. W., N.Y., NY, USA.

CONNER, Rearden, b. 1907, Southern Ireland. Writer. Publs: Shake Hands with the Devil; Rude Earth; I am Death; Men Must Live; The Sword of Love; To Kill is My Vocation; River, Sing Me a Song; Wife of Colum; The Devil Among the Tailors; My Love to the Gallows; Hunger of the Heart; The Singing Stone; The House of Cain; Kobo the Brave. Contbr. to: num. Brit. & Irish Newspapers & Periodicals; BBC; sev. Am. Periodicals; Radio Eireann; S. African Broadcasting Corp. Recip., M.B.E. Address: 25 Victoria St., Brighton BN1 3FQ, Sussex, UK.

CONNERS, Bernard F., b. 14 Sept. 1926, Albany, N.Y., USA. Businessman; Writer. Educ: B.A., St. Lawrence Univ., 1951. Publs: Don't Embarrass the Bureau (novel), 1972; Exec. Mgr., Paris Review (lit. quarterly). Mbr., var. bds. of bus. cos. Address: 60 Old Niskayuna Rd., Loudonville, NY 12211, USA.

CONNERY, Donald Stuart, b. 9 Feb. 1926, NYC, USA. Author; Writer; Political Reporter & Foreign Correspondent for Time & Life Magazines, 1951-64. Educ: A.B., Harvard Univ., 1950. Publs: The Scandinavians, 1966; The Irish, 1968; One American Town, 1972. Contbr. to: Harper's; Saturday Review; etc. Mbrships: Authors' League, N.Y.; Harvard Club, N.Y. Address: Skiff Mtn. Rd., CT 06757, USA.

CONNOR, Herbert, b. 5 Dec. 1907, Berlin, Germany. Composer; Radio Producer. Educ: Sternsches Konservatorium, Berlin. Publs. incl: Fran Mose till Schweitzer, 1948; Lyssna och spela, 1955; Cantus I–II, 1969; Samtal tonsättare, 1971; Kalender för otidensliga, 1973; Rapport från en själavandring, 1973; Nikotinmördaren, 1974; Svensk musik, 1974. Contbr. to: Svenska Dagbladet; Dagens Nyheter; Musikrevy. Mbr., Sveriges Författarförbund. Hons: Annual Writers' Award, Swedish Tonsetzergenossenschaft, 1971; Nat. Artist's Award, 1972. Address: Bultvägen 24, 126 38 Hägersten, Sweden.

CONQUEST, Robert, b. 15 July 1917, Gt. Malvern, UK. Writer. Educ: Univ. of Grenoble, France; M.A., Oxford Univ., UK. Publs: Poems, 1955; A World of Difference, 1955; Common Sense about Russia, 1960; Courage of Genius: the Pasternak Affair, 1961; Power & Policy in the USSR, 1962; Between Mars & Venus, 1962; Russia after Khrushchev, 1965; The Egyptologists (w. Kingsley Amis), 1965; The Great Terror, 1968; Arias from a Love Opera, 1969; The Nation Killers, 1970; Lenin, 1972. Contbr. to: Times Lit. Supplement; Encounter; N.Y. Times Mag.; Analog Sci. Fiction; Daily Telegraph; Commentary; & num. other jrnls. Mbrships: F.R.S.L.; Sci. Fiction Writers of Am. Hons: O.B.E., 1955; PEN Poetry Prize; Festival of Britain Poetry Prize. Address: 4 York Mansions, Prince of Wales Drive, London SW11, UK.

CONRAD, Isaac John, pen name CONRAD, Jack, b. 1912, London, UK. Commercial Foreign Correspondent, Linguist & Translator. Educ: City of London Coll.; Holborn Coll. of Law & Langs. Publs: Transl., Le Destin et La Chance, by A. Tanagras, w. Am. ed. under title of Psychophysical Elements in Parapsychological Traditions. Contbr. of transls. to var. trade & psychic jrnls. Mbrships: Fellow, Inst. of Linguists; Transls.' Guild; Transls.' Assn. of Soc. of Authors. Address: 9 Wentworth Close, Finchley, London N3, UK.

CONROY, Jack (John Wesley), pen names NORCROSS, John; BRENNAN, Tim; MORINE, Hoder, b. 5 Dec. 1899, Moberly, Mo., USA. Novelist; Editor. Critic. Encyclopedist. Educ: Univ. of Mo. Num. publs. incl: The Disinherited (novel), 1933, 1963; The Fast Sooner Hound, Slappy Hooper, (juveniles, w. A. Bontemps), 1946; They Seek A City (non-fiction, w. A. Bontemps), 1945; Ed., w. Ralph Cheyney, Unrest, annual anthols. of verse, 1929-31; Ed., w. Curt Johnson, Writers in Revolt: The Anvil Anthology, 1933-40, 1973. Contbr. to mags., newspapers. Mbr., Soc. of Midland Authors & VP for Mo. Hons: Guggenheim Mem. Fellowship for Creative Writing, 1935; James L. Dow Award, Soc. of Midland Authors, 1967; Literary Times Award, 1967; Louis M. Rabinowitz Fndn. Grant, 1968. Address: 701 Fisk Ave., Moberly, MO 65270, USA.

CONSTANDSE, Anton Levien, b. 13 Sept., 1899, Brouwershaven, Netherlands. Editor. Professor. Educ: Litt.D., Univ. of Amsterdam. Publs. incl: Principles of Atheism, 1926; Suicide of Protestantism, 1926; Aryan Culture & Prussianism, 1935; Principles of Anarchism, 1938; Image & Balance of Our Century, 1960; History of Humanism in the Netherlands, 1967; Ed., De Gids monthly review. Contbr. to: Vrÿ Nederland (weekly). Mbrships: PEN; European Soc. of Culture. Recip., Van Praag Prize for humanistic culture, 1973. Address: Zonnebloemstraat 57, Haarlem, Netherlands.

CONSTANDUROS, Denis Stephanos, b. 22 July 1910, Sutton, Surrey, UK. Script Writer. Publs: My Grandfather, 1948; BBC Classic Serials inclng: The Ambassadors, What Maisie Knew, The Spoils of Poynton (Henry James), Sense & Sensibility, Emma (Jane Austen). Contbr. to: At the Luscombes, BBC W. Reg.; BBC TV. Mbr., TV & Screenwriters Guild. Agent: Harvey Unna. Address: Squarey's, Coombe Bissett, Near Salisbury, Wilts., UK.

CONSTANT, Clinton, b. 20 Mar. 1912, Nelson, B.C., Can. Chemical Engineer; Author. Educ: B.Sc., Univ. Alta., 1935; Western Reserve Univ., USA, 1939. Publs: The War of the Universe, 1931; The Martian Menace, 1931. Contbr. to num. tech. articles & reports on astron., chem. & rocketry. Mbrships. incl: Am. Inst. Chem. Engrs.; Am. Chem. Soc.; Royal Astronomical Soc. Can.; Am. Inst. Aeronautics & Astronautics; Am. Water Works Assn.; N.Y. Acad. Scis. Hons: Fellow, Am. Inst. Chems.; Fellow, AAAS. Address: P.O. Box 1221, Atlanta, GA 30301, USA.

CONSTANTINESCU, Petre, pen name EVERAC, Paul, b. 23 Aug. 1924, Bucharest, Romania. Lawyer; Playwright. Educ: M.L. Publs. incl: (plays) The Door, 1959; Open Windows, 1959; The Discovery, 1959; Blue Eye, 1960; Nothing But Coincidences, 1966; Downstairs, 1967; Who Are You?, 1968; The Next Room, 1969; Counterpoints, 1970; A Butterfly on the Lamp, 1972; Life is Like a Wagon, 1973; The Surveyor, 1973; (essays) About Intelligence, 1969; Thesis & Antithesis, 1971; (poetry) Discursive Poems, 1971. Contbr. to var. mags. & newspapers. Mbr., Writers' Union of Romania. Hons. incl: Writers' Union Prizes, 1966, 1971; Culture Ministry Prizes, 1959, 1967, 1971. Address: Bucharest, Piata Romaná 9E, Romania.

CONWAY, Alan Arthur, b. 10 May 1920, Torquay, UK. Professor of American History; Author. Educ: B.A., M.A., London Univ.; Ph.D., Univ. of Wales. Publs: The Welsh in America, 1961; The Reconstruction of Georgia, 1966; Soldier-Surgeon: Crimean War Letters of Douglas A. Reid, 1968. Contbr. to: Histl. Assn.; Nat. Llb. of Wales Jrnl.; La. Studies; Pacific Circle; Civil War Hist.; Kan. Hist. Quarterly; British Columbia Quarterly. Address: Univ. of Canterbury, Christchurch, NZ.

CONWAY, Harry Donald, b. 3 Dec. 1917, Chatham, UK. Professor of Engineering Mechanics, Cornell University. Educ: M.A., Sc.D., Univ. of Cambridge; B.Sc., Ph.D., & D.Sc., Univ. of London. Publs: Aircraft Strength of Materials; Mechanics of Materials. Contbr. to: Jrnl. of Applied Mech.; Transactions of Am. Soc. of Civil Engrs.;

Zeitschrift angew. Math. Mech.; Zeitschrift angew. Math. Physik; Ingenieur Archiv. Mbr., Ed. Advsry. Bd., Int. Jrnl. of Mech. Scis. Address: Dept. of Mechanics, Thurston Hall, Cornell Univ., Ithaca, NY 14853, USA.

CONZE, Edward, b. 1904, London, UK. Author; Translator. Educ: Ph.D. Publs: Buddhism, 1951; Buddhist Meditation, 1956; Buddhist Thought in India, 1962; Thirty Years of Buddhist Studies, 1968. Publs. incl: (transls.) Abhisamayalankara, 1954; Vajracchedika, 1957; Buddhist Scriptures, 1959; The Large Sutra on Perfect Widsom, 1961; & num. others. Contbr. to: Jrnl. of Royal Asiatic Soc.; Hibbert Jrnl. Address: Foxwell, Marston Rd., Sherborne, Dorset DT9 4BN, UK.

COOK, Charles Thomas, b. 1886, London, UK. Baptist Minister; Consultant Editor, The Christian. Educ: D.D., Spurgeon's Bapt. Theol. Coll., London. Publs: Behold the Throne of Grace; The Billy Graham Story; London Hears Billy Graham; Tell Me about Moody. Contbr. to: The Christian; sev. other Brit. & Am. evangelical jrnls. Address: 14 Church Rd., Shortlands, Kent, UK.

COOK, Christal, b. 5 Apr. 1940, Isleworth, UK. Senior Lecturer in Religious Studies, College of Education. Educ: B.D., Univ. of London. Publs: The Face of God, 1969. Address: 100 Croham Valley Rd., South Croydon, Surrey CR2 7JD, UK.

COOK, Ramona Graham, b. San Miguel, Calif., USA. Writer. Educ: Cornell Coll.; IA.; Thomas Norman Trng. (Detroit, Mich.); D.Mus. Publs: From Boston, 1936; Hills of New England, 1946; What the Heart Creates, 1956. Contbr. to jrnls. inclng: Am. Schlr.; Sat. Evening Post; Yankee Mag.; The Villager; N.Y. Times; Christian Sci. Monitor; The Blue Moon; Am. Poetry Mag. Mbrships. incl: Authors' League; New Engl. Poetry Club; Boston Authors' Club. Address: 12 Woodcliff Rd., Wellesley Hill, MA, USA.

COOKE, Alfred Alistair, b. 20 Nov. 1908. Journalist; Broadcaster. Educ: Jesus Coll., Cambridge; Yale Univ.; Harvard Univ. Publs: (Ed.) Garbo & the Night Watchman, 1937; A Generation on Trial: USA vs Alger Hiss, 1950; Letters from America, 1951; Christmas Eve, 1952; A Commencement Address, 1954; Douglas Fairbanks: The Making of a Screen Character, 1954; (Ed.) The Vintage Mencken, 1955; Around the World in 50 Years, 1966; Talk About America, 1968; Alistair Cooke's America, 1973. Contbr. to: Guardian; NBC; BBC; Daily Herald; etc. Hons. incl: K.B.E., 1973; Peabody Award, 1972; Benjamin Franklin Medal, 1973. Address: 1150 Fifth Ave., NYC, N.Y., USA.

COOKE, Cranmer Kenrick, b. 21 Aug. 1906, Keynsham, UK. Co-ordinator of Monuments & Keeper of Antiquities, National Museums & Monuments of Rhodesia. Publs: The Rock Art of Southern Africa; A Guide to the Rock Art of Rhodesia; The Rock Art of the Federation of Rhodesia & Nyasaland (co-author); The Monuments of Rhodesia: A Bibliography of Rhodesian Archaeology from 1874. Contbr. to num. sci. jrnls. Mbrships. incl: Fellow, Soc. of Antiquaries, London; Fellow, Royal Anthropol. Soc. Address: P.O. Box 3248, Bulawayo, Rhodesia.

COOKE, Geoffrey Walter, b. 25 Aug. 1924, Sydenham, London, UK. Financial Director, Marine Engineering Company. Educ: Radio Schl. & Radio Instructors' Trng. Schl., Cranwell. Publs: Death Can Wait, 1957; Death is the End, 1965; Death Takes a Dive, 1962. Mbrships: Crime Writers' Assn; Writers' Guild. Address: 1 Manor Cottage, Down Thomas, Plymouth PL9 0AL, Devon, UK.

COOKE, Jacob Ernest, b. 23 Sept. 1924, Aulander, N.C., USA. MacCracken Professor of History, Lafayette College, Pennsylvania. Educ: Ph.D., Columbia Univ. Publs: Frederick Bancroft: Historian, 1956; Assoc. Ed., Papers of Alexander Hamilton, 15 vols., 1961-71; The Age of Responsibility, 1946-60, 1965; The Kennedy Years, 1965; Ed., Alexander Hamilton: A Profile, 1967. Mbrships. incl: Am. Histl. Assn.; Org. Am. Histns.; Columbia Univ. Seminars. Hons: Davie Schlrship., Univ. N.C., 1947; Jones Award, Lafayette Coll., 1964; Guggenheim Fellow, 1968-69; Nat. Humanities Award, 1972. Address: Dept. Hist., Lafayette Coll., Easton, PA 18042, USA.

COOKSON, Catherine Ann, pen names MARCHANT, Catherine; McMULLEN, Catherine, b. 20 June 1906, Leam Lane, S. Shields, UK. Writer. Publs. incl: Kate Hannigan, 1950; Rooney; The Garment; The Blind Miller; Hannah Massey; The Long Corridor; The Unbaited Trap; Katie

Mulholland; The Round Tower; The Nice Bloke; The Glass Virgin; Our Kate (autobiog.); The Invitation; The Dwelling Place; Feathers in the Fire; Pure as the Lily; The Mallen Trilogy; The Mary Ann Series (8 books). Mbrships: Soc. of Authors; Am. Guild of Authors. Recip., Winifred Holtby Award for Best Reg. Novel, Royal Soc. of Lit., 1968. Address: Loreto, St. Helen's Park Rd., Hastings, Sussex, UK.

COOLE, Arthur Braddan, b. 6 Jan. 1900, Birmingham, Kan., USA. Methodist Minister; Educator. Educ: A.B., Baker Univ., 1921; M.A., Univ. of Denver, 1922; Iliff Schl. of Theol.; M.S., Univ. of Denver; M.A., Calif. Coll. in China, Peiping, 1940. Publs. incl: A Commercial Geography of China, 1931; Coins in China's History, 1936, 4th ed., 1965; An Encyclopedia of Chinese Coins, vol. I, 1967, vol. II, 1973, vol. III, 1973, 6 or 7 more vols. planned. Contbr. to relig., numismatic jrnls. Address: 219 S. Williams St., Denver, CO 80209, USA.

COOMBES, Henry, b. 9 June 1909, Tewkesbury, UK. Lecturer; Teacher; Author. Educ: M.A., Queens' Coll., Cambridge. Publs: Literature & Criticism, 1953, etc.; Edward Thomas, 1956, etc.; T. F. Powys, 1960; Penguin Critical Anthology: D. H. Lawrence, 1973. Contbr. to: The Human World; The Use of Engl.; Books & Bookmen; Essays in Criticism; Southern Review, La., USA. Address: Southernwood, Daisy Bank Rd., Cheltenham, Glos., UK.

COOMBS, Joyce, pen name HALES, Joyce, b. 9 Mar. 1906, Tettenhall, Staffs., UK. Lecturer; Social Worker; Historical Researcher. Educ: Westfield Coll., Univ. of London. Publs. incl: George & Mary Sumner: Their Life & Times, 1965; Judgement on Hatcham, 1969; One Hundred Years on the Hill, 1970. Contbr. to: Times Educl. Supplement; Ch. Observer; Time & Tide; Anglican World; Scotland's Mag.; etc. Mbrships. incl: Ecclesiastical Hist. Soc.; Soc. of the Earth; Authors' Victorian Soc. Address: 2 Victoria Avenue, Finchley, London N3 1BD, UK.

COOMBS, Patricia Jane, b. 23 July, 1926, L.A., Calif., USA. Author & Illustrator, Children's Books. Educ: B.A., M.A., Univ. of Washington, Seattle. Publs: Dorrie & The Blue Witch, 1964; Dorrie & The Weather-Box, 1966; Dorrie & The Witch Doctor, 1967; Dorrie & The Wizard's Spell, 1968; Lisa & The Grompet, 1970; Dorrie & The Haunted House, 1970; Dorrie & The Birthday Eggs, 1971; Mouse Cafe, 1972; Dorrie & The Goblin, 1972; Dorrie & The Fortune-Teller, 1973; Dorrie & The Amazing Magic Elixir, 1974. Mbr., Authors' Guild of the Authors' League of Am. Hons: N.Y. Times 10 Best Illustrated Books for Mouse Cafe. Address: 178 Oswegatchie Rd., Waterford, Conn., USA.

COON, Carleton Stevens, b. 1904, Wakefield, Mass., USA. Professor & Museum Curator, Univ. of Pennsylvania. Educ: Philips Acad., Andover; Harvard; AB; MA; Ph.D. Publs: Tribes of the Rif, vol. 9, 1931; Flesh of the Wild Ox, 1933; Measuring Ethiopia, 1935; The Races of Europe, 1939; Principles of Anthropology, (w. E. D. Chapple) 1942; Races, (w. S. M. Garn & J. B. Birdsell); Reader in General Anthropology, 1948; The Mountains of Giants, vol. 23, no. 3., 1950; Caravan 1951, 1958; The Story of Man, 1953-62; The Seven Caves, 1957; The Origin of Races, 1962; The Living Races of Man, 1965. Address: 207 Concord St. W., Gloucester, MA 01930, USA.

COONE, William Richard, b. 8 Feb. 1934, Hudson, N.Y., USA. Teacher; Writer. Educ: B.A., State Univ. Binghamton, N.Y.; M.A., Cornell Univ., Ithaca, N.Y. Publs: Attica Diary, 1972. Contbr. to: N.Y. Times Sunday Sect.; N.Y. Times Book Sect.; Wilson Lib. Review; Alfred Hitchcock's Mystery Mag.; Playboy. Address: 224 Hawley Ave., Syracuse, NY 13203, USA.

COONEY, Ray, b. 1932, London, UK. Former Actor; Writer; Stage Director; Stage Producer. Publs: One for the Pot (w. T. Hilton), 1964; Chase Me Comrade, 1967; My Giddy Aunt (w. J. Chapman), 1970; Not Now Darling (w. J. Chapman), 1970; Bang Bang Beirut (w. T. Hilton), 1971; Move Over Mrs. Markham (w. J. Chapman), 1971; Why Not Stay for Breakfast (w. G. Stone), 1971; Charlie Girl; There Goes the Bride (w. J. Chapman), 1973. Mbrships: Dramatists' Guild; Soc. of West-End Mgrs.; Equity. Agent: Lawrence Fitch. Address: Suite 50, 26 Charing Cross Rd., London WC2, UK.

COOPER, Barbara, b. 1915, Loughborough, UK. Economist; Market Researcher. Educ: B.Sc.Econ., Univ. of Nottingham. Publs: Target for Malice, 1964. Drown Him

Deep, 1966; Who is my Enemy, 1967; House of Masks, 1968. Mbrships: NZ Ctr., PEN; Crime Writers' Assn. Address: P.O. Box 33, Turangi, NZ.

COOPER, Barbara Ann, b. 1929, Denbigh, UK. Author & Editor. Publs: Badminton Three Day Event; BOAC Book of Flight; Ed. & Co-author, Travellers' Digest; Ed., The Speedbird Book; Ed., Explorer 1; Ed., Explorer 2; Ed., sev. BOAC guides to Am., Pacific, & Orient; Ed., Horse Trials Handbook; Co-Ed., World Wildlife Guide; Co-Ed., World Museums Guide. Contbr. to sev. mags. & jrnls., & to TV & radio. Address: Lingwood, Grayswood, Haslemere, Surrey, UK.

COOPER, Brian Newman, b. 15 Sept. 1919, Stockport, UK. Schoolmaster; Author. Educ: Jesus Coll., Cambridge, 1938-40, 1946; M.A.(Cantab.), 1944; Cambridge Univ. Dept. of Educ., 1946-47; Dip.Ed., 1947. Publs: Where The Fresh Grass Grows, 1955; A Path to the Bridge, 1958; The Van Langeren Girl, 1960; A Touch of Thunder, 1961; A Time to Retreat, 1963; Genesis 38, 1965; A Mission for Betty Smith, 1967. Mbr., PEN. Address: 43 Parkland Close, Southlands, Mansfield, Notts., UK.

COOPER, Bryan Robert Wright, b. 6 Feb. 1932, Paris, France. Writer. Publs: North Sea Oil: The Great Gamble, 1966; The Ironclads of Cambrai, 1967; The Buccaneers, 1970; Battle of the Torpedo Boats, 1970; Alaska — The Last Frontier, 1972; Fighter, 1973; Tank Battles of World War I, 1974; Bomber, 1974; Stones of Evil, 1974. Mbrships: Writers' Guild of G.B.; London Press Club. Address: Hurst Farm House, Weald, Sevenoaks, Kent, UK.

COOPER, Colin Symons, b. 1926, Birkenhead, UK. Educational Researcher; Author; Dramatist. Publs: (plays) Riches & Rags, 1957; The Diamond Tooth, 1960; (novels) The Thunder & Lightening Man, 1968; Outcrop, 1969. Contbr. to: BBC; London Weekend TV. Mbrships: Soc. of Authors; Writers' Guild of GB. Address: 25 Warner Rd., London N8, UK.

COOPER, (Lady) Diana, (Diana, Viscountess Norwich), b. 29 Aug. 1892. Publs: (autobiogs.) The Rainbow Comes & Goes, 1958; The Light of Common Day, 1959; Trumpets from the Steep. Address: 10 Warwick Ave., London W2, UK.

COOPER, Edmund, pen name AVERY, Richard, b. 30 Apr. 1926, Marple, UK. Novelist. Educ: Didsbury Teachers' Training Coll.; Coll. of Int. Marine Telecomms. Publs. incl: The Uncertain Midnight, 1958, 4th ed., 1974; Seed of Light, 1959, 2nd ed., 1960; Transit, 1964, 4th ed., 1974; A Far Sunset, 1967, 3rd ed., 1973; The Last Continent, 1970, 3rd ed., 1974; Kronk, 1970, 2nd ed., 1972; The Overman Culture, 1971, 2nd ed., 1974; The Cloud Walker, 1973; The 10th Planet, 1973; Prisoner of Fire, 1974; The Slaves of Heaven (forthcoming). Contbr. to: London Sunday Times (Sci. Fiction Critic). Mbr., PEN. Address: "Stammers", Madehurst, Arundel, Sussex, UK.

COOPER, George William Noel, b. 21 July 1896, Hagerstown, Md., USA. Physician & Surgeon; Poet; Author. Educ: B.S., Univ. of Mich., 1919; M.D., Wayne State Univ., 1922; M.A., Western Reserve Univ., 1929. Publs: Poems For Peace, 1949; Lace of Sonnets, 1961; Russianism or Christ, 1964; History of The International Boswell Institute, 1971. Contbr. to: Gray's Anatomy, 100th Anniversary Ed.; N.Y. Times; Southern Review; Atlanta Constitution. Mbr. & Off., lit. & poetry orgs. Hons. incl: 2nd Prize for Best Book of Poetry, N.Y. Times, 1949; Chevalier de l'ordre de Palmes Academiques, 1961; Poet Laureate, 150th Anniversary Celebrations, New Orleans, La., 1968; Poet Laureate, State of La., 1973. Address: 7307 St. Charles Ave., New Orleans, LA 70118, USA.

COOPER, Jean Campbell (Mrs. V. M. Cooper), b. 27 Nov. 1905, Chefoo, N. China. Lecturer; Writer. Educ: L.L.A., St. Andrews Univ., UK. Publs: Taoism, the Way of the Mystic, 1972. Contbr. to Studies in Comp. Relig. (transls., reviews). Mbrships: Life, Royal C'wlth. Soc.; J.P. Address: Bobbin Mill, Ulpha, Broughton-in-Furness, Cumbria, UK.

COOPER, Jeffrey, b. 16 Nov. 1943, Didcot, Berks., UK. Librarian. Publs: A Bibliography & Notes on the Works of Lascelles Abercrombie, 1969. Mbrships: Lib. Assn.; Bibliographical Soc.; Printing Histl. Soc.; Pvte. Libs. Assn. Address: 160 Milton Street, Southport, Merseyside, UK.

COOPER, Jilly, b. 21 Feb. 1937, Hornchurch, UK. Journalist; Author. Publs: How to Stay Married, 1969; How to Survive from Nine to Five, 1970; Jolly Super, 1971; Jolly Super Too, 1972; Men & Supermen, 1972; Women & Superwomen, 1974. Contbr. to: Sunday Times (Columnist, 1969-); Vogue; Harpers; 19; TV & Radio Times. Agent: George Greenfield. Address: c/o Sunday Times, 200 Gray's Inn Rd., London WC1X 8EZ , UK.

COOPER, Lee Pelham, b. 4 Nov. 1926, Okla., USA. Writer. Educ: B.A., Mary Washington Coll., Univ. of Va.; Univ. of Mexico; Univ. of Heidelberg. Publs: Fun with Spanish, 1960; Fun with French, 1963; Fun with Italian, 1964; Fun with German, 1965; More Fun with Spanish, 1967; Five Fables from France, 1970; The Chinese Language, 1971; The Pirate of Puerto Rico, 1972. Contbr. to periodicals. Hons. AAUW Award, Va. State short story contest, children's div., 1959. Address: 1711 Highland Rd., Fredericksburg, VA 22401, USA.

COOPER, Lettice (Ulpha), b. 3 Sept. 1897, Eccles, Lancs., UK. Author. Educ: Lady Margaret Hall, Oxford. Publs: (novels) National Provincial, 1938; Fenny, 1953; The Double Heart, 1962; Late in the Afternoon, 1971; (biog.) Robert Louis Stevenson, 1947, 1967; Tea on Sunday, 1973; var. children's books. Contbr. to: London Mag.; Listener; Times Lit. Suppl.; Sunday Telegraph; Yorks. Post. Mbrships: PEN; V.P., Engl. Ctr.; Mgmt. Comm., Authors Soc., 1974-. Address: 95 Canfield Gardens, London, NW6 3DY, UK.

COOPER, Mae, pen names FAREWELL, Nina; COOPER-KLEIN, Nina, b. 5 June 1923, NYC, USA. Writer. Educ: Grad., Cooper Union Art Schl.; Grad., Dramatic Workshop; Bklyn. Coll. Publs: Lily Henry, 1948; w. Grace Klein: The Unfair Sex, 1953; Someone to Love, 1959; Daughter of Ishtar, 1962; Every Girl is Entitled to a Husband, 1963; Here Comes the Bride, 1964; Boy & the Square Uncle, 1966. Mbr., New Dramatists. Address: 265 Stratford Rd., Brooklyn, NY 11218, USA.

COOPER, Martin Du Pré, b. 17 Jan. 1910, Winchester, UK. Music Critic; Writer. Educ: St. Edmund Hall, Oxford; studied music w. Egon Wellesz, Vienna, 1932-34. Publs: Gluck, 1935; Bizet, 1938; Opéra Comique, 1949; French Music from the Death of Berlioz to the Death of Fauré, 1951; Russian Opera, 1951; Les Musiciens anglais d'aujourd'hui, 1952; Ideas & Music, 1966; Beethoven — the last decade, 1970. Contbr. to jrnls. inclng: The Spectator; Daily Telegraph (Music Ed., 1954-); Musical Times. Mbr., Ed. Bd., New Oxford History of Music, 1961-. Recip., CBE. Address: 12 Campden Hill Ct., London W8, UK.

COOPER, Paulette, b. 26 July 1944, Antwerp, Belgium. Writer. Educ: B.A., Brandeis Univ.; M.A., CUNY. Publs: Halloween, 1971; The Scandal of Scientology, 1971. Growing Up Puerto Rican, 1972; The Medical Detectives, 1973. Contbr. to: Sunday Times (London); N.Y. Times; Wash. Post; N.Y. Post; Christian Sci. Monitor; etc. Mbrships: Authors' League; Soc. Mag. Writers; Am. Med. Writers; Mystery Writers Am. Recip., Special Award, Mystery Writers Am. Address: 300 E. 40th St., N.Y., NY 10016, USA.

COOPER, Wendy, b. 1919, Sutton Coldfield, Warwicks., UK. Broadcaster; Freelance Journalist. Publs: Children's Books; Hair — Sexual & Social Significance; No Change — A Biological Revolution for Women. Contbr. to: Observer; London Evening News; Weekend Telegraph; Observer Colour Mag.; Good Housekeeping; Nova; Cosmopolitan; Homes & Gardens; Sunday Mirror; Guardian. Mbr., N.C.C.L. Recip., Hannen Swaffer Award, Woman Jrnlst. of Yr., 1965. Agent: David Higham Assocs. Address: 32 Vesey Rd., Sutton Coldfield, Warwicks., UK.

COOPER, William (Harry Summerfield Hoff), b. 1910, Crewe, UK. Assistant Director, Civil Service Selection Board; Novelist; Playwright. Educ: B.Sc., M.A., Cambridge Univ. Publs: Scenes from Provincial Life; The Struggles of Albert Woods; The Ever-interesting Topic; Disquiet & Peace; Young People; Scenes from Married Life; Memoirs of a New Man; You Want the Right Frame of Reference; Love on the Coast; Prince Genji (play); British Council Series, Writers & Their Work No. 115; C. P. Snow. Mbr., Savile Club. Address: 14 Keswick Rd., London SW15, UK.

COOPER, William Heaton, b. 6 Oct. 1903, Coniston, Cumbria, UK. Landscape Painter; Author. Educ: Royal Acad. Schl., London. Publs: The Hills of Lakeland, 1938, 1947; Lakeland Portraits, 1954; The Tarns of Lakeland, 1960, 1970; The Lakes, 1970. Contbr. to: Studio; BBC. Mbrships: Past Pres., Lake Artists' Soc.; Hon. Mbr., Fell &

Rock Climbing Club. Address: The Studio, Grasmere, Ambleside, Cumbria, UK.

COOPER, (Sir) William Mansfield, b. 20 Feb. 1903, Manchester, UK. Barrister-at-Law, Gray's Inn; Emeritus Professor. Educ: LL.M., Manchester Univ., 1936. Publs: Outlines of Industrial Law, 1947, 6th ed., 1972; Contbr., The United Nations: The 1st Ten Years, 1957; Hall of Residence, 1957; Modern Trends in Occupational Health, 1960; Dalton Hall, 1963; Governments & The University, 1966. Contbr. to var. legal & educl. jrnls.; Minerva; etc. Hons. incl: Knighthood, 1963; num. hon. degrees. Address: Fieldgate Cottage, 9 Station Rd., Meldreth, Royston, Herts. SG8 6JP, UK.

COOVER, Robert, b. 4 Feb. 1932, Charles City, Iowa, USA. Writer. Educ: S. Ill. Univ., Carbondale, 1949-51; B.A., Ind. Univ., Bloomington, 1953; M.A., Univ. of Chgo., 1965. Publs: (novels) The Origin of the Brunists, 1966; The Universal Baseball Association, Inc., J. Henry Waugh, Prop., 1968; Pricksongs & Descants (short stories), 1969. Contbr. to: Noble Savage; Evergreen Review; Cavalier; New Am. Review 4; Iowa Review; Tri-Quarterly; New Am. Review 12. Hons: Faulkner Award, 1966; Creative Arts Award, Brandeis Univ., 1969. Address: c/o E. P. Dutton & Co., 201 Park Ave. South, N.Y., NY 10003, USA.

COPE, Jack, b. Mooi Rivar, Natal, S. Africa. Editor; Journalist. Publs: Marie, a satire; The Fair House; The Golden Oriole; The Road to Ysterberg; The Tame Ox & Other Stories; Albino; The Man Who Doubted; The Dawn Comes Twice; The Rain Maker; (biography) Comrade Bill; (poems) Lyrics & Diatribes; (transl.) Selected Poems by Ingrid Jonker (w. W. Plomer). Contbr. to: New Yorker; Esquire; Fndr. & Ed., Contrast, S. African Lit. Quarterly; London Mag., Paris Review; The Penguin Book of S. African Verse; John Bull; Mademoiselle; Harper's; Poet's In S. Africa, etc. Mbr., PEN. Address: Sea Girt, Second Beach, Clifton, Capetown, S. Africa.

COPELAND, Thomas Wellsted, b. 10 July, 1907, E. Cleveland, Ohio, USA. Teacher. Educ: A.B., 1928, Ph.D., 1933, Yale. Publs: Our Eminent Friend Edmund Burke, 1949; A Checklist of the Correspondence of Edmund Burke (compiled w. Milton S. Smith), 1955; The Correspondence of Edmund Burke, vol. I, 1958. Hons: Litt.D., Univ. of Sheffield, UK, 1972 & Univ. of Dublin, Repub. of Ireland, 1973. Address: 251 Sunset Ave., Amherst, MA 01002, USA.

COPEMAN, George Henry, b. 19 Feb. 1922. Management Consultant. Educ: Ph.D., London Schl. of Econs. Publs: The Challenge of Employee Shareholding, 1958; The Role of the Managing Director, 1959; The Chief Executive & Business Growth, 1971; Capital as an Incentive (w. Tony Rumble), 1972; Employee Share Ownership & Industrial Stability, 1975. Mbrships: Inst. of Dirs.; Soc. of Bus. Econs.; Wider Share Ownership Counc.; Assn. of Tchrs. of Mgmt. Address: Sheridan, Woodland Way, Kingswood, Surrey, UK.

COPIC, Branko, b. 1915. Writer. Educ: Belgrade Univ. Publs. incl: A Warrior's Spring; Fighters & Fugitives; Dew on the Bayonets; Partisan Stories; sev. vols. of verse. Hons. incl: sev. Yugoslav lit. awards; Order of Meritorious Serv. to the People, 1st & 2nd class; Order of Brotherhood & Unity; 1st class; 1941 Partisan Commemoration Medal. Address: c/o Yugoslav Acad. of Scis. & Arts, Zrinski trg. II, Zagreb I, Yugoslavia.

COPLESTON, Frederick Charles, b. 10 Apr. 1907, Taunton, UK. Roman Catholic Priest; University Professor. Educ: M.A., Oxford, 1925-29; D.Phil., Gregorian Univ., Rome, Italy. Publs: A History of Philosophy, 9 vols., 1946-74; Nietzsche, 1942, 1974; Schopenhauer, 1946; Aquinas, 1955; Contemporary Philosophy, 1956, 1972; A History of Medieval Philosophy, 1972; Religion & Philosophy, 1974. Contbr. to: Mind, Philos.; Heythrop Jrnl.; Review of Metaphysics, etc. Mbrships: Fellow, Brit. Acad., 1970; Coun. & Exec. Comm., Royal Inst. of Philos.; Aristotelian Soc. Address: 114 Mount St., London W1Y 6AH, UK.

COPPAGE, George Herman, pen name JUBILATE, b. 5 Sept. 1922, Pearson, Md., USA. Poet; Cab Dispatcher. Educ: A.B., Wash. Coll.; S.T.B., Temple Univ. Publs: World Cathedralic, 1968. Contbr. to var. jrnls.; own radio prog., Jubilate Speaks, WKIK, Leonardstown, Md. Mbr., Int.

Poetry Soc. Hons. incl: Annapolis Fine Arts Fest. Silver Pitcher, Md. Poetry Soc. Poetry Reading Contest, 1970; State, area trophies, Toastmasters Int. Address: Box 154, Valhalla, Lexington Pk., MD 20653, USA.

COPPER, Basil, b. 1924, London, UK. Journalist; News Editor; Author. Publs. incl: The Dark Mirror, 1966; No Flowers for the General, 1967; Not After Nightfall, 1967; Scratch On the Dark, 1967; Die Now, Live Later, 1968; Don't Bleed on Me, 1968; The Marble Orchard, 1969; Lead File, 1970; No Letters from the Grave, 1971; From Evil's Pillow, 1971; The Vampire; In Legend, Fact & Art, 1971; The Big Chill, 1972; Strong-Arm, 1972; A Great Year for Dying, 1973; Shock-Wave, 1973; The Breaking Point, 1973; A Voice from the Dead, 1974; Ricochet, 1974; The High Wall, 1975; The Great White Space, 1975; When Footsteps Echo, 1975. Contbr. to: Argosy Mag.; num. books & anthols. Mbrships. incl: Soc. of Authors; Crime Writers' Assn. Address: Stockdoves, S.Pk., Sevenoaks, Kent, UK.

CORBETT, John Ambrose, b. 4 May 1908, Wadsley Bridge, Yorks., UK. Retired Director of Education. Publs: Essentials of Modern German Grammar, 1935, 48; Revision Exercises in German, 1937; French Word Book, 1938; Engl. version of Presse Querschnitt, by Bertil Ekholm-Erb, 1974; Basic French Grammar (w. Anne Johnson), 1975. Contbr. of transls. to: Educ., Inst. für Wissenschaftliche Zusammenarbeit, Tübingen, Germany. Address: Annables, High Halden, Ashford, TN26 3NA, UK.

CORBETT, Scott, b. 1913, Kan. City, USA. Author. Educ: B.J., Univ. of Mo. Publs. incl: (children's books) Ever Ride a Dinosaur?, Diamonds are More Trouble, Rhode Island (all 1969); What Makes a Boat Float? The Baseball Bargain, The Mystery Man, Steady Freddie (all 1970); The Hockey Trick, The Great Custard Pie Panic, The Case of the Silver Skull, Here Lies the Body, Take a Number, What About the Wankel Engine? (all 1974); (for adult) The Reluctant Landlord; Sauce for the Gander; We Chose Cape Cod; Cape Cod's Way; The Sea Fox. Address: 149 Benefit St., Providence, RI 02903, USA.

CORDELL, Alexander, b. 9 Sept. 1914, Colombo, Ceylon. Author. Publs: A Thought of Honour, 1954; Rape of the Fair Country, 1959; The Hosts of Rebecca, 1961; Song of the Earth, 1966; The Bright Cantonese, 1967; The Sinews of Love, 1968; If You Believe the Soldiers, 1974; The Fire People, 1972; Race of the Tiger, 1963; The Dream & The Destiny, 1975; 4 novels for children. Film rights sold to Rape of the Fair Country & Bright Cantonese. Contbr. to many mags., etc. Mbrships: Vice-Chmn., Swansea Writers Club; Vice-Chmn., Cardiff Writers Club. Address: Fair Country, Waen Wen, Bangor, N. Wales, UK.

COREY, Paul Frederick, b. 1903, Shelby Co., Iowa, USA. Writer. Educ: B.A., Univ. of Iowa. Publs: Three Miles Squares; The Road Returns; County Seat; Acres of Antaeus; The Red Tractor; Five Acre Hill; Shad Haul; Corn Gold Farm; Milk Flood; Buy an Acre; Build a Home; Homemade Homes; Home Workshop Furniture Projects; Holiday Homes; The Little Jeep; The Planet of the Blind. Contbr. to: SF14; Defenders of Wildlife News; Cat Fancy; Cats Mag.; Scribners; Esquire; Reader's Digest; Woman's Home Companion; etc. Mbrships: Authors Guild Inc.; Sci. Fiction Writers of Am. Agent: E. J. Carnell. Address: 267 Cavedale Rd., Sonoma, CA 95476, USA.

CORFE, Tom (Thomas Howell), b. 1928, London, UK. College Lecturer. Educ: M.A., Pembroke Coll., Cambridge; Univ. of London Inst. of Educ. Publs: History Field Studies in Durham Area, 1966; The Phoenix Park Murders: Conflict, Compromise & Tragedy in Ireland, 1879-1882, 1968; History in the Field, 1970; St. Patrick & Irish Christianity, 1973; Sunderland, a Short History, 1973; Archbishop Thomas & King Henry II, 1975. Contbr. to: Hist. Today; Irish Times; Hist. of Engl. Speaking Peoples; Times Educl. Supplement & Tchng. Hist. Address: 39 Greystoke Ave., Sunderland, UK.

CORKE, Helen, b. 1882, Hastings, Sussex, UK. Publs: A Book of Ancient Peoples, 1932; Lawrence & Apocalypse, 1933; Towards Economic Freedom, 1936; A Memoir of Jessie Chambers, 1950; Songs of Autumn, 1960; D. H. Lawrence, the Croydon Years, 1966; Neutral Ground (novel), 1968; In Our Infancy (memoir) (forthcoming). Contbr. to: Econ. jrnls.; Tex. Quarterly. Mbr., PEN. Address: Ingate, Kelvedon, Colchester, Essex, UK.

CORLET, Joyce Irving, b. 1912, Douglas, Isle of Man, UK. Journalist. Contbr. to over 150 publs; inclng. USA,

Aust., NZ, S. Africa, Norway & Switz. Mbr., Comm., Freelance Sect., Inst. of Jrnlsts. Address: 68 Greenfield Gdns., London NW2 1HY, UK.

CORLEY, Thomas Anthony Buchanan, b. 2 Aug. 1923, London, UK. Senior Lecturer in Economics. Educ: M.A., St. Edmund Hall, Oxford, 1949. Publs: The True Book about Napoleon, 1958; Democratic Despot, A Life of Napoleon III, 1961; Otto Wolff: Ouvrard, speculator of Genius (intro. & notes), 1962; Domestic Electrical Appliances, 1966; Quaker Enterprise in Biscuits: Huntley & Palmers of Reading 1822-1972, 1972. Contbr. to econ. jrnls. Mbr., Royal Econ. Soc. Address: 30 Allcroft Rd., Reading RG1 5HH, UK.

CORMACK, James Maxwell Ross, b. 1909, Aberdeen, UK. Regius Professor of Greek, University of Aberdeen. Educ: Univ. of Aberdeen; Univ. of Cambridge; Univ. of Vienna, Austria; Brit. Schl. of Archaeol., Athens, Greece; M.A. Publs: Notes on the History of the Inscribed Monuments of Aphrodisias, 1955; Ed., Monumenta Asiae Minoris Antiqua, Vol. 8, (w. W. Calder), 1962. Contbr. to: Jrnl. of Roman Studies; Jrnl. of Hellenic Studies; Annual of Brit. Schl. at Athens; Harvard Theol. Review; Classical Review; Am. Jrnl. of Archaeol. Address: 5 Royfold Cres., Aberdeen, AB2 6BH, UK.

CORNELIU, Stefanache, b. 23 Aug. 1934, Panciu, Vrancea, Romania. Writer; Editor. Educ: Dipl. in Philol., Univ. of Al. I. Cuza, 1956; Acad. Social & Pol. Scis., 1962. Publs: (all in Romanian) (novels) Tired Gods, 1969; Parallels, 1970; Beyond, 1970; Day of Forgetfulness, 1972; Wait for the Neighbour, 1974; Hope That Remains for Us, 1974; (short stories) Circle With Eyes, 1968. Contbr. to: Tribuna; Cronica; Steaua; Neue Literatur; Innostranaia Literatura (USSR); etc. Mbrships. incl: Leading Coun., Romanian Writers' Union; Jrnlsts. Union. Hons. incl: Writers' Assn. of Iasi Prize, 1968; Writers' Union of Romania Nat. Prize for Prose Writing. Address: Iasi, Str. Decebal nr. 18, ap. 6, st. A, Fl. 1, Romania.

CORNELUS, Henri Théodore, b. 22 June 1913, Vilvoorde, Brabant, Belgium. University Teacher. Educ: Lic., Roman Philol., Univ. Libre, Brussels. Publs: Kufa (novel), 1954; L'homme de Proue (novel), 1960; De sel et de terre (poems), 1967; Une île (poems), 1971; Les Hidalgos (short stories), 1971; Mer en Terre (poems), 1973; Belzébuth (novel), 1974. Contbr. to: Jrnl. des Poetes; Marginales; Synthese; Le Thyse; etc. Mbrships: Assn. of Belgian Writers; PEN. Hons. incl: Chevalier de l'Ordre de Léopold II, 1957, 1965; Int. Hans Christian Andersen Prize, 1958; 1st Class Civic Medal, 1962; 1st Class Civic Cross, 1972. Address: 23 Ave. du Vossegat, 1180 Brussels, Belgium.

CORNETT, Richard Orin, b. 13 Nov. 1913, Driftwood, Okla., USA. Educator. Educ: B.S., Okla. Bapt. Univ., 1934; M.S., Univ. of Okla., 1937; Ph.D., Univ. of Tex., 1940. Publs: Practical Physics (co-author), 1943; Algebra: A Second Course, 1945; Electronic Circuits & Tubes (co-author), 1947; Cued Speech Handbook for Parents (co-author), 1971. Contbr. to: Am. Annals of the Deaf; Sign Lang. Studies; Deaf Am.; Hearing; Tchng. Engl. to the Deaf; Jrnl. of the Am. Assn. of Phys. Tchrs. Recip., Litt.D., Jacksonville Univ., 1964. Address: Gallaudet College, 7th & Florida Ave., N.E., Wash., DC 20002, USA.

CORNFORTH, Maurice, b. 1909, London, UK. Educ: Univ. Coll., London; Trinity Coll., Cambridge; M.A. Publs: Science versus Idealism; Dialectical Materialism (3 vols.); Marxism & the Linguistic Philosophy; The Open Philosophy & the Open Society. Address: 61 Talbot Rd., London N6, UK.

CORNISH, W. R. Professor of English Law. Educ: LL.B.; B.C.L. Publs: The Jury, 1968, revised ed., 1970; Sutton & Shannon on Contracts (Ed. w. A. L. Diamond & others), 7th ed., 1970; Contbr. to: Annual Survey of C'wlth. Law; var. legal periodicals. Address: c/o London Schl. of Econs., Houghton St., London WC2, UK.

CORNWALL, Ian Wolfran, b. 28 Nov. 1909, Coonoor, S. India. Archaeologist; University Reader (Retired). Educ: B.A., St. John's Coll., Cambridge, UK, 1931; Postgrad. Acad. Dip., 1946, Ph.D., 1952, Inst. of Archaeol., Univ. of London. Publs. incl: Bones for the Archaeologist, 1956; Soils for the Archaeologist 1958; The Making of Man, 1960; (for young people) Prehistoric Animals & their Hunters, 1968; Ice Ages, 1970. Contbr. to var. profl. jrnls. Mbrships: Geols.' Assn.; Soc. Jersiaise. Hons: Carnegie

Medal, Lib. Assn., 1960; Henry Stopes Mem. Medal, Geols.' Assn., 1970. Agent: Winant Towers Ltd. Address: Cherry Lodge, Longueville Rd., St. Saviour, Jersey, Channel Islands.

CORNWELL, David John Moore, pen name LE CARRÉ, John, b. 1931, Poole, UK. Teacher; Writer. Educ: B.A., Oxford Univ., Berne Univ., Switz. Publs: Call for the Dead, 1961; A Murder of Quality, 1962. Address: c/o A. P. Watt & Son, Hastings House, Norfolk St., London WC2, UK.

CORREIA, Romeu, b. 17 Nov. 1917, Almada, Lisbon, Portugal. Bank Employee; Author. Publs. incl: Sábado Sem Sol (stories), 1947; Trapo Azul (novel), 1948; Calamento (novel), 1950; Gandaia (novel), 1952; Desporto-Rei (novel), 1955; Casaco de Fogo (play), 1955; O Vagabundo das Mãos de Oiro (play), 1960; Bonecos de Luz (novel), 1961; Jangada (play), 1963; Bocage (play), 1965; O Cravo Espanhol (play), 1969; Roberta (play), 1971; Francisco Stromp (biog.), 1973; Jose Bento Pessoa (biog.), 1974. Contbr. to: Vertice, Coimbra; Republica, Lisbon; etc. Hons. incl: Theatre Criticism Prize, 1962; Regional Press Prize, 1965; House of Press Prize, 1972. Address: Avenida D. Joao I, 11–1°Esq., Almada, Portugal.

CORRY, Percy, b. 1894, Macclesfield, Cheshire, UK. Sales Engineer; Lecturer; Actor; Producer; Managing Director (Retired). Publs: Stage Planning & Equipment, 1947; Lighting the Stage, 1954; Planning the Stage, 1961; Amateur Theatrecraft, 1961; Community Theatres, 1974. Contbr. to: Strand Elec. Jrnl. Tabs. Mbrships: Life, Assn. of Brit. Theatre Technicians; Soc. of Theatre Consultants. Address: 4 Harefield Dr., Manchester M20 8SY, UK.

CORTÁZAR, Julio, b. 1914. Writer. Publs: Bestiario (stories), 1951; Final del juego (stories), 1956; Las armas secretas (stories), 1959; Rayuela (novel), 1963; Los premios (novel), 1964; Story of Cronopios & Famas (stories); All the Fires, Fire (stories); Devil's Drool; Modelo Para Armar, 1968; Relatos (stories), 1970; Libro de Manuel (novel), 1973. Contbr. to: New World Writing; La Table Ronde; Akzente. Mbr., Jury, Casa de las Americas Award. Address: Place Général Beuret, Paris 15e, France.

CORWIN, Norman, b. 3 May 1910, Boston, Mass., USA. Writer-Producer-Director. Publs. incl: Thirteen by Corwin, 1942; Untitled & Other Dramas, 1947; Dog in the Sky, 1952; Overkill & Megalov, 1962; Lust for Life (film); Prayer for the 70's (film), 1969; Yes Speak Out Yes (cantata, commnd. by UN); The Rivalry (stage play); The World of Carl Sandburg (stage play); The Hypen (stage play); Cervantes (stage play). Contbr. to: newspapers; radio; TV. Mbr., var. film award comms. Hons. incl: Peabody Medal; Edward Bok Medal. Address: 4477 Colbath Ave., Sherman Oaks, CA 91403, USA.

COSER, Lewis, A., b. 27 Nov. 1913, Berlin, Germany. Professor of Sociology; Author; Editor. Educ: Sorbonne Univ., Paris, France; Ph.D., Columbia Univ., USA. 1954. Publs. incl: The Functions of Social Conflict, 1956; Sociological Theory (w. Bernard Rosenberg), 1957, 3rd ed., 1969; Ed., Sociology Through Literature, 1963, 2nd ed., 1972; Men of Ideas, 1965, paperback ed., 1970; Makers of Modern Social Science Series (Ed., var. vols.), 1965—; Master of Sociological Thought, 1970; Greedy Organizations, 1974. Contbr. to: Encounter; N.Y. Times Book Review; Int. Ency. Social Scis.; Ency. Britannica; etc. Address: 52 Erland Rd., Stony Brook, NY 11790, USA.

COSH, Mary, b. Bristol, UK. Freelance Writer. Educ: M.A., Oxford Univ. Publs: The Real World, 1961; Inveraray & the Dukes of Argyll (w. I. G. Lindsay), 1973. Contbr. to: Times; Times Educl. Supplement; Country Life; Glasgow Herald. Mbrships: Soc. Archtl. Histns.; Scottish Hist. Soc.; Soc. of Authors; Georgian Grp. Address: 63 Theberton St., London N1, UK.

COSIC, Dobrica, b. 1921. Novelist; Politician. Publs. incl: The Sun is Far Away; Roots; Divisions, 1961. Hons: Order of Bravery; Order of Meritorious Serv. to the People, 2nd class; Order of Brotherhood & Unity, 2nd class. Address: Fed. Assembly, Belgrade, Yugoslavia.

COSTA, Margaret Mary, married name LACY, Margaret, b. 30 Aug. 1917, Umtali, Rhodesia. Wine & Food Writer; Restauranteur. Educ: B.A., Univ. of Oxford, UK. Publs: The Country Cook, 1960; Food for the Rich (transl. of Plats Nouveaux, by P. Reboux), 1958; The Four Seasons Cookery Book, 1970, 2nd ed. 1972; London at Table,

1971. Contbr. to: Sunday Times Mag.; Gourmet; num. other Brit. & Am. mags. Mbrships: Freelance Br., Nat. Union of Jrnlsts.; Soc. of Authors. Recip., Bronze Medal for the Country Cook, Frankfurt, W. Germany, 1960. Address: 50 Well Walk, London NW3, UK.

COSTIN, Stanley Harry, b. 18 Oct. 1913, London, UK. Journalist. Educ: London Schl. of Jrnlsm. Contbr. to: Asst. Ed., Style for Men, 1946-52; Ed., Style for Men Overseas, 1952, Style for Men, 1957, Brit. Style, 1958, Style for Men Wkly., 1962; Cons. Ed., Style Wkly., 1970; London Corres., Herrenjrnl. Int. (Germany), Tailor & Men's Wear (Aust.), Southern Africa Textiles, L'Abbliamento (Italy); (articles) Men's Wear; Brit. Clothing Mfrs.; Ency. Britannica; etc. Mbrships: Press Club, London; Men's Fashion Writers' Int. (Pres., 1969-74); Nat. Union Jrnlsts. Hons: Elected Men's Fashion Writer of Yr., 1969-70. Address: Helmentor, 63 Micheldever Rd., Lee, London SE12 8LU, UK.

COSTLEY-WHITE, Hope, b. 3 Jan. 1894, Croydon, UK. Publs: St. Luke's Story of Jesus; Gloucester Story, 1947, Gloucestershire Stories, 1950; Life of Lord Dickinson, 1956; Mary Cole, 1961, paperback ed., 1973. Contbr. to: Series C, Bible Reading Fellowshop (ed., 21 yrs.); var. reviews. Address: Middle Cottage, Dinder, Wells, Somerset, BA5 3PL, UK.

COTES, Peter, occasional pen name NORTHCOTE, Peter, b. Maidenhead, Berks., UK. Theatrical Producer & Director; Critic; Biographer; Editor; Adaptor; Screenwriter; Scriptwriter. Publs: No Star Nonsense, 1949; The Little Fellow, 1951; A Handbook for the Amateur Theatre, 1957; Charles Chaplin, 1965; George Robey, 1972; The Trial of Elvira Barney, 1975. Contbr. to: Queen; Film Weekly; Stage; Plays & Players; Films & Filming; Nat. Review; Playgoer; Our Time; Spectator; etc. Mbrships: F.R.S.A.; Guild of Drama Adjudicators; Kt. of Mark Twain; Brit. Actors Equity Assn.; Assn. of Cine-Techns.; Our Society; Medico-Legal Soc.; Savage Club. Address: 27 Cathcart Rd., London SW10, UK.

COTT, Hugh Bamford, b. 1900, Ashby Magna, Leics., UK. Curator; University Lecturer. Educ: M.A., Sc.D., Selwyn Coll., Cambridge; D.Sc., Glasgow Univ. Publs: Adaptive Coloration in Animals; Zoological Photography in Practice; Uganda in Black & White; Looking at Animals: A Zoologist in Africa. Contbr. to: Proceedings of Zool. Soc., London; Proceedings of Royal Entomol. Soc.; Ibis; Photographic Jrnl.; Engrs. Jrnl.; Uganda Jrnl.; etc. Mbrships: Fellow, Royal Photog. Soc.; Fellow, Zool. Soc., London; Fndr. Mbr., Soc. of Wildlife Artists; Fellow, Inst. of Biol.; Soc. of Authors. Address: Denebanks, Netherbury, Bridport, Dorset, UK.

COTTER, Charles Henry, b. 21 Jan. 1919, Hirwaun, Wales, UK. University Teacher. Educ: B.Sc., Birbeck Coll., Univ. of London; M.Sc., Wales. Publs: The Elements of Navigation, 1953; The Principles & Practice of Radio Direction Finding, 1959; The Master & His Ship, 1962; The Apprentice & His Ship, 1963; The Physical Geography of the Oceans, 1965; The Astronomical & Mathematical Foundations of Geography, 1966; A History of Nautical Astronomy, 1968; The Complete Coastal Navigation, 1964; The Complete Nautical Astronomer, 1969; The Atlantic Ocean, 1974. Contbr. to nautical publs. Mbrships. incl: Royal Inst. Navigation; Royal Meteorol. Soc. Address: Middle Ground, Mill Rd., Lisvane, Cardiff, S. Wales, UK.

COTTERELL, Geoffrey, b. 24 Nov. 1919, Southsea, UK. Writer. Publs: Then a Soldier, 1944; This is the Way, 1947; Randle in Springtime, 1949; Strait & Narrow, 1950; Westward the Sun, 1952; The Strange Enchantment, 1956; Tea at Shadow Creek, 1958; Tiara Tahiti, 1960; Go said the Bird, 1966; Bowers of Innocence, 1970; Amsterdam, the life of a city, 1973. Address: 2 Fulbourne House, Blackwater Rd., Eastbourne, Sussex, UK.

COTTON, John, b. 7 Mar. 1925, London, UK. School Headmaster; Author; Educ: B.A., London Univ. Publs: Outside the Gates of Eden, 1969; Poetry Introduction I, 1970; Old Movies & Other Poems, 1971; Kilroy Was Here, 1975. Contbr. to: Encounter; New Statesman; Observer; Poetry (Chgo.); Poetry Review; Outposts; Transatlantic Review; Tribune; Ed., Priapus, 1962-72, Pvte. Lib., 1970—; Chmn., Poetry Soc., 1972—. Hons: Poetry Book Soc. Recommendation & Arts Coun. of GB Publ. Award, for Old Movies. Address: 37 Lombardy Drive, Berkhamsted, Herts., UK.

COTTON, L. T., b. 1922, London, UK. Consultant Surgeon. Educ: M.A., M.Ch., Univ. of Oxford; Med. Schl.,

King's Coll. Hosp., Univ. of London; F.R.C.S. Publs: A Synopsis of Surgery, 1963; A Short Textbook of Surgery (w. S. F. Taylor), 1967. Contbr. to med. jrnls. Mbrships: Fellow, Royal Soc. of Med.; Surg. Rsch. Soc.; Vascular Surg. Soc. Address: Private Wing, King's Coll. Hosp., London SE5, UK.

COTTRELL (Sir), Alan Howard, b. 17 July 1919, Birmingham, UK. Academic; Scientist. Educ: B.Sc., 1939, Ph.D., 1942, Univ. of Birmingham; M.A., Univ. of Cambridge, 1958. Publs: Theoretical Structural Metallurgy, 1948, 1955; Dislocations & Plastic Flow in Crystals, 1953; The Mechanical Properties of Matter, 1964; Theory of Crystal Dislocations, 1964; An Introduction to Metallurgy, 1967; Portrait of Nature, 1975. Mbrships: Royal Soc.; Goldsmiths Co.; US Nat. Acad. of Scis.; Royal Swedish Acad. of Scis. Recip., Harvey Prize, 1974. Address: The Master's Lodge, Jesus College, Cambridge, UK.

COTTRELL, Leonard, b. 1913, Wolverhampton, UK. Writer; TV Producer. Publs: The Lost Pharaohs; The Bull of Minos; The Anvil of Civilisation; Life Under the Pharaohs; One Man's Journey; The Mountains of Pharaoh; Lost Cities; Seeing Roman Britain; The Great Invasion; Wonders of the World; Enemy of Rome; The Tiger of Ch'in; Lost Worlds; (Ed.) Concise Encyclopaedia of Archaeology; Digs & Diggers; Realms of Gold; Five Queens of Ancient Egypt; The Warrior Pharaohs; Crete, Island of Mystery; Reading the Past; Up in a Balloon. Address: 217 Station Rd., Knowle, Warwicks., UK.

COULSON, John Hubert Arthur, pen name BONETT, John, b. 10 Aug. 1906, Benton, Northumberland, UK. Writer. Publs: (co-author w. wife, Emery Bonett) Dead Lion, 1949; A Banner for Pegasus, 1951; No Grave for a Lady, 1959; Better Dead, 1964; The Private Face of Murder, 1966; This Side Murder?, 1967; The Sound of Murder, 1970; No Time to Kill, 1972. Contbr. to: Macleans; Argosy; Woman; Mother; Britannica & Eve; Evening Standard; Toronto Star; etc. Mbrships: Garrick Club; Nat. Book League; Crime Writers' Assn. Address: 29 Upbrook Mews, London W2 3HG, UK.

COULTER, John William, b. 1888, Belfast, UK. Editor; Author; Playwright. Educ: Univ. of Manchester. Publs: The House in the Quiet Glen, 1937; Family Portrait, 1937; Radio Drama is not Theatre, 1937; Deirdre of the Sorrows, 1940; Transit Through Fire, 1942; Churchill, 1944; Turf Smoke, 1945; The Blossoming Thorn, 1946; Riel, 1962; The Trial of Louis Riel, 1969; The Drums Are Out, 1971; Deirdre, vocal & conductor's score & parts, 1972. Address: c/o Int. Copyright Bur., 26 Charing Cross Rd., London WC2, UK.

COULTHARD, Margaret, b. 1918, Cleator Moor, Cumberland, UK. Educator; Chief Examiner, Advanced Level French for London. Educ: M.A., Oxford Univ. (St. Anne's Coll.); Dip.Ed., Dept. of Educ., Oxford; Univ. of Aix-en-Provence. Publs: "O" Level French Dictation, 1962 (set of tapes, 1965); French Pictorial Composition, 1965 (edn. for Swedish schls., 1967); "A" Level French Dictation, 1966; Understanding French, 1968; Gen. Ed., Par-ci Par-la Series of French Readers; Author, 4 titles in Par-ci Par-la Series, 1970. Mbrships: MLA; Brit. Fedn. Univ. Women; Soc. of Authors. Address: 53 St. Paul's Close, Hounslow, Middx., UK.

COUMANS, Willam Karel, b. 11 Apr. 1930, Heerlen, Netherlands. Publicist. Publs: (poems) Met andere woorden, 1958; Een Stad, 1960; (anthols.) Mijn land is een gedicht, 1961; Terugblik op een uniek solist; (essays) Van Limvergse School tot Moderne Ruine. Contbr. to: Foto; What's On in Europe; Winkler Prins Ency. Mbrships: PEN; Vereniging van letterkundigen. Address: Koningsplein 62 M, Maastricht, Netherlands.

COUNIHAN, Daniel John Patrick, b. 1917, London, UK. Correspondent. Educ: St. Ignatius Coll., Lond; Hornsey Schl. of Art. Appts: Corres., Rome & Vatican, Min. of Info. & US Off. of War Info., 1944-45; Hd., News Div., Allied Info. Servs., Venezia Giulia, 1945-47; Staff, BBC News Div., 1947-; Asst. Diplomatic Corres., BBC, 1959-. Author, Unicorn Magic. Contbr. to: Times Literary Supplement; John O'London's Weekly; Tablet; Catholic Herald; Radio Times; etc. Address: 19 Powis Sq., Brighton, Sussex, UK.

COURLANDER, Harold, b. 18 Sept. 1908, Indpls., USA. Author. Educ: B.A., Univ. of Mich., 1931; postgrad.

work, Columbia Univ., 1939-40. Publs. incl: Haiti Singing, 1939; Kantchil's Lime Pit, 1950; The Hat-Shaking Dance, 1957; The Drum & the Hoe, 1960; The King's Drum, 1962; Negro Folk Music, USA, 1963; People of the Short Blue Corn, 1970; The Fourth World of the Hopis, 1971; Tales of Yoruba Gods & Heroes, 1973; A Treasury of African Folklore, 1975; (novels) The Caballero, 1940; The Big Old World of Richard Creeks, 1962; The African, 1967; The Son of the Leopard, 1974. Contbr. to: Musical Quarterly; Jrnl. of Negro Hist. Recip., var. awards, fellowships & acad. grants-in-aid. Address: 5512 Brite Drive, Bethesda, MD 20034, USA.

COURSE, Alfred George, b. 20 Feb. 1895, London, UK. Master Mariner. Educ: Brit. Master Mariner's Cert., Square Rigged (by exam.); Mbr., Inst. of Transport (by exam.). Publs: The Wheel's Kick & the Wind's Song, 1950, 3rd ed., 1968; The Deep Sea Tramp, 1960; Painted Ports, 1961; Glossary of Cargo Handling Terms, 1961, 2nd ed., 1974; Dictionary of Nautical Terms, 1962; The Merchant Navy: A Social History, 1963; A Seventeenth Century Mariner, 1965; Pirates of the Eastern Seas, 1966; Pirates of the Western Seas, 1969; Windjammers of the Horn, 1969. Contbr. to var. jrnls. Mbr., profl. orgs. Recip. sev. hons. Address: 26 Weldon Ave., Bear Cross, Bournemouth BH11 9QB, UK.

COURTNEY, Cecil Patrick, b. 1930, Belfast, UK. University Lecturer in French; Fellow & Librarian, Christ's College, Cambridge. Educ: B.A., Queen's Univ., Belfast; D.Phil., Brasenose Coll., Oxford; Ph.D., Cambridge Univ. Publs: Montesquieu & Burke, 1963. Contbr. to profl. publs. inclng: Revue d'Histoire Littéraire de la France; Revue de littérature comparée; Neophilologus; French Studies; Times Lit. Supplement. Address: 35 Kinnaird Way, Cambridge, UK.

COURTNEY, Gwendoline, b. Southampton, Hants., UK. Author; Lecturer. Publs: Torley Grange, 1935; The Grenville Garrison, 1940; The Denehurst Secret Service, 1940; Well Done, Denehurst, 1941; Sally's Family, 1946; Stepmother, 1948; Long Barrow, 1950; A Coronet for Cathie, 1950; At School with the Stanhopes, 1951; Mermaid House; The Girls of Friar's Rise, 1952; The Chiltons, 1953; The Wild Lorings at School, 1954; The Wild Lorings — Detectives, 1956; Passage of Arms (TV play). Mbrships: W. Country Writers' Assn.; Former Hon. Sec., W. of England Grp., Soc. of Authors. Address: Carigluz, Cadgwith, Helston, Cornwall, UK.

COUSINS, Albert Newton, b. 7 May 1919, Cleveland, Ohio, USA. Sociologist. Educ: A.B., Ohio State Univ., 1942; M.A., 1949, Ph.D., 1951, Harvard Univ. Publs: (contbr.) A Modern Introduction to the Family (Eds., Norman Bell & Ezra Vogel), 1960; A Society's Need . . . A University's Duty, 1967; Urban Man & Society (w. Hans Nagpaul), 1970. Contbr. to: Jrnl. Am. Bar Assn.; Am. Sociol. Review; Social Forces; Social Educ.; Indian Jrnl. Social Rsch. Mbrships. incl: Am. Sociol. Assn.; Am. Assn. Univ. Profs.; London Schl. Econs. Soc. Hons: Medal Merit U.S. Army, 1945; Fellowship Nat. Sci. Fndn., 1966. Address: 2595 Charney Rd., Univ. Heights, OH 44118, USA.

COUSINS, Geoffrey Esmond, b. 1900, London, UK. Writer on Golf & Other Sports. Publs: Golfers at Law, 1958; The Story of Scapa Flow, 1965; The Defenders, a history of the British Volunteer, 1968; A Century of Opens, 1971; An Atlas of Golf, 1974. Contbr. to var. golf mags., also to Daily Telegraph, London. Mbrships: Nat. Union of Jrnlsts.; Soc. of Authors; Press Club., London. Agent: Alec Harrison. Address: The 19th Firstway, Grand Dr., London SW20 0JD, UK.

COUSINS, Margaret, b. 1905, Munday, Tex., USA. Editor; Author. Educ: B.A., Univ. of Tex. Publs: Uncle Edgar & the Reluctant Saint; Christmas Gift; Ben Franklin of Old Philadelphia; (w. Margaret Truman) Souvenir; We were There at the Battle of the Alamo; Stories of Love and Marriage, 1961; (as Avery Johns) Traffic With Evil; The Story of Thomas Edison, 1965. Contbr. to: Pictorial Review; Good Housekeeping (Assoc.-Mng. Ed., 1942-58). Ladies Home Jrnl. (Fiction Ed., 1970-73); McCall's (Mng. Ed., 1958-61); Cosmopolitan; House Beautiful; & num. Engl. mags; Ed. Exec., var. mags. 1937-73. Mbr., Authors' League; PEN. Address: Box 1626, San Antonio, TX 78296, USA.

COUSINS, Norman, b. 24 June 1915. Editor. Educ: Teachers' Coll., Columbia Univ., USA. Publs: The Good

Inheritance, 1941; (Ed.) A Treasury of Democracy, 1941; Modern Man is Obsolete, 1945; (Ed.) Poetry of Freedom, 1946; Talks with Nehru, 1951; Who Speaks for man?, 1953; (Ed.) In God We Trust, 1958; (Ed.) March's Thesaurus, 1958; Dr Schweitzer of Lambaréné, 1960; In Place of Folly, 1961; Present Tense, 1967; The Improbable Triumvirate, 1972. Contbr. to: World Mag., (Ed.); etc. Mbrships. incl: VP, PEN; Chmn., Nat. Educ. TV; Co-Chmn., Nat. Comm. for a Sane Nuclear Policy; etc. Num. hons. incl: Benjamin Franklin Award, 1956; Eleanor Roosevelt Peace Award, 1963; UN Peace Medal, 1971. Address: 160 Silvermine Rd., New Canaan, CT 06840, USA.

COVENEY, James, b. 4 Apr. 1920, London, UK. University Professor of Modern Languages. Educ: B.A.(Hons.), Reading Univ., 1950; Docteur de l'Université de Strasbourg, France, 1953. Publs: La Légende de l'Empereur Constant, 1955; Glossary of French & English Management Terms (co-author), 1972; Le Français pour l'Ingénieur (co-author), 1974. Contbr. to: Saisons d'Alsace; Die Unterrichtspraxis; Babel; Chartered Mech. Engr.; Times Higher Educ. Supplement. Mbrships. incl: F.R.S.A.; Pres., Conference Internationale Permanente des Directeurs des Instituts Universitaires de Traducteurs et Interprètes; Trustee, Bell Educl. Trust. Address: 40 Westfield Close, Bath BA2 2EB, UK.

COVENEY, Peter James, b. 5 Aug. 1924, Aldershot, UK. Warden, Hall of Residence; Lecturer. Educ: B.A., 1945, M.A., 1948, Downing Coll., Cambridge. Publs: Poor Monkey: The Child in Literature, 1957; The Image of Childhood, 1967; Ed., Huckleberry Finn, 1966; Ed., Felix Holt, 1972. Contbr. to: Spectator; Sunday Times; Engl. Histl. Review. Mbrships: Histl. Assn.; Soc. of Authors. Address: Lincoln Hall, The University, Nottingham, UK.

COVENTRY, (Rev.) John Seton, b. 21 Jan. 1915, Deal, Kent, UK. Lecturer in Christian Doctrine. Educ: Stonyhurst Coll.; M.A., Oxford Univ.; Lic. Sacred Theol. (S.T.L.) Publs: Morals & Independence; The Breaking of Bread: Faith Seeks Understanding; The Life Story of the Mass; The Theology of Faith; Christian Truth. Mbr., Soc. of Jesus. Address: Heythrop College, Univ. of London, 11 Cavendish Square, London W1, UK.

COVILLE, Cabot, b. 1902, Wash. D.C., USA. Diplomat. Educ: A.B., Cornell Univ., Ithaca, N.Y.; Univ. of Paris, France. Publs: Corregidor, 1942; Shinto, Engine of Government, 1948. Contbr. to: Taiwan, 1943; For. Serv. Jrnl. Address: 2800 R St., N.W., Wash. D.C. 20007, USA.

COVINS, Frederick, b. 18 Feb. 1932, Birmingham, UK. Film & Theatre Author; Photographer; Antique Dealer. Publs: The Breaking Sword, 1973; The Battle for Badger's Wood, 1974; Sabbath for a Fuehrer, 1975. Contbr. of tech. features to photographic press. Address: Pipe Elm, Leigh Sinton, Malvern, Worcs., UK.

COWAN, Henry Jacob, b. 21 Aug. 1919. Professor of Architectural Science. Educ: B.Sc., 1st Class Hons., M.Sc., Manchester Univ.; Ph.D., D.Eng., Sheffield Univ. Publs. incl: The Theory of Prestressed Concrete Design, 1956; The Design of Reinforced Concrete, 1963, 3rd ed., 1975; Concrete in Torsion, 1965; The Design of Prestressed Concrete, 1966; An Historical Outline of Architectural Science, 1966; Models in Architecture, 1968; Architectural Structures, 1971; Dictionary of Architectural Science, 1973. Contbr. 200 articles, 1,000 books, reviews to jrnls.; Ed., Architectural Science Review, 1958—; Ed., Vestes, 1966—. Address: 93 Kings Rd., Vaucluse, NSW 2030, Australia.

COWAN, Lore Leni, b. Berlin, Germany. Author. Publs: Contract to Hollywood, 1932; (TV series) Stories on Stamps, 1960; (cookery) Let's Love Fish, 1966; (short stories) Children of the Resistance, 1968; Are You Superstitious?, 1968; The Wit of Women, 1969. Contbr. to: Daily Express; Picturegoer. Mbr., PEN. Agent: John Farquharson. Address: 107 Chiltern Court, Baker St., London NW1 5SX, UK.

COWAN, Peter, b. 4 Nov. 1914, Perth, W.A., Australia. University Senior Tutor. Educ: B.A., 1940, Dip.Educ., 1946, Univ. of W.A., Nedlands. Publs: (novels) Summer, 1964; Seed, 1966; (short Stories) Drift: Stories, 1944; The Unploughed Land; Stories, 1959; The Empty Street: Stories, 1965; (other) Ed., Short Story Landscape: The Modern Short Story, 1964; Spectrum One & Two (Co-Ed.), 1970; Ed., Today: Contemporary Short Stories, 1971. Recip., C'Wlth. Lit. Fund Fellowship, 1963. Address: c/o

English Dept., University of Western Australia, Nedlands, W.A. 6009, Australia.

COWARD, Roger Vilven, b. 26 Oct. 1916, Bath, UK. Auctioneer & Estate Agent. Publs: Sailors in Cages, 1967; Licence to Plunder, 1970; Where Have All the Soldiers Gone?, 1974. Mbr., Soc. of Authors. Address: The Garden Flat, Beckford, Beckford Rd., Bathwick, Bath, Somerset, UK.

COWELL, Frank Richard, b. 16 Nov. 1897, London, UK. Civil Servant; Author. Educ: B.A., King's Coll., Univ. of London, 1921; B.Sc., 1923, Ph.D., 1927, London Schl. of Econs. Publs: Culture in Private & Public Life, 1959; Values in Human Society, 1970; Cicero & the Roman Republic, 1972; Everyday Life in Ancient Rome, 1973; The Athenaeum in the Club & Social Life of London 1824-1974, 1974. Mbrships: Pvte. Lib. Soc.; Athenaeum. Recip., C.M.G., 1952. Address: Crowdleham House, Kemsing, Kent, UK.

COWEN, Frances Minto, pen names HYDE, Eleanor; COWEN, Frances, b. 27 Dec. 1915, Oxford, UK. Novelist. Publs. incl: (suspense novels) Daylight Fear; Shadow of Polperro; Secret of Arrivol; Fractured Silence; Unforgiving Minute; Hounds of Carvello; Shadow of Theale, 1974; (histl. novels) Tudor Maid, 1972; Tudor Masquerade, 1973; Tudor Mayhem, 1974; Tudor Mystery, 1974. Contbr. to: Oxford Mag.; Good Housekeeping; Woman; Woman's Weekly; Oxford Times; Oxford Mail. Mbrships: Soc. of Authors; Crime Writers' Assn.; John Evelyn Soc. Recip., Best Short Story Award, 1933. Address: Flat One, 13 Thornton Hill, Wimbledon, London SW19, UK.

COWIE, Evelyn, Elizabeth (née TRAFFORD), b. 1924, Peterborough, Northants.. UK. History Lecturer; Author. Educ: M.A., Univ. of London. Publs: Breakfasts; Left-Overs; Living Through History. Address: 38 Stratton Rd., Merton Park, London SW19 3JG, UK.

COWIE, (Captain) John Stewart, b. 1898, Mildura, Vic., Australia. Royal Naval Captain (Retired), Lawyer. Educ: RN Colls., Osborne, Dartmouth & Greenwich; Trinity Coll., Cambridge; Inns of Ct. Law Schl., Inner Temple. Publs: Mines, Minelayers & Minelaying, 1949. Contbr. to: Naval Review; Navy; R.U.S.I. Jrnl.; US Naval Inst. Proceedings; Tatler; Truth; Men Only; Fleet; Royal Gazette, Bermuda; Bermudian; Brassey's Naval Annual. Mbrships: R.U.S.I.; Navy League; Assoc., US Naval Inst.; Bermuda Tech. Soc.; Musical & Dramatic Soc.; Soc. of Arts. Recip., C.B.E. Address: 32 Mayflower Ct., P.O. Box 876, Pembroke, Bermuda.

COWIE, Leonard Wallace, b. 1919, Brighton, Sussex, UK. Lecturer on History; Writer. Educ: Univs. of Oxford, Cambridge & London; M.A.; Ph.D. Publs: Henry Newman, An American in London, 1708-43; About the Bible; Seventeenth-Century Europe; Eighteenth-Century Europe; Hanoverian England; The March of the Cross; The Reformation; Martin Luther; The Christian Calendar. Contbr. to: Victoria Co. Hist. of Wiltshire; Educl. Review; Hist. Today; Victoria Co. Hist. of York. Fellow, Royal Hist. Soc. Address: 38 Stratton Rd., Merton Park, London SW19 3JG, UK.

COWIE, Mervyn Hugh, b. 1909, Nairobi, Kenya. Founder & Former Director, Kenya National Parks; Financial Director, E. African Flying Doctor Services; Writer. Educ: Brasenose Coll., Oxford. Publs: Fly, Vulture, 1961; I Walk with Lions, 1961; Meine Freunde die Lowen, 1964; African Lion, 1966. Contbr. to var. jrnls. for 30 yrs. Mbrships: VP, Fauna Preservation Soc.; Hon. Cons., World Wildlife Fund; Inst. of Dirs.; Trustee or Mbr., var. E. African Conservation Socs. Hons: C.B.E., 1960; E.D., 1954; Gold Medal, San Diego Zoo Assn., 1972; F.C.A., 1966; Order of the Golden Ark, 1975. Address: P.O. Box 15549, Mbagathi, Nairobi, Kenya.

COWLES, Fleur, b. USA. Journalist; Writer. Educ: Pratt Inst.; LL.D., Elmira Univ. Publs: Bloody Precedent; The Case of Salvador Dali (both also French & German eds.); Tiger Flower (also Italian, German, Swedish & Portuguese eds.); Lion & Blue; Friends & Memories, 1975. Contbr. to: Treasures of the Brit. Museum; I can Tell It Now; Look Mag. (Assoc. Ed., 1947-55; For. Corres., 1955-58); Quick Mag. (Assoc. Ed., 1951-53); Flair Mag. (Ed.-in-Chief); Atlantic Monthly; Vogue; etc. Mbrships incl: Press Club; Royal Soc. of Arts; Univ. Art Mus. Coun., Univ. of Calif., Berkeley, USA; Bd. of Trustees, World Wildlife Fund. Address: A5 Albany, Piccadilly, London W1, UK.

COWLES, Virginia, b. 1912, USA. Journalist. Publs: Looking for Trouble; How America Is Governed; No Cause for Alarm; Winston Churchill: The Era & the Man; Edward VII & His Circle, 1956; The Phantom Major, 1958; The South Sea Bubble; The Kaiser, 1962; 1913: An End & a Beginning, 1965; The Russian Dagger, 1969; The Romanovs; The Rothschilds. Address: 19 Chester Sq., London SW1, UK.

COWLEY, Malcolm, b. 1898, Belsano, Pa., USA. Editor; Professor of Literature; Chancellor, American Academy of Arts & Letters. Educ: B.A.; Harvard Univ.; Univ. of Montpelier, France. Publs. incl: Exile's Return; The Literary Situation; The Faulkner-Cowley File; Blue Junaita; Collected Poems; Think Back on Us; A Many Windowed House; (Ed.) The Portable Faulkner; (Ed.) The Stories of F. Scott Fitzgerald. Contbr. to: New Republic, Lit. Ed., 1929-40; & num. mags., jrnls. & reviews. Address: Sherman, CT 06784, USA.

COWLIN, Dorothy, b. 1911, Grantham, Lincs., UK. Author. Educ: B.A., Manchester Univ. Publs: Penny to Spend; Winter Solstice; The Holly & The Ivy; The Slow Train Home; An End & A Beginning; Rowan Berry Wine; Draw the Well Dry; The Pair of Them; Greenland Seas; Woman in the Desert; Elizabeth Barrett Browning; Cleopatra. Contbr. to: Punch; Yorks. Life, & other mags.; Children's Hour, Woman's Hour, & Voice of the People, BBC. Address: Aconbury, Larpool Drive, Whitby, Yorks., UK.

COWLING, Thomas George, b. 17 June 1906, London, UK. University Professor (ret'd.). Educ: M.A., D.Phil., Brasenose Coll., Oxford. Publs: The Mathematical Theory of Non-Uniform Gases (w. S. Chapman), 1939, 3rd ed., 1970; Molecules in Motion, 1949; Magneto -Hydrodynamics, 1957, 2nd ed., forthcoming. Contbr. to: Monthly Notices & Quarterly Jrnl., Royal Astronomical Soc.; Proceedings of Royal Soc.; Nature. Mbr. &/or Fellow, var. sci. orgs. Recip., Gold Medal, Royal Stronomical Soc. Address: 19 Hollin Gdns., Leeds LS16 5NL, UK.

COWPER, Richard, pen name, MURRY, Colin, b. 1926, Dorset, UK. Educator. Educ: B.A., Brasenose Coll., Oxford; Leicester. Publs: The Golden Valley, 1958; Recollections of a Ghost, 1960; A Path to the Sea, 1961; Breakthrough, 1967; Phoenix, 1968; Domino, 1970; Private View, 1972; Kuldesak, 1972; Clone, 1973; Time out of Mind, 1973; The Twilight of Briareus, 1974; Worlds Apart, 1974; One Hand Clapping, 1975. Mbrships: Author's Soc.; Writers' Guild; Sci. Fiction Writers of Am.; Brit. Sci. Fiction Assn. Agent: A. D. Peters & Co. Address: Elm Cottage, Talygarn, Pontyclun, Glam., UK.

COX, Alfred Bertram, b. 5 Sept. 1902, Langhorne Creek, S.A. Public Accountant. Educ: Adelaide Univ. Publs: Farming is Fun, 1952 & 1973; The Other Half, 1955; The Better Half, 1957; Siestas & Fiestas, 1960; Local Government in South Australia, 1962 & 1964; Figures aren't Funny, 1967; Our First Fifty Years, 1974. Contbr. to: Aust. Post.; Aust. Broadcasting Commn.; People; TV & radio. Mbrships. incl: F.C.S.A.; F.C.I.S.; Royal Assn. of Justices; Aust. Soc. of Authors; Fellowship of Aust. Writers. Address: Cooinda, 2 Nioka Court, Beaumont 5066, S. Australia.

COX, Bertha Mae Hill, b. 10 Mar. 1901, Kosse, Tex., USA. Teacher. Educ: B.S., 1935, M.Sc., 1950, N. Tex. State Univ. Publs: True Tales of Texas, 1949; Let's Read About Texas, 1963; Our Texas, 1964; The Texans; Texans Today, 1971; Ch. Schl. lit. for United Meth. Ch. Contbr. to jrnls. & newspapers. Address: 1130 N. Winnetka, Dallas, TX 75208, USA.

COX, Betty Smith, b. 11 Nov. 1925, Richmond, Va., USA. Professor of English. Educ: Ph.B., Northwestern Univ., 1953; M.A., 1961, Ph.D., 1964, Univ. of Pitts. Publs: Cruces of Beowulf, 1971. Contbr. to: Reflections; Averett Alumni Mag. Mbrships. incl: Treas., N.C. Poetry Soc., 4 yrs.; Medieval Acad. of Am. Address: Box 877, Boiling Springs, NC 28017, USA.

COX, Charles Brian, b. 1928, Grimsby, UK. Professor of English. Educ: M.A., M.Litt., Pembroke Coll., Cambridge. Publs: The Free Spirit, 1963; Modern Poetry (w. A. E. Dyson), 1963; The Practical Criticism of Poetry, 1965; Dylan Thomas, 1967; The Black Papers on Education (w. A. E. Dyson), 1971; The Twentieth Century Mind, 1972; Joseph Conrad: The Modern Imagination, 1974. Contbr. to: Sunday Telegraph; Critical Quarterly. Address: 20 Park Gates Dr., Cheadle Hulme, Cheshire, UK.

COX, Christopher Barry, b. 1931, London, UK. University Reader. Educ: Balliol Coll., Oxford; St. John's Coll., Cambridge; M.A.; Ph.D.; D.Sc. Publs: Prehistoric Animals, 1969; Biogeography, 1973. Contrb. to: Proceedings of the Zool. Soc., London; Breviora; Am. Mus. Novitates; Geog. Bulletin, Brit. Mus. of Natural Hist.; Philosl. Transactions of Royal Soc., London. Address: Zool. Dept., King's Coll., Strand, London WC2R 2LS, UK.

COX, Constance, b. Sutton, Surrey, UK. Playwright; Television & Radio Script Writer. Publs: (plays) Vanity Fair, 1946; Madame Bovary, 1948; Northanger Abbey, 1950; Mansfield Park, 1952; Because of the Lockwoods, 1954; Lord Arthur Savile's Crime, 1963; Jane Eyre, 1964; Pride & Prejudice, 1972; Mis Letitia, 1972. Mbrships: Hon. Treas., Sussex Playwrights' Club; W. Sussex Writers' Club; Soc. of Women Jrnlsts. Hons: New Chronicle Award, for Best TV Play of the Yr., 1955; Guild of TV Screen Writers' Award for Adaptations of the Classics, 1965; Guild of TV & Screen Writers Award for the Forsyte Saga, 1966. Address: 2 Princes Ave., Hove, Sussex BN3 4GD, UK.

COX, Edith Muriel, pen name GOAMAN, Muriel, b. Bideford, Devon, UK. Former Mayor & Alderman; Author. Educ: Glos. Trng. Coll. of Domestic Sci. Publs: incl: Thomas Guy (biog.), 1959; English Clocks, 1967; Fun with Chess, 1968; Fun with Time, 1970; Fun with Travel; Old Bideford & District, 1968; Through the Ages, Food, 1968; Through the Ages, Transport, 1970; Picture Signs & Symbols; Touch Wood: The Story of Everyday Superstitions; News & Messages; Never so Good — Or how Children were Treated, 1974. Contrb. to: Municipal Review; She; Sunday Times Mag.; Pan. Mbrships: Soc. of Anthors; Nat. Book League. Address: Willow Barn, Lower Cleave, Bideford, Devon, UK.

COX, (Rev.) George Ernest Pritchard, b. 1903, Leytonstone, Essex, UK. Rector. Educ: M.A., Jesus Coll., Cambridge Univ. Publs: Torch Commentary; Gospel according to St. Matthew. Contrb. to: The Tchr.'s Commentary. Address: Beckley Rectory, Rye, Sussex, UK.

COX, Helen May, b. Auckland, NZ. Writer. Educ: Auckland Univ., (Music). Publs: The Hostess Cookbook, 1952, 9 ed.; Pressure Cooking for the Modern Home, 1955, 5 eds.; Traditional English Cooking, 1961; The Floral Art Book of Reference, 1970; Mr. & Mrs. Charles Dickens Entertain at Home, 1970. Mbr., Soc. of Authors, Sussex. Address: 25 Brunswick Terrace, Hove, Sussex, UK.

COX, John Roberts (Jack), b. 15 Jan. 1915, Worsley, Lancs., UK. Author; Consultant Editor. Educ: Univs. of Manchester & Geneva, Switz.; M.A. Publs. incl: The Outdoor Book; Camp & Trek; Lightweight Camping; The Conservation Book; The Outdoor Cookbook; Guide to Outdoor Hobbies; Modern Camping; Games, 2 vols.; Pan Guide to Pets; var. educl. handbooks & biogs.; Ed., Boys' Own Annual, 1946—. Contrb. to: Daily Telegraph; Thomson Newspapers; Sunday Times. Guardian; World Scout Bur., Geneva; Rugby Post (Ed., 1974—); also TV & radio progs. Address: Cerrig, 43 Hill View Rd., Llanrhos, Llandudno, N. Wales, UK.

COX, Naomi D., b. 14 Sept. 1904, Ravenswood, W. Va., USA. Teacher. Educ: M.A., Marshall Univ. & Athens Ohio Univ. Publs: Poverty Poems, 1968. Contrb. to poetry jrnls., anthols. Mbrships: W.Va. Poetry Soc.; Sec., Parkersburg Poetry Soc.; Lee May's Poetry Soc., Jackson Co., W. Va. Hons: 1st Prize, Nature Poetry, Little Kanawha Regional Fest., 1974; 2 awards, 1970, 4 awards, 1973, W. Va. Poetry Soc. Contests. Address: Rt. 1, Box 172, Ravenswood, WV 26164, USA.

COX, Patrick Brian, pen name as songwriter STEWART, Kenneth, b. 19 Apr. 1914, London, UK. Poet. Educ: B.A.(Hons.), 1949, Dip. in Jrnlsm., 1968, Univ. of Melbourne, Australia. Publs. incl: Hooded Falcon; Faucon Chaperonné, 1957; Singing Forest, 1958; Roses Aflame, 1965; Testament to Love, 1969; The Roseate Flame, 1971. Contrb. to num. jrnls. Mbrships: Pres., Melbourne Shakespeare Soc.; VP, Aust. Lit. Soc.; VP & Hon. Poet Laureate (1965), United Poets Laureate Int.; Regent, World Poetry Soc. Intercontinental. Hons: Trollope-Cagle World Poetry Prize, 1973. Address: G.P.O. Box 2108-S, Melbourne, Vic., 3001, Australia.

COX-GEORGE, Noah Arthur William, pen names NIJSNI, K. M.; SEMINOLA, b. 15 June 1915, Degema, Nigeria. Economist; University Teacher. Educ: B.Sc., M.Sc. & Ph.D., Univ. of London; Oxford Univ. Publs: Report on African Participation in the Commerce of Sierra Leone, 1957; Finance & Development in West Africa — The Sierra Leone Experience, 1961, revised, 1973; Studies in Finance & Development — The Gold Coast (Ghana) Experience, 1973. Contrb. to: Pub. Fin. — Finance Publiques; W. African Review; W. Africa; New C'wlth.; etc. Mbrships. incl: Royal C'wlth. Soc. Address: P.O. Box 431, Freetown, Sierra Leone, W. Africa.

COY, Harold, b. 24 Sept. 1902, La Habra, Calif., USA. Writer. Educ: A.B., Univ. of Ariz., 1924. Publs: The First Book of Presidents, 1952, 6th ed., 1973; Doctors & What They Do, 1956; The Mexicans, 1970; Man Comes to America, 1973. Mbr., Authors Guild, Inc. Hons: Thomas Alva Edison Fndn. Award for "The Americans" for special excellence in portraying America's past, 1959. Address: Altamirano 112-8, Mexico 4, D.F.

COZZENS, James Gould, b. 19 Aug. 1903, Chgo., Ill., USA. Writer. Educ: Harvard Univ., 1922-24. Publs: (novels) Confusion, 1924; Michael Scarlett: A History, 1925; Cock Pit, 1928; The Son of Perdition, 1929; S.S. San Pedro: A Tale of the Sea, 1931; The Last Adam, 1933; Castaway, 1934; Men & Brethren, 1936; Ask Me Tomorrow; or, The Pleasant Comedy of Young Fortunatus, 1940; The Just & the Unjust, 1943; Guard of Honor, 1948; By Love Possessed, 1957; Morning Noon & Night, 1968; Children & Others (short stories), 1964. Mbr., Nat. Inst. of Arts & Letters. Hons: Howells Medal, 1960; Litt.D., Harvard Univ., 1952. Address: Shadowbrook, Williamstown, MA 01267, USA.

CRABB, Edmund William, b. 28 Oct. 1912, Bridport, UK. Headmaster. Educ: Dip. Lit., Dip. Theol., London Univ. Publs: Religious Education Series, Book 1 to 8, until 1951; Living in Old Testament Days, 1962; Living in New Testament Days, 1962; Religious Education for CSE, 1966; Secret of the Plateau, 1961; Shadow in the Sunshine, 1968. Contrb. to: Spectrum; Life of Faith; Christian Grad.; Vistoria Inst. Mbrships: Assn. of Christian Tchrs.; Grads. Fellowship. Hons: Gilchrist Medal for Lit., 1938, Churton Collins Prize, 1938, London Univ. Address: 36 The Ridgeway, Kenton, Harrow, Middx. HA3 0LL, UK.

CRAGG, (Albert) Kenneth, b. 8 Mar. 1913, Blackpool, UK. Bishop; Reader in Religious Studies. Educ: B.A., M.A., & D.Phil., Jesus Coll., Oxford. Publs. incl: The Call of the Minaret, 1956; Counsels in Contemporary Islam, 1964; The Privilege of Man, 1968; Alive to God: Muslim & Christian Prayer, 1970; The Event of the Qur'ån, 1970; The Mind of the Qur'ån, 1973. Contrb. to: The Muslim World; Jrnl. of World Hist.; Ency. Britannica. Recip., sev. acad. hons. Address: Arts Bldg., Univ. of Sussex, Falmer, Brighton BN1 92N, UK.

CRAGO, Thomas Howard, b. 1907, Ballarat, Vic., Australia. Baptist Minister; Editor & Publications Director, Baptist Publications Board of Australia. Educ: L.Th., Univ. of Melbourne. Publs: Real Discipleship, The Story of F. W. Boreham; Wind in the Tree Tops; The Road Winds Up Hill; Champions of Liberty; Facing Today; Voice of Friendship. Contrb. to: Melbourne Age; Aust. Baptist; Spectator; Revelation; Ch. Admin.; Christian Educ. Address: 14 Gareth Dr., E. Burwood, Vic., Australia 3151.

CRAIG, David, b. 7 Oct. 1932, Aberdeen, Scotland, UK. University Teacher. Educ: M.A., Univ. of Aberdeen, 1954; Ph.D., Cambridge, 1959. Publs: Scottish Literature & the Scottish People 1680-1830, 1961; Ed., Moderne Prosa und Lyrik der Britischen Insaln, 1968; Ed., Selected Poems of Hugh MacDiarmid, 1970; The Real Foundation, 1973. Contrb. to: Critical Quarterly; Essays in Criticism; Mosaic; Listener; New Statesman; Scottish Studies; Times Lit. Supplement; Zeitschrift für Anglistik und Amerikanistik; Young C'wlth. Poets, 1964; Doves for the 70's, 1970, 1973; I am a Sensation, 1971, 1972, 1973. Mbr., Assn. for Scottish Lit. Studies. Address: 107 Bowerham Rd., Lancaster, UK.

CRAIG, Edward Anthony, pen name CARRICK, Edward, b. 1905, London, UK. Artist; Lecturer; Art Director; Illustrator. Educ: Italy & France. Publs: Designing for Moving Pictures, 1941; Meet the Common People, 1942; Art & Design in British Films, 1948; Designing for Films, 1949; Gordon Craig — The Story of his Life, 1968; Carini Motta's Trattato Sopra la Struttura de'Teatri, 1972. Contrb. to: Mask; Archtl. Review. Mbrships: Archtl. Assn.; F.R.S.A.; Soc. of Authors; Soc. for Theatre Rsch. Address: Cutlers Orchard, Bledlow, Aylesbury, Bucks., UK.

CRAIG, Elizabeth Josephine, b. 16 Feb. 1883, Addiewell, W. Lothian, UK. Author; Journalist. Educ: George Watson's Ladies Coll., Edinburgh. Publs. incl: Cooking with Elizabeth Craig; Economical Cookery; Simple Cookery; Enquire Within; Household Library (Set of 6); Standard Cookery; The Art of Irish Cookery; The Way to a Good Table; Woman, Wine & a Saucepan; Instructions to Young Cooks; Scandinavian Cookery; Scottish Cookery; Business Woman's Cook Book. Contbr. to var. mags. Mbrships: PEN; Press Club; Fellow, Royal Hort. Soc.; F.R.S.A.; Circle of Wine Writers. Address: St. Catherines, Botesdale, Diss, Norfolk, UK.

CRAIG, James Barkley, b. 30 Sept. 1912, West Henron, N.Y., USA. Editor; Writer. Educ: B.S., Kent State Univ., Ohio. Ed. & Contbr., Am. Forests Mag. Mbr., Soc. of Am. Foresters. Address: 7410 Arden Rd., Bethesda, MD 20034, USA.

CRAIG, (Sir) John, b. 1885, Craigdarragh, Straidarren, Co. Derry, Ireland. Principal Assistant Secretary, Treasury (Retired). Educ: LL.D., Trinity Coll., Dublin. Publs: Newton at the Mint; The Mint; A History of Red Tape. Contbr. to: Times Lit. Supplement; Econ. Review; Nature. Hons: K.C.V.O.; C.B. Address: 8 Clareville Ct., London SW7, UK.

CRAIG, Maurice James, b. 1919, Belfast, N. Ireland, UK. Former Inspector of Ancient Monuments; Poet; Author. Educ: B.A., Ph.D; Magdalene Coll., Cambridge; Trinity Coll., Dublin. Publs: Some Way for Reason (poems), 1948; The Volunteer Earl (biog.), 1948; Dublin 1660-1860, 1952; Irish Book-Bindings 1600-1800, 1954; Ireland Observed, 1970. Contbr. to: Irish Times; New Writing; Ency. Britannica; The Bell; Dublin Mag.; etc. Address: 97 Strand Rd., Dublin 4, Repub. of Ireland.

CRAIG, (Rev. Prof.) Robert, b. 22 Mar. 1917, Markinch, Fife, UK. Professor of Theology; University Principal & Vice Chancellor. Educ: M.A., 1938, B.D., 1941, Ph.D., 1950, St. Andrew's Univ., UK; S.T.M., Union Theol. Sem., N.Y., USA, 1949. Publs: The Reasonableness of True Religion, 1954; Social Concern in the Thought of William Temple, 1963; Religion: Its Reality & its Relevance, 1965; The Church: Unity in Integrity, 1966; Politics & Religion: A Christian View, 1972. On Belonging to a University, 1974. Hons: C.F., 1947; D.D., St. Andrew's Univ., 1967. Address: The Univ. of Rhodesia, P.O. Box 2702, Salisbury, Rhodesia.

CRAMPTON, Patricia Elizabeth (née Cardew Wood), b. 12 Dec. 1925, Bombay, India. Translator. Educ: M.A., St. Hugh's Coll., Oxford, UK; Fellow, Inst. of Linguists. Publs. (transls.) incl: Thor Heyerdahl's The Ra Expeditions (Norwegian); Godfried Bomans' Wily Wizard & Wicked Witch (Dutch); Dürer Today; Johannes Kepler; Immanuel Kant 1724-1974; Thomas Mann 1874-1974 (German); Mr. Bumblemoose series, 8 vols. (Dutch). Contbr. to: World Justice; German Studies; Apollo; etc. Mbrships: Comm of Mgmt. & Coun., Soc. of Authors; Coun., Inst. of Linguists; Past Chmn., Transls'. Assn.; Comm.; Transls'. Guild. Address: The Coach House, The Butts, Brentford, Middx., UK.

CRANKSHAW, Edward, b. 3 Jan. 1909. Journalist; Writer. Educ: Bishop's Stortford Coll. Publs: Joseph Conrad: Aspects of the Art of the Novel, 1936; Vienna; the Image of a Culture in Decline, 1938; Britain & Russia, 1945; Russia & The Russians, 1947; Russia by Daylight, 1951; Gestapo: Instrument of Tyranny, 1956; Russia without Stalin, 1956; Khrushchev's Russia, 1959; The Fall of the House of Hapsburg, 1963; The New Cold War: Moscow v. Peking, 1963; Khrushchev: a biography, 1966; Maria Theresa, 1969; The Hapsburgs, 1971; Tolstoy: the Making of a Novelist, 1974; (novels) Nina Lessing, 1938; What Glory?, 1939; The Creedy Case, 1954. Contbr. to: Observer, 1947-68; & num. jrnls. Mbrships: F.R.S.L. Recip., T.D. Address: Church House, Sandhurst, Kent, UK.

CRANSTON, Maurice (William), b. 8 May 1920, London, UK. Professor of Political Science. Educ: Univ. of London; Univ. of Oxford; M.A., B.Litt. Publs: Freedom — A New Analysis, 1953; Human Rights Today, 1954; John Locke, a Biography, 1957; John Stuart Mill, 1958; Sartre, 1962; Western Political Philosophers, 1964; A Glossary of Political Terms, 1964; Political Dialogues, 1969; Language & Philosophy, 1969; The New Left, 1970; The Mask of Politics, 1972. Contbr. to encys. & num. jrnls. Mbrships. incl: F.R.S.L.; Chmn., Exec. Comm., Engl. Ctr., PEN. Hons: Tom Gallon Award, 1953; James Tait Black Mem.

Prize, 1957; For. Fellow, Am. Acad. Arts & Scis., 1969. Address: 1a Kent Terrace, Regents Pk., London NW1 3RP, UK.

CRASTER, (Sir) John Montagu, b. 1901, Craster, Northumberland. Educ: Cambridge Univ. Publs: The Natural History of Dunstanburgh Castle Point; Naturalist in Northumberland, 1969. Contbr. to: The Three Northern Countiesof England; Cornhill; Chamber's Jrnl.; etc. Mbrships incl: Assoc. Sea Fisheries Comm., England & Wales (Chmn., 1949-70); Fishery Org. Soc. (Pres., 1959-69); Home Off. Advsry. Comm., Wild Birds' Protection Act, 1954-69. Hons: Kt., 1955. Address: Craster West House, Craster, Northumberland NE66, 3SR, UK.

CRATCHLEY, William Joseph, b. 16 Sept. 1908, Bristol, Glos., UK. Clerk in Holy Orders. Educ: M.A., B.Litt., Oriel Coll., Oxford; M.A., B.Sc., Ph.D., Bristol Univ.; D.D., Dublin Univ., Repub. of Ireland. Contbr. to: Expository Times; Theol.; Mod. Churchman; Oxford Dict. of the Christian Ch. Hons: Hon. Canon, Bristol & Examining Chap. to Bishop of Bristol, 1949-74; Canon Emeritus, Bristol, 1974—. Address: Amberley House, Northleach, Glos., UK.

CRATON, Michael John, b. 30 Aug. 1931, London, UK. University Teacher. Educ: B.A.(Hons.), Univ. Coll., London, 1955; M.A., 1965; Ph.D., 1968, McMaster Univ., Ont., Can. Publs: History of the Bahamas, 1962, 2nd ed., 1968; A Jamaican Plantation; The History of Worthy Park 1670-1970, 1970; Sinews of Empire; A Short History of British Slavery, 1974. Mbrships: Assn. of Caribbean Histns.; Royal C'wlth. Soc. Address: c/o Dept. of History, University of Waterloo, Ontario, Canada N2L 3G1.

CRAVEN, Margaret, b. Helena, Mont., USA. Journalist. Educ: Stanford Univ. Publs: I Heard The Owl Call My Name (on Am. Fiction Bestseller list for 1974). Contbr. of short stories to Saturday Evening Post & num. Am. mags.

CRAWFORD, Quantz L., b. 31 Oct. 1913, Cleveland, Ohio, USA. Drugless Physician (Naturopath). Educ: Dr.Chiropractic; Dr.Naturopathy; Dr.Psychol.; LL.B.; Acctcy. studies. Publs: Polio without Paralysis, 1954; Methods of Psychic Development, 1973; Hydrotherapy Simplified (chart); Rising Sign (astrol. chart), 1973. Contbr. to: Gnostica. Mbrships: Am. Naturopathic Assn.; var. relig. orgs. Address: 1022 Ridge Lake, New Orleans, LA 70001, USA.

CRAWFORD, Sallie Wallace Brown, pen name TROTTER, Sallie, b. 31 Aug. 1915, Glasgow, UK. Social Worker; State Registered Nurse; Writer. Educ: M.A., Post-grad. Dip. in Soc. Studies, Edinburgh Univ.; State Registered Nurse (England & Wales). Publs: Royal Paladin, 1950; Farewell Brave Folly, 1969; No Easy Road: a Study of the Theories & Problems Involved in the Rehabilitation of the Offender, 1970. Contbr. to: Huddersfield Examiner. Mbr., Soc. of Authors. Recip., John Craigie Cunningham Prize, Edinburgh Univ. Address: Shell Island Crafts, 36/38A Abbey St., Rhyl, Clwyd, UK.

CRAWFORD, T. G. S., b. 23 May 1945, Birmingham, UK. Government Information Officer. Publs: A History of the Umbrella, 1970. Contbr. to var. mags., UK; trade & tech. press in every continent; Cultural, educl. & lit. press in num. countries. Mbr., Intervarsity Club. Address: 9 Fullbrook Cres., Tilehurst, Reading RG3 6AX, UK.

CRAWLEY, Aidan Merivale, b. 1908, Benenden, Kent, UK. Journalist; Writer; Former Member of Parliament, Under Secretary of State for Air. Educ: M.A., Oxford Univ. Publs: Escape from Germany; De Gaulle; The Rise of Western Germany Since 1945; Reporter & Special Corres., Daily Mail, 1930-36; Fndr., ITV News, 1955; former BBC Commentator. Contbr. to: Sunday Times; Sunday Graphic; New Statesman; etc. Recip., M.B.E. Address: 19 Chester Sq., London SW1, UK.

CRAWLEY, Alan, b. 1922, Newport, Mon., UK. Educ: Leicester Coll. Publs: num. short stories, documentaries, BBC. Contbr. to: Evening News; Men Only; People; etc. Address: 66 Rodmell Ave., Saltdean, Sussex, UK.

CRAWSHAY-WILLIAMS, Rupert, b. 1908, London, UK. Reviewer of Gramophone Records. Educ: B.A., Queen's Coll., Oxford. Publs: The Comforts of Unreason, 1947; Methods & Criteria of Reasoning, 1957; Russell Remembered, 1970. Address: Castle Yard, Portmeirion, Penrhyndeudraeth, Gwynedd, UK.

CREELEY, Robert White, b. 1926, Arlington, USA. Professor of English. Educ: Harvard Univ.; Black Mtn. Coll.; Univ. of N.M.; B.A.; M.A. Publs: For Love, 1962; The Island, 1963; The Gold Diggers, 1965; Words, 1967; Pieces, 1969; The Charm, 1969; A Quick Graph, 1970; A Day Book, 1972; Listen, 1972; Contexts of Poetry, 1973. Address: Annex B, SUNY at Buffalo, Buffalo, NY 14214, USA.

CREES, Michala Kathleen, b. 27 Mar. 1928, Frome, Somerset, UK. Writer. Educ: Bristol Old Vic Theatre Schl. Publs: (plays) Shadow of the Kite, 1956; The Lasting Tune, 1970; (TV series) Crossroads, 1967-74; The Flaxton Boys, 1971; Crime Buster, 1971; (radio plays, co-author) Defeat of Varus; Madame Curie; Trojan Wars; Sword of Damocles; & num. radio & TV scripts. Mbr., Writers' Guild of GB. Address: 30 West Parade, Bristol 9, UK.

CREESE, Bethea, Writer. Publs: The Family Face; The Winter Bud; The Chequered Flag; White Laurel; Flower Piece; Evergreen Oak; The Locket; The Young Rose; Glorious Haven; Fortune Thy Foe; Beauty Queen; Little Angel; Irish Rose; Count Roger; New Girl; King of Hearts; Sea Rapture; Fire Down Below; A Rose in Wales; Damsel of Cyprus; Love for Love; Wild Jackal; Dearest & Best; Black Swan, 1974; Careers in Catering & Domestic Science, 1965. Mbrships: Soc. of Women Writers & Jrnlsts.; R.N.A. Agent: Curtis Brown Ltd. Address: Flat 14, 65 Courtfield Gdns., London SW5 0NQ, UK.

CREGAN, David Appleton Quartus, b. 1931, Buxton, Derbyshire, UK. Former Schoolmaster. Educ: B.A., Clare Coll., Cambridge Univ. Publs. incl: Ronald Rossiter; (plays) Three Men for Colverton, 1967; Transcending & the Dancers, 1968; The Houses by the Green, 1969; Miniatures, 1970; How we Held the Square, 1973; The Land of Palms & other Plays, 1974; Playbill One, 1972; A Comedy of the Changing Years; Tipper; Cast Off; The King; The Tigers in the Terrace. Contbr. to: Guardian; Contemporary Review; Plays & Players. Agent: Margaret Ramsay Ltd. Mbrships: Writer's Guild; Engl. Stage Soc. Address: 124 Briars Lane, Hatfield, Herts., UK.

CREHAN, Joseph Hugh, b. 1906, Snelland, UK. Theologian. Educ: Univ. of Oxford; Gregorian Univ., Rome, Italy; M.A.; Ph.D.; D.D. Publs: Early Christian Baptism & the Creed; Osterley Selection from the Latin Fathers; Father Thurston; Athenagoras: Embassy for the Christians; The Resurrection of the Dead; The Theology of St. John; Ed., Dictionary of Catholic Theology, 3 vols., 1962-71; Ed., sev. works by Father Thurston. Contbr. to: Theol. Studies; Jrnl. of Theol. Studies; Texte & Untersuchungen; Clergy Review; Cath. Herald; Vigiliae Christianae; The Month. Mbr., Soc. of Jesus. Address: 114 Mount St., London W1, UK.

CREMER, Jan, b. 20 Apr. 1940, Enschede, Netherlands. Author; Journalist. Educ: Acads. of Art, The Hague, Netherlands; Paris. Publs: I Jan Cremer, 1964; Jan Cremer Writes Again, 1968; I Jan Cremer Second Book; Made in U.S.A. Contbr. to: Evergreen; Cavalier; (travel Ed.) Penthouse; & sev. lit. mags. Mbrships: Fellow, Royal Geogl. Soc., London; Am. Author's Guild; Writer's Union, Netherlands; Foreign Press Assn., London; Author's League of Am. Hons: Jacob Maris Prize, 1960; Int. Book Award, Brasil, 1969; Frans Masereel Prize, 1974; Amsterdam Lit. Prize, 1967. Address: c/o Harold Matson Co., 22 E. 40th St., N.Y., NY, USA.

CRESSWELL, Helen, b. 1936, Notts., UK. Writer. Educ: B.A., King's Coll., London. Publs. incl: The Piemakers, 1967; The Signposters, 1968; The Night-watchmen, 1969; A Gift From Winklesea, 1969; At the Stroke of Midnight, 1970; The Bird Fancier, 1970; The Outlanders, 1970; Up The Pier, 1971; The Beachcombers, 1972; The White Sea Horse & other Tales of the Sea, 1972; The Bongleweed, 1973; Lizzie Dripping, 1973; Winter of the Birds, 1975. Contbr. to jrnls. & to BBC. Mbr., Soc. of Authors; PEN. Agent: A. M. Heath Ltd. Address: Old Ch. Farm, Eakring, Newark, Notts., UK.

CRICHTON, Anne O. J., b. 1920, Edinburgh, UK. Associate Professor of Health Care. Educ: Liverpool Univ.; Grad. Schl. of Bus., Columbia Univ., NYC, USA; Univ. of Wales; M.A.; Ph.D. Publs: Personnel Management in Context, 1968; Industrial Relations & the Personnel Specialists (w. P. D. Anthony), 1969; Economics of Group Practice in Saskatchewan: Vol. 1: What Price Group Practice, & Vol. II: Group Practice in the System (w. D. O. Anderson), 1973; The Community Health Centre in

Canada, Vol. III, Information Canada, 1973. Contbr. to profl. publs. Address: Dept. of Hlth. Care & Epidemiol., Fac. of Med., Univ. of B.C., Vancouver 8, B.C., Can.

CRICHTON, E(leanor) Moyra, pen name McGAVIN, Moyra, b. Angus, Scotland, UK. Former Teacher; Social Worker. Educ: Univ. of St. Andrews; Queen's Univ., Belfast; London Schl. of Econs., Univ. of London; M.A., M.Sc. Publs: Sarabel, 1961; Transl., Hal of the Ancient River — Hans Horler, 1962; The House in the Attic, 1964; Pech Gehabt, Herr Zauberer (The Wizard Who Lived in a Lighthouse); The Wizard Who Lived in a Well. Mbrships: Soc. of Authors; Brit. Assn. of Soc. Workers. Agent: Helga Greene. Address: 7 Beech Ct., 54 Fairlop Rd., Leytonstone, London E11, UK.

CRICHTON, Robert Collier, b. 30 Jan. 1925, Albuquerque, N.M., USA. Writer. Educ: B.A., Harvard Univ. Publs: The Great Imposter, 1957; The Rascal & the Road, 1961; The Secret of Santa Vittoria, 1966; The Camerons, 1971; Memoirs of a Bad Soldier, 1975. Address: 320 W. 71 St., N.Y., NY, USA.

CRICK, Bernard, b. 1929, London, UK. Professor of Politics; Editor. Educ: London & Harvard Univs.; B.Sc.(Econ.), Ph.D. Publs: American Science of Politics, 1959; Guide to Manuscripts Relating to America in Great Britain, 1960; In Defence of Politics, 1962; The Reform of Parliament, 1966; Political Theory & Practice, 1972. Contbr. to: Jt. Ed., Pol. Quarterly, 1966-; New Statesman; Guardian; Observer. Mbr., Reform Club. Address: 24 Denning Rd., London NW3, UK.

CRICK, Donald Herbert, b. 16 July 1916, Sydney, Australia. Author. Publs: Bikini Girl; Martin Place; Period of Adjustment; A Different Drummer. Contbr. to: The Australian; Sydney Morning Herald. Mbrships: Mgmt. Comm., Aust. Soc. of Authors; VP, Fellowship of Aust. Writers; Dir., Aust. Film Coun. Hons: Mary Gilmore Centenary Award, 1966; C'wlth. Lit. Fellowship, 1971 & 1973. Address: 1/1 Elamang Ave., Kirribilli, Sydney, N.S.W., Australia 2061.

CRIPPS, Matthew Anthony Leonard, b. 1913, London, UK. Former Executive Member, Regional & Government Agricultural Committees; Ecclesiastical Judge; Writer. Educ: M.A.; Oxford Univ. Publs: Agriculture Act, 1947; Agricultural Holding Act, 1948; Cripps on Compulsory Acquisition, 9th ed. Contbr. to: Ency. Britannica Yr. Books; Law Jrnl.; Observer. Hons: C.B.E.; D.S.O.; T.D.; Q.C. Address: Alton House, Felbridge, E. Grinstead, Sussex, UK.

CRISP, S. E., pen name CRISPIE, b. 1906, Walton, Suffolk, UK. Freelance Sportswriter. Educ: M.A., Univ. of Cambridge. Contbr. to: The Brit. Archer; Newsletter of the Assn. for Archery in Schls. Mbrships. incl: Soc. of Authors; Inst. of Jrnlsts.; Royal Toxophilite Soc.; Soc. of Archer-Antiquaries. Address: Rangemoor, Lytchett Matravers, Poole, Dorset BH16 6AJ, UK.

CRITCHLEY, Thomas Alan, b. 11 Mar. 1919, E. Barnet, Herts., UK. Civil Servant. Publs: The Civil Service Today, 1951; A History of Police in England & Wales, 1967, Am. ed., 1972; The Conquest of Violence, 1970; The Maul & the Pear Tree (w. P. D. James), 1971. Mbr., Reform Club. Address: 26 Temple Fortune Lane, London NW11, UK.

CROCKER, Lester Gilbert, b. 23 Apr. 1912, NYC, USA. Professor of French. Educ: B.A., 1932, M.A., 1934, N.Y. Univ.; Ph.D., Univ. of Calif., 1936. Publs. incl: An Age of Crisis. Man & World in 18th-Century French Thought, 1959; Nature & Culture. Ethical Thought in the French Enlightenment, 1963; Anthologie de la littérature française du XVIIIe siècle, 1972; Jean-Jacques Rousseau, The Prophetic Voice, 1758-78, 1973; Diderot's Chaotic Order, Approach to Synthesis, 1974. Contbr. to: 18th-Century Studies; Studies in Romanticism; Mod. Lang. Quarterly; etc. Hons. incl: Benjamin Franklin Fellow, R.S.A. (London), 1968; Nat. Book Award for Nomination, 1974. Address: 1822 Westview Rd., Charlottesville, VA 22903, USA.

CROCKER, Walter Russell, b. 25 Mar. 1902, Broken Hill, Australia. Lieutenant-Governor of South Australia. Educ: Univ. of Adelaide; Balliol Coll., Oxford; Stanford Univ. Publs: The Japanese Population Problem, 1931; Nigeria, 1936; On Governing Colonies, 1945; Self-Government for the Colonies, 1949; Nehru, 1965;

Australian Ambassador, 1971. Contbr. to: Times Lit. Supplement; Sydney Morning Herald; The Age. Recip., C.B.E., 1954. Address: The Peak Farm, Tarlee, S. Australia 5411.

CROFT, (J.) Michael, b. 8 Mar. 1922, Oswestry, UK. Theatre Director. Educ: B.A., Keble Coll., Oxford. Publs: Spare the Rod, 1954; Red Carpet to China, 1958. Recip., O.B.E., 1971. Address: 74 Bartholomew Road, London NW5, UK.

CROFT, Noel Andrew Cotton, b. 30 Nov. 1906, Stevenage, Herts., UK. Former Arctic Explorer, Soldier (Colonel) & Headmaster. Educ: Lancing Coll.; Stowe Schl.; M.A., Christ Church, Oxford; Schl. of Technol., Manchester. Publs: Under the Pole Star (w. A. R. Glen), 1937; Polar Exploration, 1939, 1947; Contbr. to: Polar Record; Geogl. Mag.; Royal Geogl. Soc. Jrnl.; Mil. Review, etc. Mbrships. incl: F.R.G.S. (Hon. Sec., 1951); Alpine Club; Chmn., Reindeer Coun. of UK; Corres: Fellow, Arctic Inst. of N. Am.; Royal Inst. of Int. Affairs. Hons: Polar Medal (Clasp Arctic 1935-36), 1942; D.S.O., 1945; Back Award, Royal Geogl. Soc., 1945, 1946; O.B.E., 1970. Address: The River House, 52 Strand-on-the-Green, London W4 3PD, UK.

CROFT-COOKE, Rupert, b. 1904, Edenbridge, Kent, UK. Author. Publs. incl: (novels) Night Out; Cosmopolis; Picaro; Same Way Home; Octopus; Brass Farthing; Harvest Moon; Fall of Man; Seven Thunders; Barbary Night; Thief Clash by Night; (autobiog.) The World is Young; The Life for Me; The Blood-Red Island; The Verdict of You All; The Gardens of Camelot; The Drums of Morning; (short stories) A Few Gypsies; (var. non-fiction) Darts; Rudyard Kipling; Buffalo Bill; Sherry; Port. Contbr. to: Poetry (Chgo.); most Brit. lit. jrnls. Recip., B.E.M. (Brit. Empire Medal). Address: c/o National & Grindlays Bank Ltd., 13 St. James's Square, London SW1Y 4LF, UK.

CROMBIE, Alistair Cameron, b. 4 Nov. 1915, Brisbane, Australia. Historian of Science; University Lecturer. Educ: M.A., Ph.D., B.Sc.; Univ. of Melbourne, Aust.; Univ. of Cambridge, UK. Publs: Augustine to Galileo: Medieval & Early Modern Science, 1952, 3rd ed., 1970; Robert Grosseteste & the Origins of Experimental Science 1100-1700, 1953, 3rd ed., 1971; Scientific Change, 1963; The Mechanistic Hypothesis & the Scientific Study of Vision, 1967. Contbr. to: Proceedings Royal Soc.; Isis; Times Lit. Supplement; Ency. Britannica; etc. Mbrships. incl: Int. Acads. for Hist. of Sci. & Hist. of Med.; Fellow, Royal Hist. Soc. Hons: Galileo Prize, 1969. Address: Orchard Lea, Boars Hill, Oxford, UK.

CROMPTON, (Mrs.) Margaret Norah, pen name MAIR, Margaret, b. 14 Sept. 1901, Clifton, Bristol, UK. Biographer; Novelist. Publs: (biog.) Passionate Search: A Life of Charlotte Brontë, 1955; George Eliot: The Woman, 1960; Shelley's Dream Women, 1967; (novels, as Margaret Mair) This was my Father, etc. Contbr. to: Contemporary Review. Mbrships: Soc. of Authors; Soc. of Women Writers & Jrnlsts.; Nat. Book League; Brontë, Soc.; Keats-Shelley Mem. Assn. Address: Ashling, 88 The Street, Shalford, Guildford, UK.

CRONIN, Archibald Joseph, b. 1896, Cardross, Dumbartonshire, UK. Physician. Educ: Glasgow Univ.; M.D.; M.B.; CH.B.; D.P.H.; M.R.C.P. Publs: Hatter's Castle; Three Loves; Grand Canary; The Stars Look Down; The Citadel; The Keys of the Kingdom; The Green Years; Shannon's Way; The Spanish Gardener; Beyond This Place; Crusader's Tomb; The Northern Light; The Judas Tree. Contbr. to: Woman's Own; John Bull; Reader's Digest; Guideposts; This Week; Am. Weekly; Ladies' Home Jrnl.; Good Housekeeping; Red Book; Cosmopolitan. Recip., D.Litt.(Hon.). Address: Champ Riond, 1815 Baugy sur Clarens, Vaud, Switz.

CRONIN, Vincent Archibald Patrick, b. 1924, Tredegar, UK. Author. Educ: B.A.; Harvard Univ.; Trinity Coll., Oxford. Publs: The Golden Honeycomb; The Wise Man from the West; The Last Migration; A Pearl to India; Guide to Paris; Louis XIV; The Italian Renaissance, 2 vols. Contbr. to: Times Lit. Supplement; Punch; Book World. Address: 44 Hyde Park Sq., London W2, UK.

CRONNE, Henry Alfred, b. 1904, Shanaghan, Co. Down, UK. Emeritus Professor of Medieval History, Univ. of Birmingham. Educ: Queen's Univ.; Belfast; Balliol Coll., Oxford; Univ. of London King's Coll. & Inst. of Histl. Rsch.; M.A. Publs: Bristol Charters, 1378-1499, 1946;

Regesta Regum Anglo-Normannorum, vols. II, III & IV (jt. Ed.), 1956-69; The Reign of Stephen, Anarchy in England, 1970. Contbr. to: Engl. Histl. Review; Hist.; Univ. of Birmingham Histl. Jrnl.; Chambers Ency.; Scottish Histl. Review; Jrnl. of Ecclesiastical Hist.; Irish Histl. Studies. Mbr., W. Country Writers' Assn. Address: Winswood Cottage, Cheldon, Chulmleigh, N. Devon, UK.

CROSBIE, Hugh Provan, pen names CARRICK, John; CROSBIE, Provan, b. 1912, Girvan, UK. Bank Manager; Author; Artist. Publs: They Shall Not Die, 1944; Richer the Dust, 1962; The Vulture, 1964; Mario, 1965; Bond of Hate, 1966; Beware the Shadows, 1967; The Killer Conference, 1968; The Young & Deadly, 1969; (as Provan Crosbie) Fairways & Foul, 1964. Contbr. to Brit. provincial press; Exhibnr. in oils & water-colours. Recip., M.C., A.I.B. (Scotland). Address: c/o Robert Hale, 63 Old Brompton Rd., London SW7 3JU, UK.

CROSBY, John, b. 1912, Milwaukee, Wis., USA. Author. Educ: Yale Univ. Publs: Out of the Blue, 1951; With Love & Loathing, 1962; Sappho in Absence, 1970; The Literary Obsession, 1973; The White Telephone, 1974; An Affair of Strangers, 1975. Contbr. to: Life; Sat. Evening Post; Collier's; Punch; Look; Atlantic Monthly. Lit. Agent: Elaine Greene Lit. Agcy. Address: Woodbourne Cottage, Hampstead Norreys, Newbury, Berks., UK.

CROSLAND, Margaret McQueen, b. Bridgnorth, Shropshire, UK. Writer; Translater. Educ: B.A., London Univ. Publs: Madame Colette, 1953; Jean Cocteau, 1955; Louise of Stolberg, 1962; My Contemporaries (anthol.), 1967; Cocteau's World, 1972; Colette: The Difficulty of Loving, 1973. Contbr. to: Times Lit. Supplement. Mbrships: PEN; Soc. of Authors. Address: The Long Croft, Upper Hartfield, Sussex, UK.

CROSS, Alan Beverley, b. 1931, London, UK. Playwright. Educ: Balliol Coll., Oxford. Publs: (plays & libretti) One More River; Half a Sixpence; Boeing-Boeing; Jorrocks; The Mines of Sulphur; The Rising of the Moon; The Owl on the Battlements; Victory. Address: c/o Curtis Brown, 13 King St., London WC2, UK.

CROSS, Alexander Galbraith, b. 29 Mar. 1908, London, UK. Ophthalmic Surgeon. Educ: Univ. of Cambridge; St. Mary's Hosp. Med. Schl., London. Co-author, May & Worth's Manual of Disease of the Eye. Contbr. to: Textbook of British Surgery; Blindness; Brit. Jrnl. of Ophthalmol.; sev. other profl. jrnls. Mbrships. incl: Pres., Fac. of Ophthalmols., 1968-71; VP, Ophthalmol. Soc. of UK; Dean, Inst. of Ophthalmol., 1967-. Address: 27 Harley St., London, W1N 1DA, UK.

CROSS, (Sir) (Alfred) Rupert (Neale), b. 1912, London, UK. Professor of English Law. Educ: D.C.L., Worcester Coll., Oxford. Publs: Evidence; Precedent in English Law; Introduction to Criminal Law (co-author); Cases on Criminal Law (co-author); Outline of the Law of Evidence (co-author). Contbr. to: Law Quarterly Review; Mod. Law Review; Criminal Law Review. Mbrship: Fellow, Brit. Acad. Address: All Souls College, Oxford, UK.

CROSS, Colin John, pen name WEIR, John, b. 12 Jan. 1928, Cardiff, UK. Journalist. Educ: B.A., Queen's Coll., Cambridge. Publs: The Fascists in Britain, 1961; The Liberals in Power 1905-14, 1963; Philip Snowden, 1966; The Fall of the British Empire, 1968; Who Was Jesus?, 1970; Adolf Hitler, 1973. Contbr. to: The Observer. Address: c/o A. D. Peters & Co., 19 Buckingham St., London WC2, UK.

CROSS, Ian, b. 1925, Wanganui, NZ. Lecturer in Literature & Journalism. Educ: Wanganui Tech. Coll. Publs: The God Boy; And the Backward Sex; After Anzac Day. Contbr. to: Landfall. Address: 85 Customhouse Quay, Wellington, NZ.

CROSS, Robert Singlehurst, b. 12 May 1925, Liverpool, UK. Publisher. Educ: M.A., Trinity Coll., Cambridge; Cert. of Merit, Royal Agricl. Coll., Cirencester. Publs: Death in Another World, 1957; A Portion for Foxes, 1958; Pai Naa (w. Dorothy Thatcher), 1959. Mbr., Election Comm., Travellers' Club. Agent: A. P. Watt & Sons. Address: Foxbury Meadow, Godalming, Surrey, UK.

CROSS, Wilbur Lucius III, b. 1918, Scranton, Pa., USA. Editor; Author; Director of Editorial Services for Continental Oil Co. Educ: B.A., Yale Univ. Publs. incl:

Challengers of the Deep, 1959; An Enduring Heritage, 1961; White House Weddings, 1968; Jobs with a Future in Computers, 1969; The Complete Book of Paper Antiques (co-author), 1973; A Guide to Unusual Vacations, 1973; over 400 articles on num. subjects & Ed. of publs. on pol., mil. operation, bus., educ., recreation, etc. Contbr. to: Reader's Digest; num. anthols.; etc. Mbrships: Authors' League Am.; Soc. Mag. Writers (former Sec.). Address: 59 Valley Rd., Bronxville, NY 10708, USA.

CROSSLEY-HOLLAND, Kevin, b. 7 Feb. 1941, Mursley, UK. Writer & Publisher. Educ: B.A., Univ. of Oxford. Publs: Havelok the Dane, 1964; King Horn, 1965; The Green Children, 1966; The Callow Pit Coffer, 1968; Transl., Beowulf, 1968; Wordhoard (w. J. P. Walsh), 1969; Transl., Storm & Other Riddles, 1970; The Pedlar of Swaffham, 1971; Pieces of Land: Journeys to 8 Islands, 1972; The Rain-Giver, 1972; The Sea Stranger, 1973; The Fire Brother, 1975; Green Blades Rising: The Anglo-Saxons, 1975. Contbr. to: Times Lit. Supplement; Times; Guardian; New Statesman; Spectator; Listener. Mbr., Lit. Panel, Gtr. London Arts Assn. Recip., Award for Best Book for Young Children, Arts Coun., 1966-68. Agent: Deborah Rogers. Address: c/o Deborah Rogers, 29 Goodge St., London WC1, UK.

CROUSE, John Oliver, b. 16 Jan. 1931, El Paso, Tex., USA. Writer; Photographer. Educ: B.A., Univ. of Miami, Fla. Contbr. to: Powerboat Mag.; Kazi, Tokyo, Japan; Nautica, Rome, Italy. Mbr., Sigma Delta Chi, profl. jrnlsm. soc. Address: 3425 N. Moorings Way, Miami, FL 33133, USA.

CROW, William Bernard, b. 11 Sept. 1895, Stratford, UK. Biologist. Educ: A.A., Oxon., 1911; M.Sc., 1920, Ph.D., 1923, D.Sc., 1929, M.Sc., Univ. Coll. of S. Wales & Mon., 1926. Publs: Mysteries of the Ancients, 18 parts, 1941-45; A Synopsis of Biology, 1960; A History of Magic, Witchcraft & Occultism, 1968; The Arcana of Symbolism, 1970. Contbr. to: New Phytol.; Annals of Botany; Jrnl. of Genetics; Med. World; Scientia; Am. Naturalist; etc. Mbrships. incl: Fellow, Linnean Soc., 1918—; Fellow, later Sci. Fellow, Zool. Soc. of London, 1928—; F.R.S.M., 1929—. Recip., num. hons. Address: 78 Broadmead Rd., Woodford Green, Essex. UK.

CROWDER, Michael, b. 1934, London, UK. Professor of History. Educ: M.A., Oxford Univ. Publs: Pagans & Politicians, 1959; The Story of Nigeria, 1959; Senegal, 1962, 1966; West Africa under Colonial Rule, 1968; Co-Ed., West African Chiefs, 1970; Ed., West African Resistance, 1970; Co-Ed., History of West Africa, 2 vols., 1972 & 1974; Revolt in Bussa, 1973; Co-Ed., Historical Atlas of Africa, forthcoming. Contbr. to: Times; Financial Times; Geogl. Mag.; W. Africa; Nigeria Mag. (Ed., 1959-62); var. acad. jrnls. Mbrships: Hon. Fellow, Histl. Soc. of Ghana. Hons: Off., Nat. Order of Senegal. Agent: Curtis Brown Ltd. Address: Dar Demdam, Rue Merrouche, Casbah, Tangier, Morocco.

CROWDER, Richard Henry, b. 7 Oct. 1909, Remington, Ind., USA. Professor of English; Author. Educ: A.B., 1931, M.A., 1933, DePauw Univ.; Yale Univ., 1936-37; Ph.D., State Univ. Of Iowa, 1944. Publs: Those Innocent Years ... James Whitcomb Riley, 1958; No Featherbed to Heaven ... Michael Wigglesworth, 1631-1705, 1962; Carl Sandburg, 1964; Frontiers of American Culture (co-ed.), 1968. Contbr. to: New England Quarterly; Bucknell Review; S. Atlantic Quarterly; Poetry; Chgo. Review; Mod. Lang. Notes; Am. Lit. Schlrship. Annual; etc. Address: 1525 Sheridan Rd., W. Lafayette, IN 47906, USA.

CROWE (Lady), Bettina Lum, pen name LUM, Peter, b. 27 Apr. 1911, Mpls., Minn., USA. Writer. Publs: Stars in Our Heaven, 1948, 1951; Fabulous Beasts, 1953; Peking, 1950-1953, 1958; The Purple Barrier, 1960; Italian Fairy Tales, 1963, 1967; Fairy Tales from the Barbary Coast, 1967; The Growth of Civilization in East Asia, 1969; Folk Tales from North America, 1973; Six Centuries in East Asia, 1973. Contbr. to: Blackwood's Mag.; Royal Ctrl. Asian Jrnl. Mbrships: Royal Ctrl. Asian Soc.; Soc. of Woman Geogs., USA. Agent: Curtis Brown. Address: Pigeon House, Bibury, Cirencester, Glos. GL7 5NT, UK.

CROWE, Sylvia, b. 15 Sept. 1901, Banbury, UK. Landscape Architect. Educ: Swanley Horticultural Coll. Publs: Garden Design, 1957; Tomorrows Landscape, 1956; Landscape of Roads, 1958; Landscape of Power, 1960; The Gardens of Mughul India (jt. author), 1972. Contbr. to

num. profl. jrnls. inclng: Archtl. Review; Country Life; Landscape Design. Mbrships. incl: F.R.I.B.A.; Inst. of Landscape Archts. Recip., D.B.E., 1973. Address: B/59 Ladbroke Grove, London W11 3AT, UK.

CROWLEY, Christine Asmussen, b. 1922, Aabenraa, Denmark. Professional Translator. Publs. (transls.): (w. Frederick C. J. Crowley) Peter Aberlard; Philosophy & Christianity in the Middle Ages — Leif Grane, 1970; Orders, Medals & Decorations of Britain & Europe — Paul Hieronymussen, 1967; Technological Forecasting in Practice; Easy Embroidery — Lis Paludan, 1974; Playing with Puppets — Lis Paludan, 1974. Address: 31 Commonfield Rd., Banstead, Surrey, UK.

CROWLEY, Desmond William, b. 11 Oct. 1920, Invercargill, NZ. University Director of Adult Education; Editor; Writer. Educ: M.A., Dip. Ed., Univ. of NZ; Ph.D., Univ. of London, UK. Publs: Ed., New Zealand Labour's Pioneering Days, 1950; The Background to Current Affairs, 1958; The Role of Colleges of Advanced Education in Australian Adult Education, 1968. Contbr. to: BBC; Aust. Broadcasting Commn.; Aust. & NZ Histl. Studies; Ed., Current Affairs Bulletin. etc. Mbrships. incl: Aust. Assn. of Adult Educ. (var. past offs.); Trustee, Sydney Mus. Applied Art & Scis., 1965-. Hons: Fellow, Aust. Coll. Educ., 1974; sev. acad. awards. Address: 1 Armstrong Street, Willoughby, N.S.W., Australia 2068.

CROWLEY, Frederick C. J., b. 1910, London, UK. Professional Translator. Publs. (transls.): (w. Christine Crowley) Peter Aberlard; Philosophy & Christianity in the Middle Ages — Lief Grane, 1970; Orders, Medals & Decorations of Britain & Europe — Paul Hieronymussen, 1967; Technological Forecasting in Practice, 1973. A.C.I.S. Recip., M.M. Address: 31 Commonfield Rd., Banstead, Surrey, UK.

CROWN, Paul, b. 19 June 1928, Braddock, Pa., USA. Retailing Executive. Educ: B.B.A., Univ. of Pitts., 1952; M.S., N.Y. Univ., 1962. Publs: Legal Protection for the Consumer, 1963; What You Should Know About Retail Merchandising, 1966; What You Should Know About Your Mailing Lists, 1973; Ed., 1st 17 books of Business Almanac Series. Address: 12 Chance St., Hicksville, NY 11801, USA.

CROWN, Sidney, b. 1924, London, UK. Consultant Psychiatrist. Educ: Middx. Hosp., London; Ph.D. Publs: Essential Principles of Psychiatry, 1971; Psychotherapy, 1973; Comments on the Case of N. E. Gorbanevskaya (essay), 1972; Pornography & Sexual Promiscuity (paper), 1973; Over 40 papers on psychol., psych. & psychosomatic topics. Contbr. to var. profl. jrnls. Mbrships: M.R.C.P.; Fellow, Royal Coll. of Psychs.; Fellow, Royal Soc. of Med.; Expmtl. Psychol. Soc.; Brit. Acad. Forensic Scis. Address: 5 Northwick Ave., Harrow, Middx. HA3 0AA, UK.

CROWTHER, George, b. 4 Mar. 1927, London, UK. Writer. Educ: Royal Acad. of Dramatic Art; M.A., Oxford Univ. Publs: Sanitized For Your Protection, 1966. Address: 7 Tackley Pl., Oxford OX2 6RR, UK.

CROWTHER, J. G., b. 1899, Lightcliffe, Yorks., UK. Journalist; Author; Former British Council Executive. Educ: Exhibnr., Trinity Coll., Cambridge. Publs: Francis Bacon, 1960; Founders of British Science, 1960; Scientists of the Industrial Revolution, 1962; Statesmen of Science, 1965; Science in Modern Society, 1967; The Social Relations of Science, 1968; Scientific Types, 1969; Fifty Years with Science, 1970; The Cavendish Laboratory 1874-1974, 1974. Contbr. to: New Sci.; Nature; etc.; Sci. Corres.; Manchester Guardian, 1928-48. Mbr., Assn. of Sci., Tech & Managerial Staffs. Address: 2 Mytre Ct., Johns Mews, London WC1N 2PA, UK.

CROZET, Charlotte, b. St. Etienne, France. Writer. Publs: Les Petites Métamorphoses, 1957; Le même piège, 1965, Engl. ed., as Girl-trap, 1968; Les amours infantiles, 1967; Marianne ou les autres, 1972. Contbr. to: Mercure de France; Nouvelle Review Française; BBC. Mbr., Association des Amis des Cahiers du Nouveau Commerce, Paris. Address: Flat 7, 23 Compayne Gdns., London NW6 3DE, UK.

CROZETTI, Ruth G. Warner (Lora), pen names WARNER-CROZETTI, R.; LORING, J. M.; O'MAHONEY, Rich, b. 18 May 1915, Indianapolis, Ind., USA. Educ: Studies in Lit., Philos., Psychol., Social Ethics. Publs: Merry Christmas, You Bastards (as Rich O'Mahoney), 1967; The Widderburn Horro, 1971 (also film); House of the Black

Death. Contbr. to: Fate Mag. Mbr., L.A. Sci. Fantasy Soc. Address: 2345 Wisteria St., Simi Valley, CA 93056, USA.

CROZIER, Brian, b. 1918, Kuridala, Qld., Australia. Director, Institute for Study of Conflict. Educ: Trinity Coll. of Music, London, UK. Publs: The Rebels, 1960; The Morning After, 1963; Neo-Colonialism, 1964; South-East Asia in Turmoil, 1965; The Struggle for the Third World, 1966; Franco, 1967; The Masters of Power, 1969; The Future of Communist Power, 1970; De Gaulle, 2 vols., 1973-74; A Theory of Conflict, 1974. Contbr. to: Daily Telegraph; Times; Nat. Review; Lugano Review; etc. Mbr., Inst. for Strategic Studies. Agent: David Higham Assoc. Address: 112 Bridge Lane, London NW11 9JS, UK.

CROZIER, Mary, b. 20 Sept. 1908, Manchester, UK. Journalist. Educ: B.A., Somerville Coll., Oxford. An Old Siek Family, 1947; Broadcasting: Sound & Television, 1958. Past contbr. to: The Tablet; The Annual Register of World Events; Radio Times; BBC Handbook; Ed. Staff, The Guardian, 1944-66. Address: 71 Priory Rd., Kew Gardens, Surrey, UK.

CRUIKSHANK, Marjorie, b. 1920, Rochdale, UK. Senior Lecturer. Educ: Ph.D., Univ. of Leeds. Publs: Church & State in English Education, 1870 to Present Day, 1963; History of Teacher Training in Scotland, 1970. Contbr. to: Brit. Jrnl. of Educl. Studies; Hist. of Educ. Quarterly, USA; Paedagogica Historica; Educl. jrnls. in Brit. & USA. Address: 105 Moss Lane, Alderley Edge, Cheshire, UK.

CRUISE O'BRIEN, Conor, b. 3 Nov. 1917, Dublin, Repub. of Ireland. Government Minister. Educ: B.A., Ph.D., Trinity Coll., Dublin. Publs. incl: Parnell & His Party, 1957; To Katanga & Back, 1962; Writers & Politics, 1965; The United Nations, 1967; Sacred Drama, 1967; Murderous Angels, 1968; (Ed.) Power & Consciousness, 1969; Camus, 1969; A Concise History of Ireland, 1972; The Suspecting Glance, (w. Maire Cruise O'Brien), 1972. Contbr. to: N.Y. Review of Books; Observer. Mbrships. incl: Royal Irish Acad.; Pro-Chancellor Dublin Univ. Address: Whitewater, The Summit, Howth, Co. Dublin, Repub. of Ireland.

CRUMP, Barry John, b. 16 May 1935, Papatoetoe, NZ. Writer. Publs: A Good Keen Man, 1961; Hang On a Minute Mate, 1962; One of Us, 1963; Two in One, 1964; Gulf, 1964; There & Back, 1965; Scrapwaggon, 1965; The Odd Spot of Bother, 1967; No Reference Intended, 1968; Warm Beer, 1969; A Good Keen Girl, 1970; Bastards I Have Met, 1971; Fred, 1972; The Best of Barry Crump, 1974. Mbr., Bahai (World Order of Baha'a Ilah). Recip., Hubert Church Award for Prose, 1963. Address: Box. 5090, Auckland, NZ.

CRYER, (Rev.) Neville Barker, pen name, FERN, Edwin, b. 23 May 1924, Accrington, UK. General Director, British & Foreign Bible Society. Educ: M.A., Hertford Coll., Oxford; Bangalore OCTU; Ridley Hall, Cambridge. Publs: God is Always Greater (transl. from German), 1963; Mary, Image of the Church (transl. from French), 1965; John Eliot (in 7 Pioneer Missionaries), 1966; Parishes with a Purpose, 1967; Experiment in Unity, 1968; By What Rite, 1969; Market Unlimited, 1972; God's Communicators, 1975. Contbr. to var. publs. Mbrships. incl: Authors Soc.; Athenaeum. Address: 5 Meadway, Epsom, Surrey KT19 8JZ, UK.

CSANADI, Imre, b. 10 Jan. 1920, Zámoly, Hungary. Writer; Publisher's Reader. Publs: Erdei Vadak, Égi Madarak (Beasts of the Wood, Birds of the Sky), 1956; Csillagforgó (Astral-round), 1966; Osszegyüjtott Versek (Collected Poems), forthcoming. Contbr. to: Magvetö publs. Mbr., Hungarian Writers' Union. Hons: József Attila Prize 1954, 1964, 1973; Kossuth Prize 1975. Address: H-1149 Budapest, Varga Gy. A.park 12/C, Hungary.

CSERES, Tibor, b. 1 April, 1915, Gyergyóremete, Romania. Writer. Educ: Cert. in Econs., Univ. of Kolozsvár. Publs: Clover Baron, 1956; Cold Days, 1963; A Wolf of a Man, 1966; Black Rose, 1967; Players & Lovers, 1970; Here on the Earth, 1973. Mbrships: Hungarian Writers' Union; Hungarian PEN. Recip., József Attila Prize (3 times). Address: 1026 Budapest, II Orló 16, Hungary.

CSERNAI, Zoltán, b. 21 Jan. 1925, Békéscsaba, Hungary. Economist. Educ: Univ. Degree in Econs. Publs: Titok a Világ Tetején (Secret on the Top of the World), 1961, also German & Czechoslovakian eds.; Az özönviz balladája (Ballad of the Flood), 1964, also German ed.;

Atleóntisz (Atlantis), 1971; Csukák, harcsák és rosszcsontok (Pikes, Silures & Scallywags), 1972. Contbr. to: SF Tájékoztató (Ed.), Sci. Fiction Bulletin, Hungarian Writers' Assn. Mbrships: Hungarian Writers' Assn.; Sci. Fiction Work Comm. Address: 1181 Budapest, Hosszuház u.10.f.3., Hungary.

CUATRECASAS, Jose, b. 19 Mar. 1903, Camprodon, Catalonia, Spain. Botanist. Educ: Lic. in Pharm., Univ. of Barcelona, 1923; Doct. in Pharm. (Botany), Univ. of Madrid, 1928. Publs: Flora & Vegetation of Macizo de Magina (Jaen, Spain), 1929; Observaciones Geobotanicas en Colombia, 1934; Prima Flora Colombiana, 3 vols., 1957, 1958 & 1959; Aspectos de la Vegetacion Natural de Colombia, 1958; A Taxonomic Revision of the Humiriaceae, 1961; Cacoa & its Allies — A Taxonomic Revision of Genus Theobroma, 1964; Brunelliaceae, Flora Neotropica, 1970. Contbr. to num. botan. jrnls. Address: Dept. of Botany, Smithsonian Instn., Wash. DC 20560, USA.

CUDDON, John Anthony, b. 1928, Southsea, UK. Writer. Educ: M.A., B.Litt., Univ. of Oxford. Publs: The Owl's Watchsong, 1960; A Multitude of Sins, 1961; Testament of Iscariot, 1962; The Acts of Darkness, 1963; The Six Wounds, 1965; The Bride of Battersea, 1967; Companion Guide to Jugoslavia, 1968. Contbr. to: Guardian; Times Lit. Supplement; Time & Tide; Tablet; Truth; Quarterly Review; Contemporary Review; Blackfriars Mag.; Times; Sunday Times; Sunday Telegraph; Observer. Address: 28c Bolton Gdns., London SW5, UK.

CUDLIPP, Reginald, b. 1910, Cardiff, UK. Newspaper Editor; Institute Director. Appts. incl: Special Corres. in USA, 1947, Features Ed., 1948-50, Dpty. Ed., 1950-53, Ed., 1953-59 News of the World; Dir., Anglo-Japanese Economic Inst., London, 1961-. Address: 342 Grand Buildings, Trafalgar Sq., London WC2, UK.

CULL, John Guinn Jr., b. 9 Nov. 1934, Venice, Ill., USA. Director, Regional Counselor Training Program & Professor, Department of Rehabilitation Counseling, Virginia Commonwealth University. Educ: B.S., 1959., M.Ed. Counseling, 1960, Texas A & M Univ.; Ph.D. Clinical Psychol., 1967, Texas Tech. Univ. Publs: Co-Author & Co-Ed. (w. R. E. Hardy), over 20 books inclng: Introduction to Rehabilitation Research; Mental Retardation & Physical Disability; Fundamentals of Criminal Behavior & Correctional Systems. Mbr., num. profl. assns. inclng: Prog. Comm., Int. Assn. of Rehabilitation Facilities; AAAS; Am. Psychol. Assn.; Am. Assn. of Workers for the Blind. Hons. incl: Nat. Citation for Contbns. to Rehabilitations Profn., Nat. Rehabilitation Assn., Las Vegas, 1974; Community Service Award, Peninsula Assn. for Retarded Children, Hampton, Va. Address: P.O. Box 499-WWRC, Fisherville, VA 22939, USA.

CULLINAN, Elizabeth, b. 1933, N.Y., USA. Writer. Educ: Marymount Coll., NYC. Publs: House of Gold, 1970; The Time of Adam (short stories), 1971. Contbr. to New Yorker Mag. Hons: Houghton Mifflin Lit. Fellowship, 1970; New Writers Award for 1970, Gt. Lakes Colls. Assn. Address: c/o The New Yorker Magazine, 25 West 43rd St., N.Y., NY 10021, USA.

CULLINGFORD, (Rev.) Cecil Howard Dunstan, b. 1904, London, UK. School Headmaster; Rural Dean. Educ: M.A., Univ. of Cambridge. Publs: Ed., British Caving; Ed., A Manual of Caving Techniques. Contbr. to: The Faith of an Evangelical; Exploring Caves; var. caving jrnls. Mbrships: Brit. Cave Rsch. Assn.; VP, Wessex Caving Club. Address: The Staithe, Beccles, Suffolk, UK.

CULLISON, Alvin Edwin, occasional pen names HANDLEMAN, Mark, & WRIGHTMAN, Alistair, b. 5 Aug. 1923, Phila., Pa., USA. Journalist. Educ: B.S., Temple Univ., Phila., Pa. Publs: Co-author of a number of books. Contbr. to: Economist; Investors Chronicle; Jrnl. of Commerce; Fin. Times; Banker; Daily Telegraph Mag.; N.Y. Times; etc. Mbrships: Overseas Press Club, N.Y.; For. Corres'. Club Japan (Sec. 1973 & formerly on Bd.). Address: c/o For. Corres'. Club of Japan, 1-2 Marunouchi, 2-chome, Chiyoda-ku, Tokyo 100, Japan.

CULLMANN, Oscar, b. 1902, Strasbourg, France. University Rector, Basle & Professor, Universities of Basle & Paris; Author. Educ: Dr. Theol., Dr. Phil., D.D., Dr. h.c.; Univ. of Strasbourg; Sorbonne Univ., Paris. Publs: (most w. sev. eds. in Engl., German, French, Swedish, Dutch, Italian,

Spanish and/or Japanese). Le problème littéraire et historique du roman pseudo-clémentin, 1930; Christ & Time, 1946; Baptism in the New Testament, 1948; Peter Disciple, Apostle, Martyr, 1952; The Christology of the New Testament, 1960; Salvation in History, 1966; Jesus & the Revolutionaries, 1970; The Johannine Group, 1975. Contbr. to acad. publs. Mbr., Inst. de France; British Acad.; Royal Dutch Acad.; Acad. Mayence. Hons: Off. of Légion d'Honneur; Comm. Palmes Académiques; Hon. Degrees, Lausanne, Manchester, Edinburgh. Address: 10A Birmannsgasse, CH 4055 Basle, Switz.

CUMING, (Rev. Canon) Geoffrey John, b. 9 Sept. 1917, Gilston, UK. Clergyman. Educ: M.A., D.D., Oriel Coll., Oxford. Publs: The World's Encyclopaedia of Recorded Music, 1952; The Durham Book, 1961; A History of Anglican Liturgy, 1969. Contbr. to: Jrnl. of Theol. Studies; Jrnl. of Ecclesiastical Hist.; New Testament Studies; Studia Liturgica; La Maison-Dieu; Theol. Address: 4 Ridgemont Close, Oxford OX2 7PJ, UK.

CUMMING, Primrose Amy, b. 1915, Kent, UK. Writer. Publs: Flying Horseman, 1959; The Mystery Trek, 1964; Foal of the Fjords, 1966; Penny & Pegasus, 1969; 17 other children's books. Contbr. to children's jrnls. & annuals. Address: Wynberg, Sandhurst, Hawkhurst, Kent, UK.

CUNLIFFE, Elaine, b. Burnley, Lancs., UK. Travel Writer. Publs: Tomorrow's Country, 1966; Unforgettable Journey, 1968; The Wandering Moon, 1969; Elaine's Australian Safari, 1970; Hi Skunks, 1975. Contbr. to: Lady; Lancs. Life; Border Life; Homes & Gdns.; House Beautiful; Scottish Field. Mbrships: Authors Soc.; Engl. Speaking Union. Address: Barr Cottage, Orchardton by Castle Douglas, Galloway, Scotland, UK.

CUNLIFFE, John Arthur, b. 1933, Colne, Lancs., UK. Teacher. Educ: Leeds & North-Western Polytechnic Lib. Schls.; Fellow, Lib. Assn. Publs: incl: The Adventures of Lord Pip, 1970; The Giant Who Stole the World, 1970; Riddles & Rhymes & Rigmaroles, 1971; Giant Kippernose & Other Stories, 1972; The Great Dragon Competition, 1973; The King's Birthday Cake, 1973; Small Monkey Tales, 1974; Farmer Barnes & the Snow Picnic, 1974; The Farmer, the Rooks & the Cherry Tree, 1975. Contbr. to: Children's Book Review; Jr. Lib. Mbr., Soc. of Authors. Agent: A. P. Watt. Address: 32 Greenside, Kendal, Cumbria LA9 4LD, UK.

CUNLIFFE-JONES, (Rev.) Hubert, b. 1905, Strathfield, N.S.W., Australia. Emeritus Professor of Theology, Univ. of Olanchester. Educ: Newington Coll., Univ. of Sydney; Camden Coll.; St. Catherine's Soc.; Mansfield Coll., Oxford; B.A.; B.Litt. Publs: The Holy Spirit; God's Truth & Power Through the Bible Today; Technology, Community & Church; The Authority of the Biblical Revelation; Deuteronomy; Jeremiah; Christian Theology since 1600, 1970. Contbr. to: Expository Times; Theol. Recip., D.D. h.c. Address: 5 Wood Rd., Manchester M16 9RB, UK.

CUNNINGHAM, Phyllis Jean, (Mrs. P. J. Cameron, b. 1914, London, UK. Editor; Author; Nurse. Educ: B.A., S.R.N., S.C.M., H.V. Cert.; Univ. of London; St. Thomas's Hosp.; Royal Coll. Nursing. Publs: Public Health for the Nursing Student (w. H. M. Cousens), 1953; A Dictionary of Midwifery & Public Health (w. G. Dodds), 2nd ed., 1963; Modern Health (w. H. S. Gear), 1965; Ed., Nursery Nursing, 1967; Ed., Principles of Health Visiting, 1967; Ed., The Nurse's Dictionary, 28th ed., 1975; The Faber Pocket Medical Dictionary (w. P. A. Riley), 1974. Contbr. to profl. jrnls. Mbr., Royal Coll. Nursing. Address: Garden Flat, 16 Priory Terrace, London NW6 4DH, UK.

CURIE, Eve, b. 1904, Paris, France. Publisher; Special Adviser to Sec.-Gen. NATO, 1952-54. Educ: B.Sc., Ph.B., Sevigne Coll., Paris. Publs: Madame Curie (different Lang. eds. throughout the world); Journey Among Warriors. Contbr. to: Cosmopolitan; Sulgrave, USA. Address: Sutton Place S., NYC, NY 10022, USA.

CURL, James Stevens, pen name ADYTUM, b. 26 Mar. 1937, Belfast, UK. Architect; Town Planning Consultant; Author. Educ: Schls. of Arch., Belfast & Oxford; Dept. of Land Use Studies, Oxford; Dipl.Arch., Dip.T.P., Oxford. Publs: European Cities & Society, 1970; The Victorian Celebration of Death, 1972; City of London Pubs (w. Timothy M. Richards), 1973; Victorian Architecture: Its Practical Aspects, 1973. Mbrships: F.S.A., London & Scotland; Assoc., Royal Inst. of Brit. Archts.; Royal Town Planning Inst.; Royal Inst. of Archts. of Ireland; Assoc.,

Royal Inc. of Archts. in Scotland. Recip., Sir Charles Lanyon Prize, 1958. Agent: A. D. Peters & Co. Ltd. Address: 52 Kingsborough Gdns., Glasgow G12 9NL, UK.

CURLEY, Daniel, b. 4 Oct. 1918, E. Bridgewater, Mass., USA. Writer. Educ: A.B., M.A., Univ. of Ala. Publs: That Marriage Bed of Procrustes (stories), 1957; How Many Angels (novel), 1958; A Stone Man, Yes (novel), 1964; In the Hands of Our Enemies (stories), 1971; Accent Anthology (co-ed. w. George Scouffas & Charles Shattuck), 1974. Contbr. to: Accent; Perspective; Epoch; Mod. Fiction Studies; Revista de Letras; etc. Mbr., Ed., Bd., Accent mag., 1955-60, currently Ed., Ascent. Hons. incl: Martha Foley Selection of Best Short Stories, 1955, 1964; O. Henry Selection, 1965; Nat. Coun. of Arts Award, 1970. Address: English Dept., University of Illinois, Urbana, IL 61801, USA.

CURLING, Bryan William Richard, pen name HOTSPUR, b. 15 Nov. 1911, Bitterne, Hants., UK. Author; Racing Journalist. Publs: British Racecourses, 1951; The Captain, the Biography of Captain Sir Cecil Boyd-Rochfort, 1970; The Grand National (w. Clive Graham), 1972. Contbr. to: Stud & Stable; Racing Corres., Daily Telegraph, 1946-65. Recip., V.R.D. Address: Fullerton Manor, Near Andover, Hants., UK.

CURPHEY, Edward George, b. 21 July 1910, Liverpool, UK. Technical Author; Translator. Educ: Univ. of Liverpool, 1930-34. Contbr. to: Chem. & Ind.; Indl. Chem.; Mfg. Chem.; Chem. Age; Rubber Age & Synthetics; Plastics; Brit. Plastics; Sci. Lubrication; Petroleum; Petroleum Times; Jrnl. of the Inst. of Petroleum; Adhesives; Chem. Products; Can. Chem. Processing; Organic Chem. Abstracts transl'd. from French & Italian. Mbrships. incl: Soc. of Authors; Inst. of Tech. Communicators; Econ. Rsch. Coun. Address: 72 Ham Rd., Worthing, Sussex, UK.

CURRAGH, Katharine, b. 1909, Bristol, UK. Educ: Bedford Coll., London Univ. Publs: Lady in to Cook. Address: Castle Yard, Portmeirion, Gwynedd, UK.

CURRAN, (Sir) Samuel Crowe, b. 25 May 1912, Ballymena, Ulster, UK. Principal & Vice-Chancellor, University of Strathclyde. Educ: M.A., B.Sc., Ph.D., Univ. of Glasgow, 1937, D.Sc., 1950; Ph.D., St. John's Coll., Cambridge, 1940. Publs: Counting Tubes (w. J. D. Craggs), 1949; Luminescence & the Scintillation Counter, 1953; Alpha, Beta & Gamma Ray Spectroscopy, 1964. Contbr. to: Nature; Physical Review; Philos. Mag.; Proceedings, Royal Soc. Mbrships. incl: F.R.S.; F.R.C.P.S.(Hon.); Athenaeum. Hons. incl: LL.D., 1968; Kt. Bachelor, 1970. Address: Univ. of Strathclyde, Royal Coll., 204 George St., Glasgow G1 1XW, UK.

CURREY, Ronald Fairbridge, b. 1894, London, UK. Lecturer. Educ: Rhodes Univ., Grahamstown, S. Africa; Trinity Coll., Oxford, UK; M.A. Publs: Coming of Age (w. others); Studies in South African Politics, Economics & Citizenship; The South African Way of Life; St. Andrew's College, Grahamstown, 1855-1955; Rhodes University, 1904-1970. Hons: M.C.; LL.D. Address: 34 Hill St., Grahamstown, S. Africa.

CURRIE, Jean, b. 1919, Streatham, UK. Creative Planner; Associate Director. Educ: Edinburgh Univ. Publs: Rhodes & the Dodecanese, 1970. Mbrships: M.I.P.A.; Former Pres., Advt. Creative Circle; Exec. Comm., Royal Acad. of Dancing; Anglo-Hellenic League. Address: 51 Norland Square, London W11 4PZ, UK.

CURTEIS, Ian, b. 1935, London, UK. Playwright. Publs: Long Voyage Out of War (trilogy of plays), 1973; The State Visit (novel), forthcoming. Stage Plays (unpubl.) incl: Inferno. Contbr. plays to TV, inclng: Beethoven; Sir Alexander Fleming; Mr. Rolls & Mr. Royce; The Folly; Second Time Round; The Regiment (series); Doomwatch (series); Owen MD (series); Barlow (series); Sutherland's Law (series); Crown Court (series); Spytrap (series); Justice (series); Hadleigh (series); The Onedin Line (series). Mbr., Writers Guild of GB. Address: c/o ALS Mgmt. Ltd., 46 Brook St., London W1Y 1YD, UK.

CURTIS, Edith Roelker, b. 29 July 1893, E. Greenwich, R.I., USA. Author. Publs: Anne Hutchinson, A Biography, 1930; Lady Sarah Lennox, An Irrepressible Stuart, 1946; A Season in Utopia, The Story of Brook Farm, 1961, 1971; Love's Random Dart (novella), 1962; Mexican Romance, 1969. Contbr. to jrnls., reviews, newspapers. Mbrships: Past Pres., Boston Br., & Past State Pres., Nat. League of Am.

Pen Women; Past Pres., Boston Authors Club; Bd. Mbr., N.H. Poetry Soc.; Past Staff Mbr., Dover, Vt., & N.H. Poetry Soc. Writers Confs. Hons: 2 prizes for A Season in Utopia, 2nd Prize, Mexican Romance, Nat. League of Am. Pen Women. Address: Box 71, Dublin, NH 034444,USA.

CURTISS, Ursula Kieran Reilly, b. 8 Apr. 1923, Yonkers, N.Y., USA. Mystery Writer. Publs: Voice Out of Darkness, 1948; The Second Sickle, 1950; The Noonday Devil, 1951; The Iron Cobweb, 1953; The Deadly Climate, 1954; The Stairway, 1955; Widow's Web, 1956; The Face of the Tiger, 1957; So Dies the Dreamer, 1960; Hours to Kill, 1961; The Forbidden Garden, 1962; The Wasp, 1963; Out of the Dark, 1964; Danger: Hospital Zone, 1966; Don't Open the Door, 1968; Letter of Intent, 1971. Contbr. to: Ladies' Home Jrnl.; Good Housekeeping; etc. Mbrships. incl: Mystery Writers of Am.; Authors League; Crime Writers' Assn. Recip., Zia Award, 1963. Address: 8408 Rio Grande Blvd., Albuquerque, NM 87114, USA.

CUSACK, Ellen Dymphna, b. 22 Sept. 1902, Wyalong, N.S.W., Australia. Writer. Educ: B.A., Sydney Univ.; Dip. Educ. Publs. incl: (novels) Come in Spinner, 1951; Southern Steel, 1953; The Sun in Exile, 1955; Heatwave in Berlin, 1961; The Sun is not Enough, 1967; The Half-Burnt Tree, 1969; A Bough in Hell, 1971; (travel) Chinese Women Speak, 1959; Holidays among the Russians, 1964; Illyria Reborn, 1966; (plays) Morning Sacrifice, 1944; The Golden Girls, 1955; (for children) Four Winds & a Family, 1948. Contbr. to newspapers & mags. Mbrships: Fellowship of Aust. Writers; Aust. Soc. of Authors; PEN. Recip., lit. awards. Address: c/o Clients Mail Dept., Bank of N.S.W., George St., Sydney, Australia.

CUSKELLY, Eugene James, b. 6 Jan. 1924. Priest. Educ: D.Theol., Gregorian Univ., Rome. Publs: A Heart to Know Thee, 1963; God's Gracious Design, 1965; No Cowards in the Kingdom, 1969. Contbr. to: Theol. Studies; Revue d'Ascetique et Mystique; Australasian Cath. Record. Mbr., Soc. of Missionaries of the Sacred Heart (Superior General since 1969). Address: Via Asmara 11, 00199 Rome, Italy.

CUSTER, Chester Eugene, b. 5 Nov. 1920, Scio, Ohio, USA. Clergyman; Editor; Writer. Educ: Univ. of Denver; A.B., Muskingum Coll.; M.Div., Garrett Theol. Sem.; M.A., Northwestern Univ. Publs: The Pilgrim Church (Ed.), 1972; All Things New (Ed.), 1973; The Descendants of Jacob & Sarah Custer, 1973; Called to Care, 1974. Contbr. to: Music Ministry; Ventures in Song; var. hymnal publs. Address: 831 Rodney Dr., Nashville, TN 37205, USA.

CUTFORTH, John Ashlin, b. 1911, Woodville, Burton-on-Trent, UK. Publisher. Educ: B.A., Univ. Coll., London. Publs: English in the Primary School; Mystery, Magic & Adventure (An anthology for ordinary boys & girls). Contbr. to: Schl. Libn.; var. newspapers & educ. jrnls. Mbr., Savage Club. Address: Masons House, Marsh Gibbon, Bicester, UK.

CUTFORTH, René, b. Woodville, Derbys., UK. Freelance Broadcaster & Journalist. Publs: Korean Reporter, 1952; Order to View, 1969. Contbr. to: Listener; Punch; New Statesman; etc.; BBC Corres., 1949-52. Address: Hosdens Farm, Gt. Maplestead, Halstead, Essex, UK.

CUTLER, Ivor. Humorist. Publs: Cockadoodledon't, 1966; Meal One, 1971, 1975; Many Flies Have Feathers, 1973; Dandruff (record), 1974; Balooky, 1975. Contbr. to: Sunday Times; Observer; Pvte. Eye; New Statesman; Poetry Review; Workshop New Poetry; Scotsman; 20th Century; Transatlantic Review. Mbrships: Equity; Performing Rights Soc.; Arts Couns. Writers in Schls. & Colls.; Mech. Copyright Performance Soc.; London Poetry Secretariat; Nat. Poetry Secretariat. Recip., Award, One of 100 Best Books in Germany, for Meal One, 1973. Address: 21 Laurier Rd., London NW5, UK.

CUTTING, Charles Latham, b. 1914, London, UK. Scientific Administrator. Educ: B.Sc., Ph.D., Queen Mary Coll., London Univ. Publs: The General Principles of Smoke-Curing Fish, 1951; The Torry Research Station Controlled Fish Smoking Kiln, 1951; Fish Saving: a History of Fish Processing From Ancient to Modern Times, 1955; The Dehydration of Fish (jt. author), 1956; Meat Chilling, Why & How (Ed.), 1972; Meat Freezing, Why & How, 1974. Contbr. to jrnls. incling: Nature; Food Technology; The Science of Food & Agriculture. Address: c/o Meat Rsch. Inst., Langford, Nr. Bristol BS18 7DY, UK.

CUTTLER, Charles David, b. 8 Apr. 1917, Cleveland, Ohio, USA. Art Historian. Educ: B.F.A., 1935, M.F.A., 1937, Ohio State Univ., Ph.D., N.Y. Univ., 1952. Publs: Northern Painting, from Pucelle to Bruegel, the XIVth, XVth & XVIth Centuries, 1968, 1973. Contbr. to jrnls. & Ency. Britannica. Address: 1691 Ridge Rd., Iowa City, IA 52240, USA.

CUYLER, Louise E., b. 14 Mar. 1908, Omaha, Neb., USA. University Professor. Educ: Eastman Schl. of Music; Univ. of Mich.; B.Mus., M.A., Ph.D. Publs: Choralis Constantinus Book III, 1950; Five Polyphonic Masses of H. Isaac, 1956; The Symphony, 1973; The Emperor Maximilian & Music, 1973. Contbr. to var. profl. jrnls. Mbrships: Mbr.-at-large, Am. Musicol. Soc.; Nat. Sec.; Int. Musicol. Soc.; Renaissance Soc. of Am.; Am. Histl. Assn. Hons: Disting. Fac. Achievement Award, Univ. of Mich., 1973; William Allen Neilson Rsch. Prof., Smith Coll., 1975. Address: School of Music of the University of Michigan, Ann Arbor, Mich., USA.

CVETKO, Martinovski, b. 25 Mar. 1930, Skopje, Yugoslavia. Editor. Publs: Lunjinci (People of the Storm), 1953; Kvečerini & Razdenuvanja (Evenings & Dawns), 1959; Prijateli (Friends), 1967; Izbrani Raskazi (Selected Stories), 1967. Contbr. to: Nov Den (New Day); Mlada Literatura (Young Lit.); Sovremenost (Mod. Time); Nostranaja Literature (For. Lit.); Svit (Light). Mbr., Writers' Union of Yugoslavia. Address: Dramska 1, Skopje, Yugoslavia.

CYRIAX, James Henry, b. 27 Oct. 1904, London, UK. Physician in Orthopaedic Medicine. Educ: Gonville & Caius Coll., Cambridge; St. Thomas's Hosp., London; L.R.C.P., 1929; M.D., 1938; M.R.C.P., 1954. Publs: Textbook of Orthopaedic Medicine, 2 vols., 1948, 6th ed., 1975; Osteopathy & Manipulation, 1949; Disc Lesions, 1953; The Shoulder, 1956; Hydrocortisene, 1957; The Slipped Disc, 1970; Cervical Spendylosis, 1971; Manipulation: Past & Present (w. E. Schiötz), 1975. Contbr. med. jrnls. Hons. incl: Heberden Prize, 1943; Gold Medal, Hosps. of Verona, 1966. Address: 32 Wimpole St., London W1 7AE, UK.

D

DAAGARSSON, Stefan, b. 14 July 1947, Bollnas, Sweden. Author; Artist. Publisher; Editor. Publs: (in Swedish) ... is to tell everything, 1968; Vigil of June, 1969; Alternatively Testament, 1970; Sluring — en bildroman, 1971; Ed., Inferi Mag., 1971—; Fndr., Publr., Bokforlaget Inferi (1st underground publ. house in Sweden), 1970—. Mbr., Swedish Union of Authors. Hons: Gavleborgs Sparbanks Kulturstipendium, 1969; Centerns Ungdomsforbunds Arets Debutant-stipendium, 1973; Gavleborgs Lans Landstings Kulturstipendium, 1973; Svenska Akademien, 1974. Address: Inferi House, Fack 69, S-820 29 Stratjara, Sweden.

da CRUZ, Daniel, pen name CROSS, T. T., b. 17 Nov. 1921, Oxford, Ohio, USA. Writer. Educ: B.S.L., Georgetown Univ. Publs: Men Who Made America, 1962; Vulcan's Hammer, 1968; Double Kill, 1973; Deep Kill, 1974; Sky Kill, 1974. Address: P.O. Box 4177, Beirut, Lebanon.

DAEM, Thelma Mary, b. 16 Nov. 1913, Banff, Alta., Can. Wife & Mother. Publs: Lucky Lure at Arrow Point, 1959; The Whistling Mountain, 1960; The Dragon With a Thousand Wrinkles, 1971; The House on the Top of the Hill, 1970; A History of Revelstoke, 1965; A Short History of Rogers' Pass, 1968. Contbr. to var. children's mags. Address: Box 505, Revelstoke, B.C., Can.

DAĞLARCA, Fazil Hüsnü, b. 26 Aug. 1914, Istanbul, Turkey. Poet. Publs: 50 vols. of poetry incling: Child & God, 1940; The Epic of Çakir, 1945; Asu, 1955; Song of Algeria, 1961; Our Vietnam War, 1966; Come On, 1968; The Blind of Vietnam, 1971. Contbr. to sev. Turkish & for. mags. & books. Mbrships: Turkish Lang. Instn.; PEN. Hons. incl: Yeditepe Prize, 1951; Poetry Prize, Turkish Lang. Inst., 1953; Turkish Award, Int. Poetry Forum, 1968; Int.

Golden Wreath Poetry Prize, Struga, Yugoslavia, 1974. Address: c/o Cem Yayinevi, Ankara Caddesi 40, Sirkeci, Istanbul, Turkey.

d'AGOSTINO, Carlo, b. 27 Feb. 1936, Genoa, Italy. Journalist-Publicist; Author. Publs: Alireport No. 1. — OV-10 Bronco, 1973; Alireport No. 2 — ZLIN 526 & Aerobatic, 1973; Aeromodelli, piccole guide Mondadori. Contbr. to: La Notte; Il Corriere dei Ragazzi; Aerei; Flaps; Tempo Sereno; Modellistica. Mbrships: Jrnlst. Assn. of Milan; Aeronautical Jrnlst. UGAI. Address: 34019 Condominio 10/M, 34019 Sistiana, Trieste, Italy.

DAHL, Arlene, b. 11 Aug. 1928, Minneapolis, Minn., USA. Actress; Designer; Beauty Consultant. Educ: Mpls. Coll. of Music; Mpls. Bus. Coll.; Univ. of Minn. Publs: Always Ask a Man, 1965; Your Beautyscope (series of 12 books), 1968; Secrets of Hair Care, 1970; Secrets of Skin Care, 1973. Contbr. to var. mags. Mbrships: Authors' League of Am., Inc.; Authors Guild, Inc. Address: 730 5th Ave., Suite 2105, N.Y., NY 10019, USA.

DAHL, Roald, b. 1916, Llandaff, S. Wales, UK. Publs: The Gremlins, 1944; Over to You, 1946; Someone Like You, 1961; Kiss Kiss, 1961; Switch Bitch, 1974; James & the Giant Peach, 1965; Charlie & the Chocolate Factory, 1965; The Magic Finger, 1966; Fantastic Mr. Fox, 1970; Charlie & the Great Glass Elevator, 1973; Danny, The Champion of The World, 1975; also film scripts inclng. You Only Live Twice, Chitty Chitty Bang-Bang. Contbr. to New Yorker. Agent: Murray Pollinger. Address: Gipsy House, Great Missenden, Bucks., UK.

DAHLBECK, Eva, b. 8 Mar. 1920, Nacka, Sweden. Actress; Author. Educ: Royal Dramatic Theatre Schl., Stockholm. Publs: Dessa mina minsta (play), 1955; Hem til Kaos (novel), 1964; S'is'ta Spegeln (novel), 1965; Den S'junde Natten (novel), 1966; Domen (novel), 1967; Med Seende Ogon (novel), 1972. Address: 35 Chemin Pont du Centenaire, CH 1214 Onex, Switz.

DAHLBERG, Edward, b. 22 July 1900, Boston, Mass., USA. Writer. Educ: Univ. of Calif., Berkeley; B.S. Columbia Univ., N.Y., 1925. Publs. incl: (novels) From Flushing to Calvary, 1932; Those Who Perish, 1934; Kentucky Blue Grass Henry Smith (short stories), 1932; Cipango's Hinder Door (verse), 1965; (other) Epitaphs of Our Time: The Letters of Edward Dahlberg, 1967; The Leafless Americans, 1967; The Carnal Myth: A Search into Classical Sensuality, 1968; The Confessions of Edward Dahlberg, 1971. Mbr., Nat. Inst. of Arts & Letters. Hons: Ariadne Fndn. Award, 1970; Cultural Coun. Fndn. Award, 1971. Address: c/o E. P. Dutton, 201 Park Ave. South, N.Y., NY 10003, USA.

DAHLLÖF, Tell Gunnar, b. 11 Mar. 1912, Mora, Sweden. Editor. Educ: Exam., Social Pol. Inst., Stockholm, 1934. Publs: Folke Bernadotte af Wisborg (contbng. author), 1949. Contbr. to: Am. Swedish Monthly, N.Y.; Svenska Dagbladet (N.Y. Corres., 1940-43); Biblis; Am.-Swedish Handbook; Columnist, Vår Industri. Mbrships: Swedish Histl. Pioneer Soc., Chgo., USA; Publicists' Club, Stockholm; Sweden Am. Fndn., ibid. Hons. incl: Snoilsky Medal, Royal Lib., 1967; LHD, Uppsala Coll., USA, 1972. Address: Malungsvägen 37, 161 42 Bromma, Sweden.

DAHRENDORF, Ralf, b. 1 May 1929, Hamburg, Germany. Professor of Sociology; Director, London Schl. of Economics. Educ: Univ. of Hamburg; London Schl. of Econs. Publs. incl: Marx in Perspective, 1953; Homo Sociologicus, 1959; Soziale Klassen und Klassenkonflict, 1957, Engl., 1959; Pfade aus Utopia, 1967; Essays in the Theory of Society, 1968; Konflict und Freiheit, 1972; The New Liberty, 1975. Contbr. to: Die Zeit; BBC, Reith Lectures, 1974. Mbrships: PEN; Commn. of the European Communities, 1970-74; Irish Acad. Hons. incl: Jrnl. Fund Award, 1966; D.Litt.; LL.D.; D.Sc. Address: London Schl. of Econs., Houghton St., London WC2A 2AE, UK.

DAICHES, David, b. 2 Sept. 1912, Sunderland, UK. Professor & Writer. Educ: M.A., Edinburgh Univ.; M.A., D.Phil., Oxford Univ.; Ph.D., Cambridge. Publs. incl: The Novel & the Modern World, revised ed., 1960; Robert Burns, 1950; Critical Approaches to Literature, 1956; Two Worlds (autobiog.), 1954; Milton, 1957; The Present Age, 1958; A Critical History of English Literature, 1960; Charles Edward Stuart, 1974. Contbr. to: New Yorker; Commentary; Poetry; etc. Mbrships: F.R.S.L.; MLA (Hon.). Hons: D.H.L., Brown Univ., USA, 1965; Doct. de l'Univ.,

Sorbonne, 1973; Scottish Arts Coun. Award, 1974. Address: Downsview, Wellhouse Lane, Burgess Hill, Sussex RH15 0BN, UK.

DAINTON, William Courtney, pen name DAINTON, Courtney, b. 1920, Turleigh, Wilts., UK. Writer. Educ: D.P.A., London. Publs: Clock Jacks & Bee Boles, 1957; The Story of England's Hospitals, 1961. Address: 34 Bourne Rd., Farncombe, Godalming, Surrey, UK.

DAINTREY, Adrian Maurice, b. 23 June 1902, London, UK. Artist. Author, I Must Say (reminiscences), 1963. Contbr. to: Punch; The Artist; Le Billet Doux. Address: 20 Randolph Rd., London W9 1AH, UK.

DAISNE, Johan, pen name of Dr. Herman THIERY, b. 2 Sept. 1912, Ghent, Belgium. Head Librarian; Flemish Author. Educ: Studied Econ. Scis., Slavic Lang. & Lit., Univ. of Ghent. Publs. incl: num. works for theatre, about film, critical essays, novels, inclng. Het zwaard van Tristan (The Sword of Tristan), 1962; De man die zijn haar kort lien knippen (The Man who had his Hair Cut Short), transl'd. into 12 langs., filmed 1965; De trein der traagheid (Un soir, un train), transl., filmed 1968; Filographic Dict. of World Lit. Contbr. to: Nieuw Vlaams Tijdschrift (New Flemish Review, co-ed.); De Periscoop. Mbrships. incl: Assn. of Flemish Writers; Assn. of Belgian Writers; Netherlands Soc. of Lit.; PEN; Flemish Royal Acad. Recip., num. hons. Address: Ottogracht 2, B 9000, Ghent, Belgium.

DAKE, Antonie Cornelis Abraham, b. 4 Mar. 1928, Amsterdam, Netherlands. Director, Television Company. Educ: Ph.D., Univ. of W. Berlin, Germany. Publs: In the Spirit of the Red Banteng, Indonesian Communists between Moscow & Peking, 1973. Address: Israelslaan 41, The Hague, Netherlands.

DAL, Erik, b. 1922, Grenaa, Denmark. Librarian (ret'd); Administrator, Danish Society for Language & Literature. Educ: Dr.phil., Univ. of Copenhagen. Publs: rsch. on Scandinavian ballads; 17th century Danish letters; Hans Christian Andersen; the history of typography & illustration. Contbr. to jrnls. inclng: Fund og Forskning; Bogvennen; Danske Studier. Mbr., sev. socs. incl: Royal Acad. of Letters & Sciences. Address: Forchhammersvej 1, 1920 Copenhagen V, Denmark.

DALE, Antony, b. 12 July 1912, Walton-on-the-Hill, Surrey, UK. Civil Servant; Chief Investigator, Historic Buildings, Department of Environment; Author. Educ: B.Litt., M.A., Oriel Coll., Oxford. Publs: Fashionable Brighton, 1947; The History & Architecture of Brighton, 1950; About Brighton, 1951; James Wyatt, 1953. Contbr. to: Archtl. Review. Mbrships: F.S.A.; Hon. Sec., Regency Soc. of Brighton & Hove, 1945—. Recip., O.B.E., 1971. Address: 33 Roedean Crescent, Brighton BN2 5RG, UK.

DALE, Celia Marjorie, b. London, UK. Publs: The Least of These; To Hold the Mirror; The Dry Land; The Wooden O; Trial of Strength; A Spring of Love; Other People; A Helping Hand; Act of Love; A Dark Corner; The Innocent Party; Mbr., PEN. Agent: Curtis Brown Ltd. Address: 35 Downside Crescent, London NW3, UK.

DALE, Margaret Jessy, pen name MILLER, Margaret J., b. 1911, Edinburgh, UK. Journalist; Children's Book Writer. Educ: B.A., Lady Margaret Hall, Oxford. Publs: Seven Men of Wit, 1960; The Queen's Music, 1961; The Powers of the Sapphire, 1962; Dr. Boomer, 1964; Mouse Tails, 1967; Willow & Albert, 1968; Gunpowder Treason, 1968; Knights, Beasts & Wonders, 1969; Emily, a Life of Emily Brontë, 1969; Plot for the Queen, 1969; Willow & Albert are Stowaways, 1970; King Robert the Bruce, 1970; Billy Saturdays, 1972. Contbr. to BBC Schls. Progs., 1948—. Mbrships: Int. PEN; Soc. of Authors; Nat. Book League. Address: 26 Greys Hill, Henley-on-Thames, Oxon. RG9 1SJ, UK.

DALE, Peter, b. 1938, Addlestone, Surrey, UK. School Head of Department. Educ: B.A., St. Peter's Coll., Oxford. Publs: Walk from the House (poems), 1962; The Storms, 1968; Mortal Fire, 1970; Villon (transl.), 1973; Mortal Fire (selected poems), 1975. Contbr. to: Times; Times Lit. Supplement; Review; Listener; Agenda; Art & Artists; Shenandoah; Tribune; etc. Mbr., A.M.A. Agent: David Highams Assoc. Address: 10 Selwood Rd., Sutton, Surrey, UK.

DALE, Reginald Rowland, b. 11 Apr. 1907, Widnes, UK. Former University Reader in Education. Educ: B.A., M.A., Univ. of Liverpool; M.Ed., Univ. of Leeds. Publs: From School to University, 1954; Down Stream: Failure in the Grammar School (w. S. Griffith), 1965; Educational Research in Britain (co-author), 1968; Mixed or Single-sex School? (3 vols.), 1969-74; Family, Class & Education (co-author), 1970. Contbr. to num. educl. & sociol. jrnls. Mbrships: Fellow, Brit. Psychol. Soc., Past Chmn., Educ. Sect.; Histl. Assn.; Assn. of Univ. Tchrs. Recip., Leverhulme Rsch. Award, 1967. Address: 81 W. Cross Lane, Swansea SA3 5LU, UK.

DALLY, Ann Gwendolen, b. 29 Mar. 1926, London, UK. Medical Practitioner (Psychiatrist). Educ: M.A., Somerville Coll., Oxford Univ.; M.B., B.S., St. Thomas's Hosp., London; D. Obst. Publs: Slim for Health, 1960; A-Z of Babies, 1961; A Child is Born (w. R. Sweering), 1966; Intelligent Person's Guide to Modern Medicine, 1967; Cicely: The Story of a Doctor, 1969; Mothers: Their Power & Influence, forthcoming; Ed., Maternal & Child Care, 1965-70. Contbr. to: Sunday Telegraph; Family Doctor; Lancet; Observer; Sunday Times; Evening News; New Humanist. Mbrships: Fellow, Royal Soc. Med.; other profl. assns. Recip., var. med. awards. Address: 13 Devonshire Pl., London W1, UK.

DALOS, György Alfrèd, b. 23 Sept. 1943, Budapest, Hungary. Literary Translator; Writer. Educ: Moscow Univ. Publs: Szauaink Szuletese (poems), 1964. Mbrships: Hungarian Assn. of Writers; PEN. Address: Lenin Krt. 101, Budapest 1067, Hungary.

DALRYMPLE, Ian Murray, b. 26 Aug. 1903. Film Producer; Writer; Director. Educ: Trinity Coll., Cambridge; LL.D. Publs. incl: (films) The Citadel; Storm in a Teacup; Coastal Command; Western Approaches; Once a Jolly Swagman; The Wooden Horse; Family Portrait; Royal Heritage; Raising a Riot; A Hill in Korea; The Admirable Crichton; London Can Take It; & num. other films & documentaries. Mbrships: Brit. Film Acad., (Chmn., 1957-8); F.R.S.A. Address: 3 Beaulieu Close, Cambridge Park, Twickenham TW1 2JR, UK.

DALRYMPLE, Jean, b. 2 Sept. 1910, Morristown, N.J., USA. Impresaria. Publs: September Child (autobiog.), 1963; Careers & Opportunities in the Theatre, 1970; The Jean Dalrymple Pinafore Farm Cookbook, 1972; The Folklore & Fact of Natural Nutrition (w. Fay Lavan), 1973; From the Last Row, 1975. Contbr. to: Reader's Digest; Mademoiselle; Seventeen; Vogue; etc. Mbrships: Dramatists' Guild; Authors' League; PEN. Address: 150 West 55th St., N.Y., NY 10019, USA.

DALTON, Dennis Morgan, b. 1929, London, UK. Executive Editor. Publs: Exec. Ed., Annuals Dept., Link House Grp. Address: Link House, Dingwall Ave., Croydon CR9 2TA, UK.

DALTON, Dorothy, b. 25 Sept. 1915, NYC, USA. Poet. Educ: B.A., Univ. of Wis. Publs: Poems, 1967; Midnight, and Counting, 1973. Contbr. to: N.Y. Quarterly; Christian Sci. Monitor; Poet (India); McCall's; Saturday Evening Post; Good Housekeeping; Southern Poetry Review; Red Cedar Review; Engl. Jrnl.; Wis. Review. Mbrships: Poetry Soc. of Am.; Ore. State Poetry Soc. Hons. incl: Writer's Digest Poetry Contest, 1970 & 1972; Ga. Poetry Soc. Award, 1973; N.Y. Poetry Forum Prize, 1973; Touchstone-Viterbo Coll., 1974. Address: 1125 Valley Rd., Menasha, WI 54952, USA.

DALY, (Most Rev.) Cahal Brendan, b. 1 Oct. 1917, Loughgiel, County Antrim, UK. Catholic Bishop of Ardagh & Clonmaenois; formerly Reader in Scholastic Philosophy, Queen's University, Belfast. Educ: B.A., M.A., Queen's Univ., Belfast; D.D., St. Patrick's Coll., Maynooth; L.Ph., Institut Catholique, Paris. Publs: Morals, Law & Life; Natural Law Morality Today; Violence in Ireland & Christian Conscience; (contbr.) Prospect for Metaphysics. Contbr. to var. relig. publs. Mbrships. incl: Relig. Advsry. Comm., BBC, N. Ireland. Address: St. Michael's, Longford, Repub. of Ireland.

DALZELL-WARD, Arthur James, b. 20 Aug. 1914, Guildford, Surrey, UK. Physician; Chief Medical Officer, Health Education Council, London. Educ: King's Coll., London; Charing Cross Hosp.; London Schl. Hygiene & Tropical Med.; M.R.C.S., L.R.C.P., F.F.C.M., D.P.H., F.R.S.H., Publs: (w. D. Pirrie) Text Book of Health Education, 1962, 2nd ed., 1975; Child Life & Health, 1970.

Contbr. to: Pergamon Press; Community Hlth.; Pub. Hlth.; Disease a Month (Chgo.); Am. Social Hlth. Assn.; Phys. Educ. Assn. of GB. Mbrships: Fellow, Coun. Mbr., Royal Inst. Pub. Hlth. & Hygiene; Brit. Med. Assn.; Fellow, Soc. Community Med. Address: Green Shutters, 631 Hurst Rd., Bexley, Kent DA5 3JP, UK.

DAMI, Aldo, b. 23 Mar. 1898, Geneva, Switz. University Professor. Educ: Univ. of Geneva; D.Litt., Univ. of Debrecen, Hungary. Publs: Tunnels, 1932; La Hongrie de Demain, 1932; Destin des Minorités, 1934; Provinces de France, 1940; La Ruthénie subcarpathique, 1944; Fatalités bulgares, 1945; Dernier des Gibelins, 1960; Refaire l'Histoire, 1973. Contbr. to: Le Monde; Esprit; Plans; La Suisse; Jrnl. de Genève; Tribune de Genève; etc. Mbrships: Chmn., Geog. Soc., Geneva; Hist. Soc., Geneva; Geneva Writers' Soc.; PEN. Hons: Hentsch French Lit. Prize, Geneva, 1923; Arthur de Claparède Geog. Prize, Geneva, 1942. Address: 16 rue de l'Ecole de Médecine, Geneva, Switz.

DANA, Margaret Bloxham, b. Verona, N.J., USA. Consumer Affairs Consultant; Journalist. Educ: N.J. State Coll.; Oberlin Coll. Publs: Behind the Label, 1939; var. buying guides. Contbr. to: Atlantic Monthly; Woman's Day; Parents' Mag.; Modern Textiles; Stores; N.Y. Times; over 110 newspapers (syndicated columns., Before You Buy, & The Consumer's Question-Box). Mbr., Bds. of Dirs., var. orgs., inclng. Am. Nat. Standards Inst. & Am. Soc. for Testing & Materials. Hons. incl: Disting. Serv. Award, Am. Apparel Mfrs. Assn., 1968; Award for Outstanding Profl. Participation, Am. Assn. Textile Technol., 1973; Meritorious Serv. Award, Standards Engrs. Soc. & Am. Soc. Testing & Materials, 1974. Address: Research Ctr., 216 King Rd., Chalfont, PA 18914, USA.

DANA, Mitchell, pen name of DANOW, Myron G., b. 26 Apr. 1947, NYC, USA. Novelist; Poet; Screenwriter. Educ: B.A. (Philos.), Yale Univ., New Haven, Conn., 1968. Publs: Beyond the Law, 1972; Town Without a Prayer, 1972; The Last Buffalo, 1973; Gun Shy, 1973; Incident in a Texas Town, 1974.

DANCE, Stanley Frank, b. 15 Sept. 1910, Braintree, Essex, UK. Music Critic; Record Producer; Author. Publs: Jazz Era, 1961; The World of Duke Ellington, 1970; The Night People, 1971; The World of Swing, 1974. Contbr. to: Jazz Hot, 1937-; Down Beat, 1937-; Jazz Jrnl., 1948-; N.Y. Herald Tribune, 1961; Saturday Review, 1962-73; Music Jrnl., 1962-. Address: 12 Oakleigh Ct., Rowayton, CT 06853, USA.

DANGERFIELD, George Bubb, b. 28 Oct. 1904, Newbury, UK. Writer; Historian. Educ: B.A., M.A., Oxon. Publs: The Strange Death of Liberal England, 1935; Victoria's Heir, 1941; The Era of Good Feelings, 1953; Chancellor Robert Livingston of New York, 1960; The Awakening of American Nationalism, 1965. Contbr. to: Am. Histl. Review; Pol. Sci. Quarterly; N. Engl. Quarterly; Va. Quarterly; The Nation. Mbrships. incl: Soc. of Am. Histns; Am. Antiquarian Soc.; The Hertford Soc. (Oxford, UK). Hons. incl: Pulitzer Prize in Am. Hist., 1954; Bancroft Prize in Am. Hist., 1954. Address: 883 Toro Canyon Rd., Santa Barbara, CA 93108, USA.

DANIEL, Hawthorne, b. 20 Jan. 1890, Norfolk, Neb., USA. Author; Editor; Lecturer. Educ: US Naval Acad.; Iowa State Coll.; Columbia Univ., N.Y. Univ. Num. publs. incl: In the Favour of the King, 1922; Ships of the Seven Seas, 1925; North America; Wheel of the Future, 1942; Judge Medina: A Biography, 1952; Ferdinand Magellan, 1964; Collab., 11 books, inclng: Misadventures of a Tropical Medico (w. Dr. H. S. Dickey), 1929; Over African Jungles (w. Martin Johnson), 1935; The Inexhaustible Sea (w. Francis Minot), 1954, 1957; A Different Kind of War (w. Vice-Admiral Milton E. Miles, USN), 1967; 15 juvenile histl. novels. Contbr. to num. jrnls., newspapers. Hons. incl: Medal of Oregon Trail Mem. Assn., 1937; US Navy War Corres. Award, 1946; Citation, Assembly of Captive European Nations, for The Ordeal of the Captive Nations (1958), 1960. Address: 37 Standish Ave., Colonial Heights, Tuckahoe, NY 10710, USA.

DANIEL, John Warwick, III, b. 3 Mar. 1902, Wash. D.C., USA. Engineering Draftsman, Retired. Educ: Corcoran Art Schl. Publs: O Coming Age!, 1940. Contbr. to poetry jrnls., USA & abroad. Mbrships: Kt. of Mark Twain, Int. Mark Twain Soc.; Hon. Mbr., Eugene Field Soc.; Hon. Mbr., Schroeder Fndn., 1941. Address: 3827 Valleybrink Rd., Atwater, L.A., CA 90039, USA.

DANIELS, Jonathan Worth, b. 1902, Raleigh, N.C., USA. Emeritus Editor. Educ: Univs. of N.C. & Columbia; A.B.; M.A. Publs: Clash of Angels; A Southerner Discovers the South; A Southerner Discovers New England; Tar Heels: A Portrait of North Carolina; The Man of Independence; The End of Innocence; Prince of Carpet Baggers; The Forest in the Future; Stonewall Jackson; Moseby; Robert E. Lee; The Devil's Backbone: The Story of the Natchez Trace; They Will Be Heard; The Time Between the Wars; Washington Quadrille; Ordeal of Ambition; The Randolphs of Virginia; White House Witness 1942-1945; The Gentlemanly Serpent. Contbr. to jrnls. Mbr., Nat. Press Club, Wash. D.C. Address: News & Observer, Raleigh, NC, USA.

DANIELSSON, Bengt Emmerik, b. 1921, Krokek, Sweden. Explorer; Anthropologist; Swedish Consul, French Polynesia. Educ: Univ. of Uppsala; Seattle Univ., Wash., USA; Ph.D. Publs: Happy Island, 1952; Work & Life on Raroia, 1956; Love in the South Seas, 1956; Forgotten Islands of the South Seas, 1957; Terry in the South Seas, 1959; Terry in Australia, 1959; From Raft to Raft, 1961; What Happened on the Bounty, 1962; Gauguin in the South Seas, 1965; La Découverte à la Polynésie, 1972; Moruroa, mon Amour, 1974; (TV script) Terry in the South Seas, 1963. Contbr. to: Jrnl. of Polynesian Soc.; Atoll Rsch. Bulletin. Address: Papehue, Paea, Tahiti, French Polynesia.

DANINOS, Pierre Charles, b. 1913, Paris, France. Writer. Publs. incl: Les Carnets du Major Thompson (Engl. ed., Major Thompson Lives in France); Le Secret du Major Thompson (Engl. ed., Major Thompson & I); Sonia, les autres et moi (Engl. ed., Life with Sonia); Les Carnets du Bon Dieu; Le Jacassin; Snobissimo; Un Certain Monsieur Blot. Contbr. to: Figaro; Punch; etc. Hons. incl: Prix Courteline for Sonia, les autres et moi; Prix Internaillie for Les Carnets du Bon Dieu. Address: 81 rue de Grenelle, Paris 7, France.

DANNATT, (James) Trevor, b. 1920, London, UK. Architect. Publs: Ed., Architects' Year Book, Vols. 3-10; Modern Architecture in Britain; Trevor Dannatt, Building & Interiors 1951-72. Contbr. to: Politiken; Guardian; Archtl. Design; Archtl. Review. Address: 28 Little Russell St., London WC1A 2HN, UK.

DANNAY, Frederic, pen name (w. Manfred B. Lee) QUEEN, Ellery; ROSS, Barnaby. Mystery Writer. Publs. incl: Roman Hat Mystery, 1929; Siamese Twin Mystery, 1933; Chinese Orange Mystery, 1934; Halfway House, 1936; Challenge to The Reader, 1938; Murder by Experts, 1947; Calendar of Crime, 1952; The Finishing Stroke, 1958; Poetic Justice, 1967; A Fine & Private Place, 1971; Ellery Queen's Crookbook, 1973; (as Barnaby Ross) Tragedy of X, 1932; Drury Lane's Last Case, 1933; (co-ed., w. Manfred B. Lee) Short Story Collections by Dashiell Hammett, O. Henry, Erle Stanley Gardner; etc. Contbr. to: Adventures of Ellery Queen TV Prog. Address: Larchmont, N.Y., USA.

DANNER, Margaret, b. 12 Jan. 1915, Chgo., Ill., USA. Poet. Educ: Roosevelt Coll.; Loyola Univ.; Northwestern Univ. Publs: Impressions of African Art Forms, 1962; To Flower: Poems, 1963; Poem Counterpoem, 1966; Ed., Brass Horses, 1968; Iron Lace, 1968; Ed., Regroup, 1969; An Do, 1970; Poets In A Bottle, 197 . Contbr. to: Poetry Mag. (asst. ed., 1956); Negro Digest (Black World); & var. other jrnls. Mbr., Am. Pen Women. Hons: Incl: Harriet Tubman Award, 1951; Midwestern Writers Prize, 1947. Address: 802 Walker Ave., Memphis, TN, USA.

DANOJLIĆ, Milovan, b. 3 July 1937, Ivanovci, Belgrade, Yugoslavia. Poet; Essayist; Translator. Educ: B.A., Belgrade Univ. Publs: Urodjenički Psalmi, 1957; Kako Spavaju Tramvaji, 1959; Balade, 1964; Lirske Rasprave, 1967; Glasovi, 1970; Rodna Godina, 1972; O Ranom Ustajanju, 1972; Onde Potok, Onde Cvet, 1973; Čistine, 1973; & num. poems transl'd from French, English & Russian. Contbr. to var. Yugoslav reviews. Mbr., Assn. Yugoslav Writers. Hons. incl: 5 Yugoslav prizes for children's poetry & transls. Address: Ranka Tajsića 40, II ulaz, Beograd, Yugoslavia.

DAPUNT, Inge, b. 13 May 1943, Landeck, Tirol, Austria. Secretary. Educ: Tchrs. Trng. Coll. Author, Vom Schtädtle und von Ländle: Im Bludazr Dialäkt. Contbr. to: (anthols.) Innsbruck '65; Innsbruck '69; Konfigurationen '69; (jrnls.) Die Diagonale; Vorarlberg; Bodensee-Hefte; Podium; Neue Wege; Literatur und Kritik; Das Fenster.

Mbr., Grazer Autorenversammlung (Graz Authors' Assn.). Address: Gabelsbergerstr. 8/5/15, 5020 Salzburg, Austria.

DARBY, Edith M., pen name GREENFIELD, Bernadotte, b. 19 Sept. 1906, Atlantic City, N.J., USA. Clerk Typist, US Government. Publs: Selma (novellette); Page Dr. Laugh. Contbr. to num. poetry anthols. (Songwriter). Mbrships: Hon. Rep., Cemtro Studi E. Scambi Int., Rome.; ASCAP; Past Chmn. for Nat. Poetry Day for State of N.J. Hons. incl: Certs. of Merit, 1970, 1973, Bronze Medal, 1970, Centro Studi E. Scambi Int.; 3rd Prize, Centennial Poem, Women's Club, Ashbury, N.J., 1970; Cert. of Merit, Silver Medal, 5th Concorso Int. di Poesia Religiosa, 1974. Address: 210 Cedarcrest Ave., Pleasantville, NJ 08232, USA.

DARBY, Henry Clifford, b. 7 Feb. 1909, Resolven, Wales, UK. Professor of Geography. Educ: B.A., 1928, Ph.D., 1931, M.A., 1932, Litt.D., 1960, St. Catherine's Coll., Cambridge. Publs: An Historical Geography of England (ed. & contbr.), 1936; The Draining of the Fens, 1940; The Domesday Geography of England (gen. ed. & contbr.), 6 vols., 1952-75; A New Historical Geography of England (ed. & contbr.), 1973. Contbr. to: geog. & histl. jrnls. Recip., sev. acad. hons. Address: 60 Storey's Way, Cambridge CB3 0DX, UK.

D'ARCH SMITH, Timothy, b. 1936, Farnborough, Hants., UK. Company Director. Publs. incl: 3 Catalogues of exhibs. for Times Bookshop, anonymously, 1961-63; Bibliography of the Works of Montague Summers, 1964; Ed., Francis Barrett, The Magus: or Celestial Intelligencer, 1967; Ed., Millard, Bibliography of Oscar Wilde, 1967; Love in Earnest, 1970. Contbr. to: Stenbook, Yeats & the Nineties, 1970. Mbrships. incl: Bibliog. Soc.; Printing Histl. Soc.; M.C.C. Address: 64A St. John's Wood High St., London NW8, UK.

D'ARCY, (Rev.) Martin Cyril, b. 1888, Bath, UK. Writer. Educ: Oxford Univ.; Gregorian Univ., Rome; M.A.; D.D.; D.Lit. Publs. incl: Thomas Aquinas; The Nature of Belief; Death & Life; The Mind & Heart of Love; Christianity & Communism; The Meeting of Love & Knowledge. Contbr. to: Month; Dublin Review; Criterion. Mbrships: Soc. of Jesus; F.R.S.L.; Athenaeum Club. Recip., LL.D. h.c. Address: 114 Mount St., London, UK.

DARLINGTON, William Aubrey, b. Taunton, Somerset, UK. Drama Critic; Author. Educ: M.A., Cambridge Univ. Publs: Alf's Button (novel), 1919, (as play), 1924, 1925; (on the theatre) Through the Fourth Wall, 1922; Literature in the Theatre, 1925; The Actor & his Audience, 1949; The World of Gilbert & Sullivan, 1950; 6001 Nights, 1960; (autobiog.) I Do What I Like, 1949; (biog.) Laurence Olivier, 1968. Contbr. to: Ency. Britannica; Punch; Strand Mag., etc.; Chief Dramatic Critic, Daily Telegraph, 1920-68; Dramatic Ed., 1925—; London Drama Corres., N.Y. Times, 1939-60. Mbrships: Soc. of Authors; League of Dramatists; Inst. of Jrnlsts. Address: Monksdown, Bishopstone, Sussex, UK.

DARNELL, Lilian Mabel, b. 1912, London, UK. Hospital Sister Tutor. Educ: Battersea Gen. Hosp.; King's Coll. (now Queen Elizabeth Coll.) of Household & Social Sci.; S.R.N., S.C.M., R.F.N., Registered Sister Tutor. Publs: Nursing — Target for Careers Series. Contbr. to: Nursing Times; Hosp. & Social Serv. Jrnl.; Women's Employment. Address: 110 Hightrees House, Nightingale Lane, Balham, London SW12, UK.

DAROW, (formerly DOUKHONINE), Anatole, b. 15 Oct. 1920, Bouy, Jaroslawl, Russia. Journalist. Educ: Inst. of Jrnlsm., Leningrad, 1938-42; Inst. of Orthodox Theol., Paris, France, 1948-50. Publs: Blocade, 1945, 2nd ed., 1964; Le Soleil Luit Quand Meme, 1959; Main Love, 1960; There is a Shore No Man, 1965; Going West — is not Easy, 1972. Contbr. to: Novoye Russkoye Slovo; Grany; La Renaissance; Voice of Am. Mbrships: Ctr. for Writers in Exile, Am. Br., PEN; Assn. of Russian Writers & Jrnlsts., Paris. Address: 34-40 78th St., Apt. 3H, Jackson Heights, NY 11372, USA.

DART, Raymond Arthur, b. 4 Feb. 1893, Brisbane, Australia. Physician. Educ: B.Sc., Univ. of Qld., 1913; M.Sc., 1915; M.B.Ch.M., Sydney Univ., 1917. Publs: Australopithecus Africanus: The Man-Ape of South Africa, 1925; Racial Origins in Bantu Speaking Tribes of South Africa, 1937; Adventures with the Missing Link (w. Dennis Craig), 1959, paperback 1961. Contbr. to: Nature & other sci. & profl. publs. Mbrships. incl: Fellow, Royal Soc. of S.

Africa, 1930–; Fellow, Inst. of Biol., 1963–; Int. Comm. of Fossil Man, 1929–; Int. Assn. Human Biols., 1968–. Hons. incl: Gold Medal, S. African Nursing Assn.; 1970; Silver Medal, Med. Assn. of S. Africa. Address: 20 Eton Park, Sandhurst, Sandton, Transvaal, S. Africa.

DARY, David Archie, b. 21 Aug. 1934, Manhattan, Kan., USA. University Professor. Educ: B.S., Kan. State Univ.; M.S., Univ. of Kan. Publs: Radio News Handbook, 1967, 1970; TV News Handbook, 1970; Manual De Noticias Radiofónicas, 1970; How to Write for Broadcast & Print, 1973; The Buffalo Book, 1974. Contbr. to num. Western hist. jrnls., articles & reviews. Mbrships: Western Hist. Assn.; Vice-Head, Radio/TV Div., Assn. for Educ. in Jrnlsm.; Mbr., Bd. Dirs., Kan. State Hist. Soc. Address: 1101 W. 27th St., Lawrence, KS 66044, USA.

DAS, Prafulla Chandra, pen name NANDAN, Subhadra, b. 22 Sept. 1927, Calcutta, India. Printer; Publisher; Bookseller; Author; Translator. Educ: Univ. of Calcutta. Publs: About 50 books, in Oriya, Bengali, Hindi & Engl. inclng: Tagore: The Poet of Light; Vivekananda: The Cosmic Conscience; Maeterlinck: The Mystic Bard; Olympic: The Light of Peace; Mother: The Divine; Transl., Jean-Christophe, by R. Rolland; Transl., Matir Maya, by K. Hamsun; Transl., Barabbas, by P. Lagerkvist; Transl., Siddhartha, by H. Hesse. Mbrships: Indian Ctr., PEN; Congress for Cultural Freedom. Recip., Bisuba Milana Lit. Prize. Address: Prafulla Press, Mohan Mahal, Chandnichouk, Cuttack – 2, Orissa State, India.

DASHTI, Ali, b. 1895. Writer; Politician; Diplomatist. Publs. incl: novels; short stories; essays; analytical work on poetry of Hafez, Saadi, Rumi, Omar Khayam & Khaghani. Contbr. to Shafaq Soekh (former Ed.). Address: The Senate, Teheran, Iran.

DASKALOV, Stoyan, b. 22 Aug. 1909, Lilyache, Bulgaria. Writer. Publs: (in Bulgarian & transl. into sev. E. European langs.) Magda's Summit, 1940; The Road, 1945; The Lipovanski Mill, 1951; Our Own Land, 1952; The Village by the Factory, 1963; The Republic of Rains, 1968. Contbr. to: September; PlamAk; SAvremennik; Literatouren Front; Narodna Cultura. Mbrships: PEN, Union of Bulgarian Writers. Hons: Prizes, Union of Bulgarian Writers, 1944, 1968, 1972; Dimitrov Prize, 1950, 1969; Honoured Cultural Worker, 1963; People's Worker in Culture, 1967. Address: Sofia, ul. Sheynovo, 21, Bulgaria.

DATHORNE, Oscar Ronald, b. 19 Nov. 1934, Georgetown, Guyana. University Professor. Educ: B.A.,1958, M.A., 1960, Univ. Of Sheffield, UK; Ph.D., 1966; Dip. Ed., Univ. of London, 1967. Publs: Dumplings in the Soup, 1963; The Scholar Man, 1964; The Black Mind, 1974; Sev. anthols. of Caribbean & African works. Contbr. to: Washington Post. Times Lit. Supplement; London Mag.; Black Orpheus. Address: 8904/Friedberg bei Augsburg, Lubastrasse 2, W. Germany.

DAUBE, David, b. 8 Feb. 1909, Freiburg, Germany. Professor of Law. Educ: Univs. Freiburg, Gottingen & Cambridge; M.A., Ph.D., D.C.L., Dr.Jur. Publs. incl: Studies in the Roman Law of Sale; The Exodus Pattern in the Bible; The Sudden in the Scriptures; Collaboration with Tyranny in Rabbinic Law; Roman Law; Civil Disobedience in Antiquity. Mbrships: F.B.A.; Soc. of Pub. Tchrs. of Law; Pres., Soc. d'Hist. des Droits de l'Antiquité, 1957. Hons: Hon. LL.D.; Dr.h.c.; Dr. Hum. Lett.h.c.; Dr.Jur.h.c.; Hon. Fellow, Oxford Univ. Ctr. for Postgrad. Hebrew Studies, Gonville & Caius Coll., Cambridge. Address: School of Law, University of California, Berkeley, Calif., USA.

D'AVANZO, Giuseppe, b. 12 Apr. 1930, Rome, Italy. Journalist. Educ: Naples Mil. Coll.; Lucerna Electronics Inst. Publs: Radar History, 1960; New Aviation, 1962; Space & Men, 1965; Mach Two, 1971; Wings & Armchairs, 1974. Contbr. to: Il Tempo; Scienze e Vita; Tuttomotori; Revista Marittima; Aviazione di Linea; Am. Aviation Publs., Wash. D.C., USA. Mbrships: Assn. Stampa Romana; Unione Giornalisti Aerospaziali Italiali; Phantom Fraternity, St. Louis, Mo., USA; Pilots Inst. Assn., Mpls., Minn.; Thousand Miles Club, Coltishall, UK. Hons: Premio di Giornalismo Aeronautico "Maria Massai", 1968, 1973. Address: 11 Via Alessandro Torlonia, Roma 00166 Italy.

DAVENPORT, John Douglas Frank, b. 21 Nov. 1929, Hitchin, UK. Automotive Journalist. Educ: Merton Coll., Oxford, 1959-61. Publs. incl: 2 books in the Adventure at Speed Series. Contbr. to: Rallies Ed., Motoring News,

1962-65, Autosport, 1966–; Ency. of Motor Sport; Safari Fever; Castrol Rally Manual I & III; Rali (Portugal); for. motoring jrnls. Mbrships: Full Mbr., Guild of Motoring Writers; Sec., Rally Pilots Assn.; Comm., Int. Rally Drivers Club; Rallies Comm., Royal Automobile Club. Address: Seven Locks, Trow Lane, Lyneham, Chippenham, Wilts. SN15 4DL, UK.

DAVENPORT, William Henry, b. 1908, Bridgeport, Conn., USA. College professor of English; Editor. Educ: A.B., Dartmouth Coll., Hanover, N.H.; A.M., Tufts Univ., Medford, Mass.; Ph.D., Yale Univ. Publs: Modern Omnibus; Dominant Types in British & American Literature; Nine Modern American Plays; Voices in Court, 1958; The Good Physician, 1962; Biography Past & Present, 1965; Engineering, 1967; The One Culture, 1970; Technology & Culture, 1972. Contbr. to: Technol. & Culture; Technol. & Soc.; Newsletter of Harvard Prog. on Pub. Conceptions of Sci. Mbr., Soc. for the Hist. of Technol. Address: 616 Purdue Dr., Claremont, Calif., USA.

DAVEY, Cyril James, b. 31 May 1911, Liverpool, UK. Methodist Minister. Publs: The March of Methodism, 1951; The Methodist Story, 1955 The Yellow Robe, 1960; Cornish Holiday, 1964; The Santi Storey, 1966; Oberammergau Holiday, 1969; 50 Lives for God, 1973; num. children's books. Address: 27 W. Hill, Epsom, Surrey, UK.

DAVEY, Gilbert Walter, b. 7 June 1913, London, UK. Insurance Company Official. Publs: Fun With Radio, 1957, 5th ed. (revised), 1969; Fun With Short-Waves, 1960, revised ed. (Fun With Short Wave Radio), 1968; Fun With Electronics, 1962, revised ed., 1972; Fun With Transistors, 1964, revised ed., 1971; Fun With Hi-Fi, 1973. Contbr. to jrnls. inclng: Practical Wireless; Radio Constructor; Boy's Own Paper (radio corres. for 21 yrs.); also to TV. Address: 36 Hillbury Ave., Kenton, Harrow, Middx. HA3 8EW, UK.

DAVICO, Oskar, b. 1909, Sabac. Writer. Publs: The Poem, 1959. Address: Internacionih brigada 39, Beograd, Yugoslavia.

DAVIDOGLU, Mihail, b. 11 Nov. 1910, Hirlau, Romania. Writer; Playwright. Educ: B.A.; Univs. of Jassy & Bucharest, 1928-32. Publs. incl: (plays) The Man in the Delta, 1947; The Miners, 1948; The Citadel of Fire, 1950; Horia, The Peasant-Leader, 1956; The Unprecedented Tempest, 1957; The Giant of the Lowland, 1958; The Black Rose, 1961; A Man in the Dark, 1965; Grandpa's Cherished Eyes, 1970; The Ancestor, 1971; The Magic Site, 1973. Mbrships: Writers' Union; Pres., Cultural Comm., Municipal Coun., Bucharest, 1956-68. Hons: 5 times winner, Vasile Alexandri Prize; var. lit. prizes; Star of Repub.; etc. Address: Cal. Victoriei 101, Etage 3, Ap. 8, Bucharest 22, Romania.

DAVIDSON, Basil, b. 1914, Bristol, UK. Historian; Novelist. Publs., about 25 books inclng: History of West Africa to 1800, 1966; The Andrassy Affair (fiction), 1968; History of East & Central Africa to 1875, 1968; The Africans, A Social & Cultural History, 1969; The Liberation of Guinè, 1969; Which Way Africa? 1971; In the Eye of the Storm; Angola's People, 1972; Black Star (Kwame Nkrumah), 1973; Can Africa Survive? Arguments against Growth Without Development, 1974; Africa in History: Themes & Outlines, 1975. Hon. Rsch. Fellow, Univ. of Birmingham. Hons: Mil. Cross; US Bronze Star. Address: 2 Palace Yard, Hereford HR4 9BJ, UK.

DAVIDSON, Eugene, b. 22 Sept. 1902, NYC, USA. Editor; Author. Educ: B.A., Yale Univ. Publs: The Death & Life of Germany, 1959; The Trial of the Germans, 1967; The Nuremberg Fallacy, 1973. Contbr. to: Modern Age (Chmn., Bd. of Publs., Ed., 1960-70); Am. Mercury; Yale Review; Am. Histl. Review; Annals of Pol. Sci.; other jrnls. & newspapers. Mbrships: Authors' Guild; PEN. Address: 1301 N. Astor St., Chgo., IL 60610, USA.

DAVIE, Elspeth, b. Ayrshire, UK. Writer. Educ: Edinburgh Coll. of Art. Publs: Providings, 1965; The Spark (short stories), 1968; Creating A Scene, 1971. Contbr. to: Cornhill; London Mag.; Transatlantic Review. Mbr., PEN. Recip., Scottish Arts Coun. Award, 1971. Address: 15 Leven Terrace, Edinburgh, UK.

DAVIE, Ian, b. 5 Apr. 1924, Edinburgh, UK. Schoolmaster. Educ: M.A., Univ. of Oxford. Publs: (poems) Piers Prodigal, 1961; A Play for Prospero, 1965; Roman Pentecost, 1970; A Theology of Speech, 1973. Contbr. to philos. & theol. jrnls. Address: Alba, Acklam, Malton, N. Yorks., UK.

DAVIES, Aneiren Talfan, b. 11 May 1909, Felindre, Henllan, UK. Pharmacist. Educ: Tech. Coll. Publs: The Colour of Saying (co-ed.), 1963 (Am. title, Dylan Thomas' Choice); Dylan: Druid of the Broken Body (co-ed.), 1964; Quite Early One Morning (ed.); num. books in Welsh. Contbr. to: Agenda. Proceedings of 11th Congress of Int. Comp. Lit. Assn.; Poetry Wales; Contemp. Poets of the Engl. Lang., 1970. Mbr., Pharmaceutical Soc., GB. Hons: O.B.E.; Welsh Arts Coun. Major Award, 1972-73; M.A. h.c., Univ. of Wales. Address: 4 Maynard Ct., Llandaff, Cardiff, UK.

DAVIES, David Margerison, pen name MARGERSON, David, b. 23 Feb. 1923, Llanelli, Wales, UK. Consultant Physician & Toxicologist; University Senior Lecturer. Educ: London Hosp. Med. Coll., F.R.C.P. Publs: Antibiotic & Sulphonamide Treatment, 1959; Medicine Today, 1961; Medicine as a Career, 1962. Ed., Adverse Drug Reaction Bulletin. Contbr. to: News Chronicle; Evening Standard; Evening News; & var. med. jrnls. Mbr., Soc. of Authors. Address: Briarsyde, Queen Rd., Consett, Co. Durham, UK.

DAVIES, David Michael, b. 5 Oct. 1929, Stroud, Glos., UK. Human Ecologist. Educ: B.A., 1952, M.A., 1955, Christ's Coll., Cambridge; Ph.D., London Univ., 1963. Publs: The Rice Bowl of Asia, 1967, 1973, USA 1968; A Journey into the Stone Age, 1969; Dictionary of Anthropology, 1972; The Influence of Teeth, Diet & Habits on the Human Face, 1972; The Last of the Tasmanians, 1973; The Centenarians of the Andes, 1974; Transportation, forthcoming. Contbr. to: New Scientist; Times; Times of India; Daily Telegraph; Sydney Morning Herald; New Knowledge. Mbrships. incl: Authors' Club; F.R.G.S.; Fellow, Royal Anthropol. Inst. Hons. incl: Winston Churchill Fellow, 1971-72; Benrus Citation Award, 1973. Agent: Press Club Ctr. Address: 88 Sussex Way, London N7, UK.

DAVIES (Rev. Canon), Ebenezer Thomas, b. 28 Oct. 1903, Pontycymmer, Wales, UK. Clergyman. Educ: B.A., M.A., Univ. of Wales. Publs: The Political Ideas of Richard Hooker, 1946; A History of the Parish of Mathern, 1947; Episcopacy & the Royal Supremacy; An Ecclesiastical History of Monmouthshire, Part I, 1952; Monmouthshire Schools & Education to 1870, 1956; Religion in the Industrial Revolution in South Wales, 1963. Contbr. to: Glamorgan Co. Hist., vol. III; Jrnl. of the Ch. in Wales Histl. Soc. (Hon. Ed., 1953-73); Glamorgan Histn. Mbr., Govng. Body, Nat. Lib. of Wales. Address: 11 Ty Brith Gdns., Usk, Gwent, UK.

DAVIES, Frederick Herbert, b. 1916, Birkenhead, UK. Educator; Author; Translator. Publs: The Servant of Two Masters, 1961; The Liar, 1963; It Happened in Venice, 1965; The Italian Straw Hat, 1967; The Spelling Mistakes, 1967; The Fan, 1968; The Lucifer Stone, 1965; Goldoni: Four Comedies, 1968; The Campiello, 1970; Three French Farces, 1973; Letters from My Windmill by Alphonse Daudet, 1975. Contbr. to: Lettres Nouvelles; Essays on John Cowper Powys, 1972. Mbrships: Soc. of Authors; Transls. Assn. Hon: Fellow Commoner, Churchill Coll., Cambridge, 1969. Agent: Margaret Ramsay Ltd. Address: 31 Bentham Close, Noctorum, Birkenhead, Merseyside, UK.

DAVIES, (Rev. Canon) George Colliss Boardman, b. 1912, Loddon, Norfolk, UK. Clerk in Holy Orders; Canon Residentiary, Worcester Cathedral. Educ: M.A., 1938, D.D., 1951, St. Catharine's Coll., Cambridge; D.D., Trinity Coll., Dublin, 1959. Publs: The Early Cornish Evangelicals, 1951; Henry Phillpotts, Bishop of Exeter, 1954; Men for the Ministry: History of the London College of Divinity, 1963. Contbr. to: Ch. Quarterly Review; Churchman. Mbr., United Oxford & Cambridge Univ. Club. Address: 10 Coll. Yard, Worcester, UK

DAVIES, Horton Marlais, b. 10 Mar. 1916, Port Talbot, UK. Professor. Educ: M.A., 1934, B.D., 1940, Edinburgh Univ., D.Phil., 1943, D.Litt., 1970, Oxon. Publs: The Worship of the English Puritans, 1948; Worship & Theology in England, 5 vols., 1961-75; Christian Deviations, 1952; Varieties of English Preaching, 1963; A Mirror of the Ministry in Modern Novels, 1959. Contbr. to Ency. Britannica; Assoc. Ed., Worship; Studie Liturgica; etc. Hons: M.A., Cambridge, 1960; D.Litt., La Salle Coll., Phila., USA, 1966; Guggenheim Memorial Rsch. Fellowship, 1960 & 1964; & others. Address: 28 Lake Ave., Princeton, NJ 08540, USA.

DAVIES, Iris, pen name RICHARDSON, Susanne, b. 4 Feb. 1936, Swansea, S. Wales, UK. Novelist. Educ: Swansea Coll. of Technol. Publs: The Green Cape, USA, 1973; Tudor Tapestry, 1974; Bride of the Thirteenth Summer, 1975; The Copper Cloud, 1975; Burn Bright Shadow, USA, 1975. Contbr. to: Woman's Own; My Wkly.; Annabel; Jackie; Loving; Love Affair; Romance; My Story; S. Wales Evening Post; Det Nye (Norway). Mbrships: Romantic Novelists' Assn.; Soc. of Women Writers & Jrnlsts. Address: 16 Major St., Manselton, Swansea, Glam., UK.

DAVIES, John Gordon, b. 20 Apr. 1919, Chester, UK. Professor of Theology; Author. Educ: B.A., 1942, M.A., 1945, B.D., 1946, D.D., 1956, Oxford Univ. Publs. incl: The Theology of William Blake, 1948, 2nd ed., 1966; Social Life of Early Christians, 1954; He Ascended into Heaven, 1958; God's Will & Gift, 1962; A Select Liturgical Lexicon, 1965; Dialogue with the World, 1967; The Secular Use of Church Buildings, 1968; Every Day God. Encountering the Holy in World & Worship, 1973. Contbr. to: Ency. Britannica; Jrnls. of Theol. Studies & Hellenic Studies; Harvard Theol. Review; etc. Address: 28 George Rd., Edgbaston, Birmingham B15 1PJ, UK,

DAVIES, Leslie Purnell, pen names incl. VARDRE, Leslie; EVANS, Morgan; BERNE, Leo; THOMAS, G. K.; PETERS, Lawrence; BRIDGEMAN, Richard; BLAKE, Robert; JEFFERSON, Ian, b. 1914, Crewe, Cheshire, UK. Optician; Writer. Educ: Manchester Univ. Publs. incl: The Paper Dolls, 1964; Man out of Nowhere, 1965; The Artificial Man, 1965; Psychogeist, 1966; Twilight Journey, 1967; The Alien, 1968; Dimension A, 1969; Genesis Two, 1969; The White Room, 1970; The Shadow Before, 1971; Give me back myself, 1972; What Did I Do Tomorrow, 1972. Contbr. to num. jrnls. Mbr., Fellow, Brit. Optical Assn. Address: Ty Newydd, Deganwy Rd., Deganwy, Conwy, Caerns. LL31 9DH, UK.

DAVIES, Louise Sarah, b. 1923, London, UK. Nutritionist; Freelance Writer; Broadcaster; College Administrator. Educ: B.Sc., Queen Elizabeth Coll., Univ. of London. Publs: See How to Cook, 1952; Easy Cooking for One or Two, 1972; Easy Cooking for Three or More, forthcoming. Contbr. to: Food Sense; Mrs. Beeton's Cookery & Household Management; Shopping List; Woman's Hour; BBC/TV. Mbr., F.A.H.E. Address: 85a Redington Rd., Hampstead, London NW3, UK.

DAVIES, Mansel Morris, b. 1913, Aberdare, Glam., UK. Professor of Chemistry. Educ: M.Sc., Ph.D., Sc.D.; Univ. Coll., Aberystwyth; Cambridge Univ. Publs: Physical Principles of Gas Liquefaction & Low Temperature Rectification; The Development of Science; Hanes Datblygiad Gwyddoniaeth (co-author); Infra-red Spectroscopy & Molecular Structure (Ed. & Contbr.); Dielectric Properties & Molecular Behaviour (Ed. & Contbr.); Eclectrical & Optical Aspects of Molecular Behaviour. Contbr. to: Dielectric & Related Processes, Vol. I, 1972, Vol. II, 1975; Reports of Chem. Soc.; var. profl. jrnls. Mbrships: Faraday Soc., Coun. Mbr., 1958-61, 1969-72; VP, 1972-75, Mbr., 1975—. Address: Talfan, Buarth Road, Aberystwyth, UK.

DAVIES, Oliver, b. 7 May 1905, London, UK. Archaeologist. Educ: B.A., 1927, M.A., 1930, Exeter Coll., Oxford; D.Litt., Univ. of Dublin, 1946. Publs: Roman Mines in Europe, 1935; Excavations at Island MacHugh, Tyrone, 1950; Natal Archaeological Studies, 1952; Archaeology in Ghana, 1961; The Quaternary in the Coastlands of Guinea, 1964; West Africa Before the Europeans, 1967; The Archaeology of the Flooded Volta Basin, 1971. Contbr. to: Annals of the Natal Mus.; S. African Archaeol. Bulletin; etc. Mbrships. incl: Royal Soc. Antiquaries, Ireland; Pres., S. African Archaeol. Soc. Address: 63 St. Patrick's Rd., Pietermaritzburg 3201, S. Africa.

DAVIES, Paul Mervyn, b. 5 Feb. 1914, York, UK. Medical Practitioner. Educ: Guy's Hosp.; M.B.; B.S.; M.R.C.S.; L.R.C.P.; D.P.H.; F.F.R. Publs: Medical Terminology in Hospital Practice (Incorporating Medical Terminology for Radiographers), 2nd ed., 1974. Mbrships: B.M.A.; Fac. of Radiols.; Brit. Inst. of Radiol.; Soc. of Authors. Recip., Territorial Decoration. Address: "Grayrigg", Hilgay Close, Guildford, Surrey, UK.

DAVIES, Rhys, b. 1903, Rhondda, UK. Author. Publs: (novels) Under the Rose; Jubilee Blues; Tomorrow to Fresh Woods; The Black Venus; The Dark Daughters; Marianne; The Painted King; The Perishable Quality; Girl Waiting in the Shade; (short stories) The Things Men Do; A Finger in Every Pie; The Trip to London; Boy with a Trumpet; The Darling of her Heart; Collected Stories; (play) No Escape; (autobiography) Print of a Hare's Foot; (biography) See Urchin; (general) My Wales; The Story of Wales. Contbr. to num. Brit. & Am. mags. & anthologies. Mbr., PEN. Recip., O.B.E. Address: c/o Curtis Brown, 13 King St., London WC2, UK.

DAVIES, Robertson, b. 1913, Thamesville, Ont., Can. Educator; Author. Educ: B.Litt. (Oxon), D.Litt., LL.D.; Upper Can. Coll.; Queen's Univ., Balliol Coll., Oxford, UK. Publs. incl: Shakespeare's Boy Actors, 1938; The Diary of Samuel Marchbanks, 1947; Fortune, My Foe, 1949; The Table Talk of Samuel Marchbanks, 1951; A Masque of Aesop, 1952; Leaven of Malice, 1954; A Mixture of Frailties, 1958; The Personal Art, 1960; Marchbanks' Almanack, 1967; Stephen Leacock, 1970; Feast of Stephen, 1970; Fifth Business, 1971; Hunting Stuart & Other Plays, 1972; The Manticore, 1973. Hons: Companion, Order of Can. Agent: Collins, Knowlton, Wing Inc. Address: The Master's Lodging, Massey College, Devonshire Place, Toronto M5S 2E1, Can.

DAVIES, Rupert Eric, b. 29 Nov. 1909, London, UK. Methodist Minister. Educ: B.A., B.D., Cantab.; M.A., Oxon. Publs: The Problem of Authority in the Continental Reform, 1946; The Catholicity of Protestantism (jt. ed.), 1951; Methodism, 1962; History of Methodism in Great Britain (jt. Ed.), 1965—; Religious Authority in an Age of Doubt, 1968; A Christian Theology of Education, 1975. Contbr. to: Times Educl. Supplement; Jrnl. of Ecclesiastical Hist.; Epworth Review. Mbr., var. relig. orgs. Recip., var. hons. Address: 27 Station Rd., Nailsea, Bristol BS19 2PD, UK.

DAVIES, (William Thomas) Pennar, b. 1911, Mtn. Ash, Glamorgan, UK. Professor of Church History. Educ: Univ. Coll., Cardiff; Balliol & Mansfield Colls., Oxford; Yale Univ., USA; B.A.; B.Litt.; Ph.D. Publs: Cinio'r Cythraul (poems); Naw Wfft (poems); Cudd fy Meiau (confessions); Anadl o 'r Uchelder (novel); Y Ddau Gleddyf (hist.); Efrydd o Lyn Cynon (poems); Caregl Nwyf (stories); Rhwng Chwedl a Chredo (criticism); Meibion Darogan (novel); y Tlws yn y Lotws (poems); Y Brenin Alltud (theol.). Contbr. to Welsh lang. publs. Mbr., Academi Gymreig. Address: Llwyn Helyg, Ffynone, Swansea, UK.

DAVIN, Daniel Marcus, b. 1 Sept. 1913, Invercargil, NZ. Publisher. Educ: M.A. & Dip.M.A., Univ. of Otago, NZ; Balliol Coll., Oxford, UK. Publs: incl: For the Rest of Our Lives, 1947, 2nd ed., 1965; Roads from Home, 1949; The Sullen Bell, 1956; Writing in New Zealand: The New Zealand Novel (w. W. K. Davin), 1956; Katherine Mansfield in Her Letters, 1959; No Remittance, 1959; Not Here, Not Now, 1970; Brides of Price, 1972; Breathing Spaces (short stories), 1975; Closing Times (Memoirs of Seven Writer Friends), 1975. Contbr. to jrnls. Mbrships: incl: F.R.S.A. Recip., M.B.E. (Mil.), 1945. Address: 103 Southmoor Rd., Oxford, UK.

DAVIN-POWER, Maurice, b. 3 Mar. 1913, Dublin, Repub. of Ireland. Medical Practitioner. Educ: M.B. Publs: (dramatic works) Shadows in the Sun; The Noon-Day Devil; Mr. Handel's Visit to Dublin; Strongbow; The General's Watch. Contbr. to: Irish Med. Times. Mbrships: incl: PEN; Soc. of Irish Playwrights (Sec.). Hons. incl: 1st Prize, 1916 Nat. Commemoration Dramatic Competition; 1st Prize, I.C.A. Int. Play Competition, 1964. Address: 33 South Circular Rd., Dublin, Repub. of Ireland.

DAVINSON, Donald, b. 20 July 1932, Middlesbrough, UK. Polytechnic Lecturer. Educ: B.Sc., D.P.A., London Univ.; F.L.A., Manchester Coll. of Sci. & Technol. Publs: Commercial Information, 1964; Academic & Legal Deposit Libraries, 1969; Periodicals, 1969; Bibliographic Organisation, 1975. Contbr. to: Assoc. Ed., New Lib. World. Mbrships: Chmn., Assn. of Brit. Lib. Schls.; Coun. Lib. Assn.; Chmn., Libnship. Bd., Coun. for Nat. Acad. Awards. Address: 133 Leeds Rd., Selby, Yorks. YO8 0JG, UK.

DAVIS, Alec, b. 7 Dec. 1912, Boston, Lincs., UK. Typographer. Educ: Dip. Jrnlsm., King's Coll., London. Publs: Type in Advertising, 1951; Package & Print, 1967; Graphics: Design into Production, 1974; The Graphic Work of Eric Fraser, 1974. Contbr. to: Penrose Annual; Archtl. Review; Design; Graphis; Country Life. Mbrships: Brit. Assn. Indl. Eds.; Comm., Printing Histl. Soc.; Hon. Mbr., Soc. Typographic Designers. Address: 6 Primrose Mansions, Prince of Wales Drive, London SW11 4ED, UK.

DAVIS, Arthur, G., b. 17 July 1915, NYC, USA. Assistant Professor of English. Educ: B.A., Univ. of Notre Dame, Ind., 1939; M.S., St. John's Univ., N.Y., 1949. Publs: Hamlet & the Eternal Problem of Man, 1964; The Royalty of Lear, 1974. Contbr. to: Humanitas. Mbrships: AAUP; Veterans of For. Wars. Address: 240 Hewes St., Brooklyn, NY 11211, USA.

DAVIS, Bertram Hylton, b. 30 Nov. 1918, Ozone Park, L.I., N.Y., USA. Professor of English. Educ: Hamilton Coll., 1937-39; B.A., 1941, M.A., 1948, Columbia Univ.; Ph.D., 1956. Publs: Johnson Before Boswell, 1960; Sir John Hawkins, The Life of Samuel Johnson, LL.D. (ed.), 1961; A Proof of Eminence: The Life of Sir John Hawkins, 1973. Mbrships. incl: MLA; Am. Soc. for 18th Century Studies; AAUP. Hons. incl: Univ. of Akron Centennial Award, 1970; LL.D., Dickinson Coll., 1974. Address: 2309 Domingo Dr., Tallahassee, FL 32304, USA.

DAVIS, Charles Alfred, b. 12 Feb. 1923, Swindon, Wilts., UK. University Professor. Educ: S.T.L., Gregorian Univ., Rome. Publs: Liturgy & Doctrine, 1960; The Study of Theology, 1962; The Making of a Christian, 1964; God's Grace in History, 1966; A Question of Conscience, 1967; Christ & the World Religions, 1970; The Temptations of Religion, 1972. Contbr. to var. jrnls. inclng: Clergy, Downside & Dublin Reviews; Studies in Relig.; New Repub.; New Statesman. Mbr., var. theol. orgs. Recip., acad. hons. Address: Dept. of Relig., Sir Geo. Williams Fac. of Arts, Concordia Univ., Montreal, P.Q., Can.

DAVIS, Derek Russell, b. 20 Apr. 1914, London, UK. University Professor of Mental Health. Educ: M.A., M.D., Clare Coll., Cambridge; Middlesex Hosp. Med. Schl. Publs: Pilot Error, 1948; Introduction to Psychopathology, 3rd ed., 1972. Contbr. to med., psych. & psychol. jrnls. Mbrships: F.R.C.P.; Fellow, Royal Coll. Psychs.; Expmtl. Psychol. Grp. (Ed., Quarterly Jrnl., 1948-57); Fndn. Schlr., former Fellow, Clare Coll. Hons: Adolf Meyer Lectr., Am. Psych. Assn., 1967. Address: 39 St. Michael's Hill, Bristol BS2 8DZ, UK.

DAVIS, Frank, pen names KOENIG, Kirk; RAMSEY, Christopher; STACEY, Sheldon, b. 16 June 1942, New Orleans, La., USA. Writer; Columnist; Photojournalist. Publs: num. How-to booklets in speciality fields; var. trade publs. for indl. corps. Contbr. to: Outdoor Life (La. Field Ed.); Sports Afield; Probe; Karate Illustrated; Black Belt (Feature Ed.); La. Conservationist (Chief Staff Writer); Nat. Rifle Assn. Conservation/Hunting Annual; Nat. Rifle Assn. Outdoor Directory; La. Woods & Water (former Ed.-in-Chief). Mbrships. incl: Outdoor Writers' Assn. of Am.; Southeastern Outdoor Press Assn. (Bd. of Dirs.); La. Outdoor Writers' Assn. (Sec.-Treas.); La. Outdoors Publng. Co., Inc. (Pres. & Chmn. of Bd.). Recip., Miles A. Coe Lit. Award. Address: 333 Dover St., Slidell, LA 70458, USA.

DAVIS, (Mrs.) Gwen, b. 11 May 1934, Pitts., Pa., USA. Writer. Educ: A.B., Bryn Mawr Coll., Pa.; M.A., Stanford Univ., Calif. Publs: Naked in Babylon, 1959; Someone's in the Kitchen with Dinah, 1962; The War Babies, 1964; Sweet William, 1967; The Pretenders, 1969; Touching, 1971; Kingdom Come, 1973; Changes (poetry), 1973; The Motherland, 1974. Mbrships: Bryn Mawr Club, Calif.; Mars Club, Paris, France. Address: 601 N. Elm Drive, Beverly Hills, CA 90210, USA.

DAVIS, Harold Eugene, pen name HED, b. 3 Dec. 1902, Girard, Ohio, USA. Historian; Educator. Educ: B.A., Hiram Coll., Ohio, 1924; M.A., Univ. of Chgo., 1927; Ph.D., Case-Western Reserve Univ., 1933. Publs. incl: History of Latin America, 1968; Hinsdale of Hiram: Pioneer Educator, 1971; Latin American Thought: An Historical Introduction, 1972, 1974; Revolutionaries, Traditionalists, & Dictators in Latin America, 1973; occasional poems. Contbr. to var. histl., educl., pol. sci. jrnls. Mbrships: Am. Histl. Soc.; Sec. Pres., Ohio Acad. of Hist.; Am. Pol. Sci. Assn. Hons. incl: Am. Univ. Fac. Author, 1950. Address: 4842 Langdrum Lane, Chevy Chase, MD 20015, USA.

DAVIS, John Frank, b. 28 Feb. 1917, Paris, France. Former Pilot, RAF; Industrialist. Educ: M.A., Univ. of Oxford. Publs: The Concorde Affair, 1970. Contbr. to: Dict. of Air Warfare. Mbrships: Companion, Royal Aeronautical Soc. Recip., mil. decorations. Address: Rock Mill, Washington, Pulborough, W. Sussex, UK.

DAVIS, John Gilbert, b. 4 Apr. 1904, London, UK. Consultant Scientist. Educ: Univ. Coll., London; Rockefeller Fellowship, Heidelberg, Germany; D.Sc., Ph.D.,

London; F.R.I.C.; F.I.F.S.T.; F.R.S.H. Publs. incl: Dairy Chemistry, 5th ed., 1953; A Dictionary of Dairying, 2nd ed., 1955, Supplementary vol., 1965; Laboratory Control of Dairy Plant, 1956; Milk Testing, 2nd ed., 1959; Cheese, vols. 1 & 2, 1965, vols. 3 & 4, 1975; Yoghourt. Contbr. to sci. & tech. jrnls., encys., symposia & int. congresses. Mbrships: Sec., Soc. Gen. Microbiol.; Pres., Soc. Applied Bacteriol., Soc. Dairy Technol.; Inst. Food Sci. Tech. Address: 52 London Rd., Reading, Berks. RG1 5AS, UK.

DAVIS, Lenwood G., b. 22 Feb. 1939, Beaufort, N.C., USA. Educational Consultant; Writer. Publs. incl: I Have A Dream: The Life & Times of Martin Luther King, Jr., 1969, 2nd ed., 1973; Blacks in the State of Oregon: 1788-1971, 1971, 2nd ed., 1974; Blacks in the Cities: 1900-1972, 1972; The History of Urban Growth & Development, 1972; Black Women in the Cities, 1972; Blacks in the Pacific Northwest: 1788-1972; The Black Family in the Urban Areas in the United States, 1973. Contbr. to num. jrnls. Mbr., sev. acad. & civic orgs. Address: P.O. Box 1011, Salisbury, NC 28144, USA.

DAVIS, Lily May, pen name (writing in collaboration w. Rosemary Davis) DAVIS, Rosemary L., b. Hull, UK. Writer. Publs: Circus in the Snow (w. R. Davis), 1959; (play) Lap of the Gods (w. R. Davis), 1968. Address: 105 Watchfield Ct., London W4 4ND, UK.

DAVIS, (Prof.) Moshe, b. 12 June 1916, Bklyn., N.Y., USA. Historian. Educ: B.A., Columbia Univ., N.Y., 1937; B.J.P., 1937, M.H.L. & Rabbinic Ordination, 1942, Tchr's. Inst. Jewish Theol. Sem. Am.; Ph.D., Hebrew Univ., Jerusalem, 1963. Publs. incl: The Emergence of Conservative Judaism, 1963; Jewish Religious Life & Institutions (latest ed.), 1971; Yom Kippur War — Israel & the Jewish People, 1974; Ed., Contemporary Jewish Civilization Series, also Hebrew publs. Contbr. to var. Jewish jrnls. Mbrships. incl: Am. Jewish Histl. Soc. (VP); Israel Histl. Soc. (Exec.). Hons. incl: D.H.L., 1974 from Hebrew Union Coll., Israel Inst. Relig. Address: Inst. Contemporary Jewry, Hebrew Univ., Jerusalem, Israel.

DAVIS, Norman, b. 1913, Dunedin, NZ. Morton Professor of English Language & Literature. Educ: M.A., Univ. of Otago; M.A., Univ. of Oxford, UK. Publs: Sweet's Anglo-Saxon Primer, 9th ed., 1953; The Language of the Pastons, 1954; Paston Letters, 1958; Beowulf (facsimile), 2nd ed., 1959; Selection from Paston Letters, 1963; Glossary to Early Middle English Verse & Prose, 1966; Sir Gawain & the Green Knight, 2nd ed., 1967; Non-Cycle Plays & Fragments, 1970; Paston Letters & Papers of the 15th Century Part I, 1971. Contbr. to profl. jrnls.; Co-Ed., Review of Engl. Studies, 1954-63. Mbrships: Fellow, Brit. Acad. Hons: NZ Rhodes Schlr., 1934; M.B.E. Address: Merton Coll., Oxford, UK.

DAVIS, Ralph Henry Carless, b. 1918, Oxford, UK. Professor of Medieval History; Editor of History. Educ: M.A., Balliol Coll., Oxford Univ. Publs: The Mosques of Cairo; The Kalendar of Abbot Samson of Bury St. Edmunds (ed.); A History of Medieval Europe; King Stephen; Regesta Regum Anglo-Normanorum, vols. iii & iv (w. H. A. Cronne). Contbr. to schrly. jrnls. Address: 56 Fitzroy Ave., Birmingham 17, UK.

DAVIS, Richard, b. London. Author; Editor; Critic. Contbr. to: 4th Pan Book of Horror Stories, 1963; Graves Give up their Dead, 1964; No Such Thing as a Vampire, 1965; Horror 7, 1965; 6th Pan Book of Horror Stories, 1965; 5th Ghost Book, 1969; 6th Ghost Book, 1970; New Writing in Horror & Fantasy, 1971; You Always Remember the First Time, 1975. Ed. & Contbr. to: Tandem Horror 2, 1968; Tandem Horror 3, 1969; Writer & Prod., Film "Viola", 1968; Years Best Horror Stories, 1971-75; Space I, Spectre I, 1974; Space II, Spectre II, 1975; Armada Sci-Fi 1 & 2, 1975; Story Ed., BBC TV "Late Night Horror", 1966-68; Critic & Reviewer, Films & Filming. Mbrships: Authors' Soc.; Screenwriters' Guild; ACTT. Address: 77 St. Quintin Ave., London W10, UK.

DAVIS, Richard Whitlock, b. 1935, Somers, Conn., USA. University Professor. Educ: Amherst Coll.; Christ's Coll., Cambridge; Columbia Univ.; B.A.; M.A.; M.Litt.; Ph.D. Publs: Dissent in Politics 1780-1830, 1971; Political Change & Continuity 1760-1885, 1972; Somers: The History of a Connecticut Town (w. Fred C. Davis), 1973. Contbr. to: Am. Histl. Review; Jrnl. of Mod. Hist.; The Histn.; Huntingdon Lib. Quarterly; Durham Univ. Jrnl. Mbrships. incl: Authors' Club, London; Soc. of Authors. Address: 7106 Waterman Ave., Univ. City, MO 63130, USA.

DAVIS, Stratford, pen name SHARMAN, Miriam, b. 1915, Glasgow, UK. Educ: M.A., Univ. of Glasgow. Publs: Death in Seven Hours; No Tears are Shed; The Troubled Mind; One Man's Secret; His Father's Ghost; Death Pays all Debts; Seeds of Violence; The Face of Danger; (TV plays) An Inch from the Heart; Late Harvest; script for Detective Game; (stage play) The Closing Net; sev. short stories, USA. Mbr., Nat. Book League. Agent: Curtis Brown. Address: Upper Kiln Farm, Leighton Buzzard, Beds., UK.

DAVIS, Sydney Charles Houghton, b. 1887, London, UK. Author; Editor. Educ: Univ. Coll., London. Publs: Car Driving as an Art: Motor Racing; Rallies & Trials; Atalanta; Controlling a Racing Car Team; The John Cobb Story; Great British Drivers; Mercedes-Benz; Cars Cars Cars; Memories of Men & Motor Cars. Contbr. to: Autocar; Motor Cycle; etc.; Sports Ed., The Autocar; Ed., Motor Racing. Address: Sutton Lodge, Clandon Rd., Guildford, Surrey GU1 2DS, UK.

DAVIS, William, b. 6 Mar. 1933, Hanover, Germany. Journalist. Educ: City of London Coll. Publs: Three Years Hard Labour, 1968; Merger Mania, 1970; The Language of Money, 1973; Have Expenses, Will Travel, 1975. Contbr. to: (ed.-in-chief) Punch; Ed., High Life (Brit. Airways In-Flight Mag.); Ed., Good Times. Mbr., Dir., City Arts Trust & Brighton Festival. Address: 23 Tudor St., London EC4, UK.

DAVITT, Thomas Edward, b. 6 May 1904, Adrian, Mich., USA. Educator; Author. Educ: A.B., Univ. of Detroit, 1932; M.A., 1936, Ph.D., 1950, St. Louis Univ. Publs: The Nature of Law, 1951; Origins of the Natural Law Tradition (co-author), 1954; Elements of Law, 1959; Basic Values in Law — A Study of the Ethico-Legal Implications of Psychology & Anthropology, 1968; Ethics in the Situation, 1970. Contbr. to: Nomos, 1960; Vanderbilt Law Review, 1960; Dict. of Christian Ethics, 1967; Human Rights, 1971. Address: 1404 W. Wisconsin Ave., Milwaukee, WI 53233, USA.

DAWES, Ben, b. 21 Apr. 1902, Burnley, Lancs., UK. University Teacher & Professor. Educ: Assoc., Royal Coll. of Sci., Imperial Coll., London; Rsch. Dip., ibid, 1924-28; D.Sci., Univ. of London, 1933. Publs: The Trematoda, 1946, 3rd ed., 1968; The Trematoda of British Fishes, 1947; Man & Animals: What They Eat & Why (A Manual of Nutrition), 1947; A Hundred Years of Biology, 1952. Org. & Ed., Advances of Parasitology, vols. 1-12, 1963-74. Contbr. to num. sci. jrnls. Mbrships: Marine Biol. Assn. of UK; Life Fellow, Linnean Soc. of London; Zool. Soc. of London; etc. Address: Rodenhurst, 22 Meadow Close, Reedley, Burnley, Lancs., BB10 2QU, UK.

DAWES, Edward Naasson, b. 30 Aug. 1914, Newtown, N.S.W., Australia. Barrister. Educ: LL.B., Univ. of Sydney, 1937. Publs: Dawes' Australian Proprietary & Private Companies — Law & Management, 1955; Cons. Ed. — 2nd ed., ibid (R.N. Purvis), 1964; Purvis on Proprietary Companies, 1973. Address: 108 Prince Alfred Parade, Newport, N.S.W. 2106, Australia.

DAWES, Frank, b. 15 Aug. 1933, Ilford, UK. Journalist; BBC Radio Producer. Publs: Not in Front of the Servants (Domestic Service in England, 1850-1939), 1973. Contbr. to: Daily Telegraph Mag. Mbrships: Soc. of Authors; Nat. Union of Jrnlsts. Address: Mariners, Dormans Pk., E. Grinstead, W. Sussex, UK.

DAWSON, Fielding. b. 2 Aug. 1930, NYC, USA. Writer; Artist. Educ: B.A., Black Mtn. Coll. Publs: An Emotional Memoir of Franz Kline, 1967; Krazy Kat/The Unveiling, 1969; Open Road, 1970; The Black Mountain Book, 1970; The Mandalay Dream, 1971; The Dream/Thunder Road, 1972; The Greatest Story Ever Told/A Transformation, 1972; A Great Day for a Ballgame, 1973; The Sun Rises into the Sky, 1974; OZ — with an X/The Battle for New York, forthcoming. Contbr. to: Boston Phoenix; N.Y. Times; Ont. Review; Art & Lit.; Black Mtn. Review; Iowa Review; Falcon; etc. Mbr., Authors' Guild Am. Address: 49 E. 19th St., N.Y., NY 10003, USA.

DAWSON, Jennifer, b. UK. Writer. Educ: B.A., St. Anne's Coll., Oxford, 1952. Publs: (novels) The Ha-Ha, 1961; Fowler's Snare, 1963; The Cold Country, 1966; Penguin Modern Stories 10 (w. others), 1972. Recip., Black Mem. Prize, 1962. Address: c/o Anthony Blond Ltd., 56 Doughty St., London WC1, UK.

DAWSON, Robert Price, b. 26 July 1918, Balt., Md., USA. Insurance Executive. Educ: Md. State Tchrs. Coll., 1938; US Infantry Schl., 1941. Author, All My Laurels, 1964. Contbr. to ins. trade mags. Mbrships: Press Club of Ore.; Willamette Writers Club, Ore. Address: 12220 S.W. Douglas, Portland, OR 97225, USA.

DAY, James Wentworth, b. 21 Apr. 1899, Exning, UK. Author; Editor; Journalist. Educ: Newton Coll., Cambridge. Publs. incl: The Lure of Speed, 1929; The Modern Fowler, 1934; Sporting Adventure, 1937; The Dog in Sport, 1938; Sport in Egypt, 1939; Farming Adventure, 1943; Harvest Adventure, 1945; Wild Wings, 1949; Rural Revolution, 1952; The Modern Shooter, 1953; A History of the Fens, 1954; The Angler's Pocket Book, 1957; A Ghost Hunters Game Book, 1958. Contbr. to num. jrnls., radio & TV on politics, the Near East, field sports, natural history, agriculture, dogs, flying, etc. Mbrships: Soc. of Authors; Inst. of Jrnlsts.; F.R.S.A. Address: Ingatestone, Essex, UK.

DAY, John Robert, occasional pen name CYCLOPS, b. 1917, Enfield, UK. Manager, London Transport Collection of Historical Relics. Educ: Univ. of London. Publs: Unusual Railways (w. B. G. Wilson), 1957; Railway Signalling Systems (w. B. K. Cooper), 1958; More Unusual Railways, 1960; Railways of Southern Africa, 1962; Railways Under the Ground, 1963; The Story of London's Underground, 1963; Railways of Northern Africa, 1964; Transport Today & Tomorrow (co-author), 1967; Trains, 1969; The Story of the Victoria Line, 1969; The Last Drop, 1971; The Story of the London Bus, 1973. Contbr. to sev. railway books & jrnls. Mbrships: M.C.I.T.; Assoc., Instn. Railway Signal Engrs. Address: 4 Lamb's Walk, Enfield, Middx., UK.

DAY, Kenneth, b. 1912, London, UK. Director, Ernest Benn Limited. Publs: The Typography of Press Advertisement; The Typographic Book (w. Stanley Morison); Book Typography, 1815-1965. Awarded O.B.E., 1971. Address: The Elephant, High St., Newport, Essex, UK.

DAY, Lillian, b. 27 June 1893, NYC, USA. Writer. Publs. incl: Paganini of Genoa; Ninon, A Courtesan of Quality; Kiss & Tell; The Youngest Profession; Murder in Time (co-author); Plays — Our Wife (w. L. Mearson); Collectors Item (w. A. Golden); Films — Our Wife, The Youngest Profession, & Living Up to Lizzie. Contbr. to num. mags. & anthols. Address: 28 rue La Fontane, Paris 75016, France.

DAY, Michael Herbert, b. 8 Mar. 1927, London, UK. Professor of Anatomy. Educ: M.R.C.S., L.R.C.P., M.B. & B.S., 1954, Ph.D., 1962, Univ. of London. Publs: Guide to Fossil Man, 1965; Fossil Man, 1969; The Fossil History of Man, 1972; Ed., Human Evolution, 1973. Contbr. to: Nature; Jrnl. of Anatomy; Listener; Am. Jrnl. of Phys. Anthropol.; Jrnl. of Human Evolution; BBC. Mbrships. incl: Anatomical Soc. of GB & Ireland; Royal Anthropol. Inst.; Soc. for the Study of Human Biol.; Am. Assn. of Phys. Anthropol.; Linnean Soc. Recip., Legg Award (for Ph.D. thesis), 1962. Address: Dept. of Anatomy, St. Thomas's Hosp. Med. Schl., Lambeth Palace Rd., London SE1 7EH, UK.

DAY, Stacey B., b. 31 Dec. 1927, London, UK. Author; Writer; Physician; University Professor. Educ: M.D., Royal Coll. Surgs. in Ireland, 1955; Ph.D., McGill Univ., Montreal, Can., 1964; D.Sc., Univ. of Cinn., USA, 1971; L.R.C.P.; L.R.C.S. Publs. incl: The Music Box (play), 1967; Poems & Etudes, 1968; Belle Chasse, 1970; Death & Attitudes towards Death, 1972; Ethics in Medicine, 1973; Molecular Pathology, 1974; Ed., Trauma: Clinical & Biological, & Communication of Scientific Information, 1975; Ed.-in-Chief, Biosciences Communications, 1975. Contbr. to & Ed., num. profl. jrnls. Mbr., num. med., profl. & civic socs. Agent: Robert Feher. Address: Sloan-Kettering Inst., 1275 York Ave., N.Y., NY 10021, USA.

DAYTON, Irene Catherine Glossenger, b. 9 Aug. 1922, Lake Ariel, Pa., USA. Poet. Educ: Grad., Roberts Wesleyan Coll. Publs: The Sixth Sense Quivers, 1970; The Panther's Eye, 1974. Contbr. to jrnls. & anthols., in USA, Europe, Japan. Mbrships: Poetry Soc. of Am.; Past Pres., 2 terms, Rochester Poetry Soc.; N.C. Poetry Soc.; Int. Platform Assn. Hons: Poetry Guinness Award, Cheltenham Fest. of Lit., UK, 1963; 1st Prize, Rochester Fest. of Relig. Arts, 1959, 1960; Finalist, Yale Univ. Younger Poets Series, 1958; Hon. Mention, Carl Sandburg Award, 1974. Address: 209 S. Hillandale Dr., E. Flat Rock, NC 28726, USA.

DEACON, Lois, b. Tamerton Foliot, Devon, UK. Author. Publs: From a Plymouth Pen, 1949; So I Went My Way, 1951; var. Hardy & Tryphena monographs, 1962—; Providence & Mr. Hardy (w. T. Coleman), 1966; George Deacon's Seven of Devon, 1970; An Angel From Your Door, 1973; Dartmoor with a Difference, 1973. Mbr., Soc. of Authors. Address: Ingledene, Meldon Rd., Chagford, Devon TQ13 8BD, UK.

DEADMAN, Ronald, b. 1919, Shoeburyness, Essex, UK. Editor. Educ: Oakley Coll., Cheltenham. Publs: Enjoying English Books, 1 & 2, 1966; Ed., The Friday Story, 1967; The Happening, 1968. Contbr. to: Teacher (Features Ed., 1966-67); Everyweek (Ed., 1967-68); Teachers' World (Ed., 1968—); New Statesman; Guardian; Educ. & Trng.; Where Mag.; BBC. Mbr., Press Coun., 1969—. Address: 54 Arundel Terrace, Barnes, London SW13, UK.

DEAKIN, (Sir) Frederick William, b. 1913, London, UK. Warden, St. Antony's Coll., Oxford Univ. Educ: M.A., Christ Ch., Oxford. Publs: The Brutal Friendship, 1962; The Case of Richard Sorge; The Embattled Mountain. Mbrships: St. James's & White's Clubs. Hons: D.S.O.; Kt., 1975. Address: Le Castellet, Var, France.

DEAKIN, Phyllis A., pen name DAQUIN, Felicity, b. Sheffield, Yorks., UK. Journalist; Broadcaster. Publs: British Section Kvindens Aarhundede (ed.), 1949; In Pride & with Promise, History of the International Federation of Business & Professional Women, 1970. Contbr. to: The Times (daily & supplements); var. women's mags.; N.Y. Times; Wash. Post; Hampshire Poets. Mbrships. incl: Soc. of Women Writers & Jrnlsts.; Press Club of London; Fndr., Hon. Sec., Nat. Fedn. of Bus. & Profl. Women's Clubs of GB. Address: 1 Burnside, Waterlooville, Hants., UK.

DEAL, Borden, pen name BORDEN, Lee, b. 12 Oct., 1922, Pontotoc, Miss., USA. Author. Educ: B.A., Univ. of Ala., Tuscaloosa, 1949; postgrad. work, Mexico City Coll., Mexico. Publs. incl: Walk Through the Valley, 1956; Dunbar's Cove, 1957; The Insolent Breed, 1959; Dragon's Wine, 1960; The Spangled Road, 1962; The Tobacco Men, 1965; A Long Way to Go, 1965; The Bookman Saga (trilogy): The Loser, 1964; Olden Times; The Least One, 1967; The Advocate, 1968; The Winner, 1973; The Other Room, 1975. Contbr. to num. mags. & anthols. Mbrships. incl: Authors' Guild; PEN. Hons. incl: J. S. Guggenheim Fellowship, 1957; Lit. Award, Ala. Lib. Assn., 1963; John H. McGinnis Mem. Award, 1966. Address: Finisterre, 712 N. Casey Key Rd., Osprey, FL 33559, USA.

DEAL, William Sanford, b. Taylorsville, N.C., USA. Minister; Professional Family Counsellor; Author. Educ: Th.B., McKinley-Roosevelt, 1942; Th.M., Defenders Sem., 1946; B.A., Taylors Univ.; 1950; Th.D., N. Bapt. Sem., Colo. Bible Coll. Sem., 1957; M.A., Pasadena Coll. Grad. Schl., 1965. Publs. incl: The Unpardonable Sin Explained, 1932; The Furnace of Affliction, 1936; Heart Talks on the Deeper Life, 1938; The Victorious Life, 1954; Baker's Pictorial Introduction to the Bible, 1961, num. eds.; Happy Married Life & How to Live It, 1967; Happiness & Harmony in Marriage, 1970; Counselling Christian Parents, 1971; Go, Christian, Go! 1974. Contbrns: Ed., The Torch; Ed. Staff Mbr., Christian Life. Address: 11326 Ranchito St., El Monte, CA 91732, USA.

DEAN, Alfreda Joan, b. 1925, Twickenham, Middx., UK. General Adviser for Primary Education (Berks.); Chief Inspector (Educ. Dept., Surrey); Former Headmistress & Lecturer. Educ: Bishop Otter Coll.; M.Ed., Univ. of Reading; Art Tchrs. Dip., Harrow Schl. of Art. Publs: Art & Craft in the Primary School, 1961; First & Second Books of Wild Flowers, 1964; Reading, Writing & Talking, 1968; Religious Education for Children, 1971; Keeping Records of Children, 1971; You & Others, 1973; Room to Learn (series), 1974; Clay in School, 1974; Ed., Exploring Your World (series). Contbr. to: 1st & 2nd Int. Reading Symposium; Techniques of Tchng.; Child Educ.; etc. Mbrships. incl: Nat. Assn. Insps. of Schls. & Educl. Advsrs.; Soc. of Authors. Address: St. Margaret's House, Mapledurham Village, Nr. Reading RG4 7TP, UK.

DEAN, Dwight Gantz, b. 9 Dec. 1918, McCluney, Ohio, USA. Professor of Sociology. Educ: A.B., Capital Univ., 1943; M.Div., Garrett Sem., 1946; M.A., Northwestern Univ., 1947; Ph.D., Ohio State Univ., 1956. Publs: Experiments in Sociology, 1963, 2nd ed., 1967; Sociology in Use, 1965 (both w. Donald M. Valdes); Dynamic Social Psychology, 1965. Contbr. to: Am. Sociol. Review; Jrnl.

Marriage & Family; Sociol. Quarterly; Phi Kappa Phi Jrnl.; etc. Mbr., num. sociol. socs. Address: 2115 Clark Ave., Ames, IA 50010, USA.

DEAN, Winton, b. 18 Mar. 1916, Birkenhead, UK. Author; Musicologist; Former Ernest Bloch Professor of Music. Educ: M.A., Univ. of Cambridge. Publs: Bizet, 1948, 3rd rev. ed., 1975; Carmen, 1949; Introduction to the Music of Bizet 1950; Franck, 1950; Hambledon v. Feathercombe, The Story of a Village Cricket Match, 1951; Handel's Dramatic Oratorios & Masques, 1959; Shakespeare & Opera, 1964; Georges Bizet, His Life & Work, 1965; Handel & the Opera Seria, 1969. Contbr. to: Grove's Dict. of Music & Musicians, 5th ed.; Ency. Britannica; etc. Mbrships: Royal Musical Assn. (Coun., 1965–), VP, 1970–); Int. Musicol. Soc.; Engl. Speaking Union. Recip., hon. R.A.M. Address: Hambledon Hurst, Godalming, Surrey, UK.

DEANE, Seamus, b. 1440, Derry City, UK. University Lecturer in English. Educ: Queen's Univ., Belfast; Pembroke Coll., Cambridge; B.A.; M.A.; Ph.D. Publs: Gradual Wars (poetry), 1972; The Adventures of Hugh Trevor by Thomas Holcroft (ed.), 1973; The Catalogues of the Libraries of Eminent Persons, vol. V, Politicians (ed.), 1974. Contbr. to: Encounter; Jrnl. of Hist. of Ideas; Revue de Litterature Comparee; Mod. Lang. Review; Studies in Burke & his Time; Times Lit. Supplement. Address: Engl. Dept., Univ. Coll., Arts Block, Belfield, Dublin 4, Repub. of Ireland.

DEANE, Shirley Joan, b. 23 Sept. 1920, Melbourne, Australia. Writer. Educ: B.A., Univ. of Melbourne. Publs: Rocks & Olives, 1953; Tomorrow is Manana, 1956, USA, 1957, Germany, 1958; The Road to Andorra, 1958, USA, 1959, Germany, 1960; The Expectant Mariner, 1962, USA, 1963, paperback ed., 1975 (serialised BBC, 1963, Aust. Broadcasting Commn., 1975); Feet in the Clouds, 1964 (serialised Aust. Broadcasting Commn., 1974); In a Corsican Village, USA, 1965; Vendetta, UK & USA, 1965; No Tears for the Dead, 1966, Denmark, 1969; Corpses in Corsica, USA, 1967. Contbr. to: Ed., Playright mag., 1971-72; Encounter; New Statesman; Cornhill Mag. Address: 53 London Rd., Canterbury, Kent, UK.

DEARMER, Geoffrey, b. 1893, S. Lambeth, UK. Writer. Educ: Westminster; Christ Ch., Oxford. Appts.: Asst. Examiner of Plays to the Lord Chamberlain, 1936-58; Ed., BBC Children's Hour, 1939-59. Publs: (novels) Saint on Holiday; They Chose to be Birds; Verse-Poems, 1915; The Day's Delight, 1922; Aught for your Comfort? , 1966; (plays) St. Paul; Three Short Plays; Tides of Invasion (script of Selsey Pageant), 1965. Mbr., Royal Victorian Order. Contbr. to var. jrnls., mags., anthols., BBC progs. Address: 68 Walsingham, St. John's Wood Park, London NW8, UK.

DEASY, Mary Margaret, b. 20 May 1914, Cinn., Ohio, USA. Writer. Educ: Mus.B., Coll.-Conservatory of Music, Univ. of Cinn. Publs: The Hour of Spring, 1948; Cannon Hill, 1949; Ella Gunning, 1950; Devil's Bridge, 1952; The Corioli Affair, 1954; The Boy Who Made Good, 1955; O'Shaughnessy's Day, 1957; The Celebration, 1963. Contbr. to: Harper's; Atlantic Monthly; New Yorker; Va. Quarterly Review; Yale Review; Mademoiselle; etc. Mbr., Authors' Guild.

DEATON, Fae Adams, b. 19 Feb. 1932, Phila., Pa., USA. Educator; Guidance Counsellor; Writer. Educ: B.Mus., Salem Coll., Winston-Salem, N.C., 1953; Univ. of Alaska, Anchorage, 1968 & 1969; Wright State Univ., Dayton, Ohio, 1971-73; Old Dominion Univ., Norfolk, Va., 1974, 1975. Ed., Writer, Scott Air Force Base Wives Club Mag., 1966-67; Ed., Native Arts & Crafts Festival Catalogue, Anchorage, Alaska, 1959; Writer, Elmendorf OUC Mag., 1967-70. Contbr. to: Old Dominion Univ. Alumae Mag.; Anchorage Times (Art & Music Reviewer & Critic); Art Publicity, Alaska Coun. on Arts. Mbrships: Nat. League of Am. Pen Women; Alaska Press Club; Tidewater Area Press Club; Am. Personnel & Guidance Assn.; Coun., Exceptional Children. Address: 176 Pickett Rd., Norfolk, VA 23502, USA.

DeBAKEY, Michael Ellis, b. 7 Sept. 1908, Lake Charles, La., USA. Surgeon. Educ: B.S., 1930, M.D., 1932, M.S., 1935, Tulane Univ., Schl. of Med., New Orleans, La. Contbr. to num. books, med. & sci. jrnls. Mbrships. incl: Pres., Harris Co. Chapt., Am. Trauma Soc., 1974; For. Mbr., USSR Med. Acad., 1974; Hon. F.R.C.S., UK; Chmn., Albert Lasker Clin. Med. Rsch. Jury Awards, 1973; Stroke Coun. Fellow, Am. Heart Assn., 1973; Trustee, China-Am.

Rels. Soc., 1973. Hons. incl: Disting. Serv. Award, Am. Soc. of Contemporary Med. & Surg., 1974; D.Sc., Hahnemann Med. Coll. & Hosp. of Phila., 1973. Address: Baylor College of Medicine, 1200 Moursand St., Houston, TX 77025, USA.

DE BEER, Esmond Samuel, b. 1895, Dunedin, NZ. Writer. Educ: M.A., New Coll., Oxford & Univ. Coll., London, UK. Publs: Ed., Diary of John Evelyn, 1st complete ed., 6 vols., UK, 1955 (Evelyn Diary, USA, 1959). Contbr. to: Hist.; Review of Engl. Studies, etc. Mbrships: F.B.A.; F.S.A.; F.R.S.L.; F.R.Histl.S. Hons: C.B.E.; D.Litt., Durham & Oxford; Litt.D., Otago. Address: 31 Brompton Square, London SW3 2AE, UK.

de BEHAULT, Maurice, b. 23 Aug. 1906, Gand, Belgium. Banker. Educ: High Financial Schl.; High Inst. for Bank & Stock Exchange Studies. Publs. incl: Symphonie finlandaise, 1954; Mademoiselle Dominique, 1959; Ca rachète pas mal de choses, 1960; Shalom Israel, 1967; Carnets de voyage satiriques, 1971. Contbr. to Belgium, French & Polish press. Mbrships: Societaire Assn. Ecrivains de Belgique; Int. Fedn. of Jrnlsts. & Writers on Tourism; var. press assns. Num. hons. incl: Prix Icare, 1954; Genet d'Or Perpignan, France, 1956; Laureat Prix Martini, 1965; Grand Prix Alain de Presles, 1971, 1973; Gold Medal, Academie de Lutèce, Paris, 1974. Address: N.1 ave. Camille Huysmans, B-2020 Antwerp, Belgium.

DE BIE, Hans, b. 24 Oct. 1936, Amsterdam, Netherlands. News Editor, Dutch Television. Educ: Press Inst. of The Netherlands. Publs: (in Dutch) ABC of Tennis, 1974; 75 years of Tennis History, 1974. Contbr. to: int. lawn tennis mags., Dutch mags., newspapers & radio; Ed., Lawn Tennis Mag. Mbrships: Org. of Jrnlsts. in Netherlands; Int. Org. of Jrnlsts.; sev. sports writers assns. Address: Cath. van Clevepark 43, Amstelveen, Netherlands.

DEBNARKIN, Andrew M., b. 21 Mar. 1918, Oćová-Zvolen, Czech. P. Engineer. Educ: Univ. Degree. Publs: Verses, 1946; With Manifesting Voice, 1952; Echoes From Overseas, 1956; Souvenir Book of the Canadian Slovak Society, 1957 & 1972. Contbr. to: Nat. News; Slovak Voice; Our Homeland. Mbr., Can. Slovak Benefit Soc. Recip., Lit. Prize 1955 Radio Free Europe, Munich. Address: 53 Longbourne Dr., Weston, Ont. M9R 2M8, Can.

DE BOER, Herman Pieter, b. 9 Feb. 1928, Rotterdam, Netherlands. Author. Educ: HBS-A, Bussum, Netherlands. Publs: Zalig zijn de Schelen (w. Betty van Garrel), 1972; De Vrouw in het Maanlicht en andere zonderlinge verhalen, 1973; Het beste van Herman Pieter de Boer: de Vestiaire van Thalia en andere verhalen, 1974. Mbrships: Maatschappij der Nederlandse Letterkunde; Vereniging van Letterkundigen. Address: Mientwei 16, Rijs-Gaasterland, Netherlands.

de BONO, Edward, b. 1933, Malta. Assistant Director of Research, Investigative Medicine; Writer. Educ: M.D., B.Sc., M.A., D.Phil., Ph.D.; Royal Univ. of Malta; Christ Church, Oxford, UK. Publs: The Use of Lateral Thinking, 1967; The Five-Day Course in Thinking, 1969; The Mechanism of Mind, 1969; The Dog Exercising Machine, 1970 (also transls. in USA, sev. European countries, Far. E., S. Am.); Children Solve Problems, 1973; PO; Beyond Yes & No, 1973; Ed., Eureka History of Inventions, 1974; CORT Thinking Programme, 1973-75; Thinking Course for Juniors, 1975. Contbr. to: Sunday Times; Sunday Mirror; Nova; Telegraph Mag.; Sci. Jrnl.; Where; Fin. Times; Nature; etc. Mbr., Med. Rsch. Soc. Agent: A.P. Watt & Sons. Address: The Cognitive Research Trust, 11 Warkworth St., Cambridge CB1 1EG, UK.

De BORN, Edith, b. Vienna, Austria. Novelist. Educ: Univ. of Vienna. Publs: 17 novels publd. by Chapman & Hall, Eyre Methuen (UK); W. W. Norton, Alfred A. Knopf (USA); Wolfgang Krüger, Hamburg, Deutscher Bücherbund, Stuttgart (transls.); Büchergemeinschaft Donauland, Vienna, Paul Zsolnay Verlag, Vienna (transls.); Nij & van Ditmar, The Hague (transls.); Editions Gerard, Marabout, Belgium (transls.). Mbrships: The Author; PEN. Address: 77 Rue du Marteau, 1040 Brussels, Belgium.

de BOURBON, Louis Adelberth (Prince-Duke of Normandy), pen names BOULENDOV, Boris; van RENKUM, Lodewÿk, b. 27 Dec. 1908, Renkum, Netherlands. Educ: J.D., Univ. of Nymegen. Publs: Het Rood v.d. hemel; Het andere lied; De Troubadour; Verzamelde Gedichten, 1974. Contbr. to: Maatstaf; Roeping; De Gemienschap, 1933-42; num. daily papers.

Hons. incl: Beethoven Prize. Address: Beethovenlaan 305, Doorwerthe, Netherlands.

DE BRAY, Reginald George Arthur, b. 1912, Leningrad, USSR. University Professor. Educ: Oriel Coll., Oxford, UK; Birkbeck Coll. & Schl. of Slavonic & E. European Studies, Univ. of London; B.A.; Ph.D. Publs: Guide to the Slavonic Languages, 1951, 2nd ed., 1969. Contbr. to: Slavonic & E. European Review, London; Study of Sounds, Tokyo; Proceedings AULLA Congress, Auckland; Eos, The Hague. Mbrships: Philol. Soc., London; I.P.A.; Phonetic Soc., Japan; I.A.L.L.S.; B.U.A.S. Address: 78 Northumberland Rd., New Barnet, Herts., UK.

DEBRECZENY, Paul, b. 16 Feb. 1932, Budapest, Hungary. Professor of Russian Literature & Slavic Languages. Educ: Eotvos Univ., Budapest; B.A. (Russian), 1953; B.A. (Hungarian), 1955; Ph.D., Univ. of London, 1959. Publs: Nikolai Gogol & his Contemporary Critics, 1966; Literature & National Identity, 1970. Contbr. to: Slavic Review; Comparative Lit.; Can. Slavic Studies; Slavic & E. European Jrnl.; etc. Mbrships: Mod. Lang. Assn. of Am.; Am. Assn. for the Advancement of Slavic Studies; Am. Assn. of Teachers of Slavic & E. European Lang. Address: 423 Dey Hall, Univ. of N. Carolina, Chapel Hill, NC 27514, USA.

DEBROT, Nicolaas, b. 4 May 1902. Physician; Writer; Governor of Netherlands Antilles. Educ: Univs. of Utrecht & Amsterdam; LL.D.; M.D. Publs: My Sister the Negro, 1935; Confession in Toledo (poetry), 1944; Poignant Summer (poetry), 1945; Pray for Camille Willocq, 1946; Clouded Existence, 1948; Those Absent (poetry), 1952; Pages from a Diary in Geneva, 1962. Hons: Kt., Order of Netherlands Lion; Grand Cross, Order of Vasco Nuñez de Balboa. Address: Gouvernementhuis, Willemstad, Duracao, Netherlands Antilles.

de BRUNHOFF, Laurent, b. 1925, Paris, France. Painter; Author of children's books. Publs: 26 books in Babar series, inclng: Babar Goes to America; Serafina the Giraffe; Anatole & His Monkey, Bonhomme; A Tue Tete; Bonhomme & the Huge Beast. Contbr. to: L'Express, Paris; Evergreen Review, N.Y.; Graphik, Germany; var. Babar films, France & USA. Address: 49 Boulevard St. Germain, Paris Ve, France.

DEBU-BRIDEL, Jacques, b. 22 Aug. 1902. Writer; Politician. Educ: Lic. en Droit, Fac. of Law, Sorbonne; Ecole Libre des Scis. Politiques. Publs. incl: Jeunes Ménages, 1935; Exil au Grand Palais, 1948; Emily Brontë (biog.), 1950; Sous la Cendre, 1951; La Grande tragédie du Monde animal, 1955; Frère esclave, new ed., 1957; Journées Révolutionnaires de Paris, vol. I, 1960, vol. II, 1961; Conjuration d'Amboise, 1963. Contbr. to num. jrnls. inclng: Notre République (Dir., 1966–). Recip., var. decorations. Address: 15 rue des Barres, Paris 4e, France.

de CAMP, Catherine Crook, b. 6 Nov. 1907, NYC, USA. Writer; Teacher. Educ: A.B., Barnard Coll., Columbia Univ., 1933; Postgrad. study, Columbia, Western Reserve & Temple Univs. Publs. incl: The Money Tree, 1972; Teach Your Child to Manage Money, 1974; Co-author, w. L. Sprague de Camp – Spirits, Stars & Spells, 1966; The Day of the Dinosaur, 1968; 3,000 Years of Fantasy & Science Fiction, 1972; Tales Beyond Time, 1973. Mbr., Authors League of Am. Hons: Darwin & His Great Discovery (w. L. Sprague de Camp) chosen Book of Month, Phila. Lib. Children's Reading Roundtable, 1974. Address: 278 Hothorpe Lane, Villanova, PA 19085, USA.

DE CARVALHO DE VALLE E. VASCONCELLOS, Antonio Serafim (Count of Souto-Vignola), pen name DA SILVA, (Prof.) J. M., b. Cavez, Portugal. Consul for Costa Rica; Consul-General for Order of the Knights of Colombo. Educ: Ph.D., Univ. of Cape Town, S. Africa. Publs. incl: Os Versos Dourados de Pitágoras; Os Milagres de Lourdes; O Homem e o Animal; O Naturismo no Lar, 2 vols.; Os Segredos da Energia; A Bondade para com os Animais; O Magnetismo Hindu; O Hipnotismo ao Alcance de Todos; Alguns Fenômenos de Levitação; House Purchase Scheme; A Strange Cocktail; Nociones de Antropologia & Fisiologia. Contbr. to sev. jrnls. Mbr., Sociedade de Estudos de Moçambique. Recip., Gold Grand Collar, Int. Acad. of Letters, Sci. & Art, Italy. K.G.O.O.C. Address: P.O. Box 731, Lourenço Marques, Mozambique.

DECAUDIN, Michel H. F., b. 22 Apr. 1919, Roubaix, France. University Professor of French Literature. Educ: Agrégé des Lettres; Dr. ès Lettres. Publs. incl: La Crise des

Valeurs Symbolistes, 1960; Le Dossier d'"'Alcools" D'Apollinaire, 1960; Panorama de XXème Siècle Français, 1964. Ed., var. works of Apollinaire. Contbr. to: La Quinzaine Littéraire; L'Info. Littéraire. Mbrships: Pres., Soc. d'Etude du XXème Siècle; Soc. des Gens de Lettres de France; Pen Club de France; Syndicat des Critiques Littéraires. Hons: Prix Léon Riotor de Critique Poétique, 1960; Prix Guizot de l'Acad. Française, 1960; Chevalier des Arts & Lettres, 1973. Address: 24 rue des Bernardins, 75005 Paris, France.

de CLIPPELE, Antoine, b. 7 Dec. 1885, Denderleeuw, Belgium. Writer. Educ: LL.D., Lic., Soc. Sci. & Pols., Univ. of Louvain. Publs: Poèmes au fil des heures, 1971; Nostalgies et Aspirations, 1971. Contbr. to: Jrnl. des Tribunaux; Le Jrnl.; La Metropole; Les Marches de France; 47 Belgian Poets (anthol.); Jrnl. de l'Acad. des Poètes; La Coupe d'Ambroisié; Les Poètes Témoins de leur Temps. Mbr., Assn. of Belgian Writers. Hons: 2nd Prize, Acad. des Jeux Floraux de Tunisie, 1946; Prix Voltaire, 1947; 1st Prize, Soc. vauclusienne des amis de Pétrarque. Address: 16 Mussenstraat, 9000 Ghent, Belgium.

DEDIJER, Vladimir, b. 4 Feb. 1914, Belgrade, Yugoslavia. Writer; Historian. Educ: Ph.D., Belgrade Univ.; M.A., Oxford, UK. Publs: War Diaries 1-3, 1945-52; Yugoslav Albanian Relations, 1948; Tito Speaks, 1952; The Beloved Land, 1962; The Road to Sarajevo, 1965; The Battle Stalin Lost, 1970; History of Yugoslavia, 1974. Contbr. to: Times Lit. Supplement; Tribune; Times; N.Y. Times; N.Y. Review of Books; etc. Mbr., Serbian Acad. of Scis. & Arts. Recip., Book of the Yr. Award, Belgrade, 1972. Address: Gorkiceva 16, 61000 Ljubljana, Yugoslavia.

DEELEY, Roger, b. 1 Jan. 1944, Rugby, Warwicks., UK. Writer. Educ: Univ. of Bristol. Publs: King's Man, 1968; By Courtesy of the Cardinal, 1970; Three Crowns for the Queen, 1972; The Byzantine Eagle, 1974. Contbr. to: Generation One, 1970; Protostars, 1971; Mags. by Thomson-Leng, IPC, Galaxy Corp., etc.; Writer/artist, Rameses, cartoon strip syndicated by Ctrl. Press Features Ltd.; BBC; ITV. Mbr., Authors' Club. Address: 50 Uphill Way, Uphill, Weston-super-Mare, Avon BS23 4TN, UK.

DEEN, Thalif, b. 11 June 1938, Colombo, Sri Lanka. Journalist. Educ: B.A., Univ. of Ceylon, 1962; M.A. (Jrnlsm.), Columbia Univ., N.Y., 1972. Publs: The Exodus of Doctors from Ceylon to the United States. Contbr. to: Ceylon Observer (Dpty. News Ed.); Hongkong Standard (Sr. Ed. Writer). Mbrships: Press Assn. of Ceylon; Hongkong Jrnlsts. Assn. Hons: Wijewardena Award for Most Outstanding Jrnlst. of Yr., Ceylon Observer, 1968; Fulbright grant to Columbia Schl. of Jrnlsm. Address: 113/28 Cotta Rd., Colombo 8, Sri Lanka.

DEERE, Alan C., b. 1917, Auckland, NZ. Air Commander, Royal Air Force. Publs: Nine Lives, 1958. Mbr., RAF Club, Piccadilly. Address: 7 Dobbins Lane, Wendover, Bucks., UK.

DE FILIPPO, Eduardo, b. 1900. Playwright; Actor; Producer. Publs: Natale in Casa Cupiello; Non ti Pago; Napoli Milionaria; Filumena Marturano; Questi Fantasmi; Le Voci di Dentro; Le Bugie con le gambe lunghe; Sabato; Domenica e Lunedi; num. other one-act plays, operas & films. Address: Via Ximenes 8, Rome, Italy.

DE FILIPPO, Giuseppe (profl. name, Peppino De Filippo), b. 24 Aug. 1903. Playwright; Actor; Producer. Publs. incl: over 60 farces; Le metamorfosi di un suonatore ambulante (musical); num. poems & songs. Address: Viale Parioli 96, Rome, Italy.

DEFORD, Miriam Allen (Mrs. Maynard Shipley), b. 21 Aug. 1888, Phila., Pa., USA. Writer. Educ: A.B., Temple Univ., 1911; Univ. of Pa. Publs. incl: Love Children (biog.), 1931; Shaker with the Wind (novel), 1942; The Overbury Affair, 1960 (Edgar Award, Mystery Writers of Am.); Penultimates (poetry), 1962; Murderers Sane & Mad, 1965 (Scroll, Mystery Writers of Am.); The Real Bonnie & Clyde, 1968; Elsewhere, Elsewhen, Elsehow (sci. fiction), 1971; Contbr. of stories, articles & verse to num. mags. & anthols.; contbr. to num. biog. dictionaries. Mbrships. incl: PEN; Mystery Writers of Am.; Sci. Fiction Writers of Am. Hons. incl: Essay Award, Comm. Econ. Dev., 1958; num. poetry prizes. Address: Ambassador Hotel, 55 Mason St., San Fran., CA 94102, USA.

de FUNIAK, William Quinby, b. 16 Nov. 1901, Birmingham, Ala., USA. Retired Professor of Law; Legal

Author. Educ: LL.B., Univ. of Va., 1924; Grad. Law Work, Univ. of Calif., 1942; LL.M., Univ. of San Fran., 1947. Publs: American Notaries Manual, 1942; Principles of Community Property, 2 vols., 1943, 2nd ed. (w. Michael Vaughn), 1971; Cases & Materials on Community Property, 1947, 2nd ed., 1969; Handbook of Modern Equity, 1950, 2nd ed., 1956; American-British Dictionary, 1963, 3rd ed., 1967; Cases on Equitable Relief, 1964. Contbr. to num. legal jrnls. Mbr., Scribes. Address: 223 Trevethan Ave., Santa Cruz, CA 95062, USA.

DEGHY, Guy, pen names FROY, Herald; GIBB, Lee, b. 1912, Budapest, Hungary. Author; Drama & Film Critic. Publs: (as Guy Deghy) Cafe Royal (w. K. Waterhouse), 1955; Noble & Manly, 1956; Paradise in the Strand, 1958; Fire Next Door, 1958; (as Herald Froy, all w. K. Waterhouse) How to Avoid Matrimony, 1957; How to Survive Matrimony, 1958; Can This be Love?, 1960; Maybe You're Just Inferior, 1961; O Mistress Mine, 1962; (as Lee Gibb, all w. K. Waterhouse) The Joneses, 1959; The Higher Jones, 1961; also film & TV scripts for Granada TV & BBC. Contbr. to: Observer; Punch. Address: 45 Fitzgeorge Ave., London W14 0SZ, UK.

DEGLMANN-SCHWARZ, Rainer Michael, b. 25 June 1941, Berchtesgaden, Germany. Journalist. Educ: Rechtsreferendar Degree in Law, Univ. of Munich. Publs: Skiing Around the World, forthcoming. Contbr. to: Bavarian Radio, Munich; S.W. Radio, Baden-Baden; Südeutsche Zeitung; Frankfurter Allgemeine; Die Welt; Neue Zürcher Zeitung; Die Zeit; Christian Sci. Monitor, USA. Mbr., Vereinigung Deutscher Reisejournalisten (Assn. of German Travel Jrnlsts.). Address: 8 Bayerstr., 824 Berchtesgaden, W. Germany.

DE GUINGAND, (Major Gen. Sir) Francis Wilfred, b. 1900, London, UK. Company Executive. Educ: R.M.C. Sandhurst. Publs: Operation Victory, 1947; African Assignment, 1953; Generals at War, 1964. Mbrships: Rand Club; Country Club; Inanda Club; Durban Country Club; London Club; Army & Navy Club; White's Club; RAC Club. Agent: David Higham & Assoc. Ltd. Address: c/o Carreras Rothmans Ltd., 27 Baker St., London W11, UK.

de HAAN, Koert, b. 24 Nov. 1899, Amsterdam, Netherlands. College Teacher of French Language & Literature (ret'd). Educ: Degree French Lang. & Lit., Study, Utrecht Univ. Publs. incl: (sci. fiction) Raket op Drift, 1957; (juvenile) De Mannen van de Swarte Draeck, 1958; (transl.) Angélique et son Amour, 1975; & num. books (some as co-author) & transls. Contbr. to: Maandblad Succes; Utrechts Nieuwsblad. Mbrships: Vereniging van Letterkundigen; Nederlands Genootschap van Vertalers. Address: Laakkade 80, The Hague, Netherlands.

de HARTOG, Jan, pen name ECKMA, F. R., b. 22 Apr. 1914, Haarlem, Netherlands. Writer. Publs. incl: De Maagd en de Moordenaar, 1938 & 4 other detective stories (as Eckma); De Ondergang van de Vrijheid, 1937 & 3 other plays; The Little Ark, 1954; The Inspector, 1961; Waters of the New World (travel), 1961; The Artist, 1963; The Hospital, 1965; The Captain, 1967; The Children, 1969; The Peaceable Kingdom, 1972. Recip., Gt. Nat. Drama Prize, 1937. Address: Atheneum Publrs., N.Y., NY, USA.

de HEREDIA y LOZANO, Manuel, b. 21 Sept. 1915, Huesca, Spain. Writer. Publs: 41 works inclng: Barro, 1958; Este Dia y Todos los Dias, 1965; El Chepa, 1972; A Beneficio del Mundo, 1973. Contbr. to: Spanish & S. Am. mags. & newspapers. Mbr., Int. Union of Official Travel Orgs. Recip., Int. Novel Prize, Mexico, 1958. Address: General Millan Astray 9-5E, Madrid 24, Spain.

DEHN, Paul Edward, b. 1912, Manchester, UK. Screenwriter; Poet. Educ: B.A., Brasenose Coll., Oxford. Publs: (poems) The Day's Alarm, 1949; Romantic Landscape, 1952; A miscellany: For Love & Money, 1956; Quake, Quake, Quake, 1961; The Fern on the Rock, 1967. Contbr. to Punch. Address: 19 Bramerton St., London SW3, UK.

DEI, Laud Alfred, b. 2 Aug. 1938, Accra, Ghana. University Lecturer. Educ: B.A., Ghana, 1964; C.E.S. (Geomorphol.), 1967, Dr. 3e Cycle (Geomorphol.), Strasbourg, France, 1969. Contbr. to: Jrnl. Tropical Geog.; Zeitschrift für Geomorphologie; Bulletin of Ghana Geogl. Assn. Address: Dept. of Geography, The University, Cape Coast, Ghana.

DEI-ANANG, Michael (Francis), b. 16 Oct. 1909. Poet; Historian; Educationist. Educ: B.A., 1936, Dip.Ed., 1938,

London Univ., UK. Publs: (poetry) Wayward Lines From Africa; Africa Speaks; Ghana Semi-Tones; Ghana Glory; Two Faces of Africa, forthcoming; (histl.) Okonkronni Augustino; Ghana Resurgent; Man's Inhumanity To Man, forthcoming; Administration of Ghana's Foreign Policy, 1956-66, forthcoming; (play) Okomfo Anokye's Golden Stool. Mbrships. incl: World Poetry Soc. Intercontinental; Int. Platform Assn., USA; Fellow, Royal Econ. Soc., UK. Hons. incl: Gold Coast Drama Award, 1954; Play performed before H.M. Queen Elizabeth II, 1961. Address: Awonkae Fie, Mampong-Akwapim, Ghana, W. Africa.

DEIGHTON, Len, b. 18 Feb. 1929, London, UK. Writer. Educ: Royal Coll. of Art, London. Publs: (novels) The Ipcress File, 1962; Horse under Water, 1963; Funeral in Berlin, 1964; The Billion Dollar Brain, 1966; An Expensive Place to Die, 1967; Only When I Larf, 1968; Bomber, 1970; Close-Up, 1972; Declarations of War (short stories), 1971; (other) Action Cook Book: Len Deighton's Guide to Eating, 1965; Où est le Garlic; or, Len Deighton's French Cook Book, 1965; Len Deighton's Continental Dossier: A Collection of Cultural, Culinary, Historical, Spooky, Grim & Preposterous Fact, 1968; Ed., London Dossier, 1967. Address: c/o Anton Felton & Ptnrs., Continuum One, 25 Newman St., London W1, UK.

DEINDORFER, Robert Greene, pen names, GREENE, Robert; DENDER, Jay; & BENDER, Jay, b. 3 July 1922, Galena, Ill., USA. Author. Educ: Univ. of Mo. Schl. of Jrnlsm. Publs: The Great Gridiron Plot, 1947; Spies & Counterspies, 1957; Confessions of a Gypsy Quarterback, 1962; Secret Service — Thirty-Three Centuries of Espionage, 1968; The Spies, 1971. Contbr. to var. anthols.; Reader's Digest; N.Y. Times; Saturday Review; Life. Mbrships: Nat. Press Club, Was. D.C.; Sec., Soc. of Mag. Writers, NYC. Address: 114 E 71st St., N.Y., NY 10021, USA.

DEISS, Joseph Jay, b. 1915, Twin Falls, Idaho, USA. Author. Educ: B.A., M.A., Univ. of Tex. Publs: A Washington Story, 1950; The Blue Chips, 1957; The Great Infidel — Frederick II of Hohenstaufen, 1963; Captains of Fortune — Profiles of Six Italian Condottieri, 1965; Herculaneum — Italy's Buried Treasure, 1966; The Roman Years of Margaret Fuller, 1969; The Town of Hercules, 1974. Contbr. to: Harper's Mag.; Mademoiselle; Cosmopolitan; Reader's Digest; Holiday; Am. Heritage. Writer-in-Residence, Currier House, Harvard Univ. Recip., Disting. Alumnus Award, Univ. of Tex., 1970; Cavaliere, Ordine della Stella della Solidarietà Italiana, Italy, 1971. Agent: Madame W. A. Bradley, Paris, France. Address: Thoreau House, Wellfleet (Cape Cod), MA 02667, USA.

DE JONG, M. G. C. J. (Theo), b. 16 July 1940, Gouda, Netherlands. Journalist. Publs: Goudse Gedichten (poetry), 1973. Contbr. to: "A.N.P.", 1958-64; "Het Parool", 1964-71; Algemeen Dagblad, 1971-74; Sijthoff Pers, 1974; Fairplay, London, UK; Sekstant, The Hague, Netherlands, Vrij Nederland, Amsterdam; Accent, ibid; Wereldkroniek, The Hague. Mbrships: Int. Perscentrum Nieuwspoort, The Hague; Nederlandse Vereniging van Journalisten. Amsterdam. Address: Lage Gouwe 160, Gouda, Netherlands.

de JOSSELIN de JONG, Kitty Henriëtte Rodolpha, b. 9 July 1903, The Hague, Netherlands. Author. Publs. incl: Het Antwoord (novel), 1931; De Appel valt niet ver van de stam (novel), 1939; Wending (novel), 1936; Ondine (poetry), 1952; Stilte voor het hart (poetry), 1960; September is een lied in blauw (poetry), 1973; & sev. short stories. Contbr. to: De Haagse Courant; Het Vaderland; etc. Mbrships: Dutch br., PEN; Soc. of Dutch Authors. Address: "de Rozenhof" 70, Epe, Netherlands.

DE LACRETELLE, Jaques, b. 14 July 1888. Author. Publs. incl: La Vie inquiète de Jean Hermelin, 1920; Silbermann, 1922; La Bonifas, 1925; Histoire de Paola Ferrani, 1929; Amour Nuptial, 1929; Le Retour de Silbermann, 1930; Les Hauts Ponts, 4 vols., 1932-35; L'Ecrivain Public, 1936; Le Pour et le Contre, 1946; Deux coeurs simples, 1953; Tiroir secret, 1959; Les Maîtres les Amis, 1959; Grece que J'aime; La Galerie des amants, 1963; Racine, 1970; (play) Une visite en été, 1952; (transls.) Precious Bane by Mary Webb & Wuthering Heights by Emily Brontë. Mbr., Acad. Française. Hons: Prix Femina, 1922; Grand Prix du Roman, Acad. Française, 1927. Address: 49 Rue Vineuse, Paris XVIe, France.

DELAET, Jean, b. 4 Jan. 1904, Forest, Brussels, Belgium. Retired Teacher of the Blind & Deaf; Former Military Observer, Air Force. Publs: Brin d'Azur, 1932; Billy Dum, 3 vols., 1936-54; Légende des Ailes, 1949; Escadrilles au Combat, 1942; Dernières Escadrilles, 1946; La Pourpre des Innocents, 1954; Le Petit Herboriste, 1968. Contbr. to: L'Avant Poste; Marginales; Audace. Mbr., Belgian PEN. Recip., sev. hon. mentions. Address: B.144 Avenue de la Mer, 8470 De Panne, Belgium.

DE LAET, Sigfried Jan Leo, b. 15 June 1914, Ghent, Belgium. University Professor. Educ: D.Ph., D.Litt.; Univs. of Ghent, Belgium & Cambridge, UK. Publs: Portorium. Etude sur l'organisation douanière chez les Romains, 1949; Archaeology & its Problems, 1957; The Low Countries, 1958; Contributions à l'étude de la civilisation des Champs d'Urnes en Flandre, 1958; De Voorgeschiedenis der Lage Landen (w. W. Glasbergen), 1959; La préhistoire de l'Europe, 1967; Prehistorische Kulturen in het Zuiden der Lage Landen, 1974. Contbr. to acad. jrnls. Hons: F.S.A.; F.S.A. (Scotland); Corres. Mbr., Prehistoric Soc. Address: Blandijnberg 2, B 9000 Ghent, Belgium.

DE LA HERA, Alberto, b. 18 Sept. 1932, Granada, Spain. University Professor. Educ: LL.D., Univ. of Navarre; Ph.D., Madrid Univ. Publs: El Regalismo Borbónico, 1963; La Cohabitación conyugal, 1966; Introducción a la Ciencia del Derecho Canónico, 1967; Pluralismo y Libertad Religiosa, 1971. Contbr. to: Apollinaris, Rome; Ius Canonicum, Navarre; L'Année Canonique, Paris; Il Diritto Ecclesiastico, Milan; Revue de Droit Canonique, Strasbourg. Mbrships: Assn. Int. di Diritto Canonico, Home; Gesellschaft für das Recht der Ostkirchen, Vienna; Assn. pour l'étude du Droit Canonique, Paris. Address: Facultad de Filosofia y Letras, Universidad de Madrid, Ciudad Universitaria, Madrid 3, Spain.

de LAIGLESIA, Alvaro, b. 9 Sept. 1922, San Sebastian, Spain. Author. Publs. incl: Un Naufrago en la Sopa, 1943; Dios le Ampare Imbecil, 1955; Libertad de Risa, 1963; Licencia para Incordiar, 1968; Se Busca Rey en Buen Estado, 1968; Nene Caca! 1969; Cuentaselo a Tu Tia, 1969; Requiem por una Furcia, 1970; El 'Sexy' Mandamiento, 1971; Mejorando lo Presente, 1971; Tocata en "Ja", 1972; Listo el Que lo Lea, 1973; Es Usted un Mamifero, 1974. Also author, plays, film scripts, radio & TV series. Ed., La Codorniz mag., 1944—. Address: Paseo de la Habana 48, Madrid, Spain.

de la MAHOTIÈRE, Stuart Renwick Robert, b. 19 Nov. 1911, London, UK. Journalist. Educ: Degree in Pol. Econ., Genoa Univ. Publs: The Common Market, 1961; The Hard Sell, 1966; Towards One Europe, 1970. Contbr. to: Port of London Mag., Accountancy; Midland Bank Grp. Newspaper; etc. Ed., The Common Market News. Mbrships: Inst. of Jrnlsts., London; Dpty. Chmn., Press Club, London, 1974; Franco-Brit. Soc.; Press Golfing Soc.; Panel of Lectrs., Inst. of Bankers. Address: 24 Thurlow Rd., Hampstead, London NW3 5PP, UK.

DELANEY, Shelagh, b. 1939, Salford, Lancs., UK. Playwright. Publs: (plays) A Taste of Honey, 1958; The Lion in Love, 1960; (films) A Taste of Honey, 1961; Charlie Bubbles, 1968; (other) Sweetly Sings the Donkey, 1963. Hons: Charles Henry Foyle New Play Award; N.Y. Drama Critics' Award; Brit. Film. Acad. Award; Robert Flaherty Award; Writers' Guild Award. Address: c/o CMA, 22 Grafton St., London W1, UK.

DE-LA-NOY, Michael, b. 3 Apr. 1934, Hessle, Yorks., UK. Author; Journalist. Publs: Before the Storm (poems), 1958; A Child's Life of Christ, 1964; Young Once Only: a Study of Boys on Probation, 1965; The Fields of Praise (anthol. of relig. poetry); 1968; A Day in the Life of God, 1971. Contbr. to: Times; Guardian; Sunday Times; Observer; Times Educl. Supplement; New Soc.; Illustrated London News; The Field; Blackwood's Mag.; Church Times; C. of E. Newspaper; Tablet; Month; Wiseman Review; Frontier; Meth. Recorder; Musical Times; Lady; New Outlook; New Humanist. Mbr., Wig & Pen Club. Address: 86 High St., Irchester, Northants., UK.

DE LARREA, Arcadio, b. 28 June 1907, Echavarri, Navarra, Spain. Ethnomusicologist. Publs: Cancionero Judio del Norte de Marrvecos, 3 vols., 1952-53; Cuentos Populares de los Judios del Norte de Marrvecos, 2 vols., 1953; El Dance Aragones y las Representaciones de Moros y Cristianos, 1953; El Folklore y la Escuela, 1956; Monumentos de la Musica Hispanoárabe, 1957; Cuentos Gaditanos, 1957; La Cancion Andaluza; El Flamenco en su Raiz, 1974. Contbr. to: Arbor; Anuario Musical; other musical jrnls. & encycs. Hons: Prizes for Nat. Folklore Rsch. 1945, Cancion Andaluza, 1960, Flamenco, 1969. Address: Rios Rosas 8—5° B, Madrid 3, Spain.

de LAUNAY, Jacques Forment, b. 28 Jan. 1924, Roubaix, France. Historian. Author. Educ: J.D. Publs: Secret Diplomacy of World War II, 1963; Major Controversies of Contemporary History, 1965; De Gaulle & His France, 1969. Address: 68 Faisanderie, B 1150 Brussels, Belgium.

DEL BURGO TORRES, Jaime, b. 11 Nov. 1912, Pamplona, Navarra, Spain. Director of Tourism, Libraries & Popular Culture. Educ: Prof. Mercantil; Periodista. Publs: Bibliografia de las Guerras Carlistas y de las Luchas Politicas del Siglo XIX, 5 vols., 1953-66; La Aventura Hispanica de los Viajeros Extranjeros del Siglo XIX, 1963; La Sucesion de Carlos II, 1967; Conspiracion y Guerra Civil, 1970; Navarra, Semblanza Emocional, 1972. Contbr. to var. Spanish & Italian jrnls. Hons: Premio Int. Literario "Bayona-Pamplona", 1962; Premio Nacional de Literatura, 1967. Address: Calle Arrieta 2—4°dcha., Pamplona, Spain.

DELDERFIELD, Eric Raymond, b. 4 May 1909. Author. Publs: Travelogue series, 1950; Lynmouth Flood Disaster, 1953; Cotswolds Villages & Churches, 1961; British Inn Signs & their Stories, 1965; Kings & Queens of England, 1966; Church Furniture, 1966; West Country Historic Houses & their Families, 3 vols., 1968, 1970, 1973; Introduction to Inn Signs, 1969; Eric Delderfield's True Animal Stories, 3 vols., 1970, 1972, 1975; Stories of Inns & their Signs, 1974. Contbr. to newspapers & periodicals, TV & radio mags. Address: Penshurst, Sarlsdown Rd., Exmouth, Devon EX8 2HY, UK.

DELDERFIELD, Ronald Frederick, b. 1912, Greenwich, UK. Novelist; Playwright; Screen & TV Script Writer. Publs. incl: The Adventures of Ben Gunn; The Dreaming Suburb; The Avenue Goes to War; Napoleon in Love; The March of the Twenty Six; There was a Fair Maid Dwelling; Seven Men of Gascony; Farewell the Tranquil Mind; A Horseman Riding By; The Green Gauntlet; The Avenue Story; Come Home, Charlie; Cheap Day Return; God is an Englishman; (plays) Worm's Eye View; All Over the Town; Peace Comes to Peckham; & sev. others incl. radio & TV serials. Contbr. to num. Brit. periodicals & newspapers. Address: Dove Cottage, Sidmouth, Devon, UK.

DELECLOS, Camille J. C., b. 27 June 1907, Stavelot, Ardennes, Belgium. Journalist & Writer. Educ: Grad., Royal Coll. of Stavelot; 5 for. langs., Royal Soc. Polyglotte, Verviers. Publs: Les Pélerins anglais de Waterloo, 1945; A travers la Roumanie nouvelle, 1962; Stavelot, Centre vivant du Tourisme culturel, 1964. Contbr. to La Revue Nationale, etc. Mbrships. incl: PEN; Soc. Royale des Ecrivains de Wallonie; Union Int. des Journalistes et Presse de langue française; Liège Delegate, Union Mondial de la Presse périodique; Fndr. & Chmn., Soc. Int. "Les Amis de G. Apollinaire". Address: 84B ave. de l'Observatoire, 4000 Liège, Belgium.

DE LEEUW, Cateau Wilhelmina, pen names HAMILTON, Kay; LYON, Jessica, b. 22 Sept. 1903, Hamilton, Ohio, USA. Portrait Painter; Illustrator; Writer; Lecturer. Publs: ca. 50 books inclng. The Dutch East Indies & the Philippines, 1943; Love is Where you Find It, 1947; From This Day Forward, 1951; William Tyndale, 1955; Fear in the Forest, 1960; Against All Others, 1961; Nurses Who Led the Way (w. A. De Leeuw), 1961; Determined to be Free, 1963; The Salty Skinners, 1964; Roald Amundsen, 1965; Truth to Tell, 1965; Benedict Arnold, 1970; Anthony Wayne, 1974. Mbrships. incl: Am. Artists Profl. League; Pen & Brush; Early Am. Inds. Assn.; Ohio Histl. Soc. Address: 1763 Sleepy Hollow Ln., Plainfield, NJ 07060, USA.

DE LERA, Angel María, pen name DE SAMANIEGO, Angel, b. 7 May 1912, Baides, Spain. Educ: Humanities & Law studies. Publs: Los clarines del miedo; La boda; Hemos perdido el sol; Tierra para morir; Bochorno; Las últimas banderas; Se vende un hombre; Los que perdimos; num. transls. in num. langs. Contbr. to: ABC; El Noticiero Universal; Historia y Vida; Gaceta Ilustrada. Hons: Alvarez Prize, Fastenrath Prize, Royal Spanish Acad. of Lang.; Planeta Prize; Galdós Novel Prize; Ateneo de Sevilla Prize. Address: Calle Londres 27, Madrid 28, Spain.

DELGADO, Alan George, b. 1909, London, UK. Author. Num. publs. incl: The Very Hot Water-Bottle,

1962; Edwardian England, 1967; Printing, 1970; A Hundred Years of Medical Care, 1970; As They Saw Her: Florence Nightingale, 1970; Victorian Entertainment, 1971; Have You Forgotten Yet? 1973; A Printbuyer's Handbook, 1974. Address: 18 Temple Fortune Lane, London NW11 7UD, UK.

DELGADO-BENAVENTE, Luis, b. 15 Oct. 1915, Getafe, Madrid, Spain. Playwright; Author. Educ: M.Litt. Plays: La voz de dentro, 1953; Presagio, 1954; Tres ventanas, 1955; Jacinta, 1956; Media hora antes, 1956. Author, El samovar hierve (short stories), 1952, Short story contbns: Antologias del humor; Antologia de cuentistas Espanoles contemporaneos, 1969. Hons. incl: Premio Calderon de la Barca, for Dias Nuestros, 1951, for Humo, 1952; Premio Ciudad de Barcelona, for Tres Ventanas, 1952; Premio Lope de Vega, for Media Hora Antes, 1955; Premio Hucha de Plata for short stories, 1972. Address: Calle de Cartagena 64, Madrid 28, Spain.

DEL MORAL MORALES, Manuel, b. 17 July 1907, Loja, Spain. Writer; Painter. Publs: Cosas de Oriente, de Corte y Cortijo; Flores y Espinas; Carro de las virtudes; El Paje y el Halcón; De la Rosa de la Alhambra; Sueño de Don Félix; La Trampa de Hefesto; El Divino Refugio, Vergel de Sabios, Locos y Poetas; Alas Rotas; Las Gracias de Sancha; Leyenda de las dos discretas estatuas; La Quiniela de Ramón; Secreto sin Confesión; Antorcha para noveles; Antorcha Literaria; Mi Doctrina. Mbrships: Fndr. Mbr., Workers Soc. of Book Writers; Soc. of Authors of Spain; Assn. of Spanish Writers & Artists. Address: Calle Goya 1, 2° C, Granada, Spain.

DEMANT, (Rev. Canon) Vigo Auguste, b. Newcastle upon Tyne, UK. Former Regius Professor of Moral & Pastoral Theology; Author. Educ: B.Sc., M.A., D.Litt.; Armstrong Coll., Newcastle, Univ. of Durham; Exeter Coll., Oxford. Publs: Christian Polity; Theology of Society; Religion & the Decline of Capitalism; The Religious Prospect; A Two-Way Religion; Our Culture (Ed. & contbr.); Christian Sex Ethics. Address: 31 St. Andrew's Rd., Old Headington, Oxford, UK.

DE MARCO, Concha, b. 23 May 1916, Soria, Spain. Poet. Educ: Lic., Natural Scis., Univ. of Madrid. Publs: (Poetry) Hora o'5, 1966; Diario de la Mañana, 1967; Acta de Identificación, 1969; Congreso en Maldoror, 1970; Tarot, 1972; Las Hilanderas, 1972; Una noche de invierno, 1974; (Prose) La Mujer española del Romanticismo, 1970. Contbr. to: Insula; Cuadernos Hispanoamericanos; La Estafeta Literaria; Urogallo; Arbol de Fuego; Cormorán y Delfín; Blanco y Negro. Recip., Juan Ramón Jimenez Criticism Prize, 1973. Address: Calle Ibiza 23, Madrid 9, Spain.

DE MARÉ, Eric Samuel, b. 10 Sept. 1910, Enfield, Middlesex, UK. Writer; Architectural Photographer. Educ: Dip., Archtl. Assn. Schl. of Arch., 1934. Publs: incl: The Canals of England, 1950; The Bridges of Britain, 1954, 1975; Penguin Handbook on Photography, 1957, 1973; Photography & Architecture, 1961; London's River, 1964; The Göta Canal, 1964; The City of Westminster, 1968; Penguin Handbook on Colour Photography, 1968, 1973; London 1851, 1973; The London Doré Saw, 1973; The Nautical Style, 1973; Wren's London, 1975. Contbr. to: Times Lit. Supplement; Book News; Guardian; RIBA Jrnl.; other profl. jrnls. Mbrships. incl: Writers Action Grp. Address: Flat 12, 63 Haverstock Hill, London NW3 4SL, UK.

DE MARTINO, Manfred Frank, b. 26 June 1924, Mineola, N.Y., USA. Psychologist. Educ: B.A., Brooklyn Coll.; M.A., Syracuse Univ. Publs. incl: The New Female Sexuality, 1969; Sex & the Intelligent Woman, 1974; Co-ed. & Contbr., Counselling & Psychotherapy with the Mentally Retarded, 1957; Ed. & Contbr., Dreams & Personality Dynamics, 1959; Ed. & Contbr., Sexual Behaviour & Personality Characteristics, 1963. Contbr. to profl. jrnls. & newspapers. Address: 115 Alpine Dr., DeWitt, NY 13214, USA.

DEMBO, L.S., b. 1929, Troy, N.Y., USA. University Professor. Educ: Syracuse Univ.; Columbia Univ.; Cornell Univ.; M.A.; Ph.D. Publs: Hart Crane's Sanskrit Charge, a Study of the Bridge, 1960; The Confucian Odes of Ezra Pound, USA 1963, UK 1964; Conceptions of Reality in Modern American Poetry, 1966; Ed., Nabokov, the Man & His Work, 1967; Criticism, Speculative & Analytical Essays, 1968; Co-Ed., The Contemporary Writer: Interviews with 16 Novelists & Poets, 1972; Co-Ed., Doris Lessing, Critical Studies, 1974. Contbr. to: Contemporary Lit. (Ed., 1966—); Am. Lit. (Ed. Bd., 1973—); Mod. Philol.; Criticism; The Nation. Mbr., MLA. Recip., Guggenheim Fellowship, 1968-69. Address: Dept. of English, Univ. of Wisconsin, Madison, WI, USA.

DE MENDELSSOHN, Peter, b. 1 June 1908, Munich, Germany. Author. Educ: Univ. of Berlin. Publs: All that Matters, 1938; The Hours & the Centuries, 1944; The Nuremberg Documents, 1946; Der Geist in der Despotie, 1953; Zeitungsstadt Berlin, 1959; The Age of Churchill, 1961; Inselschicksal England, 1965; S. Fischer und sein Verlag, 1970; Das Gewissen und die Macht, 1971; Von Deutscher Repräsentanz, 1972; Thomas Mann, 1975. Contbr. to: Süddeutsche Zeitung; Neue Rundschau; Allgemeine Zeitung. Mbrships: PEN, Engl. Ctr.; VP, PEN, German Crt.; Deutsche Akad. für Sprache und Dichtung, Darmstadt; Bavarian Acad. of Fine Arts, Munchen. Address: 8 Munich 81, Rümelinstrasse 10, W. Germany.

DE MESNE, Eugene Frederick P. C., pen name OCEAN, Julian, b. Hove, Sussex, UK. Author; Editor. Educ: London Schl. Jrnlsm.; Newspaper Inst., N.Y., USA. Publs: Contbng. Ed., Sky Blue/Grass Green, 1973; From Satan's Pit . . ., 1971, 2nd ed., 1974; Lost Moments. 1971, 2nd ed., 1974; Contbng. Ed., Rendezvous with the Sea, 1974; How Do You Tell a Woman?, 1974; The Haunting of Bella Creigh, 1975; Silhouettes by Solo, 1975; Sad Dunfrey, 1975; A Shade of Scarlet, 1975; Thoughts from 1536, 1975. Contbr. to: Northwoods Newsletter (now Jrnl.); Ed., Person to People; Ed., In-Crowd; var. other mags. Mbr., num. writers' assns. Hons: Fiction Award, Authors & Artists Int., 1974; Poetry Award, Clover Int. Soc., 1974. Address: P.O. Box 8776, Kennedy Stn., Boston, MA 02114, USA.

DEMETRIUS, James Kleon, b. 23 Aug. 1924, Chicopee Falls, Mass., USA. Colleger Professor of Greek; Author; Lecturer; Critic. Educ: B.A., Brooklyn Coll., 1948; M.A., Columbia Univ., 1949; Ph.D., Cand., ibid; Postgrad. study, N.Y. Univ., Univ. of Iowa, N.D. Univ. Publs. incl: Los Griegos en Espana, 1961; Greek Influence in Spanish Literature, 1961; A Bibliography of Greek Studies in Spain, 1962; Greek Scholarship in Spain & Latin America, 1966; Spanish Grammar Explained, 1973; Only the Stars Are Neutral, 1974; The Marvels of Modern Greek, 1974. Contbr. of over 660 book reviews, 220 articles to US, for. jrnls. Address: P.O. Box 5991, N.Y., NY 10017, USA.

DEMETRIUS, Lucia, b. 29 Sept. 1910, Bucharest, Rumania. Writer. Educ: Conservatory of Dramatic Art, Bucharest, 1931; Bucharest Univ. 1931-32. Publs. incl: (novels) Youth, 1936; Spring on the Tirnave, 1960-63; The World Begins With Me, 1968; (stories) Ilona's Wedding, 1960; Promises, 1964; At Five O'Clock Tea, 1970; I Am An Earthling, 1973; The Coming Back to Miracle, 1974; (plays) Three Generations, 1956; The Garden of God, 1966; The Crossroads without a Well, 1972; var. poems & transls. Contbr. to lit. jrnls. Mbrships. incl: Rumanian Writers' Union; PEN. Hons. incl: State Prizes, 1950, 1952. Address: Str. Matei Millo 12, Bucharest, Sect. 7, Rumania.

DEMEUSE, Pierre Joseph, b. 18 June 1909, Ans (Liege), Belgium. Journalist; Author. Educ: Univ. of Liege. Publs. incl: Suite Ardennaise, 1934; Images et Visages de l'Ardenne, 1944; Images de la Suede, 1950; Roc Brule, 1950; La Fille de Minuit, 1955; Aux Echelles du Levant, 1961; Les Amoureuses de l'Amour, 1963; La Syrie a Coeur Ouvert, 1965; 10,000 Ans d'Aventure Humaine, 1967; Aventuriers de Genie, 1969; Brulees d'Amour, 1971; A la Sueur de ton Front, 1972. Contbr. to var. reviews & mags. in Belgium, France, Sweden, Tunisia, etc. Mbrships: Assn. Gen. de la Presse belge; Assn. des Ecrivains belge. Recip., var. lit. prizes & appts. to orders of chivalry. Address: Avenue de Fléron 52, B.1190 Brussels, Belgium.

DEMING, Richard, pen names, FRANKLIN, Max; MORENO, Nick; MOOR, Emily, b. 25 Apr. 1915, Des Moines, Iowa, USA. Author. Educ: B.A., Wash. Univ., St. Louis, Miss., 1937; M.A., State Univ. of Iowa, 1939. Publs. incl: The Gallows in My Garden, 1952; Juvenile Delinquent, 1958; This Game of Murder, 1964; Man & Society: Criminal Law at Work, 1970; Jig Jake, 1971; Vida, 1972; Sleep, Our Unknown Life, 1972; Man & the World: International Law at Work, 1974; Die Naked, 1974; also 6 books under pseudonyms & 15 books as ghost-writer; over 600 short stories & novelets, var. mags. Also TV writer. Mbr., Mystery Writers of Am. Address: P.O. Box 3129, Ventura, CA 93003, USA.

DEMPSTER, Derek David, b. 1924, Tangier, Morocco. Publishing Consultant; Writer. Educ: M.A., Pembroke Coll., Cambridge. Publs: The Inhabited Universe (w. K. Gatland), 1956; The Tale of the Comet, 1958; The Narrow Margin (w. D. H. Wood), 1961. Contbr. to: Flight; Intervia; The Scotsman; Sunday Pictorial; Sunday Express; Today; Everybodys; Daily Sketch; Truth; Pvte. Pilot; The Times; Financial Times; Telegraph Mag.; BBC/TV; ATV. Mbr., Writers Guild. Agent: Curtis Brown Ltd. Address: The Coach House, Upton House, Worth, Deal, Kent, UK.

de NAHLIK, Andrew John, b. 27 Feb. 1920, Lwow, Poland. Management Consultant; Retired Wing Commander, RAF. Educ: Tech. Univ. of Lwow, 1937-39; Bath Univ., UK, 1968-69. Publs: Wild Deer, 1958; Deer Management, 1974. Contbr. to: Field, Country Life; Shooting Times; Africana; UFAW Mag.; Wild & Hund. Mbrships. incl: Brit. Inst. Mgmt.; Inst. Personnel Mgmt.; Brit. Deer Soc.; Hon. Game Warden, Kenya Game Dept. Address: c/o Lloyds Bank Ltd., Cox's & King's Branch, 6 Pall Mall, London SW1, UK.

DÉNES, Zsófia, (Mrs. József Szalatnyay), b. 14 Jan. 1885, Budapest, Hungary. Writer. Educ: Fac. of Liberal Arts, Budapest. Publs: Élet helyett órák (Hours Instead of Life), 1940, 2nd ed., 1967; Az ismeretlen Ady (The Unknown Ady), 1942; Akkor a hársak épp szerettek (The Linden Trees Were Just in Love), 1957; Zrinyi Ilona történelmi regény (Zrinyi Ilona, Historical Novel), 1959, 5th Ed., 1974; Egyszeri kaland (Adventure Happening Once), 1964; Gyalog a baloldalon (Marching On The Left Side), 1965; Párizsi körhinta (Parisian Roundabout), 1966; Szivárvány (Rainbow), 1971; Ugy, ahogy volt (As it Happened), 1974; Tegnapi uj művészek (The New Artist of Yesterday, avant-garde), 1975. Contbr. to var. jrnls. Mbr., var. orgs. Recip., sev. awards. Address: Szentháromság utca 9-11, H-1014 Budapest I, Hungary.

den HAAN, Jacques, b. 27 Mar. 1908, Rotterdam, Netherlands. Bookreviewer; Essayist; Teacher. Publs: Milleriana, 1963; Onderweg. Vallen en opstaan in de cultuurgeschiedenis, 3 vols., 1966; James Joyce, 2nd ed., 1967; Een leven als een oordeel (essays), 1968; Monnikje Lederzak en andere driestheden, 1968. Contbr. to: Het Parool; Maatstaf. Mbrships: Maatschappij der Nederlandse Letterkunde; Vereniging van Letterkundigen. Vakbond van Schrijvers. Hons: Pierre Bayle Prize, Rotterdam, 1963; Essay Prize, Jan Campertstichting, The Hague, 1970. Address: Koningin Wilhelminalaan 33, Voorburg, Netherlands.

DENHAM, Henry Mangles, b. 9 Sept. 1897, Harrow, Middlesex, UK. Naval Officer; Author. Educ: R.N. Colls., Osborn & Dartmouth; Magdalene Coll., Cambridge. Publs: Aegean; Eastern Mediterranean; Adriatic; Tyrrhenian Sea; Ionian Islands to Rhodes; Southern Turkey; Levant; Cyprus. Contbr. to: Sunday Times; Yachting World. Address: 8 Carlyle Square, London SW3, UK.

DENISON, Dulcie Winifred Catherine, pen name GRAY, Dulcie, b. Kuala Lumpur, Malaysia. Actress. Publs: Murder on the Stairs, 1957; Murder in Melbourne, 1958; Baby Face, 1959; Epitaph for a Dead Actor, 1960; Murder on a Saturday, 1961; Murder in Mind, 1963; The Devil Wore Scarlet, 1964; No Quarter for a Star, 1964; The Murder of Love, 1967; Died in the Red, 1968; Murder on Honeymoon, 1969; For Richer for Richer, 1970; Deadly Lampshade, 1971; Understudy to Murder, 1972; Dead Give Away, 1974; The Actor & His World (w. Michael Denison), 1964; Ride on a Tiger, forthcoming. Contbr. to var. mags., newspapers, etc. Mbrships: Mystery Writers' Assn.; Actors' Equity; Crime Writers' Assn. Agent: Curtis Brown Ltd. Address: 53 Chester Ct., Albany St., London NW1, UK.

DENMAN, Donald Robert, b. 7 Apr. 1911, Finchley, UK. University Professor of Land Economy. Educ: B.Sc., 1938, M.Sc., 1940, Ph.D., 1945, London Univ.; M.A., Cambridge Univ., 1948. Publs. incl: Tenant Right Valuation: In History & Modern Practice, 1942; Estate Capital: The Contribution of Landownership to Agricultural Finance, 1957; Land in the Market, 1964; Commons & Village Greens: A Study in Land Use, Conservation & Management, 1967; Land Use: An Introduction to Proprietary Land Use Analysis, 1971; The King's Vista (Persian Land Reform), 1973. Contbr. of monographs, articles & papers to acad. & profl. jrnls., & national newspapers. Fellow, Royal Inst. Chartered Surveyors. Address: 12 Chaucer Road, Cambridge, UK.

DENNEY, Ronald Colin, b. 27 June 1936, London, UK. Scientist. Educ: B.Sc., Ph.D., London Univ. Publs: Named

Organic Reactions, 1969; The Truth About Breath Tests, 1970; This Dirty World, 1971; A Dictionary of Spectroscopy, 1973; Organic Reagents for Organic Compounds, forthcoming. Contbr. to: Chem. in Brit.; Polymer; Paint & Colour Jrnl.; Jrnl. Chem. Soc.; Chem. & Ind.; Sunday Telegraph; Analyst. Mbrships. incl: Fellow Chem. Soc.; F.R.I.C. Recip., John Edward Worth Prize of Royal Soc. Promotion Health in 1965. Address: Manteo, 21 Lake View Rd., Sevenoaks, Kent, UK.

DENNIS, Benjamin Gumbu, b. 5 June 1929, Monrovia, Liberia. University Professor. Educ: A.B.; B.S.; M.A.; Ph.Ds. (Siciol. & Anthropol.). Publs: The Gbandes: A People of the Liberian Hinterland, 1973. Mbrships: Am. Sociol. Assn.; Am. Anthropol. Assn.; Rural Sociol. Soc.; African Studies Assn.; Nat. Geog. Soc.; Nat. Mbr., Smithsonian Inst.; Mid-Western Sociol. Assn. Recip., Grand Cmdr., Order of the Star of Africa, 1974. Address: 1916 Wood Lane Drive, Flint, MI 48503, USA.

DENNIS, Nigel Forbes, b. 1912, Bletchingly, UK. Editor; Poet; Playwright; Journalist. Publs: Boys & Girls Come out to Play, 1949; Cards of Identity, 1955; (plays) The Making of Moo, 1958; August for the People, 1962; Dramatic Essays, 1962; Jonathon Swift, 1970; A House in Order, 1970; (poems) Exotics, 1970. Contbr. to: Life; Harper's; Encounter; New Yorker; ed., New Republic, 1937-38; Sunday Telegraph. Agent: c/o N.Y. Review. Address: 250 W. 57th St., NYC, NY 10019, USA.

DENT, Alan Holmes, b. 7 Jan. 1905, Maybole, Ayrshire, UK. Journalist; Drama & Film Critic; Author. Educ: Glasgow Univ. Publs: Preludes & Studies (drama & lit. criticism); Nocturnes & Rhapsodies; My Dear America; The Life of Mrs. Patrick Campbell; Robert Burns in His Time; Vivien Leigh: A Bouquet; My Covent Garden, A Very Personal History of the Whole Neighbourhood, 1973. Contbr. to: Time & Tide; BBC publs.; etc. Address: 85 Aylesbury End, Beaconsfield, Bucks., UK.

DENT, Harold Collett, b. 14 Nov. 1894, Scunthorpe, Lincs., UK. Retired Teacher & Journalist; Writer. Educ: B.A., Univ. of London. Publs: A New Order in English Education, 1942; The Education Act 1944, 1944; Education in Transition, 1944; The Educational System of England & Wales, 1961; 1870-1970: Century of Growth in English Education, 1970. Contbr. to: Times Educl. Supplement; Times Higher Educ. Supplement; The Tchr.; Educ. Mbrships. incl: Assn. of Univ. Tchrs.; Assn. of Tchrs. in Colls. & Depts. of Educ.; Hon. Fellow, Educl. Inst. of Scotland; Hon. Fellow, Coll. of Preceptors. Address: Riccards Spring, Whatlington, Battle, E. Sussex, TN33 0NG, UK.

DE OBALDIA, Réné, b. 22 Oct. 1918, Hong Kong. Author; Dramatist. Publs: Midi, 1949; Les Richesses Naturelles, 1952; (novel) Tamerlan des Coeurs, 1954; (short stories) Fugue à Waterloo, 1956; (novel) Le Centenaire, 1959; Théâtre: Genousie; Le Satyre de la Villette; Le General Inconnu; L'Air du Large; Du Vent dans les Branches de Sassafras; Le Cosmonaute agricole; Sept Impromptus à Loisir; La Baby-Sitter, 4 vols., 1967-73; (poems) Innocentines, 1970. Contbr. to: Nouvelle-Revue Française; Contemporains; Bizarre; La Nef; Lettres Nouvelles; Combat; Le Figaro. Mbrships: Soc. of Dramatic Authors; Soc. of Men of Letters. Num. hons. incl: Louis Parrot Poetry Prize, 1949; Theatre Critics Prize, 1960. Address: 54 rue Saint-Lazare, 75009 Paris, France.

DE POLNAY, Peter, b. 1906. Publs. incl: Angry Man's Tale, 1938; Boo, 1941; Water on the Steps, 1943; The Umbrella Thorn, 1946; The moot Point, 1948; Out of the Square, 1950; The Next Two Years, 1951; A Beast in View, 1953; Fools of Choice, 1955; The Clap of Silent Thunder, 1957; The Scales of Love, 1958; Peninsular Paradox, 1958. Address: 33 Percy St., London W1, UK.

de RADZITZKY (d'OSTROWICK), (Baron) Carlos, b. 7 June 1915, London, UK. Writer; Jazz Critic. Educ: Cand.Philos. & Letters. Publs: Harmonika saloon, 1934; a vol d'oiseau, 1936; Dormeuse, 1937; Le fond de l'eau, 1942; Ophelie, 1955; Poèmes choisis, 1963; Désert secret, 1965; Les semeurs de feu, 1968; Le commun des mortels, 1973. Contbr. to: Marginales; Revue générale; etc. Mbrships: Gen. Sec., French Br., PEN, Belgium; Assn. of Belgian Writers; Soc. de Gens de Lettres de France; Com. du Journal des Poetes; etc. Hons: Chevalier, Ordre de Léopold II; Chevalier, Ordre de la Couronne; Chevalier, Arts & Letters of France; Prix Denayer, Acad. Royale de Belgique, 1966; Grand Prix de Poésie Commune d'Uccle,

1974. Address: Ave. Fond'Roy 110, 1180 Brussels, Belgium.

DERBY, Goldie Florence, b. 3 Oct. 1898, Ashland, Kan., USA. Housewife; Author. Publs: Greater Love (story of son killed in WWII); Rocks & Roses (relig. novel), 1957. Contbr. to: Arkansas City Daily Traveller (wkly. relig. column for over 22 yrs.). Mbrships. incl: Kan. Authors' Club; Arkansas City Authors' Club (Sec.). Hons: 1st Prize, Kan. Authors' Club Spring Contest, 1974; other lit. prizes & mentions. Address: P.O. Box 1143, Arkansas City, KS 67005, USA.

DE RENEVILLE, Mary Margaret Motley, b. 6 Jan. 1912, Godalming, Surrey, UK. Author. Publs: Devils in Waiting, 1959; Morning Glory, 1961; Home to Numidia, 1964. Contbr. to: Good Housekeeping; 20th Century; Vogue. Address: 32 Residence Argia, Rue de Parme, 64200 Biarritz, France.

DERKSEN, Leonardus Joseph, b. 5 Nov. 1926, Nijmegen, Netherlands. Journalist. Publs: Precedence for the Dead, 1962; The Chaste Passer-by, 1963; 17 ΓV plays; filmscript, '10:32'; play, Cardinalsgambit, 1971. Contbr. to: De Telegraaf. Mbr., Dutch Writers' Guild of Stage, TV Writers. Address: Vijverlaan 8, Bergen n.h., Netherlands.

de ROUGEMONT, Denis, b. 8 Sept. 1906, Neuchâtel, Switz. Writer; Professor. Educ: Univs. of Neuchâtel, Vienna & Geneva; Lic. lettres & philos. Publs. incl: Les Méfaits de l'Instruction Publique, 1929, 1972; L'Amour & L'Occident, 1939, definitive ed., 1972; L'Europe en Jeu, 1948; Vingt-huit Siècles d'Europe, 1961; Journal d'une Epoque, 1968; l'Un & le Divers, 1970; Les Dirigeants & les Finalités de la Société Occidentale, 1972; works transl'd in 17 langs. Contbr. to major mags. & jrnls., Europe, USA, Argentina, Japan. Mbr., num. cultural orgs., Europe & USA. Hons. incl: Doct. Law; Schiller Prize, 1960; Paul Tillich Award, 1969; Robert Schuman Prize, 1970. Address: 01630 St. Genis-Pouilly, France.

DERRETT, J. Duncan M., b. 1922, London, UK. Professor. Educ: D.C.L., Jesus Coll., Oxford; Ph.D., LL.D., Schl. of Oriental & African Studies, London; Barrister. Publs: The Hoysalas, 1957; Introduction to Modern Hindu Law, 1963; Religion, Law & the State in India, 1968; Law in the New Testament, 1970; Critique of Modern Hindu Law, 1970; Jesus' Audience, 1973; Dharmasastra & Juridical Literature, 1973; Henry Swinburne (1551-1624) Civil Lawyer of York, 1973. Contbr. to var. learned jrnls. Mbrships: Gray's Inn; Royal Asiatic Soc.; Studiorum Novi Testamenti Societas. Address: Chiltern House, Lee Common, Great Missenden, Bucks., UK.

DERRICK, Paul, b. 1916, Congresbury, Somerset, UK. Writer. Educ: Reading Univ. Publs: Lost Property; A Co-operative Approach to Socialism; The Company & the Community, 1964; Socialism in the Seventies?, 1970; Socialism & Inflation, 1974. Contbr. to: 60 jrnls. in UK, USA, India, NZ, Italy & Denmark inclng. New Engl. Wkly.; Lib. Mag.; Quarterly Review; var. Trade Union jrnls. Address: 30 Wandsworth Bridge Rd., London SW6, UK.

DERRIMAN, James Parkyns, b. 19 Feb. 1922, London, UK. Company Secretary & General Manager; Author. Educ: Called to Bar, Lincoln's Inn, 1947. Publs: Pageantry of the Law, 1955; Discovering the Law, 1962; Public Relations in Business Management, 1964; Company-Investor Relations, 1969. Contbr. to: The Dirs. Handbook. Mbrships: Fellow, Inst. of PR (Pres., 1973-74); Comm., Bread St. Ward Club, City of London; Bar. Assn. for Commerce, Fin. & Ind.; The Keys; Catenian Assn.; Soc. of Geneals.; etc. Appointed Freeman of City of London, 1963. Address: 34 Mossville Gdns., Morden, Surrey, UK.

DERRY, John Wesley, b. 27 Jan. 1933, Gateshead, UK. University Teacher. Educ: M.A., 1958, Ph.D., 1961, Emmanuel Coll., Cambridge. Publs: William Pitt, 1962; Reaction & Reform, 1963; The Regency Crisis & the Whigs, 1963; The Radical Tradition, 1967; Charles James Fox, 1972. Contbr. reviews to Hist.; Histl. Jrnl.; Engl. Histl. Review. Address: Dept. of Hist., Univ. of Newcastle upon Tyne, Newcastle upon Tyne NE1 7RU, UK.

DERRY, Thomas Kingston, b. 1905, Glasgow, UK. Historian; Retired Schoolmaster. Educ: M.A., Ph.D., Queen's Coll., Oxford. Publs: The European World (w. T. L. Jarman), 1950; The Campaign in Norway, 1952; The Making of Modern Britain (w. T. L. Jarman), 1956; A Short History of Norway, 1957; A Short History of Technology

(w. T. I. Williams), 1960; The United Kingdom, 1962; Britain since 1750, 1965; Europe 1815-1914, & Europe since 1914 (w. E. J. Knapton), USA 1965, UK 1966; Introducing Oslo, 1969; The Making of Britain, 2 vols. (w. M. G. Blakeway), 1968, 1969; A History of Modern Norway 1814-1972, 1973. Address: Nils Lauritssonsvei 27, Oslo 8, Norway.

DÉRY, Tibor, b. 18 Oct. 1894, Budapest, Hungary. Writer. Publs: (novels) Képzelt riport egy amerikai pop fesztiválról; Kedves boòpeer. Mbr., Magyar Irók Szövetsége. Recip., Kossuth dij, Magyar Népköztársaság Zászlórenje II. Address: 1026 Budapest, Lotz K. 20, Hungary.

DESAI, Anita, b. 24 June 1937, Mussoorie, India. Author. Educ: B.A. (Engl. lit.), Delhi Univ. Publs: Cry, the Peacock, 1963; Voices in the City, 1965; Bye-Bye, Blackbird, 1971; The Peacock Garden (for children), 1974; Where Shall We Go This Summer?, 1975. Contbr. to: Writers' Workshop; Illustrated Wkly. of India; Quest; Thought; Envoy; Harper's Bazaar. Mbr., Engl. Bd., Sahitya Akademi, New Delhi. Address: c/o Vikas Publng. House, PVT. Ltd., 5 Darya Sans, Ansari Rd., Delhi 5, India.

de STE. CROIX, Geoffrey Ernest Maurice, b. 1910, Macao, China. University Lecturer in Ancient History. Educ: B.A., Univ. Coll., London. Publs: Studies in the History of Accounting (jt. author), 1956; The Crucible of Christianity (jt. author), 1969; The Origins of the Peloponnesian War, 1972; Debits, Credits, Finance & Profits (jt. author), 1974; Studies in Ancient Society (jt. author), 1974. Contbr. to schlrly. jrnls. Mbr., Assn. of Univ. Tchrs.; Fellow, Brit. Acad.; Fellow, New Coll., Oxford. Address: "Evenlode", Stonesfield Lane, Charlbury, Oxford OX7 3ER, UK.

DE ST. MARTON, Louise Helenke, b. 18 May 1912, Kunszentmarton, Hungary. Writer. Publs: Angels & Furies, reprinted under title Come with Me. Contbr. to country newspapers. Mbrships: PEN, Sydney; Soc. of Women Writers, Aust. Address: Miami I. Waruda St., Kirribilli, Sydney, 2061, Australia.

DESANI, G(ovindas) V(ishnoodas), b. 8 July 1909, Nairobi, Kenya. Professor of Philosophy. Publs: All about H. Hatterr, (novel), 1948; Hali (play), 1950. Contbr. to: Noble Savage; Transatlantic Review; Illustrated Weekly of India. Address: Dept. of Philosophy, University of Texas, Austin, TX 78712, USA.

DESANTES GUANTER, José Maria, b. 11 Mar. 1924, Valencia, Spain, Lawyer; Scientific researcher; Professor, Fac. of Info. Scis. Educ: Ph.D., Law; Lic., Jrnlsm. Publs: El valor formativo del derecho, 1955; Macia el realismo político, 1969; La relación contractual entre autor y editor, 1970; El autocontrol de la actividad informativa, 1973; La información como derecho, 1974. Contbr. to: Bull. of Documentation of Fund for Econ. & Soc. Resch. of Spanish Confedn. of Savings Banks; Civil Law Annual; Review of Inst. of Soc. Studies of Barcelona. Mbr., Coll. of Lawyers of Madrid. Hons: Bronze Medal, Acad. Merit, 1948; Commendation, w. plaque, Order of Civ. Merit, 1962; etc. Address: Calle Capitan Haya 32 8°B, Madrid 20, Spain.

DE SAULIEU, Thierry, pen name REMEROND, b. 27 Mar. 1947, Paris, France. Journalist. Publs: Guide des Relais Routiers, 1968, 1969, 1970, 1971, 1972, 1973, 1974, 1975; Guide de la Route Facile, 1974. Contbr. to: Les Routiers; Les Maxis; Caravanier; l'Argus de l'Automobile; var. other mags. Mbrships: Assn. française de la Presse Automobile; Assn. française des Journalistes Ecrivains du Tourisme (Treas.). Recip., Royal Epaton Daphnys, Greece. Address: 24 Rue de Clichy, 75009 Paris, France.

DESBOROUGH, Vincent Robin d'Arba, b. 1914, Tunbridge Wells, Kent, UK. Archaeological Researcher & Author. Educ: B.Litt., M.A., New Coll., Oxford. Publs: Protogeometric Pottery, 1952; The Last Mycenaeans & their Successors, 1964; The Greek Dark Ages, 1972. Contbr. to: Cambridge Ancient History (rev. ed.); Annual of British Schl. of Archaeol. at Athens; Jrnl. of Hellenic Studies. Address: 13 Field House Drive, Woodstock Rd., Oxford, UK.

DESCHAMPSNEUFS, Henry Pierre Bernard, b. 7 Apr. 1911, St. Agnes, Cornwall, UK. Export Consultant & Training Specialist. Educ: B.A., Pembroke Coll., Oxford Univ. Publs: Selling Overseas, 1960; Selling in Africa, 1961;

Selling in Europe, 1963; Marketing Overseas, 1967; Exporting, 1969; Marketing in the Common Market, 1973; Presenter, BBC Radio series, A Language in your Briefcase, 1971-72. Contbr. to: Financial Times; Marketing; num. other publs. Mbr., Inst. of Export (Chmn. of Coun., 1970-71). Address: 1315 Minster House, St. James's Ct., Buckingham Gate, London SW1, UK.

DESCHNER, (Hans) Günther, b. 14 May 1941, Fürth, Bavaria, Germany. Leading Editor, Die Welt. Educ: Erlangen & Nüremburg Univs.; Leuven Univ., Belgium. Publs: Contbng. Ed., Sweite Weltkrieg, 1968; Menschen im Ghetto, 1969; Warsaw Rising, USA ed., 1972 (also Brit., Japanese, Spanish & Swedish eds.); Heydrich — A Technocrat, forthcoming. Contbr. to: Die Welt (Ed.). Mbrships: Gesellschaft für Religious- und Geistesgeschichte; Freier Deutscher Autorenverband (German Free Authors' Soc.). Address: D–483 Gütersloh 11, Joh.-Brahmsstr. 6, W. Germany.

DESCHNER, Karlheinz, b. 23 May 1924, Bamberg, Germany. Freelance Writer. Educ: Ph.D., 1951. Publs. incl: Die Nacht steht um mein Haus, 1956; Was halten Sie vom Christentum? (ed.), 1957; Abermals krahte der Hahn. Eine kritische Kirchengeschichte von den Evangelisten bis zu den Faschisten, 1962; Jesusbilder in theologischer Sicht (ed.), 1965; Kirche und Kreig. Der christliche Weg zum Ewigen Leben (ed.), 1970; Das Kreuz mit der Kirche. Eine Sexualgeschichte des Christentums, 1974. Contbr. to: konkret; das da; Pardon; Frankfurter Rundschau, etc. Recip., Ehrenmitglied des Bundes für Geistesfreiheit, Nuremberg. Address: Goethestrasse 2, 8728 Hassfurt, W. Germany.

DESMOND, Robert William, b. 1900, Milwaukee, Wis., USA. Journalist; Emeritus Professor. Educ: B.A., Univ. of Wis.; M.A., Univ. of Minn.; Ph.D., Univ. of London. Publs: Newspaper Reference Methods, 1933; The Press & World Affairs, 1937; Professional Training of Journalists, 1949. Contbr. to num. pbls. inclng: Milwaukee Jrnl.; N.Y. Herald-Tribune, Paris; N.Y. Times; Christian Science Monitor. Address: 314 Ricardo Place, La Jolla, CA 92037, USA.

des PRESLES, Claude, b. 1 Jan. 1918, Paris, France. Poet; Playwright. Educ: Law Degree. Publs. incl: (poems) Matin, 1946; Suite de Danses, 1947; L'Offrande, 1947; Preludes, 1948; Si d'Aventure . . .,1953; L'Homme de Demain, 1958; Dialogues, 1961; Le Bal, 1966; Inégal Tournoi, 1973; (plays) La Dame de Coventry, 1954; Josiane et le Bonheur, 1953; La Chemise, 1956; Point de Lendemain, 1957; La Tentation, 1966. Contbr. to La Revue Independante. Mbrships. incl: PEN; Syndicat Int. de la Critique Litteraire; Soc. des Gens de Lettres de France. Hons. incl: Prize, Soc. des Auteurs Dramatiques, 1954; Alfred Mortier Prize, Soc. des Gens de Lettres de France, 1957; Chevalier, Ordre de la Légion d'Honneur & Ordre des Arts et des Lettres. Address: 5 Avenue Emile Massard, 75017 Paris, France.

DESSÍ, Giuseppe, b. 7 Aug. 1909, Cagliari, Italy. Writer. Educ: D.Lit. Publs. incl: San Silvano, 1939; Michele Boschino, 1942; Storia del Principe Lui, 1948; I Passeri, 1955; Isola dell'Angelo, 1957; Racconti Drammatici, 1959; Il disertore, 1961; Eleonora d'Arborea, 1964; Lei era l'acqua, 1966; Paese d'ombre, 1972. Contbr. to: Il Ponte; La Nuova Antologia; Rassegna di letteratura Italiana; Il Tempo; L'Unita; Rinascita; Il Resto del Carlino; Botteghe Oscure. Mbrships: Sindacato Nazionale Scrittori; Socio SIAE. Hons. incl: Salento Prize, 1955; Puccini-Senigallia Prize, 1957; Bagutta Prize, 1962; Strega Prize, 1972. Address: Via Prisciano N.75, 00136 Rome, Italy.

DESTLER, Chester McArthur, b. 27 July 1904, Wyncote, Pa., USA. Writer; Professor. Educ: B.A., Coll. of Wooster, 1925; M.A., 1928, Ph.D., 1932, Univ. of Chgo. Publs: American Radicalism, 1865-1901, 1946; Joshua Coit, American Federalist, 1962; Roger Sherman & the Independent Oil Men, 1967; Henry Demarest Lloyd & the Empire of Reform, 1963; Connecticut: The Provisions State, 1973. Contbr. to num. jrnls. Address: 97 Meadowbrook Rd., W. Hartford, CT 06107, USA.

DETELA, Lev, b. 2 Apr. 1939, Maribor, Jugoslavia (Austrian citizen). Author. Educ: Slavic Langs. & Art Hist., Univs. of Ljubljana, & Vienna, Austria. Publs. incl: (prose) Blodnjak, 1964; Izkušnje z Nevihtami, 1967, 1973, 1974; Marijin Mojster, 1974; (poetry) Sladkor in Bič, 1969; Metaelement, 1970; Legende O Vrvohodcih in Mesečnikih, 1973; (prose & poetry) Atentat, 1966; Kraljev Kip, 1970;

1974; (plays) Junaštva, 1965; Črni Mož, 1969. Contbr. to num. lit. jrnls. & radio. Mbrships: PEN: Literarische Union, Darmstadt; Verband der slowenischen Autoren in Oesterreich. Hons: Var. Exhibits for Lit., Vienna; Prize for Novel, Univ. of Tübingen, 1970. Address: 1220 Wien, Domarstadtstr. 30/16/16, Austria.

DETHIER, Vincent G., b. 20 Feb. 1915, Boston, Mass., USA. Professor of Biology. Educ: A.B., Harvard Coll., 1936; A.M., 1937, Ph.D., 1939, Harvard Univ. Publs: Chemical Insect Attractants & Repellents, 1947; Animal Behaviour (w. E. Stellar), 1961, 3rd ed. 1970; To Know A Fly, 1962; The Physiology of Insect Senses, 1963; Fairweather Duck, 1970; Biological Principles & Processes (w. C. Villee), 1971; in preparation: Man's Plague & God's Cows (Man, Plant & Insect); The Hungry Fly — A Physiological Analysis. Contbr. to var. jrnls. Mbr., Am. Acad. of Arts & Scis.; R.S.A.; etc. Hons: Guggenheim Fellowship, 1964, 1972; & other acad. hons. Address: Dept. of Biology, Princeton Univ., Princeton, NJ 08540, USA.

de TRAZ, Georges, pen name FOSCA, François, b. 30 Aug. 30 Aug. 1881, Paris, France. Writer. Educ: Sorbonne, Paris. Publs: Bonnard, 1918; Tintoret, 1929; La peinture, qu'est-ce que c'est? , 1941; Edmond et Jules de Goncourt, 1942; Renoir, 1954; De Diderot a Valery, 1955. Contbr. to: Tribune de Geneve. Mbrships: Swiss Soc. of Writers; Hon. Mbr., Genevese Soc. of Writers. Recip., French Acad. Prize for propogation of French Lang. Address: 6 Rue des Eaux-Vives, 1207 Geneva, Switz.

DEUTSCH, Babette, b. 1895, NYC, USA. Lecturer on Poetry; Poet. Educ: B.A., Barnard Coll. Publs. incl: Banners; Honey out of the Rock; Fire for the Night; Epistle to Prometheus; One Part Love; Take them, Stranger; Animal, Vegetable, Mineral; Coming of Age: New & Selected Poems; This Modern Poetry; The Reader's Shakespeare; The Collected Poems of Babette Deutsch; Poetry in Our Time; Poetry Handbook; Mask of Silenus; Rogue's Gallery; Heroes of the Kalevala; Walt Whitman, Builder for America. Contbr. to: Nation; Poetry; Kenyon Review; Botteghe Obscure; etc. Mbrships: PEN; F.N.I.A.L. Recip., Litt.D. (Hon.). Address: 300 W. 108 St., NYC 25, N.Y., USA.

DEUTSCH, Eliot, b. 8 Jan. 1931, Gary Ind., USA. Educator. Educ: B.S., Univ. of Wis.; Ph.D., Columbia Univ. Publs: The Bhagavad Gita, 1968; Advaita Vedanta: A Philosophical Reconstruction, 1969; Humanity & Divinity, 1970; A Source Book of Advaita Vedanta, 1971; Studies in Comparative Aesthetics, 1975. Contbr. to: Jrnl. of Philos.; Int. Philos. Quarterly; Jrnl. of Aesthetics & Art Criticism. Mbrships. incl: Sec.-Treas., Soc. for Asian & Comp. Philos.; Am. Philos. Assn.; Am. Soc. for Aesthetics. Address: 4837 Kolohala St., Honolulu, HI 96816, USA.

DEVENISH, Dorothy Grace Whitty, b. 1912, Little Durnford, Wilts., UK. Writer. Publ: A Wiltshire Home. Contbr. to: Woman & Home; Woman's Wkly. Address: The Hermitage, Little Durnford, Nr. Salisbury, Wilts., UK.

DEVEREUX, Edward James Pryce, b. 30 Dec. 1899, Southport, UK. Senior Geography Master, The Mercers School, London. Educ: M.A., Cambridge. Publs: Contours (w. Boxhall), 1938, 10th ed. (revised), 1972; Mapwork with Pictures (w. M. A. Morgan): Book I — British Isles, Book II — Western Europe, Book III — Africa, Book IV — North America, Book V — British Isles; compiled An Introduction to Visual Aids. Fellow, Royal Geographical Soc. Address: 8 Highsett, Hills Rd., Cambridge CB2 1NX, UK.

DEVEREUX, Michael Pryce, b. 12 Feb. 1937, London, UK. University Careers Adviser; Former Schoolmaster. Educ: B.A., 1960, M.A., 1963, Christ's Coll., Cambridge; Postgrad. Cert. in Ed., Univ. of London, 1961. Publs: Industries in Britain, 1973; Ports in Britain (w. F. C. Evans), 1975; Future Environments in Britain — Energy, 1975. Contbr. to: Tchng. Geog. Mbrships: Geogl. Assn.; (Exec. Comm., 1963-68). Address: 96 Glebe Road, Cambridge CB1 4TA, UK.

DE VRIES, Peter, b. 27 Feb. 1910, Chgo., USA. Writer. Educ: A.B., Calvin Coll., Mich.; Northwestern Univ. Publs. incl: No But I Saw the Movie, 1952; The Tunnel of Love, 1954; Comfort Me With Apples, 1956; The Mackerel Plaza, 1958; The Tents of Wickedness, 1959; The Blood of the Lamb, 1962; Let Me Count The Ways, 1965; The Cat's Pajamas & Witch's Milk, 1968; Without a Stitch in Time, 1972; Forever Panting, 1973; The Glory of the

Hummingbird, 1974. Contbr. to: New Yorker Mag.; Poetry Mag. (Assoc. Ed., 1938). Mbr., Nat. Inst. of Arts & Letters. Address: 170 Cross Highway, Westport, Conn., USA.

DEWAR, David Ross, b. 1913, Glasgow, UK. Publs: Letters on the Ornithology of Buenos Aires, by W. H. Hudson (Ed.), 1951. Contbr. to: Uniform Edition of W. H. Hudson's Works. Address: 36 Singleton Scarp, Woodside Pk., London N12, UK.

DEWAR, Michael James Steuart, b. 24 Sept. 1918, Ahmednager, India. Professor of Chemistry. Educ: B.A., M.A., D.Phil., Balliol Coll., Oxford Univ., UK. Publs: The Electronic Theory of Organic Chemistry, 1949; Hyperconjugation, 1962; An Introduction to Modern Chemistry, 1965; The Molecular Orbital Theory of Organic Chemistry, 1969; The PMO Theory of Organic Chemistry (w. R. C. Doughery), 1975. Contbr. to num. chem. jrnls. Hons: Fellow, Am. Acad. of Arts & Scis.; Tilden Lecture of The Chem. Soc., 1954; Harrison Howe Award of The Am. Chem. Soc.; Robert Robinson Lecture of The Chem. Soc., 1974. Address: Dept. of Chem., Univ. of Texas at Austin, Austin, TX 78712, USA.

DEWAR, Peter de Vere Beauclerk-, b. 19 Feb. 1943, Tenterden, Kent, UK. Investment Manager; Registered Genealogist. Publs: The House of Nell Gwynn 1670-1974 (w. Donald Adamson), 1974. Contbr. to: Burke's Peerage; Burke's Landed Gentry. Mbrships: Fellow, Soc. of Antiquaries of Scotland; Soc. Genealogists (Comm., 1968-73); Assn. Genealogists & Record Agts. (Fndr. mbr., Hon. Dir., 1971-73); Heraldry Soc.; New Club; Puffins Club. Hons: Kt. of Malta; Appointed Falkland Pursuivant Extraord. by Lord Lyon King of Arms, 1975. Address: Whitehorn House, Milnathort, Kinross-shire KY13 7XU, UK.

DEWART, Leslie, b. 12 Dec. 1922, Madrid, Spain. Philosopher of Religion. Educ: B.A., 1951, M.A., 1952, Ph.D., 1954, Univ. of Toronto. Publs: Christianity & Revolution, 1963; The Future of Belief, 1966; The Foundations of Belief, 1969; Religion, Language & Truth, 1970. Contbr. to: Assoc. Ed., Continuum, 1964-70; Int. Dialog Zeitschrift, 1967—; Concurrence, 1968-70; Contbng. Ed., Ecumenist, 1968—; & others. Address: 14 Prospect St., Toronto, Ont. M4X 1C6, Can.

DEWDNEY, John Christopher, b. 1928, Woodford, Essex, UK. Reader in Geography. Educ: M.A., Univ. of Edinburgh. Publs: Malta — Background for Development (w. H. Bowen-Jones & W. B. Fisher), 1961; A Geography of the Soviet Union, 1965; Turkey, 1972. Contbr. to: Transactions, Inst. of Brit. Geogs.; Scottish Geogl. Mag.; Geog.; Town Planning Review; Geogl. Mag.; Sierra Leone Studies. Mbrships: Inst. of Brit. Geogs.; Royal Scottish Geogl. Soc.; Geogl. Assn.; Brit. Soc. for Middle Eastern Studies; C'wlth. Human Ecol. Coun. Address: Dept. of Geography, Science Laboratories, South Rd., Durham DH1 3LE, UK.

DEWEY, Godfrey, b. 3 Sept. 1887, NYC, USA. Author; Educator; Executive. Educ: A.B., Harvard Coll., 1909; Ed.M., 1921, Ed.D., 1926, Harvard Grad. Schl. of Educ. Publs. incl: Relative Frequency of English Speech Sounds, 1923; World English Spelling Dictionary, 1969; Relative Frequency of English Spellings, 1970; English Spelling: Roadblock to Reading, 1971. Contbr. to: sci. & educl. jrnls. Mbrships. incl: Hon. Mbr., N.Y. State Shorthand Reporters Assn.; Nat. Shorthand Reporters Assn. Address: Lake Placid Club, NY 12946, USA.

DIAMOND, Arthur Sigismund, b. 23 Dec. 1897, Leeds, UK. Master of the Supreme Court (Retired); Sociologist; Author. Educ: M.A., LL.M., LL.D., Cambridge Univ. Publs: The Law of Master & Servant, 1932, 2nd ed., 1946; Primitive Law, 1935, 2nd ed., 1950; Evolution of Law & Order, 1951; History & Origin of Language, 1959; Primitive Law, Past & Present, 1971. Address: 9 Brackwell Gardens, London NW3, UK.

DIAS, Earl J., b. 23 Mar. 1916, New Bedford, Mass., USA. Professor of English & Department Chairman; Drama, Music Critic. Educ: A.B., Bates Coll.; M.A., Boston Univ.; Grad. studies, Univ. of London, Shakespeare Inst. Publs. incl: Melodramas & Farces for Young Actors, 1956; New Comedies for Teen-Agers, 1967, 1970; Mark Twain's Letters to the Rogers Family, 1970; Henry Huttleston Rogers: Portrait of a Capitalist, 1974. Contbr. to num. profl. jrnls.; Drama Music Critic, New Bedford Standard-Times. Hons. incl: Phi Beta Kappa Reading Prize, 1937; Wilkes Fund Lectures, New Bedford Pub. Lib., 1958. Address: 52 Walnut St., Fairhaven, MA 02719, USA.

DIBLEY, Kathleen, pen names DYOU, Katherine; RALEGH, Elizabeth, b. 23 Jan. 1927, London, UK. Journalist. Publs: The Olivers, 1960; Design in the Home, forthcoming; Do-it-Yourself, forthcoming; Home Sewing Directory, forthcoming; short stories in var. mags., 1950-63; & Ed. var. mags. Contbr. to: Practical Householder (design Ed.); Home Textiles (Ed.); Good Housekeeping (Colour Advsy. Serv.); etc. Mbrships: Inst. Jrnlsts.; Inst. Pub. Rels.; Soc. Women Writers & Jrnlsts. Address: 126 Radnor Ave., Bexleyheath, Kent DA16 28Y, UK.

DIBNER, Martin, b. 5 Oct. 1911, NYC, USA. Author; Artist. Educ: B.S., Wharton Schl., Univ. of Penn., 1933; Grad. studies, Rollins Coll., 1947-48. Publs: (novels) The Bachelor Seals, 1948; The Deep Six, 1953; Showcase, 1958; Sleeping Giant, 1960; A God for Tomorrow, 1961; The Admiral, 1968; The Trouble with Heroes, 1971; (non-fiction) The Arts in California, 1966; Seacoast Maine, 1972; Portland (designer & ed.), 1972; var. French, Italian, German, Dutch & Swedish transls. Contbr. to: Esquire; Coronet; Town & Country. Mbrships. incl: Authors' League of Am.; Mark Twain Soc.; 20th Century Collect. Archives, Boston Univ. Lib. Hons. incl: Armed Forces Lit. Fellowship, 1944; Rosenwald Fellowship, 1947; Breadloaf Writers' Fellowship, 1964; State of Maine Bd. of Educ., 1973-78. Address: Mayberry Hill, Casco Village, ME 04015, USA.

DICHEV, Stefan Nikolov, b. 9 Jan. 1920, Veliko Tirnovo, Bulgaria. Writer. Publs: (in Bulgarian) For Freedom, 1954-56; Ralley, 1960; Rakovski's Youth, 1962; The Road to Sofia, 1962; The Squadron, 1968; Strongholds, 1974. Contbr. to: PlamAk; September. Mbrships: Union of Bulgarian Writers; PEN. Recip., Dimitrov Prize, 1959. Address: Sofia, ul. Midzhour, 17, Bulgaria.

DICK, Kay, pen names LANE, Edward, & SCOTT, Jeremy, b. 29 July 1915, London, UK. Publs: Fiction: By The Lake, 1949; Young Man, 1951; An Affair of Love, 1953; Solitaire, 1958; Sunday, 1962; Non-Fiction: Pierrot, 1960; Ivy & Stevie, 1971; Friends & Friendships, 1974; Ed., 3 anthols. of short stories. Contbr. to: The Windmill (Ed.); The Times; Spectator; Scotsman; Books & Bookmen; British Book News; Harpers—Queen; Times Lit. Supplement; Guardian; Observer; Daily Telegraph Mag.; Ramparts. Recip., Arts Coun. Awards, 1965, 1971, 1974. Address: Flat 5, 9 Arundel Terrace, Brighton BN2 1GA, Sussex, UK.

DICK, Margaret, b. Kelty, Fife, Scotland, UK. Writer. Publs: (novels) Point of Return, 1958; Rhyme or Reason, 1959; (lit. criticism) The Novels of Kylie Tennant-Rigby, 1966. Contbr. to: Sydney Morning Herald; The Australian. Mbrships: V.P., Int. PEN, Sydney Ctr.; Aust. Soc. of Authors. Address: c/o the Lit. Ed., The Sydney Morning Herald, G.P.O. Box 506, Sydney, Australia 2001.

DICKENS, Arthur Geoffrey, b. 1910, Hull, UK. University Professor & Administrator; Historian; Author. Educ: M.A.; D.Lit.(London); Hymers Coll., Hull; Magdalen Coll., Oxford. Publs. incl: Lollards & Protestants in the Diocese of York, 1959; Thomas Cromwell & the English Reformation, 1959; The English Reformation, 1964; Reformation & Society in 16th Century Europe, 1966; Martin Luther & the Reformation, 1967; The Counter Reformation, 1968; The Age of Humanism & Reformation, 1972; The German Nation & Martin Luther, 1974. Contbr. to: Bulletin of Inst. Histl. Rsch. (Ed.); Eng. Hist. Review; Times; num. other acad. jrnls. Mbrships. incl: Fellow, Brit. Acad.; Fellow, Royal Histl. Soc. Recip., C.M.G. Address: Inst. of Histl. Rsch., Univ. of London, Senate House, London WC1E 7HU, UK.

DICKENS, Frank, b. 1899, Northampton, UK. Research Scientist. Educ: Magdalene Coll., Cambridge; Imperial Coll., London Univ.; M.A.; Ph.D.; D.Sc. Publs: Chemical & Physiological Properties of the Internal Secretions (w. E. C. Dodds); Metabolism of Tumours by Otto Warburg (transl.). Contbr. to: Biochem. Jrnl. F.R.S. Address: 15 Hazelhurst Cres., Findon Valley, Worthing, Sussex BN14 0HW, UK.

DICKENS, Monica (Enid), b. 10 May 1915, London, UK. Writer. Publs. incl: (novels) Mariana, 1940; The Fancy, 1943; Thursday Afternoons, 1945; The Happy Prisoner, 1946; Joy & Josephine, 1948; Flowers on the Grass, 1949;

No More Meadows, 1953; The Winds of Heaven, 1955; The Angel in the Corner, 1956; Man Overboard, 1958; The Heart of London, 1961; Cobbler's Dream, 1964; Kate & Emma, 1964; The Room Upstairs, 1966; The Landlord's Daughter, 1968; The Listeners, 1970; My Turn to Make the Tea (autobiog.), 1951; (juvenile) World's End in Winter, 1972; Dora at Follyfoot, 1972. Contbr. to Woman's Own. Address: Main St., Post Office Box 386, North Falmouth, MA 02556, USA.

DICKIE, (Rev.) Edgar Primrose, b. 1897, Dumfries, Scotland, UK. Emeritus Professor; Extra Chaplain to the Queen. Educ: Edinburgh Univ.; Oxford Univ.; New Coll., Edinburgh; Marburg & Tubingen Univs., Germany; M.A.; B.D.; D.D.LL.D. Publs. incl: Revelation & Response; A Safe Stronghold; Obedience of a Christian Man; Spirit & Truth; The Seven Words from the Cross; Scottish Life & Character; The Unchanging Gospel; Remembrance; relig. works for children. Contbr. to: Scottish Jrnl. Theol.; Expository Times; Scotsman; Punch; In Our Tongues; The Professor as Preacher; etc. Mbr., Royal Overseas Club. Address: Surma, Hepburn Gdns., St. Andrews, Scotland, UK.

DICKINSON, Alan Edgar Frederic, b. 9 July 1899, Blackheath, London, UK. Writer. Educ: M.A., B.Mus., Balliol Coll., Oxford; Hon. A.R.C.M. Publs: The Art of J. S. Bach, 1936, revised ed., 1950; Beethoven, 1941; Bach's Fugal Works, 1956; Vaughan Williams, 1963; The Music of Berlioz, 1972. Contbr. to: The Music Review; The Musical Quarterly, N.Y. Mbr., Royal Musical Assn. Address: North Toutley Hall, Wokingham, Berks., UK.

DICKINSON, Harry Thomas, b. 9 Mar. 1939, Gateshead, Co. Durham, UK. University Reader in History. Educ: Univs. of Durham & Newcastle; B.A., Dip.Ed., M.A., Ph.D. Publs: Ed., The Correspondence of Sir James Clavering, 1967; Bolingbroke, 1970; Walpole & the Whig Supremacy, 1973; Ed., Politics & Literature in the Eighteenth Century, 1974. Contbr. to: Engl. Histl. Review; Bulletin Inst. Histl. Rsch.; Huntington Lib. Quarterly; Jrnl. of Brit. Studies; Hist. Today. Mbrships. incl: Fellow, Royal Histl. Soc. Address: 44 Viewforth Terrace, Edinburgh 10, UK.

DICKINSON, Patric Thomas, b. 26 Dec. 1914, Nasirabad, India. Poet. Educ: B.A., Univ. of Cambridge, UK. Publs: Theseus & the Minotaur & Poems, 1946; Stone in the Midst & Poems, 1948; A Round of Golf Courses, 1951; The Sailing Race, 1952; The Scale of Things, 1955; Poems to Remember (anthol.), 1958; The World I See, 1960; A Durable Fire (play), 1962; This Cold Universe, 1964; Poets' Choice (anthol.), 1967; Selected Poems, 1968; More than Time, 1970; Transl., The Plays of Aristophanes, 1970; A Wintering Tree, 1973; Transl., Vergil's Aeneid. Contbr. to: London Mag.; Esquire; New Statesman; Country Life; Times Lit. Supplement; BBC Radio 3. Mbr., PEN. Hons: Atlantic Award in Lit., 1948; Cholmondeley Award for Poets, 1973. Address: 38 Church Square, Rye, Sussex, UK.

DICKINSON, Peter, b. 1927, Livingstone, Zambia. Author. B.A., King's Coll., Cambridge, UK. Publs: Skin Deep, 1968; The Weathermonger, 1968; Heartsease, 1969; A Pride of Heroes, 1969; The Seals, 1970; The Devil's Children, 1970; Emma Tupper's Diary, 1971; Sleep & His Brother, 1971; The Lizard in the Cup, 1972; The Dancing Bear, 1972; The Gift, 1973; The Iron Lion, 1973; The Green Gene, 1973; The Poison Oracle, 1974. Mbr., Crime Writers' Assn., London. Agent: A. P. Watt & Son. Address: 33 Queensdale Rd., London W11, UK.

DICK-LAUDER, (Sir) George Andrew, b. 17 Dec. 1917, Poona, India. Civil Servant; Author. Publs: Let Soldiers Lust, 1963; Our Man For Ganymede, 1969; A Skull & Two Crystals, 1972. Contbr. to var. jrnls. Mbr., Edinburgh Press Club. Hons: Baronet (N.S., Can.), 1960; Kt. of Grace, Mil. & Hospitiller Order of St. Lazarus of Jerusalem, 1973. Address: 6A Succoth Gardens, Edinburgh EH12 6BS, UK.

DICKSON, (Horatio Henry) Lovat, b. 30 June 1902, Australia. Author; Publisher, 1932-67. Educ: B.A., M.A., Univ. of Alta., Can. Publs: Half-Breed, 1938; Out of the West Land, 1943; Richard Hillary, 1950; The Ante-Room, 1959; The House of Words, 1963; H. G. Wells, 1969; Wilderness Man, 1973; Radclyffe Hall At The Well of Loneliness, 1975. Mbr., Garrick Club, London. Hons: LL.D. Address: Apt. 808, 21 Dale Avenue, Toronto, Ont., Can.

DICKSON, Mora Agnes, (Mrs. Alec G. Dickson), b. Glasgow, UK. Author. Educ: Edinburgh Coll. of Art; Byam Shaw Schl. of Drawing & Painting. Publs: New Nigerians, 1960; Baghdad & Beyond, 1961; Season in Sarawak, 1962; A World Elsewhere, 1964; Israeli Interlude, 1966; Counts Us In, 1967; School in the Round, 1969; A Longhouse in Sarawak, 1971; Beloved Partner, 1974. Contbr. to: Corona; H.M.S.O. Address: 19 Blenheim Rd., London W4, UK.

DICKSON, Violet Penelope, b. 3 Sept. 1896, Gautby, Lincs., UK. Writer. Publs: Wild Flowers of Kuwait & Bahrain, 1955; Forty Years in Kuwait, 1971. Contbr. to: Jrnl Royal Ctrl. Asian Soc.; Misc. Notes: Bombay Natural Hist. Soc.; Naft Mag. B.P. Hons: Lawrence of Arabia Memorial Medal, 1961; C.B.E., 1965. Address: Seef, Kuwait, Arabia.

DI DOMENICA, Franco, b. 11 Apr. 1925, Gambatesa, Campobasso, Italy. Teacher; Lawyer; Columnist; Promoter of Fine Arts. Educ: J.D., Univ. of Naples; studies at Seton Hall Univ., N.J., USA. Publs: Un Emigrato Racconta, 1965; Come Along to Italy, 1970. Contbr. to: Spotlight, USA; Am. Review; Italian Tribune News; Il Mattino, Italy. Mbrships. incl: For. Press Assn., N.Y.; Writers, Artists & Authors of Am., N.Y.; N.J. State Tchrs. Assn.; Intercontinental Club; Hudson River Maritime Acad. (Lt.-in-Charge PR); USA Consul, Acad. Gentium, Rome & Int. Acad. of the Arts, Gela, Italy. Hons: Silver Medal, Campobasso Poetry Contest, 1966; 1st Prize, Poetry Contest, Rome, for poem Amia Madre. Address: 21 Howland Pl., Long Branch, NJ 07740, USA.

DIÉNES, André, pen name de DIENES, Andre, b. 18 Dec. 1913, Kezdivasarhely, Transylvania, Hungary (now Rumania). Artist; Photographer; Author. Publs: The Nude, 1956; Nude Pattern, 1958; Best Nudes, 1962; Sun-Warmed Nudes, 1965; Natural Nudes, 1966; Western Nudes, 1967; Nudes, My Camera & I, 1973. Address: 1401 Sunset Plaza Drive, Hollywood, CA 90069, USA.

DIERENFIELD, Richard Bruce, b. 15 Oct. 1922, Aberdeen, S.D., USA. Teacher; Author. Educ: B.A., M.Ed., Macalester Coll., St. Paul, Minn.; Ed.D., Univ. of Colo., Boulder. Publs: Religion In American Public Schools, 1962; The High School Curriculum (co-author), 1964; The Cinderella Subject: Religion In the County Secondary Schools of England, 1965; The Sociology of Religion (co-author), 1967. Contbr. to: Relig. Educ.; Jrnl. of Tchr. Educ.; Clearing House. Address: 1566 Red Cedar Rd., St. Paul, MI 55101, USA.

DIETRICH, Wilfred O., b. 22 May 1925, Burton, Tex., USA. Teacher. Educ: A.A., Blinn Coll., Brenham, Tex., 1943; B.A., Sam Houston State Univ., 1946; M.A., 1948; Univ. of Tex., A.M. Univ.; W. Tex. State Univ.; Abilene Christian Univ.; E. Tex. State Univ. Author, The Blazing Story of Washington County, 1950, revised ed., 1973. Mbrships. incl: V.P., Pres., Tex. State Tchrs. Assn.; V.P., Pres., Wash. Co. Tchrs. Assn.; Nat. Coun. Engl. Tchrs.; Tex. Coun. Tchrs. of Engl.; Tex. Jr. Coll. Assn. Address: 701 Milroy Dr., Brenham, TX 77833, USA.

DIETZ, David (Henry), b. 6 Oct. 1897, Cleveland, Ohio, USA. Editor & Author. Educ: A.B., Litt.D., Western Reserve Univ.; LL.D., Bowling Green State Univ. Publs: The Story of Science, 1931; Medical Magic, 1938; Atomic Energy in the Coming Era, 1945; Atomic Science, Bombs, & Power, 1954; All About Satellites & Space Ships, 1958; All About Great Medical Discoveries, 1960; All About the Universe, 1965; Stars & the Universe, 1968; The New Outline of Science, 1972. Mbrships: Charter Mbr. & 1st Pres., Nat. Assn. Sci. Writers. Hons. incl: Pulitzer Prize in Jrnlsm., 1936; Westinghouse Disting. Sci. Writers Award, 1945; Albert Lasker Med. Jrnlsm. Award, 1954. Address: 2891 Winthrop Rd., Shaker Heights, OH 44120, USA.

DILCOCK, Noreen, pen names FORD, Norrey; CHRISTIAN, Jill; WALFORD, Christian, b. 1907, Hull, UK. Novelist. Publs: 30 novels, 1952-69; (as Christian Walford) The Little Masters, 1969; (as Jill Christian) Master of This House, 1970; (as Norrey Ford) Someone Different, 1970; Walk Tall Country, 1973; Life Most Dear, 1974; One Hot Summer, 1974; Call to the Castle, 1974; Road of the Eagles, 1975. Adent: E. P. S. Lewin. Address: Fellside, Cartbridge Lane, Walsall WS4 1SB, UK.

DILELLO, Richard, b. 28 Sept. 1945, NYC, USA. Author; Photographer. Publs: The Longest Cocktail Party, 1972 (USA), 1973 (UK), 1975 (Japan & Netherlands). Address: 53 A Viola Rd., Suffern, NY 10901, USA.

DILKE, Christopher, b. 15 Dec. 1913, London, UK. Broadcasting Official (retired); Company Director. Educ: Trinity Coll., Cambridge. Publs: (novels) The Bridgehead; France is a Star; The Eye of the Night; A Name for Myself; The Guardian; Up And Coming; Freddle & Son; The Rotten Apple; (gen.) The Road to Dalmatia; Dr. Moberly's Mint-Mark; Letter to a King, forthcoming. Contbr. to: BBC. Address: 1 Campden Grove, London W8, UK.

DILLISTONE, Frederick William, b. 9 May 1903, Sompting, Sussex, UK. Minister of Religion. Educ: M.A., D.D., Brasenose Coll., Oxford Univ. Publs: The Structure of the Divine Society, 1951; Christianity & Symbolism, 1955; The Christian Understanding of Atonement, 1968; Traditional Symbols & the Contemporary World, 1973; Charles Raven: Naturalist, Historian, Theologian, 1975. Recip., Bampton Lectrship., Oxford Univ., 1968. Address: 15 Cumnor Rise Rd., Oxford, UK.

DILLON, Eilis (married name MERCIER), b. 1920, Galway, Ireland. Author. Publs. incl: The Bitter Glass; The Head of the Family; The Fort of Gold; The San Sebastian; The Singing Cave; The Island of Horses; The House on the Shore; Across the Bitter Sea. Contbr. to: BBC; Irish Radio. Mbrships: PEN; Soc. of Authors; Royal Dublin Soc.; Arts Coun. of Ireland. Address: (Sept.-Apr.) Villa Flores Apt. 211, 601 E. Anapamu St., Santa Barbara, CA 93103, USA, & 7 Templemore Ave., Dublin 6, Repub. of Ireland.

DİLMEN, Güngör, b, 27 May 1930, Tekirdağ, Turkey. Playwright; Stage Director. Educ: Grad., Classical Philol., Fac. of Letters, Univ. of Istanbul, 1960; postgrad. work, Yale Schl. of Drama, USA, 1961-63. Plays produced incl: Midas trilogy comprising The Ears of Midas, 1960, The Gold of Midas, 1969, The Gordian Knot, 1975; Live Monkey Restaurant, 1964; The Sacrifice, 1964; Akad's Bow, 1967; Union & Progress, 1968; Lady Bagdad, 1974; The White Gods, forthcoming; (1-act plays) Hunter Karkap, 1961; The Toes, 1964; Hamit the Potter, 1964. Mbr., Turkish Playwrights' Assn. Hons. incl: İlhan İskender Award, 1967; Yunus Nadi Award, 1970. Address: Körfezyolu Sokak 2, Kiziltoprak, İstanbul, Turkey.

DILOV, Lyuben, b. 25 Dec. 1927, Cherven Bryag, Bulgaria. Writer. Publs: (in Bulgarian) The Atomic Man, 1958; On a Spring Day, 1960; Boyan Darev's Rest, 1961; I Remember This Spring, 1964; The Stranger; The Many Names of Fear, 1967; The Rushes, 1968; My Strange Friend the Astronomer; The Road of Icarus, 1974. Contbr. to most Bulgarian mags.; TV & radio. Mbrships: Union of Bulgarian Writers; PEN; European Assn. of Sci. Fiction Writers. Hons: Prize, Dimitrov Young Communist League, 1962; Int. Award for Sci. Fiction (Poland), 1973. Address: Sofia-7, ul. Major Tompson. bl.13, vh.V, Bulgaria.

DILSON, Jesse, b. 23 Dec. 1914, Brooklyn, N.Y., USA. Science Writer & Translator. Educ: B.Sc. Publs: Electronics, 1962; The Abacus: a Pocket Computer, 1968; Curves & Automation: the Scientists' Plot, 1971. Mbrships: IEEE; Authors Guild. Address: 201 E. 30th St., N.Y., NY 10016, USA.

DI MARCO, Luis Eugenio, b. 28 Sept. 1937, Catamarca, Argentina. Economist. Educ: Ph.D., Univ. Calif.; Dr. Econs., Univ. Córdoba, Argentina. Publs: Ed., International Economics & Development, 1972; Ed., Economía Internacional y Desarrollo, 1973; Buenos Aires y el Interior, 1973; Métodos Cuantitativos y Análisis Económico, 1974. Contbr. to: Económica; Revista de Economía y Estadística; Revista de Economía. Mbrships: Argentine Econ. Assn.; Argentine Statistical Soc.; Colegio de Graduados de Economía, Córdoba. Address: Genard Pérez 543, Córdoba, Argentina.

DIMITROVA, Blaga, b. 2 Jan. 1922, Byala Slatina, Bulgaria. Writer. Publs: (in Bulgarian) Journey to Oneself, 1965, Engl. transl., 1969; A Deviation, 1967; The Last Judgement, 1969; Avalanche, 1971; Underground Sky, 1972; (plays) Doctor Faustina, 1972; An Unexpected Meeting, 1974. Contbr. to: September; PlamAk; Literatouren Front. Mbr., Union of Bulgarian Writers. Hons: Union of Bulgarian Tourists Award, 1971; Ctrl. Coun. of Trade Unions Award, 1972; Prize, Union of Bulgarian Writers, 1973. Address: Sofia, ul. Parenssov, 33, Bulgaria.

DIMOCK, Gladys Orden, b. 3 Feb. 1908, N.Y., USA. Author. Educ: B.A., Bennington Coll., Vt., USA. Publs: A Home of Our Own, 1963; The Administration of Federal Work Relief (w. A. W. Macmahon & J. D. Millett), 1941; (w. M. E. Dimock), American Government in Action, 1946; Public Administration, 1953. Contbr. to: Nat. Municipal Review; Vt. Life. Mbrships: Am. Assn. of Univ. Women; Dist. VP, Unitarian Universalist Women's Fedn. Recip., Baldwin Prize, Nat. Municipal League, 1935. Address: Scrivelsby, Bethel, VT 05032, USA.

DINES, Michael, b. 1 Feb. 1916, Manchester, UK. Businessman; Writer. Publs: Operation – Deadline, 1965; Operation – to Kill a Man, 1967; Operation – Kill or be Killed, 1969; 14 one-act plays; Currently writing for European radio and TV (specialised crime plays). Contbr. to: Jewish Life (Ed., 1965-69); Jewish Quarterly; Jewish Gazette (columnist for 10 yrs.). Mbrships: Writers' Guild of GB; Crime Writers' Assn. Recip., num. awards. Agents: Margery Vosper; David Higham Assocs. Address: White Lodge, 37 Ringley Rd., Whitefield, Manchester M25 7LH, UK.

DINGEE, Frieda Laura Hayes, b. 27 Feb. 1903, Hensonville, N.Y., USA. Educator: Educ. B.S., M.A., N.Y. Univ.; Postgrad. study, Penn State Coll., Temple Univ. Publs: Directing Learning in the Language Arts (co-author), 1948; Children Learn the Language Arts (co-author), 1959, 2nd ed., 1966. Address: 108 Wilson Ave., Kingston, NY 12401, USA.

DINGER, Aagot, b. 2 Oct. 1910, Stalheim, Norway. Psychologist; Author. Educ: studied art, psychol., philos. & lit. in France & Germany. Publs: Du skal ikke drepe! , 1971; Gudrun, 1975; also novels, poems & radio-theatre plays. Address: Norsk Forfattersentrum, Oslo; Interessen-Gemeinschaft deutschspr. Authoren, Germany; Literarische UNION, Saarbrücken, Germany. Address: Birkenstr. 23 b, 48 – Bielefeld, W. Germany.

DINGLE, Herbert, b. 1890, London, UK. Writer. Educ: Plymouth Sci. Art & Tech. Schls.; Imperial Coll. of Sci. & Technol.; D.Sc., A.R.C.S. Publs: Modern Astrophysics; Science & Human Experience; Through Science to Philosophy; Special Theory of Relativity; Science & Literary Criticism; Practical Applications of Spectrum Analysis; The Scientific Adventure; w. Viscount Samuel, A Threefold Cord; Ed., A Century of Science; Science at the Crossroads; The Mind of Emily Brontë. Contbr. to var. jrnls. Mbrships: Athenaeum Club. Address: 104 Downs Court Rd., Purley, Surrey CR2 1BD, UK.

DINHOFER, Aldred D., b. 29 May 1929, Brooklyn, N.Y., USA. Publisher; Editor; Writer. Educ: B.S., N.Y. Univ., 1956; grad. studies, Columbia Univ. Publs: Our Man in San Juan, 1964; Caribbean Here & Now, 1967, 1969, 1972; Official Guide to the Caribbean, 1970; Explore the Caribbean & Bahamas, 1971; Kids in the Kitchen, 1972. Contbr. to: Variety; Nat. Inquirer; Travel Scene; etc. Mbrships: Overseas Press Club of Puerto Rico; Japan Soc. Address: Caribbean World Communications, 1st Federal Building Suite 312, Santurce, PR 00909, USA.

DINNER, William, pen name SMITH, Surrey, b. Bournemouth, UK. Short Story Writer; Film Reader. Publs. incl: The Late Edwina Black (play, w. Wm. Morum); Little Boy Who? (play); The Astonished Guardsman (novel); The Village that Wandered (novel); No Tears for Teddy (novel). Agent: Felix de Wolfe. Address: c/o Felix de Wolfe, 1 Robert St., Adelphi, London WC2N 6BH, UK.

DINWIDDIE, Faye Love, b. 17 Sept. 1908, Paris, Tenn., USA. Journalist; Social Worker; Writer; Lecturer. Educ: Toledo Univ.; Univs. of Denver, Mich., Case Western Reserve. Publs: Song of the Mute, 1970. Contbr. to nat. radio prog., Between the Book Ends; Major Poets. Mbrships: Nat. Writers Club; Int. Black Writers Conf.; Centro Studi E. Scambi Int.; Toledo Chapt., Ohio Poetry Soc.; Eastern Ctr.; The Poetry Soc., UK; Life Mbr., Nat. Assn. for the Advancement of Coloured People. Address: 1908 Washington St., Toledo, OH 43624, USA.

DIOLÉ, Philippe Victor, b. 24 Aug. 1908, St. Maur, France. Educ: Lic. in Law, Fac. of Law, Univ. of Paris. Publs: The Undersea Adventure; 4,000 Years Under the Sea; The Sea of Sicily; The Sahara Adventure; Okapi Fever; The Errant Ark, 1974; (w. J. Y. Cousteau) Life & Death in a Coral Sea; Sunken Treasure; Whales, Mighty Monarchs of the Sea; Octopus & Squids; Diving Companions; Three Adventures; Dolphins. Contbr. to Le Figaro. Mbr., French Explorers Club. Recip., Grand Prix Walter, Acad. Française. Address: 80 rue de l'Université, Paris 75007, France.

DIOMEDE, Matthew, b. 8 June 1940, Yonkers, N.Y., USA. Teacher. Educ: Fordham Coll.; B.A., M.S., Fordham Univ. Contbr. of poetry to num. jrnls. inclng: Kansas Quarterly; Phylon; N.Y. English Record; Performing Arts Review; The Above Ground Review; The Villager; Nimrod; American Poet. Also var. anthols. Mbr., Poetry Soc. of N.H. Hons. incl: 2nd Prize, State of Maine's Writers Conf.; 1970; Dip. & Bronze Medal of Hon., Centro Studi E Scambi Int., Rome, 1972; Cert. of Merit for Outstanding Poetry, J. Mark Press, 1970. Address: 21 Botany Lane, Stony Brook, NY 11790, USA.

DIVALE, William Tulio, b. 18 Feb. 1942, NYC, USA. Anthropologist. Educ: A.A., Pasadena City Coll., 1966; B.A., UCLA, 1969; M.A., Calif. State Univ., L.A., 1971; Ph.D., SUNY, Buffalo, 1974. Publs: I Lived Inside the Campus Revolution, 1970; Warfare in Primitive Societies, 1973. Contbr. to: Behavior Sci. Rsch.; World Archaeol.; Anthropol.; Am. Ethnologist; N.Y. Folklore Quarterly; etc. Mbrships: Am. Anthropol. Assn.; Soc. for Cross-Cultural Rsch.; Northeastern Anthropol. Assn.; AAAS; Am. Sociol. Assn. Hons: C.S. Ford Cross-Cultural Rsch. Award, 1973; Ogden Mills Fellow, Am. Mus. of Natural Hist. Address: 4342 Byron Ave., Bronx, NY 10466, USA

DIVERRES, Armel Hugh, b. 4 Sept. 1914, Liverpool, UK. University Teacher. Educ: B.A., M.A., Wales; Lès L., Rennes, France; Dr., Univ. of Paris. Publs: Voyage en Béarn, 1953; La Chronique métrique attribuée a Geffroy de Paris, 1956; Vigny, Chatterton, 1967. Contbr. to: French Studies; Mod. Lang. Review; Forum for Mod. Lang. Studies; Medium Aevum; Nvouvelle Revue de Bretagne; Revue de Lit. Comparée; Archivum Linguisticum; Jrnl. of Nat. Lib. of Wales. Mbrships: incl: V.P., Brit. Br., Int. Arthurian Soc., 1963–; V.P., Soc. for French Studies, 1975; Soc. for the Study of Medieval Lang. & Lit. Recip., Officier des Palmes Acad., 1971. Address: 23 Whiteshell Dr., Langland, Swansea, UK.

DIVINE, Arthur Durham David, b. 1904, Capetown, S. Africa. Journalist. Educ: Kingswood Coll., S. Africa. Publs: Wine of Good Hope; The King of Fassaral; The Golden Fool; Boy on a Dolphin; The Nine Days of Dunkirk; The Blunted Sword; The Broken Wing; The North-West Frontier of Rome; Mutiny at Invergordon. Contbr. to: Sunday Times; Thomson Newspapers; Saturday Evening Post; John Bull; etc. Recip., O.B.E. Address: 24 Keats Grove, London NW3, UK.

DIWAKAR, Ranganath Ramachandra, b. 30 Sept. 1894, Dharwar, India. Journalist; Author. Educ: M.A., LL.B., Bombay Univ. Publs: Paramahamsa Shri Ramakrishna; Mahayogi; Saga of Satyagraha; Bihar Through the Ages; Karnatak Through the Ages; Bhagwan Buddha; The Upanishads in Story & Dialogue; Glimpses of Gandhiji; Vachana Shastra; Antaratmanige; Viswatmanige. Contbr. to: Bhavan's Jrnl.; Gandhi Marg; etc. Mbrships. incl: Indian & Eastern Newspaper Soc. (Pres., 1967); Gandhi Peace Fndn., Chmn. Address: 233 Sri Aurobindo Krupe, Sadashiv Nagar, Bangalore 560 006, India.

DIXEY, (Sir) Frank, b. 1892, Bristol, UK. Geologist; Dir., Overseas Geological Surveys (Retired). Educ: M.Sc., D.Sc., Univ. of Wales. Publs: Practical Handbook of Water Supply. Contbr. of num. official reports, memoirs & papers on geology, mineral resources & water supply, to var. jrnls. in field. Mbrships: F.R.S.; Fellow, Geolog. Soc.; Instn. of Mining & Metallurgy. Hons: K.C.M.G.; O.B.E. Address: Woodpecker Cottage, Bramber, Steyning, Sussex, UK.

DIXON, Reginald Arthur Norton, b. 1910, Lincoln, UK. Freelance Journalist & Author. Educ: Lincoln Municipal Tech. Schl. Publs: Thomas Paine, 1937; Spanish Rhapsody, 1955; So You Want a House in Spain, 1964; The Costa Brava, 1965; The Costa Blanca, 1966; The Costa del Sol, 1966; Spain, 1967. Contbr. to num. jrnls. & mags. inclng: Tit Bits; Wide World; Cornhill Mag.; Today; Men Only; Weekend; Housewife; Farmer's Weekly; Poultry World; Grower; Good Motoring; Light Car; Morris Owner; Brit. Printer. Mbr., Soc. of Authors. Address: Can Nasi, Tordera, Barcelona, Spain;

DJILAS, Milovan. Publs: Conversations with Stalin, 1962. Address: c/o Rupert Hart-Davis, 36 Soho Sq., London W1, UK.

DJURIČIĆ, Mladen, pen names MLAD-MILTIJAD; DRINČIĆ, Sava; num. others in newspapers, b. 8 Mar. 1889, Šabac, Yugoslavia. Writer. Publs. incl: U Borbi Života

(poems), 1912; Caru Rataru, 1919; Crvene zvezde, 1920; Vodozemci, 1931 (all short stories); Mrtva straža, 1939; Jadar topi brda, 1958; Odžakovići, 1963; Zviždi, Vetre! , 1963 (all novels); Istorija Jugoslovenskog Rečnog Parobrodarstva, 1965; Samoubistvo Neznanog Junaka, 1971; 40 others. Contbr. to: Srpski Književni Glasnik; Misao; num. other lit. reviews & papers (over 1,000 essays). Mbrships. incl: PEN; Authors' Assn.; Kosove Writers Club (Fndr.-Sec.). Hons: Prize, Illustrated Jrnl., 1922; French Acad. Palm, 1931; Fine Lit. Prize, Serbian Acad. Sci. & Arts, 1933. Address: 55 Hadži-Melentijeva St., 11000 Belgrade, Yugoslavia.

DMYTRYSHYN, Basil, b. 14 Jan. 1925, Poland. Professor of History. Educ: B.A., 1950, M.A., 1951, Univ. of Ark., USA; Ph.D., Univ. of Calif., Berkeley, 1955. Publs. incl: Moscow & the Ukraine, 1918-1953, 1956; USSR: A Concise History, 1965, 2nd ed., 1971; Medieval Russia: A Source Book, 900-1700, 1967, 2nd ed., 1973; Imperial Russia: A Source Book, 1700-1917, 1967, 2nd ed., 1974; Modernization of Russia Under Peter I & Catherine II, 1974. Contbr. to US, for. jrnls. Address: Dept. of Hist., Portland State Univ., Portland, OR 97207, USA.

DOBB, Maurice Herbert, b. 1900, London, UK. Emeritus Reader in Economics; College Fellow. Educ: M.A., Pembroke Coll., Cambridge; Ph.D., London. Publs. incl: Studies in the Development of Capitalism, 1946; Soviet Economic Development Since 1917, 1948; On Economic Theory & Socialism; Collected Papers, 1955; An Essay on Economic Growth & Planning, 1960; Papers on Capitalism Development & Planning, 1967; Welfare Economics & the Economics of Socialism, 1969; Theories of Value & Distribution Since Adam Smith, 1973. Contbr. to: Ency. Britannica; Ency. of Social Scis.; Econ. Jrnl.; Soviet Studies; etc. Hons: Fellow, Brit. Acad.; D.Litt., Leicester Univ. Address: Trinity Coll., Cambridge, UK.

DOBBS, Kildare Robert Eric, b. 10 Oct. 1923, Meerut, India. Writer. Educ: M.A., Jesus Coll., Cambridge, UK; Dip.Ed., Inst. of Educ., London Univ. Publs: Running to Paradise, 1961; Canada (w. Peter Varley), 1964; Reading the Time, 1968; The Great Fur Opera (w. Ronald Searle), 1970. Contbr. to: Macleans; Can. Forum; Can. Lit.; Saturday Night; Star Weekly; Reporter; Tamarack Review; Toronto Star; Toronto Globe & Mail; Times; Irish Times; London Mag. Mbrships: Bookmen, Toronto; Writers' Union of Can. Recip., Gov.-Gen.'s Award for Lit., 1962. Address: 28 Bracken Ave., Toronto, Ont., Can.

DOBOZY, Imre, b. 30 Oct. 1917, Vál, Hungary. Publs: New Seed in Cumenia (novel); Spring Wind (story); Storm (play & film); Continuation Tomorrow (play); Yesterday (film); Dawn (film); The Song of the Swain (film); Corporal & the Others (film); Eljött a Tavasz (film). Mbr., Gen. Sec., Assn. of Hungarian Writers. Hons: Kossuth Prize, Labour Order of Merit, Golden Degree, 1970. Address: Hungarian Writers' Assn., Bajza u. 18, H-1062 Budapest VI, Hungary.

DOBRACZYNSKI, Jan. b. 1910, Warsaw, Poland. Cavalry Officer; Writer; Editor, Polish Underground Magazine during WWII. Publs. incl: Invaders; Elected by Stars; The Sacred Sword; Letters of Nicodemus; The Church of Chocholow; 20th Brigade; I Came to Separate; The Great Armada; Hands of the Wall; To Drain the Sea; Men of Violence; num. transls. of works. Contbr. to: Polish Cath. jrnls. Mbrships: PEN; Société Européene de la Culture. Hons. incl: Lit. Prize, Cath. Action Inst., 1938; Wlodzimierz Pietrzak Prize, 1949 & 1953; State Lit. Prize, 1970; Reinhold Schneider Prize, W. Germany, 1972; num. mil. decorations. Agent: Agencja Autorska. Address: Warsaw 44, 42 Hetmanska St., Poland;

DOBRIANSKY, Lev E., b. 9 Nov. 1918, NYC, USA. Professor of Economics; Director, Inst. on Comparative Political & Economic Systems. Educ: B.S., 1941, M.A., 1943, Ph.D., 1951, N.Y. Univ.; Philos. Maj., Fordham Univ., N.Y., 1943; LL.D., Univ. of Munich, Germany, 1952. Publs: The Free Trade Ideal, 1954; Veblenism, a New Critique, 1957; Decisions for a Better America (co-author), 1960; The Vulnerable Russians, 1967; USA & the Soviet Myth, 1971. Contbr. to: NATO's 15 Nations; New Catholic Ency.; The Sign; etc. Mbrships: incl: AAUP; Am. Econs. Assn.; Univ. Club of Wash. Hons. incl: Freedom Fndn. Awards, 1960, 1963, 1973; Shevchenko Sci. Soc. Medal, 1965; Korean Freedom Acad. Award, 1969. Address: 4520 Kling Drive, Alexandria, VA 22312, USA.

DOBSON, Eric John, b. 1913, Roseville, N.S.W., Australia. Professor of English Language, Oxford University.

Educ: B.A., Univ. of Sydney; M.A., D.Phil., Merton Coll., Oxford, UK. Publs: English Pronunciation 1500-1700; The Phonetic Writings of Robert Robinson; The English Text of the Ancrene Riwle: MS. Cotton Cleopatra C.VI. Contbr. to: Trans. of Philological Soc.; Medium AEvum; Review of English Studies. F.B.A. Address: 9 Davenant Rd., Oxford, UK.

DOBSON, Kenneth Austin, b. 5 June 1907, Shanghai, China. Retired Colonial Service (Administration). Educ: B.A., Oriel Coll., Oxford. Publs: Mail Train, 1946; The Inescapable Wilderness, 1952; District Commissioner, 1954; Colour Blind, 1955. Mbr., Royal C'wlth Soc. Address: Priors, Jackass Lane, Keston, Kent BR2 6AN, UK.

DOBSON, Rosemary de Brissac, b. 18 June 1920, Sydney, Australia. Writer. Publs: In a Convex Mirror, 1944; The Ship of Ice, 1948; Child with a Cockatoo, 1955; Cock Crow, 1965; Rosemary Dobson (Aust. Poets Series), 1963; Focus on Ray Crooke, 1971; Selected Poems, 1973. Contbr. to: Quadrant; Southerly; Meanjin; Poetry Aust.; Tex. Quarterly; Borestone Awards; etc. Mbr., Aust. Soc. of Authors. Hons: Poetry Prize, Sydney Morning Herald, 1948; Myer Award for Poetry, 1966. Address: 61 Stonehaven Cres., Deakin, A.C.T., Australia 2600.

DODD, Arthur Edward, b. 1913, Stoke-on-Trent, UK. Poet; Playwright; Author. Educ: M.Sc., Ph.D., Univ. of London. Publs: (poetry) Poems from Belmont; Three Journeys; Words & Music; Weaver Hills; Fifth Season; (plays) The Flower-Spun Web; To Build a Bridge; Gold in Gun Street; (prose) Dictionary of Ceramics; Peakland Roads & Trackways. Contbr. to: Chambers' Ency.; Britannica Book of the Year; Poetry Review; Country Life; Listener; etc. Recip., M.B.E. Address: Hall Lodge, Upper Ellastone, Ashbourne, Derbys. DE6 2GU, UK.

DODDS, Eric Robertson, b. 1893, Banbridge, N. Ireland, UK. Classical Scholar. Educ: M.A., Univ. Coll., Oxford Univ. Publs: Select Passages Illustrating Neoplatonism; Thirty-two Poems; Journal & Letters of Stephen McKenna; Proclus, Elements of Theology; Euripides, Bacchae; Plato, Gorgias; The Greeks & the Irrational; Pagan & Christian in an Age of Anxiety; The Ancient Concept of Progress. Mbrships. incl: Inst. de France; Fellow, Brit. Acad.; Classical Assn. (former Pres.); Hellenic Soc. (former Pres.). Recip., Litt.D., Manchester, Dublin, Belfast, & Edinburgh Univs. Address: Cromwell's House, Old Marston, Oxford, UK.

DODDS, George Elliot, b. 1889, Upper Norwood, London, UK. Newspaper Executive. Educ: M.A, New Coll., Oxford. Publs: Is Liberalism Dead? , 1919; Liberalism in Action, 1922; The Defence of Man, 1947; The Logic of Liberty (w. Dr. E. Reiss), 1966. Contbr. to num. periodicals. Mbrships: Pres., Unservile State Grp.; Reform Club; Nat. Liberal; Old Millhillians. Recip., C.B.E. Address: 230 Somerset Rd., Huddersfield, UK.

DODDS, John Wendell, b. 1902, Grove City, Pa., USA. Professor. Educ: Yale Univ.; B.A., M.A., Ph.D., Litt.D., L.H.D. Publs: Thomas Southerne, Dramatist; Thackeray: a Critical Portrait; The Age of Paradox: a Biography of England 1841-51; American Memoir; Everyday Life in Twentieth Century America; The Several Lives of Paul Fejos. Contbr. to: Va. Quarterly; Pacific Spectator; Saturday Review; Huntingdon Lib. Quarterly; Sewanee Review. Mbrships: Dir., Wenner-Gren Fndn., 1954—; Pres., 1965—; Trustee, Coll. of Wooster, Ohio, 1967—; Authors' Club, London, UK. Address: 729 Frenchman's Rd., Stanford, Calif., USA.

DODGE, Ernest Stanley, b. 18 Mar. 1913, Trenton, Maine, USA. Museum Director. Educ: Harvard Univ. Publs: Gourd Growers of the South Seas, 1943; Northwest by Sea, 1961; New England & The South Seas, 1965; Beyond the Capes: Pacific Exploration from Cook to the Challenger 1776-1877, 1971; The Polar Rosses: A Biography of Sir John & Sir James Clark Ross, 1973. Contbr. to: The Am. Neptune; The New England Quarterly; Dict. of Can. Biog.; etc. Hons: Fellow, Am. Acad. of Arts & Scis.; M.A., Marlboro Coll., 1961; D.Litt., Boston Univ., 1970. Address: 161 Essex St., Salem, MA 01970, USA.

DODSON, Fitzhugh James, b. 28 Oct. 1923, Baltimore, Md., USA. Clinical Psychologist. Educ: A.B., Johns Hopkins Univ.; B.D., Yale Univ.; Ph.D., Univ. of S. Calif. Publs: How to Parent, 1970; Dr. Dodson's Whiz-Bang, Super-Ecomomy Parent's Survival Kit, 1971; How to Father, 1974. Address: 1801 S. Catalina Ave., Redondo Beach, CA 90277, USA.

DODSON, Kenneth MacKenzie, b. 11 Oct. 1907, Luanda, Angola, W. Africa. Ship's Master & Pilot; Retired Naval Officer; Author. Educ: Postgrad. courses in creative writing, Univ. of Wash., 1949-52. Publs. incl: Away All Boats, 1954; Stranger to the Shore, 1956; Hector, the Stowaway Dog, 1958; The China Pirates, 1960; From Make-Believe to Reality, 1973. Contbr. to: US Naval Inst. Proceedings; Rdrs. Digest; Nautical Mag., UK; var. newspapers & mags. in USA & UK. Mbr., Pacific Northwest Int. Writers' Conf. (VP, 1958). Hons. incl: 1st Award in Fiction, Wash. State Press Club, 1954; Cert. of Recognition, Gov.'s Invitational Writers' Day, 1966. Address: 1342 Rosario Rd., Anacortes, WA 98221, USA.

DOKE, Clement Martyn, b. 16 May 1893, Bristol, UK. Former Missionary; Professor of Bantu Languages; Author. Educ: B.A., M.A., D.Litt., etc.; Univs. of Cape of Good Hope, S. Africa, Witwatersrand, & London, UK. Publs. incl: (Transl. into Lamba) The Bible, 1959; Text Book of Zulu Grammar, 1927—; Lamba Folk Lore, 1927; Bantu Linguistic Terminology, 1935; Zulu-English Dictionary (w. B. W. Vilakazi), 1948; Text Book of Southern Sotho Grammar (w. S. M. Mofokeng), 1957; English-Zulu Dictionary (co-author), 1958. Contbr. to num. profl. jrnls.; Co-Ed., Bantu Studies & African Studies, 1924-53. Hons: Life Gov., Brit. & For. Bible Soc., 1938; D.Litt., 1971; LL.D., 1972. Address: Flat 19, Marina Hills, Keam Rd., Baysville, E. London 5201, S. Africa.

DOLBY, James Louis, b. 29 Apr. 1926, Phila., Pa., USA. Statistician; Consultant; Professor of Mathematics. Educ: A.B., Dartmouth Coll., 1946; M.A., Wesleyan Univ., 1949; Ph.D., Stanford Univ., 1966. Publs: The English Word Speculum (w. H. L. Resnikoff), 1967; The Computer & the Library (co-author), 1967; Computerized Library Catalogs (co-author), 1969; The Statistics Cum Index (w. J. W. Tukey), 1973. Contbr. to: Technometrics; Jrnl. of Lib. Automation; Language; Bulletin of Inst. Mgmt. Sci.; Jrnl. of Documentation; Ency. of Linguistics, Info. & Control; var. other profl. jrnls. Mbr., var. statistical & lib. assns. Address: 366 W. Portola Ave., Los Altos, CA 94022, USA.

DOLCI, Danilo, b. 1924, Sesana, Italy. Author. Publs: To Feed the Hungry, 1959; Report from Palermo, 1959; The Outlaws of Partinico, 1960; Outlaws, 1961. Mbrships: Nat. Inst. Urbanistica; Co-ordinator, Centro Studi di Partinico. Address: Centro Studi, Largo Scalia 5, Partinico, Italy.

DOLLINGER, Hans Karl Robert, b. 5. Feb. 1929; Biberach/Riss, Germany. Writer (History). Publs. incl: Mao und die Rote Garde, 1968; Willy, Willy! Der Weg des Menschen und Politikers Willy Brandt, 1970; Japan, die heimliche Weltmacht, 1971; Die totale Autogesellschaft, 1972; Lachen streng verboten! Die Seschichte der Deutschen im Spiegel der Karikature, 1972; Schwarzbuch der Weltgeschichte, 1973; Der Himmel hat Grenzen, 1974. Ed., Der Erste Zweite Weltkrieg in Bildern und Dokumenten, 1965; Deutschland unter den Besatzungsmächten 1945-49, 1967; & num. others. Mbr., German PEN; Verband Deutscher Schriftsteller. Address: Hochweg 6, 8031 Wörthsee-Etterschlag, W. Germany.

DOLPHIN, Reginald Charles, (Rex), b. 13 Mar. 1915, Pershore, Worcs., UK. Author. Publs: Murder Goes Nap, 1966; Driven to Kill, 1969; The Doomed Valley, 1975; num. others in 'Sexton Blake' detective series; several others under var. pseudonyms. Mbr., Crime Writers' Assn. Address: 13 Meadow Way, Hyde Heath, Amersham, Bucks., UK.

DOMARADZKI, Theodore Felix, b. 27 Oct. 1910, Warsaw, Poland. University Professor of Literature. Educ: Pol. Sci. Dip., Warsaw, 1936; M.A., Warsaw Univ., 1939; Litt.D., Rome Univ., Italy, 1941. Publs: Le Concezioni Antiche della Guerra e della Pace, 1939; Il Problema Sociale nell'Opera di B. Prus, 1941; Les Considérations de C. K. Norwid sur la Liberté de la Parole, 1971; Le Symbolisme et l'Universalisme de C. K. Norwid, 1974. Contbr. to var. acad. jrnls. inclng. Slavic & E. European Studies (Ed.). Mbrships. incl: Can. Soc. for Comp. Study of Civilizations (Pres.); Can. World Univ. Comm. (Pres.); Int. Assn. for Mod. Langs. & Lit. Hons. incl: Kt., Ordo Constantini Magni, 1973; Kt. Cmdr., Papal Order St. Gregory Gt., 1963. Address: 5601 Ave. des Cèdres, Montreal, P.Q. HIT 2V4, Can.

DOMINGUEZ ARAGONÉS, Edmundo, pen names ACAL, Luis Jacobo; O'HENRY, Henry, b. 27 Nov. 1938,

Argentona, Spain. Journalist; Editor; Lecturer; Actor. Educ: Tchr.'s Cert; Philos. & Letters, Univ. of Guadalajara. Publs: (novels) Argón 18 Inicia, 1971; Donde el agua es blanca como el gis, 1972; (factual) Crónica de una asamblea, 1972; 2 Palabras 2 (w. wife, María Luisa Mendoza), 1972; Allende el bravo (w. wife), 1973; Calzonzin Inspector (film script), 1974; Actualidad de los Partidos Políticos Mexicanos, 1975; El ladrido del cuervo (novel), forthcoming. Contbr. to: Caballero; Siete; Siempre!; Ovaciones; Ed., El Día, Solidaridad, IPN; Vice-Dir., El Gallo Ilustrado; Dir., Opinión Cultural; etc. Mbrships: PEN, Mexican br.; Mexican Assn. of Writers; etc. Address: Sabino 263, Colonia Santa María de la Ribera, México 4 D.F., México.

DOMINY, Eric Norman, b. 1918, Leeds, UK. Judo Expert. Publs: Judo — Basic Principles; Judo — From Beginner to Black Belt; Judo — Throws & Counters; Judo; Self Defence; Karate; Camping; Art of Judo; Judo: Contest Techniques; Camping at Home & Abroad. Contbr. to: Judo; & other jrnls. Mbrships: London Judo Soc.; Civil Servant Authors. Address: 18 Hamilton Way, Finchley, London N3 1AN, UK.

DOMMELSHUIZEN, Cornelis Hendrik (Cor) Jr., b. 20 Dec. 1914, The Hague, Netherlands. Cultural Adviser. Publs: Louis Bouwmeester, Een groot Nederlander (biog.), 1942; Louis Gimberg; van teen tot top (biog.), 1946; Amsterdamse Straatartisten, 1947; Gelderland à la carte, 1952; In Rok tussen de bruinhemden, 1964. Contbr. to: Het Toneel; De Toneelspiegel; Toneelschild; etc. Address: Louis Lepoutrelaan 17, 1060 Brussels, Belgium.

DONALD, Ian, b. 27 Dec. 1910, Liskeard, Cornwall, UK. Regius Professor of Midwifery. Educ: B.A., Capetown, S. Africa, 1930; St. Thomas's Hosp., London, UK; M.B.B.S., 1937; M.D., London, 1947; M.R.C.O.G., 1947; F.R.C.O.G., 1955; F.R.C.S. (Glasgow), 1958; F.C.O.G. (S. Africa), 1967. Publs: Practical Obstetric Problems, 4th ed., 1969; Chapts. in: Obstetrics & Gynecology; Marcus, Advances in Obstetrics & Gynecology, vol. I, 1967; Wells, Ultrasonics in Clinical Diagnosis, 1972; Wynn, Obstetrics & Gynecology Annual, 1972; King, Diagnostic Ultrasound, 1974. Contbr. to var. books & profl. jrnls. Mbr., num. profl. & humanitarian assns., UK & USA. Hons. incl: C.B.E., 1973; sev. profl. medals & prizes. Address: 9 Hamilton Dr., Glasgow G12 8DN, UK.

DONALD, William Spooner, b. 1 July, 1910, Carlisle, Cumberland, UK. Fishing, Manager & Secretary (Ret'd); Royal Naval Officer, 1924-49. Educ: RN Coll., Dartmouth. Publs: Stand By for Action, 1956; (plays) Hong Kong Cocktail; Pickled Salts; Singapore Slings. Contbr. to: Field; Scottish Field; Glasgow Herald; Guardian; Scotsman; Illustrated London News; Navy Yr. Book; Chambers Jrnl.; Men Only; Country Life; Sports Illustrated, Horizon, USA; Aust. Jrnl.; Auckland Herald, NZ; etc; BBC Radio 4. Mbr., Soc. of Authors. Recip., D.S.C. and Bar, 1940, 1944. Address: Troutlets, Church St., Keswick, Cumbria CA12 4DT, UK.

DONALDSON, Gordon, b. 1913, Edinburgh, UK. University Professor of History. Educ: Univs. of Edinburgh & London; M.A.; Ph.D.; D.Litt. Publs: Making of Scottish Prayer Book of 1637; Shetland Life under Earl Patrick; The Scottish Reformation; Source Book of Scottish History; Scotland: James V to James VII; Scottish Kings; Memoirs of Sir James Melville of Halhill; First Trial of Mary Queen of Scots; Scottish Historical Documents; Who's Who in Scottish History; Mary, Queen of Scots; Scotland: The Shaping of a Nation. Contbr. to jrnls. inclng: Scottish Histl. Review; Engl. Histl. Review. Address: Preston Tower Nursery Cottage, Prestonpans, E. Lothian EH32 9EN, UK.

DONCEV-KORALOV, Emil, pen name KORALOV, Emil, b. 2 Nov. 1906, Mihailovgrad, Bulgaria. Writer. Publs: Septembrists, 1945; Reflections in the Maritsa, 1951; Fellow Travellers, 1954; Restless Chronicle, 1958; The Plane-Trees Rustled, 1965; Neon Suns, 1969; Everyone has his Day, 1962. Contbr. to sev. Bulgarian mags. & newspapers. Mbrships: Union of Bulgarian Writers; PEN. Hons: Dimitrov Prize, 1952; Honoured Cultural Worker, 1967. Address: Sofia, bul. Smirnenski 2, Bulgaria.

DONCHEV, Anton, b. 14 Sept. 1930, Bourgas, Bulgaria. Writer. Publs: (in Bulgarian) Awakening (co-author), 1956; A Tale from the Time of Samouil, 1964; Time of Parting (Engl. transl.), 1967; (books for children) The Leader of the Invisible Army, 1967; The Charter. Contbr. to sev. Bulgarian lit. mags. inclng. September (Ed. Bd.). Mbr.,

Union of Bulgarian Writers. Hons: Prize, Union of Bulgarian Writers, 1961; Dimitrov Prize, 1966. Address: Sofia, ul. Geo. Milev 23, Bulgaria.

DONELSON, Irene W(itmer), (Mrs. Kenneth W.), b. 5 Mar. 1913, Placerville, El Dorado, Calif., USA. Freelance Writer; Lecturer. Educ: A.A., Univ. of Calif., Berkeley, 1932; further studies, Sacramento City Coll., 1933-34; McGeorge Schl. of Law, Univ. of Pacific, 1949-51. Publs: (w. Kenneth W. Donelson) When You Need a Lawyer, 1964; How to Handle Your Legal Problems, 1965; Married Today, Single Tomorrow: Marriage Breakup & the Law, 1969; Your Child & the Law (in preparation). Contbr. to: Coronet; Med. Econs.; Rdr.'s Digest; Signature; Mod. Maturity; etc. Mbrships. incl: Authors' League of Am.; Authors' Guild; Soc. of Mag. Writers; Calif. Writers' Club. Recip., Woman with a View Award, Copley Newspapers, 1972. Address: 2525 H St., Apt. 4, Sacramento, CA 95816, USA.

DONKER RUTGERS, Ingeborg Maria Anna, pen name I.M.A.R., b. 7 Jan. 1912, Tubbergen, Netherlands. Journalist; Public Relations Officer. Contbr. to: Algemeen Handelsblad; Haagsecourant; Algemeen Dagblad; Nieuwe Rotterdamse Courant; Volkskrant; De Groene Amsterdammer; Vrij Nederland; Delict en Delinkwent; Proces. Mbrships. incl: Dutch Union of Jrnlsts.; Coornhert Liga; Stichting Kinderhulp Zuid-Holland. Recip., Lit. Prize for Short Story, 1957. Address: 168 Springerstraat, Rotterdam 3014, Netherlands.

DONLEAVY, J. P., b. 1926, N.Y., USA. Writer. Educ: Trinity Coll., Dublin, Repub. of Ireland. Publs: (novels) The Ginger Man, 1955; A Singular Man, 1963; The Saddest Summer of Samuel S, 1966; The Beastly Beatitudes of Balthazar B, 1968; The Onion Eaters, 1971; A Fairy Tale of New York, 1973; The Unexpurgated Code, A Complete Manual of Survival & Manners, 1975; The Plays of J. P. Donleavy, 1972; Meet My Maker, The Mad Molecule (short stories), 1964. Address: Levington Park, Mullingar, Co. Westmeath, Repub. of Ireland.

DONNACHIE, Ian, b. 18 June 1944, Lanark, Scotland, UK. University Lecturer; Editor; Author. Educ: M.A., Univ. of Glasgow; M.Litt., Univ. of Strathclyde. Publs. incl: Industrial History: Scotland, 1968; Industrial Archaeology of Galloway, 1971; War & Economic Growth in Britain 1793-1815, 1973; Old Galloway, 1974; & var. essays. Contbr. to: Indl. Archaeol. (Asst. Ed., 1968—); Transp. Hist.; Explorations in Econ. Hist.; Scotsman; Scotland's Mag.; Scots Mag.; also to TV and radio (histl. progs.). Address: 21 Woodburn Terrace, Edinburgh EH10 4SS, UK.

DONNELLY, Augustine (Austin) Stanislaus, b. 1 June 1923, Port Douglas, Qld., Australia. Managing Director, Financial Company. Educ: B. Com., Univ. of Qld., 1969; & Accounting qualifs. Publs. incl: The Practice of Public Accounting, 1953, 2nd ed., 1961; Guide to Business Management, 1956; Trends in Public Accounting Practice, 1958, 2nd ed., 1964; Financial Management, 1959, 2nd ed., 1968; Profit Through Cost Analysis & Direct Costing, 1965; You & Your Money, 1966; Investing for Profit, 1969; Strategic Investing, 1973. Contbr. to num. jrnls. Mbr., var. profl. orgs. Hons: Aust. Soc. of Accts. Award for textbook Direct Costing, 1958; 1st prize award, Office Execs. Assn. of N.Y., USA. Address: 31 King Arthur Terrace, Tennyson, Qld. 4105, Australia.

DONNELLY, Dorothy, b. 7 Sept. 1903, Detroit, Mich., USA. Writer. Educ: A.B., M.A., Univ. of Mich. Publs: The Bone & the Star, 1944; The Golden Well, 1950; Trio in a Mirror, 1960; God & the Apple of His Eye, 1973. Contbr. to: Transition, Paris; Blackfriars, UK; New Yorker; Hudson Review; Poetry, Chgo.; Commonweal; Am.; Christian Century. Hons: Union League Prize, Poetry, 1954; Harriet Monroe Mem. Award, Poetry, 1957; Longview Fndn. Award, 1957. Address: 612 Lawrence St., Ann Arbor, MI 48104, USA.

DONNER, Jörn, b. 5 Feb. 1933, Helsinki, Finland. Writer; Film Director. Educ: B.A., Helsinki Univ., 1958. Publs. incl: Brev (short stories), 1954; Helsingfors-Finlands ansikte, 1961; Djävulens ansikte, Ingmar Bergmans filmer, 1962; Tapaus Naisenkuvia, 1970; Marina Maria (novel), 1972; Sverigeboken (travels), 1973; Nu Maste du, 1974. Contbr. to: Dagens Nyheter; Arena; etc. Mbr., Artists' Assn. Kiila (Chmn., 1957-58). Hons. incl: for films: Premio Opera Prima, Venice, 1963; Coppa Volpi, Venice, 1964; Finnish State Prize for Lit., 1972, for Sommar av kärlek och sorg. Address: Pohjoisranta 12, SF-00170 Helsinki, Finland.

DONNISON, David Vernon, b. 19 Jan. 1926, Yenangyaung, Burma. Research Worker; Teacher. Educ: B.A., Oxford Univ. Publs: The Neglected Child & the Social Services, 1954; Welfare Services in a Canadian Community, 1958; The Government of Housing, 1965; Social Policy & Administration (co-author), 1967; Social Policy & Administration Revisited, 1975. Recip., Litt.D., Bradford, 1973. Address: 38 Douglas Rd., London N1 2LD, UK.

DONNISON, Frank Siegfried Vernon, b. 3 July 1898, London, UK. Indian Civil Servant (Butma). Educ: M.A., Corpus Christi Coll., Oxford. Publs: Public Administration in Burma, 1953; British Military Administration in the Far East, 1956; Civil Affairs & Military Government, Northwest Europe, 1961; Civil Affairs & Military Government, Central Organization & Planning, 1966; Burma, 1970; Recip., C.B.E., 1943. Address: Lower Cross Farmhouse, East Hagbourne, Didcot, Oxon OX11 9LD, UK.

DONNITHORNE, Audrey Gladys, b. 1922, Santai, Szechuan, W. China. Economist. Educ: W. China Union Univ., Chengtu; M.A., Somerville Coll., Oxford, UK. Publs: Western Enterprise in Far Eastern Economic Development (w. G. C. Allen); China & Japan; Western Enterprise in Indonesia & Malaya (w. G. C. Allen); British Rubber Manufacturing; China's Economic System. Address: Australian National University, Canberra, A.C.T. 2600, Australia.

DONOSO, José, b. 5 Oct. 1924, Santiago, Chile. Novelist. Educ: B.A., Princeton Univ., USA. Publs: Veraneo y otros cuentos, 1955; Coronación, 1957; El Carleston (cuentos), 1959; Este Domingo, 1965; El Lugar sin Limites, 1956; El obsceno pajaro de la noche, 1969; Historia personal del "Boom", 1972; Tres novelitas Burguesas, 1973. Hons: Guggenheim Fellowship (twice); William Faulkner Fndn. Prize (for Coronación); Premio Municipal de Santiago, 1956; Premio Pedro de Oñar, 1971. Address: Calaceite, Provincia de Teruel, Spain.

DOORN, Jacoba Henriëtte, pen name DOORN, Jacqueline, b. 24 Jan. 1920, Zürich, Switz. Writer. Educ: mod. langs., Lausanne Univ.; psychol., Free Univ., Amsterdam. Publs: (novels) Grotemensen dromen niet, 1964; De Bedelaar en het Brood, 1973; (biographies) Mary Stuart (1631-1660) Een omstreden Prinses van Oranje, 1966; De Vrouw van de Stadhouder-Koning, Mary Stuart (1662-1694), 1968; Rusland en Oranje, 1974, 2nd ed., 1974. Contbr. to var. jrnls. Mbr., Vereniging van Letterkundigen Vakbond voor Schrijvers. Recip., Kosmos Eerstelingen Prijs, 1963, for Grotemensen dromen niet. Address: Parklaan 20, Bussum, Netherlands.

DOPPAGNE, Albert (Désiré Antoine), b. 29 June 1912, Leige, Belgium. University Professor. Educ: Dr. Philosophie et Lettres; Lic., Philologie romane; Lic., Histoire de l'art et archéologie. Publs: incl: Trois aspects du francais contemporain, 1966; Chasse aux belgicismes (co-author), 1971; Les Grands Feux, 1972; Nouvelle chasse aux belgicismes (co-author), 1974. Contbr. to: Langue et Administration, Brussels; La Banque des mots, Paris, France, et Linguistica Antverplana, Anvers; L'Ethnie francaise, Brussels, etc. Mbrships. incl: Comm. Royale belge de Folklore; Soc. royale de langue et de litterature wallonnes. Hons. incl: Prix de la langue francaise, Academie Francaise, 1969, 1972. Address: Rue Marie-Henriette 62, B-1050 Brussels, Belgium.

DORCY, (Sister) Mary Jean, O. P. (Frances E. Dorcy), pen name BENNETT, Jean Frances, b. 10 Mar. 1914, Anacortes, Wash., USA. Silhouette Artist; Author. Educ: A.B., Gonzaga Univ., Spokane, Wash.; M.F.A., Calif. Coll. Arts & Crafts. Publs. incl: A Shady Hobby, 1944; Mary My Mother, 1945; Our Lady's Feasts, 1945; Hunters of Souls, 1946; Crown for Joanna, 1946; Army in Battle Array, 1947; Our Lady of Springtime, 1953; Shepherd's Tartan, 1953; Fount of Our Joy, 1955; Master Albert, 1955; Our Lady's Shrines, 1956; Mary, 1958; Carrying of the Cross, 1959; St. Dominic, 1960; Never the Golden City, 1962; Saint Dominic's Family, 1964. Contbr. to N.C.W.C. Cath. newspaper syndicate, 20 yrs. Mbrships: Delta Phi Delta; Living Gall. Cath. Authors. Address: P.O. Box 280, Edmonds, WA 98020, USA.

DORMAN, Mary Elizabeth Harris, b. St. Louis, Mo., USA. Commercial Artist; Designer; Newspaper Feature Writer; Cartoonist. Educ: Hardin Coll. for Women; A.A., Kan. City Jr. Coll.; Univ. of Mich. Ext. Courses. Publs: Bitsy Books, 1971; Creative Writer (co-author), 1964; Columns, All About Names, & It's My Kind of Town;

Owner-Pres., Peppercorn Press, Inc., publng. house, 1970-73. Address: P.O. Box 304, Traverse City, MI 49684, USA.

DORSEY, John Morris, b. 19 Nov. 1900, Clinton, Iowa, USA. Psychiatrist; Professor Emeritus. Educ: B.A., M.D., M.S., Intership, Res., Univ. of Iowa; Postgrad. study, Univ. of Vienna & Psychoanalytic Inst. of Vienna. Publs. incl: The Jefferson-Dunglison Letters, 1960; Illness of Allness, 1965; American Government, Conscious Self-Sovereignty, 1969; Psychology of Language, 1971; Psychology of Political Science, 1973; Psychology of Ethics, 1974. Contbr. to health & educ. jrnls. Address: Wayne State Univ., 756 Mackenzie Hall, Detroit, MI 48202, USA.

DORTORT, David, b. 23 Oct. 1916, NYC, USA. Writer; Screenwriter; Novelist; TV & Motion Picture Producer. Educ: B.Sc., Coll. City, N.Y., 1936. Publs: (novels) Burial of the Fruit, 1947; The Post of Honour, 1949. Mbrships: Writers' Guild of Am. (Pres., Radio & TV Branch, 1954-57); Screen Writers' Guild (VP, 1952-54); Prods. Guild of Am. (Pres., 1966-68); The Caucus for Prods., Writers & Dirs. (Chmn., 1973—). Hons. incl: TV Prod. of the Year, 1967, Prods. Guild of Am.; Disting. Guest Prof., Creative Writing, Calif. State Univ., L.A. Address: 133 Udine Way, Bel-Air, L.A., CA 90024, USA.

DORWORTH, Alice Grey, pen name LYNCH, Grey, b. Oil City, Pa., USA. University Professor. Educ: B.S., Edinboro State Coll., Pa., 1939; M.S., Univ. of Pittsburgh, Pa., 1951; Ph.D., N.Y. Univ., 1956. Publs: Testing of Textiles & Non-textiles, 1955; Channels of Distribution of 4 Selected Commodities, 1956; Changeover to Computers of Accounts Receivable & Credit Departments, 1964. Contbr. to: Credit Management Yearbook, 1966. Mbrships. incl: Am. Statistical Assn.; Ops. Rsch. Soc. of Am.; Inst. of Mgmt. Sci. Address: El Mirador del Condado Condominio, 1035 Ashford Ave., Apt. 702, San Juan, PR 00907, USA.

DOUBLE, Daphne Thelma Louisa, pen name HARRIS, Daphne, b. 24 June 1909, Aucland, NZ. Cosmetician; Beauty Consultant; Manageress. Educ: Night schl. (3 yrs. Coll. & 5 yrs. study) in Engl., creative writing, art, elocution, speech & drama, music, debating. Publs: Compiler & Ed., NZ Writers & Publishers Year Book, 1965, 1969. Contbr. to NZ & Aust. newspapers & mags. Mbrships. incl: Past Pres. & Hon. Life, Penwomens Club, NZ. Inc., 1974; Past VP, NZ Playwrights Assn. Inc.; Past, NZ Women Writers Soc. Inc.; Past Organiser, Admstr., NZ. Book of the Yr. Award, 1968-69. Address: 157 Campbell Rd., Onehunga, Auckland 6, NZ.

DOUBTFIRE, Dianne Joan, b. 18 Oct. 1918, Leeds, Yorks., UK. Novelist. Educ: Dip., Slade Schl. of Fine Art; Art Tchrs. Dip., Univ. of London. Publs: Lust for Innocence, 1960; Reason for Violence, 1961; Kick a Tin Can, 1964; The Flesh is Strong, 1966; Behind the Screen, 1969; Escape on Monday, 1970; This Jim, 1974. Contbr. to: Radio Times. Books & Bookmen; Homes & Gardens; Sun; Writer. Mbrships: PEN; Soc. of Authors; Nat. Book League. Address: Folly Cottage, Ventnor, Isle of Wight, UK.

DOUGALL, Donald, b. 22 Nov. 1920, Rock Ferry, Cheshire, UK. Freelance Journalist; Broadcaster; Television Reporter. Publs: Mr. Scamplin, 1970; Mr. Scrogger's Bull, 1970; Evans' Bach Colt, 1972; Donald Dougall's TV Walkabout, 1974; (TV documentaries) The Changing Village, 1971; End of a Village School, 1972; The London Tugs, 1972; (TV series) Walkabout, 1973; My Kind of Country, 1973. Contbr. to: The Field; Farm; Trout & Salmon; Kent Life; Veterinary Practice; Folkestone Herald; Kentish Gazette; BBC Radio (Today; Woman's Hour). Mbrships: Kent & Canterbury Club.; Guild of Agricl. Jrnlsts. Address: Knowler Farm, Stelling Minnis, Canterbury, Kent, UK.

DOUGALL, Robert, b. 1913, Croydon, Surrey, UK. Freelance Writer & Broadcaster; Former BBC Television & Radio Newscaster, 1933-73. Publs: In & Out of the Box, (autobiog.), 1973. Contbr. to: Daily Mail; Sunday Express; Spectator. Mbrships: Royal Soc. for the Protection of Birds (Pres.); Royal Soc. for Lit. Recip., M.B.E. Agent: Dorothea Benson, Myddleton Agcy. Address: 4 Spaniards End, Hampstead, London NW3, UK.

DOUGLAS, Daniel Ord, b. 15 Oct. 1925, Newcastle upon Tyne, UK. College Lecturer. Educ: B.A., King's Coll., Univ. of Durham. Publs: (TV films & progs.) The Romance of Durham; Spinning the Yarn; Shakespeare's

Quatercentenary; 25 Years of Radar; Town Within a City; All the World's Their Stage; Crossroads; No Surrender; Discovering London; This Is Your Life; The Communicators; Something to Sing About; The Freewheelers; Great Occasions. Contbr. to: Times Educl. Supplement. Mbr., Writers' Guild of GB. Recip., Bronze Delfan, for 'Children Are People', 10th Int. Educl. Film Festival, Teheran, 1973. Address: 33 White Oak Drive, Beckenham, Kent, UK.

DOUGLAS, David Charles, b. 1898, London, UK. Professor of History; Author. Educ: M.A., Keble Coll., Oxford; Dr. de l'Univ., Caen, France. Publs: Social Structure of Medieval East Anglia; Feudal Documents from the Abbey of Bury St. Edmunds; English Scholars, 1939, 1951; Rise of Normandy, 1947; Gen. Ed., English Historical Documents, 1953. Contbr. to: Engl. Hist. Review; Times Lit. Supplement; etc. Mbrships: F.B.A.; Trustee, London Mus. Hons: Fellow, Keble Coll., Oxford; James Tait Black Prize, for English Scholars, 1939. Address: c/o Oxford & Cambridge Club, 71 Pall Mall, London SW1, UK.

DOUGLAS, Henry Russell, b. 1925, Bishopbriggs, Lanarks., UK. Journalist. Educ: M.A., Lincoln Coll., Oxford. Contbr. to: Liverpool Daily Post (Ldr. Writer, 1956-58; Asst. Ed., 1958-69); The Sun (Writer, 1969—); Liverpool Echo. Mbrships: F.J.I.; Inst. of Jrnlsts. (Pres., 1972-73); Press Coun.; The Media Soc. (Fndr. mbr. & 1st Treas.); United Oxford & Cambridge Club. Address: Austen Croft, 31 Austen Rd., Guildford, Surrey, UK.

DOUGLAS, Lloyd Virgil, b. 4 Aug. 1902, Brandon, Iowa, USA. Educator; Writer. Educ: B.S., M.A., Ph.D., Univ. of Iowa; LL.B., Blackstone Inst. of Law. Publs: Modern Business, 1948; The Business Education Program in the Expanding Secondary School, 1957; Teaching Business Subjects, 1958, 3rd ed., 1973; Business Education, 1963. Contbr. to: Jrnl. of Bus. Educ.; Am. Bus. Educ. Digest; Am. Bus. Educ. Yrbooks.; Bus. Tchrs. & num. other profl. publs. Mbrships. incl: Nat. Bus. Educ. Assn. (Past & Nat. Pres.); N. Ctrl. Bus. Educ. Assn. (Past Pres.); Iowa Bus. Educ. Assn. (Past Pres.); etc. Recip., num. profl. & acad. awards. Address: 1114 W. 19th St., Cedar Falls, IA 50613, USA.

DOUGLAS-HAMILTON, (Lord) James Alexander, b. 1942, Strathaven, Lanarkshire, UK. Member of Parliament. Educ: Balliol Coll., Oxford; Edinburgh Univ.; M.A., LL.B. Publs: Motive for a Mission: The Story Behind Hess's Flight to Britain, 1971. Contbr. to Jrnl. of Contemporary Hist. Mbrships: Edinburgh Town Coun., 1972-74; Hon. Pres., Scottish Amateur Boxing Assn.; New Club, Edinburgh. Agent: Peter Janson-Smith. Address: 3 Blackie House, Lady Stair's Close, Edinburgh, UK.

DOUGLAS-HOME, Charles, b. 1937, London, UK. Journalist. Publs: The Arabs & Israel, 1968; Britain's Reserve Forces, 1969; Rommel, 1973. Contbr. to: Daily Express (Pol. & Diplomatic Corres., 1962-64); The Times (Defence Corres., 1964-70, Features Ed., 1970-73, Home Ed., 1973—); BBC; Times Lit. Supplement. Mbrships. incl: Int. Inst. Strategic Studies; Royal Inst. Int. Affairs; Nat. Union of Jrnlsts. Agent: Curtis Brown. Address: The Times, P.O. Box 7, New Printing House Square, Gray's Inn Rd., London WC1X 8EZ, UK.

DOUGLASS, Paul, b. 7 Nov. 1904, Corinth, N.Y., USA. Lawyer. Educ: A.B., LL.D., Wesleyan Univ.; M.A., Ph.D., Univ. of Cinn.; studies at Univ. of Chgo.; Univ. of Berlin, Germany. Publs. incl: Practice & Procedure, Minor Courts, 1939; Story of German Methodism, 1939; Communication through Reports, 1957; How to Be an Active Citizen, 1961; New Towns, 1962. Contbr. to: Ency. Americana; Book Reviewer, Orlando Sentinel. Mbr., Nat. Press Club. Address: P.O. Box 199, W. Pawlet, VT 05775, USA.

DOUGLASS, Raymond Donald, b. 29 Dec. 1894, Gorham, Me., USA. Professor of Mathematics. Educ: A.B., 1915, A.M., 1916, Sc.D., 1941, Univ. of Me.; Ph.D., MIT, 1931; Publs: Analytic Geometry, 1950; Calculus & Its Applications, 1950; Nomographic Charts, 1950. Contbr. of chapts. to Ency. of Science & Technology, & Plant Engineering Handbook; Articles in mathl. jrnls. Address: 18 Oak Ave., Belmont, MA 02178, USA.

DOVER, Irene Amelia, b. 28 Aug. 1907, Hoddesdon, Herts., UK. Protestant Missionary; Deputationist. Educ: Bible Coll., Sydney; Missionary Bible Coll., Aust. Publs: Little Brown Boy for God, 1943; Little Brown Girl (1950's); It Happened in Western India (1950's); Pathway

Through India, 1962; Stories from India, 1967. Contbr. to: Darkness & Light (Present Ed.). Address: Rosebank, 37 Oceana Parade, Austinmer, N.S.W. 2514, Australia.

DOW, Marguerite Ruth, b. 13 June 1926, Ottawa, Ont., Can. Professor of English & Drama. Educ: B.A., Univ. Coll., Toronto Univ., 1949; B.Ed., Coll. of Educ., ibid, 1971; M.A., Schl. of Grad. Studies, ibid, 1970; Sr. Cert. in Drama, Banff Schl. of Fine Arts, Univ. of Alberta, 1956; Cert., Drama, Schl. of Fine Arts, Queen's Univ., 1955. Publs: The Magic Mask, 1966; Ed., Light from Other Windows, 1964; Co-author, Courses of Study in the Theatre Arts, 1969; Contbr., Drama Activities, 1971. Contbr. to jrnls. & textbooks. Address: 1231 Richmond St., Apt. 909, London, Ont. N6A 3L9, Can.

DOWNEY, Fairfax Davis, b. 28 Nov. 1893, Salt Lake City, Utah, USA. Writer. Educ: A.B., Yale Univ., 1916. Publs. incl: Our Lusty Forefathers; Horses of Destiny; The Guns at Gettysburg; Louisbourg: Key to a Continent; Fife, Drum & Bugle; The Red Bluecoats; Burton, Arabian Nights Adventurer; When We Were Rather Older; Mascots; Famous Horses of the Civil War; Great Dog Stories of All Time (ed.). Contbr. to: Reader's Digest; Am. Heritage; Saturday Evening Post; Smithsonian Mag.; Yankee; Army Mag. Mbrships. incl: Fellow, Co. of Mil. Histns.; Authors Guild. Recip., Class Secs. Prize for 25-Yr. Book. Address: W. Springfield, NH 03284, USA.

DOWNIE, Mary Alice Dawe, b. 12 Feb. 1934, Alton, Ill., USA. Freelance Writer. Educ: B.A.(Hons.), Univ. of Toronto. Publs: The Wind Has Wings: Poems from Canada (compiled w. Barbara Robertson), 1968; Honor Bound (w. John Downie), 1971; Scared Sarah, 1974; The Magical Adventures of Pierre. Hons: Province of Ont. Coun. for Arts Award, 1971-72; Can. Coun. Arts Bursary, 1972-73. Address: 190 Union St., Kingston, Ont., Can.

DOWNING, Richard Ivan, b. 13 Mar. 1915, Melbourne, Australia. University Professor; Chairman, Broadcasting Commission. Educ: B.A., Univ. of Melbourne; Dip. Econs., Univ. of Cambridge, UK. Publs: National Income & Social Accounts, 1970; The Australian Economy, 1973. Contbr. to var. acad. jrnls. Mbrships: Fellow, Acad. of Soc. Scis. in Aust. (Past Pres.); Chmn., Ormond Coll. Coun.; Chmn., Aust. Ballet Schl.; Trustee, Nat. Gall. of Vic.; Dir., Melbourne Theatre Co. Address: Yarra Braes Rd., Eltham, Vic. 3095, Australia.

DOYLE, Paul A., b. 6 Dec. 1925, Carbondale, Pa., USA. College Professor; Literary Critic. Educ: A.B., Univ. of Scranton, 1946; A.M., 1948, Ph.D., 1955, Fordham Univ. Publs: Author, 13 books, inclng: Pearl S. Buck: A Critical Study, 1965; Sean O'Faolain: A Critical Introduction, 1968; Paul Vincent Carroll: A Study, 1971; Evelyn Waugh: A Checklist of Primary & Secondary Material, 1972. Contbr. to num. US, for. jrnls.; Ed.-in-Chief, Evelyn Waugh Newsletter; Ed., Nassau Review; Contbng. Ed., Best Sellers; Rsch. Cons., English Literature in Transition. Address: 161 Park Ave., Williston Park, NY 11596, USA.

DRABBLE, John Frederick, b. 8 May 1906, Conisbrough, Yorks., UK. Retired Circuit Judge. Educ: M.A., Downing Coll., Cambridge; Q.C. Publs: Death's Second Self, 1971. Contbr. to: Nova; Newcastle upon Tyne Jrnl.; E. Anglian Daily Times. Mbrships: Chmn., Penal Affairs Comm.; Soc. of Friends. Address: St. Mary's Martlesham, Woodbridge, Suffolk, UK.

DRABBLE, Margaret, b. 1939, Sheffield, UK. Author. Educ: B.A., Newnham Coll., Cambridge. Publs: A Summer Birdcage; The Garrick Year; The Milestone; Jerusalem the Golden; The Waterfall. Address: c/o Weidenfeld & Nicolson, 5 Winsley St., London W1, UK.

DRACKETT, Phil, pen name KING, Paul, b. 1922, Finchley, Middx., UK. Journalist; Press & Public Relations Director. Publs. incl: Veteran Cars, 1961; Vintage Cars, 1962; Motor Rallying, 1963; Driving Your Car, 1964; Taking Your Car Abroad, 1965; International Motor Racing Book, 1967-70; Slot Car Racing, 1968; Lets Look at Motor Cars, 1966; Like Father Like Son, 1969; Rally of the Forests, 1970; Motor Racing Champions, 1973-74; The Book of the Veteran Car, 1973. Mbrships: Nat. Union of Jrnlsts.; Guild of Motoring Writers; Sports Writers Assn. Agent: Alec Harrison & Assoc. Address: 217 Lauderdale Mansions, London W9, UK.

DRAGE, Charles Hardinge, pen name CHARLES, b. 1897, Thurstaston, Birkenhead, UK. Retired Commander,

Royal Navy. Educ: M.A., Christ Church, Oxford. Publs: Two-gun Cohen; Chindwin to Criccieth; The Amiable Prussian; William King's Profession; General of Fortune; Servants of the Dragon Throne; Family Story; Taikoo; The Poon. Agent. Curtis Brown Ltd. Address: 38 Sheffield Terrace, London W8, UK.

DRAKE, Walter Raymond, b. 2 Jan. 1913, Middlesbrough, UK. Civil Servant; Author. Publs. incl: Gods & Spacemen, 1964; Spacemen in the Ancient East, 1968; Gods & Spacemen in the Ancient East, 1973; Gods & Spacemen in the Ancient West, 1974; Spacemen in the Ancient Past, 1974; Gods & Spacemen in Greece & Rome, 1975; Gods & Spacemen throughout History, 1975. Contbr. to: Flying Saucer Review; Flying Saucers; Clypeus; Lumières dans la nuit; UFO Nachrichten; Japanese Flying Saucer News; etc. Mbrships: Soc. of Authors; Soc. of Civil Serv. Authors. Address: 2 Peareth Grove, Roker, Sunderland, UK.

DRAPER, Alfred Ernest, b. 26 Oct. 1924, London, UK. Journalist; Author. Educ: N.W. London Polytechnic. Publs: Swansong for a Rare Bird, 1970; The Death Penalty, 1972; Smoke Without Fire, 1974; Edward VII, 1975. Contbr. to nat. daily newspapers & periodicals. Mbrships. incl: Ctrl. Criminal Ct. Jrnlsts. Assn.; Crime Writers Assn.; Nat. Union of Jrnlsts. Hons: Runner-up, Macmillan/Panther Crime Novel Competition, 1970. Address: 31 Oakridge Ave., Radlett, Herts., UK.

DRAPER, Peter, b. 28 Apr. 1925, Porthcawl, Wales, UK. Author. Educ: Art Schl. Publs: A Season in Love, 1961; (feature films) The System, 1964; I'll Never Forget What's'isname, 1968; The Buttercup Chain, 1970; over 80 TV plays, 1958—. Address: 1 Summer Lane, Brixham, Devonshire, UK; 155 Sutherland Ave., London W9, UK.

DRAYTON, Charles Geoffrey, b. 1924, Barbados, West Indies. Teacher; Journalist. Educ: M.A., Corpus Christi Coll., Cambridge, UK. Publs: Three Meridians, 1950; Christopher, 1959; Zohara, 1961. Contbr. to: BBC; Listener. Fellow, Inst. of Petroleum. Address: 36 Raglan St., London NW5, UK.

DRESCHER, Seymour, b. 20 Feb. 1934, N.Y., USA. Professor. Educ: B.A., CCNY, 1955; M.S., 1956, Ph.D., Univ. of Wis. Publs: Tocqueville & England, 1964; Tocqueville & Beaumont on Social Reform (ed.), 1968; Dilemmas of Democracy, 1968; Confrontation: Paris 1968 (film, co-prod. w. E. McCreary), 1971. Contbr. to: Am. Quarterly; Jrnl. of Hist. of Ideas; Jrnl. of Am. Hist.; Jewish Soc. Studies; Annales; ESC; Am. Histl. Review; Ency. Britannica. Mbr., profl. orgs. Recip., acad. hons. Address: 5550 Pocusset St., Pitts., PA 15217, USA.

DREWRY, John Eldridge, b. 4. June 1902, Griffin, Ga., USA. University Dean Emeritus (Journalism). Educ: A.B., B.J., A.M., Univ. of Ga. Publs. incl: Some Magazines & Magazine Makers, 1924; Contemporary American Magazines, 1938; Magazine Journalism: A Selected Bibliography, 1948; Journalism Enters a New Half-Century, 1951; Are We Communicating?, 1959; A Foreward Look for Communications, 1967; New Heights for Journalism, 1969. Contbr. to profl. & gen. mags.; wkly. column, Athens (Ga.) Banner-Herald, Atlanta Constitution; etc. Mbrships. incl. var. offs., Nat. Ed. Assn.; Int. Coun. of Indl. Eds. Hons. incl: Gold Key Award, Columbia Scholastic Press Assn.; Pres. Award, Ga. Press Assn.; Hon. Life Mbr., Int. Coun. of Indl. Eds. Address: 447 Highland Ave., Athens, GA 30601, USA.

DRINKWATER, Francis Harold, b. 1886, Wednesbury, Staffs., UK. Parish Priest. Educ: Cotton Coll.; Oscott. Publs: Telling the Good News; Educational Essays; Teaching the Catechism; Catechism Stories; Two Hundred Evening Sermon Notes; Seven Addresses on Social Justice; Birth Control & Natural Law; The Question of God; Our Lord's Church & Her Message; Abbreviated Catechism with Explanations. Contbr. to Cath. periodicals in UK & abroad. Agent: Brian B. Cooper, 20 Tarworth Rd., Sutton Coldfield. Address: Aston Hall, Aston-by-Stone, Staffs. ST15 0BJ, UK.

DROR, Yehezkel, b. 12 Aug. 1928, Vienna, Austria. Professor of Political Science & Public Administration. Educ: B.A., Hebrew Univ., Jerusalem; Magister Juris, ibid.; LL.M., Harvard Univ.; S.J.D., ibid. Publs. incl: Israel – High Pressure Planning (co-author), 1966; Public Policy-making Re-examined, 1968; Design for Policy Sciences, 1971; Ventures in Policy Sciences, 1971; Crazy States – A Counterconventional Strategic Problem, 1971; Diseases of Politics, forthcoming. Contbr. to: Assoc. Ed., Policy Scis.; Ed. Bd., Futures; Ed. Bd., Technol. Forecasting; Cons. Ed., Policy Scis. Book Series. Hons: Eliashiv Prize, 1957; Rosolio Prize, 1965; Levi Eshkol Prize, 1972. Address: 48 Shimoni Street, Jerusalem, Israel.

DRUCKER, Andre, b. 15 Mar. 1909, Strakonice, Bohemia. Educ: Vienna. Publs: Ach! To Be In England, 1957; A Crust of Bread, Etc., 1957; Tallula the Taxi, 1961; Little Men in a Blind Alley, 1973. Contbr. to BBC & newspapers. Address: 35 Ellesboro Rd., Harborne, Birmingham B17 8PU, UK.

DRUKS, Herbert, b. 1937, Vienna, Austria. Professor of History & International Affairs; Author. Educ: B.A., City Coll., 1958; M.A., Rutgers Univ., 1959; Ph.D., N.Y. Univ., 1964. Publs: Harry S. Truman & the Russians, 1967; From Truman through Johnson, 1971. Contbr. to: E. Europe Mag. (Assoc. Ed.). Address: P.O. Box 164, Jackson Heights, NY 11372, USA.

DRUMMOND, Humphrey, pen name ap EVANS, Humphrey, b. 18 Sept. 1922, Old Buckenham, Norfolk, UK. Educ: Trinity Coll., Cambridge. Publs: Falconry for You, 1960; Falconry in the East, 1968; Le Grand Duc, 1968; Our Man in Scotland, 1969; The Queen's Man, 1970; Falconry, 1974. Mbrships: Chmn., Scotland, Author's Sco.; PEN. Address: Megginch Castle, Errol, Perthshire, UK.

DRUON, Maurice Samuel Roger Charles, b. 1918, Paris, France. Author. Educ: Schl. of Political Sci., Faculty of Letters, Paris. Publs. incl: (novels) La Dernière Brigade, 1946; La Volupté d'Etre, 1954; Les Rois Maudits, 6 vols., 1955-60; Les Memoires de Zeus, vol. 1, L'Aube des Dieux, 1963; (short stories) Des Seigneurs de la Plaine, 1962; Le Bonheur des Uns, 1967; (essays) Lettres d'un Européen, 1944; L'Avenir en désarroi, 1968; (plays) Mégarée, 1942; Un Voyageur, 1954. Mbr., Acad. Française. Hons: Prix Goncourt, 1948; Prix de Monaco, 1966. Address: c/o Inst. de France, 23 quai de Conti, Paris 6e, France.

DRURY, Allen (Stuart), b. 2 Sept. 1918, Houston, Tex., USA. Political Correspondent. Educ: B.A., Stanford Univ., Calif., 1939. Publs: (novels) Advise & Consent, 1959; A Shade of Difference, 1962; That Summer, 1965; Capable of Honor, 1966; Preserve & Protect, 1968; The Throne of Saturn, 1971; (other) A Senate Journal, 1943-45, 1963; Three Kids in a Cart: A Visit to Ike & Other Diversions, 1965; "A Very Strange Society": A Journey to the Heart of South Africa, 1967; Courage & Hesitation: Notes & Photographs of the Nixon Administration, 1971. Hons: Pulitzer Prize, for fiction, 1960; Lit.D., Rollins Coll., Winter Pk., Fla., 1961. Address: c/o DruKill Co., Box 927, Maitland, FL 32751, USA.

DRUTEL, Marcelle Louise Marie, pen name L'AUBANELENCO, b. 24 May 1897, Marseilles, France. Writer in Langue d'Oc (dialects of Southern France). Publs: Li Desiranço, 1933; D'un Jardin, 1938; Intermezzo, 1963; De Souleù emai de luno, 1965; Li Mountjoio, 1967; Plang e Serventès, 1969; Jóusè d'Arbaud, 1971. Contbr. to: La Revue des Pays d'Oc; Calendau; Armana Prouvençau; Armana Marsihés; Lou Bartavèu; Oc; Lou Liame; Lo Gai Saber; Lou Rampau d'Oulivié. Mbrships: PEN; Felibrige; Provencal Acad. Num. hons. incl: Acad. Prize, 1947; Fabien Artigue Prize, 1958; Mireille Prize, 1959; Professorship of Letters. Address: Lou Paredoun, Ave. Pothonnier, 83.390 Cuers, France.

DUA, Ramprakash, b. 6 Oct. 1931, Kotli Loharan E., Dist. Sialkot, Pakistan. History Lecturer; Author. Educ: M.A., Pănjab Univ., Chandigarh, India, 1955; Ph.D., Indian Schl. Int. Studies, 1970. Publs: Impact of Russo-Japanese War (1905) on Indian Politics, 1966; Social Factors in the Birth & Growth of Indian National Congress Movement, 1885-1935, 1967; Anglo-Japanese Relations during First World War, 1972. Contbr. to: India Quarterly; Proceedings of Indian Hist. Congress. Address: 29 Benarsi Dass Estate, Lucknow Rd., Delhi 110007, India.

DUARTE, Paulo, b. 1899. Writer; Journalist; Anthropologist. Educ: Inst. Champagnat, France; Fac. of Law, São Paulo; Inst. d'Ethnologie & Musée de l'Homme, Paris. Publs. incl: Prisão, Exilio et Luta, 1945; Palmares pelo Avesso, 1947; Trilussa, 1955; O Espirito das Catedrais, 1958; Paul Rivet, por ele mesmo, 1960; O resto não é silencio, 1966; O Sambaqui Visto atraves de alguns Sambaquis, 1968. Contbr. to periodicals inclng: Anhambi (Fndr.). Mbr., Pres., Soc. of Writers. Address: Cuidade Universitaria, caixa Postal II.133, São Paulo, Brazil.

DUBOIS, Elfrieda Theresia, b. 1916, Vienna, Austria. Senior Lecturer; University Reader in French. Educ: M.A., D.Phil., D. es L.; Univ. of Vienna; Univ. of Birmingham, UK. Publs: Portrait of Leon Bloy, 1950; Ed., Essays presented to C. M. Girdlestone, 1960; Eighteenth Century Studies, 1969; Rapin: Reflections sur la Poetique, 1970; Critical Edition of Rotrou: Saint-Genest, 1973. Contbr. to: Claudel: A Reappraisal; The Art of The Librarian; Bulletin de la Soc. d'Etude du XVII Siècle; Durham Univ. Jrnl.; Erasmus. Address: 82 Newlands Road, Newcastle upon Tyne NE2 3NU, UK.

DU BROFF, Sidney, b. 18 July 1929, Chgo., Ill., USA. Author; Journalist. Educ: L.A. City Coll. Publs: Woe to the Rebellious Children, 1967; Black Fuse, 1975. Contbr. to: London Times; Guardian; Nation; Congress Bi-Weekly. Mbr., Brit. Soc. of Authors. Recip., 2nd Prize, Golden Hedgehog Int. Lit. Contest. Address: 7 The Corner, Grange Rd., London W5 3PQ, UK.

DUCE, Robert, b. 18 Dec. 1908, Maldon, Essex, UK. Minister of Religion; Playwright; TV & Radio Scriptwriter. Educ: City & Guilds Coll.; New Coll., London; B.Sc. Publs: Reflections of Flying Officer; Take-Off, 1951; Steps in Bible Drama, 1958; The Cross & the Sceptre (play), 1959; Hong Kong Adventure (play), 1960; Fire Over the City (play), 1962; Var. other short plays. Recip., D.D., Yankton Coll., USA, 1972. Address: 4 Dearmer House, 11 St. Alban's Ave., Bournemouth BH8 9EF, UK.

DUCHÉ, Jean, b. 17 Mar. 1915, Chabanais, Charente, France. Writer. Educ: M.A. in Law & Lit. Publs: I Said to My Wife; Not at Home; The History of France as Told to Juliette; Histoire du Monde, 5 vols.; Pecus; Le premier sexe. Mbr., S.G.D.L., Paris. Hons: Prix de l'humour, 1951; Chevalier de la Légion d'Honneur. Address: Manoir de Remauville, 77140 Nemours, France.

DUCKHAM, Alec Narraway, b. 23 Aug. 1903, London, UK. Specialist in Food & Agriculture; Writer. Educ: M.A., Dip. in Agric., Cambridge Univ. Publs: Animal Industry in the British Empire, 1932; American Agriculture, 1952; The Fabric of Farming, 1958; Agriculture Synthesis: The Farming Year, 1963; Farming Systems of the World (w. G. B. Masefield), 1970. Contbr. to agricl. & sci. papers to num. jrnls. Mbrships: Fellow, Inst. of Biol.; Agricl. Econs. Soc.; Nutrition Soc. Hons: O.B.E., 1945; C.B.E., 1950. Address: Studio Cottage, Didcot Rd., Blewbury, Oxon. OX11 9NP, UK.

DUCKHAM, Baron Frederick, b. 20 May 1933, Leeds, Yorks., UK. University Senior Lecturer in History. Educ: Univs. of Manchester & Leeds; B.A.; M.A.; Dip.Ed. Publs. incl: Yorkshire Ports & Harbours — A Short Historical Guide, 1967; The Yorkshire Ouse, 1967; A History of the Scottish Coal Industry 1700-1815, 1970; Great Pit Disasters: Britain 1700 to the Present Day (w. Helen Duckham), 1973; Learning About Land Transport, 1975. Contbr. to var. histl. & other jrnls. Mbrships: Fellow, Royal Histl. Soc.; Econ. Hist. Soc.; Histl. Assn. Recip., David Forsyth Prize, Leeds Univ., 1955. Address: c/o Dept. of History, Univ. of Strathclyde, Glasgow W1, UK.

DUCKWORTH, Marilyn, b. 10 Nov. 1935, Otahuhu, New Zealand. Writer. Educ: Queen Margaret Coll., Wellington, NZ; Victoria Univ., Wellington, NZ. Publs: A Gap in the Spectrum, 1959; The Matchbox House, 1960; A Barbarous Tongue, 1962; Over the Fence is out, 1969. Contbr. to: NZ Listener; Landfall; Mate. Mbrships: PEN. Hons: NZ Lit. Fund. Schlrship. in Letters, 1961 & 1972; Award for Achievement, 1962. Address: 27 Rimu Road, Kelburn, Wellington, New Zealand.

DUCREUX, Louis Raymond, b. 22 Sept. 1911, Marseille, France. Director of The Opera at Nancy; Former Director of Opera, Marseille & Monte-Carlo. Publs. incl: (plays) La Part du Feu, 1943; Les clefs du ciel, 1945; Un Souvenir d'Italie, 1946; L'Amour en papier, 1952; La Folie, 1960; (opera) L'Héritière. Hons: Officier de la Legion d'Honneur; Officier des Arts et Lettres. Address: Grand Theatre, 1 Rue Ste. Catherine, 54000 Nancy, France.

DUDINSTEV, Vladimir Dmitrievich, b. 29 June 1918, Kupyansk, Ukraine. Writer. Educ: Moscow Legal Inst. Publs: With Seven Brothers (collected stories), 1952; In His Place, 1954; Not By Bread Alone, 1956; Tales & Stories, 1959; A New Year's Tale, 1960; Stories, 1963; Poplar on the other Bank, 1967. Contbr. to Komsomolshay Pravda, 1946-51. Mbr., Union of Soviet Writers. Address: USSR Union of Writers, Ul. Vorovskogo 52, Moscow, USSR.

DUDLEY, Ernest, b. 1918, Dudley, Worcs., UK. Author; Broadcaster; Teacher; Naturalist. Publs. incl: Series of Dr. Morelle Mystery Novels; Leatherface; The Gilded Lily (biog.); Confessions of a Special Agent; The Scarlett Widow; Monsters of the Purple Twilight; Arthur the TV Cat; Rangi: Highland Rescue Dog; Chance & the Fire-Horses; Rufus, Story of a Fox; For Love of a Wild Thing; Scrap, the Gentle Wildcat; Series, Our Unknown Wild-Life. Contbr. to: BBC Radio & TV; most nat. newspapers; var. mags. Mbrships: Assoc. Mbr., Zool. Soc., London; Crime Writers' Assn.; Soc. of Authors; Nat. Book League. Address: 49 Hallam St., London WI, UK.

DUDLEY, Geoffrey Arthur, b. 8 Jan, 1917, Grantham, UK. Director of Studies. Educ: Univ. of Nottingham, 1935-39; B.A., Univ. of London, 1938. Publs. incl: Dreams, Their Meaning & Significance, 1956; The Right Way to Interpret Your Dreams, 1961; Rapid Reading, 1964; Use Your Imagination, 1965; Dreams — Their Mysteries Revealed, 1969; How to Be a Good Talker (w. Elizabeth Pugh), 1971; How To Interpret Your Dreams Correctly, 1973; Psychogenes Training (w. Georg Fischhof), 1974. Contbr. to: The Psychologist Mag. Address: 1 Thornton Dr., Handforth, Wilmslow, Cheshire SK9 3DA, UK.

DUDLEY-SMITH, (The Venerable) Timothy, b. 1926, Manchester, UK. Archdeacon of Norwich. Educ: M.A., Pembroke Coll., Cambridge. Publs: Christian Literature & the Church Bookstall, 1963; What Makes a Man a Christian, 1966; A Man Named Jesus, 1971. Contbr. to var. Christian periodicals & hymnbooks inclng: Crusade mag. (ed., 1955-59). Mbr., Nat. Book League. Address: Rectory Meadow, Bramerton, Norwich, UK.

DUFF, David Skene, b. 1912, E. Bridgford, Notts., UK. Writer. Publs: (biogs.) The Shy Princess: The Life of H.R.H. Princess Beatrice; The Life Story of H.R.H. Princess Louise, Duchess of Argyll; Edward of Kent: Father of Queen Victoria (w. E. M. Duff); The Life Story of H.R.H. the Duke of Cambridge; Man of God: The Story of a Norfolk Parson; Mother of the Queen; Hessian Tapestry; Victoria in the Highlands; Victorian Travels; Albert & Victoria; Elizabeth of Glamis; Whisper Louise; (novels) Loch Spy; Castle Fell; Traitors Pass. Address: Rookery Farm House, Weybread, Diss, Norfolk, UK.

DUFF, Patrick William, b. 1901, Cambridge, UK. Professor of Law. Educ: M.A., Trinity Coll., Cambridge; Munich Univ., W. Germany; Harvard Law Schl., USA. Publs: Personality in Roman Private Law. Contbr. to: Cambridge Law Jrnl.; Tulane Law Revue; etc. Hons: Fellow, Winchester Coll., UK; Hon. Bencher, Lincoln's Inn. Address: Trinity Coll., Cambridge, UK.

DUFFIELD, Anne, b. 1893, Orange, N.J., USA. Author. Publs. incl: The Lacquer Couch; The Grand Duchess; Come Back Miranda; The Golden Summer; Famietta; Castle in Spain. Address: 10 The Green, Aldbourne, Wilts., UK.

DUFFY, Maureen Patricia, b. 1933, Worthing, UK. Author; former Teacher. Educ: B.A., King's Coll., Univ. of London. Publs: That's How it Was, 1962; The Single Eye, 1964; The Microcosm, 1966; The Paradox Players, 1967; Wounds, 1969; (play) Rites, 1969; (poetry) Lyrics for the Dog Hour, 1968. Address: 24 Sunnyhill Ct., Trebovir Rd., London SW5, UK.

DUKE, Madelaine, pen name DUNCAN, Alex, b. Geneva, Switz. Author. Educ: B.Sc., M.B., Ch.B.; Univs. of St. Andrews & Edinburgh, UK; Univ. of Vienna, Austria; Fellow, Huntingdon Hartford Fndn., USA. Publs. incl: Top Secret Mission; Slipstream; No Passport; No Margin for Error; A City Built to Music; The Sovereign Lords; It's a Vet's Life; The Vet has Nine Lives; Claret Sandwiches & Sin; This Business of Bomfog; The Secret People; The Lethal Innocents; Death of a Holy Murderer, 1975. Contbr. to: Books & Bookmen; var. anthols. of short stories; med. jrnls. Mbrships. incl: Soc. of Authors; PEN. Agent: Murray Pollinger. Address: c/o Mondial Books Ltd., Norman Alexander & Co., 19 Bolton St., Piccadilly, London W1Y 8HD, UK.

DUKE-ELDER, (Sir) Stewart, b. 22 Apr. 1898, Dundee, UK. Ophthalmic Surgeon; Author. Educ: Univs. of St. Andrew's & London; M.A., D.Sc., Ph.D., M.D., LL.D. Publs: Textbook of Ophthalmology, vols. I-VII, 1932-54; System of Ophthalmology, vols. I-XV, 1958-75; Diseases of the Eye, 15th ed., 1970. Contbr. to: Proceedings of Royal Soc.; British Med. Jrnl.; Lancet; British Jrnl. of Ophthalmol.; Am., Can., French Ophthalmol. Jrnls. Hons: G.C.V.O.,

1958; Star of Jordan, 1st Class, 1958; G.C.St.J., 1960; Fothergillian Medal, 1962; Kt., Royal Order of Phoenix of Greece; 8 hon. degrees. Address: 28 Elm Tree Rd., London NW8, UK.

DULBE, Katrina Lidia, b. 21 Mar. 1907, Riga, Latvia. Assistant Professor of Slavic Languages & Literatures. Educ: Tchrs. Cert., Inst. de la Langue Francaise, Riga, 1928; LL.M., Univ. of Latvia Law Schl., 1931; Univ. of Münster, Germany; M.S., 1962; Ph.D., 1970, Schl. of Lang. & Linguistics, Georgetown Univ., USA. Publs: Termination of Leases: Paragraph 4116 of Latvian Civil Law Code, 1937; Study Relative to Paragraphs 2393-2400 of Latvian Code of Civil Law, 1937; Some Parallels to Mikhail Bulgakov's Novel The Master & Margarita, 1974. Mbr., var. profl. assns. Address: 2122 Massachusetts Ave., N.W., Apt. 708, Wash. DC 20008, USA.

DULLES, John W. F., b. 20 May 1913, Auburn, N.Y., USA. Teacher. Educ: A.B., Princeton Univ., 1935; M.B.A., Harvard Univ.; B.S.Met.E., 1943, Met.Eng., 1951, Univ. of Ariz.; Advanced Mgmt. Prog., Harvard, 1952. Publs: Yesterday in Mexico: A Chronicle of the Revolution, 1961. Vargas of Brazil: A Political Biography, 1967; Unrest in Brazil: Political-Military Crises, 1955-64, 1970; Anarchists & Communists in Brazil, 1900-1935, 1974. Contbr. to histl. reviews. Address: Box 7934 Univ. Stn., Austin, TX 78712, USA.

DU MAURIER, (Dame) Daphne, b. 1907, London, UK. Writer. Publs: The Loving Spirit; I'll Never Be Young Again; Progress of Julius; Gerald; Jamaica Inn; Rebecca; Frenchman's Creek; Hungry Hill; The du Mauriers; The King's General; The Parasites; My Cousin Rachel; Mary Anne; The Apple Tree; The Scapegoat; The Breaking Point; The Glass Blowers; The Flight of the Falcon; Vanishing Cornwall; The House on the Strand; Not After Midnight; Rule Britannia; (plays) Rebecca; The Years Between; September Tide; Castle Dor, 1962. Agent: Curtis Brown. Address: Kilmarth, Par, Cornwall.

DUMBRILLE, Dorothy Martha, (Mrs. J. T. Smith), b. 25 Sept. 1897, Crysler, Ont., Can. Housewife. Publs: Deep Doorways, 1939, reprint 1963; All This Difference, 1941, reprint 1963; Up & Down the Glens, 1944, reprint 1955; Braggart in My Step, 1956; (poetry) We Come, We Come, 1941; Last Leave, 1942; Watch the Sun Rise, 1943; Stairway to the Stars, 1946; The Battle of Crysler's Farm, 1963; A Boy at Crysler's Farm, 1967. Contbr. to: Toronto Globe & Mail (former book reviewer); num. papers & mags. Mbrships: Can. Authors' Assn.; Can. Nat. Inst. for Blind (Exec.); St. Lawrence Parks Commn. Address: Box 522, Alexandria, Ont. K0C 1A0, Can.

DUMITRIU, Petru, b. 1924, Bazias, Romania. Publisher; Editor. Educ: Univ. of Munich. Publs: Euridice, 1947; The Boyars, 1959; Meeting at the Last Judgement, 1961; Incognito, 1962; L'homme aux yeux gris, 1969. Contbr. to: S. Fischer Verlag, Frankfurt, (ed., 1963-67). Mbr., Soc. of Dramatic Authors, Paris. Address: Seilerstrasse 12, Frankfurt am Main, W. Germany.

DUMPLETON, John le Fevre, b. 1924, St. Albans, UK. Former Art Teacher & Schoolmaster; Warden, Teachers' Centres. Educ: St. Albans Schl. of Art; Adv. Dip. in Educ.(Sociol. of Educ.), Univ. of Exeter. Publs: The Art of Handwriting; Teach Yourself Handwriting; The Development of Italic Handwriting; Law & Order; Make Your Own Booklet; Illustrator; Black's Children's Encyclopedia, vol. 8. Address: 28 St. Andrew St., Tiverton, Devon, UK.

DUNBAR, Charles Stuart, b. 1900, Westminster, London, UK. Transport Consultant & Technical Journalist. Publs: Goods Vehicle Operation; Tramways in Wandsworth & Battersea; London Tramway Subway; A.B.C. of Road Haulage; Buses, Coaches & Lorries; Transport Oddities; Buses, Trolleys & Trams; Idealism & Competition: The Fares Policy of the L.C.C. Tramways; Ed., Buses Illustrated, 1949-50; Ed., Passenger Transport, 1961-63. Mbrships: F.C.I.T. Address: 9 Christchurch Rd., Malvern, Worcs. WR14 3BH, UK.

DUNBAR, Janet, b. 15 May 1901, Glasgow, UK. Writer; Broadcaster. Educ: Univ. of London. Publs: Early Victorian Woman, 1953; Golden Interlude, 1955; Flora Robson, 1960; Mrs. G. B. S., 1963; Prospect of Richmond, 1966; Peg Woffington, 1968; J. M. Barrie: The Man Behind the Image, 1970; Laura Knight, 1975. Contbr. to: Woman's Jrnl.; Times. Recip., Scottish Arts Coun. Award for J. M.

Barrie (biog.), 1971. Address: c/o Agent, Curtis Brown Ltd., 1 Crewen Hill, London W2, UK.

DUNBAR, John Greenwell, b. 1930, London, UK. Member of Staff, Royal Commission on Ancient Monuments, Scotland. Educ: M.A., Balliol Coll., Oxford. Publs: The Historic Architecture of Scotland, 1966. Contbr. to archaeol. & histl. jrnls. F.S.A. Address: Patie's Mill, Carlops, By Penicuik, Midlothian, UK.

DUNCAN, Ben (Benjamin Dillard), b. 8 Nov. 1927, Birmingham, Ala., USA. Publications Editor, National Theatre, UK; Director, Cambridge Theatre Company. Educ: B.A., Univ. of N.M., USA; M.A.(Hons.), Christ Ch., Oxford, UK. Publs: The Same Language (autobiog.), 1962; Little Friends (novel), 1965. Contbr. to: Times Educl. Supplement. Address: 11 Mill Lane, Barrington, Cambs. CB2 5QY, UK.

DUNCAN, Ronald Frederick H., b. 1914, Salisbury, Rhodesia. Author; Founder, English Stage Company. Educ: M.A. Publs. incl: (plays) The Death of Satan; The Catalyst; Two Vols. of Autobiography & many other books incl. The Mongrel & Other Poems; The Solitudes; MAN; Selected Writings of Mahatma Gandhi; The Blue Fox; Where I Live; Jan's Journal. Fndr., Devon Festival of the Arts, 1953. Address: Welcombe, Nr. Bideford, Devon, UK.

DUNCAN, William Murdoch, pen names CASSELLS, John; GRAHAM, Neill; MALLOCH, Peter; MARSHALL, Lovat; DALLAS, John, b. 18 Nov. 1909, Glasgow, Scotland, UK. Writer. Educ: M.A., Univ. of Glasgow. Publs: 220 Detective & Mystery works; many transl'd into French, Italian & German. Agent: A. P. Watt & Son. Address: c/o A. P. Watt & Son, 26/28 Bedford Row, London WC1R 4HL, UK.

DUNCAN-KEMP, Alice Monkton, b. 3 June 1901, Charleville, Qld., Australia. Grazier; Writer. Publs: Our Sandhill County, 1928-33; Our Channel County, 1961-62; Where Strange Paths Go Down, 1964; Where Strange Gods Call, 1968; We Lived with a Stone Age People. Mbr., Qld. Country Women's Assn. Address: 7 Davidson St., Oakey 4401, Qld., Australia.

DUNHAM, H. Warren, b. 24 Jan. 1906, Omaha, Neb., USA. Professor of Sociology. Educ: Ph.B., Univ. of Chgo., 1929; M.A., 1935; Ph.D., 1941. Publs: Homeless Men & Their Habitats, 1953; The Culture of the State Mental Hospital, 1960. Sociological Theory & Mental Disorder, 1959; Community & Schizophrenia, 1965; Mental Disorders in Urban Areas (co-author), 1965. Contbr. to: Am. Jrnl Sociol.; Irish Jrnl. of Med. Sci.; Annals of Soc. Psych.; Archives of Gen. Psych.; etc. Mbrships. incl: AAAS; Am. Sociol. Assn.; Mich. Acad. Arts, Scis. & Letters. Hons. incl: Fulbright Schlr., Univ. of Ain Shams, Cairo, Egypt, 1966-67; Rema Lapouse Mental Hlth. Epidemiol. Mem. Award, 1972. Address: 446 Fisher Rd., Grosse Pointe Farms, MI 48230, USA.

DUNHAM, (Sir) Kingsley Charles, b. 2 Jan. 1910, Sturminster Newton, Dorset, UK. Geologist. Educ: B.Sc., Ph.D., Univ. of Durham; M.S., S.D., Harvard Univ. Publs. incl: Geology of the Organ Mountains of New Mexico, 1936; Geology of the Northern Pennine Orefield, vol. I, 1949; Fluorspar, 1952; Geology of Moor House (w. G. A. L. Johnson), 1963; Geology of Northern Skye (w. F. W. Anderson), 1966. Contbr. to: Quarterly Jrnl. of the Geol. Soc.; Geol. Mag.; Mineral Mag.; London News; etc. Mbrships. incl: FRS; FRSE; Fellow, Geol. Soc.; Hon. FIMM; Hon. FGSA. Hons. incl: Hon. D.Sc. from 9 univs.; Kt. Bachelor, 1972. Address: 29 Bolton Gdns., London SW5 0AQ, UK.

DUNMORE, John, b. 6 Aug. 1923, Trouville, France. University Professor. Educ: B.A., Univ. of London; Ph.D., Univ. of NZ. Publs. incl: French Explorers in the Pacific, 2 vols., 1965-69; The Fateful Voyage of the St. Jean Baptiste, 1969; Meurtre a Tahiti, 1971; Norman Kirk, a portrait, 1972; An Anthology of French Scientific Prose, 1973. Contbr. to num. NZ publs.; lit. & histl. jrnls. Mbrships. incl: PEN; Exec., NZ Playwrights Assn.; NZ Prods., Dirs. & Writers Guild. Recip., Sir James Wattie Book of the Yr. Award, 1970. Address: 46 Epsom Rd., Palmerston N., NZ.

DUNN, Charles William, b. 30 Nov. 1915, Arbuthnott, UK. Professor of Celtic Languages & Literatures. Educ: A.B., McMaster Univ., 1938; A.M., 1939, Ph.D., 1948, Harvard Univ. Publs: A Chaucer Reader: Selections from the Canterbury Tales, 1952; The Highland Settler: A

Portrait of the Scottish Gael in Nova Scotia, 1953; The Foundling & the Werewolf: A Literary-Historical Study of Guillaume de Palerne, 1960; Middle English Literature, 1973. Mbrships. incl: Am. Folklore Soc.; Early Engl. Texts Soc.; Irish Texts Soc.; Medieval Acad. of Am. Hons: Can. Award, Fedn. of Arts & Scis.; Chgo. Folklore Prize. Address: 3 De Wolfe St., Cambridge, MA 02138, USA.

DUNN, John Frederick, b. 1905, Ch. Stretton, Salop, UK. Engineer. Educ: C.Eng. Publs: Exposure Meters & Practical Exposure Control, 1952; Exposure Manual, 1958, 3rd ed., 1974. Contbr. to num. engrng. & photog. jrnls. Mbrships: F.I.Mech.E.; F.I.E.E.; A.S.M.E.; F.R.P.S. Address: 1 Deneway, Bramhall, Cheshire SK7 2AR, UK.

DUNN, Peter Norman, b. 1926, Leyton, UK. University Professor of Spanish Literature. Educ: M.A., D.Litt., Univ. of London. Publs: Castillo Solorzano & the Decline of the Spanish Novel, 1952; Ed., Calderon's El alcalde de Zalamea, 1966; Fernando de Rojas & La Celestina, 1975. Contbr. to: Bulletin of Hispanic Studies; Bulletin Hispanique; MLN; Medium Aevum; Romania; Zeitschrift für Romanische Philologie; var. symposia. Mbrships: MLA of Am.; Renaissance Soc. of Am.; Assn. of Hispanists of GB; Acad. of Lit. Studies. Address: 1579 Culver Rd., Rochester, NY 14609, USA.

DUNNER, Joseph, b. 1908, Furth, Germany. Professor of Political Science. Educ: Univs. of Berlin, Frankfurt-Main, Basle, Columbia; M.A., Ph.D. Publs: The Republic of Israel; Democratic Bulwark in the Middle East; Baruch Spinoza & Western Democracy; Handbook of World History; Zu Protokoll Gegeben. Contbr. to: New Ldr.; Nation; Nat. Jewish Monthly; Midwest Jrnl. of Pol. Sci.; Univ. Bookman; Des Moines Register; Koelnische Rundschau; etc. Mbr., Harvard Fac. Club. Address: Yeshiva University, 500 W. 185 St., NY 10033, USA.

DUNNETT, Alastair MacTavish, pen names TAVIS, Alec; SINCLAIR, Duncan, b. 26 Dec. 1908, Kilmacolm, UK. Chairman/Director, Oil Exploration Company (Thomson Scottish Petroleum Ltd.). Publs: Treasure at Sonnach, 1935; Heard Tell, 1946; Quest by Canoe, 1950; Highlands & Islands of Scotland, 1951; The Duke's Day, 1970; Ed., Alistair Maclean Introduces Scotland, 1972; (plays) The Original John Mackay, 1956; Fit to Print, 1962. Contbr. to num. newspapers & mags.; Ed., The Scotsman, 1955-72. Mbrships. incl: Scottish Arts Club; Edinburgh Fest. Soc. Ltd. Hons. incl: Award for Disting. Serv. to Jrnlsm., (to The Scotsman), Univ. of Mo., USA, 1963; Best Newspaper of the Yr. (Scotsman), 1963. Address: 87 Colinton Rd., Edinburgh EH10 5DF, UK.

DUNNETT, Dorothy, pen name HALLIDAY, Dorothy, b. 1923, Dunfermline, UK. Professional Portrait Painter; Writer. Publs: Game of Kings, 1961; Queens' Play, 1964; Disorderly Knights, 1966; Dolly & the Singing Bird, 1968; Pawn in Frankincense, 1969; Dolly & the Cookie Bird, 1970; Dolly & the Doctor Bird, 1971; Ringed Castle, 1971; Dolly & the Starry Bird, 1973; Checkmate, 1975. Mbrships: PEN; Scottish Soc. of Women Artists. Agent: Curtis Brown Ltd. Address: 87 Colinton Rd., Edinburgh EH10 5DF, UK.

DUNNETT, Margaret Rosalind, b. 1909, Tunbridge Wells, UK. Writer. Educ: Dip. in Jrnlsm., London Univ. Publs. (children's novels): The People Next Door, 1961; Has Anyone Seen Emmy, 1968; The Gypsy's Grand-daughter, 1970; Maxamillian, 1972; The Boy Who Saw Emmy, 1973. Contbr. of var. stories to children's periodicals & progs. Mbr., Soc. of Authors. London. Address: Basings Cottage, Furnace Lane, Cowden, Kent, UK.

DUNNING, John Harry, b. 26 June 1927, Sandy, Beds., UK. Esmée Fairbairn Professor of International Investment & Business Studies. Educ: B.Sc.Econ., Univ. Coll., London; Ph.D., Southampton. Publs. incl: American Investment in British Manufacturing Industry, 1958; The Role of American Investment in the UK Economy, 1969; Studies in International Investment, 1970; Problems of the Small Firm in Raising External Finance, 1971; Insurance & the Economy, 1971; US Industry in Britain, 1973; (jt.-author) A New Town in Med-Wales, 1966; The Economics of Advertising, 1967; The City of London: An Economic Study, 1971; (Ed.) Multinational Enterprise, 1971; Readings in International Investment, 1972; The World's Leading Companies, 1974; Economic Analysis & the Multinational Enterprise, 1974. Contbr. to other publs. Address: Univ. of Reading, Whiteknights Park, Reading, UK.

DUNSHEATH, Percy, b. 1886, Sheffield, Yorks., UK. Electrical Engineer. Educ: M.A., Cambridge Univ.; D.Eng.. Sheffield Univ.; D.Sc.(Eng.), LL.D., London Univ. Publs. incl: Graduate in Industry, 1947; The Electric Current, 1951; Century of Technology, 1951; Electricity: How it Works, 1960; History of Electrical Engineering, 1962; Giants of Electricity, 1967. Contbr. to num. articles & papers on educ. & elec. Mbrships: IEE (Pres., 1946-47); Int. Electrotech. Commn. (Pres., 1955-58); Convocation, London Univ. (Chmn., 1949-61). Awarded C.B.E. Address: Sutton Place, Abinger Hammer, Dorking, Surrey, UK.

DUNSTER, Dave Francis Thomas, b. 26 Oct. 1926, London, UK. Lecturer; Writer. Educ: B.Sc. (Phys.), London. Publs: Semiconductors for Engineers, 1969; Dictionary of Semiconductors, 1970. Contbr. to: Electronics & Power; Design Electronics; Electronic Equipment News; Electronic Engrng.; Electronics Wkly.; etc. Mbrships: Instn. of Elec. Engrs. (Chartered Engr.); Inst. of Phys.; F.R.S.A. Address: 16 Landsown Rd., Sidcup, Kent DA14 4EG, UK.

DUNSTERVILLE, Galfrid Clement Keyworth, b. 1905, Bishopsteignton, Devon, UK. Botanist. Educ: B.Sc., Univ. of Birmingham. Publs: Venezuelan Orchids Illustrated (w. L. A. Garay), 6 vols., 1959-75; Introduction to the World of Orchids, 1962. Contbr. to: Orchid Review; Orchid Digest; Am. Orchid Soc. Bulletin. Mbrships: Am. Orchid Soc.; Rsch. Assoc., Harvard Univ. Botan. Mus. Address: Apartado 89658, El Hatillo, Caracas, Z.P. 108, Venezuela.

DUNSTONE, Maxwell Frederick, pen name DUNSTONE, Max, b. 1915, London, UK. Former Customs Officer; Writer. Publs: Cornet of Dragoons, 1960; The Customs Officer, 1970. Contbr. to: Evening News; London Opinion; Reveille; Everybody's; Radio; London Mystery Mag., etc. Mbr., Soc. of Authors. Address: 31 Grimston Ave., Folkestone, Kent CT20 2QD, UK.

DUPONT-SOMMER, André, b. 1900, Marnes-le-Coquette, France. University Professor. Educ: D. ès L., Sorbonne, Paris. Publs: The Dead Sea Scrolls: A Preliminary Survey; The Jewish Sect of Qumran & the Essenes; The Essene Writings from Qumran; and numerous books in French. Contbr. to: Jrnl. Asiatique; Revue des Etudes Juives; etc. Mbrships: l'Institut de France; Secretaire perpétuel de l'Académie des Inscriptions et Belles-Lettres; Socio Straniero della Accademia dei Lincei (Roma); Corres. Mbr., Austrian Acad. of Scis. Address: 25 quai de Conti, Paris VI, France.

DUPRE, Catherine, b. Oxford, UK. Writer. Educ: Lady Margaret Hall, Oxford. Publs: The Chicken Coop, 1967; Jelly Baby, 1968; A Face Full of Flowers, 1969; Matt Jones is Nobody, 1970; The Child of Julian Flynn, 1972. Contbr. to: Sunday Telegraph. Mbr., PEN. Recip., 2nd place, Yorks. Post Best Book of the Yr., 1967. Address: 5 Lambridge, Bath, UK.

DURACK, Mary, b. 20 Feb. 1913, Adelaide, S.A., Australia. Writer. Publs. incl: Child Artists of the Australian Bush. (w. Florence Rutter), 1952; Keep Him My Country, 1955; Kings in Grass Castles, 1959; To Ride a Fine Horse, 1963; The Courteous Savage, 1964; Kookanoo & Kangaroo, 1964; The Ship of Dreams (play), 1968; The Rock & the Sand, 1969; Swan River Saga (play), 1972. Contbr. to: Aust. Dict. of Biog.; Walkabout Mag.; Aust. Broadcasting Commn. Mbrships: Hon. Life, Fellowship of Aust. Writers; Pres., W.A. Br., 1958-63; Aust. Soc. of Authors; Hon. Life, PEN. Hons: O.B.E., 1966; C'wlth Lit. Grant, 1973. Address: 12 Bellevue Ave., Nedlands, W.A. 6009, Australia.

DURANT, Gladys May, b. 13 Sept. 1899, Southend, Prittlewell, Essex, UK. Retired Teacher of Classics. Educ: B.A.(Engl.) & B.A.Hons. (Classics, Ext.), Univ. of London. Publs: Journey Into Roman Britain, 1957; Fires of Revolt, 1957; Discovering Mediaeval Art, 1960; Landscape with Churches, 1965; Britain: Rome's Most Northerly Province, 1969. Mbr., Soc. for Promotion of Roman Studies. Address: 30 Stanley Rd., Broadstairs, Kent CT10 1DA, UK.

DURANT, William James, b. 5 Nov. 1885, North Adams, Mass., USA. Author; Professor of Latin & French. B.A., M.A., Ph.D., Columbia Univ., USA. Publs. incl: Philosophy & the Social Problem, 1917; The Story of Philosophy, 1926; Transition, 1927; Adventures in Genius, 1931; Our Oriental Heritage, 1935; The Life Of Greece, 1939; Caesar & Christ, 1944; The Age of Faith, 1950; The Renaissance, 1953. The Reformation, 1957; The Age of Louis XIV, 1963; The Age of Voltaire, 1965; Rousseau &

Revolution, 1967; Interpretations of Life, 1968; The Story of Civilization, 10 vols. (w. Ariel Durant), 1968. Recip., Pulitzer Prize, 1968. Address: 5608 Briarcliff Rd., L.A., 28, Calif., USA.

DURAS, Marguerite, b. 4 Apr. 1914. Writer. Educ: Grad. in Law, Sorbonne. Publs. incl: Le Ravissement de Lol. V. Stein; La Música (play), 1965, filmed 1967; Les Eaux et les Forêts (play), 1965; Le Vice-Consul, 1966; L'Amante Anglaise, 1967; Yes, peut-être & Le Shaga (2 plays), 1968; Détruire, dit-Elle, 1969; Susanna Andler (play), 1969; Abaha Sabana David, 1971; L'Armour, 1972; Jaune le Soleil (film), 1971; Nathalie Granger (film), 1972; La femme du Gange (film), 1973. Address: 5 rue Saint-Benoit, Paris 6e France.

DURBAND, Alan, b. 1927, Liverpool, UK. College Lecturer & English Department Head. Educ: M.A., Downing Coll., Cambridge. Publs: English Workshop — Books 1, 2 & 3, 1958; New Directions — 5 one-act plays in the modern idiom, 1961; Contemporary English — Books 1 & 2, 1962; Shorter Contemporary English, 1964; New English Books 1-4, 1966-68; Playbill One, Two, Three, 1969; Second Playbill One, Two, Three, 1973. Contbr. to jrnls. inclng: Spectator; Guardian. Mbrships: Soc. of Authors; Chmn., Merseyside Everyman Theatre Co.; Magistrate. Address: White Lodge, Hillside Dr., Woolton, Liverpool, UK.

DURBEN, Maria-Magdalena, b. 8 July 1935, Berlin, Germany. Writer; Editor; Secretary. Educ: Coll. of Educ., Erfurt; Coll. of Educ., Berlin; Mentor for Tchrs. of German Lang., Berlin. Publs: Wenn der Schnee fällt (prose w. Wolfgang Durben), 1974; Ein Stückchen von Gott (dialogue), 1974; Gruss an Taiwan (lyric w. W. Durben), 1974; Unterm Glasnadelzelt (poems), 1975. Co-Ed., UNIO. Contbr. to num. newspapers, lit. reviews, mags. & anthols. Mbrships: Lit. Union (Ctrl. Comm.); United Poets Laureate Int.; Melbourne Shakespeare Soc.; Der Turmnund; Hon. Mbr., Cosmosynthesis League, Guild of Contemporary Bards, Melbourne. Hons: Chmn., 2nd World Congress of Poets, Taipei, Taiwan, 1973; Decretum of Award, ibid., 1973; Prize, ECON Jubilee Competition, Düsseldorf, 1974. Address: D–6639 Beckingen-Saar, Schulstr. 8, W. Germany.

DURBEN, Wolfgang, pen names PASDELOUP, Jean-Marie; GRAF WILLIBALD; WENDOLIN (for art work), b. 12 Aug. 1933, Koblenz, Germany. Educ: Saarbrücken Univ.; Sorbonne Univ., Paris, France; Cambridge Univ., UK. Publs. incl: Harte Lichter (poetry), 1956; Was ist ein Gedicht? (critical essay), 1971; Manifesto for 2nd World Congress of Poets, 1973; Recolte de Patates et d'Etoiles (French poems), 1974; Wenn der Schnee fällt (w. M.-W. Durben, q.v.), 1974; Gruss an Taiwan, 1974; Ed., series "Schüler schreiben (freiwillig)", "Elèves Ecrivains". Contbr. to: UNIO (Fndr. & Co-Ed., 1963—); num. other lit. jrnls. Mbrships. incl: Lit. Union (Pres., 1956—); World Poetry Soc. Intercontinental; United Poets Laureate Int. Hons. incl: Prizes for Radio Plays, Bonn, 1969, 1970; Decretum of Award, 2nd World Congress of Poets, Taiwan, 1973; World Poetry Prize, ibid.; Doct., World Univ., Sao Paulo, Brazil, 1974. Address: D-6639 Beckingen/Saar, Schulstr. 8, W. Germany.

DURBRIDGE, Francis, b. 1912, Hull, UK. TV Producer. Educ: Birmingham Univ. Publs: Portrait of Alison; World of Tim Frazer; A Time of Day; The Scarf; My Wife Melisa, 1967; Another Woman's Shoes, 1968; Paul Temple & the Kelby Affair, 1970. Contbr. to: Radio Times; Evening News; Daily Mail; Birmingham Post; TV plays broadcast & televised in over 16 countries. Address: 14 Beamont Mews, London W1, UK.

DURDEN, Robert Franklin, b. 10 May 1925, Twin City, Ga., USA. Professor of History. Educ: A.B., 1947, M.A., 1948. Emory Univ.; Ph.D., Princeton Univ., 1952. Publs: James Shepherd Pike: Republicanism & The Americam Negro, 1850-1882, 1957; Reconstruction Bonds & 20th-Century Politics: South Dakota v. North Carolina, 1962; The Climax of Populism: The Election of 1896, 1965; The Gray & The Black: The Confederate Debate on Emancipation, 1972. Contbr. to num. histl. jrnls. Winner, Jules F. Landry Award for Best Book in Southern History or Lit., 1972; James Pinckney Harrison Vis. Prof. of Hist., Wm. & Mary Coll., 1970-71. Address: Dept. of History, Duke Univ., Durham, NC 27706, USA.

DURGNAT, Raymond Eric, pen name Green, O. O., b. 1 Sept. 1932, London, UK. Author; Professor. Educ: M.A.,

Cambridge. Publs: Nouvelle Vague — The First Decade, 1963; Greta Garbo, 1965; Luis Bunuel, 1967; Films & Feelings, 1967; Franju, 1968; The Crazy Mirror, 1969; A Mirror for England, 1970; Jean Renoir, 1974; The Strange Case of Alfred Hitchcock, 1974; Sexual Alienation in the Cinema, 1974; Durgnat on Film, 1975. Contbr. to: Art & Artists; Films & Filming; Film Comment; Books & Bookmen. Agent: Campbell, Thompson & MacLaughlin. Address: 84 St. Thomas's Rd., Finsbury Park, London N4, UK.

DURRANT, Philip John, b. 1901, Twickenham, Middlesex, UK. Fellow, Selwyn College, Cambridge University; Vice-Master & Senior Tutor (ret'd). Educ: M.A., Ph.D., Corpus Christi Coll., Cambridge Univ. Publs: General & Inorganic Chemistry, 3rd ed., 1964; Organic Chemistry, 1950; Introduction to Advanced Inorganic Chemistry (w. B. Durrant), 2nd ed., 1970; var. sci. papers. Mbr., Royal Empire Soc. Address: 16 Chaucer Rd., Cambridge, UK.

DURRELL, Gerald Malcolm, b. 7 Jan. 1925, Jamshedpur, India. Zoologist; Writer. Publs. incl: Overloaded Ark; The Bafut Beagles; My Family, & other Animals; Encounters with Animals; A Zoo in My Luggage; Birds, Beasts & Relatives, 1969; Fillets of Plaice, 1971; Catch Me a Colobus, 1972; Beasts in My Belfry, 1973; Stationary Ark, 1975; (for children) The Talking Parcel, 1974. Contbr. to: Daily Telegraph; Observer; Zoo Life; Geogl. Mag.; etc. Mbrships: F.R.G.S.; F.R.S.L.; Inst. Biol.; Fellow, Int. Inst. Arts & Letters. Recip., Conserv. Gold Medal, Zool. Soc. San Diego, USA, 1973. Address: Les Augres Manor, Trinity, Jersey, Channel Islands, UK.

DURRELL, Lawrence, b. India. Writer. Educ: St. Joseph's Coll., Darjeeling, India; St. Edmund's Coll., Canterbury, UK. Publs: Panic Spring; Cefalu; The Black Book; Reflections on a Marine Venus; Prospero's Cell; Justine; Bitter Lemons; Balthazar; Mountolive; Clea, Collected Poems; (three verse plays) Sappho; Acte; An Irish Faustus; (novels) Tune; Nunquam; Monsieur. F.R.S.L. Address: c/o National & Grindlays Bank, 13 St. James's Square, London SW1, UK.

DÜRRENMATT, Friedrich, b. 5 Jan. 1921, Konolfingen, Switz. Author; Playwright. Educ: Univs. of Berne & Zürich. Publs. incl: (comedies) Der Blinde; Romulus der Grosse; Ein Engel kommt nach Babylon; Der Besuch der alten Dame; Es steht geschrieben; Die Physikder; (radio plays) Nächtliches Gespräch mit einem verachteten Menschen; Herkules und der Stall des Augias; Das Unternehmen der Wega; (novels) Der Richter und sein Henker; Der Verdacht; (short stories) Die Panne; Der Sturz. Hons: Prix Italia, 1958; Schiller Prize, 1960; Grillparzer Prize, 1968; Art Prize, Berne, 1969; D.Litt., Temple Univ., Phila.. 1969. Address: Pertuis du Sault 34, Neuchâtel, Switz.

DURST, Paul, pen names SHANE, John; COCHRAN, Jeff, b. 1921, Archbald, Pa., USA. Writer. Educ: Colo. & Northwest Mo. State Tchrs. Colls. Publs: If I Should Die; They Want Me Dead; Ambush at North Platte; Gun Doctor; Intended Treason; Backlash; Badge of Infamy; A Roomful of Shadows; Flight of the Doves (film). Contbr. to: (films) Those Magnificent Men in Their Flying Machines; Masade; The Informer. Agent: Anthony Masters. Address: Robins Roost, Thruxton, Andover, Hants., UK.

DUTT, Rajani Palme, b. 19 June 1896, Cambridge, UK. Author; Journalist. Educ: Balliol Coll., Oxford. Publs. incl: Road to Labour Unity, 1943; Britain's Crisis of Empire, 1949; India Today & Tomorrow, 1956; Crisis of Britain & the British Empire, 1957; Problems of Contemporary History, 1963; Rise & Fall of the Daily Herald, 1964; The Internationale, 1964. Contbr. to: Ency. Britannica, 12th ed.; Ed., Workers' Wkly., 1923-24, Daily Worker, 1936-38, Labour Monthly, 1921—. Mbrships: Nat. Union of Gen. & Municipal Workers; Marx Mem. Lib. Recip., Hon. Doct., Hist. Moscow Univ., USSR, 1962. Address: 8 Highfield Ct., Highfield Rd., London NW11, UK.

DUTTON, Geoffrey Piers Henry, b. 1922, Kapunda, S. Australia. Author. Educ: B.A., Oxford Univ.; Univ. of Adelaide. Publs: The Mortal & the Marble; A Long Way South; Africa in Black & White; States of the Union; Nightflight & Sunrise; Antipodes in Shoes; Founder of a City; Flowers & Fury; Poems Soft & Loud; The Hero as a Murderer; Andy; Tamara; Tisi & The Yabby; Seal Bay; Russell Drysdale; The Literature of Australia; Tisi & the Pageant; Australia's Last Explorer. Contbr. to var. Aust. newspapers & periodicals. Address: Old Anlaby, Kapunda, S. Aust.

DUTTON, Ralph, b. 1898, Hinton Ampner, Hants., UK. Educ: Univ. of Oxford. Publs: The English Country House; The English Garden; The Land of France (w. Lord Holden); The English Interior; Wessex; The Age of Wren; London Homes; Normandy & Brittany; The Victorian Home; Chateaux of France; English Court Life; Hinton Ampner, A Hampshire Manor; Hampshire. Mbrships. incl: Histl. Bldgs. Comm., Nat. Trust; Historic Bldg. Coun., 1964-72; Trustee, Wallace Collect., 1948-69. Address: Hinton Ampner House, Alresford, Hants., UK.

DUTTON STUHLEY MANN, Delores Iola, pen name DUTTON MANN, Dee, b. 17 Nov. 1917, Mpls., Minn., USA. Outdoor Writer; Columnist; Reviewer; Founder-Composer, Composers First Productions. Publs: Minn. Outdoors Vacation & Travel Guide (annually 1959-74); Manual for Volunteer Men's Corps. Contbr. to: Sports & Recreation; Minn. Sports; Minn. Outdoors; num. Minn. newspapers; radio sports scripts. Mbrships. incl: Outdoor Writers Assn. of Am.; Dir., Publicity Chmn., Minn. Natural Beauty Coun.; Minn. Press Club; Assn. Gt. Lakes Outdoor Writers. Hons. incl: Governor's Cert. of Merit for annual mags., 1968; Award, Int. Fishing Hall of Fame (only Minn. woman honoured). Address: 1618 Calhoun Pl., Mpls., MN 55408, USA.

DUVAL, Catherine, pen name for novels DUVAL van ALTENA, Catherine, b. 11 Apr. 1922, Rotterdam, Netherlands. Author. Publs: (ghost stories) The Brides of Lannismoore, 1970; Mirror Without Reflection, 1971; Companions of Death, 1972; (novels) The Flight of the Lark, 1975; Little Agnes, 1975; (ghost stories in preparation) The Doomed; Beloved Demon. Contbr. to: Elseviers Lit. Supplement. Mbrships: Union of Writers V.V.L., Netherlands; Ghost Club, London. Address: c/o Amsterdam Boek, Wiboutstraat 129, Amsterdam, Netherlands.

DWYER-JOYCE, Alice Louise, b. 7 Sept. 1913, Birr, Ireland. Medical Practitioner. Educ: Licentiate, Royal Coll. of Physns. & Surgs., Dublin, Ireland; L.M. Publs: Pride of Inheritance, 1963; The Silent Lady, 1964; Dr. Ross of Harton, 1966; The Story of Dr. Esmond Ross, 1967; Verdict on Dr. Esmond Ross, 1968; Dial Emergency for Dr. Ross, 1969; Don't Cage Me Wild, 1970; For I Have Lived Today, 1970; Message for Dr. Ross, 1971; Cry the Soft Rain, 1972; Reach for the Shadows, 1972; The Rainbow Glass, 1973; The Brass Islands, 1974; Prescription for Melissa, 1974; The Moonlit Way, 1974; The Strolling Players, 1974. Address: "Greystones", 1 School Hill, Histon, Cambridge, UK.

DYCUS, Frances Webb, b. 18 Mar. 1919, Centerville, Tenn., USA. Poet; Essayist. Publs: (poems) Come Sit With Me, 1969; The Blue Buck Banner, 1974. Contbr. to: Christian Sci. Monitor; Tenn. Conservationist; Outdoor World; Nashville Tennessean; Improvement Era; Capper's Weekly; Old Hickory Review; Weekly Unity; Tenn. Voices Anthol. Yrbook; Fur & Feathers; Pegasus; Amber; Who Tells the Crocuses It's Spring? (anthol.); N.H. Profiles; many ch. periodicals. Mbrships: Poetry Soc. Tenn.; Tenn. Womens Press & Authors Club; United Amateur Press Assn. Address: Duck River, TN 38454, USA.

DYER, Charles, b. 2 July 1928, Shrewsbury, Salop., UK. Playwright; Novelist. Novels: Rattle Of A Simple Man, 1964; Charlie Always Told Harry Almost Everything, 1969; Staircase, 1969; Unter Der Treppe, 1970; La Crecelle, 1971. Plays: Wanted — One Body!, 1961; Time Murderers Please, 1962; Rattle of a Simple Man, 1963; Staircase, 1968; Mother Adam, 1972; Hot Godly Wind, 1973; A Loving Allelujah, 1974. Contbr. to: Plays & Players; l'Avant Scene, Paris; Sipario, Rome; The Best Plays of New York, 1963, 1968; Best Plays in London, 1963. Address: Old Wob, Chalfont St. Peter, Bucks., UK.

DYER, John Martin, b. 27 Feb. 1920, St. Louis, Mo., USA. University Professor of Marketing; Attorney at Law. Educ: A.B., St. Louis Univ., 1941; M.B.A., Pa. Univ., 1953; LL.B., 1951, J.D., 1967, Univ. of Miami. Publs: United States — Latin America Trade & Financial Relations, 1961; Export Financing (w. F. C. Dyer), 1963; Bureaucracy vs. Creativity: The Dilemma of Modern Leadership (w. F. C. Dyer), 1965; Guidelines to Operating in Latin America, 1970; The Enjoyment of Management (w. F. C. Dyer), 1971. Contbr. to: Mktng. in Latin America, by F. Dunbaugh, 1960; num. bus., econ., & Latin Am. histl. jrnls. Num. mbrships. incl: Am. Mktng. Assn.; Am. Bar Assn. Address: 7701 S.W. 52nd Ct., Miami, FL 33143, USA.

DYLAN, Bob, 24 May 1941, Duluth, Minn., USA. Songwriter; Singer; Musician. Publs: Tarantula, 1966; Writings & Drawings by Bob Dylan, 1973. Recip., D.Mus.(Hon.), Princeton Univ., 1970. Address: Box 264, Cooper Stn., N.Y., NY 10003, USA.

DYMENT, Clifford, b. 1914, Alfreton, Derbyshire, UK, d. 5 June 1971. Freelance Writer & Broadcaster; Former Film Director. Publs: Poems 1935-48, 1949; Experiences & Places, 1955; The Railway Game, 1962; Collected Poems, 1970. F.R.S.L. Recip., Atlantic Award in Lit., 1950.

DYMOKE, Juliet, b. 1919, London, UK. Film Script Reader & Historical Researcher. Publs: Sons of Tribune (children's), 1956; London in the 18th Century, 1957; The Orange Sash, 1958; Born for Victory, 1960; Treason in November, 1961; Bend Sinister, 1962; The Cloisterman, 1969; Of the Ring of Earls, 1970; Henry of the High Rock, 1971; Serpent in Eden, 1973; The Lion's Legacy, 1974. Address: Heronscroft, Burchetts Green, Berks. SL6 6QS, UK.

DYNE, Dudley Golding, b. 30 Mar. 1912, New Plymouth, NZ. Senior Journalist, Publicity & Advertising Branch, New Zealand Government Railways. Educ: Proficiency Cert. Publs: Famous New Zealand Murders, 1969. Address: 1 Halifax St., Kingston, Wellington, NZ.

DYSON, Anthony Edward, b. 1928, London, UK. University Lecturer. Educ: M.A., M.Litt., Univ. of Cambridge. Publs: Modern Poetry (w. C. B. Cox), 1963; The Practical Criticism of Poetry, 1965; The Crazy Fabric, 1965; Ed., Modern Judgments on Dickens, 1968; Casebook on Bleak House, 1969; The Inimitable Dickens, 1970; Between Two Worlds, 1972; Co-Ed., Twentieth Century Mind (w. C. B. Cox), 3 vols., 1972; Co-Ed., Education & Democracy (w. J. Lovelock), 1974; Masterful Images: Metaphysicals to Romantics (w. J. Lovelock), forthcoming. Gen. Ed., Macmillan Casebooks, 1965—. Contbr. to: Black Papers on Education (co-ed.), 1969; Critical Quarterly (co-fndr. & co-ed., 1959—); Daily Telegraph; Spectator; Listener; num. lit. jrnls. Mbrships: Critical Quarterly Soc. (co-fndr.); R.S.L. Address:Schl. of Engl. & Am. Studies, Univ. of E. Anglia, Norwich, UK.

DZHAGAROV, Georgy, b. 14 June 1925, Byala, Bulgaria. Writer; Public Worker. Publs: (in Bulgarian) (plays) The Doors are Closed, 1959; Tomorrow is also a Day, 1961; The Public Prosecutor, 1963; This Small Land, 1974; (fiction) The Problems of Life — Problems of Literature Too, 1970. Contbr. to: Literatouren Front; September; PlamAk; SAvremennik; Noviy Mir (USSR); Inostranniya Literatoura (USSR). Mbrships: Union of Bulgarian Writers; PEN. Hons: Dimitrov Prize, 1965; 'Dobri Chintoulov', 1968; People's Worker in Culture, 1971. Address: Sofia, ul. Al. Zhendov 1, Bulgaria.

E

EARLE, Olive Lydia, b. London, UK. Author; Artist; Illustrator. Educ: Nat. Acad. of Design, N.Y. Publs. incl: Birds & Their Nests; Crickets; Mice at Home & Afield; The Octopus; Paws, Hoofs & Flippers; Pigs, Tame & Wild; Robins in the Garden; State Birds & Flowers; Birds & Their Beaks; Birds of the Crow Family; Camels & Llamas; State Trees; Strange Companions in Nature; Strange Lizards; Strangler Fig; Praying Mantis; The Rose Family. Address: 154 Highview Ave., Staten Island 1, NY 10301, USA.

EAST, William Gordon, b. 1902, London, UK. Professor Emeritus of Geography. Educ: M.A., Cambridge Univ. Publs. incl: The Union of Moldavia & Wallachia, 1959; An Historical Geography of Europe; The Changing Map of Asia (co-author); The Spirit & Purpose of Geography (co-author); The Changing World (co-author); Our Fragmented World (co-author); Geography of Europe (co-author); The Caxton Atlas; The U.S.S.R.; Ed., Regions of the British Isles Series. Contbr. to: Yr. Book of World Affairs; For. Affairs; Geogl. Jrnl.; etc. Hons. incl: Murchison Award, Royal Geogl. Soc., 1971. Address: Wildwood, Danes Way, Oxshott, Surrey, UK.

EASTLAKE, William Derry, b. 1917, Brooklyn, NY, USA. Author. Publs: Go In Beauty, 1956; The Bronc People, 1958; O. Henry Prize Stories, 1959; Fiction of the Fifties; Portrait of an Artist with 26 Horses; The Bamboo Bed; Castle Keep. Contbr. to: Evergreen Review; Hudson Review; Best Am. Short Stories, 1955-57; Collier's; Saturday Evening Post; Accent; Americas; Nation; etc. Hons: D.Litt.; O. Henry Prize, 1970. Address: Route 2, Box 761A, Tucson, Ariz., USA.

EASTMENT, Winifred V. (née Phillips), b. 5 Dec. 1899, Wanstead, Essex, UK. Writer. Educ: West Ham Municipal Coll.; London Schl. of Jrnlsm. Publs: Wanstead Through the Ages, 1946, revised ed., 1969; Down at the Vicarage, 1967; Heart to Heart, 1969; Ford End: The Story of an Essex Village, 1969; We Weave as We Go (autobiog.), 1973. Contbr. to: Essex Countryside (features, reviews); & freelance jrnlsm. Mbrships: Soc. of Authors; Wanstead Histl. Soc. (Pres.). Address: 1 Spratt Hall Rd., Wanstead, London E11 2RQ, UK.

EATON, Charles Edward, b. 25 June 1916, Winston-Salem, N.C., USA. Poet; Novelist. Educ: A.B., Univ. of N.C., 1936; Princeton, 1936-37; M.A., Harvard, 1940. Publs: (poetry) The Bright Plain, 1942; The Shadow of the Swimmer, 1951; The Greenhouse in the Garden, 1956; Countermoves, 1963; On the Edge of the Knife, 1970; (short stories) Write me From Rio, 1959; The Girl from Ipanema, 1972; (novels) A Lady of Pleasure, 1972; (criticism) Karl Knaths: Paintings of Five Decades, 1974. Contbr. to many lit. publs. Mbrships. incl: Poetry Soc. Am.; New Engl. Poetry Soc. Hons. incl: The Golden Rose, New Engl. Poetry Club, 1972; O. Henry Prize Story Award, 1972; Alice Fay di Castagnole Award, Poetry Soc. Am., 1974. Address: Merlin Stone, Woodbury, CT 06798, USA.

EBBETT, Frances Eva, pen names BURFIELD, Eva; EBBETT, Eve, b. 6 June 1925, Wellingborough, Northants., UK. Author. Publs: Yellow Kowhai, 1957; A Chair to Sit On, 1958; The Long Winter, 1964; Out of Yesterday, 1965; After Midnight, 1965; The White Prison, 1966; The New Mrs. Rainier, 1967; The Last Day of Summer, 1968; Give Them Swing Bands, 1969; To the Garden Alone, 1970. Contbr. to var. mags. in NZ, UK, Aust., Sweden, Norway, Denmark, Holland & Italy. Mbr.; NZ Women Writers' Soc. Address: P.O. Box 27, Waipawa, Hawkes Bay, NZ.

EBER, Dorothy Margaret Harley, pen name EBER, Dorothy Harley, b. 18 Mar. 1930, Bromley, Kent, UK. Writer; Journalist. Educ: B.A., Trinity Coll., Univ. of Toronto, Can. Publs: The Computer Centre Party: Canada Meets Black Power — That Sir George Williams Affair, 1969; Pitseolak: Pictures out of my life, 1971; People From Our Side (w. Peter Pitseolak) 1975. Contbr. to: Can. Forum; All maj. Can. mags.; Can. Nat. Film Bd.; Int. Cinemedia. Recip., Two Awards for mag. articles, Nat. Women's Press Club. Address: 1455 Sherbrooke St. W., Apt. 1001, Montreal, Canada.

EBNER-ALLINGER, Jeannie, pen name EBNER, Jeannie, b. 17 Nov. 1918, Sydney, N.S.W., Australia. Writer. Educ: Acad. Fine Arts, Vienna, Austria, 4 yrs. Publs. incl: (poetry) Gesang an das Heute, 1952; Gedichte, 1965; (novels) Sie warten auf Antwort, 1954; Die Wildnis früher Sommer, 1958; Figuren in Schwarz & Weiss, 1962;

(short works) Der Königstiger, 1959; Die Götter reden nicht, 1961; Im Schatten der Göttin, 1963; Prosadichtungen, 1973; Protokoll aus einem Zwischenreich, 1975. transls. of 40 works from Engl. Contbr. to: Literatur & Kritik, Salzburg (publr. & ed.); num. other jrnls. & newspapers; 53 anthols. Mbrships incl: W. Pirkheimer Soc. (Bd. of Trustees); PEN (exec. comm., Austrian Ctr.). Recip. num. prizes & medals. Address: Schlossgasse 3/8, 1050 Vienna, Austria.

ECCLESTONE, Arthur, b. 10 June 1892, Wolverhampton, Staffs., UK. Headmaster, 1932-38; Inspector of Schools, 1938-57. Educ: B.A.(Hons.), M.A., London Univ.; Westminster Coll., Oxford. Publs: A Progressive English Course. Contbr. to: Times Educl. Supplement. Address: Finchfield, Widemouth Bay, Cornwall, UK.

ECONOMOU, George Demetrios, b. 24 Sept. 1934, Gt. Falls, Mont., USA. Poet; University Professor. Educ: A.B., Colgate Univ., 1956; M.A., 1957, Ph.D., 1967, Columbia Univ. Publs: The Georgics, 1968; Landed Natures, 1969; Poems for Self Therapy, 1972; The Goddess Natura in Medieval Literature, 1972. Contbr. to: Kulchur; The Nation; Chaucer Review; Com. Lit. Mbrships: MLA; Medieval Acad. of Am. Address: 606 W. 116th St., N.Y., NY 10027, USA.

EDDY, John Paul, b. 18 Jan. 1932, Glencoe, Minn., USA. Educator; Author. Educ: B.S., Univ. of Minn., 1954; M.Div., Garrett Sem., 1959; M.A., Northwestern Univ., 1960; Ph.D., Southern Ill. Univ., 1968. Publs. incl: Campus Religious Affairs, 1969; Unistar (co-author), 1970; Principles of Marketing, 1972; Action & Careers In a New Age (co-author), 1973; The Teacher & the Drug Scene, 1973; What Is Career Education? (co-author), 1975; Educational Theory & the Practice of Peace (co-author), 1975. Contbr. to: Christian Century; Coll. Mgmt.; Careers; Sci. Activities; Peace Progress; Schl. & Society; etc. Address: 2419 Simpson St., Evanston, IL 60201, USA.

EDEL, Joseph Leon, b. 1907, Pitts., Pa., USA. Professor of English; Journalist. Educ: M.A.; D.Litt.; McGill Univ., Montreal; Univ. of Paris. Publs: James Joyce; The Last Journey, 1947; Willa Cather (w. E. K. Brown), 1953; The Untried Years, 1953; The Conquest of London, 1962; The Middle Years, 1963; The Treacherous Years, 1969; (Ed.) The Complete Plays, Complete Tales & Selected Letters of James; (Ed.) The Psychological Novel, 1955; (Ed.) Literary Biography, 1957. Contbr. to: New Republic; Saturday Review; etc. Mbrships. incl: PEN; MLA; F.R.S.L.; Am. Acad. Arts & Sci.; Pres., Authors' Guild. Address: N.Y. Univ., NY 10003, USA.

EDELMAN, Maurice, b. 1911, Cardiff, UK. MP since 1945; Author; Journalist; former War Correspondent. Educ: M.A., Trinity Coll., Cambridge. Publs. incl: France: The Birth of the Fourth Republic, 1945; A Trial of Love, 1951; Who Goes Home, 1953; A Dream of Treason, 1954; The Happy Ones, 1957; A Call on Kuprin, 1959; The Minister, 1961; The Fratricides, 1963; The Prime Minister's Daughter, 1964; The Mirror: A Political History, 1966; Shark Island, 1967; All on a Summer's Night, 1969; Mbrships: PEN; Pres., Alliance Française, Off., Légion d'honneur. Address: House of Commons, London SW1, UK.

EDFELT, Bo Johannes, b. 21 Dec. 1904, Kyrkefalla, Skaraborgs län, Sweden. Author; Poet. Educ: Fil.mag., Uppsala Univ., 1930; Fil.lic., Stockholms Högskola, 1952. Publs. incl: (poetry) Högmässa, 1934; I denna natt, 1936; Vintern är lång, 1939; Elden och klyftan, 1943; Bråddjupt eko, 1947; Hemliga slagfält, 1952; Under Saturnus, 1956; Insyn, 1962; Ådernät, 1968; var. essays; transls. of lyric poetry. Contbr. to: Dagens Nyheter; Svenska Dagbladet; Bonniers Litterära Magasin; etc. Mbr., Swedish Acad.; etc. Hons. incl: Svenska Akademiens Bellmanspris, 1954, 1971; Boklotteriets stora pris, 1962; Henrik Steffens-Preis, Germany, 1967. Address: Bergviksvägen 38, 150 24 Rönninge, Sweden.

EDGARDH, Hans Bertil Hampus, b. 7 Feb. 1918, Stockholm, Sweden. Psychoanalyst. Educ: Ph.D. Publs: Ch'in Kvartetten, 1963; Hoc Est, 1966; Airy Tales, 1972. Contbr. to num. sci. & lit. jrnls. Address: Karlaplan III, 115 22 Stockholm, Sweden.

EDINBOROUGH, Arnold, b. 2 Aug. 1922, Donington, UK. Journalist; Executive. Educ: B.A., 1947, M.A., 1949, Cambridge Univ. Publs: Canada: A Panorama Book, 1966;

One Church, Two Nations (Ed.), 1967; Some Camel, Some Needle, 1974. Contbr. to: Saturday Night; Fin. Post; Can. Churchman; Can. Commentator; Illustrated London News; The Times; Shakespeare Survey; Shakespeare Quarterly. Recip., Hon. LL.D., Univ. of Guelph, Ont., 1969. Address: 10 Ancroft Pl., Toronto, Ont. M4W 1M4, Can.

EDLIN, Herbert Leeson, b. 1913, Manchester, UK. Publications Officer. Forestry Commission; Author. Educ: B.Sc.; Dip. For.; Univs. of Edinburgh & Oxford. Publs: Trees, Woods & Man; Guide to Tree Planting & Cultivation; England's Forests; Forestry; Wild Life of Wood & Forest; What Wood is That? ; Wayside & Woodland Trees; Atlas of Plant Life; The Public Park; Trees & Timbers; Woodland Crafts in Britain. Contbr. to: Forestry; Quarterly Jrnl. of Forestry; Scottish Forestry; C'wlth. Forestry Review; Ency. Britannica, etc. Recip., M.B.E., 1970. Address: 15 Howard Rd., Coulsdon, Surrey, UK.

EDLIN, John Bruce, b. 21 Aug. 1945, Invercargill, NZ. News Agency Correspondent. Contbr. to: Argus Grp. of S. Africa. Mbr., Quill Club, Salisbury, Rhodesia. Address: Box 396, Salisbury, Rhodesia.

EDLIN, Robert Nelson, b. 7 Sept. 1943, Wellington, NZ. Journalist; Editor of NZ Truth. Educ: Victoria Univ., Wellington. Contbr. to NZ Truth. Mbrships: Southland Jrnlsts.' Union (former VP); NZ Inst. Int. Affairs. Address: Rathbrook, Hukanui, RD6, Pahiatua, NZ.

EDMISTON, Helen Jean Mary, pen name ROBERTSON, Helen, b. 1913, Southport, Lancs., UK. Writer; Journalist. Educ: B.A., Univ. Coll., London. Publs: The Winged Witnesses, 1955; Venice of the Black Sea, 1956; The Crystal-gazers, 1957; The Chinese Goose, 1960; The Shake-Up, 1962; Asst. Ed., Annals of Human Genetics. Contbr. to: Music Review; Int. Jrnl. Biometeorol.; Biochemie und Physiologie der Pflanzen BPP. Mbrships: Soc. of Authors; PEN. Address: 77 Knockhall Chase, Greenhithe, Kent, UK.

EDMONDS, (Col.) Edmund W., Jr., b. 10 July 1924, Cinn., Ohio, USA. Air Force Officer. Educ: B.G.E., Univ. of Neb., Omaha; M.B.A., Geo. Wash. Univ.; Dip., Ind. Coll. of Armed Forces. Publs: The Air Force Budget, 1968, 1969, 1970, 1971, 1972, 1973 & 1974; Economic Analysis Handbook, 1973. Contbr. to: The Air Force Comptroller; Defense Mgmt. Jrnl.; Linn's Stamp News; etc. Mbr., Am. Soc. of Mil. Comptrollers. Hons. incl: Author of Yr., ASMC, 1971; US Treasury Dept. Liberty Bell Award. Address: 4110 Robertson Blvd., Alexandria, VA 22309, USA.

EDMONDS, Harry, b. 1891, Merthyr Tydfil, UK. Company Chairman. Publs. incl: North Sea Mystery; Red Desert; Riddle of the Straits; Red Invader; Trail of the Lonely River; East Coast Mystery; Wind in the East; Across the Frontiers; The Orphans of Brandenburg; A British Five-Year Plan; Yvonne; The Death Ship; Professor's Last Experiment; (poetry) Homage to Southey: The Secret Voyage; The Clockmaker of Heidelberg; The Rockets. Address: 1 Brockhill Rd., Hythe, Kent, UK.

EDMONDS, William Bentley, b. Norfolk, Va., USA. Artist; Designer. Educ: Columbia Schl. of Fine Arts, NYC; Nat. Acad. of Design, NYC. Publs: Cassandra, 1969. Address: 1444 Shakespeare Ave., Bronx, NY 10452, USA.

EDMUNDS, Pocahontas Wight, b. 8 Nov. 1904, Richmond, Va., USA. Author. Educ: A.B., Agnes Scott Coll., 1925; Cert., Alliance Francaise, Paris, 1926. Publs. incl: Legends of the N.C. Coast, 1941; The Pocahontas-John Smith Story, 1956; Tar Heels Track the Century, 1966; Virginians Out Front, 1972; Co-author, Rutherford B. Hayes, 1930, E. Harriman, 1933. Contbr. to Musical America mag. Mbr., Va. Writers Club. Address: Bonbrook, Halifax, VA 24558, USA.

EDMUNDS (Thomas) Murrell, b. 23 Mar. 1898, Halifax, Va., USA. Lawyer; Author. Educ: J.D., Univ. of Va. Novels: Sojourn Among Shadows, 1936; Between the Devil, 1939; Time's Laughter in Their Ears, 1943; Behold, Thy Brother, 1950; Passionate Journey to Winter, 1962; Beautiful Upon the Mountains, 1966; Shadow of a Great Rock, 1969. Other Publs: Moon of my Delight (3-act play), 1960; Red, White & Black (short stories), 1945; Laurel for the Undefeated (selected stories), 1964; Dim Footprints Along a Hazardous Trail (verse), 1971. Contrb. to: Anthol. of Best Mag. Verse; Va. Reader; Lyric Va. Today, vol. II;

etc. Recip., Ariz. Quarterly Poetry Award, 1963. Address: 936 St. Charles Ave., New Orleans, LA 70130, USA.

EDSTRÖM, Mauritz Natanael, b. 22 Dec. 1927, Bjärtrå, Sweden. Journalist; Writer. Educ: Inst. of Social & Pol. Scis., Stockholm, 1954. Publs: Ivar Lo-Johansson, 1954; Arne Sucksdorff, 1968; Medan världen dör, 1971. Contbr. to: Dagens Nyheter, Stockholm; var. Swedish & for. mags.; num. anthols. Mbrships: Swedish Writers Assn.; Swedish Jrnlsts. Assn.; Swedish Assn. of Film Critics. Address: Edsviksvägen 46 A, 191 45 Sollentuna, Sweden.

EDWARDS, Dorothy, b. Teddington, Middlesex, UK. Writer. Publs: 6 titles in the My Naughty Little Sister series, 1952-74; Tales of Joe & Timothy, & Joe & Timothy Together, 1969-75; 4 titles in Storychair series, 1971-72; Ed., Listen with Mother Stories, 1972; Listen, Listen! , 1972; Listen & Play Rhymes, 1 & 2, 1973; Look, See, Touch Books, 1 & 2, 1975; Read-to-Me Story Book, 1974; A Wet Monday, forthcoming; Dad's New Car, forthcoming; The Magician Who Kept a Pub, forthcoming. Contbr. to BBC Radio; TV; newspapers & mags. Mbrships. incl: Soc. of Authors; Radio Writers Assn.; Writers Action Grp. Address: c/o Methuen Children's Books, 11 New Fetter Lane, London EC4P 4EE, UK.

EDWARDS, Francis Oborn, b. 16 Jan. 1922, London, UK. Historian; Archivist; Author. Educ: B.A., London, 1947; S.T.L., Gregorian Univ., Rome, Italy; Dip.Ed., London. Publs: Seeing the Faith, 1955; The Dangerous Queen, 1964; The Marvellous Chance, 1968; Guy Fawkes: The Real Story of the Gunpowder Plot?, 1969; The Gunpowder Plot: the Narrative of Oswald Tesimond, 1973; Vatican Documents 1600-1604, forthcoming; The Elizabethan Jesuits, forthcoming. Contbr. to: The Month; Clergy Review; Jrnl. of Soc. of Archivists; Contemporary Review. Mbrships: F.S.A.(London); Fellow, Royal Histl. Soc. Address: 114 Mount St., London W1Y 6AH, UK.

EDWARDS, Gene Mary, b. 26 Dec. 1915, Hanford, Calif., USA. Library Technician. Educ: Fresno State Coll.; Visalia Jr. Coll. (later Coll. of the Sequoias); Reedley Coll. Contbr. to: (mags.) Am. Haiku; Am. Bard; Haiku Highlights; Swordsman Review; Penman Mag.; SCTH; Tweed; Mod. Haiku; (Anthols.) Ardentia Verba, 1967; Velvet Paws in Print, 1967; The Best in Poetry, 1968; Haiku & Tanka, 1969; The Wagging Tail, 1969; 6th Annual: These Are My Jewels, 1970; This Way of Life. Mrbships: Nat. Writers Club; Photographic Soc. of Am. Address: P.O. Box 298, Hanford, CA 93230, USA.

EDWARDS, Gillian Mary, b. 1918, Soham, Cambs., UK. Writer. Educ: B.A., Univ. of Reading. Publs: Sun of My Life, 1951; The Road to Hell, 1967; Uncumber & Pantaloon, 1968; I am Leo, 1969; Hogmanay & Tiffany, 1970; Tower of Lions, 1971; Hobgoblin & Sweet Puck, 1974; Accidental Visitor, 1974. Mbr., Soc. of Authors. Lit. Agent: Curtis Brown Ltd. Address: 20 Water St., Cambridge CB4 1PA, UK.

EDWARDS, Henry James (Harry), b. 1893, London, UK. Master Printer; Spiritual Healer. Publs. incl: The Science of Spirit Healing, 1945; Psychic Healing, 1948; The Evidence for Spirit Healing, 1953; The Truth about Spirit Healing, 1956; Spirit Healing, 1960; The Power of Spirit Healing, 1962; Born to Heal: The Healing Intelligence, 1965; Thirty Years a Healer, 1969; A Guide to the Understanding & Practice of Spiritual Healing, 1974. Contbr. to: The Spiritual Healer Mag. (Dir.). Mbr., Nat. Fedn. Spirit Healers. Address: The Sanctuary, Burrows Lea, Shere, Guildford, Surrey, UK.

EDWARDS, Herbert Charles, pen name EDWARDS, Bertram, b. 22 July 1912, Clerkenwell, London, UK. Schoolmaster; Author. Publs: The Restless Valley, 1955; Midnight on Barrowmead Hill (US title, The Mystery of Barrowmead Hill), 1956; Strange Traffic, 1958; Danger in Densmere, 1963; The Rise of the USA, 1968; The Burston School Strike, 1974. Address: 20 Whitehurst Ave., Hitchin, Herts. SG5 1SR, UK.

EDWARDS, Iorwerth Eiddon Stephen, b. 21 July 1909, London, UK. Egyptologist. Educ: Gonville & Caius Coll., Cambridge; M.A.; D.Litt.; F.B.A. Keeper, Egyptian Antiquities, British Museum (ret'd 1974). Publs: Hieroglyphic Texts in the British Museum, part 8, 1939; Hieratic Papyri in the British Museum, 4th Series, 1960; The Pyramids of Egypt, 1947, 1961; Treasures of Tutankhamun, 1972; (joint-Ed.) Cambridge Ancient History, 3rd ed. in progress. Contbr. to: Jrnl. of Egyptian

Archaeology; Burlington Mag.; Jrnl. of Near Eastern Studies; etc. Mbrships: F.S.A.; VP, Egypt Exploration Soc. Recip. C.B.E., 1967; C.M.G., 1973. Address: Morden Lodge, Morden Hall Rd., Morden, Surrey SM4 5JD, UK.

EDWARDS, Jane, b. 13 Mar. 1940, Niwbwrch, Anglesey, Wales, UK. Writer. Educ: Y Coleg Normal, Bangor. Publs: Dechrau Gofidiau, 1962; Byd o Gysgodion, 1964; Bara Seguryd, 1969; Epil Cam, 1972; Tyfu, 1973. Contbr. to: Storiäu'r Dydd; Taliesin; Barn; Storiäu '74; Storiäu Hamdden; Cylchgrawn BBC; Y Cymro; Y Faner; Hon; Dwedwch Chi. Hons: Winner, Novel Competition, Eisteddfod Genedlaethol, Llanelli, 1962; 1st Writer to be commissioned, Welsh Books Coun., 1964. Address: c/o Derwyn, Niwbwrch, Ynys Môn, Gwynedd, Wales, UK.

EDWARDS, Jenkin Morgan, b. 16 Dec. 1903, Llanrhystud, UK. Schoolmaster. Educ: Tchr.'s Dip. Publs: Cerddi'r Bore, 1924; Y Tir Pell, 1933; Cerddi Pum Mlynedd, 1938; Peïriannau, 1947; Cerddi'r Daith, 1954; Cerddi Hamdden, 1962; Cerddi'r Fro, 1970. Contbr. to: Y Faner; Y Traethodydd; Y Genhinen; Barn. Mbr., var. orgs. Recip., sev. hons. Address: 20 Clement Place, Barry, Glamorgan, S. Wales, UK.

EDWARDS, Jorge, b. 29 July 1931, Santiago, Chile. Writer; Chilean Chargé d'Affaires, Paris, 1971-73. Educ: Law Degree, Univ. Chile; Princeton Univ., USA. Publs: (novel) El peso de la noche, 1964; (short stories) Las Máscaras, 1967; Temas y Variaciones, 1969; Persona non grata, 1973. Contbr. to: Marcha; Coretas; Postdata; Diálogos; Atemea; Le Monde; & num. Latin Am. & Spanish mags. Mbrships: Soc. Chilean Writers; PEN. Hons: City of Santiago Prizes 1961, 1969; & 2 prizes for El Peso de la noche. Address: Basaje Forasti 19, Barcelona 6, Spain.

EDWARDS, Lynne, b. 25 June 1943, Gt. Bentley, UK. Teacher. Educ: Tchr.'s Cert., Weymouth Tchr.'s Trng. Coll. Publs: Dead As the Dodo, 1973. Address: 88 High St., Bildeston, Ipswich IP7 7EA, UK.

EDWARDS, Monica le Doux, b. 1912, Belper, Derbys., UK. Writer. Publs: The Unsought Farm; The Cats of Punchbowl Farm; The Badgers of Punchbowl Farm; Series of Romney Marsh stories, incl. Cargo of Horses; The Nightbird; Series of Punchbowl Farm stories, incl. Punchbowl Midnight; The Wanderer; (children's film serial) The Dawn Killer; (career novels, incl:) Joan Goes Farming. Contbr. to: Elizabethan; Children's Newspaper; BBC Children's Hour; Woman's Jrnl. Address: Cowdray Cross, Thursley, Surrey, UK.

EDWARDS, Philip Walter, b. 1923, Barrow-in-Furness, Lancs., UK. University Professor of English. Educ: M.A., Ph.D., Univ. of Birmingham. Publs: Sir Walter Raleigh; Shakespeare & the Confines of Art; Ed., Kyd, The Spanish Tragedy. Contbr. to: Shakespeare Survey. Address: Dept. of English, Univ. of Liverpool, Liverpool L69 3BX, UK.

EDWARDS, Ralph (H. C. R.), b. 24 June 1894, Pwllywrack, Cowbridge, Glam., UK. Adviser on Works of Art & Pictures to Historic Buildings Councils. Educ: B.A., Oxford Univ. Publs: The Dictionary of English Furniture (w. P. Macquoid), 1922-25, revised ed., 1953; Georgian Cabinet Makers (w. M. Jourdain), 1946, 3 eds.; Early Conversation Pictures, 1954; var. catalogues of exhibs. Contbr. to: Connoisseur; Burlington Mag. Mbrships: F.S.A.; Soc. of Antiquaries; Coun. Mbr., Nat. Mus. of Wales. Recip., C.B.E. Address: Suffolk House, Chiswick Mall, London W4, UK.

EDWARDS, Rex, b. 21 Oct. 1917, London, UK. Author; Scriptwriter. Publs: The Devil's Churchyard, 1958; Seven Gates to Nowhere, 1959; Coronary Case, 1964; The Dales, 1968; Dixon of Dock Green, 1974; Arthur of the Britons, 1974; The Goblet Game (play), 1968; Num. scripts for radio, TV & films. Mbrships: Writers' Guild of GB; Swedenborg Soc. Address: Finch Cottage, Finch Lane, Bushey, Herts., UK.

EDWARDS, (Richard) Cecil Churchill, b. 3 Sept. 1903, London, UK. Journalist; Editor. Publs: Bruce of Melbourne, 1966; Brown Power, 1970; John Monash, 1971; The Editor Regrets, 1972; Labor Pains, 1974. Address: 2a Hopetoun Grove, Ivanhoe, Melbourne, Vic., Australia 3079.

EDWARDS, Ronald Stanley, b. 1 May 1910, London, UK. University Professor of Economics; Business Executive; Author. Publs: Co-operative Industrial Research, 1950; Industrial Research in Switzerland, 1951; Business Enterprise (w. H. Townsend), 1958; Studies in Business Organization (w. H. Townsend), 1961; Business Growth (w. H. Townsend), 1966; Status, Productivity & Pay: A Major Experiment (w. R. D. V. Roberts), 1971. Contbr. to: Studies in Acctng.; Studies in Costing; var. profl. jrnls. Hons. incl: K.B.E.; D.Litt., Warwick Univ., 1973. Address: 49 Lowndes Square, London SW1, UK.

EDWARDS, Willard Eldridge, b. 11 Dec. 1903, Chatham, Mass., USA. Engineer, Electronics & Corrosion Prevention (retired). Educ: Grad., Mass. Radio & Telegraph Schl.; MIT; B.S.; Univ. Okla.; M.S., M.A., Litt.D., Jackson Coll., Hawaii. Publs: The Edwards Perpetual Calendar, 1943; American Samoa, 1949; The Occurrence & Prevention of Corrosion, 1963; New Year's Days are Anniversaries, 1973. Contbr. to: Mil. Engr.; Honolulu Mag.; The Am. Rationalist Mag. (Assoc. Ed.). Hons. incl: MIT Cabot Medal, 1923; Rationalist of the Year, 1969. Address: 1434 Punahou St., Apt. 622, Honolulu, HI 96822, USA.

EDWARDS, William, b. 6 Apr. 1896, Portland, Dorset, UK. Medical Practitioner (Retired). Educ: Trinity Coll., Cambridge; St. Bartholomew's Hosp.; M.D., B.Chir., B.A.(Cantab.); M.R.C.S.; L.R.C.P. Publs: The Art is Long, 1949; Home First Aid, 1969. Contbr. to: Daily Mirror; Sunday Pictorial; Sunday Graphic; Sunday People; Everywoman; Woman; Woman & Beauty; Family Dr.; etc. Mbr., Brit. Med. Assn., 1923–. Address: 9 Greville Park Ave., Ashtead, Surrey KT21 2QS, UK.

EGGER, Rowland Andrews, b. 12 Apr. 1908, Denison, Tex., USA. Teacher. Educ: A.B., 1926, LL.D., 1959, Southwestern Univ.; M.A., Southern Meth. Univ., 1927; Ph.D., Univ. of Mich., 1933. Publs. incl: Retirement of Public Employees, 1933; Organization of Peace at the Administrative Level, 1945; Research, Education & Regionalism (w. W. Cooper), 1949; Improvement of Public Administration in Pakistan, 1953; The President & Congress (w. J. P. Harris), 1963; The President of the United States, 1967, 1972; Le Métier de President, 1972; O Presidente dos Estados Unidos, 1974. Ed.-in-Chief, Int. Review Admin. Scis. Contbr. to num. profl. jrnls. & symposia. Mbr., num. profl. orgs. Recip., var. for. decorations. Address: 10556 High Hollows Dr., Dallas, TX 75275, USA.

EGGERTH, Heinrich, b. 30 Apr. 1926, Annaberg, Austria. Teacher. Publ: Am Ufer der Ereignisse, 1970. Contbr. to: Podium; Integration; Pestsäule. Mbrships: PEN; Podium. Recip., Writers' Award, Land of Lower Austria, 1970. Address: A 2734 Puchberg am Schneeberg, Neunkirchnerstr. 84, Austria.

EGLER, Frank E(dwin), b. 26 Apr. 1911, NYC, USA. Ecologist. Educ: B.S., Univ. of Chgo., 1932; M.S., Univ. of Minn., 1934; Ph.D., Yale Univ., 1936. Publs: The Programme for Tchaikovsky's Fifth Symphony — A Manuscript, 1970; The Way of Science, 1971; Contbr. to var. mags., jrnls., etc. Mbrships. incl: Fellow AAAS, Am. Geogl. Soc.; AAUP; Arctic Inst. of Am.; Ecol. Soc. of Am.; Nat. Audubon Soc. Wilderness, Wildlife Socs.; Conn. Botan. Soc.. Nature Conservancy.; etc. Address: Aton Forest, Norfolk, CT 06058, USA.

EGUDU, Romanus Nnagbo, b. 1 Feb. 1940, Ebe, Nigeria. University Teacher. Educ: B.A., Univ. of Nigeria, 1963; Ph.D., Mich. State Univ., 1966. Publs: Poetic Heritage: Igbo Traditional Verse (w. D. I. Nwoga), 1971 (in Engl., 1973); Calabash of Wisdom & Other Igbo Stories, 1973; Four Modern West African Poets, 1974. Contbr. to: Black Orpheus; Transition; Presence Africaine; African Studies; Conch; Comp. Lit. Studies; Prism Int.; Ufahamu; Nigeria Mag.; Ikenga: Jrnl.; etc. Mbrships: Nigeria Engl. Studies Assn.; Philos. Soc., Univ. of Nigeria; Soc. for the Promotion of Igbo Lang. & Culture. Hons. incl: Poetry Prize, Mich. State Univ., 1966; appointed Assoc. for W. Africa, Nat. Poetry Fndn. Inc., USA. Address: Dept. of Engl., Univ. of Nigeria, Naukka, E.C.S., Nigeria.

EHLE, John, b. 13 Dec. 1925, Asheville, N.C., USA. Writer; Producer, Documentary Films; Educator. Educ: B.A., 1949, M.A., 1953, Univ. of N.C., Chapel Hill. Publs. incl: American Adventure (26 studies of Am. character, NBCS-Radio, Radio Free Europe, Voice of Am.), 1954-56; 4 documentary films (writer/dir.); Move Over, Mountain, 1957, Kingstree Island, 1959, Lion on the Hearth, 1961, The Land Breakers, 1964, Time of Drums, 1970, The Journey of August King, 1971 (novels); The Survivor, 1968, Shepherd of the Streets, 1960, The Free Men, The Cheeses & Wines of England & France with Notes on Irish Whiskey, 1972, (non-fiction). Mbrships: Exec. Comm., Nat.

Book Comm.; Authors League; PEN. Hons: Mayflower Cup, 1965; Sir Walter Raleigh Prize, 1964, 1967, 1970; N.C. Award, 1972. Agent: Candida Donadio, N.Y. Address: 125 Westview Dr.N., Winston-Salem, NC 27104, USA.

EHRENBERG, Victor Leopold, b. 1891, Altona, Germany. University Reader & Professor of Ancient History; Author. Educ: Univs. of Göttingen, Berlin & Tübingen; D.Phil. Publs: Die Rechtsidee im früheu Griechentum; Neugründer des Staats; Ost und West; Alexander & the Greeks; The People of Aristophanes; Aspects of the Ancient World; Sophocles & Pericles; The Greek State; From Solon to Socrates; Man, State & Deity. Contbr. to: Jrnl. Hellenic Studies; Am. Jrnl. of Philol.; Historia; Gnomon; Hermes; Historische Zeitschrift; etc. Recip., Hon. D.Litt., Cambridge Univ. Address: Flat 1, 112 Fitzjohn's Ave., London NW3, UK.

EHRMAN, John Patrick William, b. 1920, London, UK. Member, Royal Commission on Historical Manuscripts. Educ: M.A., Trinity Coll., Cambridge. Publs: Grand Strategy, 1943-45, 2 vols., 1956; Cabinet Government & War, 1958; The British Government & Commercial Negotiations with Europe, 1783-1793, 1962; The Navy in the War of William III, 1963; The Younger Pitt: The Years of Acclaim, 1969. Mbrships: F.B.A.; F.S.A.; Fellow, Royal Histl. Soc.; Royal Comn. on Histl. MSS, 1973—; VP, Navy Records Soc., 1968-70, 1974—. Address: 149 Old Church St., London SW3, UK.

EIBL-EIBESFELDT, Irenäus, b. 15 June 1928, Vienna, Austria. Scientific Research Director. Educ: Ph.D., Univ. of Vienna. Publs: Galapagos (also in UK & US eds.); Im Reich der Tausend Atolle, W. Germany & UK, 1964; Ethology: Biology of Behaviour, 1970; Love & Hate, UK, 1972; ! Ko Bushmen: Aggression Control & Bonding, 1972; The Pre-Programmed Man, 1973; USA, forthcoming; The Ethological Aspects of War & Peace, 1975. Mbrships incl: Am. Soc. Mammologists; Am. Soc. Ichthyologists & Herpetologists; Charles Darwin Fndn. Address: 8135 Söcking, Starnberg, Fichtenweg 9, W. Germany.

EICHENLAUB, John Ellis, b. 7 Mar. 1922, Wash. D.C., USA. Physician; Writer. Educ: B.A., Johns Hopkins, 1942; M.D., 1945. Publs: New Approaches to Sex in Marriage, 1967; The Marriage Art, 1961; A Doctor's Secrets of Youth, Health & Long Life, 1965; College Health, 1962; The Troubled Bed, 1971; Home Remedies, 1963; Home Tonics, 1963; The Minn. Drs. Home Treasury of Unusual Stress Easers & Strong Shields against Emotional & Physical Upset, 1964. Contbr. to: Parents; Pageant; Better Homes & Gardens. Mbr: AMA. Address: 237 Med. Arts Bldg., Mpls., MN 55402, USA.

EIDSLOTT, Arnold Olav, b. 10 June 1926, Ålesund, Norway. Telephone Service Engineer. Publs: (poems) Vinden taler til den Døve, 1953; Van & Støv, 1956; Kronen av Røk, 1959; Av Dynd & Amazonas, 1963; Manes, 1965; Memento, 1967; Elegisk om Sirkus, 1970; Ved Midnatt da Havet Sank, 1971; Rekviem for Lasarus, 1973. Mbr., Norwegian Authors Assn. Hons: Gyldendal's Bequest for Norwegian Lit., 1964; Ålesund Municipal Cultural Prize, 1972. Address: Vegsundstranda 62, 6020 Vegsund, (Ålesund), Norway.

EILON, Samuel, b. 13 Oct. 1923, Israel. University Teacher. Educ: B.Sc., Israel Inst. of Technol., Haifa; Ph.D. & D.Sc., Univ. of London, UK. Publs: Industrial Engineering Tables, 1962; Elements of Production Planning & Control, 1962; Exercises in Industrial Management (jointly), 1966; Industrial Scheduling Abstracts (jointly), 1967; Inventory Control Abstracts (jointly), 1968; Distribution Management (jointly), 1971; Management Control, 1971; Applications of Management Science in Banking & Finance, 1972. Co-Ed., Omega, Int. Jrnl. of Mgmt. Sci. Contbr. to num. jrnls. Mbrships. incl: Fellow, Instn. of Mech. Engrs.; Fellow, Instn. of Prod. Engrs. Address: Dept. of Mgmt. Sci., Imperial Coll., Exhibition Rd., London, SW7 2BX, UK.

EINARSSON, Ármann Kr., b. 30 Jan. 1915, Nedridalur i Biskupstungum, Arnessyslu, Iceland. Teacher; Author (writing in Icelandic). Educ: Tchr.'s Coll., Reykjavik; Tchrs.' Univ., Copenhagen, Denmark. Publs. incl: (short stories) Hopes, 1934; (novels) The story of Jonmundur at Geisladal, 1943; The Earth is Young, 1948; Nights of July, 1951; (25 jvnle. books inclng.) Oli & Maggi in the Wilderness, 1964; Vikings on Volcano Island, 1964; Oli & Maggi on an Ice-Floe, 1965; Oli & Maggi with Gold Diggers, 1966; Oli & Maggi Find the Gold Ship, 1968; Leifur the

Lucky, 1971; Down the Chimney, 1973; (play) Children in a Bad Fix, 1971; works widely transl'd. Mbrships: Assn. of Icelandic Writers; Coun. of Writers; PEN. Recip., Norwegian Lit. Prize, Solfugl, 1964. Address: Brautarlandi 12, Reykjavik, Iceland.

EISNER, Gisela, b. 3 Apr. 1925, Berlin, Germany. Educ: B.Com., Nottingham Univ., UK, 1946; Ph.D., Manchester Univ., 1957. Publs: Jamaica 1830-1930: A Study in Economic Growth. Address: 69 Macclesfield Rd., Buxton, Derbys., UK.

EISNER, Lotte Henrietta, b. Berlin, Germany. Writer; Journalist. Educ: Ph.D. Publs: L'Ecran Demoniaque, 1952; The Haunted Screen, 1969; (Eng. transl.) 1973; F. W. Murnau, 1964. Contbr. to: Sight & Sound; sev. French, Eng. & Am. Reviews. Hons: Prix Armand Tallier 1965; Chevalier des Arts & Lettres, 1967. Address: 5 rue des Dames Augustines, 92 Neuilly sur Seine, France.

EISNER, Robert, b. 17 Jan. 1922, Brooklyn, N.Y., USA. Professor of Economics. Educ: B.S.S., CCNY, 1940; M.A., Columbia Univ., 1942; Ph.D., Johns Hopkins Univ., 1951. Publs: Determinants of Capital Expenditures, 1956; Determinants of Business Investment (w. R. H. Strotz), 1963; Some Factors in Growth Reconsidered, 1966. Contbr. to: Review of Econ. Studies; Am. Econ, Review; Quarterly Jrnl. of Econs.; Econ. Jrnl.; Bd. of Ed., Am. Econ. Review. Mbr., var. econ. socs. Address: 800 Lincoln St., Evanston, IL 60201, USA.

EISS, Albert Frank, b. 2 Feb. 1910, La Fargeville, N.Y., USA. Learning Systems Consultant. Educ: A.B., Houghton Coll., N.Y., 1933; M.A., St. Lawrence Univ., Canton, N.Y., 1942; Ph.D., N.Y. Univ., 1954. Publs: The Earth-Space Sciences (co-author), 1970; Evaluation of Instructional Systems, 1970; Individualizing Learning, 1971; Tests: Their Production & Use, 1971; Evaluating Learning, 1973. Contbr. to Sci. & Children. Mbrships: Fellow, AAAS; Nat. Sci. Tchrs. Assn.; Nat. Soc. for Perf. & Instrn. Address: P.O. Box 847, Carrollton, GA 30117, USA.

EJVEGAARD, Rolf Bertil, b. 3 Sept. 1932, Stockholm, Sweden. Assistant Professor. Educ: Ph.D., Univ. of Stockholm; Dip., Tchr.'s Coll., Stockholm. Publs: Svartvita verb, 1963; Naturvetenskapens ursprung, 1968; Samhället och bostäderna, 1969; Samhällsdebatt, 1970; Filosofi för gymnasiet, 1970-73; Indföring i filosofi, 1972; Landstingsförbundet — organisation, beslutsfattande, förhållande till staten, 1973. Mbrships: Bd., Minerva Sect., Swedish Authors' Assn., 1972—; Pres., SPF, 1969—. Address: Mellansjöv. 35, 14146 Huddinge, Sweden.

EKBAUM, Salme, b. 21 Oct. 1912, Viljandimaa, Estonia. Writer. Educ: Grad., Pharm., Univ. of Tartu. Publs: 12 novels inclng. White House, 1946; & Love & Ambition, 1972; 3 books of poetry, 1951-74; sev. plays & short stories in Estonian. Mbrships: Estonian PEN Club; Can. Ctr., PEN; Union of Estonian Writers Abroad. Recip., 3 Estonian lit. awards. Address: 98 Galbraith Ave., Toronto 16, Ont. M4B 2B7, Can.

EKERWALD, Carl-Göran, b. 30 Dec. 1923, Östersund, Sweden. Writer. Educ: M.A. Publs: Cumminfield, 1962; Wolfe-Castle, 1963; Lotus-Eaters, 1966; Polish Sugar from Norway, 1967; Saltstamper, 1969; The Ascension of Bertrand Russell, 1974. Contbr. to: Svenska Dagbladet. Mbrships: Swedish Union of Authors; Swedish Union of Dramatists. Hons: Olof Högberg Prize, 1969; Peterson-Berger Prize, 1973. Address: Bergvik, 840 40 Svenstavik, Sweden.

EKIRCH, Arthur A., Jr., b. 1915, NYC, USA. University Professor. Educ: Dartmouth Coll.; Columbia Univ.; B.A., M.A., Ph.D. Publs: The Idea of Progress in America, 1815-60; The Decline of American Liberalism; The Civilian & The Military; Man & Nature in America; The American Democratic Tradition; Voices in Dissent; Ideas, Ideals & American Diplomacy; Ideologies & Utopias: Impact of the New Deal; The Challenge of American Democracy; Progressivism in America. Contbr. to: Saturday Review; Progressive; etc. Mbrships: Am. Histl. Assn.; Org. of Am. Histns.; Soc. of Am. Histns.; Am. Studies Assn. Address: 24 Tierney Drive, Delmar, NY 12054, USA.

EKLUND, Arne S. G., b. 8 Feb. 1919, Uppsala, Sweden. Editor. Educ: M.A. Publs: A Christ in Russia, 1960; Behind the Chinese Wall, 1966. Contbr. to: Evangelii Harold, pentacostal weekly (Ed.-in-Chief); Dagen, newspaper (For. Ed.). Mbr., Swedish Publicists Club; Assn. of Swedish

Authors; Swedish Jrnlsts. Assn. Address: Finbagarvagen 5, 123 54 Farsta-Stockholm, Sweden.

EKSTRÖM, Jan Olof, b. 2 Nov. 1923, Falun, Sweden. Chairman, Board of Directors. Educ: Bach. of Econs. Publs: Döden fyller år, 1961; Döden går i Moln, 1962; Träffracken, 1963; Morianerna, 1964; Daggormen, 1965; Ålkistan, 1967; Elddansen, 1970. Mbrships: Sec., Swedish Acad. of Detection; Swedish Authors' Assn.; Int. Advt. Assn.; Swedish Assn. of Economists. Recip., Expressen Sherlock Award for best detection novel of yr., 1963. Address: Linnégatan 7, Stockholm, Sweden.

EKSTRÖM, Margareta, b. 23 Apr. 1930, Stockholm, Sweden. Writer. Educ: B.A., Stockholm Univ., 1956. Publs: Aftnar i S:t Petersburg (Evenings in St. Petersburg), 1960; Frukostdags (Breakfast Time), 1961; Flickorna (The Girls), 1963; Husliga scener (Domestic Scenes), 1964; Beringön (Bering Island), 1965; När de red omkring (Riding About), 1969; Förhallandet till främmande makter (Relations with Foreign Powers), 1972; Ord till Johanna (Words for Johanna), 1973; Människodjuren (The Human Animals), 1974. Contbr. to: Swedish Radio; Expressen. Mbrships: VP, Swedish PEN, 1969—; Ed., Swedish Film Ind., 1974. Address: Stjärnan, 740 40 Heby, Sweden.

EKVALL, Robert Brainerd, b. 18 Feb. 1898, Minchow, China. Writer; Anthropologist; Former Missionary, Explorer, Army Officer. Educ: B.A., Wheaton Coll., USA, 1920; Grad. Nyack Missionary Coll., 1922; Grad. study, Univ. of Chgo. Num. publs. incl: Cultural Relations on the Kansu-Tibetan Border, 1939; Tibetan Voices (verse), 1946, 1968; Faithful Echo, 1960; Religious Observances in Tibet: Patterns & Function, 1964; Fields on the Hoof, 1968; The Younger Brother Don Yod (co-author); A Tibetan Principality (co-author), 1969. Contbr. to num. profl. US, for. jrnls. Address: Fairfax Star Rte., Carbonado, WA 98323, USA.

EKWENSI, Cyprian, b. 1921, Nigeria, W. Africa. Teacher; Head of Features, Nigerian Broadcasting Corp. Educ: Govt. Coll., Ibadan; Chelsea Schl. of Pharmacy, London Univ.; Ph.C.; M.P.C. Publs: Ikolo the Wrestler 1947; The Leopard's Claw, 1947; African New Writing, 1947; People of the City, 1954; Jagua Nana, 1961; Burning Grass, 1962; An African Night's Entertainment, 1962; Beautiful Feathers, 1963. Contbr. to: Wide World Mag.; BBC; W. Africa. W. African Review; etc. Mbrships: PEN; Pres., S. Ona. Soc. of Nigerian Authors. Address: 32 Rumens Rd., Ikoyi, Nigeria.

ELBOGEN, Paul, b. 1894, Vienna, Austria. Author; Editor; Screenwriter. Educ: B.A., Univ. of Vienna. Publs. incl: (anthols.) Liebste Mutter; Lieber Vater; Geliebter Sohn; (other) Verlassene Frauen: Essays; Kometen des Geides; Leben als Abenteuer; Dram; The Jealous Mistress; Der dunkle Stern; Genius im Werden, 1963; Humour since Homer, 1964. Contbr. to num. jrnls. Agent: Albrecht Leonhardt. Address: 218 21st Ave., San Fran., CA, USA.

ELDER, Michael Aiken, b. 1931, London, UK. Actor; Broadcaster. Educ: Dulwich Coll.; Royal Acad. of Dramatic Art, London. Publs: Paradise Is Not Enough, 1970; The Alien Earth, 1971; The Everlasting Man, 1972; Nowhere On Earth, 1972; The Perfumed Planet, 1973; Down To Earth, 1973; A Different World, 1974; The Seeds of Frenzy, 1974; Centurian Quest, 1975. Contbr. to over 1000 Radio Broadcasts; num. TV appearances. Address: 20 Zetland Pl., Edinburgh EH5 3LY, UK.

ELEGANT, Robert Sampson, b. 7 Mar. 1928, NYC, USA. Journalist; Author. Educ: A.B., Pa. Univ., 1946; Dip. Proficiency, Inst. Far Eastern Langs. & Lit., Yale Univ., 1948; M.A., 1950, M.S., 1951, Columbia Univ., NY. Publs: China's Red Masters, 1951; The Dragon's Seed, 1959; The Center of the World, 1964, revised ed., 1968; Mao's Great Revolution, 1971; Mao vs. Chiang: The Battle for China, 1972; (novels) A Kind of Treason, 1966; The Seeking, 1969. Contbr. to num. for. & nat. publs. Mbrships. incl: Hong Kong For. Corres.' Club (Pres., VP); Asia Soc. Hons. incl: Columbia Univ. Award Disting. Serv. Jrnlsm., 1970. Address: Riverdale, Templecarrig, County Wicklow, Repub. of Ireland.

ELEKTOROWICZ, Leszek, 29 May 1924, Lvov, Poland. Writer. Educ: M.A., Jagellonian Univ., Krakow. Publs: Swiat niestworzony, 1957; Kontury, 1962; Rejterada, 1963; Zwierciadło w okruchach, 1966; Przedmo wy do ciszy, 1968; Od Londynu do Teksasu i dalej, 1970; Przechadzki Sylena, 1971; Motywy zachodnie, 1973; Gwiazdy drwiace, 1974. Contbr. to: Twórczość;

Współczesność; Życie Literackie; Literatura; Sev. for. anthols. Mbrships: Bd., Kraków Dept., Polish Writers Union; PEN; Zaiks Soc. of Authors. Address: 30-036 Krakow, Ul.Mazowiecka 8 m. 4, Poland.

ELFENBEIN, Julien, b. 12 Aug. 1897, Chgo., Ill., USA. Professor of Journalism; Writer. Educ: Univ. of Texas. Publs: Business Journalism, 1945, 1969; Businesspaper Publishing Practice, 1952, 1971; Sales Management (w. E. Leterman) 1965; Business Letters & Communications, 1967; Editor's Manual of Editorial, Production & Publishing Procedures, 1970; Handbook of Business Form Letters & Forms, 1972. Contbr. to: Jrnlsm. Quarterly; Mag. World; Writer; Engrng. Quarterly; Advt. Age; Better Editing; etc. Mbrships. incl: Nat. Press Club; Mag. Publrs. Assn.; Assn. for Educ. in Jrnlsm. Hons. incl: Jesse H. Neal Award of Merit, 1957, 1959. Address: 1028 The Parkway, Mamaroneck, NY 10543, USA.

ELIOVSON, Sima, b. 1919, Cape Town, S. Africa. Teacher. Educ: B.A., Univ. of Witwatersrand. Publs: Flowering Shrubs, Trees & Climbers, 1951; South Africa, Land of Sunshine (w. E. Eliovson), 1952; Johannesburg, The Fabulous City (w. E. Eliovson), 1954; South African Wild Flowers for the Garden, 1955; The Complete Gardening Book, 1960; Discovering Wild Flowers in Southern Africa, 1962; This is South Africa (w. E. Eliovson), 1962; Proteas for Pleasure, 1965; Bulbs for the Gardener, 1967; Gardening the Japanese Way, 1970; Namaqualand in Flower, 1972. Contbr. to: Tatler; S. African Garden & Home. Mbrships. incl: PEN; Chrmn., Johannesburg Br., Bot. Soc. of S. Africa; Tree Soc. Address: 16 N. Rd., Dunkeld W., Johannesburg, S. Africa.

ELIS, Islwyn Ffowc, b. 17 Nov. 1924, Wrexham, Wales, UK. Author. Educ: Univ. of Wales; Bala Theol. Coll.; B.A., B.D. Publs. incl: Cyn Oeri'r Gwaed (essays), 1952; (novels) Cysgod y Cryman, 1953; Ffenestri Tua'r Gwyll, 1955; Yn Ol i Leifior, 1956; Blas y Cynfyd, 1958; Tabyrddau'r Babongo, 1961; Y Blaned Dirion, 1968; Y Gromlech yn yr Haidd, 1970; Eira Mawr, 1971; Harris (play), 1973; Marwydos (short stories), 1974. Contbr. to var. jrnls. Mbrships: Welsh Acad.; Brit. Soc. of Authors. Hons: Gold Medal for Prose, Nat. Eisteddfod of Wales, 1951; Fiction Prize, Arts Coun. of GB, 1962. Address: 6 Acton Gate, Wrexham, Clwyd, Wales LL11 2PN, UK.

ELKIN, Stanley (Lawrence), b. 11 May 1930, NYC, USA. Professor of English. Educ: B.A., 1952, M.A., 1953, Ph.D., 1961, Univ. of Ill., Urbana. Publs. (novels): Boswell, 1964; A Bad Man, USA, 1967, UK, 1968; The Dick Gibson Show, 1971; (short stories): Criers & Kibitzers, Kibitzers & Criers, USA, 1966, UK, 1968; The Making of Ashenden, 1972; (filmscript): The Six-Year-Old Man, 1969; Ed., Stories from the Sixties, 1971. Contbr. to: Epoch; Views; Southwest Review, etc. Hons: Longview Fndn. Award, 1962; Prize, Paris Review, 1965; Guggenheim Fellow, 1966; Rockefeller Fellow, 1968. Address: Dept. of English, Wash. Univ., St. Louis, MO 63130, USA.

ELKINS, T. H., b. 1926, Hampstead, UK. Professor of Geography. Educ: B.A.; London Schl. of Econs.; Liège Univ. Publs: Germany, 1960, 1968; The Urban Explosion, 1973; Contbr. to: Transactions Inst. Brit. Geogs.; Geographical Jrnl.; Geog.; Geographical Mag.; Chambers' Ency. Americana; etc. Mbrship: F.R.G.S. Address: 4 King Henry's Rd., Lewes, Sussex, UK.

ELLACOTT, Samuel Ernest, b. 20 May 1911, Winkleigh, Devon, UK. Retired Schoolmaster. Educ: Portsmouth Coll. of Educ.; Southampton Univ. Publs: Ships under the Sea, 1961; Armour & Blade, 1962; Collecting Arms & Armour, 1964; The Soldier, 2 vols., 1965; The Norman Invasion, 1966; History of Everyday Things in England, vol. 5, 1968; The Seaman, 2 vols., 1970; (novel) Until You Are Dead, 1972, 1974; 8 books for Methuen Outline series. Mbrships: Past Comm., Mbr. & Deleg., Nat. Union of Tchrs.; Arms & Armour Soc. Hons: Hons. Book Award, Lib. Assn.; Runner-up, Carnegie Award for Armour & Blade, 1962. Address: Pendennis, 8 Willand Rd., West Hill, Braunton, N. Devon, EX33 1AX, UK.

ELLIN, Stanley Bernard, b. 6 Oct. 1916, NYC, USA. Author. Educ: B.A., Bklyn. Coll., 1936. Publs: Dreadful Summit, 1948; The Key to Nicholas Street, 1952; The Eighth Circle, 1952; Mystery Stories, 1956; The Winter After This Summer, 1960; The Panama Portrait, 1962; The Blessington Method & Other Strange Tales, 1964; House of Cards, 1966; The Valentine Estate, 1968; The Bind, 1970; Mirror, Mirror on the Wall, 1972; Stronghold, 1974.

Contbr. to: num. lit. jrnls. & mags. in USA & UK. Mbrships. incl: Pres., Mystery Writers of Am., 1970; Crime Writers Assn. of England. Recip., Edgar Allan Poe Award, Mystery Writers of Am., 1956, 1958 & 1960. Address: c/o Curtis Brown Ltd., 60 E. 56 St., N.Y., NY 10022, USA.

ELLIOT, John, b. 4 July 1918, Reading, UK. Writer. Educ: King's Coll., Univ. of London. Publs: A for Andromeda (w. Fred Hoyle), 1962; Andromeda Breakthrough (w. Fred Hoyle), 1964; Long River, 1967; Duel, 1969; Mogul, 1970; Fall of Eagles, 1974. Contbr. to: BBC, 1948-64, 1967-70; Creator, A for Andromeda; The Troubleshooters; Fall of Eagles. Mbrships: Soc. of Film & TV Arts; Writers' Guild. Hons: Short Film Award, Venice, 1951; Special Award, Soc. of Film & TV Arts, 1959; Shell Int. TV Award, 1970. Address: 13c Camp Rd., Clifton, Bristol BS8 3LW, UK.

ELLIOT, John Harold, b. 1900, Bridgnorth, Shropshire, UK. Publs. incl: The Brass Band Movement (w. J. F. Russell), 1936; Berlioz, 1938. Contbr. to: News Chronicle (Northern Music Critic, 1929-39); Guardian (Northern Music Critic, 1959-65); Music & Letters; Music Survey; Monthly Music Record; Halle Mag.; Radio Times; Listener; etc. Address: 8 Doone Way, Alcombe, Minehead, Somerset, UK.

ELLIOTT, Brian Robinson, b. 11 Apr. 1910, Adelaide, S.A., Australia. University Reader. Author; Editor. Educ: M.A., Univ. of Western Aust.; D.Litt., Adelaide Univ. Publs: Leviathan's Inch (novel), 1946; Singing to the Cattle (Aust. lit. essays), 1947; Ed., Coast to Coast, Australian Stories, 1948; Marcus Clarke (biog. & lit. study), 1958; The Landscape of Australian Poetry (histl. survey), 1967; Bards in the Wilderness (Colonial poetry anthol., w. Adrian Mitchell), 1970; Adam Lindsay Gordon (Colonial poets series), 1973; Marcus Clarke, For the Term of His Natural Life (reprints w. intro.), 1973. Address: 25 Glenunga Ave., Glenunga, S. Australia.

ELLIOTT, Christopher R., b. Beccles, Suffolk, UK. Journalist; Press Officer. Publs: Aeronauts & Aviators in East Anglia, Part 1, 1780s—1930s, 1971. Contbr. to: Eagle Day; The Narrow Margin; Battle Over Brit.; The Lost Prince; Young Joe, the Forgotten Kennedy; Flight Int.; Air Pictorial; Mind Alive; Sunday Times Mag.; Scots Mag.; Eastern Daily Press; E. Anglian Daily Times; Wide World; Cambridge Evening News; RAF News; E. Anglian Mag.; Sunday Companion; Hist. of WWII; etc. Mbr., Inst. of Jrnlsts. Address: Flat 4, 77 South Park Rd., Wimbledon, London SW19 8RT, UK.

ELLIOTT, George P(aul), b. 16 June 1918, Knightstown, Ind., USA. Professor of English. Educ: A.B. 1939, M.A. 1941, Univ. of Calif., Berkeley. Publs. incl: (novels) Parktilden Village, 1958; David Knudsen, 1962; In The World, 1965; Muriel, 1972; (short stories) Among the Dangs, USA, 1961, UK, 1962; An Hour of Last Things, & Other Stories, USA, 1968, UK, 1969; (poems) 14 Poems, 1964; From the Berkeley Hills, 1969; (essays) A Piece of Lettuce, 1964; Conversions, 1971; Ed., Types of Prose Fiction, 1964. Hons. incl: Guggenheim Fellow, 1961; 1970; Grant, Nat. Inst. Arts & Letters, 1969. Address: Dept. of English, Syracuse Univ., Syracuse, NY 13210, USA.

ELLIOTT, Janice, b. 14 Oct. 1931, Derby, UK. Novelist. Educ: B.A., St. Anne's Coll., Oxford. Publs: (novels) Cave with Echoes, 1962; The Somnambulists, 1964; The Godmother, 1966; The Buttercup Chain, 1967; The Singing Head, 1968; Angels Falling, 1969; The Kindling, 1970; A State of Peace, 1971; Private Life, 1972; (children's) The Birthday Unicorn, 1970; Alexander in the Land of Mog, 1973. Contbr. to: Sunday Telegraph; New Statesman; Times; Sunday Times; N.Y. Times; Harper's Bazaar; Nova; Queen; Twentieth Century. Address: Yew Tree Cottage, Partridge Green, Horsham, Sussex RH13 8EQ, UK.

ELLIOTT, Molly Galbraith, pen name DAVIES, Jay, b. 25 Oct. 1920. Freelance Journalist. Publs: Island on the Skyline, 1971. Contbr. to: NZ Herald; NZ Farmer; Christchurch Press; Auckland Star; Thursday; Eve; Int. Hotel Review; Int. Tax-free Trader; Hospitality; Travel Age W.; Pacific; NZ Woman's Wkly.; etc. Mbrships: NZ Jrnlsts. Union; Aust. Soc. of Authors; Pub. Rels. Inst. of NZ; NZ Nat. Travel Authority; Inst. of Jrnlsts., UK. Recip., Travel Award, Engl.-Speaking Union, 1966. Address: 6/40 Lake Rd., Devonport, Auckland 9, NZ.

ELLIOTT, Neil, b. 1 Mar. 1940, Sheffield, Yorks., UK. Author; Journalist; Landlord. Educ: B.S., 1961, M.S., 1962, Northwestern Univ., USA. Publs: The Golden Stairway, 1962; The Hills of Creation, 1962; Business Management, 1964; Business Law, 1965; St. Ludmilla's, 1966; The Noisy American, 1967; Sensuality in Scandinavia, 1970; The Death Doctors, 1973; The Gods of Life, 1974; My Years with Capone, 1975; Inventions that Changed the World (in preparation). Contbr. to: Playboy, N.Y. Times Mag.; Argosy; Chgo. Sunday Tribune; & var. other publs. Recip., MCA Fellowship in Creative Jrnlsm., 1958-59. Address: 41 Haywood Ave., Deepcar, Near Sheffield, Yorks., UK.

ELLIOTT, Ralph Warren Victor, b. 14 Aug. 1921, Berlin, Germany. Master of University House, Australian National University. Educ: M.A., Univ. of St. Andrew's, 1949; M.A., Univ. of Adelaide, S. Aust., 1960; F.A.H.A. Publs: Runes: An Introduction, 1959, 3rd ed., 1971; Notes on English Literature, 1960, 2nd ed., 1965; Macmillans Critical Commentaries, 1966; Chaucer's English, 1974. Contbr. to: Engl. Studies; Speculum; Times; Guardian; etc. Mbrships. incl: Aust. Coun. for Arts; Aust. Soc. of Authors; Nat. Book League; etc. Hons. incl: Emeritus Prof. of Engl., Flinders Univ. of S. Aust., 1974. Address: Univ. House, Australian National Univ., Canberra, A.C.T., Australia 2600.

ELLIOTT, William Young, b. 18 Apr. 1902, Leeds, Ala., USA. Poet; Author; Teacher; Pyrometrist. Educ: B.S., Birmingham-Southern Coll.; M.A., Univ. of Ala.; Postgrad. study, George Peabody Coll. for Tchrs. Publs: (poetry) Skylights 1, 2 & 3, 1951, 1954, 1959; Voices, 1964; Wings for the Soul, 1969; (fiction) Most Lovely Lizzie, Love Letters of a Young Confederate Soldier, 1958. Contbr. of over 300 articles & poems to var. jrnls.; also short stories in anthols. Mbrships: World Poetry Soc. Intercontinental; Ala. Writers Conclave; Ala. State Poetry Soc.; Huntsville Writers Club. Hons: Num. poetry, short story prizes, 1958—; Poet of Year, Ala. State Poetry Soc. Address: 3516 Mariposa Rd. SW, Huntsville, AL 35805, USA.

ELLIOTT-BINNS, Michael Ferrers, b. 17 Aug. 1923, N. Ladbury, UK. Barrister-at-Law. Educ: M.A., St. John's Coll., Cambridge; Middle Temple. Publs: The Layman in Church Government, 1956; A Guide to the Pastoral Measure, 1969; The Layman and His Church, 1970. Contbr. to: Ministry; Crucible. Address: Woodlands Stables, Harestone Lane, Caterham, Surrey CR3 6AL, UK.

ELLIOTT-CANNON, Arthur Elliott, pen names FORDE, Nicholas, MARTYN, Myles, b. 1919, Ashton-under-Lyne, Lancs., UK. Former Teacher; Former Publisher; Writer. Educ: St. Luke's Coll., Exeter. Publs. incl: Taking Note, 1959; Reading & Thinking; The Wild West, 1960; Australia, Diaries & Letters, 1961; Good Company, 1966; Second Verse, 1968; The Exmoor Companion, 1969; Pleasure in Reading, 1968; The Mayflower Story, 1970. Contbr. to: World Ency.; Norfolk Mag.; Woman & Home; NZ Mirror; etc. Mbr., Soc. of Authors; League of Brit. Dramatists. Address: Weymans, Gunswell Lane, S. Molton, Devon, UK.

ELLIS, Cuthbert Hamilton, pen name ELLIS, Hamilton, b. 9 June 1909, Merton, Surrey, UK. Author; Painter; Illustrator. Educ: Exeter Coll., Oxford Univ. Publs: (self-illustrated) Rapidly Round the Bend, 1959; The Splendour of Steam, 1965; The Engines that Passed, 1968; King Steam, 1971; also var. books for boys, 1939-44; Dandy Hart (novel), 1947; London, Midland & Scottish, & other vols. of railway company histories, 1953-70; The Trains We Loved; British Railway History, 2 vols. Contbr. to: Country Life; Railway Gazette; Railway Mag.; Mod. Transp.; Daily Telegraph; etc. Address: Monk's Barn, Tilmorey, Petersfield, Hants., UK.

ELLIS, David, b. 22 June 1918, Manchester, UK. Writer. Publs: (play) Make me a Widow, 1965; num. scripts for TV incl: Dixon of Dock Green; Compact; Crossroads; Emergency Ward Ten; Z Cars; Paul Temple; Spy Trap; Marked Personal; Spyder's Web; The Inside Man. Mbr., Writers Guild of GB. Address: Four Winds, Beacon Rd., Seaford, Sussex, UK.

ELLIS, Gwynn Pennant, b. Cynwyd, Wales, UK. Senior Lecturer, University of Wales. Publs: Modern Textbook of Organic Chemistry, 1966; Qualitative Organic Chemical Analysis, 1967; Medicinal Chemistry Reviews, 1972. Contbr. to: Jrnl. of the Chem. Soc.; Jrnl. of Pharm. & Pharmacol.; Jrnl. of Medicinal Chem.; Jrnl. of Applied

Bacteriol.; Co-Ed., Progress in Medicinal Chem., 1961—; etc. Mbr., Soc. of Authors. Address: Dept. of Chem., Univ. of Wales Inst. of Sci. & Technol., King Edward VII Ave., Cardiff CF1 3NU, UK.

ELLIS, Humphry Francis, b. 1907, Metheringham, Lincs., UK. Journalist; Author. Educ: M.A., Magdalen Coll., Oxford. Publs: The Papers of A. J. Wentworth (as the Vexations of A. J. Wentworth, USA); Twenty-five Years Hard; Ed., The Manual of Rugby Union Football; Mediatrics; The World of A. J. Wentworth; Co-ed., The Royal Artillery Commemoration Book 1939-45. Contbr. to: New Yorker; Countryman. Mbr., Authors Soc. Recip., M.B.E. Agent: Curtis Brown Ltd. Address: Hill Croft, Kingston St. Mary, Taunton, Somerset, UK.

ELLIS, Keith Stanley, b. 1927, Sheffield, Yorks., UK. Magazine & Freelance Writer; Author. Educ: B.A., St. John's Coll., Cambridge. Publs: Health & Happiness in Retirement; How to Make Money in Your Spare Time; The American Civil War; Warriors & Fighting Men; The Making of America; Prediction & Prophecy; Science & The Supernatural; Man & His Money; Man & Measurement; Thomas Telford, Father of Civil Engineering; Thomas Edison, Genius of Electricity. Contbr. to num. mags. Address: 3 Belmont Hill, St. Albans, Herts., UK.

ELLIS, Kenneth Leslie, b. 1924, London, UK. University Lecturer in Modern History. Educ: M.A., D.Phil., Christ Church, Oxford. Publs: The Post Office in the Eighteenth Century. Address: History Dept., North Bailey, Durham City, UK.

ELLIS, Lewis Ethan, b. 1898, Otisco, N.Y., USA. Professor of History. Educ: A.M., Syracuse Univ.; Ph.D., Univ. of Chgo. Publs: Reciprocity, 1911: A Study in Canadian-American Relationships; Print Paper Pendulum: Group Pressures & the Price of Newsprint; A Short History of American Diplomacy; Newsprint: Politics, Pressures; Frank B. Kellogg & American Diplomacy, 1925-29. Contbr. to: Miss. Valley Hist. Review; Hispanic Hist. Review. Address: Logan Lane, River Rd., New Brunswick, NJ, USA.

ELLIS, Oliver Coligny De Champfleur, pen name (jointly w. D. M. Gibbons-Turner) BRIONY, Henry, b. 7 July 1889, Sleaford, UK. Lecturer & Investigator, Forensic Science & Defence of Standard English. Educ: Univs. of Manchester & Sheffield; B.Sc., 1912; M.Sc., 1920; Ph.D., 1922; D.Sc., 1936; M.A., 1946. Publs. incl: Samson Adami, 1919; A History of Fire & Flame, 1932; Cleopatra in the Tide of Time, 1947; For English Undefiled, 1950; The Sword of the Lord, 1952; Rational Religious Belief, 1962; Rational Religious Practice, 1966; Rational Religious Conclusion, 1972. Contbr. & Ed., num. sci. & lit. jrnls. Mbrships. incl: Pres., Poetry Lovers' Fellowship; Fndr.-Mbr., VP, Poetry Soc. Inc.; F.R.I.C. Recip., sev. prizes for poetry. Address: The Old Rectory, Clee St. Margaret, Craven Arms, Salop. SY7 9DT, UK.

ELLIS, Vivian, b. 1904, London, UK. Writer. Educ: Cheltenham Coll. Publs: Faint Harmony; Zelma; Day Out; Chicanery; Ellis in Wonderland—A Hollywood Diary; I'm on a See-Saw: Autobiography; How to Make Your Fortune on the Stock Exchange; How to Enjoy Your Operation; How to Bury Yourself in the Country; How to be a Man-About-Town; Good-Bye Dollie; (children's books) Hilary's Tune; Hilary's Holidays; The Magic Baton. Contbr. to: The Rise & Fall of the Matinee Idol; Homes & Gardens; Cornhill Mag.; The Countryman; Evening Standard; Good Gardening; etc. Mbr., Garrick Club. Address: The Kennels, Holnicote, Nr. Minehead, Somerset, UK.

ELLISON, Joan Audrey Anderson, pen name ROBERTSON, Elspeth, b. 1928, Workington, Cumberland, UK. Microbiologist; Assistant Lecturer; Food Consultant. Educ: B.Sc., Queen Elizabeth Coll., London. Publs: The Great Scandinavian Cook Book (transl. & Ed.), 1966; The Findus Book of Fish Cookery, 1967; Foods of the World Series, 1969-70; The World Atlas of Food (contbng. author), 1974. Mbrship: Soc. of Chem. Ind.; Fellow, Inst. of Food Sci. & Technol.; Inst. of Food Technol.; Nutrition Soc.; Prog. Comm., Int. Wine & Food Soc. Address: 74 Doneraile St., London SW6 6EP, UK.

ELLISON, Norman Frederick, pen name NOMAD, b. 26 Apr. 1893, Liverpool, UK. Author; Broadcaster; Lecturer. Publs. incl: Down Nature's Byways, 1938; Roaming with Nomad, 1949; Adventuring with Nomad, 1950; The Wirral Peninsula, 1955, Birds of the Hilbre Island; Mammals, Reptiles & Amphibians of Lancashire & Cheshire; Marine &

Fresh Water Fishes of Lancashire & Cheshire (w. J. C. Chubb); Land & Marine Mammals of Hilbre Island, 1969. Contbr. to: Proceedings, Zool. Soc.; Cheshire Life; Liverpool Echo; etc. Mbrships incl: Fellow, Linnean Soc.; Fellowships, num. other acad. socs. Recip., Kingsley Mem. Medal, 1946. Address: 36 Mount Rd., West Kirby, Wirral, Merseyside L48 2HL, UK.

ELLISON, Ralph (Waldo), b. 1 Mar. 1914, Okla. City, Okla., USA. Professor in the Humanities. Educ: Tuskegee Inst., Ala., 1933-36. Publs: Invisible Man (novel), USA, 1952, UK, 1953; Shadow & Act (essays), USA, 1964, UK, 1966. Contbr. to: Quarterly Review of Lit.; Partisan Review; Iowa Review; Direction; New World Writing; Soon, One Morning, 1963; etc. Mbrships incl: Nat. Inst. Arts & Letters (Chmn., Lit. Grants Comm., 1964-67); Ed. Bd., Am. Scholar, 1966-69; Am. Acad. Arts & Scis.; num. trusteeships. Hons. incl: Nat. Book Award, 1953; Prix de Rome, Nat. Acad. Arts & Letters, 1955, 1956; num. docts. Address: 730 Riverside Dr., N.Y., NY 10031, USA.

ELLISON, Virginia Tier Howell, pen names MAPES, Mary A.; MUSSEY, Virginia T. H.; YUN, Leong Gor, b. 4 Feb. 1910, NYC, USA. Writer. Educ: B.A., Vassar Coll., 1932. Publs: The Exploits of George Washington, 1933; Chinatown Inside Out (w. Y. K. Chu), 1936; Falla, A President's Dog, 1941; Fun with Your Child, 1943; Surprise!, 1944; Who Likes the Dark?,1945; Training Pants, 1946; The Pooh Cook Book, 1969; The Pooh Party Book, 1971; The Pooh Get-Well Book, 1973; & other books as ghost-writer. Address: 92 Mather Rd., Stamford, CT 06903, USA.

ELLMANN, Richard, b. 1918, Highland Pk., Mich., USA. Goldsmiths' Professor of English Literature, Oxford Univ. Educ: Yale Univ.; Trinity Coll., Dublin, Repub. of Ireland; M.A., B.Litt., Ph.D. Publs: Yeats: The Man & the Masks, 1948; The Identity of Yeats, 1954; James Joyce, 1959; Eminent Domain, 1967; Ulysses on the Liffey, 1972; Golden Codgers, 1973; The Artist as Critic: Critical Writings of Oscar Wilde; Letters of James Joyce, vols. 2 & 3; Giacomo Joyce; The Critical Writings of James Joyce (Co-Ed.); The Modern Tradition. Recip., Nat. Book Award, 1959. Address: New College, Oxford, UK.

ELLMERS Judith Corrighliee, pen names LOMOND, Judy; CORIELLE, b. 26 Apr. 1925, Gisborne, NZ. Farmer; Writer. Contbr. to: NZ Weekly News; NZ Women's Weekly; NZ Farmer; poetry, Eve mag. Mbr., NZ Women Writers' Soc. Inc. Recip., Commendation. int. essay competition, Assoc. Country Women of World, 1969. Address: "Rahiri", RD 1, Te Karaka, Gisborne, NZ.

ELLNER, Charles H., b. 12 Aug. 1901, NYC, USA. Counselor-at-Law (retired). Educ: A.B., Columbia Coll., NYC, 1922; LL.B., 1925, Jur.D., Columbia Law Schl., NYC. Publs: In My Opinion — Tales from a Lawyer's Briefcase, forthcoming. Contbr. to: N.Y. State Dental Jrnl.; Columbia Law Review; L.I. Press; etc. Mbrships. incl: Fellow Int. Inst. Arts & Letters; N.Y. County Lawyers' Assn.; Queens County Bar Assn.; (former) Fellow Int. Acad. Law & Sci.; Am. Judicature Soc.; Am. Bar. Assn.; N.Y. State Bar Assn.; N.Y. State Trial Lawyers' Assn.; Acad. Pol. Sci.; N.Y. Econ. Club; N.Y. City Club. Hons. incl: Hubbard Math. Medal; Selective Serv. Medal, 1946; Arbitrator, Am. Arbitrators' Assn.; & num. acad. & profl. awards. Address: 4712 N.W. 58th St., Fort Lauderdale, FL 33319, USA.

ELSE-MITCHELL, Rae, b. 1914, Sydney, Australia. Supreme Court Judge (ret'd); Chairman, Australian Grants Commission. Educ: LL.B., Univ. of Sydney; Barrister-at-Law. Publs: Hire Purchase Law, 1941, 4th ed. 1968; Property Legislation & War Damage, 1942; Essays on Australian Constitution, 1952, 1961; Land Tax Law (N.S.W.) (co-author), 1957; Public Administration in Australia, 1958, 1968. Contbr. to: legal jrnls. inclng. Aust. Law Jrnl. (Ed., 1946-58); var. histl. & planning publs. Mbrships incl: Fellow, Royal Aust. Histl. Soc.; Pres., Coun. Lib., N.S.W., 1974-; Coun., Nat. Lib. of Aust., 1974-; Chmn., var. Royal Commns. Address: 27 Lord St., Roseville, N.S.W. 2069, Australia.

ELSEN, Albert Edward, b. 11 Oct. 1927, NYC, USA. Teacher; Scholar. Educ: A.B., 1949, M.A., 1951, Ph.D., 1955, Columbia Univ., N.Y. Publs. incl: Rodin's Gates of Hell, 1960; Purposes of Art, 1962, 3rd ed., 1972; Rodin, 1963; Auguste Rodin: Readings on His Life & Work, 1965; The Partial Figure in Modern Sculpture, Rodin to 1969; Seymour Lipton, 1972; The Sculpture of Henri Matisse,

1973; Paul Jenkins, 1973; Origins of Modern Sculpture, Pioneers & Premises, 1974. Contbr. to: Art News: Art Int.; etc. Mbrships. incl: The Coll. Art Assn. Am. (Dir., 1966-70, Sec. 1970-72, VP, 1972-74, Pres. 1974-). Hons. incl: Guggenheim Fellow, 1966-67; Sr. Fellow, Nat. Endowment Humanities, 1973-74. Address: 723 Alvarado Row, Stanford, CA 94305, USA.

ELSNA, Hebe, pen names SNOW, Lyndon; CONWAY, Laura. Publs. incl: (biogs.) A Defence of Mrs. Charles Dickens; Catherine of Braganza; (novels) The Cherished Ones; The Elusive Crown; Prelude for Two Queens; (plays) A Shade of Darkness; Mary Olivane; The Dream & the World; (as Lyndon Snow) Head of the House; Moment of Truth; (as Laura Conway) Heiress Apparent; The Unforgotten. Address: c/o Curtis Brown Ltd., 1 Craven Hill, London W2, UK.

ELSOM, John Edward, b. 1904, Westcliff-on-Sea, Essex, UK. Drama Lecturer; Theatre Critic. Educ: B.A.(Hons.), Magdalene Coll., Cambridge. Publs: Theatre Outside London, 1971; Erotic Theatre, 1973. Contbr. to: London Mag.; Theatre Quarterly; Observer; Listener. Agent: Campbell Thomson & McLaughlin Ltd. Address: 39 Elsham Road, Kensington, London W14 8HB, UK.

ELSTOB, Peter, b. 22 Dec. 1915, London, UK. Writer; Secretary-General, International PEN. Educ: Univ. Mich. Publs: Spanish Prisoner, 1939; The Flight of the Small World, 1959; Warriors for the Working Day,1960; The Armed Rehearsal, 1964; Bastogne The Road Block, 1968; The Battle of the Reichswald, 1970; Hitler's Last Offensive, 1971; Condor Legion, 1973. Contbr. to: War Monthly; Purnell's History of the 2nd World War. Mbrships: Savage Club; Soc. of Authors; PEN; Authors' Guild. Address: 22 Belsize Pk. Gdns., London NW3 4LH, UK.

ELSTON, Allan Vaughan, b. 2 July 1887, Kan. City, Mo., USA. Writer. Educ: B.S., Civ. Engrng., Univ. of Mo., 1909. Publs. incl: Timberline Bonanza, 1962; Roundup on the Yellowstone, 1962; The Landseekers, 1963; The Seven Silver Mountains, 1963; The Lawless Border, 1965; Montana Passage, 1967; Montana Manhunt, 1968; Arizona Skyline, 1969; The Big Pasture, 1970; Paradise Prairie, 1971; Saddle Up For Steamboat, 1972. Contbr. of 300 Short stories, novelets & serials to num mags., anthols. etc. Mbrships: Past Pres., Calif. Writers Guild; Western Writers of Am. Address: 2121 North Flower St., Santa Ana, CA 92706, USA.

ELSY, Mary, b. Hampstead, London, UK. Journalist; Writer. Educ: Oakley Tchrs. Trng. Coll., Cheltenham, Glos. Publs: Travels in Belgium & Luxembourg, 1966; Brittany & Normandy, 1974. Contbr. to: Sunday Telegraph; Observer; Christian Sci. Monitor; She; Petticoat; My Home & Family; Elizabethan; Travel; In Brit.; Nursery World; Odham's Children's Ency.; Children's TV, BBC. Mbr., Soc. of Authors. Address: 519c Finchley Rd., Hampstead, London NW3, UK.

ELTON, Geoffrey Rudolph, b. 1921, Tübingen, Germany. University Professor; Author. Educ: Ph.D., Univ. of London, UK; Litt.D., Cambridge Univ. Publs: The Tudor Revolution in Government; England Under the Tudors; Star Chamber Stories; The Tudor Constitution; Reformation Europe; The Practice of History; Sources of History, England 1200-1640; Political History Principles & Practice; Ed., New Cambridge Modern History, vol. 2; Modern Historians on British History, 1485-1945; Policy & Police; Reform & Renewal; Studies in Tudor & Stuart Government & Politics (2 vols.). Contbr. to: Engl. & Econ. Hist. Reviews; Hist. Jrnl.; Listener; Guardian; etc. Address: Clare College, Cambridge, UK.

ELVIN, Harold, b. 1909, Buckhurst Hill, Essex, UK. Designer of Ceramics & Furniture. Educ: Southend Schl. of Arch.; Ctrl. Arts Schl., London. Publs: The Ride to Chandigarh; A Cockney in Moscow; The Story of Canons; A Fandango for a Crown of Thorns; To Heaven with the Devil; Avenue to the Door of the Dead; Elvin's Rides; The Incredible Mile: Siberia, Mongolia, Uzbekistan, 1970; When She Cried on Friday; The Gentle Russian, 1974. Contbr. to: Punch; Men Only; Envoy; Times of India; Sunday Statesman; Hindu, Madras; The Statesman, Siam. Hons: Winner, Tom Gallon Trust Award for Fiction, 1960-61; Winner, Atlantic Award in Lit.; Winston Churchill Fellow, 1968-69. Address: 54 Kensington Ct., London W8 5DE, UK.

ELWARD, James, pen name JAMES, R., b. 22 Nov. 1928, Chgo., Ill., USA. Author; Playwright. Educ: A.B., Cath. Univ., 1950. Publs: Paper Foxhole (TV play); Upbeat (play); The Man on the Bearskin Rug (libretto for 1-act opera); Friday Night (play); Best of Friends (play); Hallelujah! (play). Contbr., Cosmopolitan mag. Active TV writer. Recip., Writers' Guild Award for Best TV Comedy Script. Address: 14 Bank St., N.Y., NY 10014, USA.

ELY, David, b. 19 Nov. 1927, Chgo., Ill., USA. Author. Educ: Univ. of N.C., 1944-45; B.A., Harvard Univ., 1949; Oxford Univ., UK, 1954-55. Publs: (novels) Trot, USA, 1963, UK, 1964; Seconds, USA, 1963, UK, 1964; The Tour, USA & UK 1967; Poor Devils, 1970; (short stories) Time Out, USA, 1968, UK, 1969. Contbr. to: Amazing; Cosmopolitan; Elks Mag.; Saturday Evening Post; Cavalier; Playboy; Ellery Queen's Mystery Mag.; Antaeus. Recip., Fulbright Schlrship, 1954. Address: Costa San Giorgio 47, Florence, Italy.

ELYTIS, Odysseus, b. 2 Nov. 1911, Heraklion, Crete. Chairman of the Board, Hellenic National Radio & Television Institute; Board Member, National Theatre. Educ: Athens Univ.; Sorbonne Univ., Paris, France. Publs. incl: Orientations, 1940; Sun the First, 1943; Six and One Remorses for the Sky, 1959; The Tree of Light, 1971; The Sovereign Sun, 1972; The Monogram, 1973; Open Book, 1974; The Siblings, 1974. Contbr. to: Verve (Paris); Mercure de France (Paris); Poetry (Chgo.); Books Abroad (Okla.). Mbrships: Assn. Int. des Critiques d'Art; European Soc. of Culture. Hons: First State Prize, Poetry, 1960; Order of Phoenix, 1965. Address: 23 Skoufa Str., Athens, 136, Greece.

EMERSON, Alfred Edwards, b. 1896, Ithaca, N.Y., USA. Emeritus Professor of Zoology, University of Chicago. Educ: B.S., M.A., Ph.D., Cornell Univ., N.Y. Publs: Termite City (w. Eleanor Fish), 1937; Principles of Animal Ecology (w. W. C. Allec, O. Park, T. Park & K. P. Schmidt), 1949; Evolution of Behaviour (w. Anne Roe & G. G. Simpson), 1958; Evolution after Darwin (w. Sol Tax & others), 1960; Science Ponders Religion (w. Harlow Shapley), 1960. Contbr. to: Am. Mus. Natural Hist.; Zoologica; etc. Mbrships: Nat. Acad. Scis.; Ecol. Soc. Am. (Pres., 1941); Soc. Study Evolution (Pres., 1960); Soc. Systematic Zool. (Pres. 1958). Recip., Sc.D.(Hon.). Address: Huletts Landing, NY 12841, USA.

EMERSON, David, b. 1900, Frome, Somerset, UK. Writer. Publs. 24 novels inclng: The Wistaria Woman, 1961; Julie & The General, 1963; Scrope & the Spinster, 1964; Sweet Orchard, 1965; The Obliging Housemaid, 1966; Young Sweetly, 1967; Old Man's Darling, 1968; Cartwright's Wicked Aunt, 1969; A Murder in the Family, 1970; Little Brother Claude, 1971; Nancy in London, 1972; Aunt Campbell's Young Man, 1973; A Nice Little Widow, 1974. Contbr. to: Westminster Gazette; Observer, 1920-30. Mbr., Soc. of Authors. Agent: Hutchinson Publng. Grp. Address: 15 St. Andrew's Rd., Burnham-on-Sea, Somerset, UK.

EMERSON, William Keith, b. 1 May 1925, San Diego, Calif., USA. Biologist; Author; Curator of Invertebrates, American Museum of Natural History. Educ: A.B., Calif. State Univ., San Diego, 1948; M.S., Univ. of Southern Calif., L.A., 1950; Ph.D., Univ. of Calif., Berkeley, 1956. Publs. incl: Wonders of the World of Shells: Sea, Land, & Fresh-water (w. M. K. Jacobson), 1971; Shells (w. A. Feininger), 1972; Traumgebilde des Meeres, Muscheln und Schnecken (w. A. Feininger), 1972; Wonders of Barnacles (w. A. Ross), 1974. Contbr. to sci. jrnls. & encys. Mbrships. incl: Pres., Am. Malacol. Union, 1961-62; Pres., Western Soc. of Malacols., 1968-69. Recip., sev. awards for rsch. Address: 10 E. End Ave., Apt. 18E, N.Y., NY 10021, USA.

EMMANUEL, Pierre, b. 3 May 1916, Gan, France. University Teacher; Broadcaster; Writer. Publs. incl: (poetry) Tombeau d'Orphée, 1941; Sodome, 1944; Le Poète fou, 1944; Visage Nuage, 1956; La Nouvelle Naissance, 1963; Ligne de Faîte, 1968; Jacob, 1970; (novel) Car enfin je vous aime; (autobiography) Qui est cet homme, 1948; (essays) La Face humaine, 1965; Choses Dites, 1970; Pour une Politique de la culture, 1971; Sophia, 1973. Contbr. to Radiodiffusion Française. Mbrships: French Acad.; Pres., PEN, 1969-71; Admnstr., Int. City of Arts. Hons. incl: Officer, Legion of Honour. Address: 61 rue de Varenne, Paris 7e, France.

EMMET, Dorothy Mary, b. 1904, London, UK. Emeritus Professor of Philosophy; Author. Educ: M.A.,

Lady Margaret Hall, Oxford. Publs: Whitehead's Philosophy of Organism; The Nature of Metaphysical Thinking; Function, Purpose & Powers; Rules, Roles & Relations; Sociological Theory & Philosophical Analysis (co-ed. w. A. Macintyre). Contbr. to: Mind; Philos.; Proceedings of Aristotelian Soc.; etc. Recip., Hon.D.Litt., Glasgow Univ. Address: 11 Millington Rd., Cambridge, UK.

EMMET, Eric Revell, b. 28 May 1909, London, UK. Schoolmaster. Educ: B.A., Brasenose Coll., Oxford Univ., 1932. Publs: An Introduction to Economics (co-author), 1939; The Use of Reason, 1960, Dutch ed., 1961; Learning to Philosophise, 1964, paperback, 1968, Dutch ed., 1968; Learning to Think, & Companion to Learning to Think, 1965, Dutch ed., 1969; 101 Brain Puzzlers, 1967, USA, 1973, also as Brain Puzzlers Delight, USA, 1968; Puzzles for Pleasure, USA, 1972; Sunday Times Brain Teasers (co-author), 1974. Contbr. to: Mind; Philos.; var. econ. jrnls. Address: Flat 2, Domum House, Domum Rd., Winchester, UK.

EMMONS, Della Gould, b. Glencoe, Minn., USA. Writer. Educ: B.S., Univ. of Minn., 1912; Creative Writing, Univ. of Wash. Publs. incl: Sacajawea of the Shoshones, 1943; Sacajawea, Spanish transl., 1949. Nothing In Life Is Free, 1953; Leschi of the Nisquallies, 1965; Jay Gould's Million Dollar Gems, 1974. Northwest History in Action, 12 Plays, 1960. Mbrships: Int. Mark Twain Literary Soc., 1943—; Nat. League of Am. Pen Women, 1944; Pacific Northwest Int. Writers, 1945—; Hons: 1st Award, Histl. Novels, 1964, Histl. Writings, 1966, Nat. League of Am. Pen Women; Reg. Award for Histl. Writings, Am. Pen Women, 1966; Torch Bearer Award, Wash. Press Women, 1973. Address: 814 N. Lawrence, Tacoma, WA 98406, USA.

EMTAGE, James Bernard de Courcey, b. Barbados, W. Indies. Writer. Educ: M.A., Magdalen Coll., Oxford Univ. Publs: Brown Sugar, 1966; Ski Fever; The Laughter Omnibus; The Pick Of The Cricketer, 1967. Contbr. to: Punch; Cricketer; Sunday Telegraph. Mbrships. incl: Author's Club. Agent: Bolt & Watson. Address: 64 Tycehurst Hill, Loughton, Essex, UK.

ENCKELL, (Valter) Mikael (Henrik), b. 2 Sept. 1932, Helsinki, Finland. Psychoanalyst; Author. Educ: M.D., 1960; Psychoanalytic Trng., Sweden, 1962-67; Psych. Trng., Finland, 1967-69. Publs: The Hidden Motive, 1962; The Reversed Visage, 1969; Across the Border of Silence, 1972; var. essays, psychoanalytic approaches to lit. & films. Hons: Svenska litteratursällskapet i Finland, 1970, 1973; State Prize, 1973. Address: Ulrikagatan 1 A 7, 00140 Helsinki 14, Finland.

ENGDAHL, Sylvia Louise, b. 24 Nov. 1933, L.A., Calif., USA. Writer; Former Computer Systems Specialist. Educ: A.B., Univ. of Calif., Santa Barbara, 1955. Publs: Enchantress From the Stars, 1970, UK ed., 1974; Journey Between Worlds, 1970; The Far Side of Evil, 1971; This Star Shall Abide, 1972, UK ed., Heritage of the Star, 1973; Beyond the Tomorrow Mountains, 1973; The Planet Girded Suns: Man's View of Other Solar Systems, 1974. Contbr. to: Horn Book Mag.; Schl. Media Quarterly; Engl. Jrnl. Recip., Newbery Hon. Book Award, 1971. Address: Box 53, Gdn. Home P.O., Portland, OR 97223, USA.

ENGEL, David (Dezsö), b. 1 Feb. 1894, Banska Bystrica, Czech. Surgeon; Scientist. Educ: M.D., Univ. of Budapest, Hungary; Univ. of Prague, Czech.; Univs. of Heidelberg, Leipzig & Kiel, Germany; Univ. of Edinburgh, UK. L.R.C.P.S., F.R.C.S., Edinburgh. Contbr. of over 60 sci. articles on cancer, surgery, orthopaedics, pathol., pharmacol., & physiol., to Brit., Am. & German jrnls. Mbrships: Brit. Med. Assn.; F.I.C.S.; Med. Bd., Shanghai Municipal Coun., China; Fndr. & Ed.-in-Chief, Folia Medica Sinica; Goethe Soc. Address: Volta Str. 64, 8044 Zurich, Switz.

ENGEL, Gilson Colby, b. 1898, Balt., Md., USA. Emeritus Professor of Clinical Surgery. Educ: B.A., D.M.; Johns Hopkins Univ.; Harvard Univ. Publs. incl: Two-plane Direction & Range Finder for Nailing Fracture of Neck of the Femur; The Creation of a Gastric Pouch following Total Gastrectomy; Carcinoma of the Stomach & Its problems; Acute Diffuse Hemorrhagic Gastritis; Reducing Mortality in Gastric Carcinoma; An Evaluation of Subtotal Gastrectomy for Gastric & Duodenal Lesions — A Post-Operative Survey of 100 Cases. Mbrships: Union League, Racquet Clubs, Phila.; Aesculapian Club, Boston. Address: 312 Lankenau Medical Bldg., Philadelphia 31, PA 19151, USA.

ENGELMANN, Bernt, b. 20 Jan. 1921, Berlin, Germany. Writer. Educ: Univs. of Cologne; Geneva, Switzerland; Paris, France (Mod. Hist., Lit., Langs., Law). Publs: Meine Freunde, die Millionäre, 1963; Meine Freunde, die Manager, 1966; Deutschland-Report, 1964; Deutschland ohne Juden, 1969; Die Macht am Rhein I & II, 1968; Krupp — Legenden und Wirklichkeit, 1970; Die vergoldeten Bräute, 1971; Das Reich zerfiel, die Reichen blieben, 1972; Wir Untertanen — Ein Deutsches Anti-Geschichtsbuch, 1973; Grosses Bundesverdienstkreuz, 1974. Mbr., PEN (VP, W. German Ctr., 1972-74); Verband deutscher Schriftsteller. Address: Haus am Wald, Berg, D-8183 Rottach-Egern, Oberbayern, W. Germany.

ENGERBRETSON, David L. pen name TRACY, David, b. 18 Feb. 1936, Tracy, Minn., USA. University Professor; Freelance Writer; Photographer. Educ: B.S., Phys. Educ., Macalester Coll., St. Paul, Minn., 1958; M.S., Univ. of Ill., 1962; Ph.D., Pa. State Univ., 1970. Contbr. to: Field & Stream; True; The Flyfisher; Fly Fisherman; TWA Ambassador; Trout; The Roundtable; Wilderness Camping; Camping Jrnl.; Greater Assn. Freshwater Fisherman; Nat. 4-H News; Ency. of Phys. Educ.; Jrnl. Assn. Mental & Phys. Rehab.; Angler's Bible; Dynamic Maturity; other jrnls. Mbrships. incl: Outdoor Writers' Assn. of Am.; Northwest Outdoor Writers' Assn. Address: 918 S. Logan St., Moscow, ID 83843, USA.

ENGH, Björg Larsen, pen names BJØRNSTAD, Marianne; BLENGH, b. 19 Mar. 1945, Oslo, Norway. Journalist. Educ: Oslo Bis. Coll. Publs: Sub-Ed., Norwegian musicians & artists, Tiden Leksikon, 1974. Contbr. to: Det Nye; Alle Kvinner; UMAG; Verdens Gang. Mbr., Norwegian Press Assn. Address: Gullkroken 9, Oslo 3, Norway.

ENGLAND, Barry, b. 1932, London, UK. Author. Publs: Figures in a Landscape, 1968; (stage plays) End of Conflict; The Damn-Givers; The Big Contract; Conduct Unbecoming; (TV plays) The Sweet War Man; The Move After Checkmate; You'll Know Me by the Stars in my Eyes. Recip., 1st Novel Award, Authors Club, 1968. Address: P.L.R., 33 Sloane St., London SW1X 9NP, UK.

ENGLEBERT, Michel Alphonse Ghislain Joseph, pen name GRAYN, Michaël, b. 24 Sept. 1937, Hannut, Belgium. Teacher of Modern Languages. Educ: M.A. Publs: Le Génie de Zola (essay, co-author), 1966; Las Mejores Historias Insolitas (Best Unusual Stories, co-author), 1966; Comme une Odeur de Soufre (Just Like a Smell of Sulphur), 1967; Las Mejores Historias de Horror (Best Horror Stories, co-author), 1969; Las Mejores Historias de Ultratumba (Best Stories from Beyond the Grave, co-author), 1973. Contbr. to: Atlanta; Hoho; Norda Prismo. Recip., Hon. distinction, Story Prize, 3rd Arts in Europe Salon, Brussels, 1966. Address: 28 rue du Curé, B-4271 Moxhe, Belgium.

ENGLISH, Elizabeth Lois, b. Macksville, Kan., USA. Author; Bank President. Educ: Kan. Univs. Publs. incl: Travel Memories of Europe; Echoes in the Wind; Leave Me My Dreams; On Wings of Psalms; The Moving Story (free verse version of the Bible); The Miracle of Miracles; Of Course, I've Faith; Wait Wait for Yet a Little Longer; Bringing Home the Greek Gods & Goddesses, 1970; Philosophics of Nature For You & Me; Children: The Blossoms of Mankind, 1974. Mbrships: Am. Poetry League; Kan. Author's Club. Recip., Hon. Ph.D., Ctrl. Christian State Coll. of Evergreen, Colo. Address: Macksville, KS 67557, USA.

ENGLISH, Isobel, b. 1923, London, UK. Author. Publs: The Key That Rusts, 1954; Every Eye, 1956; Four Voices, 1961; Gift Book (w. Barbara Jones), 1964; Life After All & Other Stories, 1973. Contbr. to: New Statesman; New Yorker; Observer; Sunday Times. Recip., Katherine Mansfield Prize, 1974, for Life After All. Address: Grove House, Castle Road, Cowes, I.O.W., UK.

ENGLISH, Ronald, b. 19 Aug. 1913, Grantham, Lincs., UK. Assistant Head Postmaster (Retired). Publs: Adventure Cycling, 1959; Cycling for You, 1964. Contbr. to: Autocar; Scotland Mag.; Lady; Countryman; etc. Mbrships: Soc. of Authors; Civ. Serv. Soc. of Authors. Address: 24 Barrowby Rd., Grantham, Lincs., UK.

ENGLUND, Guy, b. 6 June 1922, Stockholm, Sweden. Language Teacher. Publs: Evening in a Dreamed City (Short stories), 1949; Axelle, the Girl Who Sank (novel), 1959. Mbr., Swedish Assn. of Authors. Address: 10 Gläntvägen, 183 63 Täby, Sweden.

ENGSTRÖM, Clas Erik, b. 19 Mar. 1927, Härnösand, Sweden. Author. Publs. incl: On Sjunker, 1957; JS, 1961; Förrädare, Mördare, 1965; Byalaget, 1973; Fallet Klason, 1974. Contbr. to: filmscripts, TV plays. Mbrships: PEN, Past Bd. Mbr., Swedish Authors Assn.; Past Chmn., Swedish Writers Coop. Hons. incl: Swedish State Award; LRF Award; LO Award. Address: Fardume, 620 34 Lärbro, Sweden.

ENQUIST, Per Olov, b. 23 Sept. 1934, Hjoggböle, Sweden. Writer. Publs: Magnetisörens fem te vinber, 1964; Hess, 1966; Legionärerna, 1968; Sebonden, 1971; Katichalen i München, 1972. Contbr. to: Expressen; BLM; etc. Hons: BLM Prize, 1964; SvD Prize, 1966; Prize of Nordic Coun., 1969; Svenska Romanpriset, 1969. Address: Jägarvägen 1, Uppsala 752 52, Sweden.

ENRIGHT, Dennis Joseph, b. 1920, Leamington, Warwicks., UK. University Professor; Publishing Executive; Author. Educ: M.A., D.Litt., Downing Coll., Cambridge. Publs: The Laughing Hyena & Other Poems; Academic Year; The World of Dew; Aspects of Living Japan; Insufficient Poppy; Addictions; The Old Adam; Conspirators & Poets; Unlawful Assembly; Memoirs of a Mendicant Professor; Selected Poems; Shakespeare & the Students; Daughters of Earth; Man is an Onion; The Terrible Shears; Ed., A Choice of Milton's Verse. Contbr. to: Scrutiny; Essays in Criticism; Encounter; New Statesman; Listener; N.Y. Review; etc. Agent: Bolt & Watson. Address: c/o Chatto & Windus, 42 William IV St., London WC2, UK.

ENSER, A. G. S., b. 13 Feb. 1915, Nottingham, UK. Librarian (Retired), Univ. Coll., Nottingham. Publs: Branch Library Practice, 1951; Filmed Books & Plays, published by Grafton, 1952 (Supplement I, 1952, Supplement II, 1956, Supplement III, 1958, Supplement IV, 1962); Filmed Books & Plays, published by Deutsch, 1968, 3rd ed., 1975. Contbr. to: Lib. Assn. Record; Librn.; Lib. World; New Lib. World; Municipal Review; Ency. Librnship.; Sussex Mag.; Western Mail. Mbrships: Lib. Assn.; R.S.A.; Eastbourne Lit. Luncheon Soc. (Chmn. 1966-); Eastbourne Hard Hearing Assn. (Chmn.). Address: 197 King's Drive, Eastbourne, Sussex, UK.

ENSLIN, Morton Scott, b. 8 Mar. 1897, Somerville, Mass., USA. Professor of Biblical History & Literature. Educ: A.B., 1919; Th.D., 1924; Harvard Univ.; B.D., Newton Theological Instn., 1922. Publs: The Ethics of Paul, 1930, 2nd ed., 1962; Christian Beginnings, 1938; The Prophet from Nazareth, 1961, 2nd ed., 1968; Letters to the Churches, 1963; From Jesus to Christianity, 1964; Judith, 1972; Reapproaching Paul, 1972. Contbr. to: Jrnl. of Biblical Lit. (Ed., 1960-69); Crozer Quarterly (Ed., 1941-52); Harvard Theol. Review; Jrnl. of Relig.; Christian Century; Pulpit; Jewish Quarterly Review; etc. Mbrships. incl: Soc. of Biblical Lit.; Am. Theol. Soc. Address: 708 Argyle Rd., Wynnewood, PA 19096, USA.

ENSOR, Alick Charles Davidson, pen name ENSON, David, b. 27 Nov. 1906, Sheerness, Kent, UK. Solicitor; Retired Member of Parliament; Author; Farmer. Educ: Law. Soc. Schl. of Law; admitted Solicitor, 1928. Publs: I was a Public Prosecutor, 1958; Verdict Afterwards, 1960; With Lord Roberts Through the Khyber Pass, 1966. Contbr. to nat. daily newspapers; Manchester Evening News, Tit-Bits; etc. Many radio & TV appearances. Films incl: The Trials of Oscar Wilde; The Pot Carriers; Death in the Sky Above. Mbrships: Law Soc.; Past Comm. Mbr., Press Club. Address: L'Etoile d'or, 66701 Argenes-sur-Mar, France.

ENZENSBERGER, Han Magnus, b. 11 Nov. 1912. Poet; Broadcaster; Lecturer. Educ: D.Phil.; Univs. of Erlangen, Freiburg in Breisgau, Hamburg & Paris. Publs. incl: (poetry) Landesprache, 1960; Clemens Brentanos Poetik, 1961; Poems for People who Don't Read Poems, Engl. ed., 1968; Gedichte 1955-70, 1971; (essays) Politik & Verbrechen, 1964; (play) Das Verhor von Habana, 1970; (film) Durruti, 1971; (novel) Der kurze Sommer der Anarchie, 1972. Contbr. to: Kursbuch (Ed.); Stuttgart Radio (Ed., 3rd Prog.). Hons: Hugo Jacobi Prize, 1956; Kritiker Prize, 1962; Buchner Prize, 1963. Address: c/o Suhrkamp Verlag, Fach 2446, Frankfurt, W. Germany.

EÖRSI, István, b. 16 June 1931, Budapest, Hungary. Writer; Translator. Educ: M.A. Publs: Ütni az ördögöt (Beating the Devil), poems, 1956; Változatok egy közhelyre (Variations on a Commonplace), poems, 1968; Tragikomédiák (Tragicomedies), 3 plays, 1969;

Különremény (Separate Hope), poems & a play, 1971; Széchenyi és az árnyak (Szechenyi & the Shadows), play, 1973; (plays) Hordók (Barrels); Sirkö és kakaó (Tombstone & Cocoa); Huligán Antigoné (Hooligan Antigone). Contbr. to: Élet és Irodalom (Life & Lit.); Nagyvilág (lit. jrnl.). Mbrships: Hungarian Writers' Soc.; Hungarian Jrnlsts. Soc. Recip., József Attila Prize, 3rd degree, 1952. Address: 1056 Budapest, Belgrád rakpart 27, Hungary.

EPP, Eldon Jay, b. 1 Nov. 1930, Mtn. Lake, Minn., USA. University Professor of Biblical Literature; Writer. Educ: A.B., Wheaton Coll., Ill., 1952; B.D., Fuller Theol. Sem., 1955; S.T.M., Harvard Univ. Divinity Schl., 1956; Ph.D., Harvard Univ., 1961. Publs: The Theological Tendency of Codex Bezae Cantabrigiensis in Acts, 1966. Contbr. to: Harvard Theol. Review; Jrnl of Biblical Lit. Assoc.; Ed., Jrnl. of Biblical Lit., 1971—. Mbr., num. bibl. assns. Address: Case Western Reserve University, Cleveland, OH 44106, USA.

EPSTEIN, Arnold Leonard, b. 13 Sept. 1924, Liverpool, UK. Professor of Anthropology. Educ: LL.B., Queen's Univ., Belfast, 1944; Barrister-at-Law, 1948; Post-grad. studies anthropol., London Schl. Econs., 1949; Ph.D., Univ. of Manchester, 1956. Publs: Politics in an Urban African Community, 1958; Matupit: Land, Politics & Change among the Tolai of New Britain, 1969; Ed., The Craft of Social Anthropology, 1968; Contention & Dispute: Aspects of Law & Social Control in Melanesia, 1974; Joint Ed., The Politics of Dependence: Papua New Guinea 1968, 1971. Contbr. to anthropol. jrnls. Address: Schl. of African & Asian Studies, Univ. of Sussex, Falmer, Brighton, Sussex, UK.

EPSTEIN, Seymour, b. 1917, NYC, USA. Author. Educ: N.Y. Univ. Publs: Short Story 1, 1958; Pillar of Salt, 1960; The Successor, 1961; Best Short Stories of 1962, 1962; Leah, 1964; A Penny for Charity, 1965; Caught in that Music, 1967; The Dream Museum, 1971; Looking for Fred Schmidt, 1973. Contbr. to: Esquire; Redbook; Antioch Review. Hons: Edward Lewis Wallant Mem. Book Award, for novel Leah, 1964; Guggenheim Fellowship, 1965. Agent: Paul Reynolds Inc. Address: 2924 St. Monroe St., Denver, CO 60210, USA.

EPTON, Nina Consuelo, b. London, UK. Writer; Lecturer; Cheirologist. Educ: L. ès Lettres, Sorbonne, Paris, France. Publs: Islands of the Sunbird; The Valley of Pyrene; Grapes & Granite; The Palace & the Jungle; Saints & Sorcerers; Andalusia; Spain's Magic Coast; Victoria & Her Daughters; Love & the French; Love & the English; Love & the Spanish; Spanish Fiestas; Seaweed for Breakfast; Cat Manners & Mysteries; The Burning Heart. Mbr., Nat. Book League. Address: Blue Gates, 58 Vale Rd., Seaford, Sussex, UK.

ERBEN, Walter, b. 13 Oct. 1908, Leverkusen, Germany. Professor of Art. Educ: Acad. of Art, Düsseldorf. Publs: Verzauberte Stunde, 1948; Picasso und die Schwermut, 1948; Kunst und Mode, 1950; Chagall, 1956; Miro, 1960; Sardinia, 1964. Mbrships: German Sect., PEN; German Sect., Assn. of Int. Art Critics. Address: 58 Hagen, Beethovenstr. 10, W. Germany.

ERDÉLYI, József, b. 29 Dec. 1896, Feketebator, Hungary. Writer; Philologist. Publs: The Voilet Leaf, 1922; The Last Golden Eagle, 1928; The Coloured Feather, 1931; The White Tower, 1937; The Eternal Bread, 1939; Remembrance, 1940; The Musician Goat, 1941; Retrogression, 1954; The Dog-Rose Bush, 1955; The Golden Stud, 1959; The Star & the Field Cricket, 1963; The Bunch of Grapes, 1965; Evening Song, 1969; Golden Wedding, 1969; The Broomcorn Fiddle, 1969. Mbrships: PEN; Fedn. of Hungarian Writers; Fedn. of Arts of the Hungarian People's Repub. Recip., Baumgarten Lit. Prize, 1929, 1931 & 1933. Address: XII Királthágó u. 2, Budapest 1126, Hungary.

ERDÖDY, János, b. 2 Apr. 1909, Budapest, Hungary. Writer; Translator; Journalist. Publs. incl: (in Hungarian) The She-Wolf, 1957; The Fourth Horseman, 1959; Joan of Arc, 1964; Gutenberg, 1973; Requiem for Florence, 1968; Gabor Peeri, Citizen of Budapest, 1972; Servant of the Three Magi, 1970; Carnival of Venice, 1974; & more than 20 other books. Mbrships: PEN; Hungarian Writers' Assn. Recip., Hungarian Order of Liberty, Silver Medal, 1947. Address: 1077 Budapest, Dohany-u 46, Hungary.

ERHARD, Ludwig, b. 4 Feb. 1897, Fürth, Bavaria, Germany. Former Chancellor, German Federal Republic,

1963-66; University Professor of Economics. Educ: Dr.Econs., Univ. of Frankfurt/Main, 1924. Publs: (Engl. transls.) Germany's Comeback in the World Market; Prosperity Through Competition; The Economics of Success. Mbrships: Hon. Chmn., Christian Democratic Party of W. Germany; Hon. Pres. or Mbr., var. int. orgs. Hons: 23 Univ. Docts.; Citizenship of many cities; num. decorations. Address: 53 Bonn, Johanniterstr. 8, W. Germany.

ERHOLM, Ester, pen name ERHOMAA, Ester, b. 18 June 1906, Rantasalmi, Finland. Teacher; Author. Educ: Univ. Studies in Nat. Scis.; Turku Coll. of Educ. Publs: Suntion tyttö ja poika, 1948, German ed., 1952; Kirjavan koiran kuja, 1950; Hopeankirkas aika, 1957; Vihreä valtakunta, 1963; Pilvien yllä aurinko, 1963; Matleena ja pääärynäpuu, 1964 (also as TV series); Jumala on matkoilla, 1966; Kevätmorsian, 1970; Matleenan poika, 1970. Contbr. of short stories to: Kotilian Mag.; Christmas Star; etc. Mbrships: Finnish Lit. Soc.; Pirkkala Authors' Soc. Hons. incl: Alfred Kordelinin Award, 1964; Wihurin säätiön Award, 1963, 1966, 1972; Grant, Finnish Lit. Soc., 1973. Address: Voionmaankatu 69 B 29, 33300 Tampere 30, Finland.

ERICKSON, Charlotte Joanne, b. 22 Oct. 1923, Oak Park, Ill., USA. University Teacher (Reader). Educ: B.A., Augustana Coll., Ill., 1945; M.A., 1947, Ph.D., 1951, Cornell Univ.; Rsch. Fee Student, London Schl. of Econs., UK, 1948-50. Publs: American Industry & the European Immigrant, 1860-1885, 1957; British Industrialists: Steel & Hosiery, 1850-1950, 1959; Invisible Immigrants: The Adaptation of English & Scottish Immigrants in 19th Century America, 1972. Contbr. to: Explorations in Entrepreneurial Hist.; Population Studies; Am. Histl. Review. Mbrships. incl: Brit. Assn. Am. Studies (Sec.); Fellow, Royal Histl. Soc. Recip., Guggenheim Fellowship, 1966-67. Address: 30 Hartham Rd., London N7 9JG, UK.

ERIKSSON, Goran O., b. 7 Mar. 1929, Falun, Sweden. Theatre Director; Writer. Educ: Uppsala Univ. Publs: I Samma Plan, 1966; Volpone, 1968. Contbr. to: Goteborgs Handelstidning, 1956-62; Stockholms-Tidningen, 1966; Dagens Nyheter, 1968; BLM; Ord och Bild; Dialog; etc. Mbrships: Bd. Mbr., Swedish Union of Playwrights; PEN; Swedish Union of Authors; Swedish Theatre Union. Address: Kungsklippan 20 7tr., S-11225 Stockholm, Sweden.

ERIKSSON, Maj-Britt, b. 2 Dec. 1914, Stockholm, Sweden. Teacher; Writer. Publs. incl: (novels) When Each Takes His Own, 1944; The Women on Gråskär, 1954; Melody on a Hurdy Gurdy, 1956; Dyning, 1962; Legend, 1966; Åska i juli, 1969; Ophelia from Dalarö, 1972; (short stories) The Girl in the Skerry, 1944; Diary from a Skerry, 1950; From the Island, 1958; The Short Summer; Now & Then on the Skerry, 1971; Fråu Namdofjarden, 1974; (biog.) Francis from Långviksskär, 1952; Notvarp i Namdo, 1975. Mbrships: Union Swedish Writers (Comm. Mbr. 1950-70); Swedish Soc. for Protection Animals. Hons. incl: 5-yr. working schlrship. from Swedish govt. & var. other schlrships. Address: Skogsovagen 3, 13300 Saeltsjobaden, Sweden.

ERIKSSON-SABBADINI, Ing-Marie, b. 30 Sept. 1932, Hammerdal, Sweden. Writer. Educ: B.A. Publs: Märit, 1965; J Getsemane, 1968; Segerhuva, 1969; Sista slattersommaren, 1972. Contbr. to: Bonniers Lit. Mag. Mbr., Swedish Authors Assn., Stockholm. Hons. incl: Bonniers debutantstipendium, 1966; Swedish Authors Assn. Prize, 1969; Pen Clubs Award, 1971; Nordic Writer's Prize, 1972. Address: Observatoriegatan 9¹, Stockholm, Sweden.

ERITH, John, b. 14 May 1904, London, UK. Theatrical & Illustrative Photographer. Educ: St. Martin's & Slade Schls. of Art, Polytechnic Schl. of Photography, London. Publs: Erith on Portraiture, 1948; Erith on Pictorial Photography, 1951; Modern Control in Photography, 1951. Contbr. to: Mod. Photography Ency.; World's Best Photographs; var. nat. daily newspapers & publs. in UK, Europe & USA. Mbrships: Fellow, Inst. of Inc. Photographers; Former mbr., Coun. & Qualifications Bd.; Fellow, Royal Photographic Soc.; Former mbr. & Chmn., Portrait & Theatrical Panel of Qualifications Bd. Address: Smugglers House, Smugglers Walk, W. Worthing, Sussex, UK.

ERNST, Zofia, b. 22 Mar. 1918, Warsaw, Poland. Literary Translator. Educ: Fac. of Letters, Univ. of Rome, Italy. Publs. incl: Alberto Moravia: I Racconti Romani, 1957; La Romana, 1959; Italo Svevo: Una vita, 1960; G.

Tomasi di Lampedusa: Il Gattopardo, 1961, 4th ed., 1970; La Ciociara, 1961; Il Disprezzo, 1961; Federigo Tozzi: Un Osteria, 1964; La coscienza di Zeno, 1966; Gli Indifferenti, 1971; Paolo Monelli: Mussolini Piccolo Borghese, 1973. Contbr. to: Zycie Warszawy; Przekroj; Sepizki; Tyija. Mbrships: Polish Writers' Assn.; PEN; Comunita Europea degli Scrittori. Recip., Cultural Prizes, Italy, 1969, 1970. Address: Ul. Mokotowska 53 m 47, 00542 Warsaw, Poland.

ERSKINE, Dorothy Ward, b. 29 July 1896, San Mateo, Calif., USA. Writer. Educ: Univ. of Calif. Publs: (for children) Russia's Story, 1946; Big Ride, 1958; also pamphlets on conservation. Address: 233 Chestnut St., San Fran., CA 94133, USA.

ERSKINE, Margaret, b. Kingston, Ont., Can. Writer. Publs: And Being Dead; The Whispering House; I Knew McBean; Give up the Ghost; The Disappearing Bridegroom; Death of our Dear One; Dead by Now; The Voice of Murder; Sleep no More; House of the Enchantress; Case with Three Husbands; The Ewe Lamb; Case of Mary Fielding; all publd. UK & USA, also in France, Italy, Spain, Norway, Yugoslavia, etc.

ERSKINE-LINDOP, Audrey Beatrice Noel, b. London, UK. Scriptwriter; Playwright. Publs: (plays) Beware of Angels (w. D. Leslie), 1959; Let's Talk Turkey; Freeman of City of London; (other publs.) In Me My Enemy, 1948; Soldiers' Daughters Never Cry, 1949; The Tall Headlines, 1950; Out of the Whirlwind, 1951; The Singer not the Song, 1953; film 1961; Details of Jeremy Stretton, 1955; The Judas Figures, 1956; I Thank a Fool, 1958; The Way to the Lantern, 1961; I Start Counting, 1966; Sight Unseen, 1969; Journey into Stone, 1973. Recip., Prix Roman Policier, France, 1968. Address: 34 Barkston Gdns., London SW5, UK.

ERTZ, Susan, b. Walton-on-Thames, Surrey, UK. Writer. Publs. incl: Now East Now West, 1927; The Proselyte, 1933; Big Frogs & Little Frogs (short stories), 1938; Anger in the Sky, 1948; Charmed Circle, 1956; In the Cool of the Day, 1961. Mbrships: Royal Soc. of Lit.; PEN Int.; Authors Soc. Hons: Fellow, Royal Soc. of Lit., 1960. Address: 17 Sloane Court W., London SW3, UK.

ESCARPIT, Robert, b. 24 Apr. 1918, St.-Macaire, Gironde, France. University Professor. Educ: Lic.-ès-lettres, 1936; Agrégé de l'Université, 1942; Docteur-és-lettres, 1952. Publs: 30 books incl: Contes et Légendes du Mexique, 1956; Les Dieux du Patamba, 1958; L'humour, 1960; Peinture fraiche, 1960; Hemingway, 1963; Byron, 1965; Honorius Pape, 1967; Les somnambidules, 1971; L'écrit et la communication, 1973; Les Contes de la Saint Glinglin, 1973; Le Ministricule, 1974; & 7 essays. Contbr. to: Le Monde (daily columnist). Mbrships. incl: Int. Comparative Lit. Assn.; Pres., French Br., Byron Soc. Hons. incl: Prix de l'Académie de l'Humour, 1960; Prix Littéraire de Bordeaux, 1963. Address: 7 Avenue des Chasseurs, 33600 Pessac, France.

ESCOTT, Mary Lois, b. 25 Jan. 1923, Paignton, Devon, UK. Housewife. Contbr. to WRNS Mag., 1942. Mbrships: Soc. of Authors; Mothers Union. Address: Morwenna, 9 Park Rd., Redruth, Cornwall TR15 2JF, UK.

ESHELMAN, (Rev.) Byron Elias, b. 28 Oct. 1915, Red Cloud, Neb., USA. Clergyman. Educ: A.B., Emporia Kan. State Coll., 1937; M.Div., Yale Univ. Divinity Schl., 1942. Publs: Death Row Chaplain, 1962, 1972, 1975. Contbr. to: Ed., Chaps. Newsletter, Calif. Dept. of Corrections, 1951-64; Fed. Probation; Readers Digest; Calif. Living; Correctional Review; Soc. Action; etc. Mbrships: Pres., Am. Protestant Correctional Chaps. Assn., 1959-61, Am. Correctional Chap. Assn., 1960-61; Dean, Coll. of Fellows, Am. Protestant Chaps. Assn., 1970. Hons. incl: Chap. of the Yr., US Salvation Army, 1963. Address: Box 77, Occidental, CA 95465, USA.

ESKINAZI, Salomon, b. 25 Nov. 1922, Izmir, Turkey. Educator; Author. Educ: B.S. in M.E., Robert Coll., Istanbul, 1946; M.S. in M.E., Univ. of Wyo., Laramie, 1948; D.Eng., Johns Hopkins Univ., Balt., Md., 1954. Publs: Principles of Fluid Mechanics, 1952, 2nd ed., 1968; Modern Developments in the Mechanics of Continua (Ed.), 1967; Vector Mechanics of Fluids & Magnetofluids, 1967; Mechanics & Thermodynamics of our Environment, 1974. Contbr. to var. profl. jrnls. Mbrships: N.Y. Acad. of Sci.; Am. Soc. of Mech. Engrs.; AAUP; Am. Soc. of Engrng. Educ.; AAAS. Address: 300 Crawford Ave., Syracuse, NY 13224, USA.

ESKOLA, Ilmari Johannes, b. 17 Sept. 1909, Viipuri, Finland. Chief of A.R.P. (ret'd.). Publs: Kolme kunniaa, 1957; Tule Eedeniin, 1957; Lukittu ovi, 1958; Tikapuut huipulle, 1960. Mbrships: Soc. of Finnish Authors; Acad. Club. Hons: Schlrships., Finnish Acad., 1960, 1961-64, People's Educ. Fund, 1959, Finnish Culture Fund, 1960. Address: 42140 Juokslahti, Finland.

ESLÂMI NODOOSHAN, Mohammad Ali, b. 3 Oct. 1925, Nodooshan, Yazd, Iran. University Professor; Writer. Educ: LL.D., Univ. of Paris, France. Publs: We Must Not Forget Iran (essays), 1961; In Pursuit of Homa's Shadow (essays), 1965; Cloud of Time & the Cloud of Hairs (drama), 1965; Legend & Spell (novel), 1967; The Cup of Knowledge (essays), 1966; Heroes of Shahnâmeh, 1969; Legend of Legends, 1973. Contbr. to: Sokhan; Yaghmâ; Râhnema-ye-Ketâb. Mbr., Soc. for Philos. & Humanities, affiliated to UNESCO. Address: 4 Mehrân St., Pesyân Av., Tadjrish, Teheran, Iran.

ESLER, Anthony James, b. 20 Feb. 1934, New London, Conn., USA. Professor of History; Writer. Educ: B.A., Univ. of Ariz., Tucson, 1956; M.A., 1958, Ph.D., 1961, Duke Univ. Publs: The Aspiring Mind of the Elizabethan Younger Generation, 1966; Bombs, Beards & Barricades: 150 Years of Youth in Revolt, 1971; The Youth Revolution: The Conflict of Generations in Modern History (ed.), 1974; The Blade of Castlemayne (novel), 1974. Address: 1523 Jamestown Rd., Williamsburg, VA, USA.

ESPEY, John Jenkins, b. 1913, Shanghai, China. Professor Emeritus. Educ: Occidental Coll.; B.Litt., M.A., Merton Coll., Oxford, UK. Publs: Minor Heresies, 1945; Tales out of School, 1947; The Other City, 1950; Ezra Pound's Mauberley, 1955; The Anniversaries, 1963; An Observer, 1965. Contbr. to: Harper's; New Yorker; Ariz. Quarterly; Scholarly jrnls. Mbr., MLA. Address: Dept. of English, University of California, Los Angeles, CA 90024, USA.

ESPY, Willard Richardson, pen name WEDE, b. 11 Dec. 1910, Olympia, Wash., USA. Writer; Public Relations Adviser. Educ: B.A., Univ. Redlands, Calif.; Sorbonne Univ. Publs: The Bold New Program, 1951; The Game of Words, 1971; different publr., 1974; Omak Me Yours Tonight, 1974; An Almanac of Words at Play, 1975; Grandpa's Village; Contbr. to: Articles; Nation; Atlantic Monthly; Far East Review; N.Y. Times; Am. Heritage; Light Verse; This Week; Punch; Harper's; Word Ways; etc. Mbr., The Coffee House, N.Y. Recip., Gov's. Award for Lit. Excellence Wash. State, 1973. Address: 30 Beekman Pl., N.Y., NY 10022, USA.

ESSAME, Hubert, b. 1896, Exeter, UK. Retired Army Officer. Educ: Staff Coll., Quetta. Publs: The 43rd Wessex Division at War, 1952; Battle for Normandy (w. E. M. G. Belfield), 1965; Battle for Germany, 1969; Normandy Bridgehead, 1970; Battle for Europe 1918; Patton — A Study in Command, 1974. Contbr. to: Army Quarterly; US Mil. Review; Daily Telegraph Mag.; War Monthly; BBC; Westward TV. Mbr., United Serv. Club. Address: The Courtyard, West Wittering, Chichester PO20 8LQ, UK.

ESSERY, Robert John, b. 22 Nov. 1930, Birmingham, UK. Sales Director. Publs: Locomotive Liveries of the LMS, 1966; The L.M.S. Coach 1923-54, 1969; British Goods Wagons, 1970; Portrait of the LMS, 1971; The LMS Wagon, 1975. Contbr. to: Railway Modeller; Model Railway Constructor; Railway World; Model Railways. Mbrships. incl: Chmn., The LMS Soc.; Histl. Model Railway Soc. Address: 33 Ridgewood Dr., Harpenden, Herts., UK.

ESTANG, Bastard, pen name ESTANG, Luc., b. 12 Nov. 1911, Paris, France. Literary Adviser. Publs. incl: (novels) Les Stigmates, 1949; L'interogatoire, 1957; Le Bonheur et le Salut, 1961; La Fille à l'Oursin, 1971; Il était un p'tit homme, 1975; (essays) Saint-Exupéry par lui même, 1955; (poetry) Les quatre éléments, 1956; D'une Nuit Noire et Blanche, 1962; (play) Le Jour de Cain, 1967. Contbr. to: Le Figaro Littéraire; radio. Mbrships: PEN; Soc. des Gens de Lettres. Hons. incl: Chevalier de la Légion d'Honneur, 1961; Grand Prix de Littérature, Acad. Française, 1962. Address: 28 rue de l'université, Paris 7, France.

ESTES, Winston M., b. 31 Oct. 1917, Quanah, Tex., USA. Air Force Officer (ret'd.); Novelist. Educ: Tex. Technol. Coll., 1938-39. Publs: Winston In Wonderland, 1956; Another Part of the House, 1970; A Streetful of

People, 1972; A Simple Act of Kindness, 1973; Andy Jessup, (in press). Mbr., Authors' Guild of Am. Inc. Hons: Tex. Writers Round-up Award for Fiction, 1973; Border Lib. Assn. Award for Fiction, 1973; Evelyn Oppenheimer Award for Fiction, 1973. Address: 5302 Ravensworth Road, Springfield, VA 22151, USA.

ESTREICHER, Karol Jr., b. 4 Mar. 1906, Krakow, Poland. University Professor of the History of Art; University Museum Director. Educ: Ph.D., Krakow Univ. Publs. incl: (short stories) Nie Odrazu Krakow Zbudowano, 1944; 3rd ed., 1957; (novel) Krystianna, 1957 (German transl. 1958); Polish Bibliography XIX Century, vol. XI, 1975; Collegiummaius in Krakow, 1972; Biography of Leon Chwistek, Painter & Philosopher, 1969; Short History of Art, 1973, 2nd ed., 1975. Contbr. to: Nowa Polska (London), 1942-45; Rocznik Krakowski (Ed.-in-Chief, 1968-). Mbrships: PEN; Soc. Friends Art in Krakow (Pres., 1953-); Soc. Polish Art Histns. Hons: City of Krakow Prize, 1955; Jurzykowski Prize N.Y., 1972. Address; 31-008 Krakow, Jagiellonska 15, Muzeum U.J., Poland.

ESTRIN, Herman A., b. 2 June 1915, N. Plainfield, N.J., USA. Professor of English. Educ: A.B., Drew Univ., 1937; A.M., 1942, Ed.D., 1954, Tchrs. Coll., Columbia Univ. Publs. incl: The New Scientist: Essays on the Methods & Values of Science (co-author), 1962; Technical & Professional Writing: A Practical Anthology, 1963; Higher Education in Engineering in Science, 1963; Freedom & Censorship of the College Press, 1975; The American Student & His College (co-author), 1967; The American Language in the 70's (co-author), 1974. Contbr. to num. profl. jrnls. Hons. incl: Disting. Newspapers Advsr., Nat. Coun. of Coll. Publs. Advrs., 1970; Pioneer Award, Wall St. Journal, 1970; var. teaching awards inclng: Westinghouse Award, 1972. Address: 315 Henry St., Scotch Plains, NJ 07076, USA.

ETHERINGTON, Charles Leslie, b. 13 Dec. 1903, St. Catharines, Ont., Can. Organist & Choirmaster; Teacher of Music. Music Educ: Piano & Organ w. Wm. T. Thompson; Harmony w. Dr. A. Wooler, Buffalo, N.Y., USA. Publs: The Organist & Choirmaster, 1952; Protestant Worship Music: Its History & Practice, 1962. Contbr. to Jrnl. of Ch. Music, Phila., Pa., USA. Address: 41-1/2 John Street, St. Thomas, Ont. N5P 2X2, Can.

EULO, Ken, b. 17 Nov. 1939, Newark, N.J., USA. Playwright; Director. Publs: That's the Way a Champ Should Go, 1971; Bang?, 1972; Billy Hofer & the Quarterback Sneak, 1973. Contbr. to: N.Y. Times; N.Y. Post; Janus Mag.; Off-Off Broadway Mag.; Village Voice; Show Business; Back Stage. Mbrships: Dir., Playwrights Forum; Dir., O'Neill Playwrights; Artistic Dir., Courtyard Playhouse. Hons: Winner, O'Neill Summer Conf., 1971; Howard P. Foster Mem. Fund Grant, 1972; Winner, Children's Theatre Contest, Children's Theatre of Richmond, 1974. Address: 46 W. 85th St., N.Y., NY 10024, USA.

EVANS, Aeres, b. 27 Aug. 1911, Nantgaredig, Carmarthen, UK. School Teacher. Educ: Swansea Trng. Coll. Publs: Pum Drama Hanes; Yr Astronot Ifanc; Deuddeg Stori O Ddeuddeg Gwlad; Chwedlau Morgannwg; Darllen Difyr I, II & III; Chwedlau Cymru. Contbr. to: Yr Anthro; BBC; ITV. Mbrships. incl: Welsh Learners' Panel (tutor). Recip., num. awards. Address: Llwydiarth, Heol Login, Llangynnwr, Caerfyrddin (Carmarthen), UK.

EVANS, Alfred Alexander, b. 22 Aug. 1905, Bristol, UK. Professor of English; Educational Administrator; Author & Editor. Educ: B.A., 1927, Dip.Ed., 1928, M.A., 1937, Univ. of Bristol. Publs: Teaching Poetry; The Poet's Tale, 1957; Victorian Poetry, 1958; Ed., Shakespeare's King Henry IV, Parts I & II, A Midsummer Night's Dream, King Richard III, 1961-70; Contemporary (ed., verse anthol.), 1965. Contbr. to: Rschs. & Studies; Times Educl. Supplement; Fortnightly Review; var. educl. jrnls. Address: 24 Mingle Ln., Stapleford, Cambridge CB2 5BG, UK.

EVANS, Christopher Riche, b. 29 May 1931, Aberdovey, Wales, UK. Psychologist; Author. Educ: B.A., Univ. Coll., London Univ., 1960; Ph.D., Univ. of Reading, 1963. Publs: Attention, 1970; Cults of Unreason, 1973; Mind at Bay (sci. fiction anthol.), 1974; Mind in Chains (sci. fiction anthol.), 1974; Landscapes of the Night, forthcoming. Contbr. to: Sci. Am.; New Scientist; Nature; Sunday Times; Observer; Telegraph; Wash. Post; Humanist; Vogue; New Humanist; BBC; & others. Mbrships. incl: Brain Rsch. Assn. (Fndr. mbr. & Sec.); Int. Sci. Writers'

Assn. Address: 46 Queen's Rd., Teddington, Middlesex, UK.

EVANS, Dardanella Lister, pen name EVANS, Dee, b. 26 Jan. 1921, Vernon, Tex., USA. Author; Journalist; Poetess; Registered Nurse. Educ: Okla. City Univ.; Univ. of Okla. Schl. of Nursing; Ind. Univ.; Nat. Landscape & Floristry Inst., Calif. Publs: To Everything There is a Time, 1949; There's Danger in that Uniform, 1950; Emergency, Dr. Red! : The Story Behind a Fire Code, 1953; Health Museum, 1957; Health & Nutrition Book for Laymen, 1975; Num. booklets on swimming pool care & civic projs. Contbr. to: Leaves from Arcadia (poetry), 1939; Var. jrnls. Mbrships: Women in Communications, Inc.; Assoc. Bus. Writers of Am.; Nat. Writers Club; Nat. Safety Coun.; Am. Heart Assn. Address: 1273 Ragley Hall Rd., Atlanta, GA 30319, USA.

EVANS, David Stanley, b. 28 Jan. 1916, Cardiff, Wales, UK. Astronomer. Educ: B.A., Cambridge, 1937; M.A., Ph.D., 1941; Sc.D., 1971. Publs: Frontiers of Astronomy, 1946; Teach Yourself Astronomy, 1952 & later eds.; Observation in Modern Astronomy, 1968; Ed., Herschel at the Cape, 1969; The Shadow of the Telescope, 1970; External Galaxies & Quasistellar Objects, 1972. Contbr. to: Contemp. Review; Mercury; profl. jrnls. Fellowships: Inst. Physics; Royal Astron. Soc.; Royal Soc. of S. Africa. Mbrships: Am. Astron. Soc.; Int. Astron. Union Recip., McIntyre Award, Astron. Soc.; S. Africa, 1972. Address: 6001 Mountainclimb Dr., Austin, TX 78731, USA.

EVANS, Emyr Estyn, b. 1905, Shrewsbury, UK. Emeritus Professor of Geography & Irish Studies, Queen's Univ., Belfast. Educ: M.A., D.Sc., Univ. Coll., Aberystwyth. Publs: France: A Geographical Introduction; Irish Heritage; Mourne Country; Northern Ireland: British Festival Guide; Irish Folk Ways; Prehistoric & Early Christian Ireland; The Personality of Ireland. Ed., Harvest Home: The Last Sheaf. Contbr. to: Geography; archaeol. & anthropol. jrnls. Mbrships. incl: Inst. of Irish Studies (Chmn., 1965-70); F.S.A. Hons. incl: Sc.D.; Litt.D.; M.R.T.P.I.; LL.D.; Leverhulme Emeritus Fellowship, 1970. Address: 100 Malone Rd., Belfast, Northern Ireland, UK.

EVANS, George Ewart, pen name EVANS, Ewart, b. 1 Apr. 1909, Abercynon, Glam., UK. Writer. Educ: B.A., Univ. of Wales. Publs: The Voices of the Children, 1947; Ask the Fellows Who Cut The Hay, 1956; The Horse in the Furrow, 1960; The Pattern under the Plough, 1966; The Farm & the Village, 1969; Where Beards Wag All, 1970; The Leaping Hare (co-author), 1972; Acky, 1973; The Days That We Have Seen, 1975; Let Dogs Delight, 1975. Contbr. to var. lit. mags. Mbr., Exec. Oral Hist. Soc. Address: 19 The Street, Brooke, Norwich NR15 1JW, UK.

EVANS, Hilary & Mary (Husband & Wife Team), pen name (Hilary) AGARD, H. E., (Mary) b. 1935, London, UK, (Hilary) b. 1929, Shrewsbury, UK. Writers. Publs: (Hilary Evans) A World Fit for Grimsby, 1961; The Assassin, 1965; The Land of Lost Control, 1967; (Hilary & Mary Evans) Sources of Illustrations, 1972; The Victorians, 1973; John Kay of Edinburgh, 1973; The Picture Researcher's Handbook, forthcoming. Contbrs. to: Honey; Vogue; Woman; Times; Guardian; Mother. Agent: Lloyd George & Coward. Address: 11 Granville Park, London SE13 7DY, UK.

EVANS, Idrisyn Oliver, b. 11 Nov. 1894, Bloemfontein, Orange Free State, S. Africa. Civil Servant (Retired). Publs. incl: Book of Flags (w. V.-Admiral Gordon Campbell, V.C.), 1950; The Story of our World, 1957; Olympic Runner, 1957; Discovering the Heavens, 1958; The Boys' Book of the Rocks & Fossils, 1961; Exploring the Earth, 1961; Inventors of the World, 1962; Engineers of the World, 1963; Jules Verne & His Work, 1965; Benefactors of the World, 1968; The Earth, 1970; Rocks, Minerals & Gemstones, 1972. Contbr. to: Field; Motor; Cycling; Cycletouring; Landrover. Mbrships: Soc. of Authors; Fndr.-Mbr., Soc. of Civ. Serv. Authors; F.R.G.S. Address: 53 Waterer Gdns., Burgh Heath, Tadworth, Surrey KT20 5PD, UK.

EVANS, Jean, b. 20 Aug. 1929, Leicester, UK. Writer. Publs: Rival Queens; Nine Days, 1970; Royal Widow, 1971; Rebel Stuart, 1971; Jane, Beloved Queen, 1971; The White Rose of York, 1972; The Tudor Tragedy, 1972; The Divided Rose, 1972; An Heir for the Tudors, 1973; Suffolk's Queen, 1973; The Scottish Tudor, 1973; Katherine, Queen Dowager, 1974; The Rose & Ragged Staff; Henrietta Maria. Contbr. to The Writer. Mbr., Soc. of

Women Writers & Jrnlsts. Agent: David Bolt, Bolt & Watson Ltd. Address: "Sharra", Plot 1, Winchester Rd., Fair Oak, Nr. Eastleigh, Hants., UK.

EVANS, Jean Lorna, pen name JACOBY, Jean, b. 28 July, London, UK. Director, Educational Tuition Agency. Educ: B.A., Dip. Ed., London Univ. Publs: Abimbolu, 1950. Contbr. to: The Lady; Evening News; Nigerian Broadcasting Corp. Mbr., Cath. Women's League. Address: 9 Castello Ave., London SW15 6EA, UK.

EVANS, John Davies, b. 1925, Liverpool, UK. Archaeologist; Director, University Institute of Archaeology. Educ: M.A., Ph.D., Univ. of Cambridge. Publs: Malta, 1959; Excavations at Saliagos, Antiparos (w. A. C. Renfrew), 1968; The Prehistoric Antiquities of the Maltese Islands, 1971. Contbr. to var. archaeol. jrnls. Mbrships: Fellow, Brit. Acad.; Fellow, Soc. of Antiquaries; Pres., Prehistoric Soc., 1973. Address: Inst. of Archaeol., 31-34 Gordon Square, London WC1H 0PY, UK.

EVANS, Kathleen Marianne, b. 25 Feb. 1911, Pembrey, UK. Lecturer. Educ: Bedford Coll., London; King's Coll., London; B.Sc., M.A., Ph.D. Publs: Sociometry & Education, 1962; Attitudes & Interests in Education, 1965; Planning Small Scale Research, 1968; L'Action Pédagogique sur les Attitudes et les Intérêts, 1970. Contbr. to: Brit. Jrnl. of Educl. Psychol.; Educl. Rsch. Mbrships: Soc. of Authors; Assn. of Univ. Tchrs. Address: 33 Axminster Rd., Cardiff CF2 5AR, UK.

EVANS, Kenneth, b. 1917, Briton Ferry, UK. Writer. Educ: Univ. Coll., Swansea; Coll. of Commerce, Cardiff. Publs: Oasis of Fear, 1968; No Cause for Dying, 1969; Shadows of Violence, 1973; A Rich Way to Die, 1973; Blueprint to Kill, 1975. Mbr. Crime Writers' Assn. Address: 13 Kensington Pl., Newport, Gwent NPT 8GL, UK.

EVANS, Max, b. Aug. 1926, Ropes, Tex., USA. Author; Artist. Publs. incl: Southwest Wind, 1958; Long John Dunn of Taos, 1959; The Rounders, 1960; The Hi Lo Country, 1961; The Great Wedding, 1963; Mountain of Gold, 1965; Shadow of Thunder, 1967; Sam Peckinpah — Master of Violence, 1971; My Pardner, 1972; Bobby Jack Smith You Dirty Coward! , 1974; One-Eyed Sky, 1974. Contbr. over 60 short stories to nat., reg. & lit. jrnls. Mbr., W.G.A.W. Recip., City of LA Commendation Award, 1972. Address: 1111 Ridgecrest Dr. S.E., Albuquerque, NM 87108, USA.

EVANS, Philip, b. 4 Apr. 1944, Colombo, Ceylon. Editorial Director. Educ: B.A., Oxford Univ. Publs: Next Time You'll Wake Up Dead, 1972; The Bodyguard Man, 1973. Address: c/o Hodder & Stoughton Ltd., St. Paul's House, Warwick Lane, London EC4, UK.

EVANS, Robert Owen, b. 9 Sept. 1919, Chgo., Ill., USA. Professor of English & Comparative Literature; Author. Educ: A.B., Univ. of Chgo.; M.A., Ph.D., Univ. of Fla.; further educ., Harvard Univ., & Heidelberg Univ., German Fed. Repub. Publs. incl: Norfolk Billy (novel), 1952; Graham Greene: Some Critical Considerations, 1963; Milton's Elisions, 1966; The Osier Cage: Rhetorical Devices in Romeo & Juliet, 1966; Attic & Baroque Prose Style (w. J. Max Patrick), 1969; An Introduction to American Literature (translation w. L. C. Keating, Jorge Luis Borges), 1971; An Introduction to English Literature (idem), 1974. Contbr. to var. acad. jrnls. Hon. Mention, Emily Balch Clark Prize, Va. Quarterly Review, 1965. Address: 747 Zandale Dr., Lexington, KY 40502, USA.

EVANS, Ulick Richardson, b. Wimbledon, UK. University Reader & Administrator; Author. Educ: Marlborough Coll.; King's Coll., Cambridge; Sc.D.; D.Met. Publs: Metals & Metallic Compounds (4 vols.); The Corrosion of Metals; Metallic Corrosion, Passivity & Protection; An Introduction to Metallic Corrosion; The Corrosion & Oxidation of Metals: Scientific Principles & Practical Applications. Hons: C.B.E.; F.R.S. Address: 19 Manor Court, Grange Rd., Cambridge, UK.

EVANS, William, pen name AMNON III, b. 24 Nov. 1895, Tyndomen, Tregaron, Wales, UK. Cardiologist; Writer. Educ: B.S., M.D., D.Sc., F.R.C.P., London Univ. Publs: Students' Handbook of Electrocardiography, 1934; Cardioscopy, 1952; Cardiography, 2nd ed., 1954; Cardiology, 2nd ed., 1956; Diseases of the Heart & Arteries, 1964; Journey to Harley Street, 1968. Contbr. of over 100 papers on cardiology to var. jrnls. Mbr., Brit. Cardiac Soc. Hons. incl: D.Sc., Univ. of Wales; Order of Druids; K.E.D.

Prize in Pathology, 1927; Strickland Goodal Gold Medal, 1942; Sydney Body Gold Medal, 1954; 1st Leonard Abrahamson Lect., Dublin, 1963. Address: Bryndomen, Tregaron, Dyfed, Wales, UK.

EVANS DAVIES, Gloria, b. 17 Apr. 1932, Maesteg, S. Wales, UK. Poet. Publs: Words — For Blodwen, 1962; Her Name Like the Hours, 1974. Contbr. to: Times Lit. Supplement; N.Y. Times; Spectator; Listener; BBC Radio & TV; Harlech TV; var. anthols. Recip., Grants, Gulbenkian Fndn. & Royal Lit. Fund. Address: 25c High St. Superior, Brecon, Powys, S. Wales, UK.

EVANS of HUNGERSHALL, (Baron) Benjamin Ifor, b. 19 Aug. 1899, London, UK. Professor of English; Former Provost, University College, London. Educ: M.A., D.Litt., Univ. Coll., London. Publs. incl: Encounters, 1926; The Limits of Literary Criticism, 1933; Keats, 1934; Tradition & Romanticism, 1940; A Short History of English Literature, 1940; Literature Between the Wars, 1948; The Church in the Markets, 1948; The Use of English, 1949; Science & Literature, 1954; English Literature: Values & Traditions, 1962. Mbrships. incl: Vice-Chmn., Arts Coun., 1946-51; F.R.S.L.; Num. hons. incl: Officer of the Legion of Honour. Address: 1317 Minster House, St. James' Ct., Buckingham Gate, London SW1, UK.

EVENHUIS, Bert, b. 10 Jan. 1930, Groningen, Netherlands. Journalist. Publs: Het naakte bestaan, 1963; Naturisme en nudisme, 1970. Contbr. to: INF-Bulletin; La Vie au Soleil; ASA Bulletin; Naturisme; Reizen; Recreatie; Sextant; Zonnewÿzer; Schiedamse Gemeenschap; num. newspapers. Mbrships. incl: VP & PR Off., Int. Naturist Fedn., 1970—; Netherlands Jrnlsts. Soc., Amsterdam. Hons. incl: Lit. Prize, Int. Naturist Fedn. World Congress, Héliomonde, France, 1964. Address: Elzenoord 4, Vaassen, Netherlands.

EVENHUIS, Gertie, pen name SCALDIS, Eva, b. 4 Mar. 1932, Onstwedde, Groningen, Netherlands. Writer; Tutor in Dutch Language & Literature. Educ: Art Schl.; Tchrs. Coll.; B.A., Dutch Lit. Publs. incl: Verdreven vloot, 1962; Wij waren er ook bij, 1961, 6 eds.; De school van Schellebelle, 1964, Engl. transl. 1975, now in 3rd ed.; Erik en Anke, 1966-69, schl. primer in 10 parts; Draaiorgel vermist, 1969; En waarom ik niet? , 1970, Engl. transl. 1974; Verstekeling in de Sinai, 1971; Er kan nog van alles gebeuren, Dromen van vrede, 1972, transl. USA, UK, Sweden, Japan; Stefan en Stefan, 1973. Contbr. to: Trouw; Libelle; radio & TV; etc. Mbrships. incl: PEN; Nat. Writers' Guild. Hons. incl: Silver Pencil Award, 1974, for "Stefan en Stefan"; Children's Book Prize, Jan Campertstichting, for "Wij Waren er ook bij". Address: Lomanstraat 81, Amsterdam, Netherlands.

EVERDELL, Maurice Henry, b. 12 Apr. 1917, Somerset, UK. University Lecturer. Educ: B.Sc., 1938, Ph.D., 1940, Univ. Coll., Exeter. Publs: Fundamental Thermodynamics for Engineers, 1958; Introduction to Chemical Thermodynamics, 1965; Statistical Mechanics & its Chemical Applications, 1975. Contbr. to: Jrnl. of the Chem. Soc.; Nature; Jrnl. of Chem. Educ. Address: 44 High Point, Edgbaston, Birmingham 15, UK.

EVERETT, Peter, b. 1931, Hull, UK. Author. Educ: Thorne Coll. Publs. incl: The Instrument; A Day of Dwarfs; The Fetch; Negatives. Contbr. of poems to Botteghe Obscure. Address: c/o Jonathan Cape, Bedford Sq., London WC1, UK.

EVERITT, Bridget Mary, b. 1924, Burnham Market, Norfolk, UK. Publishing Editor & Distribution Manager. Educ: Ctrl. Schl. of Speech & Drama. Publs: A Cold Front, 1972. Contbr. to: Eastern World (book reviews); East West Commerce (trade digest). Agent: Winant Towers Ltd. Address: Park Cottage, Burnham Market, Norfolk, UK.

EWALD, Paul P., b. 23 Jan. 1888, Berlin, Germany. Physicist. Educ: Univs. of Cambridge, UK. Göttingen; Munich; D.Phil., 1912. Publs: Kristalle und Röntgenstrahlen, 1923; 50 Years of X-ray Diffraction, 1962; Strukturbericht (w. C. Hermann), 1931. Contbr. of num. articles to physical & crystallographic jrnls. Mbr., var. physical & Sci. Assns. Hons. degrees, T. H. Stuttgart, Germany; Univ. of Paris, France; etc.; Hon. mbr., Cambridge Philos. Soc., UK; German mineral Assn.; Soc. française de minéral. & cristallog.; etc. Corres. mbr., Göttinger Acad.; Bavarian Acad., Germany. Address: 108 Sheldon Road, Ithaca, NY 14850, USA.

EWART, Gavin Buchanan, b. 1916, London, UK. Advertising Copywriter; Freelance Writer. Educ: M.A., Christ's Coll., Cambridge. Publs: Poems & songs, 1939; Throwaway Lines, 1964; Londoners, 1964; Two Children, 1966; Pleasures of the Flesh, 1966; The Deceptive Grin of the Gravel Porters, 1968; The Gavin Ewart Show, 1971; Be My Guest, 1975; Penguin Modern Poets No. 25. Contbr. to: London Mag.; Ambit; Evening Standard; Listener; Encounter; New Statesman. Address: 57 Kenilworth Court, Lower Richmond Rd., London SW15, UK.

EWERS, John Canfield, b. 21 July 1909, Cleveland, Ohio, USA. Anthropologist. Educ: A.B., Dartmouth Coll., 1931; M.A., Yale Univ., 1934. Publs: Plains Indian Painting, 1931; Blackfeet Crafts, 1946; George Catlin, Painter of Indians & the West, 1955; The Horse in Blackfoot Indian Culture, 1955; Artists of the Old West, 1965, revised ed., 1973; Indian Life of the Upper Missouri, 1968. Contbr. to lit. & anthropol. jrnls. Mbrships. incl: Past Pres., Am. Indian Ethnohistl. Soc.; Ed. Bd., Am. W.; Former Jrnl. Ed. & Fellow, Wash. Acad. of Sci. Recip., var. acad. hons. Address: 4432 26th Rd. N., Arlington, VA 22207, USA.

EWERS, John Keith, b. 13 June 1904, Subiaco, W.A., Australia. Author. Educ: Claremont Tchrs. Coll.; London Speech Inst. Publs. incl: Money Street, 1933; Fire on the Wind, 1935; Creative Writing in Australia, 1945, revised 1956, 1959, 1962, 1966; Men Against the Earth, 1946; The Western Gateway, 1948; revised 1971; With the Sun on my Back, 1953; Modern Australian Short Stories (ed.), 1965. Contbr. to: Walkabout; Aust. Post; Westerly; etc. Mbrships. incl: Fndn. Pres., Fellowship of Aust. Writers, 1938; Regional VP, Aust. Soc. of Authors, 1963-71. Recip., C'wlth. Jubilee Lit. Comp. Award (non-fiction), 1951. Address: 2 Crossland Ct., Peppermint Grove, W. Australia 6011.

EWING, (Professor Sir) Alexander William Gordon, b. 1896, Stowting, Kent, UK. Professor in education of deaf children. Educ: M.A., Ph.D., Univ. of Edinburgh; Ph.D., LL.D., Univ. of Manchester. Publs. incl: Aphasia in Children, 1930; Handicap of Deafness (w. Irene Lady Ewing), 1938; New Opportunities for Deaf Children, 1958; Teaching Deaf Children to Talk (w. Ethel, Lady Ewing), 1964; Hearing Aids, Lipreading & Clear Speech, 1967; Hearing-Impaired Children under five, 1971. Contbr. to var. sci., med. & educ. jrnls. Recip., Kthood, 1959. Address: Horseshoe Cottage, Horseshoe Lane, Alderley Edge, Cheshire, UK.

EXMAN, Eugene, b. 1 July 1900, Morrow, Ohio, USA. Book Publisher. Retired. Educ: Ph.B., Denison Univ.; M.A., Univ. of Chgo; D.R.E.(Hon.), Middlebury Coll. Publs: The World of Albert Schweitzer, 1955; The Brothers Harper, 1965; The House of Harper, 1967. Contbr. to reviews, & Times Lit. Supplement. Address: P.O. Box 555, Barnstable, MA 02630, USA.

EXPORT, Valie, b. 17 May 1940, Linz, Austria. Artist. Educ: Design Diploma. Publs: Wien, Kompendium Wiener Aktionismus und Film, 1970; Stadt: Visuelle Strukturen, 1972. Mbrships: Filmmakers' Co-op, Vienna; Inst. of Direct Art, Vienna; Lit. Prods., Vienna; Graz Authors' Assembly. Hons: Filmpreis der Gemeinde, Vienna, 1971; Osterrichisches Staatsstipendium fur Lit. Address: 1/4/3A Grunangergrasse, Vienna 1010, Austria.

EXTON, Clive, b. 11 Apr. 1930, London, UK. Playwright; Screenwriter. Publs. incl: (TV plays) No Fixed Abode; Where I Live; Hold My Hand, Soldier; I'll Have You to Remember; The Big Eat; The Trial of Doctor Fancy; Land of My Dreams; The Close Prisoner; The Boneyard; Are You Ready for the Music?; The Rainbirds; The Crezz, 1974; Conceptions of Murder; (stage plays) Have You Any Dirty Washing, Mother Dear?; The Changing of the Guard; (films) Night Must Fall; Isadora; Entertaining Mr. Sloane; Ten Rillington Place; Running Scared; The House in Nightmare Park; Eddie & the Lucky Salt Peanut. Address: c/o A. D. Peters, 10 Buckingham St., London WC2N 6BU, UK.

EYRE, Kathleen, b. Crofton, Yorks., UK. College Lecturer; Author; Broadcaster. Publs: Sand Grown, 1960; Seven Golden Miles, 1961; The Early History of Lytham Fire Brigade, 1966; Fylde Folk — Moss or Sand, 1970; Bygone Blackpool, 1971; Lancashire Legends, 1972; Famous Lancashire Homes, 1973; Witchcraft in Lancashire, 1974; Lancashire Ghosts, 1974. Contbr. to: Summat from Home (anthol.); Nowt So Queer (anthol.); W. Lancs. Evening Gazette Annuals, 1971-74. Mbr., Lancs. Authors'

Assn. Address: "Kate's Pad", Lime Grove, St. Annes, Lytham St. Annes, Lancs., UK.

EYSENCK, Hans Jurgen, b. 4 Mar. 1916, Berlin, Germany. Professor of Psychology, University Institute of Psychiatry. Educ: B.A., 1938, Ph.D., 1940, D.Sc., 1964, Univ. of London, UK. Publs. incl: Uses & Abuses of Psychology, 1953; Sense & Nonsense in Psychology, 1957; Fact & Fiction in Psychology, 1965; Personality Structure & Measurement, 1969; Race Intelligence & Education, 1971; Psychology is about People, 1972; The Measurement of Intelligence, 1973; The Inequality of Man, 1973; The Experimental Study of Freudian Theories, 1973; Co-Ed., Encyclopaedia of Psychology, 1973. Contbr. to num. jrnls. Mbrships: Fellow, Brit. & Am. Psychol. Assns. Address: 10 Dorchester Drive, London SE24, UK.

EZHOV, Valentin Ivanovich, b. 21 Jan. 1921, Kuibyshev, USSR. Screen Writer. Educ: State Inst. of Cinematography, USSR. Publs: (co-author scripts) Our Champions, 1954; World Champion, 1955; Liana, 1956; A Man from the Planet Earth, 1968; The House of Gold, 1959; The Volga Flows, 1962; Story of a Woman Flier, 1964; Wings, 1966. Recip., Lenin Prize. Address: Mosfilm Studios, 1 Mosfilmovskaya ulitsa, Moscow, USSR.

EZQUERRA ABADÍA, Ramón, b. 22 Jan. 1904, Almuniente, Huesca, Spain. Professor of Education. Educ: D.Lit. Publs: La conspiración del Duque de Híjar (1648), 1934; Los compañeros de Hernán Cortés, 1948; Los precedentes del descubrimiento de Méjico, 1949; Gilberto de Saint-Maxent, teniente gobernador de Luidiana, 1950; La crítica de la situación de América en el siglo XVIII, 1962; Problemas de la mita de Potosí en el siglo XVIII, 1970. Contbr. to: Revista de Indias. Mbrships: Royal Geogl. Soc. Madrid (Exec. Bd); Inst. Madrilenian Studies; Inst. Fernández de Oviedo for Am. Hist. (Coun. Sci. Rsch.). Hons. incl: Nat. Prize Lit., 1933. Address: Paseo de las Delicias 45, Madrid 7, Spain.

F

FAAS, Henry Carel, pen name WANDELGANGER, b. 8 Sept. 1926, Amsterdam, Netherlands. Head, Hague Office of the Information Service of the European Communities. Educ: H.B.S., Ignatius Coll. Publs: God, Nederland en de franje, 1967; Het rode boekje van Wandelganger, 1968. Correspondent, The Daily Telegraph, 1955-70; The Observer, 1958-60; N.Y. Times, 1960-70. Mbr., Nederlandse Journalisten Vereniging; Buitenlandse Pers Vereniging. Address: Marius Bauerlaan 13, Aerdenhout, Netherlands.

FABER, John, b. 13 Feb. 1918, NYC, USA. Press Technical Representative; Author; Travel Writer. Publs: Industrial Photography, 1948; Great Moments in News Photography, 1960; Humor in News Photography, 1961; Travel Photography, 1971. Contbr. to num. profl., travel mags. w. monthly column, On the Record, Nat. Press Photographer, 13 yrs. Hons: Nat. Headliner's Award, for Great Moments in News Photography, Nat. Headliner's Club, 1961. Joseph A. Sprague Mem. Award, 1974. Address: 54 Crane Rd., Mountain Lakes, NJ 07046, USA.

FABER, Richard, b. 1924, London, UK. Diplomat. Educ: M.A., Christ Church, Oxford Univ. Publs: Beaconsfield & Bolingbroke, 1961; The Vision & the Need: Late Victorian Imperialist Aims, 1966; Proper Stations: Class in Victorian Fiction, 1971; French & English, forthcoming. Mbrships. incl: F.R.S.L. Address: c/o Foreign & Commonwealth Office, London, UK.

FABRI, Ralph, b. 23 Apr. 1894, Budapest, Hungary. Artist; Writer; Educator. Educ: B.A., Royal State Gymnasium, Budapest, 1912; Royal Univ. of Technol., Budapest; M.A., Royal Acad. of Fine Arts, Budapest, 1918; Nat. Acad. Schl. of Fine Arts, N.Y., USA. Publs. incl: Sculpture in Paper; Guide to Polymer Painting, 1966; Color, A Complete Guide for Artists, 1967; Painting Outdoors, Hist. of the Am. Watercolour Soc., 1969;

Painting Cityscapes, 1970; Artist's Guide to Composition, 1971. Contbr. to art mags.; Ed., Today's Art, N.Y.; Book Reviewer, Am. Artist Mag. Mbr., Authors Guild. Address: 54 W. 74th St., N.Y., NY 10023, USA.

FACKENHEIM, Emil Ludwig, b. 22 June 1916, Halle, Germany. Professor of Philosophy; Author. Educ: Univ. of Halle, 1937-38; Univ. of Aberdeen, UK, 1939-40; Ph.D., Univ. of Toronto, Can., 1945. Publs: Paths to Jewish Belief, 1960; Metaphysics & Historicity, 1961; The Religious Dimension in Hegel's Thought, 1967, 2nd ed., 1970; Quest for Past & Future: Essays in Jewish Theology, 1967, 2nd ed., 1970; God's Presence in History, 1970, 2nd ed., 1973; Encounters Between Judaism & Modern Philosophy, 1973. Contbr. to: Commentary; Judaism; Philosl. Quarterly; Ctr. Mag.; etc. Hons. incl: Frank & Ethel Cohen Lit. Award, 1969. Address: 563 Briar Hill Ave., Toronto M5N 1N1, Can.

FACKRE, Gabriel Joseph, b. 25 Jan. 1926, Jersey City, N.J., USA. Professor of Theology; Clergyman; Author. Educ: B.D., Ph.D., Univ. of Chgo. Divinity Schl.; further studies, Bucknell Univ. Publs: Under the Steeple, 1957; The Purpose & Work of the Ministry, 1959; The Pastor & the World, 1964; Secular Impact, 1968; Conversation in Faith, 1968; The Rainbow Sign, 1969; Humiliation & Celebration, 1969; The Promise of Reinhold Niebuhr, 1970; Liberation in Middle America, 1971; Do & Tell, 1973. Contbr. to: Christian Century; Encounter; Int. Jrnl. Relig. Educ.; etc. Address: Andover Newton Theol. School, 210 Herrick Rd., Newton Centre, MA 02159, USA.

FAHERTY, William Barnaby, pen names BRAND, Bart; BRAND, J. F., b. 17 Dec. 1914, St. Louis, Mo., USA. Clergyman; Educator; Professor of History. Educ: A.B., 1936, M.A., 1938, Ph.D., 1949, St. Louis Univ.; L.S.Th., St. Mary's Coll., Kan., 1945. Publs. incl: A Wall for San Sebastian, 1962; Living Alone: A Guide for the Single Woman, 1964; Saint Louis: University & Community, 1968; Dream by the River: Two Centuries of Saint Louis Catholicism, 1766-1967, 1973. Contbr. to num. jrnls. Mbrships: Pres., Gtr. St. Louis Histl. Soc., 1974-; St. Peter Canisius Writers' Guild, 1943-44. Recip., Cath. Press Award, 1943, 1944. Address: 3601 Lindell Blvd., St. Louis, MO 63108, USA.

FAHLSTRÖM, Öyvind Axel Christian, b. 28 Dec. 1928, Sao Paulo, Brazil. Artist. Publs: (poetry) Minneslista till Dr Schweitzer's sista updrag, 1964; Bord, 1966; (novel for Tape) Den Helige Torsten Nilsson, 1965; (essays) Om Livskonst, 1970; (film) Du Gamla du Fria, 1969. Contbr. to: Expressen, Sweden; & var. periodicals. Num. one-man exhibitions as a painter. Address: 121 2nd Ave., N.Y., NY 10003, USA.

FAINLIGHT, Ruth Esther, b. 1931, NYC, USA. Poet. Publs: (poetry) A Forecast, A Fable, 1958; Cages, UK 1966, USA 1967; 18 Poems from 1966, 1967; To See the Matter Clearly, UK 1968, USA 1969; Poems: Ruth Fainlight, Ted Hughes, Alan Sillitoe, 1971; The Region's Violence, 1973; 21 Poems, 1973; Another Full Moon, 1975; (prose) All Citizens Are Soldiers (w. husband Alan Sillitoe; transl. from Lope de Vega, Fuenteovejuna), 1969; Daylife & Nightlife (stories), 1971. Contbr. to: Times Lit. Supplement; Poetry Chgo.; Poetry Review; New Yorker; The Scotsman; Outposts. Address: 14 Ladbroke Terrace, London W11, UK.

FAIRBANK, Alfred John, b. 12 July 1895, Grimsby, Lincs., UK. Retired Civil Servant. Educ: Fellow, Ctrl. Schl. Arts & Crafts, 1933. Publs: A Handwriting Manual, 1932, 1975; A Book of Scripts, 1949; Renaissance Handwriting (co-author), 1960; Humanistic Scripts of the 15th & 16th Centuries (co-author), 1960; The Italic Hand in Tudor Cambridge (co-author), 1962; The Story of Handwriting, 1970. Contbr. to: Book Collector; Jrnl. of Soc. for Italic Handwriting. Mbrships. incl: F.R.S.A.; P.P., Soc. of Scribes & Claminators; VP, Soc. for Italic Handwriting; Soc. of Designer Craftsmen. Hons. incl: C.B.E., 1951. Address: 27 Granville Road, Hove, Sussex BN3 ITG, UK.

FAIRBURN, Eleanor, pen name CARFAX, Catherine, b. 23 Feb. 1928, Westport, Repub. of Ireland. Novelist. Educ: Grafton Acad., Dublin. Publs: (histl. novels) The Green Popinjays, 1962; The White Seahorse, 1964; The Golden Hive, 1966; Crowned Ermine, 1968; The Rose in the Spring, 1971; White Rose, Dark Summer, 1972; The Rose at Harvest End, 1974; Winter's Rose, 1976; (thrillers) A Silence with Voices, 1969; The Semper Inheritance, 1972; To Die a Little, 1972; The Sleeping Salamander,

1973. Mbr., Crime Writers Assn. Agent: Campbell Thomson & McLaughlin Ltd. Address: 199 Oxford Rd., Linthorpe, Middlesbrough, Cleveland TS5 5EG, UK.

FAIRCHILD, William, b. Cornwall, UK. Trustee, Writer's Guild of Great Britain; Dramatist. Publs: A Matter of Duty, 1943; The Swiss Arrangement, 1973; (screenplays) Morning Departure; Outcast of the Islands; The Gift Horse; The Net; Malta Story; The Seekers; Passage Home; Value for Money; John & Julie; The Extra Day; The Silent Enemy; The Horsemasters; Star. Embassy; The Darwin Adventure; Sunday Best; (stage plays) The Sound of Murder; Breaking Point; Act of Violence; Poor Horace; The Pay-Off; (TV plays) The Man With the Gun; No Mans Land; The Signal; Some Other Love. Cunningham 5101; The Break. Mbrships: Soc. of Authors; League of Dramatists; Dramatists' Club. Address: c/o I.F.A., 11 Hanover St., London W1, UK.

FAIRFAX, John, b. 21 May 1937, Rome, Italy. Adventurer. Educ: Univ. of Buenos Aires, Argentina. Publs: Vagabundos bajo el sol, 1957; Britannia, Rowing Alone across the Atlantic, 1971; Oars across the Pacific (w. S. Cook), 1972. Contbr. to: Esquire; True; Panorama; Paris Match; Neue Revue; Walkabout. Mbr., Swimming Hall of Fame, Fla., USA. Hons: Man of the Yr., UK, 1969; Benrus Citation Award, USA, 1969. Address: Flat 15, Melville Ct., Goldhawk Rd., London W12 9NY, UK.

FAIRFAX-BLAKEBOROUGH, John Freeman, b. 16 Jan. 1883, Guisborough, Yorks., UK. Author; Journalist; former Turf Official. Publs: incl: Fifty Hunt Histories; Northern Racing Records; Country Life & Sport; History of Doncaster Races; Analysis of the Turf; Humours of Village Life; Yorkshire East Riding; English Wild Animals; Paddock Personalities; Flat Racing Since 1900 (co-author); Steeplechasing (co-author); Northern Turf History, 4 vols.; 13 turf novels. Contbr. to: Spectator; Country Life; Tatler; Sporting Life; Stud & Stable; Ed., var. sporting biogs. Recip., M.C., WWI. Address: Low House, Westerdale, Whitby, Yorks., UK.

FAIRFIELD, Richard Ivan, b. 18 Nov. 1937, Gardiner, Maine, USA. Publisher; Director of a non-profit Organization. Educ: B.A., Tufts Univ., 1967; M.Div., Starr King Schl., 1969; US Int. Univ. Publs: In Search of Utopia, 1971; Communes, USA (A Personal Tour), 1972; Utopia, USA, 1972; Communes, Europe, 1972; Communes, Japan, 1973; Self-Employment Opportunities File, 1974; (forthcoming) How to Survive (& Profit From) Inflation &/or Depression; How to Save 20-50 per cent on Your Food Budget; The Guidebook to Optimal Health. Contbr. to: Green Revolution: Perspectives on Living (1973-74); Alternatives Jrnl. (1971-73); etc. Address: P.O. Drawer F, Wiscasset, ME 04578, USA.

FAIRHOLME, Elisabeth Carola, b. 1910, London, UK. Author & Illustrator. Educ: Inst. des Essarts, Territet, Sorbonne Univ., Paris, France. Publs: Sleepytails; Freaks & Fancies (w. Pamela Powell); Dinghy on the London River; Esmeralda Ahoy, USA & UK; Nobody Asked to Come. Address: Gat-E-Whing, Andreas, Isle of Man, UK.

FAIRLEY, Peter, b. 2 Nov. 1930, Kuala Lumpur, Malaya. Journalist; TV Presenter. Educ: B.A., Sidney Sussex Coll., Cambridge. Publs: Man on the Moon, 1969; The ABC of Space, 1970; Project X, 1971; Peter Fairley's Space Annual, 1972; World of Wonders Annual, 1972; A-Z of Space, 1973; British Inventions of the 20th Century, 1973; Is There Anybody Out There?, 1974. Contbr. to: TV Times; Capitol Radio; ITV. Mbr., Assn. of Brit. Sci. Writers. Address: Pacific, 149 Hayes Lane, Bromley, Kent, UK.

FALCK, Arne C.W., b. 30 Apr. 1939, Tönsberg, Norway. Author. Educ: M.A., (Lit. & Aesthetics). Publs: For Joy (novel), 1970; WDTO (Worlds Different Treaty Organization, novel), 1971; Man's Day (poems), 1972. Contbr. to most maj. Scandinavian newspapers & lit. mags. Mbr., Norwegian Soc. of Authors. Hons: City of Uppsala Cultural Prize, 1970; Conrad Mohrs Prize, 1972; Prize for Young Norwegian Authors, 1973; Knut Hamsun Prize, 1974. Address: Holtegaten 14, Oslo 2, Norway.

FALK, Stanley Lawrence, b. 11 Mar. 1927, NYC, USA. Professor of International Relations; Author. Educ: B.A., Bard Coll., Columbia Univ., 1945; M.A., 1952, Ph.D., 1959, Georgetown Univ., Wash. D.C. Publs: Bataan: The March of Death, 1962; Decision at Leyte, 1966; Liberation of the Philippines, 1971; Bloodiest Victory: Palaus, 1974; 70 Days to Singapore, 1975; 6 textbooks, nat. security affairs; contbns., var. books & encys. Contbr. to: Mil. Affairs, Pol. Sci. Qtrly., Am. Hist. Review, Can. Jrnl. of Hist., Wash. Post, Wash. Star. Address: 2310 Kimbro St., Alexandria, VA 22307, USA.

FALKNER, Annemy, pen name BELLMAN, Erik Maria, b. 9 May 1921, Hamburg, Germany. Freelance Journalist & Writer. Educ: Studied Lit. & Arch. at Univs. of Hamburg & Munich. Publs: (radio plays) Der Wiederaufbau nach dem Hamburger Brand, 1954; Michelangelo: Der Bau der Peterskirchenkuppel, 1954; Der Baumeister Fritz Schumacher, 1954; Moderner Städtebau, 1954. Contbr. to: (as regular jrnlst.) Für Sie; Constanze; Petra; Brigitte; (occasional) Süddeutsche Zeitung; Hannoversche Allgemeine Zeitung; Tages Anzeigen, Schweizer Familie, Zürich; Bild und Funk; also radio & TV. Mbr., Deutsche Journalisten-Union. Address: 2 Hamburg 65, Poppenbüttler Hauptstr. 26, W. Germany.

FALK-RØNNE, Eyvind, b. 25 May 1914, Frederiksberg, Denmark. Artist; Author. Educ: Royal Acad., Copenhagen. Publs: (opera libretti) Höst (perfs. by Den jydskhe Opera, 1950 & The Royal Theatre, 1951); Tordenvejrei (perf. by The Royal Theatre, 1959); Prins Karneval (perf. by Danish radio, 1957); Marionetterne (perf. TV, 1959); (books) At se på Kunst, 1965; Fra Kulkmalerier til Asger jorn, 1968; lär Tegning og Maling, 1969; Bogen om Tegning og Maling, 1974. Mbrships. incl: Danish Authors' Club; Danish Dramatists' Club. Address: Mothsvej 58, 2840 Holte, Denmark.

FALLA, Frank Walter, pen name SARNIAN, b. 30 Mar. 1911, St. Andrew's, Guernsey, Channel Islands. Freelance Journalist. Publs: The Silent War, 1967, 2nd ed., 1974. Contbr. to: Nat. & Sunday newspapers; Time-Life News Serv. & Mag.; BBC TV & Radio. Address: 2 Summerland, Collings Rd., St. Peter Port, Guernsey, Channel Islands, UK.

FALLA, Molly (Elayne Mary), b. 7 Sept. 1903, Te Aroha, NZ. Teacher; Author. Educ: Tchr.'s D & C Certs., Auckland Tchr.'s Coll., 1923-24. Publs: Sketchbook of New Zealand Birds, 1966; A Pocketful of Penguins, 1970; A Kea On My Bed, 1974. Contbr. to: NZ Listener; Country Life; NZ Schl. Jrnl. Mbr., NZ Women Writers' Soc. Inc. Address: 41 Kotari Rd., Day's Bay, Eastbourne, Wellington, NZ.

FALLEY, Margaret Dickson, b. 8 Nov. 1898, Minneapolis, Minn., USA. Genealogist; Author. Educ: B.S., Northwestern Univ., 1920. Publs: Richard Falley & Some of His Descendants Including Grover Cleveland, 1952; Palmer Geneaology, Pt. I, 1957; Irish & Scotch-Irish Ancestral Research, 2 vols., 1962. Contbr. to genal. jrnls. Address: 1500 Sheridan Rd., Wilmette, IL 60091, USA.

FANCOURT, Mary St. John, b. 20 Aug. 1898, Murree, India. Publs: The Peoples' Earl, 1962; They Dared to be Doctors, 1965. Contbr. to var. mags. Mbr., Soc. of Authors. Address: c/o National & Grindlays Bank Ltd., 13 St. James's Square, London SW1, UK.

FANCUTT, Walter, b. 22 Feb. 1911, Blackburn, UK. Baptist Minister. Educ: All Nations Bible Coll., London; Cntrl. Schl. of Art. Publs: The Kingsgate Pocket Poets, 8 vols., 1948; Whitchurch Baptist Church, 1952; Waterlooville Centenary, 1954; In This will I be Confident, 1957; Beyond the Bitter Sea, 1959; Escaped as a Bird, 1964; Daily Remembrance, 1966; Present to Heal, 1966; The Imprisoned Splendour, 1972; With a Strange Surprise, 1974; The Southern Baptist Association & Its Churches, 1974. Contbr. to: Bapt. Times; Wight Life; New Day. Mbrships. incl: Bapt. Union Coun.; Pres., Southern Bapt. Assn., 1950; Soc. of Authors; Radio Writers Assn. Recip., Poetry Prize, Schl. of Relig. Jrnlsm. Address: 4b St. Boniface Gardens, Ventnor, Isle of Wight, PO38 1NN, UK.

FANE, Francis Douglas, b. 16 Nov. 1909, Aberdeen, UK. Dean of Faculty, Yokohama Business College, Japan; Editor, The Asian Oceanologist. Educ: Grad. Nautical Schls.; Holder Master's Licence US Merchant Marine. Author, The Naked Warriors, 1956. Contbr. to: US Naval Inst. Proceedings; Korean Herald; The Mutual Broadcasting Co., NYC (Radio News Corres.); etc. Mbrships. incl: US Naval Inst.; Am. Soc. Advancement Sci.; For. Corres. Club. Japan; Propeller Club US (Pres. Yokohama & Tokyo Ports); Am. Japan Soc.; ArmedForces Writers' League; Asian Soc.; Royal Soc. St. George; St. Andrew's Soc. Hons: Key to City of New Orleans, 1957 & City of Torrance, Calif, 1952. Address: P.O. Box 198, Yokohama Port P.O., 231-91, Japan.

FANE, Julian Charles, b. 25 May 1927, London, UK. Author. Novels: Morning; A Letter; Memoir in the Middle of the Journey; Gabriel Young; Tug-of-War, 1975. Mbrships: F.R.S.L. Address: 32 Blenheim Terrace, London NW8, UK.

FARBER, Donald C., b. 19 Oct. 1923, Columbus, Neb., USA. Attorney; Professor. Educ: B.S. in Law, Univ. of Neb.; LL.B., J.D., Coll. of Law, ibid. Publs: From Option to Opening, 1968, 1970; Producing on Broadway, 1969, 2nd ed., 1974; Actors: Guide: What You Should Know About the Contracts You Sign, 1971; Producing, Financing & Distributing Films, 1973. Address: 230 Park Ave., N.Y., NY 10017, USA.

FARHI, Musa Moris, b. 5 July 1935, Ankara, Turkey. Writer. Educ: B.A. (Major in Humanities). Publs: The Pleasure of Your Death, 1972; also author of screenplay, The Primitives, 1960, stage play, From the Ashes of Thebes, 1969, and var. TV scripts. Mbrships: Writers Guild of GB; Soc. of Authors. Address: 32 West Hill Court, Millfield Lane, London N6 6JJ, UK.

FARLEY, George M., pen name BLUE, S. G., b. 16 Jan. 1927, Kayford, W.Va., USA. Clergyman. Publs: Nigerian Conflict, 1966; The Life & Times of Zane Grey, forthcoming. Contbr. to: Zane Grey Western Mag.; Real W.; Fur-Fish-Game; The Nat. Future Farmer; Pa. Angler; W.Va. Illustrated; Pa. Game News; Grit; var. other (esp. relig.) jrnls. Mbrships: Western Writers of Am.; Independent Assemblies of God Int. Address: 1613 Virginia Ave., Hagestown, MD 21740, USA.

FARMER, Bertram Hughes, b. 18 Dec. 1916, Malmesbury, Wilts., UK. Director, Centre of South Asian Studies; Reader in South Asian Geography. Educ: B.A., 1937, M.A., 1941, St. John's Coll., Cambridge. Publs: Pioneer Peasant Colonization in Ceylon, 1957; Ceylon: A Divided Nation, 1963; Agricultural Colonization in India Since Independence, 1974. Contbr. to: Geogl. Review; Geogl. Jrnl.; Transactions, Inst. of Brit. Geogs.; Pacific Viewpoint; Jrnl. of Dev. Studies. Mbrships: Fellow, St. John's Coll., Cambridge (Pres., 1968-71); Royal Geogl. Soc.; Inst. Brit. Geogs. (Pres., 1972). Recip., var. geogl. awards. Address: St. John's College, Cambridge CB2 1TP, UK.

FARMER, Clarence Redmond, pen name FARMER, Jack, b. 8 Mar. 1894, Pineville, Ky., USA. Retired Army Officer. Educ: Courses in Bus. Admin., Maths. Publs: Magnificent Mongrel, 1959; Philosophy & Living, 1964; Polo — King of Sports, 1972. Address: 231 W. Villaret Blvd., San Antonio, TX 78221, USA.

FARMERS, Eileen Elizabeth, pen name LANE, Elizabeth, b. 15 Nov. 1918, Nhill, Vic., Australia. Writer; Homemaker. Publs: Mad as Rabbits, 1962; Our Uncle Charlie, 1964; 2 books forthcoming. Contbr. to: Sydney Bulletin; Aust. Woman's Mirror; Vic. & N.S.W. Schl. Paper; Ideas (Melbourne Book Trade mag.). Mbrships: Fndn. mbr., Aust. Soc. of Authors; PEN; Melbourne Writers' Assn.; Poetry Lovers' Club. Hons: 2 Short Story Awards, Best One-act Play Award, num. poetry awards, Melbourne Writers' Club. Address: 70 Bradford St., Coolbinia, Perth 6050, W. Australia.

FARNSWORTH, Paul Randolph, b. 15 Aug. 1899, Waterbury, Conn., USA. University Professor Emeritus; Author. Educ: B.A., 1921, M.A., 1923, Ph.D., 1925, Ohio State Univ. Publs: Social Psychology (w. R. T. La Piere), 1936, 3rd ed., 1949; Musical Taste: Its Measurement & Cultural Nature, 1950; Social Psychology of Music, 1958, 2nd ed., 1969. Contbr. to: Am. & British Jrnls. of Psychol.; Psychol. Review; Jrnl. of Applied Psychol.; Music Educators Jrnl.; Psychol. Today; Music Jrnl.; Hinrechsen's Music Book; Jrnl. of Musicol.; Sociometry; etc. Address: 715 Salvatierra St., Stanford, CA 94305, USA.

FARR, Alfred Derek, b. 1930, Bristol, UK. Medical Laboratory Technologist; Lecturer. Educ: B.A., London Univ.; F.I.M.L.T. Publs: A Laboratory Handbook of Blood Transfusion Techniques, 1961; A Synopsis of Blood Grouping Theory & Serological Techniques, 1963; The Royal Deeside Line, 1968; The Campbeltown & Machrihanish Railway, 1969; Stories of Royal Deeside's Railway, 1971; God, Blood & Society, 1972; Let Not the Deep, 1973. Contbr. to: Ed., Med. Lab. Technol.; Nursing Mirror; Nursing Times; Brit. Hosp. Jrnl.; Vox Sanguinis; etc. Mbrships: Inst. of Med. Lab. Technol.; Gt. N. of Scotland Railway Assn. Address: "Rosslynlee", Cults, Aberdeen, UK.

FARR, Finis King, b. 31 Dec. 1904, Lebanon, Tenn., USA. Author. Educ: A.B., Princeton Univ, 1926. Publs: Frank Lloyd Wright: A Biography, 1962; Black Champion: The Life & Times of Jack Johnson, 1963; Margaret Mitchell of Atlanta, 1965; F.D.R.: A Political Biography, 1969; Chicago: A Personal History, 1972; O'Hara: A Biography, 1973; Fair Enough: The Life of Westbrook Pegler, forthcoming; (novel) The Elephant Valley, 1967. Address: c/o Brandt & Brandt, 101 Park Ave., N.Y., NY 10017, USA.

FARRAN, Roy, b. 1921. Former Printer & Publisher; Member, Alberta Legislature, & Cabinet Minister. Educ: Royal Mil. Coll., Sandhurst, UK. Publs: Winged Dagger, 1948; Jungle Chase, 1950; The Search, 1953; The Day After Tomorrow, 1958; The History of the Calgary Highlanders, 1959; Operation Tombola, 1962; Never Had a Chance, 1968. Hons: D.S.O.; M.C. Address: R.R.3, Calgary, Alta., Can.

FARRAR, Emmie Ferguson (Mrs. Franklin Floyd Farrar), b. 13 Apr. 1891, Halifax, Va., USA. Teacher. Educ: Pvte. Publs: Flower Arrangements in Virginia, 1941; Old Virginia Houses — Mobjack Bay Country, 1955; Along the James, 1957; Along the Fall Line (w. E. Hines), 1971; Northern Peninsulas (w. E. Hines), 1972. Contbr. to: Richmond Times Dispatch, Richmond News Leader (former staff mbr.). Address: 2311 Essex Rd., Richmond, VA 23228, USA.

FARRAR, Rowena Rutherford, b. 27 June 1903, Nashville, Tenn., USA. Historical Novelist. Educ: Peabody, Vanderbilt Univ., N.Y. Univ., Columbia Univ. Publs: Bend Your Heads All, 1965; A Wondrous Moment Then, 1968. Contbr. to nat. mags. & jrnls.; book reviews in newspapers; The Penwoman (Past Ed.). Mbrships: Pres., Va. Writers Club; Nat. League of Am. Pen Women; Poetry Soc. of Va. Recip., 1st Prize, for a Wondrous Moment Then, Nat. League of Am. Pen Women, 1969. Address: 1901 Hanover Ave., Richmond, VA 23220, USA.

FARRAR-HOCKLEY, Anthony Heritage, b. 8 Apr. 1924, Coventry, UK. Major-General, British Army. Educ: B.Litt., Exeter Coll., Oxford. Publs: The Edge of the Sword, 1954; (Ed.) The Commander, 1957; The Somme, 1964; Death of an Army, 1967; The War in the Desert, 1969; Airborne Carpet, 1969; General Student, 1973; Goughie: General Sir Hubert Gough, 1975. Contbr. to: Times Lit. Supplement; Hist. of the Great War; Hist. of the 2nd World War. Mbr., Int. Inst. for Strategic Studies. Address: c/o Savage Club, 86 St. James's, London W1, UK.

FARRELL, Bryan Henry, b. 23 Apr. 1923, Auckland, NZ. Geographer. Educ: B.A., Univ. of Canterbury; M.A., Univ. of Wash.; Ph.D., Univ. of Auckland. Publs: Power in New Zealand, 1962; Themes on Pacific Lands (Ed. w. M. C. R. Edgell), 1974. Contbr. to: Western Samoa (Ed. Fox & Cumberland), 1962; Man in the Pacific Islands (Ed. Ward) 1972; NZ Geog.; Econ. Geog.; Geog. Review; Jrnl. of Geog. Mbrships: Polynesian Soc.; Can. Assn. of Geographers, C'wlth. Club of Calif.; Assn. of Pacific Coast Geographers. Address: 126 Ponderosa Dr., Scotts Valley, Santa Cruz, CA 95060, USA.

FARRELL, James Gordon, b. 1935, Liverpool, UK. Author. Educ: B.A., Brasenose Coll., Oxford. Publs: The Lung, 1965; A Girl in the Head, 1967; Troubles, 1970. Contbr. to: Spectator. Address: 16 Egerton Gdns., London SW3, UK.

FARRELL, James Thomas, occasional pen name TITULESCU, Jonathan, b. 27 Feb. 1904, Chgo., Ill., USA. Novelist. Educ: Univ. of Chgo. Publs. incl: Studs Lonigan 1935; O'Meill-O'Faherty series; Tommy Gallagher's Crusade; This Man & This Woman; Boarding House Blues The Silence of History (forthcoming); (short stories) An American Dream Girl; French Girls are Vicious; (poetry) When Time was Born; Olive, 1975; Mary Anne, 1975. Contbr. to var. Am. mags. Mbrships: Authors' League of Am.; Nat. Inst. of Art & Letters. Hons. incl: Guggenheim Fellowship in Creative Writing. Address: 308 E. 79th St. N.Y., NY 10021, USA.

FARRIMOND, John, b. 1913, Hindley, near Wigan, UK Author. Publs: Dust in My Throat, 1963; The Hollow Shell 1964; Kill Me a Priest, 1965; Pick & Run, 1966; No Friday in the Week, 1967; Dust is Forever, 1969; Lay Down the

Track, 1970. Contbr. to: London Evening News; Birmingham Mail; Glasgow Herald; num. overseas papers. Address: 102 Algernon St., Hindley, near Wigan, Lancs., UK.

FARRINGTON, Benjamin, b. 10 July 1891, Cork, Repub. of Ireland. Professor of Classics; Author. Educ: B.A., Trinity Coll., Dublin; M.A., Univ. Coll., Cork. Publs: Primum Graius Homo, 1927; Science in Antiquity, 1936; Science & Politics in the Ancient World, 1939; Greek Science, 1944; Francis Bacon, Philosopher of Industrial Science, 1949, 2nd ed., 1973; The Philosophy of Francis Bacon (1603-1609), 1964; The Faith of Epicurus, 1967. Address: 8 Daniells Walk, Lymington, Hants., SO4 9PN, UK.

FARRIS, Martin Theodore, b. 5 Nov. 1925, Spokane, Wash. D.C., USA. Economist; Educator. Educ: B.A., 1949, M.A., 1950, Univ. of Mont.; Ph.D., Ohio State Univ., 1957. Publs: Domestic Transportation: Practice, Theory & Policy, (w. R. J. Sampson), 1966, 3rd ed., 1975; Modern Transportation: Selected Readings (w. P. T. McElhiney), 1967, 1973; Public Utilities Regulation, Management & Ownership (w. R. J. Sampson), 1973. Contbr. to profl. jrnls. Address: Coll. of Bus. Admin., Ariz. State Univ., Tempe, AZ 85281, USA.

FAST, Howard, pen name CUNNINGHAM, E. V., b. 11 Nov. 1914, NYC, USA. Writer. Publs. incl: Two Valleys, 1933; Strange Yesterday, 1934; The Children, 1935; Place in the City, 1937; The Last Frontier, 1941; The Unvanquished, 1942; Freedom Road, 1944; The American, 1946; Clarkton, 1947; Spartacus, 1951; Silas Timberman, 1954; The Winston Affair, 1959; April Morning, 1961; Power, 1962; The Hill, 1964; Torquemada, 1966; The Hunter & the Trap, 1967; The General Zapped an Angel, 1970; The Crossing, 1971; The Hessian, 1972. Contbr. to: Saturday Review; Saturday Evening Post; The Nation; Mag. of Fantasies & Sci. Fiction. Hons. incl: Hon. Roll of O'Brien's Best Stories, 1939; Annual Book Award, Secondary Educ. Bd., 1962. Address: 1401 Laurel Way, Beverly Hills, CA 90210, USA.

FATCHEN, Max, b. 3 Aug. 1920, Adelaide, S.A. Journalist. Publs: The River Kings, 1966; Conquest of the River, 1970; The Spirit Wind, 1973, reprinted twice 1974; Just Fancy, Mr. Fatchen, 1967. Contbr. to: Sydney Sun; Melbourne Herald; Courier Mail Brisbane; Aust. Broadcasting Corp.; Denver Post (USA). Mbrships: Aust. Jrnlst. Assn.; Aust. Soc. Authors. Recip., Commendation for children's book, The Spirit Wind by C'wlth. Lit. Bd., July 1974. Address: 15 Jane St., Smithfield, S.A.

FAUGSTAD, Åse Lilleskare, b. 3 Apr. 1941, Dale, Norway. Author. Educ: Can. mag., Univ. of Bergen, 1971. Publs: Ved mitt altar (poetry) 1966; Stilt på min tanke (poetry), 1968; Stjernene (poetry), 1974. Mbrships: Norwegian Authors' Assn.; Norwegian Authors Ctr., Artists' Soc., Bergen. Address: Holhovdvegen 4, 5280 Dalekvam, Norway.

FAULKNER, Anne Irvin, pen name FAULKNER, Nancy, b. 6 Jan. 1906, Lynchburg, Va., USA. Writer. Educ. incls: B.A., Wellesley Coll.; M.A., Cornell Univ. Publs., 23 books inclng: Rebel Drums (for young people); Pirate Quest (for young people); The Traitor Queen (for young people); Great Reckoning (for young people); Mystery of the Limping Stranger (for young people); The Witch with the Long Sharp Nose (picture book); Witches Brew (for adults); The Jade Box (for adults). Mbr., profl. orgs. Recip., Edgar Allan Poe Award, 1966. Address: 942 Rosser Lane, Charlottesville, VA 22903, USA.

FAULKNER, Peter, b. 10 July 1933, Eastbourne, Sussex, UK. University Teacher. Educ: B.A., 1956, M.A., 1960, Trinity Hall, Cambridge; M.A., Birmingham Univ., 1960. Publs: William Morris & W. B. Yeats, 1962; Ed., T. Holcroft, Anna St. Ives, 1970; Ed., William Morris: The Critical Heritage, 1973; Ed., Early Romances in Prose & Verse by William Morris, 1973. Contbr. to: Durham Univ. Jrnl.; Humanist; New Humanist; Books & Bookmen; Jrnl. of the William Morris Soc. Mbr., Brit. Humanist Assn. Recip., Peter Floud Mem. Prize, William Morris Soc., 1961, 1963. Address: Glacis, Belvidere Rd., Exeter, Devon EX4 4RU, UK.

FAULL, Lesley, b. Durban, Natal, S. Africa. Director, Cooking School. Educ: Dip., Int. Schl. of Cookery; Cert. & Dip., Cordons Bleu. Publs. incl: Buttermilk Recipes, 1964; Cream Makes the Difference, 1965; Inspired by Sugar, 1966; Their Secret was Sugar, 1967; Meat on the Menu, 1968; Rice Recipes & Curries, 1969; Cookery in South Africa — Traditional & Today, 1970; Bread, Buns, Cakes & Cookies, 1970; Milk Makes It, 1972; ABC for Cooks, 1973; Party Fare, 2nd ed., 1973; Braai & Barbecue, 3rd ed., 1974; also books in Afrikaans. Contbr. to num. mags.; Ed., Silwood Kitchen Wine; Ed., Food Monthly Newsletter. Mbr., Int. Wine & Food Soc. (Comm.). Address: Silwood, Silwood Rd., Rondesbosch 7700, S. Africa.

FAUST, Irvin, b. 11 June 1924, NYC, USA. School Guidance Counsellor. Educ: B.S., CCNY, 1949; M.A. 1952, D.Ed. 1960, Columbia Univ. Publs: Entering Angel's World: A Student-Centered Casebook, 1963; Roar Lion Roar & Other Stories, 1965; (novels) The Steagle, 1966; The File on Stanley Patton Buchta, 1970; Willy Remembers, 1971. Contbr. to: Sewanee Review; Esquire; Paris Review; Transatlantic Review; Northwest Review. Address: 417 Riverside Dr., N.Y., NY 10025, USA.

FAUVET, Jacques, b. 9 June 1914, Paris, France. Managing Editor, Le Monde newspaper. Educ: LL.B., Fac. of Law, Paris. Publs: The Cockpit of France; La France déchirée, 1957; La IVe République, 1959; Histoire du Parti communiste français, 2 vols., 1964-65. Contbr. to Le Monde. Recip., Off., Legion of Hon. Address: 5 Rue Louis Boilly, 75016 Paris, France.

FAWCETT, Brian, b. 1906, Cork, Repub. of Ireland. Engineer; Commercial Artist; Illustrator; Translator; Semi-professional Musician (Bassoon). Educ: Jamaica; USA; Civil Engr. Publs: Let Me Drive, 1950; Exploration Fawcett, 1953; The Proudest Llama, 1954; Ruins in the Sky, 1958; Railways of the Andes, 1963; Steam in the Andes, 1973. Contbr. to: Arquitecto Peruano, Lima; Turismo, Lima; Backwoods; Trains, USA; Railroad Mag., USA. Mbrships: Soc. of Authors; Fellow, Inst. Mech. Engrs.; F.R.G.S. Address: 36 Durdar Rd., Carlisle CA2 4SB, UK.

FAY, Michèle, pen name (maiden name) COTE, Michèle, b. 24 Oct. 1936, Moulins, France. Professor. Educ: B.A.; M.A. Contbr. to sev. jrnls. inclng: Quinzaine Littéraire; Esprit; Études Philosophiques; Politique Aujourd'hui. Mbr., Lit. Critics' Union. Address: 66 Rue de Rennes, Paris VIe, France.

FAYE, Jean Pierre, b. 19 July 1925. University Professor; Writer. Educ: Sorbonne Univ., Paris. Publs. incl: (novels) Entre les Rues, 1958; La Cassure, 1961; Battlement, 1962; Analogues, 1964; Les Troyens, 1970; (poems) Fleuve Renversé, 1959; Couleurs Pliées, 1965; (essays) Le Récit Hunique, 1967; Langages Totalitaires, Théorie du récit, 1972; La Critique de Langage & son Economie, 1973; Migrations des Récits sur le Peuple Juif, 1974. Contbr. to: Change (Ed., 1968); Fndr., Centre for the Analysis & Sociology of Languages, Recip., Prix Renardot, 1964. Address: Eds. Seghers-Laffont, 6 Place St. Sulpice, Paris, 6e, France.

FAZAKERLEY, George Raymond, b. 1921, Liverpool, UK. Writer. Publs: (novels) Shadow in Saffron; Kongoni; A Stranger Here; (non-fiction) Teach Yourself Window Display; Modern Interior Display. Contbr. to: Goldsmiths' Jrnl.; Furnishing World. Display; other trade jrnls. Mbrships: Soc. of Authors; Brit. Display Soc. Address: 32 Myers Rd. West, Great Crosby, Liverpool L23 0RU, UK.

FAZEKAS, László, b. 20 July 1924, Pápa, Hungary. Poet. Educ: Ph.D. Publs: A megvallatott gyermekkor, 1965; Éjféli nap, 1967; Sziklaősvény, 1973. Contbr. to: Válasz (1945-49); Kortárs; Jelenkor; Élet és irodalom. Mbr., Magyar Irók Szövetsége. Address: 1122 Budapest, Csaba-u. 10, Hungary.

FEAVER, George, b. 12 May 1937, Hamilton, Can. University Professor. Educ: B.A., Univ. of B.C., 1959; Ph.D., London Schl. of Econs., U.K., 1962. Publs: From Status to Contract: A Biography of Sir Henry Maine, 1969; Ed., Beatrice Webb's Our Partnership, 1974; The Tragedy of Black Power, 1975. Contbr. to: The New Left: Six Critical Essays, 1970; Encounter; Jrnl. of Pols.; Studies in Comparative Communism. Hons: Canada Coun. Leave Fellowships, 1970-71, 1974-75; Fellow, Am. Coun. of Learned Socs., 1974-75. Address: 1689 Allison Rd., Vancouver 8, B.C., Can.

FEDDEN, (Henry) Robin Romilly, b. 1908, Burford, Oxon., UK. Consultant, The National Trust. Educ: Magdalene Coll., Cambridge. Publs. incl: Syria, 1946;

Crusader Castles, 1950; Alpine Ski Tour: An Account of the High Level Route, 1956; Skiing in the Alps, 1958; The Enchanted Mountains, 1962; Chantemesle, 1964; The Continuing Purpose, a History of the National Trust, 1968; The White Country (verse), 1968; Churchill at Chartwell, 1969; The Giant's Causeway, 1970. Hons: C.B.E.; Hon. F.R.I.B.A. Agent: David Higham Assocs. Address: 20 Eldon Rd., London W8, UK.

FEDELLE, Estelle, b. Chgo., Ill., USA. Artist: Painter. Educ: Art Inst. of Chgo.; Northwestern Univ.; Inst. of Design; Am. Acad. of Fine Arts. Author, How to Begin Painting for Fun, 1965. Contbr. to var. art books. Mbrships: Am. Artists Profl. League; Artists Guild of Chgo.; Hons. Dir., Regent Art League, Assocs. in Art; Municipal Art League; Nat. League of Am. Pen Women. Address: 5132 West Fletcher, Chgo., IL 60641, USA.

FEDERMAN, Raymond, b. 15 May 1928, Paris, France. Professor of Literature; Writer. Educ: B.A., Columbia Univ., 1957; M.A., 1959, Ph.D., 1963, UCLA. Publs. incl: Journey to Chaos: Samuel Beckett's Early Fiction, 1965; Among the Beasts (bilingual poems), 1967; Samuel Beckett: His Works & His Critics (w. John Fletcher), 1970; Double or Nothing (novel), 1971; Amer Eldorado (novel), 1974; Surfiction (essays), (Ed.), 1974. Contbr. to: Evergreen, Partisan, N. American, Westcoast, French Reviews; Big Table; Panache; Modern Drama; Film Quarterly; Esprit (France). Le Monde (France); etc. Hons. incl: Frances Steloff Fiction Prize, 1971; Panache Expmtl. Fiction Prize, 1972. Address: 227 Depew Ave., Buffalo, NY 14214, USA.

FEDIN, Konstantin Alexandrovich, b. 27 Feb. 1892, Saratov, USSR. Novelist. Educ: D.Phil., Moscow Commercial Inst. Publs: Anna Timofsevna, 1922; The Waste Land, 1923; Cities & Years, 1924; Transvaal, 1926; Brothers, 1928; I Was an Actor, 1937; Rape of Europe, 1934; (play) Bakunin in Dresden, 1922; Sanatorium Arktur, 1940; Gorky Among Us, 1943; Return to Leningrad, 1945; Early Joys, 1945; No Ordinary Summer, 1948; Die Flamme, 1962. Mbrships. incl: Moscow Union of Soviet Writers (chmn.); Acad. of Sci., USSR; German, Acad. der Kunste. Hons. incl: Silver Medal, World Peace Coun.; Order of Lenin. Address: 52 Ul. Vorovskogo, Moscow, USSR.

FEENEY, (Rev.) Leonard, b. 15 Feb. 1897, Lynn, Mass., USA. Founder & Superior, Slaves of the Immaculate Heart of Mary; Director, St. Benedict Center. Educ: M.A., Woodstock Coll., Md., 1927; Weston Coll., 1927-29. Publs: In Towns & Little Towns, 1927; Riddle & Reverie, 1933; Fish on Friday, 1934; Boundaries, 1935; Song for a Listener, 1936; An American Woman, 1938; You'd Better Come Quietly, 1939; Survival Till Seventeen, 1941; The Leonard Feeney Omnibus, 1943; Your Second Childhood, 1945; London is a Place, 1951; Bread of Life, 1952. Address: St. Benedict Center, Still River, MA 01467, USA.

FEHR, Karl, b. 8 Aug. 1910, Berg am Irchel, Zürich, Switz. University Professor. Educ: Dr. Philos.; Higher Tchng. Dip. Publs. incl: Jeremias Gotthelfs Schwarze Spinne als christlicher Mythos, 1942; Besinnung auf Gotthelf, 1946; Jeremias Gotthelf: Mensch, Erzieher, Dichter, 3rd ed., 1953; Das Bild des Menschen bei Gotthelf, 1954; (biog.) Jeremias Gotthelf, 1954; Der Realismus in der schweiz Literatur, 1965; Josef Vital Kopp: Ein Dichter und Priesterleben im Bannkreis moderner Welt und Gottesschau, 1968; Jeremias Gotthelf: Realienbücher für Germanisten, 1967; C. F. Meyer: Realienbücher für Germanisten, 1971; Gottfried Keller: Aufschlüsse und Deutungen, 1972. Contbr. to: Germanistik; etc. Mbr., Akademische Gesellschaft schweizerischen Germanisten. Recip., Canton of Zürich Award, 1954, 1964, 1972. Address: CH-8500, Frauenfeld, Switz.

FEHRENBACH, T(heodore) R(eed), pen name FREEMAN, Thomas, b. 12 Jan. 1925, San Benito, Tex., USA. Author. Educ: B.A., Princeton Univ. Publs: Battle of Anzio, 1962; This Kind of War, 1963; Gnomes of Zurich, 1966; This Kind of Peace, 1966; FDR's Undeclared War, 1967; Lone Star, 1968; Greatness to Spare, 1968; Fire & Blood: A History of Mexico, 1973; Comanches: The Destruction of a People, 1974. Contbr. to: Saturday Evening Post; Analog; Argosy; Sunday Times, UK; Woche, Switz.; L'Express, France; var. other jrnls., USA & abroad. Mbrships incl: Tex. Inst. of Letters; Authors Guild; Sci. Fiction Writers of Am. Hons. incl: Evelyn Oppenheimer Award, 1968; Citations, Tex. House of Reps., 1969, 1973. Address: P.O. Box 6698, San Antonio, TX 78209, USA.

FEIBLEMAN, James K., b. 13 July 1904, New Orleans, La., USA. Professor of Philosophy; Author. Educ: Univ. of Va. Publs. incl: Positive Democracy, 1940; The Margitist (poetry), 1944; The Revival of Realism, 1946; The Long Habit (novel), 1948; Aesthetics, 1949; Ontology, 1951; Trembling Prairie (poetry), 1952; The Institutions of Society, 1956; The Pious Scientist, 1958; Moral Strategy, 1967; The Way of a Man (autobiog), 1970; The New Materialism, 1970; Great April (novel), 1971; The Quiet Rebellion, 1972. Contbr. of over 160 articles to profl. jrnls. Hons. incl: D.Lit., Rider Coll., 1973. Address: 1424 1st National Bank of Commerce Building, New Orleans, LA 70112, USA.

FEIFFER, Jules. Publs. incl: Boy Girl; Sick, Sick. Address: c/o William Collins Sons & Co., 14 St. James's Place, London SW1, UK.

FEIS, Herbert, b. 7 June 1893, NYC, USA, d. 2 Mar. 1972. Economist; Historian; Author. Educ: A.B., Ph.D., Harvard Coll. Publs. incl: The Sinews of Peace, 1944; Three International Episodes, 1947; The Spanish Story, 1948; The Road to Pearl Harbour, 1950; The Diplomacy of the Dollar, 1950; The China Tangle, 1953; Churchill, Roosevelt, Stalin, 1957; Between War & Peace, 1960; Japan Subdued, 1961; Foreign Aid & Foreign Policy, 1964; The Atomic Bomb & the End of World War II, 1966; Characters in Crisis, 1966; From Trust to Terror: The Onset of the Cold War, 1945-1950, 1970. Recip., Pulitzer Prize for "Between War & Peace".

FEJES, Endre, b. 15 Sept. 1923, Budapest, Hungary. Writer. Publs: Generation of Rust, 1962, 8th ed., 1973; Merry Fellows (short stories), 1966; The Liar, 1958, 2nd ed., 1973; Good Evening Summer, Good Evening Love, 1969, 3rd ed., 1973; (plays) Generation of Rust, 1963; Mocorgo, 1966; Vono, Ignac, 1969; The Marriage of Margit Cserepes, 1972; (TV plays) Good Evening Summer, Good Evening Love, 1973; The Marriage of Margit Cserepes, 1974. Contbr. to var. lit. mags. & daily papers. Mbrships: Feszek Artists' Club; Hungarian PEN. Recip., Attila Jozsef Lit. Prize. Address: Normafa ut 15/b, 1121 Budapest, Hungary.

FEKETE, Irene Anne Francis, b. 1936, Philadelphia, USA. Educational Marketing Manager, Hutchinson Publishing Group, London, UK; Executive Member, Educational Publishers' Council. Educ: Barnard Coll.; Columbia Univ., USA; Edinburgh Univ., UK; London Schl. of Econs. Publs: Zandra, UK & USA 1961; The Ornaments, 1963; Athens: Portrait of a City, 1965; Wreath for a Spy, 1967; The Ambiguous Man, 1968; Time Elsewhere (Phoenix Living Poet Series) 1970; The Common Market, 1974. Contbr. to: Cath. Tchrs' Jrnl.; Greek Life; Times Educl. Supplement; Cornhill Mag. Mbr., P.E.N. Agent: A.M. Heath & Co.

FEKETE, Sandor, b. 11 Feb. 1927, Hejoesaba, Hungary. Literary Historian; Playwright; Critic. Publs: (in Hungarian) Symposium on the Corridor, 1970; Comedy of the Man-Eater, 1971; (play) Thermidor, 1973; The Biography of Petofi, I, 1973. Mbr. Union of Hungarian Writers. Hons: Order of Liberty, 1946; Jozsef Attila Prize, 1973. Address: 1045 Budapest, Szechenyi rakpart 7, Hungary.

FELD, Michael, b. 1938, Stoke Newington, London, UK. Advertising Writer/Visualiser; Author. Publs: The Sabbatical Year, 1969; Super Shelley's Mein Kampf, 1969; Hands of the Philistines, 1974. Contbr. to: London Mag. Agent: John Johnson. Address: 38 Gerard Rd., Barnes, London SW13, UK.

FELDMAN, Irving Mordecai, b. 22 Sept. 1928, Brooklyn, N.Y., USA. Teacher. Educ: C.C.N.Y., B.S.S.S., 1950; M.A., Columbia Univ., 1953. Publs: Works & Days & other poems, 1961; The Pripet Marshes & other poems, 1965; Magic Papers & other poems, 1970; Lost Originals (Poems), 1972. Contbr. to: New Yorker; Harper's; Atlantic; Poetry, N.Y. Times; Am. Review; Harper's Bazaar; etc. Hons: Kovner Prize for Poetry, Jewish Bk. Coun. of Am., 1962; Award, Nat. Inst. of Arts & Letters, 1973; Guggenheim Fellowship, 1973. Address: Dept. of Engl., State Univ. of N.Y., Buffalo, NY 14214, USA.

FELSTEIN, Ivor, pen names STEEN, Frank; McCANN, Philip, b. 14 May 1933, Glasgow, UK. Physician; Freelance Medical Journalist. Educ: M.B., Ch.B., Univ. of Glasgow, 1956. Publs. incl: A Change of Face & Figure, 1971; Snakes & Ladders — Medical & Social Aspects of Modern

Management, 1971; Living to be a Hundred, 1973; Sex in Later Life, 1973; Sexual Pollution — Fall & Rise of Venereal Disease, 1974; The Medical Shorthand Typist (w. M. Barnard & J. Mitson), 1974. Contbr. to var. jrnls.; Cons. Ed., Brit. Jrnl. of Sexual Med. Mbrships: Brit. Geriatrics Soc.; Soc. of Authors, London. Address: 11 Kibworth Close, Whitefield, Manchester M25 7LS, UK.

FELTNER, George Frans Elof, b. 17 May 1908, Leadville, Colo., USA. Freelance Writer; Editor, The Balance Wheel for the American Association for Conservation Information. Educ: Okla. State Univ.; Int. Corres. Schls.; Alexander Hamilton Inst. Publs: A Look Back (A hist. of the Colo. Game & Fish Dept.), 1963. Contbr. to: Coors Courier (Ed.); Open Door (Ed.); The Palm (Ed.); Colo. Grocer (Asst. Ed.); Nat. Fur News (Asst. Ed.); Colo. Wildlife Fedn. News (Ed.); Colo. Outdoors (Asst. Ed.); Western Outdoor Mag. (Corres. 1963-73). Mbrships. incl: Outdoor Writers Assn. of Am.; Hon. Life., Am. Assn. for Conservation Information. Hons. incl: Int. 1st Place Award, Am. Assn. for Conservation Info. for 'A Look Back'. Address: 458 Lowell Blvd., Denver, CO 80204, USA.

FENAKEL, Judit, b. 25 June 1936; Budapest, Hungary. Journalist; Author. Educ: M.S. (Hungarian Lit.), Arts Fac., Attila József Univ., Szeged. Publs: (short stories) Dwelling Two Street, 1960; Life Is a Merry Thing, 1963; (novels) Aquarium, 1966; Ten Days in the Countryside, 1967; Stripping, 1970; Lili's Journeys, 1973; From May till May, 1974. Contbr. to: Kortárs; Uj Irás; Élet és Irodalom. Mbrships: PEN; Union of Hungarian Writers. Address: Lővölde tér 2, fsz. 3, Budapest 1071, Hungary.

FENNER, Frank John, b. 21 Dec. 1914, Ballarat, Vic., Australia. University Professor of Environmental Studies; Author. Educ: M.B., B.S., 1938, M.D., 1942, Adelaide Univ. Publs: The Production of Antibodies (w. F. M. Burnet), 1949; Myxomatosis (w. F. N. Ratcliffe), 1965; The Biology of Animal Viruses (2 vols.), 1968, 2nd ed., 1974; Medical Virology (w. D. O. White), 1970. Contbr., about 100 sci. papers, mainly acidfast bacilli, animal viruses & environmental studies, major sci. jrnls. Recip., M.B.E., 1944. Address: Centre for Resource & Environmental Studies, Australian National University, Canberra, A.C.T., Australia.

FENSHAM, Frank Charles, b. 13 Oct. 1925, Heilbron, O.F.S., S. Africa. Professor in Semitic Languages. Educ: B.A., M.A., B.D., D.D., Univ. of Pretoria; Ph.D., Johns Hopkins Univ., Baltimore, USA. Publs: Die Brief aan Hebrëers, 1962; Wetenskap en Bybelkunde, 1964; Heersers van die ou Nabye Ooste, 1970; Exodus, 1970; Die Veelkleurige kleed, 1971; Bybelse Aardryskunde, Oudheidkunde en Opgrawings, 1972. Contbr. of over 200 articles to: Jrnl. of Biblical Lit.; Jrnl. of Semitic Studies; etc.; Ed., Jrnl. of N.W. Semitic Langs.; Co-ed., Die Ensiklopedie van di Wereld. Mbrships. incl: S. African Acad. Sci. & Arts; Coun. of Fedn. of Afrikaans Cultural Socs. Address: 40 Rowan St., Stellenbosch, S. Africa.

FENTON, (Rev.) John Charles, b. 1921, Liverpool, UK. The Principal, St. Chad's College, Durham since 1965; The Principal, Lichfield Theological College, 1958-65; Vicar of Wentworth, Yorks., 1954-58. Educ: M.A., B.D., Queen's Coll., Oxford Univ.; Lincoln Theol. Coll. Publs: Preaching the Cross; The Passion According to John; Crucified with Christ; The Gospel According to Matthew; The Gospel According to John; What Was Jesus' Message. Contbr. to: Studies in the Gospels; What about the New Testament; Theol.; Jrnl. Theol. Studies; Expository Times; etc. Address: St. Chad's Coll., Durham, UK.

FENWICK-OWEN, Roderic Franklin Rawnsley, pen name OWEN, Roderic, b. 1921, London, UK. Company Director. Publs: The Desert Air Force; The Flesh is Willing; Easier for a Camel; Away from Eden; Tedder; Green Heart of Heaven; Worse than Wanton; Where the Poor Are Happy; The Golden Bubble; Roddy Owen's Africa; Beautiful & Beloved (co-author), 1974. Mbrships: Fellow, R.C.A.S.; R.G.S.; Authors' Club. Agent: David Higham Assocs. Address: Gilston Lodge, 22 Gilston Road, London SW10, UK.

FERGUSON, Arthur Bowles, b. 15 Oct. 1913, Windsor, Can. Professor of History. Educ: B.A., Univ. of Western Ont., 1935; Ph.D., Cornell Univ., USA, 1939. Publs: The Indian Summer of English Chivalry, 1960; The Articulate Citizen & the English Renaissance, 1965. Contbr. to: Jrnl. Medieval & Renaissance Studies (Assoc. Ed.); Jrnl. of Hist.

of Ideas; Renaissance Quarterly; Studies in the Renaissance; Jrnls. of Brit. & Mod. Hist. Mbrships: Am. Histl. Assn.; Renaissance Soc. of Am.; Conf. on Brit. Studies. Hons: Ford Fndn. Fellowship, 1954-55; Guggenheim Fellowship, 1971-72; Fellow of Royal Histl. Soc., 1973-. Address: 22 Lebanon Circle, Durham, NC 27705, USA.

FERGUSON, Ira Lunan, b. 27 Jan. 1904, Jackson Town, Jamaica, BWI. Clinical Psychologist. Educ: Grad. Derrick Bus. Coll., Phila., USA, 1922; B.S., Howard Univ., 1931; B.A., 1937, M.S., 1941, Univ. of Minn.; M.A., 1949; Ph.D., 1950, Columbia Univ.; LL.B., La Salle Ext. Univ., 1970. Publs. incl: The Mathematics of Dosages & Solutions for Nurses, 1956; I Dug Graves by Night to Attend College by Day, 3 vols., 1968-70; Biog. of G. Wash Carter, 1969; Which One of You Is Interracial?, 1969; Lectures in Black Studies, 1972; Don't Marry that Woman!, Or, Why Buy a Cow when Milk Is so Cheap?, 1973. Contbr. to num. profl. jrnls. Assoc. Ed., Lex et Scientia. Hons: Papers, publs., memorabilia deposited in Dr. Ira Lunan Ferguson Collect., Univ. of Wyo. Address: 2219 Clement St., San Francisco, CA 94121, USA.

FERGUSON, John, b. 2 Mar. 1921, Manchester, UK. University Professor. Educ: M.A., B.D., Cambridge Univ. Publs. incl: Religions of the Roman Empire, 1970; A Companion to Greek Tragedy, 1972; Aristotle, 1972; Sermons of a Layman, 1972; The Place of Suffering, 1972; The Open University from Within, 1975; Utopias of the Classical World, 1975; Danilo Dolci, 1975; Dictionary of Mysticism & Mystery-Religions, forthcoming; num. other books & plays. Contbr. to: Reconciliation Quarterly (jt. Ed.); Am. Jrnl. Philol.; Greece & Rome; Mod. Ch.man; etc. Mbrships: Fellow, Int. Inst. Arts & Letters; Fellowship of Reconciliation; var. relig. & classical assns. Address: Higham Cross House, Hanslope, Milton Keynes MK 19 7HP, UK.

FERGUSON, Peter Roderick Innes, b. 1933, Bromley, Kent, UK. Author. Educ: B.A., Balliol Coll., Oxford. Publs: Autumn for Heroes, 1959; Monster Clough, 1962; A Week Before Winter (In the Year of the Great Reaping), 1971. Contbr. to: Best Short Stories, 1966; Truth; Listen; Departure; Daily Telegraph Mag.; etc. Agent: John Farquharson. Address: 74 W. Riding, Bricket Wood, St. Albans AL2 3QQ, UK.

FERGUSON, Thomas, b. 1900, Falkirk, Stirlingshire, UK. Professor of Public Health. Educ: M.D., D.Sc., Edinburgh Univ. Publs: The Dawn of Scottish Social Welfare; Scottish Social Welfare 1864-1914; The Young Wage Earner; The Young Delinquent in his Social Setting; In their Early Twenties; Hospital & Community; Handicapped Youth. Mbrships: F.R.C.P.E. Address: Chowrassie, Lezayre Rd., Ramsey, Isle of Man, UK.

FERGUSSON, Adam, b. 10 July, 1932, Haddington, UK. Journalist. Educ: B.A., Trinity Coll., Cambridge Univ. Publs: Roman Go Home, 1969; A Home of Your Own (w. Rev. E. Casey), 1969; The Lost Embassy, 1972; The Sack of Bath, 1973. Contbr. to: Times (Feature Writer, 1967—); Glasgow Herald (Ldr. Writer & Diplomatic Corres. 1956-60); The Statist (Asst. Ed. & For. Ed., 1960-67); Sunday Telegraph; Illustrated London News; Crossbow; Herald Tribune; etc. Agent: Curtis Brown Ltd. Address: 9 Addison Cresc., London W14, UK.

FERGUSSON, Bernard (Lord Ballantrae), b. 6 May 1911, London, UK. Retired Soldier; Formerly Governor-General of New Zealand; Chairman, British Council; University Chancellor. Educ: Royal Mil. Coll., Sandhurst. Publs. incl: Beyond the Chindwin, 1945; The Black Watch & the King's Enemies, 1950; The Watery Maze: The Story of Combined Operations, 1961; Wavell: Portrait of a Soldier, 1961; Return to Burma, 1962; The Trumpet in the Hall, 1970. Contbr. to var. lit. jrnls. Mbrships: F.R.S.L.; F.R.G.S.; Coun., 1954-58; Soc. of Authors. Recip., D.Litt., St. Andrew's Univ. Address: Auchairne, Ballantrae, Ayrshire, UK.

FERGUSSON HANNAY, (Lady), pen name LESLIE, Doris, b. London, UK. Novelist; Historian. Educ: London; Brussels; Studied art in Florence, Italy. Publs: (novels) Full Flavour; Fair Company; Concord in Jeopardy; House in the Dust; Another Cynthia; As a Tree Falls; Paragon Street; The Marriage of Martha Todd; The Dragon's Head; Call Back Yesterday; (biogs.) Royal William; Wreath for Arabella; That Enchantress; Polonaise; The Great Corinthian; The Perfect Wife; A Toast to Lady Mary; I Return; This for Caroline; The Sceptre & the Rose; The Rebel Princess; The

Desert Queen; The Incredible Duchess. Address: c/o A. P. Watt & Son, 26-28 Bedford Row, London WC1R 4HL, UK.

FERMOR, Patrick Michael Leigh, b. 11 Feb. 1915, London, UK. Author. Publs: The Traveller's Tree, 1950; A Time to Keep Silence, 1953; The Violins of St. Jacques, 1953; Mani, 1958; (transl.) The Cretan Runner by George Psychoundakis; Roumeli. Hons: O.B.E., 1943; D.S.O., 1944; Heinemann Fndn. Prize for Lit., 1950; Kemsley Prize, 1951; Duff Cooper Prize, 1958. Address: c/o John Murray, 50 Albermarle St., London W1, UK.

FERNANDEZ DE LA REGUERA UGARTE, Ricardo, b. 1914, Barcenillas, Spain. University Professor. Educ: L. es L., Univ. of Barcelona. Publs. incl: Cuando voy a morir, 1951; Cuerpo a tierra, 1954; Perdimos el Paraiso, 1956; Vagabundos provisionales, 1959; Espionaje, 1962; transl. into sev. langs. Recip., Premio Cuidad, Barcelona. Address: Av. Gral, Mitre, 144, Barcelona, Spain.

FERNANDEZ GUTIERREZ, Julian, b. 23 Mar. 1916, Noez, Toledo, Spain. Civil Servant. Educ: Lic. in Law & Inspector of Finance. Publs. (essays): ¿Quien es Dios?, 1967, 2nd ed. 1971; ¿Que es lo Ultrahumano?, 1967; ¿Como es el Fin del Mundo?, 1968; ¿Que hay al otro Lado de la Barrera de la Muerte?, 1968; (fiction) Yo he vivido en otros Mundos; Los Anti-invasion extraterrestre; Llegaron los Extraterrestres, 1969; (novel) Historia de una Piel, 1974. Address: Clara del Rey No. 8, 7⁰-4⁰, Madrid 2. Spain.

FERNANDEZ NICOLAS, Severiano, b. 9 Sept. 1919, Leon, Spain. Lawyer. Educ: Lic. in Law, Univ. of Oviedo. Publs: Las manos vacias, 1951; Tierra de promision, 1953; Las muertes inutiles, 1960; El Desahucio, 1963; Despues de la tormenta, 1964; Las influencias, 1968; Cronica de un Juez, 1973. Mbr., Gen. Soc. of Spanish Authors. Hons. incl: Finalist, Premio Planeta, Nadal, Ondas y Ciudad de Oviedo, 1952, 1953, 1960 & 1965; Premio Selecciones de Lengua Española, 1963. Address: Avenida Reina Victoria 58—3° A, Madrid 3, Spain.

FERNEYHOUGH, Frank, b. 2 June 1911, Bucknall, Stoke-on-Trent, Staffs., UK. Professional Writer. Publs: Railways, 1948; Booking & Parcels Office Clerical Work, 1949; Railways – a Picture History, 1970; Choosing a Job on the Railways, 1973; Steam Trains Down the Line, 1975; The History of Railways in Britain, 1975; Former Ed., Brit. Railways Staff Mag., Brit. Waterways Staff Mag. Contbr. to: Chambers' Jrnl.; Housewife; Psychol.; Daily Mirror; Dean's Annuals; Engl. Digest; Musical Times; etc. Mbrships: F.R.S.A.; Authors Soc.; London Press Club; Number Ten Club. Address: 25 Rose Walk, St. Albans, Herts., UK.

FERNEYHOUGH, Roger, b. 1941, Bletchley, UK. Editorial Director; Literary Lecturer. Educ: M.A., Pembroke Coll., Oxford. Contbr. to: Times; Times Educl. Supplement; Economist; New Soc.; Jrnl. of Royal Soc. of Arts; New Sci.; Westminster Review. Fellow, Inst. of Dirs. Address: 163 Marine Parade, Brighton, Sussex, UK.

FERRER-VIDAL TURULL, Jorge, b. 2 July 1926, Barcelona, Spain, Lawyer. Educ: Lic., Law, Univ. of Barcelona; Lic., Philos. & Letters, Univ. Computense, Madrid. Publs: (novels) El Trapecio de Dios, 1954; El carro de los caballos blancos, 1957; Sábado, esperanza, 1960; Caza Mayor, 1961; Historias de mis valles, 1964; Diario de Albatana, 1967; El Racimo de uvas, 1967; Te emplazo padre, te exijo que respondas, 1974; Los papeles de Ludwig Jäger, 1974; (short stories) Sobre la piel del Mundo, 1957; Fe de vida, 1959; (biog.) Juan Maragall: vida y obra, 1970; (travel story) Viaje por la sierra de Ayllón, 1970. Contbr. to var. lit. jrnls. Hons. incl: Leopoldo Alas Prize, 1956; Correo Catalán (newspaper) Prize, 1960; Calderón Escalada Prize, 1973; etc. Address: Calle J. y F. Serrano Súñer 10, Madrid 13, Spain.

FERRIS, Paul Frederick, b. 1929, Swansea, UK. Writer. Publs. (fiction): A Changed Man, 1958; Then We Fall, 1960; A Family Affair, 1963; The Destroyer, 1965; The Dam, 1967; Very Personal Problems, 1973; The Cure, 1974; (non-fiction): The Nameless: Abortion in Britain Today, 1966; Men & Money: Financial Europe Today, 1968; The City, 1960; The Church of England, 1962; The Doctors, 1965; The New Militants, 1972; The House of Northcliffe, 1971. Contbr. to: Observer; N.Y. Times; Radio & TV; South Wales Evening Post, 1949-52. Agent: Curtis Brown. Address: 1 Craven Hill, London W2, UK.

FERTIS, Demeter George, b. 25 July 1926, Athens, Greece. University Professor. Educ: B.S., 1952; M.S., 1955, Mich. State Univ., USA; Dip., 1962, D.Eng., 1964, Athens Greece. Publs: Transverse Vibration Theory, 1961; Deflection & Vibration of Beam-like Structures of Variable & Uniform Stiffness, 1964; Dynamics of Structural Systems, vol. 1, 1971, vols. 2, 1972; Dynamics & Vibration of Structures, 1973. Contbr. to var. profl. jrnls. Mbrships: Am. Soc. of Civ. Engrs.; Nat. Commn., Am. Soc. for Testing & Mat.; Am. Soc. for Engrng. Educ. Address: 2961 Chamberlain Rd., Akron. OH 44313, USA.

FESSENKO, Tatiana, b. 20 Nov. 1915, Kiev, Russia Researcher; Author. Educ: Grad. & post-grad. studies, Univ. of Kiev, USSR. Publs: The Russian Language Under the Soviets, 1955; 18th Century Publications in the Library of Congress: a Catalog, 1961; (in Russian lang.) The Life Story of a Displaced Person, 1963; As Seen by a Tourist, 1966, Compiler & Ed., An Anthology of Russian Emigré Poetry, 1966. Contbr. to: New Russian Word (N.Y.); New Review (N.Y.); Contemporary (Toronto, Can.); Renaissance (Paris, France). Address: 3016 Que Street S.E., Washington, DC 20020, USA.

FEST, Joachim, b. 8 Dec. 1926, Berlin, Germany. Writer; Journalist. Educ: Univs. of Freiburg/Breisgau, Frankfurt & Berlin. Publs: The Face of the Third Reich, 1963; Hitler: A Biography, 1973; Ed., Publr., Frankfurter Allgemeine Zeitung. Contbr. to: Der Spiegel; Encounter, German TV & Radio. Mbr., PEN. Hons: Thomas Wolf Prize, 1971; Thomas Dehler Prize, 1973. Address: 2 Hamburg 52, Sohrhof 15, W. Germany.

FETHERSTONHAUGH, Patrick William Edward, per name FETHERSTON, Patrick, b. 10 Nov. 1928, Rotherfield, Sussex, UK. Writer. Publs: Day Off, 1955, Eighteen Quadruple Readings, 1965; Three Days after Blasphemies, 1967; Woman from Child, 1970; Natures of All Sorts, 1973; His Many and Himself, 1974. Contbr. to: Times Lit. Supplement; Ambit; Origin; New Departures. Mbrships: Brit. Soc. for Philos. Sci.; Gaberbocchus Common Room. Recip., Hon. Mbrship. Eng. Stage Soc. Address: 2 Lancaster Grove, London NW3, UK.

FIBER, Alan. Managing Director; Writer; Film & TV Scriptwriter; Broadcaster; Editorial Director; Managing Director, Business Management Advisory Services. Publs: The Independent Retailer, 1964. Be Your Own Boss, 1967. Complete Guide to Retail Management, 1972; & programme adviser, broadcaster BBC Radio & ITV, scriptwriter for film & TV on business subjects. Contbr. to int. bus. press. Mbrships: Fellow Inst. Arbitrators; Soc Authors. Address: 9 Park Grove, Edgware, Middx. HA8 7SH, UK.

FIDELSBERGER, Heinz, pen name (for med. works) HILLMANN, Heinz, b. 15 Apr. 1920, Vienna, Austria Medical Doctor; Writer. Educ: M.D., Univ. of Vienna Publs: Endstation Wohlfahrtsstaat, 1970; Sprechstunde für Gesunde und Kranke, 1971; Astrologie 2000, 1972, Lebenshilfe für Gesunde und Kranke, 1973; Sterne und Leben, 1974; Ernährung für Gesunde und Kranke, 1974, Ed., Praxis-Kurier. Contbr. to: Kurier, Vienna; Samstag, Vienna; Frauenblatt, Vienna. Mbrships: Concordia Vienna, Pres., Soc. of Astrol. in Vienna. Recip., Medizinalrat, 1974. Address: Vienna IX, Viriotgasse 6, Austria.

FIDLER, Kathleen Annie, b. 10 Aug. 1899, Coalville Leics., UK. Author; Scriptwriter; Lecturer. Educ: Tchr's. Cert. Publs: The Brydon Family Series (19 books 1944-63 in paperback 1972-73); The Dean Family Series (9 books 1953-60); Heritage of Britain Series (12 books 1952-69); Treasure of Ebba, 1968; Gold of Fast Castle, 1970; School at Sea, 1970; Flodden Field, 1971; The Thames in Story 1971; Diggers of Lost Treasure, 1972; The Boy with the Bronze Axe, 1972; The '45 & Culloden, 1973; Story of Old Inns, 1973; Haki, the Shetland Pony, 1973; Pirate & Admiral (Story of John Paul Jones), 1974. Contbr. to BBC Radio & TV, etc. Mbrships. incl: Soc. Authors; PEN: Nat. Book League. Recip., 1st Award for Flash the Sheep Dog, Moscow Film Festival, 1968. Address: Janebank Broomieknowe, Lasswade, Midlothian, UK.

FIEDLER, Leslie, b. 1917, Newark, N.J., USA Professor. Educ: N.Y. Univ.; Univ. of Wis.; Harvard; Univ. of Colo.; B.A., M.A., Ph.D. Publs. incl: Love & Death in the American Novel, 1966; The Last Jew in America, 1966 The Return of the Vanishing American, 1968; Nude Croquet & Other Stories, 1969; Being Busted, 1970; The Collected Essays of Leslie Fiedler, 1971; The Stranger in

Shakespeare, 1972; The Messengers Will Come No More, 1974. Contbr. to num. jrnls. Mbrships: AAUP; MLA; PEN. Address: Dept. of English, Annex B, State University of New York at Buffalo, Buffalo, NY 14214, USA.

FIELD, Henry, b. 1902, Chgo., Ill., USA. Museum Research Fellow. Educ: B.A., M.A., D.Sc., New Coll., Oxford Univ., UK. Pubis. incl: The Track of Man: Adventures of an Anthropologist, 1953; The Anthropology of Iraq, Iran, West Pakistan, Saudi Arabia, India, Caucasus. Address: 3551 Main Hwy., Coconut Grove, Miami, FL 33133, USA.

FIELD, Hermann Haviland, b. 13 Apr. 1910, Zurich, Switz. Educator (Professor of Urban Planning); Architect. Educ: B.A., Harvard Univ., 1933; Harvard Grad. Schl. of Design, 1932-34; Dip.Arch., Swiss Fed. Polytechnic. Inst., 1936. Pubis: Angry Harvest (novel, w. Stanislaw Mierzenski), USA 1958, 1961, UK & Poland, 1958, Germany 1959, 1962, 1964, Sweden 1959; Duck Lane (novel, w. S. Mierzenski), USA & Poland 1961. Contbr. to: Forms & Functions of 20th Century Archt.; I Was Lucky to Escape; Problems of Pediatric Hosp. Design; Evaluation of Hosp. Design; Environment & Cognition; Fortnightly Review; Listener; var. archtl. & hosp. jrnls. Mbr., var. profl. & conserv. assns. Address: 12 Old Dee Rd., Cambridge, MA 02138, USA.

FIELD, James Alfred Jr., b. 9 Mar. 1916, Chgo., Ill., USA. Historian. Educ: S.B., Harvard Univ., 1937; A.M., 1939; Ph.D., 1947; Trinity Coll., Cambridge, U.K., 1937-38. Pubis: The Japanese at Leyte Gulf, 1947; History of U.S. Naval Operations, Korea, 1962. America & the Mediterranean World, 1969. Contbr. to var. profl. pubis. Mbrships: Am. Hist. Assn.; Org. of Am. Histns.; Greta Lakes Cruising Club; Pitt Club, Cambridge. Recip., var. fellowships. Address: 612 Hillborn Ave., Swarthmore, PA 19081, USA.

FIELD, June, b. London, UK. Journalist; Author. Pubis: The Ordinary Man's Guide to Collecting Antiques, 1972; Cottages & Conversions at Home and Abroad, 1973; Collecting Georgian & Victorian Crafts, 1973; Creative Patchwork, 1974; Collecting Wisely — A Guide to the New Antiques, 1975; Restoring Property at Home and Abroad, forthcoming. Contbr. to: Financial Times; Daily Telegraph Mag.; Good Housekeeping; Diners Club Signature Mag.; Homes Abroad; Homes Overseas; Times. Mbrships: F.R.S.A.; Nat. Union Jrnlsts.; Design & Inds. Assn. Address: 43 Goodwood Court, Devonshire St., London W1N 1LS, UK.

FIELD, Mark (George), b. 17 June 1923, Lausanne, Switz. Professor of Sociology. Educ: A.B., Harvard Coll., 1948; A.M., 1950, Ph.D., 1955, Harvard Univ. Pubis: Doctor & Patient in Soviet Russia, 1957; Soviet Socialized Medicine, 1967; Social Approaches to Mental Patient Care (w. M. S. Schwartz & C. G. Schwartz, et al), 1964; Evaluating Health Program Impact: The US-Yugoslav Cooperative Research Effort (w. R. E. Berry, Jr., et al), 1974. Contbr. to: Am. Jrnl. of Sociol.; Am. Sociol. Review; Jrnl. of Int. Affairs; etc. Mbr., Int. Sociol. Assn.; etc. Address: 40 Peacock Farm Road, Lexington, MA 02173, USA.

FIELDEN, John, b. 1939, Tadcaster, Yorks., UK. Management Consultant. Educ: M.A., Worcester Coll., Oxford; A.C.A. Pubis: Planning & Management in Universities (co-author), 1973. Contbr. to: Higher Educ. Review; Surveyor; Local Govt. Fin. Address: 29 Lonsdale Rd., London SW13, UK.

FIELDING, Gabriel, pen name of BARNSLEY, Alan Gabriel, b. 25 Mar. 1916, Hexham, Northumberland, UK. Author; former Medical Practitioner. Educ: B.A., Trinity Coll., Dublin; St. George's Hosp., London; M.R.C.S. & L.R.C.P., 1941. Pubis. incl: (novels) Brotherly Love, 1954; In the Time of Greenbloom, UK, 1956, USA, 1957; The Birthday King, UK, 1962, USA, 1963; Gentlemen in Their Season, UK & USA, 1966; Collected Short Stories, 1971; (poetry) 28 Poems, 1955. Hons: Gold Medal, St. Thomas More Assn., 1963; Smith Lit. Award, 1963; Nat. Cath. Book Award, 1964; D.Litt., Gonzaga Univ., Spokane, 1967. Address: 1811 Monroe, Pullman, WA 99163, USA.

FIELDS, Alan, b. 1930, Sheffield, UK. Lecturer. Educ: B.Sc., Sheffield Univ. Pubis: Method Study, 1969; Mbrships: A.M.Inst.F.; M.I.Gas.E. Address: 69 Brookfield Rd., Bedford, UK.

FIELDS, Victor Alexander, b. 1901, Phila., Pa., USA. Professor of Voice & Diction, City College of N.Y., 1926-1969; Department Supervisor in Evening Division, 1941-65; Assistant in speech rehabilitation of disabled war veterans, Veterans' Administration, 1946-49. Educ: B.S., M.A., Ph.D. Pubis: Training the Singing Voice; The Singer's Glossary; Voice & Diction; Taking the Stage. Contbr. to: Music Jrnl. (Am.); Bulletin Nat. Assn. Tchrs. Singing: Jefferson Ency.; etc. Mbrships. incl: Comm. Surveying Handicapped Children Pub. Schls., 1936-39; Nat. Assn. Tchrs. Singing (Chmn. Nat. Advsry. Comm. on Vocal Educ., 1950-60); Nat. Educ. Assn.; Acoustical Soc. Am. Address: 9400 Atlantic Ave., Margate, NJ, USA.

FIELHAUER, Otto Magnus, pen names HABAKUK; GLASBRENNER, b. 27 May 1929, Vienna, Austria. Editor; Humourist; Cartoonist. Educ: Univ. studies. Pubis: Habakuk — Wiener Schmäh (satirical stories), 1973. Contbr. to: Kronen-Zeitung; Arbeiter-Zeitung; 20 Austrian mags. Mbrships: PEN; Fedn. of Socialist Authors (BSA). Recip., Renner Prize (Jrnlst. award), 1972. Address: 67/2 Dornbacherstr., 1170 Vienna, Austria.

FIFIELD, William, b. 1916, Chgo., Ill., USA. Radio & TV Performer; Speaker; Author. Educ: Whitman Coll., Walla Walla, Wash. Pubis: The Devil's Marchioness, 1957; Sign of Taurus, 1959; Matadora, 1960; Encyclopaedia Wines & Spirits of the World (co-author); Entretiens Avec Jean Cocteau, 1973; Jean Cocteau, 1974; The Sherry Royalty, 1975; Modigliani, 1975. Contbr. to: Arts Mag.; Playboy; Penthouse; London Mag.; Paris Review; Malahat Review; Kenyon Review; Tex. Quarterly; Caedmon Records; Harper's; Show; Yale Review; Argosy; C.B.S.; N.B.C.; BBC; sev. anthols. Recip., O. Henry Mem. Award. Agents: A. M. Heath, John Cushman, & John Johnson. Address: Sta. Eulalia de Rio, Ibiza, Baleares, Spain.

FIGES, Eva, b. Berlin, Germany. Editor; Translator. Educ: B.A., Queen Mary Coll., London. Pubis: Equinox, 1966; Winter Journey, 1967; Konek Landing, 1969; Patriarchal Attitudes, 1970; B, 1972; Days, 1974. Contbr. to: New Statesman; Nova. Mbrships: Soc. of Authors; Writers Guild of GB. Recip., Guardian Fiction Prize, 1967. Agent: Deborah Rogers. Address: 24 Fitzjohns Ave., London NW3, UK.

FIGUEROA-CHAPEL, Ramón Antonio, b. 26 Feb. 1935, Anasco, Puerto Rico. Professor of Humanities, Philosophy, Comparative French & Spanish Literature. Educ: B.S., Univ. of Puerto Rico, 1956; M.A., 1958, Ph.D., 1964, Fordham Univ., N.Y., 1964. Pubis: Poesía (poetry), 1968; Quinto Evangelio (poetry), 1969; Balbuceo (poetry), 1974; Readings in Humanities (anthol.), 2 vols., 1973-74; Contbr. to: Revista de Letras, Puerto Rico. Mbrships. incl: Ateneo Puertorriqueño; Sociedad de Escritores Puertorriqueños; Phi Kappa Phi; MLA; Am. Assns. Spanish, French Profs. Address: Miramar Towers 14L, Hernadez 721, Santurce, PR 00907, USA.

FIGUEROA de CIFREDO, Patria Dra., b. 5 Dec. 1926, Cataño, Puerto Rico. University Professor. Educ: B.A., 1941, M.A., 1957, Univ. of Puerto Rico; Ph.D., Madrid, Spain, 1963. Pubis: Apuntes Biográficos en Torno a la Vida y Obra del Dr. Cesáreo Rosa Nieves, 1965; Vida y Obra de Francisco Gonzalo Marín — Pachín Marín Héroe y Poeta, 1967; Nuevo Encuentro con la Estética de Rosa Nieves, 1969; Cinco Narraciones de Francisco Gonzalo Marín, 1973. Contbr. to: El Mundo; Revista Rumbos; Revista del Insstituto de Cultura Puertorriqueña; Boletin de la Sociedad de Bibliotecarios de Puerto Rico; etc. Mbrships. incl: AAUP; Am. Cultural Soc.; Ateneo Puertorriqueño. Address: Box 22286, UPR Station, Rio Piedras, PR 00931, USA.

FILGATE, James M., b. 1911, Louth, Repub. of Ireland. Author; British Rail Employee. Pubis: (plays) The Proposal, 1964; Broken Vows, 1957. Mbrships: Authors' Guild of Ireland; Vocational Educ. Comm., Louth County Coun.; etc. Hons: Elected Mbr., Louth County Coun. Address: 70 La Havre Towers, Weston, Southampton, UK.

FINBOW, Colin, b. 26 Nov. 1940, Ipswich, Suffolk, UK. Teacher of Film Studies. Educ: Goldsmith's Coll., Univ. of London. Pubis. incl: (radio plays) As Soon As Thursday; Tonight Is Friday; A Day Like Sunday; Outlook for Wednesday; And Now the Barley; (stage plays) The Things; Night Time for the Birds; also TV scripts for the Avengers series & Play of the Week. Contbr. to: New Radio Drama, 1966; Radio Times. Mbrships: Soc. of Authors; Radiowriters Assn. Recip., Italia Prize for radio play, And

Now the Barley, 1967. Address: c/o Margaret Ramsay, 14a Goodwin's Court, St. Martin's Lane, London WC2, UK.

FINCH, Brian, b. 25 July 1936, Wigan, Lancs., UK. Writer. TV Plays: An Arrow for Little Audrey; Rodney Our Intrepid Hero. Radio Play: I Said The Sparrow. TV Thriller: 6-part serial 'Chinese Puzzle'. Contbr. to: Pub. Eye; Hunter's Walk; Owen M.D.; Kate; Coronation St.; other Brit. TV series & serials. Mbr., Coun., Writer's Guild of GB. Address: 'Blantyre', 36 Copthall Lane, Chalfont St. Peter, Bucks., UK.

FINCH, Peter, b. 6 Mar. 1947, Cardiff, Wales, UK. Manager, Welsh Arts Council Bookshop "Oriel". Publs: Wanted, 1968; Pieces of the Universe, 1969; Cycle of the Suns, 1970; Beyond the Silence, 1970; An Alteration of the Way I Breathe, 1970; The Edge of Tomorrow, 1971; The End of the Vision, 1971; Whitesung, 1972; Blats, 1972; Antarktika, 1973. Contbr. to: Transatlantic Review; Poetry Wales; Oasis; Sixpack; Poetry Review; etc. Mbrships: Treas., Assn. of Little Presses; Coun., Poetry Soc.; Welsh Rep., Poets' Conference. Recip., Welsh Arts Coun. Bursary for experimental poetry, 1968-69. Address: 3 Heol Y Waun, Whitchurch, Cardiff CF4 1LB, UK.

FINCH, Ruth (née Tennant), b. 1930, Birkenhead, Cheshire, UK. Author. Educ: B.A., Liverpool Univ.; Sorbonne Univ., Paris, France. Publs: The Convert, 1971; That's Love (co-ed., anthol.), 1972; A Little Learning, 1973. Contbr. to: Homes & Gardens; Good Housekeeping; Woman's Jrnl.; Woman; Woman's Own; Petticoat. Mbr., Liverpool 35 Grp. Agent: Laurence Pollinger Ltd. Address: 1 Barkhill Rd., Liverpool L17 6AY, UK.

FINEBERG, S. Andhil, b. 1896, Pittsburgh, Pa., USA. Rabbi; National Consultant, National Conference of Christians & Jews, 1964-. Educ: B.A., Ph.D., D.D.; Univ. of Cinn., Columbia; Hebrew Union Coll.-Jewish Inst. of Relig. Publs: Biblical Myth & Legend; Overcoming Anti-Semitism; Punishment Without Crime; The Rosenberg Case; The Idealogical Fallacies of Communism; Are You Getting Good Neighbours? ; Deflating the Bigot. Contbr. to: Commentary; Am. Legion Mag.; Rdrs. Digest; etc. Address: 19 William St., Mt. Vernon, N.Y., USA.

FINEGAN, Jack, b. 11 July 1908, Des Moines, Iowa, USA. Professor; Author. Educ: A.B., 1928, M.A., Coll. of Bible, 1929, Drake Univ.; B.D., 1930; B.D., 1931, M.Th., 1932, Colgate Rochester Divinity Schl.; Lic. theol., Univ. of Berlin, Germany, 1934. Publs. incl: A Highway Shall Be There, 1946; Rediscovering Jesus, 1952; India Today!, 1955; Space, Atoms & God, 1959; Jesus, History & You, 1964; The Christian Church (Disciples of Christ), 1973; Encountering New Testament Manuscripts, 1974. Contbr. to: Collier's Ency.; Ency. Britannica; Interpreter's Dict. of the Bible; & var. jrnls. Hons. incl: Litt.D., Chapman Coll., 1964. Address: 1116 Cragmont Ave., Berkeley, CA 94708, USA.

FINEMAN, Irving, b. 9 Apr. 1893, NYC, USA. Writer; Engineer (ret'd.). Educ: B.S., Mass. Inst. Technol., 1917; S.B., Harvard Univ., 1917. Publs: This Pure Young Man, 1930; Lovers Must Learn, 1932; Hear, Ye Sons, 1933; Doctor Addams, 1939; Jacob: An Autobiographical Novel, 1941; Ruth, 1949; Women of Valor: The Life of Henrietta Szold, 1961. Mbr., Screen Writers Guild. Contbr. to: Harper's Bazaar; N. Am. Review; Yale Quarterly Review; The Nation; N.Y. Times Book Review; etc. Also author of screen plays. Address: Maple Hill Road, Shaftsbury, VA, USA.

FINER, Samuel Edward, b. 22 Sept. 1915, London, UK. University Professor. Educ: B.A., 1938, M.A., 1946, Trinity Coll., Oxford; M.A., Manchester, 1970. Publs. incl: Life & Times of Sir Edwin Chadwick; Local Government in England & Wales (w. Sir John Maud); Anonymous Empire; A Study of the Lobby in Great Britain; Private Enterprise & Political Power; Backbench Opinion in the House of Commons (w. H. B. Berrington & D. J. Bartholomew); The Man On Horseback — The Role of the Military in Politics; Comparative Government. Fellow, Royal Histl. Soc. Agent: Shaw Maclean. Address: All Souls College, Oxford, UK.

FINK, Merton, pen names FINCH, Matthew; FINCH, Merton, b. 1921, Liverpool, UK. Dental Surgeon; Novelist. Educ: Liverpool Univ. Publs: Dentist in the Chair, 1954; Teething Troubles, 1955; The Third Set, 1956; Hang Your Hat on a Pension, 1957; The Empire Builder, 1958; Snakes & Ladders, 1959; Solo Fiddle, 1960; Beauty Bazaar, 1961; The Match Breakers, 1962; Five are the Symbols, 1963;

Jones is a Rainbow, 1964; The Succubus, 1965; Eye with Mascara, 1966; Chew this Over, 1967; Simon Bar Cochba, 1969; Josephus Flavius, 1974. Contbr. to: Dental Prac.; BBC. Mbrships: Soc. of Authors; PEN. Agent: Laurence Pollinger. Address: 1 Barkhill Rd., Liverpool L17 6AY, UK.

FINKEL, George Irvine, pen name PENNAGE, E. M., b. 1909, South Shields, Durham, UK, d. Feb. 1975. Author; served R.A.N., 1940-58; Laboratory Manager, 1958-69. Publs: Mystery of Secret Beach; Ship in Hiding; Cloudmaker; Singing Sands; Twilight Province; Long Pilgrimage; Loyall Virginian; Journey to Jorsala; James Cook, Royal Navy (1962-70); The Peace-seekers; James Cook — A Junior Biography, 1970; James Cook, 1970; Series of Twelve Social Studies Auxiliary Readers for South Australia Education Dept., 1970; William Light, 1972; The Stranded Duck, 1973; Matthew Flinders, 1973; New South Wales, 1788-1900, 1974; Victoria — 1836-1900, 1974. Mbrships. incl: Aust. Soc. Authors (Mgmt. Comm. 1968-74). Recip., Rsch. Grant for novel from Lit. Bd. Aust. Coun. Arts.

FINKEL, Lawrence S., b. 18 Sept. 1925, NYC, USA. Educator. Educ: B.S., CCNY, 1950; M.A., Tchrs. Coll., Columbia Univ., 1951. Publs: How to Study, 1964; How to Use the Newspaper in the Classroom, 1966; The Play Is Yours: You & Drugs, 1970; Teaching English as a Second Language, 1970. Contbr. to jrnls. & encys.; Ed., num. educl. books; Speaker, var. colls. & educl. orgs. Hons: Fellowship, CCNY, 1951-53; Mbr., Educl. Advsry. Comm., N.Y. World Jrnl. Tribune, 1967. Address: 22 Trinity Ave., Spring Valley, NY 10977, USA.

FINLAY, Campbell K., b. 1909, Rangoon. Former Barrister-at-Law; Author; J.P., County Councillor; concerned with the economic & depopulation problem of the Isle of Mull, 1959-74. Educ: Eton & R.M.C., Sandhurst; called to the Bar, 1937. Publs: (children's books) We go to the Western Isles, 1959; Fisherman's Gold, 1960; Shepherd's Purse, 1961; A New Home in Kenya?, 1962; Farewell to the Western Isles, 1964; Wildcat Ginger, 1966. Author, local political articles. Contbr. to: Island of Mull — Survey & Proposals for Development, 1973. Sec., Mull & Iona Coun. of Social Serv. Address: West Ardu, Dervaig, Tobermory, Isle of Mull, Argyll PA75 6QR, Scotland, UK.

FINLAY, (Sir) Graeme Bell, Bt., b. 1917, Caerphilly, UK. Sous Juge d'Instruction & Assistant Judge of Petty Debts Court for Jersey, Channel Islands. Educ: Univ. of London; Barrister-at-Law, Gray's Inn, 1946. Publs: Proposals for an Administrative Court (co-author), 1970. Contbr. to: Justice of the Peace & Local Govt. Review; Sunday Times; Daily Telegraph. Recip., Lord Justice Holker Sr. Exhib., Gray's Inn. Address: La Campagne, Rozel, Jersey, Channel Islands, UK.

FINLAY, Ian, b. 2 Dec. 1906, Auckland, NZ. Art Historian. Educ: M.A., Univ. of Edinburgh, UK. Publs: Scotland, 1945; Art in Scotland, 1948; Scottish Crafts, 1948; History of Scottish Gold & Silver Work, 1956; The Lothians, 1960; The Highlands, 1963; The Lowlands, 1967; Celtic Art: an Introduction, 1973. Contbr. to var. lit. jrnls. Mbrships: Liveryman, Worshipful Co. of Goldsmiths, London; Former Mbr., Int. Coun. of Museums, Scottish Arts Coun.; Vice-Chmn., Scottish Arts Club; Prof. of Antiquities, Royal Scottish Acad.; Hon. Mbr., 1970; F.R.S.A., 1970. Address: Currie Riggs, Balerno, Midlothian EH14 5AG, UK.

FINLAY, Winifred Lindsay Crawford McKissack, b. 1910, Newcastle upon Tyne, UK. Writer. Educ: M.A., King's Coll., Newcastle upon Tyne. Publs: The Castle & the Cave, 1961; Alison in Provence, 1963; Mystery in the Middle Marches, 1964; Castle for Four, 1966; Adventure in Prague, 1967; Danger at Black Dyke, 1968; Cry of the Peacock, 1969; Summer of the Golden Stag, 1969; Folk Tales from the North, 1968; Folk Tales from Moor & Mountain, 1969; Singing Stones, 1970; Beadbonny Ash, 1973; Cap O'Rushes, 1974. Contbr. to: Child Educ.; BBC. Recip., Special Award, Mystery Writers of Am., 1970. Address: The Old House, Walgrave, Northampton, UK.

FINLAYSON, Roderick David, b. 26 Apr. 1904, Auckland, NZ. Writer. Educ: Seddon Technical Coll.; Auckland School of Architecture. Publs: Brown Man's Burden, 1938, 2nd ed., 1973; Sweet Beulah Land, 1942; Tidal Creek, 1948; The Schooner Came to Atia, 1952; D'Arcy Cresswell (lit. crit.), 1972; The Springing Fern, 1965. Contbr. to num. NZ jrnls. Mbr., PEN, NZ Centre.

Recip., of NZ Centennial Literary Prize, 1942. Address: 46 McLeod Road, Weymouth, Manurewa, Manukau City, NZ.

FINN, Adian William, b. 13 Sept. 1940, London, UK. Publisher of Western Equine Magazines. Educ: Studied Commercial Arts, UK, 1960-61; studied Heating & Air Conditioning Technol., E. St. Louis, Mo., USA, 1962-63. Publr./Fndr.: Can. Western Rider; Can. Quarter Horse Jrnl.; Can. Appaloosa Jrnl.; Fndr.: Burlington Post, 1965; Mtn. Advertiser, 1968; Hamilton East Ender, 1968. Mbrships: Ont. Quarter Horse Assn. (Advt. & Promotion Chmn., Quarterama Horse Show 1970-75); Dir., Am. Horse Publs., & var. equine clubs. Address: 491 Book Rd. W., Ancaster, Ont., Can.

FINNERAN, Richard John, b. 19 Dec. 1943, NYC, USA. Professor; Author; Editor. Educ: B.A., N.Y. Univ., 1964; Ph.D., Univ. of N.C., Chapel Hill, 1968. Publs: Ed., W. B. Yeats, John Sherman & Dhoya, 1969; Ed., William Butler Yeats: The Byzantium Poems, 1970; The Prose Fiction of W. B. Yeats: the Search for "Those Simple Forms", 1973; Ed., Letters of James Stephens, 1974. Contbr. to: Jrnl. Mod. Lit.; James Joyce Quarterly; Southern Humanities Review; Tulane Studies in Engl.; etc. Mbrships. incl: Int. Assn. Study of Anglo-Irish Lit. (Exec. Comm., 1973–); MLA; Chmn., Celtic Grp., 1972; S. Ctrl. & S. Atlantic MLAs. Address: English Dept., Newcomb College, Tulane University, New Orleans, LA 70118, USA.

FINNEY, David John, b. 3 Jan. 1917, Latchford, Cheshire, UK. Statistician; Biometrician. Educ: Univ. of Cambridge; Univ. of London; M.A., Sc.D. Publs. incl: Profit Analysis; Statistical Method in Biological Assay; An Introduction to Statistical Science in Agriculture; Experimental Design & Its Statistical Basis; Tecnica y Teoria Estadistica en el Diseño de Experimentos; An Introduction to the Theory of Experimental Design; Statistics for Mathematicians — An Introduction. Contbr. to var. Brit. & for. jrnls. of stats. & biol. Mbrships: F.R.S.; F.R.S.E.; Pres., Royal Statistical Soc., 1973-74; Pres., Biometric Soc., 1964-65; Int. Statistical Inst. Hons: Weldon Mem. Prize; Martini Prize. Address: 43 Cluny Drive, Edinburgh EH10 6DU, UK.

FINNEY, Gretchen L. (Mrs. Ross Lee Finney), b. 12 Dec. 1901, Browns Valley, Minn., USA. Housewife. Educ: A.B., Carleton Coll., Northfield, Minn.; M.A., Univ. of Calif., Berkeley. Author, Musical Backgrounds for English Literature, 1962. Contbr. to: Jrnl of the Hist. of Med.; Jrnl. of the Hist. of Ideas; Jrnl. of Engl. Lit. Hist.; Publs. of the MLA of Am.; Studies in Philol.; Studies in the Renaissance; Huntington Lib. Quarterly; Centennial Review of Arts & Sci.; Ency. of the Hist. of Ideas. Recip., Grants from Henry E. Huntington & Newberry Libs., 1952-53. Address: 2015 Geddes Ave., Ann Arbor, MI 48104, USA.

FINNIGAN, John, b. 17 May 1925, Bradford, Yorks, UK. Management Consultant. Educ: M.Sc., C.Eng. Publs: Industrial Training Management, 1970; The Right People in the Right Job, 1973. Mbrships: Inst. Mech. Engrs.; Inst. Personnel Mgmt.; Inst. Mgmt. Consultants. Address: 174 Bromham Rd., Bedford MK40 4BW, UK.

FIRESTONE, O. J., b. 17 Jan. 1913, Austria. Professor of Economics. Educ: M.A., McGill Univ., Can.; Doctor juris et rerum politicarum, Univ. of Vienna; Postgrad. study, London Schl. of Econs. Publs. incl: Private & Public Investment in Canada 1926-51, 1951; Problems of Economic Growth, 1965; The Public Persuader, 1970; Economic Implications of Patents, 1971; Economic Growth Reassessed (ed. & contbr.), 1972. Contbr. to Can., for. jrnls., newspapers. Address: Dept. of Econs., Univ. of Ottawa, 550 Cumberland St., Ottawa, K1N 6N5, Can.

FIRST, Ruth, b. Johannesburg, South Africa. Writer. Educ: B.A., Univ. Witwatersrand. Publs: South West Africa, 1963; 117 Days, 1965; The Barrel of a Gun: The Politics of Coups d'etat in Africa, 1970; The South African Connection (co-author), 1972; Libya: The Elusive Revolution, 1974. Contbr. to: Africa S. of Sahara; New Soc.; Dagens Hyheter (Stockholm); Guardian; Int. Affairs; Ramparts; Ufahamu. Address: 13 Lyme St., London NW1, UK.

FIRTH, (Sir) Raymond William, b. 1901, Auckland, NZ. Professor Emeritus of Anthropology, Univ. of London. Educ: Auckland Univ. Coll.; London Schl. of Econs., UK; M.A.; Ph.D. Publs. incl: Primitive Economics of the New Zealand Maori, 1929; Malay Fishermen: Their Peasant Economy, 1946; Elements of Social Organization, 1951; Ed., Man & Culture, 1957; Social Change in Tikopia, 1959; History & Traditions of Tikopia, 1961; Tikopia Ritual & Belief, 1967; Rank & Religion in Tikopia, 1970; Families & Their Relatives (co-author), 1970; The Sceptical Anthropologist, 1972; Symbols Public & Private, 1973. Contbr. to: Jrnls. of Royal Anthropol. Inst.; Oceania. Hons: Fellow, British Acad.; P.PH; LL.D; Dr. Letters; Dr. Hum. Letters; D.Sc.; Kt., 1972. Address: 33 Southwood Ave., London N6, UK.

FISCHER, Gottfried Bermann, b. 31 July 1897, Geiwitz, Germany. Publisher. Educ: Univs. of Breslau, Freiburg & Munich; Dr. of Med. Publs: Bedroht-Bewahrt (autobiog.), 1967; Briefwechsel mit Thomas Mann, 1932-55, 1971. Contbr. to: Neue Rundschau (ed.). Mbr., PEN. Hons: Goethe Plakette, Frankfurt/Main; Grosses Bundesverdienstkreuz, German Fed. Repub.; Dr. Phil.hon. causa, Univ. of Berne, Switz. Address: Casa Fischer, I 55041 Camaiore, (Lucca), Italy.

FISCHER, LeRoy Henry, b. 19 May 1917, Hoffman, Ill., USA. University Professor of History. Educ: B.A., 1939, M.A., 1940, Ph.D., 1943, Univ. of Ill., Urbana. Publs: Lincoln's Gadfly, Adam Gurowski, 1964; The Civil War Era in Indian Territory, 1974; United States Indian Agents to the Five Civilized Tribes, 1975; Civil War Sites in Oklahoma, (w. Muriel H. Wright), 1967. Contbr. to: Agricul. Hist.; Miss. Valley Histl. Review; Chronicles of Okla.; Jrnl. of Il. State Histl. Soc.; etc. Mbr., var. profl. assns. Recip., $5,000 Literary Award, Loyal Legion of the US, 1963. Address: Dept. of History, Oklahoma State Univ., Stillwater, OK 74074, USA.

FISH, Robert Lloyd, pen name PIKE, Robert L., b. 21 Aug. 1912, Cleveland, Ohio, USA. Plastics Industry Consulting Engineer; Writer. Educ: B.S., Case Schl. Applied Sci., Cleveland. Publs. incl: The Fugitive, 1962; Isle of the Snakes, 1963; Mute Witness, 1963; The Quarry, 1964; Police Blotter, 1965; Hochmann Miniatures, 1967; The Murder League, 1968; Reardon, 1970; Bank Job, 1973; A Handy Death, 1973; Memoirs of Schlock Homes, 1974. Contbr. to: Argosy; Playboy; Atlantic Monthly; Ellery Queen Mystery Mag.; Cosmopolitan; The Writer. Mbrships: Mystery Writers of Am.; Crime Writers' Assn. (UK); Authors' Guild. Hons: Edgar Awards, Mystery Writers of Am., 1962, 1969, 1971. Address: 143 Sterling Rd., Trumbull, CT 06611, USA.

FISHER, A. Stanley T., pen name SCARROTT, Michael, b. 1906, Hoima, Uganda. Chaplain & Schoolmaster. Educ: M.A., Christ Church, Oxford Univ. Publs: Anthology of Prayers; The Reach of Words (poems), 1935; Voice & Verse, 1946; The Comet, & Earlier Poems, 1948; Ambassador of Loss (novel, as M. Scarrott), 1955; Fifty Days to Easter, 1964; The History of Broadwell, 1968; The History of Kencot, 1970; Christian Records, vol. I: In the Roman Empire, 1970; The History of Westwell, 1972. Contbr. to: Notes & Queries; Teaching of Engl. in Schls. Address: 72 Rosamund Rd., Wolvercote, Oxford, UK.

FISHER, Charles Harold, b. Sidcup, Kent, UK. Chartered Mechanical Engineer. Educ: Engrng. apprenticeship; trainee, Austin Motor Co. Publs: Carburation, 4 vols., 4 eds. (1 vol. pirated in Japan); The Stromberg Injection Carburettor; Principle of the Stromberg Injection Carburettor. Contbr. to: The Automobile Engr.; num other engrng. jrnls., 1933-. Mbrships: Fellow, Inst. Mech. Engrs.; Soc. Automotive Engrs., USA. Address: Rowans, Shrewley Common, Warwicks. CV35 7AP, UK.

FISHER, Edward, b. 20 Nov. 1902, Franklin, Mass., USA. Author; Artist. Educ: S.B., Harvard Coll., 1924; M.A., Harvard Grad. Schl., 1925; further studies, Univ. of Paris, France, 1928-29; Corcoran Schl. of Art, USA, 1948-49. Publs. incl: To the Sun, 1929; Marriage in Blue, 1931; Requiem, 1933; Amazon Key, 1961; Shakespeare & Son, 1962; Love's Labours Won, 1963; The Best House in Stratford, 1965. Contbr. to: Conn. Review; Sense of Humor; New Stories; New Yorker; Scholastic; London Argosy; Bookman; etc. Hons. incl: publ. in Best British Short Stories, 1931; Kt. of Mark Twain. Address: 112 Kennedy-Warren, 3133 Conn. Ave. N.W., Wash. DC 20008, USA.

FISHER, Ernest Arthur, b. 4 Apr. 1887, Oxford, UK. Chemist; Academic & Industrial Lecturer & Researcher. Educ: B.Sc., M.A., Univ. of Oxford; D.Sc., Univ. of

London. Publs: Introduction to Anglo-Saxon Architecture & Sculpture, 1959; The Greater Anglo-Saxon Churches, 1962; Anglo-Saxon Towers, 1969; The Saxon Churches of Sussex, 1970. Contbr. to: Proceedings of Royal Soc.; Jrnl. of Agricl. Sci.; Jrnl. of Soc. of Chem. Ind.; Biochem. Soc. Jrnl.; Jrnl. of Textile Inst.; Jrnl. of Phys. Chem.; Cereal Chem. Mbrships: F.R.I.C.; Fellow, Inst. of Phys.; Gen. Comm., Brit. Assn. for the Advancement of Sci. Address: The Cottage, Akeley, Buckingham, UK.

FISHER, Muriel Ethelwyn, b. 25 July 1915, Wairarapa, NZ. School Teacher. Publs: Gardening with N.Z. Plants, Shrubs & Trees; Official History of the Borough of Birkenhead. Mbrships: Auckland Inst. & Mus.; Delegate, Nat. Coun. of Royal Forest & Bird Protection Soc. Address: 36 Kauri Rd., Birkenhead, Auckland, NZ.

FISHER, Peter Jack, b. Vienna, Austria. Author. Educ: B.Sc. Publs: Jewels, 1956; The Science of Gems, 1966; The Polio Story, 1967; The Universe, Life & Man, 1970; Das Juwelen Buch, 1967 (in German). Mbrships: Fellow Gemmol. Assn. Gt. Brit.; F.R.S.A. Address: Lantern Cottage, Liverton, Newton Abbot, Devonshire, UK.

FISHER, Richard B., b. 1919, Cleveland, Ohio, USA. Publishing Executive. Educ: B.A., M.A., Ph.D., Yale Univ. Publs: Introduction to Edgar Allen Poe: Selected Tales, 1969; A Dictionary of Drugs (w. G. A. Christie), 1971; How Drugs Work (w. G. A. Christie), 1973; The Chemistry of Consciousness, 1975. Contbr. to: Observer Colour Mag. Agent: Cassandra Carter, London Mgmt. Mbr., Brain Rsch. Assn. Address: 26 St. Paul's Road, London N1, UK.

FISHER, Verdis, b. 31 Mar. 1895, Annis, Idaho, USA. Author; Professor of English. Educ: M.A.; Ph.D.; Univ. of Utah; Univ. of Chgo. Publs. incl: The Mothers, 1943; The Golden Rooms, 1944; Intimations of Eve, 1945; Adam & the Serpent, 1947; The Divine Passion, 1948; God or Caesar, 1953; Pemmican, 1956; A Goat for Azazel, 1956; Peace Like a River, 1957; Tale of Valor, 1958; My Holy Satan, 1958; Suicide or Murder, 1962; Thomas Wolfe as I Knew Him, and Other Essays, 1963; Mountain Man, 1965; Golde Rushes & Mining Camps of the Early American West, 1968. Address: Hagerman, Idaho, USA.

FISHER, William Bayne, b. 24 Sept. 1916, Darwen, UK. University Professor; Head of Department. Educ: Univ. of Manchester; Doct., Univ. of Paris, France; Univ. of Louvain, Belgium. Publs: The Middle East — a Physical, Social & Regional Geography, 1950, num. later eds.; Malta — a Background for Development (w. H. Bowen-Jones & J. C. Dewdney), 1958; Spain (w. H. Bowen-Jones), 1962, var. later eds.; Populations of the Middle East & North Africa (w. J. I. Clarke), 1972. Contbr. to: Ed., The Cambridge History of Iran, vol. I, 1968; var. profl. jrnls. Mbrships: Past Pres., Sect E. Brit. Assn.; Royal Geog. Soc.; Brit. Geog. Assn. Recip., Murchison Award, Royal Geog. Soc., 1973. Address: Dept. of Geography, South Rd., Durham DH1 3LE, UK.

FISHLOCK, David Jocelyn, b. 1932, Bath, UK. Technology & Science Editor. Publs: Metal Colouring, 1962; The New Materials, 1967; Ed., A Guide to the Laser, 1967; Taking the Temperature, 1968; Ed., a Guide to Superconductivity, 1969; Man Modified, 1969; The New Scientists, 1971; The Business of Science, 1974. Contbr. to: New Sci. (Technol. Ed., 1962-67); Financial Times (Sci. Ed., 1967-); Weekly Energy Report (Wash.); Mgmt. Today; Metalworking Prod. (Assoc. Ed., 1959-62); etc. Mbrships. incl: Rsch & Dev. Soc.; Assn. Brit. Sci. Writers. Address: "Traveller's Joy", Copse Lane, Jordans, Bucks., UK.

FISHMAN, William J., b. 1921, Stepney, London, UK. Senior Research Fellow. Educ: Wandsworth Tchrs. Trng. Coll.; B.Sc.(Econ.), London Schl. of Econs.; Dip. Lit., London Univ. Publs: The Insurrectionists, 1970; East End Jewish Radicals, 1875-1914, 1975. Contbr. to: Hist. Today; European Judaism; E. London Arts Mag.; E. London Papers; Anglia; Hist. of the Engl. Speaking Peoples. Address: 42 Willowcourt Ave., Kenton, Harrow, Middx., UK.

FITTER, Richard Sidney Richmond, b. 1913, Streatham, UK. Naturalist. Educ: B.Sc., London Schl. of Econs. Publs. incl: London's Natural History, 1945; Pocket Guide to British Birds, 1952; The Ark in our Midst, 1959; Six Great Naturalists, 1959; Wildlife in Britain, 1963; Vanishing Wild Animals of the World, 1968; Finding Wild Flowers, 1971; Birds of Britain & Europe, (w. H. Heinzel & J. Parslow); The Wild Flowers of Britain & Northern Europe, (w. A. Fitter & M. Blamey) 1974. Contbr. to: Countryman; Observer. Mbrships: Hon. Treas., Coun. for Nature; Hon. Sec., Fauna Preservation Soc. Address: Drifts, Chinnor Hill, Oxford, UK.

FITZGERALD, Gerald Joseph, b. 8 May 1910, Chgo., Ill., USA. Reporting Broker; Writer. Educ: Univ. of Chgo.; LL.B., J.D., John Marshall Law Schl.; J.D., Blackstone Coll. of Law. Contbr. to: Limerick Ldr.; The Post (Am. newspaper); Our Navy (official USN mag.); var. other jrnls. (articles, hist. & heraldry). Address: 1400 N. Lake Shore Dr., Apt. 6-T, Chgo., IL 60610, USA.

FITZGERALD, Robert David, b. 22 Feb. 1902, Hunter's Hill, N.S.W., Australia. Land Surveyor; Poet. Educ: Qualified Land Surveyor, 1925; Fellow, Instn. of Surveyors, Aust., 1959; Publs: To Meet the Sun, 1929; Moonlight Acre, 1938; Between Two Tides, 1952; This Night's Orbit, 1953; The Wind at Your Door, 1959; Southmost Twelve, 1962; Of Some Country, 1963; Forty Years Poems, 1965. Contbr. to: The Bulletin; Meanjin; Southerly; Overland; Texas Quarterly. Hons. incl: O.B.E., for servs. to lit., 1951; Robert Frost Medallion, 1974. Address: 4 Prince Edward Parade, Hunter's Hill, N.S.W., Australia 2110.

FITZGIBBON, Constantine, b. 1919, Lenox, Mass., USA. Author. Educ: univs. in UK, France, Germany. Publs. incl: The Arabian Bird, 1949; The Iron Hoop, 1950; The Holiday, 1953; The Shirt of Nessus, 1955; The Blitz, 1957; Paradise Lost & More, 1959; When the Kissing had to Stop, 1960; The Life of Dylan Thomas, 1965; Ed., Selected Letters of Dylan Thomas, 1966; Red Hand: The Ulster Colony, 1971; A Concise History of Germany, 1972; In the Bunker, 1973; The Life of de Valera, 1974; The Golden Age, 1975; also transls. from French, German & Italian. Contbr. to newspapers & jrnls. in UK, USA & elsewhere. Mbrships: Beefsteak Club; Kildare Street Club, Dublin. Address: St. Annes, Kilziney Road, Co. Dublin, Repub. of Ireland.

FITZGIBBON, (Joanne) (Eileen) Theodora (Winifred), b. 21 Oct. 1916, London, UK. Writer. Publs: Cosmopolitan Cookery in an English Kitchen, 1952; Weekend Cooking, 1956; The High Protein Diet & Cookery Book, 1957; Country House Cooking, 1958; The Young Cook's Book, 1958; Game Cooking, 1963; The Art of British Cooking, 1964; Flight of the Kingfisher, 1967; A Taste of Ireland, 1968; Eat Well & Live Longer, 1969; A Taste of Scotland, 1970; A Taste of Wales, 1971; A Taste of England: The West Country, 1972; Theodora FitzGibbon's Cookery Book, 1972; A Taste of London, 1973; A Taste of Paris, 1974; A Taste of Rome, 1975; The Food of the Western World, 1975. Recip., sev. bronze medals. Address: Atlanta, Coliemore Rd., Dalkey, Co. Dublin, Repub. of Ireland.

FITZHARDINGE, Joan Margaret, pen name PHIPSON, Joan, b. 16 Nov. 1912, Sydney, Australia. Writer. Publs: Good Luck to the Rider, 1953; Six & Silver, 1954; It Happened One Summer, 1957; The Boundary Riders, 1962; The Family Conspiracy, 1962; Threat to the Barkers, 1963; Birkin, 1965; The Crew of the Merlin, 1966; A Lamb in the Family, 1966; Peter & Butch, 1969; The Haunted Night, 1970; Bass & Billy Martin, 1972; Polly's Tiger, 1973; The Way Home, 1973; Helping Horse, 1974. Mbr., Aust. Soc. of Authors. Hons: Book of the Yr., Children's Book Coun. of Aust., 1953, 1963; Children's Book Award, N.Y. Herald Tribune, 1964. Address: Wongalong, Mandurama, New South Wales 2792, Australia.

FITZHUGH, Louise, b. 5 Oct. 1928, Memphis, Tenn., USA. Author; Illustrator. Educ: Bard Coll.; Cooper Union; Art Students League. Publs: Suzuki Beane, 1961; Harriet the Spy, 1964; The Long Secret, 1965; Bang, Bang, You're Dead, 1969; Nobody's Family is Going to Change, 1974. Mbr., Author's Guild. Recip., Sequayah Children's Book Award, 1967. Address: c/o McIntosh & Otis, 18 East 41st St., N.Y., NY 10017, USA.

FITZLYON, Cecily April Mead, b. 1920, Langton Herring, Dorset, UK. Freelance Writer; Translator; Broadcaster. Educ: Guildhall Schl. of Music. Publs: The Libertine Librettist — A Biography of Mozart's Librettist, Lorenzo de Ponte, 1956; Price of Genius: a biography of Pauline Viardot, 1965; (transls.) Family Happiness (Tolstoy), 1953; The Devil, 1953; Ladies' Delight (Zola), 1957; Correspondence (R. Rolland R. Strauss), 1968; Embers (A. Pieyre de Mandiargues), 1970; etc. Contbr. to: Listener; London Mag.; Grove's Dict. of Music & Musicians; Encounter. Mbrships: Soc. of Authors; PEN. Address: 40 Park Drive, London NW11, UK.

FITZSIMONS, Raymund, b. Whitehaven, Cumbria, UK. Librarian. Educ: Assoc., Lib. Assn. Publs: Baron of Piccadilly, 1967; Barnum in London, 1969; The Charles Dickens Show, 1970. Contbr. to: Cornhill Mag.; Saturday Book. Address: The Retreat, The Green, Wetheral, Carlisle, Cumbria, UK.

FIXLER, Michael, b. 1927, Hungary. University Professor of English. Educ: Univ. of Wis., USA; Sorbonne Univ., Paris, France; M.A., Univ. of Oxford, UK; Ph.D. Publs: Milton & the Kingdoms of God, 1964; Ed., The Mentor Bible, 1973. Contbr. to: Commentary; The Kenyon Review; Commonweal; PMLA; RES; The Milton Ency.; Milton Studies. Mbrships: MLA of Am.; Renaissance Soc.; Fellow, Soc. for Relig. in Higher Educ. Address: 55 Fletcher St., Winchester, MA 01890, USA.

FLACH, Jacob, b. 26 Mar, 1894, Winterthur, Switz. Writer. Educ: Zurich Univ., Switz. Publs: Die Verhinderten, 1928; Minestra, 1937; Vita Vagorum, 1943; Nordischer Sommer, 1946; Wir bauen ein Marionettentheater, 1951; Brautfahrt o. Ende, 1960; Ascona, 1960; Tessin, 1965. Mbrships: Schweizer Schriftstellerverband; Zurcher Schriftsteller-Verein. Recip: Preise der Stadt, Winterthur & des Kantons Zurich. Address: Molino del Brumo, CH-6611 Arcegno, Switz.

FLACK, Elmer Ellsworth, b. 3 Oct. 1894, Mendon, Ill., USA. Minister; Theological Professor; Editor & Author. Publs: Old Testament Commentary (co-ed.), 1948; 20th Century Encyclopedia of Religious Knowledge (ed., Old Testament), 1955; Melanchthon: Selected Writings (ed.), 1962; Leaves From the Dean's Joke Book, 1971; On This Rock, 1973; The Witness of Jesus, 1973. Contbr. to: Luth. Quarterly; Interpretation; The Lutheran. Mbrships. incl: Soc. of Biblical Lit. & Exegesis; Young Men's Lit. Club. Address: 1788 W. Eldridge Ave., St. Paul, MN 55113, USA.

FLANAGAN, Patrick Joseph, b. 8 Aug. 1940, Dublin, Repub. of Ireland. Research Chemist. Educ: B.Sc., 1962, Ph.D., 1966, Univ. Coll., Dublin. Contbr. to: Jrnl. Irish Railway Record Soc.; Breifne. Mbrships: Fellow, Chem. Soc., London; Inst. of Chem. of Ireland; Irish Railway Record Soc.; Inland Waterways Assn. of Ireland. Address: 33 Fortfield Park, Terenure, Dublin 6, Repub. of Ireland.

FLANDERS, Michael, b. 1922, London, UK. Actor; Writer. Educ: M.A., Christ Church, Oxford Univ. Publs. incl: Three's Company (libretto); Transl., The Soldier's Tale; Creatures Great & Small (verse); Captain Noah & his Floating Zoo (verse); Nasrudin the Wise (prose) (verse) Penny Plain, 1951; Airs on a Shoestring, 1953; Fresh Airs, 1956; At the Drop of a Hat, 1957; At the Drop of Another Hat, 1961. Recip., O.B.E. Agent: Lister Welch Ltd. Address: 63 Esmond Rd., London W4 1JE, UK.

FLASHOFF, Ruth Eleanor, b. 16 Nov. 1909, London, UK. Retired School Principal; Journalist. Educ: Dip. in Jrnlsm. Contbr. to: The Rotorua Post; The Freelance; The Daily Telegraph, Napier; & var. others. Mbr., NZ Women Writers' Inc. Recip., Rsch. Grant (for novel in progress), Auckland Br., Fed. of Univ. Women. Address: Peniel, 9 Greenwood Rd., Havelock N., Hawke Bay, NZ.

FLEETWOOD, Frances, pen name FLEETWOOD, Frank (early works), b. 24 May 1902, London, UK. Writer. Educ: Sorbonne Univ., Paris, France. Publs: Conquest, The Story of a Theatre Family, 1953; histl. monographs on Rimini and Casertavecchia, in Italian & Engl., 1968 & 1973; Concordia, 1971; Concordia Errant, 1973; Beloved Upstart (w. V. Schuyler), 1974; Transl., U. Nobile, With the Italia to the North Pole, 1930; Transl., My Polar Flights, 1961; & var. French works inclng. 2 novels by Dekobra. Contbr. to: Times Educl. Supplement; La Piê. Hons: Hon. Mention, Gradara Int. Prize Competition, 1973; Friends of Gradara Silver Medal. Address: Via del Golfo 4, 04028 Scauri (Latina), Italy.

FLEETWOOD, Hugh Nigel, b. 14 Oct. 1944, Chichester, UK. Writer; Painter. Publs: A Painter of Flowers, 1972; The Girl Who Passed For Normal, 1973; Foreign Affairs, 1973; A Conditional Sentence, 1974. Contbr. to The Transatlantic Review. Recip., John Llewellyn Rhys Prize, 1974. Agent: Richard Scott Simon. Address: Via Clementina 11, 00184 Rome, Italy.

FLEISCHER, Wolfgang H., b. 3 June 1943, Salzburg, Austria. Writer. Publs: Unverbindliche Leidenschaften (stories), 1968; Niobe, 1969; Tripel (plays), 1971; Perpetuum mobile (multiple theatre play), 1971. Contbr.

to: Die Wiederkehr der Drachen, 1970; Erinnerungen en Heimito von Doderer, 1972; var. radio progs., criticisms & essays, S. Am. lit.; TV progs., films on mod. art & lit. Mbr., Vereinigung Hauptberuflicher Autoren (Assn. of Profl. Authors). Hons: Vienna Art Fndn. Prize, 1965; Theodor Körner Fndn. Prize, 1967. Address: Frieda Richardstr. 16, A5023 Salzburg, Austria.

FLEISCHMAN, Harry, b. 3 Oct. 1914, NYC, USA. Race Relations Administrator; Author. Educ: CCNY. Publs: We Open the Gates: Labor's Fight for Equality, 1958; Let's Be Human, 1960; Norman Thomas: A Biography, 1964, 2nd ed., 1969. Contbr. to: Ency. Yrbooks., 1971, 1972, 1973; New Ldr.; Progressive; AFL-CIO Am. Federationist; Reconstructionist; Indl. Union Digest. Address: 11 Wedgewood Ln., Wantagh, NY 11793, USA.

FLEISCHMAN, Theo, b. 1893, Antwerp, Belgium. Writer. Publs. incl: (poems) Ce vieil enfant, 1922; Archipel, 1923; (other publs.) Un curieux récit de Waterloo, 1946; Icare, 1947; Le Roi de Gand; Un qui revient de loin; Bruxelles pendant la bataille de Waterloo; Tapin tanmbour de Bonaparte en Egypte; Le Peuple aux Yeux Clairs; Napoleon & la musique; L'Epopée impériale raconté par la Grande Armée; L'Evade de Sainte-Helene; Histoires singulières; & num. radio features. Contbr. to: La Gazette, 1920; Belgian Nat. Broadcasting Inst. Hons. incl: Croix de Guerre with palm; Commander, Legion of Honour. Address: 43 Ave. Hamoir, Brussels, Belgium.

FLEISCHMANN, Harriet Drakeley, b. 11 Mar. 1904, Phila., Pa., USA. Author. Musician. Educ: B.S. in Educ., Univ. of Pa. Publs: The Great Enchantment, 1967. Address: 127 W. Queen Lane, Phila., PA 19144, USA.

FLEMING, Berry, b. 19 Mar. 1899, Augusta, Ga., USA. Writer. Educ: B.S., Harvard Coll., 1922. Publs: The Conqueror's Stone, 1927; Visa to France, 1930; The Square Root of Valentine, 1932; Siesta, 1935; To the Market Place, 1938; Colonel Effingham's Raid, 1943; The Lightwood Tree, 1947; The Fortune Tellers, 1951; Carnival, 1953; Autobiography of a Colony, 1957; The Winter Rider, 1959; The Acrobats, A Comedy in Two Acts, 1960; Lucinderella, 1964; The Make-Believers, 1973; Autobiography of a City in Arms, scheduled 1974. Contbr. to: Punch, The New Yorker; Yale Review; N.M. Quarterly. Address: 3050 Walton Way, Augusta, GA 30904, USA.

FLEMING, David James, b. 1947, Nottingham. Freelance Journalist; Scriptwriter. Educ: Corpus Christi Schl., Nottingham. Contbr. to: BBC; IPC Ltd. Mbr., Soc. of Authors. Address: 62 Connaught Gardens, Radford, Nottingham.

FLEMING, Gerald, b. 1921, Mannheim, Germany. Senior Lecturer. Educ: L.ès.L., Sorbonne, France; Inst. Français, London. Publs: Wall Pictures for Guilded Composition (w. co-op. of Fougasse); Teachers Books; Guilded Composition, 1961; Les Carré (12 cartoon films & 2 books); French Visual Grammar (w. David Langdon), 1969, 1970; Gutenberg-Jahrbuch; Busch-Jahrbuch. Contbr. to: Nat. Visual Aids Jrnl.; Schoolmaster; Govt. of India Jrnl. of Visual Aids; Praxis; Times Educl. Supplement; IRAL; DaF; Audio-visual Lang. Jrnl.; Audio-visual Instrn., USA. Address: University of Surrey, Guildford, UK.

FLEMING, John, b. 1919, Berwick-on-Tweed, UK. Educ: B.A., Trinity Coll., Cambridge Univ. Publs: Scottish Country Houses & Gardens Open to the Public, 1955; Robert Adam & His Circle in Edinburgh & Rome, UK & USA, 1962; The Penguin Dictionary of Architecture (co-author), 1966, 2nd ed., 1972. Contbr. to: Archtl. Review; Burlington Mag.; Connoisseur; Cornhill Mag. Address: Villa Marchio, Tofori, Lucca, Italy.

FLESCHER, Joachim, b. 28 Nov. 1906, Buczacz, Austro-Poland. Psychoanalyst; Psychiatrist. Educ: M.D., Vienna, 1934; Modena, 1935; State Bd., Med., 1936, Speciality Bd., Neurol. & Psych., 1938, Rome, Italy; State Bd., Med., N.Y., USA, 1957. Publs: Psicoanalisi della Vita Istintiva, 1945; Mental Health & Prevention of Neurosis, 1951; Dual Therapy & Genetic Psychoanalysis, 1966; Childhood & Destiny, 1970; Suicide & Guilt, 1971; Nazi Holocaust & Mankind's "Final Solution", 1971; Free Genetic Psychoanalysis & Prevention, 1972. Contbr. to var. sci. jrnls. Mbr., var. profl. assns. Address: 1148 5th Ave., N.Y., NY 10028, USA.

FLETCHER, Grace Nies, b. 1895, Townsend, Mass., USA. Teacher; Writer. Educ: Boston Univ.; Columbia Univ.;

Ohio Wesleyan Univ.; B.A. Publs: In My Father's House, 1956; Preachers' Kids, 1958; No Marriages in Heaven, 1960; I Was Born Tomorrow, 1961; The Whole World in His Hand, 1962; The Fabulous Flemings of Kathmandu, 1964; In Quest of the Least Coin, 1969; Merry Widow, 1970; What's Right With Us Parents?, 1972. Contbr. to Reader's Digest Book Club & Mag. Mbr., Tex. Chapt., Women in Communications. Agent: John Cushman. Address: 3301 Bellaire Drive N., Fort Worth, TX 76109, USA.

FLETCHER, John Walter James, pen name FUNE, Jonathan, b. 23 June 1937, Barking, Essex, UK. University Professor; Pro-Vice-Chancellor. Educ: B.A., M.A., Univ. of Cambridge; D.E.S., D.T.C., Univ. de Toulouse, France. Publs. incl: New Directions in Literature, 1968; Samuel Beckett: His Works & His Critics (w. Raymond Federman), 1970; Beckett: A Study of His Plays (w. John Spurling), 1972; Claude Simon & Fiction Now, 1975. Contbr. to var. lit. jrnls. Mbrships: Assn. of Univ. Profs. of French; Int. Comp. Lit. Assn. Agent: John Farquharson Ltd. Address: Univ. of East Anglia, Schl. of European Studies, University Plain, Norwich NR4 7TJ, UK.

FLETCHER, Joseph Francis, b. 10 Apr. 1905, Newark, N.J., USA. Ethicist. Educ: A.B., Univ. of W.Va.; M.Div., Berkeley Divinity Schl.; S.T.D., Univ. of London; Litt.D., Ohio Wesleyan Univ.; D.D., Berkeley, Episc. Divinity Schl. Publs: The Church & Industry, 1930; Christianity & Property, 1947; Morals & Medicine, 1954; William Temple, 1963; Situation Ethics, 1966; Moral Responsibility, 1968; Hello Lovers World, 1970; Ethics of Genetic Control, 1974. Contbr. to: Harvard Theol. Review; Harper's; Ladies' Home Jrnl.; Jrnl. of Pastoral Care; Churchman; Witness; Theol. Today; etc. Fellow, Hastings Ctr. Address: 52 Van Ness Rd., Belmont, MS, USA.

FLETCHER, Ronald, b. 1921, Hoyland, Yorks., UK. Writer. Educ: B.A., Univ. Bristol; Ph.D., London Schl. Econs. Publs: Instinct in Man, 1957; Issues in Education, 1960; The Family & Marriage in Britain, 1962; Human Needs & Social Order, 1965; The Parkers at Saltram, 1970; The Making of Sociology (3 vols.), 1971; John Stuart Mill: A Logical Critique of Sociology, 1971; The Crisis of Industrial Civilisation, 1974; Ed., The Science of Society & the Unity of Mankind, 1974; The Akenham Burial Case, 1974; What is Wrong with Higher Education, 1975. Contbr. to var. jrnls. Mbrships. incl: Brit. Sociol. Assn. Agent: Curtis Brown Ltd. Address: Cranmere, Halesworth Road, Reydon, Southwold, Suffolk, UK.

FLEW, Antony Garrard Newton, b. 11 Feb. 1923, London, UK. University Teacher. Educ: Schl. of Oriental & African Studies, London; M.A., St. John's Coll., Oxford; D.Litt., Keele. Publs: A New Approach to Psychical Research, 1953; Hume's Philosophy of Belief, 1961; God & Philosophy, 1966; Evolutionary Ethics, 1967; An Introduction to Western Philosophy, 1971; Crime or Disease, 1973. Contbr. to: Mind; Philos.; Philos. Quarterly; Praxis; Question; Studies in Philos. & Educ.; Spectator; Times Educl. Supplement; Times Higher Educ. Supplement; Daily Telegraph; Guardian; Encounter. Mbrships: Mind Assn.; Aristotelian Soc.; VP, Rationalist Press Assn. Address: 26 Alexandra Rd., Reading RG1 5PD, UK.

FLEXNER, James Thomas, b. 13 Jan. 1908, NYC, USA. Author. Educ: Lincoln Schl. of Tchrs. Coll., 1925; B.S., Harvard Univ., 1929. Publs. incl: Doctors on Horseback, 1937; The Pocket History of American Painting, 1950; Mohawk Baronet, 1959; That Wilder Image, 1962; George Washington, 1732-75, 1965; George Washington in the American Revolution, 1775-83, 1968; George Washington & the New Nation, 1783-93, 1970; 19th Century American Painting, 1970; George Washington, 1793-99, 1972; Washington: The Indispensable Man, 1974. Contbr. to num. jrnls. Mbrships. incl: Century Assn.; PEN (Pres., Am. Ctr., 1954-55); Soc. Am. Histns. (Pres., 1975–). Hons: Parkman Prize, 1955; Nat. Book Award, 1973; Special Pullitzer Prize Citation, 1973. Address: 530 E. 86th St., N.Y., NY 10028, USA.

FLITNER, David P., b. 3 Jan. 1949, Boston, Mass., USA. Student. Educ: B.A., Univ. of Maine, 1972; M.A., Univ. of Conn., 1974; current Ph.D. studies, Tufts Univ., Boston. Publs: Those People in Washington, 1973. Address: 26 Shipman Rd., Andover, MA 01810, USA.

FLORIAN, Tibor, b. 12 Apr. 1908, Selmecbanya, Hungary. Writer; Editor. Educ: Fac. of Law, Univ. of Kolozsvar, Rumania. Books pub. in Rumania, Germany, USA, incl: Above Clouds, Below Clouds, 1935; Sketches,

1936; The Stone Slabs Are Broken, 1946; New Poems, 1948; Bitter Roots, 1974. Contbr. to num. jrnls. & anthols., Europe & USA; Lit. Ed., Hungaria (weekly), Germany, 1947-49; Announcer, 1950-60, Ed., 1960-74, Radio Free Europe, NYC. Mbrships. incl: Hon. Treas., Int. PEN; Asst. Sec., Ctr. for Writers in Exile, NYC; Past Pres., Kossuth Pub. Co., Cleveland; Int. Fedn. of Jrnlsts.; Pres., Lit. Br., Arpad Acad., Cleveland; Former mbr., Rumanian, Hungarian lit. assns. Hons. incl: Silver Medal, 1964, Gold Medal, 1973, Arpad Acad. Address: 3 Mountain View Dr., New Milford, CT 06776, USA.

FLOUD, Jean Esther, b. 1915, Westcliff-on-Sea, UK. College Principal. Educ: London Schl. of Econs. & Pol. Sci.; M.A., B.Sc. (Econ.). Publs: Social Class & Educational Opportunity (w. A. H. Halsey & F. M. Martin), 1956. Contbr. to: Brit. Jrnl. of Sociol.; Sociol. Review; Brit. Jrnl. of Educ. Studies; etc. Recip., Litt.D., Leeds Univ. Address: The Principal's Lodge, Newnham College, Cambridge, UK.

FLOUD, Roderick Castle, b. 1 Apr. 1942, Barnes, UK. University Teacher. Educ: B.A., 1964, Wadham Coll., D.Phil., 1971, Nuffield Coll., Oxford Univ; M.A., Oxford & Cambridge Univs. Publs: An Introduction to Quantitative Methods for Historians, 1973; Essays in Quantitative Economic History (Ed.). Contbr. to: Econ. Hist. Review. Mbr., Coun., Econ. Hist. Soc. Address: c/o Dept. of Hist., Birkbeck Coll., Malet St., London, UK.

FLOWER, Desmond John Newman, b. 1907, London, UK. Publisher; Author; Editor; Organiser, Book Exhibitions. Educ: M.A., King's Coll., Cambridge; D.Litt. (Caen., France). Publs: The Pursuit of Poetry, 1939; History of the Argyll & Sutherland Highlanders 5th Batallion, 1959; Ed., Complete Poems of Ernest Christopher Dowson, 1934; The War, 1939-45 (co-ed. w. J. Reeves), 1960; also var. transls. from French (Voltaire, Saint Simon, etc.). Contbr. to: Times Lit. Supplement; Observer; Book Collector; The Lib. Mbr., PEN. Hons: M.C.; Officier de la Legion d'Honneur. Address: 187 Clarence Gate Gdns., London NW1, UK.

FOAKES, Grace, née PLATT, b. 1901, London, UK. Housewife. Publs: Between High Walls, 1972; My Part of the River, 1974. Address: 17 St. Denys Rd., New Middleton, Hants., UK.

FODOR, András, b. 27 Feb. 1929, Kaposmérö, Hungary. Librarian; Writer. Educ: Philos. Fac. Publs: My Way Home, 1955; Sober Morning, 1958; Seas & Hills, 1961; Turning Sky, 1964; Lines on My Face, 1967; Sunflower – Selected Translations of Poems, 1967; The Call of Silence – Selected Poems, 1969; Another Infinite, 1970; Attila József – A Biography, 1971; Double Requiem, in Memoriam Colin Mason & Lajos Fülep, 1972; The Voice of a Generation, 1973; The Captive of Time, 1974; Igor Stravinsky, 1975. Contbr. to: Kortáres; Uj Irás; Élet és Irodalom; Jelenkor; Tiszatáj. Mbrships: Sec., Poetry Sect., Hungarian Writers' Union. Hons: Attila József Prize, 1955, 1973; Cyrill & Method Prize, Bulgaria, 1974. Address: Bajcsy Zsilinszky ut 15/E, 1065 Budapest, Hungary.

FODOR, Eugene, b. 14 Oct. 1905, Léva, Hungary. Editor; Author. Educ: Lic.-ès-écon. pol., Univ. of Grenoble, France, 1927. Publs: 1936 On the Continent, 1936; Europe in 1937, 1937; France, 1951; Fodor's Travel Guides, publd. annually. Contbr. & Colomnist, Disverion mag., USA. Mbrships. incl: Soc. Am. Travel Writers; US Authors' League; Fedn. Int. des Journalistes et Ecrivains de Tourisme. Hons. incl: Grand Prix de Litterature de Tourisme, Paris, 1959; Special Award, Int. Travel Book Contest, Madrid, Spain, 1969; British Tourist Authority Award, London, UK, 1972. Address: Blue Swamp Rd., Litchfield, CT 06759, USA.

FOGG, Gordon Elliott, b. 1919, Langar, Notts., UK. Professor of Marine Biology, University College of North Wales, since 1971; Professor of Botany, Westfield College, University of London, 1960-71. Educ: B.Sc., Ph.D., D.Sc., F.R.S. Publs: The Metabolism of Algae, 1953; The Growth of Plants, 1963, 2nd ed., 1970; Algal Cultures & Phytoplankton Ecology, 1965; Photosynthesis, 1968, 2nd ed., 1972; Blue-Green Algae (w. W. D. P. Stewart, P. Fay & A. E. Walsby), 1973. Contbr. to: Jrnl. Expmtl. Bot.; Proceedings Royal Soc.; Jrnl. Marine Biol. Assn.; New Biol. Mbr., Athenaeum. Recip., LL.D. (Dundee). Address: Marine Sci. Lab., Menai Bridge, Anglesey, Gwynedd LL59 5EH, UK.

FOGHAMMAR, Stig Sverker, pen names Stig SVERKERS, ARW 493, S.F-r., Danio. Specialist writer (water plants, water hygiene, etc.); Teacher. Educ: Fil. kand., Lund Univ. & H.S., Gothenburg, 1945. Contbr. to: Grundförbättring, 1950-51; Swedish Social-Medicine Periodical, 1948-49; Pipe Installation Periodical, 1940s; Värld och Vetande, 1945; Animal & Nature, 1946-68; Akvariet, Akvarievennen, Akvariebladet, 1940s; Tidning för Sveriges Läroverk, 1930, 1940; Morgontidningen (scientific writer) 1940s; Arche Noah, Hamburg, (corres. writer); Fackläraren, 1962-68; Dagen and Vasabladet, 1974; Triumf & All about Fishing, 1973-74; Test (rabies & animal stamps). Mbrships: Assn. for Water Hygiene; Swedish Authors Assn. Hons: Schlrship., Natur & Kultur Publng. House, Stockholm, 1950; Swedish Authors Fond, Stockholm, 1973; Prize for Culture Critics, Assn. Norden, 1974. Address: Box 338, 721 07 Västeraas 1, Sweden.

FÖLDES, Anna, b. 15 Aug. 1930, Budapest, Hungary. Journalist; Author. Educ: M.A., E.L.T.E., 1952, Ph.D., 1958, Univ. Budapest. Publs: (biog.) Móra Ferenc, 1958; Bródy Sándor, 1964; (essay) Trash in Literature, 1962; (essay) Twenty Years — Twenty Novels, 1968; (essays) latest vol., The Role of the Woman: a Main Role, 1972. Contbr. to: Nök Lapja (Woman's Weekly); Szinház (theatrical review); Élet és Irodalom (lit. weekly); New Hungarian Quarterly. Mbrships. incl: Hungarian Writers' Union; Hungarian Jrnlsts.' Union. Recip., Order Labour, silver degree, 1966. Address: II Törökvész ut 8, Budapest 1022, Hungary.

FÖLDES, Michael, b. 6 Jan. 1905, Budapest, Hungary. Journalist; Writer. Publs. incl: Mélyszántás (Ploughing, play), 1951; Honvágy (Nostalgia, play), 1957; Örök szerelem (Love for ever, play), 1958; Veszélyes élet (The dangerous life, novel), 1965; A parancs (The order, novel), 1969; Hajnal Pákozdon (Struggle for liberty, novel), 1970; A Tüztorony fiai (Warriors, novel), Dimenziók és metszetek (Three hard years, novel), 1975; Virradat a város peremén (Suburban's sunrise, novel), 1974. Mbrships: PEN; Assn. of Hungarian Writers. Recip., József Attila Prize, 1950 & 1953. Address: Schönherz Zoltán u. 21, 1117 Budapest, Hungary.

FÖLDES, Péter, b. 7 May 1916, Budapest, Hungary. Writer. Publs. incl: (trilogy) Európa Homlokán, 1957, 1959, 1961; Margaréta ügy, 1966; Villa az Andrássy uton, 1969; Érik a ropogós cseresznye, 1971; (juvenile) Találkozás a föld alatt, 1956; Mókuli, 1961; A delfin lovasa, 1969; A karvalyos zászló, 1973; (sci. fiction) Az ibolya színü fény, 1956; (text book) Az ösidök regénye, 1966. Mbrships. incl: Lit. Fndn. Hungarian People's Republic; PEN; Soc. Hungarian Writers (Sec. Juvenile Sect.). Hons: József Attila Prize, 1953 & 1962. Address: Budapest 1051, V.ker., Október 6. u.19., Hungary.

FOLDI, Ernest J., pen name THE VALLEY SPORTSMAN, b. 21 Apr. 1908, Phila., Pa., USA. Newspaper Columnist; Freelance Writer; Travelog Photographer & Narrator. Educ: Metropol. Coll.; La Salle Ext. Univ.; Armour Inst. of Technol.; Grad. Schl. of Writing, USDA. Contbr. to: Va. Wildlife Mag.; Fedn. Record; Daily News-Record, Harrisonburg, Va.; Page News & Courier, Luray, Va.; Shenandoah Herald, Valley of Woodstock, Va.; WVPT-TV (educl. TV). Mbrships: Sec.-Treas., S.E. Outdoor Press Assn.; Past Pres., Va. Outdoor Writers Assn.; Outdoor Writers Assn. of Am.; Mason Dixon Outdoor Writers Assn. Address: 340 Ohio Ave., Harrisonburg, VA 22801, USA.

FONSECA, John dos Reis, b. 13 Mar. 1925, New Bedford, Mass., USA. Author; Professor of Law & Banking. Educ: A.B., Harvard Coll.; J.D., Harvard Law Schl. Publs. incl: Law of Contracts, 1965; Law of Business Organizations, 2 vols. (casebook), 1971; Environment Law (casebook), 1972; Automobile Insurance & No-Fault Law (co-author), 1974; Property & Casualty Insurance Law, 1975. Contbr. & Ed., var. ency. & jrnl. supplements; Ed.-in-Chief, Uniform Commercial Code Law Jrnl., 1968-72. Mbr., Authors League of Am. Hons: 5 Fellowships in Bus. Mgmt. Educ. Programs. Address: 26 Tamarack Lane, Clifton Knolls, Elnora, NY 12065, USA.

FOOT, Michael Richard Daniel, b. 14 Dec. 1919, London, UK. Historian. Educ: M.A., B.Litt., New Coll., Oxford; M.A., Manchester Univ. Publs: Gladstone & Liberalism (w. J. L. Hammond), 1952; British Foreign Policy since 1898, 1956; Men in Uniform, 1961; SOE in France, 1966; Gladstone Diaries, vols. I & II (Ed.), 1968, vols. III & IV (Ed. w. H. C. G. Matthew), 1975; War &

Society (Ed.), 1973. Contbr. to: Economist; Engl. Histl. Review; Ency. Brit., eds. 14 & 15. Mbrships: F.R.Hist.S. (Coun., 1970-74); Soc. of Authors. Address: Orchard Cottage, Thakeham, Pulborough, Sussex, UK.

FOOTE, Shelby Dade, b. 17 Nov. 1916, Greenville, Miss., USA. Novelist; Historian. Educ: Univ. N.C. Publs: Tournament, 1949; Follow Me Down, 1950; Love in a Dry Season, 1951; Shiloh, 1952; Jordan County, 1954; The Civil War: A Narrative, Vol. I, 1958, Vol. II, 1963, Vol. III, 1974. Mbr., Soc. of Am. Histns. Hons: 3 Guggenheim Fellowships, 1957-60; Ford Fndn. Grant; Arena Stage, Wash. D.C., 1963-64; Writer in Res., Hollins Coll., Va., 1968. Address: 542 E. Parkway S., Memphis, TN 38104, USA.

FOOTMAN, David John, b. 1895, Watchfield, Berks., UK. Retired Foreign Service Official; Emeritus Fellow. Educ: M.A., New Coll., Oxford. Publs. incl: Pemberton, 1943; Red Prelude, 1944; Pig & Pepper; Dead Yesterday. Contbr. to var. jrnls. Agent: Bolt & Watson Ltd. Address: 11A Collingham Gdns., London SW5, UK.

FOPPEMA-WOLF, Ruth Sibylle, pen name WOLF, Ruth, b. 9 Sept. 1918, Amsterdam, Netherlands. Author; Translator. Educ: Univ. of Amsterdam. Publs: Het Woord als Wapen, 1952; In Zand Geschreven, 1954; De Wieken van de Leeuwerik, 1967; Als de Morgenster Blinkt, 1969; Eleazar de Rabbÿn van Worms, 1971; Oponthoud van een Vreemdeling, 1970. Mbrships: Assn. for Netherlands Lit.; Lit. Soc.; PEN. Address: 36 Wyttenbachweg, Oegstgeest, Netherlands.

FORBES, Bryan, b. July 1926, Stratford-atte-Bow, UK. Film Director, Producer & Screen Writer. Educ: R.A.D.A. Publs: Truth Lies Sleeping, 1951; (novel) The Distant Laughter, 1972; Notes for a Life, 1974; (writer, co-prod.) The Angry Silence, 1959; (dir.) Whistle Down the Wind, 1961; (writer & dir.) The L-Shaped Room, 1962; King Rat, 1964; (writer, prod., & dir.) The Whisperers, 1966; Deadfall, 1967; dir., num. TV features. Mbrships. incl: Writers' Guild of GB; BBC, Gen. Advsry. Coun., 1966-69. Hons. incl: UN Award; Brit. Film Acad. Award; Best Screenplay Award. Address: c/o Collins, 14 St. James's Pl., London SW1, UK.

FORBES, Colin, b. 1923, Hampstead, London, UK. Author. Publs: Tramp in Armour, 1969; The Heights of Zervos, 1970; The Palermo Ambush, 1972; Target Five, 1973; Year of the Golden Ape, 1974 (all UK & USA). Mbr., Soc. of Authors. Agent: Elaine Greene Ltd.

FORBES, John Douglas, b. 9 Apr. 1910, San Fran., Calif., USA. Professor; Author. Educ: A.B., Univ. of Calif., Berkeley, 1931; M.A., Stanford Univ., 1932; A.M., 1936, Ph.D., 1937, Harvard Univ. Publs: Israel Thorndike, 1953; Victorian Architect, 1953; Murder in Full View, 1968; Death Warmed Over, 1971; Stettinius, Sr., Portrait of a Morgan Partner, 1974. Contbr. to: Am. Histl. Review; Jrnl. of Aesthetics; N.Y. Times Sunday Books; etc. Address: 3607 University Station, Charlottesville, VA 22903, USA.

FORBES, Thomas Rogers, b. 5 Jan. 1911, NYC, USA. Professor of Anatomy. Educ: B.A., 1933, Ph.D., 1937, Univ. of Rochester. Publs: The Midwife & the Witch, 1966; Chronicle from Aldgate; Life & Death in Shakespeare's London, 1971. Contbr. to num. med. jrnls. Mbrships. incl: Am. Assn. of Anatomists; Endocrine Soc.; Am. Assn. for the Hist. of Med.; Pres., VP, Beaumont Club. Hons. incl: Hon. M.A., Yale Univ., 1962. Address: Schl. of Med., Yale Univ., New Haven, CT 06510, USA.

FORBES-BOYD, Eric, b. Addleston, UK. Writer. Publs: (novels) House of Whipplestaff, 1925; Merlin Hold, 1927; A Stranger in These Parts, 1952; The General in Retreat, 1960; (travel) In Crusader Greece, 1964; Aegean Quest, 1970, 2nd ed., 1973; (children's plays) Maripoza Bung, 1929; The Deuce, 1951; The Seventeenth-Highwayman, 1951 & 1954; (Ed. anthol.) Disraeli, 1948; (plays) X03, 1926; Knight Errant (filmed as The Girl in the Night, 1931), prod. in London, 1928; Blood Royal, 1932; He Loves Me Not, 1940. Contbr. to: Sunday Times; Country Life; Christian Sci. Monitor. Mbrships: Soc. for Promotion Hellenic Studies. Address: 11 Lloyd Sq., London WC1X 9BA, UK.

FORD, Boris, b. 1917, Simla, India. University Professor. Educ: M.A., Cambridge Univ. Publs: Gen. ed., Pelican Guide to English Literature (7 vols.); Teachers' Guide to Human Rights; Britain & United Nations; Young

Writers, Young Readers. Contbr. to: Scrutiny; Encounter; Twentieth Century; New Society; New Statesman; Ed., Universities Quarterly. Address: School of Education, University of Bristol, UK.

FORD, Charles Henri, b. 10 Feb. 1919, Miss., USA. Writer; Poet. Publs: The Garden of Disorder, 1938; The Overturned Lake, 1941; Sleep in a Nest of Flames, 1949; Spare Parts, 1966; Silver Flower Coo, 1968; Flag of Ecstasy, 1972. Address: 1 W. 72nd St., N.Y., NY 10023, USA.

FORD, Douglas William Cleverley, b. 1914, Sherringham, Norfolk, UK. Senior Chaplain to the Archbishop of Canterbury. Educ: B.D., M.Th., Univ. of London. Publs. incl: Preaching Today, 1969; An Expository Preacher's Notebook, 1960; A Theological Preacher's Notebook, 1962; A Pastoral Teacher's Notebook, 1965; The Churchman's Companion, 1964; A Reading of St. Luke's Gospel, 1967; Preaching at the Parish Communion on the Gospels, 1967; On the Epistles, 1968; On the Saints' Days, 1969; Have You Anything to Declare?, 1973; Preaching on the Special Occasions, 1975. Contbr. to: Expository Times. Address: Lambeth Palace, London SE1, UK.

FORD, Edmund Brisco, University Professor; Fellow, All Souls College, Oxford. Educ: M.A., D.Sc., Wadham Coll., Oxford Univ. Publs: Mendelism & Evolution; The Study of Heredity; Genetics for Medical Students; Butterflies; British Butterflies, 1951; Moths, 1955; Ecological Genetics (French, Italian & Polish transls.); Genetic Polymorphism. Contbr. to: Heredity; Advances in Genetics; Endeavour; Nature; Symposia in Quantitative Biol., Cold Spring Harbor, USA; Proceedings of Royal Inst.; num. other profl. jrnls. Hons: F.R.S.; F.R.C.P.; Medallist, Royal Society; D.Sc., Liverpool Univ.; Hon. Fellow, Wadham Coll., Oxford. Address: 5 Apsley Rd., Oxford, UK; All Souls Coll., Oxford, UK.

FORD George H(arry), b. 21 Dec. 1914, Winnipeg, Can. Professor of English; Author. Educ: B.A., Univ. of Man.; M.A., Univ. of Toronto; Ph.D., Yale Univ., USA. Publs: Keats & the Victorians, 1944; The Pickersgill Letters, 1948; Dickens & His Readers, 1955; Double Measure: A Study of D. H. Lawrence, 1965; Jt.-Ed., The Dickens Critics, Dickens' Hard Times & the Norton Anthol. of English Literature. Contbr. to: Nineteenth-Century Fiction. Mbrships: V.P., Dickens Fellowship, London; Supvsry. Comm., Engl. Inst.; Int. Assn. of Profs. of Engl.; Sec., Lit. Club of Cinn. Hons. incl: Fellow, Am. Coun. of Learned Socs., 1959; Guggenheim Fellow, 1964. Address: Dept. of Engl., Univ. of Rochester, Rochester, NY 14627, USA.

FORD, Gordon B., Jr., b. 22 Sept. 1937, Louisville, Ky., USA. Educator; Author. Educ: A.B., Princeton Univ., 1959; A.M., 1962, Ph.D., 1965, Harvard Univ; Study at univs. of Oslo, Uppsala, Stockholm, Sofia & Madrid. Publs. incl: The Ruodlieb: The First Medieval Epic of Chivalry from 11th-Century Germany, 1965; The Wolfenbüttel Lithuanian Postile Manuscript of the Year 1573, 1965-66; Isidore of Seville's History of the Goths, Vandals & Suevi, 1966, 1970; Readings in Historical Linguistic Methodology, forthcoming. Contbr. to profl. jrnls. Address: Dept. of English Lang. & Lit., Univ. of Northern Iowa, Cedar Falls, IA 50613, USA.

FORD, Jesse Hill, Jr., b. 28 Dec. 1928, Troy, Ala., USA. Author. Educ: B.A., Vanderbilt Univ., Tenn., 1951; M.A., Univ. of Fla., 1955; Univ. of Oslo, Norway, 1961. Publs: (novels) Mountains of Gilead, 1961; The Liberation of Lord Byron Jones, USA, 1965, UK, 1966; The Feast of St. Barnabas, 1969; (short stories) Fishes, Birds & Sons of Men, USA, 1967, UK, 1968; (Play) The Conversion of Buster Drumwright, 1964; (screenplay) The Liberation of L. B. Jones, 1969. Hons: Atlantic "Firsts" Awards, 1959; Fulbright Fellow, 1961; Guggenheim Fellow, 1966; D.Litt., Lambeth Coll., Jackson, Tenn., 1966. Address: Canterfield Farm, Route 3, Humboldt, TN 38343, USA.

FORD, Lee Ellen, b. 16 June 1917, Auburn, Ind., USA. Writer; Attorney. Educ: Ph.D., Iowa State Univ., Ames; J.D., Univ. of Notre Dame, Ind. Publs: Over 200 vols. inclng: The Dog in Research, 1955; Story of Shamrock Collies, 1956; The Smooth Collie, 1957; Advanced Genetics Course, 2 vols., 1958; Animal Welfare Encyclopedia, 6 vols., 1971-74; Women's Legal Handbook Series on Job & Sex Discrimination, 7 vols.; Directory of Women Attorneys in the US, 3rd ed., 2 vols., 1974. Contbr., num. articles & papers on genetics & cytol. of the dog, to sci. jrnls. &

proceedings of sci. acads., & to Am. Kennel Club Gazette. Address: 701 S. Federal Ave., Butler, IN 46721, USA.

FORD, Percy, b. 1894, Brighton, Sussex, UK. Emeritus Professor of Economics & University Administrator; Author; Editor. Educ: B.Sc., Ph.D., London Schl. of Econs. Publs. incl: Work & Wealth in a Modern Port, 1934; Theory & Social Practice, 1969; (w. G. Ford): Guide to Parliamentary Papers; Breviates of Parliamentary Papers, 1900-54, 3 vols.; Select Lists of Parliamentary Papers, 1834-99, 1955-64, 2 vols.; Irish Dail & Senate Papers, 1922-72; Eds., Hansards Breviate 1696-1834; L. G. Hansard's Diary, 1962; (w. J. Bound): Coastwise Shipping & the Small Ports; (w. C. Thomas & T. Ashton): Survey of Southampton. Contbr. to var. econ. jrnls. Co-recip. (w. wife), Hon. LL.D. Address: 34 Orchards Way, Southampton, UK.

FORDE-JOHNSTON, James, b. 7 May 1927, Liverpool, UK. Museum Curator. Educ: B.A., 1952. M.A., 1954, Univ. of Liverpool. Publs: Neolithic Cultures of North Africa, 1959; History from the Earth, 1974; Hillforts of the Iron Age in England & Wales, 1975. Contbr. to: Archaeol. Jrnl.; Prehistoric Soc. Proceedings. Archaeologia Camboensis; Country Life; Museums Jrnl. Mbrships: F.S.A.; Fellow, Royal Anthropol. Inst.; Mbr. & Past Ed., Royal Archaeol. Inst.; Prehistoric Soc. Address: 6 Greystoke Ave., Sale, Cheshire, UK.

FORDHAM, Michael, b. 1905, London, UK. Analytical Psychologist; Editor. Educ: B.A., M.D.; Trinity Coll., Cambridge; St. Bartholomew's Hosp., London. Publs: The Life of Childhood; The Objective Psyche, 1957; New Developments in Analytical Psychology; Children as Individuals, 1969. Contbr. to: Jrnl. Analytical Psychol. (Ed.); Collected Workd of C. J. Jung (Ed.); Lib. of Analytical Psychol.; var. sci. & popular jrnls. Mbrships: F.R.C.Psych.; F.B.Ps.S.; R.S.M.; S.A.P.; Brit. Psychol. Soc.; Royal Coll. of Psych. Address: 1 St. Katharine's Precinct, Regent's Park, London NW1 4HH, UK.

FORDHAM, Peta, pen name DIONYSUS, b. Birmingham, UK. Author; Journalist. Educ: Univ. of Sorbonne, Paris, France; Birmingham Univ., UK.; B.A., Girton Coll., Cambridge Univ. Publs: The Robbers' Tale, 1965; Inside the Underworld, 1972; var. legal books. Contbr. to: Illustrated London News (Wine Corres.); Law Guardian (Leisure Ed.); Europa (Food, Wine & Travel Corres.); Consumer's Assn. (first Dir. & Ed.); most leading newspapers, mags. & weeklies. Mbrships: Circle of Wine Writers (Hon. Sec.); Press Club. Recip., Glenfiddich Medal for Wine Writing, 1971. Agent: A. P. Watt. Address: 4 Paper Bldgs., Temple, London EC4, UK.

FORD-HOUSE, Iris E., pen name FONN, Belle, b. 10 Apr. 1919, Schoepke, Pelican Lake, Wis., USA. Nursing Home Owner-Administrator. Contbr. of articles & poems to: Youth Instr.; Life & Hlth.; Listen; Our Little Friend; The Ministry; Ideals; & num. others. Mbrships. incl: Wis. Rural Writers Assn. Hons. incl: 1st Place (3 times), Poetry Div., Rhinelander Schl. of the Arts Summer Workshop. Address: Box 857, Rhinelander, WI 54501, USA.

FOREMAN, Carl, b. 23 July 1914, Chgo., USA. Film Writer; Director; Producer. Educ: Univ. of Ill., 1932-33; Northwestern Univ., 1935-36; John Marshall Law Schl., 1936-37. Publs: num. films. Mbrships: Writer's Guild of GB (Pres. 1968-); F.R.S.A. Hons: Cmdr., Order of the Phoenix, Greece, 1962; Laurel Award for Achievement in Screen Writing, Writers' Guild of Am., 1969; C.B.E., 1970; Best Brit. Screenplay Award, Writers' Guild of GB, 1972; Film Writer of the Yr., Variety Club Award, 1972. Address: 25 Jermyn St., London SW1Y 6HR, UK.

FOREMAN, Russell Ralph, b. 1921, Melbourne, Australia. Newspaper Editor; Draughtsman; Teacher. Educ: Xavier Coll., Melbourne. Publs: The Science of Appearances (co-author); Long Pig, 1958; Sandalwood Island, 1961; The Ringway Virus. Mbrships: F.I.A.L.; L.T.C.L. Address: II Corneto, 50020 Panzano-in-Chianti, Prov. Florence, Italy.

FORMAN, Harrison, b. 15 June 1904, Milwaukee, Wis., USA. Journalist; Author. Educ: B.A., Univ. of Wis. Publs: Through Forbidden Tibet, Horizon Hunter; Report from Red China; Changing China; Blunder in Asia; How to Make Money with Your Camera; The Land & People of Nigeria (w. Brenda-Lu Forman). Contbr. to: Rdr.'s Digest; Life; Look; Harper's; Collier's; Cosmopolitan; Holiday; Argosy; True; This Week; Am. Weekly; Weekend; N.Y. Times Mag.; etc. Fndr.-mbr., Soc. of Mag. Writers, N.Y. Address: 40 Central Park S., N.Y., NY 10019, USA.

FORMAN, James Douglas, b. 12 Nov. 1932, Mineola, Long Island, N.Y., USA. Author; Attorney. Educ: B.A., Princeton Univ., USA, 1954; LL.B., Columbia Univ. Law Schl., USA, 1957. Publs. incl: The Skies of Crete, 1963; Ring the Judas Bell, 1965; My Enemy, My Brother, 1969; Ceremony of Innocence, 1970; Law & Disorder, 1972; Capitalism, 1972; Socialism, 1972; Communism, 1972; Code Name: Valkyrie, 1973; The Life & Death of Yellow Bird, 1973; Fascism, 1974; Anarchism, 1975; Follow the River, 1975. Contbr. to: Can. Arms Collecting Jrnl. Recip: Lewis Carrol Award, 1971. Address: 2 Glen Road, Sands Point, NY 11050, USA.

FORMAN, Joan, b. Louth, Lincs., UK. Writer. Educl. Plays: The Turning Tide; End of a Dream; Freedom of the House; Westward to Canaan. Other publs: Princess in the Tower, 1973; Haunted East Anglia, 1974. Contbr., var. jrnls., UK & Can. Mbrships: Soc. of Authors; Educl. Writers' Grp.; League of Dramatists. Address: 4 Seton Rd., Taverham, Norwich, Norfolk, UK.

FORMAN, Robert Edgar, b. 17 July 1924, Mpls., Minn., USA. Professor of Sociology. Educ: B.A., 1948, M.A., 1949, Ph.D., 1959, Univ. of Minn., Mpls. Publs: The University & its Foreign Alumni: Maintaining Overseas Contact, (w. F. G. Moore), 1964; Black Ghettos, White Ghettos, & Slums, 1971. Contbr. to: Am. Sociol. Review; Am. Jrnl. of Sociol.; Jrnl. of Criminal Law, Criminol., & Police Sci.; Soc. Sci.; The Soc. Studies. Mbrships: Am. Sociol. Assn.; N. Ctrl. Sociol. Soc.; ΛAUP. Address: 3159 Goddard Rd., Toledo, OH 43606, USA.

FOROSTENKO, Anatole A., b. 29 Aug. 1939, Branowichi, USSR. Professor of Russian Language & Literature; Translator. Educ: B.A., Rutgers — The State Univ., 1962; M.A., Ind. Univ., 1964; Ph.D., Bryn Mawr Coll., 1972. Publs: Major Novels of Jurii German & Their Evaluation by Soviet Critics, 1972. Contbr. to: Tri-Quarterly (Northwestern Univ.); Russian Lit. Tri-Quarterly; Russian Orthodox Jrnl.; Parade. Mbr., Am. Assn. of Tchrs. of Slavic & E. European Langs. Address: Apt. 578, 17825 King's Pk. Lane, Houston, TX 77058, USA.

FORREST, (Father) Stanley John, b. 18 Feb. 1904, Whalley Range, Manchester, UK. Hon. Chaplain to the Sisters of Bethany, Bournemouth. Educ: B.A., Univ. of Leeds. Ordained, 1929. Publs: The Church in Reconstruction, 1945; Buzzards at Play, 1946; Anglican Noah's Ark, 1949; Parish Fashions, 1950; What the Vicar Likes, 1951; What's the Use, 1955; Time for a Rhyme, 1957; Chapter & Verse, 1959; Town Parsons Day, 1960; Orders in Orbit, 1962; Our Man at St. Withits, 1965; Verse from the Vestry, 1966; Parsons Playpen, 1968; Saints and Sinods, 1971; The Church Bizarre, 1973. Contbr. to: Ch. Times; & other jrnls. Address: "St. Anne", House of Bethany, St. Clement's Gdns., Bournemouth, Hants. BH1 4DZ, UK.

FORSBERG, (Charles) Gerald, b. 18 June 1912, Vancouver, B.C., Can. Former Naval Officer & Civil Servant; Writer. Publs: Long Distance Swimming, 1957; First Strokes in Swimming, 1961; Modern Long Distance Swimming, 1963. Contbr. to: Nautical Mag.; Swimming Times; Blackwoods; Brassey's Annual; sev. encys. & maritime & profl. jrnls. Mbrships: Pres., Channel Swimming Assn., 1963—; Soc. for Underwater Technol.; Nautical Inst.; Liveryman, Hon. Co. of Master Mariners; Younger Brother, Trinity House. Hons. incl: O.B.E., 1955; Marathon Swimming Hall of Fame, USA, 1965; Davids-Wheeler Award for servs. to swimming, USA, 1971. Address: c/o Barclays Bank Int., Goodenough House, 33 Old Broad St., London EC2, UK.

FORSBERG, Franklin S., b. 21 Oct. 1905, Salt Lake City, Utah, USA. Publisher; Editor; Writer. Educ: B.S., Univ. of Utah; 2 yrs. study in Sweden; M.B.A., Grad. Schl. of Bus., N.Y. Univ., USA; LL.D., Univ. of Utah. Publs: Yank, the Army Weekly, 4 vols., (hist. of WWII). Contbr. to: Field & Stream; Popular Gardening; Yank; Stars & Stripes; Advertising Age; New Homes Guide; Home Modernizing Guide; num. sportsmen's mags. Hons: D.S.M., USA; O.B.E., UK; Outstanding Jrnlst. Award, Univ. of Utah, 1974; Royal Order of Vasa, Sweden. Address: 465 Lake Ave., Greenwich, CT 06830, USA.

FORSEE, Aylesa, b. Kirksville, Mo., USA. Writer. Educ: B.S., S.D. State Univ.; Mus.B., MacPhail Coll. of Music; M.A., Univ. of Colo. Publs. incl: The Whirly Bird, 1955; Frank Lloyd Wright: Rebel in Concrete, 1959; Women Who

Reached for Tomorrow, 1960; Albert Einstein: Theoretical Physicist, 1963; William Henry Jackson: Pioneer Photographer of the West, 1964; Pablo Casals: Cellist for Freedom, 1965; Men of Modern Architecture, 1966; Headliners, 1967; Famous Photographers, 1968; Artur Rubinstein; King of the Keyboard, 1969. Mbr., Exec. Bd., Nat. Writers' Club. Hons. incl: Helen Dean Fish Award, 1956; Achievement Award, Nat. Writers' Club, 1958; Top Hand Award, Colo. Authors' League, 1966, 1969. Address: 1845 Bluebell Avenue, Boulder, CO 80302, USA.

FORSHUFVUD, Sten Gabriel Bernhard, b. 1903, Ramsele, Sweden. University Professor; Author. Educ: O.Dr., Chir-dent. d'univ. Publs: Ueber Zahnschmelz, 1941; Tandernas Halsovard, 1946; Napoleon a-t-il-été empoisonné?, 1961; Who Killed Napoleon?, 1962; Liquidation of Napoleon I & Napoleon II. Contbr. to: Annales d'Anat.path; Acta paed.scand; Acta odont; Arkiv f. Zool.; Nature; Archiv f. Toxicologie. Mbr., Svenska Tandlakar Sallskapet. Address: Ulveliden 9, Goteborg O, Sweden.

FORSSTRÖM, Ingmar, b. 24 Jan. 1935, Halsingborg, Sweden. Journalist; Writer; Translator. Educ: B.A. Publs: Danmark, 1972; Your Child from A to Ö, 1973; Approx. 35 book transls. Contbr. to Swedish mags. & newspapers. Mbrships: PEN; Swedish Publicists' Club; Swedish Jrnlsts'. Assn. Hons: Grants, Swedish Authors Fund, 1967, 1969, 1970, 1971 & 1972. Address: Holmögaddsvagen 33, S-121 56 Johanneshov, Sweden.

FORSTER, Leonard Wilson, b. 1913, London, UK. Professor of German; Fellow, Selwyn College, Cambridge. Educ: M.A., D.Phil., Trinity Hall, Cambridge Univ.; Leipzig, Bonn, Königsberg & Basle Univs. Publs: G. R. Weckherlin: zur Kenntnis seines Lebens in England; Conrad Celtis; German Poetry 1944-48; Temper of 17th Century German Literature; Penguin Book of German Verse; Janus Gruter's English Years; The Icy Fire; The Poet's Tongues. Contbr. to: German Life & Letters; Mod. Lang. Review; num. German acad. jrnls. Mbr., Athenaeum Club. Address: 49 Maid's Causeway, Cambridge, UK.

FORSTER, Raymond Robert, b. 19 June 1922, Hastings, NZ. Museum Director. Educ: B.Sc.; M.Sc.; D.Sc.(NZ). Publs: Small Land Animals of New Zealand (w. L. M. Forster), 1970; New Zealand Spiders — an Introduction (w. L. M. Forster), 1973; Spiders of New Zealand, Parts I — IV (Parts II & IV w. C. L. Wilton). Contbr. to NZ Nature Heritage, 1974-75. Mbrships: Fellow, Royal Soc. of NZ; Fellow, Art Galls. & Museums Assn. NZ. Recip., Highly Commended Watties Book of the Yr. Award, for New Zealand Spiders, 1973. Address: 100 Norfolk St., St. Clair, Dunedin, NZ.

FORSTER, Reginald Kenneth, pen name KENDAL, Robert, b. 1915, Leeds, UK. Freelance Author & Journalist. Publs: The Postmark on a Letter, 1952; Postmark Collecting, 1960; Win Prize Competitions, 1971; World Postmarks, 1973. Contbr. to: Twixt Thee & Me (anthol.), 1974; Philatelic corres., Brit. & overseas newspapers & mags.; BBC radio & TV. Mbrships: Nat. Union of Jrnlsts.; Postmark Club; Brit. Postmark Soc.; Postal Hist. Soc. of NZ. Address: 122 Scholes Park Rd., Scarborough, Yorks. YO12 6RA, UK.

FORSYTH, Frederick, b. 1939, Ashford, Kent, UK. Journalist; Author. Educ: Univ. in Spain. Publs: The Day of the Jackal, 1971, sev. eds.; The Odessa File, sev. eds.; The Dogs of War, 1974. Formerly reporter, corres., Eastern Daily Press; Reuters; Daily Express; Evening Standard; Time. Recip. of awards. Address: c/o Corgi Books, Transworld Publishers Ltd., Cavendish House, 57-59 Uxbridge Rd., Ealing, London W5, UK.

FORSYTH, William Douglass, b. 5 Jan. 1909, Casterton, Australia. Retired Diplomat. Educ: Tchrs. Coll., Melbourne; M.A., Dip. Ed., Melbourne Univ.; B.Litt., Balliol Coll., Oxford Univ., UK. Publs: Governor Arthur's Convict System, 1935 (reprinted 1975); The Myth of Open Spaces, 1942; Captain Cook's Australian Landfalls, 1970; The Post Colonial Pacific, forthcoming. Contbr. to: Econ. Record; New Guinea; Austral-Asiatic Bulletin. Mbr., Aust. Soc. of Authors. Hons: Harbison Higginbotham Prize, Melbourne Univ., 1935, 1942; O.B.E., 1955. Address: 88 Banks St., Yarralumla, ACT 2600, Australia.

FORTUIN, Herman Bernhard, pen name VRIJBUITER, b. 9 July 1911, Rotterdam, Netherlands. Head of Drama, vara Television. Educ: Univ. of Amsterdam. Publs: Spiegelt u zacht, 1939; In England staat een huis, 1946; En nu hoort u Vrijbuiter, 1946; Klein Fortuin, 1965. Contbr. to: Snoeck's Almanack; Vrij Nederland (until 1954). Mbrships: Soc. of Authors, Amsterdam; Garrick & Savage Clubs, London. Address: Zwaluwenweg 27 A., Blaricum, Netherlands.

FOSKETT, Antony Charles, b. 1926, Ilford, Essex, UK. Principal Lecturer in Library Studies. Educ: M.A., Queen's Univ., Belfast; Fellow, Lib. Assn. Publs: A Guide to Personal Indexes, 2nd ed., 1970; The Subject Approach to Information, 2nd ed., 1971; The Universal Decimal Classification, 1973. Contbr. to: Lib. World; Lib. Assn. Record; Jrnl. Documentation. Mbrships: Lib. Assn.; Assoc., Lib. Assn. of Aust.; F.I.D./C.C.C. Address: c/o S. Australian Inst. of Technol., North Terrace, Adelaide, S. Australia 5000.

FOSKETT, Douglas John, b. 1918, London, UK. Librarian. Educ: Queen Mary Coll., & Birkbeck Coll. London Univ.; M.A.; Fellow, Lib. Assn. Publs: Assistance to Readers in Lending Libraries, 1952; Information Service in Libraries, 1958 & 1967; Bibliography of Food (w. E. A. Baker), 1958; Classification & Indexing in Social Science, 1963, 1975; How to Find Out: Educational Research, 1965; Classification for a General Indexing Language, 1970. Contbr. to: Lib. Assn. Record; Library; Lib. World; Libri; Revue de la Documentation; Nature; Times Lit. Supplement; UNESCO Bulletin for Libs. Address: Univ. of London, Inst. of Educ., Malet St., London WC1, UK.

FOSTER, Brian, b. 1920, Sunderland, UK. Lecturer. Educ: M.A., Univ. of Durham; Dr., Univ. de Paris, France. Publs: The Local Port Book of Southampton 1435-6, 1963; The Changing English Language, 1968. Contbr. to: Le français moderne; Vie et Langage; French Studies; Mod. Lang. Notes; Mod. Lang. Review; Notes & Queries; Erasmus; Anglia; Engl. Studies; New Soc.; etc. Mbr., Anglo-Norman Text Soc. Address: Cestria, 20 Ardnave Cres., Bassett, Southampton, UK.

FOSTER, Carno A., b. 16 Aug. 1916, Bridgetown, Barbados, W. Indies. Road Car Inspector. Educ: Dip., Utilities Engrng. Inst., Chgo., USA. Publs: Justice in Man; A Study of Political, Social & Religious Principles of Justice, 1972. Contbr. to N.Y. Daily News. Mbrships: Off., Fosters Social Club, Pres., Grand United Order of Odd Fellows, Barbados; Trustee, Barbados Wkrs. Union; Exec. Coun.; Labor Bd.; Pres., Adelphi Civic Assn., Organizer, Block Assns., Bklyn., N.Y., USA; Off., U-Care Coord. Coun., Lafayette Gdns. Coord. Coun., Bedford-Stuyvesant Pol. League. Address: 235 Sterling St., Brooklyn, NY 11225, USA.

FOSTER, Donald Abbotts, b. 1904, King's Heath, Worcs., UK. Clergyman; Vice-Prin. Queen's Coll., Birmingham, 1930-31; Asst. Priest, Coventry Cathedral, 1931-34; Vicar St. Stephen, Bradford, 1934-39; Chaplain R.A.F.V.R., 1939-45; Vicar St. Germains, Edgbaston, Birmingham, 1945-54; Vicar Lickey, Worcs., 1954-62; Rural Dean King's Norton, 1958-62; Vicar Knowle, 1962-71; Rural Dean Solihull, 1962-68. Educ: M.A., Oriel Coll., Oxford Univ.; Ripon Hall, Oxford. Publs: An Anglican Year. Hons: Hon. Canon of Birmingham Cathedral, 1961-71; Canon Emeritus, 1971. Address: Chalcroft, Little Bridge Rd., Bloxham, Banbury, Oxon., UK.

FOSTER, Joseph Reginald, b. 20 July 1920, Wanstead, UK. International Civil Servant. Educ: B.A., 1940, M.A., 1947, Merton Coll., Oxford. Publs: incl: Modern Christian Literature, 1965; num. transls. from French, German, Dutch & Italian, inclng. Daniel Rops' What is the Bible, 1958, Bouyer's Christian Initiation, 1960, Semyonov's Siberia, 1963, Kähler's Rome & her Empire, 1963; Garzetti's From Tiberius to the Antonines, 1974. Contbr. to: Dublin Review; Downside Review; The Saints: A Concise Biographical Dictionary, 1958; German Life & Letters; German Men of Letters; Swiss Men of Letters; etc. Recip., German Govt. Prize for transl. Address: 27 rue de Bourgogne, Beggen, Luxembourg.

FOSTER, Reginald Francis, b. 13 Apr. 1896. Former Indian Army Officer; Priest; Journalist. Publs. incl: The Missing Gates, 1925; The Captive King, 1927; Confession, 1928; The Music Gallery Murder, 1928; The Secret Places, 1929; Murder from Beyond, 1930; The Dark Night, 1930; Joyous Pilgrimage, 1930; Something Wrong at Chillery, 1931; Famous Short Stories Analysed, 1932; Separate Star (autobiography), 1938; Longshanks & I, 1939; The Island,

1946; The Ancient Way, 1949; Desert Journey, 1965; The Perennial Religion, 1969; The Unknown God, 1973; & num. short stories, essays, plays etc. Address: Swan Hotel, Alresford, Hants., UK.

FOTEV, Metodija, b. 14 Mar. 1932, Ljubojno, Yugoslavia. Journalist. Publs: Potomcite na Kat, 1966; Selani i Vojnici, 1968; Golemite Skitači, 1970. Contbr. to: Razgledi. Mbrships: PEN Club of Macedonia; Macedonian Writers Soc. Hons: Oct. Prize, 1967; Nov. 13th Prize, Town of Skopje, 1969. Address; Briselska St. 33, 91 000 Skopje, Yugoslavia.

FOTHERGILL, (Arthur) Brian, b. 1921, Lytham St. Annes, Lancs., UK. Author. Educ: King's Coll., London. Publs: The Cardinal King, 1958; Nicholas Wiseman, 1963; Mrs. Jordan: Portrait of an Actress, 1965; Sir William Hamilton: Envoy Extraordinary, 1969; The Mitred Earl, 1974. Contbr. to: Ency. Britannica; New Cath. Ency.; Corvo 1860-1960 (New Quests for Corvo). Mbrships: F.S.A.; F.R.S.L.; PEN; Reform Club. Recip., Heinemann Award, 1969. Address: 5 Lansdowne Square, Hove, Sussex BN3 1HE, UK.

FOTHERGILL, Colin Arnold, b. 2 Oct. 1926, Thorpe Bay, Essex, UK. Geologist. Educ: B.Sc. 1948, Ph.D., 1954, Univ. of London. Contbr. to: Petroleum; Inst. of Petroleum Publs.; var. sci. jrnls. Mbrships. incl: Fellow, Geol. Soc. of London; Inst. of Petroleum (Coun. 1968-74); Petroleum Exploration Soc. of GB (Chmn., 1970); Brit. Nat. Comm. for Geol., Royal Soc. Address: Eves Cottage, Danbury, Essex, UK.

FOUGÈRE, Jean, b. 5 May 1914, St. Amand, Cher, France. Writer. Publs. incl: (novels) La Pouponnière, 1948; La Cour des Miracles, 1955; La Vie de Chateau, 1958; Les Petits Messieurs, 1963; Nos Tantes d'Avalon, 1968; (short stories) Un Cadeau Utile, 1953; La Belle Femme, 1971; (essays) Voulez-vous Voyager Avec Moi?, 1957; Les Nouveaux Bovides, 1966; Lettre Ouverte à un Satyre, 1969. Contbr. to: Le Figaro; Les Nouvelles Littéraires. Former VP, Soc. of Men of Letters. Hons: Grand Prix, Soc. of Men of Letters, 1968; Grand Prix de la Nouvelle, Acad. Française, 1972; Chevalier Légion d'Honneur. Address: 22 quai de Bethune, 75004 Paris, France.

FOULDS, Elfrida Vipont, pen names VIPONT, Elfrida; VIPONT, Charles, b. 3 July 1902, Manchester, UK. Publs. incl: Blow the Man Down, 1939, 1951 (USA), 1953 (UK schl. edn.) & The Heir of Craigs, 1955, 1958 (both as Charles Vipont); The Birthplace of Quarkerism (as Elfrida Vipont Foulds), 1952, rev. 73; The Story of Christianity in Britain, 1960; The Pavilion, 1969; The Elephant & the Bad Baby, 1969; Towards a High Attic, 1970; Lancashire Hotpot, 1973; Bed in Hell, 1974; George Fox & the Valiant Sixty, 1975. Mbrships: PEN; Soc. of Authors. Recip., Carnegie Medal, 1950. Address: Green Garth, Yealand Conyers, Nr. Carnforth, Lancs., LA5 9SG, UK.

FOUNTAIN, Helen Van Alstyne, pen name TYLER, Lillian, b. 15 Oct. 1906, Westfield, N.J., USA. Teacher. Publs: Star Quest, 1967; A Cage of Birds, 1970. Contbr. to num., US, for. jrnls. & anthols. Mbrships: Poetry Soc. of Am.; World Poetry Soc. Intercontinental; Acad. of Am. Poets; World Poets Resource Ctr.; N.Y. Poetry Forum; N.J. Poetry Soc.; Pa. Poetry Soc.; Poetry Fellowship of Me.; Am. Poetry League; Haiku Soc. of Am. Num. poetry hons. incl: World Poet Award, WPSI, 1970; 1st Award, Poetry Fellowship of Me., 1973, 1974; 1st Awards, N.J. Poetry Soc.; Suffield Writer-Reader Conf., 1971. Address: 23 B Maryland Ave., Cedar Glen Lakes, Whiting, NJ 08759, USA.

FOWKE, Edith Margaret, b. 30 Apr. 1913, Lumsden, Sask., Can. Associate Professor of English. Educ: B.A.(Hons.), M.A., Univ. of Sask. Publs: Folk Songs of Canada, 1954; Folk Songs of Quebec, 1957; Canada's Story in Song, 1960; Songs of Work & Freedom, 1960; Traditional Singers & Songs from Ontario, 1965; More Folk Songs of Canada, 1967; Sally Go Round the Sun, 1969; Lumbering Songs from the Northern Woods, 1970; The Penguin Book of Canadian Folk Songs, 1974. Contbr. to: Can. Forum; Can. Lit.; Jrnl. Am. Folklore; etc. Mbrships. incl. Can. Authors' Assn.; Writers' Union of Can. Hons: Can. Assn. of Children's Libns. Medal, 1970; LL.D., Brock Univ., 1974. Address: 5 Notley Pl., Toronto, Ont. M4B 2M7, Can.

FOWLER, Alastair David Shaw, b. 17 Aug. 1930, Glasgow, UK. University Professor of English Literature.

Educ: Glasgow Univ.; M.A., Edinburgh Univ., 1952; M.A., 1955, D.Phil., 1957, D.Litt., Oxford Univ., 1972. Publs: Spenser & the Numbers of Time, 1964; The Poems of John Milton (Co-Ed., w. John Carey), 1968; Triumphal Forms, 1970; Contbr. to: New Lit. Hist. (Advsry. Ed.). Mbrships: F.B.A. (1974); English Assn.; Assn. Univ. Tchrs. Hons: Carlyle Soc. (Hon. Pres.). Address: Dept. English Lit., David Hume Tower, George Square, Edinburgh EH8 9JX, UK.

FOWLER, Charles B., b. 12 May 1931, Peekskill, N.Y., USA. Journalist in the Arts. Educ: B.S., Coll. of Potsdam, SUNY, 1952; M.M. in Mus. Ed., Northwestern Univ., Evanston, Ill., 1957; D.M.A., Boston Univ. Mass., 1964. Publs: The Search for Musical Understanding (co-author), 1973. Contbr. to: Music Educators Jrnl. (Ed., 1965-70); Parks & Recreation (Ed.-in-Chief, 1973-); Musical America (Educ. Ed., 1974-); var. mags. & profl. jrnls. Mbrships. incl: Music Educators Nat. Conf.; Music Critics Assn.; Soc. for Ethnomusicol. Hons. incl: Excellence in Educl. Jrnlsm. Cert., Educl. Press Assn. of Am., 1970; Disting. Alumnus Citation, SUNY, 1972. Address: 320 Second Street S.E., Washington, DC 20003, USA.

FOWLER, Sandra, b. 4 Feb. 1937, W. Columbia, W.Va., USA. Poet; Author. Educ: Study of poetry w. Lilith Lorraine, Avalon World Arts Acad.; Palmer Inst. of Authorship, 1966. Publs: In the Shape of Sun, 1972-73. Contbr. to US, Indian jrnls. & anthols.; Contbng. Ed., Ocarina (jrnl.), Madras. Mbrships: Hon. Rep., Centro Studi E. Scambi Int.; Rep.-at-large, World Poetry Soc. Intercontinental; Avalon World Arts Acad. Hons. incl: Certs. of Merit, Avalon Int. Poetry Contests, 1963, 1964; Acad. Leonardo da Vinci, 1968, 1971; Medal of Hon., Centro Studi E Scambi Int., 1967. Address: West Columbia WV 25287, USA.

FOWLER, Will, b. 29 Aug. 1922, Jamaica, N.Y., USA. Author; Public Relations Practitioner; Composer. Publs: The Young Man from Denver, 1962; The Life & Curious Death of Marilyn Monroe, (co-author), 1974; Sev. songs. Contbr. to: Life; Colliers; Etude; Am. Wkly; Westways; Reader's Digest; Callendar; Playboy; Holiday; V.I.P. Mbrships. incl: Fndr., Gtr. L.A. Press Club; Am. Soc. of Composers, Authors & Publrs.; Cath. Press Coun. Address: 16157 Morrison St., Encino, CA 91346, USA.

FOWLES, John, b. 31 Mar. 1926, Leigh-on-Sea, UK. Author. Educ: New Coll., Oxford. Publs: The Collector, 1963; The Aristos, 1965; The Magus, 1966; The French Lieutenant's Woman, 1969; Poems, 1973. Recip., PEN Silver Pen Award, 1969; W. H. Smith Award, 1970. Address: c/o Anthony Sheil Associates, 47 Dean St., London W1, 6HX, UK.

FOX, Adam, b. 15 July 1883, London, UK. Clergyman; Schoolmaster. Educ: M.A., Univ. Coll., Oxford; Fellow, Magdalen Coll., Oxford, 1929; Canon of Westminster, 1942-63. Publs: Old King Coel (verse), 1937; God is an Artist, 1957; Dean Inge (biog.), 1960; Plato for Pleasure, reprint, 1973. Mbrships: Athenaeum, London; Headmasters' Conf., 1919-24. Hons: Sacred Poem Prize, Oxford Univ., 1929; James Tait Black Mem. Book Award, for Best Biog., 1960. Address: 4 Little Cloister, Westminster Abbey, London SW1P 3PL, UK.

FOX, Charles K., b. 9 Sept. 1908, Harrisburg, Pa., USA. Editor; Conservationist. Educ: Harrisburg Acad., 1927; Lafayette Coll., 1931. Publs: Advanced Bait Casting, 1951; This Wonderful World of Trout, 1963; Rising Trout, 1967; Gettysburg, 1972; Civil War Highlights, 1972; The Book of Lures, 1975. Contbr. to: Esquire; Outdoor Life; Fly Fisherman; etc. Mbrships: Outdoor Writers Assn. of Am.; Pa. Outdoor Writers Assn. Address: Carlisle R.D.6, PA 17013, USA.

FOX, Leonard Phillips, b. 28 Aug. 1905, Melbourne, Australia. Journalist (retired); Teacher (retired); Editor (retired). Educ: Dip.Educ., Scotch Coll.; B.Sc., Melbourne Univ. Publs: Australia & the Jews, 1939; Monopoly, 1940; Australians in Spain (co-author), 1948; Friendly Vietnam, 1958; Strange Story of Eureka Flag, 1963; Vietnam Neighbors, 1966; Gumleaves & People, 1967; E. Phillips Fox, Notes & Recollections, 1969; Eureka & its Flag, 1973; Australia Taken Over, 1974. Contbr. to: Overland; Meanjin; etc. Mbrships. incl: Fellowship Aust. Writers; Aust. Soc. Authors. Hons: Grenfell Henry Lawson Festival Awards Verse (1962), Prose (1965). Address: 10 Little Surrey St., Potts Point, N.S.W. 2011, Australia.

FOX, Levi, b. 1914, Leics., UK. Director, Educational Trust. Educ: M.A., Dr.Lit.Hum., Oriel Coll., Oxford. Publs: Leicester Castle, 1943; Coventry's Heritage, 1946, 2nd ed. 1957; The Borough Town of Stratford-upon-Avon, 1953; Correspondence of the Reverend Joseph Greene, 1965; A Country Grammar School, 1967; In Honour of Shakespeare, 1972; Shakespeare's England, 1972; Stratford, Past & Present, 1975. Contbr. to: Hist.; Shakespeare Survey; Theatre Notebook; Archives; etc. Mbrships: F.R.S.L.; F.S.A.; F.R.Hist.S. Address: Silver Birches, 27 Welcombe Rd., Stratford-upon-Avon, Warwicks., UK.

FOX, Mona Alexis, pen name BRAND, Mona, b. 1915, Sydney, Australia. Advertising Copywriter; Part-time Lecturer; Playwright. Publs: (plays) Strangers in the Land, 1956; 3 Plays, 1965; Here Under Heaven — 3 plays (Mona Brand), 1969; (children's play) Flying Saucery; num. poems, articles & short stories. Mbrships: Aust. Soc. Authors; Aust. Writers' Guild; Fellowship Aust. Writers. Recip., 1972 Moomba Festival (Melbourne) Award for Christmas Goose, children's film script. Address: 10 Little Surrey St., Potts Point, Sydney, Australia.

FOX, Paula, b. 1923, NYC, USA. Novelist; Professor (writing workshop) State University of New York at Stony Brook. Educ: Columbia Univ. Publs: Desperate Characters, 1970; The Western Coast, 1972; (for children) How Many Miles to Babylon, 1967; Portrait of Ivan, 1969; Blowfish Live in the Sea, 1970; The Slave Dancer, 1973. Mbrships: PEN; Authors' League. Hons: Guggenheim Fellowship, 1972; Nat. Inst. Arts & Letters Award, 1972; Newberry Medal, 1974 for The Slave Dancer. Agent: Robert Lescher.

FOX, Samuel, b. 18 Mar. 1905, Chgo., Ill., USA. Professor; Attorney; Certified Public Accountant. Educ: Ph.B., M.B.A., Univ. of Chgo.; LL.M., J.D., Loyola Univ., Ph.D., Univ. of Notre Dame; C.P.A., Univ. of Wis. Publs. incl: Fundamental Cost Accounting, 1958; C.P.A. Law Review, 1960; Management & the Law, 1966; Managerial Law Workbook, 1972. Contbr. to num. profl. jrnls.; Book Reviewer, Choice mag., 1968—; Drama Critic, Des Plains Times, 1955-65; Sports Ed., ibid, & Park Ridge Herald, 1946-56. Mbr., Football Writers Assn. of Am. Address: Suite 7311, John Hancock Ctr., 175 E. Delaware Pl., Chgo., IL 60611, USA.

FOXALL, Raymond, b. 26 Mar. 1916, Irlam, Lancs., UK. Author. Educ: Manchester Coll. of Commerce. Publs: Here Lies the Shadow, 1957; Song for a Prince, 1959; The Devil's Smile, 1960; The Wicked Lord, 1962; John McCormack, 1963; The Devil's Spawn, 1965; Squire Errant, 1968; The Little Ferret, 1968; Brandy for the Parson, 1970; The Dark Forest, 1972. Contbr. to: Scottish & Universal Newspapers. Mbrships: Soc. of Authors; Nat. Union of Jnrlsts. Address: The Old Crossings House, Balgowan by Tibbermore, Perthshire PH1 1QW, UK.

FOXE, Arthur Norman, b. 28 June 1902, NYC, USA. Psychiatrist; Author; Editor. Educ: M.D., Jefferson Med. Coll., 1927. Publs. incl: Dilettantism, 1930; Garbo, A Commentary on the Times (under pen name Aun Foda), 1932; The Life & Death Instincts, 1939; Studies in Criminology, 1948; Catherine Eden Moore, A New Full-Length Gainsborough, 1958; Skating for Everyone, 1966; Early Poems, 1971; Advanced Studies in Criminology, 1972; Ed., Psychomatic Aspects of Surgery, 1956; Poems of Anna Seward & Catherine Sedley, 1971. Contbr. to num. profl. jrnls. & Ed., Assoc. or Contbng. Ed., var. jrnls. inclng. Psychoanalytic Review, 1939-55, Corrective Psychiatry & Jrnl. of Social Therapy, 1958—. Address: 9 E. 67th St., N.Y., NY, USA.

FOX HUTCHINSON, Juliet Mary, pen name PHOENICE, J., b. 13 Jan. 1911, London, UK. Author. Publs: (verse novels) The Harbour; A Rainbow of Paths; (autobiog.) The Third Day; (verse) Peke Posy. Contbr. to: Homes & Gardens; Country Life; Field; Lady; Yorks. Post; Scotsman; Glasgow Herald; N.Y. Times; Herald Tribune; Christian Sci. Monitor; Chatelaine (Can.); Tablet. Mbrships: Engl. Assn.; PEN. Address: Kyloe Old Vicarage, Berwick-on-Tweed TD15 2PG, UK.

FOXWELL, Ivan, b. 1914, London, UK. Film Writer; Producer. Educ: R.M.C., Sandhurst. Publs. (screenplays): Decline & Fall (co-author); No Room at the Inn; Guilt is My Shadow; The Intruder; The Colditz Story; A Touch of Larceny; Tiara Tahiti. Contbr. to var. mags. Address: 45 Chester Square, London SW1, UK.

FOY, Louis André, pen name (on radio) TELLIER, Jacques, b. 15 June 1912, Tournan-en-Brie, France. Journalist. Educ: LL.D., Univ. of Paris; M.A., Univ. of Calif., USA. Contbr. to: Paris Presse; France Soir; Combat; Jrnl. de Génève; Agence France Presse; var. French provincial newspapers; Radio Europe No. 1. Mbrships: Pres., UN Corres.'s Assn., 1971; White House Corres.'s Assn., Wash. D.C.; State Dept. Corres.'s Assn., Wash. D.C. Hons: Kt., French Légion d'hon.; Kt., Etoile Noire du Bénin; Kt., Order of Merit, Cameroon; Cmdr., Order of Henry the Navigator, Portugal. Address: 2905 N. St. NW., Wash. DC 20007, USA.

FRAENKEL, Heinrich, pen name ASSIAC, b. 1897, Lissa, Germany. Author; Lecturer; Scriptwriter; Freelance Journalist. Publs. incl: German People Versus Hitler; Winning of the Peace; The Other Germany; A Nation Divided; The Boy Between; Farewell to Germany; Adventure in Chess; The Delights of Chess; Dover, USA, enlarged ed., 1974; (w. Rattmann) Payot Aguilera; (w. Roger Manvell) The July Plot; Dr. Goebbels; Goering; Himmler; The Incomparable Crime; Canaris; Pictorial History of the German Cinema; Rudolf Hess; Inside Hitler, 1973; 100 Days to Hitler — Seizure of Power, 1974; & works published in German. Contbr. to: New Statesman; wkly Chess column as Assiac. Agent: J. Wolfers. Address: Christopher Cottage, Thaxted, Essex, UK.

FRAME, Donald Murdoch, b. 14 Dec. 1911, NYC, USA. Teacher. Educ: B.A., Harvard Coll., 1932; M.A., 1935, Ph.D., 1941, Columbia Univ. Publs. incl: Montaigne in France, 1812-1852, 1940. Montaigne, A Biography, 1965; Montaigne's Essais: A Study, 1969; Transl., Montaigne: The Complete Works, 1957, Voltaire: Candide, Zadig, & Selected Stories, 1961, Moliere: The Misanthrope & Other Plays, 1968. Contbr. to reviews. Hons: Medal for Disting. Achievement, Am. Soc. of French Legion of Hon., 1970. Address: 401 W. 118th St., N.Y., NY 10027, USA.

FRAME, Janet, b. 28 Aug. 1924, Dunedin, NZ. Author. Educ: Otago Univ. Tchrs. Trng. Coll. Publs. incl: (novels) Owls Do Cry, 1957; The Edge of the Alphabet, 1962; Scented Gardens for the Blind, 1963; The Adaptable Man, 1965; A State of Siege, 1966; The Rainbirds, 1968 (as Yellow Flowers in the Antipodean Room, USA 1969); Intensive Care, 1970; (stories) The Lagoon, 1951, revised ed., 1961; The Reservoir & Other Stories, 1966; (poems) The Pocket Mirror, 1967. Hons: Church Mem. Award, 1951, 1954; NZ Lit. Fund Award, 1960; NZ Schlrship in Letters, 1964; R. Burns Fellowship, Otago Univ., 1965. Address: c/o Brandt & Brandt, 101 Park Ave., N.Y., NY 10017, USA.

FRANÇA, José-Augusto, b. 16 Nov. 1922, Tomar, Portugal. Art Historian; University Professor; Editor. Educ: D. ès Lettres, Paris Univ.; D.Hist., Univ. of Paris. Publs. incl: Natureza Morta, (novel) 1949; Azazel (play) 1955; Despida Breve (short stories) 1956; Une Ville des Lumières: La Lisbonne de Pombal, 1965; A Arte em Portugal no século XIX, 2 vols., 1967; A Arte em Portugal no século XX, 1974; Le Romantisme au Portugal, 1975. Contbr. to: Coloquio/Artes (Ed.); etc. Mbrships. incl: Int. Comm. of Art Hist. (Chmn. Portugal); Nat. Acad. of Fine Arts (VP, 1975); Int. Assn. of Art Critics (VP 1971-73); Int. Assn. of Cultural Freedom. Recip., Knight, Order of Arts et Lettres, France, 1973. Address: Rua Escola Politecnica 49-4-Lisbon 2, Portugal.

FRANCE, Thelma Edith Minnie, pen name BERG, Rilla, b. 31 Oct. 1907, Wellington, NZ. Nurse; Author. Educ: Wellington Tech. Coll.; Vic. Univ., Wellington; B.A., 1972. Author, The Glitter Not the Gold, 1974. Former Ed., League of Mothers Mag. Contbr. to: NZ Home Jrnl.; Weekly News; Evening Post; Hawke Bay Herald Tribune; Nelson Mail; Southland News; Relig. Mag., Aust. Mbrships: Past Sec., Treas., Comm. Mbr., NZ Women Writers' Soc.; Women Writers & Jrnlsts., London; Fedn. of Univ. Women, NZ. Address: 68 Mairangi Rd., Wadestown, Wellington 1, NZ.

FRANCIS, H(erbert) E(dward, Jr.), b. 11 Jan. 1924, Bristol, R.I., USA. University Professor; Writer. Educ: B.A., Univ. of Wis., 1948; M.A., Brown Univ., 1950. Publs: Cinco millas hasta diciembre y Como los peces, como los pajaros, como la hierba (stories), 1965; Toda la gente que nunca tuce (story collect. in Spanish), 1966; The Itinerary of Beggars (story collec.), 1973. Contbr. to: Harper's Bazaar; etc. Mrbships: Pres., Huntsville Lit. Assn., Ala.; Southeastern MLA. Hons. incl: Inclusion in Best Am. Short Stories, 1967, & Ala. Prize Stories, 1970; John H. McGinnis

Mem. Award for Best Story, 1968; Iowa Schl. of Letters Award for Short Fiction, 1973. Address: 508 E. Clinton Ave., Huntsville, AL 35801, USA.

FRANCIS, Richard Stanley, pen name, FRANCIS, Dick, b. 31 Oct. 1920, Coedcanlas, nr. Tenby, Pembrokeshire, UK. Author; former Professional Steeplechase Jockey. Publs: (autobiog.) The Sport of Queens, 1957; Dead Cert, 1962; Nerve, 1964; For Kicks, 1965; Odds Against, 1965; Flying Finish, 1966; Blood Sport, 1967; Forfeit, 1968; Enquiry, 1969; Rat Race, 1970; Bonecrack, 1971; Smokescreen, 1972; Slay-Ride, 1973; Knock Down, 1974. Contbr. to: Sports Illustrated; Copes Ency.; etc. Mbrships. incl: Crime Writers' Assn. (Chmn. 1973-74). Hons. incl. Silver Dagger Award, Crime Writers' Assn.; Edgar Allen Poe Award, Mystery Writers of Am. (Forfeit), 1970. Address: Penny Chase, Blewbury, nr. Didcot, Oxon. OX11 9NH, UK.

FRANCIS, W. Nelson, b. 1910, Phila., USA. University Professor. Educ: A.B., Harvard Coll.; M.A., Ph.D., Univ. of Pa. Publs: Ed., Book of Vices & Virtues, 1942; The Structure of American English, 1958; The English Language: An Introduction, 1965; Computational Analysis of Present-Day American English (w. Henry Kucera), 1967. Contbr. to: PMLA; Coll. Engl.; William & Mary Quarterly; Quarterly Jrnl. of Speech; Explicator; Am. Speech; Lang.; Orbis; Archivum Linguisticum; Lang. Learning; Speculum; etc. Mbrships: MLA; Linguistic Soc. of Am.; Am. Dialect Soc. Address: 45 Appian Way, West Barrington, RI 02890, USA.

FRANCOIS, André, b. 1915, Timisoara, Rumania. Author; Book Illustrator; Artist. Educ: Ecole des Beaux-Arts, Schl. of Cassandre, Paris, France. Publs: Ubu Roi; The Tattooed Sailor (drawings); The Half-Naked Knight; Crocodile Tears; Lettres des Iles Baladar (w. Jacques Prevert); Contes Drolatiques by Balzac; The Biting Eye (drawing & paintings). Contbr. to New Yorker. Mbr., Savage Club. Address: 95810 Grisy-les-plâtres, France.

FRANDSEN, Arden N., b. 4 Feb. 1902, Redmond, Utah, USA. Psychologist. University Teacher. Educ: M.S., 1929, Univ. of Utah; Ph.D., Univ. Minn., 1932. Publs: How Children Learn, 1957; Educational Psychology, 1961; 2nd ed. 1967. Contbr. to num. sci. jrnls. Mbrships: Am. Psychol. Assn.; Nat. Soc. for the Study of Educ. Address: 550 E. 6N., Logan, Utah, USA.

FRANK, Gerold, b. 1907, Cleveland, Ohio, USA. Journalist; Magazine Editor. Educ.: M.A.; Ohio State Univ.; Western Reserve Univ. Publs. incl: USS Seawolf (co-author), 1945; I'll Cry tomorrow (co-author), 1954; Too Much Too Soon (co-author), 1957; Beloved Infidel (co-author), 1959; The Deed, 1963; The Boston Strangler, 1966; An American Death: The True Story of the Assassination of Dr. Martin Luther King, Jr., 1972; Judy: A Biography of Judy Garland, 1975. Contbr. to: Nation; New Repub.; Harper's; New Yorker; etc. Mbrships. incl: Authors' League. Agent: William Morris Agcy. Address: c/o William Morris Agency, 1350 Avenue of the Americas, N.Y., NY 10019, USA.

FRANKEL, Joseph, b. 30 May 1913, Lwow, Poland. Professor of Politics. Educ: M.L., Univ. Lwow, 1935; LL.M., Univ. W. Aust.; 1948; Ph.D., Univ. London, 1950. Publs: The Making of Foreign Policy, 1962; International Relations, 1964, 2nd ed., 1969; International Politics: Conflict & Harmony, 1969, 1971; National Interest, 1970; International Theory & the Behaviour of States, 1973; British Foreign Policy 1945-1973, 1975. Contbr. to: Int. Affairs. Mbrships: Royal Inst. Int. Affairs; Int. Inst. for Strategic Studies; Pol. Studies Assn., UK; Brit. Int. Studies Assn.; London Inst. World Affairs; Univ. Assn. Contemporary European Studies. Address: The Old Rectory, Avington, Winchester, Hants, UK.

FRANKEN, Rose, (Mrs W. B. Meloney), b. 28 Dec. 1898, Texas, USA. Novelist; Playwright. Publs. incl: (novels): Pattern, 1925; Twice Born, 1935; Of Great Riches, 1937 (as Gold Pennies, UK, 1938); Claudia: the story of a marriage, 1939; Claudia & David, 1940; The Fragile Years, 1952; Rendezvous (as the Quiet Heart, UK), 1954; Return of Claudia, 1957; Antic Years, 1958; When All is Said & Done (autobiography), 1963; You're Well out of Hospital, 1966; (plays): Another Language, 1932; Claudia, 1941; Outrageous Fortune, 1944; Hallams, 1948; also var. short stories. Address: 5026 Arlington Ave., Riverdale, N.Y. USA.

FRANKENBURG, Charis Ursula, b. 1892, Isleworth, Middx., UK. Educ: Somerville Coll., Oxford; Clapham Maternity Hosp.; J.P., M.A.; S.C.M. Publs: Peter's Pages, 1920; Common Sense in the Nursery, 1922-54; Latin with Laughter, 1931; More Latin with Laughter, 1934; I'm All Right; or Spoilt Baby into Angry Young Man, 1961. Common Sense About Children: a Parent's Guide to Delinquency, 1971; Not Old, Madam, Vintage (autobiog.), 1975. Contbr. to: Guardian; Nursery World; Women in Coun. Mbrships: Magistrates' Assn.; Brit. Fedn. of Univ. Women; Soc. of Authors; Royal Coll. of Midwives; Nat. Coun. of Women. Address: 111 Marsham Ct., Marsham St., London SW1P 4LB, UK.

FRANKLIN, Alfred White, b. 2 June 1905, London, UK. Children's Physician. Educ: M.A., M.B., B.Chir., Cambridge; F.R.C.P., London. Publs: Ed., Selected Writings of Sir D'Arcy Power, 1931; Selected Writings of Sir William Osler, 1951; World Blindness, 1962; Children with Communication Problems, 1966; Selected Writings of Lord Moynihan, 1969; Ed., Concerning Child Abuse, 1975. Mbrships: Pres., Brit. Paediatric Assn., 1968-69; Pres., Sect. of Paediatrics, Royal Soc. of Med., 1964-65; Chmn., Invalid Children's Aid Assn., 1952-65. Hons: Osler Orator, Royal Coll. of Physns. of London, 1971. Address: 149 Harley St., London W1N 2DE, UK.

FRANKLIN, Ben B., b. 7 Nov. 1944, Topeka, Kan., USA. Lecture Manager. Educ: B.A., Univ. of Colo., 1967. Contbr. to: Guideposts; Nat. Enquirer; Luth. Digest; Power Life; Trail & Timberline; Christian Athlete. Mbrships: Explorers' Club, N.Y.; Adventurers' Club, N.Y.; Circumnavigators' Club; Adventurers' Club, Chgo. Address: 503 Kansas Ave., Topeka, KS 66603, USA.

FRANKLIN, Henry, b. 1906, London, UK. Lawyer; Politician. Educ: B.A., Exeter Coll., Oxford; Lincoln's Inn; Barrister-at-Law. Publs: Ignorance Is No Defence; Unholy Wedlock; Crash; Don't Go To Centa; The Flag-Wagger. Contbr. to: World Digest; Spectator; Times; BBC; etc. Address: Warren House, Warren Lane, Froxfield, Hants., UK.

FRANKLYN, Charles Aubrey Hamilton, pen name BLANCH LYON HERALD, b. 25 Aug. 1896, Brentwood, Essex, UK. Physician; Author; Genealogical Historian. Educ: St. Thomas's Hospital; Univs. of London, Oxford & Lausanne, Switz.; M.A.; M.D.; M.B.; B.S. Publs: incl: The Bearing of Coat-Armour by Ladies, 1923; English & Scottish Heraldry Compared & Contrasted, 1925; University Hoods & Robes, 1925; Genealogical History of the Families of Paulet, Berewe, Lawrence, & Parker, 750-1965, 1965; Supplement to the Paulet Book, 1969; Academical Dress from the Middle Ages to the Present Day, including Lambeth Degrees, 1970. Contbr. to num. encys. Mbrships: F.L.S.; F.S.A. (Scotland); M.R.C.S.; L.R.C.P. Recip., hon. D.Litt. Address: Wickham Hill House, Hassocks, Sussex, UK.

FRANSE, Petrus Wilhelmus, pen names BUYSMAN, F. M.; RÉTY, Michael, b. 23 Feb. 1921, Haarlem, Netherlands. TV Plays: Watchers near the Grave, 1962; A Half-Way Inn, 1963; Waiting for Johannes, 1969; Abraham, 1973. Contbr. to: Haarlems Dagblad. Mbr: Dutch Soc. of Writers. Address: Van Nonhuysstr. 17, Haarlem, Netherlands.

FRANTA, Wilmont, b. 17 Apr. 1940, Vienna, Austria. Building Engineer. Educ: Studied engrng., Tech. High Schl.; studies in Paris, Munich & Moscow. Publs: Tel-Wolle im Bauwesen, 1973; Erdölersparnis durch Bauliche Massnahmen, 1973; Technisches Handbuch '73, 1974; Ökonomie der Roofing-Platte, 1974; var. scenarios for tech. films, 1964—. Contbr. to: Architektur Aktuell; Arbeiter-Zeitung; Technische Revue; Austropublic. Mbrships. incl: Bund Sozialistischer Akademiker, Intellektueller & Künstler; Ingenieur & Architektenverein; Club der Luftfahrtpublizisten. Recip., Tech. Lit. Prize, 1969. Address: Hochhaus-Praterstern, Vienna, Austria.

FRANZÉN, Gösta, b. 14 June 1906, Soderkoping, Sweden. University Professor of Scandinavian Languages. Educ: M.A., 1929, Ph.D., 1937, Uppsala Univ.; Heidelberg Univ.; Marburg Univ. Publs: Vikbolandets by och gardnamn, 1937; Amerikansk kateder och svensk, 1947; Runo ortnamn, 1959; Laxdoelabygdens ortnamn, 1964; Faroiska batnamn, 1966; Prose & Poetry of Modern Sweden, 1969; Gustavia on Saint Barthélemy, 1974. Contbr. to: Scandinavica; Mod. Philol.; Names; etc. Mbrships. incl: Soc. Advancement Scandinavian Study

(Pres. 1958-59). Hons. incl: Kt. Order Vasa, 1950; Kt. Order N. Star (Sweden), 1962; Kt. Order St. Olaf (Norway), 1972. Address: Sunnerstavaegen 19B, 75251 Uppsala, Sweden.

FRANZEN, Lars-Olof, b. 21 June 1936, Vastra Rud, Sweden. Literary Critic. Educ: B.A. Publs: Omskrivningar (Rewritings), 1968; Danskbilder (Danish Pictures), 1971. Contbr. to: Dagens Nyheter; Swedish Broadcasting Corp. Mbrships: PEN; Swedish Authors' Union. Address: Lidnersgatan 12, 11253 Stockholm, Sweden.

FRANZERO, Carlo Maria, b. 21 Dec. 1892, Turin, Italy. Author; Journalist. Educ: LL.D., Univ. of Turin. Publs: Roman Britain, 1935; Oscar Wilde, 1937; Inside Italy, 1941; House of Mrs. Caroline, 1942; Appassionata, 1946; Memoirs of Pontius Pilate, 1948; Nero, 1954; Cleopatra, 1957; Beau Brummell, 1958; Tarquin the Etruscan, 1960. Theodora, 1961; Quartet of Biog. Works in Italian, 1965-72; Conquant'anni a Londra. Contbr. to: Daily Telegraph, 1941-46; The Spectator; Il Tempo, 1950—. Mbrships: For Press Assoc.; Società degli Autori. Recip., Grand Officer, Italian Repub. Address: Cobham Lodge, Cobham, Surrey, UK.

FRASER, Amy Stewart, b. 23 Dec. 1892. Glen Gairn, Ballater, Scotland, UK. Publs: The Hills of Home, 1973. Contbr. to: Scottish Field; Scots Mag.; Aberdeen Press & Jrnl.; Glasgow Herald; Country Fair; The Gallovidian. Mbrships. incl: Carlisle City Coun. (ret'd.); Nat. Coun. of Women, Carlisle br. (past Pres.); N.S.P.C.C., Carlisle Br. (Past Pres.); W.V.S. (County Borough Organiser). Hons: Scottish Arts Coun. Merit Award; Long Serv. Medal, W.V.S.; M.B.E., 1974. Address: Hill Crest House, Harraby Grove, Carlisle CA1 2QN, Cumbria, UK.

FRASER, Anthea Mary (née Roby), b. 18 Aug. 1930, Blundellsands, Lancs., UK. Writer. Publs: Designs of Annabelle, 1971; In the Balance, 1973; Laura Possessed, UK & USA, 1974; Home Through the Dark, UK 1974 & USA 1976; Whistler's Lane, UK & USA 1975. Contbr. to: Homes & Gardens; Woman's Own; New Idea, Aust.; Fair Lady, Femina, S. Africa; Woman's Wkly.; Cosmopolitan. Agent: Laurence Pollinger Ltd. Address: 26 Celtic Ave., Shortlands, Bromley, Kent, UK.

FRASER, (Lady) Antonia, b. 1932, London, UK. Author. Educ: Univ. of Oxford. Publs: King Arthur, 1954, 2nd ed., 1970; Robin Hood, 1955, 2nd ed., 1971; Dolls, 1963; History of Toys, 1966; Mary Queen of Scots, 1969; Cromwell Our Chief of Men, 1973; King James, 1974. Contbr. to: Fin. Times; Weekend Telegraph; Nova; Vogue; Ed., Brit. Vogue, 1964-69; Evening Standard. Mbrships: Brit. Arts Coun., 1970-72; Chmn., Soc. of Authors, 1974—. Recip., James Tait Black Mem. Award for Biog., for Mary Queen of Scots. Address: 52 Campden Hill Square, London W8, UK.

FRASER, (Sir) (Arthur) Ronald, b. 3 Nov. 1888. Former Civil Servant. Publs. incl: The Flying Draper, 1924; Flower Phantoms, 1926; The Vista, 1928; Marriage in Heaven, 1932; Tropical Waters, 1933; The Ninth of July, 1934; Miss Lucifer, 1939; The Fiery Gate, 1943; Maia, 1948; Sun in Scorpio, 1949; Beetle's Career, 1951; Glimpses of the Sun, 1952; Latin America: A Personal Survey, 1953; Lord of the East, 1956; The Wine of Illusion, 1957; A Visit from Venus, 1958; Trout's Testament, 1959; City of the Sun, 1961; The Mysteries of Chartres Cathedral (transl. from the French of L. Charpentier), 1972. Address: Swanlands, Hill Top Lane, Chinnor, Oxford, UK.

FRASER, Conon, b. 8 Mar. 1930, Cambridge, UK. Film Director. Educ: Royal Mil. Acad., Sandhurst. Publs. incl: Looking at New Zealand; The Underground Explorers; Oystercatcher Bay; Shadow of Danger; Lim of Hong Kong. Contbr. to: NZ Listener; NZ Bookworld; New Zealand's Heritage. Mbr., PEN, NZ. Address: 25 Boundary Rd., Kelburn, Wellington 5, NZ.

FRASER, Derek, b. 1940, Birmingham, UK. Senior Lecturer in History, University of Bradford, since 1973. Educ: B.A., M.A., Ph.D., Univ. Leeds. Publs: The Evolution of the British Welfare State, 1973; Urban Politics in Victorian England (forthcoming). Contbr. to: Northern Hist.; Urban Hist. Newsletter; Publs. Thoresby Soc. Mbrships: Histl. Assn.; Assn. Univ. Tchrs.; Chapel Allerton Squash Club. Address: 12 The Cres., Leeds LS17 7LX, Yorks., UK.

FRASER, Douglas Jamieson, pen name HOPE, David, b. 12 Jan. 1910. Poet. Publs: Landscape of Delight (poems in Scots & Engl.), 1967; Rhymes o' Auld Reekie, 1973. Contbr. to: Scots Mag. Burns Chronicle; Friendship Book; Fireside Book. Mbrships: Comm. Mbr., Scottish PEN; Hon. Treas., Scottish Assn. for Speaking of Verse; Hon. Sec., Edinburgh Poetry Club. Hons: Consolation Prize, Scotsman Burns Bi-Centenary Competition, 1959; Int. Who's Who in Poetry Prize, 1974. Address: 2 Keith Terrace, Edinburgh EH4 3NJ, UK.

FRASER, George MacDonald, b. 1925, Carlisle, Cumberland, UK. Writer; Former Newspaperman. Publs: Flashman, 1969; Royal Flash, 1970; The General Danced at Dawn, 1970; The Steel Bonnets, 1971; Flash for Freedom! , 1971; Flashman at the Charge, 1973; McAuslan in the Rough, 1974; The Three Musketeers (screenplay), 1974. Contbr. to: Glasgow Herald (Dpty. Ed., 1964-69); Economist; Book World; var. newspapers & mags. Mbr., Nat. Union of Jrnlsts. Agent: John Farquarson Ltd. Address: The Bungalow, Baldrine, Isle of Man, UK.

FRASER, Ian Watson, b. 23 Oct. 1907, Wellington, NZ. Minister of Religion (retired). Educ: B.A., 1927, M.A., 1928, Victoria Univ. of Wellington; B.D., Melbourne Coll. of Divinity; Univ. of Edinburgh; Univ. of Bonn, Germany; S.T.M., 1932; Th.D., 1933, Union Theol. Sem., NYC. Publs. incl: Understandest Thou?. 1946; Understanding the Old Testament, 1958; Journey into the Shadows, 1958; var. pamphlets; Contbr. to: NZ Jrnl. of Theol.; Outlook. Mbr., Hon. Sec. & Treas., Friends of the Knox Coll. Lib. Hons: C.M.G., 1973; Refugee Award, Nat. Coun. of Chs., NZ, 1970. Address: 17 Hinau St., Linden, Wellington, NZ.

FRASER, Shelagh, pen names GYLES, Sheila; SYDNEY, Carol, b. Purley, Surrey, UK. Actress; Playwright; Author. Publs: Tai-Lu Talking, 1952; Tai-Lu Flies Abroad, 1955; Come to Supper, 1956; Say Cheese, 1958; Cheeses of Old England, 1960; Carol Goes Cooking, 1962; Captain Johnnie, 1965; (plays) Judith, 1948; Always Afternoon, 1950; Sundown, 1952; Fools of Fortune, 1953; Time of Departure, 1971. Contbr. to: Scotsman; Daily Herald; Homes & Gardens; Sunday Express; BBC Woman's Hour & Today progs. Mbrships: Authors' Soc.; Brit. Actors Equity. Address: 31 Cadogan Place, London SW1, UK.

FRASER, Thomas Layton, b. 16 Mar. 1899, Hinesville, Ga., USA. Clergyman; Professor Emeritus of Bible. Educ: B.A., Davidson Coll., B.D., Th.D., Union Theol. Sem., Richmond, Va.; M.S.T., N.Y. Theol. Sem. Publs: A Survey of the Old Testament; The Life & Philosophy of Christ; The Christian Life; The Acts & Teaching of the Apostles (all coll. study guides); God & His People; With Saviour & Friend (Jr. H.S. ch. schl. mat.); The Hope of Man (short film); Jesus & The Land He Loved, 1975. Mbr., Am. Schls. of Oriental Rsch. Address: 306 Hickory St., Clinton, SC 29325, USA.

FRASER, Walter Ian Reid (Rt. Hon. Lord Fraser of Tullybelton), b. 3 Feb. 1911, Glasgow, UK. Lord of Appeal in Ordinary. Educ: B.A., Balliol Coll., Oxford, 1932; LL.B., Glasgow Univ., 1935; Queen's Coun., Scotland. Publs: Outline of Constitutional Law. Mbrships: Dean., Fac. of Advocates, Scotland, 1959-64; Judge of Court of Session, 1964-75. Address: Tullybelton House, Bankfoot, Perthshire, PH1 4DH, UK.

FRATCHER, William F(ranklin), b. 4 Apr. 1913, Detroit, Mic., USA. Professor of Law. Educ: B.A., Coll. of City of Detroit; M.A., Wayne Univ.; J.D., LL.M., S.J.D., Univ. of Mich.; Grad., Command & Gen. Staff Schl., AUS,; Univ. of Paris; Ford Fndn. Fellow, Univ. of London; Rsch. Grantee, Int. Assn. of Legal Sci., Oxford Univ. Publs. incl: The National Defense Act, 1945; Perpetuities & Other Restraints, 1954; Trusts & Estates in England, 1968; Uniform Probate Code (w. others), 1970; Fascicle on Trust, Int. Ency. Comp. Law, 1974. Contbr. to num. profl. jrnls. & Ency. Britannica. Address: Tate Hall, Columbia, MO 65201, USA.

FRATTI, Mario, b. 5 July 1927, L'Aquila, Italy. University Professor; Drama Critic; Playwright. Educ: Ph.D., Ca'Foscari Univ., Venice, Italy. Publs. incl: Masterpieces of the Modern Italian Theatre, 1967; Best Short Plays, 1967; L'Ospite Romano, 1968; Che Guevara, 1970; Mafia, 1971; Themes, 1971; La Vittima, 1972; Teatro Americano, 1972; Eleonora Duse, 1972; Roman Guest, 1973; Seducers, 1973. Contbr. to var. mags. Mbrships: Drama Desk; Outer Circle. Recip., 1st Prize for radio drama, Arta-Terme Award, 1973. Address: 145 W. 55th St., Apt. 15D, N.Y., NY 10019, USA.

FRAYN, Michael, b. 1933, London, UK. Author; Journalist. Educ: B.A., Emmanuel Coll., Cambridge Univ. Publs: The Tin Men, 1965; The Russian Interpreter, 1966; Towards the End of the Morning, 1967; A Very Private Life, 1968; Sweet Dreams, 1973; Constructions, 1974; (plays) The Two of Us, 1970; The Sandboy, 1971; Alphabetical Order, 1975. Contbr. to: The Observer (columnist 1963-68); The Guardian (reporter & columnist, 1957-63). Mbrships: F.R.S.L. Hons: Somerset Maugham Award, 1966; Hawthornden Prize, 1967; Nat. Press Award, 1970. Agent: Elaine Greene Ltd. Address: c/o Agent, 31 Newington Green, London N16 9PU, UK.

FREDBORG, Erik Lars Arvid, b. 8 Oct. 1915, Hudiksvall, Gävleborgs län, Sweden. Foreign Policy Consultant; Editor. Educ: M.A., Univ. of Uppsala; Ph.D., Univ. of Stockholm; Univs. of Vienna & Budapest, 1934-35. Publs: Bakom stålvallen, 1943; Tredje gången, 1948; Storbritannien et den ryska fragan 1918-20, 1951; Det nya Tyskland, 1953; Nationalismens oroshärdar, 1962; Problems of Southern Africa, 1965; Inflation, 1971. Contbr. to: Int. Background, Vaduz; Svensk Tidskrift, Stockholm. Mbrships: Int. Coun., European Ctr. Of Documentation & Info.; Publicistklubben, Stockholm. Address: Nr. 384, FL-9497 Triesenberg, Principality of Liechtenstein.

FREDELIUS, Claes Hjalmar, b. 24 Apr. 1945, Stockholm, Sweden. Metal Worker. Educ: Fil.kand. Publs. (novels): Monologue for Three, 1967; To Live Objectively, 1968; It's Right to Rebel, 1970. Contbr. to: Bonniers Litterära Mag.; Häften för Kritiska Studier (critical studies); Uttryck (Expression); Arbetar Kamp (Worker's Struggle). Mbrships: Soc. of Swedish Authors; Författarcentrum; Författar förlaget; Soc. of Swedish Metalworkers. Address: Ulrikagatan 2, Stockholm, Sweden.

FREDERIKSEN, Emil, b. 2 June 1902, Literary Critic. Educ: Univs. of Copenhagen, Uppsala, Lund, Berlin & Paris. Publs. incl: Fra Sazo til Hjalmar Gullberg, 1944; Ung Dansk Literatur, 1945, 1952; Johannes Jorgensens Ungdom, 1946; Den unge Grundtvig og andre Essays, 1948; Dante, 1965; Jacob Paludan, 1966; H. C. Branner, 1967; W. A. Linneman, 1969; Knuth Becker, 1970. Contbr. to: Kristeligt Dagblad, 1936-44; Berlingske Tidende, 1944-; Ed., Gads Danske Magasin, 1942-55. Address: H. A. Clausens V. 24, 2820 Gentofte, Denmark.

FREDIN, Lars Olof, b. 27 Mar. 1919, Stockholm, Sweden. Poet. Publs. incl: Utan villkor, 1944; Vindbrygga, 1954; Jordorgel, 1955; Den Blinda jorden, 1957; molnfönster, 1963; rummet, 1965; bilden, 1967; svit, 1968; i kväll i natt, 1970; ur gräsboken, 1971; Rosen, 1973; till födelse, 1973; rymd och korn, 1974; i åderträdet, 1975. Contbr. to: Bonniers Lit. Mag.; Böckernas värld, Horisont; Lyrikvännen; Ord & Bld; Arbetet; etc. Hons. incl: FIB Poetry Club Stipendium, 1970; Swedish Radio Stipendium, 1972; Swedish Acad. Stipendium, 1974. Address: Hägerstensvägen 123, 126 48 Hägersten, Sweden.

FREED, Louis Franklin, b. 13 Feb. 1903, Libau, Latvia. Psychiatrist. Educ: M.A.; M.B.; Ch.B.; M.D.; D.P.M.; D.Phil.; D.Litt. et Phil.; D.P.H.; D.T.M.&H.; D.I.H. Publs: The Problem of European Prostitution in Johannesburg, 1949; The Problem of Crime in South Africa, 1960. Contbr. to: S. African Med. Jrnl.; Med. Proceedings; Med. Chronicle. Mbrships. incl: F.R.C.Psych.; F.R.S., S.Af.; F.R.G.S.; Fellow, Royal Anthropol. Inst. & Royal Stats. Soc., London; Hon. Life Mbr., S. African Med. Assn., 1965, S. African Soc. for the Advancement of Sci., 1962. Address: 15 Lystanwold Rd., Saxonwold, Johannesburg, S. Africa.

FREEDMAN, Maurice, b. 1920, London, UK. Professor of Social Anthropology; Editor. Educ: M.A., Ph.D.; King's Coll., London; London Schl. of Econs. Publs: Social & Cultural Anthropology; Ed., Family & kinship in Chinese Soc.; Chinese Lineage & Society; Lineage Organization in Southeastern China; Chinese Family & Marriage in Singapore; Ed., A Minority in Britain; The Structure of Jewish Minorities. Contbr. to: Jewish Jrnl. of Sociol. (Mng. Ed., 1958-70, Ed., 1970-); Man; Brit. Jrnl. Sociol.; Pacific Affairs; Jrnl. Royal Anthropol. Inst.; Lit. Guide; Jewish Chronicle; Archives de Sociologie des Religions; etc. Address: Institute of Social Anthropology, 51 Banbury Road, Oxford, UK.

FREELING, Nicolas, pen name NICHOLAS, F.R.E., b. 1927, London, UK. Writer. Publs. incl: Love in Amsterdam, 1962; Because of the Cats, 1963; Valparaiso (as F.R.E.

Nicholas), UK, 1964, (as Freeling) USA, 1965; The King of the Rainy Country, 1966; The Dresden Green, 1966; Strike Out Where Not Applicable, 1967; This is the Castle, 1968; Tsing-Boum, UK, 1969 (as Tsing-Boom! , USA, 1970); Over the High Side, UK, 1971 (as The Lovely Ladies, USA, 1971); (non-fiction) Kitchen Book, 1970; Cook Book, 1971. Hons: Engl. Crime Writers Award, 1964; Grand Prix de Roman Policier, 1964; Edgar A. Poe Award, 1967. Address: Grandfontaine, 67-Schirmeck, Bas Rhin, France.

FREEMAN, Anne Hobson (Mrs. George C. Freeman, Jr.), b. 19 Mar. 1934, Richmond, Va., USA. Writer; Teacher. Educ: A.B., Bryn Mawr Coll., 1956; Fulbright Grant, London Univ., 1956-57; M.A., Univ. of Va., 1973. Contbr. of short stories & articles to nat. mags. & Richmond Mercury (newspaper). Mbr., Va. Writers Club. Hons: M. Carey Thomas Essay Prize, 1956; Mademoiselle (mag.) Fiction Contest, 1956; Mbr., Lychnos Soc., Univ. of Va., 1972. Address: 10 Paxton Rd., Richmond, VA 23226, USA.

FREEMAN, Barbara C., b. 1906, Ealing, UK. Writer & Illustrator of Children's Books. Educ: Kingston Schl. of Art. Publs: Timi, 1961; Two-Thumb Thomas, 1961; A Book by Georgina, 1962; Broom-Adelaide, 1963; The Name on the Glass, 1964; Lucinda, 1965; Tobias, 1967; The Forgotten Theatre, 1967; The Other Face, 1975. Address: Shirley, 62 Hook Rd., Surbiton, Surrey KT6 5BH, UK.

FREEMAN, David (Dave), b. 22 Aug. 1922, London, UK. Screenwriter. Educ: H.E.T., Royal Navy. Publs: (TV comedy series) Great Scott it's Maynard; Benny Hill series; Tommy Cooper series; Bedtime with Braden; Charlie Drake series; Chelsea Summer Time; Arthur Askey series; A World of his Own; The Fosset Saga; (TV plays) Deep & Crisp & Stolen; Solo for the Banker; Knock Three Times; (Screenplay) Rocket to the Moon; Fine Fettle, 1959; Robinson Crusoe (co-author), 1967; num. sketches & variety shows. Contbr. to: The Dustbinmen; other TV series. Mbr., Writers Guild, GB. Address: Pedlars Farm, Biddenden, Kent, UK.

FREEMAN, Eric Cecil, b. 10 Oct. 1913, Thornton Heath, Surrey, UK. Research Historian. Publs: The Sölva Saga, 1958, 5th ed., 1974; Nelson & the Hamiltons in Wales (w. Edward Gill), 1962. Contbr. to: Country Life; count. lit. in general. Address: Llanblethian House, near Cowbridge, Vale of Glamorgan, Wales, UK.

FREEMAN, Eugene, b. 16 Feb. 1906, NYC, USA. Professor of Philosophy, San José State Univ. Editor of The Monist (philosophical quarterly). Educ: A.B., Univ. Calif., 1926; Ph.D., Univ. Chgo., 1937. Publs. incl: The Categories of Charles Peirce, 1934; The Wisdom & Ideas of Plato (w. D. Appel), 1952, 7th ed., 1973; The Wisdom & Ideas of St. Thomas Aquinas (w. J. Owens), 1968; Spinoza, Essays in Interpretation (w. M. Mandelbaum), 1975; The Abdication of Philosophy, 1975; (contbr.) The Philosophy of Karl Popper, 1974. Contbr. to: Yale Review; Filosofia; etc. Mbrships: Am. Philosl. Assn.; Am. Metaphysical Soc.; Charles Peirce Soc.; Hons. incl: Advsr. Ed. Bd., Lib. of Living Philosophers, 1967-. Address: P.O. Box 1908, Los Gatos, CA 95030, USA.

FREEMAN, Gillian, b. 1929, London, UK. Novelist; Screen Writer. Educ: B.A., Reading Univ. Publs: The Liberty Man; Fall of Innocence; Jack Would be a Gentleman; The Story of Albert Einstein; The Campaign; The Leader; The Undergrowth of Literature; The Alabaster Egg; (films) Leather Boys; That Cold Day in the Park. Contbr. to: Guardian; London Mag.; New Statesman; Listener. Address: c/o Curtis Brown, 13 King St., London WC2, UK.

FREEMAN, Harold Webber, b. 1899, Essex, UK. Educ: M.A., Christ Ch., Oxford. Publs: Joseph & His Brethren; Down in The Valley; Fathers of Their People; Pond Hall's Progress; Hester & Her Family; Andrew To The Lions; Chaffinch's; Blenheim Orange; The Poor Scholar's Tale; Round The Island; Sardinia Re-explored. Address: c/o National Westminster Bank, Ipswich, Suffolk, UK.

FREEMAN, Ruth Lazear Sunderlin, b. 17 Apr. 1907, Penn Yan, N.Y., USA. Homemaker; Child Development Educator. Educ. incl: Cortland State Tchrs. Coll., 1928; B.S., Columbia Tchrs. Coll., 1933; Univ. of Chgo. (postgrad.). Publs. incl: Child & His Picture, 1934; Child's First Picture Book, 1940; Cavalcade of Toys, 1942; Frugal Housewife, 1957; Encyclopedia of American Dolls, 1960;

How to Repair & Dress Old Dolls, 1960; Picture Books, Yesterday & Today, 1967. Contbr. to: Am. Life Collector; educl. mags. Mbrships. incl: Smithsonion Soc.; Am. Heritage Soc. Recip., Decorative Art Book Award, 1967. Address: Old Irelandville, P.O. Watkins Glen, NY 14891, USA.

FREEMAN, Spencer, b. 10 Dec. 1892, Swansea, UK. Consulting Business Engineer; Author. Educ: Johannesburg Coll. Publs: Production Under Fire, 1968; Take Your Measure, 1972; You Can Get to the Top, 1972. Contbr. to: Sporting Life; Sporting Chronicle; var. Irish nat. newspapers. Hons: C.B.E.; Personality of the Year, Irish Racing Writers' Assn., 1973. Address: Knocklyon House, Templeogue, Dublin 14, Repub. of Ireland.

FREEMAN, Thomas Walter, b. 27 Dec. 1908, Congleton, UK. Professor of Geography, Univ. of Manchester. Educ: B.A., 1930, M.A., 1932, Univ. of Leeds; M.A., Univ. of Dublin, 1938. Publs. incl: Ireland: a general & regional geography, 1950; Pre-Famine Ireland, 1957; Geography & Planning, 1958; The Conurbations of Great Britain, 1959; A Hundred Years of Geography, 1961; The Geographer's Craft, 1967; Geography & Regional Administration, 1968; The Writing of Geography, 1971. Contbr. to: Geog. Jrnl.; Geog.; Geog. Mag.; Ed., Irish Geog., 1946-50. Mbrships. incl: Hon. Mbr., Geog. Soc. of Ireland, 1966; Pres., ibid, 1946-49; Commn. on the Hist. of Geog. Thought, Int. Geog. Union, 1968-. Address: 23 Langham Rd., Bowdon, Altrincham, Cheshire, UK.

FREITAS, Margarete Elisabeth, b. 25 July 1927, Hindenburg, Germany. University Professor. Educ: Abitur, 1947; Lib. Sci. Schl.; Commercial Coll.; For. Corres. Degree, Interpreter's Coll.; B.A., S. Ill. Univ., USA, 1963; M.A., Ph.D., 1968, Vanderbilt Univ. Publs: Deutschland ist anders (w. Harold von Hofe), N.Y., 1971. Mbrships: MLA; Am. Assn. of Tchrs. of German; S. Ctrl. MLA; Tex. Assn. of Coll. Tchrs.; Phi Beta Kappa; Phi Kappa Phi. Recip., Schlrship., Vanderbilt Univ., 1963-66. Address: Dept. of Justice, Federal Institute, Apt. 13, Reservation Point, Terminal Island, San Pedro, CA 90731, USA.

FRENCH, Alfred, b. 12 July 1916, Wolverhampton, UK. University Teacher. Educ: M.A., Selwyn Coll., Cambridge. Publs: A Book of Czech Verse, 1958; The Growth of the Athenian Economy, 1964; The Poets of Prague, 1969; The Athenian Half-Century, 1971; Czech Poetry, vol. I (Introd., R. Wellek), 1973. Contbr. to: Jrnl. of Hellenic Studies (UK); Historia (W. Germany); Slavic Review (USA); etc. Mbrships. incl: Aust. Univs. Lang. & Lit. Assn.; Czech. Soc. for Arts & Scis. in Am. Address: Classics Dept., The Univ. of Adelaide, S. Australia 5000.

FRENCH, Dorothy Kayser, b. 11 Feb. 1926, Milwaukee, Wis., USA. Writer. Educ: B.A., Schl. of Jrnlsm., Univ. of Wis. Publs: Mystery of the Old Oil Well, 1963; Swim to Victory, 1969; A Try at Tumbling, 1970; Pioneer Saddle Mystery, 1975. Contbr. to: Okla. Today; 'TEEN; Chrysler-Plymouth Spectator; Jack & Jill; Humpty Dumpty's Mag.; HiCall; Sr. Hi Challenge; Okla. Libn.; Dallas Times Herald; Mod. Baby; Christian Mother; etc. Recip., listing in Sequoyah List of recommended books for Okla. schls. & libs., 1964 & 1965. Address: 2136 Starlight Ct., Bartlesville, OK 74003, USA.

FRENCH, Frank John, b. 1919, Tadworth, Surrey, UK. Former RAF Officer. Educ: London Univ. Publs: Farewell, Gul'sary-Chingiz Aitmatov (transl. from Russian), 1970. Contbr. to var. aeronautical jrnls. Mbrships: Soc. of Authors; Inst. of Linguists. Hons: D.F.C., A.F.C.; O.B.E., 1958. Address: 10 Croutel Road, Felixstowe, Suffolk, IP11 7EF, UK.

FRENCH, (Harry Joseph) Anthony, b. 31 Jan. 1897, Dunbartonshire, Scotland, UK. Journalist. Publs: Gone For a Soldier, 1972. Contbr. to: Blackwood's "Maga". Mbrships. incl: Life Fellow, Inst. of Jrnlsts. (Exec. Comm., 1955-); London Press Club. Address: 97 Dora Rd., Wimbledon Park, London SW19, UK.

FRENCH, Warren G(raham), b. 26 Jan. 1922, Phila., Pa., USA. College Teacher; Writer. Educ: B.A., Univ. of Pa., 1943; M.A., 1948, Ph.D., 1954, Univ. of Tex. Publs. incl: John Steinbeck, 1961, revised, 1974; J. D. Salinger, 1963; The Social Novel at the End of an Era, 1966; A Filmguide to The Grapes of Wrath, (monograph), 1973; Ed., The Thirties, 1967, The Forties, 1969, The Fifties, 1971, The Twenties, 1974; Co.-Ed., w. W. Kidd — American Winners of the Nobel Literary Prize, 1968. Contbr. to num. jrnls.;

Mbr., Ed. Bd., Am. Lit. (jrnl.); Ed. Advsr., Am. Studies; Bd. of Eds., Western Am. Lit.; Contbr., annual vols., American Literary Scholarship, 1965—. Mbr. & Pres., John Steinbeck Soc. of Am. Address: Cornish Flat, NH 03746, USA.

FREND, William Hugh Clifford, pen name PHILO, b. 1916, Shottermill, Surrey, UK. University Professor. Educ: Keble Coll., Oxford; M.A., B.D., D.Phil., D.D. Publs: The Donatist Church, 1952; Martyrdom & Persecution in the Early Church, 1965; The Early Church, 1965; The Rise of the Monophysite Movement, 1972. Contbr. to: Cambridge History of Religion in the Middle East; Ed., Mod. Churchman; & var. acad. jrnls. Mbrships: F.S.A.; Fellow, Royal Histl. Soc. Recip., Hon. D.D., Edinburgh Univ., 1974. Address: Dept. of Ecclesiastical History, The University, Glasgow, UK.

FRENKIEL, Zygmunt, b. 11 Dec. 1902, Czestochowa, Poland. Journalist; Writer. Educ: Engrng. Degree, Univ. of Caën, France; Dip., Colonial Inst., Univ. of Nancy. Publs. incl: Paryz, 1937; Parlons Français, 1939; Speak English, 1946; English Letters for Poles, 1946; Polish Technician in British Industry, 1947; Be A Gentleman, 1947; The Easy Way to Speak Polish, 1948; New English-Polish Secretary, 1959; Ed., Elevator, Lift & Ropeway Engineering. Contbr. to: BBC; Ency. Britannica; Kempe's Engr. Yearbook; & var. profl. jrnls. Mbrships: Chartered Engr., Fellow, Instn. of Mech. Engrs.; Fellow, Inst. of Linguists; Inst. of Jrnlsts.; Soc. of Authors; Transls.' Assn. Hons: Off. d'Acad., 1938, Off. de l'Instrn. Pub., 1953, France. Address: 11 Rotherfield Rd., Carshalton, Surrey SM5 3DN, UK.

FRENK-WESTHEIM, Mariana, pen name FRENK, Mariana, b. Hamburg, Germany. Translator; Writer. Publs. incl: (work by Arnold Toynbee, transl. from Engl. into Spanish) México y el Occidente, 1955; (work by Juan Rulfo, transl. from Spanish into German) Pedro Paramo, Der Llano in Flammen, 1958, 2nd ed., 1964; (work by Paul Westheim, transl. from German into Spanish) Arte antiguo de Mexico, 1950, 3rd ed., 1971; original plays, stories, etc. Contbr. to: Siempre; Revista Universidad; El Cuento; etc. Mbrships. incl: PEN (Exec. Comm.); Assn. Mexican Writers (Bd. Dirs.). Hons. incl: 2 prizes for children's stories & 1 prize for puppet play from Min. Pub. Educ. Address: Av. Mexico 187-502, Mexico 11 — D.F., Mexico.

FREUD, Anna, b. 1895, Vienna, Austria. Psycho-Analyst; Director, Hampstead Child-Therapy Course & Clinic. Publs: The Ego & The Mechanisms of Defence, 1937; Infants Without Families, 1943; The Psycho-Analytical Treatment of Children, 1946; Introduction to Psycho-Analysis for Teachers; Young Children in Wartime (co-author); Normality & Pathology in Childhood, 1965. Mbr., Brit. Psycho-Analytical Soc., 1938-. Hons: C.B.E.; LL.D.; Sc.D.; M.D. Address: 20 Maresfield Gardens, London NW3, UK.

FREWER, Glyn Mervyn Louis, b. 1931, Oxford, UK. Associate Director, Advertising; Author (Children's Books). Educ: M.A., St. Catherine's Coll., Oxford. Publs: Adventure in Forgotten Valley, 1962, 3rd ed., 1968; Adventure in the Barren Lands, 1964, Am. ed., 1966; The Last of the Wispies, 1965; The Token of Elkin, 1970; Crossroad, 1970, 2nd ed., 1973; The Square Peg, 1972, 2nd ed., 1974. Contbr. to: Imagery; Birds. Mbr., Soc. of Authors. Agent: Bolt & Watson. Address: Wychwood, Stanstead Rd., Caterham, Surrey, UK.

FRICK, Elizabeth, b. 18 Jan. 1913, Marlin, Tex., USA. Library Clerk. Educ: Courses in Jrnlsm., Speedwriting, Shorthand, Typing. Publs: Edelweiss, 1966; Memories & Meditations, 1974 (poetry). Contbr. to num. mags., anthols. Mbr., Poetry Soc. of Tex. Hons. incl: Poet Laureate, Houston Pub. Lib., 1965-71; Cert. of Merit, Centro Studi E Scambi Int., Rome, 1972; 3rd Prize, Poetry Soc. of Tex. contests, 1966, 1970. Address: 212 Redan, Houston, TX 77009, USA.

FRICK, Hans Joe, b. 3 Aug. 1930, Frankfurt/Main, Germany. Author. Publs: Breinitzer oder die andere Schuld, 1965; Der Plan des Stefan Kaminsky, 1967; Das Verhör, 1969; Henri, 1970; Mulligans Rückkehr, 1972; Tagebuch einer Entziehung, 1973; Dannys Traum, Feb. 1975; Ermordung eines Verfolgers, 1975; Vor der Verabschiedung eines Gesetzes (forthcoming). Contbr. to TV & radio; var. mags. Mbrships: PEN; Verband Deutscher Schriftsteller. Address: 6 Frankfurt/Main, Morgensternstr. 36, W. Germany.

FRIDELL, Folke Ivar Walter, b. 1 Oct. 1904, Lagan, Sweden. Author. Publs: (in Swedish) Dead Man's Hand, 1946; Sinful Creation, 1948; The Grip is Hardening, 1948; The Sermon on the Mount (short stories), 1951; The Stone Face, 1962. Contbr. to var. mags. Mbr., Swedish Union of Authors. Hons: Artist State Prize, 1969. Address: Ronnasvagen 15B, 341 00 Ljungby, Sweden.

FRIEDBERG, Maurice, b. 3 Dec. 1929, Rzeszow, Poland. University Professor; Author. Educ: B.S., Brooklyn Coll., CUNY, 1951; A.M., 1953, Ph.D., 1958, Columbia Univ. Publs: Russian Classics in Soviet Jackets, 1962; A Bilingual Collection of Russian Short Stories, 1964, Vol. II (w. Robert A. Maguire), 1965; The Jew in Post-Static Soviet Literature, 1970; Ed., Leon Trotsky, The Young Lenin, 1972. Contbr. to: Commentary; Saturday Review; Midstream; & num. acad. jrnls. in USA & Europe. Mbrships. incl: PEN Am. Ctr.; Am. Assn. Advancement Slavic Studies. Hons: Appt. as Juror, Nat. Book Award, 1973. Address: 4426 Sheffield Drive, Bloomington, IN 47401, USA.

FRIEDENTHAL, Richard, b. 9 June 1896, Munich, Germany. Editor; Writer. Educ: D.Phil; Univs. at Berlin, Jena & Munich. Publs. incl: poetry; novels; short stories; biographies; Der Eroberer, 1932; Leonardo da Vinci, 1959; G. F. Handel, 1959; Goethe — His Life & Times, 1965; (travel) Die Party bei Herrn Tokaido, 1958; London zwischen gestern & morgen, 1960; (Ed.) Facts, 4 vols., 1934; Luther — His Life & Times, 1967. Contbr. to: Knaur Verlag, Berlin, (formerly Ed.). Mbr., German Acad., Darmstadt. Address: 15 Burgess Hill, London NW2, UK.

FRIEDMAN, Bruce Jay, b. 26 Apr. 1930, NYC, USA. Publishing Executive. Educ: B.J., Univ. of Mo., Columbia, 1951. Publs. (novels): Stern, USA, 1962, UK, 1963; A Mother's Kisses, USA, 1964, UK, 1965; The Dick, USA, 1970, UK, 1971; (stories) Far From the City of Class, & Other Stories, 1963; Black Angels, USA, 1966, UK., 1967; (plays): 23 Pat O'Brien Movies, 1966; Scuba Duba: A Tense Comedy, prod. 1967, publd. 1968; A Mother's Kisses, 1968; Steambath, 1970; Ed., Black Humor, 1965. Address: 11 Gateway Dr., Great Neck, L.I., NY, USA.

FRIEDMAN, Milton, b. 1912, Brooklyn, N.Y., USA. Principal Economist, U.S. Treasury Department; Paul Snowden Russell, Distinguished Service Professor. Educ: Rutgers Univ.; Univ. of Chgo.; Columbia Univ.; A.B.; M.A.; Ph.D. Publs: Capitalism & Freedom, 1962; Dollars & Deficits, 1968; The Optimum Quantity of Money & Other Essays, 1969; An Economist's Protest, 1972. Contbr. to: Newsweek; Republican Papers; The Pub. Interest. Mbrships: Mont Pelerin Soc.; Nat. Acad. Scis.; Am. Econ. Assn. (Exec. Comm.). Address: Univ. of Chgo., Dept. of Economics, 1126 E. 59th St., Chgo., IL 60637, USA.

FRIEL, Brian, b. 9 Jan. 1929, Omagh, Co. Tyrone, Repub. of Ireland. Writer. Educ: B.A., St. Patrick's Coll., Maynooth; St. Joseph's Trng. Coll., Belfast, UK. Publs: (stories) The Saucer of Larks, 1962; The Gold in the Sea, 1966; (plays) Philadelphia, Here I Come!, 1965; The Loves of Cass McQuire, 1967; Lovers, 1968; Crystal & Fox, 1970; The Mundy Scheme, 1971; The Gentle Island, 1973; The Freedom of the City, 1974; The Enemy Within, 1974; Volunteers, 1975. Contbr. to: New Yorker; Times Lit. Supplement. Recip., D.Litt., Rosary Coll., Chgo., USA. Agent: Curtis Brown. Address: Ardmore, Muff, Lifford, Co. Donegal, Repub. of Ireland.

FRIEL, George, b. 15 July 1910, Glasgow, UK. Writer. Educ: M.A., Glasgow Univ. Publs: The Bank of Time, 1959; The Boy Who Wanted Peace, 1964; Grace & Miss Partridge, 1969; Mr. Alfred, M.A., 1972; An Empty House, 1975. Contbr. to: The Adelphi; The Modern Scot; New Stories; World Review; Scottish Stories. Mbr., Writers' Guild. Hons: Scottish Arts Coun. Awards, 1969, 1972. Address: 25 Brackenbrae Rd., Bishopbriggs, Scotland, UK.

FRIES, Erik Olof Elias, b. 15 July 1900, Örtomta församling, Ostergötlands län, Sweden. School teacher. Educ: B.A., 1927, B.D., 1930, Lic. diss., 1953, Univ. Uppsala. Publs: The Piety in Verner von Heidenstam, 1934; (Contbr., Mårbacka & Öwalid II), A Conversation about Religion, 1941; Karlfeldt & the Faith of his Ancestors, 1942; (Contbr., the yearbook of the Swedish Soc. for Lit., Samlaren) Heidenstam & the Problem of Religion, 1945; Knowledge & Morality: Intuition, consciousness & conscience, 1960. Mbr., The Swedish Union of Authors. Address: Ekensbergsgatan 14 IV, 15143 Södertälje, Sweden.

FRIIS, Erik Johan, b. 5 Apr. 1913, Oslo, Norway. Editor; Publisher. Educ: B.S., St. John's Univ., Bklyn., N.Y., USA, 1938; M.A., Columbia Univ., 1946. Publs: The American-Scandinavian Foundation 1910-1960: A Brief History, 1961; Scandinavian Studies (co-Ed. & co-author), 1965; 5 transls. from the Danish, Norwegian & Swedish. Contbr. to: Am. Histl. Review; Am.-Scandinavian Review. Mbrships. incl: PEN; Fellow, Explorers' Club, N.Y. (VP). Hons: Mbr., Norwegian-Am. Hall of Hon., Decorah, Iowa; US Medal of Antarctica Serv.; Author Award, Newark Coll. of Engrng., 1973; Arts & Letters Award, Finlandia Fndn., N.Y., 1974; var. Scandinavian Orders of Chivalry. Address: 19 Shadow Lane, Montvale, NJ 07645, USA.

FRINGELI, Albin, b. 24 Mar. 1899. Teacher. Educ: Tchrs. Trng. Coll., Solothurn; Univs., Basle & Sorbonne. Publs: (poetry) Der Holderbaum; Am stille Wäg; (stories) Heimfahrt, 2nd ed., 1972; Die Zeitlosen, 1973; Mein Weg zu Johann Peter Hebel, 1961; Flucht aus der Enge; Schwarzbubenland vom Passwang ins Leimental, 1973; Schönes Schwarzbubenland, 1955; Das Amt Laufen, 1946; Der Weltverbesserer und seine Gefährten, 1975. Contbr. to & Ed. Dr Schwarzbueb, 1923. Mbrships: Swiss Writers' Assn.; Solothurn Writers' Union. Hons. incl: Johann Peter Hebel Prize, 1961; Swiss Writers' Fndn. Prize; Solothurn Art Prize, 1965; Ph.D., Basle Univ., 1969. Address: CH 4208 Nunningen, Canton of Solothurn, Switz.

FRISBY, Terence Peter Michael, b. 28 Nov. 1932, London, UK. Playwright. Publs: (plays) The Suptopians; There's a Girl in my Soup; The Bandwagon. Recip., Writers' Guild GB Award, 1970 for Best Comedy Screenplay. Address: 52 Cloncurry St., London SW6, UK.

FRISCH, Max, b. 15 May 1911, Zurich, Switz. Architect; Journalist. Educ: Zurich Univ. Publs. incl: (Plays & Novels) Blatter aus dem Brotsakc, 1940; Bin oder Die Reise nach Peking, 1945; Tagebuch mit Marion, 1947; Als der Krieg zu Ende war, 1949; Graf Oederland, 1951; Don Juan oder die Liebe zur Geometrie, 1953; Andorra, 1961 (transl. into 11 langs.); Ein Spiel, 1967; Wilhelm Tell für die Schule, 1971; Tagebuch, 1966-71, 1972. Mbr., Am. Acad. Arts & Letters. Hons. incl: German Acad. Prize, 1958; Grosser Schillerpreis Zurich, 1974. Address: CH-6611 Berzona/Tessin, Switz.

FRITZELL, Irmelin, b. 2 Feb. 1909, Ödeshög, Sweden. Author. Educ: Fil.kand. Publs: Som Vattenvallen, 1956; Återkomst (Return), 1960; Möten (Encounters), 1963; Hjärtats Höst (Heart's Autumn), 1974. Mbr., Swedish Authors' Union. Address: Karl XII str. 4, Lund, Sweden.

FROELICH, Robert Earl, b. 24 July 1929, St. Louis, Mo., USA. Professor of Psychiatry, & Assistant Dean, School of Primary Medical Care, University of Alabama. Educ: A.B., 1951, M.D., 1955, Wash. Univ., St. Louis, Mo. Publs: Medical Interviewing, 1969, 2nd ed. 1973; Film Reviews in Psychiatry, Psychology & Mental Health, 1974; Dental Office Communication, 1975. Contbr. to: Jrnl. of Med. Educ.; Mo. Med.; Hlth. Sci. TV Bulletin; Hlth. Scis. TV Source Book; Video Techniques in Psychiatric Training & Treatment, 1970; Family Practice, 1973; Clinical Pharmacy Practice, 1972; Psychological Aspects of Common Medical Problems, 1974; Sev. other sci. books & jrnls. Mbrships. incl: Chmn., Sci. Exhibs. Sub-Comm., Am. Psych. Assn.; Past Chmn., Hlth. Scis. Communication Assn.; AMA; Assn. of Acad. Psychs. Address: Schl. of Primary Med. Care, Univ. of Ala., P.O. Box 1247, Huntsville, AL 35807, USA.

FROMM, Erika, pen (maiden) name OPPENHEIMER, Erika, b. 23 Dec. 1910, Frankfurt, Germany. Professor of Psychology, University of Chicago. Educ: Ph.D., Univ. of Frankfurt. Publs: Dream Interpretation: A Dynamic Approach, (w. T. M. French), 1964; Hypnosis: Research Developments & Perspectives, (w. R. E. Shor), 1972. Contbr. to: Jrnl. of Abnormal & Soc. Psychol.; Contemporary Psychol.; Int. Jrnl. of Clin. & Experimental Hypnosis; Am. Jrnl. of Clin. Hypnosis; Am. Jrnl. of Orthopsych.; Jrnl. of Projective Techniques & Personality Assessment; etc. Mbrships. incl: Am. Psychol. Assn.; AAAS; Past Dir., Am. Orthopsych. Assn.; V.P., Soc. for Clin. & Experimental Hypnosis. Recip., sev. awards. Address: Univ. of Chgo., 5848 S. Univ. Ave., Chgo., IL 60637, USA.

FROMM, Gary, b. 27 Dec. 1933, Dortmund, Germany. Economist. Educ: B.M.E., Cornell Univ., USA; M.S., MIT; A.M., Ph.D., Harvard Univ. Publs. incl: The Brookings Quarterly Econometric Model of the U.S., 1965; Policy Simulations with an Econometric Model, 1968; Tax Incentives & Capital Spending, 1971; Public Economic Theory & Policy, 1973. Contbr. to profl. jrnls. Mbr., Nat. Press Club. Address: 4801 Dexter Terr. NW, Wash. DC 20007, USA.

FROST, Brian Reginald Thomas, b. 1926, London, UK. Educ: Univ. of Birmingham; B.Sc.; Ph.D. Publs: Nuclear Reactor Materials, 1959. Contbr. to: Progress in Metal Phys.; Pergamon Vol. V. Address: 55 Sellwood Rd., Abingdon, Berks., UK.

FROST, David Paradine, b. 7 Apr. 1939, Beccles, UK, TV Broadcaster; Writer. Educ: Caius Coll., Cambridge. Publs. incl: That Was the Week that Was; How to Live Under Labour; Talking with Frost; To England with Love (w. Antony Jay); num. TV progs.: The Frost Programme; David Frost Show; etc. Hons. incl: O.B.E.; Golden Rose, Montreux, 1967; Emmy Award, 1970. Address: 46 Egerton Crescent, London SW3, UK.

FROST, Ernest, b. 1918, Isleworth, Middlesex, UK. Lecturer in English; Novelist; Poet. Publs: The Dark Peninsula, 1949; The Lighted Cities, 1950; A Short Lease, 1953; The Visitants, 1955; Down to Hope, 1963; It's Late by My Watch, 1966; (poetry) Postcards from a Sad Holiday, 1974. Contbr. to: New Statesman; Tribune; Poetry Quarterly; Yale Review; The Observer; Music Survey; Arena; London Mag.; Times Lit. Supplement; World Review; BBC. Mbr., PEN. Agent: David Higham Assocs. Address: 2 Main St., Long Whatton, Loughborough, Leics., UK.

FROST, Helena, (Mrs. J. W. Frost), b. 6 Apr. 1943, Prague, Czechoslovakia. Linguist. Educ: Charles Univ., Prague, 1962-64; B.A., 1966, M.A., 1967, Monterey Inst. of For. Studies, Calif., USA; Ph.D., Univ. of Calif., L.A., 1973. Publs: (Dissertations) Priemy komičeskogo v četyréxaktnyx p'esax Čexova; Russian Prefixal-Suffixal Substantives with Substantival Bases, 1973. Address: P.O. Box 871, Monterey, CA 93940, USA.

FRY, Alan, b. 21 Apr. 1931, Lac le Hacha, B.C., Can. Writer. Educ: Univ. of B.C., Vancouver. Publs: Ranch on the Cariboo, 1962; How a People Die, 1970; Come a Long Journey, 1971; The Revenge of Annie Charlie, 1973; The Burden of Adrian Knowle, 1974. Address: Quathiaski Cove, B.C., Can.

FRY, Christopher, b. 18 Dec. 1907, UK. Dramatist; Former Actor, Producer, Schoolmaster. Publs: (plays) The Boy with a Cart, 1939; The First Born, 1946; A Phoenix too Frequent, 1946; The Lady's Not for Burning, 1949; Thor, with Angels, 1949; Venus Observed, 1950; A Sleep of Prisoners, 1951; The Dark is Light Enough, 1954; Curtmantle, 1961; A Yard of Sun, 1970; (transls.) Ring Round the Moon, by Jean Anouilh, 1950; The Lark, by Anouilh, 1955; Tiger at the Gates, by Jean Giraudoux, 1955; Duel of Angels, by Giraudoux, 1958; Judith, by Giraudoux, 1960; Peer Gynt, by Henrik Ibsen, 1970; (TV plays) The Brontës of Haworth, 1973; also film scripts. Mbrships. incl: F.R.S.L. Hons: Queen's Gold Medal for Poetry, 1962; Heinemann Award of R.S.L., for Curtmantle. Agent: ACTAC Ltd. Address: c/o 16 Cadogan Lane, London SW1, UK.

FRY, Rosalie Kingsmill, b. 22 Apr. 1911, Vancouver Island, B.C., Can. Writer & Illustrator. Educ: L.C.C. Ctlr. Schl. of Art, London, UK. Publs. incl: (for children) Bumblebuzz; Bandyboy's Treasure Island; Cinderella's Mouse & Other Fairy Tales; Two Little Pigs (Books 1-3); Deep in the Forest; The Little Gypsy; Pipkin the Woodmouse; The Mountain Door; Lucinda & the Painted Ball; The Echo Song; Riddle of the Figurehead; Lucinda & the Sailor Kitten; The Wind Call; Child of the Western Isles; September Island; The Castle Family; Gypsy Princess; Snowed Up; Promise of the Rainbow; Whistler in the Mist; Mungo; Secrets. Contbr. to: Lady; etc. Hons: 2 Jr. Lit. Guild Selections. Agent: Curtis Brown Ltd. Address: 1 Mountain Cottage, Llandybie, Ammanford, Dyfed SA18 2TP, Wales, UK.

FRY, William Finley, Jr., b. 25 Mar. 1924, Cinn., Ohio, USA. Physician; Psychiatrist. Educ: Bowdoin Coll., Grinnell Coll.; Univ. of Ore.; Univ. of S. Calif.; M.D., Univ. of Cinn., 1949; Univ. of Oslo (summer). Publs: Sweet Madness: A Study of Humor, 1963; Mirth Makers: Life Studies of Professional Comedy Writers. Contbr. to psych., poetry jrnls., anthols.; sev. chapts. in sci. books. Hons: Comedy Cons., Am. Conserv. Theatre Summer Inst.; San Fran., 1968. Address: 888 Oak Grove, Menlo Park, CA 94025, USA.

FRYE, (Herman) Northrop, b. 14 July 1912, Sherbrooke, Quebec, Can. Literary Critic; Professor. Educ: B.A., Toronto, 1933; M.A., Oxford, UK, 1940. Publs. incl: Fearful Symmetry: A Study of William Blake, 1947; The Well-Tempered Critic, 1963; T. S. Eliot, 1963; A Natural Perspective, 1965; The Modern Century, 1967; A Study of English Romanticism, 1968; The Stubborn Structure, 1970; The Bush Garden, 1971; The Critical Path, 1971. Contbr. to num. jrnls. Mbrships. incl: MLA; FRS Can.; Hon. Foreign Mbr., Am. Acad. of Arts & Sci. Hons. incl: R. S. Pierre Chauveau Medal, 1970; Can. Coun. Molson Prize, 1971; Companion of the Order of Can., 1972; 23 Hon. Degrees. Address: Massey Coll., 4 Devonshire Place, Toronto, Ont. M5S 2E1, Can.

FRYE, Richard Nelson, b. 10 Jan. 1920, Birmingham, Ala., USA. Professor. Educ: A.B., Univ. of Ill., 1939; M.A., 1940, Ph.D., 1946, Harvard Univ. Publs: The United States & Turkey & Iran, 1952; Iran, 1963; The History of Bukhara, 1954; The Heritage of Persia, 1962; Bukhara, 1965; Persia, 1969; The Arabs in the East, 1975. Contbr. to: Literaturnaya Gazeta, Moscow, USSR; num. Persian Lang. Jrnls.; etc. Corres. Mbr., German Archeol. Soc. Address: 546 Widener Library, Cambridge, MA 02138, USA.

FRYE, Roland Mushat, b. 3 July 1921, Birmingham, Ala., USA. Professor of English Literature. Educ: Ph.D., Princeton Univ., 1952. Publs. incl: God, Man & Satan: Patterns of Christian Thought & Life in "Paradise Lost", Pilgrim's Progress", & the Great Theologians, 1960, 2nd ed., 1972; Perspective on Man: Literature & the Christian Tradition, 1961; Shakespeare & Christian Doctrine, 1963; Shakespeare's Life & Times: A Pictorial Record, 1967; Shakespeare: The Art of the Dramatist, 1970. Contbr. to schlrly. jrnls. Mbr., profl. socs. & ed. bds. of jrnls. Address: 226 W. Valley Rd., Wayne, PA 19087, USA.

FRYER, Colin Bernard, b. 14 July 1933, Tyldesley, Lancs., UK. Ophthalmic Consultant. Educ: Liverpool Coll. of Optics; Manchester Coll. of Technol., (now Univ. of Manchester Inst. of Sci. & Technol.); F.B.O.A., F.S.O.(S.A.). Publs: Eye Health, 1965. Contbr. to: Optician; Ophthalmic Optician; Vision; Better Hlth.; var. profl. jrnls., USA & S. Africa. Mbrships: Soc. of Authors; Assn. of Optical Practitioners; Merseyside Brit. Optical Assn., (Hon. Sec. 1956-58, Vice-Chmn., 1958-59). Address: 11 Queenscourt Rd., West Derby, Liverpool Ll2 8RH, UK.

FRYSINGER, Grace Elizabeth, b. 28 Aug. 1885, Rockford, Ill., USA. Home Economist; Writer. Educ: B.Sc., Drexel Univ., 1917. Publs: Home Demonstration Work. Contbr. to: Country Gentleman; Farmer; Printer's Ink; var. other mags. Mbr., Engl. Speaking Union. Address: 3133 Connecticut Ave. N.W., Wash. DC 20008, USA.

FUCHS, Anton (Eugen) (Andreas) b. 29 Jan. 1920, Vienna, Austria. Writer. Educ: Univ. of Vienna. Publs: Deserteur, 1958; Vom Morgen in die Nacht, 1968; Imaginäre Berichte, 1974. Contbr. to: Literatur & Kritik; Zet; Podium; Word und Wahrheit; & others. Mbrships: PEN; Kogge; Carinthian Writers' Assn. Hons: Prize, Vienna Art Fund, 1967; Theodor Körner Prizes, 1968 & 1974; Lit. Prize, Carinthia, 1973. Address: A-9020 Klagenfurt, Kumpfgasse 24, Austria.

FUCHS, Daniel, b. 25 June 1909, NYC, USA. Film Scriptwriter. Educ: CCNY. Publs: (novels) Summer in Williamsburg, USA, 1934, UK, 1935; Homage to Blenholt, USA & UK, 1936; Low Company USA, 1937 (as Neptune Beach, UK, 1937); West of the Rockies, USA & UK, 1971; (stories) Stories, 1956; (Screenplays) Love Me Or Leave Me, 1955; Panic in the Streets, 1957; Jeanne Eagels, 1957. Hons: Acad. Award for Screenplay, 1956; Grant, Nat. Inst. Arts & Letters, 1962. Address: c/o Alfred A. Knopf Inc., 201 E. 50th St., N.Y., NY 10022, USA.

FUCHS, Johannes Marius, b. 10 Dec. 1905, Amsterdam, Netherlands. Writer. Educ: D. Law, Univ. of Amsterdam. Publs: Beurt — en wagenveren, 1946; Voort, in 't zadel kameraden, 1965; Gids voor Fietsers, 1968; Raadsels, rebussen en puzzels, 1970; Moord op Alfabet, 1974. Address: Herengracht 276, Amsterdam, Netherlands.

FUCHS, Lawrence Howard, b. 29 Jan. 1927, NYC, USA. Educator. Educ: B.A., NY Univ., 1950; Ph.D., Harvard Univ., 1955. Publs: The Political Behavior of American Jews, 1955; Hawaii Pono: A Social History, 1961; John F. Kennedy & American Catholicism, 1967;

Those Peculiar Americans, 1967; American Ethnic Politics, 1968; Family Matters, 1972. Contbr. to: Am. Pol. Sci. Review; Pol. Sci. Sci. Quarterly; Jrnl. of Am. Pols.; New England Quarterly; Am. Heritage. Mbrships. incl: Dir., Peace Corps, Philippines, 1961-63; Nat. Advsry. Bd. Commn. Law & Soc. Action, Am. Jewish Congress; Advsry. Bd., United World Federalists. Address: Chmn., Am. Studies Dept., Heller 68-7, Brandeis Univ., Waltham, MA 02154, USA.

FUENTES, Carlos, b. 11 Nov. 1928, Mexico City, Mexican Ambassador to France, 1975. Educ: Nat. Univ. Mexico; Institut de Hautes Etudes Internationales, Geneva. Publs: (novels & short stories) Los días enmascarados, 1954; La región más transparente, 1958; Las buenas conciencias, 1959; Aura, 1962; La muerte de Artemio Cruz, 1962; Cantar de ciegos, 1964; Zona Zagrada, 1967; Cambio de Piel, 1967; Cumpleaños, 1969; (plays) Todos los gatos son pardos, 1970; El tuerto es rey, 1971; (essays) La nueva novela hispanoamericana, 1970; Casa con dos puertas, 1971; Tiempo Mexicano, 1972. Contbr. to num. jrnls. inclng: N.Y. Times Mag.; Daedalus; Vogue; Le Monde (France); Die Zeit (Germany). Hons. incl: Fellow, Woodrow Wilson Int. Ctr. for Schlrs., Wash. D.C., 1974. Address: 20 Ave. du Président Wilson, 75116 Paris, France.

FUGARD, Athol. Actor; Playwright. Publs: The Blood Knot; Hello & Goodbye; People are Living Here; Boesman & Lena; Sizwe Banzi is Dead, 1973; The Island, 1973. Address: P.O. Box 5090, Walmer, Port Elizabeth, S. Africa.

FUKUDA, Kiyoto, b. 29 Nov. 1904, Nagasaki-ken, Hasami-ma chi, Japan. Novelist. Educ: Fac. of Lit., Imperial Univ., Tokyo. Publs: Wakakusa, 1938; Shidosya, 1946; Tenpyo no Shonen, 1958; Haru no medama (The Pupils of Spring), 1963; Aki no medama (The Pupils of Autumn), 1964; Yume wo hakobu Fune, 1967. Mbrships: Dir., Japan Writers' Assn.; Chief Dir., Japan Juvenile Writers' Assn.; PEN. Hons: Sankei Shinbun, 1958; Hans Christian Andersen Award, 1966; Noma Juvenile Lit. Prize, 1966. Address: 2-6-15 Narita-nishi Suginamiku, Tokyo, Japan.

FUKUDA, Shoji, pen name SHOJI, Kaoru, b. 19 Apr. 1937, Tokyo, Japan. Educ: LL.B., Tokyo Univ. Publs: Soshitsu (Loss), 1959; Akazukinchan ki o tsukete (Look Out, Little Red Riding Hood), 1969; Sayonara Kaiketsu Kurozukin (Farewell to the Brave Black-Masked Man), 1969. Contbr. to: Chūō Kōron; etc. Mbrships: Japanese Writers Assn.; PEN. Hons: Lit. Prize Best New Writer, 1958; Akutagawa Prize, 1969. Address: 1501 Park Mansion, 2-3-34 Mita Minato-ku, Tokyo, Japan.

FUKUDA, Tsutomu, 29 Sept. 1905, Tokyo, Japan. Professor of English Literature. Educ: Osaka For. Lang. Coll., Tchr. Trng. Inst., 1927; Litt.D., Kansei Gakuin Univ., 1968. Publs: A Study of Charles Lamb's Essay of Elia, 1964; Literary & Linguistic Travels Abroad, 1968; Sansho-Dayu & Other Stories (Engl. transl. of Japanese Lit.), 1970. Contbr. to: Poetry Nippon (Pres.); Decal; Orbis; Poet (Far E. Ed.); World of Poetry; Tweed; Ocarina; Shikai; Tantrum; Green Tree; Engl. Tchrs. Mag. Mbrships. incl: Charles Lamb Soc. Address: 3-17, 2-chome, Yakushidori, Nada, Kobe, Japan.

FUKUTAKE, Tadashi, b. 12 Feb. 1917, Okayama, Japan. Professor of Sociology. Educ: Graduated, 1940. Ph.D., 1962, Univ. of Tokyo. Publs: Man & Society in Japan, 1962; Asian Rural Society: China, India, Japan, 1967; Japanese Rural Society, 1967 & 1972; The Socio-Economic Structure of the Indian Village — Surveys of Villages in Gujarat & West Bengal (w. T. Ouchi & C. Nakane), 1964; Japanese Society Today, 1974. Mbr., Japan Sociol. Soc. (Pres., 1968-70). Recip., of The Mainichi Publication Prize, 1963. Address: 6-31-20 Daita, Setagaya-ku, Tokyo, Japan.

FULFORD, Roger Thomas Baldwin, b. 24 Nov. 1902, Flaxley, Glos., UK. Author. Educ: M.A., Worcester Coll., Oxford. Publs: Royal Dukes, 1933; George IV, 1935; The Greville Memoirs (ed. w. Lytton Strachey), 1938; The Prince Consort, 1949; Votes for Women, 1956; Hanover to Windsor, 1960; Correspondence of Queen Victoria and the Empress Frederick, "Dearest Child", 1963, "Dearest Mama", 1968, "Your Dear Letter", 1971; Samuel Whitbread, 1966; Trial of Queen Caroline, 1967. Contbr. to: Times Lit. Supplement. Recip., Evening Standard £5,000 Prize for Votes for Women, 1956. Agent: A. P. Watt. Address: Barbon Manor, Kirkby Lonsdale, Carnforth, Lancs., UK.

FULLER, Edmund, b. 1914, USA. Writer. Publs. incl: (novels) A Star Pointed North, 1946; Brothers Divided, 1951; The Corridor, USA & UK, 1963; Flight, 1970; (non-fiction) A Pageant of the Theatre, 1941, revised ed., 1965; John Milton, USA, 1944, UK, 1969; Tinkers & Genius, 1955; Man in Modern Fiction, 1958; Books with Men Behind Them, 1962; Successful Calamity, USA, 1966, UK, 1967; Commentary on Charles Williams' All Hallows Eve, 1967; God in the White House, 1968; Ed., num. anthols., collects. & relig. publs. Address: c/o Random House, Inc., 201 E. 50th St., N.Y., NY 10022, USA.

FULLER, Jean (Violet) Overton, b. 7 Mar. 1915, Iver Heath, Bucks., UK. Dealer in rare books; Author. Educ: B.A.(Hons.), London. Publs: Madeleine, 1952; The Starr Affair, 1954; Double Webs, 1958; Horoscope for a Double Agent, 1961; The Magical Dilemma of Victor Neuberg, 1965; Carthage & the Midnight Sun, 1966; Shelley (biog.), 1968; African Violets, 1968; Swinburne (biog.), 1968; Darun & Pitar, 1970; Tintagel, 1970; Noor-un-Nisa Inayat Khan GC, 1971; Conversations with a Captor, 1973; The German Penetration of SOE, 1975; The Chequered Spy, 1975. Contbr. to: Poetry Review; BBC radio progs. Mbrships: Poetry Soc.; Francis Bacon Soc. Hons: Co-winner, Manifold Chapbook Competition, 1968; Winner, Manifold Poems of the Decade Competition, 1970. Address: 6 Church Lane, Wymington, Beds., UK.

FULLER, John Harold, b. 31 May 1916, Oldham, Lancs., UK. Author; Catering Books Adviser to Publisher. Publs. incl: The Chef's Manual of Kitchen Management, 1962; The Caterer's Potato Manual, 1963; The Chef's Compendium of Professional Recipes (w. E. Renold), 1963; The Restauranteur's Guide to Guéridon & Lamp Cookery, 1964; Hotelkeeping & Catering as a Career, 1965; The Waiter (w. A. J. Currie), 1965; Ed., H. P. Pellaprat's Great Book of the Kitchen, 1967; Ed., The Theory & Practice of Catering (in press). Contbr. to: Wine & Food; Fin. Times; etc. Mbrships. incl: Hotel Catering & Institutional Mgmt. Assn. (Pres. 1972-74); Cookery & Food Assn. (VP 1968-). Hons. incl: Catering Advsr., R.A.F., (1971-). Address: Holly Lodge, The Green, Adderbury, Banbury, Oxon, UK.

FULLER, Roy Broadbent, b. 1912, Failsworth, Lancs., UK. Director, Building Soc.; Governor, BBC. Publs: My Child, My Sister; Collected Poems; Buff; New Poems; Tiny Tears; The Carnal Island; Owls & Artificers; Professors & Gods; Seen Grandpa Lately?; Catspaw. Contbr. to: London Mag.; Listener; etc. Mbrships: F.R.S.L.; Arts Coun. Poetry Panel, 1954-59; Chmn., Legal Advsry. Panel, Bldg. Soc. Assn., 1958-69; Bd., Poetry Book Soc. Ltd. 1959–. Recip., Queen's Gold Medal for Poetry, 1970. Agent: Curtis Brown Ltd. Address: 37 Langton Way, London SE23, UK.

FULLERTON, Alexander Fergus, b. 20 Sept. 1924, Saxmundham, Suffolk, UK. Writer. Educ: RN Coll., Dartmouth. Publs: Surface!, 1953; Bury the Past, 1954; Old Moke, 1954; No Man's Mistress, 1955; A Wren Called Smith, 1957; The White Men Sang, 1958; The Yellow Ford, 1959; The Waiting Game, 1961; Soldier from the Sea, 1962; The Thunder & the Flame, 1964; Lionheart, 1965; Chief Executive, 1969; The Publisher, 1970; Store, 1971; The Escapists, 1972; Other Men's Wives, 1973; Piper's Leave, 1974. Address: c/o Agent, John Farquharson Ltd., 15 Red Lion Sq., London WC1, UK.

FULTON, Robin, b. 6 May 1937, Scotland, UK. Writer. Publs: (verse) Instances, 1967; Inventories, 1969; The Spaces between the Stones, 1971; The Man with the Surbahar, 1971; Tree-Lines, 1974; (transls.) An Italian Quarter, 1966; Blok's Twelve, 1968; Five Swedish Poets, 1972; Selected Poems of Lars Gustafsson, 1972; Gunnar Harding, 1973; Tomas Tranströmer, 1974; Osten Sjöstrand, 1974; (criticism) Contemporary Scottish Poetry, Individuals & Contexts, 1974; (Ed.) Lines Review, 1967; Ten Scottish Poets, 1971; Trio; New Poets from Edinburgh, 1971; var. papers & reviews; Critical study of Tomas Tranströmer for Twayne, forthcoming.

FUMENTO, Rocco, b. 12 Feb. 1928, N. Adams, Mass., USA. Associate Professor of English. Educ: B.S., Columbia Univ., NYC, 1950; M.F.A., Univ. of Iowa, Iowa City, 1952. Publs: Devil by the Tail (novel), 1954; Tree of Dark Reflection (novel), 1962, French ed. (L'Arbre du Paradis), 1963, Spanish ed. (El Arbol de la Oscura Reflextion), 1965; Introduction to the Short Story (text), 1962. Contbr. to: Mademoiselle; Ramparts; etc. Mbr., prof. & community orgs. Recip., 3 creative writing Fellowships, Univ. of Ill. Address: 307 S. Garfield Ave., Champaign, IL 61820, USA.

FUNK, Arville Lynn, b. 11 Dec. 1929, Corydon, Ind., USA. Attorney-at-Law. Educ: B.A., Ind. Ctrl. Coll.; M.S., Butler Univ.; LL.B., J.D., Ind. Univ. Publs: Tales of Our Hoosier Heritage, 1965; Indiana's Birthplace, 1966; Our Historic Corydon, 1966; Harrison County in the Indiana Sesquicentennial, 1967; Hoosiers in the Civil War, 1967; A Sketchbook of Indiana History, 1969; The Morgan Raid in Indiana-Ohio, 1971; Squire Boone in Indiana, 1974. Contbr. to: Ind. Mag. of Hist.; Tenn. Histl. Quarterly; Ala. Hist. Quarterly; Ga. Histl. Quarterly; Filson Club Quarterly. Mbrships: Am. Bar Assn.; Ind. Bar Assn.; Harrison Co. Bar Assn. Address: R.R.5, Corydon, IN 47112, USA.

FURBANK, Philip Nicholas, b. 23 May 1920, Cranleigh, Surrey, UK. Lecturer in Literature at the Open University. Educ: M.A., Cambridge Univ., 1947. Publs: Samuel Butler 1835-1902, 1948; Italo Svevo: the Man & the Writer, 1966; Reflections on the Word "Image", 1970. Contbr. to: Listener; Guardian; Encounter; Essays in Criticism; etc. Mbrships: Fellow Emmanuel Coll. (1947-53) & Fellow King's Coll. (1970-72), Cambridge Univ. Address: 2 Regent's Park Terrace, London NW1, UK.

FURLONG, Monica, b. 1930, Harrow, Middx., UK. Publs: With Love to the Church, 1965; Travelling In, 1971. Contbr. to: Truth; Spectator; Daily Mail. Address: 21 Park Ave., Ruislip, Middx., UK.

FURLONG, Norman, b. 1907, Manchester, UK. Editor; School Librarian. Educ: A.B., Univ. of Manchester. Publs: By Reading to Writing (co-author); English Satire; Potato Riddle (co-author); Library Practice for Colleges of Education; Cataloguing Rules (co-author). Address: School Library Association, 29-31 George Street, Oxford OX1 2AY, UK.

FURLONG, Vivienne Carole, pen name WELBURN, Vivienne, b. 18 Apr. 1941, Scarborough, Yorks., UK. Writer. Educ: B.A., Univ. of Leeds; P.G.C.E. (Post Grad. Cert. of Educ.), London Univ. Inst. of Educ. Publs: Johnny So Long, & The Drag, 1967; Clearway, 1967; The Treadwheel, & Coil Without Dreams, 1975. Contbr. to: Gambit. Mbr., Soc. of Authors. Address: Flat 4, 53 Leinster Square, Bayswater, London W2, UK.

FURNESS, Audrey, b. 6 July 1911, Wallingford, Berks., UK. Writer. Educ: Ginner-Mawer Schl. of Dance & Drama. Publs: The Forbidden Cave (children's book); 12 novels, 1961-73. Contbr. to: BBC Woman's Hour; var. women's mags. Recip., selection of The Forbidden Cave as Book Soc. Choice. Address: 51 Lonsdale Road, Barnes, London SW13 9JR, UK.

FURUKAWA, Tsukasa, b. 4 Aug. 1932, Kyoto, Japan. Commercial & Technical Journalist. Educ: B.A., Rikkyo Univ., Tokyo, 1957; Am. Univ., Wash. D.C. Contbr. to: Daily News Record; Women's Wear Daily; Home Furnishings Daily; Am. Metal Market & Metalworking News; Electronic News; Supermarket News; Men's Wear. Mbr., Nichiren Shoshu Soka Gakkai (Buddhist Group). Hons: Fulbright Schlrship, 1958-59. Address: 1-4-8 Komazawa, Setagaya-ku, Tokyo, Japan.

FUSSELL, George Edwin, b. 1889, Weymouth, Dorset, UK. Writer; Agricultural Historian. Publs. incl: Farming Techniques from Prehistoric to Modern Times, 1966; The Story of Farming, 1968; Crop Nutrition, Science & Practice before Liebig, 1971; The Classical Tradition in West European Farming, 1972; Jethro Tull: His Influence on Mechanized Agriculture, 1973; James Ward, R.A., Animal Painter & His England. 1769-1859, 1974. Contbr. to var. acad. & profl. periodicals. Mbrships: Fellow, Royal Histl. Soc.; Hon. Mbr., Int. Congress of Agricl. Museums, 1969; Initiator, Brit. Agricl. Hist. Soc., 1953 (Pres., 1969-72); Econ. Hist. Soc. Recip., hon. D.Litt. Address: 55 York Rd., Sudbury, Suffolk, UK.

FYSON, Jenny Grace, pen name FYSON, J. G., b. 3 Oct. 1904, Bromley, Kent, UK. Writer. Educ: St. Swithun's Schl., Winchester. Publs: Saul & David, I & II, Religious Interludes for Schools Radio, 1952; The Three Brothers of Ur, 1964; The Journey of the Eldest Son, 1965. (Finalist, Carnegie Medal, 1964 & 1965). Contbr. to: Miscellany 5. Mbrships: Women's Int. League Peace & Freedom; Soc. Authors. Address: c/o Children's Dept., Oxford Univ. Press, 37 Dover St., London W1X 4AH, UK.

G

GABO, Naum N., b. 1890, Briansk, Russia. Sculptor. Educ: Univ. of Munich, Germany. Publs: Circle (w. B. Nicholson & L. Martin), 1937; Gabo, 1957; Of Drivers Arts, 1962. Mbrships: N.Y. Inst. of Arts & Letters; Boston Acad. of Arts & Scis., USA; Swedish Acad. Hons: Doctorate, Royal Coll. of Art, London, UK; K.B.E., 1971. Address: Breakneck Hill Rd., Middlebury, CT 06762, UK.

GABOR, Dennis, b. 1900, Budapest, Hungary. Professor, Applied Electron Physics. Educ: C.B.S., D.Sc., Techni. Univ., Budapest; Dr.Ing., Technische Hochschule, Charlottenburg, Germany. Publs: The Electron Microscope; Electronic Inventions & Their Impact on Civilisation; Inventing the Future, 1963; Innovations: Scientific, Technological & Social, 1970. Mbrships: F.Inst.P.; M.I.E.E.; F.R.S. Recip., Nobel Prize for Physics, 1971. Address: La Margioretta, Anzio, Lavinio, Viale dei Gigli, Italy.

GABOR, Mark, b. 12 Aug. 1939, NYC, USA. Writer. Educ: B.A., Reed Coll., Ore.. 1960; M.A., N.Y. Univ., 1962. Publs: The Pin-Up: A Modest History, 1972, paperback, 1973. Address: 317 E. 5th St., N.Y., NY 10003, USA.

GABRIEL, Astrik L., b. 10 Dec. 1907, Pecs, Hungary. University Professor. Educ: Ph.D. Publs: 15 scholarly books inclng: Index romain & littérature française à l'époque romantique, 1936; Die heilige Margarethe von Ungarn, 1944; The Educational Ideas of Vincent of Beauvais, 1956; Catalogue of Microfilms of One Thousand Manuscripts in the Ambrosiana, 1968; Garlandia, Studies in the History of Mediaeval Universities, 1969; Summary Bibliography of the History of Universities of Great Britain & Ireland up to 1800, 1974. Contbr. to: Am. Cath. Histl. Review; Speculum; L'Année Canonique. Mbrships. incl: Royal Histl. Soc.; Fellow, Mediaeval Acad. of Am.; C. Fellow, Inst. de France, Bavarian Acad. of Scis.; Am. Histl. Assn. Hons. incl: Prix Thorlet, Prix Dourlans, French Académie des Inscriptions, 1956; Kt., Legion of Hon., France; Kt. Cmdr., Order of Merit, Italy; Off., Palmes Académiques, France. Address: P.O. Box 578, Univ. of Notre Dame, Notre Dame, IN 46556, USA.

GABRIEL, Louise Marsh (Mrs. Cecil M.), b. 13 Jan. 1897, Arlington, Wash. D.C., USA. Writer; Teacher. Educ: W.Va. Wesleyan Coll.; Ohio Univ. Ext.; var. corres. courses. Publs: Singer On a Hilltop, 1974. Contbr. to poetry, other mags. Mbrships: Nat. Fedn. of Poetry Socs.; Past Pres., Parkersburg Chpat., W.Va. Poetry Soc.; Am. Poetry Fellowship; Am. Poetry League; Soc. of World Poets Intercontinental; Centro Studi E. Scambi Int., Rome. Hons: 1st Prize, & Nature Poetry Prize, Little Kanawha Regional, 1974; 1st Prizes, W.Va. State Contest, 1956, 1970, 2nd Prize, 1970; 1st Prize Nature Poetry Contest, 1973; 1st Prize, W.Va. Poetry Contest, 1974. Address: 3107 Custer St., Parkersburg, WV 26101, USA.

GABRIEL, Richard Alan, b. 16 Dec. 1942, Providence, R.I., USA. College Professor. Educ: A.B., Providence Coll., R.I., 1964; M.A., Univ. of R.I., 1966; Ph.D., Univ. of Mass., 1969. Publs: The Ethnic Factor in the Urban Polity, 1973; The Environment: Critical Factors in Strategy Development (w. Sylvan Cohen), 1973; Program Evaluation: A Social Science Approach, 1975. Contbr. to: Polity; Outlook; etc. Mbrships. incl: New Engl. Pol. Sci. Assn.; Am. Pol. Sci. Assn. Hons. incl: Nat. Sci. Rsch. Fellowship, 1968; Post-Doct. Rsch. Fellow, Univ. of Mass., 1974. Address: 100 Allen St., Manchester, NH 03102, USA.

GADDA-CONTI, Piero, b. 13 Feb. 1902, Milan, Italy. Writer; Journalist. Educ: LL.D. Publs: (novels) Mozzo, 1930; Gagliarda, 1932; Festa da Ballo, 1937; Adamira, 1956; La Paura, 1970; (essays) Vocazione Mediterranea, 1940; Vita di Puccini, 1955. Mbr., Rotary Club, Milan. Hons: Premio Italia Letteraria, 1930; Premio Bagutta, 1971. Address: Piazza Castello 20, Milan, Italy.

GADDIS, William, b. 1922, NYC, USA. Writer. Publs: (novels) The Recognitions, 1955; J.R., forthcoming 1975. Address: c/o Candida Donadio & Assocs., 111 W. 57th St., N.Y., NY 10019, USA.

GAGLIARDO, John G., b. 13 Aug. 1933, Chgo., Ill., USA. Professor of History. Educ: A.B., 1954, M.A., 1957, Univ. of Kansas; M.A., 1958, Ph.D., 1962, Yale Univ. Publs: Enlightened Despotism, 1967; From Pariah to Patriot: The Changing Image of the German Peasant,

1770-1840, 1969. Contbr. to: Am. Histl. Review; Jrnl. of Mod. Hist.; etc. Mbrships. incl: New Engl. Histl. Assn. (VP, 1973-74; Pres., 1974-75); Am. Histl. Assn. Address: 10 Emerson Place, Apt. 7C, Boston, MA 02114, USA.

GAHRTON, Per, b. 2 Feb. 1943, Malmö, Sweden. Writer. Educ: B.A. Publs: Children in Sweden, 1968; The Struggle for Palestine, 1970; Stand Up & Fight, Old People!, 1972; Revolution in Swedish, 1972. Contbr. to: Aftonbladet; Sydsvenska Dagbladet; Folket I Bild Kulturfront; Middle E. Int. Mbr., Swedish Authors Assn. Address: Mariagatan 7 B, 22353 Lund, Sweden.

GAIDA-GAIDAMAVICIUS, (Rev.) Pranas, pen names ZAIDYS, Pranas; CHANTIER, P., b. 26 Jan. 1914, Bajorai, Lithuania. Priest; Editor. Educ: Th.D. Publs: Homeless Man, 1951; Giant, Hero, Saint, 1954; The Great Unrest, 1961; Ed., Lithuanians in Canada, 1967. Contbr. to: Zidinys; Naujoji Romuva; Aidai; Ateitis; La Libre Belgique; Ed., Teviskes Ziburiai (The Lights of Homeland) wkly. Mbrships: Lithuanian Cath. Acad. of Sci.; Can. Consultative Coun. on Multiculturalism; Assn. for Advancement of Baltic Studies. Address: 2185 Stavebank Rd., Mississauga, Ont., L5C 1T3, Can.

GAINES, Ernest J., b. 15 Jan. 1933, Oscar, La., USA. Writer. Educ: B.A., San Fran. State Coll., 1957; Stanford Univ., 1958-59. Publs: (novels) Catherine Carmier, USA, 1964, UK, 1966; Of Love & Dust, USA, 1967, UK, 1968; The Autobiography of Miss Jane Pittman, 1971; (short stories) Bloodline, 1968. Contbr. to: Transfer, San Fran.; N.M. Quarterly. Hons: Wallace Stegner Fellowship, 1958; Grant, J.H. Jackson Fund, 1959; Grant, Nat. Endowment for Arts, 1966. Address: 998 Divisadero St., San Fran., CA 94115, USA.

GAINES, Matthew John, b. 1937, Ashington, UK. Information Officer, National Radiological Protection Board. Educ: B.Sc., Univ. of Nottingham. Publs: Atomic Energy, 1969. Address: 18 Green Ridges, Headington, Oxford, UK.

GAINHAM, Sarah, b. 1 Oct. 1922, London, UK. Writer. Publs: Time Right Deadly, 1956; Cold Dark Night, 1957; Mythmaker, 1957; The Stone Roses, 1958; Silent Hostages, 1959; Night Falls on the City, 1967; Place in the Country, 1969; Private Worlds (trilogy), 1970; Maculan's Daughter, 1974. Contbr. to: Spectator (European corres., 1957-67). Mbr., PEN. Address: A 1090 Vienna IX, Porzellangasse 7, Austria.

GAISER, Gerd, b. 15 Sept. 1908, Oberriexingen, Württemberg, Germany. Professor; Writer. Educ: Ph.D., Tübingen Univ., Königsberg; Acads. of Art, Stuttgart & Königsberg. Publs: Zwischenland, 1949; (novels) Eine Stimme hebt an, 1950; Das Schiff im Berg, 1953; Die Sterbende Jagd, 1954; Schlussball, 1957; (stories) Einmal und Oft, 1956; Gib acht in Domokosch, 1959; Am Pass Nascondo, 1960; Umgang mit Kunst, 1974. Hons: Fontane Prize, City Berlin, 1951; Lit. Prize Bavarian Acad. Fine Arts, 1955; Immermann Prize, City Düsseldorf, 1959; Raabe Prize, City Brunswick, 1961. Address: 7410 Reutlingen, Robert Koch Str. 39, W. Germany.

GALABÁRDI, Zoltán, b. 20 Jan. 1928, Nagykutas, Hungary. Reader in the Dubbing Studio, Budapest. Publs: Papsajt (Mallow, satire), 1958; Átkozottak (The Damned), 1962; Mòres (Lesson, satire), 1963; A világ rendje (The Order of the World), 1965; Egyszeregy (Elements of Arithmetics), 1968; Hetvenkedök (Blusterers), 1972. Contbr. to: Népszabadság. Mbrships. incl: Hungarian Writers' Org. Hons: Gabor Andor Prize for satirical writings, 1960; József Attila Prize, 162. Address: Kresz Géza u. 19, 1132 Budapest, Hungary.

GALAMBOS, Lajos, b. 14 Oct. 1929, Kotaj, Hungary. Writer. Educ: Univ. of Marxism. Publs: (novels) Gonosz Kátyú, 1960; Hideg van tegnap óta, 1961; Isten öszi csillaga, 1962; Mostohagyerekek, 1963; Zsilipek, 1969; Mit tudtok ti Pille Mariáról, 1969; Azok as álmok, 1970; Örök malom, 1969; Fekete Kötés, 1966; Nyilj meg ég, 1971. Contbr. to: Uj Iras. Mbrships: Bd., Alliance of Hungarian Authors; Nat. Coun. of Peace. Hons: Jozsef Attila Prize, 1962; SZOT Prize, 1960. Address: Fehérvári u. 155, H-1119 Budapest XI, Hungary.

GALAMBOSI, Làszlò, b. 2 July 1928, Berkesd, Hungary. Poet; Teacher. Publs: (poetry) Lengö fényhidak (Swinging Lightbridges), 1964; Sárkányok és tüzfak (Kites & Firetrees), 1967; A Köliliom vára (Fortress of the Stone

Lily), 1970; A láng örömei (Joys of Flame), 1972; Az irgalom ágai (Branches of Mercy), 1974; Bárany és holló (Lamb & Raven), 1975; Lepkekirály (Butterfly King), 1975. Contbr. to num. Hungarian publs. Mbrships. incl: Hungarian Writers' Union. Hons: Zrinyi Prize; Janus Pannonius Prize. Address: Pécs, Münich Ferenc u.22, Hungary.

GALAND, René, b. 27 Jan. 1923, Chateauneuf-du-Faou, France. Professor of French. Educ: Lic. ès Lettres, Univ. of Rennes, 1944; Ph.D., Yale Univ., USA, 1952. Publs: L'ame celtique de Renan, 1959; Baudelaire: poétiques et poésie, 1969; Saint-John Perse, 1972; Baudelaire as a Love Poet & Other Essays (co-author), 1969; The Binding of Proteus (co-author). Contbr. to: French Review; Romanic Review; Symposium; MLA publs.; Yale French Studies; Nouvelle Revue de Bretagne; Bulletin Baudelairien; Collier's Yr. Book; Russian Lit. Archives; Am. Legion of Honor Mag.; Bulletin of New England MLA; Nineteenth Century French Studies. Address: 8 Leighton Rd., Wellesley, MA 02181, USA.

GALANOY, Ivan Terry, b. 2 Nov. 1927, Phila., Pa., USA. Author; Journalist; Magazine Writer & Editor. Educ: B.A., Elwood Coll., L.A., Calif., 1949. Publs: Down The Tube, 1970, 1971; Tonight! 1972, 1974. Contbr. to: New Yorker; Playboy; Cosmopolitan; Rdrs. Digest; Sports Illustrated; Chgo., Ill. Tribune; etc. (over 400 published mag. articles & stories). Mbrships: Authors' Guild of Am.; Writers' Guild; ASCAP; Authors' League of Am. Hons. incl: Preceptor Award, San Fran. State Coll., 1971; Special Collections Award, Univ. of Calif., 1972; Kt. of the Mark Twain Soc., 1973. Agent: Frances Collin, Marie Rodell Agency. Address: San Fran., CA, USA.

GALATOPOULOS, Selios, b. 1932, Nicosia, Cyprus. Author. Educ: B.Sc., Univ. of London, UK. Publs: Maria Callas, 1964; Callas, La Divina: Art that Conceals Art, 1966; Italian Opera, 1971; V. Bellini: His Life & Work, 1975. Contbr. to: Music & Musicians; Contemporary Review; Mondo Lirico; Lirica Nel Mondo; Record & Recordings; BBC Radio & TV; R.T.E. (Eire); CBC (Cyprus); Opera Mag. Address: 48 Chiltern Court, Baker Street, London NW1, UK.

GALE, Daphne Frances Rumsey, b. 22 Jan. 1915, London, UK. Midwifery Superintendent, St. Thomas's Hospital; Homesister, 1st Year Student Nurses; Sister in Charge, Special Clinic. Trained, Nightingale Training Schl.; St. Thomas's Hosp.; Hosp. for Sick Children, Gt. Ormond St., London; S.R.N.; R.S.C.N.; S.C.M. Publs: Your First Baby, 1954. Contbr. to: Mother & Child (Bd., Ed. staff); sev. nursing jrnls. Mbrships: Royal Coll. of Nursing; V.A.D. Club. Address: Flat 2, Sunny Bank, 44 Sandgate Hill, Folkestone, Kent, UK.

GALE, Donald Hawking, b. 1908, Okehampton, Devon, UK. School Headmaster. Publs: Number Readiness 1-4, 1963; The Teaching of Numbers, 1963; Number Language Series 1-6, 1964, 2nd ed., 1965; Number Readiness Workbooks 1-6, 1965-70; All Over the World Assignment Cards, 1968; The Decimal Story, 1969; Global Activities 1-6, 1972. Contbr. to Teacher. Mbrships: Soc. of Authors; Head Tchrs. Assn. Address: 23 Blakesley Road, Yardley, Birmingham B25 8XU, UK.

GALE, Ramona-Ann, b. Spencer, Iowa, USA. Writer. Educ: B.Sc. Publs: Prehistoric Life, 1973; also author of a TV play & several feature programmes. Mbr., Soc. of Authors. Address: Greystones, Prior Road, Camberley, Surrey, UK.

GALE, Robert L., b. 27 Dec. 1919, Des Moines, Iowa, USA. Educator; Author. Educ: B.A., Dartmouth Coll., 1942; M.A., 1947, Ph.D., 1952, Columbia Univ. Publs. incl: Thomas Crawford, American Sculptor, 1964; Plots & Characters in Henry James, 1965; Simplified Approach to Emerson & Transcendentalism, 1966; Plots & Characters in Nathaniel Hawthorne, 1968; Plots & Characters in Edgar Allan Poe, 1970; Francis Parkman, 1973; Plots & Characters in Mark Twain, 1973. Contbr. to: Am. Lit.; 19th-Century Fiction; PMLA; Mod. Fiction Studies; etc. Mbr., MLA of Am. Address: 131 Techview Ter., Pittsburgh, PA 15213, USA.

GÁLL, István, b. 28 Dec. 1931, Budapest, Hungary. Managing Editor of Uj Irás (Literary Review). Publs: Patkánylyuk (Rat's nest, novel), 1961; Kétpárevezös szerelem (Love of Double-culler, stories), 1962; Csapda (The Trap, novel), 1966; Rohanók (The Hurryings, stories),

1968; Napimádo (The Sun-worshipper, novel), 1970; Az öreg (The Old Man, novel), 1974. Contbr. to: Kortárs; Élet és irodalom. Mbrships: PEN; Union of Hungarian Writers. Hons: József Attila Prize; Prize of Ctrl. Coun. of Hungarian Trade Unions. Address: O-utca 5.III, 1066 Budapest VI, Hungary.

GALLACHER, Tom, b. 16 Feb. 1934, Alexandria, Dunbartonshire, UK. Playwright. Major plays performed: Our Kindness to Five Persons, 1969; Mr. Joyce is Leaving Paris, 1971; Revival! 1972; Schellenbrack, 1973; Bright Scene Fading, 1973; The Only Street . . . 1973; Personal Effects, 1974. Mbrships: Fndr. Mbr., Scottish Soc. of Playwrights; Dunbarton People's Theatre. Address: c/o Dr. Jan Van Loewen Ltd., 81/83 Shaftesbury Ave., London W1, UK.

GALLAGHER, Joseph Peter O'Neill, b. 1917, London, UK. Author; Journalist/Photographer. Publs: The Prince of Thieves (w. J. J. Lynx), 1963; The Great Hohenzollern Scandal (w. J. J. Lynx), 1963; Pimpernel of the Vatican, 1967; Fred Karno — Master of Mirth & Tears, 1971; The Price of Charity — A Study of Charity Finances, 1975. Contbr. to: Press Assn.; Reuter; Express Newspapers; Brit. United Press; Irish News Agcy. (Fndr. & Gen. Mgr.); Sunday Dispatch. Mbr., Wig & Pen Club. Address: 9 Wellsmoor Gdns., Bickley, Kent, UK.

GALLAGHER, Thomas, b. NYC, USA. Author. Educ: A.B., Columbia Coll.; grad. work, New Schl. for Soc. Rsch. Publs: The Gathering Darkness, 1952; The Monogamist, 1955; Fire at Sea: The Story of the Morro Castle, 1959; Oona O', 1964; The Doctors' Story, 1967; the X-craft Raid, 1971; Assault in Norway, 1975. Contbr. to num. mags. inclng: Am. Heritage; N.Y. Mag.; Look; Redbook; Good Housekeeping; Reader's Digest. Mbrships. incl: Authors Guild. Hons. incl: Edgar Allan Poe Award, 1959. Address: 440 Riverside Dr., N.Y., NY 10027. USA.

GALLAHER, Dulcie Violet, pen name CUNDELL, Dulcie V., b. 11 Jan. 1921, Nelson, NZ. Public Servant. Educ: B.A. Studies, Canterbury Univ., Christchurch. Author, A Lamp unto our Feet, 1973. Contbr. to: NZ Broadcasting; NZ Listener; Christch. Star; NZ Herald, Auckland; NZ Womens Weekly. Mbrships: NZ Women Writers Soc.; S. Island Writers Assn.; Fndn. Mbr., Wm. Morris Singing Grp. Recip., award for short story, NZ Herald, Auckland. Address: 49 Major Horkbrook Rd., Mount Pleasant, Christchurch 8, NZ

GALLANT, Mavis, b. 1922, Montreal, Can. Writer. Publs: The Other Paris; Green Water, Green Sky. Contbr. to: New Yorker; Harper's Bazaar; Esquire; Texas Review; Glamour. Address: 83 Blvd. de Garavan, Menton-Garavan, France.

GALLEYMORE, Fanny, b. 21 May 1946, London, UK. Novelist; Film & TV Dramatist. Publs: The Orange Tree, 1970; Ground Wave Sailing, 1975. Mbr., Writers' Guild of GB. Agent: Peters & Co. Address: c/o Michael Sissons, A.D. Peters & Co., 10 Buckingham St., London WC2N 6BU, UK.

GALLICO, Paul William, b. 26 July 1897, NYC, USA. Novelist; Screen Writer; Journalist. Educ: B.S., Columbia Univ. Publs. incl: The Snow Goose, 1941; The Lonely, 1947; Jennie, 1950; Trial By Terror, 1952; Love of Seven Dolls, 1954; Ludmila, 1955; Thomasina, 1957; The Hurricane Story, 1959; Scruffy, 1962; The Day the Guinea Pig Talked, 1963; Mrs Harris, MP, 1965; The Man who was Magic, 1966; The Story of Silent Night, 1967; The Poseidon Adventure, 1969; The Zoo Gang, 1971; Honourable Cat, 1972. Contbr. to: Esquire; Argosy; etc. Address: 69 Great Russell St., London WC1, UK.

GALLUP, Donald, b. 1913, Sterling, Conn., USA. Bibliographer. Educ: B.A., Ph.D., Litt.D., Yale Univ. Publs: Ezra Pound Bibliography, 1963; T. S. Eliot Bibliography, 1969. Contbr. to: Atlantic; Book Collector; Times Lit. Supplement. Address: 216 Bishop St.-201, New Haven, CT 06511, USA.

GALOUYE, Daniel Francis, pen name DANIELS, Louis G., b. 11 Feb. 1920, New Orleans, La., USA. Journalist; Science Fiction Writer. Educ: B.A., La. State Univ., 1941. Publs. incl: Dark Universe, 1961, 2nd ed. 1971; Lords of the Psychon, 1963; The Last Leap & Other Stories, 1964; Simulacron-3 (Brit. ed., Counterfeit World), 1964; The Lost Perception, 1966; Project Barrier, 1968; The Infinite Man, 1973. Contbr. to: New Orleans States-Item; Sci. & Mech.; Popular Sci.; Num. sci.-fiction mags. in USA, UK, France,

Italy, Germany, Spain, & Japan. Mbr., Sci. Fiction Writers Assn. Hons. incl: Best Sci. Fiction Novel of 1962, Books & Bookmen, 1963. Address: 5669 Catina St., New Orleans, LA 70124, USA.

GALPIN, Brian John Francis, b. 1921, Hendon, Middlesex, UK. Barrister-at-Law; Recorder of the Crown Court; Councillor, Metropolitan Borough of Fulham 1951-59; Chairman, 1956-72, VP, 1974-, The Galpin Society. Publs: A Manual of International Law; Maxwell Interpretation of Statutes, 10th & 11th eds. Contbr. to: Halsbury's Laws of England, 3rd & 4th eds.; Ency. Forms & Precedents: Rent & Mortgage Interest Restrictions, 23rd ed.; Jrnl. Planning Law; Galpin Soc. Jrnl. Mbrships: (clubs) Travellers'; Pratt's. Address: Saint Bruno House, Charters Rd., Sunningdale, Berks., UK.

GALTON, Raymond Percy, b. 1930, Paddington, London, UK. Film & TV Scriptwriter. Publs: (book) Hancock (co-author), 1961; (films) The Rebel; The Bargee; The Spy With the Cold Nose; The Wrong Arm of the Law; Loot; Steptoe & Son Ride Again; (TV series) Hancock's Half Hour; Comedy Playhouse; Steptoe & Son; The Galton & Simpson Comedy; Casanova '73. Mbr., Screenwriters Guild. Agent: A.L.S. Management Ltd. Address: A.L.S. Management Ltd., 67 Brook Street, London W1, UK.

GAMMAGE, Allen Z., b. 27 May 1917, Cale, Ark., USA. Professor of Criminal Justice. Educ: A.S., Tarleton State Coll., Stephenville, Tex., 1936; B.A., 1938, M.A., 1945, Ph.D., 1958, Univ. of Tex., Austin. Publs: Your Future in Law Enforcement, 1961, 2nd ed., 1974; Police Training in the United States, 1963; Basic Police Report Writing, 1961; Alcoholism, Skid Row & the Police, 1972; Police Unions, 1972; Basic Criminal Law, 1974. Contbr. to: Police Mag.; Jrnl. of Criminal Law, Criminol. & Police Sci. Mbrships: Am. Soc. of Pub. Admnstrs.; Disabled Am. Veterans; Reserve Offs. Assn. of USA. Recip., Writer's Grant, Calif. State Univ., Sacramento, 1973. Address: 2613 Patton Way, Sacramento, CA 95818, USA.

GAMORAN, Mamie G., b. 17 Jan. 1900, L.I., N.Y., USA. Author. Educ: Columbia Univ.; Univ. of Cinn., Ohio; Jewish Theol. Sem. Publs: The Voice of the Prophets; With Singer & Sage; Hillel's Happy Holidays; Hillel's Calendar; Days & Ways; Funways to Holiday ; The New Jewish History, Books I, II, III, & Activity Books; Independent Learning Unit on New Jewish History, Book I; The Story of Samson Benderly; Independent Learning Units on Bible Concepts; Talks to Jewish Teachers (w. Dr. Gamoran). Contbr. to: Liberal Judaism; Reconstructionist; Jewish Spectator; Hadassah Mag.; Christian Home. Address: 229 W. 78th St., N.Y., NY 10024, USA.

GANDER, Leonard Marsland, pen name MEABEY, Leonard, b. 27 June 1902, Limehouse, London, UK. Journalist. Educ: City of London Coll. Publs: Atlantic Battle, 1941; Long Road to Leros, 1946; After These Many Quests, 1950; Television For All, 1950. Contbr. to: Daily Telegraph & Mag.; Sunday Telegraph; Times of India, Bombay. Mbrships: Press Club (Chmn., 1959-60); Savage Club; Lord's Taveners; Fellow, Royal TV Soc., 1961. Recip., 5 Campaign Medals for work as Daily Telegraph War Corres. Address: 8 Paddock Green, Rustington, Sussex BN16 3AU, UK.

GANN, Lewis Henry, b. 1924, Mainz, Germany. Senior Fellow, Hoover Institution, Stanford University, Calif., USA. Educ: M.A., B.Litt., D.Phil., Oxford Univ. Publs. incl: A History of Northern Rhodesia, Early Days to 1953, 1964; Huggins of Rhodesia: The Man & His Country (w. Michael Gelfand), 1964; A History of Southern Rhodesia: Early Days to 1934, 1965; Burden of Empire: An Appraisal of Western Colonialism in Africa South of the Sahara (w. P. Duignan), 1967; Central Africa: The Former British States, 1971; Guerrillas in History, 1971; Africa & the World at Large: An Introduction to the History of Sub-Saharan Africa from Antiquity to 1840 (w. P. Duignan), 1972; A Bibliographical Guide to Colonialism in Sub-Saharan Africa (w. P. Duignan), 1973; (co-ed. & contbr.) Colonialism in Africa 1870-1960, 5 vols., 1969-75. Contbr. to num. acad. publs. var. countries. Fellow, Royal Histl. Soc. Address: Hoover Inst., Stanford Univ., CA 94305, USA.

GANSS, Gisela, (née Rau), b. 17 Jan. 1927, Halberstadt, Germany. Interpreter; Translator; Painter. Publs: (short stories) Löwenliebe, 1969; Die Grosse Freiheit, 1969; Triff mich am alten Ort, 1973; (essays) Uber die Unmöglichkeit einen Lebenslauf zu schreiben, 1971; In Krefeld und anderswo. Contbr. to var. newspapers, mags., & art

exhibitions. Mbrships: Soc. German Authors; Citizens' Comm. (Exec.). Address: 5 Cologne 80, Piccolominstr. 433, W. Germany.

GANTNER, Neilma Baillieu, pen name SIDNEY, Neilma, b, 1922, San Fran., USA. Writer. Educ: Univ. of Melbourne, Aust.; B.A., Stanford Univ., Calif., USA. Publs: Saturday Afternoon, 1959; Beyond the Bay, 1966; The Eye of the Needle, 1970. Contbr. to: Anthol. of Aust. Humour; Aust. Signposts; Age Lit. Supplement; Meenjin. Mbrships: Aust. Soc. of Authors; Vic. Fellowship of Aust. Writers. Address: P.O. Box 497, S. Yarra, Victoria 3141, Australia.

GANZ, Paul Leonhard, b. 29 Dec. 1910, Basle, Switz. Art Historian. Educ: Ph.D., Univ. of Zurich, 1935. Publs: 16 titles, inclng: Das Wesen der franz. Kunst um späten Mittelalten, 1938; Meister Konrad Witz von Rottweil, 1947; Die Minaturen des Basler Universitätsmatrikel, 1960; Das Schweizer Haus, 1964; Die Basler Glasmaler der Spätrenaissance u. der Barockzeit, 1966; Die Basler Professorengalerie der Alten Aula, 1975. Mbr., Swiss Soc. of Authors. Address: Wiesenweg 12, Waldheim, 3652 Hilterfingen BE, Switz.

GAPERT, Werner Horst, b. 24 Nov. 1913, Danzig, Germany. Technician. Publs: Lied der Arbeit, 1934; Spuren im Sand, 1947; Licht Gerickt; Nach Feierabend, 1967; (poetry) Glaube u. Herz, 1941; (anthol.) Pegasus, 1968. Contbr. to: Danziger Hauskalender; Der Schmelztiegel; Remscheider Generalanzeiger; Rheinische Post; Um Holm und Helling. Mbr., Soc. German speaking Authors. Hons: Geneva Y.M.C.A. Prize Lyric Poetry, 1947; Steel Ind. Prize for Short Stories & Poetry, 1959; 65 Group Poetry Prize. Address: 563 Remscheid, Stockder Str. 121, W. Germany.

GAPPMAYR, Heinz, b. 7 Oct. 1925, Innsbruck, Austria. Designer. Publs: Zeichen, 1962; Zeichen II, 1964; Zeichen III, 1968; Zeichen IV, 1970; Sieben visuelle Gedichte, 1972; Visuelle Gedichte (w. Palermo: Miniaturen), 1972; texte, 1972; Quadrat (silk screen prints by Antonio Calderara), 1973. Address: 6020 Innsbruck, Liebenggstr. 16, Austria.

GARAI, Gábor, b. 27 Jan. 1929, Budapest, Hungary. Writer; Teacher of Hungarian. Educ: T.D., Tchrs. Trng. Coll., Budapest. Publs: (poems) Mediterrán ősz, 1962; Artisták, 1963; Nyárvég, 1964; B MOEM CHE BE Abi (in Russian), 1970; A szenvedély évszakai, 1973; essays: Eszköz és eszmélet, 1965; Elférünk a földön, 1973. Contbr. to: Népszabadság; Élet és Irodalom; Uj Irás; Kortárs; Budapest Radio. Mbrships: Union of Hungarian Writers; PEN. Hons: József Attila Prize, 1959 & 1962; Kossuth Prize, 1965; Pro Arte Prize, Budapest, 1970. Address: 1012 Budapest, I Mikó u.I, Hungary.

GARBUTT, Douglas, b. 1922, Manchester, UK. Professor & Head of Department of Accountancy. Educ: Manchester High Schl. of Commerce; Garnett Coll.; M.Ed., Univ. of Leicester; Dip. Ed., London; Fellow, Inst. of Cost & Mgmt. Accts.; Assoc., Chartered Inst. of Secs. Publs: Carter's Advanced Accounts (& Key), 7th ed., 1972; Simple Guide to Capital Expenditure Decisions, 1967; Planning for Profits, 1967; Training Costs, 1969; Principles of Accounts (w. E. F. Castle), 1970. Contbr. to: Mgmt. Today; Acctcy.; The Acct.; The Cost Acct.; Bus. Systems & Equipment; other profl. jrnls. Mbrships. incl: Soc. of Authors; Assn. Univ. Tchrs.; Brit. Inst. Mgmt.; Am. Assn. of Accts.; Nat. Assn. Accts. Address: Dept. of Accountancy, Univ. of Natal at Pietermaritzburg, Natal, S. Africa.

GARCIA, Joseph, b. 19 July 1937, Gibraltar. Journalist. Publs: Gibraltar Who's Who & Year Book 1974/75. Contbr. to: Gibraltar Evening Post (Ed.); Gibraltar News Agcy. (Ed.); Fin. Times, London; Sunday Times; Daily Mail. Mbrships: Int. Press Inst.; Newspaper Press Fund of GB. Address: P.O. Box 225, Vineyard House, Gibraltar.

GARCIA-ABRINES, Luis, b. 21 June 1923, Saragossa, Spain (now US citizen). Professor of Spanish Language & Literature. Educ: B.A., Univ. of Saragossa, 1945; M.A., Univ. of Madrid, 1948. Publs: Tacitus, Complete Works (co-transl. into Spanish), 1946; Critical Ed., A. Gómez de Figueroa, Alcázar Imperial de la Fama, 1951; Instrucción de Música sobre la Guitarra Española (XVII Century), 1952, 2nd ed., 1966; Así Sueña el Profeta en sus Palabras, 1960; Cuidadano del Mundo, 1974; Fndr., Ultimas Noticias 1969, Gaceta Hispana 1970 (1st Spanish newspapers in Conn.). Contbr. to: Apéndice, Guión; Revista Hispánica Moderna; other profl. jrnls. Mbr., var. profl. & musical assns. Recip., var. grants & Fellowships. Address: 205 Osborn Ave., New Haven, CT 06511, USA.

GARCÍA FONT, Juan, b. 24 Sept. 1927, Alella, Spain. Co-ordinating Editor. Educ: Lic., Philos. Publs: Historia de la ciencia, 1964; El mensaje publicitario, 1969; Paisajes del alma, 1969; Confucianismo, Taoismo, Shintoismo, 1971; Magia, Brujería, Demonología, 1974; Historia de la alquimia en España, (pending). Mbrships: Investigator, Archives of the Crown of Aragon; Past Pres., Friends Club of UNESCO, Barcelona; Lectr., Club of Friends of India. Contbr. to: Historia y Vida; Historia del Mundo (History reviews). Recip., rsch. grant, Editora Nacional, for Historia de la alquimia en España, 1971. Address: Calle Urgel 45, 3° 1a Barcelona 11, Spain.

GARCIA MARQUEZ, Gabriel, b. 1928. Writer; Journalist. Publs. incl: La hojarasca, 1955; El coronel no tiene quien la escriba, 1961; Los funerales de la Mamá Grande, 1962; La mala hora, 1962; Cien Años de Soledad, 1967; Relato de un Náufrago, 1970; Leafstorm & other stories. Contbr. to: Mundo Nuevo, Spain; Casa de las Américas, Spain; etc. Recip., Rómulo Gallegos Prize, 1972. Address: Ed. Seix-Barral, Provenza 219, Barcelona, Spain.

GARD, Joyce, pen name of REEVES, Joyce, b. 1911, London, UK. Author. Educ: B.A., Lady Margaret Hall, Oxford. Publs: Wooroo, 1961; The Dragon of the Hill, 1963; Talargain the Seal's Whelp, 1964; Smudge of the Fells, 1965; The Snow Firing, 1967; The Mermaid's Daughter, 1969; Handysides Shall Not Fall, 1975. Transl., Journey to the Centre of the Earth, by Jules Verne, 1961. Contbr. to: Miscellany Five; Transls. from French on contemporary art. Mbrships: Inst. of Contemporary Art; Royal Archaeol. Inst.; Soc. of Authors. Address: Wrens Cottage, Charing Heath, Ashford, Kent, UK.

GARDEN, Edward James Clarke, b. 1930, Edinburgh, UK. Senior Lecturer; Choir Director. Educ: Royal Acad. of Music; Univs. of London & Edinburgh; D.Mus.; F.R.C.O.; L.R.A.M.; A.R.C.M. Publs: Balakirev: A Critical Study of His Life & Music, 1967; Tchaikovsky, 1973. Contbr. to: Music & Letters; etc. Address: Norwood, Lenzie, Nr. Glasgow, UK.

GARDINER, Lillian Johnson (Mrs. Laurence B.), b. 15 Aug. 1910, Humboldt, Tenn., USA. Educ: Peabody Coll.; Falls Bus. Coll. Publs: North Carolina Land Grants in Tennessee 1778-1791, 1958; Williamson County, Tennessee, Marriages 1800-1850, 1956; Davies-Hess Family, 1960. Contbr. to geneal. jrnls.; Fndr., Publr., Tenn. Geneal. Soc. Quarterly. Mbrships: State Pres., Tenn., Nat. League of Am. Pen Women; Tenn. Women's Press & Authors Club. Address: 1863 Cowden Ave., Memphis, TN 38104, USA.

GARDINER, Patrick Lancaster, b. 17 Mar. 1922, London, UK. University Tutor (philosophy); College Fellow. Educ: B.A., (Hist) 1942, B.A., (P.P.E.), 1947, Christ Church, Oxford. Publs: The Nature of Historical Explanation, 1952; Ed., Theories of History, 1959; Schopenhauer, 1963; Ed., 19th Century Philosophy, 1969; Ed., The Philosophy of History, 1974. Contbr. to: Mind Philos.; Philosl. Quarterly; N.Y. Review of Books; Proceedings of Aristotelian Soc., Brit. Acad.; var. philosl. anthols. & jrnls. Mbrships: Soc. of Authors; Aristotelian Soc. Address: Magdalen Coll., Oxford, UK.

GARDINER-HILL, Harold, b. 14 Feb. 1891, London, UK. Consultant Physician. Educ: Pembroke Coll., Cambridge; M.A.; M.D. Publs: Clinical Involvements, 1958; Modern Trends in Endocrinology, 4th series, 1972; Compendium of Emergencies, 3rd ed., 1971; Spanish ed., 1967; Polish ed., 1974. Contbr. to: Brit. Med. Jrnl.; Lancet; The Practitioner; Country Life; Brit. Ency. Med. Practice, Endocrine Chapts.; A Hist. of Golf in Brit., Rules Chapt. Mbrships: F.R.C.P.; Royal Soc. of Med.; Assn. of Physns.; The Carlton; The Royal & Ancient, St. Andrews. Recip., M.B.E., 1919. Address: 30 Stanhope Gdns., London SW7, UK.

GARDNER, Charles, b. 1912, Nuneaton, Warwicks., UK. Publicity Manager; Author. Publs: A.A.S.F.; Come Flying With Me; Gen Book; Modern British Aircraft; History of Brooklands (Ed.); The Great Trog Conspiracy; Trogs Afloat. Contbr. to: BBC (Air Corres., 1937-39, 1946-53; War Corres., 1939-40); Aviation jrnls.; ldng. newspapers; Punch. Mbrships: Royal Aero Club; M.C.C.; A.F.R.A.C.S. Recip., O.B.E. Address: B.A.C. Ltd., Weybridge, Surrey, UK.

GARDNER, David Pierpont, b. 24 Mar. 1933, Berkeley, Calif., USA. University Administrator; Teacher; Researcher. Educ: B.A., Brigham Young Univ., 1955; M.A., 1959,

Ph.D., 1966, Univ. of Calif., Berkeley. Publs: The California Oath Controversy, 1967. Contbr. to: Educl. Record; Jrnl. for Higher Educ. Address: 202 Park Bldg., Univ. of Utah, Salt Lake City, UT 84112, USA.

GARDNER, (Dame) Helen Louise, b. 13 Feb. 1908, London, UK. University Teacher; Professor of English Literature. Educ: B.A., 1929, M.A., 1935, D.Litt., 1963, St. Hilda's Coll., Oxford Univ. Publs: The Art of T. S. Eliot, 1949; Ed., The Divine Poems of John Donne, 1952; The Metaphysical Poets, 1957; The Business of Criticism, 1959; Ed., The Elegies & Songs and Sonnets of John Donne, 1965; A Reading of Paradise Lost, 1965; Religion & Literature, 1971; The Faber Book of Religious Verse, 1972; The New Oxford Book of English Verse, 1972. Mbrships. incl: Fellow, Brit. Acad.; F.R.S.L.; Fellow, Am. Acad. Arts & Scis.; Advsry. Comm., Leverhulme Trust, 1970—. Hons. incl: C.B.E., 1962; D.B.E., 1967; R.M. Crawshay Prize, Brit. Acad., 1953; num. hon. degrees, UK & USA. Address: Myrtle House, 12 Mill St., Eynsham, Oxford OX8 1JS, UK.

GARDNER, John William, b. 1919, Clacton, Essex, UK. Freelance Science Writer. Educ: London, Southampton & Birmingham Univs.; B.Sc., Ph.D. Publs: Electricity Without Dynamos, 1963; Science Today, 1970; Atoms Today & Tomorrow, 1970; New Frontiers in Electricity, 1973. Contbr. to: Jrnl. of Phys.; Nuovo Cimento; New Sci.; Schl. Sci. Review; etc. Mbrships: F.I.M.A.; F.Inst.P.; F.I.Nuc.E.; Soc. of Authors. Address: Woodmill, Carlton, Nuneaton, Warwicks., UK.

GARDNER, Ralph D., b. 16 Apr. 1923, NYC, USA. Advertising Executive; Corporation Director. Educ: N.Y. Univ.; Colo. State Coll. Publs: Horatio Alger, Or the American Hero Era, 1964; Road to Success, 1971; Silas Snobden's Office Boy, 1973; Cast Upon the Breakers, 1974. Contbr. to newspapers & jrnls; Former Staff Mbr., Ed. & For. Corres., N.Y. Times. Mbrships: Overseas Press Club; Frankfurt (Germany) Press Club; PEN; Bibliog. Soc. of Am.; MS Soc.; Children's Lit. Assn.; Book Reviewer & Commentator, Radio Stn. WRVR, N.Y. Hons: Awards for Litt., Horatio Alger Soc., 1964, 1972. Address: 745 5th Ave., N.Y., NY 10022, USA.

GARDNER, (Robert) Brian, other name WALSH, Robert, b. 1931, Surrey, UK. Educ: Dublin Univ., Repub. of Ireland. Publs: The Big Push; German East; The Wasted Hour; Allenby; Mafeking; The Quest For Timbuctoo; The African Dream; The Lion's Cage; The East India Company; The Public Schools; (anthols.) Up the Line to Death; The Terrible Rain; Churchill in His Time. Contbr. to: Ency. Britannica; Orbis History of Guerilla Warfare.

GARE, Nene (Mrs. Frank Ellis Gare), b. 1919, Adelaide, Australia. Publs: The Fringe Dwellers, 1961, 1966; Green Gold, 1963, 1964. Contbr. to: var. Aust. women's jrnls. Mbrships: Fellowship Aust. Writers; Aust. Soc. of Authors. Agent: Winant Towers. Address: 339 Riverton Dr., Shelley Cove, WA, Australia.

GARFIELD, Brian Francis Wynne, pen names, WYNNE, Frank; GARLAND, Bennett; O'BRIAN, Frank; WYNNE, Brian, b. 26 Jan. 1939, NYC, USA. Educ: B.A., 1959, M.A., 1963, Univ. of Ariz. Publs. incl: The Arizonans, 1961; The Lawbringers, 1962; The Vanquished, 1964; Bugle & Spur, 1966; Arizona, 1969; Sliphammer, 1970; The Hit, 1971; Relentless, 1972; Death Wish, 1972; Tripwire, 1973; Kolchak's Gold, 1974; The Threepersons Hunt, 1974; The Romanov Succession, 1974; Hopscotch, 1974; Complete Guide to Western Films, 1975; also sev. screenplays. Contbr. to: Saturday Review; Books Today; etc. Mbrships. incl: Dir., Mystery Writers of Am., Inc.; Authors League; Writers Guild of Am.; Former Pres., Western Writers of Am.; Dramatists Guild. Address: P.O. Box 376, Alpine, NJ, USA.

GARFINKLE, Louis Alan, b. 11 Feb. 1928, Seattle, Wash., USA. Screenwriter. Educ: Univ. of Calif., Berkeley; Univ. of Wash.; B.A., Univ. of Southern Calif., 1948. Publs. incl: (films) The Young Guns, 1956; I Bury the Living (Killer on the Wall), 1957; Face of Fire, 1958; The Hellbenders, 1967; A Minute to Pray, A Second to Die, 1968; The Love Doctors, 1969; Beautiful Peoople, 1970; The Doberman Gang, 1972; Little Cigars, 1973. Broadway Musical: Molly, 1973; (TV Series) The Big Picture; Day in Court; Morning Court; Accused; The Dupont Show; Sheilah Graham Show; Death Valley Days. Mbrships: Dramatists' Guild; Writers' Guild of Am., West; Acad. of Motion Picture Arts & Scis. Address: 14127 Margate St., Van Nuys, CA 91401, USA.

GARFITT, Roger, b. 22 Apr. 1944, Melksham, Wilts., UK. Freelance Writer. Educ: B.A., Merton Coll., Oxford Univ. Publs: Caught on Blue (poetry), 1970; British Poetry Since 1960 (co-author), 1972; West of Elm (poetry), 1975; Two Decades of Irish Writing (co-author), 1975. Contbr. to: Times Lit. Supplement; London Mag.; The Listener; Encounter; Stand; Poetry Nation. Mbrships: Writers' Action Grp.; Writers' Guild of GB.; Lit. Panel, Southern Arts Assn. Hons: Dorothy Mauger Lit. Award, 1973; Guinness Int. Poetry Award, 1973; Eric Gregory Award, 1974. Address: c/o South Weylands Farm, Esher Rd., Walton-on-Thames, Surrey, UK.

GARFORTH, Francis William, b. 1917, Jaffna, Ceylon. Lecturer. Educ: M.A., Queen's Coll., Cambridge; B.A., London Univ. Publs: Education & Social Purpose, 1962; Ed., Locke's Thoughts Concerning Education, 1964; Ed., John Dewey Selected Educational Writings, 1966; John Locke's Of the Conduct of the Understanding, 1966; Ed., Bede's Historia Ecclesiastica, Selections, 1967; Ed., Education for the Seventies, 1969; The Scope of Philosophy, 1971; Ed., John Stuart Mill on Education, 1971. Contbr. to: Greece & Rome; Latin Tchng.; Relig. in Educ.; Studies in Educ. Mbr., Assn. of Univ. Tchrs. Address: Dept. of Educ., 173 Cottingham Rd., Hull, UK.

GARLAND, Ailsa Mary, b. London, UK. Journalist; Broadcaster. Publs: Lion's Share (autobiog.), 1968. Contbr. to: Ed., Vogue, 1960-64; Woman's Jrnl., 1964-70. Mbrships: Press Club of London; Soc. of Mag. Eds. Recip., Penna D'Oro, Rome, 1958. Agent: A. M. Heath. Address: Christmas House, Edwardstone, Colchester, UK.

GARLAND, Margaret J. C. Wolff (Mrs.), b. 5 Sept. 1907, Ionia, Iowa, USA. Educator. Educ: B.A., Iowa State Tchrs. Coll., 1928; M.A., Univ. of Iowa, 1940; Grad. study, Univs. of Wis., Minn., Kan. State, N. Iowa & Iowa State. Publs: The Good Wine, Poems Written During a Lifetime, 1972. Contbr. to: poetry, educl. jrnls.; One chapt., in Techniques of Christian Writing, 1960. Mbrships. incl: Past Pres., Waterloo-Cedar Rapids Br., Nat. League of Am. Pen Women; Judge, Iowa Poetry Assn. & Midwest Fedn. of Chaparral Poets; Iowa Poetry Assn.; Past State Chmn., Nat. Coun. of Coll. Publs: Advsrs. Hons: var. poetry prizes inclng: Poetry Achievement Award, other prizes, Iowa Poetry Day Assn., Midwest Fedn. of Chaparral Poets, Nat. League of Am. Pen Women. Address: 1309 2nd Ave. SW, Waverly, IA 50677, USA.

GARLICK, Raymond, b. 21 Sept. 1926, London, UK. Anglo-Welsh Poet. Educ: Univ. Coll., Bangor, 1944-48. Publs: A Sense of Europe: Collected poems 1954-68, 1968; An Introduction to Anglo-Welsh Literature, 1970, 2nd ed., 1972; A Sense of Time: poems & antipoems 1969-72, 1972. Contbr. to: The Anglo-Welsh Review; Poetry Wales; Planet; Transatlantic Review; etc. Mbr., Yr Academi Gymreig. Recip., Welsh Arts Coun. Lit. Prizes, 1969, 1973. Address: Hen Ysgoldy, Llansteffan, Dyfed SA33 5HA, Wales, UK.

GARNER, Alan, b. 17 Oct. 1934, Congleton, Cheshire, UK. Author. Educ: Magdalen Coll., Oxford. Publs: The Wierdstone of Brisingamen, 1960; The Moon of Gomrath, 1963; Elidor, 1965; Holly from the Bongs, 1966; The Old Man of Mow, 1967; The Owl Service, 1967; The Hamilton Hamilton Book of Goblins, 1969; Red Shift, 1973; The Breadhorse (w. A. Trowski), 1975; The Guizer, 1975; The Green Mist (dance drama), 1970; (Libretti) The Bellybag, 1971; Potter Thompson, 1972; Holly from the Bongs, 1974. Contbr. to: Times; Guardian; Times Lit. Supplement. Mbr., Soc. of Authors. Hons: Lib. Assn. Carnegie Medal, 1967; Guardian Award, 1968. Address: c/o Messrs. William Collins, 14 St. James's Place, London SW1, UK.

GARNER, Hugh, b. 1913, Batley, UK. Writer. Educ: Riverdale Tech., Toronto, Can. Publs: 7 novels; 84 short stories; book of essays. Contbr. to num. mags.; Toronto Telegram; CBC; BBC. Mbr., Assn. of Can. TV & Radio Artists. Address: 33 Erskine Ave., Apt. 1006, Toronto 12, Ont., Can.

GARNER, William, b. Grimsby, UK. Novelist. Publs: Overkill, 1966; The Deep Deep Freeze, 1968; The Us or Them War, 1969; The Puppet-Masters (Am. title: The Manipulators), 1970; The Andra Fiasco (Am. title: Strip Jack Naked), 1971; Ditto, Brother Rat! 1972; A Big Enough Wreath, 1974. Agent: Jonathan Clowes Ltd. Address: c/o Jonathan Clowes Ltd., 19 Jeffrey's Place, London NW1 9PP, UK.

GARNETT, David, b. 9 Mar. 1892, Brighton, Sussex, UK. Author. Educ: Univ. Coll. Schl., Imperial Coll. of Sci. Publs. incl: Lady Into Fox, 1922; A Man in the Zoo, 1924; Go She Must, 1927; No Love, 1929; The Grasshoppers Come, 1931; Pocahontas, 1933; Beany-Eye, 1935; War In the Air, 1942; The Golden Echo, 1953; The Familiar Faces, 1962; Aspects of Love, 1955; A Shot In the Dark, 1958; Ulterior Motives, 1966; A Clean Slate, 1971; Purl & Plain, 1973; Plough Over the Bones, 1973; The Master Cat, 1974. Contbr. to: New Statesman, 1932-39 (Lit. Ed., 1932-35). Mbrships: F.R.L.S. Hons: Hawthornden & James Tait-Black Prizes, 1923; C.B.E., 1955. Address: Le Verger de Charry, Montcuq 46-800, France.

GARNETT, Eve, b. Upper Wick, Worcs., UK. Author; Illustrator. Educ: Schl. of Painting, Royal Acad. Schls., London. Publs: (all illustrated by author) The Family from One End Street, 1937; Is It Well With the Child? (foreword by Walter de la Mare), 1938; A Book of the Seasons (anthol.), 1952; Further Adventures of the Family from One End Street, 1956; Holiday at the Dew Drop Inn, 1962; To Greenland's Icy Mountains: The Story of Hans Egede (foreword by Prof. N. Egede Block-Hoell), 1968; Lost & Found, 1974; (Illustrator) Stevenson's A Child's Garden of Verses, 1948. Contbr. to: Lib. Assn., Chosen for Children; Horn Book, USA. Mbrships: PEN; Soc. of Authors. Recip., Carnegie Gold Medal, 1938. Address: c/o Lloyds Bank Ltd., Lewes, Sussex, UK.

GARNIER, (Charlotte) Marie-Reine, b. Bourges, France. Author; Journalist. Educ: Strasbourg Univ.; Paris; Lic. és Lettres; Dr. és Lettres; B.A., St. Mary-in-the-Woods Coll., Ind., USA. Publs: Henry James et la France, 1927; Vieux Paris (w. Ch. Edwards), 1930; Ed., Cross Channel, London, 1937-40. Contbr. to: Le Mercure de France. L'Ere Nouvelle; Le Quotidien; Les Nouvelles Littéraires; Le Berry Républicain; La Vie de Rail; etc. Mbrships: Soc. des Gens de Lettres de France; Inst. of Jrnlsts., London; For. Press Assn., London. Address: 20 Talbot House, 98 St. Martin's Lane, London WC2N 4AX, UK.

GARP-STOLPE, Staffan, b. 15 Jan. 1943, Lindesberg, Sweden. Teacher; Author. Educ: Lit. studies, Univ. of Uppsala. Publs: Linser, 1971; Enosis, 1972; Den Doende, 1974. Contbr. to: Nerikes Allehanda; Uppsala Nya Tidning; Varmlands Folkblad. Mbr., Swedish Union of Authors. Address: Box 292, Persberg, Sweden.

GARRARD, (Rev.) Lancelot Austin, b. 1904, Skelbrooke, Yorks., UK. Unitarian Minister, Retired; Professor Emeritus; Author. Educ: B.D., M.A., Wadham Coll., Oxford; Marburg. Publs: Duty & the Will of God; The Historical Jesus: Schweitzer's Quest & Ours; Athens or Jerusalem? Contbr. to: The Hibbert Jrnl. (Ed., 1951-62); Jrnl. of Theol. Studies; Inquirer. Mbr., Studiorum Novi Testamenti Societas. Hons: LL.D., Emerson Coll., Boston, USA; Fellow, Manchester Coll., 1973-. Address: 13 Holmlea Rd., Goring, Reading, Berks. RG8 9EX, UK.

GARRATT, Arthur John, b. 11 Jan. 1916, Aldershot, UK. Physicist; Managing Director, Optical Company, Engineering Company, Film Company. Educ: B.Sc., London Univ. Publs: Ed., Penguin Science Survey, 1961, 1965; Ed., Penguin Technology Survey, 1966, 1967; Energy From Oil, 1968. Contbr. to: Mgmt. Today; Mgmt. Decision; Engr.; Radio Times; TV Times; Discovery; Jrnl. of Royal TV Soc.; Studio Sound; etc. Mbrships. incl: Worshipful Co. of Sci. Instrument Makers (Past Master); Inst. of Phys. (Fellow); F.R.S.A.; Soc. of Film & TV Arts; Assn. of Brit. Sci. Writers; Writers' Guild. Hons: M.B.E., 1952; Wireless World Prize, for Sci. on TV. Address: Woodruffe, Claremont Lane, Esher, Surrey KT10 9DR, UK.

GARRETT, George (Palmer), Jr., b. 11 June 1929, Orlando, Fla., USA. Writer; Professor of English. Educ: B.A., 1952, M.A., 1956, Princeton Univ. Publs. incl: (novels) The Finished Man, USA, 1959, UK, 1960; Do. Lord Remember Me, USA & UK, 1965; Death of the Fox, 1971; (short stories) King of the Mountain, USA, 1958, UK, 1959; A Wreath for Garibaldi, UK, 1969; (verse) For a Bitter Season, 1967; Ed., Contemporary Poetry Series, 1963-68; var. anthols. Contbr. to: Transatlantic Review; Hollins Critic (Co-Ed., 1968-); Contempora (Contbng. Ed., 1970-); Film Jrnl. (Contbng. Ed., 1971-). Hons. incl: Prix de Rome, Am. Acad. Arts & Letters, 1958. Address: 3600 Chateau Dr., Apt. 216, Columbia, SC 29204, USA.

GARRETT, Thomas Kenneth, b. 21 Oct. 1919, Brentford, UK. Engineer; Author. Educ: Leicester & Loughborough Colls. of Technol. Publs: The Motor

Vehicle, 1972; Valve Life, 1973. Contbr. to var. engrng. jrnls.; Worldwide. Address: 51 Crossfell Rd., Leverstock Green, Hemel Hempstead, Herts., HP3 8RQ, UK.

GARRISON, Charles J., pen name GARRISON, Chuck, b. 29 Sept. 1943, L.A., Calif., USA. Writer; Editor; Photographer. Educ: B.A., Calif. State Univ., 1968. Publs: Salt Water Fishing: Beginner to Expert, 1972; Fishing the San Diego Lakes, 1972; (Contbr.) Guidebook to Saltwater Fishing in Southern California, 1973; Complete Book of Sportfishing, 1973. Contbr. to: Field & Stream; Sports Afield; Outdoor Life; Fishing World; Garcia Fishing Annual; etc. Mbrships. incl: Outdoor Writers' Assn. Am.; Sportsfishing Assn. Calif. Hons: 1974 Eddy Award, 1st Prize for Wkly. Column; Southern Calif. Sports Coun. (Hon. Mbr.). Address: 3188 N. Hearthside St., Orange, CA 92665, USA.

GARRISON, R(ichard) Benjamin, b. 26 Feb. 1926, Kokomo, Ind., USA. Clergyman. Educ: A.B., De Pauw Univ.; B.D., Drew Theol. Sem.; M.A., Drew Univ. Grad Schl.; D.D. MacMurray Coll. Publs: Portrait of a Church: Warts & All, 1964; Creeds in Collision, 1967; The Sacraments: An Experiment in Ecumenical Honesty (w. Fr. E. J. Fiedler), 1969; Wordly Holiness, 1972; Seven Questions Jesus Asked, 1974. Contbr. to Best Sermons, Vol. IX; Collier's Ency.; relig. jrnls. Address: 1110 Mumford, Urbana, IL, USA.

GARSTEIN, Oskar Bernhard, b. 12 Nov. 1924. Professor of History. Educ: Th.B., 1950; Th.D., 1954, Ph.D., 1965, Oslo Univ., Norway. Publs: Cort Aslaksøn, 1953; Rome & the Counter-Reformation in Scandinavia, Vol. I, 1963; Catholicism in Norway (co-author), 1959; Fra Østens og Vestens Kirker, 1968; Episcolarium Commercium P. Laur. Nicolai Norvegi SJ, 1975. Address: 30 Viggo Hansteens vei, Oslo 3, Norway.

GARTEN, Hugo F., pen name KOENIGSGARTEN, H. F., b. 1904, Brno, Czech. University Tutor; Author. Educ: D.Phil., Univ. of Heidelberg, Germany; Oxford Univ., UK. Publs: (in German) Georg Kaiser, 1928; Gerhart Hauptmann, 1954; Modern German Drama, 1959. Contbr. to: Times Lit. Supplement; Drama; German Life & Letters; Oxford Companion to the Theatre. Agent: Janson-Smith. Address: 10 Priory Mansions, Drayton Gardens, London SW10, UK.

GARTNER, Chloe Maria, b. 21 March 1916, Troy, Kan., USA. Writer. Educ: Univ. Calif.; Mesa Coll., Grand Junction, Colo.; Coll. Marin, Kentfield, Calif. Publs: The Infidels, 1960; Drums of Khartoum, 1967, 2nd ed., different publr., 1968, German transl., Die Trommeln von Khartoum, 1970; Die Longe Sommer, 1970; Woman From the Glen, 1973; My Darling from the Lions, forthcoming. Contbr. to: Cosmopolitan; Good Housekeeping. Mbrships. incl: Authors' Guild. Hons. incl: Silver Medal, C'wlth. Club Calif. for The Infidels, 1960. Address: 125 Carmel Way, Menlo Pk., CA 94025, USA.

GARTON, Malinda Dean (Mrs. Fay Lester), b. Gallatin, Mo., USA. Educator. Educ: B.A., Univ. of Okla.; M.A., Colo. State Univ.; Postgrad. work in Special Educ. Publs: Teaching the Educable Mentally Retarded — Practical Methods, 3rd ed., 1974; Making Friends, with work book (elem. reader), 1965; Gartons of New Jersey & Allied Lines, 1972. Address: 508 Exchange St., Danvers, IL 61732, USA.

GARTON, Nancy, b. 1908, Northchurch, Herts., UK. Publs: Roger's Record Year, 1939; A Simple Index to the Gospels, 1949; Christian Healing for Beginners, 1955; George Müller & his Orphans, 1963. Address: Chantry Cottage, 12 Tor St., Wells, Somerset BA5 2US, UK.

GARY, Romain, b. 8 May 1914, Tiflis, Georgia. French Foreign Service; Author. Educ: Univs. of Paris & Warsaw. Publs. incl: Education Européen, 1943; Tulipe, 1946; Les Couleurs du Jour, 1952; Les Racines du Ciel, 1956; La Promesse de l'Aube, 1959, filmed, 1971; Frère Océan, 1965; La Danse de Gengis Cohn, 1967; La Tête Coupable, 1968; Le Mangeur d'étoiles, Adieu Gary Cooper, 1969; Chien Blanc, 1970; Les Enchanteurs, 1973; The Gasp, 1973; (dir.) Les Oiseaux vont mourir au Pérou, 1968. Num. hons. incl: Officer, Legion of Honour; Croix de Guerre; Prix Goncourt, 1956. Address: 1919 Outpost Dr., Los Angeles, Calif., USA.

GASCAR, Pierre, b. 13 Mar. 1916, Paris, France. Writer. Educ: B.A. Publs: Les Meubles, 1949; Les Bêtes, 1953; Les Temps des Morts, 1953; Les Femmes, 1955; Chine Ouverte, 1956; La Graine, 1956; Soleils, 1960; Le Meilleur de la Vie, 1964; Les Charmes, 1965; Les Chimères, 1969; L'Arche, 1971; Quartier Latin, 1972; Le Presage, 1972; L'Homme et L'Animal, 1974. Contbr. to: Le Figaro; La Nouvelle Revue Française; etc. Hons: Critics' Prize, 1953; Goncourt Prize, 1953; Grand Prix Littérature de L'Academie Française, 1969. Address: Abbaye de Baume Les Messieurs, Jura, France.

GASCOIGNE, (Arthur) Bamber, b. 1935, London, UK. Chairman, University Challenge TV Programme, Granada TV. Educ: M.A., Univ. of Cambridge; Yale Univ., USA. Publs: Twentieth Century Drama, 1962; World Theatre, 1968; The Great Moghuls (w. C. Gascoigne), 1971; Murgatreud's Empire, 1972; The Heyday, 1973; The Treasures & Dynasties of China (w. C. Gascoigne), 1973; Ticker Khan, 1974. Agent: Curtis Brown. Address: c/o Curtis Brown, 1 Craven Hill, London W2 3EW, UK.

GASELEE, John Stephen, b. 28 May 1933, London, UK. Freelance Journalist. Publs: Insurance, 1967. Contbr. ins. topics, to newspapers & jrnls. Mbrships: Soc. of Authors; Inst. of Jrnlsts. Recip., 2nd prize, Ins. Writer of the Yr. Award, 1972.

GASH, Jonathan, b. 30 Sept. 1933, Bolton, Lancs., UK. Doctor of Medicine. Educ: M.B.; B.S., London Univ., 1958. Publs: Pontiff (novel), 1971. Contbr. to num. medical jrnls. Address: Silver Willows, Chapel Lane, W. Bergholt, Colchester, Essex, UK.

GASH, Norman, b. 16 Jan. 1912, Meerut, India. University Professor; Historian; Author. Educ: B.A., 1933, B.Litt., 1934, St. John's Coll., Oxford; M.A., 1938. Publs: Politics in the Age of Peel, 1953; Mr. Secretary Peel, 1961; Reaction & Reconstruction in English Politics 1832-52, 1965; Sir Robert Peel, 1972. Contbr. to: Engl. & Scottish Histl. Reviews; Hist.; Histl. Jrnl.; Victorian Studies; Times Educl. & Lit. Supplements; Spectator; Contemporary Review; Philosl. Quarterly; Ency. Britannica. Fellowships: British Acad., 1963; R.S.L., 1973. Address: Gowrie Cottage, Hepburn Gdns., St. Andrews, Fife, UK.

GASKELL, (John) Philip (Wellesley), b. 1926, London, UK. Bibliographer; College Fellow, Tutor & Librarian. Educ: M.A. & Ph.D., Univ. of Cambridge. Publs: William Mason, 1951; John Baskerville, 1959; Caught! 1960; The Foulis Press, 1964; Morvern Transformed, 1968; A New Introduction to Bibliography, 1972. Contbr. to: The Lib.; Transactions of Cambridge Bibliogl. Soc.; Studies in Bibliog.; Times Lit. Supplement. Mbr., Bibliog. Soc. Address: Trinity Coll., Cambridge CB2 1TQ, UK.

GASKELL, Thomas Frohock, b. 26 Jan. 1916, Bolton, UK. Physicist. Educ: M.A., Ph.D., Cambridge Univ. Publs: Under the Deep Oceans, 1960; World Beneath the Oceans, 1964; Physics of the Earth, 1970; North Sea Oil: The Great Gamble, 1966; The Gulf Stream, 1972. Contbr. to: New Sci.; Endeavour; Ocean Ind. Mbrships: Geophys. Sec. Royal Astronomical Soc., London; VP, Inst. of Petroleum. Recip., Silver Medal, Royal Soc. of Arts, 1963. Address: 96 Belle Hill, Bexhill-on-Sea, Sussex, UK.

GASKIN, Catherine Majella, b. 2 Apr. 1929, Dundalk, Co. Louth, Repub. of Ireland. Novelist. Publs: Sara Dane, 1955; Fiona, 1970; A Falcon for a Queen, 1972; The Property of a Gentleman, 1974. Mbr., Author's Guild of Am. Address: Ballymacahara, Wicklow, Co. Wicklow, Repub. of Ireland.

GASPAR, Margit, b. 1 Aug. 1905, Budapest, Hungary. Writer. Publs: New God in Theba (play), 1946; Hamlet is Wrong (play), 1958; Step-child of the Muse, 1963 (German & Czech. eds., 1969); L'Etat c'est Moi, 1968; The Divine Spark, 1974; several plays for radio & TV. Mbrships: PEN; Int. Theatre Inst., UNESCO; Dir., Dramatic Authors Sect., Assn. of Hungarian Writers. Recip., Kossuth Prize, 1951. Address: VI Benczur utca 24, 1068 Budapest, Hungary.

GASS, William H., b. 1924, Fargo, N.D., USA. Professor of Philosophy. Educ: B.A.; Ph.D.; Cornell Univ., N.Y. Publs: Omensetter's Luck, 1966; In the Heart of the Heart, 1968; Willie Masters' Lonesome Wife, 1968; Fiction & the Figures of Life, 1970. Contbr. to: New Am. Review; New Republic; Nation; N.Y. Times Book Review; Book World; etc. Mbr., Am. Philos. Assn. Address: c/o Dept. of Philos., Washington Univ., St. Louis, MO 63130, USA.

GATES, Paul W., b. 4 Dec. 1901, Nashua, N.H., USA. Writer; College Professor. Educ: B.S., Colby Coll., 1924;

M.A., Clark Univ., 1925; Ph.D., Harvard Univ., 1930. Publs. incl: The Wisconsin Pinelands of Cornell University, 1943; 50 Million Acres: Conflicts over Kansas Land Policy, 1854-90, 1954; The Farmer's Age: Agriculture, 1815-60, 1960; Agriculture & The Civil War, 1965; History of Public Land Law Development, 1968; Landlords & Tenants on the Prairie Frontier, 1973. Contbr. to sev. histl. jrnls. Mbr., var. histl. assns. Recip., David A. Wells Prize, Harvard, 1931. Address: Dept. of History, McGraw Hall, Cornell Univ., Ithaca, NY 14850, USA.

GATHORNE-HARDY, Jonathan, b. 17 May 1933, Edinburgh, UK. Advertising Copywriter; Publisher; Bookseller; Freelance Journalist; Author. Educ: B.A., Trinity Coll., Cambridge. Publs: One Foot in the Clouds, 1961; Chameleon, 1967; The Office, 1970; The Rise & Fall of the British Nanny, 1972; Jane's Adventures In & Out of the Book, 1966; Jane's Adventures on the Island of Peeg, 1968; Jane's Adventure in a Balloon, 1975. Contbr. to: London Mag.; Times Lit. Supplement; Fin. Times; Time & Tide. Address: West Lodge, Compton Bassett, Calne, Wilts., UK.

GATTEY, Charles Neilson, b. 1921, London, UK. Author; Playwright; Lecturer. Educ: London Univ. Publs. incl: 3-Act plays: The White Falcon; The Colour of Anger; True Love — or the Bloomer. 1-act plays: Queen of a Thousand Dresses; Farewell Pots & Pans; Mrs. Adams & Eve; Mrs. Griggs Loses Her Bed; Fair Cops; biogs: The Bloomer Girls, 1967; Gauguin's Astonishing Grandmother, 1970; A Bird of Curious Plumage, 1971; The Incredible Mrs. van der Elst, 1972; Hist. novel: The King Who Could Not Stay the Tide, 1971. Address: The White House, 15 St. Lawrence Dr., Pinner, Middx., UK.

GAUDON, Jean, b. 29 May 1926, Lyons, France. Professor of French, Yale. Educ: M.A., Manchester Univ., UK; Dr. ès Lettres, Sorbonne, France. Publs: Victor Hugo, dramaturge, 1954; Victor Hugo, Choix de poèmes, 1956; Victor Hugo, Lettres à Juliette Drouet, 1964; Ce que disent les tables parlantes, 1964; Le Temps de la Contemplation, 1969. Contbr. to: Romantisme; Poétique; Le Monde; Revue d'Hist. Lit. de la France; Bulletin de la Fac. des Lettres de Strasbourg; Travaux de Linguistique et de Lit.; etc. Mbrships: Soc. Hist. Lit., Soc. Etudes Romantiques, Paris; Assn. Int. des Etudes Françaises; MLA, USA. Lauréat, Acad. Française, 1970. Address: 168 Linden St., New Haven, CT 06511, USA.

GAULDIE, William Sinclair, b. 1918, Dundee, UK. Architect. Educ: Schl. of Arch., Coll. of Art, Dundee. Publs: Looking at Scottish Buildings (w. G. Scott-Moncrieff), 1974; Fortesquieu (w. H. Scott), 1953; Architecture, 1969; The Moonstone (play, w. H. Scott), 1945. Contbr. to: Archt.'s Jrnl.; Jrnl. of Brit. Soc. of Aesthetics; Royal Inst. of Brit. Archts. Jrnl.; Illustrated Carpenter & Builder; Bldg.; BBC TV & Radio. Mbrships. incl: Fellow, Royal Inst. of Brit. Archts.; Fellow, Royal Incorp. of Archts. in Scotland (Pres., 1963-65); Broadcasting Coun. for Scotland, 1965-69. Address: c/o Gauldie, Hardie, Wright & Needham, Archts., 2 Osborne Pl., Dundee, UK.

GAUNT, Leonard, b. 26 Mar. 1921, London, UK. Editor. Publs: Commonsense Photography, 1969; Take Colour, 1970; Lens Guide, 1971; Electronic Flash Guide, 1971; Praktica Way, 1972; Photoguide to 35mm SLR, 1974; Canon Reflex Way, 1974; Praktica Book, 1975; Photoguide to 35mm, 1975; & other books on Photography. Address: 44 Hatherop Rd., Hampton, Middx. TW12 2RF, UK.

GAUNT, William, b. 5 July 1900, Hull, Yorks., UK. Art & Social Historian; Artist; Author. Educ: B.A., 1922, M.A., 1926, Worcester Coll., Oxford. Publs: Bandits In a Landscape, 1936; The Pre-Raphaelite Tragedy, 1941; The Aesthetic Adventure, 1945; num. introductions to art books. Contbr. to: Studio Connoisseur; Apollo; Burlington; Times; Times Lit. Supplement; Art News (N.Y.); Ency. Britannica. Mbr., British Sect., Int. Assn. of Art Critics. Address: 35B Lansdowne Rd., London W11 2LQ, UK.

GAUTIER, Jean-Jacques Edgar Paul, b. 4 Nov. 1908, Essomes-sur-Marne, France. Author; Dramatic Critic. Educ: B.A., Univ. of Caen; Univ. of Paris. Publs: Histoire d'un Fait divers, 1946; Vous aurez de mes nouvelles, 1956; La Chambre du Fond, 1970; Le Théâtre d'Aujourd'hui, 1972; Cher Untel, 1974; & 13 other novels. Contbr. to: Le Figaro; Elle. Mbrships: Hon. Pres., Dramatic & Music Critics Union; French Assn. of Critics; Men of Letters of France Soc.;

Dramatic Authors Soc.; Critics Circle, London, UK. Num. hons. incl: Election to French Acad., 1972; Goncourt Prize, 1946; Grand Prize de la Nouvelle, 1956; Grand Prize of Monaco for Lit., 1970. Address: 25 Quai d'Anjou, 75004 Paris, France.

GAVIN, Malcolm Ross, b. 27 Apr. 1908, Cowdenbeath, UK. University Principal (retired); Chairman Council of Royal Dental School, University of London. Educ: M.A., B.Sc., D.Sc., Glasgow Univ. Publs: Principles of Electronics (w. Prof. J. E. Houldin), 1959. Contbr. to: Brit. Jrnl. Applied Physics; Jrnl. Sci. Instruments; Electronic & Radio Engr.; etc. Mbrships. incl: Fellow, Inst. Physics (Pres. 1968-70); Fellow, Inst. Elec. Engrs.; Coun. Univ. Coll. N. Wales. Hons. incl: M.B.E., 1946; C.B.E., 1956. Address: Swn-y-Don, Penmon, Beaumaris, Anglesey LL58 8RW, UK.

GAVIN-BROWN, Wilfred Arthur, b. 10 Mar. 1904, Southampton, Hants., UK. Author; Journalist. Publs: My River, 1947; Angler's Almanac, 1949; Their Village, 1958; Successful Coarse Fishing, 1964; Death from the Hills (verse), 1966. Contbr. to: Nash's; Storyteller; Cassell's, Colour; Poetry of Today; Times; Times Lit. Supplement; Times Educl. Supplement; Spectator; Argosy; G.K. Chesterton's Wkly. Mbrships: Forty Club; Burhill Golf Club; Artists' Rifle Assn. Address: Ridgeway, Claremont Rd., Claygate, Esher, Surrey, UK.

GAWRONSKI, Jas, b. 7 Feb. 1936, Vienna, Austria. Journalist. Educ: Degree in Law, Univ. of Rome, Italy, US Chief Corres. of RAI Italian TV. Contbr. to: Affari Esteri (Italian ed. of For. Affairs). Address: 153 E. 57th St., N.Y., NY 10022, USA.

GAXOTTE, Pierre, b. 19 Nov. 1895, Revigny, Meuse, France. Writer; Journalist. Educ: Grad. Hist. & Geog., Higher Tchrs. Trng. Coll. Publs: La Revolution française, 1928; Le Siècle de Louis XV, 1933; Frederic II, 1938; La France de Louis XIV, 1945; Histoire des Français, 1951; Histoire de l'Allemagne, 1963; Paris au XVIIIᵉ siècle, 1968; Louis XIV, 1971. Contbr. to: Revue des Deux Mondes; Revue de Paris; Le Monde Moderne; La Vie française; Le Figaro; etc. Mbrships. incl: French Acad. (1963); Soc. Mod. Hist. Hons: Grand Prix, history, French Acad., 1951; Ambassador's Prize, 1963. Address: 23 rue Froidevaux, Paris XIV, France.

GAYA NUÑO, Juan Antonio, b. 29 Jan. 1913, Tardelcuende, Spain. Writer. Educ: D.Philos. & Letters, Univ. of Madrid, 1934. Publs. incl: Historia de Arte Español, 1946, 5th ed., 1973; Salvador Dalí, 1950, 2nd ed., 1954; El Santero de San Saturio, 1953, 2nd ed., 1965; Escultura Española Contemporánea, 1957; Tratado de Mendicidad, 1961; Historia del Cautivo, 1966; Bibliografía Crítica y Antológica de Picasso, 1966; Historia y Guía de los Museos de España, 1955, 2nd ed., 1968; Historia del Museo del Prado, 1969; La Pintura Española del Siglo XX, 1970, 2nd ed., 1972; Los Monstruos Prestigiosos, 1971; Cossío, Vida y Obra, 1973; Historia del Arte Universal, 1974; Juan Gris, 1974. Contbr., var. lit. jrnls. Mbr., var. lit. socs. Recip., Lázaro Galdiano Art Critics' Prize, 1974. Address: Calle Ibiza 23, 7º A, Madrid 9, Spain.

GAYDON, Alfred Gordon, b. 26 Sept. 1911, London, UK. Physicist. Educ: B.Sc., 1932, Ph.D., 1937, D.Sc., 1941, Univ. of London. Publs: Identification of Molecular Spectra (co-author), 1941, 4th ed., 1965; Spectroscopy & Combustion Theory, 1942, 2nd ed., 1948; Dissociation Energies & Spectra of Diatomic Molecules, 1947, 3rd ed., 1968; Flames, their Structure, Radiation & Temperature (co-author), 1953, 3rd ed., 1970; The Spectroscopy of Flames, 1957, 2nd ed., 1974; The Shock Tube in High-Temperature Chemical Physics (co-author), 1963; Co-Ed., Proceedings of the Eighth International Shock Tube Symposium, 1971. Mbrships: F.R.S.; Fellow, Inst. of Phys. Hons. incl: Rumford Medal, Royal Soc., 1960. Address: Dale Cottage, Shellbridge Rd., Slindon Common, Arundel, W. Sussex, UK.

GAYRE of GAYRE & NIGG, (Robert), b. Ireland. Ethnologist. Educ: M.A., Univ. of Edinburgh; Exeter Coll. Oxford; D.Pol.Sc., Palermo; D.Phil., Messina; D.Sc., Univ. of Naples. Publs. incl: Teuton & Slav on the Polish Frontier, 1944; Wassail! In Mazers of Mead, 1948; Gayre's Books, 4 vols., 1948-49; The Nature of Arms, 1961; A Case for Monarchy, 1962; Roll of Scottish Arms, part 1 (3 vols.), 1964, 1969 & 1975; Ethnological Elements of Africa, 1966; Zimbabwe, 1972; The Knightly Twilight, 1972; More Ethnological Elements of Africa, 1973; Miscellaneous Essays on Ethnology, (2 vols.), 1943-72, 1973; The Lost

Clan, 1974; British & Continental Heraldry, 1975. Contbr. to: Ency. Britannica; Engl. Ency.; etc. Mbr., Nat. Acad. of Sci., India. Recip., Bronze Medal, Inst. of Geneal., Rome. Address: Lezayre Mount, Ramsey, Isle of Man, UK.

GAZDAG, Erzsebet, pen name GAZDAG, Erzsi, b. 14 Nov. 1912, Budapest, Hungary. Freelance Writer. Educ: Univs. of Szeged & Budapest. Publs: Mesebolt, 1961; Hivogato, 1967; Tomtit in the Rain, 1971; Eferlakta kis tarisznya, 1970; One Big Chair, & some vols. of poems for children, w. music composed by Z. Kodaly. Contbr. to: Nok Lapja; Kisdobos; Mepszabadsag; Vas Nepe; Hungarian Ctrl. Press Agcy.; etc. Mbrships: Hungarian Writers' Corp.; Hungarian Repub. Art Fndn. Hons: Nivodij Publr.'s Prize, 1968; Govt. Silver Medal, 1972. Address: Petofi Sandor U.45, 9700 Szombathely, Hungary.

GEACH, Christine, pen name LOWING, Anne, b. 1930, Plymouth, UK. Writer. Publs: The Masked Ball, 1967; The Denbigh Affair, 1967; Black Midnight, 1968; Yasmin, 1969; Shadow on the Wind, 1970; The Gossamer Thread, 1971; Melyonen, 1973; The Captain's Pawn, 1975. Mbr., Romantic Novelists' Assn.; Westcountry Writers' Assn. Agent: S. Walker Lit. Agcy. Address: 6 Seaview Drive, Wembury, Plymouth PL9 0JR, UK.

GEBAUER, Manfred Ferdinand Hugo, b. 17 Oct. 1945, Komotau, Czech. Industrial Administrator. Educ: Grad. in Mktng. & Indl. Econs. Publs: Book to be in hand (lyric). Mbrships: German-lang. Authors' Soc. (IGdA); Deutscher Amateur Radio Club (DARC; call DB 7 QM); Club 68; ADAC. Address: 2F Parkstrasse, D-48 Bielefeld 17, W. Germany.

GEDDES, Alexander Benjamin, b. 4 Sept. 1904, Braemar, UK. Scientific Data Analyst, NASA, Retired. Educ: Paisley Tech. Coll. Publs: She Passed This Way, Life & Times of Mrs. H. Demetriade, 1952. Contbr. to: Chambers Jrnl. & maj. newspapers. Mbr., Soc. of Authors (UK). Address: Braeside, Mountain View, Peel, Isle of Man, UK.

GEDDES, Henry, b. 7 Apr. 1912, Dover, UK. Film Producer & Script Writer; Executive Producer & Chief Executive, Children's Film Foundation. Publs: Gorilla, 1954; (film scripts) Ali & the Camel, 1956; The Last Rhino, 1960; Eagle Rock, 1963; Son of the Sahara, 1963; Runaway Railway, 1965; Danny the Dragon, 1968; Seal Island, 1974. Contbr. to: Soc. of Film & TV Arts Jrnl.; Cinema TV Today; Kinematograph Wkly.; Sightlines. Mbrships: Soc. of Film & TV Arts; Writers Guild of GB; Past Pres., Int. Ctr. of Films for Children. Address: Brookside, Abbotsbrook, Bourne End, Bucks., UK.

GEE, Herbert Leslie, pen name GAY, Francis, b. 16 June 1901, Bridlington, Yorks., UK. Journalist; Author. Educ: City of Leeds Trng. Coll. Publs: 500 Tales to Tell Again; Telling Tales; The Shining Highway; Winter Journey; Nodding Wold; Uphill & Down; Gay Adventure; Always it is Spring; Cloud & Sunshine; And Pastures New; The Sunny Room; Bright Interlude; The Cheerful Day; Another Cheerful Day; American England; Share My Harvest; Nelson's Encyclopedia; Folk Tales of Yorkshire; many children's books inclng: The Friendly House; Caravan Joe. Address: 5 The Courtyard, Bishopthorpe, York YO2 1RD, UK.

GEE, Jack, b. 22 June 1929, London, UK. Journalist. Educ: B.A., Oxford Univ. Publs: Mirage, Arme Secrete de la Politique Française, 1970, Italian edn., Mirage, Arma Segreta della Politica Francese, 1971; Mirage, Warplane for the World, 1971, Paris Corres., Independent TV News & Flight International. Address: c/o Patrick Seale Books Ltd., 2 Motcomb St., London SW1, UK.

GEERING, Ken, b. 23 Aug. 1925, Horsted Keynes, Nr. Haywards Heath, Sussex, UK. Teacher; Freelance Journalist. Educ: B.A., M.A., P.G.C.E., Sussex Univ. Publs: Ed., It's World That Makes the Love Go Round (anthol. of poetry from Breakthru Int. Poetry Mag.); Love Poetry, 4 vols.; Nature Poetry, 4 vols.; Peace Poetry, 3 vols.; Poetry for City & Machine Age, 3 vols.; etc. Contbr. to num. lit. jrnls. Mbrships: Nat. Union of Jrnlsts.; Nat. Union of Tchrs. Address: 38 Penn Cres., Haywards Heath, Sussex, UK.

GEIERSBERGER, Erich, b. 17 May 1926, Taubenbach, Germany. Editor-in-Chief. Educ: Dip.Ing.agr.; Dr.agr. Publs: Mobilmachung der Landwirtschaft — die Maschinenbank, 1959; Der neue Weg — Agrarpolitik, Teil der Gesellschaftspolitik von morgen, 1968; Rettet das Land, 1970; Die 3te Bauernbefreiung durch den Maschinenring, 1974. Ed.-in-Chief, Landfunk (Radio) & Landwirtschaft (TV), Bavarian Broadcasting Co.; Agric. Commentator, ARD TV. Mbr., Bavarian Union of Jrnlsts. (Comm. mbr. & Chmn., Bavarian Broadcasting Sect.). Recip., Medal, Bavarian State Dept. for Land Development & Environmental Planning. Address: 8051 Kranzberg, Berg 7, W. Germany.

GEIGER, Don Jesse, b. 4 Mar. 1923, Wichita, Kan., USA. Professor of Rhetoric. Educ: B.S., M.A., & Ph.D., Northwestern Univ., Evanston, Ill. Publs: The Age of the Splendid Machine, 1961; The Sound, Sense & Performance of Literature, 1963; The Dramatic Impulse in Modern Poetics, 1967. Contbr. to var. anthols. & jrnls. inclng: Best Poems of 1958 & 1967; Jrnl. of Aesthetics of Art Criticism. Mbrships. incl: Speech Communication Assn. Recip., 4th Annual Golden Anniversary Fund Prize, SCA, 1968. Address: Rhetoric Dept., Univ. of Calif., Berkeley, CA 94720, USA.

GEISER, Christoph, b. 3 Aug. 1949, Basle, Switz. Journalist; Editor, Drehpunkt (literary review). Publs: Bessere Zeiten (Poems & Stories), 1968; Mitteilung an Mitgefangene (Poems), 1971; Hier steht alles unter Denkmalschutz (Stories), 1972; Warnung für Tiefflieger (Poems & Stories), 1974. Contbr. to: Drehpunkt; Vorwärts. Mbr., Gruppe Olten (Swiss Writers' Club); Verein der Schweizer Presse (Swiss Press Union). Hons: Förderungspreis, Canton of Berne, 1973; Award, Swiss Schiller Inst., 1974. Address: Ländteweg 1, CH-3005 Berne, Switz.

GEISMAR, Maxwell (David), b. 1 Aug. 1909, NYC, USA. Author; Critic. Educ: B.A., Columbia Coll., 1931; M.A., Columbia Univ., 1932. Publs: Writers in Crisis, 1942; The Last of the Provincials, 1947; Rebels & Ancestors, 1952; American Moderns, 1958; Henry James & The Jacobites (in England, Henry James & His Cult), 1963; Mark Twain: An American Prophet, 1970. Editor: Walt Whitman Reader, 1952; Moby Dick, 1955; Ring Lardner Reader, 1963; Emile Zola: The Naturalist Novel, 1964; Eldridge Cleaver: Soul on Ice, 1968; Mark Twain & The Three R's, 1972; & others. Contbr. to: N.Y. Times Book Review; Herald Tribune Books; Saturday Review; etc. Recip., of var. awards & fellowships. Address: Winfield, Harrison, NY 10528, USA.

GEISSLER, Christian, b. 25 Dec. 1928, Hamburg, Germany. Writer; Documentary Film Maker. Publs: Anfrage (novel), 1960; Schlachtvieh (TV play), 1963; Kalte Zeiten (novel), 1965; Ende der Anfrage (stories & plays), 1967; Das Brot mit der Feile (novel), 1973. Contbr. to: Werkhefte Katholischer Laien; Kürbiskern; Konkret; Blätter für Deutsche und Internationale Politik; Film; Plamen (Prague, Czech.); Neutralität (Basle, Switz.); Ramparts (USA). Mbrships. incl: PEN, W. Germany; German Authors Soc. (VS). Hons. incl: Premio Speciale della Rivista Milanese "Questro e Altro", 1964. Address: Brahmsallee 10, D 2000 Hamburg 13, W. Germany.

GEIST, Harold, b. 22 July 1916, Pittsburgh, Pa., USA. Clinical Psychologist. Educ: A.B., Cornell Univ., 1932; A.M., Columbia Univ., 1937; Bellevue Med. Coll.; Ph.D., Stanford Univ., 1951. Publs. incl: The Etiology of Idiopathic Epilepsy, 1962; A Child Goes to the Hospital, 1965; The Psychological Aspects of Retirement, 1968; From Eminently Disadvantaged to Eminence, 1973; Tennis Psychology, 1974. Contbr. to num. US, for. jrnls. Hons: Award for Best Article by Behavioural Sci., Am. Rehabilitation Assn., 1967. Address: 2255 Hearst Avenue, Berkeley, CA 94709, USA.

GELBER, Harry Gregor, b. 2 June 1926, Vienna, Austria. University Teacher. Educ: B.A., 1951, M.A., 1955, Cambridge Univ., UK; Ph.D., Monash Univ., USA, 1966. Publs: Australia, Britain & The EEC, 1961-63, 1966; The Coming of the Second World War, 1967; The Australian-American Alliance, 1968; Problems of Australian Defence (ed.), 1970. Contbr. to: World Pols.; Europa Archiv.; Int. Affairs; Moderne Welt; etc. Mbrships. incl: Australasian Pol. Sci. Assn.; Int. Studies Assn. Address: 68 Kooyong Koot Road, Hawthorn, Vic. 3122, Australia.

GELBER, Lionel Morris, b. 13 Sept. 1907, Toronto, Ont., Can. Historian; Writer on International Affairs. Educ: B.A., Toronto Univ., 1930; B.Litt., Balliol Coll., Oxford, 1933 (Rhodes Schlr.). Publs: The Rise of Anglo-American Friendship, 1938, reissued, 1966; Peace by Power, 1942; Reprieve from War, 1950; The American Anarchy, 1953;

America in Britain's Peace, 1961; The Alliance of Necessity, 1966; Crisis in the West, 1975. Contbr. to: Spectator; Foreign Affairs; other jrnls. in UK, USA. Mbrships. incl: Int. Inst. for Strategic Studies; Can. Inst. of Int. Affairs. Special Asst. to P.M. of Can., 1960-61. Address: 203 Richmond St., W. Toronto, Ont., Can.

GELFAND, Lawrence E., b. 20 June 1926, Cleveland, Ohio, USA. Historian; Writer. Educ: B.A., 1949, M.A., 1950, Western Reserve Univ., Cleveland, Ohio; Ph.D., Univ. of Wash., Seattle, 1958. Publs: The Inquiry: American Preparations for Peace, 1917-1919, 1963; A Diplomat Looks Back: Memoirs of Lewis Einstein, (ed.), 1968. Contbr. to: The Histn.; Western Pol. & Pacific Northwest Quarterlies; Jrnls. of Southern & Mod. Hist. Recip., Rockefeller Fndn. Fellowship, 1964-65. Address: 1437 Oakcrest Ave., Iowa City, IA 52240, USA.

GELFAND, Michael, b. 1912, S. Africa. Specialist in African Diseases. Educ: Univ. of Cape Town; Univ. of London, UK; M.D.; F.R.C.P.(London). Publs: The Sick African, 1943; Witchdoctor, 1965; The African Witch, 1967; The Philosophy & Ethics of Medicine, 1968. Hons: C.B.E. Address: Dept. of Medicine, University College, Salisbury, Rhodesia.

GELINAS, Paul J., b. 17 July 1911, Woonsocket, R.I., USA. Clinical Psychologist. Educ: B.A., Acadia Univ., Wolfville, N.S., Can.; M.A., Columbia Univ., NYC, USA; M.Sc., CCNY; Ed.D., N.Y.Univ. Publs: Wonder Book of Coins & Currency, 1966; World History for Young Readers, 1967; World Geography for Young Readers, 1967; So You Want to be A Teacher, 1967; Teenagers Can Get Good Jobs, 1968; Your Future in Psychology, 1970; The Teenager & Psychology, 1970; Teenagers Look at Sex in Nature, 1972; The Teenager in a Troubled World, 1973; Teenagers & Their Hangups, 1974. Contbr. to: Dalhousie Review; Boy's Life; Boy's World; etc. Mbrships. incl: Am. Psychol. Assn. Address: 31 W. Meadow Rd., Setauket, L.I., NY 11733, USA.

GELLÉRT, György, b. 17 Oct. 1922, Budapest, Hungary. Literary Translator. Educ: D.Econs. Publs. incl: (transls. from Russian) Works by Tolstoy, Gorky, Leskov, Korolenko, Saltikov, Goncharov, Bunin (all prose works), Leonov, Fedin, Nekrasov, Panteleiev, Aksionov, etc.; (transls. from French) La joie de Vivre by E. Zola; Catherine de Russie by Z. Oldenbourg; books of Teilhard de Chardin; & other French writers; (transls. from German) novels by modern German writers; & A Guide Book of Budapest for Russian Readers; sev. articles, forewords to transl. vols. Contbr. to num. lit. periodicals. Mbrships. incl: Hungarian Writers' Assn.; PEN. Hons. incl: Dip. Moscow, Soviet Writers' Assn., 1967, 1969, 1971. Address: 1118 Budapest, XI Somlói út. 50/A, Hungary.

GELLHORN, Martha E., b. St. Louis, Mo., USA. War Correspondent; Author. Educ: Bryn Mawr Coll., USA. Publs: The Trouble I've Seen; A Stricken Field; The Heart of Another; Liana; Wine of Astonishment; The Honeyed Peace; Two by Two; The Face of War; His Own Man; Pretty Tales for Tired People; The Lowest Trees Have Tops. Contbr. to Collier's Weekly as War Corres., Spain, 1937-38, Finland, 1939, China, 1940-1, Europe, 1943-45, Java, 1946; Reporter: Vietnam; Six-Day War. Address: c/o Morgan Guaranty Trust Co., 31 Berkeley Sq., London W1, UK.

GELLNER, Ernest André, b. 9 Dec. 1925, Paris, France. University Teacher. Educ: M.A. Oxford Univ., UK; Ph.D., London Univ. Publs: Words & Things, 1959; Thought & Change, 1964; Saints of the Atlas, 1969; Cause & Meaning in the Social Sciences, 1973; Contemporary Thought & Politics, 1973; The Devil in Modern Philosophy, 1974; Legitimation of Belief, 1975. Contbr. to: Times Lit. Supplement; Spectator; New Soc.; etc. Mbrships: Fellow, Brit. Acad.; Fellow, Royal Anthropol. Inst.; Brit. Sociol. Assn. Address: Old Litten Cottage, Froxfield, Petersfield, Hants., UK.

GELLNER, John, b. 1907, Trieste, Italy. Editor; Freelance Writer & Lecturer; Visiting Professor in Political Sciences. Educ: Dr. Law, Law Schl., Masaryk Univ., Czech. Publs: Climbers Guide through the High Tatras, 4 vols., 1936-38 (in Czech.); The Czechs & Slovaks in Canada, 1967; Canada in N.A.T.O., 1970; Bayonets in the Street, 1974. Contbr. to: Can.; Can. Def. Quarterly, 1971—; Commentator (Ed., 1964-70); Toronto Globe & Mail; Can. Aviation; other Can., US, German & Swiss publs. Mbrships:

Can. Inst. Int. Affairs; Inst. Strategic Studies. Address: R.R.3, Caledon E., Ont., Canada.

GEMMELL, Alan Robertson, b. 10 May 1913, Glasgow, UK. Professor of Biology. Educ: B.Sc., M.S., Ph.D.; Univs. of Glasgow; Leidem, Netherlands; Minn., USA. Publs: Science & the Gardener, 1962; Developmental Plant Anatomy, 1969; Sunday Gardener, 1973; Gardeners Question Time Books, 3 vols., 1964, 1966, 1974. Contbr. to: Phytopathol.; Nature; Annals of Applied Biol.; New Phytol.; Punch; John O'London's; Listener; Gardeners Chronicle; Smallholder. Mbrships: Fellow, Royal Soc. of Edinburgh, Linnean Soc., Inst. of Biol., Inst. of Wood Sci. Address: Highfield House, Aston, Nantwich, Cheshire, UK.

GEMPERLE, Karl, b. 20 July 1907, St. Gallen, Switz. Teacher (retired). Educ: Ph.D.; Grammar Schl. Tchr's. Dipl.; Sec. Schl. Tchr's. Dip. Publs: (stories & poetry) Junge Lyrik, 1932; Bunte Feier, 1938; Uns aber ruft die Zeit, 1943; Waage des Lebens, 1949. Contbr. to var. Swiss Newspapers. Mbrships: Swiss Writers' Assn.; Swiss Writers' Soc. Address: Uberlandstrasse 309, 8051 Zürich, Switz.

GENET, Jean, b. 19 Dec. 1907, Paris, France. Playwright. Publs. incl: Le Condamné à mort, 1942; Notre-Dame-des-Fleurs, 1944; Chants Secrets, 1945; Miracle de la Rose, 1946; Les Bonnes, 1947; Pompes Funèbres, 1947; Querelle de Brest, 1947; Haute Surveillance, 1949; le Journal du voleur, 1949; (plays) le Balcon, 1956; les Nègres, 1958; les Paravents, 1961; (poems) la Galère; le Parade; Un chant d'amour; le Pêcheur du Suquet. Address: c/o Rosica Colin, 4 Hereford Sq., London SW7, UK.

GENEVOIX, Maurice Charles Louis, b. 29 Nov. 1890. Author; Secretary, French Academy since 1946. Educ: Ecole normale supérieure. Publs. incl: Sous Verdun, 1914; Nuits de Guerre, 1917; La Boue, 1921; Les Eparges, 1923; La Joie, 1924; La Boite à pêche, 1926; Canada, 1945; Ceux de 14, 1950; Le Roman de Renard, 1958; Routes de l'Aventure, 1959; Jeux de Glaces, 1961; Derrière les Collines, 1963; La Forêt perdue, 1967; Bestiaire sans oubli, 1971; La Mort de Près, 1972. Hons. incl: Grand Croix, Legion of Honour, Croix de Guerre; Prix Goncourt, 1925. Address: 1 Rue de Seine, Paris 6e, France.

GENTLEMAN, David, b. 1930, London, UK. Freelance Designer & Illustrator. Educ: Royal Coll. Art, Schl. Graphic Design. Publs: Fenella in Ireland, 1967; Fenella in South of France, 1967; Fenella in Greece, 1967; Fenella in Spain, 1967; Design in Miniature, 1972. Mbrships: F.S.I.A.; A.R.C.A.; Design Coun. Hons: Royal Designer for Ind. Address: 25 Gloucester Cres., Regents Pk., London NW1, UK.

GEORGE, André, b. 31 July 1890, Blida, Algeria. Critic; Essayist; Physicist. Educ: Paris Univ. Publs. incl: Henri Poincaré, 1926; Tristan & Isolde de Wagner, 1927; L'oratoire, 1928; Mécanique quantique & Causalité, 1932; Pierre Termier, 1933; Les Nébuleuses spirales & l'Univers en expansion, 1934; Le Veritable Humanisme, 1942; Dimensions du temps, 1943; Pasteur, 1958; Napoléon & les Sciences, 1968; Vue d'ensemble de l'oeuvre de Louis de Broglie, 1973. Contbr. to: Figaro; Nouvelles Littéraires, 1945-71. Mbrships. incl: Sci. Soc., Brussels, (Pres., 1951-53); Comité du Langage Sci. Hons. incl: Croix de Guerre; Legion of Honour; Prix Binoux, Acad. des Sci. Address: Château de Gargas, 31620 Fronton, France.

GEORGE, Jean Craighead, b. 2 July, 1919, Wash. D.C., USA. Author. Educ: B.A., Pa. State Univ. Publs. incl: Vulpes, the Red Fox (w. J. L. George), 1946; The Hole in the Tree, 1957; Gull 737, 1964; Spring Comes to the Ocean, 1965; Who Really Killed Cock Robin? , 1971; Julie of the Wolves, 1972; All Upon a Sidewalk, 1974; Hook a Fish, Count a Mountain, 1975. Contbr. to: Reader's Digest; Nat. Wildlife; Nat. Hist. Mag. Hons. incl: Aurianne Award (for Dipper of Copper Creek), 1957; 3 awards (for My Side of the Mountain); World Book Award, Best Picture Book (for All Upon a Stone), 1971; Newbery Medal (for Julie of the Wolves), 1973. Address: 20 William St., Chappaqua, NY 10514, USA.

GEORGE, Norvil Lester, b. 2 Dec. 1902, Manchester, Okla., Ty., USA. Educator. Educ: B.A., 1926, M.S., 1931, Univ. of Okla.; Ed.D., Tchrs. Coll., Columbia Univ., 1947. Publs: School Custodian Manual, 1954, 1962; School Food Centers, (w. R. Heckler), 1960; Effective School Maintenance, 1969. Contbr., over 60 articles to mags. & educl. jrnls. Address: 2619 NW 67th St., Oklahoma City, OK 73116, USA.

GEORGE, Sidney Charles, b. 2 June 1898, Grimsby, UK. Author; Retired Group Captain, RAF. Publs: over 60 novels, children's books, fiction & non-fiction inclng. Jutland to Junkyard (non-fiction), 1973. Mbr., Soc. of Authors. Hons: O.B.E., 1948; M.V.O., 1953. Address: 40 Nea Rd., Highcliffe, Christchurch, Dorset BH23 4NB, UK.

GEORGE, Wilma, b. 1918, Manchester, UK. Lecturer; College Fellow & Tutor. Educ: M.A., Oxford Univ.; Cambridge Univ. Publs: Elementary Genetics, 1951; Animal Geography, 1962; Biologist Philosopher, 1963; Eating in Eight Languages, 1968; Animals & Maps, 1969; Gregor Mendel & Heredity, 1975. Contbr. to: Nature; Endeavour; Sci. Progress; Entomols.' Monthly Mag.; Brit. Jrnl. of Sociol.; Oxford Jr. Ency.; Geog. Jrnl.; Jrnl. of the Warburg & Courtauld Inst.; Folia Mendeliana; Chromosoma; Mammalia. Mbrships: Soc. Expmtl. Biol.; Genetical Soc.; Zool. Soc. of London. Agent: Peter Janson-Smith. Address: 7 Tackley Pl., Oxford, UK.

GEORGIEV, Kolyo, b. 26 Dec. 1926, Golyamo Novo, Bulgaria. Writer. Publs: (in Bulgarian) (short stories) Friends, 1966; Days of Sorrow, 1967; Possible & Impossible Confessions, 1970; Time of Struggle, Time of Love, 1974; (fiction) Judges of Oneselves, 1974; (plays) Attention, Time-Bomb, 1972; An Exceptional Chance, 1971. Contbr. to: September; PlamAk; Literatouren Front. Mbr., Union of Bulgarian Writers. Recip., Prize, Union of Bulgarian Writers, 1970. Address: bul. Al. Tolstoy, b. 10, Bulgaria.

GERALD, James Edward, b. 1906, Evant, Texas, USA. University Professor. Educ: W. Texas State Tchrs. Coll.; M.A., Univ. of Mo.; Ph.D., Univ. of Minn. Publs: The Press & the Constitution; British Press Under Government Economic Controls. Contbr. to: Jrnlst's Quarterly; The Quill; Editor & Publisher. Mbr., Assn. for Educ. in Jrnlsm. (Pres., 1952-75; Exec. Sec., 1975-). Address: 2530 Ulysses St. N.E., Minneapolis 18, MN, USA.

GÉRALDY, Paul, pen name of LEFÈVRE-GÉRALDY, Paul, b. 6 Mar. 1885, Paris, France. Poet; Playwright. Publs: (verse) Toi et Moi; Vous et Moi; (plays) Les Noces d'argent; Les Grands Garçons; Aimer; Duo; Christine, Robert & Marianne; Trois Comédies Sentimentales; Vous qui passez; (essay) L'Homme & L'Amour; (for children) Clindindin. Recip., Legion of Honour. Address: 3 rue de Martignac, Paris 73, France.

GERBER, Emil, b. 12 Sept. 1909, Zürich, Switz. Writer. Educ: Commercial Dip.; Chem. studies, Tech. Coll. Winterthur; 2 yrs., Philological Fac., Zürich; pvte. studies w. var. tchrs. Publs: Am Tor der Welt, 1934; Die Irrung des verlorenen Sohn's, 1936; Neue Lyrik (anthol.), 1936; Zwielicht (novelette), 1938; Zürcher Lyrik (anthol.). Mbrships: Swiss Assn. of Authors; Mus. Soc. Zürich. Hons: Lyric Prize, Swiss Assn. of Authors, 1936; Prize of Conrad Ferdinand Meyer Fndn., Zürich, 1939. Address: Lindhof, 8617 Mönchaltof, Switz.

GERBER, Merrill Joan, b. 15 Mar. 1938, Brooklyn, N.Y., USA. Fiction Writer. Educ: B.A., Univ. of Fla.; grad. work, Brandeis Univ. Publs: Stop Here, My Friend (short stories), 1965; An Antique Man, 1967; Now Molly Knows, 1974. Contbr. of stories to mags. inclng: Redbook; The New Yorker; Mademoiselle; Ladies' Home Jrnl.; McCalls. Mbr., Calif. Writers' Guild. Recip., Stanford Creative Writing Fellowship, 1962-63. Agent: Cyrilly Abels. Address: c/o Cyrilly Abels, Lit. Agt., 119 W. 57th St., N.Y., NY 10019, USA.

GERENCSÉR, Miklós, b. 4 Dec. 1932, Györ, Hungary. Journalist. Educ: Acad. of Applied Art; Acad. of Politics. Publs: Hátsóváros, 1958; Ember a Meszgyén, 1958; Égre Nyíló Ablak, 1959; Kerekes Kút, 1959; Szombaton Teremtett Ország, 1964; A 104 Nap, 1965; Tilalomfa, 1966; A Parancs, 1967; A Szívrabló, 1970; A Gyülölet Ellenfele, 1970; Isten Városa, 1972; Messze Mindenkitöl, 1972; Fekete Tél, 1973; Ferde Ház, 1974. Contbr. to: Népszabadság. Mbrships: Hungarian Writers Union; Nat. Union of Hungarian Newspapermen. Recip., József Attila Prize, 1959. Address: VIII Rakoczi tér 6, 1084 Budapest, Hungary.

GERGELY, Agnes, b. 5 Oct. 1933, Endrod, Hungary. Publishing House Editor. Educ: M.A., Budapest Univ. of Liberal Arts. Publs: Hátsóváros, 1958; Transl., Joyce, Chamber Music (w. I. Tótfalusi), 1958; Transl., Dylan Thomas, Portrait of the Artist as a Young Dog, 1959; Sign on my Door Jamb (poems), 1963; Lunatics (novel), 1966; Joan of Arc (poems), 1968; An Aztec Moment (poems), 1970; Transl., E. L. Masters, Spoon River Anthology, 1970; The Interpreter (novel), 1973; Selected Love Affairs (poems & transls.), 1973. Contbr. to: Élet és Irodalom; Nagyvilág. Mbrships. incl: PEN; Hungarian Artists' Econ. Fund; Hungarian Writers' Union. Recip., Hon. Fellowship in Writing, Int. Writing Prog., Univ. of Iowa, USA.

GERGELY, Mihály, b. 9 Nov. 1921, Varbó, Hungary. Writer; Editor. Publs. incl: (fiction) Örvény (Swirl), 1955; Józsáék (The Józsa Family), 1958; Atlasz, mire Rendeltettél? (Atlas, What Are You For?), 1966; Életünk, halálunk (Our Life & Death), 1972; (non-fiction) Ez a mi korank (This is our age), 1962; Röpirat az öngyilkosságról (Pamphlet on Suicides), 1969; Röpirat idegbeteg korunkról (Pamphlet on our Neurotic Age), 1970; also 9 more books. Contbr. to: Hungara Vivo (Chief Ed.); Eszperantó Magazin (Chief Ed.). Mbrships. incl: PEN; Hungarian Writers' Union (Sec. 1952-53 & 1956); Art Collectors' Club. Hons. incl: József Attila Prize, 1953; Miskolc City Lit. Award, 1972. Address: 1029 Budapest, Ördögárok utca 86, Hungary.

GERHARDIE, William Alexander, b. 21 Nov. 1895, St. Petersburg, Russia. Author. Educ: M.A., B.Litt., Worcester Coll., Oxford. Publs. incl: Futility: a Novel on Russian Themes, 1922; The Polyglots, 1925; A Bad End, 1926; Doom, 1928; Pending Heaven, 1930; Resurrection, 1934; Of Mortal Love, 1936; My Wife's the Least of it, 1938; The Romanoffs: An Historical Biography, 1940, 1971; Highlights of Russian History, 1949; (plays) Rasputin, 1960; The Fool of the Family (w. Lord Snow), 1964; Donna Quixote, 1968; (autobiography) Memoirs of a Polyglot, 1971; Collected Works, 10 vols., 1970-74. Also essays; articles; broadcasts. Recip., O.B.E., 1920. Address: 19 Rossetti House, Hallam St., Portland Pl., London W1, UK.

GERHOLM, Tor Ragnar, b. 21 Dec. 1925, Brooklyn, N.Y., USA. Associate Professor of Physics; Author. Educ: Ph.D. Publs: Fysiken och människan, 1962; Idé och samhälle, 1966; Physics & Man, 1967; Futurum exaktum, 1972. Contbr. to: Phys. Review; Nuclear Phys.; Nuclear Instruments & Methods; var. Swedish newspapers & mags. Mbr., Swedish Writers' Assn. Address: Svarthangatan 21, S-11129 Stockholm, Sweden.

GÉRIN, Winifred, (Mrs John Lock). Author. Educ: M.A., Newnham Coll., Cambridge. Publs: Anne Brontë, 1959; Branwell Brontë, 1961; The Young Fanny Burney, 1961; Charlotte Brontë, 1967; Horatio Nelson, 1970; Emily Brontë, 1971; The Brontës, 2 vols., 1973; (plays) My Dear Master, 1955; Juniper Hall, 1956. Contbr. to: Keats/Shelley Mem. Bulletin. Hons: F.R.S.L.; James Tait Black Mem. Prize, 1967; Heinemann Prize, 1968; Rose Mary Crawshay Prize, 1968. Address: 60 W. Cromwell Rd., London SW5, UK.

GERLAND-EKEROTH, Marianne Ingegerd Elisabeth, b. 29 Nov. 1924, Stockholm, Sweden. Translator (into Swedish). Educ: Fil. kand. Publs: Har du sett min lilla katt? (My own Little Cat), 1964; Hej, katt! (Hello, cat), 1969; Har du sett min lilla hund? (My own Little Dog), 1974. Translator, ca. 60 books & num. TV films. Mbr., Swedish Translators' Soc. Recip. of Translators' Merit Prize, 1971; Translators' Schlrship., 1974-78. Address: Granitvägen 11, 161 39 Bromma, Sweden.

GERMAN, Donald R., b. 11 Feb. 1931, Phila., Pa., USA. Freelance Writer; Editor. Educ: B.S., Temple Univ., Phila., 1955. Publs: The Banker's Complete Guide to Advertising, 1966; The Bank Teller's Handbook (w. J. W. German), 1970; Bank Employee's Security Handbook, 1972; Successful Job Hunting for Executives (w. J. W. German), 1974; Bank Employee's Marketing Handbook (w. J. W. German), forthcoming. Contbr. to: Bank Teller's Report; Br. Banker's Report; Tellers Mktng. Bulletin; Bank Mktng. Report; Berks. Sampler; little poetry jrnls. Mbrships: Soc. of Mag. Writers, Inc.; Berks. Poet's Workshop (Fndr.). Address: Lanesboro Mtn. Rd., Cheshire, MA 01225, USA.

GERMAN, Joan W., b. 9 Feb. 1933, Phila., Pa., USA. Freelance Writer; Publisher's Editor. Educ: Temple Univ., Phila. Publs: (all w. Donald R. German) The Bank Teller's Handbook, 1970; Successful Job Hunting for Executives, 1974; Bank Marketing Handbook, 1975. Contbr. to: Bank Teller's Report; Br. Banker's Report; Tellers Mktng. Bulletin; Bank Mktng. Report; Berks. Sampler; var. poetry jrnls. Mbrships: Pres., Berks. Br., Nat. League of Am. Pen Women, 1974-76; Fndr., Berks. Poets' Workshop. Address: Lanesboro Mtn. Rd., Cheshire, MA 01225, USA.

GERMANY, Vera Josephine, pen name GERMANY, Jo, b. Milton, Cambs., UK. Writer. Publs: Bride For a Tiger, 1973; Candles Never Lie, 1974; Black Moonlight, forthcoming. Contbr. to: Woman's Own; Lady; World Digest; BBC; etc. Mbrships: Soc. Authors; Romantic Novelists' Assn.; Soc. Women Writers & Jrnlsts. Recip., Special Merit Award in Netta Muskett Competition, 1973. Address: Verlea House, Lowfields, Little Eversden, Cambs. CB3 7HJ, UK.

GEROV, Alexander, b. 15 May 1919, Sofia, Bulgaria. Writer. Publs: (in Bulgarian) Happiness & Unhappiness, 1963; Fantastic Novellas, 1966. Contbr. to sev. Bulgarian mags., reviews & newspapers; Noviy Mir (Russia); Innostrannaya Literatura (Russia), Mbr., Union of Bulgarian Writers. Address: Sofia-26, Str. Vassil Kircov 15, Bulgaria.

GERSCHENKRON, Alexander, b. 1 Oct. 1904, Russia. Walter S. Barker Professor of Economics. Educ: Dr. rerum politicarum, Vienna, Austria, 1928. Publs: Bread & Democracy in Germany, 1943; Economic Relations with the USSR, 1945; A Dollar Index of Soviet Machinery Output, 1951; Economic Backwardness in Historical Perspective, 1962; The Stability of Dictatorships, 1963; Continuity in History & Other Essays, 1968; Europe in the Russian Mirror: Four Lectures in Economic History, 1970; Mercator Gloriosus, 1973. Mbr., var. acad. assns. Recip., var. acad. hons. Address: Dept. of Econs., M-7 Littauer Ctr., Harvard Univ., Cambridge, MA 02138, USA.

GERSON, Noel Bertram, pen names EDWARDS, Samuel & LEWIS, Paul, b. 6 Nov. 1914, Chgo., Ill., USA. Novelist; Biographer. Educ: A.B., 1934, M.A., 1935, Univ. of Chgo. Publs: Over 100 books of fiction, non-fiction, pub. in 17 countries. Mbrships: Authors Guild of Am.; Western Writers of Am. Address: 63 Pratt Ave., Clinton, CT 06413, USA.

GERSTNER, Edna Rachel, b. 17 Apr. 1914, Champa, India. Educ: A.B., Wheaton Coll., USA; M.A., Univ. of Pa.; Grad. study, Columbia. Publs: Song by the River, 1960; Idelette, 1963. Mbr., Ft. Ligonier Poetry Soc. Address: R.D. 1, Ligonier, PA 15658, USA.

GERTZ, Elmer, b. 14 Sept. 1906, Chgo., Ill., USA. Writer; Lawyer; Professor. Educ: Ph.B., Univ. of Chgo., 1928; J.D., Univ. of Chgo. Law Schl., 1930. Publs: Frank Harris: A Study in Black & White (w. A. I. Tobin), 1931; The People vs. The Chicago Tribune, 1942; American Ghettos, 1946; A Handful of Clients, 1965; Moment of Madness — The People vs. Jack Ruby, 1968; For the First Hours of Tomorrow: The New Illinois Bill of Rights, 1972; To Life, 1974. Contbr. to var. jrnls. Mbr., num. lit. & law socs. Hons: Non-Fiction Award, Friends of Lit., 1974; Award, Soc. of Midland Authors, 1969. Address: 6249 N. Albany Ave., Chgo., IL 60659, USA.

GEWEHR, Wolf, b. 12 Feb. 1939, Freiburg/Br., Germany. University Lecturer. Educ: incl: M.A., Univ. of Colo., USA, 1965; Ph.D., Univ. of Wash., 1968. Publs: incl: Reading German in the Natural Sciences, 1972, Reading German in the Social Sciences, 1972, Reading German in the Humanities, 1972, German Review & Readings, 1973, (all 4 vols. w. Wolff A. von Schmidt); Lexematische Structuren, 1974; First-Year German (w. Robert E. Helbling & Wolff A. von Schmidt), 1975. Contbr. to: Zeitschrift für Religions — und Geistegeschichte; Zeitschrift für deutsche Philologie; Deutsche Vierteljahrsschrift; Comp. Educ. Review; Handlexikon zur Literaturwissenschaft, 1974; etc. Mbr., Societas Linguistica Europaea. Address: 44 Münster, Buchenweg 3, W. Germany.

GHATALA, Elizabeth Schwenn, b. 27 Nov. 1942, Sparta, Wis., USA. Research Psychologist. Educ: B.A., 1964, M.S., 1966, Northwestern Univ., Evanston, Ill.; Ph.D., Univ. of Wis., Madison, 1970. Author, Conceptual Learning & Development — A Cognitive View, (w. H. J. Klausmeier & D. A. Frayer), 1974. Contbr. to: Jrnl. of Verbal Learning & Verbal Behavior; Jrnl. of Educl. Psychol.; Elem. Schl. Jrnl.; Educl. Technol.; Jrnl. of Expmtl. Child Psychol.; Jrnl. of Expmtl. Psychol.; Memory & Cognition; US Govt. Reports. Mbrships. incl: Am. Psychol. Assn.; Am. Educl. Rsch. Assn.; Spencer Fellow, Nat. Acad. of Educ. Address: 1785 29th St., Apt. 208, Ogden, UT 84403, USA.

GHATALA, Mohamed Habeebuddin, b. 20 June 1939, Hyderabad, India. Educator. Educ: B.Sc., Osmania Univ., Hyderabad, 1959; M.S., Kan. State Univ., Manhattan, Kan.,

USA, 1961; Ph.D., Univ. Wis., Madison, Wis., 1970. Publs: Current Issues & Approaches in Distance Education (w. C. A. Wedemeyer, R. S. Sims & B. Singh), 1974. Contbr. to: Educl. Technol.; Audiovisual Instrn.; Gyan Doot; Int. Coun. Correspondence Educ. Newsletter; Adult Leadership; etc. Mbrships. incl: Int. Coun. on Adult Educ.; Nat. Univ. Ext. Assn.; Adult Educ. Assn. USA; Indian Adult Educ. Assn. (Life Mbr.). Recip., num. acad. & debating awards. Address: 1785 29th St., Apt. 208, Ogden, UT 84403, USA.

GHILAN, Maxim, pen names MAGAL, Ran; MAGELLAN; DANIEL, A., b. 24 Mar. 1931, Lille, France. Journalist. Publs: 4 vols. of poetry in Hebrew, 1957-61; How Israel Lost Its Soul, 1974; transls. of var. lit. works from French, Engl., German & Spanish into Hebrew, Engl. & French. Contbr. to: Israel & Palestine Mthly Review, Paris (Ed.); Bul Mag., Tel Aviv (former Ed.); Haolam Hazeh Weekly, Tel Aviv (former Asst. Ed.); Engl. Desk, Jewish Telegraphic Agency, Paris Bureau; major Israeli newspapers; Anthol. Hebrew Poetry in Engl., 1968. Address: c/o Israel & Palestine Monthly Review, Boite Postale 130-10, 75463 Paris Cédex 10, France.

GHILIA, Alecu Ivan, b. 1 Mar. 1930, Sendriceni, Dorohoi, Romania. Writer. Educ: Fine Arts Inst. Publs: Relatives, 1958; Getting Out of the Apocalypse, 1961; Apassionata, 1970; Requiem for Those Alive, 1972; Devils Time, 1973. Contbr. to: Romania Literara; Luceafarul; etc. Mbrships: Writers Union of the Socialist Repub. of Romania; PEN Club. Hons: Acad. of the S.R.R. Prize, 1959; Assn. of Writers Prize, 1973. Address: Stefan Furtuna 130, Bucharest, Romania.

GHITELMAN, Hélène, b. 29 Nov. 1916, Hotin, Romania (Belgian nationality). Secretary & Translator; Poet. Educ: Univ. of Liège, Belgium. Publs: (poetry) Avec de Mots, 1962; Bresil a Nu, 1970; Vox de Sortileges, 1972. Contbr. to: Fanal, Brazil; Aonde Vamos?,'Brazil; Poesie Vivante, Switz.; Apollo; Scarabee; Signor Si; Presences, Belgium. Mbrships. incl: PEN; Casa do Poeta, Brazil; Association des Ecrivains Belges. Hons. incl: 'Première Lauréate du Prix Raymond Bath, 1973; Silver Medals, l'Union Culturelle de France, 1973, 1974; Palme d'Or du Jury de l'Académie du disque de Poésie, 1973. Address: Rue Jourdan 75, B-1060 Brussels, Belgium.

GHOSE, Zulfikar, b. 13 Mar. 1935, Sialkot, Pakistan; Author. Educ: B.A.(Keele). Publs: The Loss of India, 1964; Statement Against Corpses (w. B. S. Johnson), 1964; Confessions of a Native-Alien, 1965; The Contradictions, 1966; The Murder of Aziz Khan, 1967; Jets From Orange, 1967; The Violent West, 1972; The Incredible Brazilian, 1972; The Beautiful Empire, 1975. Address: c/o Harold Matson Co. Inc., 22 E. 40th St., N.Y., NY 10016, USA.

GIAMMARINO, Jaye, b. Brooklyn, N.Y., USA. Writer; Poet; Medical Secretary. Publs: The First Thaw, 1966; Wine in a Gold Cup, 1967; Badge of Promise, 1968; Moon Age Poets, 1970; Sun of Reflection, 1971; A Certain Hunger, 1974. Contbr. to: Major Poets; Poet Lore; PEN Women Mag.; Am. Poet; Haiku; Laurel Review; etc. Mbrships. incl: Poetry Soc. of Am.; Nat. League of Am. Pen Women; Am. Poetry League; S. & W. Lit. Assn.; World Poetry Soc. Intercontinental. Hons: 2nd Poet Laureate & Gold Cup, Am. Poets Fellowship Soc., 1967; L.H.D., Int. Acad., Hull, UK, 1970; & others. Address: 519 E. Lincoln Highway, Coatesville, PA 19320, USA.

GIBB, Jocelyn Easton, b. 1907, Pontypool, Mon., UK. Company Director. Educ: M.A., Pembroke Coll., Cambridge. Publs: An Early Draft of Locke's Essay (ed. w. R. I. Aaron), 1936; Ed., Lights on C. S. Lewis, 1965. Contbr. to: 15th Ed., Ency. Britannica; var. articles & broadcasts. Address: Mousehall, Tidebrook, Wadhurst, Sussex, UK.

GIBB, John Alexander Crawford, b. 22 Apr. 1923, Carshalton, Surrey, UK. University Lecturer. Educ: M.A., Cambridge Univ.; M.Sc., Univ. of Durham. Publs: Crop Drying, Barn & Storage Machinery, 1955; Sub-ed. & contbr., Farming, 4 vols., 1963. Contbr. to: Kempe's Engrs. Yr. Book, 1970—. Mbrships: Fellow, Instn. of Agricl. Engrs. (Hon. Ed., 1961-72, Pres., 1972-74); Am. Soc. of Agricl. Engrs.; Fellow, Royal Agricl. Socs., 1970. Address: 5 Heath Close, Wokingham, Berks., UK.

GIBBERD, Kathleen, b. 5 Mar. 1897, London, UK. Writer; Journalist. Educ: M.A., Oxford; Soc. Sci. Cert., London Schl. of Econs. Publs: Vain Adventure (novel), 1927; The People's Government & Other School

Textbooks, 1931-56; Politics on the Blackboard, 1954; No Place Like School, 1962; Teaching Religion in Schools, 1970. Contbr. to: Sunday Times; New Statesman; Guardian; Times; Times Educl. Supplement. Recip., Panton Club Prize for a 1st Novel, 1962. Address: Kent's Field, Southease, Nr. Lewes, Sussex, UK.

GIBBON, Vivian, b. 26 June 1917, Newcastle upon Tyne, UK. Educator; Dean of Education Students. Educ: B.A., Durham, 1939; Dip.Ed., 1941; Cert., Nat. Froebel Fndn. Publs: Communication & Learning in the Primary School, 1962; Beginning Mathematics, 4 Books, 1963-64; Words Your Children Use, 1964; Our World Series, 1965-70. Mbrships: ATCDE; NFF. Address: 45 The Riding, Kenton, Newcastle upon Tyne, UK.

GIBBON, William Monk, b. 15 Dec. 1896, Dublin. Poet; Author. Educ: Keble Coll., Oxford; Ph.D., Dublin Univ. Publs. incl: (poetry) The Tremulous String, 1926; The Branch of Hawthorn Tree, 1927; For Daws to Peck at, 1929; The Velvet Bow and other poems, 1971; (autobiography) Inglorious Soldier, 1968; The Brahms Waltz, 1970; (novel) The Climate of Love, 1961; (criticism) The Tales of Hoffman, 1951; Western Germany, 1955; The Rhine & its Castles, 1957; The Masterpiece & the Man, 1959. Contbr. to: Observer; Spectator; etc. Mbrships: Irish Acad. of Letters; F.R.S.L. Recip., Tailteann Silver Medal for Poetry. Address: 24 Sandycove Rd., Sandycove, Co. Dublin, Repub. of Ireland.

GIBBONS, James Gavin, b. 1922, Southampton, UK. Author. Educ: M.A., Queen's Coll., Oxford. Publs. incl: Dutch Self Taught, 1957; German Self Taught, 1958; Italian Self Taught, 1958; Spanish Self Taught, 1958; Trains Under the Channel, 1970; By Train to France, 1974; (guide books) London, 1967; Lake District, 1968; North Wales, 1968; Cornwall, 1968; Dorset & the New Forest, 1969; Yorkshire, 1969; Welsh Border, 1970; Oxford & the Shakespeare Country, 1970; South Wales, 1971; South East England, 1971; Know & Like Wales, 1975; Scotland, 1975; Ireland, 1975. Contbr. to newspapers & encys. Mbrships: Soc. of Authors; Coun., Channel Tunnel Assn. Address: Milhams, Stanley Lane, Shrewsbury, Salop. SY3 9DR, UK.

GIBBONS, Stella Dorothea, b. 1902, London, UK. Author. Educ: Univ. Coll., London. Publs. incl: Cold Comfort Farm; Roaring Tower (short stories); Nightingale Wood; The Untidy Gnome (for children); My American; Christmas at Cold Comfort Farm (short stories); The Rich House; The Bachelor; Westwood; The Matchmaker; The Swiss Summer; Ticky; Conference at Cold Comfort Farm; Fort of the Bear; Collected Poems; Beside the Pearly Water (short stories); The Shadow of a Sorcerer; Here Be Dragons; White Sand & Grey Sand; A Pink Front Door; The Woods in Winter. Mbr., F.R.S.L. Address: 19 Oakeshott Ave., London N6, UK.

GIBBS, Paula Vivien, pen name BATCHELOR, Paula, b. London, UK. Adult Education Tutor. Educ: Dip. Art Hist. Publs: Bed Majestical, 1953; Angel with Bright Hair, 1956. Address: 2a Douglas Rd., Maidstone, Kent, UK.

GIBBS, Peter Bawtree, b. 29 Aug. 1903, London, UK. Retired Engineer; Secretary, College of Education. Publs: A Flag for the Matabele, 1955; Death of the Last Republic, 1957; Crimean Blunder, 1960; Avalanche in Central Africa, 1961; The Battle of the Alma, 1963; The History of the British South Africa Police, 2 vols., 1972-74. Mbrships: F.R.S.A.; Instn. of Prod. Engrs. Recip., M.B.E. Address: 7 Heyman Rd., Bulawayo, Rhodesia.

GIBSON, Charles Edmund, b. 16 Dec. 1916, London, UK. Teacher. Educ: Wandsworth Trng. Coll., 1946-47; B.A., Open Univ., 1974. Publs: The Story of the Ship, 1949; Wandering Beauties, 1960; The Secret Tunnel, 1961, 1972; Knots & Splices, 1961; The Clash of Fleets, 1962; Be Your Own Weatherman, 1962; Daring Prows, 1963; Plain Sailing, 1963; The Ship with Five Names, 1965; With A Cross on their Shields, 1967. Contbr. to: Eagle Book of Ships & Boats; Eagle Book of Britain's Fighting Services; Ency. of Survival; Sunday Express. Mbrships: Nat. Union Tchrs.; Royal Meteorol. Soc. Agent: A. M. Heath & Co. Ltd. Address: 5 Brief St., London SE5 9RD, UK.

GIBSON, James Charles, b. 8 July 1919, Wandsworth, UK. Lecturer; Writer. Educ: Queens' & Corpus Christi Colls., Cambridge; M.A. Publs: Evelyn & Pepys, 1957; Reading Aloud, 1961; Solo & Chorus, 1964; Rhyme & Rhythm, 1965; Poetry & Song, 1976; As Large As Alone, 1969; Thomas Hardy: The Making of Poetry, 1971; Let the

Poet Choose, 1973; Ed., Romeo & Juliet, 1974; Collected Poems of Thomas Hardy, 1975. Contbr. to: Use of Engl.; Engl. Mbr., Soc. of Authors. Address: 26 St. Lawrence Forstal, Canterbury, Kent CT1 3PA, UK.

GIBSON, Quentin Boyce, b. 31 Aug. 1913, Melbourne, Australia. Teacher of Philosophy. Educ: B.A., Univ. of Melbourne; M.A., Univ. of Oxford. Publs: The Logic of Social Enquiry, 1960; Facing Philosophical Problems, 1948, rev. ed., 1961. Contbr. to: Philosophical Quarterly; The Monist; Australasian Jrnl. of Philos.; etc. Mbr., Australasian Assn. of Philos., Pres., 1945 & 1956. Address: Dept. of Philos., Faculty of Arts, Australian National Univ., Box 4, G.P.O., Canberra, A.C.T. 2600, Australia.

GIBSON, Renée Catherine, b. 16 May 1910, Balt., Md., USA. Postmaster. Educ: B.A.; Ph.D.; D.D. Publs: Journey to the Purple Mountains, 1954; Short Stories — Desert Spiritual, 1955-60; Step Away & Up to the Stars, 1956; History of National Association of Postmasters, Nevada Chapter, 1965. Columnist, Weekly News, 1956-74. Contbr. to: Radiant Living; Local papers; etc. Mbrships: Histn. & Past Pres., Nev. Chapt., Nat. Assn. of Postmasters; Md. Histl. Soc. Address: Post Office Box 308, Windmill Ranch, Beatty, NV 89003, USA.

GIBSON, Tony, b. 1919, London, UK. Director, Audio Visual & TV Centre, University of London, Goldsmiths' College, 1965-72. Educ: Queens' Coll., Cambridge; M.A. Publs: The Spare Time Book (w. Jack Singleton), 1950; Jobs & Careers, 1957; Breaking in the Future, 1964; Experiments in Television, 1967; E.T.V. on a Budget, 1969; The Use of E.T.V., 1970; The Practice of E.T.V., 1970; Closed Circuit Television Single Handed, 1972; Teachers Talking, 1973; Resources & the Teacher; as freelance writer & broadcaster, approx. 400 radio & TV progs., 1956-74. Contbr. to: Times; Guardian; Spectator; Observer; Contemporary Review; Education. Agent: A. P. Watt.

GIDAL, Sonia, b. 1922, Berlin, Germany. Writer; Press Photographer 1941-45; Arts & Crafts Teacher 1952-55. Publs: 25 vols. of My Village in .... series (w. husband as photographer), inclng: My Village in India, My Village in Thailand, My Village in Japan, My Village in Hungary, etc.; Documentary films for children's TV: My Friend Chico, 1974; The Dancing Turtles, 1974. Contbr. to educl. publishing houses, filmstrips w. sound. Mbr., Soc. Authors (London). Address: Blue Ball, Blue Ball Hill, Totnes, S. Devon, UK.

GIDDINGS, Robert Lindsay, b. 29 June 1935, Worcester, UK. Freelance Journalist; Filmwriter; Broadcaster; Playwright; Lecturer. Educ: Univ. of Bristol; B.A., 1958; M.A., 1960; Dip.Ed., 1961; M.Litt., 1967; Ph.D., Univ. of Keele, 1974. Publs: The Tradition of Smollett, 1967; British Trade Unions 1799-1939, 1970; History of England 1660-1760, 6 vols., 1967-69. Contbr. to: New Soc.; Socialist Worker; Tribune; New Knowledge; Music & Letters; Western Daily Press; Int. Socialism; Prediction; Dickens Studies Newsletter; etc. Mbrships: Soc. of Authors; Radiowriters' Assn.; Conservation Soc. Address: Somerset House, Swineford, Bristol BS15 6LW, UK.

GIEDRAITIS, Romualdas, pen name SPALIS, R., b. 31 Oct. 1915, Kaunas, Lithuania. Teacher. Educ: Degree, Univ. of Vilnius. Publs: (short stories) The Great Atonements, 1952; The Angels who Sinned, 1963; (satire) The Thirteen Calamities, 1950; Between the Earth & Heaven, 1965; (novels) The Adventures of Urehin, 1952, 1969; On the Brink, 1954; Alma Mater, 1960; The Resistance, 1969; The Girl from the Ghetto. Contbr. to Lithuanian publs. in the USA. Mbrships: Lithuanian Writers Assn., USA; Halifax Authors Circle. Recip., 1st Prize for short story, newspaper Dirva competition, USA., 1973. Address: 39 Stanley Rd., Halifax, W. Yorks., HX1 3RX, UK.

GIELGUD, Val Henry, b. 28 Apr. 1900, London, UK. Former Head of Sound Drama, BBC. Educ: Trinity Coll., Oxford. Publs. incl: Black Gallantry, 1928; The Red Account, 1939; Beyond Dover, 1940; (autobiography) Years of the Locust, 1946; How to Write Broadcast Plays, 1946; Special Delivery, 1949; High Jump, 1953; And Died So?, 1961; Years in a Mirror, 1965; A Necessary End, 1969; The Candle-Holders, 1970; (plays) Away From It all; Iron Curtain; The Bombshell; Death in Budapest; Georgeous George. Hons: O.B.E., 1942; C.B.E., 1959. Address: Wychwood, Barcombe, nr Lewes, Sussex, UK.

GIESE, Henry, b. 23 Dec. 1890, Danville, Iowa, USA. University Professor. Educ: B.S., 1919, M.S., 1927, Iowa State Coll.; Prof. Archtl. Engr., 1930. Publs: Over 200 tech. Fed. & State Bulletins; Of Mutuals & Men (history). Contbr., nun. articles to Agricl. Engrng.; Country Gentleman; Successful Farming. Address: 3507 Oakland St., Ames, IA 50010, USA.

GIGON, Fernand, b. 25 June 1908, Fontenais, Switz. Freelance Journalist. Publs: 21 books inclng: L'Epopée de la Croix-Rouge, 1943, 2nd ed. 1960; Apocalypse de l'Atome, 1958; Chine, cette Eternité, 1958; Les Américains Face au Vietcong, 1965; Vie & Mort de la Révolution Culturelle, 1969; Et Mao Prit le Pouvoir, 1969, 3rd ed. 1973; Hong-Kong, 1970; Japon, Hier & Demain, 1973; Le 400ème Chat, 1975. Address: Route de Malagnou, Case Postale 343, 1211 Geneva, Switz.

GILBERT, John Raphael, b. 1926, London, UK. Freelance Author & Editor. Educ: Columbia Univ., N.Y., USA; Univ. of London, UK; B.A. Publs: Modern World Book of Animals, 1948; Cats, Cats, Cats, 1961; Famous Jewish Lives, 1970; Tales of Ancient Rome, 1970; Charting the Vast Pacific, 1971; Pirates & Buccaneers, 1971; Highwaymen & Outlaws, 1971; National Costumes of the World, 1972; Transl., World of Wildlife, 1971-74. Address: 28 Lyndale Ave., London NW2, UK.

GILBERT, Michael Francis, b. 17 July 1912, Billinghay, UK. Solicitor; Crime Writer. Educ: LL.B., London Univ. Publs. incl: Close Quarters, 1947; They Never Looked Inside, 1948; Fear to Tread, 1953; Sky High, 1955; Blood & Judgement, 1958; The Crack in the Teacup, 1965; The Dust & The Heat, 1967; The Etruscan Net, 1969; The Body of a Girl, 1972; The Ninety Second Tiger, 1973; (plays) A Clean Kill; Windfall; (Ed.) Crime in Good Company, 1959; also radio & TV scripts. Contbr. to num. crime mags. Mbrships: Mystery Writers of Am.; Fndr., Crime Writers' Assn. Recip., TD, 1950. Address: Luddesdown Old Rectory, Cobham, Kent, UK.

GILBERTSON, Mildred Geiger, pen names GILBERT, Nan; MENDEL, Jo, b. 9 June 1908, Galena Ill., USA. Freelance Writer. Educ: Bach. Degree, Univ. of Tex. Publs: Champions Don't Cry, 1959; Academy Summer, 1960; Trouble on Valley View, 1960; Adventures of Plum Tucker, 1961; Tell a Tale of Tuckers, 1961; Then Came November, 1962; The Unchosen, 1962; Turnabout Summer, 1963; One Big Happy Family, 1963; A Knight Came Riding, 1964; A Dog for Joey, 1966; See Yourself in Print, 1967; (textbooks) The Oregon Curriculum (co-author), 1968, 1969, 1971. Mbr., Authors' Guild of Authors' League of Am. Address: 950 Park Ave, Eugene, OR 97404, USA.

GILCHRIST, Alan William, pen name COWAN, Alan, b. 1913, Sussex, UK. Writer; Schoolmaster 1946-66. Educ: B.A., Univ. London. Publs: A Kind of Truth, 1961; Nowhere to Go, 1964; A Backward Glance, 1966; Fortunately in England, 1968; Two or Three Questions, 1969; Here Be Dragons, 1972. Mbr., Soc. Authors. Recip., M.B.E. Address: 20 Forebury Ave., Sawbridgeworth, Herts., UK.

GILDER, Rosamond, b. 17 July 1891, Marion, Mass., USA. Writer; Editor. Publs: Letters of Richard Watson Guilder, 1916; John Gielgud's Hamlet, A Record of Performance, 1937; Enter the Actress, The First Woman on the Theatre, 1960; Theatre Library & Theatre Collections. Contbr. to: Theatre Arts Monthly, (ed., Drama Critic, Reviewer, 1924-48); World Theatre. Mbrships. incl: Critics Circle; Int. Theatre Inst. (Fnd., Hon. Pres.). Recip. num. hons. inclng: L.H.D., Univ. of Denver, 1969; ANTA Award, 1965. Address: 25 Gramercy Park, N.Y., NY 10003, USA.

GILL, Brendan, b. 4 Oct. 1914, Hartford, Conn., USA. Writer. Educ: B.A., Yale Univ., 1936. Publs: Death in April, 1936; The Trouble of One House, 1950; The Day the Money Stopped, 1957; Cole, 1971; Tallulah, 1972; Happy Times, 1973; Ways of Loving, 1974; Here at the New Yorker, 1975. Contbr. to: New Yorker; etc. Mbrships. incl: Municipal Art Soc. N.Y. (Chmn. Bd.); Landmarks Conservancy N.Y. (Pres.); Victorian Soc. in Am. (VP); Film Soc. Lincoln Ctr. (VP); N.Y. Soc. Lib. (Bd. Dirs.); Century Assn.; Grolier Club; Coffee House Club. Recip., Nat. Book Award, 1951. Address: c/o New Yorker, 25 W. 43rd St., N.Y., NY 10036, USA.

GILL, Crispin, b. 10 Mar. 1916, Plymouth, UK. Editor, The Countryman, 1971-; former Assistant Editor, The Western Morning News. Publs: The West Country, 1962;

Plymouth: A New History, 1966; Wreck of the Torrey Canyon, 1967; Plymouth in Pictures, 1968; Mayflower Remembered, 1970; Sutton Harbour, 1970; Ed., Dartmoor: A New Study, 1970; Isles of Scilly, 1975. Contbr. to: The Times; Financial Times; Illustrated London News; Geographical Mag.; etc. Mbrships. incl: Soc. for Nautical Rsch.; Hakluyt Soc.; Devonshire Assn.; Royal Instn. of Cornwall. Address: Greyhounds, Sheep St., Burford, Oxon. OX8 4LH, UK.

GILL, Joseph, b. 1901, Killamarsh, UK. Professor of Medieval Greek Language & Byzantine Ecclesiastic History; Author. Educ: B.A., Ph.D., S.T.L.; Gregorian Univ., Rome, Italy; Heythrop Coll., UK; Univ. Coll., London. Publs: The Council of Florence, 1959; Eugenius IV, Pope of Christian Union, 1961; Acta graeca Concilii Florentini, 1963; Personalities of the Council of Florence, 1964; Georgii Scholarii orationes in Concilio Florentino habitae, 1964; Constance et Bâle — Florence, 1965. Contbr. to: Byzantina; Byzantinische Zeitschrift; Heythrop Jrnl.; Orientalia Christiana Periodica; etc. Address: Campion Hall, Oxford OX1 1QS, UK.

GILL, Myrna Lakshmi, b. 24 May 1943, Manila, Philippines. Poet; University Instructor. Educ: B.A., Western Wash. Coll., Bellingham, 1964; M.A., Univ. of B.C., Vancouver, Can., 1965. Publs: Rape of the Spirit, 1962; During Rain, I Plant Chrysanthemums, 1966; Mind Walls, 1970; First Clearing, 1972. Contbr. to: W. Coast Review; Can. Forum; Quarry; etc. Mbr., League of Can. Poets. Recip., Can. Coun. Bursary, 1972. Address: P.O. Box 713, Sackville, N.B. E0A 3C0, Can.

GILL, Norman Thorpe, b. 11 Aug. 1909, Knaresborough, UK. Retired Head, College Biology Department. Educ: B.Sc. & Ph.D., Univ. of Leeds. Publs: Agricultural Botany (w. K. C. Vear). Contbr. to: New Phytol.; Annals of Applied Biol.; Agricl. Progress. Address: Lawnswood, Tibberton, Newport, Salop, UK.

GILLÈS, Daniel, b. 7 May 1917, Bruges, Belgium. Writer.Editor: LL.D. Publs: (novels) Jetons de présence. 1954; Le Coupons 44, 1956; Les Brouillards de Bruges, 1962; L'Etat de Grâce,1958; La Termitière, 1960; La Rouille,1970; Le Festival de Salzbourg, 1974; (biog.) Tolstoï, 1959; D. H. Lawrence, 1965; Tchékov, 1967. Mbrships: Comm., Belgian PEN; Belgian Pres., Int. Assn. of Lit. Critics. Hons: Prix Rossel, Belgium, 1951; Grand Prix de la Critique Littéraire, France, 1967. Address: 161 Ave. Churchill, 1180 Brussels, Belgium.

GILLESE, John Patrick, pen names O'HARA, Dale; SHARK, Gill, b. 1920, Omagh, Co. Tyrone, N. Ireland. Freelance Writer; Director, Literary Arts Branch, Province of Alberta. Publs: Alberta Golden Jubilee Anthology, 1955; Kirby's Gander, 1957; Chinook Arch, 1967; (films) Wings of Chance (feature); num. documentaries. Contbr. to: Teenage Tales; Heroic Heights, 1967; Singing Under Ice, 1974; Collier's Country Gentleman; Am. Wkly.; Sign; Rotarian; Star Wkly.; etc. Mbr., Can. Authors Assn. (Exec., 1945-70). Hons: Fiction Award, 1954, Non-fiction Award, 1965, Cath. Press Assn. of Am.; Vicki Metcalf Award, 1967; Alan Sangster Mem. Award, 1971; Performing & Creative Arts Award, City of Edmonton, 1972. Address: 10450 144 St., Edmonton, Alta., Can.

GILLETT, Eric Walkey, b. 1893, Bowdon, Cheshire. Writer; University Lecturer. Educ: M.A., Lincoln Coll., Oxford, UK. Publs: Poets of our Time; Normal English Prose (w. T. E. Welby); Maria Jane Jewsbury; The Literature of England (w. W. J. Entwistle); (Ed.) Elizabeth Ham: By Herself; J. B. Priestley's All About Ourselves. Contbr. to: Times; Times Lit. Supp.; Daily Telegraph; Yorkshire Post. Mbrships. incl: F.R.S.L.; PEN; M.C.C. Address: 29 Brunswick Square, Hove, Sussex, UK.

GILLETTE, Henry S., b. 29 Jan. 1915, NYC, USA. Artist; Author. Publs: Leonardo da Vinci, Pathfinder of Science, 1962; Raphael, Painter of the Renaissance, 1967. Mbr., Am. Watercolor Soc. Address: 33 Battery Place, Crugers, NY 10520, USA.

GILLIATT, Penelope Ann Douglass, b. London, UK. Writer. Educ: Queen's Coll., London; Bennington Coll., Vt., USA. Publs: One By One, 1965; State of Change, 1967; What's It Like Out, 1968 (publd. as Come Back If It Doesn't Get Better in New York, 1967); Penguin Modern Stories 5, 1970; Nobody's Business, 1972; Unholy Fools: Film & Theatre, 1972; Tati, 1975; Jean Renoir: Essays, Conversations, Reviews, 1975; (screenplay) Sunday Bloody

Sunday, 1971. Contbr. to: Guardian; The Spectator; Encore; New Statesman; Harpers Mag.; Sight & Sound; etc.; Film Critic, Observer, London, 1961-65, 1966-67; half-yearly Film Critic, New Yorker, 1967-. Hons: Best Original Screenplay, 1971: Writers' Guild of England, Writers' Guild of Am., N.Y. Film Critics, Nat. Soc. of Film Critics, nomination for Academy Award; Award for creative work in lit., Am. Acad. & Nat. Inst. Arts & Letters, 1972. Address: c/o New Yorker, 25 W. 43rd St., N.Y., NY 10036, USA.

GILLIE, Christopher, b. 1914, London, UK. Lecturer. Educ: M.A., Trinity Hall, Univ. of Cambridge. Publs: Character in English Literature, 1967; Companion to English Literature, 1971; Jane Austen: A Preface Book, 1974; English Literature 1900-1939. Contbr. to: Engl. in Educ.; Interpretations; Essays in Criticism. Mbr., Cambridge Union. Address: 1 Barton Close, Cambridge, UK.

GILLIE, Marcus Christopher Ninian, b. 22 Jan. 1914, London, UK. Teacher & Writer. Educ: M.A., Cambridge Univ. Publs: Character in English Literature, 1964; Longman's Companion to English Literature, 1972; Jane Austen: A Preface Book, 1975; Movements in English Literature, 1975. Contbr. to: Interpretations; Essays in Criticism; Delta; Use of Engl. Mbr., Cambridge Univ. Engl. Fac. Address: 1 Barton Close, Cambridge, UK.

GILLIES, Alexander, b. 1907, Sheffield, UK. Emeritus Professor of German. Educ: M.A., Sheffield Univ.; D.Phil., Göttingen Univ., Germany. Publs. incl: Herder, der Mensch und sein Werk, 1949; Ed., Wackenroder & Tieck, Herzensergiessungen eines kunstliebenden Klosterbruders, 1948, revised ed., 1966; Goethe's Faust, an Interpretation, 1957; Ed., Herder, Über die neuere deutsche Literatur, 1969; A Hebridean in Goethe's Weimar, 1969; Co-Ed., The Yr.'s Work in Mod. Lang. Studies, 1937-40; Germanic Ed., Mod. Lang. Review, 1943-60, Gen. Ed., 1955-60; Gen. Ed., Blackwell's German Texts. Mbrships: Hon. Life Mbr., Mod. Humanities Rsch. Assn.; Hon. Mbr., MLA of Am.; Authors' Club, UK. Recip., Medal, Tübingen Univ., 1973; & var. acad. hons. Address: Gates House, Ripley Rd., Knaresborough, Yorks., UK.

GILLIES, James McPhail, b. 2 Nov. 1924, Teeswater, Ont., Can. Economist; MP. Educ: B.A., Univ. of W. Ont.; M.A., Brown Univ.; Ph.D., Indians Univ. Publs: Management in the Light Construction Industry (w. F. G. Mittelbach), 1962; Capital Formation for Housing in Latin America (ed. w. W. D. Harris), 1963; Metropolis: Values in Conflict (ed. w. C. E. Elias, Jr. & S. Reimer), 1964. Contbr. to: Quarterly of Can. Studs.; Chairman, Ont. Econ. Coun., 1971-72. Address: House of Commons, Ottawa, Ont., Can.

GILLINSON, Stanley, b. 9 June 1920, Leeds, Yorks., UK. Company Director; Author. Publs: Behold a Cry, 1962, 2nd ed., 1963; The Evil Roots, 1963, 2nd ed., 1965. Contbr. to: Irish Times. Mbr., Soc. of Authors. Address: 12A Fitzgeorge Ave., Kensington, London W14 0SN, UK.

GILLMER, Thomas Charles, b. 17 July 1911, Warren, Ohio, USA. Naval Architect; Professor of Naval Architecture (Ret'd). Educ: Western Reserve Univ.; Johns Hopkins Univ.; B.S., US Naval Acad. Publs: Construction & Stability of Naval Ships, 2nd ed., 1960; Modern Ship Designs, 1970; Working Watercraft, 1972; Ships of the American Revolution, 1973; Brigs & Sloops of the American Navy, 1973. Contbr. to profl. jrnls. & yachting mags. Address: 1 Shipwright Harbor, Annapolis, MD 21401, USA.

GILLON, Adam, b. 17 July 1921, Kovel, Poland. Professor of English & Comparative Literature; Writer. Educ: M.A., Hebrew Univ., Jerusalem; Ph.D., Columbia Univ., USA. Publs: incl: Cup of Fury (novel), 1962; The Eternal Solitary: A Study of Joseph Conrad, 2nd ed., 1966; In the Manner of Haiku: Seven Aspects of Man, 1967, revised ed., 1970; The Dancing Socrates & Other Poems by Julian Tuwin, 1968; Daily Old & New, poems, 1971; Strange Mutations: In the Manner of Haiku, 1973; Summer Morn . . . Winter Weather: Poems 'Twixt Haiku & Senryu, 1975; Joseph Conrad & Shakespeare & Other Comparative Essays, 1975. Contbr. to num. US & For. jrnls. Hons. incl: Alfred Jurzykowski Award, 1968; Joseph Fels Fndn. Grant, 1969. Address: Lake Illyria, R.D.2, Box 450, New Paltz, NY 12561, USA.

GILLSAETER, Sven, b. 28 Feb. 1921, Njutaanger, Hudiksvall, Sweden. Photographer; Author. Publs: We Ended in Bali, 1959; Wave After Wave, 1964; Island After

Island; 1966; Penguins in the Wind, 1969; 5 books for children. Contbr. to: Sweden Now; Vi Weekly; Swedish Nature Mag. Mbrships: Swedish Union of Authors; Swedish Publicists Club. Address: Karlbergsvaegen 48, S-11334 Stockholm, Sweden.

GILMORE, Maeve, b. London, UK. Painter; Author. Educ: Westminster Schl. of Art, London. Publs: A World Away, 1970; Ed., A Book of Nonsense, by Mervyn Peake, 1972. Address: 1 Drayton Gdns., London SW10 9RY, UK.

GILZEAN, Elizabeth Houghton, pen names GILS, Sara; HOUGHTON, Elizabeth; HUNTON, Mary, b. 1 Mar. 1913, Lachine, P.Q., Can. Journalist; Novelist. Publs: 33 novels; Something to Do at Home, 1957; Marriage Problems; Hobbies for Housewives; Coins — A Collector's Guide. Contbr. to: Times; Birmingham Mail; Sunday Sun; Yorks. Post; Birmingham Post; Birmingham Weekly Post; Woman's Own; Annabel; Homes & Gdns.; Woman's Story; Loving; Love Affair; Good Housekeeping Ency. of Family Hlth.; Family Dr.; etc. Mbrships: Freelance Sect., Inst. of Jrnlsts & Women's Press Club, until 1959; Birmingham Writers' Grp., until 1963. Address: 4 Shepherds Mount, Compton, Newbury, Berks., UK.

GIMMELSBERGER, Erwin, b. 8 Sept. 1923, Eberschwang, Austria. Editor, Austrian Press Agency (APA). Educ: Oberrealschule. Publs: Gesang der Tulpen, 1969; Motten, 1971; Berichte für Dr. Simon, 1974; Lyrische Texte, 1974. Contbr. to: Facetten, 1968-74. Mbr., Austrian Br., PEN. Recip., Theodor Körner Prize for Lit., 1971. Address: A-5020 Salzburg, Elisabethstr. 38/2/21, Austria.

GINDIN, James, b. 23 May 1926, Newark, N.J., USA. Professor of English. Educ: B.A., Yale Univ., 1949; M.A., 1950, Ph.D., 1954, Cornell Univ. Publs: Postwar British Fiction: New Accents & Attitudes, 1962; Norton Critical Edition of Thomas Hardy's The Return of the Native (ed.), 1969; Harvest of a Quiet Eye: The Novel of Compassion, 1971. Contbr. to: var. acad. jrnls. Hons. incl: Harvest of a Quiet Eye an alternate selection, Rdr.'s Subscription Book Club, 1971. Address: 1615 Shadford Rd., Ann Arbor, MI 48104, USA.

GINGER, John, b. 1933, London, UK. Lecturer. Educ: M.A., Brasenose Coll., Oxford Univ. Publs: The Retreat from Yetunda, 1968; An Approach to Criticism, 1970; Caliban on Thursday, 1970; Nothing & a Shade, 1973. Mbr., PEN. Address: Westville, Beckford, Tewkesbury, Glos., UK.

GINGRICH, Arnold, b. 1903, Grand Rapids, Mich., USA. Editor; Publisher. Educ: B.A., Univ. of Mich. Publs: Cast Down the Laurel, 1935; The Well-Tempered Angler, 1935; Toys of a Lifetime, 1966; Business & the Arts, 1966; A Thousand Mornings of Music, 1970. Contbr. to: Esquire (Ed. 1933-45); Publs., Esquire since 1952. Mbr., Overseas Press Club. Address: 488 Madison Ave., N.Y., NY, USA.

GINIGER, Kenneth Seeman, b. 18 Feb. 1919, NYC, USA. Publisher. Educ: Univ. of Va.; NY Law Schl. Publs: The Compact Treasury of Inspiration, 1955; America, America, America, 1957; A Treasury of Golden Memories, 1958; What is Protestantism, 1965; A Little Treasury of Hope, 1968; A Little Treasury of Comfort, 1968; A Little Treasury of Healing, 1968; A Little Treasury of Christmas, 1968; The Sayings of Jesus, 1968; Heroes for Our Times, 1969. Contbr. to: Variety; True; Publrs. Weekly; Am. Weekly; NY Post; Chgo. Daily News; Chgo. Sun-Times. Mbrships. incl: PEN Am. Ctr.; Am. Inst. of Graphic Arts; Overseas Press Club of Am.; Nat. Press Club, Wash.; Writers Club, London. Recip., Chevalier, French Legion of Hon., 1964. Address: 1045 Park Ave., N.Y., NY 10028, USA.

GINSBERG, Louis, b. 1 Oct. 1895, Newark, N.J., USA. Associate Professor of English. Educ: B.A., Rutgers Univ., 1918, Columbia Univ., 1927. Publs: The Attic of the Past, 1920; The Everlasting Minute, 1937; Morning in Spring, 1970. Contbr. to: (anthols.) Mod. Am. & Brit. Poetry; Poetry: Is Appreciation & Enjoyment; Yesterday & Today; Doorways to Poetry; Twentieth Century Love Poems; This Is Am. Home Book of Mod. Verse; A Treasury of Jewish Poetry; Engl. Skills; All Around Am.; Outlook Through Lit.; N.Y. Times Book of Verse; (mags.) Atlantic Monthly; Am. Schlr.; Ann Arbor Review; Poetry (Chgo.); Sat. Review; New Yorker; Ladies Home Jrnl.; Evergreen Review & many others. Mbr., Poetry Soc. Am. Address: 490 Park Ave., Paterson, NJ 07504, USA.

GINSBURY, Norman, b. Nov. 1902, London, UK. Playwright. Educ: B.Sc., London Univ., 1922. Publs: Viceroy Sarah, 1934; Transl., Ibsen's Ghosts, 1938; An Enemy of the People, 1939; Take Back Your Freedom (w. Winifred Holtby), 1939; Transl., Ibsen's Peer Gynt, 1945 (USA 1962); The First Gentleman, 1946 (USA 1957) Transl., Ibsen's A Doll's House, 1950; John Gabrie. Borkman, 1960; Rosmersholm, 1961; Pillars of Society, 1962; Transl., Strindberg's The Dance of Death, USA 1966, UK 1967. Mbr., Dramatists' Club. Address: Barum Lodge, 25 Prideaux Rd., Eastbourne, Sussex BN21 2ND, UK.

GIRDLESTONE, Cuthbert Morton, b. 1895, Bovey Tracey, Devon, UK. Former Professor of French. Educ: Lic.-ès-Lettres, Univ. of Paris, France; M.A., Univ. ot Cambridge, UK. Publs: Dreamer & Striver, the poetry of Frederic Mistral, 1935; Mozart & his Piano Concertos, UK 1948, USA 1969; Louis François Ramond: His Life & Work, 1969; La Tragédie en Musique considérée comme Genre Littéraire, 1972; Ed., P. Claudel, L'Annonce faite à Marie; Ed., Racine, Bajazet. Address: 1 Parc de la Bérengère, St. Cloud, France.

GIRONELLA, Jose Maria, b. 31 Dec. 1917, Darnius, Gerona, Spain. Author. Publs. incl: Un Hombre, 1947; Los Cipreses Creen en Dios, 1953; Los Fantasmas de mi Cerebro, 1958; Todos somos Fugitivos, 1961; Personas, Ideas, Mares, 1963; El Japon y su Duende, 1964; China, Lagrima Innumerable, 1965; Gritos del Mar, 1968; En Asia se Muere Bajo las Estrellas, 1969; Gritos de la Tierra, 1970; Condenados a Vivir, 1971; El Mediterraneo es un Hombre Disfeazado de Mar, 1973. Contbr. to num. Spanish & Am. mags. Hons: Premio Nadal, 1946; Premio Nacional de Literatura, 1953; Premio Planeta, 1971. Address: Can Gironella, Arenys de Munt, Barcelona, Spain.

GISLASON, Vilhjalmur, b. 1897. Educator; Former dir.-gen., Icelandic State Broadcasting Corp. Educ: Reykjavík Univ. Publs. incl: Islensk endurreisn, 1923; Eggert Olafsson, 1926; Snorri Sturluson og godafraedin, 1942; Sjómannasaga, 1945; Eiríkur a Brunum, 1946; Bessastadir, 1947; Reykjavík fyrrum og nú, 1948; Brautryojendur, 1950; Allingisrímur, 1951; Mannfundir, 1954; Gamlar myndir, 1955; Tbunádarbálkur, 1968; Blod og Bladamenn 1773-1943; transl. Hugo; Dostoievsky & others into Icelandic. Address: Starhagi 2, Reykjavik, Iceland.

GITTINGS, Christine, b. Birmingham, UK. Writer. Publs: World-selection short story anthologies; series of Educational Nature Books; Dreamer's Canvas (poems). Contbr. to: Birmingham Mail; BBC; Derbyshire Countryside; Farmers' Wkly. Good Housekeeping; The Lady; Nursery World; var. children's annuals. Agents: Laurence Pollinger Ltd. Address: 47 Chestnut Rd., Moseley, Birmingham B13 9AJ, UK.

GITTINGS, Robert William Victor, b. 1911, Portsmouth, UK. Writer. Educ: Litt.D., Jesus Coll., Cambridge. Publs. incl: (poems) Matters of Love & Death, 1968; American Journey, 1972; (plays) Out of this Wood, 1955; Conflict at Canterbury, 1970; (biog. & criticism) Ed., The Living Shakespeare, 1960; Some Recollections by Emma Hardy (co-ed.), 1961; The Story of John Keats (w. Jo Manton), 1962; The Keats Inheritance, 1964; John Keats, 1968; The Odes of Keats, 1970; Selected Letters of John Keats, 1970; Young Thomas Hardy, 1975. Contbr. to: Keats-Shelley Mem. Bulletin; Keats-Shelley Jrnl. Mbr., Royal Soc. of Lit. Recip., C.B.E., 1970. Address: Dodds, East Dean, Chichester, Sussex, UK.

GJESSING, Ketil, pen name KNARK, b. 18 Feb. 1934, Oslo, Norway. Broadcasting Official. Educ: Masters Degree, Oslo Univ. Publs: Kransen et møte, 1962; Frostjern, 1968; Private Steiner Bl. A., 1970. Contbr. to: Vinduet; Samtiden; Syn og Segn; Pax; Profil. Mbrships: Den Norske Forfatterforening; Norsk Forfattersentrum. Address: Betzy Kjelsbergs, V. 15, Oslo 4, Norway.

GJURCINOV, Milan, b. 28 July 1928, Belgrade, Yugoslavia. University Professor. Educ: Doctor of Letters. Publs: Time & Expression (criticism), 1956; Presences (essays), 1963; Macedonian Writers (critical essays), 1969; Assignments (essays), 1970; Living & Dead (criticism), 1974; studies on Dostoyevsky, Chekhov & Pasternak. Contbr. to: Razgledi, Skopje; Dalo, Belgrade; Nova Makedonija, Skopje; Politika, Belgrade. Mbrships: Assn. of Slavists of Yugoslavia; Yugoslav Writers' Union; PEN (Macedonian Ctr.). Recip., 2nd October Prize for Lit.,

1970. Address: Karaorman, str. no. 22 Vodno, Skopje, Yugoslavia.

GJUZEL, Bogomil, b. 9 Feb. 1939, Cacak, Serbia. Writer. Educ: M.A.(Engl.), Univ. of Skopje; Post-grad. course, Univ. of Edinburgh, UK. Publs: poetry: Medovina (Mead), 1961; Alhemiska ruža (Alchemical Rose), 1962; Mironosnici (Libation Bearers), 1965; Bunar vo vremeto (A Well in Time), 1972; essays: Istorijata kako maštea, 1970; drama; Adam & Eve/Job, 1970-71; travel; Kuka cel svet, 1974. Contbr. to Yugoslav mags. Mbrships: PEN, Macedonian Centre (Sec., 1964-66); Macedonian Writers Union (Sec., 1970-72). Recip., Brothers Miladinov, 1965 & 1972. Address: Ivan Cankar 113a, Vlae, 91000 Skopje, Yugoslavia.

G. de LAGOS, María Concepcion, pen name LAGOS, Concha, b. 23 Jan. 1909, Córdoba, Spain. Writer; Editor. Publs. incl: La soledad de siempre, 1958; Luna de Enero, 1960; Tema fundamental, 1961; Caciones desde la barca, 1962; Los anales, 1966; El Cerco, 1971; La aventura, 1973; La vida y otros sueños, 1969; Al sur del recuerdo, 1954, 1961; Fragmentos en espiral desde al pozo, 1974. Contbr. to Spanish & S. Am. jrnls. Mbrships: Ateneo de Madrid; Real Acad. de Córdoba de Letras y Bellas Artes. Recip., Hucha de Plata, 1971. Address: Av. José Antonio 43, Madrid 13, Spain.

GLANVILLE, Brian Lester, b. 24 Sept. 1931, London, UK. Author; Journalist. Publs: Along the Arno, 1956; The Bankrupts, 1958; A Bad Streak (stories), 1961; Diamond, 1962; The Rise of Gerry Logan, 1963; The Director's Wife (stories), 1963; A Second Home, 1965; The King of Hackney Marshes (stories), 1965; A Roman Marriage, 1966; The Artist Type, 1967; The Olympian, 1969; A Cry of Crickets, 1970; The Financiers, 1972; The Thing He Loves (stories), 1973; The Comic, 1974. Contbr. to Sunday Times. Address: 160 Holland Park Ave., London W11, UK.

GLASER, Eleanor Dorothy, pen name ZONIK, E. D., b. 11 Mar. 1918, Manchester, UK. Freelance Lecturer & Drama Tutor; Adjudicator. Educ: L.R.A.M. (Lic. Royal Acad. of Music); L.G.S.M. (Lic., Guildhall Schl. of Music); Speech & Drama (Tchrs.) Publs: (plays) Up the Brook; Call the Selkie Home; Parish Pump; We're All Equal, Aren't We? ; (as E. D. Zonik) Mulligan's Shebeen. Contbr. to: Speech & Drama. Mbrships: Soc. Speech & Drama Tchrs.; Loft Theatre, Leamington Spa. Address: Childyke, Harbury, Warwicks., UK.

GLASGOW, Eric, b. 10 June 1924, Leeds, Yorks., UK. Historical Researcher. Educ: St. John's Coll., Cambridge; Manchester Univ.; M.A., Ph.D. Publs: Feargus O'Connor: Irishman & Chartist (w. Donald Read), 1961; Shelley's Debt to Greece; The Greek Factors in the Poetry of Matthew Arnold, 1973; Ed., The Legend of Kwame Nkrumah, 1973. Contbr. to: Hist.; Contemporary Review; Greek Gazette; Free Thinker; Postal Hist. Int.; Postal Hist. Bulletin. Hons: Melville Cup, Nat. Philatelic Soc., 1951-52; Lundie Reader, St. Deiniol's Lib., Hawarden, 1970, 1973, 1974. Address: 45 York Rd., Birkdale, Southport, Merseyside PR8 2AY, UK.

GLASKIN, Gerald Marcus, b. 1923, Perth, W. Aust. Author. Publs: A World of Our Own, 1955; A Minor Portrait (alternate title: The Mistress), 1957; A Change of Mind, 1959; A Lion in the Sun, 1960; The Beach of Passionate Love, 1961; A Waltz Through the Hills, 1961; Flight to Landfall, 1963; O Love, O Loneliness, 1964; No End to the Way (as Neville Jackson), 1965; The Man Who Didn't Count, 1965; A Small Selection, 1962 (alternate title: Sometimes it wasn't so nice); The Road to Nowhere, 1967; The Land that Sleeps, 1961; Turn on the Heat (play), 1967; A Bird in my Hands (memoir), 1967; Windows of the Mind, 1974; Worlds Within, 1975; Two Women: Turn on the Heat & The Eaves of Night, 1975. Mbrships: Soc. of Authors; Aust. Soc. Authors. Agent: Bolt & Watson. Address: 1 Warnham Heights, 14 Warnham Rd., Cottesloe, W.A. 6011, Australia.

GLASS, Dudley, b. 24 Sept. 1899, Adelaide, Australia. Author-Composer. Educ: B.A., Univ. of Melbourne. Publs: Australian Fantasy; The Book About the British Empire; The Spanish Goldfish; Peter Rabbit (musical play); Round the World with the Redhead Twins (verse); Engl. libretto of Carl Nielsen, Maskarade (BBC). Contbr. to: Times; Daily Telegraph; Evening News; Irish Times; Birmingham Post; Musical Opinion; N.Y. Times; Am.-Scandinavian Review; Sydney Morning Herald; Aftenposten, Oslo; etc. Mbrships incl: Int. PEN; Royal C'wlth. Soc. Hons: Lloyd Osborne

Lectr., Am.-Scandinavian Fndn.; Guest of Hon., Aust. Broadcasting Commn. Address: Savage Club, 9 Fitzmaurice Pl., London W1, UK.

GLASS, Helen B. (Mrs. Mathew J.), b. 17 Feb. 1912, Menominee, Mich., USA. Medical Technologist. Educ: B.A.; M.T. Publs: Voice Prints, 1970. Contbr. to anthols. & poetry jrnls. Mbrships: Calif. Soc. of Chaparral Poets; El Camino Poets; Sacramento Poets; Laurel Poets. Hons: 1st Prize, Ina Coolbrith Circle, 1971; 1st Prize, Robert Frost Chapt., 1973; 2nd Prize, Montalvo Competition, 1972; Hon. Mention, Chaparral State Contest, 1973, 1974; num. other prizes. Address: 10760 Carlos Way, Rancho Cordova, CA 95670, USA.

GLASS, Ruth, b. Berlin, Germany. Research Fellow & Visiting Professor in Sociology. Educ: Univs. of Geneva & Berlin; London Schl. of Econs., UK; Columbia Univ., USA; M.A. Publs: Watling, a Social Survey, 1939; The Social Background of a Plan, 1948; Urban Sociology in Great Britain, 1955; Newcomers, the West Indians in London, 1960; London's Housing Needs, 1965. Contbr. to: Town Planning Review; Archtl. Review; Population Studies; Int. Soc. Sci. Jrnl.; Planning; The Times. Mbr., Archtl. Assn. Hon: F.R.I.B.A. Address: 10 Palace Gardens Terrace, London W8, UK.

GLASSCO, John, pen names UNDERWOOD, Miles; COLMAN, George; OKADA, Hideki, b. 1909, Montreal, Can. Educ: McGill Univ. Publs: The Deficit Made Flesh, 1958; A Point of Sky, 1964; Under the Hill (w. A. Beardsley), 1959; The English Governess, 1960; Harriet Marwood, Governess, 1967; Memoirs of Montparnasse, 1970; (transl.) The Journal of Saint-Denys-Garneau, 1962; (Ed.) English Poetry in Quebec, 1964; Squire Hardman, 1966; The Temple of Pederasty, by Ihara Saikaku, 1970; The Poetry of French Canada in Translation, 1970. Contbr. to: Canadian Forum; etc. Mbr., League of Can. Poets. Address: Foster, Quebec, Can.

GLASSER, Ralph, b. 1916, Leeds, UK. Development Consultant; Lecturer in Applied Economics. Educ: B.Sc.(Econ.), London Univ.; D.Econ. & Pol. Sci., Oxford Univ. Publs: Planned Marketing — Policy for Business Growth, 1964; The New High Priesthood — Social Implications of a Marketing Orientated Society, 1967; A Nice Jewish Boy, 1968; Leisure — Penalty or Prize? , 1970; Leisure & the Pursuit of a Desirable Identity, 1973; Leisure Policy: Identity & Work, 1975. Contbr. to: Guardian; BBC; num. articles & papers in profl. jrnls. Mbrships: Soc. for Int. Dev.; Soc. of Authors. Address: c/o Agent: David Higham Assocs. Ltd., 5–8 Lower John St., Golden Square, London W1, UK.

GLASSEY, Stanley Churchill, b. 5 July 1888, Birmingham, UK. Senior English Master, Bradford Grammar School, 1919-48; Board of Education Summer School Lecturer, Oxford Univ., 1937-39; Examiner. Educ: B.A., Birmingham; M.A., Liverpool; M.A., London. Publs. incl: Groundwork of Grammar; Groundwork of English; Groundwork of Precis; Groundwork of Criticism, 1947, in USA 1974; Through Speech to Writing; Progressive Course in English Composition; Preparatory English; Creative English; Pathways to English Study. Contbr. to: Yorks. Observer; Bradford Telegraph & Argus; Radio & TV "Look North". Mbr., Soc. of Authors. Address: 160 Moreton Rd., Upton, Wirral, Merseyside, UK.

GLASSMAN, Michael, b. 12 Oct. Fastov, Russia. Educator; Writer. Educ: B.A., 1923, M.S. in Educ., 1932, CCNY, USA; J.D., N.Y. Univ. Schl. of Law, 1962. Mbr., N.Y. State Bar; Grad. study, Columbia Univ., New Schl. for Soc. Rsch.; Study of Art, Univ. of N. Ariz.; Brooklyn Mus. Art Schl.; Chautauqua Art Schl. Publs. incl: New York State: Geography, History, Government, 1949; Citizenship Education, World History, American History, 1955; The Economic World, 1962; Pollution of the Environment: Can We Survive?, 1974. Ed. & Reviser, textbooks, Barron's Educl. Series, Doubleday & Co., Globe Books Co.; Educl. Ed. & Staff Writer, N.Y. Herald Tribune, 1963-66. Address: 2666 Emory Dr. E., W. Palm Beach, FL 33406, USA.

GLASSON, Thomas Francis, b. 8 Oct. 1906, Derby, UK. Methodist Minister; Former University Lecturer in New Testament Studies. Educ: M.A., D.D., Richmond Coll., London Univ. Publs: The Second Advent: The Origin of the NT Doctrine, 1945; His Appearing & His Kingdom: The Christian Hope in the Light of its History, 1952; Greek Influence in Jewish Eschatology, 1961; Moses in the 4th Gospel, 1963; Revelation of John, 1964. Contbr. to:

Expository Times; Jrnl. of Theol. Studies; London Quarterly & Holborn Review. Mbr., Studiorum Novi Testamenti Societas. Hons: Drew Lecturer, 1968. Address: 29 Bear Cross Avenue, Bournemouth BH11 9NU, UK.

GLEASON, Dan(iel) (Patrick), b. 27 Sept. 1945, Centerville, Iowa, USA. Writer. Educ: B.A., 1967, M.F.A., 1970, Univ. of Iowa, Iowa City. Publs: The Royal & Ancient Amusement Company, 1975. Contbr. to: Ariz. Mag.; The Southern Review; Golf Mag.; Sport Mag.; Epoch; Golf Digest; Chgo. Today; N.Y. Times Mag.; Esquire. Mbr., Writers' Guild of Am. Address: 2383 Akers Mill Rd., Suite V-15, Atlanta, GA 30339, USA.

GLECKNER, Robert Francis, b. 2 Mar. 1925, Rahway, N.J., USA. University Professor & Administrator. Educ: B.A., Williams Coll., Williamstown, Mass., 1948; Ph.D., Johns Hopkins Univ., 1954. Publs: The Piper & the Bard: A Study of William Blake, 1957; Romanticism: Points of View, 1962, revised 1970, new ed., 1975; William Blake: Selected Writings, 1967, revised 1970; Byron & the Ruins of Paradise, 1967; The Complete Poetical Works of Byron, 1975. Contbr. to: Jrnl. of Aesthetics & Art Criticism; Philol. Quarterly; Criticism; Mod. Fiction Studies; Publs. of the M.L.A.; etc. Mbrships. incl: Bd. of Advsry. Eds., Am. Blake Fndn.; Charter, Am. Comm., Byron Soc. Recip., Award for best book on Blake, Poetry Soc. of Am., 1957. Address: 11879 Holly St., Grand Terrace, CA 92324, USA.

GLEDHILL, Alan, b. 26 Oct. 1895, Leeds, Yorks., UK. Emeritus Professor of Oriental Laws. Educ: Corpus Christi Coll., Cambridge; Gray's Inn. Publs: The British Commonwealth, the Development of its Laws & Institutions, vol. 6, India, 1950, 2nd ed., 1964, vol. 8, Pakistan, 1957, 2nd ed., 1967; Fundamental Rights in India, 1951; Criminal Law of the Audan & N. Nigeria, 1959. Contbr. to: Law Quarterly; Mod. Law Review; Indian Yr. Book of Int. Affairs; Jrnl. of Indian Law Inst.; Jrnl. of Burma Law Inst.; Am. Jrnl. of Legal Hist.; etc. Mbrships: Royal C'wlth. Soc.; Soc. of Pub. Tchrs. of Law. Address: 24 Chichester Ct., Rustington, West Sussex BN16 3EL, UK.

GLEN, Duncan Munro, pen name MUNRO, Ronald Eadie, b. 1933, Cambuslang, Lanarkshire, UK. Principal Lecturer, Graphic Design, Preston Polytechnic; Editor, Akros Magazine, 1965-; Dir., Akros Publications. Educ: Edinburgh Coll. of Art. Publs: Hugh MacDiarmid & the Scottish Renaissance, 1964; Stanes: A Twalsome of Poems, 1966; Kythings & other poems, 1969; Idols, 1967; Sunny Summer Sunday Afternoon in the Park? , 1969; A Small Press & Hugh MacDiarmid, 1970; The Individual & the 20th Century Scottish Literary Tradition, 1971; In Appearances — A Sequence of Poems, 1971; Clydesdale, 1971; Feres, 1971; A Cled Score, 1974; A Bibliography of Scottish Poets from Stevenson to 1974, 1974. Contbr. to var. jrnls. Mbrships: Soc. of Authors; Assn. of Small Presses; A.S.I.A. Address: 14 Parklands Ave., Penwortham, Preston, Lancs., UK.

GLENCROSS, Alan, b. 17 Dec. 1920, Warrington, Lancs., UK. Librarian; Author. Publs: Cumulated Fiction Index, 1945-1960 (w. G. B. Cotton), 1960; Grandfather's Greenwich, 1972; The Buildings of Greenwich, 1974. Fellow, Lib. Assn. Address: "Renhold", London Rd., Dunton Green, Sevenoaks, Kent, UK.

GLENDEVON, (Lord) John Adrian, b. 1912, Hopetoun, S. Queensferry, Scotland, UK. Privy Councillor; Company Director. Educ: Christ Ch., Oxford. Publs: The Viceroy at Bay, 1971. Mbr., Turf Club. Address: Durham House, Durham Pl., London SW3, UK.

GLENNON, James Aloysius, b. 24 Apr. 1900, Melbourne, Aust. Author. Publs. incl: 10 books in "Making Friends With . . ." series, 1953-64; The Heart in the Centre (novel), 1961; Australian Music & Musicians, 1968; Understanding Music, 1972. Contbr. to: Sunday Mail, Adelaide (Music Critic & Record Reviewer); var. jrnls.; radio (Programme Dir. for S. Aust. Broadcasting Comm.). Mbrships: Aust. Soc. of Authors (State VP); S. Aust. Writers' Fellowship. Address: 35 Main St., Lockleys, S. Australia 5032.

GLIAUDA, Jurgis, b. 4 July 1906, Tobolsk, Siberia. Former Attorney; Writer. Educ: Law Degree, Univ. of Lithuania. Publs: House Upon the Sand, 1952; Ora pro nobis, 1952; The Expiring Sun, 1954; The Seeds of Characters, 1955; The Throne of Bats, 1960; Agony, 1965; Under the Sigh of the Dolphin, 1966; The Sonata of Icarus, 1968; The Amphoras of Flame & Despair, 1969; Simas,

1971; On the Most Difficult Way, 1972; The Burden of Twilight, 1973; The Peaceful Morning, 1973. Mbr., Culture Club of LA Lithuanians. Hons: Draugas Book Club novel prizes, 1952, 1953, 1960, 1966, 1969; Free Lithuania Novel Prize, 1970. Address: 1304 Maltman Ave., L.A., CA 90026, USA.

GLOAG, John, b. 10 Aug. 1896, Battersea, London, UK. Author. Educ: Schl. of Arch., Regent St. Polytechnic, London. Publs. incl: English Furniture, 1934, 6th ed., 1973; A Short Dictionary of Furniture, 1952, 2nd ed., 1969; Georgian Grace, 1956, 2nd ed., 1967; Guide to Western Architecture, 1958; Victorian Comfort, 1961; Victorian Taste, 1962, 3rd ed., 1973; The Englishman's Chair, 1964; The Eagles Depart (novel), 1973. Contbr. to: Archtl. Review; Connoisseur. Mbrships: F.S.A., London; Hon. F.R.I.B.A.; Hon. Fellow, Soc. of Indl. Artists & Designers. Address: 3 The Mall, East Sheen, London SW14 7EN, UK.

GLOAG, Julian, b. 2 July 1930, London, UK. Author. Educ: Magdalene Coll., Cambridge Univ. Publs: Ed., John Gloag, The American Nation, 1954; (novels) Our Mother's House, USA & UK, 1963; A Sentence of Life, USA & UK, 1966; Maundy USA & UK, 1969. Mbrship: F.R.S.L. Address: c/o G. Borchardt Inc., 145 E. 52nd St., N.Y., NY 10022, USA.

GLOTZBACH, Andreas, b. 6 Apr. 1902, Deventer, Netherlands. Poet; Theological Writer. Publs. incl: De Piloot; De Ketter; Orkest der Ziel; Poëzie of Proza? ; Land in de Lente; Pinkster symfonie, 1952; Genesis; Lieder im Volkston; The Bible in our Tongue & in our atomical Time: a transformation of the poetical, prophetical & evangelic books, in Dutch, Engl., German. Contbr. to: Tijd & Taak; Kerk & Wereld; Hervormd Nederland; etc. Mbrships: Dutch Writers' Union. Recip., Apeldoorn Municipal Poetry Prize, 1972 & 1974. Address: 12 Chopinlaan, Apeldoorn, Netherlands.

GLOVER, Denis James Matthews, b. 10 Dec. 1912, Dunedin, NZ. Writer; Lecturer. Educ: B.A., Canterbury Univ. Coll. Publs: Sings Harry (poetry), 1951; Hot Water Sailor (autobiog.), 1962; Bedsie Book (misc. prose & poetry), 1963; (poetry) Enter Without Knocking, 1964, 2nd ed., 1971; Sharp Edge Up, 1968; Diary to a Woman, 1971. Contbr. to: Islands; Landfall; NZ Listener. Mbrships: Canterbury Univ. Coll. Coun.; NZ Lit. Fund Advsry. Comm.; Pres., Friends of Turnbull Lib., PEN (NZ Ctr.). Hons: D.S.C.(RN), 1944; Jessie McKay Award for Poetry, PEN, 1952. Address: 3/231 The Terrace, Wellington 1, New Zealand.

GLOVER, Janet Reaveley, b. 3 Dec. 1912, Cambridge, UK. Teacher; Headmistress. Educ: Degree in Hist., Somerville Coll., Oxford. Publs: The History of Lanarkshire by J. E. Wilson (co-ed.), 1937; The History of Laurel Bank School (co-ed.), 1953; The Story of Scotland, 1960, 2nd ed., 1975. Mbrships: F.R.S.A.; Pres., Assn. of Head Mistresses, 1970-72. Recip., C.B.E., 1973. Address: 185 The Green Way, Epsom, Surrey, UK.

GLOVER, John Desmond, b. 2 Feb. 1915, Australia. Professor. Educ: Ph.B., Brown Univ., 1937; M.B.A., 1939, A.M., 1942, Ph.D., 1947, Harvard Univ. Publs: Attack on Big Business, 1954; The Administrator (w. R. M. Hower & R. Tagiuri), 5th ed., 1974; Chief Executive's Handbook (w. G. Simon), 1975. Contbr. to: Harvard Bus. Review. Hon. Fellow, Univ. of Tel Aviv, Israel. Address: Harvard Bus. Schl., Soldiers Field, Baker Lib. 133, Boston, MA 02163, USA.

GLOVER, Michael, b. 1922, London, UK. Brotosh Council Member. Educ: M.A., St. John's Coll., Cambridge. Publs: Wellington's Peninsula Victories, 1963; Wellington as Military Commander, 1968; Britannia Sickens, 1970; Legacy of Glory, 1971; 1815: The Armies at Waterloo, 1973; An Assemblage of Indian Army Soldiers & Uniforms, 1973. Contbr. to: Hist. Today; Jrnl. of Soc. of Army Histl. Rsch. Agent: Peter Jansen-Smith. Address: Bidcombe, France Lynch, nr. Stroud, Glos., UK.

GLOVER, Modwena (Mrs. C. Gordon Glover), pen name SEDGWICK, Modwena, b. 2 Jan. 1916, India. Actress; Author. Educ: Ctrl. Schl. of Speech Trng. & Dramatic Arts, London, UK. Publs. incl: Jan Perry Stories, 1955; New Jan Perry Stories, 1959; The Adventures of Galldora, 1960; The Play at Pebblings Village, 1961; The Owl of Little Vetchings, 1966; The Children in the Painting, 1969; Matilda's Own Plate, 1969; A Rag Doll

Called Galldora, 1971; The Galldora Omnibus, 1973. Contbr. to num. mags. Agent: Hughes Massie Ltd. Address: The Small House, Clavering, Saffron Walden, Essex CB11 4QR, UK.

GLUBB, John Bagot, b. 16 Apr. 1897, Preston, Lancs., UK. Army Officer; Middle East Administrator; Author. Educ: Cheltenham Coll.; Royal Mil. Acad., Woolwich. Publs: The Story of the Arab Legion, 1948; A Soldier with the Arabs, 1957; Britain and the Arabs, 1959; War in the Desert, 1960; The Great Arab Conquests, 1963; The Empire of the Arabs, 1963; The Course of Empire, 1965; The Lost Centuries, 1967; Syria, Lebanon, Jordan, 1967; The Middle East Crisis, 1967; A Short History of the Arab Peoples, 1969; The Life & Times of Muhammad, 1970; Peace in the Holy Land, 1971; Soldiers of Fortune, 1973; The Way of Love, 1974. Address: West Wood, Mayfield, Sussex, UK.

GLUCKMAN, Max, b. 1911, Johannesburg, S. Africa, d. 1975. Professor of Social Anthropology. Educ: B.A., Witwatersrand Univ.; Ph.D., Exeter Coll., Oxford Univ.; M.A., Manchester Univ. Publs. incl: Economy of the Central Barotse Plain, 1941; The Judicial Process among the Barotse of Northern Rhodesia, 1955, 2nd ed. 1967; Custom & Conflict in Africa, 1956; The Ideas in Barotse Jurisprudence, 1965; Politics, Law, Ritual in Tribal Society, 1965; Contbng. Ed., Essays on the Ritual of Social Relations; Contbng. Ed., Ideas & Proceedings in African Traditional Law, 1969. Hons: Doct., Brussels Univ.; Fellow, Brit. Acad.; Hon.-For. Mbr., Am. Acad. Arts & Scis.

GLUT, Donald Frank, pen names GRANT, Don; RICHMOND, Rod; THORNE, Bradley D.; STEELE, Dale; MORRISON, Victor; ROGERS, Mick; JASON, Johnny; SPEKTOR, Dr. Adam, b. 19 Feb. 1944, Pecos, Tex., USA. Freelance Writer. Educ: B.A., Univ. of S. Calif., 1967. Publs. incl: Frankenstein Lives Again, 1971; Terror of Frankenstein, 1971; True Vampires of History, 1972; The Dinosaur Dictionary, 1972; The Frankenstein Legend: A Tribute to Mary Shelley & Boris Karloff, 1973; Bugged!, 1974. Contbr. to var. lit. publs. Mbrships: Am. Fedn. of TV & Radio Artists; Nat. Geog. Soc. Address: P.O. Box 4334, North Hollywood, CA 91607, USA.

GLYN, Sir Anthony Geoffrey Leo Simon, b. 13 Mar. 1922, London, UK. Author. Educ: Welsh Guards. Publs. incl: Romanza, 1953; The Jungle of Eden, 1954; Elinor Glyn, a biography, 1955; The Ram in the Thicket, 1957; I Can Take it All, 1959; Kick Turn, 1963; The Terminal, 1965; The Seine, 1966; The Dragon Variation, 1969; The Blood of a Britishman, 1970 (transl. into French, Spanish & Japanese, as The British in USA). Address: 6 Rue St. Louis en l'Ile, Paris 4e, France.

GLYNNE-JONES, William, b. 1907, Llanelly, UK. Writer. Publs: He Who Had Eaton of the Eagle; Farewell Innocence, Ride The White Stallion; Summer Long Ago; The Childhood Land; Brecon Adventure; Dennis & Co.; Pennants On the Main; Trail of Frozen Gold; The Magic Forefinger; Legends of the Welsh Hills; Tales of Long Ago; The Fox's Cunning; Holiday Adventure; The Boy from Fountain Gate; In Arthur's Golden Days; If Pigs Had Wings; The Golden Boy; The Buccaneers; Yukon Gold; A Time to Seek; Grandpa Blanchard's Partisans. Contbr. to num. lit. jrnls., TV, etc. Recip., Rockefeller Fndn. Atlantic Award for Lit., 1946. Address: 10 Ossian Rd., London N4, UK.

GNAROWSKI, Michael, b. 1934, Shanghai, China. Professor of English; Writer. Educ: B.A., M.A., Ph.D. Publs: Postscript for St. James Street, 1965; The Gentlemen Are Also Lexicographers, 1968; Ed., The Rising Village of Oliver Goldsmith, 1966; Three Early Poems from Lower Canada, 1969; Joseph Quesnel: Selected Poems & Songs, 1970; Archibald Lampman, 1970; Ed., Selected Stories of Raymond Knister, 1972; A Concise Bibliography of English—Canadian Literature, 1973; Gen. Ed., The Carleton Lib. Series; Series Ed., Critical Views on Canadian Writers, 1969-. Contbr. to: Waterloo Review; Culture; Ency. Am.; etc. Mbrships. incl: Can. Assn. Univ. Tchrs.; Va. Bibliog. Soc. Recip., C.D. Howe Fellowship & Rsch. Assoc. Royal Commn. Address: c/o English Dept., Carleton Univ., Ottawa, Ont. K1S 5B6, Can.

GOBAR, Ash, b. 7 Apr. 1930, Ga., USSR. Professor of Philosophy; Writer. Educ: A.B., Coll. of Wooster, USA, 1952; M.A., Univ. of Chgo., 1954; Ph.D., Univ. of Wis., 1959; Fellow, Univ. of Geneva, Switz., 1960. Publs: Philosophic Foundations of Genetic Psychology & Gestalt Psychology, 1968; Integral Philosophy, forthcoming.

Contbr. to: Philos. Today; Proceedings of Am. Philos. Soc.; Worldview; Proceedings of World Congress of Philos. Hons: Award, Am. Philos. Soc., 1967; Recognition, Outstanding Educators of Am., 1970; VP, Logic Sect., XV World Congress of Philos., 1973. Address: 989 Holly Springs Rd., Lexington, KY 40504, USA.

GODA, Gabor, b. 1 Apr. 1911, Budapest, Hungary. Writer. Publs: Honest Man, 1931; Letter from Hell, 1936; Legends, 1942; The Lies of Fascism, 1945; Before the Storm, 1946; Imposter, 1958; Collected Works, 1959; Mr Poldini, 1963; Hunting of the Devil, 1963; Flamingos, 1964; Lonesome Journey, 1965; Novel of Confessions, 1968; Concerto, 1970; Diary of an Idler, 1971; Craziness, 1973. Mbrships: PEN Club; Hungarian Writers Assn. Hons: József Attila Award, 1958, 1960 & 1971; Kossuth Prize, 1965. Address: Bimbo u. 42B, Budapest II, Hungary.

GODDARD, (Air Marshal Sir) Victor, b. 1897. Educ: Royal Naval Colls., Osborne & Dartmouth; M.A., Jesus Coll., Cambridge; Imperial Coll. of Sci. Publs: The Enigma of Menace, 1959; Flight Towards Reality, forthcoming. Address: Meadowgate, Brasted, Westerham, Kent TN16 1LN, UK.

GODDEN, Geoffrey Arthur, b. 2 Feb. 1929, Worthing, Sussex, UK. Dealer in Fine Ceramics. Publs. incl: Encyclopaedia of British Pottery & Porcelain Marks, 1964; The Handbook of British Pottery & Porcelain Marks, 1968; Coalport & Coalbrookdale Porcelains, 1970; Stevengraphs & Other Victorian Silk Pictures, 1971; Jewitt's Ceramic Art of Great Britain, 1800-1900, 1972; British Porcelain — An Illustrated Guide, 1974. British Pottery — An Illustrated Guide, 1974. Contbr. to: Connoisseur; etc. Mbrships: R.S.A.; Brit. Antique Dealers Assn. Address: 19 Crescent Rd., Worthing, Sussex, UK.

GODDEN, Rumer, b. 1907, Sussex, UK. Writer. Publs: Chinese Puzzle; The Lady & The Unicorn; Rungli-Rungliot; Black Narcissus; Gypsy Gypsy; Breakfast with the Nikolides; A Fugue in Time; The River; A Candle to St. Jude; A Breath of Air; Kingfishers Catch Fire; An Episode of Sparrows; Mooltiki; The Greengage Summer; China Court; The Battle of the Villa Fiorita; Two Under the Indian Sun; (autobiog.) In this House of Brede, 1969; short stories; children's books; biography & poetry anthologies. Contbr. to var. English & Am. publs. Agent: Curtis Brown Ltd. Address: 4 Mermaid St., Rye, Sussex, UK.

GODFREY, Dave, b. 9 Aug. 1938, Winnipeg, Man., Can. Publisher. Educ: B.A. 1960, Ph.D. 1966, Univ. of Iowa, USA; M.A., Stanford Univ., 1963; var. other Univs., USA & Can. Publs: Death Goes Better with Coca-Cola (short stories), 1967; Ed., Man Deserves Man (w. Bill McWhinney), 1967; Ed., Gordon to Watkins to You, 1970; The New Ancestors (novel), 1970. Contbr. to: Can. Short Stories, 1968; New Can. Writing, 1968. Hons: Pres.'s Medal, Univ. of Western Ont., 1965; Can. Coun. Award, 1969; Gov.-Gen.'s Award, 1971. Address: c/o New Press, 56 The Esplanade E., Toronto 1, Ont., Can.

GODFREY, Lionel Robert Holcombe, pen names MITCHELL, Scott; KENNEDY, Elliot, b. 1932, Mansfield, Notts., UK. Author. Educ: B.A., Univ. of Nottingham; Univs. of Freiburg, Germany, & Sorbonne, Paris, France. Publs. incl: Sables Spell Trouble, 1963; Deadly Persuasion, 1964; Come, Sweet Death, 1967; Double Bluff, 1968; A Knife-Edged Thing, 1969; A Haven for the Damned, 1971; The Big Loser, 1972; Rage in Babylon, 1972; Bullets Are Final, 1973; That Fatal Feeling, 1974; Never Say Dead, 1974; Dead on Arrival, 1974; Nice Guys Don't Win, 1974; Over My Dead Body, 1974. Contbr. to: Films & Filming; Int. Mag. Creatures. Mbr., Crime Writers' Assn. Address: 17 Heath Terrace, Leamington Spa, Warwicks. CV32 5NA, UK.

GODFREY, Peter, b. 8 Sept. 1917, Vereeniging, S. Africa. Journalist; Author. Educ: Witwatersrand Univ.; Univ. of S. Africa. Publs: Death Under the Table, 1954; Four O'Clock Noon (play), 1959; Radio, TV & Screen Plays. Contbr. to: (anthols.) The Queen's Awards — Fifth Series; The South African Saturday Book; The 4th Mystery Bedside Book. Creasey Mystery Bedside Book, 1972, 1974; also over 2000 short stories published in the Engl. speaking world, sev. in for. transl. Mbrships: Writers' Guild; PEN; Hon. P.R.O., Crime Writers' Assn.; N.U.J. Recip., Ellery Queen Short Story Awards, 1948, 1949, 1953. Address: 62 Richmond Hill Ct., Richmond, Surrey TW10 6BE, UK.

GODFREY, Vivian, pen name, DENNING, Melita, b. 26 Nov. 1921, London, UK. Publs: The Magical Philosophy (co-author), Vol. I, Robe & Ring, 1974, Vol. II, The Apparel of High Magick, 1975, Vol. III, The Sword & the Serpent, 1975, Vol. IV, The Triumph of Light, 1975, Vol. V, Mysteria Magica, 1975. Mbrships: Aurum Solis; Ghost Club; RILKO. Hons: Dame d'Honneur of Sovereign Mil. Order of Temple of Jerusalem, 1968. Address: BM — Sacriverb, London WC4 6XX, UK.

GODMAN, Arthur, b. 10 Oct. 1916, Hereford, UK. Author. Educ: B.Sc., Dip.Ed., Inst. of Educ., Univ. Coll., London Univ. Publs: Health Science for the Tropics, 1962; Malaysian General Mathematics, 1965; General Science Certificate Course, 1968; Chemistry, A New Certificate Approach, 1969; Junior Tropical Biology, 1970; Additional Mathematics, 1971; Physical Science, 1972; Human & Social Biology, 1973; New Certificate Physics, 1974. Contbr. to: Overseas Educ.; Hong Kong Coun. for Educl. Rsch. Mbrships: A.R.I.C.; Fellow, Royal Asiatic Soc. Address: Sondes House, Patrixbourne, Canterbury, Kent, UK.

GODSEY, John Drew, b. 10 Oct. 1922, Bristol, Tenn., USA. Clergyman; Professor. Educ: B.S., Va. Polytech. Inst., 1947; B.D., Drew Univ., 1953; D.Theol., Univ. of Basle, Switzerland, 1960. Publs: The Theology of Dietrich Bonhoeffer, 1960; Karl Barth's Table Talk, 1963; Preface to Bonhoeffer: The Man & Two of his Shorter Writings, 1965; Intro. & Epil., Karl Barth's How I Changed My Mind, 1966; The Promise of H. Richard Niebuhr, 1970. Contbr. to num. theol. jrnls. Mbr., num. theol. socs. Address: 8306 Bryant Drive, Bethesda, MD 20034, USA.

GODSIFF, Patricia Mary, pen name SAUNDERS, Patricia M., b. 21 Aug. 1915, Auckland, NZ. Writer; Poet; Critic. Educ: B.A., Univ. of NZ, Canterbury, 1938; M.A., Vic. Univ. of Wellington, 1954. Publs: (verse) Arena, 1948; Inside Looking Out, 1964; Map & Man, 1970; (Contbns. in poetry anthols.) NZ Best Poems; Discovering NZ Writing; Pacific & Other Verse; Poetry NZ; Int. Who's Who in Poetry Anthol., 1972. Contbr. to: NZ Listener; Eve's Jrnl.; London Opinion; NZ Laurel Leaves; NZ's Heritage Ency.; etc. Hons. incl: Presidential Medal, World Congress of Poets, Manila, 1969; World Poet Award, World Poetry Soc. Int., 1972. Address: 87 Agincourt St., Renwick, Marlborough, NZ.

GODWIN, Eric George, b. 1913, Vancouver, Can. Consultant Anaesthetist. Educ: Edinburgh Univ.; St Mary's Hosp., London; F.F.A.R.C.S. Publs: Anaesthesia for Nurses, 1957. Address: 17 Downs Rd., Epsom, Surrey, UK.

GODWIN, John Frederick, b. 4 Dec. 1922, Hednesford, Staffs., UK. Primary School Headmaster. Educ: Co. of Stafford Trng. Coll., 1946-48; Cert. in Educ. of Children w. Handicaps to Learning. Publs: Battling Parer (aviation hist.), 1967; Wings to the Cape (aviation hist.), 1970; Give Your Child a Better Start (pre-schl. educ. book w. kit of apparatus). Mbrships: Soc. of Authors; Nat. Assn. of Head-Tchrs. Address: 10 Church Lane, Etching Hill, Rugeley, Staffs., UK.

GOES, Albrecht, b. 22 Mar. 1908. Priest. Educ: Tübingen Univ. Publs. incl: Unruhige Nacht, 1949; Von Mensch zu Mensch, 1949; Gedichte, 1950; Das Brandopfer, 1953; Freude am Gedicht, 1954; Vertrauen in das Wort, 1955; Ruf & Echo, 1956; Genesis, 1957; Hagar am Brunnen, 1958; Rede auf Goethes Mutter, 1958; Ravenna, 1959; Aber im Winde das Wort, 1963; Das Löffelchen, 1965; Im Weitergehen, 1966; Der Knecht macht keinen Lärm, 1968; Die guten Gefahrten, 1969; Kanzelholz, 1971. Mbrships: Acad. of Arts, Berlin; German Acad. for Speech. Recip., Lessing Prize, 1953. Address: Im langen Hau 5, Stuttgart-Ruhr, W. Germany.

GOFF, Martyn, b. 7 June 1923, London, UK. Writer. Publs: The Plaster Fabric, 1956; A Season with Mammon, 1957; A sort of Peace, 1958; The Youngest Director, 1960; Red on the Door, 1962; The Flint Inheritance, 1965; Indecent Assault, 1967; A Short Guide to Long Play, 1956; A further Guide to Long Play, 1957; LP Collecting, 1959; Why Conform?, 1968; Victorian & Edwardian Surrey, 1972; Record Choice, 1974. Contbr. to: Musical Times; Books & Bookmen; etc. Mbrships. incl: Lit. Panel of the Arts Coun.; Lib. Advisory Coun.; Nat. Heritage; Savile. Address: The Studio, 11 Cheyne Gardens, Chelsea, London SW3 5QU, UK.

GOFFART, Francis-Léo, pen name de RANSART, Robert, b. 31 Jan. 1903, Lodelinsart, Belgium. Ambassador, Retired. Educ: LL.D. Publs: Inventeurs de Lumière, 1948; Le Ghibli, 1962; La Geôle de verre, 1963. Mbr., PEN & Assn. of Belgian Writers. Address: Résidence El-Nil, Chemin des Sables, 06600, Antibes, France.

GOFFMAN, Erving, b. 1922, Manville, Alta., Can. Professor of Anthropology & Sociology. Educ: B.A., Univ. of Toronto; Ph.D., Univ. of Chgo., USA. Publs: Presentation of Self in Everyday Life, 1959; Encounters, 1961; Asylums, 1961; Behavior in Public Places, 1963; Stigma, 1964; Interaction Ritual, 1967; Strategic Interaction, 1969; Relations in Public, 1971; Frame Analysis, 1974. Contbr. to: Brit. Jrnl. Sociol.; Psychiatry; Advances in Psychiatry; Am. Anthropol.; Am. Jrnl. Sociol.; Human Rels.; Grp. Processes; Disorders in Communication. Address: Dept. of Anthropol., Univ. of Pa., Phila., PA 19174, USA.

GOICHI MASHIMO, Goichi Hayashi, b. 5 May 1906, Mineyamacho, Nakagun, Kyotofu, Japan. Novelist; Essayist; Biographer. Educ: Meiji Univ., Japan. Publs: incl: Men of Kyoto, 1958; Word of Kyoto (dictionary), 1972; Spirit of Kyoto (essay), 1972; The Love & Death of Takuboku Ishikawa, 1906. Contbr. to: Kodansha; Asahi Sinbunsha; Mikasashobo; & sev. Japanese Jrnls. Mbrships: PEN; Japan Lit. Soc. Recip: Kyotosi Bunkakososha, 1969. Address: 19 Iorinocho, Ichijyoji Sakyoku, Kyotoshi, Japan.

GOLD, Herbert, b. 9 Mar. 1924, Cleveland, Ohio, USA. Writer. Educ: B.A. 1946, M.A. 1948, Columbia Univ.; Sorbonne, Paris, France, 1949-51. Publs: incl: (novels) Birth of a Hero, 1951; The Man Who Was Not With It, USA, 1956, UK, 1965; Therefore Be Bold, USA, 1960, UK, 1962; Salt, USA, 1963, UK, 1964; The Fathers, USA & UK, 1967; The Great American Jackpot, USA, 1970, UK, 1971; (stories) The Magic Will, 1971; (essays) The Age of Happy Problems, 1962; Ed., var. collects. Hons. incl: Guggenheim Fellowship, 1957; Grant, Nat. Inst. Arts & Letters, 1958; Longview Fndn. Award, 1959; Ford Fellowship, 1960. Address: 1051-A Broadway, San Fran., CA 94133, USA.

GOLD, Horace Leonard, pen names CAMPBELL, Clyde Crane; KEITH, Leigh; DELL, Dudley; STORY, Richard, b. 26 Apr. 1914, Montreal, Can. Writer; Editor. Publs: 1st-6th Galaxy Reader, 1952-62; Galaxy Science Fiction Omnibus, 1955; Five Galaxy Short Novels, 1958; Bodyguard, 1960; Mind Partner, 1961; The World that Couldn't Be, 1959; The Old Die Rich, 1955. Contbr. to: Astounding; If; Special Detective; Unknown; Superman; Batman; etc. Mbrships: Sci. Fiction Writers of Am.; Disabled Am. Veterans; Hydra. Recip: World Sci. Fiction Award, 1953. Address: 4645 Lasheart Dr., La Canada, CA 91011, USA.

GOLD, Ivan, b. 12 May 1932, NYC, USA. University Teacher. Educ: B.A., Columbia Univ., 1953; B.A., Schl. of Oriental & African Studies, London Univ., UK, 1959. Publs: Nickel Miseries (short stories), USA, 1963, UK, 1964; Sick Friends (novel), USA, 1969, UK, 1970. Contbr. to: Genesis West; Cavalier. Hons: Guggenheim Fellowship, 1963; Ingram-Merrill Fellowship, 1964; Rosenthal Award, 1964; Grant, Nat. Endowment for Arts, 1966. Address: P.O. Box 11, Woodstock, NY 12498, USA.

GOLDBERG, Gerald Jay, b. 30 Dec. 1929, NYC, USA. Novelist; Professor of English. Educ: B.S., Purdue Univ., 1952; M.A., N.Y. Univ., 1955; Ph.D., Univ. of Minn., 1958. Publs: The National Standard, 1968; The Lynching of Orin Newfield, 1970; 126 Days of Continuous Sunshine, 1972. Contbr. to: N.Y. Times Book Review. Mbr., Authors Guild. Hons: Fulbright Professorship, Univ. of Zaragoza, Spain, 1962-63; Fellow, Inst. Creative Arts, Univ. of Calif., USA, 1966-67, 1968-69; Pulitzer Prize Nominee, for The Lynching of Orin Newfield, 1970. Address: c/o Dept. of English, University of Calif., Los Angeles, CA 90024, USA.

GOLDBERG, Louis, b. 22 Feb. 1908, Melbourne, Australia. Professor Emeritus of Accounting. Educ: B. Com., 1930, M. Com. 1938, B.A., 1948, Litt.D., 1967, Univ. Melbourne. Publs: A Philosophy of Accounting, 1939, revised ed. as An Outline of Accounting, 1957; Elements of Accounting (w. V. R. Hill), 1947, later revised eds., Concepts of Depreciation, 1960; Intermediate Accounting (co-author), 1948, later eds. & Ed. of 1967 ed.; Accounting Principles, 1946; Classification of Accounts & the Planning of Accounting Systems, 1946; An Inquiry into the Nature of Accounting, 1965; S. Vaidyanath Aiyar Memorial Lectures, 1971. Contbr. to Acctng. Review; Aust. Acct.; Abacus; etc. Mbrships. incl: Aust. Soc. Accts.; Acad. Social Scis. in Aust. Recip., num. acad. awards. Address: 5 Kemsley Ct., Hawthorn, Vic. 3123, Australia.

GOLDBERG, Samuel Louis, b. 19 Nov. 1926, Melbourne, Australia. Professor of English; Author. Educ: B.A., Melbourne; B.Litt., Oxford, UK. Publs: The Classical Temper, 1961; Joyce, 1962; An Essay on King Lear, 1974. Ed., Melbourne Critical Review. Contbr. to num. lit. jrnls. Address: Dept. of English, University of Melbourne, Parkville, Vic., Australia 3052.

GOLDFARB, Ronald L., b. 16 October 1933, Jersey City, N.J., USA. Lawyer; Writer. Educ: A.B., 1954, LL.B., 1956, Syracuse Univ.; LL.M. & J.S.D. Yale Law Schl. Publs: The Contempt Power, 1963; Ransom: A Critique of the American Bail System, 1965; Crime & Publicity: The Impact of News on the Administration of Justice, (w. Alfred Friendly), 1967; After Conviction — A Review of the American Correctional System (w. Linda Singer), 1973; Jails — The Ultimate Ghetto, scheduled for 1975. Contbr. to num. jrnls. Mbr., var. legal & civic orgs. Recip., law awards. Address: 1616 H. St., N.W., Fifth Floor, Wash., DC 20006, USA.

GOLDING, William Gerald, b. 19 Sept. 1911. Author. Educ: M.A., Brasenose Coll., Oxford. Publs: Lord of the Flies, 1954, film, 1963; The Inheritors, 1955; Pincher Martin, 1956; Free Fall, 1959; The Spire, 1964; The Hot Gates, 1965; The Pyramid, 1967; The Scorpion God, 1971; (play) Brass Butterfly, 1958. Mbrships: F.R.S.L. Hons: D.Litt.; C.B.E. Address: Ebble Thatch, Bowerchalke, Wilts., UK.

GOLDMAN, Marcus Selden, b. 12 May 1894, Middletown, Ohio, USA. University Professor. Educ: A.B., Miami Univ., 1916; A.M., Univ. of Ill., 1917; Am. Field Service Fellow, Univ. of Paris, France, 1919-21; A.M., Harvard Univ., USA, 1926; Ph.D., Univ. of Ill., 1931. Publs: Sir Philip Sidney & the Arcadia, 1934; A Progressive Study of English Composition (w. B. L. Jefferson & S. E. Glenn), 1941; St. Anne & the Gouty Rector & Other Plays (w. O. R. Goldman), transl'd. from the French of H. Ghéon & H. Brochet, 1950; Poems of the Past, 1969. Contbr. to: Jrnl. of Engl. & Germanic Philol.; num. other jrnls. Mbrships. incl: MLA; Medieval Acad. of Am., Coun., 1963-67; Reserve Offs. Assn. Hons: Illinois Poetry Prize, 1917; Legion of Merit, 1946; H.H.D., Miami Univ., 1974. Address: 203 W. Mich. Ave., Urbana, IL 61801, USA.

GOLDMAN, Richard Franko, b. 7 Dec. 1910, NYC, USA. Musician; Author; Educator. Educ: B.A., Columbia Coll.; Pvte. Musical Studies w. var. tchrs. Publs: The Band's Music, 1938; Landmarks of Early American Music, 1943 & 1974; The Concert Band, 1946; The Wind Band, 1961 & 1974; Harmony in Western Music, 1965 & 1968; Translation: The Mandarin & Other Stories, 1965 & 1966. Contbr. to: The Saturday Review; The Am. Scholar; & num. others. Mbrships. incl: ASCAP. Chmn., Assn. Indep. Colls. of Music, 1970-73. Address: Peabody Inst., Baltimore, MD 21202, USA.

GOLDMAN, William, b. 12 Aug. 1931, Chgo., Ill., USA. Novelist; Screenwriter. Educ: B.A., Oberlin Coll., 1952; M.A., Columbia Univ., 1956. Publs. incl: The Temple of Gold, 1957; Soldier in the Rain, 1960; The Thing of It Is, 1967. Butch Cassidy & the Sundance Kid (screenplay), 1969; Father's Day, 1971; Wigger (jvnle), 1974; Marathon Man, 1974. Hons: Academy Award, Best Original Screenplay, 1970. Address: 740 Park Ave., N.Y., NY 10021, USA.

GOLDSMITH, Immanuel, b. 1921, Berlin, Germany. Barrister-at-Law. Educ: LL.B., London Univ., UK; called to UK Bar, 1950, Ont. Bar, 1960. Publs: Transl., The Earliest Illustrated Haggadah, 1940; Hebrew Incunables, 1948; Damages for Personal Injury & Death in Canada, 1959, 1974; Canadian Building Contracts, 1968. Contbr. to: Can. Current Law; McGill Law Jrnl.; P.T.I.C. Bulletin. Mbrships: Can. Bar Assn.; Fellow, P.T.I.C.; A.T.L.A.; Int. Comm. Jurists. Hons: Q.C., 1970. Address: 80 Kilbarry Rd., Toronto, Ont., Canada.

GOLDSMITH, John Herman Thorburn, pen name THORBURN, John, b. 30 May 1903, Manchester, UK. Civil Service Commissioner; Chairman, Civil Service Selection Board (Ret'd). Educ: Magdalen Coll., Oxford. Publs: Hildebrand, 1931, 2nd ed., 1949; Three's Company, 1932.

Contbr. to: Country Life; Salmon & Trout; Flyfishers' Jrnl. Mbrships: Royal Instn. (Mgr., 1964-67, 1968-71, VP, 1967); Flyfishers. Address: Flat 31, Marsham Ct., Marsham St., London SW1, UK.

GOLDSTEIN, Joseph, b. 7 May 1923, Springfield, Mass., USA. Professor of Law, Science & Social Policy; Author. Educ: A.B., Dartmouth, 1943; Ph.D., London Schl. of Econs., UK, 1950; LL.B., Yale Univ., USA, 1952; Grad., Western New England Inst. for Psychoanalysts, 1968. Publs: The Government of a British Trade Union, 1953; Criminal Law (w. Richard Donnelly & Richard Schwartz), 1962; The Family & the Law (w. Jay Katz), 1965; Psychoanalysis, Psychiatry & Law (w. Jay Katz & Alan Dershowitz), 1966; Crime, Law & Society (w. A. S. Goldstein), 1971; Beyond the Best Interests of the Child (w. Anna Freud & A. J. Solnit), 1973. Contbr. to var. legal jrnls. Address: Overhill Rd., Woodbridge, CT 06525, USA.

GOLEMBIEWSKI, Robert T., b. 2 July 1932, Lawrenceville, N.J., USA. Professor & Consultant. Educ: A.B., Princeton Univ., 1954; M.A., Yale Univ., 1956; Ph.D., 1958. Publs: The Small Group, 1962; Behaviour & Organization, 1962; Men Management & Morality, 1965; A Methodological Primer, 1968; Organizing Men & Power, 1967; Sensitivity Training & the Laboratory Approach, 1970, 1973; Renewing Organizations, 1972; Cases in Public Management, 1973; Individual Learning & Change in Groups, 1974. Contbr. to profl. jrnls. Mbr., of profl. orgs. Hons: Hosp. Admnstrs. Book of the Yr. Award, 1966; Am. Soc. of Trng. Dirs. Award, 1969. Address: 145 Highland Dr., Athens, GA 30601, USA.

GOLINSKI, Edith, b. 11 Dec. 1912, Preetz, Holstein, Germany. Educ: Blind Schl., Kiel. Publs: Märchen aus Wald und Feld, 1954; Der lebendige Spiegel, 1956; Blick nach innen, Erlebnisse einer Blinden, 1963; Die Sternseele, 1969; Die Blätter nahm mir der Wind, 1975. Contbr. to: Schleswig-Holsteinische Monatshefte; Heimathefte; Kieler Nachrichten; Norddeutscher Rundfunk. Mbrships: Schleswig-Holsteinischer Schriftstellerverband und Eutiner Dichterkreis; Interessengemeinschaft Deutschsprachiger Authoren; Hebbel Soc.; Fairy Tale Soc. Hons: 1st Prize, Blind Jrnl., 1955, 1956; 3rd Prize, I.G.D.A., 1970; 2nd Prize, I.G.O.A., 1974. Address: 23 Kiel, Königsweg 97, W. Germany.

GOLL, Klaus Rainer, b. 2 July 1945, Lübeck, Germany. Teacher. Educ: Studies in Educ., Kiel Univ., 1967-70 & 1974. Publs: Windstunden und andere Texte, 1973; texte über Bennen (novel), forthcoming; (contbns. in anthols.) bundes deutsch lyrik in sachen grammatik, 1974; kreatives literatur-lexicon, 1974; (anthol.) Göttinger Musenalmanach auf das Jahr 1975; num. poems set to music by Hans Kaiser. Contbr. to: die horen; das pult; Wegwarten; europäische ideen; Lübeckische Blätter; Literatur/Manuskript; ZET; etc. Mbrships: German Authors' Assn. (VS), Schleswig-Holstein; Lit. Union Inc.; Der Turmbund (Writers' Grp.), Austria; Union of German-speaking Authors. Recip., Lyric Poetry Prize, Union of German-speaking Authors, 1974. Address: D-24 Lübeck 1, Holstenstr. 40, W. Germany.

GOLUBIEW, Antoni, b. 25 Feb. 1907, Wilno, Poland. Novelist. Educ: Univ. of Wilno. Publs: (in Polish) (cycle of histl. novels) The Forest; The Coming of the New; Bad Days; Crossroads; (essays) Letters to a Friend; Searches; Carried by History; (short stories) The Road. Contbr. to: Pax, 1934-36 (Ed.); co-Ed., Tygodnik Powszechny. Hons: Cracow Reg. Prize, 1948; Readers' Prize, Odra-weekly, 1948; Pietrzak Prize, 1951. Address: Ul. Jaskólcza 4, Cracow, Poland.

GOMBERG, William, b. 6 Sept. 1911, Brooklyn, N.Y., USA. University Professor. Educ: B.S., CCNY, 1933; M.S., N.Y. Univ., 1941; Ph.D., Columbia Univ., 1947. Publs: A Labor Manual of Job Evaluation, 1947; A Trade Union Analysis of Time Study, 1948; Blue Collar World (co-auth.); New Perspectives on Poverty (co-auth.), 1965; Contbr. to: Dictionary of Am. Hist.; Wharton Quarterly; Personnel Admnstr.; Labor Hist.; Jrnl. of Occupational Med.; Jrnl. of Bus.; Trans-Action; Labor Law Jrnl.; Calif.; Mgmt. Review; Nation; Jrnl. of Acad. of Mgmt.; Monthly Lab. Review; Pol. Sci. Quarterly; etc. Recip., McKinsey Fndn. Award for Best Article, Calif. Mgmt. Review, 1961. Address: 392 Montgomery Ave., Wynnewood, PA 19096, USA.

GOMEZ GIL, Alfredo, b. 1 Nov. 1936, Alicante, Spain. Professor. Educ: Grad. study, Univ. of Granada, 1956-58;

Lic., Univ. of Madrid, 1965. Publs. incl: (poetry) Escalas Imprecisas, 1960; Pesada Arena, 1962; Brumas y Cartones, 1963; Por la Distancia, 1968; Norte, Este, Oeste y Sur, 1968; Introduccion a la Esperanza, 1971; Veinti Guatro Poemas de Nieve, 1971; Desde al Arca del Profeta, 1971; Entre Fetiches y Amuletos, 1974; El Encantador de Serpientes, 1974; (prose) El Exconde Sucanor, 1964; Chispas y Confetis, 1966; Cerebros Espanoles en USA, 1971; Erberhard Schlotter, 1973; La Vuelta de los Cerebros (sociol.), 1974; Jose de Creeft. Contbr. to num. jrnls. in Spain, Europe, USA & Latin Am. Recip., var. profl. hons. Address: Hartford Coll. for Women, 1265 Asylum Ave., Hartford, CT, USA.

GÓMEZ MESA, Luis, pen names L. G. M. & Gumucio, b. 20 Mar. 1902, Madrid, Spain. Journalist; Writer; Professor of Cinema. Educ: Lic. Law, Univ. of Madrid. Publs: Los films de dibujos animados, 1930; Cinema Educativo y cultural, 1931; Variedad de la pantalla cómica, 1932; España en el mundo sin fronteras de cine educativo, 1936; Autenticidad del Cinema, 1936; Gary Cooper: el hombre, el actor, 1961; Ladislao Vadja, 1965; El teatro y la novela en el cine español, 1967. Contbr. to: Arriba; La Estafeta Literaria; Mundo Hispánico; Arte Fotográfico; Radio Madrid. Mbrships: Cir. of Int. Union of Cinema Criticism (UNICrit); Cir. of Cinema Writers (CEC); etc. Hons: Nat. Prize of Cinema Criticism; 3 Medlas, Cir. of Cinema Writers. Address: Calle Ventura Rodriguez 15, Madrid 8, Spain.

GOMPERTZ, Geoffrey Haviland, b. 10 Oct. 1901, The Peak, Hong Kong Island. Former Business Executive; Writer. Educ: Westminster Schl. (Resident King's Scholar). Publs: China in Turmoil, 1967. Contbr. to: sev. jrnls. in the Far East before 1943. Mbrships: Overseas League; Authors' Assn. Address: "Gomshall", 19 Walls Caravan Park, Aldershot GU12 6NZ, UK.

GOMPERTZ, G.St.G. M., b. 1904, Calcutta, India. Writer. Educ: Royal Mil. Coll., Sandhurst, UK. Publs: Chinese Celadon Wares, 1958; The Ceramic Art of Korea (w. Dr. Chewon Kim), 1961; Korean Celadon & Other Wares of the Koryo Period, 1963; Korean Pottery & Porcelain of the Yi Period, 1968; Celadon Wares, 1968. Contbr. to: Burlington Mag.; Oriental Art; Artibus Asiae; Transactions of Oriental Ceramic Soc.; Transactions of the Korea Br., Royal Asiatic Soc.; Far Eastern Ceramic Bulletin; etc. Mbr., Oriental Ceramic Soc. Address: Four Points Cottage, Aldworth, Reading, Berks., UK.

GOMULICKI, Juliusz Wiktor, b. 17 Oct. 1909, Warsaw, Poland. Writer. Educ: Univ. of Warsaw; H.S. of Pol. Sci. Publs: Critical Ed., C. Norwid: Collected Works, 1971-73; Book of Polish Verse (w. J. Tuwim), 1954, 1956; Sparks & Ashes, 1959-60; An Introduction to Norwid's Biography, 1965; C. Norwid's Poems, 1966. Contbr. to: Rocznik Literacki Yrbook of Lit.; etc. Mbrships: PEN; Assn. of Polish Authors; ZAIKS. Hons: Lit. Prize of Warsaw, 1961; Prize, A. Jurzykowski Fndn., N.Y., 1971; Homo Varso-viensis' Prize, 1971; Lit. Prize of Voivodeship, Warsaw, 1974. Address: Krasinskiego 18m.3, 01-581 Warsaw, Poland.

GONZALEZ, Arturo Francis Jr., pen name GONZALEZ, Arky, b. 5 June 1928, NYC, USA. Managing Director of several companies. Educ: A.B., Brown Univ., Providence, R.I., USA, 1952. Publs: Statesman for a New Society, 1964; Prose by Professionals 1966 & 1967 (contbr.); Live Them Again, 1953 (contbr.). Contbr. to: People Mag.; Business Week; N.Y. Times; Fortune; Newsweek; Realities; Saturday Review; London Daily Express; Wash Post; etc. Mbrships. incl: Int. Inst. Strategic Studies; Overseas Press Club; PEN; Soc. Am. Travel Writers. Hons: Pacific Area Travel Assn. Mag. Award, 1967; George Hedman Travel Writing Award, 1968. Address: 104 Ardoyne House, Dublin 4, Repub. of Ireland.

GOODACRE, Elizabeth Jane, b. 24 Feb. 1929, Sydney, Australia. Writer; Lecturer. Educ: B.Sc., Ph.D., Univ. of London, UK. Publs: Reading in Infant Classes, 1967; Teachers & their Pupils' Home Background, 1968; School & Home, 1970; Children & Learning to Read, 1971; The Psychology & Teaching of Reading, 1974. Contbr. to: Tchr.'s World; Times Educl. Supplement; Educl. Rsch.; Reading. Mbrships: Brit. Psychol. Soc.; Int. Reading Assn.; Soc. of Authors. Address: 24 Brookside Crescent, Cuffley, Potters Bar, Herts. EN6 4QN, UK.

GOODERS, John, b. 1937, London, UK. Writer; Editor, Birds of the World, 1969-71; Lecturer, College of

Education, 1967-69. Educ: Southampton & London Univs. Publs: Where to Watch Birds, 1967; Where to Watch Birds in Europe, 1970; Birds of the World, 1969-70; Wildlife Photography, 1973; The Bird-Watcher's Book, 1974; Birds — A Survey of the Bird Families of the World, 1975; Wildlife Paradises of the World, 1975; TV filmscripts for wildlife series. Contbr. to: Country Life; Animals; Observer; Tchr's. World; Birds Mag. Mbrships: B.O.U.; B.T.O. Recip. Churchill Fellowship, 1970. Address: 35 Brodrick Rd., London SW17, UK.

GOODFIELD, Gwyneth June, b. 1 June 1927, Stratford-on-Avon, UK. University Professor. Educ: B.Sc., Univ. of London; Ph.D., Univ. of Leeds. Publs: The Growth of Scientific Physiology, 1960; The Fabric of the Heavens, 1961; The Architecture of Matter, 1962; The Discovery of Time, 1965; Courier to Peking, 1973. Contbr. to: Nature; Guardian; Times Educl. Supplement; Sci. Am. Mbrships: Engl. Speaking Union; Fellow, Royal Soc. Med.; F.Z.S.; AAAS. Address: c/o Tile Barn, Alfriston, Sussex, UK.

GOODMAN, Cecily, b. Newport, Gwent, UK. Publs: The Survivors (w. L. H. Hardman), 1958. Address: 24 Freeland Park, Holders Hill Rd., London NW4 1LP, UK.

GOODMAN, Jonathan, b. 1931, London, UK. Publishing Executive; Former Theatre Director & TV Producer. Publs. incl: Matinee Idylls (poetry), 1954; Chopsticks in Waltztime (play), 1959; (books) Instead of Murder, 1961; Criminal Tendencies; Hello Cruel World Goodbye, 1964; The Killing of Julia Wallace, 1969; Bloody Versicles; Posts-Mortem, 1971; Gen. Ed., Celebrated Trials Series; Ed., Trial of Ian Brady & Myra Hindley, 1973; Co-Ed., Trial of Ruth Ellis, 1974; also sev. TV scripts. Contbr. to: Med., Sci. & the Law; Police; Armchair Detective (USA); etc. Mbrships: F.R.S.A.; Brit. Acad. Forensic Scis.; Medico-Legal Soc. Agent: Charles Lavell Ltd. Address: 43 Ealing Village, London W5 2LZ, UK.

GOODMAN, Paul, b. 9 Sept. 1911, NYC, USA. Writer; Editor. Educ: B.A., CCNY, 1931; Ph.D., Chgo. Univ., 1940. Publs. incl: (novels) The Grand Piano, 1942; Parents Day, 1951; The Empire City, 1959; Making Do., 1963; (short stories) The Facts of Life, USA, 1945, UK, 1946; Adam & His Works, 1968; (plays) Three Plays, 1965; Tragedy & Comedy, 1970; (verse) The Lordly Hudson, 1963; Homespun of Oatmeal Gray, 1970; num. works of social criticism. Contbr. to: Complex (former Ed.); Partisan Review (Film Ed.); New Repub. (TV critic); Liberation (Ed., 1962-70). Hons: Harriet Monroe Prize, Poetry, 1949; var. grants & fellowships. Address: 402 W. 20th St., N.Y., NY 10011, USA.

GOODRUM, Charles A., b. 21 July 1923, Pitts., USA. Librarian. Educ: B.A., Princeton; M.S., Columbia Univ.; Wichita State Univ. Publs: I'll Trade You An Elk, 1967; The Library of Congress, 1974. Contbr. to: New Yorker; Atlantic; Christian Sci. Monitor; Lib. Jrnl.; Wilson Lib. Bulletin; Special Libs. Mbr: Special Libs. Assn. Recip. Joseph Towne Wheeler Award, Columbia Univ. Address: Congressional Research Service, Library of Congress, Washington DC, USA.

GOODSALL, Robert Harold, b. 1891, London, UK. Retired Architect. Publs: In Nelson's Day — A Story for Boys, 1914; A Beginner's Guide to Photography; Photography in Winter; Home Building, 1924; Palestine Memories 1917-18-25, 1925; Successful Portraiture; Against-the-light Photography; The Ancient Road to Canterbury; The Eastern Rother; The Arun & Western Rother; Stede Hill, the Annals of a Kentish Home; The Kentish Stour; The Medway & its Tributaries; The Widening Thames, 1965; A Kentish Patchwork; A Second Kentish Patchwork; A Third Kentish Patchwork; A Fourth Kentish Patchwork. Contbr. to: Archaeologia Cantiana; Kent Life. Mbrships. incl: Soc. of Authors; F.S.A.; Fellow, Royal Photographic Soc. Address: Stede Hill, Harrietsham, Maidstone, Kent, UK.

GOODWIN, Geoffrey Alfred, b. 1921, Dorchester-on-Thames, Oxford, UK. Educ: Wallingford County Grammar Schl. Publ: Drivecraft, 1968. Address: 75 Bath St., Abingdon, Oxon. OX14 1EN, UK.

GOODWIN, Trevor Walworth, b. 1916, Neston, Cheshire, UK. University Professor. Educ: D.Sc., Univ. of Liverpool. Publs: The Comparative Biochemistry of the Carotonoids; Recent Advances in Biochemistry; The Biosynthesis of Vitamins; Introduction to Plant Biochemistry (w. E. I. Mercer). Contbr. to var. jrnls.

Mbrships: F.R.S. Address: Dept. of Biochemistry, The Univ., Liverpool, P.O. Box 147, UK.

GOODYEAR, Stephen Frederick, pen name TAYLOR, Sam, b. 27 Mar. 1915, Southampton, UK. Schoolmaster; Researcher, Early Music & Dance. Educ: B.Sc.(Econ.); Assoc., Royal Coll. of Music. Publs: The New Recorder Tutor, Books 1-4, 1956-63; Christmas Carols, 1960; Companion Pieces to the New Recorder Tutor, 1964; Suite (Handel), 1966; Songs & Dances, Scandinavia, 1968; Commonsense Recorder Teaching, 1973. Contbr. to: The World & the School; Southern Daily Echo. Mbrships: Soc. of Authors; Musicians Union. Recip., Brit. Empire Medal, 1946. Address: White Chimneys, 29 New Rd., Hythe, Southampton SO4 6BN, UK.

GOOLD-ADAMS, Deenagh, b. 26 Dec. 1916, London, UK. Horticultural Author. Publs: The Unheated Greenhouse, 1955; The Toad in the Greenhouse, 1961; The Tortoise in the Rockery, 1965; The Cool Greenhouse Today, 1969; The Small Greenhouse, 1974. Contbr. to: var. horticultural newspapers. Address: Highfield House, Binley, Andover, Hants. SP11 6HA, UK.

GOOLD-ADAMS, Richard John Moreton, b. 1916, Brisbane, Qld., Australia. Councillor, International Institute for Strategic Studies, 1958-; Royal Institute of International Affairs, 1956-; Chairman, SS Great Britain Project, 1968-. Educ: M.A., New Coll., Oxford, UK. Publs: South Africa Today & Tomorrow; Middle East Journey; On Limiting Atomic War (pamphlet); The British Army in the Nuclear Age (pamphlet); The Time of Power — a Reappraisal of John Foster Dulles. Former contbr. to: Sunday Times; TV & Radio Commentator. Mbrships: Chmn., Brit. Atlantic Comm., 1959-62, Int. Inst. for Strategic Studies, 1963-73; Travellers' Club. Hons: C.B.E., 1974. Address: Highfield House, Binley, Andover, Hants. SP11 6HA, UK.

GOOLDEN, Barbara, b. 5 June 1900. Novelist. Publs. incl: The Knot of Reluctance, 1926; The Sleeping Sword, 1928; Sugared Grief, 1932; Young Ambition, 1938; Daughters of Earth, 1947; Strange Strife, 1952; The World His Oyster, 1955; The Ships of Youth, 1958; For Richer, For Poorer, 1959; Against the Grain, 1961; The Pebble in the Pond, 1962; The Gift, 1964; Second Fiddle, 1967; The Reluctant Wife, 1968; A Marriage of Convenience, 1969; The Snare, 1970; No Meeting Place, 1971; A Leap in the Dark, 1972; (for children) Minty & the Secret Room, 1964; Trouble for the Tabors, 1966. Address: Top End, Felcourt, East Grinstead, Sussex, UK.

GORDIMER, Nadine, b. 20 Nov. 1923, Springs, S. Africa. Author. Novels: The Lying Days, 1953; A World of Strangers, 1958; Occasion for Loving, 1963; The Late Bourgeois World, 1966; A Guest of Honour, 1971; The Conservationist, 1974. Vols. of short stories: The Soft Voice of the Serpent, 1952; Six Feet of the Country, 1956; Friday's Footprint, 1960; Not For Publication, 1965; Livingstone's Companions, 1972. Contbr. to: Encounter; London Mag.; Atlantic; New Yorker; etc. Hons: W. H. Smith Award, 1961; James Tait Black Mem. Prize, 1972. Address: 7 Frere Rd., Parktown W., Johannesburg, S. Africa.

GORDON, Anne, b. 17 Feb. 1927, Nigg, Tain, Scotland, UK. Writer. Publs: The Parish of Nigg (w. Barbara Scott); Down to the Sea (w. Jessie Macdonald). Ordinary Fellow, Bot. Soc. of Edinburgh. Hons: 1st prize awarded to Nigg Scottish Womens Rural Inst. for "The Parish of Nigg". Address: Pitcalzean Mains, Nigg, Tain, Ross & Cromarty, Scotland, UK.

GORDON, Caroline, b. 6 Oct. 1895, Trenton, Ky., USA. Writer. Lecturer. Educ: A.B., Bethany Coll., W.Va., 1916. Publs. incl: (novels) Penhally, 1931; None Shall Look Back, USA & UK, 1937; Green Centuries, 1941; The Strange Children, USA, 1951, UK, 1952; The Malefactors, 1956; The Glory of Hera, 1972; (short stories) The Forest of the South, 1945; Old Red & Other Stories, 1963; (non-fiction) Ed., The House of Fiction (w. Allen Tate), 1950, revised ed. 1960; How to Read a Novel, 1957; A Good Soldier, 1963. Hons. incl: O. Henry Prize, 1934; D.Litt., Bethany Coll., 1946, St. Mary's Coll., Notre Dame, Ind., 1964. Address: The Red House, Princeton, NJ 08540, USA.

GORDON, Cyrus Herzl, b. 29 June 1908, Phila., Pa., USA. University Professor. Educ: A.B., 1927, M.A., 1928, Univ. of Pa.; Ph.D., 1930. Publs: Smith College

Tablets, 1952; Adventures in the Near East, 1957; Hammurapi's Code, 1957; The Common Background of Greek & Hebrew Civilizations, 1965; The Ancient Near East, 1965; Evidence for the Minoan Language, 1966; Ugarit & Minoan Crete, 1966; Ugaritic Textbook, 1967; Forgotten Scripts, 1971. Contbr. to num. profl. jrnls. Mbrships. incl: Fellow, Am. Acad. of Arts & Sci.; Am. Philol. Assn.; Am. Histl. Assn.; etc. Recip., num. acad. hons. Address: 130 Dean Road, Brookline, MA 02146, USA.

GORDON, Felice, (Mrs. Norman Bogner), b. 20 Dec. 1939, London, UK. Writer; Housewife. Publs: The Pleasure Principle; The Progress of an Affair.

GORDON, George N., b. 11 Nov. 1926, NYC, USA. Author; Professor. Educ: B.S. (Dram. Arts), 1952, M.A., 1953, Ph.D. (Communications in Educ.), 1957, N.Y. Univ. Publs: Educational Television, 1965; The Language of Communications: A Logical & Psychological Examination, 1969; Classroom Television: New Frontiers in ITV, 1970; Persuasion: The Theory & Practice of Manipulative Communications, 1971; Co-author, The War of Ideas, 1973. Contbr. to var. encys. (inclng: Britannica, 1974), & jrnls. Mbrships. incl: Int. Radio & TV Soc.; The Authors' Guild. Hons. incl: Educ. Press Assn. Award, Best Feature Article, 1968; Broadcast Preceptor's Award, San Francisco State Coll., 1970. Address: 110-15 71st Road, Forest Hills, NY 11375, USA.

GORDON, Giles Alexander Esme, pen name BOSWELL, b. 1940, Edinburgh, UK. Literary Agent; Lecturer. Publs. incl: Two & Two Make One, 1966; Two Elegies, 1968; Pictures from an Exhibition, 1970; The Umbrella Man, 1971; Eight Poems for Gareth, 1971; Twelve Poems for Callum, 1972; About a Marriage, 1972; Girl with Red Hair, 1974; Farewell, Fond Dreams, 1975; Ed., Beyond the Words, 1975. Contbr. to var. lit. publs. Mbrships: Comm. of Mgmt., Soc. of Authors, 1973—; Writers' Action Grp.; Soc. of Bookmen; Writers' Guild of GB. Recip., C. Day Lewis Fellow in Writing, King's Coll., Univ. of London, 1974-75. Address: 9 St. Ann's Gdns., London NW5 4ER, UK.

GORDON, Gordon & Mildred (Husband & Wife Team), pen name THE GORDONS, (Gordon) b. Anderson, Ind., USA, (Mildred) b. 1912, Eureka, Kan. Writing Team. Educ: (both) Univ. Ariz. Publs: The Little Man Who Wasn't There; Make Haste to Live; F.B.I. Story; Campaign Train; Case File; F.B.I.; The Talking Bug (UK: Playback); The Big Frame; Captive; Operation Terror (film title: Experiment in Terror); Undercover Cat (film title: That Darn Cat); Power Play; Undercover Cat Prowls Again; Night Before the Wedding; The Informant; Catnapped! Address: 4431 Petit Ave., Encino, CA, USA.

GORDON, John Fraser, b. 1916, London, UK. Co-Director. Educ: City of London Coll. Publs. incl: The Staffordshire Bull Terrier Owner's Encyclopaedia, 1967; All About the Boxer, 1970; All About the Cocker Spaniel, 1971; The Beagle Guide, 1968; The Miniature Schnauzer Guide, 1968; The Staffordshire Bull Terrier, 1970; The Bull Terrier, 1973; The Bulldog, 1973; The Dandie Dinmont Terrier, 1973; The Pug, 1973; The Borzoi, 1974; The Irish Wolfhound, 1974; Some Rare & Unusual Breeds, 1975. Contbr. to: Dog World. Mbrships: Wig & Pen; Soc. of Authors. Hons: Freeman, City of London; Cruft's & Int. Judge of Dogs. Address: 72 Clydeway, Romford RM1 4UT, UK.

GORDON, Richard, b. 15 Sept. 1921, London, UK. Surgeon; Author. Educ: M.A.; M.B.; B.Chir., Selwyn Coll., Cambridge; St. Bart's Hospital; F.F.A.R.C.S. Publs. incl: Doctor in the House; Doctor at Sea; The Captain's Table; Doctor at Large; Doctor in Love; Doctor & Son; Doctor in Clover; Doctor on Toast; Doctor in the Swim; Nuts in May; The Summer of Sir Lancelot; Love & Sir Lancelot; The Facemaker; Surgeon at Arms; The Facts of Life; Doctor on the Boil; A Baby in the House; (play) Doctor in Love; num. films. Contbr. to: Punch; & med. jrnls. Address c/o 78 S. Audley St., London W1, UK.

GORDON-BROWN, Ian Selby, b. 14 Feb. 1925, Quetta Pakistan. Psychologist. Educ: B.A., Selwyn Coll., Cambridge, UK. Publs: World Union Goodwill (co-ed.); Participation in Industry: An Introductory Guide. Contbr. to: Beacon; var. psychol., metaphys. & indl. jrnls. Mbrships: Assoc.., Brit. Psychol. Soc. Address: 143 Talgarth Rd., London W14 9DA, UK.

GORDON WALKER, (Lord) Patrick, b. 7 Apr. 1907, Worthing, Sussex, UK. Member of the House of Lords.

Educ: M.A., B.Litt., Christ Church, Oxford Univ. Publs: Sixteenth & Seventeenth Centuries, 1935; Outline of Man's History, 1939; The Commonwealth, 1962; The Cabinet, 1970. Mbr., Reform Club. Recip., C.H., 1968. Address: 105 Frobisher House, Dolphin Sq., London SW1 3LL, UK.

GORE, Constance Florence Margaret Teresa, b. 1919, London, UK. Children's Writer. Publs: Dust & Dreams; Little Pig & the Big Potato. Contbr. to: BBC Radio: Listen With Mother; etc. Address: 8 Downs View Lodge, 186 Amhurst Rd., London E8, UK.

GORER, Geoffrey Edgar, b. 26 Mar. 1905, London, UK. Social Anthropologist. Educ: B.A., M.A., Univ. of Cambridge. Publs: The Life & Ideas of the Marquis de Sade, 1934, 3rd ed., 1964; Africa Dances, 1935; Himalayan Village, 1938, 2nd ed., 1967; The Americans, 1948; Exploring English Character, 1955; Death, Grief & Mourning, 1965. Contbr. to num. jrnls. Mbrships: Am. Anthropol. Soc.; Royal Anthropol. Soc. Address: Sunte House, Haywards Heath, Sussex RH16 1RZ, UK.

GÖRGEY, Gábor, b. 22 Nov. 1929, Budapest, Hungary. Author. Educ: Univ. of Linguistics, Budapest. Publs: (lyric poetry) Smoke & Light, 1956; Meridian, 1963; I'm Fine, Thanks, 1970; (transls.) Hunter's Fortune, 1974; (plays) One Pistol for Five (5 plays), 1969; Ararat Small (3 comedies), 1971. Contbr. to: Magyar Nemzet; Nagyvilàg; New Hungarian Quarterly; Mod. Int. Drama (Pa. Univ. Press); Confrontation (L.I. Univ.). Mbrships: PEN: Soc. of Hungarian Authors. Address: Katona J. u. 26, 1137 Budapest, Hungary.

GORHAM, Maurice Anthony Coneys, pen name RAULT, Walter, b. 19 Aug. 1902, London, UK. Writer; Director, Radio Eireann, 1953-60. Educ: B.A., Balliol Coll., Oxford Univ. Publs: The Local, 1939; Sound & Fury, 1948; Back to the Local, 1949; Television, Medium of the Future, 1949; Professional Training for Radio, 1950; Inside the Pub (co-author), 1950; Showmen & Suckers, 1951; Londoners, 1951; Broadcasting & Television since 1900, 1952; Forty Years of Irish Broadcasting, 1967; Ireland from Old Photographs, 1971; Dublin from Old Photographs, 1972. Contbr. to: newspapers, periodicals & radio. Mbrships. incl: Soc. Authors. Address: 33 Sydney Parade Ave., Dublin 4, Repub. of Ireland.

GORMAN, Ian, b. 11 May 1942, Leicester, UK. Journalist. Educ: B.A., Schl. of Oriental & African Studies, Univ. of London. Publs: The Greatest Novel of the Twentieth Century; Whither the Universe. Contbr. to: Times; Fin. Times; Sunday Times; Daily Telegraph; Sunday Telegraph; Sunday People; Nation Review; Sydney Morning Herald; Info.; New Wave; Am. Report; Earth News; Winnipeg Free Press; Daily Yomiuri; Japan Times; etc. Mbrships: For. Correspondents' Club of Japan; For. Press in Japan. Address: c/o The Foreign Correspondents' Club of Japan, 1-2 Marunouchi, 2-chome, Chiyoda-ku, Tokyo, Japan.

GORRESIO, Vittorio, b. 18 July 1910, Modena, Italy. Journalist. Educ: D. Jur., Rome Univ. Publs: Un Anno di Liberta, 1945; I Moribondi di Montecitorio, 1947; I Carissimi Nemici, 1949; I Bracci Secolari, 1951; Risorgimento Scomunicato, 1958; L'Italia a Sinistra, 1963; La Nuova Missione, 1968; Roam Ieri e Oggi, 1970; Il Sesto Presidente, 1972; Il Papa e il Diavolo, 1973. Contbr. to La Stampa, Turin. Address: Piazza Navona 106, Rome, Italy.

GOSDEN, Peter Henry John Heather, b. 1927, Fittleworth, Sussex, UK. University Teacher. Educ: M.A., Ph.D.; Emmanuel Coll., Cambridge; Univ. of London. Publs: Friendly Societies in England 1915-75, 1961; Development of Educational Administration, 1966; Educational Administration: A Bibliographical Guide, 1967; How They Were Taught: Learning & Teaching 1800-1950, 1969; The Evolution of a Profession, 1972; Self-help: Voluntary Associations in Nineteenth Century Britain, 1973. Address: The University, Leeds 2, UK.

GOSLING, Veronica, pen name HENRIQUES, Veronica, b. 1931, Hants., UK. Writer. Publs: Love from a Convict, 1954; Home is the Heart, 1955; Man in a Maze, 1957; The Face I Had, 1965; Ed., Biography of Myself by Robert Henriques. Mbrships: Authors' Assn.; PEN. Agent: Curtis Brown. Address: 29 Downshire Hill, London NW3, UK.

GOSNELL, Elizabeth (Betty) Duke Tucker, b. 21 Apr. 1921, Little Rock, Ark., USA. Educ: B.A., Duke Univ.

Publs: The Poet Who Was A Painter of Souls, 1969; Silk & Silence, 1971. Contbr. to poetry jrnls. Mbrships: Dir., World Poetry Soc. Intercontinental; Sec. & Mbr., Bd. of Trustees, South & West, Inc.; Ed., poetry column, local press; Hostess, Afterglow: The World of Poetry, KHBM AM — FM; Ldr., South & West Poetry Workshop; Poetry Soc. of Am.; Poet's Roundtable of Ark.; Ill., Ky. Poetry Socs.; Fndng. Fellow, Int. Poetry Soc., UK; United Poets Laureate Int. Hons: Winning Quatrain, South & West Poetry Fest., 1969; Citation, Select Poem, WPSI, 1970; var. other poetry prizes. Address: 803 N. Slemons St., Monticello, AR 71655, USA.

GOSSMAN, J. Lionel, b. 29 May 1929, Glasgow, UK. Teacher. Educ: M.A., Glasgow; Dip. d'Etudes Supérieures, Paris, France; D.Phil., Oxford, UK. Publs: Men & Masks: A Study of Molière. 1963; Medievalism & the Ideologies of the Enlightenment, 1968; French Society & Culture: Background for Eighteenth Century Literature, 1972. Contbr. to: MLN; Eighteenth Century Studies; Studies on Voltaire & the Eighteenth Century; Yale French Studies; French Review; PMLA. Address: Johns Hopkins Univ., Baltimore, MD 21218, USA.

GOTESKY, Rubin, b. 4 July 1906, Plosck, Poland. Educator: Editor. Educ: B.S., M.A., Ph.D., N.Y. Univ. Publs: Liberalism in Crisis, 1948; Invitation to Phenomenology (co-auth.), 1965; Struggle for Tomorrow (co-auth.), 1954; Personality: The Need for Liberty & Rights, 1967; Current Topics of Contemporary Thought, 13 vols. (co-ed. w. Ervin Laszlo), 1969-74; Social Force, Social Power & Social Violence, in Reason & Violence (ed. S. M. Stanage), 1974. Contbr. to: Knowledge & the Tchr., W. Wash. State Bull., 1965; The Aims of Educ. (ed. L. M. Brown), 1970; Philos. Review; Philos. & Phenomenol. Rsch.; Yale Review; Sat. Review; Ency. of Morals; Colliers Ency.; Ency. Am.; Ency. of Philos.; etc. Mbrships. incl: Mind. Assn.; Symbolic Logic Assn.; Pres., SSPP; Pres., IPA. Address: 4 La Plata Place, 3, Durango, CO 81301, USA.

GOTLIEB, Phyllis Fay Bloom, b. 25 May 1926, Toronto, Can. Poet; Author. Educ: B.A., M.A., Univ. of Toronto. Publs: (poetry) Within the Zodiac, 1964; Ordinary, Moving, 1969; Doctor Umlaut's Earthly Kingdom, 1974; (novels) Sunburst, 1964; Why Should I Have All the Grief? , 1969. Contbr. to: Tamarack Review; Can. Forum; Fantasy & Sci. Fiction; Galaxy; If; Amazing; Fantastic. Mbrships: League of Can. Poets; Sci. Fiction Writers of Am. Address: 29 Ridgevale Drive, Toronto, Can.

GOTTA, Salvatore, b. 18 May 1887, Italy. Novelist; Dramatist. Publs. incl: Pia, 1912; La Donna mia, 1924; Il peccato originale, 1929; Il gioco dei colori, 1932; Lilith, 1934; Amina, 1939; Tre donne innamorate, 1939; Il volto dell'umano amore, 1944; Macerie a Portofino, 1946; Domani a Te, 1950; La Saga dei Vela, 3 vols., 1955; Ilaria, 1956; Orgasmo, 1960; Aria del mio Paese, 1964; Il progresso si diverte, 1967; Murat, 1970; Il fiore de Matisse, 1972; Corradino di Svevia, 1973; Prendersi e Gasciarsi. Address: Villa Aranci, Portofino, Genoa, Italy.

GÖTZ, Gerd, pen names WERNER, Katharina; KUNZ, Dr. M., b. 19 Feb. 1929, Landau-Pfalz, Germany. Doctor, Specialist in Internal Medicine. Educ: D. Med., 1959; Univs. TBingen, Marburg & Freiburg, Heidelberg. Publs: Märchen? , 1970; Gutentaggebete Guttenachtgebete, 1973; Schönen Grüss von Detlef, 1975; Systematik und Spezial-Katalog der Marken-Heftchen BRD und Berlin, 1974. Contbr. to: Simplizissimus; Euromed; Die Horen; Das Pult; TV & radio; etc. Mbrships. incl: German Authors' Assn.; Soc. German-speaking authors; Fed. Assn. German Author/doctors. Hons. incl: 1st Prize for Short Radio Play, ARD, 1972. Address: D-433 Mülheim-Ruhr, Viktoriastr. 16, W. Germany.

GOUDGE, Elizabeth de Beauchamp, b. 24 April 1900, Wells, UK. Author. Educ: Reading Univ. Publs. incl: (novels) Island Magic, 1932; Towers in the Mist, 1936; Green Dolphin Country, 1944; The Rosemary Tree, 1956; The Child from the Sea, 1970; (short stories) White Wings, 1952; The Lost Angel, 1971; (plays) Three Plays, 1937; (children's books) Smokey House, 1938; The Little White Horse, 1946; Linnets & Valerians, 1964; (biography) God so Loved the World, 1951; Anthology of Verse & Prose: A Book of Comfort, 1964. Fellow, Royal Soc. Lit. Address: Rose Cottage, Peppard Common, Henley, Oxon., UK.

GOUGH, John Wiedhofft, b. 23 Feb. 1900, Penarth, Glam., UK. University Teacher; Author. Educ: B.A., 1922, M.A., 1926, Merton Coll., Oxford; D.Litt., 1965. Publs:

The Mines of Mendip, 1930, 2nd ed., 1967; The Social Contract, 1936, 2nd ed., 1957; John Locke's Political Philosophy, 1950, 2nd ed., 1973; Fundamental Law in English Constitutional History, 1955; The Rise of the Entrepreneur, 1969. Contbr. to: Engl. Histl. Review; Hist. Pol. Studies. Address: 28 Hill Top Rd., Oxford OX4 1PE, UK.

GOUHIER, Henri, b. 5 Dec. 1898, Auxerre, Yonne, France. Honorary University Professor. Educ: Agrégé de philos., Doct.-ès-lettres, École Normale Superieure. Publs. incl: La Pensée Religieuse de Descartes, 1924, new ed. 1972; Ed., Maine de Biran, Journal, 3 vols., 1954-57; La Pensée Metaphysique de Descartes, 1961, 2nd ed., 1969; Les Méditations Metaphysiques de J.-J. Rousseau, 1970; Pascal & les Humanistes Chrétiens, 1974; 7 books on theatre. Contbr. to: Revue Int. de Philos. (co-Ed.). Mbrships. incl: Acad. des Scis. Morales & Politiques; Assoc., Royal Belgian Acad. Recip., Grand Lit. Prize, French Acad., 1966. Address: 21 Blvd. Flandrin, 75116 Paris, France.

GOULD, James Warren, b. 14 May 1924, Boulder, Colo., USA. Professor. Educ: A.B., Univ. of Pa., 1946; Cert. des Etudes, Univ. of Paris, 1946; M.A., 1947, Ph.D., 1955, Fletcher Schl. of Law & Diplomacy. Publs: Sumatra — America's Pepperpot, 1955; Americans in Sumatra, 1960; The U.S. & Malaysia, 1969. Contbr. to: Jrnl. of S.E. Asian Studies; Western Pol. Quarterly; LA Times; US Naval Inst. Proceedings; Jrnl. of Oriental Studies; Gandhi Marg. Mbrships. incl: Fellow, Malaysian Br., Royal Asiatic Soc.; Dir., Peace Corps, Malaysia, 1964-66. Address: Scripps Coll., Claremont, CA 91711, USA.

GOULDEN, Mark, b. 1919, Clifton, Bristol, UK. Journalist; Chairman, W. H. Allen & Co., Publishers. Publs: var. works on jrnlsm.; lit.; advt.; publng. Contbr. to: Ed., Eastern Morning News; Mng. Ed., Hull Evening News; Mng. Ed., Evening News, Leeds; Mng. Ed., Sunday Referee, London; num. jrnls. in many countries. Mbrships: Press Club; Savage Club; Paternosters. Address: Mayfair House, 14 Carlos Place, London W1, UK.

GOULYASHKI, Andrey, b. 7 May 1914, Rakovitsa, Bulgaria. Writer. Publs: (in Bulgarian) Machine & Tractor Station, 1950; The Village of Vedrovo, 1952; The Golden Fleece, 1958; Seven Days of Our Life, 1965; The Adventures of Avacum Zahov, 1969; A Romantic Story, 1970; The Golden Age, 1970. Contbr. to sev. Bulgarian lit. reviews, mags., & newspapers. Mbrships: Dpty. Chmn., Union of Bulgarian Writers; PEN. Hons: Dimitrov Prize, 1950, 1951, 1959; Prizes, Union of Bulgarian Writers, 1964, 1968; Honoured Worker in Culture, 1970; Ivan Vazov Prize, 1972; Hero of Socialist Labour. Address: Sofia, bul. Biryuzov, 59, Bulgaria.

GOURDIE, Thomas, b. 18 May 1913, Cowdenbeath, UK. Handwriting Consultant; Calligrapher. Educ: Dip. Design & Crafts, Edinburgh Coll. Art. Publs: Italic Handwriting, 1955, 2nd ed., 1974; Puffin Book of Lettering, 1961; Das Schrift Schreiben, 1963; The Simple Modern Hand, 1965; Guide to Better Handwriting, 1968; Ladybird Book of Handwriting, 1968; Handwriting for Today, 1971; I Can Write, 1974; Improve Your Handwriting, 1975. Contbr. to: Sunday Times Colour Supplement; Times Educl. Supplement; Jrnl. Educl. Inst. Scotland; Lantern (S. Africa); Scots Mag. Recip., M.B.E., Servs. Educ., 1959. Address: 3 Douglas St., Kirkcaldy, UK.

GOVER, (John) Robert, b. 2 Nov. 1929, Phila., Pa., USA. Author. Educ: B.A., Univ. of Pitts., 1953. Publs: (novels) One Hundred Dollar Misunderstanding, USA & UK, 1962; The Maniac Responsible, USA, 1963, UK, 1964; Here Goes Kitten, 1964; Poorboy at the Party, 1966; J. C. Saves, 1968; Ed., W. Lowenfels, The Portable Walter, 1968. Address: 540 Picacho Lane, Santa Barbara, CA 93108, USA.

GOW, Ronald, b. 1897, Heaton Moor, UK. Research Chemist; Schoolmaster; Stage & BBC Playwright. Educ: B.Sc., Univ. of Manchester. Publs: Gallows Glorious, 1933; My Lady Wears a White Cockade, 1934; Adaptor, Love on the Dole, 1935; Ma's Bit o' Brass, 1938; (musical) Jenny Jones, 1944; Adaptor, Tess of the d'Urbervilles, 1946; Adaptor, Ann Veronica, 1949; Adaptor, The Edwardians, 1958; Mr. Rhodes, 1962; A Boston Story, 1968. Mbr., Dramatists' Club. Agent: Lawrence Fitch. Address: 9 Stratton Rd., Beaconsfield, Bucks., UK.

GOWAN, John Curtis, b. 21 May 1912, Boston, Mas., USA. Professor. Educ: A.B., 1933, Ed.M., 1935, Harvard Univ.; Ed.D., Univ. of Calif., L.A., 1952. Publs. incl: The Education & Guidance of the Ablest, 1964; Creativity: Its Educational Implications, 1967; Development of the Creative Individual, 1972; Development of the Psychedlic Individual, 1974; Trance Art & Creativity, 1975. Ed., Gifted Children Quarterly. Address: 9030 Darby Ave., Northridge, CA 91324, USA.

GOYDER, George Armin, b. 22 June 1908, London, UK. Managing Director (1935-71). Educ: London Schl. Econs. Publs: The Future of Private Enterprise, 1951, latest ed. 1954; The Responsible Company, 1961; The People's Church, 1964; The Responsible Worker, 1975. Mbrships: William Blake Trust (Fndr. Mbr.); Brit. N. Am. Comm. (Fndr.); Centre Int. Briefing (Chmn.); Reform Club. Address: Pindars, Rotherfield Greys, Henley-on-Thames, Oxon., UK.

GOYEN, William, b. 24 Apr. 1915, Trinity, Tex., USA. Author. Educ: B.A., 1937, M.A., 1939, Rice Univ., Houston, Tex. Publs. incl: (novels) The House of Breath, 1950; In a Farther Country, 1955; The Fair Sister, 1962; Come, the Restorer, 1974; (short story collects.) Ghost & Flesh, 1952; The Faces of Blood Kindred, 1960; The Collected Stories of William Goyen, 1975; (biog.) A Book of Jesus, 1973; also sev. plays. Contbr. to num. Am. & European jrnls. Mbrships: PEN; Writers' Guild; ASCAP; Dramatists' Guild. Hons. incl: Guggenheim Fellow in Creative Fiction, 1950 & 1952; McMurray Award for Best 1st Novel by a Texan, 1950. Address: 277 W. End Ave., N.Y., NY 10023, USA.

GOYTISOLO, Luis, b. 17 Mar. 1935, Barcelona, Spain. Writer. Educ: Univ. studies in Law. Publs: Las Afueras, 1958; Las Mismas Palabras, 1962; Ojos Circulos Buhos, 1971; Recuento, 1973. Recip., Premio Biblioteca Breve (for Las Afueras), 1957. Address: Balmes 441, Barcelona 6, Spain.

GRACQ, Julien, b. 27 July 1910, St. Florent le Vieil, France. Former Professor of History. Educ: Ecole Normale Superieure; Ecole des Sci. Politiques. Publs: Au château d'Argol, 1939; Un Beau Tenébreux, 1945; Le Roi Pêcheur, 1947; Liberte Grande, 1947; André Breton, 1947; La littérature a l'estomac, 1950; Le Rivage des Syrtes, 1951; Un Balcon en Forêt, 1958; Préférences; Lettrines, 1967; La Presq'ile, 1970. Address: 61 rue de Grenelle, Paris 7e, France.

GRADON, Pamela Olive Elizabeth, b. 27 Feb. 1915, Rugby, UK. University Teacher. Educ: Cheltenham Ladies' Coll.; B.A., M.A., Lady Margaret Hall, Oxford; Ph.D., London Univ. Publs: Cynewulf's Elene, 1958; Form & Style in Early English, 1971. Contbr. to: Medium Aevum, Review of Engl. Studies; Mod. Lang. Review, Engl. & Germanic Studies. Mbr: Early Engl. Text Soc. (Ed. Sec.). Address: St. Hugh's Coll., Oxford, UK.

GRAEFF, Grace Marie, b. 22 Oct. 1918, Mayville, N.Y., USA. Artist. Educ: Oberlin Conserv.; Cleveland Inst. of Music; Case Western Reserve Univ.; Jamestown Community Coll.; B.A., Empire State Coll., 1973. Publs: House Not Made With Hands, 1966. Address: RD 1, Mayville, NY 14757, USA.

GRAEME, Bruce, pen name of JEFFRIES, Graham Montague, b. 1900, London, UK. Novelist; Scriptwriter. Educ: Great War; Gray's Inn, 1930. Publs. incl: Blackshirt, 1925; Through the Eyes of the Judge, 1930; Unsolved, 1931; The Imperfect Crime, 1932; An International Affair, 1934; The Coming of Carew, 1945; And a Bottle of Rum, 1948; So Sharp the Razor, 1955; The Long Night, 1958; Almost Without Murder, 1963; Always Expect the Unexpected, 1965; Blind Date for a Private Eye, 1969; The Quiet Ones, 1970; The lady Doth Protest, 1971; Yesterday's Tomorrow, 1972; Two & Two Make Five, 1973. Address: Gorse Field Cottage, Aldington Frith, Nr. Ashford, Kent, UK.

GRAEME, Roderic, b. 1926, London, UK. Writer. Publs: the 'Blackshirt' series, 20 titles. Mbr., Crime Writers' Assn. Lit. Agent: Hutchinson & Co. Address: Bourne Farm, Aldington Frith, Nr. Ashford, Kent, UK.

GRAFF, Henry Franklin, b. 11 Aug. 1921, NYC, USA. University Professor of History; Historian; Author. Educ: B.S.S., CCNY, 1941; M.A., 1942, Ph.D., 1949, Columbia Univ. Publs: Bluejackets with Perry in Japan, 1952;

The Modern Researcher (w. J. Barzun), 2nd ed., 1970; The Adventure of the American People (w. J. Krout), 3rd ed., 1973; The Free & The Brave, 3rd ed., 1973; Ed., American Imperialism & The Philippine Insurrection, 1969; The Tuesday Cabinet: Deliberation & Decision on Peace & War under Lyndon B. Johnson, 1970. Contbr. to: N.Y. Times Book Reivew; N.Y. Times Mag.; etc. Mbrships: PEN; The Authors' Guild. Address: 47 Andrea Ln., Scarsdale, NY 10583, USA.

GRAFTON, James Douglas, b. 1916, London, UK. Radio & TV Scriptwriter. Educ: London Univ. Publs: (radio scripts) The Goon Show (originator w. Spike Milligan); over 200 comedy progs.; (TV scripts) over 300 Light Entertainment Spectaculars; over 200 situation comedies; (film) Sunstruck (co-author & prod.), 1973. Mbrships: Songwriters Guild; PRS; Writers Guild; Royal Automobile Club. Address: Burford, Byways, Selsey, Sussex, UK.

GRAHAM, Angus, b. 1892, Skipness, UK. Writer. Educ: M.A., New Coll., Oxford. Publs: Forests in the National Development, 1923; Quebec Limit Holders' Manual, 1932; The Golden Grindstone, 1935; Napoleon Tremblay, 1939. Contbr. to: Proceedings of Soc. of Antiquaries of Scotland; Jrnl. of Royal Soc. of Antiquaries of Ireland; Antiquity; Archaeol. Newsletter; Jrnl. of Forestry. Mbrships: Sec.-Treas., Quebec Forest Inds. Assn., 1925-33; Sec., Royal Comn. on Ancient Monuments, Scotland, 1935-57; Commnr., 1960-74. Address: 1 Nelson St., Edinburgh EH3 6LF, UK.

GRAHAM, Bertie Neil Grant Gordon, pen name BIDDESTONE, Neil, b. 19 Nov. 1904, Kandadola, Ceylon. Retired Tea & Rubber Planter. Publs: Hunter At Heart, 1951. Contbr. to: New Poets, 1973; Poetry Today, 1973; In Praise of God, 1973; var. planting jrnls., wildlife mags., motoring mags. & Ceylon newspapers. Mbrships. incl: Ceylon Game & Fauna Protection Soc. (VP). Recip., Prize for Essay on Planting, Ceylon, 1951. Address: c/o Post Office, Dromahair, Co. Leitrim, Repub. of Ireland.

GRAHAM, Frank Jr., b. 31 Mar. 1925, NYC, USA. Author. Educ: B.A., Columbia Coll., USA, 1950. Publs: Disaster by Default: Politics & Water Pollution, 1966; Since Silent Spring, 1970; Man's Dominion: The Story of Conservation in America, 1971; Where the Place Called Morning Lies, 1973; Audubon/Golden Primers (w. Ada Graham), 1974; Gulls: A Social History, 1975. Contbr. to: Audubon; The Atlantic; Today's Health; Am. Heritage; etc. Mbrships. incl: Authors Guild; Nat. Audubon Soc., Am. Assn. for the Advancement of Sci. Am. Inst. for Biological Sci. Recip., Disting. Achievement Award, Univ. of Maine, 1973. Address: Milbridge, ME 04658, USA.

GRAHAM, Ian James Alastair, b. 12 Nov. 1923, Campsey Ash, Suffolk, UK. Archaeologist; Research Fellow, Harvard University. Educ: B.A., Dublin Univ. Publs: Archaeological Explorations in the Department of Peten, Guatemala, 1967; Corpus of Maya Hieroglyphic Inscriptions, forthcoming. Fellow of Soc. of Antiquaries, London. Address: Chantry Farm, Campsey Ash, Suffolk, UK.

GRAHAM, John Charles Edward, b. 7 Sept. 1931, Inverness, UK. Actor; Writer. Publs: (stage plays) There Was an Old Woman; Fatal Development; (TV play) We Don't Often Lose a Boffin; 20 radio plays; radio features & short stories; Scripts for documentary & relig. films; Co-author (radio series), The Men from the Ministry; Lines from my Grandfather's Forehead. Mbrships: Writers' Guild of GB; Royal Overseas League. Address: c/o Essanay Ltd., National House, 60/66 Wardour St., London W1, UK.

GRAHAM, Stephen, b. 1884, Edinburgh, UK. Author. Publs. incl: Russia & the World, 1915; Tramping with a Poet in the Rockies, 1922; London Nights, 1925; Stalin: an Imperial Study, 1931; Life of Ivan the Terrible, 1932; Balkan Monastery, 1935; Boris Godunov, 1933; African Tragedy, 1937; Alexander of Yugoslavia, 1938; Thinking of Living, 1949; Summing-up on Russia, 1951; 100 Best poems in the Language, 1953; Pay As You Run, 1955; Part of the Wonderful Scene, 1964. Address: 60 Frith St., Soho, London W1, UK.

GRAHAM, Winston Mawdsley, b. 1939, Manchester, UK. Publs. incl: The Forgotten Story, 1945; Night Without Stars, filmed, 1950; Fortune is a Woman, 1953, filmed, 1956; Greek Fire, 1957; Marnie, 1961, filmed, 1963; The Grove of Eagles, 1963; After the Act, 1965; The Walking

Stick, 1967, filmed, 1970; Angell, Pearl & Little God, 1970; The Spanish Armadas, 1972; The Black Moon, 1973. Mbr., Soc. of Authors; Fellow, Royal Soc. Lit., 1969. Address: Abbotswood House, Buxted, Sussex, UK.

GRAHAM-BONNALIE, F. E., b. 1897, Cheshire, UK. General Practitioner; Consulting Physician. Educ: B.A., M.B., B.Ch., Christ's Coll., Cambridge; M.R.C.S., L.R.C.P., Guy's Hosp., London. Publs: Know Your Illness, 1969; Allergies, 1970; Your Doctor's Guide to Living with Stress. Mbr., Brit. Med. Assn.; Former Pres., S.W. Br. Address: 92 Spottiswoode St., Ediburgh, UK.

GRAMS, Armin, b. Oct. 1924, Chgo., Ill., USA. University Professor & Administrator. Educ: B.S., Concordia Coll., River Forest, Ill., 1947; M.A., De Paul Univ., Chgo., 1947; Ph.D., Northwestern Univ., 1952. Publs: Children & Their Parents, 1963; Facilitating Learning & Individual Development, 1966; Changes in Family Life, 1968; Sex Education: A guide for Teachers & Parents, 1969, revised 1970. Contbr. to: Luth. Educ.; Archives of Pediatrics; Jrnl. of Cons. Psychol.; Children; Nat. Parent Tchr.; Luth. Tchr.; Contemp. Psychol.; Am. Psychol.; Childhood Educ.; Child Dev. Abstracts & Bibliog.; etc. Mbrships. incl: Am. Psychol. Assn.; Soc. for Rsch. in Child Dev.; Bd. of Dirs., Int. Fedn. for Parent Educ., 1969-. Address: Blundell House, Redstone Campus, Univ. of Vt., Burlington, VT 05401, USA.

GRANASZTÓI, Pál, b. 29 Aug. 1908, Budapest, Hungary. Architect; Writer. Educ: Cert. Arch.; D.Sc. Publs: (lit.) Vallomás és Búcsú (Confession & Parting), 1961; Itthon eltem (I lived at Home), 1971; Alakok, álmok (Figures, Dreams), 1973; (archtl.) Város és építészet (Town & Architecture), 1960; Az építészet igézetében (Under the Spell of Architecture), 1966; Budapest egy építész szemével (Budapest through the Eyes of an Architect), 1971, English, French, German transls.; Ember és látvány városépítészetünkben (Man & Spectacle in Our City Planning), 1972; Építészet és Urbanisztika (Architecture & Urbanism), 1973. Contbr. to var. Hungarian periodicals. Mbrships. incl: Assn. Hungarian Archts. Hons. incl: Pro Arte Gold Medal Coun. Budapest, 1966; for arch., Hild J. medal, 1974. Address: 1068 Budapest, VI Gorkij Fasor 38, Hungary.

GRANELL, Eugenio F., b. 28 Nov. 1912, La Coruña, Spain. Writer; Professor of Spanish Literature; Painter. Educ: B.A., Inst. Nacional, Santiago de Compostela, Spain; Ph.D., New Schl. for Soc. Rsch., NYC. Publs: El hombre verde, 1944; Arte y artistas en Guatemala, 1949; Isla Cofre Mítico, 1951; La novela del Indio Tupinamba, 1959; El clavo, 1967; Lo que sucedió, 1967; Federica no era tonta, 1970; La Leyenda, de Lorca y otros escritors 1973. Contbr. to: Cuadernos; Revista Hispánica Moderna; La Torre; etc. Mbr., var. profl. assns. Hons. incl: Don Quixote Int. Award, 1967. Address: 660 W. 115th St., N.Y., NY 10025, USA.

GRANGE, Cyril, b. 17 Apr. 1900, March, UK. Technical Journalist & Photographer. Publs: The Villiers Engine, 13 eds.; Poultry Farming for a Living; Poultry Keeping Today; Poultry Feeding; Home Food Preservation; Bottling & Canning; Jam Making. Contbr. to: poultry jrnls.; 62 nat. & provincial newspapers. Mbrships: Pres., British Waterfowl Assn.; Sec., Poultry Club of GB; Chmn., Bury Naturalists' Soc.; Hon. Mbr., 4 other natural hist. socs. Address: West Hill House, Horringer Rd., Bury St. Edmunds, Suffolk, UK.

GRANHOLM, Olof Harry, b. 24 Apr. 1924, Petsma, Finland. Author. Publs: Bässpojken, 1971; Spånskottaren, 1973. Mbr., Swedish Authors of Finland Assn. Hons: Nat. Lit. Award, 1972; State Authors' Grant, 1974. Address: Trallstensvägen 23, Vasa, Finland.

GRANT, Alexander Thomas Kingdom, b. 1906. Economist, British Government, Treasury, 20 years; Fellow, Pembroke College, Cambridge, 1966-73. Educ: M.A., Univ. Coll., Oxford Univ. Publs: Society & Enterprise, 1934; A Study of the Capital Market in Britain, 1937, latest ed., 1967; The Machinery of Finance & the Management of Sterling, 1967; The Strategy of Financial Pressure, 1972. Mbr. United Oxford & Cambridge Univ. Club. Hons. incl: C.B., C.M.G., Emeritus Fellow Pembroke Coll., Cambridge Univ. Address: 66 Gough Way, Cambridge, UK.

GRANT, Doris Margaret Louise, b. 1905, Alvah, Banffshire, UK. Writer. Publs: Ed., The Hay System Cookery Book, 1936; The Hay System Menu Book, 1937;

Feeding the Family in Wartime, 1942; Your Daily Bread, 1944; Dear Housewives, 1954; Housewives Beware, 1958; Your Bread & Your Life, 1961; Your Daily Bread, revised ed., 1962; Your Daily Food, 1973. Contbr. to: Cambridge Med. Soc. Mag.; Vitalstoffe; Prevention; Here's Hlth.; Sunday Graphic; Your Environment. Mbr., Royal Motor Yacht Club. Address: Glen Huon, 59 Canford Cliffs Rd., Poole, Dorset, UK.

GRANT, Eva, b. 23 Nov. 1907, NYC, USA. Juvenile Author. Educ: N.Y. Univ.; New Schl. of Social Sci., N.Y.; Bank St. Writer's Lab., ibid. Publs: Timothy Slept On, 1964; Cecil Cat, 1967; A Cow For Jaya, 1973. Contbr. to: Instr. Mag.; Highlights for Children; Am. Nat. Red Cross; Scholastic Mags.; Ency. Britannica Educl. Corp.; Jack & Jill; Humpty Dumpty; Young World; The World of Lang.; (poetry) Lets Read More Stories; David C. Cook's Kindergarten Series. Mbr., Soc. of Children's Book Writers. Hons: 1st Prize, Narrative Poetry Contest, Cooper Hill Writer's Conf., 1972; Author Award, Newark Coll. of Engrng., 1974. Address: 255 Kingsland Terrace, S. Orange, NJ 07079, USA.

GRANT, Isabel Frances, b. Edinburgh, UK. Founder of Am Fasgadh Highland Folk Museum; Author. Publs: Everyday Life on an Old Highland Farm; Social & Economic Development of Scotland before 1603; Lordship of the Isles; Short Clan Histories of Macdonalds, Grants, Macleods; The Macleods, the History of a Clan; Highland Folkways; Angus Ug. Hons: M.B.E.; LL.D. Address: 35 Heriot Row, Edinburgh EH3 6ES, UK.

GRANT, James Russell, b. 14 Dec. 1924, Bellshill, Scotland, UK. Medical Practitioner, Social Medicine & Psychiatry. Educ: M.B. & Ch.B., Univ. of Glasgow; Inst. of Psych., Maudsley Hosp., London. Publs: (poems) Hyphens, 1958; Poems, 1959. Contbr. to: Botteghe Oscure; Prism; Fiddlehead; Trace; Saltire Review; Can. Med. Jrnl.; Can. Psych. Jrnl.; BBC; CBC. Address: 255 Creighton Ave., London N2, UK.

GRANT, John Cameron, b. 15 Dec. 1934, Edinburgh, UK. Documentary Film Writer & Producer. Educ: Royal Scottish Acad. of Music. Mbr., Lit. & Philos. Soc. Address: 37 Ladywell Way, Ponteland, Newcastle upon Tyne NE20 9TE, UK.

GRANT, John Douglas, b. 16 Oct. 1932, London, UK. Member of Parliament; Parly. Sec., Civil Serv. Dept., 1974; Parly. Sec., Min. of Overseas Devt., 1974-. Publs: Member of Parliament, 1974. Contbr. to: Daily Express (Chief Indl. Corres., 1967-70); Times; Observer; Sun; Evening News; News of World; Tribune; Labour Weekly; New Statesman. Mbrships. incl: Fabian Soc.; Nat. Union Jrnlsts; T.G.W.U. Agent: Anthony Sheil Assocs. Address: c/o House of Commons, London SW1, UK.

GRANT, John McBain, b. 15 Nov. 1923, Adelaide, S.A., Australia. Professor of Applied Economics. Educ: M.Ec., Univ. of Adelaide; Dip. Ec., Univ. of Cambridge, UK. Publs: Inflation & Company Finance (w. R. L. Mathews), 1958, 2nd ed., 1962; Topics in Accounting & Finance (co-author), 1964; Ed., Economics: An Australian Introduction (w. A. J. Hagger), 1964; Economic Institutions & Policy. An Australian Introduction (co-author), 1969. Contbr. to: Econ. Record; Banker's Mag.; Aust. Acct.; Chartered Acct.; etc. Mbrships. incl: Econs. Soc. of Aust. & NZ (Coun. mbr. & Past Pres., Tas. Br.); Assoc., Aust. Soc. of Accts. Hons: Annual Rsch. Lectr., Aust. Soc. Accts., 1964. Address: 4 Red Knights Rd., Sandy Bay, Tas., Australia.

GRANT, John Webster, b. 27 June 1919, Truro, N.S., Can. University Teacher. Educ: B.A., 1938, M.A., 1941, Dalhousie Univ., Can.; Grad. Schl., Princeton Univ.; Dip. Theol., Pine Hill Divinity Hall, 1943; D.Phil., Oxford Univ., 1948. Publs: Free Churchmanship in England, 1955; God's People in India, 1959; The Ship under the Cross, 1960; George Pidgeon: A Biography, 1962; The Canadian Experience of Church Union, 1967; The Church in the Canadian Era, 1972; Mgng. Ed., Studies in Religion/Sciences Religieuses. Mbrships. incl: Can. Histl. Assn. Hons: Rhodes Schlr., N.S., 1941; D.D., Union Coll., B.C., 1961 & Pine Hill Divinity Hall, 1962. Address: 33 Old Colony Rd., Willowdale, Ont., Canada.

GRANT, Julius, b. 1901, London, UK. Chemist. Educ: M.Sc., Ph.D., King's Coll., London; Queen Mary Coll., London. Publs: Chemical Dictionary, 4 eds.; Cellulose Pulp, 3 eds.; Science for the Prosecution: Fluorescence Analysis,

4 eds.; Laboratory Handbook of Pulp & Paper Manufacture, 2 eds.; Books & Documents; Measurement of Hydrogen Ion Concentration; Sutton's Volumetric Analysis, 13 eds.; Pregl's Quantitative Organic Microanalysis, 15 eds.; Quantitative Analysis, 15 eds.; Perkins' Quantitative Analysis, 5 eds. Mbrships: F.R.I.C.; Pres., Medico-Legal Soc.; Past-Pres., Forensic Sci. Soc. Address: 107 Fenchurch St., London EC3M 5JB, UK.

GRANT, Roderick, b. 16 Jan. 1941, Forres, Moray, Scotland, UK. Author; Journalist; Radio & TV Broadcaster. Publs: Adventure in my Veins, 1968; Seek out the Guilty, 1969; Where No Angels Dwell, 1969; Gorbals Doctor, 1970; The Dark Horizon, 1971; The Lone Voyage of Betty Mouat, 1973; The Stalking of Adrian Lawford, 1974; The Clutch of Caution, 1975. Contbr. to: BBC; Scottish TV; Times Review; Scottish Field; Scots Mag.; Shooting Times; Scotsman. Mbrships: Soc. of Authors; Radio-writers Assn.; Nat. Book League. Agent: Laurence Pollinger Ltd. Address: 3 Back Lane Cottages, Bucks Horn Oak, Farnham, Surrey, UK.

GRASHOFF, Pieter, pen names GRASHOFF, Cok; HAGEMAN, Janna G., b. 24 June 1927, Rotterdam, Netherlands. Author; Translator. Publs: Niederländische Erzähler der Gegenwart, 1966; Claudia, 26 vols., 1967-74; Floortje Bellefleur, 12 vols., 1968-75; Van Vestdijk Tot Vinkenoog, 1969; Drie Jongens, 16 vols., 1969-74; Foei! , 1970; Petra, 12 vols., 1971-75; Belinda, 12 vols., 1971-75; Tim, 6 vols., 1973-75; over 100 transls. of var. for. authors; over 150 children's books. Contbr. to: Moderne Encyclopedie der Wereldliteratuur; Het Vrije Volk; Nieuw Vlaams Tijdschrift; Tijd en Taak; Nieuwe Rotterdamse Courant; Critisch Bulletin; Litterair Paspoort; Hesse Radio. Mbr., Vereniging van Letterkundigen. Address: Copernicuslaan 13, Box 152, Spijkenisse, Netherlands.

GRASS, Gunter Wilhelm, b. 16 Oct. 1927, Danzig, Poland. Educ: Dusseldorf Kunstakademie. Publs. incl: (novels) (in German) The Tin Drum, 1959, Engl. 1962; Cat & Mouse, 1961, Engl. 1963; Dog Years, 1961, Engl. 1963; Local Anaesthetic, 1969, Engl. 1970; Gleisdreieck, 1960; Ausgefragt, 1967; Poems of Gunter Grass, 1969; (drama) Only Ten Minutes to Buffalo, 1958, Engl. 1968; Onkel Onkel, 1958, Engl. 1968; The Wicked Cooks, 1961, Engl. 1968; The Plebeians rehearse the Uprising, 1966, Engl. 1967; (prose) Dokumente zur politischen Wirkung, 1972. Mbrships. incl: PEN; Am. Acad. of Arts & Sci.; Akademie der Künste, Berlin. Hons. incl: Lit. Assn. of German Critics, 1960; Georg Büchner, 1965. Address: Niedstrasse 13, Berlin 41, W. Germany.

GRATTAN, Donald Henry, b. 7 Aug. 1926, St. Osyth, Essex, UK. BBC Executive. Educ: B.Sc.(Hons.), Univ. of London. Publs: Science & the Builder, 1962; Television & Teaching of Science, 1963; Mathematics Miscellany, 1966. Contbr. to: Times Educl. Supplement; European & C'wlth. Reviews. Mbrships: Math. Assn.; Assn. of Tchrs. of Maths.; Coun. of Open Univ.; Coun. for Educl. Technol. Address: 42 Anglesmede Crescent, Pinner, Middx., UK.

GRAU, Shirley Ann, b. 1929, New Orleans. Author. Educ: B.A., Tulane Univ., New Orleans. Publs: The Black Prince, 1955; The Hard Blue Sky, 1958; The House on Coliseum Street, 1961. Contbr. to: New Yorker; Holiday; New World Writing; etc. Address: Brandt & Brandt, 101 Park Ave., N.Y., NY, USA.

GRAVE, Elsa Margareta, b. 17 Jan. 1918, Norra Vram, Sweden. Writer. Educ: B.A., Univ. of Lund, 1940. Num. publs. incl: (poetry) Inkräktare, 1943; Bortförklaring, 1948; Lufthav, 1956; Höstfärd, 1961; Höjdförlust, 1965; Hungersöndag, 1967; Vid Nödläge, 1969; Mödrar Som Vargar, 1972; Avfall-Från & Till, 1974; (prose) Ariel, 1955; Luciafirarna, 1959; Medan vi Låg & Sov, 1966; (plays) Medusan & Djävulen, 1949; Isskåpet, 1952; Sphinxen, 1963; Krukväxterna, 1965; Fläsksabbat, 1966. Mbrships: Swedish Authors Soc.; Swedish Dramatists Soc. Recip., sev. prizes & awards. Address: Blomstervången, 30590 Halmstad, Sweden.

GRAVES, Robert Ranke, b. 24 July 1895, London, UK. Writer; Poet; Scholar. Educ: M.A., B.Litt., St. John's Coll., Oxford. Publs. incl: Goodbye To All That (autobiog.), 1929, 1957; I, Claudius, 1934; Claudius The God, 1934; The White Goddess, 1946, 1952; The Greek Myths, 1955; New Poems, 1962; Collected Short Stories, 1965; Mammon & the Black Goddess, 1965; Poetic Craft & Principle, 1967; The Crane Bag, 1969; Poems About Love, 1969; Poems 1969-70, 1970; Poems 1970-72, 1972;

Difficult Questions, Easy Answers, 1971; The Green-Sailed Vessel, 1971; Timeless Meeting, 1973. Agent: A. P. Watt & Son. Address: c/o A. P. Watt & Son., 26/28 Bedford Row, London WC1R 4HL, UK.

GRAVES, Wallace, b. 1922, Seattle, USA. University Professor; Author. Educ: B.A.; M.A.; Ph.D., Univ. of Wash. Publs: Trixie, 1971; From Word to Story, 1971. Contbr. to: Kenyon Review; Western Humanities Review; Bulletin, AAUP; Shakespeare Quarterly; Prism Int.; Nineteenth Century Fiction. Hons: Fulbright Tchr., Greece, 1957-59; Fulbright Lecturer, Sri Lanka, 1972-73. Address: c/o Don Congdon, Harold Matson Co., 22 E. 406 St., N.Y., NY 10016, USA.

GRAY, Clayton, b. 15 Mar. 1918, Montreal, Can. Writer-historian. Educ: Sir George Williams Univ.; Mus. Archival Degree, McGill Univ., Montreal; Inst. Histl. Rsch., London Univ., UK. Publs: The Montreal Story, 1949; Montreal qui disparait, 1952; Conspiracy in Canada, 1959; Le Vieux Montreal, 1964. Contbr. to: Montrealer Mag.; Montreal Star; Readers Digest; Am. Heritage; Books Abroad; Le Devoir; Weekend Mag.; etc. Mbrships. incl: PEN; Past Treas., Can. Ctr., ibid.; VP, Lake St. Louis Histl. Soc.; Histn., Soc. Montreal Mil. & Maritime Mus. Hons. incl: Cultural Affairs Grants, P.Q., 1970, 1971. Address: 1495 Ste. Croix, Montreal H41 3Z5, P.Q., Canada.

GRAY, Dulcie, b. 20 Nov. 1920, Kuala Lumpur, Malaysia. Actress. Publs. (novels): Murder on the Stairs, 1957; Murder in Melbourne, 1958; Baby Face, 1959; Epitaph for a Dead Actor, 1960; Murder on a Saturday, 1961; Murder in Mind, 1963; The Devil Wore Scarlet, 1964; No Quarter for a Star, 1964; The Actor & His World (w. M. Denison), 1964; The Murder of Love, 1967; Died in the Red, 1968; Murder on Honeymoon, 1969; For Richer For Richer, 1970; Deadly Lampshade, 1971; Understudy to Murder, 1972; Dead Give Away, 1974; Ride on a Tiger, 1975; (play): Love Affair, 1957. Contbr. to jrnls. & anthols. Mbrships. incl: Crime Writers Assn.; Mystery Writers of Am.; British Equity. Address: c/o Int. Creative Management, 22 Grafton St., London W1, UK.

GRAY, Edwyn, b. 17 July 1927, London, UK. Civil Servant. Publs: (non-fiction) A Damned Un-English Weapon, 1971; The Killing Time, 1972; The Devil's Device, 1975; (fiction) No Survivors, 1974; Action Atlantic! 1975; The Tokyo Torpedo, 1975. Contbr. to popular mags. in UK, USA & Aust., 1952—. Mbrships: Soc. of Authors; Authors' Guild Inc.; Authors' League of Am. Recip., nomination as Choice of the Month, Am. Mil. Book Club (The Killing Time). Agent: Curtis Brown Ltd. Address: 29 Cedar Ave., Hazlemere, High Wycombe, Bucks., UK.

GRAY, John, b. 9 June 1913, Kelso, Scotland, UK. Professor of Hebrew & Semitic Languages. Educ: M.A., B.D., Ph.D., Edinburgh Univ. Publs: The Keret Text in the Literature of Ras Shamra; The Legacy of Canaan; Archaeology & the Old Testament World; I & II Kings, A Commentary; The Canaanites; Joshua-Judges-Ruth, Century Bible; A History of Jerusalem; Near Eastern Mythology. Contbr. to: Palestine Exploration Quarterly; Expository Times; Jrnl. of Near Eastern Studies; Vetus Testamentum; Hibbert Jrnl.; Interpreter's Bible Dict.; Peake Commentary (new ed.); etc. Address: Inverawe, Persley, Aberdeen, UK.

GRAY, Leonard Benjamin, b. 30 Sept. 1896, Leicester, N.S., Can. Minister of Religion. Educ: B.A., Acadia Univ.; B.D., Andover Newton Theol. Schl., USA; Postgrad. study, Dartmouth Coll., Boston Univ. Publs: Coming to Grips with Life (poetry), 1971. Contbr., 500 articles, 1,000 poems, to maj. US mags., 1930—; Lectr., Schls. & Colls.; Radio Speaker & Worker, Mass. Coun. of Chs., 1961—. Mbrships: Poets Forum, Lynn, Mass.; Thoreau Soc. of Am. Hons. incl: poetry prizes, 1970, 1971, 1972, 1974; Poet of the Month; Prizes for Poems, At the Brithplace of Robert Burns, John Fitzgerald Kennedy, On the Jericho Road, Spinoza, William Wordsworth, His Best Creation. Address: 17 Johnson Rd., Saugus, MA 01906, USA.

GRAY, Michael, b. 1946, England. Journalist. Educ: B.A., Univ. of York. Publs: Song & Dance Man/The Art of Bob Dylan, 1973; Goodnight Boys & Girls/Frank Zappa in Words & Pictures (forthcoming); (play) The Great Match (w. R. Leach), 1972. Contbr. to: Guardian; Melody Maker; Rolling Stone; Let it Rock; New Humanist; Rock Mag.; Crawdaddy Mag.; Radio Times. Agent: Lorna Vestey. Address: c/o Lorna Vestey, 30 Rostrevor Rd., London SW6, UK.

GRAY, Nicholas Stuart, b. Scotland. Playwright; Novelist; Actor; Theatre Director; Illustrator. Publs. incl: (plays) Beauty & the Beast, 1951; The Tinder Box, 1951; The Imperial Nightingale, 1957; The Other Cinderella, 1958; The Seventh Swan, 1962; The Stone Cage, 1969; Gawain & the Green Knight, 1969; & 5 other plays; (novels) Down in the Cellar, 1961; Mainly in Moonlight, 1964; The Apple Stone, 1969; The Boys, 1970; Further Adventures of Puss in Boots; & Other novels; The Edge of Evening, forthcoming. Contbr. to var. mags., poetry anthols.; etc. Mbrships: Soc. Authors; Societe des Auteurs; Somerset Archeol. Soc.; Rose Soc. Hons: Am. publs. selected by Jr. Lib. Guild. Address: 20 Perrins Walk, Hampstead, London NW3, UK.

GRAY, Simon James Halliday, pen name READE, Hamish, b. 21 Oct. 1936, Hayling Island, Hants., UK. University Lecturer. Educ: B.A., Dalhousie Univ., Can.; B.A., M.A., Cambridge, UK. Publs: (novels) Colmain, 1963; Simple Pople, 1965; Little Portia, 1967; A Comeback for Stark, 1968; (plays) Wise Child, 1969; Sleeping Dog, 1969; Dutch Uncle, 1970; The Idiot, 1971; Spoiled, 1971; Butley, 1972. Contbr. to: Delta; Spectator; New Statesman; Listener; Times Lit. Supplement. Mbrships: Assn. of Univ. Tchrs.; Dramatists Guild, USA; Dramatists Soc., London. Hons: TV Drama Award, Best Play, 1969; Evening Standard Drama Award, Best Play of Yr., 1971. Address: c/o Clive Goodwin Assocs., 79 Cromwell Rd., London SW7, UK.

GRAY, Tony George Hugh, b. Dublin, Repub. of Ireland. Journalist; Freelance Writer. Publs: Starting from Tomorrow, 1965; The Real Professionals, 1966; The Irish Answer, 1967; Gone the Time, 1967; Interlude, 1968; The Record Breakers (w. Leo Villa), 1970; Psalms & Slaughter, 1972; The Orange Order, 1972; Buller (w. Henry Ward), 1974. Contbr. to: Holiday; Punch; Nova; ITV; BBC Radio. Agent: Toby Eady Assocs. Ltd. Address: 3 Broomfield Rd., Kew Gardens, Richmond, Surrey.

GRAYLAND, Eugene Charles, b. Wellington, NZ. Author; Journalist. Publs. incl: Private Presses, 1947; There Was Danger on the Line, 1954; Auckland, Queen City, 1962; Unusual Newspapers of New Zealand & Australia, 1969; Historic Coromandel (co-author), 1969; More Famous New Zealanders, 1971; Tarawera (co-author), 1971; New Zealand Disasters, paper-back ed., 1974. Contbr. to: Auckland Star (med. & sci. reporter); Hearing News (jt. Ed.); etc. Mbrships: Assoc., NZ Assn. of Scis.; Royal Soc. of NZ; Med. Jrnlsts. Assn., UK; Bookpeople; NZ Book Coun. Address: C.P.O. Box 689, Auckland, NZ.

GRAYLAND, Valerie Merle, pen names BELVEDERE, Lee; SUBOND, Valerie, b. Thames, NZ. Author. Educ: Seddon Mem. Tech. Coll., Auckland. Publs. incl: The First Strawberry, 1954; The Dead Men of Eden, 1962; Early One Morning, 1963; Baby Sister, 1964; Jest of Darkness, 1965; Coromandel Coast, 1965, & Historic Coromandel, 1969 (co-author); Farewell to a Valley, 1971; Tarawera (co-author), 1971; Thunder Beach, 1972; Fringe of Heaven, 1972; The Heights of Havenrest, 1972; The Smiling House, 1973; Return to Moon Bay, 1973; House over Hell Valley, 1974. Contbr. to: Hearing News (jt. ed.). Mbrships: PEN; Mystery Writers of Am. Address: C.P.O. Box 689, Auckland, NZ.

GRAYSON, Cecil, b. 5 Feb. 1920, Batley, Yorks., UK. University Professor. Educ: M.A., St. Edmund Hall, Oxford. Publs: Early Italian Texts (w. Prof. C. Dionisotti); Opuscoli Inediti di L.B. Alberti; Alberti & the Tempio Malatestiano; Vincenzo Calmeta: Prose e Lettere edite e inedite; L.B. Alberti, Opere volgari, 3 vols.; Life of Savonarola (transl.); Life of Machiavelli (transl.); Cinque saggi su Dante; L. B. Alberti, On Painting & On Sculpture. Contbr. to: Bibliofilia; Burlington Mag.; Engl. Miscellany; Italian Studies; Lettere Italiane; Lingua Nostra; Rinascimento; Year's Work in Mod. Langs.; etc. Mbrships: (for. mbr.) Accademia Nazionale dei Luicei; Accademia della Crusca; Accademia dell' Arcadia; etc. Recip., Premio Int. Galileo Galilei, 1974. Address: 11 Norham Rd., Oxford, UK.

GREALLY, John, b. 14 May 1934, Belfast, UK. Journalist. Educ: Heythrop Coll. Publs: Dante Comes to Town, 1969. Contbr. to: Cath. Herald (Theatre Critic 1966-68); Subeditor, Sun, 1973; Sunday Times. Address: 4 Silsoe House, Park Village East, London NW1, UK.

GREATOREX, Wilfred, b. 27 May 1921, Blackburn, UK. Writer. Publs: Arnhem (w. R. E. Urquhart); Diamond Fever. Mbrships: Writers' Guild of GB; Press Club, London; Soc. of Film & TV Arts. Hons: Writers' Guild of GB Awards for drama series scripts — The Plane Makers, 1965, The Power Game, 1967. Address: Foxwell, Berry Hill, Taplow, Bucks., UK.

GREBANIER, Bernard, b. 8 Mar. 1903, NYC, USA. Writer. Educ: B.A., CUNY, 1926; M.A., 1930, Ph.D., 1935, N.Y. Univ. Num. publs. incl: English Literature & Its Backgrounds, 2 vols., 1939-40; Mirrors of the Fire, 1946; European Literature, 2 vols., 1950-51; Introduction to Imaginative Literature, 1960; The Great Shakespeare Forgery, 1965; The Uninhibited Byron, 1970; Pegasus in the Seventies, 1973; Then Came Each Actor: Shakespearian Actors Great & Otherwise, 1975. Contbr. to num. jrnls. Mbrships: Authors Guild; PEN; The Players; Pres., N.Y. Chapt., & 1st Nat. VP, Composers, Authors & Artists of Am.; Poetry Soc. of Am. Agent: Cyrilly Abels, NYC. Address: c/o Cyrilly Abels, Lit. Agt., 119 W. 57th St., N.Y., NY 10019, USA.

GREBENIK, Eugene, b. 1919, Kiev. Editor; Principal, Civil Service College. Educ: M.Sc.(Econ.), London Schl. of Econs., UK. Publs: The Trend & Pattern of Fertility in Great Britain (w. D. V. Glass); The Population of Bristol (w. H. A. Shannon). Contbr. to var. sci. jrnls. Address: Civil Service College, Sunningdale Park, Ascot, Berks. SL5 0QE, UK.

GREBSTEIN, Sheldon Norman, b. 1 Feb. 1928, Providence, Rhode Island, USA. University Professor & Administrator. Educ: B.A., Univ. of S. Calif., 1949; M.A., Columbia Univ., 1950; Ph.D., Mich. State Univ., 1954. Publs. incl: Sinclair Lewis, 1962; John O'Hara, 1966; (Ed.). Perspectives in Contemporary Criticism, 1968; Hemingway's Craft, 1973. Contbr. to sev. jrnls. incl: Saturday Review; Am. Scholar; Book World; Univ. Review; Mod. Fiction Studies; Jrnl. of Mod. Lit. Mbrships. incl: Mod. Lang. Assn.; AAUP; Coll. Eng. Assn; Northeastern Mod. Lang. Assn. Address: State Univ. of N.Y. at Binghamton, NY 13901, USA.

GREEK, Carl Gustaf Ludvig, pen name HELLEN, Anders, b. 28 Apr. 1909, Malmoe, Sweden. Rural Dean. Educ: Theol. cand., Univ. of Lund. Publs: Pil och båge, 1950; Vad och vem? 1954; Spår till gamla brottet, 1963; En ljugande malm, 1973. Mbr., The Swedish Union of Authors. Address: Prästgården, S 260 73 Östra Ljungby, Sweden.

GREEN, Adrienne Marjorie, b. Wolverhampton, UK. Writer. Publs: The Peaceful Days (play), 1972; Heads You Win (play), 1973. Contbr. to: Radio Birmingham; BBC Radio 4; Humour-Variety Mag.; Favourite Story Mag. Mbrships: Soc. of Women Writers & Jrnlsts.; Sec., Walsall Writers Circle. Hons: Runner Up, Theodora Roscoe Award, 1974; Norrey Ford Cup for Writer of the Yr., Writers Circle, 1970, 1974. Address: 3 Charlemont Rd., Walsall, West Midlands, UK.

GREEN, Andrew Malcolm, b. 28 July 1927, Ealing, London, UK. Writer; Lecturer. Publs: Mysteries of Surrey, 1972; Mysteries of London, 1973; Mysteries of Sussex, 1973; Our Haunted Kingdom, 1973. Ghost Hunting — A Practical Guide, 1973; Haunted Houses, 1975; Ghosts of the South East, 1975. Contbr. to: Prediction; Fate & Fortune; Men Only; Surrey Life; Sussex Life; Berks. Life; Bucks. Life; Kent Life; Cornish Life; Elec. & Radio Trading; Electricity; Wireless World; etc. Mbrships: F.R.S.A.; Inst. of Jrnlsts.; Assn. of Indl. Eds.; Wig & Pen Club, London. Address: Busheygate, Battle Rd., Robertsbridge, Sussex, UK.

GREEN, Benny, b. 9 Dec. 1927, Leeds, Yorks., UK. Author. Publs: The Reluctant Art, 1962; Blame It On My Youth, 1967; 58 Minutes to London, 1969; Drums in My Ears, 1973. Contbr. to: Spectator; Punch. Dir., New Shakespeare Co. Address: c/o BBC, London W1, UK.

GREEN, Celia Elizabeth, b. 26 Nov. 1935, London, UK. Director, Institute of Psychophysical Research. Publs: Lucid Dreams, 1969; Out-of-the-Body Experiences, 1968; The Human Evasion, 1969; L'Evasione dell'Umanita, 1970; Die Flucht ins Humane, 1974; Apparitions (w. Charles McCreery), 1975. Contbr. to: Punch. Address: 118 Banbury Rd., Oxford, UK.

GREEN, David Brontë, b. 1910, Addiscombe, UK. Publs: Blenheim Palace; Gardener to Queen Anne; Grinling Gibbons; Sarah Duchess of Marlborough; Queen Anne;

Country Neighbours; In the Wood; Sir Winston Churchill at Blenheim Palace; The Official Guide Books to Blenheim Palace & to the Park & Gardens of Hampton Court & Bushey; Blenheim (battle), 1974; Children's stories. Contbr. to: Country Life; Countryman; Listener; Guardian; Connoisseur; Sunday Times. Archtl. Review. Fellow, Soc. of Antiquaries, London. Agent: Richard Scott Simon. Address: Church Hanborough, Oxford, UK.

GREEN, Dorothy, pen name AUCHTERLONIE, b. 28 May 1915, Sunderland, Co. Durham, UK. University Teacher; Writer; Journalist. Educ: B.A., 1938, M.A., 1940, Univ. of Sydney, N.S.W., Aust. Publs: Kaleidoscope (verse), 1940; Fourteen Minutes (w. H. M. Green), 1950; The Dolphin (verse), 1967; Ulysses Bound: A Study of Henry Handel Richardson & her fiction, 1973. Contbr. to: Meanjin Quarterly; Quadrant; Southerly; Hemisphere; Aust. Med. Jrnl. Mbrships: Aust. Jrnlsts. Assn.; Aust. Soc. of Authors; V.P., Canberra Br., Fellowship of Aust. Writers. Hons: Barbara Ramsden Mem. Award, 1973; Aust. Lit. Studies Fndn., 1973. Address: 52 Grayson St., Hackett, A.C.T., Australia.

GREEN, Elizabeth Adine Herkimer, b. 21 Aug. 1906, Mobile, Ala., USA. Professor of Music. Educ: B.S., Wheaton Coll.; M.Mus., Northwestern Univ. Publs: Orchestral Bowings & Routines, 1949, 1957; The Modern Conductor (coll. textbook), 1961, 1969; Teaching Stringed Instruments in Classes, 1966; The Conductor & His Score (w. N. Malko), 1975. Contbr. to music jrnls. Address: 1225 Ferdon Rd., Ann Arbor, MI 48104, USA.

GREEN, Ernest, b. 1885, Sheffield, UK. Writer. Publs: Education for a New Society, 1942, 4 eds.; Adult Education: Why This Apathy?, 1952. Contbr. to: The Jrnl., P.O. Engr's. Union; Trade Union jrnls; Education for Democracy, 1939; Education for Citizenship; Vol. 2; UNESCO Fundamental & Adult Educ. Jrnl. Mbr., Nat. Book League. Address: Guardina Court, Flat 7, Wells Promenade, Ilkley, Yorks, UK.

GREEN, George Frederick, b. 12 Apr. 1911, Old Whittington, UK. Writer. Educ: M.A., Magdalene Coll. Cambridge Univ. Publs: Land Without Heroes, 1948; Ed., Tales of Innocence, 1950; In the Making, 1952; The Power of Sergeant Stremter, 1972. Contbr. to: Winter's Tales; The Listener; Spectator; Horizon; New Writing; Life & Letters; London Mercury; num. anthols. Address: Rockwells House, Batcombe, Shepton Mallet, Somerset, UK.

GREEN, Henry, pen name of YORKE, Henry Vincent, b. 1905, Tewkesbury, Glos., UK. Company Director. Educ: Oxford Univ. Publs: (novels) Blindness, UK & USA, 1926; Living, 1929; Party Going, UK, 1939, USA, 1951; Caught, UK, 1943, USA, 1950; Loving, UK, 1945, USA, 1949; Back, UK, 1946, USA, 1950; Concluding, UK, 1948, USA, 1951; Nothing, UK & USA, 1950; Doting, UK & USA, 1952; (autobiog.) Pack My Bag, 1940. Address: c/o Hogarth Press, 40-42 William IV St., London WC2, UK.

GREEN, John Lafayette, Jr., b. 3 Apr. 1929, Trenton, N.J., USA. Educator. Educ: Bach., Miss. State Univ.; Master, Wayne State Univ.; Ph.D., studies, Rensselaer Polytechnic Inst. Publs: A System of Cost Accounting for Physical Plant Operations in Institutions of Higher Education (co-author), 1968; Administrative Data Processing in Higher Education (co-author), 1971; Budgeting in Higher Education, 1971; A New Approach to Budgeting in Higher Education (co-author), 1972. Contbr. to: Coll. & Univ. Bus. Mbrships. incl: Phi Delta Kappa; Beta Alpha Psi; Fin. Execs. Inst.; Dir., Marine Midland Bank, Eastern Div. Recip., Hon. Col.-Gov. of Ky. Address: 13 Dennin Dr., Menands, NY 12204, USA.

GREEN, Joseph Lee, b. 14 Jan. 1931, Compass Lake, Fla., USA. Technical Writer. Educ: A.A., Brevard Community Coll., 1967. Publs: The Loafers of Refuge, 1965; An Affair with Genius, 1969; Gold the Man, 1971; Conscience Interplanetary, 1972; & 40 short stories of Am. & Brit. science fiction mags. Mbrships: The Authors Guild, Inc.; Ctrl./s. Director, Science Fiction Writers of Am. Hons: Guest of Hon. (Profl. Writer), Deep South Science Fiction Conf., 1973. Address: 1390 Holly Ave., Merritt Island, FL 32952, USA.

GREEN, Julian Hartridge, b. 6 Sept. 1900, Paris, France. Author. Educ: Univ. of Va., USA. Publs. incl: Le Voyageur sur la Terre, 1926; Leviathan, 1929; Epaves, 1932; Le Visionnaire, 1934; Minuit, 1936; Journal, 2 vols., 1940; Varouna, 1940; Memories of Happy Days, 1942;

Sud, 1953; L'Ennemi, 1954; Le Malfaiteur, 1956; Le Bel Aujourd'hui, 1958; L'Autre, 1971; Ce qui reste de jour, 1972. Mbrships: French Acad.; Royal Acad., Belgium; Am. Acad. of Arts & Sci.; Hons. incl: Bookman Prize; Harper Prize; Prix de Monaco, 1951; Grand Prix Nat. de Lettres, 1966; Grand Prix, French Acad., 1970. Address: c/o Plon, 8 rue Garancière, Paris 5e, France.

GREEN, Madge, pen names DERBYSHIRE, Jane; HADDON, Sarah, b. 17 Oct. 1927, Derby, UK. Journalist; Writer. Publs: (as Jane Derbyshire) Flower Arranging, 1964; Successful Flower Arranging, 1966; The Flower Arranger & Her Garden, 1967; Pearson Book of Dried & Pressed Flowers, 1975; (as Sarah Haddon) Flower Arrangement, 1968. Contbr. to: The Flower Arranger; Amateur Gardener; Popular Gardening; Garden News; Woman's Wkly.; etc. Mbrships. incl: Aldershot Flower Arrangement Club (former Chmn.); Nat. Assn. Flower Arrangement Socs. GB (Nat. Judge). Hons: Aldershot Flower Arrangement Club (Hon. Life VP). Address: The Garland Cottage, 6, Upper Old Park Lane, Farnham, Surrey, UK.

GREEN, Michael Frederick, b. 2 Jan. 1927, Leicester, UK. Author. Educ: B.A., Open University. Publs: Stage Noises & Effects, 1958; The Art of Coarse Rugby, 1960; The Art of Coarse Sailing, 1962; Don't Print My Name Upside Down, 1963; Even Coarser Rugby, 1963; The Art of Coarse Acting, 1964; The Michael Green Book of Coarse Sport, 1965; The Art of Coarse Golf, 1967; A Roof Over My Head (The Art of Coarse Moving), 1969; Michael Green's Rugby Alphabet, 1971; The Art of Coarse Drinking, 1973. Contbr. to: Observer; Times; Daily Telegraph; Punch; BBC. Mbrships: Nat. Union of Jrnlists.; Soc. of Authors. Address: 7 St. Matthews Rd., Ealing Common, London W5 3JT, UK.

GREEN, Paul Eliot, b. 17 Mar. 1894, Lillington, N.C., USA. Writer. Educ: A.B., Univ. of N.C. Publs: over 37 books, inclng: The Field of God/In Abraham's Bosom, 1927; The Laughing Pioneer, 1933; Out of the South (15 selected plays), 1939; Salvation on a String, 1946; Dramatic Heritage, 1953; Five Plays of the South, 1963; Plough & Furrow, 1963; Home to My Valley, 1970; Trumpet in the Land, 1972; The Honeycomb, 1972. Contbr. to: Atlantic Monthly; Harpers; NY Times; Theatre Arts; Yale Review; etc. Mbrships. incl: Nat. Inst. of Arts & Letters; Pres., Nat. Theatre Conf., 1940-42; Nat. Soc. of Lit. & the Arts. Hons. incl: Pulitzer Prize, 1927; Litt.D., 6 colls. & univs. Address: Old Lystra Rd., Chapel Hill, NC 27514, USA.

GREEN, Peter Morris, pen name DELANEY, Denis, b. 22 Dec. 1924, London, UK. Professor of Classics. Educ: M.A., Ph.D., Trinity Coll., Cambridge. Publs. incl: The Expanding Eye, 1953; The Sword of Pleasure, 1957; Essays in Antiquity, 1960; Look at the Romans, 1963; The Laughter of Aphrodite, 1965; (transl.) Juvenal: The 16 Satires, 1967; Alexander the Great: a biography, 1970; The Shadow of the Parthenon, 1972; The Parthenon, 1973; A Concise History of Ancient Greece, 1973; transl. of num. works from French & Italian. Mbrships: Formerly Coun., Royal Soc. of Lit. & var. comms. for lit. prizes. Recip., Heinemann Award, 1957. Address: 1505, Sunny Vale, apt. 218, Austin, TX 78741, USA.

GREEN, Roger Lancelyn, b. 24 Nov. 1918, Norwich, UK. Author. Educ: M.A., B.Litt., Merton Coll., Oxford, 1937-42. Publs: over 50 books inclng: Andrew Lang (biog.), 1946; Tellers of Tales, 1946, revised ed., 1965; A. E. W. Mason (biog.), 1952; The Diaries of Lewis Carroll, 1953; Fifty Years of "Peter Pan", 1954; Into Other Worlds, 1957; Two Satyr Plays (from the Greek), 1957; Kipling & the Children, 1965; C. S. Lewis: A Biography, 1974. Contbr. to: Times Lit. Supplement; Jr. Bookshelf; Notes & Queries; Books & Bookmen; Kipling Jrnl. (Ed.); etc. Mbrships: Nat. Book League; PEN; Arts; William Morris Soc.; Lewis Carroll Soc.; Kipling Soc.; etc. Address: Poulton Hall, Poulton-Lancelyn, Bebington, Wirral L63 9LN, UK.

GREEN, (Rev.) Vivian Hubert Howard, b. 1915. History Tutor, Oxford Univ. Educ: M.A., 1941; D.D., 1958, Cambridge Univ. Publs. incl: The Hanoverians, 1948; From St. Augustine to William Temple, 1948; Oxford Common Room, 1957; The Swiss Alps, 1961; Martin Luther & the Reformation, 1964; John Wesley, 1964; The Universities, 1969; Medieval Civilisation in Western Europe, 1971; History of Oxford University, 1974. Contbr. to: Dictionary, Engl. Ch. Hist.; Oxford Dictionary, Christian Ch. Fellow, Royal Hist. Soc. Address: Calendars, Burford, Oxford, UK.

GREEN, William, b. 1927, London, UK. Managing Director; Managing Editor. Publs: The Air Forces of the World; The Observer's Book of Aircraft; The Observer's World Aircraft Directory; The Aircraft of the World; The Jet Aircraft of the World; Famous Fighters of the Second World War; Famous Bombers of the Second World War; The World's Fighting Planes; The Warplanes of the Third Reich. Address: High Timber, Chislehurst Rd., Chislehurst, Kent, UK.

GREENBERGER, Allen J., b. 18 Mar. 1937, Chgo., Ill., USA. Professor of History. Educ: B.A., M.A., Ph.D., Univ. of Mich. Publs: The British Image of India: A Study in the Literature of Imperialism 1880-1960, 1969. Contbr. of book reviews to Jrnl. of Asian Studies. Mbrships: Am. Histl. Assn.; Assn. for Asian Studies; Conf. of Brit. Studies; Indo-Brit. Studies Assn. Address: Department of History, Pitzer College, Claremont, CA 91711, USA.

GREENE, Carla, b. 18 Dec. 1916, Mpls., USA. Author. Publs. incl: (juvenile, Ages 4-8) Animal Doctors, 1967; Cowboys, 1972; (Ages 6-9) A Trip to the Aquarium, 1967; (Ages 8 up) Let's Learn about Lighthouses, 1969; Gregor Mendel, 1969; (Ages 9 up) Before the Dinosaurs, 1970; How Man Began, 1972; Our Living Earth, 1974; 36 books publ. in I Want to Be . . . . series, 1956-62, incl. I Want to be a Ballet Dancer; I want to be a Road Builder; I want to be a Homemaker; also biographies & travel books. Mbrships. incl: Authors' League Am.; World Geographic Soc. Hons. incl: Jr. Sci. Tchrs. Am. Award, 1972 for How Man Began; sev. other lit. awards. Address: c/o Toni Strassman, 130 E. 18th St., N.Y., NY 10003, USA.

GREENE, Frances Forester, b. 14 Oct. 1918, Lookout Mt., Ga., USA. Newspaper & Magazine Editor. Educ: Piedmont Coll., Univ. of Ala. Publs: First One Hundred Years, 1973; Assoc. Ed., Georgia Life. Contbr. to: Georgia Stories, 1969; Mag. Sect., Atlanta Jrnl. Mbr., Ga. Press Assn. Hons: var. awards & citations as Ed., Tallapoosa Journal-Beacon; Nominated by Gov. as Ga. Indl. Ambassador, 1960. Address: N. Head Ave., Tallapoosa, GA 30176, USA.

GREENE, Graham, b. 2 Oct. 1904. Author. Educ: Balliol Coll., Oxford. Publs. incl: Babbling April, 1925; Rumour at Nightfall, 1931; Stamboul Train, 1932; The Ministry of Fear, 1943; Brighton Rock, 1938; The Heart of the Matter, 1948; The Third Man, 1950; The Lost Childhood & other essays, 1951; The Quiet American, 1955; Our Man in Havana, 1958; The Comedians, 1966; (plays) The Potting Shed, 1957; Carving a Statue, 1964; (for children) The Little Fire Engine, 1950; The Little Steamroller, 1953. Contbr. to: Times; Spectator. Hons. incl: D.Litt.; C.H., 1966; Chevalier, Legion of Honour. Address: c/o The Bodley Head, 9 Bow St., London WC2, UK.

GREENE, Harris, b. 22 Oct. 1921, Waltham, Mass., USA. Writer. Educ: B.S., Boston Univ., 1943; George Washington Univ., 1953. Publs: The 'Mozart' Leaves at Nine, 1961; The Flags at Doney, 1964 (publd. in UK as "Vendetta in Rome"); The Thieves of Tumbutu, 1968; Cancelled Accounts, 1972. Mbrships: Authors League; Authors Guild of Am. Address: 3671 N. Harrison St., Arlington, VA 22207, USA.

GREENE, Maxine, b. 23 Dec. 1917, NYC, USA. College Professor. Educ: B.A., Barnard Coll., 1938; M.A., 1949, Ph.D., 1955, N.Y. Univ. Publs: The Public School & the Private Vision, 1965; Existential Encounters for Teachers, 1967; Teacher As Stranger, 1973. Contbr. to profl. jrnls. Ed., Tchrs. Coll. Record, 1965-70. Hons. Educl. Book of the Year, Delta Gamma Kappa, 1974. Address: 1080 5th Ave., N.Y., NY 10024, USA.

GREENE, Wilda Witt (Mrs. Wallace S. Greene, Jr.), b. 25 Jan. 1911, Falkville, Ala., USA. Publs: Visitation Evangelism, 1955; The Disturbing Christ, 1968. Contbr. to relig. jrnls. & Broadman Devotional Annual, 1974. Mbrships: Nashville Br., Nat. League of Am. Pen Women; Authors Guild; Tenn., Nashville Woman's Press & Authors. Address: 5020 Dovecote Dr., Nashville, TN 37220, USA.

GREENHILL, Basil Jack, b. 26 Feb. 1920, Weston-super-Mare, Somerset, UK. Director, National Maritime Museum. Educ: B.A., Univ. of Bristol. Publs: Westcountrymen in Prince Edward's Isle (w. Ann Giffard), 1967; The Merchant Schooners, 2 vols., 1968; Boats & Boatmen of Pakistan, 1972; Travelling by Sea in the 19th Century (w. A. Giffard), 1972; Westcountry Coasting

Ketches (w. W. J. Slade), 1974; A Victorian Maritime Album, 1974. Contbr. to: Times; Observer; Daily Telegraph; Christian Sci. Monitor; Country Life; var. other mags. Mbr., var. profl. assns. Recip., Award of Merit, Am. Assn. for State & Local Hist., 1968. Address: c/o National Maritime Museum, Greenwich, London SE10, UK.

GREENHOUGH, Terence, b. 15 Dec. 1944, Derby, UK. Writer. Publs: Time & Timothy Grenville, 1975; Friend of Pharaoh, 1975; The Wandering Worlds, 1975. Contbr. to: Sci. Fiction Monthly; Nebula. Address: 183 Hurst Rise, Matlock, Derbyshire, UK.

GREENWOOD, John Omerod, b. 26 July 1907, Fulham, London, UK. Lecturer; Writer. Educ: B.A., Jesus Coll., Cambridge, 1931. Publs: The Playwright, 1950; Sir Gawain & the Green Knight (transl.), 1965; Quaker Encounters vol. 1: Friends & Relief, 1975. Contbr. to: Listener; Radio Times; BBC publs.; Friend; Friends Jrnl. Mbr., Soc. of Authors. Address: 48 Mill Rd., Eastbourne BN21 2PG, UK.

GREENWOOD, Robert, b. 8 Mar. 1897, Crosshills, Yorks., UK. Author. Publs: Mr Bunting, 1940; Mr Bunting at War, 1941; The Squad Goes Out, 1943; Wagstaff's England, 1947; Mr Bunting in the Promised Land, 1949; Good Angel Slept, 1953; O Mistress Mine, 1955; A Breeze in Dinglesea, 1957; A Stone from the Brook, 1960; Spring at the Limes, 1963; Summer in Bishop Street, 1965; transl. into sev. langs. Mbr., Soc. of Authors. Address: 111 St. Andrew's Rd., Felixstowe, Suffolk, UK.

GREENWOOD, Walter, b. 17 Dec. 1903, Salford, UK. Novelist; Dramatist. Publs. incl: (novels) Love on the Dole, 1933; The Secret Kingdom, 1938; Only Mugs Work, 1938; How the Other Man Lives, 1939; So Brief the Spring, 1950; Down by the Sea, 1956; (plays) My Son's My Son (jointly), 1935; The Cure for Love, 1945, filmed 1949; Happy Days, 1959; Fun & Games, 1961; This is Your Wife, 1964; (autobiography) There Was a Time, 1967; (films) No Limit, 1935; Six Men of Dorset, 1944; Eureka Stockade, 1947; Chance of a Lifetime, 1949; The Secret Kingdom (BBC TV Serial), 1960. Address: Whitegates, Cannan Ave., Kirk Michael, Isle of Man, UK.

GREER, Germaine, b. 29 Jan. 1939, Melbourne, Aust. Writer; Journalist; Feminist. Educ: Univs. of Melbourne, Sydney & Cambridge. Publs: The Female Eunuch, 1970. Contbr. to: Listener; Spectator; Oz; Suck; etc. Address: c/o Curtis Brown, 1 Craven Hill, London W2, UK.

GREER, Herb, b. 1929, Santa Fe, N.M., USA. Playwright; Writer; Composer; Translator. Educ: B.A., Fresno State Coll., Calif.; Univ. Wash.; Univ. Coll. London; Bristol Old Vic Theatre Schl. Publs: A Scattering of Dust, 1962; The Trip, 1963; Mud Pie, 1964; Hard Journey, 1964, 2nd ed., 1972. Plays: Free Forever, 1967; Kill, Kill, 1968; Po Miss Julie, 1969; To Kill Barbarians, 1970; Embers, 1971; Kill the Kids, 1972; The New Forever Robe, 1973; Roger, Bart & Mackie, 1974; Spartan Broth, 1975; (play transl.). Magic Afternoon by Wolfgang Bauer, 1973. Contbr. to: New Directions 13. Agent: Film Rights Ltd. Address: c/o Film Rights Ltd., 113-117 Wardour St., London W1V 4EH, UK.

GREET, Kenneth G., b. 17 Nov. 1918, Bristol, UK. Methodist Minister; Secretary, Methodist Conference. Educ: D.D., Handsworth Coll., Birmingham. Publs: Situations Vacant, 1957; Man & Wife Together, 1958; Large Petitions, 1958; Applied Christianity, 1959; Social Science & the Christian, 1960; The Mutual Society, 1962; The Art of Moral Judgement, 1970. Address: 1 Central Bldgs., Westminster, London SW1, UK.

GREEVES, (Rev.), Frederick, b. 1903, Sidcup, Kent, UK. Methodist Minister; Author. Educ: B.A., Manchester Univ.; M.A., Cambridge Univ. Publs: Jesus the Son of God, 1939; The Christian Way, 1945; The Meaning of Sin, 1956; Theology & the Cure of Souls, 1960. Contbr. to: Expository Times; London Quarterly & Holborn Review. Recip., Hon. LL.D., Bristol Univ. Address: 13 Eastmead Lane, Bristol 9, UK.

GREGERSEN, Edgar Alstrup, b. 24 Apr. 1937, NYC, USA. Anthropologist. Educ: B.A., Queen's Coll., 1957; Ph.D., Yale Univ., 1962. Publs: Prefix & Pronoun in Bantu, 1967; Language in Africa, 1974. Contbr. to profl. jrnls. Address: 302 W. 12th St., N.Y., NY 10014, USA.

GREGG, Sidney John, b. 1902, Harpenden, Herts., UK. Lecturer; Reader; Senior Research Fellow. Educ: Imperial Coll., Univ. of London; D.Sc., Ph.D., B.Sc., A.R.C.S. Publs: Adsorption of Gases by Solids; Surface Chemistry of Solids; Adsorption, Surface Area & Porasity (w. K. Sing). Contbr. to sci. chem. jrnls. Address: 45 Pennsylvania Rd., Exeter, Devon, UK.

GREGOR, Arthur, b. 18 Nov. 1923, Vienna, Austria. Writer. Publs: Octavian Shooting Targets, 1954; Declensions of a Refrain, 1957; Basic Movements, 1966; Figure in the Door, 1968; A Bed by the Sea, 1970; Selected Poems, 1971; The Past Now, forthcoming, 1975. Contbr. to: New Yorker; Nation; New Repub.; Poetry; Harper's Mag.; Southern Review; Esquire; Sewanee Review; Kenyon Review; Mich. Quarterly; N.Y. Times; Quarterly Review of Lit.; Commentary; Commonweal; etc. Mbrships: PEN; Authors' Guild. Recip., 1st Appearance Prize, Poetry Mag., 1948. Address: 49 Greenwich Ave., N.Y., NY 10014, USA.

GREGOR, Howard F., b. 7 Apr. 1920, Two Rivers, Wis., USA. Geographer; Educator. Educ: B.S., 1946, M.S., 1947, Univ. of Wis., Madison; Ph.D., Univ. of Calif., L.A., 1950. Publs: Environment & Economic Life — An Economic & Social Geography, 1963; Geography of Agriculture — Themes in Research, 1970; An Agricultural Typology of California, 1974. Contbr. to: Annals of Assn. of Am. Geogs.; Geogl. Review; Econ. Geog.; Jrnl. of Geog.; Land Econs.; Sci.; Jrnl. of the W.; Only in the Form of Book Reviews (Ed.); Tijdschrift voor Economische en Sociale Geografie. Mbrships. incl: Assn. of Am. Geogs.; Am. Geogl. Soc.; Past Pres., Assn. of Pacific Coast Geogs. Address: Dept. of Geog., Univ. of Calif., Davis, CA 95616, USA.

GREGORY, Malcolm Spencer, b. 30 July 1931, Wynward, Tas., Australia. Civil Engineer; Author. Educ: B.Engrng., B.A., Ph.D., D.Eng., Univ. of Tas. Publs: Linear Framed Structures; Elastic Instability; An Introduction to Extremum Principles; Simple Digital Computing Examples. History & Development of Engineering. Contbr. to: Proceedings of Instn. Civil Engrs., London, & Am. Soc. Civil Engrs.; Civil Engrng. & Pub. Works Review; Applied Mech. Reviews of Am. Soc. Mech. Engrs. Address: 24 Esplanade, Kingston Beach, Tas., Australia.

GREGORY, Robin Edward, b. 12 Feb. 1931, London, UK. Editor; Lecturer; Writer. Educ: B.A., (Econs. & Psychol.). Publs. incl: Shorter Textbook of Human Development; (plays) Long Live the King; When the Wind Blows; Passing of Leena. Contbr. to: Musical Opinion; Orbis; Autocar; Times Educl. Supplement; Brit. Jrnl. of Educl. Psychol. Mbrships: Soc. of Authors; Brit. Psychol. Soc.; Dir., Int. Poetry Soc. Address: Rose House, Youlgrave, Bakewell, Derbys., UK.

GREMAUD, Edouard, b. 13 Nov. 1925, Vuadens, Switz. Union Official; Member of Parliament; Editor. Publs: Agriculture montagnarde et tourisme, 1965; Rapports de la Societe fribourgeoise d'economie alpestre, 1960-73; Rapports de l'Office cantonal des credits agricoles, 1963-73; Chief Ed., Agri-Journal. Mbrships: Assn. Swiss Press; Int. Assn. Agricl. Press. Address: Prof. Route des Arsenaux 22, Chemin des Grottes 12, 1700 Fribourg, Switz.

GRENELLE, Lisa, b. 22 Jan. 1905, NYC, USA. Writer; Poet; Teacher. Educ: Columbia Univ., N.Y. Publs. incl: (poetry) This Day is Ours, 1946; No Light Evaded, 1957; Self is the Stranger, 1963; On No Scheduled Flight, 1972; poems in num. anthols.; The Creating Word (prose), 1972. Contbr. to: N.Y. Times; Poetry Mag.; Coronet; Hawk & Whippoorwill; Chgo. Tribune; Sat. Evening Post; etc. Mbrships: Exec. bd., Poetry Soc. of Am., 1962-64; Chmn., poetry div., Pen & Brush Club, 1963-64; Pres., Manhattan Br., Nat. League of Penwomen, 1953-59. Hons. incl: Best Poem of Yr., Pen & Brush Club 1957 & 1969; Best Sonnet, Gustav Davidson Mem. Award, 1972. Address: 140 E. 92 St., N.Y., NY 10028, USA.

GRENVILLE, J. A. S., b. 1928, Berlin, Germany. Professor of Modern History. Educ: London Univ.; Yale Univ.; Ph.D. Publs: The Coming of the Europeans (w. J. G. Fuller), 1962; Lord Salisbury & Foreign Policy, 1964; Politics, Strategy & American Diplomacy (w. G. B. Young), 1966; Fontana History of War & Society (Ed.), 1970; The Major International Treaties, 1974; Europe Reshaped 1848-1878, forthcoming. Mbrships: Fellow, Royal Histl. Soc.; Fellow, C'wlth. Fund. Agent: David Highams. Address: 42 Selly Wick Rd., Birmingham B29 7JA, UK.

GRESS, Elsa (Judith), b. 17 Jan. 1919, Copenhagen, Denmark. Writer; Critic; Playwright; Translator; Lecturer. Educ: M.A., Univ. of Copenhagen, 1944; Columbia Univ., N.Y., USA, 1951-52. Publs: My Many Homes, 1965; Philoctetes Wounded & other Plays, 1969; Fuglefri og Fremmed (Odd Ones Out), 1971; Compania, 1975; M.I.M.I.R. & other Plays, 1975; 11 books of critical essays; 3 novels; 1 vol. of short stories. Contbr. to: Kenyon Review; Leonardo; Art of the Cinema in Europe, 1967; Renaissance of the Film, 1970; Drama Review; World of Translation, 1970; num. other publs. Mbrships. incl: Past Pres., Danish PEN; Magisterforeningen, Copenhagen. Recip., sev. prizes & medals. Address: Decenter Marienborg, 4780 Stege, Denmark.

GRESSWELL, Peter, b. 1922, Bradford, UK. Company Managing Director; Author. Publs: Houses in the Country, 1964; Environment: an Alphabetical Handbook, 1971. Mbrships: A.R.I.C.S.; F.R.S.A. Address: College House, Stanton St. John, Oxford, UK.

GREY, Beryl Elizabeth (Mrs. S. G. Svenson), b. 1927, London, UK. Prima Ballerina; Artistic Director, London Festival Ballet Co., 1968-; Lecturer & Broadcaster. Educ: Dame Alice Owens Girls Schl.; Royal Ballet Schl. Publs: Red Curtain Up, 1958; Through the Bamboo Curtain, 1965. Contbr. to dance jrnls., women's mags., TV & radio. Hons: Hon.D.Mus., Leicester Univ., 1970; C.B.E., 1973; Hon.D.Litt., City of London Univ., 1974. Address: 78 Park St., London W1, UK.

GREY, Ian, b. 5 May 1918, Wellington, NZ. Author; Editor. Educ: LL.B., Univ. of Sydney. Publs: Peter the Great, 1960; Catherine the Great, 1961; Ivan the Terrible, 1964; The First Fifty Years: Soviet Russia 1917-67; The Romanovs; Rise & Fall of the Dynasty, 1970; A History of Russia, 1970; Boris Godunov, 1973. Contbr. to: Hist. Today; Ency. Britannica. Address: 1 Linden Gdns., London W2, UK.

GRIBBLE, Leonard Reginald, b. 1 Feb. 1908, London, UK. Author; Publisher's Reader; Editor; Writer for radio & films. Publs: over 200 titles of fiction, true crime cases & belles lettres under several pen names, incl: A Diplomat Dies; The Arsenal Stadium Mystery (filmed); Famous Judges & Their Trials; Great Detective Exploits; Such Was Their Guilt; Programmed for Death; Stories of Famous Modern Trials. Contbr. to: Chambers' Ency.; Ency. Am.; Dictionary Nat. Biog. Mbrships: Press Club; Paternosters Club (Fndr. Mbr.); Crime Writers' Assn. (Fndr. Mbr.). Address: Chandons, Firsdown Cl., High Salvington, Worthing, Sussex BN13 3BQ, UK.

GRIEDER, Theodore, b. 25 Feb. 1926, Globe, Ariz., USA. Curator of Rare Books. Educ: B.A., Univ. of Southern Calif.; M.A., Ph.D., Stanford Univ.; M.L.S., Univ. of Calif., Berkeley. Publs: The Isaac Foot Library, 1963; Corpus, 1967; Fales Library Checklist, 3 vols., 1970-74; Student's First Aid to Writing, 1972; I Shall Come At You, 1973; Ed., Gale Information Guides to American Literature, English Literature, & World Literatures in English, 1974— (50 vols. planned). Contbr. to: PMLA; Notes & Queries; Restoration & 18th Century Theatre Rsch.; etc. Mbrships. incl: Grolier Club; MLA. Recip., Grants, Am. Philosl. Soc. 1965-66, Coun. on Lib. Resources 1973-74. Address: 1236 Garden St., Hoboken, NJ 07030, USA.

GRIEDER, Walter, b. 21 Nov. 1924, Basel, Switz. Illustrator; Painter. Educ: Art Schl., Basel. Publs: Pierrot, 1965; The Great Feast, 1968; The Enchanted Drum, 1969; Moritz Blunz & the Chickens, 1970; The Good Action of the Fat Children, 1972; The Big Sea Pirate Book, 1973; The Tiger & King of Apes, 1973; The Italian Marriage, 1974. Contbr. to: Graphis Annual; Graphis Poster; Graphis Record Covers; Publicity (UK). Mbr., Assn. of Swiss Graphic Designers. Hons: sev. poster prizes & 1st book prizes. Address: Bäumleingasse 16, 4051 Basel, Switz.

GRIERSON, Edward, b. 1914, Bedford, UK. Justice of the Peace; Barrister-at-Law. Educ: B.A., Exeter Coll., Oxford Univ. Publs: Reputation for a Song; The Lilies & the Bees; The Hastening Wind; Far Morning; The Second Man; The Captain General; Dark Torrent of Glencoe; A Crime of One's Own; The Massingham Affair; The Fatal Inheritance: Philip II & the Spanish Netherlands; The Imperial Dream: British Commonwealth & Empire 1775-1969; Confessions of a Country Magistrate; King of Two Worlds: Philip II of Spain. Mbr., PEN. Agent: Paul R. Reynolds, Inc. Address: Greystead, Tarset, Hexham, Northumberland, UK.

GRIESER, Dietmar, pen name ONDRUSCH, Marcel, b. 9 Mar. 1934, Hanover, Germany. Journalist; Writer. Educ: Univ. Dip. in Soc. Sci. Publs: Vom Schloss Gripsholm zum River Kwai, 1973; Schauplätze österreichischer Dichtung, 1974. Contbr. to: Frankfurter Rundschau; Frankfurter Allgemeine Zeitung; S.W. Radio; Hessian Radio. Mbr., Austrian PEN. Recip., Viktor von Scheffel Prize. Address: A-1030 Vienna, Obere Bahngasse 20, Austria.

GRIESSMAN, B. Eugene, b. 12 Aug. 1934, Spartanburg, S.C., USA. University Professor; Head, Department of Sociology & Anthropology. Educ: B.A., Tenn. Temple Coll.; B.D., New Orleans Bapt. Theol. Sem.; M.A., Baylor Univ., Dallas, Tex.; Ph.D., La. State Univ., New Orleans. Publs: Minorities, 1975. Contbng. Ed., Int. Jrnl. of Contemporary Sociol. Contbr. to: Am. Anthropol.; Southern Sociol.; Rural Sociol.; Sociol. Focus; Jrnl. of Human Rels.; Am. Forests; Le Domaine Humain. Mbrships. incl: Am. Sociol. Assn.; Southern Sociol. Soc.; Am. Anthropol. Assn.; Southern Anthropol. Soc. Rural Sociol. Soc. Address: 906 Cherokee Rd., Auburn, AL 36830, USA.

GRIEVE, Christopher Murray, pen name McDIARMID, Hugh, b. 11 Aug. 1892, Langholm, Dumfriesshire, UK. JP; Author; Journalist. Educ: Edinburgh Univ. Publs: incl: Annals of the Five Senses, 1923; Scottish Scene, 1934; (autobiography) Lucky Poet, 1943, 1972; (poetry) Penny Wheep, 1926; First Hymn to Lenin & Other Poems, 1931; The Birlinn of Clanranald, 1935; Direadh, 1939; In Memoriam James Joyce, 1957; The Kind of Poetry I Want, 1961; Collected Poems, 1920-1961, 1962; (transl.) The Threepenny Opera, 1972. Contbr. to num. Brit. & foreign newspapers & jrnls. Mbrships: PEN; MLA, Am. Address: The Cottage, Brownsbank, by Biggar, Lanarkshire, UK.

GRIFFIN, Harold John Michael, b. 28 May 1912, London, UK (Can. citizen). Editor. Publs: Alaska & the Canadian Northwest: Our New Frontier, 1944; British Columbia: The People's Early Story, 1958; Confederation & Other Poems, 1966; Now & Not Now: Selected Poems, 1973; poetry transl'd into Russian, Ukrainian, Armenian, Hungarian & Polish. Contbr. to: The Fisherman, Vancouver (Ed.); Lit. Gazette, USSR. Mbr., Can. Authors' Assn. (VP, 1965-67, 1971-73; B.C. regional rep. 1968-70, 1974—). Address: 2114 Hoskins Rd., N. Vancouver, B.C., Can.

GRIFFIN, John Howard, b. 1920, Dallas, Tex., USA. Author. Educ: Univ. of Poitiers & Ecole de Médicine, Tours, France. Publs. incl: The Devil Rides Outside, 1953; Black Like Me, 1962; Street of the Seven Angels, 1963; The Church & the Black Man, 1968; Twelve Photographic Portraits; Jacques Maritain: Homage in Words & Pictures. Contbr. to: New Voices; Spirit of Man; etc. Mbrships: Am. Soc. of Photographers in Communications; Nat. Soc. of Lit. & the Arts. Hons: Anisfield-Wolf Award, Saturday Review, 1962; Pacem in Terris Award (shared w. John F. Kennedy), 1964; Christian Culture Gold Medal, 1967. Address: 3816 W. Biddison, Ft. Worth, TX 76109, USA.

GRIFFITH, Ernest Stacey, b. 1896, Utica, NY, USA. Political Scientist. Educ: D.Phil., Oxford Univ., UK; L.H.D., Hamilton Coll.; Litt.D., W. Virginia Wesleyan. Publs: Current Municipal Problems; Modern Government in Action; American System of Government; Modern Development of City Government, 2 vols.; History of American City Government: The Colonial Period; The Conspicuous Failure 1870-1900; The Progressive Years & Their Aftermath 1900-1920; Congress: Its Contemporary Role. Mbrships: Nat. Acad., Econs. & Pol., Pres., 1957-59; Am. Pol. Sci. Assn., VP, 1958-59. Address: 1941 Parkside Drive N.W., Wash. DC, USA.

GRIFFITH, Thomas Gwynfor, b. 29 Mar. 1926, Cil-ffriw, Wales, UK. Professor of Italian Language & Literature; Author. Educ: M.A., B.Litt., Queen's Coll., Oxford; M.A., Dublin. Publs: Boccaccio: Detholion o'r Decameron, 1951; Bandello's Fiction: an Examination of the Novelle, 1955; Avventure linguistiche del Cinquecento, 1961; The Italian Language (w. B. Migliorini), 1966; Italian Writers & the "Italian" Language, 1967; Ed., Petrarch: Selected Poems (w. P. R. J. Hainsworth), 1971. Contbr. to num. jrnls.; Sr. Ed., Italian Studies. Hons: Adjudicator, Royal Nat. Eisteddfod of Wales, 1959, 1962, 1963, 1964. Address: Dept. of Italian Studies, The University, Manchester M13 9PL, UK.

GRIFFITHS, Aileen Esther, pen name PASSMORE, Aileen E., b. Wallasey, Cheshire, UK. Poet; Author; Copywriter. Educ: Wallasey Schl. of Art. Publs. incl: Mr. Bobbin's Bottle. Contbr. to: John O'London's Weekly;

Liverpool Echo; Scots Mag.; Chambers' Jrnl.; Country Life. Address: Beach View, 36 Seabank Rd., Heswall, Wirral, Cheshire, UK.

GRIFFITHS, Bruce, b. 21 Sept. 1938, Blaenau Ffestiniog, Wales, UK. University Lecturer. Educ: B.A., 1959, D.Phil., 1967, Jesus Coll., Oxford; Dip. Ling., Univ. Coll. N. Wales, Bangor, 1963. Publs: Yr Argae (transl. of Henry Bordeaux's Le Barrage), 1971; Y Claf Diglefyd (transl. of Molière's Le Malade Imaginaire), 1972; Y Dieithryn (transl. of Albert Camus' L'Etranger), 1972. Contbr. to: Forum for Mod. Lang. Studies; Taliesin; Barn; Y Genhinen; Mabon; Llwyfan; Mbrships: Welsh Acad.; Soc. for French Studies. Address: 36 Ffordd Cynan, Penrhosgarnedd, Bangor, UK.

GRIFFITHS, Charles Tom Watson, pen name BOLD, Ralph, b. 1919, Liverpool, UK. Author. Educ: Pvte. music tuition; Choral Schlr., Liverpool Cathedral. Publs: Kittens Three, 1963; The Festival of Catville, 1967; The Marigold Line, 1968. Address: Beach View, 36 Seabank Rd., Heswall, Wirral, Cheshire, UK.

GRIFFITHS, Richard Mathias, b. 21 June 1935, Barry, Glam., UK. Professor of French. Educ: B.A., 1957, M.A., Ph.D., 1961, King's Coll., Cambridge Univ. Publs: The Reactionary Revolution, 1966, French transl., 1971; Ed., Claudel: A Reappraisal, 1968; The Dramatic Technique of Antoine de Montchrestien, 1970; Marshal Pétain, 1970. Contbr. to: French Studies; Mod. Lang. Review; Revue des Sciences Humaines; Spectator; Sunday Times. Mbrships. incl: Soc. for French Studies; Soc. Huysmans; Hon. Soc. of Cymmrodorion. Address: Dept. of French, University College, P.O. Box 95, Cardiff CF1 1XA, UK.

GRIFFITHS, Sally Winefride Maude, b. 29 Dec. 1934, Haverfordwest, Pembrokeshire, UK. Author. Educ: B.Ed., St. John's Coll., York, 1975. Publs: The Tree & the Flood, 1966; Winter Day in a Glasshouse, 1968. Contbr. short stories to: Ambit, 1964/5; Transatlantic Review, 1966, 1975; Macmillan's "Winter Tales", 1974. Mbr., Writers' Action Grp. Address: Daleside, Ampleforth, York, UK.

GRIGORESCU, Ioan, b. 20 Oct. 1930, Ploiesti, Romania. Author; Journalist; Scriptwriter. Educ: Dip., Gorki Lit. Inst., Moscow, USSR, 1955; Dip., Inst. Jrnlsm., Strasbourg, France, 1960. Publs. incl: (in Romanian) Cinema Madagascar, 1956; The Obsession, 1969; The Struggle Against Sleep, 1969; Inflammable Phoenix, 1971; The World Spectacle, 1973; The Grubby Paradise, 1974; I Swear! , 1974; 8 Art Film scenarios. Contbr. to: Contemporanul (former Ed.); other lit. publs.; Radio & TV. Mbrships. incl: Scriptwriters Assn., Writers Union, Bucharest. (exec. comm.); Soc. of Authors, Paris. Hons. incl: Prix Italia, 1968; other awards for scriptwriting & prose. Address: Bucharest, 32 Boul. Primaveri, Romania.

GRIGSON, Geoffrey, b. 2 Mar. 1905, Pelynt, Cornwall, UK. Author. Educ: Oxford Univ. Publs: Several Observations; Under the Cliff, & Other Poems; The Isles of Scilly, & Other Poems; Samuel Palmer; The Crest on the Silver; The Painted Caves; The Englishman's Flora; Collected Poems; A Skull in Salop; Poems & Poets; Ingestion of Ice-Cream; Notes from a Queer Country; Discoveries of Bones & Stones, & Other Poems, 1971; Angles & Circles, & Other Poems, 1974. Contbr. to: New Statesman; Times Lit. Supplement; Guardian; Encounter; Poetry Chgo.; Listener; etc. Recip., Duff Cooper Prize, 1971. Address: Broad Town Farm, Broad Town, Swindon, Wilts., UK.

GRILLMEIER, Aloys, b. 1 Jan. 1910, Bavaria, Germany. Professor of Dogmatics. Educ. incl: Lic.Phil., Pullach Coll., 1934; Lic.Theol., Frankfurt/Main Coll., 1938; Dr. theol., Freiburg i. Br. Univ. Publs: Das Konzil von Chalkedon (Ed. w. H. Bacht & others), 1951-54; 4th ed., 1973; Der Logos am Kreuz, 1956; Christ in Christian Tradition vol. 1, 1965, 2nd ed., 1975, French transl., 1973; Wandernde Kirche u. werdende Welt, 1968; Mit Ihm u. in Ihm: Christologische Forschungen u. Perspektiven, 1975. Contbr. to: Geist u. Leben; etc. Mbr., pro oriente, Vienna i. A. Address: D-6 Frankfurt/Main 70, Offenbacher Landstr. 224, W. Germany.

GRILLO, Francesco, pen name CREPACORE, b. 19 Nov. 1898, Corigliano, Calabro, Italy. Writer. Publs: Canti Barbari, 1944; Vite e Opere di F.Pometti, 1945; Girolamo Garopoli, 1946; Il Castello ed i Conti di Corigliano, 1949; Ludovico di Durazzo e Giovanna i di Napoli, 1951; Tommaso Campanella in America, a Critical Bibliography &

a Profile, 1954, supplements 1957, 1968, 1971-72; Italia Antica e Medioevale (Calabria), 1954; Questioni Campanelliane, 1961; Profili Calabresi, 1962; Il Poeta dell'Utopia, F.Maradea, 1964; Antichità Storiche e Monumentali di Corigliano Calabro, 1966; I Duchi ed i Baroni di Corigliano, 1969; Motivi Campanelliani, 1969; La Rivoluzione Napoletana del 1799, 1972; L'Eresia Cattolica e Riformatrice di T.Campanella, 1973. Contbr. to sev. jrnls. Mbrships: Accademia Cosentina; Archivio Storico per la Calabria. Address: 3033 Middletown Rd., Bronx, NY 10461, USA.

GRIMBLE, Ian, b. 7 Aug. 1921, Hong Kong. Author; Broadcaster. Educ: B.A., Balliol Coll., Oxford, UK; Ph.D., Aberdeen Univ. Publs: The Harrington Family, 1957; The Trial of Patrick Sellar, 1962; Chief of Mackay, 1965; Denmark, 1966; The Future of the Highlands (co-ed.), 1968; Regency People, 1972; Scottish Clans & Tartans, 1973; Cochrane the Sea Wolf, forthcoming; St. Joan & the Archangel, forthcoming. Contbr. to num. mags. Mbrships: Fellow, Royal Histl. Soc.; Soc. of Authors. Address: 13 Saville Rd., Twickenham, Middx. TW1 4BQ, UK.

GRIMWADE, Andrew Sheppard, b. 1930, Melbourne, Aust. Chemical Engineer; Director, Bank. Educ: B.Sc., Trinity Coll., Melbourne; M.A., Oriel Coll., Oxford, UK. Publs: Involvement — The Portraits of Clifton Pugh & Mark Strizic, 1969. Address: 320 St. Kilda Rd., Melbourne, Victoria 3004, Australia.

GRINDROD, Muriel Kathleen, b. 4 Feb. 1902, Oxford, UK. Writer; Translator. Educ: B.A., Girton Coll., Cambridge Univ.; Sorbonne Univ., Paris, France. Publs: The Rebuilding of Italy, 1955; Italy, 1964, 2nd ed., 1966; Italy, 1968. Contbr. to: The Annual Register of World Events; Collier's Yr. Book; Int. Affairs; The World Today. Mbrships. incl: Royal Inst. Int. Affairs; Brit.-Italian Soc. (Exec. Comm.; Ed., jrnl., Rivista). Hons: O.B.E., 1962; John Florio Prize for Transl. from Italian, 1968; Commendatore of Italian Repub., 1974. Address: 45 Lancaster Grove, London NW3, UK.

GRINSELL, Leslie Valentine, b. 14 Feb. 1907, Hornsey, Middx., UK. Museum Curator of Archaeology (ret'd). Publs: Ancient Burial-Mounds of England, 1936, 2nd ed., 1953; Egyptian Pyramids, 1947; Archaeology of Wessex, 1958; Archaeology of Exmoor, 1970; Barrow, Pyramid & Tomb, 1975. Contbr. to num. archaeol. jrnls. Mbr., Prehistoric Soc. (Hon. Treas., 1947-70). Hons: M.A., Bristol Univ., 1971; O.B.E., 1972. Address: 32 Queen's Court, Bristol BS8 1ND, UK.

GRIPE, Maria Kristina, b. 25 July 1923, Vaxholm, Sweden. Author. Publs: Josefin, 1961; Hugo och Josefin, 1962; Pappa Pellerins dotter, 1963; Glasblåsarns barn, 1964; I Klockornas Tid, 1965; Hugo, 1966; Landet Utanför, 1967; Nattpappan, 1968; Glastunneln, 1969; Tanten, 1970; Julias Hus och Nattpappan, 1971; Elvis Karlsson, 1972; Elvis! Elvis!, 1973; . . . ellen dellen . . ., 1974. Mbr., Swedish Authors' Union. Hons. incl: N.Y. Herald Tribune Spring Festival Honor Book, 1966; Litteraturfrämjandets stipendium, 1968; Astrid Lindgren Prize, 1972; H.C. Anderson medal, 1974; Sveriges Författarfonds Premium för Litterär Förtjänst, 1974. Address: Fruängsgatan 37, S-611 00 Nyköping, Sweden.

GRITT, Brian Edward, pen name DRIVER, Edward, b. 1938, Ealing, Middlesex, UK. Social Services Liaison Officer; Writer; Broadcaster; Part-time Tutor, Open University. Educ: Univ. of Hull; London Schl. of Econs. Contbr. to: Family Dr.; Mental Welfare; Hosp. Jrnl. & Social Serv. Review. Mbrships: Soc. of Authors; Brit. Assn. of Social Workers; Grp. for Advancement Psychotherapy in Social Work; Assn. Disabled Profls. Address: 9 St. Michael's Rd., Welling, Kent, UK.

GROB, Gerald N., b. 25 Apr. 1931, NYC, USA. University Professor of History; Historian; Author. Educ: B.S.S., CCNY, 1951; A.M., Columbia Univ., 1952; Ph.D., Northwestern Univ., 1958. Publs: Workers & Utopia, 1961; American Ideas, 1963; The State & the Mentally Ill, 1966; Interpretations of American History, 1967, 2nd ed., 1972; American Social History Before 1600, 1970; American History: Retrospect & Prospect, 1971; Mental Institutions in America, 1973. Contbr. to var. histl. & pol. jrnls. Mbr., Ed. Bd., Bus. Hist. Review, 1972-75. Recip., Am. Assn. State & Local Hist. Annual Award for Book, The State & the Mentally Ill, 1965. Address: 821 Starview Way, Somerville, NJ 08876, USA.

GROCHOWIAK, Stanislaw, b. 24 Jan. 1934, Poland. Poet; Editor. Educ: Univs. of Poznan & Wroclaw. Publs: (poetry) Ballada rycerska, 1956; Menuet z progrzebaczem, 1956; Rozbieranie do snu, 1959; Agresty, 1963; Kanon, 1965; Totentanz in Polen, 1969; Nie bylo lata, 1970; Polowanie na cietrzewie, 1972; (novels) Plebania z magnoliami, 1956; Lamentnice, 1958; Trismus, 1963; Karabiny, 1965; (play) Rzecz na glosy, 1966. Contbr. to: Nowa Kultura, 1961-63; Kultura, 1963-72. Recip., Culture & art Prize, 1962, 1973. Address: Ul. Morszynska 3/7, Warsaw, Poland.

GROENEVELD, F. Ph. (Frits), b. 23 Dec. 1938, Wassenaar, Netherlands. Journalist. Educ: LL.B. Author of many articles in fields of environment, nature conserv., farming, planning, housing, WWII hist., etc. Contbr. to: Kredo; Milieudefensie; Chick. Mbrships: Netherlands Fedn. of Jrnlsts.; Int. Press Ctr., Nieuwspoort; Int. Fedn. of Agricul. Jrnlsts. Address: Mozartlaan 8, Leidschendam, Netherlands.

GROHSKOPF, Bernice, b. Troy, NY, USA. Writer. Educ: B.A., 1948, M.A., 1954, Columbia Univ. Publs: Seeds of Time, 1963; From Age to Age, 1968; The Treasure of Sutton Hoo, 1970, paperback ed., 1973; Shadow in the Sun, 1975; Notes on the Hauter Experiment, 1975. Contbr. short stories to: Woman's Day; Homes & Gdns. Mbrships: Author's Guild; AAUW; Richard III Soc. Hons: listed Notable Children's Books, 1963; N.J. Assn. of Tchrs. of Engl. Award, 1970. Address: 73 Buckingham Rd., Upper Montclair, NJ 07043, USA.

GROLL, Gunter, pen name GRILL, Sebastian, b. 5 Aug. 1914, Liegnitz, Germany. Author. Educ: Dr.Phil.; Univs. Vienna, Munich. Publs: De Profundis, 1946; Laterna Magica, 1947; Magie des Films, 1953; Lichter & Schatten, 1956; E.T.A. Hoffmann; Zauberspiegel, 1961. Contbr. to: Süddeutsche Zeitung (critic). Mbrships: PEN; German Writers' Union. Hons: Film Critic Prize, 1961; City Munich Lit. Prize, 1966; German Film Prize, 1972. Address: Haus Rösl, 8193 Ammerland, Germany.

GROLLMAN, Earl A., b. 3 July 1925, Balt., Md., USA. Rabbi; Author. Educ: B.A., Univ. of Cinn.; M.H.L., Hebrew Union Coll.; D.D., Portia Law Schl. Publs: Judaism in Sigmund Freud's World, 1965; Rabbinical Counselling, 1966; Explaining Death to Children, 1967; Explaining Divorce to Children, 1969; Talking About Death, 1970; Suicide: Prevention, Intervention, Postvention, 1971; Concerning Death: A Practical Guide For the Living, 1974. Mbrships: Ed. Bds., Jrnl. of Thanatology, Omega. Recip., UNESCO Trends Citation, 1971. Address: 79 Country Club Ln., Belmont, MA 02118, USA.

GRONOWICZ, Antoni. Poet; Novelist; Playwright. Educ: Ph.D. Publs: (32 books & plays inclng.) The Quiet Vengeance of Words (poetry), 1970; The United Animals (play), 1971; An Orange Full of Dreams (novel), 1972; The Hookmen (novel), 1973. Contbr. to US mags. & reviews. Mbrships: Authors League of Am.; Dramatists' Guild; Poetry Soc. of Am. PEN Am. Ctr. Address: 132 E. 82nd St., N.Y., NY 10028, USA.

GROOM, Bernard, b. 20 Sept. 1892, Crouchend, London, UK. English Teacher. Educ: M.A., Oxford Univ.; M.A., London Univ. Publs: Poems, Elkin Mathews, 1924; A Literary History of England, later reissued as A History of English Literature, 1929; A Short History of English Words, 1934; The Diction of Poetry from Spencer to Bridges, 1955; The Unity of Wordsworth's Poetry, 1966; etc. Contbr. to: Essays & Studies of the Engl. Assn.; Soc. for Pure Engl. Tracts. Recip., Bernard Groom Prize, Clifton Coll. Address: Uplands Nursing Home, Grange Park Rd., Weston-super-Mare, UK.

GROS, Bernard, b. 25 Aug. 1917, St.-Georges-sur-Fontaine, France. Teacher of Literature & Culture. Educ: Lit. studies, Univ. of Lille; Lic.-ès-Lettres; Tchng. Dip. Publs: La Littérature, 1970; Profil du "Roi se meurt", 1972; Victor Hugo, Le Voyant de Guernesey, 1975; Le Terrorisme, 1975; Profil de "L'Homme Revolté" de Camus, 1975; Bibliothèque de la Violence, 1976. Contbr. to: Réforme (Lit. Critic); Revue des Sciences Humaines; Livres de France; Mag. Littéraire. Hons: Chevalier de la Légion d'Honneur, 1970; Verly Lecoutre de Beauvais Prize, Soc. of Sci., Agric. & the Arts, Lille, 1971. Address: 16 Rue Desrousseaux, 59000 Lille, France.

GROSECLOSE, Elgin, b. 25 Nov. 1899, Waukomis, Okla., USA. Financial & Investment Counselor. Educ:

A.B., Univ. of Okla., 1920; M.A., 1924, Ph.D., 1928, Am. Univ. Publs: Money: The Human Conflict, 1934; The Persian Journey of the Reverend Ashley Wishard & His Servant Fathi, 1937; Ararat, 1939, 2nd ed., 1974; The Firedrake, 1942; Introduction to Iran, 1947; The Carmelite, 1955; The Scimitar of Saladin, 1956; Money & Man, 1961, 2nd ed., 1967; Fifty Years of Managed Money: The Story of the Federal Reserve, 1966. Contbr. to: Barron's; Wall St. Jrnl. Mbr., Authors' Guild. Hons: Am. Booksellers Award & Fndn. for Lit. Award, 1940. Address: 4813 Woodway Ln. N.W., Wash., DC 20016, USA.

GROSS, Fanny Alice, b. 1913, Lithuania. Lawyer. Educ: Univ. of S. Africa; North-Western Univ., Chgo., USA. Publs: Society & the Criminal, 1944; All God's Children, 1958; Who Hangs the Hangman, 1966. Contbr. to: Cape Argus; Cape Times; Justitia, Pretoria; Star, Forum, Johannesburg; Parents, Psychol., London; Huisgenoot, Nicro Crimonol. Jrnl., Cape Town. Mbrships: Comm. N.I.C.R.O.; PEN; Hon. Ed., Ha-Yam, organ Maritime Org. Address: Mount Carmel, Ocean View Drive, Green Point, Cape Town, South Africa.

GROSS, Feliks, b. 17 June 1906, Cracow, Poland. Professor of Sociology. Educ: Master of Jurisprudence & Public Admin., 1929, LL.D., 1931, Univ. of Cracow. Publs: Nomadism, 1936; Polish Worker, 1945; Humanistic Socialism, 1945; Foreign Policy Analysis, 1954; Seizure of Political Power, 1957; Values & Social Structure, 1967; World Politics — Tension Areas, 1967; Politics of Violence, 1973; Il Paese, Values Social Change in an Italian Village, 1974; Revolutionary Party, 1974. Contbr. to num. sociol. publs.; etc. Mbrships: Am. Sociol. Assn.; Int. Sociol. Inst.; Am. Acad. of Pol. Sci.; N.Y. Acad. of Scis.; Author's League of Am. Address: 310 West 85 St., N.Y., NY 10024, USA.

GROSS, Natan, pen name HAGRIZI, Natan, b. 16 Nov. 1919, Cracow, Poland. Film Director; Journalist. Educ: Law & Art studies, Cracow Univ., 1939; Polish Film Inst., 1945-46. Publs. incl: (3 vols. of lyrics in Polish) Selection of New Hebrew Poetry, 1947; Songs of Israel, 1948; What Remained Us of Those Days ..., 1971; Holocaust in Hebrew Poetry (co-Ed., anthol.), 1974. Contbr. to: Al Hamishmar; Kolnoa 74; Chotam; Slowo Mlodych; Nasze Stowo; Davar; Atidot; Nowiny Izraelskie; etc. Mbrships: Film Critics' Sect., Assn. Israeli Jrnlsts.; Film & TV Dirs.' Guild (Israel). Recip., Ben-Dor Prize, Davar newspaper, 1960. Address: 14 Herzog St., Givataim, Israel.

GROSSER, Alfred, b. 1 Feb. 1925, Frankfurt, Germany. Professor of Political Science. Educ: Univs. of Aix en Provence & Paris, France; agrégé de l'Univ.; Doct. ès Lettres. Publs. incl: L'Allemagne de l'Occident, 1963, Engl. transl. 1955; La Quatrième République & sa Politique Extérieure, 1961; La Politique Extérieure de la V République, 1965, Engl. transl. 1967; Au Nom de Quoi, Fondements d'une Morale Politique, 1969; L'Allemagne de Notre Temps, 1970, Engl. transl. 1971; L'Explication Politique, 1972. Contbr. to: Le Monde (pol. column); var. int. pol. publs.; German TV. Mbrships. incl: French PEN (Bd.); German PEN. Hons: Prix Drouyn de Lhuys, Acad. des Scis. Morales & Pol., 1962; Prix Broquette-Gonin, Acad. Française, 1965. Address: 8 Rue Dupleix, 75015 Paris, France.

GROSSMAN, Alfred, b. 1927, NYC, USA. Editor; Author. Educ: M.A., Harvard Univ. Publs: Acrobat Admits, 1959; Many Slippery Errors, 1963; Marie Beginning, 1964; The Do-Gooders, 1968. Contbr. to: East Europe (Ed.), 1954-61; N.Y. Times Almanac (Ed.), 1968. Address: 54 Riverside Dr., N.Y., NY, USA.

GROSSRIEDER, Hans, b. 30 Sept. 1912, Düdingen, Fribourg, Switz. Professor of German Language & Literature; Translator; Writer. Educ: Ph.D., St. Michel Coll., Univ. Fribourg. Publs: Der Stern Im Schnee, 1953; Lexikon der Weltliteratur (co-author), 1960-61; Drei Schweizer Kunstwerke in Fryburg (co-author), 1943; & num. essays on German & French lit. & art. Contbr. to: Schweizer Rundschau, Einsiedeln; Wort und Wahrheit, Vienna. Mbr., Swiss Writers' Union. Address: 2 Chemin Ste Agnès, Fribourg T, 22 19 35, Switz.

GROTTER, Kurt, b. 11 Nov. 1910, Czernowitz, Austria. Senior Television Current Affairs Editor. Educ: Bus. Dip., Univ. of Vienna; Licencié ès Scis. Commerciales, Univ. of Geneva, Switz. Productions: Eisenhower; Kennedy; De Gaulle; The Trial of Nuremburg; Stalingrad; February 1934; Austria 1945; etc. Contbr. to num. mags. &

newspapers in Austria, Italy & USA. Mbrships: Presse Club Concordia, Vienna; Austrian Union of Jrnlsts. Address: Paradis Gasse 62/1, A1190 Vienna, Austria.

GROUSSARD, Serge, b. 18 Jan. 1921, Niort, France. Journalist; Writer. Educ: Ecole Nat. d'Admin.; Ecole Libre des Sci. Politiques; Paris Univ. Publs. incl: Pogrom, 1948; Une chic fille, 1956; La Belle Espérance, 1958; La Passion du Maure, 1959; Les Chacals, 1964; Tu es Soleil, 1970; Taxi de Nuit, 1971; L'Algérie des Adieux, 1972; La Medaille de Song, 1973; La Guerre Oublié. Contbr. to: Le Figaro, Chief Reporter, 1954-62, 1969-; L'Aurore, 1962-69. Hons. incl: Legion of Honour; Croix de Guerre; Int. Prix du Grand Reportage; Prix Fémina. Address: 5 rue de Koufra, Boulogne-sur-Seine 92, France.

GROVE, Fred H., b. 4 July 1913, Hominy, Okla., USA. Writer. Educ: B.A. (Journalism), Univ. of Okla., 1937. Publs: No Bugles, No Glory, 1959; Comanche Captives, 1961; The Land Seekers, 1963; Buffalo Spring, 1967; The Buffalo Runners, 1968; War Journey, 1971; The Child Stealers, 1973; Warrior Road, 1974. Mbr., Western Writers of Am. Hons: Western Heritage Award, Nat. Cowboy Hall of Fame, 1961 & 1969; Spur Award, Western Writers of Am., 1962, 1963 & 1969; 1st Okla. Writing Award, Univ. of Okla., 1962. Address: 1005 Woodland Drive, Norman, OK 73069, USA.

GROVES, Reginald, b. 1908, London, UK. Writer; Journalist. Publs: But we Shall Rise Again, 1938; The Mystery of Victor Grayson, 1944; Rebels Oak, 1944; The Peasants' Revolt of 1381, 1947; History of West Ham Football Club, 1947; History of Chelsea Football Club, 1947; Sharpen the Sickle, 1949; Conrad Noel & the Thaxted Movement, 1968; Seedtime & Harvest, 1972; The Balham Group, 1974; Ed., World Film News, 1936-38; Ed., Cine Technician, 1950-55; Producer, Scriptwriter, Documentary films, 1938-50. Mbrships: N.U.J.; Assoc. Cine & TV Technicians; Soc. of Lab. Hist. Address: 7 Heathfield Rd., London SW18, UK.

GROVES, Sylvia Mary, b. 1904, Edgbaston, Birmingham, UK. Publ: History of Needlework Tools & Accessories, 1966, 1973, USA ed., 1973. Contbr. to: Punch; Countryman; Articles for Collectors; Country Life. Mbr., Soc. of Authors. Address: 4 Lyttelton Rd., Edgbaston, Birmingham 16, UK.

GRUBB, Frederick, b. 1932, England. Author. Educ: M.A., Ph.D., Trinity Coll., Cambridge. Publs: Title Deeds: Poems, 1961; A Vision of Reality: Studies of Modern Poetry, 1965; September Sun, 1970. Address: The Garret, 243 Haverstock Hill, London NW3, UK.

GRUBB, (Sir) Kenneth George, b. 9 Sept. 1900, Oxton, Notts., UK. Author. Educ: Marlborough Coll., 1914-18. Publs: Lowland Indians of Amazonia, 1928; Amazon & Andes, 1930; 10 other books on Latin America; World Christian Handbooks, 1949, 1952, 1957, 1962, 1968; Crypts of Power (autobiog.), 1971. Hons: C.M.G., 1942; Kt. Bach., 1953; K.C.M.G., 1970. Address: Moot Farm, Downton, Salisbury, Wilts. SP5 3JP, UK.

GRUBERG, Martin, b. 28 Jan. 1935, NYC, USA. Professor of Political Science. Educ: B.A., CCNY, 1955; Ph.D., Columbia Univ., 1963. Publs: Women in American Politics, 1968. Contbr. to: New Women: The Reference Encyclopedia of Women's Liberation, 1972; Am. Govt. '73-'74 Ency., 1972; Int. Review of Educ., 1973; Woman Speaking, 1973; Sourcebook of Am. Hist., 1973; Paper for Ctrl. Wis., Oshkosh Northwestern; Oshkosh Adv.; Lingua Franca; Am. Pol. Sci. Review; Jrnl. of Pol.; Jrnl. of Am. Hist.; Western Pol. Quarterly; Mid-Am.; Ency. Americana; etc. Address: 2020 Wisconsin St., Oshkosh, WI 54901, USA.

GRUNDY, Bill, b. 1923, Manchester, UK. Author; Playwright. Educ: B.Sc., Manchester Univ. Publs: Flower of Gloster, 1968; Up the Rams (musical documentary play), 1970; All Our Yesterdays (co-author), 1974; United We Fall (play), 1975. Contbr. to: Spectator; Punch; Daily Sketch. Mbr., Press Club. Address: The Oaks, Marple Bridge, Cheshire, UK.

GRUNDY, Rupert Francis Brooks, b. 1903, London, UK. Engineer. Educ: B.Sc., Univ. Coll., London. Publs: Builders' Materials; The Essentials of Reinforced Concrete Design. Mbrships: F.I.C.E.; F.I.Mun.E.; Royal Automobile Club. Address: The Mill House, Brigstock, Northants., UK.

GRÜNTHAL, Ivar, b. 8 June 1924, Tartu, Estonia. Doctor. Educ: M.D., Lund Univ., 1951. Publs: Uni lahtiste silmadega (Sleep with Open Eyes), 1951; Müüdid mülka põhja kadund maast (Myths About a Land That Vanished into the Swamp), 1953; Must pühapäev (Black Sunday), 1954; Meri (The Sea), 1958; Lumi ja lubi (Snow & Lime), 1960; Peetri kiriku kellad (The Bells of St. Peter's), 1962. Fndr. & Ed., The Estonian Lit. Quarterly Mana (1957-64). Mbrships: PEN; Swedish Union of Authors; Gothenburg Assn. of Authors. Recip., Henrik Visnapuu Prize, N.Y., USA, 1959. Address: Dr Lindhs 1, 413 25 Gothenburg, Sweden.

GRYLLS, R. Glynn (Lady Mander), b. London, UK. Biographer. Educ: Queen's Coll., London; M.A., Lady Margaret Hall, Oxford. Publs: Mary Shelley, 1936; Trelawny, 1939; Portrait of Rossetti, 1962. Contbr. to: Times; Sunday Times. Mbrships: PEN, Keats-Shelley Mem. Assn. Address: Wightwick Manor, Wolverhampton, UK.

GSTEIGER, Manfred, b. 7 June 1930, Twann, Berne Canton, Switz. Professor of Comparative Literature. Educ: D.Lit., Univ. Berne; Univ. Paris. Publs. incl: (poetry) Die Landschaftsschilderungen in den Romanen Chrestiens de Troyes, 1957; Literatur des Übergangs, 1963; Poesie und Kritik, 1967; Littérature Nationale et Comparatisme, 1967; Französische Symbolisten in der deutschen Literatur der Jahrhundertwende, 1972; Die zeitgenössischen Literaturen der Schweiz, 1974. Contbr. to num. acad. & lit. jrnls. Mbrships. incl: Int. Assn. Comp. Lit.; PEN. Hons. incl: Schiller Fndn. Prize, 1959; Berne Canton Prize, 1970. Address: Château 21, CH-2034 Peseux, Neuchâtel, Switz.

GSTREIN, Heinz, pen name H. G., b. 16 Dec. 1941, Innsbruck, Austria. Foreign Correspondent. Educ: Ph.D., Univ. Vienna; Univ. Innsbruck. Publs: Example Greece, 1969; Arab Socialism, 1972; The Kurdish Question, 1974; Ethiopia's Revolution, 1975. Contbr. to: Neue Zürcher Zeitung (Zürich); Die Presse (Vienna). Address: P.O. Box 1986, Ataba, Cairo, United Arab Repub.

GUARGHIAS, Aloysius, pen names IRGHEN, George; CHEN, Aloysius; IBRAHIM, Ischak, b. 12 Oct. 1933, Semarang, Java, Indonesia. Columnist; Journalist; Translator. Educ: B.A., Peking Univ., China; Grad., Diplomatic Acad., Vienna. Contbr. to: Sinar Harapan (Jakarta); Newsdom Weekly & Travelling Mag. (Hong Kong); Austrian Mil. Mag. (Vienna); Wehrkunde (Munich); The Look Mag. (Taipei); Kurier (Vienna); Biog. Mag. (Taipei). Mbrships. incl: For. Jrnlsts. Assn., Vienna; Int. Press Inst., Vienna. Address: Aspetten 27/2, A-2380 Perchtoldsdorf, Vienna, Austria.

GUDENIAN, Haig, b. 1918, Kensington, London, UK. Publisher; Former Magazine Editor. Educ: Univ. Coll. Schl., London. Contbr. to: John Bull (Chief Sub-Ed. & Asst. Ed., 1946-52); Illustrated (Asst. Ed. & Assoc. Ed., 1952-55); Ideal Home Mag. (Ed. & Mng. Ed., 1957-65.). Co-Fndr. & Dir., Gudenian, Rockall & Mayer Ltd., Publishers, Publishing, Editorial & Design Consultants. Address: 27a Frognal, London NW3, UK.

GUDMUNDSSON, Kristmann, b. 23 Oct. 1901, Borgarfjordur, Iceland. Author; Critic. Publs: 30 novels; 60 short stories; A book of gardening; Autobiog. in 4 vols.; Story of World Literature in 2 vols. Contbr. to num. mags., Norway, Denmark, Iceland. Mbrships: PEN; 12 Authors & Artists of Hon. in Iceland. Recip., Icelandic Falcon Order. Address: Post Box 615, Reykjavik, Iceland.

GUDRUN FRA LUNDI, Gudrun Arnadottir, b. 3 June 1887, Lundur, Skagafirdi, Iceland. Author. Publs. incl: Dalalif (Valley Life) vols. 1-5, 1946-51; Tengdadottirin (The Daughter-in-Law) vols. 1-3, 1952-54; Romm er su taug (Pining for Home), 1956; A okunnum slodum (In Unknown Regions), 1959; Styfdar fjardir (Pinioned Feathers) vols. 1-3, 1961-63; Hvikul er konu ast (Fickle is a Woman's Love), 1964; Dregur sky fyrir sol (Clouds Drawn Before the Sun), 1966; Gulned blod (Yellowed Leaves), 1968; Utan fra sjo (From Without the Sea) vols. 1-3, 1970-73. Contbr. of short stories, var. jrnls. Mbr., Authors Fdn. Address: c/o Leiftur h.f., Hofdatun 12, Reykjavik, Iceland.

GUEDROITZ, Prince Alexis, b. 9 June 1923, Pancevo, Serbia. Dramatic Author; Professor. Publs: Un amour sans response, 1946; "Boris Godounov" de Pouchkine, 1962; "Ivanov" de Tchekov, 1963; "L'Esprit souterrain" de Dostoievsky, 1966; "Oncle Vania" de Tchekov, 1967; "L'Idiot" de Dostoievsky, 1968; "Crime & châtiment" de Dostoievsky, 1970; "Un mois a la campagne" de Tourgueniev, 1973; "Les frères Karamazov" de Dostoievsky, 1974. Contbr. to: Revue Generale, Belgium. Mbr., PEN. Hons: Georges Vaxelaire Prize, Royal Acad. of Lang. & Lit., France, 1962; Dramatic Comps. & Authors Prize, 1968. Address: 37 Ave. Bel-Air, 1180 Brussels, Belgium.

GUÉHENNE, Jean, pen name of GUÉHENNO, Marcel, b. 25 Mar. 1890. Journalist; Educator. Educ: Ecole Normale Superieure. Publs. incl: Journal d'une Revolution, 1938; Journal des Années Noires, La Part de la France, 1949; Jean Jacques; roman & verité, 1950; Sur le Chemin des Hommes, 1964; Changer la Vie, 1964; La Mort des autres, 1968; Caliban & Propero, 1969; Carnets du vieil Ecrivain, 1971. Contbr. to: L'Europe; Vendredi; Figaro. Mbr., French Acad. Hons. incl: Legion of Honour; Croix de Guerre; Prix des Ambassadeurs; Cino del Duca Prize. Address: 35 rue Pierre-Nicole, Paris 5e, France.

GUENTHER, Charles (John), b. 29 Apr. 1920, St. Louis, Mo., USA. Poet; Translator; Librarian. Educ: A.A., Harris Tchrs. Coll.; B.A., M.A., Webster Coll. Publs: Modern Italian Poets, 1961; Selected Poems of Alain Bosquet (co-translator w. Samuel Beckett & others), 1963; Paul Valery in English, 1970; Phrase/Paraphrase (poems), 1970; Plaquette: High Sundowns (translation from J. R. Jimenez), 1974. Contbr. to: The Critic; Kenyon & Lit. Reviews; Poetry (Chgo.); etc. Book Reviewer, St. Louis Poet-Dispatch, 1953—; St. Louis Globe-Dem., 1972—. Hons. incl: James Joyce Award, Poetry Soc. of Am., 1974. Address: 2935 Russell Blvd., St. Louis, MO 63104, USA.

GUERARD, Albert (Joseph), b. 2 Nov. 1914, Houston, Tex., USA. Professor of Literature, Stanford Univ. Educ: B.A. 1934, Ph.D. 1938, Stanford Univ.; M.A., Harvard, 1936. Publs. incl: (novels) The Past Must Alter, UK, 1937, USA, 1938; Maquisard, USA, 1945, UK, 1946; Night Journey, USA, 1950, UK, 1951; The Bystander, USA, 1958, UK, 1959; The Exiles, UK, 1962, USA, 1963; (non-fiction) André Gide, USA & UK, 1951, revised ed. 1968; Conrad the Novelist, USA, 1958, UK, 1959. Contbr. to: Denver Quarterly; Partisan Review; etc. Mbr., Am. Acad. Arts & Scis. Hons. incl: Paris Review Fiction Prize, 1964; var. Fellowships. Address: Dept. of English, Stanford Univ., CA 94305, USA.

GUÉRIN, Daniel, b. 19 May 1904, Paris, France. Writer. Num. publs. incl: L'Enchantement du Vendredi Saint, 1925; La Peste Brune, 1933; Fascisme & Grand Capital, 1936; Shakespeare & Gide en correctionnelle? , 1959; Le Grain sous la Neige, 1961; L'Anarchisme, 1965; Pour un Marxisme Libertaire, 1969; Essai sur la Révolution sexuelle, 1969; Front Populaire revolution manquée, 1970; Ni Dieu ni Maître, 1971; Autobiographie de jeunesse, 1971; La Concentration économique aux Etats-Unis, 1971; Rosa Luxemburg & la spontanéité révolutionnaire, 1971; Bourgeois & bras nus, 1973; De l'Oncle Tom aux Panthéres, 1973; Ci-gît le Colonialisme 1930-1972, 1974; L'Armée en France, 1974; Introduction to selected writings Trotsky, Gauguin, Fourier. Contbr. to sev. jrnls. Address: 13 Rue des Marronniers, 75016 Paris, France.

GUERRA GARRIDO, Raul, b. 4 Apr. 1935, San Sebastian, Spain. Pharmacist. Educ: Ph.D., Univ. of Madrid. Publs (novels) Ni Hereo ni Nada, 1969; Cacereño, 1970; El Pornografo, 1971; Ay!, 1972; La Ruga de un Cerebro, 1973; Hipotesis, 1974; (tech. book) Medicamentos Españoles, 1972. Contbr. to Destino (Barcelona). Mbrships: Pres., Colegio Oficial de Framecéuticos de Guipúzcoa; Asociación de Escritores Guipuzcoanos. Hons: Prize, City of San Sebastián, 1968; Prize, City of Oviedo, 1972; Prize, Assn. of Ibero-Am. Writer, N.Y., 1973. Address: Paseo de los Olmos 5, San Sebastián, Spain.

GUEST, Anthony Gordon, b. 8 Feb. 1930, Bristol, UK. Professor of Law, King's College, University of London. Educ: M.A., St. John's Coll., Oxford Univ.; Barrister-at-law, Gray's Inn, London. Publs: Ed., Anson's Law of Contract 21st to 24th eds., 1959-75; Asst. Ed., Chitty on Contracts, 22nd ed., 1961, Gen. Ed. 23rd ed., 1968; Ed., Oxford Essays in Jurisprudence, 1961; The Law of Hire Purchase, 1966; Gen. Ed., Benjamin's Sale of Goods, 1974. Contbr. to: Law Quarterly Review; Mod. Law Review. Mbrships. incl: UN Commn. on Int. Trade Law, N.Y. & Geneva, 1968-74 (Deleg.); Garrick Club. Address: 6 Carrington House, 6 Hertford St., London W1, UK.

GUEST, Ivor Forbes, b. 14 Apr. 1920, Chislehurst, Kent, UK. Solicitor. Educ: M.A., Trinity Coll., Cambridge. Publs. incl: Napoleon III in England, 1952; The Ballet of the Second Empire, 1953-55, 2nd ed. 1974; Fanny Cerrito, 1956; Adeline Genee, 1958; The Alhambra Ballet, 1959; The Dancer's Heritage, 1960; La Fille mal gardee, 1960; The Empire Ballet, 1962; A Gallery of Romantic Ballet, 1965; The Romantic Ballet in Paris, 1966; The Pas de Quatre, 1969; Carlotta Zambelli, 1969; Dandies & Dancers, 1969; Fanny Elssler, 1970; Two Coppelias, 1970. Mbrships: Chmn., Royal Acad. of Dancing, 1969-; Vice-Chmn., Brit. Theatre Mus. Assn., 1966-; Soc. for Theatre Rsch. Address: 17 Holland Park, London W11 3TD, UK.

GUGOV, Nikola Delchev, pen name VEZHINOV, Pavel, b. 9 Nov. 1914, Sofia, Bulgaria. Writer. Publs: Second Company, 1949; For the Honour of the Fatherland, 1949; The Tracks Remain, 1959; The Boy with the Violin, 1963; With the Smell of Almonds, 1966; The Stars Above, 1966; Self-Confession, 1973; The End of Ajax, 1973. Contbr. to: September; Savremennik; Literatouren Front. Mbrships: PEN; Union of Bulgarian Writers. Hons: Dimitrov Prizes, 1950, 1951, 1971; Prize, Union of Bulgarian Writers, 1966; People's Worker of Culture, 1970; Hero of Socialist Labour, 1974. Address: Sofia, ul. Oborishte 1-a, Bulgaria.

GUICE, John David Wynne, b. 24 Mar. 1931, Biloxi, Miss., USA. Professor of History. Educ: B.A., Yale Univ., 1952; M.A., Univ. Texas, El Paso, 1953; Ph.D., Univ. Colo., 1969. Publs: The Rocky Mountain Bench: The Territorial Supreme Courts of Colorado, Montana & Wyoming 1861-1890, 1972. Contbr. to: The Am. Territorial System, 1973; Atlas of Miss., 1974; Mont. Mag. Western Hist.; Colo. Mag.; Histn.; Southern Quarterly; Am. Jrnl. Legal Hist.; etc. Mbrships. incl: Western Hist. Assn. (Mbrship. Chmn., 1972-74); Org. Am. Histns. Recip., Cert. Commendation for Rocky Mountain Bench by Am. Assn. of State & Local Hist., 1974. Address: 3010 Mesa Dr., Hattiesburg, MS 39401, USA.

GUICHARDAN, Roger Jean-Baptiste, pen name OUVARD, Jacques, b. 16 Oct. 1906, Chambery, France. Priest; Journalist. Educ: D.Th.; Lic.-ès-Lettres. Publs: Le problème de la simplicité divine en Orient et en Occident au XIV° XV siècles, 1933; Jean Traversat, héros de la résitance, 1945; La chasse aux propheties. Pourquoi je fuis les cartomanciennes, 1945; Sainteté des mamans, trans. Italian, Spanish & Portuguese, 1967; 14 novels under pen name. Contbr. to: Pélerin du XX° siècle (Ed.). Mbrships. incl: Savoie Acad.; Soc., Gens de Lettres; Soc. Cath. Writers. Hons: Prix Antoine Borrel, 1971; Off. de la Légion d'Honneur. Address: 8 Rue François 1°, Paris 75008, France.

GUIDO, Cecily Margaret, b. 5 Aug. 1912, West Wickham, Kent, UK. Archaeologist. Educ: Univ. Coll., London. Publs: Syracuse, 1958; Sardinia, 1963; Sicily: An Archaeological Guide, 1968; Southern Italy: An Archaeological Guide, 1972. Contbr. to: Archaeologia; Antiquaries Jrnl.; Antiquity; Proceedings of the Prehistoric Soc.; etc. Mbrships: Soc. of Antiquaries; Inst. of Archaeology; Prehistoric Soc.; Royal Archaeological Inst.; Soc. of Antiquaries of Scotland. Address: 3 Brook St., Bath BA1 2LN, UK.

GUINNESS, Bryan Walter (Lord Moyne), b. 27 Oct. 1905, London, UK. Writer; Company Director. Educ: M.A., Oxford Univ.; Barrister-at-Law. Publs. incl: (poetry) Under the Eyelid, 1935; Collected Poems, 1956; The Rose in the Tree, 1964; The Clock, 1973; (novels) Landscape with Figures, 1934; A Week by the Sea, 1936; Lady C's Companion, 1938; A Fugue of Cinderellas, 1956; Leo & Rosabelle, 1961; The Giant's Eye, 1964; The Engagement, 1969; (short stories) The Girl & the Flower, 1966; (autobiographical essays) Dairy Not Kept, 1975; 6 books for children, 1936-60. Contbr. to: New Statesman; Spectator; Dublin Mag.; Country Life. Mbrships. incl: F.R.S.L.; PEN; Irish Acad. of Letters. Recip., Hon. LL.D. Address: Knockmaroon House, Castleknock, Co. Dublin, Repub. of Ireland.

GUIRDHAM, Arthur, b. 1905, Workington, UK. Senior Consultant Psychiatrist (Ret'd, 1968). Educ: M.D., M.A., B.Sc., Keble Coll., Oxford; Charing Cross Hosp., London. Publs: A Theory of Disease, 1957; Christ & Freud, 1959; Man, Divine or Social, 1960; Cosmic Factors in Disease, 1963; The Nature of Healing, 1964; The Cathars & Reincarnation; The Gibbet & the Cross, 1970; Obsession, 1972; A Foot in Both Worlds, 1974. Contbr. to: Sci. of Thought Review; Man, Myth & Magic; Pulse; The Gen. Practitioner. Address: 146 High Street, Bathford, Bath, Somerset, UK.

GUIREC, Jean, b. 31 July 1898, Bordeaux, France. Writer. Publs. incl: (major novels) La Maison au bord du Monde, 1937; l'Enchantement de la Nuit, 1938; Le Crime des Indifférents, 1939; La Troisième Cour, 1948; La Cité immobile, 1951; La Fontaine des Innocents, 1957; Le Signe Féminin, 1960. Contbr. to num. lit. & acad. jrnls. Mbrships. incl: Hon. Pres., Soc. des Gens de Lettres de France; Hon. Pres., Ecrivains & Artistes de Champagne; PEN; Assn. des Ecrivains Combattants. Hons. incl: Cmdr., Légion d'Honneur, 1955; Croix de Guerre, 1918; Prix Blumenthal de Lit., 1930; Grand Prix de la Critique Poétique, 1973. Address: 40 rue de Seine, 75006, Paris, France.

GULLACE, Gino, b. 18 Aug. 1925, Ferruzzano, Reggio Calabria, Italy. Journalist; Author. Educ: Dott. in Lettere, Messina Univ.; M.A., Rochester Univ., N.Y., USA; Ph.D., Syracuse Univ., N.Y. Publs: Numero Unico, 1946; Pragmatism in Italy, 1952; American Influence on Post War Italy, 1958; I Grandi Nomi del Ventesimo Secolo (biographical studies), 1973-74. Contbr. to: Oggi: Annabella; Novella; Le Vie d'Italia & del Mondo; Enciclopedia Rizzoli-Larousse; Enciclopedia dei Ragazzi. Mbrships: Overseas Press Club, NYC; Foreign Press Assn., NYC. Address: 38 Van Ness Ct., Maplewood, NJ 07040, USA.

GULLANDER, Eric Gustaf Bertil, pen name BGr, b. 21 May 1915, Stockholm, Sweden. Author; Artist. Educ: Art studies, Stockholm, Vienna, Spain & Portugal. Publs. incl: (in Swedish) Scandinavian Butterflies, 1959, 2nd ed., 1971; Isle on the Equator, 1962; Scandinavian Moths I, 1964, 2nd ed., 1972; Linnaeus in Lapland, 1969; Linnaeus in Öland, 1970; Linnaeus in Gotland, 1971. Scandinavian Moths II, 1971; The Book of Birds by Olof Rudbeck, 1971. Contbr. to newspapers & jrnls. Mbr., Swedish Authors' Soc. Hons. incl: Cultural Prize, Swedish Authors' Soc., 1970 & 1971. Address: Finn, Malmgrens Plan 1. 121 48 Johanneshov, Stockholm, Sweden.

GULLICK, Charles Francis William Rowley, b. 1907, London, UK. Senior Research Fellow, St. Edmund Hall, Oxford. Educ: B.Litt., M.A., Queen's Coll., Oxford. Publs: Economic Geography; Oxford Economic Atlas of the World; Pictorial Atlas of the Oxford Region. Contbr. to: Geog. & geol. periodicals; Chamber's Ency. Mbr., Royal Geog. Soc. Address: Aniwa, Kirk Michael, Isle of Man, UK.

GULLICK, Etta, b. 7 Sept. 1916, Elstree, UK. Teacher. Educ: M.A., Univ. of Oxford. Publs (w. M. Hollings): The One Who Listens, 1971; It's Me, O Lord, 1972; The Shade of His Hand, 1973. Contbr. to: Clergy Review; New Fire; Mount Carmel; La Vie Spirituelle; Studi Cattolici; Dictionnaire de Spiritualité. Address: Aniwa, Kirk Michael, Isle of Man, UK.

GULLICK, John Michael, b. 6 Feb. 1916, Bristol, UK. Solicitor. Educ: M.A., Christ's Coll., Cambridge; London Schl. of Econ. Chartered Sec. Publs: Indigenous Political Systems of Western Malaya, 1960; Malaysia & its Neighbours, 1966. Contbr. to: Jrnl. of the Royal Asiatic Soc. Address: 47 Spareleaze Hill, Loughton, Essex IG10 1BS, UK.

GULSTON, Charles, b. 10 Oct. 1913, Johannesburg, S. Africa. Journalist; Author. Publs: And the Dreaming (poems), 1948; Co-Ed., South African Poetry — A New Anthology, 1948; No Greater Heritage, 1960; Eternity is for Everyman, 1971. Contbr. to: Sunday Express, Johannesburg; Natal Daily News (Mbr. Ed. Staff, 20 yrs.); Natal Mercury (Mbr. Ed. Staff, 5 yrs.); var. other S. African newspapers; Personality; The Christian Minister; Signs of the Times; other mags.; Radio S. Africa. Address: Amberwoods, 59 Everton Rd., Kloof, Natal, Repub. of S. Africa.

GUMMÉRUS, Edward Robert, pen name ERG, b. 5 Oct. 1905, Helsingfors, Finland. Author; Translator. Educ: M.A., Univ. of Helsingfors; Bach. ès Lettres, Univ. of Grenoble, France. Publs. incl: Storia Delle Letterature Della Finlandia, 1957; Italienska Vandringar, 1966; Scoperta Di Andrea Giovene, 1967; Främmande Berättelser, 1972; Palatset Med Kolonnerna, 1974; Virveln, 1975. Contbr. to var. lit. publs. Mbrships: Sveriges Författarförbund (Swedish Authors' Union); Sveriges Översättarförbund; Finlands Svenska Författarförening. Hons: Nordiska Romanpriset, 1942; Översättarpriset, 1972. Address: 78045 Björbo, Sweden.

GUNAWARDANE, Hema, b. 9 May 1924, Colombo, Sri Lanka. Journalist. Educ: B.A.; Painting, Govt. Schl. of Fine

Arts. Contbr. to: Dinamina, Sri Lanka (Staff Feature Writer, 1953–, Ldr. Writer, 1953–); Women's & Children's Pages (Ed.). Contbr. to var. mags. Mbrships: Sri Lanka Br., Royal Asiatic Soc.; Ceylon Soc. of Arts. Address: No. 30, 'Nugagahawatta', Kirulapone, Colombo 5, Sri Lanka.

GUNDRY, Dudley William, b. 1916, Falmouth, Cornwall, UK. Canon & Chancellor of Leicester Cathedral. Educ: King's College, London; B.D., A.K.C., M.Th. Publs: Religions: An Historical & Theological Study, 1958; Neils Bible Companion: Israel's Neighbours, 1959; The Teacher & the World Religions, 1968. Contbr. to: Theology; Man; Hibbert Jrnl.; Hist.; Scottish Jrnl. of Theology; (Ed.) Leicester Cathedral Quarterly. Mbr., Athenaeum. Address: 3 Morland Ave., Leicester LE2 2PF, UK.

GUNN, Donald Livingston, b. 15 Feb. 1905, Llanishen, Cardiff, UK. Zoologist. Educ: D.Sc., Univ. Coll., Cardiff; Ph.D., Birmingham Univ. Publs: The Orientation of Animals (w. G. S. Fraenkel), UK 1940, USA 1961; Behaviour of Desert Locusts & Control by Aircraft Spraying (co-author), 1948; Red Locust Control by Aircraft in Tanganyika (co-author), 1948; Pesticides, 1972-75. Contbr. to: Jrnl. of Expmtl. Biol.; Nature; Jrnl. of R.S.A.; etc. Mbrships. incl: Soc. of Authors; Soc. of Expmtl. Biol.; Fellow & Pres. (one-time Treas.), Royal Entomol. Soc.; Fellow, Inst. of Biol.; One-time Pres., Assn. Applied Biol. Hons: Medal, R.S.A., 1951; C.B.E., 1958. Address: Well Cottage, Taylors Hill, Chilham, Kent CT4 8BZ, UK.

GUNN, James, b. 12 July 1923, Kan. City, Mo., USA. Teacher; University Professor of English. Educ: B.S., 1947, M.A., 1951, Univ. of Kan. Publs. incl: Station in Space, 1958; The Joy Makers, 1961; The Immortals, 1962; Future Imperfect, 1964; The Witching Hour, 1970; The Immortal, 1970; The Burning, 1972; Breaking Point, 1972; The Listeners, 1972; Some Dreams are Nightmares, 1974; Alternate Worlds, 1975. Contbr. to var. sci. fiction & other publs. Mbrships: Pres., Sci. Fiction Writers of Am., 1971-72; Exec. Comm., Sci. Fiction Rsch. Assn. Recip., Byron Caldwell Smith Award, 1970. Address: 2149 Quail Creek Drive, Lawrence, KS 66044, USA.

GUNN, John, b. 26 Feb. 1925, Northumberland, UK. Public Relations Consultant. Educ: Royal Aust. Naval Coll.; Sydney Univ. Publs. incl: Humpy in the Hills; The Goodbye Island; Dangerous Enemies; Flying for You; Acting for You; Sailing & Ships for you; Sea Menace; The Wild Abyss; The Raging of the Sea (play); Barrier Reef by Trimaran; The Man Who Was Too Rich; The Spoils of War; Ed., The Gold Smugglers; Ed., The Gravity Stealers. Contbr. to: Times; Fin. Review; Sydney Morning Herald; A.B.C. Mbrships: Royal Sydney Yacht Squadron; P.R. Inst. Of Aust. Recip., Book of Yr. Award, Children's Book Coun., 1959. Address: 4 The Bartizan, Castlecrag, N.S.W. 2068, Australia.

GUNN, Neil Miller, b. 1891, Caithness, UK. Author. Educ: LL.D. Publs. incl: The Grey Coast; Hidden Doors; Morning Tide; The Lost Glen; Sun Circle; Highland River; Off In a Boat; Wild Geese Overhead; Second Sight; The Serpent; The Key of the Chest; The Drinking Well; The Silver Bough; The Shadow; The White Hour; Highland Pack; The Lost Chart; Bloodhunt; Other Landscape; The Atom of Delight; Storm & Precipice; Whisky & Scotland. Contbr. to Am. & Brit. periodicals. Address: Dalcraig, Kessock, Inverness, UK.

GUNNARSON, Gunnar Julius, b. 6 June 1918, Stockholm, Sweden. Editor; Author. Publs. incl: Vardagsljud – evighetsackord (essays), 1959; Ryssland 1917, 1967; Georg Lukács (biog. & critique), 1969; Lenin (biog.), 1970; Pariskommunen 1871, 1971; Social demokratiskt idiarv (history of ideas), 1971. Contbr. to Swedish periodicals. Mbrships: Swedish Authors' Union; Publicists' Club. Hons: Carl Albert Anderssons Stipend, 1971. Address: Orrmingeringen 18, 132 00 Saltsjo-Boo, Sweden.

GUNNARSSON, Gunnar, b. 18 May 1889, Iceland. Author. Publs. incl: Ströndin, 1915; Vargur í véum, 1916; Drengurinn, 1917; The Sworn Brothers, 1918, Engl. 1920; Seven Days' Darkness, 1920, Engl. 1930; Ships in the Sky I-V, 1923-28, Engl. 1937; The Night & the Dream, 1938; The Black Cliffs, 1929, Engl. 1967; Jón Arason, 1930; Vikivaki, 1932; Blindhus, 1933; Grámann, 1936; Adventa, 1937, Engl. 1940; Heidaharmur, 1940; Sálumessa, 1952; Brimhenda, 1954; & 6 vols. short stories; & 4 plays. Mbrships: Mark Twain Int. Soc; PEN; Congress of Cultural

Freedom, Iceland. Hons: Kt. of Dannebrog; Grand Cross, Order of Icelandic Falcon; Dr. Litt. Isl. h. c., 1974. Address: Dyngjuvegi 8, Reykjavik, Iceland.

GUNSTON, Bill, b. 1927, London, UK. Editor. Educ: Univ. Coll., Durham; Northampton Engrng. Coll., London. Publs: Flight Handbook, 1962; Your Book of Light, 1968; Hydrofoils & Hovercraft, 1969; The Jet Age, 1971; Transport Problems & Prospects, 1972; Transport Technology, 1972; Conquest of the Air, 1972; Bombers of the West, 1973; Shaping Metals, 1973; Attack Aircraft of the West, 1974; The Philatelist's Companion, 1975. Contbr. to: Jane's All the World's Aircraft; Brassey's Annual; etc. Mbr., Assn. of Brit. Sci. Writers. Agent: Donald Copeman. Address: Foxbreak, Courts Mount Rd., Haslemere, Surrey GU27 2PP, UK.

GUNSTON, David. Founder-Editor, Country Journal. Publs: Questions Answered About Wild Life in Britain; The Sea of Whales; Birds & You; Keenie: The Story of a Kestrel Hawk; More Adventures of Keenie; Ed., Best Nature Stories; Lawnswood Chronicles; Frenchmen's Gold; Michael Faraday – Father of Electricity; Marconi – Father of Radio; The Young Samuel Pepys; Finding Out About the Japanese; Guglielmo Marconi. Agent: Rupert Crew Ltd. Address: c/o Agent, King's Mews, Gray's Inn Rd., London WC1, UK.

GUNTER, Gordon, b. 18 Aug. 1909, Goldonna, La., USA. Marine Zoologist. Educ: B.A., La. State Normal Coll., 1929; M.A., 1931, Ph.D., 1945, Univ. of Tex. Contbr., 350 articles, sci. & profl. jrnls., & popular articles, reviews; Ed., Publs. of Inst. of Marine Sci., 1950-55; Assoc. Ed., Bulletin of Marine Sci., Gulf & Caribbean, 1961-64; Ed., Gulf Rsch. Reports, Gulf Coast Rsch. Lab., 1961. Address: P.O. Box AG, Ocean Springs, MS 39564, USA.

GUNTER, Norma, b. 11 May 1900, Covington, Ky., USA. Homemaker. Publs: The Moorpark Story, 1969; A Diamond for Moorpark, 1974. Mbrships: Ventura Histl. Soc.; Pleasant Valley Histl. Soc.; Simi Valley Histl. Soc.; Ebell of LA, 52 yrs. Address: P.O. Box 482, Moorpark, CA 93021, USA.

GUNTHER, Albert Everard, b. 1903, Heacham, UK. Retired Geologist & Administrator, International Oil Company. Educ: B.A., Univ. of Oxford. Publs: German War for Crude Oil in Europe, 1947; Rolfe Family Records, 1962; Early Science in Oxford, vol. 15, 1967; A Century of Zoology in the British Museum, 1814-1914, 1975; Life of William C. M'Intosh, F.R.S., Pioneer in Marine Biology, 1838-1931, 1976. Contbr. to: Jrnl. of the Soc. of Bibliog. & Natural Hist. Mbrships: Fellow, Geol. Soc.; F.R.G.S.; Authors' Club; Alpine Club. Address: 5 Windmill Hill, Hampstead, London NW3, UK.

GUPTA, Brijen Kishore, b. 17 Sept. 1929, Ferozpur, India. Professor of History. Educ: A.B., Dayanand Coll., 1952; A.M., Yale Univ., 1954; Ph.D., Univ. of Chgo., 1958. Publs: Sirajuddaulah & the East India Company, 1756-1757: Background to the Foundation of British Power in India, 1962, revised 1966; Indian & American Labor Legislation & Practices: A Comparative Study (w. A. P. Aggarwal), 1966; India in English Fiction, 1800-1970: An Annotated Bibliography (Ed.), 1973. Contbr. to: Mankind; Jrnl. of Asian Studies; Engl. Histl. Review; Middle E. Jrnl.; Jrnl. of the Nat. Acad. of Admin.; Jrnl. of Indian Hist.; Man & World. Mbrships: Wattumull Prize Comm., Am. Histl. Assn., 1966-69; Assn. for Asian Studies. Address: 226 Idlewood Rd., Rochester, NY 14618, USA.

GUPTA, Sudhansu, b. 17 July 1919, Calcutta, Bengal, India. Writer. Educ: M.A. Publs: (novels) Atmar Glani, 1957; Ghurni Natch, 1960; (poetry) Avhudaya, 1951; Madhukhyara, 1953; Sanchaye, 1950; Bichitra, 1955; Baliuyugar opar holta, 1968; Shimenta Shakal, 1970; Alor Avishar, 1974; (Engl. drama) Famine Fury, 1942; Raktanesha, 1950; etc. Contbr. to: Lokshevak; Janasevak; Bhasa Bharati; Shamhati; Howraah Barta; Sammelan; etc. Mbrships: Tagora Rsch. Inst., Calcutta; PEN; All India Lit. Soc.; Sec., Life Mbr., Banga Bhasa Samity; Ed., Bhabikal Jrnl., Bhabikal Sahitya Basar. Hons: Essay Prize, Delhi, 1961; Burnpur, Short Story, 1965, 1972. Address: 37 E Suren Sarker Rd., Calcutta 10, India.

GURR, Edward, b. 1905, Leicester, UK. Biologist; Writer. Educ: Coll. of Art & Tech., Leicester, UK; Chelsea Coll. of Sci. & Tech., London; Ph.D., Univ. Coll., Cork. Publs: A Practical Manual of Medical & Biological Staining

Techniques, 1953; Methods of Analytical Histology & Histochemistry, 1958; Encyclopaedia of Microscopic Stains, 1960; Staining Animal Tissues, 1962; Rational Uses of Dyes in Biology, 1965; Synthetic dyes in Biology, Medicine & Chemistry, 1971; Biological Staining Methods, 1973. Mbrships: F.R.I.C.; F.L.S.; Fellow, Inst. of Biol.; F.R.M.S.; F.S.D.C. Address: Michrome Laboratories, 42 Upper Richmond Rd. W., London SW14, UK.

GURR, Marjorie Ruth, b. 1917, Sussex, UK. Nurse; Tutor. Educ: SRN; SCM; RNT. Publs: Blood Groups (co-author). Mbrships: Royal Coll. of Nursing; Nurse Tchrs. Assn.; Examiner, Gen. Nursing Coun.; Assn. of Hlth. Careers Advsrs. Address: 25 Hillside, Southwick, Brighton BN4 4QD, UK.

GÜRSTER, Eugen, pen names STEINHAUSEN, Herrman; LEPEL, Herrman, b. 23 June 1895, Fürth, Bavaria, Germany. Writer; Former Diplomat. Educ: Ph.D., Univ. of Munich, 1921. Publs. incl: Nietzsche und die Musik, 1924; Weather Changeable (play), 1929; The Future of Freedom, 1937; The Role of Evil in History, 1939; Volk in Dunkel, 1944; Taboos unserer Zeit, 1960; Our Lost Ego, 1967; Narrheiten und Wahrheiten, 1973. Contbr. to: Die Neue Rundschau, Frankfurt; Hochland, Munich. Mbrships: PEN; Acad. of German Lang. & Lit. Hons: Bundesverdienstkreuz, 1972; Bavarian Order for Special Merits, 1974. Address: "Augustinum", Apt. 655, Stiftsbogen 74, 8 Munich 70, German Fed. Repub.

GUSTAF-JANSON, Gösta, pen name G.G-J., b. 6 Nov. 1902, Saltsjö-Duunäs, Nacka, Sweden. Writer. Educ: Univs. of Munich, Germany & Stockholm. Publs. incl: Gubben Kommer, 1934; Stora Famnen, 1937; Stampen, 1951; Över Onda & Goda, 1957; Kärlekens Decimaler, 1959; Pärlemor, 1960; Kastanjeprinsessan, 1961; Råtunaleken, 1962; Kung Vankelmod, 1963; Då Oskulden & Friden, 1968; Då Lasten var en Häxa, 1969; I Sommarns Friska Vind, 1970; De Långa Lömska Kiven, 1971; Tungt i den Branta Backen, 1972; Works transl'd into Danish, Engl., Finnish, French, Dutch, Norwegian, Spanish, Czech, German & Hungarian. Contbr. to var. jrnls., 1926–. Mbrships: PEN; Publicistklubben, Stockholm. Address: 26090 Båstad, Köpmansgat. 13, Sweden.

GUSTAFSON, Ralph Barker, b. 16 Aug. 1909, Lime Ridge, P.Q., Can. Poet; University Professor. Educ: M.A., Bishop's Univ., Can.; M.A., Oxford Univ., UK; D.Litt., Mt. Allison, Can. Publs: Flight into Darkness, 1944; Rivers among Rocks, 1960; Rocky Mountain Poems, 1960; Sift in an Hourglass, 1966; Ixion's Wheel. 1969; Pengiun Book of Canadian Verse (ed.), 1969; Theme & Variations for Sounding Brass, 1972; Selected Poems, 1972; Fire on Stone, 1974; The Brazen Tower (short stories), 1974. Contbr. to num. mags. & jrnls. Mbr., League of Can. Poets. Hons. incl: Fellowship, Can. Coun.; Univ. Poet in Residence, Bishop's Univ. Address: P.O. Box 172, N. Hatley, P.Q., Can.

GUSTAFSSON, Lars Erik Einar, b. 17 May 1936, Vasteras, Sweden. Writer. Educ: D.Phil., Univ. of Uppsala, 1961. Publs. incl: Poeten Brumbergs sista dagar och död (novel), 1969; Ballongfararna (poetry), 1962; Den nattliga hyllningen (drama), 1970; Herr Gustafsson sjalv (novel), 1971; Yllet (novel), 1973. Contbr. to Swedish, European & US reviews. Mbrships: Akad. der Wissenschaften und der Literatur, Mainz; Akad. der Künste, Berlin. Hons: Fellowship of W. Berlin, 1972. Address: Blasbogatan 8, 722 15 Vasteras, Sweden.

GUSTAITIS, Algirdas, b. 5 Oct. 1916, Mogiliavas, Lithiania. Writer; Journalist. Educ: Vilniun Univ., Lithuania; Goethe Univ., Frankfurt. Publs. incl: Tarp Sveicarijos ir Danijos, 1946; Algis Trakys ir Taksiukas Sleivys, Part I, 1959, Part II, 1962; Lietuva – Europos nugaletoja, 1961; 200.000.000 And Lithuania, 1971. Contbr. to: Ed., Hanau Lietuviai; Laisvoji Lietuva; Lietuviu Enciklopedija; Ency. Lituanica; Gabija; Pradalge; num. Lithuanian-lang. jrnls. Mbrships. incl: Hollywood For. Press Assn.; Bd., Lit. Soc., Univ. of Vytautas the Great, Kaunas, Lithuania. Recip., Hon. Lit. Award, Lithuania, 1943. Address: 1207 N. Detroit St., L.A., CA 90046, USA.

GUTH, Oscar Alphons, b. 15 July 1918, Vienna, Austria. Executive Assistant, University School of Physics. Educ: Hochschule für Welthandel, Vienna. Publs: (Prod. Ed., 17 books, inclng.) Science for High School Students, 1964; Senior Science for High School Students, 3 vols., 1966; Pioneering in Outer Space, 1970; Brain Mechanisms & the Control of Behaviour, 1972; Solar Energy Today &

Tomorrow, 1974. Contbr. of articles on int. affairs, sci. & educ. to Aust. & UK jrnls.; War Corres., United Press of Am., WWII; Asst. Ed., Egyptian Mail, Cairo, 1946-48; Ed., Aust. press & mag., 1948-60. Mbrships: Aust. Soc. of Authors; Press Club, London. Address: 3 Darling Pt. Rd., Darling Pt., Sydney 2027, Australia.

GUTHRIE, A(lfred) B(ertram), Jr., b. 13 Jan. 1901, Bedford, Ind., USA. Writer; Former Journalist. Educ: Univ. of Wash., 1919-20; A.B., Univ. of Mont., 1923. Publs: (novels) Murders at Moon Dance, USA, 1943, UK, 1961; The Big Sky, USA & UK, 1947; The Way West, USA, 1949, UK, 1950; These Thousand Hills, USA, 1956, UK, 1957; The Blue Hen's Chick, 1965; Anfive, 1971; (short stories) The Big It & Other Stories, 1960; (screenplays) Shane, 1951; The Kentuckian, 1953. Contbr. to: Esquire. Hons. incl: Litt.D., Univ. of Mont., 1949; Pulitzer Prize, 1950; Jr. Book Award, Boys' Clubs of Am., 1951; Nat. Assn. Independent Schls. Award, 1961. Address: Twin Lakes, Chateau, MT 59422, USA.

GUTHRIE, John, b. 1908, Antwerp, Belgium. Ship & Engineer Surveyor (Retired). Educ: Univ. of Strathclyde, UK. Publs: Bizarre Ships of the Nineteenth Century, 1970; A History of Marine Engineering, 1971. Mbrships: Chartered Engr.; Fellow, Inst. of Mech. Engrs.; Inst. of Marine Engrs. Address: 15 Edensor Rd., Meads, Eastbourne, Sussex, UK.

GUTHRIE, Kathleen, b. Feltham, Middx., UK. Artist. Educ: Slade Schl., London. Publs: The Magic Button; The Magic Button Goes to the Moon, 1962. Mbrships: Free Painters & Sculptors; Women's Int. Art Club. Address: 6 Mall Studios, Taskey Rd., Parkhill Rd., London NW3, UK.

GÜTT, Dieter, b. 24 Feb. 1924, Marienwerder, Germany. Journalist. Educ: M.D., Univ. of Cologne. Publs: Es Spricht Dieter Gütt, 1969; Verlorene Geschichte, 1970; Contbr. to: German TV broadcasts; Abendzeitung; Express; For. Affairs; Europa-Archiv. Mbr., Nat. Acad. of TV arts & Scis. Hons: Adolf Grimme Press Award, 1970; Bambi, 1969; Carl von Ossietzky Prize, 1970. Address: 10 W. 66 St., N.Y., NY 10023, USA.

GUTTERIDGE, Thomas Gordon Lindsay, b. 20 May 1923, Easington, Durham, UK. Writer. Educ: Art Schl. Publs: Cold War in a Country Garden, 1971; Killer Pine, 1973; Fratricide is a Gas, forthcoming. Address: 15 Howdale Rd., Downham Mkt., Norfolk PE38 9AB, UK.

GUTTSMAN, Wilhelm Leo, b. 23 Aug. 1920, Berlin, Germany. University Librarian. Educ: B.Sc., 1946; M.Sc., 1952. Publs: The British Political Elite, 1963; A Plea for Democracy, 1967; The English Ruling Class, 1969. Contbr. to: Brit. Jrnl. of Sociol.; Int. Review of Soc. Hist.; Jrnl. of Documentation; Jrnl. of Libnship. Mbr., Brit. Sociol. Assn. Address: 20 Mill Hill Rd., Norwich NR2 3DP, UK.

GUZMAN, Martin Luiz, b. 6 Oct. 1887. Journalist; Politician. Educ: Mexico Univ. Publs. incl: La querella de Mexico, 1915; Aventuras democraticas, 1929; Javier Mina, 1932; El hombre y sus armas, 1938; Memorias de Pancho Villa, 1951; Maestros rurales y Piratas y Corsarios, 1960; Necesidad de cumplir las leyes de Reforma, 1963; Febrero de 1913, 1963; Cronicas de mi destierro, 1963. Contbr. to: El Imparcial; Fndr., El Mundo, 1922; Fndr. & Dir., Tiempo, Mexico, 1942-; etc. Mbr., Nat. Commn. de los Libros de Texto Gratuitos, (Pres.). Address: Barcelona 32, Apdo. 1122, Mexico, D.F.

GWYNN, Harri, b. 14 Feb. 1913, London, UK. Broadcaster. Educ: B.A.(Hons.), Dip.Ed., M.A. Publs: Barddoniaeth Harri Gwynn, 1955; Y Fuwch a'i Chynffon, 1957. Contbr. to: Y Llenor; Taliesin; Barn; Traethodydd; etc. Mbr., Yr Acadami Gymreig. Hons: var. Eisteddfodic Crowns. Address: Tyddyn Rhuddallt, Llanrug, Caernarfon, Wales, UK.

GYÁRFÁS, Miklós, b. 6 Dec. 1915, Gyor, Hungary. Author; University Professor. Publs: The Role, 1956; Self-Portrait in Costume, 1965; It was once a Theatre, 1970; In the Workroom of the Humour, 1973; The Liontamer, 1973. Hons: József Attila, 1954; Batsányi, 1966. Address: Nógrdoli út 2/6, 1125 Budapest, Hungary.

GYLLENSTEN, Lars Johan Wictor, pen name WICTOR, Jan, b. 12 Nov. 1921, Stockholm, Sweden. Professor of Histology; Author. Educ: M.D. Publs. incl: Camera obscura (poetry, w. T. Greitz), 1946; Moderna myter (miscellany), 1949; Barnabok (novel), 1952; Senilia (novel), 1956;

Sokrates död (novel), 1960; Desparados (short stories), 1962; Juvenilia (novel), 1965; Palatset i parken (novel), 1970; Ur min offentliga sektor (essays), 1971; Grottan i öknen (novel), 1973. Contbr. to: Dagens Nyheter. Mbrships: Swedish Acad.; Nobel Comm. for Lit. Hons. incl: Lilla Nobelpriset, 1972. Address: Karlavägen 121, 115 26 Stockholm, Sweden.

GYÖRE, Imre, b. 2 Dec. 1934, Keszthely, Hungary. Poet. Educ: B.A. Publs: (poetry) Zuhogj csak ár (Rush on, Tide), 1958; Korbácsos ének (Whip-Songs), 1959; Utazás (Journey), 1962; Ünneplés médozatokkal (Celebrations with Modifications), 1965; Halá lüzö (Death Chaser), 1966; Fényem, feketeségem (My Light, My Darkness), 1967; Elöjátékok (Preludes), 1970; Balgatag leányzók (Foolish Maidens); (oratorio) Orfeo szerelme (The Love of Orfeo), 1969; (plays) Cassandra, 1973; St. Joan, 1973. Contbr. to: Magyar Nemzet. Mbr., Union Hungarian Writers. Recip., Gabor Andor Lit. Prize, 1958. Address: H-1053 Budapest, Kecskemeti utca 9, Hungary.

GYURKOVICS, Tibor, b. 18 Dec. 1931, Budapest, Hungary. Poet; Writer; Playwright. Educ: M.A., Eötvös Lorant Univ.; Prof.'s Dip., Trng. Coll. for Tchrs. of Handicapped Children, Budapest. Publs: Grafit (poems), 1961; Kenyértörés (poems), 1963; Emberfia (poems), 1965; Estére Meghalsz (play), 1969; Vaskakas (poems), 1970; Rikiki (stories), 1970; Az Öreg (play), 1971; Ne szeress, ne szeress (novel), 1971; Nagyvizit (play), 1972; Üveggolyó (stories), 1972; Isten nem szerencsejátékos (novel), 1971; Elcseréljük egymast (stories), 1972; Öszinte részvétem (play), 1973. Contbr. to jrnls. Mbr., lit. orgs. Address: Karinthy Frigyes ut 44, H-1111 Budapest, Hungary.

H

HAAVIKKO, Paavo Juhani, b. 25 Jan. 1931, Helsinki, Finland. Literary Director. Publs: (novels) Yksityisia asioita, 1960; Toinen taivas ja maa, 1961; Vuodet, 1962; (short stories) Lasi Claudius Civiliksen salaliittolaisten poydalla, 1964; (poems) Tiet etaisyyksiin, 1951; Synnyinmaa, 1955; Talvipalatsi, 1959; Puut, kaikki heidan vihreytensa, 1966; Kaksikymmenta ja yksi, 1974; (plays) Ylilaakari, 1968; Agricola ja kettu, 1968; Sulka, 1973. Hons: Pro Finlandia; Suomen Leijonan Ritarikunta. Address: c/o Otava Publng. Co., Uudenmaankatu 8-12, 00120 Helsinki 12, Finland.

HABE, Hans, b. 12 Feb. 1911, Budapest, Hungary. Writer. Educ: Univs. of Vienna & Heidelberg. Publs: Three Over the Frontier, 1936; A Thousand Shall Fall, 1941; All My Sins, 1955; Off Limits, 1957; Agent of the Devil, 1958; Ilona, 1962; The Countess, 1963; The Mission, 1966; Christopher & his Father, 1967; The Poisoned Stream, 1969; Proud Zion, 1974. Contbr. to: Welt am Sonntag; Kölnische Rundschau, Cologne; Num. other German newspapers. Mbrships: PEN; Pres., Writer's Coun. of Germany. Address: Casa Acacia, 6612 Ascona, Switz.

HABECK, Fritz, b. 8 Sept. 1916, Neulengbach, Austria. Writer. Educ: D.Jur., Vienna Univ. Publs. incl: Der Scholar vom linken Galgen, 1941; Ronan Gobain, 1956; Der Ritt auf dem Tiger, 1958; Der Kampf um die Barbacane, 1960; Der einaugige Reiter, 1963; Der Piber, 1965; Konig Artus, 1965; Salzburg-Spiegel, 1967; Francois Villon, 1969; Doktor Faustus, 1970; Johannes Gutenberg, 1971; Schwarzer Hund im goldenen Feld, 1973; (plays) Baisers mit Schlag, 1950; Marschall Ney, 1954. Contbr. to radio, Vienna. Hons. incl: Goethe Award; Austrian State Prize; Stifter Prize. Address: Grillparzerstr. 6, A-2500 Baden, Austria.

HABGOOD, (Right Rev.) John Stapylton, b. 23 June 1927, Stony Stratford, UK. Bishop of Durham; Author. Educ: M.A., Ph.D., King's Coll., Cambridge; Cuddesdon Coll., Oxford. Publs: Religion & Science, 1964. Contbr. to: Soundings (ed., A. Vidler), 1962; Jrnl. of Physiol.; Theol.; Expository Times; Frontier; Jrnl. of Theol. Studies; etc. Address: Auckland Castle, Bishop Auckland, Co. Durham DL14 7NR, UK.

HACKETT, Cecil Arthur, b. 19 Jan. 1908, Birmingham, UK. Emeritus Professor of French; Literary Critic. Educ: M.A., Emmanuel Coll., Cambridge Univ.; Doct., Univ. of Paris, France. Publs: Le Lyriame de Rimbaud, 1938; Rimbaud l'Enfant, 1948; Anthology of Modern French Poetry from Baudelaire to the Present Day, 1952, revised ed., 1965; Rimbaud, 1957; Autour de Rimbaud, 1967; New French Poetry: an Anthology, 1973. Contbr. to num. acad. jrnls. in UK, France, USA & Can. Mbr., Soc. for French Studies (Ed. Bd.). Recip., Chevalier de la Légion d'Honneur. Address: Shawford Close, Shawford, Winchester, Hants., UK.

HACKFORTH-JONES, Gilbert, b. 14 May 1900, Arkley, Herts., UK. Author & Playwright; Retired Naval Commander. Educ: Naval Colleges; Emmanuel Coll., Cambridge Univ. Publs. incl: Warriors' Playtime; Danger Below; Fish out of Water; Sweethearts & Wives; Rough Passage, 1941; Submarine Flotilla, 1940; Chinese Poison; Security Risk; All Stations to Malta; Yellow Peril; An Explosive Situation, 1973; & 13 other books; (juvenile) The Green Sailors Books; (plays, w. M. Hackforth-Jones); Sweethearts & Wives, 1948; The Policeman & the Lady; (non-fiction) True Story of Submarines; Sailing. Contbr. to: Yachtsman; etc. Address: c/o Lloyds Bank, Lymington, Hants., UK.

HACKLEMAN, Wauneta A., pen name MASON, Val, b. 7 Jan. 1915, Anderson, Ind., USA. Secretary. Educ: Ext. Courses, Glendale Community Coll., Phoenix Coll.; Grad., Fairmount Schl. of Nursing; Cert. in Jrnlsm., NIA; Reg. Med. Asst. & Lab. Techn. Publs: Soliloquies in Verse, 1965; The Candle Still Glows, 1968. Contbr. to over 40 mags., var. anthols. Mbrships. incl: State Pres., Nat. Music Chmn., Nat. League of Am. PEN Women; Nat. Treas., 3rd Nat. VP & Nat. Mbrship. Chmn., Nat. Fedn. of State Poetry Socs., Inc.; Past State Pres., Ariz. Poetry Soc. Hons: Num. nat. poetry awards inclng: Nat. Tribute Award, NFSPS; Judge, nat. poetry contests; Trophy for organizing 4 poetry socs. in Ariz. Address: 5532 Monterosa, Phoenix, AZ 85031, USA.

HADFIELD, Alan, pen name (for children's books) DALE, Robin, b. 16 May 1904, Nottingham, UK. Writer; Former Teacher; Portrait Sculptor. Educ: B.A., 1925, Dip.Ed., 1926, M.A., 1935, Fitzwilliam Coll., Cambridge. Publs. incl: (poetry) Spring in Wensleydale, 1935; Wagtails by the Way, 1939; Two Came Dancing, 1939; Love Lilts & Lyrics, 1942; Great is Diana (play), 1946; A Baker's Dozen of Sketch & Story, 1968; Ovvur t'Bar (playlet); One Man's Approach to G.B.S. (essay), 1974. Fndng. Ed., Northern Lights Quarterly. Contbr. to: Countryman; Yorks. Illustrated; Poetry Review; etc. Mbr., Soc. of Authors. Address: Foursquare, 2 New Quay St., Appledore, Devon, UK.

HADFIELD, Alice Mary (née Smyth), b. 1908, S. Cerney, Glos., UK. Librarian; Editor; Author. Educ: B.A., M.A.; St. Hilda's Coll., Oxford; Mt. Holyoke Coll., Mass., USA. Publs: King Arthur & the Round Table, 1953; An Introduction to Charles Williams, 1959; Time to Finish the Game, 1964; Williver's Luck; Williver's Quest; Williver's Return; The Cotswolds, 1966; Chartist Land Company, 1970; The Cotswolds: A New Study (Ed., w. Charles Hadfield), 1973; Ed., Oxford Dictionary of Familiar Quotations. Agent: David Higham Assocs. Ltd. Address: White Cottage, 21 Randolph Rd., London W9 1AN, UK.

HADFIELD, Ellis Charles Raymond, b. 1909, Pietersburg, S. Africa. Educ: St. Edmund Hall, Oxford, UK. Publs. incl: British Canals; The Canals of South Wales & the Border; The Canals of the East Midlands; Waterways to Stratford (w. John Norris); The Cotswolds: A New Study (w. A. M. Hadfield); The Canal Age; Atmospheric Railways; Canals of the World. Contbr. to: Econ. Hist. Review; Jrnl. of Transp. Hist.; etc. Recip., C.M.G. Agent: David Higham Assocs. Ltd. Address: White Cottage, 21 Randolph Rd., London W9 1AN, UK.

HADFIELD, Stephen John, b. 1908, London, UK. Physician. Educ: Epsom Coll.; M.A.; M.B.; B.Chir., Trinity Coll., Cambridge; St. Bartholomew's Hosp., London. Publs: Law & Ethics for Doctors. Mbrships: M.R.C.S.; L.R.C.P.; F.R.C.P., Edinburgh; Late Scottish Sec., Brit. Med. Assn. Address: 60 Greenbank Cres., Edinburgh EH10 5SW, UK.

HADLEY, Leila (Mrs. Eliott-Burton Smitter), b. 1926, NYC, USA. Writer. Publs: Give Me the World, USA & UK, 1958; How to Travel with Children in Europe, 1963; Manners for Young People, 1967; Fielding's Guide to

Travelling with Children in Europe, 1972, revised ed., 1974. Contbr. to: Palm Beach Life (Book Reviewer); Saturday Review of Lit.; Holiday; Saturday Evening Post; Venture; Travel & Camera; McCall's; Woman's Day; Town & Country. Agent: Josephine Stewart Int. Famous Agcy. Address: 1160 Fifth Ave., N.Y., NY 10029, USA.

HAEDENS, Kléber Gustave, b. 11 Dec. 1913, Equeurdreville, France. Journalist. Publs: Une Histoire de la Littérature Française, 1943; Salut au Kentucky, 1947; L'Eté finit sous les tilleuls, 1966; Adios, 1974. Contbr. to: Journal du Dimanche; Elle. Mbrships. incl: Lit. Critics Union. Hons. incl: Interallié Prize, 1966; Lit. Criticism Prize, French Acad., 1971; Novelist Prize (for Adios), French Acad., 1974. Address: La Bourdette, Aureville, 31320 Castanet-Tolosan, France.

HAENTJENS, Walter, b. 19 Apr. 1943, Hanover, Germany. Journalist; Writer. Educ: Inst. of Press Scis. Publs: (in Dutch) Along the Old Zuiderzee Towns, 1970; Dutch Traditional Craft, 1972; A Short History of Dutch Yachting, 1974. Contbr. to var. Dutch mags. Mbr., Dutch Soc. of Jrnlsts. Address: Rozenstraat 19, Alkmaar, Netherlands.

HAFEN, LeRoy R., b. 1893, Bunkerville, Nev., USA. Professor of History. Educ: Brigham Young Univ.; Univ. of Utah; Univ. of Calif.; M.A.; Ph.D.; Litt.D. Publs. incl: The Overland Mail; Pikes Peak Gold Rush; Far West & the Rockies, 15 vol. series; Western America; Ruxton of the Rockies; The Colorado Story; Life of Thomas Fitzpatrick; Colorado & its People; Mountain Men, 10 vol. series; The Joyous Journey of LeRoy R. & Ann W. Hafen (autobiog.), 1973. Contbr. to num. encys., dicts. & histl. jrnls. Mbrships. incl: Colo. Authors League; League of Utah Writers. Address: 1102 Fir Ave., Provo, UT 84601, USA.

HAFTMANN, Werner, b. 28 Apr. 1912, Glowno, Posen, Germany. Writer; Director of the Nationalgalerie. Educ: Univs. of Berlin & Göttingen, 1932-36. Publs. incl: Das Säulenmonument, 1939; Fritz Winter, 1951; Paul Klee: Wege bildnerischen Denkens, 1959, 4th ed., 1961; Malerei im 20. Jahrhundert, 1965, rev. ed., 1965; Emil Nolde: Monographie, 1958; Skizzenbuch: Zur Kultur der Gegenwart, 1961; Marino Marini: Zeichnungen, 1968; Die neue Nationalgalerie, 1969; Marc Chagall, 1972; Hans Uhlmann, 1974; Wols, 1975. Contbr. to: Die Zeit. Mbr., PEN. Hons. incl: Lessingpreis, Hamburg, 1962; Goethemedaille, Hessen, 1964. Address: Gmund am Tegernsee, Bernöckerweg 22, Oberbayern, W. Germany.

HAGA, Enoch John, pen name GRANT, C.B.S., b. 25 Apr. 1931, L.A., Calif., USA. Educator. Educ: A.A., Grant Tech. Coll., 1950; B.A., 1955, M.A., 1958, Sacramento State Coll.; Ph.D. & Dip., Calif. Inst. of Asian Studies, 1972. Publs: Understanding Automation, 1965; Automated Educational Systems (ed.), 1967; Computer Techniques in Biomedicine & Medicine (ed.), 1973. Contbr. to: Ed., Automedica; Educ. Ed., Bus. Automation Mag. & Data Processing Mag. Mbrships: Assn. for Asian Studies; Biomed. Engrng. Soc.; Fndr., Past Exec. Dir., Soc. of Data Educators; Dir., Cert. Couns. Address: 247 Edythe St., Livermore, CA 94550, USA.

HAGAN, Stella FitzThomas, pen name HAWKINS, John, b. 26 July 1908, London, UK. Teacher of English as a Foreign Language. Educ: B.A., Univ. of London. Publs: The Irish Question Today, 1941; The Green Cravat, 1959, paperback ed., 1970. Mbrships: Soc. of Authors; Nat. Book League. Address: c/o Soc. of Authors, 84 Drayton Gdns., London SW10 9SD, UK.

HAGELSTANGE, Rudolf, b. 14 Jan. 1912, Nordhausen, Germany. Author; former Journalist. Educ: Humanistisches Gymnasium, Nordhausen. Publs. incl: Es spannt sich der Bogen, 1943; Strom der Zeit, 1948; Zwischen Stern & Staub, 1953; How do you Like America?, 1957; Spielball der Gotter, 1959; Lied der Jahre, 1961; Reise nach Katmandu, 1962; Altherren Sommer, 1969; Alleingang, 1970; Venus im Mars, 1972; Der General & das Kind, 1974; (poetry) Der Kark in Prag, 1969; Gast der Elemente, 1972. Mbrships: PEN; Munich Bavarian Acad.; Acad. of Speech & Poetry, Darmstadt. Hons. incl: German Critics' Prize; Julius Campe Prize. Address: 6122 Erbach, Am Schlehdorn, W. Germany.

HAGEMANN, Sonja, pen name S. H., b. 6 Sept. 1898, Oslo, Norway. Literary Critic & Historian. Educ: Cand. Oecon., 1919, Lic., Lit. Hist., 1967, Oslo Univ. Publs. incl: Jørgen Moe, Barnas Dikter, 1963; Hjertets Geni: Henrik

Wergelands Diktning for Barn, 1964; Barnelitteratur i Norge inntil 1850, 1965; Mummitrollbøkene: En Litteraer Karakteristikk, 1967; Barnelitteratur i Norge 1850-1914, 1970; Barnelitteratur i Norge 1914-1970, 1974. Contbr. to Dagbladet (Lit. critic 1946-71); Bonniers Lit. Mag., Stockholm; Vinduet; Bok & Bibliotek; var. other jrnls. Mbrships. incl: Norwegian Authors' Soc.; Norsk Litteraturkritikerlag. Recip., Prize of Honour, Norwegian Lib. Assn., 1973. Address: Hjelmsgt. 6a, Oslo 3, Norway.

HAGGAR, Reginald George, b. 25 Dec. 1905, Ipswich, Suffolk, UK. Artist. Educ: Ipswich Schl. of Arts & Crafts; Assoc., Royal Coll. of Art, London. Publs: English Country Pottery, 1950; The Masons of Lane Delph, 1952; Staffordshire Chimney Ornaments, 1955; The Concise Encyclopedia of Continental Pottery & Porcelain; The Concise Encyclopedia of English Pottery & Porcelain (w. Wolf Mankowitz). Contbr. to: Apollo; var. encys. of antiques. Mbr., var. profl. assns. Hon: M. Univ., Univ. of Keele, 1972. Address: 337 Stone Rd., Hanford, Stoke-on-Trent ST4 8NH, UK.

HAGGARD, Raymond Gordon Rider, b. 1921, Wolverhampton, UK. Former Town Planning Consultant. Publs: Miss Ivory White, 1970. Mbrships: Instn. Civ. Engrs.; Royal Town Planning Inst. Agent: Deborah Rogers Ltd. Address: 6 Stanley Park Road, Wallington, Surrey, UK.

HAGGARD, William (Richard Henry Michael Clayton), b. 1907, Croydon, Surrey, UK. Former Indian Civil Service Official & Judge; Author. Educ: M.A., Christ Church, Oxford. Publs. incl: The Antagonists, 1964; The Powder Barrel, 1965; The Hard Sell, 1966; The Power House, 1967; The Conspirators, 1968; A Cool Day for Killing, 1969; The Doubtful Disciple, 1970; The Bitter Harvest, 1971; The Little Rug Book non-fiction), 1972; The Protectors, 1972; The Old Masters, 1973; The Kinsmen, 1974. Agent: John Farquharson Ltd. Address: Yew Tree Cottage, Farnborough St., Farnborough, Hants., UK.

HAGGARTY, John, b. 1919, Glasgow, UK. Script-writer; Film Director; Playwright. Publs: (play prods.) What Did You Do in the War, Mum?, 1971; The Puncture, 1971; Mother Peg, 1971; A Plague on all the Houses, 1971. Mbrships: Soc. of Authors; Writers' Guild of GB; Assn. of Cine & TV Technicians. Agent: Fraser & Dunlop (Scripts) Ltd. Address: 17 Ullswater Rd., London SW13 9JS, UK.

HAGGERSON, Nelson Lionel, b. 11 June 1927, Silver City, N.M., USA. Professor of Education. Educ: B.A., Vanderbilt Univ., Nashville, Tenn., 1949; M.S., 1952, Ed.S., 1956, Western N.M. Univ., Silver City; Ph.D., Claremont Grad. Schl., Calif., 1960. Publs: Secondary Education Today, 1967; To Dance With Joy, 1971. Contbr. to: Nat. Coun. for Soc. Studies Curric. Series; The Soc. Studies Ariz. Tchr.; Ariz. State Univ. Rsch. Series; sev. other profl. jrnls.; (poems in) Extension, 1968; The Other Book of Poetry, 1971; Competency Based Tchr. Educ., 1974. Mbrships. incl: Assn. of Supervision & Curric. Dev.; Nat Coun. for Soc. Studies; NEA; Ariz. Educ. Assn. Address: 132 W. Balboa Dr., Tempe, AZ 85282, USA.

HAHLO, Herman Robert, b. 3 Aug. 1905, NYC, USA. Professor of Law. Educ: Dr. Jur., Halle, Germany, 1931; LL.B., 1937, LL.D., 1964, Univ. Witwatersrand, S. Africa. Publs: South African Law of Husband & Wife, 3rd ed., 1969; Company Law Through the Cases, 2nd ed., 1969; A Case Book on Company Law, 1970; The South African Legal System (w. Prof. E. Kalin), 1968, 2nd ed., 1973. Contbr. to: Mod. Law Review; S. African Law Jrnl. Mbrships. incl: Selden Soc., London. Recip., LL.D., Univ. Witwatersrand, 1973. Address: 3450 Drummond St., Apt. 1423, Montreal, Canada.

HAIG-BROWN, Roderick Langmere, b. 1908, Lancing, Sussex, UK. Judge. Educ: LL.D. Publs: Silver; Pool & Rapid; Panther; Starbuck Valley Winter; Saltwater Summer; Mounted Police Patrol; The Tall Trees Fall; On the Highest Hill; A River Never Sleeps; Return to the River; The Western Angler; Fisherman's Spring; Fisherman's Winter; Fisherman's Summer; Measure of the Year; Captain of the Discovery; The Living Land; The Farthest Shores, 1960, Fur & Gold, 1962; The Whale People, 1962; A Primer of Flyfishing, 1964; Fisherman's Fall, 1964; The Salmon, 1974. Contbr. to var. mags. Agent: Harold Ober Assocs. Address: 2250 Campbell River Rd., B.C., Can.

HAIGH, Sheila Mary, pen name (1958-64), CHAPMAN, Sheila, b. 4 Oct. 1942, Charlton Adam, Somerset, UK.

Writer; Artist; Poet. Educ: Dip., Art Tchng., Inst. for Educ. & Bath Acad. of Fine Arts, Univ. of Bristol. Publs: A Pony & his Partner; Pony from Fire; The Mystery Pony; Ride for Freedom, 1958-64; Watch for the Ghost, 1975. Mbr., Soc. of Authors. Address: c/o Redlake Trout Farm, Somerton, Somerset, UK.

HAIGHT, Gordon Sherman, b. 6 Feb. 1901, Muskegon, Mich., USA. Teacher. Educ: B.A., 1923, Ph.D., 1933, Yale Univ. Publs: George Eliot & John Chapman, 1940; The George Eliot Letters, 7 vols., 1954-55; George Eliot: A Biography, 1968. Contbr. to US, UK, jrnls. & reviews. Mbrships: Fellow, Royal Soc. of Lit., UK; Corres. Fellow, Brit. Acad.; Fellow, Morgan Lib. Hons: James Tait Black Prize, 1969; Heinemann Award, Royal Soc. of Lit., 1969; VanWyck Brooks Award, 1969; Nat. Inst. of Arts & Letters, Am. Acad. of Arts & Letters, 1970. Address: 145 Peck Hill Rd., Woodbridge, CT 06525, USA.

HAILEY, Arthur, b. 5 Apr. 1920, Luton, Beds., UK. Author. Publs: Flight into Danger (co-author), 1958; The Final Diagnosis, 1959; Close-Up (collected plays), 1960; In High Places, 1962; Hotel, 1965; Airport, 1968; Wheels, 1971; The Moneychangers, 1975; (films) Zero Hour; Time Lock; The Young Doctors; Hotel; Airport; Wheels. Address: Lyford Cay, P.O. Box 7776, Nassau, Bahamas.

HAILSHAM OF SAINT MARYLEBONE, (Lord) Quintin McGarel Hogg, b. 1907, London, UK. Lawyer; Politician. Educ: Christ Ch., Oxford; C.H., D.C.L., LL.D., M.A. Publs: The Law of Arbitration, 1935; One Year's Work, 1944; The Law & Employers' Liability, 1944; The Times We Live In, 1944; Making Peace, 1945; The Left Was Never Right, 1945; The Purpose of Parliament, 1946; Case for Conservatism, 1947; The Law of Monopolies, Restrictive Practices & Resale Price Maintenance, 1956; A New Charter, 1969; The Devils Own Song & other verses, 1969; Science & Politics; Gen. Ed., Halsbury's Laws of England, 1970. Contbr. to num. newspapers & periodicals. F.R.S. Address: The Corner House, 13 Heathview Gdns., Putney Heath, London SW15, UK.

HAIMANN, Theo, b. 17 Nov. 1911, Koblenz, Germany. Mary Louise Murray Professor of Management Sciences, Univ. St. Louis, Mo., USA. Educ: M.B.A., Wash. Univ., St. Louis, Mo.; Ph.D., Bonn Univ., Germany. Publs: Professional Management: Theory & Practice, 1962; Supervisory Management for Hospitals & Related Health Facilities, 1965; Management in the Modern Organization, 1970; Supervision: Concepts & Practices of Management, 1972; Supervisory Management for Health Care Institutions, 1973; Management in the Modern Organization, 2nd ed., 1974; Dimensions in Modern Management, 1974. Mbrships. incl: Acad. Mgmt.; Am. Econ. Assn. Address: 4 Robin Hill, St. Louis, MO 63124, USA.

HAIN, Peter Gerald, b. 16 Feb. 1950, Nairobi, Kenya. Research Student. Educ: B.Sc., London Univ.; Sussex Univ. Publs: Don't Play With Apartheid, 1971; Radical Regeneration, 1975; (pamphlet) Radical Liberalism & Youth Politics, 1973. Contbr. to: Guardian; Times; New Soc.; Race Today. Mbrships: Young Liberals (Exec. Comm.); Liberal Party (Exec. Comm.); Anti-Apartheid Movement; Nat. Coun. Civ. Liberties; Inst. Race Rels. Address: 90 Fawe Pk. Rd., Putney , London SW15 2EA, UK.

HAINES, Geoffrey Colton, b. 1899, Barrow-in-Furness, UK. Writer. Publs: The Roman Republican Coinage by Rev. E. A. Sydenham, revised. Contbr. to: Numismatic Chronicle; The New Beacon; etc. Mbrships: F.C.A.; F.S.A.; Royal Numismatic Soc. (Hon. Treas., 1930-61); Dpty. Chmn., Royal Masonic Benevolent Inst.; Bd. of Mgmt., Royal Masonic Hosp. Recip., O.B.E. Address: 31 Larpent Ave., London SW15 6UU, UK.

HAINES, Pamela Mary, b. 4 Nov. 1929, Harrogate, Yorks., UK. Educ: M.A., Newnham Coll., Cambridge Univ. Publ: Tea at Gunter's, 1974. Contbr. to: Nova. Recip., Spectator New Writing Prize, 1971. Agent: A. D. Peters. Address: 57 Middle Lane, London N8, UK.

HAINES, William Wister, b. 1908, Iowa, USA. Writer. Educ: Culver Mil. Acad.; B.S., Univ. of Pa., 1931. Publs: (novels) Slim, 1934; High Tension, 1938; Command Decision, 1947 (also as a play); The Hon. Rocky Slade, 1957; The Winter War, 1961; Target, 1964; The Image, 1968; film scripts. Contbr. to mags. & jrnls. Lit. Agent:

Harold Ober Assocs., N.Y. Address: P.O. Box 401, S. Laguna, CA 92677, USA.

HAINING, Peter Alexander, b. 2 Apr. 1940, Enfield, Middlesex, UK. Writer & Editor. Publs. incl: Devil Worship in Britain (w. A. V. Sellwood), 1964; The Evil People, 1968; The Witchcraft Reader, 1969; A Circle of Witches, 1971; The Ghouls, 1971; The Warlock's Book, 1972; Gothic Tales of Terror, 1972; The Magic Valley Travellers, 1973; The Monster Makers, 1974; The Sherlock Holmes Scrapbook, 1974; The Hero, 1974; The Witchcraft Papers, 1974; The Illustrated History of Ghosts, 1974; Ed., Christopher Lee's New Chamber of Horrors, 1974. Mbrships: PEN; Brit. Film Inst. Address: The Hideaway, Birch Green, nr. Colchester, Essex, UK.

HAINSWORTH, Marguerite Dorothy, b. Liverpool, UK. Biologist. Educ: M.A., B.Sc., Univ. of Liverpool. Publs: Hygiene, 1967; Experiments in Animal Behaviour, UK, 1967, USA, 1968; Biological Studies Through the Microscope (Vol. I.: Motile Protista, 1972, Vol. II: Coelenterates & Their Food, 1974, Vol. III: Invertebrate Parasites & Their Free-Living Relatives, 1972). Contbr. to: Schl. Sci. Review, 9 papers, 1956-65; The Science Masters' Book, Series 4, Part 3. Mbrships: Soc. of Authors; Fellow, Inst. of Biol.; Zool. Soc. of London. Address: 31 St. Paul's Close, Hounslow, Middlesex TW3 3DE, UK.

HAIR, Ellen Eileen (Nellie), b. 22 Nov. 1913, Wellington, NZ. Writer; Journalist. Educ: Marsden Collegiate Schl., Gilby's Bus. Coll. Corres., NZ Women's Weekly, Weekly News; Staff Writer, Hawkes Bay Herald-Tribune; The Dominion; Contbr., NZ Herald, Evening Post; SE Asian, African newspapers & mags.; Writer, short stories, children's stories & poems, children's serial, The Magic Island, radio plays. Mbrships: Fndr., Life Mbr., & Hon. VP, NZ Women Writers Soc., (1932). Address: 45A Oban St. Wadestown, Wellington, NZ.

HAIRE, Wilson John, b. 6 Apr. 1932, Belfast, UK. Playwright. Publs: Within Two Shadows, 1974. Hons: George Devine Award for Drama 1971, Engl. Stage Co., 1972; Most Promising Playwrights Award for 1972, Evening Standard, 1973; Playwrighting Schlrship. for Stage Drama, Thames TV, 1974; Res. Dramatist, Royal Court Theatre, 1974. Address: 18 Lyndhurst Rd., London NW3, UK.

HAISLIP, Harvey Shadle, b. 12 July 1889, Fredericksburg, Va., USA. Retired Naval Captain, US Navy; Author; Playwright. Educ: US Naval Acad., Annapolis, Md. Publs: Sailor Named Jones, 1957; The Prize Master, 1959; Sea Road to Yorktown, 1962; Escape from Java, 1962 (historical novels); The Long Watch (play), 1952. Contbr. to mags. & US Naval Inst. Proceedings: Screen writer, maj. films. Mbrships: Authors League; Authors Guild; Writers Guild of Am. Address: 850 Webster St., Apt. 818, Palo Alto, CA 94301, USA.

HAJNAL, Gabor, b. 4 Oct. 1912, Gyepufuzes, Hungary. Writer; Poet. Educ: Univ. of Right, Budapest. Publs: (poetry) Nem istenekkel, önmagaddal, 1939; A szegény panasza, 1947; Az épülőhid, 1948; Szeptemberi nyár, 1957; Tengerre vágytam, 1959; Fényküllők, 1961; Farsangtemetés, 1963; Az idő szelelyben, 1965; Szédül az erdő, 1968; Boszorkányéj, 1971; Hüvös nyárban, 1974; (essays) A lira ma, 1968; Ihlet és mesterség, 1972; transls. of German poetry into Hungarian. Contbr. to Hungarian jrnls. Mbrships. incl: PEN. Hons. incl: József Attila Prize, 1972; Austrian Cross of Hon., Art & Sci., 1974. Address: Visegradi u. 48, 1132 Budapest XIII, Hungary.

HÅKANSON, Björn Gunnar, b. 6 Dec. 1937, Linköping, Sweden. Author; Literary Critic. Educ: Fil.kand. Publs: Rymd För Ingenting (poetry), 1962; Mot Centrum (poetry), 1963; Generalsekreteraren (prose), 1965; Kärlek I Vita Huset (poetry), 1967; Mellan Två Val (poetry), 1969; Författarmakt (essays), 1970; Fyra Resor (essay on Zambia), 1971. Contbr. to: Aftonbladet; BLM; Ord och Bild; Vinduet. Mbrships: PEN; Swedish Assn. of Authors. Recip., Aftonbladets Litteraturpris, 1967. Address: Vallstanäsvägen 32, S-19040 Rosersberg, Sweden.

HÅKANSSON, Gunvor, b. 25 July 1909, Norrköping, Sweden. Author (Children's Books); Translator. Publs: The Pomander Books, 1958-59; Ursakta mitt namn ar Trana, 1968. Contbr. to Swedish newspapers & mags. Mbr., Swedish Soc. of Authors. Hons: Pelle Jons, 1959; Swedish Authors' Union Award, 1961; Litteraturfrämjandet, 1964, 1968. Address: Torsviksvangen 33, 181 34 Lidingo, Sweden.

HAKIM, Tewfik al, b. 1902. Playwright. Publs: The Confused Sultan, 1959; Scheherezade; Pygmalion; The Cave-Dweller; You Who Are Climbing the Tree, 1963; A Magistrate's Diary; Solomon the Wise; Bird of Lebanon; Fate of a Cockroach, 1972. Mbrships. incl: Acad. of the Arabic Lang.; Higher Coun. of the Arts. Address: c/o Al-Ahram, Shalia Lal-Galaa, Cairo, United Arab Repub.

HALASZ, Robert Joseph, b. 11 June 1937, Budapest, Hungary. Editor. Educ: B.A., Univ. of Chgo., USA; M.A., Roosevelt Univ. Publs: Tiszta szívű Gyilkosok (w. Nicholas Halasz), in Hungarian, 1972. Mbr., Am. Histl. Assn. Address: 215 E. Chestnut St., Chgo., IL 60611. USA.

HALE John Rigby, b. 1923, Ashford, Kent, UK. Professor of Italian. Educ: M.A., Jesus Coll., Oxford; Johns Hopkins, USA; Harvard. Publs. incl: Machiavelli & Renaissance Italy, 1961; The Literary Works of Machiavelli (transl. & ed.), 1961; Ed., Certain Discourses Military by Sir John Smythe, 1964; The Evolution of British Historiography, 1967; Renaissance Europe, 1480-1520, 1971; Ed., Renaissance Venice, 1973. Contbr. to: The New Cambridge Modern History, Vols. I, II & III; var. lit. jrnls. Chmn., Trustees of Nat. Gall., London, 1974—. Agent: A. D. Peters. Address: c/o Dept. of Italian Studies, University College, Gower St., London WC1E 6BT, UK.

HALE, Julian Anthony Stuart, b. 27 Nov. 1940, Llandrindod Wells, Radnor, UK. Writer. Educ: M.A.(Oxon.). Publs: Elementary Reading Passages in Russian, 1967; Ceausescu's Romania, 1971; The Land & People of Romania, 1972; Radio Power, 1975. Contbr. to: Economist; Survey; Sunday Times & Daily Telegraph Colour Mags. Mbr., Nat. Union of Jrnlsts. Address: 9 Warwick Ave., London W9, UK.

HALE, Kathleen, pen name McCLEAN, Kathleen, b. Scotland. Writer; Painter. Educ: Manchester Schl. of Art; Reading Univ. Publs: Orlando's Country Peepshow; Puss-in-Boots; Orlando the Marmalade Cat Series; Henrietta, the Faithful Hen; Henrietta's Magic Egg; Manda (Murray). Contbr. to: Homes & Gardens; Child Educ.; sev. exhibitions of drawings & paintings; etc. Mbrships: Soc. of Authors; Chelsea Arts; Int. Artists; Le Petit Club Français. Address: Tod House, Forest Hill, Oxford, UK.

HALE, Nancy, b. 6 May 1908, Boston, Mass., USA. Writer; Journalist. Educ: Boston Mus. Schl. of Art. Publs. incl: Never Any More, 1934; The Earliest Dreams, 1936; The Prodigal Women, 1942; Between the Dark & the Daylight, 1943; The Empress's Ring, 1955; Heaven & Hardpan Farm, 1957; A New England Girlhood, 1958; Dear Beast, 1959; The Pattern of Perfection, 1960; The Realities of Fiction, 1962; Life in The Studio, 1969; Secrets, 1971; The Life of Mary Cassatt, 1975. Contbr. to sev. jrnls. inclng: New Yorker; Va. Quarterly; Harper's Mag. Mbrships: PEN; Authors' Guild; Authors' League of Am. Hons: Henry H. Bellaman Award, 1971; Sarah Josepha Hale Award, 1974. Agent: Harold Ober Assocs. Address: Woodburn, Route 8, Charlottesville, VA 22901, USA.

HALKIN, Simon Leo, b. 30 Oct. 1899, Dovsk, Russia. Author; University Professor Emeritus. Educ: B.A., 1926, M.A., 1928, N.Y. Univ., USA; Columbia Univ., 1930-32; D.H.L., 1947. Publs. incl: Modern Hebrew Literature: Trends & Values, 1951; Literatura Hebrea Moderna, 1968; (in Hebrew) Yehiel Ha-Hagri (novel), 1928; Ad-Mashber (novel), 1945; Collected Literary Essays & Studies, 3 vols., 1971; Adrift (short stories), 1973; var. transls. into Hebrew of works by Jack London, Maurice Maeterlinck, Walt Whitman, Shelley, Shakespeare. Mbrships. incl: Acad. Hebrew Lang.; Pres., Israel PEN. Hons. incl: Bialik Prize for Lit., 1968; State of Israel Prize, 1975. Address: Hebrew University of Jerusalem, Israel.

HALL, Alfred Rupert, b. 26 July 1920, Stoke-on-Trent, UK. Historian of Science. Educ: M.A., 1944; Ph.D., 1950; Christ's Coll., Cambridge, UK. Publs: Ballistics in the 17th Century, 1952; The Scientific Revolution, 1954; (co-ed.) A History of Technology 1953-58, From Galileo to Newton, 1962; The Cambridge Philosophical Society: A History, 1969; Correspondence of Henry Oldenberg, 1965; Brief History of Science, 1964. Contbr. to: Cambridge Histories; Sci. Am.; Annals of Sci.; BBC; etc. Mbrships: Int. Acad. of the Hist. of Sci., VP; Brit. Soc. for the Hist. of Sci.; Newcomen Soc. Recip., Silver Medal, Royal Soc. of Arts, 1974. Address: Imperial Coll., London, UK.

HALL, Angus, b. 24 Mar. 1932, Newcastle-upon-Tyne, Northumberland, UK. Writer. Publs: Love in Smoky Regions, 1962; High-Bouncing Lover, 1966; Live like a Hero, 1966; Qualtrough, 1968; Late Boy Wonder, 1969; Devilday, 1969; Long Way to Fall, 1971; On the Run, 1974; Signs of Things to Come, 1975; Monsters & Mythic Beasts, 1975. Contbr. to: Crimes & Punishment; Headlines; Books & Bookmen. Mbrships: Nat. Union of Jrnlsts; Writers Guild; Wig & Pen Club. Address: The Grey House, 96 High St., Old Town, Hastings, Sussex, UK.

HALL, Blaine R., b. 18 Feb. 1921, Clay Co., Ky., USA. President, General Insurance Business. Publs: From these Hills, Poetry, 1967; Reflections & Moods, 1969. Contbr. to Approaches; Cyclo-Flame; Am. Bard; Sev. other poetry jrnls.; Reviews in var. newspapers. Past V.P., Ky. Poetry Soc. Hons: 1st Prize, Ky. Poetry Contest, 1968; Sev. prizes, var. other poetry contests. Address: P.O. Box 508, S. Arnold Ave., Prestonsburg, KY 41653, USA.

HALL, Daniel George Edward, b. 1891, Offley, Herts., UK. Professor of History; Former Headmaster. Educ: M.A., D.Lit., King's Coll., Univ. of London. Publs. incl: Early English Intercourse with Burma, 1928, 2nd ed., 1968; Bried Survey of English Constitutional History, 1925, 2nd ed., 1939; Europe & Burma, 1945; Burma, 1950, 2nd ed., 1956; A History of South-East Asia, 1955, 3rd ed., 1968; Henry Burney: A Political Biography, 1974. Contbr. to: Hist.; Engl. Histl. Review; Pacific Affairs; etc. Mbrships: F.R.Hist.S.; F.R.A.S.; Soc. of Authors; Burma Rsch. Soc.; Royal Asiatic Soc.; Royal Histl. Soc. Address: 4 Chiltern Rd., Hitchin, Herts., UK.

HALL, Donald John, b. 1903, Oxford, UK. Solicitor of Supreme Court; Writer. Educ: M.A., Corpus Christi Coll., Cambridge. Publs: Enchanted Sand, 1932; Romanian Furrow, 1933; No Retreat, 1936; Perilous Sanctuary, 1937; This Other Eden, 1938; The Phoenix Flower: An Epic of 1939-45, 1953; The Seeming Truth, 1954; Eagle Argent, 1956; The Crowd is Silent, 1961; English Mediaeval Pilgrimage, 1965; The Ring of Words; Journey into Morning, an Epic Poem, 1972. Mbr., PEN. Recip., Romanian Order of Merit (Lit.), 1936. Address: Porth-y-Castell, Minffordd, Penrhyndeudvaeth, Merioneth, UK.

HALL, H. Duncan, b. 1891, Glen Innes, Australia. Writer; British Embassy History Adviser, 1947-56. Educ: Univs. of Sydney & Balliol Coll., Oxford, UK; M.A.; B.Litt. Publs. incl: The British Commonwealth of Nations; Drugs Limitation Convention, Historical & Technical Commentary; Mandates, Dependencies & Trusteeship; Studies of Overseas Supply (w. C. C. Wrigley); North American Supply, British Official War Histories; Commonwealth: A History of the British Commonwealth of Nations, 1971; The British Commonwealth at War (contbr. & Jt. Ed.). Contbr. to: Times; Int. Affairs; N.Y. Times; Am. Jrnl. of Int. Law; etc. Hon: "Duncan Hall Collection" to be housed in Nat. Lib. of Aust., Canberra. Address: 7501 Fairfax Rd., Bethesda, MD 20014, USA.

HALL, James Byron, b. 21 July 1918, Midland, Ohio, USA. University Provost; Author. Educ: B.A., State Univ. of Iowa, 1947; M.A., 1948; Ph.D., 1953; Kenyon Coll., Ohio, 1949. Publs: Not by the Door, 1954; The Short Story, 1955; 15x3, 1957; Racers to the Sun, 1960; Us He Devours, 1964; Realm of Fiction, 1965. Modern Culture & the Arts, 1967; Mayo Sergeant, 1967; The Hunt Within, 1973. Contbr. to anthols. Mbrships. incl: PEN; Philol. Assn. of Pacific Coast; AAUP. Hons. incl: Ore. Poetry Award, 1958; Emily Clark Balch Fiction Prize, 1967; Chapelbrook Award, 1967. Address: 1100 High St., Santa Cruz, CA 95060, USA.

HALL, Jerome, b. 4 Feb. 1901, Chgo., Ill., USA. Professor of Law; Author. Educ: Ph.D., 1922, J.D., 1923, Univ. of Chgo.; Jur.Sc.D., Columbia Univ., 1935; S.J.D., Harvard Univ., 1935. Publs. incl: General Principles of Criminal Law, 1947, 2nd ed., 1960; Living Law of Democratic Society, 1949; Studies in Jurisprudence & Criminal Theory, 1958; Comparative Law & Social Theory, 1963; Foundations of Jurisprudence, 1973. Contbr. to legal mags.; legal, philos. & soc. sci. jrnls. Mbr., profl. orgs. Recip., acad. hons. Address: Hastings Coll. of the Law, 198 McAllister St., San Fran., CA 94102, USA.

HALL, John Clive, b. 1920, Ealing, Mddx., UK. Staff Member, Encounter Magazine. Educ: Leighton Pk., Reading & Oriel Coll., Oxford. Publs: Selected Poems (w. Keith Douglas & Norman Nicholson), 1943; The Summer Dance, 1951; Edwin Muir, 1956; The Burning Hare, 1966; A House of Voices, 1973; Ed., Collected Poems of Edwin Muir; Ed.,

INTERNATIONAL AUTHORS AND WRITERS WHO'S WHO   249

Collected Poems of Keith Douglas. Address: c/o Chatto & Windus Ltd., 40 William IV St., London WC2, UK.

HALL, John Whitney, b. 23 Sept. 1916, Tokyo, Japan. Professor of History; Author. Educ: A.B., Amherst Coll., 1939; Ph.D., Harvard Univ., 1950. Publs: Japanese History: A Guide to Japanese Research & Reference Materials, 1954; Tanuma Okitsugu, Forerunner of Modern Japan, 1955; Village Japan (co-author), 1959; 12 Doors to Japan (co-author), 1965; Government & Local Power in Japan, 1966; Studies in the Institutional History of Early Modern Japan, 1968; Japan From Pre-history to Modern Times, 1970; Medieval Japan, 1974. Contbr. to: Am. Histl. Review (Ed. Bd., 1965-68). Address: Dept. of History, Yale Univ., New Haven, CT 06520, USA.

HALL, Manly Palmer, b. 1901, Peterborough, Ont., Can. President/Founder. The Philosophical Research Society, Inc. Educ: D.D. Publs. incl: Encyclopaedic Outline of Masonic, Hermetic, Qabbalistic & Rosicrucian Symbolical Philosophy; Secret Destiny of America; Story of Astrology; The Guru; Lost Keys of Freemasonry; Dionysian Artificers; The Mystical Christ; Old Testament Wisdom; Journey in Truth; Lectures on Ancient Philosophy; 12 World Teachers; Pathways of Philosophy; Reincarnation; Man, the Grand Symbol of the Mysteries. Contbr. to: Overland Monthly, 1972; Baconiana; The Annanai; num. mags. Mbrships. incl: Authors' Club; Baconian Soc., UK. Recip., Plaque to mark 50 yrs. Writing, City of L.A. Address: 3910 Los Feliz Blvd., L.A., CA 90027, USA.

HALL, Peter, b. 1932, London, UK. Professor of Geography. Educ: M.A., Ph.D., St. Catharine's Coll., Cambridge Univ. Publs: The Industries of London, 1962; London 2000, 1963, new ed., 1969; The World Cities, 1966; The Containment of Urban England, 1973; Planning & Urban Growth: An Anglo American Comparison, 1973 (w. Marion Clawson). Contbr. to: Regional Studies (Ed.); New Soc. Mbr., Royal Geogl. Soc. Agent: A. D. Peters. Address: 5 Bedford Rd., London W4 1JD, UK.

HALL, Richard, b. 1925, Margate, UK. Journalist. Educ: M.A., Keble Coll., Oxford. Publs: Kaunda, Founder of Zambia, 1964; Zambia, 1965; High Price of Principles, 1969; Discovery Africa, 1970; Stanley, 1974. Contbr. to: Observer; Guardian; Newsweek, N.Y. Fellow, Royal Geogl. Soc., London. Address: 21 Earl's Terrace, London W8, UK.

HALL, Roger Leighton, b. 17 Jan. 1939, Woodford Wells, Essex, UK. Editor; Writer. Educ: Univ. Coll. Schl., London; Dip.Tchng., Wellington Tchrs. Coll., NZ; M.A.(Hons.), Vic. Univ. of Wellington. Publs: (TV plays) Never Play Favourites; Clean-Up; Some People Get All The Luck; The Reward; The Bach; co-author of 2 series, In View of the Circumstances; co-author of sketches for Aust. A-Z; major writer for over 20 stage revues inclng. The Last Half-Crown; One in Five; also author of 12 plays for children. Contbr. to: NZ Listener; NZ Book World; Joker; Educ. Mbr., PEN. Recip., Feltex nomination for TV Writer of Yr., 1974. Address: 56 Hatton St., Wellington 5, New Zealand.

HALL, Tord Erik Martin, b. 7 Jan. 1910, Jönköping, Sweden. Assistant Professor of Mathematics. Educ: Ph.D., Univ. Uppsala. Publs: Atomer och stjärnor, 1956; Vår tids stjärnsäng, 1958; Satelliter och rymdfärder (Finnish & Norwegian edns.), 1958; Gauss Matematikernas konung (Engl. edn.), 1965; Entropi, 1966; Människan inför Kosmos, 1966; Från Ginnungagap till såpbubbla, 1970; Matematikens utveskling, 1970. Contbr. to: Svenska Dagbladet; Lychnos; etc. Mbrships: Svenska författar förbundet; Gauss-Gesellschaft E.V., Göttingen. Hons: Boklotteriets Pris, 1959; Sveriges författarfonds Pris, 1961; Aniarapriset, 1965. Address: Fyrisgatan 14, 752 22 Uppsala, Sweden.

HALL, Trevor Henry, b. 28 May 1910, Wakefield, UK. Chartered Surveyor; Company Director; Writer. Educ: M.A., Ph.D., Leeds Univ.; Coll. Estate Mgmt., London; F.R.I.C.S. Publs: The Testament of R. W. Hull, 1945; The Haunting of Borley Rectory (co-author), 1956; A Bibliography of Books on Conjuring in English 1580-1850, 1957; The Strange Case of Edmund Gurney, 1964; Sherlock Holmes, 1969; Mathematical Recreations 1633, 1969. Contbr. to: Yorks. Post (book reviewer). Mbrships. incl: Nat. Trust (former regional chmn.); Pres., Leeds Lib., 1969-. Hons. incl: J.P.; Cecil Oldman Mem. Lectr., Univ. of Leeds, 1972. Address: Carr Meadow, Thorner, Leeds, UK.

HALL, W(illiam) Douglas, b. 9 Oct. 1926, London, UK. Keeper, Scottish National Gallery of Modern Art. Educ: B.A., Univ. Coll. & Courtauld Inst. of Art, Univ. of London, 1952. Publs: Luini, 1957; Frans Hals, 1958; Holbein, 1959; Fra Angelico, 1959; Raphael, 1960; The Tabley House Papers, 1962; Giacometti, 1966; Compiler, Catalogue of Art Treasures Centenary Exhibition, Manchester, 1957; sev. other mus. publs. Contbr. to num. art jrnls. & catalogue introductions. Fellow, Mus. Assn. Address: Scottish Nat. Gall. of Mod. Art, Royal Botanic Gdn., Edinburgh, UK.

HALL, William Otterburn, b. 2 Nov. 1935, Highgate Village, London, UK. Film Columnist; Critic; Staff, London Evening News. Contbr. to: Directors in Action, 1973; San Fran. Chronicle; N.Y. Times; L.A. Times; Playgirl (USA); Thursday Mag., NZ; Ski World; BBC World Serv. & TV. Agent's Name: Murray Pollinger. Author's Address: c/o Evening News, London EC4, UK.

HALL, Willis, b. 6 Apr. 1929. Playwright. Publs: (plays) The Long & the Short & the Tall, 1959; A Glimpse of the Sea, 1959; Billy Liar (w. Keith Waterhouse), 1960; Celebration, 1961; All Things Bright & Beautiful, 1962; England Our England, 1962; Squat Betty & the Sponge Room, 1963; Say Who You Are, 1965; Whoops-a-Daisy, 1968; Children's Day, 1969; Who's Who, 1972; The Card, 1973; Saturday, Sunday, Monday, 1973; The Upper Crusts, TV series (w. Keith Waterhouse), 1973. Address: 64 Clarence Rd., St. Albans, Herts., UK.

HALLBING, Kjell Kåre, pen name MASTERSON, Louis, b. 5 Nov. 1934, Oslo, Norway. Writer. Educ: Banking & Trade Schl. Publs: The Morgan Kane series, 1966–, 76 titles inclng. Alaska Marshal, 1973; Klondike-97, 1973; The Bloody Trail to Santa Fe, 1973; Comanche, 1974. Contbr. to: Western; Alle Menn; Vi Menn (all publ'd in Oslo). Mbr., Western Writers of Am. Address: Platåveien 10, 1324 Lysaker, Norway.

HALLEN, Erik Gustaf, b. Gothenburg, Sweden. Professor of Theoretical Electrical Engineering. Educ: Chalmers Univ. Of Technol., Gothenburg; Uppsala Univ.; Sc.D. Publs: Electromagnetic Theory; Operational Calculus. Contbr. to elec. & sci. jrnls. Address: Alvagen 25, Sollentuna, Sweden.

HALLER, Mark Hughlin, b. 22 Dec. 1928, Wash. D.C., USA. Professor of History. Educ: A.B., Wesleyan Univ., 1951; M.A., Univ. of Md., 1954; Ph.D., Univ. of Wis., 1959. Publs: Eugenics: Hereditarian Attitudes in American Thought, 1963; The Peoples of Philadelphia: A History of Ethnic Groups & Lower Class Life (Ed.), 1973. Contbr. to: Jrnl. of Am. Hist.; Jrnl. of Soc. Hist. Mbrships: Am. Histl. Assn.; Org. of Am. Histns.; Am. Soc. for Legal Hist. Address: Dept. of Hist., Temple Univ., Phila., PA 19122, USA.

HALLET, Jean-Pierre, b. 4 Aug. 1927, Louvain, Belgium. Author; Explorer; Naturalist. Educ: Univ. of Brussels; Sorbonne, Paris; Study of Sociol., Agron., Tropical Med. Publs: Congo Kitabu, 1966; Animal Kitabu, 1967; Pygmy Kitabu, 1973. Contbr. to num. mags.; film narrator; TV specials.; prod., writer, Dir., Pygmies (documentary). Hons: Best Book, 1966 (Congo Kitabu), Kt. of Mark Twain, 1967. Address: 5630 W. 79th St., L.A., CA 90045, USA.

HALLETT, Graham, b. 1 Jan. 1929, Yeovil, UK. University Teacher. Educ: P.P.E., Univ. Coll., Oxford; M.A., Oxon.; Ph.D., Wales. Publs: The Economics of Agricultural Land Tenure, 1960; The Economics of Agricultural Policy, 1968; The Social Economy of West Germany, 1973. Contbr. to: Econ. Jrnl.; Pol. Quarterly. Address: 10 Coed-yr-Ynn, Rhiwbina, Cardiff, UK.

HALLGARTEN, Siegfried Solomon "Fritz", pen name HALLGARTEN, S. F., b. 6 June 1902. Author; Wine Importer & Exporter (ret'd). Educ: Dr. of Law, Heidelberg Univ.; Univ., Frankfurt a/M, Germany. Publs: Rhineland – Wineland, 1951; Alsace & its Wine Gardens, 1957; The Great Wines of Germany (w. André Simon), 1963; Guide to the Vineyards, Estates & Wines of Germany, 1974; (Contbr.) Wines & Spirits of the World, 1972; Wines of the World (Ed., André Simon), 1972. Contbr. to: Harper's Wine & Spirit Gazette; Wines & Spirits; Wine World; Deutsche Weinfach zeitung. Mbrships: PEN; Authors' Soc.; German Lawyers' Assn., W. Germany. Address: 20 Bracknell Gdns., London NW3 7ED, UK.

HALLION, Richard Paul Jr., b. 17 May 1948, Wash. D.C., USA. Curator, National Air and Space Museum, Smithsonian Institution. Educ: B.A., 1970, Ph.D., 1975, Univ. of Md. Publs: Supersonic Flight: Breaking the Sound Barrier & Beyond, 1972. Contbr. to: Astronautics & Aeronautics; Technol. & Culture; Air Enthusiast Int.; Aircraft Illustrated. Mbrships: Am. Inst. of Aeronautics & Astronautics; US Naval Inst.; Aviation, Space Writers' Assn.; Soc. for the Hist. of Technol.; Air Force Histl. Fndn. Recip., Guggenheim Fndn. Fellowship, 1973-75. Address: 1011 Marton St., Laurel, MD 20810, USA.

HALLOCK, Ruth Marie (Mrs.), b. 12 Feb. 1931, Black Diamond, Alta., Can. Newspaper Editor & Publisher; Writer. Contbr. to: Caledonia Courier (Ed. & Fndg. Publr., 5 yrs.); Terrace-Omineca Herald, Ed. & Advt. Mgr., 8 yrs.); Vancouver Sun; Vancouver Province; CBC. Hons: Award for Outstanding Jrnlsm. in Wkly Newspapers, MacMillan Bloedel Co. Ltd., 1966; Citation for Outstanding Community Serv., Terrace, B.C., 1967. Address: P.O. Box 108, Fort St. James, B.C., Can. V0J 1P0.

HALMOS, Paul, b. 19 Dec. 1911, Budapest, Hungary. Professor of Sociology. Educ: Dr. Juris, Univ. Hungary; B.A., 1945, Ph.D., 1950, Univ. of London. Publs: Solitude & Privacy, 1952, 3rd ed., 1969; Towards a Measure of Man, 1957, 2nd ed., 1958; Faith of the Counsellors, 1965, 3rd ed., 1970; Personal Service Society, 1970, 2nd ed., 1971. Contbr. to: Sociol. Review (Ed. Monographs, 1958-73); Sociol. & Social Welfare Series (Ed.). Mbr., Brit. Sociol. Assn. Hons: Charlotte Towle Lecturer, Univ. Chicago, 1971; Kincardine Lecturer, Univ. Keele, 1974. Address: Social Sci. Fac., Open Univ., Walton Hall, Milton Keynes MK7 6AA, UK.

HALSALL, Eric, b. 18 Mar. 1920, Burnley, UK. Surveyor. Publs: Hill Dog, 1961; Meg of Lonktop, 1967. Contbr. to: Farmers Guardian; Burnley Express; Yorkshire (Farming) Post; var. country mags. & BBC radio progs. Mbrships. incl: Guild of Agricultural Jrnlsts.; Mammal Soc. of GB; Dir., Int. Sheep Dog Soc.; Estate Sect., Brit. Assn. of Colliery Mgmt.; Press Off., Ribblesdale Farmers Club; Chmn., Holme Sheep Dog Trials Assn. Address: 528 Red Lees Rd., Cliviger, near Burnley, Lancs., UK.

HALTER, Carl Frederick, b. 10 Oct. 1915, Cleveland, Ohio, USA. Educator; Church Musician. Educ: Dip., Concordia Teachers' Coll., 1936; B.Mus., Baldwin-Wallace Coll., 1941; M.Mus., Northwestern Univ., 1945. Publs: The Practice of Sacred Music, 1955; God & Man in Music, 1963; The Christian Choir Member, 1959; Ed., A Handbook of Church Music (forthcoming). Contbr. to Ch. & Musical jrnls. Recip., Hon. Litt.D., 1964. Address: 1304 Forest Park Ave., Valparaiso, IN 46383, USA.

HAM, Olive Mary, b. 1918, Cheddar, UK. Teacher. Educ: B.Sc., Bristol Univ., UK. Publs: Nightingale Cottage, 1958; Off to Brittany, 1959; Aunt Matilda's Legacy, 1960. Mbr., Assn. of Assistant Mistresses. Address: 4 Parkway Dr., Bournemouth BH8 9JW, Dorset, UK.

HAMADA, Kengi, b. 18 Aug. 1900, Waimea, Kauai, USA. Writer (ret'd). Educ: Palmer Inst. of Authorship, 1922. Publs: Prince Ito (biog.), 1936; The Constant Rebel (novel), 1955; (transls.) Introduction to Contemporary Japanese Literature, 1938; The Life of an Amorous Man, 1964; Tales of Moonlight & Rain, 1971-72. Contbr. to: N. Am. Review; Studies on Japanese Culture, Japan PEN. Mbrships: Exec. Bd., Hawaii PEN Ctr.; Honolulu Press Club; Japanese Press Club, Honolulu. Address: 1742 Young St., Honolulu, HI 96814, USA.

HAMBE, Alf Gunnar, b. 24 Jan. 1931, Rävinge, Sweden. Author; Poet; Composer; Troubadour. Publs: Astronaut till häst, 1962; Visa i Molom, 1965; Gröne greven, 1967; Vraga, 1969; Fyra vindarnas hus, 1972; Se dig i vagspegeln, 1974. Contbr. to: Lyrikvännen; Svenska visor; Nordisk visbok; Den gule store viseboka 60 visor fran 60 talet. Mbrships: Sveriges Författarförbund; Författarcentrum. Hons. incl: Fritz Gustaf Grafström Award, 1965; Statens Stora Konstnärsstipendiu n, 1966, 1969 & 1973. Address: Steninge, 310 40 Harplinge, Sweden.

HAMBURGER, Michael Peter Leopold, b. 22 Mar. 1924, Berlin, Germany. University Professor; Poet; Translator. Educ: M.A., Christ Church, Oxford. Publs. incl: (poetry) Flowering Cactus, 1950; The Dual Site, 1958; Weather & Season, 1963; Penguin Modern Poets, 1969; Travelling, 1969; Ownerless Earth, 1973; (transls.) Georg

Büchner, Leonce & Lena, Lenz, Woyzeck, 1972; H. M. Enzensberger, Poems, 1966; Günter Grass, Selected Poems, 1966; Hölderlin, Poems & Fragments, 1967; Günter Eich, Journeys, 1968; Paul Celan, Selected Poems, 1972; Ed., East German Poetry, 1972; (criticism) Reason & Energy, 1957; From Prophecy to Exorcism, 1965; The Truth of Poetry, 1970; Hofmannsthal, 1973; (memoirs) A Mug's Game, 1973. Mbrships: PEN; F.R.S.L.; Berlin Acad. of Arts. Hons: Transl. Prizes, Deutsche Akad. für Sprache und Dichtung, Darmstadt, 1964; Arts Coun. of GB, 1969. Address: 34A Half Moon Lane, London SE24 9HV, UK.

HAMBURGER, Philip, b. 2 July 1914, Wheeling, W.Va., USA. Writer. Educ: B.A., Johns Hopkins Univ., 1935; M.S., Grad. Schl. of Jrnlsm., Columbia Univ., 1938. Publs: The Oblong Blur & Other Odysseys, 1949; J. P. Marquand, Esquire, 1952; Mayor Watching & Other Pleasures, 1958; Our Man Stanley, 1963; An American Notebook, 1965. Contbr. to: New Yorker mag. (Staff Writer, 1939—); The Century Assn., N.Y.; The Coffee House, N.Y. Mbrships: Coun. Mbr., Authors' Guild; PEN, Am. Ctr.; Nat. Press Club, Wash. D.C. Address: 151 E. 80th St., N.Y., NY 10021, USA.

HAMELL, (Rt. Rev. Monsignor) Patrick Joseph, b. 11 Dec. 1910, Cloughjordan, Co. Tipperary, Repub. of Ireland. Priest; University Professor of Theology. Educ: B.A., 1931, M.A., 1940, Maynooth Coll., Nat. Univ. of Ireland; D.D., Maynooth Pontifical Univ., 1937. Publs. incl: Patrology: An Introduction; Index to Irish Ecclesiastical Record 1864-1964; Maynooth Students & Ordinations 1795-1895 Index; Jacques Paul Migne; The Resurrection of the Just; The Church in Africa in St. Cyprian's Writings; Membership of the Mystical Body. Contbr. to var. theol. jrnls., etc. Co-fndr. & 1st Chmn., Irish Theol. Assn. Address: St. Brendan's, Birr, Offaly, Repub. of Ireland.

HAMELMAN, Paul William, b. 8 Oct. 1930, Hempstead, N.Y., USA. Professor of Management Science. Educ: A.B., Davis & Elkins Coll., W.Va., 1953; M.B.A., 1958, Ph.D., 1962, Univ. of Pittsburgh, Pa. Publs: Ed., Managing the University: A Systems Approach, 1972. Contbr. to: Review of Econs. & Stats.; Sloan Mgmt. Review; Jrnl. of Fin.; Jrnl. of Advt. Rsch.; Jrnl. of Mktng.; Jrnl. of Mktng. Rsch.; Socio-Econ. Planning Scis.; Jrnl. of Econs. & Bus.; Acad. of Mgmt. Jrnl.; Interfaces; Jrnl. of Long Range Planning; IEEE Transactions on Profl. Communication. Mbrships. incl: Publs. Comm., Inst. of Mgmt. Scis.; Fellow, AAAS; Am. Econ. Assn. Recip., sev. grants & fellowships. Address: 207 Eakin St., Blacksburg, VA 24060, USA.

HAMES, Jack Hamawi, b. 15 June 1920, Cairo, Egypt. Barrister. Educ: M.A., LL.B., Univ. of Cambridge, UK. Publs: Family Law. Contbr. to: Solicitors' Jrnl.; Law Times; Tax Digest; Int. Accts. Jrnl.; Law Jrnl. Recip., Q.C. Address: 10 Old Square, Lincolns Inn, London WC2, UK.

HAMIDI, Mehdi, b. 1914, Shiraz, Iran. Professor of Iranian Language & Literature. Educ: B.A., Ph.D., Tehran Univ. Publs: (poetry) Broken Talisman, 2nd ed., 1954; Ten Commandments, 1964; Beloved's Tear, 6th ed., 1970; (rsch. books) Masterpieces of Ferdowssy, 1951; Hamidi's Arooz, 1964; Paradise Wordings (2 vols.), 4th ed., 1968; Sea of Jewels (3 vols.), 6th ed., 1973. Contbr. to: Yaghma; Sapid; Keyhan newspaper; & num. Iranian newspapers & jrnls. Mbrships: Saadi Lit. Soc. Hons: 2 Prizes from Min. Educ., 1973, 1974; 2 Prizes from BBC (UK) & Iran govt. for poems on Iran. Address: Nahid St., Saltanat Abad, Do Rahi, Tehran, Iran.

HAMILTON, David, b. 5 Mar. 1940, Chertsey, Surrey, UK. Publications Manager. Educ: B.Sc.(Hons.), Reading Univ., Berks., UK. Publs: Technology, Man & the Environment, 1973. Contbr. to: New Sci. (Indl. Ed., 1967-71). Mbr., Can. Sci. Writers' Assn. Address: 14 Ellery Crescent, Ottawa, Ontario K2H 6M6, Canada.

HAMILTON, Donald (Bengtsson), b. 24 Mar. 1916, Uppsala, Sweden. Author; Photographer. Educ: B.S., Univ. of Chgo., Ill., 1938. Publs: 5 western novels; 5 mystery novels; 15 espionage novels in Matt Helm series. Contbr. to: Outdoor Life; True; Sports Afield; Yachting; Rudder; Boating; Gun World; Gun Digest; Guns; Trailer Boats. Recip., Spur Award, Western Writers of Am., 1967. Address: P.O. Box 1045, Santa Fe, NM 87501, USA.

HAMILTON, Elizabeth, b. 3 Apr. 1906, Co. Wicklow, Repub. of Ireland. Writer. Educ: M.A., London Univ., UK. Publs: The Great Teresa; The Year Returns, 1952; Simon, 1956; River Full of Stars, 1959; Put Off Thy Shoes, 1960;

An Irish Childhood, 1963; Heloise, 1966; The Desert My Dwelling Place, 1968; I stay in the Church, 1973; Cardinal Suenens: A Portrait, 1975. Contbr. to: Cath. Herald; Pax; Aylesford Review; Cath. Digest. Address: 84 Vicarage Ct., Kensington Church St., London W8 4HG, UK.

HAMILTON, (George) Ronald, b. 30 July 1909, Leeds, Yorks., UK. Schoolmaster. Educ: B.A., 1932, M.A., 1935, Magdalene Coll., Cambridge. Publs: Frederick the Great, 1936; Pendlebury & the Plaster Saints (w. Colin Badcock), 1959; Budge Firth — A Memoir & Some Sermons (ed. & co-author), 1960; Now I Remember, A Holiday History of Britain, 1964; A Holiday History of France, 1971; Summer Pilgrimage, 1973. Contbr. to: Army Quarterly; The Field; The Times. Mbrships. incl: Trustee, Armitt Lib., Ambleside. Hons: OBE; Territorial Decoration. Address: Cherry Orchard Cottage, Broad Campden, Glos., GL55 6UU, UK.

HAMILTON, Iain Bertram, b. 1920, Renfrew, UK. Editorial Director, Publishing House. Publs: Scotland the Brave; The Foster Gang; Embarkation for Cythera, 1975; Koestler, 1975. Contbr. to: Spectator (assoc. Ed., 1954-57; Ed., 1962-63); Guardian; Times Educ. Supplement. Address: 31 Highgate West Hill, London N6, UK.

HAMILTON, Max, b. 1912, Offenbach, Germany. Professor of Psychiatry. Educ: M.D., Univ. Coll., London, UK. Publs: Psychosomatics; Lectures on the Methodology of Clinical Research, 2 eds.; Readings in Abnormal Psychology. Contbr. to med., psychiatric & psychol. jrnls. Mbrships: F.R.C.P.; F.R.C.Psych.; F.B.P.S. Address: Dept. of Psychiatry, 15 Hyde Terrace, Leeds LS2 9LT, UK.

HAMILTON, William James, b. 1903, Islandmagee, Northern Ireland. University Professor of Anatomy. Educ: Queen's Univ., Belfast; M.D.; B.Ch.; D.Sc., Belfast, Glasgow; F.R.C.S.; F.R.C.O.G. Publs: Textbook of Surface & Radiological Anatomy (w. A. B. Appleton & G. Simon); Textbook of Embryology (w. J. D. Boyd & H. W. Mossman); Textbook of Anatomy (Ed.); The Human Placenta (w. J. D. Boyd). Contbr. to: British Obstetric & Gynaecological Practice; Modern Trends in Obstetrics & Gynaecology; Diseases of Ear, Nose & Throat; Jrnl. of Anatomy (former Ed.); vol. II, Marshall's Physiology of Reproduction. Address: 45 Wolsey Rd., Moor Park, Northwood, Middx., UK.

HAMILTON-EDWARDS, Gerald Kenneth Savery, b. 24 July 1906, Southsea, Hants., UK. Chartered Librarian. Educ: B.A., 1927, M.A., 1932, Keble Coll., Oxford; Dip. in Libnship., Univ. Coll., London, 1930; F.L.A., 1946. Publs: The Stevens Family of Plymouth, 1949; The Leisured Connoisseur, 1954; Twelve Men of Plymouth, 1951; In Search of Ancestry, 1966, 3rd ed., 1974; Tracing Your British Ancestors, 1966; In Search of Scottish Ancestry, 1972. Contbr. to D.N.B.,; BBC; var. mags., newspapers & jrnls. Mbr., profl. orgs. Hons: Territorial Decoration, 1946; Coronation Medal, 1953. Address: 32 Bowness Ave., Headington, Oxford OX3 0AL, UK.

HAMLIN, Bruce Gordon, b. 15 Nov. 1929, Wellington, NZ. Botanist. Educ: Wellington Tech. Coll.; Victoria Univ. of Wellington. Publs: Revision of the Genus Uncinia, 1959; Native Trees, 1962; Native Ferns, 1962. Contbr. to: Records of Dominion Museum; Royal Soc. of NZ; Tuatare; Jrnl. of Hattori Botan. Lab.; NZ Listener. Mbrships: Royal Soc. of NZ (sometime Hon. Ed. Botany); VP, Art Galleries & Museums Assn., NZ; Pres., Ed., Royal Numismatic Soc. of NZ. Address: Nat. Museum, Private Bag, Wellington, NZ.

HAMLIN, Charles Hunter, b. 16 Nov. 1890, Burkeville, Va., USA. Professor of History. Educ: A.B., Wm. & Mary Coll., 1914; M.A., Univ. of Va., 1917; Ph.D., George Peabody Coll. for Tchrs., 1941. Publs: The War Myth in U.S. History, 1927, 1954; Lobbyists & Lobbying in North Carolina Legislature, 1933; Propaganda & Myth in Time of War, 1972. Contbr. to profl. jrnls.; Dict. of Am. Hist. Address: Atlantic Christian Coll., Wilson, NC 27893, USA.

HAMLYN, Noel Tempest, b. 25 Dec. 1921, Durban, S. Africa. Writer; Journalist. Publs: South African Poetry (anthol.), 1947; Rhodesian Poetry (anthol.), 1961, 1964, 1968-69 & 1972-73; Shore of Solitude (novel), 1974. Contbr. to: Two Tone; Optima; Horizon; Rhodesia Herald (art critic); var. others. Mbrships: Rhodesian Ctr., PEN; Rhodesian Guild of Jrnlsts. Address: 45 Norton Manor, Mazoe St., Salisbury, Rhodesia.

HAMM, Marie Norstrom Roberson, b. 16 May 1917, Mpls., Minn., USA. Writer. Educ: Barnard Coll., 1935-36.

Publs. incl: The Buffet Cookbook, 1954. The Famous American Recipes Cookbook, 1955; The Second Chafing Dish Cookbook, 1963; Money in the Bank Cookbook, 1968; Italian Cookbook, 1972; Natural Foods Cookbook, 1973; Gifts From Your Kitchen, 1973; Woman's Day Encyclopedia of Cookery, 23 vols. (ed.), 1973-74. Contbr. to num. jrnls. & mags. Hons: Gold Medals for Fondue Cookbook, 1970 & The Blender Cookbook, 1971. Address: 360 East 72 St., N.Y., NY 10021, USA.

HAMMACK, Robert Dean Michael, b. 16 Nov. 1944, Du Quoin, Ill., USA. Writer-Editor. Educ: B.A., Benedictine Coll., Atchison, Kan., 1970; M.A., S.E. Mo. State Univ., Cape Girardeau, 1975. Publs: Appendix i (poetry), 1974; St. George: Universal Patron, 1975; In Wildness, 1975. Contbr. to: Nat. Stamp News (contbrn. ed.); The Independence, Jrnl. of Harry S. Truman Assn. (ed. emeritus); Second Story Mag. (fndng. ed. & publr.). Mbrships. incl: Mo. Writers' Guild. Recip., sev. awards. Address: 601 Market St., Ste. Genevieve, MO 63670, USA.

HAMMAR, (Carl Gustaf) George, b. 2 May 1906, G'öteborg, Sweden. Director of Teachers' Training College. Educ: B.A.; D.D. Publs: Christian Realism in Contemporary American Theology, A Study of Reinhold Niebuhr, W. M. Horton & H. P. Van Dusen, 1940; The Problem of Life in the Danish Dramatician Kaj Munk, 1945; Elementary Psychology, 1949; Yleinen Psykologia, 1949; Psychology, 1951; New Psychology, 1967; Teaching Psychology, 1970. Contbr. to: Ecumenical Review; var. Swedish papers & periodicals. Mbrships. incl: Swedish Union of Authors. Address: Väsbyvägen 2, 170 10 Ekerö-Stockholm, Sweden.

HAMMARBERG-ÅKESSON, Jarl, b. 22 Nov. 1940, Göteborg, Sweden. Author. Publs: Bord, duka er! 1964; "JA JA JA JA JA JA JA JA", 1966; Strålande dikter/nej så fan heller (w. Sonja Åkesson), 1967; Kändis (w. Sonja Åkesson), 1969; Brev fran Jarl, 1970; Mina kvinnor, min storfamilj, 1972; Äntra vardagen, 1973. Address: Ringarstigen 3, 161 52 Bromma, Sweden.

HAMMER, Lillian, b. Lodz, Poland. Author. Publs: Waves of Fire, 1972. Contbr. to sev. poetry anthols.; Poet Int. Monthly; Major Poets; Guaderni Di Poesia, Italy; Bitterroot I.P.F.; Mustang Review; & others. Mbrships: I.P.S.; World Poetry Soc. Intercontinental; I.C.P.A.; Soc. of Lit. Designates; Hon. VP, Centro Scombi Internazionali; etc. Hons: Award, Major Poets Chapter P.M.A.; 12 Awards, Int. & Nat. Poetry Competitions, 1968—. Address: 2820 Bronx Pk. E., Bronx, NY 10467, USA.

HAMMERSHAIMB, Erling, b. 3 Mar. 1904, Aalborg, Denmark. Professor of Semitic Philology; Former Rector, University of Aarhus. Educ: Cand. theol., 1929; M.A., 1936; Ph.D., 1941. Publs: Das Verbum im Dialekt von Ras Schamra, 1941; Amos, 1946, Engl. ed., 1970; Genesis, 1957; Some Aspects of Old Testament Prophecy, 1966. Contbr. to: Les Fouilles de Hama, Vol. IV, 1958-69. Mbrships: Nathan Söderblom Sällskapet, Uppsala, Sweden; Royal Danish Acad. Recip., Hon. Dr. Theol., Univ. of Uppsala. Address: Jens Munksvej 25, Aarhus N. 8200, Denmark.

HAMMETT, Louis Plack, b. 7 Apr. 1894, Wilmington, Del., USA. Chemist; Educator (Professor Emeritus). Educ: A.B., Harvard Coll.; Ph.D., Columbia Univ., 1923. Publs: Solutions of Electrolytes, 1929, 2nd ed., 1936; Physical Organic Chemistry, 1940, 2nd ed., 1970, & var. transls.; Introduction to the Study of Physical Chemistry, 1952. Contbr. to profl. jrnls. Mbrships: Nat. Acad. Scis.; Am. Chem. Soc.; Hon. Fellow, Chem. Soc., UK. Hons: Nicholas Medal, 1957; Norris Awards, 1960, 1966; Priestley Medal, 1961; Gibbs Medal, 1961; D.Sc., Columbia Univ., 1962; Lewis Medal, 1967; Chandler Medal, 1968; Nat. Medal of Scis., 1968. Address: 288 Medford Leas, Medford, NJ 08055, USA.

HAMMOND, Nicholas Geoffrey Lempriére, b. 15 Nov. 1907, Ayr, UK. University Teacher; Author. Educ: Fettes Coll., Edinburgh; Class I, Classical Tripos Pts. I & II, Caius Coll., Cambridge; studies, Brit. Schl. of Archaeol., Athens, Greece. Publs: A History of Greece to 322 B.C., 1959, 2nd ed., 1967; Epirus, 1967; A History of Macedonia, Vol. I, 1972; Studies in Greek History, 1973. Contbr. to: Jrnl. of Hellenic Studies; Jrnl. of Roman Studies; Greek, Roman & Byzantine Studies; etc. Hons: D.S.O., 1944; Fellow, Brit. Acad., 1968; C.B.E., 1974. Address: 3 Belvoir Terrace, Trumpington Rd., Cambridge CB2 2AA, UK.

HAMMOND, Paul Young, b. 24 Feb. 1929, Salt Lake City, Utah, USA. Political Scientist. Educ: B.A., Univ. of Utah, 1949; M.A., 1951; Ph.D., 1953, Harvard Univ., USA. London Schl. of Econs., 1952. Publs. incl: The Cold War Years: American Foreign Policy Since 1945, 1969; (co-author) American Civil Military Decisions, 1963; (co-author) Strategy, Politics, & Defence Budgets, 1962; (Co-Ed.) Political Dynamics in the Middle East, 1972. Contbr. to sev. jrnls. incl: World Politics; Am. Political Sci. Review. Mbrships: Am. Political Sci. Assn.; Int. Studies Assn.; Am. Soc. for Pub. Admin. Address: 30600 Las Estrellas Dr., Malibu, CA 90265, USA.

HAMMOND, Thomas Taylor, b. 15 Sept. 1920, Atlanta, Ga., USA. Professor of History. Educ: B.A., Univ. of Miss., 1941; M.A., Univ. of N.C., 1948; Ph.D., 1954, Columbia Univ. Publs: Yugoslavia Between East & West, 1954; Lenin on Trade Union & Revolution, 1957; Soviet Foreign Relations & World Communism: a Bibliography, 1965; The Anatomy of Communist Takeovers, 1975. Contbr. to: Foreign Affairs; Slavic Review; Nat. Geogl. Mag.; Russian Review; Am. Histl. Review. Mbrships: Am. Histl. Assn.; S. Conf. on Slavic Studies, Pres., 1966; AAUP; Am. Assn. Advancement Slavic Studies. Address: Randall Hall, Univ. of Virginia, Charlottesville, VA 22903, USA.

HAMMOND INNES, Ralph, b. 15 July 1913, Horsham, UK. Author. Publs: Wreckers Must Breathe, 1940; The Trojan Horse, 1940; Attack Alarm, 1941; Dead & Alive, 1946; The Lonely Skier, 1947; The Killer Mine, 1947; Maddon's Rock, 1948; The Blue Ice, 1948; The White South, 1949; The Angry Mountain, 1950; Air Bridge, 1951; Campbell's Kingdom, 1952; The Strange Land, 1954; The Mary Deare, 1956; The Land God Gave to Cain, 1958; Harvest of Journeys, 1959; The Doomed Oasis, 1960; Atlantic Fury, 1962; Scandinavia, 1963; The Strode Venturer, 1965; Sea & Islands, 1967; The Conquistadors, 1969; Levkas Man, 1971; Golden Soak, 1973; North Star, 1974; titles published in over 25 different langs.; serialisations. Contbr. to var. jrnls. Mbrships. incl: Coun. Soc. of Authors; PEN; Authors Guild. Address: Ayres End, Kersey, Ipswich, Suffolk IP7 6EB, UK.

HAMOD, Hamode Samuel, pen name HAMOD, Sam, b. 16 Feb. 1936, Gary, Ind., USA. Writer; Professor. Educ: B.S., 1957, M.A., 1960, Northwestern Univ., Evanston, Ill.; Ph.D., Univ. of Iowa, 1973. Publs. incl: The Holding Action, 1969; The Famous Boating Party, 1970, 2nd ed., 1973; After the Funeral Of Assam Hamady, 1971; The Famous Blue Mounds Scrapbook, 1972. Contbr. to: Settling Am. (anthol.), 1974; Surviving in Am. (Ed.); Ye Olde Town Voice (Former Fiction & Poetry Ed.); December; Kenyon Review; Gum; Noise; Mainline; Stand (UK); Ambit (UK); etc. Hons. incl: Poet-in-Residence, Pa. Pub. Schls., 1973. Address: 3111 E. 4th St., Apt. 113, Tucson, AZ 85716, USA.

HAMPTON, Christopher James, b. 1946, Fayal, The Azores. Dramatist. Educ: B.A., New Coll., Oxford. Publs: When Did You Last See My Mother?, 1967, Total Eclipse, 1969; The Philanthropist, 1970; Savages, 1974. Publs: (transls.) Marya, by Isaac Babel; Uncle Vanya, by Chekhov; Hedda Gabler, A Doll's House, by Ibsen; Don Juan, by Molière. Contbr. to: Plays of the Year. Agent: Margaret Ramsay. Address: 9 Winchester House, 16 Cambridge Pk., Twickenham, Middx., UK.

HAMPTON, Christopher Martin, b. 1929, London, UK. Lecturer in English. Educ: Guildhall Schl. of Music & Drama, London. Publs: Transl., The Fantastic Brother, 1961; Island of the Southern Sun, 1962; The Etruscans, 1969; The Etruscan Survival, 1970; An Exile's Italy, 1972; Poems for Shakespeare, 1972. Contbr. to: Group Anthol., 1963; Observer; New Statesman; Listener; London Mag.; Tribune; N.Y. Times. Mbrships: Assoc., Guildhall Schl. of Music; Coun., Poetry Soc. Address: 161 Southwood Lane, Highgate, London N6, UK.

HAMPTON, Jack Fitz-Gerald, b. Hampton, Middx., UK. Author. Educ: London Schl. of Econs. & Pol. Sci. Publs: Factory Canteens & Their Management; Canteen Cookery; Club Management Control; Catering Establishments & Prevention of Food Poisoning; Modern Angling Bibliography; Hampton on Pike Fishing. Contbr. of articles on fishing to: Field Sports; Historic Houses & Antiques; etc.; Broadcaster, Norwegian Radio, BBC Wales. Hons: Silver Medalist Int. Culinary Exhib., Frankfurt, Germany; F.H.C.I.; A.R.S.H. Address: 29 St. James's Rd., Edgbaston, Birmingham B15 2NX, UK.

HAMPTON, (Capt.) Trevor Arthur, b. 1912, Birmingham, UK. Founder & Director British Underwater Centre; Farmer; Yachtmaster & Marine Surveyor; Commissioned Royal Air Force, 1939; Bomber Command, Service Test Pilot. Educ: C.Eng.; Handsworth Tech. Coll.; Ctrl. Tech. Coll., Birmingham. Publs.: Alone at Sea, 1948; Master Diver, 1955, 3rd ed., 1970; Sailors World, 1969. Contbr. to: Yachting Monthly; Yachting World; etc. Mbrships: A.F.C.; F.Inst.P.I.; F.B.I.S.; M.R.I.N.A.; Royal Air Force Yacht Club; Royal Aero Club. Address: Lower Weeke, Warfleet, Dartmouth, Devon, UK.

HAMRE, (Lt.-Col.) Leif, b. 1914, Molde, Norway. Officer, Royal Norwegian Air Force. Educ: Flying Schl., Can.; Staff Schl., USA; Defence Coll., Norway. Publs: Otter Three Two Calling, 1960; Blue Two Bale Out, 1961; Ready for Take Off, 1962; Contact Lost, 1968; Operation Arctic, 1973. Agent: H. Aschehoug & Co. Address: Syrinveien 10, 3408 Tranby, Norway.

HAN, Seung Soo, b. 28 Dec. 1936, Chunchon, Korea. Professor. Educ: B.A., Yonsei Univ., 1960; M.P.A., Seoul Nat. Univ., 1963; D.Phil., Univ. of York, UK, 1968. Publs: The Growth & Function of the European Budget, 1971; Britain & the Common Market: The Effect of Entry on the Pattern of Manufacturing Production (w. H. H. Liesner), 1971. Contbr. to: Econ. Jrnl.; Manchester Schl. Econ. & Social Studies; Pub. Fin.; Jrnl. of World Trade Law; Economica; Asian Econs.; Korean Econ. Jrnl. Mbr., var. profl. assns. in Europe & Korea. Recip., 6th European Communities Prize (Econ. Sect.), 1971. Address: 446-10, Sokyodong, Mapogu, Seoul, Korea.

HANBURY, Harold Greville, b. 19 June 1898, Kineton, Warwicks., UK. Barrister-at-Law, Inner Temple, 1922; Law Teacher & Professor. Educ: Brasenose Coll., Oxford; D.C.L.; Q.C., 1960. Publs: Essays In Equity, 1934; Modern Equity, 1935, 10th ed., 1975; Principles of Agency, 1952, 2nd ed., 1956; The Vinerian Chair & Legal Education, 1958. Contbr. to: Law Quarterly Review; Cambridge Law Jrnl. Mbrships: Pres., Bentham Club, U.C.L., 1954; Pub. Tchrs. of Law, 1958-59; Hon. Fellow, Lincoln Coll., Oxford; Hon. Bencher, 1950. Address: Marlborough House, Falmouth, Cornwall, UK.

HANCOCK, Norman, b. 1894, London, UK. Former Chairman & Director of Newspaper Company; Writer. Publs: War from the Ranks; Interlude for John (short stories); An Innocent Grows Up (autobiog.). Mbrships: F.I.A.L.; Soc. of Authors. Hon: Recommendation by Book Soc. for An Innocent Grows Up. Address: 6 Stratford Rd., Salisbury, Wilts., UK.

HANCOCK, Ralph Lowell, b. 1903, Plainville, Ind., Usa. Writer; Photographer. Educ: Wash. Univ., St. Louis, Mo. Publs. incl: Our Southern Neighbours; Exploring American Neighbours; Opportunities in Latin America; Mexico; Desert Living; The Rainbow Republics; The Magic Land; Fabulous Boulevard; The Lost Treasure of Cocos Island; Douglas Fairbanks: The Fourth Musketeer; Baja California; The Comemoral; The Forest Lawn Story; Puerto Rico: Traveler's Guide; The Compleat Swindler. Contbr. to: Ency. Americana (Latin Am. ed.); var. trade & popular mags. & univ. publs. Address: 9697 Caminito de la Vida, San Diego, CA 92121, USA.

HANDEL, Gerald, b. 8 Aug. 1924, Cleveland, Ohio, USA. Professor of Sociology. Educ: A.B., Univ. of Chgo., 1947; A.M., 1951; Ph.D., 1962. Publs: Family Worlds (w. Robert D. Hess), 1959; Workingman's Wife: Her Personality World & Life Style (w. Les Rainwater & Richard P. Coleman), 1959; The Psychosocial Interior of the Family, 1967, 1972; The Child & Society (w. Frederick Elkin), 1972; Assoc. Ed., Jrnl. of Marriage & Family. Contbr. to: Sociol. & Soc. Rsch.; Psychol. Bull.; Merrill-Palmer Quarterly of Behaviour & Dev.; Contem. Psychol. Mbrships: Am. Sociol. Assn.; Am. Psychol. Assn.; Soc. of Study of Soc. Problems; AAUP. Address: Dept. of Sociol., City Coll., CUNY, N.Y., NY 10031, USA.

HANDLEY-TAYLOR, Geoffrey, b. 1920, Horsforth, Yorks., UK. Editor; Lecturer. Educ: Ph.D. Publs. incl: New Hyperion, 1950; Winifred Holtby Bibliography & Letters, 1955; John Gay & the Ballad Opera (co-author), 1956; The Book of the Private Press (co-author), 1958; Letters of Winifred Holtby & Vera Brittain (co-author), 1961-70; Bibliography of Iran, 1964-69; Ed., Dictionary of International Biography, 1963, 1964-65, 1966; Ed., Authors of Today, 9 vols., 1971-73. Contbr. to: Ency. Britannica. Mbrships. incl: F.R.S.L.; Pres., Lancs. Authors

Assn., 1969-72; Chmn., Gen. Coun., Poetry Soc., 1967-68. Address: National Liberal Club, P.O. Box 347, Whitehall Place, London SW1A 2HE, UK.

HANDLIN, Oscar, b. 29 Sept. 1915, NYC, USA. Historian. Educ: A.B., Bklyn. Coll., 1934, M.A., 1935, Ph.D., 1940, Harvard Univ. Publs: Al Smith & His America, 1958; Newcomers: Negroes & Puerto Ricans in a Changing Metropolis; The Americans, 1963; The Historian & the City, 1963; Fire-Ball in the Night, 1964; Popular Sources of Political Authority, 1966; America: A History, 1968; Facing Life; Youth & the Family in American History, 1971; The Uprooted, 2nd enlarged ed., 1973. Mbr., profl, orgs. Recip., awards & hon. degrees. Address: 210 Robinson Hall, Harvard Univ., Cambridge, MA 02138, USA.

HANDY, Rollo Leroy, b. 20 Feb. 1927, Kenyon, Minn., USA. University Professor. Educ: B.A., Carleton Coll., 1950; M.A., Sarah Lawrence Coll., 1951; Ph.D., Univ. of Buffalo, 1954. Publs: Methodology of the Behavioural Sciences, 1964; Value Theory & the Behavioral Sciences, 1969; The Measurement of Values, 1970; Useful Procedures of Inquiry (co-author), 1973; A Current Appraisal of the Behavioral Sciences (co-author), 1964, rev. ed., 1973; Philosophical Perspectives on Punishment (co-ed.), 1968; The Idea of God (co-ed.), 1968; The Behavioral Sciences (co-ed.), 1968. Contbr. to profl. jrnls. & the Ency. of Philosophy. Address: Fac. of Educl. Studies, SUNY at Buffalo, Buffalo, NY 14214, USA.

HANFF, Helene, b. Phila., Pa., USA. Writer. Publs: Underfoot in Show Business, 1961; 84 Charing Cross Road, 1970 (USA), 1971 (UK); The Duchess of Bloomsbury Street, 1973 (USA), 1974 (UK); & num. children's Am. Hist. books. Contbr. to: Reader's Digest; Harper's; New Yorker. Mbr., Lenox Hill, NYC, Dem. Club (Past Pres., 1970). Address: 305 E. 72nd St., N.Y., NY 10021, USA.

HANLEY, Clifford Leonard Clark, pen name CALVIN, Henry, b. 28 Oct. 1922, Glasgow, UK. Novelist. Publs. incl: Dancing in the Street, 1958; Love from Everybody, 1959; The System, 1962; It's Different Abroad, 1963; The Italian Gadget, 1966; The Hot Month, 1967; A Nice Friendly Town, 1967; The DNA Business, 1967; Miranda Must Die, 1968; The Red Haired Bitch, 1969; The Chosen Instrument, 1969; The Poison Chasers, 1971; Take Two Popes, 1972. Contbr. to: Spectator; Daily Telegraph; Times. Mbrships. incl: Glasgow Lit. & Philol. Soc. (Pres., 1965-66); PEN (Scottish Pres., 1974); Writers' Guild; Nat. Union of Jrnlsts. Address: 36 Munro Rd., Glasgow, UK.

HANLEY, Gerald Anthony, b. 17 Dec. 1916. Author. Publs: Monsoon Victory, 1946; The Consul at Sunset, 1951; The Year of the Lion, 1953; Drinkers of Darkness, 1955; Without Love, 1957; The Journey Homeward, 1961; Gilligan's Last Elephant, 1962; See You in Yasukuni, 1969; Warriors & Strangers, 1971. Address: c/o David Higham, 7-8 Lower John St., Golden Sq., London W1, UK.

HANLEY, James, b. 1901. Novelist; Playwright. Publs. incl: (novels) The Furys, New York, 1935; The Secret Journey, 1936; Hollow Sea, 1938; Our Time is Gone, 1940; The Closed Harbour, 1952; The Welsh Sonata, 1954; Levine, 1955; Another World, 1972; (essays) Soldiers Wind, 1938; Don Quixote Drowned, 1953; (stories) Men in Darkness, 1931; At Bay, 1943; Crilley, 1945; A Walk in the Wilderness, 1950; (play) Plays One, 1968. Address: c/o London Management, 235-241 Regent St., London W1A 3JT, UK.

HANNA, Paul Robert, b. 21 June 1902, Sioux City, Iowa, USA. The Lee L. Jacks Professor of Child Education (Emeritus) & The Director (Emeritus) of Stanford International Development Education Center, School of Education, Stanford Univ., Calif. Educ: A.B., Hamline Univ., St. Paul, Minn., 1924; M.A., 1925, Ph.D., 1929, Columbia Univ., N.Y. Publs. incl: Phoneme — Grapheme Correspondences as Cues to Spelling Improvement (w. Jean S. Hanna, Richard Hughes & Hugh Rudorf), 1966; Spelling: Structure & Strategies (w. Richard E. Hodges & Jean S. Hanna), 1970; & over 50 schl. social sci. textbooks. Contbr. to num. acad. jrnls. (over 100 articles). Mbrships. incl: Fellow Am. Assn. for Advancement Sci. Hons. incl: D. Pedagogy, Hamline Univ., 1937. Address: P.O. Box 430, Pescadero, CA 94060, USA.

HANQUIST, Olof (Anders Thor), b. 30 Nov. 1908, Kalmar, Sweden. Writer; Translator; Engineer. Educ: Univ. studies. Publs: Spain, 1965; Latin America (co-author),

1966; Portugal, 1968. Contbr. to: Industria; Jorden Runt. Mbr., Swedish Union of Authors. Address: Lill Jans Plan 6, 114 25 Stockholm, Sweden.

HANSEN, Hans, b. 4 Jan. 1939, Copenhagen, Denmark. Teacher. Publs: Lyd (short stories), 1965; Forsvindinger (short stories), 1967; Bim — Bam — Busse (play for children), 1971; Livsfarlige papirer (novel), 1974; Farlige Forbindelser (novel), 1975. Contbr. to: Vindrosen; Hvedekorn. Mbrships: Danish Assn. of Authors; Danish Assn. of Dramatists. Recip., Nat. Art Fndns. Production Prize, 1967. Address: Skovvej 7, 3300 Frederiksvaerk, Denmark.

HANSKI, Eino, b. 17 July 1928, Leningrad, USSR. Author. Publs: The Long Winter, 1965; The Long Journey, 1967; The Long Wait, 1968; Children of the Revolution, 1971; Hours of Freedom, 1974; Eino Hanski in the Soviet, 1974. Contbr. of radio & TV plays to Swedish Broadcasting Corp. Mbrships: Swedish Union of Authors; Swedish Union of Playwrights. Hons: Sandrews Playwright Prize, 1969; Gothenburg Cultural Grant, 1970; 5 Yr. Grant, Swedish Union of Authors, 1971-75. Address: Pölgatan 130, S-414 60 Göteborg, Sweden.

HANSON, Earl Parker, b. 16 Mar. 1899, Berlin, Germany. Geographer; Writer. Educ: B.S., Univ. of Wis., USA. Publs. incl: The Amazon, A New Frontier? , 1944; New Worlds Emerging, 1950; Transformation, the Story of Modern Puerto Rico, 1955; Puerto Rico, Land of Wonders, 1960; Puerto Rico, Ally for Progress, 1962; South from the Spanish Main, 1967. Contbr. to num. encys., jrnls.; etc. Mbrships: Fellow, Am. Geogl. Soc., 1925—; Explorers Club, 1926—; Assn. of Am. Geogs. Hons: Kt. Official, Liberian Humane Order of African Redemption; Kt., Order of the Icelandic Falcon. Address: P.O. Box 12143, Loiza Station, Santurce, PR 00914, W. Indies.

HANSON, Michael, pen name HEMAN, Nicholas, b. 1936, Eastbourne, UK. Property, Architectural & Planning Correspondent. Educ: B.Sc., Univ. of London. Publs: 2,000 Years of London, 1967; Famous Architects of the City of London, 1971. Contbr. to: The Times; Sunday Telegraph; Guardian; num. others. Mbrships. incl: Soc. of Authors; London Topograph. Soc.; Past Asst. Sec., Royal Inst. of Brit. Archts. Address: 83 Thetford Rd., New Malden, Surrey KT3 5DS, UK.

HANSON, Richard Patrick Crosland, b. 1916, London, UK. Professor of Historical & Contemporary Theology, Univ. of Manchester. Educ: Trinity Coll., Dublin, Repub. of Ireland; M.A., D.D., M.R.I.A. Publs: Commentary on 2 Corinthians; the Church of Rome, A Dissuasive (w. R. H. Fuller); Allegory & Event; Tradition in the Early Church; The Summons to Unity; Origen's Doctrine of Tradition; New Clarendon Commentary on Acts, 1967; St. Patrick: his Origins & Career, 1968; Groundwork for Unity, 1971; The Attractiveness of God, 1973; Christianity in Britain 300-700 (Ed. w. M. Barley), 1968; Ed., Pelican Guide to Modern Theology, 3 vols., 1969-70. Contbr. to num. theol. jrnls. & books. Address: 24 Styal Rd., Wilmslow, Cheshire SK9 4AG, UK.

HANSRAJANI, Kewal Ram, pen name VALLABH, Vali Ram, b. 18 Aug. 1941, Mithi, Sind, Pakistan. Translator; Writer. Educ: M.A.(Urdu), M.A.(Sociol.), LL.B. Publs: (transls. of novels into Sindhi) Ghadaar (from Urdu), 1967; The Outsider (from French); Bund Darwaza (from Punjabi); Sita Haran (from Urdu); Aag Ka Dariya (from Urdu). Contbr. to: Mehran; Sohni; Indalath; Nai Qadran; Sind Rung Publs.; Kalakar Publs.; Kahani Publs.; & var. mags. (transls. into Sindhi of over 50 short stories). Address: 2 Shamsh Chambers, 3rd Floor, Risala Rd., Hyderabad, Sind, Pakistan.

HAN SUYIN, (Mrs. Elizabeth Comber), b. 12 Sept. 1917. Author; Doctor. Educ: Univs. of Yenching, Peking, Brussels; M.B., B.S., 1948, London Univ. Publs. incl: Destination Chungking, 1942; And the Rain My Drink, 1956; The Mountain is Young, 1958; Cast but One Shadow & Winter Love, 1962; Four Faces, 1963; China in the Year 2001, 1967; The Morning Deluge, 1972; (autobiography) A Many Splendoured Thing, 1952; The Crippled Tree, 1965; A Mortal Flower, 1966; Birdless Summer: China, Autobiography, History, 1968. Address: c/o Jonathan Cape, 30 Bedford Sq., London WC1, UK.

HANY, Marieluise, b. 24 Apr. 1921, Zürich, Switz. Painter; Writer of Children's books. Educ: Ph.D. Publs: Der Haferlöwe, 1967; Daisys Tanne, 1969; Die Arche Noah,

1971; Die Geschichte vom Paradies, 1972; Der arme Fluss, 1972; Dies Land soll Dir gehören, 1973; Guten Tag Sonne, 1974. Mbrships: Soc. Swiss Female Artists; Lyceum Club, Switz. Address: Im Wingert 24, 8049 Zürich, Switz.

HAQKAUSAR, Inamul, b. 1 Apr. 1931, Kanian Kalan, Jallundar, E. Punjab. Teacher. Educ: Dip. Jrnlsm., 1953, M.A., 1954, Ph.D., 1963, Punjab Univ., Lahore. Publs: Fughani's Life & Works, 1963; The Brahmis of Quetta — Kalat (transl.), 1964; Baluchistan men Urdu, 1968; Persian Poetry in Baluchistan, 1968; Ed., Jauhar-e-Moozzam, 1970; Armaghan-e-Kausar, 1973; 3 books forthcoming. Contbr. to: Feroze Sons Urdu Ency., 2nd ed.; var. jrnls. Mbrships: Hd., Persian Soc., Govt. Coll., Quetta, 1956-70, Bazm-e-Iqbal, Quetta, 1959-70; Pakistan Writers' Guild, Karachi, 1960-. Recip., Lit. Prize, Pakistan Writers' Guild, 1969-70. Address: Government Degree College, Loralai, Pakistan.

HARBOUR, David F., pen names HARBOUR, Dave; DOUGLAS, James; SWINDELL, Doug, b. 21 Apr. 1920, Coleman, Tex., USA. Retired Colonel, US Air Force; Author. Educ: Okla. City Univ. Publs: The Flying Sportsman, 1952; Modern ABC's of Bird Hunting, 1966; Super Freshwater Fishing Systems, 1971; Hunting the American Wild Turkey, 1975. Contbng. Ed., Sports Afield Mag. Mbrships: Advsry. Bd., Nat. Wild Turkey Fedn.; Advsry. Bd., Deer Sportsmen of Am.; Outdoor Writers' Assn. of Am.; Izaak Walton League. Recip., Tex. Hall of State. Address: Rte. 1, Box 26-D, Leesburg, FL 32748, USA.

HARCOURT, (Rev. Canon) Melville, pen name CRITICUS, b. 19 Mar. 1909, Hampshire, UK. Clerk in Holy Orders. Educ: NZ Univ.; B.D., Gen. Theol. Sem. Publs: The Day Before Yesterday, 1940; A Parson in Prison, 1942; I Appeal, 1944; Tubby Clayton, A Personal Saga, 1953; Thirteen for Christ (ed. & contbr.), 1953; Portraits of Destiny, 1966. Contbr. to sev. jrnls. Recip., sev. awards & hons. Address: c/o The Midland Bank, 45 Milsom St., Bath BA1, UK.

HARDIE, Charles Dunn, b. 1911, Glasgow, UK. Professor of Education. Educ: M.A., Magdalene Coll., Cambridge Univ. Publs: Truth & Fallacy in Educational Theory; Background to modern Thought; A Minimum Vocabulary; Ed., Science in Australian Primary Schools. Contbr. to: Proceedings, Aristotelian Soc.; Mind; Philosophy; The Educand; Educl. Theory; The Philos. of Sci. Hons. incl: Henry Fellowship, Harvard Univ., USA, 1935; Bye Fellowship, Magdalene Coll., Cambridge Univ., 1936. Address: The University, Hobart, Tas., Australia.

HARDIE, Frank, b. 1911, London, UK. Steel Industry Executive. Educ: Christ Church, Merton Coll., Oxford Univ.; M.A., Ph.D. Publs: The Political Influence of Queen Victoria, 1861-1901, 3rd ed., 1963; The Political Influence of the British Monarchy, 1868-1952, 1970; The Abyssinian Crisis, 1974. Address: 18 Kensington Gate, London W8 5NA, UK.

HARDING, James, b. 30 May 1929, Bath, Somerset, UK. Author; Lecturer. Educ: Dip., Univ. de Paris, France; B.A., Univ. of Bristol, UK; Ph.D., Univ. of London. Publs. incl: Saint Saëns & His Circle, 1954; Sacha Guitery, The Last Boulevardier, 1968; The Duke of Wellington, 1968; Massenet, 1970; Rossini, 1971; The Astonishing Adventure of General Boulanger, 1971; The Ox on the Roof, 1972; Gounod, 1973; Lost Illusions: The World of Paul Léautaud, 1974; Erik Satie, 1975. Contbr. to var. lit. & musical publs. Mbrships: Classical Assn.; Assn. des Amis d'André Gide; Soc. d'Etude du XXe Siècle. Recip., Phoenix Trust Award, Soc. of Authors, 1973. Address: 3 Montagu Square, London W1, UK.

HARDING, Lowry Waring, b. 30 Oct. 1907, Harding, Va., USA. University Professor; Editor. Educ: B.A., Lynchburg Coll., 1929; M.A., Univ. of Va., 1935; Ph.D., Ohio State Univ., 1941. Publs. incl: Student Teaching in the Elementary School, 1950, 1958; Essays in Educology, 1955; Arithmetic for Child Development, 1959, 5th ed., 1969; Evaluation in Elementary School Mathematics Education, 1968, 1970; Teaching-Learning Dialogues on Elementary School Mathematics, 2 vols., 1971; Anecdota Evaluata Humorata, 1974. Contbr. to num. profl. jrnls. Address: 3077 Bembridge Rd., Columbus, OH 43221, USA.

HARDING, Richard William, b. 1939, Bristol, UK. Associate Professor. Educ: Univ. of London; Columbia Univ., USA; LL.B.; LL.M. Publs: Police Killings in Australia, 1970. Contbr. to vär. legal & criminol. jrnls. Mbr., Aust. Soc. of Authors. Address: 13 Rawson St., Subiaco, W.A., Australia.

HARDING, Walter, b. 20 Apr. 1917, Bridgewater, Mass., USA. Professor of English. Educ: B.S.Ed., Bridgewater State Coll., 1939; M.A., Univ. of N.C., 1947; Ph.D., Rutgers Univ., 1950. Publs: The Correspondence of Henry David Thoreau (Ed. w. Carl Bode), 1958; A Thoreau Handbook, 1959, 2nd ed., 1962; The Variorum Walden, 1962; A Thoreau Profile (w. Milton Meltzer), 1962, 2nd ed., 1969; The Days of Henry Thoreau, 1965; Henry David Thoreau: A Profile, 1971. Contbr. to num. lit. jrnls. Mbr., profl. orgs. Recip., Fellowship, Am. Coun. of Learned Socs., 1962-63. Address: State Univ. Coll., Dept. of Engl., Geneseo, NY 14454, USA.

HARDINGE, (The Dowager Lady Hardinge of Penshurst), Helen Mary, b. 11 May 1901, London, UK. Writer. Publs: The Path of Kings, 1952; Loyal to Three Kings, 1967; (transl. into Engl.) Gabriel Marcel's, Changement d'Esperance (Engl. title, A Fresh Hope for the World), 1950. Contbr. to: Listener; Lady; Woman; House & Gdns. Mbrships: Soc. Authors; Friends Kent Churches; Fordcombe Parochial Church Coun.; Burrswood Fellowship; Toc H. Address: South Park, Penshurst, Kent TN11 8EA, UK.

HARDINGHAM, John Frederick Watson, b. 15 June 1916, Auckland, NZ. Journalist; Editor; Author. Educ: Dip. Jrnlsm., Dip. Soc. Sci., Univ. of Auckland. Publs: The Queen in New Zealand, 1955; Bold Century, 1959; New Zealand Travel Guide, 1959; Manual of Journalism, 1967; Ed., Crime & the Community; Ed., Crime in New Zealand. Contbr. to: NZ Herald, Auckland (Ed.). Mbrships: NZ Press Assn. (Dir. & Past Chmn.); London Coun. &. NZ Exec.; C'wlth. Press Union; IPI; NZ Press Coun. Address: 45 Allendale Rd., Mt. Albert, Auckland 3, NZ.

HARDWICK, Elizabeth (Mrs. Robert Lowell), b. 27 July 1916, Lexington, Ky., USA. Adjunct Professor of English, Barnard Coll., NYC; Advisory Editor & a Founder of New York Review of Books. Educ: A.B., 1938, M.A., 1939, Univ. of Ky.; Columbia Univ., 1939-41. Publs: The Ghostly Lover (novel), 1945; The Simple Truth (novel), 1955; Ed., The Selected Letters of William James, 1960; A View of My Own (essays), 1962. Contbr. to: Partisan Review; New Yorker; Harper's. Hons: Guggenheim Fellow (fiction), 1948; 1st woman recip., George Jean Nathan Award for Dramatic Criticism, 1967. Address: 15 West 67th St., N.Y., NY 10023, USA.

HARDWICK, Michael, b. 10 Sept. 1924, Leeds, UK. Author; Playwright; Journalist; Director. Publs. incl: The Vintage Musical Comedy Book, 1973; Osprey Guide to Anthony Trollope, 1974; Upstairs Downstairs: Mr. Hudson's Diaries', 1973, & Mr. Bellamy's Story, 1974; The Inheritors, 1974; The Four Musketeers, 1975; num. books w. Mollie Hardwick inclng: The Atkinson Century (novels), 1975; num. original plays & dramatizations for radio, TV & stage. Contbr. to jrnls. & newspapers. Mbr., sev. lit. orgs. Recip., Fellow, Royal Soc. of Arts; Address: 32 Southwood Lane, Highgate Village, London N6 5EB, UK.

HARDWICK, Mollie, b. Manchester, UK. Author; Playwright; Journalist; Director. Publs. incl: Mrs. Dizzy: The Life of Mary Anne Disraeli, 1972; Upstairs Downstairs: Sarah's Story, 1973, The Years of Change, 1974, The War to End Wars, 1975, & Mrs. Bridges' Story, 1975; Emily, 1975; num. books w. Michael Hardwick inclng. The Charles Dickens Encyclopaedia; num. original plays & dramatizations for radio, TV & stage. Contbr. to mags. Mbr., lit. socs. Recip., Fellow, Royal Soc. of Arts. Address: 32 Southwood Lane, Highgate Village, London N6 5EB, UK.

HARDY, Evelyn, b. Philadelphia, Pa., USA. Writer; Broadcaster; Lecturer. Educ: B.A., Smith Coll., Mass.; London Univ., UK. Publs: Donne, A Spirit in Conflict, 1942; Swift, The Conjured Spirit, 1949; Swift: Selected Prose with Introduction, 1950; Summer in Another World, 1950; Thomas Hardy: A Critical Biography 1954; Thomas Hardy's Notebooks, 1955; Ed., Some Recollections by Emma Hardy (w. Robert Gittings), 1961; Survivors of the Armada, 1966; Midnight Festival (poems), 1968; Ed., One Rare Fair Woman: Letters of Thomas Hardy to Florence Henniker (w. F. B. Pinion), 1972. Contbr. to: London Mag.; Hist. Today; Times Lit. Supplement; Country Life; etc. Recip., Leverhulme Rsch. Grant. Address: West Wing, Bramshott Court, Liphook, Hants. GU30 7RG, UK.

HARDY, Marjorie Enid, pen name HARDY, Bobbie, b. 11 Apr. 1913, Burwood, N.S.W., Australia. Historical Researcher & Writer. Educ: B.A., Univ. of New England. Publs: Water Carts to Pipelines, 1968; West of the Darling, 1970; Their Work was Australian, 1970. Mbrships: Aust. Soc. of Authors; Royal Aust. Histl. Soc. Address: Unit 402, 349 New South Head Rd., Double Bay, N.S.W., Australia 2028.

HARDY, Richard E., b. 11 Oct. 1938, Victoria, Va., USA. Professor & Chairman, Department of Rehabilitation Counseling, Virginia Commonwealth University. Educ: B.S., Va. Polytechnic Inst. & State Univ., 1960; M.S., Va. Commonwealth Univ., 1962; Ed.D., Dipl. in Counseling Psychol.; ABPP; Nat. Award from NRA for Scholarly Works. Ed. (w. J. G. Cull), 24 books on rehab. Contbr., chapts in 35 books & num. articles in psychol., rehab. & other profl, jrnls. Num. mbrships. incl: Am. Correctional Assn.; Am. Rehab. Counselor Assn. Address: 901 W. Franklin St., Richmond, VA 23284, USA.

HARDY, Ronald Harold, b. 1919, Balham, London, UK. Author. Publs: The Place of Jackals, 1954; A Name Like Herod, 1955; Kampong, 1957; The Men From the Bush, 1959; Act of Destruction, 1962; The Iron Snake, 1965; The Savages, 1967; The Face of Jalanath, 1973. Hons: James Tait Black Mem. Book Prize, for 'Act of Destruction'; Putnam Award, USA, for 'The Savages'. Agent: Anthony Sheil Assoc. Ltd. Address: Bridle Path Cottage, Ralliwood Rd., Ashtead, Surrey, UK.

HARDY, William George, b. 1895, Oakwood, Ont., Can. Emeritus Professor of Classics. Educ: Univs. of Toronto & Chgo.; M.A., Ph.D. Publs: Son of Eli; Father of Abraham; Turn Back the River; All the Trumpets Sounded; The Unfulfilled; The City of Libertines; From Sea Unto Sea; The Greek & Roman World; other books. Contbr. to: Macleans; Can. Home Jrnl.; Tomorrow; Colliers; Saturday Evening Post; Widsor; Strand. Mbrships: Classical Assn. of Can.; Can. Authors' Assn. Hons. incl: LL.D.; Mbr., Order of Can. Address: 10828 79th Ave., Edmonton, Alta., Can.

HARE, David, b. 1947, Sussex, UK. Theatre Company Director. Educ: M.A., Cambridge Univ. Publs: (plays) Slag, 1970; The Great Exhibition, 1972; Knuckle, 1974; Lay-By (w. 6 others), 1972; Brassneck (w. Howard Brenton), 1974. Address: c/o Margaret Ramsay Ltd., 14a Goodwins Ct., St. Martin's Lane, London WC2, UK.

HARE, R. M., b. 21 Mar. 1919, Backwell, Somerset, UK. University Professor. Educ: Balliol Coll., Oxford, 1937-39, 1945-47. Publs: The Language of Morals, 1952; Freedom & Reason, 1963; Practical Inferences, 1971; Essays on Philosophical Method, 1971; Essays on the Moral Concepts, 1972; Applications of Moral Philosophy, 1972. Contbr. to var. jrnls. Mbr., Aristotelian Soc. (Pres., 1972-73). Hons: T. H. Green Prize in Moral Philos., Oxford Univ., 1950; Fellow, British Acad., 1964; Hon. Fellow, Inst. of Soc., Ethics & Life Scis., Hastings Ctr., 1974; Hon. Fellow, Balliol Coll., Oxford, 1974. Address: Saffron House, Ewelme, Oxford, UK.

HAREWOOD, (The Rt. Hon. the Earl of) (LASCELLES, George Henry Hubert), b. 1923, London, UK. Artistic Director; Managing Director, English National Opera (formerly Sadler's Wells Opera). Educ: M.A., Univ. of Cambridge. Publs: Ed. & Reviser, Kobbe's Complete Opera Book; Benjamin Britten: A Symposium. Contbr. to: Opera; Daily Mail; New Statesman; Ed., Opera, 1950-53. Mbrships. incl: Chmn., Music Advsry. Comm., Brit. Coun., 1956; Pres., Engl. Opera Grp.; Dir., Engl. Stage Co. Hons: LL.D., Univ. of Leeds., Univ. of Aberdeen; D.Mus., Univ. of Hull. Address: 3, Clifton Hill, London NW8, UK; & Harewood House, Leeds, UK.

HARGREAVES, Peter Hickman, b. 8 May 1927. Sydney, Australia. Teacher. Educ: Univs. of Liverpool, UK, & Geneva, Switz.; Huddersfield Tech. Tchrs. Trng. Coll., UK; B.A.; Dip.Ed. Publs: author, co-author, & Ed., ca. 30 adult educ. text-books, inclng. French Once a Week 1 & 2, 1961; German Once a Week, 1963; Italiano Parlato, 1965; Espanol Rapido, 1966; Spanish Once a Week, 1971; English Once a Week, 1973; Business French, 1974. Contbr. to: Daily Telegraph; Guardian; New Statesman. Mbrships: Fellow, Inst. of Linguists; Soc. of Authors; MLA; Authors' Club. Address: 1 Manor Wood Rd., Purley, Surrey CR2 4LG, UK.

HARINGTON, Dorothy Joy Nora Pepys, pen name HARINGTON, Joy, b. 22 Feb. 1914, London, UK. Writer;

TV Director. Educ: Kate Rorke's Drama Schl. Publs: Jesus of Nazareth, 1956; Paul of Tarsus, 1958. Mbrships: Soc. of Film & TV Arts; Writers' Guild; Actors' Equity. Recip., Soc. of Film & TV Arts Award for Jesus of Nazareth, as Best TV Prod. of Yr., 1956. Address: 41 Primrose Mansions, London SW11 4EF, UK.

HARKAVY, Zvi, b. 1 Feb. 1908, Ekaterinoslav, Russia. Rabbi; Librarian. Educ: B.A.; M.A.; Th.D.; Haifa Technion; Univ. of Jerusalem; Petch Tikva Yeshiva, C.S.R.A. Publs. incl: (biographies) Rambam; Rabbi Shmuel Strashun; Rabbi Reuven Katz; The Family Maskil L'eitan; Jews of Salonica; The Man; The Plant; The Animal; Scepticism of Pascal; The Secret of Happy Marriage; Judaica in Russia; Autobibliografia, 1971; Book of Ekaterinoslav-Dniepropetrovsk, 1973. Contbr. to: Ency. Judaica in Russian (Co-Ed.); & num. periodicals & jrnls. Mbrships: Religious Writers' Org. (fndr.); Religious Acads. Org. (co-fndr.). Address: P.O. Box 7031, 7 Hran St., Jerusalem 91070, Israel.

HARKER, Kenneth, b. 1927, Darlington, UK. Scientist; Writer. Educ: B.Sc., Univ. of Durham. Publs: The Symmetrians, 1966; The Flowers of February, 1970. Contbr. to: Reveille; London Opinion; Cars Illustrated; Storyteller Contest; New Worlds SF; Evening News; Evening Gazette, Middlesbrough; BBC. Mbr., Soc. of Authors. Address: 28 Cobble Carr, Guisborough, Cleveland, TS14 6NR, UK.

HARLAN, George H., b. 4 July 1916, Sausalito, Calif., USA. Naval Architect. Educ: A.A., Coll. of Marin, 1935; B.A., Univ. of Nev., Reno, 1937. Publs: Oil Lamps & Iron Ponies, 1949; Of Walking Beams & Paddle Wheels, 1951; San Francisco Bay Ferryboats, 1967. Contbr. to: Pacific Marine Review; Trains. Mbrships: Soc. of Naval Archts. & Marine Engrs.; Past Pres., Soc. of Port Engrs. of San Fran. Address: 180 Via Lerida, San Rafael, CA 94904, USA.

HARLING, Doris, b. 30 May 1908, Accrington, Lancs., UK. Writer. Contbr. to: Accrington Miscellany; Accrington Observer & Times; Lancs. Evening Telegraph. Mbrships: Lancs. Authors' Assn., 29 yrs.; Burnley & Dist. Writers Circle, 9 yrs.; attended Writers' Summer Schl., Swanick. Hons: Lancs. Authors' Assn. Prize for Dialect Verse, 1968; Short Story Award, 1967, 1970, 1971 & 1972, Ellis Cup, 1970, Burnley Writers' Circle. Address: 107 Marlborough Rd., Accrington, Lancs., UK.

HARNETT, Cynthia Mary, b. 1893, Kensington, UK. Publs: The Woolpack, 1951; The Great House; Ring Out Bow Bells; Stars of Fortune; The Load of Unicorn; Monasteries & Monks, 1963; The Writing on the Hearth, 1971, USA 1974; Mudlarks (w. Vernon Stokes); Bobtail Pup; Two & a Bit; Pets Limited; Getting to Know Dogs; var. books for younger children. Hons: Carnegie Medal, 1951; 3 Hons. Awards, N.Y. Spring Festival, 1974. Address: Little Thatch, Binfield Heath, Henley-on-Thames, UK.

HARNING, Anderz, b. 4 Apr. 1938, Hälsingland, Stocka, Sweden. Author. Publs: Fridagar, 1961; De Andra, 1963; De Maktlösa, 1964; Inte vända om, 1965; Prag-vältagen stad, 1968; Kommentar till Höss 1968, 1968; Stålbadet, 1972; Asfåglarna, 1974. Contbr. to: Göteborgs-Tidningen; Swedish Trade Union Weekly. Mbrships: Union of Swedish Authors; Svenska Publicistklubben. Hons: Gothenburg Lit. Prize, 1963; Award, Swedish Authors' Union, 1969, 1970; Annual grant, Swedish Authors' Fund, 1972—. Address: Majorsgatan 8 VI, 413 08 Göteborg, Sweden—.

HARPER, Michael Claude, b. 12 Mar. 1931, London, UK. Clergyman; Author. Educ: M.A. (Law & Theol. Tripos), Emmanuel Coll., Cambridge; Ridley Hall, Cambridge. Publs: Power for the Body of Christ, 1964; As At the Beginning, 1965; Walk in the Spirit, 1968; Spiritual Warfare, 1970; None can Guess, 1971; A New Way of Living, 1973; Glory in the Church, 1974. Address: 23 Spencer Road, East Molesey, Surrey, UK.

HARPER, Norman Denholm, b. 27 Apr. 1906, Perth, W. Australia. Historian. Educ: M.A., 1928, B.Ed., 1936, Melbourne Univ. Publs: Ed., Australia in World Affairs 1950-55 (w. G. Greenwood), 1957; Australia & the United Nations (w. D. C. S. Sissons), 1958; Our Pacific Neighbours, 1960; Ed., Australia in World Affairs 1956-60, 1963, Australia in World Affairs 1961-65, 1968 (both w. G. Greenwood); Pacific Orbit, 1968; Australia, Asia & the Pacific; Ed., Australia & the U.S., 1971; Ed., Australia in World Affairs 1966-70 (w. G. Greenwood), 1974. Contbr.

to num. profl. jrnls. Recip., var. fellowships. Address: 8 Kerr Cres., S. Camberwell, Vic. 3124, Australia.

HARRINGTON, Alan Stewart, b. 16 Jan. 1919, Newton, Mass., USA. Writer. Educ: AA.B., Harvard. Publs: The Revelations of Dr. Modesto (novel), 1957; Life in the Crystal Palace (study of life in a large corporation), 1959; The Secret Swinger (novel), 1966; The Immortalist, 1969; Psychopaths . . ., 1972; Love & Evil From a Probation Officer's Casebook (w. Dan Sakall), 1974. Contbr. to: Atlantic; Harper's; Esquire; Playboy; Penthouse; New Repub.; Nation; Chgo. Review. Mbr., PEN. Address: 2831 N. Orlando Ave., Tucson, AZ 85712, USA.

HARRINGTON, Lyn, b. 31 July 1911, Sault Ste. Marie, Ont., Can. Writer. Educ: Grad. Univ. Toronto Schl. Lib. Sci. Publs. incl: (juvenile) Stormy Summer, 1953; Ranger's Handbook, 1962; How People Live in Canada, 1964; China & the Chinese, 1966; Australia & New Zealand, 1969; The Polar Regions, 1973; Enchantment of Ontario, 1974; Kinusi, Boy Hunter of Swampy Crees, forthcoming; 4 books in collaboration with var. writers & over 2300 articles, stories & radio dramas. Contbr. to: Can. Geogl. Jrnl.; radio; etc. Mbrships. incl: Can. Authors' Assn. (VP Ont.). Recip., Sangster Award, 1969 for serv. Can. Authors' Assn. Address: 30 Beaufield Ave., Toronto M4G 3R3, Can.

HARRIS, Albert, b. 16 Feb. 1945, Phila., Pa., USA. Theatrical Director; Author. Educ: Temple Univ., Phila., Pa. Publs: Jean Anouilh's Mademoiselle Colombe (adaptor as Broadway musical play), 1975. Mbrships: Dramatists Guild, Inc.; Authors League of Am., Inc.; Soc. of Stage Dirs. & Choreographers; Actor's Equity Assn. Address: 30 Perry St., N.Y., NY 10014, USA.

HARRIS, Barbara S., (née SEGER), b. 1927, Earlville, Iowa, USA. Author. Educ: Goodman Schl. of Theatre, Chgo., Ill. Publs: Who is Julia? , 1972. Mbrships: PEN; Soroptimist Fedn. of the Ams. Inc. Agent: James Brown Assocs., N.Y. Address: 18858 Kilfinan St., Northridge, CA 91324, USA.

HARRIS, Evelyn Marjorie (Viscountess St. Davids), b. 1919, Cambridge, UK. Publishing & Press Manager, Institute of Personnel Management. Educ: B.A., Univ. of London. Publs: Married Women in Industry; Equal Pay; Ed., The Realities of Productivity Bargaining; How to Get a Job. Address: 15 St. Mark's Crescent, Regent's Pk., London NW1, UK.

HARRIS, Harold M., b. 1915, London, UK. Editorial Director, Hutchinson Publishing Group. Contbr. of detective stories & plays to var. jrnls. & BBC. Mbrships: Chmn., London Writers' Circle, 1952-61; PEN. Address: 17 Brendon House, Nottingham Place, London W1, UK.

HARRIS, Helen, (née WARREN), b. 1927, Buckfastleigh, Devon, UK. Former Dairy Adviser, National Agricultural Advisory Service. Publs: Industrial Archaeology of Dartmoor, 1968; Industrial Archaeology of the Peak District, 1971; The Bude Canal (w. Monica Ellis), 1972; The Grand Western Canal, 1973. Contbr. to: Western Morning News; Sheffield Morning Telegraph; Farmers Guardian; Country Life; etc. Address: 34 Ringer's Spinney, Oadby, Leicester, UK.

HARRIS, Herbert, b. 1920, London, UK. Author; Journalist. Publs: Who Kill to Live; Serpents in Paradise; The Angry Battalion; num. short stories published in 29 countries. Contbr. to: BBC radio; nat. newspapers; jrnls. Mbrships: Press Club; Crime Writers Assn. (Chmn., 1969). Recip., CWA Dagger, 1965. Address: c/o Press Club, London EC4, UK.

HARRIS, Hugh, b. 1897, Liverpool, UK. Former Editor & Lecturer. Educ: B.A., King's Coll., Univ. of London; M.Litt., Emmanuel Coll., Cambridge Univ. Publs: Bandello's Tragical Tales; The Greek, the Barbarian & the Slave; Questions in Philosophy; Ed., The Jewish Year Book, 1953-68. Contbr. to: The Jewish Chronicle (Lit. Ed., 1937-67); Ency. Britannica; The Times; Daily Telegraph. Mbr., PEN. Address: 149 Walm Lane, London NW2, UK.

HARRIS, John, b. 1931, London, UK. Archivist. Publs. incl: English Decorative Ironwork, 1960; Regency Furniture Designs, 1961; Lincolnshire (co-author), 1964; Italian Architectural Drawings, 1966; Buckingham Palace (co-author), 1968; The Country Seat (co-author), 1970; Sir William Chambers, 1970; A Catalogue of British Drawings for Architecture, Decoration, Sculpture & Landscape

Gardening in American Collections, 1970; The King's Arcadia, 1973. Contbr. to: Arch. Review; Country Life; Burlington Mag.; Apollo; Connoisseur; Jrnl. Soc. Archtl. Historians; etc. Mbrships: Fellow, Soc. of Antiquaries; Hon. Fellow, Royal Inst. Brit. Archts. Address: 16 Limerston St., London SW10, UK.

HARRIS, Louise, b. 28 Sept. 1903, Pawtuxet, R.I., USA. Teacher; Recitalist, Organ & Piano. Educ: B.A., Brown Univ., 1926. Publs: Comprehensive Bibliography of C. A. Stevens, 1965; "None But the Best", 1966; A Chuckle & a Laugh, 1967; The Star of the Youth's Companion, 1969; The Flag Over the Schoolhouse, 1971; C. A. Stephens Looks at Norway, 1970; Charles Adams Tales, 1972; Little Big Heart (compiled from C. A. Stephens' stories), 1974. Contbr. to: Intercontinental Biog. Mag. Address: 15 Jay St., Rumford, RI 02916, USA.

HARRIS, Marion Rose, pen names HARRIS, Rose; YOUNG, Rose; HARRIFORD, Daphne; CHARLES, Henry; ROGERS, Keith, b. 1925, Cardiff, UK. Editorial Manager. Publs: Fresh Fruit Dishes; Fact Series; Making a House a Home; Awful Slimmer; Teach Your Mother Flower Arranging. Contbr. to: Daily & Provincial newspapers; IPC women's mags. (fiction); Trade Press; S.A. Mags.; Homefinder; Homes Overseas; Real Estate Int.; Home Furnishing. Mbr., Inst. of Jrnlsts. Agent: Laurence Pollinger Ltd. Address: Walpole Cottage, Long Dr., Burnham, Bucks. SL1 8AJ, UK.

HARRIS, Mark, b. 19 Nov. 1922, Mt. Vernon, N.Y., USA. Lecturer. Educ: M.A., Univ. of Denver; Ph.D., Univ. of Minn., 1956. Publs: Trumpet to the World, 1946; City of Discontent, 1952; The Southpaw, 1953, 1963; Bang the Drum Slowly, 1956, 1973; A Ticket for a Seamstitch, 1957; Something About a Soldier, 1957; Wake Up, Stupid, 1959; Mark the Glove Boy (autobiog.), 1964, 1972; Twentyone Twice: A journal (autobiog.), 1966; The Goy, 1970; Killing Everybody, 1973. Contbr. to num. lit. jrnls., newspapers, etc. Hons. incl: L.H.D., Ill. Wesleyan Univ., 1974; Guggenheim Mem. Fndn., 1965, 1974; Nat. Endowment for the Arts, 1966. Address: 25571 Via Brava, Valencia, CA 91355, USA.

HARRIS, (Lady) Patricia Clapin, b. 14 June 1910, Cobar, N.S.W., Australia. Journalist. Publs: Accept With Pleasure, 1969; Fit for a Sultan, 1971; Dining In & Dining Out, 1973. Contbr. to: NZ Listener; NZ Book World; Thursday; Aust. Women's Wkly. Mbr., PEN. Address: Te Rama, Waikanae, New Zealand.

HARRIS, Peter Bernard, b. 31 Jan. 1929, Cardiff, Wales, UK. University Professor. Educ: B.A., Cardiff, 1950; B.Sc., London, 1953; Ph.D., London Schl. Econs., 1962; D.Litt., Natal Univ., Durban, S. Africa, 1967. Publs: Studies in African Politics, 1970; Foundations of Political Science, forthcoming; The Commonwealth, forthcoming. Contbr. to: Int. Affairs; Pacific Community; Parly. Affairs; Spectrum; World Today. Mbrships: Cambrian Soc., Durban; RAF Assn. Address: 63 Middleton Towers, 140 Pokfulam Rd., Hong Kong.

HARRIS, Robert Jennings, b. 25 Oct. 1907, Wilson County, Tenn., USA. University Teacher. Educ: B.A., 1930, Vanderbilt Univ.; M.A., 1931, Univ. of Ill.; Ph.D., Princeton Univ. Publs. incl: The Judicial Power of the US, 1940; The Constitution of the US; Analysis & Interpretation (co-author), 1953; The Quest for Equality: The Constitution, Congress & the Supreme Court, 1960; Congress & the Supreme Court, 1960; Perspectives on the South (co-author), 1967. Contbr. to: Jrnl. of Politics; Am. Political Sci. Review; etc. Mbrships. incl: VP (1950) Am. Political Sci. Assn. Address: Pavilion IX West Lawn, Charlottesville, VA 22901, USA.

HARRIS, Rosemary Jeanne, b. London, UK. Author. Educ: Courtauld Inst. of Art, Univ. of London. Publs: The Summer House, 1956; All My Enemies, 1967; A Wicked Pack of Cards, 1969; The Double Snare, 1975; (children's books) The Moon in the Cloud, 1968; The Shadow on the Sun, 1970; The Child in the Bamboo Grove, 1971; The Seal-Singing, 1971; The Bright & Morning Star, 1972; The King's White Elephant, 1973; The Lotus & the Grail, 1974; The Flying Ship, 1975. Contbr. to: Jr. Bookshelf; The Times. Mbrships: Soc. of Authors; Nat. Book League; Brit. Mus. Soc. Recip., Carnegie Medal, Lib. Assn., 1968. Address: 33 Cheyne Court, Flood St., London SW3 5TR, UK.

HARRIS, Theodore Wilson, b. 24 Mar. 1921, New Amsterdam, British Guiana. Publs: The Guyana Quartet (incl. Palace of the Peacock, 1960; The Whole Armour, 1962; The Secret Ladder, 1963); The Eye of the Scarecrow, 1965; Tumatumari, 1968; Ascent to Omai, 1970; The Sleepers of Roraima, 1970; Black Marsden, 1972; Companions of the Day & Night, 1975. Hons: C'wlth. Fellow, Univ. Leeds, 1971; Guggenheim Fellow, 1973; Henfield Writing Fellow, Univ. E. Anglia, 1974. Address: c/o Faber & Faber Ltd., 3 Queen Square, London WC1 3AU, UK.

HARRIS, Walter, b. 1925, London, UK. Life Assurance Consultant; Freelance Record Producer. Publs: Clovis, 1970; Mistress of Downing Street, 1971; Droop, 1974; The Day I Died, 1974; Vampire's Rest, 1975. Contbr. to: Penthouse; Mayfair; Daily Telegraph Mag.; Men Only; Club Int. Agent: John Farquharson. Mbr., Soc. of Authors. Address: 51 Woodlands Rd., Surbiton, Surrey, UK.

HARRISON, Brian Fraser, b. 6 Sept. 1918, Liverpool, UK. Writer; Partner, Firm of Solicitors; Captain, R.A.S.C.(T.A.), 1939-44. Publs: Advocacy at Petty Sessions, 1956, 2nd ed., 1959; Work of a Magistrate, 1964, 2nd ed., 1969; A Business of Your Own, 1968; A Business of Your Own Today, 1973. Mbrships: Soc. of Authors; Law Soc.; Justice; Brit. Legal Assn.; Inst. of Int. & Comparative Law. Recip., var. biog. listings. Address: Mouldsworth House, Mouldsworth, Chester CH3 8AP, UK.

HARRISON, David Lakin, b. 1 Oct. 1926, Sevenoaks, Kent, UK. Medical Practitioner. Educ: Clare Coll., Cambridge Univ.; St. Thomas's Hosp., London; M.A., M.B., B.Ch., Ph.D. (Cantab.). Publs: Footsteps in the Sand, 1959; Mammals of Arabia, vol. I, 1964, vol. II, 1968, vol. III, 1972. Contbr. to: Proceedings of Zool. Soc., London; The Naturalist; Bulletin of Brit. Ornithologists' Club; Annals & Mag. Natural Hist.; Durban Mus. (Novitates); Jrnl. Mammol.; Mammalia, Paris; Revue Zool. & Bot. Africaine; & num. other profl. jrnls.; Shooting Times; The Wildfowler. Mbrships. incl: Fellow, Linnean Soc. Recip., Bloomer Medal, Linnean Soc., 1968. Address: Bowerwood House, St. Botolph's Rd., Sevenoaks, Kent, UK.

HARRISON, Dex, b. 1909, Yorks., UK. Architect. Educ: Leeds Univ. Publs: Survey of Prefabrication, 1945; Standards in Building, 1947; Ed., Building Science, 1948; Ed., Specification. Contbr. to: var. tech. jrnls. Mbrships: F.R.I.B.A.; Royal Town Planning Inst. Address: 34 Holland Park Rd., Kensington, London W14, UK.

HARRISON, Elizabeth Fancourt, b. 12 Jan. 1921, Watford, Herts., UK. Author. Publs: Coffee at Dobrée's, 1965; The Physicians, 1966; The Ravelston Affair, 1967; Corridors of Healing, 1968; Emergency Call, 1970; Accident Call, 1971; Ambulance Call, 1972; Surgeon's Call, 1973; On Call, 1974; Hospital Call, 1975; paperback eds. in UK & USA. Mbrships: Assoc. Ed. & Overseas Sec., Chest & Heart Assn., 1947-72; Soc. of Authors; Romantic Novelists' Assn. (Hon. Sec. 1972—). Hons: Runner-Up, 1970, & Short-listed, 1971, 1972, 1973, Major Award, Romantic Novelists Assn. Agent: Bolt & Watson Ltd. Address: 30 Langham House Close, Ham Common, Richmond, Surrey, UK.

HARRISON, Francis Llewelyn, b. 1905, Dublin, Ireland. Professor of Ethnomusicology. Educ: M.A.; D.Mus., Oxford Univ., UK; Mus.D., Dublin Univ., Ireland. Publs: Music in Medieval Britain; The Eton Choirbook, 3 vols.; Musicology (w. others); European Musical Instruments (w. others); Fourteenth Century Motets of French Provenance; Time Place & Music. Contbr. to: New Oxford Hist. of Mus.; Annales Musicologiques; Musica Disciplina; etc. Fellow of the B.A. Lit. Agent: David Higham Assoc. Ltd. Address: Universiteit van Amsterdam, Etnomusicologisch Centrum "Jaap Kunst", Kloveniersburgwal 103, Amsterdam, Netherlands.

HARRISON, Fraser, b. 23 Oct. 1944, Stackpole, Wales, UK. Publisher. Educ: B.A., Engl. Lit., Univ. of Cambridge. Publs: The Yellow Book, an Anthology, 1974. Address: c/o Sidgwick & Jackson, 1 Tavistock Chambers, Bloomsbury Way, London WC1, UK.

HARRISON, Hank, b. 17 June 1940, Monterey, Calif., USA. Author; Poet; Technical Writer. Educ: B.A., 1964, M.A., 1969, Cert. Social Work, 1970; Coll. San. Mateo, San Fran. State Univ., Univ. Amsterdam. Publs: The Drug Crisis Handbook, 1969; The Dead Book, 1972; Secrets of the Holy Grail, 1975; scenarios for films; (works forthcoming)

Daughters of the Holy Grail; Mandala Technology; Anthem for the End of Time. Contbr. to sev. periodicals. Mbrships. incl: PEN; Am. Soc. Tech. Writers. Agent: Elaine Markson, N.Y. Address: Box 554, Fairfax, CA 94930, USA.

HARRISON, Harry (Max), pen name DEMPSEY, Hank, b. 1925, Stanford, Conn., USA. Freelance Author. Educ: Hunter Coll., N.Y. Publs. incl: Stonehenge, 1972; A Transatlantic Tunnel, Hurrah! , 1972; One Step from Earth (short stories), 1972; Best Science Fiction Stories of the Year (Ed. w. Brian W. Aldiss), 1967-; Spaceship Medic (juvenile), 1970; Ed., Astounding: The John W. Campbell Memorial Anthology, 1974. Contbr. to var. jrnls. Mbrships: Past VP, Sci. Fiction Writers of Am.; Screen Writers Guild of Am.; The Writers' Guild of GB. Recip., Nebula Award, 1974. Agent: A. P. Watt & Son. Address: c/o A. P. Watt & Son, 26/28 Bedford Row, London WC1R 4HL, UK.

HARRISON, Howard, b. 27 Sept. 1930, Bronx, NYC, USA. College Professor; Author. Educ: B.S., M.A., CUNY. Publs: Basic Facts of English Grammar, 1963; Facts of English Literature, 1964; Basic World Literature, 1967. Contbr. to: Commentary; Quartet; Jewish Life; Educ. Synopsis; N.Y. Herald Tribune; N.Y. State Educ. Mbrships: Nat. Coun. Tchrs. Engl. (USA); Dir., ibid, 1968-74; Chmn., Workload Comm., Secondary Tchrs. Engl.; MLA; Assn. of Jewish Studies. Recip., prizes, N.Y. Poetry Forum, 1973, 1974. Address: Box 113, Admin. Bldg., State Univ. of N.Y., Onenona, NY 13820, USA.

HARRISON, Kenneth Cecil, b. 29 Apr. 1915, Hyde, UK. City Librarian, Westminster. Publs: First Steps in Librarianship, 1950, 4th ed., 1973; Libraries in Scandinavia, 1961, 2nd ed., 1969; Public Libraries Today, 1963; The Library & the Community, 1963, 3rd ed., 1975; Facts at Your Fingertips, 1964, 2nd ed., 1966; British Public Library Buildings, 1966; Libraries in Britain, 1969; Public Relations for Librarians, 1973. Mbrships. incl: Pres., C'wlth. Lib. Assn., 1972-75; Pres., The Lib. Assn., 1973; Exec., Nat. Book League; VP, Int. Assn. of Metrop. City Libs. Hons: C'wlth. Fndn. Lectureship Award; Williamson Mem. Lectr., Peabody Coll., Nashville, Tenn., USA, 1969. Address: 50 W. Hill Way, London, N20 8QS, UK.

HARRISON, Michael, b. 1907, Milton, Kent, UK. Writer; Journalist. Educ: King's Coll., Schl. of Oriental & African Studies, London Univ. Publs. incl: London by Gaslight, 1963; Technical Industrial Publicity, 1969; The London That was Rome, 1971; Clarence, The Life of H.R.H. The Duke of Clarence & Avondale, K.G., 1972; London Beneath the Pavement, revised ed., 1972; Murder in the Rue Royale, 1972; The Roots of Witchcraft, 1973; The World of Sherlock Holmes, 1973. Contbr. to num. newspapers. Address: 30 Russell Ct., Woburn Pl., London WC2 H0LL, UK.

HARRISON, Molly, b. 1909, Stevenage, Herts., UK. Museum Curator; Author. Educ: Sorbonne Univ., Paris, France. Publs. incl: Picture Source Books for Social History (7 vols.); Furniture, 1953; Food, 1954; Children in History (4 vols.), 1958-62; Homes, 1960; Shops & Shopping, 1965; The English Home, 1970; Learning Out of School, 1970; People & Furniture, 1971; The Kitchen in History, 1972; On Location: Museums, 1973; Homes, 1973; Museums & Galleries, 1974; People & Shopping, 1975; Homes in Britain, 1975; Home Inventions, 1975. Contbr. to var. educl. & museol. jrnls. Mbr., Educl. Writers' Grp., Soc. of Authors, 1968-72 (Chmn., 1970-71). Recip., M.B.E. Address: The Coach House, Horse Leas, Bradfield, Berks., UK.

HARRISON, Roland Kenneth, b. 1920, Coppull, Lancs., UK. Professor. Educ: B.D., M.Th., Ph.D., D.D., Univ. of London. Publs: Personality, 1959; Healing Herbs of the Bible, 1959; Introduction to the Old Testament, 1969; Old Testament Times, 1970; The Ancient World, 1971. Contbr. to: Interpreter's Bible Dict.; Philos.; Janus; Theol. jrnls. Address: Wycliffe College, Toronto M5S 1H7, Ontario, Can.

HARRISON, Ronald George, b. 1921, Ulverston, Lancs., UK. Professor of Anatomy; Author. Educ: M.A., D.M., B.Ch., Oxford Univ. Publs: Studies on Fertility, 1954-58; Textbook of Human Embryology, 1959; The Adrenal Circulation, 1960. Contbr. to: Cunningham's Textbook of Anatomy, 10th ed., 1964; BBC; Granada ITV; var. sci. jrnls. Agent: Gabrielle Lloyd. Address: The Stables, Fernhill, Upper Brighton, Wallasey, Cheshire L45 5AW, UK.

HARRISON, Ruth, b. 24 June 1920, Kensington, London, UK. Writer. Educ: Bedford Coll., London Univ.; Dip. Royal Acad. of Dramatic Art, London; Dip. in Dramatic Art, London Univ. Publs: Animal Machines, 1964. Contbr. to: Factory Farming, 1970; Can Britain Survive? , 1971; Animals, Men & Morals, 1971; var. mags., newspapers; etc. Mbrships: Observer, Coun. of Europe Comm. of Experts on the Protection of Animals; Int. Coun., World Fedn. for the Protection of Animals; Farm Animal Welfare Advsry. Comm., Min. of Agric.; Pres., Animal Def. Soc. Recip., Felix Wankel Rsch. Award for Animal Protection, 1973. Address: 34 Holland Park Rd., Kensington, London W14, UK.

HARRISON, Sydney Gerald, b. 1924, Harrogate, Yorks., UK. Botanist; Museum Keeper. Educ: B.Sc., Leeds Univ. Publs. incl: Garden Shrubs & Trees, 1960, 1962; Handbook of Coniferae, revised 4th ed., 1966; Welsh Ferns, Clubmosses, Quillworts & Horsetails (co-author), 5th ed., 1969; The Oxford Book of Food Plants (co-author), 1969; Clinical Toxicol. (co-author), 1957; Contbr. to: Kew Bulletin; Jrnl. Royal Hort. Soc.; Jrnl. Pharm. Soc.; Quarterly Jrnl. Forestry; Welsh Med. Gazette; num. other profl. jrnls. Mbrships: Fellow, Linnean Soc., London; other profl. assns. Address: 8 Queen Wood Close, Cyn Coed, Cardiff, UK.

HARRISON, Wilfrid, b. 1909, Glasgow, UK. Professor of Politics, University of Warwick. Educ: M.A., Univ. of Glasgow; M.A., Queen's Coll., Oxford. Publs: Bentham's Fragment of Government & Principles of Morals & Legislation (Ed.); The Government of Britain, 9th ed., 1964; Conflict & Compromise; History of British Political Thought, 1593-1900; Sources in British Political Thought, 1593-1900, 1965. Contbr. to: Pol. Studies; Parliamentary Affairs; Pol. Quarterly; Chambers' Ency. Address: 93 Coten End, Warwick, UK.

HARRISON-CHURCH, Ronald James, pen name CHURCH, R. J. Harrison, b. 1915, Wimbledon, Surrey, UK. Professor of Geography, University of London; Visiting Professor, University of Wisconsin, 1956; University of Indiana, 1965, & Tel Aviv & Haifa Universities, 1972-73. Educ: B.Sc., Ph.D.; Univs. London & Paris. Publs: West Africa; Environment & Policies in West Africa; Looking at France. Contbr. to: Africa & the Islands; An Advanced Geog. of N. & W. Europe; Ency. Britannica; Chambers Ency.; Geogl. Jrnl.; Econ. Geog.; Geog. Review; Geog. Mag.; etc. Address: London Schl. Econs., London WC2A 2AE, UK.

HARRISON MATTHEWS, Leonard, b. 1901. Biologist; Author. Educ: M.A., Sc.D., King's Coll., Cambridge. Publs: South Georgia; British Amphibia & Reptiles; Wandering Albatross; Sea Elephant; British Mammals; Beasts of the Field; Animals in Colour; The Senses of Animals (co-author); The Whale; The Life of Mannals (2 vols.); Ed., Waterton's Wanderings in S. America; Introduction to Darwin's Origin of Species; Man & Wildlife. Contbr. to: num. radio & TV broadcasts; Times Lit. & Educl. Supplements; Nature; New Sci.; Endeavour; Listener; Observer; Geog. Mag.; Countryman; Field; Sunday Times; Country Fair; Punch. Fellow, Royal Soc. Address: The Old Rectory, Stansfield, Via Sudbury, Suffolk, UK.

HARROD, Leonard Montague, b. 21 May 1905, Horsham, Sussex, UK. Chartered Librarian; Book Indexer; Author. Publs: Lending Library Methods, 1933; Librarians' Glossary . . . and Reference Book, 1938, 3rd ed., 1971, updated 1975; The Libraries of Greater London, 1951; Library Work with Children, 1969. Contbr. to: Times Lit. Supplement; Lib. Assn. Record; New Lib. World; Lib. Review; Lib. Assistant; Jrnl. of Educ.; Music & Youth; Hon. Ed., The Indexer, 1964—; etc. Mbrships. incl: Lib. Assn. (Coun. Mbr., 1952-54); Am. Lib. Assn.; Soc. of Authors; Soc. of Indexers. Recip., Wheatley Medal, Lib. Assn., 1973. Address: 41 Milton Rd., Harpenden, Herts., UK.

HARROD, (Sir) Roy Forbes, b. 13 Feb. 1900, London, UK. Economist. Educ: New Coll., Oxford. Publs. incl: International Economics, 1933; Trade Cycle, 1936; Life of J. M. Keynes, 1951; Foundations of Inductive Logic, 1956; Policy Against Inflation, 1958; Reforming the World's Money, 1965; The British Economy, 1965; Money, 1969; Sociology, Morals & Mystery, 1971; Economic Dynamics, 1973. Contbr. to: Econ. Jrnl.; Quarterly Jrnl. of Econs.; Mind; Fin. Times; Times Lit. Supplement; Nihon Keiza Shimbun (Japan); etc. Hons. incl: Fellow, Brit. Acad.; Kt. Bach., 1959; Hon. Docts., Univs. of Poitiers, Coventry,

Aberdeen & Glasgow. Address: The Old Rectory, Holt, Norfolk, UK.

HARROP, Dorothy A., b. 7 Oct. 1932, Warford, Cheshire, UK. Lecturer in Bibliography. Educ: M.A., Univ. Coll., London Univ.; Fellow, Lib. Assn., Manchester Schl. of Libnship. Publs: Modern Book Production, 1968. Contbr. to: The Book Collector; Ency. of Lib. & Info. Sci.; Lib. Assn. Record; Lib. Review; Asst. Libn.; Manchester Review. Mbrships: Bibliog. Soc.; Lib. Assn.; Designer Bookbinders; Aberystwyth Bibliog. Grp. Address: Aelybryn, Llan, Llanbrynmair, Powys, Wales, UK.

HARROWER, Elizabeth, b. 8 Feb. 1928, Sydney, Australia. Writer. Publs: (novels) Down in the City, 1957; The Long Prospect, 1958; The Catherine Wheel, 1960; The Watch Tower, 1966. Contbr. to: Aust. Letters; Summer's Tales I, 1964; Mod. Aust. Writing, 1966; Aust. Writing Today, 1968. Recip., C'wlth. Lit. Fund Fellowship, 1968. Address: c/o Macmillan Co. of Australia, 107 Moray St., South Melbourne, Vic. 3205, Australia.

HARSCH, Joseph Close, b. 25 May 1905, Toledo, Ohio, USA. Journalist. Educ: B.A., Williams Coll., 1952; M.A., Corpus Christi Coll., Cambridge. Publs: The Pattern of Conquest, 1941; The Curtain Isn't Iron, 1949. Contbr. to: N.Y. Times Mag.; Harper's Atlantic; Reporter; Economist; Round Table; Times (London); Columnist, Christian Sci. Monitor, 1948—. Hons: M.A., Williams Coll., 1952; C.B.E. Address: Highland Dr., Jamestown, RI 02835, USA.

HART, (Rev.) Arthur Tindal, b. 1908, Sawbridgeworth, Herts., UK. Clergyman. Educ: M.A., D.D., Emmanuel Coll., Cambridge Univ.; Ripon Hall, Oxford. Publs: Life & Times of John Sharp, Archbishop of York; William Lloyd, Bishop, Politician, Author & Prophet; The 19th Century Country Parson; The 18th Century Country Parson; The Country Clergy in Elizabethan & Stuart Times; The Country Priest in English History; The History of St. Paul's Cathedral (co-author); Country Counting House, 1962; The Man in the Pew, 1966; The House of Kings (co-author), 1966; Church & Society 1600-1800, 1968; The Curate's Lot, 1970. Contbr. to: Ch. Quarterly; Mod. Churchman; Parson & Parish. Address: 32 Freeman Ave., Hampden Park, Eastbourne BN22 9NU, UK.

HART, Harold Eaton, b. 23 Sept. 1893, Kingston upon Thames, UK. Commercial Executive; Translator. Educ: B.A.(Econs.Tripos), 1914, M.A., 1919, Gonville & Caius Coll., Cambridge. Publs: (transls. from French) The Châteaux of France, by Francois Gebelin, 1964; The Marne, by Georges Blond, 1965. Mbrships: Soc. of Authors; Engl. Speaking Union. Hons. incl: M.C.; Chevalier de la Légion d'Honneur; Bronze Star, US Army. Address: Flat C, 203 Sandgate Rd., Folkestone, Kent, UK.

HART, Helen Mackey, b. 6 Oct. 1918, Boston, Mass., USA. Professor. Educ: B.S., Sargent Coll., Boston Univ., 1940; M.Ed., 1948, Ed.D., 1952, Boston Univ. Publs: Field Hockey: An International Team Sport, 1963; Women's Team Sports Officiating (co-author), 1964. Contbr. to profl. jrnls. & to Mass. State Curric. Guide; Coord., 12-part TV series on sports & phys. educ., WGBH-TV, Boston. Address: 764 Lynnfield St., Lynn., MA 01904, USA.

HART, Lewis Vincent, pen names HART, Lew; FRANKS, Lew; BENOIT, Frank; BENOIT, Lew, b. 3 Feb. 1929, Illogan, Cornwall, UK. Journalist. Educ: B.Sc., London Univ. Publs: In the Footsteps of Slavers, 1961; Through the Ras Ghareb, 1962; The UAR Today, 1963; In Search of the Emerald Lake, 1965; Nasser: The Man & the Myth, 1969; Chaddaffi & His Revolution, 1970. Contbr. to: Time; Life; Newsweek; Paris Match; Ogi; Egyptian Review; London Sunday Express; Observer; Manchester Guardian; Holiday; MacQueen's Ladies Home Jrnl.; Red Book; Middle E. Econ. Digest. Mbrships: Nat. Union of Jrnlsts.; F.R.Z.S. Address: 11 Ivymount Rd., West Norwood, London SE27, UK.

HARTCUP, Adeline, b. 26 Apr. 1918, Totland Bay, Isle of Wight, Hants., UK. Journalist. Educ: M.A., St. Hugh's Coll., Oxford. Publs: Angelica, 1954; Morning Faces, 1963; (transls.) The Labour & the Wounds, European Porcelain, Oriental Carpets, Historic Villas. Contbr. to: The Times; Times Educl. Supplement; Illustrated London News; etc. Mbrships: Exec. Comm., Hon. Press Off., Kent Coun. of Soc. Serv.; Comm. for Protection of Rural Kent. Address: Swanton Ct., Sevington, Ashford, Kent, UK.

HARTCUP, John, b. 1915, Elswick, UK. Writer. Educ: Freiburg Univ., Germany; Sorbonne Univ., Paris, France; London Univ., UK. Publs: Biography of Camille Desmoulins, 1950; Morning Faces, 1965. Contbr. to: Time & Tide; The Fortnightly; Staples' Modern Reading; Poetry of To-Day; Times Educl. Supplement; The Schoolmaster. Address: Swanton Court, Sevington, Ashford, Kent, UK.

HARTER, Lafayette George, Jr., b. 28 May 1918, Des Moines, Iowa, USA. Professor of Economics, Labor Arbitrator, Oregon State University. Educ: B.A., Antioch Coll., Yellow Springs, Ohio, 1941; M.A., 1948, Ph.D., 1960, Stanford Univ., Calif. Publs: John R. Commons: His Assault on Laissez-faire, 1962; Labor in America (w. J. Keltner), 1967; Economic Responses to A Changing World, 1972. Contbr. to: Western Econ. Review; Am. Econ. Review; Jrnl. of Econs. & Sociol.; Jrnl. of Econ. Issues; Land Econs.; Ore Law Review. Mbrships. incl: Am. Econ. Assn.; Am. Arbitration Assn.; Past Chapt. Pres., Ore State Employees Assn.; AAUP. Address: 3755 N.W. Van Buren St., Corvallis, OR 97330, USA.

HARTHOORN, Antonie Marinus, b. 26 Aug. 1923, Rotterdam, Netherlands. Scientist. Educ: Grad., Royal Vet. Coll., London, 1950; Ph.D., Univ. of London; D.V.Sc., State Univ. of Utrecht; D.M.V., Pharmacol. Inst., Hanover; F.R.C.V.S. Publs: The Flying Syringe — Ten years of immobilizing wild animals in Africa, 1970; Chemical Capture — A guide to the Capture of Wild Animals by Chemical Immobilization, 1975. Contbr. to: sev. textbooks; num. sci. jrnls. Mbr., Profl. orgs. Hons. incl: Gold Medal & Fellowship, Nat. Vet. Med. Assn. of GB & Ireland, 1949. Address: Dayal Bagh, 53 Ringwood Rd., Lynnwood Manor, Pretoria 0002, S. Africa.

HARTLEY, Ellen Raphael, pen name RAPHAEL, Ellen, b. 1 Jan. 1915, Dortmund, Germany. Magazine Journalist; Author. Publs: The Ellen Knauff Story, 1952, 2nd ed., different publr., 1974; Osceola — The Unconquered Indian, 1973; A Woman Set Apart (w. William B. Hartley), 1963; Eine Tapfere Frau, 1964. Contbr. to: Good Housekeeping; Redbook; Popular Mechanics; Seventeen; Sci. Digest; Boy's Life; Prism Mag.; Encounter; etc. Mbr., Soc. Mag. Writers. Address: 5747 SW 82nd St., S. Miami, FL 33143, USA.

HARTLEY, Leslie Poles, b. 1895, Whittlesey, Cambs., UK. Author. Educ: B.A., Balliol Coll., Oxford. Publs: Poor Clare, 1968; The Love Adapt, 1969; His Sister's Keeper, 1970. Contbr. to: Week-end Review; Spectator; Weekly Sketch; Observer; Time & Tide; etc. Address: Avondale, Bathford, Bath, UK.

HARTLEY, Marie, b. 25 Sept. 1905, Morley, Yorks., UK. Writer. Educ: Leeds Coll. of Art; Slade Schl. Publs: Swaledale, 1934; Wensleydale, 1936; Wharfdale, 1938; Yorkshire Tour, 1939; Yorkshire Cottage, 1942 (all w. Ella Pontefract); Yorkshire Heritage, 1950; (the following w. Joan Ingilby) Yorkshire Village, 1953; The Yorkshire Dales, 1956; The Wonders of Yorkshire, 1959; Yorkshire Portraits, 1961; Life & Tradition in the Yorkshire Dales, 1968; Life in the Moorlands of North-East Yorkshire, 1972. Contbr. to: Yorkshire Post; Country Life. Hons: M.A., Univ. of Leeds, 1968. Address: Coleshouse, Askrigg, Leyburn, Yorks., UK.

HÄRTLING, Peter, b. 13 Nov. 1933, Cemnitz, Germany. Editor; Journalist. Educ: Gymnasium, Nurtingen/Neckar. Publs. incl: (poetry) Yamins Stationen, 1955; Spielgeist-Spiegelgeist, 1962; (novels) Niembsch oder Der Stillstand, 1964; Janek, 1966; Das Familienfest, 1969; Ein Abend, Ein Nacht, Ein Morgen, 1971; Eine Frau, 1974; (play) Gilles, 1970. Contbr. to: Deutsche Zeitung & Wirtschaftszeitung; Der Monat (Ed.), 1967-70; Die Vater (Ed.). Mbrships: PEN; Acad. of Arts, Berlin; Akad. der Wissenschaften & Lit., Mainz. Hons. incl: Lit. Prize, Deutschen Industrie, 1965; Gerhart Hauptmann Prize, 1971. Address: Walldorf/Hessen, Finkenweg 1, W. Germany.

HARTMAN, (Carl) Olov, b. 7 May 1906, Stockholm, Sweden. Writer. Educ: Teol.cand., Uppsala Univ., 1932. Publs: (novels) Holy Masquerade, 1963; The Sudden Sun, 1964; Marching Orders, 1970; (plays) Profet och Timmerman (Prophet & Carpenter), 1954; Livets krona (The Crown of Life), 1956; Den brinnande ugnen (The Fiery Furnace), 1958; Marios Oro (Mary's Quest), 1963; Eld och kontrapunkt, 1967; Bäraren (On that Day), 1968; Efter oss, 1970; & var. essays & sermons. Contbr. to: Vår Lösen; Aftonbladet. Mbrships: PEN; Swedish Authors'

Union; Swedish Dramatists' Union. Hons. incl: Book Lottery Schlrship., 1958; Gustaf VI Adolfs Minnesmedalj, 1967; D.D., Univ. of Lund, 1968; Wallin Prize, 1972. Address: Kärrvägen 19, 190 30 Sigtuna, Sweden.

HARTMANN, Michael John, b. 24 July 1944, Bombay, India. Attorney; Notary Public. Educ: LL.B., London. Publs: Pepper in a Milkshake (play), 1966; Feather in a Battered Cap (play), 1972; Game for Vultures (novel), forthcoming. Contbr. to: Rhodesian Financial Gazette (film critic). Mbrships: PEN; Round Table. Recip., 1st Prize, C.A.B.S. Ctrl. African Play of the Yr. Award, 1972. Address: 5 Tomlinson Rd., Gunhill, Salisbury, Rhodesia.

HARTNACK, Johan Justus Daniel Gustav Volmer, b. 29 May 1912, Copenhagen, Denmark. Professor. Educ: M.A., 1946, Ph.D., 1950, Univ. of Copenhagen. Publs: Analysis of the Problems of Perception in British Empiricism, 1950; Wittgenstein & Modern Philosophy, 1961; Kant: Theory of Knowledge, 1967; History of Philosophy, 1973; Language & Philosophy, 1973. Contbr. to var. philos. jrnls. Mbrships: Learned Soc., Humanistic Soc., Denmark; Int. Fedn. of Socs. of Philos.; Int. Inst. of Philos. Hons: Disting. Prof., SUNY, 1973; Fac. Exchange Schlr., SUNY, 1974. Address: 6 Keystone Ct., Brockport, NY 14420, USA.

HARTON, Sibyl, b. 1898, London, UK. Educ: Goudhurst Coll., Kent; St. Mary's Coll., Paddington. Publs: A Child's Faith, 1938; The Way of the Cross, 1947; Stars Appearing, 1954; In Search of Quiet, 1955; On Growing Old, 1957; Busy my Heart with Quietude, 1961; Doors of Eternity, 1965; The Practice of Confession; The Thirteen Gold Keys; Windfall of Light. Address: Hartons Piece, West Challow, Wantage, Berks., UK.

HARTRIDGE, Hamilton, b. 1886, London, UK. Professor Emeritus of Physiology. Educ: King's Coll., Cambridge Univ.; M.A., M.D., Sc.D., M.R.C.P., F.R.P.S. Publs: Histology for Medical Students; Colours & How We See Them; Recent Advances in Physiology of Vision; Ed., Essentials of Physiology (w. Prof. D'Silva). Contbr. to: Starling, Human Physiology; num. profl. jrnls. (over 250 original articles on rsch.). Mbrships: F.R.S.; Fellow, Inst. of Physics; Hon. Mbr., Physiol. Soc., 1968. Address: 21 Frithwood Ave., Northwood, Middlesex, UK.

HARTSHORNE, Charles, b. 5 June 1897, Kittanning, Pa., USA. University Professor of Philosophy. Educ: Haverford Coll.; A.B., 1921, A.M., 1922, Ph.D., 1923, Harvard Univ. Publs. incl: The Philosophy & Psychology of Sensation, 1934, 1968; Man's Vision of God & the Logic of Theism, 1941, 1964; Reality as Social Process: Studies in Metaphysics & Civilization, 1953, 1971; Anselm's Discovery, 1965; Whitehead's Philosophy: Selected Essays 1935-1970, 1972; Born to Sing: An Interpretation & World Survey of Bird Song, 1973. Contbr. to US, UK, French, Italian, German, Spanish, jrnls. Address: 724 Sparks Ave., Austin, TX 78705, USA.

HART-SMITH, William, b. 23 Nov. 1911, Tunbridge Wells, UK. Educator; Radio Technician. Publs: (poems) Columbus Goes West, 1943; Harvest, 1945; The Unceasing Ground, 1946; Christopher Columbus, 1948; On the Level, 1950; Poems of Discovery, 1959; The Talking Clothes, 1966; Minipoems, 1974. Contbr. to most. Aust. & New Zealand lit. jrnls. & anthols., also book review, radio scripts, talks, etc. Past Pres., Poetry Soc. Aust. Hons: Wallace Crouch Gold Medal, Aust. Lit. Soc., 1959; Grace Leven Poetry Prize, 1964; Lit. Bd. Fellowship. Address: W.A. Inst. of Technol., Dept. of Engl. & Lang. Studies, Hayman Rd., Bentley West, W. Australia 6102.

HARTSTON, William Roland, b. 12 Aug. 1947, London, UK. Chess Writer. Educ: M.A., Jesus Coll., Cambridge. Publs: The Benoni, 1969, 2nd ed., 1973; The King's Indian Defence, 1969, 2nd ed., 1973; The Grunfeld Defence, 1971, 2nd ed., 1973; Korchnoi-Karpov 1974, 1974. Contbr. to: Chess; Brit. Chess Mag.; Chessplayer; Games & Puzzles. Address: 32 Malcolm Place, Cambridge CB1 1LS, UK.

HARTUNG, Ernst Johannes, b. 23 Apr. 1893, Melbourne, Vic., Australia. Professor of Chemistry. Educ: B.Sc., Univ. of Melbourne, 1913; D.Sc., 1919. Publs: The Screen Projection of Chemical Experiments, 1953; Astronomical Objects for Southern Telescopes, 1968. Fellowships: Pres., Royal Aust. Chem. Inst., 1928; Royal Stron. Soc.; Recip., David Syme Rsch. Prize, Univ. of Melbourne, 1926. Address: Lavender Farm, Woodend, Vic., Australia 3442.

HARTZELL, Raimo Kalevi, b. 24 Feb. 1941, Helsinki, Finland. TV Cameraman; Poet. Collects. of Poems: Someone's Playing the Piano, 1965; Later in the Same Summer, 1967; A Cloud Like a Dog, 1968; A Happy Spring, 1974. Contbrns. of poetry, var. Finnish cultural reviews. Mbr., Org. of Authors of Finland. Address: Kirstinkatu 2 A 4, 00530 Helsinki, Finland.

HARVEY, Celia, pen name HARVEY, Pippa, b. Preston, Lancs., UK. Poet; Housewife. Publs: Reflections, Preston Poet's Anthology. Contbr. to: Lancs. Life; Preston Jrnl.; Record; Shore (Cleveleys Poets' Mag.); Radio Blackburn. Mbrships: Lancs. Poetry Assn. (organizer); Preston Poets' Soc. (sec.); Preston & Dist. Arts Assn. (Publicity Off.). Hons. incl: Lancs. Authors' Assn. 1st Prize for Short Story, 1973; & 1st Prize for 1 Act Play, 1973; Lancs. Authors' Assn. 1st Prize Dialect Poem, 1974; Cleveleys Poets' Competition 1st Prize, 1974; Poetry Soc. (London), Arnold Vincent Bowen Competition Runner-up, 1974. Address: 8 Whitefield Rd. E., Penwortham, Preston PR1 0XJ, Lancs., UK.

HARVEY, Charles Nigel, pen name WILLOUGHBY, Hugh, b. 1916, Oxford, UK. Agricultural Adviser; Writer. Educ: M.A., Exeter Coll., Oxford Univ. Publs: The Story of Farm Buildings; Ditches, Dykes & Deepdrainage; The Farming Kingdom; Farm Work Study; (as Hugh Willoughby) Amid the Alien Corn; The History of Farm Buildings in England & Wales. Contbr. to: New Statesman; Farmer & Stockbreeder; Farmers' Wkly.; Agricl. Review; Power Farmer; Agric.; Country Life; etc. Address: 41 Corringham Rd., London NW1, UK.

HARVEY, Frank, b. 1912, Manchester, UK. Writer. Educ: B.A., St. Catharine's Coll., Cambridge. Publs: Saloon Bar, 1940; The Poltergeist, 1946; Elizabeth of Ladymead, 1949; Norman, 1963; Heavens Above! , 1963; The Day After the Fair, 1973. Mbrships: Dramatists' Club; Savage Club; Writer's Guild. Agent: Margery Vosper Ltd. Address: Mount Pleasant Cottage, East Hill, Ottery St. Mary, Devon, UK.

HARVEY, Hugh, b. 11 Sept. 1912, Worcester, UK. Science Writer. Educ: B.Sc., Stanford Univ., Calif. Publs: (contbr.) The English of Chemistry, 1972; Technological Forecasting, 1972; (Co-Ed.) Scientists in Search of their Conscience, 1973. Contbr. to: Nature; New Sci.; World Petroleum; Hydrocarbon Processing; Ocean Ind.; Sci. & Technol. Newsletter (former Ed.). Mbrships: Assn. Brit. Sci. Writers (sec.); Int. Soc. Aviation Writers (past VP); Nat. Assn. Sci. Writers, USA. Address: 6 The Spinneys, Bickley, Bromley, Kent BR1 2NU, UK.

HARVEY, John Henry, b. 1891, Basford, Notts., UK. Vice-Principal, College of Further Education. Educ: Nottingham Univ. Coll.; Univ. of Liverpool; B.Com. Publs: The Arithmetic of Commerce (1st Course); The Arithmetic of Commerce (Intermediate Course); Arithmetic for the Business Student; Practical Arithmetic with Trigonometry for Schools; Teach Yourself Commercial Arithmetic; Office Arithmetic; Nigerian eds. of The Arithmetic of Commerce, & Elements of Commerce. Contbr. to: Tech. Jrnl.; Jrnl. of Educ. Hon. Life Mbr., Assn. of Tchrs. in Tech. Instns. Address: 30 Tudor Close, Cheam, Surrey, UK.

HARVEY, John Hooper, b. 25 May 1911, London, UK. Architect; Author. Publs. incl: Dublin, 1949; The Gothic World 1100-1600, 1950; English Medieval Architects – A Biographical Dictionary Down to 1550, 1954; Edited Latin Text, with Engl. transl.: William Worcestre: Itineraries, 1969; The Master Builders, 1971; The Medieval Architect, 1972; Conservation of Buildings, 1972; Cathedrals of England & Wales, 1974; Early Nurserymen, 1975. Contbr. to: Agricl. Hist. Review; Ancient Monuments Soc. Transactions; etc. Mbrships: F.S.A. (Coun. 1959-60); F.R.S.L.; Fellow, Soc. of Genealogists. Address: 100 The Mount, York YO2 2AR, UK.

HARVEY, Margie Ballard, b. 12 July 1910, Grand Saline, Tex., USA. Poet; Freelance Fiction Writer. Contbr. to anthols: American Songbird, 1960; Bluebook of American Poetry, 1961; Treasures of Parnassus, 1962; Hearts Secrets, 1962; Fragments of Faith, 1963; American Poetry Old & New, 1965; A Burst of Trumpets, 1966; Golden Harvest, 1967; The Clover Collection of Verse, vol. 3, 1970, & vol. 5, 1972; Year Book of Modern Poetry, 1972; Lyrics of Love, 1972; Tower by the Sea, 1973; Poetry in Prayer. Mbrships: Int. Clover Poetry Assn.; Poetry Soc. of Tex.; Laurel Publrs. Int. Poetry Symposium; Int.

Poetry Soc. Address: 205 Water St., Seagoville, TX 75159, USA.

HARVEY, Olive Edythe, b. 20 Jan. 1906, Petone, Wellington, NZ. Educ: Tchrs. Cert. Publs: PM Advanced Readers, 12 supplementary readers, 1968-71; Lets Act It, Verse & Verse Plays, 1954; Action Rhymes for Juniors. Contbr. to: Child Educ.; Victorian Educ. Gazette; NZ Educ. Gazette; NZ Schl. Jrnl. Mbrships: Br. Sec., NZEI, 1945-50; Bus. & Profl. Womens Club; Wanganui Br., Nat. Coun. of Women. Address: 5 Hipango Tee, Wanganui, NZ.

HARVEY, (Rev.) Peter Noel, b. 1916, Penarth, Glam., UK. Vicar; Editor. Educ: B.A.; Univ. of Wales; St. Augustine's Coll., Canterbury. Contbr. to: Church Illustrated (Fndr., 1955, Ed., 1955-56); Anglican World (Fndr., 1960, Ed., 1960-68); SUNDAY (Fndr. & Ed., 1966-). Hon. Chap., St. Bride's, Fleet St., London, 1958-. Address: Udimore Vicarage, Rye, Sussex, UK.

HARWOOD, Alice Mary, b. 7 July 1909, W. Bromwich, UK. Author. Educ: B.A., Univ. of London. Publs: Caedmon: A Lyrical Drama, 1937; The Star of the Greys, 1939; She Had to be Queen, 1948, USA ed., The Lily & the Leopard, 1949; Merchant of the Ruby, 1950; The Strangeling, 1954; At Heart a King, 1957; No Smoke without Fire, USA, 1964; The Living Phantom, 1973. Contbr. to: Fortnightly; John O'London's Weekly; Good Housekeeping; Yorks. Post; Birmingham Post. Mbrships: Soc. of Authors; PEN; Shakespeare Club, Stratford-upon-Avon; Hon. mbr., Mark Twain Soc., USA. Address: Green Hedges, Oversley, Alcester, Warwicks., UK.

HARWOOD, Lee, b. 6 June 1939, Leicester, UK. Writer. Educ: B.A. (Engl.), Queen Mary Coll., Univ. of London. Publs: 'title illegible', 1965; The man with blue eyes, 1966; The white room, 1968; The beautiful atlas, 1969; Landscapes, 1969; The Sinking Colony, 1971; Penguin Modern Poets series, vol. 19 (w. John Ashbery & Tom Raworth), 1971; Captain Harwood's Log of Stern Statements & Stout Sayings, 1973; poetry anthols. Contbr. to: London Mag.; Paris Review; Six Pack; Boston Phoenix; etc. Mbrships: exec. coun., Poetry Soc.; Chmn., Nat. Poetry Ctr. Events Comm. Recip., Poetry Fndn. (N.Y., USA) annual award, 1967. Address: 21 Chatsworth Rd., Brighton, Sussex, UK.

HARWOOD, Ronald, b. 9 Nov. 1934, Cape Town, S. Africa. Writer. Publs: All the Same Shadows, 1961; George Washington September, Sir!, 1961; The Guilt Merchants, 1963; 2nd ed., 1969; The Girl in Melanie Klein, 1969; Sir Donald Wolfit: His Life & Work in the Unfashionable Theatre, 1971; One Day in the Life of Ivan Denisovich (screenplay & Intro.), 1971; Articles of Faith, 1973, 2nd ed., 1974. Contbr. to: Sunday Times; BBC. Mbrships: F.R.S.L.; Chmn., Writers' Guild of GB; var. offs. & comms., Arts Coun.; Prog. Dir., 1975 Cheltenham Festival of Lit. Recip., Winifred Holtby Prize, 1973. Address: c/o Agent, Felix De Wolfe & Assoc., 1 Robert St., Adelphi, London WC2N 68H, UK.

HASAN, Mehdi, b. 27 June 1937, Panipat, Brit. India. University Teacher of Journalism. Educ: M.A.(jrnlsm.). Publs: Iblaagh-I-Aam (Mass Communication), 1968, 2nd ed., 1974; Political Parties in Pakistan (in Urdu), 1974; Lack of Communication Between East & West Pakistan: 3 Causes of Succession, forthcoming. Contbr. to var. nat. newspapers. Mbrships. incl: Punjab Union of Jrnlsts.; Afro-Asian Jrnlsts. Assn. Address: Dept. of Jrnlsm., Punjab Univ., Lahore, Pakistan.

HASAN, Zafar, b. 14 Aug. 1937, Hyderabad Sind, Pakistan. Assistant University Professor of Geography; Fiction Writer (Singhi language). Educ: B.A., M.A., Univ. of Sind. Contbr. to: Ed., Dharti mag.; Sojhro; Indalath; Dharti. Mbrships: Singhi Lit. Soc.; Dir., Sind Book Ctr. Address: Dept. of Geog., Univ. of Sind, Jamshoro-Sind, Pakistan.

HASKELL, Francis James Herbert, b. 1928, London, UK. Professor of History of Art. Educ: M.A., King's Coll., Cambridge, 1951. Publs: Patrons & Painters: a study of the relations between Art & Society in the Age of the Baroque, 1963; Gericault, 1966. Contbr. to: Burlington Mag.; Jrnl. of Warburg Inst.; N.Y. Review of Books; New Statesman; etc. Fellow of the B.A. Address: c/o Trinity College, Oxford, UK.

HASKELL, Peter Thomas, b. 21 Feb. 1923, Portsmouth, UK. Civil Servant. Educ: B.Sc., Ph.D., Dip., Imperial Coll. of Sci. & Technol., Univ. of London. Publs: Insect Sounds, 1962; The Language of Insects, in Science Survey III, 1962; Sound Production in Physiology of the Insecta, vol. II, 1974. Contbr. to: Nature; New Sci.; Times Sci. Survey; Penguin Sci. Survey; Sci. News; The Listener; Sci. Jrnl.; Spon; Outlook on Agric.; etc. Mbrships: Coun., Fellow, Royal Entomol. Soc. of London; Coun. Assn. for the Study of Animal Behaviour; Fellow, Inst. of Biol.; Assoc., Royal Coll. of Sci. Recip., C.M.G., 1975. Address: 5 Alexandra Rd., Kingston upon Thames, Surrey, UK.

HASLIP, Joan, b. 27 Feb. 1912. Author; Broadcaster. Publs: Out of Focus, 1931; Grandfather Steps, 1932; Lady Hester Stanhope, 1934; Parnell, 1936; Portrait of Pamela, 1940; Lucrezia Borgia, 1953; The Sultan, Life of Abdul Hamid, 1958, 1973; The Lonely Empress, a life of Elizabeth of Austria, 1965; Imperial Adventurer, 1971. Contbr. to: London Mercury, 1929-39; BBC (Ed., European Service, 1941-45). Recip., F.R.S.L., 1958. Address: 7 Via di Doccia, Settignano, Florence, Italy.

HASLUND, Ebba, b. 12 Aug. 1917, Seattle, Wash. D.C., USA. Writer. Educ: M.A., Oslo Univ., Norway, 1941. Publs. incl: Også Vi (Short stories), 1945; (novels) Siste Halvår, 1946; Det Hendte Ingenting, 1948; Middag Hos Molla, 1951; Krise I August, 1954; Drømmen om Nadja, 1956; Hvor Går Du Vanda?, 1960; Det Trange Hjerte, 1965; Syndebukkens Krets, 1968; Aldri en Grå Hverdag (biog.), 1970; Midlertidig Stoppested (4 radio plays), 1972. Contbr. to var. Norwegian publs. Mbrships. incl: Chmn., Norwegian Authors Assn., 1971–; Chmn., Union of Authors of Books for Young People, 1965-70; V.P., PEN, 1964-68. Hons. incl: Norwegian Booksellers Prize, 1966; Riksmålprisen, 1968. Address: 52 Lillehagveien, 1310 Blommenholm, Norway.

HASSALL, William Owen, b. 1912, York, UK. Assistant Librarian, Bodleian Library. Educ: M.A., D.Phil., Corpus Christi Coll., Oxford. Publs. incl: The Cartulary of St. Mary Clerkenwell, 1949; Catalogue of the Library of Sir Edward Coke, 1950; Holkham Bible Picture Book, 1954; Wheatley Records 956-1956, 1956; They Saw It Happen (Vol. I, medieval), 1957; Who's Who in History, 1960; Douce Apocalypse (w. A. G. Hassell), 1961; How They Lived (Vol. I, medieval), 1962; Index of Persons in Oxfordshire Deeds Acquired by the Bodleian Library 1878-1963, 1966; History Through Surnames, 1967; The Holkham Library Illuminations & Illustrations in The Manuscript Library of the Earl of Leicester, 1970. Contbr. to: Connoisseur; etc. Mbr., Soc. of Antiquaries. Address: Manor House, Wheatley, Oxford, UK.

HASSELMARK, Nils-Åke, b. 22 Sept. 1934, Hunnebostrand, Göteborg, Sweden. Writer. Publs: Dikter över en brusten trädgård, 1957; Innan mörkren, 1958; Interiörmålning om vintern, 1960; Mitt i natten, glädjens hundar, 1962; Potatisätarna, 1963; Långsamma dikter, 1965; Dagar i enrum, 1971; Läppläsarens avsikter, 1974. Contbns. to anthols., Svenskt 60-tal, 1965, Ny svensk lyrik, 1965, & Lyrikantologi för universitetsbruk, 1967; Reviews in Bonniers Litterara Magasin; Contbr., Yr.-book of Scandinavian poetry, 1966. Mbr., Swedish Union of Authors. Recip., Artist's Schlrship., Swedish State, 1972-73, & Schlrship., Swedish Writers Fund, 1973-78. Address: Brännkyrkagatan 29, 117 22 Stockholm, Sweden.

HASSLER, Donald M., b. 3 Jan. 1937, Akron, Ohio, USA. Teacher; College Administrator. Educ: B.A., Williams Coll.; M.A., Ph.D., Columbia Univ. Publs: Erasmus Darwin, 1973; The Comedian as the Letter D: Erasmus Darwin's Comic Materialism, 1973. Contbr. to: Bulletin of the N.Y. Pub. Lib.; Keats-Shelley Jrnl. Mbrships: MLA; Am. Soc. for 18th Century Studies. Hons: Woodrow Wilson Fellowship; 1st Prize, Ohio Poetry Day, 1974. Address: 770 Marilyn Dr., Kent OH 44240, USA.

HASSLER, Warren W., Jr., b. 13 Jan. 1926, Baltimore, Md., USA. Professor of American History. Educ: B.A., 1951; Ph.D., 1954, Johns Hopkins Univ., USA; M.A., Univ. of Pa., 1951. Publs: General George B. McClellan: Shield of the Union, 1957; Commanders of the Army of the Potomac, 1962; Crisis at the Crossroads: The 1st Day at Gettysburg, 1970; The President as Commander in Chief, 1971. Contbr. to: N.Y. Times; Jrnl. of Politics; Am. Histl. Review; Jrnl. of Am. Hist.; etc. Mbrships. incl: Am. Histl.

Assn.; US Commn. on Mil. Hist. Address: 601 Liberal Arts Tower, Pa. State Univ., PA 16802, USA.

HASTED, Jane-Eliza, b. 1909, Madras, India. Writer. Publs: Unsuccessful Ladies, 1945; The Gentle Amazon, 1947; var. novels; also broadcast plays, talks, libretti, etc. Contbr. to S. African cultural & indl. jrnls., daily newspapers. Address: Blue Gums, P.O. Box 2, Simonstown, Repub. of S. Africa.

HASTINGS, Macdonald, b. 6 Oct. 1909, London, UK. Author. Publs. incl: (detective novels) Cork on the Water, 1951; Cork & the Serpent, 1955; Cork on the Telly, 1966; (autobiography) Jesuit Child, 1971; After You, Robinson Crusoe, 1975; (anthol.) Macdonald Hastings' Country Book, 1961, 1964; (text books) Churchill on Game Shooting, 1955, reprinted, 1971 (also French, German & US eds.); English Sporting Guns & Accessories, 1969; Wheeler's Fish Cookery Book (w. Carole Walsh), 1974; (biography) The Other Mr. Churchill, 1963; Mary Celeste, 1972; (TV series) Call the Gun Expert; Riverbeat; Voyage into England. Contbr. to: Picture Post (War Corres., WWII); Lilliput (as GULLIVER, Lemuel); Strand Mag. (Ed., 1946-49); Fndg. Ed., Country Fair, 1951-58. Address: Brown's Farm, Old Basing, Hants RG24 0DE, UK.

HASWELL, Chetwynd John Drake, pen names FOSTER, George; HASWELL, Jock, b. 18 July 1919, Penn, UK. Author; Served 21 years in Regular Army. Educ: Royal Mil. Coll., Sandhurst, 1938-39. Publs: Indian File, 1960; Soldier on Loan, 1961; The Queen's Royal Regiment, 1967; The First Respectable Spy, 1969; James II, Soldier & Sailor, 1972; British Military Intelligence, 1973; Citizen Armies, 1973; The Battle for Empire, 1975; The Concise History of the British Army, 1975. Ed., The Rose & the Laurel, jrnl. of the Intelligence Corps. Mbr., Royal United Servs. Inst. for Def. Studies. Address: The Grey House, Lyminge, Folkestone, Kent CT18 8ED, UK.

HATCH, James V., b. 25 Oct. 1928, Oelwein, Iowa, USA. Teacher. Educ: B.A., N. State Univ. of Iowa, 1949; M.A., 1955, Ph.D., 1958, State Univ. of Iowa, Ames. Publs. incl: Poems for Niggers & Crackers, 1965; Fly Blackbird, 1970; Liar, Liar, A Children's Opera, 1972; Plays By & About Women (w. V. Sullivan), 1973; Black Theatre U.S.A., 1847-1974, 1974; An Annotated Bibliography of Black American Plays (w. O. Abdallah), 1975. Contbr. to: Drama Review; Coll. Engl.; The Nation; Village Voice; Freedomways Mag.; Changing Educ.; Ararat Mag. Hons. incl: Obie Award for Best Off-Broadway Musical (Fly Blackbird), 1962; Geo. Wash. Hon. Medal Award, Freedom Fndn., 1958. Address: Engl. Dept., CCNY, 138th St. & Convent Ave., N.Y., NY 10031, USA.

HATCH, John Charles, b. 1917, Stockport, UK. Director-Emeritus, Inter-University African Studies Programme. Educ: B.A., Univ. of Cambridge, UK. Publs: The Dilemma of South Africa; New from Africa; Dwell Together in Unity; Everyman's Africa; Africa Today & Tommorrow; A History of Post-War Africa; Africa, The Re-Birth of Self-Rule; The History of Britain in Africa; Nigeria, Seeds of Disaster, 1970; Africa Emergent, 1974. Contbr. to: Ed., Third World; New Statesman; Venture; BBC. Mbr., Royal C'wlth. Soc. Agent: John Farquharson Ltd. Address: 67 Parliament Hill Mansions, Lissenden Gdns., London NW5, UK.

HATCHER, Harlan Henthorne, b. 1898, Ironton, Ohio, USA. Professor of English. Educ: M.A., Ph.D., Litt.D., LL.D., L.H.D., Ohio State Univ. Publs: The Versification of Robert Browning; Tunnel Hill; Patterns of Wolfpen; Lake Erie; The Western Reserve: The Story of New Connecticut in Ohio; A Century of Iron & Men; Creating the Modern American Novel; Central Standard Time. The Buckeye Country; The Ohio Guide; The Great Lakes; Modern Continental, British & American Dramas; Modern Dramas; A Modern Repertory; Giant from the Wilderness; The Persistent Quest for Values. Address: 631 Oxford Rd., Ann Arbor, Mich., USA.

HATCHETT, Ethel Louise, b. 5 Sept. 1892, Stephenville, USA. Associate Professor of Education; Author. Educ: B.A., Simmons Coll.; M.A., Columbia Univ. Publs: Travel by Land, Water, Air, 1935; Teaching Language Arts in Elementary Schools, 1956; Teaching Elementary School Subjects (contbng. author), 1961. Contbr. to: Tex. Outlook; Instructor. Mbrships: Nat.

League of Am. Pen Women (1st Pres., Abilene Br.); Nat. Coun. Tchrs. of Engl.; Nat. Conf. on Rsch. in Engl. Recip., Lit. Prize, Tex. State NLAPW Comm., 1973. Address: 600 Westwood Drive, Abilene, TX 79603, USA.

HAUGAARD, Erik Christian, b. 13 Apr. 1923, Copenhagen, Denmark. Author. Educ: Black Mtn. Coll. & New Schl. for Social Rsch., USA. Publs: Hakon of Rogen's Saga, 1963; A Slave's Tale, 1965; Orphans of the Wind, 1966; The Little Fishes, 1967; The Rider & his Horse, 1968; The Untold Tale, 1971; (transl.) The Complete Fairy Tales & Stories of Hans Christian Andersen, 1974. Mbrships: Soc. Authors (UK); Authors' Guild (USA); Danish Authors' Union. Hons: John Golden Loan Fund Award, 1958; Book Week Prize, 1967; Globe-Horn Book Award, 1968; Jane Addams Award, 1968; Danish Cultural Minister's Award Children's Book, 1970; Chapelbrook Fndn. Grant, 1971. Address: Toal Hall, Ballydehob, County Cork, Repub. of Ireland.

HAUGER, George, b. 1921, Thornaby-on-Tees, Yorks., UK. Lecturer in Speech & Drama. Educ: M.A., Univ. of Leeds, 1945. Publs: Ghelderode, Seven Plays I, 1960; Ghilderode, Seven Plays II, 1964; Theatre, General & Particular 1966. Contbr. to: Music & Letters; Tulane Drama Review; Theatre Arts; Adult Educ.; Speech & Drama; etc. Mbrships: League of Dramatists; Transl's. Guild. Lit. Agent: Dr. Jan van Loewen Ltd. Address: Motley, Hollybush Green, Collingham, Wetherby, Yorks., UK.

HAUGHTON, Rosemary Elena Konradin, b. 13 Apr. 1927, London, UK. Author; Lecturer; Broadcaster. Publs. incl: On Trying to be Human, 1967; The Transformation of Man, 1968; Act of Love, 1969; Love; The Theology of Experience; Tales from Eternity; The Liberated Heart; Elizabeth's; Greeting; The Carpenter's Son. Contbr. to: Commonweal; The Times; New Blackfriars; Realités; Cath. Herald; Meth. Recorder; The Month. Address: Lothlorien, Corsock, Castle Douglas, Kirkcudbrightshire, UK.

HAULOT, Arthur, b. 15 Nov. 1913, Angleur, Belgium. High Commissioner of Belgian Tourism. Publs. incl: (poems) Adolescence, 1939; D'un Monde a L'Autre, 1940; Si Lourd de Sang, 1947; Poemes pour l'Europe, 1951; Petite Suite Provencale, 1952; Poemes du Temps Retrouve, 1954; Pera, 1960; Departs, 1963; Espaces, 1967; Derives, 1969; Genese, 1972; (prose) Dachau, 1946; La Belgique Vue de Ciel, 1952; Aux Couleurs de Belgique, 1964; Tourisme et Environnement, 1975. Contbr. to: World Travel – tourisme mondial (Geneva); Rue da l'Academie Int. de Tourisme (Monaco); Vue touristique (Budapest); Journal des Poètes (Brussels). V.P., Maison Int. de Poésie. Hons: Prix Jauniaux, 1952; Brabant, 1954. Address: 95 Ave. des Ortolans, 1170 Brussels, Belgium.

HAUSCHKA, Ernst Reinhold, b. Aug. 1926, Aussig, Czechoslovakia. Librarian. Educ: Univs. of Munich & Ratisbon, Germany. Publs. incl: Weisheit unserer Zeit, 1965; Handbuch moderner Literatur im Zitat, 1968; Wortfänge, Erwägungen eines männlichen Zugvogels, 1971; Sich nähern auf Distanz, 1972; Türme einer Schweigsamen Stadt, 1973; Die Zeitbahn hinunter, 1974; Wort für Wort, 1975. Mbrships. incl: Schriftstellergruppe, Regensburg (Chmn. twice); Interessengemeinschaft deutschsprachiger Autoren (chmn. twice). Hons. incl: Sudeten-German Lit. Prize, 1973; Schubart Lit. Prize, 1974. Address: D–84 Regensburg, Bischof v. Senestrey-Str. 18, W. Germany.

HAUSER, Jacob, b. 27 Dec. 1909, Bklyn., N.Y., USA. Writer. Educ: Brooklyn Coll. Publs: Dark Metropolis, 1931; Solo (collected writings 1946-67), 6 vols.; Valentine for Venus, 1963; The Olympians, 1967; Greek Memoirs, 1967; Jacqueline, 1973. Contbr. to maj. newspapers & US jrnls.; Radio broadcasts in N.Y. & Calif. Mbrships: Poetry Soc. of Am.; Fndr. Fellow, Int. Poetry Soc. Hons: Guggenheim Travel Fellowship, 1936-37. Address: 1550 Pennsylvania Ave., Miami Beach, FL 33139, USA.

HAUSER, Marianne, b. 11 Dec. 1910, Strasbourg, France. Writer. Educ: Univ. of Berlin, Germany; Sorbonne, Paris, France. Publs: Monique, 1935; Indian Phantom Play, 1937; Dark Dominion, 1947; The Choir Invisible, 1958; Prince Ishmael, 1963; A Lesson in Music, 1964. Contbr. to: Harper's Bazaar; N.Y. Times; Herald Tribune; The Saturday Review; The Sewanee Review; etc. Mbrships: PEN, Ed. Bd., The New Writer. Hons: Rockefeller Fellow, 1955. Address:

2 Washington Square Village, Apt. 13M, N.Y., NY 10012, USA.

HAUSMANN, Manfred, b. 10 Sept. 1898. Author. Educ: Ph.D.; Univs. of Göttingen, Munich & Heidelberg. Publs. incl: Marienkind, 1927; Abel mit der Mundharmonika, 1932; Fedichte, 1949; Andreas, 1957; Kleiner Stern im Dunklen Strom, 1963; Und wie Musik in der Nacht, 1965; Wort vom Wort, 1968; Das abgründige Geheimnis, 1972; Wenn dieses alles Faulheit ist, 1972; (plays) Der dunkle Reigen, 1949; Die Zauberin von Buxtehude, 1959; (poems) Irrsal der Liebe, 1960; (essays) Tröstliche Zeichen, 1959; num. transls. from Greek, Chinese, Japanese & Hebrew. Address: Dillener Str. 49, 2820 Bremen 71, W. Germany.

HAVEL, Vaclav, b. 1936, Prague, Czechoslovakia. Playwright; Literary Manager, Balustrade Theatre, Prague, 1963-68. Publs: (plays) The Garden Party, 1963; The Memorandum, 1965; The Increased Difficulty of Concentration, 1968. Mbrships: The Union of Writers (CSSR); PEN. Address: Prague 2, Engelsovo Nabr 78, Czechoslovakia.

HAVENS, George R(emington), b. 25 Aug. 1890, Shelter Island, N.Y., USA. Professor Emeritus of French Literature. Educ: B.A., Amherst Coll., Mass., 1913; Ph.D., Johns Hopkins Univ., Balt., Md., 1917. Publs: The Age of Ideas, 1955, 2nd ed., 1962; Frederick J. Waugh, American Marine Painter, 1969. Contbr. to: Yale Review; S. Atlantic Quarterly; Sewanee Review; Fortnightly Review; Sev. profl. jrnls. Mbr., Exec. Coun., & V.P., Mod. Lang. Assn. of Am. Hons: Guggenheim Fellowship, 1930; L.H.D., Univ. of Mich., Ann Arbor, 1959; L.H.D., Ohio State Univ., Columbus, 1964. Address: 415 Glen Echo Circle, Columbus, OH 43202, USA.

HAVIGHURST, Robert James, b. 5 June 1900, Wis., USA. Social Scientist. Educ: A.B., Ohio Wesleyan Univ., 1921; Ph.D., Ohio State Univ., 1924. Publs. incl: Who Shall be Educated?, 1944; Adjustment to Retirement, 1970; To Live on This Earth: American Indian Education, 1972; Society & Education, 1975 (all co-author); Sociedad Y Educacion en America Latina, 1962; Development Tasks & Education, 1972. Contbr. to educ., psychol. & sociol. jrnls. Mbrships. incl: Gerontological Soc. (Pres., 1957); Int. Soc., Study of Behavioral Dev. Hons. incl: Thorndike Award, Am. Psychol. Assn., 1968; Meritorious Rsch. Award, Am. Educ. Rsch. Assn., 1973. Address: Dept. of Educ., Univ. of Chgo., IL 60637, USA.

HAVIGHURST, Walter, b. 28 Nov. 1901, Appleton, Wis., USA. Writer. Educ: A.B., Univ. of Denver, 1924; A.M., Columbia Univ., 1928. Publs: The Winds of Spring, 1940; The Long Ships Passing, 1942, revised ed., 1975; Signature of Time, 1949; Wilderness for Sale, 1956; The Heartland, 1962, revised ed., 1974; River to the West, 1970. Contbr. to: N. Am. Review; Am. Heritage; Am. W.; Saturday Review. Mbrships: Soc. of Am. Histns.; VP, Soc. of Midland Authors, 1969-; Bd. of Eds., Ohio Histl. Soc., 1956-60. Hons: Annual Award, Friends of Am. Writers, 1947; Award of Merit, Assn. for State & Local Hist., 1947, 1957; Am. Hist. Prize, Soc. of Midland Authors, 1970. Address: 163 Shadowy Hills Drive, Oxford OH 45056, USA.

HAVRAN, Martin, J. W., b. 12 Nov. 1929, Windsor, Ont., Can. Professor of History; Chairman. Educ: B.Phil., Univ. of Detroit, USA, 1951; M.A., Wayne State Univ., 1953; Ph.D., Western Reserve Unit, 1957. Publs: Readings in English History (co-ed.), 1967; England: Prehistory to the Present (co-author), 1968; The Catholics in Caroline England, 1962; Caroline Courtier: The Life of Lord Cottington, 1973. Contbr. to num. jrnls. Mbrships. incl: Am. Histl. Assn.; Can. Histl. Assn.; Elected Fellow of the Royal Histl. Soc., 1973. Address: Dept. of History, Randall Hall, Univ. of Va., Charlottesville, VA 22903, USA.

HAVREFOLD, Finn, b. 11 Aug. 1905, Oslo, Norway. Critic; Author. Educ: Norges Tekniske Hoyskole. Publs. incl: (novels) Til de Dristige, 1946; De gjenstridige, 1965; Bla rytter, 1968; Pilen i lyset, 1971; Under samme tak, 1972; (children's books) Drommevegen, 1953; Viggo, 1957; Grunnbrot, 1960; Putsja, 1967; Lommekniven, 1969; (plays) Jubileum, 1951; Gruppen, 1964; (biography) Helge Krog, 1959; & num. radio plays. Contbr. to: Dagbladet; Urd. Hons: Damm Prize, 1955 & 1957; Damm-Allers Film Prize, 1960; Prix Italia, 1970; Nordic Radio Prize, 1970. Address: Thomas Heftyes Gate 64C, Oslo 2, Norway.

HAWES, Frances Cooper (nee Richmond), b. 1897, Albany, N.Y., USA. Housewife. Educ: B.A., Radcliffe Coll., USA. Publs: Henry Bougham. Address: 3 Balfour Place, St. Andrews, Scotland, UK.

HAWKE, G. R., b. 1942. Napier, NZ. Professor of Economic History. Educ: Victoria Univ., Wellington; Balliol & Nuffield Colls., Oxford, UK; B.A.; B.Com.; D.Phil. Publs: Railways & Economic Growth in England & Wales 1840-1870, 1970; The Development of the British Economy, 1870-1914, 1970; Between Governments & Banks: A History of the Reserve Bank of New Zealand, 1973. Contbr. to: Aust. Econ. Hist. Review; etc. Address: 7 Voltaire St., Karori, Wellington, NZ.

HAWKES, Catharine Moira, b. Newcastle upon Tyne, UK. Travel Writer; Guide Book Author & Editor; Illustrator. Publs: (all w. John Ryder Hawkes) John & Moira Hawkes Holiday Factbook series, 1965-73; area Co-Ed. & main text co-author, Fodor's Guide to Switzerland, 1968-76. Contbr. to: Fodor's Guide to Europe; Fodor's Europe on a Budget; Fodor's Europe under 25; Shell Guide to Europe; co-author, Letts Guide to Switzerland, 1976, var. nat. & provincial newspapers, mags., travel trade jrnls. Address: 1 Lippetts Way, Catcott, Bridgwater, Somerset TA7 9HY, UK.

HAWKES, Jacquetta, b. 1910. Writer; Lecturer & Broadcaster on Archaeology. Educ: Newnham Coll., Cambridge. Publs. incl: Prehistoric Britain (w. Christopher Hawkes); (poems) A.Land Early Britain; Man on Earth; Fables; (play) Dragon's Mouth; Journey Down a Rainbow (w. J. B. Priestley); Unesco History of Mankind, vol. 1, part 1, 1963; The Dawn of the Gods, 1968; The First Great Civilizations, 1973; Ed., The Atlas of Archaeology, 1975. Mbr., UNESCO Culture Advisory Comm. Recip., O.B.E. Lit. Agent: A. D. Peters & Co. Address: Alveston, Stratford on Avon, Warwicks., UK.

HAWKES, John (Clendennin Burne), Jr., b. 17 Aug. 1925, Stamford, Conn., USA. Professor of English. Educ: A.B., Harvard Univ., 1949. Publs. incl: (novels) The Cannibal, USA 1949, UK 1962; The Lime Twig, USA 1961, UK 1962; Second Skin, USA 1964, UK 1966; The Blood Oranges, USA & UK 1971; (Stories) Lunar Landscapes, USA 1969, UK 1970; (plays) The Innocent Party: 4 Short Plays, USA 1966, UK 1967; (anthols.) Co-Ed., The Personal Voice, 1964; Co-Ed., The American Literary Anthology 1, 1968. Hons: Grant, Nat. Inst. Arts & Letters, 1962; var. Fellowships. Address: Dept. of English, Brown Univ., Providence, RI 02912, USA.

HAWKESWORTH, John, b. 1920, London, UK. Film TV Producer. Educ: B.A., Oxford Univ. Publs: (film & TV scripts) Tiger Bay; The Conan Doyle Series; (adaptations) The Million Pound Bank Note; The Elusive Pimpernel; The Goldrobbers; Upstairs Downstairs Series 1, 2, 3, 4 & 5; (novels) Upstairs Downstairs: Secrets of An Edwardian Household, 1972; Upstairs Downstairs In My Lady's Chamber, 1973. Agent: Deborah Rogers Ltd. Address: Flat 2, 24 Cottesmore Gardens, London, W8, UK.

HAWKINS, Clifford William, b. 19 Jan. 1914, Newdigate, Dorking, Surrey, UK. Senior Draughtsman. Publs: Log of the Huia, 1947, 3rd ed., 1973; Out of Auckland, 1960. Contbr. to Mariner's Mirror (Soc. for Nautical Rsch.). Mbr., Auckland Maritime Soc. (1st Chmn.). Address: 43 Aberdeen Rd., Takapuna, Auckland 9, NZ.

HAWKINS, David Frederick, b. 13 Dec. 1933, Sydney, Australia. Professor of Business Administration. Educ: B.A., 1956; M.B.A., 1958; Dr.B.A., 1962, Harvard Univ. Publs: Corporate Financial Reporting: Text & Cases, 1971; Financial Reporting Practices of Corporations, 1972. Contbr. to: Harvard Bus. Review; Bus. Hist. Review; Fin. Exec. Recip., McKinsey Award; Newcomen Award. Address: Harvard Business Schl., Baker 435, Boston, MA 02163, USA.

HAWKINS, Gordon, b. 25 July 1919, London, UK. Associate Professor of Criminology. Educ: B.A., Univ. Coll., Cardiff; Balliol Coll., Oxford Univ. Publs: The Honest Politician's Guide to Crime Control (w. N. Morris), 1970; Crime & Modern Society: America's Dilemma (w. N. Morris), 1971; Deterrence: The Legal Threat in Crime Control (w. F. Zimring), 1973. Contbr. to: The Australian (columnist). Mbrships. incl: Am. Soc. Criminol.; Aust. & NZ Soc. of Criminol.; Aust. Acad. Forensic Sci.; Soc. Pub.

Tchrs. of Law. Address: 16 Carey St., Manly, Sydney, N.S.W. 2095, Australia.

HAWLEY, William George, b. 28 July 1903, Agra, India. Chartered Engineer. Educ: Higher Nat. Cert. in Elec. Engrng., Manchester Coll. of Technol. Publs: Impulse-Voltage Testing, 1959. Contbr. to: Proceedings of the I.E.E.; Electrical Review; Railway Mag. Fellow, Inst. Elec. Engrs. Recip., I.E.E. premium, 1932. Address: Loanda, Fairmile Lane, Cobham, Surrey KT11 2DL, UK.

HAWORTH, Frieda Mary, b. 1898, Leeds, UK. Former Senior Lecturer, Froebel Educational Institute. Educ: B.Sc., Ph.D., Univ. of London. Publs: Natural History Series. Address: 22 Stonehill Rd., East Sheen, London SW14 8RW, UK.

HAWORTH-BOOTH, Michael, b. 8 July 1896, Haworth Hall, Dunswell, Hull, UK. Author; Garden Designer; Manager, Farall Publications. Publs: The Flowering Shrub Garden, 1938; The Hydrangeas, 1950, 4th ed., 1974/75; Effective Flowering Shrubs, 1951, 4th ed., 1970; The Flowering Shrub Garden Today, 1961; The Moutan or Tree Peony, 1963; The Flowering Shrub Garden, 1971; The Game of Boules (Petanque & Jeu Provençal), 1973; William Robinson, a Survey of his Life & Friends. Contbr. to: Country Life; Field; Gdnr's. Chronicle; House & Gdn.; Queen; Popular Gdng.; Amateur Gdng. Mbrships: Fellow, Linnean Soc., Royal Hort. Soc.; Chmn., W. Sussex Co. Gdn. Comm. Agent: Farall Publs. Address: Farall Nurseries, Roundhurst, Nr. Haslemere, Surrey, UK.

HAWSON, Herbert Keeble, b. 25 June 1894, Sheffield, Yorks., UK. Educ: Univ. of Sheffield. Publs: Sheffield: The Growth of a City, 1968. Mbr., Inc. Law Soc. (Pres., Sheffield Dist. Br., 1956). Hons: Lord Mayor of Sheffield, 1950-51; Freeman of City of Sheffield, 1965. Address: 67 Ranmoor Road, Sheffield S10 3JH, UK.

HAWTHORN, Geoffrey Patrick, b. 28 Feb. 1941, Slough, UK. University Lecturer. Educ: B.A., Oxford Univ., 1962. Publs: The Sociology of Fertility, 1970. Contbr. to: New Soc.; etc. Mbr., Int. Union for Sci. Study Population. Address: Churchill Coll., Cambridge CB3 0DS, UK.

HAWTHORN, Horace Boies, b. 4 Dec. 1889, Castana, Iowa, USA. College Professor; Research Sociologist. Educ: B.S., 1914, M.S., 1915, Iowa State Coll.; Ph.D., Univ. of Wis., 1922. Publs: Introduction to Sociology, 1923; Sociology in Rural Life, 1926; Sociology of World Crisis, 1947; Sociology of United Nations World, 1952; Sociology of Personality Functioning, 1954; Immortal Survival of Human Personality, 1959, 1967; Social Factors in Scholastic Writing, 1968. Mbr., Nat. Writers Club. Recip., var. hons. for Immortal Survival of Human Personality. Address: 901 S. Mulberry St., Sioux City, IA, USA.

HAWTHORNE, L. E. Jennie, b. 1916, London, UK. Lecturer in Economics. Educ: Cath. Plater Coll., Oxford. Publs: The Mystery of the Blue Tomatoes, 1958; David & the Penny Red, 1962; All About Money, 1970; Successful Writing, 1972. Address: 18 Hawthorn Rd., Wallington, Surrey, UK.

HAY, Robert Edwin, pen name HAY, Roy, b. 20 Aug. 1910, Abercorn, UK. Journalist. Publs: Annuals; In My Garden; Labour Saving Gardening; Gardening in the Modern Way. Contbr. to: Times; News of the World; Woman; Amateur Gardening; Ed., Gardener's Chronicle, 1954-69. Hons: M.B.E., V.M.H. Mbr., Farmers' Club. Address: Hurtmore Farm House, Hurtmore, Nr. Godalming, Surrey, UK.

HAYCRAFT, Howard, b. 24 July 1905. Publisher; Author. Educ: Univ. of Minn. Publs. incl: (as author, Ed., or Co-Ed.) Authors Today & Yesterday, 1933; American Authors 1600-1900, 1938; Murder for Pleasure: the Life & Times of the Detective Story, 1941; Twentieth Century Authors, 1942; British Authors before 1800, 1952; Ten Great Mysteries, 1959; Five Spy Novels, 1962; Books for the Blind: A Postscript & an Appreciation, 1965. Mbrships: Mystery Writers of Am. (Pres., 1963); Pres., Comm. for Employment of Handicapped. Address: 950 Univ. Ave., N.Y., NY 10452, USA.

HAYDEN, Mike, b. 21 Oct. 1920, NYC, USA. Author; Magazine Writer; Photo Journalist. Educ: Loomis Inst.; Univ. of Mich., 1 term; Shrivenham Univ., UK, 1 semester. Publs: Guidebook to the Northern California Coast, Vol. I: Highway 1, Vol. II: Humboldt & Del Norte, 1970;

INTERNATIONAL AUTHORS AND WRITERS WHO'S WHO

Guidebook to the Lake Tahoe Country, Vol. I: Echo Summit, Squaw Valley & California Shore, Vol. II: Alpine County, Donner-Truckee, Nevada Shore, 1971; Guidebook to the Sacramento Delta Country, 1973; Fishing the California Wilderness, 1974. Contbr. to: Sunset; Outdoor Life; Sports Afield; Field & Stream; num. other jrnls. Mbrships: Outdoor Writers' Assn. of Am.; Sierra Club; Wilderness Soc. Address: 826 E. Fourth Ave., San Mateo, CA 94402, USA.

HAYDN, Hiram, b. 1907, Cleveland, Ohio, USA. Editor; Publisher. Educ: M.A.; Ph.D.; Amherst Coll.; Western Reserve; Columbia Univ. Publs: (novels) By Nature Free; Manhatten Furlough; The Time is Noon; The Hands of Esau; (non-fiction) The Counter-Renaissance; (Ed.) The Portable Elizabethan Reader; (Ed.) the Papers of Christian Gauss; (Ed.) A Renaissance Treasury; (Ed.) A Thesaurus of Book Digests; (Ed.) Explorers in Living. Contbr. to Am. Scholar (Ed. since 1944). Address: 2 Wake Robin Rd., Westport, Conn., USA.

HAYES, Dawn M., b. 1 Jan. 1928, Weymouth, Auckland, NZ. Real Estate Company Director; Author. Publs: collect. w. Eric Lee-Johnson, artist, forthcoming. Contbr., short stories & poems to num. jrnls. & mags. inclng: NZ Listener; NZ Farmer; Arena; Poetry E.-W. Mbrships: incl: NZ Women Writers Soc. Address: 34 Bedlington St., Whangarei, NZ.

HAYES, Joseph (Arnold), b. 2 Aug. 1918, Indpls., Ind., USA. Novelist; Playwright. Educ: B.A., 1941, L.H.D., 1970, Ind. Univ. Publs: The Desperate Hours, 1954 (also play & film); Bon Voyage (w. M. Hayes), 1956 (also Disney film); The Hours after Midnight, 1957; Don't Go Away Mad, 1958; The Third Day, 1960; The Deep End, 1963; Like Any Other Fugitive, 1969; The Long Dark Night, 1974; & var. plays & films. Hons: Antoinette Perry Best Play Award for The Desperate Hours, 1955; Edgar Allen Poe Best Screenplay Award for The Desperate Hours, 1955. Address: 1168 Westway Dr., Sarasota, FL 33577, USA.

HAYES, Margaret, b. 5 Apr. 1925, London, UK. Residential Social Worker; Missionary Nurse in Zaire, 1954-72. Educ: S.R.N.; R.F.N.; S.C.M.; C.M.T. (Antwerp). Publs: Missing Believed Killed, 1966; Captive of Simbas, 1966. Contbr. to: Nursing Mirror; Canadian Nurse. Address: 49 Queen Caroline St., London W6, UK.

HAYES, Margaret Wyn, b. 16 July 1909, Wellington, NZ. Writer; Teacher of Creative Writing. Educ: Dip. Soc. Sci., Auckland Univ. Contbr. to: Eve; Thursday; NZ Women's Wkly.; Saturday, Aust. Mbrships: Aust. Soc. of Authors; Playwrights' Assn. of NZ (Inc.); NZ Women Writers' Soc. Inc. Hons: Nat. Short Story Award, 1973, Nat. TV Playwriting Award, 1974, NZ Women Writers' Assn. Address: 579 Riddell Rd., Glendowie, Auckland 5, NZ.

HAYMAN, Ronald, b. 4 May 1932, Bournemouth, UK. Writer; Theatrical Director. Educ: Trinity Hall, Cambridge Univ., 1951-54; M.A. Publs: Samuel Beckett, John Osborne, Harold Pinter, John Arden, 1968; John Whiting, Robert Bolt, 1969; Techniques of Acting, 1969; Tolstoy, 1970; Arnold Wesker, Arthur Miller, 1970; John Gielgud: A Biography, 1971; Playback, 1973; The Set-Up, 1974; Playback 2, 1974; The First Thrust, 1975. Contbr. to: New Review; Times; Drama; Theatre Quarterly; Poetry Nation; Kaleidoscope, BBC; etc. Address: 25 Church Row, London NW3 6UP, UK.

HAYMAN, Walter Kurt, b. 1926, Cologne, Germany. University Professor of Pure Mathematics. Educ: M.A., Sc.D., Univ. of Cambridge, UK. Publs: Multivalent Functions, 1958; Meromorphic Functions, 1964; Research Problems in Function Theory, 1967. Contbr. to var. jrnls. Mbrships: F.R.S.; A.R.C.S.; London Math. Soc.; Fellow, Cambridge Philosl. Soc. Address: Imperial Coll., Exhibition Rd., London SW7, UK.

HAYNES, Dorothy K., b. 12 Oct. 1918, Lanark, Scotland, UK. Writer. Publs: Winter's Traces, 1947; Robin Ritchie, 1949; Thou Shalt Not Suffer a Witch (short stories), 1949; Haste Ye Back (biog.), 1973. Contbr. to: Housewife; Lilliput; Good Housekeeping; Scots Mag.; Homes & Gardens; Glasgow Herald; Argosy; BBC; etc. Mbr., Soc. of Authors. Recip., Tom Gallon Award, 1947. Address: 14 Quarryknowe, Lanark ML11 7AH, UK.

HAYNES, Robert Vaughn, b. 28 Nov. 1929, Nashville, Tenn., USA. Professor of History. Educ: B.A., Millsaps

Coll., Jackson, Miss.; M.A., Peabody Coll., Nashville, Tenn.; Ph.D., Rice Univ., Houston, Tex. Publs: Blacks in White America Before 1865, 1972. Contbr. to: Jrnl. Miss. Hist.; Ala. Review; La. Hist. Mbrships: Am. Histl. Assn.; Southern Histl. Assn.; Assn. for Study Negro Life & Hist.; Am. Studies Assn.; Miss. Histl. Soc.; Org. Am. Histns.; Inst. Early Am. Hist. & Culture. Address: 2010 Banks St., Houston, TX 77006, USA.

HAYS, Rhys Williams, b. 16 May 1926, Cleveland, Ohio, USA. Professor of History. Educ: B.A., 1945, Ph.D., 1960, Columbia Univ.; M.Div., Union Theol. Sem., 1949; Cambridge Univ., London Univ. Publs: History of the Abbey of Aberconway, 1963; Studies in Medieval Cistercian History Presented to Jeremiah F. O'Sullivan (w. others), 1971. Contbr. to US & UK jrnls. Address: Dept. of Hist., Univ. of Wis., Stevens Point, WI 54481, USA.

HAYTER, Alethea, b. 1911, Cairo, Egypt. Former British Council Representative & Cultural Attaché. Educ: M.A., Univ. of Oxford. Publs: Mrs. Browning: a Poet's Work & Its Setting, 1962; A Sultry Month: Scenes of London Literary Life in 1846, 1965; Elizabeth Barrett Browning, 1965; Opium & the Romantic Imagination, 1968; Horatio's Version, 1972; A Voyage in Vain, 1973. Contbr. to: Times Saturday Review; Times Lit. Supplement; New Statesman; Hist. Today; Ariel. Mbrships: F.R.S.L.; Soc. of Authors. Hons: W. H. Heinemann Prize, R.S.L. (for Mrs. Browning: a Poet's Work & Its Setting); Rose Mary Crawshay Prize, Brit. Acad. (for Opium & the Romantic Imagination); O.B.E. Address: c/o Messrs. Faber & Faber, 3 Queen Square, London WC1, UK.

HAYTOV, Nikolay, b. 15 Sept. 1919, Yavorovo, Bulgaria. Writer. Publs: (in Bulgarian) (short stories) Hornbeam Foliage, 1965; Wild Stories, 1967; (plays) Haidoucks, 1968. Contbr. to sev. Bulgarian mags. & newspapers. Mbrships: Union of Bulgarian Writers; Union of Bulgarian Film Workers. Hons: Dimitrov Prize, 1969; Red Labour Banner (gold order), 1969; Honoured Worker in Culture, 1972. Address: Sofia-13, ul. Latika, 15, Bulgaria.

HAYWOOD, Charles, b. 20 Dec. 1904, Grodno, Russia. Musicologist. Educ: B.S., CCNY, USA, 1926; M.A., 1940, Ph.D., 1949, Columbia Univ.; Artist Dip., Inst. of Musical Art, 1930; Dip., Juilliard Schl. of Music, 1935. Publs. incl: James A. Bland, His Life & Songs, 1946; Modern Russian Art Songs, 1947; Cervantes & Music, 1948; Bibliog. of N. American Folklore & Folksong, 1951, rev. ed., 2 vols., 1961; Masterpieces of Sacred Songs, 1958; Folk Songs of the World, 1966; Maretzek's Revelations of an Opera Manager, 1968. Contbr. to US, for. jrnls.; Ed., Yearbook of Int. Folk Music Coun., 1968—. Hons. incl: Folger Shakespeare Lib. Fellowship, 1951; Fulbright Rsch. Prof., Vienna, Austria, 1961-62, 1967-68. Address: 145 E. 92nd St., N.Y., NY 10028, USA.

HAYWOOD, Helen Rivière, pen name RIVIÈRE, Elena, b. 28 Dec. 1907, Hampstead, London, UK. Artist; Author. Publs. incl: over 200 children's books, inclng: The Figgles Series, The Peter Tiggywig Series, 1927-72; Exploring Fossils, 1966; Noah's Ark, 1966; Looking After Pets, 1974; Prehistoric Notebook, 1975; Learning About Fruit & Flowers, 1975. Contbr. to Understanding Science. Mbr., Soc. of Authors. Recip., Celebrity Book Fair Award, Univ. of Hartford, Conn., USA, for The Noah's Ark of Rare Animals, 1967.

HAZARD, John Newbold, b. 5 Jan. 1909, Syracuse, N.Y., USA. Educator. Educ: B.A., Yale Univ., 1930; LL.B., Harvard Univ., 1934; J.S.D., Univ. of Chgo., 1939; Cert., Moscow Juridical Int., 1937. Publs: Soviet Housing Law, 1939; Law & Social Change in the U.S.S.R., 1953; The Soviet System of Government, 1957; Settling Disputes in Soviet Society, 1960; Communists & Their Law, 1969; The Soviet Legal System (w. I. Shapiro), 1962. Contbr. to law jrnls.; Bd. of Eds., Am. Jrnl. of Comparative Law. Address: 20 E. 94th St., N.Y., NY 10028, USA.

HAZEN, Allen Tracy, b. 1904, Portland, Conn., USA. Bibliographer; University Professor Emeritus of English. Educ: Yale Univ.; Harvard Univ.; B.A.; M.A.; Ph.D. Publs: Johnson's Prefaces & Dedications; Bibliography of Strawberry Hill Press; Bibliography of Horace Walpole; Catalogue of Walpole's Library. Contbr. to var. acad. jrnls. Address: 460 Riverside Dr., N.Y., NY 10027, USA.

HAZLEWOOD, Walter Gordon, b. 24 Feb. 1885, Homebush, N.S.W., Australua. Nurseryman. Publs: History of Epping, 1966; A Handbook of Trees, Shrubs & Roses, 1968. Address: 39 Austral Ave., Bee Croft, N.S.W., Australia 2119.

HAZLITT, Henry, b. 28 Nov. 1894, NYC, USA. Editor; Author; Publs. incl: Thinking as a Science, 1916 & 1969; Economics in One Lesson, 1946, num. transls.; Will Dollars Save the World? , 1947 & 1974; The Failure of the New Economics, 1959, 1973, & transls.; What You Should Know About Inflation, 1960 & 1965; The Foundations of Morality, 1964, 1972; Man vs. The Welfare State, 1969; The Conquest of Poverty, 1973. Contbr. to: N.Y. Evening Mail; N.Y. Herald; The Sun; Am. Mercury; N.Y. Times (Ed., 1934-46); Newsweek (columnist, 1946-66); The Freeman (Ed.-in-Chief, 1953). Recip., acad. hons. Address: 65 Drum Hill Rd., Wilton, CT 06897, USA.

HAZZARD, Shirley, b. 30 Jan. 1931, Sydney, Australia. Writer. Publs: Cliffs of Fall, 1963; The Evening of the Holiday, 1966; People in Glass Houses, 1967; The Bay of Noon, 1970; Defeat of an Ideal, 1973. Contbr. to New Yorker Mag. Trustee, N.Y. Soc. Lib. Hons: Award in Lit., Nat. Inst. of Arts & Letters, USA, 1966; Guggenheim Fellowship, 1974. Address: 200 East 66th St., N.Y., NY 10021, USA.

HEAD, Alice Maud, b. 3 May 1886, London, UK. Journalist. Publs: It Could Never Have Happened (autobiog.). Contbr. to: Good Housekeeping; Homes & Gardens; Country Life. Mbr., PEN. Address: 22 Whitelands House, Chelsea, London SW3, UK.

HEAD, Bessie, b. 6 July 1937, Pietermaritzburg, S. Africa. Agriculturist; Former Teacher & Journalist. Publs: (novels) When Rain Clouds Gather, USA & UK, 1968; Maru, UK & USA, 1971. Address: P.O. Box 15, Serowe, Botswana.

HEAL, Jeanne, b. 25 May 1917, Cambridge, UK. Journalist; Author; Graphologist. Educ: Ecole du Louvre, Paris, France; M.Sc. Publs: Jeanne Heal's Book of Careers for Girls, 1955; A Thousand & One Australians, 1959; New Zealand Journey, 1963; You & Your Handwriting, 1973. Contbr. to: Picture Post; Sunday Empire News; Sunday Graphic; Sydney Morning Herald, Aust.; var. UK nat. newspapers & mags. Address: 32 York Terrace West, London NW1, UK.

HEALD, Bruce Day, b. 5 June 1935, Boston, Mass., USA. Educator. Educ: A.A., Boston Univ.; B.S. (Music Educ.), Lowell State Coll. Publs: Follow the Mount, 1968, revised ed., 1970; Postmaster of the Lake, 1971. Address: RFD 2, Box 15, Meredith, NH 03253, USA.

HEALD, Timothy Villiers, b. 28 Jan. 1944, Dorchester, Dorset, UK. Journalist. Educ: Hons. Degree, Mod. Hist., Balliol Coll., Oxford. Publs: It's a Dog's Life, 1971; Unbecoming Habits, 1973; Blue Blood Will Out, 1974. Contbr. to: Times. Telegraph; Vogue; Radio Times; (formerly) Punch; Spectator; New Statesman. Address: 8 Thornton Rd., London SW14 8NS, UK.

HEALEY, Benjamin James, pen names STURROCK, Jeremy (in UK); JEFFREYS, J. G. (in USA), b. 26 June 1908, Birmingham, UK. Artist; Writer. Educ: Birmingham Univ.; Birmingham Schl. Art. Publs: Waiting For a Tiger, USA 1965, UK 1965; The Vespucci Papers, USA 1972, UK 1972, (W. Germany, Lektion Für Ladys, 1973); The Stone Baby, UK 1973, USA 1973, W. Germany 1973; A Gardener's Guide to Plant Names, USA 1972; The Village of Rogues, UK 1972, USA 1972; The Thieftaker; A Wicked Way to Die, UK 1973, USA 1973; The Wilful Lady, forthcoming UK; The Plant Hunters, forthcoming USA. Mbr., Royal Hort. Soc. Address: 19 Granard Ave., Putney, London SW15, UK.

HEALEY, Kathleen Mary, b. 18 Sept. 1912, Winton, Southland, NZ. Journalist. Publs: Growl You May, Go You Must (ghost-writer & contbr., med. anthol.), 1968; The Green & The Gold, 1975. Children's Ed., NZ Tablet, 23 yrs.; also Radio & TV scripts; ch. pageants, 1967, 1971, 1974. Mbrships: NZ Women's Writers' Soc.; NZ Playwrights' Soc. Recip., var. one-act play competition awards, nat. & local, 1948-50, 1952-55, 1957, 1962-63, 1965, 1972. Address: 112 Musselburgh Rise, Dunedin, NZ.

HEALY, James N. (James Anthony Nagle-Healy), pen name HAY, Nigel, b. 3 Aug. 1916, Cork, Repub. of Ireland. Writer; Actor; Producer. Educ: B.Comm., Nat. Univ. of Ireland. Publs: Author/Ed., The Second Book of Irish

Ballads, 1962; Ireland (Engl., German & French eds.), 1963; Author/Ed., Ballads from the Pubs of Ireland, 1965; Percy French & His Songs, 1965, paperback, 1974; Old Irish Street Ballads, 4 vols., 1967-69; The First Book of Irish Ballads (co-author), 1968; Author/Ed., Ballads from the Pubs of England, 1974; (Stage Works) Letters of a Successful T.D. (adapt.), 1971; Freeny! (w. M. Casey), 1974; var. Radio Documentaries. Contbr. to: Cork Evening Echo (52 part Hist. of Cork Stage); num. other publs. Address: 2 Lincoln Pl., Grattan Hill, Cork, Repub. of Ireland.

HEALY, John Francis, b. 1926, Plymouth, UK. Professor of Classics. Educ: M.A., Ph.D., Trinity Coll., Cambridge Univ. Publ: Cyrenaican Expeditions (w. Alan Rowe), 1955. Contbr. to: Numismatic Chronicle; Numismatic Lit.; Jrnl. Hellenic Studies; Gnomon; Actes du Congrès Int. de Numismatique. Mbrships: Fellow, Royal Numismatic Soc.; F.R.S.A.; Cambridge Union. Address: Harehill, Potter Row, Great Missenden, Bucks. HP16 9LU, UK.

HEAP, (Sir) Desmond, b. 1907, Burnley, Lancs., UK. Former Comptroller & City Solicitor to Corporation of City of London; Planning Consultant. Educ: LL.M., Manchester Univ. Publs: An Outline of Planning Law, 6th ed.; The New Towns Act; Encyclopaedia of Law of Town & Country Planning; Encyclopaedia of Betterment Levy & Land Commission. Contbr. to: Jrnl. of Planning & Environment Law. Mbrships. incl: F.R.S.A.; Law. Soc. (Pres., 1972-73); Royal Town Planning Inst. (Pres., 1955-56); Assoc., Royal Instn. of Chartered Surveyors. Recip., Hon. LL.D. Agent: Sweet & Maxwell Ltd. Address: Coward Chance, Royex House, Aldermanbury Sq., London EC2, UK.

HEARD, Anthony Hazlitt, b. 20 Nov. 1937, Johannesburg, S. Africa. Journalist. Educ: B.A. & B.A. Hons., First Class, Univ. of Cape Town, S. Africa. Publs: Ed., Cape Times (oldest continuous major daily publ. in S. Africa), 1971—. Mbr., Civil Service Club, Cape Town. Address: Cape Times, 77 Burg St., Cape Town, S. Africa.

HEARNE, John, b. 1926, Montreal, Can. Author. Educ: M.A.; Edinburgh Univ.; London Univ. Publs: Voices Under The Window; Stranger at the Gate; The Faces of Love; The Autumn Equinox; Land of the Living; Atlantic-Little Brown; Piper Verlag; Skoglunds. Contbr. to: New Statesman; Atlantic Monthly; BBC; The W. Indian Economist; Radio Jamaica; Trinidad Guardian; etc. Mbr., PEN. Address: c/o Faber & Faber, Russell Sq., London WC1, UK.

HEARNE, Reginald, b. 1929, Cork, Repub. of Ireland. Actor; Manager; Screenwriter. Educ: Royal Acad. Dramatic Art. Publs: (films) Serena; Echo of Diana; The Little Crime; The Sicilians; The Colonel's Ride; Bank Raid; also adaptation for TV work by Dumas. Contbr. to: Theatre World; var. newspapers. Address: Lion Cottage, 14 Greys Rd., Henley-on-Thames, Oxon., UK.

HEARSEY, John Edward Nicholl, b. 25 May 1928, Eastbourne, Sussex, UK. Author. Publs: The Tower, 1960; Bridge, Church & Palace, 1961; City of Constantine, 1961; London & the Great Fire, 1965; Marie Antoinette, UK & USA, 1972, paperback, 1974; Elizabeth I, 1969; Men of Power, 1970; Young Mr. Pepys, UK & USA, 1973; Voltaire, 1975. Contbr. to: Country Life; The Field; The Lady; E. Anglian Mag. Mbrships: Soc. of Authors; Nat. Book League. Address: Ross Cottage, Station Rd., Angmering, Littlehampton, Sussex, UK.

HEARST, Austine McDonnell, b. 22 Nov. 1928, Warrenton, Va., USA. Journalist. Educ: King's Smith Jr. Coll. Washington, DC, reporter & nationally syndicated columnist, 1942-52. Contbr. to: Reader's Digest & Today's Woman. Address: 810 5th Ave., N.Y., NY 10021, USA.

HEASMAN, Kathleen Joan, b. 24 June 1913, Southsea, Hants., UK. University Lecturer. Educ: M.A., Girton Coll., Cambridge Univ.; Ph.D., Bedford Coll., London Univ. Publs: Hong Kong Cost of Living Index, 1939; Evangelicals in Action, 1962; Christians & Social Work, 1965; Army of the Church, 1968; An Introduction to Pastoral Counselling, 1969; The Study of Society, 1973. Contbr. to: Hong Kong Econs. Soc.; Moral Welfare; Histl. Jrnl.; Crucible; Frontier. Mbrships: Brit. Sociol. Assn.; Women's Univ. Club. Address: The White Cottage, Leigh, Tonbridge, Kent TN 11 8HS, UK.

HEATH, Catherine, b. 17 Nov. 1924, London, UK. Senior Lecturer. Educ: M.A., St. Hilda's Coll., Oxford. Publs: Stone Walls, 1973; The Vulture, 1974; Joseph & the Goths (forthcoming). Contbr. to The Guardian. Mbrships: PEN; Anglo-Netherland Soc. Agent: Curtis Brown. Address: 14 Grosvenor Ave., Carshalton, Surrey, UK.

HEATH, Dwight B., b. 19 Nov. 1930, Hartford, Conn., USA. Professor of Anthropology. Educ: A.B., Harvard Coll., 1952; Ph.D., Yale Univ., 1959. Publs: A Journal of the Pilgrims at Plymouth — Mourt's Relation, 1963; Contemporary Cultures & Societies of Latin America, 1965, rev. ed., 1974; Land Reform & Social Revolution in Bolivia, 1969; Historical Dictionary of Bolivia, 1972. Contbr. to: Ency. Britannica; popular & profl. jrnls. Address: Dept. of Anthropol., Brown Univ., Providence, RI 02912, USA.

HEATHCOTT, Mary, pen name RAYMOND, Mary, b. 30 Sept. 1914, Manchester, UK. Journalist; Writer. Publs. incl: Take-Over, 1965; The Long Journey Home, 1967; I Have Three Sons, 1968; That Summer, 1970; Surety for a Stranger, 1971; The Pimpernel Project, 1972; The Silver Girl, 1973. Contbr. to Brit. & US mags. Mbr., Writer's Guild of GB. Agent: Harvey Unna Ltd. Address: 19 Kensington Sq., London W8, UK.

HEATH-MILLER, Mavis Blanche, pen name DUNCAN, Blanche, b. 22 Oct. 1914, Hampstead, London, UK. Author. Educ: Fay Compton Studio of Dramatic Art. Publs. incl: Always Say Good-bye; The Crescent; Scent of Summer; Disgraceful Affair, 1971; Find a Pretty Girl, 1971; Mist in the Morning, 1972; Build a High Wall, 1972; The Bitter Herb, 1973; The Mimosa Tree, 1973; The Narrow Stair, 1974; The Tall White Gates, 1974. Contbr. of short stories, articles, verse to num. mags. in 10 countries. Mbrships: Inst. of Jrnlsts.; Coun. Soc. of Women Writers & Jrnlsts. Address: North Lodge, 10 Davell Rd., Caversham Heights, Reading, UK.

HEATON, (The Very Rev.) Eric William, b. 1920, Bradford, Yorks., UK. Dean of Durham. Educ: M.A., Christ's Coll., Cambridge Univ. Publs: His Servants the Prophets, 1949; The Book of Daniel, 1956; Everyday Life in Old Testament Times, 1956 (transl'd into Italian, German, Dutch, Danish, Swedish, Hebrew); The Old Testament Prophets, 1958 (transl'd into German); Commentary on the Sunday Lessons, 1959; The Hebrew Kingdoms, 1968; Soloman's New Men, 1974. Contbr. to: Tchrs. Commentary; Jrnl. Theol. Studies; Expository Times. Address: The Deanery, Durham, UK.

HEATON, Martha, b. 21 Aug. 1896, Oxenhope, Keighley, Yorks., UK. Retired Textile Worker & Book-keeper. Publs: Sun Hill, 1968; The History of Oxenhope, forthcoming; also sev. children's plays & dialect plays pvtely. circulated. Contbr. to: Local lit. & Ch. mags. Mbrships: Yorks. Dialect Soc.; Calder Valley Poets' Soc. Hons: 1st prize, Calder Valley Soc. Annual Poetry Contest; 1st prize, Yorks Ridings Mag. Dialect Competition. Address: 6 Hawksbridge Lane, Oxenhope, Keighley, W. Yorks BD22 9QU, UK.

HEATON-WARD, William Alan, b. 19 Dec. 1919, Durham, UK. Consultant Psychiatrist; Clinical Teacher, Bristol University, Department of Mental Health. Educ: M.B., Ch.B., D.P.M., Univ. of Bristol; F.R.C.Psych. Publs: Notes on Mental Deficiency (co-author); Mental Subnormality, 4th ed., 1975; Left Behind, 1975. Mbrships: Royal Coll. of Psychs., Chmn., Mental Deficiency Sect., Chmn., S. Western Div.; BMA: Bristol Royal Medico-Chirurgical Soc. Address: 75 Pembroke Road, Clifton, Bristol BS8 3DP, UK.

HEBER PERCY, Cyril Hugh Reginald, b. 18 Dec. 1906, Hodnet, Salop., UK. Soldier (Lieutenant-Colonel); Master of Hounds & Huntsman for 22 years. Educ: Harrow Schl. Publs: Hym, 1959; While Others Sleep, 1962; Us Four, 1963. Mbrships: Master of Foxhounds Assn.; Guards Club. Hons: D.S.O.; M.C. Address: Woodlands Cottage, Ibstone, Nr. High Wycombe, Bucks., UK.

HECHTMAN, Isaac L., b. 18 Feb. 1918, Rubel, Poland. Executive Vice-President, Jewish Community Council. Educ: Ordained Rabbi, Rabbinical Sem. 'Mirer Yeshiva', 1946. Publs: Kashruth — Its Meaning & Significance. Contbr. to: Fndr. & Ed., Voice of the Vaad (Engl., French & Yiddish); Jewish Eagle, Can.; Jewish Morning Jrnl., NYC. Mbrships: Rabbinical Couns. of Am. & of Quebec; Dir.,

Beth Din D'Montreal. Address: 2615 Soissons Ave., Montreal, P.Q. H3S 1V7, Canada.

HECKEL, Robert V., b. 6 June 1925, Chgo. Heights, Ill., USA. Psychologist. Educ: B.S., 1948, M.S., 1949, Ph.D., 1955, Pa. State Univ. Publs: Psychology, The Nurse & the Patient (w. Jordan), 1963, revised ed., 1967; Applied Psychology in Dentistry (w. Greider & Cinotti), 1964; Textbook of General Psychology (w. Peacock), 1966; Pediatric Nursing (w. Latham), 1967, 2nd ed., 1972; The Return Home (w. Epps, Perry & Reeves), 1967; Crime & Delinquency (w. Mandell), 1971; Leadership & Group Dynamics, 1972; Leadership: A Brief Introduction, 1972; The Decline of Intimacy & Meaning, 1972; The Discharged Mental Patient (w. Perry & Reeves), 1973; The Rural Southern Alcoholic (w. Stenmark & Sausser), 1973. Contbr. to sev. profl. jrnls. Mbrships. incl: Am. Psychol. Assn.; AAUP. Address: Soc. Problems Rsch. Inst., Univ. of S.C., Columbia, SC 29208, USA.

HECKSCHER, August, b. 16 Sept. 1913, Huntingdon, N.Y., USA. Publicist, Public Services. Educ: B.A., Yale Univ., 1936; B.A., Harvard Univ., 1938. Publs: A Pattern of Politics, 1947; Politics of Woodrow Wilson, 1956; The Public Happiness, 1962; Alive in the City, 1974; Open Spaces of American Cities, forthcoming. Contbr. to: Christian Sci. Monitor; N.Y. Times; Va. Quarterly Review; Am. Schlr.; Owner, The Uphill Press. Mbrships. incl: Fellow, Am. Acad. Arts & Scis. Hons: D.H.L.; LL.D.; Fellow, Jonathan Edwards Coll., Yale Univ. Address: 159 E. 94 St., N.Y., NY 10028, USA.

HEDENIUS, (Per Arvid), Ingemar, b. 5 Apr. 1908, Stockholm, Sweden. Professor of Practical Philosophy. Educ: Ph.D., 1936, Docent, 1938, Uppsala Univ. Publs. incl: Sensationalism & Theology in Berkeley's Philosophy, 1936; On Law & Morals, 1941; Faith & Reason (essays), 1949; Four Virtues (essays), 1955; Yet, There Is a Day (poems), 1963; The Immoral Decency, 1969; The Doctrine of Hell, 1972; On the Conditions for Human Morality, 1972. Contbr. to: Living Philosophers, 1959; Contemporary Philosophy in Scandinavia, 1972;Inquiry; Ord och Bild; Danish Perspektiv; Personalist. Address: Norra Rudbecksgatan 12, 752 36 Uppsala, Sweden.

HEDERBERG, Hans, b. 24 July 1938, Stockholm, Sweden. Television Director. Educ: studied sociol. & pol. sci. at Univ. of Stockholm. Publs: En Liberal Attityd (A Liberal Attitude), 1963; Dagspressen I Sverige (The Daily Newspapers in Sweden), 1965; Press På Villovägar (The Press in Trouble), 1969; Detta Fantastiska Land (This Terrific Country), 1973. Mbrships: Swedish Union of Writers (SFF); Svenska Journalist Förbundet; Publicistklubben. Address: Wennerbergsgatan 6, 112 58 Stockholm, Sweden.

HEDGES, Sidney George, b. 26 Mar. 1897, d. July 1974, Bicester, Oxon., UK. Author. Publs: About 130 books of fiction; a score of volumes on each of such technical subjects as swimming, games, youth interests, world religions & other varied works incl. With One Voice; Youth Club Programmes. Swimming Complete; Swimming is for Everyone; Indoor & Community Games; Fun for the Not-so-Young; Bicester Wuz a Little Town, 2nd ed., 1974. Contbr. to: radio; B.O.P.; The Scout; & var. newspapers in USA, Can., Aust., UK. Mbrships: Royal C'wlth. Soc.; Victory Club.

HEDLUND, (Jan) Magnus (Wilhelm), b. 31 Oct. 1942, Gothenburg, Sweden. Author. Educ: Filosofie magister degree; studies in lit., Engl. & Scandinavian langs. Publs: Fluxus eller Vettvillingen i vattvällingen, 1967; Den rasande grisen (personal anthol.), 1971; Doktor Gorks sånger, 1972; Pa spaning efter den gris som flytt, 1974. Contbr. to: Dagens Nyheter; Bonniers Litterära Magasin; Vinduet; etc. Mbrships: Swedish Union of Authors; Collège de Pataphysique. Address: Övre Husargatan 35, S-413 14 Gothenburg, Sweden.

HEENAN, (The Most Rev.), John C., b. 1905, Ilford, Essex, UK. The Cardinal Archbishop of Westminster; Archbishop of Liverpool, 1956-63; Archbishop of Leeds, 1951-57. Educ: D.D., Ph.D.; St. Ignatius' Coll., Stamford Hill; Ushan Coll., Durham; Venerable Engl. Coll., Rome. Publs: Letters from Rush Green, 1936; (biog.) Cardinal Hinsley, 1944; The People's Priest, 1951; Council & Clergy, 1966; Dialogue (w. Rosemary Haughton), 1968; (autobiog.) Not the Whole Truth, 1972; A Crown of Thorns, 1974. Contbr. to: Times Lit. Supplement; The Times. Address: Archbishop's House, Westminster, London SW1P 1QJ, UK.

HEFFER, Eric Samuel, b. 12 Jan. 1922, Hertford, UK. Member of Parliament; Minister of State in Labour Government. Publs: The Agreeable Autocracies (co-author), 1960; Election 1970 (co-author), 1970; Class Struggle in Parliament, 1973. Contbr. to: New Statesman; Spectator; Tribune; Pol. Quarterly; Critica Sociale; New Pol.; New Left Review; Guardian; The Times. Agent: A. P. Watts. Address: House of Commons, London SW1A 0AA, UK.

HEGEDÜS, Géza, b. 14 May 1912, Budapest, Hungary. Writer; University Professor. Educ: D.Law, Budapest Univ. Publs. incl: Az Irástudó (The Clerk, histl. novel), 2 vols., 1946-52; Európa Közepén (In the Middle of Europe, cycle of novels), 10 books, 1954-72; A Milétoszi Hajós (The Sailor from Miletus, novel), 1956; Theseus (verse drama); A Kentaur és az Angyal (The Centaur & the Angel, essays), 1967; num. Radio & TV plays. Contbr. to: Nagyvilág; Élet és Irodalom; Népszakadság; Magyar Hirlap. Mbrships: Fedn. Hungarian Writers; Hungarian PEN. Hons: Jósef Attila Prize (twice); Order of Work, 1st & 2nd Classes. Address: 1137 Budapest XIII, Ditrói Mór utca 3, Hungary.

HEGELER, Sten, pen names BOREL, Helene; STEIN, Jan., b. 28 Apr. 1923, Copenhagen, Denmark. Psychologist. Educ: Cand. Psych., Univ. of Copenhagen, 1953. Publs. incl: Peter & Caroline; Fem sma matroser; Jorn pa Kostskole; Lise i pension; Choosing Toys for Children; co-authored w. Inge Hegeler \ Publs. incl: An ABZ of Love; Ask Inge & Sten; World's Best Slimming Diet; On Being Lonesome; XYZ of Love; Living is Loving. Contbr. to: Politiken; Aktuelt; Info.; Ed., Taenk (Danish Consumer Mag.). Mbrships. incl: Danish Psychs. Assn.; Danish Authors Assn.; Danish Jrnlsts. Assn. Recip. (w. wife), PH-Fund 1970. Address: Frederiksberg Alle 25, DK-1820 Copenhagen V, Denmark.

HEIBERG, Hans, b. 28 Jan. 1904, Oslo, Norway. Author; Critic; Former Head of Drama Department, Norwegian Broadcasting System. Educ: J.D., 1927. Publs: (novels) The Boy in a Jacket, 1931; Take that Ring & Let It Pass, 1934; (plays) The Bridge, 1945; The Feast of Memory, 1946; (biogs.) Henrik Ibsen, A Portrait, 1967; A Portrait of the poet Henrik Wergeland, 1972. Contbr. to var. daily newspapers (Cultural Ed., 1931-37, 1945-52). Mbrships. incl: Norwegian Authors' Assn., Pres., 1946-65; Norwegian State Cultural Coun., 1965-72; Norwegian Actors' Assn. Hons. incl: State Cultural Coun. Prize, 1973; Cmdr., Royal Norwegian Order of St. Olav. Address: Nils Tollers vei 5, Oslo 8, Norway.

HEIDENREICH, Charles Albert, b. 14 Oct. 1917, Stockton, Ill., USA. Professor of Psychology. Educ: A.B., Sacramento State Univ., 1953; M.A., 1955; Ed.D., Brigham Young Univ., 1965. Publs: Personality & Social Adjustment, 1968, 1970; Basic Textbook of Psychology, 1971; Dictionary of General Psychology, 1970; How to Succeed in School & College, 1973; Basic Readings in Behavior Disorders, 1969, 1972; Role of the Administrator Student & Teacher in Community College Settings, 1974. Contbr. to profl. publs. Mbrships: Phi Delta Kappa; V.P., Sacramento City Chapt., AAUP; Sacramento City Unified Tchrs. Assn. Recip., acad. hons. Address: 7324 Sunset Ave., Fair Oaks, CA 95628, USA.

HEIJERMANS, Hermine, b. 1902, Katwijk a/zee, Netherlands. Actress; Writer; Freelance Journalist. Publs. incl: De Minnaars (The Lovers); Nog meer minnaars (More Lovers); (biog.) Mijn vader Herman Heijermans (My Father Herman Heijermans). Contbr. to: Vrij Nederland; radio & TV. Mbr., Vereniging van Letterkundigen. Address: Rivierenhuis, flat 619, P. Kennedylaan, Amsterdam, Netherlands.

HEIKKINEN, Helge Birger, b. 20 Dec. 1910, Helsinki, Finland. Author. Educ: Schl. of Navigation, Rauma; Schl. of Jrnlsm., Oslo, Norway; Helsinki Univ. Publs. incl: Kap Hornin Kautta, 1947; Koululaivalla Maailman Ympäri, 1955; Jokamiehen Merenkulunopas, 5 eds. 1958-73; Suomen Joutsenesta Sumerilaislaivoihin, 1958; Vaarallisilla Vesillä, 1960; Suomen Mexrenkulkumuseo, 1961; Tornado, 1967; Veneen Hoito, 1970; Veneiden Varusteet, 1970; Meriretkeilijän Suomi, 1970; Purjehtimaan, 1971; Tuntematon Merimies, 1974. Contbr. to: Suomen Merenkulku; Ålands Sjöfart; Navigator; num. other naval jrnls. Mbrships. incl: Finnish Soc. of Authors; Assn. of Sci. & Informative Authors. Address: Bergtrollsvägen 5 A 94, 00820 Helsinki 82, Finland.

HEIMAN, Ernest Jean, b. 18 Nov. 1930, Dubuque, Iowa, USA. Teacher; Writer. Educ: B.S., 1958, M.S., 1961,

Univ. of Wis. Publs: The Dynamics of Language (co-author), 6 vols., 1971. Contbr. to Nat. Coun. of Tchrs. of Engl. Jrnl. Address: 4400 Monona Dr., Monona, WI 53716, USA.

HEIMAN, Grover George, Jr., b. 26 July 1920, Galveston, Tex., USA. Editor. Educ: B.S., Univ. of Southern Calif., Los Angeles. Publs: Jet Navigator (w. Rutherford Montgomery), 1958; Jet Tanker, 1961; Jet Pioneers, 1963; Careers for Women in Uniform (w. Virginia H. Myers), 1971; Aerial Photography, 1972. Contbr. to: Assoc. Ed., Nation's Bus.; Chief, Wash. Bur., Electronic Design Mag.; Rdrs. Digest; Pace; Nat. Aeronautics; Air Force; Armed Forces Mgmt.; etc. Mbrships. incl: Authors Guild; Authors League; Nat. Press Club, Wash. D.C. Address: 2881 Glenvale Dr., Fairfax, VA 22030, USA.

HEINESEN, William, b. 15 Jan. 1900, Thorshaven, Faroe Isles. Author. Publs: (novels) Noatun, 1938; The Black Pot, 1949; The Lost Fiddlers, 1950; Mother of the Seven Stars, 1952; Windy Dawn, 1961; The Good Hope, 1964; (stories) The Enchanted Light, 1957; The Bewitched Gamaliel, 1960; Cure for Evil Spirits, 1967; Don Juan from The Train Oil House, 1970. Mbr., Danish Lit. Acad. Recip., Scandinavian Lit. Prize, 1965. Address: Vardagöta 33, Thorshaven, Faroe Isles.

HEINLEIN, Robert Anson, b. 1907, Butler, Mo., USA. Educ: US Naval Acad., Annapolis. Publs. incl: The Green Hills of Earth; The Puppet Master; The Door into Summer; The Unpleasant Profession of Jonathan Hoag; Sixth Column; Red Planet; Time for the Stars; Have Space Suit—Will Travel; The Star Beast; Stranger in a Strange Land; & num. other novels. Contbr. to: Saturday Evening Post; Argosy; Town & Country; Colliers; etc. Mbr., Authors' Club. Address: c/o Mr. Lurton Blassingame, 60 E. 42nd St., Suite 1131, N.Y., NY 10017, USA.

HEINRICH, Willi, b. 1920, Heidelberg, Germany. Author. Publs: Das Geduldige Fleisch, 1954; Der Goldene Tisch, 1956; Die Gezeichneten, 1958; Alte Häuser sterben nicht, 1960; Gottes Zweite Garnitur, 1962; Rape of Honor, 1962; Ferien im Jenseits, 1963; Maiglöcken oder ähnlich, 1965; Mittlere Reife, 1966; Geometrie einer Ehe, 1968; Schmetterlinge weinen nicht, 1969; Jahre wie Tau, 1970; So long Archie, 1972; Liebe und was sonst noch zählt. Address: Bühlertal/Baden, Winterbach, W. Germany.

HEITNER, Robert R., b. 1 Feb. 1920, St. Louis, Mo., USA. Professor of German. Educ: B.A., M.A., Wash Univ., St. Louis; Ph.D., Harvard Univ., 1949. Publs: German Tragedy in the Age of Enlightenment, 1963; Ed., The Contemporary Novel in German. A Symposium, 1967; Ed., August Adolf von Haugwitz, Schuldige Unschuld oder Maria Stuarda, 1974. Contbr. to: The Lessing Yrbook.; Germanic Review; Ency. Americana; The German Quarterly (Ed., 1967-70); etc. Mbr., sev. acad. orgs. Address: 7840 Greenfield, River Forest, IL 60305, USA.

HEJAZI, Mohammad, b. 1899. Senator; Writer. Publs. incl: Andisheh; Ziba; Homa; Parichehr; Saghar. Address: c/o The Iranian Embassy, 16 Prince's Gate, London SW7, UK.

HELAKISA, Marja Kaarina, b. 22 June 1946, Helsinki, Finland. Writer of Children's Books; Illustrator; Translator. Educ: Helsinki Univ., 1965-69. Publs: (children's stories) Satukirja (Fairy Tale Book), 1964; Taikapuu (Magic Tree), 1968; Elli Velli Karamelli (Nelly Jelly Pretty Belly), 1973; (children's play) Schiivoavat Serafit (The Cleaning Seraphims), 1969; Salakissat (The Secret Cats), 1973; Reading Book for Primary Schls., 1974; Jrnlst., Apu (weekly mag.), 1971-72. Mbrships: Finnish Youth Writers; Finnish Writers' Soc. Hons: Topelius Prize, 1965 & Lydecken Prize, 1974 for year's best children and youth books; Weilen & Göös Prize, 1973; Finnish State Prize children's writers, 1974. Address: Unioninkatu 45 E 54, Helsinki 17, Finland.

HELANDER, Gunnar, b. 20 Mar. 1915, Vanersborg, Sweden. Dean. Educ: M.A.; M.Th. Publs. incl: Zulu Trifft den Weissen Mann, 1949; Svart Symfoni, 1953; Isingeniso (in Zulu), 1953; Big City Zulu, 1955; Svart Napoleon, 1956; Must We Introduce Monogamy, 1958. Contr. to: Handelstidningen, Göteborg. Mbrships. incl: Swedish Soc. of Authors; V.P., Defence & Aid Int.; Pres., Swedish S. Africa Comm. Recip., Kt., Royal Swedish Order of Northern Star. Address: V. Kyrkogatan 3, Vasteras, 72215, Sweden.

HELBEMAE, Gert, b. 1913, Tallin, Estonia. Editor. Publs: The Silent Man; Life Unlived; The Cuckoo's Call; The Sisters; The Black Friar; The Ship to Delos; Only Momentarily; The Fugitives; Superfluous Man; Uhvrilaiva; A Chipmunk on my Shoulder. Contbr. to: Voice of Estonia (Ed., 1947—); Tulimuld; Mana. Mbr., PEN. Address: 11 Campden Hill Mansions, London LW8 7PL, UK.

HELKA, Leena, b. 29 Dec. 1924, Rauma, Finland. Writer. Educ: M.A. Publs: (in Finnish) Prelude (poems), 1951; Just Like not Alone (stories), 1955; Tupakkirulla (fairy tales), 1957; Children's Encyclopedia, 1965; Together (novel for teenagers, co-author), 1971; (in Swedish) The Night of a Birthday (poems), 1960; Seven Sisters (poems), 1962; Half of the Animal Kingdom (poems), 1963; Foster Child (poems), 1965. Address: Valtakatu 30 A 53, 28100 Pori 10, Finland.

HELL, Johanna Wilhelmina Petronella, b. 9 Nov. 1931, The Hague, Netherlands. Writer. Publs: Het gebroken bewijs, 1967; Een huid om in te schuilen, 1970. Contbr. to: Poetry Int. 1972 (Rotterdam). Mbrships: V.V.L., Amsterdam; Poetry Workshop, Kunststichting Rotterdam. Address: Potgieterstraat 24, Zoetermeer, Netherlands.

HELLBERG, Rolf, b. 17 Nov. 1908, E. Molesey, Surrey, UK. Architect (Retired). Educ: Birmingham Schl. of Arch.; F.R.I.B.A. Publ: Shops & Stores Today (w. Ellis Somake). Mbrships: Coventry & Warwicks. Soc. of Artists (Pres.); F.R.S.A. Address: Dragonyard, Church Lane, Barford, Warwicks., UK.

HELLBOM, Ebba Sofia Kristina, b. 14 July 1912, Uppsala, Sweden. Translator. Educ: Sorbonne Univ.; Schl. Oriental Langs., Paris; Uppsala Univ. Publs. incl: Works of Karl Jaspers, Colette, C. D. Broad, Irving Stone, Ashley Montague, & scientific works translated from English, French, German & Swedish. Mbrships: Swedish League of Authors; Philos. Soc.; Dog Owners' Soc.; Swedish Soc. Protection Dogs; Nordic Anti-Vivisection Alliance. Recip., Transls. Prize Swedish Authors' Fund, 1965. Address: Artillerigatan 51, 11445 Stockholm, Sweden.

HELLER, Erich, b. 1911, Komatau, Czech. Avalon Professor in the Humanities. Educ: Dr.Jur., Prague Univ.; Ph.D., Cambridge Univ., UK. Publs: The Disinherited Mind, UK 1952, USA 1957, 1959, paperback ed., 1961; The Hazard of Modern Poetry, 1953; Enterbter Geist, 1954; The Ironic German, 1958, 1963; Thomas Mann, 1959; The Artist's Journey into the Interior, UK 1965, USA 1965, 1968 (in Germany as Die Reise der Kunst ins Innere, 1966); Essays über Goethe, 1970; Franz Kafka, UK 1974, USA 1975. Contbr. to: Times Lit. Supplement; Encounter; Cambridge Mod. Hist.; Merkur; Der Monat; Forum. Hons: Vis. Prof., Univs. of Harvard & Brandeis, USA. Address: Northwestern Univ., Evanston, IL, USA.

HELLER, Hermine, b. 10 Mar. 1921, Vienna, Austria. Writer for Radio & TV. Educ: Ph.D., Univ. of Vienna. Publs. incl: Hermann Heller, Handzeichnungen; Sturkturen in Anatomie und Landschaft, 1970; transls. of Engl. poetry (Blake, Durrell); (drama adaptation) Intermezzo by Jean Giraudoux, for Burgtheater. Contbr. to: Revue d'Histoire du Théâtre, Paris, 1961-64; (critical essays) Weltkulturen und Moderne Kunst; Die Furche; Die Presse (Vienna). Mbrships. incl: Austrian Writers' Assn.; Concordia Press Club; Foreign Corres. Club; Soc. Austrian Authors. Hons. incl: Theodor Körner Fndn. Award, 1973. Address: Hansi-Nieseweg 1, A-1130 Vienna, Austria.

HELLER, Joseph, b. 1 May 1923, Brooklyn, N.Y., USA. Writer. Educ: B.A., N.Y. Univ., 1948; M.A., Columbia Univ., 1949; Oxford Univ., UK, 1949-50. Publs: (novels) Catch-22, USA 1961, UK 1962; Something Happened, 1972; (plays) We Bombed in New Haven, USA 1968, UK 1969; Catch-22, 1971. Recip., Grant, Nat. Inst. Arts & Letters, 1963. Address: c/o Simon & Schuster, 630 Fifth Ave., N.Y., NY 10020, USA.

HELLINGA, Gerben Wytzes, pen name HELLINGER, b. 29 Dec. 1937, Samaden, Switz. Writer. Educ: Max Reinhard Seminar, Vienna. Publs: De ochtendverse Schoen, 1967; Ajax-Feyenoord, 1970; Kees de Jongen, 1971; Rudy Schokker Doesn't Cry Anymore, 1973. Contbr. to: Ave. N.R.C.; De Volkskrant; De Gids; Vrij Nederland. Recip., Henriette Rolland Holst Prize, 1972. Address: Stadhouderskade 135, Amsterdam, Netherlands.

HELLMAN, Lillian, b. 20 June 1907, New Orleans, USA. Playwright. Educ: N.Y. Univ.; Columbia Univ. Publs.

incl: (plays) The Children's Hour, 1934; Days to Come, 1936; The Little Foxes, 1939; Watch on the Rhine, 1941; The Searching Wind, 1944; Another Part of the Forest, 1946; The Lark, 1955; Toys in the Attic, 1960; (Ed.) The Selected Letters of Anton Chekhov, 1955; Dashiell Hammett, the Big Knockover, 1966; (memoir) An Unfinished Woman, 1969. Mbrships: Am. Acad. of Arts & Sci.; Acad. of Arts & Letters. Hons. incl: Gold Medal for Drama, 1964; National Book Award, 1970; LL.D.; M.A. Address: 630 Park Ave., N.Y., NY 10021, USA.

HELLMANN, Ellen, b. 1908, Johannesburg, S. Africa. Race Relations Worker. Educ: B.A., M.A., D.Phil., Univ. of Witwatersrand. Publs: Problems of Urban Bantu Youth, 1940; Handbook on Race Relations in South Africa (Ed.), 1949; Rooiyard: A Sociological Survey of an Urban Native Slum Yard, 1948, reprinted 1969. Contbr. to: St. Antony's Papers; No. 10; Jrnl. of Race Rels. & Race Rels. News. Recip., Medal, Royal African Soc., 1970. Address: 14 First Ave., Lower Houghton, Johannesburg, S. Africa.

HELLYER, Arthur George Lee, b. 16 Dec. 1902. Horticultural Journalist & Author. Publs: The Amateur Gardener, 1948; Flowers in Colour, 1955; Garden Plants in Colour, 1958; Shrubs in Colour, 1965; Gardens to Visit in Britain, 1970; All Colour Gardening Book, 1972; All Colour Book of Indoor & Greenhouse Plants, 1973; Picture Dictionary of Popular Flowering Plants, 1973. Contbr. to: Amateur Gardening; Country Life; Fin. Times. Mbrships: Fellow, Linnean Soc.; Assoc. of Hon., Royal Hort. Soc.; Coun., Royal Nat. Rose Soc. Hons: M.B.E., 1967; Victoria Medal of Hon., 1967. Address: Orchards, Rowfant, Crawley, Sussex, UK.

HELLYER, Jill, b. 17 Apr. 1925, N. Sydney, Australia. Writer. Publs: The Exile (selected verse), 1969; Not Enough Savages (novel), 1975. Contbr. to: Meanjin Quarterly; Southerly; Westerly; New Poetry (formerly Poetry Mag.); The Australian; Sydney Morning Herald; The Age; Overland. Mbrships: Aust. Soc. of Authors (Exec. Sec. 1963-1971); Poetry Soc. of Aust. Hons: Grenfell Henry Lawson Award, 1963; Poetry Mag. Award, 1965. Address: 12 Yirra Rd., Mount Colah, N.S.W. 2079, Australia.

HELM, Peter James, b. 16 June 1916, Waterfoot, UK. Teacher; Author. Educ: M.A., Cambridge Univ. Publs: Dead Men's Fingers, 1960; History of Europe, 1450-1660, 1961; Death Has A Thousand Entrances, 1962; Alfred the Great, 1963; Modern British History, 1815-1964, 1965; The Man With No Bones, 1966; Jeffreys, 1966; England Under The Yorkists & Tudors, 1471-1603, 1968; Exploring Prehistoric England, 1971; Exploring Roman Britain, 1975. Contbr. to: Ambit; Archaeol. Jrnl.; Time & Tide. Address: The Croft, Bradford-on-Tone, Taunton, Somerset, UK.

HELMFRID, Björn Hartvig, b. 20 Feb. 1915, Stockholm, Sweden. Headmaster. Educ: Ph.D. Publs: Tithe Lists as a Source for the Economic History of a Village Community 1555-1753, 1949; Stathöga, Farmers & Gentry on an East Gotland Farm, 1952; The Fortunes of Holmen Works through Four Centuries, 1954; Those at Stenhus, 1959 (studies in the golden age of Holmen works); Norrköping's Urban History 1567-1719, I & II, 1963-1973; The Hinterland of Three Towns, 1970. Contbr. to: Svenskt biografiskt lexikon. Mbrships. incl: Soc. Historic Norrköping (Pres. since 1969, Sect. since 1952). Hons. incl: E. Gotland County Coun. Cultural schlrship., 1973. Address: Slottsbrink Rönö, 61024 Vikbolandet, Sweden.

HELSZTYŃSKI, Stanisław, b. 13 Apr. 1891, Kosowo, Gostyń, Poznań, Poland. Professor of English & American Literature (Ret'd.) Essayist; Poet; Translator; Novelist. Educ: Univs. of Munich, Germany, Poznań & Warsaw, Poland; Ph.D., 1926. Publs. incl: (in Engl.) Specimens of English Poetry & Prose, 1952; Mickiewicz, Selected Poetry & Prose, 1955; Poland's Homage to Shakespeare, 1965; (in Polish) Everyman, 1933; The Man of Stratford, 1963. Contbr. to var. lit. jrnls. Mbrships: Polish Acad. of Scis.; PEN; Polish Writers' Union. Hons: Szczecin Lit. Prize, 1949; Polonia Restituta, 1956; Address: Ul. Miączyńska 56 M 26, 02-637 Warsaw, Poland.

HEMELS, Joan M. H. J., b. 2 Mar. 1944, Heino, Netherlands. Assistant Lecturer. Educ: degrees in jrnlsm. & PR; Doct., Univ. of Nijmegen. Publs. incl: Het dagbladzegel in de rariteitenkamer, 1896-1969, Rotterdam's-gravenhage, 1969; Op de bres voor de pers; De strijd voor de klassieke persvrijheid, Assen, 1969; De journalistieke eierdans. Over vakopleiding en massacommunicatie, Assen, 1972; Van perschef tot overheidsvoorlichter. De grondslagen van overheidsvoorlichting, Alphen aan den Rijn, 1973. Contbr. to var. jrnls. Mbr., num. acad. & lit. orgs. Address: Kroonsingel 23, Malden, Netherlands.

HEMLOW, Joyce, b. 1906, Liscomb, N.S., Can. Professor. Educ: Queen's Univ.; Harvard, USA; LL.D., Ph.D. Publs: The History of Fanny Burney, 1958; A Catalogue of the Burney Family Correspondence 1749-1878, 1971; The Journals & Letters of Fanny Burney (Madame d'Arblay) 1791-1840, 4 vols., 1972-73. Contbr. to: New Light on Dr. Johnson; Univ. of Toronto Quarterly; etc. Mbrships: F.R.S.C.; Engl. Speaking Union; Johnsonians', N.Y. Address: 3555 Atwater Ave., Montreal, Canada.

HEMMING, James, b. 1909, Stalybridge, UK. Writer; Lecturer. Educ: B.A., Ph.D., London Univ. Publs. incl: Democracy in School Life, 1947; Teach them to Live, 1948; The Teaching of Social Studies in Secondary Schools, 1949; Sixth Form Citizens, 1950; Mankind against the Killers, 1956; Problems of Adolescent Girls, 1960; Individual Morality, 1969; Sex & Love (w. Zena Maxwell), 1973; The Child is Right (w. Josephine Balls), 1947. Mbrships: Soc. of Authors; PEN; Brit. Psychol. Soc.; Royal Instn.; World Educ. Fellowship. Address: 31 Broom Water, Teddington, Middx., UK.

HEMPHILL, Rosemary (nee Goldie), b. 1922, Broome, Australia. Cookery Writer. Publs: Fragrance & Flavour, 1959; Spice & Savour, 1964; The Penguin Book of Spices, 1966; Look, You Can Cook, 1967; The Complete Book of Cookery, 1970; Herbs for All Seasons, 1972, 1975, Dutch transl. 1973; Herbs & Spices (w. husband J. Hemphill), 1974. Contbr. to: Aust. Gourmet Mag.; Aust. House & Garden. Mbr., Aust. Soc. of Authors. Recip., Dip. & Bronze Medal, Lit. Competition, Int. Exhib. Culinary Arts, Frankfurt, W. Germany, 1960. Address: Somerset Cottage, 745 Old Northern Rd., Dural, N.S.W. 2158, Australia.

HENDERSON, John, b. 29 Jan. 1915, Glasgow, UK. Immigration Inspector for United States of America. Educ: A.B., Hope Coll., Mich.; M.A., Niagara Univ., N.Y. Publs: 15 full-length plays, 1948—; (books) The Reachers, 1961; Now — Would You Believe, 1964; num. articles, short stories, serials, radio & TV scripts. Address: 485 Oneida Street, Lewiston, NY 14092, USA.

HENDERSON, Laurence, b. 1928, London, UK. Writer. Publs: With Intent, 1968; Sitting Target, 1970; Cage Until Tame, 1971; Major Enquiry, 1974. Contbr. to: var. mags.; BBC. Mbrships: Crime Writers' Assn.; Southend Pistol Club. Agent: Gordon Harbord. Address: 57 Crown Hill, Rayleigh, Essex, UK.

HENDERSON, Michael Ronald, b. 7 May 1942, Nelson, N.Z. Writer. Educ: Nelson Coll.; LL.B., Univ. of Canterbury, 1967; M.F.A. Cand., Univ. of Iowa, USA. Publs: New Zealand Short Stories (contbng. author), 1974. Contbr. to: Islands; Landfall; Mate; Jrnl. of Assn. of Tchrs. of Speech & Drama; N.Z. Monthly Review Mbr., PEN. Hons: Writing Bursary, Lit. Fund, N.Z., 1973; Fulbright Travel Grant, 1974. Address: P.O. Box 90, Riverside, IA 52327, USA.

HENDERSON, Philip Prichard, b. 17 Feb. 1906, Barnes, Surrey, UK. Author; Poet; Biographer. Publs: First Poems, 1930; The Complete Poems of John Skelton, 1931, 4th ed., 1964; Early Events in the Life of Anthony Price (novel), 1935; Literature & a Changing Civilization, 1935; The Poet & Society, 1939; The Letters of William Morris, 1950; The Complete Poems of Emily Brontë, 1951; Christopher Marlowe, 1952, 1974; Samuel Butler, 1953, 1967; The Life of Laurence Oliphant, 1956; Richard Coeur de Lion, 1958; William Morris: His Life, Work & Friends, 1967; Swinburne: The Portrait of a Poet, 1974. Address: 25 Christchurch Hill, London NW3, UK.

HENDERSON, William Otto, b. 1904, London, UK. University Reader (Ret'd). Educ: Downing Coll., Cambridge; Univ. of Hamburg, Germany; M.A., Ph.D. Publs. incl: The Industrial Revolution on the Continent, 1961; Studies in German Colonial History, 1962; Studies in the Economic Policy of Frederick the Great, 1963; J. C. Fischer & his Diary of Industrial England, 1966; Ed., Engels: Selected Writings, 1967; Industrial Britain under the Regency, 1968; The Industrialisation of Europe, 1969; Life of Friedrich Engels, 2 vols., 1975. Address: 11 Pinewood Ave., Thornton, Blackpool, Lancs., UK.

HENDERSON-HOWAT, Agatha Mary Dorothea, b. Selkirk, Scotland, UK. Former Sub-Editor & Archivist. Educ: Univ. of Geneva. Publs: Royal Pearl: A Biography of Queen Margaret of Scotland; Children's Book of Scottish Saints. Contbr. to: Scotland's Mag.; Glasgow Herald; Edinburgh Tatler; Archives; Ch. Quarterly Review. Mbrships: Assoc., Royal Histl. Soc.; Scottish Historical Soc.; PEN. Address: 7 Lansdowne Cres., Edinburgh 12, UK.

HENDIN, David, b. 16 Dec. 1945, St. Louis, Mo., USA. Journalist. Educ: B.S., 1967, M.A., 1970, Univ. of Mo. Publs: Everything You Need to Know about Abortion, 1971; Doctor's Save-Your-Heart Diet (w. Aileen Claire), 1972; Save Your Child's Life, 1973; Death as a Fact of Life, 1973. Contbr. to: syndicated columnist ('The Medical Consumer'); Saturday Review/Sci.; SR-World; Sci. Digest; Sci. News; Rdrs. Digest; Family News. Mbrships. incl: Nat. Assn. of Sci. Writers. Hons. incl: Claude Bernard Sci. Jrnlsm. Award, 1972; Med. Jrnlsm. Award, A.M.A., 1973; Book of the Yr., Am. Jrnl. of Nursing, 1973. Address: 21 Frederick St., Garnerville, NY 10923, USA.

HENDRICK, Thomas William, b. 1909, London, UK. Technical Author. Educ: Kingston Tech. Coll. Publs: The Modern Architectural Model; Model Making as a Career; The Viper's Nest; Corrosion & its Prevention; Monorail Structures in Concrete. Mbrships: F.R.S.A. Address: 6 Park Pl., Arundel, Sussex, UK.

HENDRY, Thomas Best, b. 7 June 1929, Winnipeg, Man., Can. Playwright. Publs: 15 Miles of Broken Glass, TV version, 1968, stage version, 1972; You Smell Good to Me, 1972; How Are Things With the Walking Wounded, 1973; Gravediggers of 1942, 1974; Doctor Selavy's Magic Theatre (record album), 1974. Contbr. to: Playbill; Can. Theatre Review; Can. Forum (Ed. bd.). Hons. incl: Can. Centennial Medal, 1967; Lt.-Gov.'s Medal, Ont., 1970; Can. Coun. Sr. Arts Award, 1974. Address: 34 Elgin Ave., Toronto, Ont. M5R 1G6, Can.

HENKIN, Louis, b. 11 Nov. 1917, Smolyan, Russia. Professor of Law & Diplomacy. Educ: A.B., Yeshiva Coll., USA, 1937; LL.B., Harvard Law Schl., 1940. Publs: Arms Control & Inspection in American Law, 1958; The Berlin Crisis & the United Nations, 1959; Law for the Sea's Mineral Resources, 1968; How Nations Behave: Law & Foreign Policy, 1968; Foreign Affairs & the Constitution, 1972; (ed.), Arms Control: Issues for the Public, 1961; World Politics & the Jewish Condition, 1972; co-ed., Transnational Law in a Changing Society, 1972. Author of num. articles in field. Fellow, Am. Acad. of Arts & Scis., 1974. Mbr., num. profl. orgs. Address: Columbia University, N.Y., NY, USA.

HENMARK, (Carl Anders Johan) Kai, b. 23 Feb. 1932, Linköping, Sweden. Author. Educ: M.A., Stockholm Univ., 1956. Publs: Resandes ensak, 1960; Säj farväl till de döda, 1961; Menuett för alefanter, 1961; En fågel av eld, 1962; Det vackra odjuret, 1963; Spott i ditt öga, 1963; T. Bullo och Fältmarskalken, 1965; I somnarens saliga dagar, 1966; Främlingen Lagerkrist, 1966; Johan utan land, 1966; O min stackars buffel, 1967; Språkstakar, 1968; Jämlikheten och samtalet, 1970; Konsten att erövra Danmark, 1971; Min liv med Emil, 1971. Contbr. to: Arbetet; B.L.M.; Var Losen. Mbrships: PEN; Swedish Union of Authors; etc. Hons: Vår Lösen Lit. Award, 1967; Gunnar Josephson Lit. Prize, 1972. Address: Pokalvägen 3II, S-11740 Stockholm, Sweden.

HENNEQUIN, Bernard, pen name BERQUIN, Jean, b. 19 Feb. 1932, Paris, France. Journalist. Educ: Lic. de Geog., Univ. of Paris, 1957. Publs: Vacances en France, 1963; Andalousie, 1967; Poitou-Guyenne, 1969. Contbr. to: Ed.-in-Chief, Touring (review of the Touring Club of France). Mbrships: Pres., French Assn. of Tourism Jrnlsts. & Writers; Touring Club of France. Address: 29 rue Duret, 75116, Paris, France.

HENNESSY, R. A. S., b. 1937, Fulham, UK. H.M. Inspector of Schools. Educ: M.A., Downing Coll., Cambridge. Publs: Transport, 1966; Factories, 1969; The Electric Railway That Never Was, 1970; Power, 1972; The Electric Revolution, 1972; Railways, 1973. Contbr. to: Railway World. Address: 40 Linden Rd., Gosforth, Newcastle upon Tyne NE3 4HB, UK.

HENNESSY, Jossleyn, b. 1903, London. Editor. Educ: New Coll., Oxford; M.A., Dip. Econs. Appts: Fndr.-Ed., World Trade, Jrnl. of Int. Chmbr. of Comm., Paris, 1928; For. Corres., Reuters, 1931-35; Chief Paris Corres., News

Chronicle, 1935-37; Dir., PR to Govt. of India, 1937-45; Inaug. Govt. of India Info. Serv., USA & Can., 1942-45; Sunday Times Corres., India & Pakistan, 1946-48; Ed.-in-Chief for Europe, Eastern Economist of New Delhi, 1953—. Publs: India & Pakistan in World Politics, 1950; India, Democracy & Education, 1955; Policy for Incomes? (w. F. W. Paish), 4th ed., 1968; Governing Elites (w. R. Wilkinson), 1969; (autobiog.) The Amazing Ancestors (vol. 1). Contbr. to: Economist; Lloyds Bank Review; Spectator; Encounter; Observer; Eastern Economist of New Delhi; Sphere; Statist; Times; New Soc.; Ency. Britannica; Ency. Americana; Int. Affairs; Review of Aust. Inst. Pub. Affairs. Recip., Chevalier, Legion of Hon. Address: 95 Linden Gdns., London W2 4EX, UK.

HENNING, Daniel Howard, b. 1 Aug. 1931, Cleveland, Ohio, USA. Lecturer. Educ: B.S., Bowling Green Univ., 1957; M.S., Univ. of Mich., 1959; Ph.D., Syracuse Univ., 1965. Publs: Co-Ed. & contbr., Environmental Policy: Concepts & International Implications, 1973; Co-Ed. & Contbr., Interdisciplinary Environmental Approaches, 1974; Environmental Policy & Administration, 1974. Contbr. to: Pub. Admin. Review; Natural Resources Jrnl.; BioSci.; var. popular mags. Mbrships: incl: Am. Soc. Pub. Admin.; Int. Coun. Environmental Law. Recip., var. fellowships & fraternal hons. Address: Govt. & Public Admin. Dept., United College, Chinese Univ. of Hong Kong, Shatin, N.T., Hong Kong.

HENREY, Madeleine, b. 13 Aug. 1906, Montmartre, Paris, France. Authoress. Publs: (autobiogs in the following sequence) The Little Madeleine, 1951; An Exile in Soho, 1952; Julia, 1971; A Girl at Twenty, 1974; Madeleine Grown Up, 1952; Madeleine Young Wife, USA 1954, UK 1960; London Under Fire 1940-45, 1969; Her April Days, 1963; A Month in Paris, 1954; Wednesday at Four, 1964; She Who Pays, 1969. Address: Villers-sur-Mer, Calvados 14 640, France.

HENRIKSON, Thomas Lars, b. 12 Apr. 1937, Stockholm, Sweden. University Teacher; Critic. Educ: Ph.D., Stockholm Univ. Publs: Nuori Otto Ville Kuusinen (co-author), 1970; Festskrift till Olof Enckell 12.3 1970 (co-author), 1970; Romantik och marxism. Estetik och politik hos oho Ville Kuusinen och Diktonius till och med 1921, 1971. Contbr. to Scand. jrnls. & newspapers; Nya Argus mag., Finland (Ed. Bd.). Mbrships: Svenska litteratursallskapet i Finland; Swedish Authors Soc.; Ed. Bd., Nya Argus mag., Finland. Address: Et. Hesperiankatu 22 A 11, 00100 Helsinki, Finland.

HENRY, Bernard, b. 18 Aug. 1902, London, UK. Publisher; Writer. Publs: Water, 1968; Fire, 1968; Air, 1969; Earth, 1969; Vikings & Norsemen, 1971; Heathrow Airport — London, 1974. Mbr., Soc. of Authors. Address: 26 St. Margaret's Rd., Ruislip, Middx. HA4 7NU, UK.

HENRY, Omer, b. 1 Jan. 1903, Sumner, Ill., USA. Former Teacher; Retired Government Servant. Educ: B.Ed., Univ. of Southern Ill. Author, Writing & Selling Magazine Articles, 1962. Contbr. to: True; Coronet; American; Popular Mech.; Am. Mercury; Am. Educ.; The Writer, Author & Jrnlst.; Writers Digest; Wash. Star; Wash. Post; Toledo Blade; Complete Love Novels; Complete Detective Novels; Friend; Daring Detective; Official Detective; Farm & Power; Fuel Oil News; Ford Truck Times; Incentive Marketing; Motel/Motor Inn Jrnl.; etc. Mbrships: Assoc. Bus. Writers of Am.; Past Pres., Writers League of Wash. Recip., Geo. Wash. Hon. Medal, for article, New National Shrine, Freedoms Fndn., 1956. Address: 8830 Sudbury Rd., Silver Spring, MD 20901, USA.

HENRY, Thomas Edward, b. 2 Feb. 1910, Derby, UK. Journalist; Company Director. Contbr. to: Former Ed.-in-Chief, Manchester Evening News. Mbrships: Int. Press Inst.; London Press Club; Manchester Club. Recip., Hon. M.A., Manchester Univ. Address: Rosenau, 22 Albert Rd., Cheadle Hulme, Cheshire, UK.

HENSCHEL, Elizabeth Georgie, b. London, UK. Writer; BBC Actress & former Announcer; Riding Instructress. Publs: The Well-dressed Woman, 1951; Thomas, a Highland Pony, 1969; Careers with Horses, 1975. Contbr. to: Riding; Horse & Pony; Light Horse; Pony; sev. other jrnls. Mbrships: incl: Soc. of Authors; Brit. Horse Soc.; Nat. Pony Soc.; Scottish Dressage Grp. Address: Alltnacriche, Aviemore, Inverness-shire, UK.

HENSEMA, Jan Henricus Hermanus, pen name J. Ha., b. 11 July 1945, Uithuizermeeden, Netherlands. Journalist.

Publs: Roos in de Regio, 1974. Contbr. to: Vrij Nederland; Huis-aan-Huis Oost Groningen. Mbrships: Nederlandse Vereniging van Journalisten; Gronings-Drentse Journalisten Vereniging. Address: Voorstraat 20, Nieuweschans (Groningen), Netherlands.

HENSHAW, James Ene, b. 29 Aug. 1924, Calabar, Nigeria. Medical Practitioner; Senior Consultant, Ministry of Health, Nigeria. Educ: M.B., B.Ch., B.A.O., Nat. Univ. of Ireland, Dublin, 1949; T.D.D., Univ. of Wales, Cardiff, UK, 1954. Publs: (plays) This is our Chance (3 plays), 1955; Children of the Goddess, 1957; Medicine for Love, 1964; Dinner for Promotion, 1967. Contbr. to sev. med. jrnls. Mbr., sev. med. socs. Hons: Henry Carr Mem. Cup (1st prize), All-Nigeria Festival of Arts, 1952; Kt. of St. Gregory the Great, Pope Paul VI, 1965. Address: 72 Yakubu Gowon Drive, Port Harcourt, Nigeria.

HENSLEY, Joseph L., b. 19 Mar. 1926, Bloomington, Ind., USA. Attorney; Writer. Educ: B.A., 1950; LL.B., 1955, Indiana Univ. Publs: Deliver Us to Evil, 1972; Legislative Body, 1972; Poison Summer, 1974; Song of Corpus Juris, 1974. Contbr. to sev. sci. fiction & mystery mags. Mbrships: Mystery Writers of Am.; Sci. Fiction Writers of Am., Chmn., Legal Comm., 1969-72. Address: 2315 Blackmore St., Madison, IN, USA.

HEPBURN, Ronald William, b. 1927, Aberdeen, UK. Professor of Philosophy. Educ: M.A., Ph.D., Aberdeen Univ. Publs: Christianity & Paradox; Metaphysical Beliefs (co-author). Contbr. to: Proceedings of the Aristotelian Soc.; Philos.; Philos. Quarterly; Jrnl. of the Hist. of Ideas, Theol.; Brit. Jrnl. of Aesthetics; Mind; Relig. Studies; Ency. of Philos. Address: Dept. of Philosophy, David Hume Tower, George Square, Edinburgh, UK.

HEPPENSTALL, (John) Rayner, b. 27 July 1911, Huddersfield, Yorks, UK. Critic; Novelist. Educ: B.A., Leeds Univ., 1933. Publs: The Blaze of Noon, 1939; The Greater Infortune, 1943-60; Four Absentees, 1960; The Fourfold Tradition, 1961; The Connecting Door, 1962; The Shearers, 1969; French Crime in the Romantic Age, 1972; Reflections on the Newgate Calendar, 1975. Contbr. to: Sunday Times; Encounter; London Mag. Recip., Retrospective Novel Award, Arts Coun., 1966. Address: 31 Churton St., London SW1, UK.

HEPPLE, Bob Alexander, b. 1934, Johannesburg, S. Africa. University College Fellow. Educ: B.A., LL.B., Univ. of Witwatersrand; M.A., LL.B., Cambridge Univ., UK; Barrister-at-Law, Gray's Inn. Publs: Race, Jobs & the Law in Britain, 1968, 2nd ed., 1970; Individual Employment Law, 1971; Public Employee Trade Unionism in the U.K., 1971; Laws Against Strikes, 1972; Tort: Cases & Materials, 1974; Bibliography of the Literature on Labour Law, 1975; Gen. Ed., Ency. of Labour Relations Law, 1972—. Contbr. to: Indl. Law Jrnl. (Ed.); Mod. Law Review; Ed., Cambridge Law Jrnl.; Inst. of Race Rels.; UN Inst. for Trng. & Rsch.; etc. Mbr., var. profl. assns. Address: Clare Coll., Cambridge CB2 1TL, UK.

HEPPNER, Sam, b. 1913, London, UK. Writer; Broadcaster; Public Relations Consultant. Publs: Background to Music, 1948; Cockie, Biography of C. B. Cochran, 1969. Contbr. to: Times; Daily Telegraph; Evening News; Woman's Jrnl.; Woman's Own; etc. Mbrships: Press Club; PEN; Soc. of Authors. Address: Literary Properties Ltd., Cobrin, Bagshot Rd., Worplesdon, Surrey, UK.

HERBERT, (Alfred Francis) Xavier, b. 15 May 1901, Geraldton, W.A., Australia. Writer. Educ: Tech. Coll., Perth; Dip. Pharmacy, Univ. of Melbourne. Publs: (novels) Capricornia, Aust. 1937, UK 1939, USA 1943; Seven Emus, Aust. & UK 1959; Soldiers' Women, Aust. 1961, UK 1962; (short stories) Larger Than Life, Aust. 1963, UK 1964; (autobiog.) Disturbing Element, Aust. & UK 1963; (forthcoming) Poor Fellow My Country. Recip., Gold Medal, Aust. Lit. Soc. Address: Redlynch, via Cairns, Qld. 4870, Australia.

HERBERT, (Edward) Ivor (Montgomery), b. 20 Aug. 1925, Johannesburg, S. Africa. Author; Journalist; Playwright; Scriptwriter. Educ: M.A., Trinity Coll., Cambridge. Publs: Eastern Windows (novel), 1953; Point-to-Point, 1964; Arkle, 1966; The Queen Mother's Horses, 1967; The Winter Kings, 1968; The Way to the Top, 1969; Night of the Blue Demands (play), 1971; Over Our Dead Bodies (novel), 1972; The Diamond Diggers (hist. S. African diamond ind.), 1972; Winter's Tale, 1973; Red

Rum, 1974; Come Riding, 1975; L'Equitation, 1975. Films incl: The Great St. Trinians' Train Robbery, 1966; num. documentaries. Contbr. to: Sunday Express; Horse & Hound; Evening News. Mbrships: Writers' Guild; Soc. of Authors; Nat. Union Jrnlsts.; Guards' Club. Address: The Old Rectory, Bradenham, Nr. High Wycombe, Bucks., UK.

HERBERT Zbigniew, b. 29 Oct. 1924, Lvov, Poland. Poet; Essayist; Playwright. Educ: Univs. of Cracow, Torun & Warsaw. Publs. incl: (in Polish) (poetry) A String of Light, 1956; Hermes, a Dog & a Star, 1957; The Study of an Object, 1961; The Inscription, 1969; Collected Verse, 1971; Mr Cogito, 1974; (plays & radio plays) The Other Room; Dramas; Cave of Philosophers; Lalek; (essays) A Barbarian in the Garden, 1963. Contbr. to: Poezja (Co-Ed.). Mbrships: Polish Writers' Assn. Hons: Prize, Polish Inst. of Sci. & Arts in Am. Lenau Int. Prize for European Lit., 1965. Address: Swierczewskiego 95/99 m. 108, Warsaw, Poland.

HERCULES, Frank Elton Mervyn, b. 12 Feb. 1917, Port-of-Spain, Trinidad, W. Indies. Author (Novelist). Publs: Where the Hummingbird Flies, 1961; I Want a Black Doll, 1967; American Society & Black Revolution, 1972. Contbr. to: N.Y. Mag.; Int. Herald Tribune; Die Zeit. Mbrships: PEN; Authors' Guild; Authors' League. Recip., Fletcher Pratt Mem. Fellowship in Prose, 1961. Address: 10 E. 138th St., Apt. 7-C, N.Y., NY10037, USA.

HERDA, D. J., b. 4 Apr. 1946, Chgo., Ill., USA. Writer; Magazine Editor. Educ: DePaul Univ.; Roosevelt Univ.; Columbia Coll.; B.A. Author, How to Process Your Photos, 1975. Contbr. to: True; The Writer; Writer's Yearbook; Am. West; Milwaukee Jrnl.; Miami Herald; Elks Mag. (Ed.); Success Unlimited; Commonweal; Communicator; Gallery; Writer, prod. & dir., sev. plays. Agent: Larry Sterning. Address: 2407 N. 44th St., Milwaukee, WI 53210, USA.

HERDAL, Harald, b. 1900. Publs. incl: Nyt Sind, 1929; Eros og Doden, 1931; Log, 1935; Mennesket, 1937; En Egn af Landet, 1939; Tusmorke, 1943; Digte i Vinteren, 1946; Drommeren, 1951; Jammersminde, 1953; Rast undervejs, 1954; Elise, 1955; Dagens gar, 1955; Det Storste, 1957; The Tin Boxes, 1958; (biography) Danish Authors, 1952; Hegnets Nattergal, 1960; Moderne Dansk for udlaendige, 1963; Den Danske Sommer, 1963; Bisser, 1964; Udvalgte Fortaellinger, 1967; Boger og pottraetter, 1970; Arbejdsdr, erindringer IV, 1970; En bibliotekslåners vandringer, 1971. Address: Folehavej 23, 2970 Horsholm, Denmark.

HERKLOTS, Geoffrey Alton Craig, b. 1902, Naini Tal, India. Biologist. Educ: Univ. of Leeds; Cambridge Univ.; M.Sc., Ph.D. Publs: Common Marine Food Fishes of Hong Kong; Vegetable Cultivation in Hong Kong; The Hong Kong Countryside, 1951; Hong Kong Birds, 1953, 1957; The Birds of Trinidad & Tobago, 1961; Vegetables in S.E. Asia, 1972. Address: Vanners, Chobham, Woking, Surrey, UK.

HERLIHY, James Leo, b. 1927, Detroit, Mich., USA. Actor; Playwright. Educ: Pasadena Playhouse, Calif. Publs: The Sleep of Baby Filbertson, 1959; All Fall Down, 1960; (plays) Crazy October, 1958; Midnight Cowboy, 1965; A Story that Ends with a Scream, 1967; Stop You're Killing Me, 1969; Season of the Witch, 1971; Blue Denim (w. William Noble), 1958. Contbr. to: Paris Review; Discovery; Eve; Mademoiselle; etc. Address: 709 Baker's Lane, Key West, Fla., USA.

HERMAN, George Richard, b. 18 Oct. 1925, St. Joseph, Mich., USA. Educ: B.S., 1951, M.A., 1956, Univ. of Kan., Lawrence. Associate Professor of English; Author. Publs: Resources for Modern Grammar & Composition (w. David Conlin), 1965, 3rd ed., 1971; Our Language Today (co-author), 1966, 2nd ed., 1971; Guide to American English (w. L. M. Myers), 4th ed., 1968. Contbr. to: Poet Lore; Colo. Quarterly; Univ. of Kan. City Review; Western Review; AAUP Bulletin; Can. Assn. Univ. Professors Bulletin. Address: Dept. of English, Arizona State University, Tempe, AZ 85281, USA.

HERMAN, Gordon Lee, b. 31 May, Spokane, Wash., USA. Poet. Educ: B.Sc., Ore. Coll. of Educ., 1957; Special Studies, Univ. of Wash. Publs: Night of Moons, 1967; Conceptions, 1974. Contbr. to: Indl. Worker; Dimensions; Dasein. Mbr., Poetry Soc. of Am. Address: South 4610 Cheatham Rd., Spokane, WA 99204, USA.

HERMANN, Istvan, b. 10 Oct. 1925, Budapest, Hungary. Professor of History of Philosophy, Budapest University. Educ: Cand. Rsch. of Philos., Acad. of Scis.,

1956; Dr.Philosl.Scis., 1969. Publs: For the Hungarian Drama, 1955; Sigmund Freud, 1964; The Problems of Decadence, 1967; The Theology of Kant, 1968; The Pseudo-art, 1969; The Problems of Socialist Culture, 1970; The Problems of Recent Culture, 1974; The Thought of G. Lukacs, 1974. Contbr. to: Comprendre; Kamera; Magyar Filozofiai Szemle; Voproszi Filozofii. Mbr., Internationale Hegel-Gesellschaft. Address: Bocskai ut 16, H-1114 Budapest, Hungary.

HERNMARCK, Carl Gustaf Michael, b. 27 Dec. 1901, Stockholm, Sweden. Retired Keeper of Decorative Art Department, National Museum, Stockholm. Educ: Fil.kand., 1927, Fil.lic., 1933, Fil.dr., 1934, Univ. of Uppsala. Publs: Georg Desmarées: Studien über die Rokokomalerei in Schweden & Deutschland, 1933; Barock-Senbarock-Gustaviansk stil — Svenskt Silversmide 1520-85, 3 vols., 1940-45; Jean Erik Rehn & det svenska konstharnverket — Fem stora gustavianer, 1944; Marieberg: En lysande representant för svenskt sjuttonhundratal, 1946; Kunglig prakt från barock & rokoko, 1948; Svenskt sjuttonhundratal, 1954; Fajans & porsalin: Svensk keramik före 1850, 1959; Les relations artistiques entre la France et la Suéde 1693-1718: Nicodéme Tessin la jeune & Daniel Cronström, Correspondence (w. R. A. Weigert), 1964. Contbr. to num. profl. jrnls. Address: Casa Calma, Linda Vista Alta, San Pedro de Alcántara, Prov. de Malaga, Spain.

HERRGÅRD, Elin, b. 18 Aug. 1907, Malax, Finland. Author. Publs: Slättbygd, 1963; Fackelblomst, 1965; Americabrevet, 1973. Contbr. to: Landsbygdens Folk. Mbrships: Finlands Svenska Författarförening; Svenska Österbottens Litteraturförening. Address: Kolmlevägen 7, 65230 Vasa 23, Finland.

HERRIOT, James, b. Glasgow, K. Veterinary Surgeon; Author. Educ: Glasgow Vet. Coll., Publs. incl: If Only They Could Talk, 1970; It Shouldn't Happen to a Vet; All Creatures Great & Small (first 2 books publd. as 1 vol.); Let Sleeping Vets Lie, 1973; Vet in Harness, 1974. Address: c/o Pan Books 18-21 Cavaye Place, London SW10 9PG, UK.

HERRMANN, Luke John, b. 9 Mar. 1932, Berlin, Germany. University Professor of the History of Art. Educ: M.A., New Coll., Oxford. Publs: J. M. W. Turner, 1963; Il paesaggio nella pittura inglese dell' Ottocento, 1967; Ruskin & Turner, 1968; British Landscape Painting of the 18th Century, 1973. Contbr. to: Burlington Mag.; Apollo; Connoisseur, etc. Mbr., Walpole Soc. (Coun.). Address: The Old Manse, Clipston, Market Harborough, Leics., UK.

HERRMANN, Thomas, b. 26 Jan. 1955, Neiderwürzbach, Saarbrücken, W. Gernamy. Businessman. Educ: Business course at Technical Coll. Publs: co-author, Book of Poems, forthcoming; Lyric Today, 1974. Mbrships: Literarische Union; Deutscher Schriftsteller Verband (German Authors' Union). Address: 6675 Niederwürzbach/Saar, Bezirksstr. 125, W. Germany.

HERSEY, Geraldine, b. 24 July 1931, London, UK. Film Executive. Publs: I Can Only Promise You Tomorrow, 1970; Kiss Your Friends Goodbye, 1971. Address: c/o Deborah Rogers Ltd., 20 Goodge St., London W1, UK.

HERSEY, John, b. 17 June 1914. Author; Lecturer, Yale University. Educ: Yale Univ., New Haven, Conn., USA; Univ. of Cambridge, UK. Publs: Men on Bataan, 1942; Into the Valley, 1943; A Bell for Adano, 1944; Hiroshima, 1946; The Wall, 1950; The Marmot Drive, 1953; A Single Pebble, 1956; The War Lover, 1959; The Child Buyer, 1960; Here to Stay, 1962; White Lotus, 1965; Too Far to Walk, 1966; Under the Eye of the Storm, 1967; The Algiers Motel Incident, 1968; The Conspiracy, 1972; The Writer's Craft, 1974; My Petition for More Space, 1974; The President, 1975. Mbrships. incl: Pres., Authors' League of Am.; Coun., Authors' Guild; Sec., Am. Acad. of Arts & Letters. Hons. incl: sev. Univ. Doctorates; Pulitzer Prize, 1945. Address: 420 Humphrey St., New Haven, CT 06511, USA.

HERSH, Burton David, b. 18 Sept. 1933, Chgo., Ill., USA. Writer. Educ: B.A. (magna cum laude), Harvard Coll.; adv. work, Univ. of Freiburg-im-Breisgau, W. Germany, & Innsbruck, Austria. Publs: The Ski People, 1968; The Education of Edward Kennedy, 1972. Contbr. to: Holiday; Esquire; Venture; Show; Horizon; Transatlantic Review; etc. Mbrships: Phi Beta Kappa, 1955; Authors' Guild. Hons. incl: Hist. & Lit. Prize, 1954, & Bowdoin Prize, 1955, Harvard; Fellow, Bread Loaf Writers' Conf., 1964; Albert Cobb Martin Mem. Lectr., Blake Schl., Hopkins, Min., 1973. Address: Box 204, Bradford, NH 03221, USA.

HERTZ, Paweł, b. 29 Oct. 1918, Warsaw, Poland. Writer. Publs: Sedan, 1948; Portret Słowackiego, 1949; Wiersze wybrane, 1955; Pieśni z rynku, 1957; Domena polska, 1961; Ład i nieład, 1964; Śpiewnik podróżny i domowy, 1969; Wieczory warszawskie, 1974. Contbr. to: Kuźnica; Odrodzenie; Nowiny Literackie; Twórczość; Tygodnik Powszechny. Mbrships: PEN (Mbr. Bd.); Union Polish Writers. Hons: Polish PEN Club Prize, 1971; Alfred Jurzykowski Fndn. Award, N.Y., 1972. Address: Nowy Świat 33 m. 15, 00-029 Warsaw, Poland.

HERVÉ-BAZIN, Jean Pierre Marie, pen name BAZIN, Hervé, b. 17 Apr. 1911, Angers, Maine et Loire, France. Journalist; Literary Critic; Novelist. Educ: Licencié-es-lettres. Publs. incl: La Tete Contre les Murs, 1949; Qui J'Ose Aimer, 1956; Au Nom du Fils, 1960; Le Matrimoine, 1967; Les Bienheureux de la Desolation, 1970; Cri de la Chouette, 1972. Contbr. to var. lit. publs. Mbrships: Soc. des Gens de Lettres de France; V.P., Syndicat des Ecrivains, 1950; PEN Club; Pres., Ecrivains de l'Ouest. Hons: Grand Priz Littéraire de Monaco, 1958; Grand Prix Int. de Poésie, 1974. Address: Le grand Courtoiseau, Trigueres, 45220 Chateaurenard, France.

HERZBERG, Judith Frieda Lina, b. 4 Nov. 1934, Amsterdam, Netherlands. Publs: Zeepost, 1963; Beendgras, 1968; Stryklicht, 1971. Contbr. to: Poetry Chgo., USA; Tirade; Hollands Maandblad. Address: Vondelstraat 75A, Amsterdam, Netherlands.

HESELTINE, Nigel, b. 1916, London, UK. Farmer. Educ: B.A.; B.Sc.; London Univ.; Trinity Coll., Dublin. Publs: Scarred Background, 1938; Dafydd ap Gwylim, 1945; Tales of the Squireachy, 1949; Inconstant Lady, 1953; From Lybian Sands to Chad, 1960; Remaking Africa, 1961. Contbr. to: World Crops; Studii Catholici. Mbrships: Int. Assn. of Agricultural Econs.; F.R.G.S.; Int. African Inst. Address: B.P. 846, Tananarive, Madagascar.

HESKETH, Phoebe, b. 29 Jan. 1909, Preston, Lancs., UK. Poet. Educ: Cheltenham Ladies' Coll. Publs: (poetry) Lean Forward, Spring!, 1948; No Time for Towards, 1952; Out of the Dark, 1954; Between Wheels & Stars, 1956; The Buttercup Children, 1958; Prayer for Sun, 1966; (prose) My Aunt Edith, 1966; Rivington, 1972; A Song of Sunlight, 1974. Contbr. to: Times; Times Lit. & Educl. Supplements; Observer; Spectator; New Statesman; Listener. Mbrships: PEN; Authors' Assn.; Exec. Comm., CPRE (Lancs.). Hons: Greenwood Prize, Poetry Soc.; FRSL, 1971. Address: Fisher House, Rivington, Nr. Bolton BL6 7SL, UK.

HESS, Albert Günter, b. 1 Mar. 1909, Prina, Germany (now US citizen). Professor of Criminology. Educ: J.D. (Ph.D.), Leipzig Univ., 1933; Cornell Univ., USA. Publs. incl: Criminal Statistics: Standard Classification of Offences, 1959; The Young Adult Offender (transl. in French, Russian & Spanish), 1965; Chasing the Dragon: A Report on Drug Addiction in Hong Kong, 1965; The Young Adult Offender: A Bibliography (co-author), 1967. Contbr. to: Am. Peoples Ency. Yearbook, 1966; num. profl. publs. & jrnls. Mbr., Authors Guild. Address: 30 Winston Woods, Brockport, NY. USA.

HESS, Manfred, b. 1898, Pirna, Saxony, Germany. Industrial Chemist. Educ: Technische Univ., Dresden; Univs. of Munich, Würzburg & Berlin. Publs: Paint Film Defects; Anstrichmaengel u. Anstrichschäden; Défauts des Peintures; Defectos de los Capas de Piutura; Metallic Corrosion Handbook (co-author). Contbr. to: Jrnl., Oil & Colour Chemists' Assn.; Paint, Oil & Colour Jrnl.; Farbe u. Lack; etc. Mbrships: F.R.I.C.; F.I.M.F.; F.T.S.C.; Assn. of Cons. Scis.; Paint Rsch. Assn.; Oil & Colour Chemists' Assn.; etc. Address: 101 Westbury Road, Northwood, Middx. HA6 3DA, UK.

HESSELL, Grace Dora Desmond, b. 27 July 1898, Walthamstow, Essex, UK. Teacher. Educ: M.A., Somerville Coll., Oxford. Publs: A Poetry Workbook, 1965. Former Br. Chmn., NZ Women Writers' Soc. Address: 1/11 Alexander St., Papakura, NZ.

HETHERINGTON, John Rowland, pen name (until 1936) ATTABOY, b. 4 Mar. 1899, Smethwick, UK. Retired Civil Servant; Bibliographical Researcher. Publs. incl: Ed., Civil Service Courier, 1932-41; Cycling for Fun, 1936; The Sense of Antiquity, 1963; Chaucer 1532-1602: Notes & Facsimile Texts, 1964, 1967; Catalogue of the Hetherington Collection of editions of the Book of Common Prayer, forthcoming; Prayers & Psalms in Quarto, forthcoming. Contbr. to num. jrnls. Mbrships. incl: Bibliog. Socs. of London, Oxford, Cambridge, Birmingham & Univ. of Va., USA. Address: 26 Vernon Rd., Birmingham B16 9SH, UK.

HETHERINGTON, Thomas Baines, pen name HETHERINGTON, Tom, b. 7 Dec. 1919, Durham City, UK. College Administrator & Lecturer; Author. Educ: B.A., 1951, M.A., 1960, Univ. of Durham. Publs: The Fighting Man, 1966; Across a Still Sleeping World, 1968; The Lion Who Fell, 1971; (BBC radio progs.) More From Ten to Eight, 1969; Pause for Thought, 1971. Mbr., Engl. Assn. Recip., Spence Watson Prize for Engl. Lit., 1951. Address: 59 Beaconsfield Rd., St. Stephen's, Canterbury, Kent CT2 7LQ, UK.

HEWETT, Anita, b. Wellington, Somerset, UK. Writer of Children's Books. Educ: Exeter Univ.; Dip. Nat. Froebel Fndn. Publs: The Elworthy Children, 1963; The Bull Beneath the Walnut Tree, 1966; The Anita Hewett Animal Story Book, 1972; Mrs. Mopple's Washing Line, 1966; Mr. Faksimily & the Tiger, 1967. Contbr. to BBC schls. broadcasting scripts, etc. Mbr., Soc. Authors. Recip., Austrian Staatpreise, 1968 for The Elworthy Children. Address: 29 Esher Rd., E. Molesey, Surrey, UK.

HEWETT, Cecil Alec, b. 1926, Laindon, Essex, UK. Planning Administrator. Educ: Univ. of Wales, Swansea. Publs: Development of Carpentry, 1969; Church Carpentry, 1974; English Cathedral Carpentry, 1974. Contbr. to: Archaeol. Jrnl.; Medieval Archaeol.; Post-Medieval Archaeol.; Country Life; Art Bulletin; Archtl. Review; Vernacular Arch.; etc. Mbrships: Vernacular Arch. Grp.; Soc. of Post- Medieval Archaeol.; A.M.S. (formerly); Assn. for Studies in Conserving Historic Bldgs.; F.R.S.A., 1973. Address: 8 Mallard Close, Kelvedon, Colchester, Essex, UK.

HEWINS, (Rev.) Geoffrey Shaw, b. 1889, Kingswood, Albrighton, nr. Wolverhampton, UK. Clergyman. Educ: B.A., Univ. Coll. of Wales; Lichfield Theol. Coll. Publs. incl: A Bibliography of Shropshire, 1922; Salopian Rambles, 1933; Midland Wanderings, 1937; Notes on Ancient Tithe Barns, 1938; Famous Trees of the Midlands, 1944; Shropshire Glimpses, 1948; Round & About the Titterstone, 1955; Villages of the Clee Hills, 1967. Contbr. to: Warwicks. Jrnl.; Worcs. Countryside; Staffs. Life; Shrops. Mag.; var. local newspapers. Address: The Old Rectory, Silvington, Cleobury Mortimer, Salop., UK.

HEWINS, Ralph Anthony, b. 16 Feb. 1909, Broadway, UK. Journalist; Author. Educ: M.A., Univ. of Oxford. Publs: Count Folk Bernadotte, 1949; Mr. Five Per Cent (C. S. Gulbenkian), 1956; The Richest American (J. Paul Getty), 1960; A Golden Dream: the Miracle of Kuwait, 1963; Quisling: prophet without Honour, 1965; The Japanese Miracle Men, 1967; biogs., in Swedish, of Count Bernadotte & King Gustaf V. Contbr. to: Farmand, Oslo; This is Japan, Tokyo; Ency. Britannica. Mbr., Press Club, London. Agent: David Higham Ltd. Address: c/o S. D. Carver, Holly Cottage, Liphook, Hants., UK.

HEWISON, William, b. 1925, South Shields, UK. Art Editor, Punch. Educ: Inst. of Educ., Univ. of London. Publs: (author & illustrator) Types Behind the Print, 1964; Mindfire, 1973. Contbr. to: Punch; Over 21. Mbrships: N.DD.; A.T.D. Address: 11 Seymour Rd., Wimbledon, London SW19 5JL, UK.

HEWITT, James, b. 9 Apr. 1928, Belfast, UK. Author. Publs: Teach Yourself Yoga, 1960; Eye-Witnesses to History Series; Nelson's Battles, 1972; Indian Mutiny, 1972; Wagon Trains West, 1973; Ireland in Revolt, 1974; Encyclopedia Yoga Practice, 1975. Contbr. to: BBC. Address: 11 Howard Rd., Dorking, Surrey, UK.

HEWITT, Joan Evelyn, b. 23 Nov. 1912, London, UK. Writer; Painter. Publs: The Glastonbury Adventure, 1946; A Pity Beyond All Telling, 1956; The Grandfather Clock, 1951. Address: 5 Dorset Rd., Windsor, Berks., UK.

HEWLETT, Richard Greening, b. 12 Feb. 1923, Toledo, Ohio, USA. Historian. Educ: Dartmouth Coll., 1941-43; Bowdoin Coll., 1943-44; M.A., 1948, Ph.D., 1952, Univ. of Chgo. Publs: The New World, 1939-46 (w. Oscar E. Anderson, Jr.), 1962; Atomic Shield 1947-52 (w. Francis Duncan), 1969; Nuclear Navy, 1946-62 (w. Francis Duncan), 1974. Contbr. to: Technol. & Culture; Mil. Affairs. Mbrships. incl: Soc. for Hist. of Technol.; Wash. Sect., Am. Nuclear Soc. Hons. incl: David D. Lloyd Prize, Harry S. Truman Lib. Inst., 1970. Address: 7909 Deepwell Dr., Bethesda, MD 20034, USA.

HEY, Nigel Stewart, b. 23 June 1936, Morecambe, UK. Writer. Educ: B.A., Univ. of Utah, USA, 1958. Publs: The Mysterious Sun, 1970; How Will We Feed the Hungry Billions?, 1972; How We Will Explore the Outer Planets?, 1973. Contbr. to: New Sci.; Indl. Rsch.; Photographic Applications; Electronic Design; Euroscience Intelligence Report (Ed.). Mbrships: Assn. Brit. Sci. Writers; Nat. Assn. Sci. Writers (USA). Int. Sci. Writers Assn.; Am. Inst. Aeronautics & Astronautics. Address: Gray's Cottage, Gray's Close, Haslemere, Surrey, UK.

HEYERDAHL, Thor, b. 6 Oct. 1914, Larvik, Norway. Author; Anthropologist. Educ: Ph.D., Univ. of Oslo. Num. publs. incl: The Kon-Tiki Expedition, 1948; Aki-Aku, The Secret of Easter Island, 1957; Sea Routes to Polynesia, 1967; The Ra Expedition, 1970; Fatu-Hiva Back to Nature, 1974; The Art of Easter Island, 1975. Contbr. to num. jrnls.; Prod., documentary films of expeditions. Hons. incl: Oscar Award for Kon-Tiki film. Address: Colla Micheri, 17020 Laigueglia, Italy.

HEYM, Stefan, b. 1913, Chemnitz, Germany; Author. Educ: Univs. of Berlin & Chicago; M.A. Publs: Hostages, 1942; Of Smiling Peace, 1944; The Crusaders, 1950; The Eyes of Reason, 1951; Goldsborough, 1961; Cannibals & Other Stories, 1958; Shadows & Lights, 1963; The Lenz Papers, 1964; Uncertain Friend, 1969; The King David Report, 1973; The Queen against Defoe & Other Stories, 1974; Funf Tage im Juni, 1974. Mbr: PEN. Agent: Mohrbooks, Zurich. Address: Tagore Strasse/9, 118 Berlin-Gruenau, German Dem. Repub.

HEYWOOD, Roland Bryon, b. 19 Nov. 1915, Ruislip, Middx., UK. Engineer. Educ: Imperial Coll., City & Guilds, 1936-38; B.Sc.; A.C.G.I., Ph.D. Publs: Designing by Photoelasticity, 1952; Designing Against Fatigue, 1962; Photoelasticity for Designers, 1969. Mbrships: C.Eng.; F.I.Mech.E.; A.F.R.Ae.S.; Edit. Bd., Jrnl. of Strain; Comm. of Stress Analysis & Strength of Components, Engrng. Scis. Data Unit. Recip., Prize for Paper Mod. Applications of Photoelasticity, Inst. of Mech. Engrs., 1948. Address: Chapel Pines, Maywood, Portsmouth Rd., Camberley, Surrey GU15 1LH, UK.

HEYWOOD, Rosalind, b. 1895, Gibraltar. Publs: The Sixth Sense, 1959, 1971 (publ'd in USA as Beyond the Reach of Sense, 1961, 1974); The Infinite Hive, 1964, 1971 (publ'd in USA as ESP: a Personal Memoir, 1963). Contbr. to: Sci. & E.S.P.; Man's Concern w. Death. Address: 3 The Drive, London SW20, UK.

HEYWOOD, Terence, b. Johannesburg, S. Africa. Author. Educ: M.A., Worcester Coll., Oxford. Publs: Background to Sweden, 1951; How Smoke Gets Into The Air (poems); Architectonic; Facing North (co-author). Contbr., num. poems to anthols., etc. Address: 42 Doneraile St., Fulham, London SW6, UK.

HEYWORTH, Peter Lawrence Frederick, b. 1921, NYC, USA. Music Critic. Educ: B.A., Balliol Coll., Oxford, UK. Publs: Ed., Berlioz, Romantic, 1972; Ed., Writings by Ernest Newman, 1972; Ed., Conversations with Klemperer, 1973. Music Critic, Times Educl. Supplement, 1952-55; Music Critic, Observer, 1955—; Gramophone Critic, New Statesman, 1956-58. Address: 32 Bryanston Sq., London W1, UK.

HIBBARD, Howard, b. 1928, Madison, Wisconsin, USA. Professor; Writer. Educ: Univs. of Wisconsin, Columbia & Harvard; Ph.D. Publs: The Architecture of the Palazzo Borghese, 1962; Bernini, 1965; Bernini e il Barocco, 1968; Florentine Baroque Art from American Collections (w. J. Nissman), 1969; Carlo Maderno, 1972; Poussin, 1974; The Holy Family on the Steps. Contbr. to: Art Bulletin (Ed.-in-Chief); Burlington Mag.; Jrnl. of the Soc. of Archtl. Histns.; Bollettino d'arte. Mbrships: Soc. of Archtl. Histns.; Renaissance Soc. of Am.; Coll. Art Assn. of Am.; Fellow, Am. Acad. of Arts & Sci. Address: 815 Schermerhorn Hall, Columbia Univ., N.Y., NY 10027, USA.

HIBBERT, Christopher M. C., b. 5 Mar. 1924, Enderby, Leics., UK. Author. Educ: M.A., Oriel Coll., Oxford. Publs. incl: The Road to Tyburn, 1957; King Mob, 1958; Wolfe at Quebec, 1959; Corunna, 1961; Benito Mussolini, 1962; The Battle of Arnhem, 1962; The Roots of Evil, 1963; Agincourt, 1964; Garibaldi & His Enemies, 1965; The Making of Charles Dickens, 1967; Charles I, 1968; London, 1969; The Dragon Wakes, 1970; The Personal History of Samuel Johnson, 1971; George IV: Prince of Wales, 1972; George IV: Regent & King, 1973; The Rise & Fall of the House of Medici, 1974. Contbr. to newspapers, profl. jrnls. & encys. Mbrships: F.R.S.L. Recip., Heinemann Award for Lit., 1962. Address: 64 St. Andrew's Rd., Henley-on-Thames, Oxon., UK.

HIBBERT, Eleanor, b. 1906, London, UK. Author. Publs. incl: (under num. pseudonyms) (as Jean Plaidy) The Rise of the Spanish Inquisition, 1959; The Murder in the Tower, 1964; The Three Crowns, 1965; The Queen's Favourites, 1966; The Third George, 1969; The Queen & Lord M, 1973; (as Eleanor Burford) Married Love, 1942; Begin to Live, 1956; Pride of the Morning, 1958; Blaze of Noon, 1958; Who's Calling, 1962; (as Ellalice Tait) Madame du Barry, 1959; This Was a Man, 1961; (as Elbur Ford) The Flesh & the Devil, 1950; (as Kathleen Kellow) Danse Macabre, 1952; (as Victoria Holt) The Shadow of the Lynx, 1972; The Curse of The Kings, 1973. Address: c/o Robert Hale, 63 Old Brompton Rd., London SW7, UK.

HICK, John, b. 20 Jan. 1922, Scarborough, Yorks., UK. University Professor; Author. Educ: M.A., D.Litt., Edinburgh Univ.; Ph.D., Cambridge; D.Phil., Oxford. Publs: Faith & Knowledge, 1957, 2nd ed., 1966; Philosophy of Religion, 1963, 2nd ed., 1973, also transl'd; Ed., Faith & the Philosophers, 1963; Ed., The Existence of God, 1963; Ed., Classical & Contemporary Readings in the Philosophy of Religion, 1964, 2nd ed., 1970; Evil & the God of Love, 1966; Christianity at the Centre, 1968; Arguments for the Existence of God, 1970; Biology & the Soul, 1972; God & the Universe of Faiths, 1973; Ed., Truth & Dialogue, 1974. Address: Dept. of Theology, Univ. of Birmingham, P.O. Box 363, Birmingham B15 2TT, UK.

HICKINBOTHAM, J. P., b. 1914, Birmingham, UK. Theological College Principal. Educ: M.A., Magdalen Coll., Oxford; Wycliffe Hall, Oxford. Publs: Conditions of Fellowship, 1948; The Open Table, 1966. Contbr. to: The Churchman; The Triumph of God; Intercommunion; Relations between Anglican & Presby. Churches; Women in Ministry. Address: Wycliffe Hall, Oxford, UK.

HICKLING, Reginald Hugh, b. 1920, Derby, UK. Legal Advisor; Attorney-General, Gibraltar. Educ: Univ. of Nottingham. Publs: The Furious Evangelist; The English Flottila; Sarawak & Its Government; Festival of Hungary Ghosts; Lieutenant Okino; Malayan Constitutional Documents (Ed.); An Introduction to the Federal Constitution. Contbr. to: Evening Standard. Mbr., PEN. Lit. Agent: David Higham Assoc. Ltd. Address: 1 Highfield Rd., Malvern, Worcs., UK.

HICKMAN, (Colonel) Arthur Selwyn, b. 6 Nov. 1900, London, UK. Retired Commissioner, British South Africa Police, Rhodesia. Publs: Men Who Made Rhodesia, 1960; Rhodesia Served the Queen, Rhodesian Forces in the Boer War 1899-1902, vol. I, 1970, vol. II, forthcoming. Contbr. to: Rhodesiana; The Outpost; Nada. Mbrships: Past Comm. Mbr., Rhodesian Ctr., PEN; Past Comm. Chmn., Rhodesiana Soc. Hons: Q.P.M.; M.B.E.; C. St. J.; Gold Medal, Rhodesian Soc., 1970; Celtic "Gwas Keyna" (Servant of St. Keyne); Bard, Gorsedd of Cornwall, 1974. Address: St. Keyne, 6 York Ave., Highlands, Salisbury N.E.69, Rhodesia.

HICKS, David, b. 1916, London, UK. Broadcasting Editor. Educ: B.A., Worcester Coll., Oxford. Publs: Calling All Beginners (in 23 langs.), 1956—; Foundations of English, 3 vols., 1956; View & Teach (Ed.), 24 TV films, 1963-66. Mbr., Int. Assn. of Tchrs. Of Engl. as a For. Lang. Address: 2 Longfield Rd., London W5, UK.

HICKS, David, b. 25 Mar. 1929, Coggeshall, UK. Designer. Educ: Central Schl. of Art, London. Publs: David Hicks on Decoration, 1966, 1972; David Hicks on Living With Taste, 1968; David Hicks on Bathrooms, 1970; David Hicks on Decoration With Fabrics, 1971; David Hicks on Decoration 5, 1972. Mbr., Ct. of Assts., Salters' Co. Address: 24 Paultons House, London SW3, UK.

HICKS, Granville, b. 9 Sept. 1901, Exeter, N.H., USA. Writer. Educ: A.B., 1923, M.A., 1929, Harvard Univ. Publs. incl: (novels) Only One Storm, 1942; There Was a Man in Our Town, 1952; (non-fiction) The Great Tradition, USA 1933, UK 1934, revised ed., 1969; Figures of Transition, 1940; Where We Came Out, USA & UK, 1954; Literary Horizons, 1970; (autobiog.) Part of the Truth, 1965. Contbr. to: New Masses (Ed. staff, 1934-39); New Leader (Lit. Cons., 1951-58); Saturday Review (Contbng. Ed., 1958-69). Hons. incl: D.H.L., Skidmore Coll., N.Y., 1968, & Ohio Univ., 1969; Litt.D., Siena Coll., N.Y., 1971; var. Fellowships. Address: Box 144, Grafton, N.Y., USA.

HIDDEN, Norman Frederick, pen name KRYPTOS, b. 24 Oct. 1913, Portsmouth, Hants., UK. Writer; Lecturer; Editor. Educ: M.A., Dip. Ed., Oxford; postgrad. work, Univ. of Mich., USA. Publs: These Images Claw (poems), 1966; Ed., Say It Aloud, 1972; Dr. Kink & his Old Style Boarding School, 1973; A Study Guide to Under Milk Wood, 1974; Ed., Over to You, 1975. Contbr. to: Workshop New Poetry (Ed.); Times Educl. Supplement; New Statesman; var. educl. jrnls.; etc. Mbrships. incl: Poetry Soc.; Advsry. Coun., Engl. Speaking Bd.; Comm., Engl. Assn. Recip., Civil List Pension, for servs. to lit., 1973. Address: 99 Pole Barn Lane, Frinton-on-Sea, Essex, UK.

HIEBERT, D(avid) Edmond, b. 21 July 1910, Corn, Okla., USA. Seminary Professor. Educ: A.B., John Fletcher Coll., 1935; Th.M., 1939, Th.D., 1942. S. Bapt. Theol. Sem. Publs. incl: Introduction to the Pauline Epistles, 1954; Introduction to the Non-Pauline Epistles, 1962; The Thessalonian Epistles, 1971; Personalities Around Paul, 1973; Mark: Portrait of the Servant, 1974; Introduction to the Gospels & Acts, 1975. Contbr. to relig. jrnls. Address: 4864 E. Townsend, Fresno, CA 93727, USA.

HIGGINBOTTOM, David, pen name FISK, Nicholas, b. 1923, London, UK. Company Director. Author. Publs: The Bouncers (illustrator & author), 1964; Making Music, 1966; Richthofen, the Red Baron, 1968; Lindbergh, the Lone Flier, 1968; Menuhin's House of Music by Eric Fenby (photographer & ed.), 1969; (children's) Space Hostages, 1967; Trillions, 1971; High Way Home, 1973; Grinny, 1973; Emma, 1974; Little Green Spaceman, 1974. Contbr. to: Daily Mirror; Strand; Lilliput; etc. Agent: A. M. Heath Address: 59 Elstree Rd., Bushey Heath, Herts., UK.

HIGGINS, Aidan, b. 1927, Co. Kildare, Repub. of Ireland. Author. Publs: Felo de Se, 1961; Langrishe, Go Down, 1966; Balcony of Europe, 1971; Images of Africa, 1971. Address: c/o Caldar & Boyars, 18 Brewer St., London W1, UK.

HIGGINS, Angus John Brockhurst, b. 1911, Narberth, Wales, UK. Professor of Theology. Educ: Univs. of Wales & Manchester; M.A.; D.D.; Ph.D. Publs: The Christian Significance of the Old Testament; The Reliability of the Gospels; The Lord's Supper in the New Testament; The Historicity of the Fourth Gospel; Jesus & the Son of Man; The Tradition about Jesus; O. Cullmann, The Early Church (Ed.); New Testament Essays (Ed.): Studies in Memory of T. W. Manson. Contbr. to: Expository Times. Scottish Jrnl. of Theol.; New Testament Studies; etc. Address: Dept. of Theol., St. David's Univ. Coll., Lampeter, Wales, UK.

HIGGINS, Dick (Richard Carter), b. 15 Mar. 1938, Cambridge, UK. Author; Publisher. Educ: Yale Coll., USA; Columbia Univ.; Manhattan Schl. of Printing, N.Y. Publs. incl: Jefferson's Birthday/Postface, 1964; A Book about Love & War & Death, Contos 1-3, 1965-69, 1972; Towards the 1970s, 1969; Ed., Fantastic Architecture (w. W. Vostell), 1971; The Ladder to the Moon, 1973; Spring Game, 1974; Modular Poems, 1974; (films) The Flaming City, 1963; Men, Women & Bells, 1968. Contbr. to num. anthols. & mod. lit. mags. Mbrships. incl: Coord. Org. Small Mags., Eds. & Publrs. (Bd. of Dirs., 1972-73); New England Small Press Assn. Recip., Fellowship, Berlin, 1975. Address: P.O. Box 26, W. Glover, VT 05875, USA.

HIGGINS, Raymond Aurelius, b. 16 Dec. 1916, W. Bromwich, UK. Senior Lecturer in Materials Technology. Educ: B.Sc., Birmingham Univ., 1937. Publs: Engineering Metallurgy, Part 1, 1957, Part 2, 1961; Materials for the Engineering Technician, 1972. Fellow, Instn. of Metallurgists. Address: 27 Springvale Ave., Park Hall, Walsall, Staffs. WS5 3QB, UK.

HIGGINS, Reynold Alleyne, b. 26 Nov. 1916, Weybridge, Surrey, UK. Archaeologist; Author. Educ: Litt.D., Pembroke Coll., Cambridge, 1938. Publs: Catalogue of Terracottas in the British Museum, 1954, 2nd ed., 1959; Greek & Roman Jewellery, 1961; Greek Terracottas, 1967; Minoan & Mycenaean Art, 1967; The Archaeology of Minoan Crete, 1973. Contbr. to: Apollo Mag.; Annual of British Schl. at Athens; Antiquaries Jrnl. Address: Hartfield, Burstead Close, Cobham, Surrey, UK.

HIGGINS, Rosalyn, b. 2 June 1937, London, UK. International Lawyer. Educ: B.A., 1958, LL.B., 1959, M.A., 1962, Girton Coll., Cambridge; J.S.D., Univ. of Yale, USA, 1962. Publs: The Development of International Law through the Political Organs of the United Nations, 1963; Conflict of Interests, 1965; The Administration of the United Kingdom Foreign Policy through the United Nations, 1966; United Nations Peacekeeping: Documents & Commentary, 3 vols., 1969, 1971, & forthcoming; Ed., Law in Movement; Essays in Honour of J. McMahon (w. J. Fawcett), 1974. Mbr., Ed. Bds., International Organization & Brit. Yrbook. of Int. Law. Recip., Cert. of Award, Am. Soc. of Int. Law, 1971. Address: c/o London Schl. of Econs., Houghton St., London WC2A 2AE, UK.

HIGGINS, Trumbull, b. 27 Sept. 1919, NYC, USA. Professor of History; Author. Educ: A.B., M.A., Ph.D., Princeton Univ. Publs: Winston Churchill & the Second Front, 1957; Korea & the Fall of MacArthur, 1960; Winston Churchill & the Dardanelles, 1963; Hitler & Russia, 1966; Soft Underbelly, 1968. Contbr. to: Am. Hist. Jrnl.; N.Y. Times Book Review; Mil. Affairs; Wash. Post. Address: 1148 5th Ave., N.Y., NY 10028, USA.

HIGGS-WALKER, James Arthur, b. 1892, Clent, Worcs., UK. Headmaster (Retired). Educ: M.A., St. John's Coll., Oxford Univ. Publs: European History, 1789-1915; Introduction to French Society in the Eighteenth Century. Contbr. of reviews to var. jrnls. Address: Long Barn, Chelwood Gate, Sussex, UK.

HIGH, Philip Empson, b. 28 Apr. 1914, Biggleswade, Beds., UK. Bus Driver. Educ: Kent Coll., Canterbury. Publs: Prodigal Son, 1963; No Truce With Terra, 1964; Reality Forbidden, 1965; The Mad Metropolis, 1966; Twin Planets, 1967; These Savage Futurians, 1967; Invader On My Back, 1968; The Time Mercenaries, 1969; Butterfly Planet, 1971; Come Hunt an Earthman, 1973; Sold — For a Spaceship, 1973; Speaking of Dinosaurs, 1974. Address: 34 King St., Canterbury, Kent, UK.

HIGHAM, Florence May Greir, b. 1896, Manchester, UK. Author. Educ: M.A., Ph.D., Univ. of Manchester. Publs: The Principal Secretary of State; 1558-1680, 1923; Charles I, 1932; King James II, 1934; Faith of Our Fathers, 1939; Lord Shaftesbury, 1945; Frederick Denison Maurice, 1947; Lancelot Andrewes, 1952; Southwark Story, 1955; Catholic & Reformed, 1962; John Evelyn Esq., 1968. Mbrships. Int. PEN; Engl. Speaking Union. Address: Coach House Flat, Beech House, Redcoats Green, Hitchin, Herts. SG4 7JR, UK.

HIGHAM, Robin (David Stewart), b. 20 June 1925, London, UK. Historian. Educ: A.B. (cum laude), Harvard Coll., Univ. of N.H.; M.A., Claremont Grad. Schl.; Ph.D., Harvard Univ. Publs. incl: Britain's Imperial Air Routes 1918-1939, 1961; Armed Forces in Peacetime: Britain 1918-1939, 1966; The Military Intellectuals in Britain: 1918-1939, 1966; A Short History of Warfare, 1966; Air Power: A Concise History, 1972; The Compleat Academic, 1975. Contbr. to: Mil. Affairs (Ed.); Aerospace Histn. (Ed.); var. profl. jrnls. Mbrships: AHA; AMI; AFHF; CBS. Recip., Aviation/Space Writers' Assn. Award, 1973. Address: 2961 Nevada Street, Manhattan, KS 66502, USA.

HIGHAM, Roger, b. 1935, Dartford, Kent, UK. Author. Publs: Island Road to Africa, 1968; Provencal Sunshine, 1969; Road to the Pyrenees, 1971; The South Country, 1972; Kent, 1974. Contbr. to: Kent Life; Blackwood's Mag.; Ch. of England Newspaper; Sturry — The Changing Scene. Agent: David Higham Assoc. Ltd. Address: 39 High St., Sturry, Canterbury, Kent, UK.

HIGHET, John, b. 1918, Glasgow, UK. Head of Social Studies Department. Educ: Glasgow Univ.; Balliol Coll., Oxford Univ.; M.A.; Ph.D. Publs: The Churches in Scotland Today; The Scottish Churches, 1960; A School of One's Choice, 1969; The Scottish Economy (co-author); The City of Glasgow (co-author). Contbr. to: Scotsman; Glasgow Herald; Brit. Jrnl. Sociol.; Soc. Serv. Quarterly. Mbr. Advsry. Coun. on Educ. in Scotland. Address: 319 Albert Dr., Glasgow G41 5EA, Scotland, UK.

HIGHSMITH, (Mary) Patricia, b. 19 Jan. 1921. Novelist, Short Story Writer. Educ: B.A., Barnard Coll., Columbia Univ., N.Y., USA. Publs: Strangers on a Train, 1949; The Talented Mr. Ripley, 1955; Deep Water, 1956; This Sweet Sickness, 1959; The Glass Cell, 1964; The Tremor of Forgery, 1968; Ripley under Ground, 1970; A Dog's Ransom, 1971; Ripley's Game, 1973; The Animal-Lover's Book of Beastly Murder, 1975. Contbr. to: Saturday Evening Post; New Review (London). Mbr., Authors Guild of Am. Hons: Mystery Writers of Am. Scroll, for The Talented Mr. Ripley, 1956; Best For. Novel Award, Crime Writers' Assn. of Gt. Britain, 1964. Address: 21 Boissiere Moncourt 77 880, France.

HIGNETT, Sean, b. 1934, Birkenhead, UK. Lecturer. Educ: M.A.; B.Phil.; Dip. Stat. Publs: A Picture to Hang on the Wall, 1966; A Cut Loaf, 1971; Var. plays & screenplays. Contbr. to: Winter's Tales; Daily Telegraph Mag.; Vogue; Scotsman; Guardian; BBC; ITV. Mbr., Writers' Guild of GB. Agent: A. D. Peters & Co. Address: c/o A. D. Peters & Co., 10 Buckingham St., London WC2, UK.

HILDESHEIMER, Wolfgang, b. 9 Dec. 1916, Hamburg, Germany. Writer. Educ: Ctrl. Schl. of Arts & Crafts, London, UK. Publs: Lieblose Legenden (short stories), 1952, revised ed., 1962; Tynset (novel), 1965; Zeiten in Cornwall (autobiog.), 1968; Masante (novel), 1972. Contbr. to: Merkur; Neue Rundschau; Akzente. Mbrships: Deutsche Akad. für Sprache & Dichtung, Darmstadt; Berliner Akad. der Künste; PEN. Hons: Film Prize of the War-Blinded, 1955; Bremer Lit. Prize, 1965; Georg Büchner Prize, 1966. Address: CH-7742 Poschiavo (GR), Switz.

HILDICK, Edmund Wallace, b. 1925, Bradford, UK. Writer. Educ: City of Leeds Trng. Coll. Publs: Bed & Work, 1962; A Town on the Never, 1963; Lunch with Ashurbanipal, 1965; Word for Word, 1965; Writing with Care, 1967; Thirteen Types of Narrative, 1968; Children & Fiction, 1970; Only the Best, USA 1973; over 40 children's books inclng. Jim Starling, 1958, Louie's Lot, 1965, Birdy Jones & the New York Heads, 1974. Ed., Kenyon Review, 1966-67. Contbr. to: Listener; Spectator; Times Educl. Supplement; Jrnl. of Educ.; Evening News; Eagle; Use of English; The Author; Books; The Writer. Address: c/o Coutts & Co., 440 Strand, London WC2, UK.

HILL, Alan John Wills, b. 1912, Barwell, Leics., UK. Publisher & Managing Director of the Heinemann Group. Educ: M.A., Jesus Coll., Cambridge. Publs: And So Was England Born (w. R. W. Finn), 1938; History in Action, 4 vols., 1963. Contbr. to: Times; Times Lit. Supplement; New Statesman; BBC. Mbrships: PEN; Garrick, Athenaeum, Lansdowne, RAF Clubs. Address: 56 Northway, London NW11, UK; New House, Rosthwaite, Borrowdale, Cumbria, UK.

HILL, Archibald Vivian, b. 26 Sept. 1886, Bristol, UK. Physiologist. Educ: Sc.D., Cambridge Univ. Publs: Living Machinery, 1927; Adventures in Biophysics, 1931; The Ethical Dilemma of Science, 1960; Trails & Trials in Physiology, 1965; First & Last Experiments in Muscle Mechanics, 1970. Contbr. to: Jrnl. of Physiol.; Proceedings of Royal Soc.; Perspectives in Biol. & Med., Chgo.; Nature, London. Mbrships: Fellow, Trinity & King's Colls., Cambridge; F.R.S., 1918; Physiol. Soc., GB; Hon. Mbr., Nat. Acad. of Scis., N.Y.; Marine Biol. Assn. Hons: Nobel Prize, Physiol. & Med., 1923; Actonian Prize, Royal Instn. Address: 11a Chaucer Rd., Cambridge CB2 2EB, UK.

HILL, Brian, pen name MAGILL, Marcus, b. 1896, Hampstead, UK. Writer. Publs: incl: Hide & I'll Find You, 1933; Correspondence Between Samuel Butler & Miss E. M. A. Savage, 1935; Samuel Butler's Notebooks (Ed., w. Geoffrey Keynes), 1951; (verse) Take All Colours, 1943; The Sheltering Tree, 1945; The Drunken Boat, 1952; The Sky Above the Roof, 1957; Fortune's Fool, 1959; Gentle Enchanter, 1960; The Trophies, 1962; (anthols.) Pleasure Garden, 1956; The Greedy Book, 1966; Such Stuff as Dreams, 1967; Julia Margaret Cameron, 1973; Collected Poems & Translations, 1974. Contbr. to var. jrnls. Mbr., Soc. of Authors. Address: 2 Grove Rd., London NW2 5TB, UK.

HILL, Christopher, b. 3 Nov. 1928, Surbiton, Surrey, UK. Writer. Publs: Scorpion, 1974; Jackdaw, forthcoming. Lit. Agent: Collins Publishers Ltd. Address: Le Presbytere, Chourgnac d'Ans, Dordogne, France.

HILL, Claude, b. 28 July 1911, Berlin, Germany. Professor of German Literature. Educ: Univs. of Gottingen & Vienna; Ph.D., Univ. of Jena, 1938. Publs: Das Drama der deutschen Neuromantik, 1938; Zwei Hundert Jahre Deutscher Kultur, 1966; Bertolt Brecht, 1974; sev. textbooks between 1948 & 1972. Contbr. to: Sat. Review; N.Y. Times; Books Abroad; German Quarterly; Symposium; Mod. Drama; Universitas; Die Zeit. Mbrships: AAUP; MLA; Am. Assn. Tchrs. of German, Am. Civil Liberties Union; Thomas Mann Ges., Zurich. Hons: Fellow, Drama Schl., Yale Univ., 1940; Fac.-Study Fellowship, Am. Coun. of Learned Socs., 1951. Address: German Dept., Rutgers Univ., New Brunswick, NJ 08903, USA.

HILL, Douglas (Arthur), pen name HILLMAN, Martin, b. 6 Apr. 1935, Brandon, Man., Can. Author. Educ: B.A.,

Univ. of Saskatchewan. Publs. incl: The Supernatural (w. Pat Williams), 1965; The Opening of the Canadian West, 1967; Georgian London, 1969-70; Bridging a Continent (as Martin Hillman), 1971; The Scots to Canada, 1972; Fortune Telling, 1972; The Comet, 1973; Coyote the Trickster (w. Gail Robinson), 1975; The English to New England, 1975. Contbr. to: Tribune (lit. Ed.); Guardian; Jewish Chronicle; Can. Forum; BBC; etc. Mbrships: Folklore Soc.; Nat. Union of Jrnlsts. & Writers Guild, UK. Recip., Can. Coun. arts grant (poetry), 1968. Address: Flat 2, 16 Haslemere Rd., London N8, UK.

HILL, Elizabeth Starr, b. 4 Nov. 1925, Lynn Haven, Fla., USA. Writer. Educ: Finch Coll., N.Y. Publs: Wonderful Visit to Miss Liberty, 1961; The Window Tulip, 1964; Evan's Corner, 1967; Master Mike & the Miracle Maid, 1967; Pardon My Fangs, 1969; Bells, A Book to Begin On, 1970. Contbr. to: Reader's Digest; New Yorker; Good Housekeeping; Harper's Bazaar; etc. Recip., ALA Notable Children's Books Choice for Evan's Corner. Agent: Brandt & Brandt. Address: Brandt & Brandt, 101 Park Ave., N.Y., NY 10017, USA.

HILL, (Sir) (James William) Francis, b. 15 Sept. 1899, Lincoln, UK. Solicitor (Ret'd). Educ: LL.M., Litt.D., Trinity Coll., Cambridge. Publs: Medieval Lincoln, 1948; Banks Family Papers, 1952; Tudor & Stuart Lincoln, 1956; Georgian Lincoln, 1966; Victorian Lincoln, 1974. Contbr. to var. jrnls. Mbrships: Pres., Nottingham Univ. Coun., 1948-67; Pro-Chancellor, 1959-72; Chancellor, 1972—; Chmn., Nat. Fndn. for Educl. Rsch., 1962-67; Pres., Lincoln Record Soc.; F.S.A.; Fellow, Royal Histl. Soc. Hons: C.B.E., 1954; Kt., 1958; Freeman of Lincoln, 1961; sev. hon. degrees. Address: The Priory, Lincoln, UK.

HILL, (John Edward) Christopher, b. 6 Feb. 1912, York, UK. University Teacher; Author. Educ: M.A., D.Litt., Balliol Coll., Oxford. Publs: The English Revolution 1640, 1940; Puritanism & Revolution, 1958; The Century of Revolution, 1961; Society & Puritanism in Pre-Revolutionary England, 1964; Intellectual Origins of the English Revolution, 1965; Reformation to Industrial Revolution, 1967; God's Englishman: Oliver Cromwell, 1970; Antichrist in 17th Century England, 1971; The World Turned Upside Down, 1972; Ed., The Law of Freedom & Other Writings of Gerrard Winstanley, 1973; Change & Continuity in 17th Century England, 1974. Address: Balliol College, Oxford, UK.

HILL, Leslie Alexander, b. 1918, Athens, Greece. Writer. Phonetician. Educ: M.A., Corpus Christie Coll., Cambridge; M.A., Univ. Coll., London. Publs: num. books on English Language & Literature. Contbr. to sev. educl. periodicals. Mbrships: Mensa; Int. Phonetic Assn.; Int. Linguistic Assn.; Soc. of Authors; Audio-Visual Lang. Assn.; Int. Assn. of Teachers of Eng. as a For. Lang. Address: La Prairie, St. Mary, Jersey, Channel Islands, UK.

HILL, Norman Llewellyn, b. 1895, Afton, N.Y., USA. Professor of International Relations. Educ: Sorbonne, Paris, France; M.A., Ph.D., Univ. of Wis., USA. Publs: incl: International Administration; The Background of European Government (w. Harold Stoke); Contemporary World Politics; If the Churches Want Peace (w. D. Lund). Contbr. to: Am. Pol. Sci. Review; Am. Jrnl. of Int. Law; Int. Conciliation (pamphlet series); var. law jrnls. Address: 232 Jackson, Berea, KY 40403, USA.

HILL, Reginald Charles, pen names MORLAND, Dick; RUELL, Patrick, b. 1936, W. Hartlepool, Co. Durham, UK. Lecturer in English. Educ: M.A., St. Catherine's Coll., Oxford Univ. Publs: A Clubbable Woman, 1970; Fell of Dark, 1971; An Advancement of Learning, 1971; An Affair of Honour (TV play), 1972; A Fairly Dangerous Thing, 1972; Ruling Passion, 1973; A Very Good Hater, 1974; (as Patrick Ruell) The Castle of the Demon, 1971; Red Christmas, 1972; Death Takes the Low Road, 1974; (as Dick Morland) Heart Clock, 1973; Albion! Albion! , 1974. Mbr., Crime Writers Assn. Address: 16 Ellers Dr., Bessacarr, Doncaster DN4 7DN, UK.

HILL, Richard Desmond, b. 1920, Bournemouth, UK. Rowing Correspondent. Educ: M.A., New Coll. Oxford. Publs: A History of St. Edward's School, 1962; Instructions in Rowing, 1963. Contbr. to Daily Telegraph. Address: Martins, School Lane, Kingston Bagpuize, Oxon., UK.

HILL, Roland Luverne, b. 18 Sept. 1904, Dawson, Minn., USA. Author; Traveller; Publisher. Educ: B.A., Long Beach State Coll., Calif. Publs: Living the Life of Rolly,

1941; I Recommend, 1944; Hillsway, 1945, 13 further eds.; In Minn. I Recommend, 1946; In Las Vegas I Recommend, 1947, 3rd ed., 1960; The Best of Hills, 1947; In Long Beach I Recommend, 1952; Hillsway's Who Who in Las Vegas, 1969; The Thirtieth Year, 1973. Contbr. to var. jrnls. Mbrships: Gall. of Living Cath. Authors; Mark Twain Soc.; Authors & Artists Guild, Chattanooga, Tenn. Address: Hillsway on Ann Lake, Mora, MN 55051, USA.

HILL, Susan, b. 5 Feb. 1942, Scarborough, Yorks., UK. Novelist; Playwright. Educ: B.A., King's Coll., Univ. of London, 1963. Publs: (novels) Gentleman & Ladies, 1969; A Change for the Better, 1969; I'm the King of the Castle, 1970; Strange Meeting, 1971; The Bird of Night, 1972; In the Springtime of the Year, 1974; (short story collects.) The Albatross, 1971; A Bit of Singing & Dancing, 1973; (collected radio plays) The Cold Country & other Plays, 1975. Contbr. to: Times; New Statesman; Listener; London Mag.; Cornhill Mag. F.R.S.L. Hons: W. Somerset Maugham Award, 1971; Whitbread Award for Fiction, 1972; John Llewellyn Rhys Prize, 1972. Address: c/o Hamish Hamilton Ltd., 90 Great Russell St., London WC1, UK.

HILL, William Charles Osman, b. 1901, Alcester, Warwicks., UK. Professor of Anatomy. Educ: M.D., Ch.B., Univ. of Birmingham. Publs: Comparative Anatomy & Taxonomy of the Primates, 8 vols., 1953-74; Man's Ancestry, 1954; Man as an Animal; The Anatomy of Callimico Goeldii, 1959; External & Visceral Anatomy of Procolobus verus, 1952; Physical Anthropology of the Existing Veddahs of Ceylon; Evolutionary Biology of the Primates, 1972. Contbr. to: Primatologia; etc. F.R.S.E. Address: Oakhurst, Dixwell Rd., Folkestone, Kent, UK.

HILLARP, Rut, b. 21 Feb. 1914, Lund, Sweden. Teacher; Poet. Educ: Ph.D. in Literature. Publs: Solens brun (The Well of the Sun), 1946; Dina händers ekon (Echoes of your hands), 1948; Båge av väntan (Bow of waiting), 1950; Blodförmörkelse (Darkening of the Blood), 1951; Sindhia (Sindhia), 1954; En eld är havet (The Sea is a fire), 1956; Kustlinje (Coastline), 1963; Ed., Socialister om Litteratur (Socialists on Literature), 1972. Mbrships: The Swedish Union of Authors; The Swedish PEN Club. Address: Siljansvägen 62, 12170 Johanneshov, Sweden.

HILLIARD, Noel Harvey, b. 6 Feb. 1929, Napier, NZ. Writer. Educ: Victoria Univ., Wellington; Wellington Tchrs. Coll. Publs: Maori Girl, 1960, 5th ed., 1973; A Piece of Land, 1963, 2nd ed., USSR 1964; Power of Joy, 1965, 2nd ed., USA 1966; A Night at Green River, 1969, 2nd ed., 1975; We Live by a Lake, 1973; Maori Woman, 1974. Contbr. to: NZ Listener; Landfall; Nat. Educ.; NZ Monthly Review; Mate; etc. Mbrships: PEN (NZ Ctr.); NZ Jrnlsts.' Union. Hons: Hubert Church Mem. Award (PEN), 1961; NZ Lit. Fund Fellowship, 1963 & 1975; Robert Burns Fellowship Lit., Otago Univ., 1971-72. Address: 28 Richard St., Titahi Bay, Wellington, NZ.

HILLIARD, Winifred M., b. 1921, Melbourne, Australia. Presbyterian Deaconess. Educ: Rolland House (Presby. Deaconess Trng. Coll.). Publs: The People in Between: The Pitjantjatjana People Ernabella, 1968. Contbr. to: Presby. Ch. Publs.; Quarterly Jrnl., Guilds of Weavers, Spinners & Dyers. Mbr., Presby. Deaconess Assn. Address: Ernabella, via Alice Springs, N.T., 5750, Australia.

HILLIER, Caroline, b. 1931, Stapleford-Tawney, Essex, UK. Writer; Translator. Educ: B.A., Univ. of Cambridge. Publs: Ed., Winter's Tales for Children 1 & 2, 1965 & 1966; Transl., Letter & Image, by Massin (w. V. Menkes), 1970; The Flood, 1971; Dialogue on an Island, 1972; Transl., Ring Roads, by P. Modiano, 1974; Transl., The Phoenicians, by G. Herm. Contbr. to: The Queen; Times; Times Lit. Supplement; Spectator. Mbr., Poetry Soc. Address: c/o Agent, Anthony Sheil Assocs. Ltd., 52 Floral St., London WC2 9DA, UK.

HILLIER, Jack Ronald, b. 1912, London, UK. Wood-Engraver; Book-Illustrator; Art Critic. Publs: Old Surrey Water Mills, 1951; Japanese Masters of the Colour-Print, 1954; Hokusai, 1955; Utamaro, 1961; Hokusai Drawings, 1966; The Japanese Print, A New Approach, 1960; Landscape Prints of Old Japan, 1960; Japanese Drawings, 1965; The Harari Collection of Japanese Paintings & Drawings, 1970; Japanese Paintings & Prints in the Collection of Mr. & Mrs. Richard P. Gale, 1970; The Uninhibited Brush: Japanese Art in the Shijo Style, 1974. Contbr. to Connoisseur. Address: 27 White Post Hill, Redhill, Surrey, UK.

HILLMAN, James, b. 1926, Atlantic City, N.J., USA. Psychologist; Analyst. Educ: Trinity Coll., Dublin; Univs. of Sorbonne, Zurich & Georgetown; M.A.; Ph.D. Publs: Emotion, 1960; Suicide & the Soul, 1964; Insearch, 1967; The Myth of Analysis, 1972; Revisioning Psychology, 1975; (Ed.) Studies in Jungian Thought. Contbr. to: Feelings & Emotions; Kundalini; Eranos JAhrbucher. Address: Zeltweg 16, Zurich 8032, Switz.

HILLMANN, Hermann Christian, b. 1910, Kiel, Germany. Senior Lecturer. Educ: Univ. of Kiel; Univ. of St. Andrews, UK; M.A. Publs: The World in March, 1939; Economic Issues; Lohnpolitik und Lohn technik heute; Britain-U.S.A.; A Survey in Key-Words; Die EWG auf dem Wege Zur Wirtschaftsunion. Contbr. to: Manchester Schl.; Economica; Econ. Jrnl.; World Affairs; Bankers' Mag.; Weltwirtschaftliches Archiv; Kyklos; Int. Affairs; Econ. Hist. Review; Jrnl. of Royal Statistical Soc. Address: 57 Foxhill Ct., Leeds 16, UK.

HILLS, George, b. 1918, Mexico City, Mexico. Writer; BBC Employee. Educ: B.A., King's Coll., Univ. of London, UK. Publs: Franco, the Man & His Nation, 1967, 1968, 1969; Spain, 1970, 1971; Broadcasting Beyond One's Frontiers, 1971; Monarquía, República, Franquismo, 1975; Rock of Contention: A History of Gibraltar, 1974. Contbr. to: Annual Register; The Tablet; Round Table; BBC; ABC. Address: 67 Bodley Rd., New Malden, Surrey KT3 5QJ, UK.

HILTON, John Buxton, pen name STANLEY, Warwick (for children's stories only), b. 8 June 1921, Buxton, Derbys., UK. Author. Headmaster, 1957-64; H.M. Inspector of Schools, 1964-70. Educ: M.A., Pembroke Coll., Cambridge 1946. Publs: The Language Laboratory in School, 1964; Death of an Alderman, 1968; Death in Midwinter, 1969; Language Teaching: A Systems Approach, 1974; Hangman's Tide, 1975; No Birds Sang, forthcoming. Contbr. to: Visual Educ.; Mod. Langs.; Young Elizabethan. Mbrships: Soc. of Authors; Crime-Writers' Assn. Recip., Robert Scarth Prize, 1952. Address: The White House, West Church St., Kenninghall, Norwich NR16 2EN, UK.

HILTON, Rodney Howard, b. 1916, Middleton, Manchester, UK. Professor of Medieval Social History. Educ: B.A., D.Phil.; Balliol & Merton Colls., Oxford Univ. Publs. incl: Leicestershire Estates in the 14th & 15th Centuries, 1947; A Medieval Society, 1968; Decline of Serfdom in Medieval England, 1969; Bondmen Made Free, 1973; The English Peasantry in the Later Middle Ages, 1975; (Ed.) Accounts of the Warwickshire Estates of the Duke of Clarence; Leger Book of Stoneleigh Abbey. Contbr. to: Engl., Econ., Agric. Hist. Reviews; Past & Present; Sci. & Soc.; Birmingham Hist. Jrnl.; Les Annales (Paris); Srednie Veka (Moscow); etc. Address: Dept. of Medieval History, Birmingham Univ., P.O. Box 363, Birmingham B15 2TT, UK.

HIMES, Chester (Bomar), b. 29 July 1909, Jefferson City, Mo., USA. Writer. Educ: Ohio State Univ., 1926-28. Publs. incl: (novels) If He Hollers Let Him Go, USA 1945, UK 1947; Lonely Crusade, USA 1947, UK 1950; The Third Generation, 1954; The Crazy Kill, USA 1959, UK 1968; All Shot Up, USA 1960, UK 1969; Pinktoes, France, 1961, USA & UK 1965; Cotton Comes to Harlem, USA & UK 1965; The Heat's On, USA & UK 1966; Run Man Run, USA 1966, UK 1967; Blind Man with a Pistol, USA & UK 1969; (autobiog.) The Quality of Hurt, 1972. Recip., Rosenwald Fellowship, 1944. Address: c/o William Morrow & Co., 105 Madison Ave., N.Y., NY 10016, USA.

HIMMELSTRUP, Kaj, b. 9 Jan. 1927, Skive, Denmark. Teacher; Dramatist. Educ: Teacher's Cert. Publs: Children of Tonacatecutli, 1967, Engl. ed., 1969; Du Store Kineser, 1969; Narrespil, 1970; Welcome to Dallas Mr Kennedy, Engl. ed., 1971; Lille Skole hvad nu?, 1972; Bønskrift til Dronning Margrethe, 1974. Num. TV & radio plays for adults & children; children's books, playscripts & books on education & culture. Contbr. to num. educl. mags. & newspapers. Mbrships: Danish Dramatist's Guild; Danish Author's Soc. Recip., 1st Prize, Danish Radioplay Competition. Address: Niels Lyhnes Alle 11, 2800 Lyngby, Denmark.

HIND, Tage, b. 16 July 1916, Sealand, Denmark. University Lecturer. Educ: M.A., Copenhagen Univ. Publs: Angels Without Trumpets, 1958; Dramaturgical Studies, 1962; Outside, 1967; Bertolt Brecht, 1968; Chekhov's The Seagull, 1970; Revolution/Theatre, 1972. Contbr. to:

Dramaturgi (Ed.); etc. Mbrships: Humanistic Soc.; Danish Dramatist's Guild. Address: 40 Kronprinsessegade, 1306 Copenhagen, Denmark.

HINDE, Cecilia Hamilton, b. 9 Aug. 1913, Singapore. Teacher. Publs: Corkey Books, Set 1, 1960; Floury Fingers, 1962, 2nd ed., 1969; Kim & Hickory Books, 1964; Flamingo Books; Budgie Books (w. A. E. Cannon), 1967; Corkey Books, Set 2, 1970; Robin & Jane Books, 1971; Time for Tea, 1973. Mbrships: Authors' Soc.; Book League; Comm., W. Country Writers' Assn. Address: 10 Marlborough Bldgs., Bath, Avon. UK.

HINDE, Richard Standish Elphinstone, b. 28 Apr. 1912, Dublin, Repub. of Ireland. Clerk in Holy Orders. Educ: M.A., Peterhouse, Cambridge, UK, 1938; M.A., 1939, B.Litt., 1948, St. Peter's Coll., Oxford; M.A., Trinity Coll., Dublin, 1962; Wycliffe Hall, Oxford. Publs: British Penal System, 1773-1950, 1951. Contbr. to Fed. Probation, USA. Mbrships: Royal C'wlth. Soc., London; Univ. Club, Dublin. Address: 17 St. Stephen's Green, Dublin, Repub. of Ireland.

HINDE, Thomas, pen name of CHITTY, (Sir) Thomas Willes, b. 1926, Felixstowe, Suffolk, UK. Educ: B.A., Univ. Coll., Oxford Univ. Publs: Mr. Nicholas; Happy as Larry; For the Good of the Company; A Place Like Home; The Cage; Ninety Double Martinis; The Day the Call Came; Games of Change; The Village; High; Bird; Generally a Virgin; Agent; Spain: an Anthology. Contbr. to: Spectator; Time & Tide; Times Lit. Supplement; Sunday Times. Mbrships: F.R.S.L.; Authors' Club; PEN. Agent: Jonathan Clowes. Address: Bow Cottage, W. Hoathly, Sussex, UK.

HINES, Barry Melvin, b. 30 June 1939, Hoyland Common, near Barnsley, Yorks., UK. Writer. Educ: Loughborough Coll. of Educ. Publs: The Blinder, 1966; A Kestrel for a Knave, 1968; First Signs, 1972. Hons: Best Brit. Screenplay, Writers Guild of GB, 1970; Yorks. Arts Assn. Fellowship in Creative Writing, Sheffield Univ., 1972-74. Address: 78 Hoyland Rd., Hoyland Common, Barnsley, Yorks., UK.

HINES, Dorothea, pen name de CULWEN, Dorothea, b. Bury St. Edmunds, Suffolk, UK. Cabaret Dancer. Publs: Love's Masquerade, 1966. Contbr. to women's mags. Mbrships: Royal Acad. of Dancing; Soc. of Authors; Romantic Novelists' Assn.; Brit. Actors' Equity Assn. Agent: Stephen Aske. Address: c/o Lloyds Bank, Cox & King's Branch, 6 Pall Mall, London SW1, UK.

HINKSON, Pamela. Novelist; Journalist. Publs. incl: Wind from the West, 1930; The Ladies' Road, 1932; The Deeply Rooted, 1935; Irish Gold, 1940; Indian Harvest, 1941; Golden Rose, 1944; The Lonely Bride, 1951. Contbr. to: Fortnightly; Cornhill; Spectator; New Statesman; Time & Tide; Observer; Sunday Times; Guardian; Country Life; etc. Address: c/o Lloyds Bank, 112 Kensington High St., London W8, UK.

HINSDALE, Harriet, b. 27 Jan. 1912, NYC, USA. Writer; Playwright; Motion Picture Story Editor. Publs: Beauty's A Charm, 1945; Robert Louis Stevenson, 1947; Be My Love, 1950, 2nd ed., 1974; Confederate Gray, 1963; Frank Merriwell's Father, 1964; Born to Rope, 1971; produced plays) El Rancho Grande; Worlds to Conquer; Ladies Unmasked; Springfield Couple (co-author); Swan Song (co-author). Mbrships. incl: co-fndr., Robert Louis Stevenson Calif. State Park; PEN (Dir., Sect.-Treas., Deleg. Annual Congress twice); Authors' League (Dramatists Guild); Calif. Writers' Guild; Screen Writers' Guild; Nat. Audubon Soc.; Laguna Beach Art Mus. Hons: The Harriet Hinsdale Robert Louis Stevenson Collection housed in Lib., Univ. of Okla., Norman; Harriet Hinsdale "Literary Memorabilia" housed in Lib., Univ. of Wyo., Laramie. Address: 256 Q Calle Aragon, Laguna Hills, CA 92653, USA.

HINTIKKA, Jaakko (Kaarlo Jaakko Juhani), b. 12 Jan. 1929, Halsingin pitaja, Finland. Philosopher. Educ: Cand.Phil., Lic.Phil., 1952, Dr.Phil., 1956, Univ. of Helsinki. Publs: Knowledge & Belief, 1962; Models for Modalities, 1969; Tieto on valtaa, 1969; Logic, Language-Games, & Information, 1973; Time & Necessity, 1973; Induzione, accettazione, informazione, 1974; Knowledge & the Known, 1974. Contbr. to: Int. Jrnl. Synthese (Ed.-in-Chief, 1965—); sev. philosl. jrnls. in Engl. Mbr. & Off., var. acad. orgs. Hons. incl: Fellow, Ctr. Adv. study in Behavioral Scis., 1970-71. Address: Mantypaadentie 13, 00830 Helsinki 83, Finland.

HINTON, Phyllis, b. Clifton, Bristol, UK. Writer; Journalist. Publs: Showing Your Horse; You & Your Horse; It's Fun to Have a Pony; The Picture Book for Young Riders; Show Horses & Ponies: What a Winner (w. John Nestle). Contbr. to: Horse & Hound (Ed. staff, 1944-51); Riding (Ed., 1952-62 & 1964-68); Country Life; The Lady; Farm & Country; The Chronicle; Go; etc. Mbrships: West Country Writers' Assn.; Inst. of Jrnlsts. Address: P.O. Box 30, Kyrenia, Cyprus.

HIRES, Clara S(heppard), b. 8 Apr. 1897, Merion, Pa., USA. Educ: Wellesley Coll.; B.A., Cornell Univ.; Tchrs. Coll., Columbia Univ.; Credits, sev. other colls. Publs: Spores. Ferns. Microscopic Illusions Analyzed, vol. I, 1965, vol. II, forthcoming. Contbr. to num. sci. jrnls. Address: 152 Glen Ave., Millburn, N.J., USA.

HIRSCH, Foster Lance, b. 20 Dec. 1943, NYC, USA. Author. Educ: B.A., Stanford Univ., 1965; M.L.A., 1966, M.H., 1967, Ph.D., 1971, Columbia Univ. Publs: Elizabeth Taylor, 1973; Edward G. Robinson, 1974; George Kelly, 1975; Tennessee Williams, 1975. Contbr. to: New Repub.; Nation; N.Y. Times; Chgo. Tribune; Village Voice; America; Variety; Film Quarterly; Film Heritage; Cinema; Shakespeare Quarterly. Address: 527 W. 113th St., N.Y., NY 10025, USA.

HIRSCH, S. Carl, b. 29 Nov. 1913, Chgo., Ill., USA. Writer. Publs: The Globe for the Space Age; The Living Community: A Venture into Ecology; Printing from a Stone: The Story of Lithography; Cities Are People; On Course; Navigating in Sea, Air & Space; Fourscore . . . & More: The Life Span of Man; This Is Automation; Riddle of Racism; Meter Means Measure, 1973; Famous American Indians of the Plains; Famous American Revolutionary War Heroes. Contbr. of articles to var. mags. & jrnls. for children. Hons. incl: Edison Awards, 1963, 1966; Jane Addams Award, 1972; Children's Reading Round Table Award, 1973. Address: 820—B Dodge Avenue, Evanston, IL 60202, USA.

HIRST, Gillian Jose Charlotte, pen name BAXTER, Gillian, b. 1938, Dartford, UK. Publs: Jump to the Stars, 1953; Tan & Tarmac, 1954; The Difficult Summer, 1955; Ribbons & Rings, 1956; Stables at Hampton, 1957; Horses in the Glen, 1958; The Perfect Horse; Knightsgate Players; Evans; Sweet Rock; Special Delivery; Pantomime Ponies; Ponies by the Sea, 1974. Mbr., Soc. of Authors. Agent: Rosica Colin. Address: Glebe View, 49 Chipstead Lane, Kingswood, Tadworth, Surrey, UK.

HIRST, Rodney Julian, b. 1920, Sheffield, UK. University Professor of Logic. Educ: M.A., Univ. of Oxford. Publs: The Problems of Perception; Human Senses & Perception (co-author); Ed., Perception & the External World; Philosophy: An Outline for the Intending Student. Contbr. to: Mind; Proceedings of the Aristotelian Soc.; Philos. Quarterly; Ency. of Philos. Address: 179 Maxwell Dr., Glasgow, G41 5AE, UK.

HITCHCOCK, Donald R., b. 31 Oct. 1930, Baltimore, Md., USA. Head of Russian Section, Department of Germanic & Slavic Languages & Literatures, University of Maryland. Educ: B.A., University of Maryland, 1952; M.A., 1954, Ph.D., 1965, Harvard. Publs: Reading the Russian Text of 'The Memoirs of a Madman' of N. V. Gogol, 1974; Ed., Zapiski sumasshedshego, by N. V. Gogol, 1974; The Appeal of Adam in Hell to Lazarus (in press). Mbrships: AAUP; Medieval Acad. of Am.; MLA; Harvard Club of Wash. Address: 3320 Toledo Place, Apt. P-4, Hyattsville, MD 20782, USA.

HITCHCOCK, Raymond John, b. 9 Feb. 1922, Calcutta, India. Author. Educ: M.A., Emmanuel Coll., Cambridge. Publs: Percy, 1969; Gilt-Edged Boy, 1971; Venus 13, 1973. Address: Abbots Worthy Mill, Winchester, Hants., UK.

HITCHMAN, Janet, b. 5 July 1916, Oulton Broad, Norfolk, UK. Writer; Broadcaster. Publs: The King of the Barbareens (autobiog.), 1960, 5th ed., 1974; They Carried the Sword (the Barnardo Story), 1966; Meeting for Burial (novel), 1968; Such a Strange Lady (biog.), 1975. Contbr. to: Observer; Times; Guardian; New Statesman; Punch; Good Housekeeping; Countryman; BBC; ITV. Mbrships: Soc. of Authors. Address: Putnams, Badwell Ash, Bury St. Edmunds, Suffolk, UK.

HIVNOR, Robert H., pen names ASKEW, Jack; PISMIRE, Osbert, b. 19 May 1916, Zanesville, Ohio, USA.

Playwright. Educ: A.B., Akron Univ.; M.F.A., Yale Univ. Publs. incl: (plays) Too Many Thumbs, 1949; The Ticklish Acrobat (comedy), 1956; The Assault upon Charles Sumner, 1966. Contbr. to: Breakout (ed., Scheville), 1973; Partisan Review; Place; New Directions Annual. Mbr., Dramatists Guild. Hons. incl: Rockefeller Grant for novel in progress. Address: 420 E. 84th St., N.Y., NY 10028, USA.

HOAGLAND, Edward, b. 21 Dec. 1932, NYC, USA. Writer; Part-time Teacher. Educ: A.B., Harvard Univ., 1954. Publs: (novels) Cat Man, 1956; The Circle Home, 1960; The Peacock's Tail, 1965; (autobiog.) Notes from the Century Before, 1969; (essays) The Courage of Turtles, 1971. Contbr. to: Noble Savage; Esquire; New Am. Review, 2 & 5; Paris Review; Transatlantic Review; New Yorker. Hons: Houghton Mifflin Lit. Fellowship, 1956; Longview Fndn. Award, 1961; Guggenheim Fellowship, 1964; Travelling Fellowship, Am. Acad. Arts & Letters, 1964; O. Henry Award, 1971. Address: 31 Jane St., N.Y., NY 10014, USA.

HOARE, Ken, b. 1929, Torquay, Devon, UK. Television Writer. Publs: (for TV) The Cage (play), 1958; Beggar My Neighbour (comedy, w. M. Sharland), 3 series, 1967-69; Mr. Digby Darling, 3 series, 1969-71; His & Hers, 2 series, 1970-71; Turnbull's Finest Half-Hour, 1972; Weren't You Marcia Honeywell? (situation comedy), 1972; The Stanley Baxter Big Picture Show (TV Special), 1973; The Stanley Baxter Moving Picture Show, 1974. Contbr. to: The Writer; Contrast; Monthly Film Bulletin. Mbrships: A.L.A.; Writers' Guild of GB. Recip., S.F.T.A. Award, Best Light Entertainment Prog. of 1973, for The Stanley Baxter Big Picture Show. Agent: Kavanagh Entertainments Ltd. Address: Silver Springs, Beazley End, Braintree, Essex, UK.

HOARE, Merval Hannah, maiden name (for publs. dating 1951 and before) CONNELLY, b. 17 June 1914, Wellington, NZ. Author. Publs: Twelve Poems, 1943; Twenty-eight Poems, 1951; Norfolk Island Poems, 1951; Rambler's Guide to Norfolk Island, 1965, 5th ed., 1974; Norfolk Island — An Outline of its History, 1774-1968, 1969; The Discovery of Norfolk Island, 1974. Mbrships: Aust. Soc. of Authors; Norfolk Is. Histl. Soc. Address: New Cascade Rd., Norfolk Is., S. Pacific.

HOARE, Robert John, b. 1921, Manchester, UK. Tutor; Librarian. Educ: Alsager Trng. Coll.; Reading Univ. Publs. incl: Understanding Through Interest, Books 1—4; Our Saints, 1—8; Write Away! Stages 1—4; The Story of Aircraft; The Old West; Messages; Words in Action, Books 1—4; Cowboys & Cattle Trails; True Mysteries; More True Mysteries; Men of the Old West; Saints; Sporting Giants; At the Bottom of the Deep Blue Sea; World War One; World War Two. Contbr. to: Tchr.; Tchrs. World; Times Educl. Supplement; etc. Mbrships: Soc. of Authors; Simmarian A.C.; Chief Sprint Coach, Berks. Amateur Athletic Assn. Address: "Karina", Wells Lane, Ascot, Berks., UK.

HOBANA, Ion, b. 25 Jan. 1931, Sînnicolaul Mare, Romania. Writer. Educ: Grad. Philology, Univ. Bucharest. Publs. incl: (fiction) The End of the Holidays, 1960, 2nd ed., 1969; (sci. fiction) The Last Veil, 1957; Men & Stars, 1963; (non-fiction) The Future Started Yesterday, 1966; Images of the Possible, 1968; Scientific Essays (w. Julian Weverbergh), 1971; (anthols.) The Golden Age of Romanian Anticipation, 1969; Fantascienza (w. Gianfranco de Turris), 1973; (stage adaptation H. G. Wells novel) The Invisible Man, Contbr. to: România Literară; Tribuna; etc. Mbr., Union Romanian Writers. Hons. incl: Romanian Writers' Union Prize, 1969 & Special Europe Award, Trieste, 1972 for The Golden Age of Romanian Anticipation. Address: Bd. Nicolae Bălcescu 24, sc.A, et 4, apt. 1, Bucharest, Romania.

HOBBS, Cecil, pen name MAUNG HAUK, b. 22 Apr. 1907, Martins Ferry, Ohio, USA. Southeast Asia Area Studies Specialist; Writer. Educ: B.A., Univ. of Ill., 1929; B.D., 1933, Th.M., 1942, Colgate-Rochester Divinity Schl. Publs: var. monographs inclng: The Burmese Family: An Inquiry into its History, Customs & Traditions, 1952; Understanding the Peoples of Southern Asia, 1967; Southeast Asia Field Trip for the Library of Congress, 1970--1071, 1972. Contbr. to var. histl. jrnls. Mbr., Bibliographical Soc. of Philippines. Hons: Lib. of Congress Awards for Meritorious Serv., 1967, for Superior Serv., 1971. Address: "Hobbs Knob", 5100 Backlick Rd., Annandale, VA 22003, USA.

HOBBS, John Sanders, b. 26 Aug. 1913, S. Molton, UK. Retired Schoolmaster. Educ: M.A., & Dip. in Anthropol., Univ. of Cambridge. Publs: General School Geography, 9

vols. Address: Cathay, 3 Stepstone Lane, Knowle, Braunton, Devon EX33 2NB, UK.

HOBBY, Bertram Maurice, b. 1905, Southampton, UK. Emeritus Fellow, Wolfson College, Oxford; Former Lecturer in Entomology. Educ: M.A., D.Phil., Queen's Coll., Oxford. Publs: Ed., Zoology of Oxford in Victoria County History of Oxfordshire, vol. 1. Contbr. to: Entomol. Monthly Mag.; Transactions & Jrnl., Soc. of Brit. Entomol.; Proceedings, Royal Entomol. Soc. of London. Mbrships: Fellow, Linnean Soc.; Fellow, Royal Entomol. Soc. of London (VP, 1948); Pres., Soc. for Brit. Entomol., 1937; Entomol. Club. Address: 7 Thorncliffe Rd., Oxford OX2 7BA, UK.

HOBHOUSE, Hermione, b. 1934, Hadspen, Somerset, UK. Tutor in Architectural History. Educ: B.A., Lady Margaret Hall, Oxford. Publs: History of the Ward of Cheap, 1963; Thomas Cubitt: Master Builder, 1971; Lost London: A Century of Demolition & Decay, 1971; History of Regent Street, forthcoming. Contbr. to: Archtl. Design; Country Life. Address: c/o Macmillan Ltd., Little Essex St., London WC2, UK.

HOBSBAUM, Philip, b. 1932, London, UK. University Lecturer in English. Educ: M.A., Downing Coll. Cambridge; Ph.D., Univ. of Sheffield; L.R.A.M.; L.G.S.M. Publs: (Ed. w. E. Lucie-Smith) a Group Anthology, 1963; The Place's Fault & Other Poems, 1964; In Retreat & Other Poems, 1966; Coming Out Fighting: Poems, 1969; A Theory of Communication, 1970; (Ed.) Ten Elizabethan Poets, 1969; A Reader's Guide to Charles Dickens, 1970. Address: Dept. of Engl., The University, Glasgow W2, UK.

HOBSBAWM, E., pen name NEWTON, Francis, b. 1917, Alexandria, Egypt. University Professor of Economic & Social History. Educ: M.A., Ph.D., Univ. of Cambridge, UK. Publs: Ed., Labour's Turning Point, 1800-1900; Primitive Rebels; The Jazz Scene; The Age of Revolution 1789-1848; Labouring Men; Bandits; Revolutionaries; Industry & Empire; Captain Swing (w. G. Rudé). Contbr. to histl. & other jrnls. Address: Birkbeck Coll., London WC1, UK.

HOBSON, Harry (Hank), pen name JANSON, Hank, b. 1907, Sheffield, UK. Author. Publs: The Gallant Affair; Death Makes a Claim; The Big Twist; Mission House Murder; Beyond Tolerance; Drop Dead; 65 other titles under pen name Hank Janson. Address: 8 Eastmearn Road, West Dulwich, London SE21, UK.

HOBSON, Katherine Thayer, b. 11 Apr. 1889, Denver, Colo., USA. Sculptor; Poet. Educ: Univs. of Leipzig, Koenigsberg & Göttingen. Contbr. to: The Craftsman Treasure of Women Poets of N.Y.; Who's Who in Poetry Anthol.; Diamond Anthol., Poetry Soc. of Am.; Anthol. of Cath. Poetry Soc. of Am.; N.Y. Times; N.Y. Herald Tribune; Poetry Digest; Am. Weave; The Churchman Hippocrene; Westminster Mag.; Step Ladder; Voices; The Tablet. Mbrships: Sec., Fine Arts Fedn., N.Y., 1952-69 Chmn., Sculpture Sect., Pen & Brush; Co-Chmn., Poetry Sect.; Poetry Soc. of Am.; Cath. Poetry Soc. of Am. Address: 27 West 67th St., N.Y., NY 10023, USA.

HOBSON, Laura Keen Zametkin, b. NYC, USA. Journalist. Educ: B.A., Cornell Univ. Publs: (for children) A Dog of His Own, 1941; (other publs.) The Trespassers, 1943; Gentleman's Agreement, 1947; The Other Father, 1950; The Celebrity, 1951; First Papers, 1964; "I'm Going to Have a Baby", 1967. Mbrships: Authors' League of Am. (Nat. Coun. Mbr.); PEN. Address: c/o Simon & Schuster, 630 Fifth Avenue, N.Y., NY 10020, USA.

HOCHHEIMER, Albert, pen name JURAT, Bert, b. 5 May 1900, Steinheim, Westphalia, Germany. Writer. Educ: Cologne Univ. Publs: Geschichte der grossen Ströme, 1954; Die Passagiere der Penelope, 1970; Abschied von den Kolonien, 1972; 20 other books for young people; 14 Radio dramas. Contbr. to: Der Bund; Die Tat (both Swiss newspapers). Mbr., PEN. Address: Via Selva Grande 4, 6942 Crocifisso-Savosa, Switz.

HOCHHUTH, Rolf, b. 1 Apr. 1931, Eschwege, Germany. Writer. Publs: (plays) Der Stellvertreter, 1963; Soldaten, 1967; Guerillas, 1970; Die Hebamme, 1972; Lysistrate und die Nato, 1974; (stories) Die Berliner Antigone, 1961; Zwischenspiel in Baden-Baden, 1974; Krieg und Klassenkrieg (essays), 1971. Recip., Berlin Art Prize, 1963. Address: 4002 Basle, Postfach 661, Switz.

HOCHWÄLDER, Fritz, b. 28 May 1911, Vienna, Austria. Playwright. Publs: (plays) Esther, 1940; Das heilige Experiment, 1942; Hôtel du Commerce, 1944; Der Fluchtling, 1945; Donadieu, 1953; Die Herberge, 1956; Der Unschuldige, 1958; Donnerstag, 1959; 1003, 1963; Der Himbeerpflücker, 1964; Der Befehl, 1968; Lazaretti, 1974. Hons: Lit. Prize, City of Vienna, 1955; Grillparzer Prize, Austrian Acad. of Sci., 1956; Anton Wildgans Prize, 1963; Austrian State Prize for Lit., 1966; Ehrenkreuz für Vissenschaft & Kunst, 1971; Ehrenring der Stadt Wien, 1972. Address: Am. Oeschbrig 27, 8053 Zurich, Switz.

HOCKE, Gustav René, b. 1 Mar. 1908, Brussels, Belgium. Author; Editor; Publisher; Newspaper Correspondent. Educ: Ph.D. Publs. incl: Das geistige Paris, 1937; Der tanzende Gott, 1948; Die Welt als Labyrinth, 1957, 4th ed., 1973; Manierismus in der Literatur, 1959, 4th ed., 1973; Der Mensch in Sein und Zeit, 1969; Leherb, Le Monde d'un Surrealiste, 1973; Verzweiflung und Zuversicht, 1974; Neomanierismus, 1975; Im Schatten der Leviathan: Lebenserinnerungen, 1975. Contbr. of over 10,000 articles on the arts to int. jrnls. & newspapers. Mbrships. incl: PEN; Deutsche Akad. für Sprache und Dichtung, Darmstadt. Hons. incl: Int. Lit. Award, Rome, 1956; 1st prize, German Kulturkreis, 1959; Commendatore & Grand Ufficiale of Italy, 1969. Address: 00045 Genzano di Roma, Via Monte Giove, Italy.

HOCKEY, Lawrence William, b. 12 June 1904, Newport, Gwent, UK. Schoolmaster, ret'd. Educ: B.A., Univ. Coll. of S. Wales & Monmouthshire, 1928; M.A., Univ. of Wales, 1956. Publs: The Undying Glory & Other Poems, 1939; Monmouthshire Poetry, 1949; W. H. Davies (biog.), 1971; more than 300 poems; articles on poets & poetry. Contbr. to: Anglo-Welsh Review; S. Wales Argus; Poetry of Today; New Schlmaster; Fiction Parade, USA; etc. Mbrships: Hon. Soc. of Cymmrodorion; Comm., Gwent Poetry Soc. (Fndr.-mbr.); Nat. Assn. of Schlmasters. Recip., 1st Prize, Engl. Lyric, Eisteddfod, Univ. of Wales, 1928. Address: 54 Beechwood Rd., Newport, Gwent NPT 8AH, UK.

HOCKING, Mary, b. 8 Apr. 1921, London, UK. Novelist. Publs: The Winter City, 1961; Visitors to the Crescent, 1962; The Sparrow, 1964; The Young Spaniard, 1965; Ask No Question, 1967; A Time of War, 1968; Checkmate, 1969; The Hopeful Traveller, 1970; The Climbing Frame, 1971; Family Circle, 1972; Daniel Come to Judgement, 1974. Mbrships: Writers' Guild of GB; Soc. of Authors. Address: 3 Church Row, Lewes, Sussex, UK.

HODELL, Åke, b. 30 Apr. 1919, Stockholm, Sweden. Author; Director, Kerberos Avant-garde Publishers. Publs. incl: Flyende Pilot, 1953; Ikaros Död, 1962; Igevär, 1963; SSVVVIIISSSCCCHHH (anthol. w. concrete, visual & sound poetry), 1964; General Bussig, 1964; Bruksanvisning för Symaskinen Singer Victoria, 1965; Orderbuch, 1965; Flat-Hatting (Lågsniff), 1966; Verner von Heidenstam, 1967; U.S.S. Pacific Ocean, a Story about the World Police, 1968; Mr. Nixon's Dreams, 1970; 13 stage plays, films, & radio & TV features, 1963-74; 11 electronic music-drama text-sound-compositions, 1967-73. Contbr. to: 4 int. anthols; 12 int. art exhibs. of concrete & other experimental poetry, 1965-72. Address: Falkenbergsgatan 5 C, III, 115 21 Stockholm, Sweden.

HODGE, Alan, b. 1915, Scarborough, Yorks., UK. Journalist; Historian; Researcher. Educ: B.A., Oriel Coll., Oxford Univ. Publs: The Long Week End (w. Robert Graves), 1940; Work in Hand (co-author), 1942; The Reader Over Your Shoulder, 1943; The Past We Share (w. Peter Quennell), 1960; Ed., The Novel Library, 1946-52; Jt. Ed., History Today, 1951–. Contbr. to: Fin. Times (Ed. writer 1946–). Address: 6 Lancaster Rd., Wimbledon, London SW19, UK.

HODGE, James Hozier, b. 1906, Edinburgh, UK. Former Company Chairman. Educ: Edinburgh Acad. Publs: (Gen. Ed.) Notable British Trials Series; War Crimes Trials Series; Ed., Famous Trials, vols. 3, 4, 5, 6 & 7. Mbr., RAF Club. Address: 3 Allermuir Rd., Edinburgh EH13 0HE, UK.

HODGE, Jane Aiken, b. 4 Dec. 1917, Boston, Mass., USA. Author. Educ: B.A., Somerville Coll., Oxford, UK; A.M., Harvard Univ., USA. Publs: Maulever Hall, 1964; The Adventurer, 1965; Watch the Wall, My Darling, 1966; Here Comes a Candle, 1967; The Winding Stair, 1968; Marry in Haste, 1969; Greek Wedding, 1970; Savannah Purchase, 1971; The Double Life of Jane Austen, 1972; Strangers in Company, 1973; Shadow of a Lady, 1974; One Way to

Venice, 1975; Rebel Heiress, 1975. Contbr. to: Hist. Today. Mbrships: Soc. of Authors; Writers' Action Grp. Agent: Bolt & Watson. Address: 23 Eastport Lane, Lewes, Sussex BN7 1TL, UK.

HODGES, Doris Marjorie, pen name HUNT, Charlotte, b. 28 Apr. 1915, Bristol, UK. Librarian; Author; Lecturer. Publs: Gemini Revenged, 1972; Gilded Sarcophagus, 1967; Cup of Thanatos, 1968; Lotus Vellum, 1970; 13th Treasure, 1972; A Touch of Myrrh, 1974; Tremayne's Wife, 1974; Chambered Tomb, 1975; A Wreath for Jenny's Grave, 1975. Contbr. to: Argosy; London Mystery Mag.; Western Daily Press; var. occult jrnls. Mbrships: Soc. of Authors; Soc. of Women Jrnlsts.; Continuative Teachers' Assn.; Crime Club. Address: 5 St. Andrew's Rd., Backwell, Bristol, UK.

HODGES, Henry W. M., b. 19 July 1920, Deddington, Oxon., UK. University Professor. Educ: St. John's Coll., Cambridge; Univ. of London. Publs: Artifacts, 1964; Technology in the Ancient World, 1970; Pottery, 1970. Contbr. to: Studies in Conserv.; Many archaeol. jrnls. Mbrships: Fellow, Int. Inst. for Conserv. of Historic & Artistic Works; Treas., 1971-74. Address: Art Conservation Programme, The Queen's University at Kingston, Kingston, Ont., Can.

HODGKIN, Robert (Robin) Allason, b. 12 Feb. 1916, Banbury, Oxon., UK. Teacher. Educ: Queen's Coll., Oxford Univ. Publs: Sudan Geography, 1951; Education & Change, 1957; Reconnaissance on an Educational Frontier, 1970. Contbr. to: Guardian; New Statesman. Mbr., Alpine Club (VP). Address: 7 Farndon Rd., Oxford, UK.

HODGKISS, Alan Geoffrey, b. 19 June 1921, Newton-le-Willows, UK. Cartographer. Publs: Maps for Books & Theses, 1970; Discovering Antique Maps, 1971; Ed. (w. J. A. Patmore), Merseyside in Maps, 1970; Contbng. Ed., Can. Cartographer. Mbrships: Comm., Soc. of Univ. Cartographers, Bulletin Ed., 1964-73; Brit. Cartographic Soc. Address: 25 Burnham Rd., Allerton, Liverpool L18 6JU, UK.

HODGSON, Peter Crafts, b. 26 Feb. 1934, Oak Park, Ill., USA. Professor of Theology. Educ: A.B., Princeton Univ., 1956; B.D., 1959; M.A., 1960, Ph.D., 1963, Yale Univ. Publs: The Formation of Historical Theology, 1966; Ferdinand Christian Baur On the Writing of Church History (ed. & transl.), 1968; Jesus — Word & Presence: An Essay in Christology, 1971; D. F. Strauss, The Life of Jesus Critically Examined (ed.), 1972-73; Children of Freedom: Black Liberation in Christian Perspective, 1974. Contbr. to relig. & philos. jrnls. Mbr., var. relig. socs. Recip., num. acad. hons. Address: 71 Brookwood Terr., Nashville, TN 37205, USA.

HODIN, Joseph Paul, b. 17 Aug. 1905, Prague, Czechoslovakia. Author; Art Critic. Educ: Charles Univ., Prague; London Univ., UK; var. Art Acads., Germany; LL.D. Publs. incl: Art & Criticism, 1944; The Dilemma of Being Modern, UK 1956, USA 1959; Henry Moore, Netherlands & Germany 1956, UK & USA 1958; Barbara Hepworth, 1961; Kokoschka, 1966; Bernard Leach, 1970; Edvard Munch, the Genius of the North, 1972; Modern Art & the Modern Mind, 1972; Bernard Stern, 1972; Manessier, 1972; Ludwig Meidner, 1973; Hilde Goldschmidt, 1974; Paul Berger-Bergner, 1974; Kokoschka & Hellas, 1975. Contbr. to: Quadrum, Brussels (UK Ed. 1956-66); Jrnl. Aesthetics & Art Criticism, USA; & others. Mbrships: incl: Int. Assn. Art Critics (Pres. Brit. Sect. 1974–). Hons. incl: 1st Prize for Art Criticism, Venice Biennale, 1954; Ph.D., Uppsala Univ., Sweden, 1969; num. European orders. Address: 12 Eton Ave., London NW3 3EH, UK.

HODSON, Henry Vincent, b. 12 May 1906, Hornsey, Middx., UK. Editor; Consultant; Author. Educ: M.A., Balliol Coll., Oxford; Fellow, All Souls Coll., Oxford, 1928-35. Publs: Economics of a Changing World, 1933; Slump & Recovery, 1929-37, 1938; Twentieth Century Empire, 1948; The Great Divide: Britain-India-Pakistan, 1969; The Diseconomics of Growth, 1972; Ed., The Annual Register of World Events, 1973–. Contbr. to: Times; Sunday Times; Sydney Morning Herald; etc. Mbrships. incl: Fellow, Inst. of Jrnlsts.; Soc. of Authors. Address: 23 Cadogan Lane, London SW1X 9DP, UK.

HOEBEL, Edward John Adamson, b. 16 Nov. 1906, Madison, Wis., USA. Anthropologist. Educ: B.A., Univ. of Wis., 1928; Univ. of Cologne, Germany, 1929; M.A., N.Y. Univ., 1930; Ph.D., Columbia Univ., 1934; Post-doctoral study, Univ. of Calif. Pubis. incl: The Cheyenne Way: Conflict & Case Law in Primitive Jurisprudence (w. K. N. Llewellyn), 1941; Anthropology: The Study of Man, 1949, 4th ed., 1972; The Comanches: Lords of the South Plains, (w. e. Wallace), 1953; The Law of Primitive Man: A Case Study in Legal Dynamics, 1954; The Cheyennes: Indians of the Great Plains, 1961. Contbr. to profl. law jrnls. Address: 2273 Folwell St., St. Paul, MN 55108, USA.

HOEFLING, Susan Joan (Brantweiner), b. 10 Nov. 1909, Cleveland, Ohio, USA. Poet. Educ: HLD, LPN. Pubis: For You — Dreamweaver Poems, 1949; For You — Melody of Life, 1962; For You — Along the Avenue, 1968. Contbr. to num. jrnls. & newspapers; also Radio & TV. Mbr., var. socs. Recip., num. awards. Address: RD 2 Mercer Road, Beaver Falls, PA, USA.

HOEKEMA, Anthony A., b. 1913, Drachten, Netherlands. Pastor; Professor of Systematic Theology. Educ: Calvin Coll., Univ. of Mich.; Calvin Theol. Sem.; Princeton Theol. Sem.; A.B., A.M., Th.B., Th.D. Pubis: The Four Major Cults, USA 1963, UK 1964; What About Tongue-Speaking? , USA 1966, UK & Netherlands 1969; Holy Spirit Baptism, USA & UK 1972; The Christian Looks at Himself, 1975. Contbr. to: Christianity Today; Calvin Theol. Jrnl.; Reformed Jrnl. Mbr., Evangelical Theol. Soc. Address: 1887 Woodcliff, S.E., Grand Rapids, MI 49506, USA.

HOFDORP, Pim (William), b. 1912, The Hague, Netherlands. Freelance Journalist; Author; Public Relations Adviser; Publicist. Educ: Commercial Univ., Rotterdam. Pubis: 15 Topographical Police Novels, all situated in The Hague (first Dutch author in this genre), 1959—; num. reprints. Agent: Mrs. J. Kempees, The Hague. Address: 12 Anthonie Heinsiusstraat, The Hague, Netherlands.

HOFF, Ursula, b. 1909, London, UK. Museum Administrator. Educ: Univs. of Frankfurt, Cologne, Munich, Hamburg & London; Dr. Phil. Pubis. incl: Charles I, Patron of the Arts, 1941; Charles Conder, His Australian Years, 1960; European Paintings before Eighteen Hundred, 1961, revised ed., 1967; Charles Conder, 1972; European Painting & Sculpture before 1800, 1973. Contbr. to: Galleries (World of Art Lib.), 1973; Apollo; Burlington Mag.; Old Master Drawing; etc. Mbrships. incl: Coun., Nat. Lib. of Aust.; Coun. Nat. Gall. of Vic.; Fellow, Aust. Acad. of the Humanities & Brit. Mus. Assn. Address: 97 Leopold St., S. Yarra, Melbourne, Australia.

HOFFMAN, Phoebe W., b. 3 Feb. 1894. Freelance Copy Editor. Educ: Columbia Univ., 1932-36. Pubis: Ebb Tide, 1972; Flame of Love, 1973. Contbr. to (anthols.): Cats in Verse, 1935; P.S.A. Golden Years Anthol., 1960; Poetry Soc. Selected Poems, 1966, 1967 & 1968; (jrnls.): Contemp. Verse, Saturday Review; N.Y. Times; Am. Poet; Am. Bard; Am. Poetry League Bull; etc. Mbrships. incl: Poetry Soc. of Am.. Hons. incl: Poet Laureate, Monterey Peninsula, Calif., 1970; Carl Sandberg Award, 1973; 1st Prize, Free Verse, Calif. Fed. Chaparral Poets' Contest, 1974. Address: 651 Sinex Ave., A-118 Pacific Grove, CA 93950, USA.

HOFFMAN, Wilhelmus Adrianus Franciscus Xaverius, pen name (for children's books) HOOGLAND, Marianne, b. 8 Apr. 1908, Gouda, Netherlands. Author; Playwright. Pubis: Haastig recht, 1937; Willibrord een held Gods, 1939; De Rebel, 1953; Anneke van het Lijsterhof, 1953; Eksters rond het erf, 1953; De weg naar Emmaüs, 1957; Noord- en Zuidnederlandse Sagen en Legenden, 1974. Contbr. to: De Volkskrant; De Goudsche Courant; Opwenteling; Brabantia. Mbrships: Soc. of Lit., Amsterdam; Royal S. Netherlands Assn. for Lit. Hist., Brussels. Address: Prins Mauritslaan 3 te, Vught, N.Br., Netherlands.

HOFFMANN, Donald, pen name ALLURED, Lloyd, b. 24 June 1933, Springfield, Ill., USA. Art Critic. Pubis: The Meanings of Architecture: Buildings & Writings by John Wellborn Root, 1973. Contbr. to jrnls.: Art Critic, Kansas City Star newspaper. Mbrships: Past Mbr., Bd. of Dirs., Soc. of Archtl. Historians; Soc. of Archtl. Historians of GB. Address: 6441 Holmes, Kansas City, MO 64131, USA.

HOFLING, Charles Kreimer, b. 22 Apr. 1920, Cinn., Ohio, USA. Psychiatrist; Medical Educator. Educ: B.A., 1942, M.D., 1946, Univ. of Cinn., Ohio. Pubis: Basic Psychiatric Concepts in Nursing (w. Madeleine Leininger, Ph.D.), 1961, 3rd ed., 1974; Textbook of Psychiatry for Medical Practice, 1963, 3rd ed., 1975; Memos to Maury (w.

Paul Ornstein, M.D.), 1968. Contbr. to: Progress in Neurol. & Psych., 1966-72; Archives of Gen. Psych.; Brit. Jrnl. of Med. Psychol.; Am. Jrnl. of Surg.; etc. Mbrships: Fellow, Am. Coll. of Psychs., Am. Psych. Assn.; Dipl., Pan-Am. Med. Assn.; Am. Psychosomatic Soc. Address: 45 Westmoreland Pl., St. Louis, MO 63108, USA.

HOFMAN, David, b. 1908, Poona, India. Member Universal House of Justice (Supreme Body Baha'i Faith) Pubis: The Renewal of Civilization, 1946; A Commentary on the Will & Testament of Abdu-l Baha, 1946; God & His Messengers, 1953. Contbr. to World Order Mag. Address: P.O. Box 155, Haifa, Israel.

HOFMO, Gunvor, b. 30 June 1921, Oslo, Norway. Author. Pubis: From Another Reality, 1948; Collected Poems, 1968; Guest on Earth, 1971. Mbr., Norwegian Authors Assn. Hons: Lit. Critic Prize, for Guest on Earth, Norwegian Lit. Critic Assn., 1972. Address: Enoks V.9, Lille Ekeberg, Norway.

HOFSTRA, Jan Willem, b. 13 Nov. 1907, Amsterdam, Netherlands. Music, Theatre, Ballet & Literary Critic. Pubis. incl: 5 novels & 1 book of poetry. Contbr. to: Elsevier's Mag.; De Tyd; Concertgebouw Preludium; Margriet, Elegance; Opera Mag.; TV Guide K.R.O.; etc. Mbrships: Govt. Coun. for Arts; Bd. Netherlands Theatre Ctr.; Theatre Schl. for Amateurs; S.E.B.A.; Theatre Dept. Conf. Dutch Lit. (Pres.); Bd. Govt. Fndn. for Lit. Hons: Kt, Order Oranje Nassau, 1972; Netherlands Soc. of Stage, TV, Radio Authors (Hon. Pres.). Dutch TV Advsr. Address: Prinsengracht 133, Amsterdam C, Netherlands.

HOGAN, Robert Goode, b. 29 May 1930, Booneville, Mo., USA. Professor of English; Author; Publisher, Proscenium Press. Educ: B.A., Univ. of Mo., 1953, M.A., 1954, Ph.D., 1956. Pubis: The Experiments of Sean O'Casey, 1960; The Independence of Elmer Rice, 1965, Betty & the Beast (play), 1967; After the Irish Renaissance, 1968; Dion Boucicault, 1968; The Fan Club (play), 1969; Eimar O'Duffy, 1972; Mervyn Wall, 1972; The Modern Irish Drama, 2 vols. (w. James Kilroy), 1974. Contbr. to: Jrnl. of Irish Lit. (Ed.). Recip., Guggenheim Fellowship for Playwriting, 1961-62. Address: Proscenium Press, P.O. Box 361, Newark, DE 19711, USA.

HOGARTH, Grace W. Allen, pen name of Mrs. Philip L Sayles, b. 5 Nov. 1905, Newton, Mass., USA. Retired Publisher; Writer. Educ: A.B., Vassar Coll., Poughkeepsie, N.Y., 1927. Pubis: A Bible ABC, 1940; This to be Love, 1949; Lucy's League, 1950; The End of Summer, 1951, John's Journey, 1952; Children of this World, 1953; The Funny Guy, 1955; As a May Morning, 1958. Contbr. to mags. concerned with children's books. Mbr., & Past Chmn., Children's Book Circle, London, UK. Address: P.O Box 23, South Freeport, ME 04078, USA.

HOGBIN, (Herbert) Ian Priestley, b. 17 Dec. 1904, Bawtry, Yorks., UK. Anthropologist. Educ: M.A., Univ. of Sydney; Ph.D., Univ. of London. Pubis: Law & Order in Polynesia, 1934, 2nd ed., 1961; Experiments in Civilization, 1958, 2nd ed., 1971; Transformation Scene, 1951; Social Change, 1958, 2nd ed., 1971; Kinship & Marriage in a New Guinea Village, 1963; A Guadalcanal Society, 1964; Studies in New Guinea Land Tenure (w. P. Lawrence), 1967; Island of Menstruating Men, 1970; Ency. of Papua New Guinea (ed., anthrop. entries), 1972; Anthropology in Papua New Guinea, 1973. Contbr. to profl. jrnls. Recip., var. acad. hons. Address: 45/204 Jersey Rd., Woollahra, Australia 2025.

HOGG, Garry (Lester), b. 5 Jan. 1902, London, UK. Writer; Lecturer. Educ: M.A., 1924; Wadham Coll., Oxford, 1924; Hon. Schl. Engl. Lang. & Lit. Pubis: Guide to English Country Houses; Castles of England; Priories & Abbeys of England; Custome & Traditions of England; Aspects of England; Facets of England; The Best of England; Museums of England; Market Towns of England; London in Colour; Cotswolds in Colour; Pageantry of Britain; The English Country Inn; Malta; Blue-Water Island; Corsica: The Fragrant Isle; The SHELL Guide to Exploring Britain; The SHELL Book of Viewpoints in England. Contbr. to: Guardian; Countryman; Country Life; etc. Address: The Coach House, Leyswood, Groombridge, Sussex, UK.

HOGG, (Brigadier) Oliver Frederick Gillilan, b. 22 Dec. 1887, Bedford, UK. Officer, Royal Artillery (Retired). Educ: Royal Mil. Acad., Woolwich; Artillery Coll. Pubis: The History of the 3rd Durham Volunteer Artillery 1860-1960, 1960; English Artillery 1326-1716, 1963; The

Royal Arsenal, 2 vols., 1963; Further Light on the Ancestry of William Penn, 1965; Clubs to Cannon, 1968; Artillery: Its Origin, Heyday & Decline, 1970; The Woolwich Mess, 2nd ed., 1971. Contbr. to: Chambers's Ency.; var. Army jrnls. Mbrships. incl: F.S.A.; Fellow, Royal Histl. Soc.; F.R.G.S.; F.R.S.A.; Fellow, Soc. Genealogists (exec. comm. 1959-62); R.A. Hist. Soc.; Soc. Army Histl. Rsch. Hons. incl: C.B.E., 1943; Leverhulme Rsch. Fellowship 1950-51. Address: 1 Hardy Rd., Blackheath, London SE3 7NS, UK.

HOGG, W(illiam) Richey, b. 3 June 1921, Vandergrift, Pa., USA. Professor of Theology; Methodist Minister. Educ: B.A., Duke Univ., 1943; B.D., 1946, Ph.D., 1951, Yale Univ. Publs: Tomorrow is Here (w. K. S. Latourette), 1948; Ecumenical Foundations, 1952, German transl. 1954; New Day Dawning, 1957; One World — One Mission, 1960, Spanish transl. 1961. Contbr. to: The History of American Methodism, 3 vols., 1964 (Mbr., Ed. Bd.); Religion in Life; Int. Review of Mission; var. relig. books & dictionaries. Hons. incl: var. Lectureships. Address: 3617 Haynie Ave., Dallas, TX 75205, USA.

HOGGART, Richard, b. 24 Sept. 1918, Leeds, Yorks., UK. International Civil Servant; Author. Educ: B.A., 1939, M.A., 1940, Leeds Univ. Publs: Auden, 1951; The Uses of Literacy, 1957; W. H. Auden — A Selection, 1961; Teaching Literature, 1963; Speaking to Each Other, vols. I & II, 1970; Only Connect (Reith Lectures for 1971), 1972. Contbr. to: Essays in Criticism; Int. Ency. of the Social Scis.; Daedelus; Ed. Bd., Univs. Quarterly; etc. Mbr., British Books Overseas Comm., British Coun., 1959-64. Hons: D.Litt., Open Univ., 1973, Bordeaux, 1975. Address: UNESCO, Place de Fontenoy, 75700 Paris, France.

HÖGMAN, Ingvar Daniel, b. 22 Feb. 1914, Gothenburg, Sweden. Teacher; Poet; Critic; Former Editor. Educ: B.A. degree. Publs: Det Blonda Landskapet (poems), 1943; Lejonets Barn (on Swedish poet Karlfeldt), 1945; Transl., T. S. Eliot, After Strange Gods, 1947; Minnesång (poems), 1950; Mälaren, 1951; Contbr. to: Stockholms-Tidningen (cultural writer 1943-60); Vår Kyrka, 1947-56 (editorial writer, & ed. Ch. of Sweden Press Agcy.); var. other newspapers & jrnls. Mbr., Swedish Soc. of Authors. Address: Väddö Folkhögskola, 760 40 Vädö, Sweden.

HOHLER, Franz, b. 1 Mar. 1943, Biel, Switz. Performer & Writer. Educ: Zürich Univ. Publs: Das Verlorene Gähnen, 1967; Idyllen, 1970; Der Rand von Ostermundigen, 1973; Fragen an Andere, 1973; Wegwerfgeschichten, 1974. Mbr., Gruppe Olten (Swiss Writers' Group). Recip., Prize, Conrad Ferdinand Meyer Inst., 1968. Address: Bergstrasse 292, Vetikon am See, Switz.

HOHNEN, David, b. 1925, London, UK. Writer; Translator; Documentary Film Narrator. Publs: Dreimal Skandinavien, 1962; Les 3 Scandinavies, 1965; A Portrait of Denmark, 1966; Danish/English, English/Danish Dictionary, 1966; transls. from Danish to Engl. of over 40 books, 60 feature films, 300 short films. Mbr., Soc. of Authors. Address: Gunderød, 2970 Hørsholm, Denmark.

HÖJER, Signe, b. 28 June 1966, Malmö, Sweden. Writer. Educ: nurse's trng.; London Schl. of Econs. Publs. incl: Africa in Our Hearts, 1962; At Home in Foreign Countries, 1964; Assam — The Rainland (w. husband, J. Axel Höjer), 1964; Leprosy (w. husband), 1966; A Miners Mansion, 1969; Wornan Power — Sex Roles & Matrilineal Traits in Asia & Africa, 1970; Mary Kingsley — Explorer in West Africa, 1973; Sitting in the Twilight; Journeys Around My Room, 1974. Contbr. to var. mags. for peace & for women. Mbr., Writers Assn. Hons: Award, Soc. for Promotion of lit., 1973; 3 awards, The Writers Foundation. Address: Lövångersgatan 7, Vällingby, Sweden.

HOJYO, Makoto, b. 5 Jan. 1918, Tokyo, Japan. Novelist; Dramatist. Educ: B.A., Waseda Univ. Publs. incl: Shunpuku (Spring Costume), 1940; Tasogare-no-Tabi (Twilight Travel), 1947; Aishunikki (Melancholy Diary), 1955; Konoyo-no-Hana (Flower of Life), 1956; Kojyo Konjaku (Tale of Castles), 1965; Akashiya no Uta (Song of Acacia), 1973; Kawabata Yasunari: Bungaku-no-Butai (Literary Background of Yasunari Kawabata), 1973. Contbr. to most maj. newspapers & mags. Mbrships. incl: Japan Writers' Assn. (Exec. Dir.); PEN, Japan (Exec. Dir.); Mus. of Japanese Mod. Lit. (Vice Chmn.). Recip., Noma Prize for Lit., 1947. Address: 5-19-4 Todoroki, Setagaya-ku, Tokyo, Japan.

HOLBRAAD, Carsten, b. 2 Dec. 1930, Odense, Denmark. University Teacher. Educ: B.Sc.(Econ.). London

Schl. of Econs., London Univ., UK; D.Phil., Univ. of Sussex. Publs: The Concert of Europe: a Study in German & British International Theory, 1815-1914, 1970; Super Powers & World Order (Ed. & contbr.), 1971; The Role of Middle Powers, 1972. Contbr. to: Coop. & Conflict; Aust. Outlook; Estudios Internacionales; Danmarks Radio. Mbr., Aust. Soc. for Latin Am. Studies. Address: 51 Hinkler St., Scullin, Canberra, A.C.T. 2614, Australia.

HOLBROOK, David Kenneth, b. 9 Jan. 1923, Norwich, UK. Author. Educ: M.A., Downing Coll., Cambridge Univ. Publs. incl: Children's Games, 1957; Imaginings (poetry), 1961; English for the Rejected, 1964; The Quest for Love, 1965; Flesh Wounds (novel), 1966; Children's Writing, 1967; Plucking the Rushes (anthol.), 1968; Old World, New World (poetry), 1969; Human Hope & the Death Instinct, 1971; Sex & Dehumanization, 1972; Ed., The Case against Pornography, 1972; Gustav Mahler & the Courage to Be, 1975; Sylvia Plath & the Problem of Existence, 1975. Contbr. to: Encounter; Critical Quarterly; Universities Quarterly; 20th Century; num. other newspapers & jrnls. Hons. incl: Keats Mem. Prize, 1973; Prize, Int. Who's Who in Poetry, 1974. Address: New Farm House, Madingley, Cambridge, UK.

HOLCROFT, Montague Harry, b. 14 May 1902, Rangiora, NZ. Journalist. Publs: The Deepening Stream, 1940; Timeless World, 1945; Discovered Isles, 1950; Dance of the Seasons, 1952; The Eye of the Lizard, 1960; New Zealand, 1963; Reluctant Editor, 1969; Graceless Islanders, 1970. Contbr. to NZ Listener. Mbr., PEN, NZ Ctr., 1946—, Pres., 5 yrs. Hons: 1st Prize, Govt. Centennial Lit. Competition, 1940; Hubert Church Awards for Prose, 1945, 1946; O.B.E., 1970. Address: A'Court Street, Sanson, Manawatu, New Zealand.

HOLDEN, David, b. 1924, Sunderland, UK. Journalist. Educ: M.A., Emmanuel Coll., Cambridge; Northwestern Univ., Ill., USA. Publs: Farewell to Arabia, 1966; Greece Without Columns, 1972. Contbr. to: The Times (Wash. corres., 1954-56; Middle East corres., 1956-60; world wide corres., 1960-61); The Guardian (roving corres., 1961-65); Sunday Times (Chief For. Corres., 1965-); N.Y. Times; Encounter; BBC; etc. Lit. Agent: Deborah Rogers Ltd. Address: 54 St. Paul's Rd., London N1, UK.

HOLDEN, Helene P., b. 20 Sept. 1935, Montreal, P.Q., Can. Writer; Book Shop Co-owner; Teacher (French & Drama). Educ: Sir George Williams Univ. Publs: The Chain, 1969; Satan, My Love, 1974. Contbr. to: Les Écrits du Canada Français. Mbrships: Writers' Union of Can.; PEN; Media Club. Address: 359 Kensington Ave., Westmount, Montreal H3Z 2H2, P.Q., Can.

HOLDEN, James Milnes, b. 2 Sept. 1918, Preston, Lancs., UK. Professor of Business Law. Educ: LL.B., 1948, Ph.D., 1950, LL.D., 1973, Univ. of London; Barrister, Lincoln's Inn, 1948. Publs: History of Negotiable Instruments in English Law, 1955; Co-Ed., Chalmers' Marine Insurance Act 1906, 5th ed., 1956; Law & Practice of Banking, Vol. 1, Banker & Customer, 2nd ed., 1974, & Vol. 2, Securities for Bankers' Advances, 5th ed., 1971; Jones & Holden's Studies in Practical Banking, 6th ed., 1971. Contbr. to: Law Quarterly Review; Mod. Law Review; Jrnl. Inst. of Bankers; Bankers' Mag.; other profl. jrnls. Hons: Hirst Essay Prize, Univ. Coll., London, 1948; Institute Prize, Inst. of Bankers, 1970. Address: Univ. of Stirling, Stirling FK9 4LA, UK.

HOLDEN, Molly, b. 7 Sept. 1927, London, UK. Poet & Writer. Educ: B.A., 1948, M.A., 1951, King's Coll., London Univ. Publs. incl: (poetry) To Make Me Grieve, 1968; Air & Chill Earth, 1971; The Country Over, 1975; (novels) The Unfinished Feud, 1970; A Tenancy of Flint, 1971; White Rose & Wanderer, 1972; Reivers' Weather, 1973; (criticism) Fool of Intellect, 1965. Contbr. to: Outposts; Poetry Review; Times Lit. Supplement; The Review; Critical Quarterly; N.Y. Times; New Statesman; Listener; Review of Engl. Lit.; BBC Radio; Victoria Co. Hist. of England. Mbrships. incl: Houseman Soc. Hons. incl: Award, Arts Coun. of Gt. Brit., 1970; Cholmondeley Award for Poets, 1972. Address: 58 Willow Rd., Bromsgrove, Worcs. B61 8PV, UK.

HOLDGATE, Martin Wyatt, b. 14 Jan. 1931, Horsham, Sussex, UK. Ecologist. Educ: M.A., Ph.D., Queens' Coll., Cambridge. Publs: History of Appleby, 1955; Mountains in the Sea, 1958; Biologie Antarctique: Antarctic Biology (jt. Ed.), 1966; Antarctic Ecology (Ed.), 1970. Contbr. to: Atlas of World Wildlife; World of Animals. sci. jrnls.

Mbrships: Fellow, Inst. of Biol., Linnean Soc., Zool. Soc. of London; F.R.S.A.; F.R.G.S. Address: 35 Wingate Way, Trumpington, Cambridge, UK.

HOLENSTEIN, Peter, b. 19 Dec. 1946, Zürich, Switz. Freelance Author & Writer; Former Journalist. Educ: Dip., Comm. Schl. Zürich, 1965. Publs: (stories) Silvia, 1972; Die Auferstehung des Josef Kellerman, 1972; Das Regenmädchen, 1972; (anthol.) Lieber Luzifer, 1974; (novel) Nochmals leben, 1975; also 150 poems, 50 short stories. Contbr. to: Zürich Woche (Ed., 1967); Sonntags-Journal (Ed., 1968); team mag. (Ed.-in-Chief, 1969-72); For. Corres., 1970-71; articles in num. other newspapers & mags. Mbrships: Swiss Authors' Union; Swiss Union of Jrnlsts.; Swiss Press Union; Freier Deutscher Authorenverband. Address: Casa Poetica, CH-6981 Termine (Ticino), Switz.

HOLFORD, Ingrid Bianchi, b. 1920, Kingston upon Thames, UK. Freelance Journalist. Educ: B.Sc.(Econ.), Univ. Coll., London. Publs: A Century of Sailing on the Thames, 1968; Interpreting the Weather, 1973. Contbr. to: Yachting Monthly; Amateur Gardening; Boat Owner; etc. Mbrships: Hon. Sec., Thames Sailing Club; Soc. of Authors; Fellow, Royal Meteorol. Soc. Address: Westonhay, 32 Hook Rd., Surbiton, Surrey, UK.

HOLLAND, Barbara Adams, b. 12 July 1925, Portland, Me., USA. Textbook Writer. Educ: M.A., 1951, Ph.D., Cand., Univ. of Pa. Publs: A Game of Scraps, 1967; Autumn Wizard, 1973; Crisis of Rejuvenation, 1975. Contbr. to reviews. Hons: Creative Artists Public Service Fellowship, N.Y. State Coun. on Arts & Nat. Endowment of the Arts, 1974. Address: 14 Morton St., Apt. 9, N.Y., NY 10014, USA.

HOLLAND, Leslie Arthur, b. 1921, London, UK. Physicist; Chartered Engineer. Educ: Acton Tech. Coll.; D.Tech.; D.Sc. Publs: Vacuum Deposition of Thin Films, 1956; The Properties of Glass Surfaces, 1964; Ed., Thin Film Micro-Electronics, 1965; Co-Ed., Vacuum Manual, 1974. Mbrships: Fellow, Inst. of Phys.; Fellow, Inst. of Elec. Engrs.; Fellow, Soc. of Glass Technol.; Exec., Int. Union of Vacuum Sci., Technol. & their Applications; Fellow, Optical Soc. Am.; Sen. Mbr., Am. Vacuum Soc. Address: Hazelwood, Balcombe Rd., Pound Hill, Crawley, Sussex RH10 3NZ, UK.

HOLLAND, Lynwood M., b. 31 Mar. 1905, Bronwood, Ga., USA. Educator; College Teacher & Administrator. Educ: A.B., A.M., Emory Univ.; Ph.D., Univ. of Ill. Publs: The Direct Primary in Georgia, 1949; State & Local Government in the United States, 1951; Georgia Government, 1965; The Warwick of the South: P. M. B. Young, 1966. Contbr. to: Am. Pol. Sci. Review; Southern Pol. Sci. Jrnl.; Nat. Municipal Review; Emory Law Jrnl. Mbrships: incl. Am. Pol. Sci. Assn.; Southern Pol. Sci. Assn. (VP); other profl. assns. & Hon. socs. Address: Bronwood, GA, USA.

HOLLAND, Margaret, b. 2 Nov. 1917, Montclair, N.J., USA. Writer. Publs: Old Country Silver, 1971; Silver, 1972. Contbr. to: Antiques (USA); Collectors Guide; Art & Antiques Weekly; etc. Mbr., Soc. of Authors. Address: The Mast Head, Frant, Tunbridge Wells, Kent, UK.

HOLLAND, Norman (James), b. 11 Oct. 1910, Warrington, Cheshire, UK. Civil Servant. Publs: Author, 70 published plays, inclng: The Militants, 1970; Daughter of the Left Hand, 1972; Watcher in the Shadow, 1973; Collections — The Magic Hat, 1941; Ten One-Act Plays, w. Foreword by Sir Ralph Richardson, 1948; Queens Most Royal, 1974. Contbr. to jrnls., anthols.; Former Lectr. in Playwriting, City Lit. Inst., London. Hons: Winner, 20 playwriting awards, 1935-74. Address: Flat 2, 13 Berkeley Place, Wimbledon, London SW19 4NN, UK.

HOLLAND, (Rt. Rev.) Thomas, b. 11 June 1908, Southport, Lancs., UK. Bishop of Salford. Educ: Ph.D., Engl. Coll., Valladolid, Spain; D.D., Gregorian Univ., Rome, Italy; Publs: Mary for Everyman, 1950; The Great Cross, 1958. Contbr. to: Beda Book; Clergy Review; Cath. Gazette; Dublin Review; Furrow; Tablet. Hons: D.S.C., 1944. Address: Wardley Hall, Worsley, Manchester M28 5ND, UK.

HOLLANDER, Hans, b. 6 Oct. 1899, Breclav, Austria (now Czechoslovakia). Writer & Lecturer on Music. Educ: Ph.D., Univ. of Vienna, Austria. Publs: Janáček, 1963; Leoš Janáček, 1964; Die Musik in der Kulturgeschichte des 19. &

20. Jahrhunderts, 1967; Musik & Jugendstil, 1974. Contbr. to num. Music Periodicals & to daily papers. Address: Gidleigh Lodge, Chagford, Devonshire, UK.

HOLLERER, Walter Friedrich, b. 19 Dec. 1922, Bavaria, Germany. Professor of Literature; Critic; Author. Educ: Ph.D.; Univs. of Erlangen, Gottingen & Heidelberg. Publs. incl: (poetry) Der Andere Gast, 1952, 1964; Ausserhalb der Saison, 1967; Systeme, 1969; (novel) Die Elephantenuhr, 1973; (other publs.) Spiele in einem Akt, 1962; Gedichte, 1964; Theorie der Modernen Lyrik, 1965; Modernes Theater auf Kleinen Bühnen, 1966. Contbr. to Akzente (Ed.); etc. Mbrships. incl: PEN; Berlin Acad. of Arts. Hons. incl: Lit. Prize, German Ind.; Fonatne Prize. Address: Heer Str. 99, 1 Berlin 19, Germany.

HOLLIDAY, Joe, pen name DALE, Jack, b. 1910, Gibraltar. Author; Editor. Publs: Dale of the Mounted (juvenile series of 12 vols.), 1950-62; Oil Trails in Headless Valley, 1953; Mosquito, 1970. Contbr. to: Toronto Star; Fin. Post; Chatelaine; Indl. Can.; Air Classics Quarterly; Airtrails; Mktng. Weekly; Ed., Can. Author & Bookman, 1959-65; etc. Mbrships: HQ Comm. Chmn., Can. Authors Assn.; Can. Aviation Histl. Soc.; Dir., Bus. Press Eds. Assn., 1964. Hons: Centennial Medal, 1967; Allan E. Sangster Mem. Award, 1973. Address: 26 Porter Cres., Scarborough, Ont. M1P 1E7, Can.

HOLLIDAY, Robert Reade, b. 1908, Manchester, UK. Motoring Writer. Publs: Norton Story; Motorcycle Parade. Mbr., Guild of Motoring Writers. Address: 7 Denehurst Gdns., London NW4 3QS, UK.

HOLLINGDALE, Stuart Havelock, b. 1910, London, UK. Head of Mathematics Dept., Royal Aircraft Establishment, 1947-67; Dir., Computer Centre, Univ. of Birmingham, 1967-74. Educ: M.A., Ph.D.; Christ's Coll., Cambridge; Imperial Coll., London: Publs: High Speed Computing; Electronic Computers (w. G. C. Tootill). Contbr. to: Jrnl. of Inst. of Navigation; var. math. & computer jrnls. Mbrships: Inst. of Maths. & its applications; Brit. Computer Soc. Address: Nedfield Hey, Lower Froyle, Alton, Hants., UK.

HOLLINGDRAKE, Sybil, b. 7 Sept. 1926, Newport, Gwent, UK. College Lecturer; Author; Dramatist. Educ: B.A., M.A., Bristol Univ. Publs: (10 one-act plays inclng.) God in my Mountain, 1961; Girl on a Threshold, 1963; The Supertramp in Monmouthshire (biog. of W. H. Davies), 1971, 2nd ed., 1973. Mbrships: Exec. Comm., Drama Assn. of Wales; Comm. of Guild of Welsh Playwrights, Mon. Drama League, Civil Defence Drama Soc., Gwent Poetry Soc. Hons. incl: Lord Howard de Walden Playwriting & Prod. Cups, BDL Festival, 1961; Guild of Welsh Playwrights' Cup, 1963; Drama Assn. of Wales Award, 1966. Address: 51 Stockton Rd., Newport, Gwent NPT 7HJ, UK.

HOLLINGSHEAD, August deBelmont, b. 15 Apr. 1907, Lyman, Wyo., USA. Professor of Sociology; Author. Educ' B.A., 1931, M.A., 1933, Univ. of Calif, Berkeley; Ph.D., Univ. of Neb., 1935. Publs: Elmtown's Youth, 1949; Two Factor Index of Social Position, 1957; Social Class & Mental Illness (w. F. C. Redlich), 1958; Trapped: Families & Schizophrenia (w. L. H. Rogler), 1965; Sickness & Society (w. R. S. Duff), 1968; Elmtown's Youth & Elmtown Revisited, 1974. Contbr. to: Am. Jrnl. of Sociol.; Rural Sociol.; Am. Sociol. Review; Marriage & Family Living; Am. Jrnl. of Psychol.; etc. Address: 19 Enoch Dr., Woodbridge, CT 06525, USA.

HOLLIS, (Rev. Canon) Gerald, b. 1919, Hull, UK. Vicar. Educ: M.A., Christ Ch., Oxford Univ.; Wells Theol. Coll. Publs: Rugger: Do It This Way. Mbr., Vincent's Club. Address: 59 Salisbury Rd., Moseley, Birmingham B13 8LB, UK.

HOLLISTER, C(harles) Warren, b. 2 Nov. 1930, L.A., Calif., USA. Professor; Author. Educ: B.A., 1951, M.A., UCLA, 1957, Ph.D., 1958, Harvard Univ. Publs. incl: Anglo-Saxon Military Institutions, 1962; Medieval Europe, 1964, 3rd ed., 1974; The Making of England, 1966, 2nd ed., 1971; Landmarks of the Western Heritage, 1967, 2nd ed., 1973; The 12th Century Renaissance, 1969; Odysseus to Columbus, 1974; River Through Time (co-author), 1975. Contbr. to: Speculum; Am. & Engl. Histl. Reviews; Econ. Hist. Review; Jrnl. of British Studies; etc. Hons. incl: Triennial Book Prize, Conf. on British Studies, 1963. Address: 4592 Via Clarice, Santa Barbara, CA 93111, USA.

HOLLOM, Philip Arthur Dominic, b. 1912, Bickley, Kent, UK. Editor; Author. Educ: F.C.C.A. Publs: The Popular Handbook of British Birds; The Popular Handbook of Rarer British Birds; A Field Guide to the Birds of Britain & Europe (co-author); Trapping Methods for Bird Ringers. Contbr. to: British Birds; Ibis; Bird Study; etc. Address: Crastock Cottage, Crastock, Woking, Surrey, UK.

HOLLOWAY, Henry Victor, b. 1 Nov. 1925, Stellenbosch, S. Africa. Journalist. Educ: B.Comm., Univ. of Stellenbosch, 1946. Publs: Spitse Op Die Sportveld (co-author), 1970; Cecil Higgs, 1974. Assoc. Mbr., S. African Acad. for Sci. & Art. Address: Kismet, 41 Third Beach, Clifton, Cape Town, S. Africa.

HOLLOWAY, James Patterson. Travel Journalist. Contbr. to: Travelnews; Manchester Evening News; Irish Times; The Lady; Jewish Chronicle; Globe & Mail (Toronto); Vancouver Sun; Winnipeg Free Press; Boston Globe; Chgo. Tribune; Off Duty. Mbrships: Royal Overseas League; Treas., Guild of Travel Writers. Hons: Tunisia Travel Award, 1972, 1974; Westtoerrisme Press Prize (Belgium), 1973. Thomson Travel Award to Jrnlsm., 1975. Address: 9 Warren Rd., Ickenham, Uxbridge, Middx., UK.

HOLLOWAY, John, b. 1920, Croydon, Surrey, UK. University Professor of Modern English; Author. Educ: M.A., D.Phil., New Coll., Oxford; D.Litt., Univ. of Aberdeen; Litt.D., Univ. of Cambridge. Publs. incl: Language & Intelligence, 1951; The Victorian Sage, 1953; The Charted Mirror, 1956; The Minute, 1956; The Fugue, 1960; The Story of the Night, 1961; The Landfallers, 1962; Wood & Windfall, 1964; The Lion Hunt, 1964; New Poems, 1970; Ed., Poems of the Mid-Century, 1957; Selections from Shelley, 1960. Contbr. to: Hudson Review; Burlington Mag.; London Mag.; Encounter; Art Int.; Essays in Criticism. Mbrships. incl: F.R.S.L. Address: Queens' College, Cambridge, UK.

HOLLOWAY, Mark, b. 10 Oct. 1917, London, UK. Writer. Educ: M.A., Trinity Hall, Cambridge Univ. Publs. incl: Heavens on Earth, A History of Utopian Communities in the United States, 1951, revised ed., 1966; William Harvey, 1957; The Objectors (co-author), 1965; Norman Douglas, A Biography, 1975. Contbr. to: Evening Standard; Books & Bookmen; Tribune; New Statesman; Times Lit. Supplement. Mbr., Soc. of Authors. Agent: A. M. Heath & Co. Ltd. Address: c/o above, 40-42 William IV St., London W1, UK.

HOLLOWAY, Percival Geoffrey, b. 23 May 1918, Birmingham, UK. Social Worker. Educ: Cert. in Soc. Sci., Southampton Univ. Publs: (poems) To Have Eyes, 1973; Rhine Jump, 1974. Contbr. to: London Mag.; Phoenix; Outposts; Anglo-Welsh Review; Orbis; Samphire; New Poetry; Tribune; Delta; Littack; Tablet; Yorkshire Post; BBC. Mbr., Prism (poetry-reading trio). Hon: Poetry Book Soc. Choice (Rhine Jump), 1974. Address: 4 Gowan Cres., Staveley, nr. Kendal, Cumbria LA8 9NF, UK.

HOLLOWAY, Teresa B., b. 17 Jan. 1906, Apalachicola, Fla., USA. Writer. Educ: Grad., Fla. State Coll. for Women, 1925; Univ. of Fla. Publs: num. novels inclng: Murder at Auction, 1961; Girl in Studio B, 1967; Nurse on Dark Island, 1969; River Nurse, 1969; Campaign for Pam, 1970. Contbr., columns, feature stories, to newspapers, mags. Mbrships: Past Pres., Jacksonville Br., Past Ed., SE Region, Nat. League of Am. Pen Women; Mystery Writers of Am. Hons. incl: Sears Fndn. Regional Award; Outstanding Lit. Contbn. Award, Nat. League of Am. Pen Women, 1966; Num. other writing awards. Address: 4349 Irvington Ave., Jacksonville, FL 32210, USA.

HOLLY, Joan Carol, pen names, HOLLY, J. Hunter; HOLLY, Joan Hunter, b. 25 Sept. 1932, Lansing, Mich., USA. Writer. Educ: B.A., Mich. State Univ. Publs: Encounter, 1959; The Green Planet, 1960; The Dark Planet, 1962; The Flying Eyes, 1962; The Grey Aliens, 1963; The Runnung Man, 1963; The Time Twisters, 1964; The Dark Enemy, 1965; The Mind Traders, 1966; The Assassination Affair (Man from U.N.C.L.E. series), 1967. Contbr. stories to jrnls. & anthols. inclng: Fantastic Mag.; Famous Sci. Fiction. Mbr., profl. orgs. Recip., acad. hons. Address: 923 W. Shiawassee, Lansing, MI 48915, USA.

HOLM, Donald Raymond, pen names HOLM, Don; DENALI, Peter, b. 3 Jan. 1918, Velva, N.D., USA. Newspaper Editor; Columnist. Educ: B.S. Publs: The Dutch Oven Cookbook, 1969; Pacific North! , 1970; 101 Best Fishing Trips in Oregon, 1971; The Complete Sourdough

Cookbook, 1972; Fishing the Pacific, 1972; The Circumnavigators, 1974; Reunion Summer (forthcoming); The Complete Salmon Book (forthcoming). Contbr. to: Outdoor Life; Field & Stream; Sports Afield; & about 50 other periodicals. Mbrships. incl: The Explorers' Club of N.Y. Hons: James H. Henshall Award, 1969 & 1970; Garcia 1st Place Award for photo-jrnlsm., 1972; N.W. Conserv. Award, 1973. Address: 9995 SW Maplecrest Ct., Beaverton, OR 97005, USA.

HOLM, Peter Röwde, b. 5 Apr. 1931, Oslo, Norway. Author. Educ: Oslo Coll. of Commerce, 1950; Nansen Schl., 1951; Commercial HS, St. Gallen, Switz., 1951-53; Cert. of Proficiency in Engl., Cambridge, 1955. Publs. incl: Innvielse ved havet, 1960; Stentid, 1962; Det plutselige landskapet, 1963; Oÿeblikkets forvandlinger, 1965; Befrielser, 1966; Diabas, 1968; Synslinjer, 1970; Sanndrömt, 1971; Isglimt, glödepunkt, 1972; Selected poems, 1973; Reisens formler, 1974. Mbrships. incl: Norwegian Union of Authors. Hons. incl: Dagbladets Poetry Prize, 1964; Norwegian Lit. Critics Prize, 1966. Address: Östre Holmensvingen 4, Oslo 3, Norway.

HOLM, Sven (Aage), pen name FARMACEUTEN, b. 15 July 1902, Copenhagen, Denmark. Pharmacist. Publs: 17 books (1 transl'd into Engl.). Address: Ahlmanns Alle 27, 2900 Hellerup, Denmark.

HOLMAN, C. Hugh, b. 24 Feb. 1914, Cross Anchor, S.C. USA. Kenan Professor of English, Univ. N.C. Educ: B.S., 1936, B.A., 1938, Presbyterian Coll., N.C., N.Y. Univ., 1939; Ph.D., Univ. N.C., 1949. Publs. incl: Thomas Wolfe, 1960, transl'd. 8 langs.; A Handbook to Literature, 1960, 3rd revised ed., 1968; Three Modes of Modern Southern Fiction: Ellen Glasgow, William Faulkner, Thomas Wolfe, 1966; The Roots of Southern Writing: Essays on the Literature of the American South, 1972; The Loneliness at the Core: Studies in Thomas Wolfe, 1975; Articles in & Ed. of var. works of schlrship., some as co-author. Contbr. to num. acad. & lit. jrnls. Mbrships. incl: MLA (Chmn., Am. Lit. Sect.). Hons. incl: L.H.D., Clemson Univ., 1969. Address: Box 2056 Chapel Hill, NC 27514, USA.

HOLMAN, Dennis, b. Lahore, India. Author; Journalist. Publs: Lady Louis, Life of the Countess Mountbatten of Burma, 1952; Noone of the Ulu, 1958; The Man They Couldn't Kill, 1960; A Sikander Sahib, 1961; The Green Torture, 1962; Bwana Drum, 1964; The Elephant People, 1967; Inside Safari Hunting, 1969; Eric & Ernie, The Autobiography of Morecambe & Wise (as Referee), 1973; The Tender Trespasser, 1975. Contbr. to num. newspapers & mags., UK & USA. Mbr., Soc. of Authors. Address: c/o John Farquharson Ltd., 15 Red Lion Sq., London WC1, UK; & Julian Bach Literary Agency Inc., 3 East St., N.Y., NY 10017, USA.

HOLMAN, Robert, b. 1936, Ilford, Essex, UK. Professor of Social Administration. Educ: Univ. Coll., Univ. of London; London Schl. of Econs.; B.A.; Ph.D.; Dip. Applied Social Studies; Cert. Social Admin. Publs: Ed., Socially Deprived Families in Britain, 1970; Unsupported Mothers & the Care of their Children, 1970; Ed., Research & Social Work, 1970; Trading in Children: A Study of Private Fostering, 1973. Contbr. to: Univs. Quarterly; Brit. Jrnl. of Social Work; Social Work Today; Policy & Pol.; Jrnl. of Social Policy; New Soc. Mbrships: Social Admin. Soc.; Ed. Bd., Brit. Jrnl. of Social Work. Address: 23 Castle Gdns., Bath BA2 2AN, UK.

HOLMBÄCK, Bure, b. 18 Mar. 1923, Backe, Sweden. Librarian; Broadcasting Investigator. Educ: Ph.D. Publs: About Sweden: A Bibliographical Outline, 1968; Det Lekfulla Alvaret, 1969. Contbr. to: Prespektiv; Horisont; Svensk Litteraturtidskrift; daily papers; radio & TV progs. Mbrships: Swedish Authors Assn.; Swedish PEN Club. Address: Lingvägen 203, S 123 59 Farsta, Sweden.

HOLMBERG, Bo, b. 8 Sept. 1930, Stockholm, Sweden. Author; Scientist. Educ: Ph.D. (Zoophysiology). Publs: 3 collections of poems, 1959-64; novels: Sondering, 1965; Kniven, 1969; Sjukdomen, 1970; Political essay: Öppet brev till Betämkare och Souensktzlande, 1972. Contbr. to: Dagens Nyheter, 1969—; num. lit. jrnls. & anthols. Mbrships: Swedish Authors' Union; (Bd., Sect. of Fiction Authors); Bd., Swedish Authors' Cooperative Edition Co., 1973-74. Address: Blåeldsvägen 59, S-16241 Vällingby, Sweden.

HOLMBERG, Margit, b. 25 May 1912, Gothenburg, Sweden. Author. Publs: 2 books of essays; 2 books of fairy stories; 6 books of children's songs, words & music; (poetry) Långt borta, 1937; Dansande sten, 1955; Regnharpa, 1957; Den läkande örten, 1961; Mänkvinna, 1963; Ättestupa, 1969; Jag en borgare, 1974. Contbr. to: Göteborgstidningen (GT); children's TV progs., Sweden & Norway, 1961-62. Mbrships: Swedish Authors' Union; Göteborgs Författarsällskap; Göteborgs Konstnärsklubb. Recip., Göteborgs stads Kulturstipendium, 1973. Address: Drakenbergst 12, 412 69 Gothenburg 5, Sweden.

HOLME, Thea, b. 27 Dec. 1903, London, UK. Broadcaster; Writer. Educ: Slade Schl. of Art, 2 yrs., Ctrl. Schl. Dramatic Art, 1 yr. Publs: The Carlyles at Home, 1965; Chelsea, 1972. Radio Progs. incl: Mansfield Park, 1973; Dear & Honoured Lady, 1974; Princess Charlotte, forthcoming. Contbr. to: Spectator; Times. F.R.S.L. Address: 13 Coleshill Village, Highworth, Wilts. SN6 7PR, UK.

HOLMES, Geoffrey Shorter, b. 17 July 1928, Sheffield, UK. Professor of History, Lancaster University. Educ: Pembroke Coll., Oxford, 1945-48; 1950-51; M.A., B.Litt. Publs: British Politics in the Age of Anne, 1967; The Divided Society (w. W. A. Speck), 1967; Ed. & Co-author, Britain after the Glorious Revolution, 1969; The Trial of Doctor Sacheverell, 1973; Religion & Party in Late Stuart England, 1974. Contbr. to: The Prime Ministers (ed. H. van Thal); History; English Historical Review; Bulletin of the Inst. of Historical Rsch.; The Times. Hons: Book of the Year, The Observer, 1967, 1973; Fellow, Royal Historical Soc., 1969. Address: Tatham House, Burton-in-Lonsdale, Carnforth, Lancs., UK.

HOLMES, Jack David Lazarus, pen name DELACHE, Jota, b. 4 July 1930, Long Branch, N.J., USA. Historian; Professor. Educ: B.A., Fla. State Univ., 1952; M.A., Univ. of Fla., 1953; Ph.D., Univ. of Tex., 1959. Publs. incl: Documentos Inéditos para la Historia de la Luisiana 1792-1810, 1963; Gayoso, 1965; José de Evia y sus Reconocimientos del Golfo de Mexico 1783-1796, 1968; New Orleans (co-author), 1970, 1972; A Guide to Spanish Louisiana 1762-1806, 1970; A History of the University of Alabama Hospitals, 1974; The 1779 "Marcha de Gálvez", 1974. Contbr. to num. histl. jrnls. Mbr., var. profl. orgs. Hons. incl: La. Lit. Award, 1966; Ala. Writers' Conclave Biog. Awards, 1966, 1967; Hackney Lit. Award, Birmingham Fest. of Arts, 1974. Address: 520 S. 22nd Ave., Birmingham, AL 35205, USA.

HOLMES, John, b. 12 May 1913, Bishopton, Renfrewshire, UK. Animal Trainer; Farmer. Educ: Edinburgh Coll. of Agriculture. Publs: Obedient Dogs, 1954; Obedience Training for Dogs, 1961; The Family Dog, 1957; The Farmers Dog, 1960; The Obedient Dog, 1975. Contbr. to: Ency. of Dogs; Daily Telegraph; The Field; Farmers Weekly; Dog World; World of Pets; The Horse; etc.; sev. radio and TV broadcasts. Prod. & Dir., A Tale of Two Pups. Mbrships: Equity; Soc. of Authors. Address: Formakin, Cranborne, Dorset BH21 5QY, UK.

HOLMES, John Clellon, b. 12 Mar. 1926, Holyoke, Mass., USA. Author. Educ: Columbia Univ, N.Y., 1943, 1945-46; New Schl., N.Y., 1949-50. Publs: (novels) Go, 1952; The Horn, 1958; Get Home Free, 1964; (essays) Nothing More to Declare, 1967. Contbr. to: Harper's; N.Y. Times Mag.; Esquire; Saturday Review; Playboy; Holiday; Glamour; Penthouse; Partisan Review; Poetry Mag. (Chgo.); Discovery; etc. Hons: Best Non-Fiction Awards, Playboy Mag., 1st Prizes, 1964, 1971, 1973, 2nd Prizes, 1970, 1972; Establishment of John Clellon Holmes Collect. of MSS, Boston Univ., 1966. Address: Box 75, Old Saybrook, CT 06475, USA.

HOLMES, Marjorie, b. 22 Sept. 1910, Storm Lake, Iowa, USA. Writer. Educ: B.A., Cornell Coll., Mt. Vernon, Iowa. Publs. incl: Ten O'Clock Scholar, 1946; Saturday Night, 1959; Follow Your Dream, 1961; I've Got to Talk to Somebody, God, 1969; Who Am I, God?, 1971; The Two From Galilee, 1972; You & I & Yesterday, 1973; As Tall as my Heart, 1974. Contbr. to: Woman's Day; Reader's Digest; etc. Mbrships. incl: Authors' League; Nat. Fed. of Press Women. Hons. incl: Women of Achievement Award, Campus Life Mag., 1973; Best Biblical Novel of the Yr., Radio Stns. of the South. Address: 1110 Shipman Lane, McLean, VA 22101, USA.

HOLMES, Philip John, b. 24 May 1945, Scunthorpe, UK. University Research Fellow, Institute of Sound &

Vibration Research; Poet. Educ: B.A., Univ. of Oxford, 1967; Ph.D., Univ. of Southampton, 1974. Publs: 3 Sections, 1971; The Experimental Characterisation of Vibration Transmission Systems Using Transient Excitation, 1974. Contbr. to: Agni Review; Jrnl. of Sound & Vibration; Grosseteste Review; Priapus; Second Aeon; Southern Arts. Address: 6 Avenue Rd., Portswood, Southampton, UK.

HOLMES, Richard, b. 5 Nov. 1945, London, UK. Writer. Educ: Churchill Coll., Cambridge Univ. Publs: Shelley: The Pursuit, 1974. Contbr. to: Times. Address: 3 Cathcart Hill, London N19, UK.

HOLMES, Richard, b. 29 Mar. 1946, Aldridge, Staffs., UK. Senior Lecturer in War Studies. Educ: M.A., Emmanuel Coll., Cambridge; N. III. Univ., USA. Publs: Borodino 1812, 1971; Bir Hakim, 1971; The English Civil War (w. Brig. P. Young), 1974. Contbr. to Purnell's History of the First World War. Mbr., RUSI. Address: 20 Heatherdale Rd., Camberley, Surrey GU15 2LT, UK.

HOLMQVIST, Lasse, b. 31 Dec. 1930, Malmo, Sweden. Television & Documentary Film Producer; Author; Entertainer. Educ: B.A., Univ. of Lund. Publs: Pa Luffen, 1967; Danmark, 1968; Vitt och Brett, 1971; Albert, 1972; Italienska Rivieran, 1973; Skane, 1974. Contbr. to Sydsvenska Dagbladet. Mbr., Swedish Union of Authors. Hons: Medal, Royal Danish Tourist Coun., 1969. Address: Varbo, 230 42 Tygelsjo, Sweden.

HOLMSEN, Sverre Ryen, b. 4 Mar. 1906, Luipaardsvlei, S. Africa. Author. Educ: Uppsala Coll., Sweden; Hermods; Pvte. study in Europe, USA, Asia, Africa & Polynesia. Publs. incl: The Island Beyond the Horizon, 1939; Polynesian Trade Wind, 1942; Singing Coral, 1946; Het Horisont, 1954; Kanariska Solvarv, 1964; Tankestrak, 1971; The Inspirators, 1973; also transls. into Engl. & other langs. Contbr. to num. jrnls. & newspapers. Mbr., Swedish Union of Authors. Hons: Schlrships., Tidens Award, 1962; Author's Fndn., 1966. Address: Hagbyholm, 190 30 Sigtuna, Sweden.

HOLROYD, Michael de Courcy Fraser, b. 1935, London, UK. Writer. Publs: Hugh Kingsmill, 1964; Lytton Strachey: The Unknown Years, 1967; Lytton Strachey: The Years of Achievement, 1968; A Dog's Life, 1969; The Best of Hugh Kingsmill, 1970; Lytton Strachey by Himself, 1971; Unreceived Opinions, 1973; The Art of Augustus John (w. Malcolm Easton), 1974; Augustus John: The Years of Innocence, 1974; Augustus John: The Years of Experience, 1975. Contbr. to: Times; N.Y. Times Book Review; Am. Scholar; Harper's; The Author; London Mag.; Sunday Telegraph. Mbrships: Soc. of Authors; Nat. Book League. Agent: A. P. Watt & Son. Address: c/o Wm. Heinemann Ltd., 15—16 Queen St., Mayfair, London W1X 8BE, UK.

HOLSBERGEN, Jan Willem, b. 3 Feb. 1915, Rotterdam, Netherlands. Writer. Educ: Acad. of Art, Rotterdam. Publs: (novels) The Gloves of Treason, 1958; Businessmen as Honest as the Day, 1967; Wimpy, the Sewing Box, 1971; (short stories) A Couple of Sparrows, 1961; (play) Brahms, the Tailor, 1967. Contbr. to: Podium; Maatstaf; de Gids; Haagsepost. Mbrships: PEN; Bd., Dutch Writers' Union. Recip., Vyverberg Reward, 1962. Address: Koestraat 10-12, Amsterdam 1001, Netherlands.

HOLT, Edgar, b. 2 Nov. 1900, Burnley, Lancs., UK. Journalist; Author. Educ: B.A., Christ Church, Oxford. Publs: The World at War, 1956; The Boer War, 1958; Protest in Arms, 1960; The Opium Wars in China, 1962; The Strangest War, 1964; The Carlist Wars in Spain, 1967; Mazzini, 1967; Risorgimento: The Making of Italy, 1970; Plon-Plon: The Life of Prince Napoleon, 1973. Contbr. to: BBC (1932-35); The Listener (Dep. Ed., 1935-37); Liverpool Daily Post (Chief Asst. Ed., 1937-47); Daily Dispatch (Asst. Ed., 1947-55); Sunday Telegraph; Ency. Britannica, 1974. Agent: A. M. Heath & Co. Ltd. Address: 184 Princes Ave., Palmers Green, London N13 6HL, UK.

HOLT, Michael, b. 7 Jan. 1929, Richmond, Surrey, UK. Writer. Educ: B.Sc., London Univ. Publs. incl: Mathematics Through Experience, 1968, 2nd ed., 1975; Science Happenings (6 vols.), 1969, 1970; Mathematics in Art, 1971; The Big Book of Puzzles, 1972; Monkey Puzzle Books (6 vols.), 1972; Let's Play Maths (co-author) 1972, 2nd ed., 1975; Maths. (12 vols.), 1973, 1974, 1975, reprint 1974; Life Cycle Books (co-author), 1974; All Round English (co-author) (2 vols.), 1974; Ready for Science (4 vols.), 1974. Contbr. to: Sunday Times; Child Educ.; Maths. in Schls.; Tchrs. World; The Math. Gazette. Mbrships: Soc. of Authors; Past Chmn., Educl. Writers' Grp. Address: The Old Parsonage, Eye, nr. Leominster, Herefordshire, UK.

HOLT, Robert Rutherford, b. 27 Dec. 1917, Jacksonville, Fla., USA. Educator; Psychologist. Educ: B.A., Princeton Univ., 1939; M.A., 1941, Ph.D., 1944, Harvard Univ. Publs. incl: Personality: Dynamics, Development & Assessment (w. I. Janis, G. Mahl, J. Kagan), 1969; Assessing Personality, 1971; LSD: Personality & Experience (co-author), 1972; Methods of Research in Clinical Psychology, 1973. Contbr. to num. profl. jrnls. Mbrships: Fellow, Am. Psychol. Assn., AAAS; AAUP. Hons: Psychol. of the Yr. Award, N.Y. Soc. of Clin. Psychols., 1973; Award, Disting. Contbns. to Clin. Psychol., Div. 12, Am. Psychol. Assn., 1974. Address: 20 East Eighth St., N.Y., NY 10003, USA.

HOLT, William, b. 1 Sept. 1897, Todmorden, Yorks., UK. Author; Artist; Radio & TV Broadcaster; Publisher. Publs: Under a Japanese Parasol, 1933; Backwaters, 1933; The Price of Adventure, 1934; I Was a Prisoner, 1934; I Haven't Unpacked, 1939; I Still Haven't Unpacked, 1953; The Weaver's Knot, 1956; The Wizard of Whirlaw, 1959; Trigger in Europe, 1966; Zu Pferd durch Europa, 1968; Ride a White Horse, 1968; Rucksack Reflections, 1971. Contbr. to: Listener; Stands Mag.; London Calling; Word Digest; Parade; Picture Post; Guardian; etc. Mbr., Soc. of Authors. Hons. incl: Radio Personality of the Yr., BBC, 1947; Kt. of Mark Twain, 1968; Arts Coun. Award for Servs. to Lit., 1974. Address: The Barn, Kilnhurst, Todmorden, Yorks., UK.

HOLTHUSEN, Hans Egon, b. 15 Apr. 1915, Rendsburg, Germany. Writer. Educ: Univs. of Tubingen, Berlin, Munich; Ph.D. Publs. incl: Hier in der Zeit (poems); Rainer Maria Rilke: a Study of his Later Poetry, 1952; The Crossing, 1959; Das Schone & das Wahre, 1958; Kritisches Verstehen, 1961; Pläydoyer für den Einzelnen, 1967; Indiana Campus, American Diary 1969; Eduard Mörike, Monograph, 1971. Contbr. to: Mercur, Munich; Atlantic Monthly; Poetry. Life Mbrships: Bavarian Acad. of Fine Arts (Pres. 1968-74); Acad. of Arts, Berlin. Hons: Kulturpreis, City of Kiel, 1956; Bavarian Order of Merit, 1973. Address: Agnesstrasse 48, Munich 40, W. Germany, & 1725 Orpington Ave., Evanston, IL 60201, USA.

HOLTTUM, Richard Eric, b. 20 July 1895, Linton, Cambs., UK. Botanist; Author. Educ: B.A., 1920; Dip.Ed., 1921, M.A., 1927, Sc.D., 1951, St. John's Coll., Cambridge. Publs: Gardening in the Lowlands of Malaya, 1953; Orchids of Malaya, 1953, 3rd ed., 1964, reprinted, 1972; Plant Life in Malaya, 1954, paperback ed., 1969; Ferns of Malaya, 1955, 2nd ed., 1968; Flora Malesiana, Series II (Pteridophyta) Vol. 1, Part 1, 1959, Part 2, 1963. Contbr. to: Kew Bulletin; Linnean Soc. Jrnl.; Malayan Orchid Review; Blumea (Leiden Univ.); Phytomorphol. (Delhi); Orchid Review (London); etc. Address: 50 Gloucester Court, Kew Rd., Richmond, Surrey TW9 3EA, UK.

HOLUJ, Tadeusz, b. 24 Nov. 1916, Cracow, Poland. Author; Journalist. Educ: Yagiellonian Univ., Cracow. Publs: Let's Swim On, Girl, 1936; Poems from Prison Camp, 1946; Trial by Fire, 1946; The Landless Kingdom, 1954-56; The End of Our World, 1958; Poems, 1960; A Tree Bears Fruit, 1963; A Rose & a Burning Forest, 1971; Eden, 1972; sona, 1972; also short stories & plays. Mbrships: PEN; Polish Writers' Union; MP. Hons: City of Cracow Prize, 1958; Min. of Arts Prize, 1962; State Lit. Prize, 1966; Trade Union Lit. Prize, 1974. Address: Ul. Emaus 14a, 30201 Cracow, Poland.

HOLYER, Erna Maria, pen name HOLYER, Ernie, b. Weilheim, Germany. Writer. Educ: A.A., San Jose Evening Coll., 1964; San Mateo Coll.; San Jose State Univ. Publs: Rescue at Sunrise, 1965; Steve's Night of Silence, 1966; A Cow for Hansel, 1967; At the Forest's Edge, 1969; Song of Courage, 1970; Lone Brown Gull, 1971; Shoes for Daniel, 1974; Und Wieder Scheint die Sonne, vols. I & II (of three), 1974. Contbr. to mags. & Ency. Britannica Schl. Lib. Address: 6893 Campisi Court, San Jose, CA 95120, USA.

HOLZHAUSEN, Carl Johan, b. 21 Feb. 1900, Göteborg, Sweden. Journalist; Author. Publs: Achilles häl (novel), 1964; The Leap (short stories), 1970; They Came from Dodona (short stories), 1972; The Dream-dog (for children), 1973; The Train Takes Twenty Minutes (novel), 1973; The Island of the Seven Cones (novel), 1974.

Mbrships: Swedish Union of Authors; Soc. of Authors, Gothenburg (Chmn., Western Region, 1963-64); Swedish Union of Jrnlsts. Hons: Short Story Competition Winner, 1945; Best Swedish Sci. Fiction Short Story Prize, European Congress, Trieste, 1967-72; Prize, Swedish Acad. of Sci. Fiction, 1974. Address: 7442 Attholmen, 441 00 Alingsås, Sweden.

HOME, (Hon.) William Douglas, b. 3 June 1912, Edinburgh. Dramatist. Educ: B.A., New Coll., Oxford; RADA. Publs. incl: (plays) Passing By, 1940; The Chiltern Hundreds, 1947; Master of Arts, 1949; The Thistle & the Rose, 1949; The Bad Samaritan, 1953; The Reluctant Debutante, 1955; The Iron Duchess, 1957; Up a Gum Tree, 1960; The Reluctant Peer, 1964; A Friend Indeed, 1966; The Secretary Bird, 1968; The Grouse Moor Image, 1968; The Jockey Club Stakes, 1970; Lloyd George Knew My Father, 1972; At the End of the Day, 1973. Address: Drayton House, E. Meon, Hants., UK.

HOMRIGHAUSEN, Elmer George, b. 11 Apr. 1900, Wheatland, Iowa, USA. Author; Theologian. Educ: Lakeland Coll., Wis.; Princeton Theol. Sem.; Chgo. Univ.; Univ. of Dubuque; B.A.; B.Th.; M.A.; Th.M.; Th.D.; D.D.; L.H.D. Publs. incl: Let the Church be the Church, 1938; Christianity in America — A Crisis, 1937; Choose Ye This Day, 1941; I Believe in the Church, 1959; Rethinking the Great Commission in an Age of Revolution, 1968. Contbr. to: Ency. Americana; Ency. of Relig. Knowledge; Theol. Today; etc. Mbrships. incl: NEA; Relig. Educ. Assn.; etc. Hons. incl: Huguenot Cross; Disting. Alumni Award, Princeton Sem., 1970. Address: 150 Leabrook Lane, Princeton, NJ 08540, USA.

HONAN, Park, b. 17 Sept. 1928, Utica, N.Y., USA. University Reader in English Literature; Author. Educ: M.A., Chgo., 1951; Ph.D., London, UK. 1959. Publs: Browning's Characters: A Study in Poetic Technique, 1961, 3rd ed., 1969; The Book, the Ring, & the Poet: A Biography of Robert Browning (w. Wm. Irvine), 1974. Mbr., MLA. Contbr. to: (Ed. or Advsry. bds.) Victorian Poetry; Victorian Studies; Studies in Browning & his Circle; Arnold Newsletter; Novel: A Forum on Fiction; Browning Soc. Notes; Complete Works of Robert Browning. Address: 35 Prospect Rd., Birmingham B13 9TB, UK.

HONE, Joseph, b. 1937, London, UK. UN Official. Educ: St. Columba's Coll., Dublin, Repub. of Ireland. Publs: The Private Sector, 1971; The Sixth Directorate, 1975; The Dancing Waiters, 1975. Contbr. to: Listener; Wash. Post; Yorkshire Post; New Statesman; Daily Telegraph; BBC (radio producer, 1963-67). Lit. Agent: Deborah Rogers Ltd. Address: Manor Cottage, Shutford, nr. Banbury, Oxon., UK.

HONE, Ralph E(merson), b. 27 July 1913, Toledo, Ohio, USA. College Professor; Dean of Humanities. Educ: B.A., 1943, M.A., 1945, Ohio State Univ.; Ph.D., N.Y. Univ., 1955. Publs: The Voice Out of the Whirlwind, 1960, 1972; John Milton's 'Samson Agonistes', 1965. Contbr. of reviews; Regular contbr., L.A. Times, 1962—. Address: Univ. of Redlands, Redlands, CA 92373, USA.

HONEY, Philip, pen names HARRISON, G. D.; PHILLIPS, H. C.; TAURUS; HART, Peter, b. London, UK. Chartered Electrical Engineer. Publs: Planning Electricity in the House, 1965; Household Electricity, 1967. Contbr. to: Elec. Times; Elec. Review; Radio & Elec. Retailing; Elec. & Radio Trading; Wireless & Electronic Retailer; Elec. Contractor & Retailer; Gas Jrnl.; Gas Serv.; Gas World; Gas Marketing; Elec. Wholesaler. Mbrships: Fellow, Instn. of Elec. Engrs.; Past Pres., Assn. of Retired Engrs.; S. Eastern Elec. Consultative Coun., 1963-71. Address: Rose Cottage, 21 The Ridings, Angmering-on-Sea, Littlehampton, W. Sussex BN16 2TW, UK.

HONEYCOMBE, Gordon, b. 1936, Karachi, British India. TV Newscaster; Actor. Educ: B.A., M.A., Univ. Coll., Oxford Univ. Publs: (play) The Redemption, 1964; (novels) Neither the Sea nor the Sand, 1969, screenplay 1972; Dragon Under the Hill, 1972; Adam's Tale, 1974. Plays (performed): The Miracles (author-dir.), 1960; Paradise Lost (author-dir.), 1961; The Golden Vision (w. Neville Smith) (BBC TV), 1968; Time & Again (Westward TV), 1975; Paradise Lost (BBC Radio), 1974. Contbr. to: Punch; Private Eye. Address: c/o Agent: A. D. Peters, 10 Buckingham St., London WC2, UK.

HONIG, Edwin, b. 3 Sept. 1919, NYC, USA. Professor of English & Comparative Literature. Publs: Garcia Lorca,

1944, (rev. ed., 1962); Dark Conceit: the Making of Allegory, 1959, 4th ed., 1972; The Gazabos: 41 Poems, 1959; Survivals: Poems, 1964; Spring Journal, Poems, 1968; Four Springs, a Poem, 1972; Calderon & the Seizures of Honor, 1972; Shake a Spear With Me, John Berryman, New Poems & a Play, 1974. Contbr. to: New Repub.; Nation; etc. Mbrships: Dante Soc.; Am. Translators Assn.; PEN. Hons. incl: Saturday Review Annual Poetry Award, 1956; Amy Lowell Poetry Schlrship, 1968; R.I. Gov.'s Award for Excellence in Arts, 1970. Address: 32 Fort Ave., Cranston, Rhode Island, USA.

HONKANEN, Hilja Loviisa Valkeapää, pen names OUTI; PELKONEN, Elina; ANNI, Mäkituvan; KARE, Kaarina; URSULA, Sanna, b. 3 June 1912, Maironiemi, Parikkala, Finland. Writer. Publs: Talo Puiden varjossa, 1945; Lohilahden kreivitär, 1946; Anna, Mäkivaaran emäntä, 1947. Contbr. to: Pellervo; Maaseudun Tulevaisuus; Nyyrikki; Perjantai; Itä-Savo. Recip., sev. awards. Address: Särkiniemi, Honkasennurkka, SF-59410 Kirjavala, Finland.

HONKANEN, Kerttu Kaarina, pen name HONKANEN, Kaarina, b. 12 Oct. 1929, Kouvola, Finland. Teacher. Educ: M.A. Publs: (in Finnish): Fairy Tales of the Black Cat, 1969; The Wonderful Adventures of Pökö-livari, 1966; Pökö-livari Going Strong, 1967; Kaitsu & Moped, 1971. Contbr. to Finnish Broadcasting Co. Mbrships: Finnish Assn. of Writers; Books for Young People in the World, Paltta; Assn. of Writers of SE Finland. Hons: Finnish Books for Young People Hons., 1967, 1970, 1972; Prize, Cultural Fund of Finland, 1967; Town of Pori Prize, 1969; Town of Kouvola Prize, 1972; Prize, Min. of Educ., Finland, 1970, 1973. Address: Kalevankatu 25, 45100 Kouvola 10, Finland.

HONNOR, Sylvia Crofts, pen name REDSTONE, Sylvia, b. 1933, Hatfield, UK. Educationist; Member, Schools Council Modern Languages Dissemination Project. Educ: B.A. (London), Univ. Coll. of S.W. (now Univ. of Exeter). Publs: De Jour En Jour, Books 1–5; Melange, 1968; Visit to France, Kit (w. B. Hearne), 1975. Ed., De Nos Jours series, 6 vols. Mbrships: Soc. of Authors; MLA; A.V.L.A. Agent: Cassell. Address: 35 Pennine Rise, Scisset, Huddersfield, UK.

HONORÉ, Anthony Maurice, b. 30 Mar. 1921, London, UK. University Professor. Educ: B.A., Univ. South Africa; D.C.L., Oxford Univ. Publs: Causation in the Law (w. H. L. A. Hart), 1959; Gains: A Biography, 1962; The South African Law of Trusts, 1967. Contbr. to: Zeitschrift der Savigny Stoflung; Law Quarterly Review; Tijdschrift voor Rechtsgeschiedenis. Address: All Souls Coll., Oxford Univ., Oxon., UK.

HONOUR, Hugh, b. 1927, Eastbourne, UK. Art Historian. Educ: M.A., St. Catharine's Coll., Cambridge. Publs: Chinoiserie, the vision of Cathay, 1961; Neo-Classicism, 1968. Contbr. to: The Connoisseur (Italian corres., 1956-61); Apollo; Architectural Review; Burlington Mag.; Country Life; Arte Veneta. Address: c/o The Travellers' Club, Pall Mall, London SW1, UK.

HOOD, Hugh John, b. 1928, Toronto, Can. Professor of English. Educ: B.A.; M.A.; Ph.D.; Univ. of Toronto. Publs: Flying a Red Kite, 1962; White Figure, White Ground, 1964; Around the Mountain: Scenes from Montreal Life, 1967; The Camera Always Lies, 1967; Strength Down Centre, 1970; A Game of Touch, 1970. Contbr. to: Kenyon Review; Esquire; Contact; Tamarack Review; Can. Forum; etc. Mbr., Can. Assn. of Univ. Teachers. Address: 4242 Hampton Ave., Montreal 261, P.Q., Canada.

HOOPER, Meredith Jean, b. 21 Oct. 1939, Adelaide, Australia. Writer. Educ: B.A., Adelaide Univ.; B.Phil., Oxford Univ., UK. Publs: Everyday Inventions, 1972; The story of Australia, 1974; More Everyday Inventions, 1975. Hons: Walter Frewin Lord Prize, 1964; Beit Prize, 1966; Aust. Children's Book of the Year Commendation, 1973. Address: 4 Western Rd., London N2, UK.

HOOPER, William Loyd, b. 16 Sept. 1931, Sedalia, Mo., USA. Music Teacher. Educ: B.A., William Jewell Coll.; M.A., Univ. Iowa; Ph.D., George Peabody Coll. for Tchrs.; Royal Coll. Music (London). Publs: Church Music in Transition, 1963; Music Fundamentals, 1966. Contbr. to: Church Musician; Music Ministry; Search; Theol. Educator. Mbrships: Music Educ. Nat. Conf.; New Orleans Music Tchrs. Assn. (Pres.); Am. Soc. Univ. Composers; Southeastern Composers League; Soc. for Promotion New

Music (England). Hons. incl: Allan Duce Philos. Award, 1953; Jesse Jones Sclr., 1960; 1st Prize Delius Composition Competition, 1973. Address: Emmanuel Baptist Church, Windmill St., Gravesend, Kent DA12 1BA, UK.

HOOVER, Helen, b. 1910, Greenfield, Ohio, USA. Metallurgist; Writer. Educ: Ohio Univ.; De Paul Univ.; Univ. of Chgo. Publs: The Long-Shadowed Forest, 1963; The Gift of the Deer, 1966; Animals at My Doorstep, 1966; Great Wolf & the Good Woodsman, 1967; A Place in the Woods, 1969; Animals Near & Far, 1970; The Years of the Forest, 1973. Contbr. to: gen., nature, & juvenile mags., USA & UK. Mbrships: Authors' Guild; Mystery Writers of Am.; Am. Assn. of Press Women. Hons. incl: Annual Achievement Award, Metal Treating Inst., 1959; Zia Award, N.M. Press Women, 1973; Blue Flame Ecol. Salute. Address: P.O. Box 89, Ranchos de Taos, NM 87557, USA.

HOPE, Alec Derwent, b. 21 July 1907, Cooma, N.S.W., Australia. Poet. Educ: B.A., Univ. of Sydney; B.A., Univ. of Oxford. Publs: The Wondering Islands, 1956; Poems, 1961; The Cave & the Spring, 1965; Collected Poems, 1966; New Poems, 1965-69, 1969; A Midsummer Eve's Dream, 1970; Dunciad Minor, 1970; Native Companions, 1974. Contbr. to: var. jrnls., Aust., UK, India, USA & Can. Mbrships: Past Pres., Aust. Soc. of Authors; Aust. Acad. of the Humanities. Recip., num. hons. inclng: Arts Coun. of GB Award, Poetry, 1965; Britannica-Aust. Award for Lit., 1965; Levinson Prize for Poetry, Chgo., 1969; O.B.E., 1972. Address: 66 Arthur Circle, Forrest, Canberra, A.C.T., Australia 2603.

HOPE, Robert Stephen Howard, b. 20 May 1915, Leyton, Essex, UK. Organising Secretary. Publs: A History of the Lord Weymouth School, Warminster, 1961, 2nd rev. ed., 1970; Warminster School Register, 1707-1895, 1972. Contbr. to: Archtl. Review. Mbrships. incl: Fellow, Royal Histl. Soc.; Wiltshire Archaeol. & Natural Hist. Soc.; Gov. & Hon. Archivist, Warminster Schl. Address: 25 Hengistbury Rd., Bournemouth, Dorset BH6 4DQ, UK.

HOPE, Ronald (Sidney), b. 4 Apr. 1921, London, UK. Educationist; Author. Educ: M.A., D.Phil., New Coll., Oxford. Publs: Spare Time at Sea, 1954, revised ed., 1974; Economic Geography, 1956, 5th ed., 1969; Dick Small in the Half-Deck, 1958; Harrap Book of Sea Verse, 1960; The Shoregoer's Guide to World Ports, 1963, reprint, 1964; Seamen & the Sea, 1965; Introduction to the Merchant Navy, 1965, 4th ed., 1973; In Cabined Ships at Sea, 1969. Contbr. to: Fairplay; etc. Recip., O.B.E., 1954. Address: Mansbridge Lodge, 207 Balham High Rd., London SW17 7BH, UK.

HOPE-SIMPSON, Jacynth Ann (née Cureton), b. 10 Nov. 1930, Birmingham, UK. Writer. Educ: Lausanne Univ., Switz.; M.A., St. Hugh's Coll., Oxford. Publs: (children's books) The Edge of the World, 1965; The Unknown Island, 1968; They Sailed from Plymouth, 1971; Save Tarranmoor! & Who Knows?, 1974; 18 others; (novels) The Unravish'd Bride, 1963; 2 others. Mbr., Soroptimist Int. Address: The Red House, Hartley Rd., Plymouth, Devon, UK.

HOPE-WALLACE, Philip Adrian, b. 6 Nov. 1911. Dramatic Critic. Educ: Balliol Coll., Oxford. Publs: A Key to Opera, 1939; pamphlets on drama, music, etc. Contbr. to var. jrnls. as music & drama critic incl: Guardian, 1946—; Times, 1935-39; Time & Tide, 1945-49.

HOPF, Alice Lightner, pen name LIGHTNER, A. M., b. 11 Oct. 1904, Detroit, Mich., USA. Writer. Educ: B.A., Vassar Coll. Publs. incl: (fiction) The Space Ark; The Day of the Drones; The Thursday Toads; Star Dog; Gods or Demons; (natural sci. & nature stories) Wild Traveller; Butterfly & Moth; Biography of a Rhino; Misunderstood Animals; Biography of an Ant, 1974; Wild Cousins of the Cat, 1975. Contbr. to: Argosy; Audobon Mag.; Boys Life; If; N.Y. Daily News; etc. Mbrships. incl: Authors Guild; Sci. Fiction Writers of Am. Recip., Best Sci. Books Award, Nat. Assn. of Sci. Tchrs., 1972. Agent: Larry Sternig Lit. Agcy. Address: 136 W. 16th St., N.Y., NY 10011, USA.

HOPKINS, Antony, b. 1921, London, UK. Composer; Conductor. Educ: F.R.C.M.; L.R.A.M. Publs: Talking about Symphonies, 1961; Talking about Concertos, 1964; Music All Around Me, 1967; Lucy & Peterkin, 1968; Talking about Sonatas, 1971. Mbrships. incl: F.R.S.A. Address: Woodyard, Ashridge, Berkhamsted, Herts., UK.

HOPKINS, (Frances) Betty, pen name JOHN, Miriam, b. 3 Oct. 1915, London, UK. Retired Director of Literary Agency; Translator. Educ: B.A., Univ. of London, 1950. Publs: (transls.) The Ermine, by Anouilh, 1956, 3rd ad., 1967; Romeo & Jeannette, by Anouilh, 1958, 2nd ed., 1967; The Orchestra, by Anouilh, 1967; Episode in the Life of an Author, by Anouilh, 1967; Prokofiev, by C. Samuel, 1971; Liszt, by C. Rostand (co-transl. under joint pen name JOHN, Victor), 1972; Les Adieux de la Grande Duchesse, by B. de Costa, 1973. Address: Elm Farm, Wickerstreet Green, Kersey, Ipswich, Suffolk, UK.

HOPKINS, Harry, b. 26 Mar. 1913, Preston, Lancs., UK. Writer. Educ: B.A., Merton Coll., Oxford. Publs: New World Arising, 1952; England is Rich, 1957; The New Look: A Social History of the 40s & 50s in Britain, 1963; Egypt, the Crucible: The Unfinished Revolution of the Arab World, 1969; The Numbers Game: The Bland Totalitarianism, 1973. Mbr., Nat. Union of Jrnlsts. Address: 61 Clifton Hill, St. John's Wood, London NW8 0JN, UK.

HOPKINS, John, b. 1938, Orange, N.J., USA. Author. Educ: Princeton Univ. Publs: The Attempt, 1968; Tangier Buzzless Flies, 1972. Contbr. to: Art & Lit.; Transatlantic Review; New Yorker; Penthouse. Agent: Peter Matson. Address: B.P. 608, Marrakech, Morocco.

HOPKINS, Kenneth, b. 1914, Bournemouth, UK. Professor of English; Author & Editor. Publs. incl: Love & Elizabeth; The English Lyric; The Poets Laureate; Inca Adventure; The Girl Who Died; She Died Because; The Forty-First Passenger; Pierce with a Pin; Body Blow; Campus Corpse; A Trip to Texas; Portraits in Satire; 42 Poems; Poor Heretic; De La Mare Selections; The Poetry of Railways, 1966; The Powys Brothers: A Biographical Appreciation, 1967; Poems, English & American, 1968; American Poems & Others, 1970; The Enfant Terrible Again, 1974. Contbr. to: Times Lit. Supplement; Poetry Review; Spectator; Punch; Time & Tide; Argosy; etc. Address: 12 New Rd., N. Walsham, Norfolk, UK.

HOPKINS, Sidney John, b. 17 Feb. 1907, London, UK. Pharmaceutical Chemist; Consultant Pharmacist, Addenbrooke's Hospital, Cambridge. Educ: London Univ. Publs: Drugs & Pharmacology for Nurses, 1963, 6th ed., 1975; Principal Drugs, 1958, 4th ed., 1973, reprinted 1974. Contbr. to: Pharm. Jrnl.; Chem. & Druggist; Mfg. Chem.; Nursing Mirror; Nursing Times; Ctrl. Off. Info.; Soap, Perfumery & Cosmetics; Medicamentos de Actualidad. Hons: M.I.M.S. Address: Throcken Holt, Wildman's Lane, Kingston, Cambridge, UK.

HOPKINSON, Alfred Stephan, b. 1908, Manchester, UK. Author. Educ: M.A., Wadham Coll., Oxford; Lincoln Theol. Coll. Publs: God at Work, 1962; Creator Spirit, 1963; Modern Man Reads the Old Testament, 1967; Rev. (co-author), 1967; The God I Want, 1967. Address: Kingsmead, Kingsgate Road, Winchester, Hants., UK.

HOPKINSON, Henry Thomas, b. 19 Apr. 1905, Manchester, UK. Author; Journalist. Educ: B.A., M.A., Pembroke College, Oxford. Publs: The Man Below, 1939; Mist in the Tagus, 1946; The Transitory Venus (short stories), 1948; Love's Apprentice, 1953; The Lady & the Cut-Throat (short stories), 1958; In the Fiery Continent, 1962; South Africa, 1964; Much Silence (co-author), 1974. Contbr. to: Picture Post (Ed., 1940-50); Lilliput (Ed., 1941-46); Drum Mag. (Ed., 1958-61). Recip., C.B.E., 1967. Address: 6 Marine Parade, Penarth, Glam. CF6 2BE, UK.

HOPPE, Arthur Watterson, b. 25 Apr. 1925, Honolulu, Hawaii, USA. Political Columnist. Educ: A.B., Harvard Coll. Publs: The Love Everybody Crusade, 1963; Dreamboat, 1964; The Perfect Solution to Absolutely Everything, 1968; Mr. Nixon & Other Problems, 1971; Miss Lollipop & the Doomsday Machine, 1973. Contbr. to: Travel & Leisure; New Yorker; Playboy. Address: San Fran. Chronicle, Fifth & Mission, San Fran., CA 94119, USA.

HOPPEN-RAM, Henderika Wilhelmina Christina, pen names HOPPEN, Harriet; WIJNSTROOM, Christy, b. 29 Mar. 1919, Bussum, Netherlands. Author. Publs: Maskerade in 't Wit, 1958; En Waarom Niet? ; Als Ik Jou Niet Had; Geen Tijd Voor Dromen; Een Jaar Ging Voorbij; Het Leven Wacht Niet; Valse Start; Wat Let Je, Annetje; Babette; Zon En Schaduw; Als Bloesem In De Wind; Wacht Niet Te Lang Tina; Het Begon Bij Kaarslicht; En Toen Kwam Die Ander; Ik Heb Op Jou Gewacht; Wist Ik Het Maar; 3 more juvenile novels forthcoming; 11 Engl. novels translated into Dutch, 1956-60. Contbr. to: De Uitkijk; var. Dutch & Aust.

Women's Weeklies. Mbr., Soc. of Lit. (V.V.L.). Address: 37 Schansweg, Rotterdam 3008, Netherlands.

HORDER, Mervyn, b. 1910, London, UK. Publisher; Editor. Educ: M.A., Trinity Coll., Cambridge. Publs: The Little Genius, 1966; Six Betjeman Songs, 1967; Ed., A Book of Love Songs, 1969; The Orange Carol Book, 1973. Address: c/o Duckworth & Co. Ltd., 43 Gloucester Crescent, London, NW1 7DY, UK.

HORECKY, Paul L, b. 8 Sept. 1913, Trutnov, Czech. Chief, Slavic & Central European Division, Library of Congress. Publs. incl: Libraries & Bibliographic Centers in the Soviet Union, 1959; (Chief Ed. & Contbr.): Russia & the Soviet Union: A Bibliographic Guide to Western Language Publications, 1965; Southeastern Europe: A Guide to Basic Publications, 1969; East Central Europe: A Guide to Basic Publications, 1969. Contbr. to: Ency. Americana; Cahiers du Monde Russe et Sovietique; etc. Mbrships. incl: Am. Lib. Assn.; Am. Assn. Advancement Slavic Studies; etc. Hons. incl: Charles Smith Schlr., Harvard Univ., 1951. Address: 2207 Paul Spring Rd., Alexandria, VA 22307, USA.

HOREMANS, Jean-Marie, b. 23 Apr. 1937, Gozée, Belgium. Professor. Educ: Lic. Philos & Letters (Roman Philol.) Ctrl. Jury, 1963. Publs. incl: André Malraux ou A la Recherche de la grandeur de l'homme, 1963; Mémoires d'un grenadier du 23ᵉ de ligne, 1968; Maurice des Ombiaux, prince des conteurs Wallons, 1968; Itinéraire poétique de Robert Goffin, 1969; Maurice Gauchez, 1969; Roger Foulon, poète de la vie et de la mort, 1971; Le Livre insolite, 1973; Un Semeur de feu: Carlos de Radzitzky, 1973. Contbr. to: Arion; Les Feuillets du Spantole; Marginales; Revue Nat., etc. Mbrships. incl: Assn. of Belgian Writers Writing in French Lang.; French PEN, Belgium. Recip., Silver Medal of Sci., Letters & Arts, Paris. Address: 75 Ave. Zaman, B 1190, Brussels, Belgium.

HORGAN, John, b. 1940, Co. Kerry, Repub. of Ireland. Editor; Senator of the Republic of Ireland. Educ: B.A., Univ. Coll., Dublin; Univ. Coll., Cork; Inc. Law Soc. of Ireland. Publs: The Church Among the People, 1969; Humanae Vitae & the Bishops, 1970. Ed., Educ. Times (Irish Times publ.). Contbr. to: Irish Times (Reporter & For. Corres. 1963-73); Commonweal; Saturday Review; Book World; Times, London; NC News Serv., Wash. D.C.; Informations Cath. Int.; N.Y. Review of Books. Address: c/o Seanad Eireann, Dublin 2, Repub. of Ireland.

HORGAN, Paul George Vincent O'Shaughnessy, b. 1903, Buffalo, N.Y., USA. Professor of English. Educ: Litt.D.; D.H.L.; New Mexico Mil. Inst. Publs. incl: The Fault of Angels; No Quarter Given; Main Line West; The Centuries of Santa Fe; Give me Possession; A Distant Trumpet; Songs After Lincoln, 1965; Memories of the Future, 1966; The Peach Stone, 1967; Everything to Live For, 1968; The Heroic Triad, 1970; Whitewater, 1970; Maurice Baring Restored, 1960. Contbr. to: Atlantic Monthly; Harper's; Saturday Evening Post; New Yorker; Am. Heritage; The Month; etc. Address: Wesleyan Univ., Middletown, CT 06457, USA.

HÖRLER, Rolf, b. 26 Sept. 1933, Uster, Switz. Teacher. Educ: Tchr. Trng., Mariaberg in Rorschach; Univ. of Zürich. Publs: Mein Steinbruch (poems), 1970; Mein Kerbholz (poems), 1970; Tagesläufe (poems), 1971; Meine Wünschelrute (lyric prose), 1972; Zwischenspurt für Lyriker, 1973; Handschriften (poems), 1973; Poems à la carte oder Monstergastmahl für Poet und Speisekarten (one-act play), 1972. Contbr. to: Neue Zürcher Zeitung; Die TAT; Der Bund; Basler Nachrichten; Spektrum; neutralität; reflexe (Ed.); (anthols.) dieses buch ist gratis; Gut zum Druck. Mbr., Gruppe Olten (Swiss Writers' Grp.). Address: Sennhüttenstr. 1, CH-8805 Richterswil, Kanton Zürich, Switz.

HORN, (John) Stephen, b. 31 May 1931, Gilroy, Calif., USA. Political Scientist. Educ: A.B.(Hons.), 1953, Ph.D., 1958, Stanford Univ.; M.Pub. Admin., Harvard Univ., 1955. Publs: The Cabinet & the Congress, 1960; Unused Power: The Work of the Senate Committee on Appropriations, 1970; Ethics in the House of Representatives: The View from the Hill (co-author), 1975; The Memorable Campaign: Hiram W. Johnson & the 1910 Campaign for the Governorship of California (co-author), forthcoming. Mbrships. incl: Exec. Bd., Stamford Alumni Assn., 1973–; Bd. Mbr., Am. Coun. on Educ., 1974–; US Commn. on Civil Rights, 1969–; Nat. Inst. of Corrections, 1973–; Inst. of Int. Educ., 1975-78.; num. acad. hons & appts. Address:

California State University, 6101 E. 7th St., Long Beach, CA 90840, USA.

HORN, Sabine, b. 10 Apr. 1918, Königsberg, E. Prussia, Germany. Writer. Publs: Aus der Stille, 1969; Das Unzerstörbare, 1972; Ein Leben im Rollstuhl (forthcoming); Geliebter Tag, Geliebte Nacht (forthcoming). Mbr., Soc. of German-Speaking Authors. Recip., Youth Prize, Königsberg, 1935. Address: Annastift-Haus Roderbruch, 3 Hanover, W. Germany.

HORNBY, John Wilkinson, pen names SUMMERS, Gordon; GRACE, Joseph; BRENT, Calvin, b. 5 Apr. 1913, Ponteland, Northumberland, UK. Writer. Publs. incl: United Nations; Forestry in Britain; Undersea World; The Sailor; Beachcombers' Bell; Mystery in Maori Land; Secret of the Valley; Amazon Adventure; Eaglets for the Legion; Song for the Saxons; Viking Fire; The Missing Cargo; The Red Scarf; Priory Island; Clowns through the Ages; Travel by Water; Gypsies; Toys through the Ages; The Adventure of UNICEF (to appear 1975); some works transl'd into Dutch. Contbr. to: Daily Mail; Radio; TV: David C. Cook Fndn.'s Publs. (USA); Bolton Evening News. Mbr., Soc. of Authors. Address: 48 Jackson Ave., Ponteland, Northumberland, UK.

HORNE, Alistair Allan, b. 9 Nov. 1925, London, UK. Author; Farmer. Educ: M.A., Jesus Coll., Cambridge. Publs: Back into Power, 1955; The Land is Bright, 1958; Return to Power, 1956; Canada & the Canadians, 1961; The Price of Glory, Verdun 1916, 1962; The Fall of Paris; The Siege & the Commune, 1870-71, 1965; To Lose a Battle, France 1940, 1969; Death of a Generation, 1970; The Terrible Year, 1971; Small Earthquake in Chile, 1972. Contbr. to var. jrnls. Mbrships: Comm. of Mgmt., Royal Lit. Fund; F.R.S.L.; Fndr., Alistair Horne Rsch. Fellowship for Mod. Hist., St. Antony's Coll., Oxford. Recip., Hawthornden Prize, 1963. Address: c/o Macmillans, 4 Little Essex St., London WC2, UK.

HORNE, Donald Richmond, b. 26 Dec. 1921, Sydney, Australia. Writer. Educ: Sydney Univ.; Canberra Univ. Coll. Publs: The Lucky Country, 1964; The Permit, 1965; The Education of Young Donald, 1967; God Is an Englishman, 1969; The Next Australia, 1970; But What if There Are no Pelicans? , 1971; The Australian People, 1972. Contbr. to var. mags. Address: 53 Grosvenor Street, Woollahra, Australia 2025.

HORNER, David, b. London, UK. Air Ministry Staff Officer. Educ: Trinity Hall, Cambridge. Publs: Through French Windows; Was It Yesterday? ; the Devil's Quill. Contbr. to: Dict. of Nat. Biog.; Life & Letters Today; Geogl. Mag. Mbrships: Brooks's & Athenaeum Clubs. Address: 5 York House, Church St., London W8, UK.

HORNER, John Curwen, b. 15 May 1922, Sandringham, Vic., Australia. Secretary. Educ: E. Sydney Tech. Coll. Publs: Dictionary of Australian History (co-author), 1970; Brutality & Aboriginal People, Racism vol. II, 1971; Vote Ferguson for Aboriginal Freedom (biog.), 1974. Contbr. to: Aust. Quarterly; Outlook; Anglican; Meth.; Race To-Day; Identity: Aboriginal News. Mbrships: Aust. Soc. of Authors; Hon. Sec., Aboriginal-Aust. Fellowship, 1958-66; Sec., Coop. for Aborigines Ltd., 1965-66; Gen. Sec., Fed. Coun. for Advancement of Aborigines & Torres Strait Islanders, 1969-70; Asst. Gen. Sec., 1972-73. Address: Irwin's Rd., East Kurrajong, N.S.W. 2758, Australia.

HORNMAN, Wim, b. 21 June 1920, Tilburg, Netherlands. Foreign Correspondent. Educ: Univ. level. Publs: I Want to Live, 1952; Sabonjo, 1950; The Whole Company, 1953; The Mask Off, 1957; The Scourge of Fear, 1959; Carnival of Contrasts, 1961; South America Again Discovered, 1963; Heroes & Fools, 1964; Poor Rats, 1965; Simba's Do Not Die, 1966; The Rebel Priest, 1968; We Want to Live, 1969; The Red Bishop, 1970; In the Grip of the Tupamaros, 1971; Children of Violence, 1973; Requiem for a Dictator, 1974. Contbr. to mags., reviews, etc., Netherlands, France. Address: Heereweg 132, Schoorl, Netherlands.

HOROVITZ, Israel, b. 31 Mar. 1939, Wakefield, Mass., USA. Author; Playwright; Scriptwriter. Educ: CUNY; Royal Acad. Dramatic Art, London. Publs: (plays) The Indian Wants the Bronx, 1968; It's Called the Sugar Plum, 1969; Collision Course, 1969; Line, 1969-71; Trees & Leader, 1971; Acrobats, 1972; The Honest-to-God Schnozzola, 1969; Morning, 1970; The Wakefield Plays,

1971-76; Germs & Shooting Gallery, 1972; Dr. Hero, 1973; (novel) Cappella, 1973; Spared, 1974; The Middle, 1974; Start to Finish, 1975; The Primary English Class, 1975; also film scripts, TV plays, num. criticisms & unpublished produced plays. Contbr. to: Le Magazine Littéraire (monthly column criticism, 1971-); Craft Horizons Mag.; Eye Mag. Mbrships. incl: Société des Auteurs; Dramatists Guild. Hons. incl: Prix de Jury, Cannes Film Fest., 1971; Lit. Award, Nat. Acad. Arts & Letters, 1972; French Critics Prize, 1973; Playwriting Award, N.Y. Coun. on Arts, 1972, 1975, & Nat. Endowment on the Arts, 1974.

HORSFALL, Jack Campbell, b. 26 Feb. 1912, Daylesford, Vic., Australia. Economist. Educ: A.B., Ormond Coll., Melbourne Univ.; A.M., Trinity Coll., Cambridge, UK. Publs: Australia: Nations of the Modern World Series; The Liberal Era. Contbr. to: Aust. Fin. Review (Ed.); New C'wlth.; Sydney Morning Herald; NZ Herald; Investors' Chronicle; Bulletin (Aust.); etc. Mbrships: Hawkes (Cambridge); Achilles Club. Address: 61 Bromby St., South Yarra, Vic., Australia.

HORSLEY, James Allen, b. 30 Mar. 1938, Martinez, Calif., USA. Financial Public Relations Specialist. Educ: A.B., Univ. of Calif. at Berkeley. Publs: God's Naked Daughter, 1972; Dance of Dismemberment, forthcoming. Contbr. to: Occident; Poet Lore. Recip., Poet Lore Award, 1968. Address: 9 Glorietta Ct., Orinda, CA 94563, USA.

HORSLEY, Phyllis Margaret, b. 1903, N. Shields, UK. Former Teacher of Modern Languages. Educ: Univ. of Durham; Univ. of Cambridge; M.A., Ph.D. Publs: Eighteenth Century Newcastle, 1970. Contbr. to: Music & Letters, 1974; Comp. Lit. Studies; etc. Address: 11 Beatty Ave., Newcastle upon Tyne NE2 3QN, UK.

HORSMAN, Ernest Alan, b. 24 Oct. 1918, Bridlington, UK. Donald Collie Professor of English. Educ: M.A., Auckland Univ. Coll., NZ, 1941; M.A., St. Catherine's Coll., Oxford Univ., UK, 1947. Publs: (Ed.) Diary of Alfred Domett, 1872-85, 1953; Jonson's Bartholomew Fair, 1960, 1965; Shakespeare, King Lear, 1973; Dickens, Dombey & Son, 1974. Contbr. to: Landfall; Islands; Aumla. Mbrships: PEN; Australian Univs. Lang. & Lit. Assn. Address: 1028 George St., Dunedin, NZ.

HORSMAN, Reginald, b. Leeds, UK. University Professor. Educ: B.A.; M.A.; Ph.D.; Univ. of Birmingham; Indiana Univ. Publs: The Causes of the War of 1812, 1962; Matthew Elliot, 1964; Expansion & American Indian Policy, 1783-1812, 1967; The War of 1812, 1969; The Frontier in the Formative Years, 1783-1815, 1970. Contbr. to: Jrnl. of Am. Hist.; Ency. Britannica; Ency. Americana; William & Mary Quarterly; etc. Mbr., Am. Histl. Assn. Address: 3548 N. Hackett Ave., Milwaukee, WI 53211, USA.

HORSPOOL, Maurice Arthur Rupert, b. 1905, Bridlington, Yorks., UK. Former Bank Manager. Publs: (plays) Julius & the Bront, 1939; Guineas for the Ghost, 1939; Nightmare's End, 1949; The Stones of St. Mary's, Scarborough (guidebook), 1972. Contbr. to: Scarborough Mercury; etc.; BBC; Theatre Window, vols. I & II; Mastery of English, vol. I. Address: Silverdale, 178 Scalby Rd., Scarborough, Yorks., UK.

HORST, Karl August, b. 10 Aug. 1913, Darmstadt, Germany. Writer. Educ: Ph.D.; Univs. of Munich, Berlin, Göttingen, Bonn. Publs. incl: Zero, 1951; Ina Seidel, Wesen & Werk, 1956; Die deutsche Literatur der Gegenwart, 1957; Das Spektrum des modernen Romans, 1959; Kritischer Führer durch die Deutsche Literatur der Gegenwart, 1962; Der Skorpion, Erzählungen, 1963; Das Abenteuer der Deutschen Literatur im zwanzigsten Jahrhundert, 1964; Zwischen den Stühlen, 1972; (Ed. & transl.) Erzähler der Welt, 24 vols., 1966-72. Contbr. to Merkur. Address: 8174 Ried/Benediktbeuern, W. Germany.

HORTON, Almon, b. 4 July, 1912, Manchester, UK. Retired Company Secretary. Publs: Amateur Journalism Survey, 11 parts, 1946; The Hobby of Amateur Journalism, Part 1, 1955; Hobby Press Guide, 1955-56; Vista, quarterly 1964—; Interlink, 1966—; Amateur Journalism in America, vol. 1, 1974. Contbr. to: The Brit. Amateur Jrnlst.; The Fossil. Mbrships. incl: Past Pres., Brit. Amateur Press Assn.; The Fossils; Lancashire Authors' Assn.; Nat. Amateur Press Assn. in Am. Address: 10 Warwick Grove, Audenshaw, Manchester M34 5QT, UK.

HORVATH, Janos, b. 7 Nov. 1921, Cece, Hungary. Professor of Economics. Educ: Ph.D., Econs., Columbia Univ., USA. Publ: China's International Grants Balance, 1974. Contbr. to: Jrnl. Econ. Lit.; Pub. Fin.; KYKLOS; Slavic Review; Southern Econ. Jrnl.; Am. Economist; Am. Jrnl. Agricl. Econs.; Antitrust Bulletin; Pol. Sci. Quarterly; Problems of Communism; Quarterly Review of Econs. & Bus.; E. Ctrl. Europe; Studies in Comp. Int. Dev. Mbr., num. profl. assns. Hons: Fellow, Hungarian Acad. of Sci., 1947; Ford Fndn. Fellow, 1962; Danforth Fellow, 1963-65. Address: Holcomb Rsch. Inst., Butler Univ., Indpls., IN 46208, USA.

HORVÁTH, László P., b. 24 Mar. 1930, Pápa, Hungary. Dramatist. Educ: Tchng. Degree in Hungarian Lang., Fac. of Liberal Arts. Publs: Márciusi Hold (poems), 1969; Pünkösdi Király (6 dramas), 1973. Mbrships: Hungarian Writers' Assn.; Magyar Népköztársaság Müvészeti Alapja. Address: Obester Street 11, 1097 Budapest, Hungary.

HOSHI, Shinichi, b. 6 Sept. 1926, Tokyo, Japan. Writer. Educ: Grad., Dept. of Agric. Chem., Tokyo Univ., 1948. publs: about 30 vols. of fantasy, sci. fiction & mystery; Bokku-chan, 1961. Contbr. to: Shösetsu Shincho; other mags. Mbrships: PEN; Mystery Writers Assn. of Japan; Sci. Fiction Writers Club of Japan; Agric. Chem. Soc. of Japan. Recip., Prize, Mystery Writers Assn. of Japan, 1968. Address: 1–2–6 Hiratsuka, Shinagawaku, Tokyo 142, Japan.

HOSKING, Eric, b. 1909, London, UK. Writer. Publs: Birds in Action (w. Cyril Newberry), 1949; Birds Fighting (w. Stuart Smith), 1955; Bird Photography as a Hobby (w. Cyril Newberry), 1961; Nesting Birds (w. Winwood Reade), 1967; An Eye for a Bird (w. Frank Lane), 1970; Wildlife Photography (w. John Gooders), 1973. Contbr. to: Country Life; Field; Brit. Birds; Birds; Animals Mag.; Shooting Times. Mbrships: Hon. F.R.P.S.; F.I.I.P.; F.Z.S.; VP, Royal Soc. for the Protection of Birds; VP, London Natural Hist. Soc. Address: 20 Crouch Hall Rd., London N8 8HX, UK.

HOSKINS, Katherine de Montalant Lackey, b. 1909, Indian Head, Md., USA. Educ: B.A., Smith Coll. Publs: (poetry) A Penitential Primer; Villa Narcisse; Out in the Open; Excursions Athenaeum. Contbr. to: Hudson Review; Quarterly Review of Lit.

HOSSENT, Harry, pen names SAVAGE, David; HOLTON, H. B., b. 12 Nov. 1916. Author; Journalist. Publs: Spies Die at Dawn; No End to Fear; Memory of Treason; Spies Have no Friends; Run for Your Death; The Fear Business; The Spy who Got Off at Las Vegas; Gangster Movies; The Great Spectaculars. Contbr. to: Motor; Service Station; Motor Trade Executive; etc. Mbr., Brit. Assn. of Indl. Eds. Agent: F. Rupert Crew. Address: 75 Abbot's Park, London Rd., St. Albans, Herts., UK.

HOTHAM, David, b. 5 Aug. 1917, Darlington, UK. Writer. Educ: B.A., Oxford Univ. Publs: The Turks, 1972. Contbr. to: Times (Corres., Saigon, 1955-57, Ankara, 1958-66, Bonn, 1966-69); Economist; Observer. Mbrships: Berwickshire Co. Coun.; Bd., River Tweed Commnrs.; New Club, Edinburgh. Agent: Anthony Sheil Assocs. Address: Milne Graden, Coldstream, Scotland, UK.

HOUGH, (Helen) Charlotte, b. 24 May 1924, Brockenhurst, Hants., UK. Artist; Writer. Publs: (for children) Jim Tiger; Morton's Pony; The Story of Mr. Pinks; The Animal Game; Algernon & Anna & Minnie; Educating Flora; A Bad Child's Book of Moral Verse; Sir Frog; Red Biddy; The Owl in the Barn; The Home-makers; The Hampshire Pig; Three Little Funny Ones; Queer Customer; Pink Pig; Bad Cat; Wonkey Donkey. Mbr., Exec. Comm., PEN. Address: 25 St. Ann's Terrace, London NW8 6PH, UK.

HOUGHTON, (Canon) Alfred Thomas, b. 11 Apr. 1896, Stafford, UK. Clerk in Holy Orders; Foundation Canon, Morogoro, Tanzania. Educ: M.A., L.Th., Univ. Coll., Durham; London Coll. of Divinity. Publs: Tailum Jan, 1931; Dense Jungle Green, 1937; In Training, 1946; The Battle of World Evangelisation; God Wills It; Preparing to Be a Missionary, 1956. Contbr. to: The Life of Faith; etc. Address: 2 Queen Elizabeth Court, Park Road, Barnet, Herts. EN5 5SG, UK.

HOUGHTON, Donald Herbert (Don), b. 2 Feb. 1930, Cormeille-en-Parisis, Paris, France. Writer; Director/ Producer, TV & Films. Publs: 7 crime novels, 1957-62;

Num. plays, serials & series, Aust. Radio & TV (Writer/Prod./Dir.), 1951-65; works for UK TV, 1965—; Screenplays for Columbia, Fox, Warners & other cos. Contbr. to: BBC; A.T.V.; Yorkshire TV; Thames TV; & others. Mbrships: Writers' Guild of Aust. (Fndn. Pres.); Writers' Guild of Gt. Brit.; A.C.T.T. Address: c/o Agent, Dalzell-Durbridge Authors Ltd., 14 Clifford St., London W1, UK.

HOUGHTON, Eric, b. 4 Jan. 1930, Shipley, Yorks., UK. Schoolteacher; Author. Educ: Cert. Educ., Univ. of Sheffield, 1952. Publs: The White Wall, 1961; They Marched with Spartacus, 1963; Summer Silver, 1963; Boy Beyond the Mist, 1967; The Mouse & the Magician, 1970; A Giant can do Anything, 1975. Mbrships: Soc. of Authors, Playwrights & Composers; Children's Writers' Grp. Recip., Jr. Book Award, Boys Clubs of Am., for They Marched with Spartacus, 1964. Address: "The Crest", 42 Collier Rd., Hastings, Sussex TN34 3JR, UK.

HOUGHTON, George William, b. 9 Sept. 1905, Perth, UK. Author. Artist; Cartoonist. Educ: Sorbonne Univ., Paris, France. Publs. incl: Golf Addict Goes East, 1967; Golf Addict Among the Scots, 1967; Better Golf — Definitely! (w. Jessie Valentine), 1967; Golf Addicts Galore (cartoons), 1968; Golfers in Orbit, 1968; Golf Addict Invades Wales, 1969; Golf with a WhippyShaft, 1969; Golf Addict in Gaucho Land, 1970; How to be a Golf Addict, 1971; Just a friendly ... (cartoons), 1973; Believe It or Not — that's Golf! , 1974. Contbr. to: Golf World; etc. Mbrships: Pres., Golf Addicts' Soc. of GB. Recip., O.B.E., 1946. Address: Coneygar House, Bridport, Dorset, UK.

HOUGHTON, Neal Doyle, b. 8 May 1895, Putnam Co., Mo., USA. University Professor of Political Science, University of Arizona. Educ: B.S. in Ed., Mo. State Tchrs. Coll., 1921; M.A., Univ. of Mo., 1923; Ph.D., Univ. of Ill., 1927. Publs: Realities of American Government, 1937; Struggle Against History: U.S. Foreign Policy in an Age of Revolution (ed. & maj. contbr.), 1968. Contbr. to num. US, for. jrnls.; Author, sev. monographs. Address: 2134 E. 6th St., Tucson, AZ 85719, USA.

HOUGHTON, (Rev.) Reginald Leighton, b. 1910, Birmingham, UK. Vicar. Educ: M.A., Durham Univ. Publs: In the Steps of the Anglo-Saxons; In the Steps of the Normans; In the Steps of St. Joan of Arc; Crusoe Game; Phantom Rider; Haunted Stable; Gallows Tor; Sealed Orders; Haunted Creek; Luck of the Ravens; Catch me a Pewit; Herons' Quests; Guide to the British Cathedrals, 1973. Address: Bartley Green Vicarage, Birmingham 32, Warwicks., UK.

HOUGRON, Jean, b. 1 July 1923. Writer. Educ: Law Faculty, Univ. of Paris. Publs. incl: Tu recolteras la Tempete, 1950; Rage Blanche, 1951; Soleil au ventre, 1952; Les Portes des l'Aventure, 1954; Les Asiates, 1954; La Terre du Barbare, 1958; Par qui le scandale, 1960; Le Signe du Chien, 1961; Histoire de Georges Guersant, 1964; Les Humiliés, 1965; La Geule Pleine de Dents, 1970; (films) Mort en Fraude, 1953; Je reviendrai à Kandara, 1955; Hons: Grand Prix du Roman, French Acad., 1953; Prix Populiste, 1965. Address: 34 rue Greneta, Paris 2e, France.

HOULDIN, Joseph Eric, b. 21 Oct. 1916, Birkenhead, UK. Professor & Head of Electronics Department, Chelsea College, London University. Educ: B.Eng., 1936, Ph.D., 1938, Univ. of Liverpool. Publs: Principles of Electronics (w. M. R. Gavin), 1959. Contbr. to: Wireless Engr.; Phys. Educ.; Jrnl. of the Instn. of Elec. Engrs.; Am. Jrnl. of Phys. Mbrships: Chmn., Electronics Grp., & Fellow, Inst. of Phys.; Fellow, Instn. of Elec. Engrs. Address: 32 Ennerdale Rd., Kew Gdns., Richmond, Surrey, UK.

HOULT, Norah, b. Dublin, Repub. of Ireland. Novelist; Journalist. Publs. incl: Poor Women, 1928; Holy Ireland, 1935; Four Women Grow Up, 1940; Scene for Death, 1943; House Under Mars, 1946; Cocktail Bar, 1950; Frozen Ground, 1952; Sister Mavis, 1953; Journey into Print, 1954; A Death Occurred, 1954; Father Home and the Television Set, 1956; Father & Daughter, 1957; Husband & Wife, 1959; Last Days of Miss Jenkinson, 1962; Poet's Pilgrimage, 1966; Only Fools & Horses Work, 1969; Not For Our Sins Alone, 1972. Address: Jonquil Cottage, Greystones, Co. Wicklow, Repub. of Ireland.

HOUNSOME, Robert Edwin, b. 1919, Brighton, UK. Freelance Writer; Public Relations Consultant. Contbr. to: Today; She; Titbits; Weekend; var. tech. jrnls.;

Reporter/Feature Writer, The Star, 1950-60; Deputy News Ed./Scriptwriter, Southern TV, 1960-62; Sometime Scriptwriter, Life With the Lyons; The Beating Heart (TV documentary). Mbrships: Inst. of P.R.; Nat. Union of Jrnlsts.; Mgmt. Bd., Poole Sports Ctr.; Comm., Wessex Export Club, Publicity Club of Bournemouth. Address: 42 Parkstone Rd., Poole, Dorset BH15 2PS, UK.

HOUSE, Ernest Robert, b. 7 Aug. 1937, Alton, Ill., USA. Educational Evaluator. Educ: A.B., Wash. Univ.; M.S., S. Ill. Univ.; Ed.D., Univ. of Ill. Publs: School Evaluation: The Politics & Process, 1973; Politics of Educational Innovation, 1974. Contbr. to: Am. Educl. Rsch. Jrnl.; Jrnl. of Educl. Psychol.; Phi Delta Kappan; Educl. Forum; Tchrs. Coll. Record; Educl. Admin. Quarterly. Mbrships: Am. Educl. Rsch. Assn.; Coun. on Exceptional Children; Am. Fedn. of Tchrs.; AAUP. Recip., Travel Study Grant, Ford Fndn., 1975. Address: 2103 Zuppke Drive, Urbana, !L, USA.

HOUSEHOLD, Geoffrey Edward West, b. 30 Nov. 1900, Bristol, UK. Author; Barrister-at-Law. Educ: Magdalen Coll., Oxford. Publs. incl: (novels) Rogue Male, 1939; Arabesque, 1948; The High Place, 1950; A Time to Kill, 1952; Fellow Passenger, 1955; Watcher in the Shadows, 1960; Thing to Love, 1963; Doom's Caravan, 1971; The Three Sentinels, 1972; (for children) The Spanish Cave, 1940; Prisoner of the Indies, 1967; (autobiography) Against the Wind, 1958; (short stories) Tales of Adventurers, 1952; The Brides of Solomon, 1958; Sabres on the Sand, 1966. Address: Church Headland, Whitchurch, Aylesbury, Bucks., UK.

HOUSEHOLD, Henry Leonard Moore, b. 1914, Dublin, Repub. of Ireland. Secretary, C.S.E. Examining Board; Former Teacher & Education Officer. Educ: B.Sc.(Econ.), Univ. of London, UK. Publs: A Preparatory Algebra; Revision Outlines of Plane Geometry; Planned Exercises in Geometry. Contbr. to: Quarterly Jrnl. of R.A. Awarded E.R.D. Address: 11 Hazelwood, Hazelwood Rd., Bristol BS9 1PU, UK.

HOUSEHOLD, Humphrey George West, b. 1906, Cheltenham, Glos., UK. Writer; Retired Schoolmaster. Educ: M.A., Cheltenham Coll. Publs: The Thames & Severn Canal, 1969. Contbr. to: The Railway Mag.; The Locomotive, Railway Carriage & Wagon Review; Country Life; Glos. Countryside; Jrnl. of Transp. Hist. Mbrships: Railway & Canal Histl. Soc.; Glos. Soc. for Indust. Archaeol. Address: 1 Marten Rd., Folkestone, Kent CT20 2JR, UK.

HOUSLOP, Norman Louis, b. 1906, London, UK. Headmaster. Educ: B.A., Univ. Coll., London. Publs: Everyday Science; Fundamental Science. Address: 27 Rodenhurst Rd., Clapham Pk., London, SW4, UK.

HOUSTON, Hugh Stewart, b. 14 June 1924, Alexandria, Scotland, UK. Academic Executive. Educ: M.A., B.Ed., Dip.Ed., Ph.D.; Wellington Coll.; Vic. Univ., NZ; Univs. of NZ, Auckland, Western Aust., & Massey (NZ). Publs: Marriage & the Family in New Zealand, 1970; Child Development, forthcoming. Contbr. to: Personality (Cons. Ed.); Aust. Jrnl. Social Issues; NZ Jrnl. of Educl. Studies; Aust. Jrnl. of Educ.; Nat. Educ.; Educ. Mbrships. incl: Fellow, Royal Soc. Arts (London); Comm. Mbr., Aust. Assn. for Rsch. in Educ.; Higher Educ. Rsch. & Dev. Soc. of Australasia; VP, Aust. Pre-Schl. Assn. Address: 26 Kinleyside Crescent, Weetangena, A.C.T., Australia 2614.

HOUSTON, James D., b. 10 Nov. 1933, San Fran., Calif. Writer. Educ: B.A., Calif. State Univ., 1956; M.A., Stanford Univ., 1962. Publs: (novels) Gig, 1969; A Native Son of the Golden West, 1971; (stories) The Adventures of Charlie Bates, 1973; Farewell to Manzanar (w. Jeanne Wakatsuki Houston), 1973; Open Field (w. John Brodie), 1974. Mbrships: Authors' Guild; Writers' Guild Am., W. Hons: Wallace Stegner Creative Writing Fellow, Stanford, 1966-67; Joseph Henry Jackson Award Fiction, San Fran., 1967; Univ. Calif., Fac. Rsch. Grant, 1972-73. Address: 2-1130 E. Cliff Dr., Santa Cruz, CA 95062, USA.

HOUWAART, Dick, b. 9 Oct. 1927, The Hague, Netherlands. Editor-in-Chief, Dagblad van het Oosten. Publs: Politiek Jaarboek, 1969, 1970, 1972; A Gouvernements Crisis, 1972; Journalism in Israel, 1973; Storm Round the Parlement, 1973; F. Weinreb — A Whitbook, 1974. Contbr. to: Tijd En Taak; Radio & TV progs., Vara, Nos, Rono. Address: Joh. v. Burenlaan 30, Almello, Netherlands.

HOVEYDA, Fereydoun, b. 21 Sept. 1924, Damascus, Syria. Diplomat. Educ: Dip., Etudes Supérieures d'Econ. Pol., Dip., Etudes Supérieures de Droit Pub., Univ. of Paris, France; LL.D., 1948. Publs: La Planification Iranienne (essay), 1949; Les Quarantaines (novel), 1962; L'Aérogare (novel), 1965; L'Historie du Roman Policier (essay), 1967; Dans Une Terre Etranger (novel), 1968; Le Losange (short stories), 1969; Les Neiges du Sinai (novel), 1973. Contbr. to: Les Cahiers du Cinema; Positif; Fiction; etc. Recip., Prix Leopold Senghor, 1973. Address: Permanent Mission of Iran to the UN, 622 Third Ave., 34th Floor, N.Y., NY 10017, USA.

HOWARD, Arthur Ellsworth Dick, b. 5 July 1933, Richmond, Va., USA. Professor of Law. Educ: B.A., Univ. of Richmond, 1954; B.A., 1961, M.A., 1965, Oxford Univ., UK; LL.B., Univ. of Va., USA, 1961. Publs: The Road from Runnymede: Magna Carta & Constitutionalism in America, 1968; Commentaries on the Constitution of Virginia, 1974. Mbr., Bd. of Eds., Am. Oxonian. Hons: Rhodes Schlrship.; 1958; Woodrow Wilson Fellow, Smithsonian Inst., 1974; etc. Address: School of Law, Univ. of Va., Charlottesville, VA 22901, USA.

HOWARD, Constance Mildred, b. 8 Dec. 1910, Northampton, UK. Embroiderer; Lecturer. Educ: Northampton Schl. of Art; Royal Coll. of Art; A.R.C.A., A.T.D. Publs: Design for Embroidery from Traditional English Sources, 1956; Inspiration for Embroidery, 1966. Mbrships: Fellow, Soc. of Designer Craftsmen; Art Wkr.'s Guild; Brit. Craft Ctr.; Coun., Embroiderers Guild; Costume Soc. Recip., M.B.E., New Year's Hons. List, 1975. Address: 43 Cambridge Rd. South, Chiswick, London W4 3DA, UK.

HOWARD, Derek Lionel, b. 6 May 1930, Brighton, UK. Director, Voluntary Agencies Council. Educ: B.Sc.(Econ.), Univ. of London; Dip. Ed., Univ. of Cambridge. Publs: British Life & Institutions; The Life of Britain; John Howard, Prison Reformer, 1958; The English Prisons, 1960; Man & Society, 1965; Prisons & Education, 1970. Contbr. to: Daily Telegraph; Times Educl. Supplement; The Teacher; BBC Radio. Mbrships. incl: Soc. of Authors; Howard League for Penal Reform; Brit. Soc. of Criminol. Hons: Cropwood Fellowship in Criminol., Univ. of Cambridge, 1969-70; J.P. Address: c/o Newham Vol. Agcys. Coun., Durning Hall, Earlham Grove, London E7, UK.

HOWARD, Elizabeth Jane, b. 1923, London, UK. Writer. Publs: (novels) The Beautiful Visit; The Long View; The Sea Change; After Julius; Something In Disguise; Odd Girl out; Portrait of Bettina (biog. w. Arthur Helps); Mr. Wrong (short stories). Contbr. to: Encounter; Queen; Vogue; Town & Country; New Yorker; Daily Telegraph; Spectator; Cosmopolitan; Daily Mail; Observer Colour Supplement; Telegraph Mag.; Evening Standard; Sunday Times; Radio Times. Agent: A. D. Peters. Address: Lemmons, Hadley Common, Barnet, Herts., UK.

HOWARD, Helen Addison, b. 4 Aug. 1904, Missoula, Mont., USA. Author; Historian. Educ: B.A., Univ. of Mont., Missoula, 1927; M.A., Univ. of S. Calif., Los Angeles, 1933. Publs. incl: War Chief Joseph, 1941-74; Northwest Trail Blazers, 1963; Saga of Chief Joseph, 1965-71; An Introduction to Pre-Missionary Indian Religion, 1974 (in Journal of the West); A Survey of American Indian Music: A Critique of 5 volumes from the Densmore Collection, 1974; Ed., American Indian Poetry, (in preparation). Contbr. to var. jrnls. Mbr., Calif. Writers' Guild; Valley Writers' Club; etc. Hons: Lecturer, American Indian Poetry, 1966-67; & others. Address: 410 South Lamer Street, Burbank, CA 91506, USA.

HOWARD, Michael Eliot, b. 1922, London, UK. College Fellow. Educ: M.A., Christ Ch., Oxford. Publs. incl: Ed., Soldiers & Governments; Disengagement iEurope; Ed., The Theory & Practice of War; The Franco-Prussian War, 1870-1871; Wellington Studies; The Mediterranean Strategy in the Second World War; Studies in War & Peace; The Continental Commitment; U.K. Official History of the Second World War; Grand Strategy, vol. IV, 1942-43. Contbr. to var. acad. jrnls., etc. Mbrships: F.B.A.; F.R.S.L.; Fellow, Royal Histl. Soc. Hons: Duff Cooper Mem. Prize, 1962; Wolfson Lit. Award for Hist., 1972. Agent: David Higham Assocs. Ltd. Address: All Souls College, Oxford OX1 4AL, UK.

HOWARD, Philip Nicholas Charles, b. 2 Nov. 1933, London, UK. Journalist. Educ: King's Schlr., Eton; B.A., Trinity Coll., Oxford. Publs: The Black Watch, 1968: The

Royal Palaces, 1970. Contbr. to: The Times; BBC. Mbr., Nat. Union of Jrnlsts. Recip., I.P.C. Award for descriptive writing, 1969; Address: Flat 1, 47 Ladbroke Grove, London W11, UK.

HOWARTH, David Armine, b. 18 July 1912, London, UK. Author. Educ: B.A., Trinity Coll., Cambridge. Publs: The Shetland Bus, 1952; Thieves Hole, 1954; We Die Alone, 1955; The Sledge Patrol, 1957; Dawn of D Day, 1959; The Shadow of the Dam, 1961; My Land & My People (Ed.), 1962; The Desert King, 1964; The Golden Isthmus, 1966; Sovereign of the Seas, 1974. Contbr. to: Sunday Times; Saturday Evening Post. Address: Wildings Wood, Blackboys, Sussex, UK.

HOWARTH, Patrick John Fielding, pen name FRANCIS, C. D. E., b. 25 Apr. 1916. Official, Royal National Lifeboat Institution. Educ: M.A., Univ. of Oxford. Publs: The Year is 1851, 1951; The Dying Ukrainian, 1953; A Matter of Minutes, 1953; Ed., Special Operations, 1954; Questions in the House, 1956; The Lifeboat Story, 1957; How Men are Rescued from the Sea, 1961; Squire, Most Generous of Men, 1963; Play Up & Play the Game, 1973; Lifeboats & Lifeboat People, 1974. Contbr. to: Hist. Today; Punch; Time & Tide. BBC. Mbrships. incl: Soc. of Authors; Inst. of Pub. Rels. Address: 912 Nell Gwynn House, London SW3, UK.

HOWARTH, Thomas Edward Brodie, b. 21 Oct. 1914, Rutherglen, Scotland, UK. Academic. Educ: M.A., Clare Coll., Cambridge Univ. Publs: Citizen King, 1961; Culture, Anarchy & the Public Schools, 1969. Contbr. to: Times Educl. Supplement. Mbrships: Pub. Schls. Commn.; Hdmasters Conf. (Chmn., 1969). Hons: M.C.; T.D. Address: Magdalene Coll., Cambridge CB3 0AG, UK.

HOWAT, Gerald Malcolm David, pen name HENDERSON-HOWAT, Gerald, b. 12 June 1928, Glasgow, UK. Schoolmaster. Educ: M.A., Univ. of Edinburgh; B.Litt., Exeter Coll., Oxford Univ.; Dip.Ed., Univ. of London. Publs: From Chatham to Churchill, 1966; Essays to a Young Teacher, 1966; The Story of Health (w. Anne Howat), 1967; The Teaching of Empire & Commonwealth History, 1967; Ed., Dictionary of World History, 1973; Documents in European History, 1789-1970, 1973; Stuart & Cromwellian Foreign Policy, 1974; Leary Constantine: A Biography, 1975. Contbr. to: Quarterly Review; The Times; Glasgow Herald; var. other jrnls. Mbr., Soc. of Authors. Fellow, Royal Historical Soc. Address: Old School House, North Moreton, Oxon., UK.

HOWATCH, Susan, b. 14 July 1940, Leatherhead, Surrey, UK. Novelist. Educ: LL.B., King's Coll., Univ. of London, 1961. Publs: The Dark Shore, 1965; The Waiting Sands, 1966; Call in the Night, 1967; The Shrouded Walls, 1968; April's Grave, 1969; The Devil on Lammas Night, 1970; Penmarric, 1971; Cashelmara, 1974. Contbr. to: The Writer. Mbrships: Mystery Writers of Am.; Authors' Guild. Address: c/o Harold Ober Associates Inc., 40 East 49th St., N.Y., NY 10017, USA.

HOWE, G. Melvyn, b. 7 Apr. 1920, Abercynon, UK. Professor of Geography. Educ: B.Sc., M.Sc., Ph.D., Univ. of Wales; D.Sc., Univ. of Strathclyde. Publs: Wales from the Air, 1957, 2nd ed., 1966; Welsh Landforms & Scenery (w. P. Thomas), 1963; National Atlas of Disease Mortality in the United Kingdom, 1963, 2nd ed., 1970; The Soviet Union, 1968; The USSR, 1972; Ed., Atlas of Glasgow & the West Region of Scotland, 1972; Man, Environment & Disease, 1972; Ed., Environmental Medicine (w. J. Loraine), 1973. Contbr. to num. profl. jrnls. Mbrships: Inst. of Brit. Geogs.; Royal Geogl. Soc.; Royal Scottish Geogl. Soc.; Royal Meteorol. Soc. Recip., Gill Mem. Prize, Royal Geogl. Soc., 1964. Address: 29 Birnam Crescent, Bearsden, Glasgow G61 2AU, UK.

HOWELLS, Roscoe, b. 27 Oct. 1919, Saundersfoot, Wales, UK. Farmer; Writer. Publs: Cliffs of Freedom, 1961; Farming in Wales, 1965; The Sounds Between, 1968; Across the Sounds, 1972; What Price Abortion?, 1973; Heronsmill, 1975. Mbrships: Guild of Agricl. Jrnlsts.; Inst. of Jrnlsts.; Farmers' Club. Address: Cwnbrwyn, St. Clears, Carmarthen SA33 4HY, UK.

HOWELLS, William White, b. 1908, NYC, USA. Professor of Anthropology. Educ: S.B., Ph.D., Harvard Univ. Publs: Mankind So Far, 1944; The Heathens, 1948; Back of History, 1954; Mankind in the Making, 1959, revised 1967; Ideas on Human Evolution, 1949-61, (Ed.), 1962; Cranial Variation in Man, 1973; Evolution of the Genus Homo, 1973; The Pacific Islanders, 1973. Address: Kittery Point, ME 03905, USA.

HOWES, Barbara, b. 1 May 1914, Boston, Mass., USA. Writer; Poet; Housewife; Anthologist. Educ: B.A., Bennington Coll., Vt. Publs. incl: (poetry) The Undersea Farmer, 1948; In the Cold Country, 1953; Light & Dark, 1959; Looking Up at Leaves, 1966; The Blue Garden, 1972; (Ed., short story anthols.) 23 Modern Stories, 1963; From the Green Antilles, 1966; The Sea-Green Horse (w. G. Jay Smith), 1970; The Eye of the Heart: Stories from Latin America, 1973. Contbr. to num. lit. & acad. jrnls. Hons. incl: Guggenheim Fellowship, 1955; Brandeis Univ. Creative Arts Poetry Grant, 1958; Lit. Award from Nat. Inst. Arts & Letters, 1971; Golden Rose Award New England Poetry Club, 1973. Address: Brook House, N. Pownal, VT 05260, USA.

HOWLETT, John Reginald, b. 4 Apr. 1940, Leeds, UK. Author; Scriptwriter. Educ: Jesus Coll., Oxford Univ. Publs: If. . . (screenplay, co-author), 1969; James Dean (biog.), 1975; Elegy For A Spy (novel), 1975. Address: Orchard House, Stone-in-Oxney, Tenterden, Kent, UK.

HOYLE, Fred, b. 1915, Bingley, Yorks., UK. Professor of Astronomy. Educ: M.A.; Emmanuel Coll., & St. John's Coll., Cambridge. Publs: Technical Papers; Nature of the Universe; Frontiers of Astronomy; Galaxies, Nuclei & Quasars; Decade of Decision; Man & Materialism; The Black Cloud; Ossian's Ride; A for Andromeda (w. John Eliot); Rockets in Ursa Major (w. G. Hoyle); Seven Steps to the Sun. Mbr., Royal Soc. Address: 1 Clarkson Close, Cambridge, UK.

HOYLES, Joseph, b. 1914, Preston, UK. Publs: Charity (play), 1935; He Was Blind, 1936; The Benevolent Despot (play), 1937; Sinbad the Sailor (pantomime), 1946; Hansel & Gretel (pantomime), 1947; Who Killed Mary Windsor?, 1947; Babes in the Wood (pantomime), 1948; Stories at Five to Ten, 1959, 3rd ed., 1964. Contbr. to: People's Jrnl.; Manchester Evening News; Oldham Chronicle; Bolton Evening News; Amateur Stage; Lancs. Evening Post. Mbr., Preston Writers' Soc. Address: 40 Isherwood St., Preston, Lancs. PR1 5HQ, UK.

HOYT, Homer, b. 14 June 1896, St. Joseph, Mo., USA. Consulting Real Estate Economist. Educ: A.B., A.M., 1913, Univ. of Kans.; J.D., 1918, Ph.D., Econs., 1933, Univ. of Chgo. Publs: One Hundred Years of Land Values in Chicago, 1933; Structure & Growth of Residential Neighborhoods in American Cities, 1939; People, Profits, Places, 1969; According to Hoyt (collected articles), 1969; Real Estate (college text), 1939, 6th ed., 1972; Urban Land Use Requirements 1968-2000, 1968. Contbr. to profl. jrnls. Hons. incl: George L. Schmutz Annual Award, Am. Inst. of Real Estate Appraisers, 1964. Address: 2939 Van Ness St. NW, Wash. DC 20008, USA.

HOYT, Murray, b. 8 Dec. 1904, Worcester, Mass., USA. Writer. Educ: A.B., Middlebury Coll.; grad. work, Columbia Univ. Publs: Does It Always Rain Here, Mr. Hoy?, 1950; Green Mountain Treasury (co-author), 1961; The Fish in My Life, 1964; The World of Bees, 1965; Jewels from the Ocean Deep, 1967; Vermont — A Special World (co-author), 1969; The Young Investor's Guide to the Stock Market, 1972; Thirty Miles for Ice Cream, 1974; Creative Retirement, 1974. Contbr. to: Saturday Evening Post; Colliers; Ladies Home Jrnl.; Woman's Day; Family Circle; Readers Digest; Good Housekeeping; etc. Mbr., Authors' Guild. Address: 8 Green Mountain Place, Middlebury, VT 05753, USA.

HRASTNIK, Franz, b. 19 Sept. 1909, Vienna, Austria. Writer; Artist; Freelance Journalist; Playwright. Educ: Univ. of Vienna. Publs: (books) Opernkonserve, 1947; The New York Book, 1953; Pekingese Flute, 1961; Pocket Museum, 1962; Faksimile, 1974; (plays) Vincent the Painter, 1946; Verschwenderin, 1953; Frl. vom Kahlenberg, 1958. Contbr. to: Neue Zürcher Zeitung; Stuttgarter Zeitung; Die Presse, Vienna. Mbrships: PEN, Austria; Concordia, Vienna. Address: A-1030 Vienna III, Dannebergplatz 16, Austria.

HRISTIC, Jovan, b. 26 Aug. 1933, Belgrade, Yugoslavia. Editor. Educ: B.A., Belgrade Univ. Publs: Poetry & the Criticism of poetry (essays), 1957; Alexandrian School (poems), 1963; Poetry & Philosophy (essays), 1964; Forms of Modern Literature (essays), 1968; Four Apocrypha (plays), 1970. Contbr. to lit. jrnls. inclng: Praxis, Yugoslavia; Dialog; Poland; Romboid, Czech.; New Lit. Hist., USA. Mbr. sev. lit. orgs. Hons: Best Radio Play,

1961; Best Theatre Play, 1965; Isidora Seculić Mem. Award, 1968. Address: Skerlićeva 26, 11000 Belgrade, Yugoslavia.

HSIUNG, Shih I., b. 14 Oct. 1902, Nanchang, Kiangsi, China. Author; President of Tsing Hua College, Hong Kong since 1963. Educ: B.A., M.A., Ph.D. Publs. incl: Lady Precious Stream, 1934; The Western Chamber, 1935; Professor From Peking, 1939; The Bridge of Heaven, 1943. Mbrships: China Soc., London. PEN (London & Hong Kong). Hons: Sec., China Soc., London. Address: The Office of the President, Tsing Hua Coll., Hong Kong.

HSU, Dixon, b. 10 Apr. 1924, Shanghai, China. Journalist; Central News Agency Correspondent in Europe. Educ: B.J., St. John's Univ., Shanghai, 1948. Mbrships: Int. Press Inst., Zurich, Switz.; Press Fndn. of Asia, Manila, Philippines; Press Club Concordia, Vienna, Austria; For. Press Club, Vienna; For. Press Assn., Taipei. Address: Central News Agcy. Inc., Vienna Office, Walfischgasse 15/9, A-1010 Vienna, Austria.

HSU, Yu, b. 11 Nov. 1908, Chekiang, China. Poet; Novelist. Educ: B.A., Peking Nat. Univ.; Univ. Paris. Publs: (poetry) Pilgrimage, 1948; Transmigration, 1952; Where Time Goes, 1958; (novels) My Love with a Ghost, 1939; A Family, 1942; The Matrimony, 1955; Of Rivers & Lakes, 1961; Time & Light, 1966; (collected short stories) Illusion, 1948; The Lamp, 1959; The Thief & the Robber, 1959; Progress of a Small Potato, 1964; (collected essays) The Spring Leeks, 1939; Ringside Sketches, 1972; Streetside sketches, 1972; (plays) Life & Death, 1940; Plays in Fantasy, 1942; (lit. criticism) Individualism & Liberalism, 1957; A Study of Chinese Classical Novels, 1969. Contbr. to var. Chinese jrnls. Mbrships. incl: PEN; Human Rights Coun., Hong Kong. Address: G.P.O. Box 13441, Hong Kong.

HUBBARD, Lafayette Ronald, b. 13 Mar. 1911, Tilden, Neb., USA. Explorer; Writer; Philosopher. Educ: Schl. of Engrng., Geo. Wash. Univ., Wash. D.C., 1932-34; postgrad. studies, Princeton Univ., 1945; Ph.D., Sequoia Univ., LA, Calif., 1950. Num. publs. incl: Fear the Ultimate Adventure, 1939; Final Blackout, 1940; Death's Deputy, 1940; Ole Doc Methuselah, 1947; Dianetics, the Modern Science of Mental Health, 1950. Contbr. to: Sportsman Pilot; Spur; Aviation; Fantasy Books; Unknown Worlds; Sci. Fiction; Detective Yarns; Western Story Mag.; Argosy; Detective Fiction Wkly.; & num. others. Mbrships. incl: Explorers' Club, N.Y.; Int. Oceanog. Fndn.; Am. Geog. Soc.; Writers' Guild (& Screenwriters' Sect.); Royal Photog. Soc., UK; Accredited to Universal News as photographer. Recip., num. civic & mil. hons. Address: 1827 19th St. N.W., Wash. DC20009, USA.

HUBBELL, Richard Whittaker, b. 13 Sept. 1914, Mt. Vernon, N.Y., USA. Communication Executive. Educ: B.A., Wesleyan Univ.; Postgrad., Columbia Univ. Publs: 4000 Years of Television, 1942; Television Programming & Production, 1945. Contbr. to: var. mags. Agent: Miss Nannine Joseph. Address: 360 First Ave., N.Y., NY 10010, USA.

HUBLER, Richard G. (Gibson), b. 20 Aug. 1912, Scranton, Pa., USA. Author; Public Relations Consultant; Journalist. Educ: A.B., Swarthmore Coll., 1934. Publs. in Fiction incl: I've Got Mine, 1945; The Chase, 1952; Man in the Sky, 1956; The Blue-and-Gold Man, 1961; South of the Moon, 1966; Love & Widsom, 1968; Wheeler (3 vols.), 1970. Other publs. incl: Lou Gehrig, 1941; Flying Leathernecks (w. John DeChant), 1944; St. Louis Woman (w. Helen Traubel), 1959; Big Eight, 1960; The Cole Porter Story, 1965; The Cristianis, 1966. Contbr. to: Atlantic; Harper's Bazaar; etc. Recip., Harper's Best War Article Award, 1941. Address: Creek Rd., Ojai, CA, USA.

HUDSON, Derek, b. 1911, London, UK. Author; Journalist. Educ: M.A., Merton Coll., Oxford. Publs. incl: Thomas Barnes of The Times; Charles Keene; Martin Tupper; James Pryde; Lewis Carroll; Sir Joshua Reynolds; Arthur Rackham: His Life & Work; The Forgotten King & Other Essays; The Royal Society of Arts, 1754-1954 (w. K. W. Luckhurst); Ed., Modern English Short Stories & Critical Essays in World's Classics; Writing Between the Lines. Kensington Palace; Munby: Man of Two Worlds. Contbr. to: The Times (Ed. Staff, 1939-49) Spectator (Lit. Ed., 1949-53) Oxford Univ. Press (Ed. Staff, 1955—); num. newspapers & jrnls. F.R.S.L. Address: 33 Beacon Hill Ct., Hindhead, Surrey, UK.

HUDSON, John Christopher, b. 6 Aug. 1900, Plumstead, London, UK. Metallurgist. Educ: D.Sc., Univ. of London; Assoc., Royal Coll. of Sci. Publs: The Corrosion of Iron & Steel, 1940; Protective Painting of Structural Steel (w. F. Fancutt), 1957, 2nd ed., 1968. Contbr. to sci. books & tech. jrnls. Mbrships. incl: Fellow, Instn. of Metallurgists; Metals Soc.; Fellow, Instn. of Corrosion Sci. & Technol.; Soc. of Chem. Ind. Hons: Sir Robert Hadfield Medal, Iron & Steel Inst., 1960; F. N. Speller Award, Nat. Assn. of Corrosion Engrs., USA, 1960; Hon. Mbr., Belgian Soc. for Study, Rsch. & Use of Materials, 1968. Address: 15 Uplands, Ashtead, Surrey KT21 2TN, UK.

HUDSON, John Pilkington, b. 24 July 1910, Derbys., UK. Professor of Horticultural Science. Educ: B.Sc. (Horticulture), M.Sc., London Univ.; Ph.D., Nottingham Univ. Publs: Control of the Plant Environment, 1957; Ed., Experimental Agriculture, 1964—. Contbr. to: Nature; Jrnl. of Horticultural Sci.; Endeavour; Span; Sci. Horticulture; etc. Mbrships: Horticultural Educ. Assn. (Past Pres., Hon. Mbr.); Soc. of Experimental Agriculture. Hons: M.B.E. (mil.), 1942; George Medal, 1943; Bar to George Medal, 1944; C.B.E., 1975. Address: The Spinney, Wrington, Bristol, UK.

HUDSON, Ronald, b. 1 Jan. 1924, Woolwich, UK. Editor; Indexer. Publs: Diary by E. B. B.: The Unpublished Diary of Elizabeth Barrett Barrett, 1831-1832 (Ed. w. Philip Kelley), 1969; A Checklist of the Correspondence of Robert & Elizabeth Barrett Browning (Co-Ed., w. Kelley), forthcoming. Contbr. to: Huntington Lib. Quarterly; Browning Inst. Studies. Mbr., Dir., Browning Inst., Inc., N.Y. Recip., commendation from Assn. of Am. Univ. Presses for design & prodn. of Diary by E E. B. B., 1970. Address: 430 E. 89th St., N.Y., NY 10028, USA.

HUDSON, Winthrop S., b. 28 Aug. 1911, Schoolcraft, Mich., USA. Professor of History. Educ: B.A., Kalamazoo Coll.; B.D., Colgate-Rochester Divinity Schl.; Ph.D., Univ. of Chgo. Publs: John Ponet (1516-1556): Advocate of Limited Monarchy, 1942; The Great Tradition of the American Churches, 1953; Understanding Roman Catholicism, 1959; American Protestantism, 1961; Religion in America, 1965, rev. ed., 1973; Nationalism & Religion in America, 1970. Contbr. to num. jrnls. Mbr., Am. Histl. Assn. Hons: Fellow, Folger Shakespeare Library, 1961, 1968. Address: 159 Rockingham St., Rochester, NY 14620, USA.

HUELIN, (Rev.) Gordon, b. 1919, London, UK. University Lecturer; Clergyman. Educ: B.D., M.Th., Ph.D., Univ. of London. Publs: On This Rock; The Story of the Christian Church; The Steep Ascent of Heaven; St. Willibrord & His Society; The Kingdom within You; The Light of the Cross; Ed., All in Good Faith; The Church & the Churches, 1970; The Cross in English Life & Devotion, 1972; Lambeth Palace, 1974. Contbr. to: Jrnl. Eccles. Hist.; Ch. Quarterly Review; New Schaff-Herzog Ency. of Relig. Knowledge; Ency. Britannica; Chambers' Ency. Mbrships: F.S.A. Address: 2 South Square, Gray's Inn, London WC1R 5HP, UK.

HUFFMAN, Laurie Nell (Alford), b. 13 April, 1916, Huntingdon, Ore., USA. Writer. Educ: matriculate of Univ. of Calif (Extension); Astrol. rsch., 1948—. Publs: A House Behind the Mint, 1969. Contbr. to: Am. Astrol.; Horoscope. Mbr., Authors' Guild. Address: 1920, Novato Blvd., Novato, CA 94947, USA.

HUGHES, Charmian Finch Noyes, b. 1916, Maskeliya, Ceylon. Educ: Royal Acad. of Dramatic Art. Publs: Gateway Guide to Eating in France (w. Spike Hughes), 1966, revised enlarged ed. publ'd. as Eating French, 1971; Gateway Guide to Eating in Italy (w. Spike Hughes), 1966, revised enlarged ed. publ'd. as Eating Italian, 1971; Cold Dishes for all Seasons (w. Spike Hughes), 1971. Agent: Richard Scott Simon Ltd. Address: Broyle Gate Farmhouse, Ringmer, Sussex, UK.

HUGHES, Cledwyn, b. 1920, Llansantffraid, Montgomeryshire, UK. Writer. Educ: Liverpool Univ. Publs. incl: The Different Drummer, 1946; Inn Closes for Christmas, 1946; Wennon, 1948; Wanderer in Wales, 1949; After the Holiday, 1949; The Northern Marches, 1950; Poaching Down Dee, 1951; Gold & Moonspray, 1952; West with the Tinkers, 1955; House in Cornfield, 1957; Royal Wales, 1957; King Who Lived on Jelly, 1958; Cheshire V.C., 1959; Ponies for Children, 1965; Making an Orchard, 1959; La Jambe de Cain, 1967; Portrait of Snowdonia, 1968; (forthcoming) Colour Book of Wales. Agent: Laurence

Pollinger. Address: 7 The Crescent, Arthog, Merioneth., UK.

HUGHES, Fiona, b. 6 Mar. 1954, Amersham, Bucks., UK. Press Photographer. Publs: Pony for Pleasure (w. Pat Smythe), 1969; Pony Problems (w. Pat Smythe), 1970. Address: The Rowan, Rabley Heath, Welwyn, Herts., UK.

HUGHES, Gervase, b. 1905, Birmingham, UK. Writer; Musician. Educ: M.A., B.Mus., Corpus Christi Coll., Oxford Univ. Publs: The Music of Arthur Sullivan, 1960; Composers of Operetta, 1962; The Pan Book of Great Composers, 1964; Dvořák: His Life & Music, 1967; Sidelights on a Century of Music, 1969; Fifty Famous Composers, 1972. Contbr. to: Opera; Music & Letters; Music & Musicians; Railway Mag. Agent: Herbert van Thal. Address: 83 Winchester Ct., London W8, UK.

HUGHES, Goronwy Alun, pen names AP ROBERT, Alun; GWENFFRWD, Alun; HUGHES, Hywel; HUGHES, H. G. A.; & others, b. 15 July 1921, Pontlotyn, Glamorgan, UK. Writer; Journalist; Translator. Educ: Univs. of Oxford, London, Liverpool; Charles Univ., Prague; Oriental Inst. of Czechoslovak Acad. of Sci.; M.A., D.Phil., C.Sc., D.Ed., D.Anthropol. Publs. incl: Bronant (short stories), 1946; Fuafatu, 1952; Rumanian Folk Art, 1954; Londyn (w. M. Novotny), 1968; Ed., Cerddi George Tattum, 1969; Men of No Property, 1971; Num. transls. Ed., Contbr., var. jrnls.; Corres., Ctrl. European jrnls. Hons: Camoes Prize, 1959, 1960. Address: Talwrn Glas, Afonwen, Mold, Clwyd CH7 5UB, UK.

HUGHES, James Quentin, b. 1920, Liverpool, UK. University Professor, Architecture, Malta; Reader, Liverpool. Educ: Liverpool Univ.; Leeds Univ.; B.Arch.; Ph.D.; Dip. Civic Design. Publs: The Building of Malta, 1956; Renaissance Architecture, 1962; Seaport, 1964; Bertotti Scamozzi; Fabbriche di Palladio, 1968; Fortress, 1969; Liverpool, 1969; Malta, 1972; Military Architecture, 1974. Contbr. to: Archtl. Review; Archtl. Forum; R.I.B.A. Jrnl.; Chambers Ency.; Times; Times Lit. Supplement; Yorks. Archaeol. Soc. Jrnl.; etc. Mbrships: F.R.I.B.A.; F.R.S.A.; Fellow, Royal Histl. Soc. Recip., M.C. & Bar. Address: Loma Linda, Criccieth, Gwynedd, UK.

HUGHES, Ken, b. 19 Aug. 1922, Liverpool, UK. Film Director; Screenwriter; Author. Publs: High Wray, 1952; The Long Echo, 1955; also film scripts & TV plays inclng: The Trials of Oscar Wilde, Cromwell, Sammy, Lenin in 1917. Contbr. to: A Variety of Short Plays; Television Playwright. Mbrships: Assn. Cine & TV Techns.; Brit. Screenwriters Guild; Brit. Actors Equity. Hons. incl: Guild of TV Producers Award, 1958; Nat. Acad. TV Arts & Scis. Award, 1959; Writers' Guild of GB Award, 1969. Address: 5 Oakhill Park Mews, Oakhill Park, London NW3, UK.

HUGHES, Owain Gardner Collingwood, b. 21 Nov. 1943, Bath, UK. Writer. Educ: M.A., Keble Coll., Oxford. Publs: The Beholding Runner, 1963-64; Hermit's Reprieve, 1969. Address: Moredrin, Talsarnau, Merioneth, UK.

HUGHES, Paul Lester, b. 25 Nov. 1915, Cedar Rapids, Iowa, USA. Teacher; Author; Researcher. Educ: B.A., Coe Coll., 1941; M.A., 1947, Ph.D., 1951; Univ. of Iowa. Publs: The Sources of Western Civilization, 1956; Crown & Parliament in Tudor-Stuart England: 1485-1714, 1959; Royal Proclamations: The Proclamations of the Early Tudors 1485-1553, 1964; Royal Proclamations: The Proclamations of the Later Tudors 1553-1586, 1966; Royal Proclamations: The Proclamations of the Later Tudors 1587-1603, 1967; Royal Proclamations: The Proclamations of King James I 1603-1625, 1974. Contbr. to: Jrnl. of Mod. Hist.; Hist.; Am. Bar Assn. Jrnl.; Am. Histl. Jrnl. Mbr., Am. Histl. Soc. Address: 240 Woodland Dr., Whitewater, WI 53190, USA.

HUGHES, Philip Edgcumbe, b. 30 Apr. 1915, Sydney, Australia. Anglican Clergyman; Professor of Theology. Educ: B.A., M.A., D.Litt., Univ. of Cape Town, S. Africa; B.D., London Univ., UK; Th.D., Aust. Coll. of Theol., Aust. Publs. incl: Commentary on Paul's Second Epistle to the Corinthians, 1962; Theology of the English Reformers, 1965; Creative Minds in Contemporary Theology (Ed. & contbr.), 1966. Contbr. to theol. jrnls. Mbrships. incl: Renaissance Soc. of Am.; Studiorum Novi Testamenti Societas; Am. Soc. for Reformation Rsch. Recip., Outstanding Educator of Am., 1973. Address: 1565 Cherry Lane, Rydal, PA 19046, USA.

HUGHES, Richard Arthur Warren, b. 19 Apr. 1900, Weybridge, Surrey, UK. Author. Educ: B.A., Oriel Coll., Oxford, 1922. Publs. incl: A High Wind in Jamaica, 1929; The Administration of War Production, Official History of the War (w. J. D. Scott), 1956; The Human Predicament, vol. I The Fox in the Attic, 1961, vol. II The Wooden Shepherdess, 1973; (for children) Gertrude's Child, 1966; Gertrude & the Mermaid, 1967. Contbr. to var. mags. in UK & USA. Mbrships: F.R.S.L.; Am. Acad. Arts & Letters (hon.); Nat. Inst. Arts & Letters, USA (hon.). Hons: O.B.E., 1946; D.Litt., Univ. of Wales, 1956; Lit. Award, 1961, Prin. Prize for Contbn. to Lit. of Wales, 1974, Welsh Arts Coun. Address: c/o Chatto & Windus, 40-42 William IV St., London WC2, UK.

HUGHES, (Robert) John, b. 28 Apr. 1930, Neath, UK. Journalist. Publs: The New Face of Africa; Indonesian Upheaval. Contbr. to num. jrnls. Mbrships: Dir., Am. Soc. Newspaper Eds.; Past Pres. & Life Mbr., For. Corres. Club of Hong Kong; Overseas Press Club, N.Y.; Authors' League; Int. Press Inst. Hons: Pulitzer Prize for Int. Reporting; Overseas Press Club Award; Nieman Fellowship, Harvard Univ. Address: 1 Norway St., Boston, MA, USA.

HUGHES, Spike (Patrick Cairns), b. 1908, London, UK. Writer. Publs: Cinderella (opera for TV), 1938; Opening Bars; Second Movement; The Art of Coarse Cricket; The Art of Coarse Bridge; The Art of Coarse Cookery; The Art of Coarse Entertaining; The Art of Coarse Language; Great Opera Houses; Out of Season; Famous Verdi Operas; Famous Mozart Operas; Famous Puccini Operas; The Toscanini Legacy; Glyndebourne; How to Survive Abroad; Ed., The International Encyclopaedia of Opera, 1974. Contbr. to: Observer; Times; Daily Express; Musical Times; Opera; etc. Agent: Richard Scott Simon Ltd. Address: Broyle Gate Farmhouse, Ringmer, Sussex, UK.

HUGHES, Ted, b. 1930. Author. Educ: Pembroke Coll., Cambridge. Publs. incl: The Hawk in the Rain, 1957; Lupercal, 1960; (Ed.) Wodwo, 1967; Poetry in the Making, 1968; Crow, 1970; (Ed.) A Choice of Shakespeare's Verse, 1971; (children's verse) Meet My Folks, 1961; The Mannerless Monster, 1964; How the Whale Became, 1963; The Iron Man, 1968; (plays) The Coming of the Kings, 1970. Contbr. to: Encounter; Observer; New Statesman; Spectator; Vogue; Harper's Bazaar; The New Yorker; Sewanee Review; Times Lit. Supplement; etc. Num. hons. incl: Somerset Maugham Award, 1960; Hawthornden Prize, 1960. Address: c/o Faber & Faber, 3 Queen Sq., London WC1, UK.

HUGHES, William Jesse, pen name NORTHERNER, b. 1912, Sheffield, UK. Teacher (Ret'd). Publs: Traction Engines Worth Modelling, 1950; A Century of Traction Engines, 1959; The Sentinel, a History of Sentinel Steam Vehicles (w. J. L. Thomas), vol. I, 1973, vol. II, 1975. Contbr. to: Model Engr.; Recreation; Model Making for Boys; Portfolios of Rd. Locomotive Soc. Mbrships: Newcomen Soc.; Past Pres., Rd. Locomotive Soc.; Soc. of Model & Expmtl. Engrs. Address: 'The Sentinel', West St., Beighton, Sheffield S19 6EP, UK.

HUGHES, Zuzana, b. 27 Apr. 1934, Turnov, Czech. Psychiatric Social Worker; Writer. Educ: Charles Univ., Prague; Univ. of Liverpool, UK; M.A.; Dip.Ed.; Dip. Translation; Dip. Allied Soc. Studies; A.A.P.S.W. Author, Poems, 1972. Contbr. to: Nové Knihý; Zlatý Máj; Svobodné Slovo, Literár-ní Noviny; etc. Mbrships: Brit. Assn. of Soc. Wkrs. Address: Talwrn Glas, Afonwen, Mold, Clwyd CH7 5UB, UK.

HUGHEY, Ruth Willard, b. 11 Sept. 1899, Gentry, Ark., USA. Educator. Educ: A.B., Galloway-Hendrix Coll., 1920; M.A., Columbia Univ., 1921; Ph.D., Cornell Univ., 1932. Publs: The Correspondence of Lady Katherine Paston — 1603-1627, 1941; The Arundel Harington Manuscript of Turod Poetry, 2 vols., 1960; John Harington of Stepney, Tudor Gentleman, 1971. Contbr. to: Review of Engl. Studies; Lib.; Renaissance Quarterly; S. Atlantic Quarterly; Brit. Soroptimist; Grad. Report. Mbrships: MLA; Renaissance Soc. of Am.; Bibliog. Soc., Univ. of Va. Recip., D.Litt., Hendrix Coll., 1939. Address: 2951 Neil Ave., Columbus, OH 43202, USA.

HUGILL, Robert, pen name GILL, Hugh, b. Gateshead on Tyne, UK. Author. Educ: B.Sc., Durham Univ. Publs: Northumberland & The Border, 1931; Cycling in the North Country; Borderland Castles & Peles, 1939, 2nd ed., 1970; Official Guide to Newcastle upon Tyne; I Travelled Through Spain, 1967; Castles & Peles of Cumberland &

Westmorland, 1975; also 4 short novels & two 1-act plays. Contbr. to: Go Mag.; var. cycling, touring & holiday mags. & jrnls. Mbrships: Newcastle upon Tyne Writers' Club; Soc. of Authors; Cyclists' Touring Club; Humanist Soc. Address: 15 Amberley Gardens, Cochrane Park, Newcastle upon Tyne NE7 7JR, UK.

HUGILL, Stan(ley James), b. 19 Nov. 1906, Hoylake, Cheshire, UK. Retired Sailor. Educ: Schl. of Oriental & African Studies, London Univ. Publs: Shanties from the Seven Seas, 1961; Sailortown, 1967; Shanties & Sailor Songs, 1969; Sailing Ships, Sailormen and Sealore, 1975. Contbr. to: Spin Folk Mag. (monthly columnist); Transl., tech. material for Japanese nautical mags. Mbrships: VP, Argonauts' Club, Liverpool, 1951—; Pres., Merseyside Folk Song Fed. Recip., 1st Prize, Seafarer lit. competition. Address: 34 Copperhill St., Aberdavey, Merioneth, Wales LL35 0HL, UK.

HUGO, Grant. Publs: Britain in Tomorrow's World: Principles of Foreign Policy, 1969; Appearance & Reality in International Relations, 1970. Contbr. to: Contemp. Review; Survival. Address: c/o Lloyds Bank Ltd., 16 St. James's St., London SW1, UK.

HUGOT, Paul Charles Emile, b. 9 June 1904, St. Denis, Reunion, Indian Ocean. Engineer. Educ: Ing., Ecole Centrale de Paris, France. Publs: La IVeme Republique, 1944; La Sucrerie de Cannes, 2nd ed., 1970, revised & transl. into Engl. as Handbook of Cane Sugar Engineering, 2nd ed., 1972. Mbrships: Int. Soc. of Sugar Cane Technologists; Queensland Soc. of Sugar Cane Technologists. Hons: Officier, Légion d'honneur; Commandeur, l'Ordre National du Merite. Address: B.P.49, St. Denis 97462, Reunion Island, Indian Ocean.

HUIE, William Bradford,-b. 1910, Hartselle, Ala., USA. Editor; Journalist. Educ: B.A., Univ. of Alabama. Publs: Mud on the Star; The Revolt of Mamie Stover; the Americanization of Emily; The Execution of Private Slovik; The Crime of Ruby Mcollum; Wolf Whistle; Hotel Mamie Stover; The Klansman; He Slew the Dreamer; The Hiroshima Pilot. Three Lives for Mississippi. Contbr. to num. mags. Address: Hartselle, Ala., USA.

HULBERT, Joan Margery, pen names ROSTRON, Primrose; ROSTRON, P. R., b. Dudley, Worcs., UK. Writer. Contbr. to: Advocate (Aust.); Birmingham Post; Cath. Times; Carriage Jrnl., USA; Chronicle of the Horse, USA; Country Life; Country Quest; E. Anglia Life; Edinburgh Tatler; Sphere; Tatler; Yachting Monthly. Mbrships: Inst. Jrnlsts.; Soc. Women Writers & Jrnlsts.; Press Club; Lansdowne Club. Address: 7 Bentinck Mansions, London W1, UK.

HULKE, Malcolm, b. 21 Nov. 1924, London, UK. Writer. Publs: The Writer's Guide, 1970; Writing for TV in the 70s, 1974; The Making of Doctor Who, 1972; var. Doctor Who children's novels, 1973-75; novel based on Crossroads, 1974; 4 further Crossroads novels, 1975; Cassell's Parliamentary Directory, 1975; many plays & series episodes, TV & radio; radio short stories & talks; jokes for The Galloping Gourmet. Contbr. to Observer. Mbrships: Former Councillor, Writers' Guild of GB; Mgmt. Comm., Aust. Writers' Guild; Crime Writers' Assn. Address: c/o Harvey Unna Ltd., 14 Beaumont Mews, Marylebone High St., London W1N 4HE, UK.

HULL, Denison Bingham, b. 25 Mar. 1897, Chgo., Ill., USA. Architect (Ret'd). Educ: A.B., 1919, M.Arch., 1923, Harvard. Publs: Thoughts on American Fox Hunting, 1958; Aesop's Fables (verse transl.), 1960; Hounds & Hunting in Ancient Greece, 1964; Digenis Akritas (verse transl.), 1972. Mbrships: VP, Chgo. Chapt., Am. Inst. of Archts.; Chgo. Soc., Archaeol. Inst. of Am. Hons: L.H.D., Lombard Coll., 1965; Gold Cross, Order of the Phoenix, Greece, 1966. Address: 342 Chestnut St., Winnetka, IL 60093, USA.

HULL, Raymond Horace, b. Shaftesbury, Dorset, UK. Writer. Publs: How to Get What You Want, 1969; Writing for Money in Canada, 1969; Tales of a Pioneer Surveyor, 1970; The Peter Principle, 1969; The Art of Making Beer, 1971; Successful Public Speaking, 1971; Home Book of Smoke Cooking Meat, Fish & Game, 1971; Gastown's Gassy Jack, 1971; Man's Best Fiend, 1972; The OFF Loom Weaving Book, 1973; OFF Wheel Pottery, 1974; Vancouver's Past, 1971; var. stage plays. Contbr. to: var. newspapers & periodicals; Anthols.; TV & Radio. Mbr., Can. Authors Assn. Agent: Barthold Fles. Address: 1703-1200 Alberni St., Vancouver, B.C., Canada V6E 1A6.

HULL, William, b. 13 Apr. 1918, Westminster, S.C., USA. Professor of Literature; Author; Poet. Educ: B.A., Furman Univ., 1938; M.A., 1940, Ph.D., 1941, Univ. of Va. Publs: Selected Poems, 1954; Dandy Brown, 1959; The Other Side of Silence, 1964; The Catullus of William Hull, revised ed., 1966; Collected Poems — 1942-68, 1970; Visions of Handy Hopper: Book I, Flood, 1970, Book II, Churn, 1971, Book III, Park, 1972, Book IV, Post, 1973, Book V, Hinge, 1974. Address: 5 First Ave., Merrick, NY 11566, USA.

HULLEY, Clarence Charles, b. 29 June 1905, Staffa, Perth, Can. Retired University Professor; Writer. Educ: B.A., M.A., Univ. of B.C., Vancouver; Ph.D., Univ. of Wash., Seattle, USA, 1943. Publs: Alaska — Past & Present, 1953, 3 eds. Contbr. to: Pacific Histl. Review; Pacific Northwest Quarterly; num. acad., histl. & geogl. jrnls. Mbrships: Am. Histl. Assn.; N.C. Lit. & Histl. Assn. Hons: sev. schlrships. bursaries, tchng. fellowships, etc. Address: 402 S. Greene St., Wadesboro, NC 28170, USA.

HULME, Hilda Mary, b. 1914, Stoke-on-Trent, UK. University Reader in English. Educ: M.A., Ph.D., Univ. Coll., London. Publs: incl: Shakespeare's Julius Caesar, 1959; Shakespeare's Richard II, 1961; Explorations in Shakespeare's Language, 1962; Shakespeare's Henry V, 1963; Introduction to Shakespeare's Language, 1972. Contbr. to: Essays in Criticism; Review of Engl. Studies; Mod. Lang. Review; Engl. Studies; Renaissance Quarterly; etc. Hons. incl: Leverhulme Fellow, 1965-66; Folger Fellow, 1966. Address: Univ. Coll., Gower St., London WC1, UK.

HULME, Thomas Joseph, b. 1919, Cannock, Staffs., UK. Senior Lecturer in Education. Educ: St. Mary's Coll. of Educ., London; Univ. of Birmingham. Publs: Junior Writing Dictionary, 1962; Find the Right Word, 1964; My Book of Words, 1970; This is Our Life, 1965; Blacks Writing Dictionary, 1972; The Dictionary of Standard English, 1973. Contbr. to Visual Educ. Mbrships: Soc. of Authors; Catenian Assn. Address: Misterton Grange, Swinford Rd., Lutterworth, Leics., UK.

HULSE, James Warren, b. 4 June 1930, Pioche, Lincoln Co., Nev., USA. Professor of History. Educ: B.A., 1952, M.A., 1958, Univ. of Nev.; Ph.D., Stanford Univ., 1962. Publs: The Forming of the Communist International, 1964; The Nevada Adventure: A History, 1965, 3rd ed., 1972; Revolutionists in London, 1970; The University of Nevada: A Centennial History, 1974. Mbr., var. profl. orgs. Address: 940 Grandview Ave., Reno, NV 89503, USA.

HULTIN, Eskil Alexis, b. 16 June 1915, Orebro, Sweden. Scientist. Educ: F.M., Lund Univ., 1941; F.L., 1947, F.D., 1950, Stockholm Univ. Contbr. to: Acta Chemica Scandinavica & other profl. jrnls. Hons: Kt., Royal Order of The North Star, 1974. Address: Arrheniuslaboratoriet, Kungl. Universitetet i Stockholm, S-10405 Stockholm, Sweden.

HULTMAN, Harald J., b. 28 July 1932, Norrtalje, Sweden. Newspaper Editor; Publicist; Writer. Educ: Sorbonne Univ., Paris, France. Publs: From a Viking Hide-out, 1964; Hemland i havet, 1965; Pressens pionjärer, 1967; Lokaltidningen i framtiden, 1968; Mot 70-talet — pressproblem idag & imorgon, 1968; Spegel & språkrör, 1970; Local News, Local Views, 1971; Första gången i Wien, 1973; Prinsen av Vasa — den siste gustavianen, 1974. Mbrships. incl: Chmn., Press Assn. of Ctrl. Sweden, 1964-68; Dist. Bd., Swedish Newspaper Publrs. Assn., 1962-71; Swedish Comm., Int. Press Inst., 1969-71; Union of For. Press in Vienna, 1971—. Address: Graf Starhemberggasse 39, A-1040 Vienna, Austria.

HUME, John Robert, b. 26 Feb. 1939, Glasgow, UK. University Lecturer; Editor; Author. Educ: B.Sc., Glasgow Univ.; Royal Coll. of Sci. & Technol. Publs: Industrial History in Pictures: Scotland, 1968; Transport History, 1968, 2nd ed., 1972; Industrial Archaeology of Glasgow, 1974. Contbr. to: Transp. Hist. (Co-Ed., 1968—); Scottish Histl. Review; Indl. Archaeol.; Ayrshire Collects.; Glasgow Herald. Mbrships. incl: Econ. Hist. Soc.; Scottish Soc. for Indl. Archaeol. (Newsletter Ed.); Scottish Railway Preservation Soc. (Chmn.). Address: 28 Partickhill Rd., Glasgow G11 5BP, UK.

HUMPHREY, William, b. 18 June 1924, Clarksville, Tex., USA. Writer. Educ: Southern Meth. Univ., Dallas;

Univ. of Tex., Austin. Publs: The Last Husband & Other Stories, USA & UK, 1953; Home from the Hill (novel), USA & UK, 1958; The Ordways (novel), USA & UK, 1965; A Time & a Place: Stories, USA 1968 (as A Time & a Place: Stories of The Red River Country, UK 1969); The Spawning Run: A Fable, USA & UK, 1970. Recip., Grant, Nat. Inst. Arts & Letters, 1962. Address: c/o Alfred A. Knopf, 501 Madison Ave., N.Y., NY 10022, USA.

HUMPHREYS, Arthur Raleigh, b. 28 Mar. 1911, Wallasey, Cheshire, UK. Professor of English; Editor; Author. Educ: B.A., 1933, M.A., 1937, Cambridge Univ.; A.M., Harvard Univ, USA, 1935. Publs. incl: William Shenstone, 1937; The Augustan World, 1954; From Dryden to Johnson (co-author), 1957; Melville, 1962; Herman Melville: White-Hacket, 1966; Shakespeare: Richard II, 1968; Shakespeare: The Merchant of Venice, 1973; Shakespeare's Art (co-author), 1973; Ed., Shakespeare's Henry IV, Part I, 1960, Part II, 1966; Henry V, 1968; Henry VIII, 1971. Contbr. to: Scrutiny; Mod. Lang. Review; Cambridge Jrnl.; Review of Engl. Studies; etc. Address: 144 Victoria Park Road, Leicester LE2 1XD, UK.

HUMPHREYS, Betty Vance, pen name of SCHNEIDER, B.V.H., b. 1927, Oakland, Calif., USA. Research Economist; Lecturer; Research & Publication Program Director. Educ: Univ. of Calif.; Univ. of London, UK; A.B., Ph.D. Publs: Labor Relations in the Pacific Coast Longshore Industry, 1956; Industrial Relations in the West Coast Maritime Industry, 1958; Industrial Relations in the California Airframe Industry, 1956; The Older Worker, 1962; Clerical Unions in the Civil Service, 1958. Contbr. to var. profl. jrnls. Mbrships: Indl. Rels. Rsch. Assn.; Soc. of Profls. in Dispute Resolution. Address: 2114 Marin Ave., Berkeley, Calif., USA.

HUMPHREYS, (His Hon. Judge) Christmas, b. 1901, London, UK. Queen's Counsel; Author. Educ: M.A., LL.B., Trinity Hall, Cambridge. Publs: The Great Pearl Robbery; Concentration & Meditation; Poems of Peace & War; Karma & Rebirth; Buddhism; Zen Buddhism; Studies in the Middle Way; Walk On; The Way of Action: A Western Approach to Zen; Buddhist Poems; Exploring Buddhism. Contbr. to: The Middle Way; Times Lit. Supplement. Mbrships: Fndr.-Pres., Buddhist Soc., 1924; Past Pres., Shakespearian Authorship Soc.; VP, World Fellowship of Buddhists. Address: 58 Marlborough Place, London NW8 0PL, UK.

HUMPHREYS, Emyr Owen, b. 15 Apr. 1919, Prestatyn, Wales, UK. Author. Educ: Univ. Coll. Wales, Aberystwyth; Univ. Coll. N. Wales, Bangor; B.A. Publs: The Little Kingdom, 1946; The Voice of A Stranger, 1949; A Change of Heart, 1951; Hear & Forgive, UK & USA 1953; A Man's Estate, UK & USA 1955; The Italian Wife, UK & USA 1957; A Toy Epic, 1958; Y Tri Llais, 1958; The Gift, 1963; Outside the House of Baal, 1965; Natives, 1968; Ancestor Worship (poems), 1970; (play) Dinas, 1970; National Winner, 1971; Flesh & Blood, 1974. Mbrships: Soc. of Authors; A.C.T.T.; Yr Academi Gymreig; Y Cymrodorion; Gorsedd y Beirdd. Hons: Somerset Maugham Award, 1953; Hawthornden Prize, 1959; Welsh Arts Coun. Prize, 1972; Gregynog Arts Fellow, 1974-75. Agent: Richard Scott Simon. Address: Ysgubor Fawr, Marianglas, Anglesey, Gwynedd, Wales, UK.

HUMPHRIES, Elsie Mary, pen name FORRESTER, Mary, b. 1905, London, UK. Former Publisher's Assistant. Educ: B.A., Univ. of London. Publs: Introduction to Great Artists, 1965; A World That Sings: The Story of the Llangollen International Music Eisteddfod, 1972. Contbr. to: Sunday Mag. Mbr., Soc. of Authors. Address: 29 Willoughby Rd., London NW3, UK.

HUMPHRIES, Helen Speirs, b. 27 May 1915, Clydebank, Scotland, UK. Teacher. Educ: Bennet Coll.; Paisley Tech. Coll. Publs: St. Margaret's series for children inclng. Margaret the Rebel; Margaret of St. Margaret's; Changes for St. Margaret's; St. Margaret's Girls Branch Out; Return to St. Margaret's; St. Margaret's Trials & Triumphs; The Strange New Girl; Prudence Goes too Far; Secrets of the Castle; The Twins Who Weren't. Address: Stuartlea, 137 Sandy Rd., Renfrew, Scotland, UK.

HUMPHRIES, Sydney Vernon, pen name VANE, Michael, b. 24 Jan. 1907 Middelburg, Cape Province, S. Africa. Surgeon (Ret'd). Educ: M.A., Pembroke Coll., Cambridge, UK; M.R.C.S., L.R.C.P., St. Thomas's Hosp.;

F.I.C.S.; F.R.C.S., England. Publs: The Hun in Africa, 1943; Snobbery Under Arms, 1944; Black Magic & White Medicine, 1958; The Life of Hamilton Bailey, 1969. Mbrships: Author's Soc.; Brit. Med. Assn. Address: c/o Barclays Bank (International) Ltd., 1 Cockspur St., London SW1Y 5BG, UK.

HUMPHRYS, Leslie George, pen name HUMPHRYS, Geoffrey, b. 22 Feb. 1921, London, UK. Headmaster. Educ: Dame Owens, Islington; Camden Coll. Publs: Time to Live, 1959; Wonders of Life, Books 1-4, 1959-61; Weather in Britain, 1963; Your Body at Work, 1963; Men Learn to Fly, 1966; Life is Exciting, 1966; Science is Exciting, Books 1-3, 1967-69; Fruit & Fruit Growing, 1969; Drinks, 1970; Men Travel in Space, 1971; Glass & Glassmaking, 1971; Motion & Power, 1974; Tools, 1975. Contbr. to: Punch; Illustrated London News; I.P.C. Mags.; Country Life; Field; etc. Mbrships: Educl. Writers Grp., Soc. of Authors; E. Anglian Writers. Address: Four Winds, Church Close, West Runton, Norfolk, UK.

HUNNINGHER, Benjamin, b. 15 Apr. 1903, Vlissingen, Netherlands. Professor of History of Dramatic Arts. Educ: Doct.Thesis, Lit., Hist. & Art Hist., Univ. of Utrecht, 1931. Publs. incl: Theatre & Education, 1946; Theatre & Realism, 1947; A Century of Dutch Theatre, 1949; The Origin of the Theatre, 1955, 2nd ed., 1961; The Theatre of Dionysos Eleuthereus, 1956; Crusade on Broadway: Ideas in American Theatre, 1963. Contbr. to: De Gids; Maatstaf; etc. Mbr., PEN. Hons. incl: J. S. Guggenheim Fndn. Fellow, 1961; Cmdr., Order of Crown, Belgium, 1965; Kt. of Order of Netherlands Lion, 1973. Address: c/o Inst. for Dramatic Art, University of Amsterdam, N.Doelenstr. 16, Amsterdam, Netherlands.

HUNT, Noreen, b. 15 Sept. 1931, Oldham, Lancs., UK. College Vice-Principal. Educ: B.A., Royal Holloway Coll., 1955; Ph.D., Inst. of Histl. Rsch., 1958; Postgrad. Cert. of Educ., Cavendish Sq. Tchr. Trng. Coll., 1959. Publs: Cluny under St. Hugh 1049-1109, 1967; Cluniac Monasticism, 1971. Contbr. to: Ampleforth Jrnl.; The Tablet; The Author; Speculum; Cistercian Studies. Mbrships: Soc. of Authors; Gen. Coun. & Exec. Comms., Inst. of Relig. of GB & Ireland; Ecclesiastical Hist. Soc. Recip., Driver Prize & Rsch. Schlrship., Royal Holloway Coll., 1955. Address: Neville's Cross Coll., Durham City DH1 4SY, UK.

HUNT, Patricia Joan, b. Sefton Park, Liverpool, UK. Local Government Officer. Publs: First Steps in Teaching, 1966; Puffin the Vicarage Cat, 1966; Sunday School Single-handed, 1967; In & Around the Church, 1969; The History of our Bible, 1969; What to Look for Inside the Church, 1970; What to Look for Outside the Church, 1971; A First Look at Churches & Chapels, 1974; A First Look at Temples & Other Places of Worship, 1974. Contbr. to: Home Words; Together; etc. Address: 7 St. John's Rd., Knutsford, Cheshire, UK.

HUNT, Robert William Gainer, b. 28 July 1923, Sidcup, UK. Research Manager, Kodak Ltd. Educ: B.Sc., D.I.C., Ph.D., & D.Sc., Univ. of London. Publs: The Reproduction of Colour, 1957, 3rd ed., 1975. Contbr. to: Jrnl. of Photographic Sci.; Jrnl. of the Optical Soc. of Am. Mbrships. incl: VP, Int. Colour Assn.; Assoc., Royal Coll. of Sci.; Fellow, Royal Photographic Soc.; F.R.S.A.; F.I.O.P.; M.R.T.S. Address: Kewferry House, 10 Kewferry Rd., Northwood, Middx. HA6 2NY, UK.

HUNTER, Alan James Herbert, b. 25 June 1922, Hoveton St. John, Norwich, UK. Author. Publs: The Norwich Poems, 1945; 22 crime novels inclng. Gently Does It, 1955; Gently in the Sun, 1959; Gently Go Man, 1961; Gently North-West, 1967; Gently with the Innocents, 1970; Gently in Trees, 1974. Contbr. to: Eastern Daily Press (Lit. Critic). Mbrships: Soc. of Authors; Crime Writers' Assn. Address: Rigby House, 4 Bathurst Rd., Norwich NR2 2PP, UK.

HUNTER, Donald, b. 1898, London, UK. Consulting Physician. Educ: London Hosp.; D.Sc., M.D., F.R.C.P. Publs: Hutchinson's Clinical Methods (co-author), 15th ed., 1968; The Diseases of Occupations, 5th ed., 1974; Health in Industry, 1959. Address: 13 Hitherwood Drive, London SE19 1XA, UK.

HUNTER, Edward, b. 2 July 1902, NYC, USA. Journalist; Author; Publisher/Editor. Publs: Guide to Peking, 1930; Brain-Washing in Red China, 1951, revised ed., 1971; Brainwashing: The Story of Men Who Defied It, 1956 (revised as Brainwashing: From Pavlov to Powers, 1960); The Story of Mary Liu, 1957; The Black Book on Red China, 1958; The Past Present: A Year in Afghanistan, 1959; In Many Voices: Our Fabulous Foreign-Language Press, 1960; Attack by Mail: A Textbook on Communist Tactics, 1961; Ed., Tactics (monthly mag., ann. bound vols.), 1964—. Contbr. to: Coronet; Esquire; Harper's; num. other mags.; formerly reporter & News Ed., var. papers USA & abroad. Mbr., Overseas Press Club. Address: 4114 North 4th St., Arlington, VA 22203, USA.

HUNTER, Evan, pen name McBAIN, Ed, b. 15 Oct. 1926, NYC, USA. Writer. Educ: B.A., Hunter Coll., N.Y., 1950. Publs. incl: (novels; as Evan Hunter) The Blackboard Jungle, 1954; Second Ending, 1956; Buddwing, 1964; The Paper Dragon, 1966; Last Summer, 1968; Sons, 1969; The Easter Man, 1972; Come Winter, 1973; (as Ed McBain) Cop Hater, 1956; Lady Killer, 1958; King's Ransom, 1959; Like Love, 1962; Ax, 1964; Doll, 1965; Fuzz, 1968; Jigsaw, 1970; Sadie When She Died, 1972; Hail To The Chief, 1973. Contbr. to: Saturday Evening Post; Playboy; Ladies' Home Jrnl.; Argosy; Cosmopolitan, etc. Recip., Mystery Writers of Am. Award, 1957. Address: c/o Scott Meredith Literary Agency Inc., 580 5th Ave., N.Y., NY 10036, USA.

HUNTER, Geoffrey Basil Bailey, b. 14 Dec. 1925, Leeds, UK. Reader in Logic & Metaphysics. Educ: M.A., New Coll., Oxford. Publs: Metalogic, 1971, rev. ed., 1973. Contbr. to: Hume (V. C. Chappell, ed.); The Is-Ought Question (w. D. Hudson, ed.); Hume & the Enlightenment (w. B. Todd, ed.); var. philos. & acad. jrnls. Address: Priormuir, St. Andrews, Fife, Scotland, UK.

HUNTER, Jim, b. 1939, Stafford, UK. Schoolmaster; Author. Educ: M.A., Gonville & Caius Coll., Cambridge; Univ. of Bristol; Ind. Univ., USA. Publs: The Sun in the Morning, 1961; Sally Gray, 1963; Earth & Stone, 1963; Modern Short Stories, 1964; The Metaphysical Poets, 1965; Gerard Manley Hopkins, 1966; The Modern Novel in English, 1966; The Flame, 1966; Modern Poets (4 vols.), 1967-68; Walking in the Painted Sunshine, 1970; Kinship, 1973; The Human Animal, 1973. Contbr. to: Time & Tide; Coll. Engl.; Spectator; Guardian; New Educ.; Listener. Agent: A. D. Peters & Co. Address: 275 High Kingsdown, Bristol BS2 8DF, UK.

HUNTER, Kristin, b. 12 Sept. 1931, Phila., Pa., USA. Freelance Writer. Educ: B.S. in Educ., Univ. of Pa., 1951. Publs: (novels) God Bless the Child, USA 1964, UK 1965; The Landlord, USA 1966, UK 1970; (play) The Double Edge, prod. 1965; (juvenile) The Soul Brothers & Sister Lou, USA 1968, UK 1971; Boss Cat, 1971; The Pool Table War, 1972; Uncle Daniel & the Raccoon, 1972. Contbr. to: Best Short Stories by Negro Writers, 1967; Negro Digest; Essence; Directions 4 (juvenile); etc. Hons. incl: Whitney Fellowship, 1959; Cheshire Cat Award, Univ. of Wis., 1971; var. other awards. Address: P.O. Box 8371, Phila., PA 19101, USA.

HUNTER, (Rt. Rev.) Leslie Stannard, b. 1890, Glasgow, UK. Former Bishop of Sheffield; Author. Educ: M.A.; D.C.L.; D.D.; LL.D.; Kelvinside Acad., Glasgow; New Coll., Oxford. Publs: John Hunter, D.D., 1921; A Parson's Job, 1931; Ed., Putting Our House in Order, 1941; Planning Ahead, 1942; The Seed & the Fruit, 1953; A Mission of the People of God, 1961; A Diocesan Service Book, 1965; Scandinavian Church, 1965; The English Church, a New Look, 1966. Hons: Cmdr., Order of Dannebrog, 1952; Freeman of City of Sheffield, 1962. Address: 55 Sefton Court, Sheffield, UK.

HUNTER, Maud Lily (Christine), b. 29 June 1910, Longtown, Cumberland, UK. Housewife; Assistant Mistress at County Primary Schools. Educ: Edge Hill Trng. Coll., Liverpool. Publs. incl: Mysterious Neighbours; Escape to Adventure, 1960; Tentenbury Manor; Michael Graham, Police Cadet; Michael Graham, Police Constable, 1962; Coutier Treasure; Laughing Water; Boy From Down Under; (series 1963-66) Bunty & Peter; The Story of Gladys Aylward; Mystery of Tentenbury Manor, 1971; Deep Waters; To Life Anew; Annalisa, 1972; Anna's Family, Bwana Masua, 1974. Contbr. to: Sunday Companion; Christian Herald; Crusade; Stirling Annual; Thomson Press. Address: 98 Helmside Rd., Oxenholme, Kendal, Cumbria, UK.

HUNTER, Norman George Lorimer, b. 23 Nov. 1899, London, UK. Author. Publs. incl: Incredible Adventures of Prof. Branestawm, 1933; 14th ed., 1974; Prof. Branestawm's Treasure Hunt, 1934, 6th ed., 1974; Puffin Book of Magic, 1968, 7th ed. as Norman Hunter's Book of Magic, 1974; The Home Made Dragon, 1971, 3rd ed., 1974; Prof. Branestawm up the Pole, 1972; Prof. Branestawm's Dictionary, 1973, 2nd ed., 1974; The Frantic Phantom, 1973; Wizards Are a Nuisance, 1973; Prof. Branestawm's Great Revolution, 1974. Contbr. to var. newspapers & mags. in UK & USA. Mbrships. incl: Soc. of Authors; Children's Writers' Circle; Assoc., Inner Magic Circle. Agent: Bodley Head. Address: Mallard Cottage, Riverside, Temple Gardens, Staines, Middx. TW18 3NH, UK.

HUNYADI, Istvan, b. 9 Mar. 1905, Budapest, Hungary. Writer; Poet. Educ: Dr. of Pol. Sci., Fac. of Law. Publs: Singing Stones, 1934; Between Two Chimes, 1937; Swinging Star, 1940; Praise of Simplicity, 1946; Step out of Yourself, 1961; Irregular Doom, 1973. Contbr. to: Kortars; Elet es Irodalom; Jelenkor. Mbrships: Union of Hungarian Writers; PEN. Address: Varga Gy. Andras park 4/a, Budapest 1149, Hungary.

HUNYADY, Joseph, b. 14 Apr. 1921, Pecs, Hungary. Writer; Translator. Educ: T.D., Budapest. Publs. incl: The Captain of Blue Mountains, 1967, 3rd ed., 1974; The Golden Horde, 1968, 2nd ed., 1972; The Sons of Sun-God, 1969; Lyon & Kid, 1970; The Storm-Bird: Biography of Petofi, 1972; Unfortunate People (short stories). Contbr. to: Pajtas; Comrade. Mbrships: Hungarian Writers' Assn.; PEN; Hungarian Jrnlsts'. Assn. Hons: Baumgarten Prize, 1948; Order of Merit "for Socialist Culture", 1971; Diploma of Homage, Xth World Youth Festival, Berlin, 1973. Address: 1122 Budapest, Maros St., 38, Hungary.

HURD, Michael, John, b. 1928, Gloucester, UK. Composer; Writer. Educ: M.A., Pembroke Coll., Oxford. Publs: Immortal Hour, 1962; Young Person's Guides, 1962, 1963, 1965; Sailors' Songs & Shanties, 1965; Soldiers' Songs & Marches, 1966; The Composer, 1968; Elgar, 1969; Vaughan Williams, 1970; Mendelssohn, 1970; Outline History of European Music, 1968; Benjamin Britten, 1966. Address: 4 Church St., West Liss, Hants., UK.

HUREAU, Jean, b. 2 Feb. 1915, Paris, France. Journalist & Holiday Travel Writer; Editor. Publs: La Tunisie, Aujourd'hui; Le Maroc, Aujourd'hui; l'Algérie, Aujourd'hui; L'Iran, Aujourd'hui; l'Espagne, Aujourd'hui; La Corse, Aujourd'hui; La Provence & la Côte d'Azur, Aujourd'hui; La Bretagne, Aujourd'hui; Gen. Ed., Les Guides Aujourd'hui (Guides for Today) series. Contbr. to: Clartés (ency.); Jeune Afrique; Revue du Touring Club de France. Mbrships. incl: Int. Fedn. of Travel Jrnlsts. & Writers (Exec. Comm.). Hons. incl: Premio Periodistas Extranjeros, Madrid, 1966; Int. Tourism Prize, 1967. Address: 2 Résidence du Parc, F-91300 Massy, France.

HURLEY, Gerald Victor, pen name HURLEY, Vic, b. 6 Oct. 1898, Springfield, Mo., USA. Retired Naval Officer; Executive; Writer. Publs: Southeast of Zamboanga, 1935; Men in the Sun Helmets, 1936; Swish of the Kris — The Military History of the Moros, 1936; Jungle Patrol — The Official History of the Philippine Constabulary, 1937; The Parthian (histl. novel); The Impact of the Bow on History, 1974. Contbr. to: Ordnance; Am.; etc. Mbr., Explorers Club, N.Y. Address: 1615 Circle Drive, Apt. 443, Lacey, WA 98503, USA.

HURLEY, William James, Jr., b. 31 Dec. 1924, Chgo., Ill., USA. University Professor; Lieutenant-Colonel, US Air Force Reserve. Educ: B.A., M.A., Depaul Univ., Chgo.; Grad., Pilot Trng. Schl.; Dip., Nat. War Coll., 1966. Publs: Dan Frontier Reading Series (for primary grades), 12 vols., 1959-74; Ed., Culturally Disadvantaged Children in the Schools Today, 1966. Mbrships. incl: AAUP; Int. Reading Assn.; Reserve Offs. Assn. of US. Recip., Ford Fndn. Fellowship, Fund for Advancement of Educ., 1960. Address: Box≠1, Palos Heights, IL 60463, USA.

HURLOCK, Elizabeth Bergner, b. 1898, Harrisburg, Pa., USA. Psychologist. Educ: Bryn Mawr Coll.; Columbia Univ.; A.B., M.A., Ph.D. Publs. incl: Modern Ways with Children; La Conducta del Nino; Child Development, 5th ed.; Personality Development; Child Growth & Development; Adolescent Development, 4th ed.; Baby's Early Years; Development Psychology, 4th ed.; Guide-posts to Growing Up. Contbr. to var. profl. jrnls. Mbrships: Sec.-Treas. & Pres., Div. on Tchng. of Psychol., Am. Psychol. Assn.; Sec.-Treas., Div. on Dev. Psychol.; AAAS; Writers' Club of Atlanta. Address: Atlanta Towers, 1270 West Peachtree St., N.W. Atlanta, GA 30309, USA.

HURRELL, Henry G., b. 1901, Plymouth, UK. Former Grain Importer; Lecturer on Natural History. Educ: M.A., Univ. of Cambridge. Publs: Atlanta My Seal, 1963; Wildlife Tame but Free, 1968; Pine Martens, 1968. Contbr. to: Western Morning News; Countryman; Brit. Birds; Countryside. Mbr., sev. natural hist. socs. Hons: J.P.; M.B.E. Address: Moorgate, S. Brent, Devon TQ10 9HN, UK.

HURREN, (Lt.-Cmdr.) Bernard John, pen name NOTT, Barry, b. 1907, London, UK. Author; Freelance Journalist; Former Press Executive. Publs: Stand Easy, 1934; Eastern med., 1943; No Specific Gravity & Second Dog, 1944-46; Fellowship of the Air: Official History of the Royal Aero Club, 1951; ABC of Atomic Energy, 1956; The Awful Motorist, 1965; Airports of the World Guide, 1970; Waterloo, as a Wargame, 1975. Contbr. to: Illustrated Guide to Brit., 1971; New Book of the Road, 1974; Rdr.'s Digest (Cons. & Contbr.); Treasures of Brit.; Engl. Ed., French Aviation Mag.; & var. nat. newspapers. Mbr., Soc. of Authors. Address: 1/43 Wilbury Rd., Hove, Sussex, UK.

HURSTFIELD, Joel, b. 1911, London, UK. Professor. Educ: D.Lit., Univ. Coll., London. Publs: The Queen's Wards; Elizabeth I & the Unity of England; Freedom, Corruption & Government in Elizabethan England, 1973; Co-Ed., Elizabeth Government & Society. Contbr. to: Official Hist. of War Series; Hist.; Law Quarterly Review; Manchester Guardian; Spectator; Times; etc. Address: 7 Glenilla Rd., London NW3, UK.

HURT, Freda Mary Elizabeth, b. 14 June 1911, Forest Hill, London, UK. Author. Publs. incl: (children's books) Clever Mr. Twink, 1953, & later books in series; The Caravan Cat, 1963; Crab Island, 1965; Benny & the Dolphin, 1968; (novels) The Body at Bowman's Hollow, 1959; So Dark a Shadow, 1967; Dark Design, 1972; Return to Terror, 1974. Mbrships: Soc. of Authors; Soc. of Women Writers & Jrnlsts. Address: 298 Pickhurst Rise, West Wickham, Kent, UK.

HUSAIN, (Syed) Mumtaz, b. 1 Oct. 1918, Para, Ghazipur, India. Teacher. Educ: M.A., Agra Univ., B.A., Allahabad Univ., B.Ed., Muslim Univ., Aligrah. Publs: Naqd-i-Hayat, 1949; Nayee Qadrain, 1953; Adabi Masayal, 1954; Nayae Tanqueedi Goshay, 1958; Adab aur Shaoor, 1962; Ghalib-Ek-Mutalaya, 1969; (forthcoming) Jadid Shaeri-ki-Jamaliyati Qadrain; Naqd-i-Harf; Life of Amir Khusroe of Delhi. Contbr. to: Naya Adab; Fanoon; Urdu; Jang Daily; Pakistan Times; Dawn; Pakistan Quarterly; etc. Mbrships. incl: Progressive Writers Assn.; Exec. Comm., Pakistan Writers' Guild. Recip., Dawood Lit. Prize, Pakistan Writers' Guild, 1970. Address: B-215/10, Federal 'B' Area, Karachi-38, Pakistan.

HUSSAINI, Asadullah Shah, b. 12 Apr. 1931, Tikhir Sind, Pakistan. Teacher. Educ: B.A., Sind Univ.; B.A., London Univ.; Ph.D., Cambridge Univ. Publs: Payam-e-Ghamgusar, 1954; Tazkira-e-Shu'ara-e-Tikhir, 1959; Ed., Kulliyate-Dilgir, 1967; Ed., Kulliyate-e-San'at, 1968; Ed., Chapara Men Charyoon; (contbr. to transl.) Maqaddima ibn Khaldun. Contbr. to: Mehran; Nai Zindhgi; Muslim World. Mbrships: Bhzm-e-Talibul-Maula; Educ. Soc., Hala; Sindhi Adabi Bd. Hons: Sindhi Adabi Bd. (Hon. Sec., 1967-70). Address: Chmn., Sind Textbook Bd., Jamshoro, Sind, Pakistan.

HUSSON, Jean Henri, b. 26 Feb. 1923, Paris, France. Writer. Publs: La Brouillerie, 1957; Les Malles, 1959; La Bête Noire, 1963; Le Cheval d'Herbeleau, 1965. Hons: Legion of Honour. Grand Prix du Roman, French Acad. Address: 34 Franklin Roosevelt, 77210 Avon, France.

HUTCHINGS, Alan Eric, b. 1910, Warrington, Lancs., UK. President, Hour of Revival Evangelistic Association. Educ: Manchester Grammar Schl. Publs: Five Past Ten; Training for Triumph. Contbr. to Evangelical Christian publs. Mbr., Nat., A.C.I.I. Hons: F.R.G.S.; LL.D. Address: 13 Lismore Rd., Eastbourne, Sussex, UK.

HUTCHINGS, Margaret Joscelyne, b. 18 Dec. 1918, Brentwood, Essex, UK. Author. Publs: Glove Toys, 1958; Modern Soft Toy Making, 1959; Dolls & How to Make Them, 1961; Toying with Trifles, 1960; The "What Shall I Do?" Series, 4 vols., 1963-66; The Book of the Teddy Bear, 1964; Making Old Testament Toys; Making New Testament Toys, 1972; Making & Using Finger Puppets, 1973; Toys from the Tales of Beatrix Potter, 1973; Modelling in Hessian; Button Box; Wool Bag, 1975. Contbr.

to most mags., etc., from time to time; BBC; L.B.C. Address: The Mimosa House, S. Weald, Brentwood, Essex, UK.

HUTCHINGS, Monica Mary (Mrs. L. G. Baber), b. 3 July 1917, Cardiff, Wales, UK. Writer. Publs: Chronicles Church Farm, 1944; Romany Cottage, Silverlake, 1945; Rural Reflections, 1946; Hundredfold, 1947; The Walnut Tree, 1948; Green Willow, 1950; The Special Smile, 1951; Dorest River, 1954; The Isle of Wight, 1956; Blue Island, 1959; Heartmender, 1960; Two for Joy, 1961; Blow the Wind Southerly, 1962; Tamarisk Summer, 1963; Man for Gill, 1964; Highway to Dreams, 1965; Thing Apart, 1966; Inside Somerset, 1964; Inside Dorset, 1965; Hardys River, 1967; Mans Dominion (w. M. Caver), 1970; Sic Guides to Wessex; Fight for Tyneham. Contbr. to var. jrnls. Mbr., Soc. Women Jrnlsts. & Writers. Address: Wheelhouse, Shore Rd., Carradale, by Campbeltown, Argyll, UK.

HUTCHINS, Maude Phelps McVeigh, b. NYC, USA. Writer; Painter; Sculptress. Educ: B.F.A., Yale Univ. Publs: Diagrammatics (w. M. J. Adler), 1932; Georgina: A Diary of Love, 1950; Love is a Pie, 1955; My Hero, 1955; The Memoirs of Maisie, 1955; Victorine, 1959; The Elevator, 1962; Honey on the Moon, 1964; Blood on the Doves, 1965; The Unbelievers Downstairs, 1967. Contbr. to: Poetry; New Yorker; Quest; Harper's Bazaar; Ramparts; New Directions; Accent; Kenyon Review; Foreground; Mademoiselle; Quarterly Review Lit.; etc. Mbrships: Author's League; Nat. Assn. of Women Painters & Sculptors; Grand Central Art Galleries. Address: 1046 Pequot Rd., Southport, CT 06490, USA.

HUTCHINSON, Ray Coryton, b. 1907, London, UK. Author. Educ: M.A., Oriel Coll., Oxford. Publs: The Answering Glory; The Unforgotten Prisoner; One Light Burning; Shining Scabbard; Testament; The Fire & the Wood; Interim; Elephant & Castle; Recollection of a Journey; The Stepmother; March the Ninth; Image of My Father; A Child Possessed; Johanna at Daybreak; Origins of Kathleen; (play) Last Train South. Hons: Sunday Times Gold Medal for Fiction, 1938; W. H. Smith Lit. Award, 1965. Agent: Curtis Brown. Address: Dysart, Bletchingley, Redhill, Surrey, UK.

HUTCHINSON, Robert, b. 11 Apr. 1924, Hutchinson, Kan., USA. Poet; Fiction Writer; Editor. Educ: A.B., Univ. of Kan., 1947; M.A., Middlebury Coll., 1950; Ph.D. cand., Columbia Univ./Union Theol. Sem., 1947-50. Publs: The Kitchen Dance, New Poetry Series, 1955; Standing Still While Traffic Moved About Me, 1971. Ed., Poems of Anne Bradstreet, 1969; Poems of George Santayana, 1970. Contbr. to num. lit. publs. Hons: Elinor Frost Poetry Schlrship., Bread Loaf Schl. of Engl., 1950; Bernard De Voto Prose Fellowship, Bread Loaf Writer's Conf., 1962; Crowell Short Story Award; Prize, Nat. Poetry Contest, Phila. Art Alliance. Address: 1437 First Ave., N.Y., NY 10021, USA.

HUTCHISON, Harold Frederick, b. 7 Nov. 1900, Sheffield, UK. Publicity Executive. Educ: M.A., Oxford Univ. Publs: Visitors' London, 1954—; The Hollow Crown, 1961; Henry V, 1967; The Poster, 1968; Edward II, 1971. Contbr. to History Today. Hons: Proxime Accessit, Chancellor's English Essay Prize, Oxford Univ., 1922. Address: 17 Cromwell Court, Cromwell Rd., Hove, Sussex, UK.

HUTCHISON, Isobel Wylie, b. 1889, Carlowrie, Kirkliston, W. Lothian, UK. Author; Botanist. Educ: Studley Hort. Coll., Warwicks. Publs: Lyrics from West Lothian, 1916; How Joy was Found, 1917; Original Companions, 1917; The Calling of Bride, 1926; (poems) The Northern Gate; On Greenland's Closed Shore; North to the Rime-Ringed Sun; Arctic Nights Entertainments; Lyrics from Greenland; The Aleutian Islands. Mbr., Royal Scottish Geog. Soc., 1934. Hons: Mungo Park Medalist; LL.D., St. Andrew's. Address: Carlowrie, Kirkliston, W. Lothian, Scotland, UK.

HUTCHISON, Sidney Charles, b. 1912, London, UK. Secretary (formerly Librarian), Royal Academy of Arts; Author. Educ: Univ. of London. Publs: The Homes of the Royal Academy, 1956; The History of the Royal Academy, 1968. Contbr. to: Ency. Britannica; Walpole Soc. Jrnl.; Museums Assn. Jrnl.; Apollo; etc. Mbrships: F.S.A.; Fellow, Museums Assn.; Arts Club, London. Recip., M.V.O. Address: 60 Belmont Close, Mount Pleasant, Cockfosters, Herts, UK.

HUTH, Angela, b. 29 Aug. 1938, London, UK. Writer. Educ: Ecole des Beaux Arts, Paris. Publs: Nowhere Girl, 1970; Virginia Fly is Drowning, 1972; Sun Child, 1975. Contbr. to: Sunday Times; Evening Standard; Cosmopolitan; London Mag.; Harpers/Queen. Mbr., Soc. of Authors. Address: Ladybird Cottage, West Stowell, near Marlborough, Wilts., UK.

HUTT, William Harold, b. 3 Aug. 1899, London, UK. Professor. Educ: B.Com., London Schl. of Econs., 1924. Publs: The Theory of Collective Bargaining, 1930; Economists & the Public, 1936; The Theory of Idle Resources, 1939; Plan for Reconstruction, 1943; Keynesianism — Retrospect & Prospect, 1963; The Economics of the Colour Bar, 1964; Politically Impossible ...?, 1971; The Strike-Threat System, 1973; A Rehabilitation of Say's Law. Contbr. to var. econ. & other jrnls., symposia, etc. Mbrships: Mont Pelerin Soc.; Phila. Soc.; Pres., Econ. Soc. of S. Africa, 1941. Prof. Emeritus, Univ. of Cape Town, 1964. Address: c/o Dept. of Economics, University of Dallas, Irving, TX 75061, USA.

HUTTON J(oseph) Bernard, b. 7 July 1911, Chrast, Czech. Author; Journalist. Lecturer. Educ: Berlin Univ., Germany; Moscow Univ., USSR. Publs. incl: Stalin, 1961; School for Spies, 1961; The Traitor Trade, 1963; Out of this World, 1965; Healing Hands, 1966; Commander Crabb is Alive, 1968; Struggle in the Dark, 1969; On the Other Side of Reality, 1969; Hess, 1970; The Great Illusion, 1970; The Fake Defector, 1970; Woman Spies, 1971; The Subverters of Liberty, 1972; The Healing Touch, 1975; (co-auth.) The Private Life of Josif Stalin, 1962; The Pain & the Glory, 1968. Contbr. to many int. mags. Mbrships. incl: Soc. of Authors; Int. Fed. of Jrnlsts.; Nat. Union of Jrnlsts. Recip., Kt. of Mark Twain, 1973. Address: 16 Beehave Lane, South Ferring, Worthing, Sussex BN12 5NN, UK.

HUXLEY, Anthony Julian, b. 1920, Oxford, UK. Writer; Editor; Freelance Photographer; Publishing Consultant. Educ: M.A., Trinity Coll., Cambridge. Publs: Orchids of Europe; Garden Terms Simplified; Flowers of Greece; Flowers of the Mediterranean (w. O. Polumin); Mountain Flowers; House Plants: Cacti & Succulents; Plant & Planet; Ed., Encyclopaedia of the World's Mountains; Encyclopaedia of the World's Oceans & Islands; Encyclopaedia of the World's Rivers & Lakes. Contbr. to: Country Life. Mbrships: F.R.G.S.; Treas., Int. Dendrol. Soc.; var. comms., Royal Horticultural Soc. Agent: John Wolfers. Address: 50 Villiers Avenue, Surbiton, Surrey, UK.

HUXLEY, Elspeth Josceline, b. 23 July 1907, London, UK. Author. Educ: Reading Univ.; Cornell Univ., USA. Publs. incl: Red Strangers, 1939; The Walled City, 1948; I Don't Mind if I Do, 1951; Four Guineas, 1954; A Thing to Love, 1954; The Red Rock Wilderness, 1957; A New Earth, 1960; The Mottled Lizard, 1962; The Merry Hippo, 1963; Forks & Hope, 1964; Back Street New Worlds, 1965; Their Shining Eldorado: A Journey Through Australia, 1967; Love Among the Daughters, 1968; The Challenge of Africa, 1971. Contbr. to: BBC; N.Y. Times; Sunday Times; Time & Tide; etc. Recip., C.B.E., 1962. Address: Green End, Oaksey, nr. Malmesbury, Wilts., UK.

HUXTABLE, (Rev.) William John Fairchild, b. 25 July 1912, Plumpton, Sussex, UK. Minister of Religion. Educ: B.A., Western Coll., Bristol, 1933; B.A., 1935, M.A., 1940, Oxford Univ. Publs. incl: The Ministry, 1943; Co-Ed., A Book of Public Worship, 1948; The Faith That Is In Us, 1953; The Promise of the Father, 1959; The Christian Doctrine of God, 1961; The Bible Says, 1962; Preaching the Law, 1964; The Preacher's Integrity, 1966; Christian Unity: Some of the Issues, 1966. Contbr. to: Congregational Quarterly; Theology; London Quarterly & Holborn Review; Int. Congl. Coun.; var. symposia. Hons: D.D., Lambeth, 1973; D.D., Aberdeen, 1973. Address: 10 Gerard Rd., Harrow, Middx., UK.

HWANG, Soon-won, b. 26 Mar. 1915, Pyongyang, Korea. Novelist. Educ: B.A., Waseda Univ., Tokyo, Japan. Publs: (novels) Live with Stars, 1950; Descendants of Cain, 1954; Of Human Graft, 1957; Trees on the Mountain Slopes, 1960; Sun & Moon, 1964; The Moving Castle, 1973; Collected Works of Hwang Soon-won, 7 vols., 1973. Contbr. to: Mod. Lit.; Lit. & Thought. Mbr., Korean Acad. of Arts. Hons: Free Asia Award, 1955; Korean Acad. Award, 1961; Samil Cultural Award, 1966; Encounter Short Story Award, 1959. Address: 55 Sadang-dong, Kwanak-gu, Seoul, Korea.

HYDE, Harford Montgomery, b. 1907, Belfast, UK. Barrister-at-Law. Educ: M.A., Magdalen Coll., Oxford; D.Litt., Queen's Univ., Belfast; Middle Temple, London. Publs. incl: Mexican Empire, 1946; The Trial of Sir Roger Casement, 1960; The Quiet Canadian, 1962; Norman Birkett, 1964; A History of Pornography, 1964; Henry James at Home, 1969; The Other Love, 1970; Their Good Names, 1970; Stalin, 1971; Baldwin, 1973; Oscar Wilde, 1975. Contbr. to: Dictionary of Nat. Biog.; Sunday Times; etc. Mbrships: Fellow, Royal Hist. Soc.; F.R.S.L.; M.R.I.A. Lit. Agent: Curtis Brown. Address: Westwell House, Tenterden, Kent, UK.

HYDE, Michael, b. 1908, Shipton-under-Wychwood, Oxon., UK. Author. Educ: Leeds Coll. of Educ. Publs: Arctic Whaling Adventures, 1955; Nootka, 1968, 3rd ed., 1974; Educational Books, 1970. Contbr. to: Guardian; BBC. Mbr., Soc. of Authors. Address: 63 Kingtree Ave., Cottingham, North Humberside, UK.

HYLAND, (Henry) Stanley, b. 26 Jan. 1914, Shipley, Yorks., UK. Television & Radio Programme Consultant & Public Relations Adviser; Former Research Librarian & Journalist. Educ: B.A., London Univ. Publs: Curiosities from Parliament, 1956; Who Goes Hang?, 1958; Green Grow the Tresses-O, 1964; Top Bloody Secret, 1968; Prod., num. maj. Current Affairs TV progs. inclng. Ministerial & other pol. broadcasts. Contbr. to num. TV & radio progs. Mbr., Crime Writers' Assn. Address: 11 The Priory, Blackheath, London SE3, UK.

HYMAN, Robin Philip, b. 9 Sept. 1931, London, UK. Publisher. Educ: B.A.(Hons.). Publs: A Dictionary of Famous Quotations, 1962; Boys' & Girls' First Dictionary, 1967; Three Bags Full, 1972; The Fairy Tale Book, 1974; also many children's books, w. Inge Hyman, inclng. Barnabas Ball at the Circus, The Magical Fish, Runaway James & the Night Owl, The Hippo who Wanted to Fly. Contbr. to: Mermaid (Ed., 1953-54). Mbrships: Soc. of Bookmen; Exec. Comm., Educl. Publr.'s Coun., 1971-; Garrick Club; MCC. Address: 101 Hampstead Way, London NW11, UK.

HYMOFF, Edward, b. 12 Oct. 1924, Boston, Mass., USA. Journalist; Editor. B.S., Boston Univ., 1949; M.A., Columbia Univ., 1950. Publs: The Mission, 1964; The Kennedy Courage, 1965; International Troubleshooter for Peace, 1965; Guidance and Control of Spacecraft, 1966; First Marine Division in Vietnam, 1967; First Air Cavalry Division in Vietnam, 1967; Fourth Infantry Division in Vietnam, 1968; The OSS in World War II, 1972. Contbr. to: Reader's Digest; Am. Legion; Argosy; True; Bulletin of the Atomic Scientists; Popular Mechanics. Mbrships. incl: Int. Inst. Strategic Studies; Nat. Press Club; Overseas Press Club; Soc. of Mag. Writers; Aviation/Space Writers Assn.; Authors' Guild. Hons. incl: Apollo Achievement Award, NASA, 1971; Non-fiction Writing Award, A/SWA, 1965; Writing Fellow, AAAS. Address: P.O. Box 92, Centuck Stn., Yonkers, NY 10710, USA.

HYSLOP, Lois Boe, b. 3 Apr. 1908, Baltic, S.D., USA. Professor of French. Educ: B.A., Augustana Coll., S.D.; M.A., Ph.D., Univ. of Wis. Publs: Baudelaire on Poe, 1952; Baudelaire: A Self-Portrait, 1957; Baudelaire as a Literary Critic, 1964; Baudelaire as a Love Poet & Other Essays, 1969; Henry Becque, 1972. Contbr. to: French Review, USA; French Studies, Oxford, UK; Bulletin Baudelairien; Kentucky Romance Quarterly. Hons: best books list, Nation Mag., 1952; Readers' Subscription Book Club, 1957. Address: 326 Hillcrest Ave., State Coll., PA 16802, USA.

IACOBAN, Mircea Radu, b. 19 Nov. 1940, Iasi, Romania. Teacher; Writer. Educ: Grad. Univ. Iasi. Publs: (stories) Estudiantina, 1962; (novel) O Mască în plus (Another Mask), 1969; (feature reports) Lumea întro picătură (The World in a Drop), 1970; (essays) Altfel despre sport (A Different View of Sports), 1972; (report) Din Azore în Antile (From Azores to Antilles), 1973; (play) Sîmbătă la Veritas (Saturday Evening at the Veritas Hotel), 1974. Contbr. to: Cronica; Radio & TV; etc. Mbrships. incl: Union Romanian Writers (Exec. Comm.). Hons. incl: Drama Prize, Romanian Writers' Union, 1973; Drama Prize of Writers' Assn. Iasi, 1970. Address: str. prof. Tafrali Nr. 4, Iaşi, Romania.

IANOSI, Ion, b. 1 May 1928, Brasov, Romania. Professor of Aesthetics. Educ: Ph.D. in Philos. Publs: Thomas Mann, 1965; Dostoyevsky — The Underground Tragedy, 1968; Dialectics & Aesthetics, 1971; The Election of Jonah, 1974; Introduction to the Philosophy of Art, 1975. Contbr. to num. mags. & jrnls. Mbrships: Soc. & Pol. Scis. Acad.; Writers Union. Recip., Lit. Hist. Prize, Writers Union, 1963. Address: Str. Architect Louis Blanc 19A, Bucharest 1, Romania.

IBRAHIMOV, Mirza Ajar-ogly, b. 5 Oct. 1911, Sarab, Iran. Politician; Writer. Educ: Inst. of Oriental Hist. Publs. incl: (plays) Hayat, 1937; Madrid, 1938; Mahabbeth, 1942; The Country Girl, 1962; A Good Man, 1965; (novels) The Day will Come, 1951; Beyuk Dayag, 1957; (scientific) Beyuk democrat, 1939; Halgilik ve realizm jabhesinden, 1962; According to Laws of Beauty, 1964; Jalil Mamed — Kuli-Zade, 1966; On the Slopes of the Murovdag, 1967; Flames are blowing, 1968. Mbrships: Acad. of Sci., Azerbaizhan; Chmn., Writers' Union, Azerbaizhan. Hons. incl: Red Banner of Labour; Order of Lenin. Address: Azerbaizhan S.S.R. Union of Writers, Baku, USSR.

ICAZA CORONEL, Jorge, b. 10 July 1906, Quito, Ecuador. Actor; Playwright; Civil Servant. Educ. Nat. Univ., Quito. Publs. incl: (plays) El Intruso, 1929; La Comedia sin Nombre, 1930; Por el Viejo, 1930; Cual Es? , 1931; Como Ellos Quieren, 1932; Sin Sentido, 1932; Flagelo, 1936; (short stories) Seis Relatos, 1952; Viejos Cuentos, 1960; (novels) En las Calles, 1935; Cholos, 1937; Huairapamuschas, 1948; El Chulla Romero y Flores, 1958. Mbrships. incl: Union of Writers & Artists; num. foreign socs. Hons. incl: First Prize for a Latin Am. Novel; First Prize, Ecuadorean Novel. Address: Rocafuerte No 12, Quito, Ecuador.

IDESTAM-ALMQUIST, Zoila Margareta Guit, b. 12 Aug. 1901, Uppsala, Sweden. Author. Educ: Exam., Etiskt Pedagogiska Inst., Uppsala. Publs: Leksakstaget, 1964; Ny i klassen, 1966; Cillas Vita Grind, 1968; Leta Efter Valter, 1969; Ansiktet I Fonstret, 1970; Sparen I Snon, 1971; Akta dej for Jan, 1974. Contbr. to newspapers. Mbr., Swedish Union of Authors. Hons: Litteraturfrämjandets Prize, 1970; Swedish Authors' Union Award, 1973. Address: Dalagatan 6 C, 111 23 Stockholm, Sweden.

IDUARTE FOUCHER, Andrés, b. 1 May 1907, Villahermosa, Tabasco. University Professor. Educ: Ph.D.; LL.D.; Univs. of Mexico, Paris, Madrid & Columbia, N.Y. Publs. incl: El. Himno a la sangre, 1928; El problema moral de la juventud mexicana, 1931; La Isla sin Veneno, 1954; Martin Luis Guzman en sus libros, 1960; Don Pedro de Alba y su Tiempo, 1962; Mexico en la nostalgia, 1965; Juarez, maximo simbolo, 1967; El Mundo Sonriente, 1968; Diez estampas mexicanas, 1971. Mbrships. incl: Nat. Inst. of Fine Arts (Dir.-Gen.); Cuban Acad. of Hist; Mexican Acad of Int. Law. Hons. incl: sev. lit. prizes; Order of Céspedes, Cuba. Address: Casa Hispanica, Columbia Univ., N.Y., NY 10027, USA.

IGGULDEN, John Manners, b. 12 Feb. 1917, Brighton, Vic., Australia, Company Director. Publs: Breakthrough, 1960; The Storms of Summer, 1960; The Clouded Sky, 1964; Dark Stranger, 1965. Mbrships: Gliding Fedn. of Aust. (Life Gov.); Port Phillip Conservation Coun. (Life Gov.). Address: R.M.B. Gleniffer Rd., Promised Land, Bellingen, N.S.W. 2454, Australia.

IGLESIAS SELGAS, Carlos, b. 25 Feb. 1920, Murcia, Spain. Lawyer; Essayist; Political Writer. Educ: Lic. Law, Univ. of Murcia; LL.D., Univ. of Madrid; Dips. in Primary Educ. & Comm. Publs: Los sindicatos en España, 1965; La via española a la democracia, 1968; Objetivos de la política

de educación, 1968; Un Regimen social moderno, 1961; Comentarios a la ley sindical, 1971; El estatuto del trabajador español en la nueva ley sindical, 1971; Las Cortes españolas, 1973. Contbr. to: Actualidad española; Revista de estudios sindicales. Mbrships: Nat. Cath. Assn. of Advtsrs.; Assn. for study of today's problems. Recip. of Francisco Franco Nat. Lit. Prize, 1965. Address: Avda. de America 25, Dpdo., Madrid 2, Spain.

IGNÁCZ, Rózsa, b. 25 Jan. 1909, Kovászna, Hungary. Writer; Translator; Former Actress. Educ: Grad., Drama Schl. Publs. incl: Anyanyelve magyar, 1937; Moneta spicciola, 1938; Született Moldovában 1940; Urak, urfiak, 1947; Torockói gyász, 1958; Prospero Szigetén, 1960; Titánia ébredése, 1964; Róza leányasszony, 1966; Argentina viharszünetben 1972; Hegyenvölgyön szánkázço diófa, 1974. Contbr. to: Vigilia; Kortárs; Nagyvilág; Jelenkor. Mbrships: PEN; Hungarian Writers Assn.; Petofi Tarsasag. Address: 1111 Budapest, Irinyi József u 43, Hungary.

IGNATOV, Rangel, b. 5 Dec. 1927, Plovdiv, Bulgaria. Writer. Publs: (in Bulgarian) (novels) A Patch of Sky for Three, 1963; Farewell Love, 1965; A Human Golgotha, 1969; (play) Court of Honour, 1974. Contbr. to: September; Literatouren Front; Narodna Cultura. Mbrships: Union of Bulgarian Writers; Union of Bulgarian Film Workers; Union of Bulgarian Jrnlsts. Hons: Prize, Dimitrov Young Communist League; Prize, Union of Bulgarian Writers; Min. of Defence Award. Address: Sofia, bul. Cherni Vruh, 25B, Bulgaria.

IGNOTUS, Paul, b. 1901, Budapest, Hungary. Freelance Writer & Broadcaster. Educ: Univ. of Budapest. Publs: Political Prisoner (autobiog.), UK, USA & France, 1959; The Paradox of Maupassant, UK & USA, 1966; Czechs, Magyars, Slovaks, 1969; Hungary, UK & USA, 1972. Contbr. to: Pol. Quarterly; Socialist Commentary; New Statesman; Sunday Times; Times Lit. Supplement; etc. Mbrships: PEN; Soc. of Authors; Soc. Européenne de Culture; Hungarian Writers' Assn. (Presidential Bd., 1956). Address: 33 Prince of Wales Mansions, Battersea, London SW11, UK.

IHIMAERA, Witi Tame, b. 7 Feb. 1944, Gisborne, NZ. Journalist; Civil Servant; Maori, & Member of Te Whanau A Kai sub-tribe of Te Aitanga A Mahaki & Rongowhakaata Tribes. Educ: Univ. of Auckland; Victoria Univ., Wellington; B.A. Publs: Pounamu, Pounamu (short stories), 1972; Tangi (novel), 1973; Whanau (novel), 1974. Contbr. to: Te Ao Hou; Te Maori; Te Awatea; NZ Listener; Islands; Landfall; Bookworld; For. Affairs Review. Mbr., PEN. Hons: 3rd Prize 1973, 1st Prize 1974, Sir J. Wattie Book of Yr. Award; Freda Buckland Award, 1973; Robert Burns Fellowship, 1975. Address: 11 Hungerford Rd., Wellington 3, NZ.

IKOR, Roger, b. 28 May 1912, Paris, France. Author; Teacher. Educ: Tchr.'s Qualification. Publs: A travers nos Déserts, 1951; Les Eaux Mêlées, 1955; Mise au net, 1957; Si le Temps (cycle of 6 novels), 1960-69; Peut-on être juif aujourd'hui, 1968; Lettre ouverte aux juifs, 1970; Le Tourniquet des Innocents, 1972; Pour une fois écoute mon enfant, 1975. Contbr. to: Figaro; Figaro Littéraire; Nouvelles Littéraires; Europe; & other lit. jrnls. Mbrships. incl: Hon. Comm., Int. League against Racism & Antisemitism; VP, Writers' Union. Hons. incl: Goncourt Prize, 1955; Albert Schweitzer Prize, 1957; Chevalier, Legion of Hon.; Off., Arts & Letters. Address: 17 Rue Alexandre Dumas, 95530 La Frette, France.

ILANGARATNE, Tikiri Bandara, b. 27 Feb. 1913, Hatarliyadda, Sri Lanka. Politician; Playright; Novelist. Publs. incl: (in Sinhalese) (Novels) Wilambeeta; Denuwara; Kathava; Thilaka; La Sanda; Thilaka & Thilaka; Nedeyo; (plays) Haramitiya; Manthri Hamuduruwo; Jataka Natyaya; Rangamandala; Handahana; Ambaryaluwo; Malsarawa; Mangala; Delova Sihina; Wivena Ginna; (short stories) Onchillawa. Address: B-20, Govt. Bungalow, Stanmore Crescent, Colombo 7, Sri Lanka.

ILERSIC, Alfred Roman, b. 14 Jan. 1920, London, UK. University Teacher. Educ: B.Com. & M.Sc.(Econ.), Univ. of London. Publs: Statistics; Government Finance & Fiscal Policy in Post-war Britain; Parliament of Commerce 1860-1960; Taxation of Capital Gains; Rate Equalisation in London. Contbr. to: Accountancy; The Accountant; Brit. Tax Review; Can. Tax Jrnl. Address: Reform Club, Pall Mall, London SW1, UK.

ILLES, Endre, b. 4 June 1902, Csütörtökhely, Hungary. Writer. Educ: Physn. Publs: Susan, 1941; The Pushings, 1942; Poison, 1943; Haughty Persons, 1946; Sharpers, 1958; Impatient Lovers, 1961; Concentric Circles, 1962; Sand-glass, 1962; The Stranger, 1965; Examination, 1968; Crayon Drawings, 1970; Two Lions, 1974; Anonymous Letters, 1974. Contbr. to: Nyugat, 1930-41; Magyar Csillag, 1941-44; Kortárs, 1958—; Uj Irás, 1961—. Mbrships: Hungarian Writers Union; PEN Club; European Community of Writers. Hons: Kossuth Prize, 1963; Pro Urbe Budapest, 1969. Address: Mányoki út 22, 1118 Budapest, Hungary.

ILLINGWORTH, Ronald Stanley, b. 7 Oct. 1909, Harrogate, UK. Paediatrician; Professor of Child Health. Educ: Univ. of Leeds. Publs. incl: The Normal Child, 6 eds.; The Normal School Child; The Development of the Infant & Young Child: Normal & Abnormal, 6 eds.; Basic Developmental Screening; The Child at School: A Paediatrician's Manual for Teachers; Babies & Young Children, 6 eds.; Lessons from Childhood: Some Aspects of the Early Life of Unusual Men & Women; Common Symptoms of Disease in Children, 5 eds.; The Treatment of the Child at Home; A Guide for Family Doctors. Contbr. to med. jrnls., books & encys. Mbrships: F.R.S.M.; Fellow, Royal Photographic Soc. Address: 8 Harley Rd., Sheffield, Yorks., UK.

ILLYES, Gyula, b. 2 Nov. 1902, Racegres, Hungary. Writer. Educ: Sorbonne, Paris, France. Publs. incl: poetry: Teremteni, 1973; Minden lehet, 1973; drama: Ujabb dramak, 1974; prose: Kharon ladikjan, 1969; Hajszalgyökerek, 1971. Contbr. to: French & Hungarian jrnls. Mbrships: PEN (VP); Presidium, Hungarian Writers' Assn., Acad. Kisfaludy, 1941-46; Acad. Hungarian, 1946-48. Hons: incl: Baumgarten Prize, 1931 & 1933; Kossuth Prize, 1948, 1953, 1970; Grand Prix de Poesie, Belgium, 1965; Herder Prize, Vienna, 1970; Cmdr., l'Ordre des Arts et Lettres, 1974. Address: 1025 Budapest, II Jozsefhegyi-u.9, Hungary.

ILOGU, (The Rev. Canon) Edmund Christopher Onyedum, pen name EDILOG, b. 25 Apr. 1920, Ihiala, Nigeria. Dean of Social Sciences, University of Nigeria; Clerk in Holy Orders. Educ: Assoc. London Coll. Div., Univ. London, 1953; S.T.M., Union Theol. Sem., N.Y., 1958; M.A., Columbia Univ., N.Y., 1959; Ph.D., State Univ. Leiden, Netherlands, 1974. Publs: West Meets East, 1955; Social Philosophy for the New Nigeria Nation, 1962; Christianity & Ibo Culture, 1974. Contbr. to: Int. Review Missions; Theol. Today; Acta Conf. papers Int. Conf. Sociol. Relig. Mbrships: Int. Assn. for Missiol. Studies; Int. Conf. Sociol. Relig. Recip., Shergold Smith Essay Prize, London Coll. Divinity, Univ. London, 1952 & 1953. Address: Dean, Fac. Social Scis., Univ. Nigeria, Nsukka, Nigeria.

IMESCH, Ludwig, pen names im Esch; Im ESCH; L.I.; L.I-E., b. 15 Aug. 1913, Randa, Bürchen, Wallis, Switz. Teacher; Journalist. Publs: (novels) Grenzwacht an Gletschern; Die Schmugglerkönigin am Geisspfad; Dürstende Erde; Professor Gramm; Ferencz der Freiheitskämpfer; also num. short stories, poems, dialect publs., radio plays & film scripts. Contbr. to: num. newspapers & jrnls. Mbrships. incl: Swiss Writers' Union; Swiss Dialect Fedn. Hons: Swiss Fedn. for Schwyzertütsch in recognition Rsch. Works & publs. in dialects. Address: Walzmühlestr. 15a, 8500 Frauenfeld TG, Switz.

IMRE, Takács, b. 31 Aug. 1926, Rábasömjén, Hungary. Editor; Writer. Publs: (poetry) Zsellérek unokája, 1955; Köangyal, 1959; A férfitánca, 1964; Elsüllyedt föld, 1969; Szertartás, 1971; (novel) Csillagok árulása, 1960. Contbr. to: Uj Irás; Jelenkor; Kortárs; Tiszatáj. Mbr., Union Hungarian Writers. Recip., József Attila Prize, 1961. Address: 8000 Székesfehérvár, Rákóczi ut 33/c, Hungary.

INDJEVA, Nevjana Todorova, b. 4 May 1929, Varna, Bulgaria. Theatre Critic; Theatrical Historian. Educ: Bulgarian Philol.; Dr. of Arts, Theatrical Theory. Publs: Theatre of Revolutionary Protest, 1966; Bojan Danovsky, 1969; On the Artistic Concepts of Geo Milev about Theatre, 1972. Contbr. to: Problems of Arts; Theatre Mag.; Sept. Mag.; Plamuk Mag.; Lit. Front Paper; Izvestija of the Inst. of Arts, Bulgarian Acad. of Scis. Mbrships: Managerial Bd., Theatrical Critics Sect., Union of Bulgarian Actors; Soc. of Bulgarian Aesthetists, Men of Letters & Arts Critics. Address: 17 Dragalevska St., Sofia, Bulgaria.

INDRIDASON, Indridi, pen names SVEINSSON, Aslakur; I DAL, Sveinn, b. 17 Apr. 1908, Fjall, S-Thing,

Iceland. Writer; Tax Official (retired). Publs: Örlög (The Fates; short stories), 1930; Dagur er lidinn (The Day is Done; biog.), 1946; Godtemplarareglan a Islandi 75 ara (75 Years of Templar Work in Iceland), 1959; AEttir Thingeyinga (Genealogy of the People of Thingeyjarsysla), vol. 1, 1969, vol. 2, 1974, vol. 3, forthcoming; Ed., Indridi Thorkelsson, Baugabrot (Broken Rings; poems), 1939; Milli hafs og heida (Between Sea & Mountain; histl. essays), 1947; Jon Arnason attraedour (Jon Arnason, octogenarian), 1955. Contbr. to: Dvöl; Idunn; Eimreidin; etc. Mbrships: Icelandic Writers' Soc.; Union of Icelandic Authors; Nat. League; Genealog. Soc. Address: Storholt 17, P.O. Box 5087, Reykjavik, Iceland.

INESON, George Hudswell, b. 1914, Doncaster, Yorks., UK. Superior of Taena Community of Oblates of St. Benedict. Educ: Schl. of Archt., London; A.A. Dip.; A.R.I.B.A. Publs: Community Journey. Contbr. to: Life of the Spirit; La Vie Spirituelle. Address: Taena Community, Upton St. Leonards, Gloucester GL4 8EB, UK.

INGATE, Mary, b. 12 Apr. 1914, Halesworth, UK. Farmer. Publs: The Sound of the Weir, 1974. Contbr. to: Homes & Gardens; Glasgow Herald; Woman's Own; Woman's Realm; Sev. Irish & Scandinavian mags.; BBC Radio; NZ Radio. Mbrships: Soc. of Authors; Crime Assn.; Soc. of Women Writers & Jrnlsts. Recip., 1st Prize, Radio Writers' Assn. Competition for Best Crime Novel by a Woman, 1974. Address: Chapel Farm, Chediston, Halesworth, Suffolk, UK.

INGHAM, Kenneth, b. 9 Aug. 1921, Harden, UK. Professor of History. Educ: M.A., D.Phil., Univ. of Oxford. Publs: Reformers in India, 1956; The Making of Modern Uganda, 1958; A History of East Africa, 1962; Ed., Foreign Relations of African States, 1974. Fellow, Royal Historical Soc. Address: The Woodlands, 94 West Town Lane, Bristol BS4 5DZ, UK.

INGILBY, Joan Alicia, b. 1911, N. Stainley, Yorks. Writer. Publs. w. M. Hartley: The Old Hand-knitters of the Dales, 1951; Yorkshire Village, 1953; The Yorkshire Dales, 1956; The Wonders of Yorkshire, 1959; Yorkshire Portraits, 1961; Getting to Know Yorkshire, 1964; Life & Tradition in the Yorkshire Dales, 1968; Life in the Moorlands of North-East Yorkshire, 1972. Contbr. to: Country Life; Yorks. Post; Dalesman. Mbrships: Yorks. Archaeol. Assn.; Assn. Yorks. Bookmen (VP); Brontë Soc. Address: Coleshouse, Askrigg, Leyburn, N. Yorks., UK.

INGLIS, Robert Morton Gall, b. 1910, Edinburgh, UK. Publisher. Publs: Ready Reckoners & Calculators; Revised Editions of the Contour Road Books of Scotland & Ireland; Popular Star Atlas; Revised Editions of Easy Guide to the Constellations; The Constellations & How to Find Them, Nortons Star Atlas. Mbr., Scottish Mountaineering Club. Address: 19 Dalrymple Cres., Edinburgh EH9 2NX, UK.

INGLIS-JONES, Elisabeth, b. London, UK. Publs: Starved Fields, 1929; Crumbling Pageant, 1932; Pay Thy Pleasure, 1939; The Loving Heart, 1942; Lightly He Journeyed, 1945; Aunt Albinice, 1948; Peacocks in Paradise, 1950; The Story of Wales, 1955; The Great Maria, 1959; The Lord of Burghley, 1964; Augustus Smith of Scilly, 1969. Contbr. to var. Welsh publs. Address: Portesbery Woods, Camberley, Surrey, UK.

INGRAM, Derek Thynne, b. 20 June 1925, Westcliff-on-Sea, Essex, UK. Journalist; Managing Editor, Gemini News Service. Publs: Partners in Adventure, 1960; The Commonwealth Challenge, 1962; Commonwealth for a Colour-Blind World, 1965; The Commonwealth at Work, 1969. Contbr. to: The Round Table; C'wlth.; Guardian; var. other newspapers. Mbrships. incl: Diplomatic & C'wlth. Writers' Assn. of Brit. (Pres., 1972-74); Ed. Bd., The Round Table; Press Club; Nat. Book League; F.R.S.A.; C'wlth Press Union; Int. Press Inst.; Nat. Union of Jrnlsts. Address: 5 Wyndham Mews, London W1H 1RS, UK.

INGRAM, George, b. 25 Jan. 1892, London, UK. Writer. Publs: Hell's Kitchen (w. DeWitt Mackenzie), 1930; Stir, 1932; Cockney Cavalcade, 1933; Stir Train, 1934; The Muffled Man, 1936; Welded Lives, 1939. Mbr., Soc. of Authors (Life). Address: 27 Finstock Rd., London W10 6LU, UK.

INGRAM-(BARRISH), Joan Rutgers, b. 13 Sept. 1917, Cape Town, S. Africa. University Lecturer; Company Director. Educ: B.A.(Hons), T.L.O.D. Publs: Die Onderste bo Vlermuisie, 1950; Waar die Liefde Woon, 1947; Marja die Kwaai Beerin, 1951; Die Hoepic se Lied, 1952; Handleiding tot die studie van die Geskiedeinis van 1814-1900, 1975. Contbr. to: Die Huisgenoot; Die Vaderland; Die Naweek; Die Jongspan; Die Brandwag; var. radio progs. Mbrships: Treas., Potchefstroom Br., Afrikaanse Skiywerskring; PEN; Life, Fndn. Simon van der Stel. Address: 3 Goetz St., Potchefstroom 2520, S. Africa.

INGRAM-BROWN, Robert, b. 4 Mar. 1911, Glasgow, Scotland, UK. Publisher. Educ: Glasgow Acad. & Strathallan Schl., Perthshire. Publs: Ed., The Nautical Mag.; Ed., Brown's Nautical Almanac. Mbrships: Fellow, Royal Astronom. Soc.; Royal Inst. of Navigation; Nautical Inst. Address: 45 Dinmont Rd., Glasgow G41 3UJ, UK.

INGRAMS, Doreen Constance, b. 14 Jan. 1906, London, UK. Retired Senior Assistant, BBC. Publs: Report on the Social & Economic Condition of the Aden Protectorate, 1949; A Time in Arabia, 1970; Palestine Papers 1917-1922: Seeds of Conflict, 1972. Contbr. to: BBC; Middle East Int.; var. other jrnls.; Author-Cons., EMC Corp., USA. Mbr., var. int. orgs. Address: 3 Westfield House, Tenterden, Kent, UK.

INGSTAD, Helge Marcus, b. 30 Dec. 1899, Meraker, Norway. Author; Explorer. Educ: Law degree. Publs. incl: Land of Feast & Famine, 1931; East of the Great Glacier, 1935; Apache-Indianerne, 1939; Kondyke Bill, 1945; Landet med De Kalde Kyster, 1948; Nunamiut; Among Alaska's Inland Eskimoes, 1951; Land under the Pole Star, 1959; Westwards to Vinland, 1965; (play) Siste Bat, 1946. Contbr. to: Nat. Geographic Mag.; etc. Mbrships. incl: Norwegian Soc. Authors; Norwegian Polar Club (Pres,); Explorer's Club (N.Y.). Hons. incl: Fridtjof Nansen Award, 1965, Univ. Oslo; The Wahlberg Award, 1968, Swedish Soc. Anthropol. & Geog.; Cmdr., Order of St. Olav. Address: Vettaliveien 24, Oslo 3, Norway.

INNES, Brian, pen name POWELL, Neil, b. Croydon, Surrey, UK. Publisher; Author. Educ: B.Sc.; M.I.O.P.; A.S.I.A.; King's Coll., London Univ.; Chelsea Schl. of Art; Ctrl. Schl. of Art; London Coll. of Printing. Publs: Book of Pirates, 1966; Book of Spies, 1967; Book of Revolutions, 1968; Book of Outlaws, 1969; Die Seeräuberei, 1969; Flight, 1970; Saga of the Railways, 1972; Explorers, 1975. Contbr. to: Ency. Britannica; Man, Myth & Magic; Brit. Printer; Facts of Print series (Ed.); etc. Mbrships. incl: Nat. Union of Jrnlsts.; Soc. of Authors; Inst. of Printing; Assoc., Soc. of Indust. Artists & Designers. Address: 74 Woodland Rise, London N10, UK.

INNES, Rosemary Elizabeth, pen name JACKSON, R. E., b. 29 Aug. 1917, Abeyne, Aberdeenshire, Scotland, UK. Former Art Teacher. Educ: Dip., Glasgow Schl. of Art; Tchrs. Cert., Jordanhill Tchrs. Trng. Ctr. Publs: The Witch of Castlekerry, 1965; The Poltergeist, 1968; Aunt Elanor, 1969; The Ashwood Train, 1970; The Street of Mars, 1971; The Wheel of the Finfolk, 1972. Mbr., PEN. Address: Learney, Torphins, Aberdeenshire, Scotland, UK.

INNES-SMITH, Robert Stuart, b. 10 Mar. 1928, Sheffield, UK. Journalist. Educ: LL.B., Sheffield Univ.; Lincoln's Inn. Publs: The Dukeries, 1953; Notable Derbyshire Houses, 1972; An Outline of Heraldry, 1973; The Dukeries & Sherwood Forest, 1974; Marlborough, 1974. Contbr. to: Derbyshire Life & Countryside; Collector's Weekly; Edinburgh Tatler, Glasgow Illustrated (Ed. Dir., 1961-69); Tatler & Bystander (Jt. Ed. & Dir., 1968-69); Royal Martyr Annual (former hon. Ed.). Mbrship: F.S.A., Scotland. Address: 195 College St., Long Eaton, Nottingham, UK.

IONESCO, Eugene, b. 13 Nov. 1912. Author; Playwright. Publs. incl: (mostly appearing in Engl. & Am. eds.) La Jeune Fille a marier, 1959; Rhinocéros (play) in collection Manteau d'Arlequin, 1959; Le Piéton de l'air, 1962; Chemises de Nuit, 1962; Le Roi se meurt, 1962; Notes & Contre Notes, 1962; Journal en Miettes, 1967; Présent passé passé présent, 1968; Jeux de Massacre (play) 1970; Macbett (play), 1972. Contbr. to var. theatrical jrnls. & author of num. essays & tales. Mbr., French Acad., 1970. Hons: Officier des Arts et Lettres, 1961; Chevalier, Legion of Honour, 1970. Address: c/o Eds. Gallimard, 5 rue Sebastien-Bottin, Paris 7e, France.

IONESCU, Ghita, b. 1913, Bucharest, Romania. University Professor of Government. Educ: Bucharest Univ. Publs: Communism in Rumania, 1964; The Breakup of Soviet Empire in Eastern Europe, 1965; The Politics of European Communist States, 1966; Between Sovereignty &

Integration, 1974. Contbr. to: Government & Opposition (Ed.); Guardian; New Soc.; World Today; Int. Affairs; Pol. Quarterly; etc. Mbr., Athenaeum Club. Agent: Shaw & Maclean. Address: Dept. of Government, The Univ., Manchester M13 9PL, UK.

IRBE, Gunars, pen name (belles-lettres only) IRBE, Andrejs, b. 10 Feb. 1924, Riga, Latvia. Sociologist. Educ: Fil. kand., Univ. of Stockholm, Sweden. Publs: Mums nav svêtvakaru (We Have No Nights of Sabbath), 1962; Marisandra kaza (Marisandra's Goat), 1966; Vientula laiva ir nošu zîme (A Lone Boat is Like a Note on a Staff), 1968; Ed. & Translated into Latvian, Contemporary Icelandic Writers, 1973. Contbr. to num. Latvian & Swedish lit. jrnls. & anthols. Mbrships: Swedish Union of Authors; Assn. of Latvian Writers Abroad; Latvian Ctr., PEN. Hons: Jānis Jaunsudrabinš Prose Prize, 1967; Work Award, Swedish Writers Fndn., 1971-74. Address: Box 1065, S-141 22 Huddinge 1, Sweden.

IRELAND, Innes, b. 1930, Brierley Hall, Yorks.. UK. Author. Publs: Motor Racing Today, 1962; All Arms & Elbows (autobiog.), 1967; Marathon in the Dust (London to Sydney), 1970. Contbr. to: Autocar (Sports Ed., 1967-70); Autosport; Daily Express. Mbrships: Montagu Motor Mus.; Country Gentleman's Assn.; Scottish Landowners Fedn.; Steering Wheel, Annabel's, Marks, Anglesay Shooting, Aston Martin Owners Clubs; CIAPGP: BRDC; BARC; BRSCC; BDC. Agent: George Greenfield. Address: Senwick House, Borgue, Kirkcudbrightshire, Scotland, UK.

IRESON, Anthony, b. 1913, Kettering, Northants., UK. Publs: Northamptonshire (County Books Series). Contbr. to: Garden News, Peterborough (Ed., 1966-70). Address: Beech Cottage, Tanners Lane, Kettering, Northants., UK.

IRETON, Glenn Forrester, b. 11 July 1906, Hammond, N.Y., USA. Editor-in Chief; Publisher; Trade Publication Writer. Educ: B.A., Colgate Univ., N.Y. Publs: Ed., Communications 70, 2 vols. Ed. & Publr., Far East Film News, 1953-61, Movie/TV Marketing, 1961—. Mbr., For. Correspondents' Club of Japan. Hons: Golden Lion, La Biennale Di Venezia, 1965; Commendation, UniJapan Film, 1963; 1st Gt. Golden Medal of Merit & Dip., MIFED, 1971; Citation, Educ. Min., Repub. of Korea, 1963. Address: Box 30, Central Post Office, Tokyo, 100-91 Japan.

IRVINE, Keith, b. 7 Aug. 1924, Ipswich, Suffolk, UK. Editor. Educ: Univs. of Manchester; London (Birkbeck); Edinburgh; Paris, France (Sorbonne). Publs: The Rise of the Coloured Races, 1970 & 1972; ed., Ency. of Indians of the Americas; World Ency. of Black Peoples; Ency. Britannica (1969-72). Contbr. to: Collier's Ency.; Washington Post; The Nation; etc. Address: 218 St. Clair River Drive, Algonac, MI 48001, USA.

IRVING, David John Cawdell, b. 1938, Hutton, Brentwood, Essex, UK. Freelance Writer. Educ: Univ. of London. Publs: The Destruction of Dresden, 1963; The Mare's Nest, 1964; The Memoirs of Field-Marshal Keitel (transl.) 1965; The Virus House, 1967; Accident — The Death of General Sikorski, 1967; The Destruction of Convoy PQ.17, 1968; Ed., Breach of Security, 1968; The Rise & Fall of the Luftwaffe, 1974; The Eighty Nine Months Biography of Hitler, 1975. Mbr., Author's Club. Agent: Max Becker. Address: 81 Duke St., London W1, UK.

IRVING, Marjorie Annette, b. 3 Sept. 1932, Blenheim, NZ. Magazine Editor. Publs: This New Zealand. Contbr. to NZ newspapers, mags. & NZ Broadcasting Corp. Mbrships: Ed., "Home & Country", NZ Country Women's Inst.; NZ Women Writers Soc.; Past Mbr., Wellington WEA Writers Club. Address: 30 Weld St., Blenheim, Marlborough, NZ.

IRWIN, David, b. 24 June 1933, London, UK. University Lecturer. Educ: M.A. The Queen's Coll., Oxford, 1956; Ph.D., Courtauld Inst. of Art, London, 1959. Publs: English Neoclassical Art, 1966; Paul Klee, 1968; Visual Arts. Taste & Criticism, 1969; Winckelmann: Writings on Art, 1972; Beunat: Designs & Ornaments of the Empire Style, 1974; Scottish Painters: At Home & Abroad 1700-1900 (co-author), 1975. Contbr. to: Apollo; Burlington Mag.; Connoisseur; Art Bulletin; etc. Mbrships. incl: F.S.A., London; F.R.S.A.; VP, Brit. Soc. for 18th Century Studies; Comm., Scottish Arts Coun. Recip., Laurence Binyon Prize, Oxford, 1956. Address: Dept. of History of Art, King's College, University of Aberdeen, Old Aberdeen AB9 2UB, UK.

IRWIN, John, b. 1917, Madras, India. Keeper, Victoria & Albert Museum. Publs: Indian Art (co-author), 1947; The Art of India & Pakistan (co-author), 1951; Shawls: A Study in Indo-European Influences, 1955; Origins of Chintz, 1970. Contbr. to: Burlington Mag.; Jrnl. of Royal Asiatic Soc. Address: Bellmans Green, Edenbridge, Kent, UK.

IRWIN, Raymond, b. 14 Mar. 1902, Huddersfield, Yorks., UK. Librarian; Professor of Library Studies. Educ: M.A., St. John's Coll., Oxford Univ. Publs: The National Library Service, 1947; Librarianship, Essays on Applied Bibliography, 1949; British Bird Books: An Index to British Ornithology, 1951; British Birds & Their Books: Catalogue of Exhibition for National Book League, 1952; The Origins of the English Library, 1958; The Heritage of the English Library, 1964; The English Library, Sources & History, 1966; & an introductory chapter in The English Library, 1958. Contbr. to: Lib. Assn. Record; Lib. Review; etc. Mbr. Lib. Assn. (Past Pres.). Hons. incl: Emeritus Prof. Lib. Studies, Univ. London; Fellow, Lib. Assn. Address. 24 Central Dr., Ansdell, Lytham St. Annes, Lancs., UK.

ISAAC, Peter Charles Gerald, b. 21 Jan. 1921, Slough, Bucks., UK. Chartered Civil Engineer; Professor of Civil & Public Health Engineering. Educ: London Univ.; Harvard Univ., USA; B.Sc.(Eng.); S.M. Publs. incl: Electric Resistance Strain Gauges (w. W. B. Dobie), 1948; Public Health Engineering, 1953; Ed., The Treatment of Trade Wastes & the Prevention of River Pollution, 1957; Waste Treatment, 1960; River Management, 1967; William Davison of Alnwick, 1968; Civil Engineering: The University Contribution, 1970; Management in Civil Engineering, 1971; Davison's Halfpenny Chapbooks, 1971; The Burman Alnwick Collection, 1973. Owner, Allenholme Press. Ed. & Publr., Bulmer Papers. Contbr. to printing & engrng. jrnls. Mbr., var. profl. assns. Address: The University, Newcastle upon Tyne NE1 7RU, UK.

ISACCS, Harold Robert, b. 13 Sept. 1910, NYC, USA. Writer. Educ: A.B., Columbia Univ., 1930. Publs. incl: No Peace for Asia, 1947; Two-Thirds of the World, 1950; Scratches on Our Minds, American Images of China & India, 1958; Emergent Americans, a Report on Crossroads Africa, 1961; The New World of Negro Americans, 1963; India's Ex-Untouchables, 1965; Ed., Straw Sandals: Chinese Stories 1918-1933, 1974; Idols of the Tribe: Group Identity & Political Change, 1975. Contbr. to: Newsweek mag. (Assoc. Ed.). Hons. incl: Anisfield-Wolf Award, 1964; Fellowship, Am. Acad. Arts & Scis., 1974. Address: 96 Farlow Rd., Newton, MA 02158, USA.

ISAKOVIC, Antonije, b. 6 Nov. 1923, Beograd, Yugoslavia. Writer. Educ: Univ. Publs: (in Yugoslavian) The Big Children, 1954; The Fern & the Fire, 1963; The Empty Hills, 1970. Contbr. to: num. Yugoslav lit. mags. Mbrships: Yugoslav Writers' Assn.; PEN. Hons: Zmajeva, 1954; Sedmi juli, 1964; Oktobarska nagrada, 1970. Address: Studentski trg 19, Beograd, Yugoslavia.

ISFELD, Jón (Kristjánsson), pen name KR., Jón, b. 5 Sept. 1908, S. Múlasýslu, Iceland. Archdeacon. Educ: Tchrs. exam., 1934; Cand. theol., 1942. Publs. incl: (for children) Bakka-Knútur, 1963; Litla Lambid (The Little Lamb), 1964; Svenni í Ási, 1964; Sonur Vitavardarins (The Lighthouse Keeper's Son), 1965; Bernskuár Adaladrengs (A Valley Childhood), 1965; Vetraraevintýri Svenna í Ási (Svenna's Winter Adventures in Ási), 1965; Kvöldstundir med Kötu Fraenku (Evenings with Cousin Kate), 1966; Gunnar & Hjördis, 1970; (for adults) Gamall Madur & Gangastúlka, 1973. Contbr. to num. Icelandic & Norwegian newspapers & mags., 1936—. Mbrships. incl: Rithöfundasamband Íslands; Prestafélag Íslands. Address: Dalgerdi, Búdardal, Iceland.

ISHAK, Fayek Matta, b. 29 Oct. 1922, Sharkia, Egypt. University Professor. Educ: B.A. Cairo Univ., 1945; Ph.D., Liverpool Univ., UK. 1962; var. Dips., Egypt & UK. Publs. incl: Literary Terms, 1963; Theories of Literary Criticism from Aristotle to the Modern Age, 2 vols., 1964; T.S. Eliot, 1965; The Mystical Philosophy of T.S. Eliot, 1971; A Complete Translation of the Coptic Orthodox Mass & the Liturgy of St. Basil (4th century) into Jamesian English (1611), 1974; Contbr. to: Bulletin; Lit. Review; etc. Mbrships. incl: Engl. Lit. Soc., Cairo (Sec.). Recip., var schlrships. & rsch. grants. Address: Dept. of English, Lakehead Univ., Thunder Bay "P", Ont. Can. P7B 5E1.

ISLAM, A. K. M. Aminul, b. 21 Dec. 1933, Dacca, India (now Bangladesh). Professor. Educ: B.A., 1952, M.A., 1954, Dacca Univ.; M.A. Archaeol., Univ. of Toronto, Ont.,

Can., 1964; Ph.D., McGill Univ., Montreal, P.Q., 1969. Publs: Bangla Shahitye Muslim Kavi- O- Kavya, 1959, 2nd ed., 1969; Ed., An Introduction to Cultural Anthropology, 1973; A Bangladesh Village: Conflict & Cohesion, 1974; Our Way: Their Way, 1974. Contbr. to: Anthropol. Quarterly; Man; Occasional Papers, Asian Studies Ctr., Mich. State Univ. Mbr., var. anthropol. assns. Recip., var. Rsch. Fellowships, 1959-67. Address: 1212 Mt. Vernon Ave., Dayton, OH 45405, USA.

ISLAS, Maya, b. 12 Apr. 1947, Cabaiguan, Las Villas, Cuba. Poet. Educ: B.A., Fairleigh Dickinson Univ., 1972. Publs: Sola . . . Desnuda . . . Sin Nombre, 1974. Contbr. to: Mirador de N.Y.; El Tiempo; Ultima Hora; El Tiempo Universal; La Voz Femenina; El Diario -La Prensa; La Lerta Nueva. Mbrships: Sec. of Correspondence, N.Y., Spanish-Am. Cultural Link. Recip., Citizen of the Yr. (Outstanding Citizen of Cabaiguan, Cuba), N.J., 1974. Address: 5800 Broadway Apt. F1, W. New York, NJ 07093, USA.

ISLER, Ursula, pen name JUCKER, Iwan, b. 26 Mar. 1923, Zürich, Switz. Writer; Journalist. Ph.D., Univ. Zürich. Publs: (fiction) In diesem Haus, 1960; Das Memorial, 1959; Porträt eines Zeitgenossen, 1962; Die Schlange im Gras, 1965; Nadine - eine Reise, 1967; Der Mann aus Ninive, 1971; Landschaft mit Regenbogen, 1975; (biog.) Rudolf Rahn, 1957; books about Zürich's hist. & sev. works on Swiss painters. Contbr. to: Neue Züricher Zeitung; Der Bund; Zürichsee-Zeitung; St. Galler Tagblatt; etc. Mbr. Swiss Writer's Union. Hons: Swiss Schiller Fndn. Award, 1961; City of Zürich Recognition Prize, 1967. Address: 14 Hornweg, 8700 Küsnacht, Zürich, Switz.

ISOTALO, Kaarlo Kustaa, b. 20 Sept. 1918, Pyhkoki, Oulun Iääni, Finland. Author. Publs. incl: Yli Karikon, 1950; Tämä meistä, 1960; Telakka, 1960; Maantie, 1961; Maa repeää, 1962; Lähin omainen, 1963; Elintilaa, 1964; Kolmen talo, 1965; Puun alla, 1966; Kuin isä ja äiti, 1967; Loikkarit, 1969; Äitiparka ja Anna, 1970; Alueuutiset, 1973; Matkalla etelästä pohjoiseen ja pain vastoin, 1974. Contbr. to: var. yr. books, etc. Mbrships. incl: Suomen Kirjailijaliitto ry; Lounais-Suomen kirjailijat ry; Killa ry; NVL ry. Hons. incl: Aleksis Kiven palkinto, 1961; Weinsteinin säätiöltä, 1962; Huttusen säätiöltä, 1963. Address: Kirkkokatu 18, 38700 Kankaanpää, Finland.

ISRAEL, Charles Edward, b. 1920, Eransville, Ind., USA. Writer. Educ: B.A.; B.H.L.; Univ. of N.C.; Univ. of Cinn. Publs: How Many Angels; The True North; etc. Contbr. to: Documentary Films; Radio & TV; etc. Address: 196 Crestwood Rd., Willowdale, Ont., Canada.

ISSAWI, Charles, b. 1916, Cairo, Egypt. University Professor. Educ: Vic. Coll., Alexandria; Oxford Univ., UK. Publs: Egypt: An Economic & Social Analysis; Egypt in Revolution; An Arab Philosophy of History; Mushkilat Qaumia; The Economic History of the Middle East; The Economic History of Iran; Issawi's Laws of Social Motion; Economics of Middle East Oil (co-author). Contbr. to: For. Affairs; Int. Affairs; Land Econs.; Milbank Mem. Fund Quarterly; Muslim World; Middle E. Jrnl. Address: 190 Prospect Ave., Princetown, NJ, USA.

ISSLER, Anne Roller, b. 25 Aug. 1892, Huntingburg, Ind., USA. Writer. Educ: B.A., DePauw Univ., Greencastle, Ind., 1915. Publs: Stevenson at Silverado (biog.), 1939; Happier for his Presence (biog.), 1949; Our Mountain Hermitage (biog.), 1950; Young Red Flicker (fiction), 1968; Mystery of the Indian Cave (fiction), 1970. Contbr. to var. jrnls. Mbrships. incl: Western Writers of Am.; Nat. League Am. Pen Women. Address: 479 Seminary St., Napa, CA 94558, USA.

ISZLAI, Zoltàn, b. 7 Nov. 1933, Szeged, Hungary. Journalist. Educ: Libn. Sect., Univ. Arts Dept. Publs: Làrmafa (poems), 1970; Csirip-Sòtàr (cycle of short stories), 1972; Kèrdèses Epizòdok (short stories), 1973; Amíg Vagyunk (poems), 1975. Contbr. to: Elet És Irodalom; Kortárs; Társadalmi szemle; Hungarian Radio, Budapest. Address: Ràth György-utca 64-66, 1122 Budapest, Hungary.

ITALIAANDER, Rolf Bruno M., b. 20 Feb. 1913, Leipzig, Germany. Explorer; University Professor. Publs. incl: The New Leaders of Africa, 1960; Dappers Afrika 1668, 1964; The Challenge of Islam, 1964; Naive Kunst aus aller Welt, 1970; Die Wassermühle, 1970; Profile & Perspektiven, 1971; Argumente kritischer Christen, 1971; Partisanen & Profeten, 1972; Sepik-Grafik, 1973; Eine

Religion für den Frieden, 1973; Spass an der Freud, 1974; (play) Ein Glied in der Kette, 1974. Mbrships. incl: Free Acad. of Art, Hamburg (co-fndr.); Am. Acads.; German Translrs.' Union. Recip., Hans Henny Jahnn Award. Address: Helwigstr. 39, Hamburg 20, W. Germany.

IVAMY, Edward Richard Hardy, b. 1 Dec. 1920, Bournemouth, UK. Professor of Law; Barrister; Author & Editor. Educ: LL.B., 1947, Ph.D., 1953, LL.D., 1967, Univ. Coll., London. Publs: General Principles of Insurance Law, 1966, 2nd ed., 1970; Fire & Motor Insurance, 1968, 2nd ed., 1973; Marine Insurance, 1969, 2nd ed., 1974; Personal Accident, Life & Other Insurances, 1973; Ed., Chalmers's "Marine Insurance Act 1906", 7th ed., 1971; Ed., Payne & Ivamy's "Carriage of Goods by Sea", 9th ed., 1972; Ed., Topham & Ivamy's "Company Law", 15th ed., 1974. Contbr. to: Jrnl. of Bus. Law; Mod. Law Review; etc. Address: 143 Bishop's Mansions, London SW6, UK.

IVENS, Michael William, pen name YORICK, b. 15 Mar. 1924, Laindon, UK. Director, Aims of Industry; Writer. Publs: Practice of Industrial Communication, 1963; Case Studies in Management, 1964; Case for Capitalism, 1967; Industry & Values, 1970; (poetry) Another Sky, 1963; Private & Public, 1968; Born Early, 1975. Contbr. to: Spectator; 20th Century (Ed.). Mbrships: Jr. Hosp. Doctors' Assn. (VP). Address: 5 Plough Place, Fetter Lane, London EC4, UK.

IWASZKIEWICZ, Jaroslav, b. 20 Feb. 1894, Kalnik, Ukraine. Writer. Educ: Kijow Univ. Publs. incl: (verse) (in Polish) Return to Europe, 1931; Olympic Odes, 1948; Dark Paths, 1957; Italian Songbook, 1974; (short stories) The Girls from Wilko, 1933; Music Stories, 1971; Gardens, 1974; (novels) Conspiracy of Men, 1930; Red Shields, 1934; Lovers from Marona, 1961; (plays) Summer in Nohant, 1937; M. Balzac's Wedding, 1959; Cosmogony, 1967. Mbrships. incl: Union of Polish Writers (Pres.); Serbian Acad. of Sci. Hons. incl: Lenin Prize; L. Reynal Prize; Prize, Minister of Culture & Art. Address: Twórczość, al. Wiejska 16, Warsaw, Poland.

IZZARD, Ralph William Burdick, b. 27 Aug. 1910, Billericay, Essex, UK. Author; Journalist. Educ: M.A., Queen's Coll., Cambridge. Publs: The Hunt for the Buru, 1949; The Innocent on Everest, 1954; The Abominable Snowman Adventure, 1955; Smelling the Breezes (w. Molly Izzard), 1958, in USA as A Walk Through the Mountains, 1959. Contbr. to num. nat. & for. jrnls. Recip., O.B.E., 1946. Address: 7 Calverley Park, Tunbridge Wells, Kent, UK.

J

JABAVU, Noni, b. Fort Hare, Cape Province, S. Africa. Broadcaster; Lecturer. Educ: Royal Acad. of Music, London, UK. Publs: Drawn in Colour, 1960. Contbr. to Radio & TV. Address: c/o Lloyds Bank Ltd., 46 Victoria St., London SW1, UK.

JACK, Ian Robert James, b. 5 Dec. 1923, Edinburgh, UK. University Reader in English Poetry; Librarian. Educ: M.A., Univ. of Edinburgh; D.Ph., Univ. of Oxford; Litt.D., Univ. of Cambridge. Publs: Augustan Satire: Intention & Idiom in English Poetry 1660-1750, 1952; English Literature 1815-1832 (vol. X, Oxford History of English Literature), 1963; Keats & the Mirror of Art, 1967; Browning's Major Poetry, 1973. Contbr. to profl. jrnls. Mbrships: Pres., Charles Lamb Soc.; VP, Johnson Soc. Hons: De Carle Lectr., Univ. of Dunedin, NZ, 1964; Warton Lectr., Brit. Acad., 1967; Fellow, Pembroke Coll., Cambridge. Address: Pembroke Coll., Cambridge CB2 1RF, UK.

JACKMAN, L. A. J., b. 1919, London, UK. Schools Museum Officer, Devon, UK. Educ: Weymouth Tch. Trng. Coll., Dorset. Publs: Marine Aquaria, 1956, new version 1974; Exploring the Seashore; Exploring the Park; Exploring the Hedgerow; Exploring the Wood; The Field, 1972; The Beach, 1974. Contbr. to: BBC educl. publs.; Tchrs. World; var. sci. jrnls. Mbrships: F.Z.S.; Marine Biol. Assn., UK. Address: 44 Old Torquay Rd., Preston, Paignton, Devon, UK.

JACKSON, Alan A., b. 12 July 1922, London, UK. Civil Servant. Publs: Rails Through the Clay (w. D. F. Croome), 1962; Volk's Railways 1883-1964, 1964; Trains of Today, 1964; Inside Underground Railways, 1964; London's Termini, 1969; Semi-Detached London, 1973. Contbr. to: Railway Mag.; Railway World; Mod. Transp.; Transp. World; Passenger Transp. Mbrships. incl: Railway Club; Victorian Soc. Address: c/o Messrs. David & Charles, Newton Abbot, Devon, UK.

JACKSON, Aubrey Joseph, b. 19 Oct. 1911, London, UK. Schoolmaster. Educ: Borough Road Coll. Publs: British Civil Aircraft 1919-1959, 2 vols., 1959; de Havilland Aircraft since 1915, 1962; Avro Aircraft since 1908, 1965; Blackburn Aircraft since 1909, 1968; British Civil Aircraft since 1919, 3 vols., 1973-74. Contbr. to: Brit. Civil Aviation News (Ed., 1949-57); Air Pictorial; Aeroplane Monthly; Air-Britain publs. Mbrships: Companion, Royal Aeronautical Soc.; Tiger Club; Rochford Hunfred Flying Grp. (Chmn.). Address: 29 Olivia Dr., Leigh-on-Sea, Essex, UK.

JACKSON, Gabriel, b. 10 Mar. 1921, Mt. Vernon, N.Y., USA. Professor of Modern History. Educ: A.B., Harvard Coll., 1942; M.A., Stanford Univ., 1950; Ph.D., Univ. of Toulouse, 1952. Publs: The Spanish Republic & the Civil War, 1965; Historian's Quest, 1969; The Making of Medieval Spain, 1972; A Concise History of the Spanish Civil War, 1974. Contbr. to profl. & histl. jrnls. Mbrships. incl: Exec. Comm., Soc. for Spanish & Portuguese Histl. Studies. Hons. incl: H. B. Adams Prize, Am. Histl. Assn., 1965-66. Address: 5959 Waverly Ave., La Jolla, CA 92037, USA.

JACKSON, Gabriele Johanna Bernhard, b. 17 Nov. 1934, Berlin, Germany. Professor of English. Educ: Hunter Coll., NYC, USA, 1951-52; B.A., Bard Coll., Annandale-on-Hudson, 1955; Royal Holloway Coll., Univ. of London, UK, 1955; Lady Margaret Hall, Oxford Univ., 1956; M.A., 1958, Ph.D., 1961, Yale Univ., USA. Publs: Vision & Judgment in Ben Jonson's Drama, 1968; Ed., Ben Jonson, Every Man in his Humor, 1970. Contbr. to: Jrnl. of Aesthetics & Art Criticism; Modern Lang. Quarterly; Ency. Americana. Recip. num. Fellowships & Scholarships. Address: Dept. of English, Temple Univ., Phila., PA, USA.

JACKSON, (Sir) Geoffrey (Holt Seymour), b. 4 Mar. 1915, Little Hulton, Lancs., UK. Diplomat; Author. Educ: M.A., Emmanuel Coll., Cambridge. Publs: The Oven-Bird, 1972; People's Prison, 1973; Surviving The Long Night, 1974. Contbr. to: Tablet; Spectator; Cath. Herald; Observer. Mbrships: Soc. of Authors; The Keys (Cath. Writers' Guild). Hons: K.C.M.G., 1971. Address: 63B Cadogan Square, London SW1X 0DY, UK.

JACKSON, Harold Thomas, b. 20 Oct. 1897, Dowdeswell, UK. Architect & Structural Engineer. Educ: Univ. of London. Publs: The Design of Structural Member, part 1, 1957, enlarged ed., 1965, part 2, 1962; The Railway Letter Posts of Great Britain, 1968, enlarged ed., 1970; The Post Office Adhesive Stamps of Great Britain, 1971. Contbr. to: Archts. Jrnl.; num. philat. & mountaineering jrnls. Mbrships. incl: Fellow, & past Chapt. Pres., Royal Inst. of Brit. Archts.; Fellow, Royal Philat. Soc.; Instn. of Structural Engrs.; GB Philat. Soc.; Pres., Railway Philat. Grp. Recip., Lister Kaye Award, 1931. Address: The Elms, Kilsby, Rugby, Warwicks., CV23 8XT, UK.

JACKSON, Joseph, b. 1924, London, UK. Barrister-at-Law (Queen's Counsel). Educ: M.A., LL.B., Queens' Coll., Cambridge Univ.; LL.M., Univ. Coll., London Univ. Publs: Formation & Annulment of Marriage, 2nd ed.; Rayden on Divorce, 6th-12th eds.; Divorce in Halsbury's Laws of England, 3rd & 4th eds.; Husband & Wife & Infants, 4th ed.; Matrimonial Finance & Taxation; English Legal History. Contbr. to: Atkins Ency. of Court Forms; Ency. Britannica; Law Quarterly Review; Can. Bar Review; Mod. Law Review; Cambridge Law Jrnl.; Law Jrnl.; Law Times; Guardian Gazette; Punch. Address: 1 Mitre Court Bldgs., Temple, London EC4, UK.

JACKSON, Nora, b. 1915, London, UK. Teacher. Educ: Furzedown Trng. Coll. Publs: Groundwork Geographies — series of 4 books for secondary modern schools on British Isles, Europe, N. America, Asia, Southern Continents; Groundwork of Physical Geography; World Wealth; A Dictionary of Natural Resources. Contbr. to: World Book Ency.; Edit. Work, Macmillan Educ. (Overseas — Nigeria, Ghana). Mbrships: A.C.P.; M.R.S.T.; F.R.G.S. Address: 58 Hill Rd., Pinner, Middx. HA5 1LE, UK.

JACKSON, Robert, b. 25 Feb. 1911, Leeds, Yorks., UK. Author; Biographer. Publs. incl: The Biography of Lord Chief Justice Hewart; Case for the Prosecution: The Biography of Sir Archibald Bodkin; Coroner; The Biography of Sir Bentley Purchase; The Crime Doctors; The Nuffield Story; The Navy's Here: The Altmark Affair (w. W. Frischauer); 30 Seconds at Quetta: The Story of an Earthquake; A Taste of Freedom: I Captained the Big Ships (w. Commodore R. G. Thelwell); One Woman's War (w. A. Mercer); Francis Camps: Famous Case Histories; & num. gardening books. Contbr. to: Illustrated. Address: 49 Cumberland Mansions, Seymour Place, London W1, UK.

JACKSON, (Right Rev.) Robert Wyse, b. 12 July 1908, Tullamore, Ireland. Clergyman (Former Anglican Bishop). Educ: Trinity Coll., Dublin; Middle Temple, UK; LL.D.; Litt.D.; D.D. Publs. incl: Jonathan Swift, dean & Pastor, 1939; The Celtic Cross (anthol.), 1950; Oliver Goldsmith: Essays, 1952; History of the Church of Ireland 1600-1932, 1953; The Best of Swift, 1967; Cathedrals of the Church of Ireland, 1970; Irish Silver, 1971; Bedell's Apocrypha, 1971; Story of Limerick, 1971; Story of Kilkenny, 1973; Miles Magrath, 1973. Contbr. to relig. & archaeol. jrnls. Mbrships. incl: Royal Irish Acad. Hons: Freeman, Limerick City. Address: Vellore, Greystones, Co. Wicklow, Repub. of Ireland.

JACKSON, Rosalee, b. 12 Apr. 1926, Wetunka, Okla., USA. Writer; Homemaker. Publs: Thinking of You (song lyric), 1945. Contbr. to: World Call; Disciple; Jr. World. Mbrships: Kan. Authors Club; Write to Sell Club; Pres., Dist. & Local Christian Women's Fellowship; Ch. Women United; Asst. Ed., Midwest Geneal. Soc. Recip., Cert. of Recognition, Famous Writers Schl. Address: 1729 Ventnor, Wichita, KS 67219, USA.

JACKSON, (Sir) William (Godfrey Fothergill), b. 28 Aug. 1917, Blackpool, Lancs., UK. Regular Army Officer. Educ: Royal Mil. Acad., Woolwich; M.A., King's Coll., Cambridge Univ. Publs: Attack in the West, 1953; Seven Roads to Moscow, 1957; Battle for Italy, 1967; Battle for Rome, 1969; Alexander of Tunis, 1971; Battle of Northern Africa, 1975. Contbr. to: Royal United Servs. Jrnl.; Royal Engrs. Jrnl. Fellow, Brit. Inst. Mgmt.; mbr., var. mil. orgs. Hons: Gold Medals for Prize Essays, Royal United Servs. Instn., 1950, 1965; O.B.E., 1957; K.C.B., 1970; M.C. & Bar. Address: c/o Williams & Glyns Bank, Whitehall, London SW1, UK.

JACKSON, William Thomas Hobdell, b. 2 Apr. 1915, Sheffield, Yorks., UK. University Professor. Educ: B.A., 1935, M.A., 1938, Sheffield Univ.; Ph.D., Univ. Wash., 1951. Publs: The Literature of the Middle Ages, 1960; Essential Works of Erasmus, 1965; Medieval Literature, a History & a Guide, 1966; An Anthology of German Literature to 1750 (w. Peter Demetz), 1967; The Anatomy of Love, The Tristan of Gottfried von Strassburg, 1971.

Contbr. to: PMLA; Euphorion; Mosaic; Mod. Lang. Quarterly; etc. Mbrships. incl: Medieval Acad. Am. (Advsry. Coun.); Acad. Lit. Studies. Hons. incl: 2 Guggenheim Fellowships 1957, 1967. Address: 90 Morningside Dr., N.Y., NY 10027, USA.

JACOB, Alaric, b. 1909, Edinburgh, UK. Journalist; Author. Publs: Seventeen, 1930; A Traveller's War, 1945; A Window in Moscow, 1946; Scenes from a Bourgeois Life, 1949; Two Ways in the World, 1962; Russian Journey: From Suzdal to Samarkand, 1969; Eminent Nonentities, 1971. Contbr. to: Daily Express; Spectator; Books & Bookmen; Hist. To-day; Pol. Quarterly. Mbr., PEN. Address: 6 Kassala Rd., London SW11 4HN, UK.

JACOB, Jessica, b. 30 May 1948, Deolali, India. Journalist. Educ: B.A., St. Xavier's Coll., Bombay Univ., 1968; M.A., Univ. of Mo., Columbia, USA, 1972. Contbr. to: Times of India, Bombay; Femina; Hindustan Standard, Calcutta. Recip., var. acad. prizes, awards & schlrships. Address: c/o Femina, The Times of India, D.N. Rd., Bombay 400001, India.

JACOBS, Arthur David, b. 14 June 1922, Manchester, Lancs., UK. Music Critic; Editor; Professor of Music; Opera Translator & Librettist. Educ: M.A., Merton Coll., Oxford Univ. Publs: Gilbert & Sullivan, 1951; A New Dictionary of Music, 1958; Ed., Choral Music, 1963; Pan Book of Opera (w. S. Sadie), 1966; A Short History of Western Music, 1972; Ed., Music Yearbooks, 1972-73 & 1973-74; Ed., British Music Yearbook, 1975. Contbr. to: Musical Times; Opera; etc. Mbrships: Nat. Union Jrnlsts.; Royal Musical Assn. Hons: McColvin Medal (UK Lib. Assn.) for outstanding new ref. work, Music Yearbook 1972-73; Yorks. Post Book Award for Short History of Western Music. Address: 53 Friars Ave., London N20 0XG, UK.

JACOBS, Francisco, pen name JACOBS, Pszisko, b. 24 July 1917, Haarlem, Netherlands. Translator in Polish & German. Publs: Verdorie, 1956 (transl. German, 1959); Theodor Jonkheer, 1956; Hamer, 1957; Hoeveel tijd vergt literair vertaalwerk? (case study), 1971. Contbr. to sev. mags. & monthlies. Mbr., Vereniging van Letterkundigen. Hons: Stipend for Hamer, 1959; Stipends for translng. studies, 1971, 1973. Address: Dr. Schaepmanstraat 48, Haarlem, Netherlands.

JACOBS, Harvey, b. 7 Jan. 1930, NYC, USA. Writer. Educ: A.B., Univ. of Syracuse, 1950. Publs: The Egg of the Glak & Other Stories, 1969; Summer on a Mountain of Spices, 1975; var. plays & screenplays. Contbr. to num. nat. mags. & jrnls.; also radio & TV. Mbrships: Writers' Guild of Am. E; TV Acad. of Arts & Scis.; Sci. Fiction Writers of Am. Hons: Earplay Award in Drama, Univ. of Wis., 1972. Address: 101 W. 12th St., N.Y., NY 10011, USA.

JACOBS, Helen Hull, occasional pen name HULL, Braxton, b. 6 Aug. 1908, Globe, Ariz., USA. Writer. Educ: Univ. of Calif., Berkeley, 1926-29; Coll. of Wm. & Mary, Williamsburg, Va., 1942. Publs. incl: Beyond the Game (autobiog.), 1936; Barry Cort (under pen name), 1938; Storm Against the Wind, 1944; Young Sportsman's Guide to Tennis, 1961; Famous American Women Athletes, 1964; Courage to Conquer, 1967; The Tennis Machine, 1972. Contbr. to num. mags. Mbrships. incl: San Fran. Press & Calif. Writers. Hons. incl: in Nat. Lawn Tennis Hall of Fame. Address: Ocean Ave., E. Hampton, NY 11937, USA.

JACOBS, Lou Jr., b. 24 July 1921, Dayton, Ohio, USA. Writer; Photographer. Educ: B.A., Carnegie-Mellon Univ., Pitts., Pa., 1942; grad., Photojrnlsm., Art Ctrl. Coll. of Design, L.A., 1950. Publs: over 30 books inclng: Shamu the Killer Whale, 1969; The Shapes of Our Land, 1970; Freelance Magazine Photography, 1970; Jumbo Jets, 1971; Contact: the First Four Minutes (w. Dr. Leonard Zunin), 1972; Space Station '80, 1973; Teenagers Inside Out (w. Eleanor Bralver), 1974. Contbr. to num. jrnls. Mbr., profl. orgs. Recip., photog. prizes. Address: 13058 Bloomfield St., Studio City, CA 91604, USA.

JACOBS, Paul, b. 24 Aug. 1918, NYC, USA. Writer. Publs: Labor in a Free Society, 1959; Old Age & Political Behaviour, 1959; The State of the Unions, 1963; Is Curly Jewish?, 1965; The New Radicals (w. Saul Landau), 1966; Prelude to Riot, 1968; Between the Rock & the Hard Place, 1970; To Serve the Devil (w. Saul Landau & Eve Pell), 1971. Mbrships: Soc. of Mag. Writers; Authors' Guild. Recip., Jrnlsm. Award, Sigma Delta Chi, 1958. Address: 2500 Filbert St., San Fran., CA 94123, USA.

JACOBS, Robert L., b. 1904, Melbourne, Australia. Former University Lecturer in Musical Appreciation; Musical Journalist; Author. Educ: B.A., Balliol Coll., Oxford; L.R.A.M. Publs: Wagner, 1934; Harmony for the Listener, 1958, paperback ed. as "Understanding Harmony", 1969; Wagner Writes from Paris (co-transl.), 1973; var. BBC Documentary features & talks. Contbr. to: Musical Review, etc. Agent: David Higham Assocs. Ltd. Address: 27 Asmuns Hill, London, NW11, UK.

JACOBS, Woodrow Cooper, b. 11 Sept. 1908, Pasadena, Calif., USA. Oceanographer & Meteorologist. Educ: A.B., Univ. of Calif. at LA., 1930; M.S., Univ. of Southern Calif., LA, 1934; Ph.D., Univ. of Calif. at LA, 1948. Publs: Survey of Instruction in Meteorology in the Colleges of the United States, 1934; Fruit-Frost Survey of Imperial Valley, California, 1941; Meteorological Results of Cruise VII of The Carnegie, 1943; Wartime Developments in Applied Climatology, 1947; Energy Exchange Between Sea & Atmosphere & Some of Its Consequences, 1951; Arctic Meteorology (w. S. Petterssen), 1956; Meteorological Satellites, 1962. Ed. or Assoc. Ed., sev. oceanol. & meteorol. jrnls. Contbr. to num. tech. & sci. jrnls., encys. & books. Address: 6309 Bradley Blvd., Bethesda, MD 20034, USA.

JACOBSEN, Gudrun, b. 30 Oct. 1930, Reykjavík, Iceland. Singer. Publs: Listamannsraunir, 1955; Gulltarin, 1957; Pilagrimsfor til Lourdes, 1961; Smafolk, 1963; Alpyouheimilio, 1964. Contbr. to: var. mags. Mbr., Assn. of Icelandic Writers. Address: Bergstadarstreet 34, Reykjavík, Iceland.

JACOBSEN, Hermann Johannes Heinrich, b. 26 Jan. 1898, Hamburg, Germany. Former Curator, University Botanic Gardens. Publs. incl: Die Sukkulenten, 1933; Succulent Plants, 1935; Mesembryanthemaceae, 1950; Kakteen und andere Sukkulenten, 1952; A Handbook of Succulent Plants, 1960; Das Sukkulenten Lexicon, 1970; Lexicon of Succulent Plants, 1975. Contbr. to jrnls. of num. int. cactus socs. Mbrships. incl: VP & Fellow, African Succulent Plant Soc.; VP, Nat. Cactus Succulent Soc.; VP, Cactus Succulent Soc., GB; Fellow, Linnean Soc., London; Hon. mbr., German Cactus Soc. Recip., Dr. rer. nat. h.c., 1963. Address: Kiel, 7 Jensendamm, W. Germany.

JACOBSON, Dan, b. 1929, Johannesburg, S. Africa. Author. Educ: B.A., Univ. of Witwatersrand, Johannesburg. Publs: The Trap, 1955; A Dance in the Sun, 1956; The Price of Diamonds, 1957; No Further West, 1959; The Evidence of Love, 1960; The Beginners, 1966; The Rape of Tamar, 1970; Inklings, 1973; The Wonder-Worker, 1973. Contbr. to: Listener; New Yorker; Guardian; Commentary USA. Address: c/o Agent, A. M. Heath & Co. Ltd., 35 Dover St., London W1, UK.

JACOBSON, Marcus A. I., pen names, MAJ, MA, b. 21 Aug. 1921, Frankenberg, Germany. Chartered Mechanical Engineer. Educ: Dip. in Applied Mech., Sheffield Univ. Publs: Know about your Tyres, 1968; Book of the Car (mech. Ed. & chief contbr.), 1970; Know about Corrosion, 1974; Money Saving Motoring (cons. Ed. & chief contbr.), 1974. Contbr. to: Jrnl. of Automotive Engrng.; Auto Design Engrng.; Proceedings, Brit. Gear Mfrs. Assn.; S.A.E. (USA). Mbrships: Fellow, I. Mech. E.; I. Prod. E.; I.M.I.; Inst of Corrosion Tech.; Inst. of Petroleum; Inst. of Metal Finishing. Address: 99 Reading Rd., Finchampstead, Wokingham, Berks., UK.

JACOBSON, Nils O., b. 19 Feb. 1937, Stockholm, Sweden. Psychiatrist. Educ: M.D., Univ. Lund, Sweden, 1968. Publs: (in Swedish) Liv efter doden? (Life Without Death?, transl'd. English & sev. langs.), 1971; Froët-Gemenskapitillväxt, 1973; Ed., 2 Swedish anthols.; Natural Ways of Healing, forthcoming. Contbr. to: Sökaren Mag. Mbr., Parapsychol. Assn. Recip., 1st Prize, 1974 Swiss Soc. Psychical Rsch. for Life Without Death & rsch. in parapsychol. Address: Dept. of Psychiatry, Huddinge Hospital, Huddinge, Sweden.

JACOBSON, Nolan Pliny, b. 27 Mar. 1909, Hudson, Wis., USA. College Professor of Philosophy & Religion. Educ: Univ. of Wis.; A.B., B.D., Emory Univ.; Ph.D., Univ. of Chgo. Publs. incl: Buddhism: The Religion of Analysis, 1970, 2nd ed., 1974; Nippondo: The Japan Way (in Japanese), 1974; Buddhism & the Modern World, forthcoming; Chapter, "The Problem of Civilisation", in Social Change (Ed., Nordskog), 1960; Chapter, "Reconceiving Science in the Unbalanced Revolution", in Science & Society: Past, Present & Future (Ed., Steneck),

1974. Contbr. to: Revue Philosophique; Eastern Buddhist; Jrnl. of Relig.; Ethics; Educl. Theory; & num. others. Mbrships. incl: AAAS; Am. Philos. Assn.; Soc. for Asian & Comp. Philos.; etc. Hons. incl: Disting. Prof. of Yr., Winthrop Coll., 1962-63; & num. rsch. & tchng. awards. Address: 1612 Clarendon Place, Rock Hill, SC 29730, USA.

JACOBSON, Rodolfo, b. 10 Nov. 1915, Berlin, Germany. Professor of Sociolinguistics. Educ: B.A., Univ. Panama; M.A., 1965, Ph.D., 1966, Univ. Mich., USA. Publs: The London Dialect of the Late Fourteenth Century, 1970; Ed., Studies in English to Speakers of Other Languages & Standard English to Speakers of a Non-Standard Dialect, 1971; Introduction to Language, 1974. Contbr. to: Acts X, XI Int. Congress Linguists; Engl. Record; Lang. Learning; Jrnl. Engl. as Second Lang.; etc. Mbrships. incl: Tchng. Engl. to Speakers Other Langs.; Am. Dialect Soc.; Nat. Assn. Bilingual Educ. Hons. incl: SUNY Award, 1970; SUNY-Cortland Deleg. XI Int. Congress Linguists, 1972. Guest Prof. Mexico, Beirut, Cairo Univs. Address: 3434 Oakdale, Apt. 1203, San Antonio, TX 78229, USA.

JACOT de BOINOD, Bernard Louis, b. 25 Feb. 1898, Sambourne, Warwicks., UK. Writer. Educ: M.A., St. John's Coll., Oxford; Barrister at Law, Inner Temple. Publs: The Longer Shadow, 1926; Trust Wesley, 1927; Frogs Feathers, 1934; Winslow Moult, 1935; Marconi (w. D. M. B. Collier), 1935; Jacqueminet, 1944; Hands of Wan Lu, 1946; Villa Mar, 1948; Night has 1000 Eyes, 1958; Tulip Tree, 1967; Jean-Marie, 1964; Moon, 1968. Contbr. of short stories to most US & UK mags. Mbr., Vincents Club, Oxford. Recip., Harvard Award for Lit., 1966. Address: Beach Hill, Buckland St. Mary, Chard, Somerset, UK.

JACQUEMARD, Simonne, b. 6 May 1924, Novelist; Journalist. Educ: Univ. of Paris. Publs: Les Fascines, 1951; Sable, 1952; Le Lecon des Ténèbres, 1954; Judith Albarès, 1958; Planant sur les Airs, 1960; Compagnons Insolites, 1961; Le Veilleur de Nuit, 1962; L'Oiseau, 1963; L'Orangerie, 1963; Les Derniers Rapaces, 1965; Dérive au Zénith, 1965; Exploration d'un corps, 1965; Navigation vers les îles, 1967. Contbr. to: Figaro Lit.; La Table Ronde. Recip., Priz Ranaudot, 1962. Address: 35 rue de la Harpe, Paris 5e, France.

JACQUENEY, Mona G., b. 15 Dec. 1914, Detroit, Mich., USA. Sociologist; Writer. Educ: A.A., Nassau Community Coll., 1965; B.A., 1967, M.A., 1971, Hofstra Univ.; Ph.D. studies (in progress), N.Y. Univ. Publs: Radicalism on Campus 1969-1971, 1972; The Golden Age Society: A Participant Observation Study of the Aged in Long Beach, N.Y. (to be publd.). Contbr. to: Police Chief; Annals Am. Acad. Pol. & Soc. Sci.; Chronicles of Higher Educ.; Educ. Digest. Mbr., var. profl. assns. Recip., T. Roosevelt Medal for Achievement in Pub. Speaking. Address: 233 E. Beech St., Long Beach, NY 11561, USA.

JACQUET-FRANCILLON, Jacques Noel, b. 31 July 1927, Vintimiglia, Italy. Journalist; Deputy Editor. Educ: Licencié en Droit; Lauréat, Fac. d'Aix-en-Provence, Concours de Droit Int. Privé, 1951. Author, Chine à Huis-Clos, 1960. Contbr. to Le Figaro. Mbrships: Assoc. Mbr., Int. Press Inst.; Nat. Press Club, Wash. D.C.; For. Press Assn., N.Y.; Assn. de la Press Diplomatique, Paris; Hon. Mbr., For. Press Assn., Tokyo. Recip., Prix Albert Londres, 1960. Address: 7 rue Marbeuf, 75008 Paris, France.

JAFFE, Abram J., b. 2 Dec. 1912, Chelsea, Mass., USA. Demographer, Specialist in Manpower & Population. Educ: Ph.D., Univ. Chicago, 1941. Publs. incl: Handbook of Statistical Methods for Demographers, 1951; Occupational Mobility in the United States, 1930-1960, 1954, latest ed., 1974; People, Jobs & Economic Development, 1959; Technology & Jobs, Automation in Perspective, 1968; Handbook of Statistical Procedures for Long Range Projections of Public School Enrollment, 1970; The Middle Years, 1971; The Retirement Dilemma, 1972. Mbrships. incl: Am. Statistical Assn. (Past Pres., N.Y. Chapt.); Fellow, Am. Assn. Advancement Sci. Address: Bur. Applied Social Rsch., 605 W. 115th St., N.Y., NY 10025, USA.

JAFFE, Aniela, b. 1903, Berlin, Germany. Analytical Psychologist. Educ: Univs. of Hamburg & Zurich, Switz. Publs: Ed., Memories, Dreams, Reflections of C. G. Jung; Co-Ed., C. G. Jung's Collected Letters; Apparitions & Precognition, 1963; The Myth of Meaning, 1970; From the Life & Work of C. G. Jung, 1971 (all originally publ'd. in German). Contbr. to: sev. Eranos-Jahrbücher; acad. jrnls. Mbrships. incl: Swiss Soc. for Practical Psychol.; Swiss

Parapsychol. Soc.; Zurich Soc. of Arts. Address: Hochstr. 73, 8044 Zurich, Switz.

JAFFE, Gabriel Vivian, pen name POOLE, Vivian, b. 1923, Nottingham, UK. Medical Writer & Editor. Educ: London Univ.; St. Thomas's Hosp., London; M.B., B.S.; M.R.C.S.; L.R.C.P. Publs: The Life Pill; Design for Loving; Promiscuity. Contbr. to: Brit. Med. Jrnl.; Brit. Jrnl. Clin. Practice; Clin. Trials Jrnl.; Lancet; Pulse; Times; Sunday Times; Financial Times; Practitioner; Hlth. Horizon; Nursing Times; Jrnl. Int. Med. Rsch.; Nursing Mirror; Bournemouth Evening Echo (Med. Corres.). Mbr., Brit. Med. Assn. Address: 7 Alum Chine Rd., Bournemouth BH4 8DT, UK.

JAHNSSON, Bengt, b. 11 June 1928, Uppsala, Sweden. Author; Theatre Critic. Educ: M.A., Univ. of Uppsala, 1955. Publs. incl: Poems of Waxio, 1955; The Death Is Growing as a Child (poems), 1960; Gulliver's Sixth Travel (novel), 1960; The Sun of Justice (poems), 1962; The Prince & the Beggar President (novel), 1969; Thresholds Are Burned Naked (poems), 1972. Address: Wittstocksgatan 19I, 115 27 Stockholm, Sweden.

JAHODA, Gloria Adelaide Love, b. 6 Oct. 1926, Chgo., Ill., USA. Author; Lecturer. Educ: B.A., 1948, M.A., 1950, Northwestern Univ. Publs: Annie, 1960; The Loving Maid, 1962; Delilah's Mountain, 1963; The Other Florida, 1967; The Road to Samarkand: Frederick Delius & His Music, 1969; River of the Golden Ibis, 1973. Contbr. to: Fla. Histl. Quarterly; Diversion; etc. Hons: Citation for Servs. to Lit., Fla. Legis., 1973; Award for Best Hist. Book of 1973, Soc. of Midland Authors, Chgo., Ill. Address: 225 Westridge Dr., Tallahassee, FL 32304, USA.

JAHODA, Gustav, b. 1920, Vienna, Austria. University Professor of Psychology. Educ: M.Sc., Ph.D., Univ. of London, UK. Publs: White Man, 1961; The Psychology of Superstition, 1969. Contbr. to profl. jrnls. Mbrships: Fellow, Brit. Psychol. Soc.; Am. Psychol. Assn. Address: Ianmyo, Peel St., Cardross, Dumbarton, UK.

JALEES, Ibrahim, b. 12 Aug. 1924, Hyderabad, India. Journalist; Author. Educ: B.A., Muslim Univ. of Aligarh, India. Publs. of short stories & novels: Four Hundred Million Beggars, 1946; Black Market, 1947; A Tale of Two Countries, 1950; Days & Nights of Prison, 1952; Free Slave (in press); Patey-Ki-Bat. Contbr. to major mags. & Newspapers in Urdu lang., Pakistan, India & Bangla Desh. Recip., Gold Medal, Southern India Urdu Lit. Soc., for Four Hundred Million Beggars, 1945. Address: 21 Bahadur Shah Market, M.A. Jinnah Rd., Karachi, Pakistan.

JALIBI, Jameel, b. 1 July 1929, Aligarh, India. Author. Educ: M.A., LL.B., Ph.D. Publs: Eliot Ke Mazameen, 1960; Pakistani Culture, 1965; Tanquid Aur Tajraba, 1967; Diwan-e-Hasan Shauqi, 1971; Diwan-e-Nusrati, 1972; Qadeem Urdu Ki Lughat, 1973; Arastoo Se Eliot Tak, 1974; Tarikh-e-Adab-e-Urdu (History of Urdu Lit. in 4 vols.), Vol. 1, 1974. Contbr. to: Naya Daur, Karachi; Saqi, Karachi; Sahifa, Lahore; Oriental Coll. Mag., Lahore; Urdu, Karachi; Auraq, Lahore, etc. Fndr. Mbr., Pakistan Writers' Guild. Recip., Nat. Lit. Prizes, 1965, 1974. Address: D-26, Block "B", N. Nazimabad, Karachi 33, Pakistan.

JAMALZADEH, S. Mohammad Ali, b. 1895, Esfahan, Iran. Writer. Publ. incl: Yeki Bud o Yeki Na bud; Ganj-i-Shaigan; Sahraiey-Mahshar; Rah Aab Nameh; Gher Az Khuda Hiechkas Nabood; Kashkool-i-Jamali. Contbr. to: Rasta Khiz. Mbr., Stockholm Peace Assn. Address: c/o Iranian Embassy, 16 Prince's Gate, London SW7, UK.

JAMES, Alan, b. 22 Aug. 1943, S. Shields, UK. Teacher. Educ: Cert. in Educ., St. John's Coll., York; B.Sc.(Econ.), London Univ.; Cert. in Biblical Studies, Newcastle Univ.; Cert. in Achievement Testing, C.G.L.I. Publs: The Post, 1970; Money, 1973; Buildings, 1975; Sir Rowland Hill & the Post Office, 1972; Newspapers & The Times in the Nineteenth Century, 1975; Living Light series, 1972; Num. titles in Blackwell's Learning Library, 1969—. Contbr. to Jrnl., Inst. of Educ., Newcastle Univ. Address: Broom Lodge, 17 Fellside, Darras Hall, Ponteland, Newcastle upon Tyne, NE20 9JP, UK.

JAMES, A(rthur) Walter, b. 30 June 1912, Southampton, UK. Journalist; Editor; Author. Educ: Keble & Magdalen Colls., Oxford; M.A.(Hons.), 1933; British Schl. at Rome, Italy. Publs: The Christian in Politics, 1962; The Teacher & His World, 1962; A Middle-class Parent's Guide to Education, 1964. Address: Cumberland Lodge, The Great Park, Windsor, Berks., UK.

JAMES, Barbara Ethel, b. Stevenage, Herts., UK. Actress. Educ: Royal Acad. of Dramatic Art. Publs: 96 short stories in 20 countries, 1958-75; Beauty that Must Die, 1961; Bright Deadly Summer, 1962; Contbr. to John Creasey's Mystery Bedside Books (anthols.), 1967, 1973; Contbr. to num. jrnls., UK & abroad. Mbr., Crime Writers' Assn. Address: Church Close, Throwleigh, Okehampton, Devon, UK.

JAMES, Betty (Mrs. Reeve-Jones), b. 30 Apr. 1918, Kingston, Surrey, UK. Author; Journalist. Publs: London on Sunday; London on $1 a Day; London & the Single Girl; London for Lovers; London for You; A Kingdom by the Sea; 1001 Money-Saving Tips. Contbr. to: Evening Standard; News of the World; Sunday Times; Woman's Realm; Good Housekeeping; She; Family Circle; In Britain. Mbr., Nat. Union Jrnlsts. Address: Walnut Tree Cottage, Herne Common, Kent CT6 7LB, UK.

JAMES, C(yril) L(ionel) R(obert), b. 4 Jan. 1901, Trinidad. Writer; Lecturer. Publs: The Life of Captain Cipriani, 1933 (abridged as The Case for W. Indian Self-Government, UK 1933); Cricket & I (w. L. N. Constantine), 1933; Minty Alley (novel), 1936; World Revolution, 1917-1936, UK & USA 1937; A History of Negro Revolt, 1938; The Black Jacobins, UK & USA 1938, revised ed., USA 1963; Mariners, Renegades & Castaways, 1953; Beyond a Boundary, UK 1963; var. short stories on W. Indian life, 1920s & 1930s; articles on cricket. Address: c/o Hutchinson & Co., 178 Gt. Portland St., London W1, UK.

JAMES, David Edward, b. 1937, Oxford, UK. Biologist; University Director of Adult Education. Educ: Univs. of Reading, Oxford, Durham, & London; B.Sc.; M.Ed.; A.B.Ps.S. Publs: Students Guide to Efficient Study, 1967; Introduction to Psychology for Teachers, Nurses & other Social Workers, 1968, 4th ed., 1973. Contbr. to: Essays in Local Govt. Enterprise, Vol. III, 1966; A Guide for Tchrs. of Nurses, 1974; The Care of the Orthopaedic Patient, 1975; num. jrnls. of adult educ. & psychol. Mbrships. incl: F.R.S.A.; Inst. of Biol.; Fellow, Royal Soc. of Hlth. Address: Way Cottage, Sandy Lane, Guildford, Surrey, UK.

JAMES, David Geraint, b. 2 Jan. 1922, Treherbert, Wales, UK. Consultant Physician, London; Professor of Medicine, Miami. Educ: M.A., 1944, M.D., 1953, Jesus Coll., Cambridge; F.R.C.P., London, 1964. Publs: The Diagnosis & Treatment of Infections, 1957. Contbr. of chapts. to var. med. textbooks, & articles on Sarcoidosis, Dermatol., Hist. of Med. & Infections, etc., in Brit. & for. med. jrnls. Mbrships. incl: For. Sec., Med. Soc. of London; Ed. Bd., Postgrad. Med. Jrnl.; Royal Soc. of Med., & num. other med. orgs. Organising Sec., var. int. med. confs. Hons. incl: Gold Medal, Inst. of Dermatol., London, 1958; Freeman, City of London, 1964. Address: 41 York Terrace East, London NW1, UK.

JAMES, Dorris Clayton, b. 13 Feb. 1931, Winchester, Ky., USA. Professor of History; Author. Educ: B.A., Southwestern-at-Memphis Coll; B.D., Louisville Presby. Theol. Sem., 1956; M.A., 1959, Ph.D., 1964, Univ. of Tex. Publs: Antebellum Natchez, 1968; The Years of MacArthur, Vol. I, 1880-1941, 1970, Vol. II, 1941-45, 1975, Vol. III, in preparation; South to Bataan, North to Mukden: The Prison Diary of Brigadier General W. E. Brougher, 1971. Contbr. to: Ency. Britannica; Am. Histl. Review; etc. Mbr., num. histl. assns. Recip., sev. acad. hons. Address: 1702 Linden Dr., Starkville, MS 39759, USA.

JAMES, M. R., pen name DANIELSON, J. D., b. 6 Dec. 1940, Wabash Co., Ill., USA. Editor; Publisher. Educ: B.S., Oakland City & Coll., 1964; Grad. studies, Univ. of Evansville, 1966-67; Cand. Magister, St. Francis Coll. Publs: Bowhunting for Whitetail & Mule Deer, forthcoming. Contbr. to: Fndr., Bowhunter Mag.; Outdoor Life; Fur-Fish-Game; Archery; Archery World; Bow & Arrow; var. crime mags. Mbrships. incl: Profl. Bowhunters Soc.; Outdoor Writers of Am.; Int. Assn. of Bus. Communicators; VP, Ft. Wayne Assn. of Bus. Eds. Hons: Ed. of the Yr., Ft. Wayne, 1969; Best Ed. Award, United Community Servs. Publs., 1970, 1971 & 1972. Address: 9713 Saratoga Rd., Ft. Wayne, IN 46804, USA.

JAMES, Noel David Glaves, b. 16 Sept. 1911, Newton, UK. Land Agent. Educ: Royal Agric. Coll., Cirencester, UK; T.D.; M.A. Publs: Working Plans for Estate Woodlands, 1948; Notes on Estate Forestry, 1949; An Experiment in Forestry, 1951; The Forester's Companion, 1955, 2nd. ed., 1966; The Trees of Bicton, 1969; The Arboriculturalist's

Companion, 1972; A Book of Trees (anthol.), 1973. Contbr. to profl. jrnls. Hons: O.B.E., 1964. Address: Blakemore House, Kersbrook, Budleigh Salterton, Devon, UK.

JAMES, Norah C., b. London, UK. Councillor. Publs: Silent Corridors; The Shadow Between; Portrait of a Patient; The Uneasy Summer; A Sense of Loss; There Is No Why; The Bewildered Heart; Love. Contbr. to: Woman's Own; Woman's Realm; Evening News; Evening Standard; Sunday Mirror; etc. Mbr., Civil Service Clerical Assn. Address: c/o National Westminster Bank, 322 Gray's Inn Rd., London WC1, UK.

JAMES, Philip Seaforth, b. 28 May 1914, Croydon, Surrey, UK. Law Professor. Educ: M.A., Trinity Coll. Oxford Univ.; Rsch. Fellow, Yale Univ., USA; Called to Bar, UK, 1939. Publs: An Introduction to English Law, 1951; General Principles of the Law of Torts, 1959; A Shorter Introsuction to English Law, 1969. Contbr. to: Mod. Law Review; Jrnl. of Bus. Law; Nat. Review; Contemporary Review. Mbr., var. profl. assns. Address: Faculty of Law, Leeds Univ., Leeds 2, UK.

JAMES, Preston Everett, b. 14 Feb. 1899, Brookline, Mass., USA. Emeritus Professor of Geography. Educ: A.B., 1920, M.A., 1921, Harvard Univ.; Ph.D., Clark Univ., 1923. Publs. incl: Outline of Geography, 1935; Latin America, 1942, 4th ed., 1969; A Geography of Man, 1950, 3rd ed., 1968; Ed., American Geography Inventory & Prospect (w. C. F. Jones), 1954; The Wide World, a Geography (w. N. Davis), 1959, 3rd ed., 1968; Ed., New Viewpoints in Geography, 1959; One World Divided, 1964, 2nd ed., 1974; All Possible Worlds, a History of Geographical Ideas, 1972. Contbr. to num. profl. jrnls. Mbr., var. profl. assns. Hons. incl: Disting. Writing Award, Nat. Coun. Geographic Educ., 1963; num. profl. hons. & degrees. Address: 379 Villa Dr. S., Atlantis, FL 33462, USA.

JAMES, William Louis Gabriel, pen name JAMES, Louis, b. 2 May 1933, Shrewsbury, Salop, UK. University Lecturer; Author. Educ: M.A., D.Phil., Jesus Coll., Oxford. Publs: Fiction for the Working Man, 1963, 2nd ed., 1974; Ed., Islands That Lie Between, 1968. Contbr. to: Victorian Studies (Advsry. Bd.); Ency. Britannica; 20th Century Studies (Ed. Bd.); Dickens Studies Annual. Mbrships: Assn. C'wlth. Lit. & Letters; F.R.S.A. Address: Elliot College, The University, Canterbury, Kent, UK.

JAMESON, Margaret Storm, b. 8 Jan. 1891, Whitby, Yorks., UK. Writer. Educ: M.A.(Hons.), Leeds Univ. Publs. incl: Modern Drama in Europe, 1920; That Was Yesterday, 1932; A Day Off, 1938; Europe to Let, 1940; Cousin Honoré, 1940; Cloudless May, 1943; Journal of Mary Harvey Russell (autobiog.), 1945; Black Laurel, 1947; The Green Man, 1952; Road from the Monument, 1962; Journey from the North, 2 vols., 1969, 1970; Parthian Words (criticism), 1970; There Will be a Short Interval. Contbr. to Times Lit. Supplement, etc. Mbrships: VP, Int. PEN; Pres., Engl. PEN, 1929-45. Recip., Hon. D.Litt., Leeds Univ. Address: c/o A. D. Peters & Co., 10 Buckingham St., London WC2, UK.

JAMES of Rusholme, (Lord) Eric John Francis, b. 1909, Derby, UK. Vice-Chancellor, University of York, 1962-73; High Master, Manchester Grammar School, 1945-62. Educ: M.A., D.Phil., Queen's Coll., Oxford Univ. Publs: (co-author) Elements of Physical Chemistry; (co-author) Science & Education; An Essay on the Content of Education; Education & Leadership. Contbr. to: Times Educl. Supplement; Guardian; etc. Mbrships. incl: Univ. Grants Comm., 1948-58; Royal Fine Arts Commn., 1973; Comm. Educ. & Trng. of Tchrs., 1971; Athenaeum Club. Hons. incl: LL.D., McGill (Montreal); LL.D., York (Toronto); D.Litt. (N.B.). Address: Penhill Cottage, W. Witton, Leyburn, Yorks., UK.

JANES, Henry Hurford, b. 1909, Chelsea, London, UK. Dramatist; Author. Publs. incl: (plays) Six One Act Plays & One Three Act Play (Gin Palace), 1937-45; Lady Must Sell, 1948; Under The Skin, 1953; var. plays for BBC & ITV; (books) Over Fifty Industrial Biographies, 1962; Red Barrel (biog.), 1963; var. booklets on histl. places & events inclng. Trafalgar Tavern Greenwich; History of Hernhill, Kent; Centenary of St. Michael's School, Hernhill. Contbr. to: Evening News; Everybody's Wkly.; Debutante; City Life; Fate; Antique Collector; etc. Agent: A. P. Watt & Son. Address: Walnut Tree House, Hernhill, Faversham, Kent ME13 9JR, UK.

JANETSCHEK, Albert, b. 27 Sept. 1925, Hochwolkersdorf, Austria. Headmaster. Educ: Grad. as Tchr., Wiener Neustadt, 1948. Publs: Botschaft der Seele, 1951; Gnade und Bewährung, 1953; Auskunft über Adam, 1968; Notration für die Zukunft, 1972; Wia Dgrisdbamzuggaln in Süwwababia, 1973. Contbr. to: Podium; Die Horen; Nebelspalter; Simplicissimus; var. other Austrian & German jrnls. (as critic). Mbrships: PEN; Die Kogge (Assn. of European Authors); Fndr. Mbr., Podium. Recip., Cultural Prize, 1964. Address: 2700-Wiener Neustadt, Haydngasse 12, Austria.

JANEWAY, Elizabeth, b. 7 Oct. 1913, Bklyn., NYC, USA. Author; Lecturer; Social Historian. Educ: A.B., Barnard Coll., N.Y. Publs: The Walsh Girls, 1943; Daisy Kenyon, 1945; The Question of Gregory, 1949; The Vikings, 1951; Leaving Home, 1953; Early Days of the Automobile, 1956; The Third Choice, 1959; Angry Kate, 1963; Accident, 1964; Ivanov Seven, 1967; Man's World, Woman's Place, 1971; Between Myth & Morning: Women Awakening, 1974. Contbr. to: Atlantic Monthly; Am. Schlr.; Saturday Review; etc. Mbrships. incl: PEN; McDowell Colony (Dir.). Hons. incl: D.Lit. Simpson Coll., 1973. Address: 15 E. 80th St., N.Y., NY 10021, USA.

JANIKOVSZKY, Eva, b. 23 Apr. 1926, Szeged, Hungary, Editor-in-Chief. Educ: B.A. Publs: (in Hungarian) Laburnum, 1962, latest ed., 1972, transl'd. German 1968, 1974; Did You Know?, 1963, latest ed., 1974, transl'd. German, Esperanto, Russian, Spanish, Serbo-Croat, Polish; If I were a Grown-Up, 1965, transl'd. 1966-74, Engl., German, French, Spanish, Swedish, Serbo-Croat, Polish, Italian; Even Granny was Young Once, 1966, transl'd. 1969 Engl., 1972 German; Happiness, 1967, transl'd. 1969 Engl.; Mir passiert immer etwas, 1972, transl'd. German, Slovak, Swedish, Danish. Mbrships: Hungarian Writers' Union; Fine Arts Fund. Recip., Deutscher Jugendbuch Preis, 1973. Address: 1071 Budapest, Bajza u. 8, Hungary.

JANIS, Irving L., b. 26 May 1918, Buffalo, N.Y., USA. Professor of Psychology. Educ: B.S., 1939, Grad. studies, 1939-40, Univ. of Chgo., & Columbia Univ., 1940-41; Ph.D., Columbia Univ., 1948. Publs: Communication & Persuasion: Psychological Studies of Opinion Change (w. others), 1953; Psychological Stress, 1958; Stress & Frustration, 1971; Victims of Groupthink, 1972. Mbr., Ed. Bd., Am. Scientist, 1969–. Chmn., Ed., Bd., Jrnl. of Conflict Resolution, 1972–. Hons. incl: Hofheimer Prize, Am. Psychiatric Assn., 1959; Fellow, Am. Acad. Arts & Scis., 1974. Address: Dept. of Psychology, Yale University, New Haven, CT 06510, USA.

JANIS, Sidney, b. 8 July 1896, Buffalo, N.Y., USA. Art Gallery Director; Writer. Publs: They Taught Themselves: American Primitive Painters of the 20th Century, 1942; Abstract & Surrealist Art in America, 1944; Picasso: The Recent Years, 1939-46 (co-author), 1946. Contbr. to var. art mags. in USA & abroad, 1940–. Address: 6 W. 57th St., N.Y., NY 10019, USA.

JANKE, Dorothy M., b. 10 Feb. 1917, Goessel, Kan., USA. Abstracter. Educ: B.A., Univ. of Kan. Contbr. to: Reader's Digest; Writer's Digest; Saturday Evening Post; Family Weekly; Wall St. Jrnl.; Grit; Am. Legion Mag.; Farm Jrnl.; Capper's Weekly. Mbrships: Kan. Authors Club; Kan. Land Title Assn.; Kan. State Histl. Soc. Recip., 1st place, light verse, Kan. Authors Club annual contest, 1955. Address: Box 336, Russell Springs, KS 67755, USA.

JANKER, Josef W., b. 7 Aug. 1922, Wolfegg, Wurttemberg, Germany. Writer. Publs: Between Two Fires, 1960; With the Back to the Wall, 1964; Stays, 1967; The Retrainer, 1971. Contbr. to: Feuilletons, Suddeutsche Zeitung, Munich; XX Olympiade-Standard, 1972. Mbrships: PEN; Chmn., Annette Droste Prize Jury. Hons: Rom Prize, German Acad., 1968; Schubart Prize, 1971; Bavarian Acad. Prize, 1974. Address: Marienburger Strasse 32, D-798 Ravensburg, W. Germany.

JANOSSY, Lajos, b. 2 Mar. 1912, Budapest, Hungary. Physicist. Educ: Vienna Univ., Austria; Ph.D., Berlin Univ., Germany. Publs. incl: Cosmic Rays & Nuclear Physics, 1948; Theory & Practice of the Evaluation of Measurements, 1965; Theory of Relativity Based on Physical Reality, 1971. Contbr. to: Magyar Fizikai Folyoirat (Ed. in Chief); etc. Mbrships. incl: Hungarian Acad., Sci. (VP 1961-71); Hungarian A.E.C. (VP); Sci. Coun., United Inst. Nuclear Rsch., Dubna. Hons. incl: Acad. Gold Medal, 1972; Copernicus Medal, 1973. Address: H-1016 Budapest, I Czako-u. 11, Hungary.

JANOWSKY, Oscar I., b. 15 Jan. 1900, Suchawola, Poland. Professor of History. Educ: B.S.S., City Coll., N.Y., 1921; M.A., 1922, Ph.D., 1933, Columbia Univ. Publs: The Jews & Minority Rights, 1933; International Aspects of German Racial Policies (w. M. Fagen), 1937; People at Bay, 1938; Nationalities & National Minorities, 1945; The JWB Survey, 1948; Foundations of Israel, 1959; Ed., The American Jew: A Reappraisal, 1964; The Education of American Jewish Teachers, 1967. Contbr. to var. jrnls. Mbrships. incl: Am. Histl. Assn.; Am. Jewish Histl. Soc.; Jewish Publn. Soc. of Am. (VP & Hon. Mbr.). Recip., num. scholastic awards. Address: 247C Mayflower Way, Rossmoor-Jamesburg, NJ 08831, USA.

JANSEN, Mogens B., b. 1930, Copenhagen, Denmark. Teacher; Psychologist; Editor; Author; Research Director. Educ: Tchr. Trng. Coll.; Copenhagen Univ. Publs: Methods of Teaching Danish, 1966-70; Five Textbook Analysis, 1966-70; num. textbooks for children and adults in Danish lang., psychol. & sci., 1960-74. Contbr. to num. Scandinavian periodicals. Chmn., Danish Reading Tchrs. Address: Nat. Inst. of Educl. Rsch., Hermodsgade 28, 2200 Copenhagen N, Denmark.

JANSEN, Peter W., b. 11 Nov. 1930, Elsdorf/Köln, Germany. Editor. Educ: Dr.Phil. Publs: Weltbezug und Erzählhaltung. Erzählwerk und dichterische Existenz Joseph Roths, 1958. Ed., Reihe Film, 1974. Contbr. to: Akzente; Merkur; Frankfurter Hefte; Die Zeit; Frankfurter Rundschau. Mbrships: Zentrum BRD, PEN; Arbeitsgemeinschaft der Filmjournalisten. Address: 7562 Gernsbach 3, Kirchstr. 16A, W. Germany.

JANSON, Marguerite, b. 18 Jan. 1904, Bienne, Berne Canton, Switz. Housewife; Writer. Educ: Dip. Bus. Publs. incl: Der Weg mit Franziska, 1945; Gestern waren wir Kinder, 1948; Ich warte auf den Morgenregen, 1950; Franziska unterm Haselbusch, 1953; (novels) Auburn und das Tal, 1955; Kleine Annie meiner Jugend, 1959 & transls. French novels into German. Mbrships: Berne Writers' Union; Assn. Swiss Writers. Hons. incl: Bienne City Art Prize, 1952; City Berne Lit. Prize, 1955; Werkjahr Pro Helvetia, 1959. Address: La Neigette, 2533 Evilard, Switz.

JANSSON, Tove, b. 9 Aug. 1914, Helsinki, Finland. Author; Painter; Illustrator. Publs: Kometen Kommer, 1946; Trollkarlens Hatt, 1948; Muminpappans Memoarer, 1950; Hur Gick det Sen?, 1952; Farlig Midsommar, 1954; Trollvinter, 1957; Vem ska Trösta Knyttet?, 1960; Det Osynliga Barnet, 1962; Pappan och Havet, 1965; Bildhuggarens Dotter, 1968; Sent i November, 1970; Lyssnerskan, 1971; Sommarboken, 1972; Solstaden, 1974. (Many transl'd. into Engl. & 21 other langs.); Bd. Mbr., Authors' Soc. Num. hons. incl: Swedish Culture Prizes, Helsinki, 1958 & 1970; Lit. Prize, Finnish State, 1963; Hans Christian Andersen Medal, 1966; Finnish State Prize, 1971. Address: Ulrikaborgsgatan 1, Helsinki 13, Finland.

JANUTA, Petronělé, pen names ORINTAITĚ, Petronělé; VAIVORYTĚ, Balé. b. 18 Feb. 1905, Liepalotai, Lithuania. Secondary School Teacher. Educ: Dip. in lit. & pedagogy, Univ. of Kaunas, Lithuania. Publs: The Hidden Wound, 1934; Daubiške's Intelligentsia, 1937; Theophilia of Kražantě, 1959; What the Sorceresses Intended, 1965; In the Woodlands of Liepalotai, 1971. Contbr. to Lithuanian anthols. & jrnls. Mbr., Lithuanian Writers' Assn. Hons. incl: "Dirva" Lithuanian Publrs. Prize for Short Story, 1973. Address: 2818 Avenel St., L.A., CA 90039, USA.

JANZON, Astrid H. M., b. 17 Apr. 1907, Jönköping, Sweden. Educational Director, State College of Nursing, Stockholm. Educ: M.A., Univ. of Stockholm, 1950. Publs: Samarbete till hälsa (Cooperation for Health), 1955, 4th ed., 1966; Statens sjuksköterskeskola 1939-69 (State College of Nursing 1939-69), 1971. Contbr. to: Tidskrift för Sveriges sjuksköterskor (Swedish Nurses' Assn. Jrnl.); Int. Nursing Review. Mbr., Minerva, Sect. for Sci. & Popular Sci. Authors, Swedish Authors' Assn. Recip., Order of the Nordic Star, 1970. Address: Rödmossevägen 5, S 123 52 Farsta, Sweden.

JAQUES, Elliott, b. 18 Jan. 1917, Toronto, Can. Professor of Sociology; Director, University Institute of Organisation. Educ: B.A., M.A., Univ. of Toronto; M.D., Johns Hopkins Med. Schl., USA; Ph.D., Harvard Univ. Publs. incl: Product Analysis Pricing (w. Wilfred Brown), 1964; Time-Span Handbook, 1964; Glacier Project Papers (w. Wilfred Brown), 1965; Progression Handbook, 1968; Work, Creativity & Social Justice, 1970. Contbr. to: Human Rels.; Int. Jrnl. of Psycho-Analysis. Mbrships: Fellow, Int.

Acad. of Mgmt., Royal Coll. o Psych.; Brit. Psychol. Soc.; Brito. Sociol. Assn. Address: Inst. of Org. & Social Studies, Brunel Univ., Uxbridge, Middx., UK.

JARCHOW, Merrill Earl, b. 25 Sept. 1910, Stillwater, Minn., USA. College Teacher & Administrator. Educ: A.B., 1930, M.A., 1933, Ph.D., 1941, Univ. of Minn. Publs: The Earth Brought Forth: A History of Minnesota Agriculture to 1885, 1949, reprinted, 1970; Carleton: The First Century (w. L. A. Headley), 1966; Private Liberal Arts Colleges in Minnesota: Their History & Contributions, 1973; Donald J. Cowling: Educator, Idealist, Humanitarian, 1974; In Search of Fulfillment: Episodes in the Life of D. Blake Stewart, 1974. Contbr. to: Am. Histl. Review; Miss. Valley Histl. Review; Minn. History. Mbrships. incl: Am. Histl. Assn.; Org. of Am. Histns. Address: 203 Oak St., Northfield, MN 55057, USA.

JARMAN, Thomas Leckie, b. 1907, London, UK. University Lecturer & Reader in History of Education. Educ: M.A., B.Litt., New Coll., Oxford; A.M., Harvard Univ., USA. Publs: The Rise & Fall of Nazi Germany; The European World, 1870-1945 (w. Dr. T. K. Derry); Landmarks in the History of Education; The Making of Modern Britain (w. T. K. Derry); Democracy & World Conflict; Socialism in Britain. Address: 6 Tyndall's Court, 48 Tyndall's Park Road, Bristol 8, UK.

JARNÉS BERGUA. Enrique, pen name JÁRBER, E., b. 30 Jan. 1919, Cascante, Spain. Soldier. Educ: Law studies; mil. studies. Publs. incl: Un silencio de tumba (also filmed), 1962; Mansa lluvia de muerte, 1963; Solo un ataúd (also filmed), 1963; El cerco invisible, 1964; Sopa de cangrejos, 1965; Mantis y Termitas, 1964; El bosque y el ratón, 1966; 5 enigmas para Mónica, 1967; Las maquinas, 1968; Cuerpos y Mentes, 1969; Relatos de un navegante, 1970. Contbr. to num. anthols., Radio & TV. Mbrships: Nat. Inst. of the Spanish Book (INLE) (Rep. Mbr., Deleg. Commn. & Coun.); Soc. of Authors of Spain; Soc. of Writers & Artists. Hons: Hucha de Plata, 1970; Hon. mention, 1970. Address: Calle de Joaquín García Morato 60, 7C, Madrid 10, Spain.

JARRETT, Arthur, b. 1919, Portsmouth, UK. Departmental Director, Medical School. Educ: Birmingham, London & Edinburgh Univs.; M.B., Ch.B.; D.Sc.; F.R.C Path.; F.R.C.P. Publs: Science & the Skin, 1964; Histology of the Skin: Psoriasis (co-author), 1965; Dermatology, a Functional Introduction, 1966; Pharmaceutical & Cosmetic Products for Topical Administration, 1969; Ed. & Co-author, Physiology & Pathophysiology of the Skin, vols. 1-3, UK & USA. Contbr. to num. jrnls. & books. Mbrships: Fellow, Inst. Biol.; Royal Soc. of Med. Address: Dermatology Dept., University Coll. Hospital Medical Schl., University St., London WC1, UK.

JARRETT, Derek, b. 18 Mar. 1928, Whyteleafe, Surrey, UK. Principal Lecturer in History, Goldsmith's College. Educ: B.A., 1951, B.Litt., 1955, M.A., 1955, Keble Coll., Oxford Univ. Publs: Britain 1688-1815, 1965; The Begetters of Revolution, 1973; (biog.) Pitt the Younger, 1974; England in the Age of Hogarth, 1974. Contbr. to: English Histl. Review. Agent: Curtis Brown Ltd. Address: 58 Beaconsfield Rd., Blackheath, London SE3 7LG, UK.

JÄRV, Harry Johannes, b. 27 Mar. 1921, Korsholm, Finland. First Librarian & Keeper of MSS, Swedish National Library. Educ: Helsinki Univ., 1944-45; Ph.Lic., Uppsala Univ., Sweden, 1954. Publs. incl: Kritik av den nya kritiken, 1953; Die Kafka-Literatur, 1961; Varaktigare än koppar, 1962; Illuminated Manuscripts, 1963; D. H. Lawrences Studier, 1964; Strindbergsfejden, 2 vols., 1968; Den seriöse konstnären, 1969; Läsarmekanismer, 1971; Mallarmé, 1972; Frihet, jämlikhet, konstnärskap, 1974; var. translations. Jt. Ed., Horisont Mag., 1954—. Contbr. to Arbetaren, 1952—. Mbrships. incl: Royal Soc. for Publn. of MSS; Finnish Soc. of Letters; Bd., Strindberg Soc., 1971—. Hons. incl: Lit. Award, Swedish Acad., 1969; Ph.D., Uppsala Univ., 1973. Address: Fyrverkarbacken 32, S-112 60 Stockholm, Sweden.

JARVIS, Arthur, b. 19 Mar. 1915, Sheffield, UK. Clerk. Publs: The Lion & the Raven, 1970. Address: 7 Nicholson Rd., Hyde, Cheshire SK14 4QH, UK.

JARVIS, Rupert Charles, b. 10 Dec. 1899, Sudbury, Suffolk, UK. Lecturer in Manuscript Studies. Educ: Univ. Berlin. Publs: The Jacobite Risings of 1715 & 1745, 1954; Customs Letter-Books of the Port of Liverpool, 1711-1813, 1954; Liverpool Registry of Merchant Ships (w. R. S. Craig), 1967; Collected Papers on the Jacobite Risings (2 vols.), 1971-72. Contbr. to: Antiquaries Jrnl.; English Histl. Review; Econ. Hist. Review; Pub. Admin.; Juridical Review; Maritime Hist.; etc. Mbrships. incl: F.S.A.; Fellow, Royal Histl. Soc. Hons. incl: Haldane Medal & Prize; Leverhulme Award; Companion Imperial Ser. Order. Address: Shelley, Station Rd., Hockley, Essex, UK.

JASTRUN, Mieczyslaw, b. 29 Oct. 1903, Korolowka, Poland. Writer. Educ: Ph.D., Cracow Univ. Publs. incl: (in Polish) Meeting in Time; History Still Fresh; The Stream & Silence; The Guarded Hour; Human Affairs; Meeting with Salomea; Poet & Courtier; Between Word & Silence; Larger than Life; Mediterranean Myth; Zone of Fruits; Poetry & Truth; In Broad Daylight; Signs of Memory; Freedom of Choice; Starry Diamond; Fighting for a word; Isle; & var. transls. from French, Russian & German. Address: ul. Iwicka 8 a m.9, Warsaw 36, Poland.

JÀVOR, Ottó, b. 7 Oct. 1925, Székesfehérvár, Hungary. Secondary School Teacher & Inspector. Educ: Grad. Univ. Budapest. Publs: (novels) Vonuljatok ki, chansonok (March Out, You Chansons), 1965; Az ember és a város (The Man & the Town), 1969; (short stories) Rossz Káderek (Bad Cadres), 1963; Talajvíz (Underground Water), 1968; A Csíkvári kerengöröl (The Cloisters of Csíkvár), 1972. Contbr. to: Kortárs; Nagyvilág; Uj Irás; Forrás; Alföld; Tiszatáj; Népszabadság; Magyar Nemzet; etc. Mbr., Hungarian Union Authors. Address: 1013 Budapest, Lánchíd u. 13, Hungary.

JAWORSKA, Wladyslawa Jadwiga, b. 14 July 1910, Rzeszow, Poland. Professor & Historian of Art; Art Critic. Educ: M.A. (mag. phil.), Jagellonian Univ., Cracow, 1934; Ph.D. (Hist. of Art), Warsaw Univ., 1960. Publs: Tadeusz Makowski: Życie i Twórczość (Life & Work), 1964; W Kregu Gaugina: Malarze Szkoły Pont-Aven, 1969; Gauguin & l'Ecole de Pont-Aven, 1971, Engl. ed. publd. UK & USA 1972. Contbr. to: Rocznik Historii Sztuki; Gazette des Beaux-Arts, Paris; Apollo, UK. Mbrships: Assn. of Histns. of Art; PEN; Int. Assn. of Art Critics (Bd. of Dirs.; Sec., Polish Sect.); Acad. Raffaello, Urbino, Italy. Hons. incl: A. Brückner's Prize, Polish Acad. of Scis., 1971; Kt. Cross Polonia Restituta, 1974. Address: Langiewicza 12 m. 4, 02-071 Warsaw, Poland.

JAY, Antony Rupert, b. 1930, London, UK. Freelance Film & TV Writer/Producer/Consultant; Chairman, Video Arts Ltd. Educ: M.A., Magdalene Coll., Cambridge. Publs: Ed., Anthology: The Pick of the Rhubarb, 1965; Management & Machiavelli, 1967; To England with Love (w. David Frost), 1967; Effective Presentation, 1970; Corporation Man, 1972; The Householder's Guide to Community Defence Against Bureaucratic Aggression, 1972; Public Words & Private Words: or, What Shall We Do About the BBC? , 1972. Agent: Curtis Brown. Address: 33 Mount Avenue, London W5 1PU, UK.

JAY, Douglas Patrick Thomas, b. 23 Mar. 1907, Woolwich, London, UK. Member of Parliament; Journalist. Educ: New Coll., All Souls Coll., Oxford Univ. Publs: The Socialist Case; 1937; Who is to Pay for the War & the Peace, 1940; Socialism & the New Society, 1962; After the Common Market, 1968. Contbr. to: Times (staff, 1929-33); Economist (staff, 1933-37); Daily Herald (City Ed., 1937-40). Address: House of Commons, London SW1A 0AA, UK.

JAY, Eric George, b. 1 Mar. 1907, Colchester, UK. Anglican Priest. Educ: B.A., 1929, M.A., 1930, Univ. of Leeds; B.D., 1937, M.Th., 1940, Ph.D., 1951, Univ. of London. Publs: The Existence of God; Origen's Treatise on Prayer; New Testament Greek: an Introductory Grammar; Son of Man, Son of God; Friendship with God. Contbr. to: Church Quarterly Review; Theol.; Can. Jrnl. of Theol. Mbrships: Can. Theol. Soc.; McGill Fac. (Montreal). Hons: Fellow of King's Coll., London, 1948; D.D., Montreal Diocesan Theol. Coll., 1964. Address: 570 Milton Street, Apt. 15, Montreal, PQ H2X 1W4, Canada.

JAY, Maurice, b. 9 July 1925, London, UK. Lecturer in Journalism; Editor. Educ: Polytechnic Schl. of Arch. Contbr. to: Design; Interior Design; Archtl. Review; Jewish Chronicle; Living Judaism; Med. News; Tchr.; Ency. Britannica. Mbrships: Soc. of Indl. Artists & Designers; Nat. Union of Jrnlsts.; Assn. of Tchrs. in Tech. Instns. Address: 1 Albert Mansions, Luxborough St., London W1, UK.

JAY, Peter Antony Charles, b. 1945, Chester, UK. Poet; Publisher. Educ: Lincoln Coll., Oxford. Publs: Adonis & Venus, 1968; The Greek Anthology, 1973; The Song of Songs (transl.), 1974; The Poems of Meleager (transl. w. Peter Whigham), 1974; The Still Unborn About the Dead (transl. w. Petre Popescu), 1974. Contbr. to: Poetry Review; Priapus; Agenda. Address: Anvil Press Poetry, 69 King George St., London SE10, UK.

JEAL, Tim, b. 27 Jan. 1945, London, UK. Author. Educ: Westminster Schl.; M.A., Christ Church, Oxford. Publs: For Love or Money, 1967; Somewhere Beyond Reproach, 1968; Livingstone, 1973; Cushing's Crusade, 1974. Contbr. to: Punch; Observer Colour Mag. Mbrships: Writers Action Grp.; Writers' Guild of GB. Hons: Runner-up, John Llewelyn Rhys Mem. Prize, 1969; Arts Coun. Bursary, 1970. Agent: Toby Eady Assocs. Ltd. Address: 2 Healey Street, London NW1, UK.

JEANNERAT, Pierre Gabriel, b. 18 May 1902, Paris, France. Retired Journalist; Art Critic. Publs: Angkor Ruins in Cambodia, 1923; Flying to 3000 B.C., 1957. Contbr. to: Daily Mail, London (Art Critic & Spec. Corres., 1935-67); & num. art mags. Mbrships: Fndr.-Mbr., Int. Assn. of Art Critics (Past Pres., Brit. Sect.); Arts Club, London. Hons: Medaille Colonial, France, 1943; O.B.E., 1947; Chevalier, Ordre de la Couronne, Belgium, 1947; Gold Medal, Int. Congress of Artists Critics & Art Histns., Rimini, Italy, 1967. Address: 7 Bryanston Sq., London W1H 7FF, UK.

JEDENBERG, Helge William, b. 1 Nov. 1908, Gothenburg, Sweden. Author; Literary Critic. Educ: Grad., Gothenburg Superior Latin Coll., 1929; Pvte. study, lit., philos., relig. & hist. of art. Publs. incl: (poetry) Beyond the Greenery, 1949; Translated Joy, 1961; Moorings, 1966; The Icons of Joy & Pain, 1968; Elegies of Eyes, 1970; The Figures of Dark & Joy, 1972; Words of Shining Dark Silver, 1973. Contbr. to Var Losen mag.; Gotesborgs-Posten. Mbrships: Swedish Union of Authors; Gothenburg Authors' Soc. Hons. incl: Gothenburg Authors' Soc. Schlrship., 1961; Gothenburg Town Schlrship., 1968; Swedish State Artistic Schlrship., 1969-70; Swedish Ch. Inst. of Culture Schlrship., 1973. Address: Ekehöjdsgatan 14, 421 68 Vastra Frolunda, Gothenburg, Sweden.

JEDRZEJEWICZ, Waclaw, b. 29 Jan. 1893, Spiczynce, Ukraine, USSR. Historian; Professor Emeritus; Author. Educ: Univ. of Cracow, Poland, 1913-14; Warsaw Schl. of Agric., 1914-17; Dip., Acad. Gen. Staff Offs., 1921-22. Publs: My Memoirs, 1914-15, 1939; Poland in the British Parliament 1939-45 (3 vols.), 1946—64; Polish-Americans in the Polish Politics, 1954; Diplomat in Berlin, Papers of Ambassador Lipski 1933-39, 1968; Diplomat in Paris, Papers of Ambassador Lukasiewicz 1936-39, 1970; Pilsudski in Tokio 1904-05, 1974. Contbr. to: Polish Review (N.Y.); etc. Mbr., Société Historique et Littéraire Polonaise (Paris). Address: 85-11 Elmhurst Ave., Elmhurst, NY 11373, USA.

JEFFARES, Alexander Norman, b. 8 Aug. 1920, Dublin, Repub. of Ireland. University Professor; Author; Editor. Educ: M.A. & Ph.D., Trinity Coll., Dublin; M.A. & D.Phil., Univ. of Oxford, UK. Publs: Yeats: Man & Poet, 1949, 2nd ed., 1962; Seven Centuries of Poetry, 1955, 2nd ed., 1960; A Commentary on the Collected Poems of Yeats, 1968; The Circus Animals, 1970; Restoration Drama, 1974; A Commentary on the Collected Plays of W. B. Yeats (w. A. S. Knowland), 1975. Contbr. to num. profl. & other jrnls. Mbrships: F.R.S.L.; F.R.S.A.; Fellow, Aust. Acad. of the Humanities; Life Chmn., Int. Assn. for the Study of Anglo-Irish Lit.; Hon. Life Fellow, Assn. for C'wlth. Lit. & Lang. Studies. Address: c/o Dept. of Engl. Studies, Univ. of Stirling, Stirling, UK.

JEFFERS, Florice Stripling, b. Bullard, Tex., USA. Bookkeeper. Educ: Corres. Courses, Jrnlsm., Okla. Univ. Var. summer workshops. Publs: Reflections, An Anthology of Prize Winning Poems by Wichita Falls Poetry Society Members, 1971. Contbr. to poetry jrnls., anthols. Mbrships. incl: Pres., Wichita Falls Poetry Soc.; Coun., Poetry Soc. of Tex.; Nat. Fedn. of State Poetry Socs.; Poet Laureate, Tex. Fedn. of Women's Clubs., 1960; Co-fndr., Acad. of Am. Poets. Hons. incl: Annual Awards, Poetry Soc. of Tex., 1963-74. Address: P.O. Box 638, Burkburnett, TX 76354, USA.

JEFFREY, Albert Hayden George, b. 1923, Sheffield, UK. Editor. Educ: B.A., Peterhouse, Cambridge Univ. Publs: Immersed Tube Tunnels, 1962. Contbr. to: Ed., Civil Engrng. & Pub. Works Review, 1957-63; Grp. Tech. Ed., Engl. Elec. Grp., 1963-69; Ed., Cement Technol. & Precast Concrete, currently. Address: 103 Whitelands Ave., Chorley Wood, Herts., UK.

JEFFREYS, Montagu Vaughan Castelman, b. 16 Dec. 1900, London, UK. University Professor & Adminsitrator; Author. Educ: M.A., Hertford Coll., Oxford. Publs. incl: (play prod.) For Amateurs & Schools (3 eds.); History in Schools: The Study of Development; Education: Christian or Pagan? ; Kingdom of this World; Glaucon: An Enquiry into the Aims of Education (3 eds.); Beyond Neutrality; Mystery of Man; Personal Values in the Modern World (3 eds.); The Unity of Education; John Locke; Education: Its Nature & Purpose; The Aims of Education; You & Other People. Mbrships. incl: Assn. of Univ. Tchrs.; Schl. Libs. Assn. Recip., C.B.E., 1953. Address: Skymers Minor, Minstead, Lyndhurst, Hants., UK.

JEFKINS, Frank William, b. 27 June 1920, London, UK. Lecturer; Author. Educ: Univ. of London; Open Univ.; B.Sc.(Econ.); B.A.; M.CAM. Publs: Copywriting & its Presentation, 1958; Wanted on Holiday, 1960; Public Relations in World Marketing, 1966; Press Relations Practice, 1968; Planned Public Relations, 1969; Advertising Today, 1971; Advertising Made Simple, 1973; Dictionary of Marketing & Communication, 1973; Marketing & PR Media Planning, 1974; Advertisement Writing, 1975. Contbr. to advt. & pub. rels. jrnls. Mbrships: CAM Soc.; Coun. mbr., Past Dir. of Studies & Chmn., Exam Bd., Inst. of Pub. Rels.; Inst. of Marketing; Brit. Assn. of Indl. Eds. Address: 84 Ballards Way, S. Croydon, Surrey CR2 7LA, UK.

JEIER, Thomas, pen name THOMAS, M. L., b. 24 Apr. 1947, Minden, Westphalia, W. Germany. Writer. Educ: Apprenticeship as Bookseller. Publs: Die Verlorenen, 1971; Der Grosse Goldrausch von Alaska, 1972; Das Western-Kochbuch, 1973; Treibt sie nach Norden! , 1973; Die Frau des Siedlers (novel), 1974; Das Versunkene Kanu (juvenile), 1974. Contbr. to: Fix & Foxi (former Ed.); Buchmarkt; Ferienland Amerika; Pop; Augsburger Allgemeine; German Radio; Ed., Western novels, Heyne Verlag. Mbr., Western Writers of Am. Recip., Friedrich Gerstäcker Award, 1974. Address: 8000 Munich 70, Wildtaubenweg 5, W. Germany.

JÉKELY, Zoltan, b. 27 Apr. 1913, Nagy-Enyed, Transylvania, Hungary. Writer. Educ: Ph.D., Fac. of Arts. Publs: (poetry) Nights, 1936; Prohibited Garden, 1957; In a Star-Tower, 1969; (novels) Medardus, 1938; Angelica & the Hermits, 1944; The Black Sailboat, 1958. Contbr. to: Kortárs; Uj Irás; Élet ès Irodalom; etc. Mbrships: PEN; Hungarian Writers' Assn.; Hungarian Anglers' Assn. Hons: Baumgarten Prize, 1939; József Attila Prize, 1971; Order of Labour, 1973. Address: Frankel Leo-utca 23, Budapest 1023, Hungary.

JELLICOE, Ann, b. 1927, Middlesbrough, UK. Playwright; Theatrical Director. Educ: Ctrl. Schl. of Speech & Drama. Publs: (plays) The Sport of My Mad Mother, 1958; The Knack, 1961; The Rising Generation, 1964; Shelley, 1965; The Giveaway, 1970; Rosmersholm (transl.), 1960; The Lady from the Sea (transl.), 1961; Der Feischutz (transl.), 1964; The Seagull (transl. w. A. Nicolaieff), 1963; Jelliplays (for children): You'll Never Guess! , 1973; Clever Elsie, 1974; A Good Thing or a Bad Thing, 1974; (guidebook) The Shell Guide to Devon (w. R. Mayne), 1975. Mbrships. incl: Soc. of Authors; George Devine Award Comm. Agent: Margaret Ramsay Ltd. Address: c/o Margaret Ramsay Ltd., 14a Goodwin's Ct., St. Martin's Ln., London WC2, UK.

JELLICOE, Geoffrey Alan, b. 8 Oct. 1900, London, UK. Landscape Architect. Educ: Archtl. Assn. Publs: Italian Gardens of the Renaissance, 1925; Gardens & Design, 1927; Studies in Landscape Design, vol. I, 1960, vol. II, 1965; vol. III, 1970; The Landscape of Man (w. Susan Jellicoe), 1975. Contbr. to num. profl. jrnls. Mbrships. incl: Inst. Landscape Archts. (Past Pres.); Royal Inst. Brit. Archts.; Royal Town Planning Inst. Address: 19 Grove Terrace, London NW5, UK.

JELLICOE, Susan, b. 30 June 1907, Liverpool, UK. Writer on Garden Subjects. Publs: Things We See: Gardens (w. Lady Allen of Hurtwood), 1953; The New Small Garden (w. Lady Allen), 1956; Modern Private Gardens (w. Geoffrey Jellicoe), 1968; Water: The Use of Water in Landscape Architecture (w. G. Jellicoe), 1971; The Gardens of Mughul India (co-author), 1972; The Landscape of Man (w. G. Jellicoe), 1975. Contbr. to: Country Life; Landscape Design. Mbr., Inst. Landscape Archts. (Hon. Assoc.). Address: 19 Grove Terrace, London NW5 1PH, UK.

JEN, Yu-wen, b. 8 Feb. 1896, Canton, China. Educator; Writer. Educ: B.A., Oberlin Coll., Ohio; M.A., Univ. Chicago, Ill. Publs. incl: (in Chinese) Studies on the Institutions of Taiping Tienkuo, 1958; Complete History of Taiping Tienkuo, 1962; Historical Record of Hung Hsiu-ch'uan, enlarged & revised ed., 1967; Taiping Tienkuo & Chinese Culture, 1968; Studies on Pai-sha Tzu, 1970; Su Jen-shan, Eccentric Genius of Kwangtung: His Life & Art, 1970; (in English) The Taiping Revolutionary Movement, 1973; The Youth of Dr. Sun Yat-sen, 1970; Ch'en Hsien-chang's Philosophy of the Natural (in Self & Society), 1970. Contbr. to num. acad. jrnls. Mbrships: Royal Asiatic Soc.; PEN. Address: 2 Stafford Rd., Kowloon, Hong Kong.

JENKINS, Alan, b. 1914, Carshalton, Surrey, UK. Journalist. Educ: M.A., St. Edmund Hall, Oxford. Publs: Castle Avalon, 1941; Absent Without Leave, 1949; The Swimming Pool, 1950; The Young Mozart, 1960; Drinka Pinta, 1970; On Site, 1971; The Stock Exchange Story, 1973; London's City, 1973; The Twenties, 1973. Mbr., Reform Club. Address: Stars Wood, High Barn, Effingham, Surrey, UK.

JENKINS, Alan Charles, b. 1914, Woodford Green, UK. Author & Journalist. Publs. incl: Between the Two Twilights, 1937; Dear Olga, 1949; Storm Over the Blue Hills, 1953; White Horses & Black Bulls, 1960; Shadow of the Deer, 1965; The Golden Band, 1967; Wildlife in Danger, 1970; Wild Swans at Suvanto; Wild Encounters; Kingdom of the Elephants. Contbr. to: Times; Evening News; Blackwood's Mag.; Animals Mag.; BBC; Birmingham Post; Western Morning News; Woman's Mirror; Aust. Broadcasting Corp.; etc. Mbr., Soc. Authors. Address: Pear Trees, Belstone, Okehampton, Devon, UK.

JENKINS, Elizabeth. Writer. Educ: Newnham Coll., Cambridge. Publs: Lady Caroline Lamb, 1932; Portrait of an Actor, 1933; Harriet, 1934; The Phoenix Nest, 1936; Jane Austen, 1938; Robert & Helen, 1944; Young Enthusiasts, 1946; Henry Fielding, 1947; Six Criminal Women, 1949; The Tortoise & the Hare, 1954; Ten Fascinating Women, 1955; Elizabeth the Great, 1958; Elizabeth & Leicester, 1961; Brightness, 1963; Honey, 1968; Dr. Gully, 1972. Address: 8 Downshire Hill, London NW3, UK.

JENKINS, Gwyn, b. 29 Oct. 1919, Neath, UK. Schoolmaster. Educ: Tchrs.' Trng. Coll. Publs: The Son of Jesse, 1961; King David, 1961; The Last Judge, 1964. Mbrships. incl: Soc. of Authors. Address: Beachley Maesmawr, Crynant, Neath, Glamorgan, UK.

JENKINS, Harold, b. 19 July 1909, Shenley, Bucks., UK. Professor of English Literature; Author. Editor. Educ: B.A., 1930, M.A., 1933, Univ. Coll., London; D.Litt. Witwatersrand, S. Africa, 1944. Publs: The Life & Work of Henry Chettle, 1934; Edward Benlowes: Biography of a Minor Poet, 1952. Contbr. to: Mod. Lang. Review; Review of Engl. Studies; The Lib.; Shakespeare Survey; Studies in Bibliog.; Jt. Gen. Ed., Arden Shakespeare, 1958—. Mbrships: Int. Assn. Univ. Profs. of Engl.; Coun. Mbr. Malone Soc. Address: 24 Brantwood Rd., London SE24 0DJ, UK.

JENKINS, Ivor, b. 25 July 1913, S. Wales, UK. Metallurgist. Educ: B.Sc. (Metallurgy), M.Sc., D.Sc., Univ of Wales. Publs: Controlled Atmospheres for the Heat-Treatment of Metals, 1946. Contbr. to: Sci. papers of Am. Soc. of Metals; Iron & Steel Inst.; Brit. Foundrymen Procs. of Int. Confs. in Europe & USA; etc. Mbrships Fellow, Inst. of Metallurgists; Fellow, Metals Soc.; Fellow Am. Soc. for Metals. Hons: C.B.E., 1970; Williams Prize Iron & Steel Inst., 1946. Address: The Grange, Onehouse Stowmarket, Suffolk, UK.

JENKINS, James Archibald, b. 1919, Glasgow, UK. Managing Director; Director. Educ: M.A., Univ. of Glasgow. Contbr. to: Electronic Engrng.; Jrnl. of TV Soc.; Jrnl. o Brit. Inst. of Radio Engrgs.; Philips Tech. Review. Mbr. Inst. of Physics. Address: The White House, Boldre Grange Lymington, Hants., UK.

JENKINS, John Geraint, b. 4 Jan. 1929, Llangrannog Dyfed, Wales, UK. Museum Keeper of Material. Educ: Univ Colls. of Wales, Swansea & Aberystwyth. Publs. incl Agricultural Transport in Wales, 1963; Traditional Country Craftsmen, 1965, 1969; The Welsh Woollen Industry, 1969 The Wool Textile Industry, 1970; Crefftwyr Ginad, 1970 The Craft Industries, 1972; Nets & Coracles, 1974. Contbr to: Ed., Folk Life, 1963—; Country Life; Local hist. jrnls etc.; TV & radio. Mbrships: F.S.A.; Fellow, Museums Assn., Royal Anthropol. Inst.; Chmn., Grp. for Reg. Studies, 1974—; Soc. of Authors. Address: St. Fagans Castle, St. Fagans, Cardiff CF5 6DY, UK.

JENKINS, John Robin, b. 11 Sept. 1912, Cambuslang, Lanarks., UK. Teacher; Writer. Educ: M.A., Glasgow Univ. Publs. incl: Happy for the Child, 1953; The Thistle & the Grail, 1954; The Cone-Gatherers, 1955; Guests of War, 1956; The Missionaries, 1957; The Changeling, 1958; Some Kind of Grace, 1960; Dust on the Paw, 1961; The Tiger of Gold, 1962; A Love of Innocence, 1963; The Sardana Dancers, 1964; A Very Scotch Affair, 1968; The Holy Tree, 1969; The Expatriates, 1971; A Toast to the Lord, 1972; A Far Cry from Bowmore, 1973. Address: 55 Mary St., Dunoon, Argyll, Scotland, UK.

JENKINS, Norman, pen name BROWN, George, b. 1910, London, UK. Journalist; Publicist; Specialist in Energy Economics. Publs: Electricity — The Answer to Nationalisation (campaign pamphlet), 1970. Ed. of: The Master Builder (Ed., 1955-65); Brit. Steelmaker (Ed., 2 yrs.); Jrnl. & Handbook, Dist. Heating Assn. (Ed., 1971—); var. engrng. jrnls. in UK, USA, etc., on energy technol. & econs.; nat. & local newspapers on total energy, heat/power generation & distribution. Hons: Valor Indl. Fellowship Award, to visit total energy installations in 6 European countries, 1965. Address: Whitehill, Ewshot, Farnham, Surrey GU10 5BS, UK.

JENKINS, Raymond Leonard, b. 1935, Oxford, UK. Comprehensive School Teacher; Lecturer. Educ: B.A., Trinity Coll., Cambridge Univ. Publs: Two Plays, 1968; The Lawbreakers, 1969. Contbr. to: Playbill Three, 1969. Mbrships: A.C.T.T.; Writers Guild of GB. Address: 187 Pitshanger Lane, London W5, UK.

JENKINS, (Rt. Hon.) Roy Harris, b. 11 Nov. 1920, Abersychan, Wales, UK. Government Minister. Educ: B.A., Balliol Coll., Oxford Univ. Publs: Pursuit of Progress, 1953; Mr. Balfour's Poodle, 1954; Sir Charles Dilke: A Victorian Tragedy, 1958; The Labour Case (paperback), 1959; Asquith, 1964; Essays & Speeches, 1967; Afternoon on the Potomac, 1972; What Matters Now, 1972; Nine Men of Power, 1974. Hons: LL.D., Leeds Univ., 1971, Harvard Univ., 1972, Pa. Univ., 1973; Dundee Univ., 1973; D.Litt., Glasgow Univ., 1972; D.C.L., Oxford Univ., 1973; Fellow, Berkeley Coll., Yale Univ., 1972; Charlemagne Prize, 1972; Robert Schumann Prize, 1972; for. mbr., Am. Acad. Arts & Sci., 1973. Address: 33 Ladbroke Sq., London W11, UK.

JENKINS, Sylvia M., b. 14 June 1936, Birmingham, UK. Adult Educator, Food Industry; Technical Writer. Educ: Grad., Ont. Inst. Studies in Educ.; Master Craftsman's Certs. in Bread Making & Flour Confectionery, Inst. Brit. Bakers, 1965. Publs: Bakery Technology: Book 1 Bread, Book 2 Cake, 1975. Contbr. to: Construction Specifier; Seaway Review; Brit. Baker; Baking Inds. Jrnl.; La Fournée; Supermarket; etc. Mbrships. incl: Fellow, Inst. Brit. Bakers; Royal Soc. Hlth.; Am. Bus. Writers' Assn. Recip., Churchill Fellowship, 1968. Address: 34-2395 Bromsgrove Rd., Mississauga, Ont., Can. L5J 1L6.

JENKINS, Vivian Gordon James, b. 1911, Port Talbot, Wales, UK. Former Schoolmaster; Sportswriter, Sunday Times. Educ: M.A., Jesus Coll., Oxford. Publs: Lions Rampant, 1956; Lions Down Under, 1960. Mbrships: Vincent's Club, Oxford; Marylebone Cricket Club; Press Club; E. India & Sports Club. Address: 28 Bowers Way, Harpenden, Herts. AL5 4EW, UK.

JENNES, Jos, b. 18 Dec. 1903, Antwerp, Belgium. Horticultural Writer. Educ: Hort. Coll., Vivoorde. Publs: Bestrijding van schadelijke dieren in de tuinbouw, 1929; Schurftziekte bij appel en peer, 1936; Planten in onze woning, 1937; Vijanden van Azalea en knolbegonia, 1937; Onze handelsbetrekkingen inzake groenten met Nederland, Duitsland, Frankrijk en Engeland, 1939; Fruitteelt in binnen-en buitebland, 1939; ABC voor het verzorgen van kamerplanten en-bloemen, 1964; ABC van de tuinier, 1966. Contbr. to: Belgische Fruitrevue — Vakblad voor de Bloemisterij-Deutsche Gärtnerbörse. Mbr., Int. Union Agricl. Jrnlsts. Address: Bergenstraat 115, 3044 Haasrode, Belgium.

JENNI, Adolfo, b. 3 May 1911, Modena, Italy. Professor of Italian Language & Literature. Educ: Litt.D., Univ. Bologna; Univ. Zurich. Publs: La sestina lirica, 1945; I recinto, 1947; Cose di questo mondo, 1957; Addio alla poesia, 1959; Il mestiere di scrivere, 1962; Quaderni di Saverio Adami, 1967; Vicende e situazioni, 1970; Recitativi, 1971; Dante e Manzoni, 1973. Contbr. to num. publs. in Italy & Switz. Mbrships: Int. Assn. Italian Lang. & Lit. Studies; Swiss Writers' Assn.; Acad. Arcadia, Rome. Hons. incl: Sev. Schiller prizes; Calabria Prize, 1974; Italia Prize, 1969. Address: Blümlisalpstrasse 12, 3074 Muri b/Berne, Switz.

JENNINGS, Elizabeth Joan, b. 1926, Boston, Lincs., UK. Writer; Former Librarian. Educ: M.A., St. Anne's Coll., Oxford. Publs: Poems, 1953; A Way of Looking, 1955; A Sense of the World, 1958; Ed., The Batsford Book of Children's Verse, 1958; Song for a Birth or a Death, 1961; The Sonnets of Michelangelo, 1961; Every Changing Shape, 1961; Recoveries, 1964; The Mind Has Mountains, 1966; Collected Poems, 1967; The Animals' Arrival, 1968; Lucidities, 1970; Relationships, 1972. Contbr. to: London Mag.; Encounter; Spectator; New Yorker; BBC Third Prog.; etc. Mbrships: Soc. of Authors; PEN. Agent: David Highams Assocs. Ltd. Address: 11 Winchester Road, Oxford OX2 6NA, UK.

JENNINGS, Gary Gayne, b. 20 Sept. 1928, Buena Vista, Va., USA. Author. Educ: Art Students League, NYC. Publs. incl: March of the Robots, 1962; The Movie Book, 1963; Black Magic, White Magic, 1964; Personalities of Language, 1965; Parades! , 1966; The Shrinking Outdoors, 1972; The Earth Book, 1974; The Treasure of the Superstition Mountains, 1974; The Terrible Teague Bunch, 1975; March of the Heroes, 1975. Contbr. to: Am. Heritage; Coronet; Cosmopolitan; Country Beautiful; Glamour; Harper's; Holiday; Nat. Geog.; N.Y. Times Book Review; Opera News; Rdrs. Digest; etc. Mbrships. incl: Authors' League of Am. Hons. incl: Funk & Wagnalls Fellowship in Prose, 1962. Address: Apartado Postal 699, San Miguel de Allende, Gto., Mexico.

JENNINGS, Paul Francis, b. 20 June 1918, Leamington Spa, UK. Copy Writer; Journalist. Publs. incl: Oddly Enough, 1951; Even Oddlier, 1952; Oddly Bodlikens, 1953; Next to Oddliness, 1955; Gladly Oddly, 1957; Idly Oddly, 1959; I Said Oddly, Diddle I? , 1961; Oodles of Oddlies, 1963; Oddly Ad Lib, 1965; I was Joking, of Course, 1968; Just a Few Lines, 1969; It's an Odd Thing But . . ., 1971; (for children) The Hopping Basket, 1965; The Great Jelly of London, 1967. Address: Hill House, Rectory Hill, E. Bergholt, Suffolk, UK.

JENNINGS, Terry John, b. 20 Apr. 1938, Sible Hedingham, UK. Lecturer. Educ: B.Sc.; Postgrad. Cert. of Educ. Publs: Mysteries of Animal Behaviour, 1967; Wild Life in the Garden, 1969; Animals in the Home & Classroom, 1971; Collecting from Nature, 1971; Background to Biochemistry, 1971; Science & Farming, 1974; Studying Birds in the Garden, 1975. Contbr. to: Schl. Sci. Review; Natural Sci. in Schls. Mbr., Soc. of Authors. Address: Elmhurst, Rectory Lane, E. Carleton, Norwich, Norfolk, UK.

JENS, Walter, b. 8 Mar. 1923, Hamburg, Germany. Novelist; Critic; Philologist. Educ: Ph.D.; Univs.of Hamburg & Freiberg. Publs. incl: (novels) Die Welt der Angeklagten, 1950; Der Blinde, 1951; Vergessene Gesichter, 1952; Das Testament des Odysseus, 1957; (essays) Statt einer Literaturgeschichte, 1957; Deutsche Literatur der Gegenwart, 1961; Zueignungen, 1962; Frensehen-Themem & Tabus, 1973; (TV plays) Die Verschwörung, 1970; Der Tödliche Schlag, 1974. Mbrships. incl: PEN; Berlin Acad. of Arts. Recip., Lessingpreis der Hansestadt Hamburg. Address: Sonnenstr. 5, 74 Tübingen, W. Germany.

JENTZ, Gaylord Adair, b. 7 Aug. 1931, Beloit, Wis., USA. Professor of Business Law. Educ: B.A., Univ. of Wis. Madison, 1953; J.D., 1957; M.B.A., 1958. Publs: Texas Uniform Commercial Code: Practical Aspects of Secured Transactions, 1968, 1972; Business Law: Text & Cases (co-author), 1968. Contbr. to: Am. Bus. Law Jrnl.; etc. Mbrships incl: Pres., Am. Bus. Law Assn.; Staff Ed. & Ed. in Chief, Am. Bus. Law Jrnl.; Pres., Tex. Assn. of Coll. Tchrs.; Dpty. Ed., Soc. Sci. Quarterly. Hons. incl: Master's Appreciation Award, 1969; Coll. of Bus. Admin. Jack G. Taylor Tchng. Excellence Award, 1971. Address: 4106 North Hills Dr., Austin, TX 78731, USA.

JEPHCOTT, Agnes Pearl, b. 1900, Alcester, Warwicks., UK. Writer. Educ: M.A., Univ. of Wales. Publs: Girls Growing Up, 1942; Married Women Working (w. Nancy Seear & John Smith), 1962; A Troubled Area, 1963; Time of One's Own, 1967; Homes in High Flats (w. Hilary

Robinson), 1971. Address: 63 Distons Lane, Chipping Norton, Oxon. OX7 5HE, UK.

JEPSON, Selwyn, b. 1899. Author. Publs. incl: The Qualified Adventurer, 1921; Rogues & Diamonds, 1925; Snaggle-Tooth, 1926; The Death Gong, 1929; Tiger Dawn, 1929; I Met Murder, 1930; Rabbit's Paw, 1932; Keep Murder Quiet, 1940; Man Running, 1948; Man Dead, 1951; The Black Italian, 1954; The Assassin, 1957; The Laughing Fish, 1960; Fear in the Wind, 1964; The Third Possibility, 1965; The Angry Millionaire, 1969; Letters to a Dead Girl, 1970; The Interrogators, 1974; (play) Dark Horizon (w. Lesley Storm), 1933; also screenplays, radio & TV plays, serials. Contbr. to mags., TV & radio in UK & USA. Agent: A. P. Watt & Son. Address: The Far House, Liss, Hants., UK.

JEREMIĆ, Dragan, b. 24 May 1925, Brdjani, Gornji Milanovac, Yugoslavia. Writer; Professor of Aesthetics & Sociology of Art. Educ: Ph.D., Belgrade Univ. Publs: (play) A Play of Life or New Paradoxes of the Actor, 1963; (essays) The Fingers of Doubting Thomas, 1964; The Critic & the Aesthetic Ideal, 1965; The Age of Anti-Art, 1970; (criticism) The Pen Like a Scalpel, 1969; (aphorisms) Both Sides, 1972. Contbr. to: The Lit. Newspaper (Chief Ed., 1970—); Contemporary (former Chief Ed., 1961-66). Mbrships: Yugoslav Writers' Union (Sec.); Int. Assn. Lit. Critics (Exec. Comm.); PEN. Recip., Milan Bogdanović for best newspaper criticism, 1974. Address: 11.000 Belgrade, Francuska 7, Yugoslavia.

JEROME, John Stewart, b. 7 Nov. 1932, Tulsa, Okla., USA. Freelance Journalist. Educ: B.A., N. Tex. State Univ., 1955. Publs: Sports Illustrated Book of Skiing, 1971; The Death of the Automobile (w. W. Norton), 1972. Contbr. to: Skiing (contbng. Ed.). Address: Franconia, N.H., USA.

JERRARD, Harold George, b. 26 Oct. 1921, Portsmouth, UK. University Professor. Educ: Univs. of London & Southampton; B.Sc., Phys.; B.Sc., Maths.; Ph.D. Publs: Introduction to Experimental Physics, 1951; Theoretical & Experimental Physics, 1961; A Dictionary of Scientific Units, 3rd ed., 1972. Contbr. to: Optics & Laser Technol.; Optics Communications: Reports on Progress in Phys. Mbrships: Fellow, Inst. of Phys.; Sec., Optical Grp., 1963-68; Chmn., 1968-72; Am. Phys. Soc. Address: Daymer House, Hook Park, Warsash, Southampton, UK.

JERROLD, Ianthe, b. 1897, London, UK. Novelist. Num. publs. incl: The Narrow Bed, 1957; My Angel, 1960; My Twin & I, 1966. Contbr. to: London Mystery Mag.; Blackwood's Mag.; Good Housekeeping; & other jrnls. Agent: A. P. Watt & Son. Address: 66c Redcliffe Gdns., London SW10, UK.

JESSUP, Frank W., b. 1909, Halling, Kent, UK. Educator; Author. Educ: M.A., LL.B., London Univ.; Barrister-at-Law, Gray's Inn. Publs: Problems of Local Government, 1949; The Cinque Ports (w. R. F. Jessup), 1952; Sir Roger Twysden 1597-1672, 1965; Background to the English Civil War, 1966; Lifelong Learning, 1969; A History of Kent, 1974; Kent History Illustrated, 1974. Contbr. to jrnls. inclng: Archaeologia Cantiana; Adult Educ.; Rewley House Papers. Mbrships. incl: Fellow, Wolfson Coll., Oxford; Fellow, Soc. of Antiquaries of London; Hon. Fellow, Lib. Assn. Address: Striblehills, Thame, Oxon., UK.

JEWELL, Derek, b. 1927, London, UK. Newspaper Publishing Director. Educ: M.A., Wadham Coll., Oxford. Publs: Man & Motor: The 20th Century Love Affair (Ed. & pt.-author), 1966; Alamein & the Desert War (Ed. & pt.-author), 1967; Come in Number One, Your Time is Up, 1971; Sellout, 1974. Contbr. to: Asst. Ed., Sunday Times 1962-63; Dpty. Ed., Sunday Times Colour Mag., 1963-68; Times; Punch; Encounter; N.Y. Times. Agent: John Farquharson Ltd. Address: 25 Spencer Rd., East Molesey, Surrey, UK.

JEWKES, John, b. 1902, Barrow-in-Furness, Lancs., UK. Professor of Economic Organization; Author. Educ: M.A.(Com.), M.A., D.Sc., Univ. of Manchester. Publs: Juvenile Unemployment (co-author); Wages & Labour in the Cotton Spinning Industry (co-author); The Juvenile Labour Market (co-author); Ordeal by Planning; The Sources of Invention (co-author); Public & Private Enterprise. Contbr. to: Econ. Jrnl.; Economica; Univ. of Chgo. Law Review; Lloyds Bank Review; etc. Recip., C.B.E. Address: Entwood, Boars Hill, Oxford, UK.

JEŻEWSKI, Bohdan O., b. 16 Feb. 1900, Warsaw, Poland. Editor; Biographer; Journalist. Educ: Schl. of Pol. Sci., Warsaw. Publs: Poles Abroad, Yr. Book & Directory, 1948, 7 eds., 1948-58; Polish Guide to London, 10 eds., 1962-75; Directory of Polish Newspapers & Periodicals in the Free World, 1962; Polonica in the British Isles (w. Dr. A. Ciechanowiecki), 1971; Chief Ed., Who's Who among Poles, & Poles Abroad Bio-bibliographical Sources, 1974—. Contbr. to Vide (Ed., 1954-55). Mbrships. incl: Polish Histl. Soc., London; Inst. of Jrnlsts.; Polish Union Jrnlsts. (Sec.-Gen., 1956-62, Vice-Chmn., 1963-64). Hons. incl: Order of Virtuti Militari. Address: 298 Northfield Ave., London W5 4UB, UK.

JHABVALA, Ruth Prawer, b. 7 May 1927, Cologne, Germany. Author. Educ: M.A., London, UK. Publs: To Whom She Will, 1955; The Nature of Passion, 1956; Esmond in India, 1958; The Householder, 1960; Get Ready for Battle, 1962; Like Birds Like Fishes, 1964; A Backward Place, 1965; A Stronger Climate, 1968; An Experience of India, 1971; A New Dominion, 1973. Contbr. to: New Yorker. Mbrships: F.R.S.L.; Authors' League of Am. Address: 1—A Flagstaff Rd., Delhi 6, India.

JIRGENSONS, Bruno, b. 16 May 1904, Adazhi, Latvia. Chemist; Emeritus Professor of Biochemistry. Educ: Univ. of Zürich, Switz., 1930; Dr.chem., 1933; Dr.chem.habil., 1934, Univ. of Latvia; Univ. of Freiburg, Germany, 1939. Publs. incl: Organic Colloids, 1958; Natural Organic Macromolecules, 1962, Russian transl., 1965; Optical Rotary Dispersion of Proteins & Other Macromolecules, 1969; Optical Activity of Proteins & Other Mocromolecules, 1973. Contbr. to sci. jrnls. Mbr., var. sci. socs. Hons. incl: Disting. Writers Award, Latvian Culture Fndn., 1959. Address: 6022 Fordham, Houston, TX 77005, USA.

JO, Yung-Hwan, b. 8 Feb. 1932, Masan, Korea. University Professor & Director of Asian Studies. Educ: B.A., Lincoln Mem. Univ.; M.A., Univ. of Tenn.; Ph.D., Am. Univ. Publs: Korea's Response to the West, 1970. Contbr. to: Asian Forum (Ed., 1970-72); Jrnls. of Pol., Peace Rsch., Int. Affairs, Asiatic Studies, Pacific Community; Asia Profile; ORBIS; Moderne Welt; Studies on Asia; Proceedings of Am. Philol. Soc.; var. Japanese, Korean & Chinese jrnls.; etc. Mbrships: Am. Pol. Sci. & Int. Studies Assns.; Assn. for Asian Studies. Hons. incl: Fulbright Fac. Grant, 1969-70; Asia Fndn. Grant, 1974. Address: Center for Asian Studies, Arizona State Univ., Tempe, AZ 85281, USA.

JOB, Jacob, b. 14 Dec. 1891. Radio Director; Writer. Educ: Ph.D.; Zürich Univ. Publs. incl: Jakob Bosshart als Erzähler, 1923; Die Jugend in der neuren deutschen Dichtung, 1932; Weg des Herzens, 1939; Italienische Städt, 1941; Sardinienfahrt, 1944; Herbst in Paris, 1945; Umbrien & Toskana, 1965; Bei Simeon dem Säulenheiligen, 1965; Autostrada del Sole, 1965; Am Mittelmeer, 1966; Im südlichen Deutschland, Fahrten durch Städte und Lande, 1969. Address: Zollikerstr. 23, 8008 Zürich, Switz.

JOBSON, Hamilton, b. 3 Apr. 1914, E. Ham, Essex, UK. Author; Retired Police Inspector. Educ: Burlington Coll. Publs. incl: Therefore I Killed Him, 1968; Naked to My Enemy, 1969; The Silent Cry, 1970; The Shadow that Caught Fire, 1972; Contract with a Killer, 1974; The Evidence You Will Hear, 1975. Mbrships: Crime Writers Assn.; Nat. Book League; PEN. Address: 43 Crosby Rd., Westcliff-on-Sea, Essex, UK.

JOELSON, F(erdinand) Stephen, b. 3 Jan. 1893, Swansea, UK. Editor; Author; Broadcaster; Publisher. Publs: Tanganyika Territory, 1920; Germany's Claims to Colonies, 1939; Compiler & Ed., num. works inclng. Settlement in East Africa, 1927; Eastern Africa Today, 1928; Eastern Africa Today & Tomorrow, 1934; Rhodesia & Eastern Africa, 1958; Fndr., East Africa & Rhodesia (wkly. jrnl.), & Ed., 1924-67. Mbrships: Past VP, Roya African Soc.; Past Gov., C'wlth. Inst.; Fellow, Inst. of Jrnlsts.; Past Coun. Mbr., Royal C'wlth. Soc., Royal Overseas League; Fndr. Mbr., C'wlth. Writers of Brit. Coun., Anglo-Rhodesian Soc. Recip., Medal for Dedicated Serv. to Africa, Royal African Soc. Address: Westwood, Cotlands, Sidmouth, Devon, UK.

JOENPELTO, Eeva, b. 17 Jan 1921, Sammatti, Finland. Author. Publs. incl: (novels) Veljen Varjo (Brother's Shadow), 1951; Johannes Vain (Johannes Only), 1952; Neito Kulkee Vetten Päällä (A Maiden Walks Over Waters), 1955; Ralli (Ralli, a Dog), 1959; Kipinöivat Vuodet, 1961

Ritari Metsien Pimennosta (A Knight From Deep Woods), 1966; Halusit Tai Et (Whether You Wish or Not), 1969; (play) Lilian Suuria Asioitia (too Big Matters), 1968. Mbrships: Union Finnish Authors (Mbr. Bd.); PEN (Pres., 1965-68). Hons: Pro Finlandia State Prizes for Veljen Varjo, 1951; Neito Kulkee Vetten Päällä, 1955; Kipinöivät Vuodet, 1961; Iiian Suuria Asioita, 1968; Halusit Tai Et, 1969. Address: Helsinki 20, Koivusaarentie 12, Finland.

JOENPOLVI, Martti Kalevi, b. 19 Apr. 1936, Käkislami, Finland. Author. Publs:Kevään kuusi päivää, 1959; Niin musta kuin multa, 1961; Roomalaiset kynttilät, 1963; Jos huonetta ei rakenna, 1965; Johanneksenleipäpuu, 1967; Kuparirahaa, 1969; Yö jona jäät vahvistuivat, 1971; Kaikki alennuksella, 1973. Mbr., Finnish Soc. of Authors. Hons: Lit. Prizes, City of Tampere, 1960, 1962 & 1972; Govt. Fellowship for Authors, 1972-74; Lit. Prize, State of Finland, 1974. Address: Maatialantie 12, 37100 Nokia, Finland.

JOGLAR CACHO, Manuel, b. 20 Mar. 1898, Morovis, Puerto Rico. Businessman; President, Cigar manufacturing company. Publs: Góndolas de Nácar, 1925; En Voz Baja, 1944; Faena Intima, 1955; Soliloquios de Lázaro, 1956; Canto a los Angeles, 1957; Por los Caminos de Día, 1958. Mbrships: Acad. of Arts & Scis. of Puerto Rico; Soc. of Puertorican Authors. Hons. incl: Grand Prize for Poetry, Acad. of Arts & Scis. of Puerto Rico, 1970; Special Prize for Poetry, Inst. of Puerto Rico of N.Y., 1974. Address: P.O. Box 913, Manatí, PR 00701, USA.

JOHNSON, Annabell (Jones), pen name JOHNSON, A. E. (jtly. w. husband), b. 18 June 1921, Kan. City, Mo., USA. Author. Educ: Wm. & Mary Coll.; Art Students' League. Publs: As a Speckled Bird, 1956; (co-author) The Big Rock Candy, 1957; The Black Symbol, 1958; Torrie, 1959; The Bear-cat, 1960; The Secret Gift, 1960; The Rescued Heart, 1961; Pickpocket Run, 1961; Wilderness Bride, 1962; The Golden Touch, 1963; A Peculiar Magic, 1965; The Grizzly, 1964; The Burning Glass, 1966; Count me Gone, 1968; A Blues I can Whistle, 1969; The Last Knife, 1971. Hons: Friends of Am. Writers Award, 1961; William Allen White Award, 1967; Western Writers of Am. Award, 1970. Address: 2925 S. Teller, Denver, CO 80227, USA.

JOHNSON, (Rev.) Aubrey Rodway, b. 23 Apr. 1901, Leamington Spa, Warwicks., UK. Emeritus Professor of Semitic Languages. Educ: Ph.D., Univ. Coll., Cardiff; London Univ.; Oxford Univ.; Halle-Wittenberg Univ., Germany. Publs: The One & the Many in the Israelite Conception of God, 1942, 2nd ed., 1961; The Cultic Prophet in Ancient Israel, 1944, 2nd ed., 1962; The Vitality of the Individual in the Thought of Ancient Israel, 1949, 2nd ed., 1964; Sacral Kingship in Ancient Israel, 1955, 2nd ed., 1967. Mbrships: Soc. for Old Testament Study (Pres., 1956); Fellow, Brit. Acad. Hons: D.D., Edinburgh Univ., 1952; D.Theol., Marburg Univ., W. Germany, 1963; & Uppsala Univ., Sweden, 1968; Burkitt Medal, Brit. Acad., 1961. Address: The Gate House, Alderley, Wotton-under-Edge, Glos. GL12 7QT, UK.

JOHNSON, B. S., b. 5 Feb. 1933. Poet; Novelist; Film Director. Educ: King's Coll., Univ. of London. Publs: incl: (poetry) Poems, 1964; Poems Two, 1972; (novels) Travelling People, 1963; Albert Angelo, 1964; Trawl, 1966; The Unfortunates, 1969; House Mother Normal, 1971; Christie Malry's Own Double-Entry, 1973; (short stories) Aren't you Rather Young to be Writing Your Memoirs?, 1973; (play) You're Human Like the Rest of Them, 1970, also filmed; (films) Up Yours Too, 1968; Paradigm, 1969. Contbr. to TV w. num. documentaries, etc. Hons. incl: Gregory Award, 1962; Somerset Maugham Award, 1967. Address: 9 Dagmar Terr., London N1 2BN, UK.

JOHNSON, Burdetta Fay Beebe, pen name BEEBE, B. F., b. 4 Feb. 1920, Marshall, Okla., USA. Author. Publs. incl: Run, Light Buck, Run, 1962; Coyote, Come Home, 1963; Assateague Deer, 1965; American Desert Animals, 1966; Ocelot, 1966; Little Red, 1966; Yucatan Monkey, 1967; Animals South of the Border, 1968; African Elephants, 1968; African Lions & Cats, 1969; African Apes, 1969; Little Dickens, Jaguar Cub, 1970. Hons: Jr. Lit. Guild selections, 1962 & 1966; 3 books made into Walt Disney films, 1962, 1963 & 1968. Address: Box 5295, Santa Fe, NM 87501, USA.

JOHNSON, Christopher George Alexander Yate Johnson, b. 1903, Edinburgh, UK. Sole Partner, Johnsons Trade Mark & Design Agents. Publs: St. Christopher — The

Patron Saint of Travellers, 3rd ed., 1938; Trade Marks & Industrial Designs: their History, Development & Protection, 1948; Industrial Designs & Trade Marks, 1959; House Style & Shop Fronts, 1961. Mbrships: F.R.S.A.; Pres., Royal Scottish Soc. of Arts, 1948-50. Address: 24 Bramdean Rise, Braid Hills, Edinburgh EH10 6JR, UK.

JOHNSON, David, b. 26 Aug. 1927, Meir, Stoke-on-Trent, UK. Writer. Educ: Sandhurst Mil. Coll. Publs: Sabre General, 1959 (Am. title, The Proud Canaries); Promenade in Champagne, 1960; Lanterns in Gascony, 1965; A Candle in Aragon, 1970; Regency Revolution: The Case of Arthur Thistlewood, 1974; 12 titles in History Jackdaw series, on Clive of India, Elizabeth Fry, The Monmouth Rebellion, The Tower of London, Duke of Marlborough, Boer War, The American Revolution, London's Police, Clipper Ships, Alfred the Great, The American Civil War, & General Gordon. Address: 47 Hantsworth Mews, London NW1 6DB, UK.

JOHNSON, David Terrence, b. 11 Sept. 1937, Kempston, Bedford, UK. Agricultural Management Lecturer; Agronomist. Educ: B.Sc., 1960, M.Sc., 1974, Reading Univ.; Nat. Dip. in Agric., 1960. Publs: Farm Planning in Malawi, 1972; A Guide to Successful Farm Management, 1972; A Guide to Profitable Maize Growing, 1974. Contbr. to: Rhodesia Agricl. Jrnl. Mbr., Agricl. Econs. Soc. Address: Mananga Agricl. Mgmt. Ctr., (C'wlth. Dev. Corp.), P.O. Box 96, Tshaneni, Swaziland.

JOHNSON, Diane, b. 28 Apr. 1934, Moline, Ill., USA. Writer. Educ: M.A., Ph.D., UCLA. Publs: Fair Game, 1965; Loving Hands at Home, 1968; Burning, 1970; Lesser Lives, 1972; The Shadow Knows, 1974. Contbr. to: Wash. Post; New Statesman. Mbrships: MLA; PEN. Recip., nomination for Nat. Book Award, 1973. Address: 46 El Camino Real, Berkeley, CA 94705, USA.

JOHNSON, Donald McIntosh, b. 1903, Bury, Lancs., UK. Medical Practitioner; Former Member of Parliament. Educ: Univ. of Cambridge; St. Bartholemew's Hosp., London; M.B.; B.Ch.; M.R.C.S.; L.R.C.P.; M.A.; Barrister-at-Law. Publs: The End of Socialism; A Doctor Regrets; Bars & Barricades; Indian Hemp, A Social Menace; A Doctor Returns; A Doctor in Parliament; The British National Health Service, Friend or Frankenstein?; A Cassandra at Westminster; Ted Heath: A Latter Day Charlemagne. Contbr. to: Spectator; Observer. Address: 55 Langley Pk. Rd., Sutton, Surrey, UK.

JOHNSON, Dorothy M., b. 19 Dec. 1905, McGregor, Iowa, USA. Writer; Magazine Editor; Professor of Journalism. Educ: B.A., 1928, Litt.D., 1973, Univ. of Mont. Publs. incl: Indian Country, 1953; The Hanging Tree, 1958; The Bloody Bozeman, 1971; The Bedside Book of Bastards (w. R. T. Turner), 1973. Contbr. to: Saturday Evening Post; Continental; Ency. Britannica; etc. Mbrships: Authors Guild; Western Writers of Am. Hons. incl: Spur Award, Best Western Short Story, 1956.

JOHNSON, Douglas (William John), b. 1 Feb. 1925, Edinburgh, UK. University Professor of French History. Educ: B.A., B.Litt., Worcester Coll., Oxford; École Normale Supérieure, Paris, France. Publs: Guizot: Aspects of French History, 1963; France & the Dreyfus Affair, 1966; France, 1969; The French Revolution, 1970; The Making of the Modern World, vol. 1, 1970, vol. 2, 1973; A Concise History of France, 1971; French History & Society (co-author), 1974. Contbr. to: New Soc.; Economist; Times Lit. & Higher Educl. Supplements; Birmingham Post. Mbr., Ed. Bd., Past & Present. Address: 29 Rudall Crescent, London NW3, UK.

JOHNSON, Edgar R., pen name JOHNSON, A. E. (jtly. w. wife), b. 24 Oct. 1912, Washoe, Mont., USA. Author; Ceramist; Sculptor. Educ: Kan. City Art Inst., Conservatory of Music; Art Students' League; N.Y. State Coll. Ceramics. Publs: (co-author) The Big Rock Candy, 1957; The Black Symbol, 1958; Torrie, 1959; The Bear-cat, 1960; The Secret Gift, 1960; The Rescued Heart, 1961; Pickpocket Run, 1961; Wilderness Bride, 1962; The Golden Touch, 1963; A Peculiar Magic, 1964; The Grizzly, 1965; The Burning Glass, 1966; Count me Gone, 1968; A Blues I can Whistle, 1969; The Last Knife, 1971. Hons. incl: William Allen White Award, 1967; Western Writers of Am. Award, 1970. Address: 2925 S. Teller, Denver, CO 80227, USA.

JOHNSON, Eyvind, b. 29 July 1900. Novelist. Publs. incl: (autobiography) Romanen om Olof, 1934-37; Grupp Krilon, 1941; Krilons Resa, 1942; Krilon sjalv, 1943;

Strändernas svall, 1946; Drommar om Rosor och eld, 1949; Molnen över Metapontion, 1957; Hans nades tid, 1961; Livsdagen lang, 1964; Stunder, vagor, 1965; (short stories) Sju liv, 1944. Mbr., Swedish Acad. Recip., Nordic Coun. Prize for Lit., 1962. Address: Vitsippsvägen 8, Saltsjöbaden 2, Sweden.

JOHNSON, (Iris) Lorene, pen name JOHNSON, Lorene Steele, b. Nashville, Kan., USA. Former Book-keeper-Secretary; Housewife. Contbr. of Short-short stories to sev. relig. mags. inclng: The Lookout; The Standard; also Radio & TV scripts, inclng. Escape from Yesterday. Mbrships: Kan. Authors Club; "Write to Sell" Club. Recip., sev. prizes for short-short & jvnle. stories, Kan. Authors' Club, 1957-71. Address: 2402 Amidon, Wichita, KS 67204, USA.

JOHNSON, James Ralph, b. 20 May 1922, Ft. Payne, Ala., USA. Artist; Author. Educ: B.S., Howard Coll., Birmingham, Ala., 1943. Publs. incl: Anyone Can Live Off the Land, 1961; Anyone Can Backpack in Comfort, 1965; Advanced Camping Techniques, 1967; Pepper, 1967; Blackie, The Gorilla, 1968; Ringtail, 1968; Moses' Band of Chimpanzees, 1969; Animal Paradise, 1969; Everglades Adventure, 1970; Southern Swamps of America, 1970; Photography for Young People, 1971; Zoos of Today, 1971; Animals & Their Food, 1972. Mbrships. incl: Western Writers of Am.; Outdoors Writers of Am. Recip., Jr. Lit. Guild selection, 1971. Address: Box 5295, Santa Fe, NM 87501, USA.

JOHNSON, Josephine (Winslow), b. 20 June 1910, Kirkwood, Mo., USA. Writer. Educ: Wash. Univ., St. Louis. Publs. incl: (novels) Now in November, USA 1934, UK 1935; Jordanstown, USA & UK 1937; Wildwood, USA 1946, UK 1947; The Dark Traveler, 1963; (short stories) Winter Orchard & Other Stories, 1935; The Sorcerer's Son & Other Stories, 1965; (verse) Unwilling Gypsy, 1936; Year's End, 1937; (essays) The Inland Island, 1969. Hons: O. Henry Award, 1934, 1935, 1942-45; Pulitzer Prize, 1935; Alumnae Citation, Wash. Univ., 1955; Award, Cinn. Inst. Fine Arts, 1964; D.H.L., Wash. Univ., 1970. Address: 4907 Klatte Rd., Cinn., OH 45244, USA.

JOHNSON, Marilue Carolyn, pen name MARILUE, b. 3 Feb. 1931, Grand Forks., N.D., USA. Writer & Illustrator of Children's Books; Artist; Sculptor. Educ: Walker Art Schl. Publs: Bobby Bear's Red Raft, 1972; Bobby Bear's New Home, 1972; Bobby Bear's Thankgiving, 1974; Bobby Bear's Christmas, 1974. Contbr. to: Ford Times; Mexican World; TV series. Address: RR 6 Tilden Woods, St. Cloud, MN 56301, USA.

JOHNSON, Pamela Hansford, b. 29 May 1912, London, UK. Writer. Publs. incl: (novels) This Bed Thy Centre, 1935; An Avenue of Stone, 1947; A Summer to Decide, 1948; Catherine Carter, 1952; The Unspeakable Skipton, 1959; An Error of Judgement, 1962; Night & Silence who is Here? , 1963; The Survival of the Fittest, 1968; The Honours Board, 1970; The Holiday Friend, 1972; (criticism) Thomas Wolfe, 1947; (plays) Proust Reconstructions, 1958; On Iniquity, 1967; Thomas Wolfe: a critical study, 1974. Mbr., PEN. Soc. for European Culture; F.R.S.L. Address: 85 Eaton Terr., London SW1, UK.

JOHNSON, Paul Emanuel, b. 1898, d. 1 Sept. 1974, Niantic, Conn., USA. Danielson Professor, Psychology & Pastoral Counselling, Boston Univ., 1957-74. Educ: A.B., M.A., S.T.B., Ph.D., D.D. Publs: Psychology of Religion; Psychology of Pastoral Care; Personality & Religion; Christian Love; Person & Counsellor, 1967; Ed., Healer of the Mind; Personality & Christian Faith (w. L. G. Colston). Contbr. to: Harvard Theol. Review; Ethics; Jrnl. Relig.; Jrnl. Philos.; Relig. Educ.; Psychol. Abstracts; Jrnl. Bible & Relig.; Am. Psychols.; Pastoral Psychol.; etc.

JOHNSON, Philip, b. 5 Oct. 1900, Congleton, Cheshire, UK. Playwright. Publs. (plays) incl: Long Shadows, 1930; Queer Cattle, 1931; Lover's Leap, 1934; One of Us, 1934; Lovely to Look At, 1937; Fish out of Water, 1941; Who Lies There? , 1946; The Door Opens, 1947. Recip., David Belasco Prize, for the best One Act Play of the Yr., 1927. Address: Wanderslore, Malden Rd., Sidmouth, Devon, UK.

JOHNSON, R(ichard) E(ugene) T(homas), b. 10 Feb. 1935, Cleveland, Ohio, USA. Library Assistant. Educ: B.A., Univ. of the Ams., Mexico, 1960; M.A., Northeastern Univ., Boston, 1973. Publs: Full Sails, 1971; Ed., Becoming Aware of Values by Bert K. Simpson, 2nd ed., 1973.

Contbr. to num. haiku jrnls. & anthols.; Contest Ed., Dragonfly Mag. Hons: Bronze medal, Centro Studi e Scambi Internazionale, 1972. Address: P.O. Box 615, San Diego, CA 92112, USA.

JOHNSON, Stowers, b. Brentwood, Essex, UK. Author; Art Collector. Educ: B.A., Queen Mary Coll., Schl. of Slavonic Studies, London. Publs. incl: London Saga, 1946; The Mundane Tree, 1947; Sonnets, They Say, 1949; Mountains & No Mules, 1949; Before & After Puck, 1953; When Fountains Fall, 1961; Gay Bulgaria, 1964; Yugoslav Summer, 1967; Turkish Panorama, 1968; Collector's Luck, 1968; The Two Faces of Russia, 1969; Agents Extra Ordinary, 1975. Contbr. to: Ed., Anglo-Soviet Jrnl., 1966-68; var. jrnls. & mags. Mbrships. incl: Hon. Treas., Poetry Soc., 1966-68; Hon. Treas., PEN., 1972-73; Soc. of Authors. Address: Corbiere, 45 Rayleigh Rd., Hutton, Brentwood, Essex, UK.

JOHNSON, Timothy, b. 18 Feb. 1942, Derby, UK. Writer. Educ: Abbotsholme Schl.; B.Sc., Imperial Coll. London. Publs: River of Time, 1967; Network Communities, 1971; Videocassettes, 1971. Contbr. to: Sunday Times; New Sci.; Fin. Times; etc. Mbrships: Nat. Union Jrnlsts.; Assn. Brit. Sci. Writers. Address: 14 Penn Rd., London N7 9RD, UK.

JOHNSON, Uwe, b. 20 July 1934, Kamién Pomorski, Pomerania. Novelist; Translator. Educ: Rostock Univ., Karl Marx Univ., Leipzig. Publs: Speculations about Jacob, 1963; Two Views, 1967; The Third Book about Achim, 1968; An Absence, 1969. Mbrships: Acad. of Arts, W. Berlin; PEN, W. Germany; German Union of Authors (V.S.). Hons: Fontane Prize of W. Berlin, 1960; Int. Prize of Lit., 1962; Georg Büchner Prize, 1971. Address: c/o Publisher, Suhrkamp Verlag, Lindenstr. 29-35, D-6 Frankfurt/Main, W. Germany.

JOHNSON, Wendell Stacy, b. 27 Dec. 1927, Kan. City, Mo., USA. Professor of English Literature; Author. Educ: B.A., Univ. of Mo., 1948; M.A., 1949, Ph.D., 1952, Ohio State Univ. Publs: The Voices of Matthew Arnold, 1961; An Introduction to Literary Criticism (w. M. K. Danziger), 1962. Gerard Manley Hopkins: The Poet as Victorian, 1968; A Poetry Anthology (w. M. K. Danziger), 1968; Words, Things & Celebrations, 1972; Sex & Marriage in Victorian Poetry, 1975. Contbr. to: Coll. Engl.; Engl Studies; Philol. Quarterly; 20th Century Lit.; Victorian Poetry; etc. Address: 360 E. 72nd St., N.Y., NY 10021; & Shell Walk, Fire Island Pines, NY 11782, USA.

JOHNS SMITH, June, pen name JOHNS, June, b. 1 June 1925, Salford, Lancs., UK. Freelance Journalist; Author; Teacher of Creative Writing. Publs: The Grasshopper Boy, 1967; Zoo Without Bars, 1969, 2nd ed. 1974; King of the Witches, 1969, 3rd ed., 1971; The Little Brother, 1970, 2nd ed., 1974; The Mating Game, 1970, 3rd ed., 1973; Black Magic Today, 1971; Practical Yoga, 1974 Mbrships: Mensa; Nat. Union Jrnlsts.; Soc. Authors; N. England Zool. Soc.; Workers' Educl. Assn. Agent: Bolt & Watson. Address: 10 Neston Dr., Upton Park, Chester, UK

JOHNSTON, Angus James, b. 5 May 1916, Chgo., Ill. USA. Historian; Teacher. Educ: B.A., Univ. of Wis.; M.A. Ph.D., Northwestern Univ. Publs: Virginia Railroads in the Civil War, 1961; The Historian's Contribution to Anglo-American Misunderstanding (co-author), 1966 Contbr. to: Jrnl. of Southern Hist.; Va. Mag. of Hist. & Biog.; Civ. War Hist. Mbrships: Am. Histl. Assn.; Org. of Am. Histns.; Histl. Assn., UK; Wis. State Histl. Soc.; Ill. St Andrew Soc.; Rolls-Royce Owners Club. Address: 1935 Highland Ave., Wilmette, IL 60091, USA.

JOHNSTON, Beryl, pen name MacGREGOR, Fiona Journalist; Author of children's books. Address: 132 Clifford's Inn, London EC4A 1BX, UK.

JOHNSTON, Ronald, b. 11 May 1926, Edinburgh, UK. Author. Publs: Disaster at Dungeness, 1964; Red Sky in the Morning, 1965; The Stowaway, 1966; The Wrecking of Offshore Five, 1967; The Angry Ocean, 1968; The Black Camels of Qashran, 1970; Paradise Smith, 1972; The Eye of the Needle, 1975. Mbrships: Coun. Mbr. & Lit. Panel Mbr. Scottish Arts Coun.; VP, Scottish PEN; Soc. of Authors Authors' Guild (USA). Address: Waverley House, Queen's Cres., Edinburgh EH9 2BB, UK.

JOHNSTON, William Denis, pen name JOHNSTON Denis, b. 18 June 1901, Dublin, Repub. of Ireland Playwright; University Professor; Barrister-at-Law. Educ

Univ. of Cambridge, UK; Harvard Law Schl., USA; Inner Temple & King's Inn, London, UK; M.A.; LL.M. Publs. incl: (plays) The Old Lady Says No! , 1929; The Moon in the Yellow River, 1931; The Dreaming Dust, 1940; A Fourth for Bridge, 1947; Strange Occurrence on Ireland's Eye, 1956; The Scythe & the Sunset, 1958; Collected Plays, 1960; (biogs.) In Search of Swift, 1959; John Millington Synge, 1965; (autobiogs.) Nine Rivers from Jordan, 1954; The Brazen Horn, 1968. Mbr., Royal Dublin Soc. Recip., O.B.E., 1945. Address: 8 Sorrento Terrace, Dalkey, Co. Dublin, Repub. of Ireland.

JOHNSTONE, Viola Mary, b. 15 Apr. 1915, Nairn, Scotland, UK. Actress; Authoress; Journalist. Educ: Old Vic Theatre Schl., London. Publs: The Hostess Cooks; Slimming Dishes; Ten Minute Cookery; Green Salads; Picnics; Enjoy Eating on a Diet (w. husband, Dr. G. J. V. Crosby), 1972. Contbr. to: Chef d'Oeuvre; The Observer; Good Eating; Tanger, Port de Maroc. Mbr., Players Theatre Club. Address: 4 Bloomsbury St., Kemp Town, Brighton BN2 1HQ, UK.

JOINER, Charles Louis, b. 1923, London, UK. Physician to Guy's Hospital; Honorary Consultant Physician, British Army. Educ: Med. Schl., Guy's Hosp., Univ. of London; M.D.; F.R.C.P. Publs: A Short Textbook of Medicine, 1962, 4th ed., 1970. Contbr. to sev. sci. jrnls.; Hon. Ed., Proceedings of Royal Soc. of Med. Mbrships: Assn. of Physns. of GB & Ireland; Royal Soc. of Med.; Harveian Soc.; European Assn. of Internal Med. Address: Ashton, Mead Rd., Chislehurst, Kent, & 152 Harley St., London W1, UK.

JOINER, Charles Wycliffe, b. 14 Feb. 1916, Iowa, USA. District Judge. Educ: B.A., 1937; J.D., 1939, Univ. of Iowa. Publs. incl: Constitutional Convention — a Means to Achieve Constitutional Reform, 1964; Fog in the Courts & at the Bar: Archaic Procedures & a Breakdown of Justice, 1969; num. legal articles & book reviews; The Civil Advocates (film), 1966. Contbr. to legal jrnls. Mbrships: incl: Bd. Dirs., Am. Judicature Soc.; Am. Trial Lawyers Assn.; Fellow, Am. Bar Fndn.; Am. Law Inst. Address: 1345 Glendaloch Circle, Ann Arbor, MI 48104, USA.

JOINER, Verna J., b. 28 Nov. 1896, Covington, La., USA. Author. Educ: Southeastern La. Univ., 1925-26 & 1951-53. Publs: From Papa & Me, 1956; This Home We Build, 1957; Growing Steady, 1959; Five Minutes to Four, 1960; Your Dating Data, 1962; What Teens Say, 1962; When Love Grows Up, 1966. Contbr. of columns & articles to relig. mags. Address: 212 N. Chestnut St., Hammond, LA 70401, USA.

JÓKAI, Anna, b. 24 Nov. 1932, Budapest, Hungary. Writer. Educ: Univ. Degree. Publs: (novels) 4447, 1968; Tartozik és követel (Debit & Credit), 1970; Napok (Days), 1972; Mindhalálig (Till Death us Parts), 1974; (plays) Fejünk felöl a tetöt (The Roof Above Our Heads), 1969; Tartozik és követel (Debit & Credit), 1971; (short stories) Kötél nélkül (Without Rope), 1969; A labda (The Ball), 1971; Szeretleink, Szerelmeink (Our Loves & Loved Ones), 1973. Mbr., Hungarian Writers' Union. Hons: József Attila Prize, 1970; Szot Prize, 1974. Address: 1074 Budapest, Dohány utca 82, Hungary.

JOKINEN, Seppo Pellervo, b. 19 Dec. 1927, Helsinki, Finland, Chief of Cultural Department, Finnish TV. Educ: M.A. Publs: Runoja (poems), 1954; Hukkumistapaus (novel), 1957; Aakkoset (poems), 1962. Mbrships: Finnish Soc. of Authors; Radio & TV Eds. Union of Finland. Address: Näyttelijäntie 6 A8, 00400 Helsinki 40, Finland.

JOLLES, Benjamin A., b. 26 Nov. 1906, Lwow, Poland. Physician; Radiotherapist. Educ: M.D., 1931, & Dip. Specialist Med. Radiol., 1936, Univ. of Florence, Italy; Intern Fndn. Curie, Paris, France, 1938; Dip. Med. Radiol., Royal Colls., London, UK, 1941; F.F.R.; F.I.Biol. Publs: Transl., Einführung in die Radiologie, 1933; Transl., Elementi di Radiologia, 1935; X-Ray Sieve Therapy in Cancer, 1953; Methods in Microcirculation Studies, 1972. Contbr. to: Brit. Jrnl. Radiol.; Clin. Radiol.; Strahlentherapie; Am. Jrnl. Roentgenol. & Radium Therapy; Lancet; Nature; other med. jrnls. Mbr., var. profl. assns. Recip., Duchess of Bedford Rsch. Fellowship. Address: 12 The Avenue, Spinney Hill, Northampton NN3 1BA, UK.

JOLLY, Cyril Arthur, b. 16 Dec. 1910, Cairo, Egypt. Author. Publs: History of Dereham Methodist Circuit, 1955; The Vengeance of Private Pooley, 1956; Henry Blogg

of Cromer, 1958, 2nd ed., 1973; S.O.S: Story of the Life-Boat Service, 1961, 2nd ed., 1974; The Spreading Flame, 1972. Mbr., Authors' Soc. Address: "Teazel Patch", Gressenhall, Dereham, Norfolk, UK.

JOLLY, William Percy, b. 2 Dec. 1922, Plymouth, UK. Scientific Author & Editor; Consultant in Electronic Instrumentation & Business Science; Biographer; University Teacher. Educ: B.Sc., Exeter Univ. Publs: Physics for Electrical Engineers, 1961; Low Noise Electronics, 1967; Cryoelectronics, 1972; Teach Yourself Electronics, 1972; Marconi, 1972; Sir Oliver Lodge, 1974. Contbr. to publs. on sci. mgmt. & investment, on electronics & tchng. Mbrships: C.Eng.; F.I.E.E.; F.I.E.R.E.; Soc. of Authors. Agent: Curtis Brown. Address: 31 The Plantation, Blackheath, London SE3, UK.

JONAS, Johanna, pen name JONAS-LICHTEN-WALLNER, Johanna, b. 5 Sept. 1914, Vienna, Austria. Writer. Educ: Univ. Vienna. Publs: (poetry) Weg durch die Zeit, 1965; Mühlviertler Sagen, 1968; Wiener Streiflichter, 1969; Die Sunduhr, 1972; Gesang im Ried, 1973; Wie weise muss man sein, um immer gut zu sein; Waldviertel, 1974; (novels) Das Osternachtwunder, 1968; Die Schuld der Lina Besenböck, 1969; Der Jäger von Birkwald, 1974; (pamphlet) Wiener Sentimentalitäten. Contbr. to num. adult & juvenile jrnls. etc. Mbrships. incl: Vienna Women's Club; Assn. Austrian Writers; Assn. Female Writers & Artists Austria. Recip., Young People's Book Competition Prize, 1965. Address: A 1040 Vienna IV, Seisgasse 18/12, Austria.

JONAS, Manfred, b. 9 Apr. 1927, Mannheim, Germany. Historian; Author. Educ: B.S.S., CCNY, 1949; A.M., 1950, Ph.D., 1959, Harvard Univ. Publs: Isolationism in America 1935-1941, 1966; American Foreign Relations in the 20th Century, 1967; Roosevelt & Churchill: Their Secret Wartime Correspondence (w. F. Loewenheim & H. Langley), 1975. Contbr. to: Am.-German, Am. Histl., Am. Pol. Sci. Reviews; Am. Studies; Jrnl. of Am. Hist.; Pol. Sci. Quarterly; & num. others. Mbr., var. histl. assns. Address: 2471 Hilltop Rd., Schenectady, NY 12309, USA.

JÓNASSON, Jakob, pen name BERSÓGLI, Bragi, b. 26 Dec. 1897, Bakkafjörður, Iceland. Teacher; Journalist; Proofreader. Educ: Agric., Commercial & Trchr. Colls. Publs: Börn Framtídarinnar, 1945; Ögróin Spor, 1952; Myndin Sem Hvarf, 1959; Myllusteinninn, 1963; Konan Sem Kunni Ad Thegja, 1965; Thar Sem Elfan Ómar, 1970; Milli Strída, at press 1974. Mbr., Icelandic Authors' Assn. Address: Gudrúnargata 1, Reykjavík, Iceland.

JONES, Alan Griffith, b. 1943, Pwll, Llanelli, UK. Senior Lecturer in German. Educ: M.A., Univ. of Oxford; Univ. of Bonn, W. Germany; Univs. of York & Birmingham, UK. Publs: 77mal England (w. R.W. Leonhardt), 1967; Anglo-German Songbook, 1968; The Germans: an Englishman's notebook, 1968; Deutsche Schüler in England (w. M. Deutschkron), 1972. Contbr. to: Anglo-German Review; Treffpunkt. Fellow, Inst. of Linguists. Address: 68 Ellenbrook Pk., Hatfield, Herts., UK.

JONES, Barbara, b. London, UK. Writer; Artist. Educ: Croydon Schl. of Art; Royal Coll. of Art (A.R.C.A.). Publs: The Isle of Wight, 1950; The Unsophisticated Arts, 1951; Follies & Grottoes, 1953, revised ed., 1974; English Furniture at a Glance, 1954, 2nd ed., 1971; Design for Death, 1967; Popular Arts of the Great War (w. Bill Howell), 1972. Contbr. to: Architect. Review; Shell Guides; etc. Mbrships: Soc. of Authors; Royal Anthrop. Inst. Address: 2 Well Walk, London NW3, UK.

JONES, Barry Owen, b. 1932, Geelong, Australia. Barrister & Solicitor; University Lecturer. Educ: M.A., LL.B., Melbourne Univ. Publs: Decades of Decision 1860-, 1965; The Penalty is Death, 1968; The Penguin Encyclopedia of People, 1970; Australian History in Photographs, 1970. Contbr. to: Bulletin (Sydney); Age; Aust.; Herald (Melbourne); var. histl. & educl. jrnls. Mbrships: Aust. Writers Guild; Aust. Soc. of Authors; A.C.T.T. Address: 37 Neerim Road, Caulfield, Victoria, Australia 3162.

JONES, Bernard, b. UK. Poet; Writer; English Lecturer. Educ: Ph.D. Publs: The Poems of William Barnes, 2 vols., 1962; William Barnes (pamphlet), 1962; John Cowper Powys (pamphlet), 1962; Thomas Cole (pamphlet), 1963; The Chanceful Season (poems), 1963; Letters of John Cowper Powys, 1970. Contbr. to: Essays on John Cowper Powys, 1972; Abinger ed. of E. M. Forster; sev. lit. jrnls.

Mbrships. incl: Soc. of Authors; Pres., Durham Univ. Engl. Soc. Hons. incl: Arts Assn. Poetry Award, 1966. Address: c/o Barclay's Bank, High Row, Darlington, Co. Durham, UK.

JONES, Charles, b. 1910, Methyr Tydfil, S. Wales, UK. Author. Publs: Book of Aphorisms; A Dose of Salts; High Wind in Glamorgan; Sauce for the Goose; My River; Come Take My Hand; Poet's Epitaph; Table D'Hote; Full Moon; The Jingle; Cabbages & Kings; The Challenger. Contbr. to: Rock & Fountain Press; Northcliffe Press; Hulton Press; Time & Tide; Adelphi; BBC; John O'London; Wales; Welsh Nation; Faner; Herald of Wales; Socialist Commentary; Planet; Rebecca. Address: West Grove, Merthyr Tydfil, S. Wales, UK.

JONES, Charles Williams, b. 23 Sept. 1905, Lincoln, Neb., USA. Emeritus Professor of English. Educ: B.A., Oberlin Coll., 1926; M.A., 1930, Ph.D., 1932, Cornell Univ. Publs: Bedae Pseudepigrapha, 1939; Writing & Speaking (jt. author), 1943; Saints' Lives & Chronicles, 1947; Medieval Literature in Translation, 1950; The St. Nicholas Liturgy, 1963; Bedae Opera Didascalica, vol. I, 1974, vol. II, in press. Contbr. to: Plan of St. Gall (chapt., The Directives of Adalhard of Corbie); reference books; acad. jrnls. Mbr., sev. profl. orgs. Recip., acad. hons. Address: 766 Spruce St., Berkeley, CA 94707, USA.

JONES, Dedwydd Skeel Harries, b. 2 Dec. 1936, Tenby, Pembs., UK. Dramatist; University Tutorial Fellow in Drama. Educ: L.S.E.; B.A., Warberg Inst. Classical Studies, London Univ., 1960. Publs: incl (plays) Owen Glyndŵr, 1970; The Women of Pilleth, 1972; Saxon, 1973; Bard, 1974; (play prods.) Service for St. Hal, 1964; Drink from an Amethyst Cup, 1967; Hearts at Night, 1968; Crucification of Black Anpag, 1972. Contbr. to: poems & articles) Poetry Review; London Welshman; Punch. Mbrships: Soc. of Authors; Welsh Acad. of Letters. Hons: Award, Arts Coun. of GB, 1964; Welsh Arts Coun. Bursary, 1964, 1967; Sunday Times Award, 1972. Address: c/o Cokaygne Publishing, 1 Portland Place, New Sq., Cambridge, UK.

JONES, Diana Wynne, b. 1934, London, UK. Playwright; Author. Educ: B.A., St. Anne's Coll., Oxford Univ. Publs: Changeover, 1970; Wilkins' Tooth, 1973; The Ogre Downstairs, 1974. Plays: The Batterpool Business, 1967; The King's Things, 1969; The Terrible Fisk Machine, 1970; (children's books) Eight Days of Luke 1975. Agent: Laura Cecil. Address: 4 Herbert Close, Oxford, UK.

JONES, Eldred Durosimi, b. 6 Jan. 1925, Freetown, Sierra Leone. College Principal. Educ: B.A., 1947, Dip.Ed., 1949, Fourah Bay Coll.; B.A.(Hons.), 1953, M.A., 1958, Corpus Christi Coll., Oxford, UK; Ph.D., Univ. of Durham, 1962. Publs: incl. The Way to Write Successful Letters, 1962; Othello's Countrymen: A Study of Africa in the Elizabethan & Jacobean Drama, 1965; The Elizabethan Image of Africa, 1971; Ed., Macbeth, 1972. Contbr. to: African Lit. Today (Ed.). Mbrships incl: Bd. of Trustees, Int. Broadcast Inst.; W. African Linguistic Soc. Hons: Criticism Prize, 1st World Festival of Negro Arts, Dakar, 1966; Fellow, Royal Soc. Arts, 1972. Address: P.O. Box 60, Fourah Bay College, University of Sierra Leone, Freetown, Sierra Leone.

JONES, Elwyn, b. 1923, Aberdare, Glam., UK. TV Dramatist & Executive; Author. Educ: London Schl. of Econs. Publs: The Last Two to Hang, 1966; Barlow in Charge, 1973; Barlow Comes to Judgement, 1974; The Barlow Casebook, 1975; The Ripper File, 1975. Contbr. to: Sunday Telegraph; Western Mail; What's On; Spectator; Radio Times (1950-57). Mbrships: Writers' Guild of GB; Soc. of Authors; Savage Club. Agent: John Farquharson. Address: 31 Abinger Rd., Bedford Park, W4 1EU, UK.

JONES, Emrys, b. 17 Aug. 1920, Aberdare, UK. Professor of Geography. Educ: B.Sc., M.Sc., Ph.D., Univ. Wales. Publs: Ed. Belfast in its Regional Setting, 1952; Social Geography of Belfast, 1960; Human Geography, 1964; Towns & Cities, 1966; Atlas of London, 1968-70; Ed., Man & His Habitat, 1971; Cities (w. E. Van Zandt), 1974; Ed., Readings in Social Geography, 1975. Contbr. to: Geog.; Geog. Jrnl.; Sociol. Review; Town Planning; Scottish Geog. Mag.; etc. Mbrships: F.R.G.S.; Reg. Studies Assn. (former Chmn.); Inst. Brit. Geogs. Address: 4 Apple Orchard, Hemel Hempstead, Herts., UK.

JONES, Emyr Wyn, b. 23 May 1907, Caernarvon, Wales, UK. Consultant Physician & Cardiologist; University

Director of Cardiological Studies; Royal Insurance Company Chief Consulting Medical Officer. Educ: M.B., Ch.B., 1928, M.D., 1930, Univ. of Liverpool; London Tchng. Hosps.; D.P.H., 1931; M.R.C.P., 1933; F.R.C.P., London, 1949. Publs: In Memoriam — Enid Wyn Jones, 1968; Cyfaredd Cof, 1970; Ar Ffiniau Meddygaeth, 1971; Ysgubau'r Meddyg, 1973. Contbr. to num. med. & lit. publs. Mbrships: Chmn., Coun., Nat. Eisteddfod of Wales; Ct., Univ. of Wales; Vice Chmn., Welsh Hosp. Bd.; Chmn., Brit. Cardiac Soc., 1968-69. Address: Llety'r Eos, Llansannan, Denbigh, Wales, UK.

JONES, Eric Lionel, b. 1936, Andover, Hants., UK. Professor of Economics. Educ: B.A., Nottingham Univ.; M.A., D.Phil., Oxford Univ. Publs: Seasons & Prices, 1964; Agriculture & Economic Growth in England, 1967; Land, Labour & Population in the Industrial Revolution, 1967; The Development of English Agriculture, 1968; Agrarian Change & Economic Development, 1969; Business Enterprise & Economic Change (co-author), 1973; Agriculture & the Industrial Revolution, 1974. Contbr. to: Econ. Hist. Review; Jrnl. Econ. Hist.; etc.; chapts. for 2 works on ornithol. Mbr., var. profl. assns. Address: The Wall House, West End Rd., Mortimer, Berks., UK.

JONES, Evan, b. 6 May 1915, LeSueur, Minn., USA. Writer. Publs: Hidden America (w. Roland Wells Robbins), 1959; The Father, 1960; Trappers & Mountain Men, 1961; The Minnesota: Forgotten River, 1963; The Plains States, 1966; Citadel in the Wilderness, 1966; American Food: The Gastronomic Story, 1975. Contbr. to: Gourmet; Travel & Leisure; Ford Times; Vista/USA. Address: c/o Robert Lescher Lit. Agt., 155 East 71st St., N.Y., NY 10021, USA.

JONES, Evan Gordon, b. 1927, Jamaica. Freelance Writer. Educ: A.B., Haverford Coll., USA; M.A., Wadham Coll., Oxford, UK; Putney Grad. Schl., USA. Publs: incl: Protector of the Indians, 1956, 1973; The Fight Against Slavery, 1975; (plays) The Spectator, 1962; Go Tell It On Table Mountain, 1973; (TV) Return to Look Behind, 1964; The Madhouse on Castle Street, 1964; A Work of Genius, 1974; The Fight Against Slavery, 1975; (films) King & Country, 1964; Modesty Blaise, 1966; Funeral in Berlin, 1967; Two Gentlemen Sharing, 1969; Outback, 1970; Night Watch, 1973. Contbr. of poems to var. mags. & anthols. Mbr., Writers Guild of GB. Address: 18 Larpent Ave., London SW15 6UU, UK.

JONES, (Everett) LeRoi, pen name BARAKA, Imamu Amiri, b. 7 Oct. 1934, Newark, N.J., USA. Theatre Director. Educ: B.A., Howard Univ., Wash. DC, 1954. Publs: incl (plays) Dutchman & The Slave, USA 1964, UK 1965; The Baptism & The Toilet, 1967; Four Black Revolutionary Plays, USA 1969, UK 1971; (novel) The System of Dante's Hell, USA 1965, UK 1966; (stories) Tales, USA 1967, UK 1969; (verse) Black Magic, USA & UK, 1969; (essays, as Baraka) Raise Race Rays Raze, 1971; Ed., var. anthols. Hons. incl: Int. Art Festival Prize, Senegal, 1966; var. Fellowships & grants. Address: Spirit House, 33 Stirling St., Newark, NJ 07102, USA.

JONES, Felix Edward Aylmer, pen name AYLMER, Felix, b. 21 Feb. 1889, Corsham, Wilts, UK. Actor. Educ: B.A., Exeter Coll., Oxford Univ. Publs: Dickens Incognito, 1959; The Drood Case, 1964. Contbr. to var. publs. (occasional reviews). Mbr., Brit. Actors' Equity Assn. (Pres., 1949-69). Hons: O.B.E., 1950; Kt. Bachelor, 1965. Address: 6 Painshill House, Cobham, Surrey, UK.

JONES, (Sir) Francis Avery, b. 31 May 1910, Briton Ferry, Glam., UK. Physician. Educ: M.D., London Univ. Publs: Ed., Modern Trends in Gastroenterology, 1952, 2nd series, 1958; Clinical Gastroenterology, 1968; The Occupational Incidence of Peptic Ulcers, M.R.C. Special Report Series No. 276 (H.M.S.O.); & num. articles on peptic ulcers & colitis in med. papers. Contbr. to: Med. Annual; Gut (Ed., 1965-69). Mbrships: F.R.C.P.; Brit. Soc. Gastroenterol. (Past Pres.); Athenaeum Club. Hons: C.B.E., 1966; Kt., 1970; M.D., Melbourne Univ. Address: 149 Harley St., London W1N 2DE, UK.

JONES, Frank H., pen name, MENTOR, b. 1899, Liverpool, UK. Accountant. Publs: incl: Guide to Company Balance Sheets & Profit & Loss Accounts; 1,000 Questions & Answers on Company Law; Book-Keeping Rapid Course; Guide to Examination Success; Jordan's Modern Book-Keeping; Student's Guide to Company Law. Contbr. to: Cert. Accts'. Jrnl.; Acct's. Wkly.; etc. Mbrships: F.C.C.A.; F.C.I.S. Address: Flat 17, Rosemount, St. Catherine's Rd., Bournemouth BH6 4AB, UK.

JONES, Glyn, b. 28 Feb. 1905, Merthyr Tydfil, UK. Schoolmaster; Author. Educ: St. Paul's Coll., Cheltenham. Publs: (novels) The Valley, the City, the Village, 1956; The Learning Lark, 1960; The Island of Apples, 1965; (short stories) The Blue Bed, 1937; The Water Music, 1944; Selected Short Stories, 1971; (poetry) Poems, 1939; The Dream of Jake Hopkins, 1954; The Beach of Falesa (libretto), 1974; Selected Poems, 1975; (non-fiction) The Saga of Llywarch the Old (transl., w. Dr. T. J. Morgan), 1955; The Dragon Has Two Tongues (criticism), 1968. Mbr., Welsh Acad. Letters (Chmn., Engl. Sect.). Hons: Premier Lit. Award, Welsh Arts Coun., 1972; D.Litt., Univ. of Wales, 1974. Address: 158 Manor Way, Whitchurch, Cardiff CF4 1RN, UK.

JONES, Goronwy John, b. 1915, Nantymoel, Glam., UK. Schoolmaster; Lecturer. Educ: Caerleon Tchrs. Trng. Coll. Publs: The Veto Controversy, 1948; Security from Aggression, 1949; Challenge to the Peacemakers, 1951; United Nations for the Classroom (co-author), 1956, revised ed., 1962; From Stalin to Krushchev, 1960; General Studies for Technical Students, 2 vols., 1965; Wales & the Quest for Peace, 1969. Contbr. to: Western Mail; New C'wlth.; UN News. Mbrships: Soc. of Authors; UN Assn., Wales (Exec. Comm.); Fellow, Royal Histl. Soc. Address: The Croft, Litchard Terrace, Bridgend, Glamorgan, UK.

JONES, Gretchen Page, b. Ninock, La., USA. Educ: Centenary Coll.; SW Inst. of Art. Contbr. to var. poetry mags., anthols. Mbrships: La. State Poetry Soc.; Charter Mbr., Shreveport Poetry Soc.; Past Publicity Chmn., Shreveport Artists & Writers Club, & Shreveport Writers Club. Hons. incl: 1st, 2nd Place, Deep S. Writers & Artists Conf., 1961 & 1962. Address: 1624 Claiborne Ave., Shreveport, LA 71103, USA.

JONES, Gwyn, b. 1907, Blackwood, Monmouth, UK. University Professor of English. Educ: M.A., Univ. Coll., Cardiff. Publs: Richard Savage; The Buttercup Field; The Still Waters; Shepherd's Hey; The Walk Hone; A Prospect of Wales; The Mabinogion; The Norse Atlantic Saga; A History of the Vikings; Kings, Beasts & Heroes; Welsh Folk Tales & Legends; Nine Icelandic Sagas; Ed., The Welsh Review. Contbr. to num. jrnls. Mbrships: Arts Coun. of GB; Chmn., Welsh Arts Coun., 1956-66; Pres., Viking Soc. for Northern Rsch., 1950-52. Hons. incl: C.B.E., 1964; Christian Gauss Award for Lit. Schlrship., 1973; Kt., Icelandic Order of the Falcon. Address: 4 Brynderwen Close, Cyncoed, Cardiff, UK.

JONES, Gwyn Owain, b. 29 Mar. 1917, Cardiff, UK. Director, National Museum of Wales; Author. Educ: M.A., D.Sc., Jesus Coll., Oxford; Ph.D., Univ. of Sheffield. Publs: Atoms & the Universe, 1956, 3rd ed., 1973; Glass, 1956, 2nd ed., 1971; (novels) The Catalyst, 1960; Personal File, 1962; Now, 1965. Contbr. to: Anglo-Welsh Review; (formerly) var. profl. phys. jrnls. Mbr., Engl. Lang. Sect., Yr Academi Gymreig. Address: New House, St. Hilary, Cowbridge, Glam. CF7 7DP, UK.

JONES, Harry Austin, pen name JONS, Hal, b. 1912, Monmouth, UK. Publs: Montana Nemesis, 1960; Cattlemans Gold, 1961; The Llano Kid, 1962; Saddle Tramps, 1963; Ghost Gunman, 1964; Mochita Stage, 1964; Alamosa Guns, 1965; Rogue Ramrods, 1965. Mbr., Soc. of Authors. Address: 11 Burnham Road, Shirehampton, Bristol, UK.

JONES, Helen Hinckley, pen name, HINCKLEY, Helen, b. 12 Apr. 1903, Provo, Utah, USA. Writer. Educ: B.S., 1924, M.S., 1928, Brigham Young Univ.; post-grad. studies at sev. univs. Publs. incl: The Mountains Are Mine, 1946; Persia Is My Heart, 1953; Reveille for a Persian Village, 1958; A Wall & Three Willows, 1967; Land & People of Iran, 1964, revised ed., 1973; Over the Mormon Trail, 1963. Mbrships: Bd. of Dirs., Calif. Writers Guild; Hon. Mbr., Pasadena Writers Club & La. Press Women. Address: 1191 E. Mendocino, Altadena, CA 91001, USA.

JONES, Ivor Wynne, b. 28 Mar. 1927, Liverpool, UK. Journalist. Educ: BBC Engrng. Schl.; Army Parachute Trng. Schl.; RAFVR Offs. Schl. Publs. incl: Money for All, The Story of the Welsh Pound, 1969; Llandudno Through the Looking Glass, 1970; Betws-y-coed, the Mountain Resort, 1972; H. M. Stanley & Wales (co-author), 1972; Shipwrecks of North Wales, 1973; Bettws-y-coed & the Conway Valley, 1974. Contbr. to Liverpool Daily Post, Alternate Ed., Day to Day in Wales column, 1955—. Mbrships: Soc. of Authors; Inst. of Jrnlsts.; Lewis Carroll Soc. Address: Pegasus, 71 Llandudno Rd., Penrhyn Bay, Llandudno, UK.

JONES, Jack Raymond, b. 11 Apr. 1922, Swansea, Wales, UK. Teacher. Educ: Dip.Ed., Bangor Normal Coll., Univ. of Wales; Dip. French Studies, Univ. of Paris, France; further studies, Univ. of Caen. Publs: Your Child At School, 1965; The Man Who Loved the Sun (Biography of Van Gogh), 1966. Contbr. to: Wales; Planet; BBC Radio. Mbr., Soc. of Authors. Address: 16 Grove Rd., Barnes, London SW13, UK.

JONES, James, b. 6 Nov. 1921, Robinson, Ill., USA. Writer. Educ: Univ. of Hawaii, 1942; N.Y. Univ., 1945. Publs: (novels) From Here to Eternity, USA 1951, UK 1952, Some Came Running, USA 1957, UK 1959; The Pistol, USA & UK, 1962; The Thin Red Line, USA 1962, UK 1963; Go to the Widow-Maker, USA & UK, 1967; The Merry Month of May, USA & UK, 1971; (short stories) The Ice-Cream Headache & Other Stories, 1968. Recip., Nat. Book Award, 1952. Address: 10 Quai d'Orléans, Ile St. Louis, Paris 4e, France.

JONES, John, b. 1924, Burma. College Fellow. Educ: M.A., Univ. of Oxford, UK. Publs: The Egotistical Sublime: A History of Wordsworth's Imagination, 1954; On Aristotle & Greek Tragedy, 1962; John Keats' Dream of Truth, 1969; The Same God, 1971; Ed., The Study of Good Letters, by H. W. Garrod, 1963. Contbr. to: Blackfriars; Observer; Times Lit. Supplement; Sunday Telegraph; New Statesman; Spectator; Proceedings of the Brit. Acad. Address: c/o Merton Coll., Oxford, UK.

JONES, Joseph Jay, b. 29 June 1908, Peru, Neb., USA. Professor of English; Author. Educ: B.Sc., Univ. of Neb., 1930; M.A., 1931, Ph.D., 1934, Stanford Univ. Publs: The Cradle of Erewhon: Samuel Butler in New Zealand, 1959; Terranglia: the Case for English as World Literature, 1965; Handful of Hong Kong (verse), 1966; Ecology XVII (verse), 1972. Contbr. to: World Lit. Written in Engl. (fndr., 1962); Am. Lit.; Am. Speech; Aust. Lit. Studies; Meanjin; Studies in the Novel. Hons. incl: Fulbright Lectureship in Am. Lit. to NZ, 1953, S. Africa 1960, Hong Kong, 1965. Address: Dept. of English, Univ. of Tex., Austin, TX 78712, USA.

JONES, Kenneth Westcott, pen name TAUNTON, Eric, b. 11 Nov. 1921, Dulwich, London, UK. Travel Writer & Author. Educ: Admiralty Signal Coll. Publs: To the Polar Sunrise, 1957; America Beyond the Bronx, 1961; Great Railway Journeys of the World, 1964; Exciting Railway Journeys of the World, 1966; By Rail to the Ends of the Earth, 1968; Romantic Railways, 1971; Business Air Traveller, 1972; Steam in the Landscape, 1972. Contbr. to: United Newspapers (Grp. travel Corres., 1960-); etc. Mbrships. incl: Inst. Jrnlsts. (Comm., London Dist., 1966-68, 1972-73); Chmn., Guild of Travel Writers, 1975-. Hons: Thomson Travel Award, 1972; Canton Valais, Switz., Tourism Prize, 1959. Address: Hillswick, Michael Rd., London SE25 6RN, UK.

JONES, Lyndon Hamer, b. 15 Apr. 1927, Bolton, Lancs., UK. Principal, South-West London College. Educ: B.A. Manchester Univ.; Post-Grad. Dip. Indl. Admin. Manchester Coll. Sci. & Technol.; Tchr's. Cert., Bolton Tech. Tchr. Trng. Coll.; Chartered Sec. Publs: (1966-67) Wages Determination; Manpower; National Income; Forms of Business Organisation & Their Finance; Economics, 1972. Contbr. to: BBC; Times Higher Educl. Supplement; Educ.; Voc. Aspects; Adult Educ.; Accts. Wkly.; Int. Acct.; Educ. & Trng.; Trng. Int; etc. Mbrships. incl: Assn. Bus. Execs. (Chmn.); Assn. Int. Accts. (Educ. Cons.). Recip., Leverhulme Exhib. Schlrship. Address: 20 Wolsey Close, Kingston upon Thames, Surrey, UK.

JONES, Madison Percy, b. 1925, Nashville, USA. Professor of English. Educ: M.A., Vanderbilt Univ.; Univ. of Fla. Publs: The Innocent; Forest of the Night; Dog Days, Best American Short Stories. Contbr. to: Sewanee Review. Mbr., S. Atlantic MLA. Address: 643 Cary Dr., Auburn, Ala., USA.

JONES, Mary R., pen name STERLING-JONES, M., b. 22 May 1913, Normandy, Mo., USA. Book-keeper; Housewife. Publs: Dear Typewriter Pal, 1968. Contbr. to: Soul & the Singer, 1968, 1969, 1971; Kan. Authors' Club Yrbook; Southwest Daily Times; Kan. City Star; Syracuse Jrnl.; Lakin Indep.; Garden City Telegram; Wichita Beacon; Pen Mag. Mbrships: Nat. Writers' Club; Kan. State Authors' Club; 7th Dist. Writers; Liberal Creative Writers. Hons. incl: 1st Prize in Poetry, Kan. Authors' Club, 1967, 1968, 1973. Address: 811 Sycamore, Liberal, KS 67901, USA.

JONES, Mervyn, b. 1922, London, UK. Author. Educ: N.Y. Univ., USA. Publs: Potbank, 1961; Big Two, 1962;

Two Ears of Corn, 1965; A Set of Wives, 1965; John & Mary, 1966; A Survivor, 1968; Joseph, 1970; Mr. Armitage Isn't Back Yet, 1971; Holding On, 1973; The Revolving Door, 1973; Strangers, 1974; Lord Richard's Passion, 1974. Contbr. to: New Statesman; Tribune; Observer. Agent: Richard Scott Simon. Address: 10 Waterside Place, London NW1, UK.

JONES, Peter, b. 12 June 1920, Wem, Shropshire, UK. Actor; Writer. Educ: Wem Grammar Schl.; Ellesmere Coll. Publs: Sweet Madness, 1953; The Party Spirit (w. John Jowett), 1954; The Rescue, 1974. Mbrships: League of Dramatists; Actors' Equity. Address: 32 Acacia Rd., London NW8 6AS, UK

JONES, Reginald Lanier, b. 21 Jan. 1931, Clearwater, Fla., USA. Professor of Education & Afro-American Studies. Educ: A.B., Morehouse Coll., Atlanta, Ga., 1952; M.A., Wayne State Univ., Detroit, Mich., 1954; Ph.D., Ohio State Univ., Columbus, Ohio, 1959. Publs: Ed., New Directions in Special Education, 1970; Ed., Problems & Issues in the Education of Exceptional Children, 1971; Ed., Black Psychology, 1972; Co-Ed. (w. I. Hendrick), Student Dissent in the Schools, 1971; Co-Ed. (w. D. MacMillan), ˉˉecial Education in Transition, 1974. Mbrships: Assn. Black Psychols. (Nat. Chmn. 1971-72); Am. Psychol. Assn.; Am. Educ. Rsch. Assn. Address: Schl. Educ., Univ. Calif., Berkeley, CA 94720, USA.

JONES, Richard, b. 1926, Rhydyfelin, UK. Journalist. Educ: Univ. Coll. of Wales, Aberystwyth; Sorbonne; Stanford Univ., Calif. Publs: The Age of Wonder (US title, The Three Suitors), 1967; The Toy Crusaders (US title, Supper with the Borgias), 1968; A Way Out, 1969; The Tower is Everywhere, 1971. Contbr. to: Times; Listener; Atlantic Monthly; BBC. Address: 120 Clapham Common West Side, London SW4, UK.

JONES, Vernon, b. 13 Oct. 1897, Portsmouth, Va., USA. University Professor. Educ: B.A., M.A., Univ. of Va., 1920; M.A., 1924, Ph.D., 1926, Columbia Univ. Publs: Character Education Through Cases from Biography, 1931; Character & Citizenship Training in the Public Schools — An Experimental Study, 1936; Character & Citizenship Education, 1950; Attitudes of College Students & Their Changes — A 37-Year Study (monograph), 1970. Contbr. to: Review of Educl. Rsch.; Jrnl. Educl. Psychol.; Ency. Educl. Rsch. Mbrships. incl: Am. Psychol., Educl. Rsch., Personnel & Guidance Assns.; Nat. Educ. Assn. Hons. incl: Am. Educl. Rsch. Assn. Award, 1940. Address: 267 Salisbury Street, Worcester, MA 01609, USA.

JONES, Virgil Carrington, b. 7 June 1906, Charlottesville, Va., USA. Writer. Educ: Va. Polytechnic Inst. & State Univ.; A.B., Jrnlsm., Wash. & Lee Univ., 1930. Publs. incl: Ranger Mosby, 1944; The Hatfields & the McCoys, 1948; Gray Ghosts & Rebel Raiders, 1956; Eight Hours Before Richmond, 1957; The Civil War at Sea, 3 vols., 1960-62; Birth of Liberty, 1963; Roosevelt's Rough Riders, 1972. Contbr. to jrnls. & newspapers. Mbr., Nat. Press Club. Hons: Meritorious Writing Award, DC Civil War Round Table, 1956; Histl. Cons., CBS-TV series, The Gray Ghost. Address: 15000 Lee Hwy., Centreville, VA 22020, USA.

JONES, Wilbur Devereux, b. 28 Sept. 1916, Youngstown, Ohio, USA. Professor of History. Educ: A.B., 1940; A.M., 1947; Ph.D., 1949. Publs: Lord Derby & Victorian Conservatism, 1956; Lord Aberdeen & the Americas, 1958; Civilization Through the Centuries, 1960; Confederate Rams at Birkenhead, 1961; Prosperity Robinson, 1967; The Peelites, 1946-57, 1972; The American Problem in British Diplomacy, 1974. Contbr. to most major Am. historical jrnls., some newspapers. Recip., Michael Award, 1956. Address: 420 S. Milledge Ave., Athens, GA 30601, USA.

JORDAN, Winthrop D(onaldson), b. 11 Nov. 1931, Worcester, Mass., USA. Professor. Educ: A.B., Harvard Univ., 1953; M.A., Clark Univ., 1957; Ph.D., Brown Univ., 1960. Publs: White over Black: American Attitudes toward the Negro, 1550-1812, 1968; The White Man's Burden: Historical Origins of Racism in the United States, 1974. Mbr., var. historical assns. Hons: Ralph Waldo Emerson Prize, Phi Beta Kappa, 1968; Parkman Prize, Soc. of Am. Histns., 1969; Nat. Book Award, 1969; Bancroft Prize, Columbia Univ., 1969. Address: 1107 Milvia St., Berkeley, CA 94707, USA.

JONES, W. R. D., b. 1924, Caerphilly, Wales, UK. Senior Lecturer in History, Caerleon College of Education; Research Officer, Schools Council. Educ: M.A.(Wales), B.Sc.Econ.(London), Univ. Coll. of S. Wales & Mon. Publs: The Tudor Commonwealth 1529-1559, 1970; Nazi Germany, 1970; The Mid-Tudor Crisis 1539-1563, 1973. Contbr. to: Wales Sect., Hist. in the Field, 1970. Mbrships: Coun., Glam. Hist. Soc. Address: Brodawel, Underwood Ave., Maesycwmmer, Hengoed, Glam., UK.

JONES-EVANS, Eric John Llewellyn, b. 2 Oct. 1898, W. Coker, Somerset, UK. Actor; Playwright; Broadcaster; Theatre Historian. Educ: M.R.C.S., L.R.C.P., St. Thomas's Hosp., Univ. of London. Publs. incl: Footlight Fever (autobiog); (plays) The Weaver of Ravelo, 1963; Murder of Nancy, 1963; The Jackal, 1964; Blue Cockade, 1964; Mr Crummles Presents, 1966; David Copperfield, 1969; Official Catalogue for the Centenary of 'The Bells' Exhibition, 1971. Contbr. to var. local jrnls. Mbr., Dickens Fellowship, London. Recip., 1st Prize, Festival of Brit. Playwriting Competition, 1951. Agents: Samuel French Ltd.; Margery Vosper Ltd. Address: The Treshams, Fawley, Near Southampton, Hants., UK.

JONSSON, Hilmar, b. 12 May 1932, Jökulsarhlith, Iceland. Chief Librarian, Keflavik Municipal Library. Educ: Sorbonne Univ., Paris, France, 1954-55. Publs: Nyjar hugvekjur, 1955; Rismál, 1964; Israelsmenn og Islendingar, 1965; Foringjar falla, 1967; Kannski verthur thú . . ., 1970; Fólk án fata, 1973. Contbr. to num. Icelandic newspapers & periodicals. Mbr., Assn. of Icelandic Authors. Address: Hátún 27, Keflavik, Iceland.

JÓNSSON, Jóhannes Helgi, pen name HELGI, Jóhannes, b. 5 Sept. 1926, Reykjavík, Iceland. Author; Former Sailor; Archivist; Secretary of Parliament. Educ: Schl. of Commerce. Publs. incl: Allra vedra von (Any Weather Whatever, short stories), 1957; Horft a hjarnid (Looked upon the Frozen Snow, novel), 1958; Hús málarans (The Painter's House, biog.), 1961; Hin hvítu segl (The White Sails, documentary novel), 1962; Svört messa (Black Ceremony, novel), 1965, also transl'd into Russian & Polish; Hringekjan (The Carousel, novel), 1969; Svipir saekja thing (Phantoms Assemble to a Conference, remembrances of nat. life); Transl., The Unknown Soldier, by V. Linna, 1971; (co-author) Íslenzkir pennar (Icelandic Pens), 1956; Bára blá (The Blue Wave), 1973. Contbr. to sev. anthols. of Icelandic Short Stories & var. mags. Mbr., Assn. of Icelandic Writers (Advsry. Comm.). Hons. incl: 1st prize, Eimreidin Mag. Short. Story Competition, 1955; Award, Icelandic Nat. Broadcasting Stn., 1971; Grant, Icelandic Cultural Min., 1972. Address: Gilsbakka, V/Ellidavatn, Reykjavík, Iceland.

JONSSON, Runer, b. 29 June 1916, Nybro, Sweden. Chief Editor; Author. Educ: Corres. courses. Publs. incl: 3 collects. of poems; 4 books of humorous short stories; 3 history textbooks; 5 books about Vicke Viking; also Rut, rysarn och de andra, 1968; Vad ger no for Johan, 1971; Vi raddar Norrgarden, 1973. Hons: Deutscher Jugendbuch Prize, 1965; var. Swedish prizes. Address: Smalandsgatan 23C, 382 00, Nybro, Sweden.

JORDAK, Karl, b. 10 Aug. 1917, Vienna, Austria. Librarian; Writer. Educ: Univ. of Vienna (German, Hist. of Art, & Philos.). Publs: Wiener Biedermeier, Begegnungen und Erlebnisse, 1960; Die Universität Wien, 1965; Das Werk des Malers F. H. Bilinski, 1968; (poems) Die veränderte Welt, 1967; Aschengewollte Schrift, 1971; Leben nur von Tod zu Tod, 1974; (radio plays) Der grosse Sturm, 1970; Sackgasse, 1973; Die Chance, 1974; (prose) Auf den Wegen Wiens, 1974. Contbr. to: Die Furche; Offenes Wort; Neue Wege; Morgen; Literatur aus Osterreich; etc.; also Austrian Radio. Mbrships: Comm. mbr., PEN, Austrian br. & Austrian Authors' Union. Hons: Award, Vienna Art Fndn., 1959; Theodor Körner Prize for Lit., 1962 & 1969; Lit. Award of Vienna, 1969. Address: Bernoullistr. 4/18, A-1222 Wien, Austria.

JORDAN, Stello, b. 17 Dec. 1914, NYC, USA. Communications Consultant; Real Estate & Investments Manager. Educ: CCNY, 1932-34; Dips., Columbia & N.Y. Univs., Queens' Coll. Publs: Ed.-in-Chief, Handbook of Technical Writing Practices, 2 vols., 1971. Contbr. to: Jrnl. Tech. Writing & Communication (Ed. Bd. Mbr.); var. engrng. & tech. communication jrnls. Mbrships. incl: Soc. Tech. Communication, Nat. Pres. 1964-65; Charter Mbr., Soc. Logistics Engrs.; Inst. of Real Estate Mgmt. Hons: Fellow, Soc. Tech. Communication, 1973. Address: 87-15 204th Street, Hollis, Queens, N.Y., NY, USA.

JORDAN, William (Bill), b. 4 Jan. 1941, Dublin, Repub. of Ireland. University Lecturer in Social Work. Educ: M.A., Christ Church, Oxford Univ.; Cert. Soc. Work, Exeter Univ. Publs: Client-Worker Transactions, 1970; The Social Worker in Family Situations, 1972; Paupers: The Making of the New Claiming Class, 1973; Poor Parents: Social Policy & the 'Cycle of Deprivation', 1974. Contbr. to: The Guardian; New Society; Soc. Work. Today. Mbr., Newton Abbot Claimants Union (Treas.). Address: 8 Knowles Hill Rd., Newton Abbot, Devon, UK.

JORDAN, Zbigniew Antoni, b. 23 July 1911, Golaszyn, Poland. Professor of Philosophy of Social Science. Educ: M.A., Univ. of Poznan, 1934; Ph.D., 1936. Publs: Mathematical Foundations of Plato's System (in Polish), 1937; The Development of Mathematical Logic & Logical Positivism in Poland Between the Two Wars, 1945, 1967; Philosophy & Ideology, 1963; Evolution of Dialectical Materialism, 1967; Karl Marx: Economy Class & Social Revolution, 1971, 1972. Contbr. to: Studia Logica; Notre Dame Jrnl. of Formal Logic; Ency. of Philos.; Marxism Communism & Western Society: A Comparative Ency.; Studies in Soviet Thought; Slavic Review. Address: Dept. of Sociol. & Anthropol., Carleton Univ., Ottawa, Ont., Can.

JORGENSEN, Mary Venn, pen name ADRIAN, Mary, b. 13 May 1908, Sewickley, PA., USA. Writer. Educ: pvte. study w. Prof. Millican, N.Y. Univ. Publs: 32 books for juvenile readers on nature, conservations & ecol., 1950-74. Contbr. to: Boys' Life; Farm Jrnl.; Jack & Jill; Grade Tchr.; Boston Post (nature columnist, for 2½ yrs.). Mbrships: Nat. Mbr., Audubon Soc.; Nat. & Int. Wildlife Fedns. Recip., The North American Bighorn Sheep selected one of best publd. in 1966, ALA. Address: 100 S.W. Vista Ave., Apt. 817, Portland, OR 97205, USA.

JOSEPH, Michael Kennedy, b. 9 July 1914, Chingford, Essex, UK. Professor of English; Author; Poet. Educ: B.A., 1933, M.A., 1934, Auckland Univ. Coll.; B.A., 1938, B.Litt., 1939. M.A., 1945, Merton Coll., Oxford, UK. Publs: (verse) Imaginary Islands, 1950; The Living Countries, 1959; Inscription on a Paper Dart, 1974; (novels) I'll Soldier No More, 1958; A Pound of Saffron, 1962; The Hole in the Zero, 1967. Mbrships: Aust. Univ. Lang. & Lit. Assn.; PEN (NZ). Hons: Hubert Church Prose Award, 1958; Jessie Mackay Poetry Award, 1959. Address: c/o English Dept., Univ. of Auckland, Private Bag, Auckland, NZ.

JOSEPH, Roger, b. 26 May 1908, Seattle, Wash. D.C., USA. Journalist. Educ: B.A., Univ. of Wash.; M.A., Univ. of S. Calif. Drama, Music Reviewer, Nevada State Jrnl., Reno Evening Gazette & contbr. to jrnls.; Entertainment Columnist. Address: 373 W. Arroyo St., Reno, NV 89502, USA.

JOSEY, Alex, b. 1910, Poole, UK. Journalist; Writer. Publs: Accident, 1939; Trade Unionism in Malaya, 1954; Socialism in Asia, 1957; Labour Laws in a changing Singapore, 1968; The Crucial Years Ahead, Republic of Singapore General Elections, 1968; Race Walking, 1968; Lee Kuan Yew, 1968; Golf in Singapore, 1969; Singapore General Elections, 1972, 1972; The Trial of Sunny Ang, 1973; Asia Pacific Socialism, 1973; The Struggle for Singapore, 1974. Mbr., Singapore Nat. Union of Jrnlsts. Address: 904 Cathay Apts., 20 Mt. Sophia, Singapore 9, Repub. of Singapore.

JOSIPOVICI, Gabriel, b. 1940, Nice, France. University Lecturer & Reader; Author. Educ: St. Edmund Hall, Oxford, UK. Publs: The Inventory, 1968; Words, 1971; The World & the Book, 1971; Mobius the Stripper: Stories & Short Plays, 1974; The Present, 1975; (plays) Evidence of Intimacy, 1972; Dreams of Mrs. Fraser, 1972; Flow, 1973; Echo, 1974. Contbr. to: Encounter; London Mag.; Transatlantic Review; Adam Int. Review; Critical Quarterly; Times Lit. Supplement. Agent: John Johnson. Address: 60 Prince Edwards Rd., Lewes, Sussex, UK.

JOUDRY, Patricia, b. 18 Oct. 1921, Spirit River, Alta., Can. Playwright. Publs: incl: (plays) The Sand Castle; Three Rings for Michele; Walk Alone Together; Semi-Detached; Valerie; The Man With the Perfect Wife; God Goes Heathen; Think Again, 1969; Now, 1970; I Ching, 1971; (novel) The Dweller On the Threshold, 1973; (non-fiction) And the Children Played, 1975; also radio & TV scripts. Mbr., Authors' League of Am. Hons: Best Play Award, Dom. Drama Festival, 1956; Prize Winner, Stratford-Globe Playwriting Competition; 1st Prize Winner, Nat. Playwriting

Seminar, London, Ont., Can. Address: Ste. Agnes de Dundee, Chateauguay Valley, Quebec, Canada.

JOUHANDEAU, Marcel Henri. Publs. incl: Marcel & e; Life of St. Philippe Neri; L'Eternel Proces; Les Argonautes. Address: 14 rue de Cal. Marchand, Paris XVIe, France.

JOUVE, Pierre Jean, b. 1887, Arras, France. Publs: Oeuvres Poétiques, I, II, III, IV; (novels) Paulina 1880; Le Monde Desert; Adventure de Catherine Crachet; La Scène Capitale; Le Don Juan de Mozart; Wozzeck. Address: 7 rue Antoine-Chantin, Paris XIVe, France.

JOVANOVSKI, Meto, b. 5 Oct. 1928, Brajčino, Macedonia, Yugoslavia. Journalist. Publs: Luman Aramijata, 1961; Zemja i Tegdba, 1964; Slana Vo Cutot Na Bademite, 1965; Svedoci, 1970; Budaletinki, 1973; several collects. of short stories. Contbr. to: Sovremenost; Razgledi; Knjzevne Novine; Politika. Mbrships: Sec., Macedonian PEN Ctr., Yugoslavia. Address: Partenij Zografski 51, 91 000 Skopje, Yugoslavia.

JOY, Edward Thomas, b. 27 Sept. 1909, London, UK. Lecturer in History, University of London; Curator, Ickworth (National Trust), Suffolk. Educ: M.A. & B.Sc.(Econ.), Univ. of London. Publs: English Furniture A.D. 43-1950, 1962; Country Life Book of English Furniture, 1964, 3rd ed. 1968; The Woodwork of Winchester Cathedral, 1964; Country Life Book of Clocks, 1967, 3rd ed. 1968; Country Life Book of Chairs, 1967, 2nd ed. 1968; Chippendale 1971; Furniture, 1972; English Antique Furniture, 1973. Contbr. to: Apollo; The Connoisseur; Country Life; Harper's Bazaar; Burlington Mag.; Furniture Hist.; Antique Collector; Antique Finder; Antiques. Address: The Rotunda, Ickworth, Bury St. Edmunds, Suffolk, IP29 5QE, UK.

JOYCE, James Avery, b. London, UK. Barrister-at-Law; University Professor; UN Consultant & former I.L.O. Official. Educ: London Schl. Econs.; Geneva Schl. of Int. Studies, Switz.; Inner Temple; LL.D.; Ph.D.; B.Sc.(Econs.). Publs. incl: World Organisation, 1945; Revolution on East River: World in the Making, 1953; Justice at Work, 1952; Red Cross International 1959; Capital Punishment: A World View, 1962; Target for Tomorrow, 1962; The Story of International Co-operation, 1964; World of Promise, 1965; Labour Faces the New Age, 1965; Decade of Development, 1965; End of an Illusion, 1968; Broken Star: Story of the League of Nations, 1970; Jobs Versus People, 1974; Ed., Population Documents, 4 vols. 1975. Contbr. to: Discovery: Contemporary Review; Brit. Weekly.; Saturday Review; Nation. Address: 7 rue de Courvoisier, Versoix, 1290 Geneva, Switz.

JOYCE, Michael, b. 10 July 1903, Saltburn-on-Sea, Yorks., UK. Bank Official. Educ: 2nd Mate's Cert., Bd. of Trade. Publs: Plato's Symposium, or The Drinking Party, 1935, 1938, 1961; Peregrine Pieram, 1936; Ordeal at Lucknow: The Defence of the Residency, 1938; My Friend H: John Cam Hobhouse, 1948; Edinburgh: The Golden Age, 1951; Edward Gibbon, 1953; Samuel Johnson, 1955. Contbr. to: London Mercury; Life & Letters; Contemporary Review; etc. Address: 68 Cornwall Gdns., London SW7, UK.

JUDAH, J(ay) Stillson, b. 7 July 1911, Leavenworth, Wash., USA. Librarian; Professor of History of Religions. Educ: A.B., Univ. of Wash., 1934; Cert. in Lib. Sci., Univ. of Calif., 1941; grad. work, Germanic & Indic langs., ibid, 1937-40, & 1946-50, & Japanese, Univ. of Colo., Navy Lang. Schl., 1944-45. Publs: Index to Religious Periodical Literature, 1949-52 (compiler & ed.), 1952; The History & Philosophy of the Metaphysical Movements in America, 1967; Hare Krishna & the Counterculture, 1974. Contbr., relig. jrnls. Mbr., sev. lib. assns. Recip., acad. hons. Address: 818 Oxford St., Berkeley, CA 94707, USA.

JUDD, Denis. b. 1938, Byfield, Northants., UK. Joint Head of History, Polytechnic of North London. Educ: B.A., Univ. of Oxford; Ph.D., Univ. of London. Publs: Balfour & the British Empire, 1968; The Victorian Empire, 1970; Posters of World War Two, 1972; The British Raj, 1972; Livingstone in Africa, 1973; George V, 1973; Someone has Blundered, 1973; The House of Windsor, 1973; The Crimean War, 1975; Edward VII, 1975; Eclipse of Kings, 1975. Contbr. to: Sunday Telegraph; Fin. Times; Daily Telegraph; New Statesman; BBC. Mbrships: Histl. Assn.; Assn. of Tchrs. in Tech. Instns. Agent: David

Highams & Assocs. Address: 20 Mt. Pleasant Rd., London NW10 3EL, UK.

JUDD, Frederick Charles, pen name LESTER-RANDS, A., b. 5 June 1914, S. Woodford, London, UK. Electronics & Audio Engineer; Technical Writer. Publs: Radio Control., 1954, revised ed., 1962; Electronic Music & Musique Concrete, 1961; Tape Recording for Everyone, 1961; Electronics Hobbies, 1962; Circuits for Audio, 1967; Electronics in Music, 1973. Contbr. over 1000 articles to tech. jrnls., now exclusive to Audio Mag. (Tech. Ed.). Mbrships: Fellow, Inst. of Sci. & Tech. Communicators; Inst. of Acoustics; Assoc., Inst. of Electronics. Recip., Norman Keith Adams Prize for Tech. Jrnlsm., Radio Soc. of GB, 1960. Address: 174 Maybank Rd., S. Woodford, London E18, UK.

JUDONG, Léo, b. 30 Nov. 1928, Hees, Belgium. Clerk; Writer. Educ: classical studies. Publs: Horizons Nouveaux (essay), 1972. Mbrships: Soc. des Gens de Lettres de France; Syndicat des jrnlsts. & écrivains; Acad. Int. de Lutèce. Recip., Silver Medal, Acad. Int. de Lutèce. Address: Place de la Gare 6, 4110 Flémalle-Haute, Belgium.

JUERGENSEN, Hans Peter, b. 21 Mar. 1930, Warder, W. Germany. Journalist. Educ: Degree in Econs.; studied LAw & Econs., Univs. of Hamburg & Bonn. Publ: So nutzt man den Wirtschaftsteil einer Tageszeitung (co-author), 1971. Contbr. to: Frankfurter Allgemeine Zeitung. Address: 157 Lake Dr., Mountain Lakes, NJ 07046, USA.

JULIUSSON, Stefan, b. 25 Sept. 1915, Hafnarfjordur, Iceland. State Inspector of Public Libraries. Educ: B.A., Carleton Coll., Northfield, Minn., USA, 1953; further studies, Cornell Univ., Ithaca, N.Y., & Univ. of Iceland, Reykjavík. Publs. incl: (novels) Westward Bound, 1950; Market Place, 1957; Twenty Four Hours, 1960; Indian Summer, 1963; Confirmation in the Autumn, 1973; (autobiog. sketches) The Huts in the Lavafield, 1972; also 9 juvenile books, 1938-69. Contbr. to var. mags. & newspapers. Mbrships. incl: Writers' Assn. of Iceland; former MP. Hons. incl: State Lit. Salary; var. prizes, Writers' & Radio Writers' Funds. Address: Brekkugata 22, Hafnarfjordur, Iceland.

JULLIG, Karl Hans, pen name GANGOLF, b. 17 Dec. 1888, Vienna, Austria. Writer; Musician. Educ: State Exam. Music. Publs. incl: plays, lyrics, novels, short stories, essays, radio plays incl. Die Gefoppten, 1949; Mozarts Tentenfass, 1952; (film) Hugo Wolf, 1964; Ghorsamster Diener Herr von Hanslick, 1966; (mystery play) Derstahlkönig, 1968; 16 Grünejahre; Die Herrgottspieler u. die Ketzer, 1971; Die Holzknechtbibel, 1973-75. Contbr. to: Unser Schaffen; Wiener Zeitung. Mbrships. incl: PEN; Austrian Writers' Assn. Hons: Prize for Advancement of Art, 1958; Theodor Körner Prize, 1959. Address: A1020 Vienna, Schreygasse 6/9, Austria.

JUNCEDA, Luis, b. 18 Mar. 1923, Luarca, Spain. Civil Servant. Educ: Commercial Trng. Publs: (humorous novels) La llaga, 1960; Cuadernos de un Sacristán, 1964; El oro y el Moro, 1970. Contbr. to: La Nueva España; Región, Oviedo. Hons: Spanish Rdrs'. Digest Prize, 1964; Cuidad de Murcia Prize, 1969. Address: Calle de Ricardo Ortiz 6, 4º1ª, Madrid 17, Spain.

JUNEJO, Abdul Jabbar, b. 26 Nov. 1935, Badin, Sind, Pakistan. Teacher. Educ: B.A., Sind Univ., 1960; M.A., 1962; Ph.D., 1974; Dip., Chinese, Peking, 1966. Publs: Kanzul Latif, 1961; Mao-je-mulk men, 1973; History of Sindhi Literature, 1973. Contbr. to local mags. Hons: Gold Medal at M.A. Degree, 1962; Sindhology Prize, 1974. Address: Dept. of Sindhi, Univ. of Sind, Jamshoro, Pakistan.

JUNEJO, Abdul Qadir, b. 1 Nov. 1945, Janhan, Tharparkar, Pakistan. School Headmaster; Writer. Educ: B.A., B.E., Sind Univ. Author, Ways, Nights & Loafers, 1973. Contbr. to monthly mags: Sohni; Sojhro; Indlath; Rooh Rehan. Mbr., Bd. Dirs., Sindhi Writers' Coop. Soc. Ltd. Address: Janhan, P.O. Fazl Bhambhro, Distt. Tharparkar, Sind, Pakistan.

JUNGER, Ernst, b. 29 Mar. 1895, Heidelberg, Germany. Writer. Publs. incl: In Stahlgewittern, 1920; Atlantische Fahrt, 1948; Heliopolis, 1949; Der Waldgang, 1951; Das Sanduhrbuch, 1954; Rivarol, 1956; Sgraffiti, 1960; Collected Works, 1960-65; Sturm, 1963; Im Granit, 1967; Ad Hoc, 1970; Annäherungen, Drogen & Rausch, 1970; Sinn u. Bedeutung, ein Figurenspiel, 1971; Philemon u.

Baucis, 1972; Die Zwille, 1973. Hons: Lit. Award, Bremen, 1956; Goslar Award, 1956; Grand Cross of Merit, 1959; Immermann Award, 1965; Freiherr vom Stein Gold Medal, 1970. Address: 7941 Wilflingen über Riedlingen, Wurtt, W. Germany.

JUNGK, Robert. Writer; University Professor. Educ: Ph.D., Univ. of Zurich, 1944; Honorarprofessor, Tech. Univ., W. Berlin, 1970—. Publs. incl: Tomorrow is Already Here, 1954; Brighter Than a Thousand Suns, 1958; Children of the Ashes, 1960; The Big Machine, 1968; Project Everyman, 1975. Mbrships: PEN, W. Germany; Bd., World Future Rsch. Assn., Paris; Hon. Pres., Manking 2000, Brussels. Hons: Hachette Prize, 1958; J. Drexel Prize, Nuremberg, 1959; Prize of the Resistance, Liege, 1961; Wilhelm Bölsche Golden Medal, Stuttgart, 1970. Address: Steingasse 31, A 5020 Salzburg, Austria.

JUTA, (Constance) Marjorie, b. 21 June 1901, Cape Town, S. Africa. Lecturer; Broadcaster; Book Reviewer. Publs: The Pace of the Ox, 1937, transls. into Dutch, German & Swedish, 1938, publd. as play Die President, 1939; I Was Lucky to Escape, 1940; Boundless Privilege, 1974. Contbr. to: The Listener, UK; Perspective, UK; Fair Lady, S. Africa. Address: Pear Tree, 37 Waterloo Rd., Wynberg, Cape, S. Africa.

JYLHÄ, Heikki, b. 21 May 1903, Maynard, Mass., USA. Editor; Author. Educ: Soc. Univ., Helsinki. Publs: Askelten kirja (poem), 1934; Delawaren pojat (novel), 1938; Ikiliikkuja (novel), 1945; Yhdeksän meren takana (poem), 1945; Portilla (for young people), 1957; Birgitta Birgerintytär (drama), 1965. Contbr. to: anthols. & books inclng. Tässä pisteessä, 1971; mags. Mbrships. incl: Author's Union of Finland; Newspapermen's Union of Finland. Recip., Uuno Kailas Prize, 1934. Address: 40950 Muurame kp. 5, Finland.

K

KABAT, Elvin Abraham, b. 1 Sept. 1914, NYC, USA. University Professor; Author. Educ: B.S., CCNY, 1932; A.M., 1934, Ph.D., 1937, Columbia Univ. Publs: Experimental Immunochemistry (w. M. Mayer & Chas. C. Thomas), 1948, 2nd ed., 1961; Blood Group Substances: Their Chemistry & Immunochemistry, 1956; Structural Concepts in Immunology & Immuno-chemistry, 1968. Contbr. of over 250 articles to var. sci. & med. jrnls. Address: 70 Haven Ave., N.Y., NY 10032, USA.

KABDEBÓ, Lóránt, b. 9 Aug. 1936, Budapest, Hungary. Literary Historian, Section Head at Petofi Literary Museum; Literary Critic. Educ: D.Litt. Publs: Biography of G. Dayka, 1969; Biography of L. Szabo, 1970, 2nd vol., 1971. Contbr. to: Napjaink (Ed. criticism); etc. Mbrships: Union Hungarian Writers; Assn. Hungarian Jrnlsts. Recip., Miskolc Lit. Prize, 1969. Address: 1146 Budapest, Dózsa György u. 19, I. 2/a, Hungary.

KABDEBO, Thomas George, b. 5 Feb. 1934, Budapest, Hungary. Librarian. Educ: B.A. (Cardiff); M.Phil.; Dip. Lib.; A.L.A. (London). Publs: Gemau Hwngaria, 1962; Attila József (poems), 1966; Gyula Illyés, Selected Poems, 1970; A Tribute to Gyula Illyés, 1968; Érettségi, 1971; Two-hearted, 1973; Magyar Odisszeuszok, 1974. Contbr. to profl. jrnls. Mbr., PEN. Hons: Winner, Short Story Contest, 1952. Address: 61 Gowan Ave., London SW6, UK.

KACHINGWE, Aubrey, b. 27 Nov. 1926, Blantyre, Malawi. Journalist; Writer; Businessman. Educ: Dip. in Jrnlsm., UK. Publs: No Easy Task, 1965. Contbr. to: African Artists (USA); BBC; Deutsch Velle (Voice of Germany); S. African & E. African mags., etc. Mbrships: Ex-Dpty.-Chmn., Rotary Club of Blantyre; Chmbr. of Comm. & Ind. of Malawi. Address: P.O. Box 729, Blantyre, Malawi.

KADAI, Heino Olavi, b. 20 Aug. 1931, Tartu, Estonia. Church Historian; Professor of Church History. Educ: B.A.,

Columbia Univ., USA, 1953; B.Th., 1958, M.Div., M.S.T., 1960, Th.D., 1969, Concordia Sem., St. Louis. Publs: Accents in Luther's Theology, 1967; Guide to Reformation Literature (w. L. W. Spitz), 1967. Contbr. to The Springfielder theol. jrnl. Address: Concordia Theol. Sem., Concordia Ct., Springfield, IL 62702, USA.

KAEL, Pauline, b. 1919, Sonoma Co., Calif., USA. Movie Critic. Educ: Univ. of Calif., Berkeley. Publs: I Lost it at the Movies, 1965; Kiss Kiss Bang Bang, 1968; Going Steady, 1970; Deeper Into Movies, 1973. Contbr. to The Citizen Kane Book, 1971. Hons. incl: LL.D., Georgetown Univ., 1972; Nat. Book Award (for Deeper Into Movies), 1973; D.Litt., Smith Coll., 1973; L.H.D., Kalamazoo Coll., 1973; Front Page Award, for best mag. column, Newswomen's Club of NY, 1974. Address: c/o The New Yorker, 25 W. 43rd St., N.Y., NY 10036, USA.

KAELBLING, Rudolf, b. 19 July 1928, Ulm, Germany. Professor of Psychiatry. Educ: M.D., Eberhard-Karls Univ., Tübingen, Germany, & Univ. of Zürich Coll. of Med., Switz., 1954; M.Sc. in psych., Ohio State Univ., Columbia, USA. 1959. Publs: Eclectic Psychiatry (w. R. M. Patterson), 1966. Contbr. of num. sci. articles to profl. publs: Address: Ohio State Univ. Hospitals, Dept. of Psych., 410 West 10th Ave., Columbus, OH 43210, USA.

KAELIN, Eugene Francis, b. 14 Oct. 1926, St. Louis, Mo., USA. Educator; Professor of Philosophy. Educ: A.B. 1949, M.A. 1950, Univ. of Mo.; Dip. d'Études Supérieures, Univ. of Bordeaux, France, 1951; Ph.D., Univ. of Ill., USA, 1954. Publs: An Existentialist Aesthetic, 1962; Art & Existence, 1970. Contbr. to: Arts in Society; Jrnl. Aesthetic Educ. Mbrships: AAUP; Am. Philosl. Assn.; Am. Soc. for Aesthetics; Soc. for Phenomenol. & Existential Philos.; Fla. Philosl. Assn. Recip., Rsch. Fellowship, Albert-Ludwigs Univ., Freiburg-im-Breisgau, W. Germany, 1964-65. Address: 604 Hillcrest St., Tallahassee, FL 32303, USA.

KAHLER, Woodland (Marquis of St. Innocent), b. 6 Feb. 1895, Dallas, Tex., USA. Writer. Educ: B.A., Yale Univ. Publs: Early to Bed; Smart; Setback; False Front; Giant Dwarf; Portrait in Laughter; The Almighty Possibility; Cravings of Desire. Contbr. to: Scribner's Mag.; World Forum. Mbrships. incl: Pres., Int. Vegetarian Union, London, UK; World League for Protection of Animals, London; Anti-Vivisection Soc., London; Beauty Without Cruelty, London; VP, Friends of Buddhism, Paris, France; Pres., Coun. of World Govt., The Hague, Netherlands. Hons. incl: Dr.'s Degree, Coll. of Applied Sci., London, UK. Chevalier de l'Ordre du Mérite, France. Address: 208 Australian Ave., Palm Beach, FL 33480, USA.

KAHN, Jack Harold, b. 2 Mar. 1904, Huddersfield, UK. Consultant Psychiatrist. Educ: M.B., Ch.B., 1928, M.D., 1948, Leeds Univ. Publs: Unwillingly to School (w. Mrs. Nursten), 1964; Human Growth & Development of Personality, 1965; The Group Process as a Helping Technique (w. Mrs. Thompson), 1970; Job's Illness: Loss, Grief & Integration, 1975. Contbr. to profl. psych. & soc. work jrnls. Mbrships: Fellow, Royal Coll. Psychs.; Fellow, Royal Soc. Med. Address: Lower Elm Lodge, Elm Row, London NW3 1AA, UK.

KAHN, Robert Irving, b. 12 Dec. 1910, Des Moines, Iowa, USA. Rabbi. Educ: B.A., Univ. of Cinn.; D.H.L., Hebrew Union Coll., Jewish Inst. of Relig. Publs: Lessons for Life, 1963; Ten Commandments for Today, 1965; The Letter & the Spirit, 1972. Contbr. to: Houston Chronicle. Mbrships. incl: Pres., Ctrl. Conf. Am. Rabbis; Nat. Chap., Am. Legion, 1959; Past Pres., B'nai B'rith; Pres., Houston Rotary Club. Hons. incl: Geo. Wash Medal, Freedoms Fndn.; Prime Minister's Medal, Govt. of Israel; Silver Beaver, Boy Scouts of Am.; Masonic Order w. 33rd Degree. Address: 1500 Sunset Boulevard, Houston, TX 77005, USA.

KAHN, Yitzhak, b. 1908, Ostrolenka, Poland. Author; Journalist; Lecturer. Publs: Spark & Flames, 1964; At the Crossroads, 1971; Literary & Theatre Criticisms & Essays. Contbr. to: Zukunft; Unzer Tsait; Unser Gedank; Dorem Africa; Goldene Keit; Letzte Nayes; Forays. Mbrships: Jewish Cultural Ctr. & Nat. Lib.; Aust. Soc. Authors. Hons: Wajzlitz — Cimerman Prize, Best Yiddish Book, 1971; Fellowship Aust. Govt., 1974. Address: 7/42 Wilgah St. E., St. Kilda, Melbourne, Australia.

KAHN-FREUND, Otto, b. 17 Nov. 1900, Franfurt am Main, Germany. Professor Emeritus; Barrister. Educ:

Dr.jur., Frankfurt; LL.M., London, UK; M.A., Oxford. Publs: The Growth in Internationalism in English Private International Law, 1960; Labour and the Law, 1972; co-Ed., Conflict of Laws (Dire & Morris), 9th ed., 1973. Contbr. to: Mod. Law Review; Law Quarterly Review; etc. Mbrships: Hon. Bencher, Middle Temple; Past Pres., Int. Soc. of Labour Law & Soc. Legislation; Assoc., Inst. of Int. Law. Hons: Dr.jur., Bonn, Brussels, Leuven, Paris & Stockholm; LL.D., Leicester. Address: Roundabouts, Shottermill, Haslemere, Surrey, UK.

KAIKO, Takeshi, b. 30 Dec. 1930, Osaka, Japan. Novelist. Educ: Grad., Osaka Ichiritsu Univ. Publs: Blue Monday, 1967; Shining Darkness, 1968; Darkness in Summer, 1972. Contbr. to: most major newspapers, weekly mags. & lit. mags. of Japan. Mbrships: PEN; Japan Writer's Assn. Hons: Akutagawa Prize, 1957; Mainichi Shuppan Bunka Prize, 1968. Address: 4-8-14 Igusa Suginami-Ku, Tokyo, Japan.

KAIL, Owen Cooke, b. 28 Apr. 1922, Bombay, India. Administrative Executive in Engineering. Educ: B.A., Ph.D. Publs: The Hill Station of Matheran, 1948; Dutch Commercial & Territorial Influence in India, 1970; Buddhist Cave Temples of India, forthcoming. Contbr. to: Jrnl. Asiatic Soc. Bombay; Our Sunday Visitor (Ind.); Times India; Illustrated Wkly. India; Mirror; Sunday Standard; Bharat Jyoti. Mbrships: Asiatic Soc. Bombay (Life Mbr.); Fellow, Royal Asiatic Soc. Gr. Brit. Address: Pushpa Vihar 1, 159 Colaba Rd., Bombay 400005, India.

KAIN, Richard Morgan, b. 19 Dec. 1908, York, Pa., USA. Professor of English. Educ: A.B., Swarthmore Coll.; M.A., Ph.D., Univ. of Chgo. Publs: Fabulous Voyager: James Joyce's Ulysses, 1947, rev., 1959; Joyce: The Man, The Work, The Reputation (w. M. Magalaner), 1956; Dublin in the Age of William Butler Yeats & James Joyce, 1962; The Workshop of Daedalus (w. R. Scholes), 1965; Susan L. Mitchell, 1972. Contbr. to var. vols. on mod. lit.; Mass. Review; Southern Review; James Joyce Quarterly; Mod. Fiction Studies; etc. Mbrships. incl: MLA; James Joyce Fndn.; James Joyce Soc. Recip., num. scholastic hons. Address: 564 Sunset Rd., Louisville, KY, USA.

KAIPAINEN, Anu Helina, b. 14 Mar. 1933, Muolaa, Finland. Author. Educ: F.M. Publs: 9 books in Finnish, inclng: Utuiset neulat, 1960; Ruusubaletti, 1965; Magdaleena ja maailman lapset, 1969. Mbrships: Writers Union of Finland; Play Writers Union of Finland; Finnish PEN. Hons: State Prize, 1967; Thanks for a Book Medal, 1967; State Prize, 1970. Address: Kasavuorentie 5B, 02700 Kauniaien, Finland.

KAISER, Ward Louis, b. 1 July 1923, Kitchener, Ont., Can. Church Official, National Council of Churches, USA. Educ: B.A., Univ. Western Ont., 1945; M.Div., Union Theol. Sem., N.Y., 1949; Emmanuel Coll., Toronto; Univs. Rutgers & Columbia. Publs. incl: Study-Action Manual on Canada, 1966; The Challenge of a Closer Moon, 1969; Intersection: Teacher's Manual, 1969; Intersection: Where School & Faith Meet, 1969; You & the Nation's Priorities (w. Charles P. Lutz), 1972. Contbr. to num. acad. relig. & secular periodicals in USA, Can. & France, more than 1000 articles. Mbrships. incl: Nat. Coun., Boy Scouts Am. (Mbr. at large). Recip., Waterloo Lutheran Univ. Award, Citation of the Yr., 1968 for servs. to educ., Can. & church. Address: 251 Diane Place, Paramus, NJ 07652, USA.

KALATHIL, Varghese, b. 31 May 1918, Thalavady, Alleppey District, India. Editor. Educ: Union Christian Coll., Alwaye; Madras Univ.; Mahraja's Coll., Trivandrum; M.A., Univ. of Travancore. Publs: Transl., Confucius, Analects; Transl., Earth & Space (U.S. Info. Serv.); Footprints of Knowledge, 1974. Contbr. to: Malayala Manorama (special Ed. 1950-55, Ed. of weekly, 1956-); Ed., Diamond Jubilee Souvenir Malayala Manorama (newspaper), 1950. Mbr., Sahitya Pravarthaka Sangam (lit. co-op.) Address: P.B. 26, Kottayam, Kerala, India.

KALICHMAN, Claire, pen name CALLIAN, Selma, b. 17 Mar. 1944, St. Gervais les Bains, France. Painter; Poet. Educ: Sorbonne Univ., Paris, 1965. Publs: L'Arpége Chimérique, 1967. Mbrships: Arts, Sciences et Lettres, Paris; Assn. des Ecrivains Belges de Langue Française. Recip., Silver Medal, Arts, Sciences et Lettres, Paris, 1970. Address: Rozemarijnstraat 24, 9000 Gent, Belgium.

KALLENBACH, W(illiam) Warren, b. 16 July 1926, Eugene, Mo., USA. Professor; Educational Research & Development Specialist. Educ: A.B., Drury Coll., 1949;

M.A., 1953, Ed.D., 1959, Stanford Univ. Publs: Education & Society, 1963; Measuring Teacher Competence: Research Backgrounds & Current Practices, 1965; The Role of the Teacher: Six Areas of Teacher Competence, 1971; Instrument for the Observation of Teaching Activities, 1972. Contbr. to educl. jrnls. Mbr., var. educl. & psychol. soc. Address: 1232 Harriet St., Palo Alto, CA 94301, USA.

KALLICH, Martin, Irvin, b. 19 Jan. 1918, Brooklyn, N.Y., USA. University Professor; Author. Educ: B.S.S., CCNY, 1938; Ph.D., Johns Hopkins Univ., 1945. Publs: The Psychological Milieu of Lytton Strachey, 1962; The American Revolution Through British Eyes, 1962; Heaven's First Law: Rhetoric & Order in Pope's Essay on Man, 1967; The Other End of the Egg: Religious Satire in Gulliver's Travels, 1970; The Association of Ideas & 18th Century Critical Theory, 1970. Contbr. to: Jrnl. of Aesthetics & Art Criticism; Tenn. Studies in Lit.; Mod. Lang. Quarterly; Studies in Burke; etc. Mbrships: MLA; Johnson Soc.; ASECS. Address: 303 Gayle Ave., DeKalb, IL 60115, USA.

KALTOVICH, Edith Lucia Rusconi, b. 13 Dec. 1925, Cordoba, Argentina. Professor; Writer; Translator. Educ: Univ. Nacional de Cordoba; M.A., Mt. Holyoke Coll., Mass., USA; Trenton State Coll.; N.Y. Univ. Publs: Romances to the Argentine Children (trnals. Dr. Alfredo Vallini), 1974; Collect Telegrams — Poems of Urgency (transl., Manuel Rueda Mediavilla), 1974. Contbr. to num. US, for. poetry & profl. jrnls. Mbrships. incl: Am. Poets Fellowship Soc.; Soc. of Children's Book Writers, Calif.; Mod. Poetry in Translation Ltd., London; Soc. Argentina de Escritores, Cordoba. Hons. incl: Appreciation Award & Trophy, 2nd World Cong. of Poets, Taipei, Taiwan, 1973; Awards, Am. Poetry Fellowship Soc., 1968-73; H.L.D., Free Univ. of Pakistan. Address: 351 East 4th St., Florence, NJ 08518, USA.

KAMEN, Kalchev, b. 31 July 1914, Kereca, Bulgaria. Writer. Publs: (in Bulgarian) The Family of Weavers, 1956-60; At Life's Source, 1962; In the new town Together, 1964; In April, 1966; Seeking My Future, 1970; Masks, 1971; Carrying the Fire, 1972; Fiery Summer, 1973; Sofia Stories, 1967. Contbr. to: September; Plamuk; Noviy Mir; New German Lit; Tvorba; Kortars; Druzhba Narodov; SAvremennik. Mbrships: Dpty. Chmn., Union of Bulgarian Writers. Hons: Dimitrov Prize, 1950; People's Cultural Worker, 1971; Ivan Vazov Prize, 1973; Hero of Socialist Labour, 1974. Address: Sofia, ul. Lyuben Karavelov, 11, Bulgaria.

KAMM, Jacob Oswald, b. 29 Nov. 1918, Cleveland, Ohio, USA. Economist. Educ: A.B., Baldwin-Wallace Coll., 1940; M.A., Brown Univ., 1942; Ph.D., Ohio State Univ., 1948. Publs. incl: Decentralization of Securities Exchanges, 1942; Making Profits in the Stock Market, 1952, 3 rev. eds.; Investors Handbook, 1954. Contbr. to profl. jrnls.; Columnist, The Plain Dealer, 1964-68; Contbng. Ed., Webster's New World Dictionary. Address: Rte. 1, Huron, OH 44839, USA.

KAMM, Josephine Mary, b. 1906, London, UK. Author. Publs: Daughter of the Desert: A Biography of Gertrude Bell, 1956; How Different from Us: A Biography of Miss Buss & Miss Beale, 1958; Hope Deferred: Girls' Education In English History, 1965; Rapiers & Battleaxes: the Women's Movement & its Aftermath, 1966; Indicative Past: a Hundred Years of the Girls' Public Day School Trust, 1971; also 22 books for young people. Mbrships. incl: Soc. of Authors; Engl. Ctr., PEN (past Exec. Comm. Mbr.); Nat. Book League (past Exec. & Nat. Coun. Mbr.). Recip., Isaac Siegel Mem. Jvnle. Award, 1963. Address: 39/67 Elm Park Gdns., London SW10 9QE, UK.

KAMPELMAN, Max M., b. 7 Nov. 1920, NYC, USA. Attorney. Educ: A.B., 1940, J.D., 1945, N.Y. Univ.; M.A., 1946, Ph.D., 1951, Univ. Minn. Publs: The Communist Party vs. the C.I.O.: A Study in Power Politics, 1957; The Strategy of Deception, 1963; Interpreting the Labour Movement, 1954. Contbr. to: World Affairs; George Washington Law Review; Columbia Jrnlsm. Review; Annals Am. Acad. Pol. & Social Sci.; Am. Perspective; Am. Jrnl. Int. Law; Minn. Review. Mbrships: Am. Bar Assn.; Fed. Bar Assn.; Dist. Columbia Bar Assn. (Comm. on Legal Ethics & Grievances, 1966-72, Comm. on Police Rels., Chmn. 1969-71); Am. Pol. Sci. Assn. (Dist. Columbia Pres. 1955, Treas. 1956-68). Address: 600 New Hampshire Ave. N.W., Wash. DC 20037, USA.

KAMPF, Harold, b. 8 Oct. 1916, Nairobi, Kenya. Personnel Manager; Solicitor; Farmer. Educ: M.A., Oxford Univ. Publs: The Man in My Chair, 1948; My Brother, O My Brother, 1953; In Search of Serenity, 1974. Contbr. to: radio; newspapers; trade mags. Mbrships: Solicitor of Supreme Ct., UK; Chmn., Counsellor, Johannesburg Marriage Guidance Soc.; Ctrl. Comm., Inst. of Personnel Mgmt., S. Africa. Address: P.O. Anerley, Natal, Repub. of S. Africa.

KANE, Nora Sophie, b. 2 Oct. 1904, Mafeking, S. Africa. Teacher; Writer. Educ: B.A., Rhodes Univ., Grahamstown. Publs: World's View: the Story of Southern Rhodesia, 1954; The Bird Woman & other Stories, 1970. Contbr. to Ency. of Southern Africa; Rhodesia Herald; Umtali Post. Mbrships: Fndr. & past Sec., PEN of Rhodesia; Co-Fndr., Rhodesian Assn. of Univ. Women, Past Nat. Pres. Address: 4 Avonfriars, Oxford Rd., Avondale, Salisbury, Rhodesia.

KANGRO, Bernard, b. 18 Sept. 1910, Estonia. Poet; Author. Educ: Mag.phil., 1938. Publs. incl: Earthbound (poems in transl.), 1951; Flucht und Bleibe (poems in transl.), 1954; Minu nägu (collect. of poetry), 1970; The Joonatan Trilogy (novels), Joonatan, kadunud veli, 1971, Ööastmes X, 1973, & Puu saarel on alles, 1973. Contbr. to jrnls. in Estonian, German, Swedish & Engl. Mbrships. incl: PEN Club; Swedish Union of Authors. Recip., sev. lit. grants. Address: Skördevägen 1, S-222 38 Lund, Sweden.

KANIN, Garson, b. 24 Nov. 1912, Rochester, N.Y., USA. Writer; Director; Producer; Playwright. Educ: Am. Acad. of Dramatic Arts. Publs: Do Re Mi, 1955; Blow Up A Storm, 1959; The Rat Race, 1960; Remembering Mr. Maugham, 1966; Cast of Characters, 1969; Where It's At, 1969; Tracy & Hepburn: An Intimate Memoir, 1971; Adam's Rib, 1972; A Thousand Summers, 1973; Hollywood: Stars & Starlets, Tycoons & Flesh-Peddlers, Moviemakers & Moneymakers, Frauds & Geniuses, Hopefuls & Has-Beens, Great Lovers & Sex Symbols, 1974. Contbr. to jrnls. & books. Mbr., profl. orgs. Recip., sev. awards. Address: Box 585, Edgartown, MA 02539, USA.

KANTOR, MacKinlay, b. 4 Feb. 1904, Webster City, Iowa, USA. Writer. Publs. incl: (verse) Turkey in the Straw, 1935; (novels) Long Remember, USA & UK, 1934; The Noise of Their Wings, USA 1938, UK 1939; Glory for Me (in verse), 1945; Don't Touch Me, USA 1951, UK 1952; Andersonville, USA 1955, UK 1956; Spirit Lake, USA 1961, UK 1962; Beauty Beast, 1968; (stories) Author's Choice, 1944; Story Teller, 1967; (autobiog.) But Look, The Morn, USA 1947, UK 1951; Missouri Bittersweet, 1969; var. juvenile works. Mbrships. incl: Soc. Am. Histns. (Fellow). Hons. incl: Pulitzer Prize, 1956; var. docts. Address: c/o Doubleday, 277 Park Ave., N.Y., NY 10017, USA.

KANTOROWICZ, Alfred, b. 12 Aug. 1899, Berlin, Germany. University Professor; Writer. Educ: D. Jur.; Univs. of Berlin, Freiberg, Munich, Erlangen. Publs. incl: (essays) In unserem Lager ist Deutschland, 1936; (play) Die Verbundeten, 1951; (other publs.) Deutsche Schicksale, 1949; Suchende Jugend, 1949; Heinrich & Thomas Mann, 1956; Meine Kleider, 1957; Spanisches Kriegstagebuch, 1966; Im 2, Drittel unseres Jahrhunderts, 1967; (Ed.) Works of H. Mann, 1951-57. Contbr. to: Vossische Zeitung, 1925-32. Address: Sierichstr. 148, 2 Hamburg 39, W. Germany.

KANYAMA, Bester, b. 24 Feb. 1932, Shamva, Rhodesia. Photographer. Publs: Kutora Mifananidzo (tips on how to take photographs, written in Shona), 1970. Contbr. to: Parade; Radio Post; Commercial Photography. Mbrships: Lic. Mbr., Inst. of Inc. Photographers, UK; Int. Inst. of Profl. Photographers. Hons: 4th Prize, Asahi Pentax Int. Photo Contest, Japan, 1964; Photographs exhibited in Municipal Mus., The Hague, Netherlands,1966. Address: P.O. Box ST.38, Southerton, Salisbury, Rhodesia.

KANZA, Thomas R. Nzenga, b. 1933, Boende, Zaire. Academic Research Fellow; Former Diplomat. Educ: M.A., B.Litt.; Univ. of Louvain, Belgium; London & Oxford Univs., UK; Harvard Univ., USA. Publs. incl: Congo, Pays de Deux Evolues (essays), 1956; Ata Ndele, 1960; Congo, 1962; Sans Rancune (novel), 1964; Conflict in the Congo (biog.), 1972; Evolution & Revolution in Africa (essays), 1973; Political Leadership & Democracy in Africa, 1974. Contbr. to: Jeune Afrique; African Affairs; African Mod. Studies; etc. Mbrships: Anglo-Belgian & Harvard Clubs. Address: St. Anthony's College, Oxford, UK.

KAPELRUD, Arvid Schou, b. 14 May 1912, Lillehammer, Norway. University Professor; Author. Educ: Cand.Th., Oslo, 1938; Dr.Th., Uppsala, 1948; further studies, Yale Univ., USA, 1949-50. Publs. incl: Baal in the Ras Shamra Texts, 1952; Central Ideas in Amos, 1956, 2nd ed., 1971; The Dead Sea Scrolls (in Norwegian), 1956, 2nd ed., 1971; Israel from the Earliest Times, 1966; The Violent Goddess, 1969; The Message of the Prophet Zephaniah, 1974. Contbr. to: Biblica, Rome, Italy; Jrnl. of Biblical Lit., N.Y., USA; Studia Theologica, Oslo, Norway; etc. Mbrships. incl: Soc. of Biblical Lit., N.Y., USA; Pres., Norwegian Lib. Assn., 1953-55. Address: Univ. of Oslo, Blindern, Oslo 3, Norway.

KAPLAN, Justin, b. 5 Sept. 1925, NYC, USA. Author. Educ: B.S., Harvard Coll., 1944; Harvard Univ. Grad. Schl. of Arts & Scis., 1944-46. Publs: Mr. Clemens & Mark Twain, 1966; Lincoln Steffens, A Biography, 1974; Mark Twain & His World, 1974. Contbr. to: Atlantic; Harper's; Saturday Review; N.Y. Times; Boston Globe; etc. Hons: Pulitzer Prize for Biog., 1967; Nat. Book Award in Arts & Letters, 1967. Address: 16 Francis Ave., Cambridge, MA 02138, USA.

KAPLAN, Robert Boris, b. 20 Sept. 1928, NYC, USA. Professor in Applied Linguistics; Associate Dean. Educ: A.B. Williamettece Univ., Salem, Ore., 1952; M.A., 1957, Ph.D., 1963, Univ. of Southern Calif. Publs. incl: Learning English Through Typewriting (w. C. W. Gay & R. D. Schoesler), 1969; Anatomy of Rhetoric: Prolegomena To A Functional Theory of Rhetoric, 1971; Hermes to Prometheus to Pandora: An Inquiry into the Development of a Unified Theory of Applied Linguistics, forthcoming. Contbr., acad. jrnls. Mbr., profl. orgs. Address: 30303 Ganado Dr., Palos Verdes Peninsula, CA 90274, USA.

KAPP, Yvonne, pen name CLOUD, Yvonne, b. 1903, London, UK. Writer. Educ: Queen's Coll., Harley St. & King's Coll., London Univ. Publs. incl: Pastiche (w. E. X. Kapp), 1926; Nobody Asked You, 1932; The Basque Children in England, 1937; The Houses in Between, 1938; transls. incl: Tales from the Calendar, Bertolt Brecht, 1961; Autobiog. of Ilya Ehrenburg, 6 vols. (w. others), 1961-66; Eleanor Marx: Vol. 1. Family Life, 1972. Contbr. to: Vogue, Paris (lit. Ed., 1927-28); Times Lit. Supplement; etc. Mbrships: Soc. of Authors; Writers' Guild of GB. Address: c/o Lloyds Bank Ltd., Highgate Village, London N6, UK.

KAR, Sisir Kumar, b. 1 Jan. 1935, Howrah, W. Bengal, India. Journalist. Educ: M.A., Calcutta Univ., 1957. Publs: (novel) Patramita (Penfriend), 1968; (short story) Bhalabasha Durer Samare (Love to a Far City), 1974; (essay) Jatiotabader ar ek nam Bandemataram; (juvenile) Gangay Bagh (Tiger in the Ganges), forthcoming. Contbr. to: Ananda Bazar Patrika; Bhakiyug; Bibaram; etc. Mbrships: Howrah Dist. Writers Conf. (Gen. Sec.); W. Bengal Union Jrnlsts. (Exec. Mbr.). Address: 14/3/1 Sri Bash Dutta Lane, Howrah-1, W. Bengal, India.

KARASLAVOV, Georgy Slavov, b. 21 Jan, 1904, Debur, Bulgaria. Writer. Publs: (in Bulgarian) (novels) A Village Correspondent, 1933; Thorn-Apple, 1938; Daughter-in-Law, 1942; Tango, 1951; Common People — a novel in 4 parts, 1952-66; (plays) A Stone in the Slough, 1959; Mother of us All, 1973; Vox Populi, 1963. Contbr. to sev. Bulgarian Mags. & Newspapers. Mbrships: PEN; Union of Bulgarian Writers. Hons: Dimitrov Prize, 1950, 1959; People's Worker in Culture, 1963; Awards: Union of Bulgarian Writers, 1944, 1968; Hero of Socialist Labour, 1964; Ivan Vazov Prize, 1973; Hero of the People's Republic of Bulgaria, 1974. Address: Sofia-Dragalevtsi, Bulgaria.

KARASLAVOV, Slav Hristov, b. 27 Mar. 1932, Debur, Bulgaria. Writer. Publs: (in Bulgarian) (play) The Salonika Brothers, 1968; (novels) Despot Slav, 1970; Ivanko's Decline, 1972. Contbr. to: September; PlamAk; Drouzhba; Obzor; Literatouren Front. Mbrships: Sec.-Gen., Union of Bulgarian Writers; PEN. Hons: Prize, Union of Bulgarian Writers, 1971; Honoured Worker in Culture, 1974. Address: bul. Emil Markov 104, bl. 24-a, vh.A, Sofia, Bulgaria.

KARASSIMEONOV, Alexander, b. 12 Sept. 1930, Sofia, Bulgaria. Writer. Publs: (in Bulgarian) The Main Witness, 1963; Friendships so Much Expected, 1966; Affection, 1969. Contbr. to: September; PlamAk; Literatouren Front. Mbrships: PEN; Union of Bulgarian Writers; Union of Bulgarian Film Workers; Union of

Bulgarian Jrnlsts. Recip., Sofia Prize, 1969. Address: Sofia, ul. Rakovski, 151-a, Bulgaria.

KARAVAEVA, Anna Alexandrovna, b. 27 Dec. 1893. Author. Publs: The Household, 1926; The Sawmill, 1928; Fires, 1943; On the Run, 1946-48; Native Hearth, 1950; Collected Works in 5 vols., 1957-58; Facts of Life, 1963; World of Yesterday, 1964; Selected Works, 1967. Mbr., USSR Union of Writers. Hons: Order of Lenin; Banner of Labour; Red Star & Badge of Honour; State Prizewinner, 1950. Address: Ulitsa Vorovskogo 52, Moscow, USSR.

KARCZEWSKA, Wanda Maria, b. 5 Dec. 1913, Wieliczaka, Poland. Writer, Educ: Classical studies, Warsaw Univ., 1931-33; Warsaw Inst. of Jrnlsm., 1934-37. Publs. incl: Lyrical Notebook, 1949; Poetry & poems, 1954; Black Horse (stories), 1959; Leave (novel), 1959; Lyrics, 1960; The Open Portrait (novel), 1962; The Weekend at the Riverside (novel), 1966; A New Poetry Selection, 1967; The Line of Light (stories), 1970; Deep Springs (novel), 1973; The Fugue with a Love Theme (novel), 1974. Contbr. to: Kultura; Nowa Kultura; Tworczosc; Polish Radio & TV; etc. Mbrships: PEN; Polish Writers' Assn.; Assn. of Authors & Stage Composers. Recip., Lit. Prize of Poznan, 1960. Address: 90-442 Lodz, Al. Kosciuszki 98 m. 12, Poland.

KARILAS, Tauno Valto, b. 20 Oct. 1900, Piippola, Finland. Author. Educ: M.A., Univ. of Helsinki, 1924; Studies in UK, Germany & France. Publs. incl: Kuolemaantuomittu majuri, 1928; Suuri kaskukirja, 1948; Robinsonista Muumipeikkoon, 1962; Selected Stories, 1951. Contbr. to weekly jrnls. Mbr., Finnish lit. socs., Int. Soc. of Young Books. Hons: Kt., 1st Class, Order of the White Lion; Kt., Order of the Rose; Topelius Prize, 1960; Hon. Chmn., Young Book Soc., 1967. Address: Fredrikinkatu 24 A 2, 00120 Helsinki 12, Finland.

KARINTHY, Ferenc, b. 2 June 1921, Budapest, Hungary. Author. Educ: Ph.D., Pazmany Peter Univ., Budapest, 1946. Publs: (novels) Szellemidezes, 1946; Spring Comes to Budapest, 1954; Epepa, 1972; (plays) Ezer Ev, 1956; Het Jatek, 1969; Steinway Grand, 1968; Hot Air, 1970; (short stories) Viz Fölött Viz Alatt, 1966. Contbr. to: Books Abroad, USA; Merian (Germany); Argosy, UK; num. Hungarian mags. Mbrships. incl: Hungarian Writers Soc.; PEN; Int. Theatre Inst. Hons: Baumgarten Prize, 1948; József Attila Prize, 1951, 1954, 1974; Kossuth Prize, 1955. Address: Menesi ut., Budapest 1118, Hungary.

KARK, Leslie, b. 12 July 1910, Johannesburg, S. Africa. Headmaster. Educ: M.A., Univ. of Oxford, UK; Barrister-at-Law, Inner Temple, London. Publs: The Fire Was Bright, 1944; Red Rain, 1946; An Owl in the Sun, 1948; Wings of the Phoenix, 1949; On the Haycock, 1957. Mbrships. incl: F.R.S.A.; Govng. Dir., Lucie Clayton Secretarial Coll. Address: 9 Clareville Grove, London SW7, UK.

KAROVSKI, Lazo, b. 17 Feb. 1927, Kavadarci, Macedonia, Yugoslavia. Professor; Writer. Educ: D.Litt. Publs: Shepherd, 1946; Bloody Blockade, 1947; Tikves's Legend, 1948; Momina Chuka, 1955; Kliment Ohridski, 1969; Naum Ohridski, 1971; (novels) Sheaves, 1971; The First Furrow, 1972. Contbr. to: Sovremenost; Razvitok; Stremez; Literaturen Zbor. Mbrships: Soc. Macedonian Writers; Soc. Yugoslav Writers. Hons: Noemvriska Prize, Bitola 1961; Civic Prize, Writers' Nights in Struga, 1963. Address: ul. Mito Hadzivasilev K-B-5/22, 91000 Skopje, Yugoslavia.

KARP, David, b. 5 May 1922, NYC, USA. Writer; Television Producer. Educ: B.Soc. Scis., CCNY, 1948. Publs: The Brotherhood of Velvet, 1952; The Girl on Crown Street, 1952; Platoon, 1952; One, 1953; The Day of the Monkey, 1954; All Honorable Men, 1956; Leave Me Alone, 1957; Enter, Sleeping, 1960; Vice-President in Charge of Revolution (co-author), 1960; The Last Believers, 1964. Contbr. to num. newspapers & mags. Mbrships. incl: Writers Guild of Am.; PEN; Dramatists Guild. Hons. incl: Edgar Award, Mystery Writers of Am., 1960; Emmy Award, Nat. Acad. TV Arts & Scis., 1964. Agent: Frank Cooper. Address: 1116 Corsica Drive, Pacific Palisades, CA 90272, USA.

KARPELES, Maud, b. 1885, London, UK. Honorary President, Intenational Folk Music Council. Publs: English Folk Songs from the Southern Appalachians, 1933; Folk Songs of Europe, 1956; Cecil Sharp, His Life & Work, 1967; Folk Songs from Newfoundland, 1970; An

Introduction to English Folk Songs, 1973; Cecil Sharp's Collection of English Folk Songs, 1974. Contbr. to: Grove's Dict. of Music & Musicians; Jrnl. of Int. Folk Music Coun. Mbrships. incl: Folklore Soc.; Engl. Folk Dance & Song Soc.; Royal Musical Assn.; Inc. Soc. of Musicians. Hons: O.B.E.; D. es L., Laval Univ.; D.Litt., Mem. Univ. of Nfld. Address: 43 Cadogan Place, London SW1, UK.

KARRER, (The Rev.) Otto, b. 30 Nov. 1888, Ballrechten, Freiberg/Br., Germany. Roman Catholic Priest; Theological Writer. Educ: Ph.D., D.Th. Publs. incl: Meister Eckehart: Das System Seiner religiösen Lehre und Lebensweisheit, 1926; John Henry Newman: Die Kirche I-II, 1945-46; Neues Testament, übersetzt u. erklärt, 1950, 4th ed., 1967; Reich Gottes, 1956; Die christliche Einheit, 1963; Das Zweite Vatikanische Konzil, 1966. Contbr. to num. acad. & theol. works & jrnls. Mbrships. incl: Official Ecumenical Dialogue Commn. Swiss Churches; Swiss Theol. Soc. Hons. incl: W. German Cross Merit, 1963; Th.D., Tübinger Univ., 1967. Address: CH-6005 Lucerne, Steinhofweg 20, Switz.

KARSH, Yousuf, b. 1908, Armenia-in-Turkey. International Photographer; Visiting Professor of Fine Arts. Publs. incl: This Is the Holy Land, 1960; These Are the Sacraments (w. Fulton J. Sheen), 1962; In Search of Greatness (autobiog.), 1962; The Warren Court (w. John P. Frank), 1965; Karsh Portfolio, 1967; Faces of Our Time, 1971. Mbrships: Corporate Mbr., Muscular Dystrophy Assn.; Trustee, Photographic Arts & Scis. Fndn.; Hon. Fellow, Royal Photographic Soc., GB. Hons: 7 degrees, Can. & USA univs.; Var. medals & awards for work for handicapped. Address: Chateau Laurier Hotel, Suite 660, Ottawa, K1N 8S7, Can.

KASCHNITZ, Marie Luise von (Mrs. Guido Kaschnitz von Weinberg), b. 31 Jan. 1901, Karlsruhe, Germany. Poet & Writer. Publs. incl: Elissa (novel) 1936; Griechische Mythen (essays) 1942; Von Menschen und Dingen (essays) 1946; Courbet (biog.) 1949; Zukunftsmusik (poems) 1952; Engelsbrücke: Romische Betrachtungen, 1955; Neue Gedichte, 1957; Lange Schatten (short stories) 1960; Dein Schweigen, Meine Stimme (poems) 1962; Wohin denn ich, 1963; Ein Wort weiter (poems) 1965; Ferngespräche (short stories) 1966; Tage, Tage, Jahre, 1968; Steht noch dahin (prose) 1970; Gespräche im All (Radio plays) 1971. Mbrships: PEN; Deutsche Akademie für Sprache und Dichtung; Akademie der Wissenschaften und der Literatur, Mainz. Hons: Buchnerpreis, 1955; Immermannpreis, 1957; Preis des Kulturkreises der deutschen Industrie. Address: Wiesenau 8, Frankfurt/Main, W. Germany.

KASER, Michael, b. 1926, London, UK. Professorial Fellow & University Reader in Economics. Educ: M.A., Univ. of Cambridge; M.A., Univ. of Oxford. Publs: Comecon, 1965, 2nd ed., 1967; Economic Development for Eastern Europe, 1968; Soviet Economics, 1970; Planning in East Europe (w. J. Zielinski), 1970. Contbr. to: Econ. Jrnl.; Income & Wealth; Soviet Studies; sev. other profl. jrnls. Address: St. Antony's Coll., Oxford, OX2 6JF, UK.

KASH, Don Eldon, b. 29 May 1934, Macedonia, Iowa, USA. Professor. Educ: B.A., 1959, M.A., 1960, Univ. of Iowa; Ph.D., 1965. Publs: The Politics of Space Cooperation, 1967; Energy Under the Oceans — A Technology Assessment of Outer Continental Shelf Oil & Gas Operations (jt.-author), 1973; North Sea Oil & Gas: Implications for Future U.S. Development (jt.-author), 1973. Contbr. to: Social Contexts of Research (Saad Z. Nagi & Ronald G. Corwin, ed.); Sci.; Chem. & Engrng. News; Bulletin of the Atomic Scis. Address: Sci. & Pub. Policy Prog., Univ. of Okla., 601 Elm, Room 432, Norman, OK 73069, USA.

KASSIRA, Anwar, b. 18 Dec. 1934, Baghdad, Iraq. University Professor; Author. Educ: B.S., Tenn. Wesleyan Coll., USA; M.A., Atlanta Univ.; Ph.D., Cath. Univ. of Am. Publs: Writings of Great Economists, 1965; Basic Concepts in Economics, Statistics & Administration, 1974. Contbr. to: Time Mag.; Economist. Mbrships: Am. Econs. Assn.; Iraqi Econs. Assn.; Nat. Soc. Sci. Honor Soc.; Va. Soc. Sci. Assn. Recip., Dean Hons., 1957. Address: 18/4/35 Masbah, Baghdad, Iraq.

KASTLE, Herbert David, pen name LEE, Herbert d'H, b. 11 July 1924, NYC, USA. Novelist. Educ: B.A., 1949, M.A., 1950, N.Y. Univ. Publs: One Thing on my Mind, 1957; Koptic Court, 1958; Camera, 1959; Bachelor Summer, 1959; The World They Wanted, 1961; Countdown to Murder, 1961; The Reassembled Man, 1964; Hot Prowl,

1965; The Movie Maker, 1968; Miami Golden Boy, 1969; Millionaires, 1972; Ellie, 1973; Cross-Country, 1975; Edward Berner is Alive Again, forthcoming; (non-fiction by Herbert d'H Lee) Surrogate Wife, 1971. Contbr. to TV. Address: 2073 Sunset Plaza Dr., L.A., CA 90069, USA.

KÄSTNER, Erich, b. 23 Feb. 1899, Dresden. Author. Educ: D.Phil.; Univs. of Leipzig, Rostock & Berlin. Publs. incl: (novels) Fabian, 1931; The Missing Miniature, 1935; A Salzburg Comedy, 1938; Emil & the Detectives, 1931; The Little Man, 1963; (poems) Herz auf Taille, 1928; Ein Mann gibt Auskunft, 1930; Die Dreisehn Monate, 1955; Eine Auswahl, 1956; (essays) Die kleine Freiheit, 1952; (plays) Emil & the Detectives, 1930; Die Schule der Diktatoren, 1956; (biography) Als ich ein kleiner Junge war, 1957; Address: Flemingstr. 52, Munich 81, W. Germany.

KATAEV, Valentin Petrovich, b. 28 Jan. 1897, Odessa, Russia. Novelist; Playwright. Publs. incl: Father, 1925; The Embezzlers, 1926; Lone White Sail, 1936; I, Son of the Working People, 1937; Son of the Regiment, 1945; The Hamlet in the Steppe, 1956; Winter Wind, 1960; (plays) Squaring the Circle, 1928; The Vanguard, 1929; Peace to Huts, War to Palaces, 1960; Waves of the Black Sea, 1961; Time of Love, 1962; Hearths of the People, 1962; Werewolf, 1963; Small Iron Door in a Wall, 1964; Floweret of Seven Colours, 1966; Holy Well, 1967. Contbr. to: Yunost (Ed.-in-Chief). Mbr., Praesidium, Union of Soviet Writers. Hons: Order of Lenin; Red Banner of Labour. Address: Ul. Vorovskogo 52, Moscow, USSR.

KATKÓ, István, b. 17 June 1923, Jász-Jákóhalma, Hungary. TV Editor of Hungarian Literature. Educ: Univ. Degree Lit.; Tchrs. Dip. Publs: (novels) Opálka és Forgószél, 1956; Piros kenyér, 1958; Félszivü Apostolok, 1958; Nap adja az árnyékot is, 1962; Szent Bertalan délutánja, 1965; Öt férfi komoly szándékkal, 1970; Vadhajtás, 1973; (short stories) Két ember az országuton; Társasutazás; (satire) Hátra arc, 1960. Contbr. to: Élet és Irodalom; Uj Irás. Mbrships: Union Hungarian Writers; PEN. Recip., Andor Gábor Prize, 1970. Address: Budapest 1085, Makarenkó u. 1, Hungary.

KATO, Shuichi, b. 19 Sept. 1919, Tokyo, Japan. Writer; Professor. Educ: M.D., Tokyo Univ. Publs: Form, Style, Tradition: Reflections on Japanese Art & Society, 1971; The Japan-China Phenomenon, 1974; Nihon Bungakushi Josetsu, 1975. Contbr. to: Asahi newspaper. Address: Setagaya-ku, Kaminoge 1-8-16, Tokyo, Japan.

KATZ, Jacob, b. 15 Nov. 1904, Magyargenes, Hungary. Professor of Social History. Educ: Ph.D., Univ. Frankfurt, Germany. Publs: Exclusiveness & Tolerance, Studies in Jewish-Gentile Relations in Medieval & Modern Times, 1961, 2nd ed., 1962; Tradition & Crisis: Jewish Society at the End of the Middle Ages, 1961, 2nd ed., 1970; (transl'd. from Hebrew) Jews & Freemasons in Europe 1723-1939, 1970; (transl'd from Hebrew) Emancipation & Assimilation Studies in Modern Jewish History, 1972; Out of the Ghetto, 1973. Contbr. to: Jrnl. of World Hist. IV; Revue des Etudes Juives CVVX; Zion; Tarbiz; Kiryat Sefer. Hons. incl: Fellow, Univ. Frankfurt; For. Mbr. Am. Acad. Arts & Scis. Address: 5 Palmach St., Jerusalem, Israel.

KATZ, Joseph, b. 1 Nov. 1910, Winnipeg, Man., Can. Professor of Education. Educ: B.A., B.Ed., M.Ed., Ph.D. Publs: Canadian Education Today, 1956; Elementary Education in Canada, 1962; Society, Schools & Progress in Canada, 1969; Education in Canada, 1974. Contbr. to: Pacific Affairs; Educ. Studies; Can. & Int. Educ.; McGill Jrnl. Educ.; Jrnl. Educ.; Tchrs. Coll. Jrnl.; Comp. Educ.; etc. Mbrships. incl: B.C. Human Rights Coun. (Chmn.); World Coun. Comp. Educ. Socs. (Chmn.); Comp. & Int. Educ. Soc. Can. (Treas.); Can. Coun. Christians & Jews (Dir.); Am. Assn. Univ. Profs.; Comp. Educ. Soc. Europe. Hons. incl: Gold Medal Educ. Univ. Manitoba, 1946. Address: 3777 Quesnelle Dr., Vancouver, B.C. V6L 2W9, Can.

KATZ, Martin, b. 1 Apr. 1929, Carmel, Calif., USA. Associate Professor of History of Russia. Educ: A.B., Stanford Univ.; M.A., Ph.D., Hist., Univ. of Calif. Publs: Mikhail N. Katkov: A Political Biography 1918-1887. Contbr. to: Can. Slavonic Papers & Polish Review. Address: Dept. of Hist., Univ. of Alta., Edmonton, Alta., Can.

KATZ, Milton, b. 29 Nov. 1907, NYC, USA. Professor of Law; Author. Educ: A.B., Harvard Univ., 1927; J.D., ibid, 1931. Publs: Cases & Materials in Administrative Law, 1947; Government Under Law & the Individual (ed. &

co-author), 1957; The Law of International Trnasactions: Cases & Materials (co-author), 1960; The Things That Are Caesars, 1966; The Relevance of International Adjudication, 1968; The Modern Foundation: Its Dual Character, Public & Private, 1968; Man's Impact on the Global Enrionment (contbr.), 1970; Federal Regulation of Campaign Finance (ed.), 1972. Address: 6 Berkeley Street, Cambridge, MA 02138, USA.

KATZ, Shemuel (Alexander), pen name SHMULIK, b. 18 Aug. 1926, Vienna, Austria. Painter; Journalist. Educ: Tech. Acad., Budapest, Hungary; Fine Arts Acad., Paris, France. Publs: On to Sinai (cartoons), 1957; The Harp has Ten Strings (cartoons), 1958; Follow the Sun to Israel (cartoons), 1961; In the Tents of Kedar (drawings), 1962; Journey in Ethiopia (drawings, w. N. Shaham), 1962; After the Deluge (cartoons), 1965; Journey in the Land of Israel (w. N. Shaham), 1966; Shemuel Katz: Paintings & Drawings, 1967; This Land we Love (drawings, w. N. Shaham), 1970; Jerusalem, Holy Business as Usual (cartoons), 1970; Jerusalem, Paintings & Drawings, 1974. Contbr. to sev. mags. Mbrships: Israel Assn. of Jrnlsts.; Israel Assn. of Painters & Sculptors. Recip., sev. medals & prizes. Address: Kibutz Gaaton 25130, Israel.

KATZ, William Loren, b. 2 June 1927, Bklyn., N.Y., USA. Historian. Educ: B.A., Syracuse Univ., 1950; M.S., N.Y. Univ., 1952. Publs: Eyewitness: The Negro in American History, 1967; Teachers' Guide to American Negro History, 1968; Five Slave Narratives, 1968; American Majorities & Minorities, 1970; The Black West, 1971; A History of Black America, 1973; An Album of the Civil War, 1974; An Album of the Reconstruction, 1974; Minorities in American History, 4 vols., Early American Slavery to Civil War, Reconstruction & National Growth, Progressive Area to Great Depression, 1974. Contbr. to var. jrnls. Recip., Gold Medal Award for Non-Fiction, 1968. Address: 34 E. 10th St., N.Y., NY 10003, USA.

KAUFELT, David Allan, b. 1939, Elizabeth, N.J., USA. Creative Supervisor, Advertising Company. Educ: Wharton Schl. of Fin. & Commerce, Univ. of Pa.; Grad. Schl., N.Y. Univ. Publs: Six Months with an Older Woman, 1973; W. H. Allen, 1974; The Bradley Beach Rumba, 1974; (Screenplay) Blood will Out (co-author), 1974; (short story) Crime of the Week, 1974. Mbr., Authors' Guild. Hon: Citation 7th Annual N.J. Writers' Conf. Agent: Owen Laster of William Morris. Address: 165 E. 60th St., N.Y., NY 10022, USA.

KAUFMAN, Gerald, b. 1930, Leeds, UK. Member of Parliament; Under-Secretary of State, Department of the Environment. Educ: M.A., Queen's Coll., Oxford. Publs: How to Live Under Labour (part-author), 1964; Ed., The Left (essays), 1966; To Build the Promised Land, 1973. Contbr. to: New Statesman; Listener; Jewish Chronicle; Sun; Tribune. Address: House of Commons, London SW1A 0AA, UK.

KAUFMAN, Morris, b. 1919, London, UK. Chemist. Educ: Chelsea Polytechnic; Dip., Imperial Coll., London; Ph.D. Publs: Recent Advances in Processing of PVC, 1962; First Century of Plastics, 1963; Giant Molecules, 1968; History of PVC, 1969; New Horizons in Education, 1970. Contbr. to: Plastics & Rubber Jrnls.; New Sci.; Times. Mbrships. incl: Fellow, Royal Inst. of Chem., Plastics Inst. Address: 5 Blackstone Rd., London NW2 6DA, UK.

KAUFMANN, Stephan George, b. 25 Mar. 1921, Vienna, Austria. Geologist. Educ: Grad., Sociol., Univ. of Vienna; Dip., Engrng. Geol., 1955. Publs: Israelogie I: Auf den Spuren Mosis, 1972; Israelogie II: Könige und Pharaonen, 1974; Europologie, forthcoming. Mbr., Concordia Club, Vienna. Address: A-1060 Vienna, Webgasse 8, Austria.

KAUFMANN, Walter, b. 1 July 1921, Freiburg, Germany. Professor of Philosophy. Educ: B.A.(Hons.), Williams Coll., 1941; M.A., 1942, Ph.D., 1947, Harvard Univ. Publs: Nietzsche, 1950, 4th ed., 1974; Existentialism from Dostoevsky to Sartre (ed.), 1956; Critique of Religion & Philosophy, 1958; From Shakespeare to Existentialism, 1959, 2nd ed., 1960; The Faith of a Heretic, 1961; Cain & Other Poems, 1962, 3rd ed., 1975; Hegel, 1965; Tragedy & Philosophy, 1968; Without Guilt & Justice, 1973; Religion in Four Dimensions, 1975. Translations into Engl.: Judaism & Christianity (Leo Baeck), 1958; Faust (Goethe), 1961; 20 German Poets, 1962; I & Thou (Buber), 1970; 25 German Poets, 1975; 11 of Nietzsche's works. Recip., Int. Leo

Baeck Prize, 1961. Address: Dept. of Philosophy, Princeton University, NJ 08540, USA.

KAUKONEN, Tauno Kalevi, b. 11 Aug. 1929, Tampere, Finland. Author. Publs: Klaani, 1963; Ken surmais suuren linnun, 1972; TV & radio plays inclng: Kihlajaiset, Aivan tavallinen ilta, & Profeetta. Mbr., Pirkkalalaiskirjailijat ry; Suomen Kirjailijaliitto ry (English Society of Authors); Suomen Näytelmäkirjailijaliitto ry (Finnish Society of Dramatists). Hons: Weilin-Göös Award, 1963 & 1972; City of Tampere Awards, 1964 & 1967. Address: Rongankatu 11 C 56, SF-33100 Tampere 10, Finland.

KAUPPINEN, Eino Ilmari, b. 26 Feb. 1910, Helsinki, Finland. University Professor of Finnish Literature. Educ: Ph.D. Publs: Koto ja Maailma, 1951; Kirjallinen Kuukauslehti, 1952; Talsteleva Sanomalehti, 1955; Runoilija ja Arvostelija, 1966; Pentti Haanpää,I, 1966. Mbrships: Soc. of Finnish Authors; Soc. of Lit. Rsch.; Finnish Lit. Soc.; Hon. mbr., Aleksis Kivi Soc. & Pentti Haanpää Soc. Address: Hiidenkiventie 1 C, 02100 Espoo 10, Finland.

KAUTTU, Raija Helena Hämetär, b. 12 Apr. 1918, Oulu, Finland. Novelist. Publs: Sankkalan kartanon rouvat, 1971; Sankkalan perijätär, 1972; Nouda hänet, Leontes, 1973; Ulrika, 1974. Contbr. to serial novels, Me Naiset, Apu. Mbrships: Suomen Kirjailijaliitto Ry; WSOY:n kirjantekijät; Kirjailijakeskus. Address: Ohjaajantie 20 A 3, 00400 Helsinki 40, Finland.

KAVLI, Guthorm, b. 1917, Trondheim, Norway. Architect; Director Administration & Architect to the Royal Palace, Oslo. Educ: D.Sc., Trondheim Univ.; Uppsala Univ., Sweden. Publs: Norwegian Architecture, Past & Present; Troenderske Trepaléer; Ed., Norwegian Art Treasures; The Royal Palace in Oslo. Contbr. to: Am.-Scandinavian Review; Burlington Mag.; Norseman; Mus.; Byggekunst; Bonytt; Kunst og Kultur; Ord och Bild; etc. Mbrships: Deleg., UNESCO Confs., Paris, France, 1952, The Hague, Netherlands, 1954; Archt., Norwegian Exhib., Edinburgh, UK, & London, 1958-59. Address: Drammensneien 1, Oslo, Norway.

KAWALEC, Julian, b. 11 Oct. 1916, Warsaw, Poland. Author. Educ: Grad., Jagellonian Univ., Cracow. Publs: Bound to the Lands, 1962; In the Sun, 1963; The Dancing Hawk, 1964; Appeal, 1968; Search for Home, 1968; To Cross the River, 1973. Mbrships: PEN; Polish Writers' Assn. Hons: Prize, Polish Eds., 1962; Prize, Polish Writers' Assn., 1962; Prize, Min. of Culture & Art, 1967. Address: 39 Zaleskiego, 31-525 Cracow, Poland.

KAY, Ernest, pen names RANDOM, Alan; LUDLOW, George, b. Darwen, Lancs., UK. Publisher; Editor; Author. Publs: Great Men, 1956, 2nd ed., 1960; Isles of Flowers: The Story of the Isles of Scilly, 1956, 3rd ed., 1975; The Wit of Harold Wilson, 1967; Pragmatic Premier: An Intimate Portrait of Harold Wilson, 1967. Contbr. to newspapers & mags. throughout the world. Mbrships: F.R.S.A., London (Life); Poetry Soc. of Am.; Accademia di Filologia Classica, Milan, Italy; Community of European Writers; United Poets-Laureate Int.; Nat. Arts Club, N.Y.; etc. Hons: U.P.L.I. Gold Medal; D.Litt.; Ph.D.; D.Journ.; Nom. Nobel Prize, 1973. Address: 11 Madingley Rd., Cambridge CB3 0EG, UK.

KAY, Lester Williams, b. 1921, Atherton, UK. Consultant Oral Surgeon & Reader in Oral Surgery, University of London. Educ: Guy's Hosp. Med. Schl., Univ. of London; M.D.S.; F.D.S.; M.R.C.S.; L.R.C.P. Publs. incl: Benign Cystic Lesions of the Jaws (w. H. C. Killey), 1972; Drugs in Dentistry, 1972; A Colour Atlas of Orofacial Diseases (w. R. Haskell), 1971; An Outline of Oral Surgery Parts 1 & 2 (w. H. C. Killey & G. R. Seward), 1971; Ed., Oral Surgery: Transactions of the 4th International Conference on Oral Surgery, 1973; The Impacted Wisdom Tooth (w. H. C. Killey), 1975; The Prevention of Complications in Dental Surgery (w. H. C. Killey), 1975. Contbr. to sev. profl. jrnls. & to sev. books on oral surg. & pathol. Mbrships. incl: Brit. Med. Assn.; Brit. Dental Assn.; Med. Jrnlsts. Assn. Address: Tympany, Beckenham Pl. Pk., Beckenham, Kent, UK.

KAY, Mara, b. Europe. Senior Copywriter. Publs: In Place of Katia, 1964; The Burning Candle, 1966; Masha, 1969; The Youngest Lady in Waiting, 1971; The Circling Star, 1973; The Storm Warning, forthcoming. Mbrships: PEN Int., London; Marquis Lib. Soc. Address: 2 Lent Ave., Hempstead, NY 11550, USA.

KAY, Robin Langford, b. 23 June 1919, Waipawa, NZ. Editor of Documents on NZ external relations, Historical Publications Branch, Department of Internal Affairs. Educ: B.A., Univ. Wellington. Publs: Official History of New Zealand in the Second World War: Italy, Vol. II, 1967; 27 (Machine Gun) Battalion, 1958; Ed., Chronology, New Zealand in the War, 1939-46, 1968; Documents on New Zealand External Relations, vol. I: The Australian-New Zealand Agreement 1944, 1972. Contbr. to: NZ's Heritage; Making of a Nation. Mbrships: NZ Acad. Fine Arts (VP); Canterbury Soc. Arts; Friends Turnbull Lib.; Wellington Histl. Assn.; Hutt Art Soc. Hons: FRSA, 1973. Address: Kerehoma, Muri Rd., Pukerua Bay, Wellington, NZ.

KAYE, Barrington, pen name KAYE, Tom, b. 1924, Blackheath, UK. University Lecturer. Educ: B.Sc., London Schl. of Econ. Publs. incl: A Manifesto for Education in Malaya, 1955; Upper Nankin Street, Singapore, 1960; Bringing Up Children in Ghana, 1962; Participation in Learning, 1970; (as Tom Kaye) It had been a Mild, Delicate Night, 1960; David, from Where He Was Lying, 1962. Contbr. to: var. profl. jrnls. Mbr., Soc. of Authors. Address: 2 St. Christophers Ct., Wellington Terrace, Clevedon, Avon BS21 7PY, UK.

KAYE, Geraldine, b. 14 Jan. 1925, Watford, UK. Writer. Educ: B.Sc.(Econ.), Univ. of London. Publs: The Pony Raffle, 1966; The Blue Rabbit, 1967; Kassim & the Sea Monkey, 1967; Tawno, Gypsy Boy, 1968; Koto & the Lagoon, 1968; Nowhere to Stop, 1972; Runaway Boy, 1972; Kassim Goes Fishing, 1972; Kofi & the Eagle,1973; Marie Alone, 1973; Joanna All Alone, 1974; Billy-hoy, 1975; A Different Sort of Christmas, 1975; Children of the Turnpike, 1975. Mbrships: PEN; Soc. of Authors; W. Country Writers' Assn.; Nat. Book League. Address: 39 High Kingsdown, Bristol BS2 8EW, UK.

KAYIRA, Legson Didimu, b. 10 May 1942, Wenya, Chitipa, Malawi. Writer; Probation Officer. Educ: Univ. of Wash.; St. Catharine's Coll., Cambridge; B.A. Publs: I Will Try, 1965; The Looming Shadow, 1967; Jingala, 1969; The Civil Servant, 1971; The Detainee, 1974. Recip., W. Coast (USA) Non-fiction Prize, 1965. Address: 23 Danbrook Rd., London SW16, UK.

KAZIN, Alfred, b. 1915, Brooklyn, N.Y., USA. Professor of Literature. Educ: B.S.S.; M.A.; Columbia Univ. Publs. incl: On Native Grounds: A Walker in the City; The Inmost Leaf; Contemporaries; (Ed.) The Portable William Blake; F. Scott Fitzgerald; Melville's Moby Dick; Introduction to Dostoevsky's Crime & Punishment; A Raw Youth; The Stories of Sholem Aleichem; The Novels of Dreiser; The Open Form: Essays for Our Time; The Works of Ann Frank; Lawrence's Sons & Lovers; Dreiser's Jennie Gerhardt. Contbr. to: Reporter; Partisan Review; N.Y. Times Book Review; etc. Address: 110 Riverside Dr., N.Y., NY, USA.

KEABLE, John Edward, b. 4 Aug. 1903, Kogarah, N.S.W., Australia. Educator. Educ: Sydney Tech. & Tchrs'. Colls. Publs: Woodworking (w. B. R. Leadbeatter), 1970; Woodworking Transparencies (w. B. R. Leadbeatter), 1972; Australian Woodworking (w. B. R. Leadbeatter), 1974. Contbr. to: Jrnl. of Inst. of Indl. Arts (Ed.); Adult Educ.; Educ. Dept. Manual Arts Bulletin. Mbrships: Inst. of Indl. Arts; N.S.W. Tchrs'. Fedn. Address: 9 Francis Street, Carlton, N.S.W., Australia 2218.

KEANE, John B., b. 1928, Listowel, Co. Kerry, Repub. of Ireland. Playwright. Publs: (plays) Sive, 1959; Sharon's Grave, 1960; Many Young Men of Twenty, 1962; The Field, 1965; Big Maggie, 1969; The Change in Mame Fadden, 1972; Moll, 1972; The Crazy Wall, 1974; (books) The Street & Other Poems, 1961; Self-Portrait, 1964; Letters of a Successful T.D., 1967; Letters of a Parish Priest, 1972. Contbr. to: Irish Times; N.Y. Times; Irish Independent; etc. Agent: May Bleazard. Address: 37 William Street, Listowel, Co. Kerry, Repub. of Ireland.

KEARNS, Francis Edward, b. 10 Aug. 1931, Brooklyn, N.Y., USA. Professor of American Literature. Educ: A.B., N.Y. Univ., 1953; M.A., Univ. of Chgo., 1954; Ph.D., Univ. of N.C., 1961. Publs: The Black Experience in American Literature, 1970; Black Identity, 1970. Contbr. to num. jrnls. inclng: Commonweal; Jrnl of Hist. of Ideas; Jahrbuch für Amerikastudien. Mbrships. incl: MLA. Recip., num. acad. hons. Address: 75 Prospect Park W., Brooklyn, NY 11215, USA.

KEATING, Henry Reymond Fitzwalter, b. 31 Oct. 1926, St. Leonards-on-Sea, Sussex, UK. Author. Educ: B.A., Trinity Coll., Dublin. Publs: Death & the Visiting Firemen, 1959; The Perfect Murder, 1964; Inspector Ghote's Good Crusade, 1966; Inspector Ghote Caught in Meshes, 1967; Inspector Ghote Hunts the Peacock, 1968; Inspector Ghote Plays a Joker, 1969; Inspector Ghote Breaks an Egg, 1970; Inspector Ghote Goes By Train, 1971; The Strong Man, 1971; Inspector Ghote Trusts the Heart, 1972; Bats Fly Up for Inspector Ghote, 1974; The Underside, 1974. Contbr. to: Crime Books Reviewer; Times. Recip., Crime Writers' Assn. Golden Dagger Award, 1964. Agent: A. D. Peters & Co. Address: 35 Northumberland Pl., London W2 5AS, UK.

KEATING, Reginald (Rex) James Thomas, b. 14 Feb. 1910, London, UK. Writer & Broadcaster; Mass Media Consultant. Publs: Nubian Twilight, 1962; Nubian Rescue, 1975. Contbr. to: Listener; UNESCO Courier; Open Univ.; Encyclopedia Britannica; BBC & other broadcasting orgs. Mbrships: Engl. Speaking Union; Royal C'wlth Soc.; Brit. Soc. for Social Responsibility in Sci. Agent: Harvey Unna Ltd. Address: Orcemont, 78120 Rambouillet, France.

KEATLEY, Sheila Marjorie, pen name AVON, Margaret, b. Birmingham, UK. Writer. Publs: The Torn Overcoat, 1962. Contbr. to var. mags. & newspapers, Brit. & overseas. Mbr., Soc. of Authors. Address: Yew Tree Cottage, Andover Rd., Wash Water, near Newbury, Berks., UK.

KECMANOVIĆ, Ilija, b. 24 July 1902, Kostajnica, Bosnia, Yugoslavia. Writer. Educ: Ph.D. Publs: Barišićeva Afera, 1954; Vuk Stefanović Karadžić, 1960; Silvije Strahimir Kranjčević, 1961; Ivo Franjo Jukić, 1973. Contbr. to: Pregled; Život; Izraz, Mod. Ency.; Istorijski Arhiv; Bibliotekarstvo; etc. Mbrships: Acad. Arts & Sci. Repub. Bosnia & Hercegovina; Assn. Yugoslav Writers; Assn. Yugoslav Transls.; PEN. Hons: 6th Apr. Prize; 27th July Prize. Address: 71000 Sarajevo, Radićeva 2, Yugoslavia.

KEDDIE, James Alfred Grant, b. 10 Nov. 1900, Tayport, Fife, UK. Retired Physician & Public Health Officer. Educ: M.D., M.B., Ch.B., St. Andrews Univ., D.P.H., Cambridge Univ.; Dip.Pub.Admin.; London Univ. Publs: The Relative Incidence of Congenital Deaf-Mutism in various Scottish Counties, 1945; The Incidence of Handicapping Defects in Children of School Age, 1949; (in jrnls.) Cerebral Palsy & Epilepsy in Childhood, 1955; Heights & Weights of Scottish Schoolchildren, 1956. Contbr. to: Brit. Jrnl. of Tuberculosis; Jrnl. of State Med.; Med. Off.; etc. Address: 11 St. Ninian's Terrace, Edinburgh 10, UK.

KEELE, Kenneth David, b. 1909, London, UK. Consultant Physician (Retired). Educ: M.D., B.S., St. Bartholomew's Hosp., London; F.R.C.P. Publs. incl: Modern Home Nursing, 1940; Anatomies of Pain, 1957; Intra-Abdominal Crises (w. N. M. Matheson), 1961; A Short History of Medicine (w. F. N. L. Poynter), 1961; William Harvey, The Man, The Physician, The Scientist, 1965; Leonardo da Vinci, forthcoming. Contbr. to: Lancet; Brit. Med. Jrnl.; Jrnl. Hist. of Med.; Jrnl. Royal Coll. Physns.; Evening Standard; etc. Mbrships incl: Assn. Physns. of GB & Ireland; Fellow, Royal Soc. Med.; num. Brit. & Int. profl. assns. Address: Leacroft House, Leacroft, Staines, Middlesex TW18 4NN, UK.

KEELEY, Edmund, b. 5 Feb. 1928, Damascus, Syria. Professor; Author; Editor. Educ: B.A., Princeton Univ.; D.Phil., Oxford Univ., UK. Publs. incl: The Libation 1959; Six Poets of Modern Greece, 1960; The Gold-Hatted Lover, 1961; Vassilis Vassilikos: The Plant, the Well, the Angel, 1964; George Seferis: Collected Poems 1924-1955, 1967; The Imposter, 1970; C. P. Cavafy: Passions & Ancient Days, 1971; Voyage to a Dark Island, 1972; Odysseus Elytis: The Axion Esti, 1974; C. P. Cavafy: Collected Poems, 1975. Contbr. to: Encounter; New Yorker; Partisan, Kenyon, Paris Reviews; N.Y. Herald Tribune, etc. Mbr., lit. & profl. orgs. Hons. incl: N.J. Authors Awards, 1960, 1968, 1970. Address: 185 Nassau St., Princeton, NJ 08540, USA.

KEELING, Derek, b. 26 Nov. 1935, London, UK. Writer & Lecturer on Photography. Educ: Royal Coll. of Sci., London. Contbr. to Brit. Jrnl. of Photography (Sci. Ed.); Photographic Applications in Sci., Technol. & Med. (USA). Mbrships: Royal Photographic Soc. of GB (Past Chmn., Lib. Comm.) Hons: Assoc. of Royal Photographic Soc. in educ. Address: 9 York Close, Shenfield, Brentwood, Essex CM15 8JZ, UK.

KEELING, Jill Annette, b. 29 Jan. 1923, Chesterfield, UK. Zoologist. Educ: B.A. in Engl., Bedford Coll., London Univ. Publs: Variations on a Theme, 1951; Ask of the Beasts, 1960; The Old English Sheepdog, 1961; Keeling's Ark (w. C. H. Keeling), 1970; Animals for Schools (w. T. K. Mills), 1973; Animal Inventions, forthcoming. Contbr. to: Chambers' Jrnl.; Countryman; Derbyshire Countryside; Woman; Tchrs'. World; etc. Mbrships. incl: Linnean Soc. of London. Address: Ctr. for Educational Zoology, Much Hadham Rd., Bishop's Stortford, Herts., UK.

KEENE, Florence Myrtle, b. 3 May 1908, Kaitaia, NZ. Teacher; Writer. Educ: Auckland Tchrs. Trng. Coll.; Auckland Univ. Publs: O Te Raki, Maori Legends of the North, 1963; Between Two Mountains, History of Whangarei, 1966; With Flags Flying (biog.), 1972; By This We Conquer (biog.), 1974. Mbrships: Pres., Northland Writers; NZ Women Writers. Address: 43 Riverside Dr., Whangarei, NZ.

KEILSON, Hans, pen names COOPER, B.; KAILAND, Alexander, b. 12 Dec. 1909, Bad Freienwalde, Germany. Pschiatrist. Educ: Univs. Berlin, Amsterdam. Publs: (novels) Das Lebengeht weiter, 1933; Komödie in Moll, 1947, Dutch ed., 1948; Der Tod des Widersachers, 1959, Dutch ed., 1961, Engl. ed., The Death of the Adversary, 1962. Contbr. to: Der Morgen, De Gemeenschap; Sinn und Form; Die Zeit; Neue Rundschau. Mbrships. incl: Netherlands Soc. for Psych.; Netherlands Soc. for Psychotherapy; Netherlands Soc. for Psycho-Analysis; PEN; German Authors in Exile Club, London. Address: Nieuwe Hilvers weg 29, Bussum, Netherlands.

KEITH, Agnes Newton, b. 6 July 1901, Oak Park, Ill., USA. Writer. Educ: B.A., Univ. of Calif. at Berkeley, 1924. Publs: Land Below the Wind, 1939; Three Came Home, 1947; White Man Returns, 1951; Bare Feet in the Palace, 1955; Children of Allah, 1966; Beloved Exiles, 1972. Contbr. to: Atlantic Monthly; Holiday; Time-Life Reading Prog., & other anthols. Mbr., Authors Guild, Inc. Recip., Atlantic Monthly Non-fiction $5,000 Award, 1939. Address: 785 Island Rd., Oak Bay, Victoria, B.C., V8S 2T8, Can.

KEITH-LUCAS, Bryan, b. 1 Aug. 1912, Cambridge, UK. Professor of Government; Author. Educ: M.A., Pembroke Coll., Cambridge; M.A., Oxford. Publs: Cripps on Compulsory Acquisition of Land (w. M. A. L. Cripps & S. Lloyd Jones), 9th ed., 1950; The English Local Government Franchise, 1952; The History of Local Government in England, 3rd ed., 1970. Contbr. to: Pub. Admin.; Cambridge Law Jrnl.; Law Quarterly Review; Econ. Hist. Review; Pub. Law; New Soc. Address: 20 King St., Canterbury, Kent, UK.

KELK, Cornelis Jan, b. 28 Aug. 1901, Amsterdam, Netherlands. Author. Educ: Univ. of Amsterdam. Publs: Jan Steen, 1932, 6th ed., 1972; Judaspenningen en Pauweveren, 1945, 5th ed., 1972; Life of Slauerhoff, 1959, abridged ed., 1971; Aards Vertier (poetry), 1965; Ik keek alleen (autobiog.), 1968; Souvenir van een zomer (novel), 1965. Contbr. to: Weekblad "De Groene Amsterdammer"; De Vrije Bladen (former Co-Ed.); De Gids (former Co-Ed.). Mbrships: PEN; Maatschappij (Leiden); Vereniging van Letterkundigen; Provinciaal Utrechts Genootschap. Hons: Dept. of Culture Award, 1960; Marianne Philips Prize, 1961. Address: Middenlaan 56, Doorwerth, Netherlands.

KELK, Fanny, pen name MONTELBAEN, Maria, b. 13 Jan. 1918, Amsterdam, Netherlands. Art Critic. Educ: Ecole du Louvre, Paris, France; Acad. de la Grande Chaumiere, Paris. Publs: Germ de Jong, 1973; Constant, 1974. Contbr. to: Elseviers' Mag.; Het Parool; Museum-journaal; Radio VARA. Mbrships: Ver Vereniging van Letterkundigen; Vereniging Nederlandse Journalisten; Assn. Int. des Critiques d'Art. Address: Kromme Waal 18, Amsterdam C, Netherlands.

KELLBERG, Aarno Antero, b. 2 Feb. 1932, Iisalmi, Finland. Teacher. Educ: Tchr. trng. coll. Publs: The Last Plays, 1964; The Koljonvirta Guerrilas, 1966; Number Four, 1970; Readers I-IV for Public Schls., 1968-69; (collab.) The Groundschool Teachers' Guidebook of the Fine Arts I-IV, 1973-74; The Groundschool Pupils' Book of the Fine Arts, 1973-74; scenarios for TV & radio; plays. Mbrships: Authors Union of Finland; Youth Authors Union of Finland; Youth Books Coun. of Finland; S.E. Authors Assn. Paltta. Hons: Min. of Educ., 1968; Cultural Fndn. of

Finland, 1968, 1971. Address: 07990 Ruotsinkylä, Finland.

KELLEY, H. N., b. 23 July 1911, Ochelata, Okla., USA. Vice President & General Manager, Oven Company. Educ: B.S., M.A., Northwestern Univ. Publs: Profile of a Parish, 1973; Conventional Murders, forthcoming. Contbr. to: var. mags.; trade jrnls. in bakery & food service fields. Mbrships: Sigma Delta Chi (jrnlsm. fraternity); Exmoor Country Club. Address: 1661 Sunset Lane, Bannockburn, Deerfield, IL 60015, USA.

KELLEY, Joanna Elizabeth, b. 23 May 1910, Murree, India. Civil Servant; Author. Educ: M.A., Cambridge Univ., 1931; Diplome pour Étrangers, Sorbonne Univ., Paris, France, 1932. Publs: When the Gates Shut, 1967. Contbr. to var. profl. jrnls. Hons: LL.D., Hull Univ., 1960; Girton Coll. Fellowship, Cambridge, 1968; O.B.E., 1973. Address: 31 Westmoreland Terrace, London SW1, UK.

KELLEY, William Melvin, b. 1937, NYC, USA. Writer. Educ: Harvard Univ. Publs: (novels) A Different Drummer, USA 1962, UK 1963; A Drop of Patience, USA 1965, UK 1966; dem, 1967; Dunsfords Travels Everywhere, 1970; (short stories) Dancers on the Sabre, USA 1964, UK 1965. Hons: Dana Reed Prize, Harvard Univ., 1960; Rosenthal Fndn. Award, 1963; Transatlantic Review Award, 1964. Address: c/o Doubleday, 277 Park Ave., N.Y., NY 10017, USA.

KELLY, Francis R., b. 1 May 1927, St. Paul, Minn., USA. Artist. Educ: Univ. of Hawaii; Acad. de la Grande Chaumiere, Paris; Central Schl. of Arts & Crafts, London. Publs: Art Restoration, 1972; The Studio & the adjust, 1975. Contbr. to: Artist; Arts Review; Art Jrnl.; Art & Artists; Connoisseur; Antique Finder; Antique Collector. Mbrships: Int. Inst. of Conservation; Hampstead Artists' Coun. Address: 18 Leinster Mews, London W2, UK.

KELLY, Gwen Nita, former pen name HEATH, Nita, b. 28 July 1922, Sydney, Australia. Writer. Educ: B.A., Univ. of Sydney. Publs: There is No Refuge, 1961. The Red Boat, 1968; What is Right? (w. M. Mackie), 1970. Contbr. to: Coast to Coast, biennial anthol. of Aust. short stories; Transition, anthol.; Aust. New Writing; & num. lit. & educl. jrnls. Mbrships. incl: Aust. Soc. of Authors; PEN (Aust.); Engl. Tchrs. Assn. Hons: Henry Lawson Award for Prose, Grenfell Festival, 1968; Commendations for short stories, Vic. Fellowship of Aust. Writers, 1965 & 1974; Guaranteed Income C'wlth. Fellowship Award, Aust. Lit. Bd., 1974-76. Address: P.O. Box 25, Armidale, N.S.W., Australia 2350.

KELLY, (Rev. Canon) John Norman Davidson, b. 13 Apr. 1909, Bridge of Allan, Scotland, UK. Anglican Priest; University Lecturer; College Principal. Educ: Glasgow Univ.; Queen's Coll., Oxford. Publs: Early Christian Creeds, 1950, 1972; Rufinus, a Commentary on the Apostles' Creed, 1955; Early Christian Doctrines, 1958; The Pastoral Epistles, 1963; The Athanasian Creed, 1964; The Epistles of Peter & of Jude, 1969; Aspects of the Passion, 1970. Mbr., Brit. Acad., 1965. Hons: D.D., Glasgow Univ., 1958; Fellow, Queen's Coll., Oxford. Address: 7 Crick Rd., Oxford, UK.

KELLY, Margaret McLaurin Ricaud, b. 22 Mar. 1910, Dillon, S.C., USA. Teacher. Educ: A.B., Winthrop Coll.; Postgrad. study, Univs. of Fla., Miami, N.C., S.C. & Duke Univ. Publs: Jack & the Flying Saucer, 1973; Poems, 1974; New Voices in American Poetry (anthol.), 1974. Address: 402 Fayetteville Ave., Bennettsville, SC 29512, USA.

KELLY, Thomas Eugene, pen name KELLY, Tim, b. 30 May 1935, Wichita, Kan., USA. Publisher. Educ: Creighton Univ., Omaha, Neb.; B.S., Univ. of Dayton, Ohio; M.S., Univ. of Kan.; Univ. of N.D. Publs: Trophy Care, 1971. Contbr. to: Outdoor Life; Sports Afield; N.D. Outdoors. Mbrships. incl: Outdoor Writers' Assn. of Am.; Nat. Taxidermists' Assn. Address: 148 Whitetail Rd., Albuquerque, NM 87122, USA.

KELSEY, Alice Geer, b. 21 Sept. 1896, Danvers, Mass., USA. Writer. Educ: B.A., Mt. Holyoke Coll., 1918. Publs. incl: Tino & The Typhoon, 1958; In the Same Country, 1958; Seven Minute Stories for Church & Home, 1958; Living & Working Together as Christians, 1960; Adventures with the Bible, 1960; New Flags Flying, 1964; Land of the Morning, 1968; The Thirty Gilt Pennies, 1968. Contbr. to many children's, educl. & relig. mags. Address: 109 Comstock Rd., Ithaca, NY 14850, USA.

KEMAL, Yasar, b. 1923, Kadirli, Adana, Turkey. Journalist; Author; Playwright. Publs. (transl'd. into Engl.) Memed My Hawk, 1961; Anatolian Tales, 1968; The Wind from the Plain, 1969; They Burn the Thistles, 1973; Iron Earth, Copper Sky, 1974; The Legend of Ararat, 1975. Mbr. & Pres., Writers' Union of Turkey. Hons: Varlik Award for Best Turkish Novel, 1956; Madarali Award for Best Turkish Novel, 1973. Address: P.K.14 Basinköy, Istanbul, Turkey.

KEMBLE, James, b. Australia. Consultant Surgeon; Urologist. Educ: Ch.M.; Sydney Univ.; St. Bartholomew's Hosp., London, UK. Publs: Idols & Invalids, 1933; Hero-Dust, 1936; Surgery for Nurses, 1949; Napoleon Immortal, the Medical History & Private Life of Napoleon Bonaparte, 1959; St. Helena during Napoleon's Exile – Gorrequer's Diary, 1969. Contbr. to: Brit. Med. Jrnl.; Sunday Times; Times Lit. Supplement; Observer; Daily Mail; Quarterly Review; etc. Mbrships. incl: F.R.C.S.; (England & Edinburgh); Fellow, Royal Soc. Med.; Soc. of Authors; Brit. Med. Assn.; Brit. Assn. Urological Surgs. Address: 24 Keswick Rd., London SW15 2JP, UK.

KEMELMAN, Harry, b. 24 Nov. 1908, Boston, Mass., USA. Writer. Educ: A.B., Boston Univ., 1930; M.A., Harvard Grad. Schl., 1931. Publs: Friday, The Rabbi Slept Late, 1964; Saturday, The Rabbi Went Hungry, 1966; The Nine Mile Walk, 1967; Sunday, The Rabbi Stayed Home, 1969; Commonsense in Education, 1970; Monday, The Rabbi Took Off, 1972; Tuesday, The Rabbi Saw Red, 1973. Mbrships: Authors' League; Dramatists' Guild. Hons: Edgar Allen Poe Award, 1964; Faith & Freedom Award. Address: Box 674, Marblehead, MA 01945, USA.

KEMPTER, Lothar, b. 1 May 1900, Zürich, Switz. Writer. Educ: D.Ph., 1929; Univs. Zürich & Berlin. Publs: Hölderlin und die Mythologie, 1929, 2nd ed., 1971; Hölderlin in Hauptwil, 1946; Das Musikkollegium Winterthur II, 1959; Aphorismen, 1973; (poetry) Schleppe und Flügel, 1974. Mbrships: Hölderlin Soc. (Dir., 1952-65); Winterthur Music Kollegium (Dir., 1938-72); Winterthur Lit. Union (Dir., 1955); Union Swiss Writers; Bd. Trustees, Martin-Bodmer Fndn. (1971-). Hons: Winterthur Town Award, 1959; Zürich Canton Award, 1972; Hölderlin Soc. (Hon. Mbr., 1974); Art Prize of Carl-Heinrich-Ernst Art Fndn., 1974. Address: CH 8408 Winterthur, Weinbergstr. 97, Switz.

KENDALL, Carlton, pen name ODLAW, Ladnek, b. 17 Aug. 1895, Oakland, Calif., USA. Author; Research Specialist; Executive. Educ: Univ. of Calif.; Travel & Rsch. Studies, London, Paris, Rome, Madrid, Geneva, Oxford, Cambridge, Yale, Harvard, Princeton, Columbia & Johns Hopkins Univs. Publs: The Truth About Korea, 1919; Caesar's Thoughts (poetry), 1973. Contbr. to num. US, for. jrnls. & poetry anthols.; Feature Writer, var. W. Coast newspapers; Cond., Literary Gossip Dept., Westward Mag. Address: 1410 Jackson St., Oakland, CA 94612, USA.

KENDALL, Carol, b. 13 Sept. 1917, Bucyrus, Ohio, USA. Writer. Educ: A.B., Ohio Univ., Athens, Ohio. Publs: The Black Seven, 1946; The Baby-Snatcher, 1952; (juvenile) The Other Side of the Tunnel, 1957; The Gammage Cup, 1959, also 2nd publr., title The Minnipins; The Big Splash, 1960; The Whisper of Glocken, 1965; also 2nd publr. Hons. incl: Ohioana Award, 1960 & Finalist Newberry Award, 1960 for The Gammage Cup. Address: 928 Holiday Dr., Lawrence, KS 66044, USA.

KENDE, Sandor, b. 27 May 1918, Budapest, Hungary. Writer. Educ: Sorbonne Univ., Paris. Publs. (in Hungarian) incl: (novels) Three Lazaruses, 1943; Sentenced to Each Other, 1946; The Sons of Lilith, 1948; The Heaven is Near, 1960; The Brothers, 1962; A Life Betrayed, 1965; Black Vacation, 1968; A Sentence Acquittal, 1968; My Friends in Love, 1970; An Extraordinary Girl, 1975; (stories) The Girl of the Seine, 1972; (play) My Friends in Love, 1973. Contbr. to: Jelenkor (lit. review). Mbr., Soc. of Writers in Hungary. Recip., awards for Culture of Socialism, 1954, 1958. Address: 7626 Pecs, Rakoczi u. 73/a, Hungary.

KENEALLY, Thomas, b. 1935, Sydney, Australia. Playwright; Novelist. Educ: studied for Priesthood & NSW Bar. Publs: The Place at Whitton, 1964; The Fear, 1965; Bring Larks & Heroes, 1967; Halloran's Little Boat (play) 1967; Three Cheers for the Paraclete, 1968; The Survivor, 1969; Childermas (play) 1969; A Dutiful Daughter, 1971; The Chant of Jimmie Blacksmith, 1972; An Awful Rose (play) 1972; Blood Red, Sister Rose, 1974. Contbr. to periodicals. Mbr., Aust. Soc. of Authors. Hons: Miles

Franklin Awards for Best Australian Novel of Yr., 1967, 1968; Captain Cook Bi-Centenary Prize, 1970; C'wlth Lit. Fellowships, 1968, 1972; Sydney Morning Herald Unesco Prize, 1972. Agent: Hope Lereche & Steel. Address: 14 Chisholm Ave., Avalon, NSW 2107, Australia.

KENKLE, Janet Everest, b. 5 Nov. 1917, Grand Rapids, Mich., USA. Kindergarten Teacher; Juvenile Author; Photographer. Educ: Grand Rapids Jr. Coll.; Univ. of Mich.; B.S., W. Mich. Univ., 1939. Publs: Once There Was A Kitten, 1951, 1962; The Kitten & the Parakeet, 1952; Christmas Kitten, 1953, 1964; Easter Kitten, 1955; Tabby's Kittens, 1956; J. Hamilton Hamster, 1957; Susie Stock Car, 1959, 1961; The Sea Cart, 1961, 1964; Schoolroom Bunny, 1965; The Raccoon Twins, 1972. Contbr. to mags., Childcraft Ency., photography jrnls. Mbr., Nat. Women's Book Assn. Hons: J. Hamilton Hamster chosen Ambassador Book by English-Speaking Union, 1957; Num. photog. hons. Address: 1360 Oakleigh Rd. NW, Grand Rapids, MI 49504, USA.

KENNEDY, Gerald, b. 30 Aug. 1907, Benzonia, Mich., USA. Methodist Bishop. Educ: A.B., Coll. of Pacific; A.N., B.D., Pacific Schl. of Relig.; S.T.M., Ph.D., Hertford Theol. Sem. Publs. incl: Lion & the Lamb, 1949; Go Inquire of the Lord, 1952; With Singleness of Heart, 1951; A Reader's Notebook, 1953; God's Good News, 1955; The Christian & His America, 1956; The Methodist Way of Life, 1958; The Marks of a Methodist, 1966; While I'm on my Feet, 1963; Who Speaks for God, 1964; The Parables, 1960; Fresh Every Morning, 1966; The Seven Worlds of the Minister, 1968; The Preacher & the New English Bible, 1972; My Third Reader's Notebook, 1973. Contbr. to var. jrnls. Recip., hon. degrees. Address: 624-C Avenida Sevilla, Laguna Hills, CA, USA.

KENNEDY, Malcolm Duncan, b. 5 Jan. 1895, Edinburgh, Scotland, UK. Specialist on Far Eastern Affairs; Former Army Officer. Educ: Royal Mil. Coll., Sandhurst, 1912-13. Publs: The Military Side of Japanese Life, 1924; Some Aspects of Japan & Her Defence Forces, 1928; The Changing Fabric of Japan, 1930; The Problem of Japan, 1935; A History of Japan, 1963; The Estrangement of Great Britain & Japan, 1969. Contbr. to: Int. Affairs; Asian Affairs; etc. Mbrships: Royal Inst. Int. Affairs; Japan Soc. of London; Royal C'wlth. Soc. Address: Inverurr, Kippford, by Dalbeattie, Kirkcudbrightshire, Scotland, UK.

KENNEDY, Robert Lee, b. 6 Jan. 1930, Compton, Calif., USA. Director of Communications, The Air Force Academy Foundation; Communications Consultant; Writer. Educ: B.A., 1956, M.A., 1971, Univ. Denver. Publs: Fundamentals of Quantity Food Preparation, Vol. I, Desserts & Beverages (w. Geraline Hardwick), 1975; Vol. II, Appetizers, Breads & Sandwiches (w. Geraline Hardwick), forthcoming; Fine Art of Business Entertaining (w. Dr. John N. Perryman), forthcoming. Contbr. to: Univ. Denver Mag.; Jrnl. Environmental Health; Schl. Food Serv. Jrnl.; & film scripts, etc. Mbrships. incl: Assoc. Bus. Writers Am. Address: 107 W. Cheyenne Rd., Colo. Springs, CO 80906, USA.

KENNELLY, Brendan, b. 17 Apr. 1936, Ballylongford, Repub. of Ireland. Professor of modern Literature. Educ: B.A., Trinity Coll., Dublin, 1961; M.A., 1963, Ph.D., 1967, Leeds Univ., UK. Publs. incl: (verse) The Rain, The Moon, 1961; The Dark About our Loves, 1962; Green Townlands: Poems, 1963 (these 3 w. Rudi Holzapfel); Let Fall no Burning Leaf, 1963; My Dark Fathers, 1964; Up and At It, 1965; Collection One: Getting Up Early, 1966; Good Souls to Survive, 1967; Dream of a Black Fox, 1968; Selected Poems, 1969; Ed., Penguin book of Irish Verse, 1970, 1972; Bread, 1971; Love-Cry, 1972; Salvation the Stranger, 1972; The Voices, 1973; (novels) The Crooked Cross, 1963; The Florentines, 1967. Contbr. to num. jrnls. Recip., A.E. Mem. Award, 1967. Address: 40 Trinity Coll., Dublin, Repub. of Ireland.

KENNET, Baron Wayland Hilton Young, b. 2 Aug. 1923. Author. Educ: Trinity Coll., Cambridge; Harvard Univ. Publs: (as Wayland Young) The Italian Left, 1949; The Deadweight, 1952; Now or Never, 1953; The Old London Churches (w. Elizabeth Young) 1956; The Montesi Scandal, 1957; Still Alive Tomorrow, 1958; Strategy for Survival, 1959; The Profumo Affair, 1963; Eros Denied, 1965; Thirty-Four Articles, 1965; (as Wayland Kennet) Preservation, 1972; (Ed.) Existing Mechanisms of Arms Control, 1965. Hons: F.R.I.B.A., 1970. Address: 100 Bayswater Rd., London W2, UK.

KENNY, Herbert A., b. 22 Dec. 1912, Boston, Mass., USA. Journalist; Book Editor. Educ: A.B., Boston Coll., 1934. Publs: 12 Birds (poetry); Suburban Man (poetry); Dear Dolphin (jvnle.); Alistare Owl (jvnle.); Cope Ann/Cope America, 1970; Literary Dublin: A History, 1974; A Boston Picture Book (w. B. Westman), 1974. Contbr. to: Mass. Review; Antioch Review; Commonweal; Cath. Ency. Mbrships: PEN; Authors' Guild; Poetry Soc. of Am.; The Speckled Band. Hons: Robert Frost Fellow in Poetry. Address: 804 Summer St., Manchester, MA 01944, USA.

KENT, Alexander, pen name of REEMAN, Douglas, b. 1925, London, UK. Author; Journalist. Publs. incl: Inclining to Crime; Stop Press Murder; The Weak & the Strong; Corpse to Cuba; The Kansas Fast Gun; Long Horn, Long Grass; Black Sunday; The Camp on Blood Island (w. Gordon Thomas); Broken Doll; Action of the Tiger; Red Red Red; Plant Poppies on my Grave; The Fall of Singapore: a New Assessment (w. I. Simson); etc. Contbr. to num. mags. & newspapers; BBC; etc. Address: c/o Scott Meredith, 44 Great Russell St., London WC1, UK.

KENT, (Ellen Louisa) Margaret, pen name KENT, Margaret, b. 15 Apr. 1894, Wells, Somerset, UK. Author. Educ: Univ. of Bristol; L.R.A.M. Publs. incl: The Cherry Tree Farm Books, 1942—; The Twins Books, 1942—; The Minute Stories, 1942; Animals of Hedge, Pond & Moor, 1944; Flowers, 1945; Pond Life, 1948; Animals of the Farm, 1949; The Seashore, 1949; At Tweedles Farm, 1949; Stories for Language Training, 1949, 1950; Four Plays with Music, 1951, 1953, 1955, 1956; The Jack-a-Nory Story Book, 1952; Two Modern Plays for Schools, 1953; The Tinker Tailor Story Book, 1955; Seaside Stories, 1957; Six Sherlocks (4 books), 1957; Kashi the Mongoose (in USA as The Lucky Thirteen), 1961; Two Dramatised Singing Games, 1963; Two-Way Songs for Infants, 1965. Contbr. to num. jrnls. Address: Meon, 3 Alexandra Way, Botley, Southampton SO3 2ED, UK.

KENWARD, Jean, b. 10 May 1920, Pangbourne, UK. Writer; Teacher. Educ: Dip., Speech & Drama, Univ. of London. Publs: Book of Rhymes; Rain; Flight of Words, 1969; The Forest, 1972; Rag Bag Book, 1973; Old Mister Hotch Potch, 1974. Contbr. to: Country Life; The Countryman; · Outposts; Poetry Review; Child Educ.; Liberal Educ.; Books. Mbr., Poetry Secretariat, Gtr. London Arts Assn. Recip., Sev. Premium Prizes, Poetry Soc. Address: 15 Shire Lane, Chorleywood, Rickmansworth, Herts., UK.

KENYON, (Dame) Kathleen Mary, b. 5 Jan. 1906, London, UK. Archaeologist. Educ: B.A., Somerville Coll., Oxford, 1928; M.A., 1933; D.Litt., 1964. Publs. incl: Excavations at Breedon-on-the-Hill, Leicester, 1950; Beginning in Archaeology, 1952; Excavations at Sutton Walls, Herefordshire, 1954; Diggin · up Jericho, 1957; Archaeology in the Holy Land, 1960; Amorites & the Canannites, 1966; Jerusalem: Excavating 3000 Years of History, 1967; Digging up Jerusalem, 1974. Contbr. to: Samaria-Sebaste, 1942, 1958; Excavations at Jericho, 1960, 1965; Antiquity; Illustrated London News; Palestine Exploration Quarterly. Mbrships incl: Hon. VP, Royal Archaeol. Inst.; Glasgow Archaeol. Soc. Hons. incl: C.B.E., 1954; D.B.E., 1973. Address: St. Hugh's Coll., Oxford, UK.

KÉPES, Géza, b. 1 Feb. 1909, Mátészalka, Hungary. Poet. Educ: Univ. Budapest; École Normale Superieure, Hungary. Publs. incl: (poetry) Gorgó mereng (Gorgon Musing), 1942; Só és bors (Salt & Pepper), 1956; Kö és festék (Stone & Colour), 1967; Viztükör (Surface of the Water), 1970; Csigaház (Snail Shell), 1973; (poetry transls.) (from Engl.) A Sziget Énekel (Songs of the Island), 1947; Elöször magyarul, 1972; Forditott Vilàg (World Turned Over), 1973; (from Finno-Ugrian langs.) Napfél és Éjfél (Midday & Midnight), 1972. Contbr. to num. reviews & jrnls. Mbrships: Finnish Lit. Soc.; Hungarian Acad. Scis. Hons. incl: Kt. Finnish Order Lion 1st class; Hungarian State Gold Medal poetry & transl.; József Attila Prizes, 1951, 1955 & 1974. Address: 1025 Budapest, Palánta utca 21, Hungary.

KERENYI, Grácia, b. 9 Sept. 1925, Budapest, Hungary. Writer. Educ: Phil.dr.; Prof. Publs: Azonosulások, 1968; Odtancowywanie poezji, 1973; Topográfia, 1975. Contbr. to: Élet és Irodalom; Vigilia; Literatura na swiecie. Mbrships: Union of Hungarian Writers; PEN; Hungarian Soc. for Classical Philol. Recip., Order for servs. rendered to propagation of Polish Culture. Address: Batthyány utca 12, 1015 Budapest, Hungary.

KERMODE, (John) Frank, b. 29 Nov. 1919, Douglas, Isle of Man, UK. University Teacher (Professor). Educ: B.A., 1940, M.A., 1947, Liverpool Univ. Publs. incl: Shakespeare's Tempest, 1954; John Donne, 1957; Romantic Image, 1957; The Living Milton; Wallace Stevens; The Sense of an Ending, 1967; Continuities, 1968; The Classic, 1975. Contbr. to: Atlantic; Commentary; N.Y. Review of Books; N.Y. Times; Partisan Review; Sewanee Review; Kenyon Review; New Lit. Hist.; Encounter; Guardian; Times Lit. Supplement; New Statesman; Listener, etc. Mbrships: Fellow, Brit. Acad.; F.R.S.L. Off., l'Ordre des Arts & des Scis. Address: King's College, Cambridge, UK.

KERNBACH, Victor, b. 14 Oct. 1923, Chişinău, Romania. Writer. Educ: B.A. Publs: (short stories) Povestiri ciudate (Strange Stories), 1967; (novels) Luntrea sublima (The Sublime Boat), 1961, latest ed., 1969; Vîntul de miercuri (The Wind of Wednesday), 1968; (poetry) Tabla de oricalc (The Tablet of Orichalc), 1971; (non-fiction) Enigmele miturilor astrale (The Enigmas of Astral Myths), 1971, latest ed., 1973. Contbr. to: România literară; Steaua; Viata româneasca; Magazin; etc. Mbr., Union Romanian Writers. Address: Drumul Taberei 57; bl.R-4, sc.B, ap.49, sec. 7, Bucharest, Romania.

KERNER, Almeric Edmund Raymond, b. Colombo, Sri Lanka. International Civil Servant. Educ: A,. Univ., Wash. D.C., USA. Publs: Ceylon: A Tourist Paradise, 1968; Anatomy of the Cod War, 1973. Contbr. to: N.Y. Times. Mbrships: Bd. Dirs., Dag Hammarskjold Mem. Schlrship. Fund, 1973; Chmn., Mbrships. & Accreditations Comm., UN Corres. Assn., 1973; Int. Study & Rsch. Grp., N.Y.; E. African Wildlife Soc., Nairobi; Ceylon Wildlife Soc., Colombo; Defenders of Wildlife Soc., Wash. D.C. Address: 435 E. 79th St., N.Y., NY 10021, USA.

KERR, Walter Francis, b. 1913, Evanston, Ill., USA. Drama Critic. Educ: Northwestern Univ., Chgo. Publs: Pieces at Eight; How Not to Write a Play; The Decline of Pleasure; The Theatre in Spite of Itself; Tragedy & Comedy; Thirty Plays hath November; Criticism & Censorship; & var. plays & adaptations. Contbr. to: Life; Saturday Evening Post; Horizon; N.Y. Times; Harper's; Commonweal. Address: 1 Beach Ave., Larchmont, NY, USA.

KERRIGAN, (Thomas) Anthony, b. 14 Mar. 1918, Winchester, Mass., USA. Writer; Translator; University Professor. Educ: Univs. of Havana, Cuba, Paris, France, Mich., USA, S. Calif., Calif., Fla., Columbia; SUNY, Buffalo. Publs. incl: (verse) At the Front Door of the Atlantic; Espousal in August; Ed. & Transl., The Selected Works of Miguel de Unamuno, 7 vols., 1969-; 2 vols. of exploration lit., 1951, 3 works by Pio Baroja, 1959; 2 vols. by Jorge Luis Borges, 1962, 1967. Contbr. to num. lit. jrnls. in Can., USA, Repub. of Ireland & Spain. Mbr., Irish PEN. Hons: Named in Directory of Fellows, Am. Coun. of Learned Socs. Address: 2 de Mayo 33, Palma de Mallorca, Baleares, Spain.

KERSHAU, Beulah Sevenney, pen name BEULAH, b. 9 Jan. 1914, Cloride, No., USA. Poet; Singer; Pianist. Publs: Poems, Vol. I, 1968, Vol. II, 1972. Contbr. to: Evansville Press; Carmi Times; Songwriters Review; Frontier News; St. Louis Globe-Democrat; Poetry Pageant. Hons. incl: 2 Awards in Int. Poetry Contests, USSR; Honor Roll, Songwriters Review. Address: Route 1, Crossville, IL, USA.

KERSHAW, Harry, pen name KERSHAW, H. V., b. 29 May 1918, Manchester, UK. Television Scriptwriter. Publs: (TV series & plays) Armchair Theatre; Shadow Squad; The Verdict is Yours; Skyport; Knight Errant; The Odd Man; Biggles; Coronation Street (Writer, Script Editor, Prod. Exec. Prod.); Pardon the Expression (Exec. Prod.); The Villains (Prod./Writer); City '68 (Prod./Writer); Family at War; Crown Court; Love Thy Neighbour; The Life of Riley (Creator/Writer). Mbr., Writers' Guild of GB. Address: 9 Bryn-y-Coed, Deganwy, Gwynedd, Wales, UK.

KERSTING, Anthony Frank, b. 7 Nov. 1916, London, UK. Architectural Photographer. Educ: Dulwich Coll., London. Publs: Portrait of Cambridge, 1955, of Oxford, 1956, of Edinburgh, 1961, of Westminster, 1964; Castles of the Crusaders, 1966; Barockkirchen in Altbayern, 1969; English Cathedrals, 1972. Contbr. to: Country Life. Mbrships: Fellow, Royal Photographic Soc.; Fellow, Royal Geog. Soc. Address: 37 Frewin Rd., London SW18 3LR, UK.

KERTESZ, Akos, b. 18 July 1932, Budapest, Hungary. Film Script Writer. Educ: Eötvös Lorand Univ. Publs: (novels) Passage, 1965; Makra, 1971; (stories) Love of Everyday, 1962; Name Day, 1973; (films) One Has to Live Every Day, 1963; Attachment, 1974. Mbrships: Assn. of Hungarian Writers; Assn. of Film Artists. Hons: Lit. Prize, Trades Union Coun., 1966; Jozsef Attila Prize, 1972. Address: Pauley Ede St. 67, H 1060 Budapest, Hungary.

KESEY, Ken (Elton), b. 17 Sept. 1935, La Junta, Colo., USA. Motion Picture Company President. Educ: B.A., Univ. of Ore., 1957; Stanford Univ., 1958-59. Publs: One Flew Over the Cuckoo's Nest, USA 1962, UK 1963; Sometimes a Great Notion, USA 1964, UK 1966; var. extracts from notebooks. Contbr. to: The Last Supplement to the Whole Earth Catalog. Hons: Woodrow Wilson Fellowship, 1958-59; Saxton Mem. Trust Award, 1959. Address: 345 Franklin St., San Fran., CA, USA.

KESSE-ADU, Kwame, b. 25 Dec. 1925, Akyem Abuakwa, Kibi, Ghana. Journalist. Publs: The Queen of the Twin Rivers (histl. novel); A Ghanaian Journalist Views America, 1968; The Birth of the Second Republic, 1969; Politics of Political Detention, 1971; Ofori Ko Banso (in Akan lang.), nos. 1 & 2 (co-author), 1973. Ed., The Gold Coast Leader, 1948, Morning Telegraph 1949-50, The Daily Guardian 1951-53, Ghana Confidential 1972-; Contbr. to: African World; The Parliamentarian; Hartford Courant, USA; The Pioneer, Kumasi (City Ed. 1954-72); Africa Bulletin, W. Germany (For. Corres.). Mbrships incl: Ghana Jrnlsts. Assn.; Ghana Assn. of Writers. Recip., Freedom of City of Knoxville, USA, 1968. Address: P.O. Box 4246, Accra, Ghana.

KESSEL, Joseph, b. 10 Feb. 1898. Writer; Journalist. Educ: Sorbonne Univ., Paris. Publs. incl: La Steppe Rouge; Les Captifs; Belle de Jour; Vent de Sable; Les Rois Aveugles; Les Enfants de Chance; La Piste Fauve; La Vallée du Rubis; Le Lion; Le Mains du Miracle, 1960; Les Alcooliques Anonymes, 1960; Pour L'Honneur, 1964; Le Coup de Grâce, 1965; Terre d'Amour & de Feu, 1965; Les Cavaliers, 1967; Des Hommes, 1972. Contbr. to: Le Matin; Figaro; Paris Soir. Mbr., French Acad. Hons: Legion of Honour, Commander; Prix des Ambassadeurs, 1958. Address: 18 rue Quentin-Bauchart, Paris 8e, France.

KESSLER, Jascha, b. 27 Nov. 1929, NYC, USA. Writer. Educ: B.A., Univ. Heights Coll., N.Y. Univ., 1950; M.A., 1951, Ph.D., 1955, Univ. of Mich., Ann Arbor. Publs: American Poems: A Contemporary Collection, 1964, 4th ed., 1972; An Egyptian Bondage & Other Stories, 1967; Whatever Love Declares (poems), 1969; After the Armies Have Passed (poems), 1970. Contbr. to num. jrnls. & mags. Mbrships: ASCAP; PEN. Recip., num. awards & hons. Address: 218 Sixteenth St., Sta. Monica, CA 90402, USA.

KESTEN, Hermann, b. 28 Jan. 1900, Germany. Author. Educ: Univs. Erlangen, Frankfurt am Main, Rome. Publs. incl: (novels in German) Joseph Breaks Free, 1930; Der Scharlatan, 1932; The Twins of Nurnberg, 1946; Der Sohn des Glücks, 1955; Bücher der Liebe, 1960; Die Abenteuer eines Moralisten, 1961; Die Zeit der Narren, 1966; Ein Mann von sechzig Jahren, 1972; (biog.) Copernicus & His World, 1948; Casanova, 1956; (short stories) Die 30 Erzählungen, 1962; (plays) Einer sagt die Wahrheit, 1930; (poetry) Ich bin der ich bin, 1974; & 35 books of plays, poems, stories, essays, anthols., more than 150 transls. publd. in 28 countries or langs. Mbr., PEN, (Pres., W. Germany). Hons. incl: Premio di Calabria, 1969; Büchnerpreis, 1974. Address: Via Brescia 29, Rome, Italy.

KESTERTON, Wilfred Harold, b. 22 July 1914, Regina, Can. University Professor of Journalism. Educ: B.A., Queen's Univ., Kingston; B.J., Carleton Univ., Ottawa. Publs: A History of Journalism in Canada, 1967; A Century of Journalism; Un Siecle de Reportage (co-ed.), 1967. Contbr. to: Queen's Quarterly; Ency. Canadiana; Ency. Americana; Can. Annual Review; Das Handbuch der Weltpresse; Can. Yrbook. Mbrships incl: Assn. for Educ. in Jrnlsm.; Lit. & Media Comm., Can. Exhibit, Brussels, 1956; Nat. Press Club Centennial Comm., 1964-68. Hons: Coronation Medal, 1953; Humanities Grant, Can. Rsch. Coun., 1953. Address: Apt. 903, Colonel By Towers, 315 Holmwood Ave., Ottawa, Can. K1S 2R2.

KETCHAM, Ralph, b. 28 Oct. 1927, Berea, Ohio, USA. Author; Teacher. Educ: A.B., Allegheny Coll. 1949; M.A., Colgate Univ., 1952; Ph.D., Syracuse Univ., 1956. Publs: Benjamin Franklin, 1965; James Madison, 1971; From Colony to Country, 1974. Contbr. to: Va. Quarterly

Review; Wm. & Mary Quarterly. Mbr., Am. Studies Assn. Recip., Nomination for Nat. Book Award, 1972. Address: 1002 Ackerman Ave., Syracuse, NY 13210, USA.

KEULS, Hans, b. 11 Sept. 1910, Amsterdam, Netherlands. Lawyer; Playwright; TV Scriptwriter. Educ: Law degree, Univ. of Amsterdam. Publs. incl: (stage plays) Plantage Tamarinda; Voor het laetst Lady Barker; Johan van Oldenbasnevelat; Confrontation on the Forum Romanum; (TV plays & serials) Stadhuis op Helten, 1960-64; The Search (w. E. Trevor), 1966; Centraal Station, 1974. VP, Soc. of Dutch Dramatists. Hons: Visser Neerlandia Prize for plays, 1965; Van der Vies Prize for plays, 1969; Hustinx Prize for Dutch/Flemish playwrights, 1972. Address: 12 Tongdean Ave., Hove, Sussex, UK.

KEY, Mary Ritchie, b. 19 Mar. 1924, San Diego, Calif., USA. Professor. Educ: M.A. 1960, Ph.D. 1963, Univ. of Tex. Publs. incl: Vocabulario Mejicano de la Sierra de Zacapoaxtla (w. Harold Key), 1953; Bolivian Indian Tribes (w. H. Key), 1967; Comparative Tacanan Phonology, 1968; Male/Female Language, 1975; Paralinguistics & Kinesics: Nonverbal Communication, 1975; The Grouping of South American Indian Languages (to be publd.) Contbr. to: Studies in Linguistics; Ethnomusicol.; Am. Anthropologist; Int. Jrnl. Am. Linguistics; Language; Linguistics; La Linguistique; other profl. publs. Mbr., var. profl. assns. Address: Program in Linguistics, Univ. of California at Irvine, Irvine, CA 92664, USA.

KEYSER, George Gustave, b. 19 Feb. 1910, Cumberland, Md., USA. Publs: Listen Softly, 1971. Contbr., over 90 poetry mags. & lit. jrnls., US, Can., Italy, India, Australia & Japan; Num. anthols. & textbooks; Assoc. Ed., Modern Haiku Mag.; Cons. Ed., Dragonfly (haiku quarterly). Mbrships: Poetry Soc. of Am.; World Poetry Soc. Intercontinental; Int. Poetry Soc.; Centro Studi E. Scambi Int.; S. & W. Lit. Assn.; Poetry Soc. of Tex.; Co-fndr., Western World Haiku Soc. Hons: Voice of the Year Award, Human Voice Quarterly, 1970; Poetry Soc. of Tex. Award, 1972; Num. awards from mags. Address: 4912 Gaston Ave., Apt. J, Dallas, TX 75214, USA.

KEYSER, James William, b. 4 May 1917, London, UK. Reader in Chemical Pathology. Educ: M.Sc.; Ph.D., Univ. of London; F.R.I.C.; Fellow, Royal Coll. Pathol. Publs: Chemistry & Therapeutics of Synthetic Drugs, 1950; Colorimetric Analysis, Vol. I (w. N.L. Allport), 1957. Contbr. to: Lancet; Brit. Med. Jrnl.; Postgrad. Med. Jrnl.; Clinical Chem.; etc. Mbr., var. profl. assns. Address: 56 Ogwen Dr., Cardiff CF2 6LL, UK.

KHAN, Ghulam Mustafa, b. 1 July 1912, Jabalpur, C.P., India. Professor. Educ: M.A., Urdu; M.A., Persian; LL.B.; Ph.D.; D.Litt. Publs. incl: Influence of Urdu on Persian, 1952; A History of Bahram Shah of Ghaznin, 1955; Hali ka dhahni Irtika, 1956; Uni Nuqoosh, 1956; A History of Persian Literature in the Indo-Pak Sub-Continent, 1972; Jami'al Qawaid, 1972; Maktubat i Sarhindi, 1972; Ed., Urdu-Sindi Dictionary, 1960; Ed., Sindhi Urdu Dictionary, 1959; Ed., Persian translation of the Koran, 1962. Contbr. to: Islamic Culture; Maarif; Azamgarh; Nagpur Univ. Jrnl.; Sind Univ. Jrnl.; Urdu; Nuqoosh, etc. Mbrships: Nagpur Univ. Ct.; Aligarh Univ. Ct. Recip., 2 lit. prizes. Address: 2 Old Univ. Campus, Hyderabad, Pakistan.

KHERDIAN, David, b. 17 Dec. 1931, Racine, Wis., USA. Poet. Educ: B.S., Philos., Univ. of Wis. Publs. incl: A Bibliography of William Saroyan, 1965; On the Death of My Father & Other Poems, 1970; Homage to Adana, 1971; Looking Over Hills, 1972; A David Kherdian Sampler, 1974; Ed., Down at the Sante Fe Depot: 20 Fresno Poets, 1970; Settling America: The Ethnic Expression of 14 Contemporary Poets, 1074. Contbr. to reviews. Address: East Chatham, NY 12060, USA.

KHOSLA, Gopal Das, b. 15 Dec. 1901, Lahore, Pakistan. Writer; retired High Court Judge. Educ: B.A., Cambridge Univ.; Barrister-at-Law, Lincoln's Inn, London. Publs. incl: Stern Reckoning, 1948; Himalayan Circuit, 1956; The Price of a Wife, 1958; The Horoscope Cannot Lie, 1961; The Murder of the Mahatma, 1963; The Last Mughal, 1969; A Taste of India, 1970; A Way of Loving, 1973; Indira Gandhi, 1974; The Last Days of Netaji, 1974. Contbr. to: Times India; Statesman; All India & BBC radio; etc. Mbr., Authors' Guild India (Pres.). Hons: short story prizes, Illustrated Wkly. India & Hindustan Times. Address: 78-G Sujan Singh Pk., New Delhi 3, India.

KHRAPCHENKO, Michail Borisovich, b. 21 Nov. 1904, Chijovka, Smolensk, Russia. Literary Scholar. Educ: Grad.,

Smolensk Univ., 1924; Post-grad., Assn. Insts. of Social Scis., 1929; Dr. Philol., 1953; Academician, 1966. Publs: N.V. Gogol, 1936; N.V. Gogol, Creative Works, 1954, 3rd ed., 1959; Leo Tolstoy as Artist, 1963, 3rd ed., 1971; The Writer as a Creative Personality & the Development of Literature, 1970, 2nd ed., 1972. Contbr. to: Znamia; Voprosi Literaturi; Russkaya Literatura. Mbr., Writers' Union of USSR. Hons: 2 Decorations, Lenin's Order, 1945, 1971; Decoration, Order of Oct. Revolution, 1974; Lenin Lit. Prize, 1974. Address: Leninski Prospect 13, Apt. 138, Moscow, USSR.

KIDNER, Frank Derek, b. 22 Sept. 1913, London, UK. Clergyman. Educ: Royal Coll. of Music, 1931-36; M.A., Christ's Coll., Cambridge, 1944. Publs: Tyndale Old Testament Commentary, Proverbs, 1964; Genesis, 1967, Psalms, Vol. I, 1973, Vol. 2, 1975. Contbr. to: Theol.; Churchman; Tyndale Bulletin. Mbrships: Soc. for Old Testament Study; Tyndale Fellowship for Biblical Rsch. Hons: Challen Gold Medal, Royal Coll. Music, 1936; Select Preacher, Univ. of Cambridge, 1957. Address: 36 Selwyn Gdns., Cambridge CB3 9BA, UK.

KIEFFER, Jean Egon, b. 20 Aug. 1913, Berlin, Germany. Art Critic; Author; Film Director. Contbr. to: Wiener Zeitung; Die Furche; Filmkunst. Mbrships: Austrian Writer's Assn.; Assn. of Austrian Film Jrnlsts. & Critics; Austrian Soc. of Film Sci. Recip., Hon. Silver Medal of Merit, Repub. of Austria. Address: 1223 Wien, Am Kaisermuehlendamm 3/78, Austria.

KIELICH, Wolf, b. 20 Dec. 1920, Djakarta, Indonesia. Television Documentary Film Producer; Journalist; Writer. Educ: Schl. of Jrnlsm., Northwestern Univ., USA. Publs: Anatomie van de Gummiknuppel, 1973; sev. books on environmental problems. Contbr. to newspapers & jrnls. Address: Zomerlaan 27, Heemstede, Netherlands.

KIELY, Benedict, b. 15 Aug. 1919, Dromore, Co. Tyrone, Repub. of Ireland. Journalist; Lecturer. Educ: Nat. Univ. of Ireland. Publs. incl: (novels) Land Without Stars, 1946; Call for a Miracle, UK 1950, USA 1951; The Cards of the Gambler, 1953; The Captain with the Whiskers, UK 1960, USA 1961; Dogs Enjoy the Morning, 1968; (short stories) A Journey to the Seven Streams, 1963; (non-fiction) Modern Irish Fiction, 1950. Contbr. to: New Yorker; Dublin Mag.; Penguin Mod. Stories 5; var. newspapers; etc. Mbrships: Irish Acad. Letters (Coun.); Am.-Irish Fndn. (Acad. Comm.). Address: c/o Irish Times, Westmoreland St., Dublin, Repub. of Ireland.

KILGOUR, Vernon Earl, b. 25 Nov. 1916, Clinton, Mass., USA. Author; Inventor. Educ: Becker Coll.; Special Student, Harvard Univ., 1945-47. Publs: The Clinton Boys & the Phantom Raider; The Clinton Boys & the Fifth Column. Ghost Writer; Agt. & Bus. Mgr., Cheney Index to Knowledge, 1945—. Address: 66 Malden St., W. Boylston, MA, USA.

KILLANIN, (Lord), pen name KILLANIN, Michael, b. 3 July 1914, London, UK. Company Director. Educ: M.A., Magdalene Coll., Cambridge; Sorbonne, Paris, France. Publs: Four Days, 1938; Sir Godfrey Kneller, 1948; Shell Guide to Ireland, 1961. Contbr. to: Daily Express, 1935; Daily Mail, 1935-39; var. jrnls., GB, Repub. of Ireland, Europe & USA. Mbrships: Royal Irish Acad.; Pres., Int. Olympic Comm. Hons: LL.D.; Var. decorations from British, French, Italian, Japanese, German, San Dominican, Columbian, Soviet & Brazilian auths. Address: 30 Lansdowne Road, Dublin 4, Repub. of Ireland.

KILLENS, John Oliver, b. 1916, Macon, Ga., USA. Writer. Educ: var. Colls.; Columbia Univ.; N.Y. Univ. Publs: (novels) Youngblood, USA 1954, UK 1956; And Then We Heard the Thunder, USA 1962, UK 1964; 'Sippi, 1967; Slaves, 1969; The Cotillion: or, One Good Bull Is Half the Herd, 1971; (play) Lower than the Angels, prod. 1965; (essays) Black Man's Burden, 1966; (filmscript) Odds Against Tomorrow. Address: c/o Simon & Schuster Inc., 630 Fifth Ave., N.Y., NY 10020, USA.

KILLEY, Homer Charles, b. 15 May 1915, Kent, UK. Professor of Oral Surgery. Educ: King's Coll. Hosp., Guy's Hosp., London. Publs. incl: Fractures of the Facial Skeleton (w. N. L. Rowe), 1955, 2nd ed., 1968; Fractures of the Middle Third of the Facial Skeleton, 1965, 2nd ed., 1971; Fractures of the Mandible, 1967, 2nd ed., 1971; Benign Cystic Lesions of the Jaws (w. L. W. Kay), 1966, 2nd ed., 1972; The Prevention of Complications in Dental Surgery (w. L. W. Kay), 1969; An Outline of Oral Surgery,

Parts I & II (co-author), 1971; The Maxillary Sinus & its Dental Implications (w. L. W. Kay), forthcoming; num. for. eds. of works. Mbr., num. profl. assns. Address: Dept. of Oral Surgery, Eastman Dental Hospital, Gray's Inn Rd., London WC1X 8LD, UK.

KILLIAN, Ray Allen, b. 9 May 1922, Catawba, Co., N.C., USA. Business Executive. Educ: A.B., Lenoir Rhyne; Grad. study, Univ. of N.C.; Geo. Wash. Univ.; Harvard Grad. Schl. of Bus. Admin.; Doctorate Bus. Admin., Lenoir Rhyne, 1973. Publs: Managers Must Lead!, 1966; Managing by Design . . . for Maximum Executive Effectiveness, 1968; The Working Woman: A Male Manager's View, 1971. Contbr. to: Am. Mgmt. Assn. publs. Address: 155 Canterbury Rd. S., Charlotte, NC 28211, USA.

KILLILEA, Marie, b. 28 June 1913, NYC, USA. Author; Lecturer; Founder of United Cerebral Palsy Association. Publs: Karen, 1952; Wren, 1954; Treasure on the Hill, 1960; With Love From Karen, 1963. Contbr. to: Reader's Digest; Family Circle; Ladies Home Jrnl. Mbrships: Int. Platform Assn.; Authors Guild; Cath. Actors Guild; Westchester Revolver & Rifle League. Hons: Christopher Awards, 1952, 1953; Golden Book Award, 1953. Address: 118 Park Avenue, Larchmont, NY 10538, USA.

KILPI, Eeva Karin, b. 18 Feb. 1928, Hiitola, Finland (now USSR). Author. Educ: M.A., Helsinki Univ., 1953. Publs: Lock of a Witch (short stories), 1959; Shores of a Blossoming Land (novel), 1960; Life To & Fro (novel), 1964; Summer & the Middle-aged Woman (short stories), 1970; Tamara (novel), 1972; Wedding-dance (novel), 1973. Mbrships: Pres., Finnish PEN, 1970-75; Bd.Mbr., Finnish Writers' Union, 1971-73. Hons: Lit. State Prizes, 1968, 1974; Lit. Prize of the City Espoo, 1974; Pro Finlandia Medal, 1974.

KILPINEN-BENSON, Inkeri, b. 15 June 1926, Heinola, Finland. Research Officer in Public Health Administration; Playwright. Educ: M.A., Univ. Helsinki, 1953; Univ. Minn., USA, 1957. Publs: (Plays, all prod. by Finnish Nat. Theatre) Atlantica, 1959; Tuntematon Potilas (Unknown Patient), 1964; Herra Johtaja (Mr. Director), 1967; Toinen, Maailma (Another World), 1972. Contbr. to: Suomen Kuvalehti; Finnish TV & radio; etc. Mbrships. incl: Finnish Dramatists Guild; Ctrl. Bd. Finnish Theatre Assns. Recip., Int. Theatre Inst. Finnish Ctr. State Prize, 1972. Address: Ylisrinne 5 as 3, 02210 Espoo, Finland.

KILROY, Thomas, b. 23 Sept. 1934, Callan, Repub. of Ireland. Writer. Educ: M.A., Univ. Coll., Dublin. Publs: The Death & Resurrection of Mr. Roche, 1968; The Big Chapel, 1971; Sean O'Casey, 1974. Mbrships: Fellow, Royal Soc. of Lit.; Irish Acad. of Letters. Hons: Guardian Fiction Prize, 1971; Heinnemann Award for Lit., 1971; Lit. Award, Irish Acad. of Letters, 1972; Am.-Irish Fndn. Award, 1974. Address: c/o Margaret Ramsey Ltd., 14a Goodwins Court, St. Martins Lane, London, UK.

KIM, Dong-Ri, b. 24 Nov. 1913, Kyung-ju, Korea. Author; Magazine Editor; Professor. Publs: Picture of a Sorceress, 1946; Literature & the Human Beings, 1948; The Story of the Yellow Earth, 1949; Reservists, 1950; A Survey of Literature, 1952; The Cross for Saphan, 1957; Existentialistic Dance, 1958; The Standard Bearer of Freedom, 1959; The Life-Size Buddha, 1963; The Sea Wind, 1963; Freedom & Life, 1966; The Sound of Magpie, 1972; The Rock, 1972; Contbr. to: Hankook Moonhak (Korean Lit.). Life Mbr., Korean Acad. of Arts. Hons. incl: Korean Acad. Arts Prize for Lit., 1958; Lit. Prize of City of Seoul, 1970; D.Litt., Chung Ang Univ. Address: 155 Hung In Dong, Sung-dong-ku, Seoul, S. Korea.

KIM, Richard, b. 13 Mar. 1932, Hamhung City, Korea. (US citizen). Writer; Adjunct Associate Professor of English. Educ: Middlebury Coll., Vt., 1955-59; M.A., Johns Hopkins Univ., 1960; M.F.A., Univ. of Iowa, 1962; M.A., Harvard Univ., 1963. Publs: (novels) The Martyred, USA & UK 1964; The Innocent, USA 1968, UK 1969; Lost Names, USA 1970, UK 1971. Mbr., Am.-Korean Fndn. (Bd. of Dirs.) Hons: Mary Roberts Rinehart Fndn. Fellowship, 1961; Ford For. Area Fellowship, 1962; Guggenheim Fellowship, 1965. Address: Leverett Rd., Shutesbury, MA 01072, USA.

KIMBLE, Vesta Baker, b. 25 Dec. 1900, Metz, W. Va., USA. Oil Company Owner. Publs: God's Gift to Me (poetry), 1960; He Leadeth Me, 1965; Booklets — Thinking of You, 1950, Our Mother, 1955, In Sympathy, 1957,

Right Living, 1964. Contbr. to poetry jrnls. & local press. Mbrships: Int. Poetry Soc.; Nat. Poetry Soc.; Tex. Poetry Soc.; Past VP, Breckenridge Poetry Soc.; Official Poet, Stephens Mem. Hosp. Aux. Address: 701 W. Hullum St., Breckenridge, TX 76024, USA.

KIMPEL, Benjamin Franklin, b. 9 May 1905, Racine, Wis., USA. Professor of Philosophy. Educ: B.A., Univ. of Wis., 1926; Ph.D., Yale Univ., 1932. Publs. incl: Religious Faith, Language, & Knowledge, 1952; Moral Principles in the Bible, 1956; Kant's Critical Philosophy, 1964; Neitzsche's Beyond Good & Evil, 1964; Schopenhauer's Philosophy, 1965; Philosophy of Zen Buddhism, 1966. Contbr. to Jrnl. for Sci. Study of Relig. Address: West St., N. Bennington, VT 05257, USA.

KING, Daniel Patrick, b. 23 Feb. 1942, Milwaukee, Wis., USA. Writer; Lecturer in Police Science & Criminal Law. Educ: Dip. in Criminalistics, Inst. of Applied Sci., Chgo., 1961; B.Sc., Univ. of Wis., 1965; Grad. Schl., Marquette Univ., 1966-68. Publs: The Right of Counsel in State Courts, 1965. Contbr. to: The Criminologist; Jrnl. of Criminal Law, Criminol. & Police Sci. (Book reviewer 1967-1972); Criminal Law Quarterly; Criminal Law Review; Baker St. Jrnl., USA; Police Jrnl., USA (Book reviewer 1964-67). Mbrships incl: Crime Writers' Assn., UK; Sherlock Holmes Soc. of London. Address: 5125 N. Cumberland Blvd., Whitefish Bay, WI 53217, USA.

KING, Francis Henry, pen name CAULDWELL, Frank, b. 4 Mar. 1923, Adelboden, Switz. Author. Educ: M.A., Univ. of Oxford, UK. Publs: To the Dark Tower, 1946; The Dividing Stream, 1951; The Widow, 1957; The Man on the Rock, 1957; The Custom House, 1961; The Last of the Pleasure Gardens, 1965; A Domestic Animal, 1969; Flights, 1973; A Game of Patience, 1974. Contbr. to: Sunday Telegraph; Spectator; Fin. Times. Mbrships. incl: F.R.S.L.; Comm., Soc. of Authors; Past Comm. Mbr., PEN; Soc. for Psychical Rsch. Hons: Somerset Maugham Prize, 1952; Katherine Mansfield Short Story Prize, 1964. Address: 19 Gordon Place, London W8 4JE, UK.

KING, Kenneth Moffat, b. 1906, San Francisco, Calif., USA. Writer. Educ: Pomona Coll., Univ. of Mich.; Univ. of Calif.; Stanford Univ.; M.A. Publs: The Stars Roll By (play); The Queen; The Book of Flight; Mission to Paradise; Six Famous Americans; Adventure Annual for Boys; Pancho Villa. Contbr. to: Elizabethan; Punch; Wide World; Daily Mail; Children's Newspaper; Heiress; etc. Address: The Studio, Great Woodcote Park, Purley, Surrey CR2 3QR, UK.

KING, Philip, b. 30 Oct. 1904, Beverley, UK. Actor; Playwright. Publs: (plays) Without the Prince; See How They Run; On Monday Next; Pool's Paradise; How Are You Johnnie; Serious Charge; Sailor Beware (w. Falkland L. Cary); Watch It Sailor; Rock a Bye Sailor; Big Bad Mouse; Murder in Company (w. John Boland); etc. Mbrships: Dramatists' Club; Savage Club; Constitutional Club. Address: 3 Woodland Way, Withdean, Brighton BN1 8BA, Sussex, UK.

KING, Ruby Thompson (Mrs.), pen name WIB, b. Johnson Co., Wrightsville, Ga., USA. English Teacher. Educ: A.B., M.A., Univ. of Ga.; Geo. Peabody Coll. for Tchrs.; Fla. State Univ.; Univ. of Edinburgh, UK. Contbr. to 7 anthols. of Am. verse & 4 int. anthols.; var. other newspapers, anthols. & mags.; Columnist, 3 newspapers. Hons: Carl Sandburg Award; Poetry Press Award. Address: POB 428, Douglas, GA 31533, USA.

KING, Rufus, pen name KING, R. G. Jr., b. 25 Mar. 1917, Seattle, Wash., USA. Attorney-at-Law. Educ: A.B. Princeton Univ., 1938; J.D., Yale Univ., 1943; Stanford Univ., Calif., 1940-41. Publs: You & I, 1940; Manifesto, 1948; Gambling & Organized Crime, 1969; The Drug Hang-Up: America's Fifty Year Folly, 1973, 2nd ed., different publr., 1974. Contbr. to num. legal periodicals. Mbrships: Am. Law Inst.; Am. Bar. Assn. (Chmn. Criminal Law Sect., 1957-62); Joint Am. Bar Assn. & Am. Med. Assn. Comm. for Narcotic Drugs (Chmn. 1953-58). Address: Woodward Bldg., Wash. DC 20005, USA.

KING, Stella, b. Birmingham, UK. Writer. Educ: Southern Coll. of Art. Publs: Once upon a Time (w. Robert Glenton), 1960; Princess Marina, Her Life & Times, 1969, USA, 1970; Biography of Yvonne Rudellat, forthcoming. Contbr. to: The Times; Beaverbrook Newspapers; N.Y. Times; Rdrs.' Digest. Address: Morar Cottage, Ridge Lane, Watford, Herts., UK.

KINGDON, Robert McCune, b. 29 Dec. 1927, Chgo., Ill., USA. Historian. Educ: A.B., Oberlin Coll., 1949; M.A., Columbia Univ., 1950; Ph.D., 1955. Publs: Geneva & the Coming of the Wars of Religion in France, 1555-1563, 1956; Geneva & the Consolidation of the French Protestant Movement, 1564-1572, 1967; Ed., Registres de la Compagnie des Pasteurs de Genève au temps de Calvin (w. J.-F. Bergier), 1962, 1964; Ed., Théodore de Bèze, Du Droit des Magistrats, 1971; Transition & Revolution, 1974. Contbr. to acad. jrnls. Mbrships. incl: Sec.-Treas., Int. Fed. of Socs. & Insts. for the Study of the Renaissance, 1967-; Exec. Bd., Renaissance Soc. Am.; Am. Hist. Soc. Address: Dept. of Hist., Univ. of Wis., Madison, WI 53706, USA.

KING-HELE, Desmond George, b. 3 Nov. 1927, Seaford, UK. Scientist. Educ: B.A., Trinity Coll., Cambridge, 1948; M.A., 1952. Publs: Shelley: His Thought & Work, 1960, 2nd ed., 1971; Satellites & Scientific Research, 1960, 2nd ed., 1962; Erasmus Darwin, 1963; Theory of Satellite Orbits in an Atmosphere, 1964; Observing Earth Satellites, 1966; Essential Writings of Erasmus Darwin, 1968; The End of the Twentieth Century?, 1970; Poems & Trixies, 1972. Contbr. to num. schlrly. jrnls. Mbr. or Fellow, sci. orgs. Recip., sev. awards. Address: 3 Tor Rd., Farnham, Surrey, UK.

KINGMA, Marten Jan, occasional pen name for jrnl. articles VAN STAPHORST, Jan, b. 30 Sept. 1906, Staphorst, Netherlands. Publicist & Public Relations Consultant. Author, Reputatie Behartiging (Caleidoscoop van de Public Relations), 1965. Contbr. to: Maatschappij Belangen; Elseviers Weekblad; Num. jrnls. & newspapers. Mbrships: Contact Centrum op Voorlichtingsgebied; Nederlands Genootschap voor Pub. Rels. Address: De Kinkhoorn, Koenestr. 81, Amerongen, Netherlands.

KINGSBURY, Phyllis May, pen name FLOWERDEW, Phyllis, b. Halifax, Yorks., UK. Educational Writer. Educ: Tchng. Dip., Southlands Coll.; Dip. in Childhood Psychol., Birmingham Univ. Publs: Wide Range Readers (co-author), 1948-54, 2nd ed., 1963-65; Stories for Sounds, 1958; Flamingo Books, 1965-66; Stories for Telling, 1966; Wide Range Interest (co-author), 1966-67; Poetry Is All Around, 1967; More Stories For Telling, 1968; New Interest Books, 1972; Trug Books, 1974; Pedro Books, 1974; Goodbye Candlelight, 1974. Mbr., Soc. of Authors. Address: Fallows, Chartway, Sevenoaks, Kent, UK.

KING TAYLOR, Lynda, b. 22 Dec. 1945, Falkirk, Stirlingshire, Scotland, UK. Industrial Psychologist; Management Journalist. Publs: Not for Bread Alone — An Appreciation of Job Enrichment, 1972; A Fairer Slice of the Cake — The Task Ahead, 1975. Contbr. to: Indl./Commercial Trng.; Educ. & Trng.; Investor's Chronicle; Trng. Jrnl. (USA); var. for. jrnls. & int. newspapers. Mbrships: Fellow, Inst. Dirs.; Assn. Bus. Execs.; Authors' Club; Friends of Tate Gall.; var. social clubs. Hons: Int. Mgmt. Speaker to S. Africa, 1973. Address: Devonport, Hyde Park, London W2, UK.

KININMONTH, Christopher, b. 24 Sept. 1917, Bramhall, Cheshire, UK. Writer. Publs: The Children of Thetis, 1949; Rome Alive, 1951; The Brass Dolphins, 1957; Travellers' Guides to Sicily, 1957; Malta, 1967; A Massacre of Innocents (co-author), 1967; Panther, 1970; Morocco, 1971; Frontiers, 1971; Maze, 1974. Contbr. to: Sunday Times; Guardian; Geograph. Mag.; UN World; Queen Mag.; Evening Standard; etc. Address: 34 Foster Rd., London W4, UK.

KINKEAD-WEEKES, Mark, b. 26 Apr. 1931, Pretoria, South Africa. University Professor. Educ: B.A., Univ. of Capetown; M.A., Oxford Univ., UK. Publs: William Golding: a critical study, 1967; Samuel Richardson: Dramatic Novelist, 1973; (Ed.) Alexander Pope, 1962; (Ed.) Twentieth Century Interpretations of The Rainbow, 1971. Contbr. to: Twentieth Century; Twentieth Century Studies; etc. Mbr., Univ. of Kent at Canterbury (Pro Vice-Chancellor). Recip., Rhodes Scholarship, 1951. Address: South Mystole House, Mystole Park, Chatham, Kent, UK.

KINNAIRD, Clark, pen names NORRIS, Edgar Poe; EARLYWINE, Hargis; ADAMS, John Paul, b. 1901, Louisville, Ky., USA. Newspaperman. Publs: This Must Not Happen Again, 1945; The Real F.D.R., 1947; Runyon First & Last, (All This & That), 1949; A Treasury of Runyon, 1961; George Washington: The Pictorial Biography, 1968; The First Century, 1968; Rube Goldberg Vs. The Machine Age, 1969. Contbr. to: Lexington Ky. Herald; Louisville

Courier-Jrnl.; Detroit Jrnl.; Detroit News; Central Press Assn. (Mgng. Ed.); Int. News Serv. (Corres.); King Features Syn. (Ed., Special Serv. & Mbr., Bd. of Dirs.); Freeman; Sat. Review; Am. Mercury; Coronet; Liberty; Argosy; Am. Weekly; Broadcaster, Televisor, C.B.S., N.B.C., A.F.R., T.N.; Syndicated Columnist, 1960—; Centennial Scrapbook; Daybook of Am. Address: 76 Mine St., Flemington, NJ 18822, USA.

KINNUNEN, Raimo J(ohannes), b. 3 Oct. 1931, Rääkkylä, Finland. Teacher; Author. Educ: Jyväskylän Tchr. Univ., 1952-1954. Publs: A Man Without His Soul, 1962; Elk-hunter, 1964; In the Open Air, 1965; The Fight of Sysmä, 1967; The Teachers of The Calling (prose poems), 1968; Wild Blood, 1968; Raju veri dramatization in the Theatre of Workers in Tampere, 1972; A Red Hag, the Blue Hair, 1973. Contbr. to: Parnasso. Mbrships: Finnish Authors' Assn.; Dramatists' Assn. of Finland. Recip., State of Finland Prize, 1969. Address: 19230 Onkiniemi, Finland.

KINOSHITA, James Otoichi, b. 3 June 1889, Totori-ken, Japan. Author. Educ: Univs. of Calif. & Southern Calif. Publs: Report on International Child Welfare Week in Tsingtau, 1924; Analysis of American Prosperity, 1930; Educational Marketing Campaign of Silk, 1934; Thrice Around the World; Rationalization of American Industry; Cherry Blossom around the World: Donation of Japanese School Children, 1973; sev. transls. Contbr. to Tsingtau Leader (Ed.); Chugai Shogyo, 1925. Fndr., Friends of the UN (Friends of the World). Address: 2056 Izumi, Komae-shi, Tokyo 182, Japan.

KINROSS, Lord (Patrick Balfour), pen name up to 1954 BALFOUR, Patrick, b. 25 June 1904, Edinburgh, UK. Author. Educ: B.A., Balliol Coll., Oxford, 1925. Publs: Society Racket, 1933; Grand Tour, 1934; Lords of the Equator, 1937; The Ruthless Innocent, 1950; The Orphaned Realm, 1951; Within the Taurus, 1954; The Century of the Common Peer, 1954; Europa Minor, 1956; Portrait of Greece, 1956; The Candid Eye, 1958; The Kindred Spirit, 1959; The Innocents at Home, 1959; Ataturk: The Rebirth of a Nation, 1964; Portrait of Egypt, 1966; The Windsor Years, 1967; Between Two Seas, 1968; Morocco (w. D. H. Gary), 1971; Hagia Sophia, 1972. Address: 4 Warwick Ave., London W2, UK.

KINSLEY, (Rev.) James, b. 17 Apr. 1922, Borthwick, Scotland, UK. Professor of English Studies. Educ: M.A., 1943, Ph.D., 1951, D.Litt., 1959, Univ. of Edinburgh; B.A., 1947, M.A., 1952, Oriel Coll., Oxford Univ. Publs: John Dryden: Poems, 4 vols., 1958; Robert Burns: Poems, 3 vols., 1968; Oxford Book of Ballads, 1969; Eds. of Dunbar, Lindsay, Galt, Alexander Carlyle; General Ed., Oxford English Novels, 1967-, & Oxford English Memoirs & Travels, 1969-. Contbr. to: Review of Engl. Studies; Mod. Lang. Review; Medium Aevum; Renaissance & Modern Studies. Mbrships: Fellow, Brit. Acad, 1971; R.S.L.; 1959; Royal Histl. Soc., 1961; Scottish Text Soc. (VP); Tennyson Soc. (VP). Address: Dept. of Engl. Studies, The University, Nottingham, UK.

KIPPHARDT, Heinar, b. 8 Mar. 1922. Dramatist. Educ: M.D., Düsseldorf. Publs: (plays) Der Hund des Generals, 1962; In der Sache J. Robert Oppenheimer, 1964; Joel Brand, Die Geschichte eines Geschafts, 1965; Die Nacht in der Chef geschlachtet wurde, 1967; Die Soldaten, 1968; (short stories) Die Ganovenfresse, 1968; (other publs) Shakespeare dringend gesucht, 1953; Der Aufstirg des Alois Piontek, 1956; Die Stühle des Herrn Szmil, 1960. Hons: Deutscher Nationalpreis, 1953; Schiller Gedachtnispreis, 1962; Hauptmann Prize, 1964; Adolf Grimme Prize, 1964; TV Prize, German Acad. of Arts. Address: Goteboldstr. 54, Munich 50, W. Germany.

KIRK, Donald, b. 7 May 1938, New Brunswick, N.J., USA. Journalist. Educ: A.B., Princeton Univ., 1959; M.A., Univ. of Chgo., 1965; Fulbright Schol., India, 1962-63; Edward R. Murrow Fellow, Coun. of For. Rels., NYC, 1974-75. Publs: Wider War: The Struggle for Cambodia, Thailand & Laos, 1971. Contbr. to jrnls. & newspapers. Mbrships: Soc. of Mag. Writers; Overseas Press Club; Authors Guild of Am.; For. Corres. Club of Japan. Hons: Page One Ward, Chgo. Newspaper Guild, 1961; Citations, Overseas Press Club, 1967, 1972, 1973. Overseas Press Club Award, for best report in any media on Asia, 1974. Address: c/o Coun. on For. Rels., 58 E. 68th St., N.Y., NY 10021, USA.

KIRK, Geoffrey Stephen, b. 3 Dec. 1921, Nottingham, UK. Regius Professor of Greek, Cambridge University.

Educ: B.A., 1946, M.A., 1948, Litt.D., 1964; Clare Coll., Cambridge Univ. Publs: Heraclitus, the Cosmic Fragments, 1952; The Presocratic Philosophers (w. J. E. Raven), 1956; The Songs of Homer, 1962; Myth, 1970; The Nature of Greek Myths, 1974. Contbr. to classical & philosl. jrnls. Mbrships: Fellow Brit. Acad. (VP, 1972); Hellenic Soc. & Classical Assn. Address: Trinity Coll., Cambridge, UK.

KIRKALDY, John Francis, b. 14 May 1908, Eastbourne, Sussex, UK. Professor of Geology. Educ: B.Sc., King's Coll., London, 1929; M.Sc.; D.Sc. Publs: Outline of Historical Geology (w. A. K. Wells), 1948; General Principles of Geology, 1954; Rocks & Minerals in Colour, 1963; Fossils in Colour, 1967; Geological Time, 1971. Contbr. to profl. jrnls. inclng: Quarterly Jnrl. of Geol. Soc.; Proceedings of Geols. Assn.; Geol. Mag. Mbr., var. geol. assns. Address: 36 Heath Dr., Potters Bar, Herts., UK.

KIRK-GREENE, Anthony Hamilton Millard, pen names CAVERHILL, Nicholas; & H. M. S., b. 16 May 1925, Tunbridge Wells, UK. University Lecturer. Educ: B.A., 1949, M.A., 1954, Univ. of Cambridge; M.A., Univ. of Oxford, 1967. Publs: Adamawa Past & Present, 1958; Barth's Travels in Nigeria, 1962; Principles of Native Administration, 1965; The Emirates of Nigeria, 1966; Lugard & the Amalgamation of Nigeria, 1968; Crisis & Conflict in Nigeria, 1971; West African Narrative, 1973. Contbr. to: Times Lit. Supplement; Engl. Histl. Review; Africa; African Affairs; Jrnl. of Mod. African Studies; sev. other jrnls. on African matters. Mbrships: incl: Coun., African Studies Assn., 1966-69; Royal African Soc. Hons. incl: Harkness Fellowship, 1958-59; M.B.E., 1963. Address: St. Antony's Coll., Oxford, UK.

KIRKMAN, William Patrick, b. 23 Oct. 1932, Samastipur, India. Secretary, University Appointments Board. Educ: B.A., 1955, M.A., 1959, Univ. of Oxford, UK; M.A., Univ. of Cambridge. Publs: Unscrambling an Empire, 1966. Contbr. to: Africa Contemporary Record, 1973-74; Times; Times Lit. Supplement; Fin. Times; Int. Affairs; BBC. Mbrships: Fellow, Wolfson Coll., Cambridge; Chmn., Standing Conf. of Univ. Appts. Servs., 1971-73; Ctrl. Coun., Royal C'wlth Soc.; Royal Inst. of Int. Affairs. Address: 19 High St., Willingham, Cambridge CB4 5ES, UK.

KIRKPATRICK, Samuel, A., b. 24 Oct. 1943, Harrisburg, Pa., USA. Political Scientist. Educ: B.S., Shippensburg State Coll., Pa., 1964; M.A., 1966, Ph.D., 1968, Pa. State Univ. Publs: Urban Political Analysis: A Systems Approach (co-author), 1972; The Social Psychology of Political Life (co-author), 1972; Quantitative Analysis of Political Data (co-author), 1974. Contbr. to: Midwest Jrnl. Pol. Sci.; Pub. Opinion, Western Pol., Social Sci., Sociol. Quarterlies; Midwest Review Pub. Admin., Pol. Sci. Annual; etc. Mbrships: incl: Pres.-Elect, Southwestern Pol. Sci. Assn.; Am. Sociol. Assn. Address: Bureau of Govt. Research, Univ. of Oklahoma, 455 W. Lindsey, Room 304, Norman, OK 73069, USA.

KIRKUP, James, b. 23 Apr. 1928, South Shields, UK. Poet; Dramatist; Travel Writer. Educ: B.A., King's Coll., Univ. of Durham. Publs. incl: (poetry) The Drowned Sailor, 1948; A Correct Compassion, 1952; The Descent Into the Cave, 1956; Refusal to Conform, 1964; Paper Windows, 1967; The Body Servant, 1972; Zen Gardens, 1973; Scenes from Sesshu, 1974; (prose) The Only Child, 1956; Tokyo, 1966; Bangkok, 1968; Hong Kong, 1969; Japan Behind the Fan, 1970; Heaven, Hell & Hara-kiri, 1974; also transls. of plays, poetry & prose from mod. & medieval French, German, Italian, Spanish, etc. Address: BM-Box 2780, London WC1V 6XX, UK.

KIRSCH, Robert, pen names DUNDEE, Robert; BANCROFT, Robert, b. 18 Oct. 1922, Coney Island, N.Y., USA. Author. Educ: B.A., 1949, M.A., 1951; Univ. Calif., L.A.; Litt.D., Univ. Redlands, Calif., 1970. Publs: (novella) Do Not Go Gentle, 1958; (novels) In the Wrong Rain, 1959; Madeleine Austrian, 1960; The Wars of Pardon, 1965; (novels, as Robert Dundee) The Restless Lovers, 1960; Pandora's Box, 1961; Inferno, 1962; (novels, as Robert Bancroft) The Castilian Rose, 1961; Knight of the Scimitar, 1962; (history) West of the West (w. William Murphy), 1968. Contbr. to: N.Y. Times; Saturday Review; L.A. Times (chief book critic); etc. Mbrships. incl: PEN. Address: 50 Church Rd., Richmond, Surrey, UK.

KIRST, Hans Hellmut, b. 5 Dec. 1914, Osterode, Germany. Former Farmer; Writer. Publs. incl: Galgenstrick, 1951; 08/15 (trilogy), 1954; Keiner Kommt davon, 1957;

Fabrik für Offiziere, 1960; Nacht der Generale, 1962; Aüfstand der Soldaten, 1965; Die Wölfe, 1967; Held im Türm, 1970; transl. into num. langs. Mbrships: PEN; Authors' Guild, USA. Recip., Edgar Allen Poe Special Award, USA, 1965. Address: Caslano bei Lugano, San Michele, Casa 7, Switz.

KIRSTINÄ, Väinö (Antero), b. 29 Jan. 1936, Tyrnävä, Finland. Writer. Educ: Fil.kand., Univ. of Helsinki, 1963. Publs. incl: Lakeus (poems), 1961; Luonnollinen tanssi (poems), 1965; Ed., Kirjoittajan tyot (writers' handbook), 1968; Talo maalla (poems), 1969; Säännöstelty eutanasia (poems), 1973; transls. of Baudelaire, Breton, Quintana; etc.; also var. essays, articles & lit. criticisms. Contbr. to: Parnasso; Chief Ed., Kirjailija. Mbrships: Soc. of Finnish Writers, 1963-; Pres., Nuoren Voiman Liitto, 1972-. Hons: Finnish State Lit. Prize, 1964; Govt. Fellowship for Authors, 1970-73. Address: Tammelanpuistok 5-7 C 32, 33500 Tampere 50, Finland.

KIŠ, Danilo, b. 22 Feb. 1935, Subotica, Yugoslavia. Writer; Translator. Educ: B.A., Belgrade Univ. Publs: Mansarda (attic), 1963; Psalm 44, 1963; Bašta, pepeo (The Garden, Ashes), 1965; Rani jadi (Youthful Griefs), 1970; Peščanik (Sand-Glass), 1972; Poetika (Poetics), 1972, book 2, 1974; Contbr. to: Delo; Kniževnost; Vidici; Forum. Mbrships: Writers' Soc., Yugoslavia; Soc. Lit. Transls., Serbia; PEN. Recip., NIN Prize, 1973, for best Yugoslav novel of 1972 (Peščanik). Address: Ranka Tajsića 40, ulaz III, 11000 Belgrade, Yugoslavia.

KISER, Clyde Vernon, b. 22 July 1904, Bessemer City, N.C., USA. Demographer. Educ: A.B., 1925, A.M., 1927, Univ. of N.C.; Ph.D., Columbia Univ., 1932. Publs. incl: Sea Island to City, 1932; Group Differences in Urban Fertility, 1942; Co-author, Social & Psychological Factors Affecting Fertility, 5 vols., 1946-58; The Fertility of American Woman, 1958; Ed., Research in Family Planning, 1962. Contbr. to profl. jrnls. & encys. Address: 605 N. 14th St., Bessemer City, NC 28016, USA.

KISIELEWSKI, Stefan, pen name KISIEL, b. 7 Mar. 1911, Warsaw, Poland. Writer; Critic; Composer. Educ: 3 dips. (music; composition; piano), Conservatoire of Warsaw; Polish lit. studies, Warsaw Univ. Publs incl: 100 Times with Head Against the Wall, Paris (essays), 1972; Matter Mixed, London 1973; Brain & Music, 1974. Contbr. to: Sygodnik Powszechny; Ruch Muzyczny. Mbrships: Composers' Union; Writers' Union; Presidium, Authors' Union. Hons: Music Prize, Cracow, 1956; Jurzykowski Fndn. Award, USA, 1973. Address: 00-582 Warsaw, Al I Armii 16 m.11, Poland.

KISJÓKAI, Erzsébet Mária (pen name), b. Budapest, Hungary. Writer. Publs: 36 books inclng. Bérház (Building, novel), 1953; Áldott bilincs (Blessed Handcuffs, poems), 1956; A gyertyáknak égni kell (The Candles Must Be Lit, novel), 1957; The Writing on the Wall (novel), 1958; Lázadás (Woman Against Fate, novel), 1958 & 1959; Tulipántos láda (The Painted Box, play), 1959; A császárnö pávája (The Peacock of the Empress, mystery), 1961; Ének Stuart Máriához (Mary Stuart), 1962; Counsel For the Defense (novel), 1970; Az Édenkert titkai (Secrets of Paradise, travel book), 1973. Mbrships. incl: PEN; Acad. of Art, USA; Helicon Soc., Can.; Hon. VP, Kodály Acad., USA. Hons: Radio Free Europe, Munich, 1953; Gold Medal, Cleveland, USA, 1965. Address: Tesselschade Laan 6, Hilversum, Netherlands.

KISNER, Jacob, pen names KISNER, Jack; SMALLWOOD, Jason, b. 30 Apr. 1926. Poet; Editor; Writer; Research Director, Moneytree Publications, 1972-. Educ: Harvard Univ. Ext.; Mass. State Univ.; Burdett Coll.; Cambridge Ctr. for Adult Educ.; Boston Mus. Fine Arts. Publs: I am Hephaestus, 1970; (plays) First Came Paula; Speak of the Devil; The Monkey's Tail; (TV plays) The Late Mr. Honeywell; A World Apart. Contbr. to: Dorchester Herald (Fndr., Ed., Publr.); Ed., Crossroads, Can.; Am. Ed., View, Can.; etc. Mbrships. incl: Exec. Comm., Wilson MacDonald Poetry Soc., Can.; Am. Newspaper Guild; Fndr., Acad. Am. Poets; Bd. of Dirs., NY Poetry Forum. Recip., num. lit. awards & hons. Address: 750 Park Ave., N.Y. NY 10021, USA.

KISSEIH, (Justice) Victor Emmanuel Amate, b. 4 Feb. 1926, Odumase-Krobo, Ghana. Judge of the High Court of Judicature; Ghana Civil Service since 1961, Lands Officer (Legal), Lands Dept.; Senior State Attorney, 1966; Principal State Attorney, 1971; Chief State Attorney, 1973. Educ: Univ. Coll., Gold Coast; LL.B., Hull Univ.,

UK, 1959; called to Bar, Middle Temple, London, 1960. Publs: (primary schl. textbook) Nilee Tsofa. Mbrships. incl: Soc. Friends Mentally Retarded Children (Life Mbr. & Treas.); Ghana Boy Scouts Assn. (Mbr. Supreme Coun. & Asst. Nat. Treas.); Presby. Trng. Coll., Akropong-Akwapim (Mbr. Mgmt. Comm.). Address: 12 Third Ave., The Ridge, Accra, Ghana.

KISSI-AFARE, Samuel, b. 19 Sept. 1934, Obo-Kwahu, Ghana. Journalist; Businessman. Educ: sev. dips., Trade Union Coll., Moscow, USSR, 1961-62, & Kwame Nkrumah Ideological Inst., Winneba, 1963-65. Contbr. to: The Echo (Fndr., currently Ed.). Mbrships. incl: Bd. of Dirs., Ghana Broadcasting Corp., 1970-1972; Exec. Mbr., Ghana Br., C'wlth Press Union, 1971-; Vice-Chmn., Ghanaian Guild of Eds. Address: Echo Publs. Ltd., P.O. Box 3460, Accra, Ghana.

KITABATAKE, Miyo, pen name YAHO, b. 5 Oct. 1903, Aomori, Japan. Novelist. Educ: Jissen Women's Univ. Publs: Mō-hitotsuno-hikariwo (More Light!), 1948; Akutarewarashi Poko (Poko, a Naughty Boy), 1953; Togūhi (The Crown Princess), 1966; Oni-wo-kau Goro (Goro who keeps a Demon), 1971. Contbr. to: Asahi; Sincho. Mbrships: Japan Profl. Lit. Artists Assn.; PEN; Japan Women's Lit. Assn. Hons: Sankei Prize & Noma Prize, both for Juvenile Lit., 1972. Address: 1405 Wakamatsu, Kamakura-yama, Kamakura-shi 248, Japan.

KIVIMAA, Arvi, b. 6 Sept. 1904, Hartola, Finland. Writer; Former Dir., National Theatre. Publs. incl: First Poems, 1925; Katu Nousee Taivaaseen, 1928; Passacaglia, 1950; Most Beautiful Poems (selection), 1958; Manhatten, 1959; Joenrannan Puu, 1961; Samothraken Nike, 1964; Prokonsuli ja Keisari, 1969; Teatterin Humanismi, 1972; Kasvoja Valohämystä, 1974. Contbr. to num. for. publs. Mbrships. incl: PEN, Finland (Chmn., 1936, 1954-57); Assn. Finnish Writers; Scandinavian Theatre Coun. (Pres., 1963-69). Hons. incl: Prof., 1958, Ph.D., 1973, Helsinki Univ.; H. Steffens Prize, Hamburg, 1971; num. decorations. Address: SepänKatu 15B, 00150 Helsinki 15, Finland.

KIVISTÖ, Pentti Eino Johannes, b. 11 Aug. 1922, Lappee, Finland. Foreman; Author. Publs: Pictures in a Grave (poems), 1952; Water-grey Organ (novel), 1956; Hero (novel), 1958; The Masks (play), 1965. Contbr. to: Kansan Työ, 1953-57; Suomalainen Suomi, 1958-60; Etelä-Saimaa, 1970-74; Karjalan Aamu, 1970-71. Mbrships: Finnish Soc. of Authors; Union of Finnish Critics. Hons: Lit. Prize, Borough of Lauritsala, 1957; Lit. Prize, Finnish Soc. of Authors, 1957; Soc. of Young Spirit Award, 1969. Address: Lauritsalantie 73, 53300 Lappeenranta 30, Finland.

KLASS, Philip J., b. 8 Nov. 1919, Des Moines, Iowa, USA. Technical Journalist; Avionics Editor. Educ: B.S. (Elec. Engrng.), Iowa State Univ., 1941. Publs: UFOs — Identified, 1968; Secret Sentries in Space, 1971; UFOs Explained, 1975; Sr. Avionics Ed., Aviation Wk. & Space Technol. Mag. Mbrships: Fellow, Inst. Elec. & Electronics Engrs.; AAAS; Nat. Press Club; Aviation/Space Writers Assn. Address: 560 "N" St. S.W., Wash., DC 20024, USA.

KLEIN, Alexander, b. 12 Nov. 1923, Szibo, Hungary. Public Relations Executive; Film Writer-Producer. University Teacher; Editor; Writer. Educ: B.S., CUNY, 1942. Publs. incl: Armies for Peace, 1950; Courage is the Key, 1953; The Empire City, 1955; Grand Deception, 1955; The Counterfeit Traitor, 1958, filmed 1962; The Double Dealers, 1959; The Fabulous Rogues, 1960; The Magnificent Scoundrels, 1961; Rebels, Rogues, Rascals, 1962; That Pellet Woman, 1965; Natural Enemies, 1970; Dissent, Power & Confrontation, 1972; (co-author, film) Shalom, Baby! , 1975. Contbr. to: num. anthols., text-books, & gen., lit. & acad. jrnls. Mbrships. incl: Co-Fndr., Arden House Annual Convocations on For. Policy, 1947-. Recip., num. film & lit. awards. Address: 521 W. 112th St., N.Y., NY 10025, USA.

KLEIN, Philip S., b. 10 June 1909, Allentown, Pa., USA. Historian. Educ: A.B., Franklin Coll., 1929; A.M., Univ. of Chgo., 1933; Ph.D., Univ. of Pa., 1938. Publs: Pennsylvania Politics 1817-1832 — A Game Without Rules, 1941; History of the US (co-author), 1951; President James Buchanan (biog.), 1962; A History of Pennsylvania (co-author), 1973. Contbr. to: Am. Hist. Review; Jrnl. of Am. Hist.; Pa. Hist.; Pa. Mag. of Hist. & Biog. Mbrships: Sec., Pres. & Exec. Coun., Pa. Hist. Assn.; Hist. Soc. of Pa.; Am. Hist. Assn.; Org. of Am. Histns. Address: Dept. of History, 601 Liberal Arts Tower, Pennsylvania State Univ., Univ. Park, PA 16802, USA.

KLINGENSMITH, Don Joseph, b. 1 Apr. 1901, Lovilia, Iowa, USA. Pastor. Educ: A.B., John Fletcher Coll., 1928; M.A., Okla. State Univ., 1941; M.Div., Garrett Sem., 1947. Publs: The New Testament in Everyday English, vol. 1, 1967, 3rd ed., 1969; The New Testament in Everyday English, 1974. Contbr. to var. Ch. mags. Mbrships. incl: Nat. Writers' Club; United Amateur Press; Am. Civil Liberties Union; Nat. Assn. of Evangelicals; World Gospel Mission 1000 Club; Wycliffe Assocs.; Hon. Chief & Councilman, Ponca Indians. Address: 206 Collins Ave., Mandan, ND 58554, USA.

KLOSEK, Judi, family name BASSO, b. 17 Sept. 1944, NYC, USA. Writer/Editor. B.A., Hunter Coll., N.Y.; Assoc. degree of Design, N.Y. Schl. of Design. Publs: (TV Documentary) Voices of Dissent; Ed-in-Chief, Designer Mag. Contbr. to: Future Hawaii. Mbrships incl: World Future Soc.; Nat. Home Fashions League. Recip., NSID Award for Outstanding Reporting, 1973. Address: 2060 Pacific Ave., San Fran., CA 94109, USA.

KNAPP, Bettina L., b. 9 May 1926, NYC, USA. College Professor; Author. Educ: B.A., Barnard Coll.; M.A., Ph.D., Columbia Univ. Publs: incl: Louis Jouvet, Man of the Theatre, 1957; Aristide Bruant. A Biography, 1968; Jean Genet. A Critical Study of His Writings, 1968; Antonin Artaud, Man of Vision, 1969; Jean Cocteau. A Critical Study of His Writings, 1970; Jean Racine, Mythos & Renewal in Modern Theatre, 1971; Celine, Man of Hate, 1974; Off Stage Voices, 1975; That Was Yvette (co-author). Contbr. to: Yale Theatre; Mod. Drama; Studies in the 20th Century; Drama & Theatre; Books Abroad; etc. Address: Hunter Coll., 68th St. & Park Ave., N.Y., NY 10021, USA.

KNAPTON, Ernest John, b. 31 Aug. 1902, Queensbury, Yorks., UK. Professor of History Emeritus; Writer. Educ: B.A., Univ. of B.C., Can., 1925; B.A.(Hons.), Oxford Univ., UK, 1928; M.A., Harvard Univ., USA, 1931; Ph.D., Harvard Univ., 1934. Publs. incl: The Lady of the Holy Alliance, 1939; France Since Versailles, 1952; Empress Josephine, 1963; Europe & the World Since 1914 (w. T. K. Derry), 1966; France, An Interpretive History, 1971; Revolutionary & Imperial France, 1972. Contbr. to num. histl. jrnls. Hons. incl: D.Litt., Wheaton Coll., Norton, Mass., 1972. Address: Fox Hill Rd., Chatham, MA 02633, USA.

KNEBEL, Fletcher, b. 1 Oct. 1911, Dayton, Ohio, USA. Writer. Educ: B.A., Miami Univ., Oxford, Ohio, 1934. Publs: Night of Camp David, 1965; Vanished, 1968; Trespass, 1969; Dark Horse, 1972; The Bottom Line, 1974; (books w. Charles Bailey II) No High Ground, 1960; Seven Days in May, 1962; Convention, 1964. Contbr. to: Look (1951-71). Mbrships: Gridiron Club (Wash. D.C., Pres., 1964); Nat. Press Club (Wash. DC). Hons. incl: D.Litt., Miami Univ., 1964; LL.D., Drake Univ., Des Moines, Iowa, 1968. Address: 208 Edgerstoune Rd., Princeton, NJ 08540, USA.

KNEPLER, Henry, b. 8 May 1922, Vienna, Austria. Professor of English. Educ: B.A. & M.A., Queen's Univ., Ont., Can.; Ph.D., Univ. of Chgo., USA. Publs: What Is the Play, 1967; The Gilded Stage, 1968; Man About Paris, 1970. Contbr. to: Modern Drama; Queen's Quarterly; Coll. Engl.; Modern Philol.; Leonardo. Address: 1344 Madison Park, Chicago, Il., USA.

KNIGHT, Alanna, b. Northumberland, UK. Novelist; Tutor in Creative Writing. Publs. incl: Legend of the Loch, 1969; So You Want to Write, 1971; Lament for Lost Lovers, 1972; The White Rose, 1973; A Stranger Came By, 1974; The Passionate Kindness — the Story of R. L. Stevenson & Fanny Osbourne, 1974; stage play on R. L. Stevenson performed at Edinburgh Festival, 1973. Contbr. to num. mags. world-wide, radio & TV. Mbrships. incl: Aberdeen Writers' Circle (jt. chmn.); Soc. Women Writers & Jrnlsts.; F.S.A. (Scotland); Hons: 1st novel Award, R.N.A., 1968; Short Story Award, United Writers' Assn., 1971. Address: 374 Queen's Rd., Aberdeen AB1 8DX, UK.

KNIGHT, Bernard, pen name PICTON, Bernard, b. 3 May 1931, Cardiff, Wales, UK. Senior Lecturer & Consultant in Forensic Pathology. Educ: M.D., B.Surg., Welsh Nat. Schl. of Med., Univ. of Wales; Barrister at Law, Gray's Inn. Publs: The Lately Deceased, 1963; Thread of Evidence, 1965; Mistress Murder, 1966; Russian Roulette, 1968; Policemans Progress, 1969; Tiger at Bay, 1970; Murder Suicide or Accident, 1971; Lion Rampant, 1972; Legal Aspects of Medical Practice, 1972; Deg y Dragwyddoldeb, 1972; Edefyn Brau, 1973; chapts. in num.

textbooks. Contbr. to num. newspapers; also radio & TV. Mbrships. incl: Soc. of Authors; Crime Writers Assn.; Writers Guild of GB. Address: 28 Ty Gwyn Crescent, Penylan, Cardiff, Wales, UK.

KNIGHT, Bertram, b. 21 Mar. 1904, Northampton, UK. Schoolmaster; Author. Publs: Sending Messages, 1970; Time to Look Around, 1971. Contbr. to var. educl. jrnls. Address: Byways, Ecton, Northampton, UK.

KNIGHT, Damon, b. 19 Sept. 1922, Baker, Ore., USA. Anthologist. Publs. incl: (novels & short stories) Hell's Pavement, 1955; A for Anything, 1959; In Deep, 1963; Off Center, 1965; Turning On, 1966; (biog. & criticism) In Search of Wonder, 1956, 2nd ed., 1967; Charles Fort: Prophet of the Unexplained, 1970; (anthols.) Now Begins Tomorrow, 1963; Beyond Tomorrow, 1965; The Metal Smile, 1968; Dimension X, 1970; The Golden Road, 1973; A Shocking Thing, 1974; also transls. from French lang. Contbr. to: Galaxy; Analog; Playboy; etc. Mbrships: Sci. Fiction Writers of Am.; Milford Sci. Fiction Writers' Conf. Recip., Hugo Award, 1954. Address: Box 8216, Madeira Beach, FL 33738, USA.

KNIGHT, George Richard Wilson, b. 19 Sept. 1897, Sutton, Surrey, UK. Emeritus Professor of English Literature. Educ: B.A., 1923, M.A., 1931, St. Edmund Hall, Oxford Univ. Publs. incl: The Wheel of Fire, 1930; The Imperial Theme, 1931; The Burning Oracle, 1939; The Starlit Dome, 1941; The Crown of Life, 1947; Lord Byron: Christian Virtues, 1952; The Mutual Flame, 1955; The Golden Labyrinth, 1962; Ibsen, 1962; Byron & Shakespeare, 1966; Neglected Powers, 1972. Contbr. to: Times Lit. Supplement; 20th Century; Contemp. Review; Review of Engl. Studies; etc. Mbrships. incl: F.R.S.L.; Fellow, Int. Assn. Arts & Letters; Engl. Assn. Hons. incl: C.B.E.; var. hon. degrees. Address: Caroline House, Streatham Rise, Exeter EX4 4PE, UK.

KNIGHT, Hugh McCown, b. 16 Nov. 1905, Baltimore, Md., USA. Newspaper Columnist & Editorial Artist (retired). Publs: A Simplified Guide to Collecting American Coins (written & illustrated), 1959. Contbr. to: Page One Mag.; Numismatist; Sunday Chicago Sun-Times; etc. Mbrships. incl: Am. Numismatic Assn.; Chicago Coin Club; Ctrl. States Numismatic Soc. Address: 7434 W. 111th St., Worth, IL 60482, USA.

KNIGHT, John, b. 22 Mar. 1906, Trinidad. Author. Publs: Straight Lines & Unicorns, 1960. Contbr. to: Agenda; Ambit; Dublin Mag.; Listener; Mass. Review; Outposts; Poetry (Chgo.); Poetry Review; Phoenix; Spectator; Times Lit. Supplement; var. anthols.; etc. Mbr., Soc. of Authors. Address: The Canyalk, Bosorne, St. Just, Penzance, Cornwall TR19 7NS, UK.

KNIGHTS, Lionel Charles, b. 15 May 1906, Grantham, UK. University Teacher. Educ: B.A., M.A., Ph.D., Selwyn Coll. & Christ's Coll., Cambridge. Publs: Drama & Society in the Age of Jonson, 1937; Exploration: Essays in Criticism, 1946; Some Shakespearean Themes, 1959; An Approach to Hamlet, 1960; Further Explorations, 1965; Public Voices: Literature & Politics, 1971; Ed., Metaphor & Symbol (w. Basil Cottle), 1960. Contbr. to: Scrutiny; The Criterion; Southern Review; Sewanee Review; N.Y. Review of Books; etc. Mbrships: Mbr. of Univ. Tchrs.; Royal C'wlth Soc. Hons: Dr., Univ. of Bordeaux, 1964; Dr., Univ. of York, 1969; D.Litt., Manchester, 1974. Address: 57 Jesus Lane, Cambridge CB5 8BS, UK.

KNOBLOCH, Edgar, b. 11 Nov. 1927, Prague, Czech. Lawyer; Economist. Educ: LL.D., Charles Univ., Prague; Orient Inst., Prague. Publs: The Heart of Asia, 1961; The Art of Central Asia, 1965; The Death of Tamerlane (novel), 1965; Beyond the Oxus, 1972. Contbr. to: Archéologia, Paris; Geogl. Mag., London; Ctrl. Asian, Archtl., & Contemporary Reviews, London. Address: 4ème Avenue No. 3, 1330 Rixensart, Belgium.

KNOLL, Helmfried, b. 18 Jan. 1930, Vienna, Austria. Bank Correspondent for Foreign Languages. Educ: Dip., Inst., transls. & interpreters, Univ. of Graz. Publs. incl: Von meinen Wanderpfaden, 1967; Erwandte Heimat- erlebte Fremde, 1969; Wanderungen rings um Wien, 1972; Gipfel und Wege zwischen Salzburg und Bad Ischl, 1973; Vom Nordwald bis zur Puszta, 1974; Erlebte Geschichte im Land unter der Enns, forthcoming; (transls. from Spanish) Der Rebell, 1965; Aus einem fernen Land, 1968; Känguruhmädchen für alles, 1970. Contbr. to: Wiener Zeitung; Auto-Touring; Kurier; Bergwelt; Alpinismus; etc.

Mbr., IGdA (lit. soc.). Recip., List of Hon. Fed. Min. of Educ., 1968. Address: Bauernfeldgasse 10/1, A-1190 Vienna, Austria.

KNOOP, Faith Yingling (Mrs. Werner Caldwell Knoop), b. Elgin, Ill., USA. Educ: Trenton State Coll.; ext. study, var. colls. & univs. Publs: Arkansas: Yesterday & Today, 1935, 1947; Quest of the Cavaliers: De Soto & the Spanish Explorers, 1940; Zebulon Pike, 1950; Lars & the Luck Stone, 1950, 1958; Kuni of the Cherokees, 1957; Amerigo Vespucci, 1966; Francisco Coronado, 1967; Vasco Numez de Balboa, 1969; Sir Edmund Hillary, 1970; over 200 stories & articles. Mbrships. incl: Nat. League Am. Pen Women (Little Rock Br. Treas.); Nat. Soc. Arts & Letters; Women's Nat. Book Assn. Address: 6 Ozark Point, Little Rock, AR 72205, USA.

KNOWLES, Asa Smallidge, b. 15 Jan. 1909, Northwest Harbor, Me., USA. University President. Educ: A.B., Bowdoin Coll., 1930; Harvard Bus. Schl.; A.M., Boston Univ., 1935. Publs: Co-author, Industrial Management, 1944; Ed.-in-Chief, Handbook of College & University Administration, 2 vols., 1970; Co-author & Ed., Handbook of Cooperative Education, 1971. Address: Northeastern Univ., 360 Huntingdon Ave., Boston, MA 02115, USA.

KNOWLES, John, b. 1926, Fairmont, W. Va., USA. Editor. Educ: M.A., Yale Univ. Publs: A Separate Peace. Contbr. to: Holiday; Saturday Evening Post; Cosmopolitan; Reader's Digest. Address: c/o Holiday, Independence Sq., Phila., Pa., USA.

KNOWLES, Malcolm Shepherd, b. 24 Aug. 1913, Livingston, Mont., USA. Professor of Adult Education. Educ: A.B., Harvard Coll., 1934; M.A., 1949, Ph.D., 1960, Univ. of Chgo. Publs: Informal Adult Education, 1950; How to Develop Better Leaders (w. Hulda Knowles), 1955; Introduction to Group Dynamics (w. Hulda Knowles), 1959; Handbook of Adult Education in the US (Ed.), 1960; The Adult Education Movement in the US, 1962; Higher Adult Education in the US, 1969; The Modern Practice of Adult Education: Andragogy vs. Pedagogy, 1970; The Adult Learner: A Neglected Species, 1973. Contbr. to: num. jrnls. in field. Mbrships. incl: Authors Guild; Adult Educ. Assn. of the USA; Am. Rsch Assn.; AAUP. Address: 1506 Delmont Dr., Raleigh, NC 27606, USA.

KNOWLTON, Edgar Colby, Jr., b. 14 Sept. 1921, Delaware, Ohio, USA. Professor of European Languages. Educ: A.B., 1941, A.M., 1942, Harvard Univ.; Ph.D., Stanford Univ., 1959; var. summer schls. Publs: Transl., Sá de Meneses, The Conquest of Malacca, 1971; V. Blasco Ibáñez (w. A. Grove Day), 1972; Transl., Almeida Garrett, Camoëns, 1972. Contbr. to: Books Abroad; Romance Philol.; Romance Notes; Am. Speech; Tamil Culture; Linguist; Studies in Short Fiction; Boletim do Instituto Luís de Camoës; num. other profl. jrnls.; Honolulu Advertiser (Concert reviews 1957-61). Mbrships incl: MLA (bibliog. comm. 1969-). Hons. incl: Translation Prize, Secretaria de Estado da Informação & Turismo, Portugal, 1970-71. Address: 1026 Kalo Pl. Apt. 403, Honolulu, HI 96814, USA.

KNOX, Raymond Anthony, b. 23 Sept. 1926, Wellington, NZ. Editorial Director; Journalist. Educ: Victoria Univ., Wellington. Publs: (Ed., partworks) New Zealand's Heritage, 1971; New Zealand Today, 1973; New Zealand's Nature Heritage, 1974. Contbr. to: NZ Listener (short stories, articles, columns, book & opera reviews; Feature Writer, 1956, Chief Reporter, 1964); Here & Now; NZ Nat. Review; NZ Broadcasting Corp. (radio documentaries, talks, criticism); TV Documentary on NZ novelists. Mbr., Paremata Residents' Assn. (Sec., 1971, 1972). Hons: Toured GB as Guest of C'wlth Relations Office, 1965. Address: 1 Bayview Rd., Paremata, Wellington, NZ.

KNOX, Robert Buick, b. 10 Oct. 1918, Banbridge, Down, UK. Professor of Ecclesiastical History. Educ: M.A., B.D., Presby. Coll., Belfast; B.A., Ph.D., London Univ. Publs: James Ussher, Archbishop of Armagh, 1967; Voices from the Past: History of the English Conference of the Presbyterian Church of Wales, 1969; Wales & "Y Goleuad" 1869-1879, 1969. Contbr. to: Studies in Ch. Hist.; Scottish Jrnl. of Theol.; Expository Times. Mbr., Ecclesiastical Hist. Soc. Address: Westminster College, Cambridge, UK.

KNOX, William (Bill), pen names MacLEOD, Robert; WEBSTER, Noah; KIRK, Michael, b. 20 Feb. 1928, Glasgow, UK. Author; Journalist. Publs. incl: To Kill a Witch, 1971; Whitewater, 1974; A Burial in Portugal, 1973; All Other Perils, 1974; (non-fiction) Court of Murder: Famous Trials at Glasgow High Court, 1968. Contbr. to: BBC; Scottish TV; etc. Mbrships: Soc. of Authors; Mystery Writers Am.; Crime Writers Assn.; Past Pres., Assn. of Scottish Motoring Writers. Address: 55 Newtonlea Ave., Newton Mearns, Glasgow G77 5QF, UK.

KNOX-JOHNSTON, Robin, b. 17 Mar. 1939, Putney, Surrey, UK. Master Mariner; Company Director; Author. Publs: A World of My Own, 1969; Robin Round the World, 1970. Contbr. to: True (USA); Yachting World; Yachting Monthly. Mbr., Savage Club. Recip., C.B.E., 1969. Address: Cherry Trees, School Lane, Hamble, Hants., UK.

KNUTSSON, Rolf Erik Anund, b. 25 Feb. 1929, Stockholm, Sweden. Director & Producer, Swedish Broadcasting Corporation; Author. Educ: Swedish Film Inst. Film Schl., 1966-68. Publs: Att vara samman i sin kropp iakttagen, 1964; Förändring, 1966; Torkel 5 år, 1968, Engl. transl., 1970; Dahlbergs demonstrerar, 1969; Beroende av digg för sina liv, 1969; Josefine 5, Zimbabve Afrika, 1971, Danish transl., 1974; 5 TV dramas. Mbrships: Swedish Union of Authors; Swedish Assn. of Jrnlsts. Recip., 1st Prize, Prix Danube, Bratislava, 1971, for TV drama. Address: Rådjursvägen 14, S-170 10 Ekerö, Sweden.

KOBAYASHI, Masako, pen name MATSUNO, Masako, b. 12 July 1935, Niihama-shi, Japan. Writer. Educ: B.A., Waseda Univ., 1958; M.L.S., Columbia Univ., 1960. Publs: A Pair of Red Clogs, 1960; Taro & the Tofu, 1962; Chie & the Sports Day, 1965; Taro & the Bamboo Shoot, 1963; My Goldfish, 1972; Cryboy Nakitaro, 1974; Rabbits in Flowers, 1975. Address: 23-1, 1-chome Furuedai, Suita-shi, Osaka, Japan.

KOBLER, Jasper F., b. 6 Apr. 1928, Niagara Falls, N.Y., USA. Professor of American Literature. Educ: B.S., 1949, B.A., 1951, La. State Univ.; M.A., Univ. of Houston, 1959; Ph.D., Univ. of Texas, Austin, 1968. Articles: Hemingway's The Sea Change: A Sympathetic View of Homosexuality, Ariz. Quarterly, 1970; Francis Macomber as 4-letter Man, Fitzgerald/Hemingway Annual, 1972; Lena Grove: Faulkner's Still Unravish'd Bride of Quietness, Ariz. Quarterly, 1972; Let's Run Catherine Barkley up the Flagpole & See Who Salutes, The CEA Critic, 1974; Faulkner's A Rose for Emily, the Explicator, 1974. Mbr., S. Ctrl. MLA. Address: P.O. Box 13561, North Texas Station, Denton, TX 76203, USA.

KOC, Robert Joseph, b. 11 Apr. 1914, Vienna, Austria. Author; Lyricist. Publs: Landschaft der Seele (poems), 1947; Rückkehr von den Meeren (poems & prose), 1959; Vindobona (poems), 1961; Die Unbeschuhten (prose), 1964; Yü-lung-shan: Gesang am Jadedrachenberg, 1969; Weltabend: 5 Gespräche über eine Stadt, 1971; Verhülltes Wort (prose), 1972; Brieftagebuch, 1973; Perceval (novella), 1974; Ed., Blätter für das Wort. Contbr. of num. essays to periodicals & jrnls. Mbrships: PEN; Österreichischer Schriftstellerverband (Austrian Authors' Soc.). Hons: Schlrship., Brit. Coun., Vienna, 1947; Lit. Prize of Vienna, 1960. Address: 1020 Wien, Wittelbachstr. 4/19, Austria.

KOCH, Claude Francis, b. 28 Nov. 1918, Phila., Pa., USA. Professor of English. Educ: B.S., La Salle Coll.; M.A., Univ. of Fla.; Niagara Univ.; Univ. of Pa. Publs: Island Interlude, 1951; Light in Silence, 1958; Kite in the Sea, 1964; Casual Company, 1965. Contbr. to: Sewanee Review; Southern Review; Antioch Review; Northwest Review; Delta Review; Four Quarters; Ave. Hons: Dodd-Mead Fellowship, 1949; Sewanee Review Fellowship, 1957; Rockefeller Fndn. Fellowship, 1965; Linback Award for Disting. Tchng., 1968; La Salle Coll. Centenary Award, 1965. Address: 128 W. Highland Ave., Phila., PA 19118, USA.

KOCH, James H., b. 5 Mar. 1926, Milwaukee, Wis., USA. Author; Poet. Educ: B.A., Carleton Coll., 1949; postgrad. studies, 1949-52, Woodrow Wilson Fellow, 1949, Princeton Univ. Publs. incl: Pitfalls in Issuing Public Bonds, 1963, 2nd ed., 1974; A Selected, Annotated Bank Marketing Bibliography, 1968, 2nd ed., 1971; Advertising & Promotion Practices of Full Service Banks, 1970; How Banks Can Use Direct Mail As an Effective Marketing Tool, 1973. Contbr. to: Direct Mktng.; Bank Mktng.; Country Property News; Golden Yr.; Diamond Anthol. of Poetry Soc. of Am.; etc. Mbrships. incl: Poetry Soc. of Am.; Direct Mktng. Writers' Club. Address: 1020 Park Ave., N.Y., NY 10028, USA.

KOESTLER, Arthur, b. 5 Sept. 1905, Budapest, Hungary. Author. Educ: Univ. of Vienna, Austria. Num. publs. incl: Spanish Testament, 1938; Darkness at Noon, 1940; Scum of the Earth, 1941; Arrival & Departure, 1943; The Yogi & the Commissar, 1945; The God that Failed (co-author), 1950; The Trail of the Dinosaur, 1956; The Sleepwalkers, 1959; The Act of Creation, 1964; Drinkers of Infinity, 1968; The Case of the Midwife Toad, 1971; The Roots of Coincidence, 1972; The Challenge of Chance (co-author), 1973; The Heel of Achilles, 1974. Contbr. to: Ency. Britannica; Ency. of Philos.; Encounter; Sunday Times; Observer; N.Y. Times. Mbrships: F.R.S.L. Hons: LL.D., 1968; Sonning Prize, Univ. of Copenhagen, Denmark, 1968; C.B.E., 1972; Companion of Lit., 1974. Address: c/o A. D. Peters, 10 Buckingham St., London WC2, UK.

KOFLER, Werner, b. 23 July 1947, Villach, Carinthia, Austria. Writer. Educ: Tchr.'s Trng. Coll., 4 yrs. Publs: Local Circumstances, 1973; Analo & Other Comics, 1973; Autobiography, 1975; Örtliche Verhältnisse (radio play, broadcast by var. stns. in Germany, Austria & Holland). Contbr. to: Literatur und Kritik; Neues Forum; Manuskripte, Graz; Akzente, Cologne; Tintenfisch, Berlin; etc. Mbrships: Austrian Union of Jrnlsts.; Graz Authors' Assn.; Autorenbuchhandlung. Hons: Lyrics Studentship Lit. Prize, Austrian Univ., 1969; Exhibnr., Austrian State Exhib. for Lit., 1972-73. Address: Hetzgasse 8/24, A-1030 Vienna 3, Austria.

KOGAN, Bernard Robert, b. 16 May 1920, Chgo., Ill., USA. Professor of English. Educ: B.A., 1941; M.A., 1946, Univ. of Chgo.; Ph.D. 1953. Publs: The Chicago Haymarket Riot: Anarchy on Trial, 1959; Darwin & His Critics, 1960. Contbr. reviews to: Showcase, Chgo. Sun-Times. Mbrships: MLA, Am.; AAUP; Nat. Coun., Tchrs. of Engl.; Phi Beta Kappa. Address: 9034 N. Bennett Ave., Evanston, IL 60203, USA.

KOIVISTOINEN, Eino Hannes, b. 10 May 1907, Kuopio, Finland. Author; Master Mariner. Educ: Navigation Inst., Master, 1938; Navy Reserve Offs.' Schl., 1941. Publs: 14 books & 5 plays in Finnish; Engl. transl. incl: Swelling Sails, Notes of a Voyage Around the World, 1970; Taurua of Tahiti (play). Contbr. to Navigation of Finland, 1938-55. Mbrships: Life Mbr., Authors League of Finland; Dramatists League of Finland. Hons: Winner, TV play writing contest, 1960; State Prize of Lit., for The Old Tramp (novel), 1974. Address: Kalliolankatu 3, Kotka, Finland.

KOKOSCHKA, Oskar, b. 1 Mar. 1886, Pöchlarn, Austria. Artist; Writer. Educ: Vienna Sch. of Ind. Art. Publs. incl: A Sea Ringed with Visions, 1962; (autobiography) Mein Leben, 1972; London Views. British Landscapes, 1972; (plays) Morder, Hoffnung der Frauen, 1907; Der brennende Dornbusch, Hiob, 1911; Orpheus & Eurydice, 1916. Num. one-man exhibitions; Fndr., Int. Summer Acad. of Fine Arts, Salzburg. Num. hons. incl: C.B.E., 1959; Rome Prize, 1960; Erasmus Prize, 1960; D.Litt. Address: 1844 Villeneuve, Vaud, Switz.

KOLANKIWSKY, Mykola, b. 19 June 1912, Paniwci, Ukraine. Editor; Publisher; Writer. M.A., Theol. Acad. of Lviv., Ukraine, 1936. Publs: Bombs in the Gay Manner, 1947; Ambassadors, 1968; Contbr. to num. mags. & newspapers in Europe & Can.; fndr. & Ed., We and the World. Hon. Mbr., Soc. of the Architects of Lviv. Address: Niagara Falls Art Gallery & Museum, Queen Elizabeth Way, Niagara Falls, Ont., Can.

KOLBER, Sandra, b. 7 June 1934, White Plains, N.Y., USA. Poet; Scriptreader. Educ: B.A., McGill Univ., Montreal, Can. Publs: Bitter Sweet Lemons & Love, 1967; All There is of Love, 1969. Contbr. to: Canadian; Anglo-Jewish Press. Mbrships: Can. Circle; PEN; C.A.P.A.C. Address: 100 Summit Circle, Montreal, P.Q., Can.

KOLJEVIĆ, Svetozar, b. 9 Sept. 1930, Banja Luka, Yugoslavia. Professor of English Literature. Educ: Dip., Fac. of Philos., Belgrade, 1954; M.Litt., Cambridge, 1957; Ph.D., Zagreb, 1960. Publs: Trijumf inteligencije, 1963; Yugoslav Short Stories, 1966; Humor i mit, 1968; Naš junački ep, 1974. Contbr. to: Književnost; Izraz; Letopis Matice srpske. Mbrships: Assns. of Writers & of Lit. Transls., Bosnia & Herzegovina; PEN, Belgrade Ctr. Hons. incl: City of Sarajevo Lit. Award, 1969. Address: Višnjik 9, 71 000 Sarajevo, Yugoslavia.

KOLOZSVARI GRANDPIERRE, Emil, b. 15 Jan. 1907, Kolozsvár, Hungary. Writer. Educ: D.Phil. Publs. incl: A rosta, 1932; A nagy ember, 1935; Alvajárók, 1938; Tegnap, 1942; Szabadság, 1945; Lófö és kora, 1946; Lelkifinomságok, 1948; Mérlegen, 1950; A csodafurulya, 1954; A törökfejes kopja, 1955; A büvös kaptafa, 1957; Legendäk nyomában, 1959; Párbeszéd a sorssal, 1962; A burok, 1964; Dráma félvállról, 1966; Szellemoi galeri, 1968; Utolsó hullám, 1972; Harmazcseppek, 1974. Contbr. to: Kortárs; Uj Irás; Jelenkor; Former Ed., Magyarok. Mbr., PEN. Hons: Baumgarten Lit. Prizes, 1938 & 1942; József Attila Lit. Prize, 1969. Address: II Palánta-utca 20a, 1025 Budapest, Hungary.

KOLSTOE, Oliver Paul, b. 28 Feb. 1920, Canton, S.D., USA. Professor. Educ: B.A. in Edic., State Coll., N.D. 1941; M.S., Psychol., Univ. of N.D., 1948; Ph.D., Educl. Psychol. & Special Educ., State Univ. of Iowa, 1952. Publs: A High School Work Study Program for Mentally Subnormal Students (w. R. M. Frey), 1965; Teaching Educable Mentally Retarded Children, 1970; Mental Retardation: An Educational Viewpoint, 1972; College Professoring: Through Academia with Gun & Camera, 1975. Contbr. to profl. jrnls. Address: 1618 Lakeside Dr., Greeley, CO 80631, USA.

KOMAROVSKY, Mirra. Professor Emeritus; Lecturer in Sociology. Publs: Co-author, Leisure: A Suburban Study, 1934; The Unemployed Man & His Family, 1940, 3rd ed., 1972; Women in the Modern World, 1953 & 1972; Common Frontiers of the Social Sciences, 1957; Blue-Collar Marriage, 1964, 1967. Articles incl: Functional Analysis of Sex Roles, Am. Sociol. Review, 1950; Continuities in Family Research, Am. Jrnl. of Sociol., 1956; Cultural Contradictions & Sex Roles: The Masculine Case, Am. Jrnl. of Sociol., 1973; Some Problems in Role Analysis. Am. Sociol. Review, 1973. Patterns of Self Disclosure, Jrnl. of Marriage & the Family, 1974. Mbrships: Past Pres., Am. Sociol. Assn.; mbr., num. sociol. socs. Address: Barnard Coll., Columbia Univ., N.Y., NY, USA.

KOMLÓS, Aladár, b. 10 Dec. 1892, Alsósztregova, Hungary. Professor; Author. Educ: Ph.D., univ., Hungary. Publs. incl: Gyulaitól a marx.kriti (study) – Római kaland (novel), 1933, 3rd ed., 1973; Irók és elvek (studies), 1937; Reviczky Gy. (study), 1955; Vajda János (study), 1956; Tegnap ésma (studies), 1956; Reggeltöl estig (poems), 1963; Petöfitöl Adyig (study), 1969; Vereckétöl Dévényig (studies), 1972. Contbr. to: Nyugat; Korunk; Toll; Századunk; Szép Szó; Uj Irás; Élet és Irodalom, etc. Mbr., PEN. Hons: Gold Medals, Order of Labour, 1960, 1967, 1972; State Prize, 1972. Address: II Lajos u.37.II.8, 1023 Budapest, Hungary.

KON, Kanichi, b. 8 Dec. 1909, Hirosaki, Aomori, Japan. Novelist; Poet. Educ: Wased Univ., Tokyo. Publs: (novels) A Verse of Seagulls; A Verse of Dragons; A Verse of Phantom Flowers; Wallflowers; Under the Boots; Pier No. 13 (filmed, 1958); Unsinkable Battleship Nagato; (biog.) A Life of the Poet, Kojirō Fukushi; (poetry anthol.) Mississippi Flows into Sumida; (essay) Verse of Nalives. Contbr. to: Mainichi; Bungei-Shunjyu; & num. daily & wkly. newspapers. Mbr., PEN. Recip., Naokis Prize for Wallflowers, 1957. Address: Minato-kul 11-19, Tokyo, Japan.

KONING, Alexander Christiaan, b. 19 Dec. 1949, Stad-Delden, Netherlands. Lawyer; Trade Union Leader. Educ: LL.M., Univ. of Utrecht. Publs: Collected Poems, 1973; Collections to Church Ceremonies, 1974; Ik verwerp, 1975. Contbr. to: Vraagteken; Stentor; Trophonios. Mbr., PEN, Netherlands. Address: Asch van Wijckskade 6a, Utrecht, Netherlands.

KONKLE, Janet Everest, b. 5 Nov. 1917, Grand Rapids, Mich., USA. Kindergarten Teacher; Juvenile Author; Photographer. Educ: Grand Rapids Jr. Coll.; Univ. of Mich.; B.S., W. Mich. Univ., 1939. Publs: Once There Was a Kitten, 1951, 1962; The Kitten & the Parakeet, 1952; Christmas Kitten, 1953, 1964; Easter Kitten, 1955; Tabby's Kittens, 1956; J. Hamilton Hamster, 1957; Susie Stock Car, 1959, 1961; The Sea Cart, 1961, 1964; Schoolroom Bunny, 1965; The Raccoon Twins, 1972. Contbr. to: Childcraft Ency.; var. mags. & photography jrnls. Mbrships: A.C.E.I.; Nat. Women's Book Assn. Hons: J. Hamilton Hamster chosen Ambassador Book by English-Speaking Union, 1957; Num. photog. hons.; Permanent collect. MSS in Univ. of S. Miss. Address: 1360 Oakleigh Rd. NW, Grand Rapids, MI 49504, USA.

KONNYU, Leslie, b. 28 Feb. 1914, Tamasi, Hungary. Geographer-Cartographer. Educ: Elem. Tchrs. Dip., 1933; Secondary Tchrs. Dip., 1944; B.M.E., 1954; Cartographer's Dip., 1957; M.A., Geog., 1965. Publs. incl: Bond of Beauty (poems), 1959; Against the River (poems), 1961; A History of American Hungarian Literature, 1962; J. Xantus, Hungarian Geographer in America, 1965; A Condensed Geography of Hungary, 1971; 21 books in Hungarian, 1 in German, 1 in French. Contbr. to newspapers & reviews. Mbrships: Int. PEN; Mo. Writers Guild; Treas., St. Louis Writers Guild; VP, St. Louis Poetry Ctr. Address: The American Hungarian Review, 5410 Kerth Rd., St. Louis, MO 63128, USA.

KONOPKA, (Baron) Feliks Ignacy Leon, b. 17 July 1888, Brén, Kraków, Poland. Author; Poet; Translator. Educ: Jagellonian Univ. & Acad. of Fine Arts, Kraków. Publs. incl: Words in Darkness, 1929; The Last Autumn, 1972; (transls. — into Polish) F. Schiller, The Robbers, 1964; J. W. v. Goethe, Selected Poems, 1955, 1968; Goethe, Faust I & II, 1962, 1968; J. de la Fontaine, Fables, 1955, 3rd ed., 1971; P. Verlaine, 26 Poems, 1975; (into French verse) A. Fredro, La Vengeance, 1955; A. Mickiewicz, Sonnets de Crimée, 1973, 1975; C. K. Norwid, Choix de Poèmes, 1974; (into French prose) C. K. Norwid, Poignée de Sable; ad Leones!, 1974. Contbr. to: Czas; Ateneum; Verbum; Pologne Littéraire; etc. Mbrships: PEN; Assn. of Polish Men of Letters. Hons. incl: Prize, PEN, 1963. Address: ul. Krupnicza 8/2, 31-123 Kraków, Poland.

KONVITZ, Milton Ridvas, b. 12 Mar. 1908, Safad, Israel. Professor. Educ: B.S., N.Y. Univ., 1928; M.A., 1930; J.D., 1930; Ph.D., Cornell Univ., 1933. Publs: Alien & Asiatic in American Law, 1946; Constitution & Civil Rights, 1947; On the Nature of Value, 1946; Civil Rights in Immigration, 1953; Fundamental Liberties of a Free People, 1957; A Century of Civil Rights, 1961; Expanding Liberties, 1966; Religious Liberty & Conscience, 1968; Bill of Rights Reader, 1954, 1973; Judaism & Human Rights, 1972; Recognition of Emerson, 1972. Contbr. to profl. jrnls. Mbrships incl: Am. Philos. Assn.; Am. Bar Assn.; Am. Studies Assn. Recip., num. hon. degrees. Address: 16 the Byway, Forest Home, Ithaca, NY 14850, USA.

KOOLE, Willem, b. 10 May 1935, Rotterdam, Netherlands. Journalist. Educ: Univs. of Utrecht & Rotterdam; Fellow, Salzburg Seminar in Am. Studies, 1964. Contbr. to: Economisch Dagblad. Mbrships: Contact-Centrum Voorlichtingsgebied; Nederlandse Vereniging Journalisten; Former mbr., Nederlands Genootschap voor PR, & Parlementaire Pressclub. Address: Pioenweg 11, The Hague, Netherlands.

KOOYKER-ROMYN, Johanna Maria, pen name KOOIKER, Leonie, b. 20 Oct. 1927, Markelo, Netherlands. Writer. Publs: Het Malle Ding van Bobbistiek, 1970; De Boevenvangers, 1972; Het Laantje met de Lindeboom, 1972; De Diamant van de Piraat, 1972; De Dochter van die Schilder op de Berg, 1973; De Heksenteen, 1974; Je Hart of je Heerlykheid. Mbr., Vereniging van Letterkundigen. Recip., Gold Pencil Award, 1971 for best children's book. Address: Bos 17, Papendrecht, Netherlands.

KOPS, Bernard, b. 28 Nov. 1926. Writer. Educ: London Schls. Publs: Poems, 1955; Poems & Songs, 1958; An Anemone for Antigone, 1959; Erica, I Want to Read You Something, 1967; (novels) Awake for Mourning, 1958; Yes from No Man's Land, 1967; The Dissent of Dominick Shapiro, 1967; By the Waters of Whitechapel, 1970; Partners, 1975; (plays) David, It is Getting Dark, 1959; The Dream of Peter Mann, 1959; Four Plays, 1964; The Boy Who Wouldn't Play Jesus, 1965; (autobiog.) The World is a Wedding, 1964 & Breakdown, 1976. Contbr. to var. anthols. Recip., Arts COun. Award for Lit., 1975. Address: Flat 1, 35 Canfield Gdns., London NW6, UK.

KORG, Jacob, b. 21 Nov. 1922, NYC, USA. Professor of English. Educ: B.A., CCNY, 1943; M.A., 1947, Ph.D., 1952, Columbia Univ. Publs: George Gissing, A Critical Biography, 1963; Dylan Thomas, 1965; The Force of Few Words, 1968; Poems of Robert Browning (ed.), 1972. Contbr. to: Am. Schlr.; Univ. of Toronto Quarterly; The Nation; Antioch Review; Commentary; etc. Mbr., MLA. Address: Department of English, University of Wash., Seattle, WA 98195, USA.

KORHERR, Helmut Karl, b. 29 Mar. 1950, Vienna, Austria. Doctoral Student of Theatre; Dramatist. Educ: Univ. of Vienna. Publs: (prods., w. Wilhelm Pellert) Der Teufel schläft nicht (morality play), 1973; Die Nachtgeher

(radio play), 1973; Dr. Tschicker und Herr Heut (radio play), 1973; Jesus von Ottakring (folkdrama), 1974; ... und sie wissen, was sie tun (drama), 1974; (children's story in anthol.) Der Weihnachtsmann, 1974. Contbr. to: Impulse mag. Mbr., PEN. Hons. incl: Film Promotional Prize, City of Vienna, 1973; Theodor Körner Prize for Lit., 1973. Address: Herbststr. 61/25, 1160 Vienna, Austria.

KORINETZ, Juri, b. 14 Jan. 1923, Moscow, USSR. Writer; Poet; Painter. Educ: Moscow Maxim Gorky Institute of Literature. Publs: (novels) There, Far Beyond the River, 1968, publ. in Engl., Italian, Dutch, Swedish, Danish, Norwegian, Czech, Bulgarian, German; Greetings from Werner, 1972, German title In der Mitte der Welt; Volodya's Brothers, 1974, German ed.; (poetry) Saturday in Monday, 1966; Four Sisters, 1970. Contbr. to: Murzilka; Kostyor; Detskaya Literatura; Jahrbuch der Kinderliteratur (W. Germany). Mbr., PEN. Hons. incl: 1st Prize Lenin Anniversary Award USSR, 1966 for There, Far Beyond the River, also same book UNESCO Award, 1973; W. German Award, best youth book, 1973. Address: Moscow A-319, Krasnoarmeiskaja 21 — 108, USSR 125 319.

KORN, K(urt) Theodore, b. 8 July 1913, Hamburg, Germany. Retired Methodologist. Educ: Dr.rer.nat. (Sc.D.), Hanseatisch Univ., 1934. Publs: Die Rationelle Gestaltung der Chemischen Produktion, 1934; Manhood of Industrial Engineering, 1952. Contbr. to: Topical Time (columnist); Western Stamp Collector; Air Post Jrnl.; UNTOPicalist (former ed.); Ergonetics (former ed.); The Clevelander; Jrnl. of Indust. Engrng.; The Champion; UNSU Review; etc. Address: Box 35, Reynoldsburg, OH 43068, USA.

KÖRNER, Stephan, b. 26 Sept. 1913, Ostrava, Czech. Professor of Philosophy. Educ: Jur. Dr., Charles Univ., Prague; Ph.D., Trinity Hall, Cambridge Univ. Publs: Kant, 1955; Conceptual Thinking, 1955; The Philosophy of Mathematics, 1960; Experience & Theory, 1966; What is Philosophy? , 1969; Catgorial Frameworks, 1970. Contbr. to schlrly. jrnls. inclng: Ratio (Ed., 1961—); Mind; Proceedings of the Aristotelian Soc. Mbr., num. schlrly. orgs. Address: 10 Belgrave Rd., Bristol BS8 2AB, UK.

KORNHAUSER, William, b. 5 Feb. 1925, Chgo., III., USA. Professor of Sociology. Educ: B.A., 1948, M.A., 1950, Ph.D., 1953, Univ. of Chgo. Publs: The Politics of Mass Society, 1959, UK ed. 1960, Japan 1961, Argentina 1970; Scientists in Industry, 1962. Contbr. to: Am. Jrnl. of Sociol.; Jrnl. of Social Issues; Minerva. Mbrships: Am. Sociol. Assn.; Am. Soc. of Pol. & Legal Philos. Hons: Fellow, Social Sci. Rsch. Coun., 1951-52, Ctr. for Adv. Study in Behavioral Scis., 1954-55, Adlai Stevenson Inst. Int. Affairs, 1968-70. Address: Dept. of Sociology, University of Calif., Berkeley, CA 94720, USA.

KORODA, Miklós, b. 6 June 1909, Budapest, Hungary. Writer. Educ: Budapest Univ. of Econs. Publs. (novels): The World is a Dream, 1939; Enlightenment, 1942; The Adventures of Christopher Karacs (a picaresque tetralogy) 1959-69; A Tower of Fools — Novel of the Medieval Craftsmen of Buda, 1974. Contbr. to: Horizon; Contemporary; etc. Mbrships. incl: Hungarian Writers' Union; Hungarian Artists' Econ. Fund; PEN. Hons: Franz Joseph Prize for Lit., 1940; Govt. Prize for Labour, 1969. Address: 1014 Budapest, 1 Uri utca 37, Hungary.

KORTEN, David Craig, b. 30 July 1937, Longview, Wash., USA. University Professor; Consultant. Educ: A.B., 1959, M.B.A. 1961, Ph.D., 1968, Grad. Schl. of Bus., Stanford Univ. Publs: Planned Change in a Traditional Society: Psychological Problems of Modernization in Ethiopia, 1972. Contbr. to: Studies in Family Planning; Jrnl. of Applied Behavioral Sci.; Harvard Bus. Schl. Bulletin; Jrnl. Cross-Cultural Psychol.; Air Univ. Review; Comp. Educ. Review; Jrnl. of Conflict Resolution. Mbr. num. profl., civic & int. orgs. Hons. incl H. Hoover Fellowship, 1960-61; Ford Fndn. Fellowship, 1962-64; Allied Chem. Co. Fellowship, 1966-67. Address: 2327 Cascade Way, Longview, WA 98632, USA.

KORTNER, Peter, pen name HOFER, Peter, b. 4 Dec. 1924, Berlin, Germany. Freelance writer. Educ: B.A., UCLA, USA. Publs: Jim for Sale, 1970; A Slightly Used Woman, 1973; Breakfast With a Stranger, 1975; (films) There's A Girl in My Soup (additional dialogue); Some You Win . . . (sole writer). Mbrships: Writers Guild of GB, Grosvenor House Gymnasium & Swimming Pool Club. Recip., 2 Emmy Awards, Hollywood, Calif., USA. Address: 156 Holland Road, London W14 8BE, UK.

KORTOOMS, Antonius Johannes, pen name KORTOOMS, Toon, b. 23 Feb. 1916, Deurne, Netherlands. Author; Journalist. Educ: Tchrs. Sem. Publs: Liefde in Peelland, 1947; De Zwarte Plak, 1948; Beekman en Beekman (trilogy), 1949-50; De kleine Emigratie, 1951; Deze Jongeman, 1952; Parochie in de Peel, 1952; Ditzwarte goud, 1954; Mijn kinderen eten turf, 1959; Zon over de Peel, 1966; Help, de dokter verzuiptl , 1968; En nu de keuken in! , 1971; Turf in m'n ransel (autobiography), 1974. Contbr. to: Panorama. Mbr., Assn. of Authors (V.V.L.). Address: Plantsoenlaan 12, 1542 Bloemendaal, Netherlands.

KOS, (KOSCH), Erih (Erich), b. 15 Apr. 1913, Sarajevo, Yugoslavia. Educ: Law Degree, Belgrade Univ. Publs: Best Years, 1955; Big Mac, 1956; Il tifo, 1958; Ice & Snow, 1961; Sparrows of Van Pe, 1962; First Person Singular, 1962; Nets, 1967; Mixed Society, 1969; Dossier Hrabak, 1971; Why Not? , 1971; Novels, short stories, essays. Contbr. to: Savremenik; Knjizevne novine; etc. Mbrships: Assn. of Writers of Yugoslavia; PEN. Hons: Book of Yr. Lit. Prize, Assn. of Writers, 1958; Oct. Prize, Town of Belgrade, 1964; NIN Critics' Prize, 1968; 7 July Prize for Lit., Repub. of Serbia, 1974. Address: Jovanova 32b, Belgrade, Yugoslavia.

KOSINSKI, Jerzy Nikodem, pen name NOVAK, Joseph, b. 14 June 1933, Lodz, Poland. Novelist. Educ: M.A. Publs: (non- fiction) The Future is Ours, Comrade, 1960; No Third Path: A Study of Collective Behaviour, 1962; (fiction) The Painted Bird, 1965; Steps, 1968; Being There, 1971; The Devil Tree, 1973; Cockpit, 1975. Contbr. to: The Am. Schlr.; N.Y. Times. Mbrships: Pres., Am. Ctr., PEN, 1973-; Bd., Nat. Writers' Club; Bd., Int. League for the Rights of Man. Hons. incl: Best For. Book Award (for The Painted Bird), Paris, France, 1966; Nat. Book Award (for Steps), 1969; Award in Lit., Nat. Inst. of Arts & Letters, 1970. Address: 18-K, 60 W. 57th St., N.Y., NY 10019, USA.

KOSKIMIES, (Kaarlo) Rafael, b. 9 Feb. 1898, Savonlinna, Finland. University Professor; Writer. Educ: Ph.Mag., 1920; Ph.D., 1923. Publs: Theorie des Romans, 1935; Elävä Kansalliskirjallisuus, 3 vols., 1944-49; Porthanin aika, 1956; Y.S. Yrjö-Koskinen, 2 vols., 1968-74; Aleksis Kivi, 1974. Contbr. to: The Review Aika; Valvoja-Aika (Chief Ed., 1932-41); Uusi Suomi. Mbrships: Past Pres., Finnish Acad. of Sci. & Letters; Finnish Soc. of Lit. Hons: Prize, E. Aaltonen Fndn., 1950; Prize, Finnish Acad. of Sci. & Letters, 1969; Prize, Wihuri Fndn., 1970. Address: Lutherink. 12 A 11, 00100 Helsinki 10, Finland.

KOSSOBUDZKI, Leszek Wincenty Roman, pen name KOS, Wincenty, b. 19 July 1930, Cracow, Poland. Editor; Journalist; Translator. Educ: M.A., Warsaw Univ.; Jagellonian Univ., Cracow. Publs. incl: prefaces, epilogues, commentaries, contbr. to works of Flaubert, 1954; Stendhal, 1955; R. Coelho Lisboa, 1956; P.-A. Lesort, 1957; R.-M. Albérès, 1958; F. Mauriac, 1958; (authors transl'd into Polish) R. Dorgelès, 1958; A. Robbe-Grillet, 1959; J. Cayrol, 1960; N. Kazantzakes, 1962; G. Simenon, 1969; C. Feld, 1969; A. Appia, 1974; Ed., Guide to the Academy of Mining & Metallurgy of Cracow, 1972; Collected Works of J. Meissner, forthcoming. Contbr. to var. sci. & rsch. publs. Mbrships. incl: PEN. Address: 12 Stachowicza St., 30-103 Cracow, Poland.

KOSTELANETZ, Richard (Cory), b. 14 May 1940, NYC, USA. Writer. Educ: A.B., Brown Univ., 1962; M.A., Columbia Univ., 1966; Fulbright Schl., King's Coll., Univ. of London. Publs: The Theatre of Mixed Means, 1968; Master Minds, 1969; Visual Language, 1970; In the Beginning, 1971; The End of Intelligent Writing, 1974; Recyclings: Volume One, 1974. Contbr. to num. US. for. jrnls.; Compiler, num. anthols. incing: On Contemporary Literature, 1964, rev. ed., 1969; Possibilities of Poetry, 1970; In Youth, 1972; Essaying Essays, 1974. Mbr., Am. PEN. Hons: Guggenheim Fellowship, 1967-68; Pulitzer Fellowship in Critical Writing, 1965. Address: 242 E. 5th St., N.Y., NY 10003, USA.

KOSTIUK, Hryhory, pen name PODOLIAK, Boris, b. 12 Oct. 1902, Kamyanets-Podilsky, Ukraine. Educ: Fac. of Hist. & Lit., Univ. of Kiev, 1925-29; Rsch. Inst. of Hist. & Theory of Lit., Kharkiv, 1929-32. Publs: Panas Mirny, 1930; The Fall of Postyshev, 1954; Stalinist Rule in the Ukraine: A Study of the Decade of Mass Terror (1929-1939), 1960; Theory & Reality, 1971; Volodymyr Vynnychenko & His Last Novel, 1971; Chronicle of Literary Life in Diaspora, 1971. Contbr. to var. lit. jrnls.

Mbrships: Ukrainian Writers' Assn. in Exile, Slovo; PEN, Ctr. for Writers in Exile; Ukrainian Acad. of Arts & Scis., USA; Inst. for the Study of the USSR. Address: 69 Monona Ave., Rutherford, NJ 07070, USA.

KOSTOV, Vladimir, b. 22 Sept. 1932, Bitola, Yugoslavia. Professor. Educ: Fac. of Philos., Univ. of Skopje. Publs: Faces with Disguises, 1967; Mara's Wedding, 1968; A Play (collection of short stories), 1969; New Reason, 1970. Contbr. to: Razgledi; Sovremenost. Mbr., Yugoslav Writers' Soc. Hons: November Prize, Town of Bitola, 1967 & 1969; 1st of May Prize, Repub. of Yugoslavia, 1968. Address: Zgrada I, No: 20, Aleksandar Turundzev St., 97000 Bitola, Yugoslavia.

KÖSZEGI, Imre, b. 4 Feb. 1903, Koszeg, Hungary. Novelist. Educ: D.Jur. Publs: Budavár ostroma, 1945; A pesti lány, 1958; Ágyudörges Budaörsnél, 1967; A lázadó trónörökös, 1969; Tollas Konty, 1971; A kincstaláló, 1973; & Hungarian transls. works Cronin, L. Green, B. Toy, G. Young, etc. Contbr. to: Világ; Magyar Nemzet; Az Est (1923-38); etc. Mbrships: Assn. Hungarian Writers; PEN; Assn. Hungarian Jrnlsts. Recip., Medal Labour, 1973. Address: 1124 Budapest, Levendula u. 6/a, Hungary.

KOTHARI, Hemraj, b. 10 Nov. 1933, Sujangarh, India. Editor; Engineer & Management Consultant. Educ: B.Sc., Darjeeling, 1953; studies in Europe in Engrng., Jrnlsm. & Mgmt. Publs. incl: A.I.E. Handbook, 1958; Kothari's World of Reference Works, 1963; Directory of Company Secretaries, 1969; Who's Who In India, 1973. Contbr. to: (Fndr.-Ed.) What's On In Calcutta; Profl. Engr.; & num. mags. Mbrships incl: (Pres.) Engr.'s Club; Inst. of Int. Affairs; (VP) The Engr.'s Guild. Hons: Deleg., var. Nat. & Int. Confs. inclng. Asia Assembly. Address: Kothari Publs., 12 India Exchange Pl., Calcutta-700001, India.

KOTOWICZ, Caroline S., b. 26 July 1918, Milwaukee, Wis., USA. Poet. Publs. inc.: Anthology of American Poets, 1963, 1964, 1965, 1966, 1969, 1970 & 1971; Poems out of Wisconsin, 1967; New Poems out of Wisconsin, 1969; Spring Anthology, 1969, 1970, 1971, 1972, 1973; 9 Muses, 1971; 9 Muses, 1972; Selected Poems, 1972; Selected Poems, 1973; Clover Collection of Verse, 1974. Contbr. to: S. Milwaukee Voice Jrnl. (Poetry Ed.); Ideals; Wis. Trails. Mbrships. incl: Clover Leaf Int. Assn.; Poets Laureate Int.; Ariz. State Poetry Soc.; The Int. Poetry Soc.; etc; Hons: A.P.F.S., IV Poet Laureate; World Poet Award Winner, 1970; & num. others. Address: 215 Fairview Ave., S. Milwaukee, WI 53172, USA.

KOVÁCS, E. Kálmán, b. 16 June 1912, Orosháza, Hungary. Author. Educ: B.A., Univ. of Budapest. Publs: (novels) An Unlucky Bloke, 1941; The Blacksmith of Kakasszik, 1947; A Night in Luxembourg Garden, 1949; (plays) Three Poor Chaps, 1947; The Battle at Kakasszik, 1949; (essays) George Dozsa, 1946; Father Bem, 1947. Contbr. to: Napjaink; Uj Aurora. Mbrships. incl: Soc. of Hungarian Writers; PEN; Hungarian Soc. of Hist. of Lit.; Soc. of Hungarian Histns.; Assn. for Promotion of Social & Natural Scis. Recip., Order of Labour. Address: 5 Comenius Street, H-3950 Sárospatak, Hungary.

KOVÁCS, György, b. 27 Apr. 1911, Cusmed, Romania. Editor; Author. Educ: Univs. of Aiud & Cluj. Publs. incl: Varjak a falu felett, 1934; Erdelyi tél, 1938; Boszorkány, 1946; Bekülö Erdely, 1947; Foggal es körömmel (sev. eds. & transl. into German, French & Czech.), 1949; Bünügy, 1956; Dali Jóska rózsája, 1957; Ozsdola leánya, 1959; Katonasir, 1960; Santa Ielkek, 1961; Falusi, Kaland, 1961; Hínár, 1964; Bánat és bor, 1966; Kozmáne szép asszony, 1969; Döglött gránát, 1970; Pusztulás, 1971. Contbr. to: Igaz Szo (Ed.-in-Chief). Recip., State Prize, 1952. Address: Srada Mihai Viteazul 6, Tirgu Mures, jud. Mures, Romania.

KÖVESI, Christina, b. 9 May 1945, Vienna, Austria. Playwright. Educ: Vienna Acad. of Music; Vienna Univ. Publs: Familienglück, 1966; Haben Sie auch einen Schutzendel?, 1967; Die Goldene Flöte, 1968; Smeraldina, 1969; Der Weyland Casperl, 1970; Der Rauchfangkehrer auf dem Regenbogen, 1971; Pfeffermaus, 1972; Drei Zwillinge, 1972; Die beiden Nasen der Wahrheit, 1974. Contbr. to: Die Presse, Vienna. Mbr., Austrian Authors' Assn. Address: Nussdorferstr. 30, A-1090 Vienna, Austria.

KOVNER, Abba, b. 14 Mar. 1918, Sevastopol, USSR. Writer. Publs: incl: (vols. of poetry in Hebrew) Ad Lo Or, 1947; Preida me-ha-Darom, 1949; Admat ha-Hol, 1961; Mi-Kol ha-Ahavot, 1965; Ahoti Ketana; Hupah ba-Midbar; Lehakat ha-Ketsev Mofiah al Har Grizim; Ha-Sefer ha-Katan; (prose in Hebrew) Panim el Panim: She-at ha-Efes; Panim el Panim: Ha-Tsomet; Contbr. to: Isreli Lit. Mags., Midstream, N.Y. Chmn., Hebrew Writers' Assn. of Israel, 1970. Hons: Israel Prize for Lit., 1970; Brenner Award for Poetry; Shlonsky Award; Am. Jewish Congress Culture Award; Remembrance Award, World Union of the Survivors of Bergen-Belsen, N.Y., 1970. Address: Kibbutz Ein ha-Horesh, Israel.

KOWALEWSKA, Maria, b. 11 Oct. 1901, Vilna, Russia (now USSR). Writer: Author & Translator of Children's Books. Educ: Grad., Poznan Univ. Publs: The Mysterious Note, 1956; About Fik & Myk & a House Made of Sticks, 1958; The Strange Events in Zawodzie, 1960; The Voice of Nature (w. M. Kownacka), 1963; The Crazy Courtyard, 1963; Following the Thread, 1969; The Black Claw from the Wild Jungle, 1970; Sapcio & Pufcio from the Steep Bank, 1972; The Little — it is Me, 1972; I Wanted to be a Star, 1973; The Guests, 1974; Over 25 books transl.'d from Russian. Contbr. to num. Polish children's mags. Mbrships: Polish Writers' Union; PEN; ZAIKS Soc. of Authors. Recip., sev. lit. prizes. Address: ul.Boya 4 m.34, 00-621 Warsaw, Poland.

KOWALSKI, John J., b. 8 Oct. 1928, Worcester, Mass., USA. Teacher; Writer; Poet. Educ: A.B., Emerson Coll.; Ed.M., Worcester State Coll. Contbr. to jrnls. & newspapers. Mbrships: Fndr., Acad. of Am. Poets; Fellow, Int. Poetry Soc. Address: 118 Algonquin Dr., Wallingford, CT 06492, USA.

KOZIEBRODZKI, (Count) Leopold B., b. 10 Dec. 1906, Podhajczyki, Poland. Lawyer; Economist; Political Scientist. Educ: LL.M., Univ. of Warsaw, 1928; LL.D., Univ. of Paris, France, 1956. Publs: Le Droit d'Asile, 1962; Polish Civil Law (No. 18 of Law in Eastern Europe) (co-author), 1973. Contbr. to: Am. Jrnl. of Comp. Law. Mbrships: Am. Soc. of Int. Law; Am. Econ. Assn.; Am. Political Sci. Assn.; Am. Fin. Assn. Address: 1500 Oakview Dr., McLean, VA 22101, USA.

KRAFT, Charles Howard, b. 15 July 1932, Waterbury, Conn., USA. Professor of Anthropology. Educ: B.A., Wheaton Coll., 1953; B.D., Ashland Theol. Sem., 1960; Ph.D., Hartford Sem. Fndn., 1963. Publs: incl: A Study of Hausa Syntax, 3 Vols., 1963; An Introduction to Spoken Hausa (textbook, workbook & tapes), 1965; Where Do I Go From Here? (co-author), 1966; Teach Yourself Hausa (co-author), 1973; Spoken Hausa: Introductory Course (co-author), 1974; Hausa Reader, 1974. Contbr. to: Practical Anthropol.; Jrnl. of African Langs.; Theol., News & Notes; Evangelical Missions Quarterly; etc. Hons. incl: Fulbright-Hays Ctr. Fac. Award, 1967. Address: 1200 Lyndon Street, S. Pasadena, CA 91030, USA.

KRAMER, Frank Raymond, b. 2 Jan. 1908, Baraboo, Wis., USA. Professor of Classics. Educ: B.H., M.A., Ph.D., Greek & Latin, Univ. of Wis. Publs: Voices in the Valley: Mythmaking & Folk Belief in the Shaping of the Middle West, 1964. Contbr. to num. profl. jrnls. & reviews. Address: 25 Lincoln Rd., Tiffin, OH 44883, USA.

KRAPIVA, pen name of APRAKHOVICH, Kondrat Kondratyevich, b. 6 Mar. 1906, Nizok, Minsk, USSR. Writer. Educ: Byelorussia Univ. Publs: incl: Nettles, 1925; Fables, 1927; (plays) Who Laughs Last, 1939; The Larks Sing, 1951; Men & Devils, 1958; (satirical Poem) The Bible, 1926; Collected Works, 4 vols., 1963; Forty Fables, 1966. Mbr., Byelorussian S.S.R. Acad. of Sci. (VP, 1956—). Hons: State Prize, 1941, 1950, 1971; Order of Lenin, 3 times; Red Banner of Labour; Red Star. Address: c/o Writers' Union, Minsk, Byelorussia, USSR.

KRAR, Stephen Frank, b. 20 July 1924, Mor, Hungary. Teacher; Technical Author. Educ: Tchr. Trng. Course, Univ. Toronto, Can., 1954-55. Publs: incl: Machine Shop Training, 1962, 2nd ed., 1967, Spanish ed., 1971; Technology of Machine Tools, 1969, French ed., 1972; Measurement & Layout, Transparency Book 2, 1970; Turning Technology, 1971; Threads & Testing Instruments, Transparency Book 3, 1972; Grinding Technology, 1973; Cutting Tools, Transparency Book 4, 1973; Metallurgy, Transparency Book 5, 1974; Machine Shop Operation, Visutext Series, 1974. Mbrships. incl: Ont. Voc. Educ. Assn. (Pres., 1964). Recip., Award, 1972 for Sales exceeding 100,000 copies Machine Shop Trng. Address: 420 Fitch St., Welland, Ont. L3C 4W8, Can.

KRASINSKI, Janusz, b. 5 July 1928, Warsaw, Poland. Writer. Publs: Haracz Szarego Dnia, 1959; Jakie Wielkie

Slonce, 1962; Wozek, 1966; Skarga, 1968; Zywiol Dotad nie Znany, 1973; Czapa i Inne Dramaty, 1973; (play prods.) Czapa czyli smierc na raty (Death in Instalments), 1966; Filip z prawda w oczach, 1968; Wkrotce nadejda bracia, 1968; Sniadanie u Desdemony, 1973. Contbr. to: Dialog; Kultura; Miesiecznik Literacki. Mbrships: PEN; Treas., Polish Writers' Union; VP, Polish Dramatic Writers' Club. Hons: Stanislaw Pietak Award, 1967; Polish Radio Listeners' Award, 1973; Krzyz Kawalerski Orderu Odrodzenia Polski, 1974. Address: Niemcewicza 7/9 m. 92, 02-022 Warsaw, Poland.

KRASLOW, David, b. 16 Apr. 1926, NYC, USA. Journalist. Educ: CCNY, 1943-44; A.B., Univ. of Miami, 1948; Nieman Fellow, Harvard Univ., 1961-62. Publs: A Certain Evil (co-author), 1965; The Secret Search for Peace in Vietnam (co-author), 1968. Mbrships: Nat. Press Club; Gridiron Club; Fed. City Club; Sigma Delta Chi. Hons: Raymond Clapper Mem. Award for disting. Wash. corres., & Geo Polk Mem. Award for disting. int. reporting, both 1969; Dumont Award for int. reporting. Address: 2316 N. Gate Terr., Silver Spring, MD 20906, USA.

KREIS, Erna, pen name MODENA, Maria, b. 24 Sept. 1899, St. Gallen, Switz. Housewife. Educ: Zürich Univ. Publs: Sonette der Liebe, 1937; Irrfahrt des Herzens, 1940; Neue Märchen, 1941; Der Barde Iraner und seine Märchen, 1943; (poetry) Die Sonette um Dorian Sun, 1945; Musik des Lebens, 1948; Heimat im Süden, 1959; (plays) Sappho, 1951; Orpheus & Eurydike, 1951; Franz von Assisi, 1954; Paulus der Apostel, 1956, (tales & legends) Der goldene Fisch, 1958; (poems) Die Verwandlung der Schiffe, 1963; (tales & legends) Der Regen bogen, 1969; Tavasami, 1972, 2nd ed., 1973. Contbr. to anthols., reviews etc. Mbrships. incl: PEN; Am. Int. Inst. Hons. incl: Gold Medal, Academia il Mondo Libero. Address: Waldeckweg 15, Binningen, Switz.

KRENKEL, John H., b. Atlanta, Ill., USA. Educator. Educ: B.S., in Educ., Ph.D., Univ. of Ill.; M.A., Claremont Grad. Schl. Publs: Illinois Internal Improvements 1818-1848, 1958; Richard Yates Civil War Governor, 1966; Richard Yates the Younger, Governor & Congressman, 1968; Life & Times of Joseph Fish Mormon Pioneer, 1970. Contbr. to jrnls. & encys.; Reviews in histl. jrnls. Address: 619 E. Erie, Tempe, AZ 85282, USA.

KRENZ-SENIOR, Ethel Rosabelle, pen name MIRANDA, Maria, b. 7 May 1903, Willemstad, Curaçao, Dutch Antilles. Author. Educ: Univ. Amsterdam. Publs: De Verwachting. Contbr. to De Tyd (Amsterdam). Mbrships: PEN; Société des Écrivains Vaudois. Address: Ch. de la Résidence 4, 1009 Pully, Switz.

KREPPS, Robert Wilson, b. 1919, Pittsburgh, Pa., USA. Author. Educ: Univ. of Pittsburgh; Westminster Coll., Pa., A.B. Publs: The Field of Night; The Courts of the Lion; Tell it on the Drums; Earthshaker; Gamble My Last Game; Baboon Rock; The Big Gamble, 1961; El Cid, 1961; Boy's Night Out, 1962; Taras Bulba, 1962; Send Me No Flowers, 1964; Stagecoach, 1966; Hour of the Gun, 1967; Fancy, 1969. Contbr. to: Saturday Evening Post; Collier's; John Bull; Argosy; Bluebook; etc. Address: 1488 40th Ave. N.E., St. Petersburg, FL 33703, USA.

KREUDER, Ernst, b. 29 Aug. 1903, Zeitz, Germany. Author. Educ: Frankfurt Univ. Publs: (novels) Die Gesellschaft vom Dachboden, transl. into Engl., French & Swedish, 1946; Schwebender Weg, 1947; Die Unauffindbaren, 1948; Herein ohne anzuklopfen, 1954; Agimos oder die Weltgehilfen, 1959; Spur unterm Wasser, 1963; Tunnel zu vermieten, 1966; Hörensagen, 1969; (poems) Sommers Einsiedelei, 1956. Mbrships: Lit. Acad., Mainz; German Acad. of Speech, Darmstadt; PEN. Recip., Büchner Prize, 1953. Address: Mühltalstr. 135, 61 Darmstadt, W. Germany.

KREY, Laura Letitia, pen name EVERETT, Mary, b. 18 Dec. 1890, Galverton, Tex., USA. Writer. Educ: B.A., Univ. of Tex. Publs: And Tell of Time, 1938; On the Long Tide, 1940; Contbr. to: Craft of Fiction, 1942; Twentieth Century English, 1946. Mbrships. incl: Inst. of Letters, Tex.; Philosoph. Soc., Tex.; United Daughters of the Confederacy. Recip., Hon. Medal, Mary Baldwin Coll., Staunton, Va. Address: 4203 Wilshire Parkway, Austin, TX 78722, USA.

KRIEZA, Miroslav, b. 7 July 1893. Writer; Director, Yugoslav Lexicographical Institute. Publs. incl: The Return of Phillip Latinovicz; On the Verge of Reason; Flags; (short stories) God Mars of Croatia; (plays) In Agony; Golgotha; The Glembaj Cycle; Aretaeus; (other) The Ballads of Petrica Kerempuh; Beisetzung in Theresienburg; Essays, 6 vols.; Collected Poems, 7 vols.; Europaisches Alphabet. Address: c/o Yugoslav Lexicographical Inst., Zagreb, Yugoslavia.

KRIGE, Uys, b. 4 Feb. 1910, Bontebokskloof, Swellendam, S. Africa. Writer. Educ: B.A., Univ. Stellenbosch. Publs: (non-fiction) The Way Out, 1946; (short stories) The Dream & the Desert, 1953; Orphan of the Desert, 1967; (anthols.) Poems of Roy Campbell, 1960; Olive Schreiner, 1968; The Penguin Book of South African Verse (Co-Ed., w. Jack Cope), 1968; (4 1-act plays) The Sniper, 1962; (play) The Two Lamps; & 26 books of plays, poems, short stories, essays, autobiog. etc. in Afrikaans. Contbr. to more than 60 anthols., reviews & periodicals in many countries, both Engl. & Afrikaans. Recip., num. acad. hons. Address: P.O. Box 25, Onrust River 7201, S. Africa.

KRISHER, Bernard, b. 9 Aug. 1931, Frankfurt, Germany. Correspondent. Educ: B.A., Queen's Coll.; Adv. Int. Reporting Prog. Cert., Columbia Univ. Publs: Draftee's Confidential Guide (w. Alan Levy & James Cox), 1957, revised 1965. Mbr., For. Corres. Club of Japan. Address: c/o Newsweek, Asahi Bldg., 6-6-7 Ginza, Chuo-ku, Tokyo, Japan.

KRISHNA MURTHY, Venkatraman, pen names KOWSIKAN; VANDU MAMA, b. 1 July 1926, Arimasam, Pudukottai, Tamil Nadu, S. India. Journalist; Author. Publs. incl: (short story collects.) Veenayin Natham, 1962; Secretary Uma, 1962, 1964; Adimayin Thiyagam, 1962, 1969; (histl. novel) Bhamini Pavai, 1965; (soc. novels) Thoorathu Pachai, 1967; Uyir Sirippu; (biogs.) Rajaji, 1968, 1970; Dr. Radha Krishnan (forthcoming); over 50 children's books. Contbr. to ldng. Tamil and children's mags. Mbr. Children's Writers' Assn., Madras. Hons: Prizes for short story competitions. Address: Plot C, 270 Fourth Ave., Ashok Nagar, Madras 600083, S. India.

KRISTENSEN, Sven Möller, b. 12 Nov. 1909, Darum, Jutland. Editor; Literary Critic; Writer. Educ: Ph.D., Copenhagen Univ. Publs: Aestetiske studier i dansk fiktionsprosa 1870-1900, 1938; Digteren og samfundet I-II, 1942,-45; Amerikansk litteratur 1920-40, 1942; Dansk litteratur 1918-1950, 1950; En musaik af moderne dansk litteratur, 1954; Digtningens Teori, 1958; Digtning og Livssyn, 1959; Vurderinger, 1961; Den dobbelte Eros, 1966; (essays) litteratursociologiske, 1970; (Ed.) Frammede digtere: det 20 aahundrede, 1967-78. Contbr. to: Land og Folk, 1945-53; Ed., Athenaenm; Dialog, 1950-53. Mbrshins: Danish Acad.; Norwegian Acad. of Sci. Address: Copenhagen Univ., Vingaards allé 53, 2900 Hellerup, Denmark.

KRISTENSEN, Tom, b. 4 Aug. 1893, London, UK. Literary Critic; Author. Educ: Copenhagen Univ. Publs. incl: (poems) Mirakler, 1922; Paafuglefjeren, 1922; Verdslige Sange, 1927; De forsvundne Ansigter, 1953; Den sidste Lygte, 1954; (novel) Haervaerk, 1930; (essays) Mellem Krigene, 1946; Til Dags Dato, 1953; Den evige Uro, 1958; I min Tid, 1963; Beger, beger, beger, 1967; (autobiography) En Bogorms Barndom, 1953; Abenhyerlige Forliesen, 1966; (short stories) Vindrosen, 1934; Hvad er Heta? , 1946. Contbr. to: Politiken. Mbrships: Danish Soc. of Authors; Danish Acad. Hons: Knight of Dannebrog; Holberg Medal; Aarestrup Medal. Address: Torelore, Thurø, Denmark.

KRISTJÓNSDÓTTIR, Jóhanna, pen name KRISJÓNSDÓTTIR, Hanna, b. 14 Feb. 1940, Reykjavík, Iceland. Journalist. Educ: Grad., Univ. of Iceland, Reykjavík, 1964. Publs: 'Ast 'A Raudu Ljósi, 1960; Segdu Engum, 1963; Midarnir Voru Prir, 1967. Contbr. to: Morgunbladid newspaper; num. mags. Mbr., Writers' Union of Iceland. Address: Drafnarstigur 3, Reykjavík, Iceland.

KRLE, Risto, b. 3 Sept. 1900, Struga, Yugoslavia. Playwright. Publs: Antica, 1950; Millions of Sufferers, 1972; Money Is Murder, 1958. Mbr., Assn. of Macedonian Writers. Recip., 11 Oktomvri Prize, 1966. Address: Pariska No. 5, 91000 Skopje, Yugoslavia.

KROG, Eustace Walter, b. 31 Oct. 1917, Leighton Buzzard, Beds., UK. Director, Rhodesia Literature Bureau. Publs: Ed., African Literature in Rhodesia, 1966; Outdoor Book for Rhodesia, forthcoming. Contbr. to: Bundu Book 4, Rock Climbing; Teacher in New Africa; Tchrs' Forum; other educl. mags.; Rhodesia Calls; Rhodesian Caravanner & Outdoor Life; Alpine Jrnl. (Rhodesian corres.); Mountain Club of Rhodesia Jrnl. (Ed.). Mbrships incl: PEN. Recip., Book Ctr. of Rhodesia Lit. Award (on behalf of Rhodesia Lit. Bur.), 1974. Address: 6 Clairwood Rd., Alexandra Park, Salisbury, Rhodesia.

KROHN, Aarni Leopold, b. 7 July 1930, Helsinki, Finland. Secretary-General, Culture Organisation of Finland. Educ: Univ. of Helsinki. Publs: Kurkikohtaus (Meeting of Cranes), (poems), 1962; Minä olen Bobrikov (I am Bobrikov), (novel), 1964; Tsaarin Helsinki (The Czar's Helsinki), 1967; Kuka on tuo mies (Who is that Man), (novel), 1971. Mbrships: Finnish Soc. of Authors; Int. PEN Club; Culture Org. of Finland; Authors of Helsinki. Hons. incl: Finnish Acad. Award, 1969; Wihuri Fndn. Award, 1972; 2nd Prize for Libretto, Savonlinna Opera Fest., 1974. Address: Kivelänkatu 1 C 5, Helsinki 26, SF-00260, Finland.

KROLOW, Karl, b. 11 May 1915. Poet; Essayist. Educ: Univs. of Gottingen & Breslau. Publs: (poetry) The Signs of the World, 1952; Wind & Time, 1954; Days & Nights, 1956; Foreign Bodies, 1959; Selected Poems, 1962; Invisible Hands, 1962; Collected Poems, 1965; (essays) Aspects of Contemporary German Lyric Poetry, 1961; Schattengefecht, 1964; Poetisches Tagebuch, 1966; (transl.) Contemporary French Lyric Poetry; Spanish Poems of the 20th Century. Mbrships: PEN; Acad. of Fine Arts of Bavaria: German Acad. of Speech; Mainzer Acad. for Lit. Recip., Buchner Prize, 1956; Grosser Niedersachsischer Kunstpreis, 1965. Address: 61 Darmstadt, Alexandraweg 5, W. Germany.

KRONEGGER, Maria Elisabeth, b. 23 Sept. 1932, Graz, Austria. Professor of French & Comparative Literature. Educ: Transl. of French Lit., 1953, Tchrs. Exam., 1960, Kark Franzens Univ., Graz.; Dip. in Contempt. Lit., Sorbonne, Paris, 1954; M.E., Kan. Univ., USA, 1958; Ph.D., Fla. State Univ., 1960. Publs: James Joyce & Associated Image Makers, 1968; Impressionist Literature, 1973. Contbr., acad. jrnls. Mbrships. incl: Int. & Am. Comparative Lit. Assns. Recip., sev. rsch. grants. Address: Mich. State Univ., Dept. of Romance Langs., Wells Hall 502, East Lansing, MI 48823, USA.

KROON, Dirk, b. 9 May 1946, Schiedam, Netherlands. Writer. Educ: D.Litt., Univ. Leiden. Publs: (poetry) Materiaal voor morgen, 1968; Hutselen met het gras, 1972; De getekende dag, 1973; In het voorbijgaan, 1974. Contbr. to: De Gids; Wending; Kentering; Yang; Dietsche Warande en Belfort; Raam; & num. anthols.; etc. Mbrships: Dutch Writers' Union; PEN; Ctr. Aesthetics. Address: Stresemannplaats 177, Rotterdam 3014, Netherlands.

KROYER, Peter Emil, b. 15 Mar. 1919, Blundellsands, Lancs., UK. Writer. Educ: M.A., Univ. of Oxford, 1947; Univ. of Florence, Italy. Publs: Poems in The Threshold, 1936, 1937; The Story of Lindsey House, Chelsea, 1955. Mbr., Danish Club, London, UK. Recip., D.F.C., 1944. Address: Via Canto alle Gracchie 8, 50020 San Michele a Torri, Scandicci, Firenze, Italy.

KRUEGER, John Richard, b. 14 Mar. 1927, Fremont, Neb., USA. Professor of Uralic & Altaic Studies. Educ: B.A., Geo. Wash. Univ., 1948; Ctrl. Asian Inst., Univ. of Copenhagen, Denmark, 1952-54, 1968, 1972; Ph.D., Univ. of Wash., Seattle, USA, 1960. Publs: Introduction to Classical Mongolian (w. K. Grønbech), 1955; Poetical Passages in the Erdeni-yin Tobci, 1961; Chief Ed., Mongolia & the Mongols, vol. I, 1971; The Kalmyk-Mongolian Vocabulary in Stralenberg's 1730 Geography, 1975. Contbr. to: Ctrl. Asiatic Jrnl.; Jrnl. of Am. Oriental Soc.; Names. Mbrships. incl: Mongolia Soc.; Fndr., Tibet Soc.; Am. Oriental Soc.; Inner Asia Soc. Address: P.O. Box 606, Bloomington, IN 47401, USA.

KRÜGER, Horst, b. 17 Sept. 1919, Magdeburg, Germany. Author. Educ: Philos. & lit. studies, Univs. of Berlin & Freiburg. Publs: Das Zerbrochene Haus (novel), 1966; Deutsche Augenblicke (essays), 1969; Fremde Vaterländer (travel essays), 1971; Zeitgelächter (miscellany), 1973; Ostwest — Passagen (new travel essays), 1975. Contbr. to: Badische Zeitung (former lit. critic); Die Zeit; Frankfurter Allgemeine; Merkur; Neue Rundschau; S.W. Broadcasting Corp., Baden-Baden (former prog. ed.). Mbrships: PEN German Ctr.; Deutsche Akad. für Sprache und Dichtung, Darmstadt. Hons: Thomas Dehler Lit. Prize, 1970; J.H. Merck Prize for lit. essays, Deutsche Akad., 1972; Berlin Critic's Prize, 1973. Address: 6 Frankfurt am Main 70, Hainerweg 21/4, W. Germany.

KRUSE, Hinrich, b. 27 Dec. 1916, Toftlund, Denmark. Teacher. Educ: Tchrs. Trng. Coll., Kiel, 1936-38. Publs: Weg un Umweg, 1958; Mitlopen, 1961; Dat Gleis, 1967; Gustern is noch nich vorbi, 1969; Station 45, 1973. Mbrships: Schleswig-Holsteinischer Schriftstellerverband, Kiel; Futiner Kreis. Hons: Hans Bottcher-Preis fur Horspiels, Stiftung FVS, Hamburg, 1965; Quickborn-Preis, Hamburg, 1974. Address: 2351 Braaku, Neumunster, W. Germany.

KRUSS, James Jacob Hinrich, pen name POLDER, Markus, b. 31 May 1926, Heligoland, Germany. Writer. Educ: Tchrs'. degree. Publs: The Lighthouse on the Lobster-Cliffs, 1956; My Greatgrandfather & I, 1959; The Happy Islands behind the Winds, 1960; Eagle & Dove, 1961; Timm Thaler, 1962; 3 x 3, 1963. Contbr. to German Radio & newspapers. Mbrships: PEN; Deutscher Schriftstellerverband. Hons: Deutscher Jugendbuchpreis, 1960, 1964; Hans Christian Andersen Award, 1968. Address: Casa Montañeta, La Calzada, Las Palmas de Gran Canaria, Spain.

KRUUSE, Jens, b. 6 Apr. 1908, Odense, Denmark. Literary Critic; Author. Educ: M.A., 1931, Ph.D., 1934, Copenhagen; further studies, Cambridge, UK, Paris, France. Publs: Det Følsomme Drama, 1934; Min Hat Sidder Skaeut (autobiog.), 1951; Min Lykkelige Barndom (autobiog.), 1966; Som Vanvid (contemporary hist.), 1967; Hvad Der Bor i Dit Hjerte (novel), 1973; Et Kvarters Tid (novel), 1975. Contbr. to var. mags. & jrnls. Mbrships: Fndr./Pres., Danish Lit. Critics' League; Learned Soc. of Aarhus. Hons: Golden Laurels Award for Leading Author of Yr., 1968; Lakeroe Award of Scandinavia, 1968. Address: Horhavevej 40, 8270 Højbjerg, Denmark.

KRZYWICKA, Irena, b. 28 May 1904, Yenisieisk, Russia. Polish Writer. Educ: M.A., Warsaw Univ. Publs: Pierwsza krew (novel), 1930; Co odpowiadac doroslym na drazliwe pytania? (essays), 1936; Rodzina Martenow (novel), 1948; Mrok, polmrok i swiatlo (short stories), 1969. Contbr. to: Wiadomosci Literackie, 1925-39; Robotnik, 1936-39 & 1947-48; Wiadomosci, 1965-. Mbrships: Polish PEN; Polish Assn. of Writers. Hons: Golden Cross of Merit, 1946; Off., Polonia Restituta, 1956. Address: 33 avenue Voltaire, 91440 Bures sur Yvette, France.

KUBLY, Herbert Oswald, b. 26 Apr. 1915, New Glarus, Wis., USA. Author; Journalist; Educator. Educ: B.A., Univ. of Wis. Publs. incl: Men to the Sea (play), 1944; Inherit the Wind (play), 1948; American in Italy, 1955; Easter in Sicily, 1956; Varieties of Love, 1958; Italy, 1961; The Whistling Zone, 1963; Switzerland, 1964; At Large, 1964; Gods and Heroes, 1969; Perpetual Care (play), 1974; The Duchess of Glover, 1974. Contbr. to: The Saturday Review; N.Y. Times Book Review; Time; Life; Vogue; Esquire; etc. Mbrships. incl: Dramatists' Guild of Am. (Sec., 1947-49); Coun. for Wis. Writers. Hons: Nat. Book Award, 1956; Citation, Univ. of Wis., 1962; Wis. Coun. for Writers, 1st Prize, 1970. Address: Wilhelm Tell Farm, New Glarus, WI 53574, USA.

KUBRICK, Stanley, b. 26 July 1928. Film Writer & Director. Educ: City Coll of NY. Films: Fear & Desire, 1952; Killer's Kiss, 1954; The Killing, 1956; Paths of Glory; Spartacus; Lolita, 1962; Dr. Strangelove, 1964; 2001: A Space Odyssey, 1968; A Clockwork Orange, 1971; Barry Lyndon, 1975. Recip., num. awards. Address c/o Louis C. Blau, 9777 Wilshire Blvd., Beverly Hills, Calif., USA.

KUCHARSKI, Jan Edward, pen name KAJOT, b. 26 Dec. 1914, Sosnowiec, Poland. Writer. Publs. incl: Lésne godziny, 1957; Co komu z lasu, 1962; Dwa brzegi rseki, 1970; (for children) Piotruś szuka przyjaciele, 1971; Moja babcia czarownica, 1974. Contbr. to: Miesięcznik Literacki; Kultura; Literature. Mbrships: PEN, Warsaw; Assn. of Polish Writers; Assn. of Polish Jrnlsts. Hons: Prize, Assn. of Polish Writers for Short Story, 1950; Prize, Min. of Culture & Art, 1960; Prize, wkly. Swiatowid, 1962. Address: ul. Koronowska 15 a, 02-905, Warsaw, Poland.

KUEHNEL T-LEDDIHN, (Ritter von) Erik M, pen names HOMME de LETTRES; VITEZOVIC, Tomislav; CAMPBELL, Francis S.; O'LEARY, C.F., b. 31 July 1909, Tobelbad, Styria, Austria. Author; Lecturer; Painter. Educ: Dr.pol.sci., Budapest, Hungary. Publs. incl: Gates of Hell, 1933; Night over the East, 1935; Liberty or Equality, 1952; Menace of the Herd, 1943; Black Banners, 1954; Die Gottlosen, 1962; Timeless Christian, 1970; Amerika-Leitbild im Zwilicht, 1971; Leftism, 1974; Luftschlösser Lügen und Legenden, 1972; Das Rätsel

Liebe, 1974. Contbr. to: Nat. Review (N.Y.); Cath. World (N.Y.); Commonweal; The Tablet; La Table Ronde (Paris); Criticon (Munich); etc. Mbrships: Am. Geog. Soc.; Kts. of Malta. Recip., 2nd Prize, Entraide Sociale, Paris, 1936. Address: A-6072 Lans, Tyrol, Austria.

KUENNE, Robert Eugene, b. 29 Jan. 1924, St. Louis, Mo., USA. Professor of Economics; Author. Educ: B.J., Univ. of Mo., 1947; B.A., 1948, M.A., 1949, Wash. Univ.; M.A., 1951, Ph.D., 1953, Harvard Univ. Publs: The Theory of General Economic Equilibrium, 1963; The Attack Submarine: A Study in Strategy, 1965; The Polaris Missile Strike: A General Economic Systems Analysis, 1966; Monopolistic Competition Theory: Studies in Impact, (ed.), 1967; Microeconomic Theory of the Market Mechanism: A General Equilibrium Approach, 1968; Eugen von Böhm-Bawerk, 1971. Contbr. to: Wall St. Jrnl.; N.Y. Times; var. profl. jrnls. Address: 63 Bainbridge St., Princeton, NJ 08540, USA.

KÜHNER, Hans, b. 16 Apr. 1912, Eisenach/Thüringen, Germany. Historian. Educ: Studies in Hist. of Music, Art, Lit. & Hist., Munich, Florence, Rome. Publs: (music) Hector Berlioz — Charakter und Schöpfertum, 1952; Grosse Sängerinnen der Klassik und Romantik, 1954; Verdi, 1961, 6th ed., 1974; (hist.) Caterina Sforza, 1957; Index Romanus, 1963; Die Päpste, 1963; Die Cäsaren, 1964; Neues Papstlexikon, 3rd ed., 1965; Tabus der Kirchengeschichte, 3rd ed., 1971; Gezeiten der Kirche, 1971; Latium, Land um Rom, 3rd ed., 1974. Contbr. to var. radio stns., jrnls., encys. etc. Mbrships: PEN; Verband Deutscher Schriftsteller; Int. Schutzverbandes deutsch-prachiger Schriftsteller. Address: 8572 Berg/Thurgau, Switz.

KUHNS, William A., b. 20 Jan. 1943, Cleveland, Ohio, USA. Writer. B.A., Univ. of Dayton, 1966. Publs: Exploring the Film (w. Robert Stanley), 1968; Environmental Man, 1969; The Electronic Gospel, 1969; The Post-Industrial Prophets, 1971; Movies in America, 1973; The Reunion, 1973; The Moving Picture Book, 1975. Contbr. to: New Orleans Review; Dialogist; Psychol. Today; Playboy. Mbr., Author's Guild. Recip., Media & Methods Maxi Award, 1971. Address: R.R.1, Alcove, P.Q. J0X 1A0, Can.

KUIC, Ranka, b. 15 June 1925, Sarajevo, Yugoslavia. University Professor. Educ: Dip. in Engl., Fac. of Philol., Belgrade, 1951; M.A., Bristol Univ., 1954; Dr. Lit. Scis., Univ. of Ljubljana, 1956. Publs: about 200 inclng. The Art of Translating Poetry, 1963; P. B. Seli. Poezija, 1964; Revoluc. misao P. B. Selija: V. Godvin i T. Pein, 1968; Kolridz Pesme, 1969; Seli. Pesme, 1969; V. B. Jeits. Poezija, 1969; Blejk. Lirika, 1972; In the Path of Tito (transl.), 1972; Antologija Engl. Romant. Poezije, 1974; Selijevi Pogledi na Politiku. Relig. i Poeziju, 1974. Contbr. to sev. newspapers & mags. Mbrships. incl: PEN, London; Shelley Keats Assn., USA; Int. Assn. Transls., The Hague; Writers Assn. of Yugoslavia; VP, Assn. of Lit. Transls., Belgrade. Hons. incl: Nagrada Milos N. Duric, 1974. Address: 167a Bulevar Revolucije, 11000 Belgrade, Yugoslavia.

KUIMBA, Giles, b. 5 Oct. 1936, Charter Dist., Rhodesia. School Teacher; Writer. Educ: Primary Tchrs.' Higher Cert. Publs: (in Shona lang.) Gehena Harina Moto, 1965; Tambaoga Mwanangu, 1968. Contbr. to: Prize Mag. (in Engl., for African rdrship.); African Serv., Rhodesia Broadcasting Corp. (Radio Announcer, 1965-69). Recip., 2nd prize, Rhodesia Lit. Bur. Competition, for Gehena Harina Moto, 1963. Address: 15 Muuyu Lane, Mufakose Township, P.O. Mufakose, Salisbury, Rhodesia.

KUKLICK, Bruce, b. 13 Mar. 1941, Philadelphia, Pa., USA. Writer; Editor. Educ: B.A., 1963, M.A., 1965, Ph.D., 1968, Univ. of Pa. Publs: Josiah Royce: An Intellectual Biography, 1972; American Policy & the Division of Germany, 1972. Contbr. to: Am. Quarterly (Ed.); Hist. & Theory. Mbrships: Am. Histl. & Philosl. Assns.; Am. Studies Assn. Address: Department of History, University of Pennsylvania, Philadelphia, PA 19174, USA.

KULNCEWICZ (OWA), Maria Z., b. 30 Oct. 1899, Samara, Russia. Writer. Educ: Nancy Univ., France; Krakow Univ., Poland; Warsaw Univ. Publs. incl. Cudzoziemka (The Stranger), 1936, transl. into 14 langs.; Klucze (The Keys), 1943, Poland 48, transl. into 4 langs.; Lesnik (The Forester), 1953 Paris, 57 Warsaw, transl. into Engl.; Gajoliwny (The Olive Grove), 1961 Warsaw, 62 USA; Tristen, 1967 Warsaw, 74 USA, transl. into 4 langs.; Fantomy, autobiog., 1971 Warsaw: The Kowalski family

(1st radio novel in Europe), 1938. Contbr. to num. mags. Mbrships. incl: PEN; Fndr. & 1st Pres., PEN Centre for Writers in Exile. Hons. incl: Nat. Grand Prize, Lit., Warsaw, 1974. Address: Kazimierz Dolny, Nr. Lublin, Poland.

KUNCEWICZOWA, Maria, b. 30 Oct. 1899, Samara, Russia. Writer; Professor of Polish Literature. Educ: Warsaw Univ. Publs. incl: (in Polish) Alliance with a Child; Face of a Man; Maiden Love; Two Moons; The Stranger (transl. into sev. langs.); Everyday; Herod's Town; The Keys; The Conspiracy of the Absent; The Forester, 1954; At Home & in Poland, 1958; The Discovery of Patusan, 1959; The Olive Grove, 1961; Don Quixote & the Nurses, 1966; Phantoms, vol. I, 1971, Natura, vol. II, 1974. Mbr., PEN. Hons: Lit. Prize, Warsaw, 1937; Pietrzak Prize, 1966. Address: Old Kennels, Flint Hill, VA 22627, USA.

KUNDERA, Milan, b. 1 Apr. 1929, Brno, Czechoslovakia. Writer. Educ: Acad. of Music & Dramatic Arts, Prague. Publs: (poetry) Man a Broad Garden, 1953; The Last May, 1955; (drama) The Owners of the Keys, 1962; Deux oreilles deux mariages, 1969; (short stories) Ridiculous Loves, 1963; The Second Book of Ridiculous Loves, 1965; The Third Book of Ridiculous Loves, 1969; (novels) La vie est ailleurs, 1973; The Joke, 1967. Contbr. to: Literární noviny; Listy. Mbr., Union of Czechoslovak Writers. Hons. incl: Klement Gottwald State Prize, 1963; Union of Writers' Prize, 1967; Prix Médicis, 1973.

KÜNG, Andres, b. 13 Sept. 1945, Ockelbo, Sweden, (nationality Estonian). Writer. Educ: Civilekonom, Stockholm Schl. of Econs. Publs. incl: Latin-amerika – reform eller stagnation? (Latin America — Reform or Stagnation?), 1969; Jordens förtryckta (Oppressed of the Earth), 1970; Estland — en studie i imperialism (Estonia – A Study in Imperialism), 1971; Vad händer i Baltikum? (What Happens in the Baltic States?), 1973; Att så socialism och skörda fascism: Fallet Chile (To sow Socialism & Reap Fascism: The case of Chile), 1974. Mbr., Swedish Authors' Soc.; Estonian PEN; Swedish Jrnlsts'. soc. Recip., Cultural Award, Estonian Comm., Sweden, 1974. Address: Regementsg. 52 A, S-217 48 Malmö, Sweden.

KUNITZ, Stanley J., 29 July 1905, Worcester, Mass., USA. Poet; Educator. Educ: M.A., Harvard Univ. Publs. incl: (verse) Intellectual Things, 1930; Passport to the War, 1944; Selected Poems, 1958; The Testing Tree, 1971; The Terrible Threshold, 1974; The Coat Without a Seam, 1974. (editions) Living Authors, 1931; Authors Today & Yesterday, 1933; British Authors Before 1800, 1952; XX Century Authors, 1955; Poems of John Keats, 1964; European Authors 1000-1900, 1967; (transl.) Poems of Akhmatova, 1973; Story under Full Sail by A. Voznesensky, 1974. Mbr., Nat. Inst. of Arts & Letters. Hons. incl: Garrison Medal, 1926; Pulitzer Prize, 1959. Address: 157 W. 12th St., N.Y., NY 10011, USA.

KUNNAS, Kirsi, b. 14 Dec. 1924, Helsinki, Finland. Author; Poet. Publs: (poems) Villi Omenapuu, 1947; Uivat saaret, 1950; Tuuli nousee, 1953; Vaeltanut, 1956; (for children) Tiitiäisen satupuu, 1956; Tiitiäisen tarinoita, 1957; Nikkar tikkarin mäellä, 1960. Puu Puu ja Käpypoika, 1972; Aikamme aapinen, 1967; Aikamma lukukirja, 1968. Hons: State Prize, 1957; Tampere City Prize, 1957, 1972; Arvid Lydecken Award, 1972; Pro Finlandia Medal, 1973. Address: 34110 Lakiala, Finland.

KÜNNEMANN, Horst Heinz, pen names PLATHE; HEINO, b. 30 June 1929, Berlin, Germany. Lecturer; Teacher; Translator; Author; Editor. Educ: Tchrs. Trng. Coll., Berlin. Publs: Wasa-Schicksal eines Schiffe, 1966, also Italian transl.; Wigwams, Büffel, Indianer, 1968; Kinder & Kulturkonsum, 1972, 2nd ed., 1974; Drachen, Schlangen, Ungeheuer, 1970; Cowboys, Colts und Wilder Westen, 1972; Profile zeitgenössischer Bilderbuchmacher, 1972; Safari zu den Massais, 1973; Das grosse Seeräuberbuch, 1973, also Danish transl.; co-author, sev. other books. Contbr. to: Jugendliteratur; Schl. Lib. Jrnl. (N.Y.); etc. Mbrships. incl: German Writers' Union; Int. Rsch. Soc. Youth Lit. Hons. incl: 2nd Prize Concours Critics Children's Lit., Prague, 1967. Address: 2 Hamburg 72, De Beern 5, W. Germany.

KUNOSKI, Vasil, b. 20 Nov. 1916, Debar, Yugoslavia. Editor of Nǎs Svet Children's Magazine. Educ: Tchrs. Trng. Coll. Publs: (juvenile) Volšebno Livče (Magic Leaf), 1950; Zajče Bez Opavče (Tail-less Bunny), 1956; Strašno, Postrašno, Najstrašno (Dreadful, More Dreadful, Most Dreadful), 1963; Predraznióni Večeri (Pre-holiday Evenings), 1960; Zgodi i Nezgodi (Happenings & Incidents),

1971. Contbr. to all Major Yugoslav children's publs. Mbrships: PEN; Assn. Sci. Fiction Writers Yugoslavia. Hons: Mlado Pokolenje Prize, 1971; 11th Oct. Prize, 1972; 13th Nov. Prize, 1963. Address: ul. Dimitar Pandilov Br. 18, Skopje, Yugoslavia.

KUNZ, Johannes, b. 2 Jan. 1947, Vienna, Austria. Journalist; Press Adviser to the Austrian Federal Chancellor. Publs: Ich Bin Der Meinung (Witze and Anekdoten über Bundeskanzler Bruno Kreisky), 1974. Contbr. to: Bis Ende; Austrian radio; etc. Mbrships. incl: Jrnlsts. Union; Union Parliamentary Eds.; Concordia Press Club. Address: 1190 Vienna, Traklgasse 8/31, Austria.

KUNZEL, Franz Peter, b. 31 Mar. 1925, Königgrätz, Bohemia. Writer; Translator. Publs: Der Sozialismus mit menschlichem Gesicht (w. A. Kusak), 1969; Übersetzungen aus dem Tschechischen und dem Slowakischen nach 1945 (bibliob.), 1969. Contbr. to: Süddeutsche Zeitung, Munich; Frankfurter Allgemeine Zeitung, Frankfurt; Bavarian Radio. Hons: Translation Prize, Czech. Writers' Assn., 1968; Translation Decoration, Cultural Comm. of BDI, 1971; Decoration, Bavarian Acad. of Fine Arts, 1972. Address: Egenhoferst. 24, 8031 Puchheim b. Munich, W. Germany.

KUPRANEC, (The Rev.) Orest Franko, b. 16 June 1924, Drohobych, Ukraine. Ukrainian Catholic Priest. Educ: Ph.D. Publs: Guagninus Toponymy of 1611, 1954; Ex Historia Ecclesiae Orthodoxae in Polonia, 1955; Poloniae Tentamina Unionis apud Orthodoxos, 1957; Anathemized Hetman Mazepa, 1958; The Orthodox Church in Poland in the Period between the Wars 1918-1939, 1974; The Ukrainian Catholic Seminary in Hirschberg, Culemberg, 1975. Contbr. to num. theol. & other jrnls. Mbrships. incl: Ukrainian Theol. Soc., Rome; Assn. Ukrainian Catholic Press; Can. Assn. Slavists. Address: 3100 Weston Road, Weston, Toronto, Ont. M9M 2S7, Can.

KURKO, Kaarlo Sakari, pen names HARA, Paul; GUENARD, C.; MORAND, Rene, b. 10 Oct. 1899, Pieksämäki, Finland. Author. Publs: 17 books inclng. The Legions of Sahara, 1933; The Liberation Battles of Lithuania, 1935; The Military Operations for the Conquest of St. Petersburg, 1919-21, 1942; Ingermanland in the Clutches of the G.P.U., 1943; The Trip through the Tropic, 1946; The 350 Year Memorial Publication of the Church of Ingermanland, 1960; The Polish Battles in 1920 & the Contemporaneous Struggles of the White Russian Army in the Territory of the Ukraine, forthcoming; Väestönsuojelua Kirkonkylässä (play). Contbr. of over 1600 articles to: Maaseudun tulevaisuus; Hakkapeliitta; Suomen kuvalehti; Yhteishyvä; etc. Mbrships: Authors' Union of Finland; French-Finnish Soc. Hons: Schlrship., State of Finland, 1935 & 1943; French Legion of Honour, 1949. Address: Välskärinkatu 9A8, 00260 Helsinki 26, Finland.

KURLENTS, Alfred, b. 19 Dec. 1902, Valga, Estonia. High School Teacher; Editor; Professor; Librarian. Educ: M.A., Univ. of Tartu, 1931; B.L.S., McGill Univ., Montreal, Can., 1952; Ph.D., Univ. of Montreal, 1962. Publs: Loterii meetod (The Way to Win), 1929; Der Eltern Schatz, 1933; Kindluseehitajad (Builders of the Castle), 1938; Satire & Humour in the Russian Bylinas & Estonian Folksongs, 1962; Karl Rumor, 1963; Transl., 10 books of fiction from Russian into Estonian; Ed.-in-Chief, Estonians in Canada, 1975. Contbr. to: Queen's Quarterly; Can. Slavic Studies; Tulimuld. Mbrships: Can. & Estonian Ctrs., PEN; Can. Lib. Assn.; Estonian Learned Soc. of Am.; Hoosier Folklore Soc. Address: 4376 Circle Rd., Montreal, P.Q., H3W 1Y5, Can.

KUROKAWA, Shozo, b. 30 Nov. 1930, Tokyo, Japan. University Teacher. B.A., Waseda Univ., Tokyo; M.A., Univ. of Hawaii. Publs: Learn Japanese, Pattern Approach, vol. 3, 1963; Advanced Japanese, Parts I & II, 1974. Contbr. to: Jrnl. of Assn. of Teachers of Japanese; Educ. Perspectives, Jrnl. of Coll. of Educ., Univ. of Hawaii. Mbrships: Assn. of teachers of Japanese; PEN; Kokugogakkai; Phonetic Soc. of Japan; Int. Sociolinguistic Assn., Rsch. Comm.; Int. Documentation Centre, mbr. Bd. of Dirs.; Hawaii Assn. of Lang. Teachers. Address: Dept. of E. Asian Langs., 1890 East West Rd., Honolulu, HI 96822, USA.

KURTZ, Carmen, b. 18 Sept. 1911, Barcelona, Spain. Writer. Publs. incl: Duermen bajo las Aguas, 1954; La vieja ley, 1956; El Desconocido, 1956; Detrás de la piedra, 1958; Al lado del hombre, 1961; El último camino, 1961; En la oscuridad, 1963; El Becerro de Oro, 1964; Las Algas, 1966; En la Punta de los Dedos, 1968; Entre dos oscuridades, 1969; Al otro lado del mar, 1973; El Viaje, 1974; El

Regreso, forthcoming; also 13 children's novels. Contbr. to: Bilbao's Bank "Diana" (Lit. Guide). Hons. incl: Ciudad de Barcelona Prize, 1954; Planeta Prize, 1956; Leopoldo Alás Award Finalist, 1961; C.C.E.I. Children's Book Award, 1963, 1966; Lazarillo Children's Book Award, 1964; Ateneo de Sevilla Award Finalist, 1973. Address: Calle Ciudad de Balaguer 65, 3º-2a, Barcelona, Spain.

KURTZ, Paul, b. 21 Dec. 1925, Newark, N.J., USA. Professor; Author; Editor. Educ: B.A., 1948, N.Y., Univ.; M.A., 1949, Ph.D., 1952, Columbia Univ. Publs. incl: Decision & the Condition of Man, 1965; American Philosophy in the 20th Century, 1966; A Catholic Humanist Dialogue, 1972; The Humanist Alternative, 1973; The Fullness of Life, 1974. Contbr. to profl. jrnls.; Ed., The Humanist (jrnl). Address: c/o The Humanist, 923 Kensington Ave., Buffalo, NY 14215, USA.

KURZMAN, Dan, b. 27 Mar. 1927, San Fran., Calif., USA. Author; Foreign Correspondent. Educ: B.A., Univ. of Calif., Dip., Sorbonne, Paris. Publs: Kishi & Japan: The Search for the Sun, 1960; Subversion of the Innocents, 1963; Santo Domingo: Revolt of the Damned, 1965; Genesis 1948: The First Arab-Israel War, 1970; The Race for Rome, 1975. Contbr. to: Saturday Review; Wash. Star-News. Mbrships: Overseas Press Club of Am.; PEN; Nat. Press Club, Wash. D.C.; State Dept. Corres. Club; Tokyo For. Corres. Club; Overseas Writers Club, Wash. D.C. Hons: Best Book on For. Affairs, Overseas Press Club Award, 1963; Front Page Award, Int. Reporting, Wash. Post, 1964; George Polk Mem. Award, L.I. Univ., 1965; Dan Kurzman Collect. estab., Boston Univ., 1966. Address: c/o Maxwell Aley Assocs., 145 E. 35th St., N.Y., NY 10016, USA.

KUŠAN, Ivan, b. 30 Aug. 1933, Sarajevo, Yugoslavia. Writer. Educ: Acad. of Fine Arts. Publs: (Juvenile novels in Engl.) The Mystery of Green Hill, 1962; Koko & the Ghosts, 1966; The Mystery of the Stolen Painting; (in Serbo-Croat) 3 novels, 2 books of short stories, & sev. juvenile books. Contbr. to num. Yugoslav mags. Hons: Lit. Awards, Zagreb City, 1961 & 1971; First Yugoslav Candidate for Andersen Prize, 1974; Num. juvenile prizes in Yugoslavia. Address: Draškovićeva 13, 41000 Zagreb, Yugoslavia.

KUSCHEL, Gerald, b. 18 July 1930, Trenton, N.J., USA. Professor of Education; Writer. Educ: B.S., Rider Coll., 1952; M.A., 1959, P.D., 1960, Columbia Univ.; Ed.D. Publs: Discord in Teacher-Counsellor Relations, 1967; Fact & Folklore: Social & Psychological Foundations of Teaching (w. C. Madon), 1974. Contbr. to: Am. Schl. Bd. Jrnl.; Counsellor Educators & Supvsrs. Jrnl.; & others. Address: 10 Earl Rd., Melville, NY 11746, USA.

KUSNIEWICZ, Andrzej, b. 30 Nov. 1904, Kowenice, Ukraine. Writer. Educ: M.A. Publs: (poetry) Words of hatred, 1956; Candle-end for the devil, 1959; Private Time, 1962; (novels) Corruptics, 1961; Eroica, 1963; On the Way to Corinth, 1964; King of the Two Sicilies, 1970; Spheres, 1971; Weightlessness, 1973. Contbr. to: Miesiecznik Literacki; Polish Radio. Mbrships: Polish Writers Union; Sec., Polish Br., PEN; Assn. of Polish Jrnlsts. Hons. incl: Lit. Prize, Polish Min. of Culture, 1971; Polish Nat. Prize, 1st Class, 1974. Address: 02-594 Warsaw, Brunn St. 28/57, Poland.

KUTCHINSKY, Berl, b. 14 Aug. 1935, Aarhus, Denmark. Senior Lecturer. Educ: Candidatus Psychologiae, 1961. Publs: Studies on Pornography & Sex Crimes in Denmark, 1970; Law, Pornography & Crime: The Danish Experience, 1975. Contbr. to: Jrnl. of Social Issues; Int. Jrnl. of Criminol. & Penol.; Archives of Sexual Behavior (Ed. Bd.). Mbrships: Dir., Inst. of Criminal Sci.; Scandinavian Rsch. Coun. for Criminol.; Danish Psychols'. Assn.; Decriminalization Comm., Coun. of Europe; Rsch. Comm. for Sociol. of Law, Int. Sociol. Assn. Address: Institute of Criminal Science, 17 Rosenborggade, DK-1130 Copenhagen K, Denmark.

KUWABARA, Takeo, b. 10 May 1904, Tsuruga, Japan. Writer; Critic. Educ: B.A., Kyoto Univ., Japan, 1928. Publs. incl: Reality & Fiction, 1943; Introduction to Literature, 1950; Conquest of Chogolisa, 1959; Encyclopaedia of Diderot & d'Alembert, 1954; French Revolution, 1959; Comparative Study of Bourgeois Revolutions, 1964; Nakae Chomin, 1966; Theories of Literature, 1967; Selected Works, 1968-72. Contbr. to: Diogenes (Comm. Mbr.); Sekai. VP, PEN, Japan. Recip., Asahi Prize, 1975. Address: 421 Tonodan-Yabunosita, Kamikyo-ku, Kyoto, Japan 602.

KUYLENSTIERNA, Krister, b. 28 Apr. 1903, Sperlingsholm, Sweden. Writer; Lecturer. Publs: Fräckheten var mitt Vapen, 1937; Mediceerna, 1939; Babels Torn, 1952; Allt är Guld som Glimmar, 1953; Bland Röda & Vita i Guatemala. Contbr. to: Allers; Vecko Journalen; Idun. Mbr., Cercle Suedois, Paris, France. Address: 13 Chemin du Ruisselet, 1009 Pully, Switz.

KUZMOWYCZ, Olha, pen name OKA, b. 24 Nov. 1917, Lviv, Ukraine. Journalist. Educ: Grad., Schl. of Jrnlsm., Warsaw, Poland, 1938. Contbr. to: Yunak, Toronto, Can. (Ed.-in-Chief 1967-); Plastovyj Shlakh, Toronto (Ed.); Ukrainian Jrnlst., N.Y. (Ed.); Svoboda, Jersey City, N.J. (Corres. Ed.). Mbrships: Fedn. Ukrainian Jrnlsts. in the Free World (Sec.-Gen.); Ukrainian Jrnlsts. Assn. of Am. (Sec. Gen.). Address: 221 Fire Island Ave., Babylon, NY 11702, USA.

KVAALE, Reidun (Margit), pen name ERGO, b. 18 Mar. 1927, Rena, Norway. Journalist. Educ: Western Coll. for Women, Oxford, Ohio, USA, 1 yr.; Acad. of Jrnlsm., Norway, 1952-53. Contbr. to A-Magasinet (Sunday mag. supplement of Aftenposten); Drammens Tidende; Norsk Dameblad; Billedbladet Na. Recip., Press Prize, Norges Industriforbund (Fedn. of Norwegian Inds.), 1970. Address: Gravdalsveien 12 M, Oslo 7, Norway.

KWAK, Chong Won, b. 13 May 1915, Koryong Goon Sangrim Myeun, Korea. Professor; University President. Educ: D.Litt., Nihon Univ., Japan. Publs: The Investigation of a New Pattern Human, 1955; A Companion for Speculation, 1962; What Is a Literature?, 1959; Sentence Dictionary, 1961. Contbr. to num. jrnls. Mbr. & Auditor, Korean Lit. Writers Assn. Hons: Presidential Citation for Lit., 1967, 1968; Prize, Nat. Acad. of Arts, 1969; Citizen Medal, Camellia Citation, 1970. Address: 409-58 Chung-Neung Dong, Sung-Bukku, Seoul, Korea.

KWAMI, Frederick Baldwin, pen name KAKABIKU, b. 10 Oct. 1909, Keta, Gold Coast (Ghana). Teacher; Publisher; Writer. Educ: Akropong-Akwapim Presby. Trng. Coll., 1931-34. Publs. incl: Megafa Konyi O, 1952; Kakabiku Yearly Almanacs, 1960-; Open Sesame, 1970; Living Aphorisms II; Eweawo Fe Blemanyawo. Contbr. of poems to Ghana broadcasting servs. Mbr., Ghana Assn. of Writers. Address: Flamboyant Garden, P.O. Box 30, Agbozume V.R., Ghana.

KYLE, Duncan, b. 11 June 1930, Bradford, UK. Author. Publs: A Cage of Ice, 1970; Flight into Fear, 1972; A Raft of Swords, 1974 (in USA as: The Suvarov Adventure, 1973); Terror's Cradle, 1975. Address: Oak Lodge, Valley Farm Rd., Newton, Sudbury, Suffolk, UK.

KYLE, Elisabeth (Agnes M. R. Dunlop). Novelist; Writer of books for children. Publs. incl: (novels) The Begonia Bed, 1934; The White Lady, 1941; The Pleasure Dome, 1943; The Skaters' Waltz, 1944; Conor Sands, 1952; Forgotten as A Dream, 1953; Mirror Dance, 1970; The Scent of Danger, 1971; The Silver Pineapple, 1972; (for children) Vanishing Island, 1942; The Lintowers, 1951; The House of the Pelican, 1954; Maid of Orleans, 1957; The Money Cat, 1958; The Eagle's Nest, 1961; Love is for the Living, 1966; The Song of the Waterfall, 1969; The Stilt Walkers, 1972. Address: 10 Carrick Park, Ayr, Scotland, UK.

KYLE, George M., b. 30 Dec. 1925, Hardin Co., Tenn., USA. Journalist; Editor. Educ: B.S. (Jrnlsm.). Contbr. to: Ed., Ala. Conservation, 1952-59; Ed., Outdoor Recreation Action, 1966-74; Pk. Maintenance Mag.; Southern Lumberman; Southern Outdoors; Life Mag.; Field & Stream; Jrnl. of Soil & Water Conservation. Mbrships: Outdoor Writers Assn. of Am.; Chmn., Outdoor Recreation Tech. Study Comm., 1962-63, Reg. Rep., Nat. Outdoor Recreation Div., 1972—, Soil Conservation Soc. of Am.; Recreation Facilities Costs Nat. Comm., Nat. Recreation & Pk. Assn. Hons: Am. Motors Nat. Profl. Conservation Award, 1960; Superior Serv. Award, Dept. of the Interior, 1974. Address: 3431 Charleston St., Annandale, VA 22003, USA.

KYUCHOUKOV, Prodan, pen name PETROV, Ivaylo, b. 19 Jan. 1923, Bdintsi, Bulgaria. Writer. Publs: (in Bulgarian) Baptism, 1953; Nonka's Love, 1956; Ground Swell, 1961; Small Illusions, 1963; Before I was Born, 1968; Confused Notes, 1971; Before I was Born & After, 1971; Devil's Tails, 1972. Contbr. to: September; PlamAk. Hons: Dimitrov Prize, 1972; Honoured Worker of Culture, 1974. Address: Sofia, kv. Iztok, bl. 3-A, Bulgaria.

L

LA BARRE, Weston, b. 13 Dec. 1911, Uniontown, Pa., USA. Anthropologist. Educ: A.B., Princeton Univ., 1933; Ph.D., Yale Univ., 1937; Rsch. Intern, Menninger Clinic, 1938. Publs. incl: The Human Animal, 1954; Materia Medica of the Aymara Indians, 1959; They Shall Take Up Serpents: Psychology of the Southern Snake-handling Cult, 1962; Normal Adolescence: Its Dynamics & Impact, 1968; The Ghost Dance: Origins of Religion, 1970. Contbr. to var. profl. jrnls. Mbr., Am. Anthrop. Assn.; & others. Recip., var. acad. awards. Address: Dept. of Anthropol., GM Duke Stn., Durham, NC 27706, USA.

LACHICA, Eduardo, b. 5 Apr. 1932, Manila, Philippines. Journalist. Educ: B.Litt., Ateneo de Manila Univ.; Assoc. Nieman Fellow, Harvard Univ., 1967-68. Publs: The Huks: Philippine Agrarian Society in Revolt, 1971. Contbr. to: Depthnews (Japan Ed., news serv. of Press Fndn. of Asia); The Australian, Sydney; Christian Sci. Monitor. Mbr., Bd., For. Corres. Club of Japan, 1974-75. Recip. Manila Rotary Club Award for Investigative Jrnlsm., 1970. Address: c/o For. Corres. Club of Japan, 1-2 Marunouchi 2-chome, Chiyoda-ku, Tokyo, Japan.

LACRETELLE, Jacques Amaury Gaston de, b. 14 July 1888, Cormatin, France. Writer. Publs. incl: Silbermann, 1922; La Bonifas, 1925; Amour nuptial, 1930; L'Ecrivain public, 1936; Le pour et le contre, 1946; Idées dans un chapeau, 1946; Deux coeurs simples, 1953; Tiroir secret, 1959; Les Maîtres & les amis, 1959; La Galerie des amants, 1964; (transl.) Precious Bane by Mary Webb; Wuthering Heights by Emily Bronte. Mbr., French Acad. Hons: Commander, Legion of Honour; Grand Prix, French Acad., 1930. Address: 49 rue Vineuse, Paris 16e, France.

LACRUZ, Mario, b. 13 July 1929, Barcelona, Spain. Publisher. Publs: El Inocente, 1952; La Tarde, 1954; El Ayudante del Verdugo, 1971. Hons: Premio Simenon, 1951; Prize of the City of Barcelona, 1955. Address: Mandri 66, Barcelona 6, Spain.

LADAME, Paul Alexis, b. 21 July 1909, Geneva, Switz. Journalist; University Professor; Press Officer. Educ: Grad., Inst. Int. Studies; Dr. Pol. Sci., Geneva Univ. Publs: Le Destin du Reich, 1945; L'Assemblée générale des Nations Unies, 1949; Les Fossoyeurs de l'Occident, 1950; Le Rôle des Migrations dans le Monde Libre, 1958; Theorie de la Demagogie, 1963; La Désinformation, 1968. Contbr. to: Jrnl. de Genève; num. other jrnls.; Swiss Broadcasting Corp. (Dipl. Commentator, 1945-52). Mbrships. incl: PEN; Soc. des Arts, Genève; Int. Assn. of Pol. Sci. Address: "Les Grangettes", CH-1299 Commugny, Switz.

LAEDERACH, Monique, b. 16 May 1938, Les Brenets, Neuchâtel, Switz. Teacher. Educ: B.A., Univ. of Neuchâtel. Publs: (poems) L'étain la source, 1970; Pénélope, 1971; Ballade des faméliques baladins de la grande tanière, 1974. Mbr., PEN. Address: Rue du Lac 28, CH-2014 BÔLE (Ne), Switz.

LAESTADIUS, Lars-Levi, b. 26 Dec. 1909, Umea, Sweden. Theatrical General Manager. Educ: B.A., Univ. of Upsala, 1936. Publs: Stenen vill falla (The stone wants to fall), 1936; Herr Blink går över alla gränser (Mr. Blink oversteps all bounds), 1943; Herrgården (The manor-house), 1945; Melodi på lergök (Melody on toy occarina), 1946; Sönderslagen spegel (Broken mirror), 1948. Mbrships: Swedish Union of Authors; Swedish Union of Dramatists. Recip., Konstnärsstipendium, 1972 & 1973. Address: Häradsgatan 2 B, 252 59 Helsingborg, Sweden.

LaFEBER, Walter Frederick, b. 30 Aug. 1933, Walkerton, Ind., USA. Noll Professor of History, Cornell University. Educ: A.B., Hanover Coll., 1955; M.A., Stanford Univ., 1956; Ph.D., Univ. of Wis., 1959. Publs: The New Empire: An Interpretation of American Expansion, 1860-1898, 1963; John Quincy Adams & American Continental Empire, 1965; America, Russia & the Cold War, 1967, 2nd revised ed., 1972; The Creation of the American Empire (co-author), 1973; The American Century: Americans in the Twentieth Century (co-author), 1974. Mbr., Am. Histl. Assn. Recip., acad. hons. Address: Hist. — McGraw Hall, Cornell Univ., Ithaca, NY 14853, USA.

LAFFEATY, Christina, pen names CARSTENS, Netta; FORTINA, Martha, b. 28 Apr. 1932, Johannesburg, S. Africa. Publs. incl: The Reluctant Bride, 1966; Dark

Pursuer, 1967; Stormy Oasis, 1968; Prisoner of Fate, 1968; Road to Destiny, 1969; Broken Journey, 1969; The Passion & the Pain, 1970; Uneasy Eden, 1970; Mistress of Mooralee, 1971; Nor Pride Nor Pity, 1972; Sugar Angel, 1972; Clouds Over Castile, 1973; The Beckoning Dream, 1974; Kathryn of Tamerlaine, 1974. Contbr. to: BBC; Evening News; Parade; Mother; My Weekly. Mbr., Crime Writers' Assn. Address: 98 Cat Hill, East Barnet, Herts., UK.

LAFFERTY, Blanche Gertrude, b. 3 Feb. 1877, Slate Lick, Pa., USA. Teacher; Poet. Educ: Grad., Slippery Rock State Coll., Pa., 1902; further studies, Temple Univ., Phila. Publs: Poems in var. anthols., 1969, 1970, 1971, 1974; Poetry to Ponder, 1969; A Treasury of Poems From My Sunset Years, 1973. Contbr. to: Norristown Times Herald; Butler Argus; Kinnelon Times; Pequannock Argus; Boonton Times; Mtn. Lakes News; Newark Sunday News. Mbrships: N.J. Poetry Soc.; Int. Clover Poetry Assn.; Soc. of Lit. Designates, Wash.D.C. Recip., Author's Award, Newark Coll. of Engrng., for A Treasury of Poems From My Sunset Years. Address: 35 Bartholdi Ave., Butler, NJ, USA.

LAFFIN, John, b. 21 Sept. 1922, Sydney, Australia. Military & Political Historian; Novelist; Poet. Educ: D. Litt. Publs: 75 books incing: Middle East Journey, 1956; Digger, 1958; The Walking Wounded, 1959; Scotland the Brave, 1963; Codes & Ciphers, 1964; British Campaign Medals, 1964; Jackboot, 1965; Tommy Atkins, 1966; The Hunger to Come, 1966 & 1970; Women in Battle, 1967; Anatomy of Captivity, 1968; New Geography, 1967, 1968-69, 1970-71; Surgeons in the Field, 1970; Fedayeen: The Arab-Israeli Dilemma, 1973; Letters from the Front, 1914-18, 1973; The Arab Mind, 1974; The French Foreign Legion, 1974. Contbr. to newspapers & mags. Mbr., Soc. of Authors. Address: Oxford House, Brampton Bryan, Bucknell, Salop, UK.

LAFONT, Robert, b. 16 Mar. 1923, Nimes, France. University Professor. Educ: D.Lit. Publs. incl: (poetry) Aire Liure, 1974; Dire, 1962; (novels) Tua Culpa, 1974; Tè Tu Tèieu, 1968; Li Maires D'Anguilas, 1966; (theatre) Teatre Claus, 1969; Ramon VII, 1967; La Loba, 1959; (linguistics) L'Ortografia Occitana, 1971; La Phrase Occitane, 1967; (cultural history) Baroques Occitans, 1974; Trobar, 1972; (politics) La Revendication Occitane, 1974; Lettre Ouverte Aux Français, 1973. Contbr. to var. jrnls. Mbr., Institut D'Etudes Occitanes. Hons. incl: Prix Théodore-Aubanel, 1959. Address: 14 Rue Parmentier, 30000 Nimes, France.

LAGERSTROM, (Ake) Bertil (Georg), b. 29 May 1916, Upsala, Sweden. Journalist; Author. Educ: Upsala Univ., 1935-39. Publs: (novels) Rag-dolls, 1943; Grass Widower, 1945; The Bewitched Ditch, 1946; (plays) Nachspiel, 1963; The Glass Wall, 1967, 3rd ed. 1970; Jericho, 1970; The Flamingo Marsh, 1970; (musical radio play) The Musical Alley, 1958; sev. children's books; Svartloga, the Story of an Island, 1959; Ships from the Seven Seas, 1962; About 150 short stories; About 40 works translated from Engl., French, & German. Contbr. to num. Swedish, other Scandinavian, German, French, Italian, & Japanese mags. Address: Sodra Kungsvagen 216A, 181 62 Lidingo, Sweden.

LAGUERRE, Enrique A., pen names PRADO, Alberto; UROYAN, Luis, b. 3 May 1906, Moca, Puerto Rico. University Professor. Educ: B.A., Univ. of Puerto Rico, 1938; M.A., 1941; Ph.D., Columbia Univ., N.Y., USA, 1954. Publs: La llamarada, 1935; Solar Montoya, 1941; El 30 de febrero, 1942; Le resaca, 1949; Los dedos de la mano, 1951; La ceiba en el tiesto, 1956; El laberinto, 1957; Cance sin río, 1962; El fuego y su aire, 1970. Contbr. to: El Mundo; Revista Ibero-am. (USA); Anales (Spain). Mbrships incl: PEN; Ateneo de P.R.; Soc. of Writers. Hons. incl: h.c., Cath. Univ. & Univ. of P.R.; Medal of Hon., Philol. Studies, Univ. of P.R. Address: Calle 7 7-22 Villa Rica, Bayamón, Puerto Rico 00619.

LA GUMA, (Justin) Alex(ander), b. 20 Feb. 1925, Cape Town, S. Africa. Author; Freelance Journalist. Publs: A Walk in the Night, 1962, 2nd ed. 1973; And A Threefold Cord, 1965; The Stone Country, 1968, 2nd ed., 1974; In the Fog of The Seasons' End, 1972. Contbr. to var. jrnls. Mbrship: Deputy Sec.-Gen., Afro-Asian Writers Assn. Recip., Lotus Award for Lit., Afro-Asian Writers Assn., 1969. Address: 36 Woodland Gdns., London, N10 3UA, UK.

LAGUNA-DIAZ, Elpidio, b. 15 Feb. 1945, Río Piedras, Puerto Rico. Professor of Spanish Literature. Educ: B.A.,

Univ. of Puerto Rico, 1966; M.A., St. John's Univ., N.Y., 1968; Ph.D., CUNY, 1974. Publs: El Tratamiento del Tiempo Subjetivo en la Obra de Gabriel Miró, 1969; Pablo (prose poems), 1969; Sombra Azul (prose poems), 1970; Eduardo Barrios o la Estética del Silencio, 1972; var. transls. Contbr. to: Asomante; Sin Nombre; Isla Literaria (all Puerto Rico); Mensaje de Nueva York; var. Spanish lang. newspapers. Mbrships. incl: MLA; Soc. de Autores Puertorriqueños. Hons: A.T. Huntington Medal, 1967; 1st Prize Short Story, Revista Mensaje, 1969; 1st Prize Essay, Int. Contest, Iberoamerican Writers & Poets Guild, 1972. Address: Rutgers Univ., Conklin Hall, Newark, NJ 07102, USA.

LAHIRI, Amar, b. 15 Oct. 1907, Deoghar, India. Journalist. Educ: B.A., Univ. of Calcutta. Publs: Japanese Modernism & Japan Talks (in Engl.), 1940; Mikado's Mission (in Engl.), 1941; Said Subhas Bose (in Engl.), 1946; Ein Inder Sieht Berlin (An Indian Sees Berlin, in German), 1964. Contbr. to num. newspapers & mags. in Japan, Burma, India & UK, currently chief European corres. for DEMPA grp., Tokyo & N.Y. Mbrships. incl: For. Pres. Corres. Assn. of Berlin (W.). Address: Schaper Strasse 14, 1000 Berlin 15, W. Berlin, Germany.

LAHOVÁRY, Paul, b. 30 July 1909, Bucharest, Rumania. Advocate. Educ: LL.B. Publs: Elemente Monografice ale Pietii Amza, 1937; Le Miroir d'Obsidiane, 1938; In Umbra Marelui Flaubert, 1939; Casa Terekov, 1940; Hypérion, 1943; Caleidoscop Suedez, 1944; Craiu Nou (novel), 1947; Vântoasele (novel), 1953. Contbr. to: Vremea; Universul Literar; Convorbiri Literare; Revista Fundatiilor Regale; Bilete de Papagal; Da si Nu. Mbrships: Swedish Union of Authors; Swedish Union of Language Masters; Swedish Union of Authorized Translators. Recip., Remus Cioflec for Best Novel of the Yr. (Craiu Nou), Bucharest, 1947. Address: Vintrosagatan 54, 124 47 Bandhagen, Sweden.

LAHR, John, b. 12 July 1941, Los Angeles, USA. Writer. Educ: B.A., Yale Univ.; Worcester Coll., Oxford, UK. Publs: Notes On a Cowardly Lion, 1969; Up Against the Fourth Wall, 1971; A Casebook on Harold Pinter's "The Homecoming" (co-author), 1971; Acting Out America, 1972; Astonish Me, 1973; The Autograph Hound, 1973; Hot to Trot, 1974. Contbr. to: Village Voice. Mbrships: PEN; N.Y. Drama Critics Circle. Recip., George Jean Nathan Award, 1970. Address: 418 East 88th St., N.Y., NY 10028, USA.

LAHTINEN, Reino Johannes, b. 8 Jan. 1918, Helsinki, Finland. Playwright. Over 200 plays for theatre, TV & radio inclng: Only Human Beings, 1956; The Worthless People, 1959; Henrik & Kate, 1962; A Thunder-Storm in the Autumn, 1965; Country Life, 1973. Mbrships: Finnish Authors' Union; Finnish Dramatists' Union (Bd. Mbr., 1964-71); Lit. Coun. of Finnish State, 1971-73. Hons: Best Finnish Radio Play Prize, 1965; Pro Finlandia Decoration, 1971. Address: Kylmänojankatu 8 A 20, 37100 Nokia, Finland.

LAITHWAITE, Eric Roberts, b. 14 June 1921, Atherton, Lancs., UK. Chartered Electrical Engineer; Professor of Heavy Electrical Engineering. Educ: B.Sc., 1949, M.Sc., 1950, Univ. of Manchester; Ph.D., 1957; D.Sc., 1964. Publs: Induction Machines for Special Purposes, 1966; Propulsion Without Wheels, 2nd ed., 1970; The Engineer in Wonderland, 1967; Linear Electric Motors, 1971; Exciting Electrical Machines, 1974. Contbr. to profl. & trade jrnls. Mbrships. incl: FRSA; var. engrng. assns. Recip., award, Royal Soc., 1966. Address: Dept. of Elec. Engrng., Imperial Coll. of Sci. & Technol., Exhibition Rd., London SW7 2BT, UK.

LALIĆ, Ivan V., b. 8 June 1931, Belgrade, Yugoslavia. Writer; Editor; Translator. Educ: M.A., Zagreb Univ. Publs: (poems) Vreme, Vatre, Vrtovi, 1961; Čin, 1963; Krug, 1968; Izabrane i Nove Pesme,1969; Fire Gardens, (in Engl.), 1970; A Szerelem Müvei (in Hungarian), 1971; Temps, Feu, Jardins (in French), 1973; (essays) Kritika i Delo, 1971; transls. from Engl., Am. French & German poetry. Contbr. to: Knjizevnost (Co-ed.); other lit. mags. & jrnls. Mbrships: Yugoslav Writer's Union (Sec.-Gen., 1961-64); PEN (Sec., Serbian Ctr.). Hons. incl: Zmaj Prize, 1961; Pro Litteris Hungaricis, 1970. Address: Internacionalnih Brigada 39, 11000 Belgrade, Yugoslavia.

LAMB, Beatrice Pitney, b. 12 May 1904, Morristown, N.J., USA. Author. Educ: B.A., Bryn Mawr; M.E., Columbia Univ. Publs: India: A World in Transition, 1963, 4th ed., 1975; India (illustrated), 1965; The Nehrus of India: Three Generations of Leadership. Contbr. to: Am. Pol. Sci. Quarterly; pamphlets for League of Women Voters; Ed., UN News, 1945-49. Mbrships: Assn. of Asian Studies; Asia Soc.; Soc. of Women Geogs. Address: 672 Oenoke Ridge, New Canaan, CT 06840, USA.

LAMB, Dana Storrs, b. 4 Jan. 1900, Bklyn., N.Y., USA. Investment Manager. Educ: Dartmouth Coll.; Williams Inst. Pol., Princeton Univ.; B.S. Publs: On Trout Streams & Salmon Rivers, 1963; Bright Salmon & Brown Trout, 1964; Wood Smoke & Watercress, 1965; Not Far From the River, 1967; Some Silent Places Still, 1969; Sporting Etchings Commentary, 1970; Green Highlanders & Pink Ladies, 1971; Where the Pools are Bright & Deep, 1973. Contbr. to: Fly Fishers Jrnl., London; Atlantic Salmon Jrnl., Montreal; Anglers' Club Bulletin, N.Y. Mbr., Century Assn. Address: 141 Sunken Meadow Rd., Northport, NY 11768, USA.

LAMB, Geoffrey Frederick, pen name BALAAM, b. Lewisham, London, UK. Former Schoolmaster & Lecturer; Author. Educ: M.A., Kings Coll., London Univ. Publs. incl: Modern Action & Adventure; Modern Adventures in Air & Space; Modern Adventures at Sea; The South Pole; The Pegasus Book of Magicians; Card Tricks; Mental Magic; Table Tricks; Secret Writing; Magic Charms & Talismans; (text-books) English for General Certificate; Practical Work in Précis & Comprehension; (biog.) Franklin: Happy Voyager; (as Balaam) Chalk in My Hair; Come out to Play. Mbrships. incl: Soc. of Authors; Magic Circle. Address: Penfold, Legion Lane, Kings Worthy, Winchester, Hants., UK.

LAMB, John William, b. 15 July 1896, Derby, UK. Canon & Prebendary of York Minster. Educ: M.A., Trinity Coll., Dublin; M.A., Ph.D., Univ. of Leeds. Publs: St. Wulstan, Prelate & Patriot: a Study of his Life & Times, 1933; The Archbishopric of Lichfield (787-803), 1964; The Archbishopric of York: the Early Years, 1967; The Archbishopric of Canterbury: from its Foundation to the Norman Conquest, 1971. Contbr. to Ency. Britannica. Hon: Archbishopric of Canterbury nominated as one of 1st 3 Books of Yr., Ch. Times, 1971. Address: 61 St. James Rd., Bridlington, North Humberside, YO15 3PQ, UK.

LAMBERT, Derek William, pen name FALKIRK, Richard, b. 1929, London, UK. Journalist; Novelist. Publs: The Sheltered Days (autobiog.), 1965; Angels in the Snow, 1969; The Kites of War, 1969; For Infamous Conduct, 1970; The Twisted Wire, 1972; The Chill Factor, 1973; Blackstone, 1972; Blackstones Fancy, 1973; Beay Blackstone, 1973. Contbr. to var. newspapers & mags. Mbr., Nat. Union of Jrnlsts. Agent: Desmond Elliot. Address: c/o Desmond Elliot, Arlington Books, 38 Bury St., St. James, London SW1 6AU, UK.

LAMBERT, (Madame Gaillard), Olga Stephanie Françoise, pen name LAMBERT, Françoise, b. 7 Sept. 1915, Brussels, Belgium. Journalist; Author. Publs: Je Restaure, 1970; Décoration de Halls & Entrées, 1971; Conflits (novel), 1972; La Perle Espagnole (novel), 1972; La Décoration du Coin-Repas, 1973; Soirées à l'Espagnole, 1973; Recevoir à l'Orientale, 1974. Contbr. to: Le Nouvel Illustre. Mbrships: Soc. des Gens de Lettres; Sec.-Gen., Jrnlsts' Mutual Aid Assn. Address: 14 Square Desaix, 75 Paris 15e., France.

LAMBOT, Isobel Mary, pen names TURNER, Mary; INGHAM, Daniel, b. 21 July 1926, Birmingham, UK. Writer. Educ: B.A., Liverpool Univ., Tchng. Cert., Birmingham Univ. Publs: 15 thrillers inclng: Watcher on the Shore, 1972; Grip of Fear, 1974; The Justice Hunt, 1975. Contbr. to: Woman's Own; Homes & Gardens; Woman's Realm. Mbrships: Crime Writer's Assn.; PEN; Writer's Guild; Soc. of Authors. Address: 14 Stafford Rd., Lichfield, Staffs., UK.

LAMBRICK, Hugh Trevor, b. 20 Apr. 1904. Indian Civil Servant (retired); Fellow, Oriel College, Oxford. Educ: M.A., D.Litt., Oriel Coll., Oxford. Publs: Sir Charles Napier & Sind, 1952; John Jacob of Jacobabad, 1960; History of Sind, vol. 1, 1964; The Terrorist, 1972; Sind Before the Muslim Conquest, 1973. Contbr. to: Geographical Jrnl.; Listener; History of the English Speaking Peoples; Jrnl. of the Oriental Inst., Baroda; Karachi Morning News; var. books & encys. Fellow, Soc. of Antiquaries, London, & Royal Geographical Soc. Address: Picketts Heath, Boars Hill, Oxford, UK.

LAMMING, George (Eric), b. 1927, Barbados. Novelist. Publs: In the Castle of My Skin, UK & USA 1953; The Emigrants, UK 1954, USA 1955; Of Age & Innocence, 1958; Season of Adventure, 1960; Water with Berries, 1972; The Pleasures of Exile, 1960; verse publd. in num. anthols. Hons: Guggenheim Fellowship, 1954; Kenyon Review Fellowship, 1954; Maugham Award, 1957. Address: c/o Longman, 74 Grosvenor St., London W1, UK.

LAMONT, Corliss, b. 28 Mar 1902, Englewood, N.J., USA. Author; Educator. Educ: A.B., Harvard Univ., Cambridge, Mass., 1924; Ph.D., Columbia Univ., NYC, 1932. Publs: The Illusion of Immortality, 1935; You Might Like Socialism, 1939; Freedom is As Freedom Does: Civil Liberties Today, 1956; The Philosophy of Humanism, 1965; Freedom of Choice Affirmed, 1967; Voice in the Wilderness, Essays of Fifty Years, 1974. Contbr. to: The Humanist; The Nation; Science & Society; N.Y. Times; Jrnl. of Philos. Mbrships. incl: Hon. Chmn., Am. Humanist Assn.; V.P., Poetry Soc. of Am.; Sec., Jrnl. of Philos. Address: 315 W. 106 St., #15C, N.Y., NY 10025, USA.

LAMONT, William Dawson, b. 3 Feb. 1901, P.E.I., Can. Retired University Teacher. Educ: M.A., Univ. of Glasgow, UK.; D.Phil., Balliol Coll., Oxford. Publs: Introduction to Green's Moral Philosophy, 1934; Principles of Moral Judgement, 1946; The Value Judgement, 1955; The Early History of Islay, 1966; Ancient & Medieval Sculptured Stones of Islay, 1968, 1972; Moral Philosophy, 1975. Contbr. to: Proceedings of Aristotelian Soc.; Mind; Philos.; Scottish Studies; Proceedings of Royal Irish Acad. F.S.A. Scot. Recip.. hon. D.Litt., Univ. of E. Africa. Address: 37 Kirklee Rd., Glasgow G12 0SP, UK.

LAMPE, Augusta, b. 22 June 1911, former Dutch E. Indies. Dental Surgeon. Educ: Univ. of Utrecht. Publs: Bloemen voor Nippon, 1973. Mbrships: World Union of Med. Writers (U.M.E.M.); Dutch Writers Union (V.V.L.). Hons: Prize for TV Play & for Radio Play, Ctr. for Dutch Drama, Amsterdam, 1970; 2 Prizes for Radio, 1971; Prize for TV Play, 1972. Address: Valkenburglaan 35, Flat A-14, Oosterbeek, Gld., Netherlands.

LAMPLUGH, Lois, b. Barnstaple, Devon, UK. Writer. Publs: The Pigeongram Puzzle, 1955; Nine Bright Shiners, 1955; Vagabonds' Castle, 1957; Rockets in the Dunes, 1958; The Sixpenny Runner, 1960; Midsummer Mountains, 1961; The Rifle House Friends, 1965; The Linhay on Hunter's Hill, 1966; The Fur Princess & the Fir Prince, 1969; Mandog, 1972. Contbr. to Western Morning News. Mbr., W. Country Writers' Assn. Address: Springside, Bydown, Swimbridge, Devon EX32 0QB, UK.

LAMPTEY, Jonathan Kwesi, b. 10 May 1909, Secondi, Ghana. Teacher. Educ: B.Sc., London Univ.; B.Sc., Exeter Univ. Publs: Towards a National Science Policy, 1971. Contbr. to: Ghana Sci. Tchrs. Jrnl. Mbrships: F.R.G.S.; Fellow, Royal Econ. Soc.; Hansard Soc.; Life, Ghana Sci. Tchrs. Assn. Address: P.O. Box 4942, Accra, Ghana.

LANCASTER, Bruce Morgan, b. 5 Oct. 1923, Miss., USA. Diplomat; University Lecturer. Educ: B.S., Miss. State Univ., 1943; grad. study, Duke Univ., 1946-47; Mbr., Royal Coll. of Defence Studies, 1970; Ph.D., Am. Univ., 1974. Publs: Spoils System Diplomacy, forthcoming. Contbr. to: Southern Growth Policies Review; Am. For. Serv. Jrnl.; Soc. Scis. Quarterly. Mbrships. incl: Am. Pol. Sci. Assn. Recip., acad. & profl. hons. Address: Box 333, Rte. 1, Starkville, MS 39759, USA.

LANCASTER, Henry Oliver, b. 1 Feb. 1913, Sydney, N.S.W., Australia. University Professor (Mathematical Statistics). Educ: Univ. of Sydney; London Schl. of Hygiene & Tropical Medicine, UK; B.A., Ph.D., M.D., B.S., D.Sc. Publs: Bibliography of Statistical Bibliographies, 1968; The Chi-Squared Distribution, 1969; An Introduction to Medical Statistics, 1973. Contbr. to: Medical Jrnl. of Aust.; Biometrika; Jrnl. Royal Statistical Soc.; Annals of Mathematical Statistics; Aust. Jrnl. Statistics (Ed. 1959-71); Int. Statistical Review. Hons: Fellow, Aust. Acad. of Sci. Address: Dept. of Mathematical Statistics, Univ. of Sydney, Sydney, N.S.W., Australia 2006.

LANCASTER, Osbert, b. 4 Aug. 1908. Artist; Writer. Educ: Lincoln Coll., Oxford; Slade Schl., London. Publs. incl: Progress at Pelvis Bay, 1936; Pillar to Post, 1938; Classical Landscape with Figures, 1947; The Saracen's Head, 1948; Private Views, 1956; The Year of the Comet, 1957; Signs of the Times, 1961; All Done From Memory (autobiography), 1964; Graffiti, 1964; Temporary Diversions, 1968; Sailing to Byzantium, 1969; Meaningful Confrontations, 1971; Theatre in the Flat, 1972; The Littlehampton Bequest, 1973; & designed num. sets for opera. Recip., C.B.E. Address: 12 Eaton Sq., London SW1, UK.

LANCASTER BROWN, Peter, b. 13 Apr. 1927, Leeds, Yorks., UK. Author. Publs: Twelve Came Back, 1957; Call of the Outback, 1970; What Star Is That?, 1971; Astronomy In Colour, 1972; Coast of Coral & Pearl, 1972; The Seas & Oceans in Colour, 1973; Comets, Meteorites & Men, 1973; Australia's Coast of Coral & Pearl, 1974; Star & Planet Spotting, 1974; Planet Earth in Colour, 1975; Megaliths, Men & Myths, 1975; Travellers in the Outback (forthcoming). Contbr. to: Blackwoods; New Sci.; Nature; Tchr. Mbrships: Soc. of Authors; Brit. Sci. Writers; Int. Astronl. Union; F.R.G.S.; Fellow, Royal Astronomical Soc. Address: "Karlsvik", 30 Eghams Wood Road, Beaconsfield, Bucks., UK.

LANCE, Leslie. Novelist; Farmer. Publs. incl: Springtime for Sally; Bright Winter; Bride of Emersham; The House in the Woods; The New Lord Whinbridge; Now I Can Forget; The Love that Lasts; Return to Kingsmere; No Summer Beauty. Contbr. to: IPC; Thomsons. Address: c/o Samuel Walker Literary Agency, 199 Hampermill Lane, Oxhey, Watford, Herts., UK.

LANCTOT, Gustave, b. 1883. Archivist; Writer. Educ: B.Litt.; LL.M.; D.Litt.; Q.C.; Univs. of Montreal, Paris & Oxford. Publs. incl: Contes populaires canadiens, 1923; Les Archives du Canada, 1926; Situation politique de l'Eglise canadienne, 1942; Trois ans de guerre, 1943; Jacques Cartier devant l'histoire, 1947; Histoire du Canada des origines au Traité de Paris, vol. I, 1959, vol. II, 1963, vol. III, 1964; Le Canada & la Revolution américaine, 1965; Montréal sous Maisonneuve, 1966. Mbrships. incl: Pres., Ottawa Hist. Soc.; formerly Pres., Royal Soc. of Canada. Hons: M.C.; LL.D.; Order of Canada. Address: 5642 Woodbury Ave., Montreal, Canada.

LAND, Barbara Neblett, b. 11 July 1923, Hopkinsville, Ky., USA. Writer; Editor. Educ: B.A., Univ. of Miami, Fla., 1944; M.S., Columbia Univ., 1946. Publs. incl: Jungle Oil (co-author), 1956; The Quest of Isaac Newton, (co-author) 1960; The Quest of Johannes Kepler, 1963; Lee: A Portrait of Lee Harvey Oswald (co-author), 1967; The Telescope Makers, 1968; Evolution of a Scientist, 1973. Contbr. to: NY Times; Look; Sci. World; Book of Knowledge (ency.); etc. Mbrships: Authors Guild; Authors League of Am. Hons. incl: Sloane-Rockefeller Fellowship, 1959. Address: Unit 20, 36 Jerdanefield Road, St. Lucia (Brisbane), Queensland, Australia 4067.

LAND, Myrick Ebben, b. 25 Feb. 1922, Shreveport, La., USA. Writer; Editor; Lecturer. Educ: B.A., UCLA, 1945; M.S., Columbia Univ., 1946. Publs: (novels) Search the Dark Woods, 1955; Quicksand, 1969; Last Flight, 1975; (plays) The Cage Door, 1972; At the Lakehouse, 1973; (non-fiction) The Fine Art of Literary Mayhem, 1963; Lee: A Portrait of Lee Harvey Oswald, 1967. Contbr. to: NY Times Mag.; World; This Week; Look Mag.; Listener; Coronet; etc. Mbrships. incl: Authors Guild; Univ. of Qld. Club. Hons: Pulitzer Travelling Fellowship, Columbia Grad. Schl. Jrnlsm., 1946; Mystery Writers of Am. Nomination, 1969. Address: Unit 20, 36 Jerdanefield Road, St. Lucia, Queensland, Australia 4067.

LANDAU, Edwin Maria, pen name DEVIN, Marius, b. 20 Sept. 1904, Coblenz, Germany. Scholar; Translator; Journalist. Educ: Doctor's degree, Univ. of Breslau, 1927. Author, Claudel, 1966, 2nd ed. 1973. Transl., Claudel, Mallarmé, Malègue, Jammes, Cocteau, Molière, Racine, Corneille, & Voltaire. Contbr. to Claudel Studies, Dallas, USA. Mbrships. incl: PEN; Paul Claudel Soc.; Pres., Swiss Assn. of Friends of Paul Claudel; Fndr., Int. Rsch.-Ctr. for Claudel Studies, Univ. of Zurich; For. Press Assn. of Switz. Recip., Chevalier, Order of Arts & Letters, France. Address: Beustweg 7, CH-8032 Zurich, Switz.

LANDAU, Rom, b. 17 Oct. 1899. Sculptor; Professor of Islamic Studies. Publs. incl: God is My Adventure, 1935; Of No Importance, 1940; The Wing, 1945; Sex Life & Faith, 1946; Odysseus, 1948; Human Relations, 1949; Invitation to Morocco, 1950; Portrait of Tangier, 1952; Among the Americans, 1954; An Outline of Moroccan Culture, 1957; Arab Contribution to Civilization, 1958; Islam & The Arabs, 1958; The Kasbas of Southern Morocco, 1969; The Alaouites: the cultural contribution of King Hassan II,

1970. Contbr. to Radiodiffusion Marocaine. Mbr., World Congress of Faiths, 1936-44. Hons: L.H.D.; Order of Ouissam Alaouite. Address: c/o Faber & Faber, 3 Queen Sq., London W1, UK.

LAND BUTLER, Anna Mabel, b. 7 Oct. 1901, Phila., Pa. USA. Teacher; Author; Journalist. Educ: Temple Univ., Phila.; Univ. of Md.; Trenton State Coll. Publs: Album of Letters — Unsent, 1952; Touchstone, 1961; High Noon, 1971. Contbr. to: sev. poetry anthols. & jrnls. inclng. Am. Poets & Today's Poets; newspapers; profl. & club jrnls. inclng. "Responsibility" (past ed.) & Nat. Link Jrnl. (past assoc. ed., Eastern Area). Mbr., num. civic, profl. & lit. orgs. Recip., num. profl., lit. & club hons. Address: 410 N. Kentucky Ave., Atlantic City, NJ 08401, USA.

LANDER, Jack Robert, b. 15 Feb. 1921, Hinckley, Leics., UK. University Professor; Author. Educ: B.A., M.A., M.Litt., Pembroke Coll., Cambridge. Publs: The Wars of the Roses, 1965; Conflict & Stability in Fifteenth Century England, 1969. Contbr. to: Engl. & Am. Histl. Reviews; Hist.; Speculum; Can. Jrnl. of Hist.; Bulletin Inst. Histl. Rsch.; Bulletin John Rylands Lib. Address: Apt. 620, University Towers, 1201 Richmond St., London, Ont. N6A 3L6, Can.

LANDHEER, Bart, b. 30 Jan. 1904, Rotterdam, Netherlands. Professor of International Relations; Author. Educ: Univ. of Leyden; Ph.D., Soc. Sci., Univ. of Vienna, Austria. Publs. incl: The Netherlands, 1943; Mind & Society, 1952; Pause for Transition, 1957; The Role of Knowledge in the World System, 1974; Ed., European Yearbook, vols. I-XX. Contbr. to: Co-existence (Ed. Bd); World '70 (Ed. Bd.); num. Am., Dutch, German, Italian, French & Polish jrnls. Mbrships: Soc. Européene de Culture, Venice (Coun.); Vredesopbouw (Bd.); PEN. Address: Vleysmanlaan 10, Wassenaar, Netherlands.

LANDHEER, Jo, b. 16 Oct. 1900, Rotterdam, Netherlands. Poetess. Publs: Golven, 1925 & 1930; Donkere Vruchten, 1937; Verzamelde Gedichten, 1941; Enkele Nieuwe Gedichten, 1950; Verzamelde Gedichten, 1954; Zestien Gedichten, 1964. Contbr. of poems to: Helikon; De Gids; Maatstaf; PEN — Quarterly of the Neths. Mbrships: PEN; Maatschappij der Nederlandse Letterkunde. Address: De Schansenberg, Beekbergerweg 46, Loenen o/d Veluwe, Netherlands.

LANDIS, Lincoln, b. 5 Aug. 1922, Logansport, Ind., USA. Foreign Policy Analyst. Educ: DePauw Univ., 1940-42., B.S., West Point, 1945; M.A. Columbia Univ., 1959; Cert., Command & Gen. Staff Coll., 1963; PhD., Georgetown Univ., 1969. Publs: Politics & Oil: Moscow in the Middle East, 1973; Contbng. Ed., Science & Technology in National Security, 1975. Contbr. to: World Affairs; The New Middle East; Europa Archiv, Bonn; Newsday; Wash. Star-News; Copley News Serv. Mbrships: Pi Sigma Alpha; Am. Soc. Pol. & Soc. Scis. Hons. incl: Sr. Rsch. Fellow, Ctr. for Strategic & Int. Studies, Georgetown Univ. Address: 5014 25th Rd. North, Arlington, VA 22207, USA.

LANDIS, Paul H., b. 5 Mar. 1901, Cuba, Ill., USA. Emeritus Professor of Sociology. Educ: B.A., M.A., Ph.D. Publs. incl: (coll. texts) Social Problems: In Nation & World, 1959; Population Problems, 2nd ed., 1954; So This is College, 1954; Social Control, revised ed., 1956; Introductory Sociology, 1958; Making the Most of Marriage, 5th ed., 1975; (H.S. texts) Social Living, 3rd ed., 1958; Problems of Social Living, 3rd ed., 1958; Your Marriage & Family Living, 3rd ed., 1969; Sociology, new ed. 1972. Pres., Am. Rural Sociol. Soc., 1946. Recip., Disting. Alumni Award, Greenville Coll., 1970. Address: 411 S. Blaine, Moscow, ID 83843, USA.

LANDQUIST, John, b. 3 Dec. 1881, Stockholm, Sweden. Professor of Psychology. Educ: Ph.D., Uppsala Univ. Publs. incl: The Will, 1908; Essays, 1913; Gustav Froding, 1916; Knut Hamsun, 1917; The Living Past, 1919; Knowledge of Man, 1920; Henri Bergson, 1928; Modern Swedish Literature in Finland, 1929; Humanism, 1931; The Unity of the Soul, 1938; Psychology, 1940; History of Pedagogy, 1941; As I remember them, 1949; In Youth, 1957; Charles Darwin, Life & Work, 1959; Art & Politics, 1970. Contbr. to: Dagens Nyheter; Aftonbladet. Address: Villavagen 19, Stocksund, Sweden.

LANDSBERGIS, Algirdas. b. 23 June 1924, Kybartai, Lithuania. Teacher. Educ: Kannas Univ., 1941-44; J. Gutenberg Univ., Mainz, Germany, 1946-49; B.A.,

Brooklyn Coll., USA, 1951; M.A., Columbia Univ., 1960. Publs: Kelione (The Journey) (novel), 1955; Five Posts in the Market Place (play), 1969; The Last Picnic (play), 1974. Contbr. to: Books Abroad; Literary Review; Arena; Contbng. Ed., Ency. of World Drama, 1972. Mbrships. incl: PEN-in-Exile (Chmn., Am. Br.); Dramatists Guild, Inc.; Authors League of Am., Inc. Hons: Daily Draugas Novel Prize, Chgo., 1953; Drama Award, Ohio Lithuanian Cultural Assn., 1957; Play Award, LA Drama Assn., 1970. Address: 87-20 125 St., Richmond Hill, NY 11418, USA.

LANDSTRÖM, Bjorn Olof August, pen name STENMAN, Karl Stefan, b. 21 Apr. 1917, Kuopio, Finland. Writer; Illustrator. Publs: Regina och Gullkronan, 1951; Skeppet i Flaskan, 1952; Havet utan ände, 1953; Vägan til Vinland, 1954; Skeppet (The Ship), 1961; Vägen til Indien (The Quest for India), 1964; Columbus, 1966; Egyptiska skepp (Ships of the Pharaohs), 1970. Mbrships. incl: Finnish & Swedish Writers Unions. Hons. incl: Ph.D., Uppsala, 1971; Pro Finlandia Medal, 1972. Address: Högbergsgatan 15 B 14, 00130 Helsinki 13, Finland.

LANE, Carla, pen name of HOLLINS, Romana, b. Liverpool, UK. TV Scriptwriter; Playwright; Broadcaster. Publs: (TV Comedy Series) Liver Birds (over 50 episodes); Bless This House; Mother Makes Three; No Strings; Going, going, gone free; (Play) Liver Bird, 1974. Contbr. to: Radio & TV (BBC). Mbrships: Writers Guild of GB. (Comm., Northern Br.); Liverpool Writers Club (Past Chmn.); Dir., Radio City (Independent Radio) Ltd., Recip., Pye Award, 1974. Address: Sandfield Park, West Derby, Liverpool, UK.

LANE, Frank Walter, b. 15 Aug. 1908, London, UK. Broadcaster & Lecturer; Publisher's Reader; Photographer. Publs: Animal Wonder World, 1951; Nature Parade, 1954; Kingdom of the Octopus, 1957, 1974; The Elements Rage, 1965; An Eye for a Bird (w. E. Hosking), 1970; (as photographer) The African Ark (w. R. J. Prickett), 1974. Address: Drummoyne, Southill Lane, Pinner, Middx. HA5 2EQ, UK.

LANE, Frona, pen name NEAL, Anorf, b. 29 Nov. 1903, Austin, Tex., USA. Writer; Teacher; Dramatist. Educ: LA State Coll.; Univ. of Calif., LA; Cumnock Schl. of Expression; Sawyer Commercial Coll. Publs. incl: Apples of Gold, 1945; The Third Eyelid, 1951; Make Believe, 1955; One Prayer Not Wasted, 1972; Eve Made Wise, 1974. Contbr. to num. poetry jrnls. & Calif. newspapers. Mbrships: Pres., San Diego Br., Nat. League of Am. Pen Women; Past Pres., Calif. Fedn. of Chaparral Poets. Hons: Poetry Prizes from orgs. in Calif., Tex., La., Midwest; Montalvo Competition in Lit.; Alice Benton Nat. Dramatic Monolog Award; Confederate Rsch. Award, num. others. Address: 1400 El Norte Parkway, San Marcos, CA 92069, USA.

LANE, Jane. Author. Publs. incl: Undaunted, 1934; England for Sale, 1943; Gin & Bitters, 1945; London Goes to Heaven, 1947; Parcel of Rogues, 1948; Dark Conspiracy, 1952; The Sealed Knot, 1952; Sow the Tempest, 1960; From the Snare of the Hunters, 1968; The Young & Lonely King, 1969; The Questing Beast, 1970; Sir Devil-May-Care, 1971; (books for children) The Escape of the King, 1950; The Escape of the Princess, 1962; The Return of the King, 1964; The Champion of the King, 1966; (biographies & histories) Titus Oates, 1949; Puritan, Rake & Squire, 1950; Cat Among the Pigeons, 1959. Address: Kingsbury, 97 Sea Rd., Angmering-on-Sea, Sussex, UK.

LANE, Margaret, b. 23 June, 1907. Novelist; Biographer; Journalist. Educ: M.A., St. Hugh's Coll., Oxford. Publs. incl: Faith, Hope, No Charity, 1935; At Last the Island, 1937; Walk into my Parlour, 1941; Where Helen Lies, 1944; The Brontë Story, 1953; A Calabash of Diamonds, 1961; A Night at Sea, 1964; A Smell of Burning, 1965; Purely for Pleasure, 1966; The Day of the Feast, 1968; Frances Wright & the Great Experiment, 1971. Contbr. to: Daily Express, 1928-31; Daily Mail, 1932-38. Mbr., Women's Press Club, (Pres., 1958-60). Recip., Prix Femina, 1935. Address: Blackbridge House, Beaulieu, Hants., UK.

LANG, André, b. 12 Jan. 1893, Paris, France. Author. Publs. incl: Le Responsable, 1921; Voyage en zigzags dans la République des Lettres, 1922; Les Trois Henry, 1930; Mes Deux Femmes, 1932; Tiers de Siècle, 1935; L'Homme libre, ce Prisonnier, 1947; Le Voyage à Turin, 1956; Une vie d'orages: Mme. de Stael, 1958; Le septième ciel, 1958; Bagage à la Consigne, 1961; Pierre Brisson, 1967; La Société & l'Ecrivain, France (1900-1930), 1975. Mbrships:

Dramatists' Soc.; Men of Letters Soc.; Assn. of Combatant Writers; Hon. Pres., Cinema & TV Critics' Assn. Hons. incl: Eve Delacroix Prize, 1961; Off., Legion of Hon. Address: 15 Rue Lakanal, 75015 Paris, France.

LANG-DILLENBURGER, Elmy, pen name LANG, Elmy. b. 13 Aug. 1921, Pirmasens, Germany. Author; Translator; Journalist. Educ: Interpreter's Dip. Publs: (poetry) Mitternachtsspritzer, 1970; (novel) Frühstück auf französisch, 1971; (radio play) Die Verfolgung, 1974; (play) Der Fall Chardon; (radio story) Dani und Heseki reisen zur Erde, 1975; Short stories. Contbr. to: Lady Int.; Der Literat. Mbrships: Union German Writers; Europäische Autorenvereinigung Die Kogge. Address: 678 Pirmasens, Lemberger Str. 20, W. Germany.

LANGDON, John (Franklin) (Coasten), pen names GANNOLD, John; RUSSELL, Rex, b. 20 Jan. 1913, W.L.A., Calif., USA. Writer. Publs: The Blue Men, 1950; Vicious Circuit, 1953; S.S.Silverspray, 1958; 36 Hours!, 1965; The Fix, 1972; The Night of the Fox, 1974. Contbr. to num. anthols. inclng: Tales for Males, 1945; Various Temptations, 1955; O. Henry Prize Stories, 1957; Best American Short Stories, 1957; New Horizons, 1970; & to num. mags. inclng: Story Mag.; Clipper; Mast; Paris Review; Mag. of Fantasy & Sci. Fiction. Mbrships: Authors League of Am.; Authors Guild of Am.; Writers Guild of Am.W. Hons. incl: 1st Prize, Paris Review Short Story Contest, 1956. Address: Apartado Postal No. 9, Tepoztlan, Morelos, Mexico.

LANGDON, Robert Adrian, b. 3 Sept. 1924, Adelaide, Austrialia. Historian. Publs: Tahiti: Island of Love, 1959, 4th ed., 1972; The Lost Caravel, 1974. Contbr. to: Pacific Islands Monthly; Jrnl. of Pacific Hist. Mbrships: Hakwyt Soc.; Soc. des Oceanistes, Paris; Soc. des Études Oceaniennes, Tahiti; Polynesian Soc., Wellington. Address: 15 Darambal St., Aranda, A.C.T., Australia 2614.

LANGE, Per, b. 30 Aug. 1901, Hörsholm, Denmark. Author. Educ: Matriculation in Hist. of Art & Lit., Univ. of Copenhagen, 1919. Publs: (poems) Kaos og Stjernen, 1926; Forvandlinger, 1929; Orfeus, 1932; Udvalgte Digte, 1953; I Bjergene, 1971; (essays) Spejlinger, 1953; Ved Musikkens Taerskel, 1957; Samtale med et Aesel, 1961; Samlede Essays, 1964; Om Krig of Krigsmaend, 1966; Dyrenes Maskerade, 1970. Contbr. to: Sind og Samfund; Berlingske Tidende; Vindrosen. Hons: Henri Nathansens Födselsdagslegat, 1941; Det Ancher'ske Legat, 1950; Louisianaprisen, 1959. Address: Dr. Olgas Vej 5, II, DK-2000 Copenhagen F., Denmark.

LANGE, Victor, b. 13 July 1908, Leipzig, Germany. University Professor & Author. Educ: M.A., Univ. of Toronto; Ph.D., Leipzig Univ. Publs: Die Lyrik und ihr Publikum im England des 18. Jahrhunderts, 1934; Kulturkritik und Literaturbetrachtung in Amerika, 1938; Modern German Literature, 1945, 1968; Humanistic Scholarship in America, 1968; The Age of Revolution, 1976. Contbr. to: Yale Review; New Repub.; Life Int.; Saturday Review; Neue Rundschau; etc. Mbrships. incl: Pres., Int. Assn. of Germanic Studies, 1965-70; Pres., Am. Assn. of 18th Century Studies, 1975; VP, MLA of Am. Hons. incl: Cmdrs. Cross, Order of Merit, German Fed. Repub.; Goethe Medal in gold, Goethe Inst. Address: 230 E. Pyne Bldg., Princeton Univ., Princeton, NJ 08540, USA.

LANGFORD, Gerald, b. 20 Oct. 1911, Montgomery, Ala., USA. Professor of English. Educ: B.A., 1933, M.A., 1934, Ph.D., 1940, Univ. of Va. Publs: Alias O. Henry, 1957; The Richard Harding Davis Years, 1961; The Murder of Stanford White, 1962; Ingénue Among the Lions, 1965; Faulkner's Revision of "Absalom, Absalom!", 1971; Faulkner's Revision of "Sanctuary", 1972. Mbrships: MLA; Tex. Inst. of Letters. Address: 1711 Pearl St., Austin, TX, USA.

LANGLEY, Lee, (Miss) b. Calcutta, India. Writer. Publs: The Only Person, 1972; Sunday Girl, 1973. Contbr. to: Guardian; Daily Telegraph; London Evening Standard. Mbr., Writers Guild of GB. Address: 6 Chislehurst Rd., Richmond, Surrey, UK.

LANGLEY, Noel A., b. 25 Dec. 1911, Durban, S. Africa. Author-Playwright. Educ: Univ. of Natal. Publs. incl: (plays) Queer Cargo; Cage me a Peacock; The Burning Bush; The Walrus & the Carpenter, 1941; The Snow Queen, 1967; (films) The Wizard of Oz, 1938; They Made me a Fugitive, 1946; The Search for Bridey Murphy, 1957; (other publs.) Hocus Pocus, 1941; The Music of the Heart,

1946; Nymph in Clover, 1948; Tales of Mystery & Revenge, 1950; An Elegance of Rebels, 1960; The Loner, 1967; My Beloved Teck, 1970; A Dream of Dragon Flies, 1972. Address: c/o Writers' Guild of Am., Hollywood, Calif., USA.

LANGLEY, Stephen Gould, b. 25 Dec. 1938, Gardner, Mass., USA. College Professor; Theatre Manager. Educ: Cert., Ctrl. Schl. of Speech & Drama, London, UK, 1959; B.A. 1960, M.A. 1961, Emerson Coll., Boston; Ph.D., Univ. of Ill., 1966. Publs: Theatre Management in America, 1974; Producers on Producing, 1974. Contbr. to: Cape Playbill; Cape Cod Compass; Theatre Technol.; etc. Mbrships: AAUP; US Inst. for Theatre Technol.; Authors' League of Am.; Dramatists Guild; Coun. of Stock Theatres; Assoc. Couns. of the Arts. Address: Box 1527 GPO, Brooklyn, NY 11202, USA.

LANGSAM, Walter Consuelo, b. 2 Jan. 1906, Vienna, Austria. University President & Historian (Ret'd). Educ: B.A., CCNY, USA, 1925; M.A., 1926, Ph.D., 1930, Columbia Univ. Publs. incl: The World Since 1914, 1933, 6th ed., 1948; Documents & Readings in the History of Europe Since 1918, 1939, 3rd ed., 1969; Francis the Good: The Education of an Emperor (1768-1792), 1949; Historic Documents of World War II, 1958; Where Freedom Exists, 1967; An Honor Conferred, A Title Awarded, A History of the Commercial Club of Cincinnati, 1880-1972, 1973; The Common Market: Problems & Prospects, 1974. Mbr., Pres., The Lit. Club of Cinn. Address: 621 Library, Univ. of Cinn., Cinn., OH 45221, USA.

LANOUX, Armand, b. 24 Oct. 1913, Paris, France. Writer. Num. publs. incl: Bonjour Monsieur Zola, 1954; Le Commandant Watrin, 1956; Quand la Mer se retire, 1963; Le Violon dans le feu, 1967; Maupassant, le bel ami, 1967; La Polka des canons, 1971; Le Coq rouge, 1972; 1900, la Bourgeoisie absolue, 1973; Le Berger des abeilles, 1974; Paris 1925, 1975. Mbrships. incl: Sec. Gen., Goncourt Acad.; VP, French PEN; VP, Authors & Dramatists Soc. Address: 7 Route de Malnoue, 77420 Champs-sur-Marne, France.

LANTZ, J. Edward, b. 7 June 1911, Edgerton, Ohio, USA. Clergyman; Professor. Educ: A.B., DePauw Univ., 1934; M.Div., Yale Univ. Div. Schl., 1938; M.A., Univ. of Mich., 1942; Univ. of Chgo.; Litt.D., Evangelical Bible Coll. & Sem., 1969. Publs. incl: Stories to Grow By, 1953; Church Councils in the South, 1956; Plays for Happier Homes (co-author), 1957; Reading the Bible Aloud, 1959. Contbr., over 100 articles, num. book reviews, to jrnls. Mbrships: Pres., Atlanta Writers Club; Ga. Writers Assn.; Dixie Coun. of Authors & Jrnlsts. Address: 1040 Springdale Rd. NE, Atlanta, GA 30306, USA.

LANTZ, Robert, b. 20 July 1914, Berlin, Germany. Literary & Talent Agent. Educ: Univ. Berlin. Publs. incl: (play) L'Inconnue de la Seine. Mbr., PEN. Recip., Austrian Reich Prize, 1934 for L'Inconnue de la Seine. Address: The Lantz Off. Inc., 114 E. 55th St., N.Y., NY 10022, USA.

LANTZ, Ruth Cox, b. 11 Jan. 1914, Gainesville, Fla., USA. Teacher; Writer; Artist. Educ: A.B., Emory Univ., 1934; Yale Univ. Art Schl., 1934-35; Pratt Inst., N.Y., 1935; M.A., Univ. of Mich., 1942. Publs: Bible Characters in Action (w. Edward Lantz), 1955; Plays for Happier Homes (w. Edward Lantz), 1957. Ed., The Shepherdess, 1949-58. Contbr. to var. lit. publs. Mbrships: Atlanta Writers Club; Ga. Writers Assn.; Dixie Coun. of Authors & Jrnlsts.; Chmn., Atlanta Br. Creative Writing Grp., AAUW, 1969, 1974. Hons: Marel Brown Poetry Award, 1972; Atlanta Writers Club Juvenile Story Award, 1973. Address: 1040 Springdale Rd. N.E., Atlanta, GA 30306, USA.

LÁNYI, Sarolta, b. 6 June 1891, Székesfehérvár, Hungary. Poet; Translator. Educ: Tchrs. Trng. Coll. Publs: Ajándék (Present), 1912; Távozó (In Departure), 1914; Napjaim (My Days), 1921; Számlálatlan evek (Uncounted Years), 1947; Kései ajándek (Late Present), 1950; Őszi kert (Autumn Garden), 1956; Énekszó (Songword), 1962; Múlt és jelenidő (Past & Present Tense), 1966; Téli hajnal (Winter Dawn), 1971; Feledni kár (It's Wrong to Forget), 1975. Mbrships: PEN; Hungarian Writers' Assn. Hons: Baumgarten Prize, 1948; József Attila Prize, 1950, 1972; Gold Order Work, 1956, 1961, 1966; Order Red Flag Work, 1971. Address: H-1126 Budapest XII, Hollósy Simon u.34, Hungary.

LAPATI, Americo D., b. 2 Nov. 1924, Providence, R.I., USA. University Professor. Educ: A.B., 1945, S.T.B., 1947,

St. Mary's Sem. & Univ., Balt., Md.; M.A., 1951, Ph.D., 1958, Boston Coll., Chestnut Hill, Mass. Publs: A High School Curriculum for Leadership, 1961; Orestes A. Brownson, 1965; John Henry Newman, 1972; Education & the Federal Government: A Historical Record, 1975. Contbr. to: New Scholasticism; Mod. Schlman.; Notre Dame Jrnl. of Educ. Mbrships. incl: Philos. of Educ. Soc.; Am. Educl. Studies Assn. Hons. incl: Fulbright Schlr., Italy, 1964; Outstanding Educator of Am. Award, 1972. Address: School of Education, Catholic Univ. of America, Wash. DC, USA.

LAPESA, Rafael, b. 1908, Valencia, Spain. University Professor. Educ: Madrid Univ. Publs: Historia de la Lengua Española, 1942, 1951, 1955; Asturiano y Provenzal en el Fuero de Avilés, 1948; La trayectoria poética de Garcilaso, 1948, 1968; La obra literaria del Marqués de Santillana, 1957; De la Edad Media a nuestros días, 1967. Mbrships: Real Acad. Espanola; MLA, USA; Hispanic Soc. of Am.; Nat. Acad. of Letters, Uruguay; Am. Assn. of Teachers of Spanish & Portuguese. Address: Residencia de Profesores 3, Calle de Isaac Peral, Madrid 15, Spain.

LAPONCE, Jean Antoine, b. 4 Nov. 1925, Decize, France. Teacher. Educ: Dip., Inst. of Pol. Studies, Paris, 1947; Ph.D., U.C.L.A., 1956. Publs: The Protection of Minorities, 1961; The Government of France under the Fifth Republic, 1962; People vs. Politics, 1970. Contbr. to: Can. Jrnl. of Pol. Sci.; Am. Pol. Sci. Review; Western Pol. Quarterly; Comp. Pols.; Revue Française de Sci. Pol.; Pol. Studies; Comp. Pol. Studies; Brit. Jrnl. of Pol. Sci. Mbrships. incl: Pres., 1973-76, Exec. Comm., 1966-70 & 1970-75, Int. Pol. Sci. Assn.; Pres., Can. Pol. Sci. Assn., 1972-73; Exec. Coun., Soc. Sci. Rsch. Coun. of Can., 1966-69. Address: Dept. of Pol. Sci., Univ. of B.C., Vancouver 8, B.C., Can.

LAPPALAINEN, Kauko Kalevi, b. 11 Apr. 1940, Oulu, Finland. Author; Poet; Translator. Educ: B.A. in Educ., Ariz. State Univ., USA, 1964; Helsinki Univ. Publs. incl: poetry, 1 novel in Finnish; Outside the Alphabets (in Engl.), 1966; Trans., The Europeans, by Henry James, 1967. Contbr. of poetry & transls., Finland, US jrnls. & anthols. Mbrships: Finnish Soc. of Authors; Finnish Transls. Soc. Hons. incl: Num. prizes & grants, Finland; Author Fellowship, City of Helsinki, 1969; Vis. Author, Bulgarian Soc. of Authors, Varna, 1969; Mbr., Int. Writers Conf., Lahti, 1968. Address: Kanneltie 5 B 14, 00420 Helsinki 42, Finland.

LAPPALAINEN, Seppo Kelevi, b. 15 Oct. 1936, Polvijärvi, Finland. Writer. Educ: People Educl. Inst. Publs: (novels) Miljoonamiesten suku, 1971; Suomessa olen minä syntynyt 1972; Maailmanrannan rellut, 1974; Tonkkakuninkaat, 1969; Asekätkijät, 1964; (drama) Kummikuntavieraat. Contbr. to: Parnasso; Pellervo; Maaseudun Tulevaisuus; Suomenmaa. Mbrships: Suomen Kirjailifaliitto; Suomen Arvostelijainliitto. Address: 83960 Kinahmo, Finland.

LARESE, Dino, b. 26 Aug. 1914, Amriswil, Switz. Teacher. Educ: Tchrs. Trng. Coll., Kreuzlingen. Publs: Toggenburger und Thurgaue Sagen, 1963; Im Hause nebenan, Märchen, 1968; Regula, Jugendbuch, 1963; Beggnungen mit Schweizer Komponisten, 1974. Mbrships PEN; Rotary Club. Recip., East-Swiss Radio Prize. Address: Postfach 15, CH8580, Amriswil, Switz.

LARKIN, John Alan, b. 29 July 1936, Sharon, Conn., USA. Historian; University Professor. Educ: B.A., 1958; M.A., 1961; Yale Univ; Ph.D., N.Y. Univ., 1966. Publs. incl: The World of Southeast Asia (w. Harry J. Benda), 1967; The Pampangans: Colonial Society in a Philippine Province, 1972. Contbr. to schlrly. jrnls. inclng: Jrnl. of Asian Studies; Jrnl. of S.E. Asian Hist. Mbrships. incl: Am. Histl. Assn.; Am. Anthropol. Assn.; Assn. of Asian Studies. Address: Dept. of Hist., SUNY/B-Ellicott Complex, Red Jacket Quadrangle, Buffalo, NY 14261, USA.

LARKIN, Philip Arthur, b. 9 Aug. 1922. Poet; Novelist; Librarian. Educ: M.A., St. John's Coll., Oxford. Publs: (poems) The North Ship, 1945; The Less Deceived, 1955; The Whitsun Weddings, 1964; (Ed.) The Oxford Book of Twentieth Century English Verse, 1973; (novels) Jill, 1946, 1964; A Girl in Winter, 1947; (essays) All What Jazz, 1970. Contbr. to Daily Telegraph, 1961-71. Mbrships: F.R.S.L. Hons: The Queen's Gold Medal for Poetry, 1965; D.Litt. Address: c/o Univ. of Hull, Hull, Yorks., UK.

LARNER, Jeremy, b. 20 Mar. 1937, Olean, N.Y., USA. Writer. Educ: A.B., Brandeis Univ., Mass., 1958; Univ. of Calif., Berkeley, 1958-59. Publs: Drive, He Said (novel), USA, 1964, UK, 1965; The Addict in the Streets (w. R. Tefferteller), USA, 1965; UK, 1966; The Answer (novel), 1968; Ed., Poverty, (w. I. Howe), 1968; Nobody Knows: Reflections on the McCarthy Campaign of 1968, 1970; (screenplays) Drive, He Said (w. Jack Nicholson), 1970; The Candidate, 1971. Contbr. to: Paris Review; Harper's. Mbr., Ed. Bd., Dissent Mag. Hons. incl: Delta Novel Prize, 1964; Aga Khan Prize, Paris Review, 1964. Address: c/o Candida Donadio, III W. 57th St., N.Y., NY 10019, USA.

LARNI, Martti, b. 22 Sept. 1909, Helsinki, Finland. Writer. Num. publs. incl: Lahella Syntia (Close to Sin), 1946, filmed in 1954; Neljas nikama (The Fourth Vertebra), 1957, transl. into 21 langs.; Tasta ei puhata julkisesti (One Does Not Speak in Public of This), 1964, transl. into 5 langs. Mbrships: Past Chmn., Hon. Mbr., Finnish Writers Union; Fndr. Mbr., Finnish Jrnlsts. Union (1940). Hons: Pro Finlandia Medal, 1965; 1st Prize, Int. Satire Competition, Aleko, Sofia, 1967. Address: Perhekuja 4, 00680 Helsinki, 68, Finland.

LARSEN, Egon, b. 13 July 1904, Munich, Germany. Writer. Publs: Men Who Changed the World, 1952; An American in Europe: Count Rumford, 1953; Men Who Fought for Freedom, 1958; Atomc Energy: the First Hundred Years, 1958; A History of Invention, 1961; 4th ed. 1971; The Cavendish Laboratory, 1962; Laughter in a Damp Climate (anthol.), 1963; The Deceivers, 1966; Strange Sects & Cults, 1971; Radio & Television, forthcoming. Contbr. to: Radio Munich; Süddeutsche Zeitung, Munich; other European newspapers. Mbrships: Int. PEN; Soc. of Authors; Writers Guild. Recip., Diesel Medal (silver), 1963. Address: 34 Dartmouth Rd., London NW2 4EX, UK.

LARSEN, Lawrence H., b. 18 Jan. 1931, Racine, Wis., USA. Professor of History. Educ: B.S., Lawrence Univ., 1953; M.S., Univ. of Wis., 1955; Ph.D. 1962. Publs: The President Wore Spats: A Biography of Glenn Frank, 1965; Factories in the Valley: Neenah-Menasha 1870-1915 (w. Charles N. Glaab), 1969; Aspects of American History 1776-1970, 2 vols. (w. Robert L. Branyan), 1970; Urban Crisis in Modern America (w. Robert L. Branyan), 1971; The Eisenhower Administration 1953-1961: A Documentary History, 2 vols. (w. Robert L. Branyan), 1971. Contbr. to profl. jrnls. Mbrships: Org. of Am. Histns.; State Hist. Soc. of Wis. Address: 428 E. 65th Terrace, Kansas City, MO, USA.

LARSEN, Michael Frederick, b. 8 Jan. 1941, NYC, USA. Literary Agent. Educ: B.A., CCNY. Publs: California Publicity Outlets, 1972. Mbrships: Publicity Club of San Fran. Bay Area; Bay Area CCNY. Address: 1029 Jones, San Francisco, CA 94109, USA.

LARSEN, Peter, b. 24 Oct. 1933, Berlin, Germany. Photographer; Author. Publs: Young Africa, 1964; Boy of the Masai, 1964; Boy of Nepal, 1970; Boy of Dahomey, 1970; United Nations — At Work throughout the World, 1970; Boy of Bolivia, 1971; Museums of Israel, 1975; Three Faces of Jerusalem, 1975. Mbrships: Former Fellow, Royal Photographic Soc., Royal Geogl. Soc.; Assoc., Am. Soc. Mag. Photographers; Nat. Union of Jrnlsts.; Profl. Photographers of Am. Recip., Jerusalem Seal of Quality. Address: 373 Chiswick High Rd., London, W4, UK.

LARSON, Lorentz, b. 5 Nov. 1894, Wildwood, N.J., USA. Writer. Educ: B.A. Publs: Nya skolor i USA, 1931; Ungdom läser. En undersökning över läsintresserna hos barn och ungdom, åldern 7-20är, 1947; Maskplockare Andersson, 1950; Barn och serier, 1954; Segla Sakta, 1960; Blå Skuggan, 1965. Contbr. to: Barn och Kultur; Bookbird, Mbr., Svenska Författarförbundet. Recip., Ph.D.(h.c.), Uppsala, 1969. Address: Anderssons väg 3, 31100 Falkenberg, Sweden.

LARSSON, Knut (Georg Valdemar), b. 3 Sept. 1910, Malmö, Sweden. Author; Archivist. Publs: Ute blommar rosmarin, 1948; Röd lykta, 1950; Eldslägga, 1951; Av jord, 1959; Det röda och det blå, 1961; Efterdyning, 1969. Mbrships: Swedish Union of Authors; Skånes Författarsällskap. Hons: Awards, Bd., Swedish Union of Authors, Readers Circle Fund, & the Book Lottery, 1959; Sjöbergs Schlrship., 1960; 6 Awards, Swedish Authors Fund, 1960-72; Cultural Schlrship., Malmö City, 1964. Address: Edward Lindahlsgatan 14 C, 217 42 Malmö, Sweden.

LARSSON, Maj Gudrun, b. 1 Jan. 1914, Toarp, Sweden. Author. Publs: Möte på Perrong (poetry), 1963; Blågul Akvarell (poetry), 1968; Finlandsresa (essays), 1971; Water Colors (poetry in Engl. transl.), 1971; Kvinnor i Tidspegel (political hist.), 1973. Contbr. to: Lyrikvännen; Perspektiv; Horisont; Studiekontakt; Impuls; Budkavle; Land. Mbrships: Swedish Union of Authors; Göteborgs Författarsällskap. Hons: Karin Collin award, 1968; Litteraturfrämjandets stipendium, 1971; Swedish Authors' Fund, 1973; Falköpings Tidnings Cultural award, 1974. Address: Luttra, 521 00 Falköping, Sweden.

LÁRUSDÓTTIR, Elinborg, pen name SUNNA, b. 12 Nov. 1891, Skagafjord, Iceland. Housewife. Educ: Icelandic State Tchrs. Coll., Reykjavik. Publs: Over 30 books inclng: Förumenn, 3 vols., 1938-40; Simon i Nordurhlid, 1945; Horfnar Kynslódyir, 4 vols., 1960-64. Contbr. to The Icelandic Canadian. Mbr. & Past Treas., Assn. of Icelandic Authors. Address: Vitastigur 8A, Reykjavik, Iceland.

LASKI, Marghanita, b. 24 Oct. 1915. Author. Educ: Somerville Coll., Oxford. Publs. incl: (novels) Love on the Supertax, 1944; Little Boy Lost, 1949; The Victorian Chaise-Longue, 1953; (play) The Offshore Island, 1959; Ecstasy: A Study of some Secular & Religious Experiences, 1961; Domestic Life in Edwardian England, 1964; The Secular Responsibility, 1967; Jane Austen & Her World, 1969; George Eliot & Her World, 1973. Contbr. to: Radio & TV progs. incl. Kipling's Engl. Hist., 1973. Address: c/o David Higham Associates, 5-8 Lower John St., London W1, UK.

LASKI, Philip Michael, b. 5 Aug. 1918, Manchester, UK. Writer; Historian. Educ: B.S., l'Ecole des Hautes Etudes Internationales, Geneva, Switz. Publs: Magritte, 1961; Ed.-in-Chief, The Millionaire's Diary, 1967-68; The Trial & Execution of Madame du Barry, 1969. Contbr. to: Le Peintre (London Corres., 1966-); UNESCO News. Assoc. Mbr., Writers' Guild of GB. Address: c/o Winant, Towers Ltd., Clifford's Inn, Fetter Lane, London EC4, UK.

La SOR, William Sanford, b. 25 Oct. 1911, Phila., Pa., USA. Clergyman; Professor. Educ: A.B., Univ. of Pa., 1931; Th.B., 1934 Th.M., 1943; Princeton Theol. Sem., M.A., Princeton Univ., 1934; Ph.D., Dropsie Univ., 1949; Th.D., Univ. of S. Calif., 1956. Publs: Amazing Dead Sea Scrolls, 1956, revised ed., 1959; Great Personalities of the Old Testament, 1959; Great Personalities of the New Testament, 1961; Church Alive!, 1972; Dead Sea Scrolls & the New Testament, 1972; Handbook of New Testament Greek, 2 vols., 1973. Contbr. to relig. jrnls. Mbr., var. bibl. socs. Address: 1790 E. Loma Alta Dr., Altadena, CA 91001, USA.

LASZLO, Anna, b. 5 Jan. 1922, Budapest, Hungary. Writer. Educ: Dip. Dramaturgy, Acad. Dramatic Art. Publs. (short stories) New-Years Eve, 1959; Woodpecker on the Water, 1965; Colourful Morning, 1973; (biog.) Alexander Hevesi, 1960, 2nd ed., 1973; (novels) Expecting You next Tuesday, 1963; The Perfidious, 1967; Final Report, 1969. Contbr. to: Kortars, Jelenkor; Alfold; Nagyvilag; Elet es Irodalom, var. newspapers. Mbrships: Hungarian Writers' Union; PEN. Recip., var. radio & lit. competition prizes. Address: Tulipan utca 15, H-1022 Budapest, Hungary.

LASZLO, Ervin, b. 12 June 1932, Budapest, Hungary. Professor of Philosophy. Educ: Artist Dip., Franz Liszt Acad. of Music, Budapest, 1947; Doct. ès-Lettres et Sciences Humaines, Sorbonne, Paris, France, 1970. Publs. incl: Essential Society, 1963; Beyond Scepticism & Realism, 1966; System Structure & Experience, 1969; The Systems View of the World, 1972; Introduction to Systems Philosophy, 1972, 2nd ed., 1973; A Strategy for the Future, 1974. Contbr. to: Scientia; Philos. of Sci.; Main Currents in Mod. Thought; Futurist; etc. Hons. incl: Pro Arte Award, Pres. of Hungary, 1947; Exceptional Achievement Award, Lisbon, 1959. Address: Maple Beach Road, Geneseo, NY 14454, USA.

LATHAM, E(dward) Bryan, b. 7 May 1895, London, UK. Timber Consultant. Publs: Timber, An Historical Survey of its Development & Distribution; Victorian Staffordshire Portrait Figures; Timber from Forest to Man; History of Timber Trade Federation of United Kingdom; Territorial Soldiers' War; Trebartha, the House by the Stream. Contbr. to Ency. Britannica; Timber Trades Jrnl.; Empire Forestry Review; Unasylva. Mbrships. incl: Past Pres., Timber Dev. Assn.; Past Pres., Timber Trade Fedn., UK.; VP, Commonwealth Forestry Assn.; Past Pres., Inst. of Wood Sci. Address: Trebartha House, Launceston, Cornwall, UK.

LATHAM, Frank Alexander, b. 3 Jan. 1924, Spital, Cheshire, UK. Timber Importer. Publs: Timber Town (the history of the Liverpool Timber Trade), 1967; Alpraham, The history of a Cheshire Village, 1969; Tilstone Fearnall, The history of a Cheshire Village, 1970; Tiverton, The history of a Cheshire Village, 1971; Ed. & Rsch. Organizer, Tarporley, The history of a Cheshire Village, 1973. Contbr. to Timber Trades Jrnl. Address: Hilbre Grange, Alpraham, Tarporley, Cheshire, UK.

LATHAM, Jean Gudrun Rucker, b. 5 Jan. 1910, London, UK. Writer. Publs: Dolls' Houses, a personal choice, 1969; Victoriana, 1971; The Pleasure of Your Company, 1972; Miniature Antiques, 1972; Happy Families, 1974. Contbr. to: Antique Dealer & Collection Guide; Silver; Popular Guide to Antiques. Mbrships: Authors Soc.; Nat. Book League. Address: Dark Lane House, Marlborough, Wilts., UK.

LATYSHEV, Igor Aleksandrovich, b. 9 May 1925, Smolensk, USSR. Specialist in History & Political Life of Japan. Educ: Dr. of Histl. Scis., 1967. Publs: 6 books in Russian. Contbr. to var. Soviet pol. & Sci. mags. Mbrships: Jrnlst.'s Assn. of USSR; For. Press Corres.'s Club of Japan. Address: Dept. of Asia & Africa, Pravda Editorial Office, Pravda St. 24, Moscow, USSR.

LAUNERT, Edmund, b. 28 Feb. 1926, Mühlhausen/Thür., Germany. Principal Scientific Officer, Ministry of Agriculture, UK. Educ: Dr.rer.nat., Univ. of Munich; Univ. of Jena. Publs: Gramineae, Pt. 1, Flora Zambesiaca, 1971; Sommerblumen, 1972; Gartenstauden, 1972; Gebirgsflora in Farben, 1974; Sommergrüne Gartengehölze und Rosen, 1974; Immergrüne Gartensträucher und Nadelbäume, 1974; Scent & Scent Bottles, 1975; & sev. transls. into Engl. Contbr. to: Antique Dealers' Guide; Seal; Connoisseur; jrnl. of the Glass Circle. Mbrships. incl: Regensburgische Botanische Gesellschaft. Recip., Scheffel Prize for Lit., 1949. Address: 15 Halford Rd., Richmond, Surrey, UK.

LAURENCE, (Jean) Margaret, b. 18 July 1926, Neepawa, Man., Can. Writer. Educ: B.A., Univ. of Man., 1947. Publs. incl: A Tree for Poverty (anthol.) 1954; (novels) This Side Jordan, 1960; The Stone Angel, 1964; A Jest of God, 1966; The Fire-Dwellers, 1969; (stories) The Tomorrow-Tamer, 1963, USA 1964; A Bird in the House, 1970; (non-fiction) The Prophet's Camel Bell, 1963 (as New Wind in a Dry Land, USA, 1964); Long Drums & Cannons, UK, 1968, USA, 1969. Contbr. to: Holiday; Maclean's (travel articles). Hons. incl: Gov.-Gen.'s Award, 1967; Sr. Fellowship, Can. Coun., 1967. Address: Elm Cottage, Beacon Hill, Penn, Bucks., UK.

LAURENT, Emmanuel, pen name RENAULT, b. 29 May 1899, Wasmes, Hainaut, Belgium. Journalist. Publs: Le Grisou, 1938; Les Mysteres de la Mine, 1942; Le Stigmate Bleu, 1954; La Bande Noire de l'Entre- Sambre-et-Meuse: Coecke & Goethals etaient-ils Innocents?, 1972; var. pamphlets of popular hist. on Hainaut. Contbr. to: Le Moustique; Samedi; num. other articles in newspapers & jrnls. Mbr., S.A.B.A.M. (Soc. of Belgian Authors).Hons: Golden Palm, Order of the Crown, 1963; Medal of the City of Brussels, 1973. Address: rue Jean d'Ardenne 24, 1050 Brussels, Belgium.

LAURENT, Jacques, pen name SAINT-LAURENT, Cecil. b. 5 Jan. 1919, Paris, France. Author; Journalist. Educ: Faculté des Lettres, Paris. Publs. incl: (as C. Saint-Laurent) Caroline chérie; Lucrèce Borgia; Ici Clotilde; Les Passagers pour Alger; Les Agités d'Alger; A Simon l'honneur; L'Histoire imprévue des dessous féminins; (as J. Laurent) Les Corps Tranquille; Paul & Jean-Paul; Le petit canard; Lettre ouverte aux étudiants; Les Bêtises; Dix perles de culture. Contbr. to: Arts, (Pres., 1954-59); Fndr., La Parisienne; has written for the cinema. Recip., Prix Goncourt. Address: Presses de la Cité, 8 rue Garancière, Paris 6e, France.

LAURENTI, Joseph Lucian, b. 10 Dec. 1931, Hesperange, Luxembourg. Professor of Spanish & Italian. Educ: B.A., 1958, M.A., 1959, Univ. of Ill., Urbana; Ph.D., Univ. of Mo., Columbia. Publs. incl: Estudios sobre la novela picaresca espanola, 1970; Los prologos en las novelas picarescas espanolas, 1971; Literary Relations between Spain & Italy, 1972; The World of Federico García Lorca, 1974. Contbr. to jrnls. in field. Mbrships. incl: Int. Assn. of

Hispanists. Recip., Order of Don Quixote, Sigma Delta Pi, 1972. Address: Dept. of For. Langs., Ill. State Univ., Normal, IL 61761, USA.

LAURENTS, Arthur, b. Brooklyn, N.Y., USA. Writer; Stage Director. Educ: B.A., Cornell Univ., Ithaca, N.Y. Publs: (plays) Home of the Brave (Brit. title, The Way Back); The Bird Cage; The Time of the Cuckoo (Brit. title, Summer Madness); A Clearing in the Woods; Invitation to the March; The Enclave; (libretti for musicals) West Side Story; Gypsy; Anyone Can Whistle; Do I Hear a Waltz? ; Hallelujah, Baby! ; (novel) The Way We Were; (screenplays) Caught; Rope; The Snake Pit; Anastasia; The Way We Were. Mbrships. incl: Coun., Dramatists Guild; PEN; Authors Guild; Screenwriters Guild. Recip., Sidney Howard Playwriting Award, 1946. Address: Quogue, NY 11959, USA.

LAVATER-SLOMAN, Mary Helen, b. 14 Dec. 1891, Hamburg, Germany. Biographer. Publs. incl: J. C. Lavater, 1939; Catherine the Great, 1941; Die Grosse Flut, 1943; Einsamkeit, Annette von Droste-Hlf., 1950; Herrin der Meere (Elizabeth I), 1956; Goethen Eckermann, 1959; Konigin Christine v. Schweden, 1966; Das Gold von Troja, H. Schliemann, 1969; Lowenherz (Lion-Heart), 1972. Contbr. to: Neue Zurcher Zeitung; Berner Bund; Du; Merian; Atlantis; etc. Mbrships: PEN; Swiss Soc. for Lit. Hons: Schiller Prize of Zurich; 2 Prizes of town of Winterthur, Canton of Zurich; Int. Prize of Lake Constance. Address: Hochstrasse 40, 8044 Zurich, Switzerland.

LAVIN, Mary, b. 11 June 1912, E. Walpole, Mass., USA. Writer; Farmer. Educ: M.A., Nat. Univ. of Ireland, Dublin. Publs. incl: Tales from Bective Bridge, 1942; The House in Clewe Street, 1945; The Great Wave, 1961; In the Middle of the Fields, 1967; The Stories of Mary Lavin, 2 vols., 1964-73; Happiness, 1969; The Second Best Children in the World, 1972; A Memory, 1972. Contbr. to: New Yorker; Atlantic Monthly. Mbrships. incl: Past Pres., Irish Acad. of Letters; Past Pres., PEN. Hons: D.Litt.; James Tait Black Mem. Prize (for Tales from Bective Bridge); Katherine Mansfield Prize (for The Great Wave); Gold Medal, Eire Soc., 1974; Gregory Medal, 1975; Arts Award, Royal Meath Assn., 1975. Address: The Abbey Farm, Bective, Co. Meath, Repub. of Ireland.

LAVINE, John M., b. 20 Mar. 1941, Duluth, Minn., USA. Publisher-Editor, Lavine Newspaper Group. Educ: B.A., Carleton Coll., Northfield, Minn., 1963; Grad. Schl., Univ. of Minn., Mpls., 1963. Contbr. to: Murphy Newspapers, 1962; Wall St. Jrnl., 1963; United Press Int.; Assoc. Press; Worldview; King Features (editorials syndicated to 250 newspapers), 1964-68. Mbrships: Am. Soc. of Newspaper Eds.; Nat. Conf. of Ed. Writers. Recip., Outstanding Young Man of Wis., Wis. Jaycees, 1967. Address: Lavine Newspaper Group, 20-22 W.Ctrl. St., Chippewa Falls, WI 54729, USA.

LAW, Bessie Trull, b. 3 June 1892, Union, N.C., USA. Publs: With My Memories, 1973; Loveliness Around Us, 1974. Contbr. to poetry jrnls. & mags. Mbrships: Charter Mbr., N.C. Poetry Soc.; Hon. Mbr., Greensboro Writers; Am. Poetry League; Centro Studi E Scambi Int., Rome; World Poetry Soc.; Nat. Writers Club. Hons: Cert. of Merit, 1959, 1960, Silver Cup, 1960, Greensboro Writers; Gold Cup, 1961, Cert. of Merit, 1962, Burlington Writers; Cert. of Merit, Centro Studi E Scambi Int., 1969. Address: 912 Forest Hill Dr., Greensboro, NC 27410, USA.

LAWFORD, (Lt.-Col.) James Philip, b. 1915, Peking, China. Senior Lecturer, R.M.A. Sandhurst, 1967-. Educ: Clare Coll., Cambridge; M.A. Publs: Solah Punjab, (part-author) 1967; Charge, (co-author) 1967; History of the British Army, (co-ed.) 1970; Wellington's Masterpiece, (co-author) 1972; 30th Punjabis, 1972; Wellington's Peninsular Army, 1973; Victoria 1813, 1973. Mbr., Soc. for Army Histl. Rsch. Agent: London Management. Address: Shapley Heath, Winchfield, Bastingstoke, Hants., UK.

LAWLOR, John James, b. 5 Jan. 1918, Plymouth, UK. Professor of English Language & Literature. Educ: Magdalen Coll., Oxford, 1936-39. Publs: The Tragic Sense in Shakespeare, 1960; 'Piers Plowman': an Essay in Criticism, 1962; Ed., Patterns of Love & Courtesy: Essays in Memory of C. S. Lewis, 1966; To Nevill Coghill from Friends (w. W. H. Auden), 1966; Chaucer, 1969; Ed., The New University, 1968; Ed., Higher Education: Patterns of Change in the 1970s, 1972. Contbr. to: Review of Engl. Studies; Mod. Lang. Review; Medium Aevum, Speculum, etc. Mbrships. incl: Fellow, Soc. of Antiquaries. Recip.,

D.Litt. Address: 14 Church Plantation, Keele, Staffs. ST5 5AY, UK.

LAWRENCE, Berta, b. North Marston, Bucks., UK. Teacher of French & English. Educ: B.A.(Hons.), Univ. of London; Dip.Ed., Univ. of Reading. Publs: A Somerset Journal, 1951; Quantock Country, 1952; The Bond of Green Withy, 1954; The Nightingale in the Branches, 1955; Coleridge & Wordsworth in Somerset, 1970; Somerset Legends, 1973. Contbr. to: Western Morning News; Countryman; Exmoor Review; Bulletin of Charles Lamb Soc.; Child Educ.; Lady; Sydney Morning Herald; BBC; Radio Eireann; etc. Mbrships: Soc. of Authors; PEN; Comm. Mbr., W. Country Writers' Assn. Address: 17 Wembdon Hill, Bridgwater, Somerset, UK.

LAWRENCE, Henry Lionel, b. London, UK. Writer (Fiction & Films). Publs: The Children of Light, 1960 (filmed as These are the Damned by J. Losey); The Sparta Medallion, 1961. Contbr. to: Guardian, etc. Mbrships: Inst. Practitioners in Advt.; Writers Guild of GB; Former Ed., Red Herrings, Crime Writers Assn. Address: c/o Winant Towers Ltd., 14 Cliffords Inn, London EC4, UK.

LAWRENCE, Jerome, b. 14 July 1915, Cleveland, Ohio, USA. Playwright; Author; Director. Educ: B.A., Ohio State Univ. Publs. incl: (plays, w. Robert E. Lee) Inherit the Wind, 1955, num. eds. & transls. in 30 langs.; Auntie Mame, 1957; The Gang's All Here, 1960; The Night Thoreau Spent in Jail, 1972; Jabberwock, 1974; 15 others; num. Radio & TV plays & series, 1938-; (biog.) Actor: The Life & Times of Paul Muni, 1974, UK 1975. Contbr. to: Saturday Evening Post; Theatre Arts; etc. Mbrships: Am. Playwrights Theatre (Pres. & Co-fndr.); num. other profl. orgs. Hons: Peabody Awards, 1949, 1952; num. other awards & citations; var. degrees. Address: 21056 Las Flores Mesa Dr., Malibu, CA 90265, USA.

LAWRENCE, Jodi, pen name, FERRARO, Jodi, b. 7 Sept. 1938, Bristol, Pa., USA. Writer. Educ: A.B., Univ. of Southern Calif.; further studies, Univ. of Copenhagen, Denmark. Publs: Survival Kit, 1970; Alpha Brain Waves — A Study of Biofeedback, 1972; Off the Beaten Track in Hawaii, 1972; Search for the Perfect Orgasm, 1973; Signet, 1974. Contbr. to: Readers Digest; N.Y. Times; Today's Film-maker; Western Lit. Review, etc. Mbrships: Soc. of Mag. Writers; Overseas, L.A. Press Clubs; Writers' Unit — Actors' Studio; Authors' Guild of Am. Hons. incl: Lowell Drama Prize; Am. Corp. Pub. Broadcasting & Radio Amsterdam Int. Drama Award. Address: 10858 Fruitland Dr., Studio City, CA 91604, USA.

LAWRENSON, Thomas Edward, b. 19 Sept. 1918, Middlewich, Cheshire, UK. University Professor. Educ: B.A., Manchester Univ., 1939; M.A., 1947; Ph.D., 1953. Publs: Hall of Residence — Saint Anselm Hall in the University of Manchester, 1957; The French Stage in the Seventeenth Century, 1957; Lesage's Crispin Rival de son Maître (ed.), 1961; Lesage's Turcaret (ed.), 1969; Modern Miscellany Studies in Honour of Eugène Vinaver (ed.), 1969. Contbr. to: Theatre Rsch./Recherches/Théâtrales; French Studies; Mod. Langs. Review; etc. Recip., Chevalier de l'Ordre Nationale du Mérite, 1972. Address: Whitecroft, Blackwood End, Ellel, Lancaster LA2 0QB, UK.

LAWSON, Donald E., pen name LAWSON, Don, b. 20 May 1917, Chgo., Ill., USA. Encyclopedia Editor; Author. Educ: B.A., 1939, Litt.D., 1970, Cornell Coll., Mt. Vernon, Iowa; Writers' Workshop, Univ. of Iowa, 1941. Publs. incl: A Brand for the Burning (novel), 1961; Young People's History of America's Wars, 6 books 1963-74; Frances Perkins, 1967; The Lion & the Rock, 1970. Contbr. to: Argosy; Adventure; Family Circle; Story. Mbrships: Cliff Dwellers; Chgo. Press Club; Chgo. Lit. Club. Address: 1122 Lunt Ave., Chgo., IL 60626, USA.

LAWSON, Joan, b. 30 Jan. 1908, London, UK. Teacher; Author; Dance Critic. Educ: Leningrad Choreographic Acad., Russia. Publs: European Folk Dance, 1953; Mime, 1957; Dressing for the Ballet, 1958; Classical Ballet, 1960; A History of Ballet, 1964; The Teaching of Classical Ballet, 1973; Teaching Young Dancers, 1974. Contbr. to: Dancing Times (Critic 1940-64); Ency. Brit.; Oxford Jr. Ency. Mbrships: Fellow, Vice-Chmn., Imperial Soc. of Tchrs. of Dancing; Critics Circle. Address: 11 Hallswelle Rd., London W11 0DH, UK.

LAWSON, Richard Henry, b. 11 Jan. 1919, San Fran., Calif., USA. Professor of German. Educ: B.A., 1941, M.A., 1948, Univ. of Ore.; Ph.D., UCLA, 1956. Publs: Edith

Wharton & German Literature, 1974. Contbr., chapts. to books, articles in US, for. jrnls. Address: Dept. of Germanic & Slavic Langs. & Lits., San Diego State Univ., San Diego, CA 92182, USA.

LAWSON-WOOD, Denis, b. 27 Dec. 1906, Chiswick, London, UK. Clerk in Holy Orders; Lecturer on Acupuncture. Educ: Inter. LL.B., London Univ. ext.; Western Orthodox L.Th., 1952; Ph.D., Glaston, 1954; Dr. of Acupuncture, 1974. Publs: Chinese System of Healing, 1959; Judo Revival Points, 1960; Glowing Health, 1961; First Aid at Your Fingertips, 1963; Acupuncture Handbook, 1964; Five Elements of Acupuncture, 1965; Atlas of Acupuncture, 1967; The INcredible Healing Needles, 1974. Mbrships. incl: Fellow, Acupuncture Assn., 1960—; Registered Manipulative Therapist, until 1969; Tunbridge Wells Writers' Circle. Address: 4 Cumberland Walk, Royal Tunbridge Wells, Kent, UK.

LAWTON, Harold Walter, b. 27 July 1899, Stoke-on-Trent, UK. Emeritus Professor of French. Educ: B.A., 1921, M.A., 1923, Univ. Coll. of N. Wales; Doct. de L'Université, Univ. of Paris, 1926. Publs: Térence en France au XVIe Siècle. Tome I: Editions & Traductions, 1926, reprinted 1970, Tome II: Imitation & Influence, 1972; Handbook of French Renaissance Dramatic Theory, 1949, reprinted 1972; Ed., J. Du Bellay, Poems, 1961. Contbr. to: Modern Lang. Review; French Studies; Revue du XVIe Siècle; Revue de Littérature Comparée; Bibliothèque d'Humanisme & Renaissance. Hons: Médaille d'Argent de la Reconnaissance Francaise, 1946; Officier d'Académie, 1948. Address: 4 Timberbank, Vigo Village, Meopham, Kent, UK.

LAXNESS, Halldor Kilijan, b. 23 Apr. 1902. Writer. Publs. incl: The Great Weaver of Cashmere, 1927; Salka Valka, 1934; Independent People, 1939; The Atom Station; Paradise Reclaimed; The Fish Can Sing; (play) Independent People, 1972; (transl. into Icelandic) Hemingway's Farewell to Arms; Voltaire's Candide. Hons. incl: Nobel Prize for Lit., 1955; Sonning Prize, 1969. Address: P.O. Box 664, Reykjavik, Iceland.

LAZAREVIĆ, Branislav L., b. 2 Dec. 1910, Beograd, Yugoslavia. Writer. Publs: Urezi na dlanu, 1930, 2nd ed. 1970; Jedan čovek sam, 1939; Vrapci u gradini, 1951; Svirajka od zove, 1953, 2nd ed. 1967; Akvareli, 1954, 2nd ed. 1965; Rat mravinjaka, 1959. 2nd ed. 1966; Avantura, 1959, 2nd ed. 1971; Zakonik, 1959, 2nd ed. 1963; Lutke, 1960, 2nd ed. 1968; U čizmama, 1961, 2nd ed. 1972; Škola za ptice, 1964; Srušeno vreme, 1966; Čudnovati krojač, 1971; Prasnaga, 1973. Contbr. to sev. Yugoslav & other jrnls. Mbrships: PEN; Assn. of Serbian Writers. Address: Kosovska 30, 37000 Kruševac, Yugoslavia.

LAZEROWITZ, Morris, b. 22 Oct. 1907, Lodz, Poland. Educator; Writer. Educ: A.B., 1933, Ph.D., 1936, Univ. of Mich., USA. Publs: The Structure of Metaphysics, 1955; Studies in Metaphilosophy, 1964; Philosophy & Illusion (w. A. Ambrose), 1968; Psychoanalysis & Philosophy (Contbr. & Co-Ed. w. C. Manly), 1970; G. E. Moore, Essays in Retrospect (Contbr. & Co-Ed. w. A. Ambrose), 1970; Lugwig Wittgenstein, Philosophy & Language (Contbr. & Co-Ed. w. A. Ambrose), 1972; Philosophical Theories (w. A. Ambrose), 1975. Contbr. to US, UK jrnls. Address: Newhall Rd., Conway, MA 01341, USA.

LÊ, Tât Diù, b. 2 Aug. 1942, Hà-Dông, Viêtnam. Writer. Publs: Khoi Hành, 1964; Kè Tình Nguyên, 1965; Quay Trong Gió Lôc, 1965; Dêm Dài Môt Dòi, 1966; Ngùòi Da, 1967; Phá Núi, 1968; Nhûng Giọt Mùc, 1970. Contbr. to: Bách-Khoa; Van; Dông Phuong; Thòi Nay. Mbr., PEN. Hons: Long Story Prize, PEN, 1966; Nat. Lit. & Art Prize, 1971. Address: 225B Binh Thoi Phu Tho, Saigon II, S. Vietnam.

LEADBEATTER, Bruce Robert, b. 19 Sept. 1927, Alstonville, N.S.W., Australia. Lecturer in Industrial Arts. Educ: Sydney Tchrs. Coll., 1946-47; A.S.T.C. Manual Arts, Univ. of N.S.W., 1961-63. Publs: Resource Units in Industrial Arts (co-author), 1963; Woodworking (w. Keable), 1970; Woodworking Transparencies (w. Keable), 1972; Australian Woodworking (w. Keable), 1974. Contbr. to: Manual Arts Bulletin; Indl. Arts Educ. Mbrships: VP, E. Sydney Inst. of Indl. Arts; Woodwork Syllabus Comm., N.S.W. Dept. of Educ., 1962-68. Recip., 1st Prize, Indl. Arts Inst. Design Contest, 1968. Address: 59 Turton Ave., Belmore, 2192 Sydney, Australia.

LEAN, Arthur Edward, b. 17 Dec. 1909, Laurium, Mich., USA. University Professor of Education. Educ: A.B., 1930, Ph.D., 1948, Univ. of Mich.; A.M., Columbia Univ., 1934. Publs: John Dewey & the World View (co-author, co-ed.), 1964; And Merely Teach: Irreverent Essays on the Mythology of Education, 1968. Contbr. to School & Society; Phi Delta Kappan. Address: 1112 Chautauqua, Carbondale, IL 62901, USA.

LEANDER, Sigfrid, pen name S. L., b. 25 Feb. 1893, Stockholm, Sweden. Retired Educator; Author. Educ: Fil.kand., Univ. of Lund, 1932. Publs: Folkbildning — Vad är det?, 1953; Under Arbetareinstitutets Tak, 1955; Hundra År i Blekinge, 1963; Utsikt över Karlskrona, I-II, 1970; En Folkbildares Bibliografi, 1920-1972, 1973; Folk & Bildning: Jämförande Studier, 1974. Mbr., Swedish Union of Authors. Hons: Karlskrona Stads Kulturstipendium, 1963; Blekinge Läns Landstings Kulturpris, 1967; Anton Nyströms award, 1970; Swedish Authors' Fund Award, 1970; Socrates Prize, 1973. Address: Stortorget 14, II, 111 29 Stockholm, Sweden.

LEASE, Richard Jay, b. 10 Dec. 1914, Cherokee, Ohio, USA. Police Officer; Professor. Educ: Wittenberg Coll.; B.A., 1937, M.A., 1961, Univ. of Ariz.; Grad. studies, Ind. Univ., Louisville Univ., Ariz. State Univ. Publs: Alcohol & Road Traffic: Problems of Enforcement & Prosecution (co-author), 1963; New Horizons in Police Efficiency, Methods & Personnel Selection. Contbr. to num. police & forensic jrnls., & newspapers; Ed., Gen. Sect. of What's New, jrnl. of Am. Acad. of Forensic Scis. Hons: US Rep. on Panel, 5th Int. Conf. on Alcohol & Rd. Traffic, Freiburg, Germany, 1969; Paper presented, 6th Int. Conf. of Forensic Scis., Edinburgh,1972. Address: 2145 Boise Dr., Las Cruces, NM 88001, USA.

LEASOR, Thomas James, b. 20 Dec. 1923. Author; Company Director. Educ: Oriel Coll., Oxford. Publs. incl: (novels) Not Such a Bad Day, 1946; NTR-Nothing to Report, 1955; Spylight, 1966; Passport for a Pilgrim, 1968; A Week of Love, 1969; Never Had a Spanner on Her, 1970; Follow the Drum, 1972; Mandarin Gold, 1973; The Chinese Widow, 1974; (non-fiction) The Red Fort, 1956; War at the Top, 1959; Bring out Your Dead, 1961; Rudolph Hess: The Uninvited Envoy, 1961; Singapore: the Battle that Changed the World, 1968. Contbr. to num. Brit. & Am. mags., newspapers & jrnls. Recip., Order of St. John. Address: Swallowcliffe Manor, Salisbury, Wilts., UK.

LEATHAM, Louis Salisbury, b. 16 Nov. 1902, Salt Lake City, Utah, USA. Banker. Educ: Univ. of Utah Ext. Div.; Cmd. & Gen. Staff Coll., AUS. Publs: The Letham or Leatham Family, 1955; The Joshua Salisbury Family, 1961; Karl S. Little, Utah's Mister Credit Union, 1963. Contbr. to jrnls. in UK., Australia & Utah, & newspapers. Address: 546 DeSoto St., Salt Lake City, UT 84103, USA.

LEAVITT, Jerome Edward, b. 1 Aug. 1916, Verona, N.J., USA. College Professor. Educ: B.S., Newark State Coll., N.J., 1938; M.A., NY Univ., NYC, 1942; Ed.D., Northwestern Univ., Evanston, Ill., 1952; Tchrs. Coll., Columbia Univ., Univ. Colo., Univ. Arizona. Publs. incl: The Beginning Kindergarten Teacher, 1965, 2nd ed., 1971; Ed., Nursery, Kindergarten Education, 1958; Terrariums & Aquariums, (w. Huntsburger), 1961; America & Its Indians, 1961; By Land, By Sea, By Air, 1969; The Battered Child, 1974; Rocks From the Sky (w. Lang), 1975. Contbr. to num. acad. jrnls. Mbrships. incl: Assn. Childhood Educ. Int. (Life Mbr.); Nat. Soc. for Study Educ. Address: 1338 E. Almendra Dr. Fresno, CA 93710, USA.

LEBEL, Robert, b. 1904, Paris, France. Art Expert, French Courts of Justice; Pres., French Chamber of Art Experts. Educ: Sorbonne; Dip., Ecole du Louvre. Publs: Leonard de Vinci, 1952; Marcel Duchamp, 1959 (also publd. UK); Gericault, 1960; La Double Vue, 1964; L'Envers de la Peinture, 1964; L'Oiseau Caramel, 1969; Traité des Passions, 1972. Contbr. to: Preuves; L'Oeil; Art & Artists; etc. Recip., Prix du Fantastique, 1965. Addres: 16 Blvd. Raspail, Paris 75007, France.

LEBO, Dell, pen name (in India), LEBO, Deli, b. 6 Aug. 1922, NYC, USA. Psychologist. Educ: B.A., N.Y. Univ., 1949; M.A., 1951, Ph.D., 1956, Fla. State Univ. Publs. incl: Poems & Verse by Dell Lebo, Book I, The Metaphysical Poetry, Book II, The Three Cornered Habit, 1966; Religion in the Poetry of Dell Lebo, 1969. Contbr. to profl. jrnls.; 200 sci. articles, poetry, in USA, Italy, UK, India & Japan; Ed., Jacksonville Poetry Quarterly; Writer, Perf., TV show Psychologist's Notebook, 1959; Weekly TV prog., 1968-69;

Author, 3 McGraw-Hill 'Sound Seminars'. Mbrships. incl: Fndr., Arcane Order, 1950; Hon. US Rep., Centro Studi E Scambi, Rome, 1969-71; Fndng. Fellow, Int. Poetry Soc.; World Poetry Soc. Intercontinental; VP, Dylan Thomas Poetry Club. Hons. incl: Dip. di Benemerenza, 1967, Silver Medal of Hon., 1967, Gold Medal of Hon., 1969, Centro Studi E Scambi; Var. other poetry awards, US, UK & Italy. Address: Child Guidance Clinic, 1635 St. Paul Ave., Jacksonville, FL 32207, USA.

LEBOWITZ, Albert, b. 18 June 1922, St. Louis, Mo., USA. Lawyer. Educ: A.B., Wash. Univ., St. Louis, 1945; LL.B., Harvard Law Schl., 1948. Publs: (novels) Laban's Will, USA & UK, 1966; The Man Who Wouldn't Say No, 1969. Contbr. to: Perspective mag., St. Louis (Co-Ed., 1961—). Address: 743 Yale Ave., University City, MO 63130, USA.

LE CAIN, Errol, b. 1941, Singapore. Film Designer & Animator. Educ: St. Joseph's Inst., Singapore. Publs: King Arthur's Sword, 1968; The Cabbage Princess, 1969; The White Cat, 1973. Address: c/o Associated Freelance Artists, 19 Russell St., London WC2B 5HP, UK.

LE CLEZIO, Jean Marie Gustave, b. 13 Apr. 1940. Writer. Educ: Nice Univ., France. Publs: The Interrogation, 1963; Fever (short stories), 1965; Le Déluge, 1966; L'Exrase Matérielle, 1967; Terra Amata, 1967; La Guerre, 1970; Haï, 1971; The Book of Flights, 1972; Les Géants, 1973. Recip., Prix Renaudot, 1963. Address: c/o Eds. Gallimard, 5 rue Sébastien-Bottin, Paris 7e, France.

LE COMTE, Edward (Semple), b. 28 May 1916, NYC, USA. University Professor of English. Educ: A.B., Columbia Coll., NYC; M.A., Ph.D., Columbia Univ., N.Y.; Publs: Endymion in England: The Literary History of a Greek Myth, 1944; Yet Once More: Verbal & Psychological Pattern in Milton, 1953, 2nd ed. 1969; Dictionary of Last Words, 1955; The Long Road Back, 1957, 2nd ed. 1958; He & She, 1960, 2nd ed., 1961; A Milton Dictionary, 1961, 2nd ed., 1969; Grace to a Witty Sinner: A Life of Donne, 1965; The Notorious Lady Essex, 1969, 2nd ed., 1970; The Man Who was Afraid, 1969; Milton's Unchanging Mind: Three Essays, 1973; Poets' Riddles: Essays in Seventeenth-Century Explication, 1974. Mbrships: Milton Soc. of Am.; Renaissance Soc. of Am.; Authors Guild. Address: Box 113, N. Egremont, MA 01252, USA.

le COMTE, Willy, b. 7 July 1907, Amsterdam, Netherlands. Journalist; Publisher; Author. Educ: HBS/III, The Hague. Publs: "England-Spiel"; Espionage & Contra-Espionage, 1947. Contbr. to Economisch Dagbland. Mbrships. incl: Int. Press Club; Netherlands Soc. of Jrnlsts.; NEPAB Netherlands Econ. Press & Advsry. Bur. (ed.-in-chief, newsletter). Recip., Export Prize of Yr., 1970. Address: Villa "De Sonnebergh", 27, Utrechtseweg, Oosterbeek, Netherlands.

LEE, Beverly S., b. 6 July 1934, Honolulu, Hawaii, USA. Graduate Student. Educ: R.N., St. Luke's Hosp., NYC; B.A., Univ. of Hawaii, Honolulu. Publs: The Easy Way to Chinese Cooking, 1963. Mbr., bds. of sev. univ. women's clubs. Address: 1550 Wilder Ave., A110, Honolulu, HI 96822, USA.

LEE, Chia, b. 9 Jan, 1918, Soochow, China. Foreign Correspondent; Writer; Columnist. Educ: Shanghai Univ.; Tokyo Imperial Univ., Japan. Publs. incl: Dreamy Picture (transl. of Heine's poems), 1943; As I Saw It (transl. of Rossevelt Jr.'s book on the War & China), 1945; Politics in Japan Since Yoshida, 1960. Contbr. to: Pure Lit., Taipei; Chung-Wai Monthly, Taipei; Ro-Man, Japan; Seikai Orai, Japan; Toki-no-Kadai, Jadai, Japan; Yomiuri Weekly, Japan; etc. Mbrships: For. Correspondents' Club in Japan; Pres., ibid., 1963-64; Treas. & Dir., 1964-74. Address: 705, Habitation, 3-9, Sanbancho, Chiyoda-ku, Tokyo, Japan.

LEE, Chin Y., b. 23 Dec. 1917, Hunan, China. Novelist. Educ: B.A., S.-W. Assoc. Univ., China; F.M.A., Yale Univ., USA. Publs: Flower Drum Song, 1957; Lover's Point, 1959; Madam Goldenflower, 1961; A Corner of Heaven, 1962; The Sawbwa & His Secretary, 1963; The Virgin Market, 1965; The Land of the Golden Mountain, 1968; Days of the Tong Wars, 1974. Contbr., var. mags. Mbrships: Authors' League of Am.; Dramatists' Guild of Am. Hons: Calif. C'wlth. Club Gold Medal for Fiction, 1957; Box Off. Blue Ribbon Award. Address: 5333 Ellenvale Ave., Woodland Hills, CA 91364, USA.

LEE, (Sir) Henry Desmond Pritchard, b. 30 Aug. 1908, Nottingham, UK. President, Hughes Hall, Cambridge; Former Headmaster, Clifton, Winchester. Educ: Corpus Christi Coll., Cambridge, 1927-31; Fellow, ibid., 1933-48. Publs: Zero of Elea, 1936; Aristotle Mateorologica, 1952; Plato Republic, 1955, 2nd ed., 1974; Plato Timaeus & Critias, 1971. Contbr. to: Classical Quarterly; Greece & Rome. Mbrships: Headmasters Conf.; Chmn., ibid., 1959, 1960, 1967; Athenaeum Club. Recip., Hon.Litt.D., Nottingham Univ., 1963. Address: 8 Barton Close, Cambridge, UK.

LEE, James Michael, b. 29 Sept. 1931, NYC, USA. Professor of Religious Education. Educ: A.B., St. John's Univ., 1955; A.M. & Ed.D., Columbia Univ. Publs. incl: Catholic Education in the Western World, 1967; The Purpose of Catholic Schooling, 1968; Toward a Future for Religious Education, 1970; The Shape of Religious Instruction, 1971; The Flow of Religious Instruction, 1973; Forward Together, 1973. Contbr. to relig. jrnls. Mbrships. incl: Relig. Educ. Assn.; Am. Educl. Rsch. Assn. Address: 52088 Harvest Dr., South Bend, IN 46637, USA.

LEE, John Alexander, b. 3 Oct. 1891, Dunedin, NZ. Bookseller; Politician. Publs: Children of the Poor, 1934; The Hunted, 1936; Civilian into Soldier, 1937; Socialism in New Zealand, 1938; Shining with the Shiner, 1944; Simple on a Soapbox, 1963, 1964; Shiner Slattery, 1964; Rhetoric at the Red Dawn, 1965; Delinquent Days, 1967; Mussolinis Millions, 1971; Political Notebooks, 1973. Mbrships: Pres., Labour Party, Auckland; Pres., PEN. Hons: D.C.M.; LL.D., Otago Univ., 1964. Address: 48 Seaview Terrace, Mt. Albert, Auckland, NZ.

LEE, John F., b. 12 Mar. 1885, Andrew Co., Mo., USA. Banker; Lawyer; Farmer. Educ: Grad., Univ. of Mo.; Admitted to Bar, 1926. Publs. incl: Selected Poems, 1957; Sweet Harmony, 1962; Number Six, 1966; Hued Blocks, 1968; Anchors, 1970; Old Missouri, 1973; We Pause to Ponder, 1974. Address: 1201 Price, Savannah, MO, USA.

LEE, Laurie, b. 26 June 1914, Stroud, Glos., UK. Poet; Writer. Publs: (poetry) The Sun My Monument, 1944; The Bloom of Candles, 1947; My Many-Coated Man, 1955; (radioplay) The Voyage of Magellan, 1948; (travel) A Rose for Winter, 1955; (essay) The Firstborn, 1964; (autobiography) Cider with Rosie, 1959; As I Walked Out One Midsummer Morning, 1970. Hons: Atlantic Award, 1947; William Foyle Poetry Prize, 1956; W. H. Smith Award, 1960. Address: 49 Elm Park Gdns., London SW10, UK.

LEE, O-Young, b. 15 Jan. 1934, A-San, Korea. Professor, Ewha Women's University; Editor. Educ: B.A., 1956, M.A., 1959, Seoul Nat. Univ. Publs: (essays & criticism) The Literature in Resistance, 1958; The Lane of Intelligence, 1959; In this Earth & In that Wind, 1963; The Place where the Wind Sits, 1964; When a Leaf Sways in the Wind, 1966; Korea & the Koreans, 6 vols., 1969; From that Spinning Wheel, the Fatal Yarn, 1972; My Son, This is your Fatherland, 1973; (novel) The General's Moustache, 1966. Contbr. to Literature & Thought (Ed.-in-Chief). Mbrships: Korean Writers' Assn.; Korean Coun., PEN. Address: 1-115 Sung-Buk Dong, Sung-Buk Ku, Seoul, Korea.

LEE, Polly Jae Gardiner, pen names GARDINER, Jae; LEE, Gardiner, b. Toledo, Lucas, Ohio, USA. Author; Photographer. Educ: Univ. of Hawaii. Publs: Giant. Contbr. to: Viva; San Fran. Examiner; Ohio Wholesale Wine Dealers Annual. Address: P.O. Box 1679, San Fran., CA 94101, USA.

LEE, Robert, b. 28 Apr. 1929, San Fran., Calif., USA. Educator; Theologian; Author. Educ: B.A., Univ. of Calif., Berkeley; M.A., Pacific Schl. of Relig., Berkeley; B.D., Union Theol. Sem., N.Y.; Ph.D., Columbia Univ. Publs. incl: Social Sources of Church Unity, 1960; Religion & Leisure in America, 1964; The Church & the Exploding Metropolis, 1966; The Schizophrenic Church, 1969; The Spouse Gap (w. M. Casebier), 1971. Contbr. to num. soc. & relig. jrnls. Mbrships incl: Fellow, Soc. for Relig. in Higher Educ. Hons. incl: Sr. Fellow, East-West Ctr., 1972-73. Address: Inst. of Ethics & Society, San Fran. Theological Sem., San Anselmo, CA, USA.

LEE, Robert E(dwin), b. 15 Oct. 1918, Elyria, Ohio, USA. Playwright; Lecturer. Theatre Arts, University of California, Los Angeles, 1967—. Educ: Northwestern, Ohio Wesleyan, Western Reserve & Drake Univs. Plays (all w. Jerome Lawrence) incl: Look, Ma, I'm Dancin', (musical) first produced NYC, 1948; Inherit the Wind, first produced Broadway 1955; Auntie Mame, first produced Broadway 1956 (musical adaptation 'Mame' first produced Broadway 1966); Only in America, first produced Broadway 1959; A Call on Kuprin, first produced Broadway 1961; Dear World, (musical) first produced Broadway 1969; The Incomparable Max, first produced Broadway 1971. Filmscripts (w. Jerome Lawrence): Auntie Mame, 1959; Inherit the Wind, 1960; radio & TV progs. Mbrships. incl: Co-Fndr., Bd. of Govs., Am. Playwrights Theatre, 1963—; Co-Fndr., Bd. of Trustees, Margo Jones Award Inc., 1960—; Dramatists Guild; Acad. Motion Picture Arts & Scis.; Nat. Acad. TV Arts & Scis. Recip., num. awards (4 for Inherit the Wind). Agent: Harold Freedman, Brandt & Brandt. Address: 15725 Royal Oak Rd., Encino, CA 91316, USA.

LEE, Virginia Wilson, b. 25 Aug. 1907, Hominy, Okla., USA. Teacher; Librarian. Educ: B.S., 1948, M.Ed., 1956, Univ. of Houston, Tex.; Publs: The Lords Valley, 1963; Derrick Tall, 1972, Spanish ed., 1974. Contbr. to: Tex. Outlook, 1958; Anthol. of Am. Short Stories, 1961; Nev. Libs., 1968-74; Beating Wings, 1970. Mbrships: Pres., Nev. Assn. Schl. Libns., ALA, 1972-74; Nat. & State Deleg., 1966-74; Pres., Lyon Co., NEA, 1965-67; Writers' Coop., Can. Address: P.O. Box 162, Fernley, NV 89408, USA.

LEE, William Rowland, b. Uxbridge, Middx., UK. Author; Teacher Trainer; Lecturer. Educ: M.A., London Univ.; Ph.D., Prague Univ., Czech. Publs. incl.: Teach Yourself Czech (w. Z. Lee), 1959; Simple Audio-Visual Aids to Foreign Language Teaching (w. H. Coppen), 1968 rev.; Language-Teaching Games & Contests, 1969; The Argonauts English Course (w. L. Koullis), 1965-73; The Dolphin English Course, 1970-74. Contbr. to: Engl. Lang. Tchng. Jrnl. (Ed.). Mbrships. incl: Int. Assn., Tchrs. of Engl. as a For. Lang. (Fndr. & Chmn.). Recip., Hon. Fellowship, Trinity Coll. of Music, London, 1972. Address: 16 Alexandra Gdns., Hounslow, Middx. TW3 4HU, UK.

LEE, Ying, pen name MIAO, Yung Yu Kwun, b. 18 Apr. 1927, Canton, China. Editor. Educ: B.A., Kwungtung Nat. Univ. Publs: Critical Reviews of Chinese Poetry, 1960; About the Arts, 1964; Heart Song, 1970; The Clouded Peak, 1975. Contbr. to: Asia Int.; Current Lit. Mbr., PEN. Address: Emerald Court 158, 2 Nga Tsin Wai Road, Kowloon, Hong Kong.

LEEDS, Morton Harold, b. 15 May 1921, NYC, USA. Government Executive. Educ: B.S.Sc., CCNY, 1944; M.A., Grad.Fac., New Schl. for Soc. Rsch., 1948; Ph.D., ibid, 1950. Publs: Aging in Indiana, 1959; The Aged, The Social Worker & The Community, 1961; Geriatric Institutional Management (w. Herbert Shore), 1964; Washington Colloquium on Science & Society, 2nd series, 1967; Jackstones (poetry), 1970; Outgrowing Self-Deception (w. Gardner Murphy), 1974. Contbr. of articles & poems to jrnls. & chapts. to books. Mbr., sev. profl. orgs. Address: 6219 Lone Oak Dr., Bethesda, MD 20034, USA.

LEEDY, Paul D., b. 4 Mar. 1908, Harrisburg, Pa., USA. University Professor. Educ: A.B., Dickinson Coll., Carlise, Pa., 1930; M.A., Univ. of Pa., 1938; Ph.D., N.Y. Univ., 1958. Publs: The Wonderful World of Books (co-auth.), 1952; Reading Improvement for Adults, 1956; Read with Speed & Precision, 1963; Improve Your Reading, 1963; Perspectives in Reading, 1964; A Key to Better Reading, 1968; Practical Research: Planning & Design, 1974. Contbr. to: Psychol. Abstracts; Vital Speeches of the Day; Schl & Soc.; Jrnl. of Reading; etc. Mbrships. incl: Int. Reading Assn. Recip., Fndrs. Day Award for Disting. Serv., N.Y. Univ., 1958. Address: 3690 38th St., N.W., Wash. DC 20016, USA.

LEEMING, Owen, b. 1 Aug. 1930, Christchurch, NZ. Writer. Educ: B.A., M.A., Univ. of Canterbury, NZ. Publs: White Gardenia (TV biog.), 1968; Order (radio play), 1969; Yellow (radio play), 1970; The Quarry Game (stage play), 1970; Reefer's Boys (radio play), 1971; Venus Is Setting (poems), 1972. Contbr. to: London Mag.; Landfall; Islands. Recip., Katherine Mansfield Menton Mem. Fellowship, 1970. Address: 21 Rue de 1a Liberté, 13980 Alleins, France.

LEES, John David, b. 27 Aug. 1936, Bury, Lancs., UK. University Teacher. Educ: B.A. Oxon.; M.A., Mich., USA; Ph.D., Manchester, UK. Publs: The Committee System of the U.S. Congress, 1967; The Political System of the United States, 1969, 1974; (co-ed.) Political Parties in Modern Britain, 1972; (co-ed.) Committees in Legislatures: A Comparative Analysis, 1975. Contbr. to: Parliamentary

Affairs; Jrnl. of Am. Studies; Govt. & Opposition; Pub. Admin; New Outlook; Pol. Studies; Int. Affairs; Dictionary of World Hist.; Rivista Italiana de Scienza Pol. Mbrships: Pol. Studies Assn.; Comm., Brit. Assn. for Am. Studies; Am. Pol. Sci. Assn. Recip., 1965 Gilbert Campion Award. Address: 25 Larchwood, Keele Univ., Staffs. ST5 5BB, UK.

LEFCOE, George, b. 18 Feb. 1938, Jersey City, N.J., USA. Law Professor. Educ: B.A., Dartmouth Coll.; LL.B.(J.D.), Yale Law Schl. Publs: Land Development Law, 1966, 2nd ed., 1974; Land Finance Law, 1969; Introduction to American Land Law, 1974. Contbr. to law jrnls. inclng: Yale Law Jrnl.; Stanford Law Review; Southern Calif. Law Review. Mbr., Fla. Bar Assn. Address: 972 Ocean Front, Santa Monica, CA 90403, USA.

LEFEBVRE, Jean-Jacques, pen name CONSTANT, Philippe, b. 4 Aug. 1905, St-Philippe-de-Laprairie, Can. Archivist. Educ: Litt.B., Univ. of Montreal, 1926. Publs. incl: Les Canadiens-Français d'aujourd'hui, 1940; William Smith (1769-1847) son History of Canada, 1946; Le Canada, l'Amérique, 1954, 2nd ed. 1968; Sir Wilfrid Laurier, sa famille, 1969; La Famille Lamarre, de Longueuil, 1970; La Famille Bourassa, de Laprairie, 1971. Contbr. to: Revue du Barreau; Revue du Notariat; Bulletin des Recherches historiques; Québec Hist.; & num. other histl. jrnls. Num. mbrships. incl: Past Sec. & VP, Soc. Hist. Montréal; Past Pres.. Quebec Libns. Assn. Address: 3540 rue Durocher (15), Montreal 130, Can.

LEFF, Gordon, b. 9 May 1926, London, UK. Professor of History. Educ: B.A., Ph.D., King's Coll., Cambridge; Litt.D. Publs: Bradwardine & the Pelagians, 1957; Mediaeval Thought, 1958; The Tyranny of Concepts, 1961; Gregory of Rimini, 1961; Richard Fitzralph, 1963; Heresy in the Later Middle Ages, 2 vols., 1967; Paris & Oxford Universities in the 13th & 14th Centuries, 1968; History & Social Theory, 1969; William of Ockham; The Metamorphosis of Scholastic Discourse, in press. Contbr. to: Engl. Histl. Review; Encounter; Times Lit. Supplement; etc. Address: The Sycamores, 12 The Village, Strensall, York YO3 8XS, UK.

LEFF, Vera, b. 24 July 1913, Edinburgh, UK. Writer. Publs: (non-fiction) The School Health Service (w. S. Leff); From Witchcraft to World Health (w. S. Leff); Health & Humanity (w. S. Leff); The Search for Sanity (w. S. Leff); The Greatness of London; Scunthorpe — our Town; Riverside Story (The History of the Borough of Bermondsey); The Story of Tower Hamlets; (fiction) The Struggle; The Wife of the Prisoner; Sev. BBC broadcasts. Contbr. to: Better Health; Parents; The Hosp.; Humanist. Mbr., Humanist Soc. Address: 598 Finchley Rd., London NW11, UK.

LEFFELAAR, Hendrik Louis, b. 20 Jan. 1929, Amsterdam, Netherlands. Journalist. Educ: LL.B., LL.M., Univ. of Leiden. Publs: Het Kaartenhuis in Dixie, 1958; Leven op Rantsoen, 1959; Through a Harsh Dawn, 1963; Israel: De Langste Week, 1967. Contbr. to: De Gids; Literair Paspoort. Hons: Citation, Reina Prinsen Geerligs Prize, 1955. Address: 6401 32nd St. N.W., Wash., DC 20015, USA.

LEFLAR, Robert A., b. 22 Mar. 1901, Siloam Springs, Ark., USA. Law Teacher. Educ: B.A., Univ. of Ark., 1922; LL.B., 1927, S.J.D., 1932, Harvard Univ., Publs: American Conflicts Law, 3rd ed., 1968; The First 100 Years: Centennial History, University of Arkansas, 1972; Appellate Judicial Opinions, 1974. Contbr. to: Harvard Law Review; N.Y. Univ. Law Review; other legal jrnls. Mbrships. incl: Ark. Constitutional Convention (Pres. 1968-70); Commission on Uniform State Laws, 1945—; Phi Beta Kappa. Recip., Am. Bar Fndn. Award for Legal Rsch., 1969. Address: 1717 W. Center St., Fayetteville, AR 72701, USA.

LE GALLIENNE, Eva, b. 11 Jan. 1899, London, UK. Actress; Director, Founder of Civic Repertory Company. Educ: Sevigne Coll., Paris, France. Publs. incl: (autobiog.) At 33, 1934; With a Quiet Heart, 1953; (transls.) Six Plays of Henrik Ibsen, 1957; Seven Tales of Hans Christian Andersen, 1959; The Wild Duck & Other Plays, 1961; The Nightingale, 1965; The Little Mermaid, 1971; (theatre) The Mystic in the Theatre, 1966; (play) Alice in Wonderland (w. Florida Friebus), 1932; (children's story) Flossie & Bossie, 1949. Contbr. to num. publs. Mbrships. incl: Actors' Equity Assn.; Dramatists' Guild. Hons. incl: Soc. Arts & Sci. Gold Medal, 1934; Women's Nat. Press Club Outstanding Woman of the Year Award, 1947; Recip. many acad. hons. Address: N. Hillside Rd., Weston, CT 06880, USA.

LEGUM, Colin, b. 3 Jan. 1919, Kestell, Orange Free State, S. Africa. Journalist; Author; University Lecturer. Publs. incl: Attitude to Africa (co-author), 1951; Must We Lose Africa?, 1954; Bandung, Cairo & Accra, 1958; Congo Disaster, 1960; Pan-Africanism: A Political Guide, 1962, 2nd ed., 1965; Ed., Africa Handbook, 1963, 3rd ed., 1968; South Africa: Crisis for the West, (w. M. Legum), 1964; Ed., Aambia — Independence & After, 1966; The Bitter Choice (co-author), 1968; The Africa Contemporary Record, 1969, 7th ed., 1975. Contbr. to: The Observer (Africa & C'wlth. Corres., 1949—, Assoc. Ed., 1969—); BBC Radio & TV, etc. Address: 15 Denbigh Gardens, Richmond Surrey, UK.

LEHMANN, John Frederick, b. 2 June 1907, Bourne End, Bucks., UK. Poet; Critic; Biographer; Editor; Publisher; University Professor. Educ: Eton; Trinity Coll., Cambridge. Publs. incl: A Garden Revisited, 1931; Evil Was Abroad, 1938; New Writing in Europe, 1940; Forty Poems, 1942; The Age of the Dragon, 1951; Ancestors & Friends, 1962; Collected Poems, 1963; (autobiography) The Whispering Gallery, 1955; I Am My Brother, 1960; The Ample Proposition, 1966; A Nest of Tigers (The Sitwells in Their Times), 1968; Virginia Woolf & Her World, 1975; Ed. var. anthologies. Contbr. to: London Mag., (Ed.); New Writing, (Ed.); Orpheus, (Ed.); BBC; etc. Mbrships. incl: Pres., Royal Lit. Fund, 1966—; Alliance Française in GB, 1955-63; F.R.S.L. Hons. incl: Legion of Honour, C.B.E. Address: 85 Cornwall Gdns., London SW7, UK.

LEHMANN, Rosamund Nina. Novelist. Educ: Girton Coll., Cambridge. Publs: Dusty Answer, 1927; A Note in Music, 1930; Invitation to the Waltz, 1932; The Weather in the Streets, 1936; (play) No More Music, 1939; The Ballad & the Source, 1944; The Gypsy's Baby, 1946; The Echoing Grove, 1953; The Swan in the Evening, 1967. Address: 70 Eaton Sq., London SW1, UK.

LEHMANN, William C(hristian), b. 29 Nov. 1888, Slater, Iowa, USA. Retired Professor of Sociology. Educ: B.A., Lakeland Coll., Sheboygan, Wis., 1910; B.D., Vanderbilt Univ., 1917; M.A., 1919; Ph.D., Columbia Univ., 1930. Publs: Adam Ferguson & the Beginnings of Modern Sociology, 1930; John Miller of Glasgow 1735-1801: His Life & Thought & His Contributions to Sociological Analysis, 1960; Henry Home, Lord Kames & the Scottish Enlightenment, 1971; Scottish Contributions to Early American Life & Culture, forthcoming. Contbr. to profl. jrnls. Mbrships: Am. Sociol. Soc.; AAUP. Address: 2200 19th St., N.W., apt. 805, Wash. DC 20009, USA.

LEHMBERG, Stanford Eugene, b. 23 Sept. 1931, McPherson, Kan., USA. Historian. Educ: B.A., 1953, M.A., 1954, Univ. of Kan., Ph.D., Cambridge Univ., UK, 1956. Publs: Sir Thomas Elyot, Tudor Humanist, 1960; Sir Walter Mildmay & Tudor Government, 1965; The Reformation Parliament, 1529-1536, 1970; Sir Thomas Elyot, The Book Named the Governor (ed.). Contbr. to: Engl. Histl. Review; Histl. Jrnl.; Renaissance Quarterly; Can. Jrnl. of Hist.; etc. Mbr. & Pres., Minn. Br., Engl.-Speaking Union. Address: Dept. of History, University of Minnesota, Minneapolis, MN 55455, USA.

LEIGHTON, Alexander Hamilton, b. 17 July 1908, Phila., Pa., USA. Professor of Social Psychiatry. Educ: B.A., Princeton Univ., 1932; M.A., Cambridge Univ., 1934; M.D., Johns Hopkins Univ., 1936. Publs. incl: Human Relations in a Changing World, 1949; My Name is Legion, 1959; An Introduction to Social Psychiatry, 1960; Psychiatric Disorder Among the Yoruba (co-author), 1963; The Character of Danger, 1963; Come Near (novel), 1971. Contbr. to schlrly. jrnls. Mbr., num. profl. orgs. Recip. num. acad. hons. Address: Harvard Schl. of Pub. Hlth., 677 Huntington Ave., Boston, MA 02115, USA.

LEIS, Henry Patrick, Jr., b. 12 Aug. 1914, Saranac Lake, N.Y., USA. Surgeon; Clinical Professor. Educ: B.S., Fordham Univ., 1936; M.D., N.Y. Med. Coll., 1941. Publs: Diagnosis & Treatment of Breast Lesions, 1970; num. chapter contbns. inclng. The Second Breast; Changing Concepts in Breast Cancer; The Search for the High Risk Patient; etc. Contbr. to: Jrnl. of Breast (Assoc. Ed.); Jrnl. of Int. Surgery (Cons. Ed., Oncology); Jrnl. Soc. for Acad. Achievement (Ed. Bd.); & num. med. jrnls. Mbrships. incl: AAAS; AAUP; WHO; Am. Med. Writers' Assn.; Int. Platform Assn.; (Fellowships) Am. Coll. Surgeons; Int. Coll. Surgeons (Hon.); N.Y. Acad. Med.; Royal Soc. Health, UK.

Hons: Kt., Mil. & Hosp. Order of St. Lazarus of Jerusalem, 1971; Alumni Medal, N.Y. Med. Coll., 1973; & num. others. Address: 147-03 5th Ave., Whitestone, NY 11357, USA.

LEISTER, Lois Anderson, b. 14 Oct. 1928, New Kensington, Pa., USA. Contbr. to: Better Camping Mag.; Modern Images; Jean's Jrnl.; Am. Poet; Prairie Poet; United Poets; Cyclo-Flame. Mbr., Md. Poetry Soc. Hons: 1st Prize, Spenserian Sonnet Contest, 1969; 1st Prize, Quatrain Contest, 1970; 1st Prize, Ballad Contest, 1970; Num. ed. staff citations for excellence. Address: 4112 Ryon Rd., Upper Marlboro, MD 20870, USA.

LEITER, Robert David, b. 2 June 1922, NYC, USA. Professor of Economics. Educ: B.S., CCNY, 1941; M.A., 1944, Ph.D., 1947, Columbia Univ. Publs. incl: Labor Problems & Trade Unionism, 1952, 5th ed. (new title, Labor Economics & Industrial Relations), 1962; The Teamsters Union: A Study of its Economic Impact, 1957; Featherbedding & Job Security, 1964; Modern Economics, 1969, 3rd ed., 1971; Costs & Benefits of Education (ed.), 1974. Contbr. to num. profl. jrnls. Pres., Metrop. Econ. Assn., NYC, 1957-58. Recip., Rockefeller Fndn. Award, 1954-56. Address: 263 West End Ave., N.Y., NY 10023, USA.

LEJEUNE, Jean, b. 18 June 1914, Herstal, Belgium. Professor, University of Liège. Educ: B.A., 1936, Ph.D., 1938, Agrégé de l'enseignement supérieur, 1948, Univ. de Liège. Publs: La Formation du Capitalisme Moderne dans la Principauté de Liège au XVIe Siècle, 1939; Liège et son Pays. Naissance d'une Patrie (XIIIe — XIVe s.), 1948; La Principauté de Liège, 2nd ed., 1949; Les Van Eyck, Peintres de Liège et de sa Cathédrale, 1956; Liège et l'Occident, 1958; Pays sans Frontière (Aix-la-Chapelle, Liège, Maastricht), 1958; Art Mosan aux XIe & XIIe s., 1961; Liège & Bourgogne, 1968; Liège de la Principauté à la Métropole, 3rd ed., 1974. Contbr. to sev. histl. jrnls. Mbr., sev. histl. socs. & comms. Hons. incl: Michel Perret Prize, Inst. of France, 1941; Rouveroy Prize, Free Soc. of Emulation, 1960. Address: Rue du Rêwe, 2 bis, 4000 Liège, Belgium.

LeMASTER, J. R., b. 29 Mar. 1934, Pike Co., Ohio, USA. Professor of English. Educ: B.S., Defiance Coll., 1959; M.A., 1962; Ph.D., 1970, Bowling Green State Univ. Publs: Poets of the Midwest, 1966; The Heart Is a Gypsy, 1967; Children of Adam, 1971. Contbr. of poetry & articles to num. jrnls. Mbrships. incl: S. & W. Lit. Soc.; Ky. State Poetry Soc. Recip., S. & W. Publ. Award, 1970. Address: Dept. of Engl., Defiance Coll., Defiance, OH 43512, USA.

LEMBKE, Janet Nutt, b. 2 Mar. 1933, Cleveland, Ohio, USA. Housewife. Educ: A.B., Middlebury Coll., Vt., 1953. Publs: Bronze & Iron: Old Latin Poetry from its Beginnings to 100 B.C., 1973; Transl. & Ed., Aeschylus, Suppliants, 1975. Contbr. to: Arion; Publrs. Wkly.; Carleton Miscellany; Minn. Review; Sparrow; N.M. Quarterly; Poetry Northwest; etc. Mbr., PEN (Am. Ctr.). Recip., Fellowship, Ford Fndn. Nat. Transl. Ctr., Austin, Tex., 1968-69. Address: 6 Snowflake Lane, Westport, CT 06880, USA.

LENGYEL, Balázs, b. 21 Aug. 1918, Budapest, Hungary. Literary Critic; Editor. Educ: Dr. of Pol. Sci. Publs: A mai magyar lira, 1948; Ezüstgaras, 1955; Hagyomány és kisérlet, 1971; A török Magyarországon, 1972; Verseskönyvről verseskönyvre, 1975. Contbr. to: Élet és Irodalom. Mbrships: Hungarian Authors Assn.; PEN Club. Address: Naphegy utca 28, Budapest 1, Hungary.

LENGYEL, Cornel Adam, b. 1 Jan. 1915, Fairfield, Conn., USA. Author. Publs. incl: American Testament: The Story of a Promised Land, 1956; Four Days in July, 1958; I, Benedict Arnold: The Anatomy of Treason, 1960; Presidents of the USA, 1961; Ethan Allan & the Green Mountain Boys, 1961; Three Plays, 1964; Fifty Poems, 1965; The Declaration of Independence, 1969; The Creative Self, 1971. Contbr. to: Poet Lore; Coast; Argonaut; Menorah Jrnl.; Poet; var. lit. anthols.; etc. Mbrships. incl: Poetry Soc. of Am.; World Poetry Soc.; Authors Guild; AAUP. Hons. incl: Alice Fay di Castagaola Award, Poetry Soc. of Am., 1971. Address: Adam's Acres W., Georgetown, CA 95634, USA.

LENGYEL, József, b. 4 Aug. 1896, Marcali, Hungary. Writer. Educ: Univ. Publs: Prenn's Drifting; Acta Sanctorum; From Beginning to End; The Judge's Chair; Confrontation. Recip., Kossut Prize, 1964. Address: 1014 Budapest 1, Toth A. Setany 30, Hungary.

LENGYEL, Menyhert Melchior, b. 12 Jan. 1880, Hungary. Writer; Dramatist. Publs. incl: libretto for Bartok's The Miraculous Mandarin; (play) Typhoon, 1907; (film scripts) To Be or not To Be; Angle; Cat; Ninochka. Recip., Grand Prix, Rome, 1963. Address: Via Porta Pinciana 16a, Rome, Italy.

LENGYEL, Péter, b. 4 Sept. 1939, Budapest, Hungary. Novelist. Educ: Budapest Univ. of Scis. Eötvös Loránd. Publs: transls. of works by Salinger, Hemingway, Moravia, Pirandello, etc.; Két sötétedés, 1969; Ogg második bolygója, 1971; Mellékszereplök, forthcoming. Contbr. to: Kortars; Uj Iras; Elet es Irodalom. Mbrships: Hungarian Writers Assn.; Exec. Comm., Hungarian PEN. Hons: 2nd Prize for Short Story, Reg. Concours for Young Writers, Ctrl. & Eastern Europe, Int. PEN & Int. Writers Fund. Address: Branyiszko 25, 1026 Budapest, Hungary.

LENZ, Siegfried, b. 17 Mar. 1926. Writer. Educ: Univ. of Hamburg. Publs: (novels) es waren Habichte in der Luft, 1951; Duell mit dem Schatten, 1953; So Zärtlich War Suleyken, 1955; Der Mann im Strom, 1957; Brot & Spiele, 1959; Stadtgespräch, 1963; Deutschstunde, 1968; Das Vorbild, 1973; (stories) Jäger des Spotts, 1958; Das Feuerschiff, 1960; (plays) Zeit der Schuldlosen, 1961; Das Gesicht, 1963; Haussuchung, 1967. Contbr. to: Die Welt, 1949-51. Hons: Hauptmann Prize, 1961; Bremer Lit. Prize, 1962. Address: Oberstr. 72, Hamburg 13, W. Germany.

LEON, (His Honour) Henry Cecil, pen name CECIL, Henry, b. 19 Sept. 1902. Former County Court Judge; Chairman, British Copyright Council. Educ: King's Coll., Cambridge; Barrister-at-Law. Publs. incl: (fiction) Full Circle, 1948; Ways & Means, 1952; Brothers in Law, 1955, film, 1957; Much in Evidence, 1957; Sober as a Judge, 1958; The Buttercup Spell, 1971; The Wanted Man, 1972; Truth with Her Boots On, 1974; (non-fiction) Know About English Law, 1965; The English Judge, 1970; (plays) A Woman Named Anne, 1970; The Tilted Scales, 1970. also TV series Brothers in Law; Mr. Justice Duncannon & num. radio plays. Recip., M.C. Address: 6 Gray's Inn Sq., London WC1, UK.

LEONARD, Edith Marian, b. 2 Nov. 1896, San Bernardino, Calif., USA. Counselor; Author; Emeritus Professor. Educ: A.B., Nat. Coll. of Educ., Evanston, Ill.; M.A., Claremont Coll. Grad. Schl., Calif.; grad. studies, Northwestern Univ., Evanston, 1939. Publs. incl: Foundations of Learning in Childhood Education (w. D. D. VanDeman & L. E. Miles), 1963; Basic Learning in the Language Arts (w. VanDeman & Miles), 1965; through FAITH the VICTORY (w. D. D. VanDeman), 1967, 2nd ed., 1971. Contbr., articles to educl. jrnls. & chapts. to books. Mbr., num. profl. orgs. Address: P.O. Drawer JJ, Santa Barbara, CA 93102, USA.

LEONARD, Elmore, b. 11 Oct. 1925, New Orleans, La., USA. Novelist; Screenwriter. Educ: Ph.B., Univ. of Detroit. Publs., 11 novels, inclng: Hombre, 1961; The Moonshine War, 1969; Valdez Is Coming, 1969; Fifty-Two Pickup, 1974; Mr. Majestyk, 1974. Has had 11 novels or screenplays accepted for motion picture prodn. Mbrships: Writers Guild of Am., W.; Authors Guild; Western Writers of Am. Address: 420 Suffield, Birmingham, MI 48009, USA.

LEONARD, Hugh, b. 9 Nov. 1926, Dublin, Repub. of Ireland. Playwright. Publs. incl: (stage plays) The Big Birthday, 1956; A Leap in the Dark, 1957; Stephen D., 1960; The Quick & the Dead, 1966; The Au Pair Man, 1967; Da, 1973; Summer, 1974; (TV plays) The Second Wall; Love Life; Silent Song; (TV series) Me Mammy; (TV adaptations) Dombey and Son; The Moonstone; Wuthering Heights; Country Matters; Father Brown etc. Contbr. to: Books & Bookmen; Plays and Players; Hibernia Mbrships. incl: PEN; Dramatist's Club; Writers' Guild. Hons: Italia Award for Silent Song, 1966; Jacobs TV Award. Address: Killiney Heath, Killiney, Co. Dublin, Repub. of Ireland.

LEONHARDT, Rudolf Walter, b. 9 Feb. 1921, Altenburg, Thuringia, Germany. Journalist. Educ: Ph.D., Bonn Univ., 1950; Univs. Cambridge, London. Publs: 77 mal England, 1957, transl'd into Spanish, 1964; Xmal Deutschland, 1961, transl'd into Engl., Italian, Spanish, 1964; Reise in ein fernes Land (w. Marion Graefin Doenhoff & Theo Sommer), 1964, transl'd into Japanese, 1965; Wer wirft den ersten Stein, 1969; Drei Wochen und drei Tage in Japan, 1970; Deutschland, 1972; Argumente, 1974; Heines Mädchen und Frauen, 1975. Contbr. to: Die Zeit; Neue Zürcher Zeitung; Guardian; Sunday Times;

Times Lit. Supplement; N.Y. Times. Address: 2 Hamburg 50, Elbchaussee 81, W. Germany.

LEONOV, Leonid Maximovich, b. 31 May 1899, Moscow, Russia. Writer. Educ: Moscow Univ. Publs: Barsuky, 1924; The Thief, 1927; Sotj, 1930; Skutarevsky, 1932; Road to the Ocean, 1936; The Ordinary Man, 1941; Lenushka, 1943; The Fall of Velikoshumsk, 1944; The Golden Car, 1946; Sazancha, 1959; Mr. McKinley's Flight, 1961; Eugenia Ivanovna, 1963; Plays, 1964. Mbrships: USSR Acad. of Sci.; USSR Union of Writers. Hons. incl: State Prize, 1942; Lenin Prize, 1957; Order of Lenin. (4 times); Red Banner of Labour; etc. Address: Union of Soviet Writers, 52 Ulitsa Vorovskogo, Moscow, USSR.

LEONTIEF, Wassily, b. 5 Aug. 1906, Leningrad, Russia. Professor of Economics. Educ: Dept. of Econs., Univ. of Leningrad, 1925; Ph.D., Univ. of Berlin, Germany, 1928. Publs: The Structure of American Economy, 1919-39, 1941; Studies in the Structure of the American Economy, 1953; Input-Output Economics, 1966; Essays in Economics, 1966. Contbr. to var. acad. jrnls. Address: Littauer 309, Harvard University, Cambridge, MA 02138, USA.

LEOV, Jordan, b. 29 Aug. 1920, Titov Veles, Yugoslavia. Deputy Public Defence Lawyer, Macedonia. Educ: Fac. of Law. Publs. incl: (play) Blossoming Jasmine, 1957; short stories Stronger than Death, 1952; The Lost World, 1957; (novels) Bosom Friends, 1956; Deaf Dawns, 1960; Poppy, 1964; Anthology of Pain, 1968; (TV play) Romance of the Hanged Man, 1972. Contbr. to: Prosveta (Chief Ed.); Nova Macedonia; Sovremenost; Razgledi; Macedonian Review. Mbrships: Soc. of Writers, Yugoslavia; Cultural & Educl. Assn. of Macedonia (VP); PEN. Recip., Kliment Ohridski Prize, Soc. of Writers, Macedonia. Address: Mito Xadzivasilev 48 Vlez IV st. 20, 91000 Skopje, Yugoslavia.

LE PATOUREL, John, b. 29 July 1909, Guernsey, Channel Islands, UK. Emeritus Professor, University of Leeds. Educ: M.A., Ph.D., Jesus Coll., Oxford Univ. Publs: The Medieval Administration of the Channel Islands, 1937; The Manor & Borough of Leeds, 1957; The Building of Castle Cornet, Guernsey, 1958. Contbr. to: Engl. Histl. Review; History; Revue du Nord. Mbrships: Fellow, Royal Histl. Soc. (VP, 1968-70). Hons: Doct., Univ. of Caen, 1957; Fellow, Brit. Acad., 1972. Address: Westcote, Hebers Ghyll Dr., Ilkley, W. Yorks. LS29 9QH, UK.

LERNER, Alan Kjay, b. 31 Aug. 1918, NYC, USA. Theatrical Writer; Producer. Educ: Harvard Univ. Prods. incl: (stage) The Patsy, 1942; Brigadoon, 1947; Paint Your Wagon, 1951; My Fair Lady, 1956; Camelot, 1960; On a Clear Day You Can See Forever, 1964; Coco, 1969; (films) An American In Paris, 1951; Gigi, 1958; My Fair Lady, 1964; Camelot, 1968; Paint Your Wagon, 1969; On a Clear Day You Can See Forever, 1970. Mbrships: Dramatist's Guild of Am., (Pres., 1958-63); Pres., Commn. for a Nat. Cultural Centre, Wash. Address: 745 Fifth Ave., N.Y., NY 10022, USA.

LERNER, Laurence David, b. 12 Dec. 1925, Cape Town, S. Africa. University Teacher; Writer. Educ: B.A., 1944, M.A., 1945, Cape Town; B.A.(Hons.), 1949, Cambridge, UK. Publs: (poetry) Domestic Interior, 1959; The Directions of Memory, 1964; Selves, 1969; A.R.T.H.U.R., 1974; (fiction) The Englishmen, 1959; A Free Man, 1968; (criticism) The Truest Poetry, 1960; The Truthtellers, 1967; The Uses of Nostalgia, 1972; An Introduction to English Poetry, 1975. Contbr. to: Encounter; London Mag.; New Statesman; Sunday Times; Essays in Criticism; Critical Quarterly; etc. Address: 232 New Church Rd., Hove, Sussex, UK.

LERNER, Max, b. 20 Dec. 1902, Ivenitz, Russia. Editor; Universtiy Professor. Educ: B.A.; M.A.; Ph.D.; Univs. of Yale & Wash. Publs. incl: It is Later Than You Think, 1938; Ideas are weapons, 1939; Ideas for the Ice Age, 1941; Public Journal, 1945; The World of the Great Powers, 1947; Actions & Passions, 1948; The Unfinished Country, 1959; Education & a Radical Humanism, 1962; The Age of Overkill, 1962; Tocqueville's Democracy in America, 1966; Tocqueville & American Civilization, 1969. Contbr. to: Ency. of the Social Sci.; Ed., Nation, 1936-38; N.Y. Post; New Republic; etc. Mbr., Nat. Emergency Coun. Address: 445 E. 84th St., N.Y., NY 10028, USA.

LERNER, Robert Earl, b. 8 Feb. 1940, NYC, USA. Professor of History. Educ: B.A., Univ. of Chgo.; M.A.,

Ph.D., Princeton Univ. Publs: The Age of Adversity: Europe in the Fourteenth Century, 1968; The Heresy of the Free Spirit in the Later Middle Ages, 1972; One Thousand Years: Western Europe in the Middle Ages, (co-author), 1974. Contbr. to: Speculum; Am. Histl. Review; Ch. Hist.; French Histl. Studies; Modern Philol.; Archiv für Kulturgeschichte; Deutsches Archiv für Erforschung des Mittelalters. Mbrships: Mediaeval Acad. of Am.; Am. Histl. Assn. Hons. incl: Nat. Endowment for the Humanities Rsch. Fellow, 1972. Address: Dept. of History, Northwestern Univ., Evanston, IL 60201, USA.

LERNER, Warren, b. 16 July 1929, Boston, Mass., USA. Professor of History. Educ: B.S., Boston Univ., 1952; M.A., 1954, Ph.D., 1961, Columbia Univ. Publs: The Soviet World in Flux (co-ed. w. C. M. Foust), 1967; A Students Guide to Western Civilization, 1968; Karl Radek: The Last Internationalist, 1970; Studies in the Development of Soviet Foreign Policy (ed.), 1973. Contbr. to: S. Atlantic Quarterly; Law & Contemporary Soc.; Studies on the Soviet Union; Am. Histl. Review. Address: Center for International Studies, 2101 Campus Dr., Duke University, Durham, NC 27706, USA.

LERNET-HOLENIA, Alexander, b. 21 Oct. 1897, Vienna, Austria. Novelist; Playwright. Publs. incl: Ollapotrida, 1926; Die Abenteuer eines jungen Herrn in Polen, 1931; Die Standarte, 1934; Der Mann im Hut, 1937; Die Trophae, 1946; Mars in Widder, 1947; Das Feuer, 1949; Die Wege der Welt, 1952; Der junge Moncada, 1954; Der Graf Luna, 1955; Mayerling, 1960; Naundorff, 1961; Das Halsband der Königin, 1962; Götter & Menschen, 1964; Die Weisse Dame, 1965; Pilatus, 1967; Die Hexen, 1969; Die Geheimnisse des Hauses Österreich, 1971; Die Beschwörung des Herrn, 1973. Address: Hofburg, Vienna I, Austria.

LE ROI, David, b. 28 Jan. 1905, San Fran., Calif., USA. Research & Feature Critic, Look & Learn, Fleetway Publications, 1961-. Educ: Sydney Univ.; M.A.; B.Sc.; F.I.A.L. Publs. incl: Boy's Book of Jets, 1952; Boy's Book of Flight, 1957; Nuclear Power, 1959; Jet Propulsion; Radio, Radar & Television; Man Made Materials, 1960; Story of Agriculture; Story of Medicine, 1960; Eagle Book of Modern Wonders; A Thousand Answers to a Thousand Questions; How we get & use Oil, 1962; Aluminium Today; Science in the Twenty-First Century; Modern Inventions; Look at Roads; Treasure Book of Animals; Wonders of Nature; 1001 Questions & Answers; The Channel Tunnel, 1969; Inner Space; New Ideas for this Modern Age; In the Days of the Dinosaurs. Mbrships. incl: Inst. of Jrnlsts.; Nat. Union of Jrnlsts.; Soc. of Authors. Contbr. to: Liverpool Daily Post; New Scientist; Pictorial Educ.; Hospital Times; etc. Address: 12 Kirklees Rd., Thornton Heath, Surrey CR4 6HP, UK.

LESER, Norbert Franz, b. 31 May 1933, Oberwart, Burgenland, Austria. University Professor. Educ: LL.D., Univ. of Vienna, 1958. Publs: Zwischen Reformismus und Bolschewismus. Der Austromarxismus als Theorie und Praxis, 1968; Die Odyssee des Marxismus, 1971; Sozialismus zwischen Relativismus und Dogmatismus, 1974. Contbr. to: Int. Jrnl. of Contemporary Hist.; Kölner Zeitschrift für Soziologie; Salzburger Nachrichten. Mbrships: Vice-Chmn., Hans Kelsen Inst., Vienna; Co-Dir., Inst. for Pol. Sci., Univ. of Salzburg. Recip., Karl Renner Prize for pol. jrnlsm., 1967. Address: Vienna 16, Gablenzg. 82-86/8, Austria.

LESHAN, Eda J., b. 6 June 1922, NYC, USA. Writer. Educ: B.S., Tchrs. Coll., Columbia Univ.; M.A., Clark Univ. Publs: How to Survive Parenthood, 1965; The Conspiracy Against Childhood, 1967; Sex & your Teenager, 1969; Natural Parenthood, 1970; How do your Children Grow; What Makes Me Feel this Way, 1972; The Wonderful Crisis of Middle Age, 1973. Contbr. to: Rdrs. Digest; Redbook; McCalls; N.Y. Times Mag.; Woman's Day. Mbrships: Am. Psychol. Assn.; Assn. for Humanistic Psychol.; Am. Fed. of TV Artists; Nat. Acad. of TV Arts & Scis. Hons: Woman of the Yr., Brandies Univ. Womens Comm., 1973; Citation for Pub. Enlightenment, Homosexual Community Counselling Ctr., 1974. Address: 263 West End Ave., N.Y., NY 10023, USA.

LESHINSKY, Tania, b. 3 Sept. 1920, Uman, Russia. University Teacher of Russian & German Literature. Educ: A.M., Harvard Univ., 1943; Univ. Vienna. Publs: The Russian Novel, 1951; The Landing, 1953; (novel) L'Ombra Ribelle, 1960. Contbr. to: Am. Slavic Review: Collier's Ency.; Aufbau; Basler Nachrichten; Elle; Femina. Mbrships: Schweizerischer Schriftsteller Verband, Zürich; Int.

Schutzverband deutschsprächiger Schriftsteller, Zürich. Address: Mühleback Strasse 41, 8008 Zürich, Switz.

LESINS, Knuts, b. 28 Mar. 1909, St. Petersburg, Russia. Pianist; Music Teacher; Writer; Journalist. Educ: M.A., Latvian State Conservatoire of Music, Riga, 1932. Publs: (in Latvian) Omens in the Dark, 1938; Faces & Problems in Latvian Music, 1939; The Seal of Love, 1943; Reflections, 1946; Things That Arrange Themselves, 1948; The Wine of Eternity, 1949; John the Musician, 1950; The Proud Hearts, 1952; Dead End Street, 1955; Under Foreign Stars, 1956; The Last Home, 1957; Sunset in the Grass, 1962; (in Engl.) The Wine of Eternity, 1957. Contbr. to: Short Stories Int.; Arena; sev. Latvian jrnls. Mbrships: Nat. Writers' Club; PEN; Latvian Press Assn. Recip., Hon. Mention, Minn. Centennial Disting. Book Competition, USA, 1957. Address: 4824 14th Ave. S., Mpls., MN 55417, USA.

LESLIE, Anita, b. 21 Nov. 1914, London, UK. Author. Publs: Life of Rodin, 1939; Train to Nowhere, 1947; Love in a Nutshell, 1952; The Fabulous Leonard Jerome, 1954; Mrs. Fitzherbert, 1962; Jennie — Lady Randolph Churchill, 1968; Edwardians in Love, 1972. Address: Oranmore Castle, Co. Galway, Repub. of Ireland.

LESLY, Philip, b. 29 May 1918, Chgo., Ill., USA. Counsel to Management on Public Affairs & Mass Communications. Educ: B.S., Northwestern Univ., 1940. Publs: Public Relations: Principles & Procedures (co-author), 1945; Public Relations in Action, 1947; Public Relations Handbook, 1950, 3rd ed., 1967; Everything AND the Kitchen Sink, 1955; Lesly's Public Relations Handbook, 1971; The People Factor, 1974. Contbr. to: Ind. Week; The Freeman; Nat. Observer; PR Jrnl.; PR Quarterly; Vital Speeches; Podium Review; Jrnl of Marketing; Wall St. Jrnl. Mbr., var. profl. assns. Address: 33 N. Dearborn St., Chgo., IL 60602, USA.

LESSING, Doris, b. 22 Oct. 1919, Kermanshah, Iran. Writer. Num. publs. incl: The Grass is Singing, 1950; Martha Quest, 1952; A Proper Marriage, 1954; The Habit of Loving, 1957; A Ripple from the Storm, 1958; The Golden Notebook, 1962; A Man & Two Women, 1963; African Stories, 1964; Landlocked, 1965; Particularly Cats, 1967; The Four-Gated City, 1969; Briefing for a Descent Into Hell, 1971; The Temptation of Jack Orkney, 1972; The Summer Before the Dark, 1973; This Was the Old Chief's Country, 1973; The Sun Between Their Feet, 1973; The Memoirs of a Survivor, 1974. Contbr. to num. jrnls. Mbrships: Hon., Am. Acad. Arts & Letters, & Nat. Inst. Arts & Letters, 1974; Hon. Fellow, MLA, 1974; Inst. of Cultural Rsch. Recip., Somerset Maugham Award, 1957. Agent: Curtis Brown.

LESTER, Reginald Mounstephens, b. 1 Oct. 1896, Hawkhurst, Kent, UK. Author & Chartered Journalist. Publs. incl: Practical Astronomy, 1944; Air Training Course: Meteorology, 1944; The Householder & The Law, 1947; Building or Buying a House, 1947; House Purchase, 1948; Everybody's Weather Book, 1948; Weather Prediction, 1949; In Search of the Hereafter, 1952, 2nd ed., 1956; Observer's Book of Weather, 1955; Christianity in the New Age, 1966. Contbr. to: Fin. Times (Estate Mkt. Corres., 1946-68); Homefinder (Ed., 1946-56); Sailors News (Ed., 1946-59. Mbrships. incl: Inst. Jrnlsts. (past Pres.); Fellow Royal Meteorol. Soc. Address: 57 Petitor Rd., Torquay, Devon TQ1 4QF, UK.

LESYTCH (-KIRSHAK), Wadym, b. 25 Feb. 1909, Ustia Zelene, Ukraine. Journalist; Editor. Educ: Mag. jur.; Dip., Schl. of Jrnlism. Publs: (poetry) Lirychnyi zoshyt, 1953; Rozmova z bat'kom, 1957; Kreidiane kolo, 1960; Kamiani luny, 1964; Vybrani poezii 1930-65, 1965; Predmetnist' nizvidkil', 1972; (essay) Nykyfor z Krynytsi, 1971. Contbr. to: Literaturno-Naukovyi Vistnyk; Arka; Kyiv; Arena; Slovo; Lysty do Pryiateliv; Suchasnist. Mbrships: Bd., Am. Br., PEN, Ctr. for Writers in Exile; Bd., SLOVO, Assn. of Ukrainian Writers in Exile. Address: c/o Ukrainian Acad. of Arts & Sciences in US, Inc., 206 West 100 St., N.Y., NY 10025, USA.

L'ETANG, Hugh Joseph Charles James, b. 23 Nov. 1917, London, UK. Editor. Educ: B.A., B.M., B.Ch., St. John's Coll., Oxford Univ.; St. Bartholomew's Hosp.; Harvard Schl. of Pub. Hlth., USA; Dip. in Indl. Hlth. Publ: The Pathology of Leadership, 1969. Contbr. to: The Practitioner (Ed.); Hist. of Medicine; Brassey's (Armed Forces) Annual; Jrnl., Royal United Servs. Inst. for Defence Studies; Army Quarterly; Jrnl. of Alcoholism. Mbrships:

Fellow, Royal Soc. Med.; Mil. Commentators' Circle (Hon. Sec.); Sherlock Holmes Soc. of London. Address: 27 Sispara Gdns., West Hill Rd., London SW18 1LG, UK.

LEUPEN, Herbert, b. 13 Feb. 1934, Amsterdam, Netherlands. Writer. Publs: 10 books since 1962, inclng: Muis in de Melk, 1969; Daho Zonder Tulband, 1969; Mag Ik Effe Ademhalen, 1970; Robert Townsend's Up the Organization (transl. into Dutch), 1970; Sporen van Gebruik, 1975; Maat 38, 1975. Contbr. to: Ave.-Literair; Muziek Expres. Address: Loodskotterhof 63, Amsterdam N, Netherlands.

LEVER, (Sir) Tresham Joseph Philip, Bt., b. 3 Sept. 1900, Leicester, UK. Author. Educ: M.A., Univ. Coll., Oxford. Publs: The Life & Times of Sir Robert Peel, 1942; The House of Pitt, 1947; Godolphin, His Life & Times, 1952; The Letters of Lady Palmerston (ed.), 1957; The Herberts of Wilton, 1967; Lessudden House, Sir Walter Scott & the Scotts of Raeburn, 1971; Clayton of Toc H, 1971. Contbr. to jrnls. & Times Lit. Supplement. Mbrships: Fellow, Royal Soc. of Lit.; Pres., Bronte Soc. Address: Lessudden, St. Boswells, Roxburghshire, UK.

LEVI, Paolo, b. 20 July 1919, Genova, Italy. Writer. Educ: Bachelorship. Publs. incl: (plays) Legittima difesa, 1952; Gli dei dipietra, 1956; Lastrico d'inferno, 1958. Hons: Microfono d'argento, for radio dramas, 1952; Premio St. Vincent, 1952, 1958/59; Premio Marzotto, 1956; Premio Riccione, 1958. Address: Via Ronciglione 20A, 00191 Rome, Italy.

LEVIN, Alvin Irving, b. 22 Dec. 1921, NYC, USA. University Professor; Educator; Composer-arranger, motion pictures, TV & theatre, 1945-65. Educ: B.M., Univ. of Miami, 1941; M.A., Calif. State Univ., 1955; Ed.D., Univ. of Calif., 1968. Publs: My Ivory Tower, 1950; Symposium: Values in Kaleidoscope, (monograph) 1973; Happy Land, (music-drama) 1971; (film scripts): Main Street Symphony, 1960; No Escape, 1961; The Last Judgment, 1961. Contbr. &/or compiler, sev. US Dept. of Educ. reports/reviews. Mbrships. incl: Fndr. & Pres., Alvin Irving Levin Philanthropic Fndn., L.A., 1973-; Bd. of Overseers, Calif. Schl. Profl. Psychol., 1974-; Int. Coun. on Educ. for Tchng.; Am. Statistical Assn.; AAUP. Address: 12416 Magnolia Blvd., N. Hollywood, CA 91607, USA.

LEVIN, Deana, b. 15 July 1906, London, UK. Teacher; Writer. Educ: B.A., London. Publs: Children in Soviet Russia, 1942; Soviet Education Today, 1959, 2nd ed., 1963; Leisure & Pleasure of Soviet Children, 1966; Moscow, Leningrad, Kiev: A Guide, 1973.

LEVIN, Meyer, b. 8 Oct. 1905, Chgo., Ill., USA. Novelist. Educ: Ph.B., Univ. of Chgo., USA. Publs: Reporter, 1929; Frankie & Johnny, 1930; Yehuda, 1931; The Golden Mountain, 1932; The New Bridge, 1933; The Old Bunch, 1937; Citizens, 1940; My Father's House, 1947; In Search, 1950; Compulsion, 1956; Eva, 1959; The Fanatic, 1964; The Stronghold, 1967; Gore & Igor, 1969; The Settlers, 1972; The Obsession, 1974. Contbr. to: Esquire; New Yorker; N.Y. Times Mag.; Commentary; Saturday Review; etc. Mbrships: PEN; Authors League. Address: Herzlia On Sea, Israel.

LEVINE, (Albert) Norman, b. 22 Oct. 1924, Ottawa, Ont., Can. Writer. Educ: B.A. 1948, M.A., 1949, McGill Univ., Montreal; King's Coll., London, UK, 1949-50. Publs: The Tightrope Walker (verse), 1950; The Angled Road (novel), 1952; Canada Made Me, 1958; One Way Ticket (short stories), 1961; Ed., Canadian Winter's Tales, 1968; From a Seaside Town (novel), 1970; I Don't Want to Know Anyone Too Well (short stories), 1971. Contbr. to: Spectator; Harper's Bazaar; etc. Hons: Fellowship, 1959, Arts Award, 1969, Can. Coun. Address: 45 Bedford Rd., St. Ives, Cornwall, UK.

LEVINE, Isaac Don, b. 1 Feb. 1892, Mozyr, Russia. Writer; Editor. Publs: The Russian Revolution, 1917; Yashka (w. Maria Botchkareva), 1918; The Resurrected Nations, 1919; The Man Lenin, 1924; Stalin, 1931; Mitchell: Pioneer of Air Power, 1943; The Mind of an Assassin, 1959; I Rediscover Russia, 1964; Intervention, 1969; Eyewitness to History (autobiog.), 1973. Contbr. to: Review of Reviews; Current History; Forum; Saturday Evening Post; Life; Rdr.'s Digest; New Repub.; etc. Address: Box 351, Waldorf, MD 20601, USA.

LEVINSON, Boris Mayer, b. 1 July 1907, Kalvarijah, Lithuania. Clinical Psychologist. Educ: B.S., City Coll.,

CUNY, USA, 1937; M.S., Schl. of Educ., ibid, 1938; Ph.D., N.Y. Univ., 1947. Publs: Problems of Jewish Religious Youth, 1959; Pet-Oriented Child Psychotherapy, 1970; Pets & Human Development, 1972. Contbr. to: Jrnl. of Genetic Pyschol.; Jrnl. of Clin. Psychol., Mental Hygiene; Psychol. Reports; Nat. Humane Review; Jrnl. of the Am. Vet. Med. Assn.; Mod. Vet. Practice; Perceptual & Motor Skills. Address: 86-35 Queens Blvd., Apt. 1-K, Elmhurst, NY 11373, USA.

LEVINSON, Maurice, b. 1911, Bessarabia, Russia. London Taxi Driver; Author; Journalist; Lecturer. Publs: The Trouble with Yesterday, 1946; The Desperate Passion of Henry Knopp, 1962; Taxi! 1963; The Woman from Bessarabia, 1964. The Taxi Game, 1973. Contbr. to: New Statesman; Evening Standard; Homes & Gardens; Penthouse; etc. Ed., Taxi Newspaper. Address: 9 Maxted Park, Harrow-on-the-Hill, Middx., UK.

LÉVIS MIREPOIX, Duc Antoine de, b. 1 Aug. 1884. Author. Educ: Paris Univ. Publs. incl: (novels) Le papillon noir; Le seigneur inconnu; Le voyage de Satan; Montségur; (memoirs) La touche Tréville à Naples; La Politesse; (historical non-fiction) François Ier; Les Trois femmes de Philippe Auguste; Sainte Jeanne de France; La France de la Renaissance; Les guerres de Religion; Vieilles races & temps nouveaux; Grandeur et Misère de l'Individualisme Français; Saint Louis, roi de France. Mbr., French Acad. Hons: Gobert Hist. Prize; Commander, Legion of Honour; Croix de Guerre. Address: 30 rue de Berri, Paris 8e, France.

LEVI-STRAUSS, Claude, b. 28 Nov. 1908, Brussels, Belgium. Professor. Collège de France, Paris; Anthropologist. Educ: Agrégé de Philosophie, 1931; D.Litt., 1948. Publs: Les Structures élémentaires de la parenté, 1949; Race et histoire, 1952; Tristes Tropiques, 1955; Anthropologie structurale, 1958; Le Totémisme aujourd'hui, 1962; La Pensée sauvage, 1962; Le Cru et le cruit, 1964; Du Miel aux cendres, 1967; L'Origine des manières de table, 1968; L'Homme nu, 1971; Anthropologie structurale deux, 1973. Mbrships. incl: French Acad.; Nat. Acad. of Sci. of USA; Brit. Acad. Hons. incl: Erasmus Prize, 1973; Gold Medal, 1967, Nat. Ctr. Sci. Rsch.; num. acad. hons. Address: 2 rue des Marronniers, 75016 Paris, France.

LEVY, Alan, b. 10 Feb. 1932, NYC, USA. Author; Foreign Correspondent. Educ: A.B., Brown Univ., Providence, R.I., 1952; M.S., Columbia Grad. Schl. of Jrnlism., N.Y., 1953. Publs. incl: Operation Elvis, 1960; Kind-Hearted Tiger, 1964; The Culture Vultures, 1968; God Bless You Real Good: My Crusade with Billy Graham, 1969; Rowboat to Prague, 1972; Good Men Still Live, 1974. Contbr. to: N.Y. Times; Harper's; Atlantic; Horizon; Cosmopolitan; Rdrs. Digest; Sat. Review; ARTnews; etc.; also to sev. anthols. Mbrships. incl: PEN Am. Ctr.; Overseas Press Club Am.; Soc. of Mag. Writers; Authors Guild. Recip., New Repub. Younger Writer Award, Wash. D.C., 1958. Address: Albertgasse 59/7, A-1080 Vienna VIII, Austria.

LEVY, Benn Wolfe, b. 1900. Farmer; Dramatist. Educ: Univ. Coll., Oxford. Publs. incl: This Woman Business; Mud & Treacle; Art & Mrs. Bottle; The Devil; Evergreen; Hollywood Holiday (w. John van Druten); Springtime for Henry; The Poet's Heart; The Jealous God; Clutterbuck; Return to Tyass; Cupid & Psyche; The Rape of the Belt; The Tumbler; Public & Confidential; The Marriage. Mbrships: House of Commons, 1945-50; Arts Coun. (exec.), 1953-61. Recip., M.B.E. Address: Cote House, Aston, Oxon., UK.

LEVY, Isaac Jack, b. 21 Dec. 1928, Rhodes, Italy (now Greece). University Professor. Educ: B.A., Emory Univ., USA, 1957; M.A., Univ. of Iowa, 1959; Ph.D., Univ. of Mich., 1966. Publs: Co-Ed., Hispanic Studies; Sephardic Ballads & Songs in the United States, 1959; Prolegomena to the Study of the "Refranero Sefardi", 1969; Ed., American Society of Sephardic Studies, 1969; Ed., The Sephardic Scholar, II, 1972-73. Contbr. to: Southern Israelite; S.C. Educ. News; Romance Notes; Revista Iberoamericana; Hispania; etc. Mbrships. incl: MLA; Am. Soc. Sephardic Studies; S.C. Conf. For. Lang. Tchrs. Recip., var. rsch. grants & acad. awards. Address: 4201 Sandwood Drive, Columbia, SC 29206, USA.

LEVY, Lillian Rae (Berliner), b. 16 Mar. 1918, Chgo., Ill., USA. Journalist; Author. Educ: Univ. of Chgo., 1937-38. Publs: Space: Its Impact on Man & Society, 1965; Science News Yearbook, 1969-70. Contbr. to: Harper's

Ency. of Sci.; Japanese Ency.; Saturday Review; Family Hlth.; Saturday Evening Post; MacLean's of Can.; Pioneer Women; Chgo. Jewish Forum, etc. Mbrships: Nat. Press Club; Wash. Press Club; Am. Newspaper Women's Club. Address: 4609 Norwood Drive, Chevy Chase, MD 20015, USA.

LEWIS, Cecil Arthur, b. 29 Mar. 1898, Birkenhead, Cheshire, UK. Broadcaster; Writer. Publs: Broadcasting From Within, 1924; Sagittarius Rising, 1936 (paperback, 1969); The Trumpet in Mine, 1938; Challenge to the Night, 1938; Self Portrait (diaries & jrnls. of Charles Ricketts, R.A.), 1939; Pathfinders, 1943; Yesterday's Evening, 1946; Turn Right for Corfu, 1973; Never Look Back, 1974; The Unknown Warrior, play transld. from French of Paul Raynal, 1930. Recip., Mil. Cross, 1916. Address: c/o Nat. Westminster Bank, 97 Strand, London WC2, UK.

LEWIS, Clifford, pen name (w. Mary Lewis) BERRISFORD, Judith M., b. 1912, Stoke-on-Trent, UK. Author. Publs: (w. Mary Lewis) Many children's books inclng. series about Taff, a Welsh sheepdog; Skipper, a white Alsatian; Jackie & her cousin Babs. Address: 38 Hawes Drive, Deganwy, Gwynedd, Wales, UK. See also under LEWIS, Mary.

LEWIS, Dillwyn, b. 15 Oct. 1930, Cardiff, UK. Headmaster. Educ: Tchng. Dip., Monmouthshire Coll. of Educ., Caerleon, 1954; Univ. of Wales. Publs: A History of Beddau & District, 1965; The History of Llantrisant, 1966, revised ed., 1974; The Llantrisant Investiture Book, 1969; A History of Tonyrefail, 1971; Llantrisant & Llantwit Fardre Rural District Council – Official Guide, 1972; Fndr.-Ed., The Glamorgan Log, Nat. Union of Tchrs. County Mag., 1968-74. Mbrships: Pub. Rels. Off., Glamorgan Co. Assn., 1971-74; Pub. Rels. Off., Mid Glamorgan Co. Assn., 1974–. Address: 12 Llantrisant Rd., Beddau, Pontypridd, Glamorgan CF38 2BB, UK.

LEWIS, Eiluned, b. Newtown, Montgomeryshire, UK. Writer; Former Journalist; J.P. Educ: M.A., Westfield Coll., London Univ. Publs: Dew on the Grass, 1934; The Land of Wales (w. Peter Lewis), 1937; The Captain's Wife, 1943; In Country Places, 1951; The Leaves of the Tree, 1953; Honey Pots & Brandy Bottles, 1954; Selected Letters of Charles Morgan, with Memoir, 1967; also two books of verse. Contbr. to Country Life; News Chronicle; Sunday Times, 1931-6. Recip., Book Guild Gold Medal. Address: Rabbits Heath Cottage, Bletchingly, Surrey, UK.

LEWIS, Hywel David, b. 21 May 1910, Llandudno, Gwynedd, UK. University Professor. Educ: B.A., 1932, M.A., 1934, Univ. Coll., Bangor; B.Litt., Jesus Coll., Oxford, 1935. Publs: Morals & the New Theology, 1947; Morals & Revelation, 1951; Contemporary British Philosophy, Vol. III (ed.), 1956; Our Experience of God, 1959; Freedom & History, 1962; Clarity is not Enough (ed.), 1962; Teach Yourself the Philosophy of Religion, 1965; World Religions (w. R. L. Slater), 1966; Dreaming & Experience, 1968; The Elusive Mind, 1969; The Self & Immortality, 1973. Contbr. to: Mind; Philos.; Ethics; Ed., Relig. Studies; etc. Mbr., var. philos. assns. Recip., num. acad. hons. Address: 1 Normandy Pk., Normandy near Guildford, Surrey, UK.

LEWIS, Janet (Mrs. Yvor Winters), b. 17 Aug. 1899, Chgo., Ill., USA. Writer. Educ: A.A., Lewis Inst., Chgo.; Ph.B., Univ. of Chgo. Publs: Novels: The Invasion, 1932; The Wife of Martin Guerre, 1941; Against a Darkening Sky, 1943; The Trial of Søren Qvist, 1947; The Ghost of Monsieur Scarron, 1959; Goodbye, Son (stories), 1946; Poems, 1924-44, 1950. Contbr. to: New Yorker; New Republic; Transition; This Quarter; Poetry: Chicago; McCalls; Saturday Evening Post; Southern Review; Sewanee Review; Former Mbr., PEN. Hons: Shelley Memorial Award, 1946; Gold Medal, Commonwealth Club of San Francisco, 1947; Guggenheim Fellow, 1950-51. Address: 143 W. Portola Ave., Los Altos, CA 94022, USA.

LEWIS, Mary, pen names HOPE, Amanda, & (w. Clifford Lewis) BERRISFORD, Judith M., b. 1921, Stoke-on-Trent, UK. Author. Educ: Manchester Univ. Publs: The Small Shrub Garden; Rhododendrons & Azaleas; The Wild Garden; The Very Small Garden; The Young Gardener; Gardening on Lime; Window Box & Container Gardening; (w. Clifford Lewis): Many children's books inclng. series about Taff, a Welsh sheepdog; Skipper, a white Alsatian; Jackie & her cousin Babs. Contbr. to var. mags. Address: 38 Hawes Drive, Deganwy, Gwynedd, Wales, UK. See also under LEWIS, Clifford.

LEWIS, Min, b. 1919, Newport, Mon., UK. Antique Dealer; Established Pram, Doll & Toy Museum. Educ: Art Coll. Publs: Laugharne & Dylan Thomas, 1967; History of Perambulators in Infantilia, 1971. Contbr. to: S. Wales Evening Post; Country Quest; local Carmarthen papers & mags. Address: The Pram, Doll & Toy Museum, Bath, Rd., Beckington, Bath, Somerset, UK.

LEWIS, Norman. Author. Educ: Intelligence Corps, 1939-45. Publs: Sand & Sea in Arabia, 1938; Samara, 1949; Within the Labyrinth, 1950; A Dragon Apparent, 1951; Golden Earth, 1952; A Single Pilgrim, 1953; The Day of the Fox, 1955; The Volcanoes Above Us, 1957; The Changing Sky, 1959; Darkness Visible, 1960; The Tenth Year of the Ship, 1962; The Honoured Society, 1964; A Small War Made to Order, 1966; Every Man's Brother, 1967; Flight from a Dark Equator, 1972. Address: c/o Wm. Collins Sons, 14 St. James' Place, London SW1, UK.

LEWIS, Saunders, b. 15 Oct. 1893. Writer; Dramatist. Educ: M.A., Liverpool Univ. Publs. incl: (plays) The Eve of St. John, 1921; Buchedd Garmon, 1937; Amlyn ac Amig, 1940; Gan Bwyll, 1952; Brad, 1958; Esther, 1960; Cymru Fydd, 1967; Problemau Prifysgol, 1968; (novels) Monica, 1930; Merch Gwern Hywel, 1964; (poetry) Mair Fadlen, 1937; Byd a Betws, 1941. (criticism) A School of Welsh Augustans, 1924; Daniel Owen, 1936; Ysgrifau Dydd Mercher, 1945; (political) Canlyn Arthur, 1938; (transl.) Molière: Doctor er ei Waethaf, 1924; Beckett: With aros Godot, 1970. Contbr. to Radio. Address: 158 Westbourne Rd., Penarth, Glamorgan, UK.

LEWIS-SMITH, Anne Elizabeth, b. 14 Apr. 1925, London, UK. Writer & Poet. Publs: The Seventh Bridge, 1963; The Beginning, 1964; Flesh & Flowers, 1967; Dandelion, 1970. Contbr. to: Aerostat (Ed.); Envoi (Ed., Mbr. Bd.); & more than 40 mags. in UK, USA, Can., Israel, India, etc. Mbrships: PEN; London Press Club; Brit. Balloon & Airship Club (Comm. Mbr.); Poetry Soc.; Balloon Fedn. Am.; Poetry Day London (Engl. Dir., Chmn., 1967, 1970). Address: Primrose Cottage, Peppard Common, Henley-on-Thames, Oxon., UK.

LEWTY, Marjorie, b. 8 Apr. 1906, Wallasey, UK. Author. Publs: Never Call it Loving, 1958; The Imperfect Secretary, 1959; Dental Nurse at Denley's, 1968; The Extraordinary Engagement, 1972; All Made of Wishes, 1974. Mbr., Romantic Novelists Assn. Address: 21 Woodcote Rd., Leamington Spa, Warwicks., UK.

LEYPOLDT, Martha, b. 2 Oct. 1918, Hanover, Ont., Can. Professor. Educ: B.A. Linfield Coll., 1944; M.R.E., N. Bapt. Theol. Sem., 1949; M.A., Univ. of Chgo., 1959; Ed.D., Ind. Univ., 1964. Publs: 40 Ways to Teach in Groups, 1967, German ed., 1970; Learning Is Change, 1971. Contbr. to relig. & educl. jrnls. Address: 274 B Murray Place, King of Prussia, PA 19406, USA.

LI, Shu-t'ien, b. 10 Feb. 1900. Professor Emeritus; Consulting Engineer; Author. Educ: B.S.(C.E.), Nat. Peiyang Univ., China, 1923; Ph.D., Cornell Univ., USA, 1926. Publs: 16 books & over 700 papers, monographs & rsch. reports. Contbr. to profl. jrnls. Mbrships. incl: World Open Univ. (Chmn. & Pres. 1972-); var. profl. assns. Recip. num. hons. Address: P.O. Drawer 5505, Orange, CA 92667, USA.

LIBERAKI, Margarita, b. 1919, Athena, Greece. Novelist; Dramatist. Educ: Athens Univ. Publs: The Trees, 1947; The Straw Hats, 1950; Trois Etés, 1950; The Other Alexander, 1952; (plays) Kandaule's Wife, 1955; The Danaids, 1956; L'Autre Alexandre, 1957; Le Saint Prince, 1959; La Lune a Faim, 1961; Sparagmos, 1965; Le Bain de Mer, 1967; Erotica, 1970; (film scripts) Magic City, 1953; Phaedra, 1961. Address: 7 rue de L'Eperon, Paris 6e, France.

LIDDELL, (John) Robert, b. 13 Oct. 1908, Tunbridge Wells, Kent, UK. University Teacher; Lecturer. Educ: B.A., 1931, B.Litt. 1933, M.A., 1935, Oxford Univ. Publs. incl: (novels) Kind Relations, 1939 (as Take This Child, USA, 1939); Unreal City, 1952; An Object for a Walk, 1966; The Deep End, 1968; The Stepsons, 1969; (short stories) Watering Place, 1945; The Last Enchantments, UK, 1948, USA, 1949; (non-fiction) A Treatise on the Novel, UK, 1947, USA, 1948; Aegean Greece, 1954; The Novels of Jane Austen, UK & USA, 1963; Mainland Greece, 1965. Mbrship: F.R.S.L. Address: c/o Barclays Bank, High St., Oxford, UK.

LIDMAN, Hans (Gustav Otto), b. 22 Aug. 1910, Sveg, Harjedalen, Sweden. Author. Publs: 50 books inclng: Den sjungande dalen, 1954; Laxögat, 1959; Pärlugglans skog, 1960; Äventyr i norr, 1963; Mina lyckliga år, 1964; Solen och frosten, 1965; Kamrat i norr, 1966; I Tinomaras spår, 1967; Under silverbågen, 1968; Tusen vingar, 1970; Napp i norr, 1971; Lim-Johan, 1971; Gudanatt, 1972; Resa in i solen, 1973; Olle Nordberg, en nordisk faun, 1974. Contbr. to: Horisont; Från Jaktmarker och Fiskevatten; Svenska Dagbladet; num. anthols. Mbrships. incl: Assn. of Swedish Authors; Assn. of Authors of Norrland. Hons. incl: Medal, Gustav Adolf Acad., Uppsala, 1952; hon. mbr., Nation Gästrike-Hälsinge, Uppsala, 1960; Silver Cup for Cultural Achievement, Savings Bank of Gävleborg Province, 1961. Address: Box 28, 828 00 Edsbyn, Sweden.

LIDMAN, Sara, b. 30 Dec. 1923, Sweden. Writer. Educ: Uppsala Univ. Publs. incl: Tjärdalen, 1953; Hjortronlandet, 1955; Aina, 1956; Regnspiran, 1958; Bära Mistel, 1960; Jag o min son, 1961; Med fem diamanter, 1964. Address: Jungmansgrand 2, Stockholm SV, Sweden.

LIEBENOW, J. Gus, b. 4 May 1925, Berwyn, Ill., USA. Former Director of African Studies & VP for Academic Affairs, Indiana University. Educ: B.A., 1949, M.A., 1950, Univ. of Ill.; Harvard Univ., 1951-52; Ph.D., Northwestern Univ., 1955. Publs: African Attitudes toward Agriculture, Education & Rural Transformation, 1968; Liberia: The Evolution of Privilege, 1969; Colonial Rule & Political Development in Tanzania, 1971; chapts. in num. other books on Africa. Contbr. to: Am. Pol. Sci. Review; Jrnl. African Admin.; etc. Mbrships. incl: Fndg. Fellow, African Studies Assn. (Exec. Bd.) Recip., num. rsch. Fellowships. Address: 633 Raven Crest R. 12, Bloomington, IN 47401, USA.

LIEDGREN, Jan, b. 12 May 1938, Östersund, Sweden. Dental Surgeon; Author. Educ: Lic. Practitioner, 1962. Publs: Som I Går, 1962; Kön, 1966; Den Gåtfulla Bomben, 1974. Contbr. to: Helsingborgs Dagblad; Tidskrift; Dental Review; Apollonia. Mbrships: Swedish Soc. of Authors; Coop. of Swedish Published Authors (Författarförlaget); Authors' Center (Författarcentrum). Recip., Swedish Soc. of Authors Award (Författarfonden), 1974. Address: Kaptensvägen 3, S 13210 Saltsjö-Boo, Sweden.

LIEGEOIS, Fernand, pen name MIRABAUX, Alain, b. 10 Jan. 1925, Lens, Belgium. Teacher at International School. Publs: (novels) A L'Ombre de la Lumière; Les Pousse-cailloux du Seigneur; (fables) Le Chemin de la Croix; Le Tour de Saint Vincent; (non-fiction) Lamartine, cet Inconnu; La Grotte de Lascaux. Contbr. of lit. & histl. criticism to jrnls. & newspapers. Mbrships: L'Acad. Luxembourgeoise; l'Acad. de Mâcon. Hons: 2nd Place, Grand Prix Vérité, Paris, 1961; Prize for Arts, Sci. & Lit., French Govt., 1972. Address: rue du Nouveau Monde, 5A a 7400 Soignies, Belgium.

LIFFNER, Axel G-A., b. 6 Nov. 1919, Karlskrona, Sweden, Literary Editor. Publs: Opus 0, 09, 1947; Semikolon, 1951; Glanslöst, 1956; Frivaro, 1962; Cypern u p a , 1966; Vardagsbulder, 1969. Mbr., Bd., Swedish PEN, 1960-71. Recip., Carl Emil Englund Prize for Poetry, 1970. Address: St. Paulsgatan 19, 116 47 Stockholm, Sweden.

LIFQUIST, Rosalind C., b. 5 June 1903, Henning, Minn., USA. Consumer Economics Specialist, Ret'd. Educ: Dip., Univ. of Wis., 1921; B.A., 1935, M.S., 1937, Univ. of Minn. Author, agric. bulletins, inclng: Food Guide for Older Folks, Planning Food for Institutions, What Makes Food Prices; Var. rsch. reports & contbns. to mags. Charter Mbr., Capital Women's Press Club. Address: 1727 Mass. Ave. NW, Washington, DC 20036, USA.

LIFSHIN, Lyn L., b. Burlington, Vt., USA. Poet. Educ: B.A., Syracuse Univ., N.Y.; M.A., Univ. of Vt.; Grad. study, var. Univs. Publs: Why is the House Dissolving, 1968; Leaves & Night Things, 1970; Black Apples, 1970, 2nd ed., 1973; Lady Lyn, 1970; Moving by Touch, 1972; Tentacles, Leaves, 1972; Museum, 1973; 40 Days, Apple Nights, 1974; The Old House on the Croton, 1974; Audley End, 1974; The Old House, Plymouth, 1974; Shaker Poems, 1974; Selected Poems, 1974; All the Women Poets, 1974. Contbr. to var. lit. jrnls. Hons. incl: Harcourt Brace Fellowship, 1968; Poetry MS Award, 1968; Hart Crane Memorial Award, 1968; MacDowell Fellow, 1973. Address: 2142 Appletree Lane, Niskayuna, NY 12309, USA.

LIGGETT, Clayton Eugene, b. 23 Feb. 1930, Aberdeen, S.D., USA. Teacher. Educ: B.A., Buena Vista Coll., Iowa,

1952; Postgrad. studies, State Univs. of Iowa & Calif. at San Diego, Univs. of Wyo. & Calif. at Berkeley. Publs: The Theatre Student; Concert Theatre, 1970. Contbr. to: Dramatics; Am. Educl. Theatre Assn. Jrnl. Address: 1078 Evergreen Dr., Encinitas, CA 92024, USA.

LIGHTSTONE, Albert Harold, b. 28 Nov. 1926, Ottawa, Can. Professor of Mathematics. Educ: B.Sc., Carleton Coll., Ottawa, 1952; M.A., Univ. of N.B., Fredericton, 1953; Ph.D., Univ. of Toronto, 1955. Publs: The Axiomatic Method, 1964; Concepts of Calculus, 2 vols., 1965, 1966; Symbolic Logic & the Real Number System, 1965; Fundamentals of Linear Algebra, 1969; Linear Algebra, 1969. Contbr. to: Zentralblatt für Mathematik; Maths. Mag.; Am. Math. Monthly. Mbr., Math. Assn. Am. Address: Dept. of Maths., Queen's Univ., Kingston, Ont., Can.

LILJEQUIST, Gösta Hjalmar, b. 20 Apr. 1914, Norrköping, Sweden. Professor of Meteorology. Educ: B.Sc., Lund Univ., 1936; Ph.D., Uppsala Univ., 1957. Publs: Arktisk utpost. The story of the Swedish-Finnish-Swiss Expedition to North-Eastland 1957-58, 1960; Meteorologi, 1962; Populär meteorologi, 1966, 2nd ed., 1970; Klimatologi, 1970; Meteorological section in Lodén K. (w. O. Mathiesen), 1971; Jordens klimat, 1974. Contbr. to var. meteorol. mags. Mbrships. incl: Swedish Union of Authors. Address: Meteorologiska institutionen, Uppsala, Sweden.

LILLI, Laura, b. 11 Mar. 1937, Rome, Italy, Journalist. Educ: Ph.D., Univ. of Rome, 1960. Publs: Zeta O Le Zie, 1972; James Bond E La Critica (contbng. author), 1966; (introduction) Evelyne Sullerot's Demain Les Femmes, Italian ed., 1966; (introduction & notes) Herbert Von Borch's Die Unfertige Gesellschaft, Italian ed., 1966. Contbr. to: Quarto Mondo; Compagna; Il Mondo; L'Espresso; Panorama; La Stampa. Address: Largo Goldoni, 47 — Roma, Italy.

LILLY, Doris, b. 26 Dec. 1927, L.A., Calif., USA. Author. Publs: How To Marry A Millionaire, 1951; How To Make Love in Five Languages, 1964; Those Fabulous Greeks: Onassis, Niarchos & Livanos, 1970. Contbr. to: Cosmopolitan; Vogue; Esquire; Harpers Bazaar; N.Y. Post (columnist for 7 yrs.); etc. Address: 301 East 62nd St., N.Y., NY 10021, USA.

LILLY, Isabella Purvis, pen names ALLAN, Ann; COUSIN ANN, b. 18 Nov. 1907, Wyndham, NZ. Writer. Publs: Go Ye Out, 1943; A Child's Prayer, 1944; When We Pray, 1946; Life upon Life, 1954; Rhythm Thoughts, 1957; Streamlined Thoughts, 1965; poems; children's stories. Contbr. to: Childrens Ed., Outlook; NZ Home Jrnl.; Engl. Christian Herald; NZ Herald; N. Shore Gazette; N. Shore Times-Advertiser; Forest & Bird, etc. Mbrships. incl: Sec., Auckland Presby. Mins. Wives Assn.; Sec., Auckland Penwomens Club; NZ Women Writers Assn. Winner, var. competitions. Address: Flat 5, 2 Saltburn Rd., Milford 9, Auckland, NZ.

LIM, (York) Quan, b. 12 Feb. 1935, Sun Wai City, Kwantung, China. Journalist. Publs: I Came from China, 1950; Our Land — Canada, 1956; Guide to Canadian Immigration & Citizenship, 1958; History of the Chinese in Canada, 1958. Contbr. to: Ctrl. Daily News, Great China Evening News, Overseas News, all Taipei, Taiwan; Newdom Weekly, Travel Mag., Overseas Chinese Daily News, Hong Kong Times, all Hong Kong; Chinese Voice Daily, New Repub. Daily, Chinatown News, all Vancouver, B.C., Can. Mbrships incl: Chinese Can. Citizens' Assn. (Sec. Chinese Benevolent Assn., Vancouver (Publicity Dir). Recip., Special Servs. Award, Fedn. of Overseas Chinese Assn., 1969. Address: 2640 Prince Albert St., Vancouver, B.C. V5T 3X3, Can.

LIMANI, Same, pen name ŽARNOSKI, b. 1 Jan. 1935, Zirovnica, Yugoslavia. Teacher. Educ: Tchrs.' Coll. Publs: Raspukani bigori (Burst Bitternesses), 1970; Iskri vo izgasneta pepel (Sparks in Smouldering Ashes), 1971; Ne grači tazna ptico (Do not Croak, Mournful Bird), 1973. Contbr. to The Contemporary. Mbrships: Macedonian Writers' Club; Ed. Bd., The Contemporary mag. Recip., Kliment Ohridski Award, 1973. Address: 91255 Žirovnica, Makedonska, Yugoslavia.

LIMBACHER, James L., b. 30 Nov. 1926, St. Marys, Ohio, USA. Librarian; Teacher. Educ: B.A., M.A., Bowling Green Univ.; M.S. in Ed., Ind. Univ.; M.S. in L.S., Wayne State Univ. Publs: Using Films, 1967; Four Aspects of the

Film, 1969; A Reference Guide to Audiovisual Information, 1973; Film Music: From Violins to Video, 1974; Shadows on the Wall, 1975; Feature Films on 8mm & 16mm (annual); Library Film Ratings. Contbr. to film jrnls: Monthly column, Previews Mag.; Educl. TV series, Shadows on the Wall, 1974; Script Writer, film series Our Modern Art — The Movies, 1972—. Hons: Gold Medal, for script of The Man Called Edison, Atlanta Film Fest.; Mich. Libn. of Yr. Award, 1974. Address: Morley Manor, Apt. 1201, 21800 Morley Ave., Dearborn, MI 48124, USA.

LINARES-BECERRA, Concha, b. 22 May 1910, Madrid, Spain. Educ: Lang. & Music studies. Publs. incl: Por qué me casé con el, 1933; Diez días millonaria, 1934; La novia de la Costa Azul, 1935; Opereta, 1937; La conquista del hombre, 1937; A sus ordenes, mi Coronel!, 1939; Mientras llega la primavera, 1939; Cita en el paraíso, 1940; Maridos de lujo, 1941; Muchachas sin besos, 1943; A Nueva York por un piso, 1946; El matrimonio es asunto de dos, 1949; La hora prohibida, 1953; El miedo nos une, 1954; Niebla desde la frontera, 1957; La vida secreta de una señora, 1961; Escándalo en mi Universo, 1963; La extrema llamada, 1968; La manzana era inocente, 1971. Contbr. to var. mags. & newspapers. Mbr., var. socs. Address: Calle Vallehermoso 22, Madrid 15, Spain.

LIND, Levi Robert, b. 29 July 1906, Trenton, N.J., USA. University Professor of Classics. Educ: A.B., 1929, A.M., 1932, Ph.D., 1936, Univ. of Ill. Publs. incl: Ed. & Transl. of var. works inclng. The Epitome of Andreas Vesalius, 1949, 2nd ed., 1969; Virgil's Aeneid, 1963; Problemata Varia Anatomica: The University of Bologna MS 1165, 1968; Johann Wolfgang von Goethe, Roman Elegies & Venetian Epigrams, 1974; Ovid, Tristia, 1975. Contbr. to: Classical Jrnl.; Classical Philol.; etc. Mbrships. incl: Am. Philol. Assn.; Medieval Acad. of Am. Hons. incl: Fellow, Am. Coun. Learned Socs., 1940—. var. acad. grants. Address: 1714 Indiana St., Lawrence, KS 66044, USA.

LINDARS, Barnabas (Frederick Chevallier), b. 11 June 1923, Leighton Buzzard, UK. Lecturer in Divinity; Priest of Church of England. Educ: St. John's Coll., Cambridge, 1942-46, Westcott House, 1946-48; B.A., 1945, M.A., 1948, B.D., 1961, D.D., 1973. Publs: New Testament Apologetic, 1961; Ed. & Contbr., Words & Meanings, 1968; Behind the Fourth Gospel, 1971; Gospel of John (New Century Bible), 1972; Ed. & Contbr., Christ & Spirit in the New Testament, 1973; co-author, Témoignage de l'évangile de Jean, 1974. Contbr. to: New Testament Studies; Theol.; etc. Mbrships: Studiorum Novi Testamenti Societas; Soc. Old Testament Study. Address: Divinity School, St. John's St., Cambridge CB2 1TW, UK.

LINDAY, Ryllis Elizabeth Paine, b. 3 June 1919, Mt. Iron, Minn., USA. Teacher Aide; Author. Educ: Wis. State Superior, Wis.; Marylhurst, Portland Community Coll. Publs: Look at Me, 1959; Now I Am Two, 1963. Contbr. to: Together; Ore. Sprtsman. Mbrships: Treas., Alpha Kappa; Clackamas Co. Election Bd., 12 yrs. Address: 660 S.W. 10th St., Lake Oswego, OR 97034, USA.

LINDBERG, Karl Sivert, pen name VEITS, Ulf, b. 27 Mar. 1933, Stockholm, Sweden. Teacher. Educ: Fil. mag. Publs: (poetry) Vädur, 1956; Skola, 1961; Kvast, 1966; (short stories) Odlorna, 1958; Återkomst, 1959; Medan Tya levde, 1964; Lugn som en filbunke, 1974. Mbrships: Swedish Authors' Union; Författarcentrum; Socialistiska Skolarbetare; Chmn., Solnalärarnas Ombudsförsamling. Address: Ankdammsgatan 19, 171 43 Solna, Sweden.

LINDBERGH, Anne Spencer Morrow, b. 1906, USA. Air Explorer; Author. Educ: Smith Coll., Northampton, Mass., USA. Publs: North to the Orient, 1935; Listen, the Wind, 1938; The Wave of the Future, 1940; The Steep Ascent, 1944; Gift from the Sea, 1955; The Unicorn, 1958; Dearly Beloved, 1963; Earth Shine, 1970; (autobiography) Hour of Gold, Hour of Lead, 1973. Hons: Cross of Honour, US Flag Assn.; Hubbard Gold Medal, Nat. Geographical Soc. Address: Scott's Cove, Darien, CT 06820, USA.

LINDE, (Per Johan) Ebbe (Fredrik), b. 27 Sept. 1897, Kolmarden, Sweden. Author; Former Dramatic Critic; Former University Teacher in Electrochemistry; Former Psychological Scientist. Educ: Phil.Lic. Publs: Dikter O-III, 1924-36; Brott & straff, 1930; Brudsporre, 1931; Senapskornet, 1934; Isljuset, 1939; Gyllenåsnan, 1947; Vision & Eko, 1957; Dagboksålder, 1969; Works by Brecht, Ionesco, Jimenez, Apollinaire, Lope de Vega, & sev. classic authors transl'd into Swedish (w. introductions). Contbr. to: Ny Tid; Bonniers Litterära Magasin; Dagens Nyheter.

Mbrships: PEN; Union of Swedish Authors; Swedish Union of Dramatists. Address: Häradsvägen 1, 610 23 Kolmården, Sweden.

LINDE, Gunnel, b. 14 Oct. 1924, Stockholm, Sweden. Author; Television Director & Producer. Publs. incl: Tacka vet jag Skorstensgränd (Chimney Top Lane), 1959; Osynliga klubben och Kungliga spöket (The Invisible League & The Royal Ghost), 1960; Den vita stenen (The White Stone), 1964; Med Lill-Klas i kappsäcken (Pony Surprise), 1965; Löjliga familjerna, 1971; Jag är en varulvsunge, 1972. Contbr. to radio, TV, anthols. & jrnls. Mbrships. incl: Swedish Union of Writers; Swedish Jrnlsts. Assn. Recip., sev. grants & lit. awards. Address: Grindavägen 9, 185 00 Vaxholm, Sweden.

LINDÉN, Erik Hugo Emanuel, pen names RISTARE, Bo; LOWÖ, Hans, b. 17 June 1918, Björnlunda, Sweden. Railway Official; Writer. Publs: Min själ har en längtan (poetry), 1956; Norrlandslyriker (anthol.), 1958; Jorden och skuggorna (poetry), 1964; 27 lyriker (anthol.), 1964; Tvärsnitt (anthol.), 1965; Pegas (anthol.), 1966; Poesi 67 (anthol.), 1967; Ångermanländsk lyrik (anthol.), 1967; Fjorton diktar (poetry), 1974. Contbr. to: Perspektiv (lit. reporter, 1960—); Nya Norrland (lit. reporter, 1960—); Skribent (ed., 1958-73). Mbrships. incl: Swedish Union of Authors. Recip., Katarinastiftelsen schlrship., 1971. Address: Junkergatan 14 b.v., S 126 53 Hägersten, Sweden.

LINDER, (Alfhild) Marianne, b. 7 July 1919, Stockholm, Sweden. Author; Lyric Poet; Reciter; Translator; Teacher. Educ: B.A., Univ. of Stockholm, 1947. Publs: Brunnarna (The Wells), 1950; De röda lutorna (The Red Lutes), 1951; Chonchet, Djävulen & Döden (Chonchet, the Devil & Death), 1954; Ros & bröd (Rose & Bread), 1965; Ed., Studiegrupp Poesi 67, 1967. Contbr. to num. lit. & other jrnls. & anthols. Mbrships. incl: Assn. of Swedish Authors, 1954; Fndr., Swedish Sect., Int. Lit. Union, 1958, Pres., 1971—; Lit. Translators Sect., 1971. Strindberg Soc. Hons. incl: 1st Poetry Prize, Review Clarté, 1956; Int. 1st Poetry Prize, Lit. Union, 1968; num. awards & schlrships. Address: Heleneborgsgatan 50, III, S-117 32 Stockholm, Sweden.

LINDGREEN, Jørgen, b. 27 Aug. 1936, Odense, Denmark. Author; Dramatist. Publs: Vaerftet, 1966; Vaerftet (radio play), 1970; Huset i Baggården (TV play), 1971; Kobberburet (radio play), 1972; Stillerlisten (radio play), 1972; Hvor er Viggo (TV play), 1973; Tillidsmanden (radio play), 1975; Jul på slottet (TV play), 1975; Atomer på Naesset (novel), 1975. Mbr., Fedn. of Danish Dramatists. Recip., 2 Govt. Art Fund Grants. Address: Skjoldsvej 4, 5200 Odense V, Denmark.

LINDGREN, Astrid, b. 14 Nov. 1907, Vimmerby, Sweden. Author. Publs. incl: Pippi Långstrump, 1945; Mio min Mio, 1954; Lillebror och Karlsson pa Taket, 1955; Rasmus på luffen, 1956; Rasmus Pontus och Toker, 1957; Barnen på Bråkmakargatan, 1958; Sunnanäng, 1959; Madicken, 1960; Lotta på Bråkmakargatan, 1961; Karlsson på Taket Flyger igen, 1962; Emil i Lönneberga, 1963; Vi på Saltkråkan, 1964; Nya hyss av Emil i Lönneberga, 1966; Karlsson på Taket smyger igen, 1968; Än lever Emil i Lönneberga, 1970; Bröderna Lejonhjärta, 1973. Mbrships: Acad. of the Nine; PEN; Union of Swedish Authors Hons. incl: Int. Hans Christian Andersen Award, 1958; N.Y. Herald Tribune Spring Book Fest. Award, 1959; Swedish Acad. Gold Medal, 1971. Address: Dalagatan 46, Stockholm, Sweden.

LINDGREN, Barbro, b. 18 Mar. 1937, Stockholm, Sweden. Author. Publs: Loranga, Masarin Och Dartanjang (for children), 1969; Felipe, 1970; Jättenhemligt (for children), 1971; Eldvin, 1972. Hons: Heffaklumpen, 1971; Astrid Lindgrenprizet, 1973. Address: Stora Söderby 19500 Märsta, Sweden.

LINDGREN, Sören Gotthard, b. 13 Mar. 1935, Kyrkslätt, Finland. Journalist. Educ: Sociol. & Pol. Sci. studies, Univ. of Helsinki, Finland; Finnish Lang. studies, Univ. of Stockholm, Sweden. Publs. of poetry: Ornament, 1954; De tolo, 1957; Exil, 1958; Abals död, 1959; Politiska dikter, 1969. Contbr. to: Nya Argus; Vasabladet. Mbrships: Finlands svenska författareförening; Sveriges författarförbund. Address: Box 79 (Meionvägen 31), S-170 10 Ekerö, Sweden.

LINDGREN-UTSI, Ethel John, pen name LINDGREN, b. 1 Jan. 1905, Evanston, Ill., USA. Editor; Research Worker. Educ: B.A., 1927, M.A., 1930, Ph.D., 1936,

Cambridge Univ. Publs: Ed., The Study of Society: Methods & Problems (w. Sir F. Bartlett; Prof. M. Ginsberg; Dr. R. H. Thouless), & contbr. of chapter "The Collection & Analysis of Folklore" to same, 1939. Contbr. to: Brit. Jrnl. of Psychol.; Jrnl. of Royal Ctrl. Asian Soc. & Am. Anthropol. Mbrships. incl: Royal Inst. of Int. Affairs; Royal Asiatic Soc.; Royal Geog. Soc.; Zoolog. Soc., London. Address: Sunbourn, Harston, Cambridge, CB2 5NZ, UK.

LINDSAY, Cressida Anne, b. 22 Oct. 1930, London, UK. Author. Publs: No Wonderland, 1960; Fathers Gone to War & Mothers Gone to Pieces, 1963; No John No, 1966; Fathers & Lovers, 1969. Contbr. to var. publs. Hons: Gemini Trust; Arts Coun. Address: The Old Rectory, Scoulton, Norfolk NOR 21X, UK.

LINDSAY, Jack, b. 20 Oct. 1900, Melbourne, Australia. Author. Educ: B.A., D.Litt., Qld. Univ. Publs: works incl. poetry, drama, novels (histl. & contemporary), lit. & art criticism, biog., ancient & medieval hist., archaeol., hist. of sci., transls. from ancient Greek & Latin, & from French, Russian, etc. Mbrships: Fellow of Royal Soc. of Lit.; Fellow of Ancient Monument Soc. Hons: Aust. Lit. Soc. Gold Medal, 1960; Soviet Order of Merit (Znak Pochota) for transl. of Russian poetry. Address: 40 Queen St., Castle Hedingham, Halstead, Essex, UK.

LINDSAY OF DOWHILL, (Sir) Martin, pen name LINDSAY, Martin, b. 22 Aug. 1905, London, UK. Author; Former Member of Parliament. Publs: Those Greenland Days, 1932; The Epic of Captain Scott, 1933; Sledge, 1935; So Few Got Through, 1946; Three Got Through, 1946; The House of Commons, 1947; Shall we Reform the Lords?, 1950. Contbr. to: Country Life; House & Gdn.; The Observer; The Listener; The Spectator; Country Gentleman's Mag.; Army Quarterly & Brit. Army Review. Hons. incl: C.B.E.; D.S.O. Address: The Old Vicarage, Send, Nr. Woking, UK.

LINDSEY, David, b. 1 Dec. 1914, Waldwick, N.J., USA.. University Professor of History. Educ: B.A., Cornell Univ., 1936; M.A., Pa. State Univ., 1938; Ph.D., Univ. of Chgo., 1950. Publs: Ohio's Western Reserve, 1955; "Sunset" Cox, 1959; An Outline History of Ohio, 2nd ed., 1960; Abraham Lincoln & Jefferson Davis, 1960; Andrew Jackson & Henry Clay, 1963; Andrew Jackson & John C. Calhoun, 1973; Americans in Conflict, 1974. Contbr. to: Mankind; Wash. Post; L.A. Times; Am. Hist. Illustrated. Mbrships. incl: Am. Histl. Assn.; Org. of Am. Histns. Recip., 2 Fulbright lectureships & var. grants. Address: Calif. State Univ., 5151 State Univ. Dr., L.A., CA 90032, USA.

LINDSJÖ, Inga Britta, b. 29 Jan, 1922, Härnösand, Sweden. Author. Educ: Fil.kand. Publs: Som i havets mussla, 1949; Det fattas ett par linser, 1951; Har någon sett Kornelius, 1952; Jag vill röra vid ljuskronan, 1953; Fabian Sjölejon, 1959; Morsan, 1963; Människan och hans hustru, 1967; Nöjd. Bilder från ett storföretag, 1970; Festplatsen, 1973. Mbr., Swedish Authors' Union. Address: Sankt Olofsgatan 43 B, 753 30 Uppsala, Sweden.

LINDSLEY, Mary Frances, b. NYC, USA. Poet; Author. Educ: A.B., Hunter Coll., NYC; M.A., Columbia Univ. Publs. (Verse): Uncensored Letter, 1949; Grand Tour, 1952; Promenade, 1965; Pomp & Circumstance, 1966; Pax Romana, 1967; Selected Poems, 1967; Otma, 1968; Rosaria, 1969; Workday of Pierre Toussaint, 1970; Circe & the Unicorn, 1971; The Masquers, 1972; One Life, 1973; Anarch's Hand, 1974; (Short Stories): Beyond Baker Street (w. Dr. I. L. Jaffee), 1973. Mbrships. incl: Poetry Soc. of Am.; N.Y. Poetry Forum; United Poets Laureate Int. Hons. incl: Bronze medal, 1966, Silver medal, 1967, Accademia Leonardo da Vinci, Rome, 1966. Address: 13361 El Dorado 201 H, Seal Beach, CA 90740, USA.

LING, Trevor Oswald, b. 17 Feb. 1920, London, UK. Professor of Comparative Religion. Educ: M.A., Univ. of Oxford, 1949; Ph.D., Univ. of London, 1960. Publs: Buddha, Marx & God, 1967; A History of Religion East & West, 1969; Buddhist Dictionary, 1970; The Buddha: Buddhist Civilization in India & Ceylon, 1973. Contbr. to: S. Asia Review; Religion; New Community; Population Studies. Mbrships. incl: Royal Asiatic Soc.; Royal Soc. for India, Pakistan & Ceylon; Int. Assn. for the Hist. of Relig. Address: Dept. of Comparative Religion, Univ. of Manchester, Manchester M13 9PL, UK.

LINKLATER, Magnus Duncan, b. 1942, Orkney, UK. Editor, Sunday Times Colour Magazine, 1972–. Educ:

Eton; Trinity Hall, Cambridge; B.A. Publ: Hoax — The Inside Story of the Howard Hughes-Clifford Irving Affair, (co-author w. Lewis Chester & Stephen Fay) 1972. Address: 31 Gibson Sq., London N1, UK.

LINNER, Birgitta, b. 25 Oct. 1920, Ystad, Sweden. Marriage Guidance Counsellor; Author; Lecturer. Educ: Law degree, Lund Univ., 1946; Dip., Trng. Inst., Clin. for Pastoral Counselling & Psychotherapy, 1954; Dip., Grp. Psychotherapy, Inst. of Educ., Stockholm Univ. Publs: Sex & Society in Sweden, 1968, 1972; Sex & Personal Relationship, 1972. Contbr. to: Am. Jrnl. of Orthopsych.; Advances in the Biosciences 10, 1973. Mbrships incl: Swedish Assn. for Grp. Psychotherapy; For. Affiliate, Am. Assn. of Marriage Counsellors; Am. Orthopsych. Assn.; Int. Fed. of Women Lawyers, Zonta. Address: Svartmunkegränd 2 A, SF 20 100 Åbo 10, Finland.

LINNMAN, Gunnel Margareta Sofia, b. 9 Jan. 1918, Stockholm, Sweden. Natural History Museum Curator. Educ: Ph.D. Publs: Stora Karlsö (co-author), 1973; Educl. & popular sci. books on geol., biol., etc. Contbr. to: Svensk Naturvetenskap; Fauna och flora; Svensk Botanisk Tidskrift; Geologiska Föreningens Förhandl.; Publs. of Svenska Turistföreningens, Sveriges Geologiska Undersöknings, Swedish Broadcasting Co.; Stockholmstidningen; Vi; etc. Mbrships: Vice-Chmn., Geol. Sect., Sveriges Naturvetareförbund; Geol. Soc., Sweden; Swedish Authors' Union. Address: Swedish Museum of Natural History, 10405 Stockholm 50, Sweden.

LINS, Osman, b. 5 July 1924, Vitória de Santo Antao, Pernambuco, Brazil. College Professor; Author. Educ: Ph.D. Publs: O Visitante, 1955; Os Gestos, 1957; O Fiel e a Pedra, 1961; Nove, Novena, 1966; Guerra sem Testemunhas — o Escritor, sua Condição e a Realidade Social, 1969; Avalovara, 1973; sev. plays. Contbr. to lit. jrnls. Mbr., Soc. Brasileira de Autores Teatrais. Hons: Prize Fábio prado, 1954; Prize Coelho Neto, 1955; Prize Monteiro Lobato, 1957; Nat. Prize of Comedy, 1961; Prize José de Anchieta, 1967. Address: Alameda Lorena, 289, apt. 141, 14°, 01424 São Paulo, S.P.-Brazil.

LINSENMEYER, Helen Walker (Mrs.), b. 3 Mar. 1906, Energy, Ill., USA. Writer; Retired Librarian & Cataloguer. Educ: S. Ill. Univ. Carbondale, 1925; Santa Ana Coll., 1965-68; Calif. State Univ., Fullerton, 1967-70. Publs: From Fingers to Finger Bowls: A History of California Cookery, 1972; (works in progress) An Autobiography; Cookbook of Family Recipes; History of Fruits & Vegetables in the United States; The Early French in Illinois. Mbrships: Huthmacher House Assn.; Grand Tower, Ill. (Sec.); Jackson Co. Histl. Soc. Honoured at Annual Orange Co. (Calif.) Authors' Dinner, 1973. Address: Box 272, Grand Tower, IL 62942, USA.

LINSKILL, Doris Joy, pen name TREVOR, Joy, b. 13 Feb. 1908, Woodford Green, Essex, UK. Stage & Film Artist. Publs: Love & Life (novel, as Nita Bevis), 1937; Two Plays: The Moon Chase, & The Fate of Yesterday, 1973. Contbr. to Kaleidoscope; New Poets; Contemporary Poets; Our National Heritage, 1974. Mbr., Equity. Address: 74 Crest Rd., Cricklewood, London NW2, UK.

LINSSEN, Robert Léon, b. 11 Apr. 1911, Brussels, Belgium. Author. Publs: La reconstruction de l'Homme, 1940; L'homme devant l'Infini, 1944; Etudes psychologiques C. G. Jung et Krishnamurti, 1949; De l'amour humain à l'amour divin, 1950; Le Destin du XXeme siècle, 1949; Bouddhisme Zen et Taoisme, 1953; Spiritualité de la Matiere, 1960; L'Eveil suprême 1969; Le Zen, 1970; Living Zen, 1955. Contbr. to: Dir., Etre Libre; The Middle Way; The Mountain Path. Mbrships: Soc. des Gens de Lettres de France; PEN; Belgian Assn. of Writers. Recip., Grand Prix du Livre, La Louviere, 1940. Address: 20 rue P. de Deken, Brussels, 1040 Belgium.

LIN YUTANG, b. 10 Oct. 1895, Changchow, China. Author; Philologist. Educ: M.A.; Ph.D.; Univs. of Harvard & Leipzig. Publs. incl: My Country & My People, 1936; The Importance of Living, 1937; With Love & Irony, 1941; A Leaf in the Storm, 1942; Between Tears & Laughter, 1943; Peace is in the Heart, 1950; The Unexpected Island, 1954; Lady Wu, 1957; Secret Name, 1959; Red Peony, 1962; The Pleasures of a Non-Conformist, 1963; Juniper Loa, 1964; Flight of the Innocents, 1965; The Chinese Theory of Art, 1967. Contbr. to: China Critic; Lun Yu; This Human World; Yuchoufeng. Address: 315 E. 65th St., N.Y. NY 10021, USA.

LIPPARD, Lucy Rowland, b. 14 Apr. 1937, NYC, USA. Writer. Educ: B.A., Smith Coll., 1958; M.A., N.Y. Univ. Inst. of Fine Arts, 1962. Publs: Philip Evergood, 1966; Pop Art, 1966; Surrealists on Art, 1970; Dadas on Art, 1971; Changing: Essays in Art Criticism, 1971; Tony Smith, 1972; Six Years: The Dematerialization of the Art Object, 1973. Contbr. to art mags. Recip., sev. acad. hons. Address: 138 Prince St., N.Y., NY 10012, USA.

LIPSCOMB, William Nunn, Jr., b. 9 Dec. 1919, Cleveland, Ohio, USA. Professor of Chemistry. Educ: B.S., Univ. of Ky., 1941; Ph.D., Calif. Inst. of Technol., 1946. Publs: Boron Hydrides, 1963; Nuclear Magnetic Resonance Studies of Boron & Related Compounds (w. G. R. Eaton), 1969. Contbr. to num. sci. jrnls. Mbrships. incl: Am. Crystallographic Assn.; Am. Chem. Soc.; Am. Phys. Soc. Recip., num. acad. hons. Address: Dept. of Chemistry, Harvard Univ., 12 Oxford St., Cambridge, MA 02138, USA.

LIPTÁK, Gábor, b. 30 June 1912, Budapest, Hungary. Writer. Educ: B.A.; M.A. Publs. incl: Aranyhíd, 1961; Regélö Dunántul, 1964; Vallomások a Balatonról, 1969; Sárkányfészek, 1969; Amiröl a kövek beszélnek. Contbr. to var. wkly & monthly publs., Hungary. Mbrships: Hungarian Writers Union; PEN. Recip., Silver Medal, Hungarian Order of Labour. Address: 8230 Balatonfüred, Petöfi S.u.36.sz., Hungary.

LISTER, Raymond George, b. 28 Mar. 1919, Cambridge, UK. Director of Architectural Metalworking Firm. Publs. incl: The British Miniature, Silhouettes; The Muscovite Peacock; The Loyal Blacksmith; Decorative Wrought Ironwork in Great Britain, 1957; Decorative Cast Ironwork in Great Britain, 1960; Edward Calvert, 1962; Victorian Narrative Paintings, 1966; William Blake, 1968; Samuel Palmer & His Etchings, 1969; A Title to Phoebe, 1972; British Romantic Art, 1972. Contbr. to: Climbers' Club Jrnl.; Irish Book; Blake Studies; etc. Mbrships. incl: F.R.S.A.; Royal Soc. Miniature Painters, Sculptors & Gravers (Pres., 1970—); Fedn. Brit. Artists (Gov., 1972—); Pvte. Libs. Assn. (Pres., 1971-74). Agent: Stephen Aske. Address: Windmill House, Linton, Cambridge CB1 6NS, UK.

LISTER, Richard Percival, b. 23 Nov. 1914, Nottingham, UK. Writer. Educ: B.Sc., Manchester Univ. Publs: The Way Backwards, 1950; The Oyster & the Torpedo, 1951; Rebecca Redfern, 1953; The Idle Demon, 1958; The Rhyme & the Reason, 1963; The Questing Beast, 1965; A Journey into Lapland, 1965; Turkey Observed, 1967; The Secret History of Genghis Khan, 1969; One Short Summer, 1974. Address: 120 Hatherley Ct., Hatherley Grove, London W2, UK.

LISTON, Hattye Eileen Hinton, b. 24 Feb. 1924, Rocky Mount, N.C., USA. Paraprofessional Training Program Director; Associate Professor of Psychology; Psychologist. Educ: B.S., N.C. Coll., Durham; M.S., N.Y. Univ., NYC; Certs., Yale Univ. & Dept. of Pub. Hlth., Univ. of N.C., Chapel Hill. Publs: How to Study & Learn, 1965. Mbr., profl., acad. & community orgs. Recip., grant to train paraprofessionals, Nat. Inst. of Mental Hlth. Address: 1213 Eastside Dr., Greensboro, NC 27406, USA.

LITT, Iris, b. 18 Mar. 1928, NYC, USA. Writer. Educ: B.A., Ohio State Univ.; Univ. de las Americas, Mexico City. Contbr. to Writer's Digest & Ency. of Advertising; Monthly column in The Writer; Poetry in poetry jrnls.; Ed. Writer, Calling All Girls, Miss America (mags.); Guest Ed., Mademoiselle mag. Mbrships: Poetry Soc. of Am.; Copy Club of N.Y. Hons: Award for Coll. Poetry, Atlantic Monthly mag., 1947; 2nd prize for Poetry, Nat. League of Am. Pen Women, Boston br., 1974. Address: 252 W. 11th St., Garden Floor, N.Y., NY 10014, USA.

LITTLE, Alan Macnaughton Gordon, b. 13 Oct. 1901, Great Crosby, Lancs., UK. Classical Scholar; Teacher. Educ: B.A., M.A., Cambridge Univ., UK; Ph.D., Yale Univ., USA. Publs: Myth & Society in Attic Drama, 1942, 1967; Roman Perspective Painting & the Ancient Stage, 1971; A Roman Bridal Drama at the Villa of the Mysteries, 1972. Contbr. to: Am. Jrnl. of Archaeol.; Am. Art Bulletin; Harvard Studies in Classical Philology; Yale Doura Studies. Mbr., Archaeol. Inst. of Am. Address: Apt. 304, 3041 Sedgwick St. NW, Wash. DC 20008, USA.

LITTLE, Bryan Desmond Greenway, b. 22 Feb. 1913, Deal, Kent, UK. Author; Lecturer. Educ: Jesus Coll., Cambridge; M.A. Publs. incl: The Building of Bath, 1947; Cheltenham, 1952; The City & County of Bristol, 1954; The Monmouth Episode, 1956; Crusoe's Captain, 1960; English Historic Architecture, 1964; Portrait of Somerset, 1969; Birmingham Buildings, 1971; The Colleges of Cambridge, 1973; Sir Christopher Wren (biog.), 1975. Contbr. to: Country Life; Geogl. Mag., Cath. Herald; Archt. & Bldg. News; Birmingham Post. Mbrships: Soc. of Authors; VP, W. Country Writers' Assn. Address: c/o National Westminster Bank, 32 Corn St., Bristol 1, UK.

LITTLE, Kenneth Lindsay, b. 19 Sept. 1908, Liverpool, UK. Social Anthropologist. Educ: M.A., Cantab.; Ph.D., London. Publs: Negroes in Britain, 1946; The Mende of Sierra Leone, 1951, revised ed., 1967; Race & Society, 1952; West African Urbanization, 1965; African Women in Towns, 1973; Urbanization as a Social Process, 1974. Contbr., sev. profl. jrnls. Mbrships: incl: Assoc., Soc. Anthropols.; Royal Anthropol. Inst.; Int. African Inst. Recip., num. acad. hons. Address: 4 West Mains Rd., Edinburgh, UK.

LITTLE, Thomas Russell (Tom), b. 1911, Tynemouth, UK. Managing Director, Tom Little Associates Ltd.; European Rep., Saudi Press Agency. Publs: Egypt; Modern Egypt; High Dam at Aswan; South Arabia; The Arab World Today. Contbr. to: The Times; The Economist; The Observer; The World Today; The Middle East Jrnl.; The Middle East Forum (Beirut); The Annual Register of World Events; The Middle East; A Political & Economic Survey. Address: ESR Cottage, Whitchurch, Reading RG8 7EX, Berks., UK.

LITTLEDALE, Freya (Lota), b. NYC, USA. Freelance Author & Editor. Educ: B.S., Ithaca Coll., N.Y.; N.Y. Univ. Grad. Schl. of Arts & Scis. Publs. incl: The Magic Fish, 1967; King Fox & Other Old Tales, 1971; Timothy's Forest (w. Harold Littledale), 1969; Ed., A Treasure Chest of Poetry, 1964; Andersen's Fairy Tales, 1966; Chosts & Spirits of Many Lands, 1970; Strange Tales from Many Lands (anthol.), 1975. Mbrships: Authors' Guild Inc.; Authors' League of Am. Hons: Ghosts & Spirits of Many Lands selected as one of Children's Books of Yr., Child Study Assn. Am., 1970. Address: 305 E. 86th St., N.Y., NY 10028, USA.

LITTLER, Sir Emile, b. 9 Sept. 1903. Theatrical Impresario; Producer; Author; Company Director. Prods. incl: Victoria Regina; The Night & The Music; Claudia; Annie Get Your Gun; The Love Birds; The Happiest Millionaire; Signpost to Murder; The Right Hon. Gentleman; 1066 & All That; Lilac Time. Publs: (co-author) Cabbages & Kings; Too Young to Marry; Love Isn't Everything; & 10 Christmas pantomimes. Address: Palace Theatre, Shaftesbury Ave., London W1, UK.

LITVINOFF, Emanuel, b. 30 June 1915, London, UK. Library Director; Journalist; Broadcaster. Publs: (verse) Conscripts, 1941; The Untried Soldier, 1942; A Crown for Cain, 1948; (novels) The Lost Europeans, USA, 1959, UK, 1960; The Man Next Door, UK, 1968, USA, 1969; (short stories) Journey Through a Small Planet, 1972; var. TV plays, 1966-71. Contbr. to: Penguin Mod. Stories 2, 1969; Guardian; Listener; Jews in Eastern Europe (Fndr.). Address: 36 Byron Ct., Mecklenburgh Sq., London WC1, UK.

LITWAK, Lee E., b. 28 May 1924, Detroit, Mich., USA. Professor of English. Educ: B.A., Wayne State Univ., Detroit, 1948; Columbia Univ., 1948-51. Publs: (novels) To the Hanging Gardens, USA, 1964, UK, 1966; Waiting for the News, USA, 1969, UK, 1971; (non-fiction) College Days in Earthquake Country (w. Herbert Wilner), 1971. Contbr. to: Midstream; Partisan Review; Esquire; Nugget; Commentary. Hons: Award, Longview Fndn., 1958; Award, Nat. Endowment for Arts, 1968; Daroff Mem. Prize, 1970; Guggenheim Fellowship, 1970. Address: 1933 Greenwich St., San Fran., CA 94123, USA.

LIU, Leo Yueh-yun, b. 3 Apr. 1940, Canton, China. Assistant Professor of Political Science. Educ: B.A., Nat. Taiwan Univ., Taipei, 1962; M.A., Univ. of Hawaii, Honolulu, 1965; M.L.S., Univ. of Western Ont., London, Can., 1968; Ph.D., Univ. of Alta., Edmonton, 1970. Author, China as a Nuclear Power in World Politics, 1972. Contbr. to: Dalhousie Review; China Report; Asian Studies & Int. Problems. Mbrships. incl: Can. Pol. Sci. Assn.; Can. Lib. Assn. Address: Dept. of Pol. Sci., Brandon Univ., Brandon, Man., Can.

LIU, Wu-chi, pen name HSIAO, Hsia, b. 27 July 1907, Wu-chiang, China. Professor. Educ: Nat. Tsing Hua Univ.,

Peking; B.A., Lawrence Univ., Appleton, Wis., USA; Ph.D., Yale Univ.; London Univ., UK. Publs: Confucius, His Life & Time, 1955; A Short History of Confucian Philosophy, 1955; An Introduction to Chinese Literature, 1966; Su Man-shu (World Authors Series), 1972; Ed. & Transl., Sunflower Splendour, An Anthology of Chinese Poetry (w. Irving Y. C. Lo), 1975. Contbr. to: Tsing Hua Jrnl. of Chinese Studies; Comparative Lit.; Funk & Wagnall Ency.; The Ency. of Philos.; Biograph. Dict. of Repub. China; Dict. of Oriental Lits.; & var. other encys. Address: Dept. of E. Asian Languages and Literature, Goodbody Hall, Indiana Univ., Bloomington, IN 47401, USA.

LIVERANI, Giuseppe, b. 17 Sept. 1903, Faenza, Italy. Museum Director; Editor; Ceramics Expert & Lecturer. Publs. incl: Catalogo delle Porcellane dei Medici, 1936; La Maiolica Italiana dalle Origini sino alla Comparsa della Porcellana Europea, 1957, Swedish ed. 1958, UK, USA, Can. & German eds. 1960; Selezioni di Opere del Museo Internazionali delle Ceramiche di Faenza, 1963; La Manifattura di Doccia nel 1760, 1972; Ed., review Faenza. Contbr. to: num. encys., dicts., books & jrnls. Mbr., num. histl. & ceramic assns. Hons. incl: Dip. & Gold Medal, Schl. of Culture & Art, 1967; Cmdr., Order of Repub., 1974. Address: Via Martiri Ungheresi 4, 48018 Faenza, Italy.

LIVERSIDGE, (Henry) Douglas, b. 12 Mar. 1913, Swinton, Yorks., UK. Journalist; Author. Publs: White Horizon, 1951; The Last Continent, 1958; The Third Front, 1960; The Whale Killers, 1963; Saint Francis of Assisi, 1968; Peter the Great, 1968; Lenin, 1969; Joseph Stalin, 1969; Saint Ignatius of Loyola, 1970; The White World, 1972; Queen Elizabeth II, 1974. Contbr. to num. jrnls. & newspapers. Address: 56 Love Lane, Pinner, Middx. HA5 3EX, UK.

LIVINGS, Henry, b. 20 Sept. 1929, Prestwich, UK. Playwright. Educ: Univ. of Liverpool. Publs: Stop It Whoever You Are, 1961; Big Soft Nellie, 1961; Nil Carborundum, 1962; Kelly's Eye, 1963; Eh?, 1964; Little Mrs. Foster Show, 1966; Good Grief!, 1968; Honour & Offer, 1969; Pongo Plays 1-6, 1971; This Jockey Drives Late Nights, 1972; ffinest ffamily in the Land, 1973. Mbrships: Brit. Actors' Equity; Writers' Guild of GB; Dobcross Band Club; The Film Exchange Manchester. Hons: Evening Standard Drama Award, 1961; Britannia Award, 1963. Address: 33 Woods Lane, Dobcross, Oldham, Lancs., UK.

LIVINGSTON, Braniff I., pen name BABCOCK, G., b. 2 July 1946, Dallas, Tex., USA. Travel Writer. Educ: B.A., M.A., Cazenovia, 1968; Ph.D., Onassis Univ., NYC, 1973. Publs: A History of the R.M.S. Caronia, 1974; A Guide to Trans-Atlantic Air Travel, 2nd revised ed., 1974. Contbr. to: N.Y. Times; Arts Mag. Mbrships. incl: Inter-Continental Club for Travel Writers; Int. Air Transport Assn. (VP, PR, 1971, 1973, 1974). Recip., Award, Int. Air Travel Assn., Disting. Travel Reportage. Address: 317 W. 99th Street, Apt. 3B, N.Y., NY 10025, USA.

LIVINGSTON, Myra Cohn, b. 17 Aug. 1926, Omaha, Neb., USA. Poet; Author; Teacher. Educ: B.A., Sarah Lawrence Coll., Bronxville, N.Y. Publs. incl: Ed., A Tune Beyond Us: A Collection of Poems, 1968; A Crazy Flight & Other Poems, 1969; Speak Roughly to Your Little Boy: An Anthology of Parody & Burlesque, 1971; The Malibu & Other Poems, 1972; What a Wonderful Bird the Frog Are: An Assortment of Humorous Poetry & Verse, 1973; The Poems of Lewis Carroll, 1973; The Way Things Are & Other Poems, 1974; Come Away, 1974. Mbrships. incl: Authors' Guild; PEN; Soc. of Children's Book Writers. Hons. incl: Notable Book Award, S.Calif. Coun. of Lit., 1973. Address: 9308 Readcrest Dr., Beverley Hills, CA 90210, USA.

LIVINGSTONE, Douglas, b. 23 May 1934, London, UK. Playwright. Educ: Bristol Univ.; Royal Acad. of Dramatic Art. Publs. incl: (TV plays) I Remember the Battle; Cry Baby Bunting; Nora; I Can't See My Little Willie; Competition; If You Could See What I Can See; A Touch of the Victoriana's; Mummy & Daddy; After Loch Lomond; Constance Lytton; (dramatizations) Wessex Tales (Thomas Hardy); Clayhanger (Arnold Bennett). Mbrships: Writers Guild of GB; Brit. Actors Equity. Address: 16 Riverview Gdns., London SW13, UK.

LLOYD, D. Tecwyn, b. 22 Oct. 1914, Llawrybetws, Merionethshire, N. Wales, UK. University Lecturer. Educ: B.A., Univ. of Wales, Bangor; M.A. (Liverpool). Publs: Erthyglau Beirniadol, 1947; Safle'r Gerbydres, 1970; Lady Gwladys a Phobl Eraill, 1971. Contbr. to: Taliesin, Jrnl. of Welsh Acad. of Letters (Ed., 1965–); Poetry Wales; Y Genhinen; Llên Cymru; Trivium; Y Traethodydd; Ysgrifau Beirniadol; Analecta Eremotica; etc. Mbrships. incl: Yr Academi Gymreig; Lit. Comm., Nat. Eisteddfodd of Wales; Hon. Soc. of Cymmrodorion; Keats-Shelley Mem. Assn.; Hellenic Soc. Hons: Lit. Awards, Welsh Arts Coun., 1971, 1972. Address: Garth Martin, Ffordd Llysonnen, Caerfyrddin, Dyfed, UK.

LLOYD, Richard Dafydd Vivian Llewellyn, pen name LLEWELLYN, Richard, b. Wales, UK. Author. Publs. incl: How Green Was My Valley, 1939; None but the Lonely Heart, 1943, 1968; A Flame for Doubting Thomas, 1954; The Flame of Hercules, 1957; Warden of the Smoke & Bells, 1958; Chez Pavan, 1959; A Man in a Mirror, 1961; Sweet Morn of Judas' Day, 1964; Down Where the Moon is Small, 1966; The End of the Rug, 1968; But We Didn't Get the Fox, 1970; White Horse to Banbury Cross, 1972; The Night is a Child, 1972; Bride of Israel, My Love, 1973; (plays) The Scarlet Suit, 1962; Ecce, 1972. Address: c/o Michael Joseph, 52 Bedford Sq., London WC1, UK.

LLOYD, Wyndham E. B., b. 1901, London, UK. Chest Physician. Educ: Winchester Coll.; Gonville & Caius Coll., Cambridge; St. Bartholomew's Hosp., London; M.A.; M.R.C.S.; L.R.C.P.; D.P.H. Publs: A Hundred Years of Medicine, 1936, revised 1968. Address: The Small House, Coffinswell, Newton Abbot, Devon, UK.

LLYWELYN-WILLIAMS, Alun, b. 27 Aug. 1913, Cardiff, Wales, UK. Director of Extra-Mural Studies, University College of N. Wales. Educ: M.A., Wales. Publs: Cerddi, 1944; Pont y Caniedydd, 1956; Crwydro Arfon, 1959; Y Nos, y Niwl, a'r Ynys, 1960; Crwydro Brycheiniog, 1964; Y Llenor a'i Gymdeithas, 1966; Nes Na'r Hanesydd? 1968; Ed., Tir Newydd, 1935-39. Contbr. to: Times Lit. Supplement; Poetry Wales; The Welsh Review; Transactions Hon. Soc. Cymmrodorion; Taliesin; Y Traethodydd; Lleufer; (Y Llenor). Mbrships. incl: Yr Acad. Gymreig; N. Wales Arts Assn.; Hon. Soc. Cymmrodorion; Dir., Harlech TV Ltd., & Welsh Theatre Co. Recip., Ellis Griffith Memorial Prize, 1960-61. Address: Pen-y-Lan, 55 Ffordd Belmont, Bangor, Gwynedd, Wales, UK.

LO, Chin-Tang, b. 27 July, 1929, Lungsi, Kansu, China. University Professor of Chinese Literature. Educ: B.A., 1952; M.A., 1956; Ph.D., 1961; Nat. Taiwan Univ. Publs: The History of Chinese Short Songs, 1956; Essential Record of Bibliography of Various Dynasties, 1959; The Study of Synopsis of Yuang Drama, 1961; A Study of the Dramatists of Ming Dynasty, 1966; (transl.) Early Chinese Literature, 1969. Contbr. to: China Monthly; Continent Mag.; Ming-Pao Monthly; Jrnl. Oriental Studies; Lit. World; Tamkang Review, etc. Recip., acad. hons. Address: Dept. of E. Asian Lit., Univ. of Hawaii, Honolulu, HI 96822, USA.

LO, Hsiang-lin, b. 19 Oct. 1906, Shing Ning Co., Kwangtung Province, China. Professor of Chinese (Retired). Educ: B.A., 1930; Dip. in Hist., Grad. Schl., Nat. Tsing Hua Univ., Publs. incl: A Study of Chinese Genealogies, 1971; A General History of China, 2 vols., 15th ed., 1972; The Ancestry & Upbringing of Dr. Sun Yat-sen, 1972; Fu Ping-ch'ang (1896-1965), & Modern China, 1973. Contbr. to var. jrnls. Mbrships: Pres., Chinese PEN Ctr. of Hong Kong; Hong Kong Br., Royal Asiatic Soc. Hons: Hon. Prof., Dept. of Chinese, Univ. of Hong Kong, 1968; Chung-shan Publ. Award, Min. of Educ., Chinese Nat. Govt., 1972. Address: 22 MacDonnell Rd., 1st Floor, Hong Kong.

LO, Ki-lp, b. 15 Jan. 1925, Peking, China. Principal, Kwang Hsia College; Editorial Chairman. Educ: Bach., Chinese Univ. of Hong Kong. Publ: The Red Books of Communist China, 1971. Contbr. to: Chung Hing Mag. & Newspaper. Mbrships: Chinese PEN Ctr. of Hong Kong; Standing Dir., Kowloon Chmbr. of Comm.: Standing Councillor, World Christian Children Welfare Assn. Hon., Glorious of Literature, Fishing Ind. & Commercial Gen. Assn., 1971. Address: 550 Nathan Rd., 10th Floor, Front Blk, Kowloon, Hong Kong.

LO, Ngar Ying, pen name TSUI, Ying, b. 16 Dec. 1938, Canton, China. Writer. Educ: Sing Kung Univ. Publs. incl: Two Faced Beauty, 1968; A Splendid Dream, 1968; Red, Yellow Blue White & Black, 1973. Contbr. to: Home Life Jrnl.; Sing Tao Pictorial; Wah Kiu Yat Po; Sing Tao Jih Pao; Tintin Yat Po. Mbrships: Comm., Chinese PEN Ctr. of Hong Kong; Vice Comm., Lo Clan's Assn.; Permanent Dir., S. China Athletic Assn.; Comm., Hong Kong Civic Assn. Address: H16 Hilltop Mansion, 60 Cloudview Rd., North Point, Hong Kong.

LO, Winston Wan, b. 12 Apr. 1938, Kwangtung, China. University Professor. Educ: B.A., Univ. of Hong Kong; Ph.D., Harvard Univ., USA. Publs: Life & Thought of Yeh Shih (1150-1223). Contbr. to: Monumenta Serica Philosophies; E. & W. Address: 3052 Corrib Drive, Tallahassee, FL 32303, USA.

LOADES, David Michael, b. 19 Jan. 1934, Cambridge, UK. University Lecturer. Educ: B.A., 1958, M.A. & Ph.D., 1961, Emmanuel Coll., Cambridge. Publs: Two Tudor Conspiracies, 1965; The Oxford Martyrs, 1970; Politics & the Nation, 1450-1660, 1974. Contbr. to: Jrnl. of Ecclesiastical Hist.; Transactions of the Royal Histl. Soc.; Archiv Für Reformationsgeschichte. Mbrships. incl: Ecclesiastical Hist. Soc.; Royal Histl. Soc. Recip., acad. awards. Address: Oatlands, Farnley Mount, Durham City, UK.

Lo BELLO, Nino, pen names incl. TORNATA, Ben, b. 8 Sept. 1921, NYC, USA. Author; Freelance foreign correspondent. Educ.: B.A., Queens Coll., NY, 1947; M.A., N.Y. Univ., 1948. Publs: The Vatican Empire, 1969; The Varican's Wealth, 1971; Vatican, USA, 1973. Contbr. to: N.Y. Times & Los Angeles Times (book reviewer); num. mags. & newspapers. Mbrships: Overseas Press Club., Am.; For. Press Club., Vienna, Austria; Soc. of Mag. Writers, N.Y., USA. Hon: on N.Y. Times Best Seller List, June 1969. Address: Lenaugasse 24, 3400 Weidling bei Vienna, Austria.

LOCK, Dennis Laurence, b. 15 Sept. 1929, London, UK. Chief Organisation & Methods Officer. Educ: H.N.C. Applied Phys., Acton Tech. Coll. Publs: Project Management, 1968; Ed., Director's Guide to Management Techniques, 1970; Industrial Scheduling Techniques, 1971; Ed., Engineer's Handbook of Management Techniques, 1973; Ed., Financial Management of Production, forthcoming; Factory Administration Handbook (co-author & advsry. ed.), forthcoming. Contbr. to: New Scientist; Director; other profl. jrnls. Mbrships: Assoc., Brit. Inst. Mgmt.; Fellow, Physical Soc.; Fellow, Inst. of Prod. Control. Address: 29 Burston Dr., Park Street, St. Albans, Herts. AL2 2HR, UK.

LOCKARD, W. Duane, b. 26 Nov. 1921, Owings, W. Va., USA. Professor of Political Science; Writer. Educ: B.A., 1947, M.A., 1948, Yale Univ.; Ph.D., 1952. Publs: New England State Politics, 1959; The Politics of State & Local Politics, 1963; New Jersey Governor, 1964; Toward Equal Opportunity, 1968; The Perverted Priorities of American Politics, 1971. Contbr. to: Nation; Am. Pol. Sci. Reviews; Pol. Sci. Quarterly; Reporter; Soc.; Pol. Studies. Address: 120 Fitz Randolph Rd., Princeton, NJ 08540, USA.

LOCKE, Edwin Allen, III, b. 15 May 1938, NYC, USA. Psychologist. Educ: B.A., Harvard Univ., 1960; M.A., 1962, Ph.D., 1964, Cornell Univ. Publs: Task Experience as a Source of Attitudes (w. P. E. Breer), 1965; Principles of Effective Study, in press. Contbr. to profl. jrnls. Mbrships: Md. Psychol. Assn.; N.Y. Acad. of Scis.; Acad. of Mgmt.; Fellow, Am. Psychol. Assn. Address: Coll. of Bus. & Mgmt., Univ. of Md., College Park, MD 20742, USA.

LOCKE, Elsie Violet, b. 17 Aug. 1912, Hamilton, NZ. Writer. Educ: B.A., Auckland Univ. Publs: The Runaway Settlers, 1965; The End of the Harbour, 1968; Growing Points & Prickles 1920-60, 1972; series of booklets for children on soc. hist. of NZ. Contbr. to: Landfall; Islands; NZ Listener; NZ Schl. Jrnl.; etc. Mbr., Aust. Soc. of Authors. Recip., Katherine Mansfield Award for essay in Landfall, 1959. Address: 392 Oxford Terr., Christchurch, 1, NZ.

LOCKE, Francis Philbrick, b. 1 May 1912, Lincoln, Neb., USA. Journalist (Retired). Educ: A.B., Harvard Coll., 1933; Nieman Fellow, Harvard, 1946-47. Contbr. to: Free World; Reporter; Common Sense. Mbrships: Former Mbr., Am. Soc. of Newspaper Eds.; Nat. Conf. of Edit. Writers. Hons: Sigma Delta Chi Nat. Prize for edit. writing, 1946; Trans-World Airlines Award for edit. writing, 1957. Address: 7368 W. Westwood Drive, Riverside, CA 92504, USA.

LOCKETT, Marjorie L., b. 8 Sept. 1922, Watertown, Wis., USA. Travel Writer; Editor. Educ: Lakeland Coll., Wis. Publs: (Area ed.) Fodor's Guide to Mexico; (fndr. & ed.) Travel Hotline Mexico; (ed.) 3 English Language mags. for foreign tourists: Guide Mexico (City), Guide Sureste, Guide Acapulco. Contbr. to: The News (Mexico); Chgo. Tribune;

& num. mags. in Mexico. Mbrships: Am. Soc. of Bus. Writers; Foreign Corres. Assn. Address: Rio Atoyac 26-4, Mexico 5, D.F., Mexico.

LOCKLEY, Ronald Mathias, b. 8 Feb. 1903, Cardiff, Wales, UK. Writer; Naturalist. Publs. incl: Dream Island, 1930; Birds of the Sea, 1945; The Island Farmers, 1946; Letters from Skokholm, 1947; The Golden Year, 1948; The Charm of the Channel Islands, 1950; The Nature Lover's Anthology, 1951; Bird-Ringing (w. Rosemary Russell), 1953; Sea-Birds (w. James Fisher), 1954; The Pan Book of Cage Birds, 1961; Britain in Colour, 1964; The Private Life of the Rabbit, 1964; Animal Navigation, 1967; The Book of Bird-Watching, 1968; The Island, 1969; Man Against Nature, 1970; The Naturalist in Wales, 1970; Seal Woman, 1974; Ocean Wanderers, 1974. Contbr. to popular & sci. jrnls. Address: Cole Pk., Malmesbury, UK.

LODGE, David, b. 28 Jan. 1935, London, UK. University Lecturer. Educ: B.A. 1955, M.A. 1959, Univ. Coll., London Univ.; Ph.D., Birmingham Univ., 1967. Publs. incl: (novels) The Picturegoers, 1960; Ginger, You're Barmy, UK, 1962, USA, 1965; The British Museum is Falling Down, UK, 1965, USA, 1967; Out of the Shelter, 1970; (non-fiction) Language of Fiction, UK & USA, 1966; Ed., Jane Austen's Emma: A Casebook, 1968; The Novelist at the Crossroads (essays), 1971; Ed., Modern Literary Criticism, 1972; Co-author, var. plays. Contbr. to: Weekend Telegraph. Recip., Harkness C'wlth. Fellowship, 1964. Address: Dept. of English, Birmingham Univ., Birmingham B15 2TT, UK.

LOEB, Ethel Wile, b. 13 Feb. 1910, NYC, USA. Writer; Columnist. Educ: Columbia Univ.; Schl. of Jrnlsm. Reporter, Soc. Ed., Stringer, var. N.Y., Md. newspapers; Radio & TV Documentary Supvsr., VP Sound Studies, Inc., 1948-69; Columnist, Frederick (Md.) News Post, 1974—. Mbr., Past Bd., Mbr., Am. Newspaper Women's Club; Am. Women in Radio & TV. Address: Wellcome Farms, Rt. 2, Frederick, MD 21701, USA.

LOENING, Sarah Larkin, b. 9 Dec. 1896, Nutley, N.J., USA. Publs: Three Rivers, 1934; The Trévals, A Tale of Quebec, 1936; Radisson, 1938; Dimo (in French), 1940; Joan of Arc, 1951; The Old Master & Other Tails, 1958; Mountain in the Field, 1972. Mbr., Pen & Brush. Address: First Neck Lane, Southampton, NY 11968, USA.

LOETSCHER, Lefferts Augustine, b. 24 July 1904, Dubuque, Iowa, USA. Church Historian; Editor; Author. Educ: A.B., Princeton Univ., 1925; Th.B., 1928, Th.M., 1929, Princeton Theol. Sem.; A.M., 1932, Ph.D., 1943, Univ. of Pa. Publs. incl: The Broadening Church, A Study of Theological Issues in the Presbyterian Church since 1869, 1954; Ed.-in-Chief, 20th-Century Encyclopedia of Religious Knowledge, 2 vols., 1955; The Problem of Christian Unity in early 19th-Century America, 1969. Contbr. to var. encys. Mbr., var. Ch. assns. Address: 140 Ross Stevenson Circle, Princeton, NJ 08540, USA.

LÖFGREN, Ulf J. G., b. 13 Oct. 1931, Umeå, Sweden. Author & Illustrator of Children's Books. Educ: B.A., Univ. of Uppsala, 1957. Publs. incl: Det underbara trädet, 1969, USA ed. (The Wonderful Tree), 1970; Färgtrumpeten, 1969; Patriks snabbverkstad, 1969; Den flygande orkestern, 1969; Ett, två, tre, 1970; Vi åker året runt, 1971; Precissomduvill, 1971; Patriks cirkus, 1971; Vem stoppar trafiken? 1973; Den förtrollade draken, 1973. Contbr., Swedish TV (series). Mbrships: Coun. Chmn., Soc. of Swedish Illustrators; Coun. Mbr., Swedish Authors' Fund. Hons. incl: Award, Swedish Soc. of Lit., 1969; Bronze medal, Leipzig Book Fair, 1971. Address: Bovägen 33, 18143 Lidingö, Sweden.

LOFTS, Norah, Pen Name, CURTIS, Peter, b. 27 Aug. 1904. Author. Publs. incl: (as Norah Lofts) I Met a Gypsy, 1935; White Hell of Pity, 1937; Silver Nutmeg, 1947; A Calf for Venus, 1949; The Lute Player, 1951; Bless this House, 1954; Scent of Cloves, 1958; Heaven in Your Hand, 1959; The House at Old Vine, 1961; The Concubine, 1964; Lovers all Untrue, 1970; The Lost Ones, 1969; A Rose for Virtue, 1971; Charlotte, 1972; Nethergate, 1973; Crown of Aloes, 1974; (as Peter Curtis) Dead March in Three Kevs, 1940; Lady Living Alone, 1944; The Devil's Own, 1959. Address: Northgate House, Bury St. Edmunds, Suffolk, UK.

LOGAN, Joshua, b. 5 Oct. 1908, Texarkana, Tex., USA. Film & Stage Director. Educ: Princeton Univ. Prods. incl: (stage) On Borrowed Time, 1938; I Married an Angel, 1938;

Two for the Show, 1939; Higher & Higher (co-author), 1939; Charlie's Aunt; Happy Birthday, 1945; Mister Robert= (co-author), 1948; South Pacific (co-author), 1949; Wish you were Here (co-author), 1952; Picnic, 1953; The World of Suzie Wong, 1958; Look to the Lilies, 1970; (films) I Met My Love Again, 1937; Picnic, 1955; Sayonara, 1957; South Pacific, 1957; Fanny, 1960; Camelot, 1966; Paint Your Wagon, 1968. Recip., Puli·zer Prize. Address: 435 E. 52nd St., N.Y., NY 10022, USA,

LOGUE, Christopher, Pen Name VICARION, Count Palmiro, b. 23 Nov. 1926. Playwright; Screenwriter; Songwriter; Poet. Publs. incl: (verse) Wand & Quadrant, 1953; Weekdream Sonnets, 1955; The Man Who Told His Love, 1958; The Arrival of the Poet in the City, 1963; ABC, 1966; The Words of the Establishment Songs, 1966; New Numbers, 1969; Twelve Cards, 1972; (plays) The Trial of Cob & Leach, 1959; Antigone, 1961; (screenplays) The End of Arthur's Marriage, 1963; Savage Messiah, 1972; (as Count Palmiro Vicarion) Lust, a pornographic novel, 1957; (Ed.) Count Palmiro Vicarion's Book of Limericks, 1957. Contbr. to: Private Eye; Times; Vogue; etc. Address: 18 Denbigh Close, London W11, UK.

LOINGER, Silvia Mary, pen name SIMALO, b. 2 Sept. 1917, Vienna, Austria. Author. Educ: Coll. studies. Publs: Irgendwann, 1967; Irgendwo, 1969. Mbrships: Österreichischer Schriftstellerverband (Austrian Authors' Soc.); Presseclub Concordia (Union of Austrian Writers & Jrnlsts.); Hon. mbr., European-Am. Cultural Soc., Eurafolk; Hon. mbr., Int. Union, Upholders of Civilization. Address: Alserstr. 65, 1080-Wien, Austria.

LOMBARD, Alf, b. 8 July 1902, Paris, France. Retired Professor of Romance Philology. Educ: Ph.D., Uppsala Univ., Sweden, 1931. Publs. incl: The Languages of Europe & of the White Race (in Swedish), 1926; Les Constructions Nominales dans le Français Moderne, 1930; La Prononciation du Roumain, 1935; Southern Swedish & Central Swedish (in Swedish), 1945; Le Verbe Rounmain, Étude Morphologique, 2 vols., 1954-55; Ed. & Reviser, K. Nyrop, Manuel Phonétique du Francais Parlé, 1963; The Destinies of Latin in the East (in Swedish), 1967; Roumanian Grammar (in Swedish), 1973; La Langue Roumaine, 1974. Fndr. & Ed. (1940-70) collect. Études Romanes de Lund (23 vols.). Contbr. to num. linguistic jrnls. Mbr., num. learned socs., Sweden & abroad. Recip., num. academic & cultural hons.; Mélanges de Philologie offerts à A. Lombard, publ'd. in his hon., 1969. Address: Nehrmans väg 16, 223 60 Lund, Sweden.

LOMPOLO, Jouni Kaarlo, pen name ORIGO, b. 24 Sept. 1936, Kittilä, Finland. Editor. Educ: 1st part, Exam. of Arch., Tech. Inst., Helsinki. Publs: Ikuisia ajatuksia, 1967; Käytöksen kultainen kirja, 1971; Hullunkuriset perheet, 1973. Contbr. to Helsingin Sanomat. Mbrships: Suomen Sanomalehtimiesliitto; Suomen Kirjailijaliitto; Suomen Näytelmäkirjailijaliitto. Address: Franzeninkatu 20 A 15, 00500 Helsinki 50, Finland.

LONDZIN, Victor, pen name LESZCZA, Jan, b. 20 May 1918, Zabrzeg, Silesia, Poland. Mechanical Designer. Educ: Univ. of Munich, Germany. Publs: Czas obłąkany (Time of Insanity), 1947; Konie drewniane (Wooden Horses), 1967; Szkicownik (Sketch Book), 1969. Contbr. to: Polish Student Abroad Mag. (Co-Ed., Contbr.); The Chronicle (Co-Ed., Contbr., lit. sect.); (poetry & poetry transls.) Culture, Paris; News, London; Poets & Painters Press, London; Subjects, N.Y.; Anthol. of Mod. British & Am. Poetry, N.Y., 1958 & 1965; etc. Mbrships: Polish Lit. Club, W. Germany (Sec., co-fndg. mbr.); Polish Union of Jrnlsts., London. Address: 1447 Aura Way, Los Altos, CA 94022, USA.

LONG, Beatrice Powell, pen names LONG, Bee Bacherig, POWELL, Patsy, TRIXIE, b. 8 Oct. 1907, Pittsboro, Miss., USA. Poet; Writer. Educ: Bowling Green Bus. Univ.; Univ. of Tenn. Evening Classes. Publs: Reflections, 1964; Where Treasures Lie, 1967. Contbr. to poetry jrnls., other mags., anthols. in USA, UK, Italy, India. Mbrships. incl: Pres., Poetry Soc. of Tenn.; Rep., Centro Studi E Scambi, Rome; Poets' Roundtable of Arkansas; Acad. of Am. Poets; Tenn. Woman's Press & Authors' Club; World Poetry Soc. Intercontinental. Hons. incl: Author Memorial Plaque, Memphis, 1965; 1st Prize, Haiku, Nat. Fedn. of State Poetry Socs., 1973. Address: 103 Eastland Dr., Memphis, TN 38111, USA.

LONG, Donald Stuart, pen name LONG, D. S., b. 5 Jan. 1950, Walla Walla, Wash., USA (of NZ parentage). Writer;

Publisher; Teacher of the deaf. Educ: B.A., Dip.Ed.; Univ. of Canterbury, NZ; Christchurch Tchrs. Coll. Publs: Borrow Pit (poems), 1971; Poems From the Fifth Season, 1975; Contemporary Maori Writing (co-ed. of anthol.), forthcoming. Contbr. to: Edge (Ed.); Kayak; Prism Int.; Makar; Mate; Chelsea; Cafe Solo; Poetry Aust.; New Poetry; Ploughman; Ark River Review; Westerly; New Argot; etc. Mbrships: COSMEP; COSMEPA; PEN; Assn. of Handcraft Painters; NZ Book Coun. Address: P.O. Box 25042, Victoria St., Christchurch, New Zealand.

LONG, James Scott, b. 11 Aug. 1892, York, Pa., USA. Distinguished Professor of Chemistry. Educ: Ch.E., 1914, M.S., 1915, Lehigh Univ.; Ph.D., Johns Hopkins Univ., 1922. Publs: Chemical Calculations (co-author), 1923, 10 eds.; Qualitative Analysis (w. others), 1923; Elementary Experiments on the Non-Metals (w. others), 1923; Treatise on Protective Coatings (co-author), 10 books in 5 vols. Contbr., 145 papers in US & for. jrnls.; Holder, 20 patents. Address: 2267 Habersham Dr., Clearwater, FL 33516, USA.

LONG, John Frederick Lawrence, b. 1917, London, UK. Head, Soviet Foreign Policy & Military Affairs Section, Radio Liberty, Munich, Germany, 1964-68; Headmaster, Munich International School, 1968-74; Principal, Community High School, Tehran, 1974. Educ: Queen's Coll., Cambridge; M.A. Publ: Modern Russia: An Introduction. Contbr. to: The Times. Financial Times; Economist; etc. Address: c/o Community Schl., Box 1505, Tehran, Iran.

LONG, John J., b. 3 July 1933, Niagara Falls, N.Y., USA. Broker; Cattle Farmer. Educ: B.S., Niagara Univ. Contbr. to: Ed., Conservation Courier; monthly column in N.Y. State Conservation Coun. Comments. Mbrships: Outdoor Writers Assn. of Am.; Sec.-Treas., N.Y. State Outdoor Writers Assn. Address: 1953 Balmer Rd., Ransomville, NY 14131, USA.

LONGFORD, Elizabeth, b. 30 Aug. 1906, London, UK. Writer. Educ: B.A., 1931, M.A., 1941, Lady Margaret Hall, Oxford. Publs: Jameson's Raid, 1960; Victoria R.I., 1964; Wellington — The Years of the Sword, 1969; Wellington — Pillar of State, 1972; The Royal House of Windsor, 1974; Winston Churchill, 1974. Contbr. to: New Statesman; Spectator; Books & Bookmen; Sunday Times Mag.; Horizon, USA; Victorian Studies, USA; N.Y. Times. Mbrships. incl: F.R.S.L. Hons. incl: James Tait Black Mem. Prize for Victoria R.I., 1964; Hon. D.Litt., Sussex Univ., 1970; C.B.E., 1974. Address: 18 Chesil Ct., Chelsea Manor St., London SW3 5QP, UK.

LONGLEY, Michael, b. 27 July 1939, Belfast, UK. Arts Administrator. Educ: Degree, Classics, Trinity Coll., Dublin, Repub. of Ireland, 1963. Publs: No Continuing City, 1969; An Exploded View, 1973; Ed., Causeway: The Arts in Ulster, 1971. Contbr. to: Encounter; New Statesman; Listener; Times Lit. Supplement; London Mag.; Honest Ulsterman; Poetry Nation; Irish Times; etc. Recip., Eric Gregory Award for Poetry, 1965. Address: 18 Hillside Pk., Belfast 9, UK.

LONGMATE, Norman Richard, b. 15 Dec. 1925, Newbury, UK. BBC Official. Educ: B.A., 1950, M.A., 1954, Worcester Coll., Oxford. Publs: King Cholera, 1966; The Waterdrinkers, 1968; How We Lived Then, 1971; If Britain Had Fallen, 1972; The Workhouse, 1974; The Real Dad's Army, 1974; The G.I.s, forthcoming; Target 53: Coventry, forthcoming. Contbr. to: The Observer mag.; The Sunday Telegraph; BBC Radio broadcasts. Address: c/o Hutchinsons, 3 Fitzroy Sq., London W1, UK.

LOOMIE, Albert Joseph, b. 29 July 1922, NYC, USA. Historian. Educ: B.A., Loyola Univ., Chgo., 1944; M.A., Fordham Univ., 1949; S.T.L., Woodstock Coll., 1953; Ph.D., London Univ., 1957. Publs: The Spanish Elizabethans, 1963; Toleration & Diplomacy, 1963; Guy Fawkes in Spain, 1972; Spain & the Jacobean Catholics, Vol. I, 1603-12, 1973. Contbr. to: Bulletin of Inst. of Historical Rsch.; English Historical Review; Revue Belge de Philol. & d'Histoire. Mbrships. incl: Corresp. Fellow, Real Acad. de la Historia, Madrid; Fellow, Royal Historical Soc., UK; Am. Historical Assn. Hons. incl: Guggenheim Fellow, 1965-66. Address: Dept. of History, Fordham Univ., N.Y., NY 10458, USA.

LOOS, Anita, b. 26 Apr. 1893. Screen Writer. Publs. incl: (novels) Gentlemen Prefer Blondes, 1925; The Whole Town's Talking; The Fall of Eve; Cherries are Ripe; The

Social Register; A Mouse is Born, 1950; This Brunette Prefers Work, 1956; No Mother to Guide Her, 1961; (autobiography) A Girl Like I, 1966; (films) Red Headed Women; Blossoms in the Dust; I Married an Angel; The Pirate; (plays) Happy Birthday, 1946; Gentlemen Prefer Blondes, 1949; Mama Steps Out; They Met in Bombay; A Girl Like I, 1966. Address: c/o Avon Books, 959 Eighth Ave., N.Y., NY 10019, USA.

LÓPEZ DE SERANTES, Josefina, pen name MIREYA, b. 6 Apr. 1922, La Coruña, Spain. Publs: Entre el amor y el orgullo; Deber sagrado; Un sueño de Amor; El misterio de Foremerte; El buen papa Juan. Contbr. to: El Ideal Gallego; La voz de Galicia; El faro de Vigo; Lecturas; Hogar y Moda; Siluetas; Mujer. Mbrships: Nat. Inst. of the Spanish Book; Soc. of Authors of Spain. Hons: Story Prize, 1948, La Región Prize, 1952, El Ideal Gallego; Ivory Tower Prize for Celos, 1950; Radio Prize Petición de Mano, 1955. Address: Calle Madrid 136, 2°, La Coruña, Spain.

LOPEZ QUINTÁS, Alfonso, b. 21 Apr. 1928, Mugardos, Coruna, Spain. Professor of Philosophy & Aesthetics. Educ: San Juan de Poyo Coll., Pontevedra, Spain; Univs. of Salamanca & Madrid; also studied at univs. in Germany, UK, Austria & Italy. Publs. incl: Metodología de lo Suprasensible, 1966; El triángulo hermenéutico, 1971; Romano Guardini y la dialéctica de lo viviente, 1966; Diagnosis del Hombre Actual, 1966; Hacia un Estilo Integral de Pensar: vol. 1, Estetica, 1967, vol. 2, Metodologia. Antropologia, 1967; Pensadores Cristianos Contemporaneos: vol. 1, Haecker, Wust, Ebner, Przywara, Zubiri, 1968; Filosofia Española Contemporanea, 1970; El Pensamiento Filosofico de Ortega Y D'Ors, 1972. Contbr. to reviews & jrnls. Mbr., profl. orgs. Recip., acad. hons. Address: Madre de Dios, 39, Madrid — 16, Spain.

LOPEZ RUBIO, José, b. 13 Dec. 1903, Motril, Spain. Playwright; Film & TV Scenarist; Translator. Educ: Law studies, Univ. of Madrid. Publs. incl: Un trono para Cristy, 1956; La novia del espacio, 1956; Las manos son inocentes, 1958; Diana está comunicando, 1960; Esta noche, tampoco, 1961; Nunca es tarde, 1964; El corazón en la mano, 1972; (TV) Al filo de lo imposible, 1971. Contbr. to var. lit. jrnls. Mbrships: incl: Admin. Coun., CISAC; Circle of Cinema Writers. Hons. incl: Nat. Theatre Prize for El Corazón en la mano, 1972; Nat. TV Prize for Al filo de lo imposible, 1971; Nat. Cinema Prize for Eugenia de Montijo, Nada menos que todo un hombre, etc. Address: Calle Requena 5, Madrid 13, Spain.

LORANT, Stefan, b. 22 Feb. 1901, Budapest, Hungary. Editor; Author. Educ: Acad. of Econs., Budapest; Harvard Univ., USA; LL.D.; M.A. Publs. incl: I Was Hitler's Prisoner, 1935; The New World, 1946; The Presidency, 1951; The Life of Abraham Lincoln, 1954; The Life & Times of Theodore Roosevelt, 1959; Pittsburgh: The Story of an American City, 1964; The New World: The First Pictures of America, 1965; The Glorious Burden: The American Presidency, 1968; Fighting for the New World, 1972; The Road to Tyranny: Germany from Bismarck to Hitler, 1973; Sieg Heil, An Illustrated History of Germany from Bismarck to Hitler, 1974. Contbr. to: Weekly Illustrated; Life; Look; Lilliput; Picture Post, USA; etc. Address: Fairview, Lenox, MA 01240, USA.

LORAYNE, Harry, b. 4 May 1926, NYC, USA. Memory Training Expert; Founder & President, Harry Lorayne School of Memory, NYC. Publs: How to Develop a Super-Power Memory, 1956; Secrets of Mind Power, 1961; Miracle Math, 1966; Instant Mind Power, 1967; Memory Isometrics Course, 1968; Mental Magnetism Course, 1969; Good Memory: Good Student!, 1972; 10 books on card magic. Contbr. to mags. & newspapers. Agent: William Morris. Address: 62 Jane St., N.Y., NY 10014, USA.

LORCK-FALCK, Ewen, b. 19 June 1934, Steinkjer, Norway. Grammar School Teacher; Correspondence School Headmaster. Educ: Cand. philol., 1971. Publs: (poetry) Før Midnatt, 1964; Vår tanke — vår skjebne, 1966; Gruppe 66, 1966; Gruppe 67, 1967; Trøndsk lyrikk, 1966, 1967; Under ein ny himmel, 1968; (sci. treatise) Bertram Dybwad Brochmann og samtiden, 1971. Contbr. to: Vårt Blad; Aftenposten; Østlendingen; Adresseavisen; Samfunnsliv. Mbrships: Norwegian Soc. of Authors; Ctr. of Authors; PEN; Nordic Assn. Recip., Prof. Welhaven's Award, 1971. Address: Elverum Gymnas, 2401 Elverum, Norway.

LORD, Gigi, b. NYC, USA. Social Worker; Poet. Educ: B.S., M.A., N.Y. Univ.; Grad. study, Columbia Univ. Schl. of Soc. Work. Publs: Toppling After Itself, 1969. Contbr.

to num. poetry jrnls. Mbrships: Poetry Soc., UK; Poetry Soc. of Am.; Pa. Poetry Soc. Hons: 1st Place Award, Toppling After Itself, Nat. Fedn. of State Poetry Socs.; Premium Award, Poetry Soc., UK, 1969; Henry Rago Award, N.Y. Poetry Forum, 1973. Address: 55 E. 21st St., Brooklyn, NY 11226, USA.

LORD, Robert Needham, b. 18 July 1945, Rotorus, NZ. Writer. Educ: B.A., Victoria Univ., Wellington, Dip.Tchng., Wellington Tchrs. Coll. Publs: (plays) It Isn't Cricket, 1971; Balance of Payments, 1972; Meeting Place, 1972; Nativity, 1973; Well Hung, 1974; Heroes & Butterflies, 1974; I'll Scream if I Want To, 1975; Glitter & Spit, 1974; Dead & Never Called Me Mother, 1975; (radio plays) Moody Tuesday, 1972; Friendship Centre (TV), 1973; The Body in the Part, 1973; Blood on my Sprigs, 1973. Mbrships: PEN; Aust. Writers Guild; Actors Equity NZ. Hons: Katherine Mansfield Young Writers' Award, 1969; Queen Elizabeth II Arts Coun. of NZ Travel Award, 1974. Address: Apt. 12, "Norman", 43 W. 93rd Street, N.Y., NY 10025, USA.

LORD, Walter, b. Oct. 1917, Baltimore, Md., USA. Author. Educ: B.A., Princeton Univ., 1939; LL.B., Yale Univ., 1946. Publs: The Fremantle Diary, 1954; A Night to Remember, 1955; Day of Infamy, 1957; The Good Years, 1960; A Time to Stand, 1961; Peary to the Pole, 1963; The Past That Would Not Die, 1965; Incredible Victory, 1967; The Dawn's Early Light, 1972. Contbr. to: Am. Heritage; N.Y. Times Book Review. Mbrships. incl: Authors League (Coun.); Authors Guild; ASCAP. Hons: Summerfield G. Roberts Award, 1961; Annual Book Award, Colonial Dames of America, 1973. Address: 116 E. 68th St., N.Y., NY 10021, USA.

LORD, William Jackson Jr., b. 10 May 1926, Milam, Tex., USA. Academician. Educ: B.B.A., 1950, M.B.A., 1953, Univ. of Tex.; Ph.D., Univ. of Ill., 1961. Publs: How Authors Make a Living, 1962; Functional Business Communication, 1968, 2nd ed., 1974. Contbr. to: Jrnl. of Bus. Communication; ABCA Bulletin; Social Sci. Quarterly. Mbrships: Pres., Am. Bus. Communication Assn., 1974; Fellow, 1974. S.W. Fedn. of Acad. Disciplines. Hons: Grant, Authors League of Am., 1959; Tchng. Excellence Award, Coll. of Bus. Coun. & Students Assn., 1965-66, 1969-70; UT Chmbr. Fellow, Austin Chmbr. of Comm., 1974. Address: 3500 Hillbrook Drive, Austin, TX 78731, USA.

LORING, Elisabeth Ann, pen name ELISABETH ANN, b. 12 May 1915, London, UK. Editor; Journalist. Publs: (romantic novels) Night After Bond Street; Bronze Angel; etc. (health) Beauty Adorned; Elisabeth Ann's Book of Beauty; Slim. Contbr. to: Sunday Dispatch (Woman's Ed.); Good Housekeeping (Woman's Ed.; former Beauty Ed.); Modern Wkly. (Woman's Ed.); Times; Doctor on Holiday & at Leisure (Ed.) Lab-Lore (Ed.). Mbrships: Cookery & Food Assn.; Med. Jrnlsts. Assn. Address: Flat 4, Crofton House, 1 New Cavendish St., London W1M 7RP, UK.

LOSADA MARTÍN, Juan, num. pen names incl. MARTYN, John L., b. 24 Nov. 1922, Madrid, Spain. Journalist; Author. Publs: Crimenes y criminales españoles, 1963; El mundo alucinante del crimen, 1967; La sociedad de masas en el socialismo escandinavio, 1967; Perfiles humanos de la cuidadanía, 1968; Sintesís del pensamiento de Pablo Iglesias, 1974; Alfa de Centauro, 1974. Contbr. to: num. mags & newspapers in Madrid; El Socialista, Toulouse; Avanti, Rome; La Vanguardia & Revista Socialista, Buenos Aires; Ibérica, N.Y. Mbr. & Writer for Spanish Socialist Workers Party. Address: Calle Reyes Católicos 18, El Escorial, Spain.

LOSHAK, David, b. 6 Apr. 1919, Pinner, UK. Art Historian; University Teacher, Art History. Educ: Acad. Dip., Univ. of London; M.A., N.Y.Univ., USA. Publs: The Art of Thomas Girtin, (w. T. Girtin), 1954; Catalogue of G. F. Watts Exhibition, Tate Gallery, London, 1954. Contbr. to: An Introduction to Literature & the Fine Arts, 1950; Critique; Burlington Mag.; Coll. Art Jrnl.; Victorian Studies; Konsthistorisk Tidskrift; Ency. Britannica. Address: Visbygade 8, 2100 Copenhagen Ø, Denmark.

LOSHAK, David Leslie Ivor, b. 16 Apr. 1933, Harrow, UK. Journalist. Educ: B.A., Univ. of Oxford, 1955. Author, Pakistan Crisis, 1971. Contbr. to: Contemporary Review; Daily Telegraph; New Nation; Am. Med. News; Aust. Med. Assn. Gazette; num. other jrnls.; BBC; Can. Broadcasting Corp. Mbrships: Nat. Union of Jrnlsts.; Dev. Jrnlsts. Assn.; Med. Jrnlsts. Assn. Address: 164 Burbage Rd., London SE21 7AG, UK.

LOSS, Louis, b. 11 June 1914, Lancaster, Pa., USA. Professor of Law. Educ: B.S., Univ. of Pa., 1934; LL.B., Yale Univ., 1937. Publs: Securities Regulation, 1951, 2nd ed., 6 vols., 1961, 1969; Blue Sky Law, 1958. Contbr. to: Harvard Law Review; Yale Law Jrnl.; Revue Int. de droit comparé; etc. Mbrships incl: Reporter, Fed. Securities Code, Am. Law Inst.; Coun., Sect. of Corp. Banking & Bus. Law, Am. Bar Assn.; Fellow, Am. Acad. Arts & Scis.; Am. Bar Fndn.; Soc. Pub. Tchrs. of Law, UK; Assn. of Bar of N.Y. Recip., A.M., Harvard, 1953. Address: 39 Meadow Way, Cambridge, MA 02138, USA.

LÖSSER-DÄHMLOW, Margarete Caroline, pen name DÄHMLOW, Margarete C., b. 17 Sept. 1897, Neckarsulm, Germany. Contractor; Owner, Iron Wholesale Dealer. Educ: Commercial Coll. Publs: Num. novellas & short stories (serious & light), 1927—. Contbr. to: Diozösan -Bildungswerk, Rottenbeurg, Guideposts (Brit. ed.). Mbr., Hamburg Authors' Soc. Address: 235 Neumünster 2, Strandallee, W. Germany.

LOTTMAN, Eileen, pen name WILLIS, Maud, b. 15 Aug. 1927, Mpls., Minn., USA. Writer. Educ: Univ. of Iowa, Iowa City. Publs: The Hemlock Tree, 1975; Summersea, 1975. Contbr. to: Publrs. Wkly.; Village Voice; Harper's Mag. Bookletter; Detroit News; Providence Jrnl.; & others. Address: 890 W. End Ave., N.Y., NY 10025, USA.

LOUGHARY, John William, b. 6 Nov. 1930, Omak, Wash., USA. Counseling Psychologist. Educ: B.S., Univ. of Ore., 1952; M.A., 1956; Ph.D., 1958; State Univ. of Iowa. Publs: Counseling in Secondary Schools, 1961; Counseling, A Growing Profession (ed. & contbr.), 1965; Man Machine Systems in Education (ed. & contbr.), 1966; Counseling Information System (jt. author), 1967; Requirements of Educational Information Systems During the Next Two Decades (co-ed.), 1968; Career Survival Skills (co-author), 1974; That Isn't Quite What I Had in Mind (co-author), 1974. Contbr. to jrnls. Mbr., profl. orgs. Address: Coll. of Educ., Univ. of Ore., Eugene, OR 97403, USA.

LOUHIJA, Aura Ellen, b. 4 Mar. 1923, Vaasa, Finland. Writer. Educ: B.A. Publs: Episode (novel), 1962; Hannuli (novel), 1971; To Be With All Along (novel), 1973; Matti & Mathilda (documentary play), 1974. Mbrships: Finnish Soc. of Youth Lit.; Finnish Dramatists' Soc.; Finnish Soc. of Authors. Hons: Youth Lit. Coun. Award, 1971; State Lit. Award, 1974. Address: Ulvilantie 7 b E 42, 00350 Helsinki 35, Finland.

LOUNAJA, Matti Heikki, b. 12 Apr. 1912, Kiuruvesi, Finland. Forestry Technician; Novelist. Educ: Forestry Inst. Publs: Pitkin varsitietä, 1950; Lautta chittaa kylän, 1951; Maaton mies (short stories), 1952; Peittyneet jäljet, 1954; Kurjet palaavat, 1955; Jäätyneet tiet, 1956; Vihreän kullan maa, 1961; Tämä päivä, 1962; Peni, ystäväni, 1966. Mbr., Assn. of Finnish Authors. Address: 75200 Juuka, 1. kp. Finland.

LOUNELA, Pekka, b. 20 Aug. 1932, Helsinki, Finland. Author. Publs. incl: 4 vols. of poetry; 2 vols. of essays; 4 anthols. of int. & Finnish jokes; num. radio & TV plays; Idän kääntöpiiri, 1962; Mies joka ampui kissan, 1970; Romppasen perheen Ruotsiin muutto, 1972. Mbrships: Pres., Radio Drama & Lit. Experts Grp., OIRT — Int. Org. of Radio & TV, 1968-74; Pres., Union of Northern Dramatists Socs., 1972-74, Soc. of Dramatists, 1969—, Eino Leino Soc.; Organizer, Lahti Int. Writers Reunion, 1965-71. Recip., Drama Prize, Govt. of Finland, 1973. Address: Peukaloisentie 4 E, 00820 Helsinki 82, Finland.

LOUP, Thérèse (Mrs. Harvey), pen name ROBERT, Dominique, b. 9 Dec. 1931, Estavayer-le-Lac, Switz. Teacher. Publs: Soif, 1963; Un Air de Flûte, 1965; Ermites & Batisseurs, 1967; Enganes, 1969; Num. poems put to music. Mbrships: Swiss Writers' Soc.; Writers' Soc. of Fribourg; Writers' Soc. of Vaud; Lyceum Club. Address: 5 Chemin des Allières, 1012 Lausanne, Switz.

LOURENS-KOOP, Adriana Luberta Klazina, Pen name TOUSSAINT, Jacky, b. 24 June 1920, Amersfoort, Netherlands. Housewife. Educ: Univ. studies in Classical langs. Publs. incl: (transls.) Three came to Ville Marie (by Alan Sullivan), 1947; The Dreamer-chants (by Harold Robbins), 1950; The Way West (by A. B. Guthrie), 1952; Mara, Daughter of the Nile (by E. J. McGraw), 1953; Ze kunnen het niet laten, 1975. Contbr. to: Boulevard mag., 1972-74. Mbr., Vereniging Van Letterkundigen (lit. soc.). Recip., Hon. Mention, Fontijn Prize, 1974, for Ze kunnen

het niet laten. Address: Toussaintplein 18a, Alphen a/d Rijn, Netherlands.

LOUWEN, Jan, pen name VIKING, Ted, b. 26 May 1924, Amsterdam, Netherlands. Journalist. Publs. incl: sev. theatre plays, 1957-60; Operatie Amazone (Operation Amazone), 1968; Grafrozen voor McGregor (Grave-roses for McGregor), 1968; De geparfumeerde sarcophaag (The perfumed Sarcophagus), 1970; Poppenspel in Praag, 1970; Misdaad volgens polis (Crime by Policy), 1971; Slalom met de dood (Slalom with Death), 1971; Moorden op z'n Venetiaans, 1973. Contbr., articles & short stories to var. mags. Mbrships: Dutch Union of Jrnlsts.; Mederlandse Vereniging van Letterkundigen. Address: Putterweg 3, Wapenveld (gem. Heerde), Netherlands.

LOVELACE, Earl, b. 1935, Trinidad. Civil Servant. Publs: (novels) While Gods Are Falling, UK, 1965, USA, 1966; The Schoolmaster, UK & USA, 1968. Recip., B.P. Independence Award, 1965. Address: c/o Henry Regnery Co., 114 W. Illinois St., Chgo., IL 60610, USA.

LO VERDE, Giuseppe, b. 2 Aug. 1906, Hamburg, Germany. Lawyer; University Professor; Journalist. Educ: Doct. Law, 1929, Doct. Pol. Scis., 1931, Univ. of Palermo, Italy. Publs. incl: I Dominions Britannici, 1931; Die Lehre vom Staat im neuen Italien, 1931; Il Nazionalsocialismo, 1939. Contbr. to num. jrnls.; German Radio & TV. Mbrships incl: Ordine degli Avvocati, Rome. Recip., Prize, Agnelli Fndn., 1939. Address: 19 rue du General Colonieu, 92 Rueil-Malmaison, France.

LOVINESCU, Horia, b. 20 Aug. 1917. Theatre Director; Playwright. Educ: Bucharest Univ. Publs: (in Romanian) Jean Arthur Rimbaud; (plays) Destroyed Citadel, 1954; Inn at the Crossroads, 1955; Boga Sisters, 1957; Above All, 1959; Feber, 1960; The Man who Lost his Humanity, 1961; The Paradise, 1962; The Death of An Artist, 1964; The Man Instead, 1966. Mbrships: PEN; Theatre Coun.; Romanian Writers' Union. Recip., State Prize & other Romanian Awards. Address: C.I. Nottara Theatre, 20 Bulevardul Magheru, Bucharest, Romania.

LOW, Jean Barclay, b. 8 Dec. 1903, Motherwell, UK. Academic Tutor; International Public Speaker. Educ: M.A., Glasgow. Publs: No Green Pastures, 1937. Contbr. to educl. jrnls., lit. mags. & nat. newspapers. Mbrships. incl: Scottish Comm. Mbr., Soc. of Authors. Address: 35 The Paddocks, Oatlands Chase, Weybridge, Surrey, KT13 9RL, UK.

LOW, Lois Dorothea, pen names LOW, Dorothy Mackie; PAXTON, Lois, b. 15 July 1916, Edinburgh, UK. Author. Publs: (as Dorothy Mackie Low) Isle for a Stranger, 1962; Dear Liar, 1963; A Ripple on the Water, 1964; The Intruder, 1965; A House in the Country, 1968; To Burgundy & Back, 1970; (as Lois Paxton) The Man Who Died Twice, 1968; The Quiet Sound of Fear, 1971; Who Goes There?, 1972; Double Yellow Line (forthcoming). Contbr. to Brit. & European women's mags. Mbrships: Romantic Novelists Assn. (Chmn., 1969-71); Crime Writers Assn.; Nat. Book League. Address: High View, Shawcross Rd., W. Runton, Norfolk, UK.

LOWELL, Robert Traill Spence, Jr., b. 1 Mar. 1917, Boston, Mass., USA. Poet; Playwright. Educ: B.A., Harvard Univ. Publs: Land of Unlikeness, 1944; Lord Weary's Castle, 1946; The Mills of the Kavanaughs, 1951; Life Studies: New Poems & an Autobiographical Fragment, 1959; Imitations, 1961; For the Union Dead, 1964; Near The Ocean, 1967; The Voyage, 1968; Prometheus Bound, 1970; Notebook, 1970; History, 1973; For Lizzie & Harriet, 1973; The Dolphin, 1973; (plays) The Old Glory, 1964; Benito Cereno, 1967. Hons: Pulitzer Prize, 1947, 1974; Prize, Am. Acad., of Arts & Letters; Nat. Book Award, 1959. Address: c/o Faber & Faber, 3 Queen Sq., London WC1, UK.

LOWENFELS, Walter, b. 10 May 1897, NYC, USA. Poet. Publs. incl: USA. With Music (play), 1930; Thou Shalt Not Overkill (poetry), 1968; In the Time of Revolution: Poems from our Third World (ed.), 1969; The Writing on the Wall: Protest Poems, Whitman to Today (ed.), 1969; The Poetry of My Politics (prose), 1969; The Tenderest Lover: Whitman's Erotic Poems (ed.), 1970; The Life of Fraenkel's Death (prose, w. Howard McCord), 1970; The Revolution Is To Be Human (prose), 1973; From the Belly of the Shark (ed.), 1974; Reality Prime (prose), 1974. Address: Boulder Dr., Peekskill, NY 10566, USA.

LOWNDES, Robert Augustine Ward, pen names (over 50) incl. MORLEY, Wilfred Owen; KENT, Mallory; GREY, Carol, b. 4 Sept. 1916, Bridgeport, Conn., USA. Editor; Writer. Publs: Mystery of the Third Mine, 1953; The Duplicated Man (w. J. Bluh), 1959; The Puzzle Planet, 1961; Believer's World, 1961; Three Faces of Science Fiction, 1973. Contbr. to mags. Mbrships: Sci. Fiction Writers of Am.; Baker St. Irregulars. Hons: Guest of Hon., for contbn. to fantastic fiction, 'Lunacon, 1969, Boskone, 1973. Address: 717 Willow Ave., Hoboken, NJ 07030, USA.

LOWRY, Joan, pen name CATLOW, Joanna, b. 17 July 1911, Kendal, UK. Writer. Publs: Sisters to Simon, 1955, German ed., 1957; The Sapphire Smoke, 1957; The Night of the High Wind, 1960; The Enchanted Land, 1963. Contbr. to: Sydney Morning Herald. Mbr., W. Country Writers' Assn. Address: Buckleigh House, Westward Ho! N. Devon EX39 1BJ, UK.

LOWRY, Nelson Jr., b. 1 May 1926, Provo, Utah, USA. Critic; Scholar; University Professor of Comparative Literature. Educ: A.B., Harvard Univ., 1947; Ph.D., Yale Univ., 1951. Publs: Baroque Lyric Poetry, 1961; Co-Ed., The Disciplines of Criticism: Essays in Literary Theory, Interpretation, & History, 1968; Ed., Cervantes: A Collection of Critical Essays, 1969. Contbr. to: Italian Quarterly (Co-Fndr. & Assoc. Ed., 1956–); Lexicon der Weltliteratur im 20 Jahrhundert; Ency. Poetry & Poetics; Comp. Lit.; Yale Review; Ency. of Lit. in 20th Century; Dict. of Mod. Lit.; etc. Mbrships. incl: MLA; Int. Comp. Lit. Assn.; Dante Soc. of Am.; PEN. Recip., Guggenheim Fellowship, 1961-62. Address: 1837 Yale Station, New Haven, CT 06520, USA.

LOWRY, Robert James, b. 28 Mar. 1919, Cinn., Ohio, USA. Writer. Educ: Univ. of Cinn. Publs: Casualty, 1946; Find me in Fire, 1948; The Wolf that Fed us, 1949; The Big Cage, 1949; The Violent Wedding, 1953; Happy New Year, Kamerades! , 1954; What's Left of April, 1956; The Last Party, 1956; New York Call Girl, 1958; The Prince of Pride Starring, 1959; Party of Dreamers, 1962. Contbr. to: Horizon (England); Collier's; The Am. Mercury; Time; N.Y. Times; L'Europeo (Italy). Recip., 3rd Prize, O. Henry Mem. Award Stories, 1950. Address: 3747 Hutton St., Cincinnati, OH 45226, USA.

LUARD, Nicholas Lamert, b. 26 June 1937, London, UK. Author. Educ: Sorbonne Univ., France; M.A., Cambridge Univ., UK; M.A., Univ. of Pa., USA. Publs: The Warm & Golden War, 1967; The Robespierre Serial, 1975. Contbr. to num. mags. & jrnls. Address: 10 Wilbraham Pl., London SW1, UK.

LUBIN, Georges Lucien, b. 24 Jan. 1904, Ardentes, Indre, France. Writer. Publs: La Terre a soif, 1934; Changer de peau, 1936; Maxime Rasquin, 1951; Correspondance de George Sand, 10 vols., 1964-74; George Sand en Berry, 1967; Oeuvres autobiographiques de George Sand, 2 vols., 1970-71; Album Sand, 1973. Mbrships: Pres., Soc. of Friends of Maurice Rollinat; Bur., Lit. Hist. Soc. of France; Bur., Int. Assn. of French Studies. Hons: Chevalier, Légion d'Honneur, 1970; Prize, Acad. Française, 1965, 1970; Prize, l'éd. critique, 1967. Address: 50 quai Alphonse Le Gallo, 92100 Boulogne sur Seine, France.

LUCAS, John, b. 26 June 1937, Exeter, UK. University Lecturer. Educ: B.A., 1959, Ph.D., 1964, Univ. of Reading. Publs: Tradition & Tolerance in 19th Century Fiction, 1966; The Melancholy Man, 1970; Literature & Politics in the 19th Century, 1971; About Nottingham, 1971; A Brief Bestiary, 1972; Arnold Bennett, 1974. Contbr. to: Spectator; Essays in Criticism; Critical Quarterly; Tribune; Transatlantic & Oxford Reviews; Renaissance & Mod. Studies; etc. Mbrships: Nat. Book League; Young Writers Assn.; E. Midlands Arts Assn. (Cons.). Address: 19 Devonshire Ave., Beeston, Notts., UK.

LUCAS, Robert, b. 8 May 1904, Vienna, Austria. Author; Journalist. Educ: Dr.Phil.(Sci.), Univ. of Vienna. Publs: Teure Amalia, vielgeliebtes Weib! Die Briefe des Gefreiten Hirnschal, 1946; Frieda Lawrence, 1972; (plays) Das Jahr 48, 1928; Das Grosse Festspiel, 1931; War & Peace (stage adaptation of Tolstoi's novel), 1943; (film script) The Diary of Mr. Pim, 1932. Contbr. to: Die Politische Bühne (Ed.); Neue Freie Presse (London Chief Corres.); Glasgow Herald; BBC (Chief Scriptwriter in German Serv., 1938-67); etc. Recip., M.B.E., 1966. Address: Calton Cottage, Renfrew Road, Kingston Hill, Surrey, UK.

LUCE, Clare Boothe. Writer; Diplomat. Publs. incl: (plays) Abide with Me, 1935; The Women, 1936; Kiss the Boys Good-Bye, 1938; Margin for Error, 1939; Child of the Morning, 1952; Stuffed Shirts; Europe in the Spring. Contbr. to: Vanity Fair, (former Mgng. Ed.). Recip., Hammarskjöld Prize, 1966.

LUCIA, Ellis (Joel), b. 6 June 1922, Watsonville, Calif., USA. Author; Freelance Writer. Educ: B.A., Pacific Univ. Publs. incl: The Saga of Ben Holladay, 1959; Klondike Kate, 1962; Tough Men, Tough Country, 1963; The Big Blow, 1963; This Land Around Us, 1969; Mr. Football: Amos Alonzo Stagg, 1970; Owyhee Trails, 1973; The Big Woods, 1975. Contbr. to: N.Y. Times; True; Argosy; Ford Times; Northwest; LA Times; Empire; Westways; Am. Forest; Sunset; Parade; True W.; etc. Mbrships: Western Writers of Am.; Authors' Guild of Am. Hons. incl: D.Litt., Pacific Univ., 1965; Western Heritage Award, 1974. Address: P.O. Box 11507, Portland, OR 97211, USA.

LUDLUM, Robert, b. 25 May 1927, NYC, USA. Novelist. Educ: B.A., Wesleyan Univ., 1951. Publs: The Scarlatti Inheritance, 1971; The Osterman Weekend, 1972; The Matlock Paper, 1973; The Rhinemann Exchange, 1974; The Road to Gandolfo (as Michael Shepheard), 1975; Trevayne — A Novel (as Jonathon Ryder), 1973. Mbr., Authors Guild & The Players. Hons: Book of the Month Selections, 1971, 1972, 1973; Full Selection, The Lit. Guild, 1974. Address: c/o Henry Morrison, Inc., 50 W. 10th St., N.Y., NY 10011, USA.

LUDWIG, Jack, b. 30 Aug. 1922, Winnipeg, Man., Can. University Professor of English; Playwright; Author. Educ: B.A., Univ. of Man., Winnipeg, 1944; Ph.D., UCLA, USA, 1953. Publs. incl: Recent American Novelists, 1962; The Great Hockey Thaw, 1974; Stories British & American (co-ed), 1953; Soundings: New Canadian Poets (co-ed.), 1970; (poetry) Homage to Zolotova, 1974; (novels) Confusions, 1963; Above Ground, 1968, 2nd ed., 1974; A Woman of Her Age, 1973. Contbr. to: Tamarack Review; Atlantic Monthly; Midstream; London Mag.; var. anthols. of short stories. Hons. incl: O. Henry Short Stories Awards, 1961, 1965; Can. Coun. Awards, 1962, 1967. Address: Writing Program, Banff Ctr., Alberta, Can.

LUH, Bor Shiun, b. 13 Jan. 1916, Shanghai, China. Food Scientist & Technologist. Educ: B.S., Chiao Tung Univ., Shanghai, 1938; M.S. (Food Sci.), Ph.D. (Agricl. Chem.), Univ. of Calif., Berkeley, USA. Publs: Baby Food, 1971; Commercial Fruit Processing (w. J. G. Woodroof), 1975; Commercial Vegetable Processing (w. J. G. Woodroof), 1975. Contbr. to: D. K. Tressler & M. A. Joslyn (Eds.), Fruit & Vegetable Juice Processing Technology, 2nd ed. 1971 (chapts. 8, 9, 10); Jrnl. of Food Sci.; Food Technol.; Confructa; Jrnl. Sci., Food & Agric., UK; Plant Physiol.; Calif. Agric. Mbr. var. profl. assns. Hons. incl: Cons. to FAO 1969, & UN Indl. & Dev. Org. 1972. Address: Dept. of Food Science & Technology, Univ. of California, Cruess Hall, Davis, CA 95616, USA.

LUHAR, Tribhuvandas Purushottamdas, pen name SUNDARAM, b. 22 Mar. 1908, Mia-Matar, Broach, India. Educ: Grad. in Arts, Gujarat Vidyapith, Ahmedabad. Publs. incl: (poetry) Kavya Mangala, 1933; Vasudha, 1940; Yatra, 1951; (short stories) Hirakani, 1938; Piyasi, 1940; (prose & criticism) Dakshinayan, 1934; Arvachin Kavita, 1946; Avalokana, 1965; Chidambara, 1968. Contbr. to: Dakshina; Sanskriti; Kumar, etc. Mbrships. incl: Majlis; Progressive Writers Assn; Lekhak Milan (var. offs. in each, 1934-45). Hons. incl: Ranjitram Gold Medal, 1934; Narmad Gold Medal, 1955; Sahitya Acad. Nat. Award, 1968. Address: Dakshina Karyalaya, Sri Aurobindo Ashram, Pondicherry 605002, India.

LUITING, Ton, b. 16 July 1936, Hilversum, Netherlands. Broadcasting Critic & Journalist; Poet. Publs: (poems) Heldere Nevel, 1964; (poems) In mantels van tandulees, 1971; (biography) Ontmoeting met Paul de Vree, 1971; (poems) Twee-schaar, 1972; (poems) Nektar, 1974. Contbr. to: Lotta Poetica; Ons Erfdeel; De Tafelronde. Mbrships: Lit. Union; Ed. Bd., Kruispunt-Sumier; Sec., Poetry Workgroup; Genootschap v. Nederlands Schrÿvende Aforisten. Address: Korenbloemstraat nr. 6, Hilversum, Netherlands.

LUKÁCS, Imre, b. 4 Feb. 1908, Devecser, Hungary. Journalist. Contbr. to: Filateliai Szemle; Ruházati Munkás. Mbrships: Fedn. of Hungarian Jrnlsts.; Hungarian Writers Assn.; Hungarian Philatelic Assn. Address: Amerikai ut. 19. II. 1., Budapest 1145. XIV, Hungary.

LUKE, Peter Ambrose Cyprian, b. 12 Aug. 1919, St. Albans, UK. TV Producer & Writer. Educ: Byam Shaw Schl. of Art; Atelier André Lhote, Paris. Publs: The Play of Hadrian VII, 1968; Sisyphus & Reilly, an autobiography, 1972; (play) Hadrian the Seventh; Prods. incl: (TV plays) Small Fish are Sweet, 1958; Pigs Ear with Flowers, 1960; Roll on Bloomin' Death, 1961; Devil a Monk Wou'd Be, 1966; (films, writer & dir.). Anach Cuan, 1967; Black Sound— Deep Song, 1968. Contbr. to: BBC; ABC TV; Reuters News Desk, 1946-47. Hons: Order of St. John; M.C. Address: La Almona, El Chorro, Prov. de Malaga, Spain.

LUNDBERG, (Sven Gunnar) Ingemar, pen name BERGLUND, Sven G., b. 27 Sept. 1927, Falkenberg, Sweden. Author. Educ: Gothenburg Univ.; Lund Univ.; Reykjavik Univ., Iceland. Publs: Anush, 1952; Utsikt mot trädgården, 1955; Resan till Timbuktu, 1957. Contbr. to: Dagens Nyheter; Svenska Dagbladet; Expressen; Aftonbladet; Kvälls-Posten; Vecko-Journalen; Ord och Bild; Sydsvenska Dagbladet; Stockholms-Tidningen; Göteborgs-Posten; etc. Mbr., Swedish Writers' Assn. Address: Galtås 2, Glommen 50, Sweden.

LUNDBLAD, Jane Kristina, b. 28 May 1905, Vänersborg, Sweden. Writer; Translator. Educ: Dip. d'Études Françaises, Univ. of Montpellier, France, 1924; Columbia Univ., USA, 1945-46; Fil. Dr., Uppsala Univ., Sweden, 1948. Publ: Nathaniel Hawthorne & European Literary Tradition, 1947. Contbr. to: Göteborgs Handels— & Sjöfarts Tidning; Svenska Dagbladet; Swedish Radio. Mbrships: Swedish Assn. Univ. Women (past pres.); Swedish PEN; Publicistklubben; Zonta Club. Address: Karlavägen 54, VI, 11449 Stockholm, Sweden.

LUNDGREN, Paul Arthur, pen name McCUTCHEON, James, b. 4 Jan. 1925, Kan. City, Mo., USA. Rare Book Seller; Art Dealer. Educ: Univ. of Okla.; Law Schl., ibid.; Miss. Coll.; Wichita State Univ. Publs: Black Ulysses, 1974. Contbr. to: Inscape Mag. (Assoc. Ed.); Boys Life; Adventure; Fifteen Western Tales; True West; VFW Mag.; Kan. Mag.; Kan. Quarterly; Tall Windows; New Pacific; Wichita Eagle—Beacon Newspaper. Mbrships: VP, Kan. Authors; Club; Kan. State Histl. Soc.; Am. Inter-Profl. Assn.; Tokeka Club, B.P.O.E. Address: 217 Fillmore St., Topeka, KS 66606, USA.

LUNG, Chu-Yung, pen name FUN-CHI, b. 28 Nov. 1904, Peng-Kiang, Hu-Nan, China. Professor. Educ: B.A. Publs: The Origin & Development of Chinese Literature, 1937; Research for Poetics, 1942; Collection of Poems Composed in My Hong Kong Living; Lung Fun-Chi's Chinese Paintings & Calligraphic Albums, 1973. Contbr. to: Asian Poetry Forum; Hwa Kiu Yap Po; etc. Mbrships: Chinese PEN Ctr., Hong Kong; Sec., Metropolis Mil. Schl. Alumni Assn., Hong Kong. Address: 4/F, I — C, Sai Yeung Choi St., Kowloon, Hong Kong.

LURIE, Alison, b. 3 Sept. 1926, Chgo., Ill., USA. University Lecturer in English. Educ: A.B., Radcliffe Coll., 1947. Publs: V.R. Lang: A Memoir, Germany, 1959; (novels) Love & Friendship, UK & USA, 1962; The Nowhere City, UK, 1965, USA, 1966; Imaginary Friends, UK & USA, 1967; Real People, USA, 1969, UK, 1970; The War Between the Tates. Hons: Yaddo Fndn. Fellowship, 1963, 1964, 1966; Guggenheim Fellowship, 1965; Rockefeller Grant, 1968. Address: Dept. of English, Cornell Univ., Ithaca, NY 14850, USA.

LUSTIG, Arnost, b. 21 Dec. 1926, Prague, Czechoslovakia. Writer; Screenwriter; Visiting Professor of Literature. Am. Univ. Film & Creative Writing. Educ: M.A., Jrnlsm., Czech.; degree in Pol. & Soc. Scis., 1954. Publs. (stories): Night & Hope, 1958; Diamond of the Night, 1959; The Street of the Lost Brothers, 1959; Nobody will be Humiliated, 1964; The White Birches in Fall, 1965; The Bitter Smell of Almonds, 1968; (novels): Dita Saxova, 1962; A Prayer for Katherina Horovitzova, 1963; Darling, 1969; (essay): Aesthetics of Reportage. Mbrships. incl: Authors Guild of Am.; PEN; Soc. European Writers; Union Czech. Writers (Ctrl. Comm. & Presidium, 1963-69). Awards: 3 for A Prayer for Katherina Horovitzova; 2 for Diamond of the Night; 1 for Night & Hope. Address: 4000 Tunlaw Rd. N.W., Apt. 825, Wash. DC, USA.

LUTOUR, Lou, b. St. Louis, Mo., USA. Educator; Broadcaster; Poet-Evangelist. Educ: A.B.; M.F.A.; M. in Spec. Ed.; D.D.; Special Trng., Speech, Broadcasting & Jrnlsm. Publs: Speech Reveals Culture, 1960; Poetry — The Power & the Glory, 1967; Treasure House, 1970; Poetic

Verses of Our Lady of Lourdes, 1972; God-in-Me, 1973. Contbr. to poetry mags. & maj. negro press, US & Bermuda. Num. mbrships. incl: Life Mbr., Poetry Soc. of England; United Poets Laureate Int., World Congress of Poets; Fndr., World Poets Resource Ctr., Inc. Hons. incl. over 150 awards, 10 hon. doctorates, US & for. Address: 1270 Fifth Ave., N.Y., NY 10029, USA.

LUTYENS, Mary, b. 31 July 1908. Writer. Educ: Queen's Coll., London. Publs. incl: (fiction) Perchance to Dream, 1935; Rose & Thorn, 1936; A Path of Gold, 1941; Together & Alone, 1942; And Now There is You, 1953; The Lucian Legend, 1955; Meeting in Venice, 1956; Cleo, 1973; (autobiography) To Be Young, 1959; (for children) Julie & the Narrow Valley, 1944; (Ed.) The Only Revolution, 1970; The Penguin Krishnamurti Reader, 1970; The Urgency of Change, 1971; (Biography) The Ruskins & the Grays, 1972; & num. serials as Esther Wyndham. Contbr. to: Apollo; Cornhill. Address: 2 Hyde Park St., London W2, UK.

LUTZER, Erwin Wesley, b. 3 Oct. 1941, Colfax, Can. Minister of Religion. Educ: Th.B., Winnipeg Bible Coll., Can.; Th.M., Dallas Theol. Sem., USA; M.A., Chgo Grad. Schl. of Theol.; M.A., Loyola Univ. Publs: The Morality Gap, 1972; How in this World can I be Holy?, 1975; 3rd book, forthcoming. Contbr. to: Eternity Mag.; Moody Monthly; Christianity Today, Bibliotheca Sacra. Mbr., Evangelical Theol. Soc. Address: 5142 Jarlath Ave., Skokie, IL 60076, USA.

LUXTON, Lewis Varley, pen name CUTHBERTSON, C.C. de C., b. 21 Sept. 1940, Adelaide, Australia. Consultant. Educ: B.A., 1963; M.A., 1968; Pembroke Coll., Cambridge Univ., UK. Publs: Essays, 1959; Essays, 1963; Ed., The Letters of Charles Le Grice, 1966-74, 1974; Collected Letters, 1970-74, 1974; Ed., Jack Elliot's Adventures in South Africa (w. Margaret Stanborough), 1974; Trade Practices Manual, 1974. Contbr. to: Melburnian; The Age. Mbrships. incl: Melbourne Club. Address: 20 Kensington Rd., S. Yarra, Vic. 3141, Australia.

LYALL, Gavin Tudor, b. 9 May 1932. Former Journalist; Author. Educ: B.A., Pembroke Coll., Cambridge. Publs: The Wrong Side of the Sky, 1961; The Most Dangerous Game, 1964; Midnight Plus One, 1965; Shooting Script, 1966; Venus with Pistol, 1969; Blame the Dead, 1972; (Ed.) Freedom Battle: The RAF in World War II, 1968. Contbr. to: Picture Post, 1956-67; BBC, 1958-59; Sunday Times, 1959-63. Address: 14 Provost Rd., London NW3, UK.

LYBECK, (Carl Mikael) Sebastian, b. 3 Aug. 1929. Poet. Educ: Aabo Acad., Finland, 1947-49; Finnish Cadet Schl., Helsinki, 1949-51; Jrnlst. trng., Finnish Cadet Schl., Helsinki, 1951-52; Helsinki Univ., 1953-54. Publs. incl: (poems): Jorden har alltid sitt ljus, 1958; Dikter fran Lofoten, 1961; Liten stad vid havet, 1963; Mitt i den nordiska idyllen, 1973; Aar det liv i ditt liv? 1974; (children's books): Latte Igelkott reser till Lofoten, 1957; Als des Fuchs seine Ohren verlor, 1966; Naar Elefanten tog Tanten, 1967; num. transls. in sev. langs. Mbrships. incl: Writers' Ctr., Sweden (num. lecture tours 1967—); an initiator of Co-op. Writers' Publ., Sweden, 1970—. Hons: sev. schlrships. from Finland & Sweden & Writers' Orgs. Address: Morgonbrisv. 2c, S-451 00 Uddevalla, Sweden.

LYKIARD, Alexis, b. 2 Jan. 1940, Athens, Greece. Writer. Educ: B.A., 1962, M.A., 1966, King's Coll., Cambridge. Publs: (novels) The Summer Ghosts, 1964; Zones, 1966; A Sleeping Partner, 1967; Strange Alphabet, 1970; The Stump, 1973; Instrument of Pleasure, 1974; (transls.) Lautréamont's Maldoror, 1970; The Piano Ship, 1974. Vols. of poetry: Robe of Skin, 1969; Eight Lovesongs, 1972; Greek Images, 1973; Lifelines, 1973; (prose) Ed., Wholly Communion, 1965; Ed., Best Horror Stories of Sheridan LeFanu, 1970; Ed., The Horror Horn — Best Ghost Stories of E. F. Benson, 1974. Mbrships: Soc. of Authors; Lit. Panel, Arts Coun. of G.B. Address: c/o A.D. Peters & Co., 10 Buckingham St., London WC2N 6BU, UK.

LYMAN, Irene Vera Ponting, b. Wellingborough, Northants., UK. Novelist. Educ: Nottingham Coll. of Art. Publs: The Well in the Wood; To Have Thy Love; House of the Golden Cupid; Minarets in the Moonlight; Dark Isle of Love; Trail of the Firebird. Contbr. of poetry to var. mags. Mbrships: Soc. of Authors; Romantic Novelists Assn.; West Country Writers Assn.; Caravan Club; Co. of Veteran Motorists; Siamese Cat Club; Fndr. Mbr., Int. Poetry Soc. Recip., 1st Prize for Essay on Italy, Italian Govt. Address:

Plas Meudon, Maenporth Rd., Mawnan, Falmouth, Cornwall, UK.

LYNCH, Stanislaus, b. 19 Oct. 1907, Ballyjamesduff, Co. Cavan, Repub. of Ireland. Author; Breeder of Connemara Ponies & Hunters. Publs: (poems) Hoof-Prints on Parchment; Rhymes of an Irish Huntsman; (prose) Echoes of the Hunting Horn; From Foal to Tally-Ho! ; Hounds Are Running; A Hunting Man's Rambles. Contbr. to: Country Life; Field; Tatler; Chronical (USA); etc. Mbrships. incl: PEN (Chmn. 1971-72); Irish Olympic Horse Soc. & Show Jumping Assn., Ireland (Fndr. Chmn.). Hons. incl: Gold Medal, Int. Grand Chapt. Saint Hubert, Vienna, 1959; Olympic Dip. for Epic Lit., 1948, 1952. Address: The Glebe, Balrothery, Balbriggan, County Dublin, Repub. of Ireland.

LYNE, Michael Charles Edward, b. 12 Sept. 1912, Upton Bishop, Herefordshire, UK. Artist. Publs: Homes Hounds & Country, 1937; Litter to Later on, 1974; A Parsons Son, 1974; The Home in Action (w. Henry Eynmalen). Contbr. to: The Field; Country Life. Address: Dunfield House, Fairford, Glos., UK.

LYNGBIRK, Jytte, b. 14 Mar. 1935, Frederiksberg, Denmark. Author. Publs: Anne, 1961; Ingen at Følges med, 1962; Menneske i Mørke, 1963; Gensyn med Virkeligheden, 1965; To Dage i November, 1966; Rejse med Kit, 1969; Charlotte, 1969; Tre Skvespil for Børn, 1970; Allan og Maya, 1971; Skyggerne ved Søen, 1972; Kit Vivas (esperanto), 1973; Sidste Forår, 1974; Radio plays for children, 1959-69; var. theatrical works for children. Contbr. to: Ishøj Theater (plays). Mbrships: Danske Dramatikeres Forbund; Dansk Forfatterforening. Address: Brentedalen 8, Tranegilde, 2630 Tastrup, Denmark.

LYON, Marjorie (Mrs. W. L. Meredyth-Starmer), b. 8 Aug. 1914, Wallasey, Cheshire, UK. Writer; Lecturer; Adjudicator. Educ: M.A.; F.T.C.L.; F.R.S.A.; L.R.A.M. Publs: Junior Anthology for the Younger Verse Speaker, Books 1-2; The Lovely Lady of Bethlehem; To Banbury Cross; Over the World so Wide; Dream Come True; Where the Golden Apples Grow; There & Back Again. Contbr. to BBC Radio; Recital tours, USA. Address: Little Somerville, 5 Foxley Lodge, Dale Rd., Purley, Surrey CR2 2EA, UK.

LYON, Ruth Alta, b. 23 Nov. 1913, Moline, Ill., USA. Writer; Editor; Associate Editor, Call to Prayer. Educ: B.A., Ctrl. Bible Coll., Springfield, Mo., 1958. Publs: The Eighth Wonder of the World, 1958. Contbr. to: Advance Mag.; Pentecostal Evangel; Reach Out (Ed.); Christ for All (Ed.). Address: 909 Woodridge St., Springfield, MO 65803, USA.

LYONS, Enid Muriel, b. 9 July 1897, Duck River, Tas., Australia. Writer. Educ: Tchr.'s Trng. Coll. Publs: So We Take Comfort, 1965; The Old Haggis, 1970; Among the Carrion Crows, 1973. Mbr., Aust. Soc. of Authors. Recip., Dame Grand Cross, Order of the Brit. Empire, 1935. Address: "Home Hill", 77 Middle Rd., Devonport, Tas., Australia.

LYSHOLM, Gustaf Adolf, b. 10 Mar. 1909, Stockholm, Sweden. Author. Publs: Nu Snöar det på Östermalm, 1965; Bostonvalsernas Stad, 1966; Röster från Ödemarken, 1967; Stad med Lykttändare & Hästar, 1969; När Jag var Femton År, 1973. Mbrships: Swedish PEN; Soc. of Swedish Authors. Recip., Hon. Prize for Authors & Artists, City of Stockholm, 1970. Address: Regeringsgatan 76, 111 39 Stockholm, Sweden.

LYTLE, Andrew Nelson, b. 26 Dec. 1902, Murfreesboro, Tenn., USA. Novelist; Former Editor, Sewanee Review. Educ: B.A., Vanderbilt Univ., Nashville, Tenn., 1925. Publs: Bedford Forrest & his Critter Company, 1931; The Long Night, 1936; At the Moon's Inn, 1941; A Name for Evil, 1947; The Velvet Horn, 1957; Novella & Four Stories, 1958. Contbr. to: Hound & Horn; Am. Review; Sewanee Review; Va. Quarterly Review; Kenyon Review; Daedalus; Southern Review; Nat. Review. Hons. incl: D.Litt., Kenyon Coll., 1965; D.Litt., Univ. of Fla., 1970; D.Litt., Univ. of the S., 1972. Address: Monteagle S., S. Assembly, Monteagle, TN 37356, USA.

LYTTON, David, b. 1927, S. Africa. Freelance Writer. Publs: (novels) The Goddam White Man, UK, 1960, USA, 1961; A Place Apart, UK & USA, 1961; The Paradise People, UK & USA, 1962; The Grass Won't Grow Till Spring, 1964; The Freedom of the Cage, 1966; (short stories) A Tale of Love, Alas, & Other Episodes, 1969. Address: c/o The Bodley Head, 9 Bow St., London WC2, UK.

LYTTON, Hugh, b. 26 Sept. 1921, Nuremberg, Germany. Professor of Educational Psychology. Educ: Univ. of Nottingham; B.A. (German), 1941; B.A. (French), 1949; Univ. of London; Ph.D.(Psychol.), 1966; M.A.(Psychol.), 1953, Univ. of Liverpool. Publs: School Counselling & Counsellor Education in the United States — a report, 1968; Guidance & Counselling in British Schools (ed. w. M. Craft), 1969, 2nd ed., 1974; Creativity & Education, 1971. Contbr.xto profl. jrnls. Mbrships. incl: Fellow, Brit. Psychol. Soc. Address: 3911 Vardell Rd., Calgary, Alta. T3A 0C3, Can.

M

MA, Jacob K. J., b. 12 Feb. 1923, Shansi Prov., Repub. of China. Newspaper Correspondent. Educ: B.J., Nat. Funtan Univ., Shanghai. Publs: Looking at the World from Taiwan, 1969, in 6th ed.; Practical News Coverage, 1971. Contbr. to: United Daily News; Econ. Daily News. Mbrships: Int. Press Inst.; For. Press Assn., N.Y. Address: One Sherman Square, Apt. 4G, N.Y. NY 10023, USA.

MA, John Ta-jen, b. 22 Feb. 1920, Wenchow, China. Librarian; Author. Educ: B.A., Nat. Ctrl. Univ., 1944; Postgrad. Schl. of Jrnlsm., Chungking, China, 1945; M.A., Univ. of Wis., USA, 1948; M.L.S., Columbia Univ., 1958. Publs: A Test of Disputed Authorship; Ch'en Tzu-chia & Chu Tzu-chia, 1968; Elementary Chinese for American Librarians: A Simple Manual, 1968; East Asia: A Survey of Holdings at the Hoover Institution on War, Revolution, & Peace, 1971. Contbr. to: Jrnl. of Asian Studies; Issues & Studies; etc. Mbr. & Dir., Am. Assn. of Tchrs. of Chinese Lang. & Culture. Address: P.O. Box 2464, Stanford, CA 94305, USA.

MAATTANEN, Sakari, b. 12 Aug. 1938, Wiipuri, Finland. Journalist. Educ: World Press Inst., St. Paul, Minn. Publs: The Case of (Max) Jakobson, 1973. Contbr. to: Helsingin Sanomat. Mbrships: Fellow, World Press Inst. Alumni & For. Press Assn., NYC; Finnish Press Assn. Recip., 3 Story of the Yr. Awards, Finland. Address: Ilkantie 13 A 1 00400 Helsinki 40, Finland.

MacARTHUR, David Wilson, pen name WILSON, David, b. 29 Aug. 1903, Glasgow, Scotland, UK. Author. Educ: M.A.(Ordinary), M.A.(Hons.), Glasgow Univ. Publs. incl: They Sailed for Senegal, 1938; The River Windrush, 1946; Traders North, 1951; The Desert Watches, 1954; Simba Bwana, 1956. Contbr. to: Colliers; Saturday Evening Post; Strand; etc. Mbrships: Inc. Soc. of Authors, London; Fellow, Ancient Monuments Soc.; Former Mbr., Royal Toxophilite Soc.; Royal Gourock Yacht Club. Address: Ridigita Farm, P.O. Box 411, Marandellas, Rhodesia.

McARTHUR, Harvey King, b. 9 May 1912, Billingsville, Mo., USA. Professor. Educ: Ph.B., Wheaton Coll., Ill., 1933; Th.B., Westminster Theol. Sem., Phila., Pa., 1937; S.T.M. 1940, Ph.D., 1941, Hartford Sem. Fndn.; Further study, var. univs., USA & abroad. Publs: New Testament Sidelights, 1960; Understanding the Sermon on the Mount, 1969, Brit. ed., 1961; The Quest Through the Centuries, 1966; In Search of the Historical Jesus, 1969, Brit. ed., 1970. Contbr. to var. profl. jrnls. Mbrships. incl: Soc. of Biblical Lit. Recip., var. study grants. Address: 90 Sherman St., Hartford, CT 06105, USA.

MACAULEY, Robie (Mayhew), b. 31 May 1919, Grand Rapids, Mich., USA. Magazine Fiction Editor. Educ: A.B., Kenyon Coll., Ohio, 1941; M.F.A., Univ. of Iowa, 1950. Publs: The Disguises of Love (novel), USA, 1952, UK, 1954; The End of Pity & Other Stories, USA, 1957, UK, 1958; Technique in Fiction (w. George Lanning), 1964; Ed., Gallery of Modern Fiction: Stories from the Kenyon Review, 1966. Contbr. to: Kenyon Review (Ed., 1959-66); Playboy (Fiction Ed., 1966—). Mbr., PEN. Hons. incl: Furioso Fiction Prize, 1949; Guggenheim Fellowship, 1964; O. Henry Award, 1967. Address: 1323 Sandburg Terrace, Chgo., IL 60614, USA.

MACBETH, George Mann, b. 19 Jan. 1932, Shotts, Lanarks., UK. Poet. Educ: M.A., New Coll., Oxford. Publs.

incl: Collected Poems 1958-70; 1971; Shrapnel, 1973; My Scotland, 1973; A Poet's Year, 1973; The Transformation, 1975; The Samurai, 1975. Editor: The Poet's Voice; New Comment; Poetry Now. Recip., Sir Geoffrey Faber Mem. Award. Address: c/o BBC, Broadcasting House, London, W1, UK.

McCABE, Eugene, b. 7 July 1930, Glasgow, UK. Playwright. Educ: B.A., Univ. Coll., Cork, Repub. of Ireland. Publs: (plays) King of the Castle, 1964; Breakdown, 1966; Swift, 1969. Contbr. to: Irish Writing; Hibernia; Dublin Mag.; Threshold; Lit. Sect., Irish Press. Hons: Irish Life Drama Award, 1964; Screen Play Award, Prague Int. TV Festival, Czech., 1974. Address: Drumard Clones, Co. Monaghan, Repub. of Ireland.

McCABE, John C., III, B. 14 Nov. 1920, Detroit, Mich., USA. Writer. Educ: Ph.B., Univ. of Detroit, 1947; M.F.A., Fordham Univ., 1948; Ph.D., Shakespeare Inst., Univ. of Birmingham, UK, 1954. Publs: Mr. Laurel & Mr. Hardy, 1961, 4th ed., 1968; George M. Cohan: The Man Who Owned Broadway, 1973; The Comedy World of Stan Laurel, 1974. Contbr. to: Variety; Detroit News. Address: Box 363, Mackinac Island, MI 49757, USA.

McCABE, Joseph E., b. 23 Apr. 1912, Western Pa., USA. Clergyman; Educator. Educ: A.B., Muskingum Coll.; M.A., Ohio State Univ., 1940; B.Th., Princeton Theol. Sem., 1943; M.Th., 1947; Ph.D., Univ. of Edinburgh, UK., 1951. Publs: The Power of God in a Parish Program, 1959; Service Book for Ministers, 1961; Challenging Careers, in the Church, 1966; Your First Year at College, 1967; Reason Faith & Love, 1972; Better Pastoring & Preaching, 1973. Mbrships: Past Chmn., Bd. of Trustees, Beirut Coll. of Women, Lebanon; Commn. on Ecumenical Mission & Rels., United Presby. Ch.; Chmn., Fulbright Selection Comm. of Iowa; Trustee, Coe Coll. & Hoover Pres. Lib. Address: 163 Thompson Dr., S.E., Cedar Rapids, IA 52403, USA.

McCAIN, William David, b. 29 Mar. 1907, Bellefontaine, Miss., USA. University President. Educ: B.S., Delta State Univ.; M.A., Univ. of Miss.; Ph.D., Duke Univ.; Litt.D., Miss. Coll. Publs. incl: The United States & the Republic of Panama, 1937; The Story of Jackson: A History of the Capital of Mississippi, 1821-1951, 1953; An Outline of Four Generations of the Family of Henry Fox (1768-1852) and His Wife, Sarah Harrell Fox (1772-1848) of South Carolina & Mississippi, 1971; Eight Generations of the Family of John Shaw (1788-1858) & His Wife, Nancy Worthy Shaw (1788-1846) of North Carolina, South Carolina & Mississippi, 1974. Num. mbrships. incl: Fellow, Past Pres., Fndng. Mbr., Soc. of Am. Archivists; Ed., Jrnl. of Miss. Hist., 1939-56. Contbr. to histol. jrnls. Address: Southern Stn., Box 1, Hattiesburg, MS 39401, USA.

McCALL, Edith, b. 5 Sept. 1911, Charles City, Iowa, USA. Writer. Educ: M.A., Univ. of Chgo., 1949. Publs. incl: Log Fort Adventures, 1958; Steamboats to the West, 1959; Men on Iron Horses, 1960; Wagons Over the Mountains, 1961; Gold Rush Adventures, 1962; Pioneer Show Folk, 1963; Cowboys & Cattle Drives, 1964; Pioneer Traders, 1964; Ports in the Wilderness, 1968; English Village in the Ozarks, 1969; Stalwart Men of Early Texas, 1970; People & Our Country, forthcoming; var. series, textbooks, social studies books & supplementary rdrs. Mbrships. incl: Authors' Guild; Authors' League of Am.; Mo. Writers' Guild. Recip., Mo. Writers' Guild Award, 1960. Address: P.O. Box 255, Hollister, MO 65672, USA.

McCARTHY, Mary, b. 21 June 1912, Seattle, Wash., USA. Author. Educ: B.A., Vassar Coll. Publs. incl: The Company She Keeps, 1942; The Oasis, 1949; The Groves of Academe, 1952; Venice Observed, 1956; Memories of a Catholic Girlhood, 1957; On the Contrary, 1961; The Group, 1963; Vietnam, 1967; Hanoi, 1968; Birds of America, 1971; Medina, 1972; The Seventeenth Degree, 1974; The Mask of State, 1974. Contbr. to: New Yorker; Encounter; Harper's; N.Y. Review of Books. Mbrships: Authors' League of Am.; Nat. Inst. Arts & Letters; Am. Acad. Arts & Scis. Hons. incl: Horizon Award; Guggenheim Fndn. Fellowships, 1949, 1959; Degrees, Syracuse Univ., 1973, Hull Univ., 1974. Address: 141 rue de Rennes, Paris 6, France.

McCARTHY, Shaun Lloyd, pen name CORY, Desmond, b. 16 Feb. 1928, Lancing, Sussex, UK. University Lecturer in English Literature. Educ: M.A., St. Peter's Coll., Oxford; Ph.D., Wales. Publs: The Johnny Fedora Series, 14 titles inclng: Deadfall, 1965; The Night Hawk, 1970; Take my

Drum to England, 1971; The Circe Complex, 1975; (films) Deadfall (w. Bryan Forbes); England Made Me (w. Peter Duffell). Contbr. to: UWIST Review, 1968-72 (Ed.). Mbrships: Fellow, Inst. of Linguists; Fellow, Inst. of Arts & Letters, Geneva. Address: c/o John Farquharson Ltd., 15 Red Lion Square, London WC1R 4QW, UK.

McCARTHY, Virginia T., (Mrs. John H. McCarthy III), b. St. Louis, Mo., USA. Syndicated Columnist. Educ: B.A., Maryville Coll. Writer of "Woman's Place", a weekly syndicated column on working women which appears in 14 newspapers incl. The Omaha World-Herald, Omaha, Neb., Suburban Newspapers Inc., Donnelly Publications Inc. & The Penny Saver, Pinehurst, Mass.. Contbr. to: N. Am. Newspaper Alliance; St. Louis Post-Dispatch; etc. Mbrships: Nat. Fedn. Press Women; Mo. Press Women; Bd. of Dirs., Mo. Writers' Guild; Pres., St. Louis Writers' Guild; Press Club Metrop. St. Louis. Hons. incl: 8 Awards 1969-74, Mo. Press Women for "Woman's Place". Address: 8709 Sierra Dr., St. Louis, MO 63117, USA.

McCLEERY, William, b. 15 Sept. 1911, Hastings, Neb., USA. Playwright. Educ: A.B., Univ. of Neb. Plays: Hope for the Best, 1945; Parlor Story, 1947; Good Housekeeping, 1950; A Play for Mary, 1951; The Lady Chooses, 1955; The Guest Cottage, 1956; Love Out of Town, 1964; Good Morning, Miss Dove, 1965. Books: Wolf Story, 1947; The Way to Go (co-author), 1974. Exec. Ed., Assoc. Press Feature Serv., 1935-37; Sunday Ed., PM newspaper, NYC, 1939-45; Assoc. Ed., Ladies' Home Jrnl., 1958-63; Ed., University, A Princeton Quarterly, 1964—. Address: 317 Edgerstoune Rd., Princeton, NJ 08540, USA.

McCLELLAND, Vincent Alan, b. 3 Mar. 1933, Clitheroe, Lancs., UK. Professor of Education. Educ: B.A., 1954, Dip.Ed., 1956, Sheffield; M.A., 1955; M.A., Birmingham, 1958; Ph.D., Sheffield, 1968. Publs: Cardinal Manning: His Public Life & Influence 1865-92, 1962; English Roman Catholics & Higher Education 1830-1903, 1973. Contbr. to: New Catholic Ency.; num. acad. & profl. jrnls. Mbrships. incl: Hist. of Educ. Soc.; Cath. Record Soc. Address: c/o Dept. of Educ., Univ. Coll., Cork, Repub. of Ireland.

McCLUNE, Gregory William, b. 16 Mar. 1945, Belfast, N. Ireland, UK. Attorney; Playwright. Educ: B.A., 1965, LL.B., 1968, Univ. of Cape Town, S. Africa; Admitted as Attorney of High Court of Rhodesia, 1974. Publs: (plays produced) The Arab Party, 1965; Last Night We Were Four, 1966; With Courage This Day, 1969. Contbr. to: Responsa Meridiana — The Changing Nature of Dilictual Liability, 1967. Mbrships: PEN, Rhodesian br.; Law Soc. of Rhodesia. Hons: Caltex Play of the Yr. Award, Rhodesia, 1966; Cabs Play of the Yr. Award, Rhodesia, 1969. Address: 14 Glamis Road, Hatfield, Salisbury, Rhodesia.

McCLUNEY, Gregory D., b. 27 Dec. 1946, Kansas City, Mo., USA. Advertising Executive. Educ: B.S., Univ. of Kan., Lawrence. Contbr. to: Engl. Review; Outdoor Life; TWA Ambassador; Advt. Age; Kan. City Star & Times. Mbrships. incl: Am. Bus. Writers; Assn. of Indl. Advertisers; Aviation & Space Writers' Assn.; Am. Advt. Fedn. Hons: Addy Awards (5), 9th Dist. Am. Advt. Fedn.; 1st Place, Mo. State Univ. Speechwriter's Day; Award of Achievement, Nat. Agricl. Mktng. Assn. Address: 224 Bayview Dr., Lee's Summit, MO 64063, USA.

McCLURE, James Howe, b. 9 Oct. 1939, Johannesburg, South Africa. Writer. Publs: The Steam Pig, 1971; The Caterpillar Cop, 1972; Four & Twenty Virgins, 1973; The Gooseberry Fool, 1974. Mbr., Crime Writers' Assn. Recip., Gold Dagger, Crime Writers' Assn., best crime novel 1971. Agent: A. D. Peters & Co., 10 Buckingham St., London WC2N 6BU. Address: 14 York Rd., Headington, Oxford OX3 8NW, UK.

McCOMB, Billie Pile, pen name PILE, Billie, b. 4 Oct. 1913, Blackwell, Okla., USA. Private Nurse. Educ: L.R.N.; Famous Authors Schl. Contbr. to: Cherokee Repub.; Holton Recorder, Kan.; Bailey Ctr. Index, Kan.; Wellington News, Kan.; Leon News, Kan.; China Grove Times, N.C.; Madison Press, Ohio; Jrnl. of Am. Med.; Charley Jones Joke Book (all carrying humorous column, Part Plagarism). Mbrships: Sec., Kan. Authors Club, 1964; Int. Typographical Union Aux., 1954-57, 1965-. Address: 303 S. Hydraulic Ave., Wichita, KS 67211, USA.

McCOMB, Frederick Wilson Henry, var. pen names, b. 9 Feb. 1927, Belfast, UK. Author; Journalist. Publs: The Story of the M.G. Sports Car, 1972; Veteran Cars; the formative years of motoring, 1974. Contbr. to: Ency. of Motor Sport, 1971; Car Facts & Feats, 1971; Milleruote Ency., 1975; Asst. Ed., Autosport, 1953-55; Ed., Autocourse, 1957-58; Ed., Safety Fast, 1959-64; Old Cars, USA; num. other motoring jrnls. Mbrships: Guild of Motoring Writers; Inst. of Adv. Motorists; BSM High-Performance Club. Address: St. Peter's Cottage, E. Marden, Chichester, W. Sussex, UK.

McCONKEY, James R., b. 2 Sept. 1921, Lakewood, Ohio, USA. Professor of English. Educ: B.A., Cleveland Coll., 1943; M.A., Western Reserve Univ., 1946; Ph.D., Univ. of Iowa, 1953. Publs: The Novels of E. M. Forster, 1957; Night Stand, 1965; Crossroads, 1968; A Journey to Sahalin, 1971. Contbr. to: New Yorker; Yale Review; Hudson Review; Sewanee Review. Mbr.: Am. PEN. Hons. incl: Award for Essay, Nat. Endowment for the Humanities, 1968; Guggenheim creative writing Fellowship, 1969-70. Address: R.D. 1, Trumansburg, NY 14886, USA.

McCONNELL, James Vernon, b. 26 Oct. 1925, Okmulgee, Okla., USA. Professor of Psychology. Educ: B.A., La. State Univ., 1947; M.A., 1954, Ph.D., 1956, Univ. Tex. Publs: Psychology (w. Allen Calvin, M. Scriven, J. Gallagher, C. Hanley & F. J. McGuian), 1961; Ed., The Worm Re-Turns, 1965; Contbr., Ed., Psychology Today: An Introduction, 1970; Co-Ed., Science, Sex & Sacred Cows, 1971; Understanding Human Behavior, 1974. Contbr. to: Esquire; Road & Track; Ency. Britannica Yearbook (1973); & num. sci. fiction mags. & sci. jrnls. Mbrships. incl: Fellow Am. Psychol. Assn.; Am. Assn. for Advancement Sci. Recip., Rsch. Career Dev. Award, HIH, 1963-68 (Nat. Inst. Health). Address: 4101 Thornoaks Rd., Ann Arbor, MI 48104, USA.

McCORD, Howard Lawrence, b. 3 Nov. 1932, El Paso, Tex., USA. Professor of English. Educ: B.A., Univ. of Tex. at El Paso, 1957; M.A., Univ. of Utah, 1958. Publs: The Spanish Dark, 1965; Fables & Transfigurations, 1967; Longjaunes His Periplus, 1968; The Life of Fraenkel's Death, 1969; The Fire Visions, 1970; Gnomonology: A Handbook of Systems, 1971; Maps, 1971; The Diary of a Young Girl, 1972; Mirrors, 1973; Friend, 1974; Selected Poems, 1974. Contbr. to var. lit. jrnls. Mbrships: PEN; Poetry Soc. of Am. Hons. incl: Borestone Mountain Poetry Award, 1969; Hart Crane & Alice Crane Williams Fndn. Award for Poetry, 1970; D. H. Lawrence Fellow, 1971. Address: Dept. of English, Bowling Green Univ., Bowling Green, OH 43403, USA.

McCORMICK, George Donald King, pen names McCORMICK, Donald; DEACON, Richard, b. 9 Dec. 1911, Rhyl, Flintshire, UK. Publs: The Mystery of Lord Kitchener's Death, 1959; The Identity of Jack the Ripper, 1959; The Mask of Merlin, 1963; Pedlar of Death, 1965; Madoc & the Discovery of America, 1966; John Dee, 1968; A History of the British Secret Service, 1969; A History of the Russian Secret Service, 1972; A History of the Chinese Secret Service, 1974. Mbr., Soc. of Authors. Address: Flat 11, Lion House, Carlton Hill, Exmouth, Devon, UK.

McCORMICK, Mary, (Thelma), b. 24 Feb. 1908, Vincennes, Ind., USA. Retired Civil Service Clerk; Poet. Publs: Fourteen Poems, 1965; Harp on the Willow Tree, 1969. Contbr. to: (essays) Grass Roots; Cyclo Flame; Hoosier Challenger; (poems) Ocarina; Paperman; Grass Roots; Avalon Anthol.; Cyclo Flame; New Athanaeum; Candor; The Am. Friend; The Houyhnhnm Scrapbook; Cyclotron; Hoosier Challenger; Poets' Bulletin; Mobile Press; Drovers Telegram; Columbus Citizen; Snowy Egret; Denver Post; num. other anthols. & lit. jrnls. Mbrships. incl: Avalon World Arts Acad.; The Pensters; Ala. Poetry Soc.; Writers' Conclave. Hons. incl: Citations, Avalon World Arts Acad.; Award of Merit, Ala. Writers' Conclave; etc. Address: 3205 Riverside Dr., Mobile, AL 36605, USA.

McCORMICK, Victoria, pen name GREEN, Janet, b. 4 July 1914, Hitchin, Herts., UK. Author. Publs. incl: (plays) Lighten Our Darkness; Murder Mistaken; Matilda Shouted Fire; (screenplays) The Clouded Yellow; Eye Witness; Sapphire; Victim; Life for Ruth (w. J. McCormick); Seven Women; A Month to Kill (Italian TV); Rosalie is Dead (forthcoming); (novel) My Turn Now, 1971. Contbr. to var. mystery anthols. Mbrships. incl: Dramatists' Guild, N.Y.; Mystery Writers of Am. Hons. incl: British Acad. Award, 1959; Prix Femina du Cinema; Edgar, Mystery Writers of Am. (all for Sapphire, 1959). Address: 20 Grove Ct., Beaconsfield, Bucks., UK.

McCOURT, Edward (Alexander), b. 10 Oct. 1907, Mullingar, Ireland. Professor of English. Educ: B.A., Univ. of Alta., Can., 1932; B.A. 1934, M.A. 1947, Oxford Univ., UK. Publs. incl: (novels) Music at the Close, 1947; The Wooden Sword, UK & Can., 1956; Walk through the Valley, UK, 1958; Fasting Friar, 1963 (as The Ettinger Affair, UK, 1963); (non-fiction) The Canadian West in Fiction, 1949; The Road Across Canada, Can., USA & UK, 1965; Remember Butler, UK & Can., 1967; The Yukon & the Northwest Territories, Can., 1969, UK, 1970; num. short stories. Recip., Ryerson Award, 1947; Address: Dept. of English, Univ. of Saskatchewan, Saskatoon, Sask., Can.

McCULKEN, (Brother) Francis Joseph, pen name DOYLE, Lynn C., b. 11 Nov. 1904, Phila., Pa., USA. Religious Teacher, Catholic Order, The Marianists. Educ: B.S., Univ. of Dayton, Ohio, 1928; M.Litt., Univ. of Pittsburgh, Pa., 1958. Publs. incl: Mary's Troubador, The Late Rev. Al Seitz, S.M., 1950; Mary's Iron Major, The Late Rev. John Ott, S.M., 1952. Contbr. to: Maryknoll Mag.; The Shield; The Messenger; The Apostle of Mary; The Marianist Educator. Mbr., Marianist Writers' Guild. Address: St. John's Home, 144 Beach 111th St., Rockaway Park, NY 11694, USA.

McCULLAGH, Sheila Kathleen, b. 3 Dec. 1920, Surrey, UK. Writer. Educ: Univ. of Leeds. Publs: The Griffin & Dragon Pirate Books series, 1958-; One, Two, Three & Away! series, 1964-; Flightpath to Reading Series, 1974-; Into New Worlds, 1974. Contbr. to educl. jrnls. Mbr., Soc. of Authors. Address: Treveor, Croft Todn, Nancledra, Penzance, Cornwall, UK.

McCUTCHAN, Philip Donald, occasional pen name MacNEIL, Duncan, b. 13 Oct. 1920, Cambridge, UK. Author. Educ: Royal Mil. Coll., Sandhurst. Publs. incl: Poulter's Passage, 1967; The Screaming Dead Balloons, 1968; The Day of the Coastwatch, 1968; The Bright Red Businessman, 1969; The All-Purpose Bodies, 1969; Man, Let's Go On, 1970; Hartinger's Mouse, 1970; Half a Bag of Stringer, 1971; This Drakotny, 1971; The German Helmet, 1972; The Oil Bastards, 1972; Pull My String, 1973; Call for Simon Shard, 1974; Coach North, 1974; Beware Beware the Bight of Benin, 1974; A Very Big Bang, 1975; By Command of the Viceroy, 1975; (under pen name) Drums Along the Kyber, 1969; Lieutenant of the Line, 1970; Sadhu on the Mountain Peak, 1971; The Gates of Kunarja, 1972; The Red Daniel, 1973; Subaltern's Choice, 1974. Address: c/o Barclay's Bank Ltd., 90 Osborne Rd., Southsea, Hants. PO5 3LW, UK.

McCUTCHEON, W. A., b. 1934, Belfast, N. Ireland, UK. Keeper of Technology & Local History, Ulster Museum, 1968–. Educ: Queen's Univ., Belfast; M.A.; Ph.D.; F.S.A.; F.R.G.S. Publs: The Canals of the North of Ireland, 1965; Railway History in Pictures: Ireland, Vol. 1, 1969, Vol. 2, 1971; Travel & Transport in Ireland, (co-author) 1973. Contbr. to: Ulster Folklife; Ulster Jrnl. of Archaeol.; Economic Hist. Review; Irish Geography; Geographical Jrnl.; Technol. & Culture; Trans. of the Newcomen Soc.; Jrnl. of Industrial Archaeol.; var. vols. of essays on Irish indl. & commercial hist. Mbrships. incl: Royal Geographical Soc.; Newcomen Soc.; Soc. for the Study of the Hist. of Technol. (USA). Address: Ulster Museum, Botanic Gdns., Belfast, Northern Ireland, UK.

McDANIEL, Charles Ainsworth, b. 28 Aug. 1930, NYC, USA. Television Dramatist. Educ: Am. Acad. of Dramatic Arts; Univ. of London; UCLA. Has written for all major Am. dramatic TV shows. Scripts for Marcus Welby, M.D.; Kung Fu; Name of the Game; Judd for the Defense; etc.; also Beyond This Place There Be Dragons (NBC movie of the week). Major Screenplays: Neighbours. Mbrships: Writers' Guild of Am.; Am. Acad. of TV Arts & Scis.; Dramatists' Guild. Address: 621 S. Barrington, Los Angeles, CA 49, USA.

McDANIEL, Esther Koerner, b. 18 Nov. 1906, Mt. Vernon, Ind., USA. Writer; Poet. Educ: Lockyear's Bus. Coll. Publs: Rainbow to the Storms, 1964. Contbr. to num. poetry jrnls. & reviews. Mbrships: Nat. League of Am. Pen Women; World Poetry Soc.; South & West, Inc.; Poetry Soc. of Alaska; Assoc., Poetry Soc. of Tex.; Ore. State Poetry Soc.; Ozark Writers Guild. Hons. incl: 1st Prizes, Poetry & Short Stories, Alaska, Colo., Ark., Miss., Calif., La., Ore. above socs. & others. Address: 850 Hillview Dr., Ashland, OR 97520, USA.

McDARRAH, Fred W., b. 5 Nov. 1926, Brooklyn, N.Y., USA. Photographer; Picture Editor. Educ: Grad., N.Y.

Univ., 1954. Publs: Ed., The Beat Scene, 1960; The Artist's World in Pictures, 1961; Greenwich Village, 1963; New York, New York, 1964; The New Bohemia (w. John Cruen), 1966; Sculpture in Environment, 1967; Guide for Ecumenical Discussion (w. James J. Young), 1970; Museums in New York, 2nd ed., 1973; Ed., Saturday Review Executive Desk Diary, 1962-64. Contbr. to: Village Voice (Picture Ed., 1971–); Infinity; Culture Hero. Recip., num. awards for photography. Address: 505 W. Broadway, N.Y., NY 10012, USA.

McDONALD, Erwin Lawrence, pen name HANKINS, Clabe, b. 31 Oct. 1907, London, Ark., USA. Editor/Writer. Educ: Assoc., Sci., Ark. Polytechnic Coll., Russellville, 1934; B.A., Ouachita Bapt. Univ., Arkadelphia, Ark., 1943; Master of Divinity, S. Bapt. Theol. Sem., Louisville, Ky., 1947; D.Litt., Georgetown Coll., Ky., 1958. Publs. incl: 75 Stories & Illustrations from Everyday Life, 1964; Across the Editor's Desk, 1966; Stories for Speakers & Writers, 1970; Sixty Years of Service — History of Rotary Club of Little Rock, Ark., 1974. Mbrships: Former Pres., S. Bapt. Press Assn.; Former Mbr., Exec. Bd., Assoc. Ch. Press. Address: 1419 Garland Ave., North Little Rock, AR 72116, USA.

McDONALD, Hugh Dermot, b. 29 Oct. 1910, Dublin, Ireland. Professor of Philosophy of Religion & Theology. Educ: B.A., B.D., Ph.D., D.D., Univ. of London. Publs: Ideas of Revelation: 1700-1860; Theories of Revelation: 1860-1960; I & He; Jesus: Human & Divine; The Church & its Glory; Living Doctrines of the New Testament; Freedom in Faith. Contbr. to: Scottish Jrnl. of Theol.; Harvard Theol. Review; Spectrum; Faith & Thought; New Baker Dictionary of Ethics; New Dictionary of the Ch.; Zondervan Pictorial Ency. of the Bible. Mbr., Royal Inst. of Philos. Address: 'Fairhaven', 43 The Rough, Newick, Sussex BN8 4NS, UK.

McDONALD, Lucile Saunders, b. 1 Sept. 1898, Portland, Ore., USA. Journalist. Educ: Univs. of Ore. & Wash.; Columbia Univ. Publs: 23 books, mainly juvenile, inclng. Coast Country, 1966; The Mystery of the Long House & The Stolen Letters (both w. Z. Ross), latest ed. 1970; Garden Sass, 1971; Swan Among the Indians, 1972; The Arab Marco Polo: Ibn Battuta (forthcoming). Contbr. to Seattle Times Sunday Mag. (staff mbr., 23 yrs.). Mbrships: Women in Communications; Authors' Guild of Am.; Seattle Free Lances; Western Writers of Am. Hons. incl: Gov.'s Writers' Day Awards, 1967, 1973; Wash. State Presswomen Torchbearer Award, 1971. Address: 3224 109th Ave., Bellevue, WA 98004, USA.

MACDONALD, Robert William, b. 18 Dec. 1922, Wantagh, N.Y., USA. Government Official. Educ: B.A., Clark Univ., Worcester, Mass., 1948; M.A., Brown Univ., Providence, R.I., 1951; Ph.D., Georgetown Univ., Wash. D.C., 1962. Publs: Ed., Inside the Arab Mind, 1960; Morocco: A Politico-Economic Analysis, 1961; The League of Arab States: A Case Study in Regional Organization, 1965; Contbr., Alliances, 1970. Mbrships. incl: Am. Pol. Sci. Assn.; Middle East Inst.; World Assn. for Pub. Opinion Rsch.; Am. For. Serv. Assn.; Alexandria Hist. Soc. Address: 219 Wolfe St., Alexandria, VA 22314, USA.

MacDONALD, Simon Gavin George, b. 5 Sept. 1923, Beauly, Inverness, UK. University Professor of Physics; Author. Educ: M.A., Edinburgh Univ.; Ph.D., Univ. of St. Andrews. Publs: Problems & Solutions in General Physics, 1967; Physics for Biology & Premedical Students, 1970; Physics for the Life & Health Sciences, 1975. Contbr. to: Acta Cryst.; Zeit für Krist; Chem. in Ind.; New Worlds; D. C. Thomson Pubs. Mbr., Soc. of Authors. Address: 10 Westerton Ave., Dundee DD5 3NJ, UK.

MacDONALD DOUGLAS, Ronald Angus, pen names MacDONALD Angus, IOLAIR, An Sean, b. 1906, Edinburgh, Scotland. Literary Journalist. Publs: Strangers Come Home; The Sword of Freedom; The Scots Book; The Irish Book; The Closed Door; (plays) The Red Laugh; The Woman Beyond. Contbr. to: Num. Scottish, Engl., & Am. mags. & jrnls.; Former Ed., Catalyst mag.; BBC. Mbrships. incl: Soc. of Authors; PEN; League of Dramatists; Fellow, Int. Inst. of Arts & Letters; Radiowriters' Assn. Address: Tigh an Uillt, Wilton Dean, Hawick, Roxburghshire, UK.

McDONNELL, Virginia (Bleecker), pen name McDONNELL, Jinny, b. 24 Nov. 1917, Short Hills, N.J., USA. Author; Registered Nurse. Educ: R.N., Samaritan Schl. of Nursing, Troy, N.Y. Publs. incl: Doctors & Nurses, 1962; Your Future in Nursing, 1963; Olympic Duty, 1965;

paperback, 1969; Dee O'Hara, Astronauts Nurse, USA, Can. & UK, 1965; The Ski Trail Mystery, 1966; County Agent, 1968; Careers in Hotel Management, 1971; Silent Partner, 1972; The Deep Six, 1974; num. short stories & articles. Mbrships. incl: Authors' Guild & League; Mystery Writers of Am. Recip., Hons. from City of Hope & Leukemia Soc. Address: 79 Hudson Park Rd., New Rochelle, NY 10805, USA.

McDOUGALL, Colin Malcolm, b 13 July 1917, Montreal, P.Q., Can. University Administrator. Educ: B.A., McGill Univ., 1940. Publs: Execution (novel), 1958. Contbr. of short stories, articles & reviews to var. jrnls. Mbrships: F.R.S.A. Hons: Gov.-Gen's. Award for Fiction, 1959, 1st Prize. P.Q. Lit. Contest, 1959, Beta Sigma Phi 1st novel Award; Womens' Can. Club Prize; Pres's. Medal, Univ. of W. Ont. Address: 433 Lansdowne Ave., Montreal 214, P.Q., Can.

McDOWELL, Edwin Stewart, b. 13 May 1935, Somers Point, N.J., USA. Editorial Writer. Educ: B.S., Temple Univ., Phila., 1959. Publs: Portrait of an Arizonan, 1964; Three Cheers & a Tiger, 1966. Contbr. to: Wall St. Jrnl. (staff mbr.); num. other newspapers, jrnls. & mags. (articles & reviews). Mbrships. incl: Mont Pelerin Soc.; Nat. Conf. Ed. Writers. Address: c/o Wall Street Journal, 22 Cortlandt St., N.Y., NY 10007, USA.

McDOWELL, Frederick P. W., b. 29 May 1915, Phila., Pa., USA. Professor of English. Educ: B.S., 1937, M.A., 1938, Univ. of Pa; M.A., 1947, Ph.D., 1949, Harvard Univ. Publs: Ellen Glasgow & the Ironic Art of Fiction, 1960; Elizabeth Madox Roberts, 1962; Caroline Gordon, 1966; Ed., The Poet as Critic, 1966; E. M. Forster, 1969; E. M. Forster: An Annotated Bibliography of Secondary Writings about Him, 1975. Contbr. to: Publs of MLA; Criticism; Contemporary Literature, Wis.; Journal of Modern Lit.; & num. other jrnls. Mbrships. incl: MLA; Shaw Soc., London; N.Y. Shavians; Ellen Glasgow Soc.; Joseph Conrad Soc. Recip., Sr. Fellowship, Nat. Endowment for Humanities, 1973-74. Address: 1118E Court St., Iowa City, IA 52240, USA.

McELWEE, William Lloyd, b. 13 Sept. 1907, London, UK. Schoolmaster; Academic Lecturer. Educ: Marburg Univ., 1925-26; B.A., Christ Ch., Oxford, 1930. Publs: The Struggle for Supremacy in Germany (w. A. J. P. Taylor); The Reign of Charles V, 1935; The Murder of Sir Thomas Oxbury, 1952; The Story of England. 1952; England's Precedence, 1603-1688, 1956; The Wisest Fool in Christendom, 1958; Britain's Lowest Years, 1918-40, 1962; History of England, Teach Yourself Series, 1960; Battle of D-Day, 1965. Contbr. to: Sunday Telegraph; New Statesman; Daily Telegraph. F.R.S.L. Address: 99 Winchester Rd., Micheldever, Hants., UK.

MacEOIN, Gary, b. 12 June 1909, Curry, Co. Sligo, Repub. of Ireland. Writer. Educ: B.A., Univ. of London, 1942; M.A., 1943, Ph.D., 1951, Nat. Univ. of Ireland; Barrister-at-Law, King's Inns, Dublin. Publs. incl: Cervantes, 1952; Latin America: The Eleventh Hour, 1962; Colombia, Venezuela & the Guianas, 1965; What Happened at Rome, 1966; Revolution Next Door: Latin America in the 1970s, 1971; Northern Ireland, Captive of History, 1974; No Peaceful Way: Chile's Struggle for Dignity, 1974. Contbr. to num. jrnls. & symposia. Mbrships. incl: O'seas Press Club of Am.; Inst. of Journalists, UK. Hons. incl: Award, Cath. Press Assn. of US, 1974. Address: 820 S. Langley Ave., Apt. 101, Tucson, AZ 85710, USA.

MACESICH, George, b. 27 May 1927, Cleveland, Ohio, USA. Professor of Economics; Director, Center for Yugoslav-American Studies, Research and Exchanges. Educ: A.A., 1951, B.A., 1953, Geo. Wash Univ; M.A., 1954; Ph.D., Univ. of Chgo., 1958. Publs. incl: Financing Industrial & Regional Development: American Experience with the Small Business Administration 1955-65, 1972; Monetary & Financial Organization for Growth & Stability: The U.S. & Yugoslavia, 1972; Money & Finance in Contemporary Yugoslavia (w. D. Dmitrijević), 1973. Contbr. to num. profl. jrnls. & publs. Mbr., var. profl. assns. Address: Center for Yugoslav-American Studies, Research & Exchanges, 930 West Park Ave., Florida State University, Tallahassee, FL 32306, USA.

McEVOY, , Marjorie, b. York, UK. Novelist. Publs: (novels) Softly Treads Danger, 1963, 2nd ed., 1969; The Grenfell Legacy, 1968; Ravensmount, 1974; The Wych Stone, 1974. Contbr. to: Caravan; Mod. Caravan; Co. Gentleman's Estate Mag.; BBC; etc. Mbr., R.N.A., London.

Address: 54 Miriam Ave., Somersall, Chesterfield, Derbys. S40 3NF, UK.

MAC EWEN, Gwendolyn, b. 1 Sept. 1941, Toronto, Ont., Can. Poet; Novelist. Publs: The Rising Fire, 1963; Julian the Magician, 1963; A Breakfast for Barbarians, 1966; The Shadow Maker, 1969; King of Egypt, King of Dreams, 1971; The Armies of the Moon, 1972; Noman, 1972; The Magic Animals, selected poems, 1975. Recip., The Gov. Gen.'s Award, 1970. Address: c/o MacMillan Publishers, 70 Bond St., Toronto, Ont., Can.

McFARLANE, James Walter, b. 12 Dec. 1920, Sunderland, UK. University Teacher; Author. Educ: M.A., B.Litt., St. Catherine's Univ., Oxford. Publs: Ibsen & the Temper of Norwegian Literature, 1960; The Oxford Ibsen, 8 vols., 1960-75; Henrik Ibsen: a critical anthology, 1970. Contbr. to: Scandinavica (Ed.); Mod. Lang. Review; Times Lit. Supplement; German Life & Letters; Ency. Britannica. Mbrships: F.R.S.A.; Soc. of Authors; Assn. Univ. Tchrs. Address: The Croft, Stody, Melton Constable, Norfolk NR24 2EE, UK.

MACFARLANE, Robert Gwyn, b. 26 June 1907, Worthing, UK. Pathologist; Emeritus Professor of Clinical Pathology. Educ: St. Bartholomew's Hosp. Med. Schl., Univ. of London; M.D.; B.S.; M.R.C.S.; M.A.(Oxon). Publs. incl: Human Blood Coagulation & its Disorders (w. R. Biggs), 1953, 3rd ed., 1963; Treatment of Haemophilia & Other Coagulation Defects (Ed. w. R. Biggs), 1966; Ed., The Haemostatic Mechanism in Man & Other Animals, 1970. Contbr. to var. books, encys. & sci. jrnls. Mbrships: F.R.S.; Coun., 1960-61; F.R.C.P. Hons: C.B.E., 1964; Cameron Prize, Edinburgh Univ., 1967. Address: Mallie's Cottage, Opinan, Laide, Achnasheen, Ross-shire, UK.

McFARLANE, Shona Graham, b. 27 Mar. 1930, Gore, NZ. Artist; Journalist. Educ: Dunedin Tchrs. Coll.; Hammersmith Schl. of Art, London, UK; Schl. of Art, Goldsmiths Coll., London. Publs: Dunedin: Portrait of a City (author & illustrator), 1971; Mixed Media (author & illustrator), 1975. Mbrships: Coun. Mbr., Queen Elizabeth II Arts Coun. of NZ; Past Pres., Dunedin Civic Arts Coun.; Otago Art Soc. Inc.; Coun. Mbr., Dunedin Pub. Art. Gall. Soc., Otago Early Settlers' Assn., Otago Theatre Trust. Hons. incl: M.B.E., 1973; Nat. Bank Art Award, 1974. Address: 28 Ings Ave., St. Clair, Dunedin, NZ.

MACFIE, Alec Lawrence, b. 29 May 1898, Glasgow, UK. University Professor Emeritus. Educ: M.A., LL.B., D.Litt., Univ. of Glasgow. Publs: Theories of the Trade Cycle, 1934; An Essay on Economy & Value, 1936; Economic Efficiency & Social Welfare, 1943; The Individual in Society (Papers on Adam Smith), 1967. Contbr. to: Econ. Jrnl.; Scottish Jrnl. of Pol. Econ.; Oxford Univ. Papers; Cambridge Jrnl.; Economica; Jrnl. of Hist. of Ideas (USA); Ethics (Univ. of Chgo.); Hibbert Jrnl.; etc. Recip., Hon. LL.D., Univ. of Glasgow. Address: 21 Tannoch Drive, Milngavie, Glasgow G6Z 8AY, UK.

McGAHERN, John, b. 12 Nov. 1934, Dublin, Repub. of Ireland. Teacher; Professor of Literature. Educ: Univ. Coll., Dublin. Publs: (novels) The Barracks, UK, 1963, USA, 1964; The Dark, UK, 1965, USA, 1966; (short stories) Nightlines, UK, 1970, USA, 1971; (play) Sinclair, prod. 1972; var. TV plays. Hons: A.E. Mem. Award, 1962; Macauley Fellowship, 1964; Awards, Arts Coun., 1966, 1968, 1971. Address: c/o Faber & Faber Ltd., 3 Queen Square, London WC1, UK.

McGANN, George T., b. 9 July 1913, NYC, USA. Journalist. Educ: Univ. of Notre Dame, Ind. Publs: The Game of Billiards, 1965; Court Hustler, 1973. Contbr. to: Esquire Mag.; World Tennis Mag.; The Bulletin (Sydney, Aust.). Mbrships. incl: For. Press Assn., NYC; Nat. Press Club, Wash. DC; Overseas Press Club, NYC. Recip., Danzig Trophy for outstanding tennis writing, 1969. Address: 71-26 Juno St., Forest Hills, NY 11375, USA.

McGERR, Patricia, b. 26 Dec. 1917, Falls City, Neb., USA. Writer. Educ: A.B., Univ. of Neb., 1936; M.A., Columbia Univ. Grad. Schl. of Jrnlsm., 1937. Publs: Pick Your Victim, 1946; Seven Deadly Sisters, 1947; Catch Me If You Can, 1948; Save the Witness, 1949; Follow, as the Night, 1950; Death in a Million Living Rooms, 1951; The Missing Years, 1953; Fatal in my Fashion, 1954; Martha Martha, 1960; My Brothers Remember Monica, 1964; Is there a Traitor in the House, 1964; Murder is Absurd, 1967; Stranger with my Face, 1968; For Richer for Poorer will Death, 1969; Legacy of Danger, 1970; Daughter of

Darkness, 1974. Contbr. to mags. Mbrships: Bd. Dirs., Mystery Writers Am.; Authors League Am. Hons: Grand Prix de Litt. Policiere, France, 1952; 1st Prize, Ellery Queen's Mystery Mag., 1967. Address: 5415 Conn. Ave., N.W., Wash. D.C. 20015, USA.

McGILL, Thomas E(merson), b. 26 Sept. 1930, Sharon, Pa., USA. Professor; Writer. Educ: B.A., Youngstown State Univ., 1954; M.A., 1957, Ph.D., 1958, Princeton Univ. Author, Readings in Animal Behavior, 1965, 2nd ed., 1973. Contbr. to: Sci.; Jrnls. of Comp. & Physiol. Psychol.; Ency. Americana; Am. Psychol.; Behaviour; Animal Behaviour. Address: Green River Rd., Williamstown, MA 01267, USA.

McGIVERN (Rev.), James Sabine, S. J., b. 27 July 1908, Edmonton, Atla., Can. Member, Society of Jesus; Professor. Educ: Jesuit Sems., Guelph, Montreal, Toronto, Can.; Valkenburg, Holland; Feldkirch, Austria; B.A., Ph.D.; M.A., Univ. of Toronto, 1949. Publs: Royal Engineers in British Columbia, 1960; Shadows Over Huronia (ed.), 3 eds., 1965; Your Name & Coat of Arms, 1969-70; The Huron Relation of 1635 (co-author), 1971. Contbr. to: Weekly Columnist, Toronto Telegram; etc. Ed., The Martyr's Shrine Message & Scottish Genealogical Helper (quarterlies). Recip., M.B.E. Address: Regis Coll., 3425 Bayview Ave., Willowdale, Ont., Can.

McGOVERN, Bernard Stephen Patrick, pen name MAC, b. 3 Oct. 1921, Leeds, UK. Local Government Officer. Educ: Army Cert. of Educ. Publs: Playleadership, 1973; The Playleaders Handbook, 1975; Sociological & Educational Implications of Playleadership. Contbr. to: Pks. & Sportsgrounds Mag.; Times Educl. Supplement. Mbrships: Fndr. Mbr., Inst. of Playleadership; Exec. Comm.; Ed., Inst. Mag., 1972; Fellow, Nat. Assn. Recreation Ldrs.; Treas.; Pres., 1961-68; Assoc., Swimming Tchrs. Assn.. 1961; Examiner, Kent Br., Royal Life Saving Soc.; Int. Playground Assn. Address: Play Leadership Scheme, Amenities Dept., Town Hall, Lewisham, London SE13, UK.

MACGREGOR, James Murdoch, pen name McINTOSH, J. T., b. 14 Feb. 1925, Paisley, UK. Journalist. Educ: M.A., Aberdeen Univ. Publs. incl: A Cry to Heaven, 1960; The Iron Rain, 1962; Wine Making for All, 1966; Beer Making for All, 1967; Time for a Change, 1967; Six Gates from Limbo, 1968; Take a Pair of Private Eyes (w. Peter O'Donnel), 1968; A Coat of Blackmail, 1970; Transmigration, 1970; Flight from Rebirth, 1971; The Cosmic Spies, 1972; The Suiciders, 1972; Galactic Takeover Bid, 1973. Address: 63 Abbotswell Dr., Aberdeen, UK.

MacGREGOR-HASTIE, Roy Alasdhair Niall, b. 28 Mar. 1929, Prague, Czech. Author. Educ: B.A., Univ. of Manchester; M.F.A., Univ. of Iowa, USA. Publs. incl: (biographies) Khrushchev, 1959; Mao Tse-tung, 1960; Pope John XXIII, 1962; Pope Paul VI, 1963; (other) The Mechanics of Power, 1965; The Day of the Lion, 1966; Anthology of Contemporary Romanian Poetry, 1969; The Last Romantic, 1972. Contbr. to: Punch; Poetry Review; Mod. Poetry in Transl.; & other lit. jrnls.; major Engl. lang. newspapers. Mbrships. incl: PEN; Soc. of Authors; Translators Assn. Hons. incl: Transl. Prizes (Poetry), European Community of Writers, 1969, 1972; Fellowship in Creative Writing, Univ. of Iowa, 1973. Address: c/o Savage Club, 86 St. James' St., London SW1, UK.

McGREW, Janice Weggener, pen name (poetry) McGREW, Jan, (professional articles) WAGGENER, Janice (biog.), McGREW Janice W., b. Humboldt, Neb., USA. Professor of Psychology of Handicapped Children. Educ: A.B., 1930, M.A., 1934, Univ. of Denver; Ph.D. Cand., Univ. of N. Colo. Contbr. to state, nat., poetry anthols., textbooks on speech pathol., profl. jrnls. Mbrships: Nat. Fedn. of State Poetry Socs.; State, local offs., Poetry Soc. of Colo.; Ariz. State Poetry Soc. Hons: Prizes, num. hon. mentions, Colo. state poetry contests. Address: Box 71, Kiowa, CO 80117, USA.

McGUIGAN, F. Joseph, b. 7 Dec. 1924, Okla. City, USA. Professor of Psychology; Author. Educ: B.A., 1945, M.A., 1949, UCLA; Ph.D., Univ. of Southern Calif., 1950. Publs. incl: Experimental Psychology, 1960, 2nd ed., 1968; Psychology (w. A. D. Calvin), 1961; The Biological Basis of Behavior, 1963; Thinking: Studies of Covert Language Behavior, 1966; Contemporary Studies in Psychology (w. Paul J. Woods), 1972; Contemporary Approaches in Conditioning & Learning (co-ed. w. D. B. Lumsden), 1973; Principles of Covert Behavior — A Study in the Psychophysiology of Thinking (in preparation). Contbr. to var. psychol. jrnls. Address: Dept. of Psychology, Hollins College, VA 24020, USA.

McGURN, Barrett, b. 6 Aug. 1914, NYC, USA. Spokesman, United States Supreme Court, Washington D.C. Educ: A.B., 1935, Hon. Litt.D., 1958, Fordham Univ. Publs. incl: YANK — The GI Story of the War (co-author), 1947; The Overseas Press Club Cookbook (co-author), 1962; Decade in Europe, 1959; A Reporter Looks at the Vatican, 1962; A Reporter Looks at American Catholicism, 1967; Heroes of Our Times (co-author), 1968. Contbr. to: Reader's Digest; Commonweal; etc. Mbrships. incl: Pres., 1963-65, Life Gov., Overseas Press Club of Am. Hons. incl: Best Am. For. Corres., Overseas Press Club, 1957. Address: 5229 Duvall Dr., Westmoreland Hills, MD 20016, USA.

McHALE, Philip John, b. 28 July 1928, Birmingham, UK. Playwright; Secondary School Teacher. Educ: Auckland Tchrs. Trng. Coll.; London Univ., UK; Massey Univ., NZ. Publs: Inside Broadcasting, 1968; Collected Plays, 1969; No Flowers & Other Plays, 1970; Communications & the Post Office, 1970; Stories for Reading Aloud, 1973. Contbr. to radio, TV & newspapers. Mbrships: Brit. League of Dramatists; Soc. of Authors. Hons: 1st award, Brussels Film Festival, 1958; Award of Merit, Antwerp, 1959; Award of Merit, Chgo., 1959. Address: 24 Inglis St., Auckland 10, NZ.

McHALE, Tom, grew up Scranton, Pa., USA. Writer. Educ: Temple Univ., Phila., grad. 1963; Univ. of Pa.; Univ. of Iowa. Publs: (novels) Principato, USA, 1970, UK, 1971; Farragan's Retreat, USA & UK, 1971. Address: c/o Viking Press, 625 Madison Ave., N.Y., NY 10022, USA.

MACHIN, Evelyn Louise, b. 17 Jan. 1915, Stoke Bishop, Bristol, UK. Teacher. Educ: Lady Margaret Hall, Oxford; Extra-mural Dip. Archaeol., Univ. of London. Contbr. to: Lady; BBC; etc. Mbr., Soc. of Women Writers & Journalists.

MACHLIS, Joseph, pen name (for fiction) SELCAMM, George, b. 11 Aug. 1906, Riga, Latvia. Writer; Professor of Music. Educ: B.A., CCNY, USA, 1927; Cert. in Piano, Inst. of Musical Art, 1928; M.A., Columbia Univ., 1937. Publs: The Enjoyment of Music, 1955, 3rd ed., 1970; Introduction to Contemporary Music, 1961; American Composers of Our Time, 1964; Music: Adventures in Listening, 1966; Let's Listen to Music, 1975; (novels) The Night is for Music, 1965; 57th St., 1971. Mbr., PEN, USA. Address: 310 E. 55th St., N.Y., NY 10022, USA.

McHUGH, Arona, b. 8 Aug. 1924, Boston, Mass., USA. Novelist; Freelance Writer. Educ: B.A., Univ. of Iowa, 1950; M.S., 1951; M.A. work, Columbia Univ. Publs: A Banner with a Strange Device, 1964, UK, 1965; The Seacoast of Bohemia, USA, 1965, UK, 1966; The Luck of the Van Meers, USA & UK, 1969; The Calling of the Mercenaries, USA, 1973, UK, 1975. Mbrships: PEN; Authors' Guild. Hons: Bernard De Vote Fellowship in Fiction Writing, 1967; McDowell Colony Fellowship, 1969; Edward Albee Fndn. Fellowship, 1972. Address: c/o Paul Reynolds Inc., 12 E. 41st St., N.Y., NY 10017, USA.

McHUGH, Ivy Cecil Stuart, b. 1 Sept. 1902, Kuala Lumpur, Malaysia. Wife & Mother. Publs: Food, Flowers & Wine (w. Helen Cox); Floral Art Book of Reference (w. H. Cox); Mr. & Mrs. Charles Dickens Entertain at Home (w. H. Cox); Knock on the Nursery Door. Contbr. to: BBC Radio & TV; Indep. TV; Cheshire Life; Glos. Life; Field; Popular Gardening; Daily Telegraph; Wilts. & Glos. Standard. Mbr., West Country Writers' Assn. Address: Baunton Fields, Cirencester, Glos. GL7 7BB, UK.

MacINNES, Colin, b. 1914, London, UK. Writer. Publs. incl: (novels) City of Spades, UK, 1957, USA, 1958; Absolute Beginners, UK, 1959, USA, 1960; Mr. Love & Justice, UK, 1960, USA, 1961; All Day Saturday, 1966; Westward to Laughter, UK, 1969, USA, 1970; Three Years to Play, UK & USA, 1970; (non-fiction) England, Half English (essays), UK, 1961, USA, 1962; London: City of My Dreams, 1962; Australia & New Zealand (w. the Eds. of Life), USA, 1964; Sweet Saturday Night, UK, 1967. Address: c/o MacGibbon & Kee Ltd., 3 Upper James St., London W1R 4BP, UK.

MacINNES, Helen, b. 7 Oct. 1907, Glasgow, UK. Novelist. Publs. incl: Above Suspicion, 1941; Assignment in Brittany, 1942; Horizon, 1946; Friends & Lovers, 1947; Rest & Be Thankful, 1949; Neither Five nor Three, 1951; I & My True Love, 1953; Pray for a Brave Heart, 1955;

North from Rome, 1958; Decision at Delphi, 1960; The Venetian Affair, 1963; Home is the Hinter, 1964; The Double Image, 1966; The Salzburg Connection, 1968; Message from Malaga, 1971; The Snare of the Hunter, 1973. Recip., Wallace Award. Address: Jefferys Lane, E. Hampton, NY 11937, USA.

McINTOSH, Kinn Hamilton, pen name AIRD, Catherine, b. 20 June 1930, Huddersfield, UK. Writer. Publs: The Religious Body, 1966; A Most Contagious Game, 1967; Henrietta Who? , 1968; The Complete Steel, 1969; A Late Phoenix, 1971; His Burial Too, 1973. Mbrships: Crime Writers' Assn.; Soc. of Authors. Address: Invergordon, Sturry, Canterbury, Kent CT2 0NG, UK.

MacINTOSH, Phoebe-Joan, pen name MacINTOSH, Joan, b. 23 June 1924, Wellington, NZ. Writer. Publs: Wreck of the Tararua, 1970; Never a Dull Moment, 1974. Mbrships: Aust. Authors' Soc.; NZ Women Writers' Soc. Address: 28 Alamein St., Riverton, Southland, NZ.

MacINTYRE, Elisabeth (Mrs. Elisabeth Eldershaw), b. Sydney, NSW, Australia. Writer; Artist. Publs. incl: Katherine Who Lives in Australia; Mr. Koala Bear; Jane Likes Pictures; Ambrose Kangaroo; Hugh's Zoo; The Affable, Amiable, Bulldozer Man; Ninji's Magic; The Purple Mouse, 1975. Hons: Aust. Picture Book of Yr. Award, circa 1964; Lit. Fellowship, Aust. Coun. of Arts, 1973-75. Address: c/o Jo Stewart, I.C.M., 1301 Avenue of the Americas, N.Y., NY 10019, USA.

MACKAY, Ian Reay, b. 22 Mar. 1922, Melbourne, Vic., Australia. Medical Researcher. Educ: Univ. of Melbourne; M.B., B.S., M.D. Publs: Autoimmune Diseases: Pathogenesis, Chemistry & Therapy (w. F. M. Burnett), 1963; The Human Thymus (w. G. Goldstein), 1969. Contbr. to num. textbooks & profl. jrnls., Australia, Europe, USA, UK. Hons: Searle Lectr., Am. Assn. for Study of Liver Diseases, 1960. Address: 3 Beamsley St., Malvern, Vic. 3144, Australia.

McKELLAR, (Thomas) Peter Huntly, b. Dunedin, NZ. University Professor of Psychology. Educ: M.A., Otago Univ.; Ph.D., Univ. Coll., London, UK. Publs: Text Book of Human Psychology, 1952; Imagination & Thinking, 1957, 3rd ed., 1967; Experience & Behaviour, 1968. Contbr. to profl. jrnls. Mbrships: Fellow, Brit. & NZ Psychol. Socs. Address: 4 Pitt St., Dunedin, NZ.

MACKELWORTH, Ronald Walter, b. 7 Apr. 1930, London, UK. Sales Manager. Publs: Firemantle, 1968; Tiltangle, 1971; Starflight 3000, 1972; Year of the Painted World, forthcoming. Contbr. to var. Sci. Fiction anthols. & sales mags. Mbrships: Fellow Inst. Profl. Salesmen; Intelligence Corps Comrades Assn.; Raynes Park Old Boys' Soc. Address: 3 Glendale, Woodberry Lane, Rowlands Castle, Hants., UK.

MACKENZIE, Andrew Carr, b. 30 May 1911, Oamaru, NZ. Journalist. Educ: Wellington Coll., 1924-28. Publs: The Unexplained, 1966 UK, 1970 USA; Frontiers of the Unknown, 1968 UK, 1970 USA; Apparitions & Ghosts, 1971 UK, 1972 USA; A Gallery of Ghosts (anthol.), 1972 UK, 1973 USA; Riddle of the Future, 1974 UK, 1975 USA. Contbr. to: Jrnl., Soc. for Psychical Rsch. Mbr., Coun., Soc. for Psychical Rsch. Address: 18 Castlebar Park, London W5 1BX, UK.

MACKENZIE, (John Anderson) Ross, b. 26 Aug. 1927, Edinburgh, UK. (Now US citizen). Professor of Church History. Educ: M.A., Edinburgh Univ., 1949; B.D., 1952, Ph.D., 1962, New Coll., Edinburgh; Teol. lic., Univ. of Lund, Sweden, 1964; studies at var. other univs. Publs. incl: Called Christian, Named Church, 1972; The Word in Action, 1973; Trying New Sandals, 1974. (transl.) Wingren, Man & the Incarnation, 1959; Wingren, Creation & Law, 1961. Reicke, The Gospel of Luke, 1964; Persson, Sacra Doctrina, 1970. Contbr. to: Corpus Dict. of Western Churches, 1970; Interpretation; Ch. Hist.; Jrnl. of Presby. Hist. Address: Union Theological Seminary, 3401 Brook Rd., Richmond, VA 23227, USA.

MacKENZIE, Norman Hugh, b. 8 Mar. 1915, Salisbury, Rhodesia. University Professor of English. Educ: B.A., 1934, M.A., 1935, Rhodes Univ., SA; Ph.D. (Union Schol.), Univ. of London, 1940. Publs: Hopkins (Writers & Critics Series), 1968; The Poems of Gerard Manley Hopkins (co-ed.), 1967; Poems of G. M. Hopkins (ed.), 1974. Contbr. to profl. jrnls. in UK, USA & Can. Mbrships. incl: Life Mbr., Yeats Soc.; Int. Pres., Hopkins Soc. Hons: Milner

Mem. Prize, Hist., 1933. Address: Dept. of English, Queen's Univ., Kingston, Ont., Can.

MacKENZIE, Ossian, b. 26 July 1907, Hampden, Me., USA. Educator. Educ: B.A., Univ. of Mont., 1928; Harvard Univ., 1928-31; J.D., Fordham Law Schl., 1938; Admitted, N.Y. State Bar, 1938; LL.D., Rider Coll., 1962. Publs: The American Association of Collegiate Schools of Business, 1916-66 (co-author), 1966; Correspondence Study in the United States (co-author), 1969; The Changing World of Correspondence Study (co-author), 1970. Contbr. to profl. jrnls. Address: Rutgers Univ., Camden, NJ 08102, USA.

MACKENZIE-GRIEVE, Averil Salmond, b. 3 Apr. 1903, Rotherfield, Sussex, UK. Writer; Engraver. Publs: The Last Years of the English Slave Trade, 1940; Transl., Camillo Spreti, Description of the Island of Malta in 1794; The Great Accomplishment; Aspects of Elba; Clara Novello; A Race of Green Ginger; Time & Chance; 4 novels; var. transl. from French, German & Italian. Contbr. to: Chambers Ency.; Times Lit. Supplement; Country Life; Sunday Times; Saturday Book; New English Review; Crown Colonist; Future; Harpers. Mbr., Soc. of Authors. Hon: Off., Order of St. John of Jerusalem (for contbns. to Order's History). Address: George Hill House, Robertsbridge, Sussex, UK.

MACKERRAS, Colin Patrick, b. 26 Aug. 1939, Sydney, N.S.W., Australia. Professor of Modern Asian Studies. Educ: B.A., Melbourne Univ., 1961; B.A., Aust. Nat. Univ., 1962; M.Litt., Cambridge Univ., UK, 1964; Ph.D., Aust. Nat. Univ., 1970. Publs: China Observed 1964-1967, (w. N. Hunter), 1968; The Uighur Empire According to the T'ang Dynastic Histories, 1972; The Rise of the Peking Opera, 1770-1870, 1972; Jt.-Contbng. Ed., Essays on the Sources for Chinese History, 1973. Contbr. to: China Quarterly; Ctrl. Asiatic Jrnl.; other profl. jrnls. Mbrships. incl: Assn. for Asian Studies, Inc.; Am. Acad. of Political & Soc. Sci. Address: School of Modern Asian Studies, Griffith Univ., Nathan, Qld., Australia 4111.

MACKESY, Piers Gerald, b. 15 Sept. 1924, Cults, Aberdeenshire, UK. Fellow of Pembroke College, Oxford; Historian. Educ: B.A., Christ Ch., Oxford, 1950; D.Phil., Oriel Coll., Oxford, 1953; Harkness Fellow, Harvard Univ., USA, 1953-54. Publs: The War in the Mediterranean, 1803-10, 1957; The War for America, 1775-83, 1964; Statesmen at War: The Strategy of Overthrow, 1798-99, 1974. Contbr. to: Jrnl. of Royal United Serv. Instn.; Yale Review; Hist. Today. Fellow, Royal Histl. Soc. Hons. incl: Vis. Fellow, Inst. for Adv. Study, 1961-62; Huntington Lib., 1967-68; Vis. Prof., Calif. Inst. of Technol., 1967. Address: Bull Hill House, Chadlington, Oxford, UK.

MACKIE, Albert David, pen name, MacNIB, b. 18 Dec. 1904, Edinburgh, UK. Journalist. Educ: M.A., Edinburgh Univ. Publs: Poems in Two Tongues, 1928; Sing a Sang o'Scotland, 1944; A Call from Warsaw, 1944; Gentle like a Dove, 1951; The Hearts, 1959; Scottish Pageantry, 1968; The Scotch Comedians, 1973; The Scotch Whisky Drinker's Companion, 1973. Contbr. to: Scotland's Mag.; Scots Mag.; TV Times; Akros; Lines. Mbrships: Nat. Union of Jrnlsts.; Soc. of Authors. Address: 27 Blackford Ave., Edinburgh EH9 2PJ, UK.

MACKIE, Philip, b. 26 Nov. 1918, Broughton, Lancs., UK. Writer. Educ: B.A., Univ. Coll., London. Publs: Hurrah! The Flag, 1957; All the Way Up, 1970; Napoleon & Love, 1974; The Organization, 1974; (plays) The Whole Truth, 1956; Open House, 1958; The Key of the Door, 1959; The Big Killing, 1962. Contbr. to Jrnl. of Soc. of Film & TV Arts. Mbrships: Writers' Guild of GB (Past Exec. Councillor); Dramatists' Club; Soc. of Authors; PEN. Hons: Award, Writers' Guild of GB, 1968, 1972; Award, Critics' Circle, TV, 1972. Address: Siddington Old Rectory, Cirencester, Glos., UK.

McKIE, Ronald Cecil Hamlyn, b. 11 Dec. 1909, Toowoomba, Qld., Australia. Journalist. Educ: Univ. of Qld. Publs: This Was Singapore, 1942; Proud Echo, 1953; The Heroes, 1960; Malaysia in Focus, 1963; The Company of Animals, 1965; Bali, 1969; Singapore, 1972; The Mango Tree (novel), 1974. Mbrships: Aust. Soc. Authors; PEN. Hons: C'wlth Lit. Fund Grant, 1970; Grant, Lit. Bd., Aust. Coun. for the Arts, 1974. Address: 147 Sutherland St., Paddington, Sydney, Australia 2021.

McKIM, Audrey, b. 15 Oct. 1909, Edmonton, Alta., Can. Writer (Children's Books); Teacher; Editor. Educ: Tchrs. Coll., Edmonton. Publs: Here Comes Dirk, 1951;

Lexy O'Connor, 1953; Andy & the Gopher, 1959; Sun Hee & the Street Boy, 1962; China's Way, 1973; & 15 others. Mbrships: Can. Authors' Assn.; Can. Women's Press Club. Hons: Hon. Mention, Little. Brown's Award for Best Can. Book for Children, 1959; Vicki Metcalfe Award (for contbn. to Can. children's lit.), 1969. Address: Apt. 307, 49 Glen Elm Ave., Toronto, Ont. M4T 1V2. Can.

MACKINTOSH, Ian, b. 26 July 1940, Inverness, UK. TV Writer; Novelist. Educ: Royal Acad., Inverness; Britannia Royal Naval Coll., Dartmouth. Publs: A Slaying in September, 1967; Count Not the Cost, 1967; A Drug Called Power, 1968; The Man from Destiny, 1969; The Brave Cannot Yield, 1970; Warship, BBC drama series (creator, Ed.). Mbrships: Writers' Guild of GB, Crime Writers' Assn.; Assn. of Dirs. & Prods. Address: c/o Christopher Busby Ltd., 44 Gt. Russell St., London WC1B 3PA, UK.

MACKSEY, Kenneth, b. 1st July 1923, Epsom, UK. Author. Educ: Staff Coll., British Army. Publs: The Shadow of Vimy Ridge, 1965; Armoured Crusader, 1967; Crucible of Power, 1969; Tank, 1970; Tank Warfare, 1971; Guinness Book of Tank Facts & Feats, 1972; Guinness History of Land Warfare, 1973; Battle, 1974; The Partisans of Europe in the Second World War, 1975; The Guinness History of Sea Warfare, 1975; Gudenan, Panzer General, 1975. Contbr. to sev. mags. Mbr., R.U.S.I. Recip., George Knight Clowes Essay, 1956, 1958. Address: Whatley Mill, Beaminster, Dorset, UK.

MACKWORTH, Cecily, b. Llantillio Pertholey, UK. Writer. Publs: I Came out of France, 1942; A Mirror for French Poetry, 1946; François Villon, 1947; The Mouth of the Sword, 1950; The Destiny of Isabelle Eberhardt, 1952; Springs Green Shadow, 1954; Guillaume Apollinaire & the Cubist Life, 1961; English Interludes, 1974. Contbr. to: Horizon; Life & Letters Today; Cornhill; Poetry Quarterly; Preuves; Critique; Europe; Les Lettres nouvelles. Mbrships: PEN; Int. Assn. of Lit. Critics; Soc. of Authors. Address: 21 rue Charles V, Paris 4, France.

MACLACHLAN, (The Rev.) Lewis, b. 7 Nov. 1894, Blackford, Perthshire, UK. Minister of Religion. Educ: M.A., Univ. Glasgow; Westminster Coll. Theol., Cambridge. Publs: Religion for the Non-religious, 1931; Prayers of World Fellowship, 1941; The Faith of Friendship; Fellowship of Reconciliation, 1942; Intelligent Prayer, 1946; Defeat Triumphant, 1947; Teaching of Jesus on Prayer, 1952; How to Pray for Healing, 1956; Commonsense about Prayer, 1962; 21 Steps to Positive Prayer, 1965; Miracles of Healing, 1968. Contbr. to: Relig. Press; etc. Address: 1 The Shieling, Cliff Dr., Canford Cliffs, Poole, Dorset BH13 7JG, UK.

McLAREN, John, b. 7 Nov. 1932, Melbourne, Australia. Lecturer in English. Educ: B.A., B.Ed., Melbourne; M.A., Monash. Publs: Our Troubled Schools, 1968; Dictionary of Australian Education, 1974; Dream & Reality — Man & the Environment in Australian Fiction, 1974-75. Contbr. to: Overland; Critical Review, Melbourne Studies; Segment. Mbrships. incl: Fellowship of Aust. Writers; Aust. Soc. of Authors. Address: P.O. Box 128, Toowoomba, Qld., Australia 4350.

MACLEAN, Alistair, b. 1922. Novelist. Educ: Glasgow Univ. Publs. incl: H.M.S. Ulysses, 1956; Ice Station Zebra; When Eight Bells Toll; Night Without End; The Guns of Navarone; Puppet on a Chain, 1969; Caravan to Vaccares, 1971; Bear Island, 1971; Captain Cook, 1972; The Way to Dusty Death, 1973; Breakheart Pass, 1974; (screenplays) Where Eagles Dare; Deakin; Caravan to Vaccares; When Eight Bells Toll. Mbr., Lloyd's. Address: c/o Wm. Collins Sons, 14 St. James' Place, London SW1, UK.

McCLEAN, Allan Campbell, b. 18 Nov. 1922, Walney Island, Barrow-in-Furness, UK. Novelist. Publs: The Hill of the Red Fox, 1955; The Islander, 1962; The Glasshouse, 1968; The Year of the Stranger, 1971. Hons: Frederick Niven Award for Best Scottish Novel 1959-62 (The Islander); Scottish Arts Coun. Award, 1972 (The Year of the Stranger). Address: Anerley Cottage, 16 Kingsmills Rd., Inverness, UK.

McLEAN, Donald James, b. 18 Jan. 1905, Broken Hill, N.S.W., Australia. Teacher; Journalist. Educ: Sydney Tchrs. Coll. Publs: (fiction) No Man is an Island, 1955; Nature's Second Sun, 1955; (education) It's People that Matter, 1969; The Changing Orient, 1974. Contbr. to: Sydney Morning Herald Weekend Mag. Mbr., Aust. Soc. of Authors.

Recip., Carnegie Travelling Scholarship, 1953-54. Address: 34 The Point Rd., Woolwich, N.S.W., Australia 2110.

MacLEAN, Katherine, b. 22 Jan. 1925, Glen Ridge, N.J., USA. Writer (short stories & novels). Educ: B.A., Barnard Coll., N.Y., 1950; Postgrad. studies, Univ. of Conn. 1965; Goddard Coll., 1974. Publs: Cosmic Checkmate (w. Charles DeVet), 1960; The Diploids (sci. fiction collect.), 1961, 1973; The Man in the Bird Cage (novel), 1971; Missing Man (sci. fiction novel), 1975. Contbr. to: Astounding Sci. Fiction; Galaxy Sci. Fiction; The Reporter; Fantasy & Sci. Fiction; Analog. Mbrships. incl: AAAS; Mensa; Soc. for Gen. Systems Rsch; Sci. Fiction Writers of Am.; Sci. Fiction Rsch. Assn. Recip., Nebula Award for Best Novella, Sci. Fiction Writers of Am., 1972. Address: 30 Day St., S. Portland, ME 04106, USA.

MacLEISH, Andrew, b. 30 Aug. 1923, Phila., Pa., USA. Professor of English & Linguistics. Educ: M.A., Univ. of Chgo., 1951; Ph.D., Univ. of Wis., 1961. Publs: The American Revolution Through British Eyes, 1962; Oedipus: Myth & Drama, 1967; The Middle English Subject-Verb Cluster, 1969; A Glossary of Grammar & Linguistics, 1972. Contbr. to: Coll. Engl.; PLMA; TESOL Quarterly; Pacific Speech; etc. Mbrships: Ling. Soc. Am.; Midwest MLA. Address: Dept. of Engl., Univ. of Minn., Mpls., MN 55455, USA.

MacLEISH, Archibald, b. 7 May 1892. University Professor; Government Administrator. Educ: B.A., Yale Univ.; LL.B., Harvard Univ. Publs. incl: (verse) The Happy Marriage, 1924; Public Speech, 1936; America was Promises, 1939; (prose) Streets in the Moon, 1926; The Irresponsibles, 1940; A Time to Speak, 1941; Poetry & Opinion, 1950; Freedom is the Right to Choose, 1951; Poetry & Experience, 1961; The Eleanor Roosevelt Story, 1965; A Continuing Journey, 1968; (poetry) Collected Poems, 1952; The Wild Old Wicked Man & Other Poems, 1968; The Human Season, 1972. Mbrships. incl: Am. Acad. of Arts & Letters (Pres., 1953-56); UNESCO, 1946. Hons. incl: Commander, Legion of Honour; LL.D. Address: Conway, MA 01341, USA.

McLELLAN, Alden, IV, b. 3 Mar. 1936, Meridian, Miss., USA. Financial Planner; Estate Planner; Scientific Consultant; Educ: B.A., 1960, M.A., 1964, Univ. of Calif., Berkeley; Ph.D., Univ. of Nev., 1967; Profl. Engr., State of Wis., 1972. Publs: A Table of the Riemann Zeta Function & Related Functions, 1968; The Upper Atmospheric Environment of the Supersonic Transport, 1971, 2nd ed., 1973. Contbr. to: Nature; Phys. Review; Solar Physics; Il Nuova Cimento; Maths. of Computations; Zeitschrift für Naturforschung; Jrnl. of Spacecraft & Rockets; other profl. jrnls. & publs. Mbr., var. profl. & honor socs. Address: 2020 Kendall Ave., Madison, WI 53705, USA.

McLELLAN, Robert, b. 28 Jan. 1907, Linmill, Lanark, UK. Playwright. Educ: Glasgow Univ. Publs: (plays) Jeddart Justice, 1934; The Changeling, 1935; The Carlin Moth, 1946; Toom Byres, 1947; Torwatletie, 1950; The Hypocrite, 1970; Jamie the Saxt, 1971; (gen.) The Isle of Arran. Contbr. to: Scotsman; Scottish Field; New Alliance, etc. Mbrships: League of Dramatists (Past Chmn., Scottish Sub-Comm.); Soc. of Authors (Past Chmn., Scottish Sub-Comm.); Scottish Soc. Playwrights; Hon. VP, Lallans Soc., 1972—. Hons: Poetry Prize, 1956, Drama Bursary, 1968, Scottish Arts Coun. Address: High Corrie, Isle of Arran, KA27 8JB, UK.

McLENDON, James, Nelson, b. 7 Mar. 1942, Gainesville, Fla., USA. Author. Educ: Fla. State Univ., Tallahassee, 1960-61; E. Tenn. State Univ., Johnson City, 1962-64; Ark. State Tchrs. Coll., Conway, 1965; Fla. Atlantic Univ., Boca Raton, 1966-67. Publs: Papa: Hemingway in Key West, 1972; Andros Island: A Contemporary History, 1974 (50 part periodical serial). Contr. to: Saturday Evening Post; Holiday; Writer's Digest; num. newspaper Sunday mags. & trade jrnls. Recip., 1st Prize, Writer's Digest Short-Story Contest, 1968. Agent: Jay Garon-Brooke & Assoc., Inc. Address: c/o above, 415 Central Park West, N.Y., NY 10025, USA.

MacLENNAN, Hugh, b. 20 Mar. 1907, Glace Bay, Can. Writer. Educ: B.A, Dalhousie Univ.; B.A. Oxford Univ., UK; Ph.D., Princeton Univ., USA. Publs. incl: (novels) Two Solitudes, 1945; The Precipice, 1948; The Watch that Ends the Night, 1959; Return of the Sphinx, 1967; (non-fiction) Oxyrhyncus, 1935; Cross Country, 1949; Thirty & Three, 1954; Seven Rivers of Canada, 1962; Rivers of Canada, 1974. Contbr. to: Maclean's; Harper's; etc. Mbrships. incl:

Royal Soc. of Can.; Royal Soc. of Lit., UK. Hons. incl: Gov.-Gen.'s Awards for Lit., 1945, 1948, 1949, 1954, 1959; Molson Prize, Can. Coun., 1966; Companion, Order of Can., 1967. Address: 1535 Summerhill Ave., Montreal 109, P.Q., Can.

MacLEOD, Ellen Jane, pen name ANDERSON, Ella, b. 17 May 1918, Glasgow, UK. Author. Publs: 14 youth books, 1956-71, & 5 romantic novels, 1963-74. Contbr. of serials & short stories to var. publs. Mbr., Soc. of Authors. Address: 12 Montgomery Place, Bucklyvie, Stirlingshire, FK8 3NF, UK.

McLEOD, James Richard, b. 8 Jan. 1942; Spokane, Wash., USA. College English Instructor. Educ: B.A., Univ. of Wash., 1966; M.A., E. Wash. State Coll., 1969. Publs: Theodore Roethke: A Manuscript Checklist, 1971; Theodore Roethke: A Bibliography, 1973; Theodore Roethke, forthcoming. Contbr. to: Northwest Review; Mirror Northwest. Mbrships. incl: Nat. Coun. of Tchrs. of Eng.; Bd. of Dirs., Wash. Poets' Assn., 1973-75. Hons: Outstanding Young Educator, Spokane Valley Chmbr. of Comm., 1969. Address: 1212 Ash, Coeur d'Alene, ID 83814, USA.

MacLEOD, Jean Sutherland, pen name AIRLIE, Catherine, b. 20 Jan. 1908, Glasgow, UK. Novelist. Publs. incl.: The Wild MacRaes (as Catherine Airlie); Sugar Island, 1964; The Wolf of Heimra, 1965; The Moonflower, 1967; The Joshua Tree, 1968; Moment of Decision, 1970; The White Cockade (histl. romance); The Dark Fortune (histl.); Time Suspended, 1973; The Restless Years. Contbr. to: Woman & Home; Woman's Own; Woman's Weekly. Mbrships: Romantic Novelists' Assn.; St. Andrew Soc., York. Recip., Histl. Award, R.N.A., 1962. Address: Tigh-an-Rudha, Kilmelford, by Oban, Argyll, UK.

MacLEOD, Norman Wicklund, b. 1 Oct. 1906, Salem, Ore., USA. Poet; Novelist; Editor; Professor. Educ: B.A., Univ. of N.M., 1930; M.A., Columbia Univ., 1936; grad. work, var. univs. Publs: (poems) Horizons of Death, 1934; Thanksgiving before November, 1936; We Thank You All the Time, 1941; A Man in Midpassage, 1947, Pure as Nowhere, 1952; (novels) You Get What You Ask For, 1939; The Bitter Roots, 1941. Contbr. to: Red Clay Reader; Southern Poetry Review, Chelsea; num. other lit. jrnls. Mbrships: Fndr.-Dir., Y.M.H.A. Poetry Ctr., NYC, 1939-42; PEN; N.C. Writers' Conf. Hons. incl: Horace Gregory Award, 1972; Lit. Prog. Fellowship, Nat. Fndn. for the Arts, 1974-75. Agent: Robert P. Mills. Address: P.O. Box 756, Pembroke, NC 28372, USA.

Mac LIAMMOIR, Micheál, b. 25 Oct. 1899, Cork, Repub. of Ireland. Actor; Designer; Playwright. Publs. incl: The Importance of Being Oscar, 1960; Talking About Yeats, 1965; (plays) Ford of the Hurdles, 1928; Where Stars walk, 1940; III Met by Moonlight, 1946; The Mountains Look Different, 1948; A Slipper for the Moon, 1954; (Autobiography) All for Hecuba, 1946; Put Money in Thy Purse, (diaries), 1954; Each Actor on his Ass, 1962; (poems in Irish) Blath Agus Taibhse, 1964; (travel) Ireland, 1966; W. B. Yeats & His World (w. Eavan Boland), 1971. Address: 4 Harcourt Terrace, Dublin 2, Repub. of Ireland.

MacLOW, Jackson, b. 12 Sept. 1922, Chicago, Ill., USA. Poet; Composer; College Teacher. Educ: A.A., Univ. of Chgo., 1941; B.A., Brooklyn Coll., 1958. Publs. incl: The Twin Plays, 1966; Verdurous Sanguinaria (play), 1967; August Light Poems, 1967; 22 Light Poems, 1968; 23rd Light Poem, 1969; The Pronouns, 1971; Stanzas for Iris Lezak, 1972; 4 Trains, 1974. Contbr. to num. anthols., US & Europe, & jrnls., US, Mexico, Canada, Japan, UK, France, W. Germany, Netherlands, Belgium & Italy. Mbr., PEN Am. Ctr. Hons. incl: Creative Artists Pub. Serv. Prog. Fellowship, 1974;. Mbr., poetry panel, CAPS, 1974-75. Address: 1764 Popham Ave., Bronx, NY 10453, USA.

MacMAHON, Bryan Michael, b. 29 Sept. 1909, Listowel, Co. Kerry, Repub. of Ireland. Teacher. Educ: St. Patrick's Trng. Coll., Drumcondra, Dublin. Publs: The Lion Tamer & Other Stories, 1948; Children of the Rainbow, 1950; The Red Petticoat & Other Stories, 1955; The Honey Spike, 1967; Here's Ireland, 1971; Peig (transl.), 1974. Contbr. to: Bell; Partisan Review; Sign; Lamp. Mbrships. incl: Pres., Irish PEN, 1972-73; Irish Acad. of Letters. Hons: Bell Award, 1945; Cath. Press Award, USA; LL.D., Nat. Univ. of Ireland, 1972. Address: 38 Ashe St., Listowel, Co. Kerry, Repub. of Ireland.

McMANUS, Kay, b. 4 July 1922, Nottingham, UK. Writer. Publs: Raven, 1966; Listen and I'll Talk, 1969. Contbr. to: BBC Radio & TV; Granada TV; etc. Mbrships: PEN; Soc. of Authors; Writers' Guild of GB. Recip., Joseph Cowen Mem. Prize, Univ. of Durham, 1961. Address: Flat 2, The Old House, 22 Town St., Leeds 7, Yorks LS7 4NB, UK.

MacMILLAN, David Neil Stirling, b. 9 Oct. 1925, Airdrie, UK. Historian. Educ: M.A., Glasgow Univ., 1949; Ph.D., Sydney Univ., Aust., 1963. Publs: The Sydney Scene (w. A. Birch), 1963; Scotland & Australia, 1788-1850, 1967; Australian Universities, 1968; Canadian Business History, 1972. Contbr., sev. profl. jrnls. Mbrships: Fellow, Royal Aust. Histl. Soc., 1968—; Dir., Bus. Archives Coun. of Can., 1968—. Address: c/o Dept. of Hist., Trent Univ., Peterborough, Ont., Can.

McMILLAN, James, pen name CORIOLANUS, b. 30 Oct. 1925, Glasgow, Scotland, UK. Journalist; Author. Educ: M.A., Glasgow Univ. Publs: The Glass Lie, 1965; The American Take-Over of Britain (w. Bernard Harris), 1967; The Honours Game, 1969; Anatomy of Scotland, 1970; Roots of Corruption, 1972; The British Genius (w. Peter Grosvenor), 1973. Contbr. to: Rdrs'. Digest. Mbr., Press Club. Address: "Thurlestone", Fairmile Park Rd., Cobham, Surrey, UK.

McNAMARA, Barbara Willard, pen name O'CONNOR, Elizabeth, b. 31 Aug. 1913, Dunedoo, NSW, Australia. Author. Publs: Steak for Breakfast, 1958; The Irishman, 1960; Find a Woman, 1963; The Chinee Bird, 1966; A Second Helping, 1969. Recip., Miles Franklin Lit. Award, 1960. Address: Kangerang, Chartus Towers, N. Queensland, Australia.

McNAMARA, Lena Brooke, pen name MACK, Evalina, b. 13 May 1890, Norfolk, Va., USA. Artist; Writer. Educ: Corcoran Art Schl., Wash. D.C.; Pa. Acad., Phila., Pa. Publs: Death of a Portrait; Miniature Murders; The Corpse in the Cove; Death Among the Sands; Penance was Death, 1964; Pilgrim's End, 1967. Mbrships: Norfolk Soc. of Arts; Irene Leache Mem. Art Soc.; Mystery Writers of Am. Address: 512 Colonial Ave., Norfolk, VA 23507, USA.

McNAMARA, (Father) William, b. 14 Feb. 1926, Providence, R.I., USA. Priest; Retreat Master; Lecturer; Writer; Director, Spiritual Life Institutes of America. Educ: B.A., Cath. Univ. of Am., Wash. DC, 1951; M.A., Boston Coll., 1955. Publs: Manual for Retreat Masters, 1960; The Art of Being Human, 1962; The Human Adventure: Contemplation for Everyman, 1974; Mount of Passion, 1975. Contbr. to: Call to Adventure, 1967; Spiritual Psychols., 1975; Ave Maria; Cath. Mind; Relig. Educ.; Desert Call; New Cath. World; Alive; Ed., Spiritual Life, 1955-62. Mbr., Advsry. Bd., Esalen Inst., 1965-69. Address: Spiritual Life Inst., Star Route 1, Sedona, AZ 86336, USA.

McNAMEE, Mary Dominica, b. 7 Aug. 1894, Sault Ste. Marie, Mich., USA. Emeritus of College of Notre Dame, Belmont. Educ: B.A., Dominican Coll., San Rafael, Calif.; M.A., Stanford Univ. Publs: Willamette Interlude, 1968; Light in the Valley, 1968. Mbrships: Classics Assn. of Am.; Calif. Histl. Assn.; Teilhard Ctr. for the Future of Man, London. Recip., Hons., San Fran. Browning Soc. Address: 2992 Lasuen Drive, Carmel, CA 93921, USA.

McNEAL, Robert Hatch, b. 8 Feb. 1930, Newark, N.J., USA. Professor of History. Educ: B.A., Yale Univ.; M.A., & Ph.D., Columbia Univ. Publs: The Bolshevik Tradition. Lenin, Stalin, Khrushchev, 1964, red. ed., The Bolshevik Tradition. Lenin, Stalin, Khrushchev, Brezhnev, 1974; Resolutions & Decisions of the Communist Party of the Soviet Union 1898-1964. vols. I-IV (gen. ed.), 1974. Mbrships: Am. Histl. Assn.; Am. Assn. for Advancement of Slavic Studies. Address: Dept. of Hist., Univ. of Mass., Amherst, MA 01002, USA.

McNEILL, Donald Burgess, b. 1911, Belfast, UK. Lecturer in Physics; Director, McNeill Group Ltd. Educ: M.Sc., Ph.D., Queen's Univ., Belfast. Publs: Introduction to Experimental Physics; Theoretical & Experimental Physics; Dictionary of Scientific Units; Ulster Tramways & Light Railways; Coastal Passenger Steamers & Inland Navigations in the North of Ireland; Irish Passenger Steamship Services; Great Southern & Western Railway. Mbrship: Fellow, Inst. Phys. Address: 8 Marcello Park, Newtownards, Co. Down, Northern Ireland, UK.

McNEILL, William H., b. 31 Oct. 1917, Vancouver, B.C., Can. Professor of History. Educ: B.A., 1938, M.A., 1939, Univ. of Chgo., USA; Ph.D., Cornell Univ., 1947. Publs. incl: The Greek Dilemma, War & Aftermath, 1947; History Handbook, 1949 (rev. as History Handbook of Western Civilization, 1953, new ed., 1969); Past & Future, 1954; World History in Maps (co-author), 1960, new ed., 1963; The Rise of the West, 1963; A World History, 1967; Readings in World History (co-author), vols. I-X, 1968-73; The Shape of European History, 1974; Venice. the Hinge of Europe, 1081-1797, 1974. Contbr. to encys. & profl. jrnls. Hons: National Book Award, 1964; num. grants for rsch. & writing. Address: Dept. of History, Univ. of Chgo., 1126 E. 59th St., Chgo., IL 60637, USA.

McNEISH, James, b. 23 Oct. 1931, Auckland, NZ. Writer. Educ: B.A. Publs: Fire under the Ashes, 1965; Mackenzie, 1970; The Mackenzie Affair, 1972; Larks in a Paradise, 1974. Contbr. to: Observer, UK; NZ Listener. Mbr., Bridge in NZ Trust (Dir.). Recip., Katherine Mansfield Award, 1973. Address: c/o George Greenfield, John Farquarson Ltd., 15 Red Lion Square, London WC1R 4QW, UK.

McQUOWN, Frederic Richard, b. 4 Jan. 1907, London, UK. Barrister-at-Law; Horticultural Writer & Broadcaster. Educ: M.A., Christ Ch., Oxford Univ. Publs: Pinks, Selection & Cultivation, 1955; Intelligent Gardening, 1958; Plant Breeding for Gardeners, 1963; Carnations & Pinks, 1965, 1970; Fine-Flowered Cacti, 1965, 1971; The Dictionary of Indoor Plants in Colour (to be publd. USA as The Dictionary of House Plants, co-author), 1975. Contbr. to: Reader's Digest Ency. Garden Plants & Flowers, 1971; Amateur Gardening; BBC; etc. Mbrships. incl: Gray's Inn; Fellow, Linnean Soc., London. Address: 48 Cumbrian Gdns., London NW2 1EF, UK.

McRAE, Kate, b. 6 May 1939, Ealing, London, UK. Journalist. Educ: M.A., Univ. of Edinburgh, 1961; Lic., Royal Schls. of Music, 1968. Contbr. (feature articles & music criticisms) to Hongkong Standard. Publs: Adaptations of 2 novels into radio scripts for serialization on Radio Hongkong. Mbr., Hongkong Jrnlsts' Assn. Recip., Wkly. Short Story Prize, China Mail, 1971. Address: c/o Barclays Bank, Royal Parade, Hanger Lane, London W5, UK.

MacVICAR, Angus, b. 28 Oct. 1908, Duror, Argyll, UK. Author. Educ: M.A., Glasgow Univ. Publs: over 60 books inclng. (fiction) The Purple Rock, 1933; The Lost Planet series (for children), 1952-65; (non-fiction) Salt in My Porridge 1971; Heather in My Ears, 1974. Contbr. to newspapers, mags., Radio & TV. Mbr., Soc. of Authors. Address: Achnamara, Southend, Campbeltown, Argyll, UK.

McWHINEY, Grady, b. 15 July 1928, Shreveport, La., USA. Professor of American History. Educ: B.S., Centenary Coll., 1950; M.A., La. State Univ., 1951; Ph.D., Columbia Univ., 1960. Publs. incl: Reconstruction & the Freedom (ed.), 1963; Grant, Lee, Lincoln & the Radicals (ed.), 1966; To Mexico with Taylor & Scott 1845-1847 (ed.), 1969; Braxton Bragg & the Confederate Defeat, 1969; Southerners & Other Americans, 1973. Contbr. to: Jrnl. of Southern Hist.; Negro Hist. Bulletin; Civil War Hist.; Ency. Americana; etc. Recip., var. acad. & lit. awards. Address: Dept. of Hist., Wayne State Univ., Detroit, MI 48202, USA.

MADAY, Bela Charles, b. 3 Nov. 1912, Prague, Czechoslovakia. Anthropologist. Educ: Ph.D., Pázmány Univ., Budapest, Hungary, 1937. Publs. incl: Bibliography for the Study of East Central & Southeast Europe, 1971; Ed., Anthropology & Society, 1975; also Ed. & Author, var. Area Handbooks & Language Texts. Contbr. to: Current Anthropol.; Am. Anthropol.; E. European Quarterly; Ethnologia Europaea; Annals of N.Y. Acad. of Scis.; World Anthropol.; etc. Mbrships. incl: Fellow, Am. Anthropol. Soc.; Anthropol. Soc. of Wash.; Soc. for Med. Anthropol.; VP, Am. Hungarian Fndn.; Dir., Hungarian Rsch. Ctr. Address: 4258 49th Street, Washington, DC 20016, USA.

MADDEN, (Albert) Frederick McCulloch, b. 27 Feb. 1917, Bracadale, Skye, UK. University Teacher & Administrator. Educ: B.A. 1938, B.Litt. 1939, Christ Ch., Oxford; M.A., 1946; D.Phil., 1950. Publs: British Colonial Developments, 1953; Essays in Imperial Government, 1963; Imperial Constitutional Documents, 1966. Contbr. to: Engl. Histl. Review; Jrnl. of C'wlth. Hist. Mbrships: Fellow, Royal Histl. Soc.; Vice-Chmn., Bd., Mod. Hist., 1968-71 & 1973. Recip., sev. acad. hons. Address: The Oaks, Shotover Hill, Headington, Oxford, UK.

MADDEN, David, b. 25 July 1933, Knoxville, Tenn., USA. Writer. Educ: M.A., San Fran. State Coll. Publs: The Beautiful Greed, 1961; Wright Morris, 1964; The Poetic Image in Six Genres, 1969; Cassandra Singing, 1969; The Shadow Knows, 1970; James M. Cain, 1971; Brothers in Confidence, 1972; Bijou, 1974; Ed. of 6 books. Contbr. to: Kenyon Review; Mass. Review; Saturday Review; New Repub.; Epoch; Jrnl. of Aesthetics & Art Criticism; Mod. Fiction Studies; Critique; Film Quarterly; Southern Poetry Review. Mbrships. incl: Soc. for Study of the Cinema; Popular Culture Assn.; Screen Writers' Guild; Authors' League; Soc. for the Study of Southern Lit. Hons. incl: Rockefeller Grant in Fiction, 1969. Address: 614 Park Blvd., Baton Rouge, LA 70806, USA.

MADIA, Chunilal Kalidas, b. 12 Aug. 1922. Writer; Journalist. Educ: H.L. Coll. of Commerce, Ahmedabad, India. Publs. incl: (in Gujarati) (novels) Vyajanos Varas; Liludi Dharati; Kumkum Ane Ashaka; (short stories) Padmaja; Champo Ane Kel; Tej Ane Timir; Roop-Aroop; Antasrota; (plays) Rangada; Vishavimochan; Raktatilak; Shoonyashesh; (poems) Sonnet; (criticism) Granthagarima; Shahamrig; Suvarnamrig. Contbr. to: Prabhat; Navsaurashtra; Ed., Varta; Ed., Ruchi; Lit. Ed., Sandesh. Mbrships: PEN; Congress of World Writers. Hons: Narmad Gold Medal, 1951; Ranajitram Gold Medal, 1957. Address: B-213, Chandralok, Manav Mandir Rd., Malabar Hill, Bombay 6, India.

MADISON, Charles A., b. 16 Apr. 1895, Kiev, Russia. Editor. Educ: A.B., Univ. of Mich.; M.A., Harvard Univ. Publs: Critics & Crusaders, 1947, 2nd ed., 1959; American Labor Leaders, 1950, 2nd ed., 1961; Leaders & Liberals in 20th Century America, 1961; The Owl Among Colophons, 1966; Book Publishing in America, 1966; Yiddish Literature, 1968; Eminent American Jews, 1970; Irving to Irving: Author-Publisher Relations, 1974. Contbr. to: Poet Lore; The Nation; Yale Review; Va. Quarterly Review. Address: 231 E. 76th St., N.Y., NY 10021, USA.

MADSEN, Svend Åge, b. 2 Nov. 1939, Arhus, Denmark. Author. Publs: Besoget (novel), 1963; Otte Gange Orphan (short stories), 1965; Saet Verden er Til (novel), 1971; Dage med Diam (novel), 1972. Hons: Louisianna Prize, 1967; Danish Acad. Prize, 1972. Address: Vestre Strandallé 154 b, Dk-8240 Risskov, Denmark.

MAGARSHACK, David, b. 1899, Riga, Russia. Biographer. Educ: Riga Schl. & London Univ.; B.A. Publs. (biogs.): Chekhov, 1952; Turgenev, 1954; Gogol, 1957; Dostoevsky, 1962; Stanislavsky, 1950; Pushkin, 1967; (criticisms): Chekhov the Dramatist, 1952; Stanislavsky on the Art & the Stage, 1950-61; (transls.): Dostoevsky, 1951-60; Leskov, 1962; Turgenev, 1960; Gogol, 1960; The Real Chekhov, 1972. Contbr. to: New Writings; New Statesman; Times Educ. Supplement; NY Times; etc. Agent: Curtis Brown Ltd. Address: 49 Willow Rd., Hampstead, London NW3, UK.

MAGER, Nathan H., b. 8 June 1912, NYC, USA. Publisher. Educ: B.C.S., N.Y. Univ., 1932; Grad. study, Columbia Univ., N.Y. Univ. Schl. of Fin. Publs. incl: Legal, Political & Business Guide, 1940; Practice Tests for All Jobs, 1948; The Office Encyclopedia, 1955; Conquest without War, (w. J. Katel), 1961; How to Work with Tools & Wood, 1965; Encyclopedic Dictionary of English Usage, 1974. Address: 1013 E. Lawn Dr., Teaneck, NJ 07666, USA.

MAGGIO, Joseph Alan, b. 19 Mar. 1938, Atlantic City, N.J., USA. Writer. Educ: B.A., Univ. of Miami, Fla.; 100-ton Masters Lic. for sailing vessels. Publs: Company Man, 1972; Survive a Recent Sorrow (a novel about the collapse of America), 1975. Contbr. to: Life; Newsweek; Fiction Review; World-wide jrnls & newspaper supplements; for. corres. covering wars in Viet Nam, Biafra, Mid-East & Congo. Mbrships: Authors' Guild of Am.; Marine Corps.; Combat Correspondence Assn. Hons: Coast Guard Jrnlsm. Award; Nominated by Miami Beach Sun for Ernie Pyle Award for 6-part series on starving senior citizens on prosperous Miami Beach. Address: Chinese Junk Ming-Hai, Pier 2 — Slip 23, Dinner Key Marina, Coconut Grove, FL, USA.

MAGNER, James Edmund Jr., b. 16 Mar. 1928, NYC, USA. Professor of English; Poet. Educ: B.A., Duquesne Univ., 1957; M.A., Univ. of Pitts., 1961; Ph.D., 1966. Publs: Toiler of the Sea, 1965; Although there is the Night, 1968; Gethsemane, 1969; John Crowe Ranson: Critical Principles & Preoccupations, 1971; The Dark is Closest to

the Moon, 1973. Contbr. to: Coll. Engl.; Mediterranean Review; New Engl. Review; Hiram Review; Pale Horse Review; Christian Century; etc. Mbrships: AAUP; Nat. Coun. Tchrs. of Engl.; MLA; Ohio Poets Assn. Hons: Nominated for Pulitzer Prize, 1965, 1968, 1974; Geo. E. Grauel Mem. Fellowship for Writing & Rsch., 1970. Address: Engl. Dept., John Carroll Univ., Cleveland, OH 44118, USA.

MAGNUSSON, Magnus, b. 1929, Reykjavik, Iceland. Freelance Broadcaster, 1968—; Editor, Bodley Head Archaeologies, 1971—; Author, Translator. Educ: Jesus Coll., Oxford; B.A.(Oxon). Publs: (transl. w. Hermann Palsson) Njal's Saga, 1960; The Vinland Sagas, 1965; King Harald's Sagas, 1966; Laxdaela Saga, 1969; transl. 5 books by Halldor Laxness; (transl.) Golden Iceland, by Samivel, 1967; Introducing Archaeology, 1972; Viking Expansion Westwards, 1973. Contbr. to: Business Scotland; Spectator; Listener; Iceland Review. Agent: Deborah Rogers Ltd. Address: Blairskaith House, Balmore-Torrance, Glasgow G64 4AX, Scotland, UK.

MAGOON, Eaton "Bob" Jr., b. 24 June 1922, Honolulu, Hawaii, USA. Real Estate Executive; Songwriter; Playwright. Educ: B.A., Yale Univ.; N.Y. Univ. Law Schl. for 2 yrs.; Hastings Coll. of Law for ½ yr.; Univ of Calif., Berkeley; Columbia Univ. Author, musical comedies: 49th Star; 13 Daughters; Heathen; Paradise! Paradise! Mbrships: ASCAP; Dramatists' Guild; Authors' League of Am.; Am. Guild of Authors & Composers. Address: 3633 Diamond Head Rd., Honolulu, HI 96816, USA.

MAHER, Sean, b. 15 Jan. 1932, Tullamore, Co. Offaly, Repub. of Ireland. Office Manager; Author; Artist. Publs: The Road to God Knows Where, 1972 (autobiography depicting life as boy travelling the road, & schl. life); Paintings of road life in Ireland. Contbr. to var. Irish papers & Irish Radio. Address: The Caravan, Monastery Rd., Clondalkin, Co. Dublin, Repub. of Ireland.

MAHONY, Patrick Frederick, b. 11 Feb. 1911, London, UK. Author; Lecturer; Lit. Asst. to Maurice Maeterlinck, 1940-47. Publs: Out of the Silence, 1948; Unsought Visitors; You Can Find A Way, 1950; Magic of Maeterlinck, 1952; Barbed Wit & Malicious Humor, 1956; Breath of Scandal; Who's There?; Escape into the Psychic World. Contbr. to: N.Y. Times; L.A. Times; Harper's Mag.; King Features Syndicate; Psychic Mag.; num. learned jrnls. Hons. incl: Nat. Soc. of Arts & Letters Award, 1970; Drama Award of Distinction, Alpha Phi, Redlands Univ., Calif. Address: 5885 Locksley Pl., Hollywood, CA 90068, USA.

MAHR, (Allen) David, b. 7 Jan. 1910, Belleville, Ill., USA. Government Postal Clerk; Poet. Educ: Courses at McKendree Coll. & Mo. Univ. Contbr. to: Cycloflame, San Angelo, Tex.; Southwest Times, Ft. Smith, Ariz.; var. anthols. Mbrships. incl: McKendree Writers' Conf., Ill.; St. Louis Poetry Ctr.; Avalon Writers, Tex.; Ariz. Poetry Soc.; Manifold, UK. Hons. incl: Award for contbns. to Afro-Am. Lit., Sigma Gamma Rho, St. Louis, 1974. Address: 4838 Cote Brilliante, St. Louis, MO 63113, USA.

MAICAS BORRELL, Abelardo, pen name MAICAS, Victor, b. 17 Sept. 1917, Valencia, Spain. Publs: Caminar y Contar (short stories), 1952; Dignidad (novel), 1952; Días y Sueños (tales), 1963. Contbr. to var. lit. jrnls. in Spain, S. Am., & N.Y.; short stories in Antología de Cuentos de Hoy, etc. Mbrships: Hon. Mbr., Assn of Cultural Exchange, Matto Grosso, Brazil; Advsr., Spanish-Am. Acad. Zenith de Heredia. Recip. of Escritores Valencianos Prize (Valencia Writers), 1958. Address: Gran Via Fernando el Católico 49, Valencia 8, Spain.

MAIER, Paul Luther, b. 31 May 1930, St. Louis, Mo., USA. Professor; Author; Campus Chaplain. Educ: B.A., 1952, B.D., 1955, Concordia Sem., St. Louis, Mo.; M.A., Harvard Univ., 1954; Ph.D., Univ. of Basle, 1957. Publs: Caspar Schwenckfeld, 1959; A Man Spoke, A World Listened — The Story of Walter A. Maier, 1963; Pontius Pilate, 1968; First Christmas, 1971; First Easter, 1973; The Flames of Rome, 1975. Contbr. to: Christian Herald; N.Y. Times Book Review. Mbrships. incl: Am. Histl. Assn. Address: 919 Dobbin Dr., Kalamazoo, MI 49007, USA.

MAILER, Norman Kingsley, b. 31 Jan. 1923, USA. Author; Journalist. Educ: B.S., Harvard Univ. Publs. incl: The Naked & the Dead, 1948; The Deer Park, 1955, Play, 1967; The Presidential Papers, 1963; An American Dream, 1964; The Armies of the Night, 1968; Miami & the Siege of Chicago, 1968; Moonshot, 1969; A Fire on the Moon,

1970; The Prisoner of Sex, 1971; Existential Errands, 1972; St. George & the Godfather, 1972; Marylin, 1973; (poems) Deaths for the Ladies, 1962. Contbr. to: Dissent; Co-Fndr., Village Voice. Hons: Nat. Book Award, 1969; Pulitzer Prize, 1969. Address: 128 Willow St., Brooklyn, NY, USA.

MAILLART, Ella, b. 20 Feb. 1903, Geneva, Switz. Traveller; Writer. Publs: Parmi la Jeunesse Russe, 1932; Des Monts Célestes aux Sables Rouge, 1934; Oasis Interdites, 1937; Gypsy Afloat, 1942; Cruises & Caravans, 1942; The Cruel Way, (transl. into Swedish, Dutch, French, Spanish etc.), 1947; Ti-Puss; The Land of the Sherpas. Mbr., F.R.G.S., London. Address: 10 Ave. Vallette, Geneva, Switz.

MAIN, Jackson Turner, b. 6 Aug. 1917, Chgo., Ill., USA. Teacher. Educ: B.A., Univ. of Wis., 1939; M.A., 1940; Ph.D., 1949. Publs: The Antifederalists: Critics of the Constitution 1781-1788, 1961; The Social Structure of Revolutionary America, 1965; The Upper House in Revolutionary America, 1967; Political Parties before the Constitution, 1973; The Sovereign States 1775-1783, 1973. Contbr. to: Jrnl. of Am. Hist.; Wm. & Mary Quarterly. Mbrships: Coun., Inst. for Early Am. Hist. & Culture; Am. Hist. Assn.; Org. of Am. Histns.; Am. Antiquarian Soc.; Wis. Hist. Soc.; N.Y. Hist. Soc.; Fellow, Am. Coun. of Learned Socs., 1962-63. Address: 3 Coraway Rd., Setauket, NY 11733, USA.

MAIS, Stuart Petre Brodie, b. 4 July 1885. Journalist; Broadcaster; Novelist; Lecturer. Educ: Christ Church, Oxford. Publs. incl: April's Lonely Soldier, 1916; Lovers of Silver, 1918; Why We Should Read, 1920; England of the Windmills, 1931; These I Have Loved, 1933; Walking at Week-Ends, 1935; Light Over Lundy, 1938; Listen to the Country, 1939; Youth after the War, 1943; I Return to Ireland, 1948; I Loved You Once, 1949; Buffets & Rewards, 1952; Dutch Holiday, 1960; Greek Holiday, 1962; Round Britain Coach Holiday, 1963; This Delicious Madness, 1968; All Change, 1972. Contbr. to: Daily Express; Evening News; Daily Telegraph. Mbrships: F.R.S.A. Address: Flat 20, Bliss House, Finches Gdns., Lindfield, Haywards Heath, Sussex, UK.

MAJOR, Alan Percival, pen name JOHN, Dane, b. 26 May 1929, Gillingham, Kent, UK. Writer; Author. Educ: Intermediate & Final City & Guilds Certs. for Typography, 1948, 1950. Publs: Coast, Estuary & Seashore Life, 1973; Collecting World Sea Shells, 1974; Collecting Fossils, 1974; Collecting & Studying Mushrooms, Toadstools & Fungi, 1975. Contbr. to num. Brit. & overseas publs. of all types. Address: 32 Bramley Ave., Thanington, Canterbury, Kent, CT1 3XW, UK.

MAJOR, James Russell, b. 7 Jan. 1921, Riverton, Va., USA. Historian. Educ: B.A., Va. Nil. Inst., 1942; M.A., 1948, Ph.D., 1949, Princeton Univ. Publs: The Estates General of 1560, 1951; The Deputies to the Estates General of Renaissance France, 1960; Representative Institutions in Renaissance France, 1421-1559, 1960; The Western World — Renaissance to the Present, 1966, 2nd ed., 1971; Bellièvre, Sully & the Assembly of Notables of 1596, 1974. Contbr. to: Am. Histl. Review; the Jrnl. of Mod. Hist.; etc. Mbrships. incl: Ed. Bd., Jrnl. of Mod. Hist., 1966-69. Address: Dept. of Hist., Emory Univ., Atlanta, GA 30322, USA.

MAJOR, Otto, b. 4 Apr. 1924, Budapest, Hungary. Author; Journalist. Educ: Fac. of Arts, Univ. Pázmány Peter, Budapest, 1948. Publs: Magyar Atlantisz (cycle of novels), 7 vols., 1955-60; Játék a tükörrel (short stories), 1962; (novels) Tibériási Justus, 1965; A nagy Herodes, 1968; Szent Kelemen vallomásai, 1970; Szerelem és halál a Kapucinus utcában, 1973. Contbr. to: Tükör (Art Dir.); var. lit. reviews. Mbrships: Assn. of Hungarian Authors; PEN. Hons: József Attila Lit. Prizes, 1953, 1956. Address: Szalag utca 7, 1011 Budapest, Hungary.

MAKAVEJEV, Dušan, b. 13 Oct. 1932, Belgrade, Yugoslavia. Film Director; Screenwriter. Educ: Grad., Univ. of Belgrade, 1955; Belgrade Acad. for Film, Theatre, Radio & TV, 1955-59. Publs: Poljubac za drugaricu parolu, 1964; Montaža atrakcija, S.M. Eisenstein (ed.), 1964; WR: Mysteries of the Organism, 1972. Contbr. to: Politika, Belgrade; Književne novine, Belgrade; Filmska kultura, Zagreb; Ekran, Ljubljana; Film Quarterly (USA); Positif, Paris. Hons: Oct. Award, City of Belgrade, 1968; L'Age D'Or Award, Brussels, 1973. Address: 5 rue Bezout, Paris 75014, France.

MAKELA, Jukka L., b. 5 Feb. 1917, Oulu, Finland. Author. Publs: Salaista palapelia, 1964; Salaisen sodan saatosta, 1965; OsKu, 1966; Helsinki liekeissa, 1967; Lumi palaa, 1968; Marokon Kauhu, 1969; Lumitiikeri, 1970; Taipaleenjoki, 1971; Kannas salamoi, 1972; Terasvyory Kannaksella, 1973; Aunuksen savut, 1974. Translations: Hemligt krig (in Swedish), 1966; Im Rucken des Feindes (in German), 1967; OsKus fjarrpatruller (in Swedish), 1969. Mbrships: Finnish Soc. of Authors; Culture Org. of Finland. Address: Vaskivuorentie 4 D 25, 00440 Helsinki 44, Finland.

MALAMUD, Bernard, b. Apr. 1914, Brooklyn, N.Y., USA. University Lecturer; Author. Educ: N.Y. City Coll.; Columbia Univ.; B.A.; M.A. Publs. incl: The Natural, 1952; The Assistant, 1957; A New Life, 1961; The Fixer, 1966; Pictures of Fidelman, 1969; The Tenants, 1972; (short stories) The Magic Barrel, 1957; Idiots First, 1963; Rembrandt's Hat, 1973. Num. short stories for Atlantic; Esquire; Partisan Review; New Yorker; etc. Mbrships: Nat. Inst. of Arts & Letters; Am. Acad. of Arts & Sci. Hons. incl: Daroff Mem. Award, 1958; Nat. Book Award, 1959, 1967; Pulitzer Prize, 1967. Address: Bennington Coll., Bennington, VT 05201, USA.

MALERBA, Luigi, b. 11 Nov. 1927, Parma, Berceto, Italy. Writer. Publs: La Scoperta Dell'Alfabeto, 1963; Il Serpente, 1966; Salto Mortale, 1968; Il Protagonista, 1973; Le Rose Imperiali, 1974; Mozziconi, 1975. Contbr. to: Corriere Della Sera; Il Mondo; Il Caffè; Playboy. Hons: Selezione Campiello Prize, 1966; Ninfa d'Oro, 1966; Sila Prize, 1969; Médicis Etranger Prize, 1970. Address: Via Tor Millina 31, Rome, Italy.

MALGONKAR, Manohar Dattatray, b. 12 July 1913, Bombay, India. Writier. Educ: B.A.(Hons.), Bombay Univ. Publs: (novels) Distant Drum, 1960; Combat of Shadows, 1962; The Princes, 1963; A Bend in the Ganges, 1965; Spy in Amber, 1970; The Devil's Wind, 1972; (short stories) A Toast in Warm Wine, 1974; In Uniform, forthcoming; (histl. works) Kanhoji Angrey, 1959; Puaras of Dewas, 1963; Chatrapatis of Kolhapur, 1971. Contbr. to: Life Int.; Times Lit. Supplement; Orientations; Illustrated Wkly. of India. Address: P.O. Jagalbet, Londa, S.C. Railway, Belgaum District, Karnataka State, India.

MALHERBE, François Ernst Johannes, b. 3 May 1894, Paarl, S. Africa. Emeritus Professor of Netherlands & Afrikaans Literature. Educ: M.A., Stellenbosch; Litt.D., Univ. of Amsterdam, Netherlands. Publs: Humor in die algemeen en sy uiting in die Afrikaanse Letterkunde, 1924; Lewensvorme, 1941; Klassieke Meesters van die Renaissance, 1944; Wending en Inkeer, 1948; Afrikaanse lewe en letterkunde, 1958; Blye Dae: An Autobiography, 1975. Contbr. to: Ons Eie Boek (Chief Ed.); var. mags., S. Africa & abroad. Mbrships. incl: PEN; S.A. Akademie vir Wetenskap en Kuns. Hons. incl: Stal Prize for Lit. Sci. Address: 9 Rowan St., Stellenbosch, Repub. of S. Africa.

MALHERBE, Vertrees Canby, b. 10 Dec. 1927, Wash. D.C., USA. Teacher. Educ: B.A., Wellesley Coll., Mass.; Secondary Tchrs. Dip., Univ. of Cape Town, S. Africa. Publs: What They Said: 1795-1910 History Documents, 1971; Eminent Victorians in South Africa, 1972; Film strip & Commentary for Nat. Film Bd. Mbrships.incl: S. African PEN Ctr., Cape (Comm.); Histl. Soc. of Cape Town. Address: Rooi Dak, Baker Rd., Kenilworth, Cape Province (7700), S. Africa.

MALHOTRA, Madan Lal, b. 14 Sept. 1915, Lahore, India (now Pakistan). Lecturer. Educ: Grad., 1936, M.A., 1938, Punjab Un''. Publs: Straws in the Wind, 1967; Quirks of Fate, 1970; Bridges of Literature, 1971; The Fifth Wheel, 1974. Contbr. to: Illustrated Weekly of India; Caravan; Jrnl. of Indian Writing in Engl.; Banasthali Patrika; Tchr. Today; Literary Criterion; etc. Recip., Rajasthan Govt. Disting. Serv. Merit Award, for critical & creative work in Engl., 1969 & 1974. Address: "The Shelter", 4-B, Mayur Colony, Ajmer (Rajasthan), India.

MÄLK, August, b. 4 Oct. 1900, Island Oesel, Estonia. Writer. Educ: Univ. of Tartu, Dorpat. Publs: 43 works inclng. Surnud majad (histl. novel), 1934; 6 novels on fishermen & coastal life, 1932-44; Tee kaevule (2 part psychol. novel), 1952-53; Jumalaga, meri! (short stories), 1967. Mbrships: Chmn., Assn. of Estonian Writers Abroad; Swedish Writers' Union; PEN. Address: Klubbacken 30, IV, 126 56 Stockholm-Hägersten, Sweden.

MALLEA, Eduardo, b. 14 Aug. 1903, Argentina. Writer; Journalist. Publs. incl: Cuentos para una Inglesa Desesperada, 1926; La cuidad junto al Rio Inmovil, 1936; Fiesta en Noviembre, 1938; Meditación en la Costa, 1940; Las Aguilas, 1941; Los Enemigos del Alma, 1950; La Torre, 1951; Chaves, 1953; La vida blanca, 1960; Las travesías, 1962; La barca de hielo, 1967; La Penúltima Puerta, 1970; Gabriel Andaral, 1971; Triste piel del universo, 1971. Contbr. to: La Nación. Mbrships. incl: Bd. of Dirs. of Sur & Realidad; Former Pres., Argentine Soc. of Writers. Hons. incl: First Nat. Prize for Lit., 1947, 1970. Address: Posadas 1120, Buenos Aires, Argentina.

MALLINSON, Vernon, b. 16 Feb. 1910, Barnsley, UK. Professor of Comparative Education. Educ: B.A., Univ. of Leeds, 1931; M.A., 1936; Univ. of Lyon, France, 1930. Publs: Teaching a Modern Language, 1953; None can Be Called Deformed, 1956; Introduction to the Study of Comparative Education, 1957, 4th ed., 1975; Power & Politics in Belgian Education, 1963; Modern Belgian Literature, 1966; Belgium, 1969. Contbr. to: Mod. Langs.; Comparative Educ. Review; Comp. Educ.; Int. Review of Educ.; etc. Fndr. Mbr., Comparative Educ. Soc. in Europe; Pres., Brit. Sect., 1968. Hons: Officer, Order of Leopold, 1972. Address: 19 Alpha House, Kendrick Rd., Reading, Berks., UK.

MALLOWAN, (Dame) Agatha Mary Clarissa, pen names CHRISTIE, Agatha; WESTMACOTT, Mary; b. 15 Sept. 1890, Torquay, UK. Writer. Publs: over 80 novels inclng. The Mysterious Affair at Styles, 1920; Poirot Investigates, 1924; The Murder of Roger Ackroyd, 1926; Murder at the Vicarage, 1930; The Hound of Death, 1933; Murder on the Orient Express, 1934; The A.B.C. Murders, 1935; Appointment with Death, 1938; Hercule Poirot's Christmas, 1938; Ten Little Niggers, 1939; The Body in the Library, 1942; The Labours of Hercules, 1947; Crooked House, 1949; After the Funeral, 1953; 4.50 from Paddington, 1957; A Caribbean Mystery, 1964; 3rd Girl, 1966; Passenger to Frankfurt, 1970; Nemesis, 1971; Elephants can Remember, 1972; Postern of Fate, 1973; Poirot's Early Cases, 1974. Hons: C.B.E., 1956; D.B.E., 1971; D.Litt., Exeter Univ. Address: Winterbrook House, Wallingford, Oxon., UK.

MALM, Johan Einar Fredrik, b. 6 July 1900, Botkyrka, Sweden. Author. Educ: M.A., Univ. of Uppsala, 1928. Publs: (Poetry) Dikter 1920-32, 1933; Än Flyga Svanarna, 1937; Pejlingar, 1939; Valda Dikter, 1940; Ankargrund, 1941; Något att Förlora, 1945; Ingenting Lever Länge, 1950; Hundvakt, 1953; Dikter (selected), 1956; Förbjuden Utflykt, 1958; Sprängda Horisonter, 1964; Fäste i Vinden, 1965; (Prose) I Kalle Schevens Skärgård, 1950; Uppsala i Mitt Hjärta, 1955; Alle Mans Skärgård, 1958; Biljett till Bodensjön, 1959; Berömda Indianhövdingar, 1960; Dödsdans i Dakota, 1961; Skärgårdsfresk, 1963; De Kämpade Förgäves, 1967; Skärgård Genom Tusen År, 1969; Sitting Bulls Krig, 1970. Contbr. to: Svenska Dagbladet. Mbrships: Swedish Authors' Union; PEN. Address: Götgatan 8 B, Norrtälje, Sweden.

MALM, William Paul, b. 6 Mar. 1928, La Grange, Ill., USA. Musicologist. Educ: B.M., 1948, M.M., 1950, Northwestern Univ; Ph.D., UCLA, 1959. Publs Japanese Music & Musical Instruments, 1959; Nagauta: The Heart of Kabuki Music, 1963; Music Cultures of the Pacific, the Near East, & Asia, 1967. Contbr., var. profl. jrnls. Mbrships. incl: Soc. for Ethnomusicol.; Bd., Asian Music Soc. Recip., var. acad. hons. Address: School of Music, Univ. of Mich., Ann Arbor, MI 48104, USA.

MALMQUIST, Eve Karl Theodor, pen name EM, b. 15 Nov. 1915, Malmö, Sweden. Professor of Educational Research. Educ: Phil.kand., Phil.lic., Univ. of Lund; Dr.Phil., Univ. of Stockholm; & grad. studies in USA. Publs. incl: Prevention of Reading Disabilities, 1969; Teaching of Reading in the Elementary School, 1973; Les Difficultés d'apprendre à lire, 1973; Läs- och skrivsvårigheter hos barn, 1973; Förderung legasthenischer Kinder in der Schule, 1974. Contbr. to num. profl. jrnls. Mbrships. incl: Dir., Int. Reading Assn., 1966-74; Mbr., Assn. of Swedish Authors; Chmn., Comm., Int. Book Year, 1972. Hons. incl: Co-author, one of 25 best educl. books, Phi Lampba Theta, USA, 1972. Address: Drottninggatan 35, 58227 Linköping, Sweden.

MALONE, Dumas, b. 10 Jan. 1892, Coldwater, Miss., USA. Historian. Educ: A.B., Emory Univ., 1910; B.D., Yale, 1916; M.A., 1921; Ph.D., 1923. Publs. incl: The Public Life of Thomas Cooper, 1926; Edwin A. Alderman:

A Biography, 1940; Jefferson & His Time 5 vols. (Jefferson the Virginian, 1948); Jefferson & the Rights of Man, 1951; Jefferson & the Ordeal of Liberty, 1962; Jefferson the President: 1st Term, 1970; Jefferson the President, 2nd Term, 1974); The Story of the Declaration of Independence, 1954; Thomas Jefferson as Political Leader, 1963; Empire for Liberty. Mbr., var. profl. socs. Hons. incl: Wilber Lucius Cross Medal, Yale, 1972; John F. Kennedy Medal for Contbn. to Hist., Mass. Hist. Soc., 1972. Address: 2000 Lewis Mountain Rd., Charlottesville, VA 22903, USA.

MALPASS, Eric, b. 14 Nov. 1910, Derby, UK. Author. Publs: Beefy Jones, 1957; Morning's at Seven, 1965; At the Height of the Moon, 1967; Oh My Darling Daughter, 1970; Fortinbras has Escaped, 1970; Sweet Will, 1973; The Cleopatra Boy, 1974; A House of Women, 1975. Contbr. to: Argosy; BBC. Mbrships: Pres., Nottingham Writers' Club; Pres., Derby Writers' Guild. Hons: Winner, Observer Short Story Competition, 1954; Palma d'Oro, Italy, 1960; Goldene Leinwand, Germany, 1969. Address: Broadleaves, 216 Breedon St., Long Eaton, Nottingham, UK.

MALRAUX, André, b. 3 Nov. 1901, Paris, France. Novelist; Politician. Publs. incl: Lunes en papier, 1921; Royaume farfelu, 1928; La Voie royale, 1930; La Condition humaine, 1933; Les Noyers de l'Altenburg, 1943; Psychologie de l'art, 3 vols., 1947-49; La Monnaie de l'Absolu, 1949; La Métamorphose des dieux, 1957; Antimémoires, 1967; Le Triangle Noir, 1970; Les Chênes qu'on abat, 1971; La Tête d'Obsidienne. Mbr., Am. Acad. of Arts & Sci. Hons. incl: Croix de Guerre (4 palmes); D.S.O.; Legion of Honour. Address: 2 rue d'Estienne d'Orves, 91370 Verrieres-le-Buisson, France.

MALRAUX-GOLDSCHMIDT, Clara. Writer. Publs.: Le Livre de Comptes, 1930; Portrait de Griselidis, 1945; La maison ne fait pas Crédit; Par de plus longs chemins; La Lutte inégale; Le bruit de nos pas, 1963; Nos Vingt ans, 1966. Address: 12 Sq. Albin Cachot, Paris, France.

MALSBARY, George Elmer, b. 9 Feb. 1917, L.A., Calif., USA. Medical Technologist. Educ: Med. Technol. Schl., USN; L.A. City Coll., 2½ yrs. Contbr. to: True Frontier; Westerner; Pioneer W.; Golden W.; Gt.W.; Berkeley, Calif. Gazette; San Jose, Calif. Mercury-Sun. Mbr., Western Writers of Am. Address: 3573 Terrace Way, Apt. 42, Lafayette, CA 94549, USA.

MALSTER, Robert, b. 21 Apr. 1932, Norwich, Norfolk, UK. Journalist. Publs: Wreck & Rescue on the Essex Coast, 1968; Wherries & Waterways, 1971; Saved from the Sea, 1974. Contbr. to: Ships Monthly; E. Coast Digest; E. Coast Mariner (Ed.); etc. Mbrships: Soc. for Nautical Rsch.; Norfolk Nautical Soc. Address: 23 Bixley Rd., Ipswich, Suffolk IP3 8PH, UK.

MAMALAKIS, Markos J., b. 30 Oct. 1932, Salonika, Greece. University Professor of Economics. Educ: LL.D., Univ. Salonika, 1955; Ludwig-Maximilian Univ., Munich, 1955-57; M.A., 1959, Ph.D., 1962, econs., Univ. Calif. Publs: Essays on the Chilean Economy (w. Clark Reynolds), 1965; Theory of Sectorial Clashes (in Spanish), 1966; The Growth & Structure of the Chilean Economy. From Independence to Allende, 1975; Historical Statistics of Chile, 1840-1967 (Vols. I, II, III, IV). Contbr. to: Latin Am. Rsch. Review; Economia Internazionale; Jrnl. Dev. Studies; etc. Mbrships. incl: Am. Econ. Assn.; Int. Assn. for Income & Wealth. Recip. num. acad. fellowships & grants. Address: 2977 N. Shepard Ave., Milwaukee, Wis., USA.

MAMATEY, Victor S(amuel), b. 19 Feb., 1917, N. Braddock, Pa., USA. Professor of History. Educ: Dip., Comenius Univ. Czechoslovakia, 1938; A.M., Harvard Univ., USA, 1941; Ph.D., Univ. of Paris, France, 1949. Publs: The United States & East Central Europe, 1914-1918, 1957; Soviet Russian Imperialism, 1964; World in the Twentieth Century (w. G. Bruun), 5th ed., 1967; Rise of the Habsburg Empire, 1526-1815, 1971; The History of the Czechoslovak Republic, 1918-48 (w. R. Luza), 1973. Mbr., var. profl. assns. Hons: G.L. Beer Prize, Am. Histl. Assn., 1958; Guggenheim Fellow, 1959. Address: 142 Spruce Valley Rd., Athens, GA 30601, USA.

MANCHESTER, William, b. 1 Apr. 1922, Attleboro, Mass., USA. Writer. Educ: B.A., Univ. of Mass., 1946; A.M., Univ. of Mo., 1947; L.H.D., Univ. of Mass., 1965. Publs. incl: Disturber of the Peace, 1951; The City of Anger, 1953; Shadow of the Monsoon, 1956; Beard the Lion, 1958; A Rockefeller Family Portrait, 1959; The Long

Gainer, 1962; Portrait of a President, 1962; The Death of a President, 1967; The Arms of Krupp, 1968; The Glory & the Dream, 1932-72, 1974. Contbr. to periodicals & Ency. Britannica. Mbr., Authors Guild. Hons. incl: Hammarskjold Prize, 1967; Overseas Press Club Award, 1968; Univ. of Mo. Hon. Award for Disting. Serv. to Jrnlsm., 1969. Address: Wesleyan Univ., Middletown, CT 06457, USA.

MANDA, Donald Moses, b. 25 Jan. 1944, Chintenche, Malawi. Author; Community Developer. Educ: B.A.; Dip.C.D.; now reading for M.Ed. Recip., Burney Prize, Univ. of Manchester, UK., 1972. Address: Dept. of Community Development, P.O. Box 5700, Limbe, Malawi.

MANDEL, Loring, pen names MILLER, Karl; BELL, Christopher, b. 5 May 1928, Chgo., Ill., USA. Dramatist. Educ: B.S., Univ. of Wis., 1949. Publs: sev. plays. Contbr. to: Playboy Mag.; N.Y. Times; Radio; TV. Mbrships: VP, Coun., Writers' Guild of Am., East; Dramatists' Guild; ASCAP; Nat. Collegiate Players. Hons: Emmy Award, Outstanding Writing Achievement, 1967-68; Sylvania Award, Outstanding Contbn. to Creative TV — Original Drama, 1959; 25th Anniversary Award, Nat. Acad. TV Arts & Scis., 1973.

MANDEL, Oscar, b. 24 Aug. 1926, Antwerp, Belgium. Playwright. Educ: B.A., N.Y. Univ.; M.A., Columbia Univ.; Ph.D., Ohio State Univ. Publs: A Definition of Tragedy, 1961; The Theatre of Don Juan, a Collection of Plays & Views, 1963; Chi Po & the Sorcerer — A Chinese Tale for Children & Philosophers, 1964; The Fatal French Dentist, 1967; The Gobble-Up Stories, 1967; Seven Comedies by Marivaux, 1968; Five Comedies of Medieval France, 1970; The Collected Plays of Oscar Mandel, 2 vols., 1970-72; Three Classic Don Juan Plays, 1971; Simplicities: 51 poems, 1974. Contbr. to: Am. Scholar; Lit. Review; etc. Mbr., MLA. Address: 979 Casiano Rd., L.A., CA 90049, USA.

MANDER, John, b. 1932. Assistant Literary Editor, New Statesman, 1960—; Editorial Advisor, Encounter, 1965-73. Educ: Eton & Trinity Coll., Cambridge. Publs: Berlin: The Eagle & the Bear, 1959; The Writer & Commitment, 1961; Berlin: Hostage for the West, 1962; Great Britain or Little England? , 1963; Static Society: The Paradox of Latin America, 1969; Elegiacs (poems), 1972; Our German Cousins, 1974. Contbr. to: Encounter; New Statesman; Observer; Sunday Times; Guardian, etc. Address: 6 Duncan Terrace, London N1, UK.

MÁNDY, Iván, b. 23 Dec. 1918, Budapest, Hungary. Writer. Publs: (Short stories) The 21st Street, 1948; Movies of old, 1966; A Man's Dream, 1971; (novels) The Wives of Fabulya, 1959; On the Field's Perimeter, 1963; What About Old Boy?, 1972. Mbrships: PEN Club; Hungarian Writers Assn. Hons: Baumgarten Prize, 1948; József Attila Prize, 1969. Address: Mező Imre u. 25, 1081 Budapest VIII, Hungary.

MANEV, Todor Subev, pen name ZIDAROV, Kamen, b. 16 Sept. 1902, Draganovo, Bulgaria. Writer. Publs: (in Bulgarian) (play) King's Mercy, 1949; (prose) For the sake of Honour, 1957; Blockade, 1960; Ivan Shishman, 1962; Kaloyan, 1969; Boyan the Magician, 1971. Contbr. to: September; PlamAk; Literatouren Front. Mbrships: PEN; Union of Bulgarian Writers. Hons: Dimitrov Prize, 1950; People's Worker in Culture, 1970; Hero of Socialist Labour, 1974. Address: Sofia, ul. V. Kolarov, 3, Bulgaria.

MANFRED, Frederick Feikema, b. 6 Jan. 1912, Rock Township, Doon, Iowa, USA. Writer; University Writer in Residence. Educ: B.A., Calvin Coll., Mich., 1934. Publs. incl: The Golden Bowl, 1944; Boy Almighty, 1945; The Primitive, 1949; The Giant, 1951; Morning Red, 1956; Conquering Horse, 1959; Wanderlust (tril.), 1962; The Man Who Looked like the Prince of Wales, 1965; Winter Count (poems), 1966; Eden Prairie, 1968; Conversations with Frederick Manfred, 1974. Contbr. to sev. gen. & acad. jrnls. Mbrships: Authors' League; PEN; Soc. Midland Authors; The Players. Recip., lit. awards. Address: Luverne, MN 56156, USA.

MANGIONE, Jerre (Gerlando), b. 20 Mar. 1909, Rochester, N.Y., USA. Professor of English. Educ: B.A., Syracuse Univ., N.Y., 1931. Publs: Mount Allegro (novel), 1943; The Ship & the Flame (novel), 1948; Reunion in Sicily, 1950; Night Search, 1965 (as To Walk the Night, UK, 1967); Life Sentences for Everyone (fables), USA & UK, 1966; A Passion for Sicilians, 1968; America is also Italian, 1969; The Dream & the Deal, 1971. Contbr. to:

Time; N.Y. Herald Tribune, & New Repub. (book reviews, 1930s); Monthly Review (Ed.-in-chief, 1945-48). Recip., num. grants & fellowships. Address: 1939 Panama St., Phila., PA 19103, USA.

MANGOCHE MBEWE, Mathurino Valentino Bwirani, b. 11 June 1934, Jumpha Village, Dedza, Malawi. Teacher. Educ: B.A., Univ. of Unisa; Dip. Educ., Univ. of Durham; Cert. in Educl. Planning; Cert. in Dev. Admin. Publs: Notebook of Chichewa for Visitors, 1971; Ulalo, I & II, Chichewa Primers for Primary Schools, 1971. Recip., profl. award. Address: P.O. Box 171, Zomba, Malawi.

MANHATTAN, Avro, b. 6 Apr. 1914, Milan, Italy. Author. Educ: Sorbonne, Paris, France; London Schl. of Econs., UK. Publs: The Vatican in World Politics, 1950; The Dollar & the Vatican 1956; Vatican Imperialism In the 20th Century, 1966; Catholic Power Today, 1968; Catholic Imperialism & World Freedom, 1972; Religious Terror in Ireland, 1972; The Vatican Billions — 2000 Years of Wealth Accumulation, 1973. Contbr. to var. jrnls. Mbrships: Soc. of Authors, London; PEN, London; Royal Soc. of Lit.; Life Mbr., Brit. Interplanetary Soc. Hons: Grand Cross, Kts. of Bethlehem, 1955; Kt., Kt. Templars, 1972. Address: 24 Ansdell Terrace, Kensington, London W8, UK.

MANHOLD, John Henry, b. 20 Aug. 1919, Rochester, N.Y., USA. Pathologist. Educ: B.A., Univ. of Rochester, 1940; D.M.D., Harvard Univ., 1944; M.A., Wash. Univ., 1956. Publs. incl: Introductory Psychosomatic Dentistry, 1956; Outline of Pathology, 1960; Clinical Oral Diagnosis, 1964. Contbr. to med., psychol., dental & interdisciplinary jrnls.; var. anthols. Mbrships. incl: Treas., Acad. of Psychosomatic Med.; Int. Assn. of Dental Rsch.; AMA; AAAS. Address: 83 Cranford Pl., Teaneck, NJ, USA.

MANHOOD, Harold Alfred, b. 6 May 1904. Writer. Publs: Nightseed, 1928; Apples by Night, 1932; Crack of Whips, 1934; Fierce & Gentle, 1935; Sunday Bugles, 1939; Lunatic Broth, 1944; (novel) Gay Agony, 1930; Selected Stories, 1947; A Long View of Nothing, 1953. Address: Holmbush, Nr. Henfield, Sussex, UK.

MANIKKA ARACHCHI, Sisira Kumara, pen name DESHABANDU, Vansanatha, b. 22 Jan. 1924, Weligama, Sri Lanka. Writer; Journalist. Educ: Sastra Visárada Dip., 1951. Publs. incl: Onna Ohomai Uné, 1964; Apé Pothè Ohoma Nethé, 1965; Má Dutu Vietnámaya, 1968; Ságarayak Meda Amana Ratak Eta, 1970; Yanu Kee Hein, 1971; Kiyaga Magiya (poems), 1972; Siri Lanka Illanka, 1974. Contbr. to var. nat. daily & wkly. papers. Mbrships: Fndr. Pres., Liberal Writers' Org., Sri Lanka; Former VP & Gen. Sec., Press Assn. of Ceylon. Hons: Award for Best Film Script, Janata competition, 1954; Lit. Award, 1963. Address: 676 High Level Rd., Nugegoda, Sri Lanka.

MANKIEWICZ, Don M(artin), b. 20 Jan. 1922, Berlin, Germany. Freelance Writer. Educ: B.A., Columbia Univ., USA, 1942; Columbia Law Schl. Publs: (novels) See How They Run, 1951; Trial, USA & UK, 1955; It Only Hurts a Minute, USA, 1966, UK, 1968; (screenplays) Trial, 1955; I Want to Live, 1958; var. TV plays. Contbr. to: New Yorker (Reporter, 1946-48). Mbr., TV Acad. of Arts & Scis. (Bd. of Govs., N.Y. Chapt.). Recip., Harper Novel Prize, 1954. Address: 115 Minnesota Ave., Long Beach, L.I., NY 11561, USA.

MANKIEWICZ, Joseph Leo, b. 11 Feb. 1909, Wilkes-Barre, Pa., USA. Film Writer, Director & Producer. Educ: B.A., Columbia Univ. Prods. incl: (script) If I had a Million; Forsaking all others; (prod.) Philadelphia Story; Woman of the Year; Keys of the Kingdom; (script & dir.) Letter to Three Wives; All About Eve; The Barefoot Contessa; Guys & Dolls; The Quiet American; Cleopatra; No Way Out; (dir.) House of Strangers; Five Fingers; Suddenly Last Summer; La Bohème; There Was a Crooked Man, 1969; Sleuth, 1972. Mbrships. incl: Pres., Screen Dirs'. Guild. Hons. incl: Oscar, 1949, 1950; Order of Merit, Italy. Address: Long Ridge Rd., Bedford, NY 10506, USA.

MANKOWITZ, Wolf, b. 7 Nov. 1924. Author; Playwright. Educ: M.A.(Engl. Tripos), Downing Coll., Cambridge. Publs. incl: (novels) Make Me An Offer, 1952; A Kid for Two Farthings, 1953; Laugh Till You Cry, 1955; Cockatrice, 1963; The Biggest Pig in Barbados, 1965; Penguin Wolf Mankowitz, 1967; (plays) The Bespoke Overcoat & Other Plays, 1955; (musical plays) Expresso Bongo, 1958; Belle, 1961; Pickwick, 1963; Passion Flower Hotel, 1965; Stand & Deliver, 1972; (films) The Millionairess, 1960; The Long & The Short & The Tall,

1961; Casino Royale, 1967; The Hebrew Lesson, 1972. Address: Simmonscourt Castle, Donnybrook, Dublin 4, Repub. of Ireland.

MANN, Francis Anthony, b. 10 June 1914, Bolton, UK. Journalist. Educ: Balliol Coll., Oxford; B.A. Oxon. Publs: Where God Laughed: The Sudan To-day, 1954; Well Informed Circles, 1961; Zelezny: Portrait Sculpture 1917-70, 1970; Tiara, 1973. Contbr. to: Daily Telegraph; Sunday Telegraph; Daily Telegraph Mag.; Punch; World Book Ency., US; BBC; Italian TV; CBC; etc. Mbrships: Past Pres., Anglo-Am. Press Assn. of Paris; Inst. of Jrnlsts., London; Assne. della Stampa Estera, Rome. Address: 58018 Porto Ercole (Gr.), Italy.

MANN, Leonard, b. 15 Nov. 1895, Melbourne, Vic., Australia. Writer. Educ: LL.B., Univ. of Melbourne, 1920. Publs: (novels) Flesh in Armour, 1932; Human Drift, 1935; A Murder in Sydney, UK & USA, 1937; Mountain Flat, UK, 1939; The Go-Getter, 1942; Andrea Caslin, UK, 1959; Venus Half-Caste, UK, 1963; (verse) The Plumed Voice, 1938; Poems from the Mask, 1941; The Delectable Mountains, 1944; Elegiac & Other Poems, 1957. Mbrships: Fellowship of Aust. Writers (Pres., 1938, 1941); Aust. Soc. Authors (Coun.). Hons: Aust. Lit. Soc. Award, 1932; Crouch Award, 1941; Grace Leven Award, 1957. Address: Ferncroft, Greenthorpe Rd., Olinda, Vic. 3788, Australia.

MANN, Thaddeus Robert Rudolph, b. 4. Dec. 1908, Lwow, Poland. Physiologist; Biochemist; Professor of Physiology of Reproduction. Educ: M.D., Univ. of Lwow; Ph.D. & Sc.D., Univ. of Cambridge, UK. Publs: Biochemistry of Semen, 1954; Biochemistry of Semen & of the Male Reproductive Tract, 1964. Contbr., about 250 papers, to var. sci. jrnls. Mbrships: incl: Fellow, Royal Soc.; Biochem. Soc.; Physiol. Soc.; Soc. of Expmtl. Biol. Hons. incl: C.B.E., 1962; Dr.vet.med., Univ. of Ghent, Belgium, 1971; Dr.sci.nat., Jagellonian Univ., Cracow, Poland, 1973. Address: Unit of Reproductive Physiol. & Biochem., Downing St., Cambridge CB2 3EZ, UK.

MANNES, Marya, pen name, SEC, b. NYC, USA. Writer. Publs: Message From a Stranger, 1948; More in Anger, 1958; Subverse, 1959; The New York I Know, 1961; But Will It Sell?, 1964; They, 1968; Out of My Time, 1971; Uncoupling (w. Norman Sheresky), 1972; Last Rights, 1974. Contbr. to num. mags. & newspapers inclng: N.Y. Times; Sat. Review; Atlantic; Newsweek; Chgo. Tribune. Mbrships: PEN; Authors' Guild. Recip., var. awards & hon. degrees inclng: Am. Jewish Congress Nat. Women's Div. Award, 1969. Address: c/o Harold Ober Assocs. (agent), 40 E. 49th St., N.Y., NY, USA.

MANNIN, Ethel, b. 11 Oct., 1900, London, UK. Writer; Journalist. Publs. incl: (novels) Sounding Brass; Ragged Banners; Linda Shawn; Rolling in the Dew; The Dark Forest; The Burning Bush; The Lady & the Mystic; Bitter Babylon; The Midnight Street, 1969; Free Pass to Nowhere, 1970; (travels & memoirs) South to Samarkand; An American Journey; England for a Change; England at Large, 1970; (essays) Common Sense & the Child; Women & the Revolution; Loneliness: a Study of the Human Condition; (autobiography) Young in the Twenties — a Chapter of Autobiography, 1971; Stories from My Life, 1973. Address: Oak Cottage, 27 Burghley Rd., London SW19, UK.

MANNING, Olivia, b. Portsmouth, Hants., UK. Writer. Publs: (General) The Remarkable Expedition, 1947; Extraordinary Cats, 1967; (short stories) Growing Up, 1948; My Husband Cartwright, 1956; A Romantic Hero, 1967; (novels) Artist among the Missing, 1949; School for Love, 1951; A Different Face, 1953; The Doves of Venus, 1955; The Great Fortune, 1960; The Spoilt City, 1962; Friends & Heroes, 1965; The Play-Room, 1969; The Rain Forest, 1974. Contbr. to: New Statesman; Observer; Sunday Times; Vogue; Harper's Bazaar; The Spectator; Encounter. Mbr., Authors Soc. Address: 3/71 Marlborough Place, London NW8, UK.

MANNING, Rosemary, pen names VOYLE, Mary; DAVYS, Sarah, b. 9 Dec. 1911, Weymouth, Dorset, UK. Writer. Educ: B.A., London Univ. Publs: (for adults) Remaining a Stranger; Look, Stranger; The Chinese Garden; Man on a Tower, A Time & a Time; (for children) Green Smoke; Dragon in Danger; Dragon's Quest; Boney was a Warrior; A Grain of Sand. Mbr., Soc. of Authors. Address: 20 Lyndhurst Gdns., London NW3 5NR, UK.

MANOLESCU, Nicolae, b. 27 Nov. 1939, Ramnicu-Valcea, Romania. Literary Critic. Educ: Ph.D. Publs: Contemporary Romanian Literature (w. D. Micu), 1965; Unfaithful Readings, 1966; Metamorphosis of the Poetry, 1968; Maiorescu's Contradiction, 1970; Themes, 1971. Contbr. to: Contemporanul, 1962-72; Romania Literara, 1972–. Mbrships: Writers' Union of Romania. Recip., Prize of Writers' Union, 1970. Address: aleea Lotrioara 3, Bucharest, Romania.

MANOUVRIEZ-LEROY, Simone Hortense, pen name DE LA GOULETTE, Simone, b. 1 Oct. 1897, Merlemont, Belgium. Novelist; Poet; Author of Dramatic Art. Publs: Guide des Promenades des distractions et de la gastronomie d'Olloy-sur-Viroin, 1972. Contbr. to: Cahiers Wallons; Le Bourdon; Guetteur Wallon. Mbrships: Rèlis Namurwès; Royal Assn. of French Writers, Brussels; Royal Assn. of Wallon Lit., Liège, Charleroi; Commission Culturelle de Wallonie; Sabam. Hons: 1st Prize, Wallon Song, AREF, Brussels, 1967; 3rd Prize, Moureau, AREW Charleroi, 1968. Address: 1 Autre cote de l'eau, 6382 Olloy-sur-Viroin, Belgium.

MANOV, Emil, b. 29 July 1918, Sofia, Bulgaria. Writer. Publs: (in Bulgarian) Captured Flock, 1947; The End of the Delias, 1954; Unauthentic Case, 1963; Galatea's Flight, 1963; Steep Slopes, 1965; Letters from Sofia, 1970; The Director's Son, 1973; (play) The Nameless Street, 1972. Contbr. to: PlamAk; September. Mbrships: PEN; Union of Bulgarian Writers. Hons: Prize, Union of Bulgarian Writers, 1948; Honoured Worker of Culture, 1965. Address: Sofia, ul. Rakovski 151, Bulgaria.

MANSELL, George Hennah, b. 1911, Hastings, Sussex, UK. Administrative Director, IPC Electrical-Electronic Group, 1972–; Chairman, PPITB Periodical Publishing Committee. Publs: Gen. Ed., High Buildings in the United Kingdom; Gen. Ed., Your House on View; The Houses we Build. Contbr. to: Annual Register of World Events; U.I.A. Review. Mbrships: Deleg. for Info. to the Coun., Int. Union Archts., 1972–; R.I.B.A.; M.Inst.R.A. Address: 28 Dorset Rd., London SW19, UK.

MANSFIELD, Harvey C., Sr., b. 3 Mar. 1905, Cambridge, Mass., USA. Political Scientist; Educator. Educ: B.A., 1927, M.A., 1928, Cornell Univ.; Ph.D., Columbia Univ., 1932. Publs: The Lake Cargo Controversy, 1932; The Comptroller General, 1939; A Short History of OPA, 1949; Arms & the State (w. W. Millis & H. Stein), 1958. Contbr. to: books in field inclng: The New Political Economy: The Public Use of the Private Sector, 1975; profl. jrnls. & reviews. Mbr., profl. & civic orgs. Address: 430 W. 116th St., N.Y., NY 10027, USA.

MANSON, Cecil Murray, b. 20 Jan. 1896, London, UK. Journalist; Broadcaster; Sculptor & Painter; Photographer. Publs: (all w. Celia Manson): Tides of Hokianga, 1956; Dr. Agnes Bennett, 1960; Curtain-raiser to a Colony, 1962; The Lonely One, 1963; The Adventures of Johnny van Bart, 1965; Pioneer Parade, 1966; I Take Up My Pen, 1971. Contbr. to: Daily Mail; London Calling; BBC; NZ Broadcasting Corp.; NZ Listener; Dominion; Christchurch Press; Auckland Weekly; Newsweek. Mbr., PEN. Address: Tara Hill, Kereru Rd., Day's Bay, Eastbourne, Wellington, NZ.

MANTLE, Winifred Langford, pen name LANG, Frances, b. 15 Feb. 1911, Merry Hill, nr. Wolverhampton Staffs., UK. Author; Former University Lecturer & Teacher. Educ: B.A.(Hons.), M.A.(Oxon.). Publs: 52 works of gen., histl. & children's fiction since 1951, inclng. Jonnesty, 1973; Milord Macdonald, 1973. Contbr. to: Times Educl. Supplement; var. women's mags., UK, Scandinavia, Can., etc. Mbrships: Soc. of Authors; Romantic Novelists' Assn. Recip., Romantic Novelists' Award, 1961. Address: 7 The Parklands, Finchfield Hill, Wolverhampton WV3 9DG, UK.

MANTOV, Dimitur, b. 13 Jan. 1930, Bossilkovo, Bulgaria. Writer. Publs: (in Bulgarian) Awakening, 1956; Kaloyan, 1958; Ivan Assen II, 1960; The Price of Silence, 1962; The Happy One, 1963; The Big Day, 1966; Devil's Carousel, 1971; Han Kroum, 1973; Yuvigi Han Omourtag. Contbr. to: September; PlamAk. Address: Sofia, bul. Vazov VL., 12, Bulgaria.

MANUEL, Frank Edward, b. 12 Sept. 1910, Boston, Mass., USA. Professor of History. Educ: A.B., 1930, A.M., 1931, Ph.D., 1933, Harvard Univ. Publs: The New World of Henri Saint-Simon, 1956; The Eighteenth Century

Confronts the Gods, 1959; The Prophets of Paris, 1962; Isaac Newton, Historian, 1963; Shapes of Philosophical History, 1965; A Portrait of Isaac Newton, 1968; Freedom from History (essays), 1971; The Religion of Isaac Newton, 1974. Contbr. to profl. jrnls. Mbrships incl: Fellow, Am. Acad. Arts & Scis. Hons: Guggenheim Fellow, 1957-58. Address: 29 Washington Sq. W., N.Y., NY 10011, USA.

MANVELL, Roger, b. 10 Oct. 1909, Leicester, UK. Author; Lecturer. Educ: B.A., Ph.D., Univ. of London; D.Litt., Univ. of Sussex, 1971. Publs. incl: Film, 1944; New Cinema in Britain, 1969; Shakespeare & the Film, 1971; Films & the Second World War, 1974; The Dreamers (novel), 1957, 1964; (biog.) Doctor Goebbels, 1959; Herman Göring, 1962; The July Plot, 1964; Heinrich Himmler, 1965; Rudolph Hess, 1971, 1973; Inside Adolf Hitler, 1973; (these biogs. w. H. Fraenkel) Ellen Terry, 1968; Sarah Siddons, 1970; Charlie Chaplin, 1974. Ed.-in-Chief, Int. Ency. of Film, 1972. Contbr. to var. encys. Recip., Hon. D. Litt., Univ. of Leicester, 1974. Address: Hennerton Lodge, Wargrave, Reading RG108PD, UK.

MANWELL, Reginald Dickinson, b. 24 Dec. 1897, Harford, Pa., USA. Biologist; University Professor. Educ: A.B., A.M., Amherst Coll.; Sc.D., Johns Hopkins Univ. Scl. of Hygiene & Pub. Hlth. Publs: Practical Malariology (w. others), 1946, rev. ed., 1963; Introduction to Protozoology, 1961, rev. ed., 1968; The Church Across the Street, 1949, rev. ed., 1962. Contbr., num. sci. papers to profl. jrnls. Address: Hoag Lane, Fayetteville, NY 13066, USA.

MANZ, Hans, b. 16 July 1931, Wila, Zürich, Switz. Teacher. Educ: Tchr. Trng., Oberseminar, Zürich. Publs: Lügenverse, 1965; Dreissig Hüge, 1966; Konrad, 1969; Worte kann man drehen, 1973; Ess- und Trinkgeschichten, 1973. Contbr. to: Tages- Anzeiger- Magazin. Mbr., Gruppe Olten (Swiss Writers' Grp.). Address: Im Allmendli, 8703 Erlenbach, Switz.

MAPP, Alf Johnson, Jr., b. 17 Feb. 1925, Portsmouth, Va., USA. Author; Historian; University Professor. Educ: A.B., Coll. of William & Mary, 1961. Publs: The Virginia Experiment: The Old Dominion's Role in the Making of America, 1957, 2nd ed., 1974; Frock Coats & Epaulets, 1963, 1972; America Creates Its Own Literature, 1965; Just One Man, 1968; The Golden Dragon: Alfred the Great & His Times, 1974. Contbr. to reviews & histl. jrnls.; Writer, TV & film scripts. Mbrships. incl: Ed. Bd., Jamestown Fndn.; Bd. of Eds., Va. Independence Bicentennial Comm.; Pres., Poetry Soc. of Va.; Va. Writers Club, Nat. Ed. Bd. Hons: Pulitzer nominee, 1953; "Ten Best" List, Am. Histl. Publ. Soc., 1963. Address: 225 Grayson St., Portsmouth, VA 23707, USA.

MARAI, Sándor, b. 11 Apr. 1900. Poet; Novelist. Publs. incl: Versek; Panaszkönyv; A mészáros; Zendülök; Idegen emberek; Csutora; Egy Polgár vallomàsai; Bébi, vagy az elsö szerelem; A szegények iskolàja; Bolhapiac; Istenek nyomában; Válás Budán; Kabala; Napnyugati örjárat A négy évszak; A sziget; Müsoron kivül; Sèrbödöttek; transl. into num. langs. Address: 100 Park Terrace W., N.Y., NY 10034, USA.

MARAINI, Dacia, b. 13 Nov. 1936. Author. Educ: Florence & Rome. Publs: La Vacanza, 1962; L'Età del Malessere, 1962; (poems) Crudelta All' Aria Aperta, 1966; (novel) A Memoria, 1967; (plays) La famiglia normale, 1967; Il ricatto a teatro, 1968; (other) Memoirs of a Female Thief, 1973. Recip., Formentor Prize. Address: Lungotevere Della Vittoria 1, Rome, Italy.

MARANGWANDA, John Weakley, b. 23 Sept. 1924, Chiweshe Tribal Trust Land, Rhodesia. Civil Aviation Agent. Publs: Kumazivandadzoka, 1959. Contbr. to: Rhodesia Herald; local newspaper. Mbrships: Chmn., Mazoe Burial Soc. Address: 2625 Jerusalem, New Highfield, P.O. Highfield, Salisbury, Rhodesia.

MARCEAU, Félicien, pen name of CARETTE, Louis, b. 16 Sept. 1913, Cortenberg, Belgium. Author; Playwright. Educ: Law Fac., Louvain Univ. Publs: (plays) L'Oeuf, 1956; La Bonne Soupe, 1958; La Preuve par Quatre, 1964; Madame Princess, 1965; Le Babour, 1969; L'Homme en Question, 1973; (novels) Bergère Légère, 1953; Les Elans du Coeur, 1955; Creezy, 1969; Le Corps de mon Ennemi, 1975; (essay) Balzac et Son Monde, 1955; (Memoirs) Les Années Courtes, 1968. Mbr., Jury du Prix Médicis. Hons: Prix Pelman du Théâtre, 1954; Prix Interallié, 1955; Prix

Goncourt, 1969; Grand Prix Prince Pierre de Monaco, 1974. Address: c/o Editions Gallimard, 5 Rue Sébastien-Bottin, Paris 75007, France.

MARCH, Rosemary, occasional pen name DEREK, Helen, b. 11 Nov. 1936, London, UK. Freelance Writer. Educ: Maidenhead Coll. Contbr. to: Times; Guardian; Daily Telegraph; Good Housekeeping; She; Reader's Digest; TV Times; Country Gentlemen's Mag.; Off Duty, USA; Am. Forests; Sci. Digest. Mbr., Thames Valley Writers' Soc. (Chmn.). Address: The Elms, Chalkhouse Green, Reading, Berks., UK.

MARCSON, Simon, b. 8 Oct. 1910, Winnipeg, Man., Can. Professor of Sociology. Educ: A.B., 1936, A.M., 1941, Ph.D., 1950, Univ. of Chgo., USA. Publs: The Scientist in American Industry, 1960; Automation, Alienation & Anomie, 1970. Contbr. to: Am. Sociol. Review; Am. Jrnl. of Sociol; Social Forces; Am. Anthropol.; Technol. & Culture; Social Sci. & Med.; Sci. & Technol.; Am. Sci.; Am. Behavioral Sci.; IRE Transactions. Fellowships: Am. Sociol. Assn.; Am. Anthropol. Assn.; Soc. for Applied Anthropol.; AAAS; Mbr., Int. Sociol. Assn. Recip., Fulbright Schlrship., 1959-60. Address: 36 Marion Rd., Princeton, NJ 08540, USA.

MARCUS, Aage, b. 31 Dec. 1888. Former Librarian, Royal Academy of Fine Arts, Copenhagen. Publs. incl: Mester Eckehart, 1917; Bibliography of the History of Danish Art, 1935; Leonardo da Vinci, 1940; Den blaa Drage, 1941; Billedkunsten, 1942; Danish Portrait Drawings, 1950; Christian Mysticism, 1953; Rejse i Sverige, 1956; Hellas, 1958; Höduft og Havluft, 1958; Det hellige Land, 1959; Damske Levnedsböger, 1965; Religionernes Digtning, 1967; Den Lange Vej, 1969. Address: Hørsholm, Denmark.

MARCUS, Frank, b. 30 June 1928, Breslau, Germany. Playwright; Theatre Critic. Educ: St. Martin's Schl. of Art. Publs: The Formation Dancers, 1964; The Killing of Sister George, 1965; Mrs. Mouse, Are You Within?, 1968; The Window, 1970; Notes on a Love Affair, 1972; Blank Pages, 1973. Contbr. to: Sunday Telegraph; Plays & Players; London Mag.; etc. Mbrships: Arts Coun. (Drama Panel); League of Dramatists (exec. comm.); Critics' Circle. Hons: Best Play of Yr. Awards, 1965, from Evening Standard, Plays & Players, & London Critics (in Variety). Address: 42 Cumberland Mansions, Nutford Pl., London W1, UK.

MAREK, Veronika, b. 19 Dec. 1937, Budapest, Hungary. Writer; Illustrator. Educ: Univ. of Budapest. Publs., illustrated by author, incl: Boribon, 1958; Laci és az oroszlán, 1961; A csunya kislány, 1963; Boribon és Annipanni series, 1972-75; sev. other books for children. Contbr. to: Kisdobos; Hungarian Radio & TV; Pannonia Animated Studio. Mbrships: Hungarian Writers' Assn.; UNIMA. Address: H-1027 Budapest, Frankel Leo ut 1, Hungary.

MARGERIT, Robert, b. 25 Jan. 1910, Brive, France. Author. Publs. incl: L'Ile des perroquets; Mont-Dragon; Le Vin des vendangeurs; Par un été torride; Le Dieu nu; La Femme forte; Le château des bois noirs; La Malaquaise; Les Amants; La Terre aux loups; L'Amour & le temps; Les Autels de la peur; Un Vent d'acier; Les hommes perdus; Waterloo. Hons: Legion of Honour; Prix Renaudot, 1951; Grand Prix du Roman, 1963; Nat. Order of Merit. Address: 46 rue Spontini, Paris 16e, France.

MARGOLD, Stella K., b. NYC, USA. Journalist; Radio Broadcaster. Educ: B.A., 1931, M.A., 1932, Ph.D. Cand., Univ. of Mich. Publs: Let's Do Business with Russia — How We Can & Why We Should; Housing Abroad; Export Credit Insurance in Europe Today. Contbr. to num. bus. & trade jrnls., newspapers; etc. Mbrships: Overseas Press Club; UN For. Press Assn.; UN Corres. Assn. Address: 765 Amsterdam Ave., N.Y., NY 10025, USA.

MARGUERITTE, Bernard Jean Edmond, b. 18 May 1938, Paris, France. Journalist. Educ: lic. és lettres, Sorbonne, Paris. Publs: "le Bloc le l'est à l'heure du choix"; The Other Poland, forthcoming. Contbr. to: Le Monde; L'Express: Radio Europe-1; Radio Suisse-Romande. Address: ul. Rakowiecka 59A m. 5, Warsaw, Poland.

MARGULL, Hans Jochen, b. 25 Sept. 1925, Tiegenhof, Danzig. University Professor. Educ: S.T.M., NY Theol. Sem., 1950; Dr. theol., 1958, Dr. theol. habil., 1960, Hamburg Univ. Publs: Theologie der missionarischen Verkündigung, 1959; Hope in Action, 1962; Aufbruch zur

Zukunft, 1962. Contbr. to: Die Religion in Geschichte und Gegenwart. Mbrships: Chmn., Dialogue Working Grp., World Coun. of Chs., 1969-75; Kuratorium des Hansischen Goethepreises. Address: Jenischstrasse 29, D 2 Hamburg 52, W. Germany.

MARIANOWICZ, Antoni, b. 4 Jan. 1924, Warsaw, Poland. Writer. Educ: Diplomatic-Consular Schl., Warsaw. Publs: Over 20 books inclng: Plamy na sloneczku (poems), 1957; Krolowa Bona umarla (poems), 1973; sev. plays & musicals; radio & TV scripts; transl. from Engl., French & German; children's books; anthols. Contbr. to: Variety (USA); Szpilki; Przekroj; Literatura. Mbrships: Polish Writers' Union; PEN; Polish Jrnlsts. Union; Polish Soc. of Authors (ZAIKS). Hons. incl: Offs. Cross. Polonia Restituta; Golden Cross of Merit. Address: Sniadeckich 1/15 m. 17, 00-654 Warsaw, Poland.

MARINO, Adrian, b. 5 Sept. 1921, Iasi, Romania. Literary Critic. Educ: B.A., M.A., Geneva Univ., Switz.; Dr. Docent, Univ. of Bucharest, Romania. Publs: Life & Work of Alexandru Macedonski, 1967, 1968; Introduction in Literary Criticism, 1968; Modern, Modernism, Modernity, 1969; Dictionary of Literary Ideas, I (A-G), 1973; ¡Olé! España, 1974; Criticism of Literary Ideas, 1974. Contbr. to Cahiers Roumains d'Etudes Littéraires (in French, Engl. etc.). Mbrships: Union of Romanian Writers; Assn. Int. de Lit. Comparée; Soc. Française d'Etude du XVIIIe Siècle. Hons: B.P. Hasdeu Prize, S.S.R. Acad., 1968; Prize, Union of Romanian Writers, 1969. Address: Cluj-Napoca, 72 Rákoczi St., Romania.

MARÍN PÉREZ, Pascual, b. 16 June 1917, Cieza, Murcia, Spain. Magistrate; University Professor. Educ: Grad. & Dr., Law; Grad. & Dr., Pol. & Econ. Sci. Publs. incl: Introducción a la Ciencia del Derecho, 1959, 3rd ed., 1974; La crisis del contrato, 1964; Política Del Derecho, 1966; Lo que vi en la República Arabe Unida, 1966; El nuevo Código civil portugués, 1966. Contbr. to var. profl. & lit. publs. Mbrships: Assn. Henry Capitant des amis de la Culture Juridique Française; Real Acad. de Jurisprudencia y Legislación; Inst. de Estudios Políticos. Address: Cea Bermúdez 68, 2nd Group, 2nd Floor A, Madrid, Spain.

MARK, Irving, b. 3 June 1908, NYC, USA. Professor Emeritus of History; Attorney. Educ: B.A., CCNY, 1929; M.A., Columbia Univ., 1931; LL.B., N.Y. Law Schl., 1933; Ph.D., Columbia Univ., 1940. Publs: Agrarian Conflicts in Colonial New York, 1711-1775, 1940, 2nd ed., 1965; Ed., The Faith of our Fathers: an Anthology Expressing the Aspirations of the American Common Man 1790-1860 (w. E. L. Schwaab), 1952; Great Debates, U.S.A. (& Teacher's Answer Key), 1969. Contbr. to num. profl. jrnls. Hons. incl: Comm.in-Aid of Creativity, Monmouth Coll., 1970, LL.D., ibid, 1973. Address: 4084 Bedford Ave., Brooklyn, NY 11229, USA.

MARK, Paul J., pen name JÄGER, Joseph, b. 11 Oct. 1931, Sur, Grisons, Switz. Accountant. Publs: Randsteine, 1968; Ed., Ondra Lysohorsky (anthol.). Contbr. to: UNIO, Saarbrücken; Poésie, Vivante, Geneva; Die Tat, Zürich. Mbr., Lit. Union, Saarbrücken. Address: Buchholzstrasse 119, CH-8053 Zürich, Switz.

MARKANDAYA, Kamala (Purnalya), b. 1924, India. Writer. Educ: Madras Univ. Publs: (novels) Nectar in a Sieve, UK, 1954, USA, 1955; Some Inner Fury, UK, 1955, USA, 1956; A Silence of Desire, UK & USA, 1960; Possession, India, UK & USA, 1963; A Handful of Rice, UK & USA, 1966; The Coffer Dams, UK & USA, 1969. Recip., Award, Nat. Assn. Independent Schls., USA, 1967. Address: c/o John Farquarson Ltd., 15 Red Lion Square, London WC1, UK.

MARKER, Frederick J(oseph), Jr., b. 10 Oct. 1936, Medford., Mass., USA. University Professor, Toronto. Educ: A.B., Harvard Univ., 1958; Univ. of Copenhagen, Denmark, 1958-63; D.F.A., Yale Univ., 1967. Publs: Hans Christian Andersen & the Romantic Theatre, 1971; The Scandinavian Theatre, A Short History, (w. L. L. Marker), 1975; Revels History of Drama in English, 1750-1880, (part author), 1975; Transl., Tumult, by Johannes Allen, 1969, US Ed. as Relations, 1970; Ed. & Transl., The Heibergs, 1971. Contbr. to: Theatre Survey; Theatre Notebook; Quarterly Jrnl. of Speech; Educl. Theatre Jrnl.; Anderseniana; Ibsen Yrbook.; Scandinavica; Theatre Rsch. Mng. Ed., Mod. Drama, 1972—. Mbrships. incl: ASTR; Int. Fedn. for Theatre Rsch, Recip., sev. fellowships & grants. Address: 144 Banbury Rd., Don Mills, Ont. M3B 2L3, Can.

MARKER, Lise-Lone (Christensen), b. 23 Sept. 1934, Aalborg, Denmark. University Professor, Toronto. Educ: Mag. art., Univ. of Copenhagen, 1961; Ph.D., Yale Univ., 1968. Publs. incl: David Belasco, Naturalism in the American Theatre, 1975; The Scandinavian, A Short History (w. F. J. Marker), 1975; Revels History of Drama in English, 1750-1880 (co-author), 1975. Contbr. to: Theatre Survey; Quarterly Jrnl. of Speech; Theatre Rsch.; Mod. Drama (Assoc. Ed., 1972—); other profl. jrnls. Mbrships. incl: Int. Fedn. for Theatre Rsch.; ASTR; SASS. Recip., sev. fellowships & grants. Address: 144 Banbury Rd., Don Mills, Ont. M3B 2L3, Can.

MARKFIELD, Wallace (Arthur), b. 12 Aug. 1926, Brooklyn, N.Y., USA. Writer. Educ: B.A., Brooklyn Coll., 1947; N.Y. Univ., 1948-50. Publs: (novels) To an Early Grave, USA, 1964, UK, 1965; Teitlebaum's Window, USA, 1970, UK, 1971. Contbr. to: New Leader (Film critic, 1954-55); Partisan Review; Commentary. Hons: Guggenheim Fellowship, 1965; Grant, Nat. Endowment for the Arts, 1966. Address: c/o Alfred A. Knopf Inc., 201 E. 50th St., N.Y., NY 10022, USA.

MARKO, Kurt, b. 20 July 1928, Scheibbs, Austria. University Professor. Educ: Ph.D., 1954. Publs: Sic et Non. Kritisches Wörterbuch des sowjetrussischen Marxismus-Leninismus der Gegenwart, 1962; Sowjethistoriker zwischen Ideologie und Wissenschaft, 1964; Evolution wider Willen. Die Sowjet- ideologie zwischen Orthodoxie und Revision, 1968; Dogmatismus und Emanzipation in der Sowjetunion, 1971; L'intellighenzia sovietica tra la critica e il dogma, 1972; Pragmatische Koexistens Partnerschaft von Ost und West? , 1973. Contbr. to num. acad. & pol. jrnls. Mbr., PEN. Address: A-1010 Vienna 1, Johannesgasse 22/13, Austria.

MARLAND, Michael, b. 28 Dec. 1934, London, UK. Headmaster. Educ: Christ's Hosp.. London; B.A., Sidney Sussex Coll., Cambridge. Publs: Spotlight, 1966; Following the News, 1967; Towards the New Fifth, 1969; Head of Department, 1970; Theatre Choice, 1972; The Experience of Work, 1973; Pastoral Care, 1974; The Question of Advertising, 1974; The Craft of the Classroom, 1975. Contbr. to: Times Educl. Supplement. Address: 22 Compton Terrace, London N1 2UN, UK.

MARLOW, Joyce Mary, b. 27 Dec. 1929, Manchester, UK. Author. Publs: The Peterloo Massacre, 1969; The Tolpuddle Martyrs, 1971; Captain Boycott & the Irish, 1973; The Life & Times of George I, 1973. Mbr., Soc. of Labour Hist. Address: Magnolia Cottage, East Lane, Bedmond, Watford WD5 0QG, UK.

MARLOWE, Dan J., pen name SANDAVAL, Jaime, b. 10 July 1914, Lowell, Mass., USA. Writer. Publs. incl: Killer With A Key, 1959; The Name of the Game is Death, 1962; The Vengeance Man, 1965; The Raven is a Blood Red Bird, 1967; Operation Flashpoint, 1970; Operation Checkmate, 1970; Operation Hammerlock, 1974. Contbr., short stories to var. mags. & book reviews to Detroit Free Press. Mbrships. incl: Crime Writers Assn., UK.; Am. Authors Guild. Recip., Edgar Allan Poe Award for best suspense novel, Mystery Writers of Am., 1970. Address: 123 N. First St., Harbor Beach, MI 48441, USA.

MARLOWE, Derek, b. 21 May 1938, London, UK. Writer. Educ: London Univ. Publs: A Dandy in Aspic, 1966; Memoirs of a Venus Lackey, 1968; A Single Summer with L.B., 1969; Echoes of Celandine, 1971; Do You Remember England?, 1972; Somebody's Sister, 1974. Mbrships: Writers' Guild of GB; Soc. of Authors. Hons: Award for Best TV Documentary Script, Writers' Guild, 1971; Emmy Award for TV script, Search for the Nile, USA, 1972. Address: Foscombe, Ashleworth, Glos., UK.

MARÓTI, Lajos, b. 18 Nov. 1930, Budapest, Hungary. Writer; Literary Director, Publishing. Educ: Theol. Univ. of Benedictines, Pannonhalma; Degree, Physics & Maths., Eötvös Lóránt Univ. of Scis., Budapest. Publs: (in Hungarian) The Sightless, The Monastery, Hippi Aquarium (novels); 3 vols. of poetry, 2 vols. of essays; The Night After the Last, St. Martin's Summer (plays). Mbrships: Hungarian Assn. of Writers; PEN. Address: Kökörcsin u.19, 1113 Budapest XI, Hungary.

MARR, (Rev.) Ronald James, b. 14 Mar. 1933, Caledonia, Ont., Can. Editor. Educ: Grad., Prairie Bible Inst., Three Hills, Alta. Contbr. to: The Christian Inquirer (Ed.); The Evangelical Christian; Fe. Address: 131 S. Mill St., Ridgeway, Ont., Can. L0S 1NO.

MARSH, Henry, pen name SAKLATVALA, Beram, b. 15 Sept. 1911, Manchester, UK. Author. Educ: B.A., Univ. Coll., London. Publs. incl: Phoenix & Unicorn, 1954; Air Journey, 1967; The Christian Island, 1970; The Origins of the English People, 1969; Dark Age Britain, 1970; Documents of Liberty, 1971; The Origins of the English People, 1972; The Caesars, 1972; Slavery & Race, 1974; some transls. Contbr. to: London Mercury; New Statesman; Hist. Today. Mbrships: Dean of Studies, Working Man's Coll., 1952-61; Vice Prin., 1961-66. Address: 18 Grosvenor Place, London SW1X 7HS, UK.

MARSH, John, b. 5 Nov. 1904, Brighton, Sussex, UK. College Principal. Educ: M.A., D.Phil., Mansfield Coll., Oxford; also Edinburgh Univ. Publs: The Living God, 1942; The Fulness of Time, 1952; Trans., Stauffer, Theology of the New Testament, 1955; A Year with the Bible, 1957; Amost & Micah, 1959; Trans., Bultmann, History of the SYNOPIC Tradition, 1963; Pelican Commentary on John, 1967. Mbrships: Soc. for N.T. Study; Soc. of O.T. Study. Hons. incl: Chmn., Congl. Union of Engl. & Wales, 1962-63; Moderator, Free Ch. Fed. Coun., 1970-71; C.B.E., 1964. Address: Rannerdale Close, Buttermere, Cockermouth, Cumbria CA13 9UY, UK.

MARSH, John, pen names HARLEY, John; ELTON, John, b. 8 Aug. 1907, Halifax, UK. Author. Educ: Leeds Univ. Publs: The Young Winston Churchill, 1956, USA, 1973; Clip a Bright Guinea; Monk's Hollow; Hate Thy Neighbour; The Four Doctors. Contbr. to: Country Life; Yorks. Life; Yorks. Ridings Mag.; most nat. Brit. newspapers. Mbrships: Soc. of Authors; PEN; Crime Writers' Assn.; Press Club; Fndr., Halifax Authors' Circle. Address: Chalfont, Rawson Ave., Halifax, W. Yorks., UK.

MARSH, John Leslie, b. 3 Nov. 1927, Morristown, N.J., USA. College Professor. Educ: A.B., Syracuse Univ., 1950; M.A., 1953; Ph.D., 1959, Univ. of Pa. Publs: American Literature, A Televised Approach, 1965; English Literature, A Televised Approach, 1966; A Student's Bibliography of American Literature, 1971; The Grandin Opera House, or Theatre on the Kerosene Circuit, 1973. Contbr. to: Jrnl. of Popular Culture; W. Pa. Hist.; Players; Mil. Uniforms in Am. Mbrships: Am. Studies' Assn.; Popular Culture Assn.; Co. of Mil. Histns. Recip., Edinboro Fndn. Hon. Award, 1973. Address: P.O. Box 25, Edinboro, PA 16412, USA.

MARSH, (Dame) Ngaio, b. 23 Apr. 1899, Christchurch, NZ. Theatre Producer; Novelist. Educ: Canterbury Univ., NZ; Coll. Schl. of Art, Christchurch, NZ. Publs. incl: A Man Lay Dead, 1934; Enter a Murderer, 1935; Vintage Murder, 1937; Death & the Dancing Footman, 1942; Died in the Wool, 1945; Final Curtain, 1947; Opening Night, 1951; Scales of Justice, 1955; Off with His Head, 1957; False Scent, 1960; Dead Water, 1964; Death at the Dolphin, 1967; Clutch of Constables, 1968; When in Rome, 1969; Tied up in Tinsel, 1972; Black as He's Painted, 1974; (autobiography) Black Beech & Honey Dew, 1966. Address: 37 Valley Rd., Cashmere, Christchurch 2, NZ.

MARSHALL, Alan, b. 2 May 1902, Noorat, Vic., Australia. Author. Publs. incl: Tell Us About the Turkey, Jo, 1946; Pull Down the Blind, 1949; Bumping Into Friends, 1950; People of the Dreamtime, 1952; I Can Jump Puddles, 1955; How's Andy Going, 1956; The Gay Provider, 1961; In Mine Own Heart, 1963; These were my Tribesmen, 1965; Whispering in the Wind, 1969; Pioneers & Painters, 1971; Fight for Life, 1972; Short Stories, 1973; Hammers over the Anvil, 1975; works publd. in 24 countries. Mbrships. incl: Fellowship of Aust. Writers; Coun. Mbr., Aust. Soc. of Authors; Life Mbr., Aust. Folklore Soc. Hons: C'wlth. Lit. Fund Fellowships, 1954, 1961; O.B.E., 1972; Hon. LL.D., Melbourne Univ., 1972. Address: "Gurrawilla," 13a Potter St., Black Rock, Victoria, Australia 3193.

MARSHALL, Bruce, b. 24 June 1899, Edinburgh, UK. Writer. Educ: M.A., St. Andrews & Edinburgh Univs.; B.Comm., Edinburgh Univ. Publs. incl. Father Malachy's Miracle, 1931; All Glorious Within, 1945; The White Rabbit, 1952; The Bishop, 1970; The Black Oxen, 1970; Urban the Ninth, 1973. Contbr. to: Saturday Evening Post; Cosmopolitan. Mbr., Scottish Inst. of Chartered Accts. Recip., Wlodmiertz Prize, Poland, 1959. Address: c/o Lloyds Bank, 6 Pall Mall, London SW1, UK.

MARSHALL, Catherine. Publs: Beyond Ourselves; Christy; God Loves You; Man Called Peter; Prayers of Peter Marshall; To Live Again; Under Sealed Orders; Claiming God's Promises; Something More. Address: c/o Peter Davies Ltd., 15-16 Queen St., London W1X 8BE, UK.

MARSHALL, Elizabeth Margaret, pen name SUTHERLAND, Elizabeth, b. 24 Aug. 1926, Kemback House, Cupar, UK. Author. Educ: Cert. in soc. sci., Edinburgh Univ. Publs: Lent Term, 1973; The Seer of Kintail, 1974. Contbr. to newspapers & mags. Mbrships. incl: Glasgow Writers' Circle. Recip., Constable Fiction Trophy, 1972. Address: St. John's Rectory, 21 Swinton Rd., Baillieston, Glasgow 69, UK.

MARSHALL, James, b. 12 May 1896, NYC, USA. Attorney-at-Law. Educ: LL.B., Columbia Univ., 1920. Publs: Ordeal by Glory, 1927; Swords & Symbols: The Technique of Sovereignty, 1939, 2nd ed., 1969; The Freedom to be Free, 1943; Law & Psychology in Conflict, 1966; Intention — In Law & Society, 1968. Contbr. to: Pol. Sci. Quarterly; Columbia, Va., Harvard Law Reviews; Harper's; Atlantic; Saturday Review; Am. Schlr.; Psychol. Today; etc. Mbrships. incl: Exec. Bd., PEN Am. Ctr.; Hon. VP, Am. Jewish Comm.; Bd., Partisan Review, etc. Hons. incl: Gold Medal, Pub. Educ. Assn., 1952; Holmes-Munsterberg Award, Int. Acad. Forensic Psychol., 1973. Address: 430 Park Avenue, N.Y., NY 10022, USA.

MARSHALL, John David, b. 7 Sept. 1928, McKenzie, Tenn., USA. Librarian. Educ: B.A., Bethel Coll.; M.A., Grad study, Fla. State Univ. Publs. incl: Books-Libraries-Librarians, 1955; Of, By, & For Librarians, First Series, 1960, Second Series, 1974; Louis Shores: A Bibliography, 1964; A Fable of Tomorrow's Library, 1965; Library in the University, 1967. Book Review Ed., Jrnl. of Lib. Hist.; Contbng. Ed., Southern Observer, 1953-66; Gen. Ed., Shoe String Press Contributions to Library Literature Series. Address: 802 E. Main St., Murfreesboro, TN 37130, USA.

MARSHALL, John Norman, b. 6 May 1905, Walton-on-Thames, Surrey, UK. Author & Journalist. Publs. incl: The Weaving Willow, 1953; Recreation-Motoring, 1954; Sussex Cricket, A History, 1959; The Duke Who Was Cricket, 1961; Man, Oh Man, 1965; Lord's, 1969; Headingley, 1970; Old Trafford, 1971; Off-Duty Winemaking, 1974; Contbr., Late Extra, 1950; Fleet Street, 1960; The Boundary Book, 1965; Best Cricket Stories, 1966; Duleep, 1967; All you Need to Know About Drinks (Wine Section), 1973. Contbr. to: Evening News, London; Guest Publs. (Mags.); Good Housekeeping: Wine Mine. Mbrships. incl: Press Club, London (VP, former Chmn.). Address: Church House, Thakeham, Pulborough, Sussex, UK.

MARSHALL, Jonathan, b. 9 Mar. 1931, London, UK. Playwright; Journalist; Author. Publs: How to Survive in the Nick, 1974; Thoughts from a Prison Cell, 1975; The Reformation of a Criminal, 1975. Contbr. to: Soc. Servs. Paper; Frontsheet; Sunday Times. Mbrships: Coun., Howard League; Chmn., Old Lag's Soc. Address: c/o Dr. Jan van Loewen, 81-83 Shaftesbury Ave., London W1, UK.

MARSHALL, Michael Eric, b. 1936, Lincoln, UK. Chaplain, London University, 1964-69; Vicar, All Saints' Church, London, 1969—. Educ: Christ's Coll., Cambridge; Cuddesdon Theological Coll., Oxford; M.A.(Cantab). Publ: A Pattern of Faith (co-author), 1966. Address: All Saints' Vicarage, 7 Margaret St., London W1, UK.

MARSHALL, Paule, b. 9 Apr. 1929, Brooklyn, N.Y., USA. Writer. Educ: B.A., Brooklyn Coll., 1953. Publs: Brown Girl, Brownstones (novel), USA, 1959, UK, 1960; Soul Clap Hands & Sing (short stories), 1961; The Chosen Place, The Timeless People (novel), USA, 1969, UK, 1970. Hons: Guggenheim Fellowship, 1961; Rosenthal Award, 1962; Ford Theatre Award, 1964; Grant, Nat. Endowment for Arts, 1966. Address: c/o Harcourt, Brace & Jovanovich, 757 Third Ave., N.Y., NY 10017, USA.

MARTI, René, b. 7 Nov. 1926, Frauenfeld, Thurgau, Switzerland. Assistant Director, Zurich Municipal Government; Teacher & Translator, English & French; Proprietor, New Press Agency; Editor, "Leben und Umwelt" & "Schweizer Frauenkorrespondenz". Publs: Das unauslöschliche Licht (Novelle), 1955; French transl. 1975; Dom des Herzens (poems), 1967; Die fünf Unbekannten (stories & poems), 1971; Der unsichtbare Kreis (stories), 1974; stories & poems in var. anthols. Contbr. to var. newspapers. Mbrships: Schweizerischer Schriftstellerverband; Former mbr., Bd. of Dirs., Zürcher Schriftstellerverein; Regensburger Schriftstellergruppe;

Fndg. mbr. & former acting chmn., Interessengemeinschaft deutschsprachiger Autoren; Literarische Union, Saarbrücken; Verein der Schweizer Presse. Address: Haus am Herterberg, Haldenstr. 5, CH-8500 Frauenfeld, Switzerland.

MARTIN, Aurel, b. 15 May 1926, Jibou, Romania. Literary Historian & Critic; Director of Publishing House. Educ: B.A., Univ. of Cluj-Napoca. Publs: Contemporary Poets, Vol. I, 1967, Vol. II, 1971; Romanian Literature, 1972; Introduction to N. Filimon's Work, 1973; Metonymies, 1974; Pro Patria, 1974. Contbr. to: Romanian Encyclopaedic Dict., Vols. I-IV, 1962-66; Little Encyclopaedic Dict., 1972; Ed., Young Writer, Morning Star, Lit. Review; var. newspapers, TV; etc. Mbrships: Leading Bur., Romanian Writers' Union; Leading Coun., Romania Cultural Assn., Romania — GB Friendship Assn. Address: Bucuresti, Calea Grivitei 163, Sectorul 8, Romania.

MARTIN, Bengt, b. 24 May 1933, Stockholm, Sweden. Author. Publs. incl: Langsamvakenramsan, 1964; Den mjuka klon, 1966; Det skönaste, 1967; Sodomsäpplet, 1968; Nejlikmusslan, 1969; Finnas till, 1970; Party för lyckliga ostar, 1973; Joakim I & II, 1974. Contbr. to: Folkbladet Daily News, Östgöten; Swedish TV. Mbr., Swedish Authors Soc. Hons. incl: Litteraturfrämjandets Prize, 1970; Mag. Vi's Prize, 1970. Address: Radmansgatan 69 III, 113 60 Stockholm, Sweden.

MARTIN, Bernard, b. 13 Mar. 1928, Seklence, Czech. University Professor of Jewish Studies. Educ: B.A., Univ. of Chgo., USA, 1947; M.H.L., Hebrew Union Coll., 1951; Ph.D., Univ. of Ill., 1961. Publs. incl: Prayer in Judaism, 1968; Ed., Contemporary Reform of Jewish Thought, 1968; Ed., A Shestov Anthology, 1970; Great Twentieth Century Jewish Philosophers, 1970; A History of Judaism, 1974; transls. incl: Israel Zinberg, A History of Jewish Literature, 5 vols., 1972-74. Contbr. to: Am. Jewish Archives; Jrnl. of Ctrl. Conf. of Am. Rabbis (Ed., 1974—); Judaism; Theol. Today; etc. Mbr. & Off., var. Jewish & acad. orgs. Address: Dept. of Religion, Yost Hall, Case Western Reserve University, Cleveland, OH 44106, USA.

MARTIN, Ernest Walter, b. 31 May 1914, Shebbeow, Devon, UK. Author. Publs: The Secret People, 1954; Where London Ends, 1958; The Tyranny of the Majority, 1961; The Book of the Village, 1962; The Book of the Country Town, 1962; The Shearers & the Shorn, 1965; Country Life in England, 1966; Comparative Development in Social Welfare, 1972. Contbr. to: The Observer; New Blackfriars; New Soc.; Sociol. Review; Aryan Path; BBC radio & TV. Mbrships: Writers' Guild of GB; Soc. Welfare Hist. Grp., USA; Hon. Rsch. Fellow, Univ. of Exeter, 1974. Recip., Civil List Pension for servs. to lit. & soc. hist., 1972—. Address: Editha Cottage, Black Torrington, Beaworthy, Devon EX 21 5QF, UK.

MARTIN, Francis Xavier, b. 2 Oct. 1922, Ballylongford, Co. Kerry, Repub. of Ireland. Historian. Educ: B.A., 1949, M.A., 1952, Univ. Coll., Dublin; B.D., Gregorian Univ., Rome, Italy, 1951; Ph.D., Peterhouse, Cambridge, UK, 1959. Publs. incl: Friar Nugent: a Study of Francis Lavalin Nugent, 1569-1635, 1962; Ed., Leaders & Men of the Easter Rising, Dublin 1916, 1967; The Scholar Revolutionary: Eoin MacNeill, 1867-1945, & the Making of the New Ireland (Ed. w. F. J. Byrne), 1973. Contbr. to var. schlrly. jrnls. etc. Mbrships: Irish MSS Commn., 1963—; Royal Irish Acad., 1967—; Trustee, Nat. Lib. of Ireland, 1971—. Recip., Royal Irish Acad. Prize, 1952. Address: Augustinian House of Studies, Ballyboden, Dublin 14, Repub. of Ireland.

MARTIN, George Whitney, b. 25 Jan. 1926. NYC, USA. Writer. Educ: B.A., Harvard Coll., 1948; Trinity Coll., Cambridge, UK, 1949-50; LL.B., Univ. of Va. Law Schl., USA, 1953. Publs: The Opera Companion: A Guide for the Casual Operagoer, 1961; The Battle of the Frogs & the Mice: An Homeric Fable, 1962; Verdi: His Music Life & Times, 1963; The Red Shirt & the Cross of Savoy: The Story of Italy's Risorgimento, 1748-1871, 1969; Causes & Conflicts: The Centinnial History of the Association of the Bar of the City of New York 1870-1970, 1970. Contbr. to: Yale Review; About the House; Opera News; Wash. Post. Mbrships: Century Assn., N.Y.; Grolier Club. Address: 333 E. 68th St., N.Y., NY 10021, USA.

MARTIN, John Bartlow, b. 4 Aug. 1915, Hamilton, Ohio, USA. Writer; Ambassador; University Professor of Journalism. Educ: B.A., DePauw Univ., 1937. Publs. incl:

Why Did They Kill, 1953; Break Down the Walls, 1954; The Deep South Says Never, 1957; The Pane of Glass, 1959; Overtaken By Events, 1966; The Life of Adlai E. Stevenson, 1975. Contbr. to: Harper's; Reader's Digest; Saturday Evening Post; Life; Look; etc. Mbrships: Century Assn., N.Y.; Fed. City Club, Wash. Hons: Sigma Delta Chi Mag. Award, 1950, 1956; Benjamin Franklin Mag. Award, 1953, 1955, 1956, 1957; L.H.D. Knox Coll., 1974. Address: 185 Maple Ave., Highland Park, IL 60035, USA.

MARTIN, José Luis, pen name (for fiction) YUNKEL, Ramar, b. 11 July 1921, Vega Baja, Puerto Rico. Professor of Spanish-American Literature. Educ: B.A., 1942, M.A., 1953, Univ. of Puerto Rico; Ph.D., Columbia Univ., USA, 1965. Publs. incl: Arco y Flecha, 1961; La Poesia de José Eusebio Caro, 1966; Romancero del Cibuco, 1970; El Retorno, 1972; Crítica Estilística, 1973; Literatura Hispanoamericana Contemporánea, 1973; La Narrativa de Vargas Llosa, 1974. Contbr. to num. Spanish lang. & lit. jrnls. Mbrships. incl: MLA; Inst. of Iberoam. Lit.; Hispanic Inst. of the U.S. Recip., var. acad. hons. Address: 666 West End Ave., (Apt. 5-c), N.Y., NY 10025, USA.

MARTIN, Nancy (Mrs. A. E. Salmon), b. Croydon, UK. Author. Publs. incl: The Post Office: from Carrier Pigeon to Confravision, 1969; Four Girls in a Store, 1971; Fire Service Today, 1972; William Carey, The Man Who Never Gave Up, 1974; Search & Rescue, The Story of the Coastguard, 1974; Careers in the Post Office (forthcoming); Prayers for Children & Young People (forthcoming). Mbrships. incl: Authors' Soc.; Women's Press Club of London (Past Chmn.); Pres., Fndr., Croydon Writers' Circle. Recip., Berwick Sayers Award, Croydon, 1966-67. Address: Garden House, Church Lane, Fittleworth, Pulborough, Sussex, UK.

MARTIN, Ralph Guy, b. 4 Mar. 1920, Chgo., Ill., USA. Author. Educ: Grad., Schl. of Jrnlsm., Univ. of Mo., 1941. Publs. incl: Boy from Nebraska, 1946; The Human Side of FDR (co-author), 1960; Man of the Century: Winston Churchill, (co-author), 1961; The Bosses, 1964; Wizard of Wall Street, 1965; The GI War, 1967; A Man for All People, 1968; Jennie: The Life of Lady Randolph Churchill, 2 vols., 1969, 1971. Contbr. to: New Repub. (Assoc. Ed., 1945-48); Newsweek Mag. (Assoc. Ed., 1953-55), House Beautiful (Exec. Ed., 1955-57); etc. Mbrships. incl: Authors' League of Am.; Authors' Guild; Dramatists' Guild; Overseas Press Club. Address: Gabriele Dr., E. Norwich, NY 11732, USA.

MARTIN, Richard Milton, b. 12 Jan. 1916, Cleveland, Ohio, USA. Professor of Philosophy. Educ: A.B., Harvard Univ., 1938; M.A., Columbia Univ., 1939; Ph.D., Yale Univ., 1941. Publs. incl: Towards a Systematic Pragmatics 1959; Intension & Decision, A Philosophical Study, 1963; Belief, Existence, & Meaning, 1969; Logic, Language, & Metaphysics, 1971; Events, Reference, & Logical Form; Whitehead's Categoreal Scheme & Other Papers. Contbr. to num. schlrly. jrnls., reviews etc. Mbrships: Exec. Comm. & Coun., Assn. for Symbolic Logic, 1950-53; Exec. Comm., E. Div., Am. Philos. Assn., 1964-67. Address: Paxhurst, Tuxedo Park, NY 10987, USA.

MARTINEAU, Gilbert, b. 26 July 1918, Rochefort-sur-Mer, France, Diplomat, French Foreign Service. Educ: St. Etienne Coll., France. Publs: La Vie à St.-Hélène au Temps de Napoléon; Napoleon's St. Helena; Napoléon se rend aux Anglais (transl. publd. UK & USA); Napoléon & l'Empire. Contbr. to Le Figaro. Mbrships: Soc. des Gens de Lettres de France; Authors' Soc., London; Assn. des Ecrivains Combattants. Hons. incl: Prix du Cercle de l'Union, Paris, 1971. Address: Consul de France, Longwood House, Island of St. Helena, South Atlantic Ocean.

MARTÍNEZ-DELGADO, Luis, b. 12 Mar. 1894, Bogotá, Colombia. Writer; Historian; Lawyer. Educ: Fac. of Law & Pol. Scis., Bogotá; Law studies, Paris, France. Publs. incl: Historia de Colombia, 2 vols., 1885-95 & 1895-1910; A propósito del Dr. Carlos Martínez-Silva: Capítulos de Historia Política; Panamá, su Separación de Espana: su Incorporación a la Gran Colombia; Su independencia de Colombia: el canal interoceánico de Panamá; Documentos y Correspondencia del General José María Obando, 4 vols.; Episódios de la vida del General Obando; Ed., Historia Extensa de Colombia, 30 vols. Contbr. to num. lit. jrnls. Mbr., num. acads. Address: Carrera 16A, 46, 21 Bogotá, Colombia.

MARTINI, Teri, b. 4 June 1930, Teaneck, N.J., USA. Teacher. Educ: B.S., Trenton Tchrs. Coll., 1952; M.A.,

Columbia Univ., 1964. Publs: The True Book of Indians, 1954; The True Book of Cowboys, 1955; Mystery of the Hard Luck House, 1965; The Lucky Ghost Shirt, 1971; Patrick Henry, Patriot, 1972; The Mystery of the Woman in the Mirror, 1973; John Marshall, 1974. Contbr. to: The Grade Tchr.; Childcraft Ency.; Young Miss; Teen Mag. Mbrships: Authors' Guild; Women's Nat. Book Assn.; Soc. of Children's Book Writers. Address: 216 Overlook Ave., Leonia, NJ, USA.

MARTINSEN, Ella Lung, b. 6 Jan. 1901, Dominion Creek, Yukon Territory, Can. Author; Poet. Publs: Black Sand & Gold, 1956-67; Trail to North Star Gold, 1969. Contbr. to: The Alaska Book; Alaska Mag.; Alaska Sportsman Mag. Mbrships. incl: Pres., Santa Barbara Br., Nat. League of Am. Pen Women; Alaska Club; Int. Alaska-Yukon Club. Hons. incl: Gold Plaque for 2 gold rush books, Santa Barbara Br., Nat. League of Am. PEN Women. Address: 3033 Lomita Rd., Santa Barbara, CA 93105, USA.

MARTÍN VIGIL, José Luis, b. 28 Oct. 1919, Oviedo, Spain. Educ: Lic. Philos. & Theol.; Lic. Classical Humanities. Publs. incl: La vida sale al encuentro, 1956; Tierra brava, 1958; Cierto olor a podrido, 1960; Sexta galería, 1962; Los curas comunistas, 1965; Un sexo llamado débil, 1967; Sentencia para un menor, 1971; Primer amor, primer dolor, 1972; Nación de muchachos, 1973; No hay lugar para inocentes, 1974. Contbr. to: Cuadernos para el Diálogo; Gaceta del Norte. Mbrships: Soc. of Authors of Spain; Assn. of Spanish Writers & Artists. Hons: Ciudad de Oviedo Prize, 1962; Perez Galdós Prize, 1965. Address: Calle Velázquez 75, Madrid 6, Spain.

MARVEL, Carl Shipp, b. 11 Sept. 1894, Waynesville, Ill., USA. Chemist. Educ: A.B., M.S., Ill. Wesleyan Univ., Bloomington, Ill., 1915; A.M., Univ. of Ill., Urbana-Champaign, 1916; Ph.D., 1920; D.Sc., Ill. Wesleyan Univ., 1946. Publs: An Introduction to the Organic Chemistry of High Polymers, 1959; Ed.-in-Chief, Organic Syntheses, vol. 5, 1925 & vol. II, 1931. Contbr. to: Jrnl. of Am. Chem. Soc.; Jrnl. of Polymer Sci.; Jrnl. of Organic Chem. Mbrships. incl: Nat. Acad. of Sci.; Am. Philos. Soc.; Am. Chem. Soc.; AAAS; Am. Acad. Arts & Scis. Hons. incl: D.Sc., Univ. of Ill., 1963; Dr. h.c., Univ. of Louvain, Belgium, 1970. Address: 2332 E. 9th St., Tucson, AZ 85719, USA.

MARWICK, William Hutton, b. 16 Oct. 1894, Creektown, Old Calabar, Nigeria. Lecturer; Author. Educ: M.A., Edinburgh Univ. Publs: Economic Developments in Victorian Scotland, 1936; Scotland in Modern Times, 1964; A Short History of Labour in Scotland, 1967. Contbr. to: Econ. Hist. Review; Univ. of Edinburgh, Scottish Labour Hist. Soc. Jrnls.; Book of Old Edinburgh Club; Jrnl. of Friends' Histl. Soc.; Records of Scottish Ch. Hist. Soc. Address: 5 Northfield Crescent, Edinburgh EH8 7PU, UK.

MARWIG-RUBIN, Anny Marie, b. 14 Dec. 1893, Eiderstedt, Germany. Author. Publs: Kalle Vips & Klara, 1940; Kalle Stensopp on Adventure, 1941; The King's Galleon, 1942; The Tide, 1949; The Ant Bettina, 1950; To Go North, 1951; Mattje, 1952; Una Marina, 1956; In Ethiopia, 1957; Come With Me to Africa, 1959; School Holidays in Africa, 1962; The Land Under the Wind, 1971. Contbr. to Swedish & for. newspapers & mags. Mbrships: Swedish Writers' Union; German Writers' Union. Hons: Sev. prizes, Swedish Writers' Union, Stockholm & for. newspapers; Grants, Fredr. Ström's Mem. Fund, 1966; Travel Grants, 1962, 1963, 1971, 1973. Address: Ringvägen 2, 11726 Stockholm, Sweden.

MARX, Anne, b. Bleicherode am Harz, Germany. Poet; Author; Lecturer; Critic; Translator; Editor. Educ: Med. Schls., Heidelberg, Berlin; Var. US colls. Publs. incl: Ein Büchlein: German Lyrics; Into the Wind of Waking, 1960; The Second Voice: A Collection of Poems, 1963; By Way of People, 1970; A Time to Mend, 1973. Contbr. to mags., reviews, poetry jrnls. & anthols. in US, UK, France, Italy & Switz. Mbrships. incl: Life Mbr., Past Off., Exec. Bd., Poetry Soc. of Am.; Nat. Poetry Ed., other offs. Nat. League of Am. Pen Women; Acad. of Am. Poets; Fedn. of State Poetry Socs. Num. hons. incl: Fellowships, Poetry Soc. of Am.; N.Y. Writers Conf.; Greenwood Prize, Poetry Soc. of GB, 1966; Cecil Hemley Mem. Award, Poetry Soc. of Am., 1974. Address: 315 The Colony, Hartsdale, NY 10530, USA.

MARX, Gerhard Otto, b. 10 May 1936, Hagen, Germany. Journalist. Educ: B.A., M.A., Ambassador Coll.,

USA. Publs: An Examination of the Germanic Love of Nature, 1969; The Historical Roots of the Herrenvolk Concept, 1969; The Origin of Antisemitism, 1970; Anglo-Saxon Mythology & the Christian Nativity Festival, 1972; The Decline of the Judaic Element in Orthodox Christianity to 1517 A.D., 1974. Contbr. to: Die Reine Wahrheit (News Ed., 1961-63); The Plain Truth (Contbng. Ed., 1964-74); Radio & TV Scriptwriter, The World Tomorrow. Mbrships: Inst. of Jrnlsts., London, UK; Assn. of Am. Corres., London. Address: 27 Salisbury Rd., Harpenden. Herts. AL5 5AR, UK.

MASCALL, Eric Lionel, b. 12 Dec. 1905, Sydenham, Kent, UK. Professor, Historical Theology, retired. Educ: B.A., 1927, M.A., 1931, B.D., 1943, D.D., 1958, Cambridge Univ.; M.A., B.D., 1945, D.D., 1948; Oxford Univ.; B.Sc., London Univ., 1926. Publs. incl.: Christian Theology & Natural Science, 1956; The Importance of Being Human, 1958; The Secularisation of Christianity, 1965; The Openness of Being, 1971. Contbr. to: Jrnl. of Theol. Studies; Ch. Quarterly Review; New Blackfriars; etc. Mbr., Fellow, Brit. Acad. Hons: num. acad. hons. inclng. Emeritus Prof., King's Coll., London, 1974—. Address: 30 Bourne St., London SW1, UK.

MASIYE, Agrippa Viane, b. 8 Oct. 1931, Gwanda, Rhodesia. Teacher. Educ: Primary Tchrs'. Cert.; Adv. Theol. Cert. Publs: Imfundiso Yobukristu, 1967; Koze Kukufice Lawe, 1970; Wangithengisela Umntanakhe, 1972; You & the Church, 1972. Contbr. to: Evangelical Visitor, USA; Two Tone (Rhodesian poetry jrnl.); Good words. Mbrships. incl: Ndebele & Shona Writers' Assn. (Vice-Chmn.); PEN, Rhodesia; Christian Writers' Club (Sec.). Hons. incl: 3rd Prize, Lit. Competition, Rhodesia Lit. Bur., 1967; 4th Prize, Lit. Competition, 1968. Address: P.O. Box 2020, Bulawayo, Rhodesia.

MASOLIVER, Liberata, b. 18 Jan. 1911, Sabadell, Spain. Publs. incl: Efún, 1954; Un camino lleva a la cumbre, 1955; Los Galiano, 1957; Selva verde, selva negra, 1958; Barcelona en Llamas, 1960; La Mujer del Colonial, 1961; Pecan los Buenos, 1962; Maestro Albanil, 1963; Nieve y Alquitrán, 1964; La Retirada, 1966; Casino veraniego, 1967; Telóni, 1968; La Bruixa, 1969; Hombre de Paz, 1970; Dios con nosotros, 1971; Los miniamores de Angelines, 1972; Estés donde estés, 1973. Contbr. to: Barna; Sabadell; Diario del Valles; 4 novels serialized in La Prensa. Mbr., Assn. of Spanish Writers & Artists. Hons. incl: Elisenda de Montcada Prize, 1954; La Prensa Prize, 1974; etc. Address: Paseo Valldoreix 6, San Cugat, Spain.

MASON, Bruce Edward George, b. 28 Sept. 1921, Wellington, NZ. Writer; Actor. Educ: Vic. Univ. Coll. Publs: Theatre in Danger (w. J. Pocock), 1957; The Pohutukawa Tree, 1960, 5th ed. 1974; The End of the Golden Weather, 1962, 3rd ed. 1974; Awatea, 1970; Zero Inn, 1970; New Zealand Drama, 1973. Contbr. to: NZ Listener; NZBC Arts Review; Landfall; S.E. Asia Quarterly; NZ Slavonic Jrnl. Mbr., Downstage Theatre, Wellington. Hons: Winner, Nat. Playwright Competition, 1958; State Schlrship. in Letters, 1973. Address: 14 Henry Street, Wellington 3, NZ.

MASON, Douglas Rankine, pen name RANKINE, John, b. 26 Sept. 1918, Hawarden, Flintshire, UK. Headmaster. Educ: B.A., Manchester Univ. Publs. incl: (as John Rankine) The Blockade of Sinitron, 1964; Interstellar Two Five, 1966, 3rd ed., 1968; Binary "Z", 1969, 2nd ed., 1970; Operation Umanaq, 1973; (as Douglas R. Mason) From Carthage Then I Came, 1966; Ring of Violence, 1968, 2nd ed., 1969; The Tower of Rizwan, 1968; Matrix, 1970; Satellite 54-0, 1971; Horizon Alpha, 1971; The Phaeton Condition, 1973, 2nd ed., 1974; The End Bringers, 1973. Mbrships: Soc. of Authors; Nat. Assn. of Head Tchrs. Address: 16 Elleray Park Road, Wallasey, Merseyside L45 0LH, UK.

MASON, Francis Kenneth, b. 1928, Blackheath, Surrey, UK. Managing Director, Alban Book Services Ltd. Educ: RAF Coll., Cranwell, 1948-51. Publs: Hawker Aircraft Since 1920, 1961; The Hawker Hurricane, 1962; The Gloster Gladiator, 1963; Battle over Britain, 1969; Air Facts & Feats, 1970; Know Britain, 1972; Know Aviation, 1973; Ed., Ribbons & Medals, 1974; Dictionary of Military Biographies, 1974. Contbr. to: Flying Review; Flight. Mbrships: Fellow, Royal Histl. Soc.; Assoc., Royal Aeronautical Soc. Address: Havering, 147 London Rd., St. Albans, Herts. AL1 1TA, UK.

MASON, Haydn Trevor, b. 12 Jan. 1929, Saundersfoot, Wales, UK. University Professor. Educ: B.A., Univ. of

Wales, 1949; A.M., Middlebury Coll., 1951; D.Phil., Oxford Univ., 1960. Publs: Pierre Bayle & Voltaire, 1963; Ed., Marivaux, Les Fausses Confidences, 1964; Ed. & Transl., Leibniz-Arnauld Correspondence, 1967; Ed., Voltaire, Zadig & Other Stories, 1971; Voltaire, 1975. Contbr. to: Times Lit. Supplement; French Studies; Mod. Lang. Review; Romanic Review; Stendhal-Club; etc. Mbrships. incl: Assn. Univ. Profs. of French; other profl. assns. Address: Schl. of European Studies, Univ. of E. Anglia, Norwich NR4 7TJ, UK.

MASON, Madeline, b. 24 Jan. 1913, NYC, USA. Author; Poet. Publs: Poems: Hill Fragments, 1936; The Cage of Years, 1949; At the Ninth Floor: A Sonnet Sequence in a New Form, 1958; Sonnets in a New Form, 71; The Challengers, 75; (stories) Riding for Texas, 1936, 1938; Trans., Kahill Gibran's The Prophet; Memoirs: As I Knew Them. Contbr. to: Ladies Home Jrnl.; Harpers Bazaar; Sat. Review; N.Y. Times; etc. Mbrships. incl: V.P., Poetry Soc. Am.; Nat. League Am. PEN Women; N.Y. Pres., Composers Authors & Artists of Am., 1962-64. Hons. incl: Diamond Jubilee Award of Distinction in Poetry, Nat. League Am. PEN Women, 1958; Composers Authors & Artists Award of Distinction, 1964. Address: Hotel Seville, 22 E. 29th St., N.Y., NY 10016, USA.

MASON, Malcolm John, b. 19 Dec. 1912, Pahiatua, NZ. Chartered Accountant; Writer. Educ: B.A.; B.Com.; Dip. Soc. Scis.; profl. qualifications. Publs: The Way Out, 1946; The Water Flows Uphill, 1954; Why Not Japan? , 1965. Contbr. to NZ publs. Mbr., PEN (Pres., NZ Ctr., 1962-65). Address: 29 Everest St., Khandallah, Wellington, NZ.

MASON, Philip, pen name WOODRUFF, Philip, b. 19 Mar. 1906, London, UK. Writer. Educ: B.A., 1927, M.A., 1952, D.Litt., 1972, Balliol Coll., Oxford Univ. Publs: (as Philip Woodruff) Call The Next Witness; The Wild Sweet Witch; The Island of Chamba; Whatever Dies; Colonel of Dragoons; The Sword of Northumbria; Hernshaw Castle; The Founders; The Guardians; (as Philip Mason) An Essay on Racial Tension; Commonsense about Race; The Birth of a Dilemma; Year of Decision; Prospero's Magic; Patterns of Dominance; Race Relations; A Matter of Honour, 1974; Kipling: The Glass, the Shadow & the Fire, 1975. Hons. incl: Fellow, Schl. of Oriental & African Studies, 1970; D.Sc., Bristol, 1971. Address: Hither Daggons, Cripplestyle, Alderholt, nr. Fordingbridge, Hants., UK.

MASON, Richard, b. 16 May 1919. Author. Publs: The Wind Cannot Read, 1947. The Shadow of the Peak, 1949; The World of Suzie Wong, 1957; The Fever Tree, 1962. Address: c/o A.M. Heath & Co. Ltd., 35 Dover St., London W1, UK.

MASSEY (Sir), Arthur, b. 5 Jan 1894, Keighley, UK. Physician. Educ: M.B.Ch.B., Univ. of Leeds, 1920; M.D., 1924. Publs: Epidemiology & Air Travel, 1933; Ed., Modern Trends in Public Health, 1949. Contbr. to med. publs. Mbrships. incl: V.P. & Hon Fellow, Royal Soc. of Hlth.; Hon. Fellow, Am. Pub. Hlth. Assn.; Brit. Med. Assn. Hons: C.B.E., 1941; Hon. Physn. to King George VI, 1950-52; Hon. Physn. to H.M. The Queen, 1952-53; Kt., 1956. Address: 93 Bedford Gardens, London, W8, UK.

MASTERMAN, (Sir) John Cecil, b. 12 Jan. 1891, Kingston Hill, Surrey, UK. Former Provost, Worcester College, Oxford. Educ: Worcester Coll., Oxford. Publs. incl: An Oxford Tragedy, 1933; Fate Cannot Harm me, 1935; Marshal Ney, 1937; The Case of the Four Friends, 1957; Bits & Pieces, 1961; The XX system in the War of 1939 to 1945, 1972; On the Chariot Wheel, (autobiog.), 1975. Mbrships. incl: BBC Gen. Adv. Coun.; ATV Educl. Adv. Comm., 1961-67; Vice-Chancellor, Oxford Univ., 1957-58. Hons. incl: O.B.E.; LL.D.; D.C.L.; Royal Order of Crown of Yugoslavia; Kt., 1959. Address: 6 Beaumont St., Oxford, UK.

MASTERS, John, b. 26 Oct. 1914, India. Writer; Retired Army Officer. Educ: Royal Mil. Coll., Sandhurst, UK. Publs. incl: (novels) Nightrunners of Bengal, 1951; The Deceivers, 1952; Bhowani Junction, 1954; Coromandel! , 1955; Far, Far the Mountain Peak, 1957; Fandango Rock, 1959; To the Coral Strand, 1962; Trial at Monomoy, 1964; Fourteen Eighteen, 1965; The Breaking Strain, 1967; The Rock, 1970; (autobiog.) Bugles & a Tiger, 1956; The Road Past Mandalay, 1961; Pilgrim Son, 1971 (all except last also publd. USA.). Hons: D.S.O., 1944; O.B.E., 1945. Address: c/o Michael Joseph Ltd., 52 Bedford Square, London WC1, UK.

MASTERS, William Walter, pen name MASTERS, W. W., b. 12 July 1894, Yeovil, UK. Educator. Educ: B.D., Kelham Hall. Publs: Airways, 1926; Eleven, 1928; Murder in the Mirror, 1931. Mbrships: Soc. of Authors; NALGO. Address: "Turners", Haslemere, Surrey GU27 2NJ, UK.

MATABWA, Charles January, b. 6 June 1943, Thyolo Dist., Malawi. Laboratory Technician. Educ: Dip. in Lab. Technol. Publs: Equilibrium Moisture Content of Seasoned Wood in Malawi, Part II Specific E.M.C. Values for Important Species. Address: Soil Productivity Rsch. Unit, P.O. Box 5748, Limbe, Malawi.

MATANE, Paulias Nguna, b. Sept. 1932, Rabaul, Papua New Guinea. Permanent Secretary, Ministry of Business Development, Papua New Guinea. Publs. incl: Kum Tumun of Morj, 1966; A New Guinean Travels Through Africa, 1971; What Good is Business?, 1972; Bai Bisnis I Helpim Yumi Olsem Wanem?, 1973; My Childhood in New Guinea, 1972; Two New Guineans Travel Through Southeast Asia, 1974; Aimbe the Challenger, 1974. Contbr. to: New Guinea Writing; Jrnl. of Educ., Papua New Guinea. Mbrships. incl: Pres., Rotary Club, Port Moresby, 1973-74. Recip., Forsyth Prize, 1955. Address: Box 3383, Port Moresby, Papua New Guinea.

MATEVSKI, Mateja, b. 13 Mar. 1929, Istanbul, Turkey. Poet; Theatre Critic; Journalist; Director General, Radio-Television Skopje. Educ: Fac. of Arts, Lit. Dept.; post-grad. degree in theatre, Paris, France. Publs: Rains (poetry), 1956; Equinocium, 1963; Sunset, 1969; Nebie e tramonti (in Italian), 1969; Papblo Neruda (ed. & transl.), 1972; F. G. Lorca (ed. & transl.), 1974; Poems (bilingual, Macedonian & Serbian), 1974. Contbr. to jrnls. inclng: Young Lit. (ed.); Reviews (ed.). Mbr., lit. orgs.; Recip., sev. awards. Address: Partenija Zografski 49, 91000 Skopje, Yugoslavia.

MATHER, Jim, pen name DURHAM, Stanley, b. 12 Feb. 1913, Lanchester, Durham, UK. Journalist; Horticultural & Agricultural Consultant. Publs: Ed., Daily Mirror's Mr. Digswell Gardening Book (2 issues); Growing Food for the Freezer; The Casual Gardener. Contbr. to: Sunday Mirror (Gardening Ed.); Daily Mirror; The Greenhouse (former Ed.); var. gardening mags. Mbrships. incl: Fellow, Royal Hort. Soc.; Press Club; Inst. Jrnlsts. (Pres., 1973-74). Recip., Emergency Reserve Decoration. Address: The Ridge, Churt, Surrey GU10 2LU, UK.

MATHIAS, Peter, b. 10 Jan. 1928, Somerset, UK. Chichele Professor of Economic History. Educ: B.A., 1951; M.A., 1955; Cambridge Univ.; M.A., Oxford Univ., 1969. Publs: The Brewing Industry in England, 1700-1830, 1959; English Trade Tokens, 1962; Retailing Revolution, 1967; The First Industrial Nation, 1969; USA & Japanese eds., 1971; Science & Society 1600-1900 (ed.), 1972; Debates in Economic History (gen. ed.), 1967–. Contbr. to schlrly. jrnls. Mbrships: Pres., Int. Econ. Hist. Assn.; var. other histl. orgs. Address: All Souls Coll., Oxford, UK.

MATHIAS, Roland, b. 4 Sept. 1915, Talybout-on-Usk, Breconshire, UK. Poet; Editor; Critic. Educ: B.A., 1936, B.Litt., 1939, Jesus Coll., Oxford; M.A., 1944. Publs: Break in Harvest, 1946; The Roses of Tretower, 1952; The Eleven Men of Eppynt, 1956; The Flooded Valley, 1960; Whitsun Riot, 1963; Absalom in the Tree, 1971; Vernon Watkins, 1974. Contbr. to: Poetry Wales; Planet; Spirit; Poetry Now; Ed., The Anglo-Welsh Review, 1961–. Mbrships: Engl. Sect., Yr Academi Gymreig; Pres., S. & Mid-Wales Writers' Assn., 1972–; Welsh Arts Coun., 1974–. Recip., Welsh Arts Coun. Prize for Poetry, 1972. Address: Deffrobani, Macscelyn, Brecon LD3 7NL, Powys, UK.

MATHIESSEN, Peter, b. 22 May 1927, NYC, USA. Writer; Explorer. Educ: Sorbonne, Paris, France, 1948-49; B.A., Yale Univ., 1950. Publs: Race Rock (novel), 1954, UK 1955; Partisans (novel), USA, 1955, UK, 1956; Wildlife in America, USA, 1959, UK, 1960; The Cloud Forest, USA, 1961, UK, 1962; Raditzer, USA, 1961, UK, 1962; Under the Mountain Wall, USA, 1962, UK, 1963; At Play in the Fields of the Lord (novel), USA, 1965, UK, 1966; The Shorebirds of North America, 1967; Oomingmak, 1967; Sal Si Puedes, 1970; Blue Meridian, 1971; Fndr. & Ed., Paris Review. Mbr., N.Y. Zool. Soc. (Trustee). Hons. incl: Atlantic Firsts Award, 1951. Address: Bridge Lane, Sagaponack, L.I., NY 11962, USA.

MATHIS, Byron Claude, b. 10 Mar. 1927, Longview, Tex., USA. University Professor. Educ: B.A. 1949, M.A. 1950, Tex. Christian Univ.; Ph.D., Univ. of Tex., 1956.

Publs: Psychological Foundations of Education — Learning & Teaching (co-author), 1970; Ed., Profiles in College Teaching: Models at Northwestern (w. W. C. McGaghie), 1972. Contbr. to: Contemporary Psychol.; Psychol. in the Schls.; Jrnl. Educl. Rsch. Mbrships incl: Fellow, Am. Psychol. Assn., & AAAS. Address: 9350 Nashville Ave., Morton Grove, IL 60053, USA.

MATHUR, Dinesh C., b. 9 Dec. 1918, Jodhpur, India. Professor of Philosophy. Educ: M.A. 1941, LL.B. 1942, Agra Univ.; A.M. 1954, Ph.D. 1955, Columbia Univ., USA. Publs: Modern Logic: Its Relevance to Philosophy (co-author), 1969; Naturalistic Philosophies of Experience, 1971. Contbr. to: Indian Jrnl. Pol. Sci.; Philosl. Quarterly; Jrnl. of Philos.; Quest; Diogenes; etc. Mbrships: All India Philosl. Congress (formerly Exec. Comm.); Am. Philosl. Assn. Hons: Fulbright Schlr., 1954-55; Fellowships, Columbia Univ. & SUNY. Address: 24 Trefoil Lane, Brockport, NY 14420, USA.

MATIHALTI, Hellevi Marja-Liisa Salminen, pen name SALMINEN, Hellevi, b. 19 Feb. 1941, Lapua, Finland. Educ: Grad., Commercial Coll., 1960. Publs: (in Finnish) Baby, 1962; The Gray Rain of September, 1964; A Hedgehog of Paper, 1967; Allison, 1972; What's the Matter, Saila?, 1974 (all juvenile books). Contbr., columns, articles & TV criticism to Finnish newspapers. Mbrships: Finnish Soc. of Authors; Finnish Provincial Authors; Finnish Soc. of Critics; Finnish Juvenile Authors. Address: Kp 13, 62200 Kauhava, Finland.

MATKOVIĆ, Ljiljana, b. 9 Dec. 1938, Zagreb, Yugoslavia. Writer; Translator. Educ: B.A., 1961, M.A., 1964, Univ. of Zagreb. Publs: Traganje za blizinama (In Search of Closeness), 1971; Žena i Crkva (Woman & Church), 1973; Ti nisi sišao s križa (You didn't Come Down from the Cross), 1974; Da bi i oni živjeli (They Want to Live Too), 1974. Contbr. to: Telegram; Ency. Moderna; Kana; Glas Koncila; Marulić; Crkva u svijetu; Obnovljeni život. Mbrships: Soc. of Croatian Lit. Transls.; Bd., Croatian Lit. Soc. of St. Cyrillus & Methodius; Int. Assn. of Women & Home Page Jrnlsts. Address: Amruševa 9/1, 41000 Zagreb, Yugoslavia.

MATLOFF, Maurice, b. 18 June 1915, NYC, USA. Historian. Educ: B.A., Columbia Coll., N.Y., 1936; M.A., 1937, Ph.D., 1956, Harvard Univ.; Cert., Russian Area Studies, Yale Univ., 1944. Publs: Washington Command Post (contbr.), 1951; Strategic Planning for Coalition Warfare, vol. I, 1941-42 (co-author), 1953, vol. II, 1943-44 (author), 1959; Command Decisions (co-author), 1959; Total War & Cold War (co-author), 1962; Recent Interpretations in American History (co-author), 1962; Readings in Russian History (co-author), 1962; Theory & Practice of War (co-author), 1965; D-Day (co-author), 1971; Soldiers & Statesmen (co-author), 1973. Gen. Ed., American Military History, 1969; contbr. to var. jrnls. Recip., Meritorious Civilian Service Medal, 1965. Address: 4109 Dewmar Ct., Kensington, MD 20975, USA.

MATSON, Emerson, N., b. 23 May 1926, Seattle, Wash., USA. Public Relations Consultant. Educ: Univ. of Wash.; Metropol. Bus. Coll. Publs: Longhouse Legends, 1968; Legends of the Great Chiefs, 1972; Agricl. Motion Picture Scripts inclng. Partners in Wheat, 1974. Contbr. to: Former newspaper Ed. Mbr., Seattle Free Lance Writers. Hons: 1st Prize, Trade-fiction sect., Phila. Book Show, (for Longhouse Legends), 1969; MS of Longhouse Legends included in Kerlan Collect., Walter Lib., Univ. of Minn., 1971. Address: 11015 Bingham Ave. E., Tacoma, WA 98446, USA.

MATSSON, Ragnar, b. 15 Oct. 1913, Stockholm, Sweden. Teacher. Educ: Ph.D. Publs: Tystnad klockan tio, 1955; Sommaren är ljuvlig för ungdomen, 1957; Berättaren i Mangskog, 1970. Contbr. to: Horisont; Nordisk Tidskrift; Svensk litteraturtidskrift. Mbr., Swedish Authors Union. Address: Hangarvägen 3/2, 183 62 Täby, Sweden.

MATSUI, Tadashi, b. 5 Oct. 1926, Kyoto, Japan. Publisher. Educ: Grad., Doshisha Univ. Publs: What is a Picture Book?, 1973. Mbrships: Organizer, Int. Comm. Biennale of Illustrations, Bratislava; Japan Book Publrs. Assn.; Working Comm., Tokyo Book Dev. Ctr., UNESCO; Editol. Soc. of Japan. Hons: Sankei Award for Children's Books, 1965; Silver Plaque (awarded by Czech. in connection w. the B.I.B.), 1974. Address: 1-5 Kugayama 1-chome, Suginami-ku, Tokyo, Japan.

MATSUMOTO, Shigeharu, b. 2 Oct. 1899, Osaka, Japan. Writer; Business Executive. Educ: B.A.; Univs. of

Tokyo, Yale, Vienna, Geneva & Wisconsin. Publs. incl: (Ed.) (In Japanese) A Documentary History of American People, 1950-58; (transl.) Albert Thomas' Histoire Anecdotique du Travail, 1928; C. A. Beard's The Republic, 2 vols., 1948-9; A basic History of the United States (w. K. Kishimura), 2 vols., 1954-56; Lectures on aspects of American Culture by D. Riesman, 1962. Mbrships: Inst. of Asian Econ. Affairs; Pres., Japanese Assn. for Am. Studies, 1952-67; Bd., Japan Broadcasting Corp. Recip., First Class Order of the Sacred Treasure. Address: Int. House of Japan, 11-16, 5-chome, Roppongi, Minato-ku, Tokyo, Japan.

MATTHEWS, J(ohn) H., b. 11 Sept. 1930, Swansea, UK. University Professor. Educ: B.A., Wales, 1949; B.A., 1951; Dr. de l'Univ., Montpellier, France, 1955. Publs. incl: Les deux Zola, 1957; Péret's Score: Vingt Poèmes de Benjamin Péret, 1965; An Introduction to Surrealism, 1965; An Anthology of French Surrealist Poetry, 1966; André Breton, 1967; Surrealist Poetry in France, 1969; Surrealism & Film, 1969; Theatre in Dada & Surrealism, 1974; The Custom-House of Desire: A Half Century of Surrealist Stories, 1975; Benjamin Péret, 1975. Contbr. to: Symposium (Ed., 1965-); Ed. Bd. Mbr., Books Abroad, Dada/Surrealism, Phases (Paris), etc. Address: 123 Pine Ridge Rd., Fayetteville, NY 13066, USA.

MATTHYSSEN, Joannes Michael, pen name, MARYNEN, Joannes, b. 20 Apr. 1902, Borgerhout-Antwerp, Belgium. Bank Director. Educ: special studies related to commerce & fin. Publs. incl: (in sev. langs.): Vluchtende Verten, 1961; Amerika-Impressies, 1962; Kosmos, 1962; Spiralen, 1964; Stemmen, 1965; Kontinenten, 1965; Diagonaal, 1966; Spektraal, 1968; Intermezzo, 1970; Integraal, 1971; Universum, 1972; Fataal, 1972; Horizonten, 1973; Stimmen, 1974. Contbr. to num. jrnls. Mbr., sev. lit. orgs. Recip. num. state & poetry awards & hons. Address: Cederlaan 4, B — 2610 Wilrijk, Belgium.

MATTINGLEY, Christobel Rosemary, b. 26 Oct. 1931, Adelaide, Australia. Librarian; Writer. Educ: B.A., Univ. of Tas.; Cert of Proficiency, Lib. Trng. Schl., Pub. Lib. of Vict.; Registration Cert., Lib. Assn. of Aust. Publs. incl: Windmill at Magpie Creek, 1971; The Picnic Dog, 1970; Worm Weather, 1971; Emu Kite, 1972; The Surprise Mouse, 1974; The Battle of the Galah Trees, 1974; Show & Tell, 1974. Contbr. to Aust. Children's Libs. Newsletter. Mbrships: Assoc. Lib. Assn. of Aust.; Aust. Soc. of Authors; Children's Book Coun. of Aust. Hons. incl: Highly Commended, Children's Book of Yr. Award, Aust., 1972; Aust. Lit. Bd. Fellowship, 1975. Address: 18 Allendale Grove, Stonyfell, S.A., Australia 5066.

MATTSON, Asko Erik Vilhelm, pen name MARTINHEIMO, Asko, b. 28 Sept. 1934, Finland. Author; School Teacher. Publs: (for young people) Tulvanlityn päämaja, 1965; Taivas rautaa, 1966; Melkein seitsemän, 1967; Polttaa polttaa..., 1968; Pilkku päässä, 1970; Pääkallokiitäjä, 1971; Etäisyys M 31, 1973; also 2 TV & 7 radio plays for young people. Hons: State Prizes, 1969 & 1972; H. C. Andersen Dip. of Merit, Int. Bd. on Books for Young People, 1971. Address: Myllärinkatu 6 A 9, 37100 Nokia, Finland.

MATUTE, Ana Maria, b. 26 July 1925, Barcelona, Spain. Novelist. Num. publs. incl: Los Abel, 1948; Pequeno Teatro, 1954; Los hijos muertos, 1958; Tres y un sueno, 1961; Algunos muchachos, 1968; La torre vigia, 1971; Children's books — El pais de la pizarra, 1956; Paulina, 1960; Caballito loco, 1960; Elm polizon de 'Ulisses', 1965. Contbr. to periodicals. Hons. incl: Cafe Gijon Prize, 1952; Planeta Prize, 1954; Critics Prize, 1959; Fastenrath Prize, Royal Spanish Acad., 1969; Runner-up, Int. Hans Christian Andersen Award, 1970; Highly Commended Author, ibid, 1972. Address: Santiago Rusiñol 15, Sitges, Spain.

MATZ, Samuel Adam, b. 1 July 1924, Carmi, Ill., USA. Food Scientist. Educ: B.A., Evansville Univ., 1948; M.S., Kan. State Univ., 1950; Ph.D., Univ. of Calif., 1958. Publs: Chemistry & Technology of Cereals as Food & Feed, 1959; Bakery Technology & Engineering, 1960, 1972; Water in Foods, 1965; Food Texture, 1962; Cereal Science, 1969; Cereal Technology, 1970; Cookie & Cracker Technology, 1968. Address: 916 Kehoe Dr., St. Charles, IL 60174, USA.

MAUGHAM, (Lord) Robin, b. 17 May 1916, London, UK. Writer. Educ: B.A., Trinity Hall, Cambridge Univ. Publs. incl: Come to Dust, 1945; Nomad, 1947; Approach to Palestine, 1947; North African Notebook, 1947; The Servant, 1948; Behind the Mirror, 1955; The Man with Two

Shadows, 1958; The Slaves of Timbuktu, 1961; November Reef, 1962; The Green Shade, 1966; Somerset & All the Maughams, 1966; The Second Window, 1968; The Wrong People, 1970; Escape from the Shadows, 1972; The Last Encounter, 1972; The Barrier, 1973; The Black Tent & Other Stories, 1974; The Sign, 1974. Mbr.. Garrick Club. Address: Casa Cala Prada, Santa Eulalia del Rio, Ibiza, Baleares, Spain.

MAUGHAN, A. M., b. Darlington, Co. Durham. Company Director. Publs: Monmouth Harry, UK & USA, 1956; Young Pitt, 1974. Contbr. to: Holiday; Woman's Jrnl. Mbr., Engl. Speaking Union. Address: 2 Ryton Sq., Sunderland SR2 7UF, UK.

MAULNIER, Thierry, pen name of TALAGRAND, Jacques Louis, b. 1 Oct. 1909. Journalist; Playwright. Educ: Ecole Normale Supérieure, Paris. Publs. incl: (plays) Antigone, 1944; Jeanne & les Juges, 1949; La Maison de la Nuit, 1953; Le Sexe & le Néant, 1960; Signe du feu, 1960; (prose) Nietzche, 1933; Racine, 1934; Violence & Conscience, 1945; la Ville au fond de la mer, 1967; Lettre aux Américains, 1968; l'Honneur d'être juif, (w. G. Prouteau), 1970. Contbr. to: l'Action Française; Figaro; Combat; La Revue de Paris; Co-Fndr., La Table Ronde. Mbr., French Acad. Hons: Legion of Honour; Grand Prix, French Acad., 1959; Prix Pelman, 1959. Address: 3 rue Yves-Carriou, 92 Marnes-la-Coquette, France.

MAURER, David W., b. 12 Apr. 1906, Wellston, Ohio, USA. Professor of Linguistics. Educ: B.A., 1928, M.A., 1929, Ph.D., 1936, Ohio State Univ.; post-doct. studies, Univs. of Mich. & Mexico. Publs. incl: The Big Con, 1940, rev. ed., 1962; Whiz Mob, 1964; Mencken, The American Language (abridged w. Raven McDavid), 1964; Narcotics & Narcotic Addiction, 4th ed., 1973; The American Confidence Man, 1974; Kentucky Moonshine, 1974. Contbr. to: Ency. Britannica; Ency. Americana; num. books, symposia, profl. jrnls., etc. Mbrships. incl: MLA; Am. Dialect Soc. (Pres., 1968-69). Hons. incl: Fulbright Professorships at Univs. in Germany & Italy. Address: 4124 Nachand Lane, Louisville, KY 40218, USA.

MAURIAC, Claude, b. 25 Apr. 1914. Journalist; Critic. Educ: D.Jur. Publs. incl: (essays) Aimer Balzac; André Breton; Marcel Proust par Lui-Même; Conversation avec André Gide; Hommes & Idées d'Aujourd'hui; La Littérature Contemporaine; (novels) Toutes Les Femmes Sont Fatales, 1957; Le Dîner en ville, 1959; L'Agrandissement, 1963; (plays) La Conversation, 1964; Femmes Fatales, 1966; l'Oubli, 1966; Ici, Maintenant, 1971; Un autre de Gaulle 1944-54, 1971. Contbr. to: Figaro; Figaro Lit. Hons: Prix Sainte-Beuve, 1949; Prix Médicis, 1959.

MAXEINER, Rudolf, b. 20 Jan. 1924, Frankfurt/Main, Germany. Journalist; Chief of Press. Educ: Agricultural Engineer. Publs: Über Zeit und Raum: Die Geschichte des Raiffeisenverbandes Rhein-Main, 1873-1973, 1973. Contbr. to: DLG — Mitteilungen; Der Hessenbauer; Raiffeisenkurier Rhein-Main; Hessen Radio. Mbr., Verband deutscher Agrarjournalisten. Address: D 6079 Sprendlingen, Kurtschumacherring 80, W. Germany.

MAXWELL, (Ian) Robert, b. 10 June 1923, Selo Slatina, Czechoslovakia. Scientific Publisher; Former M.P. Publs: Ed., Information USSR, 1963; Ed., The Economics of Nuclear Power, 1965; Public Sector Purchasing, 1968; Man Alive (co-author), 1968; (films, co-prod.). Mozart's Don Giovanni, 1954; Bolshoi Ballet, 1957; Swan Lake, 1968. Mbr., Coun. of Europe (Vice-Chmn., Sci. & Technol. Comm., 1968). Kennedy Fellow, Harvard Univ., USA, 1971. Address: Headington Hill Hall, Oxford OX3 0BW, UK.

MAXWELL, William, b. 16 Aug. 1908, Lincoln, Ill., USA. Journalist. Educ: B.A., Univ. of Ill., Urbana, 1930; M.A., Harvard Univ., 1931. Publs: (novels) Bright Center of Heaven, 1934; They Came Like Swallows, USA & UK, 1937; The Folded Leaf, USA, 1945, UK, 1946; Time Will Darken It, USA, 1948, UK, 1949; The Château, 1961; (short stories) Co-author, Stories, 1956; The Old Man at the Railroad Crossing & Other Tales, 1966; (non-fiction) The Heavenly Tenants, 1946; Ancestors, 1971. Contbr. to New Yorker (staff mbr., 1936–). Mbr.. Nat. Inst. Arts & Letters. Hons. incl: Award, Friends of Am. Writers, 1938. Address: 544 E. 86th St., N.Y., NY 10028, USA.

MAY, Charles Paul, b. 23 Nov. 1920, Bedford, Iowa, USA. Writer; Photographer. Educ: B.A., Drake Univ., 1947; M.A., Okla. State Univ., 1948. Publs. incl: Box Turtle Lives in Armor, 1960; A Book of Canadian Animals, 1962; Women in Aeronautics, 1962; A Second Book of Canadian Animals, 1964; Animals of the Far North, 1964; Central America, 1966; A Book of Canadian Birds, 1967; Great Cities of Canada, 1967; The Early Indians, 1971; Stranger in the Storm, 1973; Oceania, 1973; Probation, 1974. Contbr. to: N.Y. Times; St. Louis Post-Dispatch; Pitts. Post-Gazette; Chgo. Tribune; San Fran. Examiner; Toronto Star; Toronto Telegram; Ottawa Citizen; Vancouver Sun; Lib. Jrnl.; Saturday Night; etc. Mbrships: Pres., Forum of Writers for Young People, 1968-69; Dir., St. David's Christian Writers' Conf., 1974-75. Recip., 2nd Prize, Juvenile, 27th Annual Book Show, Phila., 1972. Address: P.O. Box 548, Ansonia Stn., N.Y., NY 10023, USA.

MAY, Derwent James, b. 29 Apr. 1930, Eastbourne, UK. Journalist; Author. Educ: M.A.(Oxon.). Publs: (novels) The Professionals, 1964; Dear Parson, 1969; The Laughter in Djakarta, 1973. Contbr. to: Lit. Ed., Listener, 1965—; Observer; Encounter; Times Lit. Supplement; etc. Address: 201 Albany St., London NW1, UK.

MAY, Gita, b. 16 Sept. 1929, Brussels, Belgium. Professor of French Literature. Educ: B.A., Hunter Coll., NYC, 1953; M.A., 1954, Ph.D., 1957, Columbia Univ. Publs: Diderot & Bandelaire, Critiques d'Art, 1957, 3rd ed., 1973; De Jean-Jacques Rousseau à Madame Roland, 1964, 2nd ed., 1974; Madame Roland & the Age of Revolution, 1970. Contbr. to: Romantic Review (Mbr., Ed. Bd.); Publs. of MLA; French Review; L'Esprit Créateur; Symposium. Hons. incl: Chevalier, Ordre des Palmes Académiques, France, 1968; Van Amringe Disting. Book Award, 1971. Address: 404 W. 116th St., N.Y., NY 10027, USA.

MAY, Robin (Robert Stephen), b. 26 Dec. 1929, Deal, Kent, UK. Writer; Journalist; Former Actor. Publs: Operamania, 1966; Theatremania, 1967; The Wit of the Theatre, 1969; Who's Who in Shakespeare, 1972; Companion to the Theatre, 1973; The American West, 1974; Wolfe's Army, 1974. Contbr. to: Contemporary Review; Scottish Opera Mag.; Look & Learn; Annals of Wyoming. Mbrships. incl: Nat. Union of Jrnlsts.; English Westerners' Soc. Address: 23 Malcolm Rd., London SW19 4AS, UK.

MAYER, Martin, b. 14 Jan. 1928, NYC, USA. Writer. Educ: A.B., Harvard Univ., 1947. Publs: Wall Street: Men & Money, 1955; The Experts (UK title, The Candidate), 1955; Madison Avenue, USA, 1958; The Schools, 1961; The Lawyers, 1967; All You Know Is Facts, 1969; About Television, 1972; The Bankers, 1975. Contbr. to: Esquire; Fortune; Commentary; Harper's; Cosmopolitan; Think; Art News; High Fidelity; Musical Am.; N.Y. Times Mag.; Life; Saturday Evening Post; TV Guide; etc. Mbrships: Authors' Guild; Book Table, Century. Address: P.O. Box 478, Shelter Island, NY 11964, USA.

MAYER, Sydney Louis, b. 2 Aug. 1937, Chgo., Ill., USA. Lecturer & Historian. Educ: B.A., 1962, M.A., 1963, Univ. of Mich.; Yale Univ., 1963-65; London Schl. of Econs., UK, 1966-71. Publs: MacArthur, 1971; MacArthur in Japan, 1973; Directors Guide to the USA (w. J. A. Holmes), 1973; European Manuscript Sources of the American Revolution, 1974; Co-Ed., The World of South East Asia, 1970; Ed., World War One, 1973; Ed., World War Two, 1973; Compiler, World War One, & World War Two (w. A. J. P. Taylor), 1974. Contbr. to: Hist. of WW1; Hist. of the 20th Century; Hist. of WWII; Historia; War Monthly; Cons. Ed., Ballantine's Hist. of the Violent Century series. Mbrships: F.R.G.S.; Savage Club. Address: 38 Glebe Place, London SW3, UK.

MAYER-KOENIG, Wolfgang, b. 28 Mar. 1946, Vienna, Austria. Secretary to Austrian Federal Chancellor; Author & Political Writer. Educ: Study of Classic, German Philol. & Hist. of Art. Publs: Sichbare Pavillons, (poetry), 1969; Stichmarken (long poems), 1969; Vorläufige Versagung (selection), 1975. Contbr. to: Basler Nachrichten; Salzburger Nachrichten; Die Zukunft, Vienna; Neue Wege; Anstoss und Aspekte; Colloquia Germanica, Ky., USA; Der Neue Tag; Kölnische Rundschau; Berliner Tagesspiegel; Rheinische Post; Meanjin Quarterly, Australia; num. TV & radio progs. Mbrships. incl: Int. Robert Musil Soc. (Exec. Dir.); Fndr., Austrian Univ. Cultural Ctr. "Literarische Situation"; var. educl. orgs. Recip., Theodor Körner Prize for Lit., 1973. Address: A-1170 Vienna, Hernalser Gürtel 41, Austria.

MAYES, Edythe Beam, b. 9 May 1902, Kingsmountain, N.C., USA. Writer. Educ: Lenoir Rhyne Coll.; Juilliard

Schl. of Music; Columbia Univ.; Grad. Schl. of Writing, N.Y. Univ. Publs: Washington — God's Workshop, 1973; Gift, 1973; Butterflies, 1974. Contbr. to var. lit. publs. Mbrships: Poetry Soc. of S.C.; Am. Poetry Fellowship Soc.; Am. Poetry League; United Amateur Press; Life Danae Mbr., Clover Int. Poetry Assn. Hons: Poem of Yr. Award, 1970; Writer of Yr. Award, 1971; Cert. of Merit for Poem, 1972; 2 Prizes for Poems, Clover Int. Poetry Competition, 1974. Address: 358 Clark Ave., Staten Island, NY 10306, USA.

MAYFIELD, Julian, b. 6 June 1928, Greer, S.C., USA. Writer; University Teacher. Educ: Lincoln Univ., Pa. Publs: (novels) The Hit, USA, 1957, UK, 1959; The Long Night, USA, 1958, UK, 1960; The Grand Parade, USA, 1961, UK, 1962; (play) 417, 1954; (screenplay) Co-author, Uptight, 1968; Ed., The World Without the Bomb: The Papers of the Accra Assembly, 1963. Contbr. to African Review (Fndg. Ed., 1964-66). Recip., Rabinowitz Fellowship, 1967. Address: Chaka Farm, R.F.D. 2, Spencer, NY 14883, USA.

MAYHEW, Alan Harding, b. 13 Dec. 1934, Hayes, UK. Architect. Educ: Dip., Arch., Polytechnic, London; Dip., Tropical Studies, Archtl. Assn., London. Publs: Manual of Tropical Housing & Building: Part 1, Climatic Design (co-author), 1974. Contbr. to: Archt.'s Jrnl.; Jrnl. of the Univ. of Cape Coast, Ghana. Mbrships: Assoc., Royal Inst. of Brit. Archts.; Archtl. Assn.; Assoc., Ghana Inst. of Archts. Address: 10 Danby Terrace, Exmouth, Devon, UK.

MAYHEW, David Raymond, b. 18 May 1937, Putnam, Conn., USA. College Professor of Political Science; Author. Educ: B.A., Amherst Coll., 1958; Ph.D., Harvard Univ., 1964. Publs: Party Loyalty Among Congressmen: The Difference Between Democrats & Republicans 1937-1952, 1966; Congress: The Electoral Connection, 1974. Address: Political Science Dept., Yale Univ., New Haven, CT 06520, USA.

MAYNARD, Merrill A., b. 29 Mar. 1918, Newburyport, Mass., USA. Poet. Educ: Harvard Univ. Publs: They Sing in the Night, 1953; Come Walk with Me, 1956; My Cup Runneth Over, 1973. Mbrships: New Engl. Poetry Club; Poetry Soc. of Am.; Dir., Braille Poets' Guild. Address: 171 Washington St., Taunton, MA, USA.

MAYNE, Richard John, b. 2 Apr. 1926, London, UK. Author. Educ: B.A., M.A., Ph.D., Trinity Coll., Cambridge. Publs: The Community of Europe, 1962; The Institutions of the European Community, 1968; The Recovery of Europe, 1970; The Europeans, 1972; Europe Tomorrow (Ed.), 1972; The New Atlantic Challenge (Ed.), forthcoming; Father of Europe, forthcoming. Contbr. to: Encounter; Times Lit. Supplement; Listener; New Statesman; etc. Mbrships: Trustee, 1964—, Dir., 1971-73, Fed. Trust for Educ. & Rsch. Address: c/o Commission of the European Communities, 20 Kensington Palace Gdns., London W8 4QQ, UK.

MAYO, Bernard, b. 9 July 1920, Leicester, UK. Professor of Philosophy. Educ: B.A., M.A., Magdalen Coll., Oxford. Publs: Logic of Personality, 1952; Ethics & the Moral Life, 1956; Ed., Analysis, 1956-65; Ed., Philos. Quarterly, 1973-. Contbr. to num. philos. jrnls. Mbrships: Aristotalian Soc.; Brit. Soc. for Philos. of Sci. Address: 4 Maynard Rd., St. Andrews, Fife, UK.

MAYR, Ernst, b. 5 July 1904, Kempten, Germany. Professor of Zoology. Educ: Cand.Med., Univ. of Greifswald, 1925; Ph.D., Univ. of Berlin, 1926. Publs. incl: Systematics & Origin of Species, 1942; Methods & Principles of Systematic Zoology, 1953; Animal Species & Evolution, 1963; Principles of Systematic Zoology, 1969; Populations, Species & Evolution, 1970. Mbrships. incl: Pres., Am. Ornithols. Union, 1956-57; Pres., Am. Soc. of Naturalists, 1962-63; Pres., Soc. of Systematic Zool., 1966. Hons. incl: Walker Prize, Boston Mus. of Sci., Mass., 1971; Nat. Medal of Science, 1970; var. acad. medals & hon. degrees. Address: Harvard Univ., Museum of Comparative Zoology, Cambridge, MA 02138, USA.

MAZLISH, Bruce, b. 15 Sept. 1923, NYC, USA. Historian. Educ: B.A., Columbia Coll., 1944; M.A., 1947; Ph.D., 1955; Columbia Univ. Publs: The Western Intellectual Tradition: From Leonardo to Hegel (co-author), 1960; Psychoanalysis & History, 1963; The Railroad & the Space Program: An Exploration in Historical Analysis, 1965; The Riddle of History: The Great Speculators from Vico to Freud, 1966; In Search of Nixon: A Psychohistorical Study, 1972; James & John Stuart Mill.

Father & Son in the 19th Century, 1975. Contbr. to jrnls. Fellow, Am. Acad. of Arts & Scis. Recip., acad. hons. Address: 3 Channing Circle, Cambridge, MA 02138, USA.

MAZOUR, Anatola G(regory), b. 24 May 1900, Kiev, Russia. Emeritus Professor of History. Educ: A.B., Univ. of Neb., 1929; M.A., Yale Univ., 1930; Ph.D., Univ. of Calif., Berkeley, 1934. Publs: The First Russian Revolution 1825; Outline of Modern Russian Historiography; Russia: Past & Present; Finland Between East & West; The Romanov Dynasty; Men & Nations (w. J. People); Economic Development of the SSSR; The Writing of History of the Soviet Union; Women in Exile: Wives of the Decembrists. Contbr. to: Am. Hist. Review; Mod. Hist.; Le Monde; Review of Ctrl. European Affairs; Pacific Hist. Review. Mbrships. incl: Am. Hist. Soc.; AAUP; Am. Slavic Soc. Recip., Hon. LL.D., Univ. of Neb., 1963. Address: 781 Frenchman's Rd., Stanford Univ., CA 94305, USA.

MBITI, John Samuel, b. 30 Nov. 1931, Kitui, Kenya. Clergyman; Professor. Educ: B.A. (London), Makerere Univ., Kampala, Uganda; A.B., Th.B., Barrington Coll., R.I., USA; Ph.D., Cambridge, UK. Publs: Akamba Stories, 1966; African Religions & Philosophy, 1969; Poems of Nature & Faith, 1969; Concepts of God in Africa, 1970; New Testament Eschatology in an African Background, 1971; The Crisis of Mission in Africa, 1971; Love & Marriage in Africa, 1973; The Voice of Nine Bible Trees, 1973; Introduction to African Religion, 1975; The Prayers of African Religion, 1975. Contbr. to: Worldview; Presence; Africa Theol. Jrnl.; etc. Mbr., Studiorum Novi Testamenti Soc. Recip., Hon. L.H.D., Barrington Coll., R.I., 1973. Address: The Ecumenical Inst., 1298 Caligny, Switz.

MEACHAM, Harry Monroe, b. 19 July 1901, Petersburg, Va., USA. Writer; Critic. Educ: St. Johns Coll., Va. C'wlth. Univ. Publs: The Caged Panther: Ezra Pound at St. Elizabeth's, 1967; 100 Years of Alaska Poetry (co-ed.), Lyric Virginia Today, vol. II, (co-ed.). Contbr. to: Poetry Critic, Richmond (Va.) News Leader; Ed., The Detonator; Assoc. Ed., Paideuma; etc. Mbrships. incl: Poetry Soc. of Am.; Past Pres., Poetry Soc. of Va., Va. Writers Club; Hon. Life Mbr., New England Poetry Club, Poetry Soc. of N.H.; Chmn., Advsry. Bd. for Affiliated Socs., Acad. of Am. Poets. Hons: Hon. Chancellor, Nat. Fedn. of State Poetry Socs., 1969-70; Disting. Serv. to Poetry Citation, Lyric Mag., 1970. Address: 350 N.Blvd., Petersburg, VA 23803, USA.

MEAD, Russell, b. 1 Jan. 1935, Pueblo, Colo., USA. Educational Administrator. Educ: A.B., Dartmouth Coll., USA. Publs: If a Heart Rings, Answer, 1964; Tell me Again about Snow White, 1966. Contbr. to var. educl. jrnls. Mbrships: Assn. of Am. Rhodes Schlrs.; Nat. Assn. of Media Educators. Recip., Elinor Frost Playwright, 1956. Address: 238 Main St., Concord, MA 01742, USA.

MEAD, Stella. Journalist; Author. Educ: Univs. of Toulouse & Berlin. Publs: The Land of Legends & Heroes; The Land of Happy Hours; The Land Where Stories Grow; The Land Where Dreams Come True; Princes & Fairies; Great Stories from Many Lands; The Land of Never-Grow-Old; Rama & Sita; The Shining Way; Morning Light; Golden Day; Under the Sun; Traveller's Joy; Magic Journeys. Contbr. to var. Engl. & Am. jrnls. Address: c/o NatWest Bank, Wembley Park, Middx., UK.

MEADE, James Edward, b. 23 June 1907. University Professor. Educ: M.A., Oriel Coll., Oxford; M.A., Trinity Coll., Cambridge. Publs. incl: Public Works in their International Aspect, 1933; The Economic Base of a Durable Peace, 1940; Planning & the Price Mechanism, 1948; A Geometry of International Trade, 1952; Problems of Economic Union, 1953; The Control of Inflation, 1958; The Growing Economy, 1968; The Controlled Economy, 1972. Mbrships: Am. Econ. Assn.; Am. Acad. of Arts & Sci.; Coun., Royal Econ. Soc., (VP, 1966—). Hons: C.B., 1947; F.B.A., 1951. Address: 38 High St., Little Shelford, Cambs., UK.

MEALEY, Michael Palmer, b. 16 May 1940, Oakland, Calif., USA. Journalist. Contbr. to: Oakland (Calif.) Tribune; San Fran. Examiner; Concord (Calif.) Transcript; currently Tokyo Bur. Chief, McGraw Hill World News. Mbrships: For. Corres. Club of Japan; Am. Newspaper Guild. Recip., Bronze Star for coverage of Viet Nam war for Pacific Stars & Stripes, US Army, 1965. Address: McGraw Hill World News, Rm. 1528 Kasumigaseki Bldg., 3-2-5 Kasumigaseki, Chiyoda ku, Tokyo, Japan.

MEANS, Florence Crannell, b. 15 May 1891, Baldwinsville, N.Y., USA. Author. Educ: Univ. of Denver; McPherson Coll. Publs: 41 books inclng. Rafaelo & the Consuelo; A Candle in the Mist, 1931; Rainbow Bridge; Tangled Waters, 1936; Shuttered Windows, 1938; Across the Fruited Plain; Teresita of the Valley; The Moved-Outers, 1945; The House under the Hill; The Silver Fleece; The Rains Will Come; Knock at the Door, 1957; Borrowed Brother; But I Am Sara; It Takes All Kinds; Our Cup Is Broken; Smith Valley, 1973. Hons. incl: Nat. Award, Child Study Assn., 1945; Emmy Award, 1957. Address: 595 Baseline Rd., Boulder, CO, USA.

MEANS, Marianne Hansen, b. 13 June 1934, Sioux City, Iowa, USA. Political Columnist. Educ: B.A., Univ. of Neb., 1956; Geo. Wash. Univ. Publs: The Woman in the White House, 1963. Mbrships: White House Corres.'s Assn.; Women's Nat. Press; Phi Beta Kappa; Delta Delta Delta; Theta Sigma Phi; Kappa Tau Alpha; Gamma Alpha Phi Club. Recip., Front Page Award, N.Y. Newspaper Women, 1962. Address: 1521 31st St., NW Washington, DC 20007, USA.

MEARES, Ainslie Dixon, b. 3 Mar. 1910, Melbourne, Vic., Australia. Psychiatrist. Educ: M.D., B. Agric. Sci., Univ. of Melbourne; D.P.M.; Fellow, Aust. & NZ Coll. of Psychiatrists. Publs: The Medical Interview, 1957; Hypnography, 1957; The Door of Serenity, 1958; Marriage & Personality, 1958; The Introvert, 1958; Shapes of Sanity, 1960; A System of Medical Hypnosis, 1961, 2nd ed., 1972; The Management of the Anxious Patient, 1963; Relief without Drugs, 1967, 2nd ed., 1969; Where Magic Lies, 1968; Strange Places, Simple Truths, 1969, 2nd ed., 1973; Student Problems & a Guide to Study, 1969; The Way Up, 1970; Dialogue with Youth, 1973; The New Woman, 1974. Address: 99 Spring St., Melbourne, Vic., Australia 3000.

MECHTEL, Angelika, b. 26 Aug. 1943, Dresden, Germany. Author. Publs: Gegen Eis und Flut (Poems), 1963; Die feinen Totengräber (Stories), 1968; Kaputte Spiele (Novel), 1970; Hochhausgeschichten (Stories), 1971; Friss Vogel (Novel), 1972; Das gläserne Paradies (Novel), 1973; Die Blindgängerin (Novel), 1974. Contbr. to: Publikation; Simplicissimus; Kürbiskern. Mbr., German PEN; Verband Deutscher Schriftsteller; Dortmunder Gruppe 61. Hons: Förderpreis für Literatur, Nuremberg, 1970; Förderpreis des Kulturkreises im BDI, 1970; Tukan-Literaturpreis, Munich, 1971. Address: 8061 Einsbach/München, Haus 36, W. Germany.

MEDLICOTT, William Norton, b. 11 May 1900, Wandsworth, Surrey, UK. University Professor; Historian; Editor. Educ: M.A., D.Lit. (London), D.Litt.(Wales); Univ. Coll. & Inst. of Histl. Rsch., Univ. of London. Publs. incl: The Congress of Berlin & After, 1938; The Economic Blockade, Vol. I, 1952, Vol. II, 1959; Contemporary England 1914-64, 1967; Bismarck & Germany, (co-author), 1971; The Lion's Tail: An Anthology of Criticism & Abuse (co-author), 1971. Contbr. to: Engl. Histl. Review; Hist.; Int. Affairs; etc. Mbrships: var. profl. orgs.; ed. bds. of sev. profl. jrnls. Hons. incl: Fellow, Univ. Coll., London, 1960—. Address: 2 Cartref, Ellesmere Road, Weybridge, Surrey, UK.

MEDVEI, Victor Cornelius, b. 1905, Budapest, Hungary. Associate Chief Assistant (Endocrine), St. Bartholomew's Hospital, London, 1941—; Principal Medical Officer, H.M. Treasury. Educ: St. Bartholomew's Hospital; M.D.; F.R.C.P. Publs: Mental & Physical Aspects of Pain, 1949; The Medical & Psychological Aspects of Scientific Work, 1964. Contbr. to: Chambers Ency.; Ency. of Sports Medicine; Lancet; Practitioner. Mbrships: Pres., Harveian Soc. of London; PEN. Address: 38 Westmoreland Terrace, London SW1, UK.

MEEK, Ronald Lindley, b. 27 July 1917, Wellington, NZ. Professor of Economics. Educ: LL.M., 1939, M.A., 1946, Univ. of NZ; Ph.D., Cambridge Univ., 1949. Publs: Studies in the Labour Theory of Value, 1958; The Economics of Physiocracy, 1962; Economics & Ideology, 1967; Figuring Out Society, 1972; Turgot on Progress, Sociology & Economics, 1973; Precursors of Adam Smith, 1973. Contbr. to: Econ. Jrnl.; Economica; Scottish Jrnl. of Pol. Econ.; Sci. & Soc.; Hist. of Pol. Econ.; etc. Mbrships: Ed. Bd., Adam Smith's Works & Correspondence, 1958—; E. Midlands Reg. Econ. Planning Coun., 1967—; Bd. Dirs., Leicester Theatre Trust. Address: 27 The Fairway, Oadby, Leics., UK.

MEEUS, Marcel, pen name CREMER, Samuel, b. 15 Sept. 1934, Leuven, Belgium. Journalist. Educ: Langs.; Jrnlsm.; Inst. of Hort. Contbr. to: Libelle Rosita; De Boer; Levend Land; Bij de Haard; Tuinbouwberichten; Fleur; Sect. Gardeners' News. Mbrships: Union Presse Periodique Belge; Belgian sect., Fedn. of Int. Agricl. Jrnlsts. Address: Brabanconnestraat 82, B — 3000 Leuven, Belgium.

MEHAR, Mumt. b. 9 Mar. 1942, Sukkur-Sind, Pakistan. Journalist. Educ: B.A., Univ. of Sind; M.A., Univ. of Karachi. Publs: A Collection of Short Stories in Sindhi; A Collection of Articles in Sindhi. Contbr. to: Naeen Zindagi; Mehran; Sohini; Sojhro. Mbrships: Sindhi Writers Soc.; People's Literary Soc. Address: c/o Al-Karim Laundry, Ido-Lane, Tannery Rd., Layri Oits, Karachi 2, Pakistan.

MEHL, Roger Adolphe, b. 10 May 1912, Relanges, France. Professor of Ethics & Religious Sociology, University of Strasbourg. Educ: M.A.; D.Th. Publs: La Condition du Philosophe chrétien, 1947; Le Vieillissement & la Mort, 1956; La Rencontre d'Autrui, 1956; De l'Autorité des Valeurs, 1957; Société & Amour, 1961; Traité de Sociologie du Protestantisme, 1965; Pour une éthique sociale chrétienne, 1967; Les Attitudes Morales, 1971. Contbr. to sev. relig. & philosl. jrnls. Mbrships. incl: Ctrl. Comm., Ecumenical Coun. of Chs.; Societas Ethica. Hons. incl: D.D., Univ. of Glasgow, UK, 1967; D.D., Univ. of Basle, Switz., 1971. Address: 6 Rue Blessig, 67000 Strasbourg, France.

MEHNERT, Klaus, b. 10 Oct. 1906, Moscow, Russia. Writer; Radio, TV Commentator; Professor Emeritus of Political Science. Educ: Univs. of Tubingen, Munich, Berlin, Calif. (Berkeley); Ph.D., Hist., Univ. of Berlin, 1929. Publs: num. books, the following transls. into Engl. & approx. 12 other langs.: Youth in Soviet Russia, 1933; Soviet Man, 1960; Peking & Moscow, 1963; China Returns, 1972; Other Engl. transls. incl: The Russians in Hawaii: 1804-1819, 1939; Stalin Versus Marx, 1952; Peking & the New Left, 1969; Moscow & the New Left, 1975. Contbr. to jrnls. Address: 7291 Schömberg, bei Freudenstadt, W. Germany.

MEHTA, Rustam, b. 4 June 1912, Bombay, India. Chief Editor & Manager, Book Publishers. Educ: M.S., Univ. of Bombay; Ph.D., Univ. of Birmingham, UK. Publs: Handicrafts & Industrial Arts of India, 1960; Masterpieces of Indian Sculpture, 1968; Kama-Chumbana, 1969; Konarak: The Sun-Temple, 1969; Masterpieces of Indian Textiles, 1970; Masterpieces of Indian Bronzes & Metal Sculpture, 1971; The Female Form in Indian Art, 1972; Masterpieces of Indian Temples, 1974; Masterpieces of Indo-Islamic Architecture. Address: Nagin Mahal, 82 Veer Nariman Rd., Bombay 400 020, India.

MEHTA, Ved Parkash, b. 21 Mar. 1934, Lahore, India. Writer. Educ: B.A., Pomona Coll., USA, 1956; B.A., 1959, M.A., 1962, Balliol Coll., Oxford Univ., UK; M.A., Harvard Univ., USA, 1961. Publs. incl: Face to Face, 1957; Walking the Indian Streets, 1960, rev. ed., 1971; Fly & the Fly-Bottle, 1963; The New Theologian, 1966; Delinquent Chacha (novel), 1967; Portrait of India, 1970; John is Easy to Please, 1971; Daddyji, 1972; (num. eds. & transls. of works). Contbr. to: New Yorker Mag. (Staff Writer, 1961—); num. Am., Brit. & Indian newspapers & mags., 1957—. Mbrships. incl: Century Assn., NYC. Hons. incl: Secondary Educ. Annual Book Award, 1958; D.Litt., Pomona Coll., 1972. Address: c/o The New Yorker Magazine, 25 W. 43rd St., N.Y., NY 10036, USA.

MEICHSNER, Dieter, b. 14 Feb. 1928, Berlin, Germany. Writer. Educ: Berlin Univ. Publs: Versucht's nochmal mit uns!, 1948; Weisst Du, warum? 1952; Die Studenten von Berlin, 1954; num. radio plays & 16 TV plays. Mbrships: Acad. of Art, Hamburg; PEN. Hons: Schiller Prize, Baden-Württemberg, 1959; Alexander Zinn Prize, Hamburg. Address: Rögenweg 31, D-2 Hamburg 67, W. Germany.

MEIER, Gerhard (Werner), b. 20 June 1917, Niederbipp, Berne, Switz. Author. Publs: (poetry) Das Gras grünt, 1964; Im Schatten der Sonnenblumen, 1967; Einige Häuser nebenan, 1973. Prose Publs: Kübelpalmen träumen von Oasen, 1969; Es regnet in meinem Dorf, 1971; Der andere Tag, 1974. Contbr. to: Neue Zürcher Zeitung; Basler Nachrichten; Nationalzeitung; Der Bund; Weltwoche; etc. Mbrships: Bernese Authors' Assn.; Gruppe Olten (Swiss Writers' Grp.). Hons. incl: Lit. Prizes, Canton of Berne, 1964, 1968, 1971; Commission, Pro Helvetia, 1970; Award, Swiss Schuller Inst., 1970; Lit. grant, City of Bern, 1973. Address: Lehnweg 17, CH4704 Niederbipp, Switz.

MEIER, Henk J., pen names SANDERS, Robert; WARNER, Kim, b. 28 Mar. 1937, Groningen, Netherlands. Writer. Educ: dr.soc.sc. Publs. incl: Political Yearbook, 1967; Menswaardig Sterven; IJS in Het Vuur; Albainn; Ratio-Yearbook. Contbr. to var. jrnls. Mbrships. incl: Writers Union; Jrnlsts. Union. Hons. incl: Hon. Creative Award, 1970; Typ. Critical Prize, 1971; Silver chanter of Daily World, 1973. Address: P.O. Box 45, Amsterdam, Netherlands.

MEIER, Herbert, b. 29 Aug. 1928, Solothurn, Switz. Writer. Educ: Dr.Phil.; Univs. of Basle & Fribourg; Univ. of Vienna, Austria. Publs. incl: (plays) Die Barke von Gawdos, 1954; Der König von Bamako, 1960; Skorpione (TV play), 1964; Rabenspiele, 1970; Stauffer-Bern, 1974; Dunant, 1975; (novels) Ende September, 1959; Verwandtschaften, 1963; Stiefelchen, 1970; (stories) Anatomische Geschichten, 1973. Contbr. to: Neue Zurcher Zeitung, Zurich; Schweizer Monatshefte; etc. Mbrships. incl: Schweizer Schriftsteller "Gruppe Olten"; Hofmannsthal Gesellschaft, Frankfurt. Hons. incl: Bremer Literaturpreis, 1955; C. F. Meyer Preis, 1964; Preise der Stadt und des Kantons Zurich, 1957, 1969, 1970, 1972. Address: Muhlehalde 21, CH-8032 Zurich, Switzerland.

MEILEN, Wilm-Artur, pen name MEILEN, Bill, b. 16 Sept. 1932, Cardiff, UK. Associate Professor of Drama. Educ: Trinity Coll., London; F.T.C.L.; L.T.C.L.; Cardiff Coll. of Music & Drama. Publs: The Division, 1967; Moving On, 1968; The Bullpen, 1968; Eyes of Grass, 1969; K.K.K., 1969; Delta Two, 1970. Regular broadcaster, poetry progs., CKUA, Alta., Can.; Writer, TV, film, stage plays, short stories, poetry, features. Dir./Admstr., Poets of Alta. Contest, 1974. Address: 608 College Plaza II, 8210-111 St., Edmonton, Alta., Can.

MEIN, Margaret, b. 29 Feb. 1924, Preston, Lancs, UK. Lecturer in French. Educ: B.A., Lady Margaret Hall, Oxford, 1945; Dip. in Educ., Oxford, 1946; B.A., London Ext. Fr. Cl., 1950; Ph.D., Bedford Coll., London Univ., 1953. Publs: Proust's Challenge to Time, 1962; A Foretaste of Proust: A Study of Proust & his Precursors, 1974. Contbr. to: Adam; Aust. Jrnl. of French Studies; Bulletin de la Société des Amis de Proust; Comp. Lit.; Entretiens sur Gide; Entretiens sur Valéry; L'Esprit Createur; Europe; Forum for Mod. Lang. Studies; French Review; French Studies; Mod. Lang. Review; Romantic Review. Mbrships. incl: MLA; Soc. of French Studies; Société des Amis de Proust; Société des Amis de Gide. Address: 63 Manor Rd., Old Woodstock, Oxford OX7 1XR, UK.

MELAMED, Zhak Nissim, pen name DRAGOMIR, Assenov, b. 15 May 1926, Mihaylovgrad, Bulgaria. Writer. Publs: (in Bulgarian) (novels) The Large Stone House, 1963; The Fruit of the Winds, 1966; A Profession for Angels, 1974; (plays) Roses for Doctor Shomov, 1967; Birthday, 1965; Saturday Evening Walk, 1969; Hot Nights in Arkadia, 1970; Examinatioons, 1970. Contbr. to: PlamAk; September. Mbr., Union of Bulgarian Writers. Hons: Prize, Union of Bulgarian Writers, 1970; Dimitrov Prize, 1974. Address: Sofia ul. Ivaylo 28, Bulgaria.

MELCHER, Gil (Gilbert Wayne), pen names AACHEN, C.V.; McCALL, Craig; BURT, Gill; G.W.M., b. 27 Feb. 1910, Manchester, Okla., USA. Public Relations Executive; Author. Educ: B.S., Creighton Univ., 1933; Wichita State Univ., 1935; Univ. of Colo., 1937; Univ. of Ala., 1945. Publs: The Prisoners Handbook, 1942-43. Ed. &/or Contbr. to: consumer publs.; gen. & trade mags.; etc. Mbrships. incl: Fndr., Pres., Creighton Press Club; Life., Kan. Authors' Club.; Neb. Writers Guild.; Outdoor Writers Assn. of Am.; AAAS; Am. Acad. of Pol. & Soc. Sci.; Acad. of Pol. Sci. Hons. incl: Outstanding Citizen Award, Gulf Shores, Ala., 1949; Lions int. 100% Gov's Award, 1971. Address: 202 Fort Morgan Parkway, Gulf Shores, AL 36542, USA.

MELCHINGER, Siegfried, b. 22 Nov. 1906, Stuttgart, Germany. College Professor Emeritus. Educ: Univ. of Tübingen; Univ. of Munich. Publs: Theater der Gegenwart, 1956; Drama zwischen Shaw und Brecht, 1958; Schauspieler, 1965; Geschichte des politischen Theaters, 1971; Das Theater der Tragödie, 1974. Mbr., PEN. Address: 7821 Höchenschwand, Strittberg, W. Germany.

MELCHIOR, Ib Jorgen, b. 17 Sept. 1917, Copenhagen, Denmark (US citizen). Author; Motion Picture Writer, Director & Producer. Educ: Cand. phil., Copenhagen Univ., 1937. Publs. incl: (novels) Order of Battle, 1972; Sleeper Agent, 1975; (play) Hour of Vengeance, 1962; (film scripts) The Angry Red Planet, 1959; Journey to the 7th Planet, 1962; Robinson Crusoe on Mars, 1964; The Time Travelers, 1964; Ambush Bay, 1966; (TV scripts) Men into Space series, 1959-60; The Outer Limits, 1965; over 40 documentaries; var. transls. of Ibsen. Contbr. to: Great Dog Stories of All Times; 1962; num. other anthols. & jrnls. Mbrships. incl: Authors' Guild; Writers' Guild of Am.; MS Soc.; Acad. of Sci. Fiction (hon. mbr.). Recip., sev. nat. awards for documentary awards & dramas. Agent: H.N. Swanson Inc. Address: 8228 Marmont Lane, L.A., CA 90069, USA.

MELLANBY, Kenneth, b. 26 Mar. 1908, Barrhead, UK. Scientist, Research Worker. Educ: B.A., Univ. of Cambridge; Ph.D., Univ. of London; Sc.D., Univ. of Cambridge. Publs: Scabies, 1943, 2nd ed., 1973; Human Guinea Pigs, 1945, 2nd ed., 1973; The Birth of Nigeria University, 1958; Pesticides & Pollution, 1967; The Mole, 1970; The Biology of Pollution, 1972. Contbr. to: Times; Minerva; New Scientist. Mbrships: Pres., Inst. of Biol., 1972-73; Pres., Assn. for the Study of Animal Behaviour, 1968. Hons: D.Sc., Univ. of Ibadan; D.Sc., Univ. of Bradford; D.Sc., Univ. of Leicester. Address: Hill Farm, Wennington, Huntingdon, UK.

MELLOAN, George Richard, b. 10 Nov. 1927, Greenwood, Ind., USA. Editor. Educ: B.S., Butler Univ., Indpls., Ind., 1950. Contbr. to: Wall St. Jrnl. (Dpty. Ed., Ed. Page; also theatre & opera reviews). Mbrships: Nat. Conf. Ed. Writers; N.Y. Assn. of Theatre Critics, Eds. & Reporters. Address: 265 Kimball Ave., Westfield, NJ 07090, USA.

MELLOR, David P., b. 19 Mar. 1903, Launceston, Tas., Australia. Chemist; Retired Professor of Chemistry. Educ: B.Sc., 1926, M.Sc., 1928, Univ. of Tas.; D.Sc., 1946; Fellow, Royal Aust. Chem. Inst. Publs: Role of Science & Industry (vol. V, C'wlth. Offl. War Hist.), 1958; Chelating Agents & Metal Chelates (ed. w. F. P. Dwyer), 1964; The Evolution of the Atomic Theory, 1971. Contbr. to: Chemistry in Space Research, 1972; sci. periodicals in field. Mbrships. incl: Bd. of Trustees, Aust. Mus. Recip., sev. awards. Address: Unit 10, Lynholm Court, 199 Pacific Highway, Lindfield, N.S.W., Australia 2070.

MELLOR, Geraldine, b. 1910, Bedford, UK. Journalist; Lecturer. Educ: Assoc., London Acad. Music. Contbr. to: Brit. Philatelic Press; Pulse Int.; Country Quest; Herts. Countryside; Home Cos. Newspapers Ltd.; European, nat. provincial & Irish newspapers. Mbr., Women's Press Club. Address: 9 Highfield Ave., Harpenden, Herts. AL5 5UB, UK.

MELVILLE, Alan, b. 9 Apr. 1910. Former TV Producer; Screen Writer; Playwright. Educ: Edinburgh Acad. Publs. incl: (revues) Sky High, 1941; A La Carte, 1948; Hulla Baloo (co-author), 1972; (plays) Top Secret, 1949; Simon & Laura, 1954; Mrs. Willie, 1955; Change of Tune, 1959; Marigold, 1959; Fuender Bitte Melden, 1966; Demandez Vicky, 1966; (films) Hot Ice, 1952; All for Mary, 1955; (novels) Death of Anton, 1936; Warning to Critics, 1939; (autobiography) First Tide, 1945; Myself When Young, 1956; Merely Melville, 1970; (TV series) What's My Line?, Before the Fringe; Misleading Cases. Address: c/o Eric Glass, 28 Berkeley Sq., London W1, UK.

MEMBRECHT, Steven, b. 13 June 1937, Amersfoort, Netherlands. Author; Psychology Teacher; Psychotherapist. Educ: Grad., Social Acad., Amsterdam, 1960. Publs: Waiting for the Sun, 1961; The End Will Come, 1962; The Spacious Prison, 1964; The Jump Into the Net, 1965; 27 Stories from the Homosexual Sphere, 1969; On Homosexuality, 1969; Death Comes to Life, 1970; The Violet Brains, 1972; I Should Go to America Once, 1972; The Comeback of Hannibal Stip, 1975. Contbr. to var. papers, radio & TV. Mbrships: Former Bd. Mbr., PEN; Soc. of Dutch Writers. Hons: De Reina Prinsen Geerligs Prize, 1962; Die Kogge Förderpreis, Germany, 1966. Address: le Bloemdwarsstraat 15", Amsterdam-C, Netherlands.

MEMMI, Albert, b. 15 Dec. 1920, Tunis. University Professor. Educ: Univs. of Algiers & Sorbonne. Publs. incl: The Pillar of Salt, 1953; Strangers, 1955; Anthologie des ecrivains nord-africains, 1955; Colonizer, Colonized, 1957; Portrait of a Jew, 1962; Le français & le racisme, 1965; The Liberation of the Jew, 1966; Dominated Man, 1968; The Scorpion, 1970. Recip., Order of Nichan Iftikhar. Address: 5 rue Saint Merri, Paris 4e, France.

MEMON, Hameed Sindhi, b. 12 Oct. 1939, Naushahroferoz, Nawabshah, Sind, Pakistan. University

Controller of Examinations. Educ: B.A.(Hons.), M.A., LL.B. Publs: (short stories in Sindhi) Semi, 1959; Udaswadiyoon, 1967. Contbr. to: Marvee (Asst. Ed., 1959-60); Rooh-Rehan (Ed., 1960-69); Marvee Weekly (Assoc. Ed., 1972-73); Naeen Zindagi; Mehran; Sohni; Agte-Quadam. Mbrships: Sindhiadabi Sangat Sind; Sec., Hyderabad Br., Sindhiadabi Sangat Sind. Recip., Badal Awards, Best Ed. of Yr., 1960-1967.

MENDELSOHN, Everett I., b. 28 Oct. 1931, NYC, USA. Professor of the History of Science. Educ: A.B., Antioch Coll.; M.A., Ph.D., Harvard Univ. Publs: Heat & Life, 1964; Ed., Human Aspects of Biomedical Innovation, 1971; Ed., Science & Values, 1974. Contbr. to: Ed., Jrnl. of the Hist. of Biol.; Ed. Bd., Sci. Studies & Sci., Med. & Man. Mbrships: incl: VP, AAAS; Acad. Int. d'hist. des scis. Address: Holyoke Ctr. 838, Harvard Univ., Cambridge, MA, USA.

MENDEZ-LEITE VON HAFE, Fernando, b. 5 Aug. 1905, Oporto, Portugal. Writer; Historian; Technical Director, Film Studios; Consulting Engineer. Educ: Mechanical Engrng. degree. Publs: (in Spanish) The Cinema & Its Mysteries, 1934; The American Cinema, 1942; The French Cinema, 1942; The Secrets of the Cinema, 1950; Synthetic History of the Cinema, 1950; History of the Spanish Film, 2 vols. Contbr. to num. jrnls., Europe, Mexico; Translator. Mbrships: Motion Picture Writers Guild of Spain; Comité International des Recherches Historiques Cinématographiques, Paris. Hons: Spanish Nat. Awards for motion picture books, Min. of Info., 1965; Awards, Motion Picture Writers Guild, 1950, 1965, 1967. Address: Fuente del Berro 23, Madrid 9, Spain.

MENDOZA ROMERO, María Luisa, pen names CHINA; CATAY. b. 17 May 1934, Guanajuato, Mexico. Journalist; Author; Scriptwriter; Teacher. Educ: Philos. & Letters; Grad., Interior Design; Grad. Scenarist. Publs. incl: Crítica de la Crítica, 1966; Con Él, Conmigo, con Nosotros Tres, 1971; (select. of columns) La O por lo Redondo, 1971; (pamphlet) Crónica de Chile, 1972; (lects.); Oiga Usted!, 1973; Que pasa con el teatro en México?, 1971; Maquinita de Hacer Ruido (pvte. ed.); 2 Palabras 2 (essay, w. husband, Edmundo Domínguez Aragonés), 1971; Allende el Bravo (w. husband); De Ausencia (novel), 1974; El Perro del Escribano & Las Cosas, forthcoming. Contbr. to: El Sol de México; Siempre; Las Américas; TV Commentator. Recip., num. prizes. Address: Sabino 263, Colonia Santa Maria de la Ribera, México 4 D.F., México.

MENEN, Aubrey, b. 22 Apr. 1912, London, UK. Author. Educ: Univ. Coll., London. Publs. incl: Upon This Rock, 1972; Cities in the Sand, 1973; Fonthill, 1974; The New Mystics (w. Graham Hall) 1974. Contbr. to: N.Y. Times Mag.; Horizon; New Yorker; Vogue; Harper's Bazaar; Holiday; Travel & Leisure; Home & Gardens; McCall's; etc. Address: c/o William Morris Agency Inc.; 1350 Ave. of the Americas. N.Y., NY 10019, USA.

MENZIES, Elizabeth Grant Cranbrook, b. 24 June 1915, Princeton, N.J., USA. Author; Photographer. Publs: Before the Waters: the Upper Delaware Valley, 1966; Princeton Architecture: A Pictorial History of Town & Campus (co-author), 1967; Millstone Valley, 1969. Contbr. to: Ency. Americana; Princeton Alumi Weekly; Princeton Hist. Mbrships: N.J. Histl. Soc.; Stony Brook-Millstone Watersheds Assn.; Nat. Audubon Soc. Address: 926 Kingston Rd., Princeton, NJ 08540, USA.

MÉRAS, Phyllis Leslie (Mrs. Thomas Cocroft), b. 10 May 1931, Brooklyn, N.Y., USA. Journalist. Educ: B.A., Wellesley Coll., Mass., 1953; M.S., Grad. Schl. of Jrnlsm., Columbia Univ., NYC, 1954; Inst. of Advanced Int. Studies, Geneva, Switz., 1957. Publs: First Spring: A Martha's Vineyard Journal, 1972; A Yankee Way with Wood, 1975. Contbr. to: N.Y. Times Mag.; Saturday Review; The Nation; Yankee; Odyssey; Travel Mag.; Book World; Contbng. Ed., The Vineyard Gazette. Hons: Swiss Govt. Exchange Fellowship, 1957; Pulitzer Grant, to do work in critical jrnlsm., 1967. Address: W. Tisbury, Mass., USA.

MERCATANTE, Anthony Stephen, b. 29 Jan. 1940, Bklyn., N.Y., USA. Writer. Educ: B.A., CUNY; St. Peter's Coll., Oxford, UK, Summer 1974. Publs: Ed., The Harper Book of Christian Poetry, 1972; Zoo of the Gods: Animals in Myth, Legend & Fable (illustrated by author), 1974. Contbr. to: Gentlemen's Quarterly Mag. Address: 15 Abingdon Square, N.Y., NY 10014, USA.

MERCER, David Stuart, b. 27 June 1928, Wakefield, UK. Playwright. Educ: B.A., Dunelm, 1953. Publs: The Generations, 1964; Ride a Cock Horse, 1966; Three TV Plays, 1966; Belcher's Luck, 1967; The Parachute, 1967; On the Eve of Publication, 1970; Flint, 1970; After Haggerty, 1970; The Bankrupt, 1974; Duck Song, 1974. Mbrships: Writers' Club; Dramatists' Club. Hons: Writers' Guild Award (Best TV Play), 1962, 1967, 1968; Evening Standard Drama Award, 1965; Brit. Film Acad. Award, 1965. Address: 37 Hamilton Gdns., London NW8, UK.

MERCER, Marilyn, pen name FRENCH, Jane, b. 10 June 1923, White Plains, N.Y., USA. Editor; Writer. Educ: B.A., Smith Coll., 1945. Publs: Adultery for Adults (w. Joyce Peterson), 1967. Contbr. to: McCalls; Glamour; Rdrs. Digest; Family Circle; House & Gdn.; Saturday Evening Post; NY Mag.; Cosmopolitan; Ladies' Home Jrnl.; Harpers; Cath. Digest; etc. Mbrships: Am. Soc. of Mag. Eds.; Newswomen's Club; Authors' Guild. Address: 340 E. 64th St., N.Y., NY 10021, USA.

MERI, Veijo (Vaino Valvo), b. 31 Dec. 1928, Viipuri, Carelia, Finland. Author. Educ: Histl. studies, Univ. of Helsinki. Publs. The Manila Rope, 1957; 10 novels; 4 collects. of short stories; 6 plays; 2 books of essays; biog. of Aleksis Kivi, 1973; transl.; poems of Francois Villon, 1974. Hons: 6 Finnish State Prizes; Finnish State Sillanpaa Prize, 1963; Lit. Prize of Nordic Coun., 1973. Address: Pyorokiventie 9 A 2, Helsinki 83, Finland.

MERL, Dorothea, b. 19 July 1920, Innsbruck, Austria. Author. Educ: Univ. of Innsbruck. Publs: Der Paradiesvogel, 1971; Bis an die Rosenwolke, 1973. Contbr. to: Der Schlern; Mitteilungen des Oesterreichischen Alpenvereins; Brennpunkte; etc. Mbrships: Der Turmbund; Acad. Sect., Austrian Alpine Soc. Recip., Student Lit. Competition Prize, Austrian Coll. —Innsbruck Coll. Soc., 1950-59. Address: Goethestr. 13/III, A 6020 Innsbruck, Austria.

MERLE, Robert, b. 29 Aug. 1908, Professor of English Literature. Educ: Sorbonne Univ., Paris. Publs: Oscar Wilde, 1948; Week-end à Zuydcoote, 1949; La Mort est mon métier, 1953; L'Ile, 1962; Un Animal doue de raison, 1967; Derrière la vitre, 1970; Malevil, 1972; (plays) Flamineo, 1953; Nouveau Sisyphe; (essays) Moncada, 1965; Ben Bella, 1965; & var. transl. Recip., Croix du Combattant, 1945. Address: Le Bousquest de la Malonie, Marquay, Dordogne, France.

MEROW, Erva Loomis, b. 23 Sept. 1922, Jackson, Wis., USA. Special Education Teacher. Educ: B.S. Publs. incl: Northwest Passage, 1959; Sherlock Bones, 1961; Wisconsin Lore, 1961; On Stage, Children, 1963; Golden Prize, 1965; Here, Boy, 1965; Pony, 1965; The Seagull & Me, 1972; Breakfast with Paul (play), 1965; Little Lulu: Surprise for Mother, 1974. Contbr. to var. profl. & lit. publs. Mbrships: Wis. Coun. of Writers; Nat. Assn. of Mental Retardation. Hons: 1st Prize, Play, Jade Ring Prize, Wis. Reg. Writers Assn., 1962; Title of Danae, Int. Clover Poetry Assn., 1974. Address: 601-71st St., Kenosha, WI 53140, USA.

MERRENS, H. Roy, b. 21 July 1931, Salford, Lancs., UK. Professor; Toronto Harbour Commissioner. Educ: B.A., Univ. Coll., London, 1954; M.A., Univ. of Md., USA, 1957; Ph.D., Univ. of Wis., 1962. Publs: Colonial North Carolina in the Eighteenth Century: A Study in Historical Geography, 1964. Contbr. to: Can. Cartographer; Econ. Geog.; Geogl. Review; Wm. & Mary Quarterly; S.C. Histl. Mag.; Jrnl. Southern Hist.; etc. Mbrships incl: Can. Assn. Geogs.; Am. Geogl. Soc.; Assn. Am. Geogs.; Org. of Am. Histns. Recip., Guggenheim Fellowship, 1966-67. Address: 48 Waverley Rd., Toronto 8, Ont., Can.

MERRICK, Hugh (Harold A. MEYER), b. 23 June 1898. Retired Executive, Overseas Rediffusion. Educ: Westminster Schl. & Christ Church, Oxford, UK. Publs. incl: Companion to the Alps, 1974; (novels): Pillar of the Sky; Out of the Night; Anthology; The Perpetual Hills; (transl.): To the Third Pole, Prof. G. O. Dyhrenfurth; The Everest Lhotse Adventure, Albert Eggler; The White Spider, Heinrich Harrer; North Face in Winter, Toni Hiebeler; Alps & Alpinism, Paul Lukan; (autobiog.): Kurt Diemberger; (poetry): Sonnets to the Argentine; (as H. A. Meyer): Athletics by Members of the Achilles Club; Modern Athletics by the Achilles Club. Contbr. to: John O'London's; The Sphere; Country Life; Field; Alpine Jrnl.; etc. Mbrships. incl: Nat. Liberal Club; Alpine Club. Address: 22 Empire House, S. Kensington, London SW7, UK.

MERRIL, Judith, b. 21 Jan. 1923, N.Y., USA. Radio Writer. Educ: B.A., Rochdale Coll., Toronto, Can., 1970. Publs. incl: (novels) Shadow on the Hearth, 1950; The Tomorrow People, 1960; Outpost Mars (w. C. M. Kornbluth), 1952; Gunner Cade (w. C. M. Kornbluth), 1952; (short stories) Out of Bounds, 1960; Daughters of Earth, 1969; Survival Ship, 1973; Ed., The Year's Best SF, 1960-66. Contbr. to var. sci. fiction mags. Mbrships: Sci. Fiction Rsch. Assn.; ACTRA, Toronto; Writers' Union of Can.; Edit. Bd., Inst. for Twentieth Century Studies. Address: c/o Spaced Out Library of Toronto Public Libraries, 566 Palmerston Ave., Toronto, Ont., Can.

MERRILL, Jean Fairbanks, b. 27 Jan. 1923, Rochester, N.Y., USA. Writer. Educ: B.A., Allegheny Coll., 1944; M.A., Wellesley Coll., 1945; Fulbright Schlr., Univ. of Madras, India, 1952-53. Publs. incl: Henry, the Hand-Painted Mouse, 1951; Boxes, 1953; The Travels of Marco, 1956; A Song for Gar, 1960; The Superlative Horse, 1961; The Pushcart War, 1964; Red Riding, 1968; Mary, Come Running, 1970; The Toothpaste Millionaire, 1972; Maria's House, 1974; The Girl Who Brightened Up the World, 1975. Contbr. to: Vermont Life. Mbr., Authors' Guild. Hons. incl: Lewis Carroll Shelf Awards, 1963, 1965; Boys' Club of Am. Jr. Book Award, 1965. Address: Angel's Ark, 29 S. Main St., Randolph, VT 05060, USA.

MERRILL, John Nigel, b. 19 Aug. 1943, London, UK. Writer; Lecturer. Publs: Walking in Derbyshire, 1969; Motoring in Derbyshire, 1970; Legends of Derbyshire, 1972; Famous Derbyshire Homes, 1973; Peak District Walks No. 1 — For the Motorist, 1973; Peak District Walks No. 2 — For the Rambler, 1974; Legends & Folklore of the Midlands, 1974; Explore Derbyshire by Car, 1974; Legends & Folk History of the N.W., 1974. Contbr. to: Scots Mag.; Derbys. Life & Countryside; Mountain Life; In Brit.; This England; The Lady; Scotland's Mag. Mbr., Soc. of Authors (Sec., Northern Grp.). Address: "Cadgwith", 6 Farwater Close, Dronfield, Sheffield S18 6RE, UK.

MERRILL, Wilfred Kerner, b. 5 Nov. 1903, Chgo., Ill., USA. Retired Park Ranger. Educ: Grad., US Sea Trng. Bur.; Grad., var. F.B.I. schls., sev. Nat. Pks. Publs: All About Camping, 1962, rev., 1965; Getting Out of Outdoor Trouble, 1965; The Hunter's Bible, 1968; The Hiker's & Backpacker's Handbook, 1971; The Survival Handbook, 1971. Contbr. to: F.B.I. Law Enforcement Bulletin; Western Outdoors. Mbrships: Life Mbr., Tuolumne Co. Peace Offs. Assn.; Life Mbr., Nat. Rifle Assn.; & others. Address: Rancho Sonora Estates, Rte. 4 Box 830-77, Sonora, CA 95370, USA.

MERWE, Jaap Van De, b. 14 Sept. 1924, Rotterdam, Netherlands. Writer. Educ: Leyden Univ. Publs: 't Oproer Kraait (songbook), 1969; Gij Zijt Kanalje (a century of ditties), 1974; (plays) Tehuis, 1972; Jungle Opera, 1974; Cheerful Guerrilla, 1974. Contbr. to: De Nieuwe Linie; Vara radio & TV (songs, documentaries, adaptations of Steptoe & Son, a Till Death Us Do Part); Amsterdam theatres (satirical intimate revues). Mbrships: Bd., Assn. Dutch Theatre, Radio & TV Script Writers; Bd., Dutch Br., Int. Theatre Inst. Address: 47 Michelangelostraat, Amsterdam, Netherlands.

MERZ, Natasha, pen name SAGAR, Krishna, b. 22 Dec. 1932, Hong Kong. Writer; Journalist. Educ: B.A., Univ. of Oxford, UK. Publs: My School in India, 1960; sev. books for children; 250 short stories & essays. Contbr. to: Schweizer Illustrierte; Der Zürichbieter; Ringier Verlag; sev. mags. & newspapers. Mbr., Swiss Writers' Assn. Hons: Prizes, STEO Fndn., Switz., 1970 & 1972; Prize, Neue Zürcher Zeitung, 1971. Address: Schaffhauserstr. 136, CH-8302 Kloten, Switz.

MESSENT, Claude John Wilson, b. 26 July 1899, Norwich, UK. Clerk in Holy Orders. Publs: Old Cottages & Farm Houses of Norfolk, 1928; Parish Churches of Norfolk & Norwich; Carstone; Lych-Gates in Eastern England; The Architecture on the Royal Estate of Sandringham. Contbr. to: E. Anglaian Mag.; Eastern Daily Press. Mbrship: Assoc., Royal Inst. of Brit. Archts. Address: The Gable, Brundall Rd., Blofield, Norwich, Norfolk NOR 84Z, UK.

MESZOCY, Miklos, b. 19 Jan. 1921, Szekszard, Hungary. Writer. Educ: Grad. in Law & Pols. Publs: Az Atléta Halála (Paris, 1965; Budapest & Munich, 1966, Copenhagen, 1967; Prague, 1970; Saulus, (Budapest & Paris, 1968, Munich, Warsaw & Leipzig, 1970, Helsinki, 1974, Barcelona, 1975). Contbr. to: Kortárs; Uj Irás; Élet és Irodalom; Jeklenkor; Uj Symposion; Hid; Literatur und

Kritik; Akzente; Neue Rundschau. Mbr., PEN Club. Address: Varosmajor u. 48, Budapest 1122 XII, Hungary.

METHLING, Finn Ludvig, b. 8 Aug. 1917, Frederiksberg, Denmark. Playwright; Author. Educ: M.A. Publs: var. plays, 1950-75. Mbrships: Chmn., Danish Dramatists' Union, 1968-73. Hons: Antony Cross, 1951; Polish Radio & TV Prize, 1961; Holberg Medal, 1962. Address: Kratmosevej 12, DK-2950 Vedbaek, Denmark.

MEWS, Hazel, b. 25 Dec. 1909, London, UK. Librarian; Lecturer. Educ: M.A., D.Litt., King's Coll., Univ. of London. Publs: Frail Vessels: Woman's Role in Women's Novels from Fanny Burney to George Eliot, 1969; Reader Instruction in Colleges & Universities, 1972. Contbr. to Lib. Assn. Record. Mbrships: Fellow, Lib. Assn.; Royal C'wlth. Soc. Address: 12 Morden College, Blackheath, London SE3 OPW, UK.

MEYER, George Rex, b. 15 Mar. 1928, Croydon, N.S.W., Australia. Educationalist. Educ: B.A., B.Sc., M.Ed. (Sydney); Ph.D. (London); F.A.C.E. Publs. incl: Field Work in Animal Biology (w. M. A. Besly), 1954; Practical Work in Biology (w. others), 1965; Science & the Environment of Man (w. R. Cull & K. S. McDonnell), 1965; Objective Tests in Science (w. R. Cull & K. S. McDonnell), 1967; Chmn., Ed. Bd., Nat. Sci. Curriculum Mats. Project. Contbr. to profl. jrnls. Address: P.O. Box 154, Beecroft, NSW 2119, Australia.

MEYER, Michael, A., b. 15 Nov. 1937, Berlin, Germany. Professor of Jewish History; Author. Educ: B.A., Univ. of Calif., L.A., USA; Ph.D., Hebrew Union Coll.-Jewish Inst. of Relig. Publs: The Origins of the Modern Jew, 1967; Ideas of Jewish History, 1974. Contbr. to: Commentary; Judaism; Am. Histl. Review; Jewish Social Studies. Hons: Frank & Ethel Cohen Award for Book on Jewish Thought, 1967; Hilberry Prize, Wayne State Univ. Press, 1967. Address: 3101 Clifton Ave., Cinn., OH 45220, USA.

MEYER, Michael Leverson, b. 11 June 1921, London, UK. Author; Translator. Educ: M.A., Christ Ch., Oxford Univ. Publs. incl: Contbng. Ed., Eight Oxford Poets, 1941; Ed., Collected Poems of Sidney Keyes, 1945; The End of the Corridor (novel), 1951; The Ortolan, 1968; Henrik Ibsen; The Making of a Dramatist, 1968; Henrik Ibsen: The Farewell to Poetry, 1971; Henrik Ibsen; The Top of a Cold Mountain, 1971; num. transls. of plays of Ibsen & Strindberg. Contbr. to: Times Lit. Supplement; Times; Sunday Times. Mbrships. incl: F.R.S.L. Hons: Gold Medal, Swedish Acad., 1964; Whitbread Biog. Prize, 1971. Address: 4 Montagu Sq., London W1H 1RA, UK.

MEYER, Nicholas, b. 24 Dec. 1945, NYC, USA. Author; Scriptwriter. Educ: Univ. of Iowa. Publs. incl: The Love Story Story; Target Practice; The Seven-Per-Cent Solution, 1974; (film script) The Invasion of the Bee-Girls. Address: c/o E. P. Dutton & Co., Inc., 201 Park Ave. S., N.Y., NY 10003, USA.

MEYNELL, Laurence W., pen names ETON, Robert, TRING, Stephen, b. 9 Aug. 1899, Wolverhampton, UK. Former Schoolmaster; Author. Publs. incl: (as L. W. Meynell) Blue Feather, 1928; The Evil Hour, 1947; The Man No One Knew, 1951; Bridge Under the Water, 1955; The Abandoned Doll, 1960; More Deadly than the Male, 1964; The Curious Crime of Miss Julia Blossom, 1970; The End of the Long Hot Summer, 1972; (as Robert Eton) The Pattern, 1934; The Dragon at the Gate, 1948; (as Stephen Tring, for children) The Old Gang, 1951; Penny Dreadful, 1952; Nurse Ross Takes Over, 1958. Contbr. to: Time & Tide (Lit. Ed., 1958-60). Address: 9 Clifton Terr., Brighton, Sussex, UK.

MICHAEL, George Edward, b. 29 Aug. 1919, Rochester, N.H., USA. Antiquarian; Writer; Lecturer. Educ: Emerson Coll. Publs: Antiquing with George Michael, 1967; Treasury of New England Antiques, 1969; Treasury of Antiques of the Federal Period, 1971; Basic Book of Antiques, 1974. Contbr. to: Boston Sunday Globe (Antiques Ed.); Antiques Gazette (Ed.); Yankee Mag. (Antiques Cons.); Public TV Antiques progs. (Host 1963-). Mbrships: Nat. Trust for Historic Preservation; Washington Crossing Fndn.; Am. Assn. Museums; Int. Platform Assn. Address: 12 Evergreen Dr., Merrimack, NH 03054, USA.

MICHAEL, Wolfgang F., b. 23 Feb. 1909, Freiburg, Germany. University Professor. Educ: Ph.D., Munich Univ., 1934. Publs: Die Anfaenge des Theaters in Freiburg i. B,

1934; Die geistlichen Prozessionsspiele in Deutschland, 1947; Frühformen der deutschen Buehne, 1963; Das deutsche Drama des Mittelalters, 1971. Contbr. to: Speculum; Jrnl. of Engl. & Germanic Philol.; Daphnis; Germanic Review; etc. Mbrships: MLA; Medieval Acad. of Am.; Am. Assn. of Teachers of German. Hons: Verdienstkruez I Klasse der Bundesrepublik Deutschland, 1972; Goethe Medal, Goethe Inst., 1972. Address: Dept. of Germanic Langs., Univ. of Texas in Austin, TX 78712, USA.

MICHAELIS, Anthony R., b. 22 Aug. 1916, Berlin, Germany. Scientist; Writer; Executive Editor, Interdisciplinary Science Reviews. Educ: B.Sc., Imperial Coll.; Ph.D., London Univ. Publs: Research Films, 1956; From Semaphore to Satellite, 1965; Scientists in Search of Their Conscience, 1973. Contbr. to: Daily Telegraph (Sci. Corres., 1963-73); sci. mags. & jrnls. Address: 18 Park Place Villas, London W2, UK.

MICHELOUD, Pierrette, b. 6 Dec. 1920, Vex, Valais, Switz. Poet. Educ: Fac. of Theol., Lausanne; Univ. of Zurich; Univ. of Paris, France. Publs. incl: Suspended Points, 1953; This Double Face, 1959; Passionately, 1960; The Child of Salmacis, 1963; Valais of the Heart, 1964; As the Wind Goes, 1966; All the Day All the Night, 1974. Contbr. to: Chief Ed., Les Pharaons. Mbrships: Comm. Dir., Assn. of French Lang. Writers; Acad. Int. du Culture Française, Brussels; Soc. of Men of Letters, France; Swiss Soc. of Writers. Hons: Prize, Schiller Fndn., 1964; Rhodes Lit. Prize, 1965; Edgar Poe Prize, 1973. Address: 5 rue Perronet, 75007 Paris, France.

MICHELSEN, Hans Günter, b. 1920, Hamburg, Germany. Playwright. Publs: (plays) Stienz, 1963; Feieraband 1 & 2, 1963; Lappschiess, 1964; Drei Akte, 1965; Helm, 1965; Frau L, 1966; Planspiel, 1969; Drei Hörspiele, 1971; (radio play) Episode, 1964. Hons: Forderpreis des Gerhart-Hauptmann-Preises, 1963; Hauptmann Prize, Berlin, 1965; Lit. Prize, Freien Hansestadt Bremen, 1967. Address: Lindenstr. 35, Frankfurt am Main, W. Germany.

MICHENER, James Albert, b. 3 Feb. 1907. Former University Professor; Author. Educ: B.A.; M.A.; Univs. of Pa., Va., Harvard, Ohio State & St. Andrews, Scotland, UK. Publs. incl: Unit in the Social Studies, 1940; Tales of the South Pacific, 1947; The Voice of Asia, 1951; Sayonara, 1954; The Bridge at Andau, 1957; The Hokusai Sketchbook, 1958; Hawaii, 1959; Caravans, 1963; The Source, 1965; Iberia, 1968; The Drifters, 1971; The Fires of Spring, 1972; Centennial, 1974. Mbr., Pres. Kennedy's Food for Peace Prog. (Chmn., 1961). Hons: Pulitzer Prize, 1947; Einstein Award, 1967. Address: Box 125, Pipersville, PA 18947, USA.

MICKLEM, (Rev.) Nathaniel, b. 1888, London, UK. Minister, United Reformed Church; Principal Emeritus Mansfield Coll., Oxford; Wilde Lecturer, Natural & Comparative Religions. Educ: M.A., D.D., New Coll., Oxford; LL.D., Mansfield Coll., Oxford. Publs. incl: Religion, 1948; Law & the Laws, 1952; The Box & the Puppets, 1957; A Religion for Agnostics, 1965; Behold the Man, 1969. Mbr., Authors' Club. Hons: Companion of Hon., 1937; Select Preacher, Oxford, 1960; Patron, Liberal Int., 1973. Address: Sheepstead House, Abingdon, Oxon., UK.

MIDDLETON, Christopher, b. 10 June, 1926, Truro, Cornwall, UK. University Teacher. Educ: B.A., 1951, M.A.; D.Phil., 1954; Oxford Univ. Publs: Torse 3, Poems, 1949-61, 1962; Nonsequences/Selfpoems, 1965; Our Flowers & Nice Bones, 1969; The Fossil Fish, 1970; Briefcase History, 1972; The Lonely Suppers of W. V. Balloon, 1975. Mbr., W. German Acad. Arts. Recip., Sir Geoffrey Faber Mem. Prize, 1963. Address: Rt. 8, Box 168, Austin, TX 78746, USA.

MIDDLETON, Drew, b. 1913, NYC, USA. Educ: Syracuse Univ., N.Y. Publs. incl: The British, 1957; The Sky Suspended, 1960; The Glorious Sunset, 1963. Contbr. to N.Y. Times. Address: c/o Martin Secker & Warburg Ltd., 7 John St., London WC1, UK.

MIDDLETON, Nigel Gordon, b. 24 Jan. 1918, Sheffield, Yorks., UK. Sociologist. Educ: Sheffield City Coll. of Educ.; Off. Cadet Corps, Royal Artillery, Shrivenham; B.Sc.(Econ.), London Schl. of Econs.; M.Phil., Post Grad. Schl., London Schl. of Econs. Publs: When Family Failed, 1970; A Place for Everyone — A History of

State Education, 1975. Contbr. to: Staff Writer, Union Jack; Ed., Crown News; Jrnl. of Educl. Studies; Med. Off. of Hlth.; Co. Couns. Gazette; Hlth. Visitor. Mbrships: Fndr. Chmn., Inst. of Hlth. Educ.; Brit. Sociol. Assn.; Maj., Royal Army Educ. Corps. Address: "Dunrock", Waterloo Bay, Glenarm Rd., Larne, Co. Antrim, UK.

MIDDLETON, O(sman) E(dward), b. 25 Mar. 1925, Christchurch, NZ. Writer. Educ: Auckland Univ., 1946, 1948; Sorbonne, Paris, France, 1955-56. Publs: (verse) Six Poems, 1951; (short stories) Short Stories, 1953; The Stone & Other Stories, 1959; (juvenile) From the River to the Tide, 1964. Hons: Award, 1959; Schlrship, 1965, NZ Lit. Fund; Hubert Church Award, 1964; Robert Burns Fellowship, Univ. of Otago, 1970. Address: c/o Dept. of English, Univ. of Otago, Dunedin, NZ.

MIDDLETON, Stanley, b. Bulwell, Nottingham, UK. College Head of English. Educ: B.A., London Univ., 1940; M.Ed., Univ. of Nottingham, 1952. Publs. incl: A Serious Woman, 1961; The Just Exchange, 1962; Two's Company, 1963; Him They Compelled, 1964; Terms of Reference, 1966; The Golden Evening, 1968; Wages of Virtue, 1969; Apple of the Eye, 1970; Brazen Prison, 1971; Cold Gradations, 1972; A Man Made of Smoke, 1973; Holiday, 1974. Mbrships: PEN; Writers' Guild of GB, Recip., Booker Prize (shared w. Nadine Gardiner), 1974. Address: 42 Caledon Rd., Sherwood, Nottingham NG5 2NG, UK.

MIEDZYRZECKI, Artur A, b. 6 Nov. 1922, Warsaw, Poland. Poet; Novelist; Essayist; Literary Critic. Educ: Univ. of Paris, France, 1946-49. Publs. incl: (poems) Namiot z Kanady, 1943; Strony przydrozne, 1945; Selected Poems, 1957, 2nd ed., 1971; Noc darowana, 1960; Piekne Zmeczenie, 1962; Zamówienia, 1968; (prose) Opowieści mieszkańca namiotów, 1957, 2nd ed., 1965; Powrót do Sorrento, 1958; Śmierć Robinsona, 1963; Poezja dzisiaj, 1964; Dialogi i sasiedztwa, 1971; Zlota Papuga, 1971. Poetry Ed., Nowa Kultura, 1956-58; Ed., Poezja, 1965-68. Mbrships: PEN; Bd., Polish Writers' Union, 1956-67, VP, 1965-67. Hons: Fellowship, Harvard Int. Seminar, 1965; Prize, Polish PEN, 1971. Address: Warsaw, Marszalkowska 68-47, Poland.

MIHÁLYI, Gabor, b. 1 July 1923, Košice, Czechoslovakia. Journalist. Educ: M.A., 1951; Cand. for Lit. (Ph.D.), 1962. Publs: Molière, 1954; Roger Martin du Gard, 1960; Végjáték (Endgame — Survey of Modern West-European & American Drama), 1971. Ed. of: Nagyvilág. Contbr. to Szinház; Kritika; New Hungarian Quarterly; Mod. Drama (Kan. Univ., USA). Mbrships: Unions of Hungarian Writers & Jrnlsts.; Hungarian PEN; Hungarian Soc. for Hist. of Lit; Hungarian Theatre Inst. Address: II. Törökvész ut 8, Budapest, 1022, Hungary.

MIHAYLOV, Radoslav, b. 10 Mar. 1928, Kalimantsi, Bulgaria. Writer. Publs.: (in Bulgarian) The Hour of Truth, 1965; Judgement, 1967; The Big Family, 1970; Explosion, 1971; The Bells of September, 1973; The First Volleys, 1973. Contbr. to: PlamAk; September. Mbr. Union of Bulgarian Writers. Address: Sofia-30 ul. Poroy 20, Bulgaria.

MIHAYLOVA, Lilyana, b. 11 May 1939, Plovdiv, Bulgaria. Teacher of Bulgarian Language. Publs: (in Bulgarian) Women, 1966; House on a Bend, 1969; The Ship, 1972; Open Up, It's Me, 1972. Contbr. to: PlamAk; September; Obzor; Literatouren Front. Mbr.. Union of Bulgarian Writers. Hons: Order of Cyril & Methodiy — II degree, 1969; Silver Ring, Evening News, 1972; Grand Prize, Varna Film Festival, 1973. Address: gr. Pernik, bul. Tolbouhin 12/11, Bulgaria.

MIKES, George, b. 1912, Siklos, Hungary. Author. Educ: LL.D., Univ. of Budapest. Publs. incl: How to be an Alien; How to Scrape Skies; Wisdom for Others; Milk & Honey; Down with Everybody; Shakespeare & Myself; Über Alles; Little Cabbages; Italy for Beginners; Switzerland for Beginners; East is East; How to be Inimitable; Tango; Mortal Passion; How to Unite Nations; Book of Snobs (w. Duke of Bedford); How to be Affluent; Eureka; Not by Sun Alone; Boomerang; The Prophet Motive; The Land of the Rising Yen; Humour in Memoriam; The Spy Who Died of Boredom. Contbr. to: Encounter; Sunday Times; Times Lit. Supplement; Punch; etc. Mbr., PEN. Address: c/o Andre Deutsch, 105 Great Russell St., London, WC1, UK.

MIKHALKOV, Sergei Vladimirovich, b. 12 Mar. 1913, Moscow, USSR. Poet; Playwright; Children's Writer. Publs. incl: (in Russian) Uncle Steve, 1936; Collected Works, 2 vols., 1936; (plays) Tom Kenti, 1938; Red Neckerchief,

1947; I Want to Go Home, 1949; Lobsters, 1952; Sombrero, 1958; A Monument to Oneself, 1958; Campers, 1959; Collected Works, 4 vols., 1964; My Friend & I, 1967; In the Museum of Lenin, 1968. Mbr., USSR Union of Writers (Chmn., 1970–). Hons. incl: Order of Lenin (twice); Red Banner of Labour; Red Star; Lenin Prize, 1970. Address: USSR Union of Writers, ulitsa Vorovskogo 52, Moscow, USSR.

MIKKOLA, Marja-Leena, b. 18 Mar. 1939, Salo, Finland. Writer. Educ: B.A., Helsinki Univ. Publs: Naisia, 1962; Tyttö Kuin Kitara, 1964; Etsikko, 1967; Liisa ja Veikko Ihmemaassa, 1969; Raskas Puuvilla, 1971; Lääkärin Rouva, 1972. Contbr. to: Parnasso; Kulttuurivihkot. Mbrships: Writers' Union of Finland; Bd. Mbr., Union of Cultural Workers; Hon. Mbr., Eino Leino Soc. Recip., State Lit. Prize, 1973. Address: 4 Linja 17-19 C 22, 00530 Helsinki 53, Finland.

MILBURN, Robert Leslie Pollington, b. 1907, Cullercoats, Northumberland, UK. Master of the Temple. Educ: Univ. of Cambridge; Univ. of Oxford; M.A. Publs: Saints & their Emblems in English Churches, 1952; Early Christian Interpretations of History, 1954. Contbr. to: Ch. Quarterly Review; Jrnl. of Theol. Studies. Address: The Master's House, Temple, London EC4, UK.

MILDENBERGER, Wolfgang Ernst, b. 14 Jan. 1923, Freiberg i. Br., Germany. Educ: Ph.D., Univ. of Freiberg i. Br., 1950. Publs: Der Hauptmann vom Wald, 1953; Drei Fetzen blauer Himmel, 1975. Mbrships: Swiss Authors' Union; Pres., Literarischer Club, Zürich. Hons: Scheffelpreis, 1941; Award for Dialect Poetry, Province of Südbaden, 1952. Address: Carl Spittelerstr. 174, 8053 Zürich, Switz.

MILES, Elton Roger, b. 25 May 1917, Coryell, Tex., USA. Professor of English. Educ: A.B., Baylor Univ.; M.A., N. Tex. State Univ.; Ph.D., Univ. of Tex. Publs: Regional Culture in the Southwest, 1953; Lucky Seven: Autobiography of a Cowman, 1957; The Way I Heard It: Tales of the Big Bend, 1959; Southwest Humorists, 1969. Contbr. to jrnls. in field. Mbr., Tex. Folklore Soc. (Pres.). Address: 505 E. Hendryx Ave., Alpine, TX 79830, USA.

MILGRAM, Gail Gleason, b. 14 June 1942, S. Amboy, N.J., USA. Educator. Educ: B.S., Georgian Ct. Coll., Lakewood, N.J., 1963; M.Ed., 1965, Ed.D., 1969, Rutgers Univ., N.B., N.J. Publs: The Teenager & Alcohol, 1970; The Teenager & Smoking: Tobacco & Marijuana, 1972; The Teenager & Sex, 1974; An Annotated Bibliography of Alcohol Education Material, 1975. Contbr. to: Jrnl. of Alcohol & Drug Educ.; Jrnl. of Studies on Alcohol. Address: 15 Dobson Rd., E. Brunswick, NJ 08816, USA.

MILLAR, James Primrose Malcolm, pen name WHITE, G. A., b. 17 Apr. 1893, Edinburgh, UK. General Secretary, National Council of Labour Colleges; Editor, Plebs, & Plebs Textbooks. Publs: Education for Emancipation, 1926; We Did Not Fight, (co-author), 1935; Trade Union Education — Some Vital Issues, 1960; The Vest Pocket Speaker, 1961; History of the Labour College Movement, (co-author). Contbr. to: Plebs; Forward; Scotsman; Times; Bulletin for the Study of Labour History. Address: 5 Mount Boone, Dartmouth, Devon, UK.

MILLAR, Kenneth, pen name MACDONALD, (John) Ross, b. 13 Dec. 1915 Los Gatos, Calif., USA. Educ: B.A., Univ. of Western Ont., 1938; M.A., Ph.D., Univ. of Mich., 1938-51. Publs: incl: The Dark Tunnel, 1944; Blue City, 1947; The Moving Target, 1949; The Way Some People Die, 1951; Find a Victim, 1954; The Galton Case, 1959; The Wycherly Woman, 1961; The Chill, 1964; Black Money, 1966; The Instant Enemy, 1968; The Goodbye Look, 1968; The Underground Man, 1971; Sleeping Beauty, 1973. Contbr. to: Esquire; Cosmopolitan; N.Y. Times Mag. & Book Review; Sports Illustrated. Mbrships: Mystery Writers of Am. (Pres.); Authors League; Writers Guild West; Crime Writers Assn., UK. Hons. incl: Silver & Gold Dagger Awards, Crime Writers Assn., 1965-66; Grand Master Award, Mystery Writers of Am., 1974. Agent: Harold Ober Assocs. Address: 4420 Via Esperanza, Santa Barbara, CA 93105, USA.

MILLAR, Margaret Ellis Sturm, b. 5 Feb. 1915, Kitchener, Ont., Can. Novelist. Educ: Univ. of Toronto. Publs. incl: The Invisible Worm, 1941; The Devil Loves Me, 1942; The Iron Gates, 1945; It's All in the Family, 1948; Do Evil in Return, 1950; Rose's Last Summer, 1952; Wives & Lovers, 1954; Beast in View, 1955; An Air that Kills,

1957; The Listening Walls, 1959; A Stranger in my Grave, 1960; How Like an Angel, 1962; The Fiend, 1964; The Birds & the Beasts were There, 1967; Beyond this Point are Monsters, 1970. Contbr. to: Cosmopolitan. Mbr., Mystery Writers of Am. (Pres.). Recip., Edgar Allen Poe Award, 1957. Agent: Harold Ober Assocs. Address: 4420 Via Esperanza, Santa Barbara, CA, 93105 USA.

MILLEN, Bernard, b. 1920, London, UK. Managing Director Universal Public Relations Pty. Ltd. (Sydney) since 1967. Educ: Goldsmiths Coll., London. Publs: The Great Barrier Reef, 1958; Discovering Modern Australia, 1963. Contbr. to: Radio Australia; Book Knowledge; John Bull; Daily Express; Evening News; Melbourne Sun News-Pictorial; Melbourne Herald; Melbourne Age; Sydney Morning Herald; Adelaide News; Walkabout; etc. Mbrships: Royal Geogl. Soc.; Aust. Jrnlsts.' Assn. Address: 9 Margaret St., Fairlight, NSW 2094, Australia.

MILLER, Arthur, b. 17 Oct. 1915. Playwright. Educ: B.A., Univ. of Mich. Publs: The Man who Had All the Luck, 1943; Situation Normal, 1944; Focus, 1945; All My Sons, 1947; Death of a Salesman, 1949; The Crucible, 1953; A View from the Bridge, 1955; A Memory of Two Mondays, 1955; Collected Plays, 1958; After the Fall, 1964; Incident at Vichy, 1964; (short stories) I don't Need You Anymore, 1967; (plays) The Price, 1968; The Creation of the World & Other Business, 1972; (Screenplay) The Misfits, 1959; In Russia (w. Inge Morath), 1969. Mbr., PEN (Pres., 1965-69). Hons. incl: Pulitzer Prize, 1949; Antoinette Perry Award, 1953; Gold Medal, Am. Acad. of Arts & Letters, 1959. Address: c/o Int. Famous Agency, 1301 Ave. of the Americas, N.Y., NY 10019, USA.

MILLER, Benjamin F., b. 10 Sept. 1907, Fitchburg, Mass., USA, d. 1971. Research Physician; Medical School Professor. Educ: Med. Degree, Harvard Med. Schl.; Chem. Engr., MIT. Publs: You & Your Doctor, 1948; Ed., When Doctors Are Patients, 1952; The Complete Medical Guide, 1956; Man & His Body, 1960; Modern Medical Encyclopedia, 1964; Good Health, 1966; Modern Medical Encyclopedia of Baby & Child Care, 1966; Family Health Guide & Encyclopedia, 1970; Investigating Your Health, 1971; Encyclopedia & Dictionary of Medicine & Nursing, 1972; The Family Book of Preventive Medicine, 1972; Freedom from Heart Attacks, 1972. Contbr. of 130 sci. papers to jrnls. Recip., Francis Amory Prize, Acad. Arts. & Scis.. 1962.

MILLER, Christian (née Grant), b. 1920, Monymusk, Scotland, UK. Writer. Publs: The Champagne Sandwich, 1969. Contbr. to var. newspapers, mags., & radio. Mbr., Soc. of Authors. Agent: A.M. Heath & Co. Address: Old Stables, Newtown, Newbury, Berks., UK.

MILLER, Clement A., b. 29 Jan. 1915, Cleveland, Ohio, USA. Musicologist. Educ: B.Mus., M.Mus., Cleveland Inst. Music; M.A., Western Reserve Univ.; Ph.D., Univ. of Mich. Publs: Heinrich Glarean: Dodecachordon, 1965; Franchinus Gafffurius: Practica Musicae, 1968; Johannes Cochlaeus: Tetrachordum Musices, 1970; Sebald Heyden: De Arti Canendi, 1971; Hieronymus Cardanus: Writings on Music, 1973. Contbr. to: Musical Quarterly; Musica Disciplina; Jrnl. Am. Musicol. Soc. Mbrships: Am. Musicol. Soc.; Medieval Acad. of Am.; Lute Soc. of Am.; Royal Music Assn. Recip., Guggenheim Fellowship Award, 1974-75. Address: 1481 S. Belvoir Blvd. Cleveland, OH 44121, USA.

MILLER, Don Ethan, b. 25 Dec. 1947, NYC, USA. Writer. Educ: B.A.(cum laude), Dartmouth Coll., 1968. Publs: Bodymind, 1974. Contbr. to: Boston Phoenix; Prevention; etc. Fellow of the MacDowell Colony, Peterborough, N.H. Address: 325 West 86th St., NYC, NY 10024, USA.

MILLER, Donald George, b. 1909, Braddock, Pa., USA. Professor of New Testament; President, Theological Seminary; Editor; Pastor. Educ: Greenville Coll., Ill.; Biblical Sem., N.Y.; N.Y. & Basel Univs.; A.B., S.T.B., S.T.M., M.A., Ph.D. Publs: Conqueror in Chains; Fire in Thy Mouth; The Way to Biblical Preaching; The Nature & Mission of the Church; The Gospel According to Luke; The Gospel According to John & the Johannine Epistles; The Authority of the Bible. Contbr. to: Ed., Interpretation, 1947–; Assoc. Ed., Layman's Bible Commentary, 1957–; var. other theol. jrnls. Address: Poplar Hill, Line Bridge Rd., Whiteford, MD 21160, USA.

MILLER, Donald Lane, b. 14 May 1918, Pittsburgh, Pa., USA. Communications Executive. Educ: A.B., Kenyon

Coll., 1940. Publs: Strategy for Conquest, 1966; The People Who Brought Us Liberty, 1975. Mbr., Nat. Press Club, Wash. D.C. Address: 309 Green St., Alexandria, VA 22314, USA.

MILLER, Dora O., pen names MILLER OF DILLER; D.O.M., b. 6 Feb. 1898, Diller, Neb., USA. Columnist; Freelance Writer & Poet. Publs: num. historic, patriotic, relig. & comic pageants, pefd. var. cities, USA. Contbr. to: Neb. Writers Guild Anthol.; Jefferson Co. Ch. Mag.; Midwest Chaparral Poets Mag.; Midlands Mag. of Omaha World Herald; Omaha World Herald; Neb. Centennial Anthol.; Lincoln Jrnl.; etc. Mbrships. incl: Nat. Fedn. of Press Women Inc.; Nat. Chmn., ibid, Women's Writing Contest; Neb. Fedn. of Press Women; Sec.-State Chmn., ibid, Women's Writing Contest; Neb. Writers Guild. Recip., Women of Achievement Award, Neb. Press Women, 1957; var. nat. awards, Nat. Fedn. of Press Women Writing Contests. Address: Box 67, Diller, NB 68342, USA.

MILLER, E. Willard, b. 17 May 1915, Turkey City, Pa., USA. Professor of Geography; Associate University Dean. Educ: B.S., Clarion State Coll., 1937; A.M., Univ. of Neb., 1939; Ph.D., Ohio State Univ., 1942. Publs: Global Geography (ed.), 1957; The World's Nation: An Economic & Regional Geography (co-author), 1958; A Geography of Manufacturing, 1962; An Economic Atlas of Pennsylvania, 1964; Exploring Earth Environments: A World Geography, 1964; Mineral Resources of the United States, 1967; Energy Resources of the United States, 1967; A Geography of Industrial Location, 1970; Socioeconomic Patterns of Pennsylvania: An Atlas, 1975. Contbr. to: Econ. Geog.; Profl. Geographer; Jrnl. of Geog.; Sci. Monthly; etc. Mbrships. incl: Assn. of Am. Geogs.; Fellow, AAAS, Nat. Coun. for Geog. Educ. Address: 845 Outer Dr., State Coll., PA 16801, USA.

MILLER, Edward John, b. 29 Sept. 1914, Ealing, UK. Libraries Adviser, National Trust; Writer. Educ: B.A., London Univ. Publs: Prince of Librarians: The Life & Times of ntonio Panizzi of the British Museum, 1967; That Noble Cabinet: A History of the British Museum, 1974. Contbr. to var. acad. jrnls. Mbrships: Fellow, Soc. of Antiquaries; Royal Histl. Soc.; Hon. Soc. of Cymmrodorion; Bibliog. Soc.; etc. Address: 37 Aldbourne Rd., London W12 0LW, UK.

MILLER, Gordon Wesley, b. Quorn, Australia. University Professor. Educ: Univ. of Melbourne; Univ. of London, UK; B.A.; Ph.D. Publs: Success, Failure & Wastage in Higher Education, 1970; Higher Education Research in Australia & New Zealand, 1970; Educational Opportunity & the Home, 1971. Contbr. to: Times; Univs. Quarterly; Jrnl. Educl. Psychol. Mbrships: Brit. Sociol. Assn.; Brit. Psychol. Soc.; Inc. Soc. of Authors, Playwrights & Composers; F.R.S.A. (Life); Assn. Univ. Tchrs. Address: Univ. of London, Inst. of Education, Malet St., London WC1, UK.

MILLER, Harry George, b. 15 Feb. 1941. Associate Professor of Education. Educ: B.A., Carroll Coll., Waukesha, Wis., 1963; M.E., 1967; Ed.D., 1970; Univ. of Neb., Lincoln. Publs. incl: A Course in American Government, 1969; Using Levels of Questions in the Social Studies, 1971; Strong Confrontation as an Educational Technique, 1971; Assessment for Accountability & Revision in Social Studies, 1973; Beyond Facts: Objective Ways to Measure Thinking, 1975. Contbr. to var. profl. jrnls. Mbrships. incl: Pub. Adult & Continuing Educ. Assn. Address: 2020 Norwood Dr., Carbondale, IL 62901, USA.

MILLER, Helen Hill, b. 1899, Highland Pk., Ill., USA. Writer. Educ: Bryn Mawr Coll.; Oxford Univ.; Univ. of Chgo.; B.A., Dip. Econ. & Pol. Sci., Ph.D. Publs: Greek Horizons; Sicily & the Western Colonies of Greece; Bridge to Asia; The Greeks in the Eastern Mediterranean; Greece; The Case for Liberty; George Mason, Constitutionalist; Realms of Arthur, 1969; Greece Through the Ages, 1971; Historic Places Around the Outer Banks, 1974. Contbr. to: Economist; etc. Mbrships: Wash. Press Club; Overseas Writers, Wash. Agent: Marie Rodell. Address: 2810 P St. N.W., Washington, DC 20007, USA.

MILLER, Henry Arthur, b. 1910, Liverpool, UK. Engineer; Author; Lecturer. Educ: C.G.I.A.; C.Eng.; M.I.E.E.; Liverpool Inst.; Liverpool Coll. of Technol. Publs. incl: Luminous Tube Lighting, 1945; Electronic Devices, 1948; Electrical Installation Practice, Vol. 1, 1960, Vol. 2, 1962, Vol. 3, 1965; Practical Wiring, Vols. 1 & 2, 1969; Electrical Craft Studies, Vols. 1 & 2, 1970; 30 Engineering

Workbooks; Q & A on Electric Wiring; Domestic Electrical Equipment. Contbr. to: Sci. Abstracts, Elec. Review; etc. Mbrships: F.R.S.A.; Soc. of Authors; Soc. of Arts; MENSA; C.G.I.A. Assoc.; etc. Address: 4 Newhaven Close, Cromer, Norfolk, UK.

MILLER, Henry Valentine, b. 26 Dec. 1891, NYC, USA. Writer. Publs. incl: Tropic of Cancer; Black Spring; The Cosmological Eye; The Angel is My Watermark; Obscenity & the Law of Reflection; Henry Miller Miscellanea; Sexus; Nights of Love & Laughter; A Devil in Paradise; The Intimate Henry Miller; The Henry Miller Reader; To Paint is to Love Again; In Defense of Freedom to Read; Order & Chaos; Henry Miller in Conversation; My Life & Times; On Turning Eighty. Contbr. to most major mags., USA & Europe. Mbrships: Acad. of Arts & Scis., USA; Cmdt., Ordre d'Arts & Lettres, Paris, France. Recip., Book of Yr. Award, Italy. Address: 444 Ocampo Drive, Pacific Palisades, CA 90272, USA.

MILLER, James Edwin, Jr., b. 9 Sept. 1920, Bartlesville, Okla., USA. Professor of English. Educ: M.A., 1947, Ph.D., 1949, Univ. of Chgo. Publs: A Critical Guide to Leaves of Grass, 1957; Start with the Sun: Studies in the Whitman Tradition, 1960; Walt Whitman, 1962; Reader's Guide to Herman Melville, 1962; F. Scott Fitzgerald: His Art & His Technique, 1964; J. D. Salinger, 1965; Quests Surd & Absurd: Essays in American Literature, 1967; Word, Self, Reality: The Rhetoric of Imagination, 1972; Theory of Fiction: Henry James, 1972. Mbrships: Pres., Nat. Coun. of Tchrs. of Engl., 1970; M.L.A. Address: Dept. of Engl., Univ. of Chgo., 1050 E. 59th St., Chgo., IL 60637, USA.

MILLER, John Perry, b. 26 Mar. 1911, Lynn, Mass., USA. Professor of Economics. Educ: B.A., 1932, M.A., 1934, Harvard Univ.; Ph.D., 1937. Publs: Unfair Competition: A Study in Criteria for Control of Trade Practices, 1941; Pricing of Military Procurements, 1949; The New England Economy, 1951; The Economic Outlook for the Naugatuck & Farmington River Valleys in the State of Connecticut, 1956; Index of Economic Journals; Cartels, Competition & Their Regulation, 1962. Contbr. to acad. jrnls. Mbrships. incl: Am. Econ. Assn.; Royal Econ. Soc. Recip., num. acad. hons. Address: Box 2038, New Haven, CT 06521, USA.

MILLER, Jon, b. 14 July 1921, Southend, Essex, UK. Naturalist; Television Presenter & Researcher. Educ: Photo. Dip., Reimann Schl. of Photography, London. Publs: Of Fish & Men, 1958, 1960; Mountains in the Sea, 1972; How to Keep Unusual Pets, 1975; How to Fool Your Brain, 1975. Contbr. to: The Geog. Mag.; How Annual; Look In; Illustrated Weekly of India. Fellow, Zool. Soc., London. Address: Albia House, Gillan, Manaccan, Nr. Helston, Cornwall TR12 6HJ, UK.

MILLER, Max Cameron, b. 1 Oct. 1908, Oxford, UK. Actor. Publs: (play) Lights that go Out, 1932; (radio play) Death Takes a Week End, 1935; (revues) Bodger on Broadway, 1941; Two's Company, 1954; (children's play) The Cloth With the Insects On (w. Jean McConnell), 1948; & one-act plays, radio scripts, etc. Mbrships: BBC Club; Brit. Actors' Equity Assn.; Brit. Actors' Benevolent Fund. Address: Graystone, 162 Thundersley Pk. Rd., Benfleet, Essex SS7 1EN, UK.

MILLER, Merle, b. near Montour, Iowa, USA. Editor; Author; Journalist. Educ: State Univ. of Iowa; London Schl. Econs., London, UK. Publs. incl: Island 49; That Winter; Day in Late September; On Being Different: What It Means to be a Homosexual; Plain Speaking: An Oral Biography of Harry S. Truman; Warm Feeling; other books, film scripts, TV plays. Contbr. to num. mags. Hons. incl: On Nonfiction Bestseller List for 1974 (for Plain Speaking). Address: c/o G. P. Putnam's Sons, 200 Madison Ave., N.Y., NY 10016, USA.

MILLER, Robert C., b. 1899, Blairsville, Pa., USA. Director of Learned Society (Retired). Educ: Greenville Coll.; Univs. of Ill. & Calif.; A.M.; Ph.D. Publs: The Sea, USA & UK, 1966. Mbrships: Fellow, AAAS; Calif. Acad. of Scis. Address: Calif. Acad. of Sciences, San Fran., CA 94118, USA.

MILLER, Stuart, b. 28 Dec. 1937, NYC, USA. Educator. Educ: A.B., Oberlin Coll., 1958; Univ. of Florence, Italy, 1958-59; M.A., 1961, Ph.D., 1963, Yale Univ., USA. Publs: Measure, Number & Weight: A Polemical Study of the College Grading Problem, 1967; The

Picaresque Novel, 1968; Hot Springs, 1971. Contbr. to: Intellectual Digest Mag.; Learning Mag.; Popular Psychol. Mag.; Cross-Talk Mag.; Synthesis. Mbr., MLA. Hons. incl: Fulbright Fellowship, 1958-59; Haskell Fellowship, Oberlin Coll., 1963. Address: 3847-21 St., San Fran., CA 94114, USA.

MILLETICH, Helmut Stefan, b. 21 Nov. 1943, Winden, Austria. Schoolteacher. Educ: Grad., 1961, M.A., 1967, Univ. of Vienna. Publs: (fiction) Immer saugende Erde, 1970; (poem cycle) Protokolle zur Steinigung, 1972; (poems) Träume steten Wachens, 1974; (score & record) Oberwarter Messe (textbook). Contbr. to: Pannonia; Volk und Heimat; Austrian Radio (O.R.F.). Mbrships: Gen. Sec., Austrian PEN, Burgerland; Vice-Dir., European Liszt Ctr. Address: A-7000 Eisenstadt, Kirchäckergasse 6/4, Austria.

MILLETT, Mervyn Richard Oke, b. 16 May 1910, Sydney, Australia. Scientific Researcher; Editor. Educ: B.A., Univ. of Melbourne. Publs: Australian Eucalypts, 1969; Native Trees of Australia, 1971. Contbr. to: Aust. Book Review; Austr. Fin. Review; Search; The Aust. Student; The C'wlth. Profl.; Your Garden; Aust. Sci. Tchrs.' Jrnl. Mbrships. incl: Linnean Soc. of N.S.W.; Aust. Soc. of Authors; Ed.-in-Chief, Profl. Offs. Assn., Aust. Pub. Serv.; Aust. & NZ Assn. for the Advancement of Sci. Address: 72 McNicol Rd., Tecoma, Vic., Australia 3160.

MILLIGAN, Terence Alan, pen name MILLIGAN, Spike, b. 1918, India. Comedian; Writer. Publs: Silly Verse for Kids; Dustbin of Milligan; Little Pot Boiler; Bed Sitting Room; Goon Show Script Books, vols. 1 & 2; Book of the Goons; A Book of Bits; Milliganimals; Badd Twit Lion; Bedside Milligan; Puckoon; Adolph Hitler, My Part in his Downfall (war memoirs, vol. I), 1972; Small Dreams of a Scorpion; Badjelly the Witch; Rommel? Gunner Who? (war memoirs, vol. II), 1974; Dip the Puppy — Monster Jelly; Transports of Delight. Address: 9 Orme Ct., London W2, UK.

MILLINGTON, Terence Alaric, b. 1922, Barrow-in-Furness, UK. Lecturer & Consultant in Mathematics Education. Educ: B.Sc.; Dip.Ed., King's College & Inst. of Educ., Univ. of London; F.I.M.A. Publs: Dictionary of Mathematics, 1966, 1972, 1975; Living Mathematics (6 books) 1967, 1970, 1971, 1972; Mathematics Courses for Use with Overhead Projectors, 1971; History of Mathematics Filmstrips, 1971, 1972, 1973, 1975; Mathematics Through School, 1972. Contbr. to: Educ. for Teaching; The Teacher; UNESCO reports; etc. Mbrships: Math. Assn.; Inst. Maths. & its Application; Tchrs. of Maths; Soc. of Authors; A.T.C.D.E.; A.U.T. Address: 10 Creswick Walk, Hampstead Garden Suburb, London NW11 8AN, UK.

MILLS, A.R., b. 1930, Essex, UK. Publisher. Educ: Dip. Engl. Lit., London Univ. Publs: Middle Distance Running, 1961; Portrait of Moscow, 1965; Portrait of Leningrad, 1967; Ed., Two Victorian Girls, 1966; The Halls of Ravenswood, 1967; Two Victorian Ladies, 1969; Radio, drama, talks etc. Contbr. to: Essays in Criticism; etc. Mbrships: Press Club; Amateur Athletic Assn. Address: 1 Warley Rd., Woodford Green, Essex, UK.

MILLS, Dennis Richard, b. 1931, Winthorpe, Notts., UK. University Staff Tutor. Educ: Univs. of Nottingham, Manchester & Leicester; M.A., Ph.D. Publs: The English Village, 1968; Ed., English Rural Communities, 1973. Contbr. to: E. Midland Geog.; Agric. Hist. Review; Local Histn.; Tchr.; Times Educl. Supplement; etc. Address: c/o Open University Regional Office, 143 Derby Rd., Nottingham, UK.

MILLS, Edward David, b. 1915, London, UK. Architect. Educ: Polytechnic Schl. of Arch.. London. Publs: The Modern Factory; The Modern Church; The New Architecture in Great Britain; Architects Details, 5 vols.; Factory Building; The Changing Work Place. Contbr. to: Archt. & Bldg. News; Archtl. Design; Archtl. Review; Industriebau; R.I.B.A. Jrnl.; etc. Mbrships: F.R.I.B.A. (Coun. mbr., 1954-62, 1963-69); F.S.I.A. Hons: C.B.E.; Bossom Rsch. Fellow, 1953; Churchill Fellow, 1969. Address: Gate House Farm, Newchapel, Lingfield, Surrey, UK.

MILLS, Ruth Ina, b. 24 Apr. 1914, Pittsfield, Mass., USA. Professor of Education. Educ: B.A., Rockford Coll., 1941; M.Ed., Mass. State Tchrs. Coll., 1946; Ed.D., Univ. of Md., 1959. Publs: So You Don't Want to Raise a Brat!. 1971. Address: 215 Vermillion St., Athens, WV 24712, USA.

MILLS, (William) Mervyn, b. 23 Feb. 1906, London, UK. Senior Air Historian (ret'd.), Ministry of Defence. Educ: King's Coll., London Univ. Publs: (novels) The Long Haul; Tempt Not the Stars; The Winter Wind; (plays) Nelson of the Nile; The Tree of Heaven; (TV plays) Dance Without Music; The Queen of Spades (adaptation); (Radio plays) The Skull; Peter Simple (series); The Lost World (adapted series); Paul Jones; Mexican Gold; (histl. works) Royal Air Force Operations in Libya, the Western Desert & Tunisia July 1942 to May 1943; RAF Operations from Malta June 1940 to May 1945. Mbr., Soc. of Authors. Hons: Mention in Despatches, 1945. Address: 95 Priory Road, London N8 8LY, UK.

MILLWARD, John Scandrett, b. 1924, Swansea, Wales, UK. Headmaster. Educ: M.A., Merton Coll., Oxford. Publs: Portraits & Documents of the Sixteenth Century; Portraits & Documents of the Seventeenth Century; Portraits & Documents of the Eighteenth Century (w. H. P. Arnold-Craft). Address: Loughborough Grammar Schl., Loughborough, Leics. LE11 2DU, UK.

MILNE, Alexander Taylor, b. 1906, Finchley, UK. Journal Director. Educ: M.A., Univ. Coll., London. Publs: Writings on British History: an annual bibliography, 1934-45, 8 vols., 1937-60; Catalogue & Index of Bentham Manuscripts; Centenary Guide to Publications of the Royal Historical Society; Ed., Librarianship & Literature, 1969; Historical Study in the West (part-author). Contbr. to: Am. Histl. Review; Bulletin of Inst. of Histl. Rsch.; Engl. Histl. Review; Hist.; etc. Fellow, Royal Histl. Soc. Address: 9 Frank Dixon Close, Dulwich, London SE21 7BD, UK.

MILNE, Charles Ewart, b. Dublin, Repub. of Ireland. Sailor; Works Clerk; Journalist; Estate Manager; Writer; Poet. Publs. incl: Forty North Fifty West, 1938; Letter from Ireland, 1940; Listen Mangan, 1941; Jubilo, 1945; Boding Day, 1947; Diamond Cut Diamond, 1950; Elegy for a Lost Submarine, 1951; Galion, 1953; Life Arboreal, 1953; Garland for the Green, 1962; Time Stopped, 1967. Contbr. to: Irish Press; Irish Times; Dublin Mag.; Poetry Review; World Review; Kilkenny Mag.; Spectator; New Statesman; Times; Sunday Times; London Mag.; Life & Letters; Tribune; Poetry Chicago; Johns Hopkins Review; Transatlantic Review; Oxford Book of Irish Verse. Mbr., Soc. of Authors. Address: 46 De Parys Ave., Bedford, UK.

MILNE, Lorus Johnson, b. 1912, Toronto, Ont., Can. Professor of Biology. Educ: M.A., Univ. Toronto; Ph.D., Harvard Univ. Publs. incl: (all w. M. J. Milne) Famous Naturalists, 1952; Animal Life, 1959; Plant Life, 1959; The Balance of Nature, 1960; Because of a Tree, 1963; Growth & Age, 1964; Living Plants of the World, 1967; The Ages of Life, 1968; When the Tide Goes Far Out, 1970; The How & Why of Growing, 1972; Invertebrates of North America, 1972; The Animal in Man, 1973; Because of a Flower, 1974. Contbr. to: N.Y. Times; Science. Mbrships. incl: Am. Assn. Advancement Sci.; Am. Soc. Zools. Address: 1 Garden Lane, Durham, NH 03824, USA.

MILNE, Margery Joan, b. 1915, NYC, USA. Professor of Biology. Educ: M.A., Ph.D.; Hunter Coll.; Columbia Univ.; Radcliffe Coll. Publs: (all w. L. J. Milne) A Multitude of Living Things, 1947; The Biotic World & Man, 1952, 3rd ed., 1965; The Mating Instinct, 1954; The Lower Animals, 1960; The Mountains, 1963; The Valley, 1963; The Crab that Crawled Out of the Past, 1965; Gift from the Sky, 1967; The Phoenix Forest, 1968; The Ages of Life, 1968; The Nature of Animals, 1969; The Nature of Plants, 1971. Contbr. to: Harper Ency. Sci.; N.Y. Times; etc. Mbrships. incl: Audubon Soc. Address: 1 Garden Lane, Durham, NH 03824, USA.

MILNER, Ian Frank George, b. 6 June 1911, Oamaru, NZ. University Professor, Charles University, Prague. Educ: M.A., Canterbury Univ., NZ, 1933; B.A., Univ. of Oxford, UK, 1937; Univs. of Calif. & Columbia, USA, 1937-39. Publs. incl: New Zealand's Interests & Policies in the Far East, 1940; The Structure of Values in George Eliot, 1968. Transls. from Czech incl: Silesian Songs, by P. Bezruč, 1967; Selected Poems of Miroslav Holub (w. G. Theiner), 1967; Although, poems by Miroslav Holub (w. Jarmila Milner), 1971; Selected Poems by Vladimír Holan (w. J. Milner), 1971. Contbr. to num. lit. books & jrnls. Mbrships: Dickens Fellowship; Circle of Mod. Philol., Prague. Hons. incl: Rhodes Schlrship., 1934; Petr Bezruč Prize, 1967. Address: Lopatecká IIa, Prague 4 – Podolí, Czechoslovakia.

MILNER, Nina Marion (née Blackett), pen name FIELD, Joanna, b. 1900, London, UK. Psychoanalyst;

Writer. Educ: B.Sc., University Coll., London Univ. Publs: (as J. Field) A Life of One's Own, 1934; An Experiment in Leisure, 1937; (as Marion Milner) The Human Problem in Schools, 1938; On Not Being Able to Paint, 1950, 1957; The Hands of the Living God, 1969. Contbr. to: Int. Jrnl. Psychoanalysis. Address: 12 Provost Rd., London NW3 4ST, UK.

MILTON, John R., pen names GARRARD, Christopher; LEWIS, Carson, b. 24 May 1924, Anoka, Minn., USA. Professor of Western American Literature; Editor. Educ: B.A. & M.A., Univ. of Minn., Mpls.; Ph.D., Univ. of Denver, Colo. Publs: The Loving Hawk, 1962; The Tree of Bones, 1965; This Lonely House, 1968; Conversations with Frank Waters, 1971; Oscar Howe: The Story of an American Indian, 1972; The Tree of Bones and Other Poems, 1973; The Blue Belly of the World, 1974; Crazy Horse, 1974. Contbr. to: S. Dakota Review (Ed.); & sev. Western Am. jrnls. Mbrships. incl: Pres., Exec. & Ed. Bds., Western Lit. Assn.; Chmn., S.D. Affiliated Soc., Acad. of Am. Poets. Recip., Wurlitzer Fndn. Fellowship, 1965. Address: 630 Thomas St., Vermillion, SD 57069, USA.

MINAHAN, John, b. 30 Apr. 1933, Albany, N.Y., USA. Magazine Editor & Publisher. Educ: Cornell Univ. 1955-57; Harvard Univ. 1957-58; Columbia Univ. 1959-60. Publs: A Sudden Silence (novel), USA 1963, UK 1964; The Passing Strange (novel), USA, 1965, UK, 1966; The Dream Collector, 1972; Transl., Cafarakis, The Fabulous Onassis, 1972; Jeremy (novel), USA, 1973, UK, 1974; What Makes Buddy Drum˚(biog.), forthcoming. Contbr to: Time mag. (Staff writer, 1960-61); N.Y. Times; The American Way (Ed. 1974-). Recip., Doubleday Award, 1960. Agent: Lucy Kroll Agcy. Address: 200 E. 84th St., N.Y., NY 10028, USA.

MINCHINTON, Walter Edward, b. 29 Apr. 1921, London, UK. Professor of Economic History. Educ: B.Sc., London Schl. of Econs., 1947. Publs: The British Tinplate Industry: A History, 1957; The Trade of Bristol in the 18th Century, 1957; Politics & the Port of Bristol in the 18th Century, 1963; Devon at Work: Past & Present, 1974; (Ed.), Essays in Agrarian History, 2 vols., 1968; Industrial South Wales 1750-1914, 1969; The Growth of English Overseas Trade in the 17th & 18th Centuries, 1969; Wage Regulation in Pre-Industrial England, 1972. Contbr. to publs. in field. Mbrships. incl: Coun., Econ. Hist. Soc., 1954-66; Chmn., Brit. Agric. Hist. Soc., 1968-71; Fellow, Royal Hist. Soc. Address: 53 Homefield Rd., Exeter EX1 2QX, UK.

MINGAY, Gordon Edmund, b. 20 June 1923, Long Eaton, Derbys., UK. University Professor. Educ: B.A., Univ. of Nottingham, 1952; Dip.Ed., 1953; Ph.D., 1958. Publs: English Landed Society in the 18th Century, 1963; The Agricultural Revolution 1750-1880, 1966; Britain & America: A Study of Economic Change 1850-1939, 1970; Ed., Agric. Hist. Review. Contbr. to: Econ. Hist. Review; Agric. Hist. Review; Times Lit. Supplement. Mbrships: Royal Hist. Soc.; Agric. Hist. Soc.; Econ. Hist. Soc. Address: Mill Field House, Selling Court, Selling, Faversham, Kent, UK.

MINNEY, Rubeigh James, b. 1895, Calcutta, India. Journalist; Editor; Film Scriptwriter; Film Producer. Educ: King's Coll., London, UK. Publs. incl: No. 10 Downing St., 1963; I Shall Fear No Evil, 1966; The Two Pillars of Charing Cross, 1967; The Bogus Image of Bernard Shaw, 1969; The Tower of London, 1970; Hampton Court, 1971; Rasputin, 1972; Puffin Asquith, 1973; (plays) Clive of India (w. W. P. Lipscomb); Gentle Caesar (w. Osbert Sitwell). Contbr. to: var. newspapers & mags.; BBC. Mbrships: Writers' Guild; Authors' Soc. Address: Hook House, Cousley Wood, Wadhurst, Sussex, UK.

MINOGUE, Kenneth Robert, b. 11 Sept. 1930, Palmerston, NZ. Reader in Political Science, London School of Economics. Educ: B.A., Univ. of Sydney, Aust.; B.Sc., London Schl. of Econs., UK. Publs: The Liberal Mind, 1963; Nationalism, 1967; The Concept of a University, 1973. Contbr. to: Star; London Opinion; Pol. Studies; London Trend; 20th Century Am. Schlr.; Spectator; Encounter; Times Lit. Supplement; Times Higher Educl. Supplement. Address: 71 Lonsdale Rd., London SW13 9DA, UK.

MIRET-MAGDALENA, Enrique, b. 12 Jan. 1914, Zaragoza, Spain. Professor of Morals; Author. Educ: D.Sc., Univ. Inst. of Theol. Publs: Que eran los secerdotes obreros?, 1966; Metodo de Formacion y Accion, 1966;

Nuevos Catolicos, 1966; Cristianismo para el Pueblo, 1968; El Celibato del Clero, perdurara?, 1968; Catolicismo para manana, 1974. Contbr. to: Triunfo; Cuadernos para el Dialogo; Vida Neuva; Infrmations Catholiques Internationales; Gentleman; Pueblo; Hechos y Dichos; etc. Address: Galileo 102, Madrid, Spain.

MIRODAN, Alexandru, b. 5 June 1927, Budeasa, Arges, Romania. Playwright. Educ: Grad., Lyceum, Bucharest, 1945; Fac. of Philos., Univ. of Bucharest, 2 yrs. Publs. incl: Theatre, 1965; Theatre, Vols. I & II, 1971; Theatre (new short plays), 1973; (plays) The Journalists, 1956; The Famous 702, 1961; The Head of the Soul Office, 1964; The Transplantation of the Unknown Heart, 1969; The Mayor of the Moon, 1969. Contbr. to: Contemporanul; Theatre; Cinema. Mbrships: Union of Romanian Writers; Film Assn. of Romania; Theatre & Music Assn. Hons: Cultural Dept. Prize for Theatre, 1959; Romanian Acad. Prize for Theatre, 1962. Address: Str. Galati 8, Bucharest, Romania.

MIRUS, Ludmilla, pen names EGGER, Ellen (until 1964), MIRUS-KAUBA, Ludmilla (currently), b. 10 Mar. 1905, Mistelbach, Austria. Author of children's books. Educ: Dipl. rer. merc., Coll. of Commerce, Vienna, 1927; Studied at Univ. of Vienna, 1927-28. Publs: In diesem Sommer begann das Leben, 1964; Der kleine Engel, 1969; Geschichten von der kleinen Nel, 1972; Tiere, die uns begegnen, 1972; Inges wunderbare Reise mit dem Luftballon, 1974; Minh, aus dem Dorf des glücklichen Drachen, 1975. Contbr. to children's progs.. Bavarian radio. Mbrships: Free German Authors' Union; German Writers' Union. Address: August-Mohl-Str. 34, D 867 Hof/Saale, W. Germany.

MISHEV, Georgy, b. 2 Nov. 1935, Yoglav, Bulgaria. Journalist; Film Scriptwriter. Publs: (in Bulgarian) Stories of the Ossum River, 1963; Adamites, 1966; Matriarchy, 1966; Distancing, 1973. Contbr. to: September; PlamAk; Literatouren Front. Mbr., Union of Bulgarian Writers. Address: Sofia 37-pancherevo, ul.2nd, 3, Bulgaria.

MISHRA, Vishwa Mohan, b. 12 Nov. 1937, India. Professor. Educ: B.A., M.A., Univ. of Patna, India; M.A., Univ. of Georgia; Ph.D., Univ. of Minn. Publs: Communication & Modernization in Urban Slums, 1972; Basic News Media & Techniques, 1973. Contbr. to: Jrnlsm. Quarterly; Reading Rsch. Quarterly; Gazette; Indian Jrnl. of Social Rsch.; Human Org. Mbrships: AAUP; Sigma Delta Chi; Kappa Tau Alpha. Address: 2176 Donovan Place, Okemos, MI 48864, USA.

MISIRKOVA-RUMENOVA, Kata, b. 14 Sept. 1930, Postol, Greece. Librarian; Author. Publs. incl: Childhood of Misirkov, 1964; I Love My Town, 1967; Fire's Song, 1968; Wrestling, 1972; Hot Land, 1972; The Boys of Vardor's Land, 1972; Vida & a Construction, 1974; (plays) Autumnal Meeting; Janidokema; Not Denouncement; Meeting. Contbr. to: Nova Makedonija; Stremež; Razgledi; Sovremenost; etc. Mbrships: Macedonian Authors' Soc. (Mgmt. Comm.); Yugoslav Authors' Soc.; PEN; Yugoslav Libns. Soc. Hons: Lit. Prizes for Wrestling & The Boys of Vardor's Land, 1972; Awards for four dramas, 1973. Address: st. Pirinska Nr. 28/IV, 91000 Skopje, Yugoslavia.

MISTLER, Jean, b. 1 Sept. 1897. Civil Servant; Writer. Educ: Ecole Normale Supérieure, Paris. Publs. incl: La Symphonie inachevée; Hoffmann le fantastique; A Bayreuth avec Richard Wagner; Le Bout du monde; Les Orgues de Saint Sauveur; Gaspard Hauser; La Route des étangs. Contbr. to: L'Aurore, 1954–; Revue de Paris, 1928-40. Mbr., French Acad. Address: 11 rue de l'Université, Paris 7e, France.

MITCHELL, Adrian, b. 24 Oct. 1932, London, UK. Writer; Journalist. Educ: Christ Church, Oxford Univ., 1952-55. Publs. incl: (verse) Ed., Oxford Poetry (w. R. Selig), 1955; Poems, 1964; Out Loud, UK & USA, 1968; Ride the Nightmare, 1971; (plays) The Ledge, prod. 1961; Marat/Sade (adapted from P. Weiss), UK, 1964, USA, 1965; The Criminals (adapted from J. Triana), prod. 1967; Tyger (adapted from W. Blake), prod. 1971; (novels) If You See Me Comin', UK, 1962, USA, 1963; The Bodyguard, UK, 1970, USA, 1971. Contbr. to: Peace News; Black Dwarf; var. newspapers. Hons: Gregory Award, 1961; Transl. Award, PEN, 1966. Address: c/o Jonathan Cape Ltd., 30 Bedford Square, London WC1, UK.

MITCHELL, (Charles) Julian, b. 1 May 1935, Epping, Essex, UK. Writer. Educ: B.A., 1958, M.A., 1962, Oxford Univ. Publs: Ed., Light Blue, Dark Blue (anthol.), 1960;

Introduction (co-author, short stories), 1960; (novels) Imaginary Toys, 1961; A Disturbing Influence, 1962; As Far As You Can Go, 1963; The White Father, UK, 1964, USA, 1965; A Circle of Friends, UK, 1966, USA, 1967; The Undiscovered Country, UK, 1968, USA, 1970. Mbr., Arts Coun. Lit. Panel, 1966-69. Hons: Harkness Fellowship, 1959; Rhys Mem. Prize, 1965; Maugham Award, 1966. Address: 68 Christchurch St., London SW3, UK.

MITCHELL, David John, b. 24 Jan. 1924, London, UK. Freelance Journalist & Author. Educ: M.A., Trinity Coll., Oxford Univ. Publs: Women on the Warpath: Story of Women of the First World War, 1966; The Fighting Pankhursts, 1967; 1919 Red Mirage, 1970; The Pankhursts, 1970. Contbr. to: Horizon Hist. of Brit. Empire, 1973; Hist. Today; Horizon; Mankind; Times; Daily Telegraph Mag.; Sunday Telegraph; New Statesman. Address: c/o Hope, Leresche & Steele, 11 Jubilee Pl., London SW3 3TE, UK.

MITCHELL, Edward B., b. 28 Jan. 1937, Aurora, Ill., USA. College professor. Educ: B.A., Beloit Coll., Beloit, Wis., 1959; Ph.D., Univ. of Conn., 1963. Publs: Continental Short Stories: The Modern Translation (w. Rainer Schulte), 1968; Nineteenth-Century American Short Stories (w. William Holmes), 1970; Henry Miller: Three Decades of Criticism, 1971. Contbr. to: Tex. Studies in Lit. & Lang.; Critique; Am. Lit. Address: Dept. of Engl., Ohio Univ., Athens, OH 45701, USA.

MITCHELL, (Sister) Elaine, pen name MICHAUD, E. G., b. 25 Mar. 1920, Tomahawk, Wis., USA. Dietitian. Educ: A.B., Aquinas Coll., Dietary Cert., N. Easton Coll.; Gabriel Richard Inst.; Braille & Lip Reading Tchr.; Cert. of Garontol.; Cert. of Theol. Publs: Love Has Many Voices (anthol.), 1972. Contbr. to: Nat. Anthol. for Tchrs. & Libns.; Int. Who's Who in Poetry Anthol.; Intercontinental Poetry Anthol. Mbrships. incl: Midwest Chapt., Nat. Writers Club.; Int. Chmn., Poetry Readings, IPA. Recip., sev. tchng. & writing awards. Address: 205 Carrier N.E., Grand Rapids, MI 49505, USA.

MITCHELL, Geoffrey Duncan, b. 5 June 1921, Lancaster, UK. Professor of Sociology. Educ: B.Sc.(Econ.), London Schl. of Economics. Publs: Neighbourhood & Community (co-author), 1954; Sociology: The Study of Social Systems, 1959, 2nd ed., 1970; A Hundred Years of Sociology, 1968; Ed., A Dictionary of Sociology, 1968; Ed., Sociology: An Outline for the Intending Student, 1970. Contbr. to: Brit. Jrnl. of Sociol.; Sociol. Review; Human Rels. Address: Dept. of Sociology, Amory Bldg., Univ. of Exeter, Exeter EX4 4RJ, UK.

MITCHELL, Gladys, b. 19 Apr. 1901, Cowley, Oxford, UK. Author. Educ: Dip., European Hist., Univ. of London. Publs: Dance to Your Daddy, 1969; Gory Dew, 1970; Lament for Lets, 1971; A Hearse on May-Day, 1972; The Murder of Busy Lizzie, 1973; A Javelin for Jonah, 1974; Winking at the Brim, 1974; Convent on Styx, 1975. Mbrships. incl: Soc. of Authors; Crime Writers' Assn.; Detection Club. Address: 1 Cecil Close, Corfe Mullen, Wimborne, Dorset, BH21 3PW, UK.

MITCHELL, (Sir) Harold Paton, b. 21 May 1900, Fife, Scotland, UK. Company Director; former M.P. for Brentford & Chiswick, 1931-45. Educ: R.M.C., Sandhurst; M.A., Univ. Coll., Oxford; D. ès Sci. Politiques, Univ. of Geneva. Publs: Downhill Ski-Racing, 1931; Into Peace, 1945; In My Stride, 1951; Europe in the Caribbean, 1963; Caribbean Patterns, 1967 & 1972; The Spice of Life, 1974. Contbr. to: Current Hist.; Int. Jrnl. Can. Inst. of Int. Affairs; Calif. Inst. of Int. Studies. Hons: Knight Commander Polonia Restituta, 1943; Polish Cross of Valour, 1945; Baronet, 1945; LL.D. Address: Château de Bourdigny, 1242 Geneva, Switz.

MITCHELL, Jean Brown, b. 26 July 1904, Manchester, UK. University Lecturer (Retired). Educ: M.A., Newnham Coll., Cambridge. Publs: Historical Geography, 1954; Ed., Great Britain: Geographical Essays, 1962. Contbr. to Ency. Britannica, 15th ed., 1974. Mbrships: Inst. of Brit. Geogs.; Royal Geog. Soc.; Royal Scottish Geog. Soc.; Soc. of Antiquaries of Scotland; Econ. Hist. Soc.; Univ. Women's Club. Address: 8 Buckingham Terrace, Edinburgh EH4 3AA, UK.

MITCHELL, Jerome, b. 7 Oct. 1935, Chattanooga, Tenn., USA. Professor of English & American Literature. Educ: B.A., Emory Univ., 1957; M.A., 1959, Ph.D., 1965, Duke Univ.; Univ. of Bonn, Germany, 1957, 1961-62 &

1965. Publs: Thomas Hoccleve — A Study in Early 15th-Century English Poetic, 1968; Hoccleve's Minor Poems (rev. w. A. I. Doyle), 1970; Chaucer the Love Poet (ed. w. Wm. Provost), 1973. Contbr. to: Engl. Lang. Notes; Mod. Land. Quarterly; Jrnl. of Engl. & Germanic Philol.; Studies in Scottish Lit.; Studies in Medieval Culture; Assoc. Ed., S. Atlantic Bull., S. Atlantic MLA. Address: Dept. of Engl., Univ. of Ga., Athens, GA 30602, USA.

MITCHELL, Joseph, b. 27 July 1908, Robeson Co., N.C., USA. Magazine Writer. Educ: Univ. of N.C., Chapel Hill, 1925-29. Publs: My Ears Are Bent (newspaper articles), 1938; (short stories) McSorley's Wonderful Saloon, USA, 1943, UK, 1946; Old Mr. Flood, 1948; The Bottom of the Harbor, USA, 1959, UK, 1961; Joe Gould's Secret, 1965. Contbr. to: N.Y. Herald Tribune (Reporter, 1929-31); N.Y. World Telegram (Reporter, 1931-38); New Yorker (Staff Writer, 1938—). Mbr., Nat. Inst. Arts & Letters. Recip., Grant, Nat. Inst. Arts & Letters, 1970. Address: c/o The New Yorker, 25 W. 43rd St., N.Y., NY 10036, USA.

MITCHELL, Julian, b. 1 May 1935, Epping, UK. Writer. Educ: B.A., M.A., Oxford. Publs: Imaginary Toys, 1961; A Disturbing Influence, 1962; As Far As You Can Go, 1963; The White Father, 1964; A Circle of Friends, 1966; The Undiscovered Country, 1968; Jennie, Lady Randolph Churchill (w. Peregrine Churchill), 1974. Contbr. to num. Brit. weeklies; etc. Hons: John Llewellyn Rhys Mem. Award; Somerset Maugham Award. Address: c/o Clive Goodwin, 79 Cromwell Rd., London SW7, UK.

MITCHELL, W(illiam) O(rmond), b. 13 Mar. 1914, Weyburn, Sask., Can. Writer. Educ: Univ. of Man., 1932-34; B.A., Univ. of Alta., 1942. Publs: (novels) Who Has Seen the Wind, USA, 1947, UK, 1948; Jake & the Kid, 1961; The Kite, 1962; The Vanishing Point, 1972; (short story) The Black Bonspiel of Wullie MacCrimmon, 1965 (also as play in Three Worlds of Drama, 1966); var. plays, CBC, 1947—. Contbr. to: Maclean's Mag. (novel, The Alien, serialized 1953-54); Atlantic. Hons: Maclean's Novel Award, 1953; Pres.'s Medal, Univ. of Western Ont., 1953; Leacock Medal, 1962. Address: 3031 Roxboro Glen Rd., Calgary, Alta., Can.

MITCHELL, Yvonne, b. 7 July 1925, London, UK. Writer; Actress. Publs: The Same Sky (play), 1953; Actress, 1957; The Bedsitter, 1959; Frame for Julian, 1960; A Year in Time, 1964; The Family, 1967; Martha On Sunday, 1970; God Is Inexperienced, 1974; (children's) Cathy Away, 1964; Cathy at Home, 1965; But Wednesday Cried, 1974. Hons: TV Actress of the Yr., 1952; Festival of Brit. Prize for Best Play, 1953; Brit. Film Acad. Award, 1956; Berlin Festival Award, Best Film Actress, 1957; Best Actress Award, Variety Club of GB, 1957. Address: Domaine du Plan-Sarain, La Roquette-sur-Siagne, 06550 France.

MITCHISON, Naomi, b. 1897, Edinburgh, UK. Writer. Publs. incl: The Corn King & the Spring Queen; Black Sparta; Memoirs of a Spacewoman; Karensgaard; When We Become Men; Friends & Enemies; The Family at Ditlabong; Sunrise Tomorrow; The Young Alexander; The Young Alfred the Great; Return to Fairy Hill; Cleopatra's People; African Heroes; Small Talk; A Life for Africa; Solution Three; All Change Here; num. others. Contbr. to: New Statesman; Guardian; Glasgow Herald; Scotsman; New Scientist; Saltire Review; Scots Mag.; Reporter; etc. Mbr., PEN. Agent: David Higham. Address: Carradale, Campbelltown, Argyll, Scotland, UK.

MITFORD, Jessica, b. 11 Sept. 1917. University Professor. Publs: (autobiography) Hons & Rebels, 1960; The American Way of Death, 1963; The Trial of Dr. Spock, 1970; Kind & Unusual Punishment, 1973. Address: 6411 Regent St., Oakland, Calif., USA.

MITGANG, Herbert, b. 20 Jan. 1920, NYC, USA. Journalist; Author. Educ: LL.B., St. John's Univ. Schl. of Law, 1942. Publs: The Return, 1959; Freedom to See: TV & the 1st Amendment, 1962; The Man Who Rode the Tiger, 1963; America at Random (Ed.), 1968; The Letters of Carl Sandburg (Ed.), 1970; Washington, DC, in Lincoln's Time (Ed.), 1971; Spectator of America (Ed.), 1971; Abraham Lincoln: A Press Portrait, 1971; Working for the Reader, 1972; Get These Men Out of the Hot Sun, 1972; The Fiery Trial, A Life of Lincoln, 1974. Contbr. to: Am. Heritage; New Repub.; Atlantic; Progressive; Commonweal; Observer; Telegraph. Mbrships. incl: Pres., Authors' Guild of Am., 1970—; Coun., Authors' League, 1965—; US

Deleg., Int. Exec. Comm., PEN, London. Hons. incl: Gavel Award, Am. Bar Assn., 1963, 1969. Address: N.Y. Times, 229 W. 43rd St., N.Y., NY 10036, USA.

MITRA, Sisirkumar, b. 5 Dec. 1901, Konnagar, W. Bengal, India. Teacher; Writer. Educ: Calcutta Univ.; Bengal Nat. Univ. Publs: Sri Aurobindo: A Homage (w. Tan Yun-Shan), 1940; Cultural Fellowship of Bengal, 1946; The Vision of India, 1949; The Liberator — Sri Aurobindo, India & the World, 1954; The Dawn Eternal, 1954; Resurgent India, 1963; A Marvel of Cultural Fellowship, 1967; History as the Future, 1968; India: Vision & Fulfilment, 1972; Sri Aurobindo, 1972. Contbr. to: Mod. Review, Calcutta; Indian Review, Madras; Visya-Bharati Quarterly; Prabuddha Bharata; Triveni; Mother India. Mbr., Coun., Sri Aurobindo Int. Ctr. of Educ. Winner, All-India Essay Competition, 1924. Address: Sri Aurobindo Ashram, Pondicherry 605002, S. India.

MITRU, Alexandru, pen name of PÎRAIANU, Alexandru, b. 6 Nov. 1914, Craiova, Rumania. Writer; Literature Teacher, Educ: Univ. of Bucharest. Pubs. incl: Muntele de Aur, 1954, 4th ed., 1974; În ţara legendelor, 1956, 3rd ed., 1973; Poveşti cu tîlc, 1956, 4th ed., 1973; Legendele Olimpului, 2 vols., 1960-62, 5th ed., 1973; Marile legende ale lumii, 2 vols., 1963-65; Săgeata căpitanului Ion, 1967, 2nd ed., 1969; Povestiri despre Păcală şi Tîndală, 1975. Contbr. to num. lit. & children's jrnls. Mbrships. incl: Bucharest Writers' Assn.; Rumanian Writers' Union; Exec. Comm., Dept. of Lit. for Children. Num. hons. incl: Short Story Prize, Min. of Culture, 1949; Rumanian Writers' Union Prize, 1968; Prize, Rumanian Acad., 1972; Rdrs.' Trophy Cup, 1974. Address: 7000, Bucharest III, 20, str. Vişinilor 2, Rumania.

MIURA, Hiroshi, b. 19 Oct. 1930, Tokyo, Japan. Editorial Writer. Educ: B.A., Univ. of Kyoto. Publs: The Sleeping Rose, 1969. Contbr. to: Sankei Shimbun. Mbr., Japan PEN. Address: Kodan-Jyutaku 54-2, 4-8-2 Tamadaira, Hino-shi, Tokyo, Japan.

MIURA, Shumon, b. 12 Jan. 1926, Tokyo, Japan. Novelist. Educ: Grad., Tokyo Univ. Publs: Miniature Garden, 1967; Sacrifice, 1972. Contbr. to: Shincho; Bungakukai; Gunzo; etc. Mbrships: Bd. of Dirs., Japan Writers' Assn.; Japan PEN. Recip., Shincho Lit. Prize, 1967. Address: 3-5-13 Denenchotu Ohtaku, Tokyo, Japan.

MIXTER, Russell L., b. 1906, Williamston, Mich., USA. Teacher. Educ: Wheaton Coll.; Mich. State Univ.; Univ. of Ill.; Ph.D. Publs: Ed., Evolution & Christian Thought Today, 1959. Contbr. to: Former Ed., Jrnl. of Am. Sci. Affiliation; Christian Life; Christianity Today. Mbr., AAAS. Address: 1006 North President, Wheaton, IL 60187, USA.

MIYAMOTO, Kenji, b. 17 Oct. 1908, Yamaguchi, Japan. Chairman of Presidium, Central Committee of Communist Party of Japan. Educ: Grad., Tokyo Imperial Univ. Publs. incl: Problems of Democratic Revolution, 1947; Advance towards Freedom & Independence, 1949; Twelve Years' Letters, 1952; World of Yuriko Miyamoto, 1954; Prospects of Japanese Revolution, 1961; The Path of Our Party's Struggle, 1961; Actual Tasks & the Communist Party of Japan, 1966; Selection from Literal Critiques of Kenji Miyamoto, 1968; The Road towards a New Japan, 1970; Standpoint of the Communist Party of Japan, 1972; Dialogues with K. Miyamoto, 1972; K. Miyamoto with Pressmen, 1973; Abashiri Note, 1975. Address: Central Committee of the Communist Party of Japan, Sendagaya 4-26-7, Shibuya-ku, Tokyo, Japan.

MIZENER, Arthur, b. 3 Sept. 1907, Erie, Pa., USA. University Professor; Author. Educ: B.S., Princeton Univ.; 1930; A.M., Harvard Univ., 1932; Ph.D., Princeton Univ., 1934. Publs: The Far Side of Paradise: A Biography of Scott Fitzgerald, 1951, 2nd ed., 1965; The Sense of Life in the Modern Novel, 1967; Twelve Great American Novels, 1968; The Saddest Story: A Biography of Ford Madox Ford, 1971; Scott Fitzgerald & His World, 1972. Contbr. to: N.Y. Times; Book Review; Southern, Sewanee & Kenyon Reviews; Atlantic Monthly; Harper's. Address: Dept. of English, Cornell Univ., Ithaca, NY 14850, USA.

MIZNER, Elizabeth Howard, pen name, HOWARD, Elizabeth, b. 24 Aug. 1907, Detroit, Mich., USA. Author. Educ: A.B., A.M., Univ. of Mich.; Grad. work, Wayne State Univ. Publs: Sabina, 1941; Adventure for Alison, 1942; Dorinda, 1944; Summer under Sail, 1947; North Winds Blow Free, 1949; Peddler's Girl, 1951; Candle in the Night, 1952; A Star to Follow, 1954; The Road Lies West, 1955;

A Girl of the North Country, 1957; The Courage of Bethea, 1959; Verity's Voyage, 1964; Winter on Her Own, 1968; Wilderness Venture, 1973. Address: 9692 W. Bay Shore Rd., Traverse City, MI 49684, USA.

MOAT, John, b. 1936, Mussoorie, India. Writer. Educ: M.A., Univ. of Oxford, UK. Publs: 6d Per Annum (verse), 1966; Heorot (novel), 1968; A Standard of Verse, 1969; Thunder of Grass, 1970; The Tugen & the Toot, 1973. Contbr. to: BBC; Listener; etc. Co-Fndr., Arvon Fndn. Address: c/o A.D. Peters & Co., 10 Buckingham Gate, London WC2, UK.

MOBERG, Zeth Agarth, b. 25 Nov. 1925, Borås, Sweden. Advertising Copywriter. Educ: Schl. of Jrnlsm., Syracuse Univ., USA; Journalisthögskolan, Gothenburg; Univ. of Gothenburg; Swedish Schl. of Arts & Crafts. Publs: Rönnflöjten, 1965; Kontaktmannen, 1969. Mbr., Swedish Union of Authors. Recip., Schlrship., Swedish Fund of Authors, 1972. Address: Stureplatsen 3, 411 39 Gothenburg, Sweden.

MOCH, Jules, b. 15 Mar. 1893, Paris, France. Former Prime Minister of France; Engineer. Educ: Schl. Marine Engrng. Publs: Paix en Algérie, 1961; Le Pont sur la Manche, 1962; Non à la force de frappe, 1964; Histoire du rearmément allemand, 1965; Recontres avec Darlan et Eisenhower, 1968; Destin de la Paix, 1969; Rencontres avec Léon Blum, 1970; Rencontre avec de Gaulle, 1971; Le Front populaire, grand espérance, 1971; Socialisme de l'Ere atomique, 1973. Contbr. to: Le Midi Libre; etc. Hons. incl: Cmdr. Legion d'Honneur; Croix de Guerre, 1914-18, 1939-45 (5 citations); Medaille de la Résistance avec rosette; Norwegian Croix de Guerre. Address: 97 Boulevard Murat, 75016 Paris, France.

MODIANO, Patrick Jean, b. 30 Aug. 1945, Boulogne-Billancourt, France. Novelist. Publs: La Place de l'Etoile, 1968; La Ronde de Nuit, 1969; Les Boulevards de Ceinture, 1972. Hons: Prix Roger Nimier, 1968; Prix Felix Fénéon, 1969; Grand Prix, French Acad., 1972. Address: 29 rue Daubigny, Paris 17e, France.

MOELLER, Dorothy Wilson, b. 14 Nov. 1902, Dawson, N.D., USA. Writer. Educ: B.A., Univ. of Iowa. Publs: Good Morning, Doctor! (ghost for Dr. W. A. Rohlf), 1938; Speech Handicapped School Children (Ed. w. Wendell Johnson), 1967; Living with Change: the Semantics of Coping (w. Wendell Johnson), 1972. Contbr. to: Asha; Rehab. Record; Books at Iowa. Mbrships: Women in Communications, Inc.; Ed., Iowa Voter, League of Women Voters; Nineteenth Century Study Club. Hons: Leadership Award, Alpha Phi Omega, 1950; Headliner Award, Women in Communications, Inc., 1973. Address: 623 East College St., Iowa City, IA 52240, USA.

MOEN, Arve Sverre, b. 2 Nov. 1912, Asnes, Norway. Editor; Author. Educ: Examen Artium, 1932; Cand. Jur. (Ex. in Law), Univ. of Oslo, 1936; studies in art hist., 1936-39. Publs: Storm i vannglass (short stories), 1945; Døden er et Kjaertegn (novel), 1948; Edvard Munch — samtid og miljø, 1957, kvinnen og eros, 1958, landskap og dyr, 1959; Gullalderens mestere, 1964; Du store verden så liten, 1966. Contbr. to var. jrnls., also Ency. Britannica. Mbr., sev. lit. orgs. Address: Langerudsvingen 27, Oslo 11, Norway.

MOFFETT, Samuel Hugh, b. 7 Apr. 1916, Pyongyang, Korea. Missionary; Educator. Educ: A.B., Wheaton Coll., 1938; Th.B., Princeton Theol. Sem., 1942; Ph.D., Yale Univ., 1945. Publs: Where'er the Sun, 1953; The Christians of Korea, 1962; Joy for an Anxious Age, 1966; The Biblical Background of Evangelism, 1968. Contbr. to jrnls. & Concise Dictionary of Christian World Mission. Address: Presbyterian Mission, CPO Box 1125, Seoul, Korea.

MOGHAL, Ghulam Nabi, b. 12 Mar. 1942, Hyderabad, Sind, Pakistan. Public Servant. Educ: B.A., Univ. of Sind, 1966. Publs: (selections of short stories in Sindhi lang.). Nuan Shaher, 1966; Raat-Ja-Nen, 1969. Contbr. to: Mehran; Naren Zindagi; Sohni; Rooh Rehan; Maruara; Naeen Duniya; Koonj. Address: F/765 Farid Mohalla, West Kacha, Hyderabad, Sind, Pakistan.

MOHAN, K. R. K., b. 18 Nov. 1933, Masulipatam, Andhra Pradesh State, India. Government Postal Official; Author. Educ: B.A. Publs. incl: Mani Manjiralu (in Telugu), 1963; Tomorrow's Truths about the Moon Told Today (in Engl.), 1964; Tushara Binduvulu (Telugu), 1964; Devata, 1964; Kanuvippu, 1965; Gabbilaalu, 1965. Contbr. to:

Indian Express, Vijayawada; Deccan Chronicle, Hyderabad; Bhovan's Jrnl., Bombay; Child Welfare, Hyderabad; var. publs., Telugu lang. Mbrships. incl: Telugu Sec., Nat. Coun. Indian Writers, Hyderabad; Chmn., William Mem. Lit. Soc., Hyderabad. Hons. incl: 1st Prize, All India Radio Essay Writing Competitions, 1973, 1974. Address: Plot No. 12, P & T Colony, Gaddiannaram, Hyderabad 500 036, India.

MOHAN, (The Rev.) Talbot G., b. 1895, Torquay, Devon, UK. Church of England Clergyman; Secretary, Church Pastoral Aid Society; formerly Vicar of Holy Trinity, Islington, London. Educ: St. Edmund Hall, Oxford; Wycliffe Hall, Oxford. Publs: Your Bereavement, 1958; Parochial Patronage, 1962. Mbr., Royal C'wlth. Soc. Address: 18 Uplands Way, Sevenoaks, Kent, UK.

MOHOLY, Lucia, b. Austria. Publisher; Editor; Lecturer. Writer; Educ: Prague Univ.; Acad. of Graphic Art, Leipzig; Bauhaus Schl. of Design, Weimar & Dessau. Publs: Bauhaus Books (collaborator, 1924-30; A Hundred Years of Photography, 1939; Who Is Who in Graphic Art (co-ed.), 1962; Moholy-Nagy Marginal Notes, 1972. Contbr. to: Nature; Research; Times; Times Lit. & Educl. Supplements; Burlington Mag.; Jrnl. of Documentation; Coll. Art Jrnl. (USA); etc. Mbrships: Royal Photog. Soc. of GB; Soc. of Authors; Lib. Assn.; Philosophische Gesellschaft, Zurich; Assn. Int. des Critiques d'art; Swiss Brit, Soc. Address: Rotfluhstr. 10, 8702 Zollikon ZH, Switz.

MOHRMANN, Christine A.E.M., b. 1 Aug. 1903, Groningen, Netherlands. Professor of Greek & Latin. Educ: Dr., Classical Philol., Univ. of Nijmegen. Publs: Atlas of the Early Christian World; Liturgical Latin; Etudes sur le latin des Chrétiens, 3 vols.; etc. Contbr. to: Vigiliae Christianae; Revue des Etudes Latines; etc. Mbrships: Sec. Gen., Permanent Int. Comm. of Linguists; Soc. de Linguistique, Paris; Hon. Mbr., Linguistic Soc. of Am. Hons: Hon. degrees, Univ. Cattolica del Sacro Cuore, Milan, Italy, Univ. of Ireland, Dublin, Repub. of Ireland, Univ. de Nice, France, Univ. de Gand, Belgium. Address: St. Annastraat 40, Nijmegen, Netherlands.

MOHRT, Michel, b. 28 Apr. 1914, Morlaix, France. Writer. Educ: Degree, Law, Univ. of Rennes. Publs: Montherlant, "Homme libre", 1943; Le répit, 1947; Mon Royaume pour un cheval, 1949; Les Nomades, 1951; Le Serviteur fidèle, 1953; Le Nouveau roman américain, 1955; La Prison maritime, 1961; La Campagne d'Italie, 1967; L'Ours des Adirondacks, 1969; L'Air du large, 1970; (play) Un jeu d'enfer, 1970; Deux Indiennes à Paris, 1974. Contbr. to: N.R.F.; Revue des Deux Mondes; Le Monde; Le Figaro; Sunday Times. Hons: Grand Novel Prize, for La Prison maritime, French Acad., 1962; Grand Lit. Criticism Prize, for L'air du large, 1970. Address: 4 bis rue du Cherche-Midi, Paris, France.

MOIR, James, b. 1908, Workington, Cumberland, UK. Acoustical Consulting Engineer. Educ: Rugby Coll. of Technol. Publs: High Quality Sound Reproduction; High Fidelity Sound Reproduction. Contbr. to: Wireless World; Hi-Fi News; I.E.E. Jrnl.; A.E.S. Jrnl.; Audio Engrng.; F.M./T.V.; Stereo Review; Electronic Engrng.; Electronics. Mbrships. incl: Fellow, Inst. Elec. Engrs.; Fellow, Audio Engrng. Soc., USA.; Am. Phys. Soc.; Am. Acoustical Soc.; Brit. Kine & TV Soc.; var. offs., Inst. Elec. Engrs.; Chmn., Brit. Sect., Audio Engrng. Soc. Hons. incl: I.E.E. Premium for paper on Acoustics of Cinema Auditoria, 1941. Address: 16 Wayside, Chipperfield, Herts. WD4 9JJ, UK.

MOK, Maurits, b. 7 Nov. 1907, Haarlem, Netherlands. Author. Publs: (novels) Badseizoen; Niemandsland; De Ontmaskering; (poems) Kaas- en Broodspel; Gedenk de Mens; Avond aan Avond; Met Job geleefd; Grondtoon; (children's books) Dr. Kwekkeltee, 6 vols. Contbr. to: Haagsche Courant, The Hague (reviewer); num. Flemish publs. Mbrships: Dutch PEN Ctr.; Dutch Soc. Authors. Hons: Poetry Prize of Amsterdam, 1957; Award, Fndn. of Artists in the Resistance, 1958; Henriette Roland Holst Prize, 1962; Marianne Philips Prize, 1968. Address: Voorstraat 101, Delft, Netherlands.

MOLINARI, Ricardo E., b. 20 Mar. 1898. Poet. Educ: Argentina. Publs. incl: El Huesped y la Melancolía, 1946; Días donde la Tarde es un Pájaro, 1954; Unida Noche, 1957; El Cielo de las Alondras y las Gaviotas, 1963; Una sombra antigua Canta, 1966; La Hoguera Transparente, 1970; La Escudilla, 1973; (complete works) Las Sombras del Pájaro tostado, 1974. Recip., all poetry prizes in Argentina. Address: Julián Alvarez 2092, Buenos Aires 25, Argentina.

MOLLENHOFF, Clark Raymond, b. 16 Apr. 1921, Burnside, Iowa, USA. Newspaper Correspondent. Educ: LL.B., J.D., Drake Univ. Law Schl., 1944; Nieman Fellow, Harvard Univ., 1949-50; Eisenhower Exchange Fellow, 1960-61. Publs: Washington Cover-up, 1962; Tentacles of Power, 1965; Despoilers of Democracy, 1965; The Pentagon, 1967; George Romney — Morman in Politics, 1968; Strike Force, 1972. Contbr. to: Look; Harper's; Atlantic; New Repub.; Nation. Mbrships. incl: Gridiron Club; Nat. Press Club. Hons. incl: Nat. Headliner Award, 1960; William Allen White Award, 1964; Drew Pearson Fndn. Award, 1973. Address: 5704, 32nd St. N.W., Washington, DC 20015, USA.

MÖLLERSTEDT, Gunnar, pen name AHM, George, b. 12 Dec. 1932, Mora, Sweden. Television Producer. Educ: Fil. Mag. Publs: (poetry) Näsvissla Boken, 1960; Apteringar, 1963; (novels) Vikarien, 1961; I själva verket, 1963; Den ofrånkomlige, 1965. Address: S:t Sigfridsgatan 58, 412 66 Gothenburg, Sweden.

MOLLO, Victor, b. 1909, St. Petersburg, Russia. Bridge Correspondent & Bridge Editor. Educ: Univ. of London, UK. Publs: Streamlined Bridge; Card Play Technique (w. N. Gardener); Bridge for Beginners (w. N. Gardener); Bridge Psychology, 1958; Will You be my Partner, 1959; Bridge: Modern Bidding, 1961; Bridge in the Menagerie, 1965; The Bridge Immortals, 1967; Victor Mollo's Winning Double, 1968; Bridge: Case for the Defence, 1970; Best of Bridge (w. E. Jannersten), 1973; Bridge in the Fourth Dimension, 1974; (pocket guides) Winning Bidding; Winning Conventions; Winning Defence. Mbr., Soc. of Authors. Address: 801 Grenville House, Dolphin Square, London SW1, UK.

MOLLOY, Paul George, b. 4 July, 1923, Winnipeg, Man., Can. Writer; Daily Columnist with The Chicago Sun-Times. Educ: B.A., Univ. Man. Publs: And Then There Were Eight, 1963; A Pennant for the Kremlin, 1965; All I Said Was . . ., 1968. Contbr. to Am. & Can. mags. Mbr., Authors' Guild Am. Hons: Nat. Headliner Award, 1960; Chicago's Outstanding Jrnlst. Award, 1961; George Washington Honor Medal, 1965 & 1970. Address: Chicago Sun-Times, 401 N. Wabash Ave., Chicago, IL 60611, USA.

MOLNÁR, Gábor, b. 2 Dec. 1908, Budapest, Hungary. Writer; Naturalist. Publs: 21 books, inclng: Kalandok a braziliai őserdőben, 1940; Az óriáskigyók földjén, 1955; Jaguárországban, 1960; A Fehér arany vadonában, 1961; Pálmakunyhó az őzerdőben, 1963; A dzsungel doktora, 1967; Biborkiskó, 1969; Négy hágó szilavadonában, 1970; Gyémántmosók, 1972; Éjbe zuhant évek, 1973; Én kedves Amazoniám, 1975. Contbr. to: all major Hungarian reviews & newspapers. Mbrships. incl: Hungarian Writers' Assn.; PEN Club; Art Fndn. of Hungarian People's Repub.; Hungarian Geog. Soc.; Assn. of the Blind. Hons. incl: Order of Hungarian People's Repub., silver. Address: Őzike utca 30, 1121 Budapest XII, Hungary.

MOLNAR, George, b. 25 Apr. 1910, Nagyvarad, Hungary. Associate Professor. Educ: Dip. in Archtl. Engrng., Tech. Univ., Budapest. Publs: Statues, 1954; Insubstantial Pageant, 1959; Postcards, 1961; Molnar at Large, 1968; The People's Suit, 1974. Contbr. to: Sydney Morning Herald; Quadrant. Hons: O.B.E.; F.R.A.I.A. Mbrships. incl: Fellow, Royal Aust. Inst. of Arch. Address: 22 Wolseley Rd., Point Piper, N.S.W., Australia 2027.

MOLNÁR, Géza, pen name CZIBUS, Csaba, b. 6 Nov. 1923, Rakospalota, Hungary. Writer. Publs: Szerelmes kisinas, 1956; Hullámverés, 1958; Márta, 1959; Város a felhők alatt (trilogy), 1964-71; Sárkányok fiai, 1969; Vasárnap mindig esik az eső, 1970; Kulvárosi barangolás, 1974. Contbr. to: Kortárs; Uj Irás; Élet és Irodalom; Forrás; Népszabadság; Népszava. Mbrships: Hungarian Writers' Assn.; PEN Club. Hons: József Attila Prize; SZOT Prize. Address: Frakno-utca 14/a, 1115 Budapest, Hungary.

MONAGHAN, James, b. 19 Mar. 1891, West Chester, Pa., USA. Author; Editor. Educ: A.B., Swarthmore Coll., 1913; M.A., Univ. of Pa., 1918; Litt.D., Monmouth Coll., 1947. Publs. incl: Lincoln Bibliography 1839-1939, 2 vols., 1943; The Overland Trail, 1947; Civil War on Western Border, 1956; Australians & the California Gold Rush, 1966; Chile, Peru & the California Gold Rush, 1973. Contbr. to: Dict. Am. Hist.; Atlas of Am. Hist., var. histl. jrnls.; Ed., Am. Trails series, 1947-49; Histl. Rsch. Ed., Exec. Dir., State Histn., Ill. State Histl. Lib. & Soc., 1939-51. Recip., C'wlth. Club of Calif. Best Book Award,

1973. Address: 8 W. Constance Ave., Apt. C-2, Santa Barbara, CA 93105, USA.

MONCRIEFF, Robert Wighton, b. 1903, Preston, Lancs., UK. Industrial Research & Development Worker; Consultant; Author. Educ: B.Sc., Manchester Univ. Publs: The Chemical Senses: Mothproofing; Odour Preferences; Man-made Fibres; Wool Shrinkage & its Prevention; The Chemistry of Perfumery Materials; Odours, 1970; The Nature of Gravitation (pvte). publ.), 1972. Contbr. to: Jrnl. of Applied Physiol.; Am. Jrnl. of Psychol.; Jrnl. of Physiol.; Perfumery Essential Oil Record; etc. Address: The Gables, Hambrook, Chichester, Sussex, UK.

MONCURE, Jane Belk (Mrs. James A. Moncure), b. 16 Dec. 1926, Orlando, Fla., USA. Educator. Educ: B.S., Va. C'wlth. Univ., 1952; M.A., Columbia Univ., 1954. Publs: Pinny's Day at Playschool, 1955; Bunny Finds a Home, 1962; Flip, the True Story of a Dairy Farm Goat, 1964; Try on a Shoe, 1973; Play With Me Alphabet Books (series of 5), 1973; How Do You Feel?, 1974; Winter Is Here, 1975; Spring Is Here, 1975; Summer Is Here, 1975; Fall Is Here, 1975; "Wait! " Says His Father, 1975. Mbrships. incl: Pres., Va. Assn. for Early Childhood Educ., 1958-60; Southern Assn. for Children Under 6; Nat. Assn. for Educ. of Young Children. Address: 1046 Briarcliff Rd., Burlington, NC 27215, USA.

MONELLI, Paolo, b. 15 July 1894. Journalist; Novelist. Educ: D.Jur., Bologna Univ. Publs. incl: Le Scarpe al sole, 1921, 1955; 1965; Questo mestieraccio, 1928; La guerra è bella ma è scomoda, 1929; Barbaro dominio, 1933; Il ghiottone errante, 1935, 1947; Roma, 1943, 1945, 1963; Naja parla, 1947; Mussolini piccolo borghese, 1950; Nessuna nuvola in cielo, 1957; Avventura nel primo secolo, 1958; Il vero bevitore, 1963; Ombre Cinesi, 1965. Contbr. to: La Stampa; Il Monod; Tempo; Espresso; France Soir; etc. Num. hons. incl: Croix de Guerre, Belgium; Saint Vincent Grand Prix, 1960. Address: Via Venti Settempre 3, 00187 Rome, Italy.

MONET, Jacques, b. 26 Jan. 1930, Saint-Jean, P.Q., Can. Jesuit Priest; Professor. Educ: B.A., Univ. of Montreal; Ph.L. & Th. L., Coll. de l'Immaculée-Conception, Montreal; M.A. & Ph.D., Univ. of Toronto. Publs: The Last Cannon Shot. A Study of French Canadian Nationalism, 1837-1851, 1969. Contbr. to: Can. Histl. Review; Histoire Sociale/Soc. Hist.; Histl. Papers. VP., Can. Histl. Assn. Address: Dept. of Hist., Univ. of Ottawa, Ottawa, Ont., Can.

MONIGATTI, Charles Rex Ivan, b. 11 June 1923, Nelson, NZ. Public Relations Consultant; Editor. Educ: M.A.; Dip. in Jrnlsm. Publs: New Zealand Sensations, 1962; New Zealand Headlines, 1963; From Bells to Blazes, 1965; Fruitful Years, 1966; Switch On, 1970; Energy on the Move, 1972. Contbr. to num. NZ jrnls. Mbr., PR Inst. of NZ. Address: 25 Braithwaite St., Karori, Wellington, NZ.

MONKHOUSE, Francis John, b. 1914, Workington, Cumbria, UK. Geographer. Educ: Emmanuel Coll., Cambridge; London Univ. Inst. of Educ.; M.A.; D.Sc. Publs. incl: The Belgian Kempenland, 1949; Principles of Physical Geography, 1954; Study-Guide in Physical Geography, 1956; Landscape from the Air, 1959; A Regional Geography of Western Europe, 1959; Europe: A Geographical Survey, 1961; Dictionary of Geography, 1965; North America (w. H. R. Cain), 1970; Climber & Fellwalker in Lakeland (w. J. S. Williams), 1972; The Man-made Landscape (w. A. V. Hardy), 1974. Contbr. to: Geog.; Econ. Geog.; Scottish Geog. Mag.; Jrnl. of Geog. Address: Crag Farm House, Ennerdale, Cleator, Cumbria CA23 3AS, UK.

MÖNNICH, Horst, b. 8 Nov. 1918, Senftenberg/Lausitz, Germany. Author. Educ: Berlin Univ. (Drama & German Studies). Publs: Die Autostadt (novel), 1951; Das Land ohne Träume, 1954; Erst die Toten haben ausgelernt (novel), 1956; Reise durch Russland, 1961; Der Vierte Platz (novel), 1962 & 1973; Einreisegenehmigung, 1967; Aufbruch ins Revier, Aufbruch nach Europa, 1971; Hiob im Moor (radio play), 1966; Quarantäne im Niemandsland (radio play), 1972; Ein Dortmunder Agent, 1974. Contbr. of num. plays to all maj. German TV & Radio Stns. Mbrships: PEN, German Ctr.; German Authors' Assn. (VS); Gruppe 47. Hons. incl: Ernst Reuter Prize, 1967 & 1970; Int. Radio Drama Ctr. Award, 1973. Address: 8211 Breitbrunn am Chiemsee, Wolfsbergerstr. 25, W. Germany.

MONOSZLÖY, Dezső, b. 28 Dec. 1923, Budapest, Hungary. Writer. Educ: Grad., Law Fac., Pázmány Péter Univ. Publs: Egből üzenek, 1941; Gombostűk háborúja, 1944; Égetett sienna, 1947; Csak egyszer élünk, 1959; Virrasztó szerelem, 1964; Töltésszimmetria, 1965; Villamos alatt, 1965; Csók, 1966; Aranykor, 1967; Sivatag, Tetovált angyalok, 1968; A milliomos halála, 1969; Aranymecset, 1973. Contbr. to: Encounter; Presse; Literatur & Kritik; Pestsäule; Die Welt; Neue Zürcher Zeitung; Kortárs; Alföld; Irodalmi Szemle; Híd; sev. other E. European mags. Recip., Madách Prize, 1966. Address: A-1010 Vienna, Fleischmarkt 20/2/5, Austria.

MONROE, Keith, pen names COCHRAN, Rice; KEITH, Donald, b. 22 Aug. 1917, Detroit, Mich., USA. Writer. Educ: Stanford Univ.; UCLA. Publs: Use Your Head in Tennis, 1950; How to Succeed in Community Service, 1962; California, 1963; The Rock That Burns, 1965; Space: A New Direction for Mankind, 1969; Art in Persuasion, 1973; In Search of Ancient Mysteries, 1974; Other Men's Sons, 1975. Contbr. to: Harper's Mag.; New Yorker; N.Y. Times Sunday Mag.; Reader's Digest; Fortune. Mbrships: Authors' Guild; Soc. of Mag. Writers. Address: 11965 Montana Ave., L.A., CA 90049, USA.

MONRO-HIGGS, Gertrude, pen name MONRO, Gavin, b. Wimbledon, Surrey, UK. Former School Principal. Publs: Who Killed Amanda" 1967; A Bent for Blackmail, 1968; Marked with a Cross, 1968; Trip to Eternity, 1970. Contbr. to: BBC; sev. mags. & children's anthols.; The Horse-Lovers' Book. Mbrships: Crime Writers' Assn.; Chmn., W. Sussex Writers' Club, 1971-74. Address: Holmleigh, Kentwyns Drive, Kerves Lane, Horsham, Sussex, UK.

MONSARRAT, Ann Whitelaw, (Mrs. Nicholas Monsarrat), b. 8 Apr. 1937, Walsall, Staffs., UK. Writer. Publs: And The Bride Wore..., UK, 1973, USA, 1974. Contbr. to: Daily Mail, 1958-72; The Sun, 1970-72. Address: San Lawrenz, Gozo, Malta.

MONSARRAT, Nicholas John Turney, b. 22 Mar. 1910, Liverpool, UK. Writer; Broadcaster. Educ: Trinity Coll., Cambridge. Publs. incl: Think of Tomorrow, 1934; The Whipping Boy, 1936; My Brother Denys, 1948; The Cruel Sea, 1951; The Tribe that Lost its Head, 1956; The Ship that Died of Shame, 1959; The Pillow Fight, 1965; Richer than All His Tribe, 1968; The Kappillan of Malta, 1973; (autobiography) Life is a Four-Letter Word, vol. I, 1966, vol. II, 1970. Mbr., F.R.S.L. Hons: Heinemann Prize for Lit., 1951; Coronation Medal, 1953; Order of St. John of Jerusalem, 1973. Address: 15 Triq Il-Wileg, San Lawrenz, Gozo, Malta.

MONSEY, Derek, b. 28 Mar. 1935, Bridlington, UK. Writer. Publs: Its Ugly Head, 1959; The Hero Observed, 1960; Mia, 1965; The Adulterer, 1966; The Big Picture, 1967; An Affair, 1973; August for the Family, 1974. Address: Domaine du Plan-Sarrain, La Roouette sur Siaque, A.M., France.

MONTAGNES, E. Ian, b. 11 Mar. 1932, Toronto, Ont., Can. General Editor, University of Toronto Press. Educ: B.A., M.A., Univ. of Toronto. Publs: An Uncommon Fellowship — The Story of Hart House, 1969; Cold Iron & Lady Godiva — Engineering Education at Toronto 1920-1972 (co-ed. w. Robin S. Harris), 1973. Contbr. to: Can. Lit.; Scholarly Publishing; Sec., Assn. of Can. Univ. Presses. Address: Editorial Dept., Univ. of Toronto Press, Toronto, Ont. M5S 1A6, Can.

MONTAGU, (The Hon.) Ewen Edward Samuel, b. 29 Mar. 1901, London, UK. Queen's Counsel; Judge (Retired); Judge Advocate of the Fleet (Retired). Educ: Harvard, USA; M.A., LL.B., Trinity Coll., Cambridge, UK. Publs: The Man Who Never Was, 1953; The Archer-Shee Case, 1974. Mbrships: Former Pres., United Synagogue, Anglo-Jewish Assn.; Former Chmn., Gen. Purpose Comm., Royal Yachting Assn.; Chmn., Pioneer Hlth. Ctr. Recip., C.B.E. Address: 24 Montrose Ct., Exhibition Rd., London SW7 2QQ, UK.

MONTAGU, Ivor, b. 23 Apr. 1904, London, UK. Writer; Film Producer. Educ: Royal Coll. of Sci., London; King's Coll., Cambridge. Publs: Table Tennis Today, 1923; Table Tennis, 1936; The Traitor Class, 1940; Plot Against Peace, 1952; Land of Blue Sky, 1956; Film World, 1964; Germany's New Nazis, 1967; With Eisenstein in Hollywood, 1968; The Youngest Son, 1970. Contbr. to: Daily Wkr.; Labour Monthly; Marxism Today; Times; Manchester Guardian; Sunday Graphic; etc. Mbrships: Fndr. Pres., Int. Table Tennis Fedn.; Life V.P., Engl. Table Tennis Fedn.; Hon. Mbr., Writers' Guild. Address: Old Timbers, Verdure Close, Watford WD2 7NJ, UK.

MONTAGU OF BEAULIEU, (3rd Baron) Edward John Barrington Douglas-Scott-Montagu, b. 20 Oct. 1926, London, UK. Founder Trustee of Beaulieu Museum Trust. Educ: New Coll., Oxford. Publs: The Motoring Montagus, 1959; Lost Causes of Motoring, 1960; Jaguar, A Biography, 1961; The Gordon Bennett Races, 1963; Rolls of Rolls-Royce, 1966; The Gilt & the Gingerbread, 1967; Lost Causes of Motoring: Europe, vol. I, 1969, vol. II, 1971; More Equal than Others, 1970; History of the Steam Car, 1971; Man and the Automobile: A Social History; Ed., Veteran & Vintage Mag. Mbrships: Coun., Nat. Heritage; Pres., Southern Tourist Grp.; Press., Assn. of Brit. Transport Museums; V.P., Transport Trust; Guild of Motoring Writers; Inst. of Journalists. Address: Palace House, Beaulieu, Hampshire, UK.

MONTANELLI, Indro, b. 22 Apr. 1909. Journalist; Writer. Educ: Univs. of Florence & the Sorbonne, Paris. Publs: Storia di Roma, 1957; Storia dei Greci, 1958; Incontri, 1961; Garibaldi, 1962; Gente qualunque, 1963; Dante e il suo secolo, 1964; Italia dei secoli bui, 1965; (plays) I sogni muoiono all'alba (also filmed); Il Generale della Rovere (also filmed); Kibbutz. Contbr. to: Corriere della Sera, 1939-73; Fndr., Il Giornale, 1974. Hons: Bagutta Prize; Marzotto Prize. Address: Piazza Navona 93, Rome, Italy.

MONTEFIORE, Hugh William, b. 12 May 1920, London, UK. Bishop of Kingston-on-Thames; former University lecturer & College Fellow & Dean. Educ: M.A., St. John's Coll., Oxford; M.A., B.D., Sidney Sussex Coll., Cambridge. Publs: Beyond Reasonable Doubt, 1962; Commentary on the Epistle to the Hebrews, 1964; Truth to Tell, 1966; The Question Mark, 1968; Can Man Survive? , 1970; Doom or Deliverance, 1972; Ed., Changing Directions, 1974. Contbr. to: (books) Soundings; We Became Anglicans; Journeys in Belief; (jrnls.) Theol.; New Testament Studies; Novum Testamentum. Address: White Lodge, 23 Bellevue Road, London SW17, UK.

MONTEITH, (Rev.) Lionel, b. 6 Aug. 1921, Brighton, UK. Psychotherapist; Clinic Director; Minister of Religion. Educ: Dip.Th., Univ. of London, 1957; Cert. for Ordination, New Coll., London, 1958; studied w. Drs. P. L. Backus & L. Haas. Contbr. to lit. jrnls. in UK, USA, Can., Australia, NZ, S. Africa, Argentina & India, inclng: Poetry Commonwealth (Int. Poetry Jrnl., ed., 1948-53); Reform; Outposts; Variegation; Can. Poetry Mag.; Southerly; Arena; Trek; Engl. Folios; Voice of Ahimsa. Mbrships. incl: Fellow, Int. PEN. Address: The Lincoln Mem. Clin. for Psychotherapy, 77 Westminster Bridge Rd., London SE1 7HS, UK.

MONTES AGUILERA, Francisco, pen name ZAHORI, b. 22 Aug. 1916, Almeria, Spain. Naval Official. Publs. incl: Isabel de Barreto, Adelanto del Mar del Sur, 1960; Un Marino español, El Conde de Barcelona, 1966; Cadiz trascendente, forthcoming; La Hija de Ascara, forthcoming. Contbr. to: ABC; Semana; Sonata Gallega; Spes; Formacion. Mbrships. incl: Royal Hispano-Am. Acad.; San Romualdo Acad. of Scis., Letters & Arts. Hons. incl: Lucio Cornelio Balbo; El Puerto de Cadiz, Avanzada de Europa. Address: Calle Eladio Lopez Vilches, Num. 7-3⁰ Izquierda, Madrid 33, Spain.

MONTES DE OCA, Marco Antonio, b. 3 Aug. 1932, Mexico City, Mexico. Professor of Spanish Literature; Cultural Adviser to Government; Editor. Publs. incl: Ruina de la infame babilonia, 1953; Contrapunto de la fé, 1955; Pliego de testimonios, 1956; Delante de la luz cantan los pájaros, 1959; On the ruins of Babylon, 1964; Vendimia del Juglar, 1965; Autobiografía, 1967; Poesía Reunida, 1970; Astillas, 1973; Se llama como quieras, 1974; Lugares donde el espacio cicatriza, 1974; El surco y la brasa, 1974. Contbr. to: Le Monde; Hispanic Arts; Cuadernos; etc. Mbrships: Fndr. & Sec., PEN of Mexico; VP, Assn. of Writers of Mexico; Latin-Am. Community of Writers. Hons. incl: Nat. Mazatlán Prize, 1966; Guggenheim Grant, 1967-68, 1970-71. Address: Filosofía y Letras 52, Copilco-Universidad, Mexico 20 D.F., Mexico.

MONTGOMERIE, William, b. 1904, Glasgow, UK. Editor. Educ: Univs. of Glasgow & Edinburgh; M.A., Ph.D. Publs: Via: Squared Circle; New Judgments, Robert Burns; Hogarth Book of Scottish Nursery Rhymes (ed. w. N. M. Montgomerie); A Book of Scottish Nursery Rhymes (ed. w. N. M. Montgomerie); Well at the World's End. Contbr. to: Review of Engl. Studies; Hibbert Jrnl.; Scottish Studies; Folk-Lore; Jrnl. of Folk Dance & Song Soc.; New Brit. Poets; Ed., Burns Chronicle, 1950, Scots Chronicle, 1951;

etc. Address: 131 Warrender Park Rd., Edinburgh EH9 1DS, UK.

MONTGOMERY, Brian, b. 1903, London, UK. Writer; Borough Councillor, 1971-1974; Retired Diplomat, Army Officer & Instructor. Educ: Royal Mil. Coll., Sandhurst. Publs: A Field-Marshal in the Family (biog.), 1973, Am. ed., 1974. Contbr. to var. lit mags. Mbrships: Soc. of Authors; Pakistan Soc.; Army & Navy Club. Recip., M.B.E. Address: 11a The Gateways, Chelsea, London SW3 3HX, UK.

MONTGOMERY, Elizabeth Rider (Mrs. Arthur Julesberg), b. 12 July 1902, Huaras, Peru (of Am. parentage). Writer. Educ: Western Wash. Coll.; UCLA. Publs. incl: (jvnle. non-fiction) Keys to Nature's Secrets, 1946; Alexander Graham Bell, 1963; Hans Christian Andersen, 1968; William C. Handy, Father of the Blues, 1968; Henry Ford, 1969; Gandhi, 1970; Walt Disney, 1971; Duke Ellington, 1972; Dag Hammarskjöld, 1973; Indian Patriots, 1974; Super Showmen, 1974; (jvnle. fiction) Sally Does It, 1940; Mystery of Edison Brown, 1960; Two Kinds of Courage, 1966; also var. schl. textbooks, plays, etc. Recip., nat. prizes for sev. plays. Address: 10203 47th Ave. S.W., D2, Seattle, WA 98146, USA.

MONTGOMERY, John, b. 14 Apr. 1916, Edinburgh, UK. Author. Publs: Two Men & a Dog; Mr. Sparrow; Foxy; Village Green; My Friend Foxy; Your Dog; Abodes of Love; Royal Dogs; Toll for the Brave; The Twenties; The Fifties; 1900: The End of an Era; The Christmas Cat; Foxy & the Badgers; Looking after your Cat; Comedy Films; The World of Cats; Florence Nightingale; Arthur, The Television Cat. Ed., Pan Book of Animal Stories; Ed., Pan Book of Cat Stories. Contbr. to: Guardian; Sunday Times; Observer; Evening Standard; Woman's Own; Saturday Book. Agent: A. D. Peters. Address: c/o above, 10 Buckingham St., London WC2, UK.

MONTGOMERY, Mamie Elizabeth Wakefield, pen name WAKEFIELD, Elizabeth, b. 18 Apr. 1891, Seattle, Wash., USA. Piano Teacher; Practical Nurse. Educ: Pvte. music study; studied nursing, Mpls. Chirpractic Coll. Hosp., 1 yr. Publ: James Jays Takes a Case, 1972. Contbr. to: Listen; Youth's Instructor; Guide; MV Prog. Kit; Review & Herald (all Takoma Park, Wash.); Braille Publ.; Youth Happiness; (both Lincoln, Neb.). Mbr., Seventh Day Adventist Ch. Address: 700 Reserve, Apt. 2-3, Hot Springs, AR 71901, USA.

MONTGOMERY, Marion, b. 16 Apr. 1925, Tomaston, Ga., USA. Teacher; Writer. Educ: A.B., M.A., Univ. of Ga. Publs: (novels) The Wandering of Desire, 1962; Darrell, 1964; Ye Olde Bluebird (novella), 1967; Fugitive, 1974; (poetry) Dry Lightning, 1960; Stones from the Rubble, 1965; The Gull & Other Georgia Scenes, 1969; (criticism) Ezra Pound: A Critical Essay, 1970; T. S. Eliot: An Essay on the American Magus, 1970; The Reflective Journey Toward Order: Essays on Dante, Wordsworth, Eliot, & Others, 1973. Address: English Dept., Univ. of Ga., Athens, GA 30602, USA.

MONTGOMERY, Ruth Shick, b. Sumner, Ill., USA. Author; former Political Columnist. Educ: Purdue Univ., Ind. Publs: Once There was a Nun, 1962; Mrs. LBJ, 1964; A Gift of Prophecy, 1965; A Search for the Truth, 1966; Flowers at the White House, 1966; Here & Hereafter, 1968; Hail to the Chiefs, 1970; A World Beyond, 1971; Born to Heal, 1972; Companions Along the Way, 1974. Contbr. to num. mags. Mbrships. incl: Wash. Press Club (Pres., 1950-51); Mrs. Roosevelt's White House Press Conf. Assn. (Pres., 1944-45). Hons. incl: Best non-fiction award, Ind. Univ., 1966; George R. Holmes Jrnlsm. Award, 1957; LL.D., Baylor Univ. & Ashland Coll. Address: Apartado 923, Cuernavaca, Mor., Mexico.

MOODIE, Graeme Cochrane, b. 27 Aug. 1924, Dundee, UK. Professor of politics. Educ: M.A., Univ. of St. Andrews, 1943; Harkness Fellow, Princeton Univ., USA, 1949-51; M.A., Oxford Univ., 1953. Publs: Some Problems of the Constitution (w. Geoffrey Marshall), 1959, 5th ed., 1971; The Government of Great Britain, 1961, 3rd ed., 1971; Opinions, Publics, & Pressure Groups (w. G. Studdert Kennedy), 1970; Power & Authority in British Universities (w. Roland Eustace), 1974. Contbr. to: Pol. Studies; Parliamentary Affairs; Times Higher Educl. Supplement. Address: Dept. of Politics, University of York, Heslington, Yorks., UK.

MOODY, Harold Leonard Birch, b. 22 Apr. 1919, Gosforth, UK. Teacher; Lecturer. Educ: B.A., 1941, M.A.,

1944, Univ. of Cambridge; Univ. of London. Publs: Facing Facts, 1966; A Peacock Selection, 1967; Selected Readings, 1968; Literary Appreciation, 1968; Varieties of English, 1970; The Teaching of Literature in Developing Countries, 1971; The Walls & Gates of Kano City, 1974. Contbr. to: Univs. Quarterly; W.African Jrnl. of Educ.; Nigeria Mag.; London Educ. Review; Engl. Lang. Tchng. Mbrships: Soc. of Authors; Nat. Assn. of Tchrs. of Engl.; Int. Assn. of Tchrs. of Engl. as a For. Lang. Address: Fairfield Barn, Slaidburn Rd., Bentham via Lancaster, UK.

MOODY, Henry Laurence, b. 1 Mar. 1907, Whitehead, Co. Antrim, UK. Author. Publs: The Lantern Men, 1951; The Young Kings, 1960, 2nd ed. 1962; Some Must Die, 1964; No More to the Woods, 1967; Comet in a Red Sky, 1968; The Ruthless Ones, 1969; Conquistador, 1969; The Small War, 1970; The Roxton Kibbutz, 1971; The Dark-eyed Client, 1974; The Austrian Butterfly, 1975; (film) What Became of Jack & Jill, 1972. Contbr. to: Century of Histl. Stories; Evening News; Belfast Telegraph. Address: 44 Bawnmore Rd., Belfast, UK.

MOODY, Theodore William, b. 26 Nov. 1907, Belfast, UK. Professor of Modern History, University of Dublin since 1939. Educ: M.A., Ph.D.; Univs. London, Queen's, Belfast. Publs. incl: Ulster Plantation Papers, 1608-13, 1938; Thomas Davis, 1814-45, 1945; Queen's Belfast, 1845-1849: The History of a University (w. J. C. Beckett), 1959; Ed. & Contbr., The Fenian Movement, 1968; Historical Studies, VI, 1968; Ed., Michael Davitt's Leaves from a Prison Diary, reprinted, 1972; The Ulster Question, 1603-1973, 1974. Contbr. to var. acad. jrnls. etc. Mbrships. incl: Fellow Royal Histl. Soc.; Irish MSS Comm. Recip., Hon. D.Litt., Queen's Univ., Belfast, 1959. Address: Trinity Coll., Dublin, Repub. of Ireland.

MOORCOCK, Michael, b. 1939, Mitcham, Surrey, UK. Writer; Editor; Performer/Composer. Publs: The Eternal Champion Cycle, 1963-75; Behold the Man, 1969; The Final Programme, 1969; The Chinese Agent, 1970; A Cure for Cancer, 1971; English Assassin, 1972; Breakfast in the Ruins, 1972; An Alien Heat, 1972; The Hollow Lands, 1975; Ed., New Worlds Mag., 1963-73, Best of New Worlds Series, 1967-74; New Worlds Fair, (record album) 1975. Contbr. to: New World; Books & Bookmen; Sunday Times; etc. Mbrships. incl: Writers' Guild; Sci. Fiction Writers' Am. Hons. incl: Nebula Award, 1967; Brit. Fantasy Award, 1967; August Derleth Fantasy Award, 1971, 1972, 1973. Agent: Anthony Sheil Assocs. Address: c/o 52 Floral St., London WC2, UK.

MOORE, Alex, b. London, UK. Teacher & Demonstrator of Ballroom Dancing. Publs: Ballroom Dancing, 1936; Popular Variations, 1969; The Revised Technique of Ballroom Dancing, 1973. Contbr. to: Dancing Times; Mod. Dance. Mbrships: Chmn., Imperial Soc. of Tchrs. of Dancing; Pres., Int. Coun. of Ballroom Dancing. Address: Zeeta Dance Studios, 13 Penrhyn Rd., Kingston on Thames, Surrey KT1 2BZ, UK.

MOORE, Brian, b. 25 Aug. 1921, Belfast, UK. Novelist. Publs: The Lonely Passion of Judith Hearne, 1955; The Feast of Lupercal, 1957; The Luck of Ginger Coffey, 1960; An Answer from Limbo, 1962; The Emperor of Ice Cream, 1965; I Am Mary Dunne, 1968; Fergus, 1970; The Revolution Script, 1971; Catholics, 1972; The Great Victorian Collection, 1975. Hons: Award, Authors' Club of GB, 1956; P.Q. Lit. Prize, 1958; Guggenheim Fellowship, 1959; Gov. Gen. of Can.'s Award for Fiction, 1961; Grant, US Nat. Inst. of Arts & Letters, 1961; Sr. Fellowship, Can. Coun., 1962; W. H. Smith Award, 1972; Regents Prof. of Engl., UCLA, 1974-75. Address: c/o Collins, Knowlton, Wing, 60 East 56th St., N.Y., NY 10022, USA.

MOORE, Dan Tyler, b. 1 Feb. 1908, Wash. D.C., USA. Director General, International Platform Association; Writer; Lecturer. Educ: Grad., Sheffield Sci. Schl., Yale Univ., 1931. Publs: The Terrible Game, 1957; Cloak & Cipher, 1962; Wolves, Widows & Orphans, 1967; Lecturing for Profit, 1967. Contbr. to jrnls. inclng: Sat. Evening Post; Collier's; Reader's Digest; Redbook; True; Talent. Mbr., num. clubs. Hons: Sat. Evening Post — Best Short Stories of 1956; Winner, Teenage Book Award, 1957. Address: 2564 Berkshire Rd., Cleveland Heights, OH 44106, USA.

MOORE, Donald, b. 7 May 1923, Loughborough, UK. Concert Manager. Publs: Where Monsoons Meet; The Sacrifice & Other Stories; Far Eastern Agent; We Live in Singapore; All of One Company; The Sumatra; The Striking Wind; Judgement of Oleron; Highway of Fear; The First 150 Years of Singapore; The Magic Dragon. Address: 15G Balmoral Park, Singapore 10, Repub. of Singapore.

MOORE, Doris Langley. Founder, Museum of Costume, Bath. Publs. incl: The Technique of the Love Affair; A Winter's Passion (novel); E. Nesbitt (biog.); The Woman in Fashion; The Child in Fashion; The Vulgar Heart; Pleasure, A Discursive Guide Book; My Caravaggio Style (novel); Marie & the Duke of H. (biog.); Fashion Through Fashion Plates; The Late Lord Byron (biog.); Lord Byron — Accounts Rendered (biog.); All Done by Kindness (novel), 1951. Contbr. to: Sunday Times; etc. Hons: O.B.E., 1971; F.R.S.L., 1974. Address: 5 Prince Albert Rd., London NW1, UK.

MOORE, Edward Carter, b. 12 Feb. 1917, Mt. Clemens, Mich., USA. University Vice Chancellor & Professor. Educ: B.A., Western Mich. Univ., 1938; M.A., 1946, M.A., 1947, Ph.D., 1950, Univ. of Mich. Publs: American Pragmatism: Peirce, James & Dewey, 1961; Studies in the Philosophy of Charles Sanders Peirce (ed. w. Richard Robin), 1964; William James, 1965; The Essential Writings of Charles S. Peirce, 1972. Contbr. to: Ed., Transactions of Charles S. Peirce Soc. (Ed., 1965-70); profl. & acad. jrnls. Mbrships. incl: Nat. Pres., Charles S. Peirce Soc., 1964-66; Am. Philos. Assn.; Philos. of Sci. Assn. Address: Indiana Univ.—Purdue Univ. at Indpls., Rm. 106A, Admin. Bldg., 355 N. Lansing St., Indpls., IN 46202, USA.

MOORE, Edward J., b. 2 June 1935, Chgo., Ill., USA. Playwright; Actor. Educ: Goodman Theatre, Chgo., Ill. Publs: The Sea Horse, 1974. Mbrships: Fndr., N.Y. Playwrights' Workshop; Screen Actors' Guild; Am. Fedn. of TV & Radio Artists; Actors' Equity Assn.; Drama Guild. Recip., Vernon Rice Outstanding New Playwright 1974 Award; The Sea Horse, Otis Guernsey's Ten Best Plays of 1973-74. Address: Apt. 3A, 11 Carmine St., N.Y., NY 10014, USA.

MOORE, Eva Beate, pen name MAY, b. 11 May 1925, Mannheim, Germany. Author; Composer. Educ: Grad., Kindergarten Tchrs.' Coll., Melbourne. Publs: Of This & That, 1973; Thank You, God, 1973; Don't Tell Me About Goldilocks! , 1974. Mbr., Soc. of Women Writers. Address: 2 Willoby Ave., Glen Iris, Vic., Australia 3146.

MOORE, (The Worshipful Chancellor the Rev.) Evelyn Garth, b. 6 Feb. 1906, London, UK. Chancellor; Barrister-at-Law; Clerk in Holy Orders; College Fellow. Educ: M.A., Trinity Coll., Cambridge Univ.; Gray's Inn. Publs: An Introduction to English Canon Law, 1967; Ecclesiastical Law in Halsbury's Laws of England (co-author), 3rd ed.; Kenny's Cases on Criminal Law, 8th ed. w. supplement; Christianity & Psychical Research, forthcoming. Contbr. to: Ency. Britannica; Chambers's Ency.; Law Quarterly; Theol.; Cambridge Law Jrnl.; Ch. Times; etc. Address: Corpus Christi Coll., Cambridge, UK.

MOORE, Gerald, b. 30 July 1899, Watford, UK. Pianist; Accompanist to Singers & Instrumentalists. Educ: Univ. of Toronto, Ont., Can. Publs: The Unashamed Accompanist, 1943; Singer & Accompanist, 1953; Am I too Loud? 1962; The Schubert Song Cycles, 1975. Contbr. to: Careers in Music. Mbrships: Pres., Int. Soc. of Musicians, 1962. Hons. incl: C.B.E., 1954; Royal Acad. of Music, 1962; D.Litt., Univ. of Sussex, 1968; Mus.D., Univ. of Cambridge, 1973; & num. others. Address: Beechwood Cottage, Penn Bottom, Penn, High Wycombe, Bucks., UK.

MOORE, Harry T., b. 1908, Oakland, Calif., USA. University Professor. Educ: Chgo., Northwestern & Boston Univs.; Ph.D. Publs. incl: The Novels of John Steinbeck, revised ed. 1968; The Life & Works of D. H. Lawrence, USA & UK; Co-Ed., The Achievement of D. H. Lawrence; The Intelligent Heart, USA & UK, 1956, 1960; The Collected Letters of D. H. Lawrence, UK & USA; The World of Lawrence Durrell; 20th Century German Literature, USA, 1967, UK, 1971; 20th Century French Literature, USA, 1966, paperback 1967, UK 1969; Age of the Modern, 1971. Contbr. to: N.Y. Times Book Review; Saturday Review; New Repub.; etc. Mbrship: F.R.S.L. Address: 922 S. Division, Carterville, IL 62918, USA.

MOORE, Mary (née Galbraith), pen name OSBORNE, Helena, b. 1930, Oxford, UK. Writer. Educ: M.A., Lady Margaret Hall, Oxford Univ. Publs: The Arcadian Affair (publd. in USA as The Golden Guild of Tiryns), 1969; Pay-Day (publd. in USA as My Enemy's Friend), 1972. Contbr. to: Cornhill; Argosy; Woman's Jrnl.; etc. Recip., Mary Elgin Award for Fiction, 1969. Agent: Bolt &

Watson. Address: Touchbridge, Boarstall, Aylesbury, Bucks., UK.

MOORE, Pamela Robinson, b. 28 Mar. 1903, Duluth, Minn., USA. Actress; Social Worker. Educ: A.B., Radcliffe Coll., 1924; Special Studies, Sorbonne Univ., Paris, France, 1924; Master of Social Work, Univ. of Wash., USA, 1949. Contbr. to: (creative writing) Poets' Guild; Essence; Plume & Sword; Haiku Highlights; Scimitar & Song; Boston Herald; Radcliffe Quarterly; San Diega Union; Young Crusader; My Weekly; (profl.) Adult Educ. Assn. of Am.; Survey Midmonthly; Social Work; Nat. Jrnl. of Rehab.; Adult Ldrship. Mag.; & num. others. Mbrships. incl: Pres., Western Guild of Social Workers; Seattle Press Club. Hons: 5th Prize, Poetry Sect., 1968, Writers Digest Annual Contest; Prizes for Haiku, Haiku Highlights Mag.; etc. Address: P.O. Box 49, University Station, Seattle, WA 98105, USA.

MOORE, Peter Gerald, b. 5 Apr. 1928, Richmond, Surrey, UK. Professor of Statistics & Deputy Principal, London Business School. Educ: B.Sc., Univ. Coll., London, 1949; Ph.D., Princeton Univ., USA, 1955. Publs: Principles of Statistical Techniques, 1958; Statistics & the Manager, 1966; Basic Operational Research, 1968; Risk & Business Decision, 1972. Contbr. to: Fin. Times; other profl. jrnls. Mbrships: VP, Fellow, Inst. of Actuaries, 1972-; Fellow, Royal Statl. Soc. (Hon. Sec., 1968-74). Hons. incl: J.D. Scaife Medal, Inst. of Prod. Engrs., 1964; Guy Medal, Royal Statl. Soc., 1970. Address: London Bus. Schl., Sussex Place, London NW1 4SA, UK.

MOORE, Rayburn Sabatzky, b. 26 May 1920, Helena, Ark., USA. Teacher & Scholar; Author. Educ: B.A., 1942, M.A., 1947, Vanderbilt Univ.; Ph.D., Duke Univ., 1956. Publs: Constance Fenimore Woolson, 1963; Ed., For the Major, & Selected Short Stories of Constance Fenimore Woolson, 1967; Paul Hamilton Hayne, 1972. Contbr. to: Ga. Review (Ed. Bd.); Am. Lit.; Am. Quarterly; S. Atlantic Quarterly; Southern Lit. Jrnl.; S. Atlantic Bulletin; etc. Mbrships. incl: Exec. Comm., Gen. Topics VI, & Norman Foerster Prize Comm., Am. Lit. Sect., MLA; Exec. Coun., Soc. for Study of Southern Lit.; Poe Studies Assn. Address: Dept. of English, Univ. of Georgia, Athens, GA 30602, USA.

MOORE, Ruth, b. St. Louis, Mo., USA. Writer. Educ: A.B., M.A., Wash. Univ., St. Louis; D.Litt., McMurray Coll. Publs: Man, Time & Fossils; The Earth We Live On; Charles Darwin; The Coil of Life; Evolution (in Life Nature Series), 1962; Niels Bohr: The Man, His Science, & the World They Changed; Ape Into Man (w. Sherwood L. Washburn), 1974. Contbr. to: Ency. Britannica; Brit. Yearbook; Harper's; New Repub. Mbrships: Chmn., Prairie Ave. Historic Dist.; Commn. on Chgo. Archtl. & Histl. Landmarks; Women's Nat. Press Club. Address: 860 Lake Shore Drive, Chgo., IL 60611, USA.

MOORE, Sally Christine, b. 1943, Birmingham, UK. Journalist. Publs: The Hunt, 1966. Mbrships: Nat. Union of Jrnlsts.; Soc. of Authors; Songwriters' Guild. Address: Daily Mirror, Holborn Circus, London EC1, UK.

MOORE, Una Katherine, b. 25 Apr. 1898, Hampstead, London, UK. Teacher. Educ: M.A., Lady Margaret Hall, Oxford. Publs: Kipling & the White Mau's Bucku, 1965; Family Fortunes, 1965; Cordial Relations, 1966; Women, 1970; Victorian Wives, 1974. Contbr. to: Blackwoods. Mbr., Cowdray Club. Address: Riverside House, Shoreham, Sevenoaks, Kent, UK.

MOORE, Virginia, b. 11 July 1903, USA. Writer. Educ: B.A., Hollins Coll.; M.A., Ph.D., Columbia Univ. Publs. incl: Not Poppy, 1927; Sweet Water & Bitter, 1931; Distinguished Women Writers, 1934; Homer's Golden Chain, 1935; The Life & Eager Death of Emily Brontë, 1936; Virginia is a State of Mind, 1943; Ho for Heaven, 1946; The Unicorn: William Butler Yeats' Search for Reality, 1954; The Whole World, Stranger, 1957; Scottsville on the James, 1969. Contbr. to: Sat. Review of Lit.; Atlantic Monthly; Harpers Mag.; Yale Review; etc. Mbr., Pen & Brush Club. Recip., Hollins Medal. Address: Cliffside, Scottsdale, VA 24590, USA.

MOORE, Wilfred George, b. 8 May 1907, Burton-on-Trent, UK. Author. Educ: B.Sc., Univ. of London; F.R.G.S. Publs: The Geography of Capitalism, 1938; The World's Wealth, 1947; A Dictionary of Geography, 1949; Essential Geography – 4 books, 1956-60; Children Far & Near, 15 books, 1958-66; New

Visual Geography – 17 books, 1959-72; The Penguin Encyclopaedia of Places, 1971; Find The Answer Geography, 1973. Contbr. to: Schoolmaster; Tchrs. World. Address: Fouroaks, 34 Copsewood Way, Northwood, Middlesex, UK.

MOOREHEAD, Alan, b. 22 July 1910, Melbourne, Aust. Writer. Educ: Melbourne Univ. Publs. incl: A Year of Battle, 1943; African Trilgy, 1944; Eclipse, 1945; The Rage of the Vulture, 1948; The Traitors, 1952; Rum Jungle, 1953; A Summer Night, 1954; Gallipoli, 1956; The Russian Revolution, 1958; No Room in the Ark, 1959; The White Nile, 1960; The Blue Nile, 1962; Coopers Creek, 1963; The Desert War, 1965; Darwin & the Beagle, 1969; A Late Education, 1970. Hons: C.B.E.; Duff Cooper Award, 1956; Sunday Times Gold Medal, 1956; Royal Soc. of Lit. Award, 1963. Address: c/o Nat. Bank of Australasia, Aust. House, Strand, London WC2, UK.

MOORHOUSE, Frank Thomas, b. 21 Dec. 1938, Nowra, Australia. Short Story Writer. Educ: Var. courses, Univ. of Qld. Publs: Futility & Other Animals, 1969; The Americans, Baby, 1972; The Electrical Experience, 1974. Contbr. to: Bulletin; Southerly. Mbrships: Aust. Jrnlsts.' Assn.; Aust. Soc. of Authors; Ewenton Club. Hons: Banjo Paterson Short Story Prize, 1964; Henry Lawson Short Story Prize, 1970; State of Vic. Short Story Prize, 1970; Aust. Lit. Fellowship, 1973. Address: GPO Box 4430, Sydney, Australia.

MOORHOUSE, Geoffrey, b. 29 Nov. 1931, Bolton, Lancs., UK. Writer. Publs: The Other England, 1963; The Press, 1963; Against All Reason, 1969; Calcutta, 1971; The Missionaries, 1973; The Fearful Void, 1974. Contbr. to: Guardian (Chief Features Writer 1958-70); Times; Listener. Mbrship: F.R.G.S. Agent: A. P. Watt & Son. Address: c/o agent: 26-28 Bedford Row, London WC1R 4HL, UK.

MOORMAN, John Richard Humpidge, b. 4 June 1905, Leeds, UK. Bishop of Ripon. Educ: M.A., D.D., Emmanuel Coll., Cambridge. Publs: Sources for the Life of St. Francis of Assisi, 1940; Church Life in England in the Thirteenth Century, 1945; A New Fioretti, 1946; B. K. Cunningham: A Memoir, 1947; St. Francis of Assisi, 1950; The Grey Friars in Cambridge, 1952; A History of the Church in England, 1953, 1973; The Path to Glory, 1960; Vatican Observed, 1967; A History of the Franciscan Order, 1968; The Franciscans in England: 1224-1974, 1974. Contbr. to: Engl. Histl. Review; The Thomist; Ampleforth Jrnl.; Book Collector; The Libn.; Theol. Recip., Litt.D., Leeds & St. Bonaventure, USA. Address: Bishop Mount, Ripon, N. Yorks., HG4 5DP, UK.

MORAES, Dominic, b. 19 July 1938. Poet; Writer. Educ: Jesus Coll., Oxford. Publs. incl: A Beginning, 1957; Gone Away, 1960; The Tempest Within, 1972-73; The People Time Forgot, 1972; A Matter of People, 1974; (autobiography) My Son's Father, 1968; also books of poems & travels in India. Recip., Hawthornden Prize, 1957. Address: c/o UN Fund for Pop. Activities, 485 Lexington Ave., N.Y., NY 10017, USA.

MORAN, (Lord) Charles McMoran Wilson, b. 10 Nov. 1882, Skipton-in-Craven, Yorks., UK. Physician. Educ: M.D., London Univ. Publs: Anatomy of Courage, 1945, 2nd ed., 1967; Winston Churchill: Struggle for Survival, 1967. Mbrships: Pres., Royal Coll. of Physns., 1941-50; Dean, St. Mary's Hosp. Med. Schl., 1920-45. Address: 25 Bryanston Sq., London W1H 7FL, UK.

MORAN, Patrick Alfred Pierce, b. 1917, Sydney, N.S.W., Australia. Professor of Statistics. Educ: M.A., D.Sc., Sc.D., Univ. of Sydney. Publs: The Theory of Storage, 1959; The Random Process of Evolutionary Theory, 1962; Introduction to Probability Theory, 1968. Contbr. to var. sci. jrnls. F.A.A. Address: Australian National University, Box 4, G.P.O., Canberra, A.C.T., Australia.

MORAND, Paul, b. 13 Mar. 1889, Paris, France. Diplomat; Novelist. Educ: Univs. of Paris & Oxford. Publs. incl: (novels) Green Shoots, 1921; Lewis & Irene, 1924; Rien que la terre, 1926; Champions of the World, 1928; France la douce, 1933; Bucharest, 1935; Vie de Maupassant, 1942; Journal d'un attaché d'Ambassade, 1949; Bains de Mer, 1960; Le Prince de Ligne, 1964; Nouvelles des yeux, 1965; Journal d'un attaché, 1970; Venises, 1971. Mbr., French Acad. Recip., Legion of Honour. Address: Château de l'Aile, Vevey, Switz.

MORAVIA, Alberto, b. 28 Nov. 1907. Writer; Journalist. Publs. incl: (novels) Gli Indifferenti, 1929; La Mascherata, 1941; La Romana, 1947; L'Amore Coniugale, 1949; Il disprezzo, 1954; La noia, 1961; L'Attenzione, 1965; (plays) Teatro, 1958; Il dio Kurt, 1967; La Vita è Gioco, 1970; (short stories) La bella vita, 1935; I Raconti, 1954; L'Automa, 1963; Il Paradiso, 1970; Io e lui, 1971; (essays) L'Uomo, Come fine, 1965; A quale tribù appartieni, 1974; (travel) La rivoluzione culturale in Cina, 1967. Mbr., PEN (Pres., 1959). Address: Lungotevere della Vittoria 1, Rome, Italy.

MORAY WILLIAMS, Ursula, b. 19 Apr. 1911, Petersfield, Hants., UK. Writer of Children's Books; Justice of the Peace for County of Worcestershire, Chairman of Juvenile Branch, Evesham. Publs. incl: (juvenile) Adventures of the Little Wooden Horse, 1938; The Nine Lives of Island Mackenzie, 1959; The Three Toymakers Series; The Noble Hawks; A Picnic with the Aunts, 1973; The Line, 1974; & more than 60 other children's stories & plays. Contbr. to: Puffin Post; Cricket USA & UK; & BBC Jackanory Prog., 5 plays. Recip., Honor Book Award 1972, for The Three Toymakers Series, USA. Address: Court Farm, Beckford, nr. Tewkesbury, Glos., UK.

MOREAU, David Merlin, pen name MERLIN, David, b. 1927, Cairo, Egypt. Company Chairman. Educ: M.A., Jesus Coll., Cambridge. Publs: The Simple Life, 1962; That Built-In Urge, 1963; Summer's End, 1966; Look Behind You, 1973. Contbr. to: Guardian; Bedside Guardian; Sunday Times; Financial Times; Dir.; New Sci.; Ideal Home; Vogue; Aust. Financial Review; etc. Mbrships: F.R.S.M.; Soc. of Authors; Inst. of Dirs.; Fellow, Chem. Soc.; Brit. Inst. Mgmt. Address: Rowley Cottage, Langley Park, Bucks. SL3 6DT, UK.

MOREAUX, Michel, b. 6 Feb. 1947, Lodelinsart, Belgium. Teacher of Latin & Greek. Educ: Lic., Classical philol., oriental langs., State Univ. of Liège. Publs: Sourires mouillés, roses givrées, 1971; Destins en filigrane, 1973; Nocturnales, 1974; & num. other poems & tales. Contbr. to: Jrnl. de Charleroi; Lunatique; Nouvelle Gazette; Grand Angle; L'Atrium des Poètes; Flammes vives, etc. Hons. incl: Palme D'Or for 25 poems. Acad. du Disque; Gold Medal, Int. competition, Paris for fantasy tale, A Munich un Soir, 1973; Prix Fraternité for poem, Complainte pour un monde, 1973. Address: rue des Déportés 10, B 6050, Lodelinsart, Belgium.

MORECROFT, John Henry, b. 26 Sept. 1907, Dover, UK. Journalist. Publs: co-author, The Old Bailey, 1970; White Tie Tales (a collection of after-dinner anecdotes by the famous), 1974. Life Mbr., Nat. Union of Jrnlsts. Address: 164 The Gateway, Dover, Kent CT16 1LJ, UK.

MOREL, Dighton. Publs: Moonlight Red, 1960; The Little Perisher, 1961; Autumn Fair, 1962; The Son, 1963. Address: c/o Martin Secker & Warburg Ltd., 14 Carlisle St., Soho Square, London W1V 6NN, UK.

MORENO BÁEZ, Enrique, b. 19 Sept. 1908, Seville, Spain. University Professor. Educ: Lic. es-Lettres, Madrid, 1932; M.A., Oxford, 1936; Ph.D., Cambridge, 1943; Dr. es-Lettres, Madrid, 1948. Publs: Lección y sentido del "Guzmán de Alfarache", 1948; Nosotros y nuestros clásicos, 1961, 2nd ed., 1971; Reflexiones sobre el "Quijote", 1968, 3rd ed., 1974. Los cimentos de Europa, 1971. Contbr. to num. jrnls. Mbr., Assn. Int. de Hispanistas. Recip., acad. hons. Address: Plazuela de Feijoo, 1, 1, Santiago de Compostela, Prov. de la Coruña, Spain.

MORETTI, Marino, b. 18 July 1885. Novelist; Poet. Publs. incl: I Pesci fuor d'acqua, 1914; Il Sole del Sabato, 1916; La voce di Dio, 1920; I puri di cuore, 1924; L'Andreana, 1935; La vedova Fioravanti, 1940; I coniugi Allori, 1946; Il fiocco verde, 1948; Il Pudore, 1950; Il Tempo Migliore, 1952; Uomini soli, 1954; La camera degli Sposi, 1958; Tutte le Novelle, 1959; Romanzi della mia terra, 1961; Tutti i ricordi, 1962; Anna degli Elefanti, 1963; Tutte le poesie, 1966; Romanzi dell'Amorino, 1967; L'Ultima Estate, 1969; Tre Anni e un Giorno, 1971. Contbr. to: Corriere della Sera. Address: Cesenatico (Forli), Italy.

MOREY, Frederick Lotharo, b. 16 April, 1924, Cinn., Ohio, USA. Professor of English. Educ: A.B. & B.S., Ashland Coll., Ohio, 1955; M.A., Univ. of Md., Coll. Pk., 1966; Ph.D., Howard Univ., Wash. D.C., 1970. Publs: Ed., Emily Dickinson Bulletin, 1968—; Ed., Higginson Journal of Poetry, 1971—; Dickinsonic & Other Poems, 1972; The

Fifty Best Poems of Emily Dickinson, 1974. Contbr. to: Papers of the Bibliographical Soc. of Am.; Thought; Markham Review. Mbrships. incl: VP, Nat. Fedn. of State Poetry Socs.; Past Pres., Md. State Poetry Soc.; MLA; Eds. of Learned Jrnls. Address: 4508 38th St., Brentwood, MD 20722, USA.

MORGADO, Benjamin, b. 14 Nov. 1909, Coquimbo, Chile. Lecturer. Educ: Tchr. Trng. Publs. incl: (verse) Cascada silenciosa, 1926; Un hombre triste en el fondo del mar, 1938; Distancia y cielo, 1956; Algunos sonetos, 1966; (prose) Esquinas, 1927; Muro de lágrimas, 1955; Alcance de nombre, 1957; El hombre en el tiempo, 1959; 9 cuentos, 1967; La gente vive y sufre, 1970; (theatre) El hombre del Brazo Encogido, 1935; Petróleo; Alguién viene de lejos; (essays) Literatura Japonesa, 1973; Teatro Japonés, 1974. Contbr. to: Occidente. Mbrships: Pres., Union of Am. Writers (S. Am.); Hon. Mbr. & Dir., Soc. of Playwrights of Chile, etc. Hons. incl: Nat. Theatre Prize, 1965. Address: Casilla 9641, Mac Iver 376, dep. 52, Santiago de Chile, Chile.

MORGAN, Arthur Ernest, b. 20 June 1878, Cinn., Ohio, USA. Engineer; Educator; Author. Publs. incl: My World, 1927; The Seedman, 1932; The Long Road, 1936; The Small Community, 1942; Edward Bellamy — A Biography, 1944; Nowhere Was Somewhere, 1946; Bottom-Up Democracy, 1954; Search for Purpose, 1955; It Can Be Done, 1962; Observations, 1968; Dams & Other Disasters, 1971; The Making of the TVA, 1974. Contbr. to: Atlantic Monthly; Harper's; N.Y. Times; var. mags. Mbrships. incl: Fellow, AAAS; Am. Sociol. Soc.; Am. Soc. Civil Engrs. Hons: 7 acad. degrees; Disting. Alumni Award, St. Cloud State Coll., Minn., 1974. Address: Box 243, 114 E. Whiteman, Yellow Springs, OH 45387, USA.

MORGAN, Bryan Stanford, b. 1923, London, UK. Freelance Writer. Educ: B.A., St. Catharine's Coll., Cambridge Univ. Publs. incl: (novels) Vain Citadels, 1947; Rosa, 1949; The Sacred Nursery, 1951; The Business at Blanche Capel, 1954; Pepe's Island (co-author), 1965; (non-fiction) The End of the Line, 1955; Fastness of France, 1962; Electronics at Work, 1965; Explosions & Explosives, 1967; The Rolls & Royce Story, 1971; Men & Discoveries in Mathematics, 1972; Early Trains, 1973; Ed., The Great Trains, 1973. Contbr. to: Take Home Books; Factory Mgr.; Scope; Railway Mag.; Mod. Railways; Model Engr.; etc. BBC. Address: 12 Princedale Rd., London W11, UK.

MORGAN, Dan, b. 24 Dec. 1925, Holbeach, Lincs., UK. Writer; Managing Director, Menswear Retail Company. Publs: Guitar, 1965; The Minds series, 1967; The Venturer Twelve series (w. John Kippax), 1974-; The Country of the Mind (in mind series), 1975. Contbr. to: New Worlds; Vision of Tomorrow; New Writings in SF; Alfred Hitchcock Mystery Mag.; etc. Mbr., Soc. of Authors. Address: 1 Chapel Lane, Spalding, Lincs. PE11 1BP, UK.

MORGAN (Rev.), Dewi, b. 5 Feb. 1916, Pengam, Wales, UK. Priest. Educ: B.A., Univ. Coll., Cardiff; St. Michael's Theol. Coll., Llandaff. Publs. incl: Expanding Frontiers, 1957; 1662 & All That, 1961; Seeds of Peace, 1965; Arising from the Psalms, 1966; Ed., They Became Christians, 1966; Ed., Faith in Fleet Street, 1967; God & Sons, 1967; The Printed Word (w. Michael Perry), 1969; Church in Transition, 1970; Phoenix of Fleet Street, 1973; Book of the Year, Soc. for Propagation of the Gospel, 10 yrs. Contbr. to: Radio & TV; Everymans Ency.; Ency. Americana; Daily Mail Yr. Book; Quarterly Intercession Paper (Ed.); num. newspapers & jrnls. Mbrships. incl: Press Club (Chap.); Inst. of Jrnlsts. (Chap.); Publicity Club, London (Chap.). Address: St. Bride's Rectory, Fleet St., London EC4Y 8AO, UK.

MORGAN, Dyfnallt, b. 4 May 1917, Merthyr Tydfil, Wales, UK. University Lecturer. Educ: M.A., Dip. in Educ., Univ. of Wales. Publs: Gwŷr Llên Y Ddeunawfed Ganrif, 1966; Ed., Gwŷr Llên Y Bedwaredd Ganrif Ar Bymtheg, 1968; Y Llen A Myfyrdodau Eraill, 1967; Rhyw Hanner Teunctid, 1971; D. Gwenallt Jones, 1972. Contbr. to: Barn; Planet; Poetry Wales; Porfeydd; Taliesen; Y Cymro; Y Faner; Y Genhinen; Y Traethodydd; Y Tyst. Mbr., Yr Academi Gymreig. Recip., Royal Hist. Eisteddfod of Wales Crown Award, 1957. Address: Cilan, Ffordd Garth Uchaf, Bangor, Gwynedd, UK.

MORGAN, (The Hon. Sir) Edward James Ranembe, b. 25 Mar. 1900, Warwick, Qld., Australia. Lawyer. Educ: LL.B., Univ. Adelaide, 1920. Publs: Lamps and Vineleaves

(w. C. R. Jury & V. F. Knowles), 1919; The Adelaide Club 1863-1963, 1963; Early Adelaide Architecture (w. S. H. Gilbert), 1969. Mbr., Aust. Soc. Authors. Hons: Kt., 1952; Bundey Prize Engl. Verse, Univ. Adelaide, 1921. Address: 155 Kermode St., N. Adelaide, S. Australia.

MORGAN, Edwin (George), b. 27 Apr. 1920, Glasgow, UK. University Reader in English. Educ: M.A., Glasgow Univ., 1947. Publs. incl: The Vision of Cathkin Braes, 1952; Poems from Eugenio Montale, 1959; Ed., Collins Albatross Book of Longer Poems, 1963; Emergent Poems, 1967; Proverbfolder, 1969; Wi the Haill Voice, 1972; From Glasgow to Saturn, 1973; The Whittrick, 1973; Essays, 1974. Contbr. to jrnls., newspapers. Hons: Cholmondeley Award for Poets, 1968; Scottish Arts Coun. Books Awards, 1968, 1973; Magyar PEN Mem. Medal, 1973. Address: 19 Whittingehame Court, Glasgow G12 0BG, UK.

MORGAN, Elaine Neville, b. 7 Nov. 1920, Pontypridd, UK. Writer. Educ: M.A., Lady Margaret Hall, Oxford. Publs: The Descent of Woman, 1972. Hons: Playwriting Award, Cheltenham Lit. Festival, 1955; Writers' Guild Award for Best TV Dramatization, 1974. Address: 24 Aberffrwd Rd., Mountain Ash, Glam., UK.

MORGAN, Joe Warner, b. 7 July 1912, Lafayette, Ind., USA. Editor. Educ: A.B., Knox Coll., Galesburg, Ill. Publs: Expense Account, 1958; Amy, Go Home, 1964. Mbrships: Phi Delta Theta; Sigma Delta Chi, Soc. of Profl. Jrnlsts. Address: 66 Cleary Ct., San Fran., CA 94109, USA.

MORGAN, John Stewart, b. 11 May 1911, Rotherham, Yorks., UK (now Can. citizen). Social Worker; Educator. Educ: B.A., 1932, M.A., 1937, Jesus Coll., Oxford Univ.; Dip. Ed., Armstrong Coll., Univ. of Durham (now Newcastle Univ.), 1933. Publs: Eating Out, 1946; Contbng. Ed., Welfare & Wisdom, 1965; Comparative Social Administration (co-author), 1967; (contbr.) Jenkins, Social Security in International Perspective, 1968. Contbr. to profl. jrnls. in Can., UK & USA. Mbrships: Authors' Club, London, UK; num. profl. & civic orgs. Hons: LL.D., Memorial Univ., Nfld., Can., 1966; D.Litt., Lincoln Mem. Univ., Tenn., USA, 1967; Can. Centennial Medal, 1967; A.M., Univ. of Pa., 1971. Address: 712 W. St. Andrews Rd., Phila., PA 19118, USA.

MORGAN, Judith Ann, pen names KRAGEN, Jinx; MORGAN, Jinx, b. 9 June 1939, Napa, Calif., USA. Writer. Educ: B.A., Stanford Univ. Publs: Saucepans & the Single Girl, 1965; The How to Keep Him (After You've Caught Him) Cookbook, 1968. Contbr. to: Ladies Home Jrnl.; Bon Appetit; Nat. Observer; Var. TV prods. Mbrships: Writers' Guild of Am.; Royal C'wlth. Soc. Address: 5301 Broadway Terrace, Oakland, CA 94618, USA.

MORGAN, Kenneth O., b. 1934, London, UK. Modern Historian. Educ: B.A., M.A., D.Phil., Oriel Coll., Oxford. Publs. incl: Wales in British Politics, 1886-1922, 1963, 2nd ed., 1970; British General Election 1964 (part-author), 1965; Freedom or Sacrilege? , 1966; The Age of Lloyd George, 1971; (part-author) Lloyd George: Twelve Essays, 1971; Lloyd George, 1974; Keir Hardie: Radical & Socialist, 1975. Contbr. to: Jrnl., Contemporary Hist.; Hist. Jrnl.; Pol. Studies; Pol. Sci. Quarterly; Welsh Hist. Review (Ed., 1965—); etc. Mbrships: Fellow, Royal Histl. Soc.; Bd. of Celtic Studies; Coun., Univ. Coll. of Wales. Address: Queen's Coll., Oxford, UK.

MORGAN, Marabel, b. 25 June 1937, Crestline, Ohio, USA. Author; Founder, Marriage Enrichment Programme; Public Speaker. Educ: Ohio State Univ. Publs: The Total Woman, 1973. Hon: No. 1 best-selling book, N.Y. Times & Publisher's Weekly, 1974. Address: P.O. Box 380277, Miami, FL 33138, USA.

MORGAN, Marie Griffin, b. 1 Dec. 1914, Nahunta, Ga., USA. Editor; Publisher. Educ: Assoc. Degree, Abraham Baldwin Agricl. Jr. Coll., 1937; B.S.H.E., Univ. of Ga., 1939; Univ. of Kan., 1947-48. Publs: The Writers Directory, 1971-73. Mbrships: Ga. Press Assn.; Nat. Press Assn.; Int. Platform Assn.; Int. Writers; Chapt. Bd. VP, Colonial Dames of 17th Century, 1975-77; Ga. State Treas., 1972-75; Chapt. Pres., United Daughters of the Confederacy; Dist. Dir.; State Chap. Hons. incl: Home Maker of the Yr., Baldwin Alumni; Woman of Yr., Bus. & Profl. Women; Outstanding Unit Pres. in State, Am. Legion Aux. Address: Route 3 Davis Rd., Tifton, GA 31794, USA.

MORGAN, Michael Croke, b. 13 Oct. 1911, Guildford, Surrey, UK. History Teacher. Educ: M.A., Oxford Univ.

Publs: Freedom & Compulsion, 1954; Cheltenham College, 1968; Lenin, 1971; Foreign Affairs 1886-1914, 1973. Contbr. to: Ency. of World Hist. Mbrships: Histl. Assn.; Engl. Speaking Union. Address: Worlds End House, Bristol BS8 4TH, UK.

MORGAN, Richard Ernest, b. 17 May 1937, Centre Co., Pa., USA. Professor of Government. Educ: A.B., Bowdoin Coll., 1959; M.A., 1961; Ph.D., 1967, Columbia Univ. Publs: The Politics of Religious Conflict, 1968; Ed., The American Political System: Introductory Readings (w. James E. Connor), 1971; The Supreme Court & Religion, 1972; Series Ed., Short Studies in American Politics. Contbr. to: Westin & Pritchett, The Third Branch of Government, 1963; Kurland, Supreme Ct. Review, 1973; New Ldr.; Procs. Acad. Pol. Sci. Recip., var. Fellowships. Address: Bowdoin Coll., Brunswick, ME 04011, USA.

MORGAN, Stanley, b. 10 Nov. 1929, Liverpool, UK. Writer. Educ: Liverpool Inst. Publs: The Sewing Machine Man, 1969; Octopus Hill, 1970; The Debt Collector, 1970; The Courier, 1971; Come Again Courier, 1972; Tobin Takes Off, 1973; Mission to Katuma, 1973; Tobin on Safari, 1973; Tobin in Paradise, 1974; Tobin in Trouble, 1974; The Fly Boys, 1974; Tobin for Hire (to appear 1975); Tobin in Las Vegas (to appear 1975); The Fly Boys in London (to appear 1975); The Russ Tobin Bedside Guide, (to appear 1975). Agent: Desmond Elliott. Address: Ardeen, The Curragh, Co. Kildare, Repub. of Ireland.

MORGAN, Thomas Christopher, pen name MUIR, John, b. 20 Mar. 1914, Preston-on-Severn, Shrewsbury, UK. Farmer. Publs: The Devil's Post Office, 1955; Creatures of Satan, 1956; Crook's Turning, 1957. Contbr. to: Farmer & Stockbreeder; Dairy Farmer; Shropshire Star; Shropshire Jrnl.; Express & Star; The Field. Mbr., Coun. of Nat. Farmers' Union of England & Wales. Address: Preston-on-Severn, Uffington, Shrewsbury, UK.

MORGAN, Verne, b. Sidcup, UK. Actor-Producer-Director of Stage, Films & TV. Publs: English People Speak Like This (w. B. Morgan), 1952; English Idiom, 1953; Complete Pantomimes, 1966-74; Yesterday's Sunshine, 1974; The Sun Still Shone, 1975; Everyday English, 1975; num. short stories, theatre scripts, & one-act plays. Contbr. to: Sunday Express; Evening News; Rdr.'s Digest; Engl. Digest. Mbr., Brit. Actors' Equity. Address: 14 Victoria Rd., London SW14 8EX, UK.

MORGAN-WITTS, Max, b. 27 Sept. 1931, Detroit, Mich., USA. Author; TV & Film Producer-Director. Educ: Acad. of TV & Radio Arts, Toronto. Publs: The Day Their World Ended, 1969; Earthquake — The Destruction of San Francisco, 1971; Shipwreck — The Strange Fate of the Morro Castle, 1972; Voyage of the Damned, 1974. Contbr. to The Listener. Mbrships. incl: Royal Soc. of Lit.; Am. Authors' Guild. Hons: Kt. of Mark Twain, 1970; Edgar Allen Poe Award, 1972. Address: c/o Jonathan Clowes Ltd., 19 Jeffrey's Place, London, NW1 9PP, UK.

MORGENSTERN, Oskar, b. 24 Jan. 1902, Goerlitz, Silesia, Germany. Educator; Economist. Educ: Doct. rer. pol., Vienna Univ., Austria, 1925. Publs. incl: Wirtschaftsprognose, 1928; The Limits of Economics, 1937; On the Accuracy of Economic Observations, 1950; Predictability of Stock Market Prices (w. C. W. J. Granger), 1970; Long Term Projections of Power (co-author), 1973. Contbr. to: Econ. Activity Analysis, (Ed.), 1954; Naval Rsch. Logistics Quarterly (co-Ed.); Zeitschrift für Nationalokonomie (co-Ed.); num. tech. jrnls. Mbr., econ. orgs. Hons: F.D. Converse Award, 1967; num. Docts. & Fellowships. Address: 94 Library Pl., Princeton, NJ 08540, USA.

MORICE, Anne, pen name SHAW, Felicity, b. 1918, Birchington, Kent, UK. Author. Publs: Death in the Grand Manor, 1970; Murder in Married Life, 1971; Death of a Gay Dog, 1971; Murder on French Leave, 1972; Death & the Dutiful Daughter, 1973; Death of a Heavenly Twin, 1974; Killing with Kindness, 1974; Nursery Tea & Poison, forthcoming. Mbr., Petit Club Français. Address: Rose Farm House, Turville Heath, Henley-on-Thames, Oxon., UK.

MORICE, Stella Margery, b. 18 Sept. 1901, Gisborne, NZ. Kindergarten Teacher (Retired). Publ: The Book of Wiremu, 1944, 5 eds. Contbr. to Engl. mags. & NZ newspapers. Mbr., Gisborne Art Soc. Recip., Esther Glen Medal, Lib. Assn. (for Book of Wiremu), 1946. Address: 121 Fox St., Gisborne, NZ.

MORISON, Samuel Eliot, b. 9 July 1887, Boston, Mass., USA. Historian. Educ: Litt.D., Harvard Univ. Publs. incl: John Paul Jones; Admiral of the Ocean Sea; Christopher Columbus, Mariner; Oxford History of the American People; Old Bruin: Commodore Matthew C. Perry; Growth of the American Republic, 1950; European Discovery of America: The Northern Voyages, 1971; Samuel de Champlain: Father of New France, 1972; European Discovery of America: The Southern Voyages, 1974. Mbrships. incl: F.B.A. Hons. incl: LL.D. Univs. Oxford, Harvard, Yale & Columbia; Pulitzer Prize, 1943 for Admiral of the Ocean Sea & 1960 for John Paul Jones. Address: Good Hope, Northeast Harbor, ME 04662, USA.

MORITA, Yuzo, b. 12 June 1940, Sukumo, Japan. Writer. Educ: B.Sc., Tokyo Univ. of Agric., 1964. Publs: (in Japanese) The People of the World, 1968; The Courageous Japanese, 1969; Australia the Futureland, 1970; In Search of the Origin of the Japanese, 1973; (in Engl.) Yugoslavia, 1973. Contbr. to: The Sun; Asahi Graphic; Mainichi Graphic; Wkly. Post. Mbrships: Pres., Japan Youth Travel Club; Chmn., Youth Friendship Assn. Inc. Address: 396-1 Tanoura, Sukumo-shi, Kochi Pref., Japan.

MORLAN, John E., pen name ADAMS, John, b. 12 Oct. 1930, Abilene, Tex., USA. University Professor of Instructional Technology; Overseas Projects Director; Media Specialist. Educ: B.S., M.Ed., Abilene Christian Coll., Tex.; Ed.D., Tex. Tech. Univ. Publs. incl: Teaching the Disadvantaged Child (co-author), 1968; Preparation of Inexpensive Teaching Materials, 1973; Classroom Learning Centers, 1974; var. musical compositions. Contbr. to var. profl. jrnls. Mbrships: Assn. for Educl. Communication & Technol.; Nat. Sci. Tchrs. Assn.; Broadcast Music Inc. Address: Dept. of Instructional Technology, San Jose State Univ., San Jose, CA, USA.

MORLAND, Nigel, pen names FORREST, Norman; DONAVAN, John; SHEPHERD, Neal; McCALL, John Corey; DANE, Mary; GARNETT, Roger; KIMBERLEY, Hugh; DE SOLA, John, b. London, UK. Writer; Editor. Publs. incl: Fingerprints, 1935; Hangman's Clutch, 1954; Background to Murder, 1955; This Friendless Lady, 1957; Science in Crime Detection, 1958; An Outline of Sexual Criminology, 1966; A Pattern of Murder, 1966; Ed., Papers from the Criminologist, 1970; & about 290 crime novels. Ed., The Criminologist, 1966—; Ed., Int. Jrnl. Forensic Dentistry, 1974-; Ed., Forensic Photography, 1972—. Contbr. to var. nat. & int. newspapers & periodicals. Mbrships. incl: Press Club; Crime Writers' Assn. (Co-Fndr.). Address: c/o Cassell & Co. Ltd., Red Lion Sq., London WC1, UK.

MORLEY, Robert, b. 26 May 1908. Actor; Dramatist. Publs: Goodness How Sad, 1937; Staff Dance, 1944; Edward My Son (w. Noel Langley), 1948; The Full Treatment (w. Ronald Gow), 1952; Hippo Dancing, 1954; Six Months Grace (w. D. Hamilton), 1957; Robert Morley: Responsible Gentleman (w. S. Stokes), 1966; also appeared in num. plays & films incing: The African Queen; Oscar Wilde; The Loved One; Song of Norway; Cromwell; When Eight Bells Toll; (plays) Halfway up the Tree; How the Other Half Loves. Recip., C.B.E. Address: Fairmans, Wargrave, Berks., UK.

MÖRNE, (Signe) Barbro, b. 6 Feb. 1903, Esbo, Finland. Librarian; Writer. Publs: Tystnadens spaar, 1923; Bild och syn, 1927; Dikter, 1933; Trädet i vinternatten, 1942; Jag bands av aarets tider, 1948; Läggspel, 1950; Dikter i urval, 1970; (fiction) Gaarden som försvann, 1966; Filips resa runt jorden, 1948. Contbr. to var. poetry jrnls. Mbr., Finlands svenska författareförening. Hons: State Lit. Prizes, 1927 & 1952; Finlands Stadsförbund förtjänsttecken för bibliotekstjänstgöring, 1966. Address: Helsingforsvägen 15, 02700 Grankulla, Finland.

MÖRNER, Carl Magnus Birgersson, b. 31 Mar. 1924, Mollösa, Sweden. Director; Historian. Educ: Ph.D., Univ. of Stockholm, 1954. Publs: The Political & Economic Activities of the Jesuits in the La Plata Region: The Hapsburg Era, 1953, Spanish ed., 1968; Race Mixture in the History of Latin America, 1967, Swedish & Spanish eds., 1969, French ed., 1971; La Corona española y los foráneos en los pueblos de indios de América, 1970. Contbr. to: Hispanic Am. Hist. Review; Latin Am. Rsch. Review; Jahrbuch für Geschichte Lateinamerikas; Anuario de Estudios Americanos; Historia Mexicana, etc. Mbrships: Soc., Scandinavian Assn. for Rsch. on Latin Am.; Sec., Coord. Comm., European Latin Am. Histns. Recip., Premio

Loubet, 1957. Address: Askrikevägen 17, S 181 46, Lidingö 1, Sweden.

MORONEY, John R., b. 29 Jan. 1939, Dallas, Tex., USA. Professor of Economics, Tulane University. Educ: B.A., Southern Meth. Univ., Dallas, Tex., 1960; Ph.D., Duke Univ., Durham, N.C., 1964. Author, The Structure of Production in American Manufacturing, 1972. Contbr. to: Am. Econ. Review; Jrnl. of Pol. Economy; Jrnl. of Money, Credit & Banking; Southern Econ. Jrnl.; Western Econ. Jrnl.; Jrnl. of Reg. Sci.; Indl. & Labor Rels. Review; Quarterly Review of Econs. & Bus.; Metroeconomica. Mbrships. incl: Am. Econ. Assn.; Royal Econ. Soc.; Econometric Soc.; Exec. Comm., Southern Econ. Assn. Fellow, Inst. of Pub. Utilities. Hons. incl: Fac. Rsch. Fellowship, Soc. Sci. Rsch. Coun., 1969. Address: 4735 Carondelet St., New Orleans, LA 70115, USA.

MORPURGO, Jack Eric, b. 18 Apr. 1918, London, UK. University Professor; Author. Educ: Christ's Hospital; Univ. of N.B., Can.; Wm. & Mary Coll., Va., USA; Inst. of Histl. Rsch., London Univ., UK; King's Coll., Newcastle; B.A., D.Litt., Lit.D., D.H.L. Publs. incl: Charles Lamb & Elia, 1949; The Last Days of Shelley & Byron, 1952; Ed., Keats, Poems, 1953; History of the United States (w. R. B. Nye), 1955; Rugby Football: An Anthology, 1958; The Road to Athens, 1963; Venice, 1944; Cobbett: A Year's Residence in USA, 1964; Ed., Cooper, The Spy, 1968; Treasures of the British Museum (w. others), 1972; Barnes Wallis: A Biography, 1972. Contbr. to lit. jrnls. Mbrships. incl: PEN; Soc. of Bookmen. Address: Cliff Cottage, 51 Cliff Rd., Leeds LS6 2EZ, UK.

MORRAH, Dermot Michael Macgregor, b. 26 Apr. 1896. Arundel Herald Extraordinary; Journalist. Educ: New Coll., Oxford. Publs. incl: If It Had Happened Yesterday, 1930; The British Red Cross, 1944; The Work of the Queen, 1958; To Be a King, 1968; (for King George's Jubilee Trust) The Royal Family in Africa, 1947; The Royal Family, 1950; (play) Chorus Angelorum, 1937; (films) Royal Heritage, 1953. Contbr. to: Daily Mail; Times; Daily Telegraph. Mbrships. incl: Commonwealth Press Union; Brit. Red Cross Soc.; Chmn., Circle of Wine Writers, 1964-66; F.S.A. Address: 131a Ashley Gdns., London SW1, UK.

MORRAH, Patrick Arthur Macgregor, b. 31 July 1907, Shanklin, Isle of Wight, UK. Journalist. Educ: M.A., Christ Ch., Oxford. Publs: 1660: The Year of Restoration, 1960; Alfred Mynn & the Cricketers of his Time, 1963; The Golden Age of Cricket, 1967; The History of the Malayan Police. Contbr. to: Daily Telegraph; Sunday Telegraph. Mbrships: Soc. of Authors; PEN; MCC; United Oxford & Cambridge Univ. Club; Queens Club. Address: 07 Beatty House, Dolphin Sq., London SW1, UK.

MORRELL, David, b. 1943, Kitchener, Ont., Can. Associate Professor. Educ: St. Jerome's Coll., Univ. of Waterloo, Ont.; Pa. State Univ., USA; M.A., Ph.D. Publs: First Blood, 1972. Contbr. to: Ellery Queen's Crookbook, 1974; Ellery Queen's Mystery Mag.; Jrnl. of Gen. Educ. Recip., Disting. Recognition Award, Friends of Am. Writers, 1973. Agent: Henry Morrison. Address: 1421 Laurel St., Iowa City, IA 52240, USA.

MORRELL, W. P., b. Auckland, NZ. Professor of History (Retired). Educ: M.A., D.Litt., Univ. of Otago; D.Phil., Balliol Coll., Oxford, UK. Publs. incl: British Colonial Policy in the Age of Peel & Russell, 1930, 1966; The Provincial System in New Zealand, 1932, revised ed., 1964; The Gold Rushes, 1940, 1968; British Colonial Policy in the Mid-Victorian Age: South Africa, New Zealand, the West Indies, 1969; The Anglican Church in New Zealand: A History, 1973. Contbr. to Chambers's Ency. Mbrships: Life Fellow, Royal C'wlth. Soc.; Fellow, Royal Histl. Soc. Address: 20 Bedford St., St. Clair, Dunedin, NZ.

MORRILL, George Percival, b. 14 May 1920, Montclair, N.J., USA. Author; Editor. Educ: B.A., M.A., Wesleyan Univ., Middletown, Conn. Publs: Dark Sea Running, 1960; The Multimillionaire Straphanger, A Biography of John Emory Andrus, 1971; Snow, Stars & Wild Honey, 1975. Contbr. to: Saturday Evening Post; Cosmopolitan; McCall's; Colliers Argosy; Vt. Life; Reader's Digest; etc. Mbr., Socratic Lit. Soc. Recip., Colliers Star Story, 1949. Agent: Brandt & Brandt. Address: Thayer Rd., Higganum, CT 06441, USA.

MORRIS, Clifford Eric, b. 29 Oct. 1940, Cardiff, UK. Senior Lecturer in International Relations, Military

Academy. Educ: B.A., St. Davids Univ. Coll., Lampeter; Postgrad. Dip. in Educ., Univ. Coll., Cardiff; M.A., Univ. of Leicester. Publs: Blockade: Berlin & the Cold War, 1973; Tanks — An Illustrated History, 1975. Contbr. to: Wirtschaft und Gesellschaft im Industriezeitalter (Int. Ency. of Econ. & Soc. Instns.). Mbrships: Int. Inst. for Strategic Studies; Royal United Servs. Inst. for Defence Studies. Address: Dept. of War Studies & Int. Affairs, Royal Mil. Acad. Sandhurst, Camberley, Surrey, UK.

MORRIS, Colin, b. 1916, Liverpool, UK. Writer; Producer; Director; Actor; Interviewer, BBC TV. Publs: (stage play prods) Desert Rats, 1945; Italian Love Story, 1945; Reluctant Heroes, 1950; (TV plays) The Unloved, 1954; Who, Me, 1959; Jacks & Knaves, 1960; Women in Crisis, 1963; The Newcomers, 1965; King of the River, 1967; Walk with Destiny, 1974; (TV serials) Reluctant Bandit, 1966; The Dragon's Opponent, 1973; (TV series) The Carnforth Practice, 1974; num. dramatized documentaries, 1954-74. Contbr. to: Evening Standard; Sunday Mirror. Hons: Atlantic Award in Lit., 1946; 4 Best Script Awards, 1955, 1956, 1958 & 1961. Agent, Dr. Jan Van Loewen Ltd. Address: 75 Hillway, London N6, UK.

MORRIS, David Elwyn, b. 1920, London, UK. Solicitor. Educ: M.A., Brasenose College, Oxford. Publs: China Changed My Mind, 1947; The End of Marriage, 1971; Pilgrim Through This Barren Land, 1974. Contbr. to: Marriage For & Against, 1972. Mbr., The Law Soc. Address: Woodstock, Bois Avenue, Chesham Bois, Amersham, Bucks., UK.

MORRIS, David Henry St. Lawrence, pen names, MORRIS, David; MORRIS, David St. L.; LAWRENCE, David, b. 25 Nov. 1920, Handsworth, UK. Educ: St. John's Coll., Cambridge. Publs: Frame This Picture, 1946; The Money in Your Pocket, 1957; Dead Orchid, 1958; Death Has Two Hands, 1958; Cry for Tomorrow (forthcoming). Contbr. to: Britannia & Eve; The Onlooker, India. Hons. incl: J.P., 1966—; Mayor, 1963-65; Hon. Alderman, 1974 of Cheltenham. Address: Chadwick, 145 Old Bath Rd., Cheltenham, Glos., UK.

MORRIS, Denis Edward, b. 1907, Woodford Green, Essex, UK. Radio Programme Controller (Retired). Publs: Poultry Keeping for Profit; Poultry for Profit & Pleasure; The French Vineyards; Guide to the Pleasures of Wine, 1973. Contbr. to: Harper's Bazaar; Int. Hotel Review; Birmingham Post; Wine Corres., Daily Telegraph, Field. Mbrships: Coun., Lord's Taverners, 1961-66; Chmn., Nat. Cricket Assn., Press & P.R. Comm., 1968-72; Chmn., Shoreham Constituency, Conservative Assn., 1971—. Recip., O.B.E. Address: Little Nepcote, Findon, Worthing BN14 0SN, UK.

MORRIS, Desmond, b. 1928, Purton, Wilts., UK. Author; Former Curator of Mammals. Educ: B.S., D.Phil.; Birmingham & Oxford Univs. Publs: The Behaviour of the Ten-Spined Stickleback; The Story of Congo; Curious Creatures; The Biology of Art; Monkeys & Apes; The Big Cats; The Mammals: A Guide to the Living Species; Men & Snakes (co-author); Men & Apes; Men & Pandas; Zootime; Ed., Primate Ethology; The Naked Ape; The Human Zoo; Patterns of Reproductive Behaviour; Intimate Behaviour. Contbr. to: Behaviour; Brit. Birds; Zoo Life; New Sci.; Brit. Jrnl. Animal Behaviour; etc. Address: Wolfson College, Oxford, UK.

MORRIS, Donald R., b. 1924, Frankfurt a/M., Germany. Former Operations Officer, C.I.A.; News Analyst. Educ: B.S.(E.E.), U.S. Naval Acad., Annapolis, Md. Publs: China Station, USA & UK, 1951; Warm Bodies, USA & UK, (re-titled All Hands on Deck), 1957; The Washing of the Spears, USA & UK 1965. Contbr. to: Naval Inst. Proceedings; Reporter; Atlantic; True; Argosy; Houston Post (staff mbr. 1972-); Radio & TV. Mbr., Mensa. Address: The Houston Post, Houston, TX 77001, USA.

MORRIS, Geoffrey Christopher, b. 24 Jan. 1906, Gt. Bookham, Surrey, UK. University Director of Studies in History. Educ: M.A., King's Coll., Cambridge Univ. Publs: The Journeys of Celia Fiennes; Introduction to Life Under the Tudors; Political Thought in England, Tyndale to Hooker; The Tudors; The Laws of Eccles Polity; Western Political Thought, Vol. I — Plato to Augustine, 1967. Contbr. to: Pol. Ideas; Il Pensiero Politico; Histl. Jrnl.; Time & Tide; etc. Mbrships: Fellow, Royal Histl. Soc.; Princeton Inst. for Advanced Study, USA, 1956 & 1966; Huntington Lib. Address: 5 Merton St., Cambridge, UK.

MORRIS, Helen, b. 1909, Dundee, UK. College Lecturer. Educ: M.A., Girton Coll., Cambridge Univ. Publs: Portrait of a Chef., 1938, reprinted 1975; Elizabethan Literature, 1958; series, Notes on English Literature: King Lear, 1965, Richard II, 1966, Antony & Cleopatra, 1968, Romeo & Juliet, 1970; Where's that Poem? , 1967, revised & enlarged, 1974. Contbr. to: Army Quarterly; Wine & Food; Huntington Lib. Quarterly; Shakespeare Studios. Mbrships: Royal C'wlth. Soc.; A.T.C.D.E. Address: 5 Merton St., Cambridge, UK.

MORRIS, James D., b. 10 Jan. 1927, Meadow, S.D., USA. University Professor. Educ: B.S., Northern State Coll.; M.A., Ed.D., Univ. of N.D. Publs: Project Method in Business Education, 1973; Business & Economic Education, 1974; Conceptual Development in Business Education, forthcoming. Contbr. to: Balance Sheet; Bus. Educ. World; Jrnl. of Bus. Educ. Mbrships: incl: Vis. Sci. Prog., Am. Assn. Higher Educ. Address: 1634 Makiki St., Honolulu, HI 96822, USA.

MORRIS, Jan, pen name MORRIS, James, b. 2 Oct. 1926, England. Writer. Educ: M.A., Univ. of Oxford. Publs: Coast to Coast; Sultan in Oman; Coronation Everest; The Presence of Spain; Venice; Oxford; The Hashemite Kings; Cities; Places; Pax Britannica; Heaven's Command; Conundrum. Mbrship: Fellow, Royal Soc. of Lit. Recip., Heinemann Award, Royal Soc. of Lit., 1960. Address: Trefan Bach, Fforest, Abergavenny, Gwent, Wales, UK.

MORRIS, Jean, pen name O'HARA, Kenneth, b. 15 Jan. 1924, Sevenoaks, Kent, UK. Author; Dramatist. Educ: B.A.(Hons.), London Univ. Publs. incl: Man & Two Gods, 1953; Half of a Story, 1956; The Adversary, 1959; The Blackamoor's Urn, 1962; A Dream of Fair Children, 1966; The Monarchs of England, 1975. Contbr. to: BBC Radio & TV. Mbr., PEN. Recip., Arts Coun. of GB Drama Bursary, 1955. Address: 2 Langham House Close, Ham Common, Richmond, Surrey, UK.

MORRIS, John, b. 27 Aug. 1895, Gravesend, UK. Author; Broadcaster. Educ: M.A., M.Sc., King's Coll., Cambridge. Publs: Living with Lepchas, 1938; Traveller from Tokyo, 1943; The Phoenix Cup, 1947; (Ed.) From the Third Programme, 1956; Hired to Kill, 1960; A Winter in Nepal, 1963; Eating the Indian Air, 1968. Contbr. to: BBC, Controller Third Prog., 1952-58; Mt. Everest Exped., 1922, 1936. Hons: C.B.E.; Murchison Mem. Award, Royal Geographical Soc., 1929. Address: 21 Friday St., Henley-on-Thames, Oxon., UK.

MORRIS, John Humphrey Carlile, b. 1910, Wimbledon, London, UK. University Reader, Oxford; Fellow, Magdalen Coll. Educ: Christ Ch., Oxford, 1928-32; B.A., 1931; B.C.L., 1932; D.C.L., 1949. Publs: Cases in Private International Law; Ed., Theobald on Wills; Gen. ed., Dicey's Conflict on Laws: Chitty on Contracts; The Rule Against Perpetuities (w. Prof. W. Barton Leach); The Conflict of Laws. Contbr. to: Law Quarterly Review; Harvard Law Review; Mod. Law Review; Cambridge Law Jrnl. Address: Magdalen College, Oxford, UK.

MORRIS, John Wesley, b. 14 Nov. 1907, Billings, Okla., USA. Geographer (Professor). Educ: B.S., Univ. of Okla., Norman, 1930; M.S., Okla. State Univ., Stillwater, 1934; Ph.D., Geo. Peabody Coll. for Tchrs., Nashville, Tenn., 1941. Publs: Oklahoma Geography, 1953, 3rd ed., 1962; World Geography, 1958, 3rd ed., 1971; Historical Atlas of Oklahoma, 1965, 2nd ed., 1974; Methods of Geographic Instruction, 1968; The Southwestern United States, 1970. Contbr. to: Landscape; Profl. Geographer; Soc. Sci. Quarterly; Soil Sci.; Jrnl. of Geog.; The Grade Tchr. Address: 833 McCall Dr., Norman, OK, USA.

MORRIS, Katharine, b. Nottingham, UK. Writer. Publs: New Harrowing; The Vixens Cub; Country Dance; The House by the Water; The Long Meadow. Mbrships: Shakespeare Reading Soc.; Engl. Speaking Union; Institut Français. Address: Bleasby, Nottingham, UK.

MORRIS, Leon Lamb, b. 1914, Lithgow, NSW, Australia. College Principal. Educ: Univs. of Sydney & Melbourne, Aust., & London & Cambridge, UK; M.Sc.; M.Th.; Ph.D. Publs. incl: Commentary on I Corinthians; The Apostolic Preaching of the Cross; The Biblical Doctrine of Judgement; Commentary on Luke; Commentary on Revelation; Commentary on I & II Thessalonians; Studies in the Fourth Gospel; The Cross in the New Testament; Commentary on John; about 20 others. Address: Ridley Coll., Parkville, Vic., Australia 3052.

MORRIS, Louise Elizabeth Burton, b. 6 Dec. 1905, Arleston, Panola Co., Tex., USA. Editor; Author; Certified Genealogist; Heraldist; Lecturer. Educ: Okla. City Univ.; Okla. Univ.; Samford Univ., Ala.; Brigham Young Univ.; Nat. Archives Inst. of Geneal. Rsch., Wash. D.C. Publs. incl: Founders & Patriots of the Republic of Texas, 1963; Primer of Genealogical Research, 1965, 3rd ed., 1974; Lineages & Genealogical Notes, 1967. Contbr. to: The Quarterly (Pres.-Ed.); & num. other jrnls. Mbrships. incl: F.S.A. (Scotland); F.H.G.; F.M.H.S.; etc. Recip., Hon. Ph.D. Address: "Hacienda Tejas", 2515 Sweetbrier Dr., Dallas TX 75228, USA.

MORRIS, Margaret, b. 1891, London, UK. Founder of Ballet Company; Author. Publs: Margaret Morris Dancing, 1925; The Notation of Movement, 1928; Ski-ing Exercises, 1934; Maternity & Post Operative Exercises, 1936; Tennis by Simple Exercises, 1937; Basic Physical Training, 1937; My Galsworthy Story, 1967; My Life in Movement, 1969; Creation in Dance & Life, 1970; The Art of J. D. Fergusson, a Biased Biography, 1974. Address: 2 Manchester Sq., London W1, UK.

MORRIS, Richard, b. 26 Feb. 1909. Actor-Producer; Writer; Poet. Publs: Cocktails With the Captain; Norfolk Island (1-act plays); Considered Trifles, 1967; Désarmer ou Mourir, 1969; Poor Byron (biog); The Rat Race, 1967, 1974; Decline & Rise, (3-act plays) 1973; Equity Speeches, 1951-57; La Mort sur la Route est Evitable; lyrics, sonnets, short stories, playlets. Mbrships: Past Organizing Sec., Shaw Soc.; Past Comm. Mbr., John O'Londons Lit. Circle; Pres., Geneva Arts Club; Cons. Mbr., Cartel des Théâtres de Genève; Pres., Assn. des Amis du Musée d'Instruments Anciens de Musique. Winner, Poetry Recital, London Civil Defence Contest, 1944. Address: Riverrun, 1295 Tannay, Switz.

MORRIS, Thomas Baden, b. 30 Apr. 1900, Godstone, Surrey, UK. Novelist; Playwright. Publs. incl: (novels) Blind Bargain, 1957; So Many Dangers, 1960; Murder on the Loire, 1964; Wild Justice, 1965; Orchids With Murder, 1966; Shadows on Abu Simbel, 1967; Undying Serpent, 1970; The Muddy Leaf Mystery, 1971; The Horns of Truth, 1972; Third Time Unlucky, 1973; (3-act plays) The Beautiful One, 1938; Murder Without Men, 1944; The Song of the Morning, 1949; Frost on the Rose, 1951; The Nine Days, 1953; Island of Sirens, 1957; Deserted Night, 1961; The Crooked Tree, 1963; (plays for BBC) Nefertiti's Daughter; Too Dear for My Possessing; Bitter Beauty. Address: 6 Sion Hill Place, Bath BA1 5SJ.

MORRIS, Wright Marion, b. 1910, Central City, Neb., USA. University Lecturer; Author. Educ: Crane Coll., Chgo.; Pomona Coll., Calif. Publs. incl.: The Deep Sleep, 1954; Cause for Wonder, 1963; One Day, 1965; In Orbit, 1967; God's Country & My People, 1968; Wright Morris: A Reader; Fire Sermon, 1971; War Games, 1971; Love Affair: A Venetian Journal, 1972; A Life, 1973; About Fiction, 1975. Contbr. to: Harper's Bazaar; N.Y. Times Mag.; Living Novel; etc. Hons: Guggenheim Fellowship in Photography, 1942, 1946, in Lit., 1954. Nat. Book Award, 1956. Address: 341 Laurel Way, Mill Valley, CA 94941, USA.

MORRISON, David Ralston, b. 4 Aug. 1941, Glasgow, UK. Librarian. Educ: Strathclyde Univ.; Assoc., Lib. Assn. Publs: Essays on Neil H. Gunn (ed.), 1971; Essays on Fionn MacColla (ed.), 1973; The Idealist & Other Stories, 1973; The Hammer & Thistle (w. Alan Bold), 1974. Contbr. to poetry anthols. & lit. jrnls. inclng: Scotia Review (ed., 1972); Lines Review; Akros; New Edinburgh Review. Address: 33A Huddart St., Wick, Caithness, UK.

MORRISON, John Gordon, b. 1904, Sunderland, UK. Writer. Publs: (short stories) Sailors Belong Ships, 1947; Black Cargo, 1955; Twenty-three, 1962; Selected Stories, 1972; Australian By Choice, 1973; (novels) The Creeping City, 1949; Port of Call, 1950. Contbr. to: Meanjin; Overland; etc. Mbrships: Aust. Fellowship of Writers, Vic.; Aust. Soc. of Authors. Hons: C'wlth. Lit. Fund Fellowships, 1947, 1949; Gold Medal, Aust. Lit. Soc., 1963. Address: Flat 5, 127 Brighton Rd., Elwood, Victoria 3184, Australia.

MORRISON, Nancy (Agnes) Brysson Inglis, pen name: BRYSSON MORRISON, N., b. Scotland, UK. Author. Publs: The Gowk Storm, 1933; These Are My Friends, 1946; The Winnowing Years, 1950; The Hidden Fairing, 1951; The Following Wind, 1954; The Other Traveller, 1957; Mary Queen of Scots, 1960; Thea, 1963; The Private Life of Henry VIII, 1964; Haworth Harvest: The Lives of the Bröntes, 1969; King's Quiver; the Last 3 Tudors, 1972; True Minds: The Marriage of Thomas & Jane Carlyle, 1974. Hons: Recommended by Book Soc., 1933, 1951; 1st Niven Award, 1950; Lit. Guild Award, USA, 1960. Lit. Agent: John Johnson. Address: The Caledonian Club, 112 Princes St., Edinburgh EH2 3AQ, UK.

MORRISON, Thomas James, pen name MUIR, Alan, b. Glasgow, UK. Filmwriter; Novelist. Publs: The Truce Breaker, 1929; Tony Potter, 1930; The Cairn, 1935; The Queen of Spades, 1936; It's Different Abroad, 1939; Death Comes on Derby Day, 1939; They're Home Again, 1946; (film scripts) The Stars Look Down, 1939; Ice Cold in Alex, 1959; The Pot Carriers, 1965; (original film scripts) Stop Press Girl, 1948; Petticoat Pirates, 1962. Contbr. to: Tatler; Sketch; Argosy. Mbrships: Writers' Guild of GB; Fndr. Mbr., Screenwriters' Assn. Address: 244 Finchley Rd., London NW3, UK.

MORRISON, Tony, b. 1936, Hampshire, UK. Zoologist; Writer; TV Film Producer. Educ: B.Sc., Univ. of Bristol. Publs: Steps to a Fortune, (co-author), 1967; Animal Migration, 1973; Land Above the Clouds, 1974. Contbr. to: Observer; Daily Telegraph. Mbrships. incl: Fauna Preservation Soc.; Fellow, Royal Geogl. Soc. Flamingo Survival Grp., I.C.B.P., Smithsonian Instn. Address: 48 Station Rd., Woodbridge, Suffolk, UK.

MORSE, Elsa Peters, pen name PETERS, E. Gordon, b. 2 Apr. 1895, NYC, USA. Researcher on History of Money; Author. Publs: Tomorrow's Money (w. Felix J. Frazer), 1948; The Key to World Peace & Plenty, 1960. Contbr. to: Soviet Woman; The Tragedy of Am. Educ. Recip., 1st Prize, Int. Inst. for Peace Contest, Vienna, Austria, for A New Civilization — Peace With Abundance, 1963. Address: 5655 Anza St., Sutro Heights, San Fran., CA 94121, USA.

MORTIMER, James Edward, b. 1921, Bradford, UK. Former Member, London Transport Executive & National Board for Prices & Incomes; Chairman, Conciliation & Arbitration Service. Educ: Ruskin Coll., Oxford. Publs: A History of the Association of Engineering & Shipbuilding Draughtsmen, 1960; British Trade Unions Today (w. C. Jenkins); The Kind of Laws the Unions Ought to Want (w. C. Jenkins); Industrial Relations; Trade Unions & Technological Change, 1971; History of the Boilermakers' Society, vol. I. 1834-1906, 1973; num. booklets on trade union subjects. Contbr. to Tribune & Personnel Mgmt. Address: Conciliation & Arbitration Service, Cleland House, Page St., London SW1, UK.

MORTIMER, John Clifford, b. 21 Apr. 1923. Barrister; Q.C.; Playwright. Educ: Brasenose Coll., Oxford. Publs. incl: (plays) The Dock Brief & Other Plays, 1959; The Wrong Side of the Park, 1960; Two Stars for Comfort, 1962; A Voyage Round My Father, 1970; Collaborators, 1973; (novels) Charade, 1947; Like Men Betrayed, 1953; Three Winters, 1956; (Film Script) John& Mary, 1970; (ballet scenario) Home, 1968. Contbr. to: Evening Standard; Observer; New Statesman. Recip., Italia Prize, 1958. Address: 16a Blomfield Rd., London W9, UK.

MORTIMER, Johnnie, b. 2 July 1930, Clare, Suffolk, UK. Scriptwriter. Publs: (films, w. Brian Cooke) Father Dear Father; No Sex Please We're British; Man About the House; (TV) Man About the House; Father Dear Father; Cribbins; Tommy Cooper Hour; Life with Cooper; etc.; (Radio) Men from the Ministry; Round the Horne; etc. Contbr. to: The Listener. Mbrships: Writers' Guild of GB; Cartoonists' Club of GB. Address: c/o Fraser & Dunlop Scripts Ltd., 91 Regent St., London W1R 8RU, UK.

MORTIMER, Penelope (Ruth), b. 1918, Rhyl, N. Wales, UK. Writer; Critic. Educ: London Univ. Publs. incl: Johanna (as P. Dimont), 1947; A Villa in Summer, UK, 1954, USA, 1955; The Bright Prison, UK, 1956, USA, 1957; Daddy's Gone A-Hunting, UK, 1958 (as Cave of Ice, USA, 1959); Saturday Lunch with the Brownings, UK, 1960, USA, 1961; The Pumpkin Eater, UK, 1962, USA, 1963; My Friend Says It's Bullet-Proof, UK, 1967, USA, 1968; The Home, UK, 1971, USA, 1972; (screenplay) Bunny Lake is Missing (w. J. Mortimer), 1965. Contbr. to: Observer (Film Critic, 1967-70). Address: 134 Loudoun Rd., London NW8, UK.

MORTIMER, Raymond, b. 25 Apr. 1895. Writer. Educ: Balliol Coll., Oxford. Publs: Channel Packet, 1942; Manet's Bar aux Folies-Bergères, 1944; Duncan Grant, 1944. Contbr. to: Sunday Times (Lit. Critic). Hons: C.B.E.; Chevalier, Legion of Honour. Address: 5 Canonbury Pl., London N1, UK.

MORTIMER, Robert Cecil, b. 6 Dec. 1902, Bristol, UK. Bishop of Exeter, 1949-73. Educ: B.A., Keble Coll., 1925, M.A., Christ Ch., Oxford, 1929; B.D., 1939; D.D., 1947. Publs: Origins of Private Penance, 1939; Elements of Moral Theology, 1947; Christian Ethics, 1950; Western Canon Law, 1953. Mbrships. incl: Pres., Woodard Corp., 1954-73. Hons: Fellow, Keble Coll., 1951; Hon. Student, Christ Ch., 1964. Address: The Old Rectory, Newton Reigny, Penrith, Cumbria CA11 0AY, UK.

MORTIMER, (Major) Roger Francis, b. 1909, London, UK. Former Officer, Coldstream Guards; Racing Correspondent; Broadcaster. Publs: Anthony Mildmay; The Jockey Club; The Derby Stakes; Twenty Great Horses; History of Steeplechasing (co-author); Great Horses of the World. Contbr. to: Sunday Times; The Racehorse; The Brit. Racehorse. Address: Budds Farm, Burghclere, Newbury, Berks., UK.

MORTON, Arthur Leslie, b. 4 July 1903, Hengrave, Suffolk, UK. Writer. Educ: B.A., Peterhouse, Cambridge. Publs: A People's History of England, 1938; Language of Men, 1945; The English Utopia, 1952; The British Labour Movement (w. George Tate), 1956; The Everlasting Gospel: a Study in the Sources of William Blake; The Life & Ideas of Robert Owen; Socialism in Britain; The Matter of Britain, 1966; The World of the Ranters, 1970. Contbr. to: Criterion; Left Review; Listener; Marxist Quarterly; Mod. Quarterly; New Engl. Weekly; Our Time; Sci. & Soc.; Marxism Today; etc. Agent: Lawrence & Wishart. Address: The Old Chapel, Clare, Suffolk, UK.

MORTON, Frederic, b. 1925, Vienna, Austria. Writer. Educ: B.S., M.A. Publs: The Darkness Below, 1950; Asphalt & Desire, 1953; The Witching Ship, 1961; The Rothschilds, 1962. Contbr. to: N.Y. Times; Book Review; Holiday Mag.; Esquire; Atlantic Monthly; Reporter; Nation. Mbrships: Authors' Guild; PEN. Address: c/o Secker & Warburg,14 Carlisle St.. London W1V 6NN, UK.

MORTON, George Fletcher, b. 1882, Macclesfield, Ches., UK. Educator. Educ: Cambridge Univ.; London Schl. of Econs.; M.A.; B.Sc. Publs: Childhood Fears; Hike & Trek; Hike & Hero; Madhouse for the Million; Highlands & Backwoods. Contbr. to: Yorks. Post; New Engl. Review; B.O.P.; etc. Address: Uplands, Shipham, Winscombe, Somerset, UK.

MORTON, Henry Vollam, b. 25 July 1892, Ashton-under-Lyne, UK. Author; Journalist. Publs. incl: The Heart of London, 1925; The Call of England, 1928; In Search of Wales, 1932; Blue Days at Sea, 1932; Our Fellow Men, 1936; Women of The Bible, 1940; Middle East, 1941; In the Steps of Jesus, 1953; A Stranger in Spain, 1954; This is Rome, 1960; This is the Holy Land, 1961; The Waters of Rome, 1966; A Traveller in Italy, 1969. Contbr. to: (pre WWI) Daily Mail; Daily Express; Daily Herald; Ed., Empire Mag. Mbr., F.R.S.L. Hons: Order of Phoenix, Greece, 1937; Order of Merit, Italy, 1965. Address: Schapenberg, Somerset W., Cape Province, Repub. of S. Africa.

MORTON, John Cameron Andrieu Bingham, pen name BEACHCOMBER, b. 7 June 1893, Tooting, UK. Journalist. Educ: Univ. of Oxford. Publs: The Bastille Falls; Brumaire; Saint-Just; Marshal Ney; The Dauphin; Ste. Thérèse of Lisieux; Pyrenean; Camille Desmoulins; The Gascon; Sobieski; Springtime; The Dancing Cabman; The Death of the Dragon. Address: Melleray, Sea Lane, Ferring, Worthing, W. Sussex, UK.

MORTON, Lena Beatrice, b. 15 June 1901, Flat Creek, Ky., USA. University Professor of English. Educ: B.A., M.A., Univ. of Cinn.; Grad. Dip. in Educ.; Ph.D., Western Reserve Univ.; Cert. of Completion in Engl., Univ. of London, UK. Publs: Negro Poetry in America, 1925; Farewell to the Public Schools . . . I'm Glad We Met, 1952; Man Under Stress, 1960; My First Sixty Years, 1965; The Influence of the Sea on English Poetry from the Anglo-Saxon Period to the Victorian Period, 1975. Contbr. to var. lit. publs. Mbrships: MLA; AAUP; Hon. Mbr., Int. Mark Twain Soc., 1952; Fellow, Int. Inst. of Arts & Letters, 1952. Address: 3256 Beresford Ave., Cincinnati, OH 45206, USA.

MORTON, Miriam, b. 14 June 1918, Kishinev, USSR. Writer; Translator. Educ: B.S., Univ. of N.Y., USA. Publs. incl: The Arts & the Soviet Child; The Aesthetic Education of Children in the USSR, 1972; Said the Racoon to the Moon, 1974; (Ed. & Transl.) From Two to Five, 1963; A Harvest of Russian Children's Literature (anthol.), 1967;

The Moon Is Like a Silver Sickle: A Celebration of Poetry by Soviet Children, 1972; (Transl.) Zoo Babies, 1973. Contbr. to: N.Y. Times Book Review; Horn Book Mag.; New World Review; etc. Recip., Notable Book Award, Am. Lib. Assn., 1967. Address: 61 Stockton Rd., Kendall Park, NJ 08824, USA.

MORTON, Richard Alan, b. 22 Sept. 1899, Liverpool, UK. Emeritus Professor of Biochemistry; Author. Educ: Ph.D., D.Sc., Univ. of Liverpool. Publs: Vitamins (vol. 9, International Encyclopaedia of Nutrition); Quinones in Biochemistry, 1965; History of the Biochemical Society, 1969); Biochemical Spectroscopy, 2 vols., 1975. Contbr. to: Jrnl. of Chem. Soc.; Biochem. Jrnl.; Brit. Jrnl. of Nutrition; Nature. Mbrships: F.R.S. (Coun., 1959-61 & 1970-72); F.R.I.C. (Coun., 1958-60, VP, 1960-62). Hons. incl: Meldola Medallist, 1930; D.Sc., Univ. of Wales; Sc.D., Univ. of Dublin. Address: 39 Greenhill Rd., Liverpool L18 6JJ, UK.

MOSBLECH, Berndt, b. 1 Sept. 1950, Duisburg, German Fed. Repub. Publisher. Publs: Ich erinnere . . ., 1973; Wo enden eigentlich die Schlafgrenzen? (lyrical prose), 1973; für Günter Eich (lyrical plaque), 1974; silbernes Lyrikplakat, 1974; Gedanken an einen einziger Sommer (lyrical prose w. 3 lithographs by Jean Cocteau), 1974; Die Aufzeichnungen des Morandinus Morandin (lyrical prose), 1975; Ikarus, (lyrical prose) 1975; Ed., var. anthols. Mbrships: Verband deutscher Schriftsteller; Int. Autorenvereinigung "Die Kogge"; Dir., Literarische Werkstatt, Duisburg, 1971—. Recip., Malkasten Lit. Prize, Düsseldorf, 1973. Address: Elisabethstr. 18, 41 Duisburg 11, W. Germany.

MOSCATI, Sabatino, b. 1922, Rome, Italy. Academic. Educ: Pontifical Biblical Inst.; Litt.D., Rome Univ. Publs: Ancient Semitic Civilizations, 1957; The Semites in Ancient History, 1959; The Face of the Ancient Orient, 1960; The World of the Phoenicians, 1968. Contbr. to: Jrnl. of Near Eastern Studies; Jrnl. of Biblical Lit.; Jrnl. of Bible & Relig.; Cath. Biblical Quarterly; Orientalia; Biblica; Sefarad; Archiv Orientalni; Museon; Rivista degli Studi Orientali; Rendiconti Accad. Lincei; etc. Mbrships: Academia dei Lincei; Pontifica Accademia d'Archeologia; Pres., Italian Acad. Union. Address: Via Vigliena 10, 00192 Rome, Italy.

MOSELEY, George V. H., III, b. 6 Sept. 1931, W. Point, N.Y., USA. College Teacher. Educ: B.A., Univ. of Colo., 1954; M.A., Yale Univ., 1960; D.Phil., St. Antony's Coll., Oxford Univ., UK, 1970. Publs: China: From Empire to People's Republic, 1968; The Party & the National Question in China, 1966; A Sino-Soviet Cultural Frontier: The Ili Kazakh Autonomous Chou, 1966; The Consolidation of the South China Frontier, 1973. Mbr., Assn. for Asian Studies. Address: 14 Oak Shade Rd., Sterling, VA 22170, USA.

MOSELEY, Maboth, b. UK. Writer. Educ: pvte. Publs: Irascible Genius, Life of Charles Babbage, 1964, Am. ed., 1970; also four novels. Contbr. to var. newspapers & mags.; Past Ed., Computer Survey. Mbr., Soc. of Authors. Address: 51 Beaufort Mansions, Beaufort St., London SW3 5AF, UK.

MOSER, Thomas Colborn, b. 1923, Connellsville, Pa., USA. University Professor; Writer. Educ: A.B.; M.A.; Ph.D., Univ. of Pitts.; Purdue; Harvard. Publs: Joseph Conrad: Achievement & Decline; Wuthering Heights: Text, Sources, Criticism; Lord Jim: A Critical Edition. Contbr. to: Nineteenth Century Fiction; Daedalus; Mosaic; Tex. Studies in Lit. & Lang. Address: 812 Esplanada Way, Stanford, CA, USA.

MOSES, Elbert Raymond Jr., b. 31 Mar. 1908, New Concord, Ohio, USA. Professor Emeritus. Educ: A.B., Univ. of Pitts., Pa.; M.Sc., Ph.D., Univ. of Mich., Ann Arbor. Publs: A Guide to Effective Speaking, 1956, 1957; Phonetics; History & Interpretation, 1964. Contbr. to: Am. Speech & Hearing Assn. Mag.; Jrnl. of Am. Speech; Speech Monographs. Mbrships: Am. Speech & Hearing Assn.; Am. Acad. of Arts & Scis.; Int. Soc. of Phonetic Scis.; Int. Phonetic Assn.; Speech Assn. of Am. Address: 18 Fairview Ave., Clarion, PA 16214, USA.

MOSKVITIN, Jurij Robert, b. 6 Jan. 1938, Copenhagen, Denmark. Author. Educ: Pianist-Composer, Grad., Hon. Dip., Royal Danish Conserv. of Music; M.A. (Philos.), Univ. of Copenhagen. Publs: Essay on the Origin of Thought, 1974. Contbr. to: Dagbladet Politiken. Mbrships: Pres., Det Neo-Platoniske Selskab (Neo-Platonic Soc.); Danish

Authors' Union. Address: Chr. Winthersvej 23, 1860 Copenhagen K, Denmark.

MOSLEY, Leonard, b. Manchester, UK. Former Correspondent, Drama & Film Critic; Author. Publs: The Reich Marshal; Power Play; On Borrowed Time; Hirohito; Curzon; Duel for Kilimanjaro; The Last Days of the British Raj; Faces from the Fire; 14 other histories, biogs., & novels. Contbr. to: N.Y. Times; Daily Telegraph. Recip., O.B.E. Agent: Curtis Brown Ltd. Address: Les Arches, Les Hauts de St. Paul, 06 St. Paul de Vence, France.

MOSLEY, Nicholas, (Lord Ravensdale), b. 25 June 1923, London, UK. Writer. Educ: Eton Coll.; Balliol Coll., Oxford Univ. Publs: (novels) Spaces of the Dark, 1951; The Rainbearers, 1955; Corruption, 1958; Meeting Place, 1962; Accident, 1966 (filmed); Assassins, 1967; Impossible Object, 1969 (filmed); Natalie Natalia, 1971; (non-fiction) African Switchback, 1958; The Life of Raymond Raynes, 1961; Experience & Religion, 1967; The Assassination of Trotsky, 1972 (filmed). Address: 9 Church Row, Hampstead, London NW3, UK.

MOSS, (Very Rev.) Basil, b. 1918, Salford, Lancs., UK. Clergyman; Former Director of Ordination Training. Diocese of Bristol. Educ: M.A., Univ. of Oxford. Publs: Clergy Training Today, 1964; Crisis for Baptism, 1966. Contbr. to: Ch. Quarterly Review; Theol.; sev. other relig. jrnls. Address: Provost's Lodge, St. Philip's Place, Birmingham B3 2PP, UK.

MOSS, Howard, b. 1922, NYC, USA. Editor; Author. Educ: Univs. of Mich., Wis., Harvard & Columbia; B.A. Publs. incl: The Wound & the Weather, 1946; The Toy Fair, 1954; A Swimmer in the Air, 1957; A Winter Come, A Summer Gone, 1960; The Magic Lantern of Marcel Proust, 1962; Second Nature, 1968; Writing Against Time, 1969; Selected Poems, 1971; The Poet's Story, 1973; Instant Lives, 1974; Buried City, 1975. Contbr. to: New Yorker; Poetry Mag.; N.Y. Times Book Review; Harper's; N.Y. Quarterly; etc. Mbrships: PEN; Writer's Guild; Nat. Inst. of Arts & Letters. Recip., Nat. Book Award in poetry, 1972. Address: 27 W. 10th St., N.Y., NY 10011, USA.

MOSS, Peter, b. 1921, Marlborough, Wilts., UK. Writer. Publs: Our Own Homes through the Ages, 1956; Meals through the Ages, 1958; Sports & Pastimes through the Ages, 1962; Town Life through the Ages, 1970; The Media; Violence & Punishment; Medicine & Morality, 1974; Today's English, vols. 1 & 2, 1968; History Alive Books 1-6, 1967; Tombstone Treasure, 1966; Hermit's Hoard, 1966; Die Schlangenbande, 1966; World History 1900-1974, 1975. Contbr. to BBC World Serv. Mbr., Soc. of Authors. Agent: Mark Paterson. Address: Brook Cottage, Ripe, Lewes, Sussex, UK.

MOSS, Stirling, b. 1929, London, UK. Racing Driver. Publs: In the Track of Speed; Stirling Moss' Book of Motor Racing; Stirling Moss' Second Book of Motor Racing; Le Mans '59; My Favourite Car Stories. Contbr. to: Sunday Times. Mbrships. incl: Arts Theatre; Brit. Racing Drivers' Club; Brit. Racing & Sports Car Club. Address: Stirling Moss Ltd., 46 Shepherd St., London W1, UK.

MOSSE, Werner, b. 5 Feb. 1918, Berlin, Germany. University Teacher. Educ: M.A., Ph.D., Corpus Christi Coll., Cambridge, UK. Publs: The European Powers & the German Question 1848-1871, 1958; Alexander II & the Modernisation of Russia, 1959; Ed., Entscheidungsjahr 1932, 1965; Ed., Deutsches Judentum in Krieg und Revolution 1916-1923, 1971; Liberal Europe: The Age of Bourgeois Realism 1848-1875, 1974. Contbr. to: Ency. Britannica; Engl. Histl. Review; Histl. Jrnl. Fellow, Royal Histl. Soc. Address: Dawn Cottage, Ashwellthorpe, Norwich, Norfolk, UK.

MOSSKIN, Peter, b. 6 Mar. 1945, Stockholm, Sweden. Writer; Musician. Educ: B.A. Publs: Ett par jeans i Medelhavet, 1968; Ungdomsupproret, 1969. Mbr., Swedish Writers Assn. Address: Vasterfors 71, 780 41 Gagnef, Sweden.

MOTLEY, Mary Margaret, (pen name), b. 1912, Godalming, Surrey, UK. Writer. Publs: Devils in Waiting; Morning Glory, 1961; Home to Numidia, 1964. Contbr. to: Housewife; Homes & Gardens. Agent: David Higham Assocs. Address: 32 Residence Argia, Rue de Parme, 64200, Biarritz, France.

MOTT, Michael Charles Alston, b. 8 Dec. 1930, London, UK. Writer; Teacher. Educ: Oriel Coll., Oxford Univ.; B.A., London Univ. Publs: (poetry) The Cost of Living, 1957; The Tales of Idiots, & New Exile, 1959; A Book of Pictures, 1962; Absence of Unicorns, Presence of Lions, 1976; (novels) The Notebooks of Susan Berry, 1962, USA 1963, paperback 1964; Helmet & Wasps, 1964; (children's novels) Master Entrick, 1965, USA 1966, paperbacks 1967, 1968; The Blind Cross, 1968, USA 1969. Contbr. to: Poetry; Kenyon Review (poetry Ed., 1967-70); Poem; Southern Review; Encounter; num. other lit. jrnls. & poetry anthols. Mbrships: F.R.G.S. Agent: A. D. Peters. Address: c/o English Dept., Emory Univ., Atlanta, GA 30322, USA.

MOTT, (Sir) Nevill Francis, b. 1905. Publisher; Author. Educ: M.A., St. John's Coll., Cambridge. Publs. incl: An Outline of Wave Mechanics, 1930; The Theory of Atomic Collisions (w. H. S. W. Massey), 1933; The Theory of the Properties of Metals & Alloys (w. H. Jones), 1936; Wave Mechanics & its Applications (w. I. N. Snedden), 1948; Elements of Wave Mechanics, 1952; Atomic Structure & the Strength of Metals, 1956; Electronic Properties of Non-Crystalline Materials (w. E. A. Davis), 1971; Metal-Insulator Transitions, 1974. Contbr. to: Philos. Mag. (past Ed.); Taylor & Francis Ltd., Sci. Publrs. (Chmn., 1965–). F.R.S. Address: 31 Sedley Taylor Rd., Cambridge, UK.

MOTTRAM, Anthony John, b. 8 June 1920, Coventry, UK. Director of National Tennis Development. Publs: Quick Ways to Better Tennis; Modern Lawn Tennis; Improve Your Tennis; Play Better Tennis. Mbrships: All England Club; Edgbaston Priory Club; Earlsdon Club. Address: 3 Coombe Hill Glade, Kingston, Surrey, UK.

MOTTRAM, Vernon Henry, b. 1882, Tewkesbury, UK. Retired Professor of Physiology. Educ: M.A., Univ. of Cambridge. Publs: Manual of Histology; Food & the Family; Functions of the Body; Food & the Principles of Dietetics (w. R. Hutchinson & G. G. Arnold); Healthy Eating; Physical Basis of Personality. Contbr. to: Jrnl. of Physiol.; Biochem. Jrnl.; Schl. & Coll.; & sev. other jrnls. Address: Waterhouse, Monkton Combe, Bath, Somerset, UK.

MOUAT, Kit, b. 1 Mar. 1920, Croydon, UK. Poet; Author; Freelance Journalist; Bookseller. Publs: What Humanism is About, 1963, German transl., Leben in Dieser Welt, 1964; Time Smoulders & Other Poems, 1971; Poems of an Angry Dove, forthcoming. Contbr. to: World Med.; Guardian; Tribune; Oz; Humanist; Freethinker; Viewpoint; Scrip; Headland; BBC radio & TV; etc. Mbr., Writers' Guild GB. Address: Mercers, High St., Cuckfield, Sussex RH1 7JU, UK.

MOUCHET, Charles Michel, b. 21 Mar. 1920, Geneva, Switz. Writer. Educ: Univ. of Geneva. Publs: Le Mot Poésie, 1953; De Natura (transl. of Lucrèce), 1954; 17 Poèmes, 1955; Débris, 1958; Morte ou Vive (essai poétique), 1969; Marches, 1973; Arabesques, 1974. Contbr. to: Cooperation; Rencontre. Mbrships: PEN; Swiss Soc. of Writers. Recip. Blondel Prize, Univ. of Geneva, 1945. Address: 14 Cours de Rive, 1204 Geneva, Switz.

MOULD, Daphne D. C. Pochin, b. 15 Nov. 1920, Salisbury, Wilts., UK. Author; Aerial Photographer. Educ: B.Sc., 1943, Ph.D., 1946, Univ. of Edinburgh. Publs: The Roads from the Isles, 1950; Scotland of the Saints, 1952; West – over Sea, 1953; Ireland of the Saints, 1953; The Rock of Truth, 1953; The Mountains of Ireland, 1955; Irish Pilgrimage, 1955; The Celtic Saints, 1956; The Irish Dominicans, 1957; Peter's Boat, 1959; The Angels of God, 1961; The Irish Saints, 1963; Ireland from the Air, 1972; The Aran Islands, 1972; (in preparation) Valentia Island; Irish Monasteries. Contbr. to: Irish Times; Ireland of the Welcomes; Countryman; U.S. Catholic; & other jrnls. Address: Aherla House, Aherla, Co. Cork, Repub. of Ireland.

MOULD, George, b. 29 Nov. 1894, Bury, Lancs., UK. Retired as Chief Regional Officer, Central Office of Information, 1962. Publs: They Build a City (play), 1937; Lancashire's Unknown River, 1970; Manchester Memories, 1972. Contbr. to: Daily Mail; Manchester Evening News; & other papers. Mbrships: Manchester Press Club (Hon.); Nat. Union Jrnlsts. (Life); Civil Serv. Club (Life); Over Wyre Probus Club (Fndn. mbr., past Chmn.). Hons: Member, Victorian Order; O.B.E. Address: 3 Fylde Court, Esplanade, Knott End on Sea, Fleetwood FY6 0BD, UK.

MOULD, H. K. Journalist. Educ: Regent St. Schl. of Jrnlsm. & Mod. Langs., London, UK, 1950. Contbr. to: Vox Populi, Accra, Ghana, 1943; Gold Coast Spectator, Accra, Ghana; Ed., African Morning Post, 1950-61; Ed., Weekly Advertiser, 1968—. Recip., Schlrship., Gold Coast Govt., 1950. Address: Weekly Advertiser, P.O. Box 6109, Accra-North, Accra, Ghana.

MOULE, (Rev.) Charles Francis Digby, b. 1908, Hangchow, China. Professor of Divinity; Fellow, Clare College, Cambridge. Educ: M.A., Emmanuel Coll., Cambridge; Ridley Hall (Anglican Theol. Coll.), Cambridge. Publs. incl: An Idiom Book of New Testament Greek, 1953; Commentary on the Epistles to the Colossians & to Philemon, 1957; The Birth of the New Testament, 1962. Contbr. to: Ency. Brit.; Biblisch—Historisches Handwörterbuch; Jrnl. Theol. Studies; etc. Mbrships: Am. Soc. for Biblical Lit.; Studiorum Novi Testamenti Societas. Hons: Fellow, Brit. Acad.; D.D., St. Andrews Univ.; Fellow, Emmanuel Coll., Cambridge, 1972—; Canon Theologian, Leicester Cathedral, 1955—. Address: Clare Coll., Cambridge, UK.

MOULT, Thomas, b. Mellor, Derbys., UK. Poet; Critic; Editor; Novelist; Lecturer. Publs. incl: Snow Over Elden, 1920; The Comely Lass, 1923; Barrie, 1928; Mary Webb, 1932; (poetry) Down Here the Hawthorn, 1921; Brown Earth, 1922; Derbyshire in Prose & Verse, 1929; (autobiography) Wind in the Trees; (Ed.) Playing For England, by Jack Hobbs, 1931; Cricket is My Life, by Len Hutton, 1949. Contbr. to: Sunday Times; Observer; Engl. Review; Manchester Guardian; etc. Mbr., Poetry Soc. (Pres.). Recip., Carnegie Prize. Address: The Mill House, Finchingfield, Braintree, Essex, UK.

MOUNTFORD, (Sir) James Frederick, b. 1897, W. Bromwich, Staffs., UK. Former University Professor & Vice Chancellor; Author. Educ: D.Litt.; Univ. of Birmingham; Oriel Coll., Oxford. Publs: Quotations from Classical Authors in Medieval Glossaries, 1925; The Scholia Bembina, 1943; Outline of Latin Prose Composition, 1942; British Universities, 1966; Keele: an Historical Critique, 1972; eds. of: Kennedy's Latin Primer, 1930; Arnold's Latin Prose, 1938; Sidgwick's Greek Prose, 1951. Contbr. to classical & educl. jrnls. Hons: Litt.D.; D.C.L.; LL.D. Address: 11 The Serpentine, Liverpool L19 9DT, UK.

MOUSSA, Pierre Louis, b. 1922, Lyons, France. Banker. Educ: Ecole Normale Supérieure, Paris; Inst. for Political Sci. Studies, Paris. Publs: Les Chances Economiques de la Communauté Franco-Africaine, 1957; Les Nations Prolétaires, 1959; L'Economie de la Zone Franc, 1961; Les États-Unis et les Nations Prolétaires, 1965. Address: c/o Banque de Paris et des Pays-Bas, 3 Rue d'Antin, 75083 Paris Cédex 02, France.

MOUSTIERS, Pierre Jean, b. 13 Aug. 1924. Author. Educ: L.en D.; Univs. of Aix-Marseilles & Neuchâtel. Publs: Le journal d'un geôlier, 1957; La Mort du Pantin, 1961; Le Pharisien, 1962; La Paroi, 1969; L'Hiver d'un Gentilhomme, 1971; (plays) Les Epreuves de Rembrandt, 1957; L'Argent de Poche, 1963; (essay) Henri Bazin ou le romancier en mouvement, 1973. Contbr. to: Nice-Matin; Radio-Marseille. Hons: Hommes & Lectures Prize, 1962; Grand Prix de sport. lit.; Grand Prix du Roman, French Acad., 1969; Prix des Maisons de la Presse, 1972; Resistance Medal. Address: Campagne Sainte Anne, Blvd. des Acacias, 83 Toulon, France.

MOUTAFCHIEVA, Vera Petrova, b. 28 Mar. 1929, Sofia, Bulgaria. Writer. Publs: A Chronicle of Troubled Times, 1965-66; The Case of Jamme, 1967; The Knight, 1970; Levski in Court, 1972; The Trial, 1973; Belote for Two, 1974. Contbr. to sev. lit. reviews & newspapers. Mbrships: PEN; Union of Bulgarian Writers. Address: Sofia, kv. Iztuk, ul. Latinka, 77 vh.B, Bulgaria.

MOW, Anna B. (Mrs. Baxter M. Mow), b. 31 July 1893, Daleville, Va., USA. Former Teacher; Missionary; Author. Educ: B.A.; M.R.E.; M.Th. Publs: Say 'Yes' to Life, 1961; Your Child, 1963; Going Steady with God, 1965; Your Teenager and You, 1967; So Who's Afraid of Birthdays, 1969; The Secret of Married Love, 1970; Your Experience & the Bible, 1973. Hons: D.D., 1959; Va. State Mother of Yr., 1973. Address: 1318 Varnell Ave. N.E, Roanoke, VA 24012, USA.

MOWAT, David William, b. 1943, Cairo, Egypt. University Fellow in Drama. Educ: B.A., New Coll., Oxford, UK. Prods: (plays) Jens, 1965; Anna-Luse, 1968;

Purity, 1969; The Others, 1970; Inuit, 1970; John, 1971; Phoenix-and-Turtle, 1972; My Relationship with Jayne, 1973; Come, 1973; The Collected Works, 1974; Main Sequence, 1974; The Memory Man, 1974; The Love Maker, 1974. Publs: Anna-Luse & other plays, 1970; The Others, 1973; Four Stories (New Writers XI), 1974. Contbr. to Encounter. Agent: Dr. Jan Van Loewen Ltd. Address: c/o Dr. Jan Van Loewen Ltd., 81-83 Shaftesbury Ave., London W1V 8BX, UK.

MOWAT, Farley McGill, b. 12 May 1921, Belleville, Ont., Can. Author. Educ: B.A., Univ. of Toronto. Publs. incl: People of the Deer, 1952; The Regiment, 1955, new ed., 1973; The Grey Seas Under, 1959; Owls in the Family, 1961; Never Cry Wolf, 1963, new ed., 1973; Curse of the Viking Grave, 1966; Canada North, 1967; Sibir, 1970, new ed., 1973; Wake of the Great Sealers, 1973; Top of the World Trilogy: Ordeal by Ice, 1960, new ed., 1973, The Polar Passion, 1967, new ed., 1973, Tundra, 1973. Contbr. to num. mags. & reviews. Mbr., Can. Writers' Union. Hons. incl: sev. lit. awards; 3 degrees. Address: 25 John St., Port Hope, Ont., Can.

MOWATT, Ian, b. 15 Nov. 1948, Oban, Argyll, UK. College Lecturer. Educ: M.A.(Hons.), St. Andrews Univ., 1971; M.A., Univ. of Pa., USA, 1973. Publs: Just Sheaffer, or Storms in the Troubled Heir, 1973. Contbr. to Pa. Review. Recip., Thovron Schlrship., 1971-73. Address: 15 Langcraigs Terrace, Glenburn, Paisley, Renfrewshire, Scotland, UK.

MOWRER, Edgar Ansel, b. 8 Mar. 1892, Bloomington, Ill., USA. Newspaperman; Author. Educ: B.A., Univ. of Mich., 1913; Univs. of Chgo. & Paris, France. Publs. incl: Immortal Italy, 1922; The Future of Politics, 1930; The Dragon Awakes, 1938; Global War (w. M. Rajchman), 1942; The Nightmare of American Foreign Policy, 1948; Challenge & Decision, 1950; An End to Make-Believe, 1961; Triumph & Turmoil, 1968; Umano & the Price of Lasting Peace (w. Lilian T. Mowrer), 1973. Contbr. to num. newspapers & mags. Mbrships. incl: Century Assn., NYC; Off., Legion of Honour, France, 1936; Authors League of Am. Recip., Pulitzer Prize for Best Foreign Corres., 1932. Address: Wonalancet, NH 03897, USA.

MOWRER, Lilian T(homson), b. London, UK. Writer. Educ: Liverpool Univ.; Sorbonne, Paris, France; Rome, Italy. Publs: Journalist's Wife, 1937; Arrest & Exile, 1940; Riptide of Aggression, 1942; Concerning France, 1944; The U.S. & World Relations, 1952; The Indomitable John Scott of Long Island, 1960; I've Seen it Happen Twice, 1969; UMANO and Price of Lasting Peace (w. Edgar A. Mowrer), 1973. Contbr. to: New Yorker; Town & Country; Sat. Review. Mbrships: Am. Newspaper Womens Club, Wash. D.C.; Soc. of Geneals., UK.; Tamworth Arts Coun., N.H. Address: Wonalancet, NH 03897, USA.

MOY, Ragnhild Margrethe, pen name MØY, b. 15 Apr. 1944, Orkdal, Norway. Journalist. Educ: Norwegian Jrnlst. Schl. Contbr. to: Aftenposten. Address: Ammerudveien 29 A, Oslo 9, Norway.

MOYNAHAN, Julian b. 1925, Cambridge, Mass., USA. Professor of English. Educ: B.A., 1947; M.A., 1951, Ph.D., 1957, Harvard Univ. Publs: Sisters & Brothers, 1961; The Deed of Life, 1963; Pairing Off, 1969; Vladimir Nabokov, 1971; Garden State, 1973. Contbr. to: Observer; N.Y. Times Book Review; Listener; New Statesman; Wash. Post; Book World; etc. Mbrships: MLA; AAUP; Assn. of Univ. Teachers (Brit.); Am. Comm. on Irish Studies. Hons: Ingram-Merrill Fndn. Award, 1971; Nat. Endowment for the Arts Award, 1967; Nat. Endowment for the Humanities Award, 1972. Address: 3439 Laurenceville Rd., Princeton, NJ 08540, USA.

MOYNE, (Baron) Bryan Walter Guinness, pen name GUINNESS, Bryan, b. 27 Oct. 1905, London, UK. Brewer; Writer. Educ: M.A., Christ Church, Oxford; Barrister-at-Law. Publs. incl: 23 Poems, 1931; Landscape with Figures, 1934; A Week by the Sea, 1936; Reflexions, 1947; Story of a Nutcracker, 1953; Collected Poems, 1956; Priscilla & the Prawn, 1960; Leo & Rosabelle, 1961; The Girl with the Flower, 1966; The Engagement, 1969; The Clock, 1973. Mbrships. incl: Gov., Nat. Gallery of Ireland; F.R.S.L.; Irish Acad. of Letters. Address: Biddesden House, Andover, Hants., UK.

MOYNIHAN, John Dominic, b. 1932, London, UK. Journalist. Publs: The Soccer Syndrome, 1966; Not All a Ball, 1970; Park Football, 1970. Contbr. to: Daily

Telegraph; Sunday Telegraph (Dpty. Lit. Ed.); New Statesman; Guardian; Observer; Queen; Evening Standard; Daily Express; The Sun; etc. Mbr., Sportswriters' Assn; Football Writers' Assn. Address: 4 Kildare Terrace, London W2, UK.

MPHAHLELE, Ezekiel, b. 17 Dec. 1919. University Teacher; Writer. Publs. incl: Man Must Live; (short stories) The Living & the Dead; (autobiography) Down Second Avenue; (essays) The African Image; Voices in the Whirlwind; (other) The Wanderers; In Corner B. Contbr. to: Drum mag., 1955. Address: Dept. of Engl., Univ. of Denver, Denver, CO 80210, USA.

MRÓWCZYŃSKI, Bolesław, b. 22 July 1910, Lodz, Poland. Writer. Publs: Dutur z Rajskiego Ogrodu, 1958; Plama na Złotej Puszczy, 1958; Cién Montezumy, 1961; Błękitny trop, 1961; Bartochowie, 1965; Miecz Kagenowy, 1968. Mbrships: PEN; Związek Literatów Polskich. Address: 02-586 Warszawa, Dąbrowskiego 69a m.83, Poland.

MROZEK, Slawomir, b. 1930, Poland. Former Cartoonist & Journalist. Publs. incl: The Elephant, 1957; (short stories) The Rain, 1962; The Ugupu Bird, 1968; (plays) The Police, 1958; What a Lovely Dream, 1963; Let's Have Fun, 1963; The Death of the Lieutenant, 1963; Striptease, 1964; Tango, 1964; On the High Seas, 1970; Vatzlav, 1970; The Happy Event.

MSISKA, Stephen Kauta, b. 28 Dec. 1914, Livingstonia, Malawi, C. Africa. Minister of Region. Educ: Dip. Theol., New Coll., Edinburgh, UK. Publs: African Traditional Religion in Malawi, 1967; Infant Baptism (Tymbuka), 1970; Practical Theology, 1973. Contbr. to: London Illustrated News; Ministry (S. Africa); Unity. Mbrships: Relig. Rsch., E. & Ctrl. Africa; World Rsch. on Marriage, Uganda. Recip., Prize for Unity Mag., C.C.A.P. Theol. Coll., Malawi. Address: Ulanda House, Chilulu F.D. School, P/B Ngonga, P.O. Rumphi, N. Region, Central Africa.

MUDIE, Ian, b. 1911, Hawthorn, S.A., Australia. Former Editor-in-Chief of Publishing House; Lecturer; Author. Publs. incl: Corroboree to the Sun, 1940; This is Australia, 1941; The Australian Dream, 1943; The Christmas Kangaroo, 1946; The Blue Crane, 1959; Riverboats, 1961; The North-Bound Rider, 1963; Rivers of Australia, 1966; Look, the Kingfisher, 1970; Australia Today, 1970; Glenelg Sketchbook, 1974. Contbr. to newspapers & mags. Mbrships: Past Fed. Pres., Fellowships of Aust. Writers; C'wlth. Lit. Fund Fellow & Lectr.; Past Reg. VP, Aust. Soc. of Authors. Address: 8 Bristol St., Glenelg S., S.A., Australia 5045.

MUELLER, Christian, b. 3 Feb. 1945, Zurich, Switz. News Correspondent. Educ: Doct. of Philosl. Fac., Bonn Univ., German Fed. Repub.; Univ. of Munich; Univ. of Zurich, Switz. Publs: Oberst i.G. Stauffenberg: Eine Biographie, 1970. Address: 1-31-21 Okamoto, Setagaya-ku, Tokyo 157, Japan.

MUELLER, Gerhard O. W., b. 15 Mar. 1926, Eigenrieden, Germany. Professor of Law; Educator-Criminologist; Author. Educ: J.D., Univ. of Chgo., 1953; LL.M., Columbia Univ., 1955. Publs: Criminal Law & Procedure (w. J. Hall), 1965; International Criminal Law (w. E. M Wise), 1965; Comparative Criminal Procedure (w. le Poole), 1969; Crime, Law & the Scholars, 1969. Contbr. to: Challenge; Wall St. Jrnl.; & var. major legal & criminol. jrnls. Address: 40 Washington Square South, N.Y., NY 10012, USA.

MUELLER, Robert Emmett, b. 4 Apr. 1925, St. Louis, Mo., USA. Writer; Artist. Educ: B.S.E.E., M.I.T., 1948; B.A., N.Y. Univ., 1951. Publs: Inventivity, 1963; Inventor's Notebook, 1964; Eyes in Space, 1965; Science of Art, 1967. Contbr. to: Art in Am. Recip., Fellowship, Breadloaf Writers' Conf., 1968. Address: Britton House, Roosevelt, NJ 08555, USA.

MUELLER, William R(andolph), b. 10 July 1916, Balt., Md., USA. Educator; Director, Humanities Institute. Educ: A.B., Princeton Univ.; M.A., Ph.D., Harvard Univ. Publs: The Prophetic Voice in Modern Fiction, 1959, 1966; John Donne: Preacher, 1962, 1963; The Testament of Samuel Beckett (w. J. Jacobsen), 1964, 1966; Ionesco & Genet: Playwrights of Silence (w. J. Jacobsen), 1968; Celebration of Life: Studies in Modern Fiction, 1972. Contbr. to: Huntington Lib. Quarterly; Coll. English; Publications, MLA; Mod. Lang. Quarterly; Bulletin, AAUP; other profl.

jrnls. Mbr., AAUP. Recip., var. Fellowships. Address: The Humanities Inst., Box 515, Brooklandville, MD 21022, USA.

MUFTEE, Mumtaz, b. 12 Sept. 1905, Lahore, Pakistan. Retired Civil Servant. Educ: B.A., Punjab Univ. Publs: Unkehi (short stories), 1940; Gehmagehmi (short stories), 1942; Ghubare — (essays), 1943; Chup (short stories), 1947; Ismaraen (short stories), 1952; Guriya Ghar (short stories), 1956; Nizam Saqqa (plays), 1958; Alipur Ka Aeli (autobiog.), 1964; Piaz Ke Chilke (character studies, 1968; Labbaik (reportage), 1974. Contbr. to sev. jrnls. Mbr., var. orgs. Address: 514 F6/1 Islamabad, Pakistan.

MUFTI, Masud, b. 10 June 1934, Gujrat, Pakistan. Civil Servant. Educ: Dip., Pub. Admin., Cambridge Univ.; M.A., Punjab Univ.; Dips., Int. Affairs, Jrnlsm. Publs: (in Urdu) Mohaddab Shisha (short stories), 1964; Sar-i-Rahe (humour), 1964; Khilone (novella), 1969; Rag-i-Sang (short stories), 1970. Contbr. to all Urdu mags. Mbr., Pakistan Writers Guild. Hons: Nat. Prize, Pakistan Writers Guild, 1970. Address: Commissioner, Rawalpindi Div., 1 Civil Lines, Rawalpindi, Pakistan.

MUGGERIDGE, Malcolm, b. 1903, Sanderstead, UK. Journalist. Writer; Television Personality. Educ: M.A., Univ. of Cambridge. Publs: Winter in Moscow, 1933; The Thirties, 1940; Affairs of the Heart, 1949; Muggeridge Through the Microphone, 1969; Tread Softly For You Tread on My Jokes, 1968; Jesus Rediscovered, 1969; Something Beautiful for God, 1971; Paul: Envoy Extraordinary, (w. A. Vidler), 1972; Chronicles of Wasted Time: part 1, The Green Stick, 1972, part 2, The Infernal Grove, 1973. Address: Park Cottage, Robertsbridge, E. Sussex, UK.

MUGGESON, Margaret Elizabeth, pen names DICKINSON, Margaret; JACKSON, Everatt, b. 30 Apr. 1942, Gainsborough, UK. Writer. Educ: Lincoln Tech. Coll. Publs: Pride of the Courtneys, 1968; Brackenbeck, 1969; Portrait of Jonathan, 1970; (as Everatt Jackson) The Road to Hell, (forthcoming). Contbr. to: Lincolnshire Life; Parade; Art & Craft Educ. Mbr., Soc. of Authors. Address: 'The Laurels', 3 Norwood Rd., Skegness, Lincs., UK.

MÜHLETHALER, Hans, b. 9 July 1930, Zollbrück, Emmental, Switz. Writer. Educ: Primary Schl. Tchr. Publs: Zutreffendes ankreuzen, 1967; Ausser Amseln gibt es noch andere Vögel, 1969. Mbr., Gruppe Olten (Swiss Writers' Grp.). Recip., Lit. Award, Bern. Address: Siedlung Halen 43, 3037 Stuckishaus, Switz.

MUIR, Augustus, b. Carluke, Ont., Can. Author. Educ: M.A., Edinburgh Univ. Publs. incl: The Third Warning; The Blue Bonnet; The Black Pavilion; The Red Carnation; The Man who Stole the Crown Jewels; The Sands of Fear; The Bronze Door; Castles in the Air & other novels; The Vintner of Nazareth; How to Choose & Enjoy Wine; The History of the Fife Coal Company, & other indl. & mercantile hists.; Regimental History of the Royal Scots; The Intimate Thoughts of John Baxter, Bookseller; The Story of Jesus for Young People. Contbr. to: Scotsman; & var. newspapers & periodicals. Address: 48 St. John's Rd., Stansted, Essex, UK.

MUIR, Barbara Kenrick, pen name KAYE, Barbara, b. 4 Aug. 1908, Saxmundham, Suffolk, UK. Writer. Publs: No Leisure to Repent, 1947; The Gentleys, 1948; Pleasant Burden, 1949; Black Market Green, 1950; In Whose Custody, 1951; Festival at Froke, 1951; Champion's Mead, 1951; Rebellion on the Green, 1953; Neighbourly Relations, 1954; London-Lychford Return, 1955; Minus Two, 1962; Live & Learn, 1970. Contbr. to: Essex Wkly. News (Feature Writer, 1960-62); Good Housekeeping; Housewife; Guardian; Everybody's; Home & Country; etc. Mbr., Nat. Book League. Agent: John Farquharson Ltd. Address: Scriveners, Blakeney, Holt, Norfolk, UK.

MUIR, Frank, b. 5 Feb. 1920. Writer; Broadcaster. Served RAF, 1940-46. Publs: Call My Bluff (w. Patrick Campbell), 1972; You Can't Have Your Kayak & Heat It, 1973; Prods: (w. Denis Norden) Take it From Here; Bedtime With Braden; And So to Bentley; Whack-O; The Seven Faces of Jim; & num. TV revues, scripts, panel games, etc. Recip., Screenwriters' Guild Award, 1961. Address: Anners, Thorpe, Egham, Surrey, UK.

MUIR, Marie Agnes, pen names KAYE, Barbara; BLAKE, Monica, b. 25 Aug. 1904, Sheffield, UK. Author. Publs. incl: Dear Mrs. Boswell; Princess of Mexico;

Torridons' series (as Marie Muir); Footsteps in the Dark; Fire on the Mountain; The Girl in Room 750 (as Barbara Kaye); Prisoner of the Sun (as Monica Blake). Contbr. to var. mags. Mbrships: PEN (Hon. Sec., Scottish Ctr., 1959-69); Soc. Authors. Address: Gable Cottage, Aberlady, E. Lothian, UK.

MUIR, Percy, b. 1894, London, UK. Antiquarian Bookseller. Publs: Points from a Bibliographer's Notebook, 1931; Book Collecting as a Hobby, 1944; Minding My Own Business, 1956; English Children's Books, 1954; Printing & the Mind of Man, 1967; Victorian Book Illustration, 1970. Contbr. to: New Paths in Book Collecting, 1934; Talks on Book Collecting; Walter de la Mare, a Tribute; Memoirs of James II; Colophon, Book Collector. Mbrships: Life Pres. of Hon., Int. League of Antiquarian Booksellers; Past Pres. & Life Mbr. of Hon., Antiquarian Booksellers Assn., Soc. de la Librairie Ancien & Mod. Address: Scriveners, Cley Rd., Blakeney, Norfolk, UK.

MUIRDEN, Bruce Wallace, b. 31 May 1928, Melbourne, Australia. Journalist; Ministerial Press Secretary. Educ: Melbourne & Adelaide Univs. Publs: The Puzzled Patriots, 1968. Contbr. to Aust. Humanist (Ed.); Nation Review (Corres.). Mbrships: Aust. Jrnlsts.' Assn.; Fndr., Humanist Soc. of S.A. Address: 219 Kensington Rd., Kensington, S.A., Australia 5068.

MUJICA LAINEZ, Manuel, b. 11 Sept. 1910, Buenos Aires, Argentina. Writer; Journalist. Educ: Paris & Univ. of Buenos Aires. Publs: Glosas Castellanas, 1936; Miguel Cane, padre, 1942; Vida de Aniceto el Gallo, 1943; Canto a Buenos Aires, 1943; Vida de Anastasio el Pollo, 1947; Misteriosa, Buenos Aires, 1951; Los Idolos, 1953; La Casa, 1954; Bomarzo, 1962; El Unicornio, 1965; Crónicas Reales, 1967; De Milagros y de Melancolías, 1968; Cécil, 1973. Contbr. to: La Nacíon, 1932—. Mbrships: Argentine Acad. of Letters; Nat. Acad. of Fine Arts. Hons. incl: John F. Kennedy Prize; Fort Glori Prize. Address: O'Higgins 2150, Buenos Aires, Argentina.

MUKERJEE, Amiya Bhusan, b. 3 Feb. 1918, India. Professor of Medicine. Educ: M.B.B.S., 1940; M.R.C.P., London, 1944; M.D., Calcutta, 1945; F.R.C.P., London, 1970. Contbr. of num. articles to: Jrnl. of Indian Med. Assn. (sr. Assoc. Ed. 1969-72, Hon. Ed. 1972-); Calcutta Med. Jrnl.; Jrnl. of Indian Med. Assn.; Bulletin, Calcutta Schl. of Tropical Med.; Indian Heart Jrnl.; Jrnl. Indian Med Profn.; Indian Practitioner; Indian Med. Forum; Jrnl. Assn. of Physns. of India; & other med. jrnls. Recip., num. schlrships., prizes & medals. Address: 79/2 Lower Circular Rd., Calcutta 14, India.

MULHOLLAND, Brendan, b. 1933, Dublin, Repub. of Ireland. Journalist. Educ: Municipal Coll., Burnley, Lancs., UK. Publs: Almost a Holiday, 1966; The Commuter, 1967. Contbr. to: Daily Herald (staff mbr. 1957-61); Daily Mail (staff mbr. 1961-67); Sunday Express (staff mbr. 1967-). Mbr., Nat. Union Jrnlsts. Address: 36 Althorp Rd., London SW17, UK.

MULIKITA, Fwanyanga Matale, b. 1928, Mongu, Zambia. Minister of Education; Zambia's First Ambassador to UN, 1964-66; Permanent Secretary Education, 1966-68; Cabinet Minister from 1969; Minister of Power Transport & Works, 1971-73. Educ: B.A.; M.A.; Fort Hare Univ. Coll., Univs. Stanford & Columbia, USA. Publs: Batili Ki Mwanaka, 1958; Shaka Zulu, 1967; A Point of No Return, 1967; Simbilingani Wa Libongani; A Wise Fool & Other Stories. Address: P.O. Box RW 93, Lusaka, Zambia.

MULKERNE, Donald James Dennis, b. 14 Oct. 1921, New Bedford, Mass., USA. College Professor. Educ: B.S. & Ed.M., Boston Univ.; Ed.D., Columbia Univ., N.Y. Publs: Economic & Social Geography, 1958; The Term Paper: Step by Step, 1965; How Do You Spell It? , 1965; Office Administration & Procedures, 1965; Civil Tests for Typists, 1970. Contbr. to: Jrnl. of Bus. Educ.; The Secretary; Bus. Educ. World; Bus. Educ. Forum. Mbrships: Albany Chapt. Pres., Admnstv. Mgmt. Soc., 1966; Assn. for Systems Mgmt.; Nat. Secs. Assn. Int. Address: SUNY at Albany, 1400 Wash. Ave., Albany, NY 12222, USA.

MULLETT, (The Rev.) John St. Hilary, b. 1925, Sheffield, UK. Church of England Clergyman; Rector, Que Que, Rhodesia, 1952-60; Vicar, Bollington, Cheshire, 1961-69; Proctor, Convocation of York. Educ: M.A., St. Catharine's Coll., Cambridge Univ.; Lincoln Theol. Coll. Publs: One People One Church One Song, 1969. Contbr. to: Prism; Parish & People. Mbrships: Nat. Church Assembly, 1966-70; C. of E. Synod, since 1971; Wirral Dist. Educ. Comm., since 1973; Royal Coll. Organists; Soc. St. Albans & St. Sergius; Int. Fellowship for Rsch. Hymnol. Address: St. Saviour's Vicarage, 16 Bidston Rd., Oxton, Birkenhead, Cheshire, UK.

MULLIGAN, Hugh A., pen name HAM, b. 23 Mar. 1925, NYC, USA. Senior Correspondent, The Associated Press. Educ: B.A., Marlboro Coll., Vt., 1948; M.S., Boston Univ., 1951; M.A., Harvard Univ., 1951. Publs: The Torch is Passed, 1963; Kelso, a Horse (co-author); Lightning Out of Israel, 1967; No Place to Die, 1967. Contbr. to: Readers' Digest; Time Mag.; Life Mag.; Cath. Digest; Life Mag., Ed. & Publr.; Quill; Wash. Post Mag.; etc. Mbrships: Overseas Press Club Am. (Mbr. Bd. Govs.); Authors' League Am.; London Lib. Hons. incl: D.H.L. Marlboro Coll., 1973; Overseas Press Club Annual Award for Reporting, 1968. Address: 19 Campbell Ct., Queens Gate Gdns., London SW7, UK.

MULLINGS, Peter Coningsby, b. 17 Dec. 1928, Ashton-upon-Mersey, UK. TV Producer & Director. Educ: St. Bede's Coll., Manchester; Pa. State Univ., USA. Publs: Chapt., Lighting the Stage in Handbook for the Amateur Theatre, 1957. Contbr. to: Soc. of Film & TV Arts Jrnl.; Amateur Photographer; Coins; TV in the Univ. Mbrships: Assn. of Brit. Sci. Writers; Royal Instn. of GB; Royal Photographic Soc.; Soc. of Film & TV Arts; Savage Club; Chelsea Arts Club. Address: 2 Penrith Ave., Sale, Cheshire, UK.

MULLINS, Edwin, b. 14 Sept. 1933, London, UK. Author; Journalist; Film-maker. Educ: M.A., Merton Coll., Oxford Univ. Publs: Alfred Wallis, 1967; Braque, 1969; The Pilgrimage to Santiago, 1974. Contbr. to: Sunday Telegraph; Guardian; Daily Telegraph Mag.; Fin. Times; BBC Radio & TV. Mbrships: Int. Assn. Art Critics (former Treas., Brit. Sect); Soc. Authors; Writers' Action Grp. Address: 7 Lower Common St., London SW15 1BP, UK.

MUMFORD, Lewis, b. 19 Oct. 1895, Flushing, N.Y., USA. University Professor. Educ: Univs. of N.Y. & Columbia. Publs. incl: Story of Utopias, 1922; The Golden Bay, 1926; Faith for Living, 1940; The Condition of Man, 1944; Values for Survival, 1946; Art & Technics, 1952; The Highway & the City, 1963; The Urban Prospect, 1968; The Pentagon of Power, 1970; Interpolations & Forecasts 1922-72, 1972. Contbr. to: Dial; Sociolog. Review; Am. Caravan. Mbrships. incl: Am. Acad. of Arts & Letters (Pres., 1963-65); Am. Philosoph. Soc.; Nat. Inst. of Arts & Letters. Hons. incl: Nat. Medal for Lit., 1972; LL.D. Jefferson Mem. Medal, 1972; & num. other awards. Address: Amenia, N.Y., NY 12501, USA.

MUNAWWAR, Muhammad, b. 27 Mar. 1923, Bhera, Pakistan. Teacher; Writer; Translator. Educ: M.A. Publs: Meezan-i-Iqbal, 1972; Ghubar-i-Tamanna, 1974; Aulad-i-Adam, 1974; (transls.) Alfitnatul Kubra, 1959; Adeeb, 1960; Al-Akhbar-ut-Tiwal, 1964; Siasatnamah, 1961; Teen Musalman Phalsoof 1972. Contbr. to num. newspapers & mags. Mbrships. incl: Ctrl. Iqbal Comm., Lahore; Muslim Educl. Congress, ibid; Mng. Comm., Dyalsingh Trust Lib., ibid.; Comm. Of Courses, Bd. of Inter & Second. Educ., ibid. Address: Dept. of Urdu, Govt. College, Lahore, Pakistan.

MUNBY, Alan Noel Latimer, b. 25 Dec. 1913, London, UK, d. 26 Dec. 1974. Librarian; Author. Educ: M.A., Litt.D., Cambridge Univ. Publs: The Alabaster Hand & other Ghost Stories, 1949; Phillipps Studies, 5 vols., 1951-60; The Cult of the Autograph Letter, 1962; Connoisseurs & Mediaeval Miniatures, 1972. Contbr. to: Times Lit. Supplement; The Library; Book Collector. Mbrships: Bibliog. Soc. (Pres., 1974-75); Cambridge Bibliog. Soc. (Pres.).

MUNBY, Lionel Maxwell, b. 7 May 1918, Leeds, UK. Extra Mural University Tutor; Author; Editor. Educ: M.A., Hertford Coll., Oxford. Publs. incl: Pictorial History Book; Herts. Population Statistics 1563-1801, 1964; Marxism & History, a Bibliography, 1967; East Anglian Studies, 1968; Madingley Hall, 1970; Ed., The Luddites & Other Essays, 1971; Ed., City & County History Series, 1973—. Contbr. to: Amateur Histn. (Ed., 1955-67); Local Histn. (Ed., 1968—); Short Guides to Records in Hist. (Ed., 1962-70); Our Hist. (Ed., 1963-70); also sev. for. histl. jrnls. Mbrships: Histl. Assn.; Standing Conf. for Local Hist.; Workers' Educ. Assn. Address: 16 Carisbrooke Rd., Cambridge CB4 3LR, UK.

MUNFORD, William Arthur, b. 27 Apr. 1911, London, UK. Librarian. Educ: B.Sc. Econ., Ph.D., London Schl.

Econs. Publs: Penny Rate, 1951; William Ewart, M.P., 1960; Edward Edwards, 1963; L. S. Jast, 1966; J. D. Brown, 1968. Contbr. to var. libnship. jrnls. Mbrships incl: Lib. Assn. (Hon. Sec., 1951-55). Address: 11 Manor Ct., Pinehurst, Grange Rd., Cambridge CB3 9BE, UK.

MUNIZ-ROMERO, Carlos, b. 17 Aug. 1930, Rosal de la Frontera, Huelva, Spain. Jesuit Priest; University College Director. Educ: Lic., Philos.; theol. studies. Publs: Los caballeros del hacha, 1971; El llanto de los buitres, 1971; Seis poetas granadinos posteriores a García Lorca (contbng. author), 1973; Ed., Relatos Vandaluces, 1973. Contbr. to: Reseña; Proyeccion; Razon y Fe. Mbrships: Soc. of Jesus; Ateneo de Málaga. Recip., Premio Angel Ganivet, 1970. Address: Plaza de San Ignacio 4, Malaga, Spain.

MUNJANJA, Amos Munemo, b. 12 Feb. 1932, Mondoro-Hartley, Rhodesia. Writer; Editor, African Farmers' Journal. Educ: B.A. Cand., Univ. of S. Africa, Pretoria. Publs: Tsumo neMadimikira (Shona proverbs & idioms), 2 vols., 1965-69; (novel) Rinamanyanga Hariputirwi (Evil Will Out), 1971; Zvirahwe (Shona riddles), 1972; Num. gospel tracts. Contbr. to: Advance; Champ Review; Outpost; Rhodesia Herald; Moto. Mbrships: Fndr., Salisbury African Drama Assn.; Provisional Coun., Christian Coll. of Southern Africa; Exec. Mbr., Evang. Fellowship of Rhodesia; TV Workshop. Recip., 2 prizes, Rhodesia Lit. Bur., for book on Shona proverbs, 1965, & for novel, 1971. Address: 83 Mutamba Dr., P.O. Mufakose, Salisbury, Rhodesia.

MUÑOZ-HILDALGO, Alfredo (Florencio), b. 3 Nov. 1918, Madrid, Spain. Professor of Psychology; Theologian. Educ: Ph.D.; Th.D.; studies at Univs. of Madrid, St. Thomas, Philippines, Hong Kong, Rome, Amsterdam & in USA. Publs. incl: La Espada & la Rosa, 1949, 1956; Hombre, Mujer, Amer, 1953; Varones; Divorcio Espiritual; Matrimonio, Dicha o Angustia, 1962. Contbr. to: Unitas, Manila; Ecclesia; Mundo Cristiano; Tercer Programa; etc.; var. newspapers. Mbrships incl: Inst. de Ciencias de la Familia (Dir.); Ctr. de Orientacion Familiar (Pres.). Hons. incl: Awards from Spanish Radio, 1953, & TV, 1963. Address: Avenida Generalisimo 74.12.E., Madrid 16, Spain.

MUNRO, Alice, b. 10 July 1931, Wingham, Ont., Can. Writer. Educ: Univ. of Western Ont., 1949-51. Publs: Dance of the Happy Shades (short stories), 1968; Lives of Girls & Women (novel), 1971. Contbr. to: Can. Forum; Tamarack Review; Queen's Quarterly; Montrealer. Recip., Gov.-Gen.'s Award for Lit., 1969. Address: 1648 Rockland, Victoria, B.C., Can.

MUNRO, Hugh Macfarlane, pen names WYVIS, Ben; JASON; FARLANE, Jason, b. Govan, Glasgow, UK. Writer. Publs: Who Told Clutha, 1958; Clutha Plays a Hunch, 1959; A Clue for Clutha, 1960; The Clydesiders, 1961; Tribal Town, 1964; Clutha & the Lady, 1973; Get Clutha, 1974. Contbr. to: Brit., Can., Australasian, etc. radio & TV. Mbrships: PEN; Soc. of Authors; Nat. Union Jrnlsts.; Crime Writers' Assn. Agents: Curtis Brown Ltd.; John F. Gibson, UK; Daniel P. King, USA; Gertrud Schaefer, W. Germany. Address: Ealasaid, 21 Eglinton St., Saltcoats, Ayrshire, UK.

MUNRO, Ian S., b. 1914, Glasgow, UK. Senior Lecturer, Aberdeen College of Education. Educ: M.A., Univ. of Glasgow. Publs: Leslie Mitchell: Lewis Grassic Gibbon, 1966; Ed., A Scots Hairst, 1967; The Island of Bute, 1973; (stage adaptation) Sunset Song, 1964; About 25 radio plays broadcast by BBC. Contbr. to: Scotsman; Radio Times; Aberdeen Press & Jrnl.; Scottish Educl. Jrnl. Agent: S.C.O.T.T.S. Address: Braeside, Catterline, Stonehaven, Kincardineshire, UK.

MUNROE, Elizabeth Lee, pen name GRENELLE, Lisa, b. 22 Jan. 1910, NYC, USA. Teacher; Writer; Poet. Educ: Columbia Univ. Publs: This Day is Ours, 1946; No Light Evaded, 1957; Self is the Stranger, 1963; No Scheduled Flight, 1973. Contbr. to: Educl. Forum; Saturday Evening Post; N.Y. Times; N.Y. Herald Tribune; Chgo. Herald Tribune; Lyric; Yankee; Spirit; etc. Mbrships. incl: Mbr., 1964—, Exec. Bd., 1962-64, 1972—, Poetry Soc. of Am.; Pres., Manhattan Br., Am. Pen Women, 1953-59. Hons. incl: Gustav Mem. Sonnet Prize, Poetry Soc. of Am., 1972. Address: 140 E. 92nd St., N.Y., NY 10028, USA.

MUNSEY, Cecil Richard Jr., pen name RICHARDSON, C., b. 21 May 1935, Portsmouth, N.H., USA. Educational Administrator. Educ: B.A., M.A., San Diego State Univ.; Ph.D., US Int. Univ., San Diego. Publs. incl: The Illustrated Guide to Collecting Bottles, 1970; The Illustrated Guide to

the Collectibles of Coca-Cola, 1972; Disneyana: Walt Disney Collectibles, 1974. Contbr. to num. mags. 7 jrnls. (ed.) Calif. Assn. for the Gifted Communicator; Jrnl. of the Fedn. of Histl. Bottle Clubs, (ed.); Nat. Bottle Gazette, (ed. 1968-9); etc. Mbrships. incl: Authors' Guild; Nat. Assn. for Gifted Children. Recip: Valley Forge Teachers' Medal, 1965. Address: 13541 Willow Run Rd., Poway, CA 92064, USA.

MUNTEANU, Romul, b. 18 Mar. 1926, Calanul Mic, Romania. Professor of Comparative Literature. Educ: B.A., Cluj Univ.; M.A., Karl Marx Univ., Leipzig. Publs: Bertolt Brecht, 1966; The Tragic Farce, 1970; Literary Portraits, 1972; Diary of Readings, 1973; The Modern French Novel, 1973; The European Culture of the Enlightenment, 1974. Contbr. to: Steaua; Romania Literara; Transilvania; Saptamina; Cahiers roumains d'études littéraires. Mbrships: Bur., Writers' Union of Romania. Hons: Criticism Prizes, Writers' Union (1971) & Saptamina. Address: Str. Gramont 12, Bucharest V, Romania.

MUNTZ, (Isabelle) Hope, pen name LANGLAND, William, b. 8 July 1907, Toronto, Can. Medievalist; Historical Novelist. Educ: Ctrl. Schl. Arts & Crafts, London; Westminster & Chelsea Polytechnics; Toronto Schl. Art. Publs: The Golden Warrior, 1948, 4th ed., 1974; The Carmen de Hastingae Proelio, 1972. Contbr. to: Graya; etc. Mbrships: F.S.A.; Fellow Royal Histl. Soc.; Fellow Ancient Monuments Soc.; Battle & Dist. Histl. Soc. (Pres.); Kent Archaeol. Soc.; Sussex Archaeol. Soc.; E. Yorks. Archaeol. Soc.; E. Yorks. Histl. Soc. Address: c/o Messrs. Chatto & Windus Ltd., 40-42 William IV St., London WC2, UK.

MUNTZING, Arne, b. 2 Mar. 1903, Gothenburg, Sweden. Professor of Genetics. Educ: Ph.D., Univ. of Lund, 1930; Rsch. Assoc., Univ. of Calif., USA, 1933-34. Publs: Genetics: Basic & Applied, 4 eds., (transl'd. into English, Russian & German), 1953-71. Contbr. of num. papers to Hereditas & many for. jrnls. Mbrships: Acads. of Sci., Sweden, Finland, Denmark & Germany; Socs. of Genetics & Botany, USA, Scotland, Japan, India, Egypt & Sweden. Hons: Gen. Prize, Univ. of Engrng., Stockholm. 1973; Lit. Prize, Minerva, 1970; Darwin Medal, Acad. of Sci., Germany, 1959. Address: Inst. of Genetics, Univ. of Lund, Sweden.

MURAJI UCHIKI, Tamotsu Uchiki, pen name MURAJI UCHIKI, b. 21 Apr. 1904, Aza, Shimokarako, Higashimatsuyamashi, Saitama Prefecture, Japan. Writer. Educ: Waseda Univ. Publs. incl: History of the Tribe, 1938; Gate of Spring, 1942; The Spirited Mountain Range, 1953; Sixteen Years of Age, 1959; The Garden of the Heavens (6 vols.), 1972. Contbr. to var. lit. jrnls. Mbrships: Japan Authors' & Writers' Assn.; PEN; Dir., Japan Juvenile Lit. Authors' & Writers' Assn. Hons: Shōgakukan Lit. Prize, 1957; Saitama Prefectural Cultural Prize, 1972; Zensen Lit. Merit Prize, 1973; Min. of State for Educ. Lit. Prize, 1973. Address: 13-3 Aza, Nakai, Hannoshi, Saitama Prefecture, Japan.

MURAKAMI, Yoshio, b. 12 Dec. 1937, Tokyo, Japan. Journalist. Educ: B.A., Keio Univ., Tokyo, 1960; M.A. (Int. Rels.), 1961, M.A. (Law & Diplomacy), 1962, Ph.D., 1964, Fletcher Schl. of Law & Diplomacy. Publs: Japan & America (co-author w. staff of Asahi Shimbun), 1971, Engl. transl., 1972; num. transls. Contbr. to: Asahi Jrnl; Weekly Asahi (both in Japanese). Mbr., For. Corres. Club. of Thailand. Recip., Joseph C. Grew Schlrship., Fletcher Schl. of Law & Diplomacy, 1962-64. Address: 2-4 Yumino-cho, Okayama City, Japan 700.

MURARI, Timeri N., b. 29 July 1941, Madras, India. Journalist. Educ: Loyola Coll., Madras Univ.; B.A., McGill Univ., Montreal, Can. Publs: The Marriage, 1973; The New Savages, 1975. Contbr. to: The Guardian; Sunday Times; Observer Mag.; Penthouse Mag.; Nova; Washington Post. Mbr., Nat. Union Jrnlsts. Agent: A.M. Heath. Address: 195 Chatsworth Ct., Pembroke Rd., London W8, UK.

MURAWSKI, Benjamin J., b. 20 Jan 1926, Pittsfield, Mass., USA. Psychologist; Director, Psychological Testing Laboratory; Associate Professor of Psychology. Educ.: A.B., Clark Univ., Worcester, Mass., 1949; Ph.D., Harvard Univ., 1954. Publs: The Gynecologic Patient: A Psycho-Endocrine Study, 1962; Psychosomatic Aspects of Gynecologic Disorders: Seven Psychoanalytic Case Studies, 1969. Contbr. to: Jrnl. Applied Physiol.; Archives Int. Med.; Jrnl. Fertility & Sterility; Psychophysiol.; etc. Mbrships. incl: Fellow, Mass. Psychol. Assn.; Mass. Bd.

Certification in Psychol. Recip., Trng. & Dev. grant, Fndn.'s Fund for Rsch. in Psych., 1955-58. Address: Peter Bent Brigham Hosp., 721 Huntington Ave., Boston, MA 02115, USA.

MURCH, Edward William Lionel, b. 1920, Plymouth, UK. Writer. Publs.: The Poet of Goosey Fair; Things That Go Bump; The Thin Red Line; The Parting Shot; Morning, Noon & Night; Spring Flowers for Marguerite; The Trials of Captain Savage; On the Hill; The Journey of the Star; Caroline, Five Minutes from the Sea; Tell it to the Wind; The Dipper; The Beggars of Bordeaux; No Name in the Street; Saint Germaine; Wits' End; The Last Blue Mountain; Beyond the Stars. Fellowships: F.R.S.A.; F.I.A.L. Address: Heatherdene, Dousland, Yelverton, Devon, UK.

MURDOCH, Jean Iris, b. 15 July 1919, Dublin, Repub. of Ireland. Novelist; Philosopher; University Lecturer. Educ: Somerville Coll., Oxford. Publs. incl: Sartre, Romantic Rationalist, 1953; Under the Net, 1954; The Sandcastle, 1957; The Bell, 1958; A Severed Head, 1961, (play, 1963); The Time of the Angels, 1966; The Nice & the Good, 1968; Bruno's Dream, 1969; A Fairly Honourable Defeat, 1970; The Sovereignty of Good, 1970; An Accidental Man, 1971; The Black Prince, 1973; (plays) The Servants & the Snow, 1970; The Three Arrows, 1972. Contbr. to: Aristotelian Soc. Papers. Address: Cedar Lodge, Steeple Aston, Oxon., UK.

MURENA, H. A., b. 14 Feb. 1923, Buenos Aires, Argentina. University Lecturer in Philosophy. Publs. incl: (poetry) La vida nueva, 1951; El Círculo de los paraísos, 1958; F.G. un bárbaro entre la belleza, 1972; (novels) La fatalidad de los cuerpos, 1955; Nimas Nimenos, 1969; Caina Muerte, 1971; (play) el juez, 1953; (essays) El pecado original de América, 1954; El nombre secret, 1969; La cárcel de la mente, 1970; (short stories) El centro del infierno, 1956; El coronel de caballeria, 1970. Address: San José 910, Buenos Aires, Argentina.

MURI, Sigurd, b. 17 July 1927, Sjøholt, Norway. Architect; Author. Educ: Norwegian Tech. Univ., Trondheim. Publs: Kom Til Granada, 1962; Kvile På Steinar, 1970; Norske Kyrkjer, 1971; Sett Gjennom Gitter, 1974. Contbr. to var. jrnls. Mbr., Norwegian Authors' Assn. Recip., Gift of Hon., Gjelsvik Fund, 1970. Address: Brusetvegen 51, 1364 Hvalstad, Norway.

MURPHY, Dervla, b. 1931, Cappoquin, Co. Waterford, Repub. of Ireland. Writer. Publs: Full Tilt, 1965; Tibetan Foothold, 1966; The Waiting Land, 1967; In Ethiopia with a Mule, 1968. Contbr. to: Irish Times; Cornhill Mag.; Daily Telegraph; Blackwoods Mag. Address: Clairvaux, Lismore, Co. Waterford, Repub. of Ireland.

MURPHY, Michael Joseph, b. 2 July 1913, Liverpool, UK. Folklorist. Publs: At Slieve Gullion's Foot, 1942; Mountain Year, 1964; Slieve Gullioners; Folktales from Ulster, 2 vols.; The Green Book; Tyrone Folk Quest, 1973; Folktales of the North of Ireland, 1975; plays produced in Belfast, London, & Dublin. Contbr. to: Dublin Mag.; The Bell; Irish Writing; Threshold; BBC; Ulster TV; R.T.E. Address: 7 St. Patrick's Pk., Dromintree, S. Armagh, N. Ireland, UK.

MURPHY, Peter Anthony, b. 5 Aug. 1945, Melbourne, Australia. Teacher. Educ: B.A., Dip. in Educ., Monash Univ., Vic.; Assoc. Dip. in Librarianship, Royal Melbourne Inst. of Technol., Vic. Publs: Escape Victim & Other Poems, 1974; Moon Landscape & Other Stories, 1975; Jo Being (opera libretto), 1975. Contbr. to: Westerly; Nation Review; Aust.; Makar; Hemisphere; Fields; Saturday Club Book of Poetry; Ploughman; Aust. Jrnl. of Adv. Educ.; Dhara, India; Gargantua, UK; Cave, NZ; Mate, ibid. Mbr., Fellowship of Aust. Writers. Recip., Commendation, State of Vic. Short Story Award, 1974. Address: 3 The Panorama, Eaglemont, Vic., Australia 3084.

MURPHY, Thomas Bernard, b. 23 Feb. 1935, Tuam, Co. Galway, Repub. of Ireland. Playwright. Educ: Tchrs. Dip. Publs: (plays) The Fooleen (A Crucial Week In The Life of A Grocer's Assistant), 1968; A Whistle In The Dark, 1970; The Morning After Optimism, 1973; The Orphans, 1974; Famine; The White House; On The Outside (w. Noel O'Donoghue); On the Inside; The Vicar of Wakefield (adaptation); The Sanctuary Lamp; TV plays & screenplays. Mbrships: Bd. of Dirs., Irish Nat. Theatre (The Abbey Theatre); Fndr. mbr., Moli Prod. Co.; Writers' Guild of GB. Recip., Irish Acad. of Letters Award, for Distinction

in Lit., 1972. Address: 32 Highfield Rd., Dublin 6, Repub. of Ireland.

MURRAY, Blanche Geraldine, pen name, WARRINER, Geraldine, b. 15 Aug. 1923, Romford, Essex, UK. Freelance Writer. Contbr. to: Parents; Western Mail; Manchester Evening Chronicle; Birmingham Post & Mail. Publs: Annabel. Mbrships: Soc. of Authors; Royal Horticultural Soc. Address: La Meule, 17 Hardwick Rd., Sutton Coldfield, W. Midlands B74 3BY, UK.

MURRAY, David Stark, pen name BROWN, Irwin, b. 1900, Barrhead, UK. Consultant Pathologist; Author. Educ: B.Sc.(Hons.), M.B., Ch.B., Glasgow Univ. Publs. incl: Man's Microbic Enemies, 1934; Science Fights Death, 1936; Health for All, 1942; The Anatomy of Man & Other Animals, 1954; Medical Care & Family Security (w. E. D. Lear), 1962; India — Which Century, 1967; Why a National Health Service, 1971; International Medical Care (co-author), 1972; Blueprint for Health, 1973. Contbr. to: Med. Today & Tomorrow (Ed., 1937-69); other profl. jrnls. Mbrships: Fellow, Royal Soc. Med.; Fellow, N.Y. Acad. of Scis. Recip., acad. hons. Agent: A.M. Heath & Co. Address: 34 Denmark Ave., London SW19 4HQ, UK.

MURRAY (Rev) Edmund Joseph, C.S.C., b. 14 Apr. 1907, Bridgeport, Conn., USA. Priest; Educator; Historian. Educ: A.B., Notre Dame Univ., 1934; B.Th., Holy Cross Coll.; Ph.D., Univ. Coll., Cork, Nat. Univ. of Ireland, 1953. Publs: Basic Irish History to Poynings Law, 1965; Fundamental Irish History from Earliest Days, 1974. Contbr. to var. reviews & newspapers. Address: P.O. Box 511, Notre Dame Univ., Notre Dame, IN 46556, USA.

MURRAY, Jesse George, b. 28 Dec. 1909, St. Louis, Mo., USA. Journalist; Author. Educ: Chaminade Coll., St. Louis, Mo.; Northwestern Univ., Chgo., Ill. Publs: New Horizons, 1943; History of Rehabilitation of Austria, 5 vols., 1951; The Madhouse on Madison Street, 1965; The Legacy of Al Capone, 1964; (plays) Townsend Goes to Town, 1939; Off the Record, 1941. Contbr. to: Chgo. Herald & Examiner; Rocky Mtn. News; Toronto Star; Evanston Daily News—Index; Chgo. Am.; Chgo. Today. Mbrships: Authors' League of Am.; Am. Newspaper Guild; Chgo. Newspaper Reporters Assn. Address: Elk Ranch, Eureka Springs, AR, USA.

MURRAY, Jim (James Patrick), b. 29 Dec. 1919, Hartford, Conn., USA. Journalist. Educ: B.A., Trinity Coll., Hartford, Conn., 1943. Publs: The Best of Jim Murray, 1965; The Sporting World of Jim Murray, 1968. Contbr. to: Sports Illustrated (Fndr. & Ed., 1953-61; Sat. Evening Post; Golf Digest; Golf Mag.; Life; Playboy. Mbrships: VP, L.A. Press Club; Nat. Assn. of Sportscasters & Sportswriters. Hons. incl: Sportswriter of Yr., 1964, 1966, 1967, 1968, 1969, 1970, 1971, 1972, 1973, 1974; Nat. Headliners' Award, 1965. Address: 430 Bellagio Terr., L.A., CA 90049, USA.

MURRAY, John Joseph, b. 1915, Bath, Me., USA. Professor of History. Educ: Univ. of Me.; Ind. Univ.; U.C.L.A.; A.B.; M.A., Ph.D. Publs: A Student Guidebook to English History; An Honest Diplomat at the Hague; Sjumakternas Expedetion Till Ostersjon, 1953; The Heritage of the Middle West; Amsterdam in the Age of Rembrandt, 1967; George I, the Baltic & the Whig Split of 1717, 1969; Antwerp in the Age of Plantin & Breughel, 1970. Contbr. to: Huntington Lib. Quarterly; Jrnl. of Mod. Hist.; Am. Hist. Review; Jrnl. of Ctrl. European Affairs; Bijdragen Voor Geschiedenis der Nederlanden; Histn.; Annals of the Am. Acad. of Pol. & Soc. Sci. Mbrships. incl: Fellow, Royal Histl. Soc. Address: 2318 26th St. S.E., Cedar Rapids, IA, USA.

MURRAY, Katherine Maud Elisabeth, b. 3 Dec. 1909, Cambridge, UK. Retired College Principal. Educ: B.A., B.Litt., Somerville Coll., Oxford; M.A., Cambridge by incorporation. Publs: Constitutional History of the Cinque Ports, 1935; Register Daniel Rough, 1945. Mbrships: Fellow, Royal Histl. Soc., until 1974; F.S.A.; Chmn., Coun., Sussex Archaeol. Soc.; Pres., Sussex Record Soc. Address: Upper Cranmore, Heyshott, Midhurst, Sussex, UK.

MURRAY, William Hutchinson, b. 18 Mar. 1913, Liverpool, UK. Author. Publs: Mountaineering in Scotland, 1947; The Story of Everest, 1953; Highland Landscape, 1962; The Hebrides, 1966; The West Highlands of Scotland, 1968; The Islands of Western Scotland, 1973. Mbrships: Countryside Commn. for Scotland; Chmn., Scottish

Countryside Activities Coun.; V.P., Alpine Club; PEN. Hons: Mungo Park Medal, Royal Scottish Geog. Soc., 1950; Lit. Award, USA. Educl. Bd., 1954; O.B.E., 1966. Address: Lochwood, Loch Goil, Argyll, UK.

MURRAY-BROWN, Jeremy, b. 1932, Nathiagali, India. Freelance Writer & Director. Educ: M.A., New Coll., Oxford, UK. Publs: Ed., The Monarchy & its Future, 1969; Kenyatta, 1972. Contbr. to: New Soc.; Listener; Daily Telegraph; Life & Work. Agent: A. D. Peters & Co. Address: 35 Brook Green, London W6, UK.

MURRAY-SMITH, Barbara, b. 21 Apr. 1924, Melbourne, Vic., Australia. Author; Journalist. Educ: Toorak Coll., Mt. Eliza, Vic.; studied at Melbourne Conservatorium (Speech & Drama). Publs: Australian Guide to Etiquette, 1971. Contbr. as social columnist to: Melbourne Truth; Southern Cross; Toorak Times; The Green Place mag. Address: 4 Canberra Rd., Toorak, Melbourne, Vic., Australia 3142.

MURRELLS, Joseph, pen name TEMPLE, Edith, b. 1904, London, UK. Professional Manager; Songwriter; Author. Publs: (songs) Count Your Blessings, 1946; Those Were the Days, 1946; Mia Mantilla, 1948; Panis Angelicus (Heavenly Bread), 1949; I Know You're Mine, 1953; Engagement Waltz, 1955; (biogs.) Daily Mail Book of Golden Discs, 1966; Book of Golden Disc, 1975. Contbr. to: Sunday Telegraph; Daily Mail; New Musical Express; Melody Maker; Daily Mirror; Daily Express; Rolling Stone. Mbrships: Songwriters' Guild of GB; Performing Rights Soc. Ltd. Agent: Barrie & Jenkins. Address: 35 Beechfield Rd., Harringey, London N4 1PD, UK.

MURROS, (Irja) Helena, b. 27 May 1914, Pukkila, Finland. Translator of novels; Poet. Publs: (poetry) Lapsi ja kankaankutoja, 1938; Kuparimalja, 1941; Viikatteen kuu, 1943; Tyttö ja tähdet, 1948; Ruoho kukkii, 1953. Mbr., Finnish Authors' Soc. Recip., Mikael Agricola Medal, 1965. Address: Töölöntorinkatu 3 B 37, 00260 Helsinki 26, Finland.

MURRY, Colin, pen name COWPER, Richard, b. 1926, Dorset, UK. Writer. Educ: Rendcomb Coll.; Brasenose Coll., Oxon. Publs: The Golden Valley, 1958; Recollections of a Ghost, 1960; A Path to the Sea, 1961; Private View, 1971; One Hand Clapping, 1974. Contbr. to: Arts Review; Anglo-Welsh Review. Mbrships: Authors' Soc.; Brit. Sci. Fiction Assn.; Sci. Fiction Writers of Am. Agent: A. D. Peters & Co. Address: Elm Cottage, Talygarn, Pontyclun, Glam., UK.

MUSGRAVE, Clifford Walter, b. 26 July 1904, London, UK. Librarian; Museums Director; Author. Publs: Royal Pavilion, 1959; Regency Furniture, 1961; Adam & Hepplewhite Furniture, 1966; Life in Brighton, 1970. Contbr. to: Connoisseur; Burlington Mag.; Country Life; Antiques (USA); Antique Collector. Mbrships: Regency Soc. (VP); Hon. mbr., Georgian Grp. Recip., Hon. D.Litt., Sussex Univ. Address: 25a St. Peter's Rd., E. Blatchington, Seaford, Sussex, UK.

MUSGROVE, Frank, b. 16 Dec. 1922, Nottingham, UK. University Professor. Educ: B.A., Magdalen Coll., Oxford; Ph.D., Univ. of Nottingham. Publs: The Migratory Elite, 1963; Youth & the Social Order, 1964; The Family, Education & Society, 1966; Society & the Teacher's Role, 1969; Patterns of Power & Authority in English Education, 1971; Ecstasy & Holiness, 1974. Contbr. to: Econ. Hist. Review; Africa; Sociol. Review; Brit. Jrnl., Educl. Psychol.; Brit. Jrnl., Sociol.; Brit. Jrnl., Social & Clin. Psychol.; etc. F.R.S.A. Address: 11 Oakwood Dr., Prestbury, Cheshire, UK.

MUSHIN, William Woolf, b. 1910, London, UK. University Professor of Anaesthetics; Writer. Educ: London Hosp. Med. Coll. Publs: Brachial Plexus Block; Anaesthesia for the Poor Risk; Physics for the Anaesthetist, 3rd ed.; Thoracic Anaesthesia, 2nd ed.; Automatic Ventilation of the Lungs, 3rd ed. Contbr. to: Brit. Med. Jrnl.; Lancet; Anaesthesia; Brit. Jrnl. Anaesthesia. Hons: C.B.E.; M.A.; F.R.C.S.; F.F.A.R.C.S.; M.B.B.S. Address: Dept. of Anaesthetics, Welsh National Schl. of Medicine, Heath Park, Cardiff CF4 4XN, UK.

MUSTILA, Jouko Eemeli, b. 14 Feb. 1931, Messukyla, Finland. Author. Educ: Inst. of Soc. Scis. Publs: (in Finnish) Slow Polka; Stranger in the Attic; Gay October (novels); Boys & the Emperor's League (juvenile). Contbr. to Koti-Posti mag. Mbr., Assn. of Writers in Finland. Hons:

1st Prize, Short Story Contest, Karjalan Aamu mag. Address: Pikkukyla, 05400 Jokela, Finland.

MUSTO, Barry, pen name SIMON, Robert, b. 1930, Birmingham, UK. Sales Promotion Manager; Author. Publs: The Lawrence Barclay File, 1969; Storm Centre, 1970; The Fatal Flaw, 1970; (as R. Simon) The Sunless Land, 1972; Codename Bastille, 1972; No Way Out, 1973; The Weighted Scales, 1973. Mbrships: PEN; Crime Writers' Assn. Agent: John F. Gibson. Address: 'Thistles', Back Lane, Little Addington, Northants., UK.

MUTHARIKA, Bingu Wa, b. 24 Feb. 1934, Chisoka, Thyolo, Malawi. Economist. Educ: B.Com.; M.A., Econs. Publs: Toward Multinational Economic Co-operation in Africa, 1972; Time to Say Goodbye; From Dependency to Self-Reliance. Contbr. to: African Dev.; Afrika Spectrum; Interecons. Mbrships: Sec./Treas., Addis Ababa Chapt., Soc. for Int. Dev.; Fellow, Royal Econ. Soc., London; Royal African Soc., ibid; Sec., Addis Ababa Club, Lions Int. Address: United Nations, Economic Commn. for Africa, P.O. Box 60008, Addis Ababa, Ethiopia.

MUUSS, Rolf Eduard, b. 26 Sept. 1924, Tating/Eiderstedt, Germany. College Professor & Administrator. Educ: Tchng. Dip., Pädagogische Hochschule, Flensburg-Mürwik, 1951; M.Ed., Western Md. Coll., 1954; Ph.D., Univ. of Ill., 1957. Publs: First Aid for Classroom Discipline Problems, 1962; Theories of Adolescence, 1962, enlarged 2nd ed., 1968, enlarged 3rd ed., 1975; Adolescent Behavior & Society: A Book of Readings, 1971, revised ed. forthcoming. Contbr. to: Jrnl. of Educl. Psychol.; Child Dev.; Jrnl. of Personality; Jrnl. of Expmtl. Educ.; Jrnl. of Educl. Rsch.; Educl. Forum; etc. Mbrships. incl: Fellow, Am. Psychol. Assn.; Treas., Md. Psychol. Assn., 1971-73; Eastern Psychol. Assn. Address: Goucher Coll., Towson, MD 21204, USA.

MYCIELSKA, (Countess) Gabriela, (wife of Stanislas, Knight of Malta), b. 29 Sept. 1907, Kraków, Poland. Translator; Advocate. Educ: mag. jur. Publs: num. transls. from French & German into Polish, inclng. de Beauvoir's Le Deuxième sexe, Mauriac's Genitrix, Alfred Döblin's Der blaue Tiger, Hermann Kestea's Casanova; Ernst Schnabel's Der sechste Gesang, & num. other stories from Thomas Mann, Anna Seghers, Heinrich Böll, Louis Aragon, Heinrich Heine, Albrecht Goes, Tadeusz Zielinski, etc. Contbr. to Polish lit. jrnls. Mbrships: Assn. of Polish Writers; PEN; ZAIKS; Exec., Polish-Austrian Soc. Address: ul. Florianska 27/2, 31-019 Krakow, Poland.

MYER, Kenneth, b. London, UK. Freelance Industrial Video Correspondent. Educ: M.A., Pembroke Coll., Cambridge. Contbr. to: Guardian; BBC; Video & Film Communications; var. specialized jrnls. Address: Two Bridges, Portsmouth Road, Esher, Surrey, UK.

MYERS, Alexander Reginald, b. 3 Nov. 1912, Huddersfield, Yorks., UK. University Professor. Educ: B.A., 1934, M.A., 1935, Univ. of Manchester; Ph.D., Univ. of London, 1956. Publs: England in the Late Middle Ages, 1952, 8th ed., 1971; The Household of Edward IV, 1959; English Historical Documents, 1327-1485, 1969; London in the Age of Chaucer, 1972. Contbr. to num. histl. jrnls. Mbrships: Fellow, Royal Histl. Soc.; Fellow, Soc. of Antiquaries; Pres., Histl. Assn. of GB., 1973-76; Coun., Royal Histl. Soc., 1970-74. Recip., Mark Hovell Book Prize, 1935. Address: Schl. of Hist., The Univ., P.O. Box 147, Liverpool L69 3BX, UK.

MYERS, Bernard Samuel, b. 4 May 1908, NYC, USA. Art Historian; Teacher; Publisher. Educ: Sc.B., 1928, A.M., 1929, Ph.D., 1933, N.Y. Univ.; Brevet, Inst. d'Art & Archaeol., Sorbonne, France, 1931. Publs. incl: Encyclopedia of Painting, 1955, revised eds., 1961, 1970; Mexican Painting in Our Time, 1956; The German Expressionists (sev. langs.), 1957; Art & Civilization, 1957, 2nd ed., 1967; McGraw-Hill Dictionary of Art (w. S. D. Myers), 1969; Dictionary of Twentieth Century Art (w. S. D. Myers), 1974. Contbr. to var. jrnls., reviews, etc. Mbrships: Coll. Art Assn.; Pres., Treas., Inst. of Fine Arts Alumni Assn., 1973–. Address: 82 Willow St., Brooklyn Heights, NY 11201, USA.

MYERS, David, b. 8 Dec. 1925, London, UK. Cartoonist. Educ: Sir John Cass Tech. Inst.; St. Martin's Schl. of Art, London; Nat. Dip. in Design. Publs: (author & artist) The Drawing Machine TV Series, 1963. Contbr. to: Punch; Daily Express; Evening News; Mirror; Sketch; Evening Standard; TV commercials. Mbr., Cartoonists' Club of GB. Address: Rosefield House, Tatsfield, Westerham, Kent, UK.

MYERS, Hortense, b. 15 July 1914, Indpls., Ind., USA. Journalist. Educ: B.S., Butler Univ. Publs: (w. R. E. Thompson) Robert F. Kennedy, The Brother Within, 1962; (w. Ruth Burnett) Carl Ben Eielson, Young Alaskan Pilot, 1961; Cecil DeMille, Boy Dramatist, 1963; Vihjalmur Stefansson, Young Arctic Explorer, 1966; Edward R. Murrow, Young Newscaster, 1969; Vincent Lombardi, Young Football Coach, 1971; Joseph Pulitzer, Young Journalist, 1975. Mbrships. incl: Nat. Fedn. Press Women (Pres., 1962); Woman's Press Club of Ind. (Pres., 1954-56). Recip., Newsman of Yr. Award, Indpls. Press club, 1972. Address: 7839 W. 56th St., Indpls., IN 46254, USA.

MYERS, Jacob M., b. 25 Oct. 1904, York Co., Pa., USA. Clergyman; Educator. Educ: A.B., Gettysburg Coll., 1927; B.D., 1930, S.T.M., 1931, Luth. Theol. Sem., Gettysburg, Pa.; S.T.D., Temple Univ., 1937; Ph.D., Johns Hopkins Univ., 1946. Publs. incl: The Anchor Bible, vol. 12 — I Chronicles, vol. 13 — II Chronicles, vol. 14 — Ezra-Nehemiah, 1965, vol. 42 — I & II Esdras, 1974; Invitation to the Old Testament, 1967; The World of The Restoration, 1968. Contbr. to var. theol. publs. Mbr., var. profl. assns. Recip., Litt.D., Gettysburg Coll., 1967. Address: 141 Seminary Ave., Gettysburg, PA 17325, USA.

MYERS, Martin, b. 7 Dec. 1927, Toronto, Ont., Can. Writer. Educ: B.A., Univ. of Toronto, Ont.; M.A., Johns Hopkins Univ., Balt., Md., USA. Author, The Assignment, 1971, 2nd ed. 1972. Contbr. to: CBC Radio; Dialogue; Stimulus; Toronto Life; Toronto Star; Can. Mag.; Maclean's. Mbrships: Can. Writers' Union; Authors' Guild; Can. Authors' Assn.; Assn. of Can. TV & Radio Artists. Address: 5 Sandpiper Ct., Don Mills, Ont., M3A 3G7, Can.

MYERS, Robert Manson, b. 29 May 1921, Charlottesville, Va., USA. Professor of English. Educ: B.A., Vanderbilt Univ., 1941; M.A., Columbia Univ., 1942; Ph.D., 1948; M.A., Harvard Univ., 1943. Publs: Handel's Messiah: A Touchstone of Taste, 1948; From Beowulf to Virginia Woolf, 1952; Handel Dryden & Milton, 1956; Restoration Comedy, 1961; The Children of Pride: A True Story of Georgia & the Civil War, 1972. Conbr. to: MLA Publs.; Musical Quarterly; Harvard Theol. Review; Va. Mag. of Hist. & Biog. Mbrships: MLA; Am. Soc. for 18th Century Studies. Hons. incl: Nat. Book Award in Hist., 1973; Annual Fndrs. Award, Confederate Mem. Lit. Soc., 1973; Special Commendation, Ga. Hist. Commn., 1973. Address: 2101 Connecticut Ave., N.W., Wash. DC 20008, USA.

MYERS, Rollo Hugh, b. 23 Jan. 1892, Chislehurst, UK. Author; Musicologist. Educ: M.A., Univ. of Oxford. Publs: Music in the Modern World, 1939; Erik Satie, 1948, French transl. 1959; Debussy, 1948; Introduction to the Music of Stravinsky, 1951; Ravel: Life & Works, 1960; Emmanuel Chabrier & His Circle, 1969; Modern French Music, 1971. Transls: Cock & Harlequin, by J. Cocteau, 1921; A Call to Order, by J. Cocteau, 1924; 40,000 Years of Music, by J. Chailley, 1956. Contbr. to: Grove's Dictionary of Music; Ency. Britannica; Encyclopédie de la Pléiade; Music & Letters; Musical Quarterly; num. other musical jrnls. Mbr., Royal Musical Assn. Recip., Officier d'Académie, 1948. Address: c/o Savile Club, 69 Brook St., London W1, UK.

MYERS, Thora Wallis, b. 9 Jan. 1908, Ashtead, Surrey, UK. Journalist. Publs: Which Career for You? ; Ed., The Rucksack Book; Ed., The Guider, 1948-67. Contbr. to: Daily Mail Yr. Book; Children's Newspaper; Christian Herald; The Guide. Address: 39 Hans Pl., London SW1X 0JZ, UK.

MYERS, Wendy, b. 1941, Sheffield, UK. Student Nurse. Publs: Seven League Boots, 1969. Contbr. to: Pulse; Guy's Hosp. Nurses' League Jrnl. Mbr., Student Nurses Assn. Address: 34 Derwent Ave., Hatch End, Pinner, Middlesex, UK.

MYHILL, Henry, b. 26 Oct. 1925, Leicester, UK. Author. Educ: M.A., Oxford; Univs. of Cambridge, Grenoble, Sorbonne, Madrid, Zaragoza, Perugia, Innsbruck, Rennes, Lisbon. Publs: Introducing the Channel Islands, 1964; The Spanish Pyrenees, 1966; The Canary Islands, 1968; Brittany, 1969; Portugal, 1972; North of the Pyrenees, 1973. Contbr. to: Stock Exchange Gazette; Fin. Times; Sunday Telegraph; Motor Caravanner; Motor Caravan & Camping; Caravanning; num. part-works, etc.

Address: c/o Mrs. F. Turner, L'Ancrage, Gorey Harbour, Jersey, Channel Islands.

MYKLE, Agnar, b. 8 Aug. 1915, Norway. Novelist; Short Story Writer. Educ: Univ. of Econ. & Political Sci., Bergen. Publs: (in Norwegian) The Rope Ladder, 1947; The Hotel Room, 1951; It's all the same to me, said the boy, 1953; Lasso Round the Moon, 1955; Puppet Theatre, a manual, 1956; The Song of the Red Ruby, 1956; Cross My Heart, 1958; Rubicon, 1965; The Book of the Century, 1967; A Man & His Sink, 1968. Address: Asker, Norway.

MYLES JONES, Iwan, b. 4 Sept. 1921, Mtn. Ash, Glam., UK. Writer; Retired Teacher. Educ: Subsid. B.Sc., Cardiff Univ., 1943; Qualified Registered Tchr., Cardiff Coll. of Educ., 1948. Contbr. to: Western Mail; Storyteller; Dragons & Daffodils, 1960; BBC Wales. Mbrships: Former Mbr., Authors' Soc.; Llantwit Maj. Art Soc. Address: Y Fan Lâs, 6 Waterfall Mews, Ham Manor Private Park, Llantwit Major, Glam., UK.

MYRDAL, Jan, b. 19 July 1927, Stockholm, Sweden. Publisher; Columnist. Publs. incl: (novels) Hemkomst, 1954; Jubelvar, 1955; Att bli och vara, 1956; (essays) Söndagsmorgen, 1965; Skriftställning, 1968, II, 1969, III, 1970, IV, 1973; (autobiography) Rescontra, 1962; Samtida bekännelser, 1964; (books in Engl.) Report from a Chinese Village, 1965; Angkor: an essay on art & imperialism, 1970; China: the revolution continued, 1971; Gates to Asia, 1971. Contbr. to: Stockholms-Tidningen; Aftonbladet; Chmn. & Publ. Folket i Bild/Kulturfront. Address: Fagervik, S-150 30 Mariefred, Sweden.

N

NABOKOV, Vladimir, b. 23 Apr. 1899, St. Petersburg, Russia. Author. Educ: B.A., Trinity Coll., Cambridge, UK, 1922. Publs. incl: The Real Life of Sebastian Knight, 1941; Bend Sinister, 1947; Pale Fire, 1952; Lolita, 1958; Invitation to a Beheading, 1959; The Gift, 1963; The Defense, 1964; Eugene Onegin (transl. w. commentary), 1964; Despair, 1966; Speak Memory, 1966; ADA, 1969; Mary, 1970; Glory, 1971; Poems & Problems, 1971; Transparent Things, 1972; Strong Opinions, 1973; Look at the Harlequins! , 1974; Tyrants Destroyed, 1975. Contbr. to: New Yorker; Atlantic Monthly; Playboy; Esquire. Address: c/o Weidenfeld & Nicolson, 11 St. John's Hill, London SW11 1XA, UK.

NAGAMATSU, Sadamu, b. 31 Mar. 1904, Kikusui Town, Kumamoto Prefecture, Japan. Professor of English Literature; Writer. Educ: Grad., Fac. of Engl. Lit., Tokyo Univ., 1928. Publs. incl: Ulysses (transl. from James Joyce), 1931; Living in the Country (novel), 1956; The Definitive Works of Nagamatsu Sadamu, 1972; Man, This Contradictory but Beautiful Animal (essays); Studies in Classic American Literature (transl. from D. H. Lawrence), 1974. Contbr. to: Shincho; Kodo; Young English Student; Sev. Japanese newspapers. Mbrships: Japanese Writers' Soc.; Japanese PEN. Recip., Kumamoto Nichi-Nichi Newspaper Lit. Prize (Kumanichi Bungaku Sho). Address: No. 199, 4 Chome, Izumi, Kumamoto City, Japan.

NAGANOWSKI, Egon, b. 31 Mar. 1913, Innsbruck, Austria. Literary Critic; Translator. Educ: Ph.D. Publs. incl: Anna Seghers, 1955; The Magic Key. A Story on the Life & Works of Martin Andersen Nexø, 1958; Telemachus in the World Labyrinth. On the Works of James Joyce, 1962, Hungarian ed., 1975; Robert Musil (monograph), 1975; Var. transls. of German, Austrian & Helvetian lit. Contbr. to var. lit. jrnls. Mbrships: Polish Writers Assn.; PEN; James Joyce Fndn., Tulsa, USA; Int. Musil Gesellschaft, Vienna, Austria. Recip., Lit. Prize of Poznań, 1971. Address: 61-816 Posnań, ul. Ratajczaka 42 m.15, Poland.

NAGAOKI, Makoto, b. 31 Jan. 1904, Osaka City, Japan. Chairman, University School of Humanities; Professor of Japanese Literature. Educ: B.A., Dept. of Aesthetics, Tokyo Imperial Univ. Publs: A Woman in Osaka, 1949; A Goodman Father, 1965; Contbr. to Asahi Jrnl. of Broadcasting. Mbrships: PEN; Japan Soc. of

Letters; Japan Soc. of TV & Radio Writers. Hons: Osaka Prefectural Award of Arts, 1956; 10th Cultural Prize of Broadcasting, 1959; Osaka-citizen Prize for Cultural Achievements. Address: Konda, 7-2-13, Habikino-shi, Osaka, Japan.

NAGLE, Elizabeth, b. 2 Aug. 1918, Manchester, UK. Writer. Educ: Berlitz Schl., Lausanne, Switz.; Queens Secretarial Coll., London, UK. Publs: Veterans of the Road, 1955; Old Cars the World Over, 1958; The Other Bentley Boys, 1964. Contbr. to: Veteran Car (Ed., 1966-68). Mbrships: Veteran Car Club (Sec., 1952-57, Hon. Life Mbr.); other car clubs. Address: Tile Cottage, Brook, Lyndhurst, Hants. SO4 7HD, UK.

NAGY, Peter, b. 12 Oct. 1920, Budapest, Hungary. University Professor. Educ: Ph.D., University Pázmány, Budapest. Publs: Reception of the French Classic Drama in Hungary, 1943; Móricz Zsigmond, 1953; Szabó Dezsö, 1963; Libertinage et Révolution, 1975; several volumes of literary & theatre criticism. Contbr. to: Irodalomtörténet; Kritika: New Hungarian Quarterly; etc. Mbrships: Corres. Mbr., Hungarian Acad. of Scis.; ICLA; ILCA; PEN. Hons: József Attila Prizes, 1953, 1954. Address: Árnyas ut 40, 1121 Budapest, Hungary.

NAIDOO, Morganathan Ramsamy, b. 15 Sept. 1936, Pinetown, S. Africa. College Lecturer in Geography & Head of Department. Educ: B.A., Dip. Ed., Univ. of Natal, Durban; B.A.(Hons), Univ. of S. Africa, Pretoria. Publs: A Secondary Geography of Zambia (w. M. Mumbwe), 1969; Lands & Peoples of Central Africa (w. W. D. Michie & E. D. Kadzombe), 1973; A Systematic Geography Workbook, Books I & II, 1975. Mbr., Zambia Geogl. Assn. Address: 7896 Thelma Street, La Salle 690, Province Quebec, Canada.

NAILON, Philip, b. Bradford, Yorkshire, UK. Reader in Management Studies; Writer. Educ: B.Sc.; M.Phil.; F.H.C.I.M.A. Publs: Case Studies in Hotel Management (w. R. Doswell), 1967, 2nd ed., 1973; Bibliography of Hotel & Catering Operation (w. V. Bootle), 1970. Address: Dept. of Hotel, Catering & Tourism Mgmt. Univ. of Surrey, Guildford, Surrey, UK.

NAIPAUL, Shiva, b. 1945, Trinidad, W. Indies. Writer. Educ: Queen's Royal Coll., St. Mary's Coll., Trinidad; Univ. Coll., Oxford, UK. Publs: Fireflies, 1970; The Chip-Chip Gatherers, 1973. Contbr. to: Penguin Modern Stories 4, 1970; Spectator; New Statesman; London Mag.; Times Lit. Supplement. Hons: Jock Campbell — New Statesman Award, 1970; John Llewellyn Rhys Prize, 1970; Winifred Holtby Prize, Royal Soc. of Lit., 1970; Whitbread Award for Fiction, 1973. Agent: Curtis Brown Ltd. Address: c/o Andre Deutsch Ltd., 105 Great Russell St., London WC1, UK.

NAIPAUL, Vidiadhar Surajprasad, b. 17 Aug. 1932. Former Broadcaster; Writer. Educ: B.A., Univ. Coll., Oxford. Publs: The Mystic Masseur, 1957; The Suffrage of Elvira, 1958; Miguel Street, 1959; A House for Mr. Biswas, 1961; The Middle Passage, 1962; Mr. Stone & the Knights Companion, 1963; An Area of Darkness, 1964; The Mimic Men, 1967; A Flag on the Island, 1967; The Loss of El Dorado, 1969; In a Free State, 1971; The Overcrowded Barracoon, 1972. Contbr. to: BBC; New Statesman. Hons. incl: Somerset Maugham Award, 1961; Hawthornden Prize, 1964; Booker Prize, 1971. Address: c/o André Deutsch, 105 Gt. Russell St., London WC1, UK.

NAIRNE, Charles John Campbell, b. 1909, Perth, UK. Editor, Local Councils Review since 1973; Asst. Ed., John O'Lundon's Wkly, 1935-41; BBC Publs. 1946-69; Ed., Radio Times, 1968-69. Educ: B.A., London Univ. Publs: (novels) One Stair Up; Stony Ground; The Little Valley of God (transl.); The Secret Holiday (transl.); The Trossachs & the Rob Roy Country. Contbr. to: Chambers' Ency.; Guardian; Glasgow Herald; Scots Mag.; Tablet; Municipal Jrnl.; Local Govt. Chronicle; etc. Address: Tanglewood Cottage, Brittains Lane, Sevenoaks, Kent, UK.

NAKAMIKADO, Yuko, b. 4 Feb. 1923, Tokyo, Japan. Journalist. Educ: Tsuda Coll., Tokyo; Tokyo Univ. Inst. of Jrnlsm.; Northwestern Univ., Ill. Contbr. to: Reuters Ltd. Mbrships: For. Corres. Club of Japan; Observer Mbr., Japanese Prime Mins. Off. Press Club. Address: Reuters, 9th Floor Kyodo Tsushin Kaikan, 2 Aoi-cho, Akasaka, Minato-ku, Tokyo, Japan.

NAKAMURA, Yasuo, b. 26 Apr. 1919, Tokyo, Japan. Director, Kyoto Prefectural Research Institute of Education. Educ: Tokyo Phys. Sci. Coll. Publs: Noh to Nohmen no Sekai, 1962; Noh to Nohmen no Sekai, 2nd Series, 1963; Nippon no Dento: Noh, 1967; Noh no Men, 1969; Nippon no Koten-geino: Noh, 1969; Noh, 1971; Noh E Kagami, 1973; & others. Contbr. to: Geinoshi Kenkyu (Hist. of Performing Arts); Bungaku (Literature); Kanze; Sado Mag.; Noh-men Kogei (Craft of Noh-Men). Mbrships: Japanese Soc. of Dramatics; Soc. for the Study of Hist. of the Performing Arts. Hons: Prize for publ., Noh no Men, Japanese Theatrical Acad., 1970. Address: 58-9 Tojiin Kitama-machi, Kita-ku, Kyoto City, 603 Japan,

NAKARAI, Toyozo W., b. 16 May 1898, Kyoto, Japan. Honoured Professor of Old Testament, Emmanuel School of Religion. Educ: A.B., Kokugakuin Univ.; A.B., A.M., Butler Univ., USA; Ph.D., Univ. of Mich.; Postdoctoral studies, ibid, Univ. of Chgo., Hebrew Union Coll., others. Publs: Japanese Conversation, 1922; A Study of the Kokin-shu, 1930; Biblical Hebrew, 1951; An Elder's Public Prayers, 1968. Contbr. to profl. jrnls. Address: Drawer Q, Milligan College, TN 37682, USA.

NAKOV, Atanas Fotinov, pen name NAKOVSKI, Atanas, b. 31 Aug. 1925, Sofia, Bulgaria. Writer. Publs: (in Bulgarian) Maria Against Piralkov, 1962; A Street Beyond the River, 1964; The Endless Street, 1968; The World in the Evening & in the Morning, 1973. Contbr. to sev. lit. reviews, mags. & newspapers. Mbr. Union of Bulgarian Writers. Recip., Prizes, Union of Bulgarian Writers, mags. & newspapers. Mbr. Union of Bulgarian Writers. Recip. Prizes, Union of Bulgarian Writers, 1970-73. Address: Sofia, bul. Evlogi Georgiev, 116, Bulgaria.

NALL, Frances M. (Mrs. T. Otto), b. 18 Nov. 1902, Mt. Union, Iowa, USA. Writer. Educ: B.A. DePauw Univ.; M.A., Univ. of Ill., D.Litt., Iowa Wesley Coll., 1959. Publs: When Are We Patriotic?, 1940; One World — One Family, 1946; Let's Get Together, 1946; The Globe, a Neighbourhood, 1944; The Church Through the Centuries, 1949; One Church for One World, 1951; It Happened This Way, 1956; The Church in Today's World, 1960. Contbr. to num. ch. mags.; Ed., Meth. Ch. Bulletin, 1943-60. Mbrships: Nat. League of Am. Pen Women; Women's Press Assn. Address: 2509 Wynnewood Dr., Clearwater, FL 33515, USA.

NANDA, Bal Ram, b. 11 Oct. 1917, Rawalpindi, India. Historian; Biographer. Educ: M.A. Publs: Mahatma Gandhi: A Biography, 1958; The Nehrus: Motilal & Jawaharlal, 1962; Ed., Nehru & the Modern World, 1967; Ed., Socialism in India, 1967; Gokhale, Gandhi & the Nehrus, 1974. Contbr. to Ency. Britannica. Mbrships: Indian Coun. World Affairs (Exec. Coun., 1963-69). Indian Histl. Records Commn. Recip., Fellowship, Rockefeller Fndn., 1964. Address: C.II/63, Dr. Zakir Husain Marg., New Delhi 110003, India.

NARAYAN, Rasipuram Krishnaswami, b. 10 Oct. 1906. Publs: (novels) Swami & Friends, 1935; The Bachelor of Arts; The Dark Room; The English Teacher; Mr. Sampath; The Financial Expert; Waiting for the Mahatma; The Guide, 1958; The Man-Eater of Malgudi, 1961; Gods, Demons & Others, 1964; The Sweet-Vendor, 1967; Ramayana, 1972; (short stories) An Astrologer's Day; The Lawley Road; A Horse & Two Goats; (autobiography) My Days, 1974. Address: 15 Vivekananda Rd., Yadavagiri, Mysore 2, India.

NARAYN, Deane, b. 18 July 1929, Manchester, UK. Writer. Educ: M.A., Christ Church, Oxford Univ. Publs: The Small Stradivari (novel), 1961; An Edge of Pride (novel), 1964. Contbr. to: Saturday Review, (N.Y.); Detroit Free Press (Mich.); The Strad (London); Illustrated Times of India (Bombay); etc. Address: 209 Brompton Rd., Knightsbridge, London SW3 2EJ, UK.

NARPATI, B., b. 12 Dec. 1920, Phillaur, India. Financial Journalist. Educ: Punjab Univ. Publs: The Monetary System: its components & some trade issues, 1973. Contbr. to: Contemporary Review, London; Statist. Mbrships: Inst. of Jrnlsts., London; Press Club, ibid.; Nat. Book League; Soc. of Authors; Profl. Exec. Servs. Address: c/o Institute of Journalists, 1 Whitehall Pl., London SW1A 2HE, UK.

NASH, Paul, b. 2 Sept. 1924, Newcastle upon Tyne, UK. Professor; Author; Editor; Consultant. Educ: B.Sc.(Econ.), London Schl. Econs., 1949; Cert. Ed., London Univ. Inst. of Educ., 1950; Dip. Ed., 1952; M.Ed., Toronto Univ., Can., 1955; Ed.D., Harvard Univ., USA,

1959. Publs: The Educated Man: Studies in the History of Educational Thought, 1965; Authority & Freedom in Education: An Introduction to the Philosophy of Education, 1966; Culture & the State: Matthew Arnold & Continental Education, 1966; Models of Man: Explorations in the Western Educational Tradition, 1968; History & Education: The Educational Uses of the Past, 1970; A Humanistic Approach to Performance Based Teacher Education, 1973. Contbr. to var. profl. jrnls. Address: Boston Univ., 264 Bay State Rd., Boston, MA 02215, USA.

NASR, Seyyed Hossein, b. 7 Apr. 1933, Tehran, Iran. University Chancellor & Professor of History of Science & Philosophy. Educ: B.S., MIT, USA, 1954; Ph.D., Harvard, 1958. Publs: Three Muslim Sages, 1964; An Introduction to Islamic Cosmological Doctrines, 1964; Ideals & Realities of Islam, 1966; Islamic Studies, 1967; Science & Civilization in Islam, 1968; The Encounter of Man & Nature, 1968; Sufi Essays, 1972. Contbr. to profl. jrnls. Mbrships: Inst. int. de philos.; Dir., Imperial Iranian Acad. Philos.; Int. Soc. for Hist. of Religs.; Middle Eastern Assn. Recip., Royal Book Award, Iran. Address: Shemiran, Amaniyah, Pahlavi Ave., 25 Farkhar St., Tehran, Iran.

NATHAN, Robert Gruntal, b. 2 Jan. 1894, N.Y., USA. Novelist; Former Lecturer in Poetry. Educ: Harvard Univ. Publs. incl: Peter Kindred, 1919; There is another Heaven, 1929; Selected Poems, 1935; Dunkirk, 1940; Morning in Iowa, 1944; Married Look, 1950; The Snowflake & the Starfish, 1959; The Wilderness Stone, 1961; The Devil with Love, 1963; The Mallot Diaries, 1965; Stonecliff, 1967; Mia, 1970; The Elixir, 1971; Summer Meadows, 1973; Evening Song, 1973; (plays) Sleeping Beauty, 1950; Juliet in Mantua, 1966. Mbrships: PEN; VP, Nat. Inst. of Arts & Letters; Acad. of Am. Poets; Acad., Motion Picture Arts & Sci. Address: 1240 N. Doheny Dr., Hollywood 69, Calif., USA.

NATHUSIUS, Marie-Sophie, b. 19 June 1906, Amsterdam, Netherlands. Writer. Educ: Ballet & Drama trng. Publs: novels: De Partner, 1954, reprinted 1970; Mijnheer Goed, 1959; Een Gat In De Tijd, 1966; histl. novel: Rahel, 1974; TV play for the Vara, 1974 transl. from French, German & Engl., into Dutch, for radio, theatre & psychol. books. Contbr. to sev. Dutch newspapers. Mbrships: PEN (bd., Dutch centrum, 1967-74); Maatschappij der letteren, Netherlands & Die Kogge, Germany. Hons: Municipal Prize for novel, Amsterdam, 1955; Van der Vies Prize for play: Interview, 1965. Address: Prinses Margrietlaan 5, Amstelveen, Netherlands.

NATUSCH, Sheila Ellen, b. 1926, Invercargill, NZ. Botanist. Educ: M.A., Univ. of Otago. Publs: Native Plants, 1956; Native Rock, 1959; Stewart Island, (w. N. S. Seaward), 1962; Animals of New Zealand, 1967; A Bunch of Wild Orchids, 1968; Brother Wohlers, 1969; New Zealand Mosses, 1969. Contbr. to: Wellington Botan. Soc. Bulletin; NZ Plants & Gdns.; NZ Listener; Marine News. Mbrships. incl: Wellington Botan. Soc.; Royal Soc. of NZ; NZ Ship & Marine Soc. Address: 46 Ohiro Bay Parade, Wellington 2, NZ.

NAUGHTON, Bill, b. 12 June 1910, Ballyhaunis, Co. Mayo, Ireland (UK subject). Publs: A Roof Over Your Head (autobiog.), 1945; (novels) Rafe Granite, 1947; One Small Boy, 1957; Alfie 1966; Alfie Darling, 1970; (short stories) Late Night in Watling Street & Other Stories, 1959; The Goalkeeper's Revenge, 1961; (plays) Alfie, prod. 1963; All in Good Time, prod. UK, 1963, USA, 1965, publd. 1964; Spring & Port Wine, prod. UK, 1965 (as Keep it in the Family, prod. USA, 1967), publd. 1967; He Was Gone When We Got There, prod. 1966; Lighthearted Intercourse, prod. 1971; (juvenile) Pony Boy, 1966. Address: Craigton, Orrisale Rd., Ballasalla, Isle of Man, UK.

NAUMČESKI, Volče, pen name DANOSKI, b. 18 Jan. 1916, Prilep, Yugoslavia. Writer. Publs: Spring is Coming, 1939; Macedonian Bouquet, 1941; A Waving Flag, 1950; The Stork Came, 1951; The Poem of Evil, 1951; Visiting with the Dwarfs, 1952; Holyday, 1955; Spring & Fall, 1958; The Last Flight, 1960; Verses, 1961; Sunshine Tears, 1966; Golden Leaves, 1967; Lighting Bugs, 1967; Seventy Flowers, 1970; Fragrant Play, 1973. Contbr. to num. Macedonian & Yugoslav publs. Mbrships: PEN; Assn. Inventors. Hons: Award best children's book, Struga Evenings of Poetry, 1967; 11th Oct. Award Lit. achievement, 1972. Address: 29 Noemvri br. 37, 91000 Skopje, Yugoslavia.

NAVARRA, John Gabriel, b. 3 July 1927, Bayonne, N.J., USA. Professor. Educ: A.B., 1949, M.A., 1950, Ed.D., 1954, Columbia Univ. Publs. incl: Experimenting in Science, 1955, 1961; Our Noisy World, 1969; Earth Science, 1971; Drugs & Man, 1973; Science in the Elementary School, 1975; Sr. author, var. educl. prog. series inclng. The Young Scientist, 1971, & Junior High Science Program, 1973; num. books in InvestiGuide & InvestiVision series, 1967-69. Contbr. to: Sci. Educ.; Sr. High Schl. Newsletter; Classroom Sci. Bulletin; etc. Mbr. num. profl. orgs. Recip., 24th Recognition Award, Sci. Educ., 1961. Address: P.O. Box 647, Farmingdale, NJ 07727, USA.

NAVARRETE, Raúl, b. 5 Nov. 1942, Arandas, Jalisco, Mexico. Writer. Publs: Aquí, allá, en esos lugares (novel), 1966; Autobiografía, 1968; Luz que se duerme (novel), 1969; El oscuro señor y la señora (novel), 1973. El sexto día de la creación (stories & poems), 1974. Fndr.-Mbr., Writers' Assn. of Mexico. Hons: Decario del Centro Mexicano de Escritores, 1965-66; Premio Nacional de Literaturea Carlos Trouyet, 1970. Address: Unidad Loma Hermosa, Edificio No. 14-A-402, Col. Irrigación, México 10, D.F.

NAYLER, Joseph Lawrence, b. 18 Jan. 1891, Glasgow, UK. Aeronautical Scientist. Educ: M.A., Peterhouse, Cambridge Univ.; C. Eng. Publs: Aviation of Today, 1930; Flight Today, 1936; Modern Aircraft Design, 1950; High Speed Flight, 1956; Handbook of the Aircraft Industry, 1958; Dictionary of Aeronautical Engineering, 1959; Dictionary of Astronautics, 1964; Aviation: Its Technical Development, 1965; Dictionary of Mechanical Engineering, 1967; Newnes Engineers Pocket Book, 1971. Contbr. to: Kemps Engrs. Yr. Book, 1974; var. sci. & gen. jrnls. Mbrships: Fellow, Royal Aeronautical Soc., Am. Inst. Aeronautics & Astronautics, & Brit. Interplanetary Soc.; Brit. Fire Servs. Ltd. (Hon.). Address: Craigton, Claremont Rd., Claygate, Surrey KT10 0PL, UK.

NDLOVU, Elkanah Milton, b. 14 Dec. 1913, Gwanda Dist., Rhodesia. Teacher. Educ: Primary Tchrs'. Cert. Publs: Inhlamvu Zase Ngodlweni, 1962; Umdengosiba, 1973; Okungatshayelwa Mathambo. Recip., Lit. Prizes, 1957, 1959. Address: Lupane Mission, P.O. Box 25, Lupane, Rhodesia.

NEAL, Bernard George, b. 1922, Wembley, UK. Professor of Engineering Structures. Educ: Sc.D., Trinity Coll., Cambridge. Publs: The Plastic Methods of Structural Analysis; Structural Theorems & Their Applications. Contbr. to: Philos. Trans. Royal Soc.; Jrnl. Inst. of Civ. Engrs.; Jrnl. of Aeronautical Scis. Mbr., All England Lawn Tennis Club. Address: Imperial College of Science & Technology, South Kensington, London SW7, UK.

NEAL, Eric Victor, b. 1913, King's Lynn, UK. Teacher; Head, Geography & Social Studies Department, Abbotsford School, Ashford; Author. Publs: Tricky Words & More Tricky Words, (w. Hemming), 1958; Five Thousand Years of Music Making, 1961; Where the Money Goes, 1963; Making Music, 1964; A Sentence Dictionary, 1965; Lenin & the Bolsheviks, 1965; Explorers, 1966; Exercises with your Dictionary, 1966. Mbrships: Soc. of Authors; F.R.G.S. Address: 120 Fordbridge Rd., Ashford, Middx. TW15 3RU, UK.

NEAL, Ernest Gordon, b. 20 May 1911, Boxmoor, Herts., UK. Teacher. Educ: M.Sc., Ph.D., London Univ. Publs: Exploring Nature with a Camera, 1946; The Badger, 1948; Woodland Ecology, 1953; Topsy & Turvy My Two Otters, 1961; Uganda Quest, 1971; Biology for Today (w. K. R. C. Neal), 1974. Contbr. to: Field; Country Life; Illustrated London News; Times; Sunday Times; Wildlife. Mbrships: Chmn., Somerset Trust for Nature Conserv.; Chmn., Mammal Soc.; Brit. Ecol. Soc.; Fellow, Inst. of Biol., 1968. Hons: Stamford Raffles Award, Zool. Soc. of London, 1965; Wildlife Photographer of the Yr. Award, Animals Mag., 1969. Address: Mansell House, Milverton, Taunton, Somerset TA4 1JU, UK.

NEAL, Harry Edward, b. 4 May 1906, Pittsfield, Mass., USA. Freelance Writer. Publs. incl: Writing & Selling Fact & Fiction, 1949; Communication — From Stone Age to Space Age, 1960; Treasures by the Millions, 1961; The Hallelujah Army, 1961; Diary of Democracy, 1962; The Industrial Revolution, 1964; Nonfiction — From Idea to Published Book, 1964; The Virginia Colony, 1969; Oil, 1970; Of Maps & Men, 1970; The Story of the Secret Service, 1971. Contbr. to num. jrnls. Mbrships. incl: Authors Guild,

Authors League of Am.; Soc. of Mag. Writers; Children's Book Guild of Wash. D.C. Address: 210 Spring St., Culpeper, VA 22701, USA.

NEAL (Sister) Marie Augusta, (Helen C. Neal), b. 22 June 1921, Brighton, Mass., USA. Teacher; Researcher. Educ: A.B., Emmanuel Coll., Boston; M.A., Boston Coll.; Ph.D., Harvard Univ. Publs: Values & Interests in Social Change, 1965; Articles in: The Changing Sister, 1965; The New Nun, 1968; Vows but no Walls, 1968; Women in Modern Life, 1968; Religion in America, 1968; Church as Mission, 1969. Contbr. to: Sociological Analysis; Review of Relig. Rsch.; Jrnl. for the Scientific Study of Relig.; Social Compass; Concilium. Recip., Ford Fndn. Grant for Monograph on Changing Structures of Relig. Orders. Address: 400 The Fenway, Boston, MA, USA.

NEAL, Mary Julia, b. 15 Aug. 1905, Auburn, Ky., USA. English Teacher; Author. Educ: B.S., M.A., W. Ky. Univ.; Grad. study, Univ. of Mich., Syracuse Univ. Publs: By Their Fruits, 1947, 1974; Journal of Eldress Nancy (ed.), 1963; The Shaker Image (co-author), 1964. Contbr. to var. jrnls. Hons. incl: Southern Lit. Fellowship, 1960; Lectr., Shaker Exhib., Phila. Mus., of Art. 1962; Participant, Shaker confs. Address: 1523 Park St., Bowling Green KY 42101, USA.

NEALE, Walter Castle, b. 9 Aug. 1925, NYC, USA. Professor of Economics. Educ: A.B., Princeton Univ., 1947; M.A., Columbia Univ., 1948; Ph.D., Univ. of London, UK, 1953. Publs. incl: India: The Search for Unity Democracy & Progress, 1965; Economic Change in Rural India: Land Tenure & Reform in Uttar Pradesh 1800-1955, 1962. Contbr. to: Trade & Market in the Early Empires, 1957; Land Control & Social Structure in Indian History, 1969; Frontiers of Development Administration, 1971; Studies in Economic Anthropology, 1971; Jrnl. of Asian Studies; Indian Econ. Jrnl.; Land Econs.; Quarterly Jrnl. of Econs.; etc. Address: 2307 Laurel Ave., Knoxville, TN 37916, USA.

NEAME (Lt.-Gen. Sir), Philip, b. 12 Dec. 1888, Faversham, Kent, UK. Army Officer. Educ: Royal Military Acad., Woolwich; Imperial Defence Coll. Publs: German Strategy in the Great War, 1923; Playing with Strife (autobiography), 1946. Contbr. to: R.E. Jrnl.; The Sapper; The Field; var. other mags. & newspapers. Recip., num. military, civil & sporting hons. Address: The Kintle, Selling Court, Faversham, Kent, UK.

NEDELKOVSKI, Mile, b. 25 Nov. 1935, Prilep, Yugoslavia. Writer. Educ: Acad. of Film, Theatre, Radio & TV, Ljubljana. Publs: Ulaviot od Prespa, 1965; Peštara, 1968; Topli Buri, 1969; Eretikon-Erotikon, 1969; Pepelaši, 1970; Trnenki, 1972; Trijumfot na Trojanskiot konj, 1973. Contbr. to: all major Yugoslav mags. & reviews. Mbrships: Writers Soc. of Macedonia; Soc. of Film Workers of Socialist Repub. of Macedonia. Recip., Kočo Racin Prize, Struga, 1969. Address: ul. "700" No. 11, 91000 Skopje, Yugoslavia.

NEDERVEEN HENDRIKS, Wietske, b. 25 May 1936, Zwijndrecht nr. Dordrecht, Netherlands. Teacher. Educ: Paedagogische Acad.; Royal Conserv. of Music, Netherlands. Publs: Dierenvertelboek (animal stories), 1968, 3rd ed., 1972; Vrolýke Dierenvertelboek (jt. author), 1973. Contbr. to: Dordts Dagblad (music & art reviewer); Dordtboek (poems); sev. mags. Mbr., Vereninging voor Letterkundigen. Recip., Prize for Poetry, Quod Novum (univ. weekly), 1974. Address: Korte Geldersekade 2, Dordrecht, Netherlands.

NEDONCELLE, Maurice, b. 30 Oct. 1905, Roubaix, France. Roman Catholic Priest; University Professor. Educ: Doct.-ès-lettres, Sorbonne; Ph.D., Univ. of Paris; Doct. Theol., Strasbourg. Publs. incl: La Philosophie religieuse en Grande-Bretagne de 1850 à nos jours, 1934; La Réciprocité des Consciences, 1942; La Philosophie religieuse de Newman, 1946; Introduction à l'Esthétique, 1953; Prière humaine, prière divine, 1962; Explorations personnalistes, 1970; Intersubjectivité & ontologie, 1974; var. transls. in Engl. Contbr. to philosl. jrnls. Mbrships. incl: Inst. de France (corres. mbr.). Recip., Doct. h.c., Univ. of Louvain & other acad. hons. Address: 29 Faubourg National, 67000 Strasbourg, France.

NEEDHAM, Joseph, b. 1900, Clapham, London, UK. Emeritus Sir William Dunn Reader in Biochemistry; Member, Faculties of Biology & of Oriental Studies, Cambridge University; Master of Caius College. Educ: Oundle; Caius Coll., Cambridge. Publs: Science &

Civilisation in China, 7 vols.; Heavenly Clockwork; Chemical Embryology; Biochemistry & Morphogenesis; The Sceptical Biologist; Time, the Refreshing River; Within the Four Seas; The Grand Titration; The Development of Iron & Steel Technology in China. Mbrships: F.R.S.; F.B.A. Recip., Sc.D. Address: Master's Lodge, Gonville & Caius Coll., Cambridge CB2 1TA, UK.

NEEDLEMAN, Morriss H(amilton), b. 2 July 1907, Bklyn., N.Y., USA. Educator. Educ: A.B., 1931; M.S., 1939. Publs. incl: An Outline-History of English Literature: To Dryden, 1936; An Outline-History of English Literature: Since Milton, 1938; Survey-History of English Literature, 1938; American Literature, 1945; A Manual of Pronunciation, 1949; Biology for All (co-author), 1950; Handbook for Practical Composition, 1968; Basic Reading-Spelling Communication Vocabulary, & Teacher's Manual, 1970; The Needleman Basic Communication Vocabulary of 2,000 Words, 1972; Ed. & Ghostwriter, num. books & manuals. Mbrships. incl: Nat. Coun. of Tchrs. of Engl.; Int. Reading Assn. Address: 2991 S. Garden Dr., Apt. 308, Lake Worth, FL 33460, USA.

NEF, John Ulric, b. 13 July 1899, Chgo., Ill., USA. Author. Educ: Harvard Univ.; Ph.D., Robert Brookings Grad. Schl. Publs. incl: The Rise of the British Coal Industry, 1932; Industry & Government in France & England, 1940; The United States & Civilization, 1942, 2nd ed., 1967; The Universities Look for Unity, 1943; La Route de la Guerre Totale, 1949; War & Human Progress, 1950; The Birth of Industrial Civilization & the Contemporary World, 1954 (in French); Cultural Foundations of Industrial Civilization, 1958; The Conquest of the Material World, 1964; Search for Meaning, 1973. Contbr. to profl. jrnls. Mbrships: Cosmos Club; F Street Club, Wash. D.C.. Address: 2726 N St. Northwest, Wash. DC 20007, USA.

NEGALHA, Jonas, b. 26 Apr. 1933, Azores. Professor; Journalist. Educ: Ph.D., Litt.D., H.D., Ped.D., Psych.D., Soc.D., Sc.D., D.D. Publs: The Shortest Day, 1971; African Poems, 1971; The Shipwreck, 1974; Num. works of poetry, transls., anthols., sci. articles, thesis; Poems translated into num. langs. Contbr. to num. lit. jrnls. Mbrships: World Poetry Soc.; Cercle Int. de la Pensée & des Arts Français; Ctr. Studi e Scambi Int.; Accad. Leonardo Da Vinci. Hons. incl: Nominated for Nobel Prize in Litt., 1971; & for Nobel Peace Prize, 1974; Grand Prix Humanitaire Français, Chevalier du Mérite Français, 1973. Address: Caixa Postal 7244, Sao Paulo 01000, Brazil.

NEIDLE, Michael, b. 8 Jan. 1911, London, UK. College Lecturer; Writer. Educ: T.Eng. (C.E.I); F.I.T.E.; A.S.E.E. (Dipl.) Publs: Pictorial Guide to Electrical Installation Practice, 1961, 2nd ed., 1973; Electrical Installation Technology, 1970, 2nd ed., 1975; Electrical Contracting & Management (Ed. & co-author), 1973; Electric Wiring of Buildings (co-author), 1974; Installation & Regulations, 1974; Questions & Answers on Electric Wiring, 1975. Contbr. to: Elec. Times; Builder; Chambers Ency.; I.E.E. Jrnl., etc. Mbrships: Assoc., Instn. Elec. Engrs.; Instn. Elec. & Electronic Techn. Engrs. Address: 26 Elmer Gdns., Edgware, Middx., UK.

NEIHARDT, John Gneisenau, b. 8 Jan. 1881, Sharpsburg, Ill., USA. Author; Poet. Educ: Nebraska Normal Coll. Publs. incl: The Divine Enchantment, 1900; The Dawn Builder, 1911; The Stranger at the Gate, 1913; The Song of Hugh Glass, 1915; The Splendid Wayfaring, 1920, 1970; The Song of the Indian Wars, 1925; Collected Poems, 1926; Black Elk Speaks (transl. into num. langs.), 1932; The Cycle of the West, 1949; Lyric & Dramatic Poems, 1965; All is But a Beginning, 1972. Mbrships. incl: Nat. Inst. of Arts & Letters; Acad. of Am. Poets. Hons. incl: Litt.D.; LL.D.; Thomas Jefferson Award, 1968. Address: Skyrim Farm, Route 7, Columbia, Mo., USA.

NEIL, (Rev.) William, b. 13 June 1909, Glasgow, UK. Reader in Biblical Studies, University of Nottingham. Educ: Univ. of Glasgow; Heidelberg Univ., Germany; M.A.; B.D.; Ph.D.; D.D. Num. publs. incl: The Rediscovery of the Bible, 5th ed., 1962; The Life & Teaching of Jesus, 1965; The Plain Man Looks at the Bible, 8th ed., 1972; The Truth about the Early Church, 1970; The Truth about the Bible, 1972; The Acts of the Apostles (New Century Bible), 1973; Concise Dictionary of Religious Quotations, 1975; What Jesus Really Meant, 1975; Gen. Ed., Knowing Christianity, 1964—. Contbr. to: Cambridge History of the Bible; Sev. theol. jrnls. Address: Hugh Stewart Hall, The Univ., Nottingham, UK.

NEIMARK, Paul, b. 13 Oct. 1934, Chgo., Ill., USA. Writer. Educ. incl: B.A., Roosevelt Univ. Publs: 15 books inclng. She Lives! , 1971. Contbr. 4,200 articles to: N.Y. Times; Reader's Digest; etc. Recip., M.K. Cooper Award for best human relations book, 1971. Address: 920 Ridgewood Place, Highland Park, IL 60035, USA.

NEKRASOV, Victor PItonovich, b. 17 June, 1911, Kiev, USSR. Actor; Journalist; Writer. Educ: Inst. of Engrng. & Architecture, Kiev. Publs: In the Trenches of Stalingrad, 1946; The Native Town, 1954; First Journey, 1958; Vassia Konakoff, 1960; Kira Georgievna, 1962; Both Sides of the Ocean, 1962; A Month in France, 1965; Distance of 12,000 Kilometres, 1965; Travels in Different Measurements, 1967. Hons: Stalin Prize for Lit., 1947; Badge of Honour; Red Star. Address: Ukrainian Branch, USSR Union of Writers, Kiev, USSR.

NELISSEN, Jean, b. 2 June 1936, Geleen, Netherlands. Journalist. Publs: Vedetten Van de Weg, 1971; Hemel en Hel op een Stukje Leer, 1973; Sterren van een Boetbalnatie, 1974. Address: Wilhelminasingel 82, Maastricht, Netherlands.

NÉLOD, Gilles, b. 6 Aug. 1922, Brussels, Belgium. Teacher of Classics & Philosophy. Educ: B.A.; Tchng. Qualification. Publs: Empédocle d'Agrigente, essay, 1959; Panorama du Roman historique, essay, 1969; Les Poings, histl. stories, 1974; Histoire et Histoires, essay in Lettres vivantes, 1975. Contbr. to: Marginales; La Revue Nationale; Tribune Laïque; La Pensée & les Hommes; Présence Francophone. Mbrships. incl: PEN; Belgian Writers' Assn.; Belgian & For. Periodical Jrnlsts. Assn.; Royal Assn. of Walloon Dialect & French-speaking Writers. Hons. incl: Laureate, French Nat. Acad. of Hist., 1964; Jean Savant Medal, 1964; Premium, Govt. of Brabant Province, 1972. Address: Avenue des Volontaires 14, 1040 Brussels, Belgium.

NELSON, Cordner Bruce, b. 6 Aug. 1918, San Diego, Calif., USA. Writer; Editor. Educ: A.B., Univ. of the Pacific. Publs: The Jim Ryan Story, 1967; The Miler, 1969; Track & Field: The Great Ones, 1970; Runners & Races: 1500 & Mile, 1973. Contbr. to mags.; Ed., Track & Field News, 1948-72. Hons: The Jim Ryan Story chosen one of best books for young adults, Lib. Jrnl. Address: Box 6476, Carmel, CA 93921, USA.

NELSON, Ethel Florence, pen name Nina, b. 1923, St. Johns, Nfld., Can. Lieder Singer; Writer. Educ: Mem. Univ., St. Johns, Nfld.; Royal Acad. of Music, London. Publs: Shepheards Hotel, 1960; Your Guide to Egypt, 1964, to Lebanon, 1965, to Jordan, 1966, to Syria, 1966, to Czechoslovakia, 1968, to Malta, 1969; Holland, 1970; Mena House, 1970; Denmark, 1973; Tunisia, 1974; Belgium & Luxembourg (in preparation), 1975. Contbr. to: Egyptian Radio & TV. Mbrships. incl: Royal Overseas League; Guild of Travel Writers. Address: The Knowle, Crown Lane, Virginia Water, Surrey GU25 4HW, UK.

NELSON, Gwendoline Ethel, pen name PRIESTWOOD, Gwen, b. 26 May 1923, London, UK. Housewife. Publ: Through Japanese Barbed Wire, USA 1943, UK & India, 1944. Contbr. to: N.Y. Jrnl. American, 1943; Trend Mag., 1945, The Onlooker, 1946, Bombay, India. Mbr., PEN. Address: Stone House, Lac Manitou Sud, R.R. 1, Ste. Agathe des Monts, P.Q., Can.

NELSON, John Robert, b. 21 Aug. 1920, Winona Lake, Ind., USA. Clergyman; Educator. Educ: A.B., DePauw Univ., 1941; B.D., Yale Univ., 1944; D.Theol., Univ. of Zürich, Switz., 1951. Publs: The Realm of Redemption, 1951; One Lord, One Church, 1958; Christian Unity in North America, 1958; Criterion for the Church, 1963; Crisis in Unity & Witness, 1968; No Man is Alien, 1971. Contbr. to: Christian Century (Ed.-at-Large); Jrnl. Ecumenical Studies (Assoc. Ed.); Religion in Life; Theol. Studies; etc. Mbrships. incl: Fellow, Am. Acad. Arts & Scis., & Soc. Européenne de Culture. Recip., var. hon. docts. Address: 480 Jamaicaway, Boston, MA 02130, USA.

NELSON, Julius, b. 15 Aug. 1910, Berezina, Russia. Teacher. Educ: B.S., Ind. Univ. of Pa.; M.A., Tchrs. Coll., Columbia Univ. Publs: Artyping, 1939, 3rd ed., 1974; Stylebook for Typists, 1945; Brief Typing, 1954, 1962; Faster Typing, 1959, 1969; Typewriting Mini-Drills, 1967; Typewriter Mystery Games, vol. 1, 1951, vol. II, 1954, vol. III, 1959, vol. IV, 1962, vol. V, 1964, vol. VI, 1969, vol. VII, 1973; Teaching Typewriting Today, 1973. Contbr., monthly column, Jrnl. of Bus. Educ., 1939—; Gregg Writer.

Address: 3200 Southgreen Rd., Baltimore, MD 21207, USA.

NELSON, Lawrence Emerson, b. 25 July 1893, Clinton, Mo., USA. University Teacher; Author; Museum Curator; Administrator. Educ: A.B., William Jewell Coll., 1915; A.M., Univ. of Kan., 1921; Ph.D., Stanford Univ., 1925; Litt.D., Univ. of Redlands, Calif., 1971; L.H.D., Sioux Falls Coll., 1972. Publs: Our Roving Bible, 1945; Studying Civilization (co-author), 1949; Redlands: Biography of a College, 1958; Only One Redlands, 1963; It's A Great Day (co-author), 1970. Contbr. to var. philatelic, religious & secular mags. Mbrships: PEN; Past Pres., Calif. Writers Guild; Past Chmn., Redlands Writers Week. Address: 811 N. University St., Redlands, CA 92373, USA.

NELSON, Michael Harrington, pen name STRATTON, Henry, b. 4 Oct. 1921, Maidstone, Kent, UK. Writer; TV Scriptwriter & Interviewer. Publs: Knock or Ring, 1957; A Room in Chelsea Square, 1958; When the Bed Broke, 1961; Captain Blossom, 1972; Captain Blossom Soldiers On, 1974; (as Henry Stratton) Blanket, 1960. Author of var. TV plays. Address: 1 New Cottages, Nep Town, Henfield, Sussex, UK.

NELSON, Truman John Seymour, b. 18 Feb. 1911, Lynn, Mass., USA. Novelist; Historian. Publs. incl: The Sin of the Prophet, 1952; The Passion by the Brook, 1953; The Surveyor, 1960; Documents of Upheaval, 1966; The Torture of Mothers, 1965; The Right of Revolution, 1968; The Old Man, 1973; Sev. anthologies incl: Thoreau in our Season; The New Left; Literature in Revolution; Black Titan; John Brown Reader. Contbr. to: Ramparts; N.Y. Times Book Review; Nation; Saturday Review; Guardian; Etc. Mbrships: Thoreau Soc.; Essex Inst. Recip., Humanities Award, Pan-African Assn., 1964. Address: 23 Olive St., Newburyport, MA, USA.

NELVIN, Åsa Kerstin, b. 3 June 1951, Gothenburg, Sweden. Clerk; Actress. Educ: Swedish Acad. Dramatic Art, 1967-68. Publs: De Vita Björnana (The White Bears), 1969; Det Lilla Landet (The Little Country), 1971. Mbr., Swedish Union of Authors. Hons: Schlrships., Swedish Authors' Fund, 1971, 1974; Schlrships., Schöldström Fund, 1973. Address: AB Norstedts & Söners Förlag, Box 2052, 103 12 Stockholm, Sweden.

NEMEROV, Howard, b. 1 Mar. 1920, NYC, USA. Teacher; Writer. Educ: B.A., Harvard, 1941. Publs. incl: (verse) Mirrors & Windows, 1958; New & Selected Poems, 1960; The Next Room of the Dream, 1962; The Blue Swallows, 1967; Gnomes & Occasions, 1973; (fiction) The Melodramatists, 1949; Federigo: of the Power of Love, 1954; The Homecoming Game, 1957; A Commodity of Dreams & Other Stories, 1959; Stories Fables & Other Diversions, 1971; (non-fiction) Poetry & Fictional Essays, 1963; Journal of the Fictive Life, 1965; Reflexions of Poetry & Poetics, 1972. Mbrships incl: Nat. Inst. Arts & Letters; Fellow, Am. Acad. Arts & Scis. Hons. incl: St. Botolph's Club, Boston Prize for Poetry, 1968; Frank O'Hara Mem. Prize, Poetry, 1971. Agent: The Margot Johnson Agcy. Address: 6970 Cornell Ave., St. Louis, MO 63130, USA.

NEMES, György, b. 26 Mar. 1910, Debrecen, Hungary. Writer; Novelist; Journalist. Educ: B.A.(Econ. Scis.), Dip.Econs. Publs: (novels) Canaan, 1963; A Single Moment, 1965; Net, 1967; In Flagranti, 1968; No Secret, 1970; Hurry! , 1972; David & Clotild, 1972; (short stories) Twelve Short Stories, 1967; No Entry, 1974. Contbr. to: Élet és Irodalom; Nagyvilág; Kortárs; Uj Irás. Mbrships: Hungarian Writers' & Jrnlsts'. Assns.; PEN; Hungarian UNO Soc.; Hungarian Bibliophil. Soc. Hons: József Attila Prize; Rózsa Ferenc Prize. Address: Palánta utca 1/a, 1025 Budapest, Hungary.

NÉMETH, Laszló, b. 18 Apr. 1901, Nagybánya, Hungary (now Romania). Writer. Educ: Med. Univ. Publs: Gyàsz, 1935; Bün, 1936; Berzsenyi, 1937; Utolsò Kisèrlet, 1937-41; Kèszülödès, Minöség forradalma, Kisebbségben, 1942; Zsigmond Mòricz, 1943; Az èrtelmisèg Hivatàsa, 1943; Iszony, 1947; Égetö Eszter, 1956; Törtènelmi dràmàk, 1957; Tàrsadalmi dràmàk, 1958; Mai tèmàk, 1963; Sajkodi estèk, 1961; Kisérletezö Ember, 1963; Irgalom, 1965; Unpublished Essays, 1968; Collected Works, 1968—; Transls. of Shakespeare, Tolstoy, Ibsen, etc. Contbr. to: Tanu; Válasz. Hons: Kossuth Prize, 1957; Herder Prize, 1965. Address: 1026 Budapest, Szilàgyi Erzsèbet 79, Hungary.

NEPOMUCKA, Krystyna, pen names NEP; LECHICKA, Beata; DWORAKOWSKA, Krystyna; BUBULKIEWICZ, Nepomucen, b. Warsaw, Poland. Educ: Degrees in Law & Art. Publs: Małżeństwo niedoskonałe, 1960, 3rd ed., 1972; Rozwód niedoskonały, 1962. 3rd ed., 1972; Obraczka ze słomy, 1966; Samotność niedoskonała, 1971, 3rd ed., 1972; Miłość niedoskonała, 1974. Contbr. to: Przekrój; Wiadomości Londyńskie; Chłopska Droga; Za i Przeciw. Mbrships: PEN; Polish Lit. Soc.; Polish Printing Assn. Hons: Premiera Miesąca. 1972, Premiera Roku, 1972, Polish Radio. Address: Madalińskiego 21 m 17, 02-513 Warszawa, Poland.

NESBIN, Esther Caroline Winter, b. 5 Aug. 1910, Denver, Colo., USA. Librarian. Educ: B.A., 1931; Lib. Sci. Cert., 1932, Univ. of Buffalo. Publs: Shaker Literature in the Grosvenor Library, 1940; Library Technology Study Manuals, 4 vols., 1974. Contbr. to Calif. Garden Mag. Mbrships: Calif. Assn. of Schl. Libns.; Escondido Histl. Soc.; Vista Ranchos Histl. Soc. Hons: Award for Outstanding Serv. to Educ., Consuelo Lodge, Free & Accepted Masons, 1965; Award for Outstanding Serv. to Educ., Escondido Chmbr. of Comm., 1972. Address: P.O. Box 102, San Marcos, CA 92069, USA.

NESBITT, Marion, b. 28 Dec. 1900, South Boston, Va., USA. College Professor. Educ: B.S., M.A., Ed.D., Columbia Univ. Publs: A Public School for Tomorrow, 1953, paperback ed., 1967; Captain John Smith's Page, 1957; Virginia's History & Geography (co-author), 1965; The Land of Virginia, 1973. Contbr. to: Educl. Leadership; Childhood Education; Nat. Educ. Assn. Jrnl. Mbrships. incl: Va. Writers' Club; English Speaking Union. Address: 1100 West Ave., Richmond, VA 23220, USA.

NESIN, Aziz, b. 26 Dec. 1915, Istanbul, Turkey. Writer. Educ: Acad. of War. Author, 62 books, transl'd. into 18 langs. Mbr., Turkish Writers Syndicate. Hons. incl: 4 First Prizes, Int. Humour Contest, 1956, 1957, 1966 & 1969; Prize for Theatre, Turkish Lang. Inst., 1970. Address: Kadiköy, Feneryolu, Alageyik Sokak 7, Istanbul, Turkey.

NESTLE, John Francis, pen name FALCON, b. 27 July 1912, Winterbourne, Sutton, Surrey, UK. Equestrian Correspondent; Horse Photographer. Educ: Grad., Sandhurst, 1934; Dip. as riding instr., Inst. of the Horse. Publs: Show Horses & Ponies: What Makes a Winner (w. Phyllis Hinton), 1973. Contbr. to nat. newspapers & equestrian jrnls. in UK, USA & Australia, inclng: Horse & Hound; Riding; The Light Horse; The Horse World; Hoofs & Horn. Mbrships. incl: Inst. of Jrnlsts; Royal Dublin Soc.; Brit. Show Pony Soc.; W. Country Writers' Assn. Address: P.O. Box 30, Kyrenia, Cyprus.

NETHERCLIFT, Beryl Constance, pen name MASCALL, Margery D., b. 1911, Woodford Green, Essex, UK. Author. Publs: No Road Runs By, 1935; Greensleeves, 1939; The Snowstorm, 1967; Castle Steep, 1970; The Certain Spring, 1971. Contbr. to: Sussex Co. Mag.; Christian Sci. Monitor; children's publs., women's jrnls., etc. Mbrships: Soc. of Authors; Archaeol. Soc. Address: 83 Graham Ave., Brighton, Sussex, UK.

NETTELL, Richard Geoffrey, pen name KENNEGGY, Richard, b. 1 Nov. 1907, Mansfield, Notts., UK. Writer. Publs: Wait for the Wagon, 1938; Drive the Dead Leaves, 1940; Midsummer Spring, 1943; Rum & Green Ginger, 1946; Brose & Butter, 1947; Garfin's God, 1948; Hearthstone Heart, 1952; Girl in Blue Pants, 1967; Naked to Mine Enemy, 1968. Contbr. to anthols. & jrnls. inclng: BBC Late Night Story; Woman's Illustrated; Books & Bookmen. Address: Adgeston, Sandown, Isle of Wight, UK.

NEUBERGER, Albert, b. 15 Apr. 1908, Wurzburg, Germany. Emeritus Professor of Chemical Pathology. Educ: M.D., Univ. of Wurzburg; Ph.D., Univ. of London,xUK. Contbr. to: Biochem. Jrnl.; Proceedings of Royal Soc.; Sev. other learned jrnls. Mbrships. incl: Med. Rsch. Coun., 1962-66; Chmn., Govng. Body, Lister Inst. of Preventive Med., 1971—; Pres., Assn. of Clin. Biochems.; Fellow, Royal Soc.; Fellow, Royal Coll. of Pathols.; F.R.C.P. Hons: C.B.E., 1964; LL.D., Univ. of Aberdeen, 1967; Ph.D., Jerusalem Univ., 1968. Address: 22 W. Heath Ave., London NW11, UK.

NEUBERGER, Egon, b. 27 Feb. 1925, Zagreb, Yugoslavia. Professor of Economics. Educ: B.A., Cornell Univ., USA, 1947; M.A., 1949, Ph.D., 1958, Harvard Univ. Publs: The USSR & the West as Markets for Primary Products: Stability, Growth, & Size, 1963; Co-Ed.,

International Trade & Central Planning: An Analysis of Economic Interactions, 1968; co-Ed., Perspectives in Economics: Economists Look at their Fields of Study, 1971; co-Ed., Urban & Social Economics in Market & Planned Economies, 2 vols., 1974. Contbr. to num. profl. jrnls. Mbrships. incl: Jt. Comm. on Eastern Europe, Am. Coun. of Learned Socs. & Soc. Sci. Rsch. Coun.; Planning Comm., Comm. on Comparative Urban Econs. Address: Box 523, 5 Somerset Court, E. Setauket, NY 11733, USA.

NEUFELD, Peter Lorenz, b. 4 Feb. 1931, Whitewater, Man., Can. Journalist. Educ: B.A.; B.Ed.; M.Ed.; Ph.D. Publs: Aurora, 1968; The Invincible White Shepherd, 1970; Prairie Vistas, 1973. Contbr. to: Brandon Sun; Winnipeg Tribune; Western Producer; North/Nord. Mbrships. incl: Can. Authors Assn.; Hist & Sci. Soc. of Man. Recip., Plaque for rsch. & writing involving German Shepherd Dogs (Alsations), White Shepherd Club of Can., 1972. Address: Box 81, 317 — 1st Ave. S.W., Minnedosa, Man., Can.

NEUFFER, Claude Henry, b. 2 Nov. 1911, Abbeville, S.C., USA. Professor of American & Southern Literature; Editor. Educ: B.S., Clemson Univ.; M.A., Univ. of S.C.; Univs. of Va. & Wis. Publs: The Christopher Happoldt Journal (w. Bachman & Audubon), 1960; The Name Game: From Oyster Point to Keowee (co-author), 1972; (co-ed.) Purely Original Verse by J. Gordon Coogler, 1974; (fndr.-ed.) Names in South Carolina, annual place-name jrnl., 1954—. Contbr. to: Am. Speech; Names; Southern Folklore; Georgia Review; etc. Mbrships. incl: Am. Name Soc.; S. Atlantic MLA; pres., S.C. Soc. Address: 4532 Meadowood Rd., Columbia, SC 29206, USA.

NEUGEBOREN, Jay, b. 30 May 1938, Bklyn, N.Y., USA. Novelist. Educ: B.A., Columbia Univ., 1959; M.A., Ind. Univ., 1963. Publs: Big Man, 1966; Listen Ruben Fontanez, 1968; Corky's Brother, 1969; Parentheses: An Autobiographical Journey, 1970; Sam's Legacy, 1974. Contbr. to: Esquire; N.Y. Times Book Review; Sport; Transatlantic Review; Mass. Review; New Am. Review; etc. Mbrships: PEN; Phi Beta Kappa. Recip., Fellowship in Creative Writing, Nat. Endowment for the Arts, 1973-74. Address: 252 River Drive, North Hadley, MA 01035, USA.

NEUMANN, Robert, b. 22 May 1897, Vienna, Austria. Author. Educ: Univ. of Vienna. Publs: ca. 36 books, transl'd into 26 langs., inclng. (in Engl.) Flood, 1930; Ship in the Night, 1932; Zaharoff: The Armaments King, 1935; A Woman Screamed, 1938; By the Waters of Babylon, 1939; 23 Women, 1940; Mr. Tibbs Passes Through, 1943; Inquest, 1945; Children of Vienna, 1946; Blind Man's Buff, 1949; Shooting Star & Circe's Island, 1954; The Plague House Papers, 1958; The Dark Side of the Moon, 1961; Hitler, Pictorial History of the 3rd Reich, 1962; Festival, 1963; later books in German. Mbrships. incl: Int. VP, PEN; Hon. Pres., Austrian PEN; Deutsche Akad. für Sprache und Dichtung, Darmstadt. Hons. incl: Austrian Cross of Hon. 1st Class Arts & Scis.; Medal of Hon., 1st Class, City of Vienna. Address: Villa Belmonte, Locarno-Monte, Switz.

NEUMEYER, Martin Henry, b. 8 Oct. 1892, Jackson, Mo., USA. Emeritus Professor of Sociology; Emeritus Editor, Sociology & Social Research. Educ: A.B., DePauw Univ., Greencastle, Ind., 1919; B.D., Garrett Theol. Sem., Evanston, Ill., 1921; A.M., Northwestern Univ., Ill., 1922; Ph.D., Univ. of Chgo., 1929. Publs: Community & Society (w. L. D. Osborn), 1933; Leisure & Recreation (w. E. S. Neumeyer), 1936, 2nd ed., 1958; Juvenile Delinquency in Modern Society, 1949, 3rd ed., 1961; Social Problems in a Changing Society, 1953. Contbr. to: Social Sci. (Ed. bd.); Pacific Sociol. Review; Soc. Problems. Mbrships. incl: Am. Sociol. Assn.; Past Pres., Pacific Sociol. Assn. Address: 6263 La Tijera Blvd., L.A., CA 90056, USA.

NEUSTATTER, Walter Lindesay, b. 7 Dec. 1903, Munich, Germany. Consulting Psychiatrist. Educ: Univ. Coll. & Hosp., London; M.D.; B.Sc. Publs: Modern Psychiatry in Practice, 1934; The Early Treatment of Mental & Nervous Disorders, 1939; Psychological Disorder & Crime, 1955; The Mind of the Murderer, 1960; Psychiatry in Medical Practice. Contbr. to: Lancet; Brit. Med. Jrnl.; Guy's Hosp. Reports; Medico-legal Jrnl.; Med., Sci. & the Law; Brit. Ency. Med. Prac.; etc. Mbrships: VP, Medicolegal Soc.; Acad. Forensic Sci.; Fellow, Royal Coll. of Psychs.; F.R.C.P. Address: 128 Harley St., London W1, UK.

NEVANLINNA, Sinikka Sisko, pen names, KALLIO-VISAPÁÁ, Sinikka -1958, KALLIO, Sinikka 1958-, b. 2 Feb. 1917, Rauma, Finland. Author; Translator.

Educ: M.A., Helsinki Univ., 1939. Publs: (novels) Vahasydän, 1946; Kolme Vuorokautta, 1948; Kaislakerttu, 1950; (poetry) Siivet, 1946; Neljästi Minä Palaan, 1948; Sils-Maria, 1950; (essays) Santiagon Simpukka, 1952; Kuvista ja Kuvaamisesta, 1955; (short stories) Puita, 1966; num. transls. of novels, poetry & Philos. from sev. langs. into Finnish. Contbr. to sev. Finnish mags. Mbrships. incl: PEN (Bd, Finland, 1949-56). Recip., sev. transl. prizes. Address: Bulevardi 9 A 19, 00120 Helsinki 12, Finland.

NEVILLE, Barbara Alison, pen name CANDY, Edward, b. 22 Aug. 1925, London, UK. Graduate Student; Writer. Educ: M.B., B.S.; Univ. Coll., London; Univ. Coll. Hosp. Med. Schl. Publs: (detective stories) Which Doctor, 1953; Bones of Contention, 1954; Words for Murder Perhaps; (novels) The Graver Tribe, 1958; A Lady's Hand, 1959; A Season of Discord, 1964; Strokes of Havoc, 1965; Parent's Day, 1967; Doctor Amadeus, 1969. Contbr. to: Times (reviews). Mbrships: Writers Action Grp.; Electro-Encephalographic Soc. Recip., Arts Coun. Award, 1967. Address: 2 Mile End Rd., Newmarket Rd., Norwich NR4 7QY, UK.

NEVILLE, Derek, pen name SALT, Jonathan, b. 18 Nov. 1911, London, UK. Author. Publs. incl: (fiction) Bright Morrow; Burning Leaves; Strange Fortune; (poetry) A First Selection; A Second Selection; A Third Selection; The Light Without a Name; Put Off Thy Shoes; Youth's Logic; Breaking Through; (hist.) Blackburn's Isle; (nature stories) Footprints on the Grass; Honky; Honey; (philos.) Windows; (relig.) The Garden of Silence. Contbr. to over 225 jrnls. inclng: Punch; Pick of Punch; Blackwoods; Chambers Jrnl.; London Opinion; Woman's Own. Address: Itteringham Mill, Itteringham, Norwich, Norfolk, UK.

NEVIN, Edward Thomas, b. 5 Feb. 1925, Pembroke Dock, UK. University Teacher. Educ: B.A., Univ. Coll. of Wales Aberystwyth, 1949; M.A., 1951; Ph.D., Corpus Christi Coll., Cambridge, 1952. Publs: The Problem of the National Debt, 1953; The Mechanism of Cheap Money, 1954; Textbook of Economic Analysis, 1952, 4th ed., 1975; Capital Funds in Jnder-developed Countries, 1960; Introduction to Micro-Economics, 1973. Contbr. to: Econ. Jnrl.; Economica; Oxford Econ. Papers. Mbrships: Royal Econ. Soc.; Chmn., Assn. of Univ. Tchrs. of Econs, 1971-74. Address: 31 Rotherslade Rd., Langland, Swansea, UK.

NEWALL, Venetia June, b. 1935, London, UK. Folklorist; Lecturer. Educ: M.A.; Sorbonne Univ., Paris, France; Univ. of St. Andrews, UK. Publs: An Egg at Easter: A Folklore Study, 1971; The Folklore of Birds & Beasts, 1971; Ed., The Witch Figure, 1973; Encyclopaedia of Witchcraft & Magic, 1974; Folklore, Myths & Legends of Britain (co-author), 1973; Gen. Ed., The Folklore of the British Isles series, 1973; The Folklore of London (w. R. Buchanan), 1975. Contbr. to num. folklorist & other jrnls. Mbrships: incl: PEN; Int. Ed. Advsry. Bd., Studies,in Folklore; Sec., Folklore Soc.; Couns. Soc. for Folklife Studies; F.R.G.S.; Int. Folk Music Coun. Agent: A. P. Watt & Son. Address: Dept. of Engl., Univ. Coll., London Gower St., London WC1E 6BT, UK.

NEWBOLT, Peter, b. 21 Oct. 1923, London, UK. Typographer; Book Designer; Editor; Photographer. Educ: Univ. of Oxford. Publs: Praise of Books (anthol.), 1955. Contbr. to: Time & Tide; The Connoisseur; Homes & Gardens; Book Design & Production; TV Times; Country Life; sev. tech. publs. Mbrships: Inst. of Jrnlsts.; F.R.S.A. Address: High St., Cley, Holt, Norfolk, UK.

NEWBY, Eric, b. 6 Dec. 1919, London, UK. Writer. Publs: The Last Grain Race, 1956; A Short Walk in the Hindu Kush, 1958; Something Wholesale, 1962; Slowly Down the Ganges, 1966; Grain Race: Pictures of Life Before the Mast in a Windjammer, 1968; The Wonders of Britain (co-author), 1968; The Wonders of Ireland (co-author), 1969; Love & War in the Apennines, 1971; Ganga, Sacred River of the Hindus, 1974; The Michell Beazley World Atlas of Exploration, forthcoming. Mbrships: F.R.S.L. (1973); Assn. of Cape Horners. Recip., M.C., 1945. Address: Pear Tree Court, Harbertonford, Totnes, Devonshire TQ9 7TA, UK.

NEWBY, Percy Howard, b. 1918, Crowborough, UK. Director of Programmes, BBC Radio. Educ: St. Paul's Coll., Cheltenham. Publs: A Journey to the Interior; Agents & Witnesses; Mariner Dances; The Snow Pasture; The Young May Moon; A Season in England; A Step to Silence; The Retreat; The Picnic at Sakkara; Revolution & Roses; Ten

Miles from Anywhere; A Guest & His Going; The Barbary Light; Something to Answer For, 1968; A Lot to Ask, 1973. Hons: Atlantic Award for Lit., 1946; Somerset Maugham Prize, 1949; Booker Prize, Yorks. Post Fiction Award, 1969; Booker Prize, 1969. Agent: David Higham Assocs. Address: Upton House, Cokes Lane, Chalfont St. Giles, Bucks., UK.

NEWCOMER, James William, b. 14 Mar. 1912, Gibsonburg, Ohio, USA. Educator. Educ: Ph.B., Kenyon Coll., 1933; M.A., Univ. of Mich., 1938; Ph.D., Univ. of Iowa, 1953. Publs: Liberal Education & Pharmacy, 1960; Maria Edgeworth the Novelist, 1969; Maria Edgeworth, 1973; Celebration (libretto for orch., chorus, soloists), 1973. Contbr. to: Bicentennial Collect. of Tex. Short Stories, 1974; Scots Mag.; Descant; 19th Century Fiction; Eire-Ireland; Cimarron Review; Arlington Quarterly; Classical Jrnl.; Jrnl. of Higher Educ.; etc. Mbrships. incl: MLA; Am. Comm. for Irish Studies; Irish Am. Cultural Inst.; Edgeworth Soc. Address: 1100 Elizabeth Blvd., Fort Worth, TX 76110, USA.

NEWHOUSE, Edward, b. 10 Nov. 1911, Budapest, Hungary. (US citizen). Publs: (novels) You Can't Sleep Here, 1934; This Is Your Day, 1937; The Hollow of the Wave, USA 1949, UK, 1950; The Temptation of Roger Heriott, USA, 1954, UK, 1955; (short stories) Anything Can Happen, 1941; The Iron Chain, 1946; Many Are Called, USA, 1951, UK, 1952. Contbr. to New Yorker, 1936—. Recip., var. mil. hons. Address: Upper Nyack, NY 10960, USA.

NEWLON, Clarke, b. Griswold, Iowa, USA. Journalist; Retired US Air Force Officer (Colonel). Educ: Grinnell Coll.; Univ. of Neb. Publs: 1001 Questions Answered About Space, 1961; Famous Pioneers in Space, 1962; LBJ The Man from Johnson City, 1964; The Fighting Douglas MacArthur, 1965; Space Age Dictionary, 1965; Famous Mexican Americans, 1972; The Men Who Made Mexico, 1973; Police Dogs in Action, 1974. Contbr. to: Colliers; Saturday Evening Post; Reader's Digest; etc. Hons: Jr. Lit. Guild selection for Police Dogs in Action, 1974. Address: 3714 Massachusetts Avenue NW, Washington, DC 20016, USA.

NEWMAN, Daisy Neumann, b. 9 May 1904, Southport, Lancs., UK. Author. Publs: Now that April's There, 1945; Diligence in Love, 1951; The Autumn's Brightness, 1955; Mount Joy, 1968; A Procession of Friends: Quakers in America, 1972; I Take Thee, Serenity, 1975. Contbr. to: Sat. Review; Ladies' Home Jrnl.; New Yorker. Mbr., Friends Hist. Assn. Address: 1 Bayberry Rd., Hamden, CT 06517, USA.

NEWMAN, G. F., b. London, UK. Writer. Publs: Sir, You Bastard, 1970; Billy, 1971; The Abduction, 1972; You Nice Bastard, 1972; The Player & The Guest, 1972; The Split, 1973; Three Professional Ladies,x1973; The Price, 1974. Mbr., Writers Guild of GB. Address: Cullinagh, Dunmanway, Co. Cork, Repub. of Ireland.

NEWMAN, Leonard Hugh, b. 1909, Bexley, Kent, UK. Managing Director, Natural History Photographic Agency; Author. Publs: Butterfly Farmer; Transformations of Butterflies & Moths; Butterfly Haunts; British Moths in their Haunts; Looking at Butterflies; Nature Parliament (w. Peter Scott & James Fisher); The Observer's Book of Insects (w. E. F. Linssen); Man & Insects, 1965; Ants from Close-up, 1967; The Complete British Butterflies in Colour, 1968. Contbr. to: Field; Country Life; Countryman; Das Tier, Germany; Int. Wildlife, USA. Mbrships. incl: F.R.H.S. Address: Betsoms, Westerham, Kent, UK.

NEWMAN, Leslie Arthur, b. 15 Aug. 1904, Maulden, Beds., UK. Minister of Religion. Educ: B.A., London Univ.; Ph.D., Durham Univ. Publs: Highways in the Byeways; Gypsy Tells her Story; News from the North; The Master Enters; A Plan for Living. Contbr. to: Meth. Recorder; Preacher's Mag.; Brighton Argus. Address: 141 Surrenden Rd., Brighton, Sussex, UK.

NEWMAN, Loretta Marie, b. 29 July, 1911, Kansas City, Mo., USA. Musician; Educator; Psychologist. Educ: B.M., Univ. of Rochester, N.Y., 1933; M.A., Univ. of Kan. City, 1943; M.A., Calif. State Univ., Long Beach, 1957. Publs: College Health Course Syllabus, (co-author), 1955; College Orientation Manual, (co-author), 1957; College Reading & Study Improvement, 1964, 4th ed. 1975; Building Basic College Reading Skills, 1964, 4th ed. 1975. Contbr. to: Claremont Coll. Reading Conf., 1966; Western

Coll. Reading Assn. Proceedings, 1969, 1971, 1972, 1973, 1974. Mbrships. incl: Past Sec., Western States Coll. Reading Assn.; Calif. Tchrs. Assn. Recip., sev. musical & other awards. Address: 3210 Merril Dr., Torrance, CA 90503, USA.

NEWNHAM, Wilfred Henry, b. 2 Mar. 1916, Shepparton, Vic., Australia. Programme Director. Educ: Assoc., Fed. Inst. Accts., Australasian Inst. Secs. Publs: Melbourne — Biography of a City, 1956; Melbourne Sketchbook, 1967; Victoria Illustrated, 1970; Historic Hotels of Adelaide, 1971; Kangaroo Island Sketchbook, 1975. Contbr. to: Listener; Everybody's; Herald, Sun & Age (Melbourne). Mbrships: Aust. Writers' Soc.; Royal Vic. Histl. Soc.; Royal Geogl. Soc., S.A.; Nat. Trust, S.A.; Profl. Offs.' Assn. Address: 3 Indra Terrace, Brighton, S.A., Australia.

NEWSOME, David Hay, b. 15 June 1929, Leamington Spa, UK. Headmaster. Educ: M.A., Emmanuel Coll., Cambridge. Publs: A History of Wellington College 1859-1959, 1959; Godliness & Good Learning. Four Studies on a Victorian Ideal, 1961; The Parting of Friends, 1966; Bishop Westcott & the Platonic Tradition, 1969; Two Classes of Men. Platonism in English Romantic Thought, 1974. Contbr. to: The Rediscovery of Newman; The Victorian Crisis of Faith, 1970; Theol.; Ency. Britannica; Jrnl. of Theol. Studies; Jrnl. of Ecclesiastical Hist.; etc. Mbrships: Fellow, Royal Histl. Soc.; Fellow, Emmanuel Coll., Cambridge, 1959-70. Address: Headmaster's House, Christ's Hosp., Horsham, W. Sussex, UK.

NEWSTEAD, Gordon Henry, b. 1 July 1917, Cairo, Egypt. Emeritus Professor, Aust. Nat. Univ.; Assoc. Commissioner, Tasmanian Hydro Electric Commission. Educ: M.E.E., Univ. of Melbourne. Publs: General Circuit Theory, 1959; An Introduction to the Laplace Transformation (w. J. C. Jaeger), 3rd ed., 1968. Contbr. to: Ency. Americana, 1972; Int. Dictionary of Geophysics, 1967; Nature; Proceedings of the Inst. Elec. Engrs. Address: 81 Davey St., Hobart, Tas., Australia 7000.

NEWTH, Mette Cecilie, b. 31 Jan. 1942, Oslo, Norway. Artist. Educ: Dip. in Ceramics, State Schl. of Art & Crafts, Norwegian Acad. Fine Arts. Publs: The Little Viking, 1969; Tiny Terror, 1975. Contbr. to Norwegian Broadcasting & BBC. Mbr., Norwegian Children's Book Union (Bd.). Recip., Grant for Writers of Children's Books, Oslo City, 1972. Address: Paal Bergs Vei 74, 1349 Rykkinn, Norway.

NEWTON, Earle Williams, b. 10 Apr. 1917, Cortland, N.Y., USA. Educator; Editor; Librarian; Curator. Educ: A.B., Amherst Coll., 1938; A.M., Columbia Univ., 1939; Ph.D., Inst. for Adv. Studies in Educ., 1973. Publs: Before Pearl Harbour, 1942; The Vermont Story, 1749-1949, 1949. Former Ed., Am. Heritage, Vt. Life, Hist. News, Vt. Quarterly, Touchstone; Spain & Her Rivals (co-ed.), 1970; etc. Mbrships: Sec., Am. Assn. for State & Local Hist., 1946-53; Sec., Soc. of Am. Histns., 1947-50; ALA. Hons: Cmdr., Order of Isabela la Catolica, 1965; Order of Merit, 1968, Spanish Govt. Address: College of the Americas, 105 W. Gonzalez St., Pensacola, FL 32501, USA.

NEWTON, Kenneth, b. 15 Apr. 1940, London, UK. University Teacher. Educ: B.A., Univ. of Exeter; Ph.D., Univ. of Cambridge. Publs: Opportunities After 'O' Level, 1965; The Sociology of British Communism, 1969. Contbr. to: Brit. Jrnl. of Pol. Sci.; Sociol.; Jrnl. of Pol.; Policy & Pol.; Acta Sociologica; Race; Pol. Studies. Mbrships: Pol. Studies Assn.; Brit. Sociol. Assn. Hons: Vis. Fellowship, Coun. of European Studies; Rsch. Fellowship, Am. Coun. of Learned Socs. Address: Nuffield College, Oxford OX1 1NF, UK.

NEWTON, Norman, b. 1929, Vancouver, B.C., Can. Radio Producer; Former Freelance Writer & Actor. Publs: The House of Gods, 1961; The One True Man, 1963; The Big Stuffed Hand of Friendship, 1969; Thomas Gage in Spanish America, 1969; Stage Plays; Fire in the Raven's Nest, 1973. Contbr. to: Contemporary Verse; Can. Poetry; Times Lit. Supplement; Can. Lit.; Essays in Criticism; Can. Forum; Alphabet; N.Y. Times. Address: 1236 W. 27th Ave., Vancouver 9, B.C., Can.

NEWTON, Robert Henry Gerald, b. 1903, London, UK. Retired. Educ: B.A., Magdalene Coll., Cambridge. Publs: Acting Improvised; Magic & Make-Believe; Show With Music; Exercise Improvisation; Together in Theatre; Ed., Twenty Minute Theatre; Ed., Miller's Medley; A Creative Approach to Amateur Theatre; Improvisation Steps Out;

Improvisation Project & Practice. Contbr. to: Drama; Amateur Stage; Town & Country Planning; Theatre & Stage; Theatre Arts Monthly; Visvabharati Quarterly; Adult Educ. Address: 3 Crawley Lane, Pound Hill, Crawley, Sussex RH10 4EB, UK.

NEY, James Walter Edward Colby, b. 28 July 1932, Nakuru, Kenya. Educator. Educ: A.B., 1955, A.M., 1958, Wheaton (Ill.) Coll.; Ed.D., Univ. of Mich., 1963. Publs. incl: Readings in the Philosophy of Science, 1969; Readings in American Society, 1969; Exploring in English, 1972; Progress in English, 1972; Adventures in English, 1972; American English for Japanese Students, 1973; Linguistics, Language Teaching & Composition in the Grades, 1974. Contbr. to num; lit. & educl. jrnls. Mbrships. incl: Mod. Langs. Assn.; Linguistic Soc. of Am. Address: Engl. Dept., Room 504, Lang. & Lit. Bldg., Coll. at Univ. St., Tempe, AZ 85281, USA.

NEY, Norbert, b. 30 June 1951, Eutin/Holstein, W. Germany. Editor; Writer. Contbr. to: (poetry anthols.) Words of the Living, 1973, 1974; My Favourite Poem, 1973; Workshop foligraf; Literatur/Manuskript; Ed., Zikade. Mbrships: Unio Cir.; Circle of the Friends of the Oldenburger Hefte. Address: 75 Karlsruhe 1, Post Box 4606, Lessing St. 56, W. Germany.

NEZNAKOMOV, Petar, b. 12 Oct. 1920, Sliven, Bulgaria. Writer. Publs: (in Bulgarian) Friday Again, 1947; In Those Days, 1960; Attila; The Scourge of God, 1961; The Petrovs, 1963; The Mystery Ship, 1967; The Painlevé Case, 1970. Contbr. to: September; Plamak; Nasha Rodina; Literatouren Front; Sturshel. Mbrships: Union of Bulgarian Writers; Union of Bulgarian Film Workers; Union of Bulgarian Jrnlsts. Hons: Silver Ring, Evening News, 1966; Choudomir Prize, 1970; Prize, Dimitrove Young Communist League, 1974. Address: Sofia-13, kv. Iztok, bl. 5, vh.B, Bulgaria.

NGHIÊM XUÂN, Viêt, pen name (for poetry) XUÂN VIÊT, b. 10 Jan. 1913, Tây-Mô, Hâ-Dông, Vietnam. Professor, Law Faculty, Saigon. Educ: LL.D. Publs: (poetry, in Vietnamese) Prelude, 1949; The Eternal Meeting, 1954; Transl. into French, Kim Vân Kiêù (Vietnamese nat. poem, w. Xuân Phúc), 1961; The Nine Dragon Hymn (in Engl.), 1966; La Trahison des Maîtres (politics, in French), 1972. Former contbr. to: (Saigon mags.) Tû Do (Liberty); Thanh Niên (Youth). Mbr., PEN (former VP & Gen. Sec., Saigon). Address: 136 B/C Lê Vǎn Duyêt, Saigon, S. Vietnam.

NGUGI, Wa Thiong'o James, b. 1936. Novelist. Educ: Univs. of Makerere & Leeds. Publs: (play) The Black Hermit, 1962; Weep Not Child, 1964; The River Between, 1965; A Grain of Wheat, 1967; Homecoming, 1972; Secret Lives, 1974. Address: c/o Heinemann Educl. Books, 48 Charles St., London W1, UK.

NGUYEN, Dang Liem, b. 6 Feb. 1936, Cho-Lon, S. Vietnam. Associate Professor of Indo-Pacific Languages. Educ: M.A., Univ. of Mich., USA, 1961; Lic.-es-Lettres, Univ. of Saigon, S. Vietnam, 1962; Ph.D., Aust. Nat. Univ., 1966. Publs. incl: English Pronunciation for Vietnamese, 1962; English Grammar, A Combined Tagmemic & Transformational Approach, 1966; A Contrastive Grammatical Analysis of English & Vietnamese, 1967; Intermediate Vietnamese, Vols. I & II, 1971; Ed., Studies in Southeast Asian Linguistics, 1973. Contbr. to: Hemisphere; Van-Hoa Nguyet-San (Min. of Educ., Saigon); etc. Hons. incl: Univ. of Hawaii Rsch. Coun. Grants, 1970, 1971. Address: 7081 Kamilo St., Honolulu, HI 96825, USA.

NGUYEN VAN LOC, b. 24 Aug. 1922, Vinh-Long, Vietnam. Lawyer; Writer; Politician. Educ: LL.M.; Univs. of Montpellier & Paris. Publs: Uprising, 1946; Rank, 1948; New Recruits, 1948; Poems on Liberation, 1949; Recollections of the Green Years, 1960; Free Tribune, 1966; Poisonous Water, 1971. Mbrships: Vietnam Red Cross; Inter-Schls. Assn.; Vietnam Assn. for Protection of Human & People's Rights; Barristers Fraternity; Former Prime Minister of S. Vietnam. Address: 162 Gia Long, Saigon, Vietnam.

NHÂT-TIÊN, Bùi, b. 24 Aug. 1936, Hanoi, Vietnam. Novelist. Publs: Devastated Threshold, 1961; The Curtain Raiser, 1962; Pearl Hands, 1965; The Unsound Sleep, 1966; Our Beloved Country, 1968; A Gift from the River, 1973; etc. Contbr. to: Ed. in Chief, Mod. Schl., The Young; Culture of Today; New Wind; Orient; Lit.; Rsch. in Lit.; Gen. Knowledge. Mbrships: Nat. Coun. of Culture & Educ.,

1974-78; Vice Chmn., Vietnamese Ctr., PEN. Recip., Nat. Lit. Prize for Novels, for Devastated Threshold, 1962. Address: No. 159 Thiều Tri, Phú Nhuận, Saigon, Vietnam.

NIBLETT, William Roy, b. 25 July 1906, Keynsham, Somerset, UK. University Professor. Educ: B.A., Univ. of Bristol; B.Litt., Univ. of Oxford. Publs: Education & the Modern Mind, 1954; Christian Education in a Secular Society, 1960; Ed., Moral Education in a Changing Society, 1963; Universities Between Two Worlds, 1974; Ed., The Sciences, The Humanities & The Technological Threat, 1975. Contbr. to: Times Higher Educ. Supplement; Univs. Quarterly; Guardian; Fortnightly; Modern Churchman. Recip., C.B.E., 1970. Address: Pinfarthings, Amberley, Stroud, Glos. GL5 5JJ, UK.

NICHOL, David McGregor, b. 29 Dec. 1911, Dundas, Ont., Can. Journalist. Educ: B.A., 1932, M.A., 1933, Univ. of Mich., USA. Contbr. to: This is Germany, 1950; Cavalcade of Europe, 1960. Recip., William the Silent Award for Jrnlsm., 1952. Address: 1 Matthews Oast, Plough Lane, Upper Harbledown, Canterbury, CT2 9AR, UK.

NICHOLAS, Barry, b. 6 July 1919, London, UK. Professor of Comparative Law; Author. Educ: M.A., Oxford Univ. Publs: Introduction to Roman Law, 1962; Jolowicz's Historical Introduction to Roman Law, 3rd. ed., 1972. Contbr. to var. legal & classical jrnls. Address: Brasenose College, Oxford, UK.

NICHOLAS, Herbert George, b. 8 June 1911, Treharris, Glam., UK. University Teacher. Educ: M.A., New Coll., Oxford; Yale Univ. Publs: The American Union, 1948; The British General Election of 1950, 1951; To the Hustings, 1956; The United Nations as a Political Institution, 1959, 5th ed., 1975; Britain & the United States, 1963; Tocqueville's De la Democratie en Amerique (ed.), 1961. Contbr. to: Listener; Econ.; Reporter; Yale Review; Encounter; Times. Mbrships: incl: Fellow, Brit. Acad., 1969; Brit. Assn. for Am. Studies; Royal Histl. Soc.; Am. Histl. Assn.; Recip., Hon. D.C.L., Univ. of Pitts., 1968. Address: New Coll., Oxford, UK.

NICHOLS, Beverley. Writer. Educ: Balliol Coll., Oxford. Publs. incl: Prelude; Patchwork; Women & Children Last; A Village in a Valley; Verdict on India; The Tree that Sat Down; All I Could Never Be, 1949; Merry Hell, 1951; Death to Slow Music, 1957; The Rich Die Hard, 1958; Murder by Request, 1960; A Case of Human Bondage, 1966; The Art of Flower Arrangement, 1967; (plays) Mesmer; Shadow of the Vine; The Sun in My Eyes, 1969; The Wickedest Witch in the World, 1971; Father Figure, 1972; Down the Kitchen Sink, 1974. Address: c/o Eric Glass, 28 Berkeley Sq., London W1, UK.

NICHOLS, Jeannette Paddock, b. Rochelle, Ill., USA. Professor of History. Educ: M.A.; Ph.D.; LL.D.; Columbia Univ., N.Y. Publs: History of Alaska; The United States in the 20th Century; The Republic of The United States, Short History of American Democracy, Growth of American Democracy, 3 vols., (w. Roy F. Nichols); James Styles & George Stuart; (ed. w. James Randall) Democracy in the Middle West. Contbr. to: Am. Hist. Review; N.Y. Times Book Review; Ency. Am.; Political Sci. Quarterly; etc. Mbr., Int. Fed. of Univ. Women. Address: Hist. Dept., Univ. of Pa., Phila., PA 19104, USA.

NICHOLS, Peter Richard, b. 1927, Bristol, UK. Writer. Educ: Bristol Old Vic Schl.; Trng. Coll. Publs: A Day in the Death of Joe Egg, 1967; The National Health, 1970; Forget-me-Not Lane, 1971; Chez Nous, 1974; The Freeway, 1975; var. TV & Film scripts, 1950-67. Contbr. to: Six Granada Plays, & New Granada Plays, 1963-64; The TV Dramatist, 1973. Agent: Margaret Ramsay Ltd. Address: 17 Dartmouth Row, London SE10, UK.

NICHOLS, Ruth, b. 1948, Toronto, Ont., Can. Author. Educ: Univ. of B.C., Vancouver; McMaster Univ., Hamilton, Ont.; B.A.; M.A. Publs: A Walk Out of the World, 1969; Ceremony of Innocence, 1969; The Marrow of the World, 1972. Mbrships. incl: VP, India's Medal for Creative Writing, 1962; Fellow, Can. Coun., 1971-74. Recip., Book of the Yr. Award, Can. Assn. of Children's Libns. Address: c/o The MacMillan Co. of Can. Ltd., 70 Bond St., Toronto, Ont., Can.

NICHOLSON, Gerald William Lingen, b. 6 Jan. 1902, Weston-Super-Mare, UK. Soldier; Military Historian; Educ: B.A., Queen's Univ., Kingston, Ont., Can., 1931; B.Paed.,

Ont. Coll. of Educ., 1935. Publs. incl: The Fighting Newfoundlanders, 1963; The White Cross in Canada: A History of St. John Ambulance, 1967; More Fighting Newfoundlanders, 1969; The Gunners of Canada: The History of the Royal Regiment of Canadian Artillery, vol. I, 1967, vol. II, 1972. Contbr. to: Can. Army Jrnl.; Can. Histl. Review. Mbrships: Sec., Can. Histl. Assn., 1957-61; Royal United Serv. Instn. Recip., J. B. Tyrrell Gold Medal, Royal Soc. of Can., 1968. Address: 1101 Bronson Place, Ottawa, Can.

NICHOLSON, Hubert, b. 23 Jan. 1908, Hull, UK. Novelist; Former Journalist. Publs: Half My Days & Nights (autobiog.), 1941; New Spring Song (poems), 1943; Here Where the World is Quiet, 1944; A Voyage to Wonderland (essays), 1947; The Sacred Afternoon, 1949; Little Heyday, 1954; The Mirage in the South (poems), 1955; Sunk Island, 1956; Mr. Hill & Friends, 1960; Patterns of Three & Four, 1965; The Lemon Tree, 1970; Dead Man's Life, 1971; Ella, 1973. Contbr. to: PEN anthols.; Guinness Book of Poetry; Grigson's Poetry of the Present; Best Poems of 1955; The Terrible Rain (war poems); var. jrnls. & mags. Mbrships: Fellow, PEN; Fellow, Int. Inst. of Arts & Letters; Life, Nat. Union of Jrnlsts. Address: Kertch Cottage, 3 Albert Rd., Epsom, UK.

NICHOLSON, Joyce, b. 1 June 1919, Melbourne, Australia. Publisher; Writer. Educ: B.A., Melbourne Univ. Publs: Our First Overlander, 1944; Adventure at Gull's Point; Gull's Point & Pineapple; Man Against Mutiny, 1966; Freedom for Priscilla, 1974. Contbr. to: Aust. Audio Visual News; Ed., Austn. Bookseller & Publr. Mbrships: PEN; Aust. Soc. of Authors; Royal Histl. Soc. of Vic.; Lyceum. Recip., 2nd Prize, Victorian Centenerary Histl. Lit. Competition. Address: 26 Fordholm Rd., Hawthorn 3122, Melbourne, Australia.

NICHOLSON, Lillie Margaret, pen name A VAGABOND SCHOOLMARM, b. 1 July 1892, Burrton, Kan., USA. Teacher. Educ: B.S., Hays State Tchrs., Kan., 1929; Master's degree, Kan. State Univ., 1934; Master Tchr.'s Cert., Kan. Univ., 1954. Publs: Zig Zags; Compilation of Weekly Columns in the Newton Kansan, 1952-55; Freedom Has a Happy Ring (contbng. author), 1959. Contbr. to var. lit. jrnls. Mbrships: Kan. State Tchrs. Assn.; Nat. Ret'd Tchrs.' Assn.; Creative Writers' Club, Newton, Kan.; Kan. Authors' Club; S.D. Poetry Soc. Recip., Prize for Article in Freedom Has a Happy Ring, Kan. Bulletin for Pub. Schls., 1959. Address: 818 Spruce St., Newton, KS 67114, USA.

NICHOLSON, Margaret Beda, pen name YORKE, Margaret, b. 1924, Surrey, UK. Author; Librarian. Publs: Summer Flight, 1957; Pray Love Remember, 1958; Christopher, 1959; Deceiving Mirror, 1960; The China Doll, 1961; Once a Stranger, 1962; The Birthday, 1963; Full Circle, 1965; No Fury, 1967; The Apricot Bed, 1968; The Limbo Ladies, 1969; Dead in the Morning, 1970. Contbr. to: Homes & Gardens. Mbrships: Soc. of Authors; Crime Writers' Assn. Address: Oriel Cottage, Long Crendon, Bucks., UK.

NICHOLSON, Norman Cornthwaite, b. 8 Jan. 1914, Millom, UK. Author. Publs: Five Rivers; The Pot Geranium; The Old Man of the Mountains; William Cowper, 1951; H. G. Wells; Cumberland & Westmorland; Provincial Pleasures; Man & Literature; The Lakers, 1955; Selected Poems, 1966; Portrait of the Lakes, 1963; Greater Lakeland, 1969; A Local Habitation, 1972; Wednesday Early Closing, 1975; Ed., The Penguin Anthology of Religious Verse. Contbr. to: Times Lit. Supplement; Ch. Times. Hons: Heinemann Prize, 1945; M.A., Univ. of Manchester, 1958; Cholmondeley Award, 1967; Soc. of Authors Travel Award, 1973; M.A., Open Univ., 1975. Agent: David Higham Assocs. Address: 14 St. George's Terrace, Millom, Cumbria, UK.

NICHOLSON, Roy Stephen, Sr., b. 12 July 1903, Wallahall, S.C., USA. Clergyman; Administrator; Educator. Educ: Ctrl. Wesleyan Acad.; Th.B., Ctrl. Schl. of Relig.; Pvte. study & ext. sources. Publs. incl: Wesleyan Methodism in the South, 1933; The History of the Wesleyan Methodist Church, 2 rev. ed., 1951, 1959; Studies in Church Doctrines, 1943, 1958; Arminian Emphases, 1962; A Valid Theology for Our Day, 1963. Contbr. to jrnls. & var. books. Address: 2035 Melody Lane, Brooksville, FL 33512, USA.

NICK, Dagmar, b. 30 May 1926, Breslau, Germany. Writer. Publs: (poetry) Märtyrer, 1947; Das Buch Holofernes, 1955; In den Ellipsen des Mondes, 1959; Zeugnis und Zeichen, 1969; (prose) Einladung nach Israel,

1963; Einladung nach Rhodos, 1967; Israel, gestern und heute, 1968. Mbrships. incl: German Authors' Assn. (VS); PEN. Hons. incl: Ehrengabe zum Gryphius Prize, 1970. Address: Uhlandstr. 3, 7501 Karlsbad 1, W. Germany.

NICKELS, Sylvie, b. 10 Oct. 1930, Neuchâtel, Switz. Travel writer. Publs: The Young Traveller in Finland, 1962; Travellers' Guide to Finland, 1965; Assassination in Sarejevo, 1966; The Young Traveller in Yugoslavia, 1967; Caxton & the Early Printers, 1968; Travellers' Guide to Yugoslavia, 1969; Scott & the Discovery of the Antarctic, 1972; The Vikings (in preparation); Iceland (in preparation); Co-ed., Finland, an Introduction, 1973. Contbr. to: Financial Times. Daily Telegraph; Country Life; Illustrated London News; A.A. touring books. Mbrships: Guild of Travel Writers; Royal Geog. Soc.; Nat. Book League. Address: 29 Northfield, Girton, Cambridge CB3 0QG, UK.

NICKSON, Hilda, pen names PRESSLEY, Hilda; PRESTON, Hilary, b. 18 Nov. 1912, Maltby, Rotherham, Yorks., UK. Writer. Publs: 56 novels, 1957—. Mbrships: V.P., Romantic Novelists' Assn.; Sec., E. Anglian Writers. Address: "Artilda", The Street, Dilham, N. Walsham, Norfolk, UK.

NICOL, Davidson Sylvester Hector Willoughby, pen name NICOL, Abioseh, b. 14 Sept. 1924, Freetown, Sierra Leone. Ambassador. Educ: B.A. 1946, M.A., M.D., Ph.D., Christ's Coll., Cambridge Univ., UK. Publs: Alienation: An Essay, 1960; Africa: A Subjective View, 1964; The Truly Married Woman & Other Stories, 1965; Two African Tales, 1965; Africanus Horton, 1969 (as Black Nationalism in Africa, 1967, USA, 1969). Contbr. to num. verse anthols. Mbr., num. civic, educl. & int. orgs. Hons. incl: Independence Medal, Sierra Leone, 1961: C.M.G., 1964; var. docts., UK & USA. Address: High Commission of Sierra Leone, 33 Portland Pl., London W1, UK.

NICOL, Donald MacGillivray, b. 1923, Portsmouth, Hants., UK. University Professor of Byzantine & Modern Greek. Educ: M.A., Ph.D., Pembroke Coll., Cambridge; Brit. Schl. of Archaeol., Athens. Publs: The Despotate of Epiros, 1957; Meteora, The Rock Monasteries of Thessaly, 1963; The Byzantine Family of Kantakouzenos (Cantacuzenus) ca. 1100-1460: a Genealogical & Prosopographical Study, 1968; The Last Centuries of Byzantium, 1261-1453, 1972; Byzantium: its Ecclesiastical History & Relations with the Western World, 1972. Contbr. to: Cambridge Medieval Hist.; Ency. Britannica; sev. acad. jrnls. Mbr., Royal Irish Acad. Address: King's Coll., Univ. of London, Strand, London WC2R 2LS, UK.

NICOL, Eric Patrick, pen name JABEZ, b. 28 Dec. 1919, Kingston, Ont., Can. Writer. Educ: M.A., Univ. of B.C., 1948; Univ. of Sorbonne, Paris, France. Publs. incl: Sense & Nonsense, 1948; The Roving I, 1951; Shall we Join The Ladies? , 1955; Girdle Me a Globe, 1957; In Darkest Domestica, 1959; History of Canada, 1960; Russia Anyone? , 1963; Space Age Go Home, 1964; 100 Years of What? , 1966; A Scar is Born, 1968; Vancouver, 1970; Still a Nicol; Letters to My Son; (plays) Regulus; Like Father, Like Fun. Contbr. to: Can. Broadcasting Corp.; Recip. Leacock Award for Humor, 1951, 1955, 1957. Address: 3993 W. 36th Ave., Vancouver V6N 2S7, Can.

NICOLAEFF, Ariadne, b. Odessa, USSR. Producer; Writer; Translator. Publs: (plays) Lock & Key, 1956; The Promise by Arbuzov (transl.); Ivanov by Chekov (transl.); The Twelfth Hour by Arbuzov (transl.); Confession at Night by Arbuzov (transl.); The Third Wife, 1973; A Month in the Country by Turgenev (transl.), 1974. Contbr. to: Times; BBC Talks; Evening Standard; Theatre Newsletter. Agent: John Cadell Ltd. Address: BM-Box 8855, London WC1V 6XX, UK.

NICOLE, Christopher Robin, pen names YORK, Andrew; GRANGE, Peter; CADE, Robin, b. 7 Dec. 1930, Georgetown, Guyana. Author. Educ: Fellow, Can. Bankers' Assn. Publs. incl: West Indian Cricket, 1957; Off White, 1959; Ratoon, 1962; The Amyot Trilogy, 1965; The West Indies, 1965; White Boy, 1966; The Eliminator series, 1967-; The Thunder & the Shouting, 1969; Caribee, 1974; The Fear Dealer, 1974; The Devil's Own & The Fascinator, 1975. Mbrships. incl: Crime Writers' Assn.; Authors' Guild, Am. Inc. Address: S. Grange de Beauvoir, St. Peter Port, Guernsey, Channel Islands, UK.

NICOLL, Allardyce, b. 1894, Glasgow, UK. Professor of English. Educ: M.A.; Univ. of Glasgow. Publs: The

Development of the Theatre; Film & Theatre; The theory of Drama, Masks, Mimes & Miracles; Stuart Masques & the Renaissance Stage; British Drama; World Drama; A History of English Drama, 1660-1900, 6 vols.; The Elizabethans; The Works of Cyril Tourneur; Shakespeare; The English Stage; The World of Harlequin; Theatre & Dramatic Theory; English Drama, 1900-30. Ed., Shakespeare Survey, 1948-65. Contbr. to: Times Lit. Supp.; Mod. Lang. Review; etc. Recip., sev. hon. degrees. Address: Wind's Acre, Colwall, Malvern, Worcs., UK.

NICOLSON, Lionel Benedict, b. 6 Aug. 1914, Sevenoaks, Kent, UK. Editor; Author. Educ: B.A., Balliol Coll., Oxford. Publs: Hendrick Terbrugghen, 1958; Wright of Derby, Painter of Light, 1968; Georges de la Tour (w. Christopher Wright), 1974. Contbr. to: Burlington Mag.; Observer; New Statesman. Hons: M.V.O., 1947; C.B.E., 1971. Address: 45 B, Holland Park, London W11, UK.

NICOLSON, Robert, b. Glasgow, UK. Writer. Publs: Love Is a Sickness, 1938; The Gradual Day, 1950; Mrs. Ross, 1961; The Whisperers, 1961 2nd ed., 1966; A Flight of Steps, 1966, 2nd ed., 1967. Contbr. to: Best Short Stories, 1937; Adelphi Mag.; London Mercury; Spectator; Glasgow Herald; also short stories, radio & TV. Recip., M.B.E., 1972. Address: 66 Kelvin Drive, Glasgow G20 8QN, UK.

NIEBURG, Harold L., b. 26 Nov. 1927, Phila., Pa., USA. University Professor. Educ: Ph.B., 1947; A.M., 1952, Ph.D., 1961, Univ. of Chgo. Publs: Nuclear Secrecy & Foreign Policy, 1964; In the Name of Science, 1966; Political Violence: The Behavioral Process, 1969; Culture Storm: Politics & the Ritual Order, 1973; La violenza politica, 1974. Contbr. to: Annals of Am. Acad. of Pol. & Soc. Sci.; Current; Jrnl. of Conflict Resolution; Nation; Am. Behavioral Sci.; Am. Econ. Review; Dissent; Sci.; World Pols.; etc. Mbrships: AAAS; Am. Pol. Sci. Assn.; N.W. Pol. Sci. Assn. Address: RD 2, Rockwell Rd., Vestal, NY 13850, USA.

NIELSEN, Torben, b. 22 Apr. 1918, Vedslet, Denmark. Author. Publs: Gry, 1969; Aret Rundt, 1970; Tilfaeldet Lisa Kjeldsen, 1971; Taendstikleg, 1972; Mig og Min Bedstemor, 1972; 30 Meter Ned, 1973; Galgesangen, 1973; Nitten Røde Roser, 1973; Hvad Laver Politiet? , 1973; Nold Og Gangsterne, 1974; Enkejagt, 1975.Mbr., Danish Authors' Club. Recip., Edgar Allan Poe Prize, for Nitten Røde Roser, 1974. Address: Grumstrup, 8732 Hovedgård, Denmark.

NIEMINEN, Anna-Maija, pen name RAITTILA, Anna-Maija, b. 23 July 1928, Joensuu, Finland. Writer. Educ: B.Th. Publs: (collects. of poems) Ruiskukkaehtoo, 1947, 4th ed., 1961; Sateenkaari, 1968; Sinitiaisten Tanssi, 1969; Keskipäivän Pilvi, 1972; Anna Meidät Kaikki Toisillemme, 1974. Contbr. to: Communion. Mbrships: Soc. of Writers, Finland; Soc. of Transls., Finland; PEN. Hons: 2 State Prizes, Hungary & Finland, 1971; 2 Publrs. Lit. Prizes, 1968, 1972. Address: Kimmeltie 26 C 24, 02100 Tapiola, Finland.

NIEMINEN, Hannu Pertti, b. 29 June 1929, Vaasa, Finland. Teacher. Educ: Tchrs.' Trng. Coll., Helsinki. Publs. incl: Kiinalaisia kertojia (prose, transl. from Chinese), 1958; Syksyn ääni (poetry, transl. from Chinese), 1966; Rautaportista tulevat (lyrics), 1968; Virralla (poetry, transl. from Chinese), 1970; Niin kiire tässä elämässä (lyrics), 1972; Mao Tse-tung, Runot (poetry, transl. from Chinese), 1973; transls. of over 30 dramas. Contbr. to sev. mags. Mbrships: Finnish Soc. of Authors; Soc. of Transls. Recip., num. prizes. Address: SF-05510 Päivärinta, Finland.

NIENABER, Gabriël Stephanus, b. 12 Nov. 1903, Fauresmith, S. Africa. Professor of Afrikaans. Educ: M.A. & M.Ed., Univ. of Orange Free State; D.Phil. & Litt., Univ. of Ghent, Belgium. Publs: Oor die Afrikaanse taal, 1934; Klaas Waarzegger se samespraak, 1940; Oor Afrikaans, part 1, 1949, part 2, 1953; Bluettes by Charles Etienne Boniface, early Natal author & wit, 1963; Hottentots, 1963; Afrikaanse etimologieë (w. Prof. S.P.E. Boshoff), 1967; Louis Meurant, 1968; Afrikaans in die vroeë jare, 1971. Contbr. to num. jrnls. & books. Mbr. profl. orgs. Recip. many hons. Address: Woodhouseweg 57, Scottsville, Pietermaritzburg 3201, Repub. of S. Africa.

NIENABER, Petrus Johannes, pen names, van NIEKERK, I. R.; de VILLIERS, Ryno B.; ROUSSEAU, J. J., b. 1 Oct. 1910, Fauresmith, Bloemfontein, S. Africa.

Professor; Institute Director. Educ: B.A. & M.A., Univ. of S. Africa; D.Litt. et Phil., Amsterdam, Netherlands. Publs: Geskiedenis van die Afrikaanse Letterkunde (co-author), 1941; Bibliografie van Afrikaanse Boeke, 7 vols., 1943-71; Bronnegids by die studie van die Afrikaanse Taalen Letterkunde, 6 vols., 1947-69; Perspektief en Profiel, 1951. Contbr. to var. periodicals. Mbr., sev. profl. orgs. Recip., sev. hons. Address: c/o Nat. Afrikaans Lit. Mus. & Rsch. Ctr., P.O. Box 517, Bloemfontein, Repub. of S. Africa.

NIESEWAND, Peter, b. 30 June 1944, Johannesburg, S. Africa. Journalist. Publs: In Camera, 1973. Contbr. to: The Guardian (reporter, 1973—); Daily Mail; Observer; C'wlth.; Africa Report; Africa Confidential; BBC; former Rhodesia Corres. for var. agcys. & broadcasting Cos. Mbr., Nat. Union Jrnlsts. Hons: IPC Int. Jrnlst. of the Yr., 1974. Agent: John Farquarson Ltd. Address: c/o The Guardian, 192 Gray's Inn Rd., London WC1X 8EY, UK.

NIGHTINGALE, Gay, b. Sydenham, London, UK. Writer. Educ: London Univ.; Open Univ. Publs: ABC of Potted Plants, 1973; (part-author) Michael Barratt's Down-to-Earth Gardening Book, 1974. Contbr. to: Garden News. Mbrships: Fellow, Royal Horticultural Soc. Address: Lavender House, 47 Lechmere Ave., Chigwell, Essex, UK.

NIJHUIS, Harry, pen name (wine & beer-making publs.), WIJNHUIS, Herman, b. 28 Sept. 1941, Zutphen, Netherlands. Journalist. Educ: Journalism at College. Publs: Thuis gemaakte landwijnen en bier (Home-made wines & beers), 1973; prose writing in literary series. Contbr. to: Boererij-Magazine; sev. hobby mags. Mbr., NVJ Amsterdam (Dutch Union of Jrnlsts.). Address: Maandagsdijk 2, Barchem (Gld), Netherlands.

NIKLAUS, Robert, b. 18 July 1910, London, UK. Professor of French, Univ. of Exeter. Educ: Univ. of London; B.A.; Ph.D.; L.ès.L. Publs: Rousseau, Rêveries du Promeneur Solitaire; Marivaux, Arlequin poli par l'amour, (w. T. Niklaus); Diderot, Pensées Philosophiques; Diderot, Lettre sur les aveugles; Diderot & Drama; French Prose Composition; French Unseens; Beaumarchais Le Barbier de Séville; A Literary History of France; The Eighteenth Century; Gen. Ed., Textes Français Classiques & Modernes. Contbr. to: Ency. Britannica; Chambers Ency.; Mod. Lang. Review, etc. Mbrships: incl: Pres., Soc. for French Studies, 1968-70; Treas., Int. Soc. for 18th Century Studies, 1968—. Hons: Dr., Univ. of Rennes, France; Off., Ordre National du Mérite. Address: 17 Elm Grove Rd., Topsham, Exeter, Devon, UK.

NIKOLAI, Lorraine C., b. 20 Feb. 1910, Wausau, Wis., USA. Sales Representative. Contbr. to: Rib Mountain Echoes, Vol. I, 1963, Vol. II, 1967; Wausau Writers' Anthol. Vol. I, 1974; Wausau Daily Record Herald; Times Review. Mbrships: Wausau Writers Grp. (23 yrs.); Wis. Regional Writers' Assn.; var. civic & Ch. orgs. Hons: Cert., Int. Who's Who in Poetry, UK; Cert. of Lit., Centro Studi e Scambi Int., Rome, Italy. Address: 701 Humboldt Ave., Wausau, WI 54401, USA.

NIKOLENKO, Lada, b. 18 Dec. 1917, Leningrad, USSR. Art Historian. Educ: B.Phil., Inst. of For. Langs., Leningrad; M.A., Inst. of Fine Arts, N.Y. Univ., USA. Publs: Francesco Ubertini called il Bacchiacca; Wie Staub aus der Steppe. Contbr. to: Sovremennik; Gazette des Beaux Arts; The Connoisseur; Apollo; Pantheon; Grani; Sev. Russian emigré jrnls. Former mbr., Collage Art Assn. of Am. Address: 8 Munich 21, Geyerspergerstr. 38, W. Germany.

NIKULA, Karl Oscar, b. 31 May 1907, Vasa, Finland. University Professor of History. Educ: M.A., 1928, Ph.D., 1934, Abo Akademi. Publs: Svenska skärgardsflottan 1756-1791, 1933; Tenala och Bromarf socknars historia, 1938; Augustin Ehrensvärd, 1960; Abo stads historia 1721-1809, 1972; Abo stads historia 1809-1856, 1974. Mbrships: Rsch. Mbr., Finska historiska samfundet, 1952; Societas Scientiarum Fennica, 1953; K.Hum. Vetenskapssamfundet i Lund, 1965; Rsch. Mbr., Turn hist. Yhdistys, 1967. Hons: Falckenska priset, 1939, Hedvig von Schantz pris, 1961, Eklund-Modeenska priset, 1974, Svenska litt.sällskapet i Finland. Address: Slottsg.28 A, 20100 Abo 10, Finland.

NILSON, Amabel Rhoda, pen name NILSON, Bee, b. 22 Nov. 1908, Rotherham, NZ. Author; Retired Lecturer in Nutrition. Educ: BH Sc., Otago Univ.; Dip. Ed., Univ. of London, UK; State Registered Dietician. Publs: Penguin Cookery Book, 1952; Book of Meat Cookery, 1962;

Cooking for Special Diets, 1964; Herb Cookery, 1974; Bee Nilson's Slimming Guide, 1974. Mbrships: Brit. Dietetic Assn.; NZ Dietetic Assn.; Soc. of Authors. Address: 43A Coolhurst Rd., London N8 8ET, UK.

NILSSON, Nils Åke, b. 1 Sept. 1917, Karlskrona, Sweden. Professor of Russian Language & Literature. Educ: Ph.D., 1950. Publs: Gogol et Pétersbourg, 1954; Ibsen in Russland, 1958; Russian Heraldic Virši, 1964; Studies in Chekhov's Narrative Technique, 1968; The Russian Imaginists, 1970; Rysk Litteratur från Tjechov till Solsjenitsyn, 1973; Osip Madel'štam: Five Poems, 1974. Contbr. to: Russian Literature (ed.); Stockholm Slavic Studies (ed.); Scandolslavica (co-ed.). Mbrships: Royal Acad. of Letters, Hist. & Antiquities; Int. Dostoevsky Soc. (Pres.); AILLS (Pres.). Recip., Elsa Thulin Transl. Prize, 1965; Address: Tegnérlunden 12, 113 59 Stockholm, Sweden.

NIN, Anaïs, b. 21 Feb. 1903, Paris, France. Writer. Publs: D. H. Lawrence: An Unprofessional Study, 1932; House of Incest, 1936; Winter of Artifice, 1939; Under a Glass Bell; Ladders to Fire; Children of the Albatross (1940s); The Four-Chambered Heart; A Spy in the House of Love (1950s); Seduction of the Minotaur, 1961; Collages, 1964; Diary, 5 vols., 1966— (vols. I & II also recorded by the author for Spoken Arts Inc.). Contbr. to: Travel Leisure; Playgirl; Westways; MS. Mbrships: PEN; Acad. of Arts & Letters, 1974. Hons: Prix Sevigné, 1970; Doct., Phila. Coll. of Art, 1971; Doct., Dartmouth Coll. Address: Box 26598, L.A., CA 90026, USA.

NINEHAM, Dennis Eric, b. 27 Sept. 1921, Southampton, UK. University Teacher. Educ: B.A., M.A., B.D., Oxford Univ.; B.D., Cambridge Univ. Publs: A New Way of Looking at the Gospels, 1961; The Gospel of St. Mark, 1963; Ed., Studies in the Gospels, 1966; Ed., The Church's Use of the Bible, 1963. Contbr. to: Jrnl. Theol. Studies; Expository Times; Theol.; Biblica; etc. Hons: D.D. Birmingham Univ.; D.D. Berkeley Divinity Schl., New Haven, Conn., USA. Address: Keble Coll., Oxford OX1 3PG, UK.

NISBET, Stanley Donald, b. 26 July 1912, Isafjordur, Iceland. Professor of Education. Educ: M.A., 1934, M.Ed., 1940, Edinburgh Univ. Publs: Purpose in the Curriculum, 1957. Contbr. to: Mental Measurements Yrbook.; Brit. Jrnl. of Educl. Psychol.; Scottish Educl. Studies. Mbrships: Royal Soc. of Edinburgh; Brit. Psychol. Soc. Address: 6 Victoria Park Corner, Glasgow G14 9NZ, UK.

NISH, Ian H., b. 1926, Edinburgh, UK. Reader in International History. Educ: Edinburgh Univ.; London Univ.; M.A.; Ph.D. Publs: The Anglo-Japanese Alliance, 1962; The Story of Japan, UK & USA 1968; Alliance in Decline, 1972. Mbrships: Assn. Asian Studies; Histl. Assn. Address: Oakdene, Charlwood Dr., Oxshott, Surrey, UK.

NITYANANDAN, Perumpilavil Madhava Menon, b. 4 Nov. 1926, Palghat, Kerala, India. Mechanical Engineer; Company Director. Educ: B.Eng. (Mech.), Madras Univ., 1947. Publs: The Long, long days, 1960. Contbr. short stories & articles to: Illustrated Weekly of India; Times of India. Mbrships: incl: Gears Comm., Indian Standards Inst.; Zonal Comm., Indian Soc. of Tribol.; Nat. Productivity Coun. of India; Alliance Française of Madras. Address: "The Wabe", 15 Arundalenagar, Madras 60041, India.

NIVEN, Sir (Cecil) Rex, b. 20 Nov. 1898, Otaru, Japan. Administrator; Author. Educ: B.A., M.A., Balliol Coll., Oxford, UK. Publs: A Short History of Nigeria, 1937- (13 eds.); How Nigeria Is Governed, 1950; My Life (w. late Sardauna of Sokoto), 1962; Nine Great Africans, 1964; War of Nigerian Unity, 1970. Hons: M.C., 1918; C.M.G., 1953; Kt. Bach., 1960. Address: Old Cottage, Hope Road, Deal, Kent, UK.

NIVEN, David, b. 1 Mar. 1910. Actor; Producer. Educ: R.M.C. Sandhurst. Publs: Round the Rugged Rocks, 1951; The Moon's a Balloon, 1971. Films: Wuthering Heights; Dawn Patrol; Raffles; The Elusive Pimpernel; Silken Affair; The Little Hut; Bonjour Tristesse; Separate Tables; Ask any Girl; The Guns of Navarone; The Best of Enemies; 55 Days at Peking; The Pink Panther; Prudence & the Pill; Before Winter Comes; The Brain; The Statue; King, Queen, Knave. Hons: Acad. Award, 1959; NY Critics' Award, 1960. Address: c/o Coutts & Co., 440 Strand, London WC2, UK.

NIXON, Joan Lowery, b. 3 Feb. 1927, L.A., Calif., USA. Author; Instructor in Creative Writing. Educ: B.A.,

Univ. of S. Calif.; Elem. Educ. Credential, Calif. State Coll. Publs. incl: Mystery of the Haunted Woods, 1967; Mystery of the Secret Stowaway, 1968; Delbert, the Plainclothes Detective, 1971; The Alligator Under the Bed, 1974; The Secret Box Mystery, 1974; The Mysterious Red Tape Gang, 1974; This I Can Be, 1975; People & Me, 1975. Contbr. to var. writers' confs. Mbrships: Charter Mbr., Assoc. Authors of Children's Lit., Soc. of Children's Book Writers. Hons: Jr. Lit. Guild Selection, 1974. Address: 8602 Shadowcrest, Houston, TX 77036, USA.

NKETIA, J. H. Kwabena, b. 22 June 1921, Mampong Ashanti, Ghana. Professor. Educ: B.A., Univ. of London, 1949. Publs: Funeral Dirges of the Akan People, 1955; African Music in Ghana, 1962; Drumming in Akan Communities, 1963; Folk Songs of Ghana, 1963; The Music of Africa, 1974. Contbr. to: Ethnomusicol.; African Music; Daedalus; Jrnl. of the Int. Folk Music Coun. Mbrships: Soc. for Ethnomusicol.; Hon. Fellow, Royal Anthropol. Inst.; Fellow, Ghana Acad. of Arts & Sci.; Int. Soc. for Music Educ. Hons: Grand Medal, Govt. of Ghana, 1968; Osborne Award, African Music Soc. Address: Inst. of African Studies, Univ. of Ghana, Legon, Ghana.

NOBBS, David Gordon, b. 13 Mar. 1935, Orpington, UK. Writer. Educ: B.A., Univ. of Cambridge. Publs: The Itinerate Lodger, 1965; Ostrich Country, 1968; A Piece of the Sky is Missing, 1969; The Death of Reginald Perrin, 1975; Num. TV Comedy scripts inclng: The Two Ronnies; Sez Les. Agent: Jonathan Clowes. Address: 195 High St., Barnet, Herts., UK.

NOBLE, Barbara Margaret, b. 1907, Hendon, Middx., UK. Writer. Publs: The Years That Take the Best Away, 1930; The Wave Breaks, 1932; Down by the Salley Gardens, 1935; The House Opposite, 1943; Doreen, 1946; Another Man's Life, 1952. Contbr. to films (London story ed., 20th Century-Fox, 1940-50). Mbr., PEN. Address: Greythorpe, Packhorse Rd., Gerrards Cross, Bucks., UK.

NOEL, Sterling, b. 28 Mar. 1903, San Fran., Calif., USA. Writer; Editor. Educ: Univ. of Calif.; Columbia Univ.; Univ. of Paris. Publs: I Killed Stalin, 1951; Few Die Well, 1953; To Paris with Love, 1954; Hydra-Head, 1955; Storm Over Paris, 1955; Run for Your Life, 1958; Prelude to Murder, 1959; We Who Survived, 1959; Empire of Evil, 1961. Contbr. to jrnls. & mags.; Columnist, Hearst newspapers. Mbr., Dramatists Guild, Authors League of Am. Address: c/o Agent, Robert P. Mills Ltd., 156 East 52nd St., N.Y., NY 10022, USA.

NOEL HUME, Ivor, pen name AKERMAN, Richard, b. 1927, Chelsea, London, UK. Archaeologist. Publs: Archaeology in Britain, 1953; Treasure in the Thames, 1956; Great Moments in Archaeology, 1957; Here Lies Virginia, 1963; 1775: Another Part of the Field, 1966; Historical Archaeology, 1969; Artifacts of Colonial America, 1970; All the Best Rubbish, 1974; (as R. Akerman) The Charlestown Scheme, 1971; The Truth about Fort Fussocks, 1972. Contbr. to: Connoisseur; Antiques; Country Life; Apollo; Illustrated London News; Listener; etc. Mbrships: F.S.A. Agent: A. P. Watt; Curtis Brown. Address: P.O. Box 1711, Williamsburg, VA 23185, USA.

NOËL-PATON, Margaret Hamilton, b. 21 Jan. 1896, Bombay, India. Writer. Publs. incl: Tales of a Grand-daughter — A Memoir of the Artist Sir Noël Paton, Queen's Limner for Scotland 1866-1901, 1970; 3 books of verse; sev. short plays. Contbr. to radio progs. & jrnls. inclng: Blackwood's Mag.; Scots Mag.; Good Housekeeping; Country Life. Mbr., Soc. of Authors. Address: Braecot, Hopeman, Elgin, Moray IV30 2SL, UK.

NOLAN, Jeannette Covert, b. 1897, Evansville, Ind., USA, d. 10 Dec. 1974. Former University Lecturer. Publs: Florence Nightingale; Gather Ye Rosebuds; Joan of Arc; Sudden Squall; Abraham Lincoln. Agent: N. G. Macintosh. Address: 25 Northview Drive, Indianapolis, Indiana, USA.

NOLAN, William Francis, b. 6 Mar. 1928, Kansas City, Mo., USA. Author. Publs: 30 books, inclng: Adventure on Wheels, 1959; Barney Oldfield, 1961; Phil Hill: Yankee Champion, 1962; John Huston: King Rebel, 1965; Logan's Run, 1967; Dashiell Hammett: A Casebook, 1969; Space for Hire, 1971; Alien Horizons, 1974; Hemingway: The Last Days of the Lion, 1974; The Ray Bradbury Companion, 1975. Contbr. to: Prairie Schooner; Sports Illustrated; Playboy; Coronet; Rd. & Track; L.A. Times; Alfred Hitchcock's Mystery Mag.; etc. Mbrships. incl: 1st

Printings of Am. Authors Comm., Writers Guild of Am.; Film Comm., Mystery Writers of Am. Hons. incl: Edgar Allan Poe Award, 1970 & 1972. Address: 1337½ S. Roxbury Dr., Los Angeles, CA, USA.

NOONAN, Michael John, b. 19 Sept. 1921, Christchurch, NZ. Author: Radio, TV, & Screen Scriptwriter. Educ: Univ. of Sydney, Aust. Num. publs. incl: In the Land of the Talking Trees, 1946; The Golden Forest, 1947; The Patchwork Hero, 1958; Flying Doctor, 1961; Flying Doctor on the Great Barrier Reef, 1961; The December Boys, 1963; Air Taxi, 1967; The Pink Beach, 1969; Flying Doctor under the Desert, 1969; The Sun is God, 1973; num. radio & TV plays. Mbrships: Soc. of Authors; Writers Guild of GB; Soc. of Aust. Writers (London); Aust. Soc. of Authors; Authors Guild of Am. Address: 231 Park West, London W2 2QL, UK.

NOOTHOVEN VAN GOOR, Mary, b. 28 Dec. 1911, Amsterdam, Netherlands. Painter. Educ: Conservatoire of Music, Amsterdam. Publs: Sarabande, 1952, 6 later eds. under title Het meisje Jennifer (The Girl Jennifer); Vrome Heidenen (Pious Heathen), 1954. Mbr., Soc. of Authors. Address: Stichtstraat 7, Amsterdam Zuid, Netherlands.

NORBECK, Edward, b. 18 Mar. 1915, Prince Albert, Sask., Can. (now US citizen). Anthropologist; University Professor. Educ: B.A., 1948, M.A., 1949, Ph.D., Anthropol., 1952, Univ. of Mich. Publs: Takashima, a Japanese Fishing Community, 1954; Pineapple Town — Hawaii, 1959; Religion in a Primitive Society, 1961; co-ed., Prehistoric Man in the New World, 1964; Changing Japan, 1965; Sr. Contbng. Ed., The Study of Personality, 1968; Religion & Society in Modern Japan, 1970; Sr. Contbng. Ed., The Study of Japan in the Behavioral Sciences, 1970; Religion in Human Life, 1974. Contbr. to profl. jrnls. Recip., num. fellowships & scholarships. Address: 2420 Locke Lane, Houston, TX 77019, USA.

NORDAHL, June Olga, b. Jersey City, N.J., USA. Writer; Poet; Singer; Songwriter; Bible Schlr. Educ. incl: A.B., Geo. Wash. Univ., Wash. D.C., 1950; Georgetown Law Ctr., Wash. D.C., 1959-64. Publs: Love Is A Silver Door (poetry), 1964; Life Is But A Bubble (poetry), 1964; The Woman On A Cloud, An Invocation to Aphrodite (poetry), 1965; The Boy From Lemuria, Companion to Women on a Cloud (poetry), 1965; Once Each Spring (play), 1966; The Black Widow (play), 1967. Contbr. to jrnls. & newspapers. Mbrships. incl: Am. Newspapers Women's Club. Hons. incl: Pres. Medallion for Ldrship., George Wash. Univ., 1957; Address: 2060 Mountain Ave., Scotch Plains, NJ 07076, USA.

NORDEN, Denis, b. 6 Feb. 1922. Scriptwriter; Broadcaster. Served RAF, 1942-45. Prods: (w. Frank Muir) Take it From Here; Bedtime with Braden; And so to Bentley; Whack-O; The Seven Faces of Jim; (films, w/out Frank Muir) The Bliss of Mrs. Blossom; Buona Sera Mrs. Campbell; The Best House in London; Every Home Should Have One; Twelve Plus One; The Statue; num. TV & radio panel games, revues & scripts. Recip., Screenwriters' Guild Award, 1961. Address: 170 Piccadilly, London W1, UK.

NORDEN, Heinz, b. 1905, London, UK. Author; Editor; Translator. Educ: Univ. of Chgo., Ill., USA. Publs: Einstein on Peace, (w. O. Nathan), 1960. Transl: About 50 works inclng: Friedlander, Early Netherlands Art, 14 vols., 1967; Ritter, The Sword & the Scepter, 4 vols., 1969; Vol. 2, Notebooks of Paul Klee. Ed: Modern Age Books; Book of Knowledge; Limited Ed. Club; Spectrum; Saturday Review. Contbr. to: Debunker; Scholastic; N.Y. Times Mag.; Saturday Review; Mensa Jrnl.; Med. Tribune; Chem. Age; Insight. Mbrships. incl: PEN; Fellow, Inst. of Linguistics; Transls. Assn.; Am. Transls. Assn.; Soc. of Authors. Address: 3A Greenaway Gdns., London, NW3, UK.

NORDENBERG, Reidar, b. 16 Oct. 1923, Arvika, Sweden. Journalist. Publs: Lönnträdet, 1965; Du Joakim, 1966; Resenärerna, 1967; Hjärtspecialisten, 1971. Mbr., Swedish Authors Assn. Address: Hantverksgatan 11 A, 671 00 Arvika, Sweden.

NORDWALL, Ove Björnson, b. 19 Mar. 1938, Stockholm, Sweden. Music Producer. Educ: Stockholm Univ. Publs: Fran Mahler till Ligeti, 1965; Det omöjligas konst, 1966; Igor Stravinsky, 1967; Ligeti-dokument, 1968; Witold Lutoslawski, 1968, Swedish ed., 1969; György Ligeti — Eine monographie, 1971; Béla Bartók, 1972; sev. anthols., transls. & eds. Contbr. to: Scandinavian daily newspapers, & music pubis. in num. countries. Mbrships: Swedish Authors' Soc.; Bd., Sect. for Free Writers on Cultural Subjects; Swedish Sect., Int. Soc. for Contemp. Music. Recip., Swedish Great Award for Writers, 1971, 1972. Address: Österlångatan 14, S-111 31 Stockholm, Sweden.

NORELL, Gösta Gerhard, b. 24 Sept. 1924, Sundsvall, Sweden. Teacher; Precentor. Educ: Royal Acad. of Music, Stockholm, 1946-49; M.A., Univ. of Lund, 1970; Libn., 1973. Publs: Gömda Vägar (Hidden Ways, poems), 1968; Metamorfoser (Metamorphoses, poems), 1968; Strängarna (Chords, poems), 1970; Människans Dröm (The Dream of Man, poems & prose), 1974; Himlens ruiner (Ruins of Heaven, poems), 1975. Mbrships: Swedish Union of Authors; Swedish Union of Tchrs.; Swedish Union of Ch. Musicians. Address: 86041 Liden, Box 22, Sweden.

NORENG, Harald, b. 25 Apr. 1913. Hisöy, Norway. Professor of Scandinavian Literature. Educ: Ph.D., Univ. Oslo, 1949. Publs: Nils Kjoer, Fra radikal til reaksjonoer, 1949; Christian Braunmann Tullin, 1951; Björnstjerne Björnsons dramatiske diktning, 1954; Björnsons skuespill pa svensk scene, 1967; Christian Braunmann Tullins Yamtlige Skrifter (ny utgave) I-III, 1972—; Co-Ed., Norsk Riksmaalsordbok I-IV, 1958. Contbr. to: Edda; Nordisk Tidskrift; etc. Mbrships. incl: Det norske videnskaps-akademi i Oslo; Yelskapet til vitenskapenes fremme, Bergen; The Crabtree Fndn., London; Vetenskaps-Societeten, Lund. Hons. incl: Visiting Prof., Lund, 1954-55; Int. Assn. Scandinavian Studies (Pres. 1968-70). Address: Øvre Kalfarli 4, 5000 Bergen, Norway.

NORGATE, Matthew, b. 10 May 1901, London, UK. Writer; Broadcaster; Lecturer. Publs: Revelations of a Soviet Diplomat by Grigory Bessedovsky (transl.), 1930; Not So Savage, 1975. Contbr. to: Essays of the Year, 1930; Shots in the Dark, 1951; Penguin Film Review, 1948-50; Woman's Hour, 1969; Evening Standard; Daily Express; Guardian; Spectator; Listener; Ed., Critics' Circular, 1952-64; etc. Mbrships: Hon. Gen. Sec., Critics' Circle, 1952-64. 1975—; Hon. Treas., 1964-69; Pres., 1947-48; Chmn., Film Sect., 1946-47; Coun.; Chmn., var. comms., Savage Club. Recip., Freeman of the City of Norwich, 1972. Address: 7 Lloyd Sq., London WC1X 9BA, UK.

NORGATE, Walter Matthew Le Grys, b. 1901, London, UK. Drama & Film Critic; Radio Journalist; Freelance Broadcaster. Publs: Transl., Revelations of a Soviet Diplomat, by B. Bessedovsky, 1928. Contbr. to: Nation & Athenaeum; Tribune; Truth; Evening Standard; Daily Express; Guardian; Listener; Films & Filming; Referee; Time & Tide; Spectator; Essays of the Yr.; Shots in the Dark; Woman's Hour; Penguin Film Reviews; W. End Theatre Progs. Mbrships: Critics' Circle; Radio Writers' Assn.; Savage Club. Agent: Herbert van Thal. Address: 7 Lloyd Square, London WC1, UK.

NORMAN, Eva Elisabeth, b. 3 July 1945, Borlänge, Sweden. Teacher. Educ: M.A. (Lit., German, Philos.). Publs: (novels) Status Quo, 1970; Den längsta da, 1971; Eftersläckning, 1973; (TV dramas) Den längstada; Oskar Nilsson, 1972. Mbrships: Swedish Authors' Union. Författarcentrum; Swedish Union of Playwrights; Swedish PEN. Address: Spelmansgatan 23, 78100 Borlänge, Sweden.

NORMAN, Frank (John), b. 9 June 1930, Bristol, UK. Novelist; Playwright. Publs. incl: Soho Night & Day, 1966; The Monkey Pulled His Hair, 1967; Barney Snip: Artist, 1968; Banana Boy, 1969; Norman's London, 1969; Lock 'Em Up & Count 'Em, 1971; Dodgem-Greaser, 1971; The Lives of Frank Norman (Penguin Anthol.), 1972; One of Our Own, 1973; Much Ado About Nuffink, 1974; (plays) Fings Ain't Wot They Used T'Be, 1959; A Kayf Up West, 1964; Insideout, 1969; Costa Packet, 1972. Contbr. to var. mags. & newspapers. Recip., Evening Standard Drama Award, 1960. Agent: Richard Scott Simon Ltd. Address: 5 Seaford Ct., 222 Great Portland St., London W1, UK.

NORMAN (Jean), Birger Isak, b. 30 July 1914, Kramfors, Sweden. Writer. Publs: Sanger vid floden, 1951; Vandringsutställning, 1953; Franvarons ring, 1956; Resa genom dagrar, 1960; Ön, 1963; Strykfagel, 1964; Samhället som dikt, 1966; Adalen 31, 1968; Mannen i backspegeln, 1969; Vinterfiske, 1970; Sol, vad vill du mig?, 1971; Löken, 1972; Utanför Eden, 1974. Contbr. to: Metallarbetaren; Kommunalarbetaren; Arbetet. Mbr., Swedish Authors' Assn. Recip., Litteraturfrämjandet stora pris, 1971. Address: Tengdahlsgatan 4, 116 41 Stockholm, Sweden.

NORRIS, Francis Hubert, pen name DIOPTRIC, b. 1909, London, UK. Company Director; Polytechnic Lecturer. Educ: Dartford Tech. Coll.; London Schl. of Photo-Engraving; Dip., Paper Technol. Publs: Paper & Paper Making; The Nature of Paper & Board. Contbr. to: Paper; Trade Press. Address: 3 The Ridge, Whitton, Middx., UK.

NORRIS, Hoke, b. 8 Oct. 1913, Holly Springs, N.C., USA. Publicist; Author. Educ: B.A., Wake Forest Coll.; Univ. of N.C.; Harvard Univ.; Univ. of Chicago. Publs: (novels) All the Kingdoms of the Earth, 1956; It's Not Far But I Don't Know the Way, 1968; Ed., We Dissent, Essays about the South, 1962. Contbr. to: Playboy; Redbook; Rogue; Genesis; Cavalier; December; Saturday Review; Columbia Jrnlsm. Review; Chicago Tribune Mag. Mbrships: Chicago Press Club; Soc. Midland Authors; Friends Lit.; Authors' Guild. Hons: Friends Lt. Award, 1957; Soc. Midland Authors Award, 1968. Address: 1701 N. North Park Ave., Chicago, IL 60614, USA.

NORRIS, James Alfred, b. 1929, London, UK. Broadcasting Administrator. Educ: M.A., St. Catharine's Coll., Cambridge. Publs: The First Afghan War 1838-1842, 1967. Contbr. to: S. Asian Review, 1967—. Mbrships. incl: BBC Club; Soc. of Authors. Address: Devon Cottage, Bessels Green, Sevenoaks, Kent, UK.

NORRIS, Louis William, b. 3 Feb. 1906, Columbus, Ohio, USA. Educator. Educ: B.A., Otterbein Coll., 1928; S.T.B., 1931, Ph.D., 1937, Boston Univ.; Harvard Univ.; Univ. of Berlin. Publs: Polarity: A Philosophy of Tensions Among Values, 1956; The Good New Days, 1956. Contbr. to: Saturday Review; Vital Speeches; Educ. Record; Liberal Educ., etc. Mbrships. incl: Am. Philosl. Assn.; AAUP; NEA; Int. Assn. of Univ. Profs.; Nat. Acad. Relig. (Treas. 1947-50); AAAS. Hons. incl: LL.D., 1953; Disting. Service Award, 1973; Otterbein Coll.; Litt.D., MacMurray Coll., 1960; L.H.D., Baldwin Wallace Coll., 1972. Address: 4443 Ellicott St., N.W. Wash. DC 20016, USA.

NORRIS, Luther, b. 29 Aug. 1920, Richmond, Ind., USA. Publisher. Publs: Sourdough Tales, 1946; Fascinating Alaska, 1947; The Saga of Alaska, 1948; Ed., The Non-Canonical Sherlock Holmes, 1974; Publr., The Sherlockian Doyle, 1973, The Mission That Failed, 1973, & Beyond Baker Street, 1974. Contbr. to: Asia Calling. Mbrships. incl: Crime Writers Assn., UK; Mystery Writers of Am.; Gtr. LA Press Club; Sherlock Holmes Soc. of London; The Baker St. Irregulars; Edgar Wallace Soc.; Sax Rohmer Soc.; Lord Warden, Praed St. Irregulars; The King of Scandinavia's Own Sherlockian. Recip., Irregular Shilling, Baker St. Irregulars, 1956. Address: 3844 Watseka Ave., Culver City, CA 90230, USA.

NORRIS, Phyllis Irene, b. 7 May 1909, Salisbury, UK. Writer. Publs: The House of the Lady-Bird, 1946; The Polkerin Mystery, 1949; The Cranstons at Sandly Bay, 1949. Address: Rooftree, 49 Hulse Rd., Salisbury, Wilts. SP1 3LU, UK.

NORTH, Edmund H., b. 12 Mar. 1911, NYC, USA. Screen Writer. Educ: Culver Mil. Acad.; Stanford Univ. Publs. (motion pictures): One Night of Love, 1934; I Dream Too Much, 1935; Young Man with a Horn, 1950; In a Lonely Place, 1950; The Day the Earth Stood Still, 1951; Cowboy, 1958; Sink the Bismarck! , 1960; Damn the Defiant, 1962; Patton, 1970. Mbrships: Writers Guild of Am., W.; Pres., Screen Br., Writers Guild of Am., 1956-57. Hons: Valentine Davies Award, Writers Guild of Am., 1967; Screen Writers Guild Awards, 1934, 1970; Acad. Award, 1970. Address: 212 N. Carmelina Ave., L.A., CA 90049, USA.

NORTH, Eleanor Beryl, b. Mercer, USA. Poet; College Professor; Lecturer. Educ: A.B. & M.A., Pa. State Univ.; grad. studies, Oxford, Cambridge & London Univs., UK, Sorbonne, Paris, France, & Harvard Univ., USA. Publs: Break of Dawn, 1928; Fall 'O Dew, 1936; Star Dust, 1942; Grace Notes, 1953; My Heart Sings, 1969; High Tide, 1973. Contbr. to num. anthols. & poetry mags. inclng: Am. Poet; Sea to Sea in Song; Ch. Advocate; Oracle. Mbrships. incl: Hon. VP, Centro Studi E Scambi Internazionali, Rome, Italy; Lit. Cons., Int. Poetry Soc., UK. Recip., num. awards. Address: 204 E. Hamilton Ave., Apt. 14, State Coll., PA 16801, USA.

NORTH, Joan Marian, b. 15 Feb. 1920, Hendon, London, UK. Writer. Educ: King's Coll., Univ. of London. Publs: Emperor of the Moon, 1956; The Cloud Forest, 1965, 1966; The Whirling Shapes, 1967; The Light Maze,

1971. Mbrships: Buddhist Soc., London; Soc. of Authors; Coll. of Psychic Sci. Address: 8 Grey Close, London NW11 6QG, UK.

NORTHAM, Lois Edgell, pen name NEILSON, Lois, b. 7 Oct. 1912, Bournemouth, Hants., UK. Teacher; Editorial Assistant; Social Worker. Educ: Nat. Froebel Fndn. Higher Cert., Bedford Froebel Coll. Publs: The Money Family; The Kingsway Reading Scheme. Contbr. to: Times of Ceylon; Colombo Broadcasting Corp.; BBC London; Child Educ.; Nursery World; var. women's mags. Address: Cidermill Lodge, Newdigate, near Dorking, Surrey, UK.

NORTHCOTT, (Rev.) Cecil, b. 1902, Devon, UK. Writer. Educ: Ph.D., Cambridge Univ. Publs: Who Claims the World? ; John Williams sails on; Change Here for Britain; Southward Ho! ; Guinea Gold; Whose Dominion; Glorious Company; Venturers of Faith; Robert Moffat; Voice Out of Africa; Pioneer in Africa; Religious Libert. Contbr. to: Daily Telegraph (Churches Corres.). Address: 34 Millington Rd., Cambridge, UK.

NORTON, Alan R., b. 1911, London, UK. Psychiatrist. Educ: Univ. of Oxford; St. Thomas's Hosp.; D.M.; F.R.C.Psych. Publs: The New Dimensions of Medicine, 1969; Drugs, Science & Society, 1973. Contbr. to: Brit. Med. jrnl.; Economist; World Med. Mbr., Royal Soc. of Med. Address: 15 Dartmouth Row, London, SE10, UK.

NORTON, Andre Alice, pen name NORTH, Andrew, b. Cleveland, Ohio, USA. Writer. Publs: 78 books (inclng. num. juvenile) in fields of Adventure, Mystery, Historical & Science Fiction; Ed., 5 anthols. Mbrships: Am. Pen Women; Women in Communication; Am. Authors League; Sci. Fiction Writers of Am. Hons: Plaque of Hon., Netherlands Govt., 1947; Invisible Little Man (s-f) Award, 1963; Hon. Headliner of Yr., Women in Communication, 1963; Hon. Book, Boys Clubs of Am., 1965. Address: 2588 Lake Howell Lane, Maitland, FL 32751, USA.

NORTON, Graham Peter George, b. 24 Mar. 1935, Penzance, Cornwall, UK. Lecturer; Writer. Educ: B.A., Stanford Univ., Calif., USA; B.Sc.(Econ.), London Schl. of Econs., UK. Publs: Discovering Victorian London, 1969; London Before the Blitz, 1970. Contbr. to: Sunday Times; Times; Country Life; Round Table; Illustrated London News. Mbrships: Nat. Union Jrnlsts.; Royal C'wlth. Soc.; Engl. Speaking Union. Address: 1(b) Glenshaw Mansions, Priory Rd., London NW6 3NR, UK.

NORTON, Lucy, b. 25 July 1902, Long Melford, Suffolk, UK. Writer. Educ: Roedean Schl.; Royal Coll. of Art. Publs: (transl): Journal of Eugène Delacroix, 1951; (Ed. & transl): Saint-Simon at Versailles, 1958 & Historical Memoirs of the Duc de Saint-Simon, 3 vols., 1967, 1968, 1972. Contbr. to: Apollo Mag.; Country Life. Mbrships: The Strachey Trust (Chmn.); Soc. of Authors. Address: 81 Oakwood Court, London W14 8JF, UK.

NORTON, Peter John, b. 9 Jan. 1913, Buriton, Hants., UK. Artist; Teacher of Painting; Writer. Publs: The End of the Voyage; The Special Train; Figureheads; State Barges. Mbr., Soc. for Nautical Research. Address: 1 The Square, Compton, Chichester, Sussex PO18 9HA, UK.

NORVELLE, Lee, b. 1892, Pendleton, Ky., USA. University Professor; Chairman, Board of Directors, All Ways Travel, Inc. Educ: Taylor Acad., Ind.; Iowa & Cornell Univs.; A.B., M.A., Ph.D. Publs: The Will to Speak Effectively; Speaking Effectively (co-author); Dramatization of the Hoosier Schoolmaster. Contbr. to: Theatre Arts; Speech Monographs; N.Y. Times; Cue; Indpls. Star; Nat. Theatre Conf. Quarterly; Players Mag.; etc. Mbrships: Am. Educl. Theatre Assn. (Pres. 1938-39); Nat. Theatre Conf. (Pres. 1942-44). Hons: Award of Merit, Am. Theatre Assn., 1972; Award of Excellence, Am. Coll. Theatre, 1973. Address: Apts. 120-122, Univ. Apt. West, Bloomington, IN, USA.

NORWOOD, Hayden Eugene, b. 29 Sept. 1907, Providence, R.I., USA. News Journalist. Educ: B.A., Lehigh Univ., Pa.; M.A., Cornell Univ., N.Y. Publs: They Met at Mrs. Bloxom's (novel), 1938; Death Down East (novel), 1939; The Marble Man's Wife (biog.), 1947; An Owl in the House, (reminiscence), 1959. Contbr. to: Story Mag.; Va. Quarterly Review; Esquire. Address: 1427 Westgate Dr., Bethlehem, PA 18017, USA.

NORWOOD, Victor George Charles, pen names BOWIE, Jim, RUSSELL, Shane, CANSFIELD, Paul; TYRONE, Paul;

DARK, Johnny; BAXTER, Shane; JANSON, Hank, b. 21 Mar. 1920, Scunthorpe, Lincs., UK. Author; Explorer; Mineral Prospector. Educ: B.A., Sheffield Coll., 1939; Dip. Lit., Bennett Coll., 1947. Publs. incl: (non-fiction) Man Alone, The Long Haul; Jungle Life of Guiana; Jungle Treasures; (fiction) Journey of Fear; The Headhunters; The Dark Star; The Earth in Dark; The Terror; Cry of the Beast; Temple of the Dead; The Skull of Kanaima. Contbr. to num. publs. Mbrships: Royal Soc. of Lit.; 1st Chmn. & Fndr., N. Lincs. Writers Circle. Recip., num. acad. hons. Address: 194 W. Common Lane, Westcliff, Scunthorpe, S. Humberside DN17 1PD, UK.

NOSSACK, Hans Erich, b. 30 Jan. 1901, Hamburg, Germany. Writer. Educ: Univ. of Jena. Publs: (stories) Interview mit dem Tode, 1947; Begegnung im Vorraum, 1963; (novels) Spätestens im November, 1955; Spirale, 1956; Der Jüngere Bruder, 1958; Der Fall d'Arthez, 1968; Dem Unbekannten Sieger, 1969; Bereitschaftsdienst, 1973; (play) Die Rotte Kain, 1950; (essays) Pseudo-autobiographische Glossen, 1971. Contbr. to: Merkur. Mbrships: PEN; Acad. of Scis. & Lit., Mainz; Free Acad. of Arts, Hamburg; Deutsche Akad. Für Sprache und Dichtung, Darmstadt. Hons: Georg Büchner Prize, 1961; Wilhelm Raabe Prize, 1963; Orden des Pour le mérite, 1973; Zinn Prize, Hamburg, 1974. Address: Hansastr. 20, 2 Hamburg 13, W. Germany.

NOSSAL, Frederick Christian, b. 23 Dec. 1927, Vienna, Austria. Journalist. Educ: St. Aloysius Coll., Sydney, Aust. Publs: Dateline – Peking, 1962. Contbr. to: Pakistan Economist; Commerce, Bombay; Far Eastern Econ. Review, Hong Kong; S. China Morning Post, Hong Kong; Montreal Star; Christian Sci. Monitor; N.Y. Times; Chgo. Sun-Times; Daily Telegraph; Associated Newspapers Ltd., Sydney; Melbourne Herald; Toronto Globe & Mail, etc. Mbrships. incl: Can. Inst. Int. Affairs; Soc. for Int. Dev. Address: 10401 Riverwood Dr., Potomac, MD, USA.

NOTT, David, b. 11 Oct. 1928, Liverpool, UK. Freelance Journalist; Newspaper Correspondent. Educ: Tripos I (Mod. Langs.), Tripos II (Law), St. Catharine's Coll., Cambridge, 1949-52. Publs: Angels Four, 1972; Into the Lost World, 1975. Contbr. to: (Corres. in N. of S. Am., Caribbean & Ctrl. Am.) Daily Telegraph, Economist, Latam Econ. Report, Bolsa Int. Review, etc.; num. other newspapers & mags. Address: Ed. Las Churuatas, Calle Maury, Los Naranjos, Las Mercedes, Caracas 106, Venezuela.

NOTT, Kathleen (Cecilia), b. London, UK. Writer. Educ: King's Coll., London Univ.; B.A., Somerville Coll., Oxford Univ. Publs. incl: (novels) Mile End, 1938; An Elderly Retired Man, 1963; (verse) Landscapes & departures, 1947; Poems from the North, 1956; Co-Ed., New Poems, 1957, 1957; Creatures & Emblems, 1960; (non-fiction) The Emperor's Clothes, 1954; A Clean Well-Lighted Place, 1960; Objections to Humanism (co-author), 1963; A Soul in the Quad, 1969; Philosophy & Human Nature, 1970; Ed., Int. PEN Bulletin of Selected Books, 1960–. Mbr., PEN (VP, UK Ctr.). Recip., Bursary, Arts Coun., 1968. Address: 6 Newlands Rd., Horsham, Sussex, UK.

NOURISSIER, François, b. 18 May 1927, Paris, France. Writer; Journalist. Educ: Ecole libre des Sci. politiques, Paris. Publs. incl: L'Eay grise, 1951; Lorca, 1955; Le Corps de Diane, 1957; Bleu comme la nuit, 1958; Un petit bourgeois, 1964; Une Histoire française, 1966; Le Maître de Maison, 1968; The French, 1970; Cartier-Bresson's France, 1971; Contbr. to: La Parisienne, 1956-58 (Ed.); Vogue; Les Nouvelles Lits. Le Point; L'Express. Hons. incl: Félix Fénéon Prize, 1952; Grand Prix du Roman, French Acad., 1966; Prix Femina, 1970; Address: 23 rue Henri Heine, 75016 Paris, France.

NOVAK, Michael, b. 9 Sept. 1933, Johnstown, Pa., USA. Philosopher; Associate Director in the Humanities, Rockefeller Foundation. Educ: Gregorian Univ., Rome, Italy; Cath. Univ., Wash. DC, USA; Harvard Univ.; A.B.; B.T.; M.A. Publs. incl: The Open Church, 1964; Belief & Unbelief, 1965; A Time to Build, 1967; A Theology for Radical Politics, 1969; Naked I Leave, 1970; The Experience of Nothingness, 1970; The Rise of the Unmeltable Ethnics, 1972; A Book of Elements, (w. K. Laub-Novak), 1972; Choosing Our King, 1974. Contbr. to philosl., theol., & other jrnls. Hons. incl: LL.D.; D.Litt. Agent: Sterling Lord. Address: The Rockefeller Fndn., 111 W. 50th St., N.Y., NY 10020, USA.

NOVOMESKÝ, Ladislav, b. 27 Dec. 1904, Budapest, Hungary. Journalist; Writer. Educ: Teacher's Coll., Modra. Publs: (in Czech) (poetry) Sunday, 1927; Rhomboid, 1932; The Open Window, 1935; Saints Behind the Village, 1939; Villa Theresa, 1963; 30 Minutes to Town, 1963; The Unexplored World, 1964; From there & Others, 1970. Contbr. to: Pravda chudoby; Halônoviny; Ludovy denník; Slov-zvesti; Tvorba; DAV; etc. Mbrships: incl: Assn. of Slovak Writers; Slovak Writers' Union; Slovak Nat. Coun. Hons. incl: Nat. Artist, 1964; Klement Gottwald Order, 1968; Order of Lenin; Red Banner of Labour (twice) Address: Bratislava, Martincekova 32, Czechoslovakia.

NOWLAN, Alden, b. 25 Jan. 1933, Windsor, N.S., Can. Writer. Publs: The Rose & the Puritan, 1958; A Darkness in the Earth, 1959; Wind in a Rocky Country, 1961; Under the Ice, 1961; The Things Which Are, 1962; Bread, Wine & Salt, 1967; Miracle at Indian River, 1968; The Mysterious Naked Man, 1969; Playing the Jesus Game, 1970; Between Tears & Laughter, 1971; Various Persons Named Kevin O'Brien, 1973; I'm A Stranger Here Myself, 1974. Contbr. to: Reader's Digest; Maclean's Mag.; Weekend Mag. Mbrships: League of Can. Poets; Writers' Union of Can. Hons: Guggenheim Fellowship, 1967; Gov.-Gen.'s Award for Poetry, 1968; D.Litt., Univ. of N.B., 1971. Address: c/o Dept. of Engl., Univ. of New Brunswick, Fredericton, N.B., Can.

NUMANO, Allen Stanislaus Motoyuki, pen name CORENANDA, A.L.A., b. 3 Nov. 1908, Yokohama, Japan. Writer; Translator; Violinist; Industrial Designer; Pioneer in Field of Mentalogy. Educ: Worcester Coll., Oxford Univ., UK; Royal Coll. of Music, London. Publs: Transl., L. P. Lochner, Fritz Kreisler, 1959; Transl., Maymie R. Krythe, All About Christmas, 1962; Transl., Fairbanks-Morse Opposed Piston Engine Instructions 3800 D8/9, 1964; (as Corenanda) Music & Reminiscences, forthcoming. Contbr. to: Times of Ceylon; Mainichi; Japan Times; On Music & Life; Music & Criticism; etc. Mbrships: Soc. of Authors, UK; Transls.' Assn.; Am. Transls.' Assn.; Fellow, Inst. Linguists, UK. Address: P.O. Box 2442, Honolulu, HI 96804, USA.

NUMMI, Lassi (Lauri Juhani Yrjönpoika), b. 9 Oct. 1928, Helsinki, Finland. Author; Literary Editor. Publs: (poems) Vuoripaimen, 1949; Taivaan ja maan merkit, 1956; Kuusimittaa, 1963; Keskipäivä, delta, 1967; (prose) Maisema, 1949; Viha, 1952; Runoilijan kalenteri, 1968. Contbr. to: Uusi Suomi; Y.V. Monthly Mag. Mbrships: Bd., Writers' Union of Finland, 1964- (Pres., 1969-72); Bd., PEN, 1969-; Union of Finnish Critics; Eino Leino Soc. Hons: State Lit. Prize, 1950, 1964, 1968; Pro Finlandia Medal. Address: Ulvilantic 11 B A 4, 00350 Helsinki 35, Finland.

NUNN, William Curtis, pen names, CURTIS, Will; & TWIST, Ananias, b. 2 June 1908, Georgetown Tex., USA. Professor of History. Educ: B.A., S.W. Univ., Tex., 1928; M.A., 1931, Ph.D., 1938, Univ. of Tex. Publs. incl: Escape from Reconstruction, 1956, 1974; Texas Under the Carpetbaggers, 1962; Peace Unto You (as Will Curtis), 1970; Snide Lights of Texas History (as Ananias Twist, w. M. Potter), 1959; Ten Texans in Gray (ed.), 1968. Contbr. to book reviews to histl. jrnls.; wkly. column, Be Still, in var. Tex. newspapers. Address: 3801 South Dr., Ft. Worth, TX 76109, USA.

NUSBAUM, Loretta Willene Hinson, b. 30 June 1915, Carthage, Mo., USA. Postal Clerk; Writer; Editor. Publs: These I Love, 1967. Contbr. to poetry, espec. haiku, jrnls., US & abroad. Mbrships. incl: World Poetry Soc. Intercontinental; Acad. of Am. Poets; Am. Haiku Soc.; Western World Haiku Soc.; Centro Studi E. Scambi Int., Rome; United Amateur Poets; Idaho Poets & Writers Giild; Midwest Chaparral Poets; Ed., Student Sect., Modern Haiku. Hons. incl: Haiku awards; 3rd Prize, Nat. League of Am. Pen Women, 1973. Address: Box 141, Bern, KS 66408, USA.

NUTTALL, Geoffrey Fillingham, b. 1911, Colwyn Bay, UK. Lecturer in Church History. Educ: Balliol & Mansfield Colls., Oxford; M.A., D.D. Publs. incl: The Holy Spirit in Puritan Faith & Experience; Christian Pacifism in History; The Visible Saints, 1640-60; Richard Baxter; The Faith of Dante Alighieri; (co-ed) From Uniformity to Unity, 1662-1962. Contbr. to: Jrnl. of Ecclesiastical Hist.; Jrnl. of Theol. Studies; Archiv für Reformationsgeschichte; Evangelisches Kirchenlexicon. Mbr., Penn. Recip., Hon. D.D., Wales. Address: 2 Brim Hill, London N2 OHF, UK.

NUTTALL, Kenneth, b. 14 July, 1907, Whitworth, Lancs., UK. Schoolmaster. Educ: City of Leeds Trng. Coll. Publs: Your Book of Acting, 1957, 1972; Let's Act, Books 1—4 & Tchrs. Book, 1959; Play Production for Young People, 1963; Young Actors, Books 1, 2 & Tchrs. Book, 1965; Four Plays from History, 1965; Four Plays for Christmas, 1965; Services we Use, 1966; Co-auth., Reading Routes, 1974. Mbr., Nat. Book League. Address: 23 Madeira Ave., Worthing, Sussex BN11 2AT, UK.

NUTTIN, Joseph (Remi), b. 7 Nov. 1909, Zwevegem, Belgium. Psychologist; Dean, Faculty of Psychology, University of Louvain. Educ: Dr. in Philos. & Letters, Univ. of Louvain, 1941; Dr. Philos. in Psychol., 1941. Publs. incl: Psychoanalysis & Personality, 1962; Primary Mental Abilities in Children, 1965; Reward & Punishment in Human Learning, 1968; Pleasure & Reward in Human Motivation & Learning, 1973; Ed., Louvain Psychol. Series Studia Psychologica. Contbr. to num. jrnls. Mbrships. incl: Pres., Psychol. Commn., Nat. Fndn. Rsch. in Belgium; Pres., Int. Union Psychol. Sci., 1972—; Acad. Scis., Belgium. Hons. incl: Cmdr., Order of Leopold; Gt. Off., Order of Crown. Address: 112 Tiensestraat, Louvain, Belgium.

NYANAPONIKA, b. 12 July 1901, Hanau/Main, Germany. Buddhist Monk. Educ: Classical Coll., Germany. Publs. incl: The Heart of Buddhist Meditation, 1962; Abhidhamma Studies, 1962; The Power of Mindfulness, 1968; 12 Writings & transls. of Buddhist texts in The Wheel series; sev. writings & transls. in German. Mbrships: Co-fndr. & Pres., Buddhist Publ. Soc., Kandy; Fellow, World Acad. of Art & Sci. Address: Forest Hermitage, Kandy, Sri Lanka.

NYBERG, Helmer V., b. 20 Feb. 1907, Jönköping, Sweden. Retired Teacher; Author. Educ: Tchng. certs., Linköping, 1932. Publs: Jordrök (Earth Smoke), 1938; Under Nyet (Under the New Moon), 1942; Under Vardträdet (Under the Guardian Tree) (cantata), 1942; Ed., The Coal-Carrier & The Dancer, 1960; Ed., Tao in my Heart, 1962; Samtal med Osynlig (Dialogue with the Unseen), 1967; Ed., Bortom & Här (Beyond & Here) (w. S. Hagliden), 1968. Contbr. to: Hemmets Veckotidning, Malmö. Mbr., Swedish Soc. of Authors. Recip., Grant from Sveriges Författarfond, 1974. Address: Ceresgatan 4, 552 48 Jönköping, Sweden.

NYE, Douglas Charles (Doug.), b. 18 Oct. 1945, Guildford, Surrey, UK. Writer; Journalist. Publs. incl: British Cars of the '60s, 1970; The Lotus Story 1961-71, 1972; Racing Cars, 1972; Carl Benz: father of the Automobile, 1973; Racing Drivers Manual, 1973; Motor Racing, 1974; Motor Racing Mavericks, 1975; Great Racing Cars, 1975; The Racing Tyrrells, 1975. Contbr. to: Autosport; Auto Sport, Japan; Illustrated Motor Sport, Sweden; Autosprint, Italy; Sports Car World, Aust.; Technicar, S. Africa; Auto Visie, Netherlands; Player Yr. Book; etc. Mbrships. incl.: Guild of Motoring Writers. Address: 8 Broomwood Way, Lower Bourne, Farnham, Surrey GU10 3LP, UK.

NYE, Robert, b. 1939, London, UK. Author; Critic. Publs: Juvenilia I, 1961; Juvenilia II, 1963; Doubtfire, 1967; Tales I Told my Mother, 1969. March has Horse's Ears, 1966; Taliesin, 1966; Beowulf, 1968; Wishing Gold, 1970; Poor Pumpkin, 1971; A Choice of Sir Walter Raleigh's Verse, 1972; A Choice of Swinburne's Verse, 1973; The English Sermon, 1750-1850, 1975; Three Plays, 1975; (poetry) Darker Ends, 1969; The Seven Deadly Sins — A Masque, 1974. Contbr. to: Times; Spectator; Guardian; Encounter; Listener; Observer; N.Y. Times; Atlantic Monthly; Poetry Nation; BBC Radio; etc. Address: 18 Lonsdale Terr., Edinburgh EH3 9HL, UK.

NYGARDSHAUG, Gert, b. 22 Mar. 1946, Tynset, Norway. Writer. Educ: Studies in Philosophy, History & Sociology, Univ. of Oslo. Publs: Impulser (poetry), 1966; Paxion (poetry), 1971; Et bilde et verktøy (poetry), 1974. Mbrships: Den Norske Forfatterforening (Norwegian Union of Authors); Norsk Litteraturkritikerlag (Norwegian Literary Critics' Assn.). Address: Vallervn. 128, 1346 Gfettum, Norway.

NYGREN, Anders, b. 1890, Gothenburg, Sweden. Former Bishop of Lund. Educ: Th.S. & D.D., Univ. of Lund. Publs: Religiost Apriori, 1921; Dogmatikens Vetenskapliga Grundlaggning, 1922; Filosofisk & Kristen Etik, 1923; Agape & Eros, I, 1932, II, 1938; Commentary on Romans, 1949; Christ & His Church, 1955; Meaning & Method, Prolegomena to a Scientific Philosophy of Religion

& Scientific Theology, 1972. Hons: D.D., Sopron Univ., Hungary, 1947; D.D., Rock Island, Ill., USA, 1948; D.D., Univ. of Aberdeen, UK, 1948; D.D., Heidelberg Univ., W. Germany, 1950; D.D., Toronto Univ., Can., 1954; D.D., Knox Coll., Toronto, 1954; D.D., Helsinki Univ., Finland, 1963; Royal Prize, Swedish Acad., 1974. Address: Helgonavagen 10, Lund, Sweden.

NYSTROM-NERMAN, Ingrid Maria, b. 1 Dec. 1917, Kristinehamm, Sweden. Librarian. Educ: Lib. Schl. Stockholm. Publs: (poems) Vattenspegal, 1944; Kamé, 1946; Dropper av sten, 1948; Glesnader, 1957. Mbr., Swedish Authors' Union. Recip., Cultural Award, City of Boras, 1966. Address: Karlagatan 12, 502 33 Borås, Sweden.

O

OAKES, Philip, b. 31 Jan. 1928, Burslem, Staffs., UK. Writer; Journalist. Publs: Unlucky Jonah, 1952; Exactly What We Want, 1955; The Godbotherers, 1969; In The Affirmative, 1969; Experiment at Proto, 1973; Married/Singular, 1974. Contbr. to: London Mag.; Sunday Times; New Statesman; Cosmopolitan. Address: Pinnock Farm House, Pluckley, Kent, UK.

OAKESHOTT, Walter Fraser, b. 1903, Lydenburg, S. Africa. School Master; Former Rector, Lincoln College, Oxford. Educ: M.A., Balliol Coll., Oxford. Publs: incl: Men Without Work (co-author), 1938; Classical Inspiration in Medieval Art, 1949. The Queen & the Poet, 1960; Mosaics of Rome, 4th to 14th Century, 1968; Sigena: Romanesque Paintings in Spain & The Artists of the Winchester Bible, 1972. F.B.A. Recip., Hon. LL.D., Lincoln Coll., Oxford, 1953. Address: Old School House, Eynsham, Oxford, UK.

OAKLEY, Charles Allen, b. 30 Sept. 1900, Portsmouth, Hants., UK. Industrial Psychologist. Educ: B.Sc., M.Ed., Glasgow Univ. Publs: Handbook of Vocational Guidance, 1935; Scottish Industry Today, 1937; Men at Work, 1944; Scottish Industry, 1953; Ed., Commercial Apprenticeships, 1962; The Last Tram, 1962; Where We Come In, 1964; The Second City, 1967; Dear Old Glasgow Town, 1974; History of a Faculty, 1974. Ed., Glasgow Chmbr. of Comm. Jrnl., 1949–, Glasgow Corp. Indl. Handbook, 1958–. Address: 3a Cleveden Dr., Glasgow G12 0RZ, UK.

OAKLEY, Kenneth Page, b. 17 Apr. 1911, Amersham, UK. Palaeoanthropologist; Former Deputy Keeper, Department of Palaeontology, British Museum. Educ: B.Sc., 1933; Ph.D., 1938; D.Sc., 1955, Univ. of London. Publs: Man the Tool-Maker, 1949, 6th ed. 1971; Fluorine Dating Method, 1951; Solution of the Piltdown Problem, 1953; The Problem of Man's Antiquity, 1964; Frameworks for Dating Fossil Man, 1964, 3rd ed. 1969; Decorative & Symbolic Uses of Vertebrate Fossils, 1975; Sr. Ed., Catalogue of Fossil Hominids, 1967-75. Contbr. to: Nature; Science; Antiquity; Man; Perspectives on Human Evolution 1972. Mbrships: F.G.S.; F.S.A. Hons: Fellow, Brit. Acad., 1957; Fellow, Univ. Coll., London, 1958. Address: Flat 2, Islip Place, Islip Rd., Oxford, OX2 7SR, UK.

OAKLEY, Mary Ann B., b. 22 June 1940, Buchannon, W. Va., USA. Attorney. Educ: B.A., Duke Univ., 1962; M.A., 1970; J.D., 1974, Emory Univ. Publs: Elizabeth Cady Stanton, 1972. Contbr. to: Emory Law Jrnl.; Family Law Quarterly. Mbrships: Am. Bar Assn.; Am. Judicature Soc. Hons: Phi Beta Kappa; Order of the Coif; Scribes. Address: 15 Peachtree St. N.E., Suite 902, Atlanta, GA 30303, USA.

OAKLEY, Stewart Philip, b. 1931, Kenton, Middx., UK. Senior Lecturer in History. Educ: M.A., Lincoln Coll., Oxford; Ph.D., L.S.E. Publs: The Story of Sweden, 1966; The Story of Denmark, 1972. Contbr. to: History; Engl. Hist. Review; Scandinavica; Collier's Ency. Mbr., Hist. Assoc. Address: 24 Branksome Rd., Norwich, NR4 6SW, UK.

OATES, John Claud Trewinard, b. 24 June 1912, Gloucester, UK. Librarian. Educ: M.A.; Reader, Histl. Bibliography, Univ. Lib., Trinity Coll., Cambridge. Publs: A

Catalogue of the Fifteenth-Century Printed Books in the University Library Cambridge, 1956; Shandyism & Sentiment 1760-1800, 1968. Contbr. to: Ed., The Lib.; Transactions of the Bibliographical Soc., 1953-60; The Book Collector; etc. Mbrships: Pres., Bibliographical Soc., 1970; Cambridge Bibliographical Soc.; Bibliographical Soc. of Va.; Trustee, Laurence Sterne Trust. Hons: Sandars Reader in Bibliography, Cambridge Univ., 1952, 1964. Address: 144 Thornton Rd., Cambridge, UK.

OATES, Joyce Carol, b. 16 June 1938, Lockport, N.Y., USA. Associate Professor of English. Educ: B.A., Syracuse Univ., N.Y., 1960; M.A., Univ. of Wis., 1961. Publs: incl: (short stories) By the North Gate, 1963; The Wheel of Love, USA, 1970, UK, 1971; (novels) With Shuddering Fall, USA, 1964, UK, 1965; A Garden of Earthly Delights, USA, 1967, UK, 1970; Expensive People, USA, 1968, UK, 1969; Them, USA, 1969, UK, 1971; Wonderland, USA, 1971, UK, 1972; (plays) Sunday Dinner, prod. 1970; 2 vols. of verse. Hons. incl: O. Henry Award, 1967; O. Henry Special Award,, 1970; Rosenthal Award, 1968; Nat. Book Award, 1970. Address: Dept. of English, Univ. of Windsor, Windsor, Ont., Can.

OATTS, (Col.) Henry Augustus, b. 1898, Roslin, UK. Educ: Royal Mil. Coll., Sandhurst. Author, Loch Trout. Contbr. to: The Field; Sev. other jrnls. Address: Cuil Lodge, Kilmelford, Oban, Argyll, UK.

OATTS, Lewis Balfour, b. 6 Apr. 1902, Roslin, UK. Retired Army Officer. Educ: Royal Mil. Coll., Sandhurst. Publs: Proud Heritage, 4 vols., 1952, 59, 61, 63; Jungle in Arms, 1965; I Serve, 1966; The Highland Light Infantry; 1969; Emperor's Chambermaids, 1973. Mbrships: Fellow, Soc. of Antiquaries of Scotland; Queen's Bodyguard for Scotland. Recip., DSO, 1946. Address: Temple House Bungalow, Arbury, Nuneaton, Warks., UK.

O'BALLANCE, Edgar, b. 17 July 1918, Dalkey, Co. Dublin, Ireland. Author; Military Commentator; Journalist. Publs. incl: Arab-Israeli War, 1948, 1956; The Sinai Campaign 1956, 1959; The Red Army of China, 1962; The Red Army of Russia, 1964; The Greek Civil War, 1966; Arab Guerilla Power, 1974; The Electronic War in the Middle East, 1974; War in Vietnam, 1974; Secret War in the Sudan, 1975; The Communist Insurgent War; The Indo-China War; The Third Arab-Israeli War. Contbr. to: Sunday Telegraph; Sunday Times; Wash. Post; Times; BBC; num. pol. & mil. jrnls. worldwide. Mbrships. incl: Nat. Union Jrnlsts. Agent: K. B. O'Ballance. Address: 1 Cedar Tree Rd., Arnold, Nottingham, UK.

OBENHAUS, (Rev.) Victor, b. 1903, Superior, Wis., USA. Professor; Clergyman. Educ: Oberlin Coll.; Union Theological Sem.; Columbia Univ.; M.A.; B.D.; B.A.; Ed.D. Publs: The Hebrew Prophets & America's Conscience; The Responsible Christian; Church & Faith in Mid-America; Religion in American Culture (co-author); Ethics for an Industrial Age; And See the People; Suburban Religion. Contbr. to: Christian Century; Nation; Social Action; Rural Sociology. Mbrships: Am. Soc. of Christian Ethics; Am. Sociological Assn.; Soc. for the Scientific Study of Relig.; Relig. Rsch. Assn. Address: 5549 Woodlawn, Chgo., IL, USA.

OBERLÄNDER, Hans, b. 29 Nov. 1899, Berlin, Germany. Educator; Journalist. Educ: Ph.D. Publs: Die Jugend siegt, 1919; Kampf, 1923; Der Leise Klang, 1936; Rhythmus Eines Schicksals, 1962. Contbr. to: Neue Politik, Hamburg; Lübecker Nachrichten. Mbrships: Fränkischer Kreis; Deutsche Friedens Union. Address: 24 Lübeck, Moltkeplatz 3, W. Germany.

OBERLIN, Cirs, b. 30 Mar. 1919, Berne, Switz. Surgical Dentist. Educ: Dr. med. dent. Publs: Kalibaba oder die Elternlosen (novel), 1969; Alle sind Niemand (poems), 1972. Contbr. to: Merkur; etc. Mbrships: Gruppe Olten (Swiss Writers' Group); Kogge. Recip., Award, Berne, 1969. Address: 8050 Zürich, Hofwiesenstr. 330, Switz.

OBEY, André, b. 1892, Douai, France. Administrator, Comédie Française; Musical & Stage Director. Educ: B.A. & LL.B., Univ. of Lille. Publs: Le Joueur de Triangle; L'Apprenti Sorcier; (plays) Noé; L'Homme de Cendres; Une fille pour au Vent; Frost at Midnight. Mbr., PEN. Address: L'Hirondelle, 49730 Montsoreau, France.

OBIECHINA, Emmanuel Nwanonye, b. 20 Sept. 1933, Nkpor, Nigeria. University Lecturer in English. Educ: B.A., Univ. Coll., Ibadan, Nigeria; Ph.D., Cambridge Univ., 1966.

Publs. incl: Literature for the Masses, 1971; Onitsha Market Literature, 1972; Igbo Traditional Life, Culture & Literature (w. M. J. C. Echeruo), 1971; An African Popular Literature: A Study of Onitsha Market Pamphlets, 1973; (forthcoming) Culture, Tradition & Society in the West African Novel. Contbr. to: African Lit. Today; Nigeria Mag.; African Forum; Rsch. in African Lit.; Conch; etc. Mbrships.incl: Nigerian Eng. Studies Assn.; MLA (Nigeria); Nigerian Acad. of Arts, Sci. & Technology. Address: Dept. of Eng., Univ. of Nigeria, Nsukka, Nigeria.

OBOLENSKY, Dimitri, b. 1918, Petrograd, Russia (now Leningrad, USSR). Professor of Russian & Balkan History, University of Oxford. Educ: M.A. & Ph.D., Univ. of Cambridge. Publs: The Bogomils, 1948; Ed. & Transl., The Penguin Book of Russian Verse, 1962; Ed., A Historical Russian Reader (w. J. Fennell), 1969; The Christian Centuries, Vol. 2, The Middle Ages (w. D. Knowles), 1969; The Byzantine Commonwealth, 1971; Byzantium & the Slavs, 1971. Contbr. to: Oxford Slavonic Papers; Slavonic & E. European Review; Dumbarton Oaks Papers; E. Christian Review. Mbrships: F.B.A.; F.S.A.; Fellow, Royal Histl. Soc. Address: 29 Harbord Rd., Oxford, UK.

O'BRIAN, Jack, b. 16 Aug. 1921, Buffalo, N.Y., USA. Writer; Radio Commentator. Educ: D.Litt., Niagara Univ., Niagara Falls, N.Y. Contbr. to: Harper's Bazaar; Cosmopolitan; Readers Digest; etc. Hons. incl: Twice nominated for Pulitzer Prizes; Christophers Award; Am. Legion Award; VFW Award; Cath. War Veterans Award; Morality in Media Award. Address: 225 E. 73rd St., N.Y., NY 10021, USA.

O'BRIEN, Cyril Cornelius, pen name WILSON, Crane, b. 22 Mar. 1906, Halifax, N.S., Can. Educator; Psychologist. Educ: B.A., St. Mary Univ., Halifax, 1926; L.Mus., McGill Univ., 1931; D.Paed., Univ. of Montreal, 1937; D.Mus., 1950; Ph.D., Univ. of Ottawa, 1944. Publs: The Problem Drinker in Industry (co-auth.), 1950; Management of Addictions (co-auth.), 1955; Contemporary Studies in Industrial Psychology, 1969. Contbr. to: Guest Ed., Educ.; Schl. & Soc.; Am. Jrnl. of Psychol.; & num. others. Fellowships incl: Int. Inst. of Arts & Letters; Am. Psychol. Assn.; AAAS; Royal Soc. Arts, London. Hons. incl: Kt. Cmdr., Order of St. Bridget of Sweden, 1968. Address: P.O. Box 666, Edmonton, Alta, T5J 2K8, Can.

O'BRIEN, Edna, b. 15 Dec. 1932, Tuamgraney, Co. Clare, Repub. of Ireland. Writer. Educ: Lic., Pharmaceutical Soc. Ireland. Publs. incl: (novels) The Country Girls, UK & USA, 1960; The Lonely Girl, UK & USA, 1962; Girls in their Married Bliss, UK, 1964, USA, 1968; August is a Wicked Month, UK & USA, 1965; Casualties of Peace, UK, 1966, USA, 1967; A Pagan Place, UK & USA, 1970; (short stories) The Love Object, UK, 1968, USA, 1969; (screenplays) The Girl with Green Eyes, 1964; Three into Two Won't Go, 1968; Zee & Co., 1972. Hons: Kingsley Amis Award, 1962; Novel Award, Yorks. Post, 1971. Address: c/o A. M. Heath, 35 Dover St., London W1, UK.

OCAMPO, Victoria. Writer; Publisher. Publs. incl: De Francesca a Beatrice, 1924; Domingos en Hyde Park, 1936; San Isidro, 1941; Lawrence de Arabia y otros ensayos, 1951; Virginia Woolf en su diario, 1954; Tagore en las barrancas de San Isidro, 1961; Dialogos con Borges, 1969; Dialogos con Mallea, 1969; & num. transl. incl: Camus; William Faulkner; Dylan Thomas; Graham Greene. Contbr. to: Sur (Ed.). Mbrships: PEN (VP); Fndr., Argentine Women's Union; Pres., Comm. of Letters, Nat. Fndn. for the Arts. Hons. incl: Legion of Honour; C.B.E. Address: Elortondo 1811, San Isidro, Buenos Aires, Argentina.

OCKENGA, (Rev.) Harold John, b. 6 July 1905, Chgo., Ill., USA. Educator. Educ: B.A., Taylor Univ.; D.D., Princeton Seminary; M.A., Ph.D., Univ. of Pitts. & num. other degrees & doctorates. Publs. incl: These Religious Affections, 1937; Our Protestant Heritage, 1938; Have You met these Women, 1940; Every one that Believeth, 1942; The Comfort of God, 1944; Our Evangelical Faith, 1946; The Spirit of the Living God, 1947; Power Through Pentecost, 1959; Preaching in Thessalonians, 1963; Faith for a Troubled World, 1970. Contbr. to: Christianity Today; United Evangelical Action. Address: 624 Bay Rd., Hamilton, MA 01936, USA.

O'CONNELL, Charles Christopher, b. 21 Dec. 1917, Cork, Ireland. Managing Director, Arklow Knitwear. Educ: Mod. Langs., Cork Schl. of Commerce. Publs: Light over Fatima, 1947; The Vanishing Island, 1957; The Miracle Maker, 1960; The Stubborn Heart, 1964; many serials

republd. as paperbacks; short stories transl. into sev. for. langs. Contbr. to num. jrnls., mags., etc. inclng: Atlantic Monthly; Woman's Day (Aust.); Woman's Own; Argosy; BBC; RTE. Mbr., Soc. of Authors. Address: "Sidda Ville", Rosebank, Douglas Rd., Cork, Repub. of Ireland.

O'CONNOR, Garry Peter, b. 31 Jan. 1938, Edgware, London, UK. Playwright; Theatre Critic. Educ: B.A., King's Coll., Cambridge; Ecole Jacques Lecoq, Paris, France. Publs: Le Théâtre en Grande-Bretagne, 1966; The Musicians (play), 1969; I Learned in Ipswich How to Poison Flowers (play), 1970; French Theatre Today, 1975; transls. of sev. plays. Contbr. to: Queen Mag. (TV critic, 1964-1966); Financial Times (theatre critic, 1966-1974); BBC; etc. Mbrships. incl: Nat. Union of Jrnlsts. Hons. incl: 1st Prize, Playwriting Competition, 1974. Address: Victoria Terr., Deddington, Oxon, UK.

O'CONNOR, Patrick Joseph, pen name FÍACC, Padraic, b. 15 Apr. 1924, Belfast, N. Ireland. Poet. Educ: St. Joseph's Seminary, Callicoon, N.Y. Publs: By the Black Stream, 1969; Odour of Blood, 1973; The Wearing of the Black, 1974. (anthologies) New Irish Poets, 1948; Modern Irish Poetry, 1972; Choice, 1973; Ten Irish Poets, 1974. Contbr. to: Hibernia; Irish Times; BBC; Irish Press; Capuchin Annual; Poetry Ireland; etc. Recip., George Russell (AE) Mem. Prize, 1957. Address: 43 Farmley Park, Glengormley, Newtown Abbey, Co. Antrim, N. Ireland.

ODA, Makoto, b. 2 June 1932, Osaka, Japan. Author. Educ: B.A., Univ. of Tokyo; Harvard Univ., USA. Publs: Nandemomiteya Ro (I Want to see Everything, criticism & essay), 1961; Amerika (novel), 1962; Daichi To Hoshi Kagayaku Tenno Ko (The Children of the Earth & Starry Heaven), 1963; Doro No Sekai (The World of Med), 1965; Gendaishi (Modern History), 1968; Ga-To (G — Island), 1973; Yonaoshi No Rinri To Ronri (Ethics & Logics of Revolution, criticism & essay). Contbr. to var. jrnls. Mbrships: Japan Writers' Assn.; PEN. Address: 90 Dogashiba-cho, Tennoji-ku, Osaka, Japan.

O'DEA, Marjory Rachel, b. 31 July 1928, Melbourne, Aust. Public Servant; Principal Science Adviser, International Activities Section, Policy Division, Department of Science. Educ: B.A. & Dip.Ed., Univ. of Melbourne. Publs: Six Days Between a Second, 1969; Of Jade & Amber Caves, 1974. Contbr. to: The Australian; Canberra Times; Aust. Quarterly; Aust. Jrnl. of Sci. Mbrships: Fellowship of Aust. Writers; Aust. Soc. of Authors. Recip., Poetry Aust. Prize, Poetry Soc. of Aust., 1968. Address: 58 Barada Crescent, Aranda, A.C.T., Australia 2614.

ÖDEEN, Mats, b. 24 May 1937, Stockholm, Sweden. Playwright. Publs: The Girl in the Cage, prod. 1969; Innocence & Arsenic, prod. 1973; sev. other stage & radio plays. Mbr., Sec., Swedish Union of Playwrights. Address: Rindögatan 52, 115 35 Stockholm, Sweden.

ØDEGÅRD, Knut, b. 6 Nov. 1945, Molde, Norway. Author. Educ: Univ. of Oslo. Publs (in Norwegian): The Dreamer, the Wanderer, the Source, 1967; Concert in a White House, 1968; The Boarding-House, 1970; The Dark Rain, 1972 (poetry); The Bird & the Dream (prose, for children), 1974; Hljómleikar í hvítu húsi (poetry), 1973; Transl., anthol. Faroese Poetry, 1974; Transl., Hungarian, Icelandic poems. Contbr. to jrnls. Mbrships: Past Bd. Mbr., Norwegian Soc. of Authors; Bd. Mbr., Norwegian Soc. of Lit. Critics; European Soc. of Culture, Venice. Hons: Norwegian State Working Schlrship., 3 yrs. Address: Anders Rørholts v.2, 3100 Tønsberg, Norway.

ODELBERG, (Carl Victor) Wilhelm, b. 1 July 1918, Gustafsberg, Sweden. Chief Librarian, Royal Swedish Academy of Sciences. Educ: Ph.D., Stockholm Univ., 1954. Publs: (in Swedish) The Life & Times of Vice-Admiral Carl Olof Cronstedt, 1954; The History of Sicily, 1957; The Surrender of Sveaborg, 1958; Ed., var. historical MSS; Ed., Yearbook Les Prix Nobel, 1968—. Contbr. to: Historisk Tidskrift; Personhistorisk Tidskrift; Svenska Dagbladet. Mbrships. incl: Royal Swedish Acad. of Scis.; Swedish Assn. of Special Libs. (Chmn., 1961—). Address: Kungl. Svenska Vetenskapsakadeien, S— 104 05, Stockholm 50, Sweden.

ODELL, Robin Ian, b. 19 Dec. 1935, Totton, UK. Editor & Publications Manager. Publs: Jack the Ripper in Fact & Fiction, 1965; Humanist Glossary, (w. T. Barfield), 1967; Exhumation of a Murder, 1975. Contbr. to: The Humanist; Crime & Punishment. Mbrships: Soc. of Authors; Crime Writers' Assn. Hons: FCC Watts Mem. Prize, 1957;

Int. Humanist & Ethical Union Prize, 1960. Address: 15 Churchill Cresc., Sonning Common, Reading, Berks. RG4 9RU, UK.

ODLUM, Doris Maude, b. 1890, Folkestone, UK. Consultant Psychiatrist. Educ: M.A., Oxford; B.A., London; F.R.C.Psych.; D.P.M.; Royal Free Hosp.; St. Mary's Hosp., London. Publs: Psychology, The Nurse & The Patient; Journey Through Adolescence; The Mind of Your Child. Contbr. to: Brit. Med. Jrnl.; Lancet; Practitioner; Family Doctor; etc. Mbr., European League for Mental Hygiene (Past Pres.) Address: Ardmor, 11 Cliff Drive, Canford Cliffs, Poole, Dorset, UK.

O'DONNELL, Margaret Jane, b. 20 May 1899, Carlisle, Cumberland, UK. Teacher (Retired). Educ: B.A. 1920, M.A. 1923, Durham Univ. Publs: Feet on the Ground: An Approach to Poetry, 1946; Anthology of Contemporary Verse, 1953; Fair Words: An English Language Course, 1958; Anthology of Commonwealth Poetry, 1963. Address: 11 Brunton Cres., Carlisle CA1 2AX, Cumbria, UK.

O'DONNELL, Michael, b. 20 Oct. 1928, Sheffield, UK. Editor. Educ: B.A., M.B., B.Chir., Trinity Hall, Cambridge Univ.; St. Thomas' Hosp., London. Publs: Cambridge Anthology, 1952; The Europe We Want, 1971. Contbr. to: Daily Telegraph; Daily Telegraph Mag.; Sunday Times Mag.; Vogue; Times; Daily Mail; Daily Mirror; New Sci.; Ed., World Med.; Woman; Pvte. Eye; BBC Radio & TV; Brit. & Am. TV Cos. Mbrships: Gen. Med. Coun.; Fellow, Royal Soc. of Med.; Brit. Med. Assn.; Med. Jrnlsts.' Assn. Named Med. Jrnlst. of the Yr., 1973. Address: Cedar Tree House, Weybridge Park, Weybridge, Surrey, UK.

O'DONNELL, Peadar. Writer. Educ: St. Patrick's, Dublin. Publs: Storm Islanders, 1925; Adrigoole, 1928; The Knife, 1930; The Gates Flew Open; On the Edge of the Stream, 1934; Salud; An Irishman in Spain, 1937; The Big Windows, 1955; Mbr., Irish Acad. of Letters; Address: 176 Upper Drumcondra Rd., Whitehall, Dublin, Repub. of Ireland.

O'DONOVAN, Joan Mary, b. 1914, Mansfield, UK. Educator; Writer. Educ: Furzedown Teacher Training Coll. Publs: Dangerous Worlds; The Visited; Shadows on the Wall; The Middle Tree; The Niceties of Life; She, Alas! ; Little Brown Jesus. Mbr. Soc. of Authors. Agent: A. P. Watt & Son. Address: County Educ. Office, New Rd., Oxford OX1 1NA, UK.

O'DONOVAN, John Purcell, pen name MARSH, Andrew, b. 29 Jan. 1921, Dublin, Repub. of Ireland. Author; Playwright. Publs: Shaw & the Charlatan Genius, 1965; The Shaws of Synge Street (play), 1966; Copperfaced Jack (play), 1967. Contbr. to: Dublin Evening Press; Radio Telefis Eireann; BBC. Mbrships: Chmn., Soc. of Irish Playwrights, 1974-75; VP, Royal Irish Acad. of Music. Address: 21 Barnhill Ave., Dalkey, Co. Dublin, Repub. of Ireland.

ODROWĄŻ-PIENIĄŻEK, Janusz, b. 2 July 1931, Opatowice, Poland. Writer; Museum Director. Educ: M.A., Warsaw Univ.; Postgrad. studies, Univ. of Montreal, Can. Publs: Opowiadania Paryskie (Paris Stories), 1963; Teoria fal (poems in prose), 1964; Ucieczka z cieptych krajów (Escape from the Tropics), 1968; Matżeństwo z Lynda Winters albo Pamiatka po Glorii Swanson, 1971, 2nd ed. 1972; Cocktail u Ksiezny Gieorgijew, 1971, 2nd ed. 1972; Party na calle Guatemala, 1974; var. scientific works. Contbr. to var. Polish lit. reviews. Mbrships. incl: Union of Polish Writers; PEN; Assn. Polish Authors & Composers. Address: 02-036 Warsaw, Uniwersytecka 1 m. 2, Poland.

OË, Kenzaburo, b. 1935. Writer. Publs: (In Japanese) The Catch, 1958; Pluck the Flowers, Gun the Kids, 1958; Our Age, 1959; Screams, 1962; The Perverts, 1963; Hiroshima Notes, 1963; Adventures in Daily Life, 1964; A Personal Matter, 1964, Engl. ed., 1969; Football in the First Year of Mannen, 1967. Hons: Akutagawa Prize, 1958; Shinchosa Lit. Prize, 1964; Tanizaki Prize, 1967. Address: 585 Seijo-machi, Setagaya-Ku, Tokyo, Japan.

OERLEMANS, Jacques Willem, b. 22 May 1926, Velsen, Netherlands. Assistant Professor of Modern History, University of Amsterdam. Educ: M.A. & Ph.D., Univ. of Amsterdam. Publs: (poems) De verte tussen ons in, 1962; Autoriteit en vrÿheid 1800-1914, 1966; Authority & Freedom — A historical inquiry into resistance against the industrial society, 1970. Contbr. to Nieuwe Rotterdamse

Courant. Mbrships: Soc. of Netherlands Authors; Netherlands Histl. Assn. Recip., Fellowship, Netherlands Inst. for Adv. Study in the Humanities & Soc. Scis. Address: Varleweg 6 (Rhoon), Rotterdam — 22, Netherlands.

OESTERLE, John Arthur, b. 12 June 1912, Grand Rapids, Mich., USA. Professor of Philosophy. Educ: Ph.D., Univ. of Detroit, 1937; Ph.L., 1940, Ph.D., 1943, Laval Univ., Quebec City, Can. Publs: Logic: The Art of Defining & Reasoning, 1952, revised ed., 1963; Ethics: The Introduction to Moral Science, 1957; Treatise on Happiness, 1963; Treatise on the Virtue, 1966. Contbr. to jrnls. Recip., var. acad. hons. Address: 1127 N. Eddy St., S. Bend, IN 46617, USA.

O'FAOLAIN, Sean, b. 1900. Former Director, Arts Council of Ireland. Educ: M.A.; D.Litt.; Nat. Univ. of Ireland; Harvard Univ. Publs. incl: Midsummer Night Madness, 1932; Life Story of de Valéra, 1933; A Born Genius, 1936; A Purse of Coppers, 1937; An Irish Journey, 1939; Story of Ireland, 1943; The Irish, 1948; The Short Story, 1948; The Vanishing Hero, 1956; I remember, I Remember, 1962; Vive Moi, 1965; The Heat of the Sun, 1966; The Talking Trees, 1970; (play) She Had to Do Something, 1938; (Biography) The Great O'Neill, 1942; Newman's Way, 1952. Address: 17 Rosmeen Park, Dunlaoire, Dublin, Repub. of Ireland.

OFFEN, Ronald Charles, b. 2 Oct. 1930, Chgo., Ill., USA. Author; Freelance Editor, Drama Critic, & Book Reviewer. Educ: A.A., Wright Jr. Coll., 1950; M.A., Univ. of Chgo., 1967. Publs: Dillinger: Dead or Alive? , (co-author), 1970; Cagney, 1973; Brando, 1974. Contbr. to: Poetry; Carleton Miscellany; Prairie Schooner; Poetry Ed., Chgo. Daily News; Poetry Ed., Dec. Mag. Mbrships: Authors Guild; Chgo. Press Club. Recip., 1st Prize, Acad. of Am. Poets, 1957. Address: 1637 W. Chase Ave., Chgo., IL 60626, USA.

OFFERLE, Mildred, b. 3 Jan. 1912, Barnum, Minn., USA. Teacher. Educ: Dip., Duluth State Coll., 1932; B.S., Mankato State Coll., 1966. Publs: Crystal Wells, 1950; The Long Cry, 1960; Moods & Thoughts, 1970. Contbr. to num. jrnls. & newspapers. Mbrships: World Poetry Soc. Intercontinental; Hon. Rep., Centro Studi E. Scambi Int.; Am. Poetry League; League of Minn. Poets. Hons. incl: Margaret Miller Pettingill Mem. Award, 1950; Placed, Minn. Centennial Poetry Contest, 1958; var. other poetry awards. Address: 105 3rd St. SW., Madelia, MN 56062, USA.

O'FLAHERTY, Liam, b. 1896, Aran Islands. Novelist. Educ: Nat. Univ. of Ireland. Publs. incl: Mr. Gilhooley, 1926; The Life of Tim Healy, 1927; The Assassin, 1928; A Tourist's Guide to Ireland, 1929; Two Years, 1930; I Went to Russia, 1931; The Puritan, 1932; Shame the Devil, 1934; Hollywood Cemetry, 1935; Famine, 1937; Short Stories of Liam O'Flaherty, 1937; Land, 1946; Two Lovely Breasts, 1948; Insurrection, 1950; The Short Stories of Liam O'Flaherty, 1956.Address: c/o A. D. Peters, 10 Buckingham St., London WC2, UK.

O'FLANAGAN, Petronella, b. 26 June 1909, Dublin, Repub. of Ireland. Writer; Radio Producer. Educ: Diploma in Home Econ., London. Publs: Fodor's Woman's Guide to Europe, 1953; Fish Recipes, 1956; Encyclopaedia of Ireland, 1968. Contbr. to: Irish Press; Sunday Press; Daily Sketch; Cinn. Post; Providence Visitor; Woman's Life; Personality Parade; Finnish, Swedish, Aust. & South African mags.; South African Radio; etc. Mbrships: PEN; Soc. of Authors; Soroptimists Int.; United Arts Club, Dublin. Producer, Jacob's Award Winning Radio "Feature" Programme, 1973, 1975. Address: 27 Anglesea Rd., Ballsbridge, Dublin 4, Repub. of Ireland.

OGDEN, Brian John, b. 26 June 1936, Watford, UK. Teacher; Church Army Officer. Educ: Proficiency Cert., Relig. Knowledge, Univ. of London. Publs: The Kings & I, 1968; Eyes Right, 1969; Sing to the King, 1970; Homes, 1970; A Class of their Own, 1971; Hands, 1972; Christian Family Festivals, 1973. Address: 54 High St., Overstrand, Cromer, Norfolk, UK.

OGNALL, Leo H, pen names CARMICHAEL, Harry; HARTLEY, Howard, b. 1908, Montreal, P.Q., Can. Novelist. Publs: Over 80 novels inclng. A Slightly Bitter Taste; The Condemned; Murder by Proxy; Suicide Clause; Post Mortem; Flashback; Cry on my Shoulder; The Secret of Simon Cornell; The Eye of the Hurricane; Routine Investigation; Counterfeit; Portrait of a Beautiful Harlot.

Mbrships. incl: Soc. of Authors; PEN; Crime Writers' Assn.; W. Riding Medico-Legal Soc. Address: 18 Avondale Ct., Shadwell Lane, Leeds 17, Yorks., UK.

O'GORMAN, Francis, b. 12 Sept., Urmston, Lancs., UK. University Lecturer in History. Educ: Leeds Univ., 1959-62; Cambridge Univ., 1962-65. Publs: The Whig Party & the French Revolution, 1967; Edmund Burke: His Political Philosophy, 1973; The Rise of Party in England: The Rockingham Whigs, 1760-82, 1975. Contbr. to: Economist; Eng. Histl. Review; Hist.; Government & Opposition; Studies in Burke & his Times; Jrnl. of 18th Century Studies; etc. Mbrships: Royal Histl. Soc.; Histl. Assn. Address: 17 Oughtrington Lane, Lymm, Cheshire, UK.

O'GORMAN, Frank, b. 1940, Manchester, UK. University Lecturer in History. Educ: Univs. of Leeds & Cambridge; B.A.; Ph.D. Publs: The Whig Party & the French Revolution, 1967; Edmund Burke: His Political Philosophy, 1973; The Rise of Party in England 1760-1782, The Rockingham Whigs, 1975. Contbr. to: Govt. & Opposition; Studies in Burke & his Time. Address: 17 Oughtrington Lane, Lymm, Cheshire, UK.

O'GRADY, Desmond Michael, b. 11 Dec. 1929, Melbourne, Aust. Journalist; Author. Educ: B.A., Melbourne. Publs: Eat from God's Hand (non-fiction), 1965; A Long Way from Home (short stories), 1966; Deschooling Kevin Carew (novel), 1974. Contbr. to: Quadrant; Southerly; Overland; Meanjin; Tex. Quarterly; Lit. Review; Sunday Times, London; N.Y. Times; The Critic; Il Mondo; Tempo Presente. Mbrships: Assn. della Stampa Estera in Italia; Aust. Soc. of Authors; Fellowship of Aust. Writers. Recip., Quadrant Short Story Award, 1961. Address: Via Bartolomeo Gosio 77, 00191 Rome, Italy.

O'GRADY, Francis Dominic, b. 24 Apr. 1909, NSW, Aust. Writer. Publs: The Golden Valley, 1955; Goonoo Goonoo, 1956; Hanging Rock, 1957; No Boundary Fence, 1960; Wild Honey, 1961; The Sun Breaks Through, 1964. Contbr. to: Dictionary of Aust. Biog. Mbrships: Royal Aust. Histl. Soc.; Town Clerks' Soc. of NSW. Recip. V. Guy Kable Award, 1948. Address: 21 Karilla Ave., Lane Cove, NSW, Australia 2066.

O'GRADY, John, pen names CULOTTA, Nino; O'GRADA, Sean, b. 9 Oct. 1907, Waverley, NSW, Aust. Author. Educ: Ph.C., Sydney Univ. Publs: They're a Weird Mob, 1957; Cop This Lot, 1960; No Kava for Johnnie, 1961; Gone Fishin', 1962; The Things They Do to You, 1963; Aussie English, 1965; O'Grady Sez, 1969; Are You Irish or Normal? , 1970; So Sue Me, 1970; Aussie Etiket, 1971; It's Your Shout Mate, 1972; Smoky Joe, 1972; Survival in the Doghouse, 1973; Gone Gougin', 1974. Mbrships: Councillor, Aust. Soc. of Authors; PEN; Jrnlsts.' CLub, Sydney. Address: 68 Algernon St., Oatley, NSW 2223, Australia.

O'HARA, Monica, b. Liverpool, UK. Journalist. Publs: Understanding the Causes & Treatment of Kidney Failure, 1975. Contbr. to: Liverpool Echo; Family Doctor; D. C. Thomson, Dundee; Warrington Guardian Series; (former ed.) Liverpool Observer Group. Mbrships: Med. Jrnlsts. Assn. Address: Meols Lodge, 27 Meols Dr., Hoylake, Wirral, Merseyside, UK.

OHBAYASHI, Kiyoshi, b. 25 Apr. 1908, Tokyo, Japan. Novelist; Dramatist; Scriptwriter. Educ: B.A., Keio Univ. Publs: Tada Kimi Yueni, 1960; Kono Chi Hatsurumade, 1962; Ano Nami no Hatemade, 1965; Tsubasayo Itsu no Hini, 1971. Mbrships: Pres., Writers' Guild of Japan; PEN; Chmn., Japanese Broadcast Writers' Assn.; Hons: Noma Bungei Shō, 1943; Shiju Hō Shō (Order of Cultural Merit), 1972. Address: 5 — 26 — 1/Shimouma Setagaya-ku, Tokyo, Japan.

O'HIGGINS, (Rev.) James, S. J., b. 21 Aug. 1915, Birstall, nr. Leeds, UK. Tutor in Modern History. Educ: M.A., D.Phil., Oxford Univ.; S.T.L., Heythrop Coll. Publs: Anthony Collins, the Man & his Works, 1970. Contbr. to: Jrnl. of Theol. Studies. Address: Campion Hall, Oxford, UK.

O'HIGGINS, Paul, b. 5 Oct. 1927, Dublin, Repub. of Ireland. Lecturer & Director of Studies in Law; Fellow, Christ's College, Cambridge. Educ: Trinity Coll. Dublin; Clare Coll., Cambridge, UK; M.A., LL.B., Ph.D.; Barrister-at-Law, Dublin & Lincoln's Inn, London. Publs.

incl: Censorship in Britain, 1972; Ency. of Labour Relations Law, 1972. (co-ed. w. B. A. Hepple); Workers Rights, 1975; Bibliography of Literature relating to British & Irish Labour Law (w. B. A. Hepple & J. Neeson), 1975. Contbr. to: Cambridge Law Jrnl.; New Soc.; Indl. Law Jrnl.; Brit. Yearbook of Int. Law; etc. Hons. incl: Gilbert Murray Prize (shared), 1968; VP, Inst. Shop Acts Admin., 1974. Address: Christ's Coll., Cambridge CB2 3BU, UK.

ÖHRN, Bertil, b. 17 Feb. 1906, Häverö, Sweden. Publs: Fågelsjöar i Södra & Mellersta Sverige, 1940; Fågelregioner, 1961; Barrskogsfåglar, 1963; Fåglarna & Människan, 1965; Fågelsjöar i Mosaiknatur, 1968. Mbr., Sveriges Författarföbund. Address: Odensgatan 1, 752 22 Uppsala, Sweden.

OJA, Hannes, b. 29 Mar. 1919, Martna Co., Estonia. Cost Accountant; Author. Educ: Uuemoisa Agricl. Coll., Estonia. Publs: Inward Beats, 1955; Marks on the Sands of Thought, 1964; On the Footbridge of Feelings, 1967. Contbr. to: Tulimuld; Mana; Pohjala Tahistel; Meie Elu; Vaba Eestlane, etc. Mbrships: PEN Can. Ctr.; Estonian PEN Ctr. in Exile; R.S.L.; Assn. of Estonian Authors in Exile; Estonian Lit. Soc. & Cultural Coun. in Can.; Inst. for Estonian Lang. & Lit., Stockholm. Recip., Estonian Lit. Prize for On the Footbridge of Feelings, 1968. Address: 186 Cleveland St., Toronto, Ont. M4S 2W6, Can.

OJO, G. J. A., b. 1930, Ado-Ekiti, Nigeria. University Lecturer. Educ: M.A. & Ph.D., Nat. Univ. of Ireland, Dublin. Publs: Yoruba Culture, 1966; Yoruba Palaces, 1966; Sev. schl. geogl. textbooks. Ed., Nigerian Geogl. Jrnl., 1967-68. Mbrships. incl: Pres., Nigerian Geogl. Assn., 1971-73; Pres., Nigerian Nat. Comm. for Int. Geogl. Union, 1971-74; Am. Geogl. Soc.; Assn. of Am. Geogs.; AAAS. Address: Univ. of Ife, Ile-Ife, Nigeria.

OKAFOR-OMALI, Dilim, b. 7 Jan. 1927, Pt. Harcourt, Nigeria. Auto-Engineer. Educ: Wandsworth & Paddington Tech. Colls.; A.M.I.M.I.; A.M.I.T.A. Publs: A Nigerian Villager in Two Worlds, 1965. Address: 12 Carr St., Enugu, E. Ctrl. State, Nigeria.

ÓLA, Árni, b. 2 Dec. 1888, Kelduhverfi, N. Iceland. Journalist; Author. Publs. incl: Excursions in Iceland, 4 vols., 1944-72; History of Reykjavík, 7 vols., 1950-68; Historic Places in Iceland, 5 vols., 1961-71; Icelandic Traditions, 3 vols., 1964-73. Contbr. to: Lesbók Morgunblaðsins (wkly, Ed. 25 yrs.). Hons: Order of the Falcon, 1973; honoured by municipalities of Reykjavík & Snaefell Dist. Address: Kleppsvegur 36, Reykjavík, Iceland.

OLAUSSON, Rune Erland, pen name ALM, Monica, b. 19 July 1933, Göteborg, Sweden. Author. Publs: over 20 books (novels, essays, biogs., & children's books), inclng: 7 books about horses & riding under name of Monica Alm, Veteranen (novel), 1962, & Mord pa TV (Murder on TV, novel), 1974; ed. of about 10 anthols. of short stories by Swedish writers. Contbr. to TV, newspapers & Weekly mags. Mbrships: Swedish Union of Authors; Swedish Drama Writers. Recip., Gold Prize, Best TV-script, 1967. Address: Bromsvagen 2, 184 00 Akersberga, Sweden.

OLBY, Robert, b. 1933, Beckenham, UK. Lecturer, University of Leeds. Educ: Univ. of London; Univ. of Oxford; M.A.; D.Phil. Publs: Origins of Mendelism, 1966; Charles Darwin, 1967; The Path to the Double Helix, 1974; Contbr. to: Brit. Jrnl. for the Hist. of Sci.; Annals of Sci.; Jrnl. of Chem. Educ. Mbr., Ed. Bd., Annals of Sci. Address: Chevin Cottage, W. Chevin Rd., Otley, W. Yorks., UK.

OLDENBOURG, Zoë, b. 31 Mar. 1916. Writer. Educ: Sorbonne Univ., Paris. Publs: Argile & Cendres, 1946; La Pierre angulaire, 1953; Bûcher de Montségur, 1959; Les Brûlées, 1961; Les Cités charnelles, 1961; Essai historique sur les Croisades, 1963; Catherine de Russia, 1965; Saint Bernard, 1969; La Joie des Pauvres, 1970. Mbr., Jury, Prix Femina, 1961-. Recip., Prix Femina, 1953. Address: 35 rue Poussin, Paris 16e, France.

OLDHAM, Frank, b. 1903, Leicester, UK. Retired Headmaster; Justice of the Peace. Educ: King's Coll., London Univ.; St. John's Coll., Cambridge Univ.; M.A.; B.Sc. Publs: Thomas Young, Philosopher & Physician, 1933; General Physics, 1939; Thomas Young (w. A. Wood), 1954; Physics for Today (w. E. Langton), 1962. Contbr. to: Les Inventeurs Célèbres, 1950. Mbrships: Fellow, Inst. Physics. Address: 19 Dingle Rd., Bournemouth, UK.

OLEDAL, Brita, b. 10 Jan. 1906, Hovby, Lidköping, Sweden. Teacher of Housekeeping. Educ: Fredrika Bremer Soc.'s Sem. of Country Housekeeping, Rimforsa; Cordon Bleu, Paris, France. Publs: Bakom slutna ögonlock, 1960; I mörko lande, 1962; Lyckans ögonglas, 1967; Livstycket, 1969; Då log Sara, 1971; Skottår, 1973; Kurragömma med Alfred, 1974. Mbrships: Swedish Writers' Soc.; Swedish Soc. of the Blind. Hons. incl: Cultural Prize, Arvika Rotary Club, 1965; Nya Wermland-Tidningens Cultural Prize, 1967. Address: Talken, S 670 30 Edane, Sweden.

OLIVER, F. R., b. 1932, Nairobi. Exeter University Reader in Economic & Social Statistics. Educ: St. John's Coll., Cambridge Univ.; Balliol & Nuffield Colls., Oxford Univ.; M.A.; D.Phil. Publs: The Control of Hire Purchase, 1961; What do Statistics Show, 1964. Contbr. to var. econ. & stat. jrnls. Address: Mardon Hall, Streatham Dr., Exeter, UK.

OLIVER, (Rev.) John, b. 1935, London, UK. Vicar; Writer. Educ: M.A.; M.Litt., Gonville & Caius Coll., Cambridge. Publs: The Church & Social Order, 1968. Contbr. to: Theology; Crucible. Address: South Molton Vicarage, Devon, UK.

OLIVER, Leslie Claremont, b. 5 Feb. 1909, London, UK. Consultant Neurosurgeon. Educ: Guy's Hosp. Med. Schl.; Univ. of London; M.B., B.S., London; F.R.C.S. (England); Fellow. Am. Coll. Surgeons. Publs: Essentials of Neurosurgery, 1952; Parkinson's Disease & its Surgical Treatment, 1953; Basic Surgery, 1958; Parkinson's Disease, 1967; Removable Intracranial Tumours, 1969. Contbr. to: Techniques in British Surgery, 1950; Royal Northern Operative Surgery, 1951; Modern Treatment Year Book, 1959; var. sci. jrnls. (56 articles). Mbr., var. profl. bodies. Address: 94 Harley St., London W1N 1AF, UK.

OLIVER, Paul (Hereford), b. 1927, Nottingham, UK. Head, Department of Arts & History, Architectural Association School of Architecture. Educ: A.T.D. & N.D.D., Goldsmith's Coll., London. Publs: Bessie Smith, 1959, sev. eds.; Blues Fell this Morning, 1960, sev. eds.; Conversation with the Blues, 1965, sev. eds.; Screening the Blues, 1968, 2nd ed. 1970; The Story of the Blues, 1969 (sev. eds.); Savannah Syncopators: African Retentions in the Blues, 1970; Ed., Blues Paperbacks Series, 1970; Ed., Shelter & Society, 1970; Ed., Shelter in Africa, 1971; Ed., Shelter in Greece, (w. O. Doumanis), 1974; Ed., Shelter, Sign & Symbol, 1975. Contbr. to sev. archtl. & jazz jrnls & books. Mbr., Archtl. Assn. Address: Cott Farm, Dartington, Totnes, Devon, TQ9 6HA, UK.

OLIVER, Richard Alexander Cavaye, b. 1904, Lockerbie, UK. Former Pro-Vice-Chancellor, University of Manchester. Educ: Univ. of Edinburgh; Stanford Univ., Calif., USA; M.A.; B.Ed.; Ph.D. Publs: Educational Guidance of the School Child, (co-author), 1936; Research in Education, 1946; Occasional Publications of the Joint Matriculation Board, 1954-67. Contbr. to: Africa; Brit. Jrnl. of Psychol.; Yr. Book of Educ.; Univs. Quarterly. Mbr. & Fellow, Brit. Psychol. Soc. Address: Waingap, Crook, Kendal, Cumbria, LA8 9HT, UK.

OLIVER, Robert Tarbell, b. 7 July 1909, Sweet Home, Ore., USA. Research Professor Emeritus of International Speech. Educ: A.B., Pacific Univ., 1932; M.A., Univ. of Ore., 1932; Ph.D., Univ. of Wis., 1937. Publs. incl: The Psychology of Persuasive Speech, 1942, revised 1957, 1968; Korea: Forgotten Nation, 1944; Verdict in Korea, 1955; Culture & Communication, 1962; History of Public Speaking in America, 1965; Effective Speech, 5th ed., 1970; Communication & Culture in Ancient India & China, 1971. Contbr. to: Quarterly Jrnl. of Speech; Reader's Digest; Sewanee Review; Am. Mercury; True; Current Hist.; New Ldr.; Vital Speeches of the Day; etc. Mbrships. incl: VP, Pres., Speech Communication Assn. of Am.; Advsry. Comm., Am.-Korean Soc.; Dir. of Publs., Pres., Speech Assn. of the Eastern States. Hons. incl: LL.D., Pacific Univ., 1949; Pres. Medal. Repub. of Korea, 1959. Address: 601 Ridge Ave., State Coll., PA 16801, USA.

OLIVER, Roland Anthony, b. 30 Mar. 1923, Srinagar, Kashmir. Professor of the History of Africa. Educ: M.A., Ph.D., King's Coll., Cambridge Univ. Publs: The Missionary Factor in East Africa, 1952; Sir Harry Johnston & the Scramble for Africa, 1957; Ed., The Dawn of African History, 1961; A Short History of Africa (w. J. D. Fage), 1962; Ed., A History of East Africa (w. G. Mathew), 1963; Africa since 1800 (w. A. E. Atmore), 1967; Ed., The Middle Age of African History, 1967; Ed., The Jrnl. of

African History (w. J. D. Fage), 1960-1973; Africa in the Iron Age (w. B. M. Fagan), 1975; Gen. Ed., Cambridge History of Africa, in 8 vols., 1975. Mbrships: Royal African Soc.(Coun.); Acad. Royale des Sciences d'Outremer, Brussels (corres. mbr.). Recip., Haile Selassie Prize Trust Award, 1966. Address: 7 Cranfield House, Southampton Row, London WC1, UK.

OLIVERA, Miguel Alfredo, b. Buenos Aires, Argentina. Writer; Professor. Educ: Prof. Phil. Lit. Publs: Hojas Secas, poems, 1938; Agonia, polyglot review, 1938-1946; La Ifigenia de Goethe, 1939; Camila O'Gorman, an Argentine Tragedy, 1960; Sapphô, o de la Educaciòn, 1969; Oda a Leandro, poem, 1970; El Collar de la Paloma, poems, 1974; El Ramo de Olivos, novel, 1974; Transls. into Spanish of verse by Sappho, Goethe, Cocteau, Rilke, T. S. Eliot, L. Durrell, Christopher Fry, Shelley & Shakespeare. Contbr. to num. Argentine jrnls. Mbrships. incl: Pres., Argentine Ctr., PEN; Engl. Ctr., PEN; Argentine Soc. of Writers. Address: Calle Basavilbaso 1396, Buenos Aires, Argentina.

OLLERENSHAW, (Dame) Kathleen, b. 1 Oct. 1912, Manchester, UK. Mathematician. Educ: M.A., D.Phil., Somerville Coll., Oxford. Publs: The Education of Girls, 1961; The Girls' Schools, 1966; Returning to Teaching, 1974. Contbr. to num. nat. & profl. jrnls. on rsch. in maths., educ.; financing local govt. Mbrships incl: Chmn., Jt. Comm., Royal Northern Coll. of Music, Manchester, 1958—; Coun., Univ. of Salford, 1964—; F.I.M.A.; Comm. of Inquiry, Local Govt. Fin., 1974—. Hons: D.B.E., 1971; F.C.P., 1974; O.St.J., 1974; acad. hons.; Lord Mayor of Manchester, 1975-76. Address: 2 Pine Rd., Manchester M20 0UY, UK.

OLSEN, Bjorn Gunnar, b. 7 Apr. 1942, Halden, Norway. Writer. Publs: Ved skjulegtedet, 1967; Fløyelshjertene lieg Enindringen oundetvakel, 1971; Spøkelsesly, 1972; Reisen tilbake, 1972-1973; Gå ikke i stillhet, 1972-1973; Under kirkegårdsstjernen, 1974. Hons: Mads Wiel Nygaards legat, 1972; State 3-year writing grant. Address: Labyveven 29, 1750 Halden, Norway.

OLSEN, Thomas Carl Morrell, pen name MORRELL, John, b. 7 May 1912, Glasgow, Scotland, UK. Wine Correspondent & Journalist. Publs: Taste of Death, 1942; Wines of the World, 1975. Contbr. to: Homes & Gardens; Good Housekeeping; Scotsman; Signature; Cheshire Life; About Wine; Wine Mine; Gen. Practitioner; Pulse; etc. Mbrships: Press Club; Wig & Pen; Brontë Soc.; Circle of Wine Writers; Confrerie des Vignerons de Saint Vincent de Macon et Bourgogne; Pairie d'Arbois; Gouste-vin de Rouen. Address: Valserine, Thorkhill Gdns., Thames Ditton, Surrey, UK.

OLSON, Bernhard Emanuel, b. 27 Feb. 1910, Winburne, Pa., USA. Educator; Director of Interreligious Affairs. Educ: A.B., Coll. of Emporia, Kan., 1938; B.D., Drew Theol. Sem., Madison, N.J., 1942; Ph.D., Yale Univ., 1959. Publs. incl: Faith & Prejudice, 1963; The Meaning & Conduct of Dialogue (w. D. M. Kelley), 1970; Homework for Christians, 1970; Public Aid for Nonpublic Education, 1971. Ed., Dialogue, 1967-; annual bibliogs. Books for Brotherhood & Paperbacks on Inter-group Rels. Contbr. to: Relig. Educ.; other profl. jrnls. Mbr., num. relig. & civic orgs. Hons: Anisfield-Wolf Award, Saturday Review, & Nat. Mass Media Brotherhood Award, Nat. Conf. Christians & Jews (both for Faith & Prejudice) 1964. Address: 799 Barth Dr., Baldwin, L.I., NY 11512, USA.

OLSON, Philip G., b. 16 Feb. 1934, Racine, Wis., USA. Professor; Chairman, Department of Sociology. Educ: B.A., 1954, M.A., 1956, Univ. of Ariz.; Ph.D., Purdue Univ., 1959. Publs: America as a Mass Society, 1963; The Study of Modern Society, 1970. Contbr. to Am. Sociol. Review. Mbrships: Coun., Sect. on Community, Am. Sociol. Assn., 1974-77; State Rep., Midwest Sociol. Soc.; Bd., 1974-76; Chmn., Comm. of Consultants on Local Arrangements, Alpha Kappa Delta; Sigma Xi. Address: Dept. of Sociology, University of Missouri-Kansas City, 5100 Rockhill Rd., Kansas City, MO 64110, USA.

OLTMANS, Willem Leonard, b. 10 June 1925, Huizen, Netherlands. Journalist; Lecturer. Educ: NOIB Nijenrode Castle; Yale Univ., USA, 1950. Publs: De Verraders, 1968; Grenzen an de Groei, 1973, 1974; Den Vaderland Getrouwe, 1973; Reflections on Limits to Growth, 1973; On Growth: The Crisis of Exploding Population & Resource Depletion, 1974; Die Grenzen des Wachtums, 1974. Contbr. to: Nieuwe Rotterdamse Courant; Algemeen Handelsblad; De Telegraaf; Elseviers Weekblad; Vrij

Nederland; Groene Amsterdammer; De Nieuwe Linie; Grote Provinciale Dagblad Pers; Times of Indonesia; Indonesian Observer; United Asia. Mbr., Netherlands Fedn. of Jrnlsts. Address: Amerbos 205, Amsterdam, Netherlands.

OLYNYK, Roman, pen name RAKHMANNY, Roman, b. 26 Dec. 1918, Lviv, Ukraine. Journalist; Broadcaster. Educ: M.A., Univ. of Toronto, Can.; Ph.D., Univ. of Montreal. Publs: Blood & Ink, USA 1960; Along the Fiftieth Parallel, Can. 1969; Not by Word Alone: A Dialogue, Can. 1971; Fire & Cinders, 1974. Contbr. to: Can. Slavonic papers; Jrnl. Int. Affairs; Suchasnist, Munich (Assoc. Ed.). Mbrships: Can. Assn. Slavists; Ukrainian Free Acad. of Scis., Can.; Ukrainian Sci. Soc. of T. Shevchenko, Can.; Czechoslovak Soc. of Arts & Scis. in U.S.; PEN; Can. Consultative Coun. on Multiculturalism. Hons: 1st Prize, Ukrainian Jrnlsts. Assn. of Am., 1972; Taras Shevchenko Award, Can., 1974. Address: 211 Sheraton Dr., Montreal, P.Q. H4X 1N7, Can.

O'MALLEY, Raymond Morgan, b. 1909, London, UK. University Lecturer in Education. Educ: Trinity Coll., Cambridge; London Inst. of Educ. Publs. incl: One-Horse Farm, 1948; Introducing Chaucer, 1967; London Street Life, 1967; (w. R. Cave) Living with Other People, 1967, Living with the Mass Media, 1967, Education for Personal Responsibility, 1967; (w. D. Thompson) Rhyme & Reason, 1957, English 1-5, 1955-59, Poetry 1-5, 1961-63, The Tree in the Wood 1-4, 1966, English for the Living 1 & 2, 1949-51. Contbr. to: Scrutiny; Times Educ. Supplement. Address: 8 Hills Ave., Cambridge CB1 4XA, UK.

OMAN, Carola Mary Anima, b. 1897, Oxford, UK. Writer. Publs: Nelson, 1948; Sir John Moore, 1953; David Garrick, 1958; Mary of Modena, 1962; Ayot Rectory, 1965; Gascoyne Heiress, 1968; Wizard of the North, 1973. Mbrships: F.S.A.; F.R.S.L.; F.R.Hist. Soc.; Pres., Herts. Br., Brit. Red Cross, 1947-1958; Trustee, Nat. Portrait Gall., 1956, Nat. Maritime Mus., 1955. Address: Bride Hall, Welwyn, UK.

OMARI, T. Peter, b. 1930, Mpraeso, Ghana. Chief, Social Development Section, UN Economic Commission for Africa. Educ: Ctrl. State Univ., Wilberforce, Ohio, USA; Univ. of Wis.; B.A.; M.Sc.; Ph.D. Publs: Marriage Guidance for Young Ghanaians, 1962; Social Work in West Africa, 1962; Basic Course in Statistics for Sociologists, 1962; Kwame Nkrumah: Anatomy of an African Dictatorship, 1970. Contbr. to: Brit. Jrnl. of Sociol.; Soc. Forces; int. Jrnl. of Human Rels. Mbr., Am. Sociol. Assn. Address: c/o University of Ghana, P.O. Box 25, Legon, Accra, Ghana.

OMMANNEY, Francis Downes, b. 22 Apr. 1903, London, UK. Marine Biologist. Educ: B.Sc., Ph.D., Univ. London; Royal Coll. Sci. Publs: South Latitude, 1938; North Cape, 1939; The House in the Park, 1944; The Ocean, 1949; The Shoals of Capricorn, 1952; Isle of Cloves, 1955; Eastern Windows, 1956; Fragrant Harbour, 1961; The Fishes, 1963; A Draught of Fishes, 1965; The River Bank, 1966; Collecting Sea Shells, 1968; Lost Leviathan, 1971. Contbr. to: Geogl. Mag.; Sunday Times; etc. Hons: Sunday Times Gold Medal, 1938 for South Latitude; Int. PEN Club, Silver Pen Award, 1971 for Lost Leviathan. Address: c/o Nat. Westminster Bank Ltd., Royal Garden Br., 55 Kensington High St., London W8, UK.

O'MORRISON, Kevin, b. St. Louis, Mo., USA. Playwright. Educ: Ill. Mil. Schl. Publs: (TV plays) The House of Paper, 1959; And Not a Word More, 1960; A Sign for Autumn, 1962; (stage plays) The Long War, 1965; The Morgan Yard, 1971; The Realist, 1974. Mbrships: The Players; Dramatists' Guild, Inc.; Authors' League of Am.; Writers' Guild of Am. Address: 239 East 18th St., N.Y., NY 10003, USA.

O'NEIL, Terrence (William), b. 31 Mar. 1928, Coventry, UK. Journalist. Publs: Christmas Countdown, & Other Poems; Fragments & Splinters; Awe & Majesty; Saki. Contbr. to var. jrnls. Mbrships: Barbican Poetry Circle (Press Off.); Little Baddow Arts Ctr. Address: 9 Claremont Close, London N1 9LT, UK.

O'NEILL, Ana Maria, b. 7 Mar. 1894, Aguadilla, Puerto Rico. Teacher. Educ: A.B., Univ. of Puerto Rico, 1924; A.M., Columbia Univ., N.Y., 1927; Rochdale Inst., 1939; Ariz. State Univ., 1952-1953; Columbia Univ., 1956-1957. Publs: Ethics for the Atomic Age, 1948; Un Dianóstico del Sistema Educativo, 1958; Cuerpo y Alma del Cooperativismo, 1961; Psicología de la Comunicación, 7th ed., 1973. Mbrships. incl: AAUP; Past Pres., Comm. on

Ethics, Psychols. Assn. of Puerto Rico; Hon. Mbr., Asoc. de Maestros de Puerto Rico; Asoc. de Graduadas de la Univ. de Puerto Rico. Hons. incl: Vawter Fndn. Award, 1938; Award, Co-op. League of the US; Pergamino de Reconocimiento, 1955; Prof. Emeritus, 1961, Hon. Ph.D., 1973, Univ. of Puerto Rico. Address: 121 O'Neill St., Hato Rey, PR 00918, USA.

O'NEILL, Michael J. A., b. 1 Mar. 1913, Dublin, Repub. of Ireland. University Professor. Educ: A.B., Fordham Univ., N.Y., USA, 1937; A.M., 1950, Ph.D., 1952, Univ. Coll., Dublin, Repub. of Ireland. Publs: Lennox Robinson, 1964; James Joyce Miscellany (Ed. w. M. Magalaner), 1962; Holloway's Abbey Theatre (Ed. w. R. Hogan), 1967; Holloway's Irish Theatre (Ed. w. R. Hogan), 3 vols., 1969, 1970, 1971. Contbr. to var. profl. jrnls. Mbrships: Fellow, Royal Soc. of Antiquarians of Ireland; Soc. for Theatre Rsch., London; Can. Assn. of Univ. Tchrs. Hons: Can. Coun. Awards, 1966, 1967; Can. Coun. Leave Fellowship, 1969-70. Address: 175 Waller St., Ottawa K1N 6N5, Ont., Can.

ONETTI, Juan Carlos, b. 1 July 1909. Writer; Editor. Publs: El pozo, 1939; Tierra de nadie, 1941; Para esta noche, 1943; La vida breve, 1950; Un sueño realizado y otros cuentos, 1951; Una tumba sin nombre, 1959; Los adioses, 1954; La cara de la desgracia, 1960; Jacob y el otro, 1961; El Astillero, 1961; El infierno tan temido, 1962; Tan triste como ella, 1963; Juntacadáveres, 1965. Contbr. to: Marcha (Ed., 1939-42); Ed., Vea y Lea, 1946-55. Recip., Nat. Lit. Prize of Uruguay, 1963. Address: Gonzalo Ramirez 1497, Montevideo, Uruguay.

ONG, Walter Jackson, b. 30 Nov. 1912, Kan. City, Mo., USA. Priest, Society of Jesus; Professor of English; Professor of Humanities in Psychiatry. Educ: B.A., Rockhurst Coll., Kansas City, 1933; Ph.L., 1940, M.A., 1941, S.T.L., 1948, St. Louis Univ.; Ph.D., Harvard Univ., 1955. Publs. incl: Frontiers in American Catholicism, 1957; Ramus, Method, & the Decay of Dialogue, 1958; The Barbarian Within, 1962; The Presence of the Word, 1967; Knowledge & the Future of Man (Co-author & Ed.), 1968; Rhetoric, Romance & Technology, 1971. Contbr. to num. philosl., lit., & theol. jrnls. Num. mbrships. incl: Pres., Milton Soc. of Am., 1967; MLA; Cambridge Bibliographical Soc.; Fellow, Am. Acad. of Art & Scis. Address: St. Louis Univ., St. Louis, MO 63103, USA.

ONIANS, Richard Broxton, b. 11 Jan. 1899, Liverpool, UK. Researcher; University Professor; Writer. Educ: B.A., M.A., Univ. of Liverpool; Ph.D., Trinity Coll., Cambridge. Publs: The Origins of European Thought about the Body, the Mind, the Soul, the World, Time & Fate, New Interpretations of Greek, Roman & Kindred evidence, also of some basic Jewish & Christian beliefs, 1951, 2nd enlarged ed., 1954. Contbr. to acad. jrnls. Mbrships. incl: Soc. of Authors; Life, Hellenic Soc.; Life, Cambridge Philol. Soc.; Past Chmn., Nat. Campaign Comm. for Expansion of Higher Educ.; Past Chmn., Jt. Standing Comm. & Conf. on Lib. Coop. Recip., acad. awards. Address: Stokesay, 21 Luard Rd., Cambridge CB2 2PJ, UK.

ONSLOW, John, b. 1906, Garmston, UK. Retired Army Officer; Former Cattle Rancher, B.C., Can. Educ: Royal Mil. Coll., Sandhurst, UK. Publs: Bowler Hatted Cowboy, 1962; Fire in the Desert, 1964; The Stumpfs, 1966; Stumpf & the Cornish Witches, 1969. Contbr. to: Blackwoods Mag.; Argosy; Look & Learn. Address: Hurst Farm, Loxwood, Billinghurst, W. Sussex, UK.

OOKA, Shohei, b. 1909, Tokyo, Japan. University Teacher; Critic; Novelist; Translator. Educ: Univ. of Kyoto. Publs. incl: (in Japanese) Memories of a Prisoner of War, 1949; A Woman of Musashino Plain, 1950; Fires of the Plain, 1951; Oxygen, 1953; Diary of Hamlet, 1955; Battle of Leyte, 1971; (transl.) Chartreuse de Parme by Stendhal, 1949; etc. Hons: Yokomitsu Prize, 1940; Yomiuri Prize, 1952; Mainichi & Shincho Prize, 1961; Mainichi-Gejitsu Prize, 1972. Address: 7-15-12 Seijo, Setagaya-ku, Tokyo, Japan.

OORTHUYS, Casparus Bernardus, b. 1 Nov. 1908, Leiden, Netherlands. Photographer. Publs: Rotterdam — dynamic town; Photobook of Dutch costume; The Beauty of the Netherlands; Amsterdam, its Beauty & Character; Mensen-people, 1969; Het laatste jaar 1944-45 (The last year of the war), 1970. Mbr., Profl. Union of Photographers. Recip., Kt., Orange Order, 1971. Address: 925 Prinsengracht, Amsterdam, Netherlands.

OOSTERLOO, Jan Hendrik, b. 23 July 1911, Delft, Netherlands. Art Critic. Publs: De Meesters van Delft (The Masters of Delft; Life & Works of the Delft Painters of the 17th Century), 1948; Onder het puin stierf hat geluk (novel), 1960; Sander (novel), 1963; De toekomstligt weer open (novel), 1965; Zon aan de overzÿ (novel), 1968; Delft in foto's (introduction), 1968. Contbr. to daily & weekly papers. Mbr., Int. Perscentrum "Nieuwspoort", The Hague. Address: Oude Delft 46, Delft, Netherlands.

OPIE, Iona, b. 13 Oct. 1923, Colchester, UK. Author. Publs: (all w. husband Peter Opie) I Saw Esau, 1947; The Oxford Dictionary of Nursery Rhymes, 1951; The Oxford Nursery Rhyme Book, 1955; The Lore & Language of Schoolchildren, 1959; Puffin Book of Nursery Rhymes, 1963; Children's Games in Street & Playground, 1969; The Oxford Book of Children's Verse, 1973; The Classic Fairy Tales, 1974. Hons: M.A., Oxford Univ., 1962; Coote-Lake Medal (w. Peter Opie), 1960; European Prize (w. Peter Opie), City of Caorle, 1964; Chgo. Folklore Prize (w. Peter Opie), 1970. Address: Westerfield House, West Liss, Hants., UK.

OPIE, Peter, b. 25 Nov. 1918, Cairo, Egypt. Author. Publs: I Want to Be, 1939; Having Held the Nettle, 1945; The Case of Being a Young Man, 1946; 7 other works w. wife (see OPIE, Iona). Contbr. to: Ency. Britannica; Chambers Ency.; New Cambridge Bibliog. of Engl. Lit.; etc. Mbrships: Pres., Folklore Soc., 1963-1964; Pres., Anthropol. Sect., Brit. Assn., 1962-1963. Hons: Chosen Book Competition, 1946; Silver Medal, R.S.A., 1953; M.A., Oxford Univ., 1962; 3 awards jointly w. wife (see OPIE, Iona). Address: Westerfield House, West Liss, Hants., UK.

OPPENHEIMER, Christine Backus, b. 9 July 1920, Marseilles, France. Writer (poetry). Educ: B.A., Calif. Secondary Tchng. Cert., Univ. of Calif. at L.A., USA. Publs: Building the Bridge, 1964. Contbr. to: N.Y. Times; Mass. Review; Cyclo-Flame; Bitterroot; Portland Oregonian; Am. Weave; North Am. Mentor; Cardinal Quarterly. Mbrships. incl: Nat. League Am. Pen Women; Int. Platform Assn.; Acad. of Am. Poets; Wis. Fellowship of Poets. Hons. incl: 1st Prize, Calif. Olympiad of the Arts, 1964, 1968; Gold Medal, United Poets Laureate Int., Philippines, 1968. Address: 22 Miller Park, Chautauqua, NY 14722, USA.

ORDISH, George, b. 1904, London, UK. Pest Control Specialist. Educ: B.Sc.(Econ.), Univ. of London; Dip. Hort. Publs. incl: Untaken Harvest, 1952; Garden Pests, 1956; The Living House, 1960; The Last of the Incas (w. E. Hyams), 1963; Man, Crops & Pests in Central America, 1964; Biological Methods of Crop Pest Control, 1967; Ladies Only (w. Pearl Binder), 1972; The Great Wine Blight, 1973; John Curtis, Pioneer of Pest Control, 1974; A Year in the Life of a Butterfly, forthcoming; (transls.) The Mask of Medusa, by Caillois, 1963; Animal Societies, by Chauvin, 1968. Contbr. to: Illustrated London News; Listener; Wine & Food; Gardener's Chronicle. Mbrships: Soc. of Authors; Assn. of Applied Biols.; Guild of Agricl. Jrnlsts. Agent: Deborah Owen. Address: c/o Deborah Owen, 78 Narrow St., London E14, UK.

ORDOÑEZ, Valeriano, S. J., pen name IS-ORVAL, b. 28 Nov. 1924, Torres del Río Navarra, Spain. Priest; Teacher; Vocational Guidance Counsellor; Poet; Lecturer. Educ: Lic., Philos. & Letters, Spain & Colombia; Lic., Theol.; M.A., Greek & Latin Humanities. Publs. incl: (in French, German, Engl.): Intenta vivir cantando, 2nd ed., 1972; Intenta orar cantando, 3rd ed. 1970; Intenta descubrir hermanos, 3rd ed. 1974; Cerca de Tí, 1967; La Legión de Loyola, 1958 (Is-Orval); Hasta encontrar el camino, 1964; La otra juventud, 3rd ed., 1967; Horizontes para siempre, 1968; La Juventud sonrie a la muerte, 1957; Los Santos noticia diaria, 1973. Contbr. to num. mags. & newspapers. Mbr., var. socs. & insts. Recip., 1st Prize, Specialist Poetry for Anthols., Mérida, Venezuela, 1950. Address: Calle Bergamín 32, Pamplona, Spain.

OREL, Harold, b. 31 Mar. 1926, Boston, Mass., USA. Professor of English. Educ: B.A., Univ. of N.H., 1948; M.A., 1949, Ph.D., 1952, Univ. of Mich. Publs. incl: The World of Victorian Humor, 1961; Thomas Hardy's Epic-Drama: A Study of the Dynasts, 1963; Thomas Hardy's Personal Writings: Prefaces, Literary Opinions, Reminiscences, 1966; The Development of William Butler Yeats, 1885-1900, 1968; English Romantic Poets & The Enlightenment: Nine Essays on a Literary Relationship: Studies in Voltaire & Eighteenth Century, 1973; Irish History & Culture: Aspects of a People's Heritage, 1975. Contbr. to num. lit. jrnls. V.P., Thomas Hardy Soc., UK. Address: 713 Schwarz Rd., Lawrence, KS 66044, USA.

ORGAN, Troy Wilson, b. 25 Oct. 1912, Edgar, Neb., USA. University Professor. Educ: B.A., Hastings Coll.; B.D., McCormick Theol. Sem.; M.A., Ph.D., Univ. of Iowa. Publs: An Index to Aristotle, 1949; The Examined Life, 1956; The Self in Indian Philosophy, 1964; The Art of Critical Thinking, 1965; The Hindu Quest for the Perfection of Man, 1970; Hinduism, 1974. Mbrships: Am. & Ohio Philosl. Assns; Indian Philosl. Congress. Hons: Ford Fndn. Fellowship, 1952; Fulbright Fellowship to India, 1958, 1965; Disting. Prof. & Baker Awards, Ohio Univ., 1965. Address: 65 Second Street, Athens, Ohio, USA.

ORGLAND, Ivar, b. 13 Oct. 1921, Oslo, Norway. University Lecturer; Poet; Translator. Educ: Master's Degree, Univ. of Oslo, 1949; Dr.'s Degree, Univ. of Iceland, 1969. Poetry Publs. incl: Lilje og sverd, 1950; Mjød og malurt, 1959; Jørannatten, 1963; Villhonning, 1966; Nattstill fjord, 1973. 20th Century Icelandic Poetry Translations incl: Eg sigler i haust, 1955; Enno syng vårnatti, 1959; Krystallar, 1965; Stilt vaker Ijoset, 1972; Så fløder havet inn, 1974. Contbr. to: Syn og Segn; Samtiden; Vinduet (Norway); Helgafell (Iceland); Ord och Bild (Sweden); Horisont (Finland); etc. Mbrships: PEN; Norwegian Assn. of Authors. Hons. incl: Sunnmørsprisen, 1974. Address: Lerkevegen 27, 1370 Asker, Norway.

ORIGO, Iris M., b. 15 Aug. 1902, Birdlip, Glos., UK. Writer. Publs: Leopardi, 1935; Tribune of Rome, 1938; War in Val D'Orcia, 1947; The Last Attachment, 1949; The Merchant of Prato, 1957; Images & Shadows; The Vagabond Patt. Contbr. to: Times Lit. Supplement; Hist. Today; Atlantic Monthly; Speculum; etc. Mbrships: F.R.S.L. Hons: Isabella d'Este Medal; L.D., D. Wheaton Coll. & Smith Coll., Mass. Address: 30 Monte Savello, Rome 00186, Italy.

O'RILEY, Ivan Walter, b. 19 July 1923, Wellington, NZ. Journalist. Publs: Giant in the Sun, 1968; Thunder in the North, 1970; The Hunt for Mineral Treasure, 1971; Perth, A City of Light, 1971; Boobs in the Bush, 1974; Adelaide Hills in Colour, 1974; Batavia Road, 1975; Australia's Scenic Wonders, 1975; Australia's Living Past, 1975. Contbr. to: Signature; Reader's Digest; Australasian Post; Pix/People; Rendezvous. Mbrships: Aust. Soc. of Authors; Fellowship of Aust. Writers; Aust. Jrnlsts. Assn.; Aust. Photographic Soc. Address: 11 Hoadley St., Mawson, Canberra, A.C.T., Australia 2607.

ORKENY, Istvan, b. 5 Apr. 1912, Budapest, Hungary. Writer; Playwright. Publs: (short stories) The Dance of the Sea, 1941; Snowstorm, 1951; The Duchess of Jerusalem, 1962; One Minuit Stories, 1963; (plays) The Tott Family; Cat's Game, 1973. Mbr., PEN. Hons: Jozsef Attila Prize, 1953 & 1963; Kossuth Prize, 1972; Grand Prix de L'Hunour Noir, France, 1970. Address: Pasareti ut 39, 1026 Budapest, Hungary.

ORLAND, Henry, b. 23 Apr. 1918, Saarbrücken, Germany. College Professor. Educ: B.M., 1949, M.M., 1950, Ph.D., 1959. Northwestern Univ., USA. Publs: Flut (Flood), German poetry, 1947; Symphonic Sound Ideals between 1750 & 1850 & their Cultural Background, 1960. Contbr. to mags.; Lit. & Music Critic, St. Louis Post-Dispatch & St. Louis Globe-Democrat (newspapers). Mbr., ASCAP. Hons. incl: Chgo. Critics Award, 1952. Address: 21 Bon Price Terr., St. Louis-Olivette, MN 63132, USA.

ORLANDIS, Jose, b. 29 Apr. 1918, Palma de Mallorca, Spain. University Professor. Educ: LL.D, Univ. of Madrid; D. Canon Law, Univ. Lateranense, Rome. Publs: El espiritú de verdad, 1961; El Poder Real y la secesión al trono en la Monarquía visigoda, 1962; Estudios sobre Instituciones Monásticos medievales, 1971; La Iglesia Antigua y Medieval, 1974; Historia social y económica de la España visigoda, 1974. Contbr. to: Anuario de Historia del Derecho Español; Anuario de Estudios medievales; Ius Canonicum; Scripta Theologica; etc. Mbrships: Inst. of Ch. Hist., Univ. of Navarre; Past Pres., Spanish Soc. of Monastic Studies; Past Pres., Aragon Soc. of Soc. Scis. Address: Biblioteca de Humanidades, Universidad de Navarra, Pamplona, Spain.

ORLANDO, Ruggero, pen name CALZOLARI, Gino, b. 5 July 1907, Verona, Italy. Member of Parliament; Broadcasting Journalist. Educ: Univs. of Rome & Naples; Dr. in Maths., 1929. Publs: Carlo Pisacone, 1935; The Remaking of Italy (co-author), 1942; L'Inghilterra è un castello in aria, 1955; Gli anni dell'aquila, 1968; Gli Haiku dello Zodiaco, 1970; Qui Nuova York, 1971. Contbr. to: Europeo, Milan. Mbrships: Past V.P., UN Correspondents

Assn., N.Y., USA; Exec. Comm.; V.P., For. Press Assn., ibid, 1971. Hons: For. Jrnlsm. Award, UCLA, 1967; St. Vincent Prize for Jrnlsm., 1971; Premio Stampa, Mantua, 1973. Address: Camera dei Deputati, Roma, Italy.

ORLOFF, Arthur Ellsworth, b. 25 Nov. 1908, NYC, USA. Screen, Television, & Radio Writer. Educ: A.B., 1928, LL.B., 1931, Fordham Univ., N.Y. Publs: Num. screen, TV, & radio scripts, for all major film studios, CBS Radio Network, & other prods., 1936—. Mbrships: Sev. Comms., & Past Dir., Writers Guild of Am., W.; For. Film Award Nominating Comm., Acad. of Motion Picture Arts & Scis.; Acad. of TV Arts & Scis. Address: 2318 Coldwater Canyon Dr., Beverly Hills, CA 90210, USA.

ORLOVITZ, Gil, b. 7 June 1918, Phila., Pa., USA. Writer; Editor. Publs. incl: (verse) Concerning Man, 1947; Keep to Your Belly, 1952; The Diary of Dr. Eric Zeno, 1953; The Papers of Professor Bold, 1958; Selected Poems, 1960; The Art of the Sonnet, 1961; Couldn't Say, Might be Love, 1969; (novels) Milkbottle H, UK, 1967, USA, 1968; Ice Never F, UK, 1970; (short stories) The Story of Erica Keith & Other Stories, Poems & a Play, 1957; Ed., Award Avant-Garde Reader, 1965. Contbr. to: Quarterly Review of Lit.; Lit. Review (plays). Address: 924 W. End Ave., N.Y., NY 10025, USA.

ORMESSON, Comte Jean d', b. 1925. Journalist; International Official. Educ: Ecole Normale Supérieure, Paris. Publs: L'Amour est un plaisir, 1956; Du côté de chez Jean, 1959; Un amour pour rien, 1960; Au revoir & merci, 1966; Les Illusions de la mer, 1968; La Gloire de l'Empire, 1971. Contbr. to: Le Monde; France-Soir; Paris Match; Ed.-in-Chief, Le Figaro, 1974—; Diogenes. Mbrships: French Acad.; Control Comm. of Cinema, 1962-69; Coun. ORTF, 1960-62; Delegate to var. int. confs. Recip., Grand Prix du Roman, French Acad., 1971. Address: 10 ave. du Parc-Saint-James, 92200 Neuilly-sur-Seine, France.

ORMOND, Willard Clyde, b. 19 Mar. 1906, Rigby, Idaho, USA. Magazine Writer; Author. Educ: Brigham Young Univ.; Art Inst. of Chgo. Publs. incl: Hunting in the Northwest, 1948; Hunting Our Biggest Game, 1956; Hunting Our Medium Size Game, 1958; Bear, 1961; Complete Book of Hunting, 1962; Complete Book of Outdoor Lore, 1964; Outdoorsman's Handbook, 1970; Co-author, sev. other outdoor books. Contbr. to num. sporting mags.; Contbng. Ed., Am. Rifleman mag., 7 yrs.; Outdoor column, Post Register, Idaho, 29 years. Hons: 1st Place, Nat. Sportsmen's Outdoor Story Contest, 1927; 3rd Place, Writer's Digest Nat. Fiction Contest, 1937. Address: Rt. 2, Box 70—A, Rigby, ID 83442, USA.

ORPAZ, Yitzhak, b. 15 Nov. 1923, Zinkow, USSR. Newspaper Editor; Writer. Educ: Univ. of Tel-Aviv. Publs: Eisev Pere, 1959; Or Bead Or, 1962; Mot Lysanda, 1964; Zeid Hazvia, 1966; Nemalim, 1968; Masa Daniel, 1969; Shalosh Novelot, 1972; The Death of Lysanda, 1970. Contbr. to: Al Hamishmar; Haaretz; New Outlook; Now; Stand. Recip., Asher Barash Prize, 1962; Talpir Prize, 1967. Address: 191a Ben-Yehuda St., Tel-Aviv, Israel.

ORR, Clyde Jr., b. 1921, Lewisburg, Tenn., USA. Professor of Chemical Engineering; Writer. Educ: B.S.; M.S.; Ph.D.; Univ. of Tenn.; Ga. Inst. of Tech. Publs: Fine Particle Measurement; Between Earth & Space; Particulate Technology, 1966. Mbrships: Am. Chem. Soc.; Am. Inst. of Chem. Engrs. Address: 5091 Hidden Branches Circle, Dunwoody, GA 30338, USA.

ORR, James Edwin, b. 15 Jan. 1912, Belfast, UK. Professor of History; Universities' Missioner. Educ: D.Phil., Univ. of Oxford; Ed.D., Univ. of Calif., USA; D.Theol., Serampore Coll., India; D.D., Univ. of S. Africa, Pretoria. Publs: The Second Evangelical Awakening in Britain, 1949; Full Surrender, 1951; Faith That Makes Sense, 1960; The Light of the Nations, 1965; A Hundred Questions about God, 1969; The Flaming Tongue, 1973; The Fervent Prayer, 1974. Mbrships. incl: F.R.S.L.; Fellow, Royal Histl. Soc.; Am. Histl. Assn. Address: 11451 Berwick St., L.A., CA 90049, USA.

ORSI, Ferenc, b. 17 Apr. 1927, Barcs, Somogy, Hungary. Journalist; Dramatist; Writer. Publs: Aranylakodalom, 1957; Kincses Baranya, 1963; Szinhaz rivalda nelkul, 1965; Romolusz e Remusz, 1966; A Tenkes kapitanya, 1967; Zrinyi, 1973; also 10 TV plays & 9 stage plays. Contbr. to: Kortars; Uj iras; Pajtas; etc. Mbrships: Hungarian Writers' Union; Hungarian Journalists' Union; Feszek Club. Hons: Alexandria Jury Prize, 1962; Golden

Nimfa Award, Monte Carlo, 1964. Address: Alig utca 6/b, I, Budapest 1132, Hungary.

ORSLER, Michael, b. 1931, Woolpit, Suffolk, UK. Schoolmaster. Educ: B.A., Univ. Coll., Leicester. Publs: The Imperial Room, 1967; The Big Dig, 1970; Rhumb Line, 1971. Contbr. to: Manchester Guardian; New Yorker. Agent: Christopher Busby. Address: Fuchsias, Fornham-All-Saints, Bury St. Edmunds, Suffolk, UK.

ORTEGA CUENTAS, Julio Cesar, b. 29 Sept. 1942, Casma, Peru. Professor of Literature. Educ: D.Litt., Cath. Univ. of Peru, 1967. Publs: De este reino, 1964; Teatro, 1965; La contemplacion y la fiesta, 1969; Mediodia, 1970; Figuracion de la persona, 1971; Relato de la Utopia, 1973. Contbr. to: Textos en el aire (Series Dir.), 1973; Editorial del Instituto de Cultura (Dir.), 1974. Mbrships: Latin-Am. Lit. Expert, UNESCO Prog. of Cultural Studies, 1968-74; Vis.Prof., Univ. of Pitts., USA, 1969, Yale Univ., 1970, Univ. of Tex., 1973. Address: Domingo Elias 160-B, Miraflores, Colombia, S. America.

ORTHOFER, Peter Bernd, pen names HAGEL, Jan; BERND, Peter, b. 17 June 1940, Berlin, Germany. Author; Satirist. Educ: Univ. studies in Philos. & Psychol. Publs: Lieben und Liebenlassen; Österreich hat immer Saison; Das Wandern ist des Deutschen Lust; Als wärs ein Stück von ihm; Liebe unter 6 Augen; Make Love; Mensch ärgere dich doch. Contbr. to num. leading Austrian & German mags. & newspapers. Mbrships: PEN; Assn. of Dramatists & Composers (Comm.); Union of Profl. Authors (Comm.); Creative Club, Austria. Address: Wollzeile 21, A — 1010 Vienna, Austria.

ORTON, Thora Margaret, pen name COLSON, b. Murree, Pakistan. Writer; Former Toy Designer. Educ: Rachel McMillan Trng. Coll., Deptford, UK. Publs: Rinkin of Dragon's Wood, 1965, Am. ed., 1965, German (transl.) ed., 1966. Contbr. to: The Christian Sci. Monitor. Address: Riverslea, Tywyn, Gwynedd, N. Wales, UK.

ORTZEN, Leonard Edwin, (Len), b. 1912, London, UK. Freelance Author & Translator. Educ: Sorbonne, Paris, France. Publs: The Gallic Land, 1952; Just Across the Channel, 1954; Your Guide to the Loire Valley, 1968; Stories of Famous Disasters at Sea, 1969; North African Writing, 1970; Famous Lifeboat Rescues, 1971; Famous Arctic Adventures, 1972; Stories of Famous Submarines, 1973; Stories of Famous Sea Raiders, 1973; Stories of Famous Shipwrecks, 1974; Imperial Venus, 1974; Stories of Great Exploration, 1975. Contbr. to: UNESCO Features; Realities; New Statesman; London Mag. Mbr., Soc. of Authors. Address: Ivy Cottage, Leonard Stanley, Stonehouse, Glos., UK.

ORVIL, Ernst, b. 12 Apr. 1898, Oslo, Norway. Author; Poet; Dramatist. Publs: 13 novels; 12 books of poems; 7 comedies & tragedies; 4 books of short stories. Mbrships: PEN, Oslo; Norwegian Authors' Soc., Oslo; Norwegian Dramatists' Assn., Oslo. Address: Vibes G., 21 Oslo 3, Norway.

OSBORN, (Sir) Frederic James, b. 26 May 1885, London, UK. City Developer. Publs: New Towns after the War, 1918, 1942; Green-Belt Cities, 1946, 1949; Can Man Plan? & other Verses, 1959; The New Towns: Answer to Megalopolis (w. A. Whittick), 1963, 3rd ed. 1975; Letters of Lewis Mumford & Frederick Osborn, 1971. Contbr. to: Town & Country Planning (Ed., 1949-65); var. tech. jrnls. & newspapers. Mbrships. incl: Town & Country Planning Assn., GB (Pres.); Int. Fedn. Housing & Planning (VP). Hons. incl: Kthood., 1956; Gold Medal, Royal Town Planning Inst., 1963; Howard Mem. Medal, 1968. Address: 16 Guessens Rd., Welwyn Garden City, Herts, UK.

OSBORN, George Howard, b. 1911, London, UK. Chemist. Educ: Tech. Coll., Brighton; Univ. of London. Publs: Analysis of Aluminium Alloys, 1947; Synthetic Ion-exchangers, 1955; Walks in Dorset, 1974; Exploring Ancient Dorset, 1975. Contbr. to: Nature; Analyst; Jrnl. Chem. Soc.; Metallurgia; Jrnl. Soc. Chem. Ind.; Chem. in Britain. Address: Cherry Tree Cottage, Merley Ways, Wimborne, Dorset, UK.

OSBORNE, Charles, b. 24 Nov. 1927, Brisbane, Australia. Author; Critic; Musicologist. Educated pvtely. Publs: Kafka, 1967; 50 Works of English Literature We Could Do Without (w. Brigid Brophy & Michael Levy), 1967; Swansong (poems), 1968; The Complete Operas of Verdi, 1969; Ned Kelly, 1969; The Concert Song

Companion, 1974; Ed. & Transl., sev. other vols. Contbr. to: Radio & TV; London Mag.; Times Lit. Supplement; New Statesman; Spectator; Guardian; Sunday Times; etc. Mbrships: Dir., Poetry Int.; Sec., Poetry Book Soc.; Lit. Dir., Arts Coun. of GB. Address: c/o Agent, Richard Scott Simon Ltd., 36 Wellington St., London WC2, UK.

OSBORNE, (Mrs.) Dorothy G., pen name ARTHUR Gladys, b. 1917, London, UK. Founder, Secretary of Art Group; Author. Publs: Lin & the Legend; Kanoka of the Pirates; (as Gladys Arthur) The Other Side of the Mountain; (as Dorothy Osborne) The Secret of Old White Horn; Trouble at Keemaha Falls; Ann, Jerry & the Knights Valiant. Contbr. to: Christian Herald; Christian; Our Own Mag.; Animal Ways; King's Messenger; Discoverer; Cheerio; Ch. Army Gazette; Young Soldier; Boys & Girls; BBC; Busy Bees; Woman's Outlook; Statesman; etc. Address: Avalon, Newton St. Cyres, Exeter, UK.

OSBORNE, Geoffrey, b. 10 Mar. 1930, Gravesend, Kent, UK. Journalist; Author. Publs: The Power Bug, 1968; Balance of Fear, 1968; Traitor's Gait, 1969; Checkmate for China, 1969; Death's No Antidote, 1971; A Time for Vengeance, 1974; Yet Here's a Spot, 1976. Contbr. to: Bristol Evening Post (Chief Sub-Ed., 1962–); Argosy; Reveille; London Evening News; John Creasey's Mystery Bedside Book; Aust. Women's Wkly.; num. other overseas mags. Mbrships: Soc. of Authors; Crime Writers' Assn.; PEN. Address: Paguera, 15 Stoneyfields, Easton-in-Gordano, nr. Bristol, Avon, BS20 0LT, UK.

OSBORNE, Harold, b. 1 Mar. 1905, London, UK. Writer; Editor. Educ: M.A., Cambridge Univ. Publs. incl: Foundations of the Philosophy of Value, 1933; Theory of Beauty, 1952; Indians of the Andes, 1952, USA 1973; Bolivia: A Land Divided, 1954, 3rd ed., 1964; Aesthetics & Criticism, 1955; Ed., Aesthetics & The Modern World, 1968; Aesthetics & Art Theory, 1968, USA 1970, Portuguese transl., 1970; South American Mythology, 1968; The Art of Appreciation, 1970; Ed., The Oxford Companion to Art, 1970; Ed., Aesthetics, 1972; Ed., The Oxford Companion to the Practical Arts (to appear 1975). Contbng. Ed., Brit. Jrnl. of Aesthetics; Cons. Ed., and/or Contbr. to var. aesthetic jrnls. Address: 90A St. John's Wood High St., London NW8, UK.

OSBORNE, John, b. 6 Apr. 1911, Birmingham, UK. Dentist. Educ: L.D.S. & M.D.S., Univ. of Birmingham; Ph.D., Univ. of Sheffield. Publs: Dental Mechanics for Students, 1939, 6th ed. 1970; Acrylic Resins in Dentistry, 1943, 3rd ed. 1948; Partial Dentures, 1954, 4th ed. 1974. Contbr. to: Brit. Dental Jrnl.; Int. Dental Jrnl.; Aust. Dental Jrnl. Mbrships: Pres., Hosps. Grp., Brit. Dental Assn.; Int. Dental Fedn. Address: Vesey Cottage, Warlands Lane, Shalfleet, Newport, Isle of Wight, UK.

OSBORNE, John James, b. 1929, London, UK. Playwright; Actor. Publs. incl: (plays) Look Back in Anger; The Entertainer; Epitaph for George Dillon; The World of Paul Slickey; A Subject of Scandal & Concern; Luther; Under Plain Cover; Inadmissible Evidence; A Patriot for Me; A Bond Honoured; Time Present; The Hotel in Amsterdam; West of Suez; Hedda Gabler (adaptation); A Sense of Detachment; A Place Calling Itself Rome; The Picture of Dorian Gray; The End of the Old Cigar; Watch It Come Down; (TV plays) The Right Prospectus; Very Like a Whale; The Gift of Friendship; Jill & Jack; (films) Tom Jones; Moll Flanders. Contbr. to Declaration. Agent: Robin Dalton Assocs. Address: c/o 11 Hanover St., London W1, UK.

OSBORNE, Margaret, b. 1909, Wimbledon, Surrey, UK. Dog Breeder; Author. Educ: L.R.A.M.; L.R.C.M. Publs: The Collie, 1957; The Shetland Sheepdog, 1959; Collies, 1961; Know Your Welsh Corgi. Contbr. to: Dog World; Our Dogs; Shetland Sheepdog Mag., USA. Mbrships: Ladies Br., Kennel Club (var. comms.). Address: Shiel, Stockbury, Sittingbourne, Kent, UK.

OSER, Jacob, b. 1915, NYC, USA. University Professor; Author. Educ: B.S.; M.A.; Ph.D.; Univs. of Ill.; Columbia. Publs: Economic History of Modern Europe (co-author), 1953, & Spanish ed.; Must Men Starve? The Malthusian Controversy, 1956, & Spanish ed.; Promoting Economic Development: with Illustrations from Kenya, 1967; Economics: Reality through Theory (co-author), 1973; Henry George, 1974; Evolution of Economic Thought, 3rd ed., 1975. Contbr. to: Jrnl. Farm Econs.; Social Rsch.; Current Econ. Comment; Jrnl. Econ. Hist.; Indian Jrnl. Econs.; Am. Jrnl. Econs. & Sociol. etc. Mbr., Assn. for Evolutionary Econs. Address: South Rd., Clinton, NY 13323, USA.

OSERS, Ewald, b. 13 May 1917, Prague, Czech. Broadcasting Administrator. Educ: Charles Univ., Prague; B.A., Univ. of London, UK. Publs. incl: (transls.) The Correspondence between Richard Strauss & Hugo von Hofmannsthal, 1961; The Secret Conferences of Dr. Goebbels 1939-43, 1970; Three Czech Poets, 1971; Selected Poems by Ondra Lysohorsky, 1971; With the Volume Turned Down & Other Poems by Reiner Kunze, 1973; num. others. Contbr. to: London Mag.; Stand; Contemp. Lit. in Transl.; Observer; Poésie Vivante; etc. Mbrships. incl: Coun., 1973–, Fellow, Inst. of Linguists; Vice-Chmn., 1970, Chmn., 1971, Transls. Assn; PEN. Int.; Poetry Soc. Recip., Schlegel-Tieck Transl. Prize, 1971. Address: 33 Reades Lane, Sonning Common, Reading RG4 9LL, UK.

O'SHAUGHNESSY, John, b. 29 Aug. 1927, Lancs., UK. University Professor; Author. Educ: M.A. Publs: Business Organization, 1956; Analysing & Controlling Business Procedures, 1959; Evaluate Your Sales Force, 1972; Inquiry & Decision, 1973. Contbr. to Jrnls. of Marketing & Retailing, USA. Address: 76 High St., Blunham, Beds., UK.

OSHIMA, Shotaro, b. 28 Sept. 1899, Toyama, Japan. Emeritus Professor of English Literature. Educ: B.A., D.Litt., Waseda Univ., Tokyo; Merton Coll., Oxford, UK, 1937-1939. Publs. incl: Poetic Imagination in English Literature, 1953; Studies in Modern Irish Literature, 1956; Collected Poems of Yeats (Japanese transl.), 1958; Yeats, the Man & the Poet, 1961; W. B. Yeats & Japan, 1965; Journeys & Scenes: Poems, 1968; Poems, 1972. Contbr. to var. lit. jrnls.; (articles) Yeats & the Japanese Theatre, 1965; Jack B. Yeats, 1971; Synge in Japan, 1971. Mbrships: Dir., Japan Poets Club, 1959-; Pres., Yeats Soc. of Japan, 1965-. Hons: Tributes in Prose & Verse, 1970; Order of Merit, Emperor's Spring Awards, 1974. Address: 34-4 Nishisugamo, 2-chome, Toshima-ku, Tokyo, Japan.

OSMANCZYK, Edmund Jan, b. 10 Aug. 1913, Jagielno, Poland. Journalist; Writer. Publs. incl: (in Polish) Polish Affairs, 1946; Prussian Documents, 1947; Germany 1945-50, 1951; The Contemporary America, 1960; The Interesting History of UN 1945-1965, 1965; It was a year 1945 . . ., 1970; Our Europe, 1971; Poles of the Rodlo Sign (w. Helena Lehr), 1972; Encyclopaedia of International Relations & the UN, 1974; (verse) The Struggle is Victorious, 1945. Contbr. to num. newspapers & jrnls. as corres. Mbrships: PEN; Polish Writers' Union. Hons. incl: State Prize, 1955; Order of Builders of People's Poland, 1972. Address: Plac Zamkowy 8/5, Warsaw, Poland.

OSMOND, Edward, b. Orford, UK. Freelance Illustrator; Art School Teacher. Publs: A Valley Grows Up, 1953; From Drumbeat to Tickertape, 1960; The Artist in Britain, 1961; Animals of Central Asia, 1967; Animals of the World & Animals of Britain, 3 vols.; Exploring Fashions & Fabrics; People of the Grasslands; People of the Deserts; People of the Jungle Forests; People of the High Mountains; People of the Lonely Islands; People of the Arctic. Mbrships. incl: Soc. of Indl. Artists & Designers; Soc. of Authors. Recip., Carnegie Award, 1953. Address: Downland Cottage, Lullington Close, Seaford, E. Sussex, UK.

OSMOND, Laurie, b. London, UK. Writer; Artist; Sculptor. Publs: The Thames Flows Down, 1957. Contbr. to var. jrnls. Mbrships: Soc. of Authors; Sussex Authors. Address: Downland Cottage, Lullington Close, Seaford, E. Sussex, UK.

OSTERLING, Anders Johan, b. 13 Apr. 1884, Hälsingborg, Sweden. Author; Critic. Educ: Lund Univ., Sweden. Publs. incl: Preludier, 1904; Arets visor, 1907; Bäckahästen, 1909; Facklor i stormen, 1913; Idyllernas bok, 1917; De sju strängarna, 1922; Jordens heder, 1927; Tonen fran havet, 1933; Skånska utflykter, 1934; Dagens gärning I-III, 1920, 1921, 1931; Minnetsvägar, 1967. Contbr. to: Svenske Dagbladet, 1919-35; Stockholms-Tidningen, 1936-66. Mbrships: Swedish Acad.; PEN (Swedish Pres.); Chmn., Nobel Lit. Prize Comm., 1921–. Address: Blockhusringen 39, 15125 Stockholm, Sweden.

OSTRO, Ernest Albert, b. 13 Aug. 1938, Bremen, Germany. Journalist; Writer. Educ: A.B., Harvard Univ. Publs: What Your Mayor Does, 1970. Contbr. to: The Progressive, USA; The Month, UK; The Tablet, UK; Anthony Messenger, USA; Crosscurrents, USA. Mbrships.

incl: Nat. Press Club, Wash. D.C.; For. Press Assn., London. Recip., award for best mag. article, Cath. Press Assn. of Am. Address: Pugs Corner, Abinger Common, Nr. Dorking, Surrey, UK.

O'SULLIVAN, Dermot Alexis, b. 13 July 1929, Cork, Repub. of Ireland. Writer. Educ: B.Sc., M.Sc., Ph.D., Univ. Coll., Cork; postgrad., Univ. of Calif. at Berkeley, USA. Contbr. to: Chem. & Engrng. News; Environmental Sci. & Technol. Mbrships: Nat. Assn. Sci. Writers Inc. (USA); Am. Chem. Soc.; Chem. Soc.; Assn. Brit. Sci. Writers; Wig & Pen Club. Address: 5 Mostyn Road, London, SW19, UK.

OSVÁT, Erzsébet, b. 21 Mar. 1913, Beregovo, USSR. Nursery Rhyme & Tale Writer. Educ: Tchrs. Trng. Coll. Publs: Csivi-csivi, Megérkeztünk (Chirp-chirp, Here We Are), 1959; Csipkebokor Vendéget Vár (Guest-Waiting Briar), 1962; Fogócska (Tig-tag), 1966; Kiskelep (Clattering Storkling), 1973. Contbr. to: Kisdobos; Dörmögö Dömötör; Nök Lapja; Népszabadság; Népszava. Mbr., Hungarian Writers Union. Recip., Order of Labour (silver), 1973. Address: 1098 Budapest, IX, Távíró u. 23/II.1, Hungary.

OTHMER, Donald Frederick, b. 11 May 1904, Omaha, Neb., USA. Distinguished Professor of Chemical Engineering, Polytechnic Institute, Brooklyn, NY. Educ: B.S., Univ. Neb., 1924; M.S., 1925, Ph.D., 1927, Univ. Mich. Publs: Co-Ed., Kirk-Othmer Encyclopedia of Chemical Technology, 1st ed., 17 vols., 2nd ed., 24 vols., Spanish ed., 16 vols., 1947-72; Tech. Ed., UN Report, Technology of Water Desalination, 1964; Fluidization, 1956; Fluidization & Fluid Particle Systems (co-author). Contbr. to num. Am. & for. tech. jrnls., etc. (more than 325 articles on chem. engrng., phys. chem. processes, thermodynamics, extractive metallurgy, etc.); Inventor & Author, over 110 patents; Lectr.. num. int. congresses. Mbrships. incl: Fellow, AAAS; Hon. Life Mbr., NY Acad. Scis. Hons. incl: Tyler Award, 1958; D.Eng., Univ. Neb., 1962; Honor Scroll, Am. Inst. Chems., 1970; Disting. Cons. Award, 1975. Address: 333 Jay St., Bklyn., NY 11201, USA.

OVERBY, George Robert, b. 21 July 1923, Jacksonville, Fla., USA. University President. Educ: B.A., 1951, Ph.D., 1966, Fla. State Univ.; M.Ed., 1959, Specialist in Ed., 1963, Univ. of Fla. Publs: A Critical Review of Selected Issues Involved in the Establishment & Functioning of the National Council for Accreditation of Teacher Education from Its Origin through 1965, 1967; Author, Constitution, Bylaws & Code of Ethics of Christian Warriors for Christian Education, Inc. Contbr. to profl. jrnls.; Ed., Christian Education & Christian Educator (jrnls.). Mbrships: Special Cons., Special Comm., Am. Assn. of Colls. for Tchrs. Educ. & others. Hons: Commendation for Bylaws; etc., above. Address: PO Drawer C, Cape Canaveral, FL 32920, USA.

OVERHOFF, Julius, b. 12 Aug. 1898, Vienna, Austria. Writer. Educ: Vienna Univ.; J.D., Cologne Univ., W. Germany. Publs: Ein Buch von der Stadt Soest, 1935; Die Pflugspur (Collected Poems), 1935, 2nd ed., 1962; Eine Familie aus Megara (novel), 1948, 2nd ed., 1965; Reise in Lateinamerika, 1953; Die Welt mit Dschingiz-Chan (novel), 1959; Die Herabkunft der Granga, 1964. Contbr. to: PEN Almanach; Merkur (Munich); Neue deutsche Hefte (Berlin); & others. Mbr., PEN; etc. Hons: Willibald Pirkheimer Medal, 1969. Address: 673 Neustadt 19, Roemerweg 47, W. Germany.

OVERMAN, Frances Elizabeth Henson, b. 9 Mar. 1913, Eddyville, Ky., USA. Freelance Writer. Educ: A.B., Murray State Univ.; Union, Western State of Northwestern Univs.; Univs. of Tenn. & Wis. Contbr. to num. profl. jrnls. Mbrships. incl: Hon. Mbr., Tau Kappa Alpha Forensic Fraternity; Int. Comm., Fine Arts Sect., Centro Studi E. Scambi Internazionale. Hons. incl: Citation, Study of Am. Judicial System, 1971. Address: 109 Pelham Rd., Oak Ridge, TN 37830, USA.

OVERMAN, Michael, b. 1920, Devizes, Wilts., UK. Journalist; Editor; P.R. Officer; Technical Author. Educ: Royal Mil. Acad., Woolwich. Publs: Roads Bridges & Tunnels, UK & USA 1967, Germany 1969, France 1970. Water — Solutions to a Problem of Supply & Demand, UK & USA 1968, Sweden 1969, France 1970; Science Against Crime (w. Stuart Kind), 1971; Marc Brunel & the Tunnel, 1971; Understanding the Computer, 1972; Understanding Telecommunications, 1974; Understanding Energy, 1975;

Man the Bridge Builder, 1975. Address: The Meusings, Church End, Walkern, Herts., UK.

OVINGTON, John Derrick, b. 14 May 1925, Spennymoor, UK. First Assistant Secretary, Australian Government Department of the Environment & Conservation. Educ: B.Sc., 1945, Ph.D., 1947, D.Sc., 1964, Univ. of Sheffield. Publs: Woodlands, 1965. Contbr. to: Ecol.; Applied Ecol.; New Phytol.; Oikos; Annals of Bot. Num. mbrships.incl: Fellow, Inst. of Biol.; Fellow, Forestry Soc.; F.R.S.A.; Ecol. Soc.; VP, Ecol. Commn., Int. Union for Conservation of Nature. Recip., Emeritus Professorship, Aust. Nat. Univ., 1965. Address: 18 Downes Pl., Hughes, Canberra, A.C.T., Australia 2605.

OWAIN, Owain, b. 11 Dec. 1929, Pwllheli, Gwynedd, Wales, UK. Educator. Educ: B.Sc., Univ. of Wales; Dip. Ed.; ARIC. Publs: Amryw Ddarnau, 1969; Bara Brith, 1971; Hei Ho, 1972; Y Byd a'i Bethau, 1972; Y Peiriant Pigmi, 1973; Rho Gynnig, 1974; Yr Ymlusgiaid, 1974. Contbr. to: Y Cymro; Y Faner; Barn; Y Wawr; Taliesin; Wales Sci. Bulletin; Y Genhinen; etc. Mbrships: Founding Chmn., Clwb y Gader; Past Pres., Cymdeithas Rhieni Bangor; Founding Ed., Tafod y Ddraig; Founding Ed., Gofod. Hons: 1st Prize, short story competition, Barn, 1968; 1st Prize, children's book competition, W.J.E.C., 1969; Num. prizes, Nat. Eisteddfod, 1970—; Annual Lit. Prize, Welsh Acad., 1972. Address: "Cil Enlli", Faenol Isaf, Tywyn, Gwynedd LL 36 ODW, Wales, UK.

OWEN, Alun Davies, b. 24 Nov. 1926. Former Actor; Playwright. Publs. incl: (plays) Two Sons, 1957; The Rough & Ready Lot, 1958; A Little Winter Love, 1963; The Goose, 1967; There'll Be Some Changes Made, 1969; (films) The Criminal, 1960; A Hard Day's Night, 1964; (other publs.) Three TV Plays, 1961; Progress to the Park, 1962; The Rose Affair, 1962; A Little Winter Love, 1964; Maggie May, 1964; (TV plays) After the Funeral, 1960; Dare to Be a Daniel, 1962; The Hard Knock, 1962; The Stag, 1963; The Other Fella, 1966; The Winner, 1967; The Fantasist, 1967; Male of the Species, 1969. Address: c/o Felix de Wolfe, 61 Berkeley House, 15 Hay Hill, London W1, UK.

OWEN, Benjamin Evan, b. 1918, London, UK. Teacher. Educ: Birmingham Training Coll. Publs: (Ed.) Blackwell's Junior Poetry Books, 1960; The Night Sky, 1965; What Happened Today, vols. 1-3, 1966; (Ed.) Pergamon Poets, 1968; (Ed.) Athena Books, 1968; Carford Readers, 1970; Checkers, 4 Titles, 1973-74. Contbr. to: Fortnightly; Outposts; Contemporary Review; Birmingham Post; Oxford Mail; Times Supplements; Use of Engl.; Teacher; Teacher's World; etc. Address: 35 High St., Watlington, Oxford OX9 5PZ, UK.

OWEN, Charles, b. 14 Nov. 1915, Brighton, UK. Writer; Management Consultant; Retired Navy Officer. Educ: R.N. Colls., Dartmouth & Greenwich. Publs: Independent Traveller, 1966; Britons Abroad, 1968; The Maltese Islands, 1969; The Opaque Society, 1970; The Great Trains (of Europe), 1973; No More Heroes, 1975. Contbr. to var. jrnls. & mags. Mbr., Soc. of Authors. Recip., D.S.C., 1943. Address: c/o A. P. Watt, 26 Bedford Row, London WC1R 4HL, UK.

OWEN, David Elystan, b. 1912, Kingston-on-Thames, Surrey, UK. Museum Director. Educ: Ph.D.; B.Sc. Publs: Story of Mersey & Deeside Rocks, 1939; History of Kirkstall Abbey, 1955; Water Highways, 1967; Water Rallies, 1969; Water Byways, 1973. Contbr. to: BBC; var. publs. Mbrships: Fellow, Museums Assn.; F.G.S. Recip., C.B.E., 1972. Address: Manchester Museum, The Univ., Manchester M13 9PL, UK.

OWEN, Douglas David Roy, b. 1922, Norton, Suffolk, UK. University Professor of French; Editor. Educ: Univs. of Nottingham & Cambridge; M.A.; Ph.D. Publs: Fabliaux (w. R. C. Johnston), 1957; The Evolution of the Grail Legend, 1968; The Vision of Hell, 1970; Ed., Arthurian Romance: Seven Essays, 1970; Transl., The Song of Roland, 1972; Two O.F.Gauvain Romances (w. R. C. Johnston), 1972; The Legend of Roland, 1973; (Ed.), Chrétien de Troyes, Arthurian Romances, 1975; Noble Lovers, 1975. Contbr. to: Forum for Mod. Lang. Studies (Ed.); & profl. jrnls. Mbrships. incl: Int. Arthurian Soc.; Soc. Rencesvals; Soc. for French Studies. Address: 7 W Acres, St. Andrews, Fife, UK.

OWEN, Gail Lee, b. 29 Nov. 1937, Fort Benton, Mont., USA. Writer. Educ: B.S., Webb Inst., Glen Cove, N.Y.;

M.A., Univ. of Neb. Publs: The Betterment of Man, 1974. Contbr. to: Int. Review of Social Hist. (Netherlands); Histl. Jrnl. (GB); Slavonic & E. European Review (GB); Int. Review of the Hist. of Banking (Italy); Histl. Abstracts. Mbrships: Am. Histl. Assn.; Mensa; Common Cause; dir., Concerned Citizens for a Quality Environment. Address: 7001 Bitterroot Rd., Route 5, Missoula, MT 59801, USA.

OWEN, Jack, pen name DYKES, Jack, b. 1929, Flamborough, Yorks., UK. Civil Servant. Publs: The Taste of Yesterday, 1969; Pig in the Middle, 1970; Harpoon to Kill, 1972. Address: 46 Kingsway, Cottingham, Yorks HU16 5BB, UK.

OWEN, John Elias, b. 1919, Manchester, UK. Sociologist. Educ: Duke Univ., Durham, N.C., USA; Univ. of London, UK; Univ. of Southern Calif. L.A., USA; M.A.; Ph.D. Publs: Sociology in East Pakistan, 1962; L. T. Hobhouse, Sociologist, 1974. Contbr. to: Introduction to Sociology; Frontiers of Social Science; Contemporary Sociology; Nat. & Engl. Review; Brit. Weekly; Aryan Path; New Leader; Christian Century; Sociology & Social Rsch.; num. other jrnls. Address: Sociol. Dept., Ariz. State Univ., Tempe, AZ 85281, USA.

OWEN, Rowland Hubert, b. 3 June 1903, Armagh, N. Ireland, UK. Retired Civil Servant; Organist & Choirmaster Educ: B.A., LL.B., Trinity Coll., Dublin, Repub. of Ireland Publs: Economic Surveys of India, 1949, 1952; Insurance Aspects of Children's Playground Management, 1966, Children's Recreation: Statutes & COnstitutions, 1967. Mbr., Surrey Organists' Assn. (Pres.-elect). Hons: C.M.G., 1948; US Medal of Freedom. Address: Oak Tree Cottage, Holdfast Lane, Haslemere, Surrey, UK.

OWEN, Thomas, b. 22 July 1910, Louvain, Belgium Writer. Educ: LL.D. Publs: Hotel Meuble, 1943; Le Livre Interdit, 1944; Le Jeu Secret, 1950; Ceremonial Nocturne, 1968; La Truie, 1972; Pitie pour les Ombres, 1973; La Cave aux Crapauds, 1974; Le Rat Kavar, 1975. Contbr. to: Fiction (Belgium); Mystere Mag.; Marginales; etc. Address: 74 Av. Eugene Demolder, 1030 Brussels, Belgium.

OWENDOFF, Robert Scott, b. 16 Mar. 1945, Wash. D.C., USA. US Naval Officer. Educ: B.S., US Naval Acad., 1968. Publs: Better Ways of Pathfinding, 1964; Sun Is Your Guide, 1968; Self-Orienting Sundial, 1968. Contbr. to mags. Address: 11156 Byrd Dr., Fairfax, VA 22030, USA.

OWENS, Joseph, b. 17 Apr. 1908, Saint John, N.B., Can. Clergyman. Educ: Pontifical Inst. Medieval Studies; Licentiate, 1946, Doct., 1951. Publs: The Doctrine of Being in the Aristotelian Metaphysics, 1951; St. St. Thomas & the Future of Metaphysics, 1957; A History of Ancient Western Philosophy, 1959; An Elementary Christian Metaphysics, 1963; The Wisdom & Ideas of St. Thomas Aquinas (w. Eugene Freeman), 1968; An Interpretation of Existence, 1968. Contbr. to num. acad. publs. Mbrships. incl: Royal Soc. Can. (Sec. Sect. II, 1969-72); Am. Philosl. Assn. Recip., Aquinas Medal, 1972. Address: Pontifical Inst. Medieval Studies, 59 Queen's Park Cres., E, Toronto M5S 2C4, Can.

OWENS, Rochelle, b. 2 Apr. 1936, Brooklyn, N.Y., USA. Playwright; Poet. Publs: Not be Essence that Cannot be, 1961; Salt & Core, 1968; Futz & What Came After, 1968; I am the Babe of Joseph: Stalin's Daughter, 1971; Poems from Joe's Garage, 1973; The Karl Marx Play & Others, 1974; The Joe 82 Creation Poems, 1974. Contbr. to: The Partisan Review; The Village Voice; Exile (Can.). Mbrships: ASCAP; Dramatists' Guild; Authors' Guild; New Dramatists' Committee. Hons. incl: Obie Award for Disting. Playwright, 1967-68; Creative Artists Pub. Serv. Grant, 1973; Obie Award Nomination for Best Play, 1973; Nat. Endowment for Arts, 1974; ASCAP Award, 1974. Address: 606 W. 116 St., N.Y. NY 10027, USA.

OWIREDU, Peter Augustus, b. 22 Aug. 1926, Cape Coast, Ghana. Educationist (Headmaster). Educ: B.A. (Engl., Latin, Pure Maths.), 1952, Dip.Ed., 1953, Univ. of London, UK. Publs: Education & the Social Order, 1955; Some Reflections on Education in the Gold Coast, 1955; Towards a Common Language for Ghana, 1957; English for West African, 1958; Matrilineal Inheritance among the Akans — Today & Tomorrow, 1959; The Changing Role of Chiefs in Ghana, 1959; Nine Years at Apam, 1968; The 10th Year at Apam, 1969; Apass Comes of Age, 1974. Contbr. to: Daily Graphic; Evening News; Ghanaian Times; Ashanti Pioneer; Ashanti Times; Ed., Adisadel Mag., 1950; also var. reviews, etc. Mbrships. incl: Assoc. Mbr., Ghana

Hist. Soc.; Moral Re-armament Grp.; VP, Voluntary Workcamps Assn.; Ghana Teaching Service (Advisory Comm., Ctrl. Region). Hons: Patron, Ghana UN Assn.; Hon. Mbr., Hansard Soc. for Parliamentary Govt., UK. Address: Apam Secondary Schl., P.O. Box 29, Apam, Ghana.

OZ, Erdal, b. 21 Mar. 1935, Yildizeli, Sivas, Turkey. Writer. Educ: Fac. of Law, Univ. of Ankara. Publs: Yorgunlar (short stories), 1960; Odalarda (novel), 1960; Kanayan (short stories), 1973; Yaralisin (novel), 1974. Contbr. to: var. newspapers & mags. Mbrships: Turkish Writers' Syndicate; Turkish Lang. Inst. Address: Pasalimani, Nacak Sokak 21/16, Kuzguncuk, Istanbul, Turkey.

ÖZDOĞRU, Nüvit, b. 5 May 1925, Istanbul, Turkey. Actor; Director. Educ: B.A., Robert Coll., Istanbul, 1946; M.A., Wash. State Univ., 1953; Grad. Work, Univ. of Wis., 1950-53. Publs: Our Turkish, 1958; Siğil Tas Olsa (poems), 1966; Turkish Language Today, 1974; (transls.) The Neighbourhood by Ahmet Kutsi Tecer, 1964; The Ballad of Ali of Keshan by Haldun Taner, 1970; Bedel by Arthur Miller, 1970; Dry Summer by Necati Cumali, 1971. Contbr. to: Milliyet; Cumhuriyet; Aksam; Short Story Int.; Reader's Ency. of World Drama. Mbrships: Turkish Playwrights' Assn.; Int. Theatre Inst.; UNESCO; etc. Address: Güliz Ap. D. 1, Çamlik Yolu, Etiler, Istanbul, Turkey.

P

PACEY, W(illiam) C(yril) Desmond, b. 1 May 1917, Dunedin, NZ. University Professor & Administrator. Educ: B.A., Univ. of Toronto, Ont., Can., 1938; Ph.D., Univ. of Cambridge, UK, 1941. Publs: Frederick Philip Grove, 1945; Book of Canadian Stories, 1947; Creative Writing in Canada, 1952; The Cow with the Musical Moo, 1952; Hippity Hobo & the Bee, 1952; The Picnic & Other Stories, 1958; Ten Canadian Poets, 1958; Our Literary Heritage, 1967; Ethel Wilson, 1968; Essays in Canadian Criticism, 1969; Major Canadian Writers, 1974; Waken, Lords & Ladies Gay, 1974. Contbr. to num. jrnls. incing: Dalhousie Review; Fiddlehead; Am. Lit.; Ariel. Mbrships. incl: Assn. of Can. & Quebec Lit. Hons: D.Litt., Mt. Allison Univ., N.B., 1973; D.Litt., Univ. of N.B., 1973. Address: 249 Winslow St., Fredericton, N.B., Canada.

PACHAI, Bridglal, b. 30 Nov. 1927, Ladysmith, S. Africa. Professor. Educ: B.A.; M.A.; Ph.D.; N.T.D. Publs: History of 'Indian Opinion', 1961; The International Aspects of the South African Indian Question, 1971; The Early History of Malawi (Ed.), 1972; The History of the Nation: Malawi, 1973; Livingstone Man of Africa (Ed.), 1973. Mbrships. incl: Ed. Bds., Jrnl. of Soc. Sci., Univ. of Malawi (Chmn. of Bd.), & Transafrican Jrnl. of Hist., Kenya. Recip., var. hons. Address: Dalhousie Univ., Halifax, N.S., Can.

PACHECO, José Emilio, b. 30 June 1939, Mexico City, Mexico. Writer. Educ: Nat. Univ. of Mexico. Publs. incl: (poetry) Los elementos de la noche, 1963; El reposo del fuego, 1966; No me Preguntes cómo pasa el tiempo, 1969; Irásy no volverás, 1973; (novel) Morirás lejos, 1967; (short stories) La sangre de Medusa, 1958; El viento distante, 1963, 1969; El principio del placer, 1972; (eds.) Antología del modernismo, 1970; New Poetry of México, 1970; var. transls. Contbr. to var. lit. jrnls. Mbr., PEN. Hons: Magda Donato Prize, 1968; Nat. Poetry Prize, 1969; Xavier Villaurrutia Prize, 1973. Address: Reynosa 63, Mexico City Z.P. 11, Mexico.

PACK, Stanley Walter Croucher, b. 14 Dec. 1904, Portsmouth, UK. Writer & Lecturer; retired Royal Navy Captain. Educ: M.Sc., D.I.C., A.C.G.I., St. John Coll., Malta; Imperial Coll., London; RN Coll., Greenwich. Publs: Anson's Voyage, 1948; Weather Forecasting, 1948; Admiral Lord Anson, 1960; The Battle of Matapan, 1961, 2nd ed., 1968; Windward of the Caribbean, 1964; The Wager Mutiny, 1965; Britannia at Dartmouth, 1967; Sea Power in the Mediterranean, 1971; Night Action off Cape Matapan, 1972; The Battle for Crete, 1973; Cunningham the

Commander, 1974; The Battle of Sirte, forthcoming; Operation Torch, forthcoming. Contbr. to var. mags., etc. Mbrships. incl: Royal Ocean Racing Club. Hons: C.B.E., 1957; A.D.C. to H.M. Queen Elizabeth, 1957-60; Off. Legion Merit USA, 1948. Address: Strete, Dartmouth, Devon, UK.

PACKARD, Vance, b. 22 May 1914, Granville Summit, Pa., USA. Author. Educ: B.A., Pa. State Univ.; M.S., Columbia Univ. Publs: The Hidden Persuaders, 1957; The Status Seekers, 1959; The Waste Makers, 1960; The Pyramid Climbers, 1962; The Naked Society, 1964; The Sexual Wilderness, 1968; A Nation of Strangers, 1972. Contbr. to: Atlantic; N.Y. Times Mag.; Reader's Digest; etc. Mbrships: Author's Guild; Am. Sociol. Assn.; Soc. of Mag. Writers. Recip., Disting. Alumni Awards, Columbia & Pa. State Univs. Address: 87 Mill Rd., New Canaan, CT, USA.

PACKE, Michael St. John, b. 1916, Eastbourne, Sussex, UK. Author. Educ: M.A., Magdalene Coll., Cambridge Univ. Publs: First Airborne, 1948; The Life of John Stuart Mill, 1954, 1955; The Bombs of Orsini, UK, 1957, USA, 1958, Netherlands, 1959. Contbr. to: Collier's Ency. Address: 6 The Brecque, Alderney, Channel Islands, UK.

PACKER, James Innell, b. 1926, Twyning, UK. Associate Principal, Trinity College, Bristol. Educ: M.A. & D.Phil., Univ. of Oxford. Publs: Fundamentalism & the Word of God, 1958; Evangelism & the Sovereignty of God, 1961; God Has Spoken, 1965; Growing Into Union, (co-author), 1970; Knowing God, 1973. Contbr. to: The Churchman; sev. other jrnls. Mbrships. incl: Soc. for the Study of Theol. Recip., Tyndale Fellowship for Biblical Rsch. Address: Trinity Coll., Stoke Hill, Bristol, BS9 1JP, UK.

PACKER, Joy (Lady Packer, née Petersen), b. 1905, S. Africa. Writer; Former Journalist. Educ: Univ. of Cape Town. Publs: Pack & Follow, 1945; Grey Mistress, 1949; Apes & Ivory, 1953; (autobiog. trilogy) Home from Sea, 1963; The World is a Proud Place, 1966; Deep as the Sea, 1975; (novels) Valley of the Vines, 1955; Nor the Moon by Night, 1957; The High Roof, 1959; The Glass Barrier, 1961; Man in the Mews, 1965; The Blind Spot, 1967; Leopard in the Fold, 1969; Veronica, 1970; Boomerang, 1972. Address: 101 Grosvenor Sq., College Rd., Rondebosch, Cape Town, Repub. of S. Africa.

PACKETT, Charles Neville, b. 25 Feb. 1922, Bradford, UK. Incorporated Insurance Broker. Publs. incl: Guide to the Republic of San Marino, 1958, 2nd ed., 1964; History of the Greek Order of St. Dennis of Zante, 1962; Diamond Jubilee History of Ionic Lodge No. 3210, 1966; Guide to Tongatapu Island, Kingdom of Tonga, 1969, 2nd ed., 1971; Guide to the Republic of Nauru, 1971; A History & A to Z of Her Majesty's Lieutenancy of Counties (1547-1972) with particular reference to the West Riding of Yorkshire, 1973; Bradford Corps Directory, St. John Ambulance, 1974. Num. mbrships. incl: F.R.S.A.; F.R.G.S.; F.C.I.B.; A.C.I.I.; Num. hons. incl: Cmdr., Order of St. Agatha, Repub. of San Marino, 1970; O.St.J., 1971; M.B.E., 1974. Address: San Marino, 15 Fairway, Tranmere Pk., Guiseley, Leeds, LS20 8JT, UK.

PACO d'ARCOS, Joaquim, b. 14 June 1908, Lisbon, Portugal. Writer. Publs. incl: The Last Hero; Ana Paula; Anxiety; United States 1942; The Road to Sin; Triple Mirror; Imperfect Poems; Churchill — The Statesman & the Writer; The Captive Doe; Memoirs of a Banknote; Cela 27; The Long Arm of Justice; Not Too Exemplary Tales. Contbr. to: Ocidente, Lisbon; Mod. Age, Chgo.; Figaro Litteraire, Paris; etc. Mbrships. incl: Portuguese Soc. of Writers (Chmn., 1963-65); PEN; Hon. Mbr., Soc. des Gens de Lettres de France. Hons. incl: Cmdr. of Infante D. Henrique, Portugal; Cmdr. of Victorian Order, GB; Chevalier de la Légion d'honneur, France; var. lit. prizes. Address: Avenida Antonio Augusto de Aguiar 38, 4°, Lisbon 1, Portugal.

PACURARIU, Francisc, b. 2 Jan. 1920, Teaca, Romania. Diplomat; Romanian Ambassador. Educ: M.D. Publs: An Introduction to Latin-American Literature, 1966; Outlines for a Portrait of Latin America (essays), 1967; Contemporary Spanish-American Profiles (essays), 1968; Simple Spy-Glass (poems), 1972; An Anthology of the Pre-Columbian Literature, 1973; The Uprising of the Drawer of Circles (poems), 1974; The Labyrinth (novel), 1974. Contbr. to: Romania Literara; Viata Romaneasca; Steaua; Transilvania; Tribuna; Secolul XX. Mbrships. incl: Romanian Writers' Union; Bucharest Writers' Assn. Recip.,

Bucharest Writers' Assn. Prize, 1974. Address: Strada Herastrau 38, Bucharest, Romania.

PAETEL, Karl Otto, b. 23 Nov. 1906, Charlottenburg, Berlin, Germany. Foreign Correspondent; Author; Translator. Educ: Univ. level. Publs. incl: Schriften der Jungen Nation, Vols. 1-5, 1935-39; Nazi Deutsch: Glossary of Contemporary German Usage (co-author), 1940; Ernst Juenger — Weg und Wirkung, 1949; The Reign of the Black Order in the Third Reich (co-author), 1954; Jugendbewegung und Politik, 1961; Versuchung oder Chance, 1965. Contbr. to: Nuernberger Nachrichten; Die Furche, Vienna; etc. Mbrships: PEN; Int. Writers Assn., Zurich. Hons: Sueddeutsche Rundfunk Citation, 1956; Medal of Merit, 1st Class, German Fed. Repub., 1965. Address: 68-49 Burns St., Forest Hills, NY 11375, USA.

PAGACZEWSKI, Stanislaw, b. 9 July 1916, Cracow, Poland. Writer. Educ: Jagiellonian Univ., Cracow. Publs: A Civil Red Day, 1959; Devil's Stone, 1961; Night Birds, 1962; Haw Drops, 1965; Kidnapping of Baltazar Sponge, 1966; An Imp Inn, 1968; Anna of Southern Seas, 1969; Let's Take the Waters, 1972. Mbrships: Polish Writers Assn; PEN. Address: 9/5 Biernacki St., Cracow, Poland.

PAGANO, Leo, b. 13 Mar. 1920, Amsterdam, Netherlands. Public Relations Officer. Educ: Amsterdam Univ. Publs: Helsinki 1952: Report of the Olympic Games; Football Encyclopedia, 1955; Football Yearbooks (International), 1954, 1955, 1956, 1957; Australia: Land for Immigrants, 1958; Developments in Dutch New Guinea, 1959. Contbr. to Dutch radio & newspapers. Mbrships: Fed. of Netherlands Jrnlsts.; Dutch Fed. for P.R. Address: Gen. Spoorlaan 4, Voorschoten, Netherlands.

PAGET, (Arthur) Gordon Westwood, b. 22 Feb. 1893, Chiswick, Middx., UK. Clerk in Holy Orders. Educ: M.A., St. Chad's Coll., Durham Univ.; Ely Theol. Coll. Publs: A Short History of Hedenham Church & Parish, 1936, 2nd ed., 1974; The Organ in Norwich Cathedral, 1942. Contbr. to: Organ Quarterly; Musical Opinion; Cathedral News (Bury St. Edmunds). Fellow, Royal C'wlth. Soc. Address: The Flat, The Provost's House, St. Edmundsbury, Suffolk, UK.

PAGET, Julian Tolver, b. 11 July 1921, London, UK. Retired Army Officer; Public Relations Executive. Educ: M.A., Christ Church, Oxford Univ. Publs: Counter-Insurgency Campaigning, 1967; Last Post: Aden 1964-67, 1969. Contbr. to var. mil. publs. Address: 4 Trevor St., London SW7 1DU, UK.

PAGET, Robert Ferrand, b. 1890, Watford, UK. Bio-chemical Engineer; Archaeologist. Educ: Ph.D., London Univ. Publs: In the Footsteps of Orpheus, 1967; Central Italy: An Archaeological Guide, 1970; Cumae & Roman Baiae, 1972. Contbr. to: Jrnl. of Roman Studies; Latomus; Newsweek; Der Spiegel; Vergilius. Address: 104 Gaetano De Rosa, 1.80070 Bacoli, Naples, Italy.

PAGNOL, Marcel, b. 28 Feb. 1895. Author; Playwright. Film Prods. incl: Topaze, 1932; Cigalon, 1934; La fille du puisatier, 1940; Manon des sources, 1952; Les Lettres de mon moulin, 1954. Publs. incl: La petite fille aux yeux sombres, 1919; La gloire de mon père, 1958; Le château de ma mère, 1960; L'eau des collines, 1963; Le masque de fer, 1965; (plays) Marius, 1929; Fanny, 1932; Judas, 1953; Fabien, 1956; (transl.) Hamlet; Midsummer Night's Dream; Bucolique de Virgile. Address: 16 square du Bois-de-Boulogne, Paris 16e, France.

PAHL, R. E., b. 1935, London, UK. Professor of Sociology. Educ: St. Catharine's Coll., Cambridge Univ.; London Schl. of Econs.; M.A.; Ph.D. Publs: Urbs in Rure, 1965; Ed., Readings in Urban Sociology, 1968; Patterns of Urban Life, 1970; Whose City? , 1970; Managers & Their Wives (w. J. M. Pahl), 1971, 1972; Series Ed., Penguin Sociology. Contbr. to: Sociol. Review; Sociol.; Sociol. Inquiry; Sociologia Ruralis; Urban Studies; New Society. Mbr., Brit. Sociol. Assn. (Ed. Bd., official jrnl. Sociology 1970-1972). Agent: A. D. Peters. Address: Patrixbourne Lodge, nr. Canterbury, Kent, UK.

PAHLEN, Kurt, b. 26 May 1907, Vienna, Austria. Writer; Musicologist; Conductor; Composer; Former Director, Buenos Aires Opera House; Former University Professor, Montevideo. Educ: Ph.D. & Mus.D., Univ. of Vienna, 1929. Publs: 22 books inclng: Music of the World, a History, 1944; The Magic World of Music, 1945; Introduction to Music, 1952; Tschaikowsky, 1957; Opera of the World, 1964; Symphony of the World, 1968; Great Singers, 1970; The Mozart Book, 1971; Music Therapy, 1974; Johann Strauss, 1975; Children & Music, 1975; 3 operas. Contbr. to: La Prensa; El Dia; sev. Swiss, German, & Austrian jrnls. Mbr., PEN. Hons. incl: Cross for Arts & Sci., 1st class, Austria. Address: CH-8708 Männedorf, Zurich, Switz.

PAIK, Chull, pen name of PAIK, Se-chull, b. 18 Mar. 1908, N. Pyong-an Province, Korea. Literary Critic. Educ: Grad., Tokyo Educl. Coll., Japan. Publs. incl: History of the Trend of Modern Korean Literature, 1946; An Introduction to Literature, 1953; Whole History of Korean Literature, 1957; A Collection of Paik's Works, 1969; My Literary Memoirs, 1974. Contbr. to all Korean mags. Mbrships: Int. PEN (Pres., Korean Ctr.); Korean Writers' Assn.(exec. Bd.); Inst. of Korean Studies (Pres.). Hons. incl: Doct., Chung-ang Univ., Seoul; Lit. Award, Korean Acad. Arts, 1971. Address: San 83-19, Huksok-dong, Kwanak-ku, Seoul 151, Korea.

PAIN, Frank, b. 4 Mar. 1895, High Wycombe, UK. Teacher of Wood Turning. Publs: The Practical Wood Turner. Contbr. to: The Wood Worker. Address: 64 Chairborough Rd., High Wycombe, Bucks., UK.

PAINE, Lauran, (numerous pseudonyms), b. 25 Feb. 1916, Duluth, Minn., USA. Author. Over 500 books incl. Westerns; Romances; Mysteries; Adventure; etc.; Biographies incl: Benedict Arnold; Simon Bolivar; Saladin; John Burgoyne; etc. Address: Fort Jones, CA 96032, USA.

PAINTER, Raymond, b. 1934, London, UK. Financial Journalist. Publs: Fortunes to be Made, 1970; Your Money & You, 1972. Contbr. to: Daily Express (fin. jrnlst., 1950-66); Investment (Ed., 1966-67); Weekly News; Woman & Home; Pulse; etc. Agent: Rupert Crew Ltd. Address: 11 Matfield Close, Bromley, Kent, BR2 9DY, UK.

PAINTON, Ivan Emory, pen name ZARELLIO, Florian, b. 7 Aug. 1909. Artist; Poet; Painter. Educ: Northwestern State Univ., Alva, Okla.; O.B.U., Shawnee, Okla. Publs: Basic Art, 1967; Reflections From the Inner Room (poetry), 1969; The Ballad of Old Pogue, 1969; Whispers in the Night (poetry), 1971; Portrait & Figure Painting by the Method of Anatomical Analogy, 1974. Contbr. to: Dictionary of Int. Biog. Mag., 1970; Int. Who's Who in Poetry Anthol.; var. newspapers, jrnls. throughout USA. Recip., Hon. Ph.D., Colo. Christian Coll. Address: Studio of Fine Arts, Orion, Fairview, OK 73737, USA.

PAISH, Frank Walter, b. 1898, Croydon, Surrey, UK. Retired Professor & Economic Consultant. Educ: M.A., Trinity Coll., Cambridge Univ. Publs: Insurance Funds & their Investment (w. G. L. Schwartz), 1934; The Post-war Financial Problem, 1950; Business Finance, 1953; Studies in an Inflationary Economy, 1962; Ed., Benham's Economics, 7th ed. 1964, 8th ed. 1967, 9th ed. (w. A. J. Culyer), 1973; How the Economy Works, 1970. Contbr. to: Economica; Econ. Jrnl.; Scottish Jrnl. of Pol. Econ.; Banker; Irish Banking Review; etc. Recip., M.C. Address: Shoreys, Ewhurst, Cranleigh, Surrey, UK.

PAKKANEN, (Anja) Kaija, b. 11 Dec. 1915, Leppävirta, Finland. Author (Children's Books). Educ: State Nursing Schl. Publs: Missu löytää ratkaisun, 1953; Tuntematon Gisela, 1958; Vimperin pihan Ilona, 1959; Kapteeni Mikko ohoi, 1966; Sebastianin tytär, 1970; Tule, sanoi Tomtom, 1972; plays for radio, TV & theatre. Contbr. to: Yhteishyvä Mag. (Ed., Jr. Sect., 1956-1965). Mbrships: Suomen Kirjailijaliitto; Int. Contbr. to: Yhteishyvä Mag. (Ed., Jr. Sect., 1956-1965). Mbrships: Suomen Kirjailijaliitto; Int. Bd. on Books for Young People; Suomen Nuorisokirjailijat; Suomen Kääntäjäin Yhdistys. Hons: Book for the Young (Nuorten Kirja) Prize, 1954, 1960, 1967, 1968; Tauno Karilas-Prize, 1971. Address: 02170 Espoo 17, Haukitie 6, Finland.

PÁKOLITZ, István, b. 18 Sept. 1919, Paks, Tolna Shire, Hungary. Editor. Educ: Tchrs., Trng. Coll.; Lorand Eotvos Univ. Fac. of Arts. Publs: Maria Stuart (transl. from Schiller), 1959; (poetry) Three Poets, 1954; Vintage, 1958; Lullaby, 1961; Light & Shade, 1962; Evening Song, 1963; Long-Sighted, 1965; Just Mátyás King, 1966; Which is Possible, 1969; Sign, 1971; Dandelion, 1972; Greenish-Gold, 1973; Crowns, 1974. Contbr. to: Nice Verses; Jelenkor; Kortárs; Élet és Irodalom; Nök Lapja; Magyar Nemzet; Népszava; etc. Mbrships: Hungarian Writers' Soc.; Hungarian Jrnlsts.' Soc. Hons. incl: József Attila Prize, 1963; Hungarian Trades Union Coun. Prize, 1974. Address: Rakoczi ut 72, 7622 Pecs, Hungary.

PÁL, József, b. 6 Oct. 1923, Zalaegerszeg, Hungary. Librarian. Publs: Sing-song, 1954; Honey-Extractor, 1960; From Behind Blue Window, 1967; Ice-Pipe, forthcoming. Mbrships: Soc. of Hungarian Writers; Assn. of Hungarian Libs. Address: Veres Péter utca 22, 7624 Pécs, Hungary.

PALACIOS, Leopoldo-Eulogio, b. 31 Jan. 1912, Madrid, Spain. Professor of Logic. Educ: Fac. of Arts., Univ. of Madrid. Publs: La Prudencia Política, 1945; El Mito de la Nueva Cristiandad, 1951; Don Quijote y la Vida es Sueño, 1960; Filosofía del Saber, 1962; El Juicio y el Ingenio y otros ensayos, 1967; Salutación y otros poemas, 1972. Contbr. to num. jrnls. Mbr., sev. acad. orgs. Hons. incl: Nat. Prize for Lit., 1945. Address: Ministro Ibañez Martin, 2, Madrid — 15, Spain.

PALAVESTRA, Predrag, b. 14 June 1930, Sarajevo, Yugoslavia. Writer; Institute Director. Educ: Ph.D., Belgrade Univ. Publs: The Anthology of the Postwar Serbian Poetry, 1955; The Literary Themes, 1958; The Defense of Criticism, 1961; Serbian & Croatian Poetry in XX Century, 1964; The Literature of Young Bosnia, 2 vols., 1965; New Evangelists, 1968; The Currents of Tradition, 1971; Serbian Postwar Literature 1945-1970, 1972; Early Expressionism in Serbian Poetry, 1973. Contbr. to & Ed. of var. lit. periodicals. Mbrships: VP, Serbian Ctr., PEN; Yugoslav Writers Union. Recip., sev. awards. Address: Bulevar Revolucije 225/IV, 11050 Belgrade, Yugoslavia.

PALEN, Jennie, M., b. Samsonville, N.Y., USA. Certified Public Accountant; Writer; Poet; Ghost Writer; Poetry Critic. Educ: B.C.S., N.Y. Univ. Publs. incl: Moon Over Manhattan (poems), 1949; Report Writing for Accountants, 1955; Good Morning, Sweet Prince (poems), 1957; Stranger, Let Me Speak (poems), 1964; Encyclopedia of Accounting Forms & Reports, 1964; Encyclopedia of Auditing Techniques, 1966. Contbr. to num. anthols., jrnls. & tech. books. Mbrships. incl: Nat. League of Am. Pen Women; Brooklyn Poetry Circle; Pa. Poetry Soc.; Women's Press Club, N.Y.; Poetry Soc. of Am. Recip., num. lit. awards. Address: 26 E. Tenth St., N.Y., NY 10003, USA.

PALESTRANT, Simon S, pen names STRAND, Paul E.; STEVENS, S.P.; EDWARDS, Stephen, b. 8 July 1907, NYC, USA. Artist; Author. Educ: Dip., Pratt Inst. Art Schl., 1929; B.S., N.Y. Univ., 1935; M.S. in Educ., CCNY, 1937. Publs. incl: Block Prints, 1931; Working with Plastics, 1947; Toymaking, 1951; Lamps & Lampshade Making, 1951; Tailoring & Dressmaking, 1952; Car Owner's Fix-It Guide, 1952; Mechanism & Devices, 1954; Mechanisms & Machines, 1956; Games On the Go, 1974. Contbr. to var. profl. jrnls. Mbrships: Tchrs. Union; AAUP; Authors' League of Am.; Writers' Guild of Am., E.; TV Writers' Grp.; Nat. Acad. TV Arts & Scis.; Mystery Writers of Am.; Crime Writers' Assn., GB. Address: 185 West End Ave., N.Y., NY 10023, USA.

PALLE, Albert Jacques, b. Le Havre, France. Journalist. Educ: B.A., Sorbonne, Paris. Publs: L'Expérience, 1959; Les Marches, 1962; Les Chaudières à la Lune, 1964. Mbr., Société de Paris. Recip., Th. Renaudot Prize. Address: 21 Rue du Vieux Colombier, Paris 6, France.

PALM, Anders L., b. 9 Sept. 1940, Stockholm, Sweden. Author; Journalist. Educ: M.A.. Publs: Mars — vi kommer! (Mars — the New Frontier!), 1971. Contbr. to: FIB-aktuellt; Se; Saxons veckotidning. Mbr., Swedish Authors' Union. Address: Stavsjövägen 34, 125 41 Älvsjö, Sweden.

PALME, Sven Jacob Arved, b. 1 Feb. 1941, Uppsala, Sweden. Computer Expert. Educ: B.Technol., Royal Inst. of Technol., Stockholm, 1964; M. Computer Sci., 1968. Publs: Beware of MRA, 1962; Free Abortion, 1964; Learning FORTRAN after ALGOL, 1970; An Innocent Girl from the Countryside, 1970; Bombs in Stockholm, 1971; The Bank Robber, 1972; Programming Languages, 1972; Female Murder, 1974; Computers & Society, 1974. Contbr. Soc. Democratic Party, 1960-; Swedish Soc. for Info. Processing; Swedish Union of Authors. Address: Soc. Democratic Party, 1960—; Swedish Soc. for Info. Processing; Swedish Union of Authors. Address: Skeppargatan 73, S 115 30 Stockholm, Sweden.

PALMER, Alan Warwick, b. 28 Sept. 1926, Ilford, Essex, UK. Schoolmaster. Educ: M.A., B.Litt., Oriel Coll., Oxford Univ. Publs: Independent Eastern Europe (w. C. A. Macartney), 1962; A Dictionary of Modern History, 1962, paperback ed., 1964; Yugoslavia, 1964; The Gardeners of

Salonika, 1965; Napoleon in Russia, 1967; The Lands Between, 1970; Metternich, 1972; Russia in War & Peace, 1972; Life & Times of George IV, 1972; Alexander I, 1974; Frederick the Great, 1974. Contbr. to: Oxford Slavonic Papers; Hist. Today; Hist of 20th Century; Hist of WWI (Ed. Co-ord.). Agent: Peter Janson-Smith. Address: 4 Farm End Woodstock, Oxford OX7 1XN, UK.

PALMER, Arnold, b. 1929, Latrobe, Pa., USA. Professional Golfer. Educ: Wake Forest Univ. Publs: Situation Golf; My Game & Yours; Portrait of a Professional Golfer; Arnold Palmer's Golf Book; Go for Broke. Mbr., Profl. Golfers' Assn. of Am. Address: Box 52, Youngstown, Pa., USA.

PALMER, Arthur Montague Frank, b. 1912, Northam, UK. Electrical Engineer; Member of Parliament. Educ: Brunel Coll. of Technol. Publs: Future of Electricity Supply; Modern Norway; Law & the Power Engineer. Contbr. to: New Statesman; Socialist Commentary; New Sci.; Times; Elec. Review. Mbrships: C.Eng.; Fellow, Instn. of Elec. Engrs.; M.Inst.F. Address: 14 Lavington Ct., London SW15, UK.

PALMER, Beryl Marian, b. 24 Mar. 1930, Rossland, B.C., Can. Writer. Publs: The White Boar, 1969; The Wrong Plantagenet, 1972. Mbr., Can. Authors' Assn. Address: 2590 W. 43rd Ave., Vancouver, B.C. V6N 3H7, Can.

PALMER, Cedric King, b. 13 Feb. 1913, Eastbourne, Sussex, UK. Composer; Author. Educ: Royal Acad. of Music. Publs: Music, 1944; Compose Music, 1947; The Musical Production, 1953; The Piano, 1957; Orchestration, 1964; The ABC of Church Music, 1967. Mbrships. incl: Soc. of Authors; Savage Club. Address: Clovelly Lodge, 2 Popes Grove, Twickenham TW2 5TA, UK.

PALMER, Ethel Margaret, pen name PALMER, Peggy, b. 27 Nov. 1894, Baldwin City, USA. Schoolteacher. Educ: B.A.; M.S. Contbr. to: Poet Int.; Int. Clover Poetry Assn.; Kan. Kernels; Maize This Wk. Mbrships: Kan. Author's Club; Recording Sec., Dist. 3 Authors' Club; Recording Sec. & Treas., Local Writers' Club; NEA; AAUW; ADK; OES; UPW. Address: 101 W. Maple St., Independence, KS 67301, USA.

PALMER, Frederick Richard Green, b. 30 Jan. 1936, Blackpool, UK. Painter; Writer; Lecturer. Educ: Goldsmiths Coll. Schl. of Art, Univ. of London; N.D.D., A.T.C. Publs: Art & the Young Adolescent, 1970; Visual Awareness, 1972; Sequences, 1973; Monoprint Techniques, 1975; (series of slidefolios) Looking Around, 1969-70; Write a Story, 1969-70. Contbr. to: Thames TV; Ed., 3 Arts Quarterly, 1960; BBC; var. mags. Mbr., Educl. Writers Grp. Exec. Comm., Soc. of Authors. Address: 9 Kingswood Pl., London SE13, UK.

PALMER, Joan Lilian, b. 12 Oct. 1934, London, UK. Journalist. Publs: Magazine Editing & Publishing, 1973; Animals, All Famous, Mostly Friendly, 1974. Contbr. to: Memo Mag.; Pitman periodicals; Argus Press (Ed. Staff); Dog News (Hon. Ed.). Mbrships: Nat. Union of Jrnlsts.'; Inst. of Jrnlsts.; Wig & Pen Club. Address: Green Castle, Goudhurst, Kent TN17 1JN, UK.

PALMER, Joseph Mansergh, b. 1912, Alverstoke, Hants., UK. Naval Officer; Editor. Educ: Royal Naval Coll., Dartmouth. Publs: Sunda Passage, 1964. Contbr. to: Navy Int. (Ed.); Navy (Ed., 1964-70); British Reader's Digest (Ed. Cons.). Address: River Hall Farm, Biddenden, Kent, UK.

PALMER, Madelyn, pen name PETERS, Geoffrey, b. 12 Nov. 1910, Adelaide, Australia. Civil Servant. Publs: Dead Fellah, 1961; The Claw of a Cat, 1964; The Eye of a Serpent, 1965; The Twist of a Stick, 1966; The Flick of a Fin, 1967; The Mark of a Buoy, 1967; The Chill of A Corpse, 1968; Fareham Creek, 1974. Mbr., Crime Writers' Assn. Address: 14 Park Lane, Fareham, Hants., UK.

PALMER, Marian (Mrs.), b. 1930, Rossland, B.C., Can. Author. Publs: The White Boar, USA & Can., 1968, UK, 1969; The Wrong Plantagenet, USA & UK, 1972. Mbr., Can. Authors' Assn. Agent: A. D. Peters & Co. & Harold Matson & Co. Inc., N.Y. Address: 2590 W. 43rd Ave., Vancouver, B.C., V6N 3H7, Can.

PALMER, Norman D., b. 25 June 1909, Hinckley, Me., USA. University Professor. Educ: A.B., Colby Coll., 1930; M.A., 1932, Ph.D., 1936, Yale Univ. Publs: The Irish Land

League Crisis, 1940; International Relations: The World Community in Transition (w. H. C. Perkins), 1953; The Indian Political System, 1961; South Asia & United States Policy, 1966; Elections & Political Development: The South Asian Experience, 1975. Contbr. to: Am. Pol. Sci. Review; Jrnl. of Int. Affairs; Pol. Studies; Int. Studies; New Leader; Asian Survey; Orbis; etc. Mbrships. incl: Nat. Pres., Int. Studies Assn., 1970-71; Am. Pol. Sci. Assn. Hons. incl: L.H.D., Colby Coll., 1955; M.A., Univ. of Pa., 1971. Address: 1110 Signal Hill Lane, Berwyn, PA 19312, USA.

PALMER, Peter John, b. 20 Sept. 1932, Melbourne, Australia. Teacher. Educ: B.A., 1953; Ed.B., 1967, Melbourne Univ. Publs: The Past & Us, 1957; The 20th Century, 1965; Confrontation, 1971; Interaction, 1973; Expansion, 1974. Address: 12 Bettina St., E. Burwood, Victoria, Australia 3151.

PALMER, Raymond Edward, b. 1 Apr. 1927, Bristol, UK. Author; Journalist. Bristol Evening Post, 1949-50; Comtel Reuters, 1952-54; Associated Press, USA, 1954-67. Contbr. to: Sunday Times; Observer; Reader's Digest; Penthouse; Cosmopolitan; Telegraph Mag.; N.Y. Times; L.A. Times; Chgo. Tribune; Saturday Review; etc. Address: One Lyme Farm Rd., Lee, London SE12, UK.

PALMER, Robert, E.A., b. 15 Aug. 1932, Boise, Idaho, USA. Professor of Classical Studies. Educ: B.A., 1953; M.A., 1954; Ph.D., 1956, Johns Hopkins Univ. Publs: The King & the Comitium: A Study of Rome's Oldest Public Document, 1969; The Archaic Community of the Romans, 1970; Roman Religion & Roman Empire, 1974. Contbr. to: Am. Jrnl. of Philology; Hesperia; Historia; Jrnl. of Indo-European Studies; Athenaeum; Am. Jrnl. of Archaeology; Phoenix; Rivista Storica dell'Antichita; Rivista di Filologia e Istruzione Classica. Address: 720 Williams Hall CU, Dept. of Classical Studies, Univ. of Pa., PA 19174, USA.

PÁLSSON, Hermann, pen name CADWR, b. 26 May 1921, Saudanes, Iceland. University Reader. Educ: Cand. mag., Univ. of Iceland; B.A., Univ. Coll., Dublin. Publs. incl: Sidfraedi Hrafnkels Sogu, 1966; Helgafell, 1967; Art & Ethics in Hrafnkel's Saga, 1971. Transls: (w. M. Magnusson): King Harald's Saga, 1966; Laxdaela Saga, 1969; (w. Paul Edwards) Gautrek's Saga, 1968; Arrow-Odd, a Medieval Novel, 1970; The Book of Settlements, 1972; Hrolf Gautreksson, 1972; Eyrbyggja Saga, 1973; (w. D. Fox) Grettir's Saga, 1974; (alone) Hrafnkel's Saga & other Icelandic Stories, 1971; The Confederates, 1974. Contbr. to: Ency. Britannica; Le Moyen Age; Skírnir. Mbr., Medieval Acad. of Am. Address: 14 Royal Terrace Mews, Edinburgh EH7 5BZ, UK.

PAMOJA, Imani, b. 3 Feb. 1947, Dallas, Tex., USA. Writer; Teacher; Editor. Educ: Bishop Coll., Dallas, Tex. Publs: Gittin Our Minds, Our Shit, Our People Together; Voices From the South (w. Elihue Smith); The Face of America. Contbr. to: Today's Black World; Body & Soul Bazaar; Black Scene. Mbrships: Co-Dir., Uhuru Family; Sec., Assn. of Advancing Artists & Writers; Ed., Newsletter, S. Black Cultural Alliance; Acting Dir., Uhuru Cultural Dev. Ctr.; Poetry Soc. of Tex.; Centro Studi E Scambi; Am. Biograph. Assn.; Int. Platform Assn. Recip., var. poetry awards; num. biograph. listings. Address: c/o Akini Isi Publishing Co., P.O. Box 26057, Dallas, TX 75226, USA.

PANKHURST, Richard Keir Pethick, pen name R. K. P. P., b. 3 Dec. 1927, Hampstead, UK. Historian; Educator. Educ: B.Sc., 1949, Ph.D., 1954, London Schl. of Econs. Publs. incl: William Thompson, Britain's Pioneer, Feminist & Cooperator, 1954; An Introduction to the Economic History of Ethiopia, 1961; Travellers in Ethiopia, 1965; State & Land in Ethiopian History, 1966; An Introduction to the History of the Ethiopian Army, 1967; Economic History of Ethiopia, 1968. Contbr. to var. jrnls. Recip., Haile Selassie I Trust Prize for Ethiopian Studies, 1973. Address: P.O. Box 1896, Addis Ababa, Ethiopia.

PAPACONSTANTINOU, Theophylactos, b. 10 July 1905, Monastir, Serbia. Journalist. Educ: Bach.Pedagogy, 1927; Master of Letters, Hist. & Philos., 1930, Univ. of Athens. Publs. incl: Against the Current, 1949; Anatomy of the Revolution, 1952; The New Line of Communism, 1956; Jon Dragoumis & the Political Prose, 1957; Problems of Our Era, 6th ed., 1960; The Battle of Greece, 2nd ed., 1966. Contbr. to: Gt. Hellenic Ency., 1928-34; Nat. Broadcasting Inst., 1950-53, 1959-64; Nea Hestia; var. newspapers. Mbrships. incl: Union of Athens Daily Newspaper Jrnlsts.; Hellenic Soc. for Humanistic Studies.

Hons: Athens Acad. Prize, 1953; Cmdr., Royal Order of Phoenix, 1965; Kt.Cmdr., Royal Order George I, 1972. Address: 23 Agias Philotheis, Philothei, Athens, Greece.

PAPAKONGOS, Kostis, b. 24 July 1936, Pachtouri, Mts. of Pindos, Greece. Author. Educ: Inst. of Drama, Athens, 2 yrs. Publs: Poetry: Non-Crucified, 1956; South, 1966; Polar Night, 1970; Tourist Guide, 1970; Portraits, 1973; Ostraka, 1973; Ashakt Janpad & Other Poems, 1973; Prose: Waves of Rhodes, 1969. Contbr. to: Aftonbladet, Dagens Nyheter, Stockholm; Information, Copenhagen. Mbr., Swedish Authors' Union. Recip., Schlrship., Swedish Fndn. of Authors, 1974-78. Address: Sigtunag. 6, III, ÖG, 113 22 Stockholm, Sweden.

PAPPAGEOTES, George Christos, b. 10 Feb. 1926, Almyros, Greece, d. 6 Mar. 1963. Professor; Editor. Educ: B.S., 1951, M.A., 1952, Columbia Univ., USA; Ph.D., 1955. Publs: Say it in Greek, 1956; Say it Correctly in Greek, 1957; Cortina's Modern Greek in 20 Lessons, 1959; Modern Greek Readers, expmtl. ed., 1960; Modern Greek in a Nutshell, 1961; Modern Greek Literary Gems, 1962; Japan & China by Nikos Kazantzakis (transl.), 1963; The Story of Modern Greek Literature, 1972; Modern Greek Reader, 1975. Contbr. to ency., dictionaries, & var. periodicals & newspapers. Mbrships: Educl. Coun. Greek Archdiocese, 1958; profl. orgs. Recip. profl. hons.

PARANDOWSKI, Jan, b. 1895, Lwow, Poland. Professor of Literature. Educ: Lwow Univ. Publs. incl: Mythology, 1922; Eros on Olympus, 1925; Two Springs, 1927; King of Life, 1929; The Olympic Discus, 1932; Visits & Encounters, 1934; Heaven in Flames, 1936; Three Signs of Zodiac, 1938; Mediterranean Hour, 1949; Alchemy of the Word, 1950; Sundial, 1953; Petrarca, 1955; Essays, 1956; Voyages, 1959; Return to Life, 1961; September Night, 1962; Loose-Leaves, 1967; Acacia, 1967; Reflexions, 1975; Pres., PEN. Address: Warsaw, Zimorowicza 4, Poland.

PARASURAM, T. V., b. 1 Apr. 1923, Tattamangalam, Kerala, India. Journalist; Author. Educ: Nieman Fellow, Harvard Univ., 1958-59. Publs: Defending Kashmir (co-author), 1949; A Medal for Kashmir, 1958. Contbr. to: Indian Express; var. Indian & Am. jrnls. Recip., Chaman Lal Jrnlsm. Award, 1972. Address: Indian Express Newspapers, 5853 Nebraska Ave. N.W., Wash. DC 20015, USA.

PARES, Marion Stapylton, pen name Campbell, Judith, b. 1914, W. Farleigh, Kent, UK. Writer. Publs: Family Pony, 1962; The Queen Rides, 1965; Police Horses, 1967; World of Horses, 1969; Horses & Ponies, 1970; World of Ponies, 1970; Anne – Portrait of a Princess, 1970; Family on Horseback, 1972; Princess Anne & Her Horses, 1972; Elizabeth & Philip, 1972; The Champions, 1973; Royalty on Horseback, 1974. Contbr. to: Woman's Own; Sunday Times; Horse & Hound; Field; Light Horse; Look & Learn; Farmer's Weekly. Agent: A.M. Heath & Co. Ltd. Address: Studfall Ridge, Lympne Hill, Hythe, Kent, UK.

PARGETER, Edith Mary, pen name (for thrillers) PETERS, Ellis, b. 28 Sept. 1913, Horsehay, Shropshire, UK. Author. Publs. incl: Reluctant Odyssey, 1946; Warfare Accomplished, 1947 (war trilogy); The Soldier at the Door, 1954; The Heaven Tree, 1960; The Green Branch, 1962; The Scarlet Seed, 1963; A Bloody Field by Shrewsbury, 1972; Sunrise in the West, 1974; num. thrillers; transls. from Czech. Contbr. to gen. mags. Mbrships. incl: Soc. of Authors; Mystery Writers of Am.; Crime Writers' Assn. Hons. incl: Edgar Award of Mystery Writers of Am. for best thriller of year, 1962 (for Death & the Joyful Woman). Address: Parkville, Park Lane, Madeley, Telford, Shropshire, UK.

PARHAM, William Thomas, b. 1913, London, UK. Writer. Publs: Von Tempsky – Adventurer, 1969; Island Volcano, 1973. Contbr. to: NZ Herald; Christchurch Star; Auckland Star; Histl. Review; NZ Broadcasting Corp. Mbr., Whakatane Histl. Soc. Address: 19 Dell Ave., Remuera, Auckland 5, NZ.

PARIKH, Rasiklal Chhotalal, pen name MUSIKARA, b. 20 Aug. 1897, Sadara, Gandhinagar Dist., India. Teacher; Researcher. Educ: B.A., Univ. of Bombay. Publs. incl: (hist.) Gujaratni Rajadhanio, 1958; Kavyaprakasa-samketa named Kavyadarsa of Someswara Bhatt, 1959; (lit. works) Bharatanu Natyasastra, 1944; Ananda-mimansa, 1961; Parishadni Atmavyakti, 1963; Purovacana ane Vivecana, 1965. Contbr. to: Ed., Quarterly Puratattva; Yugadharma; Jt. Ed., Prasthana. Mbrships: Sec., Gjuarat Puratattva

Mandir; Dir., B.J. Inst. of Learning & Rsch., 1938-68. Recip., Sahitya Acad. Prize, 1960. Address: 11 Bharatiniwas Society, Ellisbridge, Ahmedabad-380006, India.

PARK, June (Mrs. Mardall), b. 4 June 1920, London, UK. Architect; Writer. Educ: Dip., Archtl. Assn. Publs: Houses & Bungalows, 1958; Houses for To-day, 1971. Contbr. to archtl. mags. Mbrships: Archtl. Assn.; Royal Inst. Brit. Archts. Address: 7 Fitzroy Park, London N6 6HS, UK.

PARK, Kyung Lee (pen name), b. 28 Oct. 1926, Kyung-Nam Chung-Moo, Korea. Writer. Publs: The Calculation, 1955; A Drifting Island, 1959; The Apothecary Kim's Daughter (histl. tragedy), 1962; The Mart & the Battlefield (novel), 1964; The Land (epic novel), 1969. Contbr. to: Mod. Lit.; Lit. & Thought. Mbrships: Battlefield (novel), 1964; The Land (epic novel), 1969. Contbr. to: Mod. Lit.; Lit & Thought. Mbrships: PEN; Assn. of Korean Men of Letters. Hons: Third New Lit. Talent Prize, 1957; Korean Lit. Woman Prize, 1965; Wol-Tan Lit. Prize, 1973. Address: 768-6 Jung-loong Dong, Sungbook-Gu, Seoul, Korea.

PARK, Roy Hampton, b. 1910, Dobson, N.C., USA. Publisher; Editor. Educ: B.S., N.C. State Univ.. Raleigh. Publs: Ed.-in-Chief, Duncan Hines Guide Books; Adventures in Good Eating; Lodging for a Night; Vacation Guide; Guide to the Middle Atlantic States; Duncan Hines Food Odyssey (co-author); Adventures in Good Cooking. Contbr. to: This is The South (Ed.). Address: Terrace Hill, Ithaca, NY 14850, USA.

PARKER, John, b. 1906, Bristol, UK. Politician. Educ: M.A., St. John's Coll., Oxford. Publs: Independent Worker & Small Family Business, 1931; New Trends in Socialism, 1936; 42 Days in the Soviet Union, 1946; Labour Marches On, 1948; Newfoundland, 1950; 12 Modern Yugoslav novels (Ed.) 1958—; Harold Wilson, 1964; Willy Brandt, 1966. Contbr. to: Public Enterprise; Pol. Quarterly; New Statesman; etc. Mbr., Fabian Soc., Gen. Sec., 1939-45, Hon. Sec., 1954-71, Chmn., 1950-53, VP, 1971—. Address: 4 Essex Ct., Temple, London EC4, UK.

PARKER, Marion Dominica Hope (Sister Mary Dominic of the Cross), also DOMINIC, Mary & HOPE, Marion, b. 29 June 1914, Christchurch, NZ. Eremitical Contemplative of the Order of Preachers. Educ: B.A., M.A., Canterbury Univ., NZ; B.Litt., Oxford Univ., UK. Publs: Language & Reality, 1949; The Slave of Life: A Study of Shakespeare & the Idea of Justice, 1955; Media of Communication: Art & Morals, 1970; (transls.); Latourelle, Theology, Science of Salvation, 1969; Daniélou, The Crisis in Intelligence, 1970; Christ & the Church, Signs of Salvation, 1972; Laurentin, Has Our Faith Changed?, 1972. Contbr. to: NZ New Writing, 1944, 1945; Mass for Young People, 1973. Recip., Hilda Mathieson Prize, 1948. Address: 27 Grosvenor Rd., Richmond, Surrey TW10 6PE, UK.

PARKER, Nancy Winslow, b. 18 Oct. 1930, Maplewood, N.J., USA. Illustrator; Painter; Writer of children's books. Educ: B.A., Mills Coll., Calif., 1952; Art Students League & Schl. of Visual Arts, NYC. Publs: The Man With the Take-Apart Head, 1974; The Party at The Old Farm, 1975; (illustrator) Oh, A-Hunting We Will Go, 1974; Warm as Wool, Cool as Cotton, 1975. Address: 51 E. 74th St., N.Y., NY 10021, USA.

PARKER, (Rev.) Thomas Henry Louis, b. 28 Sept. 1916, Hayling Island, UK. Lecturer in Systematic Theology. Educ: M.A., Emmanuel Coll., Cambridge, 1942; D.D., 1961. Publs: The Oracles of God, 1947; Doctrine of the Knowledge of God, 1952, 1959, 1970; Portrait of Calvin, 1954; Calvin's New Testament Commentaries, 1971; Karl Barth, 1970. (Ed.) English Reformers, 1966; (Ed.) Essays in Christology for Karl Barth, 1956; Service in Christ, 1966; Contbr. to: Chambers' Ency.; Jrnl. of Theological Studies; Erasmus; etc. Mbrships: Soc. of Authors; Renaissance Soc. Address: 3 Union Pl., Stockton Rd., Durham, UK.

PARKER, (Rev.) Thomas Maynard, b. 1906, London, UK. College Fellow. Educ: M.A., D.D., Exeter Coll., Oxford Univ. Publs: The Re-Creation of Man, 1940; The English Reformation to 1558, 1950; Christianity & the State in the Light of History, 1955. Contbr. to: New Cambridge Mod. Hist., Vol. III; Augustinus Magister; History; Engl. Histl. Review; etc. Mbrships: F.S.A.; Fellow, Royal Histl. Soc. Address: University Coll., Oxford OX1 4BH, UK.

PARKER, (William George) Derek, b. 27 May 1932, Looe, Cornwall, UK. Writer; Broadcaster. Publs: The Fall of Phaethon, 1954; Company of Two, 1955; Byron & His World, 1968; The Question of Astrology, 1970; Ed., Selected Letters of Edith Sitwell, 1970; The Compleat Astrologer (w. Julia Parker), 1971; The Compleat Lover (w. Julia Parker), 1972; The Westcountry, 1973; Donne & His World, 1974; Familiar to All, 1974. Contbr. to: The Times; The Listener; New Statesman; Guardian; Sunday Telegraph; Ed., Poetry Review, 1965-70. Mbrships: Comm. of Mgmt., Soc. of Authors & Royal Lit. Fund; Chmn., Radiowriters Assn., Soc. of Authors. Address: 37 Campden Hill Towers, London W11 3QW, UK.

PARKES, Alan Sterling, b. 10 Sept. 1900, Rochdale, UK. Chairman, Galton Foundation; Consultant, International Planned Parenthood Federation; Former Biologist. Educ: M.A., Sc.D., Cambridge Univ.; Ph.D., Manchester Univ.; D.Sc., London Univ. Publs: Internal Secretions of the Ovary, 1929; (Ed.) Marshall's Physiology of Reproduction, 4 vols., 1952-66; Sex, Science & Society, 1966; Patterns of Human Reproduction, 1975. Contbr. to num. sci. jrnls. Ed., Jrnl. of Biological Science. Mbrships. incl: Endocrinol. Sect., Royal Soc. of Med., Pres., 1949-50; Comp. Med. Sect., Pres., 1962-63; Chmn., Soc. for the Study of Fertility, 1950-52, 1964-66. Hons: CBE, 1956; Kt., 1968. Address: 11 Adams Rd., Cambridge CB3 9AD, UK.

PARKES, Colin Murray, b. 1928, London, UK. Consultant Psychiatrist. Educ: Westminster Med. Schl.; Univ. of London; M.D.; M.B.; B.S.; D.P.M.; M.R.C.Psych. Publs: Bereavement: Studies of Grief in Adult Life, 1972, German & Swedish transls., 1974. Contbr. to: Jrnl. of Psychosomatic Rsch.; Brit. Med. Jrnl.; Psychosomatic Med.; Soc. Sci. & Med.; Psychiatry; Brit. Jrnl. of Med. Psychol. Mbrships: Royal Coll. of Psych.; Brit. Assn. of Soc. Psych.; Assn. for the Study of Animal Behaviour; Chmn., Cruse; Chmn., Clin. Rsch., Tavistock Inst. Address: Unit for the Study of Psycho-Social Transitions, The Tavistock Inst. of Human Rels., 120 Belsize Lane, London NW3 5BA, UK.

PARKES, (Rev.) James William, pen name HADHAM, John, b. 22 Dec. 1896, Guernsey, Channel Islands. Clergyman; Scholar. Educ: M.A., D.Phil., Oxford; M.A., Cambridge. Publs. incl: The Jew & His Neighbour, 1930; The Conflict of the Church & the Synagogue, 1934; The Jew in the Medieval Community, 1938; The Foundations of Judaism & Christianity, 1960; A History of the Jewish People, 1962; Whose Land?, A History of the Peoples of Palestine, 1969; (as John Hadham) Good God, 1940; Commonsense about Religion, 1961. Contbr. to var. encys. & jrnls. Mbr.: Jewish Histl. Soc. of Eng. (Pres. 1949-51). Address: Netherton, Iwerne Minster, Blandford, Dorset DT11 8LY, UK.

PARKES, Roger Graham, b. 15 Oct. 1933, Chingford, Essex, UK. Novelist; Scriptwriter. Educ: Nat. Dip. Agricl., Royal Agricl. Coll., Cirencester. Publs: Death Mask, 1970; Line of Fire, 1971; The Guardians, 1973; The Dark Number (w. Edward Boyd), 1973. Mbrships: Writers' Guild GB; Writers' Action Grp.; Royal Agricl. Coll. Address: Cartlands Cottage, Kings Lane, Cookham Dean, Berks. SL6 9AY, UK.

PARKHILL, Wilson, b. 14 Sept. 1901, Bklyn, N.Y., USA. Headmaster; Educational Consultant. Educ: A.D., Williams Coll., Williamstown, Mass.; A.M., Columbia Univ. N.Y. Publs: The Constitution Explained, 1948; Independent School Operation (co-author); Var. Am. Hist. Texts for use in pub. schls. Mbrships. incl: Past Pres., Headmaster Assn.; Past Pres., Country Day Schl. Headmasters' Assn. Recip., L.H.D., Williams Coll. Address: Belgrade, ME 04917, USA.

PARKINSON, Cyril Northcote, b. 30 July 1909, Barnard Castle, Co. Durham, UK. Author. Educ: M.A., Cambridge; Ph.D., London. Publs. incl: Edward Pellew Viscount Exmouth, 1934; War in the Eastern Seas, 1954; Parkinson's Law: The Pursuit of Progress, 1958; The Law and the Profits, 1960; In-laws & Outlaws, 1962; East & West, 1963; Mrs. Parkinson's Law, 1968; The Law of Delay, 1971; The Fur-lined Mousetrap, 1972; Devil to Pay, 1973; Industrial Disruption, 1973; Big Business, 1974; The Fireship, 1975. Contbr. to: Economist; Ency. Britannica; etc. Mbrships. incl: Royal Histl. Soc.; Soc. for Nautical Rsch. Recip., Julian Corbett Prize, London Univ., 1936. Address: Les Caches Hall, St. Martins, Guernsey, Channel Islands.

PARKINSON, Frederick Charles Douglas, b. 1916, Ilford, Essex, UK. Editor; Publishing Executive; Former Art School Principal. Publs: Type Identification Charts. Contbr. to: Artist, Art Review, Artist's Guide (Mng. Ed., 1948—); Pictures & Prints (Mng. Ed., 1962-70); Helmsman (Ed., 1962-66); Art News; Art; var. yachting jrnls.; etc. Mbrships: Arts Club; Chelsea Arts Club; Royal Cinque Ports Yacht Club. Address: Knollys Cottage, Willesborough Lees, Near Ashford, Kent, UK.

PARKINSON, (Rev.) John, b. 1930, Cleckheaton, Yorks., UK. Clergyman. Educ: Leicester Univ.; Assoc., London Coll. Divinity; Chaplain to the Forces. Publs: Kingdom Come, 1970; Ed., New Venture. Mbr., Royal C'wlth. Soc.; United Soc. for Christian Lit. (Metrop. Sec., 1959-62). Address: The Vicarage, Kenton, Exeter, UK.

PARKINSON, Roger, b. 1939, Skipton, UK. Writer; Journalist. Educ: M.A., King's Coll., London. Publs: The Origins of World War One; The Origins of World War Two; The American War of Independence; Clausewitz; (all 1970); The Hussar General, 1975; Zapata, 1975; Moore of Corunna, 1975; Peace for Our Time, 1972; Blood, Toil, Tears & Sweat, 1973; A Day's March Nearer Home, 1974; The Peninsula War, 1973; The Desert War, 1975. Mbrships: Inst. for Strategic Studies; Pres., Assn. of Yorkshire Bookmen. Agent: Campbell, Thomson & McLaughlin. Address: Barras, Masongill, Carnforth, Lancs., UK.

PARKINSON, Thomas Francis, b. 24 Feb. 1920, San Fran., Calif., USA. Professor of English. Educ: A.B., 1945; M.A., 1946, Univ. of Calif., Berkeley; Ph.D., 1948. Publs: W. B. Yeats, Self-Critic, 1951; Men, Women, Vines, 1959; A Casebook on the Beat, 1961; Masterworks of Prose, 1961; W. B. Yeats, The Later Poetry, 1964; Thanatos, 1965; Robert Lowell, 1968; Protect the Earth, 1970; Homage to Jack Spicer, 1971; W. B. Yeats, 1972; What the Blind Man Saw, 1974. Contbr., lit. jrnls. inclng. N.Y. Times Book Review. Recip., num. acad. hons. Address: 1001 Cragmont, Berkeley, CA 94708, USA.

PARKMAN, Sydney Muller, b. 1895, Mumbles, Glam., UK. Author. Publs: East of Singapore; Accidental Adventurer; Account Closed; Sunk Without Trace; Plunder Bar; Night Action; Tide Watchers; Ship Ashore; Uncharted; Acting Second Mate; Facts About Floyd; Passing of Tony Blunt; Seven Days Hard; Cuban Legacy; Captain Bowker; Life Begins Tomorrow; The Singing Crow (w. N. Scarlyn Wilson). Contbr. to: Cornhill Mag.; Brit. Weekly; Daily & Evening Press. Address: 244 St. Helens Rd., Hastings, Sussex, UK.

PARKS, Rena Ferguson, b. 17 Jan. 1888, Pendleton, Ore., USA. Adult Educator. Educ: Univ. of Ore.; Ore. State Univ.; Univ. of Pa. Publs: The Changing Land, 1970; Miniature Profiles, 1973; Furrows in the Sun, 1973. Contbr. to var. jrnls., lit. mags. & newspapers. Mbrships: Dept. of Adult Educ., NEA; Ore. Pub. Hlth. Assn.; Ore. State Poetry Assn. 1965—; Portland Verse Weavers Soc., 1936-65; Ldr., Workshop for Poetry, Ctrl. Lib., Ore. Hons. incl: Top Hons., Ore. State Poetry Contests; Winner, Verseweavers Special Recognition Contest, 1964; Sweep Stake Ribbon, Centennial Yr. Poetry Exhibit, State Fair, Salem, Ore., 1965. Address: 709 S.W. Clay St., Portland, OR 97201, USA.

PARMANN, Øistein, b. 10 Mar. 1921, Oslo, Norway. Author; Publisher. Educ: Univ. of Oslo. Publs. incl: 3 novels; Norwegian Sculpture; History of the Norwegian Art & Craft School, 1969; Marcello Haugen, 1974. Mbrships: Norwegian Acad. of Lang. & Lit.; PEN. Recip., Award, City of Oslo, 1968. Address: Rute 16, Nesoddtangen 1450, Norway.

PARMELEE, Alice, b. 1903, N.Y., USA. Religious Writer. Educ: B.A., Bryn Mawr Coll., Pa., USA. Publs: Building the Kingdom; Fellowship of the Church; Patriarchs, Kings & Prophets; A Guidebook to the Bible; All the Birds of the Bible; They Beheld His Glory. Mng. Ed., Episcopal Ch. Annual, 1942-55. Address: 26 E. 81 St., N.Y., NY 10028, USA.

PARODI, Anton Gaetano, b. 19 May 1923, Calabria, Italy. Journalist; Playwright. Educ: Univs. of Turin & Genoa. Plays incl: Il Gatto; Il nostro scandalo quotidiano; L'ex-maggiore Hermann Grotz; Adolfo o della nagia; Filippo l'Imposte; Una corda per il figlio di Abele; Quel pomeriggio di domenica; Una storia della notte; Pioggia d'estate; Cielo di pietra; I giorni dell'Arca; Quello che dicono. Contbr. to Unità, Budapest, 1964—. Hons. incl:

Premio Nazionale di teatro Riccione, 1959, 1965. Address: Via Benvenuto Cellini 34/7, Genoa, Italy.

PARONEN, Samuli, b. 23 May 1917, Virolahti, Finland, d. 26 Aug. 1974. Novelist. Publs: Kesä Aataminkylässä, 1964; Kuolismaantie, 1967; Lallinkorven leipä, 1968; Tämä on huone 8 (short stories), 1969; Kaivos, 1970; Huone puutalossa, 1971; Laiva, 1972; Kapina, 1973; Kortteeri, 1974; Aphorism collection, 1974. Contbr. to mags. Mbr., Finnish Authors Union. Hons. incl: State Prize for Lit., 1972.

PARRAS, Tytti Kristiina, b. 28 Jan. 1943, Helsinki, Finland. Writer. Educ: Univ. of Tampere (Press & Mass Communications). Publs: Jojo, 1968; Rakkaat, 1970. Mbrships: Finnish Authors' Union; Pirkkalaiskirjailijat von Tampere. Hons: J. H. Erkko Award, best first novel, 1968; Best First Novel Prize, Otava, 1968. Address: Kuninkaankatu 39 A 22, 3320 Tampere 20, Finland.

PARRINDER, (Rev.) Edward Geoffrey, b. 30 Apr. 1910, New Barnet, Herts., UK. University Professor. Educ: London Univ.; Montpellier Univ.; M.A.; D.D.; Ph.D. Publs. incl: West African Religion, 1949, 2nd ed. 1961; African Traditional Religion, 1954, 3rd ed. 1974; Worship in the World's Religions, 1961, 2nd ed. 1974; African Mythology, 1969; Avatar & Incarnation, 1970; A Dictionary of Non-Christian Religions, 1971; The Indestructible Soul, 1973; The Bhagavad Gita: A Verse Translation, 1974; The Wisdom of the Forest, 1975; many of foregoing titles transl'd. Contbr. to profl. jrnls. Mbr., var. profl. assns. Recip., Hon. D.Litt. Address: 31 Charterhouse Rd., Orpington, Kent, UK.

PARROTT, Arthur Wilson, b. 1908, Timaru, Canterbury, NZ. Biologist; Museum Curator. Publs: Sea Anglers' Fishes of New Zealand; Big Game Fishes of New Zealand; The Queer & Rare Fishes of New Zealand; Sea Anglers' Fishes of Australia; Animals of New Zealand, forthcoming. Contbr. to: Stamp Monthly (Stanley Gibbons Mag.); NZ Nature Heritage, 1974; Transactions Royal Soc. of NZ; NZ Entomologist; Linnean Soc., N.S.W., Aust. Mbrships: Royal Soc. of NZ; other profl. assns. Address: Lochiel, 446 Atawhai Dr., Nelson, NZ.

PARROTT, Ian, b. 5 Mar. 1916, London, UK. University Professor; Composer; Author. Educ: Royal Coll. of Music, 1932-34; New Coll., Oxford, 1934-37, D.Mus., 1940; M.A., 1941. Publs: Pathways to Modern Music, 1947; A Guide to Musical Thought, 1955; Method in Orchestration, 1957; The Music of "An Adventure", 1966; The Spiritual Pilgrims, 1969; Elgar (Master Musicians Series), 1971. Contbr. to: Musical Times; Music & Letters; MGG, etc. Address: Henblas, Abermad, Aberystwyth SY23 4ES, Dyfed, UK.

PARRY, (Rev.) Geraint Wynne, b. 27 Sept. 1916, Caernarfon, Wales, UK. Methodist Minister. Educ: Hartley Victoria Coll., Manchester. Publs: (in Welsh) A Heuo'r Gwynt, 1965; Rhaid Croesi Afon Drin, 1967; Potelaid O Foddion, 1970; Storiau Awr Hamdden, 1974; (TV play) Dyn Diarth, 1971. Contbr. to: Eurgrawn. Address: Merton Villa, Tywyn, Gwynedd, Wales, UK.

PARRY, Hugh Jones, pen name CROSS, James, b. 10 Mar. 1916, London, UK. Sociologist; Author. Educ: A.B., Yale Univ., New Haven, Conn., USA, 1937; M.A., Columbia Univ., N.Y., 1939; Ph.D., Univ. of Southern Calif., L.A., 1949. Publs: Public Opinion in Western Europe, 1953; Root of Evil, 1957, 3rd ed. 1959; The Dark Road, 1959, 4th ed. 1969; The Grave of Heroes, 1961, 3rd ed. 1969; To Hell for Half a Crown, 1967, 2nd ed. 1970. Contbr. to: Int. Jrnl. of Opinion & Attitude Rsch.; Sci. Monthly; Pub. Opinion Quarterly; Archives of Gen. Psych.; sev. other sci. jrnls.; Saturday Evening Post; Cavalier; Playboy; sev. mystery story mags. & anthols. Mbrships. incl: Am. Sociol. Assn.; Authors' League; Mystery Writers of Am. Recip., sev. prizes & awards. Address: 4814 Falstone Ave., Chevy Chase, MD 20015, USA.

PARRY, Marian, b. 28 Jan. 1924, San Francisco, Calif., USA. Illustrator. Educ: B.A., Univ. of Calif. at Berkeley, 1946; studies of etching & stone engraving. Publs. incl: (self-illustrated) Die Vogel, Switz., 1967, transl'd. by author as The Birds of Basel, 1969; Roger & the Devil, 1972; (as illustrator) Exercises in Perspective, 1956; Aristophanes, Birds, 1959; City Mouse — Country Mouse, 1970; M. Ginsberg, The Lazies, 1973; B. Levin, The Zoo Conspiracy, 1973; C. Pomerantz, The Long-Tailed Rat, 1975. Contbr. to: Atlantic Monthly; Sci. Am.; etc. Recip.

var. awards for The Birds of Basel. Address: 60 Martin St., Cambridge, MA 02138, USA.

PARRY, Thomas, b. 14 Aug. 1904, Carmel, Caerns., UK. University College Principal (Retired). Educ: M.A., D.Litt., Univ. Coll., Bangor. Publs: History of Welsh Literature, Welsh ed., 1944, Engl. transl., 1955; Gwaith Dafydd ap Gwilym, 1954; Ed., Oxford Book of Welsh Verse, 1962. Contbr. to: Transactions, Hon. Soc. Cymmrodorion; Yorks. Celtic Studies; etc. Mbrships: Fellow, Brit. Acad. Hons: LL.D., Univ. of Wales; D.Litt. Celt., Univ. of Ireland. Address: Gwyndy, 2 Victoria Ave., Bangor, Gwynedd, UK.

PARRY-JONES, Daniel, b. 12 Oct. 1891, Llangeler, Wales, UK. Clergyman. Educ: B.A., St. David's Coll., Lampeter. Publs: Welsh Country Upbringing, 1948; Welsh Country Characters, 1952; Welsh Legends & Fair Lore, 1953; Welsh Children's Games & Pastimes, 1961; My Own Folk, 1972. Mbr., Yr Academi Gymreig (Engl. Sect.). Address: 18 Allt-Yr-Yn Cres., Newport, Gwent NPT 5GD, UK.

PARRY-WILLIAMS, (Sir) Thomas Herbert, b. 21 Sept. 1887, Rhyd-ddu, UK, d. 3 Mar. 1975. Emeritus Professor of Welsh Language & Literature. Educ: M.A. & D.Litt., Univ. Coll. of Wales; D.Litt., Univ. of Oxford; Ph.D., Univ. of Freiburg, Germany; Sorbonne, Paris, France. Num. publs. incl: Phonology of Welsh & Breton, 1913; The English Element in Welsh, 1923; Ysgrifau, 1928; Pedair Cainc y Mabinogi, 1937; Lloffion, 1942; Welsh Poetic Diction, 1947; Islwyn, 1948; Ugain o Gerddi, 1949; Sir John Rhys, 1954; Myfyrdodau, 1957; Ymhél â Phrydyddu, 1958; Pensynnu, 1966. Contbr. to: Bulletin of the Bd. of Celtic Studies; Major Welsh lang. jrnls. Mbrships. incl: Past Pres.. Nat. Lib. of Wales; Past Pres., Royal Nat. Eisteddfod of Wales. Hons. incl: LL.D., Univ. of Wales; Medal, Hon. Soc. of Cymmrodorion, 1951. Address: Wern, N. Rd., Aberystwyth, Dyfed, UK.

PARSLOE, Guy, b. 5 Nov. 1900, Stroud Green, UK. Author; Administrator. Educ: London Univ. Publs. incl: The English Country Town; (Ed.) Guide to the Historical Publications of the Societies of England & Wales 1929-43; Wardens' Accounts of the Worshipful Company of Founders of the City of London 1497-1681; Minute Book of the Corporation of Bedford 1647-1664; Contbr. to Brit. Welding Jrnl. (Ed., 1954-67). Mbrships: Inst. of Hist. Rsch., 1927-43; Sec.-Gen., Inst. of Welding, 1948-66, VP, 1966-69; Pres., Jr. Inst. of Engrs., 1966-67. Address: 1 Leopold Ave., London SW19, UK.

PARSLOW, Percy, b. 1914, Kingston, Surrey, UK. Jeweller; Breeder of Small Mammals. Publs: Practical Hamster Keeping, 1967; Hamsters, 1969. Mbrships: Nat. Hamster Coun. (Pres., Judge); Southern Hamster Club (Pres.). Address: Parslows Hamster Farm, Great Bookham, Leatherhead, Surrey, UK.

PARSONS, Christopher James, b. 5 Aug. 1941, Epsom, Surrey, UK. Lecturer in Further Education. Educ: Nottingham Univ.; London Univ.; B.A., Ph.D. Publs: Written Communication for Business Students (w. S. J. Hughes), 1970; Theses & Project Work, 1973; Literary Use in Further Education, 1973. Mbrships: Soc. of Authors; Assn. for Liberal Educ.; Nat. Assn. for the Tchng. of Engl. Address: 12 Pagoda Ave., Richmond, Surrey, UK.

PARSONS, Denys, b. 1914, London, UK. Head, Press & Public Relations Section, The British Library. Educ: M.Sc., Univ. of London. Publs: It Must Be True; All Too True; True to Type; What's Where in London; Funny Ha Ha & Funny Peculiar; The Directory of Tunes & Musical Themes. Contbr. to Jrnl. of Soc. for Psychical Rsch. Agent: A. M. Heath & Co. Ltd. Address: 21 Kingsley Pl., London N6 5EA, UK.

PARSONS, Edward, pen name ONLOOKER (for sporting events only), b. 9 Dec. 1900, Burwash Common, Sussex, UK. Retired Officer (Royal Marines, & NZ Regular Force). Publs: Owning, Training & Racing Horses, 1974; Bible-back (auto-biog.), 1974; The 'Sport of Queens' & Royal Marines (to appear 1975). Contbr. to: Cookery & Food Review, UK; Catering, NZ; Hoofbeats, NZ; other catering, racing & cricket publs. Mbrships: Fellow, Cookery & Food Assn. (past Chmn., NZ Div.); PEN; var. ex-serv. & racing orgs. Recip., Silver Medal, Cookery & Food Assn. Address: 48 Bollard Ave., Avondale, Auckland 7, NZ.

PARSONS, John Arthur, b. 27 Sept. 1926, London, UK. Public Relations Consultant; Professional Photographer. Publs: A Fisherman's Year, 1974. Contbr. to: Engl., Aust., NZ angling mags., 1943-73; Christchurch Press & Taupo Times (weekly angling column), currently. Address: P.O. Box 860, Taupo, NZ.

PARSONS, Kitty, b. Stratford, Conn., USA. Writer; Watercolorist. Educ: Tchrs. Coll., Columbia Univ.; Boston Univ.; Chgo. Univ.; Pratt Inst.; Am. Acad. of Dramatic Art. Publs: Do You Know Them?, 1922; Stories of People Worth While, 1924; Ancestral Timber (ballads), 1957; Down to Earth (light verse), 1964; Up & Down & Roundabout (juvenile verse), 1967; Your Husband or Mine (light verse), 1970. Contbr. to num. reviews, newspapers. Mbrships. incl: Nat. League of Am. Pen Women; Boston Authors Club; Vt. League of Writers; Am. Poetry League; Poetry Socs. of N.H., Ky., Pa. & Va. Num. hons. incl: 7 Prizes for plays, poems, articles, unpublished books, Am. League of Am. Pen Women, 1956-73; Poetry Awards, socs. in Pa., Ky., N.C., Okla., Ala., & Deep South Writers Conf. Address: Box 27, Rockport, MA 01966, USA.

PARSONS, Richard Augustus, b. Bay Roberts, Nfld., Can. Barrister; Solicitor; Author. Educ: Bach. Civil Law, McGill Univ., Montreal, 1921. Publs: Reflections, 1954; Reflections, Books I & II, 1958; The Village Politicians, 1960; Sea Room, 1963; The Rote, 1965; The Village & Wayside, 1967; Interludes, 1970; The Tale of a Lonesome House, 1971; The Legend of the Isle, 1973. Mbr., Ed. Bd., Chitty's Law Jrnl. Recip., Hon. D.Litt., Mem. Univ. of Nfld., 1974. Address: 34 Queen's Rd., St. John's, Nfld., Can.

PARTRIDGE, Eric Honeywood, b. 6 Feb. 1894, Waimata Valley, Gisborne, NZ. Writer. Educ: B.A., M.A., Univ. of Qld.; B.Litt., Univ. of Oxford, UK. Publs: The French Romantics' Knowledge of English Literature, 1924; Eighteenth Century English Romantic Poetry, 1924; Songs & Slang of the British Soldier: 1914-1918 (w. J. Brophy), 1931; A Dictionary of Slang & Unconventional English, 1937, 7th ed. 1970; Usage & Abusage, 1947; A Dictionary of Forces Slang (co-author), 1948; A Dictionary of the Underworld, British & American, 1950; Origins, 1958; A Dictionary of Catch Phrases, British & American (in progress). Contbr. to: The Guardian; Sunday Times; Books & Bookmen. Recip., Hon. D.Litt., Univ. of Qld. Address: 34 Orpington Rd., Winchmore Hill, London N21 3PG, UK.

PARTRIDGE, Frances Catherine, b. 15 Mar. 1900, London, UK. Translator. Educ: Honours degree, Newnham Coll., Cambridge Univ. Publs: Ed., Greville Diaries (w. R. Partridge), 8 vols., 1938. Num. transls. inclng. works by B. Ibañez, M. Asturias, A. Carpentier, J. Kessel. Mbrships: Soc. of Authors; Handel Soc.; Botanical Soc., GB. Address: 16 W. Halkin St., London SW1, UK.

PASCAL, Roy, b. 1904, Birmingham, UK. University Professor of German. Educ: M.A., Litt.D., F.B.A., Pembroke Coll., Cambridge. Publs: Social Basis of the German Reformation; The Nazi Dictatorship; Shakespeare in Germany; The Growth of Modern Germany; The German Sturm und Drang; The German Novel; Design & Truth in Autobiography; German Literature in the 16th & 17th Centuries; From Naturalism to Expressionism. Contbr. to: Goethe Soc.; German Life & Letters; Mod. Lang. Review; etc. Mbr., Assoc. of Univ. Tchrs., Pres., 1944-45. Address: 102 Witherford Way, Birmingham 29, UK.

PASMANIK, Wolf, b. 3 May 1924, Tarnapol, Poland. Educ: Ph.D., Lit. Inst. of Soviet Writers, Univ. of Moscow, 1944. Publs: 3 books of Yiddish poetry — Flowers, 1939; My Home, 1947; My Songs, 1971. Contbr. to jrnls. in Poland, France, Argentina, USA. Mbrships: PEN; Am. Poets Assn.; Poets & Writers of Am. Hons: PEN Club Prize for Yiddish Poetry; Lisa & Willir Shor Poetry Grant. Address: 350 E. 67th St., N.Y., NY 10021, USA.

PASO GIL, Alfonso, b. 12 Sept. 1926, Madrid, Spain. Educ: Lic., Philos. & Letters, Univ. of Madrid; Jrnlst., Fac. of Info. Scis. Publs. incl: (plays) Los pobrecitos, 1957; El cielo dentro de casa, 1958; El canto de la cigarra, 1961; Usted puede ser un asesino, 1958; La corbata, 1964; En el Escorial, cariño mío, 1968; El armario, 1969; Nerón-Paso, 1969; (novels) Solo diecisiete años, 1969; Cálida Josefina, 1973. Contbr. to: num. mags. & jrnls. Mbrships: Counslr., Soc. of Authors of Spain; Rep. Sen. of Spain, Int. Inst. & Acad. of Authors. Hons. incl: Nat. Theatre Prize, 1957, 1961; Alvarez Quintero Prize, Spanish Royal Acad., 1960; Medal of Profl. Merit, 1973. Address: Calle Peña del Sol, 32, Madrid 34, Spain.

PASOLINI, Pier Paolo, b. 1922. Poet; Writer; Film Director. Publs. incl: Poesie a Casarsa, 1942; La meglio Gioventu, 1954; Ragazzi di Vita, 1955; Le Ceneri di Gramsci, 1957; Una Vita violenta, 1959; Passione & Ideologia, 1960; Theorem, 1968; (films) Mamma Roma, 1962; Edipo Re, 1968; Theorem, 1968; Porcile, 1969; Medea, 1970; Decamerone, 1971; I Racconti di Canterbury, 1972; (play) Orgia, 1969. Hons: Silver Bear, Berlin, 1971; Golden Bear, 1972; Special Jury Prize, Cannes, 1974. Address: Via Eufrate 9, Rome, Italy.

PASSMORE, John Arthur, b. 9 Sept. 1914, Manly, Australia. Professor of Philosophy. Educ: M.A., Univ. of Sydney. Publs: Ralph Cudworth, 1950; Hume's Intentions, 1952; A Hundred Years of Philosophy, 1957; Philosophical Reasoning, 1961; The Perfectibility of Man, 1970; Man's Responsibility for Nature, 1974. Contbr. to: Encounter; Art Int.; Quadrant; Mind; Philos. Review; etc. Mbrships: For. Hon., Am. Acad. of Arts & Scis.; Pres., Aust. Acad. of Humanities; VP, Inst. Int. de Philos.; Dir., Aust. Elizabethan Theatre Trust. Recip., Mackie Medal, Aust. Assn. for Advancement of Sci., 1965. Address: 6 Janz Cres., Manuka, Canberra, Australia.

PASSUTH, László (Ladislas), b. 15 July 1900, Budapest, Hungary. Novelist. Educ: Dr. of Law & Pol. Sci. Publs. incl: The Rain God Weeps Over Mexico; Monteverdi; Imperia; The Porphyrogenitos; Lagoons; 25 novels in 12 langs. Mbrships: VP, Hungarian PEN; Union of Hungarian Writers. Address: Rózsehegy utca 1, H-1024 Budapest II, Hungary.

PASTAN, Linda, b. 27 May 1932, NYC, USA. Poet. Educ: B.A., Radcliffe Coll., Mass.; M.L.S., Simmons Coll., Boston, Mass.; M.A., Brandeis Univ., Waltham, Mass. Publs: A Perfect Circle of Sun, 1971; Aspects of Eve, 1975. Contbr. to: Harpers; The Nation; The New Repub.; Am. Scholar; Quarterly Review of Lit. Mbr., Poetry Soc. of Am. Address: 11710 Beall Mtn. Rd., Potomac, MD 20854, USA.

PATAI, Raphael, b. 22 Nov. 1910, Budapest, Hungary. Educator; Anthropologist. Educ: Dr.Phil., Univ. of Budapest, 1933; Ph.D., Hebrew Univ. of Jerusalem, 1936. Publs: Ed., Herzl Yearbook, vols. I-VII, 1958-71; Ed., Studies in Biblical & Jewish Folklore (w. F. L. Utley & D. Noy), 1960; Ed., The Complete Diaries of Theodor Herzl, 5 vols., 1960; Hebrew Myths (w. Robert Graves), 1964; Ed., Myth & Legend of Ancient Israel (Angelo Rappaport), 3 vols., 1967; Ed., Women in the Modern World, 1967; The Hebrew Goddess, 1967; Golden River to Golden Road: Society, Culture & Change in the Middle East, 3rd ed., 1969; Tents of Jacob: The Diaspora Yesterday & Today, 1971; Myth & Modern Man, 1972; Ency. of Zionism & Israel, 2 vols., 1971; The Arab Mind, 1973; The Myth of the Jewish Race (w. Jennifer P. Wing), 1975. Address: 39 Bow St., Forest Hills, NY 11375, USA.

PATCHETT, Mary Elwyn, b. Sydney, Australia. Writer. Publs: Roar of the Lion; Rebel Brumby; Stranger in the Herd; The Long Ride; Ajax the Warrior; Farm Under the Sea; Quarter Horse Boy; Warrimco; Tiger in the Dark; Summer on Wildhorse Island; Wild Brother; The Proud Eagles; The Last Warrior. Mbrships: Soc. of Aust. Writers: F.Z.S. Agent: Bolt & Watson. Address: 235 Latymer Ct., London W6, UK.

PATEL, Baburao, b. 4 Apr. 1904, Maharashtra, India. Editor; Film Producer. Publs: Grey Dust; Burning Words; The Sermon of the Lord; Prayer Book; Rosary & the Lamp; Homoeopathic Lifesavers for Home & Community; (films) Kismet; Mahananda; Bala Joban; My Darling; Maharanee; Draupadi; Gvalan. Contbr. to: Filmindia, (Fndr. & Ed.); Ed., Mother India. Address: Girnar, Pali Hill, Bombay 50, India.

PATERSON, Adolphus Anang, b. 19 Sept. 1927, Labadi, Accra, Ghana. Journalist. Educ: Dip., Multi-Nat. For. Jrnlsts. Proj., Ind. Univ., Bloomington, USA, 1962-63. Contbr. to: Africa Report; Time; Progress Int.; Daily Telegraph Mag.; BBC; Daily & Sunday Telegraphs; Ashanti Pioneer (former columnist); Ashanti Times. Mbrships. incl: Ghana Jrnlsts. Assn.; Am. Profl. Jrnlsts. Soc. Address: 15-70, Off Teshie Rd., Labadi, Accra, Ghana.

PATERSON, Alistair Ian Hughes, b. 28 Feb. 1929, Nelson, NZ. Educationist; Dean, General Studies, New Zealand Police Department. Educ: Victoria Univ. of Wellington; Auckland Univ.; B.A.; Dip., Educ.; Dip., Tchng. Publs: Caves in the Hills, 1965; Birds Flying, 1973; Ed., Mate mag. Contbr. to: Arena; Edge; Poetry Aust.; Mate;

Poetry NZ; Poet; Landfall; NZ Bookworld; Thursday Mag. Recip., Nat. Poetry Award, Penwomen's Club, 1968. Address: P.O. Box 10153, The Terrace, Wellington, NZ.

PATERSON, Donald Edgar, b. 13 Feb. 1935, Nelson, NZ. Legal Counsel to Ombudsman; Professor of Law. Educ: B.A., LL.M., Univ. of Wellington, NZ; J.S.D., Yale Univ. Law Schl. Publs: Introduction to Administrative Law in NZ, 1966; How to Minimise Income Tax & Death Duties, 2nd ed., 1968. Contbr. to: NZ Law Jrnl.; NZ Univs. Law Review; Otago Law Review; Rydge's Bus. Jrnl. Mbrships: NZ Law Soc.; Wellington Dist. Law Soc. Address: 12 Paddington Grove, Karori, Wellington, NZ.

PATERSON, Neil, b. 1916, Greenock, Scotland, UK. Author; Screenwriter. Educ: M.A., Edinburgh Univ. Publs: The China Run, 1948; Behold thy Daughter, 1950; And Delilah, 1951; Man on the Tight-Rope, 1953; A Candle to the Devil, 1975; (screenplays) The Kidnappers; High Tide at Noon; The Shiralee; Room at the Top; The Spiral Road. Mbrships. incl: Vice-Chmn., Scottish Arts Coun. (Chmn., Lit. Comm.); Arts Coun. of GB; Chmn. of Prod., Films of Scotland; Gov., Nat. Film Schl.; Dir., Grampian TV; Gov., Pitlochry Festival Theatre; Former Gov., Brit. Film Inst. Hons: Atlantic Award in Lit., 1946; Oscar Award, Am. Film Acad., 1960. Address: St. Ronans, Crieff, Perthshire, UK.

PATERSON, Robert, b. 25 Oct. 1908, Ashington, UK. Teacher. Educ: Tchrs. Trng. Coll., Oxford. Publs: English for Today, I & II, 1946; English with a Purpose, I – IV, 1956. Contbr. to: Tchrs. World; Schoolmaster; Pictorial Educ.; Natal Tchrs. Jrnl., Grade Tchr., USA. Mbr., Nat. Assn. of Hd. Tchrs. Address: "Linksfield", 5 Claremont Gdns., Whitley Bay, Northumberland, UK.

PATERSON, Thomas Thomson, b. 29 Sept. 1909, Buckhaven, Fife, UK. University Professor. Educ: B.Sc., Edinburgh Univ.; M.A., Ph.D., Cambridge Univ. Publs. incl: Studies in the Ice Age in the Himalayas, 1939; Prehistory of the Punjab, 1958; Glasgow Ltd., 1960; Management Theory, 1966; Fundamentals of Management, 1970; Job Evaluation, 1972; Manual for Job Evaluation, 1972; Decision Dynamics, 1975; Decision Systems, 1975. Contbr. to profl. jrnls. (100 papers, num. articles). Mbrships: Fellow, Royal Soc. Edinburgh. Agent: Shaw Maclean. Address: Dept. of Economics & Commerce, Simon Fraser Univ., Burnaby 2, B.C., Can.

PATERSON, Timothy Norman, b. 4 Apr. 1934, Nuwara Eliya, Ceylon. Translator; Lexicographer; Writer. Educ: Mbr., Inst. of Linguists. Publs: (transls.) The Flood in Florence (Bonechi), 1966; Pre-Roman Figurines, 1970; (dicts.) Italian-English Section Bilingual Dictionary (letters I, N, O, S, T, U, V, Z), 1971; English-Italian Section Compact Dictionary (letters A – Z), 1974. Contbr. to: La Sicilia; L'Aurora. Mbrships: Transls.' Guild, Inst. of Linguists; Transls'. Assn., Soc. of Authors; Assn. Nazionale Italiana Traduttori. Address: Viale del Poggio Imperiale 23, 50125 Florence, Italy.

PATERSON, William, b. 1926, Middx., UK. Director of Public Relations. Publs: Industrial Publicity Management, 1968. Contbr. to var. mgmt. jrnls. Mbr., For. Press Assn.; M.I.P.R. Recip., M.Cam., 1975. Address: The Lodge, West Dr., Harrow Weald, Middx., UK.

PATEY, (Very Rev.) Edward Henry, b. 1915, Newton Abbot, UK. Dean of Liverpool; Author. Educ: M.A.; Hertford Coll., Oxford; Westcott House, Cambridge. Publs: Boys & Girls Growing Up; Holy Communion in a Divided Church; Religion in the Club; Worship in the Club; A Doctor's Life of Jesus; Young People Now; Enquire Within; Look out for the Church; Burning Questions; Don't Just Sit There. Mbr., Oxford Union Soc. Address: The Cathedral, Liverpool L1 7A2, UK.

PATON, Alan Stewart, b. 11 Jan. 1903, Pietermaritzburg, South Africa. Writer. Educ: B.Ed.; B.Sc., Univ. of Natal. Publs: Cry, The Beloved Country, 1948; Too Late the Phalarope, 1953; South Africa & Her People, 1955; South African Transition, 1956; Debbie Go Home, 1960; Hofmeyr, 1965; Instrument of the Peace, 1968; Kontakion for You Departed, 1969; Apartheid & the Archbishop, 1973. Contbr. to: sev. jrnls. & mags. Pres., Liberal Party of South Africa, 1954-68. Recip. sev. hon. degrees & doctorates; Freedom Award of USA, 1960. Address: P.O. Box 278, Hillcrest, Natal, Repub. of S. Africa.

PATON, (Canon) David Macdonald, b. 1913, Hendon, Middx., UK. Clergyman. Educ: M.A., Brasenose Coll., Oxford Univ. Publs: Blind Guides? , 1939; Christian Missions & the Judgment of God, 1953; Anglicans & Unity, 1962; Ed., S.C.M. Press, 1956-59. Contbr. to: Essays in Anglican Self-Criticism; Ministry of the Spirit; Reform of the Ministry; Asia Handbook. Address: 17 Brunswick Rd., Gloucester GL1 1HQ, UK.

PATRICK, John, b. 17 May 1905. Dramatist. Publs. incl: (plays) The Willow & I, 1942; The Hasty Heart, 1945; The Teahouse of the August Moon, 1953; It's Been Wonderful, 1965; Everybody's Girl, 1966; Scandal Point, 1967; A Barrel full of Pennies, 1970; Macbeth Did It, 1971; The Dancing Mice, 1971; Anybody Out There? , 1972; The Savage Dilemma, 1972; (films) Three Coins in the Fountain, 1954; A Many Splendoured Thing, 1955; High Society, 1956; The World of Suzie Wong, 1960; Shoes of the Fisherman, 1968. Hons. incl: Pulitzer Prize, 1954; Screen Writers' Guild Award, 1957; Foreign Corres. Award, 1957. Address: Hasty Hill Farm, Haverstraw Rd., Suffern, NY, USA.

PATTEN, Brian, b. 1946, Liverpool, UK. Writer. Publs: Little Johnny's Confession, 1967; Penguin Modern Poets, No. 10, 1967; Notes to the Hurrying Man, 1969; The Elephant & the Flower, 1970; The Irrelevant Song, 1971; Jumping Mouse, 1972; The Unreliable Nightingale, 1973; Ed., The House That Jack Built, 1973. Contbr. to: Vogue; Sunday Times; Books & Bookmen. Address: c/o George Allen & Unwin, 40 Museum St., London WC1, UK.

PATTERSON, Alfred Temple, b. 1902, Newcastle upon Tyne, UK. Emeritus Professor. Educ: M.A., Univ. of Durham. Publs. incl: Radical Leicester; The Other Armada; The University of Southampton Centenary History; A Selection from the Southampton Corporation Journals, 1815-35, & Borough Council Minutes, 1835-47; A History of Southampton 1700-1914: Vol. I: An Oligarchy in Decline, 1700-1835; Vol. II: The Beginnings of Modern Southampton, 1836-67; Southampton: A Biography; Ed., The Jellicoe Papers; Jellicoe; Tyrwhitt of the Harwich Force. Contbr. to var. jrnls. Fellow, Royal Histl. Soc. Agent: Curtis Brown Ltd. Address: The Sele, Stoughton, Chichester, UK.

PATTERSON, Edward M., b. 1920, Bangor, N. Ireland, UK. Scientist. Educ: B.Sc., M.Sc., D.Sc.; Queen's Univ. of Belfast; Univ. of St. Andrews. Publs: Belfast & Co. Down Railway, 1958; Great Northern Railway of Ireland, 1962; Donegal Railways, 1962; Lough Swilly Railway, 1964; Ballycastle Railway, 1965; The Ballymena Lines, 1968; Clogher Valley Railway, 1972. Contbr. to num. sci. jrnls. Mbrships: Royal Irish Acad.; Fellow, Royal Soc.; Edinburgh; F.R.S.A. Address: 25 Caldwell Rd., West Kilbride, Ayrshire, KA23 9LF, UK.

PATTERSON, Helen Temple, b. 31 Jan. 1904, Bredbury, Cheshire, UK. University Lecturer (Retired). Educ: M.A., Manchester Univ.; Dip. d'Etudes Supérieures, Fac. des Lettres, Lille, France; F.I.A.L., Zurich, Switz. Publs: Critical Edition of Voltaire's Traité de Métaphysique, 1937; Poetic Genesis, 1960; The Sum of History (transl. of Bilan de l'Histoire by René Grousset w. A. Temple Patterson), 1951. Contbr. to: Revue de l'hist. littéraire; Revue Mod.; French Studies; Mod. Lang. Review; etc. Mbrships: Life Fellow, Int. Inst. of Arts & Letters; Mod. Humanities' Rsch. Assn. Address: The Sele, Stoughton, Chichester, Sussex, UK.

PATTERSON, Merrill Reeves, b. 27 Jan. 1902, Jersey City, N.J., USA. University Administrator; Teacher; Consultant. Educ: B.S., Wesleyan Univ.; A.M., Brown Univ.; Ph.D., Yale Univ.; Litt.D. (Hon.), Marietta Coll. Publs: Sumner Lincoln Fairfield: A Biographical Study (1803-1844), 1933. Contbr. to var. mags. & histl. jrnls. Address: 411 5th St., Marietta, OH 45750, USA.

PATTERSON, Orlando Horace Lloyd, b. 5 June 1940, Westmoreland, Jamaica. Professor of Sociology. Educ: Univ. of W. Indies, 1959-62; (External), B.Sc., London Univ., UK; Ph.D., London Schl. Econs., 1962-65. Publs: The Sociology of Slavery, 1967; The Children of Sisyphus (novel), 1964; An Absence of Ruins, 1967; Die the Long Day, 1972. Contbr. to: Times Lit. Supplement; Pub. Interest; Brit. Jrnl. of Sociol. Mbr. of Sorokin Award Comm., Am. Sociol. Assn. Hons: Prose Prize, Dakar Festival of Negro Arts, 1966; A.M., Harvard Univ., USA, 1971. Address: 15 Shephard St., Cambridge, MA 02138, USA.

PATTERSON, Raymond Murray, b. 13 May 1898, Darlington, UK. Cattle Rancher; Hunter; Guide; Writer. Educ: B.A., 1921, M.A., 1958, Univ. of Oxford. Publs: The Dangerous River, 1954; The Buffalo Head, 1961; Far Pastures, 1963; Trail to the Interior, 1966; Finlay's River, 1968. Contbr. to: Hudson's Bay Record Soc. series, Vol. XVIII; Blackwoods; Country Life; The Beaver. Hons: Award for biographical writing, Wash. State Press Club, 1955; Award for prose writing, Lib. Dev. Commn. & B.C. Lib. Assn., 1972. Address: 2685 Queenswood Dr., Victoria, B.C. V8N 1X6, Canada.

PATTERSON, William Lorenzo, b. 27 Aug. 1891, San Fran., Calif., USA. Lawyer. Educ: B.A. Publs: We Charge Genocide; The Crime of Government Against the Negro People, 1951; The Man Who Cried Genocide, 1971. Recip., Lenin 100th Anniversary Medal. Address: 101 W. 147th St., N.Y., NY 10039, USA.

PATTINSON, Nancy Evelyn, pen name ASQUITH, Nan, b. Barnsley, Yorks., UK. Novelist. Publs. 21 novels inclng: The Quest; Garden of Persephone; Out of the Dark; The Girl from Rome. Contbr. to: Woman's Own; The Lady; Pony; Honey; Woman's Realm; My Weekly; Elizabethan; etc. Mbrships: Romantic Novelist's Assn.; The Author. Address: Willow Cottage, Old Barn Close, Willingdon Village, Eastbourne, Sussex BN20 9HJ, UK.

PATTON, James Welch, b. 1900, Murfreesboro, Tenn., USA, d. 17 May 1973. Professor of History. Educ: A.M., Ph.D.; Vanderbilt Univ.; Univ. of N.C. Publs: Unionism & Reconstruction in Tennessee; The Women of the Confederacy (co-author); Ed., Messages, Addresses & Public Papers of Governor Luther H. Hodges, Vol. I, 1960, Vol. II, 1962, Vol. III, 1963. Contbr. to: Travels in the Old South; Jrnl. Southern Hist.; Dict. of Am. Hist.; Collier's Ency.; etc. Address: 614 East Franklin St., Chapel Hill, NC, USA.

PAU, Shiu Yau, b. 11 May 1892, Yokohama, Japan. Principal & Chief Professor, Lai Ching Art Institute, Hong Kong. Educ: Kyoto City Univ. of Arts, Japan, 1915; Paintings & Arts Univ., 1918, Japan. Publs: Poetry for Chinese Paintings, 1966; Poetry for Landscape Paintings, 1968; Poetry for Bird Paintings, 1970; How to Appreciate the Masterpieces in the Old Palace, 1974. Contbr. to: Lit. World; Jih Hua Yuek Poa (Japan); var. Hong Kong newspapers. Mbr., PEN. Hons: All China Arts Exhib. Prize, 1909; All Japan Arts Exhib. Prize, 1918. Special Prize, Kyoto City Univ., 1915; Address: Lai Ching Art Institute, Causeway Bay Paterson Bldg., Block A—1, 4th Floor, Paterson St., Hong Kong.

PAUGH, Richard Lewis, b. 29 June 1925, Akron, Ohio, USA. Journalist (Travel, Conservation & Recreation). Educ: Ohio State Univ. Publs: Teen-age Fishing Clinics, 1969. Contbr. to: 14 newspapers & mags. of syndicated columns on outdoor subjects, conserv. & the environment. Mbrships: Outdoor Writers' Assn. of Am.; Outdoor Writers of Ohio (VP 1964, Pres. 1965, Conven. Chmn. 1975); Sigma Delta Chi; Soc. Profl. Jrnlsts.; Press Club of Ohio. Hons. incl: Best Weekly Outdoor Columns, 1964, 1965, 1967, 1968, 1969, 1970; Outdoor Writers' Man of the Yr., 1965; Best Environmental Columns, 1970; Master's Citation, Am. Soc. Conserv. Writers, 1972. Address: 2860 Minerva Lake Rd., Columbus, OH 43229, USA.

PAUK, Walter, b. 1 May 1914, New Brit., Conn., USA. Professor of Education. Educ: A.B., Univ. of Conn., 1949; Ph.D., Cornell Univ., 1955. Publs: How to Take Tests, 1969; How to Read Factual Literature, 1970; How to Read Creative Literature, 1970; Reading for Facts, 1974; Reading for Ideas, 1974; Six-Way Paragraphs, 1974; How to Study in College, 2nd ed., 1974; A Skill at a Time Series, 1975; Reading in English for Arab Students, 1975. Contbr. to profl. jrnls. Mbr., profl. orgs. Recip. acad. hons. Address: Reading Study Ctr., 375 Olin Hall, Cornell Univ., Ithaca, NY 14853, USA.

PAUL, Aileen, b. 2 June 1917, Waycross, Ga., USA. Writer; Consumer Specialist; TV & Radio Performer. Publs: Kids Cooking: A First Cookbook for Children, 1970; Kids Gardening: A First Indoor Gardening Book for Children, 1972; Kids Camping, 1973; Candies, Cookies & Cakes, 1974; Kids Cooking Complete Meals, 1975. Contbr. to: Christian Sci. Monitor; N.Y. Times; Bergen Bulletin; Press Jrnl.; Beachcomber. Mbrships. incl: Authors' Guild; Acad. of TV Arts & Scis.; Am. Women in Radio & TV; Coop. Inst. Assn.; Int. Radio & TV Soc. Hons: Schl. Lib. Jrnl. Citation, 1970; AM Broadcaster of Yr. Award, Am. Women in Radio & TV, 1973. Address: 121 Gladwin Ave., Leonia, NJ 07605, USA.

PAUL, Betty, b. 21 May 1921, Hendon, Middx., UK. Scriptwriter; Actress. Publs: (stage plays) What About Stanley, 1965; Law & Order Gang, 1971; about 50 TV credits. Mbrships: Writers Guild of GB; Brit. Equity. Address: 90 Coleherne Ct., London SW5, UK.

PAUL, Elisabeth, Lillian, b. 30 July 1910, Reigate, Surrey, UK. Writer. Publs: A Faithful Witness, 1966. Mbrships: Hon. Sec., Sudan Church Assn. Address: The Forge, Sandford Saint Martin, Oxon. OX5 4AG, UK.

PAUL, Jan S., b. 2 Apr. 1929, Iowa City, USA. Specialist, Technical Communications. Educ: A.A., Bakersfield Coll.; B.Sc., Pacific Int. Univ., Calif.; B.A., Calif. State Univ.; M.Sc., Univ. of Chgo.; Ph.D., Phoenix Univ., Italy; D.Sc., Univ. of Calif. Publs. incl: Knotted String, 1967; Lintens, 1970; A Twilight of Honour, 1975. Contbr. to: Sci. Digest; Writer's Digest; Popular Mechanics; sev. poetry anthols. inclng. Best Poets of 20th Century, 1974; etc. Mbrships. incl: Author's Guild of Am., Dramatist's Guild of Am. Hons. incl: Poet of the Yr., 1974; Pulitzer Noms., 1967, 1970; Dr., Org. for Higher Ed., 1974. Address: P.O. Box 6488, Bakersfield, CA 93306, USA.

PAUL, Leslie Allen, b. 30 Apr. 1905, Dublin, Repub. of Ireland. Author; Lecturer. Publs. incl: Angry Young Man, 1951; Sir Thomas More, 1953; English Philosophers, 1953; Transition from School to Work, 1962; Alternatives to Christian Belief, 1967; A Church by Daylight, 1973; The Waters & The Wild, 1975. Contbr. to: BBC; C.B.C.; A.B.C.; Christian Century; World's Children; Jrnl. Indl. Rels.; etc. Mbrships. incl: Simone Weil Mem. Comm. (Hon. Sec., 1956-59); Fellow, Indl. Welfare Soc., 1960-62; F.R.S.L.; R.I. Philos.; VP, Philosl. Soc.; Soc. of Authors. Recip., Atlantic Award in Lit., 1946. Address: 6 Church Croft, Madley, Hereford HR2 9LT, UK.

PAULISSEN, Martin, b. 11 Apr. 1912, Arnhem, Netherlands. Journalist. Publs: Moderne Propaganda, 1946; Geest contra Geweld (Spirit v. Violence), 1948; Drankenboek (Book of Beverages), 1962-63, 1965-66, 1967-68; Over Wijnen (About Wines), 1973. Contbr. to: Dutch & German Trade Papers; Dutch Radio & TV; UNO Press, Amsterdam. Mbrships: Int. Fedn. of Tourism Journalists & Writers; Nederlandse Vereniging van Journalisten; Contact-Centrum op Voorlichtingsgebied. Address: Van Deventerlaan 9, Voorburg 2111, Netherlands.

PAULS, John P., b. 28 Apr. 1916, Paulopol, Russia. Professor of Russian Language & Literature, Univ. of Cinn. Educ: M.A., Warsaw Univ., 1939; Ph.D., Univ. Munich, 1947. Publs: Ideology of Cyrillo-Methodians & its Origin, 1954; Pushkin's Poltava, 1962; Chekhov's Names, 1974. Contbr. to: Names; Slavic & E. European Jrnl.; Weiner Slav. Jahrbuch; Slavia Orientalis; Ukrainian Review; Books Abroad. Mbrships. incl: Am. Assn. Tchrs. Slavic & E. European Langs.; Am. Name Soc. Recip., Von Humboldt Fellowship, Univ. Vienna, 1943-45. Address: 3422 Lyleburn Pl., Cinn., OH 45220, USA.

PAULSEN, Wolfgang, b. 21 Sept. 1910, Düsseldorf, Germany. University Professor; Critic. Educ: Univs. of Tübingen; Bonn; Berlin; Leipzig; Ph.D., Univ. of Berne, Switz., 1934. Publs: Expressionismus und Aktivismus, 1935; Georg Kaiser: Die Perspektiven seines Werkes, 1960; Die Ahnfrau: Zu Grillparzers früher Dramatik, 1962; Versuch über Rolf Bongs: Der Schriftsteller als Dichter, 1973; Ed., Bonaventura, Nachtwachen; Franz Grillparzer, Die Jüdin von Toledo. Contbr. to: Germanistik, Tübingen; The Germanic Review. Mbrships. incl: MLA of Am.; Deutsche Schiller Gesellschaft. Address: 49 Maplewood Drive, Amherst, MA 01002, USA.

PAULSON, Arvid, b. 14 Feb. 1888, Helsingborg, Sweden. Actor; Author; Translator. Privately educated. Publs. incl: The Story of Don Quixote (w. C. Edwards), 1922; Contbr. to Luck by Lothrop Stoddard, 1929; Transl., num. Strindberg, Ibsen plays; Transl., Ed., Letters of Strindberg to Harriet Bosse, 1959, 1961; The Strindberg Reader, 1968; Strindberg's novels, The Natives of Hemse, The Scapegoat, Days of Loneliness, The Dance of Death, Parts I, II, 1971, 1974. Transl. in num. anthols. Mbrships. incl: PEN; Am. Transls. Assn. Hons. incl: Gold Medal, Swedish Acad., 1964; Twice cited in US Congressional Record for scholarly attainment, transls. of Strindberg, Ibsen, 1967, 1968. Address: 5606 9th Ave., Brooklyn, NY 11220, USA.

PAUST, Marian (Mrs.), b. 5 Feb. 1908, Richland Ctr., Wis., USA. Writer; Poet. Educ: B.S., Univ. of Wis. Publs: Honey to be Savored, 1968; Everybody Beats A Drum, 1970. Contbr. to num. anthols., poetry jrnls. Mbrships: Nat. League of Am. Pen Women; State Bd. Mbr., Wis. Fellowship of Poets; Wis. Reg. Writers Assn.; Coun. of Wis. Writers, Inc.; Acad. of Am. Poets; Nat. Fedn. of State Poetry Socs.; Wis. Acad. of Scis., Arts & Letters. Hons: Poet Laureate, Wis., 1956, 1969; State Writers Cup Award, 1960; 2 Jade Rings, 2 Bard's Poet's Chair Special Awards. Address: Rt. 4, Box 484, Fox Hollow Rd., Richland Ctr., WI 53581, USA.

PAVLOVSKI, Bożin, b. 7 Jan. 1942, Svan, Yugoslavia. Publisher; General Editor. Educ: Univ. of Skopje. Publs: (novels) A Play with Love, 1964; Miladin from China, vols. I & II, 1967, 1968; The Macedonian People behind the Equator, 1970; Duva, 1973; (short stories) Ludisti, 1967. Mbr., PEN. Hons: Racin's Prize, 1967; Youth Prize (Mladost), 1973. Address: Maxim Gorki 18, Skopje, Yugoslavia.

PAVLOVSKI, Jovan, b. 10 Sept. 1937, Tetovo, Yugoslavia. Journalist. Educ: univ. degree in Yugoslav Lit. Publs: August (poetry), 1962; Medea (poetry), 1969; Miso, iso.so, o (poetry for children), 1972; This Radiovce (novel), 1972; Identity (poetry), 1974; The Worm Sun (novel), 1974. Contbr. to many periodicals. Mbrships: Macedonian Assns. of Jrnlsts. & Writers. Hons: Best Macedonian Radio Play, 1969; Racine Prize, Best Macedonian Novel, 1972; RTV Skopje Prize for Best Book for Children, 1972. Address: "Ivan Agovski" No. 1/I, 91000 Skopje, Yugoslavia.

PAVLOWITCH, Stevan K., b. 1933, Belgrade, Yugoslavia. Senior Lecturer. Educ: Univs. of Paris & Lille, France; Univ. of London, UK; Lic.ès L., B.A., M.A. Publs: Anglo-Russian Rivalry in Serbia 1837-39, 1961; Yugoslavia, 1971. Contbr. to: E. Chs. Review; Annales; European Studies Review; Slavonic & E. European Review; Rass. Stor. del Risorg.; Trib. de Genève; Gaz. de Lausanne; Survey; Slavic Review; Review of Study Ctr. for Yugoslav Affairs; Revue d'Athènes; etc. Address: University of Southampton, Southampton, Hants. SO9 5NH, UK.

PAWLE, (Shafto) Gerald (Strachan), b. 1913, Bishop's Stortford, UK. Editorial Director, Beaverbrook West of England Newspapers. Publs: Squash Rackets, 1951; The Secret War, UK & USA 1956; The War & Colonel Warden, UK & USA 1963. Contbr. to: Beaverbrook Newspapers; Daily Telegraph; Western Morning News; BBC; ITV; South Africa Broadcasting Corp. Mbr., Press Club. Address: Treworgan, Mawnan, Falmouth, Cornwall, UK.

PAXTON, John. Editor, The Statesman's Year-Book. Appts: Hd., Econs. Dept., Millfield Schl., 1952-63; Asst. Ed., 1964-68, Dpty. Ed., 1968, The Statesman's Year-book; Ed., 1969—; Sr. Cons. Ed., The Macmillan Press Ltd., 1970—. Publs: Trade in the Common Market Countries, (w. A. E. Walsh) 1965; The Structure & Development of the Common Market, 1968; Trade & Resources of the Common Market & EFTA, 1970; Smuggling, (w. John Wroughton) 1971; Into Europe, (w. A. E. Walsh) 1972; Everyman's Dictionary of Abbreviations, 1974; World Legislatures, 1974; The Statesman's Year-Book World Gazetteer, 1975; Competition Policy, (w. A. E. Walsh) 1975; European Political Facts 1918-73, (w. C. Cook) 1975; The Developing Common Market, 1975. Contbr. to: Keesing's Contemporary Archives; Times Lit. Supplement; etc. Mbrships: Soc. of Authors; PEN. Address: c/o The Macmillan Press Ltd., 4 Little Essex St., London WC2R 3LF, UK.

PAYN, W. H., b. 1913, Somerton, Suffolk. Publs: Ornamental Waterfowl, 1957, 3rd ed. 1974; The Birds of Suffolk, 1962. Fellow, Linnean Soc. Recip., M.B.E. Address: Hartest Place, Bury St. Edmunds, Suffolk, UK.

PAYNE, Donald Gordon, pen names MARSHALL, James Vance; CAMERON, Ian, b. 1924, London, UK. Author. Educ: Charterhouse, Oxford. Publs: Walkabout, 1959; The Lost Ones, 1961; Wings of the Morning, 1962; A River Ran Out of Eden, 1963; Lodestone & Evening Star, 1966; The Mountains at the Bottom of the World, 1973; The Wind at Morning, 1973; Magellan & the First Circumnavigation of the World, 1974. Contbr. to: Reader's Digest; Book of the Month Club. Agent: David Higham Assoc. Address: Pippacre, Westcott Heath, Dorking, Surrey, RH4 3JZ, UK.

PAYNE, Ernest Alexander, b. 19 Feb. 1902, London, UK. Baptist Minister of Religion; Author. Educ: B.A., B.D., London Univ.; M.A.; B.Litt., Oxford Univ. Publs. incl: Harry Wyatt of Shansi, 1895-1938, 1939; The Church Awakes, 1942; The Free Church Tradition in the Life of England, 1944, 3rd ed., 1965; The Fellowship of Believers, 1945, 2nd ed., 1952; The Baptists of Berkshire, 1951; James Henry Rushbrooke, 1954; The Baptist Union: A Short History, 1959, 2nd ed., 1964; Free Churchmen, Unrepentant & Repentant, 1965; Out of Great Tribulation: Baptists in the U.S.S.R., 1974. Contbr. to: Congregational & Baptist Quarterlies; Theol. Recip., C.H., 1968. Address: Elm Cottage, 21 Manor Rd., Pitsford, Northants., UK.

PAYNE, Laurence, b. 5 June 1919, London, UK. Actor; Writer. Publs: Nose on My Face, 1961; Too Small For His Shoes, 1962; Deep and Crisp and Even, 1964; Birds in the Belfry, 1966; Spy For Sale, 1969; Even My Foots Asleep, 1971. Address: 3d Grosvenor Hill, Wimbledon, London SW19, UK.

PAYNE, Stanley G(eorge), b. 9 Sept. 1934, Denton, Tex., USA. Professor of History. Educ: Ph.D., Columbia Univ., 1960. Publs: Falange: A History of Spanish Fascism, 1961; Politics & the Military in Modern Spain, 1967; The Spanish Revolution, 1970; A History of Spain & Portugal, 2 vols., 1973; Basque Nationalism, 1974. Contbr. to: Am. Hist. Review; Jrnl. of Mod. Hist.; Jrnl. Contemp. Hist. Mbrships: Am. Hist. Assn.; Soc. for Spanish & Portuguese Hist. Studies. Fellowships: Soc. Sci. Rsch. Coun., 1958, 1961, 1970; Guggenheim Fndn., 1962; Am. Coun. of Learned Socs., 1971. Address: 3917 Plymouth Circle, Madison, WI 53705, USA.

PAYNTER, William Henry, b. 3 Jan. 1901, Callington, Cornwall, UK. Writer; Broadcaster. Publs: History of St. Mary's Church Callington; Primitive Physic: John Wesley's Book of Old Fashioned Cures & Remedies (ed.); Guide to Callington; Guide to Liskeard; Daniel Gumb — The Cave-Man Mathematician; History of Bishop Trelawney; John Allen's History of Liskeard (ed. & revised). Looe — History & Guide. Contbr. to: London & provincial press; var. mags. & jrnls.; BBC & ITV. Mbrships: Soc. of Authors; Mus. Assn.; Bard of Cornish Gorsedd (bardic name Whyler Pystry); Curator, Cornish Mus., Looe, Cornwall. Address: Janola, Miners Way, Addington, Liskeard, Cornwall, UK.

PAZ, Octavio, b. 31 Mar. 1914, Mexico City, Mexico. Writer; Poet; Essayist; Visiting Professor, Harvard Univ.; Mexican Foreign Service, 1962-63. Publs. incl: (in Spanish) (poetry) Salamandra, 1962; Versiones y Diversiones, 1974; (prose) Apariencia desnuda, 1973; Los Hijos del Limo, 1974; El Mono Gramatico, 1974; (in English) (poetry) Sun-stone, 1970; Eagle or Sun, 1970; Configurations, 1971; Renga, 1972; Early Poems, 2nd ed., 1973; (prose) Claude Levi Strauss: An Introduction, 1970; The Other Mexico, Critique of the Pyramid, 1972; Alternating Current, 1973; Conjunctions & Disjunctions, 1974; The Bow & the Lyre, 1974; Children of the Mire, 1974; Ed., Plural (lit. & pol. review), 1971-72. Recip., Grand Prix Int. de Poésie, Belgium, 1963. Address: Lerma 143, Mexico, S, D.F.

PEACH, Lawrence du Garde, b. 14 Jan. 1890, Sheffield, UK, d. 31 Dec. 1974. Writer; Dramatist. Educ: M.A., Manchester Univ.; Ph.D., Sheffield Univ. Publs: num. plays & short stories. Contbr. to: Punch; num. newspapers. Mbrships: Authors Soc.; Dramatists Club. Hons: O.B.E.; D.Litt. Address: Foolow, Eyam, Via Sheffield, UK.

PEACOCK, (Major) Basil, b. 2 Apr. 1898, Newcastle-upon-Tyne, UK. Emeritus Dental Specialist; Special Reserve & Territorial Officer (1916-47). Educ: L.D.S., R.C.S.; Med. Coll., Durham Univ.; Newcastle Dental Schl. Publs: Prisoner on the Kwai, 1966; Peacock's Tales, 1968; History of The Royal Northumberland Fusiliers, 1970; Discursive Dentist, 1972; Tinker's Mufti, 1974. Contbr. to: Blackwood's Mag.; Brit. Dental Jrnl.; BBC Radio. Mbrships: Brit. Dental Assn.; Civil Serv. Club. Hons: M.C.; Territorial Decoration. Agent: Shaw Maclean. Address: 11 Harcourt Field, Wallington SM6 8BA, Surrey, UK.

PEACOCK, Ronald, b. 22 Nov. 1907, UK. Professor of German; College Administrator. Educ: B.A., 1929, M.A., 1930, Leeds Univ.; Litt. D.; Dr.phil., Marburg Univ., Germany. Publs: Hölderlin, 1938, 73; The Poet in the Theatre, 1946, revised ed., 1960; The Art of Drama, 1957, US ed., 1974; Goethe's Major Plays, 1959, 3rd ed., 1970; Criticism & Personal Taste, 1972. Contbr. to: Times Lit. Supplement; Listener; Manchester Guardian; Mod. Lang.

Review; German Life & Letters; Euphorion; etc. Mbrships. incl: PEN; MLA; Engl. Goethe Soc.; Mod. Humanities Rsch. Assn. Recip., Goethe-Institut Gold Medal, 1969. Address: Bedford Coll., Regents Park, London NW1 4NS, UK.

PEACOCKE, Arthur Robert, b. 29 Nov. 1924, Watford, UK. University Lecturer; College Dean. Educ: M.A., B.Sc., D.Phil., D.Sc., Oxford Univ.; B.D., Birmingham Univ.; Sc.D. (by incorporation), Cambridge Univ. Publs: The Molecular Basis of Heredity (w. R. B. Drysdale), 1965; Science & the Christian Experiment, 1971; The Osmotic Pressure of Biological Macromolecules, 1974. Contbr. to: New Sci.; Zygon; Mod. Churchman. Mbrships: Sec., Brit. Biophys. Soc.; Athenaeum. Recip., Lecomte du Noüy Int. Prize, 1973. Address: Clare Coll., Cambridge, UK.

PEAKE, Lilian, pen name EPTON, Lilian, b. 25 May 1924, London, UK. Writer. Publs. incl: No Friend of Mine, 1972; Familiar Stranger, 1973; Man In Charge, 1973; Till the End of Time, 1973; A Sense of Belonging, 1974; Master of the House, 1974; The Dream on the Hill, 1974; The Impossible Marriage, 1974. Contbr. to: Bucks. Free Press; Woman; etc. Mbrships: Soc. of Authors; Soc. of Women Writers & Jrnlsts.; Romantic Novelists' Assn. Address: 48, Dungannon Chase, Thorpe Bay, Southend-on-Sea, Essex SS1 3NJ, UK.

PEARCE, Ann Philippa, b. Great Shelford, UK. Writer. Educ: M.A., Girton Coll., Cambridge. Publs: Minnow on the Say, 1954; Tom's Midnight Garden, 1958; Mrs. Cockles' Cat, 1961; A Dog so Small, 1962; The Children of the House, (w. Sir Brian Fairfax-Lucy), 1968; The Elm Street Lot, 1969; The Squirrel Wife, 1971; Beauty & the Beast, 1972; What the Neighbours Did & Other Stories, 1972; Lion at School, 1973. Contbr. to: Times Lit. Supplement; BBC; Guardian; Scriptwriter-Producer, BBC Schls. Dept., 1945-58. Mbr., Soc. of Authors. Address: c/o Kestrel Books, 17 Grosvenor Gdns., London SW1, UK.

PEARCE, Brian Leonard, pen names REDMAN, Joseph; FARNBOROUGH, B.; HUSSEY, Leonard, b. 1915, Weymouth, UK. Freelance Lecturer & Translator; Writer. Educ: B.A., Univ. Coll., London. Publs: Pamphlets on Labour Movement History; The Communist Party & the Labour Left (1925-29); Early History of the British Communist Party; (transls.) Preobrazhensky: The New Economics; Mandel: Marxist Economic Theory; Trotsky: Results & Prospects; Lublinskaya: French Absolutism; Rodinson: Islam & Capitalism; Emmanuel: Unequal Exchange. Contbr. to: Stand; Engl. Lang. Tchng.; Labour Review; etc. Mbrships. incl: Transls. Assn. Address: 42 Victoria Rd., New Barnet, Herts., UK.

PEARCE, Brian Louis, b. 4 June 1933, Acton, London, UK. Librarian; Author; Poet. Publs. incl: The Eagle & the Swan (play), 1966; The Argonauts & Other Poems, 1970; Requiem for the Sixties (verse), 1971; Twickenham College of Technology: the First Thirty-Five Years 1937-72, 1974; var. vols. of verse, verse-drama, family & local hist. Contbr. to: Enigma; Envoi; Expression Poetry Quarterly; Guardian; Outposts; Poesie Vivante; Poetry Review; Tribune; Ed., Expression, Richmond Poetry Grp. Jrnl., 1965-67; Ed., Quarto Poets Series, 1973-. Recip., 5th-6th Place Award, Poetry Soc.'s 1-Act Verse Play Contest, 1964. Address: 72 Heathfield S., Twickenham, Middx. TW2 7SS, UK.

PEARCE, Donn, b. 28 Sept. 1928, Croydon, Pa., USA. Novelist; Screen Writer; Journalist. Publs: Cool Hand Luke, 1965; Pier Head Jump, 1972; Dying in the Sun, 1974. Contbr. to: Playboy; Esquire; Penthouse; True; Gall.; Oui. Mbrships: Writers Guild of Am.; Screen Actors Guild; Acad. of Motion Picture Arts & Scis. Hons: Fellowship, Breadloaf Writers Conf., 1965; Nominated for Acad. Award, 1967. Address: 2443 Whale Harbor Lane, Fort Lauderdale, FL 33312, USA.

PEARCE, Noira Margaret, b. 29 Dec. 1919, Toowoomba, Qld., Australia. Teacher. Educ: B.A., Univ. of Qld. Publs: Flower Fairies' Secrets, 1963. Contbr. to: The Mountain Gazette; The Advertiser. Mbr., Aust. Soc. of Authors. Address: Dunolly, 1 Warne St., Katoomba, N.S.W., Australia 2780.

PEARCE, Raymond Maplesden, pen name MAPLESDEN, Ray, b. 25 Nov. 1894, Manchester, UK. Retired Medical Practitioner; Writer. Educ: T.D., M.B., Ch.B., Victoria Univ., Manchester. Publs: Doctor Allen G.P., 1938; Deplorable Doctors, 1965; Slender Threads (co-author, play). Contbr. to Brit. Med. Jrnl. Mbrships: Manchester Press Club; Soc. of Authors. Address: Flat No. 1 Market Cross House. Aldeburgh. Suffolk IP15 5BJ. UK.

PEARCE, Thomas Matthews, b. 22 May 1902, Covington, Ky., USA. Professor Emeritus of English. Educ: B.A., Univ. of Mont., 1923; M.A., 1925, Ph.D., 1930, Univ. of Pitts. Publs. incl: Lane of the Llano, 1936; Southwest Heritage (w. others), 1938, 3rd ed., 1972; Signature of the Sun (w. M. Major), 1950; New Mexico Place Names, 1965; Mary Hunter Austin, 1965; Oliver La Farge, 1972. Contbr. to reviews. Hons: Rsch. Grants, Henry E. Huntingdon Lib. & Univ. of N.M. Address: 1712 Sigma Chi Rd. N.E., Albuquerque, NM 87106, USA.

PEARCE, Winifred Mary, b. 1892, Gt. Yarmouth, UK. Author. Publs: Five Missionary Biographies for Children; Five School Tales; Don Percy; Knight in Royal Service. Contbr. to: Life of Faith; Engl. Churchman; Crusade; other relig. jrnls. Address: 8 Northstead Rd., Tulse Hill, London SW2, UK.

PEARLMAN, Moshe, b. 23 Mar. 1911, London, UK. Writer. Educ: B.Sc.(Econ.), London Schl. Econs. Publs: Collective Adventure, 1938; Mufti of Jerusalem, 1947; Adventure in the Sun, 1948; The Capture & Trial of Adolf Eichmann, UK 1962, USA 1963; Ben Gurion Looks Back, UK & USA, 1965; Historical Sites in Israel, USA 1966, 1969; The Zealots of Masada, USA 1967, UK 1968; Jerusalem: A History of 40 Centuries (co-author), USA & UK, 1969; Pilgrims to the Holy Land (co-author), USA & UK, 1970; In the Footsteps of Moses, USA 1973, UK 1974; The Maccabees, USA & UK, 1974. Address: 16 David Marcus St., Jerusalem, Israel.

PEARSON, Bill (William Harrison), b. 18 Jan. 1922, Greymouth, NZ. University Teacher. Educ: B.A., M.A., Univ. of Canterbury; Ph.D., King's Coll., Univ. of London. Publs: Frank Sargeson's Collected Stories 1935-63 (Ed.), 1963; Coal Flat, 1963; Henry Lawson Among Maoris, 1968; Roderick Finlayson, Brown Man's Burden & Later Stories (Ed.), 1973; Fretful Sleepers & Other Essays, 1974. Contbr. to: Landfall; Islands; NZ Monthly Review; Jrnl. of Pacific Hist. Mbrships. incl: Patron, Univ. of Auckland Maori Club, 1959-66. Jt. Recip., Landfall Rdrs. Award, 1960. Address: Engl. Dept., Univ. of Auckland, Auckland, NZ.

PEARSON, Frederick Keith, b. 1929, Manchester, UK. College Lecturer in Automobile & Agricultural Engineering. Educ: Chelsea Coll.; Bolton Trng. Coll. Publs: Douglas Southern Electric Tramway, 1954; Snaefell Mountain Railway, 1955; Manx Electric Railway, 1956; Douglas Bay Tramway, 1956; Isle of Man Tramways, 1970. Contbr. to: Mod. Tramway; Railway Mag.; I.M.I. Jrnl.; Jrnl. of the Manx Mus. Address: 15 Raybourne Ave., Poulton le Fylde, Blackpool FY6 7RT, UK.

PEASE, Jane Hanna, b. 26 Nov. 1929, Waukegan, Ill., USA. Professor of History. Educ: A.B.(magna cum laude), Smith Coll., Northampton, Mass.; M.A., Ph.D., Univ. of Rochester, N.Y. (all w. William H. Pease): Black Utopia: Negro Communal Experiments in America, 1963; 2nd ed., 1972; The Antislavery Argument (co-Ed.), 1965; Bound with Them in Chains: A Biographical History of the Antislavery Movement, 1972; They Who Would Be Free: Blacks' Search for Freedom, 1830-1861, 1974. Contbr. to: Jrnls. of Am., Southern, Negro Hist.; Am. & New England Quarterlies; etc. Mbrships. incl: New England, Am., Southern Histl. Assns.; Org. Am. Histns. Recip., sev. rsch. grants. Address: Dept. of History, Univ. of Maine, Orono, ME 04401, USA.

PEASE, William Henry, b. 31 Aug. 1924, Winchenden, Mass., USA. Professor of History. Educ: B.A.(cum laude), Williams Coll., Williamstown, Mass.; M.A., Univ. of Wis., Madison; Ph.D., Univ. of Rochester, N.Y. Publs. (all w. Jane H. Pease): Black Utopia: Negro Communal Experiments in America, 1963, 2nd ed., 1972; The Antislavery Argument (co-Ed.), 1965; Bound with Them in Chains: A Biographical History of the Antislavery Movement, 1972; They Who Would Be Free: Blacks' Search for Freedom, 1830-1861, 1974. Contbr. to: Jrnls. of Am., Southern, Negro Hist.; etc. Mbrships. incl: New England, Am., Southern Histl. Assns.; Org. Am. Histns. Recip., sev. rsch. grants. Address: Dept. of History, Univ. of Maine, Orono, ME 04401, USA.

PEATE, Iorwerth Cyfeiliog, b. 27 Feb. 1901, Glan-llyn, Llanbryn-Mair, Wales, UK. Welsh Folk Museum Curator (retired). Educ: M.A., D.Sc., Univ. of Wales. Publs. incl: The Welsh House, 1940, 3rd ed., 1946; Clock & Watch Makers in Wales, 1945, 2nd ed., 1960; Tradition & Folk Life, 1972; Cymru a'i Phobl; Y Crefftwr yng Nghymru; Canu Chwarter Canrif. Contbr. to var. profl. & lit. jrnls.

Mbrships: Former Pres., Sec. H (Anthropol.), Brit. Assn. for the Advancement of Sci.; F.S.A., London; 1st Pres., Soc. for Folk Life Studies. Hons: D.Litt. Celt., Univ. of Ireland, 1960; D.Litt., Univ. of Wales, 1970. Address: Maes-y-coed, St. Nicholas, Cardiff CF5 6SG, UK.

PECCORINI, Francisco L(etona), b. 27 Nov. 1915, San Miguel, El Salvador. University Professor. Educ: Dip. in Classics, Colegio de S. Ignacio de Loyola, Spain, 1939; Lic. Philos. 1942, Lic. Theol. 1950, Colegio de S. Francisco Javier, Spain; Ph.D., 1958, Univ. Comillas, Spain. Publs: Gabriel Marcel: La Razon de Ser en la Participacion, 1959; El Ser y los Seres según Santo Tomás de Aquino, 1961; El Hombre en Perspectiva Ontológica, 1963; Los Fundamentos Ultimos de los Derechos del Hombre, 1964; A Method of Self-Orientation to Thinking, 1970; La Voluntad del Pueblo en la Emancipación de El Salvador, 1972. Contbr. to profl. jrnls. Mbrships incl: Acad. Nacional de Historia, San Salvador; Medieval Acad. of Am. Address: 10059 Los Caballos Ct., Fountain Valley, CA 92708, USA.

PÉCHY, Blanka, b. 21 Sept. 1894, Pécs, Hungary. Writer; Literary Translator; Actress. Educ: Dipl., Acad. of Theatre Art, 1914. Publs: Mari Jászai, 1958, 3rd ed., 1971; Regény, 1963, 2nd ed., 1964; The Faithful Unfaithful Ones, 1969, 2nd ed., 1973; Hard to Speak, 1974. Contbr. to var. Hungarian jrnls. Mbrships: Hungarian Writers' Assn.; PEN; Linguistic Assn.; Fndr. Mbr., Ferenc Liszt Assn.; Chmn., Performers' Dept., Actors' Assn. Hons: Merited Artist of Hungarian People's Repub., 1958; Labour Award, 1959; TUC Award, 1963; Dips., Acad. of Theatre Art, 1964, 1974; Gold Medal of Labour Awards, 1964, 1969, 1974. Address: Bajza utca 1, 1071 Budapest, Hungary.

PECK, Merton Joseph, b. 17 Dec. 1925, Cleveland, Ohio, USA. Professor of Economics. Educ: A.B., Oberlin Coll., 1949; M.A., 1951, Ph.D., 1954, Harvard Univ. Publs. incl: The Maintenance of Way Employment on U.S. Railroads, 1957; Avoidable Costs of Passenger Train Service, 1957; Competition in the Aluminium Industry, 1961; Weapons Acquisition: An Economic Analysis (w. F. M. Scherer), 1962; Technology, Economic Growth & Public Policy (w. R. Nelson & E. Kalachek), 1967; Economic Aspects of Television Regulation, 1973. Mbr., Am. Econ. Assn. Address: Yale Univ., Dept. of Econs., 37 Hillhouse Ave., New Haven, CT 06520, USA.

PEDLEY, Robin, b. 11 Aug. 1914, Grinton, UK. Professor of Education. Educ: M.A., Ph.D., Univ. of Durham. Publs: Comprehensive Schools Today, 1955; Comprehensive Education, 1956; The Comprehensive School, 1963, revised ed., 1969; The Comprehensive School (in Hebrew, W. J. Orring), 1966; The Comprehensive University, 1969. Contbr. to var. educl. jrnls. Address: Annerley, Waters Green, Brockenhurst, Hants., UK.

PEDRETTI, Erica, b. 25 Feb. 1930, Sternbeck, Czech. Writer. Educ: School of Arts & Crafts, Zürich (Silversmith). Publs: Harmloses, bitte (prose), 1970; Heiliger Sebastian (novel), 1973. Contbr. to: Weltwoche; Neue Zürcher Zeitung; Basler Nachrichten. Mbr., Gruppe Olten (Swiss Writers' Grp.). Hons: Prix Suisse, 1970; Sponsorship, Schiller Inst., 1971; Book Prize, Canton of Berne, 1973. Address: 5 Rue du College, CH 2520 La Neueville, BE, Switz.

PEEL, Derek, b. 1924, Delhi, India. Biographical & Historical Researcher; Freelance Journalist. Publs: Without the City Wall (w. Hector Bolitho), 1952; A Pride of Potters, 1957; A Garden in the Sky, 1960; The Drummonds of Charing Cross, 1967. Contbr. to: Illustrated London News; Times; Braemar Book; etc. Mbr., Soc. of Authors. Address: 1 St. Nicholas Rd., Brighton, Sussex, UK.

PEEL, Edwin Arthur, b. 11 Mar. 1911, Liverpool, UK. Professor of Educational Psychology. Educ: B.Sc., Leeds Univ.; M.A., Ph.D., D.Lit., London Univ. Publs: The Psychological Basis of Education, 1956, 2nd ed., 1967; The Pupil's Thinking, 1960; The Nature of Adolescent Judgment, 1971; The Quality of Thinking in Secondary School Subjects (Ed. & Contbr.), 1972. Contbr. to var. profl. jrnls. & books of readings. Mbrships: Fellow, Brit. Psychol. Soc.; Pres., 1960-61; Assn. of Child Psychol. & Psych.; Fellow, Ctr. for Adv. Study in the Behavioral Scis., Palo Alto, Calif., USA, 1963-64, 1968-69. Address: 47 Innage Rd., Northfield, Birmingham B31 2DY, UK.

PEEL, Hazel Mary, pen name PEEL, Wallis, b. 1930, London, UK. Writer. Publs: Fury, Son of the Wilds, 1959; Pilot the Hunter, 1962; Pilot the Chaser, 1964; Easter the

Showjumper, 1965; Jago, 1966; Night Storm the Flat Racer, 1966; Dido & Rogue, 1967; Gay Darius, 1968; Untamed, 1969; Law of the Wild, 1974; Land & Power, 1975. Contbr. to: Courier; She; Riding; Elizabethan; Honey; Petticoat; Animal Ways; Reveille. Mbr., Soc. of Authors. Agent: London Independent Books Ltd.

PEEL, Marie Eugene, b. 1922, London, UK. Critic & Educational Writer. Educ: M.A., Newnham Coll., Cambridge. Publs: Criticism in Practice, 1964; Seeing to the Heart, 1967; (Ed.). The Family of Man, 1973; Making Sure of Language (co-author), Books I & II, 1975; (Ed.). Selected Poems of Peter Redgrove, 1975. Contbr. to: Child Educ.; Use of Engl.; Books & Bookmen. Address: 80 St. George's Sq., London SW1V 3QX, UK.

PEETERS, Gerardus Henricus, b. 3 Jan. 1928, Rotterdam, Netherlands. Editor. Publs: De vlam van Men-kau-ra, 1959; Evert loopt in de val, 1959; Het geheim van Moortgat, 1961; Omnibus van Paultje, 1963; Strand en Duin, 1972; Wei-en waterland, 1972; Bart en Hanneke, 1975; several radio plays & plays for children. Mbr., Vereniging van letterkundigen. Address: Delftlaan 71, Haarlem, Netherlands.

PEGGE, Cecil Denis, b. 1902, Briton Ferry, S. Wales, UK. Film Researcher; Writer. Educ: M.A., Magdalene Coll., Cambridge Univ. Publs: Construction, 1930; Bombay Riots, 1932; Obsidian (poems), 1934; The Fire, 1943; The Flying Bird, 1955; Tribute, 1966. Contbr. to: Fear No More (anthol.), 1941; Poetry Review; Blackwood's Mag.; Audio-Visual Communication Review; Univ. Film Jrnl.; Nature; Jrnl. Mental Sci. Mbrships: Cambridge Union Soc.; Authors' Soc. Address: c/o Barclays Bank Ltd., Benet St., Cambridge, UK.

PEHRSON, Howard Virgil, pen names KING, David; WESTON, Matt, b. 22 Nov. 1914, Marshall, Minn., USA. Educ: B.A., Univ. of Minn. Publs: The Brave & the Damned, 1966; The Expendables, 1966; Desert Danger, 1967; Trojan Tank Affairs, 1967; Two Faced Enemy, 1967; Target for Tonight, 1968; Desert Mascarade, 1968; Stars & Swipes Forever, 1969; Outlaw Doc, 1969; Butch Cassidy the Sundance Kid & the Wild Bunch, 1970; Morgan, 1970; Morgan's Revenge, 1971; There was a Crooked Man, 1972. Contbr. to engrng. jrnls & num. newspapers. Address: P.O. Box 2204, Casper, WY 82601, USA.

PEIERLS, (Sir) Rudolf Ernst, b. 5 June 1907, Berlin, Germany. Theoretical Physicist. Educ: Ph.D., Leipzig Univ., 1929; D.Sc., Manchester Univ., 1935; Berlin Univ.; Fed. Inst. of Technology, Zurich. Publs: The Laws of Nature, 1955; Quantum Theory of Solids, 1955. Contbr. to sev. sci. jrnls.; Ed. Bd., Contemporary Physics. Mbrships: F.R.S.; Nat. Acad. of Scis., USA; Inst. of Physics, London; Am. Acad. of Arts & Scis. Recip. C.B.E., 1946; Kt., 1968. Address: Farleigh, Orchard Lane, Old Boar's Hill, Oxford OX1 5JH, UK.

PELLATON, Jean-Paul, b. 10 Aug. 1920, Porrentruy, Switz. Professor. Educ: B.A. Publs: Cent Fleurs et un Adjudant, 1953; Quinze Jours avec Bob, 1955; Le Visiteur de Brume, 1960; Vitraux du Jura, 1968; Les Prisons et leurs Clés, 1973; Un Jardinier de Banlieue, 1975. Contbr. to: Coopération, Basle; Serv. de presse suisse. Mbrships: Swiss Writers Soc.; Jurassian Inst. Hons: Prix OSL, 1950; Paul Budry Prize, 1969; Prize for prose, Soc. jurassiene d'Emulation, 1973. Address: 16 chemin de l'Etang, 2800 Delémont, Switz.

PELLERITE, James John, b. 30 Sept. 1926, Clearfield, Pa., USA. Professor of Flute; Concert Flautist. Educ: Wayne State Univ.; Juilliard Schl. of Music; Schl. of Music, Ind. Univ. Publs: A Handbook of Literature for the Flute, 1963, rev. ed., 1966; A Modern Guide to Fingerings for the Flute, 1964, 2nd rev. ed., 1973; A Notebook of Techniques for a Flute Recital, 1966; Performance Methods for Flautists, 1967. Contbr. to: Woodwind World; Instrumentalist Mag. Mbrships. incl: V.P., Nat. Flute Assn., 1973-74. Recip., var. profl. & acad. hons. Address: 109 N. Glenwood Ave. W., Bloomington, IN 47401, USA.

PELLERT, Wilhelm, b. 26 Jan. 1950, Vienna, Austria. Student. Educ: Dr. cand., Univ. of Vienna. Publs: (plays, w. Helmut Korherr) Dr. Tschicker und Herr Heut, 1973; Der Teufel Schläft Nicht, 1973; Die Nachtgeher, 1973; . . . Und Sie Wissen, Was Sie Tun, 1974; Jesus Von Ottakring, 1974; (co-author of screenplay) Die Ersten Tage, 1971. Contbr. to: Impulse; Anthol. of the Best German Children's Stories.

Mbrships: PEN; Fndr. Mbr., Vienna Film Club. Hons: Theodor Körner Prize for Lit., 1973; Film Promotional Prize, City of Vienna, 1973. Address: A-1130 Vienna, Erzbischofgasse 25-29/10/5, Austria.

PELLING, Henry Mathison, b. 27 Aug. 1920, Birkenhead, Cheshire, UK. University Lecturer; Assistant Director of Research, History Faculty. Educ: B.A., M.A., Ph.D., St. John's Coll., Cambridge; M.A., Oxford. Publs: Origins of the Labour Party, 1954, 2nd ed., 1965; British Communist Party, 1958, 2nd ed., 1974; American Labor, 1960; Modern Britain, 1885-1955, 1960; Short History of the Labour Party, 1961, 4th ed., 1972; History of British Trade Unionism, 1963, 2nd ed., 1971; Social Geography of British Elections, 1885-1910, 1967; Britain & the Second World War, 1970; Winston Churchill, 1974. Contbr. to jrnls. Fellow, St. John's Coll., Cambridge. Address: St. John's Coll., Cambridge CB2 1TP, UK.

PELTZ, Isac, b. 12 Feb. 1899, Bucharest, Romania. Writer. Educ: Theol. Publs. incl: (novels) The Road of Vacaresti, 1933; Arson at the Lindens' Inn, 1934; The Dying of the Youthful Age, 1936; On All Fours, 1936; The Nights of Miss Mili, 1937; Good Country, 1937; The Dry Boots, 1937; The Game of Life & Death, 1939; Bleeding Israel, 1945; The Girls' Crossing, 1948; Max & His World, 1957. Contbr. to var. maj. Romanian lit. mags. & reviews, 1918–. Mbr., Romanian Writers' Union. Hons: Prize for Novel, Soc. of Romanian Writers, 1929; Order of Cultural Merit, 1st class, 1969; Groper Lit. Prize, Israel, 1973. Address: str. Traian 21, Bucharest – Sector 4, Romania.

PELZ, Lotte Auguste, b. 6 Apr. 1924, Vienna, Austria. Former Teacher & Writer. Educ: Lib. exam.; Dip. Educ. Publs: (all w. Werner Pelz) God is no More, 1963, German ed. 1965, paperback 1968; True Deceivers, 1966; I Am Adolf Hitler, UK 1969, USA 1971. Address: Bryn Coch, Llanfachreth, nr. Dolgellau, Gwynedd, N. Wales, UK.

PELZ, Werner, b. 25 Sept. 1921, Berlin, Germany. Senior Lecturer in Sociology; Former Anglican Clergyman. Educ: External B.A., London Univ., UK; G.O.E., Lincoln Theol. Coll.; Ph.D., Bristol Univ. Publs: God Is No More (w. Lotte Pelz), 1963, USA 1964, paperback 1966; Distant Strains of Triumph, 1964; True Deceivers (w. L. Pelz), 1966; I Am Adolf Hitler, 1969; The Scope of Understanding in Sociology, 1974. Contbr. to: Listener; Guardian. Address: 107 Mayona Rd., Montmorency, Melbourne, Vic., Australia 3094.

PEMÁN, José Maria, b. 1897, Cadiz, Spain. Author. Educ: Univs. of Seville & Madrid. Publs. incl: Elegía de la Tradición de España, 1931; El Divino Impaciente, 1933; Nieve en Cadiz; Edipo; Antogona; Hombre Nuevo; & num. essays, poems, novels & plays. Mbrships: Argentine Acad. of Letters; Lisbon Acad. of Sci.; Hispanic Soc. of Am.; Acad. of Cuba; Acad. of Puerto Rico. Hons. incl: Juan March Prize, 1957; Grand Cross, Order of Alfonso X; Grand Cross of Merit, Peru; Grand Cross, Order of Merit, Ecuador. Address: Felipe IV, No. 9-3, Madrid 14, Spain.

PEMBA, Tsewang Yishey, b. 5 June 1932, Gyantse, Tibet. Surgeon. Educ: M.B., B.S., Univ. Coll. Hosp., London Univ., 1955; F.R.C.S., 1967. Publs: Young Days in Tibet, 1956; Idols on the Path, 1966. Mbrships: Brit. Med. Assn.; F.R.C.S., Edinburgh. Recip., Hallett Prize, Royal Coll. of Surgs., England, 1966. Address: Panoma House, P.O. Darjeeling, W. Bengal, India.

PEMBERTON, John, b. 1912, Romford, Essex, UK. Professor of Social & Preventive Medicine. Educ: Univ. Coll. & Hosp., London Univ.; M.D.; F.R.C.P.; Dip. Pub. Hlth. Publs: The Health of the Eldery at Home (co-author); Ed., Recent Studies in Epidemiology; Will Pickles of Wensleydale, 1970. Address: 44 Osborne Park, Belfast, N. Ireland, UK.

PEMBLE, Edna Rosalie, b. 1902, Broken Hill, N.S.W., Australia. Company Manager & Part-Owner; Writer. Educ: Stott & Hoare Bus. Coll. Publs: Play Better Squash, 1969. Contbr. to: Aust. Author; Nat. Geogl. Mag.; Aust. Broadcasting Commn. Mbrships: Aust. Soc. of Authors; Master Carriers Assn., N.S.W. Address: 79 Saunders Bay Rd., Caringbah, N.S.W., Australia 2229.

PENDER, Lydia Kathleen, b. 29 June 1907, London, UK. Writer of Children's Books. Educ: Sydney Univ., Aust. Publs: (stories) Barnaby & the Horses, 1961; Dan McDougall & the Bulldozer, 1963; Sharpur the Carpet Snake, 1967; Barnaby & the Rocket, 1972; (verse) Marbles

in My Pocket, 1957; Brown Paper Leaves, 1971. Contbr. to: Schl. Mag. (N.S.W. Educ. Dept. Publ.); Reading Time (Jrnl. C.B.C. Aust.); similar publs. in Vic., Qld., W.A.; & anthols., radio, TV, etc. Mbrships: Children's Book Coun. Aust. (N.S.W. Br., past Hon. Sec.); Aust. Soc. Authors. Hons: C.B.C. Picturebook of Yr. Award, Commendations 1968 & 1973. Address: 33 Elva Ave., Killara, NSW, 2071, Australia.

PENDLE, George, b. 20 Feb. 1906, London, UK. Woollen Exporter. Educ: M.A., Corpus Christi Coll., Oxford Univ. Publs: Much Sky, 1932; Argentina, 1955; Paraguay: A Riverside Nation, 1956; Uruguay, 1957; South America: A Visual Geography, 1958; The Land of People of Chile, 1960; Peru, 1966; History of Latin America, new ed. (paperback), 1975. Contbr. to BBC (Special Corres., 1955). Address: 60 Third Ave., Frinton-on-Sea, Essex, UK.

PENDLEBURY, Bevis John, b. 6 June 1898, Handsworth, UK. Teacher. Educ: B.A., 1920, M.A., 1921, Univ. of Birmingham. Publs. incl: Dryden's Heroic Plays: A Study of the Origins, 1923; English Lyrical Types, 1934; Revision Course of French Grammar, 1940; English Test Papers, 1949; A Grammar School English Course, 4 vols., 1956-58; Comprehension & Comment, 1968; Advanced Comprehension & Comment, 1969; English Practice for Middle Forms, 1970; The Art of the Rhyme, 1971; Short stories broadcast by BBC, 1955 & 1956. Contbr. to: Times Educl. Supplement; Punch. Mbr., Inc. Assn. of Asst. Masters. Address: 8 King's Rydon Close, Stoke Gabriel, Totnes, Devon, TQ9 6QG, UK.

PENDOVSKI, Branko, b. 27 May 1927, Kocani, Yugoslavia. Editor. Educ: Fac. of Philos. Publs: Igra (Game), 1956; Skali (scales), 1964; Smrtta na ordenot (The Death of the Order), 1969; Dramas: Studenti (Students); Pod piramidata (Below the Pyramid); Potop (Deluge); Precek (Reception), 1974. Contbr. to: Razgledi; Nova Makedonija. Mbrships: Soc. of Writers of Yugoslavia; Macedonian PEN. Address: ul Georgi Skrizevski br. 22, Skopje, Yugoslavia.

PENFIELD, Wilder, b. 26 Jan. 1891, Spokane, Wash., USA. Neurophysiologist; Neurosurgeon. Educ: Litt.B., Princeton Univ., 1913; B.A., 1916, M.A. & B.Sc., 1920, D.Sc., 1935, Univ. of Oxford; M.D., Johns Hopkins Univ., 1918. Num. publs. incl: Ed., Cytology & Cellular Pathology of the Nervous System, 1932; Manual of Military Neurosurgery, 1941; Epileptic Seizure Patterns (w. K. Kristiansen), 1950; The Torch, 1960; The Second Career, 1963; Man & his Family, 1967; Science, the Arts & the Spirit, 1970. Contbr. to num. profl. jrnls. Mbrships. incl: F.R.S.; num. med., surg., neurol., & other sci. socs. Num. hons. incl: 2 Rhodes Schlrships; 32 hon. degrees; C.M.G., 1943; O.M., 1953; Companion, Order of Can., 1967. Address: Montreal Neurol. Inst., 3801 Univ., Montreal, P.Q., H3A 2B4, Can.

PENNANEN, Lea Airi-Sirkka, pen name PIKKUMÖLLIÄINEN, Leena, b. 16 Oct. 1929, Ihantala, Suomi, Finland. Radio Editor. Educ: Mag. phil., Helsinki Univ. Publs. incl: (children's books) Me leijonat; Piilomaan pikku aasi; (contbng. author to anthols.) The Work of a Writer; The Creative Word & Society; & num. radio plays for children. Contbr. to num. mags. Mbrships: Chmn., Assn. of Writers for Young People in Finland; Bd. of Dirs., Fitera Writers Guild; Finnish Writers Union; Assn. of Finnish Playwrights; Assn. of Transls. in Finland; Bd. of Dirs., Lit. Bd. for Young People. Address: Kauppalantie 7, 00320 Helsinki 32, Finland.

PENNINGTON, Albert Joe, b. 29 Oct. 1950, Van Buren, Mo., USA. Farmer; Writer. Educ: Univ. of Ark. Publs: Ozark National Scenic Riverways, 1967; Big Boy, The Story of a Dog, 1970. Contrbt. to: Fur, Fish & Game; Full Cry; Ozark Mountaineer. Address: Fremont, MO 63941, USA.

PENNINGTON, Donald Henshaw, b. 15 June 1919, Cheshire, UK. Fellow, Tutor, Balliol Coll., Oxford. Educ: B.A. (Hist.), Balliol Coll., Oxford. Publs: Members of the Long Parliament (w. D. Brunton), 1954; The Committee at Stafford (w. I. A. Ross), 1957; Seventeenth Century Europe, 1970. Contbr. to: History Today; Engl. Histl. Review; History. Fellow, Royal Histl. Soc. Address: Balliol College, Oxford, UK.

PENNINGTON, Eunice Catherine Randolph, b. 16 Feb. 1923, Pleasant Site, Fremont, Mo., USA. Author; Librarian. Educ: B.A.; M.S. Publs: History of Carter County, 1959;

Perry, The Pet Pig, 1966; Ozark National Scenic Riverways (co-author), 1967; History of Ozarks, 1971; Master of the Mountains, 1971; Lady Bird Mystery, 1974. Contbr. of num. articles to newspapers & mags. Hon. Life Mbr., Eugene Field Poetry Soc. Recip., Doctorate, Colo. Christian Coll., 1974. Address: Fremont, MO 63941, USA.

PENNY, David George, b. 5 Sept. 1950, Crayford, Kent, UK. Educ: Portsmouth Polytechnic; Derby Coll. of Technol. Publs: The Sunset People, 1975. Contbr. to Galaxy. Mbrships: Brit. Sci. Fiction Assn.; Nat. Hang-Gliding Assn. Agent: E. J. Carnell Lit. Agcy. Address: 44 High St., Welshpool, Powys, Wales, UK.

PENROSE, Edith Tilton, b. 1914, LA, USA. University Professor; Author. Educ: A.B.; M.A.; Ph.D.; Univ. of Calif.; Johns Hopkins Univ. Publs: Economics of International Patent System, 1951; The Theory of the Growth of the Firm, 1959, 4th ed., 1969; Large International Firm in Developing Countries, 1969; Growth of Firms, Middle East Oil & Other Essays, 1971. Contbr. to: Econ. Jrnl.; Am. Econ. Review; Jrnl. Dev. Studies; Economica; Middle E. Econ. Survey; Jrnl. Econ. Hist.; Bus. Econ. Review; etc. Mbrships: Royal Econ. Soc.; Soc. for Int. Dev.; Soc. Brit. Orientalists; Am. Econ. Assn. Address: 15 Chaldon Way, Coulsdon, Surrey, UK.

PENROSE, Harald, b. 12 Apr. 1904, Hereford, UK. Author. Educ: London Univ.; Dipl., Engrng. & Aeronautics; C.Eng. Publs: I Flew with the Birds, 1949; No Echo in the Sky, 1958; Airymouse, 1967; British Aviation: the Pioneer Years, 1966, Great War & Armistice, 1969, The Adventuring Years, 1973. Contbr. to: Blackwoods; Flight; Yachting World; Yachts & Yachting; Aeroplane; etc. Mbrships: Fellow, Royal Aeronautical Soc.; Royal Instn. of Naval Archts.; Soc. of Authors; Coun. for Protection of Rural England. Recip., O.B.E. Address: Nether Compton, Sherborne, Dorset, UK.

PENZLER, Otto M., b. 8 July 1942, Hamburg, Germany. Writer; Editor. Educ: Univ. of Mich., Ann Arbor; N.Y. Univ. Publs: Attacks of Taste, (co-ed.), 1971; The Detectionary, (co-author), 1971; ABC's Wide World of Sports Encyclopedia, (co-author), 1973; Encyclopedia of Mystery & Detection, (co-author), 1975. Compiler, with introduction, Raffles Revisited, by B. Perowne, 1974. Contbr. to: The Baker St. Jrnl.; The Armchair Detective; Lit. Guild Mag.; Phoenix; N.Y. Daily News. Mbrships: Mystery Writers of Am.; Baker Street Irregulars; Writers Guild of Am. Address: 2771 Bainbridge Ave., N.Y., NY 10458, USA.

PEPERS, Anna Elisa, pen name, van der STEEN, Maria, b. 11 July 1906, Hamont, Belgium. Author. Publs: Totale Uitverkoop (novel); Balans (novel); Sintels rapen (poetry); Laat maar (poetry); Kwelwater (poetry); Geen paniek (poetry); Zeg het stannelend (poetry). Contbr. to num. jrnls. inclng: De Wereldkroniek; De Nieuwe Stem; Kentering; Kruispunt Sumier; Vers-Univers; Naar Morgen. Mbr., Vereniging van Letterkundigen. Address: Cannenburglaan 176, The Hague, Netherlands.

PEPPER, Joan, pen name ALEXANDER, Joan, b. 1920, Southborough, UK. Writer. Publs: Fly Away Paul; The Choice & the Circumstance; Carola; Lewis' Wife; Thy People, My People, 1967; Where Have All the Flowers Gone? , 1969; Strange Loyalty, 1969; Bitter Wind, 1970. Contbr. to: BBC; Argosy; London Mystery Mag.; etc. Mbr., PEN. Address: c/o Lloyd's Bank, Cox's & King's Branch, 6 Pall Mall, London SW1, UK.

PERCIVAL, Alicia Constance, b. 13 May 1903, London, UK. Lecturer; Author. Educ: M.A., Dip.Ed., Univ. of Oxford; D.Phil., Univ. of London. Publs: The English Miss, To-day & Yesterday, 1938; Victorian Best-seller, 1947; Youth Will be Led, 1951; Origins of the Headmasters' Conference, 1969; Alice in New Zealand, 1971; Very Superior Men, 1973; Aunt Margaret, 1974. Contbr. to: English; Folklore; Times Educl. Supplement; & other educl. jrnls. Mbrships. incl: Comm. of Mgmt., Engl. Assn.; PEN; Royal C'wlth. Soc. Recip., Medal, Poetry Soc. Address: 21 Maunsel St., London SW1P 2QN, UK.

PERCIVAL, Allen Dain, b. 23 Apr. 1925, Bradford, UK. Principal, Guildhall School of Music & Drama; Author. Educ: Mus.B., Magdalene Coll., Cambridge. Publs: The Orchestra, 1956; The Teach Yourself History of Music, 1961; The Court of Elizabeth I (w. Rachel Percival), 1974. Contbr. to: Musical Times; Music Tchr.; Music in Educ.; Educ.; etc. Address: 7 Park Parade, Cambridge, UK.

PERCY, Douglas C., b. 5 May 1914, Toronto, Ont., Can. Clergyman; Teacher. Publs: Stirrett of the Sudan, 1949; Hidden Valley, 1951; When the Bamboo Sings, 1956; Beyond the Tangled Mountain, 1960; Flight to Glory, 1966; 2 vols., Gabartarwar Litafi mai Tsarki (Hausa Lang.). Contbr. to: Evangelical Recorder (Ed.); Eternity Mag.; Moody Monthly; Gospel Herald. Mbr., Authors' Guild of Am. Recip., 2nd Prize, Zondervan Int. Fiction Contest, 1951. Address: 73 Binswood Ave., Toronto, Ontario M4C 3N8, Can.

PERCY, Walker, b. 28 May 1916, Birmingham, Ala., USA. Writer. Educ: B.A., Univ. of N.C., Chapel Hill, 1937; M.D., Columbia Univ., 1941; Intern Bellevue Hosp., N.Y., 1942. Publs: The Moviegoer, USA, 1961, UK, 1963; The Last Gentleman, USA, 1966, UK, 1967; Love in the Ruins: The Adventures of a Bad Catholic at a Time Near the End of the World, USA & UK, 1971. Hons: Nat. Book Award, 1962; Grant, Nat. Inst. Arts & Letters, 1967. Address: Old Landing Rd., Covington, LA, USA.

PERDIGUERO PEREZ, Fernando, pen name PIN, Oscar, b. 29 Nov. 1929, Madrid, Spain. Writer; Chemical Engineer. Publs: Cuando no hay Guerra da gusto, 1953; Los Naufragos del Queen Enriqueta, 1954; El Pobre de pedir millones, 1956; El Rey y Mary Pepi, 1959; El Regalo, 1962. Contbr. to num. jrnls. inclng: La Codorniz. Recip., Dos Estrellas Prize, 1962. Address: Caleruega, 14, Madrid – 33, Spain.

PEREIRA, Harold Bertram, b. 31 May 1890, Calcutta, India. Journalist. Educ: A.B., Univ. of Calcutta. Publs: The Food of Kings, 1938; The Colour of Chivalry, 1950; Aircraft Badges & Markings, 1955; Royal Beasts, 1956; Playing Cards of the World, 1967; The Arab Horse, 1969; Seals, 1971; The Glory of Glass, 1972; Man & the Stars, 1972. Contbr. to: Illustrated London News; Aeronautics; Aeroplane; Flight. Mbrships: Fellow, Inst. of Jrnlsts. & Heraldry Soc. Address: 22 Thornton Ave., Streatham Hill, London SW2 4HG, UK.

PEREIRA, Michael Nicholas O'Donnell, b. 1928, London, UK. Professional Soldier until 1964. Publs: A River Grown Deep, 1959; An Angel Came Down, 1965; Mountains & a Shore: A Journey through Southern Turkey, 1966; Stranger in the Land, 1967; An Echo from Silence, 1968; Istanbul: Aspects of a City, 1968; When One Door Shuts, 1969; The Fifth Answer, 1969; Pigeon's Blood, 1970; East of Trebizond, 1971; The Singing Millionaire, 1972; Across the Caucasus, 1973; Masquerade, 1973; Second Cousin Twice Removed, 1974. Contbr. to: Observer. Agent: A. P. Watt & Son. Address: c/o ibid, 26-28 Bedford Row, London WC1, UK.

PEREIRA, Wilfred Dennis, b. 1921, London, UK. Company Director. Publs: Time of Departure, 1956; Serene Retreat, 1957; Johnson's Journey, 1958; The Lion & the Lambs, 1959; North Flight, 1959; Lark Ascending, 1960; The Cauldrons of the Storm, 1961; Arrow in the Air, 1963; The Wheat from the Chaff, 1967; An Uncertainty of Marriages, 1969; Aftermath 15, 1973; The Charon Tapes, 1975. Address: Woodfold Cottage, Down Hatherley, Glos., UK.

PERELMAN, Sidney Joseph, b. 1 Feb. 1904. Writer. Educ: Brown Univ., USA. Publs. incl: Dawn Ginsbergh's Revenge, 1929; Parlor, Bedlam & Bath, 1930; Look Who's Talking, 1940; The Dream Department, 1943; Keep it Crisp, 1946; Chicken Inspector No. 23, 1967; Baby, It's Cold Inside, 1970; (plays) All Good Americans, 1934; The Night Before Christmas (w. L. Perelman), 1941; One Touch of Venus (w. Ogden Nash), 1943; The Beauty Part, 1963; (films) (co-author) Monkey Business, 1931; Horsefeathers, 1932. Contbr. to New Yorker. Mbrships: Screenwriters' Guild; Dramatists' Guild. Recip., Best Screenwriter Award, 1956. Address: Erwinna, Bucks Co., PA 18920, USA.

PEREZ-RIOJA, Jose Antonio, b. 16 Feb. 1917, Granada, Spain. Librarian; Author. Educ: Dr. Classic Philol. (cum laude), Univ. of Madrid. Publs. incl: El Humorismo, 1949; Gramática de la lengua española, 1953, 9th ed., 1970; El estilo de "Azorin", 1965; Estilistica, 1967; Diario de Cadiz, 1968; Sintesis del Arte Universal, 1971; Radiografia de la Cultura, 1972; Guia Literaria de Soria, 1973. Contbr. to: Bellas Artes; Hispania; Arbor; Celtiberia; ABC; etc. Mbr., var. lit. & cultural orgs. Hons. incl: Azorin Prize, 1963; Feijoo Prize, 1964; Marqueses de Taurisano Prize, 1968. Address: c/o Dr. Fleming, 5 Casa de Cultura, Soria, Spain.

PERHAM, (Dame) Margery Freda, b. 1895, Lancashire, UK. Retired Reader in Colonial Administration, University of Oxford. Educ: M.A., Univ. of Oxford. Publs: Major Dane's Garden, 1924; Native Administration in Nigeria, 1937; The Government of Ethiopia, 1948; Lugard, 2 vols., 1956-60; The Colonial Reckoning, the Reith Lectures for 1961, 1962; African Outline, 1966; Colonial Sequence, 2 vols., 1967-70; African Apprenticeship, 1974. Contbr. to: The Times; Int. Affairs; & other jrnls. Hons. incl: D.C.M.G.; C.B.E.; D.Litt.; F.B.A.; D.C.L.; LL.D. Address: 5 Rawlinson Rd., Oxford, UK.

PERKINS, Edward A., Jr., b. 23 Sept. 1928, Portland, Ore., USA. University Administrator & Professor. Educ: B.A., Univ. of Wash., 1953; M.A., Stanford Univ., 1956; Ed.D., Ore. State Univ., 1963. Publs: Executive Typewriting, 1966; Practice for Professional Typing, 1968; Typing for the Air Force, 1971; Mimeograph Instruction Series, 1972; Fluid Instruction Series, 1972; Reprographics in Business Education, 1972. Contbr. to var. num. & mgmt. jrnls. Mbrships. incl: Nat. Bus. Educ. Assn.; Histn., Western Bus. Educ. Assn., 1966. Recip., acad. awards. Address: Route 2, Box 556, Pullman, WA 99163, USA.

PERKINS, James Oliver Newton, b. 11 July 1924, Bedford, UK. University Professor. Educ: M.A.; Ph.D., St. Catharine's Coll., Cambridge. Publs. incl: Sterling & Regional Payment Systems, 1956; Britain & Australia: Economic Relationships in the 1950's, 1962; International Policy for the World Economy, 1969; Australia in the World Economy, 1969; Macro-economic Policy in Australia, 1971; The Banks & the Capital Market, 1970; The Sterling Area, the Commonwealth & World Economic Growth, 1970. Contbr. to: Econ. Record. Mbrships: Econ. Soc. of Aust. & NZ; Int. Econ. Assn. Address: 18 Riddle St., Bentleigh, 3204, Vic., Australia.

PERKINS, Margaret, b. 8 Aug. 1926, Manchester, UK. Teacher; Lecturer. Educ: Tchrs. Cert., Sheffield Coll. of Educ.; Assoc., London Coll. Music (Speech & Drama) & New Era Acad.; Fellow, Victoria Coll. of Music. Publs: Fog by Night, 1966; Omega to Alpha, 1968; Speech Mastery in Fifteen Lessons, 1970; Yoga for Women's Lib, 1972; People — Trees & Places, 1974; Ed., Yorkshire Poets, 1971, 1972. Contbr. to: Poetry for Peace; Poetry for the City; Halifax Evening Courier; Star, Sheffield; etc.; var. anthols. Mbrships. incl: Yorks. Poets Assn. (Chmn., 1970—); Sheffield Writers Club (Vice- Chmn., 1974). Address: 64 Broomgrove Rd., Sheffield S10 2NA, UK.

PERKINS, Michael, b. 3 Nov. 1942, Lansing, Mich., USA. Poet. Educ: B.A., Ohio Univ., 1963; New Schl. for Soc. Rsch.; CCNY. Publs: The Blue Woman, 1966; Shorter Poems, 1968; Renie Perkins, 1969. Contbr. to: The Nation; N.Y. Quarterly; Choice; Poems One Line & Longer (anthol.). Address: c/o Harold M. Wit, Allen & Co., 30 Broad St., N.Y., NY, USA.

PEROWNE, Stewart Henry, b. 1901, Worcester, UK. Civil Servant. Educ: M.A., Corpus Christi Coll., Cambridge; Harvard Univ., USA. Publs. incl: The One Remains, 1954; The Life & Times of Herod the Great, 1956; Hadrian, 1960; Caesars & Saints, 1962; Death of the Roman Republic, 1969; Roman Mythology, 1969; The Siege within the Walls, Malta 1940-43, 1970; Rome, 1971; The Journeys of St. Paul, 1973; The Caesars' Wives: Above Suspicion? , 1974. The Archaeology of Greece & the Mediterranean, 1974. Contbr. to: Times; Ency. Britannica; Collier's Ency. Mbrships. incl: F.S.A. Hons: O.B.E.: Kt., St. J. Address: 44 Arminger Rd., London W12 7BB, UK.

PERRIN, Noel, b. 1927, New York, USA. Writer. Educ: M.Litt.; Williams Coll., Mass.; Trinity Hall, Cambridge, UK. Publs: A Passport Secretly Green, 1961; Dr. Bowdler's Legacy, 1970; Amateur Sugar Maker, 1972; Vermont in all Weathers, 1973. Contbr. to: New Yorker; Punch; Harper's; Yale Review. Address: Dept. of English, Dartmouth Coll., Hanover, N.H., USA.

PERRY, Charles Stuart, b. 11 Mar. 1908, Melbourne, Vic., Australia. Librarian. Educ: LL.B. Publs: Litany of Beauty, 1934; NZ Writers' Handbook, 1952; The Indecent Publications Tribunal, 1965; No Mean City, 1969. Contbr. to: Times Lit. Supplement; NZ Listener; Otago Law Review. Mbrships. incl: Pres., 1952-53, Fellow, Hon. Life Mbr., NZ Lib. Assn.; Fellow, Lib. Assn.; Pres., NZ Ctr., PEN, 1950-52; Dpty. Mbr., 1970-72. Full Mbr., 1964-70, Indecent Publs. Tribunal. Address: 66 Salamanca Rd., Wellington 5, NZ.

PERRY, Gordon Arthur, b. 20 Sept. 1914, Hindolvestone, Norfolk, UK. Educational Publishing Consultant; Author; Editor. Educ: Univ. of Reading. Publs. incl: Soils, 1965; Plant Life, 1965; The Farmer's Crops, 1966; Progressive Biology, Book 1, 1967, Book 2, 1968, Book 3, 1970; Villages & Village Life, 1970; Minerals, Mines & Mining, 1970; Police & the Police Service, 1974; Shops, Stores & Markets, 1975; Councils & Local Government, 1975. Contbr. to: Rural Studies Jrnl.; Norfolk Life. Mbrships: Assn. of Tchrs. in Colls. & Depts. of Educ.; Nat. Assn. of Environmental Educ. Address: 14 St. Andrew's Close, Holt, Norfolk, UK.

PERRY, Grace, b. 26 Jan. 1927, Melbourne, Aust. Poet; Editor. Educ: M.B.; B.S., Sydney Univ. Ed., Medical Practitioner; Founder & Ed., Poetry Australia. Publs: (poetry) Red Scarf, 1963; Frozen Section, 1967; Two Houses, 1969; Black Swans at Berrima, 1972; Berrima Winter, 1974. Contbr. to: BBC; Commonwealth; Poetry Today; Etc. Mbrships: PEN; Aust. Soc. of Authors; Aust. Book Publishers' Assn. Address: South Head Press, 350 Lyons Rd., Five Dock, Australia 2046.

PERRY, Linette Purbi, b. Srinagar, Kashmir, India. Commercial Artist; Writer; Copywriter. Educ: Sch., Colwyn Bay, UK; Univ. of Punjab, India; Dip., Fine Arts, Slade Schl. of Art, London, UK, 1949. Publs: (screenplay) The Secret Place, 1957; (novel) All the Wrong People, 1961; (TV plays): Uncle Jonathan, 1969; A Measure of Malice, 1969; The Family is a Vicious Circle, 1970. Address: c/o P.L. Representation Ltd., 33 Sloane St., London, SW1X 9NP, UK.

PERRY, (The Ven.) Michael Charles, b. 5 June 1933, Ashby de la Zouch, UK. Archdeacon. Educ: M.A., Trinity Coll., Cambridge Univ.; Westcott House, ibid. Publs: The Easter Enigma, 1959; The Pattern of Matins & Evensong, 1961; The Churchman's Companion, 1963; Meet the Prayer Book, 1963; Crisis for Confirmation, 1968; The Printed Word, 1969; Sharing in One Bread, 1973; The Resurrection of Man, 1975. Contbr. to: Ch. Quarterly (Ed., 1968-71); Expository Times; Theol.; Jrnl. Theol. Studies; View-Review; Mod. Churchman. Mbrships: Studiorum Novi Testamenti Soc.; Soc. Psychical Rsch.; Soc. for Study of Theol. Address: 7 The College, Durham, UK.

PERRY, Owen William, b. 24 Jan. 1922, London, UK. Head of Department of General & Professional Studies, Lewes Technical College; Writer. Educ: B.Sc., London Univ. Publs: Mathematics for O Level, 1965; Numerical Examples for "A" Physics, 1965; Enjoying Science, 1967; Multiple Choice Tests for 'O' Level Mathematics, 1972. Mbrships: Soc. of Authors; Ct. of Electors; Convocation. Agent: Mark Patterson. Address: 119 Southdown Rd., Seaford, Sussex, UK.

PERRY, Ritchie John Allen, b. 7 Jan. 1942, King's Lynn, UK. Writer. Educ: St. John's Coll., Oxford. Publs: The Fall Guy, 1972; Nowhere Man, 1973; Ticket to Ride, 1973; Holiday with a Vengeance, 1974; Your Money & Your Wife, 1975. Mbr., Crime Writers Assn. Address: Innisfree, 10 Park Hill, Dersingham, Norfolk, UK.

PERRY, Thelma Davis, b. 15 Apr. 1906, Wagner, Okla., USA. Journalist. Educ: A.B., J.D., M.A., 1936, Howard Univ.; Ph.D. cand., Univ. of Chgo., 1950. Publs: Culture of a Contemporary All-Negro Community (w. Mozell C. Hill), 1943; History of the American Teachers Association, 1975. Contbr. to: Negro Hist. Bulletin; Jrnl. of Negro Hist.; Social Forces; Southwestern Jrnl.; Jrnl. of Social Psychol.; etc. Mbrships: Acad. of Pol. Sci.; Assn. of Social Sci. Tchrs.; Assn. for the Study of Negro Life & Hist.; DC Bar; Nat. Lawyers Club. Hons. incl: Recognition Cert., Bus. & Profl. Women's League, Inc., 1960. Address: 1407 14th St., N.W., Wash., DC 20005, USA.

PERSSON, (Nils) Bertil Alexander, b. 10 Nov. 1941, Trelleborg, Sweden. Clergyman; Educator; Author. Educ: M.A.; B.Litt.; D.D. Publs. incl. var. schl. texts; Ord till de unga, 1967; Gud är här tillstädes. Ett kompendium över den svenska psalmboken och dess historia, 1967; Kulter Sekter Samfund, 1970; Min. Gudstjänstbok, 1971; "Från dogmat till evangeliet". Till minne av 100-årsdagen av professor Emanuel Linderholms födelse den 4 april 1972, 1972; A Contribution to The Unity in Christ, 1974; Sovjetisk religionspolitik av idag, 1974. Ed., Religion och Kultur; FLR-Aktuellt; Trosinformation. Contbr. to: Dagen; Svenska Posten; Göteborgs Veckotidning; etc. Mbr., Swedish Union of Authors. Address: Box 748, 171 07 Solna 7, Sweden.

PERSSON, Per Erik, b. 16 Feb. 1923, Fämjö, Sweden. Professor of Systematic Theology. Educ: Fil.kand., 1952, Teol.dr., 1957, Univ. of Lund. Publs. incl: Evangelisch & Römisch-katholisch, 1961; Roman & Evangelical, 1964; Repraesentatio Christi, 1966; Sacra doctrina, 1970. Contbr. to: Ed., Svensk teologisk kvartalskrift. Ecumenical Review; Lutheran World; Materialdienst des konfessionskundlichen Instituts. Mbrships: Royal Soc. of Letters of Lund; Faith & Order Commn., World Coun. of Chs. Address: P.H. Lings väg 3, S-223 65 Lund, Sweden.

PERTWEE, Michael H. R., b. 1916, London, UK. Publs: Name Dropping (autobiog.), 1974. (plays) Death on the Table (w. Guy Beauchamp), 1938; The Paragon (co-author), 1948; Four Musketeers (co-author), 1967; She's Done It Again, 1969; Don't Just Lie There, Say Something, 1971; A Bit Between the Teeth, Adaptor, Birds of Paradise.; (films): Laughter in Paradise; Happy Ever After; The Naked Truth; Strange Bedfellows; A Funny Thing Happened on the Way to the Forum; Salt & Pepper; One More Time. Mbr., Savile Club. Agent: I.F.A. Address: 34 Aylestone Ave., London NW6, UK.

PERUTZ, Kathrin, b. 1 July 1939, NYC, USA. Writer. Educ: B.A., Columbia Univ.; M.A., N.Y. Univ. Publs: The Garden, 1962; A House on the Sound, 1964; The Ghosts, 1966; Mother is a Country, 1968; Beyond the Looking Glass, 1970; Marriage is Hell, 1972. Contbr. to: Voices, 1965; N.Y. Spy, 1967; America the Beautiful, 1968; Books & Bookmen; The Elizabethan; Daily Telegraph Mag.; Vogue; Am. Scholar; Cosmopolitan; Harper's; Mademoiselle; New York; N.Y. Times; Newsday; Phila. Inquirer; Seventeen; Viva. Address: 16 Avalon Rd., Great Neck, NY 11021, USA.

PESCHLER, Eric A., b. 7 Aug. 1922, Kimratshofen, Bayern. Journalist. Educ: Studied German Philol. Publs: Wider Die Traegen Herzen, 1954; Privat in Moskau, 1964; Das Kalte Paradies, 1972. Contbr. to Swiss TV. Mbrships: Ctr. for German-speaking Authors Abroad, PEN; Pres.. Int. Comm. German-speaking Writers. Address: 9501 Hosenruck Am Nollen, Switz.

PESIN, Harry, b. 16 Oct. 1919, NYC, USA. Advertising Executive; Author; Photographer. Educ: B.B.A., CCNY. Publs: My Little Brother Gets Away With Murder, 1958; The Acropolis Is A Nice Place To Visit But I Wouldn't Want To Live In The Eiffel Tower, 1963; Sayings To Run An Advertising Agency By, 1966; Why Is A Crooked Letter, 1969; Welcome, Stranger & Partners, 1974. Mbrships: ASMP; Soc. of Photogs. in Communications; Copy Club. Address: P.O. Drawer 350, Rancho Santa Fe, CA 92067, USA.

PETCH, James Alexander, b. 1900, Sunderland, UK. Educator. Educ: M.A., Pembroke Coll., Oxford; LL.D. Publs: Fifty Years of Examining; Before Admission; G.C.E. & Degree. Contbr. to: Ency. Britannica; etc. Mbrships: F.S.A.; Pres., Lancs. & Chrs. Antiquarian Soc., 1958-65. Address: Willow Cottage, Bucknell, Salop, UK.

PETER, Laurence Johnston, b. 16 Sept. 1919, Vancouver, B.C., Can. Author; Lecturer. Educ: B.A., M.Ed., Western Wash. State Coll.; Ed.D., Wash State Univ. Publs: Prescriptive Teaching, 1965; The Peter Principle (w. Ray Hull), 1969; The Peter Prescription, 1972; Competencies for Teaching System, 1975. Contbr. to: IBM Think; Clearing House; Educ. Panorama; Chem. Engrng.; LA Times; Psychol. Today, etc. Mbrships incl: PEN; Can. Psychol. Assn.; AAUP; Authors' Guild; I.P.A.; Phi Delta Kappa. Recip., Rsch. Awards. Address: 2332 Via Anacapa, Palos Verdes Estates, CA 90274, USA.

PETER, Lily, b. Marvell, Ark., USA. Farmer; Writer. Educ: B.S., Memphis State Univ.; M.A., Vanderbilt Univ.; Hon. L.H.D., Moravian Coll., 1965. Publs: The Green Linen of Summer, 1964; The Great Riding, 1966; The Sea Dream of the Mississippi, 1973. Contbr. to jrnls & newspapers. Mbrships: Nat. League of Am. Pen Women; Poets Roundtable of Ark.; Nat. Soc. of Arts & Letters; Poetry Socs. of Tex., Tenn. & Ga. Hons: Gold Cup, Ark. Authors & Composers Soc., 1967; Gold Cup, Poetry Soc. of Okla., 1967; Gemstone Award, Poetry Soc. of Tenn., 1972; & num. other lit. prizes. Address: Rt. 2, Box 69, Marvell, AR 72366, USA.

PETERKIEWICZ, Jerzy, b. 1916, Fbaianki, Poland. Professor & Head of the Department of East European Languages & Literatures, University of London. Educ: Univ. of Warsaw; St. Andrews Univ., UK; King's Coll., Univ.

of London; M.A.; Ph.D. Publs. incl: The Knotted Cord, 1953; Polish Prose & Verse, 1956, 1970; Antologia liryki angielskiej, 1958; Isolation, 1959; Five Centuries of Polish Poetry (w. Burns Singer), 1960, 1970; The Quick & the Dead, 1961; That Angel Burning at my Left Side, 1963; Inner Circle, 1966; Green Flows the Bile, 1969; The Other Side of Silence, 1970. Contbr. to: Sunday Times; Times Lit. Supplement; Encounter; London Mag.; Listener; Slavonic Review; 20th Century; & other lit. jrnls. Address: c/o Christy & Moore, Ltd., 52 Floral St., London WC2, UK.

PETERS, Donald Leslie, pen name (for fiction) PETERS, Leslie, b. 17 Aug. 1925, Lincoln, Neb., USA. School Counsellor. Educ: B.S., 1953, M.Ed., 1955, Mont. State Univ. Publs: For Thinking Teens, 1967; Homeroom Guidance activities, 1968; Stories for Thinking Teens, 1968; The Time of Your Life, 1975. Contbr. to: Good Housekeeping; Boys' Life; Am. Girl; Scouting; Woman's Own, UK; Woman's Day, Aust.; etc. Mbrships. incl: Nat. Pres.. Am. Schll. Cnslr. Assn., 1970-71. Hons. incl: Wall St. Jrnl. Student Achievement Award, 1953; Silver Beaver, BSA, 1956. Address: 139 Birchwood Drive, Billings, MT 59102, USA.

PETERS, Heinz Frederick, b. 18 Jan. 1910, Dresden, Germany. Professor of German & Comparative Literature, Portland State College. Educ: Univ. of London, UK; Ph.D., Univ. of Munich, Germany, 1933. Publs: Rainer Maria Rilke: Masks & the Man, 1960; My Sister, My Spouse: A Biography of Lou Andreas-Salome, 1962; Lou: Das Leben der Lou Andreas-Salome, 1964. Contbr. to: Am. Schlr.; Germanic Review; German Quarterly; Mod. Lang. Quarterly. Mbrships: Am. Assn. of Tchrs. of German; MLA; AAUP. Hons: O.M., Fed. Repub. of Germany, 1959; Goethe Medal, Goethe Inst., 1962. Address: 9175 Monterey Pl., Portland, OR 97225, USA.

PETERS, Richard Stanley, b. 1919, Missouri, United Provinces, India. University Professor of the Philosophy of Education. Educ: Univs. of Oxford & London, UK; B.A.; Ph.D. Publs: Brett's History of Psychology, 1953; Hobbies, 1956; The Concept of Motivation, 1958; Social Principles & the Democratic State (w. S. I. Benn), 1959; Ethics & Education, 1966; Ed., The Concept of Education, 1967; Perspectives on Plowden, 1969; The Logic of Education (w. P. H. Hirst), 1970; Reason, Morality & Religion, 1972; Authority, Responsibility & Education, revised ed., 1973; Ed., The Philosophy of Education, 1973; Reason & Compassion, 1973; Psychology & Ethical Development, 1974. Address: Inst. of Educ., Malet St., London WC1E 7HS, UK.

PETERSEN, William John Henry, b. 30 Jan. 1901, Dubuque, Iowa, USA. Historical Writer; Professor of American & Iowa History. Educ: B.A., Univ. of Dubuque, 1926; M.A., 1927, Ph.D., 1930, Univ. of Iowa. Publs. incl: Steamboating on the Upper Mississippi, 1937; Iowa: The Rivers of Her Valleys, 1941; Looking Backward on Hawkeyeland, 1947; The Story of Iowa, 2 vols., 1952; The Pageant of the Press, 1962; A. T. Andreas Atlas of Iowa in 1875, 1970. Contbr. to: Waterways Mag.; Papers in Ill. Hist.; Scribner's Dict. of Am. Hist.; var. encys., newspapers & profl. jrnls. Mbr., profl. orgs. Hons: Iowa Lib. Assn. Award; Award of Merit, Am. Assn. State & Local Hist. Address: 329 Ellis Ave., Iowa City, IA 52240, USA.

PETERSON, Hans, b. 26 Oct. 1922, Varing, Sweden. Author. Publs: ca. 80 books for children & adults. Magnus books, 1958-63; Liselott, 1962-65; Pelle Jansson, 1970-72; Elise books, 1971, 1972, 1973; (for the handicapped) Elin, 1973; Halge & Anni, 1974; books publd. in USA, UK, Can., Norway, Denmark Finland, Iceland, Poland, Faroe Islands, Germany, Netherlands, France, USSR, Japan, Yugoslavia & Lithuania. Mbrships: Swedish Authors' Assn.; sev. other Swedish lit. Socs. Hons. incl: German Children's Book Prize, 1958; Nil Holgersson Prize, 1959; Swedish State Prize, sev. times; Gothenburg Town Prize. Address: Marstrandsgatan 21, 417 24 Gothenburg, Sweden.

PETERSON, (Karl) Ivar (Sigvard), b. 17 Apr. 1912, Krogsered, Sweden. Columnist. Contbr. to jrnls., newspapers & TV, inclng: Land, Stockholm; Kvalls-Posten, Malmö; Dagens Nyheter, Stockholm; Svenska Dagbladet, Stockholm; Göteborg-Posten. Mbrships: Swedish Assn. of Jrnlsts.; Swedish Publicist-Klubb; Chmn., Swedish Org., Int. Fedn. of Agricl. Jrnlsts.; Swedish Parliamentary Jrnlsts. Club. Address: Genvägen 3, 18234 Danderyd, Sweden.

PETERSON, Merrill D., b. 31 Mar. 1921, Manhattan, Kan., USA. Historian; Educator. Educ: B.A., Univ. Kan.,

1943; Ph.D., Harvard Univ.. 1950. Publs: The Jefferson Image in the American Mind, 1960; Democracy, Liberty & Property: The State Constitutional Convention Debates of the 1820's, 1966; Thomas Jefferson & the New Nation: A Biography, 1970; James Madison: A Biography in His Own Words, 1974; The Portable Thomas Jefferson, 1975. Contbr. to: Va. Quarterly Review, etc. Mbrships: Am. Histl. Assn.; Org. Am. Histns.; Southern Histl. Assn.; Soc. Am. Histns., etc. Recip., Bancroft Prize in Am. Hist., 1961. Address: 1817 Yorktown Dr., Charlottesville, VA 22901, USA.

PETERSSON, Robert Torsten, b. 14 June 1918, Berkeley, Calif., USA. Professor; Writer. Educ: B.A., Univ. of Calif. Publs: Sir Kenelm Digby: The Ornament of England, 1956; (ed.) King Richard II, 1957; The Art of Ecstasy: Teresa, Bernini, and Crashaw, 1970. Contbr. to: Colliers' Ency.; Yale Review; Jrnl. of the Am. Acad. of Relig.; Yale Studies in the Hist. of Sci.; Daedalus; Renaissance Quarterly. Mbrships: MLA; Renaissance Soc.; Guild of Scholars; Milton Soc. of Am. Recip. Nat. Cath. Book Award, 1971. Address: 63 Dryads Green, Northampton, MA 01060, USA.

PETHYBRIDGE, Roger William, b. 1934, Skipton, Yorks., UK. University Lecturer, Russian & E. European Studies. Educ: M.A., Oxford Univ.; Docteur ès Sc. Politiques, Grad. Inst. Int. Studies, Geneva, Switz. Publs: A Key to Soviet Politics, the Crisis of the Anti-Party Group, 1962; A History of Post-War Russia, 1966; The Spread of the Russian Revolution — Essays on 1917, 1972; The Social Prelude to Stalinism, 1974. Address: University College, Singleton Park, Swansea, UK.

PETIT de MURAT, Ulyses, b. 7 Jan. 1907, Buenos Aires, Argentina. Writer; Lecturer. Educ: Univ. Argentina. Publs: Conmemoraciones (Commemorations), 1929; Rostros (Faces), 1931; Marea de lágrimas (Tide of Tears), 1935; Las Islas (The Islands), 1935; El Balcón Hacia la Muerte (Balcony to Death), 1942; Aprenoizaje de la Soledad (Apprenticeship of Solitude), 1943; Ultimo Lugar (Last Place), 1964; Carta a los Jóvenes del Ano 2000 (Letter to the Young Men of the Year 2000), 1971; & about 90 film scripts. Contbr. to: La Nación; La Opinión (L.A.); etc. Mbrships. incl: Argentine Writers' Soc. (former Pres. & VP). Hons. incl: Nat. Award for Contbn. Lit., 1972. Address: Avenida Federico Lacroze 2764-5, Piso-21, Buenos Aires, Argentina.

PETITPIERRE, Jacques, b. 9 Jan. 1890, Corcelles, Neuchatel, Switz. Lawyer; Writer; Historian. Educ: Fac. of Law, Univ. of Neuchatel. Publs: Patrie Neuchateloise, 5 vols., 1934-72; Le Mariage de Mendelssohn, 1937 (Engl. transl., 1948); Neuchatel & la Suisse devant l'Europe en 1856, 1958. Contbr. to Swiss, French, Dutch & Japanese jrnls. Mbrships. incl: Soc. des Ecrivains suisses; Soc. des Ecrivains neuchâtelois & jurassiens; PEN; Socs. d'hist. neuchateloise, & suisse romande. Hons: Prize, Soc. d'hist. du Canton de Neuchatel; Gold Medal, Off., Soc. Lettres Arts & Scis., Paris, France. Address: Evole 2, 2000 Neuchâtel, Switz.

PETRAKIS, Harry Mark, b. 5 June 1923, St. Louis, Mo., USA. Freelance Writer & Lecturer. Educ: Univ. of Ill., Urbana, 1940-41. Publs: (novels) Lion at my Heart, USA & UK, 1959; The Odyssey of Kostas Volakis, 1963; A Dream of Kings, USA, 1966, UK, 1967; (short stories) Pericles on 31st Street, 1965; The Waves of Night & Other Stories, 1969; (screenplay) A Dream of Kings, 1969; (biog.) The Founder's Touch, 1965; (autobiog.) Stelmark, 1970. Hons: Atlantic Firsts Award, 1957; Benjamin Franklin Citation, 1957; Award, Friends of Am. Writers, 1964; Award, Friends of Lit., 1964; D.H.L., Univ. of Ill., 1971. Address: 80 East Rd., Dune Acres, Chesterton, IN 46303, USA.

PETRIE, (Sir) Charles Alexander, b. 20 Sept. 1895, Liverpool, UK. Writer. Educ: M.A., Corpus Christi Coll., Oxford. Publs. incl: History of Government, 1929; Mussolini, 1931; Spain, 1934; Bolingbroke, 1937; When Britain Saved Europe, 1941; Chapters of Life, 1950; Scenes of Edwardian Life, 1965; Don John of Austria, 1967; King Charles III of Spain, 1971; A Historian Looks at His World, 1972; The Great Tyrconnel, 1973. Contbr. to: Outlook, 1925-8; Engl. Review; Empire Review; New Engl. Review, Mgng. Ed., 1945-50); Illustrated London News. Mbrships. incl: Hispanic Soc. of Am.; F.R.Hist.S. Hons. incl: C.B.E.; Ph.D. Address: 190 Coleherne Court, London SW5, UK.

PETRIE, Rhona, pen name of DUELL, Eileen-Marie, b. 1922, St. Leonards-on-Sea, UK. Probation Officer; Teacher;

Writer. Educ: Univ. London. Publs: Death in Deakins Wood, 1963; Murder by Precedent, 1964; Running Deep, 1965; Dead Loss, 1966; Foreign Bodies, 1967; Maclurg Goes West, 1968; Despatch of a Dove, 1969; Come Hell & High Water, 1970; Thorne in the Flesh, 1971. Contbr. to: Ellery Queen's Mystery Mag.; etc. Mbrships: Crime Writers' Assn.; Nat. Book League. Address: c/o John Farquharson Ltd., 15 Red Lion Sq., London WC1R 4QW, UK.

PETROCELLI, Orlando R., b. 10 Oct. 1930, NYC, USA. Publisher. Educ: Bklyn. Coll. Publs: Ed., Best Computer Papers of 1971, 1971; The Pact, 1973; Olympia's Inheritance, 1974. Contbr. to: The Trentonian (book reviewer); Book World — Chgo. Tribune (reviews). Mbrships: Authors' Guild; Players Club. Address: 174 Brookstone Dr., Princeton NJ 08540, USA.

PETROLAY, Margit, b. 11 Nov. 1908, Budapest, Hungary. Writer. Educ: Univ. Fac. of Arts. Publs: A Paradicsom Dombja (novel), 1941; A Sárkányok Lovagja (novel for the young), 1956; Erdei kalács (story book), 1966, 1973; Legenda Aurea (transl.), 1942. Contbr. to mags. for the young, tchng. jrnls. Mbrships: Soc. of Authors; PEN. Address: Budapest 1032, Zápor u.63, Hungary.

PETRY, Ann (Lane), b. 12 Oct. 1912, Old Saybrook, Conn., USA. Writer. Educ: Ph.G., Univ. of Conn., 1931; Columbia Univ., 1943-44. Publs: (novels) The Street, USA, 1946, UK, 1947; Country Place, USA, 1947, UK, 1948; The Narrows, USA, 1953, UK, 1954; (juvenile) The Drugstore Cat, 1949; Harriet Tubman: Conductor on the Underground Railroad, 1955 (as a Girl Called Moses, UK, 1960); Tituba of Salem Village, 1964; Legends of the Saints, 1970; (short stories) Miss Muriel & Other Stories, 1971. Mbr., Authors League of Am. (Sec., 1960). Recip., Houghton Mifflin Lt. Fellowship, 1946. Address: c/o Russell & Volkening Inc., 551 Fifth Ave., N.Y., NY 10017, USA.

PETRY, Ray C., b. 2 July 1903, Eaton, Ohio, USA. Church Historian; Medievalist; Emeritus Professor. Educ: B.A., Manchester Coll., Ind., 1926; M.A., 1927, Ph.D., 1932, Univ. of Chgo. Publs. incl: Late Medieval Mysticism, 1957; History of Christianity, vol. I, 1962; Medieval & Renaissance Studies, vol. I (jt. author), 1966; Essays in Divinity, vol. I (jt. author), 1968; S. Bonaventura, vol. II (jt. author), 1973. Contbr. to relig. & histl. jrnls. & encys. Mbr., relig. & histl. orgs. Recip., acad. hons. Address: 543 Quinault Apt., 1615 Circle Dr., Lacey, WA 98503, USA.

PETTERSSON, Bengt Karl, b. 30 May 1915, Visby, Sweden. Professor of Ecological Botany. Educ: Ph.D. Publs: Natur på Gotland, 1946; Gotlands Orkidéer, 1951; The Vallhagar Country: Some Natural Features Relating to its History, 1955; Dynamik & Konstans i Gotlands Flora & Vegetation, 1958. Contbr. to: Dagens Nyheter, Stockholm. Mbrships. incl: Swedish Union of Authors; Swedish Botanical Soc. (mbr. of Bd. & Ed. staff). Recip., Linnaeus Prize, 1959. Address: Bofinksvägen 6 D, S—902 37 Umea, Sweden.

PETTERSSON, H. Bertil N., pen name MALM, Margaretha, b. 16 Apr. 1932, Stockholm, Sweden. Author. Publs. incl: Utkast, 1958; Dagbok, 1962; Rekviem, 1963; Insnitt, 1967; Valda dikter, 1968; Under molnen, 1970; Berättelser kring Slentrianen, 1972; Handen på hjärtat, 1973; (poetry as Margaretha Malm) Dagar utanför tiden, 1961; Ingenstans vaknar gud, 1963; Inte den du söker, 1959; (transl.) In This Well-Known Season by Robin Fulton, 1973; & 7 other books. Mbr., Swedish Union Authors. Recip., sev. prizes & grants. Address: Ronnebygatan 55, S-702 28 Örebro, Sweden.

PETTIGREW, Thomas Fraser, b. 14 Mar. 1931, Richmond, Va., USA. Professor of Social Psychology & Sociology. Educ: B.A., Univ. of Va., 1952; M.A., 1955, Ph.D., 1956, Harvard Univ. Publs: Christians in Racial Crisis: A Study of the Little Rock Ministry (w. E. Q. Campbell), 1959; A Profile of the Negro American, 1964; Racially Separate or Together, 1971; Ed., Racial Discrimination in the United States, 1975. Contbr. to: N.Y. Times Mag.; New Repub.; New Soc.; etc. Mbrships. incl: Pres., Soc. for the Psychol. Study of Soc. Issues, 1967-68. Address: 1330 Wm. James Hall, Harvard Univ., Cambridge, MA 02138, USA.

PETTIT, Philip Noel, b. 20 Dec. 1945, Ballygar, Co. Galway, Repub. of Ireland. University Teacher. Educ: B.A., M.A., Nat. Univ. Ireland; Ph.D., Queen's Univ., Belfast;

M.A., Cambridge Univ. Publs: On the Idea of Phenomenology, 1969; The Concept of Structuralism, 1975. Contbr. to Cambridge Review (Ed., 1973-75); etc. Mbrships: Mind Assn.; Rish Philosl. Soc. Address: Trinity Hall, Cambridge, UK.

PETTITT, George A., b. 7 June 1901, Oakland, Calif., USA. Educator. Educ: A.B., 1926, Ph.D., 1940, Univ. of Calif. Publs: So Boulder Dam Was Built, 1935; Primitive Education in North America, 1946; The Quileute of La Bush, 1950; Twenty-Eight Years in the Life of a University President, 1966; Clayton: Not Quite Shangri-La, The Story of a California Town, 1969; Prisoners of Culture, 1970; Berkeley, The Town & Gown of It, 1973. Contbr. to: Calif. Monthly; Am. Folklore Jrnl.; Ency. Britannica; Univ. Explorer (radio broadcast). Address: 1429 Euclid Ave., Berkeley, CA 94708, USA.

PETTIWARD, Daniel, pen name R. D., b. 7 Nov. 1913, Polzeath, Cornwall, UK. Freelance Journalist & Critic. Educ: B.A., Univ. Coll., Oxford, UK. Publs: Truly Royal, 1939; Money for Jam, 1956. Contbr. to: Punch; London Mystery Mag.; Drama Critic, Southern Evening Echo, 1962—; Daily Telegraph Mag.; BBC; etc. Address: 48a The Close, Salisbury, Wilts. SP1 2EL, UK.

PETUCHOWSKI, Jakob Josef, b. 30 July 1925, Berlin, Germany. (US citizen 1954—). Educator; Clergyman; Lecturer. Educ: B.A., Univ. of London, UK, 1947; B.H.L., 1949, M.A. & Rabbinic Ordination, 1952, Ph.D., 1955, Hebrew Union Coll., USA. Publs: The Theology of Haham David Nieto, 1954, 2nd ed., 1970; Ever Since Sinai, 1961, 2nd ed., 1968; Prayerbook Reform in Europe, 1968; Heirs of the Pharisees, 1970; Contributions to the Scientific Study of Jewish Liturgy, 1970; Understanding Jewish Prayer, 1972. Contbr. to: Ency. Britannica; Ency. Int.; Ency. Judaica; num. relig. jrnls. Recip., Hon. F.H.L., Maimonides Coll., Winnipeg, Can., 1959. Address: 7836 Greenland Pl., Cinn., OH 45237, USA.

PEVSNER, (Sir) Nikolaus B.L., b. 1902. Emeritus Professor, History of Art; Former University Teacher. Educ: Ph.D. Publs: The Baroque Architecture of Leipzig; Italian Painting from the End of the Renaissance to the Rococo; Academies of Art Past & Present; Pioneers of Modern Design; Outline of European Architecture; The Buildings of England, 46 vols.; The Englishness of English Art; Studies in Art, Architecture & Design; Some Architectural Writers of the Nineteenth Century. Address: 2 Wildwood Terrace, North End, London NW3, UK.

PEYPERS, Ankie, b. 29 Sept. 1928, Amsterdam, Netherlands. Author. Publs: (poetry) October, 1951; Taal en teken, 1956; Woorden als jij, 1963; Binnenland, 1967; tussen tekst en uitleg, 1968; drempel van ontheemden, 1971; over derwisj en het nabije westen, 1974; (novels) Geen denken aan, 1961; Tussentijds, 1966; De vallei van obermann, 1969. Contbr. to var. Dutch & Flemish reviews. Mbrships: Bd., PEN; Union of Writers; Soc, of Dutch Lit.; Bd., Coun. of Arts. Recip., Anne Frank Prize, 1962. Address: Zuider Parallelweg 9, Velp (G), Netherlands.

PEYRE, Henri, b. 21 Feb. 1901, Paris, France. University Professor; Author. Educ: Agrégation, 1924; Doct. ès Lettres, 1932. Publs: 40 books, of which latest Qu'est-ce que le Symbolisme? , 1974. Contbr. to 50 Am. & French reviews. Mbrships: Past Pres., MLA; Past Pres., Am. Assn. Tchrs. of French; Am. Philos. Soc.; Am. Acad. of Arts & Scis. Hons: 12 Degrees; sev. prizes, French Acad. Address: Yale Station, New Haven, CT, USA.

PEYREFITTE, Pierre Roger, b. 17 Aug. 1907. Former Diplomat; Writer. Educ: B.A.; Toulouse Univ.; Schl. of Political Sci., Paris. Publs. incl: Les Amitiés Particulières. 1944-5; Le Prince de Neiges, 1947; L'Oracle, 1948; Les Ambassades, 1951; La Fin des Ambassades, 1953; Jeunes Proies, 1956; Chevaliers de Malte, 1957; L'Exilé de Capri, 1959; Le Spectateur Nocturne, 1960; La Nature du Prince, 1963; Les Juifs, 1965; Notre Amour, 1967; Les Américains, 1968; Des Français, 1970; La Coloquiste, 1971; Manouche, 1972. Address: 9 Ave. du Maréchal Maunoury, Paris 16e, France.

PEYTON, Kathleen Wendy (née Herald), pen name PEYTON, K. M., b. 1929, Birmingham, UK. Educ: Manchester Art Schl. Publs: Sabre, 1947; The Mandrake, 1949; Crab the Roan, 1953; Windfall, 1963; The Maplin Bird, 1964; The Plan for Birdsmarsh, 1965; Thunder in the Sky, 1966; Flambards, 1967; Fly by Night, 1968; The Edge of the Cloud, 1969; Flambards in Summer, 1969;

Pennington's Seventeenth Summer, 1970; The Beethoven Medal, 1971; A Pattern of Roses, 1972; Pennington's Heir, 1973. Mbr., Soc. of Authors. Address: Rookery Cottage, North Fambridge, Essex, UK.

PFEIFER, Lillian E., b. 16 July 1907, Ft. Morgan, Colo., USA. Writer. Educ: Hastings, Neb. Bus. Coll. Publs: Jubilee Anthology, 1955; The Wolfers, 1967. Contbr. to: Jr. Mag.; Can. Travel Bur.; CBC; Western Prod.; Alta. Poetry Book; Times Press, 1942-53. Mbr., Can. Author's Assn. (Pres., 1962-64). Recip., Jessie Drummond Boyd Award for Poetry, Alta. Yr. Book, 1974. Address: 36 Waterloo Dr. S.W., Calgary, Alta., T3C 3E8, Can.

PFEIFFER, C. Boyd, pen name FLETCHER, Scott, b. 5 Aug. 1937, Balt., Md., USA. Writer; Photographer; Editor. Educ: B.A., Gettysburg Coll., 1960. Publs: Field & Stream Fishing Guide (w. L. James Bashline), 1972; Tackle Craft, 1974; Shad Fishing, 1975; Guide to Salt Water Fishing. Contbr. to num. sporting jrnls. Mbrships: Outdoor Writers Assn. of Am.; Mason-Dixon & Va. Outdoor Writers Assns.; Dir., Pa. Outdoor Writers Assn. Hons. incl: Award for Best Newspaper Column, Nat. Hunting & Fishing Day, 1973; Best Newspaper Column Award, Recreation Vehicle Assn., 1974. Address: 9306 Joey Drive, Ellicott City, MD 21043, USA.

PHAM, Van Ky, b. 10 July 1916, Quinhon, Vietnam. Novelist; Playwright. Educ: Inst. Chinese Studies, Univ. Paris. Publs: (novels) Frères de Sang, 1947; Celui qui régnera, 1954; Les yeux courroucés, 1958; Les Contemporains, 1959; Perdre la demeure, 1961; Des Femmes assises çà et là, 1964; Mémoires d'un Eunuque, 1966; (poetry) Fleur de jade, 1945; Poème sur Soie, 1961; (short stories) L'Homme de nulle part, 1946; (play) Le Rideau de pluie, 1974. Mbrships. incl: Soc. Authors & Playwrights, Paris; European Soc. Culture. Recip., Grand Prix du Roman de l'Académie Française, 1961. Address: 62/2 Avenue du Général de Gaulle, 94700 Maisons-Alfort, France.

PHELAN, John Leddy, b. 19 July 1924, Fall River, Mass., USA. Professor of History. Educ: A.B., Harvard Univ., 1947; Ph.D., Univ. of Calif., at Berkeley, 1951. Publs: The Millennial Kingdom of the Franciscans in the New World, 1956, 2nd ed., 1970; The Hispanization of the Philippines: Spanish Aims & Filipino Responses, 1565-1700, 1959, 2nd ed., 1967; The Kingdom of Quito in the Seventeenth Century, Bureaucratic Politics in the Spanish Empire, 1967. Contbr. to: Hispanic-Am. Historical Review; The Americas; Boletin de Historia & Antigüedades, Bogota. Corresp. Mbr., Acad. Colombiana de Historia, & Acad. de Historia de la Republica del Ecuador. Address: 5457 Lake Mendota Drivice, Madison, WI 53706, USA.

PHELAN, Josephine, b. 23 Feb. 1905, Hamilton, Ont., Can. Librarian. Educ: M.A., B.L.S., Univ. Toronto. Publs: The Ardent Exile, 1951; The Boy Who Ran Away, 1954; The Bold Heart, 1956; The Ballad of D'Arcy McGee, 1967. Mbr., Can. Authors' Assn. Hons: Gov. Gen's. Award, Creative Non-fiction, 1952; Univ. B.C. Medal Popular Biog., 1952. Address: 49 Thorncliffe Pk. Dr., Apt. 407, Toronto M4H 1L1, Can.

PHELAN, Mary Kay, b. 30 June 1914, Baldwin City, Kan., USA. Writer. Educ: B.A., De Pauw Univ., Ind.; M.A., Northwestern Univ., Ill. Publs: The White House, 1962; The Circus, 1963; Mother's Day, 1965; The Fourth of July, 1966; Mr. Lincoln Speaks at Gettysburg, 1966; Election Day, 1967; Four Days in Philadelphia, 1776, 1967; Midnight Alarm: The Story of Paul Revere's Ride, 1968; Probing the Unknown: The Story of Dr. Florence Sabin, 1969; The Great Chicago Fire, 1971; Martha Berry, 1971; Mr. Lincoln's Inaugural Journey, 1972; The Story of the Boston Tea Party, 1973; The Burning of Washington, 1814, 1975. Address: 2524 Lorton Ave., Davenport, IA 52803, USA.

PHELAN, Nancy Eleanor, b. 2 Aug. 1913, Sydney, Australia. Writer. Educ: Sydney Univ.; Conservatorium Music, Sydney. Publs: Atoll Holiday, 1958; The River & the Brook, 1961; Welcome the Wayfarer, 1965; Serpents in Paradise, 1967; Pillow of Grass, 1969; A Kingdom by the Sea, 1969; Some Came Early, Some Came Late, 1970; The Chilean Way, 1973; Nina, A Russian Cookery Book (co-author); & 9 books on Yoga. Contbr. to: Sydney Morning Herald Lit. Supplement (book reviewer); etc. Hons. incl: Lit. Grant for 3 yrs. by Lit. Bd. Aust. Coun. Arts, 1973. Address: 2 Byron Hall, 97 Macleay St., Potts Point 2011, N.S.W., Australia.

PHELPS, Donald (Norman), b. 13 Dec. 1929, Bklyn., N.Y., USA. Essayist; Editor & Publisher. Educ: B.A., Brooklyn Coll., 1951. Publ: Covering Ground, 1969. Contbr. to: For Now (Ed. & Publr.); Nat. Review; Minn. Review; New Leader; Nation; Mulch; The Second Coming; Kulchur; Film Culture; Moviegoer; Vort. Address: 644 Chauncey St., Bklyn., NY 11207, USA.

PHELPS BROWN, Ernest Henry, b. 1906, Calne, Wilts., UK. University Professor, Economics of Labour. Educ: Wadham Coll., Oxford. Publs: The Framework of the Pricing System, 1936; A Course in Applied Economics, 1951; novel: The Balloon, 1953; The Growth of British Industrial Relations, 1959; The Economics of Labour, 1962; A Century of Pay (w. M. H. Browne), 1968; Pay & Profits, 1968. Address: 16 Bradmore Rd., Oxford OX2 6QP, UK.

PHIBBS, Richard, b. 1911, Boyle, Repub. of Ireland. Writer. Educ: Jesus Coll., Cambridge; Univ. Coll., London; B.A. Publs: Transl., The White Llama, 1938; The Lottery Ticket, 1940; Cockle-Button-Cockle-Ben, 1940; Buried in the Country, 1947; Henry Jane of Farrenhaven, 1949; Abram Brown, 1955. Contbr. to: Now; The Bell; Adelphi. Mbrships: Soc. of Authors; PEN. Address: 56 Sutherland St., London SW1, UK.

PHILIP, Kathleen, b. 14 June 1914, Isle of Gigha, Argyll, UK. M.A., Glasgow, 1936; M.Ed., Aberdeen, 1951. Publs: Victorian Wantage, 1969; Reflected in Wantage, Part I, 1970, Part II, 1971; Black Wantage, 1972; Memoirs of Sarah Jane Harris, 1973; The Cherry Barn, 1974. Address: 22 Belmont, Wantage OX12 9AS, UK.

PHILIPP, Elliot Elias, b. 1915, London, UK. Obstetrician & Gynaecologist. Educ: Univ. of Cambridge; Middx. Hosp., Univ. of London; Univ. of Lausanne, Switz. M.A.; M.B.; B.Ch.; F.R.C.S. Publs: Ed., Scientific Foundations of Obstetrics & Gynaecology for Students, 2nd ed. Contbr. to: Sunday Times; News Chronicle; Lancet; BBC; ITV; CBS. Mbrships: Fellow, Royal Coll. of Obstetricians & Gynaecols.; Royal Soc. of Med. Recip., Chevalier, Legion of Hon., France. Address: 27 Harley House, London NW1 5HE, UK.

PHILLIPS, Anthony Charles Julian, b. 1936, Falmouth, Cornwall, UK. College Chaplain. Educ: King's Coll., London Univ.; Gonville & Caius Coll., Cambridge Univ.; B.D.; A.K.C.; Ph.D. Publs: Ancient Israel's Criminal Law, 1971; Deuteronomy, 1973. Contbr. to: Vetus Testamentum; Theology; S. African Outlook; Words & Meanings; Jrnl. Semitic Studies. Mbr., Soc. of Old Testament Studies. Address: St. John's Coll., Oxford, UK.

PHILLIPS, David Lindsay, b. 27 Nov. 1914, Dundee, UK. Writer. Publs: The Lichty Nichts, 1962; The Exploits of Wiselike Ned, 1963; Hud Yer Tongue, 1964; My Dundee, 1971; Oor Dundee, 1972; No Poets' Corner in the Abbey, 1971; M'Gonagall & Tommy Atkins, 1973; Jimmy Shand, 1975. Contbr. to: Scots Mag.; People's Jrnl.; other Scottish periodicals. Address: 8 Quarryside, Dundee, Scotland, UK.

PHILLIPS, Dewi Zephaniah, b. 1934, Wales, UK. Professor of Philosophy. Educ: B.A., M.A., Univ. Coll., Swansea; B.Litt., St. Catherine's Coll., Oxford. Publs: The Concept of Prayer, 1965; Faith & Philosophical Enquiry, 1970; Death & Immortality, 1970; Moral Practices (w. H. O. Mounce), 1970; Sense & Delusion (w. Ilham Dilman), 1971; Gen. Ed., Studies in Ethics & the Philosophy of Religion (all Routledge & Kegan Paul); Athronyddu am Grefydd, 1974; Religion & Understanding (ed.); Morality & Purpose; Saith Ysgrif ar Grefydd. Contbr. to: Mind; Analysis; Philos.; Philos. Quarterly; Ratio; etc. Address: 45 Queen's Rd., Sketty, Swansea, UK.

PHILLIPS, E. Hereward, b. 1905, Birmingham, UK. Journalist; Fundraising Consultant. Publs: Fundraising Techniques, 1969. Contbr. to: Yorks. Post (former Ed. Staff); Evening Standard (former Ed. Staff). Mbrships: F.I.P.R.; M.I.J.; Press Club. Address: 11 Ravenscroft Park, Barnet, Herts. EN5 4ND, UK.

PHILLIPS, Ian Marcus David, b. 9 Feb. 1951, Oxford, UK. Editor. Contbr. to: Autosport (Ed.); Autocourse; Autosport Annual. Mbrships: Brit. Racing & Sports Car Club; Brit. Automobile Racing Club; Steering Wheel Club. Address: 19 Buller Rd., London NW10, UK.

PHILLIPS, (Rev. Canon) John Bertram, b. 16 Sept. 1906, London, UK. Clergyman; Author. Educ: M.A.,

Cambridge, 1933; D.D., Lambeth, 1966. Publs. incl: Letters to Young Churches, 1947; The Gospels in Modern English, 1952; Plain Christianity, 1954; New Testament Christianity, 1956; The Church Under the Cross, 1956; Is God at Home?, 1957; The New Testament in Modern English, 1958; A Man Called Jesus, 1959; Good News, 1963; Four Prophets, 1963; Ring of Truth, 1967; Through the Year with J. B. Phillips (Ed., D. Duncan), 1974. Recip., Hon. D.Litt., 1970. Address: Golden Cap, 17 Gannetts Park, Swanage, Dorset BH19 1PF, UK.

PHILLIPS, Margaret Mann, b. 1906, Kimberworth, Yorks., UK. University Reader in French. Educ: B.A., M.A., Somerville Coll., Oxford; Univs. of Paris & Bordeaux; D. d'Université. Publs: Outgoing, 1936; Erasme et les Débuts de la Réforme française, 1934; Within the City Wall, 1943; Erasmus & the Northern Renaissance, 1949; The Adages of Erasmus, 1964. Contbr. to: Mod. Lang. Review; etc. Address: 103 Ditton Rd., Surbiton, Surrey, UK.

PHILLIPS, Mary, b. 26 Jan. 1936, Bridgwater, UK. Translator. Educ: B.A., M.A., New Hall, Cambridge. Publs: (transls.) The Wonderful World of Nature, 1962; The Wonders of Wildlife in Europe, 1963; The Social Function of Industrial Design, 1970. Contbr. to: Int. Socialism; Socialist Worker. Mbr., Transls'. Assn. Address: 66 Longland Court, Avondale Square, London SE1, UK.

PHILLIPS, Michael Joseph, b. 2 Mar. 1937, Indpls., Ind., USA. Teacher; Poet. Educ: B.A., Wabash Coll., Crawfordsville, Ind., 1959; M.A., Ind. Univ., Bloomington, 1964, Ph.D., 1971; C.A., Oxford Univ., UK, 1969, 1971; further studies, var. univs., USA, UK, France. Publs. incl: Girls, Girls, Girls, 1967; Three Poems of the Cross, 1970; Four Gothic Twilight Poems, 1971; Concrete Sonnets, 1972; Love, Love, Love, 1973. Contbr. to: Am. Poets; Mass. Review; Poetry People; Prairie Poets; Love Woman; Out of Sight; Alphabet Anthol.; Golden Harvest; Timeless Treasures; etc. Recip., Nat. Endowment for the Arts Poetry Reader. Address: 5103 N. Park Ave., Indpls., IN 46205, USA.

PHILLIPS, Olga Somech, pen name (on Daily Sketch) OLGA, b. 1901, Manchester, UK. Author; Lecturer. Educ: Clarendon House, Southport; Hampstead Conservatoire, London. Publs: Solomon J. Solomon, 1931; St. Giles & Elsewhere: Tales of Jewish Life, 1936; Isaac Nathan, 1937; The Bayswater Synagogue (w. Hyman A. Simons), 1963; The Boy Disraeli, 1968; World of Wonder. Contbr. to: Look & Learn; Jewish Chronicle; Daily Sketch. Mbrships: var. Jewish & civic orgs, Royal Soc. of Lit., 1940-. Address: 4 Perceval Ave., London NW3, UK.

PHILLIPS, Peter Edward, b. 1903, Aberdare, Glam., UK. Formerly Deputy Headmaster, boys' school. Educ: M.A., Univ. of Wales, Aberystwyth. Publs: French Literary Appreciation (w. J. B. Davies). Address: 8 Glan Nant St., Aberdare, Glam., UK.

PHILLIPS, Stella, b. 26 Dec. 1927, Devonport, Devon, UK. Librarian; Author. Publs: Down to Death, 1967; The Hidden Wrath, 1968; Death in Arcady, 1969; Death Makes the Scene, 1970; Death in Sheep's Clothing, 1971; Yet She Must Die, 1973; Dear Brother, Here Departed, 1975. Contbr. to var. mags. & radio progs. Mbrships: Crime Writers' Assn.; Lib. Assn. (Assoc.). Address: 33 Bishopton Avenue, Stockton-on-Tees, Cleveland, UK.

PHILLIPSON, Herbert, b. 16 Mar. 1911, Staincross, Yorks., UK. Clinical Psychologist; Writer. Educ: B.A., Hull Univ.; M.A., London Univ. Publs: Education: A Search for New Principles, 1942; The Object Relations Technique, 1955; Interpersonal Perception (co-author), 1966. Contbr. to: Brit. Jrnl. Med. Psychol.; Brit. Jrnl. Proj. Psychol. Mbrships: Fellow, Brit. Psych. Soc.; Hon. VP, Brit. Soc. Proj. Psych. Address: Castle Bytham, Nr. Grantham, Lincs., UK.

PHILLPOTTS, Mary Adelaide Eden, b. Ealing, UK. Writer. Publs. incl: Illyrion & Other Poems, 1916; Man, a Fable, 1922; The Friend, 1923; A Marriage, 1928; The Atoning Years, 1929; Yellow Sands, 1930; The Youth of Jacob Ackner, 1931; The Growing World, 1934; The Gallant Heart, 1939; The Round of Life, 1940; Our Little Town, 1942; From Jane to John, 1943; The Adventurers, 1944; The Lodestar, 1946; Stubborn Earth, 1951; A Song of Man, 1959; Panorama of the World, 1969; (plays) Akhnaton, 1926; Laugh with Me, 1938. Address: Cobblestones, Kilkhampton, Bude, Cornwall, UK.

PHILP, Dennis Alfred Peter, b. 10 Nov. 1920, Cardiff, UK. Writer. Publs: Antiques Today; Antique Furniture; Furniture of the World; (plays) Beyond Tomorrow; The Castle of Deception; Love & Lunacy. Contbr. to: Collectors' Guide; Antique Finder; Art & Antiques. Mbrships: Brit. Antique Dealers' Assn.; Furniture Hist. Soc. Agent: Margery Vosper. Address: 22 Kelvin Rd., Roath Park, Cardiff, UK.

PHILP, (Rev.) Howard Littleton, b. 1902, Helland, Cornwall, UK. Canon. Educ: Univs. of Birmingham, London & Oxford; B.A.; Ph.D.; B.Litt. Publs: The Frustration of Will: Acts & Conation; Freud & Religious Belief; Jung & the Problem of Evil. Fellow, Brit. Psychol. Assn. Address: 55 The Close, Salisbury, Wilts., UK.

PHILPS, Frank R., b. 1914, Potters Bar, UK. Retired Consultant Cytologist. Educ: M.D.; D.P.H.; F.R.C.Path.; Univ. Coll. Hospital. Publs: A Short Manual of Respiratory Cytology, 1963; Watching Wildlife, 1968. Contbr. to: Brit. Jrnl. of Cancer; Brit. Med. Jrnl. Mbr., Brit. Med. Assn. Recip., M.B.E. Address: Sparrow Hall, Brentor, Tavistock, Devon, UK.

PHIPPS, Grace May, b. Shirley, Christchurch, NZ. Writer. Educ: Schl. of Art, Christchurch Univ. Publs: Marriage with Eve, 1955; The Women of the Family, 1956; The Life for Louise, 1957; Concerning Eve, 1959; A Nurse Like Kate, 1960; The Young Wife, 1962; Two Sisters in Love, 1966; Doctor on the Scene, 1967; The Tenderhearted Nurse, 1968; No Wife for a Parson, 1969; Marriage While You Wait, 1970; The Bridal Boutique, 1971; And Be My Love, 1972; The Doctor's Three Daughters, 1973; We Love You, Nurse Peters, 1974; Maternity Hospital, 1975. Address: 30 Hamilton Ave., Fendalton, Christchurch 4, NZ.

PHIPPS, (Rt. Rev.) Simon Wilton, b. 1921, Furneux Pelham, Herts, UK. Bishop of Lincoln. Educ: M.A., Trinity Coll., Cambridge. Publs: God on Monday, 1966. Recip., M.C. Address: Bishop's House, Eastgate, Lincoln, UK.

PHYTHIAN, Brian A., b. 15 May 1932, St. Helens, Lancs., UK. Headmaster; Author. Educ: B.A., M.A., Univ. of Manchester; B.Litt., Wadham Coll., Oxford. Publs: R.B. Sheridan, 1964; Manchester Grammar School 1515-1965, 1965; Starting Points, 1967; Considering Poetry, 1970; Concise Dictionary of English Idiom, 1973; Ed., Henry V, 1975; Concise Dictionary of Slang, 1975. Contbr. to Use of Engl. Address: Langley Park School for Boys, Beckenham, Kent, UK.

PICARD, Barbara Leonie, b. 1917, Richmond, UK. Writer. Publs. incl: The Odyssey of Homer, 1952; Tales of the Norse Gods & Heroes, 1953; Stories of King Arthur & His Knights, 1955; Ransom for a Knight, 1956; The Iliad of Homer, 1960; Lost John, 1962; Hero Tales of the British Isles, 1963; One is One, 1965; The Young Pretenders, 1966; Twice Seven Tales, 1968; Three Ancient Kings, 1972; Tales of Ancient Persia, 1972. Address: c/o Oxford Univ. Press, Ely Ho., 37 Dover St., London W1, UK.

PICARD, Dorothy Young, pen name CROMAN, Dorothy Young, b. 25 Dec. 1906, Waverly, Wash., USA. Author. Educ: Reed Coll., Portland, Ore., 2 yrs. Publs: Mystery of Steamboat Rock, 1956; Five Readers for Slow Learners: Something to Do (2 books), World of Wonder, Gather Around (2 books), 1962-71. Mbrships: Seattle Br., Nat. League of Am. Pen Women; Authors Guild, Inc. Address: P.O. Box 181, Nespelem, WA 99155, USA.

PICARD, Hymen W(illem) J(ohannes), pen name PICARD, Eve, b. 20 June 1910, Driebergen, Netherlands. Author. Educ: LL.M.; M.A. Publs: Sev. books in Dutch, 1935-46; Gentleman's Walk, 1968; Grand Parade, 1969; Masters of the Castle, 1972; Man of Constantia; Lords of Stalplein, 1974. Contbr. to S. African Broadcasting Corp. Mbr., PEN. Address: 1204 Silverstream, Disa Pk., Highlands Estate, Cape Town, Repub. of S. Africa.

PICCARD, Jacques, b. 28 July 1922, Brussels, Belgium. Oceanologist; Deep Sea Explorer & Technical Research Consultant. Educ: Acad. Degree, Univ. of Geneva, Switz., 1946; Dip., Grad Inst. Int. Studies, Geneva, 1947. Publs. incl: De la Stratosphere aux Abysses, 1957; Profondeur 11,000 Metres, 1961; Un Univers Mysterieux, 1962; Le Mesoscaphe Auguste Piccard, 1968; Voyages au Fond des Oceans, 1970; The Sun Beneath the Sea, 1971; also var. sci. papers. Mbrships. incl: Life Mbr., Nat. Geographic Soc., Wash. D.C., USA; Hon. Mbr., Soc. Acad. Vaudoise, Lausanne, Switz. Hons. incl: Gold Medal, Royal Geographic

Soc., Belgium, 1971; Off., Order of Leopold, Belgium, 1972. Address: 19 Avenue de l'avenir, CH-1012 Lausanne, Switz.

PICKARD BAILEY, Phyllis Marguerite, b. 1904, London, UK. Writer; Teacher. Educ: Froebel Inst., UK; Univ. Coll., London. Publs: Praktische Kinderpsychologie, 1951; I Could a Tale Unfold, 1961; The Activity of Children, 1965; Time for Reading, (w. C. Obrist), 1967; The Psychology of Developing Children, 1970. Mbr. Brit. Psychological Soc. Agent: Dorothea Benson. Address: Coin de Terre, La Corbiere, Guernsey, Channel Islands.

PICKERING, Frederick Pickering, b. 10 Mar. 1909, Bradford, UK. Emeritus Professor of German; Writer. Educ: B.A.; Ph.D.; Univs. of Leeds & Breslau. Publs: Ed., Christi Leiden in einer Vision geschaut, 1952; The Anglo-Norman Text of the Holkham Bible Picture Book, 1971; (monographs) Literature & Art in the Middle Ages, 2nd ed., 1970; Augustinus oder Boethius?, 2 vols., 1967 & 1975; Course-Book University German, 1968. Contbr. to: Euphorion; Zeitschrift für Deutsche Philologie, etc. Address: Arborfield Ct., Arborfield Cross, Berks., UK.

PICKERING, Margaret Fanny, pen name HARLAND, Elizabeth M., b. 11 Mar. 1904, Norfolk, UK. Writer. Publs. incl: The Houses in Between, 1936; Farmer's Girl, 1942; Penguin Guide to Norfolk & the Isle of Ely, 1949; Diary of a Country Housewife: weekly articles in Eastern Daily Press, 1949−, book form 1951, reprint 1974; book on linen industry w. special ref. to Norfolk, forthcoming. Contbr. to: Farmers' Weekly; Norfolk Fair; Eastern Daily Press; radio; TV. Mbrships. incl: East Anglian Writers; Coun., Norfolk & Norwich Archaeol. Soc. Address: Hope House, Hindolveston, Dereham, Norfolk, UK.

PICKERING, Robert Easton, b. 12 Feb. 1934, Carlisle, UK. Writer. Educ: B.A., Queen's Coll., Oxford. Publs: Himself Again (w. Am. ed. as The Uncommitted Man), 1966; In Transit, 1968. Address: 07150 Lagroce, France.

PICKERSGILL, John Whitney, b. 23 June 1905, Wyecombe, Ont., Can. Writer. Educ: B.A., 1926, M.A., 1927, Univ. of Man.; B.Litt., Oxford Univ., UK, 1953. Publs: The Mackenzie King Record, Vols. I-IV (Vols. II-IV w. D. F. Forster), 1960-70; The Liberal Party, 1962; Le Parti Liberal, 1963. Contbr. to var. newspapers & mags. Mbrships: Can. Inst. of Int. Affairs; Can. Histl. Assn.; Pol. Sci. Assn. Hons: LL.D., Mem. Univ. of Nfld., 1967, Univ. of Man., 1967; D.C.L., Bishop's Univ., 1967; Companion of the Order of Can., 1970. Address: 550 Maple Lane, Ottawa, Ont., Can.

PICKLES, Dorothy Maud, b. 1903, Bridlington, UK. Lecturer; Broadcaster. Educ: M.A.; B.Sc.(Econ.); Univs. of Leeds, Paris & London. Publs: The French Political Scene, 1937; France Between the Republics, 1946; France: the First Years of the Fourth Republic, 1953; France: The Fourth Republic, 1954; The Fifth French Republic, 1960; Algeria & France, 1963; France, 1964; The Uneasy Entente, 1966; Introduction to Politics, 1951, 1967; Democracy, 1970; The Government & Politics of France, (2 vols.) 1972, 1973. Contbr. to: World Today; Annual Register; Int. Affairs; Contemporary Reviews; etc. Address: White Hatch, 29 Detillens Lane, Limpsfield, Oxted, Surrey, UK.

PICKLES, William, b. 1903, Bradford, UK. Reader in Political Science; Former BBC Producer. Educ: M.A.; Univs. of Leeds & Sorbonne, Paris. Publs: Is France a Democracy & France Faces Fascism, (both w. Dorothy Pickles) 1940; The French Constitution of October 1958, 1959; Not With Europe, 1962; How Much has Changed, 1967; Where do we come in? 1975; 3 transls. Contbr. to: La Nef; Politique Etrangère; Public Law; Int. Affairs; Politica; Int. Review; Jrnl. of Common Market Studies; etc. Mbr., Political Sci. Assn. Address: White Hatch, 29 Detillens Lane, Limpsfield, Oxted, Surrey, UK.

PICKUP, Beth Walmsley, b. Morris Green, Bolton, UK. Writer. Educ: Bolton Tech. Coll. Publs: num. under pen names. Contbr. to: Eadon's Press; Gerrad's Publ. of Lancs. Prose & Verse; Enterprize Fndn.; Oldham Chronicle; Red Rose & Record mags.; The Lady; BBC Radio 3 & 4; local radio; Lancs. Life, etc. Mbrships. incl: Lancs. Authors Assn.; Preston Poets' Soc.; Fndr. Mbr., Leyland Writers' Assn.; Women's 1st (Past Press Corres. & Hon. Treas.) Hons. incl: 1st winner, Preston Poets' Mackenzie Trophy, 1965, 1969; Awards for Prose, Poetry & Short Story. Address: Innisfree, School Lane, Euxton, Chorley, Lancs. PR7 6JL, UK.

PIDOUX, Edmond, b. 25 Oct. 1908, Mons, Belgium. Professor. Educ: Licence ès lettres, Lausanne Univ. Publs. incl: (plays) Ni le Sang ni la Loi, 1954; Le Vendredi de Robinson, 1974; (essays); L'Afrique à l'âge ingrat, 1956; Voir la Montagne, 1970; (poetry): La Ligne d'Ombre, 1966; Africaines, 1969; De David à Jonas, 1969; L'espace d'un moment, 1975. Contbr. to Les Alpes. Mbrships. incl: Soc. des auteurs et compositeurs dramatiques; Acad. Rhodanienne des Lettres. Hons. incl: drama prize, l'Eglise de Genève, 1951; poetry prize, L'Expression française, 1963; Soc. des poètes et artistes de France, 1966. Address: 7 chemin du Moléson, 1012 Lausanne, Switzerland.

PIECHOWSKI, Jerzy, b. 31 Mar. 1936, Płock, Poland. Novelist; Essayist. Educ: Master of Classic Philol., Warsaw Univ., 1960. Publs: Cien Sprawy, 1962; Sekretarz Piłata, 1966; Drzewo Gorczycy, 1968; Rzym Pfonie, 1969; Znak Salamandry, 1970; Gwiazdy z Kraju Połnocy, 1972; Swiadkowle i Trukciciele, 1972; Źrenice Mroku, 1973; Trzeecia Pokusa, 1974; Spotkanie 2 Minotaurem, 1974/75. Contbr. essays to jrnls. Mbrships: PEN; Union of Polish Writers. Recip., Pietrzak Prize, 1967. Address: ul. Międzynarodowa 46/48A m. 226, 03-922 Warsaw, Poland.

PIEPER, Josef, b. 4 May 1904, Elte, Westphalia, Germany. University Professor; Writer. Educ: D.Ph.; Univs. of Berlin & Muenster. Publs: Vom Sinn der Tapferkeit; Zucht u. Mass; Uber die Gerechtigkeit; Musse und Kult; Glueck u. Kontemplation; Über das Ende der Zeit; Hoffnung u. Geschichte; Tod. u. Unsterblichkeit; Ueber die Liebe. Contbr. to: Hochland; Folia Humanistica; La Table Ronde; Universitas; Review of Pols. Mbr., PEN. Hons: Dr. theol., Munich, 1964, Muenster, 1974. Address: Malmedy-Weg 10, D44 Muenster, Westphalia, W. Germany.

PIERARD, Richard Victor, b. 29 May 1934, Chgo., Ill., USA. Professor of History. Educ: B.A., 1958, M.A., 1959, Calif. State Univ., L.A.; Ph.D., Univ. of Iowa, 1964. Publs: Protest & Politics (co-author), 1968; The Unequal Yoke, 1970; The Cross & The Flag (co-author), 1972; Politics: A Case for Christian Action (co-author), 1973. Contbr. to: The Reformed Jrnl.; The Other Side; Christianity Today. Recip., Fulbright Schlrship., Univ. of Hamburg, Germany, 1962-63. Address: Dept. of History, Indiana State Univ., Terre Haute, IN 47809, USA.

PIERCE, Ovid Williams, b. 1 Oct. 1910, Weldon, N.C., USA. Teacher; Writer. Educ: B.A., Duke Univ., 1932; M.A., Harvard Univ., 1938. Publs: The Plantation, 1953; On a Lonesome Porch, 1960; The Devils Half, 1968; The Wedding Guest, 1974. Contbr. to: N.Y. Times Book Review; Holiday Mag.; South West Review; Longview Jrnl. Hons: Sir Walter Raleigh Award, 1954, 1960; State of N.C. Award, 1968; O. Max Gardner Award, 1973; Halifax Resolves Award, 1974. Address: Box 2681, Greenville, NC, USA.

PIERHAL, Armand, b. 27 July 1897, Thessalonica, Greece. Writer; Journalist. Educ: Studies at Univ. of Lausanne; Studied Music, Paris. Publs: Jeunes Morts chéris des Dieux, 1938; La Chartreuse de Tonar, 1956; De Dixeu Vivant (essays), 1941; Le Combat de Pitiers, 1949; L'Antimachiavel, 1951; Le diable est un imbecile, 1962; Maximes Alexandrines (poems), 1969. Contbr. to: Le Figaro; Les Nouvelles Littéraires; La Croix; L'Ambe; Temps Présent; L'Art Vivant; La Nef. Mbrships incl: PEN; Comm., Soc. Gens de Lettres; Assn. of Cath. Writers; Artistic & Scientific Press. Hons: Chevalier de la Légion d'honneur; Off., l'Ordre Nat. du Mérité; Archon-Despérouse Prize, 1970. Address: 234 Blvd. Pereire, 75017 Paris, France.

PIERRE, Andrew J., b. 1934, Vienna, Austria. Senior Research Fellow, Council on Foreign Relations; Author. Educ: Ph.D.; C.E.P.; M.I.A.; B.A.; Columbia Univ.; Inst. d'Etudes Pols., Paris; Schl. of Int. Affairs; Amherst Coll. Publs: Nuclear Politics: The British Experience with an Independent Strategic Force, 1939-70, 1972. Contbr. to: Brit. & European Security, 1973; After Czech., 1970; Survival; For. Affairs; The World Today, etc. Mbrships: Int. Inst. for Strategic Studies; Arms Control Assn.; Am. Pol. Sci. Assn.; Int. Studies Assn.; Fedn. of Am. Scis., etc. Address: 697 W. End Ave., Apt. 11E, N.Y., NY 10025, USA.

PIERSON, George Wilson, b. 22 Oct. 1904, NYC, USA. Emeritus Professor of History; Author. Educ: B.A., 1926, Ph.D., 1933, Yale. Publs: Tocqueville & Beaumont in America, 1938, abridged, 1959; Yale College, an Educational History, 1871-1921, 1952; Yale: The University College, 1921-37, 1955; The Education of

American Leaders, 1969; The Moving American, 1973; Gustave de Beaumont: Lettres d'Amérique (co-Ed.), 1973. Contbr. to: Am. Univs. in 19th Century, 1950; histl. & educl. jrnls. Mbrships: Fellow, Am. Acad. Arts & Scis.; Am. Hist. Assn.; Century Assn.; etc. Hons. incl: Dr. Humanities, 1974; other acad. awards. Address: 176 Ives St., Mt. Carmel, CT 06518, USA.

PIEYRE DE MANDIARGUES, André, b. 14 Mar. 1909, Paris, France. Poet; Novelist. Publs. incl: L'Etudiante, 1946; Les Incongruités monumentales, 1948; Les Masques de Léonor Fini, 1951; Astyanax, 1956; Les Monstres de Bomarzo, 1957; Feu de braise, 1959; Sugai, 1960; L'Age de craie, 1961; Sabine, 1964; Beylamour, 1965; Les Corps illuminés, 1965; Larmes de généraux, 1965; La Marge, 1967; Ruisseau des Solitudes, 1968; Le Marronnier, 1968; Mascarets, 1971; Bona l'amour & la peinture, 1971; Le Cadran lunaire, 1972. Hons: Critics Prize, 1951; Prix Goncourt, 1967; Address: 36 rue de Sévigné, Paris 13e, France.

PIHERA, Lawrence James, b. 9 Jan. 1933, Cleveland, Ohio, USA. Advertising Writer. Educ: Univ. of Hawaii; Cooper Schl. of Art. Publ: Making of a Winner, 1972. Contbr. to: Today's Autosports; Rdr.'s Digest; Cappel's Crafts; Dayton USA Mag.; McCall Spirit. Mbrships: Fine Arts Commn.; Fine Arts Assn.; Dayton Advt. Club; Art Ctr., Dayton (Treas.). Hons. incl: 1st Place, Advt. Writing (newspaper), 1970, 1971; 1st Place, Advt. Writing (TV), 1974. Address: 1605 Ambridge Rd., Centerville, Ohio, USA.

PIHLAJAMAA, Heimo Tuomo Elias, b. 10 Feb. 1936, Veteli, Finland. Educ: Lit. studies, Helsinki Univ. Publs: Yksin Tein, 1966; Kafuri, 1968; Talven Ohjelma, 1969; Toukokuu, 1970; Elamaa Lansi-Venajalla, 1971. Contbr. to: Parnasso, Finland; Kentering, Netherlands-Belgium. Mbrships: Finnish Socs. of Authors, Translators, Critics; Finnish PEN Ctr. Recip., Finnish State Prize in Lit., 1969.

PIKE, Edgar Royston, b. Enfield, Middlesex, UK. Author. Publs: Encyclopaedia of Religion & Religions; Human Documents series (Industrial Revolution in Britain, Victorian Golden Age, Age of the Forsytes, Lloyd George Era, Adam Smith's Time); Adam Smith; Mohammed; Republican Rome; Ancient India, Lands of the Bible; Charles Darwin; Finding out about the Babylonians; Britain's Prime Ministers; The World's Strangest Customs. Ed. Exploring the Past series; Pathfinder Biographies; Thinker's Library; Thrift Books; World Digest, 1950-60. Mbrships incl: Esher Local Hist. Soc. (Pres. 1968-). Address: 14 Hinchley Dr., Esher, Surrey, UK.

PILCHER, Rosamunde E., pen name FRASER, Jane, b. 22 Sept. 1924, Lelant, Cornwall, UK. Author. Publs. incl: Sleeping Tiger; On My Own; The End of the Summer; Another View; The Day of the Storm, 1975. Contbr. to: Woman & Home; Woman; Woman's Own. Recip., 2nd Prize, Romantic Novelists Assn., 1970. Agent: Curtis Brown Ltd. Address: Over Pilmore, Invergowrie, Dundee, UK.

PILIKIAN, Hovhanness Israel, pen names GALE, John; PILI, Giovanni; PILL, John, b. 15 Apr. 1942, Nineveh, Iraq. Educ: B.A., Am. Univ., Beirut, Lebanon; Dip., Univ. of Munich, W. Germany. Publs: My Hamlet, 1961; Mahumodo, Prince of Darkness, 1964; The Copy for Mahumodo, 1965; Kabuki or Noh?, 1975. Contbr. to: Drama (quarterly); Ency. Britannica. Address: 20 Norman Court, 395 Nether St., London N3 1QG, UK.

PILINSZKY, János, b. 27 Nov. 1921, Budapest, Hungary. Poet; Writer. Educ: Univ. of Budapest. Publs: Trapéz és korlát, 1946; Harmadnapon, 1959; Nagyvárosi ikonok, 1970; Szálkák, 1972; Grossstadt-Jkonen, 1972; Végkifejlet, 1974. Contbr. to: Új Ember; Élet és irodalom; Kortárs; Les lettres nouvelles; Etudes; Esprit; Merkur; Akzente; Ensemble; Literatur und Kritik; Wort und Wahrheit; etc. Mbrships: Hungarian PEN; Bavarian Acad. of Fine Arts, Munich, Germany, 1973. Hons: Baumgarten Prize, Budapest, 1947; Bourse Gabriel Marcel, Paris, France, 1970; József Attila Prize, Budapest, 1971. Address: Hajós-u.1, 1065 Budapest VI, Hungary.

PILISUK, Marc, b. 19 Jan. 1934, NYC, USA. Professor of Public Health. Educ: B.A., Queens Coll., NYC, 1955; M.A., 1956, Ph.D., 1961, Univ. of Mich; post-doct. trng., Psychol. Clinic, Univ. of Calif., Berkeley, 1972-73. Publs: Ed., The Triple Revolution: Social Problems in Depth (w. R. Perrucci), 1968, 2nd rev. ed., 1971; Ed., Poor Americans: How the White Poor Live (w. Phyllis Pilisuk),

1971; International Conflict & Social Policy, 1972; How We Lost the War on Poverty (w. Phyllis Pilisuk), 1973. Contbr. to profl. jrnls. Hons. incl: Essay Award, Soc. for Psychological Study of Social Issues, 1965. Address: 494 Cragmont Ave., Berkeley, CA, USA.

PILKINGTON, Betty (Alsterlund), b. 9 Mar. 1912, Moline, Ill., USA. Journalist. Educ: A.B., Smith Coll.; Univ. of Mich. Publs. (contbng. author): American Authors (1600-1900), 1938; Twentieth Century Authors, 1942. Contbr. to: This Week; N.Y. Herald Tribune Sunday Mag.; Nation; New Repub.; Christian Sci. Monitor; Commonweal; Insiders' Newsletter; Gemini News Serv., London; Pacifica Radio. Mbrships: UN Correspondents Assn.; For. Press Assn.; Former Mbr., Authors' League. Address: 321 East 45, N.Y., NY 10017, USA.

PILLER, Ernst, b. 20 Feb. 1943, Vienna, Austria. Bank Manager. Educ: Commercial acad.; Dip. & Ph.D., Univ. of World Trade, Vienna. Publs: Kreditgenossenschaften in Österreich — Ihre Dynamik und ihre Stellung im Rahmen des Kreditgewerbes (Co-operative Credit Associations in Austria — Their Dynamics & their Situation in the Austrian Banking System), 1970. Contbr. to: Österreichisches Bank-archiv; fin. columns of most Austrian daily newspapers. Mbrships: Presseclub Concordia; profl. assns. Address: A-1020 Wien 2, Taborstr. 98/18, Austria.

PILLEY, A. Thadé, b. 1909, Paris, France. Conference Interpreter; Language Consultant; Consultant Editor. Educ: M.A., St. John's Coll., Oxford, UK. Publs: Backchat in 4 Languages, 1950; Chit-Chat in French, 1955. Contbr. to: New Linguist (Cons. Ed., 1973-74). Mbrships: Hon. Pres., Polyglot Fedn.; Prin., Linguists' Club; VP, Inst. of Linguists; MLA; Franco-Brit. Soc. Address: 1 Elvaston Mews, London SW7, UK.

PILPEL, Harriet Fleischl, b. 2 Dec. 1911, NY, USA. Lawyer. Educ: B.A., Vassar Coll.; LL.B., J.D., Columbia Law Schl. Publs: Your Marriage & the Law, 1952, 1964; Rights & Writers, (w. Theodora Zavin) 1960; A Copyright Guide, (w. Morton David Goldberg) 1960; Know Your Rights, (w. Minna Post Peyser) 1965. Contbr. to: Publisher's Weekly (co-authors, column 'You Can Do That'); var. mags. on marriage & family law, civil liberties, status of women, etc; Columbia Law Review (Articles Ed.) Address: 70 E. 96th St., N.Y., NY 10028, USA.

PINCHER, (Henry) Chapman, b. 29 Mar. 1914, Ambala, India. Special Writer on Defence & Politics. Educ: B.Sc.; King's Coll., London; Mil. Coll. of Sci. Publs. incl: Breeding of Farm Animals, 1946; Into the Atomic Age, 1947; Evolution, 1950; Not with a Bang, 1965; The Giantkiller, 1967; The Penthouse Conspirators, 1970; Sex in Our Time, 1973; The Skeleton at the Villa Wolkonsky, 1975. Contbr. to: tech. jrnls. Address: Lowerhouse Farm, Ewhurst, Surrey, UK.

PINE, Leslie Gilbert, pen name MOORSHEAD, Henry, b. 22 Dec. 1907, Bristol, UK. Author; Barrister-at-Law. Educ: B.A., London Univ., 1931; Barrister-at-Law, Inner Temple, 1953. Publs. incl: A Guide to Titles, 1959; The Genealogists Encyclopedia, 1969; Princes of Wales, 2nd ed., 1970; The New Extinct Peerage, 1972; The Highland Clans, 1972; The Middle Sea, 1973; Teach Yourself Heraldry & Genealogy, 4th ed., 1974. Contbr. to:(Past Ed.) Burke's Peerage & other biog. ref. books; num. encys., newspapers, mags. & jrnls. Mbrships. incl: F.J.I.; F.R.G.S.; F.R.A.S.; F.S.A.Scotland; F.A.S.; Royal Soc. St. George. Hons. incl: Freeman, City of London; Liveryman of Glaziers' Co. Address: Hall Lodge Cottage, Brettenham, Ipswich, Suffolk IP7 7QP, UK.

PINES, Maya (Mrs. J. N. Froomkin). Journalist; Author. Educ: B.A., M.S., Columbia Univ. Publs: Retarded Children Can Be Helped (w. C. Capa), 1957; Health & Disease (w. R. Dubos), 1965; Revolution in Learning: the Years from Birth to Six, 1967, 1969; The Brain Changers: Scientists & the New Mind Control, 1973, 1974. Contbr. to: Life Mag. (Reporter, 1952-60); Harper's Mag.; N.Y. Times Mag.; McCall's, etc. Mbr., Soc. of Mag. Writers. Address: 4724 32nd St. N.W., Washington, DC 20008, USA.

PINGET, Robert, b. 19 July 1919. Former Barrister & Painter. Publs: Fantoine & Agapa, 1951; Mahu ou le Matériau, 1952 Le Renard & la Boussole, 1955; Graal Flibuste, 1957; Baga, 1958; Le Fiston, 1959; Lettre morte, 1959; Clope au dossier, 1961; L'Inquisitoire, 1962; Quelq'un, 1965; Autour de Mortin, 1965; Le Libera, 1968; La Passacaille, 1969; (plays) La Mnaivelle, 1960; Architruc,

1961; L'hypothèse, 1961; Hons: Critics Prize, 1963; Prix Femina, 1965. Address: 4 rue de l'Université, Paris 7e, France.

PINION, Francis Bertram, b. 4 Dec. 1908, Glinton, Peterborough, UK. University Reader & Administrator; Author & Editor. Educ: M.A., Cambridge Univ.; Dip. Ed., Oxford Univ. Publs: A Hardy Companion, 1968, 2nd ed., 1974; One Rare Fair Woman (w. Evelyn Hardy), 1972; A Jane Austen Companion, 1973; Ed. & contbr., Thomas Hardy & the Modern World, 1974; Ed., Hardy's Two on a Tower, 1975; A Brontë Companion, 1975. Contbr. to: Times Lit. Supplement; Notes & Queries; Review of Engl. Studies. Mbrships: VP, Thomas Hardy Soc. Address: 65 Ranmoor Crescent, Sheffield S10 3GW, UK.

PINKERTON, Marjorie Jean, b. 15 June 1934, Chgo., Ill., USA. Librarian and Instructor in Library Science. Educ: B.A., Carroll Coll., Wis., 1956; M.A., Univ. of Wis., 1964; M.A., Univ. of Mo., 1973. Publs: Outdoor Recreation & Leisure: A Reference Guide & Selected Bibliography (w. J. R. Pinkerton), 1969. Contbr. to: Revista Iberoamericana, (Mexico). Mbrships: ALA; Mo. Lib. Assn.; Mo. Assn. of Schl. Libns.; Beta Phi Mu. Recip., Joycee Wives Outstanding Young Woman of Columbia Award, 1969. Address: 1014 Westport Dr., Columbia, MO 65201, USA.

PINNER, Erna, b. 1896, Frankfort on Main, Germany. Author & Illustrator of Animal Life. Publs: Curious Creatures, 1951; Born Alive, 1959; Unglaublich und doch Wahr, 1964. Contbr. to: Die Weltwoche; Zuerich; Die Tat; Naturwissenschaftliche Rundschau Stuttgart; Radio Cologne. Mbrships: PEN; Ctr. of German-speaking Authors Abroad. Address: 3 Cleve House, 7-9 Cleve Rd., London NW6 3RN, UK.

PIÑON, Nelida, b. 3 May 1936, Rio de Janeiro, Brazil. Writer; Professor of Creative Writing. Educ: Grad., Fac. of Philos., Cath. Univ., Rio de Janeiro. Publs: (novels) Guia-Mapa de Gabriel Arcanjo, 1961; Madeira Feita Cruz, 1963; Fundador, 1969; A Casa da Paixão, 1972; Tebas do meu coração, 1974; (short stories) Tempo das frutas, 1966; Sala do armas, 1973. Contbr. to: Histórias de Amor Maldito; Antologia de Contos Brasileiros de Bichos; Mundo Nuevo, Paris, France; Mundus Artium, USA; Contemporary Latin-Am. Lit., USA; Tri Quarterly, USA; Suplemento Literario do Minas, Brazil; Vozes; etc. Address: Av. Bartolomeu Mitre 33, Apt. 601, Leblon, 20.000 Rio de Janeiro, Brazil.

PINTER, Harold, b. 10 Oct. 1930, London, UK. Playwright. Publs. incl: (plays) The Room, 1957; The Dumb Waiter, 1957; The Birthday Party, 1957; A Slight Ache, 1958; The Caretaker, 1959; Night School, 1960; The Dwarfs, 1961; The Collection, 1962; The Lover, 1962; The Homecoming, 1965; Landscape, 1969; Silence, 1969; Old Times, 1970; Monologue, 1972; (screenplays) The Servant, 1963; The Pumpkin-Eater, 1964; Accident, 1967; A la Recherche du Temps Perdu, 1972; (Dir.) Exiles, 1970; Butley, 1971, film, 1973; & var. TV plays. Hons. incl: C.B.E. Address: 7 Hanover Terrace, London NW11, UK.

PINTO, Jacqueline, pen (maiden) name BLAIRMAN, Jacqueline, b. 16 Sept. 1927. Housewife. Publs: Triplets at Royders, 1950; A Rebel at St. Agatha's 1952; The Headmistress in Disgrace, 1952; Moses Mendelssohn, 1960. Contbr. to: Homes & Gardens, 1954-57 (Sub-Ed.,). Address: 89 Uphill Rd., Mill Hill, London NW7 4QD, UK.

PIONTEK, Heinz, b. 15 Nov.1925. Author. Educ: Theologisch-Philosophische Hochschule, Dillingen, Germany. Publs. incl: (poetry) Die Furt, 1952; Die Rauchfahne, 1953; Wassermarken, 1957; Mit einer Kranichfeder, 1962; Klartext, 1966; (prose) Vor Augen, 1955; Aus meines Herzens Grunde, 1959; John Keats: Poems, 1960; Kastanien aus dem Ferer, 1963; Neue deutsche Erzählgedichte, 1964; Manner die Gedichte machen, 1970; Die Erzählungen, 1971; Deutschegedichte seit 1960, 1972; Helle Tage anderswo, 1973. Mbr., Bavarian Acad. of Fine Arts. Hons. incl: Berlin Prize for Lit., 1957; Rom-Preis, 1960. Address: Dülferstr. 97, 8000 Munich 50, W. Germany.

PIOTROWSKI, Andrzej, b. 30 Nov. 1931, Lwów, USSR. Publisher. Educ: Master's degree in philol., Warsaw Univ. Publs: (verse) Oczy śniegu (Eyes of Snow), 1956; Przerazenia (The Horrors), 1959; Nasze stwarzanie światów (We Are Creating Worlds), 1963; Ballady o obojgu (Ballade about Two of Us), 1965; Zuzanna w Kąpieli (Susanna in the bath), 1967; Do ziemi (Into the Earth), 1969;

Swiadectwa (Testimonies), 1971; (prose) Prósba o Annę (Asking for Anne), 1962; transls. from Czech, Slovak, Russian & Engl. Contbr. to Polish lit. mags. Mbrships. incl: Union of Polish Writers. Recip., Young Authors Award, 1957. Address: ul. Dygasińskiego 14 m.8, 01-603 Warsaw, Poland.

PIRANI, Max, b. 4 Aug. 1898, Melbourne, Aust. Professor of Music; Pianist. Publs: Life of Czerny; Mendelssohn; Bruch; Life of Emanuel Moor. Contbr. to: Can. Press. Mbr. Royal Philharmonic Soc. Hons: R.A.M.; R.C.M. Address: Harting, Petersfield, Hants., UK.

PIRENNE, Maurice Henri Leonard, b. 30 May 1912, Verviers, Belgium. University Lecturer in Physiology; Writer. Educ: M.A., Dr.Sc., Liège Univ.; Max Planck Inst. für Physik, Berlin; Princeton & Columbia Univs.; Sc.D., Cambridge. Publs: The Diffraction of X-Rays & Electrons by Free Molecules, 1946; Vision & the Eye, 2nd ed., 1967, French transl. w. revisions, 1972; Optics, Painting & Photography, 1970, Spanish transl., 1974. Contbr. to: Jrnl. Gen. Physiol.; Jrnl. of Physiol., etc. Mbrships. incl: Soc. Royale des Sci. de Liège, 1972; Fellow, former Phys. Soc. Recip., Prix Walthère, 1937. Address: 75 Blenheim Drive, Oxford, OX2 8DL, UK.

PIRIE, David Tarbat, b. 4 Dec. 1946, W. Pennard, Somerset, UK. Writer. Educ: B.A., Univ. of York; Univ. of London. Publs: Samuel Fuller's Films (co-author), 1969; Rogar Corman: The Millenic Vision (co-author), 1970; A Heritage of Horror: The English Gothic Cinema, 1972. Contbr. to: Time Out; Sight & Sound; Monthly Film Bulletin; Cinema Rising; Oz; Int. Times; Film Jrnl.; Fantastique. Mbr., Nat. Union of Jrnlsts. Address: c/o Time Out, 374 Grays Inn Rd., London WC1 X8BB, UK.

PITFIELD, Thomas Baron, b. 5 Apr. 1903, Bolton, Lancs., UK. Composer. Publs: The Poetry of Trees, 1947; Limusicks, c. 1949; Words Without Songs, 1951; Musicians Notes for Guitarist, 1959; Recording a Region, forthcoming. Contbr. to: The Listener; Country Life; The Countryman; The Artist; Ches. Life; Lancs. Life; Yorks. Life; Musical Times; Musical Opinion; Ch. Music; The Inquirer. Mbr., Composers' Guild of GB. Recip., F.R.M.C.M. Address: 21 East Downs Rd., Bowdon, Altrincham, Ches., UK.

PITTENGER, William Norman, b. 23 July, 1905, Bogota, N.J., USA. Clergyman; Professor of Theology. Educ: S.T.B.; S.T.M.; S.T.D.; D.D. Publs. incl: The Christian Sacrifice, 1951; The Word Incarnate, 1959; Process Thought & Christian Faith, 1968; Time for Consent, 1970; Making Sexuality Human, 1970; The Holy Spirit, 1974; & more than 50 other books. Contbr. to: Expository Times; Church Quarterly Review; Jrnl. Theol. Studies; Brit. Jrnl. Sexual Med.; Encounter; etc. Mbrships: Am. Theol. Soc. (former Pres.); Faith & Order Commn. World Coun. Churches (former Chmn.). Address: King's Coll., Cambridge, UK.

PITTER, Ruth, b. 7 Nov. 1897, Ilford, UK. Poetess. Publs: First Poems, 1920; Persephone in Hades, 1931; A Mad Lady's Garland, 1934; A Trophy of Arms, 1936; The Spirit Watches, 1939; The Rude Potato, 1941; The Bridges, 1945; Pitter on Cats, 1946; Urania, 1951; The Ermine, 1953; Still by Choice, 1966; Poems 1926-66, 1968. Contbr. to: BBC TV Brains Trust; Woman; Punch; etc. Hons: Hawthornden Prize, for A Trophy of Arms, 1937; William Heinemann Award, 1954; Queen's Gold Medal for Poetry, 1955; Companion of Lit., 1974. Address: The Hawthorns, Long Crendon, Aylesbury, Bucks., UK.

PITZ, Henry C., b. 16 June 1895, Phila., Pa., USA. Artist; Writer; Educator. Educ: Grad., Phila. Mus. Schl. of Art & Spring Garden Inst.; D.Litt., Ursinus Coll. Publs. incl: Pen, Brush & Ink, 1949; Ink Drawings Techniques, 1957; Illustrating Children's Books, 1963; The Brandywine Tradition, 1969; Frederic Remington (ed.), 1972; A Plethora of Art — The Creative Life of Howard Pyle, 1975. Contbr. of over 100 articles to US & UK jrnls. & newspapers; Assoc. Ed., Am. Artist (jrnl.), 1942–. Address: 3 Cornelia Place, Chestnut Hill, Phila., PA 19118, USA.

PLAISTED, Thais Margaret (Miss), b. 14 Jan. 1898, San Fran., Calif., USA. Author; Lecturer; Parliamentarian. Educ: A.B., Radcliffe Coll., 1920; A.M., 1930, Grad. study, Univ. of S. Calif. & UCLA, Univ. of Calif. Publs: An Integrated Course in American History: Syllabus, Projects, Map Studies, 1933-35; An Integrated Course in Art Appreciation, 1935; Parliamentary Law Exercises, 1967;

Thomas Jefferson: Parliamentarian, 1974. Contbr. to profl. jrnls. Hons: Hon. Mention, Eugene Field Soc., St. Louis, Mo., 1943; Var. other lit. hons., S. Calif. Woman's Press Club, 1943, 1944, 1956. Address: 701 S. Gramercy Dr. No. 210, L.A.. CA 90005, USA.

PLANCHON, Roger, b. 12 Sept. 1931, Ardèche, France. Theatrical Director; Playwright; Director, National Popular Theatre, France. Publs: (plays) Le Remise, 1961; Pattes blanches, 1964; Bleus, Rouges ou les Libertins, 1967; Dans le Vent, 1968; L'Infâme, 1970; Le Conchon Noir. Recip., Croix de Guerre. Address: Théâtre de la Cité, 8 Place de la Libération, Villeurbanne (Rhône), France.

PLANT, Jack (John Albert Stanley), b. 7 May 1926, Shorncliffe, Folkestone, Kent, UK. Schoolmaster. Educ: Tchrs. Cert., Wymondham Coll., Norfolk; Dip., Schl. Hygiene, Royal Inst. of Pub. Health & Hygiene. Publs: (jvnle. novels) Moppy's Great Adventure, 1956; Spy Trail to Danger, 1962; The League of the Purple Dagger, 1963; (textbooks) Let's Act It, 1958; The Discovery Plays (w. John Anderson), 1961-63; Contbr. to: Storyteller; London Evening News; Bolton Evening News; Singapore Free Press; Home Chat; Utusan Melayu; Mickey Mouse Wkly. Mbrships: Lektor, Brit. Ctr., Stockholm, Sweden, 1955-57; Camp Supvsr., Children's Country Holidays Fund, 1952-65. Address: c/o 76 Greenfield Rd., Folkestone, Kent CT19 6ER, UK.

PLANTE, David, b. 1940, Providence, R.I., USA. Writer; Teacher. Educ: B.A.; Boston Coll.; Univ. of Louvain, Belgium. Publs: The Ghost of Henry James, 1970; Slides, 1971; Relatives, 1972; The Darkness of the Body, 1974; (transl. w. N. Stangos) Argo, by A. Embiricos, 1967. Contbr. to: Transatlantic Review; Penguin Mod. Stories. Mbr., Writer's Action Group. Agent: Deborah Rogers. Address: c/o Deborah Rogers, 29 Goodge St., London W1, UK.

PLATER, Alan, b. 1935, Jarrow-on-Tyne, UK. Full-time Writer, 1961–. Educ: King's Coll., Newcastle; Univ. of Durham. Publs: Close the Coalhouse Door, 1969; And a Little Love Besides, 1973; You & Me — Four Plays, 1973; TV, Radio & Stage Plays; Films. Contbr. to: In A Few Words; Playbill Three; Sunday Times; Tribune; Theatre Choice; New Statesman; Time Out; Poetry mags. Mbr., Writers' Guild of GB. Agent: Margaret Ramsay Ltd. Address: 133 Westbourne Ave., Hull, E. Yorks., UK.

PLATT, Desmond Christopher Martin, b. 1934, Canton, China. University Professor; Writer. Educ: M.A., D.Phil., Oxford. Publs: Finance, Trade & Politics in British Foreign Policy, 1968; The Cinderella Service: British Consuls since 1825, 1971; Latin America & British Trade, 1806-1914, 1972. Contbr. to: Econ. Hist. Review; Past & Present; Pol. Studies; Inter-Am. Econ. Affairs; Jrnl. Latin Am. Studies, etc. Mbrships: Fellow, Royal Histl. Soc.; Fellow, Queens' Coll., Cambridge, & St. Antony's Coll., Oxford; Soc. for Latin Am. Studies (Chmn., 1973-75). Address: 19 Linton Rd., Oxford, UK.

PLATT, Harrison Gray, b. 27 Apr. 1902, Portland, Ore., USA. Editor; Lexicographer. Educ: B.A., Reed Coll., Portland, Ore., 1925; Yale Univ.; M.A., Harvard Univ., 1927. Publs: Current Expressions of Fact & Opinion (w. P. G. Perrin), 1941; Mng. Ed., Dictionary of Military Terms, 1943; Mng. Ed., World Book Encyclopedia Dictionary, 1963; Ed. in Chief, Harcourt Brace Intermediate Dictionary, 1968; Ed. in Chief, Harcourt Brace School Dictionary, 1968, 1972. Contbr. to var. jrnls. & newspapers. Mbrships: Former Mbr., MLA, Miss. Valley Histl. Assn., Geogl. Soc. Address: 160 East 48 St., N.Y., NY 10017, USA.

PLATT, Philip S., b. 26 Nov. 1889, Scranton, Pa., USA. Public Health Administrator & Social Welfare Worker. Educ: B.A., M.A., & Ph.D., Yale Univ., New Haven, Conn.; C.P.H., Harvard Univ.. Cambridge, Mass.; M.P.H., Harvard Schl. of Pub. Hlth. Publs: Health Survey of 86 Cities, (co-author), 1925; The Appraisal Form for Administrative Health Practice, 1927; Voluntary Health Agencies — an interpretive study, 1945; Ed., Madison's (Ct.) Heritage, 1954. Contbr. to: Am. Jrnl. of Pub. Hlth.; Survey Graphic. Mbrships. incl: Fellow, Am. Pub. Hlth. Assn.; Pres. & Hon. Pres., Conn. Soc. for Prevention of Blindness. Recip., Order of King Albert, Belgium. Address: P.O. Box 812, Madison, CT 06433, USA.

PLAUE, Ernst Maximilian, pen names BECK, Maximilian; WITTHAUER, Ernest, b. 25 Apr. 1929,

Vienna, Austria. Journalist. Publs: Ohne Bügelfalte, 1954; Der Mörderkam, alsdie Sonne brannte, 1968. Contbr. to: ORF Radio & TV; Revue; Euromed; var. newspapers & periodicals. Mbrships: Jrnlsts.' Trade Union; Journalisten-Gewerkschaft; Presseclub Concordia; Club der Luftfahrtpublizisten; Chmn., Union of Austrian Criminal Jrnlsts. Address: Elisabeth-Allee 95d, Haus 24, 1130 Wien, Austria.

PLAUT, W. Gunther, b. 1 Nov. 1912, Münster, Germany. Rabbi; Author. Educ: LL.B., 1933, Dr.iuris utr., 1934, Berlin; M.H.L., Rabbi, Cinn., Ohio, USA, 1939. Publs. incl: The Book of Proverbs — A Commentary, 1961; Judaism & the Scientific Spirit, 1962; The Rise of Reform, 1963; The Growth of Reform, 1964; The Case for the Chosen People, 1965; Genesis — a Commentary, 1974. Contbr. to newspapers, mags. & jrnls. inclng: Toronto Globe & Mail (columnist); Commentary; Sci. Forum. Mbr., relig. & civic orgs. Recip., D.D., Cinn., 1964. Address: 1950 Bathurst St., Toronto, Ont. Can.

PLEAT, Susan Ruth, b. 1943, Nottingham, UK. TV Writer. Educ: B.A., St. Anne's Coll., Oxford Univ. Publs: (TV plays) The Wind Blew Her Away, 1970; The Silver Collection, 1971; The Outsider, 1971; I Wouldn't Tell On You, Miss, 1972; Passengers, 1973; Brenda, 1973; The String Tying Machine, 1973; Mary, Mary, 1974. Contbr. to: (TV Drama series) Coronation Street; Kate; Within These Walls; Inigo Pipkin/Pipkins (childrens' educl.). Agent: Mrs. Francis Head. Address: Flat 23, Lapwing Ct., Lapwing Lane, Didsbury, Manchester 20, UK.

PLECHL, Pia Maria, b. 24 Jan. 1933, Baden bei Wien, Austria. Educ: Ph.D., Univ. of Vienna, 1955. Publs: Ein gutes Land, 1966; Kreuz und Äskulap, 1967; Das Marchfeld, 1969; Gott zu ehrn ein vatterrunser pett, 1970; Traumstrassen durch Österreich, 1972; Land der Berge, vol. 1, 1973, vol. 2, 1973, one vol. ed., 1974; Baden, 1974. Contbr. to: Die Presse (Chief Ed.); Anthol. of Lower Austrian Lit. Mbrships: Authors' & Presseclub Concordia; VP, Cath. Jrnlsts'. League, Vienna; Austrian Fedn. of Univ. Women. Hons: Medal of Österreichischer Burgenverein, 1966; Spanish Nat. Prize for For. Essayists, 1967. Address: 1130 Vienna XIII, Stuweckengasse 10, Austria.

PLEYDELL, Susan, b. Kinross-shire, UK. Writer. Educ: L.R.A.M. (Piano), Royal Coll. of Music, London. Publs: Summer Term, 1959; A Festival for Gilbert, 1960; The Glen Varroch Gathering, 1960; Good Red Herring, 1962; A Young Man's Fancy, 1962; Griselda, 1964; The Road to the Harbour, 1965; Jethro's Mill, 1974; Pung of Dragons, 1975. Contbr. of short stories to most maj. mags. in UK & overseas. Address: (Agent), c/o A. M. Heath & Co. Ltd., 40-42 William IV St., London WC2, UK.

PLOMER, William (Charles Franklyn), b. 10 Dec. 1903, Pietersburg, Transvaal, S. Africa. Writer. Publs. incl: (novels) Turbott Wolfe, UK & USA, 1926; The Case is Altered, UK & USA, 1932; Museum Pieces, UK, 1952, USA, 1954; (verse) Notes for Poems, 1927; Selected Poems, 1940; Collected Poems, 1960; Taste & Remember, 1966; Celebrations, 1972; 5 vols. of short stories, 1927-49; 4 plays, w. music by Benjamin Britten; var. autobiogl. works. Mbrships. incl: F.R.S.L.; Poetry Soc., London (Pres., 1968—). Hons: D.Litt., Durham Univ., 1958; Queen's Gold Medal for Poetry, 1963; C.B.E., 1968. Address: c/o Jonathan Cape Ltd., 30 Bedford Square, London WC1, UK.

PLOMLEY, Roy, b. Kingston-upon-Thames, UK. Playwright; Broadcaster. Publs: All Expenses Paid, 1951; Devil's Highway, 1952; Half Seas Over, 1953; Lock, Stock & Barrel (w. A. Swinson), 1957; We'll All Be Millionaires! , 1958; The First Time I Saw Paris; Tax Free (w. A. Menzies), 1960; The Best Hotel in Boulogne, 1961; The Shiny Surface, 1963; Everybody's Making Money Except Shakespeare; Home & Dry, 1964; The Lively Oracles, (w. J. Allegro), 1965; Moonlight Behind You, 1967; You're Welcome to my Wife, (transl'd. from French), 1971; Just Plain Murder, 1972; Murder for Two, (transl'd. from French), 1973; Desert Island Discs, 1975. Contbr. to BBC. Mbrships: Past Chmn., Exec. Comm., Radio & TV Writers Assn.; Past Chmn., Exec. Comm., Radiowriters Assn. Address: 91 Deodar Rd., London, SW15, UK.

PLOTTEL, Jeanine Parisier, b. 21 Sept. 1934, Paris, France. College Professor. Educ: B.A., Barnard Coll., USA; M.A., Ph.D., Columbia Univ. Author, Les Dialogues de Paul Valéry, 1960. Contbr. to: PMLA; French Review; Dada/Surrealism; Books Abroad; Revue Dada Surréalèssme.

Mbrships: MLA; Am. Assn. of Tchrs. of French; Assn. Int. des Etudes Françaises; Syndicat des Jrnlsts. & des Ecrivains. Address: 21 East 79th St., N.Y. NY 10021, USA.

PLOWMAN, Allan William, b. 1915, Barnet, Herts., UK. Editor; Journalist. Educ: M.A., Queen's Coll., Oxford Univ. Publs: Canterbury, 1935; Animated Display, 1959; Display Techniques, 1966. Ed., Glass Age; Wine Correspondent; Catering & Hotel Management; The Freezer Family. Address: Le Chalet, School Close, Cryers Hill, nr. High Wycombe, Bucks., UK.

PLUCKROSE, Henry Arthur, pen name COBBETT, Richard, b. 23 Oct. 1931, London, UK. Teacher; Author; Editor. Publs. incl: Let's Make Pictures; Let's Use the Locality; Churches; Castles; Houses; Cathedrals & Abbeys; Creative Art & Craft; Introducing Acrylic Painting; Introducing Crayon Techniques; Creative Themes; Open School, Open Community; Ed., A Craft Collection; Ed., Art & Craft Today; Ed., Book of Crafts; Ed., Starting Point; Ed., Altogether, 2 vols.; Ed., Art & Craft in Educ., monthly jrnl. Address: 3 Butts Lane, Danbury, Essex, UK.

PLUMMER, Clare Emsley, pen name EMSLEY, Clare, b. 23 Sept. 1912, Coventry, UK. Author. Publs. incl: Painted Clay, 1947; Keep Thy Heart, 1948; The Fatal Gift, 1951; Unjust Recompense, 1953; Flame of Youth, 1957; Call Back Yesterday, 1958; The Long Journey, 1959; Doctor Michael's Bondage, 1962; A Nurse's Sacrifice, 1962; A Surgeon's Folly, 1963; Doctor at the Crossroads, 1966; Nurse Catherine's Marriage, 1967; Sister Rachel's Vigil, 1968; An Island for Doctor Phillipa, 1969; Chris Baynton, SRN, 1971; A Time to Heal, 1972; Highway to Fate, 1973; Strange Marriage, 1974; A Heart's Captivity, forthcoming. Address: 9 King Edward Ave., Worthing, Sussex BN14 8DB, UK.

PLUMMER, Gladys, b. 1891, London, UK. Colonial Education Officer (Retired). Educ: B.A., Univ. Coll., London; London Day Trng. Coll. for Tchrs.; var. Tchr. Trng. Colls.; Tchrs. Dip. Publs: About Your Food, 1940; The Teaching of Domestic Subjects in Africa, 1940; My Bible Story, series of 16, 1963; Stories from the Bible, series of 3, 1964; When Jesus was a Boy, series of 4, 1966; God & One Redhead: Mary Slessor of Calabar (w. Carol Christian), 1970. Recip., O.B.E. Address: 51 Moira Ct., London SW17, UK.

PLUMPP, Sterling D., b. 30 Jan. 1940, Clinton, Miss., USA. College Teacher; Creative Writer. Educ: St. Benedict's Coll., 1960-62; B.A., Roosevelt Univ., 1968. Publs: Portable Soul, 1969; Half Black, Half Blacker, 1970; Black Rituals, 1972; Muslim Men, 1972; Steps to Break the Circle, 1975. Contbr. to: Black World Mag.; Black Books Bulletin. Mbrships: NAACP; Centro Studi e Scrambi Internazionali, Address: 6921 S. Oglesby Ave., Chgo., IL 60649, USA.

POCOCK, Hugh Raymond Spilsbury, b. 18 Sept. 1904, Charlton, Kent, UK. Retired Executive, Petroleum Co. Educ: M.A., Univ. of Oxford. Publs: The Conquest of Chile, 1968; The Memoirs of Lord Contanche, 1975. Contbr. to: Bulletin of the Société Jersiaise; The Field; This England. Address: Les Niémes, St. Peter, Jersey, Channel Islands, UK.

PODHORETZ, Norman, b. 1930, Brooklyn, N.Y., USA. Editor-in-Chief, Commentary Magazine. Educ: Columbia Univ., N.Y.; Jewish Theol. Sem. of Am., N.Y.; Univ. of Cambridge, UK; A.B.; B.A.; B.H.L.; M.A.; L.H.D. Publs: Doings & Undoings; The Fifties & After in American Writing, 1964; Ed., The Commentary Reader, 1966; Making It, 1968. Contbr. to: Commentary, Partisan Review; Scrutiny; New Yorker. Address: c/o Commentary, 165 E. 56th St., N.Y., NY 10022, USA.

POERTNER, Paul, b. 25 Jan. 1925, Elberfeld, Germany. Writer. Educ: Univ. of Cologne. Publs: Wurzelwerk, 1960; Tobias Immergruen, 1963; Scherenschnitt, 1963; Gestern, 1965; Einkreisung, 1968; Umrisse, 1968; Spontanes Theater, 1973; Ed., Experiment-Theater, 1960; Ed., Literatur-Revolution 1910-1925, 1960-62. Mbrships: PEN; German Writers Assn. Recip., 2 lit. prizes. Address: CH-8126 Zumikon, Fadacher 12, Switz.

POETHEN, Johannes, b. 13 Sept. 1928, Wickrath, Nordrhein-Westfalen, Germany. Writer. Publs: (poems) Risse des himmels, 1956; Ankunft und echo, 1961; Im namen der trauer, 1969; Gedichte 1946-1971, 1973.

Contbr. to: Deutsche Zeitung; Stuttgarter Zeitung. Mbrships: PEN; Comm. Mbr., German Writers' Union. Hons: Hugo Jacobi Poetry Prize, 1959; Forderpreis der Stadt Koln, 1962; Forderpreis zum Immermann Preis der Stadt Dusseldorf, 1967. Address: Zur Schillereiche 23, 7000 Stuttgart — 1, W. Germany.

POGUE, Forrest Carlisle, b. 17 Sept. 1912, Eddyville, Ky., USA. Historian. Educ: A.B. Murray State Coll., Ky., 1931; M.A., Univ. of Ky., 1932; Ph.D., Clark Univ., 1939. Publs. incl: The Supreme Command, 1954; George C. Marshall: Education of a General, 1880-1939, 1963; George C. Marshall: Ordeal & Hope, 1939-1942, 1966; George C. Marshall: Organizer of Victory, 1943-45, 1973. Contbr. to var. publs. Mbrships: Am. Histl. Assn.; Soc. of Am. Histns.; Pres., Am. Mil. Inst.; Former Pres., Am. Comm. on the Hist. of the Second World War, Oral Hist. Assn. Recip., D.Litt., Wash. & Lee Univ., 1970; LL.D., Murray State Univ., Ky., 1970. Address: River House, 1111 Army-Navy Drive, Arlington, VA 22202, USA.

POHL, Frederick, b. 26 Nov. 1919, NYC, USA. Writer. Publs: The Space Merchants (w. C. M. Kornbluth), 1953; The Age of the Pussyfoot, 1968; The Gold at the Starbow's End, 1972. Contbr. to: Playboy; Galaxy; Fantasy & Sci. Fiction; If.; etc. Mbrships: Pres., Sci. Fiction Writers of Am., 1974—; Am. Astronautical Soc.; N.Y. Acad. of Scis.; Brit. Interplanetary Soc. Hons: Hugo Awards (Best Ed., 1966, 1967 & 1968; Best Short Story, 1973); Edward E. Smith Mem. Award, 1966. Address: 386 W. Front St., Red Bank, NJ 07701, USA

POINDEXTER, Joseph Boyd, pen name ADAMS, Sam, b. 4 July 1935, NYC, USA. Editor. Educ: A.B., Harvard Univ. Contbr. to: Business Week; N.Y. Times; Dun's Review; Art News. Mbr., N.Y. Financial Writers' Assn. Address: 49 West 75th St., N.Y., NY 10023, USA.

POLACK, Albert Isaac, b. 4 Apr. 1892, Bristol, UK. Schoolteacher. Educ: M.A., Univ. of Cambridge. Publs: Tolerance: Can it be Taught? , 1950; Jesus in the Background of History (w. W. W. Simpson), 1957. Contbr. to: Common Ground. Address: 4 Guthrie Rd., Clifton, Bristol BS8 3EZ, UK.

POLAK, Alfred Laurence, b. 1900, London, UK. Educ: B.A., Birkbeck Coll., Univ. of London. Publs: Legal Fictions, 1945; Second Thoughts, 1951; Puffs, Balloons & Smokeballs, 1955; Late Sittings, 1957. Contbr. to: Justice of the Peace; London Musical Events; Assoc. Ed., Family Law; Engl. Address: 128 Grove End Gdns., London NW8, UK.

POLAND, Dorothy Elizabeth Hayward, pen names FARELY, Alison; HAMMOND, Jane, b. 1937, Barry, UK. Civil Servant. Publs: Crown of Splendour; Devils Royal; The Lion & the Wolf; Last Roar of the Lion; Leopard from Anjou; Throne of Wrath; King Wolf; Kingdom under Tyranny; Last Howl of the Wolf; The Hell Raisers of Wycombe; Fire & the Sword; The Golden Courtesan; Shadow of the Headsman. Address: Horizons, 95 Dock View Rd., Barry, S. Glam. CF6 6PA, UK.

POLANOWSKI, Tadeusz, b. 7 Oct. 1922, Warsaw, Poland. Writer; Research Librarian. Educ: Master in Pol. Sci., Warsaw, 1952; Rsch. Libn. Dip., Bibliotekshögskolan, Sweden, 1974. Publs. incl: num. transls. from German, French, Engl. into Polish; Kolce bez róż, 1955; Taniec wśród fuków, 1957; Wybrałem fry-wolność, 1961; Chodzące klatki, 1964. Contbr. to: Szpilki; Świat; Światowid; Przegląd kulturalny; Wiadomości, London. Mbrships: Polish Writers Union, 1950-70; Swedish Union of Authors, 1972—. Recip., Polish TV Annual Prize for musical serial on old for. folksongs, 1968. Address: Selmedalsvägen 32, 2 tr., 126 55 Hägersten, Sweden.

POLE, Jack Richon, b. 14 Mar. 1922, London, UK. Historian; Vice-Master, Churchill College, Cambridge, 1975. Educ: B.A., Oxford Univ.; Ph.D., Princeton Univ., USA; M.A., Cambridge Univ. Publs: Political Representation in England & the Origins of the American Republic, 1966; Ed. & Introduction, The Advance of Democracy, 1967; Ed., The Revolution in America: Documents of the Internal Development of America in the Era of the Revolution, 1754-1788, 1970; Foundations of American Independence, 1971; Ed., Slavery, Race & Civil War in America, 1975; The Decision for American Independence, 1975; Jefferson Memorial Lecture, Berkeley, Calif., USA, 1971. Contbr. to: Am. Hist. Review; Jrnl. Southern Hist.; etc. Mbrships. incl: Coun. of the Senate, Cambridge Univ., 1970-74; Coun.,

Inst. of Early Am. Hist. & Culture, Williamsburg, Va., USA, 1974-77; Fellow Royal Histl. Soc.; Am. Histl. Assn. Hons. incl: Fellow Histl. Soc. Ghana, 1967; Ramsdell Award, Southern Histl. Assn., 1959. Address: Churchill Coll., Cambridge, UK.

POLEVOI, Boris Nikolaevich, b. 17 Mar. 1908, Moscow, USSR. Journalist; Writer. Educ: Kalinin Ind. Coll. Publs. incl: (in Russian) The Hot Shop, 1939; Blood-stained Stone, 1942; Till Their Last Breath, 1943; We Are Soviet People, 1948; He Came Back, 1949; Gold, 1950; American Diaries, 1956; Far Behind the Lines, 1958; All Men are Brothers, 1960; Meetings on the Cross-roads, 1961; Our Lenin, 1962; On the Wild Shore, 1963; Doctor Vera, 1966; In Great Offensive, 1966; Nuremberg Diaries, 1959. Contbr. to: Pravda; ed., Yunost. Mbrships. incl: USSR Union of Writers; Bd., Union of Soviet Jrnlsts. Hons. incl: Order of Lenin (twice); Gold Medal, World Peace Coun. Address: 13 Begovaya St., Apt. 113, Moscow, USSR.

POLIAKOV, Leon, b. 1910, Leningrad, USSR. Writer. Educ: D. ès L., Sorbonne Univ., Paris, France. Publs: Harvest of Hate, 1956; History of Antisemitism, 3 vols., 1975; The Aryan Myth, 1975. Agent: Anthony Gornall. Address: 35 Ave. Kennedy, 91300 Massy, France.

POLITZER, Heinz, b. 31 Dec. 1910, Vienna, Austria. Professor of German; Author. Educ: German & Engl. Philol., Univs. of Vienna & Prague, 1929-34; Ph.D., Bryn Mawr Coll. Grad. Schl., Univ. of Pa., USA, 1950. Publs. incl: Amerika erzählt (German transl., Am. Anthol.), 1958, 8th ed., 1969; Die gläserne Kathedrale (poems), 1959; Frana Kafka: Parable & Paradox, 1962, 2nd ed., 1966; Franz Grillparzer oder das abgründige Biedermeier, 1972; Hatte Ödipus einen Ödipus-Komplex? Versuche zum Thema Psychoanalyse und Literatur, 1974. Contbr. to num. lang. & lit. jrnls. Mbrships. incl: PEN; MLA; Int. Schnitzler Rsch. Assn. Recip., lit. hons. & medals. Address: Dept. of German, Univ. of Calif., Berkeley, CA 94720, USA.

POLLARD, Hugh Mortimer, b. 1915, Symonstone, UK. Writer; Educator. Educ: M.A., Oxford Univ.; Ph.D., Liverpool Univ. Publs: Pioneers of Popular Education, 1956; (Ed.) Religious Education in Secondary Schools, 1961. Contbr. to: Current Hist.; Manx Museum Jrnl. Prin., St. Martin's Coll., Lancaster since 1963. Address: Pollard Row, Symonstone, Nr. Burnley, Lancs., UK.

POLLARD, John Richard Thornhill, b. 1914, Exeter, UK. Senior Lecturer in Classics. Educ: Univ. Coll., Exeter; Exeter Coll., Oxford; T.D., M.A., B.Litt. Publs: Journey to the Styx; Adventure Begins in Kenya; Africa for Adventure, African Zooman; Wolves & Werewolves, 1964; Helen of Troy, 1965; The Long Safari, 1967; Seers, Shrines & Sirens, 1965; The Aeneid translated C. Day Lewis, Appreciation, 1969. Contbr. to: Horace The Minstrel; Bonavia-Hunt; Ency. Britannica; Oxford Class Dict.; Times; Field; Ibis; E.A. Standard; etc.; Gilbert Harding, by his Friends. Mbrships: F.Z.S.; M.C.C. Address: Chiffchaffs, Hwfa Rd., Bangor, Caernarvonshire, UK.

POLLEY, Judith Anne, pen names LUELLEN, Valentina; HAGAR, Judith; Kent, Helen, b. 15 Sept. 1938, London, UK. Writer. Publs. incl: The Flowering Desert, 1970; Madelon, 1970; A Man for Melanie, 1970; The King's Cavalier, 1971; Dangerous Deception, 1972; Castle of the Mist, 1972; The Secret of Val Verde, 1974; The King's Shadow, 1975. Contbr. to: Womans' Realm; Fleetway Paperbacks; Pan. Mbr., Romantic Novelists' Assn. Address: Stoke Cottage, Wolverton, Nr. Basingstoke, Hants., UK.

POLLINGER, Gerald John, b. 1925, New Malden, Surrey, UK. Authors' Agent & Company Director, Pearn, Pollinger, & Higham Ltd.; Director, Laurence Pollinger Ltd. Educ: Univ. of Southampton. Publs. (w. William Green): The Aircraft of the World; The World's Fighting Places; The Observer's Book of Aircraft; The Scottie Book of Model Railways; Model Railways as a Pastime; Famous Aircraft of the World; Strange but Flew. Contbr. to: Aviation Book Reviewer; Air Pictorial. Address: c/o Laurence Pollinger Ltd.

POLLINS, Harold, b. 1924, London, UK. University Lecturer; Writer. Educ: B.Sc., London Schl. of Econs. Publs: Social Change in South-West Wales (co-author), 1954; Britain's Railways: an Industrial History, 1971; Trade Unions in Great Britain (co-author), 1973. Contbr. to: Economica; Econ. Hist. Review; Jewish Jrnl. Sociol.; E. London Papers; Colliery Engrng.; Race. Mbrships: Soc. Indl. Tutors; Assn. Univ. Tchrs. Address: 4 Court Close, Kidlington, Oxford, UK.

POLLOCK, (Rev.) John Charles, b. 1923, London, UK. Clergyman; Writer. Educ: M.A., Trinity Coll., Cambridge; Ridley Hall, Cambridge. Pubs. incl: A Cambridge Movement, 1953; Earth's Remotest End, 1960; Hudston Taylor & Maria, 1962; Moody Without Sankey, 1963; The Keswick Story, 1964; The Christians from Siberia, 1964; Billy Graham, 1966; revised ed., 1969; The Apostle, 1969; A Foreign Devil in China, USA 1971, UK 1972; George Whitefield & the Great Awakening, US 1972, UK 1973; Wilberforce, 1975. Contbr. to: Churchman; C. of E. Newspaper; Christianity Today; Sunday Telegraph. Mbr., Engl. Speaking Union. Agent: Curtis Brown Ltd. Address: Rose Ash House, South Molton, Devon, UK.

POLNER, Zoltan, b. 24 Jan. 1933, Szeged, Hungary. Journalist. Educ: Cert. Tchr.; D.Phil. Pubs: Szigorú vallomás (Severe Statement), 1962; A szívetekre bízom (I Entrust it to your Hearts), 1966; Egyetlen hangszer (Single Instrument), 1971. Contbr. to Where is Vietnam? American Poets, 1969. Mbr., Assn. of Hungarian Writers. Recip., Lit. Prize, City of Szeged, 1971. Address: 6721 Szeged, Szücs u 17, Hungary.

POLO LOPEZ-BERDEAL, Carlos, b. 24 Oct. 1905, Mondoñado, Spain. Navy Chaplain. Educ: Sem., St. Catalina, Mondoñada. Pubs: El Gran Idiota (3-act comedy), 1955; Las Sieta Palabras, 1958; Galicia, En sus Hombres de Hoy, 1971. Contbr. to: Hoja del Lunes, Vigo; Derrotas. Mbrships: Soc. Gen. de Autores de España; Ateneo de Madrid; Fndr., Spanish Assn. of Writers on Tourism; V.P., Asociacion Española de Humanologia; Hon., Vigo Press. Address: Calle Padre Jesus Ordoñez 5 dpdo., Madrid 2, Spain.

POLSON, Cyril John, b. 1901, Wolverhampton, Staffs., UK. Emeritus Professor of Forensic Medicine. Educ: M.D., Univ. of Birmingham; Barrister-at-Law, Inner Temple. Pubs: The Disposal of the Dead, 3rd ed.; Essentials of Forensic Medicine, 3rd ed.; Clinical Toxicology (co-author), 2nd ed.; The Scientific Aspects of Forensic Medicine. Mbrships: F.R.C.P.; F.R.C.Path.; Pres., Brit. Acad. of Forensic Scis., 1974-75; Pres., Brit. Assn. in Forensic Med., 1963-65; Authors' Club. Address: 16 Tewit Well Rd., Harrogate, Yorks., UK.

POLVIANDER, Anni Kyllikki, pen names POLVA, Anni; HEINO, Kyllikki, b. 6 Jan. 1915, Raivola, Finland. Pubs: over 30 novels & num. books for girls aged 10-14, inclng. Tiina series, 1955-74. Mbr., Finnish Authors' Soc. Address: Kurjenkaivonkenttä 5A12, SF-20500 Turku 50, Finland.

POMADA, Elizabeth Lucy, b. 12 June 1940. Literary Agent; Writer; Reviewer. Educ: B.S., Cornell Univ., 1962. Pubs: California Publicity Outlets, 1972; Places to Go with Children in Northern California, 1973. Contbr. to: San. Fran. Chronicle; Calif. Living; Am. Artist; McCall's; Mankind; San. Fran.; etc. Address: 1029 Jones, San. Fran., CA 94109, USA.

POMERANS, Arnold Julius, b. 27 Apr. 1920, S. Africa. Translator. Educ: B.Sc. Pubs: 124 transls. inclng. Heisenberg, de Broglie, Taton, Rostand, Piaget, Huizinga, Geyl. Clavelin, Slijper, Rosendorfer & Coh-Bendit. Mbr., Soc. of Authors. Address: Battle House, Polstead Heath, Colchester, Essex, UK.

POMIANOWSKI, Jerzy, b. 13 Jan. 1921, Lodz, Poland. Writer; University Professor of Polish Literature; Translator; Screenplay Writer. Educ: M.D., Univ. of Moscow, USSR, 1947. Pubs: Z Widowni (essays), 4 vols., 1953-63; Koniec i poczatek (novel), 1955, 4th ed. 1962; Babel, 1973; Guida alla moderna letteratura polacca, 1973; Benia der König (play), 1974. Contbr. to: Wórczość; Nowa Kultura; Dialog; Les Temps Modernes; La Fiera Letteraria; Settanta; Literatura. Mbrships: Polish Br., PEN; Polish Writers' Union; Past Pres., Polish Br., Union Mondial des Écrivains-Medicins. Hons: Nat. Award of Poland, 1955; First Prize, Polish Min. of Culture & the Arts, 1962. Address: Via Annia Faustina 1, 00153 Rome, Italy.

POMOGÁTS, Béla, b. 22 Oct. 1934, Budapest, Hungary. Research worker, literary science. Educ: M.A., Univ. of Budapest. Pubs: Kuncz Aladár, 1968; Déry Tibor, 1974. Contbr. to: Literatura; Irodalomtörtenet; Kortárs; Jelenkor; Magyar Mühely (Paris). Mbr., Union of Hungarian Writers. Address: Budapest 1065, Nagymezo utca 28, Hungary.

POND, Grace Isabelle, b. 20 May 1910, St. John's Wood, London, UK. Educ: Pitman's Coll. Writer on Cats. Pubs: The Observer's Book of Cats, 1959; Cats, 1962; Cat Lovers' Diary; The Perfect Cat Owner, 1966; The Complete Cat Guide, 1968; The Long-Haired Cats, 1968; Batsford Book of Cats, 1969; Cats, 1970; Champion Cats of the World, 1972; The Complete Cat Encyclopaedia, 1972; The Cat Lover's Bedside Book, 1974; The Long-haired Cat (w. M. Calder), 1974. Contbr. to: The Treasury of Cats, 1972; Cats & Cat Care, 1973; Our Cats; Fur & Feather; Sunday Times. Mbrships: Fellow, Zoological Soc.; Hon. Organizer, Nat. Cat Club Show; Int. Cat Club. Address: Barbeeches, Buchan Hill, Crawley, Sussex, UK.

POND, Thomas William, b. 1927, London, UK. Editor; Publisher; Writer. Pubs: The Hamster Handbook, 4th ed.; The Golden Hamster; International Directory of Translators & Interpreters, 1967. Contbr. to: Middlesex Times; Automation; All Pets, etc. Address: 5 Norbreck Parade, N. Circular Rd., London NW10 7HR, UK.

PONIATOWSKA, Elena, b. 19 May 1933, Paris, France. Journalist; Author. Pubs: Lilus Kikus, 1954; Meles y Teleo, 1956; El Retiro, 1957; Palabras Cruzadas, 1961; Todo Empezo el Domingo, 1963; Los Cuentos de Lilus Kikus, 1967; La Jornada, 1968; Hasta no Verte Jesus Mio, 1969; La Noche de Tlatelolco, 1970. Contbr. to: Antologia de Cuentistas Mexicanos; Diez Cuentos Mexicanos Contemporaneos; Rojo de Vida y Negro de Muerte; Novedades; Siempre; Nivel; Plural; Dialogos; etc. Mbr., var. profl. orgs. Hons. incl: Turismo Frances Prize, 1965; Mazatlan Prize, 1970; Villaurrutia Prize, 1970; Periodistico Prize, 1973. Address: Cerrada del Pedregal No. 79, Coyoacan, ZP 21 Mexico D.F., Mexico.

PONSONBY, D(oris) A(lmon), pen names RYBOT, Doris, TEMPEST, Sarah, b. 23 Mar. 1907, Devonport, UK. Writer. Educ: Shrewsbury H.S.; Villabelle, Neuchâtel, Switz. Pubs, incl: (as Doris Rybot) (fiction): Romany Sister, 1960; A Japanese Doll, 1961; (non-fiction): My Kingdom for a Donkey, 1963; A Donkey & a Dandelion, 1966; It Began Before Noah, 1972; (as D. A. Ponsonby) (fiction): Family of Jaspard, 1950; Bells Along the Neva, 1964; The Forgotten Heir, 1969; The Heart in the Sand, 1970; Flight from Hanover Square, 1972; The Gamester's Daughter, 1974; (non fiction): The Lost Duchess, 1958; A Prisoner in Regent's Park, 1961. Mbrships: W. Country Writers' Assn., Life, London Lib. Address: c/o Curtis Brown Ltd.

POOLE, Gray Johnson, pen name GRAY, Betsy, b. 26 Sept. 1906, Phila., Pa., USA. Writer. Educ: Johns Hopkins Univ., Balt., Md., 3 yrs. Pubs. incl: Weird & Wonderful Ants (w. husband Lynn Poole), USA 1961, UK, 1963; Insect Eating Plants, 1963; Electronics in Medicine, 1964; One Passion, Two Loves, USA, 1966, UK, 1967; Men Who Pioneered Inventions, 1969; Architects & Man's Skyline, 1972; Nuts from Forest, Orchard & Field, 1974; num. for. lang. eds. of works. Contbr. to: Ency. Britannica; Nation's Bus.; Look; etc. Mbrships. incl: Calif. Writers Guild (VP, 1975); PEN. Recip., Robert E. Sherwood Award (TV documentary), 1956. Address: 1417 Amherst Ave., L.A., CA 90025, USA.

POOLE, Josephine, b 1933, London, UK. Writer. Pubs: A Dream in the House, 1961; Moon Eyes, 1965; 1967; The Lilywhite Boys, 1968; Catch as Catch Can, UK 1969, USA 1970; Yokeham, 1970; Billy Buck, UK & USA 1972. Contbr. to Miscellany Five. Mbrships: Soc. of Authors; PEN. Agent: A. P. Watt & Son. Address: Poundisford Lodge, Poundisford, Taunton, Somerset, UK.

POOLEY, Robert C., b. 25 Mar. 1898, Brooklyn, N.Y., USA. Emeritus Professor of English. Educ: B.A., M.A., Univ. of N. Colo.; Ph.D., Univ. of Wis. Pubs: Teaching English Usage, 1946, 2nd ed., 1974; Teaching English in Wisconsin, 1948; Teaching English Grammar, 1957; (ed.-in-chief) America Reads series. Contbr. to: Engl. Jrnl.; Elem. Engl.; Am. Speech; Coll. Engl.; Lit. & Life, series. Mbrships: Wis. Engl. Coun., (pres., 1938); Nat. Coun. of Teachers of Engl., (pres., 1941); Nat. Conf. on Rsch. in Engl., (pres., 1938). Hons: W. Wilbur Hatfield Award, 1950; Award of Merit, Wis. Coun. of Teachers of Engl. Address: 1580 Arcadia Dr., Jacksonville, FL 32207, USA.

POP, Simion, b. 25 Sept. 1930, Varaiu, Romania. Writer; Journalist. Educ: Stefan Gheorghiu Acad. of Soc. Pol. Scis.; Schl. of Lit., Bucharest. Pubs. incl: Paralela 45, book I, 1958, book II, 1970; Triunghiul, 1964, 2nd ed., 1967; Criza de timp, 1969; Nord, 1971; The Marry Cemetry, 1972; Marsul Alb, 1974. Contbr. to: Romania Literara; Marginales Review (Brussels); Introduction to

Romanian Lit. (USA); Jugend der Welt; etc. Mbrships. incl: PEN; F.I.J.E.T.; Romanian Writers' Union; Romanian Jrnlsts'. Union; Int. Tourism Agcy., Monte Carlo. Hons. incl: Romanian Acad. Prize, 1958; Writers' Union Prize, 1967. Address: 8 D. Onciul St., Bucharest 3, Romania.

POPA, Marian, b. 15 Sept. 1938, Bucharest, Romania. Professor of Comparative Literature. Educ: Univ. doctorate. Publs: Homo Fictus, 1968; Modele si Exemple, 1971; Dictionar de Literatura Romana Contemporana, 1971; camil Ptrescu, 1972; Calatorii — Le Epocii Romantice, 1972; Forma ca Deformare, 1974; Comicology, 1975. Contbr. to: Luceafarul; Saptamina; etc. Mbr., Writers' Union of Romania. Address: VI, str. Carol Davila 59, Bucharest, Romania.

POPE, Arthie Walling, b. 27 Apr. 1930, Crockett, Tex., USA. Teacher; Counsellor. Educ: B.A., Stephen F. Austin State Univ., Nocogdachoes, Tex., 1970; M.A., Inst. Technológica de Estudios Superiores, Monterrey, Mexico, 1974. Contbr. to newspapers & jrnls. inclng: S. & W.; But an Echo; Bapt. Standard; Quitaque Post; The Helper; Focus. Mbrships. incl: Poetry Soc. of Tex. Recip., sev. prizes for short stories & poems. Address: 3605 South St., Nocogtoches, TX 75961, USA.

POPE, Dudley Bernard Egerton, b. 29 Dec. 1925, Ashford, Kent, UK. Naval Historian; Author; Former Journalist. Publs: (naval hist.) Flag 4, 1954; The Battle of the River Plate, 1956; 73 North, 1958; England Expects, 1960; At 12 Mr. Byng Was Shot, 1962; The Black Ship, 1963; Guns, 1965; The Great Gamble, 1972; (fiction) Ramage, 1965; Ramage & the Drum Beat, 1967; Ramage & the Freebooters, 1968; Governor Ramage R.N., 1973; Ramage's Prize, 1974. Mbrships: Soc. for Nautical Rsch.; Navy Record Soc.; Royal Ocean Racing Club; Royal Temple Yacht Club; Ocean Cruising Club. Address: Yacht Ramage, c/o Peter Janson-Smith Ltd., 31 Newington Green, London N16 9PU, UK.

POPE-HENNESSY, (Sir) John Wyndham, b. 1913, London, UK. Writer; Dir., Victoria & Albert Museum, London, 1967-73. Educ: Balliol Coll., Oxford. Publs. incl: Sassetta, 1939; Sienese Quattrocento Painting, 1947; Nicholas Hilliard, 1949; paolo Uccello, 1950; Fra Angelico, 1952; Italian Gothic Sculpture, 1955; Italian Renaissance Sculpture, 1958; Italian High Renaissance & Baroque Sculpture, 1963; The Portrait in the Renaissance, 1967; Essays on Italian Sculpture, 1968; Raphael, (Wrightsman Lectures), 1970. Contbr. to: Burlington Mag. Recip., C.B.E. Address: 41 Bedford Gdns., London W8, UK.

POPESCU, Christine, pen name PULLEIN-THOMPSON, Christine, b. 1 Oct. 1930, Wimbledon, Surrey, UK. Author. Publs: 50 books for children since 1948 incl: We Hunted Hounds; Ride by Night; The First Rosette; For Want of a Saddle; The Phantom Horse Series; The Eastmans Move House; Nigel Eats his Words; Robbers in the Night; Dog in a Pram; A Day to Remember; Good Riding; (anthols. & collects.) A Pony Scrap Book; The Christine Pullein-Thompson Book of Pony Stories (forthcoming). Mbrships: Authors' Soc.; Bix Parish (Councillor). Address: Highfield, Middle Assendon, Henley-on-Thames, Oxon., UK.

POPESCU, Julian John Hunter, pen name HUNTER, John, b. 4 July 1928, Oxford, UK. BBC Senior Monitor. Educ: B.Com., Univ. of London; Dip.Ed., Univ. of Reading. Publs: An Elementary Italian Grammar, 1961; The Danube, 1961; The Volga, 1962; The Po, 1962; Let's Visit the USSR, 1967; Italian for Commerce, 1968; Let's Visit Yugoslavia, 1968; Let's Visit Rumania, 1969; Let's Visit Czechoslovakia, 1970; Read About France, 1970. Contbr. to Oxford Jr. Ency. Mbrships: Phyllis Ct. Club, Henley-on-Thames; Assn. of Broadcasting Staff. Address: Highfield, Middle Assenden, Henley-on-Thames, Oxon., UK.

POPHAM, Hugh, b. 1920, Seaton, Devon, UK. Writer. Educ: B.A., Corpus Christi Coll., Cambridge. Publs: Against the Lightning, 1944; The Journey & the Dream, 1945; To the Unborn — Greetings, 1946; Beyond the Eagle's Rage, 1951; Sea Flight, 1954; Cape of Storms, 1957; Monsters & Marlinspikes, 1959; The Sea Beggars, 1961; The Shores of Violence, 1963; The House at Cane Garden, 1966; Gentleman Peasants, 1968; The Somerset Light Infantry, 1968; Into Wind, 1969; The Dorset Regiment, 1970. Contbr. to: Blackwoods; Yachts & Yachting. Mbrships: Soc. of Authors; PEN. Address: Thatchways, Nutbourne, Chichester, Sussex, UK.

POPMA, Murk Albrecht Johan, b. 31 Mar. 1940, Apeldoorn, Netherlands. Librarian; Poet. Publs: Buitenstaander, 1966; Klaagliederen, 1971; Het naakte bestaan, 1974. Address: De Pauwentuin 8, Amstelveen, Netherlands.

POPOV, Vassil, b. 29 July, 1930, Mindya, Bulgaria. Writer. Publs: (in Bulgarian) Short Stories, 1959; The Small Mine, 1962; The Man & the Earth, 1962; The Roots, 1967; A Hero's Time, 1968; The Beautiful Mankind, 1971; Times Eternal, 1973. Contbr. to: September; PlamAk; Suvremennik; Literatouren Front. Mbr. Union of Bulgarian Writers. Recip. Reward of Cyril & Methodiy — I degree, 1974. Address: Sofia, bul. Hristo Botev, 15, Bulgaria.

POPPER, (Sir) Karl Raimund, b. 28 July 1902, Vienna, Austria. Writer; Professor Emeritus, London Univ. Educ: Ph.D., Vienna Univ. Publs. incl: Logik der Forschung, 1934, 5th ed., 1973; The Open Society & Its Enemies, 1945, 11th ed. 1974; The Poverty of Historicism, 1957, 8th ed. 1974; The Logic of Scientific Discovery, 1959, 7th ed. 1974; Conjectures & Refutations, 1963, 5th ed., 1974; Objective Knowledge, 1972, 3rd. ed., 1974; The Philosophy of Karl Popper, Library of Living Philosophers, ed. P.A. Schilpp, 1974; Publs. in 16 langs. Contbr. to num. acad. jrnls. Mbrships incl: F.B.A.; Corres., Inst. de France; Hon. For. Mbr., Am. Acad. Arts & Scis.; Int. Acad. for the Philos. of Sci.; Hon. Fellow, London Schl. of Econs.; Hon. Mbr., R.S.N.Z. Hons. incl: Kthood, 1965. Address: Fallowfield, Manor Rd., Penn, Bucks., UK.

PÖRN, Gustav Ingmar, b. 19 Aug. 1935, Korsholm, Finland. University Lecturer in Philosophy. Educ: Fil. mag., 1960, Fil. lic. 1964, Åbo Acad.; studies at Oxford Univ., UK, 1961-62; Ph.D., Univ. of Birmingham, 1968. Publs: The Logic of Power, 1970; Elements of Social Analysis, 1971. Contbr. to philosl. jrnls. Address: Dept. of Philosophy, Univ. of Birmingham, P.O. Box 363, Edgbaston, Birmingham B15 2TT, UK.

PORTAL, Marta, b. 10 Aug. 1930, Nava, Spain. Journalist; Writer. Educ: Lic., Info. Scis. (Jrnlsm.). Publs: (novels) A tientas y a ciegas, 1966; El Malmuerto, 1967; A ras de las sombras, 1968; Ladridos a la luna, 1970; El buen camino, 1974; (essay) El Maíz: grano sagrado de America, 1970; (short stories) La veintena, 1972; (forthcoming) Proceso narrativo de la revolución mexicana. Contbr. to: ABC (daily newsmag.); Pyresa Cuadernos Hispano-americanos. Mbrships: Off. Register of Jrnlsts. Assn. of Spanish Writers & Artists. Hons: Planeta Prize, 1966; March Fndn. Schlrships. for study, 1968, rsch. for forthcoming book, 1971; Fellow, Inst. of Hispanic Culture, 1973. Address: Calle Claudio Coello 69-B, Madrid 1, Spain.

PORTEOUS, Leslie Crichton, b. 22 May 1901, Leeds, UK. Author; Journalist. Publs: Farmer's Creed, 1938; Teamsman, 1939; Land Truant; The Cottage, 1941; Changing Valley, 1950; Derbyshire, 1950; Chuckling Joe, 1954; Peakland, 1954; Lucky Columbell, 1959; The Beauty & Mystery of Well-Dressing, 1959; Toad Hole, 1960; Richard Jeffries, 1965. Contbr. to: Manchester Guardian; Rdr's. Digest, Farmers Wkly.; Countryman. Address: Two Dales, Matlock, Derbys., UK.

PORTEOUS, Norman Walker, b. 1898, Haddington, UK. University Professor of Hebrew & Semitic Languages; College Principal; Author. Educ: M.A., B.D., Edinburgh Univ.; M.A., Oxford; D.D., St. Andrew's; Univs. of Berlin, Tübingen & Münster, Germany. Publs: Das Alte Testament: Daniel, 1965; Living the Mystery, collected essays, 1967. Contbr. to: Record & Revelation; Old Testament & Mod. Study; Peake's Commentary on the Bible. Address: 3 Hermitage Gdns., Edinburgh EH10 6DL, UK.

PORTER, David John, b. 16 Apr. 1948, Lowestoft, Suffolk, UK. Writer; Director, Children's Theatre Company. Educ: New Coll. of Speech & Drama, London; D.D.A. (London); L.R.A.M. (Speech & Drama); A.D.B. Plays: Fifty Minutes, 1965; Cages for Laughter, 1968; The Flower, 1969; Saint Rosa, I Die, 1969; Your Moods, 1970; The Beach Map, 1970; Her Majesty's Seaweed, 1971; Voyage Next Door, 1972; A Mortlake Pageant, 1972. Contbr. to: Phoenix; Pervarsity; Outlook. Mbrships: Soc. of Authors; League of Dramatists; Vivid Children's Theatre; Brit. Children's Theatre Assn. Recip., Husson Mem. Prize for Creative Writing, London, 1970. Address: Kolme, Irex Rd., Pakefield, Lowestoft, Suffolk, UK.

PORTER, Enid, b. 1910, Westcliff-on-Sea, Essex, UK. Curator, Folk Museum. Educ: B.A., Univ. Coll., London;

Cavendish Square Trng. Coll., London. Publs: Ed., Tales from the Fens, 1963; Sixty Years a Fenman; Fenland Railwayman; Fenland Memories; Cambridgeshire Customs & Folklore, 1969; Folklore of East Anglia, 1974. Contbr. to: Folk Life: Folklore; Countryman; E. Anglian Mag.; Cambs., Peterborough & Hunts. Life. Mbrships: Folklore Soc.; Folk Life Studies. Address: Museum Cottage, Northampton St., Cambridge, UK.

PORTER, Hal, b. 16 Feb. 1911, Albert Park, Melbourne, Australia. Author. Publs. incl: Elijah's Ravens, 1968; The Actors: An Image of the New Japan, 1968; Eden House, 1969; Mr. Butterfly & Other Tales of New Japan, 1970; Selected Stories, 1971; The Right Thing, 1971; It Could Be You (ed.), 1972; Fredo Fuss Love Life, 1974; In An Australian Country Graveyard, 1974; The Extra, 1974. Contbr. to var. mags. Hons. incl: 6 C'wlth. Lit. Fund Fellowships, 1956-76; Ency. Britannica Award, 1967; Adelaide Advertiser Lit. Competitions, 1964, 1966, 1968; Sydney Jrnlsts. Club, 1963, 1964. Address: "Glen Avon", Garvoc, Vic., Australia 3265.

PORTER, Joshua Roy, b. 7 May 1921, Godley, Cheshire, UK. Clerk in Holy Orders; University Professor of Theology. Educ: B.A., M.A., Merton Coll., Oxford. Publs: World in the Heart, 1944; Moses & Monarchy, 1963; The Extended Family in the Old Testament, 1967; Ed.& Contbr., Proclamation & Presence, 1970; Contbr., Promise & Fulfilment, 1963; Source Book of the Bible for Teachers, 1970; Tradition & Interpretation, 1975. Contbr. to var. theol. jrnls. Mbrships: Comm., Soc. for Old Testament Study; Soc. for Biblical Lit.; Assn. of Brit. Orientalists. Address: Queen's Building, Univ. of Exeter, Exeter, Devon, UK.

PORTER, Joyce, b. 1924, Marple, Cheshire, UK. Former WRAF Officer; Author. Educ: B.A., Univ. of London. Publs. incl: Dover One, 1964; Dover Two, 1965; Dover Three, 1965; Sour Cream with Everything, 1966; Dover & the Unkindest Cut of All, 1967; The Chinks in the Curtain, 1967; Rather A Common Sort of Crime, 1970; Dover Strikes Again, 1970; Only with a Bargepole, 1971; A Meddler & Her Murder, 1972; It's Murder with Dover, 1973. Contbr. to: The Writer; Ellery Queen's Mystery Mag. Mbrships: Crime Writers' Assn.; Mystery Writers of Am. Agent: Curtis Brown Ltd. Address: 68 Sand St., Longbridge Deverill, Nr. Warminster, Wilts., UK.

PORTER, Katherine Anne, b. 15 May 1890, Indian Creek, Tex., USA. Writer. Publs: (short stories) Flowering Judas, 1930; The Leaning Tower, 1944; Collected Stories, 1965; (essays) The Days Before, 1952; Collected Essays, 1970; (other publs.) Pale Horse, Pale Rider, 1939; Ship of Fools, 1962; A Christmas Story, 1968; Noon Wine; (transl.) French Song Book, 1933; The Itching Parrot (from Spanish), 1942. Mbrships: Nat. Inst. of Arts & Letters, N.Y.; Nat. Acad. of Arts & Letters. Hons. incl: D.Litt.; Emerson-Thoreau Medal; Pulitzer Prize, 1966. Address: Apts. 1517-1518, 6100 Westchester Park Dr., Coll. Park, MD 20740, USA.

PORTWAY, Christopher John, b. 30 Oct. 1923, Halstead, Essex, UK. Travel & Fiction Writer. Publs: Journey to Dana, 1955; Forbidden Frontier, 1962; The Pregnant Unicorn, 1969; Corner Seat, 1972; Double Circuit, 1974; All Exits Barred, 1971; Lost Vengeance, 1973; The Tirana Assignment, 1974. Contbr. to: Daily Telegraph; Daily Express; Sunday Times; Times; Guardian; Jewish Chronicle; Country Life; Geogl. Mag.; Blackwoods Mag.; Railway Mag.; Trains & Railways; Railway World; etc. Mbrships: Inst. of Jrnlsts.; Guild of Travel Writers; E. Anglian Writers; Globetrotters Club; World Expeditionary Assn. Address: Jasan, White Ash Green, Halstead, Essex CO9 1PD, UK.

POSNANSKY, Merrick, b. 8 Mar. 1931, Bolton, UK. Professor of Archaeology; Author. Educ: B.A.; Ph.D.; Dip. in Prehistoric Archaeol.; Univ. of Nottingham; Peterhouse, Cambridge. Publs: The Nile Quest, 1962; Prelude to East African History, 1966; Twilight Tales of the Black Baganda by Mrs. Fisher (Ed., new ed. w. introduction), 1971. Contbr. to: Archaeol.; Uganda Jrnl. (Ed., 1962-66); Man; Azania. Mbrships. incl: Museums Assn. of Middle Africa (Fndr. Pres., 1959-61); Museums Assn. of Tropical Africa (VP, 1961-64); Prehistoric Soc.; Uganda Soc. (Pres., 1964); Ghana Mus. & Monuments Bd. (com., 1967-73); Ghana Histl. Soc., 1968-72; Ed. Bd., W. African Jrnl. Archaeol. Recip., acad. awards. Address: Univ. of Ghana, P.O. Box 3, Legon, Ghana.

POSNER, Ernst, b. 9 Aug. 1892, Berlin, Germany. Archivist; Historian. Educ: Ph.D., Univ. of Berlin, 1920. Publs: American State Archives, 1964; Archives & the Public Interest, 1967; Archives in the Ancient World, 1972. Contbr. to: Am. Archivist; Am. Histl. Review; Indian Archives; Historische Zeitschrift. Mbrships: Am. Histl. Assn.; Am. Assn. for State & Local Hist.; Soc. of Am. Archivists, (Pres., 1955-56). Hons: Waldo G. Leland Prize, 1965,-1973; Award of Distinction, Am. Assn. for State & Local Hist., 1963. Address: Am. Kalchrain, CH 6315 Oberägeri, Switz.

POSNER, Michael Vivian, b. 1931, London, UK. Economic Adviser, Department of Energy. Educ: M.A., Balliol Coll., Oxford Univ. Publs: Italian Public Enterprise (w. S. J. Woolf), 1966; Fuel Policy, 1973. Contbr. to: Managed Econ.; Unfashionable Econs. Hons: Visiting Prof., USA, 1957-58; Fellow, Pembroke Coll., Cambridge Univ., 1960-. Address: Okyamie, Bulmer, York YO6 7BL, UK.

POSTER, Cyril Dennis, b. 5 Sept. 1924, London, UK. Educationist; Author. Educ: B.A., M.A., Cambridge Univ; Postgrad. & Adv. Certs. in Educ., London Univ. Publs: Read, Write, Speak, 1964; Times & Seasons, 1966; The School & the Community, 1970. Contbr. to: Headship in the 1970s (symposium, Ed. Bryan Allen), 1969; New Soc.; Where. Address: Parsonage Farmhouse, Parsonage Chase, Minster, Sheppey, Kent, UK.

POSTHUMUS, Cyril, b. 1918, Sunbury, UK. Motoring Journalist. Publs: Miniature Car Construction; How to build a Scale-Model Monoposto Alfa Romeo; (co-author) The Racing Car Development & Design; Sir Henry Segrave; The British Competition Car; The Land Speed Record; The German Grand Prix; World Sports Car Championship; Vintage Cars. Contbr. to: Ency. of the Automobile (Italy); On Four Wheels; Motor; Road & Track (USA); Ed., Motor Racing, 1967-69; Ed., Autoworld, 1967-70. Mbrships: Inst. of Jrnlsts.; Inst. of Adv. Motorists; Guild of Motoring Writers. Address: 35 Stane Way, Ewell, Surrey KT17 1PN, UK.

POTOK, Chaim, b. 17 Feb. 1929, NYC, USA. Writer. Educ: B.A., Yeshiva Univ., 1950; M.H.L., Jewish Theol. Seminary, 1954; Ph.D., Univ. of Pa., 1965. Publs: The Chosen, 1967; The Promise, 1969; My Name is Asher Lev, 1972. Contbr. to: Commentary; Saturday Review; N.Y. Times Book Review; Special Projects Ed., Jewish Publ. Soc. of Am. Mbr., PEN. Address: 1528 Walnut St., Phila., PA 19102, USA.

POTTER, Denis Christopher George, b. 17 May 1935. Playwright; Journalist. Educ: B.A., New Coll., Oxford. Publs: (plays) The Glittering Coffin, 1960; The Changing Forest, 1962; The Nigel Barton Plays, 1968; Son of Man, 1970; (novel) Hide & Seek, 1973; (TV plays) Stand Up Nigel Barton; Where the Buffalo Roam; A Beast with Two Backs; Paper Roses; Casanova; Follow the Yellow Brick Road; Only Make Believe. Contbr. to: Sun, 1964; Daily Herald, BBC. Address: Morecambe Lodge, Duxmere, Ross on Wye, Herefordshire, UK.

POTTER, George Richard, b. 6 Aug. 1900, Norwich, UK. Retired Professor of Medieval History. Educ: M.A. & Ph.D., Univ. of Cambridge. Publs: Sir Thomas More, 1925; Autobiography of Ousâme, 1931; Short History of Switzerland, 1955. Contbr. to: Engl. Histl. Review; Hist. Today; Bulletin of John Rylands Lib.; Hist.; Cambridge Medieval Hist. Mbrships: F.S.A.; Fellow, Royal Histl. Soc.; Past Pres., Histl. Assn. Hons. incl: Cultural Attaché, Brit. Embassy, Bonn, W. Germany, 1955-57. Address: Herongate, Derwent Lane, Hathersage, Sheffield, S30 1AS, UK.

POTTER, Jeremy, b. 1922, London, UK. Publisher; Novelist. Educ: M.A., Queen's Coll., Oxford. Publs: Hazard Chase, 1964; Death in Office, 1965; Foul Play, 1967; The Dance of Death, 1968; A Trail of Blood, 1970; Going West, 1972; Disgrace & Favour, 1975. Address: c/o Constable & Co., 10 Orange St., London WC2, UK.

POTTER, Margaret, pen names NEWMAN, Margaret; BETTERIDGE, Anne, b. 21 June 1926, London, UK. Writer. Educ: M.A., St. Hugh's Coll., Oxford Univ. Publs. incl: (as Anne Betteridge) The Foreign Girl, 1960; Return to Delphi, 1964; The Truth Game, 1966; Shooting Star, 1968; Sirocco, 1970; The Girl Outside, 1971; Journey From a Foreign Land, 1972; The Sacrifice, 1973; A Time of Their Lives, 1974; The Stranger on the Beach, 1974; (juvenile, as Margaret Potter) Sandy's Safari, 1971; The

Story of the Stolen Necklace, 1974; Trouble on Sunday, 1974. Contbr. to var. jrnls. & mags. Recip., Major Award Romantic Novelists' Assn., 1967. Address: c/o Hurst & Blackett, 3 Fitzroy Square, London, UK.

POTTER, Simeon, b. 1898, London, UK. Professor of English (Retired). Educ: Univ. of London; Oxford Univ.; M.A., B.Litt., Ph.D. Publs: Everyday English; An English Vocabulary; An English Grammar; The Outlook in English Studies; Our Language; Cheshire Place-Names; Modern Linguistics; Language in the Modern World; Changing English. Contbr. to: Jt. Ed., The Language Library; Anglia; Mod. Språk; Medium Aevum; Mod. Lang. Review; Review of Engl. Studies; Times Lit. Supplement; etc. Mbrships: Hon. Fellow, Inst. of Linguists; F.R.S.L. Address: Maze Cottage, Hampton Court Rd., East Molesey, Surrey KT8 9BY, UK.

POUCHER, William Arthur, b. 22 Nov. 1891, Horncastle, Lincs., UK. Consulting Chemist, ret'd.; Author. Educ: London Univ. Publs: Perfumes, Cosmetics & Soaps, 3 vols., 1923, 8th ed., 1974; 13 Art Books on the British hills, 1940-50; 8 Art Books on Britain, Ireland & the Dolomites, 1943-63; 4 Pictorial Guides to the Lake District, Wales, Scotland & the Pennines, 1960-66, num. eds. Contbr. to: sev. art books; Country Life; Photographic Jrnl.; mountaineering jrnls. Mbrships: Fellow, Royal Photographic Soc.; Fellow, Pharmaceutical Soc. Recip., Gold Medal Award, Am. Socs. Cosmetic Chems., 1954. Address: 4 Heathfield, Reigate Heath, Surrey, UK.

POULET, Georges, b. 1902, Chenee, Belgium. University Professor. Educ: St. Servais Coll.; Univ. of Liège; Ph.D.; D.Litt.; LL.D. Publs: Etudes sur le Temps humain; La Distance interieure; Les Metamorphoses du Cercle; La Conscience critique, 1972. Mbrships. incl: Am. Acad. of Arts & Scis.; Royal Acad. of Belgium. Recip., Hon. Docts., Univs. of Edinburgh, Geneva & Nice. Address: Villa Orangini, Ave. Brancolar 119, Nice, France.

POULSEN, Ezra James, b. 26 Dec. 1889, Paris, Idaho, USA. Educator; Writer; Publisher. Educ: Utah State Agric. Coll. Ext.; A.B., 1917, Grad. Study, Brigham Young Univ. & Univ. of Utah. Publs. incl: Songs for the Toilers, 1922; Birthright (novel), 1950; Almira Cozzens Rich, 1954; James Poulsen — A Faithful Dane; Robert Price; A Star Has Fallen & Other Poems; Behold, The Sun Rises (novel), 1972. Contbr. to num. jrnls. & mags. Mbrships: Int. Inst. of Arts & Letters; Utah Acad. of Arts & Scis.; Utah Poetry Soc., Inc. Address: 587 First Ave., Salt Lake City, UT, USA.

POULTER, Scott Larry, pen name POULTER, S. L., b. 27 Oct. 1943, Peoria, Ill., USA. Publisher; Editor; Poet. Educ: Currently studying at Univ. of Wis. Publs: The Glass Partition, 1972; Distant Thunder, 1974; A Collection of Time, 1975. Contbr. to: Fine Arts Review; Choice; Poetry Venture; Quartet; Hawk & Whippoorwill Recalled; The Lyric; Grande Ronde Review; & num. others. Mbrships incl: Poetry Soc. of Am.; Haiku Soc. of Am.; IMPACT; Wis. Fellowship of Poets; Wis. Regional Writers Assn. Hons. incl: Awards, Jade Ring Poetry Competitions, 1971, 1973, 1974; Competition Awards, Wis. Regional Writers Assn., 1971, 1973; 250 Dollar Award, Wis. Coun. for Writers; Trophy Award, Wis. Fellowship of Poets, 1974. Address: 1527 W. Mitchell St., Milwaukee, WI 53204, USA.

POUND, John Pickman, b. 5 Jan. 1916, Edinburgh, UK. Research Engineer. Educ: St. Martins Schl.; Allhallows Schl. Publs: Practical R. F. Heating for the Wood Industry, 1957; Radio Frequency Heating in the Timber Industry, 1973. Contbr., over 250 articles to profl. jrnls. Address: 133 Thornton Rd., Cambridge CB3 0NE, UK.

POWELL, Anthony Dymoke b. 21 Dec. 1905, London, UK. Writer. Educ: Balliol Coll., Oxford. Publs. incl: Venusberg, 1932; From a View to a Death, 1933; John Aubrey & His Friends, 1948; A Buyer's Market, 1952; The Acceptance World, 1955; At Lady Molly's, 1957; Casanova's Chinese Restaurant, 1960; The Kindly Ones, 1962; The Soldier's Art, 1966; Books Do Furnish a Room, 1971; Temporary Kings, 1973; (plays) The Garden God, 1971; The Rest I'll Whistle, 1971. Hons. incl: Croix de Guerre; James Tait Black Mem. Prize; D.Litt. Address: The Chantry, Nr. Frome, Somerset, UK.

POWELL, Caryll Nicolas Peter, b. 1920, Johannesburg, S. Africa. Author. Educ: M.A., Peterhouse, Cambridge. Publs: The Hills Remain; The Drawings of Henry Fuseli; From Baroque to Rococo; Fuseli's Nightmare, 1973; The Sacred Spring, 1974. Contbr. to: Burlington Mag.; The

Listener. F.R.S.L. Recip., D.S.O. Agent: David Higham Assoc. Ltd. Address: c/o British Council, 10 Spring Gdns., London SW1A 2BN, UK.

POWELL, Dilys, b. 20 July, 1901, Bridgnorth, UK. Film Critic. Educ: B.A., Somerville Coll., Oxford. Publs: Descent from Parnassus, 1934; Remember Greece, 1941; The Traveller's Journey is Done, 1943; An Affair of the Heart, 1957; The Villa Ariadne, 1973. Contbr. to: Sunday Times. Mbrships: F.R.S.L. Recip., C.B.E., 1974. Address: 14 Albion St. London W2 2AS, UK.

POWELL, (Rev.) Gordon, b. 1911, Warrnambool, Aust. Clergyman; Writer. Educ: Melbourne Univ.; Glasgow Univ.; M.A.; B.D. Publs: Two Steps to Tokyo, 1945; Personal Peace & Power, 1949; Happiness is a Habit, 1954; The Blessing of Belief, 1956; The Secret of Serenity, 1959; Freedom from Fear, 1960; New Solutions to Difficult Sayings of Jesus, 1962; Surprise Treasure, 1965. Contbr. to: Communion Messages; Reader's Digest. Address: Quaker Hill, Pawling, N.Y. NY 12564, USA.

POWELL, (Rev.) Ivor, b. 1910, Crosskeys, UK. Official Evangelist, Baptist Union. Publs: We Saw It Happen; Black Radiance; Silent Challenge; Broad Horizons; God's Little Ones; Theology; Bible Cameos; Bible Pinnacles; Bible Treasures; Bible Windows; Bible Highways; This I Believe; John's Wonderful Gospel; Luke's Thrilling Gospel; The Rising of the Son; Don't Lose That Fish. Recip., D.D., Trinity Coll., Dunedin, Fla., 1972. Address: 612 Surf View Dr., Santa Barbara, CA 93109, USA.

POWELL, Lester, b. 14 June 1912, London, UK. Author. Educ: St. Andrew's Coll., Dublin. Publs: A Count of Six, 1948; Shadow Play, 1949; Spot the Lady, 1950; Still of Night, 1952; The Black Casket, 1953; The Big M, 1973. Contbr. to radio & TV in UK, Am., Can., Germany, Italy, etc. Mbrships: Writers' Guild GB (former Reg. Chmn.). Address: 6 Oxford St., Dartmouth, Devon, UK.

POWELL, Neil, b. 11 Feb. 1948, London, UK. Teacher. Educ: B.A. (Engl. & Am. Lit), 1969; postgrad. rsch. in Engl. poetry, 1969–71, M.Phil., 1974, Univ. of Warwick. Publs: Henry V: A Commentary, 1973; Suffolk Poems, 1975. Contbr. to: New Statesman; Encounter; Critical Quarterly; Outposts; Phoenix; Poetry Review; Univs. Poetry; The Use of Engl.; Workshop New Poetry; etc. Mbr., Soc. of Authors. Recip., Eric Gregory Award for poetry, 1969. Address: 15 The Town, Great Staughton, Huntingdon, Cambs. PE19 4BB, UK.

POWELL, Violet Georgiana, b. 13 Mar. 1912, London, UK. Journalist; Writer. Publs: Five Out of Six (autobiog.) 1960; A Substantial Ghost; The Literary Adventures of Maude ffoulkes, 1967; The Irish Cousins; The Books & Background of Somerville & Ross, 1970; A Compton-Burnett Compendium, 1973. Contbr. to: Times; Sunday Times; Evening Standard; Punch; The Queen. Address: The Chantry, nr. Frome, Somerset, UK.

POWELL-FROISSARD, Lily, b. 10 Sept. 1925, Berlin, Germany. Writer; Editor; Translator. Publs: The Bird of Paradise, 1970; Co-Ed., The Horseman's Dictionary of International Reference (w. husband, Jean Froissard). Contbr. to: Light Horse; Riding; Dressage; The Chronicle of the Horse; etc. Recip., James Tait Black Mem. Prize for Best Novel of 1970. Address: 23 Rue de Vaugirard, Paris VI, France.

POWELL-SMITH, Vincent, pen names JUSTICIAR; ELPHINSTONE, Francis; SANTA MARIA, b. 28 Apr. 1939, Westerham, Kent, UK. University Lecturer; Management Consultant; Editorial Adviser. Educ: Birmingham Univ.; Inns of Ct. Schl. of Law; Int. Fac. Comp. Law, Luxembourg; LL.M.; D.Litt.; LL.B.; Dip. Com. Publs. incl: Case Books on Land Law, 1968, Industrial Law, 1969 (w. R. S. Sim); Casebook on Contract, 1972; The Building Regulations Explained & Illustrated (w. W. S. Whyte), 1973; Questions & Answers on the Safety & Health At Work Act, 2 eds., 1974; Law of Boundaries and Fences, 1975; Questions & Answers on the New Employment Law, 1975; books on heraldry. Contbr. to: Law Students' Annual & Mng. Ed. Ency. of Bldg. Law & Controls (Former Ed.); & Var. jrnls. Mbrships incl: F.R.S.A.; F.F.B. Recip., Grand Prix Humanitaire de France, 1970. Agent: Hope, Leresch & Steele. Address: Links Edge, 2 Bankart Ave., Leicester LE2 2DB, UK.

POWER, (Marie) Elaine, b. 8 Nov. 1931, Auckland, NZ. Bird & Animal Artist. Publs: Small Birds of the New

Zealand Bush, 1970; Waders in New Zealand, 1971; New Zealand Water Birds, 1973. Mbrships: Ornithol. Soc. of NZ; Royal Forest & Bird Protection Soc. of NZ Inc.; Auckland Inst. & Mus.; Soc. of Wildlife Artists of Australasia. Address: 18 Lake View Rd., Takapuna, Auckland, NZ.

POWER, Patrick C., b. 14 May 1928, Dungarvan, Waterford, Repub. of Ireland. Teacher & Lecturer. Educ: B.A., M.A., Ph.D., Univ. Coll., Galway; Tchrs. Trng. Cert. & Dip., Irish Christian Brothers Trng. Schls. Publs: The Story of Anglo-Irish Poetry, 1967; A Literary History of Ireland, 1969; Transl. & Ed., Brian Merriman, The Midnight Court, 1971; Transl., Flann O'Brien, The Poor North, 1973; Book of Irish Curses, 1974. Contbr. to: Dublin Mag.; Irish Times. Mbr., Taisce (Irish Conserv. Soc.). Address: Ballyneale, Carrick-on-Suir, Co. Tipperary, Repub. of Ireland.

POWERS, Edwin, b. 19 Feb. 1896, NYC, USA. Teacher; Researcher. Educ: A.B., Williams Coll., 1919; LL.B., N.Y. Law Schl., 1924; M.A., Dartmouth Coll., 1930. Publs: A Report on the Development of Penological Treatment at Norfolk Prison Colony in Massachusetts (w. Commons & Yahkub), 1940; An Experiment in the Prevention of Delinquency, (w. Helen Witmer), 1951; The Basic Structure of the Administration of Criminal Justice in Massachusetts, 1955, 6th ed., 1973; Crime & Punishment in Early Massachusetts: A Documentary History, 1966. Contbr. to var. profl. publs. Mbr., var. profl. assns. Address: 17 Andrina Rd., W. Yarmouth, MA 02673, USA.

POWERS, J(ames) F(arl), b. 8 July 1917, Jacksonville, Ill., USA. Writer. Educ: Northwestern Univ., Chgo., 1938-40. Publs: Prince of Darkness & Other Stories, USA, 1947, UK, 1948; The Presence of Grace (short stories), USA & UK, 1956; Morte d'Urban (novel), USA & UK, 1962. Mbr., Nat. Inst. Arts & Letters. Hons: Grant, Nat. Inst. Arts & Letters, 1948; Guggenheim Fellowship, 1948; Rockefeller Fellowship, 1954, 1957, 1967; Nat. Book Award, 1963. Address: c/o Doubleday & Co., 277 Park Ave., N.Y., NY 10017, USA.

POWICKE, Michael Rhys, b. 2 Oct. 1920, Manchester, UK. Professor of History. Educ: M.A., Oxford Univ., UK. Publs: Military Obligation in Medieval England, 1962; The Community of the Realm, 1972. Contbr. to: Speculum; Am. Histl. Review. Mbrships: Royal Histl. Soc.; Medieval Acad. of Am. Address: 145 Briar Hill Ave., Toronto M4R 1H8, Ont., Can.

POYNTER, John Riddoch, b. 13 Nov. 1929, Coleraine, Aust. Professor of History. Educ: M.A., Magdalen Coll., Oxford; Ph.D., Univ. of Melbourne. Publs: Russell Grimwade, 1967; Society & Pauperism: English Ideas on Poor Relief 1795-1834, 1969; Alfred Felton, 1974. Contbr. to: Histl. Studies. Mbrships: Fellow, Acad. of Social Sci. in Aust.; Fellow, Aust. Acad. of the Humanities. Dpty. Vice-Chancellor (Rsch.) Univ. of Melbourne, 1975—. Address: 4 Manningtree Rd., Hawthorn, Vic., Australia 3122.

POZO FERNANDEZ, Fortunato, pen name OZOP, b. 2 Apr. 1906, Villalobos de Campos, Spain. Police Commissioner. Educ: Dipl., Criminal Rsch. & Forensic Toxicol., Schl. of Legal Med., Univ. of Madrid; studies at Spec. Tech. Schl. Publ: Manual de Vigilancia de Caza y Pesca, 1960, 3rd ed., 1972. Contbr. to: Investigación; Policia; Estudios penitenciarios; Asst. Ed. & Owner, Funcionarias. Mbrships: Soc. of Authors of Spain; Assn. of Spanish Writers & Artists. Address: Calle Navas de Tolosa 5, 1º, Madrid 13, Spain.

PRACHT-FITZELL, Ilse Johanna, Elfriede, b. 2 June 1926, Cologne, Germany. Writer. Educ: Univ. of Cologne, 1947-50; Rutgers Univ. Grad. Schl., 1959-61. Publs: Gedichte, eine Auswahl, 1973. Contbr. to: (in USA) Lyrica Germanica; Lyrik und Prosa; German-American Studies; (in W. Germany) Das Boot; Pages; Das Pult; (Austria) Heilbronner Stimme (w. Germany); Oldenburger Hefte; Unio; Das Literarische Wort. Mbrships: Assn. of German Lang. Authors, Ohio, USA; Literarische Union; Interessengemeinschaft deutschsprachiger Autoren, W. Germany. Address: 46 Ridgeview Rd., Jamesburg, NJ 08831, USA.

PRAGER, Theodor, b. 17 May 1917, Vienna, Austria. Economist. Educ: B.Com., 1939, Ph.D., 1943, Univ. of London, UK. Publs: There's Work for All (w. Michael Young), 1945; Märchen und Wahrheit von der Wirtschaft, 1953; Wirtschaftswunder oder keines? 1963; Konkurrenz und Konvergenz, 1972; Schwerpunkte und Tendenzen der britischen Wirtschaftsforschung, 1974; Zwischen London und Moskau, 1974. Contbr. to var. jrnls. in Austria, UK, USA & Italy. Hons: Sir Henry Premchand Book Prize, London, UK, 1939; Award, Theodor Körner Inst., Vienna, Austria, 1962; Overseas Fellow, Churchill Coll., Cambridge, UK, 1973. Address: 1100 Vienna, Vivaldi-Gasse 3, Austria.

PRATER, Douglas Clifford Rouse, b. 19 July 1917, London, UK. School Headmaster. Educ: Worcester Coll. of Educ. Publs: Look at your Atlas, Book 1, 1966, Book 2, 1969; Look at your Bible Old Testament, 1973; Look at your Bible New Testament, 1973. Contbr. to: Times Educl. Supplement. Mbrships: Pres., St. Albans Br., Nat. Assn. of Hd. Tchrs., 1973-74. Address: Crantock, 11 Newberries Ave., Radlett, Herts, UK.

PRATOLINI, Vasco, b. 19 Oct. 1913. Writer. Publs: Via de' Magazzini, 1942; Cronaca familiare, 1947; Cronache di poveri amanti, 1947; Le ragazza di San Frediano, 1950; Metello, 1955; Lo Scialo, 1960; La constanza della ragione, 1963; Allegoria e Derisione, 1966. Hons: Lugano Prize, 1947; Viareggio Prize, 1955; Feltrinelli Prize, 1957; Marzotto Prize, 1963. Address: Via Tolmino 12, Rome, Italy.

PRATT, John, pen name WINTON, John, b. 1931, Hampstead, London, UK. Lt. Commander R.N. (retired). Educ: St. Paul's Schl., London; Royal Naval Coll., Dartmouth; Royal Naval Engrs. Coll., Plymouth. Publs: We Joined the Navy, 1959; We Saw the Sea, 1960; Down the Hatch, 1961; Never Go To Sea, 1963; All the Nice Girls, 1964; H.M.S. Leviathan, 1967; The Forgotten Fleet, 1970; Freedom's Battle; The War at Sea 1939-45, 1967. Contbr. to: Cheshire Life; Liverpool Daily Post. Mbr., Soc. of Authors & PEN. Address: c/o The Chartered Bank, 2 Regent St., London SW1, UK.

PRATT, John Clark, b. 19 Aug. 1932, St. Albans, Vt., USA. Professor of English. Educ: B.A., Univ. of Calif., Berkeley; M.A., Columbia Univ.; Ph.D., Princeton Univ. Publs: The Meaning of Modern Poetry, 1962; John Steinbeck, 1970; Ed., Ken Kesey, One Flew Over the Cuckoo's Nest, 1973; The Laotian Fragments, 1974. Contbr. to: Hemingway in our Times, 1974; Northwest Review; Denver Post. Mbrships. incl: The Coffee House, NYC; MLA. Recip., Fulbright Sr. Fellowship, Univ. of Lisbon, 1974. Address: Dept. of English, Colorado State Univ., Fort Collins, CO 80521, USA.

PRATT, Mildred Claire, b. 18 Mar. 1921, Toronto, Ont., Can. Artist. Educ: B.A., Victoria Coll., Univ. of Toronto, 1944; Int. Studies, Columbia Univ., USA, 1944-45. Publs: Haiku, 1965; The Silent Ancestors, 1971. Contbr. to: Families; Can. Forum; Fiddlehead; Haiku Mag.; Am. Haiku; Haiku Highlights; Haiku W. Mbrships: Can. Soc. of Graphic Art; Can. Soc. of Painter-Etchers & Engravers; Ont. Geneal. Soc. Address: 5 Elm Ave., Apt. 7, Toronto M4W 1N1, Ont., Can.

PRATT, Thursa A., b. Henrietta, Ky., USA. Retired Cosmetology Teacher. Educ: Univ. of Cinn.; W.Va. Wesleyan Coll.; Moler System of Colls. Contbr. to: Am. Poets Fellowship League; Sea to Sea in Song; Poet Int. Monthly; Am. Poets Fellowship; Prairie Poet; United Poets; Oakhill Press; Echoes of W.Va. Poetry; La. P.S. Anthol.; Ky. P.S. Anthol.; Willowsong; Andrews: Adventurers; Poets' Crossroads; Cinn. Times-Star; Strophes; Del. Valley Rose Newsletter; Am. Poetry League Anthol.; & others. Mbrships. incl: Chancellor, Nat. Fed. of State Poetry Socs., 1974; Pres., W.Va. Poetry Soc., 1971-75; Acad. Am. Poets; Tex., La. & Ky. State Poetry Socs. Address: 1625 Oak St., Parkersburg, WV 26101, USA.

PRAZ, Mario, b. Rome, Italy. Emeritus Professor of English Language & Literature. Educ: Litt.D., Dr. Jur., Univs. of Rome & Florence. Publs: Unromantic Spain; The Romantic Agony; Storia della Letteratura inglese; The Flaming Heart; The House of Life; Conversation Pieces; The Hero in Eclipse in Victorian Fiction; An Illustrated History of Furnishing; On Neoclassicism; Mnemosyne. Contbr. to: London Mercury; Criterion; Engl. Studies; Corriere della Sera; La Stampa; Il Tempo; Il Giornale; Critique; L'Arc; Art News; Southern Review; other lit. jrnls. Mbrships: Socio Nazionale Academia dei Lincei; PEN. Hons: K.B.E.; Litt.D. degrees, Univs. of Cambridge, UK, Paris Sorbonne & Aix-Marseille, France. Address: Via Zanardelli 1, Rome 00186, Italy.

PREBBLE, John Edward Curtis, b. 1915, Edmonton, UK. Writer. Publs. incl: Where the Sea Breaks, 1944; The

Edge of Darkness, 1948; Age Without Pity, 1950; The Mather Story, 1954; The Brute Streets, 1954; The High Girders, 1956; My Great-Aunt Appearing Day, 1958; The Buffalo Soldiers, 1959; Culloden, 1961; The Highland Clearances, 1963; Glencoe, 1966; The Darien Disaster, 1968; The Lion in the North, 1971; Spanish Stirrup, 1973; Mutiny: Highland Regiments in Revolt, 1975. Contbr. to: var. newspapers & jrnls. Mbrships: F.R.S.L.; PEN; Soc. of Authors; Writers' Guild. Agent: Curtis Brown. Address: Shaw Coign, Alcocks La., Burgh Heath, Tadworth, Surrey, UK.

PREDA, Marin, b. 5 Aug. 1922, Silistea Nova, Romania. Writer. Publs: Encounter in the fields, 1948; The Moromets, 1955; The Wastrels, 1962; The Intruder, 1967; Impossible Return, 1972; The Great Recluse, 1973; The Delirium, 1975. Mbrships: Romanian Writers' Union (VP); Romanian Acad. (Corres. mbr.). Hons: Labour Order 1st Class; Star of R.S.R., 2nd Class; Cultural Merit, 1st Class. Address: Dr. Herescu 4, Bucarest, Romania.

PRESCOTT, Dorothea Mildred, b. London, UK. Writer; Editor. Educ: B.A., London Univ. Publs: series of 14 books for the School Assembly; Stories of Peter the Fisherman; Zacchaeus; Noah & His Ark; The Two Little Houses; Jesus & the Four Kind Friends; Ten Little Silver Coins; New Old Bible Stories, 1946; New Idea for Tony, 1948; Tony's Gang on Holiday, 1950; David the Dauntless, 1952; A New Day (Compiler). Mbrships: Zonta Club of London; Brit. Fedn. of Univ. Women. Address: c/o The Blandford Press, Link House, West St., Poole, Dorset BH15 1LL, UK.

PRESCOTT, Frederick, b. 11 Aug. 1904, London, UK. Physician. Educ: King's Coll., London; Middlesex Hosp. Med. Schl., London; M.Sc.; Ph.D.; F.R.I.C.; M.R.C.P. Publs: Modern Chemistry, 1932; Organic Chemistry, 1938; Intermediate Chemistry, 1940; Vitamins in Medicine, 1942; Control of Pain, 1964; Anti-Microbial Agents in Medicine, 1974. Contbr. to med. jrnls. inclng: Brit. Med. Jrnl.; Lancet; Jrnl. of Am. Med. Assn. Mbrships: incl: F.R.S.M.; BMA: Brit. Pharmacol. Soc. Address: Coombe Ridge, Churt, Farnham, Surrey GU10 2LQ, UK.

PRESCOTT, H(ilda) F(rances) M(argaret), b. 22 Feb. 1896, Latchford, Cheshire, UK. Writer. Educ: B.A., Lady Margaret Hall, Oxford Univ.; M.A., Manchester Univ. Publs incl: (novels) The Unhurrying Chase, UK & USA, 1925; Son of Dust, UK, 1932, USA, 1956; Dead & Not Buried, UK & USA, 1938; The Man on a Donkey: A Chronicle, UK, 2 vols., 1952; USA, 1952; (non-fiction) Spanish Tudor UK & USA, 1940, revised ed. 1953; Friar Felix at Large, USA, 1950 (as Jerusalem Journey, UK, 1954); Once to Sinai, UK, 1957, USA, 1958. Mbrship: F.R.S.L. Hons: Black Mem. Prize, 1941; Christopher Medal, 1953; D.Litt., Durham Univ., 1957. Address: Orchard Piece, Charlbury, Oxon., UK.

PRESLEY, James, b. 13 Jan. 1930, Nash, Tex., USA. Writer. Educ: B.A., E. Tex. Univ., 1950; M.A., Univ. of Tex., 1955; grad. work, Univ. of Ams., 1955, Univ. of Tex., 1956-58. Publs: Center of the Storm; Memoirs of John T. Scopes (w. John T. Scopes), 1967; Please, Doctor, Do Something! (w. Joe D. Nichols), 1972; Vitamin B6; The Doctor's Report (w. John M. Ellis), 1973; Public Defender (w. Gerald W. Getty), 1974; Human Life Styling (w. John C. McCamy), 1975. Contbr. to: N.Y. Times Mag.; Tex. Observer (contbng. Ed.). Recip., Anson Jones Award for Excellence in Med. Writing, 1971. Address: Route 6, Box 415, Texarkana, TX 75501, USA.

PRESS, John Bryant, b. 11 Jan. 1920, Norwich, UK. British Council Officer. Educ: M.A., Corpus Christi Coll., Cambridge. Publs: The Fire & the Fountain, 1955; Uncertainties, 1956; The Chequer'd Shade, 1957; Guy Fawkes Night, 1958; Rule & Energy, 1963; A Map of Modern English Verse, 1969; The Lengthening Shadows, 1971; Ed., Poetic Heritage. Contbr. to Southern Review. F.R.S.L. Recip., Heinemann Award, 1959. Address: 1 Beaumont Pl., Oxford OX1 2PJ, UK.

PRESS, Sylvia, b. NYC, USA. Radio Script Editor; Publicity & Special Events Director, New York Radio Station. Educ: Hunter Coll., Columbia Univ., N.Y., A.B. Publs: The Care of Devils; Un' Ossessione Americana; Four Days to Gay Head, 1973; Creator, Press Clippings, & other radio progs. Agent: Int. Famous Agcy. Inc. Address: London Terrace, 445 W. 23rd St., N.Y., NY 10011, USA.

PRESSER, Sem, b. 21 Nov. 1917, Amsterdam, Netherlands. Photojournalist. Publs: travel guides, Riviera,

1952, Paris, 1953, Spain, 1953, Belgium, 1954, Ardennes, 1956; Wandelingen langs de Riviera (stories), 1960; Quatre photographes neerlandais de France, 1963; Vier even hier, 1964. Contbr. to: Nieuwe Revu, Amsterdam; De Journalist; De Telegraaf; etc. Mbrships. incl: Fedn. of Netherlands Artists Orgs.; Netherlands Assn. of Photojrnlsts. (Pres.); Netherlands Assn. of Jrnlsts.; Bd., World Press Photo. Recip., Golden Medal, Biennale Venice, 1959. Address: Vondelstraat 96, Amsterdam, Netherlands.

PREST, Wilfred, b. 3 May 1907, York, UK. Emeritus Professor. Educ: B.A., 1930, M.A., 1934, Leeds Univ.; M.A.(Com.), Manchester Univ., 1932; M.Com., Univ. of Melbourne, Aust., 1943. Contbr. to: Economics of Australian Industry, 1963; Australian Economy, 1963; Accounting Frontier, 1965; Contemporary Australia, 1969; Econ. Record; Aust. Quarterly; Round Table; Growth; Annual Reports of C'wlth. Grants Commn.; Jrnl. of C'wlth. Pol. Studies; etc. Mbrships: C'wlth. Grants Commn., 1963-65; Past Pres., Econ. Soc. of Aust. & NZ; Royal Econ. Soc.; Am. Econ. Assn. Hons: Vis. Rsch. Fellow, Aust. Nat. Univ., 1973-75; C.B.E., 1965. Address: 71 Dendy St., Brighton, Vic. 3186, Australia.

PRESTON, Ivy Alice, b. 11 Nov. 1914, Southburn, Timaru, NZ. Writer. Publs: 23 novels (some transls. into Norwegian, Dutch & Italian) inclng: The Silver Stream (autobiog.), 1959; None So Blind, 1961; Rosemary for Remembrance, 1962; Ticket of Destiny, 1965; Interrupted Journey, 1968. Contbr. to var. jrnls. Mbrships. incl: Romantic Novelists Assn.; NZ Women Writers; Pres., Timaru Writers Guild. Address: 95 Church St., Timaru, S. Canterbury, NZ.

PRESTON, Richard Arthur, b. 4 Oct. 1910, Middlesbrough, UK. Professor of History; University Administrator; Author. Educ: B.A., 1931, M.A., 1932, Leeds Univ.; Ph.D., Yale Univ., USA, 1936. Publs: Gorges of Plymouth Fort, 1953; Men in Arms, 1956, 3rd ed., 1970; Royal Fort Frontenac (co-author), 1958; Kingston Before the War of 1812, 1959; Canada in World Affairs 1959-61, 1965; Canada & Imperial Defense, 1967; Ed., Contemporary Australia, 1969; Canada's RMC, 1969; Ed., The Influence of the United States on Canadian Development, 1972; For Friends at Home, 1974. Contbr. to: Am. & Can. Histl. Reviews; Int. & Can. Army Jrnls.; Can. Defence, Queen's, Univ. of Toronto Quarterlies; Ont. Hist.; etc. Address: Duke Univ., Durham, NC, USA.

PRESTON, (Rev. Canon) Ronald Haydn, b. 1913, Bristol, UK. Clergyman; University Professor; Writer. Educ: B.Sc.; M.A.; London Schl. Econs.; St. Catharine's Soc.; Ripon Hall, Oxford. Publs: Christians in Society; The Revelation of St. John the Divine; Ed., Technology & Social Justice, 1971; Industrial Conflicts & Their Place in Modern Society, 1974; Perspectives on Strikes, 1975. Contbr. to: Guardian; Theol., etc. Address: The University, Manchester M13 9PL, UK

PRETORIUS, Johannes Loduvicus, b. 9 Apr. 1938, Pretoria, S. Africa. Publisher. Educ: M.A., Dev. Admin.; B.A., Africa Studies; B.A., African Law & Admin. Publs: Nyimbo Zosaiwalika, 1971. Contbr. to Early History of Malawi, 1973. Mbr., Nat. Fauna Preservation Soc. of Malawi. Address: Claim, P.O. Nkhoma, Malawi.

PREUSS, Roger, b. 29 Jan. 1922, Waterville, Minn., USA. Author; Artist. Educ: B.F.A., Mpls. Coll. of Art & Design. Publs: Wildlife of America (Official Almanac/Calendar), annually since 1955; Outdoor Horizons, 1957; American Wildlife, 1964; This is Minnesota, 1965; Minnesota Today, 1965. Contbr. to: Nat. Wildlife; Sports Review; Today's Art; Western Can. Outdoors; Sports & Recreation; Vol.; Outdoorsman; Look; Pioneer; Am. Farm; Picture; Ducks Unlimited; Capital; Conservation Digest; Sports Afield. Mbrships. incl: Outdoor Writers Assn. of Am.; Gt. Lakes Outdoor Writers; Minn. Poets, Authors & Artists; Int. Inst. of Arts & Letters. Num. hons. incl: Book Recommendation, ALA, 1957; Wildlife Writer of the Yr. Award, 1955; Minn. Centennial Award, 1958. Address: 2224 Grand Ave., Mpls., MN 55405, USA.

PREUSSLER Otfried, b. 20 Oct. 1923, Reichenberg i. B., Bohemia. Writer, Children's Books & Plays. Educ: Study of pedagogy. Publs. incl: Der kleine Wasserman, 1956; Die kleine Hexe, 1958; Der Rauber Hotzenplotz, 3 vols., 1962, 1969, 1973; Das Kleine Gespenst, 1966; Krabat, 1971; (60 for. lang. eds. in 26 langs., above & others). Contbr. to radio & TV, W. Germany, Austria, Switz. Mbrships: PEN; Histl. Co. of Children's Books; Int. Bd., Books for Young People;

Int. Youth Lib., Munich. Hons: German State Children's Prize, 1963, 1972; Int. Hans Christian Andersen Prize, 1972; European Prize for Children's Books, Univ. of Padua, 1973; Dutch Prize, 1972, 1973. Address: Postfach 168, D-8201 Stephanskirchen, W. Germany.

PREVERT, Jacques, b. 4 Feb. 1900, Neuilly-sur-Seine, France. Writer. Educ: Ecole communale, Paris. Publs. incl: Paroles; Histoires; Spectacle; La Pluie & le beau temps; (screenplays): L'Affaire est dans le sac; Drôle de drame; Quai des brumes; Le jour se lève; Les enfants du paradis; Lumière d'été; Les Visiteurs du Soir; Les Portes de la Nuit; Les Amants de Vérone; La Bergère & le Ramoneur; Notre-Dame de Paris; & num. songs. Address: 82 blvd. de Clichy, Paris 18e, France.

PRICE, Alfred Walter, b. 1936, Cheam, UK. Retired Officer, Royal Air Force; Author. Publs: Instruments of Darkness, 1967; Luftwaffe, 1970; Aircraft versus Submarine, 1973; Battle over the Reich, 1973. Spitfire at War, 1974. Contbr. to: Sunday Express; RAF Quarterly; Aircraft Profiles. Mbrships: Fellow, Royal Histl. Soc.; Royal United Servs. Instn. Recip., L. G. Groves Mem. Prize for Aircraft Safety, 1963. Address: c/o Agent, Campbell Thomson & McLaughlin Ltd., 80 Chancery Lane, London WC2, UK.

PRICE, Beverley Joan, pen name RANDELL, Beverley, b. 9 Dec. 1931, Wellington, NZ. Author; Editor. Educ: B.A., Univ. of NZ. Publs: PM Commonwealth Readers (16 books), 1964; Methuen Caption Books (24 books), 1965; Methuen Number Story Caption Books (16 books), 1967; PM Felt Books (8 books), 1967; A Guide to the Ready to Read Series & supporting books, 1969; Meg & Mark Books (8 books, co-author), 1969; John the Mouse who Learned to Read, 1970; Methuen Story Readers (42 books), 1972; PM Listening Skillbuilders (24 books), 1972; Methuen's Country Books (8 books), 1973; First Phonics (28 books), 1974; PM Animal Books (8 books, co-author), 1974; PM Creative Workbooks (8 books), 1974; Ed., sev. series of infant readers. Address: 38 Alexandra Rd., Hataitai, Wellington 3, NZ.

PRICE, Christine Hilde, b. 1928, London, UK. Author; Illustrator. Educ: Vassar Coll., Poughkeepsie, N.Y., USA. Publs: Three Golden Nobles, 1951; The Dragon & the Book, 1953; Song of the Wheels, 1956; David & the Mountain, 1959; Made in the Middle Ages, 1961; Made in the Renaissance, 1963; The Valiant Chattee-Maker, 1965; Made in Ancient Greece, 1967; Made in Ancient Egypt, 1970; Heirs of the Ancient Maya, 1972; Talking Drums of Africa, 1973; Made in West Africa, 1975. Mbrships. incl: PEN; Soc. of Women Geogs. Address: R.F.D.I., Castleton, Vt., USA.

PRICE, David John, b. 9 Apr. 1943, Wallasey, UK. Journalist. Educ: B.Sc., Univ. of London, 1964; B.A., Ambassador Coll., 1968. Publs: The Arab Challenge, 1975. Contbr. to: The Plain Truth; Worldwide News. Mbrships: F.R.S.A.; Inst. of Jrnlsts.; Royal Inst. of Int. Affairs. Address: 60 Tollgate Rd., Colney Heath, St. Albans, Herts. AL4 0PY, UK.

PRICE, (Edward) Reynolds, b. 1 Feb. 1933, Macon, N.C., USA. Associate Professor of English. Educ: A.B., Duke Univ., Durham, N.C., 1955; B.Litt., Oxford Univ., UK, 1958. Publs: (novels) A Long & Happy Life, USA & UK, 1962; A Generous Man, USA, 1966, UK, 1967; Love & Work, USA & UK, 1968; (short stories) The Names & Faces of Heroes, USA & UK, 1963; Permanent Errors, USA, 1970, UK, 1971; (verse) Late Warning, 1968; Ed., The Archive, 1954-55; Advsry. Ed., Shenandoah. Hons. incl: Faulkner Fndn. Prize, 1963; Nat. Endowment for Arts Fellowship, 1967. Address: 4813 Duke Stn., Durham, NC 21106, USA.

PRICE, Ernest Maurice, b. 20 Apr. 1906, Old Colwyn, UK. Technical College & University Lecturer. Educ: B.Sc.(Tech.), M.Sc.(Tech.), Victoria Univ. of Manchester. Publs: (w. Dr. H. Buckingham) Principles of Electronics, 1953; Principles of Electrical Measurements, 1955; Electro-Technology, Vol. II, 1956, Vol. III, 1959. Fellow, Inst. of Elec. Engrs. Address: 18 Windermere Rd., Bradford BD7 4RQ, UK.

PRICE, Joseph Henry, b. 6 June 1924, Rochdale, Lancs., UK. University Teacher. Educ: Pembroke Coll., Oxford Univ., 1941-42 & 1947-48; M.A. Publs: The Gold Coast General Election of 1951, 1951; Political Institutions of West Africa, 1967, revised ed. 1975; Comparative

Government, 1970, revised ed. 1975. Contbr. to: Pol. Studies; Islamic Review; Guardian; Economist; W. Africa; W. African Review. Mbrships: Brit. Inst. Mgmt.; Nigerian Inst. Mgmt.; var. pol. sci. assns. Address: The Old Vicarage, Cragg Vale, Hebden Bridge, W. Yorks. HX7 5TB, UK.

PRICE, Lucie Harris Locke, pen name LOCKE, Lucie, b. 22 Feb. 1904, Valdasta, Ga., USA. Artist; Poet. Educ: H. Sophie Newcomb Coll., Tulane Univ., New Orleans, La Publs: (poetry) Naturally Yours, Texas (self-illustrated), 1949; Seize the Ring, 1972. Contbr. to: Mitre Press Spring Anthol., 1967; Cyclo-Flame; Quaderni di Poesia; Bitterroot; (formerly) Discovery; Flame; etc. Mbr., Poetry Soc. of Tex. Hons. incl: var. prizes, Southwest Writers Confs., 1945-66; Diploma di Benemerenza, Academia Leonardo da Vinci, Rome, Italy, 1967, 1968, 1972; Avalon Presidential Citation, 1969; Hon. Mention, Nat. Fedn. of State Poetry Socs. Inc., 1972. Address: 401 Southern St., Corpus Christi, TX 78404, USA.

PRICE, Stanley, b. 12 Aug. 1931, London, UK. Writer. Educ: M.A., Gonville & Caius Coll., Cambridge Univ. Publs: Crusading for Kronk, 1960; Just for the Record, 1961; A World of Difference, 1962; The Biggest Picture, 1964. Plays: Horizontal Hold, 1967; The Starving Rich, 1973; Exit Laughing, 1974; The Two of Me, 1975. Films: Arabesque, 1966; A Fistful of Life, 1968; Gold, 1974; Shout at the Devil, 1975. Contbr. to: Life Mag., N.Y. (reporter 1957-60); Observer (Staff mbr. 1964-65); N.Y. Times; Punch; New Statesman; Plays & Players; Sunday Telegraph (Staff mbr. 1963). Mbrships: Dramatists Guild, USA; Writers' Guild of Gt. Brit. Address: 21 Hillside Gdns., London N6, UK.

PRICE, Victor Henry John, b. 10 Apr. 1930, Newcastle, N. Ireland. BBC Official. Educ: B.A., Queen's Univ., Belfast. Publs: The Death of Achilles, 1964; The Other Kingdom, 1964; Caliban's Wooing, 1966; (transl.) The Plays of Georg Buchner, 1971. Address: 18 Cambridge Park, Twickenham, Middx. TW1 2JE, UK.

PRICE, Willard, b. 1887, Peterborough, Can. Explorer; Writer. Educ: Case Western Reserve Univ., Cleveland, Ohio, USA; Columbia Univ., N.Y.; M.A.; Litt.D. Publs: 36 books incl. The Japanese Miracle; The Amazing Mississippi; Incredible Africa; The Amazing Amazon; Roving South; Japan's Islands of Mystery; Barbarian; Riptide in the South Seas; Ancient Peoples at New Tasks; The Negro Around the World; American Influence in the Orient; (boys' books) Amazon Adventure; South Sea Adventure; Underwater Adventure; Volcano Adventure; Whale Adventure; Elephant Adventure; Safari Adventure; Gorilla Adventure; Cannibal Adventure. Contbr. to Ency. Britannica & num. jrnls. Address: 814-N. Alhambra, Laguna Hills, Calif., USA.

PRIDER, Rex Tregilgas, b. 22 Sept. 1910, Narrogin, W. Australia. Professor of Geology. Educ: B.Sc., Univ. of W.A., 1930; Ph.D., Cambridge Univ., UK, 1939. Publs: Elements of Geology for Australian Students (w. E. de C. Clarke & C. Teichert), 1944, 4th ed., 1967; Elementary Practical Geology (w. E. de C. Clarke & C. Teichert), 1946, 4th ed., 1968. Mbrships. incl: Pres., Geol. Soc. of Aust., 1958-59. Hons: Lyell Fund, Geol. Soc. of London, 1951; Medal, Royal Soc. of W.A., 1970. Address: Dept. of Geol., Univ. of W.A., Nedlands, W. Australia 6009.

PRIEGO LOPEZ, Juan, b. 1 Feb. 1899, Madrid, Spain. Retired Army Colonel. Educ: Infantry Acad.; Adv. War Acad.; Fac. of Law, Univ. of Madrid. Publs: Síntesis de la Independencia, 1947; Literature militar española y universal, 1956; Historia militar contemporánea, 1961; Guerra de la Independencia, 3 vols., 1964-74. Contbr. to: Diccionario de Historia de España in Occidente; Ejercito; Revista de Historia militar. Mbr., Nat. Inst. of the Spanish Book. Address: Calle Clara de Rey 60, 2ºA, Madrid, Spain.

PRIESTLEY, H. E., b. 1901, Bradford, Yorks., UK. Lecturer; Author. Educ: M.A., Leeds Univ.; M.Ed., Leeds Univ.; Ph.D., London Univ. Publs. incl: John Stranger, 1960; Finding Out About Anglo-Saxon England, 1964; The Awakening World (1750-1966), 1967; Britain Under the Romans, 1967; The English Home: A History of the Smaller English House, 1970; Heraldic Sculpture: The Work of James Woodford, 1972; The Book of 1874— A Daily Diary of Events, 1973; Ancient & Roman Britain, 1975. Contbr. to Essex Countryside. Mbr., Soc. of Authors. Address: 8 Loten Rd., Benfleet, Essex SS7 5DD, UK.

PRIESTLEY, John Boynton, b. 13 Sept. 1894. Writer. Educ: M.A.; LL.D.; D.Litt.; Trinity Hall, Cambridge. Publs.

incl. (novels): The Doomsday Men; Let the People Sing; Low Notes on a High Level; Saturn over the Water; The Shapes of Sleep; Lost Empires; Salt is Leaving; (essays): Midnight on the Desert; Thoughts in the Wilderness; Man & Time; Essays of Five Decades, 1969; (plays): When We are Married; Take the Fool Away; The Glass Cage; Time for the Conways; (criticism): The Art of the Dramatist; Literature & Western Man; & num. TV plays. Contbr. to: BBC. Mbrships. incl: PEN; Int. Theatre Inst.; Nat. Theatre Bd., 1965-67. Address: Kissing Tree House, Alveston, Stratford-upon-Avon, Warwicks., UK.

PRIME, Derek James, b. 20 Feb. 1931, London, UK. Minister of the Gospel. Educ: M.A., Emmanuel Coll., Cambridge; S.Th., Lambeth Dip. in Theol. Publs: A Christian's Guide to Prayer, 1964; A Christian's Guide to Leadership, 1966; Questions & Answers on the Christian Faith, 1967; This Way to Life, 1968; Tell Me the Answer (series). Address: 11 Midmar Gdns., Edinburgh EH10 6DY, UK.

PRIME, Honor Mary Corderoy, b. 1904, Bristol, UK. Teacher & University Coach. Educ: B.A., Univ. Coll., London; Cambridge Trng. Coll. for Women. Publs: Moonface, 1961; Moonface & Matthew, 1963; Matthew's Ear, 1964. Mbrships: Soc. of Authors; Soc. of Women Writers & Jrnlsts.; Brit. Fedn. Univ. Women. Address: 7 Surrenden Close, Brighton 8EB, Sussex, UK.

PRIMMER, Phyllis Cora, b. 10 July 1926, Collingwood, Ont., Can. Writer. Educ: Cert., Christian Educ., Canadian Bible Coll., Regina, Sask. Publs: Till Night Is Gone, 1953; At the River's Turning, 1960; Beyond the Bend, 1965; Walk into the Wind (forthcoming). Mbr., Simcos Co. Hist. Assn. Address: Shanty Bay, Ont., Can.

PRIMOST, Sydney Simon, b. 6 Aug. 1900. Chartered Accountant. Publs: Voyage up the Amazon; Lion Smacked his Head; Golden Eagle Street; The Pools of the Gods; Ed., Harcourtier. Mbr., PEN. Recip., Fellowship & Hon. Life Mbrship., Am. Int. Acad. Address: Grande Vue, W. Heath Rd., London, NW3, UK.

PRINCE, Peter, b. 1942, Bromley, Kent, UK. Writer; Writer-in-Residence, Vauxhall Manor School, SE11, 1973-74; Editor BBC Publishing Ltd., 1969-71. Publs: Play Things, 1972; Dogcatcher, 1974; (TV plays) Notes from the Underground, 1974; The Floater, 1975. Contbr. to: New Statesman; Let it Rock; Observer. Mbr., Writers' Action Grp. Recip., Somerset Maugham Award, 1973. Agent: A. D. Peters & Co. Address: 21 Macaulay Ct., Macaulay Rd., London SW4, UK.

PRING, Julian Talbot, b. 28 Oct. 1913, London, UK. University Teacher. Educ: M.A., Balliol Coll., Oxford; Ph.D., London Univ. Publs: Grammar of Modern Greek, 1950; Colloquial English Pronunciation, 1959; Oxford Dictionary of Modern Greek (Greek-English), 1965. Address: Dept. of Phonetics, University College, London WC1, UK.

PRINGLE, John Martin Douglas, b. 28 June 1912, Hawick, Scotland, UK. Journalist. Educ: M.A., Lincoln Coll., Oxford. Publs: China Struggles for Unity, 1937; Australian Accent, 1958; On Second Thoughts, 1972; Have Pen: Will Travel, 1973. Contbr. to: Encounter; Times Lit. Supplement. Address: 27 Bayview St., McMahon's Point, N. Sydney, N.S.W., Australia 2060.

PRINS, Sonja, pen names KOOPMAN, Wanda; DAAMS, P. J. L.; LENORMAND, S.; ALBRECHT, Willi, b. 14 Aug. 1912, Haarlem, Netherlands. Author. Publs: Proeve in strategie (as Wanda Koopman), 1933; De groene jas, 1949; Brood en rozen, 1953; Het geschonden aangezicht, 1955; Nieuwe proeve in strategie, 1957; Notities, 1973; Dagboekgedigten, 1974. Contbr. to: De Gids; Maatstaf; De Nieuwe Stem; Front (Fndr., Ed.). Mbrships. incl: Dutch Writers' Union. Address: Boshut, Eikenlaan 6, Baarle-Nassau (NB), Netherlands.

PRINZ ZU LÖWENSTEIN-WERTHEIM-FREUDEN-BERG, Hubertus Friedrich, b. 14 Oct. 1906, Schönwörth Castle, near Kufstein, Tyrol, Austria. Writer; Historian; Political Analyst. Educ: Univs. of Munich, Hamburg, Geneva, Berlin; LL.D., Hamburg Univ., 1928. Publs. incl: The Child & the Emperor, The Lance of Longinus, Eagle & Cross (relig. tril.), 1945-47; Nato: The Defence of the West, 1961; Deutsche Geschichte, 4th ed., 1962 (sev. langs.); Towards the Further Shore, 1968; (novel) Kaiser Ohne Purpur, 1975. Contbr. to var. scholarly jrnls. etc. Mbrships:

Pres., Free German Authors' Assn.; Brit. Soc. of Authors. Recip., D.Litt., Hamline Univ., St. Paul, Minn., USA, 1943. Address: 53 Bonn-Bad Godesberg, Lahnstrasse 50, W. Germany.

PRIOR, Allan, b. 1922, Newcastle-upon-Tyne, UK. Writer. Publs: A Flame in the Air; The Joy Ride; The One-Eyed Monster; One Away; The Interrogators; The Operators; The Loving Cup; The Contract; Paradiso. Mbrships: PEN; Savage Club. Address: 24 Waverley Rd., St. Albans, Herts., UK.

PRITCHETT, Victor Sawdon, b. 16 Dec. 1900, Ipswich, UK. Critic; Author. Publs. incl: Marching Spain; Shirley Sanz, Nothing Like Leather; It May Never Happen; The Living Novel; Books in General; When My Girl Comes Home; The Key To My Heart; Foreign Faces; New York Proclaimed; The Living Novel & Later Appreciations; Dublin; Blind Love; George Meredith & English Comedy, 1970; Balzac, 1973; The Camberwell Beauty, 1974; (autobiography) A Cab at the Door, 1968; Midnight Oil, 1971. Mbrships. incl: PEN; Am. Acad. of Arts & Letters; F.R.S.L. Recip., C.B.E. Address: 12 Regent's Park Terr., London NW1, UK.

PRIZEMAN, John Brewster, b. 15 Nov. 1930, Little Bookham, UK. Architect. Educ: Archtl. Assn. Schl. of Archts., London; AA dip.; R.I.B.A.; MSIA. Publs: Kitchens, 1966; European Interiors, 1969; Living Rooms, 1970; Your House — the outside view, 1975. Contbr. to: Observer; Times; Sunday Times; Daily Express; Daily Mail; Daily Telegraph; Guardian; House & Garden. Address: 53 Upper Montagu St., London W1H 1FQ, UK.

PROCHNOW, Herbert Victor, b. 19 May 1897, Wis., USA. Banker; Writer. B.A.; M.A.; Ph.D.; Univ. of Wis.; Northwestern Univ., Chgo. Publs. incl: The Public Speaker's Treasure Chest, 1942; Term Loans & Theories of Bank Liquidity, 1949; Effective Public Speaking, 1960; Practical Bank Credit, 1963; World Economic Problems & Policies, 1965; The Five-year Outlook for Investment Rates in the US & Abroad, 1972; Speaker's Source Book, 1001 Quips, Stories & Illustrations for All Occasions, 1973. Contbr. to Chgo. Tribune, 1968-70. Mbr., Chgo. Assn. of Commerce & Ind., (Pres., 1964,—65). Hons. incl: Cross of the Order of Merit of Germany, 1968. Address: 2950 Harrison St., Evanston, IL 60201, USA

PROCKTER, Noel James, b. 15 Dec. 1910, Lingfield, UK. Horticultural Consultant; Journalist; Author. Publs: Simple Propagation, 1950; Garden Hedges, 1960; Climbing & Screening Plants, 1973. Contbr. to: Amateur Gardening; The Sun; Radio. Mbrships. incl: Fellow, Linnean Soc. of London; Royal Hort. Soc.; Garden Hist. Soc. Address: 110 Malthouse Rd., Crawley, W. Sussex, RH10 6BH, UK.

PROCTOR, Dorothea Hardy, b. 18 July 1910, Calhan Ranch, Colo., USA. Poet; Painter; Sculptor; Housewife. Educ: Univ. of Tulsa. Publs: Listening For Absolutes, 1968; The Delight of Being Poems/Sculptures, 1971. Mbrships. incl: Tulsa Poetry Quarterly; Writers Club T.U.S. & W. Inc.; Nat. Fedn. of Poetry Socs.; Okla. Writers Assn.; Tuesday Writers; Tulsa Poets; Poetry Soc. of Okla. Hons. incl: Best Book Award, Arts Coun., for The Delight of Being; many prizes for poetry & sculpture; Doct. Artes y Cultura, Honoris Causa, Spain. Address: 1542 E. 34th St., Tulsa, OK 74105, USA.

PROCTOR, Ian, b. 12 July 1918, Ealing, London, UK. Industrial Designer; Company Director. Educ: London Univ. Publs: Racing Dinghy Handling, 1948; Racing Dinghy Maintenance, 1949; Sailing: Wind & Current, 1953; Boats for Sailing, 1967. Contbr. to: Yachts & Yachting; Daily Telegraph (yachting corres. for 11 yrs.). Mbrships: Fellow, Soc. of Indl. Artist & Designers & Royal Soc. of Arts; Hamble River, Warsash, Hayling Island & Aldenham Sailing Clubs. Recip., sev. design awards. Address: Fenmead, Brook Ave., Warsash, Southampton, UK.

PROCTOR, Raymond Lambert, b. 18 Oct. 1920, Bearden, Tenn., USA. Associate Professor of European & Middle Eastern History. Educ: B.S. Mil. Sci., Univ. of Md. Madrid Campus, Spain, 1960; M.A. 1962, Ph.D. 1966, Univ. of Ore., Eugene. Publs: Agonía de Un Neutral, Spain 1972; Agony of a Neutral & the Blue Division, 1974. Contbr. to: Jrnl. of Modern Hist.; Mil. Affairs; Aerospace Histn. Mbrships incl: Am. Mil. Inst.; Inst. Aerospace Studies. Hons: Fac. Study Grants, Univ. of Idaho Rsch. Coun., 1968, 1970, 1973; honoured by Spanish Chief of State, 1973. Address: Hist. Dept., Univ. of Idaho, Moscow, ID, USA.

PROFFER, Ellendea C., b. 24 Nov. 1944, Phila., Pa., USA. Editor; Publisher. Educ: A.B., Univ. of Md., 1966; A.M., 1968, Ph.D., 1970, Ind. Univ. Publs: Zoikina kvartira (Russian ed.), 1971; Diaboliad & Other Stories, 1972; The Early Plays of Mikhail Bulgakov, 1972. Contbr. to: Ed., Russian Lit. Triquarterly; TriQuarterly; Can.-Am. Slavic Studies; Books Abroad. Mbr., Am. Assn. for the Advancement of Slavic Studies. Address: 2901 Heatherway, Ann Arbor, MI, USA.

PROKOSCH, Frederic, b. 17 May, 1906, Wisconsin, USA. Writer. Educ: B.A., Haverford Coll.; M.A., King's Coll., Cambridge, UK; Ph.D., Yale Univ., USA. Publs. incl: The Asiatics, 1935. Contbr. to num. jrnls. Hons: Guggenheim Fellowship, 1936; Fulbright Fellowship, 1951; Harper Prize for Novels, 1937; Monroe Prize for Poetry, 1941. Address: Ma Trouvaille, 06 Plan de Grasse, France.

PROSS, Harry, b. 2 Sept. 1923, Karlsruhe, Germany. Writer; Professor. Educ: D.Phil., Univ. of Heidelberg, 1949; Postgrad. Studs., Stanford Univ., USA. Publs: Die Zerstörung der deutschen Politik, 1959; Literatur und Politik, 1961; Moral der Massenmedien, 1967; Publizistik, 1970; Medienforschung, 1972; Politische Symbolik, 1974; etc. Contbr. to: Deutsche Rundschau; Neue Rundschau; etc. Mbr., PEN; ISDS Zürich; VS; VDW. Address: D-8999 Weissen Post Weiler/Allgäu, W. Germany.

PROUSSIS, Costas M., b. 26 June 1911, Angastina, Cyprus. Professor; Author. Educ: Lic.Philos., Univ. of Athens, Greece, 1934; Ph.D., Univ. of Chgo., USA, 1951. Publs. incl: Grammar of Modern Greek, 1934; Kostis Palamas, 1943; Aesthetic Culture, 1946; Cyprus Prose, 1949; The Athenian Iliad, 1951; The Novels of A. Terzakis, 1966; Folklore & Cyprus, 1972; (co-author) The Educated Man, 1965; The Voice of Cyprus, 1965; Fiction in Several Languages, 1968; Poems of Cyprus, 1970. Contbr. to var. profl. jrnls. Mbrships. incl: Am. Philol. Assn.; Classical Assn. of New England; MLA. Hons. incl. Acad. of Athens Award, 1946. Address: 11 Lehigh Rd., Wellesley, MA 02181, USA.

PRUGH, Jeffery Douglas (Jeff), b. 15 Sept. 1939, Pitts., Pa., USA. Journalist, Los Angeles Times. Educ: Glendale Coll., Calif., 1958-60; B. Jrnlsm., Univ. of Mo., 1962. Publ: The wizard of Westwood (biog.) (w. Dwight Chapin), 1973. Contbr. to: Sports Illustrated; People; Time; World Tennis; (anthols.): Best Sports Stories, 1971; Action, 1971. Mbrships: U.S. Basketball Writers' Assn. (Past Pres.); Southern Calif. Football Writers (Past Pres.); Sigma Delta Chi. Hons. incl: 3rd Prize 1967, 2nd Prize 1972; 1st Prize 1973, Calif.-Nev. Assoc. Press Writing Contest; 1st Prize, San Fernando Valley Press Club, L.A., 1970; 1st Prize, Greater L.A. Press Club, 1973. Address: 6110 Canterbury Dr., Fox Hills, CA 90230, USA.

PRYCE-JONES, David Eugene Henry, b. 15 Feb. 1936, Vienna, Austria. Author. Educ: B.A., M.A., Oxford Univ., UK. Publs: Owls & Satyrs, 1961; The Sands of Summer, 1962; Next Generation, 1963; Quondam, 1965; The Stranger's View, 1967; The Hungarian Revolution, 1969; Running Away, 1971; The Face of Defeat, 1973; The England Commune, 1974. Contbr. to: Daily Telegraph Mag.; Spectator; etc. Address: c/o A.D. Peters, 10 Buckingham Street, London WC2, UK.

PRYOR, Adel, b. 2 Dec. 1918, Haugesund, Norway. Writer; Housewife. Publs: (novels) Tangled Paths, 1959; Clouded Glass, 1961; Hidden Fire, 1962; Out of the Night, 1963, 3rd ed., 1971; Hearts in Conflict, 1965; Forgotten Yesterday, 1966; Valley of Desire, 1967; Sound of the Sea, 1968. Norwegian ed., 1975; Free of a Dream, 1969, German ed., 1973; Her Secret Fear, 1971. Hons: Engl. Composition Prize, 1934; Sir William Thorne award for Engl., 1937; Short Story Contest Award, 1946. Address: 8 Iona St., Milnerton, Cape, Repub. of S. Africa.

PRYOR, Hubert C., b. 18 Mar. 1916, Buenos Aires, Argentina (U.S. Citizen). Editor; Writer. Educ: Schl. of Jrnlsm., Univ. of London. Contbr. to: Modern Maturity; NRTA Jrnl.; Look; Science Digest; Medical World News. Mbr., Am. Soc. of Mag. Eds. Address: Office: 215 Long Beach Blvd., Long Beach, CA 90801, USA; Home: 44 Paloma Ave., Long Beach, CA 90803, USA.

PUCKLE, Owen Standidge, b. 2 June 1899, Romford, Essex, UK. Research Engineer. Educ: The Polytechnic, Regent St., London. Publs: Television Reception (transl. from German of Manfred, Baron von Ardenne w. additional chapt.), 1936; Time Bases, 1943, (transl. into Russian,

French, Dutch), 8th ed., 1952; An Introduction to the Numerical Control of Machine Tools (w. J. R. Arrowsmith), 1964. Contbr. to num. profl. & other jrnls., UK & abroad. Mbrships: Fellow, Instn. of Elec. Engrs.; Radio Sect. Comm., ibid., 1945-48; Fellow, Royal TV Soc., 1936; Coun.; Chmn., 3 yrs. Hons. incl: M.B.E., 1945; Duddell Premium, Instn. of Elec. Engrs., 1942. Address: Pigeon House Cottage, Grove Rd., Beaconsfield HP9 1UP, UK.

PUDDEPHA, Derek Noel, b. 1930, Birmingham, UK. Local Authority Press Officer. Educ: Worcester Cathedral King's Schl. Publs: Fly Fishing Is Easy, 1968; Coarse Fishing Is Easy, 1970. Contbr. to Angling Press. Address: 15 Quantock Rd., Weston-super-Mare, Avon, UK.

PUDNEY, John, b. 1909, Langley, Bucks., UK. Publisher; Writer. Publs: (Childrens' books) Fred & I Series; The Hartwarp Series; Poetry: Collected Poems, 1957; Spandrels, 1969; Take This Orange, 1971; Selected Poems 1967-73, 1973; (fiction) The Long Time Growing Up, 1971; (non-fiction) De Lessep's Canal, 1968; Crossing London's River, 1972. Brunel & His World, 1974; London Docks, 1975; (plays) Ted (TV); The Little Giant, A Musical Documentary, (stage), 1973. Agent: David Higham Assocs. Address: 4 Macartney House, Chesterfield Walk, Greenwich Park, London SE10 8HJ, UK.

PUE, Thomas William, b. 3 Feb. 1915, Brandon, Man., Can. Editor; Publisher. Editor of Alberta Farm Life (Weekly newspaper) & 16 other Alberta community newspapers. Mbrships: Edmonton Press Club, Western Can. Farm Writers' Assn. Address: 10026 - 109 Street, Capilano Cres., Edmonton, Alta., Canada.

PUECHNER, Ray, pen names VICTOR, Charles B.; TIGER, Jack; HADDO; Oliver; PEEKNER, Ray. b. 12 Aug. 1935, Milwaukee, Wis., USA. Educ: B.S., Marquette Univ. Publs: The Whole Sky Burned, 1968; The LSD & Sex & Censorship & Vietnam Cookbook, 1968; Can't Help Being Beautiful, 1972; A Grand Slam, 1973. Contbr. to: Saturday Review; North Am. Review; The Smith; LA Free Press; var. other mags. Mbrships: Sci. Fiction Writers of Am.; Coun. for Wis. Writers. Address: Ray Peekner Literary Agency, 2625 N. 36th St., Milwaukee, WI 53210, USA.

PUERTO, Carlos, b. 29 Mar. 1942, Madrid, Spain. Scriptwriter. Educ: Degree superior. Publs: Tiempo sin Angela, 1965; No he Muerto Todavia, 1967; Agonizante Sol, 1969; Matrimonio y Cine, 1970; Algo de Tierra Mojada, 1966; Las Edades del Amor, 1968; El Nuevo Silencia, 1970; La Mujer del Ano 2000, 1970. Contbr. to: Triunfo; Informaciones; Ya; La estafeta literaria. Mbr., Circle of Writers of Cenema. Hons: Cuidad de Leon Prize; Literoy Prize. Address: Camino de Vinateros 139, Madrid 30, Spain.

PUGH, John Charles, b. 9 Jan. 1919, Bristol, UK. Professor of Geography, University of London. Educ: M.A., Univ. of Cambridge; Ph.D., Univ. of London. Publs: Land & People in Nigeria, (w. K. M. Buchanan), 1955; A Short Geography of West Africa, (w. A. E. Perry), 1960; West Africa, (w. W. B. Morgan), 1969; Surveying for Field Scientists, 1975. Contbr. to var. sci. jrnls. Mbrships. incl: F.R.I.C.S.; Geol. Soc. of London; Inst. of Brit. Geogs.; Royal Geogl. Soc.; Royal Commonwealth Soc. Address: King's Coll., Strand, London WC2R 2LS, UK.

PUIG, Manuel, b. 28 Dec. 1932, Gen. Villegas, Argentina. Novelist. Educ: studies philos. for 3 yrs., Univ. of Buenos Aires, & film direction for 1 yr., Centro Sperimentale di Cinematogrfia, Rome. Publs: La traición de Rita Hayworth, 1968, USA ed., Betrayed by Rita Hayworth, 1973; Boquitas pintadas, 1969, USA ed., Heartbreak tango, 1973; The Buenos Aires Affair, 1973, USA ed., 1975. Contbr. to: Plural, Mexico; Review, N.Y. Hons: novels given disting. mention by N.Y. Times, 1971, ALA, 1971 & 1973, & Le Monde, 1969. Address: Violeta 8, Coyoacán, México 21 DF.

PUIGVERT, Antonio, b. 23 Apr. 1905, Barcelona, Spain. Urological Surgeon. Educ: M.D. Publs. incl: Atlas de Urografia, 1933; Tratado de Urografia Clinica, 1944; La Tuberculosis Urinaria y Genital Masculina, 1958; Tratado de Operatoria Urologica, 1971. Contbr. to: Anales de la Fundacion Puigvert; Archivos Espanoles de Urologica (Fndr.); Assoc. Ed. over 20 med. jrnls. Mbr., over 30 profl. orgs. Hons. incl: Order of Merit for Rsch & Invention, 1963; Legion of Honour, 1968; Premier Prize, Nat. Acad. of Med., Madrid; num. others. Address: Fundacion Puigvert, Cartagena 340, Barcelona — 13, Spain.

PUJALS, Esteban, b. 26 Dec. 1911, Vilaseca, Spain. Professor of English Literature. Educ: Lic. Letters, Univ. of Barcelona; Dr. Letters, Univ. of Madrid; Ph.D., Univ. of London. Publs: Espronceda y Lord Byron, 1951; Transl. & Ed., Dylan Thomas: Poemas, 1955; España y la Guerra de 1936 en la poeía de Roy Campbell, 1959; Drama, pensamiento y poesía en la literatura inglesa, 1965; El romanticismo inglés, 1969; La poesía inglesa del siglo XX, 1973. Contbr. to: Arbor; Atlántida; Filología Moderna; Nuestro Tiempo; Revista de Literatura. Mbrships: Int. Assn. of Univ. Profs. of Engl.; Byron Soc. Hons: Menéndez Pelayo Prize, 1949; Cross of Civil Merit, 1960. Address: Ministro Ilbáñez, Martín 3, Madrid 15, Spain.

PULASKI, Mary Ann Spencer, b. 9 Sept. 1916. Psychologist; Lecturer. Educ: B.A., Wellesley Coll., 1938; M.A., Queens Coll., 1958; Ph.D., CUNY, 1968. Publs: Learning to Use Our Language, 1967; Understanding Piaget: An Introduction to Children's Cognitive Development, 1971; Step by Step Guide to Correct English, 1974. Contbr. to: Child Dev.; Psychol. Today; & educl. film strips, etc.; The Child's World of Make-Believe (Ed., Jerome Singer), 1974. Mbrships. incl: Nassau Co. Psychol. Assn. (Pres. & Treas.); N.Y. State Psychol. Assn. (Mbr. Exec. Bd.); Jean Piaget Soc. (Bd. Dirs.). Hons: Fellow Am. Psychol. Assn., 1974; Durant Schlr., Wellesley Coll., 1937. Address: 19 Lynn Rd., Port Washington, NY 11058, USA.

PULLEIN-THOMPSON, Josephine Mary Wedderburn, pen name, MANN, Josephine, b. Wimbledon, UK. Author. Publs., 16 books for children & num. others for adults, inclng: Gin & Murder; They Died in the Spring; Murder Strikes Pink; Race Horse Holiday; All Change; Historical Anthology: Horses & their Owners, 1970; A Place with Two Faces, 1972; Proud Riders, 1973; Ride Better & Better, 1974; Black Beauty's Clan, 1975. Mbrships: Crimewriters' Assn.; PEN; Soc. of Authors; Brit. Horse Soc. Recip., Ernest Benn Prize, 1961. Address: 16 Knivet Rd., London SW6 1JH, UK.

PUMPHREY, George Henry, b. 11 Apr. 1912, Flint, UK. Principal Lecturer in Education. Publs: Story of Liverpool's Public Services, 1939; Look After Yourself, 1939; Look After Others, 1945; Trouble at the Grange, 1945; Good Manners, 1946; Juniors, 1949; The Childrens' Book of Folk Tales, 1950; Grenfell of Labrador, 1955, Am. ed., 1956; Children's Comics, 1955; Comics & your Children, 1956; What Children think of their Comics, 1957; Conquering the English Channel, 1965. Contbr. to var. educl. jrnls. Mbrships. incl: Soc. of Authors; Royal Inst. of Pub. Hlth. & Hygiene. Address: 10 Rose Ave., Retford, Notts., UK.

PURCELL, Theodore Vincent, b. 6 June 1911, Evanston, Ill., USA. Jesuit, Roman Catholic Priest; Professor of Industrial-Organizational Psychology. Educ: A.B., Dartmouth Coll., 1933; A.M., 1945, Lic. Theol., 1946, Loyola Univ., Chicago, Ill.; A.M., 1950, Ph.D., 1952, Harvard Univ. Publs: The Worker Speaks His Mind on Company & Union, 1953; Blue Collar Man, 1960; Cases in Business Ethics, 1968; The Negro in the Electrical Industry, 1971; Blacks in the Industrial World: Issues for the Manager, 1972. Contbr. to num. acad. publs. Mbrships. incl: Indl. Rels. Rsch. Assn.; Am. Psychol. Assn. (Fellow, Div. Indl. & Org. Psychol.). Recip., num. acad. hons. Address: Loyola Univ. of Chicago, Chicago, IL, USA.

PURCELL, (Rev. Canon) William Ernest, b. 1909, Bradford, Yorks., UK. Religious Broadcaster; Cathedral Canon. Educ: B.A., Univ. of Wales; M.A., Keble Coll., Oxford. Publs: These Your Gods; Onward Christian Soldier; Pilgrims Programme; A Plain Man Looks at Himself; Behold Thy Glory; Woodbine Willie; Fisher of Lambeth; Him We Declare; Portrait of Soper; British Police in a Changing Society. Agent: David Higham Assoc. Address: 10 College Green, Worcester, UK.

PURDAY, Herbert Frank Percy, b. 6 June 1887, Bromley, Kent, UK. Mechanical Engineer; Designer; Writer. Educ: Assoc., City & Guilds Inst.; B.Sc. Publs: Diesel Engine Design, 1919, 5th ed., 1948; Streamline Flow, 1949; Diesel Engine Designing, 1962; Linear Equations in Applied Mechanics. Mbr., Instn. Mech. Engrs. Address: 13 Southdown Rd., Southwick, Sussex BN4 4FT, UK.

PURDOM, Thomas E., b. 19 Apr. 1936, New Haven, Conn., USA. Writer. Educ: Lafayette Coll., Easton, Pa. Publs: (non-fiction) Adventures in Discovery, 1969; (fiction) Reduction in Arms, 1971; The Barons of Behaviour, 1972. Contbr. to: Phila. Bulletin; Univ. Pa.

News Bur.; Analog.; Galaxy; Mag. Fantasy & Sci. Fiction; Amazing Stories; American Libs.; Kiwanis Mag.; var. anthols. incl. Future Quest; This Side of Infinity; World's Best SF, 1st series; & sci. filmscripts, etc. Mbrships. incl: Sci. Fiction Writers' Am. (VP 1970-71, 1971-72); World Future Soc.; Am. Civil Liberties Union. Hons: Visiting Asst. Prof. Engl., Temple Univ., Phila., Spring 1971 & 1972; MSS & papers on deposit Temple Univ. Lib. Address: 4734 Cedar Ave., Phila., PA 19143, USA.

PURDUM, Herbert R., b. 4 Aug. 1921, Dover, Ohio, USA. Writer. Educ: B.A., Univ. of Southern Calif., L.A. Publs: My Brother John, 1966, 3rd ed. 1971; A Hero for Henry, 1968, 2nd ed. 1969; About 100 radio scripts; About 200 TV scripts; 2 motion picture screenplays. Mbr., Writers' Guild of Am., W. Recip., Spur Award, for My Brother John, Western Writers of Am., 1966. Address: 1301 N. Sparks St., Burbank, CA 91506, USA.

PURDY, James, b. 1923. Editor; Writer. Publs. incl: (novels): 63: Dream Palace, 1956; Color of Darkness, 1957; Malcolm, 1959; The Nephew, 1960; Cabot Wright Begins, 1963; Sleepers in Moon-Crowned Valleys, Pt. I, Jeremy's Version, 1970; Pt.II, The House of the Solitary Maggot, 1971; I am Elijah Thrush, 1972; (play): Children is All, 1962; (stories & poems): An Oyster is a Wealthy Beast, 1967; Mr. Evening, 1968; On the Rebound, 1970; The Running Sun, 1971. Address: 236 Henry St., Brooklyn, NY 11201, USA.

PURDY, Richard Little, b. 1904, Middletown, N.Y., USA. Professor Emeritus of English. Educ: B.A., Ph.D., Yale Univ. Publs: The Larpent Manuscript of the Rivals, 1935; Thomas Hardy, A Bibliographical Study, 1954; Ed., Thomas Hardy's Our Exploits at West Poley, 1952; Ed., Far from the Madding Crowd, 1957. Contbr. to: Times Lit. Supplement; etc. Mbrships: Fellow, Berkeley Coll., Yale Univ., 1933—; Athenaeum Club; Elizabethan Club. Address: 245 Whitney Ave., New Haven, CT 06511, USA.

PURSER, Philip, b. 28 Aug. 1925, Letchworth, UK. Journalist. Educ: M.A., St. Andrews Univ., 1950. Publs: Peregrination 22, 1962; Four days to the Fireworks, 1964; The Twentymen, 1967; Night of Glass, 1968; The Holy Father's Navy, 1971; The Last Great Tram Race, 1974. Contbr. to: Sunday Telegraph; Daily Telegraph mag.; Contrast; The Listener; Nova; Vogue; Holiday Mag (USA); etc. Mbrships: Soc. of Authors; Critics' Circle. Recip., I.P.C. Critic of the Yr. Award, 1965. Address: Hillside, Lois Weedon, Towcester, Northants., UK.

PURTON, Rowland, W., b. 1925, London, UK. Headmaster. Educ: Westminster Coll. Publs: 43 books, inclng: Surrounded by Books, 1962, enlarged ed., 1970; English for Work & Play, vols. 1-4, 1966-67; Trailblazer 1: Forests & 3: Farming, 1969; Let's Look at Maps & Mapmaking, 1971; Churches & Religions, 1972; Know Your Town: Buildings Around Town, People Around Town, Trade Around Town & Looking Around Town, 1972; Rivers & Canals, 1972; Markets & Fairs, 1973; Day by Day, 1973; Parks & Open Spaces, 1975. Contbr. to num. educl. jrnls. Mbrships. incl: Schl. Lib. Assn. Address: 61 Windsor Rd., London E7 0QY, UK.

PUSEY, Merlo John, b. 3 Feb., 1902, Woodruff, Utah, USA. Writer; Editor. Educ: A.B., Univ. of Utah, 1928. Publs: The Supreme Court Crisis, 1937; Big Government: Can We Control It? , 1945; Charles Evans Hughes (biog.), 2 vols., 1951; Eisenhower The President, 1956; The Way We Go To War, 1969; The USA Astride the Globe, 1971; Eugene Meyer (biog.), 1974. Contbr. to: Atlantic; Harper's; Saturday Evening Post; Yale Review; Am. Mercury; Forum; Wash. Post (Assoc. Ed., 1946-71—); etc. Mbrships: Am. Pol. Sci. Assn.; Cosmos & Nat. Press Clubs, Wash. DC. Hons. incl: Pulitzer & Bancroft Prizes for biog., 1952; Litt.D., Brigham Young Univ., 1952; Gavel Award, Am. Bar Assn., 1960. Address: Route 2, Dickerson, MD 20753, USA.

PUTLAND-VAN SOMEREN, Elisabeth Jacoba, pen name van SOMEREN. Liessje, b. 9 Sept. 1913, Groningen, Netherlands. Author; Lecturer. Educ: B.A., Univ. of Amsterdam. Publs: Escape from Holland, 1941; The Young Traveller in Holland, 1948; Ann & Peter in Holland, 1959; Ann & Peter in Belgium, 1962; Erica, 1962; Umpire to the Nations — Hugo Grotius, 1965; Continental Cookbook, 1970. Contbr. to mags. & radio in UK, Holland & Can. Mbrships: Soc. of Authors; PEN; Writers Action Grp. Address: Flat 4, 42 Castelnau, London SW13 9RU, UK.

PUTRAMENT, Jerzy, b. 14 Nov. 1910, Minsk, USSR. Educ: Univ. of Vilno. Publs: (in Polish) (Poems) War & Spring, 1944; Selected Verse, 1951; (novels) Reality, 1948; September, 1952; Crossroads, 1954; Stepchildren, 1965; The Boar; The Forest; Pretty Believers; Half Century of Memoirs; To Be Oneself, 1968; Boldyn, 1969; Lipca, 1973; & num. short stories. Contbr. to: Kultura; Miesiecznik Literacki; Chief Ed., Wspolczesność; Ed., Literatura. Mbr., Union of Polish Writers (V. Chmn., 1959—). Hons. incl: State Prize, 1953,—55, 1964. Address: Zarzad Glowny ZLP, Krakowskie Przedmiescie 87/89, Warsaw, Poland.

PUVAČIĆ, Dušan, b. 6 Apr. 1936, Banjaluka, Yugoslavia. Writer; Literary Critic. Educ: Univ. Belgrade. Editor of Savremenik; many translations of English criticism into Serbian. Contbr. to: Književne novine (Ed., 1962-69). Književnosi; Iraz; Nin; Relations; Books Abroad; Tri-Quarterly; etc. Mbrships: PEN (Sect. Serbian Ctr., 1969-73); Assn. Serbian Writers; Assn. Lit. Transls. Serbia. Address: Univ. of Lancaster, Dept. of Central & S.E. European Studies, Lonsdale Coll., Lancaster, UK.

PUZDROWSKI, Edmund Franciszek, b. 2 Jan. 1942, Kartuzy, Poland. Journalist; Publicist. Educ: M.S., Univ. of Nicholos Kopernik, Toruń. Publs: (poetry) Koło, 1966; Rzecz kaszubska, 1968; Niezmienność, 1968; Betonowy dom, 1971; Wiersze domowe, 1972; Sztuka podnoszenia palców, 1974; Przyszedłem wypełnić, 1975; (story) Białe sa słowa miłości, 1970; Contbr. to: Twórczość; Litery. Mbrships: Polish PEN; Union of Polish Writers. Hons: Prize, Competition for Writers under 30 from E. & Middle European Countries, Int. Writers Fund, London, UK, 1965; Prize, Poetry Festival, Łódź, 1966. Address: Ul. Gdyńska 7 b m.30, 80-340 Gdańsk, Poland.

PUZO, Mario, b. 1920, NYC, USA. Writer; Former Government Official. Educ: New Schl. for Soc. Rsch., NY; Columbia Univ. Publs. (novels): The Dark Arena, USA, 1955, UK, 1971; The Fortunate Pilgrim, USA, 1965, UK, 1966; The Godfather, USA & UK, 1969; (juvenile): The Runaway Summer of Davie Shaw, 1966; (autobiog.): The Godfather Papers & Other Confessions, 1972; num. articles. Address: c/o G.P. Putnam Sons Inc., 200 Madison Ave., N.Y., NY 10016, USA.

PYBUS, Rodney, b. 1938, Newcastle-upon-Tyne, UK. Television Scriptwriter; Part-time Adult Education Tutor. Educ: Gonville & Caius Coll., Cambridge Univ. Publs: In Memoriam Milena, 1973. Contbr., primarily of poetry, to: Stand; Times Lit. Supplement; Encounter; European Judaism; BBC 1 TV 'Full House'; Phoenix; Planet (Wales). Mbrships: Writers Action Grp.; A.C.T.T.; Vice-Chmn., Lit. Comm., Northern Arts. Address: 52 Fern Ave., Jesmond, Newcastle-upon-Tyne NE2 2QX, UK.

PYLES, Thomas, b. 5 June 1905, Frederick, Md., USA. Retired University Professor. Publs: Words & Ways of American English, 1952; The English Language — A Brief History, 1968; English — An Introduction to Language (w. J. Algeo), 1970; The Origins & Development of the English Languages, 2nd ed., 1971. Contbr. to: Saturday Review; N.Y. Times Mag.; PMLA; Mod. Lang. Notes. Mbrships. incl: MLA; Linguistic Soc. of Am.; Am. Dialect Soc. Address: 629 N.E. Boulevard, Gainesville, FL 32601, USA.

PYM, Dora Olive, b. 1O Dec. 1890, Rugby, UK. University Lecturer. Educ: M.A., Girton Coll., Cambridge. Publs: Readings from the Literature of Ancient Rome, 1922; Readings from the Literature of Ancient Greece, 1924; Salve per Saecula, 1936; Outlines for Teaching Greek Reading, 1946; Tom Pym, a Portrait, 1952; Alive on Men's Lips (w. Nancy Silver), 1953; Free Writing, 1956; The Tragedy of Dido & Aeneas, 1970. Mbrships: Life, Sometime Mbr. of Coun., Classical Assn.; Hon., Jt. Assn. of Classical Tchrs. Address: 591 Finchley Rd., London NW3, UK.

PYNCHON, Thomas, b. 8 May 1937, Glen Cove, NY, USA. Writer. Educ: B.A., Cornell Univ., 1958. Publs: (novels) V, USA & UK, 1963; The Crying of Lot 49, USA, 1966, UK, 1967. Hons: Faulkner Award, 1964; Rosenthal Mem. Award, 1967. Address: c/o J. B. Lippincott Inc., E. Washington Square, Phila., PA 19105, USA.

Q

QUANDOUR, Mohy I., b. 6 Mar. 1938, Amman, Jordan. Businessman; Film Producer, Director & Screenwriter. Educ: B.A., 1960, Earlham Coll., Richmond, Ind.; M.A., 1961, Master of Int. Studies, 1962, Claremont Grad. Schl., Calif.; Ph.D., 1964, Claremont Univ. Ctr. Publs: The Skyjack Affair, 1970; Rupture, 1971; Trois Petits Tours, 1972. Mbrships. incl: Screen Writers Guild of Am.; Dirs. Guild of Am.; Independent Film Prods. Assn., Hollywood; Int. Advt. Assn. Address: 3518 Cahuenga Blvd. W., Hollywood, CA 90068, USA.

QUANDT, Richard E., b. 1 June 1930, Budapest, Hungary. Professor of Econometrics. Educ: B.A., Princeton Univ., 1952; M.A., 1955, Ph.D., 1957, Harvard Univ. Publs. incl: Microeconomic Theory: A Mathematical Approach 1958, 2nd ed. (w. J. M. Henderson), 1971; The Demand for Travel: Theory & Measurement, 1970; Nonlinear Methods in Econometrics (w. S. M. Goldfeld), 1972. Contbr. to: num. econ. jrnls. Mbrships. incl: Fellow, Econometric Soc., 1968; Am. Econ. Assn. Address: 162 Springdale Rd., Princeton, NJ 08540, USA.

QUARTEY, Leonard Michael, b. 4 Sept. 1921, Keta, Volta, Ghana. Horticulturist; Curator Grounds & Gardens Organization, Botanical Gardens, University of Ghana; Teacher. Educ: Cert. Hort., Univ. Pa.; N. London & Croydon Polytechnics. Publs: (Contbr.) The Gardener's Directory (by J. W. Stephenson), 1960; The Flowering Trees of the World (by Edwin Manninger), 1962; The Flowering Vines of the World (by Edwin Manninger), 1970. Mbrships: Assoc. Royal Hort. Soc. (elected, 1959); Am. Hort. Soc. (elected, 1962); Fellow, Linnean Soc. (elected, 1972). Address: Univ. Ghana, P.O. Box 55, Legon, Ghana.

QUAYLE, Eric, b. 14 Nov. 1921, Bootle, Lancs., UK. Author. Educ: Aston Commercial Schl., Birmingham. Publs: Ballantyne the Brave, 1967; The Ruin of Sir Walter Scott, 1968; The Collector's Book of Books, 1971; The Collector's Book of Children's Books, 1971; The Collector's Book of Detective Fiction, 1972; The Collector's Book of Boys' Stories, 1973; Old Cook Books — An Illustrated History, 1975. Contbr. to num. mags., jrnls., etc. Mbr., Soc. Authors. Address: Carn Cobba, Zennor, St, St. Ives, Cornwall, UK.

QUDOOSI, Aijazul Haque, b. 15 July 1905, Jullundur, India. Writer; Editor. Educ: Acad. Degrees, Relig. & Oriental Learning, Madarssah Mazahirul Uloom, Saharanpur, & Madarssah Diniyat Sarkar Alee, Hyderabad, Deccan. Publs. incl: Tazkirai Soofiyae Sind, 1959, Punjab 1962, Bengal 1965, Sarhad 1966; Sh. Abdul Quddous Gangoohi & His Teaching, 1961; Urdu Translation of Tozak Jehangiri, Parts I & II, 1970; History of Sind, (2 vols.) 1971-74; Iqbal Key Mehboob Sofia, 1975. Contbr. to: Jang; Hurriyat; Anjam; Monthly Riaz; Alrahim; Alwali; Package; etc. Mbr., Pakistan Writers' Guild. Hons. incl: Dawood Lit. Award, Pakistan Writers' Guild, 1968. Address: 457/5 Qudoosi Manzil, Liaquatabad, Karachi-19, Pakistan.

QUENAU, Raymond, b. 21 Feb. 1903. Editor; Writer. Educ: Univ. of Paris. Publs: Le Chiendent, 1933; Odile, 1937; Un rude hiver, 1940; Pierrot, mon ami, 1942; Exercices de style, 1947; L'instant fatal, 1948; Petite Cosmogonie Portative, 1950; Le dimanche de la vie, 1952; Zazie dans le Métro, 1959; Le Chien à la Mandoline, 1965; Les Fleurs bleues, 1965; Une histoire modèle, 1966; Courir les Rues, 1967; Battre la Campagne, 1968; Le Vol d'Icare, 1968; Fendre les Flots, 1969; Le Voyage en Grèce, 1973; Dir. & Ed., Ency. de la Pléiade. Mbr., Acad. Goncourt. Address: c/o Gallimard, 5 rue Sebastien-Bottin, Paris, France.

QUENNELL, Peter, b. 9 Mar. 1905, Bickley, Kent, UK. Former Professor of English Literature. Educ: Balliol Coll., Oxford. Publs. incl: The Sign of the Fish, 1960; Ruskin: The Portrait of a Prophet, 1952; Shakespeare: the poet & his background, 1963; Aspects of 17th Century Verse; (Ed.) Memoirs of William Hickey; Byron: A Self Portrait (1798-1824); Mayhew's London Labour & the London Poor; Alexander Pope: the Education of Genius, 1968; Romantic England, 1970; Marcel Proust, 1971; Samuel Johnson, His Friends & Enemies, 1972. Contbr. to: Cornhill Mag. (Ed., 1944-51); Ed., Hist. Today. Address: 388 Strand, London WC2, UK.

QUEST, Rodney, b. 27 May 1897, Bolton, UK. Barrister-at-Law. Publs. Men Are Different, 1932; Secret Establishment, 1961; Venus of Samos, 1962; Just Off Bond Street, 1963; Countdown to Doomsday, 1966; The Fenton Affair, 1967; The Cerberus Murders, 1969; Murder with a Vengeance, 1971; Death of a Sinner, 1971. Address: 96 Gregories Rd., Beaconsfield, Bucks., UK.

QUICK, Vivien Muriel Ann, b. 5 Oct. 1919, Codsall, UK. Writer. Publs: Diet Reform Cookbook (w. W. C. Quick), 1952; Everywoman's Wholefood Cookbook, 1974. Contbr. to: Southern Observer; Health for All Mag. Mbr., Vegetarian Soc. Address: Kilmarth, Elmer Rd., Elmer Sands, Bognor Regis PO22 6JA, UK.

QUICK, William Clifford, b. 23 Apr. 1902, Liskeard, UK. Naturopath; Osteopath. Educ: M.Sc., Univ. of Bristol. Publs: Diet Reford Cookbook (w. V. Quick), 1952; Everywoman's Wholefood Cookbook (w. V. Quick), 1974; Bronchitis & Emphysema, 1968; Sinusitis; forthcoming, Cystitis. Contbr. to: Health for All Mag., Hon Ed., 1961-70; Brit. Naturopathic Jrnl.; Osteopathic Review. Mbrships: Soil Assn.; Brit. Naturopathic & Osteopathic Assn.; Vegetarian Soc. Address: Kilmarth, Elmer Rd., Elmer Sands, Bognor Regis PO22 6JA, UK.

QUIGLEY, Aileen, pen names LINDLEY, Erica; FABIAN, Ruth, b. 1930, Luton, Beds., UK. Writer. Educ: Univ. Coll., B.A., London. Publs: King's Pawn, 1971; Child of Fire, 1971; Shadow of Dungeon Wood, 1972; Rose Brocade, 1972; Bloodstone, 1972; Scent of Violets, 1973; Devil in Holy Orders, 1973; King Bastard, 1973; Court Cadenza, 1974. Contbr. to: My Weekly; BBC Morning Story; BBC Woman's Hour; Woman's Day, Aust.; Allers, Norway, Sweden, Denmark. Mbr., Soc. of Authors. Agent: Campbell Thomson & McLaughlin Ltd. Address: 14 Newquay Rd., Park Hall, Walsall, Staffs., UK.

QUIGLEY, John, b. 30 Sept. 1928, Glasgow, UK. Company Director (Wines & Spirits); Author. Publs: To Remember with Tears, 1963; The Bitter Lollipop, 1964; The Secret Soldier, 1966; The Golden Stream, 1970; The Last Checkpoint, 1971; King's Royal, 1975. Address: White Court, Killearn, Stirlingshire, UK.

QUIGLEY, Martin S., b. 24 Nov. 1917, Chgo., Ill., USA. Writer; Educator; Publisher. Educ: A.B., Georgetown Univ., 1939; M.A. 1973, Ed.D. 1975, Columbia Univ. Publs: Great Gaels, 1944; Roman Notes, 1946; Magic Shadows: The Story of the Origin of Motion Pictures, 1948; Ed., New Screen Techniques, 1953; Catholic Action in Practice (co-author), 1962; Films in America (co-author), 1970. Contbr. to: Motion Picture Herald; Motion Picture Daily (Ed.-in-chief); Ency. Britannica; Mid-50s Motion Picture Technol.; num. mags. (articles on films & family life educ.). Address: Quigley Publishing Co. Inc., 1270 6th Ave., N.Y., NY 10020, USA.

QUIGLY, Isabel Madeleine, b. 17 Sept. 1926, Ontaneda, near Santander, Spain. Writer. Educ: B.A., Newnham Coll., Cambridge, UK. Publs: The Eye of Heaven (novel), 1955; Charlie Chaplin, the Early Comedies; Pamela Hansford Johnson (Writers & their Work series); Many transls. from Italian, Spanish & French. Contbr. to: Times Lit. Supplement; Encounter; Fin. Times; Guardian; Spectator (Film Critic, 1956-66) Tablet. Mbrships: Comm. of Mgmt., Soc. of Authors, 3 yrs.; Exec. Comm., Transls.' Assn., 3 yrs.; Chmn., 1973; Exec. Comm., PEN, 6 yrs.; Permanent PEN Rep., Nat. Coun., Nat. Book League; Assoc., Newnham Coll., Cambridge. Recip., Florio Prize, 1966. Address: Tower Cottage, Fletching, Uckfield, Sussex, UK.

QUIN, Ann (Marie), b. 17 Mar. 1936, Brighton, Sussex, UK. Part-time Secretary. Publs: (novels) Berg, UK, 1964, USA, 1966; Three, UK, 1966, USA, 1968; Passages, 1966; Tripticks, 1972. Contbr. to: Nova; El Corno Emplumado, Mexico City; Transatlantic Review. Hons: D. H. Lawrence Fellowship, Univ. of N.M., USA, 1964; Harkness Fellowship, 1964-67; Arts Coun. Grant, 1969. Address: 22 Lansdowne Rd., London W11, UK.

QUINN, (Rev.) James, b. 1919, Glasgow, UK. Priest; Writer. Educ: Univ. of Glasgow; Heythrop Coll., Oxon.; M.A. Publs: Our Lady in Scripture & Tradition, 1960; New Hymns for all Seasons, 1969; The Theology of the Eucharist, 1973. Mbr., Soc. of Jesus. Address: 28 Lauriston St., Edinburgh EH3 9DJ, UK.

QUINN, John Michael, b. 27 Nov. 1922, Co. Tyrone, Ireland. Priest; Educator; Institute Associate Director.

Educ: B.A., Villanova Univ., 1945; M.A., 1949, Ph.D., 1960, Cath. Univ. of Am. Publs: The Doctrine of Time in St. Thomas Aquinas, 1960; The Concept of Time in St. Augustine, 1965; The Thomism of Etienne Gilson: A Critical Study, 1971. Contbr. to: New Scholasticism; The Thomist; Augustinianum. Mbr., var. relig. & philos. orgs. Address: Villanova Univ., Villanova, PA 19085, USA.

QUIRK, (Charles) Randolph, b. 12 July 1920, Lambfell, Isle of Man, UK. Professor of English Language & Literature; Author. Educ: M.A., Ph.D., D.Lit., London Univ. Publs. incl: An Old English Grammar (w. C. L. Wrenn), 1955, 2nd ed., 1958; The Teaching of English (w. A. H. Smith), 1959, 2nd ed., 1964; The Use of English, 1962, 2nd ed., 1968; Essays on English Language — Mediaeval & Modern, 1968; A Grammar of Contemporary English (co-author), 1972; A University Grammar of English (w. S. Greenbaum), 1973; The Linguist & the English Language, 1974. Contbr. to: Lang.; Jrnl. of Linguistics; Listener; etc. Mbrships. incl: Philol. Soc.; Linguistic Assn. of GB; Linguistic Soc. of Am. Address: 62 Talbot Rd., Highgate, London N6 4RA, UK.

QUIRK, Lawrence Joseph, b. 9 Sept. 1923, Lynn, Mass., USA. Author; Journalist; Editor-Publisher. Educ: B.A., Suffolk Univ., Boston, Mass., 1949; Grad. Study, Boston Univ., 1949-50. Publs. incl: Films of Joan Crawford, 1968; Robert Francis Kennedy, 1968; Films of Ingrid Bergman, 1970; Films of Paul Newman, 1971; Films of Fredric March, 1971; Films of William Holden, 1973; The Great Romantic Films, 1974; Films of Robert Taylor, 1975; Films of Ronald Colman, 1975. Ed. & Publr.-Owner, Quirk's Reviews. Contbr. to num. film publs.; N.Y. Times. Address: 74 Charles St., N.Y., NY 10014, USA.

QUIROGA, Elena, Spanish Writer. Publs: Viento del Norte, 1951; La Sangre, 1952; Algo Pasa en la Calle, 1954; La Enferma, 1954; La Careta, 1955; Plácida, La Joven, 1956; La Ultima Corrida, 1958; Tristura, 1960; Escribo tu Nombre, 1965. Hons: Nadal Prize, 1950; Critics' Prize, 1960. Address: Real Acad. de la Hist., Léon 21, Madrid 14, Spain.

QUIXLEY, Joan Muriel Edmund, b. 4 Dec. 1913, Lincoln, UK. Nurse Tutor. Educ: Univ. of London; Nightingale Schl., St. Thomas' Hospital; Royal Coll. of Nursing. Publ., Obstetrics & Gynaecology for Nurses, 1956. Address: 18 Castle Garden, Petersfield, Hants., GU32 3AG, UK.

QURESHI, Ishtiaq Husain, b. 1903, Patiali, India. Minister of Education, Pakistan; Vice-Chancellor, Karachi University. Educ: Univ. of Delhi; Univ. of Cambridge; UK; M.A.; Ph.D. Publs: The Administration of the Sultanate of Delhi; The Muslim Community of the Subcontinent of India & Pakistan: A Historical Analysis; The Pakistani Way of Life; The Struggle for Pakistan; The Administration of the Mughul Empire; Ulema in Politics; Education in Pakistan. Contbr. to: Sources of Indian Tradition; Jrnl. of Pakistan Hist. Soc.; Pakistan Horizon; Hist. of Freedom Movement; For. Policies in a World of Change; etc. Address: Zeba Manzar, Shahid-I-Millat Rd., Karachi — 5, Pakistan.

R

RABIN, Chaim, b. 22 Nov. 1915, Giessen, Germany. University Professor of Hebrew; Author. Educ: B.A., 1937; Dip. Oriental Studies, 1938; Ph.D., 1939; D.Phil., 1942; Hebrew Univ. of Jerusalem; Schl. of Oriental Studies, London; Christ Ch., Oxford. Publs. incl: Everyday Arabic (co-author), 1940; Everyday Hebrew, 1942; Arabic Reader, 1947; Hebrew Reader, 1948; The Zadokite Documents, 1954; Qumran Studies, 1957; A Short History of the Hebrew Language, 1974. Contbr. to: Ency. Britannica; Enci. dello Spettacolo; Hebrew Ency.; Ency. Judaica; etc. Mbrships: Hebrew Lang. Acad.; Israel Assn. for Applied Linguistics. Address: P.O. Box 7158, Jerusalem 91070, Israel.

RABON, Florence Graham, b. 22 July 1906, Key West, Fla., USA. Writer, Public Relations. Educ: B.S., Fla. State Univ. Writer, relig., drama, music, feature articles, for Miami Herald newspaper. Contbr. to Key West Citizen. Mbrships: Nat. League of Am. Pen Women; Bd. of Dirs., Fla. PR Assn. Address: P.O. Box 1243, Key West, FL 33040, USA.

RADCLIFFE, Donald Vane, b. 23 Mar. 1920, Belle Plaine, Iowa, USA. Freelance Writer. Educ: B.S., Iowa State Univ., Ames Iowa. Publs: Instructing Older Trainees, 1970; Motivation & the Disadvantaged, 1971; To See or Not, 1974; & short stories incl. Song of the Simidor. Contbr. to: Comtemporary Surgery (Assoc. Ed., 1972-73); Annals Opthalmol. (Assoc. Ed., 1968—); Jrnl. Cryosurgery (Assoc. Ed., 1967-70); Contemporary Therapy (Assoc. Ed., 1974—); Hearing Aid Jrnl. (Ed.); Dental Team; Fishing Gazette; Future; Gas Inds.; Incentive Mktng.; etc. Mbrships: Am. Med. Writers' Assn.; Assoc. Bus. Writers Am. Hons: Song of the Simidor included in Martha Foley Best Am. Short Stories, 1967. Address: 5615 N. Wayne Ave., Chicago, IL 60660, USA.

RADCLIFFE, (Rev.) Lynn James, b. 14 Apr. 1896, Cornwall, N.Y., USA. Clergyman. Educ: B.A., Wesleyan Univ., 1919; M. Div., Boston Univ., 1922; Grad. Schl., Harvard Univ., 1922-23; D.D., Syracuse Univ. 1937, Wesleyan Univ. 1962. Publs: Making Prayer Real, USA 1952, UK 1956; Seven Steps Toward Spiritual Progress, 1953; With Christ in the Garden, 1959; With Christ in the Upper Room, 1960. Contbr. to: Racism: A World Issue, 1947; Sermons, The Upper Room, 1962; The Christian Advocate; Zions Herald. Mbr., Cinn. Lit. Club, 1950-61. Hons. incl: Book of the Yr. Prize, Ohio Lib. Assn., 1953. Address: 21 Ferndale Rd., Madison, NJ 07940, USA.

RADDALL, Thomas Head, b. 13 Nov. 1903, Hythe, Kent, UK. Author. Publs: His Majesty's Yankees, USA 1942, UK 1944; Roger Sudden, USA 1945, UK 1946; Pride's Fancy, USA 1946, UK 1948; The Nymph & the Lamp, USA 1950, UK 1951; Tidefall, USA 1953, UK 1954; The Wings of Night, USA 1956, UK 1957. Hons: Gov.-Gen's. Award, Can., 1944, 1948, 1957; Lorne Pierce Gold Medal, Royal Soc. of Can., 1956; Order of Can., 1971. Address: 44 Park St., Liverpool, N.S., Can.

RADDATZ, Fritz J., b. 3 Sept. 1931, Berlin, Germany. University Teacher; Writer. Educ: D.Phil.habil. Publs. incl: Kurt Tucholsky — Bildbiographie, 1961; Verwerfungen — 6 literarische Essays, 1971; Erfolg oder Wirkung — Schicksale politische Publizisten in Deutschland, 1972; Georg Lukacs, Monographie, 1973; Paul Wunderlich — Das graphische Werk, 1974; Karl Marx, Eine politische Biographie, 1975; also author, 10 TV- films. Contbr. to: Merkur; Akzente; Frankfurter Heete; Neue Rundschau; Zeit; Spiegel; Suddeutsche Zeitung; Frankfurter Allgemeine Zeitung; var. anthols. Mbrships: PEN; Pres., Kurt Tucholsky Fndn. Address: Leinpfad 109, 2 Hamburg 60, W. Germany.

RADEMACHER, Gail, b. 18 Feb. 1945, Highland Park, Ill., USA. Playwright. Educ: B.A. (German lit.). Drama prods: Ladies' Day, 1970; The Death of Kikoss, 1970; Guns & Butter (adaptation, 3 playlets by Cervantes), 1971; Helen (from Euripides), 1971; Medea (from Euripides), 1972; Oedipus Tyrannus (from Sophocles), 1974; The Highwaymen (adaptation of Schiller's Die Röuber), 1974. Address: 20 Norman Court, 395 Nether St., London N3, UK.

RADEV, Milcho, b. 4 Apr. 1925, Stanke Dimitrov, Bulgaria. Writer. Publs: (in Bulgarian) Along the footway, 1960; Saturday Evening, 1960; Once More Yesterday, 1974. Contbr. to: Literatouren Front. Mbrships: Union of Bulgarian Writers; Union of Bulgarian Jrnlsts. Hons: Prize, Union of Bulgarian Writers, 1962; Sofia Prize, 1966. Address: Sofia, ul.VL.Poptomov, 48, Bulgaria.

RADICE, Betty, b. 1912, East Yorks., UK. Tutor in Classics, English Literature & Philosophy; Editor, Penguin Classics since 1964. Educ: B.A., St. Hilda's Coll., Oxford. Publs. incl: (Ed. & transl.) The Letters of the Younger Pliny, 1963; Terence: The Brothers & Other Plays, 1965; Phormio & Other Plays, 1967; Livy: The War with Hannibal, 1965; Pliny: Letters & Panegyrics, 1969; Erasmus, Praise of Folly, 1970; The Letters of Abelard & Heloise, 1974; Who's Who in the Ancient World, revised ed., 1973. Contbr. to: Arion; Greece & Rome; etc. Mbrships: Classical Assn.; Roman Soc.; Royal Soc. of Lit. Address: 65 Cholmeley Cresc., London N6, UK.

RADICHKOV, Yordan, b. 16 Oct. 1929, Kalimanitsa, Bulgaria. Writer. Publs: (in Bulgarian) Hot Noon, 1965; Ferocious Mood, 1965; Unlighted Yards, 1966; Goatbeard, 1967; Gunpowder Primer, 1969; Rock Art, 1970; Small Fatherland, 1974. Contbr. to: September; PlamAk; SAvremennik; Obzor; Literatouren Front. Mbr., Union of Bulgarian Writers. Hons: Dimitrov Prize, 1971; Honoured Worker in Culture, 1972; Prizes, Union of Bulgarian Writers, 1965, 1966, 1968. Address: Sofia, bul. Tolbouhin, 27, Bulgaria.

RADLEY, Eric John, b. 12 June 1917, Ratnapura, Sri Lanka. Farmer. Educ: B.A., Dip.Ed., Univ. of London. Publ: Notes on Economic History. Contbr. to: Country Diary; Forest of Dean Newspapers. Address: Elton Farm, Newnham-on-Severn, Glos., UK.

RADLEY, Jack Augustus, b. 27 June 1907, Portsmouth, UK. Consulting Scientist. Educ: Portsmouth Coll. of Tech. & Sci. Publs: Fluorescence Analysis in Ultraviolet Light, 1933, sev. eds.; Starch & its Derivatives, 1940, 3rd ed. (2 vols.), 1953, 4th ed., 1968; Photography in Crime Detection; The Manufacture & Technology of Starch & its Derivatives, 1975. Contbr. to: Food Manufacture; Discovery; Analyst die Starke; Chemical Age; Chemist & Druggist; etc. Mbrships: F.R.I.C.; Soc. of Dyers & Colourists; Soc. of Chemical Ind. Address: 220-222 Elgar Rd., Reading, Berks., UK.

RADNITZ, Brad Irwin, b. 22 Oct. 1933, Brooklyn, N.Y., USA. Television & Motion Picture Writer. Educ: B.S., Northwestern Univ. Motion Picture & TV Credits: McHale's Navy, 1966, 1967; Lucy, 1966; Mission Impossible, 1967; To Die in Paris, 1968; The Reluctant Spies (TV Movie of the Wk.), 1969; Family Affair, 1969, 1970; To Rome with Love, 1970; McMillan & Wife, 1972; Hec Ramsey, 1973; Columbo, 1974; Get Christy Love; Caribe, 1975. Mbrships. incl: Writers' Guild Am. (Coun. Bd. Dirs., 1972, 1973; Bd. Dirs., Prod., Writers' Guild Am. Pension Plan, Health & Welfare Plan; Co-Chmn., Negotiating Comm., 1972, 1973); Acad. TV Arts & Scis. Address: 18049 Coastline Dr., Malibu, CA 90265, USA.

RADOEV, Ivan, b. 30 Mar. 1927, Pordim, Bulgaria. Repertory Director, Theatre of Sofia. Publs: (in Bulgarian) (plays) The World is Small, 1956; A Justinian Coin, 1959; Romeo, Juliet & Oil, 1965; Red & Brown, 1971; Sadal & Orpheus, 1971. Contbr. to: Literatouren Front; Narodna Kultura; Teatar. Mbrships: PEN; Union of Bulgarian Writers. Address: Sofia, bul. Biriuosov, 55, Bulgaria.

RADWANSKI, Pierre Arthur, pen name AL VAN-GAR, b. 4 Jan. 1903, Latoszyn, Poland. Professor of Anthropology; Writer. Educ: L.Ph., Jagellonian Univ., Cracow, 1926; D.Sc., 1931. Author, Man The Known, 1966, Japanese ed., 1970, Engl. abridged ed., 1972. Contbr. to: Royal Anthropol. Inst. of GB & Ireland; Bull. of Polish Inst. of Arts & Scis., N.Y. Mbrships. incl: N.Y. Acad. of Scis.; Royal Anthropol. Soc. of Belgium; Past Sec. Gen., Polish Inst. of Arts & Scis. Hons. incl: Award of Queen Elisabeth of Belgium, 1951; Grant, Can. Coun., 1966; Nominee for Nobel Peace Prize, 1969; Silver Medal, UK, 1973. Address: 5050 Roslyn Ave., Apt. 31, Montreal H3W 2L2, Can.

RADZINOWICZ, (Sir) Leon, b. 15 Aug. 1906, Lodz, Poland. Professor of Criminology. Educ: M.A., Geneva, Switz.; M.A.; LL.D., Cambridge Univ., UK; LL.D., Rome, Italy; LL.D., Cracow, Poland. Publs: History of English Criminal Law, 4 vols., 1948-68; In Search of Criminology, 1961; Ideology & Crime, 1966; Crime & Justice (Ed., w. Marvin Wolfgang, 3 vols., 1971; Cambridge Studies in Criminology, 33 vols. Contbr. to maj. legal & criminol.

reviews. Hons: Fellow, Brit. Acad.; Hon. For. Mbr., Am. Acad. of Arts & Scis.; James Barr Prize, Harvard Law Schl., USA, 1950; Kt., Order of Leopold, Belgium, 1930; Coronation Medal, 1953; Kt., UK, 1970. Address: 21 Cranmer Rd., Cambridge, UK.

RADZYMINSKA, Józefa, pen name MIECZYSŁAWA, b. 1 June 1921, Warsaw, Poland. Writer. Educ: Acad. of Pol. Sci., Warsaw. Publs. incl: The Line of Blood (poetry), 1944; A Tale About Strangers (poetry), 1953; Another Earth (prose), 1964; The Most Important Thing (prose), 1966; Night Over Us (prose), 1966; The Heavy Ring (poetry), 1969; Roses From Fire (prose), 1969; Second Time Ashes (prose), 1970; The White Eagle on Rio de la Plata (prose), 1971. Contbr. to Polish, Engl., Spanish & Italian lang. jrnls. Mbrships. incl: Union of Polish Writers; PEN. Hons. incl: 3 Prizes for Novels, 1955, 1956, 1958. Address: Broniewskiego 14/29, 01-771 Warsaw, Poland.

RAE, Isobel Falconer, b. 1902, London, UK. Writer. Educ: M.A., Girton Coll., Cambridge. Publs: The Strange Story of Dr. James Barry; Knox the Anatomist; Charles Cameron, Architect to the Court of Russia, 1971. Contbr. to radio & to Scottish newspapers & other publs. Address: Dunlugas Cottage, Nairn, UK.

RAE, John Malcolm, b. 20 Mar. 1931, London, UK. School Headmaster; Author. Educ: M.A., Sidney Sussex Coll., Cambridge, 1955; Ph.D., Dept. of War Studies, King's Coll., London, 1965. Publs: The Custard Boys, 1960; Conscience & Politics, 1970; The Golden Crucifix, 1974; The Treasure of Westminster Abbey, 1975; (film script) Reach for Glory (co-author). Contbr. to: Times Lit. Supplement. Recip., UN Award, for Reach for Glory, 1962. Address: Westminster School, 17 Dean's Yard, London, SW1P 3PB, UK.

RAE, Margaret Doris, pen name RAE, Doris, b. 13 Jan. 1907, Newccastle upon Tyne, UK. Writer. Publs: Sings the Nightingale, 1956; The Whispering Wind, 1958; The Music & the Splendour, 1959; Serenade to a Nurse, 1962; Bright Particular Star, 1962; Magic Spring, 1965; The Constant Star, 1966; Flame of the Forest, 1969; Honeysuckle in the Hedge, 1973; The Spirit & the Fire, 1974; Duet in Low Key, 1974. Address: 79 Cheviot View, Ponteland, Northumberland NE20 9BH, UK.

RAEBURN, Antonia Dora, b. 27 Oct. 1934, London, UK. Historian. Educ: Art Tchr.'s Dip., Inst. of Educ. Univ. of Bristol. Publs: The Militant Suffragettes, 1973, 2nd ed., 1974; The Suffragette View, 1975. Contbr. to: The Times; Times Educl. Supplement. Address: Dovecote Cottage, Membland, Newton Ferrers, Plymouth, Devon, UK.

RAFFEL, Burton Nathan, b. 27 Apr. 1928, NYC, USA. Writer; University Teacher. Educ: B.A., Brooklyn Coll., 1948; M.A., Ohio State Univ., 1949; J.D., Yale Univ., 1958. Publs. incl: Short Story 3 (w. others), 1960; Poems from the Old English, 1960; Beowulf, 1963; Anthology of Modern Indonesian Poetry, 1964; From the Vietnamese, 1969; Mia Poems, 1968; The Complete Poetry & Prose of Chairil Anwar, 1970; Russian Poetry under the Tsars, 1971; Introduction to Poetry, 1971; Why Re-create, 1973; Horace: Ars Poetica, 1974. Address: 765 Harrison St., Denver, CO 80206, USA.

RAGAN, Samuel Talmadge, b. 31 Dec. 1915, Berea, N.C., USA. Editor-Publisher; Television Performer. Educ: B.A., Atlantic Christian Coll., 1936. Publs: The Tree In The Far Pasture (collected poems), 1964; The New Day, 1964; Dixie Looked Away, 1965; Free Press & Fair Trial, 1967; Back to Beginnings (w. Elizabeth S. Ives), 1969; To The Water's Edge (collected poems), 1972. Contbr. to: World Book Ency. (contbng. ed.); var. mags. Mbr., num. press assns. Hons. incl: Arnold Young Award, best book of poetry, 1964 & 1972. Address: 255 Hill Rd., Southern Pines, NC 28387, USA.

RAGHUBIR SINH, b. 23 Feb. 1908, Laduna, Sitamau, Ctrl. India. Author; Historian; Former M.P. & State Administrator. Educ: B.A., 1928, LL.B., 1930, M.A., 1933; D.Litt., 1936, Agra Univ., U.P. Publs: (Hindi) Purva-Madhyakalin Bharat (hist.), 1932; Malwa men Yugantar (hist.), 1938; Shesh Smritiyan (essays), 1939, 4th ed., 1966; Purva-Adhunik Rajasthan (hist.), 1951; Maharana Pratap (biog.), 1973; (English) Malwa in Transition, 1936; Indian States & New Regime, 1938; Durga Das Rathor (biog.), forthcoming. Contbr. to: Sarswati; Nagari Pracharini Patrika. Mbrships. incl: PEN, Indian br.; Royal Asiatic Soc., UK (Life). Hons: Mangla Prasad Prize, 1945;

U.P. Govt. Prize, 1954. Address: "Raghubir Niwas", Sitamau, (Malwa — M.P.), 458-990, India.

RAHIKAINEN, Kalevi Ferdinand, b. 3 Apr. 1927, Koskenpää, Finland. Author. Educ: Working People's Acad.; Drawing Schl., Turku Art Soc. Publs: (poetry) Hyvaa huomenta, 1958; Kuin maa, 1958; Vaiti minussa, 1962; Paikka maassa, 1969; Asiakirja, 1970. Pois Päin, 1972; EKAlogia, 1973; (novels) Aurinko on vielä nuori, 1962; Kaikki Se, 1966; Minä Urho ja Mao, 1973. Contbr. to var. Finnish mags. & newspapers. Mbrships: Finnish Soc. of Authors; Finnish Soc. of Critics. Address: Postipuuntie 5 A 5, 02600 Espoo 60, Finland.

RAHNEMA, Zain-Alabedin, b. 6 Dec. 1894, Karbala, Mesopotamia (now Iraq). Former Iranian Ambassador to France, Lebanon, Syria & Jordan; Former Vice-Premier; Writer & Author. Publs: The Pyambar (The Messenger), 1962, 21 eds.; Translation & Commentary of the Holy Quran, 3 vols. Contbr. to: Nowbabahr; Rahnema. Mbrships: Gen. Sec., Iranian PEN; Ency. Britannica Writers Grp. Recip., Cmdr., Order of Arts & Letters, France. Address: 219 Niavaran Ave., Kuye Ranema, Teheran, Iran.

RAINBOW, Bernarr, b. 2 Oct. 1914, London, UK. Lecturer in Music Education. Educ: Trinity Coll. of Music, London; Leicester Univ.; M.Ed.; Ph.D.; F.T.C.L.; L.R.A.M.; A.R.C.M.; L.G.S.M. Publs: Music in the Classroom, 1956, 2nd ed., 1971; The Land without Music, 1967; Handbook for Music Teachers, 1968; The Choral Revival, 1970. Contbr. to: Grove's Dictionary; Dictionary of Liturgy & Worship; Musical Times; Music in Educ.; Jrnl. of Educ.; etc. Mbrships: Bd. of studies in Music, London Univ.; Chmn., Tonic Solfa Assn.; Dir., Curwen Inst. Address: 6 Townshend Terr., Richmond, Surrey, UK.

RAINIO, Kullervo, b. 10 Aug. 1924, Jyväskylä, Finland. Professor, Social Psychology; Member of Parliament. Educ: Ph.D., Helsinki Univ., 1955. Publs. incl: (poems) Nurkkapöydässa, 1945; Lapsellinen yksinpuhelu, 1946; Tietämättä mistään, 1950; Nämä kuvat, 1958; Leadership Qualities, 1955; A Stochastic Theory of Social Contacts, 1962; Group Maze, 1972; Sosiaalipsykologian oppikirja (w. Klaus Helkama), 1974. Contbr. to: Quality & Quantity. Mbrships: Suomen Kirjailijaliitto; Suomen Psykologinen Seura (Chmn., 1958-59); Assn. Int. de Psychologie Appliquée; European Assn., Expmtl. Social Psychol. Address: Petaksentie 44, 00630 Helsinki 63, Finland.

RAINWATER, Dorothy Thornton, b. 14 Sept. 1918, Ardmore, Okla., USA. Writer. Educ: B.A., Univ. of Okla. Publs: American Silver Manufacturers, 1966; American Spoons, Souvenir & Historical, 1968; American Silverplate, 1972; Sterling Silver Holloware, 1973. Contbr. to: Antiques; Antiques Jrnl.; Antiques Trader; Jewelers' Circular — Keystone; The Magazine Silver; The Spinning Wheel; Western Collector. Mbrships: Nat. Sci. Fair (Int. Coun.); Hawaiian Acad. of Sci. (Chmn., Inter-Soc. Sci. Educ. Coun.); Hawaiian State Sci. Fair; AAUW. Address: 2805 Liberty Pl., Bowie, MD 20715, USA.

RAJAN, Mannaraswamighala Sreeranga, b. 4 Aug. 1920, Badikayalapalli, Andhra Pradesh, India. Professor of International Organization; Editor, India Quarterly & Foreign Affairs Reports (monthly), Indian Council World Affairs. Educ: M.A., 1943, Litt.D., 1963, Mysore Univ.; M.A., Columbia Univ., N.Y., 1952. Publs: United Nations & Domestic Jurisdiction, 1958, 2nd ed., 1961; The Post-War Transformation of the Commonwealth, 1965; India in World Affairs, 1954-56, 1964; Non-alignment, India & the Future, 1970; India's Foreign Relations During the Nehru Era: Some Studies, forthcoming. Contbr. to: Int. Org. (Boston); etc. Mbr., Indian Coun. World Affairs, New Delhi (Mbr. Exec. Commn). Hons: Asian Fellow, Aust. Nat. Univ., Canberra, 1971-72. Address: Schl. Int. Studies, Jawaharlal Nehru Univ., New Mehrauli Rd., New Delhi 110057, India.

RAKENG, Oddrar, pen name Orak, b. 24th Jan. 1939, Tistedal, Norway. Journalist. Publs: 4 children's books, 1966-69; Vi som gar kjerrereien, 1970; Det nye diktet, 1971; Fargesendinger, 1973. Mbrships: Norwegian Union of Journalists; Norwegian Press Union; Assn. of Young People's Authors; Norwegian Author's Assn.; Norwegian Authors' Ctr. Recip., 1st Prize for best poem in Profil, 1961. Address: Hertug Skules reg 30, 2600 Lillehammer, Norway.

RAKOFF, ALVIN, b. 6 Feb. 1927, Toronto, Can. Film & Television Director. Educ: B.A., Univ. of Toronto.

Contbr. plays (adaptations & originals) to BBC, Anglia & Thames TV. Mbrships: Pres., Assn. of Dirs. & Prods.; Soc. of Film & TV Arts; Assn. of Cinematographers & TV Techns.; Writers' Guild of GB. Address: 1 The Orchard, London W4 1JZ, UK

RAKOS, Sandor, b. 25 Nov. 1921, Ujfehértó-Kálmánháza, Hungary. Poet. Publs: The Dog Answers, 1946; Manhood, 1952; In the Courtyard of the Fire, 1957; The Proceeding of the Poor, 1959; Gilgamesh (transl.), 1960; Trees, In Storm, 1962; The Message of the Claytables, A Sumerian Anthology (transl.), 1963; Circles Enlarging, 1965; Silence Worth a Cry, 1969; A Naked Face, 1971; The Present of the Memory, 1973. Contbr. to: Nagyvilág; Kortárs; Alföld; Élet és irodalom. Mbrships: Union of Hungarian Writers; Hungarian PEN. Hons: József Attila Prize, 2nd degree, 1958, 1st degree, 1963; Order of Labour, Silver Grade, 1971 Address: Gorkii fasor 3 H-1071 Budapest VII, Hungary.

RALPHS, Sheila, b. 1923, Abergavenny, UK. Senior University Lecturer; Writer. Educ: B.A., Bedford Coll., London. Publs: Etterno Spiro: A Study in the Nature of Dante's Paradise; Dante's Journey to the Centre: Some Patterns in his Allegory. Contbr. to: Mod. Lang. Studies; Ency. Britannica. Address: Italian Dept., Manchester University, Manchester, UK.

RAMA, Carlos M., b. 26 Oct. 1921, Montevideo, Uruguay. Editor; Lawyer; Professor of Universal History. Educ: Univs. of Montevideo & Paris. Publs: incl: La Historia y la Novela, 1947; Ensaya de Sociologica Uruguaya, 1956, L'Amerique Latine, 1959; La religion en el Uruguay, 1964; Sociologia del Uruguay, 1965; Los afro-uraguayos, 1967; Sociologia de America Latina, 1970. Contbr. to: Nuestro Tiempo, (Ed., 1954-6); Ed., Gacetilla Austral, 1961—; El Siglo Ilustrado. Hons: Order of Liberation, Spain; Officier des Palmes Acad., France. Address: Coronel Alegre 1340, Montevideo, Uruguay.

RAMANUJAN, A. K., b. 16 Mar. 1929, Mysore, India. University Professor. Educ: B.A.; M.A.; Ph.D. Publs: The Striders, 1966; The Interior Landscape (transl. from Classical Tamil), 1967; Relations, 1972; Speaking of Siva (transl. from Medieval Kannada), 1973. Contbr. to: Poetry; London Mag.; N.Y. Times; etc. Hons: Poetry Soc. Recommendation, 1966; Tamil Writers' Assn. Award, 1969; Nat. Book Award Nominee, 1974. Address: 1130 E 59th St., Univ. of Chgo., Chgo., IL 60673, USA.

RAMAZANI, Rouhollah K., b. 21 Mar. 1928, Tehran, Iran. University Professor. Educ: LL.M., Schl. of Law, Econs. & Pol. Sci., Univ. of Tehran, 1951; Dept. of Pol. Sci., Univ. of Ga.; S.J.D., Schl. of Law, Univ. of Va., 1954. Publs: The Middle East & the European Common Market, 1964; The Foreign Policy of Iran, 1500-1941; A Developing Nation in World Affairs, 1966; The Northern Tier: Afghanistan, Iran & Turkey, 1966; The Persian Gulf: Iran's Role, 1972, reprinted, 1973; Iran's Foreign Policy, 1941-73: A Study of Foreign Policy in Modernizing Nations, 1975. Contbr. to num. acad. jrnls. Mbr., var. legal assns. Address: Cabell Hall 232, Univ. of Va., Charlottesville, VA, USA.

RAMIREZ-DE-ARELLANO, Diana Teresa Clotilde, b. 3 June 1919, NYC, USA. Poet; Writer; Literary Critic; Professor. Educ: B.A., Univ. of Puerto Rico, Rio Piedras, 1941; M.A., Columbia Univ., N.Y., 1946; Ph.D., Univ. of Madrid, Spain, 1962. Publs: Los Ramirez de Arellano de Lope de Vega, 1954; Caminos de la creacion poetica en Pedro Salinas, 1956; Angeles de Ceniza, 1958; Un vuelo casi humano, 1960; Poesia Contemporánea en Lengua Española, 1961; Privilegio, 1965; Del Señalado oficio de la muerte, 1974. Contbr. to num. poetry & other jrnls. Mbrships. incl: PEN; Puerto Rican Writers Assn.; Soc. of Puerto Rican Authors; Fndr. & Hon. Pres., Ateneo Puertorriqueno de Nuevo York. Recip., num. awards & prizes. Address: 23 Harbor Circle, Centerport, L.I., NY 11721, USA.

RAMM, Eva, b. 23 Nov. 1925, Bergen, Norway. Editor; Novelist. Educ: Cand. Psychol. Publs: Med Stöv Pâ Hjernen, 1958; Engel Pâ Vidvanke, 1962; Kvinnekall Og Mannefall, 1965; Noe Mâ Gjöres, 1968; En Gang Var Himmelen Blâ, 1970; Mors Tre Hoder, 1973. Mbrships: Norwegian Authors' Assn.; Ungdomslitteraturens forfatterlag; PEN; Norsk Parapsykologisk forening. Address: Kirkeveien 74 D, Oslo 3, Norway.

RAMMURTY, Annavarapu Venkat, b. 8 Aug. 1950, Jami, Andhra Pradesh, India. Journalist. Educ: B.Sc.,

C.M.D. Coll., Bilaspur; M.Sc., Govt. Coll. of Sci., Raipur. Contbr. (in Hindi, Kannada, & Gujarati langs.) to: Dharmayug; Karmaveer; Kismet; Vigyan Pragati, mostly on sci. subjects. Address: Sub-Ed., Dharmayug, The Times of India Bldg., Dr. Dadabhai Naoroji Rd., Bombay 400001, India.

RAMS, Edwin M., b. 31 Dec. 1922, Chgo., Ill., USA. Urban Economic Consultant. Educ: B.S., Northern Ill. Univ.; LL.B., LL.M., Jur.D., John Marshall Law Schl. Publs: Condemnation Appraisal Handbook, 1963; Principles of City Land Values, 1964; Valuation for Eminent Domain, 1973; Real Estate Appraising Handbook, 1975; Analysis & Valuation of Retail Locations, 1975. Contbr. to: The Appraisal Jrnl.; Lincoln Law Review; Tech. Valuation; S. African Jrnl. of Econs.; etc. Mbrships. incl: Am. Econ. Assn.; N. Ill. Univ. Fndn.; Lambda Alpha (Pres., 1965-67). Recip., Arthur A. May Mem. Award, 1966. Address: 12112 Lerner Pl., Bowie, MD 20715, USA.

RAMSDEN, E. H. Art Historian. Publs: An Introduction to Modern Art, 1940, 2nd ed., 1949; Twentieth Century Sculpture, 1949; Sculpture: Theme & Variations, 1953; The Letters of Michelangelo (transl., annotator, Ed.), 2 vols., 1963; Michelangelo (Masters Series), 1966; Michelangelo, 1971; Come — Take This Lute, forthcoming. Contbr. to jrnls. inclng: Apollo; Country Life; Burlington; Polemic; Horizon; Studio; World Review; Werk. Mbrships. incl: Soc. of Authors. Address: 30 Mallord St., London SW3, UK.

RAMSDEN, Herbert, b. 20 Apr. 1927, Manchester, UK. University Professor. Educ. incl: B.A. (French), 1948; B.A. (Spanish), 1949, M.A., 1953, Manchester Univ.; Dr. en Fil. y. Let., Madrid Univ., Spain, 1954. Publs. incl: Weak-Pronoun Position in the Early Romance Languages, 1963; Azorin's 'La ruta de Don Quijote', 1966; The 1898 Movement in Spain, 1974; The Spanish 'Generation of 1898', 1974. Contbr. to: Anales Galdosianos; Bulletin of Hispanic Studies; etc. Mbrships. incl: Nat. Coun. for Mod. Langs. (Hispanic rep., 1972). Hon: Kemsey Travelling Fellow, 1951-52. Address: Grove House, Grove Lane, Cheadle Hulme, Cheshire, UK.

RAMSEY, Norman Foster, b. 27 Aug. 1915, Wash. D.C., USA. Higgins Professor of Physics; Research Administrator; Author. Educ: A.B., Columbia Univ., 1935, M.A., 1939, Ph.D., 1940; B.A., Cambridge Univ., UK, 1937, M.A., 1940, Sc.D., 1954; M.A., Sc.D., Oxford Univ., 1973. Publs: Experimental Nuclear Physics, 1953; Nuclear Moments, 1953; Molecular Beams, 1956; Quick Calculus, 1965; Nuclear Interaction in Molecules (Science in Progress 13). Contbr. to: Phys. Review; & other sci. jrnls. Hons: Lawrence Award, 1960; Pavisson- Germer Prize, 1974. Address: Lyman Laboratory of Physics, Harvard Univ., Cambridge, MA 02138, USA.

RAMSEY, Robert W., b. 9 Oct. 1912, Memphis, Tenn., USA. Professor; Writer. Educ: B.A., Univ. of Ark., 1935; M.A., Univ. of Ariz., 1949. Publs: Fire in Summer, 1942; The Mockingbird, 1951; Fiesta, 1955. Address: Dept. of English, Univ. of Ariz., Tucson, AZ, USA.

RAMSKILL, Valerie Patricia, pen name BROOKE, Carol, b. Plymouth, UK. Publs: Light & Shade, 1947; To Reach the Heights, 1948; Devils' Justice, 1948; Simon & Monica, 1950; As Others See Us, 1952; The Changing Tide, 1952; Bitter Summer, 1954; No Other Destiny, 1955; The Way of Life, 1956; The Day Returns, 1957; To Each his Own, 1958; Shadow of the Past, 1960; For Promised Joy, 1962; This Day's Madness, 1962; Till all the Seas, 1964; Deceivers Ever, 1965. Contbr. to Heiress Mag. Address: Armadale, Mellor Brow, Mellor, Nr. Blackburn, Lancs., UK.

RANCE, Janet Mary (née Maxtone Graham), pen name GRAHAM, Janet, b. 1928, London, UK. Writer. Educ: St. James's Secretarial Coll., London. Contbr. to: Reader's Digest; The Guardian; Sports Illustrated (USA); Science Digest; Holiday; Good Housekeeping. Mbrships: Soc. of Mag. Writers, USA; The London Lib. Agent: J. A. Maxtone Graham. Address: Jessamine Cottage, Streatley, Reading, Berks., UK.

RANCE, Peter, b. 1923, London, UK. Headmaster. Educ: Loughborough Coll., UK. Publs: Teaching by Topics, 1968; Record Keeping in Progressive Primary Schools, 1970; Teaching Sailing, 1975. Mbrships: Soc. of Authors; Inst. of Royal Engrs. Recip., TT.D. Address: School House, Birch Green, Nr. Hertford, Herts., UK.

RAND, Ayn, b. 2 Feb. 1905, St. Petersburg (now Leningrad), USSR. (US Citizen). Writer; Editor. Educ: Grad., Univ. of Leningrad, 1924. Publs. incl: (novels) We the Living, USA & UK, 1936; The Fountainhead, USA 1943, UK 1947, screenplay 1949; (non-fiction) For the New Intellectual, 1961; The Virtue of Selfishness, 1965; Introduction to Objectivist Epistemology, 1967; The Romantic Manifesto, 1970; The New Left, 1971; (play) Night of January 16th, 1936; Ed., The Objectivist, 1962-71, The Ayn Rand Letter, 1971—. Recip., D.H.L., Lewis & Clark Coll., Portland, Ore.. 1963. Address: The Ayn Rand Letter, 201 E. 34th St., N.Y., NY 10016, USA.

RAND, Michael John, b. 19 Aug. 1927, Mildenhall, Suffolk, UK. Pharmacologist. Educ: B.Sc., 1949, M.Sc., 1955, Univ. of Melbourne, Aust.; Ph.D., Univ. of Sydney, 1957. Publs: Textbook of Pharmacology (w. others), 1968; An Introduction to the Physiology & Pharmacology of the Autonomic Nervous System (co-author), 1969, 1973. Contbr. to num. sci. & med. jrnls. & books. Mbr., var. profl. assns. Address: 8. 6/46 Lansell Rd., Toorak, Vic., Australia 3142.

RANDALL, Anthony Asheton, b. 7 Aug. 1923, Horsham, UK. Solicitor. Educ: London Univ. Publs: To Catch a Spy, 1965; Ride a Tiger, 1965; Flashpoint, 1966; Suicide Passage, 1967. Contbr. to: BBC; Escort; Creasey Mystery Mag.; London Mystery Mag.; Titbits; Parade; Weekly Post; Secrets; Carnival; Columba; C.W.A. Anthology; & foreign publs. Mbrships: Law Soc.; Crime Writers' Assn. Address: Willow, Chamberlaines, Kinsbourne Green, Harpenden, Herts., UK.

RANDALL, Florence Engel, b. 18 Oct. 1917, Bklyn., N.Y., USA. Author. Educ: N.Y. Univ.; Pratt Inst., N.Y. Publs: Hedgerow, 1967; The Place of Sapphires, 1969; The Almost Year, 1971; Haldane Station, 1973; A Watcher in the Woods (novel), forthcoming. Contbr. to: Harper's Mag.; Virginia Quarterly; Redbook; Good Housekeeping; Ladies' Home Jrnl.; Cosmopolitan; The Writer; Seventeen; Ingenue; Chatelaine. Mbr., Authors' League of America. Recip., Am. Lib. Assn. Notable Book, 1971. Address: 88 Oxford Blvd., Great Neck, NY, USA.

RANDALL, John Herman, b. 1899, Grand Rapids, Mich., USA. Professor of Philosophy. Educ: Columbia Coll.; Columbia Univ.; A.B., A.M., Ph.D. Publs: Making of the Modern Mind; Our Changing Civilization; Religion & the Modern World; Nature & Historical Experience; Role of Knowledge in Western Religion; Aristotle: The Career of Philosophy, 1962, 1965; Plato: Dramatist of the Life of Reason, 1970; Hellenistic Ways of Deliverance & the Making of the Christian Synthesis, 1970. Contbr. to: Ed., Jrnl. of Philos.; Jrnl. of Hist. of Ideas; etc. Mbrships: Pres., E. Div., Am. Philos. Assn., 1956, Renaissance Soc. of Am., 1955-56. Address: 15 Claremont Ave., N.Y., USA.

RANDALL, Neville Bennett, b. 28 June 1916, Hampstead, UK. Journalist. Educ: B.A., St. John's Coll., Oxford. Publs: Thou Bleeding Piece of Earth, 1964; Life after Death, 1975. Contbr. to: Daily Mail. Address: Miller's Cottage, Trumpet Hill, Reigate, Surrey, UK.

RANDALL, Rona, b. Birkenhead, Cheshire, UK. Novelist; Journalist. Publs. incl: The Silver Cord, 1963; The Willow Herb, 1965; The Arrogant Duke, 1966; Knight's Keep, 1967; Jordan & the Holy Land (travel), 1968; Broken Tapestry, 1969; The Witching Hour, 1971; Silent Thunder, 1972; Glenrannoch, 1973; Dragonmede, 1974; The Watchman's Stone, 1975. Contbr. to: Woman; My Home; Good Housekeeping; Daily Telegraph; var. women's mags., C'wlth. & Scandinavia, etc. Mbrships: PEN; Soc. of Authors; Crime Writers' Assn. of GB. Hons. incl: Romantic Novelists' Assn. of GB Major Award, 1969; Lit. Guild of Am. & Doubleday Book Club Selections, for Dragonmede, 1974. Address: Walnut House, Ticehurst, Wadhurst, Sussex TN5 7JB, UK.

RANDELL, Beverley Joan, b. 1931, Wellington, NZ. Author & Editor of Children's Books; Teacher. Educ: B.A., Univ. of NZ.; Dip. Tch. Publs. incl: Caption Books (series of 24), 1964; Number Story Caption Books (series of 16), 1965; Story Readers (series of 72), 1966; PM Listening Skillbuilders (series of 24), 1971; Meg & Mark Books (co-author, series of 9), 1972; PM Country Readers (co-author, series of 18), 1970; Methuen Country Books (co-author, series of 8), 1974; Methuen First Phonetics (series of 28), 1974; John the Mouse Who Learned to Read, 1971; PM Creative Workbooks, 1971-74; PM Animal Books (co-author, series of 8 books), 1974; Commonwealth

Readers (series of 16), 1966; & Ed. of sev. other series of infant reading books. Mbrships: PEN; NZ Women Writers Soc.; Aust. Soc. Authors. Address: 38 Alexandra Rd., Hataitai, Wellington, NZ.

RANDOLPH, Michael Richard Spencer, b. 1925, London, UK. Editor. Educ: The Reader's Digest (UK edition), 1957—; Director, The Reader's Digest Association Ltd., 1966—. Educ: Queen's Coll., Oxford. Mbr., Press Club; F.R.S.A. Address: The Reader's Digest, 25 Berkeley Sq., London W1X 6AB, UK.

RANKIN, Herbert David, b. 21 June 1931, Belfast, N. Ireland, UK. Professor of Classics. Educ: Trinity Coll., Dublin, Repub. of Ireland. Publs: Plato & the Individual, 1964; Petronius the Artist, 1971. Contbr. to var. classical jrnls. Mbrships. incl: Soc. for the Promotion of Hellenic Studies; Mind Assn. Address: Classics Dept., Univ. of Southampton, Southampton SO9 5NH, UK.

RANSEMAR, Erik, b. 22 Oct. 1926, Karlskrona, Sweden. Editor. Educ: Socionom DSI, Göteborg, 1964. Publs. incl: O, Vandringsman (novel), 1959; Byn vid de två vägarna (novel), 1960; Främlingstid (poetry), 1962; Ransemars byrå (aphorisms), 1967; En dikt til Marx (poetry), 1971; En dag i december i Sverige (poetry), 1972; Ord denna explosiva vara (poetry), 1973. Mbrships: Swedish Union of Authors; Swedish Assn. of Jrnlsts. Recip., Göteborg City Cultural Schlrship. Address: Murarstigen 7, 150 24 Rönninge, Sweden.

RANSFORD, Oliver Neil, pen name WYLCOTES, John, b. 25 Apr. 1914, Bradford, UK. Consultant Anaesthetist. Educ: M.D., Univ. of London; F.F.A.R.C.S.; D.A.; Middlesex Hosp., London. Publs: Livingstone's Lake, 1966; The Battle of Majuba Hill, 1967; The Rulers of Rhodesia, 1968; Bulawayo, 1968; The Battle of Spion Kop, 1969; The Slave Trade, 1971; The Great Trek, 1972. Contbr. to: Lancet; Jrnl. of Tropical Med.; Personality; Blackwoods; Rhodesiana. Mbrships. incl: Rhodesiana Soc. Hons. incl: Rhodesiana Gold Medal, 1972. Address: 8 Heyman Rd., Bulawayo, Rhodesia.

RANSOM, Harry Howe, b. 14 May 1922, Nashville, Tenn., USA. Professor, Political Science. Educ: A.B., Vanderbilt Univ., 1943; A.M., 1949, Ph.D., 1954, Princeton Univ. Publs: Central Intelligence & National Security, 1958; Can American Democracy Survive Cold War? , 1963; An American Foreign Policy Reader, 1965; The Intelligence Establishment, 1970. Contbr. to: World Politics; N.Y. Times Mag,; etc. Mbrships. incl: Int. Inst. for Strategic Studies; Am. Pol. Sci. Assn. Recip., 4 acad. hons. Address: Dept. of Pol. Sci., Vanderbilt Univ., Nashville, TN 37235, USA.

RANSOM, Jay Ellis, b. 12 Apr. 1914, Missoula, Mont., USA. Author. Educ: B.A., Univ. Wash., Seattle, 1935; Univs. Mont., Calif. Publs. incl: Arizona Gem Trails & the Colorado Desert of California, 1955; Petrified Forest Trails, 1955; The Rock-Hunter's Range Guide, 1962; Fossils in America, 1964; A Range Guide to Mines & Minerals, 1964; The Gold Hunter's Field Book, 1975; Gems & Minerals of America, 1975. Contbr. to approx. 100 trade, tech., rsch., nat., histl., quarterlies, mags., jrnls. (more than 500 articles). Mbrships. incl: Am. Anthropol. Assn.; Am. Folklore Soc.; Explorers Club, N.Y.; Northwest Outdoor Writers Assn. (VP, 1975). Hons. incl: Wash. State Author, 1965; Ore. State Author, 1975. Address: 1821 E. 9th St., The Dalles, OR 97058, USA.

RANTA-RONNLUND, Sara, b. 27 Nov. 1903, Puoltsa, Kiruna, Sweden. Author. Publs: Nadevalpar, 1971; Najder, 1972; Njoalpassoner, 1973. Mbr., Swedish Authors' Union. Recip., Uppsala Kulturstipendium, 1972. Address: Hagundagatan 19, S-75238 Uppsala, Sweden.

RAO, Raja, b. 21 Nov. 1909, Hassan, India. Writer. Educ: Aligarh Univ.; Univ. of Madras; Sorbonne Univ., Paris. Kanthapura, 1938; The Cow of the Barricades, 1947; The Serpent & the Rope, 1960; The Cat & Shakespeare, 1964. Hons: Sahitya Akademi Prize for Lit., 1964; Padma Bhushan (India), 1970. Address: 1808 Pearl St., Austin, TX 78701, USA.

RAPHAEL, Frederic Michael, b. 14 Aug. 1931, Chgo., Ill.; USA. Novelist; Screenwriter. Educ: M.A., Cambridge Univ., UK, 1954. Publs. incl: (novels) The Earlsdon Way, 1958; The Limits of Love, UK 1960, USA 1961; Lindmann, UK 1963, USA 1964; Orchestra & Beginners, UK 1967, USA 1968; Like Men Betrayed, UK 1970, USA

1971; Who Were You With Last Night?, UK 1971; (screenplays) Nothing but the Best, 1964; Darling, 1965; Two for the Road, 1967; Far from the Madding Crowd, 1967; A Severed Head, 1971. Contbr. to Sunday Times, 1962—. Fellow, Royal Soc. of Lit. Hons: Brit. Screen Writers' Award, 1965, 1966, 1967; Brit. Acad. Award, 1965; US Acad. Award, 1966. Address: The Wick, Langham, Colchester, Essex, UK.

RAPIN, Simone, b. 16 June 1901, Lausanne, Switz. Actress; Singer; Stage Producer; Teacher of Dramatic Art. Educ: B.A., M.Sc., Univ. of Lausanne. Publs. incl: Une Jeune Fille Juive, 1955; L'Année de l'Amour, 1957, 2nd ed., 1973; Mon Lac, 1962; Une Nuit dans Chillon, 1965; L'Enfant Victorieux, 1965; La Symphonie du Partir, 1967; Cette France, 1972; Petite Galerie Marcel Proust, 1973; Mon Italie, 1973; L'Oeil du Temps, 1974; (plays) La Trève de Dieu; La Journée a Plus de 24 Heures. Contbr. to: Masques & Visages; Cahiers Luxembourgeois; Poésie Vivante; sev. other French-lang. jrnls. Mbrships. incl: Berrichonne Acad.; Pontzen Int. Acad. of Naples; VP, Geneva Arts Club. Fndr., Simone Rapin Prize for Poetical Plays. Recip., sev. awards & prizes. Address: 16 Blvd. des Philosophes, Geneva 1205, Switz.

RAPOPORT, Janis Beth, b. 22 June 1946, Toronto, Ont., Can. Writer; Publishing Consultant; Freelance Editor. Educ: B.A., Univ. of Toronto, 1967. Publs: Within the Whirling Moment, 1967; Foothills, 1973; Jeremy's Dream, 1974. Contbr. to: Globe & Mail; Can. Forum; Tamarack Review. Mbrships: Book Publrs.' Profl. Assn.; Exec. Mbr. responsible for organizing courses in profl. dev., 1972-74; Dir., Can. Periodical Publrs. Assn., 1974-75. Address: 36 Tarbert Rd., Willowdale, Ont., Can.

RASK, Lars Arvid, b. 22 Feb. 1926, Kinnekulle, Sweden. Author; Educator. Publs: Någon färdas, 1954; Jokkmokk, 1965; Vi upptaker Sverige, 1969; Vi och vildmarken, 1970; Lule älu och Letsi, 1972. Mbrships. incl: Swedish Union of Authors. Recip., Tilldelad Första Prize, 1972. Address: Box 577, 960.30 Vuollerim, Sweden.

RASKIN, Ellen, b. 13 Mar. 1928, Milwaukee, Wis., USA. Writer & Illustrator of Children's Books. Educ: Univ. Wis. Publs. incl: Nothing Ever Happens on My Block, 1966; Silly Songs & Sad, 1967; Spectacles, 1968; Ghost in a Four-room Apartment, 1969; And It Rained, 1969; The World's Greatest Freak Show, 1970; The Mysterious Disappearance of Leon (I, mean Noel), 1971; Franklyn Stein, 1972; Who. Said Sue, Said Whoo?, 1973; Figgs & Phantoms, 1974. Hons. incl: Bklyn. Mus. Art Books for Children Citation, 1973, 1974; Soc. Illustrator's Citation Merit, 1966, 1970, 1971; Boston Globe-Horn Book Award: Honor Book, 1973; Newbery Hon., 1975. Address: 12 Gay St., N.Y., NY 10014, USA.

RASMUSSEN, Steen Eiler, b. 1898, Copenhagen, Denmark. Retired Professor of Architecture. Educ: Royal Acad. of Fine Arts, Copenhagen. Publs: London, the Unique City; Towns & Buildings; Experiencing Architecture. Address: Dreyersvej 9, 2960 Rungsted Kyst, Denmark.

RASTENIS, Nadas, b. 4 Jan. 1891, Stagalenai, Vilnius, Lithuania. Attorney-at-Law; Poet; Translator. Educ: LL.B., Schl. Law, Boston Univ., 1924; Harvard Univ.; Johns Hopkins Univ. Publs. incl: (poetry) War's Curse, 1941; (Lithuanian) The Holiday of Three Roses, 1955; (transl. into Engl.) The Forest of Anykciai by Baranauskas, 1956; The Seasons, by Doenaltis, 1967; (transls. from Russian) White Night & Parting by Pasternak; (transls. into Lithuanian) Venus & Adonis by Shakespeare; Rubaiyat of Omar Khayyam, by Fitzgerald; & many poems & folk songs from Lithuanian into Engl. Contbr. to: Scimitar & Song; Laurel Leaves. Mbrships. incl: Lithuanian Writers' Assn. (1945—); United Poet Laureates Int. Hons. incl: Nominated for Nobel Peace Prize, 1967. Address: 818 Hollins St., Baltimore, MD 21201, USA.

RATERMANIS, J. B., b. 30 June 1904, Latvia. Professor of French Language & Literature. Educ: Bach., lic. ès lettres, Lille, France; M.A., Dr.philol. & philos., Univ. of Latvia, Riga. Publs: Etude sur le style de Baudelaire, 1949; Etude sur le comique dans le thâtre de Marivaux, 1961; The Comic Style of Beaumarchais, 1961; Beaumarchais, Le Mariage de Figaro, édition critique, 1968; Essai sur les formes verbales dans les tragédies de Racine, 1972. Contbr. to: Français Moderne; French Studies; Philol. Quarterly. Mbrships: MLA; Am. Assn. of Tchrs. of French. Hons: Fellowship of Am. Coun. of Learned Socs.,

1963, 1965. Address: 2376 Ron Way, San Diego, CA 92123, USA.

RATKÓ, József, b. 9 Aug. 1936, Budapest, Hungary. Librarian. Educ: B.A., (Hungarian Lit.). Publs: Without Fear, 1966; Unarmed, 1968; Sharing Our Bread, 1970; My Illegitimate Dead, 1975. Contbr. to: Új Irás; Tiszatáj; Alföld; Kortárs; Napjaink. Mbr., Hungarian Writers' Union. Recip., József Attila Prize, 1969. Address: Nagykálló, Hungary.

RATNER, Marc Leonard, b. 19 Jan. 1926, NYC, USA. Professor of English & American Literature. Educ: B.A., Fordham Univ., 1950; M.A., Univ. of Pa., 1951; Ph.D., N.Y. Univ., 1958. Publ: William Styron: A Study, 1973. Contbr. to: Harpers Mag.; Am. Lit.; Mass. Review. Mbrships: MLA; Am. Studies Assn. Address: 1325 Brewster Dr., El Cerrito, CA 94530, USA.

RATTIGAN, (Sir) Terence, b. 10 June 1911, London, UK. Dramatic Author. Educ: Harrow & Trinity Coll., Oxford. Publs. incl: First Episode, 1934; French Without Tears, 1936; After the Dance, 1939; Flare Path, 1942; While the Sun Shines, 1943; The Winslow Boy, 1946; The Browning Version, 1948; The Deep Blue Sea, 1952; Variation on a Theme, 1958; Ross, 1960; Man & Boy, 1963; A Bequest to the Nation, 1970. Films incl: Quiet Wedding; Way to the Stars; The Sound Barrier; The Winslow Boy; Separate Tables; The V.I.P.'s; The Yellow Rolls-Royce; Goodbye, Mr. Chips. TV plays incl: The Final Test, 1962; Heart to Heart, 1962; Nelson, 1966. Hons: C.B.E., 1968; Knighted, 1971; Ellen Terry Award, 1946 & 1948; New York Critics' Award, 1947. Address: c/o Dr., Jan Van Loewen Ltd., 81/83 Shaftesbury Ave., London W1, UK.

RAU, Chalapathi, pen names, MAGNUS; M. C., b. Waltair, Vizag, India. Journalist; Editor. Educ: B.L., M.A., Madras Univ. Publs: Fragments of a Revolution, 1965; Gandhi & Nehru, 1966; The Press in India, 1967; Nehru for Children, 1968; All in All, 1969; Jawaharlal Nehru, Biography, 1973; The Press, 1974; The Romance of the Newspaper, 1974. Contbr. to: New Statesman, London; Mainstream, India. Mbrships. incl: Fndr.-Pres., Fedn. of Working Jrnlsts., India. Recip., sev. hon. degrees. Address: Nat. Herald, 15A Bahadurshah Zafar Mong, New Delhi, India.

RAUBENHEIMER, George Harding, pen name HARDING, George, b. 1923, Pretoria, S. Africa. General Manager; Chief Pilot. Publs: North of Bushman's Rock, 1965; Dragon's Gap, 1967; The Gun Merchants, 1969; The Skytrap, 1972; (screenplay) Mr Kingstreets War (co-writer), 1970. Mbrships: S. African Mil. Hist. Soc.; S. African Air Force Assn. Address: 19 Lystanwold Rd., Saxonwold, Johannesburg 2001, Repub. of S. Africa.

RAUTAPALO, Tauno Erik, pen names RAUTAPALO-RAPP, T.; TUURI, Tauno, b. 29 Nov. 1914, Helsinki, Finland. Author; Painter. Educ: Var. Art Schls. Publs: 18 books incing: Ahoy, Main Sail Up!, 1944; People, 1945; In Wild Lapland, 1946; Finn the Archer, 1946; King of the Ring, 1946; Brave Boys, 1949; Hippu's Adventures in the Gold Fields, 1950; Gold-Diggers, 1957; Bearskin, 1958; Pena Tells a Story, 1963; Men in the Trenches, 1967; Ed., Adam. Contbr. to var. mags. Mbrships. incl: Finnish Author Soc.; Authors of Helsinki; Authors of Finnish Jvnle. Lit. Hons. incl: Topelius Prize, 1950. 1st Prize, Jvnle. Novel Competition (2nd Prize, Scandinavian Finals), 1963. Address: Näyttelijäntie 3A 13, 00400 Helsinki 40, Finland.

RAVEGNANI, Guiseppe, b. 13 Oct. 1895. Critic; Journalist. Publs: Uomini Visti, 2 vols.; (transl.) Antologia di Novelle Catalane; & num. critical works. Contbr. to: Il Resto del Carlino; Ed., Il Corriere Italiano; Il Regno; Ed., La Fiera Letteraria; La Stampa; Corriere della Sera; Dir., Il Corriere Padano, Il Gazzettino, La Gazzetta di Venezia; Lit. Ed., Epoca; & num. other papers. Address: Piazza Morbegno 5, Milan, Italy.

RAVEN, Ronald William, b. 28 July 1904, Coniston, UK. Consulting Surgeon. Educ: St. Bartholomew's Hospital, Univ. of London; M.R.C.S., L.R.C.P.; 1928; F.R.C.S., 1931. Publs. incl: Treatment of Shock, 1942; Surgical Care, 1952; Cancer in General Practice (jointly), 1952; Handbook on Cancer for Nurses & Health Visitors, 1953; Cancer & Allied Diseases, 1955; Modern Trends in Oncology, 2 vols., 1973. Contbr. to: Brit. Ency. Med. Practice; Operative Surgery; & num. papers on surgical subjects. Mbrships. incl: Coun., Royal Coll. Surgeons;

Chmn., Marie Curie Mem. Fndn.; N.Y. Acad. Sci. Hons. incl: O.B.E., 1946; Legion of Honour, 1952. Address: 29 Harley St., London W1N 1DA, UK.

RAVEN, Ruth Margaret Janey, b. 1895, Ringwould, Kent, UK. Publs: Bible Lessons for the Sunday Nursery. Address: The Hermitage, Lyddington, nr. Uppingham, Rutland, UK.

RAVEN, Simon (Arthur Noel), b. 1927. Author; Critic; Playwright. Educ: M.A., Univ. of Cambridge. Publs: The Feathers of Death, 1959; Brother Cain, 1959; Doctors Wear Scarlet, 1960; The English Gentleman, 1961; Close of Play, 1962; Boys Will Be Boys, 1963; The Rich Pay Late, 1964; Friends in Low Places, 1965; The Sabre Squadron, 1966; Fielding Grey, 1967; The Judas Boy, 1968; Places Where They Sing, 1970; Sound the Retreat, 1971; Come Like Shadows, 1972. Bring Forth The Body, 1974; sev. plays & TV dramatisations inclng: The Pallisers (from Trollope's 6 Palliser novels). Mbr., Horation Soc. Agent: Curtis Brown Ltd. Address: c/o Blond & Briggs Ltd., 56 Doughty St., London WC1N 2LS, UK.

RAVENHILL, Adrian Francis, b. 1932, Gloucester, UK. Marketer of Audio-Visual Aids; Former Mission Worker. Educ: M.A., Pembroke Coll., Cambridge; M.A., Trinity Coll., Dublin; Baptist Coll., Dublin. Publs: Transl., Secret of Happiness, 1965; Transl., Call to Indonesia, 1972. Mbr., Soc. of Authors. Address: 55 Tuffley Cres., Gloucester, UK.

RAWLINS, Dennis, b. 20 Mar. 1937, Baltimore, Md., USA. Writer. Educ: B.A., Harvard Univ., 1959; M.A., Boston Univ., 1962. Publs: Peary at the North Pole, Fact or Fiction, 1973; The Deep Planets, forthcoming. Contbr. to: Nature; U.S. Naval Inst. Proceedings; & var. tech. jrnls. in US, Scandinavia & UK. Mbrships: Fellow Royal Astronomical Soc., London. Hons: private papers preserved US Nat. Archives, Wash. DC. Agent: Wm. Morris, NYC. Address: St. Paul Ct., Apt. 413-F, 3120 St. Paul St., Baltimore, MD 21218, USA.

RAWLS, (Woodrow) Wilson, b. 24 Sept. 1913, Scraper, Okla., USA. Former Carpenter; Writer; Lecturer. Publ: Where the Red Fern Grows, 1961, paperback 1974. Contbr. to Saturday Evening Post (serialization of Where the Red Fern Grows as The Hounds of Youth). Mbr., Int. Platform Assn. Hons: Where The Red Fern Grows named as Lit. Guild Selection for Young Adults, 1961. Address: 551 11th St., Idaho Falls, ID 83401, USA.

RAWSON, Claude Julien, b. 8 Feb. 1935, Shanghai, China. Professor. Educ: M.A., B.Litt., Oxon. Publs: Henry Fielding, 1968; Focus: Swift (Ed.), 1971; Henry Fielding & the Augustan Ideal Under Stress, 1972; Gulliver & the Gentle Reader, 1973; Fielding, A Critical Anthology (Ed.), 1973; Yeats & Anglo-Irish Literature: Critical Essays by Peter Ure (Ed.), 1974. Contbr. to acad. jrnls. inclng: Essays in Criticism; Mod. Lang. Review; Review of Engl. Studies; 18th-Century Studies. Mbrships. incl: Pres., Brit. Soc. for 18th-Century Studies, 1974. Address: Dept. of Engl., Univ. of Warwick, Coventry CV4 7AL, UK.

RAWSON, Nicholas, b. 9 Dec. 1934, Porthmadog, N. Wales, UK. Author. Educ: B.A.; Milton Keynes Coll. of Educ.; Ruskin Coll.; Keble Coll., Oxford. Publs: Texts in New Writers 3 (co-author), 1963; Shards, 1973. Contbr. to: Transatlantic Review; Diagonal (German); Signature Poetry Anthol. Recip., Arts Coun. of GB Writers' Award, 1971. Agent: John Calder. Address: Guards Hill, Brampton, Cumbria, UK.

RAWSON, Wyatt Trevelyan Rawson, b. 2 Jan. 1894, London, UK. Teacher; Author. Educ: B.A., Cambridge Univ. Publs: A New World in the Making (Ed.); The Freedom We Seek (Ed.); The Werkplaats Adventure; Life of Kees Boeke; The Way Within; The Story of the New Education. Contbr. to: The New Era; The Seeker; Light. Mbrships: Engl. Speaking Union; London Lib.; Royal Inst. of Int. Affairs; Elder, Soc. of Friends (Quakers). Address: 44 Vineyard Hill Rd., London SW19, UK.

RAY, Cyril, b. 16 Mar. 1908, Manchester, UK. Author. Educ: Jesus Coll., Oxford Univ. Publs. incl: Scenes & Characters from Surtees, 1948; The Pageant of London, 1958; Merry England, 1960; Regiment of the Line, The Story of the Lancashire Fusiliers, 1963; The Wines of Italy, 1966; In A Glass Lightly, 1967; Lafite, 1968; Bollinger, 1971; Cognac, 1973; Ed., The Gourmet's Companion, 1963; Best Murder Stories, 1965; The Compleat Imbiber,

1956-71. Mbrships: Hon. Life Mbr., Nat. Union of Jrnlsts.; Fndr. & Pres., Circle of Wine Writers. Hons. incl: 1st Wine & Food Socs. André Simon Award, 1964; Trofeo de Bologna, 1967; Cavalière dell' ordine al merito della Repub. Italiana; Chevalier dl Mérité Agricole, France. Glenfiddich Award. Address: Delmonden Manor, Hawkhurst, Kent, UK.

RAY, Dorothy Jean, b. 10 Oct. 1919, Cedar Falls, Iowa, USA. Writer; Anthropologist. Educ: B.A., Univ. of N. Iowa; Grad. work, Radcliffe Coll., Cambridge, Mass., Univ. of Wash., Seattle. Publs: Artists of the Tundra & the Sea, 1961; Eskimo Masks: Art & Ceremony, 1967; Graphic Arts of the Alaskan Eskimo, 1969; The Eskimo of Bering Strait, 1650-1898, 1975. Contbr. to: Alaska; Alaska Jrnl.; Beaver; Arctic Anthrop.; Polar Notes, Dartmouth; Names; etc. Mbrships: Soc. of Woman Geogs.; Am. Anthrop. Assn.; Sec.-Treas., Alaska Div., AAAS. Address: P.O. Box 586, Port Townsend, WA 98368, USA.

RAY, Mary Eva Pedder, b. 14 Mar. 1932, Rugby, UK. Civil Servant; Writer. Educ: London Dip. Social Studies; Cambridge Cert. Relig. Knowledge; Birmingham Coll. Art & Craft; Coll. of the Ascension, Selly Oak, Birmingham. Publs: The Voice of Apollo, 1964; The Eastern Beacon, 1965; Standing Lions, 1968; Spring Tide, 1969; Living in Earliest Greece, 1969; Shout Against the Wind, 1970; A Tent for the Sun, 1972; The Ides of April, 1974; Sword Sleep, 1975. Address: Pandora, 24 Richmond Dr., Herne Bay, Kent, UK.

RAY, Sibnarayan, b. 20 Jan. 1921, Calcutta, India. Teacher; Writer. Educ: M.A., Calcutta Univ.; M.A., Melbourne Univ., Aust. Publs. incl: Explorations, 1956; Sahityachinta, 1955; Prabaser Journal, 1958; Moumachitantra, 1961; Kathara Tomar Mon, 1967; Gandhi India & The World, 1970; Autumnal Equinox, 1973; Kavir Nirvasan, 1973; I Have Seen Bengal's Face, 1974. Contbr. to var. jrnls. Mbrships: Fellow, Inst. of Histl. Studies, Calcutta, 1970; Life Mbr., S. Asian Studies Assn. of Aust. & NZ, 1974; PEN. Hons. incl: Rockefeller Fndn. Fellowship, 1956-58. Address: The Crest, 14 Fuller St., Bulleen, Vic. 3105, Australia.

RAYBURN, Robert Gibson, b. 14 Jan. 1915, Newton, Kan., USA. Clergyman; Educator. Educ: A.B., Wheaton Coll., Ill.; Th.B., Th.M., Omaha Presby. Theol. Sem.; Th.D., Dallas Theol. Sem., Tex. Publs: Fight the Good Fight, 1956; What About Baptism?, 1957. Contbr. to: Christianity Today; Presby. Jrnl.; Presbyterian, Covenant Sem. Theol. Review. Mbrships: Evangelical Theol. Soc.; Hymn Soc. of Am.; Mil. Chaps. Assn. Address: 12330 Conway Rd., St. Louis, MO 63141, USA.

RAYMOND, Diana Joan, b. 25 Apr. 1916, Blackheath, London, UK. Novelist. Educ: Cheltenham Ladies Coll. Publs: The Small Rain; Between the Stirrup & the Ground; Stranger's Gallery; The Five Days; Guest of Honour; The Climb; People in the House; The Noonday Sword; Front of the House; Are You Travelling Alone; The Best of the Day; Incident on a Summer's Day. Mbr., Soc. Authors. Agent: A. P. Watt & Son. Address: 22 The Pryors, East Heath Rd., London NW3, UK.

RAYMOND, Patrick, b. 25 Sept. 1924, Cuckfield, Sussex, UK. RAF Officer; Writer. Educ: Dartington Hall; Grad., RAF Staff Coll., 1962, Jt. Servs. Staff Coll., 1965. Publs: A City of Scarlet & Gold, 1963; The Lordly Ones, 1966; The Sea Garden, 1970; The Last Soldier, 1974. Address: 24 Chilton Rd., Chesham, Bucks., UK.

RAYNER, Claire, pen names LYNTON, Ann; BRANDON, Sheila, b. 22 Jan. 1931, London, UK. Writer. Educ: State Registered Nurse. Publs: over 40 books inclng: Mothers & Midwives; What Happens in Hospital; Parents' Guide to Sex Education; Home Nursing & Family Health; Woman's Medical Dictionary; (novels as Sheil Brandon) The Lonely One; Private Wing; (juvenile) Shilling a Pound Pears; The House on the Fen, transl. into Swedish, Finnish & Icelandic; Lady Mislaid; The Performer Series: Gower Street, Haymarket, Paddington Green, transl. into German, Dutch, French. Contbr. to num. mags., jrnls., TV & radio. Mbr., Soc. of Authors & Medical Jrnlsts. Assn. Recip., Gold Medal, Royal Northern Hosp., London. Agent: Michael Horniman. Address: c/o A. P. Watt & Son., 26-28 Bedford Row, London WC1R 4IH, UK.

RAYNER, John Desmond, b. 1924, Berlin, Germany. Rabbi; Senior Minister, Liberal Jewish Synagogue, St. John's Wood, London since 1961; Minister, South London Liberal Jewish Synagogue, 1953-57. Educ: M.A.,

Emmanuel Coll., Cambridge Univ. Publs: Towards Mutual Understanding between Jews & Christians, 1960; Service of the Heart; Co-Ed., Union of Liberal & Progressive Synagogues, 1967; Co-Ed., Gate of Repentance, 1973. Contbr. to: Pointer; etc. Mbr., B'nai Brith (1st Lodge of England). Hons: VP, Leo Baeck Coll. Address: 18 Armitage Rd., London NW11 8RA, UK.

RAYNES, (Lady) Frederica Rozelle Ridgway, née PIERREPONT, pen name CASTWEAZLE, Eleanor, b. 17 Nov. 1925, Keighley, UK. Writer. Publs: North in a Nutshell, 1968; Maid Matelot, 1971. Contbr. to: Sunday Express; Kentish Express; Kent Life; Sussex Life; Yachting Monthly; Nottingham Observer. Mbrships. incl: F.R.S.A.; Nat. Union of Jrnlsts.; Royal Naval Sailing Assn. Address: 88 Narrow St., London E14, UK.

RAYNOV, Bogomil, b. 19 June 1919, Sofia, Bulgaria. Professor of History of Arts. Publs: (in Bulgarian) The Inspector & the Night, 1964; Roads to Nowhere, 1966; Mr Nobody, 1967; Nothing Better than bad weather, 1968; The Great Boredom, 1971; A Naive Middle-Aged Man, 1973; A requiem for a Nogood Woman, 1974. Contbr. to sev. mags., reviews & newspapers. Mbrships: PEN; Dpty. Chmn., Union of Bulgarian Writers. Hons: Dimitrov Prize, 1952, 1959; Prize, Union of Bulgarian Writers, 1960, 1966, 1968, 1969; Honoured Worker in Culture, 1965; People's Worker in Culture, 1971. Address: Sofia, ul. Neofit Rilski 48, Bulgaria.

REA, (Rev.) Fred(erick) Beatty, b. 31 May 1908, Dublin, Repub. of Ireland. Methodist Minister. Educ: Univ. of Dublin; Edgehill Theol. Coll.; B.A.; B.D.; Dip.Ed. Publs: Alcoholism: Its Psychology & Cure, 1954; Ed., Southern Rhodesia: The Price of Freedom, 1964; We Would See Jesus, 1971. Contbr. to Looking at Ireland, 1937. Address: Wesley Manse, Belvedere, Salisbury, Rhodesia.

READ, Brian, (Ahier), b. 1927, Jersey, Channel Islands. Public Relations Officer, Local Government. Educ: De La Salle Coll., Jersey. Publs: The Long Chase, 1963; The Empty Cottage, 1963; A Friend For Anna, 1966; The Water Wheel, 1970; Healthy Cities, 1970; Lucy and the Chinese Eggs, 1971; The Water We Used, 1972; Men of Iron, 1974. Agent: Laurence Pollinger Ltd. Address: 50 St. Mark's Rd., Henley-on-Thames, Oxon. RG9 1LW, UK.

READ, David Haxton Carswell, b. 2 Jan. 1910, Cupar, Fife, Scotland, UK. Minister of Religion. Educ: B.D., New Coll., Edinburgh, 1936; M.A., Univ. of Edinburgh, 1932. Publs. incl: The Pattern of Christ, 1967; Holy Common Sense, 1966, 1968; The Presence of Christ, 1968; Virginia Woolf Meets Charlie Brown, 1968; Christian Ethics, 1968, 1969; Giants Cut Down to Size, 1970; Religion Without Wrappings, 1970; Overheard, 1971; Curious Christians, 1972; An Expanding Faith, 1973; Sent from God, 1974. Contbr. to num. relig. publs. Mbrships. incl: Dir. & Sec., Fndn. for the Arts, Relig. & Culture; Inst. for Relig. & Soc. Studies. Hons. incl: D.D., Yale Univ., 1959; D.D., Hope Coll., 1969; L.H.D., Trinity Univ., 1972. Address: 1165 5th Ave., N.Y. NY 10029, USA.

READ, Donald, b. 31 July 1930, Manchester, UK. Professor of Modern English History; Author. Educ: Univ. Coll., Oxford, 1949-54. Publs: Peterloo, the Massacre & its Background, 1958; Feargus O'Connor, Irishman & Chartist (w. E. Glasgow), 1961; Press & People, Opinion in Three English Cities, 1961; The English Provinces 1760-1960, 1964; Cobden & Bright, 1967; Edwardian England, 1972; Ed., Documents from Edwardian England, 1973. Address: Darwin College, Univ. of Kent, Canterbury, Kent, UK.

READ, Elfreida, b. 2 Oct. 1920, Vladivostok, Russia. Writer of Children's Books. Educ: Shanghai Pub. Schl. for Girls. Publs. incl: The Dragon & the Jadestone, 1958, 2nd ed., 1971; The Magic of Light, 1959; The Enchanted Egg, 1963, 2nd ed., 1965; The Spell of Chuchuchan, 1966, 2nd ed., 1967; Magic for Granny, 1967; Twin Rivers, 1968; No-One Need Ever Know, 1971; Brothers by Choice, 1974; & poetry, plays. Hons. incl: B.C. Award poetry, 1965; Chancel Drama Competition 10 Best Plays Selection Award; 1st place, Can. Centennial Contest for children's stories, 1967; Jr. Lit. Guild Book Month Selection, Brothers by Choice, Aug. 1974. Address: 2686 W. King Edward Ave., Vancouver, BC V6L 1T6. Can.

READ, Jan (John Hinton), b. 18 Nov. 1917, Sydney, Australia. Writer. Educ: Trinity Coll., Glenalmond; Emmanuel Coll., Cambridge; B.Sc., Univ. of St. Andrews. Publs. incl: History for Beginners (w. Antonio Mingote),

1960; The Wines of Spain & Portugal, 1973; The Moors in Spain & Portugal, 1974; (film scripts) The Blue Lamp; White Corridors; Street Corner; First Men in the Moon; (TV scripts) Robin Hood; Dr. Finlay's Casebook; Danger Man; Sherlock Holmes; The Borderers. Contbr. to: Jrnl. of Chem. Soc.; Burlington Mag.; Hollywood Quarterly; Hist. Today; etc. Recip., Writers' Guild Award for Best TV Series, Dr. Finlay's Casebook. Address: 18 Lowndes Square, London SW1, UK.

READ, Leonard Edward, b. 26 Sept. 1898, Hubbardston, Mich., USA. Foundation President. Educ: Grad., Ferris Inst., Big Rapids, Mich., 1917. Publs. incl: Elements of Libertarian Leadership, 1962; Anything That's Peaceful, 1964; The Free Market & Its Enemy, 1965; Deeper Than You Think, 1967; Accent on the Right, 1968; Let Freedom Reign, 1969; Talking to Myself, 1970; Then Truth Will Out, 1971; To Free or Freeze, 1972; Who's Listening? , 1973; Having My Way, 1974; Castles in the Air, 1975. Contbr. to trade & commercial periodicals. Mbrships. incl: Am. Econ. Assn. Recip., Litt.D., Grove City Coll., Pa. Address: Hillside, Irvington-on-Hudson, NY 10533, USA.

READ, Piers Paul, b. 7 Mar. 1941. Author. Educ: M.A., St. John's Coll., Cambridge Univ. Publs: (novels) Game in Heaven with Tussie Marx, 1966; The Junkers, 1968; Monk Dawson, 1969; The Professor's Daughter, 1971; The Upstart, 1973; (TV plays) Coincidence, 1968; The House on Highbury Hill, 1972; (radio play) The Family Firm, 1970. Mbrships: Inst. Contemporary Arts (Coun., 1971-73); Soc. of Authors (Comm. of Mgmt., 1973); F.R.S.A. Hons: Harkness Fellow, 1967-68; Sir G. Faber Mem. Prize, 1968; Hawthornden Prize, 1969; Somerset Maugham Award, 1969. Address: 8 Ravenscourt Rd., London W6 0UG, UK.

READE, Brian Edmund, b. 13 Jan. 1913, St. Marychurch, Torquay, UK. Art Historian; Deputy Keeper, 1958-1973, Department of Prints & Drawings, Victoria & Albert Museum. Educ: B.A., 1934, M.A., 1938, King's Coll., Cambridge Univ. Publs: Edward Lear's Parrots, 1948; The Dominance of Spain, 1951, transls. in Dutch, German & French; Regency Antiques, 1953; Art Nouveau & Alphonse Mucha, 1963; Aubrey Beardsley, 1966; Ballet Designs & Illustrations, 1967; Beardsley, 1967, German transl., 1969; Ed., Sexual Heretics, 1970; Louis Wain, 1972; (poetry) Eye of a Needle, 1971. Contbr. to: Burlington Mag.; Psychol. Today (USA); Hist. Today; Antigonish Review; etc. Address: 6 Abingdon Villas, London W8, UK.

READER, (William Henry) Ralph, b. 25 May 1903, Crewkerne, UK. Theatrical Producer; Author; Composer; Actor. Publs: It's Been Terrific, 1952; Great Oaks, 1953; Oh Scouting is a Boy, 1956; The Gang Show Story, 1957; Ralph Reader Remembers, 1974. Contbr. to: My Weekly; Scouting; Readers Digest; etc. Hons: M.B.E., 1946; C.B.E., 1957; Dutch Medal of Merit, 1974. Address: 203 Sherrock Gdns., Hendon, London NW4 JJ, UK.

READER, William Joseph, b. 20 Nov. 1920, Weston-super-Mare, UK. Freelance Historian. Educ: B.A., Ph.D., Jesus Coll., Cambridge Univ. Publs: Men & Machines (w. C. H. Wilson), 1958; Professional Men, The Rise of the Professional Classes in 19th Century England, 1966; The Weir Group: A Centenary History, 1971; Architect of Air Power, The Life of 1st Viscount Weir, 1968; Imperial Chemical Industries: A History vol. I, The Forerunners, 1970, vol. II, The First Quarter Century, 1975; Life in Victorian England, 1964; Hard Roads & Highways, 1964; The Middle Classes, 1972; Victorian England, 1974. Contbr. to: Bus. Hist. Review; Bus. Hist.; Hist. Today; Mgmt. Today. Mbrships: Fellow, Royal Histl. Soc.; Soc. Authors. Address: 67 Wood Vale, London NW10 3DL, UK.

READY, William Bernard, b. 16 Sept. 1914, Cardiff, UK. University Librarian; Writer; Professor of Bibliography. Educ: B.A.(Hons.), Univ. of Wales, 1939; Assoc., Lib. Assn. of GB, 1938; Dip. in Educ., Balliol Coll., Oxford, 1946; M.A., Univ. of Man., Can., 1948; Dip. in Adv. Lib. Admin., Rutgers Univ.; M.L.S., Univ. of Western Ontario. Publs: The Great Disciple, 1951; The Poor Hater, 1958; The Tolkien Relation, 1968; Necessary Russell, 1969; Notes on the Hobbit & the Lord of the Rings, 1970. Contbr. to var. jrnls. Mbr., var. profl. assns. Hons. incl: Fellow, Royal Soc. of Can., 1974. Address: Office of the University Librarian, McMaster University Library, Hamilton, Ont., Can.

REARDON, (Rev.) Bernard Morris Garvin, b. 9 Apr. 1914, London, UK. Minister of Religion; University Teacher (Reader & Head of Department, Religious Studies).

Educ: M.A., Keble Coll., Oxford; Ripon Hall, Oxford. Publs: Henry Scott Holland, 1962; Ed., Scott Holland, Fibres of Faith, 1962; Religious Thought in the Nineteenth Century, 1967; Liberal Protestantism, 1968; Roman Catholic Modernism, 1970; From Coleridge to Gore, 1971; Liberalism & Tradition: Aspects of Catholic Thought in Nineteenth Century France, 1975. Contbr. to: Studia Patristica; Jrnl. of Theol. Studies; Jrnl. of Ecclesiastical Hist.; other theol. jrnls. Address: Dept. of Religious Studies, The Univ., 2 The Grove, Newcastle upon Tyne NE12 9PE, UK.

REBELLO, Luiz-Francisco, b. 10 Sept. 1924, Lisbon, Portugal. Playwright; Dramatic Critic; Lawyer. Educ: Law. Publs: (plays in Portuguese) World Began at 5.47 pm, 1947; The Forthcoming Day, 1953; Someone Must Die, 1956; Love is Urgent, 1958; Birds with Broken Wings, 1959; Condemned to Live, 1963; Freedom, Freedom, 1974; (essays, history) Modern Theatre, 1957; Pictures of Contemporary Theatre, 1961; A Story of Portuguese Drama, 1968; Game for Men, 1971. Contbr. to: Primer Acto; Il Dramma; Enciclopedia dello Spettacolo. Dialog. Mbrships. incl: Portuguese Soc. Authors (Pres.); Int. Theatre Inst. Hons: Portuguese Writers' Assn. Drama Prize, 1964; Portuguese Acad. Scis., elected 1972. Address: Avenida Duque de Loulé 31, Lisbon 1, Portugal.

RECHY, John (Francisco), b. 10 Mar. 1934, El Paso, Tex., USA. Writer. Educ: B.A., Tex. Western Coll., El Paso; New Schl. for Soc. Rsch., N.Y. Publs: (novels) City of Night, USA 1963, UK 1964; Numbers, 1967; This Day's Death, USA & UK 1970. Recip., Longview Award, 1961. Address: c/o Grove Press, 80 University Pl., N.Y., NY 10003, USA.

RECKITT, Basil Norman, b. 12 Aug. 1905, St. Albans, UK. Retired Company Director & Chairman. Educ: Uppingham Schl.; M.A., King's Coll., Cambridge Univ. Publs: History of Reckitt & Sons Ltd., 1951; Charles I & Hull, 1952; The Lindley Affair, 1972. Mbr., Hull Univ. Pro-Chancellor & Chmn. Coun. Hons: LL.D., Hull Univ., 1967; D.L., Humberside. Address: The Elms, Roos, nr. Hull, UK.

RECKTENWALD, Lester Nicholas, b. 2 Sept. 1902, Hartford, Minn., USA. College Professor. Educ: B.S., M.A., Univ. of Minn.; Univ. of Wis.; Columbia Univ. Publs: Hail Tomorrow, 1944; Guidance & Counseling, 1953; The Psychological Inventory, 1956; (monographs) Meaning & Structure of Personality; Classifactory Approach to Personality; Developmental Approach to Personality; Interaction & Personality; Differential Personality Patterns; Assessment of Personality; Representative Theories. Contbr. to profl. jrnls. Mbrships. incl: Am. Psychol. Assn.; Life Fellow, Int. Inst. of Arts & Letters. Recip., var. hons. Address: 480 Quigley Rd., Wayne (Strafford), PA 19087, USA.

REDDY, T. Ramakrishna, b. 1 July 1937, Kanganambanda, A.P., India. Teacher. Educ: B.A.(Hons.), 1958, M.A., 1959, Univ. of Mysore, India; Ph.D., Univ. of Ky., USA, 1966. Publs: India's Policy in the United Nations, 1968. Mbr., Am. Pol. Sci. Assn. Address: RFD 4, Box 745, Ogden, UT 84403, USA.

REDER, Philip, b. 1924, London, UK. Director of Music, Parmiter's School. Educ: A.G.S.M.; A.R.C.M.; Guildhall Schl. Music. Publs: The Man Who Grew Matches, 1962; Music & Rhythm for Junior & Senior Classes, 1966; French, Prussian Marches, 1967; Epitaphs, 1969; Ed., Great Piano Virtuosos, Von Lenz, 1972. Contbr. to: Music in Educ.; Tchrs.' World; Times Educl. Supplement; Music Tchr. Mbrships: Soc. Authors; Piano Perfs. Club. Address: 37 Overton Dr., Wanstead, London E11, UK.

REDFERN, George B., b. 24 May 1910, Clarksville, Ohio, USA. School Administrator. Educ: A.B., Wilmington Coll., Wilmington, Ohio; Ed.M., Ed.D., Univ. Cinn., Cinn., Ohio. Publs: How to Appraise Teaching Performance, 1957; Improving Principal-Faculty Relationships, 1966; The School Administrator & Negotiation, 1968; How to Evaluate Teaching: A Performance Objectives Approach, 1972. Contbr. to: New Directions for Educ.; Educl. Admin. Quarterly; Nat. Elem. Prin.; Educl. Leadership. Mbrships. incl: Am. Assn. of Schl. Admnstrs.; Am. Assn. Schl. Personnel Admnstrs. (Past Pres.); Nat. Educ. Assn. Hons. incl: Disting. Prof., Nat. Acad. for Schl. Execs., AASA. Address: 8111 Lewinsville Rd., McLean, VA, USA.

REDFERN, Walter David, b. 1936, Liverpool, UK. Reader, Reading University. Educ: M.A., Ph.D., Cambridge Univ.; Ecole Normale Superieure, Paris. Publs: The Private World of Jean Giono, 1967; Paul Nizan, 1972. Contbr. to: Romanic Review; French Review; Symposium; Times Lit. Supplement; Nouvelle Revue Française; Europe; Jrnl. European Studies. Address: 8 Northcourt Ave., Reading, Berks., UK.

REDGRAVE, (Sir) Michael Scudamore, b. 20 Mar. 1908. Actor; Author. Educ: M.A., Magdalene Coll., Cambridge. Publs: Actor's Ways & Means, 1953; Mask or Face, 1955; The Mountebank's Tale, 1959; (plays) The Seventh Man, 1936; The Aspern Papers, 1959; Circus Boy, 1963; theatrical prods. incl: Hamlet; Merchant of Venice; King Lear; Uncle Vanya; The Master Builder; films incl: Fame is the Spur; The Dam Busters; The Loneliness of the Long Distance Runner; & num. others. Hons: Kt.; C.B.E.; Order of Dannebrog, 1955. Address: 35 Lower Belgrave St., London SW1, UK.

REDGRAVE, Paul, b. 28 Feb. 1920, Bradford, Yorks., UK. Schoolmaster. Educ: M.A., St. Catherine's Coll., Oxford Univ. Publs: Full Fathom Six, 1959, 2nd ed., 1961; The Ballad of Childe the Hunter. Contbr. to: Black Belt Mag. (Brit. Corres.); BBC talks; etc. Recip., Spender Essay Prize, Oxford Univ., 1950. Address: Yeoland House, Clearbrook, Yelverton, Devon, UK.

REDGROVE, Peter, b. 1932, Kingston, Surrey, UK. Scientific Journalist & Editor; Resident Writer, Falmouth Schl. of Art, Cornwall, UK, 1966—. Educ: Queens' Coll., Cambridge Univ. Publs: The Collector, 1960; The Nature of Cold Weather, 1961; At the White Monument, 1963; The Force, 1966; Dr. Faust's Sea-Spiral Spirit, 1972; In the Country of the Skin, 1973; Hermaphrodite Album (w. Penelope Shuttle), 1973; The Terrors of Dr. Treviles (w. Penelope Shuttle), 1974; Sons of My Skin: Poems 1954-74, (Ed., w. Introduction by Marie Peel), 1975. Recip., Guardian Fiction Prize, 1973 for In the Country of the Skin. Address: c/o Routledge & Kegan Paul, Broadway House, 68-74 Carter Lane, London EC4, UK.

REDMAN, Lister Appleton, b. 2 Jan. 1933, Blackburn, Lancs., UK. Schoolmaster. Educ: M.A. (Physics), The Queen's Coll., Oxford; M.A., (Educ.), Lancaster Univ. Publs. incl: Nuclear Energy, 1963; Essential Elementary Physics, 1967, 2nd ed., 1970; The Physics Teaching Handbook, 1971; A-Level Physics Comprehension, book 1, 1972, book 2, 1974; The Young Student's Laboratory Guide, 1972; Getting to Know Physics, Book 1, 1973, 2 & 3, 1974, 4 & 5, 1975. Contbr. to: Schl. Sci. Review; Physics Tchr., USA.; Succes, Netherlands; etc. Mbrships. incl: Fellow, Inst. of Physics. Address: 6 Miletas Place, Fairhaven, Lytham St. Annes, Lancs. FY8 1BQ, UK.

REDMAN, Theodore Francis, b. 1916, Wallasey, Cheshire, UK. Obstetrician & Gynaecologist. Educ: Univ. of Manchester; T.D.; M.B., Ch.B.; F.R.C.S.E.; F.R.C.O.G. Publs: Lecture Notes on Midwifery, 1958, 3rd ed., 1975. Contbr. to: Brit. Med. Jrnl.; Lancet; other profl. jrnls. Address: 87 Old Park Rd., Leeds 8, UK.

REECE, Alys, pen name WINGFIELD, Susan, b. Bury St. Edmunds, UK. Supervisor of an Adult Training Centre. Publs: To My Wife — 50 Camels, 1965; The Goat Bag (as Susan Wingfield). Mbrships: Soc. Authors; PEN. Agent: Messrs. Campbell Thomson & McLaughlin Ltd. Address: Bolton Old Manse, Haddington, E. Lothian, UK.

REECE, Benny Ramon, b. 7 Dec. 1930, Asheville, N.C., USA. Professor of Classical Languages. Educ: A.B., Duke Univ., 1953; M.A. 1954, Ph.D. 1957, Univ. of N.C.; Univ. of Munich, 1957-58. Publs: Documents Illustrating Cicero's Consular Campaign, 1967; Plautus: Epidicus, 1967; Learning in the Tenth Century, 1968 reprinted 1972; Sermones Ratherii Episcopi Veronensis, 1969. Contbr. to: Am. Jrnl. Philol.; Transactions Am. Philol. Assn.; Am. Philosl. Soc. Yrbook; Latomus; Classical Folia; Furman Studies. Mbrships: Am. Philol. Assn.; Classical Assn. of Middle West & South; Am. Philosl. Soc. Hons: Num. Fellowships, inclng. Southeastern Inst. for Medieval Studies, 1965, & Coop. Prog. in Humanities, Duke Univ., 1966-67. Address: Cottonfields, Route 3, Greenville, SC 29609, USA.

REED, Alexander Wyclif, b. 7 Mar. 1908, Auckland, NZ. Publisher. Publs. incl: Myths & Legends of Maoriland; Myths & Legends of Australia; Myths & Legends of Fiji; Myths & Legends of Polynesia, 1974; Treasury of Maori

Folklore; Place Names of Australia; Place Names of New Zealand, 1975; Concise Maori Dictionary; Illustrated Encyclopedia of Maori Life; Illustrated Encyclopedia of Aboriginal Life; Wonder Tales of Maoriland. Mbrships: Polynesian Soc.; PEN. Hons. Esther Glen Medal, 1947; Christopher Medallion, 1974. Address: 22 Fairview Cres., Kelburn, Wellington, N.Z.

REED, (Sir) Alfred Hamish, b. 30 Dec. 1875, Hayes, Middx., UK. Author; Publisher. Publs: The Story of New Zealand, 1945, 12th ed., 1970; The Story of Otago, 1947; The Gumdigger, 1948; The Story of Canterbury, 1949; The Story of the Kauri, 1953; The Four Corners of New Zealand, 1954; The Story of Early Dunedin, 1956; The Story of Northland, 1956; The Story of Hawke's Bay, 1958; Walks in Maoriland Byways, 1958; The Story of a Kauri Park, 1959; Heroes of Peace & War in Early New Zealand, 1959; Florence Nightingale, 1960; From North Cape to Bluff on foot at 85, 1961; From East Cape to Cape Egmont on foot at 86, 1962; From Sydney to Melbourne on Foot, 1965; Anthony Trollope in New Zealand, 1969; Ben & Eleanor Farjeon, 1973; The Happy Wanderer, 1974. Hons: M.B.E., 1948; C.B.E., 1962; Kt. Bach., 1974. Address: 153 Glenpark Ave., Dunedin, N.Z.

REED, Ishmael, b. 22 Feb. 1938, Chattanooga, Tenn., USA. Writer; Publishing Executive. Educ: Univ. of Buffalo, N.Y., 3 yrs. Publs: (novels) The Free-Lance Pallbearers, USA 1967, UK 1968; Yellow Back Radio Broke-Down, USA 1969, UK 1971; Mumbo-Jumbo, USA 1972; (verse) Catechism of D Neoamerican HooDoo Chuck, UK 1970; Conjure, USA 1972; Ed., 19 Necromancers from Now, USA 1970. Address: 6 Bret Harte Way, Berkeley, CA 94708, USA.

REED, Kit (Lillian Craig), b. 7 June 1932, San Diego, Calif., USA. Writer. Educ: B.A., Coll. of Notre Dame of Md., Balt., 1954. Publs: Mother Isn't Dead She's Only Sleeping, 1961; At War As Children, 1964; The Better Part, 1967; Mr. Da V & Other Stories, 1967; When We Dream (juvenile), 1967; Armed Camps, 1970; Cry of the Daughter, 1971; Tiger Rag, 1973; Fat (anthol.), 1975. Contbr. to jrnls. & anthols. inclng: Transatlantic Review; Cosmopolitan. Hons. incl: Guggenheim Fellow, 1964-65; 5-yr. grant, Abraham Woursell Fndn., 1965-70. Address: 45 Lawn Ave., Middletown, CT, USA.

REED, Maud Dorothy, b. London, UK. Filmstrip Producer. Publs: Angela at School, 1946; New Girl at Fir Trees, 1948; It Was Candy's Idea, 1955; Candy Finds the Clue, 1958; Candy Does It Again, 1960; Candy in the Alps, 1964; A Hundred Dreamtime Tales, 1967; Making Sound Filmstrips, 1969; (plays) The Devil in Antioch; A World Invisible. Contbr. to BBC. Address: 36 Southview Dr., Worthing, Sussex, UK.

REED, S. Kyle, b. 17 Apr. 1922, Knoxville, Tenn., USA. Professor of Industrial & Personnel Management; Consultant. Educ: N.C. State Univ.; B.S., Univ. of Tenn., Knoxville; Ph.D., Univ. of Edinburgh, UK; Post-doct. studies, Univ. of Mich., USA. Publs: Production Scheduling Simulation, 1971. Contbr. to: Factory; Advanced Mgmt.; Southern Jrnl of Bus.; Tenn. Town & Country; Tenn. Survey of Bus.; Am. Prod. & Inventory Control Soc. Quarterly Bulletin. Mbr. var. profl. assns. & fraternities. Hons. incl: Ford Fndn. Fellowship, 1962; Fndn. for Econ. Educ. Fellowship, 1963; Alcoa Fndn. Fellowship, 1964. Address: 504 David Lane, Concord, TN 37720, USA.

REED, Stanley William, b. 1911, Plaistow, London, UK. Consultant on Regional Development British Film Institute since 1972; Director British Film Institute, 1965-72. Educ: Coll. St. Mark & St. John, Chelsea. Publs: The Cinema; How Films are Made; A Guide to Good Viewing. Contbr. to Ency. Britannica; etc. Address: 54 Felstead Rd., Wanstead, London E11, UK.

REEMAN, Douglas Edward, pen name KENT, Alexander, b. 15 Oct. 1924, Thames Ditton, UK. Author. Publs. incl: Path of the Storm, 1966; The Deep Silence, 1967; The Pride & the Anguish, 1968; To Risks Unknown, 1969; The Greatest Enemy, 1970; Enemy in Sight, 1970; The Flag Captain, 1971; Against the Sea (non-fiction), 1971; Rendezvous-South Atlantic, 1972; Sloop of War, 1972; Command a King's Ship, 1973; Go In and Sink, 1973; The Destroyers, 1974; Signal — Close Action, 1974; Richard Bolitho — Midshipman, 1975; Blaze of Glory, 1975. Contbr. to var. nautical mags. Mbrships. incl: Soc. for Nautical Rsch.; Royal Naval Sailing Assn. Address: c/o The Hutchinson Grp., 3 Fitzroy Sq., London W1P 6JD, UK.

REES, Brinley Roderick, b. 1919, Tondu, Glam., UK. Professor of Greek. Educ: M.A., Ph.D., Merton Coll., Oxford Univ. Publs: The Merton Papyri, 1959; The Use of Greek, 1960; Papyri from Hermopolis, 1964; Lampas (w. M. E. Jervis), 1970; Classics for Intending Students, 1970; Aristotle's Theory & Milton's Practice: Samson Agonistes, 1972. Contbr. to: Oxford Classical Dictionary; Jrnl. Egyptian Archaeol.; Classical Review; Greece & Rome; Classical Philol.; Eos; Jrnl. John Rylands Lib.; Didaskalos; Latin Tchng.; Man Myth & Magic; Handbook for Hist. Tchrs.; etc. Mbrships. incl: Classical Assn.; Egypt Exploration Soc.; Hellenic Soc. Address: 1 Russell Rd., Moseley, Birmingham B13 8RA, UK.

REES, David, b. 1928, Swansea, UK. Writer. Educ: B.A., Univ. Coll., Swansea, Univ. of Wales. Publs: Korea: The Limited War, 1964; The Age of Containment, 1967; Harry Dexter White, 1974. Address: c/o Macmillan London, Ltd., Little Essex St., London WC2, UK.

REES, Ennis, b. 17 Mar. 1925, Newport News, Va., USA. Poet; Professor of English. Educ: A.B., William & Mary Coll.; M.A., & Ph.D., Harvard Univ. Publs: The Tragedies of George Chapman: Renaissance Ethics in Action, 1954; The Odyssey of Homer (transl.), 1960; The Iliad of Homer (transl.), 1963; Poems, 1964; Fables from Aesop, 1966; Selected Poems, 1973. Contbr. to: Jrnl. of Engl. & Germanic Philol.; Sewanee Review; Prairie Schooner; Arion; Red Clay Reader; Outposts; Children's Digest. Address: Engl. Dept., Univ. of S.C., Columbia, SC 29208, USA.

REES, Leslie, b. 1905, Perth, Australia. Formerly Deputy Director of Drama, Australian Broadcasting Commission. Educ: B.A.; Univs. W. Aust. & London. Publs: Modern Short Plays, 1951, Spinifex Walkabout, 1953; Westward from Cocos, 1956, & Coasts of Cape York, 1960 (all w. Coralie Rees); Mask & Microphone, 1963; People of the Big Sky Country, 1970; (juvenile) Shy the Platypus, 1943; Boy Lost on Tropic Coast, 1969; Digit Dick on the Great Barrier Reef, 1970; (non-fiction) The Making of Australian Drama: A Historical & Critical Survey from the 1830's to the 1970's, 1973; & 25 other books. Mbrships. incl: Int. PEN; Pres., Sydney Ctr., PEN, 1968—. Address: 4/5 The Esplanade, Balmoral Beach 2088, NSW, Australia.

REES, William. b. 1887, Brecon, UK. Emeritus Professor of History. Educ: Univ. Coll., Cardiff; London Schl. of Econs.; M.A.; D.Sc.; D.Litt. Publs: South Wales & the March 1284-1415; Map of South Wales & Border in the 14th Century; An Historical Atlas of Wales; Cardiff — A History of the City; A Bibliography of the History of Wales, 1931 (jt. author); Order of St. John in Wales, 1953; Industry Before the Industrial Revolution, 2 vols., 1968. Mbrships. incl: F.S.A.; Former Mbr. of Coun. & VP, F.R.Hist.Soc.; Ct. & Coun., Nat. Mus. of Wales; Ct., Nat. Lib. of Wales. Recip., Kt., Order of St. John. Address: 2 Park Rd., Penarth, Glam. CF6 2BD, UK.

REESE, Max M., b. 11 Aug. 1910, Surrey, UK. Historian. Educ: B.A. (Mod. Hist.), Merton Coll., Oxford, 1932. Publs: The Tudors & Stuarts, 1940; Shakespeare: his World & his Work, 1953; The Cease of Majesty, 1961; The Puritan Impulse, 1975; Ed., Shakespeare: 1 Henry IV; Henry V; Elizabethan Verse Romances; Gibbon's Autobiography. Address: 7 Mowatt Rd., Grayshot, Hindhead, Surrey, UK.

REES-MOGG, William, b. 1928, Bristol, UK. Editor & Director, The Times. Educ: M.A., Balliol Coll., Oxford. Publs: Sir Anthony Eden; His Majesty Preserved; The Reigning Error. Contbr. to: Financial Times; Sunday Times (var. ed. posts., 1960-67); Times; Director. Mbr., Garrick Club. Address: 3 Smith Sq., London SW1, UK.

REEVE, Edith, pen name SIMON, Edith, b. 18 May 1917, Berlin, Germany. Novelist. Historian; Painter; Sculptor. Publs: (novels) The Chosen, 1940; Biting the Blue Finger, 1942; Wings Deceive, 1944; The Other Passion, 1947; The Golden Hand, 1952; The Past Masters, 1953, 2nd ed. (title The House of Strangers), 1954; The Twelve Pictures, 1955; The Sable Coat, 1958; The Great Forgery, 1961; (history) The Piebald Standard, 1959; The Making of Frederick the Great, 1963; The Reformation, 1967; The Saints, 1968; Luther Alive, 1968; The Anglo-Saxon Manner, 1972. Contbr. to: Ency. Britannica; Horizon (USA). Mbr., Soc. Authors. Address: 11 Grosvenor Cres., Edinburgh EH12 5EL, UK.

REEVE, F. D., b. 18 Sept. 1928, Phila., Pa., USA. Author. Educ: A.B., Princeton Univ.; Ph.D., Columbia Univ. Publs: The Red Machines, 1968; In the Silent Stones (verse), 1968; Just Over the Border, 1969; The Brother, 1971; The Blue Cat (verse), 1972; White Colors, 1973. Contbr. to: Kenyon; Poetry; Book World; N.Y. Times; Book Review; New Yorker; Yale Review; Mich. Quarterly; N. Am. Review; Occident; Little Mag. etc. Mbrships: PEN; Conn. Acad. of Arts & Scis. Recip., Lit. Award, Am. Acad. Arts & Letters/Nat. Inst., 1970. Address: Higganum, CT, USA.

REEVE-JONES, Alan Edmond, pen name ALLEN, Edmund, b. 22 Sept. 1914, Bergen, Norway. Author; Journalist. Educ: Hymers Coll.; Berlin Univ. Publs: London Pubs, 1962; A Dram Like This, 1974; A Bluffer's Guide to Philosophy, 1975; The Dance Crazes, 1975. Contbr. to: In Brit.; Automobile Assn. publs.; BBC; ITV; etc. Mbrships: Performing Right Soc.; Writers' Guild of GB; Brit. Actors' Equity Assn.; Mech. Copyright Protection Soc. Recip., Kt. of Mark Twain, 1970. Address: Walnut Tree Cottage, Herne Common, Kent CT6 7LB, UK.

REEVES, James, b. 1 July 1909. Freelance Author & Broadcaster. Educ: M.A., Cambridge Univ. Publs. incl: The Wandering Moon, 1950; The Critical Sense, 1956; The Idiom of the People, 1958; Collected Poems, 1960; Understanding Poetry, 1965; The Cold Flame, 1967; The Trojan Horse, 1968; Ed., Chaucer, Lyric & Allegory, 1970; Maeldun the Voyager, 1971; How to Write Poems for Children, 1971; How the Moon Began, 1971; The Path of Gold, 1972; Poems & Paraphrases, 1972; The Voyage of Odysseus, 1973; The Forbidden Forest, 1973; Complete Poems for Children, 1973; Ed., num. anthols. & vols. of Poetry. Address: Flints, Rotten Row, Lewes, Sussex, UK.

REEVES, Marjorie Ethel, b. 17 July 1905, Westbury, Wilts., UK. University Teacher. Educ: St. Hugh's Coll., Oxford; Westfield Coll., London Univ.; M.A.; PhD.; D.Litt. Publs: Growing Up in a Modern Society; Three Questions in Higher Education; Then & There Series: The Medieval Town; Elizabethan Court; other titles; The Influence of Prophecy in the Later Middle Ages, 1969; The Figurae of Joachim of Fiore, 1973. Contbr. to: Medieval & Renaissance Studies; Speculum; Traditio; New Era; Times Educl. Supplement; Recherches de Theol.. Ancien & Medievale; Medievalia & Humanistica. Mbrships: Fellow, Brit. Acad.; Fellow, Royal Histl. Soc.; Histl. Assn. Address: 38 Norham Rd., Oxford OX2 6SQ, UK.

REEVES, Trevor Edward, b. 24 Nov. 1940, Dunedin, NZ. Publisher; Editor; Writer. Educ: Univ. of Otago; King Edward Polytech.; Dip. Indl. Admin., A.N.Z.I.M. Publs: Stones (poems), 1972; Hibiscuits (poems), 1973. Contbr. to: (articles) Ariel, Can.; Aarhus, C'wlth. Newsletter (Denmark), etc.; (poems) Cave (Ed. Cons.); Landfall; Argot; New Argot; Freed; Frontiers; Edge (Contbng. Ed.); Mate; Arena; NZ Listener; etc. (all NZ); Expression; Sat. Club Book of Poetry, etc. (all Aust.); W. Coast Poetry Review; Second Coming (Ed. Cons.), etc. (all USA); Streetword, UK. Mbrships. incl: NZ Lit. Fund Advsry. Comm.; PEN; NZ Book Coun. Address: 61 Mornington Rd., Dunedin, NZ.

REGENASS, René, b. 15 May 1935, Basle, Switz. Writer; Editor. Educ: Basle Univ. Publs: Der Besuch blieb meist über Nacht, 1969; Wir haben das Pulver nicht erfunden, uns gehören nur die Fabriken, 1971; Alle Wege bodenlos, 1972; Wer Wahlplakate beschmiert, beschädigt fremdes Eigentum, 1973; Die Sitzung (play), 1964; Triumph ist eine Marke, 1975. Contbr. to: Nat.-Zeitung, Basle; Basler Nachrichten; Drehpunkt; Neutralität. Mbr., Gruppe Olten (Swiss Authors' Club). Recip., of Lyric Award of Canton of Baselland, 1972. Address: Grimselstr. 5, CH-4000, Basle, Switz.

REHDER, Helmut, b. 22 June 1905, Bergedorf, Hamburg, Germany. Professor of German Language & Literature, University of Texas. Educ: Ph.D., Univ. of Heidelberg, 1929. Publs: Die Philosophie der Unendlichen

Landschaft, 1932; 14 major textbooks in German (co-author), 1944-74; J. N. Meinhard n.s. Überzungern, 1953; Co-Ed., Goethe's Faust, 2 vols., 1954-55. Contbr. to sev. German & Am. lit. & other profl. jrnls. Mbrships. incl: MLA; Past Pres., S. Ctrl. MLA; Am. Assn. of Tchrs. of German. Recip., Order of Merit of W. German Repub., 1st Class, 1972. Address: Rte. 10, Box 11, Austin, Area 512, TX 78736, USA.

REICHARDT, Jasia, b. Warsaw, Poland. Writer; Exhibition Organiser. Educ: Old Vic Theatre Schl. Publs: Victor Pasmore, 1962; Pin, 1962; Yaacov Agam, 1966; The Computer in Art, 1971; Cybernetics, Art & Ideas (Ed.), 1971; series of 13 monographs, Art in Progress. Contbr. to: Ed., Monthly ICA Bulletin, 1964-68; Asst. Ed., Art News & Review, 1958-60; Concepts of Modern Art, 1974; Nature; BBC; New Sci.; etc. Mbrships. incl: Nat. Union of Jrnlsts.; Art Critics Int. Assn.; Expmtl. Projs. Comm., Arts Coun., 1970-74. Address: 12 Belsize Pk. Gdns., London NW3 4LD, UK.

REICHELT, Hans-Peter, pen names EPPENDORFER, Hans; HAPER, Matthias, b. 10 June 1942, Lütjenburg, Germany. Writer; Journalist. Educ: Coll. Dip. in Jrnlsm. Publs: Lyrik, 1972; Versuch über die Pubertät (w. H. Fichte), 1974. Contbr. to: Zeit Konkret; das da; Radio; also lectures at Studio-Bühne, Kiel; Corso-Theater, Neumünster; Theater Im Zimmer, Hamburg; etc. Mbrships: Verband Deutscher Schriftsteller (German Authors' Union); Deutsches Journalisten Union; Die Wendeltreppe, Hamburg (lit. cabaret). Address: 2 Hamburg 20, Woldsenweg 6, W. Germany.

REICHEN, Charles-Albert, b. 18 Aug. 1907, Frutigen, Switz. University Professor of Philosophy; Writer. Educ: Lic. es-lettres; Agrégation de l'Univ. Publs: La Fin du Monde est pour demain (Doomsday for tomorrow), 1947; l'Art musical et son évolution (Musical Art & its Evolution), 1956; Histoire de l'Astronomie (A History of Astronomy), 1962; Histoire de la Chimie (A History of Chemistry), 1963; Histoire de la Physique (A History of Physics), 1964; Rythmes Inactuels (Poems of Yesternight), 1965, 1966. Chief Ed., Jeunesse Mag./Jugendwoche, 25 yrs. Mbrships. incl: PEN; Swiss Soc. of Authors. Address: 13 Route du Signal, 1080 Lausanne, Switz.

REID, Alastair, b. 22 Mar. 1926, Whithorn, UK. Writer. Educ: M.A., Univ. of St. Andrews, 1949. Publs: 8 children's books; Ounce Dice Trice, 1958; Oddments, Inklings, Omens, Moments, 1959; Passwords, 1963; transls. of the work of Jorge Luis Borges, Pablo Neruda & other Latin Am. poets. Contbr. to: New Yorker (Staff Writer); Atlantic Monthly; Listener. Mbrships: Poetry Soc.; Scottish Arts Club. Recip., Guggenheim Fellowships, 1955-56 & 1956-57. Agent: John Wolfers. Address: c/o John Wolfers, 3 Regent St., London WC1, UK.

REID, James Malcolm, b. 10 Apr. 1902, Boulder, Colo., USA. Book Publisher; Director. Educ: B.A., Dartmouth Coll., 1924. Publs: poetry: A Closer Look (w. John Ciardi & Laurence Perine), 1963; 100 American Poems of the Twentieth Century (w. Lourence Perrine), 1966; An Adventure in Textbooks, 1969. Contbr. to: Engl. Jrnl.; Dartmouth Alumni Mag.; Ridgefield Press. Address: Kent Hills, Kent, CT 06757, USA.

REID, John, b. 4 Dec. 1915, Guelph, Ont., Can. Writer. Publs: Horses With Blindfolds, 1968; The Faithless Mirror, 1974; The Lost Child, 1975. Contbr. to: Youth Today; Wyndham Lewis in Canada; Homage to Ronald Duncan; Ephemerat. Mbr., Assn. of Can. TV & Radio Artists. Recip., Chancellorship, Fergusson Coll. Address: 169 Castlefield Ave., Toronto, Ont. M4R 1G6, Can.

REID, John Gilbert, b. 18 Mar. 1899, Blockley, UK. Historian. Educ: A.B., Hamilton Coll., USA, 1921; M.A., 1931, Ph.D., 1934, Univ. of Calif., Berkeley. Publs: Pickwickians Abroad (as Dier Treblig Nhoj), 1913; The Manchu Abdication & the Powers, 1908-1912, 1935; Far East Ed., Foreign Relations of the United States, for years 1928-49 (Dept. of State Series), 1939-71. Contbr. to Chinese; US jrnls. Hons: Penfield Schol. in Int. Affairs, Diplomacy & Belles Lettres, 1935-36. Address: 4804 Tecumseh St., College Park, MD 20740, USA.

REID, (The Rev.) John Kelman Sutherland, b. 1910, Leith, UK. Professor of Christian Dogmatics, University of Aberdeen since 1966; Co-Ed., Scottish Journal of Theology since 1947; Secretary Joint Committee on New English Bible, 1949—. Educ: M.A., D.D.; Univs. Edinburgh,

Heidelberg, Marburg, Basle, Strasbourg. Publs: The Authority of Scripture, 1957; Our Life in Christ, 1963; Presbyterians & Unity, 1965; Christian Apologetics, 1969; Transl. & Ed., Calvin's Theological Treatises, 1954; Calvin's Concerning the Eternal Predestination of God, 1961. Hons: C.B.E.; T.D. Address: Don House, 46 Don St., Aberdeen AB2 1UU, UK.

REID, Loren Dudley, b. 1905, Gilman City, Mo., USA. Professor of Speech, University of Missouri. Educ: B.A.; M.A.; Ph.D.; Grinnell Coll., Univ. Chicago, Univ. Iowa. Publs: Charles James Fox, 1969; First Principles of Public Speaking; Ed., American Public Address; Teaching Speech, 4th ed.; Speaking Well, 3rd ed. Contbr. to: Quarterly Jrnl. of Speech; Speech Monographs; Parly. Affairs; etc. Mbrships. incl: Fellow Royal Histl. Soc.; Hansard Club (London). Hons. incl: Winans Award, 1969; Golden Anniversary Award, 1970; Disting. Prof. Awards, Univ. Mo., 1970, 1971. Address: 200 E. Brandon Rd., Columbia, MO 65201, USA.

REID, Louis Arnaud, b. 1895, Ellon, Aberdeenshire, UK. Emeritus Professor of Philosophy; Author. Educ: M.A., Ph.D., D.Litt., Univ. of Edinburgh. Publs: Knowledge & Truth; A Study in Aesthetics; Creative Morality; Preface to Faith; Ways of Knowledge & Experience; Rediscovery of Belief; Philosophy & Education; Meaning in the Arts. Contbr. to: Mind; Philos.; Proceedings of Aristotelian Soc.; Hibbert Jrnl.; Brit. Jrnl. Educl. Studies. Address: 50 Rotherwick Rd., London NW11, UK.

REID, Meta A. C. J., pen name REID, Meta Mayne, b. Yorks., UK. Writer; Housewife. Educ: B.A., Manchester Univ. Publs. incl: Phelim & the Creatures, 1952; All Because of Dawks, 1954; Carrigmore Castle, 1954; Tiffany & the Swallow Rhyme, 1955; Sandy & the Hollow Book, 1961; The Tinker's Summer, 1967; The House at Spaniards' Bay, 1965; The Silver Fighting Cocks, 1966; The Glen Beyond the Door, 1968; The Two Rebels, 1969; Beyond the Wide World's End, 1972; Plotters of Pollnashee, 1973; (poetry) No Ivory Tower, 1974; & about 80 BBC radio scripts. Contbr. to num. mags. & newspapers. Mbr., PEN (Belfast Chmn., 1960, Irish Pres., 1969-71). Recip., Poetry Prize & Trophy, Listowel Writers Wk., Co. Kerry, Repub. of Ireland, 1974. Address: 30 Ballymullan Rd., Crawfordsburn BT19 1JG, UK.

REID, Randall, b. 4 Oct. 1931, Paso Robles, Calif., USA. College Teacher & Writer. Educ: B.A., San Fran. State Coll., 1959; M.A., 1961, Ph.D., 1966, Stanford Univ. Publs: The Fiction of Nathanael West: No Redeemer, No Promised Land, 1968; (novel) Lost & Found, forthcoming. Contbr. to: New Am. Review; Carolina Quarterly; etc. Hons: Woodrow Wilson Fellowship 1954-60; NDEA Fellowship, 1965-66; NEH Fellowship for Younger Humanists, 1972-73; Short story Detritus included in Prize Stories 1973; The O. Henry Awards, 1973. Address: Deep Springs Coll., Deep Springs, CA 89010, USA.

REID, Robert, b. 20 Apr. 1933, Cleckheaton, UK. Author. Educ: M.A., Christ Ch., Oxford; M.Sc., Queen's Univ., Can.; Ph.D., Queens' Coll., Cambridge. Publs: Tongues of Conscience, 1969; Marie Curie, 1974; Microbes & Men, 1974. Address: 22 Colet Gardens, London W14, UK.

REID, Victor Stafford, b. 1 May 1913, Kingston, Jamaica. Journalist. Publs: New Day, 1948; The Leopard, 1957; Sixty Five, 1962; The Young Warriors, 1964; Mount Ephraim, 1968; The Jamaicans, 1975. Contbr. to sev. mags. & jrnls. Mbrships: Chmn., Jamaica Nat. Trust Commn.; VP, Caribbean Conserv. Assn.; Former Pres., Jamaica Lib. Assn. Hons: Musgrave Medal, 1955; Can. Coun., 1958-59; Guggenheim Fellowship, 1959-60. Address: Pump Farm, Rock Hall, Jamaica, W. Indies.

REID BANKS, Lynne, (Mrs. Chaim Stephenson), b. 1929, London, UK. Reporter; Scriptwriter; Author; Playwright. Educ: Italia Conte Schl.; R.A.D.A. Publs: The L-Shaped Room, 1960; An End to Running, 1962; Children at the Gate, 1968; The Backward Shadow, 1971; One More River, 1972; Two is Lonely, 1973; Sarah & After, 1975. Contbr. to: Indep. TV News (Reporter/Scriptwriter, 1954-61); Sunday Observer; Spectator; Sunday Telegraph; Good Housekeeping; Ladies Home Jrnl.; Cornhill. Agent: Bolt & Watson Ltd.

REIF, Rita, b. 12 June 1929, NYC, USA. Newspaper Reporter & Antiques Columnist. Educ: B.S., Fordham Univ.; M.A., Grad. Schl. of Arts & Scis., Columbia Univ.

Publs: Living With Books, 1968, 2nd ed., 1973; The Antiques Collector's Guide to Styles & Prices, 1970; Treasure Rooms of America's Mansions, Manors & Houses, 1970; Home: It Takes More Than Money, 1975. Contbr. to: N.Y. Mag.; Art News. Hons: Dorothy Dawe Awards for Disting. Reporting, 1969, 1970, 1971; Press Award, Nat. Soc. of Interior Designers. Address: 57 W. 58th Street, N.Y., NY 10019, USA.

REIGER, George Wesley, b. 7 Apr. 1939, Brooklyn, N.Y., USA. Conservation Editor, Field & Stream; Senior Editor, International Wildlife & National Wildlife. Educ: A.B., Princeton Univ., N.J., 1960; Law Schl., Univ. of Va., Charlottesville, 1962; M.A., Columbia Univ., N.Y., 1964. Publs: Ed., Zane Grey: Outdoorsman, 1972; Profiles in Saltwater Angling, 1973; Ed., Fishing With McClane, 1975. Contbr. to: Audubon; Field & Stream; Fishing World; Int. Wildlife; Motor Boating & Sailing; Nat. Wildlife; New Sci.; Salt Water Sportsman; Sea Frontiers; Sci. Digest; Wash. Post. Mbrships: Nat. Wildlife Fedn.; Outdoor Writers' Assn. of Am. Address: Heron Hill, Locustville, VA 23404, USA.

REIJONEN, Tuuli, pen name TUULIPUU, b. 19 Oct. 1904, Tempere, Finland. Newspaper Editor; Critic; Columnist. Publs: People on the Eastern Frontier, 1941; Faces, 1948; Through Water & Fire, 1959; The Mosaic of the Carelian Isthmus, 1969; plays, novels, short stories. Contbr. to periodicals, mags. & cultural publs. Mbrships: Union of Finnish Writers; PEN; Union of Finnish Playwrights; Union of Finnish Newspaper Ed.; etc. Hons: 1st Prize, Int. Competition of Short Story Writers, N.Y. Herald Tribune, 1952; Pro Finlandia Medal. Address: Mannerheimintie 85, D 103, 00270 Helsinki 27, Finland.

REILLY, David Robin, b. 3 Jan. 1928, Everton, Hants., UK. Writer. Educ: Wellington Coll.; Royal Mil. Acad., Sandhurst. Publs: The Rest to Fortune, 1960; The Sixth Floor, 1969; Wedgwood Jasper, 1972; Wedgwood: The Portrait Medallions, 1973; The British at the Gates, 1974; British Watercolours, 1974. Contbr. to: Ency. Britannica; Collins' Ency. Knowledge. Address: c/o Curtis Brown.

REILLY, Noel Marcus Prowse, b. 1902, Pinner, UK. Economist; Former Financial Counsellor, British Embassy, Washington; Former UK Alternate Director, World Bank. Educ: M.A., Univ. of Cambridge; B.Sc.(Econ.) & Ph.D., Univ. of London. Author, The Key to Prosperity. Contbr. to: Spectator; Christian Sci. Monitor. Recip., C.M.G. Address: N. Sandwich, NH 03259, USA.

REIMANN, Arnold Luehrs, b. 3 July 1898, Adelaide, Australia. Retired Research Professor of Physics. Educ: B.Sc., 1919, D.Sc., 1935, Univ. of Adelaide; Ph.D., Univ. of Berlin, Germany, 1926. Publs: Thermionic Emission, 1934; Vacuum Technique, 1952; Physics, 2 vols., 1971; Physics, vol. III: Moderm Physics, 1973. Contbr. to: Annalen der Physik; Zeitschrift der Physik; Philosl. Mag.; Proceedings of the Phys. Soc. of London; Proceedings of the Royal Soc. of London (A). Memberships: Fellow, Inst. of Phys. & Phys. Soc. of London; Fellow, Aust. Inst. of Phys.; Fellow, Royal Soc. of Qld., Pres., 1955. Address: 52 Lucinda St., Taringa, Brisbane, Australia 4068.

REINDORP, (Rt. Rev.) George Edmund, b. 1911, Goodmayes, Essex, UK. The Lord Bishop of Salisbury. Educ: Trinity Coll., Cambridge; Westcott House; M.A.; D.D. Publs: What About You?, 1956; No Common Task, 1957; Putting It Over, 1961; Over to You, 1964; Preaching through the Christian Year, 1973. Contbr. to: Ch. Times (Theol. advsr., 1957-61). Address: Church House, Crane St., Salisbury, Wilts., UK.

REINEMANN, John Otto, b. 10 Oct. 1902, Frankfurt am Main, Germany. Criminologist. Educ: LL.D., Univ. of Frankfurt a. M., 1926; State Bar Exam., Berlin, 1928; Postgrad. study, Univ. of Pa., USA. Publs: The Challenge of Delinquency (co-author), 1950; Carried Away: Recollections & Reflections, 1975. Contbr. to profl. jrnls.; Ed., The Quarterly of Pa. Assn. of Probation, Parole & Correction, 1962—. Address: 21 W. Phil-Ellena St., Phila., PA 19119, USA.

REISCHAUER, Edwin Oldfather, 15 Oct. 1910, Tokyo, Japan. University Professor; Author. Educ: A.B., Oberlin Coll., 1931; M.A., 1932, Ph.D., 1939, Harvard Univ.; studies in France, Japan, China, 1933-38. Publs. incl: Japan Past & Present, 1946, 3rd ed., 1963; The United States & Japan, 1950, 3rd ed., 1965; Wanted: An Asian Policy, 1955; Beyond Vietnam: The United States & Asia, 1967; Japan: The Story of a Nation, 1970, 2nd ed., 1974; East

Asia; Tradition & Transformation (co-author), 1973; Toward the 21st Century: Education for a Changing World, 1973. Contbr. to: For. Affairs; N.Y. Times Mag.; For. Pol.; etc. Hons. incl: LL.D., Harvard, Yale, Chgo., Mich., etc. Address: 1737 Cambridge St., Room 503, Cambridge, MA 02138, USA.

REKIMIES, Erkki (Vilho Kalevi), b. 21 Nov. 1923, Kouvola, Finland. Educ: Mod. Lit. Studies, Univ. of Helsinki; Finnish Army Offs. Schl. Publs. incl: Pahakurun aavesusi, 1954; Hannu Rautapaita, 1955; Suurten metsien vaeltaja, 1956; Jouko Vakivahaa, 1957; Tapporahat, 1959; Turman korpit, 1960; SOS—Hanhikari, 1962; Hopeakynsi, 1968; Tuomas ja tykkivene, 1968; Susi-Rolf, Martti ja mina, 1970. Nakymaton intiaani, 1972. Contbr. of column to Kouvolan Sanomat newspaper. Hons. incl: Int. H.C. Andersen Prize, 1962; Jagt den Wolf Lit. Prize of State of Austria, 1967. Address: Okantie 14, 45720 Kuusankoski 2, Finland.

REMINI, Robert Vincent, b. 17 July 1921, NYC, USA. Historian; Educator. Educ: B.S., Fordham Univ.; M.A., Ph.D., Columbia Univ. Publs: Martin Van Buren & the Making of the Democratic Party, 1959; The Election of Andrew Jackson, 1963; Andrew Jackson, 1966; Andrew Jackson & the Bank War, 1969; The Age of Jackson (ed.), 1972; We, the People: A History of the United States (w. James I. Clark), forthcoming. Contbr. to: Am. Histl. Review; Ency. Britannica; Commonweal; Ed. Bd. of Jrnl., Org. of Am. Histns., 1969-72. Recip., sev. acad. grants & awards. Address: Dept. of Hist., Univ. of Ill., Chgo. Circle, Chgo., IL 60680, USA.

REMPT, Jan Dirk, pen name MERKRID DE JONG VAN HAGE, T.P., b. 14 Sept. 1907, Purmerend, Netherlands. Journalist; Director & Editor of International Press Agency. Educ: Law dip., Univ. of Leyden. Publs. incl: Cadeaustelsel, 1931; Reis naar Engeland, 1946; Emigratie: Kansen voor Jonge Nederlanders, 1947; All About Australia (co-author), 1952; Aan de Rande der Wereld: Een Hollandse Emigrant in Australia, 1953. Contbr. to: Aust. & Dutch farm jrnls.; Dutch Fin. Daily News; Aust. Depts. Immigration & Trade; AVRO Broadcasting Stn. & Radio Nederland Wereldomroep, Netherlands. Mbrships: Aust. Jrnlsts. Assn.; Aust. Soc. of Authors; PEN; etc. Address: 55-75 Fowler Rd., Illawong via Menai, Sydney, Australia.

RENAULT, Mary, pen name of CHALLANS, Mary, b. 4 Sept. 1905, London, UK. Writer. Educ: M.A., St. Hugh's Coll., Oxford Univ.; S.R.N., 1936. Publs. incl: (novels) Purposes of Love, UK 1939 (as Promise of Love, USA 1940); North Face, UK & USA 1948; The Charioteer, UK 1953, USA 1959; The Last of the Wine, UK & USA 1956; The King Must Die, UK & USA 1958; The Bull from the Sea, UK & USA 1962; The Mask of Apollo, UK & USA 1966; Fire from Heaven, UK & USA 1970; The Persian Boy. Mbrships: F.R.S.L.; PEN (Pres., S. Africa, 1961). Hons: Award, Nat. Assn. Independent Schls., USA, 1963; Silver Pen Award, 1971. Address: c/o Longman Grp. Ltd., 74 Grosvenor St., London W1, UK.

RENDEL, (Sir) George William, b. 1889. Diplomat (Ret'd). Educ: M.A., Queen's Coll., Oxford, UK. Publs: The Sword & The Olive, 1957. Mbrships: Chmn., Singapore Constl. Commn., 1953-54; Travellers Club. Recip., K.C.M.G. Address: 5/24 Lennox Gardens, London SW1, UK.

RENDELL, Isabel Mary, b. 18 Jan. 1907, Long Buckby, Northants., UK. School Teacher. Educ: B.A., Univ. London; Univ. Coll. Southampton. Publs: (Nativity play) The First Good Joy. Contbr. to: Somerset Archaeol. & Natural Hist. Proceedings; Poetry Quarterly; Sussex County Mag. Mbrships: Somerset Archaeol Soc.; Yeovil Archaeol. Soc. (Comm. Mbr.). Address: 1 Greystones Ct., Hendford Hill, Yeovil BA20 2RG, UK.

RENDELL, Joan, b. Launceston, Cornwall, UK. Writer; Lecturer; Radio & TV Broadcaster. Educ: Pvte. Schl. & Ealing Schl. Art. Publs: Collecting Matchbox Labels, 1963; Flower Arrangement with a Marine Theme, 1967; Matchbox Labels, 1968; Collecting Natural Objects, 1972, USA ed., 1973; County Crafts; Your Book of Corn Dollies; Collecting from Nature, forthcoming. Contbr. to num. publs. Mbrships: Brit. Matchbox Label & Booklet Soc. (Hon. Ed., 1952–); Launceston Floral Art Group (Life Mbr. & Fndr. Chmn.); Japan Soc. London (Life Mbr.). Hons: M.B.E. Address: Tremarsh, Launceston, Cornwall, UK.

RENÉRIUS, Hans-Evert, pen name RENÉ, Hans Evert, b. 8 Dec. 1941, Habo, Jönköping, Sweden. Teacher. Educ: Fil.Mag. & Fil.Kand., Univ. of Gothenburg; Teol.Kand., Univ. of Lund. Publs: Debut 64, 1964; Poems, transl'd by M.Allwood & C.Richards, 1971; Vi måste lära (We must Learn), 1973; Poesin är du, 1974. Contbr. to: Scholasticus; Jönköpings-Posten; Smålands-Folkblad; Götheborgske Spionen; Göteborgs-Tidningen; Vår Lösen; Horisont; Teaterrecensent i Jönköpings-Posten (theatre critic); sev. anthols. Mbrships: Swedish, Småland, & Gothenburg Socs. of Authors. Address: Asperög. 5b, 414 74 Gothenburg, Sweden.

RENLING, (Bernt) Halvdan, b. 12 Oct. 1924, Malå, Västerbotten, Sweden. Author. Publs: Vargsommar, 1956; Bergakväll, 1960; Immer, 1962; Legend vid Silvano, 1964; Dikter När sångaren skall komma, 1966; Skadare, 1968; Det idealiska sömnmedlet, en studie kring neurosedyn (w. E. Ransemar), 1970; Medvän här, 1973. Recip., Swedish Authors' Club Prize, 1974. Address: G. Brogatan 21, II, 111 20 Stockholm, Sweden.

RENO, Ottie Wayne, b. 7 Apr. 1929, Pike Co., Ohio, USA. Common Pleas Judge; Attorney-at-Law. Educ: Assoc. in Bus. Admin., 1949, LL.B., 1953, Franklin Univ., Ohio; J.D., Capital Univ., Columbus, 1966. Publs: The Story of Horseshoes, 1963; Pitching Championship Horseshoes, 1971, revised ed., 1975. Mbr., legal orgs. Hons: 11 times Ala. State Champion at Pitching Horseshoes. Address: Rte. 5 — Box 305, Lucasville, OH 45648, USA.

RENOIR, Jean, b. 15 Sept. 1894, Paris, France. Film Producer; Writer. Educ: Univ. d' Aix-en-Provence. Publs: Orvet, 1953; Renoir, My Father, 1962; The Notebooks of Captain Georges, 1966; (films incl.) Nana; Madame Bovary; La Grande Illusion; La Règle du Jeu; Le Déjeuner sur l'Herbe; Le Testament de Docteur Cordellier, 1959; Le Caporal Epinglé, 1961; Le Petit Theâtre de Jean Renoir, 1969; (theatrical prods.) Orvet; Carola. Jules César. Mbrships. incl: Cinemathèque Français (VP); Am. Acad. Arts & Scis. Hons. incl: Legion of Honour; Croix de Guerre; Prix Charles Blanc, 1962. Address: 1273 Leona Dr., Beverly Hills, CA 90210, USA.

RENOLD, Penelope, b. 5 May 1916, Manchester, UK. Secretary/Director, Book & Information Centre; Translator; Freelance Historian. Educ: B.A., M.A., Univ. Coll., London; Inst. of Histl. Rsch. Publs: The Wisbech Stirs, 1595-1598 (vol. 51 Cath. Record Soc.), 1958; Letters of William Allen & Richard Barret, 1572-1598 (vol. 58 Cath. Record Soc.). Mbrships. incl: Royal Histl. Soc.; Cath. Record Soc. Address: 6 Forest Side, Worcester Park, Surrey KT4 7PB, UK.

RENSHAW, Charles Bailey, b. Sale, Cheshire, UK. Writer. Publs: Articles describing annual 1000-mile walks in Europe & over 700 places stayed at in Switz., Italy & S. France. Mbrships: Life mbr., Soc. of Authors; Royal Photographic Soc.; Royal Automobile Club. Address: c/o National Westminster Bank Ltd., 1 New Bond St., London W1, UK.

RENSHAW, Patrick Richard George, b. 1936, London, UK. University Lecturer; Former Journalist. Educ: M.A., Jesus Coll., Oxford, 1956-59, Queen's Coll., 1959-60; Northwestern Univ., Ill., USA, 1960-61. Publs: The Wobblies: the Story of Syndicalism in the United States, 1967, Italian transl., 1971, Japanese transl., 1974; The General Strike, 1975. Contbr. to: Illustrated Hist. of Am. People, vol. 13, 1975; Jrnl. Am. Studies; Hist. Today; Guardian; etc. Mbrships. incl: B.A.A.S.; Soc. for Study of Labour Hist. Agent: Curtis Brown. Address: 8 Swaledale Road, Sheffield S7 2BY, Yorks.. UK.

RENVALL-KROKFORS, Saga Viola Magdalena, b. 6 Apr. 1905, Tammerfors, Finland. Lecturer. Educ: Univ. degree. Publs: (poems) Inom kretsen, 1929; Juni, 1931; En stjärna var det, 1933; Mot synranden, 1936; Livsvilja, 1942; Väg och vinge, 1947; Möte med tystnaden, 1950; Osynlig närhet, 1954; Manbrev, 1957; Innerst, 1962; 99 dikter (urval), 1965; Bla vind, 1969; Varfrudag, 1972; Sev. books for children. Mbrships: Swedish Authors' Assn. of Finland; S.W.Br., Finnish Authors' Soc. Hons: Author's grant; 2 Swedish Lit. Awards. Address: 21600 Pargas, Trädgardsgatan 4, Finland.

RENVOIZE, Jean, b. London, UK. Writer. Publs: The Masker, 1960; A Wild Thing, 1970; Children in Danger, 1974; The Net, 1974. Agent: David Higham Assocs. Address: 13 Christchurch Hill, London NW3, UK.

RÉNYI, Péter, b. 15 Sept. 1920, Temesvár, Románia. Journalist; Art Critic; Essayist. Publs: Messages from "Free Land", 1957; Debating, 1967; Our 25 Years (with his wife), 1970; Debate Continuing, 1972. Contbr. to: Népszabadság; Filmkultura; Kritika; Kortárs; Interpress-Graphik; etc. Mbrships: Hungarian Writers' Assn.; PEN; Assn. Hungarian Jrnlsts.; Hungarian Coun. Film Art. Hons: Kner Izidor Fndn., 1939; Rózsa Ferenc Prize, 1960; József Attila Prize, 1963. Address: 1137 Budapest, XIII Szt. István Park 26, Hungary.

RESTON, James Barrett, b. 3 Nov. 1909, Clydebank, UK. Journalist. Educ: B.A., Univ. of Ill., 1932. Publs: Prelude to Victory, 1942; The Artillery of the Press, 1967; Sketches in the Sand, 1967. Contbr. to: N.Y. Times. Hons. incl: Pulitzer Prizes (jrnlsm.), 1945, 1957; 18 hon. degrees. Address: 3124 Woodley Rd. N.W., Wash. DC 20036, USA.

REUTER, George S., Jr., b. 9 Feb. 1920, Holden, Mo., USA. Educational Administrator. Educ: B.A., in Ed., B.S., M.S. in Ed., Ctrl. Mo. State Univ.; Ed.D., Univ. of Mo.; Postdoctoral study, Harvard Univ. Publs: One Blood, 1964; Democracy & Quality Education, 1965; Eastern Baptist College, Yesterday, Today & Forever, 1966; Achieving Quality Education, 1971; Emergency School Assistance Program Seminars, 1972. Contbr. to jrnls. Address: P.O. Box 376, Portageville, MO 63873, USA.

REUTERSWÅRD, Maud, b. 19 Feb. 1920, Stockholm, Sweden. Radio & TV Producer; Author. Educ: Studied Educ. at Univ. for 2 years. Publs: Solvända, 1962; Svenska landskapsblommor, 1966; Dagar med Knubbe Du har ju pappa, Elisabet, 1971; Han - där, 1972; Ta steget, Elisabet, 1973; När man heter Noak, 1974; & num. plays for children. Mbrships: Swedish Authors' Union; Writers' Centre; Union of Journalists; Radio Producers' Assn. Recip., "Heffaklumpen" award, best book of 1972. Address: De Geersgatan 14, 115 29 Stockholm, Sweden.

REVEL, Jean-François, b. 19 Jan. 1924. University Teacher; Columnist. Educ: Ecole Normale Supérieure; Sorbonne Univ., Paris. Publs: (novel) Histoire de Flore, 1957; (essays) Pourquoi des Philosophes? , 1957; Pour L'Italie, 1958; Le Style du Général, 1959; Sur Proust, 1960; La Cabale des Devots, 1962; En France, 1965; Contrecensures, 1966; Histoire de la Philosophie Occidentale, vol. I, 1968, vol. II, 1970; Ni Marx ni Jésus, 1970; Les Idées de notre Temps, 1972. Contbr. to: L'Express, 1966—. Address: 55 Quai de Bourbon, Paris 4e, France.

REW, (Rev.) Harold, b. 17 Feb. 1898, Swansea, Glam., UK. Canon of Llandaff; Author. Educ: Off.'s Mil. Schl.; Univ. of London; Coll. of Resurrection, Mirfield, Yorks. Publs: At One, 1936; The Steep Ascent, 1937; The Dullness of Our Blinded Sight, 1949; Ode to Youth, 1957; also poetry. Contbr. to: Welsh Churchman. Hons: Hon. Canon Libn., Llandaff Cathedral, 1961-1970; Chevalier de l'Ordre des Palmes Académiques, France, 1964. Address: 3 The Cathedral Green, Llandaff, Cardiff, UK.

REXROTH, Kenneth, b. 22 Dec. 1905, South Bend, Ind., USA. Author. Publs. incl: In What Hour, 1940; Art of Worldly Wisdom, 1949; 100 Poems from The Japanese, 1955; The Homestead Called Damascus, 1962; An Autobiographical Novel, 1966; Collected Shorter Poems, 1967; The Collected Long Poems of Kenneth Rexroth, 1968; 100 More Chinese Poems; The Orchid Boat: the Women Poets of China (w. Ling Chung), 1973; The Elastic Retort, 1973. Contbr. to: Saturday Review; N.Y. Times; Nation; etc. Mbr., Nat. Inst. of Arts & Letters. Hons. incl: Shelley Mem. Award. Address: 1401 E. Pepper Lane, Santa Barbara, CA 93103, USA.

REY, Henri François, b. 31 July 1919. Former Journalist & Broadcaster; Writer. Educ: Lic. de Phil., Univ. of Montpellier. Publs: La Fête Espagnole, 1958; La Comédie, 1960; Les Pianos Mécaniques, 1962; Les Chevaux Masqués, 1965; Le Rachdingue, 1967; Opéra pour un tyran, 1967; Halleluya, ma vie, 1970; Le Barbare, 1972. Address: 44 rue Boissonade, Paris 14e, France.

REYMOND, Marie-Louise, b. 7 June 1885, Pully, Switz. Novelist. Publs: (novels) Le Miracle; Cendrine (transl. into Dutch & German); Hors du Jeu? ; Kianga; La Cloche de Bois; Le Feu Saluda; L'Oiseau de l'Aube; Marco; Le Chant du Loup; (children's stories) Le Prince Jean; Briquet d'Argent; Les Ailes d'Or; Vive le Soleil! Contbr. to: Illustré; Pour Tous; Images du Monde; etc. Mbrships. incl: Soc. Lamartine et de l'Amitié littéraire franco-suisse,

Geneva; Soc. des Ecrivains suisses; Soc. des Gens de Lettres de France. Hons: Prix de 'Reflets', Geneva; Prix d'Arts et Lettres, Lausanne. Address: Ave. des Cerisiers 31, 1009 Pully, Switz.

REYNA, Ruth, b. 31 July 1904, Pioneer, Ohio, USA. Philosopher; Indologist; Editor; Writer. Educ: B.A., Univ. S. Calif.; M.A., Fla. State Univ., 1958; Ph.D., Poona Univ., India, 1961. Publs: Reincarnation and Science, 1973; Introduction to Indian Philosophy, 1971; Concept of Maya from the Vedas to the 20th Century, 1962; The Philosophy of Matter in the Atomic Era, 1963; Aum Dictionary of Oriental Philosophy (2 vols.), 1975; num. short stories. Contbr., over 300 articles & monographs on Oriental subjects; Assoc. Ed., Marathi Ency. of Philos. Mbrships. incl: Phi Beta Kappa; Univ. Women of India; Tchrs. Assn., Panjab Univ., India. Address: 165 South Olive St., Lake Elsinore, CA 92330, USA.

REYNER, John Hereward, b. 25 June 1900, Manchester, UK. Electronic Engineer; Founder & Managing Director, Furzehill Laboratories Ltd., 1927-64. Educ: B.Sc.; D.I.C.; A.C.G.I. City & Guilds Engrng. Coll.; London Univ. Publs: Modern Radio Communication, 1923, reissued as Radio Communication (w. P. J. Reyner), 1960, 3rd ed., 1972; Cathode Ray Oscillographs, 1941, 5th ed., 1959; Ed., Radio & Electronics Handbook, 1959; The Universe of Relationships, 1960; Psionic Medicine, 1974; The Diary of a Modern Alchemist, 1974; The Age of Miracles, 1975. Mbrships: F.I.E.E.; I.E.E.E. (Life Mbr.). Address: Bramleys, Butlers Cross, Aylesbury, Bucks., UK.

REYNOLDS, Alfred Christopher, b. 21 May 1911, Brinscall, UK. Art & Biology Teacher. Educ: Assoc., Royal Coll. of Art, London. Publs: Small Creatures in my Back Garden, 1965, 3rd ed., 1973; The Pond on my Window-Sill, 1969, 3rd ed., 1973; Creatures of the Bay, 1974, 2nd ed., 1975. Contbr. to: Entomols.' Monthly Mag.; Wildlife Mag.; Miscellany Four; Christmas Anthol.; Ency. of Gardening. Mbrships: Sci. Fellow, Zool. Soc. of London; E. African Wild Life Soc. Address: 40 Fitzroy Ave., Kingsgate, Broadstairs, Kent, UK.

REYNOLDS, Barbara Eva Mary, b. 13 June 1914, Bristol, UK. University Professor. Educ: B.A. (French), B.A. (Italian); Ph.D., Univ. Coll., London; M.A., Cambridge Univ. Publs: The Linguistic Writings of Alessandro Manzoni, 1950; Dante, Paradise (transl. w. Dorothy Sayers), 1962; Cambridge Italian Dictionary, 1962; Dante, La Vita Nuova (transl.), 1969; Ariosto, Orlando Furioso (transl.), 1975; Concise Cambridge Italian Dictionary, 1975. Mbrships. incl: Hon., Lucy Cavendish Coll., Cambridge. Hons: Edmund Gardner Prize, 1962; Silver Medal, Italian Govt., 1962; Silver Medal, Province of Vicenza, 1971. Address: 26 Parkside, Wollaton, Nottingham, UK.

REYNOLDS, Ernest Randolph, b. 13 Sept. 1910, Northampton, UK. Writer; Lecturer. Educ: B.A., London Univ., 1930; Ph.D., Cambridge Univ., 1934. Publs: Early Victorian Drama, 1936, 2nd ed., 1965; Modern English Drama, 1949; Mephistopheles & the Golden Apples (poetic fantasy), 1943; The Plain Man's Guide to Antique Collecting, 1963; The Plain Man's Guide to Opera, 1964; Collecting Victorian Porcelain, 1966; Northamptonshire Treasures (essays), 1972. Recip., Kirke White Poetry Prize, Nottingham Univ., 1930. Address: 43 Wantage Rd., Northampton, UK.

REYNOLDS, Gordon, b. 1921, Hull, UK. Editor; Organist & Choirmaster; Professor of Marmony; Broadcaster. Publs: Oxford School Music Books; Beginners's Series; Oxford Instrumental Series; A Young Teachers' Guide to Class Music; Organo Pleno; The Choirmaster in Action; Full Swell. Ed., Music in Education, 1961—. Address: 12 Ashley Gdns., Petersham, Surrey, UK.

REYNOLDS, John, b. 1899, Sydney, Australia. Director of Mining Companies; Author. Publs: The Discovery of Tasmania, 1642; Sir Edmund Barton, First Australian Prime Minister, Biography, 1948; Sir Edward Braddon, Biographical Sketch, 1951; Launceston: The History of an Australian City, 1969; Men & Mines, A History of Australian Mining 1788-1971. Mbrships. incl: Press., Fellowship of Aust. Writers (Tasmanian Br.), 1953-60, 1967-69; Chmn., Tasmanian Histl. Rsch. Assn., 1956, 1969 sessions. Address: "Merrington", 10 Knocklofty Terr., W. Hobart, Tasmania, Australia 7000.

REYNOLDS, Louis Bernard, b. 23 Feb. 1917, Verdery, S.C., USA. Minister of Religion; Editor. Educ: B.A., Fisk Univ., Nashville, Tenn., 1958; M.A., Howard Univ. Schl. of Relig., Wash. DC, 1968. Publs: Dawn of a Brighter Day, 1945; Little Journeys into Storyland (w. C. L. Paddock), 1947; Look to the Hills, 1960; Great Texts from Romans, 1972; Bible Answers to Today's Questions (w. R. H. Pierson), 1974. Contbr. to: Signs of the Times; These Times; Review & Herald; Kan. City Call. Mbrships. incl: NAACP; Bd. of Dirs., Assoc. Ch. Press. Hons. incl: LL.D., Union Bapt. Sem., Birmingham, Ala., 1970. Address: 7510 Dundalk Rd., Takoma Pk., MD 20012, USA.

REYNOLDS, Philip Alan, b. 15 May 1920, Worthing, UK. University Professor of Politics; Writer. Educ: B.A., 1940, M.A., 1950, Oxford. Publs: War in the Twentieth Century, 1951; British Foreign Policy in the Interwar Years, 1954; Introduction to International Relations, 1971. Contbr. to: New Cambridge Mod. Hist., Vol. XII, 1968; Studies in Pols., Nat. & Int., 1970; Slavonic Review; Hist.; Pol. Quarterly; Pol. Studies; World Survey; Int. Quarterly; Brit. Int. Studies Assn. Jrnl.; etc. Mbrships: Chmn., Brit. Coord. Comm. for Int. Studies; Int. Pol. Sci. Assn.; Royal Inst. Int. Affairs; etc. Address: Fylde Coll., Univ. of Lancaster, Lancaster LA1 4YF, UK.

REY-STOLLE, Alejandro,·pen name XAVIER, Adro, b. 31 July 1910, Santiago, Spain. Lecturer; Writer. Educ: Philos. & Letters; Theol.; Psychol. Publs. incl: (novels) El último tedeum; Las cuentas de una vida; Mar de fondo, 2 eds.; El hombre que tenía dos almas; Almas Hundidas, 4 eds.; El otro cura; Nirmala, 3 eds.; El otro curso, 3 eds.; Abismos de papel, 4 eds.; (biogs.) Bonifacio VIII, Iglesia y Estado; Carlos María, 13 eds.; (travel) España en Africa, ayer y hoy; (essays) Tres caras del matrimonio; Cuando el matrimonio juega su baza, 6 eds.; El otro Dios; La otra Iglesia; Fracasos de Dios. Contbr. to num. lit. jrnls. Mbr., var. lit. socs. Address: Calle Palau 3, Barcelona 2, Spain.

RHEE, H. Albert. Sociologist. Educ: B.Litt., M.A., St. Catherine's & St. Antony's, Oxford. Publs: Agriculture & Industry (w. J. R. Bellerby), 1956; Office Automation in Social Perspective, 1968; Human Ageing & Retirement, 1974 (Span. & Germ. transls. 1975). Contbr. of num. sociol. articles to var. profl. jrnls. Mbrships: Ctr. de Recherches s. l. Inst. Int., Geneva; Oxford Univ. Grad. Ctr.; Société suisse de sociologie; Int. Comm. for Occupational Mental Health; Swiss Gerontol. Soc. Address: Rue du Vidollet 12, CH-1202 Geneva, Switz.

RHODES, Albert, b. 1918, Sheffield, Yorks., UK. Managing Director of Rhodes Engineering Ltd. Educ: Chesterfield Coll. Technol. Publs: Butter on Sunday, 1964; A Summer of Yesterday, 1967; Calico Bloomers, 1968; Shout into the Wind, 1975; (stage play) Don't Whistle for Me; (radio play) A'napple & A'norange. Mbrships: Soc. Authors; Writers' Summer Schl. Agent: John Farquharson. Address: Applegarth, The Bent, Curbar, nr. Sheffield, Derby, UK.

RHODES, (Rev.) Clifford Oswald, b. 1911, UK. Rector. Educ: St. Peter's Hall, Oxford; Wycliffe Hall, Oxford; M.A. Publs: The New Church in the New Age; Mass Communications & the Spirit of Man; Musical Instruments & the Orchestra; The Awful Boss's Book; Authority in a Changing Society (Ed.); The Necessity for Love, the history of Interpersonal Relations. Former Ed., Record, 1946-49; C. of E. Newspaper, 1949-59; Business, 1960-63. Address: The Rectory, Somerton, Oxf., UK.

RHODES, James Eric Wynfield, b. 1888, Prestwich, Lancs.. UK. Former College Lecturer. Educ: Royal Tech. Inst., Salford; Municipal Schl. of Technol., Manchester; London Univ.; B.Sc.; Ph.D. Publs: Micropetrology for Beginners; Phase Rule Studies; Concise Physical Chemistry. Mbrships: F.R.I.C.; F.G.S. Address: 14 Penlands Vale, Steyning, Sussex, UK.

RHODES, Richard Lee, b. 4 July 1937, Kansas City, USA. Writer. Educ: B.A., Yale Univ., 1959. Publs: The Inland Ground: An Evocation of the American Middle West, 1970; The Ungodly: A Novel of the Donner Party, 1973; The Ozarks, 1974. Contbr. to: Playboy; Harper's; Esquire; Atlantic Monthly; Reader's Digest; Redbook; N.Y. Times Book Review; Chicago Tribune Book World; Nat. Observer. Recip., John Guggenheim Mem. Fndn. Fellowship, 1974-75. Address: 5015 Walnut, Apt. D, Kansas City, MO 64112, USA.

RHYMES, (Rev. Canon) Douglas Alfred, b. 26 Mar. 1914, Devon, UK. Clerk in Holy Orders; Vicar of Camberwell, London; Hon. Canon, Southwark Cathedral, London. Educ: B.A. (Philos.), Birmingham Univ.; Ripon Hall Theol. Coll., Oxford. Publs: Laymans Church (co-author), 1962; No New Morality, 1963; Prayer in the Secular City, 1968; Through Prayer to Reality (USA only), 1974. Contbr. to: New Christian; Prism; New Statesman; Celebration; Franciscan; New Spirtuality; etc. Address: St. Giles Vicarage, Benhill Rd., London SE5 8RB, UK.

RHYS, Jean (Mrs. Jean Hamer), b. 1894, Dominica, W. Indies. Writer. Educ: Royal Acad. Dramatic Art, UK. Publs: (novels) Postures, 1928 (as Quartet, USA 1929); After Leaving Mr. Mackenzie, UK & USA 1931; Voyage in the Dark, UK 1934, USA 1935; Good Morning, Midnight, 1939; Wide Sargasso Sea, UK & USA 1966; (short stories) The Left Bank & Other Stories, UK & USA 1927; Tigers are Better-Looking, 1968. Contbr. to: Penguin Mod. Stories, 1, 1969. Hons: Arts Coun. Bursary, 1967; Smith Lit. Award, 1967; Heinemann Award, 1967. Address: c/o André Deutsch Ltd., 105 Great Russell St., London WC1, UK.

RICCIUTI, Edward R., b. 27 May 1938, NYC, USA. Writer. Educ: B.A., Univ. of Notre Dame; Cert., Sloan-Rockefeller Adv. Sci. Writing Fellow, Columbia Univ. Grad. Schl. of Jrnlsm. Publs: Catch a Whale by the Tail, 1969; An Animal for Alan, 1970; Shelf Pets, 1971; The American Aligator, Its Life in the Wild, 1972; Killers of the Seas, 1973; Dancers on the Beach, 1973; Donald & the Fish that Walked, 1974; To the Brink of Extinction, 1974; Do Toads Give You Warts? , 1975. Contbr. to: Audubon; Parade; Signature; Argosy; Sci. World; Animal Kingdom; etc. Mbrships: Bds. of Dirs., Am. Alligator Coun. & Conn. Zool. Soc.; Soc. of Mag. Writers; Nat. Assn. of Sci. Writers. Address: RFD 3 Box 39, Roast Meat Hill, Killingworth, CT 06417, USA.

RICE, (Rev.), Brian K., pen name VIGILANS, b. 1932, Sutton, Surrey, UK. Birmingham Diocesan Director of Education. Educ: Peterhouse, Cambridge; Jerusalem; Univ. of Chgo.; Lincoln; M.A.; B.D.; S.T.M. Publs: What is Christian Giving? , 1958; Stewardship & Evangelism, 1963; Christianity & the Affluent Society, 1966. Contbr. to: Ch. Times; other jrnls. Mbrships: Ch. Commrs.; One; GB-USSR Assn. Address: 44 Vernon Rd., Edgbaston, Birmingham B16 9SH, UK.

RICE, Joan Odette, b. 15 Aug. 1919, London, UK. Author & Lecturer. Educ: Manor House Schl.; Maida Vale H.S. Publs: All About Clubs, 1974. Contbr. to var. women's mags. & BBC. Mbrships: Soc. Authors; Soc. Women Writers (Coun. Mbr.); Radio Writers' Assn.; Royal Air Force Club. Recip., Gold Medal for Public Speaking, London Acad. Music & Dramatic Art. Agent: Mary Irvine. Address: Popefield, 2 Cross Lane, East Common, Harpenden, Herts. AL5 1BT, UK.

RICE, Ross Richard, b. 13 Jan. 1922, Shenandoah, Iowa, USA. Professor of Political Science. Educ: Creighton Univ.; Northern Iowa Univ.; M.A. 1949, Ph.D. 1956, Univ. of Chgo. Publs: Western Politics (w. Frank Jonas), 1961; Extremist Politics, 1964; Politics in the American West (w. F. Jonas), 1969. Contbr. to: Am. Pol. Sci. Review; Western Pol. Quarterly (book review Ed.). Mbrships incl: Am. Pol. Sci. Assn.; Western Pol. Sci. Assn. (Exec. Comm.; Bd. of Eds.); Am. Acad. Pol. & Soc. Sci.; Int. Platform Assn. Recip., Rsch. Grant for work on career of Senator Carl Hayden. Address: 108 W. Palmcroft Dr., Tempe, AZ 85282, USA.

RICH, Rowland William, b. 10 Mar. 1901, London, UK. Professor & Principal, College of Education (Ret'd). Educ: Univ. Coll., London, 1919-21; London Day Trng. Coll., 1921-22; M.A.; Ph.D. Publs: Training of Teachers in England & Wales during the Nineteenth Century, 1933, reprinted 1972; The Teacher in a Planned Society, 1950. Address: 65 Cheriton Rd., Winchester, Hants. SO22 5AY, UK.

RICH, Stephen Peter, b. 8 Jan. 1942, Stratford, UK. Playwright. Educ: Alleyn's Coll. of God's Gift, Dulwich, London. Publs. incl: (theatre) The Emperor Henry IV (transl. Enrico IV by Luigi Pirandello, produced N.Y., 1972, London, 1973); Farewell to All Our Fans, 1975. (TV) The Critic, 1968; Breakdown; Retribution; The Ring; Fallen Star; Lots of Friends in the Big City; etc. (films) Mister Precious & Master Percy; (non-fiction) Be an Inventor, 1970. Mbrships: Writers' Guild of Gt. Brit.; Authors' Soc.; Dramatics Guild N.Y. Recip., Arts Coun. Bursary, 1966. Address: P. L. Representation, 33 Sloane St., London SW1, UK.

RICHARDS, Alfred Luther, b. 12 Jan. 1939, Balt., Md., USA. Educational Psychologist; Writer. Educ: B.A., 1962, M.A., 1969, Stetson Univ., Fla.; M.Ed., Univ. of Fla.; 1971; Ph.D., Union Grad. Schl., Ohio, 1972. Publs. incl: Homonovus: The New Man (w. Anne C. Richards), 1973; Perceptual Psychology: A Humanistic Approach to the Study of Persons (co-author), 1975. Contbr. to: Jrnl. of Humanistic Psychol.; New Voices in Educ., etc. Mbrships incl: Sec., Colo. Chapt., Assn. for Humanistic Psychol., 1973-4; AM. Humanist Assn. Recip., First Prize Award, for Make These Dry Bones Live, 1964. Address: 1533 9th Ave., Greeley, CO 80631, USA.

RICHARDS, Alun, b. 27 Oct. 1929, Pontypridd, Glam., UK. Author; TV Playwright. Educ: Univ. Coll. of Wales. Publs: The Elephant You Gave Me, 1963; The Home Patch, 1966; A Woman of Experience, 1969; Home to an Empty House, 1974; Dai Country (stories), 1974; Collected Plays, 1975. Mbr. & Chmn., Welsh Sect., Writers' Guild of GB. Recip., Arts Coun. Prize for Dai Country, 1974. Address: 326 Mumbles Rd., Swansea, UK.

RICHARDS, Christine-Louise, b. 11 Jan. 1910, Radnor, Pa., USA. Artist; Composer; Author; Publisher. Educ: Study of art & piano, US & Europe. Publs: The Blue Star Fairy Book of Stories for Children, 1950; The Blue Star Fairy Book of More Stories for Children, 1969 (author & illustrator of both); num. song lyrics. Address: Springslea, P.O. Box 185, Morris, NY 13808, USA.

RICHARDS, Denis, b. 1910, London, UK. Writer. Educ: B.A., 1931, M.A., 1935, Trinity Hall, Cambridge Univ. Publs: Royal Air Force, 1939-45 (w. H. St. G. Saunders), 3 vols.; Modern Europe; Modern Britain (w. J. W. Hunt); Britain Under the Tudors & Stuarts; Britain, 1714-1851 (w. Anthony Quick); The Modern Age (w. Evan Cruikshank); Offspring of the Vic: A History of Morley College; Britain & the Ancient World (w. J. A. Bolton); Britain, 1851-1945 (w. Anthony Quick), 1967; Twentieth Century Britain, 1968; Medieval Britain (w. A. E. Ellis), 1973. Contbr. to var. jrnls. Mbrships. incl: PEN; Arts Club; Soc. Authors. Recip., C. P. Robertson Mem. Trophy, 1954 for Royal Air Force 1939-45. Address: 16 Broadlands Rd., London N6, UK.

RICHARDS, Horace Gardiner, b. 21 Mar. 1906, Phila., Pa., USA. Geologist. Educ: A.B., 1929; M.S., 1929; Ph.D., 1932. Publs: Animals of the Seashore, 1938; Record of the Rocks, 1953; Geology of the Delaware Valley, 1956; Cretaceous Fossils of New Jersey, vol. I, 1958, vol. II, 1962; The Story of Earth Science, 1959; Annotated Bibliography of Quaternary Shorelines, vol. I, 1965, vol. II, 1970, vol. III, 1974. Contbr. of 282 titles to sci. jrnls. Mbrships. incl: Fellow, Geol. Soc. of Am.; Paleontol. Soc.; Pres., Int. Commn. of Shorelines. Hons. incl: Pres.'s Award, Am. Assn. of Petroleum Geols., 1945. Address: 509 Woodland Terrace, Phila., PA 19104, USA.

RICHARDS, Ivor Armstrong, b. 26 Frb. 1893. Literary Critic; Professor of English Literature. Educ: M.A.; D.Litt.; Magdalene Coll., Cambridge. Publs. incl: Principles of Literary Criticism, 1924; Practical Criticism, 1929; Basic Rules of Reason, 1933; Basic English & its Uses, 1943; Nations & Peace, 1947; The Wrath of Achilles, 1950; The Screens & Other Poems, 1960; Why so, Socrates? , 1963; Poetries & Sciences, 1970; Internal Colloquies: Collected Poems to 1970. Hons. incl: C.H.; Loines Award for Poetry, 1962; Emerson-Thoreau Medal, 1970. Address: Magdalene Coll., Cambridge, UK.

RICHARDS, Peter Godfrey, b. 20 Aug. 1923, Richmond, Surrey, UK. University Professor. Educ: B.Sc.(Econ.), Univ. of London, 1945; Ph.D., Univ. of Southampton, 1955. Publs: Delegation in Local Government, 1955; Honourable Members, 1959; Patronage in British Government, 1963; Parliament & Foreign Affairs, 1967; The New Local Government System, 1968; Parliament & Conscience, 1970; The Back-benchers, 1972; The Reformed Local Government System, 1973. Contbr. to: Pol. Quarterly; Pol. Studies; Parly. Affairs; Pub. Law; Pub. Admin. Mbrships: Coun., Hansard Soc.; Study of Parl. Grp.; Royal Inst. of Pub. Admin.; Pol. Studies Assn. Address: Dept. of Politics, The University, Southampton, UK.

RICHARDS, Raymond, b. 1906, Macclesfield, UK. Chairman & Managing Director, Dominion Tea Plantation Co. Ltd. Educ: M.A. Publs: The Lesser Chapels of Cheshire, 2 vols.; The Manor of Gawsworth; Old Cheshire Churches, 1974. Mbrships. incl: F.S.A.; F.R.Hist.S.; Athenaeum Club;

Royal Mersey Yacht Club. Address: Gawsworth Hall, Near Macclesfield, Cheshire, UK.

RICHARDS, Ronald Charles William, pen name SADDLER, Allen, b. 15 Apr. 1923, London, UK. Writer; Journalist. Publs: Great Brain Robbery, 1965; Gilt Edge, 1966; Talking Turkey, 1968; Betty, 1974. Contbr. to: Guardian; Plays & Players; radio plays in drama broadcasts; Ed., The Western Front. Mbrships: Chmn., W. Country Br., Writers' Guild of GB, 1974; Nat. Union of Jrnlsts. Address: 6 South St., Totnes, Devon TQ9 5DZ, UK.

RICHARDS, Stanley, b. 23 Apr. 1918, Bklyn., N.Y., USA. Playwright; Editor; Anthologist. Educ: Columbia Univ.; Feagin Schl. Drama. Publs. incl: (plays) Through a Glass, Darkly; August Heat; Sun Deck; Tunnel of Love; Journey to Bahia; O Distant Land; Mood Piece; Mr. Bell's Creation; The Proud Age; Once to Every Boy; Half-Hour, Please; Know Your Neighbor; Gin & Bitterness; The Hills of Bataan; District of Columbia; Ed., 8 books, The Best Short Plays 1968-1975; & num. other anthols. Contbr. to var. theatrical jrnls.; etc. Mbrships: Dramatists Guild; Soc. Theatre Rsch. (London). Recip., 3 US Dept. State Grants for work in theatre in Chile & Brazil, 1960-62. Address: 420 E. 72nd St., N.Y., NY, USA.

RICHARDS, William Leslie, b. 28 May 1916, Capel Isaac, Llandeilo, UK. Schoolmaster. Educ: B.A., M.A., Dip. in Educ., Univ. of Wales. Publs. incl: Yr Etifeddion, 1956; Telyn Teilo, 1957; Llanw a Thrai, 1958; Cynffon o Wellt, 1960; Gwaith Dafydd, 1960; Llwyd o Fathafarn, 1964; Dail yr Hydre, 1968; Adledd, 1973; Cymraeg Heddiw (w. others), 4 vols., 1965-69; Co-ed., Y Cawr o Rydcymerau, 1970. Contbr. to Welsh-lang. jrnls. Mbr., Cymmtodorion Soc. Hons: T. E. Ellis Essay Prize, 1939; Sir Ellis Griffith Mem. Prize, Univ. of Wales, 1964-65; Hon. Druid, Gorsedd of Bards, 1971. Address: Heulfryn, 12 Thomas St., Llandeilo, Dyfed SA19 6LB, UK.

RICHARDSON, Evelyn May, b. 16 May 1902, Shag Harbour, N.S., Can. Former Teacher. Educ: Dalhousie Univ., Halifax, N.S. Publs: We Keep a Light, 1945, latest ed., 1974 (as We Bought an Island, 1953, 1954); Desired Haven, 1953; No Small Tempest, 1957; My Other Islands, 1960; Living Island, 1965. Contbr. to: Dalhousie Review; Saturday Night; Atlantic Advocate; Down E.; Yankee; CBC scripts. Mbr., Can. Authors' Assn. Hons: Gov. Gen.'s Award for Creative Non-fiction, 1945; Ryerson Press All Can. Fiction Award, 1953; Dip. of Hon., Mexico, 1960. Address: Barrington, N.S., Can.

RICHARDSON, Geoffrey Alan, b. 27 July 1936, Preston, Lancs., UK. Educator. Educ: M.A., Cantab., 1958; Cert.Ed., Exeter Univ., 1959; Dip.Ed.Man., Sheffield Poly Mgmt. Ctr., 1973. Publs: Case Studies in the Australian Environment, 1970. Contbr. to: Geography; Scottish Geog. Mag.; Times Educl. Supplement. Address: Glenmoor Cottage, Westwood Dr., Ilkley, Yorks., UK.

RICHARDSON, Joanna, b. London, UK. Biographer; Critic. Educ: M.A., St. Anne's Coll., Oxford. Publs. incl: Fanny Brawne, 1952; Rachel, 1956; Théophile Gautier: his Life & Times, 1958; Sarah Bernhardt, 1959; The Everlasting Spell: a study of Keats & his Friends, 1963; Edward Lear, 1965; George IV: a Portrait, 1966; Creevey & Greville, 1967; Princess Mathilde, 1969; Verlaine, 1971; Stendhal: a critical biography, 1974; Victor Hugo, 1976. Contbr. to: BBC; Times Lit. Supplement; Sunday Times; Spectator; New Statesman; Mod. Lang. Review; N.Y. Times Book Review; Wash. Post; etc. Fellow & Coun. Mbr., R.S.L. Address: 55 Flask Walk, London NW3, UK.

RICHARDSON, Mozelle Groner, b. 26 Jan. 1914, Hereford, Tex., USA. Housewife. Publs: Portrait of Fear, 1971; Curse of Kalispoint, 1971; The Masks of Thespis, 1973; Candle in the Wind, 1973; The Song of India, 1975. Mbrships: Authors' Guild; Mystery Writers of Am. Recip., Writers' Award, Okla. Univ., 1973. Address: 1704 Elmhurst, Okla. City, OK 73120, USA.

RICHARDSON, Ralph Cyril Hastings, b. 1902, Marton, NZ. Engineer. Educ: Canterbury Coll. Publs: The Commissioning of Electrical Plant & Associated Problems. Address: P.O. Box 2628, Wellington, NZ.

RICHARDSON, Robert Galloway, b. 2 Oct. 1926, London, UK. Consultant Medical Editor & Author. Educ: M.A., B.M., B.Ch., Brasenose Coll., Oxford; Middlesex Hosp., London. Publs: The Surgeon's Tale, 1958; Surgery: Old & New Frontiers, 1968; The Surgeon's Heart, 1969,

USA ed. (The Scalpel & the Heart), 1970; The Abominable Stoma: A Historical Survey of the Artificial Anus, 1973; Larrey: Surgeon to Napoleon's Imperial Guard, 1974. Mbrships: F.R.S.M.; B.M.A.; Brit. & Int. Socs. for Hist. of Med.; Soc. of Authors. Address: The Old Cottage, 258 Bromley Rd., Shortlands, Kent BR2 0BW, UK.

RICHARDSON, William Arthur Ridley, b. 27 July 1924, London, UK. Schoolmaster & University Lecturer. Educ: B.A., & Dip.Ed., Univ. of Oxford. Publs: Transl., Brazil: A Brief History, by A. J. Lacombe, 1954; Ed., Modern Spanish Unseens, 1964, 2nd ed., 1968; Ed., El agua envenenada, by F. Benítez, 1968; Ed., Los de abajo, by M. Azuela, 1973; Transl., The Population of Latin America: A History, by N. Sánchez-Albornoz, 1974. Mbr., Soc. for Latin Am. Studies. Address: Schl. of Humanities, Flinders Univ. of S. Aust., Bedford Pk., SA, Australia 5042.

RICHARTZ, Walter E., b. 14 May 1927, Hamburg, Germany. Writer. Educ: Dr. rer. nat.(Chem.). Publs: Prüfungen eines braven Sohnes, 1966; Tod den Ärtzten, 1969; Noface, 1973. Mbrships: PEN; German Authors' Assn. (V.S.). Address: Otto-Kämper-Ring, 6079 Buchschlag bei Sprendlingen, W. Germany.

RICHEY, Elinor (Mrs. E. Hilmer Soderberg), b. 6 Dec. 1920, Braxton, Miss., USA. Instructor in Creative Writing; Editor; Speaker on architectural preservation. Educ: B.S., W. Va. Univ., 1942; M.S., Northwestern Univ., 1943. Publs: The Ultimate Victorians of the Continental Side of San Francisco Bay, 1970; Remain to be Seen: Historic California Houses Open to the Public, 1973; Bathbreaking Women, 1975. Contbr. to: New Yorker; Harper's; Antioch Review; Saturday Review; Reporter; Am. Heritage; Am. West; etc.; essays & articles publd. in sev. anthols. & textbooks. Mbrships: Fndr., Urban Care Architl. Heritage Comm. of Berkeley, 1971; Bd. of Dirs., Calif. Writers Club. Recip., var. annual awards for news & feature writing. Address: 3080 Claremont Ave., Berkeley, CA 94705, USA.

RICHLER, Mordecai, b. 27 Jan. 1931, Montreal, P.Q., Can. Writer. Educ: Sir G. Williams Univ., Montreal. Publs. incl: (novels) Son of a Smaller Hero, Can. & UK 1955, USA 1965; A Choice of Enemies, Can. & UK 1957; The Apprenticeship of Duddy Kravitz, UK, Can. & USA 1959; The Incomparable Atuk, UK & Can. 1963 (as Stick Your Neck Out, USA 1963); Cocksure, Can., UK & USA 1968; St. Urbain's Horseman, Can., UK & USA 1971; (short stories) The Street, Can. 1969, UK 1972; var. screenplays; Ed., Can. Writing Now, 1970. Hons. incl: Paris Review Prize, 1969; Gov.-Gen.'s Award, 1969; var. Fellowships. Address: Hillcrest, Kingston Hill, Surrey, UK.

RICHMAN, Alvin, b. 6 Aug. 1935, Wash. DC, USA. Research Specialist. Educ: B.S., MIT, 1957; M.I.A., Columbia Univ., 1959; Ph.D., Univ. of Pa., 1968. Publs: (monographs) A Scale of Events Along the Conflict-Cooperation Continuum, 1967; Curve of Conflict-Cooperation Events in Soviet-American Relations August 1945—November 1950, 1969. Contbr. to: Jrnl. of Int. Affairs; Sociol. of Educ.; Int. Interactions; Richard Merritt (Ed.), Communications in International Politics, 1972. Mbr., profl. orgs. Recip., acad. hons. Address: 5311 38th St., N.W., Wash. DC 20015, USA.

RICHMAN, Barry, M., b. 18 Mar. 1936, Montreal, Can. Professor of Management & International Business. Educ: B.Comm., McGill Univ., 1958; M.S., 1959, Ph.D., 1962, Columbia Univ., USA. Publs. incl: Soviet Management: With Significant American Comparisons, 1965; A Firsthand Study of Industrial Management in Communist China, 1967; Industrial Society in Communist China, 1969, 1972; Leadership, Goals & Power in Higher Education (w. R. Farmer), 1974; Management & Organizations (w. R. Farmer), 1975. Contbr. to US & for. jrnls. & mags. Address: Grad. Schl. of Mgmt., UCLA, L.A., CA 90024, USA.

RICHMOND, Hugh Macrae, b. 20 Mar. 1932, Burton-on-Trent, Staffs., UK. Professor of English. Educ: B.A., Emmanuel Coll., Cambridge Univ., 1954; D.Phil., Wadham Coll., Oxford Univ., 1957. Publs: The School of Love, 1964; Shakespeare's Political Plays, 1967; Shakespeare's Sexual Comedy, 1971; Renaissance Landscapes, 1973; The Christian Revolutionary, 1974. Contbr. to: P.M.L.A.; Mod. Philol.; Shakespeare Quarterly; Comparative Literature; Studies in the Lit. Imagination; etc. Mbrships. incl: Renaissance Soc. of Am.; Comparative Lit. Assn. Recip., sev. acad. hons. Address: Dept. of Engl., Univ. of Calif., Berkeley, CA 94720, USA.

RICHMOND, Oliffe Legh, b. 1881, London, UK. Professor of Humanity (Ret'd). Educ: M.A., King's Coll., Cambridge. Publs: Propertius, 1926; Challenge to Faith; Thames Symphony; The Farther View. Contbr. to: Times Lit. Supplement; Guardian; var. classical jrnls. Address: 3 Silchester Hall, Silchester Common, nr. Reading, UK.

RICHTER, Derek, b. 14 Jan. 1907, Bath, UK. Medical Consultant; Managing Ed., Journal of Neuropsychiatry, 1956-70. Educ: M.A.; Ph.D.; Magdalen Coll., Oxford Univ. Univ. Munich. Publs: Perspectives in Neuropsychiatry; Schizophrenia; Somatic Aspects; Metabolism of the Nervous System; Aspects of Learning & Memory, 1966; The Challenge of Violence. Contbr. to var. sci. books & jrnls. Mbrships: M.R.C.P.; Fellow Royal Coll. Psych.; Int. Brain Rsch. Org. (1972 Sec.-Gen.); Mental Health Trust & Rsch. Fund (1970 Trustee). Recip., 1970 Simmelweis Medal, Budapest. Address: Deans Cottage, Deans Lane, Walton-on-the-Hill, Surrey, UK.

RICHTER, Hans Peter, b. 28 Apr. 1925, Cologne, Germany. University Professor of Scientific Methods & Sociology; Author. Educ: Dr. rer. pol.; Univs. of Cologne, Bonn, Mainz, Tübingen. Num. publs. incl: Karussell und Luftballon, 1958 (Uncle & his Merry-go-round, 1959); Hans kauft ein, 1961; Birgitta, 1963; Nikolaus, 1965; Damals was es Friedrich, 1968; I was there, 1971; Katzen haben Vorfahrt, 1973; Mohammed, 1974; Saint-Just, 1975; num. transls. Contbr. to: Frankfurter Hefte; Deutsche Rundschau; Die Zeit. Hons. incl: Jugendbuch Preis, 1961; Cité Int. des Arts, Paris, 1965, 1966. Address: Franz-Werfel-Str. 58, D-65 Mainz, W. Germany.

RICHTER, Hans Werner, b. 12 Nov. 1908. Writer. Publs. incl: Die Geschlagenen, 1949; Spuren im Sand, 1953; Du Sollst nicht Töten, 1955; Linus oder der Verlust der Würde, 1958; Almanach der Gruppe 47, 1947-1962, 1962; Bestandsaufnahme-Eine deutsche Bilanz, 1962; Walther Rathenau-Reden & Schriften, 1964; Plaedoyer für eine neue Regierung oder Keine Alternative, 1965; Menschen in freundlicher Umgebung, 1965; Doda, 1966; Blinder Alarm, 1970; Rose weiss, Rose rot, 1971. Address: München-Pasing, 7 Rembrandtstr., W. Germany.

RICHTER, Harvena, b. 13 Mar. 1919, Reading, Pa., USA. Writer; Educator. Educ: B.A., Univ. of N.M.; M.A., Ph.D., N.Y. Univ. Publs: The Human Shore, 1959; Virginia Woolf: The Inward Voyage, 1970. Contbr. to: Saturday Evening Post; New Yorker; Atlantic; Christian Sci. Monitor; etc. Mbrships. incl: Authors' Guild; Authors' League; MLA. Recip., Writing Fellowships at Yaddo, MacDowell Colony, Wurlitzer Fndn. Address: c/o Paul R. Reynolds, 12 E. 41st, N.Y., NY 10017, USA.

RICK, Kenneth K., b. 1924, London, UK. Producer; Director; Writer; Lecturer. Educ: Polytech., Regent St. Publs: almost 2000 TV, cinema & radio commercials; documentaries for BBC TV; sponsored documentaries for non-theatrical exhib.; scripts for audio-visual presentations. Contbr. to: Advertisers Weekly; Royal TV Soc. Jrnl.; A.C.T.T. Jrnl.; Inst. of Practitioners in Advtng. Jrnl.; Broadcast TV Mail. Mbrships: Soc. of Motion Picture & TV Engrs.; A.C.T.T.; I.P.A. Address: 61 N. End House, Fitzjames Ave., W. Kensington, London W14 0RX, UK.

RICKARDS, Colin William, b. 15 Dec. 1937, Purley, Surrey, UK. Journalist; Managing Editor, Caribbean Business News, Toronto. Publs: Caribbean Power, 1963; Buckskin Frank Leslie — Gunman of Tombstone, 1964; Bowler Hats & Stetsons, 1966, 2nd ed., 1970; Charles Littlepage Ballard — Southwesterner, 1966; The Man from Devil's Island, 1968; Mysterious Dave Mather, 1968; How Pat Garrett Died, 1970; The Gunfight at Blazer's Mill, 1974; (contbr.) Over the Air, 1962; (contbr.) Latin America & the Caribbean, 1967. Contbr. to: Books & Bookmen; Look & Learn; Tally Sheet; Old West; Fin. Times; etc. Mbrships: Engl. Westerner's Soc.; Western Writers Am. Address: Apt. 715, 15 Vicora Linkway, Don Mills, Ont. M3C 1A7, Can.

RICKARDS, Maurice, b. 1919, London, UK. Author. Publs: Posters at the Turn of the Century; Posters of the 1920s; Banned Posters; Posters of the First World War; Posters of Protest & Revolution; Ed., Engine Driving Life; New Inventions; Brews & Potions; The Pye Book of Science; Offbeat Photography; The World Saves Life; The World Fights Fire; The World Communicates; The World Fights Crime; The Rise & Fall of the Poster; Take Notice;

Where They Live in London. Mbr., Soc. Indl. Artists. Address: 10 Fitzroy Square, London W1P 5AH, UK.

RICKELL, Walter Leroy, pen names, FREDRIC, Keith; BEAVERS, Col. H. O., b. 6 Dec. 1937, Harrisburg, Pa., USA. Writer; Photographer; Graphic Designer. Contbr. to: Guns; Guns & Ammo; Gun World; Gun Digest; Petersen Books; Rock & Gem; Westerner; Horse & Rider; Western Horseman. Mbrships: Outdoor Writers Assn. of Am.; NRA Life Mbr. Address: 920 N. Reese Pl., Burbank, CA 91506, USA.

RICKERT, John E., b. 18 Apr. 1923, Rutland, Vt., USA. Educator. Educ: A.B., Stanford Univ., 1951; BFT — Am. Grad. Schl. Int. Mgmt., 1953; M.A., Rutgers Univ., 1958; Ph.D., Clark Univ., 1960. Publs. incl: A Vocabulary for Indexing & Retrieving Urban Literature, 1968; Ed., Urban & Regional Information Systems for Social Programs, 1968; Ed., Urban & Regional Information Systems; Federal Activities & Specialization Systems, 1969—; Service Systems for Cities, 1969—; Past, Present & Future, 1970—; Information Systems & Political Systems, 1972—; Information Research for an Urban Society, vols. I & II, 1973; num. monographs. Contbr. to: Annals Assn. Am. Geogs.; Fine Arts; etc. Mbrships. incl: Urban & Reg. Info. Systems Assn. (VP); Am. Geogl. Soc. Address: 539 Boston Ave., Egg Harbor City, NJ 08215, USA.

RICKETTS, Ralph Robert, b. Simla, India. Writer. Educ: Magdalen Coll., Oxford. Publs: A Lady Leaves Home; Camilla; The Manikin; Love in Four Flats; Henry's Wife; We Are Happy. Address: Old Alresford Lodge, Alresford, Hants., UK.

RICKWORD, John Edgell, b. 22 Oct. 1898, Colchester, Essex, UK. Poet; Writer. Educ: Pembroke Coll., Oxford. Publs: (poetry) Behind the Eyes, 1921; Invocations to Angels, 1928; Twittingpan, 1930; Complete Poems, 1975; (prose) Rimbaud: The Boy & the Poet, 1924, 2nd ed., 1963; Love One Another (fiction), 1930; Essays & Opinions, 1921-31, 1974. Contbr. to: Times Lit. Supplement; New Statesman; London Mercury; Ed., The Calendar of Modern Letters, 1925-27; Left Review, 1935-37; Our Time, 1944-47. Hons: Special Award, Arts Coun., 1966; Civil List Pension for servs. to lit., 1968. Address: c/o. Carcanet Press, 266 Councillor Lane, Cheadle Hulme, Cheshire SK8 5PN, UK.

RIDDELL, Patrick, b. 1904, Belfast, UK. Author; Playwright; Newspaper Columnist. Publs: I Was An Alcoholic, 1955; Fire Over Ulster, 1970; The Irish Are They Real, 1972; Could I Help Being Irish, 1975; (stage plays) The House of Mallon; Mr. Labby's Last Case; Defence in Depth; The Music Room; pioneered radio drama serial w. adaptation of Dumas' The Count of Monte Cristo, London, 1938; about 70 radio plays, 1926—. Contbr. to: Sunday News; Ulster TV; Daily Express; N.Y. Times; Belfast Telegraph; etc. Mbr., Soc. of Authors. Address: 31 Derryvolgie Ave., Belfast BT9 6FN, UK.

RIDDLE, Donald Husted, b. 22 Jan. 1921, Bklyn., N.Y., USA. College President. Educ: A.B., 1949, M.A., 1951, Ph.D., 1956, Princeton Univ. Publs: The Problems & Promise of American Democracy (Ed. & co-author), 1964, 2nd ed. entitled Contemporary Issues in American Democracy, 1969; The Truman Committee: a Study in Congressional Responsibility, 1964; American Society in Action (Ed.), 1965. Contbr. to: Nation; Police Chief; Am. Govt. Annual, 1965-66; Pub. Opinion Quarterly; Chgo. Jewish Forum. Mbrships. incl: Pres., Acad. of Criminal Justice Scis., 1970-71; N.Y. State Regents Reg. Coord. Coun. for Postsecond. Educ., NYC. Address: 45 E. 89th St., N.Y., NY 10028, USA.

RIDDOLLS, Brenda Harks, pen name ENGLISH, Brenda H., b. Sleights, Whitby, N. Yorks., UK. Novelist. Educ: M.R.C.S.; L.R.C.P. Publs: (regional novels of Whitby dist.) Into the North, 1966; The Gabriel Hounds, 1966; These Yellow Sands, 1967; The Goodly Heritage, 1968; The Proper Standard, 1969; Crying in the Wilderness, 1970; Hob of High Farndale, 1971; Sins of the Fathers, 1972; This Freedom, 1973; Except Ye Repent, 1974. Mbr., Soc. Authors. Address: Groves Bank, Sleights, Whitby, N. Yorks., UK.

RIDEOUT, Roger William, b. 9 Jan. 1935, Bromham, Beds., UK. Professor of Labour Law & Vice-Dean Faculty of Laws, University College, London; Barrister. Educ: LL.B., Ph.D., Univ. Coll., London. Publs: The Right to Membership of a Trade Union, 1963; Principles of Labour

Law, 1972; Practice & Procedure of the National Industrial Relations Court, 1973; Trade Unions & the Law, 1973. Contbr. to: Mod. Law Review; Current Legal Problems; etc. Mbrships: Gray's Inn; Soc. Pub. Tchrs. of Law. Address: 63 Wood Lane, Highgate, London N6 5UD, UK.

RIDGE, Antonia, b. Amsterdam, Netherlands. Author; Radio Writer; Broadcaster. Publs: (num. for. eds.) Family Album; Cousin Jan; By Special Request; Grandma went to Russia; Thirteenth Child; For Love of a Rose; The Man who painted Roses — P. J. Redouté; Engl. text, 27 French & Dutch books for children; Engl. books for children; num. radio & TV plays, UK & abroad; Engl. lyrics for Obernkirchen Children's Choir inclng. song Happy Wanderer. Contbr. to sev. mags. Mbrships: Soc. of Authors; Song Writers Guild of GB; French Soc. of Authors. Recip., Writers' Guild of GB award for best radio play, 1969. Address: 5 Cranbrook Dr., Esher, Surrey KT10 8DL, UK.

RIDGWAY, Athelstan, b. 28 Oct. 1912, Birkenhead, Cheshire, UK. Administrator, Writers' Weekend School, 1965—; Freelance Journalist; Short Story Writer. Contbr. to: Contemporary Review; London Evening News; Tit-Bits; Lilliput; Men Only; Sunday Times; Daily Mail. Mbr., Press Club. Address: Le Vauquiedor Manor, Guernsey, Channel Islands, UK.

RIDLER, Anne (Barbara), b. 30 July 1912. Author. Educ: King's Coll., London Univ. Publs. incl: (verse) Poems, 1939; The Nine Bright Shiners, 1943; The Golden Bird, 1951; A Matter of Life & Death, 1959; Selected Poems, USA 1961; Some Time After, 1972; (plays) Cain, 1943; Henry Bly & Other Plays, 1950; The Trial of Thomas Cranmer, 1956; Who Is My Neighbour, 1963; (anthols.) Ed., A Little Book of Modern Verse, 1941; Best Ghost Stories, 1945; (criticism) Ed., Shakespeare Criticism, 1919-35; Ed., Shakespeare Criticism 1935-60, 1963; var. libretti. Address: 14 Stanley Rd., Oxford, UK.

RIDLEY, Arnold, b. 7 Jan. 1896, Bath, UK. Dramatist; Actor; Producer. Educ: Bristol Univ. Publs: Keepers of Youth, 1929; (plays incl.) The Brass God, 1921; The Ghost Train, 1925; Third Time Lucky, 1929; Headline, 1934; Out Goes She (w. B. Merivale), 1939; Peril at End House (w. A. Christie), 1940; Easy Money, 1947; Beggar My Neighbour, 1951; You, My Guests! , 1956; Geranium, 1957; Bellamy (w. A. Armstrong), 1959; High Fidelity (w. C. Wallis), 1964; Festive Board, 1970; (films incl.) Royal Eagle (also dir.), 1935; Blind Justice, 1935; The Seven Sinners, 1936; var. articles & short stories. Address: c/o Hughes Massie & Co., 69 Gt. Russell St., London WC1, UK.

RIDLEY, Florence H., b. 13 Nov. 1922, Murfreesboro, Tenn., USA. Professor. Educ: B.A., Randolph Macon Woman's Coll., 1944; M.A., Vanderbilt Univ., 1952; Ph.D., Harvard, 1957. Publs: Surrey's Translation of Vergil's Aeneid (ed.), 1963; Chaucer's Prioress & the Critics, 1965; Selected Poems of William Dunbar (ed.), 1969; The Middle Scots (ed.), vol. IV, A Manual of the Writings in Middle English (Albert Hartung, ed.), 1973. Contbr. to profl. jrnls. inclng. Studies in Scottish Lit. Mbrships. incl: Medieval Acad. of Am.; Early Engl. Text Soc. Address: Dept. of Engl., Rolfe Hall, UCLA, L.A., CA 90024, USA.

RIDLEY, Geoffrey Norman, b. 1905, London, UK. Scientist. Educ: B.Sc., Univ. of London. Publs: Man Studies Life; De Mensch en de Levensproblemen; Man: The Verdict of Science; Your Brain & You. Contbr. to: Lit. Guide (now Humanist); Schl. Sci. Review. Address: 49 Oarside Dr., Wallasey, Merseyside, UK.

RIDLEY, Jasper Godwin, b. 25 May 1920, West Hoathly, Sussex, UK. Author. Educ: Sorbonne Univ., Paris, France; Magdalen Coll., Oxford, UK. Publs: Nicholas Ridley, 1957; Thomas Cranmer, 1962; John Knox, 1968; Lord Palmerston, 1970; Mary Tudor, 1973; Garibaldi, 1974. Mbrships: F.R.S.L.; PEN; Soc. of Authors; Sussex Authors. Recip., James Tait Black Mem. Prize, for Lord Palmerston, 1970. Address: The Strakes, West Hoathly, E. Grinstead, Sussex, UK.

RIDOUT, Ronald, b. 1916, Farnham, Surrey, UK. Author. Educ: B.A., Oxford. Publs: over 300 titles inclng. English Today, 1948; International English, 1961; World-Wide English, 1966; English Proverbs Explained, 1967; Books for Me to Write in, 1968; English Now, 1970; Fun with Words, 1974; Dragon Puzzle Books, 1975; Puzzle It Out, 1975. Mbrships: Soc. of Authors; Soc. of Bookmen. Agent: AA. P. Watt & Son. Address: Stile House, Vicarage Lane, Haslemere, Surrey, UK.

RIECK, Max Karl Friedrich, pen name SVEDIN, Peter, b. 16 Mar. 1918, Nutteln, Mecklenburg, Germany. Poet; Author; Educator. Educ: Studies at Univs. of Hamburg & Prague, Czech. Publs: Heidhexe/Moorbrand/ Almenglühen (histl. novel); sev. vols. of poetry in High & Low German; Maja Trimurlis der Wanderer (philos. novel), forthcoming. Contbr. to: frei schaffender. Mbr., German Authors' Union (VS). Address: 3472 Beverungen 1, Ulmenweg 18, W. Germany.

RIEGEL, Robert Edgar, b. 1897, Reading, Pa., USA. Professor of History. Educ: Carroll Coll., Waukesha, Wis.; Lawrence Univ., Appleton, Wis.; Univ. of Wis.; A.M.; Ph.D.; LL.D. Publs: The Story of the Western Railroads, 1926; America Moves West, 1930; United States of America, 1947; Young America, 1949; The American Story (w. D. F. Long), 2 vols., 1955. Contbr. to: Am. Histl. Review; Miss. Valley Histl. Review; Current Hist.; Dictionary of Am. Biog. Address: 6 Ledyard Lane, Hanover, NH, USA.

RIEMENS, Hendrik, b. 25 Oct. 1908, Amsterdam, Netherlands. Diplomat; Author. Educ: D.Econ. Sci., Amsterdam Univ. Publs: The Amortisation Syndicate, 1935; Les Pays-Bas dans le monde, 1939; The Netherlands' Story of a Free People, 1944; Le Pays-Bas, 1945; The Financial Development of the Netherlands, 1949; Perspectives in the Netherlands, 1958; L'Europe devant l'Amerique latine, 1962; Latin America, 1963; Mexico, 1964; Belgium, Country of Contrasts; Present-day problems in Latin America, 1969. Contbr. to Int. Spectator, Hague (Ed.). Address: Julianalaan 84, Overveen, Netherlands.

RIESMAN, David, b. 22 Sept. 1909, Phila., Pa., USA. Professor. Educ: A.M., Harvard Coll., 1931; LL.B., Harvard Law Schl., 1934; Grad. study, 1934-35. Publs: The Lonely Crowd, 1950, 1953, 1961; Individualism Reconsidered, 1954; Thorstein Veblen, 1954; Constraint & Variety in American Education, 1956; Abundance for What? & other Essays, 1964; Conversations in Japan, 1967; The Academic Revolution (w. C. Jencks), 1968, 1975; Academic Values & Mass Education, 1970, 1975. Contbr. to: Encounter; Am. Scholar; other profl. jrnls. Mbrships. incl: Century Assn.; Am. Acad. Arts & Scis. Hons: Prize, Am. Acad. Arts & Letters, 1960; Best Book in Field of Higher Educ., Am. Coun. on Educ., 1968, 1973. Address: 380 William James Hall, Harvard Univ., Cambridge, MA 02138, USA.

RIESS, Curt, pen names MARTIN, C. R.; AMSTEIN, Martin; & others, b. 21 June 1902, Würzburg, Germany. Writer. Educ: Univs. of Munich; Berlin; Heidelberg; Paris (Sorbonne), France. Publs: 72 books inclng: Total Espionage, 1941; Das hat's noch einmal, 1955; Göbbels, 1948; The Berlin Story, 1953. Contbr. to: Stern; Paris Match; Esquire; Saturday Evening Post. Mbr., PEN, London, UK. German PEN, Darmstadt. Hon. D.Phil. Address: CH 8127 Scheuzen auf der Forch, Zürich 950393, Switz.

RIFBJERG, Klaus, b. 15 Dec. 1931, Copenhagen, Denmark. Literary Critic; Author. Educ: Univs. of Princeton & Copenhagen. Publs: incl: (novels) Den Kroniske Uskyld, 1958; Operaelsken, 1966; Arkivet, 1967; Lonni Og Karl, 1968; Marts 1970, 1970; Til Spanien, 1971; Brevet til Gerda, 1972; (short stories) Rejsende, 1969; Den Syende Jomfru, 1972; (non-fiction) Udviklinger, 1965; Ar, 1970; Narrene, 1971; Svaret Blaeser i Vinden, 1971; & poetry. Contbr. to: Information; Politiken. Hons. incl: Danish Acad. Award; Nordic Coun. Award. Address: Tesseboelle, 4681 Herfoelge, Denmark.

RIGBY, Fred Frankland, b. 13 Feb. 1904, Westhoughton, UK. Clerk in Holy Orders. Educ: B.Sc., M.A., M.Ed., Univ. of Manchester. Publs: Elementary Change Ringing, 1946; Discussion on Marriage, 1954; Anglicanism for Parents, 1962; Can We Imitate Jesus Christ, 1964; Sex, Law & Love, 1966; Life & Growth (co-author), What Christian Marriage Means; Problems of Personal Relationships; Playing the Recorders; To Our Lady of Bromsberrow, 1970. Contbr. to: Theology; Crucible; Church Times. Address: Little Court, Longhope, Glos., UK.

RIGG, Robinson Peter, b. 13 Jan. 1918, Blackpool, Lancs., UK. Vice-President, Public Relations & Advertising, Insurance Company. Educ: A.B., Liverpool Univ. Publs: Audiovisual Aids & Techniques in Management & Supervisory Training, 1969. Contbr. to: Dirs. Handbook; Fin. Times; Bus. Admin.; Indl. Advt. & Mktng.; Film User (U.K.); Univ. Film Assn. Jrnl. (USA); Handelsblatt (W. Germany); num. others. Mbrships incl: Fellow, Royal Photog. Soc.; Inst. of PR; Inst. of Dirs.; Soc. of Authors;

PR Soc. of Am.; Mich. Shores; Chgo. Press. Address: 1234 Isabella St., Evanston, IL 60201, USA.

RIJDES, Barend, pen name OPDENCAMPE, F. C., b. 5 Apr. 1910, Neerbosch, Netherlands. Author. Educ: L.H.D., Leyden Univ. Publs: Het Derde Beeld, 1943, 1945; Orpheus (poems), 1944, 1947; De Burgemeester, 1961; Ramth, 1962; Een Bedolven Bestaan, 1967; Bitterkoekjes (aphorisms), 1968; Palaia (poems), 1969; Een Rijtuig in de Sneeuw, 1971. Mbr., PEN. Hons: Reisbeurs der Nederlandse Regering, 1953, 1963; Aanmoedigingsprijs C.P.N.B., 1954. Address: Prins Mauritslaan 121, Overeen, Netherlands.

RILEY, Edward C., b. 5 Oct. 1923, Mexico City, Mexico. Professor of Hispanic Studies. Educ: B.A., M.A., Queen's Coll., Oxford. Publs: Cervantes's Theory of the Novel, 1962; Suma Cervantina (ed., w. J.B. Avalle-Arce), 1973. Contbr. to: Times Lit. Supplement; Mod. Lang. Review; Bulletin of Hispanic Studies; Comp. Lit.; Anales Cervantes; Filologia; etc. Mbrships. incl: Mod. Humanities Rsch. Assn.; Assn. of Hispanists; Soc. for Latin Am. Studies. Address: Dept. of Hispanic Studies, David Hume Tower, George Sq., Edinburgh EH8 9JX, UK.

RIMMINGTON, Gerald Thorneycroft, b. 18 Mar. 1930, Leicester, UK. Professor of Education. Educ: M.A., Leicester Univ., 1959; B.Sc., 1956, Ph.D., 1964, Univ. London; M.Ed., Nottingham Univ., 1972. Publs: Malawi, A Geographical Study (w. J. G. Pile), 1965; The Resources of the Shubenacadie-Stewiacke Area of Nova Scotia, 1966; Social Studies: A Creative Direction (w. Lillian M. Logan), 1969; Teaching the Social Sciences (w. R. D. Traill & Lillian M. Logan), 1972. Contbr. to: Geogl. Jrnl.; Nyasaland Jrnl.; Comp. Educ.; etc. Mbrships. incl: Fellow, Royal Geogl. Soc.; Can. Assn. Profs. Educ.; Leics. Archaeol. & Histl. Soc. Address: Dept. Educ., Mt. Allison Univ., Sackville, N.B., Can.

RINCÓN GUTIÉRREZ, Maria Eugenia, b. 26 Sept. 1926, San Esteban de Gormaz, Spain. Professor of Catalan Literature, Autonomous University of Madrid. Educ: Lic., Philos. & Letters, Barcelona Univ.; Ph.D., Complutense Univ. of Madrid. Publs: (poetry) Tierra Secreta, 1962; Corazón en Órbita, 1963; Frontera de la Sombra, 1968, 2nd larger ed., 1973; Boca sin tiempo, 1974; (prose) Ideologia Literaria de Gregorio Marañón (Ph.D. Thesis), 2 vols., 1976. Contbr. to: Poesia Española; Argensola; Agora; Espadana; Levante; ABC; Provincias; Alaluz (Calif., USA). Hons: Poetry Prize, for Corazón en Órbita, Coun. of Province of Valencia, 1963; Grant, March Fndn., 1968. Address: Calle Claudio Coello, 69—A, 4º—A, Madrid 1, Spain.

RINGSTAD, Muriel Esther Proctor, b. 24 July 1896, Snohomish, Wash., USA. Teacher. Educ: A.B., M.Ed., Univ. of Wash.; M.L.S., Univ. of N.Y. Publs: Adventures on Library Shelves, 1968; Claiming a Right, 1972. Contbr. to: PHP Int.; Secret Place; Moments with God; Church Sunday Schl. Papers; Wash. Wonderland; Highlights; Ideals. Mbrships: Nat. Writers' Club; Christian Writers Int.; Oregon Christian Writers; Western Rsch. Assocs. Recip., Golden Acorn PTA Award. Address: 1300 S. 7th St., Kelso, WA 98626, USA.

RINGWALD, Donald Charles, b. 3 Apr. 1917, Kingston, N.Y., USA. Financial Manager. Publs: Hudson River Day Line, 1965; The Mary Powell, 1972. Contbr. to: Am. Neptune; Marine News; N.Y. Folklore Quarterly; Ships & the Sea; Steamboat Bill; Telescope; Ulster Co. Gazette; Kingston Daily Freeman. Mbrships. incl: Steamship Histl. Soc. of Am., Inc. (Ed., Quarterly Jrnl., 1955-60, Ed.-inChief, 1961-66; Pres., 1973—); num. marine & histl. assns. Address: P.O. Box 7015, Albany, NY 12225, USA.

RINHART, Floyd Lincoln, b. 24 Sept. 1915, Newark, N.J., USA. Author. Educ: Randolph Macon Acad. Publs: American Daguerreian Art, 1967; American Miniature Case Art, 1969; America's Affluent Age, 1971. Contbr. to: Art in Am.; Antique's Jrnl.; Modern Photography; Camera 35; Ed., The New Daguerreian Jrnl. Mbrships: Royal Photog. Soc.; The Daguerreian Soc. Address: Rte. 3, Box 340, Melbourne Beach, FL, USA.

RINHART, Marion Hutchinson, b. 20 Feb. 1916, Bradley Beach, N.J., USA. Author. Publs: American Daguerreian Art, 1967; American Miniature Case Art, 1969; America's Affluent Age, 1971. Contbr. to: Art in Am.; Antiques Jrnl.; Modern Photography; Camera 35; Ed., New Daguerreian Jrnl. Mbr., The Daguerreian Soc. Address: Rte. 3, Box 340, Melbourne Beach, FL, USA.

RINKOFF, Barbara Jean, pen name RICH, Barbara, b. 25 Jan. 1923, NYC, USA. Author. Educ: B.A., N.Y. Univ. Publs. incl: A Map is a Picture, 1965; The Dragon's Handbook, 1966; Elbert, The Mind Reader, 1967; Birthday Parties Around the World, 1967; The Family Christmas Book, 1969; Name: Johnny Pierce, 1969; Harry's Homemade Robot, 1969; The Pretzel Hero, 1970; Tricksters & Trappers, 1970; The Case of the Stolen Code Book, 1971; Guess what Grasses Do, 1972; The Watchers, 1972; Let's Go to a Jetport, 1973; Guess what Trees Do, 1974; No Pushing — No Ducking, 1974; Red Light Says Stopı, 1974; Guess what Rocks Do, 1975. Recip., 5 Book of the Yr. Awards, Child Study Assn. Address: 25 Langland Dr., Mt. Kisco, NY 10549, USA.

RINNE, Reino, b. 17 July 1913, Kuusamo, Finland. Author. Publs: Tunturit hymyilevät, 1945; Tie päättyy tunturin laella, 1946; Erämaan omia ihmisiä, 1949; Kullanhuuhtoja, 1955; Anna minulle atomipommi, 1970; Ihminen evp., 1970; Sähkeitä tähdistä, 1971; Olen puhunut, 1973; Koillismaan Kuusamo, 1973; Kaukopuheluja, 1974. Mbrships: Soc. of Finnish Authors; Finnish Nature Soc.; Rotary Club, Kuusamo. Recip., Prize, Finnish State Lit., 1970, 1971. Address: Kitkantie 4, 93600 Kuusamo, Finland.

RINSER, Luise, b. 30 Apr. 1911, Pitzling, Bavaria, Germany. Writer. Educ: Degree in Psychology & Education. Publs: 25 books (transl'd into 20 langs.) inclng. Die gläsernen Ringe, 1940; Mitte des Lebens, 1950; Daniela, 1953; Ein Bündel weisser Narzissen (short stories), 1956; Abenteuer der Tugend, 1957; Tobias, 1968; Baustelle (diary), 1971; Grenzübergänge (diary), 1973; Hochzeit der Widerspruche (letters), 1973; Der schwarze Esel, 1974; Philemon (play) & num. essays. Contbr. to: Neue Zeitung, Munich, 1945-52 (lit. critic). Mbrships: PEN; Acad. of Arts, Berlin; German Authors' Union (VS). Address: Rocca di Papa, Prov. Roma, Via di Marino 49, Italy.

RINTALA, Paavo Olavi, b. 20 Sept. 1930, Viborg, Finland. Author. Publs: My Grandmother & Mareshall Mannerheim, 1961, 2nd ed., 1962; Leningrad Symphony, 1941-1942, 1968. Contbr. to: Kaleva Mag. (Columnist); Sozialistiskaja Industria, Moscow. Hons: Lenin 100 yr. Medal; & Lit. prizes Finland, 1955, 1962, 1965, 1972, 1973. Address: 02430 Masala, Finland.

RIOS, Juan, b. 28 Sept. 1914, Lima, Peru. Poet; Dramatist. Publs: Cancion de Siempre, 1941; Malstrom, 1941; La Pintura Contemporanea en el Peru, 1946; Teatro I, 1961; Ayar Manko, 1963. Contbr. to Oiga. Mbr., Peruvian Acad. of Spanish Langs. Hons: Nat. Prize for Playwriting, 1946, 1950, 1952, 1954, 1960; Nat. Poetry Prize, 1948, 1953. Address: Dos de Mayo 657, Miraflores, Lima 18, Peru.

RIPLEY (Rev.), Francis Joseph, pen name LANCASTER, George, b. 26 Aug. 1912, St. Helens, UK. Clergyman. Educ: Up Holland Coll., Wigan. Publs. incl: A Blueprint for Lay Action, 1944; Souls at Stake (w. F. S. Mitchell), 1948; This Is the Faith, num. ed., 1950, rev. ed., 1974; A Priest for Ever, 1960; The Mary Potter Story, 1963; The Apostolate of the Laity, 1966; Pope Paul Speaks, 1968; Jubilee Talks to Legionaries, 1972. Contbr. to relig. jrnls.; Mgr. & Ed., Catholic Gazette, 1954-60; Ed., Catholic Truth, 1961-71; Chmn., Ed. Bd., Faith Mag. Mbrships. incl: Soc. of Authors; Past Dir., Cath. Info. Ctr., Liverpool. Hons: The Last Gospel, 1961, nominated Spiritual Book of Year, 1962. Address: Ch. of St. Oswald & St. Edmund, Ashton-in-Makerfield, Wigan, WN4 9NP, UK.

RIPLEY, Randall B., b. 24 Jan. 1938, Des Moines, Iowa, USA. Professor of Political Science. Educ: B.A., DePauw Univ., 1959; M.A., 1961, Ph.D., 1963, Harvard Univ. Publs: Public Policies & Their Politics, 1966; Party Leaders in the House of Representatives, 1967; Majority Party Leadership in Congress, 1969; Power in the Senate, 1969; The Politics of Economic & Human Resource Development, 1972; Legislative Politics U.S.A. (Co-Ed.,). 3rd ed., 1973; American National Government & Public Policy, 1974; Congress, 1975. Contbr. to jrnls. Mbr., profl. orgs. Address: Dept. of Pol. Sci., Ohio State Univ., Columbus, OH 43210, USA.

RIPLEY, S. Dillon, b. 20 Sept. 1913, NYC, USA. Zoologist; Museum Director; Author. Educ: B.A., Yale Univ., 1936; Ph.D., Harvard Univ., 1943; M.A., Yale Univ., 1961; Sc.D., 1974. Publs: Trail of the Money Bird, 1942; Search for the Spiny Babbler, 1952; A Paddling of Ducks, 1957; Ornithological Books in Yale Library (w. L.

Scribner), 1961; A Synopsis of the Birds of India & Pakistan, 1961; The Land & Wildlife of Tropical Asia, 1964; Handbook of the Birds of India & Pakistan (w. Sálim Ali), Vols. I-X, 1968-74; The Sacred Grove, 1969. Contbr. to: Smithsonian Mag.; N.Y. Times Book Review; Jrnl. of World Hist.; Int. Zoo Yearbook; Am. Sci.; Auk; Ibis; Condor; etc. Address: 2324 Massachusetts Ave. N.W., Wash. DC 20560, USA.

RIPOLL ARBÓS, Luis, b. 30 Aug. 1913, Palma de Mallorca, Spain. Editor; Journalist. Educ: Info. Scis.; Shorthand. Publs. incl: Letras Mallorquinas, 2 vols.; La Catedral de Mallorca; La Pintura Mallorquina en el siglo XIX, 3 vols.; Cocina de las Baleares; (in Mallorquin) Llibre de bons Amonestaments; Llibre de cuina Mallorquina; Llibre de Plats Dolços Mallorquins; Llibre de Vins, Licors i per necessari. Contbr. to: Destino; Columnist & Ed., Diario de Mallorca; Sub-Dir., Majorca Daily Bull. Mbrships: Press Assn. of Balearic Isles; Majorcan Cir.; Fomento del Turismo de Mallorca; Fine Arts Cir.; etc. Hons. incl: Siurell de Plata Prize, Palma, 1969; Flor d'Ameller Prize, 1971. Address: Calle Calatrava 68, Palma de Mallorca, Baleares, Spain.

RIPPON, (Rt. Hon.) Aubrey Geoffrey Frederick, b. 1924, nr. Bath, Somerset, UK. MP for Hexham; Queen's Counsel; Minister of Technology, 1970; Chancellor of the Duchy of Lancaster, 1970-73; Secretary of State for the Environment, 1973-74. Educ: M.A., Brasenose Coll., Oxford Univ. Publs. incl: Forward from Victory, by Four Young Conservatives, 1943; The Rent Act, 1957; The Landlord & Tenant Temporary Provision Act, 1958; The Responsible Society (co-author). Contbr. to legal & pol. publs. Mbrships: Carlton Club; M.C.C. Address: Ellwood, Barrasford, Hexham, Northumberland, UK.

RITCHIE, Cicero Theodore, b. 9 Apr. 1914, Halifax, N.S., Can. Geologist. Educ: B.Sc., Balhousie Univ., Halifax. Publs: The Willing Maid, 1957; Black Angels, 1958; The First Canadian: The Story of Samuel de Champlain, 1962; Runner of the Woods: Story of Pierre Radisson, 1964. Contbr. to: Ency. Britannica, 1973. Mbrships: Assn. Profl. Engrs., Ont.; Bd. of Trade of Metrop. Toronto. Address: 37 Henry St., Kentville, N.S., Can. B4N 2L3.

RITCHIE, (Rear Admiral) George Stephen, b. 30 Oct. 1914, Burnley, Lancs., UK. Hydrographic Surveyor. Educ: Royal Naval Coll., Dartmouth, 1928-31. Publs: Challenger, 1957; The Admiralty Chart, 1967. Contbr. to jrnls., inclng: Geog. Mag.; Jrnl. of Navigation; Int. Hydrographic Review. Mbrships. incl: Fellow, Royal Instn. of Chartered Surveyors & Royal Inst. of Navigation. Hons. incl: D.S.C., 1942; C.B., 1967; Silver Medal, Royal Soc. of Arts, 1970; Gold Medal, Royal Geog. Soc., 1972. Address: St. James, Ave. Princesse Alice, Monte Carlo, Principality of Monaco.

RITCHIE, John Charles Forster, b. 1917, Dumfries, Dumfriesshire, UK. Aircraft Navigation Superintendent. Publs: Aircraft Navigation Aids, 1968. Liveryman, Guild of Air Pilots & Air Navigators. Address: 34 Waldegrave Gdns., Strawberry Hill, Twickenham, Middx., UK.

RITCHIE-CALDER, Peter Ritchie, (Baron of Balmashannar), b. 1 July 1906, Forfar, UK. Senior Fellow, Center for the Study of Democratic Institutions, Calif., USA, 1972—; Journalist; Author. Educ: M.A. (Edinburgh), 1961. Publs. incl: The Birth of the Future, 1934; Men Against the Jungle, 1954; Ten Steps Forward, 1958; From Magic to Medicine, 1959; Living with the Atom, 1962; Two-Way Passage, 1964; Man & the Cosmos, 1968; Leonardo & the Age of the Eye, 1971; Pollution of the Mediterranean, 1972. Contbr. to: News Chronicle; Daily News; New Statesman; etc. Mbrships. incl: Assn. of Brit. Sci. Writers (Fndr. Mbr.). Hons. incl: C.B.E., 1945; Created Life Peer, 1966; Gollancz Award, 1969. Address: Box 4068, Santa Barbara, Calif., USA.

RITSCHEL, Karl Heinz, b. 20 Jan. 1930, Oberaltstadt, Czechoslovakia. Journalist; Writer; Chief Editor, Salzburger Nachrichten. Educ: Dr.phil., 1959; cand. jur. Publs. incl: Südtirol — ein europäisches Unrecht. Eine Geschichte der Südtirolfrage, 1960, 1964; Eine Stadt erzählt: Venedig, 1969; Kreisky: Der Pragmatiker — Sozialdemokrat ohne Dogma, 1972; Unbekanntes Italien — Le Marche, die Marken, 1974; China — eine Momentaufnahme, 1974; Julius Raab — der Staatsvertragskanzler, 1975; Stichwort Österreich, 1975. Mbrships: Austrian PEN; Pres., PEN Club, Salzburg; VP, Presseklub Concordia; Vereinigung der Parlamentsredakteure. Hons. incl: Leopold Kunschak Prize, 1970; Award, Fedn. Int. des Rédacteurs en Chef, Paris, 1970. Address: 5020 Salzburg, Hugo v. Hofmannsthalstr. 32, Austria.

RIVE, Richard Moore, b. 1 Mar. 1931, Cape Town, S. Africa. Lecturer in English Literature. Educ: B.A., 1962, B.Ed., 1968, Univ. of Cape Town; M.A., Columbia Univ., USA, 1966; D.Phil., Oxford Univ., UK, 1974. Publs: African Songs (short stories), 1963; Emergency (novel), 1964; Quartet (short stories), 1964; Compiler, Modern African Prose, 1964; works widely transl'd. Contbr. to num. mags, in Africa, Europe, Asia, NZ & USA. Hons. incl: Fairfield Fndn. Fellowship for lit. contbn., 1963-64; Winner, S. African Short Story Competition (The Visits), 1970; Winner, BBC Play Competition (Make Like Slaves), 1971. Address: 2 Selous Ct., Rosmead Ave., Claremont, Cape Town, Repub. of S. Africa.

RIVERA, Feliciano, b. 24 Nov. 1932, Morley, Colo., USA. Philologist. Educ: B.A., Univ. of N.M., 1961; M.A., Univ. of Colo., 1962; M.A., Univ. of Denver, 1964; Ph.D., Univ. of Calif., 1969. Publs. Mexican/American Source Book, 1969; The Chicanos, 1972; Le Raza, 1974. Contbr. to: Immigration Review; Pacific Coast/Am. Histns.; Calif. Histl. Review. Mbrships: Danforth Assoc.; Am. Histl. Assn. Address: History Dept., San José State University, San José, CA 95114, USA.

RIVERS, Patrick, b. 1920, London, UK. Journalist; Marketing Executive, The Thomson Organization, 1963-72; Magazine Editor, K.G. Murray Publishing Co. (Sydney, Aust.), 1954-59. Publs: The Restless Generation, 1972; Politics by Pressure, 1974; The Survivalists, 1975. Contbr. to: Guardian; New Soc.; New Internationalist; Africa Report; Travel Trade Gazette; Latin Am. Mbrships: Conserv. Soc.; Alternative Soc. Agent: John Farquharson Ltd. Address: Field Gate, Brockweir, Chepstow, Gwent NP6 7NN, UK.

RIVERS, William L., b. 17 Mar. 1925, Gainesville, Fla., USA. Teacher; Author. Educ: B.A., 1951, M.A., 1952, La. State Univ.; Ph.D., Am. Univ., 1960. Publs: The Opinionmakers, 1965; The Adversaries: Politics & the Press, 1970; Responsibility in Mass Communication (w. Wilbur Schramm), 1969; Other Voices: The New Journalism in America (w. Everette Dennis), 1974; Writing: Craft & Art, 1975; Finding Facts: Interviewing, Observing, Using Reference Sources, 1975. Contbr. to: N.Y. Times Mag.; Saturday Review; etc. Mbrships. incl: Authors' League Am.; Nat. Press Club. Recip. Disting. Rsch. Award for The Opinionmakers, 1966. Address: Dept. Communication, Stanford Univ., Stanford, CA 94305, USA.

RIVETT, Rohan Deakin, b. 16 Jan. 1917, Melbourne, Australia. Journalist. Educ: B.A., Melbourne Univ.; Balliol Coll., Oxford. Publs. incl: 3 books on cricket; Behind Bamboo, 1946; The Community & the Migrant, 1953; Australian Citizen, 1965; Australia: Modern World Series, 1968; Writing About Australia, 1969; David Rivett: Fighter for Australian Science, 1972. Contbr. to: Nation Review; Canberra Times; Le Monde; Times; Sunday Times; Statesman (India). Mbrships: Pres., Melbourne Press Club, 1974-75; Hon. Life, Adelaide Press & Int. Press Inst.; Coun., Aust. Soc. Authors, 1966-75. Recip., C'wlth. Lit. Awards, 1967, 1972. Address: 147 Wattle Valley Rd., Camberwell, Vic., Australia 3142.

RIVKIN, Ellis, b. 7 Sept. 1918, Balt., Md., USA. Professor of Jewish History. Educ: B.A., 1941, Ph.D., 1946, Johns Hopkins Univ., Balt., Md.; B.H.L., Balt Hebrew Coll., 1944. Publs: Leon de Modena & the Kol Sakhal, 1952; The Dynamics of Jewish History, 1970; The Shaping of Jewish History: A Radical New Interpretation, 1971. Contbr. to encys. & num. theol. & histl. jrnls. Mbrships. incl: Am. Histl. Soc.; Fellow, AAAS; Medieval Acad. of Am.; Soc. of Biblical Lit.; Assn. of Jewish Studies. Hons. incl: Simon Guggenheim Fellowship, 1962-63; D.H.L., Balt. Hebrew Coll., 1975. Address: Hebrew Union Coll., Jewish Inst. of Relig., 3101 Clifton Ave., Cinn., OH 45220, USA.

RIZVI, Saiyid Athar Abbas, b. 10 July 1921, Jaunpur, India. University Teacher. Educ: M.A., Ph.D., D.Litt., Agra Univ. Publs. incl: Source Book of Medieval Indian History (in Hindi), 10 vols., 1954-62; Haqaiq-i-Hindi (in Hindi), 1957; Swatantra Dilli (in Hindi), 1957; Freedom Struggle in U.P., 6 vols., 1957-61; Muslim Revivalist Movements in Northern India, 1965; Alakhbani (in Hindi), 1971; Fathpur Sikri, 1972; Fathpur Sikri, a Major Study, 1975; Religious & Intellectual History of the Muslims in Akbar's Reign, 1975. Contbr. to num. other books & jrnls. Mbr., Aust. Acad. Humanities (Coun. 1973-74). Hons. incl: var. awards for works in Hindi, 1956-65; var. Fellowships. Address: Dept. of Asian Civilizations, Aust. Nat. Univ., Box 4, P.O., Canberra, A.C.T. 2600, Australia.

ROA BASTOS, Augusto, b. 12 June 1917, Asuncion, Paraguay. Writer. Publs: El trueno entre las hojas, 1953; Hijo de hombre, 1960; El Baldío, 1966; Madera quemada, 1967; Moriencia, 1971; Cuerpo presente y otros cuentos, 1971; Yo el Supremo, 1974. Address: Panamá 929-pis 8º— Dto. 26, Buenos Aires, Argentina.

ROA GARCIA, Raúl. Professor; Minister of Foreign Affairs, Cuba. Publs: Historia de las Doctrinas Sociales, 1948; Quince Años Después, 1950; Viento Sur, 1953; Retorno, 1953; Retorno a la Alborada, 1964. Recip., Nat. Jrnlsm. Award, Justo de Lara, 1954. Address: Ministerio de Asuntos Exteriores, Havana, Cuba.

ROBBE-GRILLET, Alain, b. 18 Aug. 1922, Brest, France. Author; Film Director. Educ. as Agricultural Engineer. Publs: Les Gommes, 1953; Le Voyeur, 1955; La Jalousie, 1957; Dans le Labyrinthe, 1959; L'Année Dernière à Marienbad, 1961; L'Immortelle, 1963; La Maison de Rendez-vous, 1965; Projet pour une Révolution à New York, 1970; Glissements Progressifs du Plaisir, 1974. Address: 18 blvd. Maillot, 92200 Neuilly-sur-Seine, France.

ROBBINS, Harold, pen name of KANE, Francis, b. 21 May 1916, N.Y., USA. Author. Publs: Never Love a Stranger, 1948; The Dream Merchants, 1949; A Stone for Danny Fisher, 1952; Never Leave Me, 1953; 79 Park Avenue, 1955; Stiletto, 1960; The Carpetbaggers, 1961; Where Love Has Gone, 1962; The Adventurers, 1966; The Inheritors, 1969. Address: Le Cannet, Cannes, France.

ROBBINS, Keith Gilbert, b. 9 Apr. 1940, Bristol, UK. University Teacher. Educ: M.A., D.Phil., Magdalen & St. Antony's Coll., Oxford. Publs: Munich 1938, 1968; Sir Edward Grey, 1971. Contbr. to: Histl. Jrnl.; Int. Affairs; Slavonic & E. European Review; Jrnl. of Contemp. Hist.; Jrnl. of Ecclesiastical Hist.; Jrnl. of Imperial & C'wlth. Hist.; European Studies Review. Mbrships: Fellow, Royal Histl. Soc.; Eccles. Hist. Soc.; Histl. Assn.; Assn. of Contemp. Histns. Address: Hafod Fadog, Aber Rd., Llanfairfechan, Gwynedd, UK.

ROBBINS, Rossell Hope, b. 22 July 1912, Wallasey, UK. Scholar. Educ: Lic., Guildhall Schl. of Music, London, 1932; B.A., 1933, Dipl. Ed., 1934, Univ. of Liverpool; Ph.D., Cambridge, 1937. Publs. incl: Index of Middle English Verse (w. Carleton Brown), 1943; Christopher Marlowe: Dr. Faustus, 1948; The T. S. Eliot Myth, 1951; Secular Lyrics of the XIVth & XVth Centuries, 1952; Early English Christmas Carols, 1961; Supplement to the Index (w. J. Cutler), 1965; The Chaucerian Apocrypha, 1973; Poems Dealing with Contemporary Conditions, 1975. Contbr. to: num. lit., musicol. philol. & histl. jrnls. Mbrships. incl: var. offs., MLA of Am.; Mod. Humanities Assn.; F.R.S.L., 1958. Address: Katsbaan Onderheugel, 6163 Shear Rd., Saugerties, NY 12477, USA.

ROBERTHALL, (Lord) Robert Lowe, b. 1901, Tenterfield, Australia. Economist. Educ: Univ. of Qld.; Magdalen Coll., Oxford, UK; B.Eng.; M.A. Publs: Earning & Spending; The Economic System in a Socialist State. Contbr. to: Oxford Econ. Papers; Econ. Jrnl.; other profl. jrnls. Mbrships. incl: Royal Econ. Soc. (Pres., 1958-60). Hons: K.C.M.G., 1954; C.B. Address: 34 Maunsel St., London SW1, UK.

ROBERTIELLO, Richard C., b. 20 July 1923, NYC, USA. Psychiatrist; Psychoanalyst. Educ: B.A., Harvard Univ., 1943; M.D., Columbia Univ., 1946; Cert. Psychoanalyst, N.Y. Med. Coll., 1954. Publs: Voyage from Lesbos, 1959; A Handbook of Emotional Illness & Treatment, 1961; The Analyst's Role (co-author), 1963; Sexual Fulfillment & Self-Affirmation, 1964. Contbr. to: Forum; Physician's World; The Village Voice. Mbrships. incl: Exec. Bd., Soc. for Sci. Study of Sex; Fellow, Am. Psychiatric Assn.; Fellow, Am. Inst., Psychotherapy & Psychoanalysis. Address: 49 E. 78th St., N.Y., NY 10021, USA.

ROBERTS, Arthur Owen, pen name MEGO, Al, b. 7 Jan. 1923, Caldwell, Idaho, USA. Professor of Philosophy & Religion. Educ: B.A., Geo. Fox Coll., 1944; B.D., Nazarene Theol. Sem., 1951; Ph.D., Boston Univ., 1954; Harvard Univ. Publs: Through Flaming Sword, 1959; Move Over, Elijah, 1967; Early Quaker Writings (Ed., w. Hugh Barbour), 1973; Listen to the Lord, 1974. Contbr. to: American Quakers Today (Ed., Edwin B. Bronner), 1966; Quaker Understanding of Christ & of Authority, 1974; Quaker Relig. Thought; Christianity Today; Eternity;

Banner; Evangelical Friend; Quaker Life; etc. Address: 2514 Roberts Lane, Newberg, OR 97132, USA.

ROBERTS, Betty Katherine Winkler, b. 29 Aug. 1926, Ronceverte, W.Va., USA. Editor, National & International Publication. Educ: Registered Nurse, St. Luke's Hosp. Schl. of Nursing, NYC, 1947; B.A., Univ. of Pitts., 1962; M.A., Marshall Univ., Huntingdon, W.Va., 1970. Contbr. to: Jrnl. of Rehabilitation (Ed.). Mbrships: Nat. Press Club; Am. Newspaper Women's Assn.; Advt. Club Metrop. Washington; Soc. Nat. Assn. Publs: Edpress Assn. Address: 4504 Commons Dr., Annandale, VA 22003, USA.

ROBERTS, Brian, b. 19 Mar. 1930, London, UK. Writer. Educ: London Univ. Publs: Ladies in the Veld, 1965; Cecil Rhodes & the Princess, 1969; Churchills in Africa, 1970; Diamond Magnates, 1972; The Zulu Kings, 1974. Contbr. to var. S. African & Brit. newspapers & mags. Address: Gum Tree Cottage, Teubes Rd., Kommetjie, Cape, Repub. of S. Africa.

ROBERTS, Carol A., b. 5 Mar. 1933, Pottsville, Pa., USA. Teacher. Educ: M.S., Temple Univ., Phila., Pa.; M.A., Bread Load Schl. of Engl., Middlebury, Vt. Author, A Mebish Named Lovable, 1972. Contbr. to: S. & W.; Prize Poems, Pa. Poetry Soc.; Prize Poems, Nat. Fedn. of State Poetry Socs.; Centro Studi E. Scambi Int.; A Goodly Heritage. Mbrships: A.A.U.P.;. N.E.A.; Pa. State Educ. Assn.; Nat. Fedn. of State Poetry Socs.; Pa. Poetry Soc.; Pres., Keysner Poets, 1973-74; Acad. of Am. Poets; Harrisburg M.S. Club. Hons: 1st Prize, Short Story, Harrisburg M.S. Club, 1973; Grand Prize, Pa. Poetry Soc., 1974. Address: 308 Arbys Rd., Harrisburg, PA 17109, USA.

ROBERTS, Cecil, b. 1892, Nottingham, UK. Journalist; Lecturer; Former War Correspondent. Educ: Univ. Coll.; LL.D. Publs: Scissors, 1923, Sails of Sunset, 1924; The Love Rack, 1926; Spears Against Us; Pilgrim Cottage; Victoria Four-Thirty; A Terrace in the Sun; The Remarkable Young Man; Love is Like That; And So to Bath; And So to America; Gone Rustic; Gone Rambling; Gone Afield; Gone Sunwards; Half Way; One Year of Life; Portal to Paradise; Collected Poems, 1960; Autobiography, 5 vols. (The Growing Boy; Years of Promise; The Bright Twenties; Sunshine & Shadow; The Pleasant Years). Hons: Freedom, City of Nottingham; Hon. Citizen of Alassio; Gold Medal of Rouse. Address: c/o Hodder & Stoughton, Warwick Lane, London EC4, UK.

ROBERTS, Denys Tudor Emil, b. 19 Jan. 1923, London, UK. Barrister-at-Law. Educ: M.A.; B.C.L.; Wadham Coll., Oxford. Publs: Smuggler's Circuit; Beds & Roses; The Elwood Wager; The Bones of the Wajingas; How to Dispense with Lawyers. Address: Victoria House, Hong Kong.

ROBERTS, Edna, pen names HILTON, Josephine; FINLAY, Michael; OWEN, Richard, b. 3 Nov. 1912, Blacko, nr. Nelson, Lancs., UK. Journalist. Contbr. to more than 250 magazines incl: Good Housekeeping; Christian Herald; Woman's Wkly.; Lady; Christian; & BBC & Radio Blackburn. Mbrships: Burnley & Dist. Writers' Circle (Pres. & Fndr. Mbr.); Lancs. Authors' Assn.; Yorks. Poets' Assn.; Pennine Assn. for Arts. Hons: Batty Cup, Writer of the Yr. Award, 1969; Burnley Writers' Circle Top Prizewinner for Radio & Jrnlsm. annually 1956-73. Address: 22 Reedley Grove, Reedley, nr. Burnley, Lancs. BB10 2LA, UK.

ROBERTS, Elizabeth Mauchline, b. 1936, Barrow-in-Furness, Lancs., UK. Teacher; Research Worker. Educ: B.A., Bristol Univ.; Inst. of Educ., London Univ. Publs: Lenin & the Downfall of Tsarist Russia, 1966; Stalin, Man of Steel, 1968; Roosevelt, 1970; Mao Tse Tung & the Chinese Communist Revolution, 1970; Gandhi, Nehru & Modern India, 1974. Contbr. to: World Questions. Address: 105 Barton Rd., Lancaster, UK.

ROBERTS, Eric, pen name ROBIN, b. 5 Apr. 1914, London, UK. Writer & Broadcaster. Publs: Adventure in the Sky, 1960; Oddities of Animal Life, 1962; Animal Ways & Means, 1963; (plays) Whose Deal?, 1957; Murder by Arrangement, 1961; Ring for Hartley, 1963. Contbr. to: Punch; She; Woman's Own; BBC Radio & TV; Brit. Forces Radio; etc. Address: Gatesgarth, Overstone, Northants. NN6 0AG, UK.

ROBERTS, Francis Warren, b. 3 Dec. 1916, Menard, Tex., USA. University Professor & Administrator. Educ: A.B., 1938, D.Litt.(Hon.), 1972, Southwestern Univ.;

Ph.D., Univ. of Tex., Austin, 1956. Publs: Bibliography of D. H. Lawrence, 1962; Complete Poems of D. H. Lawrence (co-Ed.), 1964; D. H. Lawrence & His World (co-author), 1966; Phoenix II Uncollected, Unpublished & Other Prose Work by D. H. Lawrence (co-Ed.), 1968. Contbr. to: Tex. Quarterly; Jrnl. of Mod. Lit.; Renaissance & Mod. Studies. Mbrships. incl: Mod. Humanities Rsch. Assn.; Tex. State Histl. Assn.; Tex. Inst. of Letters. Hons. incl: Theta Sigma Chi Roundup Award, 1963. Address: 2305 Windsor Rd., Austin, TX 78703, USA.

ROBERTS, H. V. Molesworth, b. 1896, Lewisham, London, UK. Librarian; Architectural Historian; Professional Indexer. Educ: Strand Schl.; King's Coll., London Univ. Publs: Sub-ed., Catalogue of R.I.B.A. Library, 2 vols., 1937-38; 3 Guides to Surrey Churches: Beddington, 1931, 1938, Wallington 1937, Carshalton 1958, 1961, 1966; Italian Romanesque Architecture (MS); The British National Press: English words classified by subject and date (MS). Contbr. to: Enciclopedia Italiana; Builder; Archt. & Bldg. News; Archtl. Review. Address: Percy Gdns., Worcester Park, Surrey, UK.

ROBERTS, Irene, pen mane ROWLAND, Iris; HARLE, Elizabeth; SHAW, Irene; CARR, Roberta b. 27 Sept. 1925, Leyton, London, UK. Writer. Publs: Squirrel Walk, 1961; Morning Star, 1962; Golden Rain, 1963; Golden Flower, 1964; Valley of Bells, 1965; Shadows on the Moon, 1966; Jungle Nurse, 1967; The Olive Branch, 1968; Surgeon in Tibet, 1969; Orange Blossom for Tara, 1970; The Golden Pagoda,1971; Sister Julia, 1972; The Throne of Pharaohs, 1973. Contbr. to var. mags. in Europe & USA. Hon. Life Mbr., W. Essex Writers Club. Address: Alpha House, Higher Town, Malborough, Devon TQ7 3RL, UK.

ROBERTS, John Anthony Storm, pen name ROBERTS, John Storm, b. 24 Feb. 1936, London, UK. Writer & Journalist. Educ: M.A., Christ Church Coll., Oxford Univ. Publs: A Land Full of People: Kenya Today, 1967, 2nd ed., 1968; Black Music of Two Worlds, 1972, 3rd ed., 1974; (part author) Music in Africa Ency., 1974; Africa World Book Year Book, 1974-75; (radio) The English on the Riviera, 1967; The Union Man, 1968; Top of the Pops, 1969; (film script) Countdown at Kusini, 1972. Contbr. to: Stereo Review; Crawdaddy; Village Voice; Africa Report (US); Melody Maker; Black Music; Geogl. Mag.; Drum Mag.; Prism Int.; Transition; etc. Mbr., Authors' Guild Am. Address: 123 Congress St., Bklyn., NY 11201, USA.

ROBERTS, Sonia Leslie, pen names TREVOR, Charlotte; LESLIE, Robert, b. 23 Oct. 1934, Surbiton, Surrey, UK. Journalist. Publs: Ballet Annual, 1955; History of Birdcage, 1972; Keeping Pet Birds, 1972; Deep Freeze Secrets, 1973; Story of Islington, 1974; Gem Collecting, 1974. Address: 36 Wilton Sq., London N1, UK.

ROBERTS, William Geoffrey, b. 6 Oct. 1929, London, UK. Petroleum Technologist. Educ: Highgate Schl.; M.A., Trinity Hall, Cambridge Univ. Publs: Quest for Oil, 1970, 2nd ed., 1975. Address: Chimneys, Rosemary Lane, Thorpe, Egham, Surrey TW20 8QE, UK.

ROBERTS-JONES, Philippe John, pen name (poetry) JONES, Philippe, b. 8 Nov. 1924, Brussels, Belgium. Chief Curator; University Professor. Educ: Doct., Philos. & Letters, Univ. of Brussels. Publs. incl: (poetry) Amour et autres Visages, 1956; Graver au vif, 1971; Etre selon, 1973; (essays) De Daumier à Lautrec, 1960; Honoré Daumier — Moeurs conjugales, 1967; Du Réalisme au Surréalisme, 1969; Magritte poète visible, 1972; Bruegel — La chute d'Icare, 1974. Contbr. to: Cahiers du Sud; Courrier du Ctr. Int. d'Etudes Poétiques; Gazette des Beaux Arts; Jrnl. des Poètes; Marginales; Quadrum. Mbrships. incl: Admnstr.; PEN; Int. Assn. of Art Critics. Recip., num. hons. Address: 66 rue Roberts-Jones, 1180 Brussels, Belgium.

ROBERTSON, Colin, b. 1906, Hull, Yorks., UK. Writer. Educ: Tech. Coll., Bradford; Sloane Schl., Chelsea. Publs: The Devil's Lady; Two Must Die; Peter Gayleigh Flies High; Venetian Mask; The East Lake Affair; Who Rides a Tiger; Murder Sits Pretty; Time to Kill; Dark Money; The Green Diamonds; The Devil's Cloak. Mbrships: Soc. of Authors; Crime Writers' Assn. Address: St. Christopher's, 23 Sutherland Ave., Bexhill, Sussex, UK.

ROBERTSON, Mima Simpson Taylor, b, 1901, Dunfermline, Fife, UK. Author. Publs: Bitter Bread; The Castilian. Contbr. to People's Friend. Address: 15 Cameron St., Dunfermline, Fife, UK.

ROBILLIARD, Robin Virginia, b. 17 Feb. 1934, Hastings, NZ. Sheep Farmer's Wife. Educ: Trng. as Registered Gen. Nurse, Christchurch Pub. Hosp. Publs: A Birthday at the Lighthouse, 1967; Paul of the Timber Mill, 1967; Kay of the Tobacco Farm, 1967; Dayle Lives in a Country Town, 1967; Sarah at the Festival of Arts, 1968; P.M. Country Readers, 1968, 1969; Children of Golden Bay, 1969; A Dairy Farm Family, 1970; An Apple Orchard Family, 1970; Morning till Night, 1970; People at Work series, 1974; The Country Books, UK 1974. Mbrships: PEN; Aust. Soc. of Authors. Address: Rocklands, R.D. Takaka, Nelson, NZ.

ROBIN, (Rev.) Arthur de Quetteville, b. 1929, Melbourne, Australia. Clergyman. Educ: Cert. of Applied Chem., Royal Melbourne Inst. of Technol., 1950; Th.L., Ridley Coll., 1953; B.A., Univ. of Melbourne, 1958; B.A., 1961, M.A., 1965, Univ. of Cambridge, UK; Ph.D., Univ. of W.A., 1971. Publs: Charles Perry, Bishop of Melbourne, 1967. Contbr. to: Aust. Dict. of Biog.; Dict. of World Hist.; Jrnl. of New Testament Studies; Jrnl. Eccles. Hist.; Studies in Hist., Univ. of W.A. Mbr., Royal Vic. Histl. Soc. Recip., Hulsean Prize, Univ. of Cambridge, UK, 1965. Address: 236 La Trobe Terrace, Geelong, Vic., Australia.

ROBINS, Denise, b. London, UK. Novelist. Publs: 167 novels inclng: House of the Seventh Cross; Khamsin; Time Runs Out; Dark Corridor; Arrow in the Heart; I Should have Known; The Snow Must Return; A Love Like Ours; Forbidden; Love & Desire & Hate; Wait for Tomorrow; Laurence, My Love; etc., etc; Hist. Novels incl: Gold for the Gay Masters; Dance in the Dust; etc; Autobiography, Stranger than Fiction. Contbr. to: Radio; TV (serialist); num. mags., inclng. She; also newspapers (Letter Columnist). Address: 15 Oathall Rd., Haywards Heath, Sussex RH16 3EG, UK.

ROBINSON, Antony Meredith Lewin, b. 11 Oct. 1916, Swindon, Wilts., UK. Library Director. Educ: B.A., Rhodes Univ., Grahamstown, 1937; Dip. in Libnship., Univ. Coll., London, 1939; Ph.D., Univ. of Cape Town, 1961. Publs: None daring to make us afraid, 1962; Thomas Pringle's Narrative of a residence in South Africa (ed.), 1966; Systematic bibliography, 1966, 2nd ed., 1971; The Letters of Lady Anne Barnard to Henry Dundas from the Cape & elsewhere (ed.), 1973; Francois Le Vaillant: Traveller in South Africa, 1781-1784 (co-ed.), 1973. Contbr. to: Dict. of S. African Biog.; Standard Ency. of S. Africa. Mbr., var. lib. orgs. Address: 136 Camp Ground Rd., Newlands, Cape Town, S. Africa.

ROBINSON, Eric Henry, b. 1924, Calne, Wilts., UK. University Professor. Educ: M.A., Jesus Coll., Cambridge. Publs. incl: Rhyme & Reason; John Clare: The Shepherds Calendar (co-Ed.); Selected Poems & Prose of John Clare; Frederick Martin: Life of Clare (co-Ed.); Partners in Science: James Watt & Joseph Black (co-Ed.); Science & Technology in the Industrial Revolution (co-author); James Watt & the Steam Revolution (co-author). Contbr. to: Guardian; Listener; Hist. Today; Histl. Jrnl.; Annals of Sci.; Math. Gazette; Technol. & Culture; etc. Hons: Simon Rsch. & Guggenheim Fellowships. Agent: Curtis Brown Ltd. Address: Dept. of History, Univ. of Mass., USA.

ROBINSON, Howard, b. 1885, Redwood Falls, Minn., USA. University Professor of History (Ret'd); Author. Educ: M.A.; Ph.D.; LL.D.; Hamline Univ.; Columbia Univ. Publs: Development of the British Empire, 1924; History of Great Britain, 1927; Bayle the Sceptic, 1931; The British Post Office, a History, 1948; Britain's Post Office, 1953; A History of the New Zealand Post Office, 1964; Carrying British Mails Overseas, 1964. Contbr. to: Ency. of Social Scis.; Compton's Ency. Life Mbr., Royal Histl. Soc. & Am. Histl. Assn. Address: 75 Elmwood Place, Oberlin, OH 44074, USA.

ROBINSON, Jack Fay, b. 7 Mar. 1914, Wilmington, Mass., USA. Clergyman. Educ: A.B., Univ. of Mont., 1936; B.D., Crozer Theol. Sem., 1939; A.M., Univ. of Chgo., 1949. Author, The Growth of the Bible, 1969. Mbrships: Int. Platform Assn.; Am. Soc. of Ch. Hist. Address: P.O. Box 4578, Chgo., IL 60680, USA.

ROBINSON, Kenneth Dean, b. 1909, Manchester, UK. Headmaster (Ret'd), Bradford Grammar School, 1963-74; Headmaster, Birkenhead School, 1946-63. Educ: Corpus Christi Coll., Oxford Univ. Publs: Septimus (w. R. L. Chambers); Latin Way. Contbr. to: Times Educ. Supplement; Liverpool Daily Post. Address: Lane House, Cowling, W. Yorks. BD22 0LX, UK.

ROBINSON, Kenneth Ernest, b. 9 Mar. 1914, London, UK. University Teacher & Administrator. Educ: M.A., Hertford Coll., Oxford; London Schl. of Econs. Publs: Ed., Five Elections in Africa (w. W. J. M. MacKenzie), 1960; Ed., Essays in Imperial Government (w. A. F. Madden), 1963; The Dilemmas of Trusteeship, 1965; co-Ed., A Decade of the Commonwealth, 1966. Contbr. to: Univ. Co-operation & Asian Development; L'Europe du XIX et XX Siècle, Tome 7; Int. Affairs; Pol. Studies; Pub. Admin.; Am. Pol. Sci. Review; Listener; Economist. Mbrships. incl: Fellow, Royal Histl. Soc.; Corres. mbr., Acad. des Scis. d'outre mer, Paris. Hons: LL.D., Chinese Univ. of Hong Kong, 1969; C.B.E., 1971; D.Litt., Univ. of Hong Kong, 1972. Address: 10c St. Augustine's Rd., London NW1 9RN, UK.

ROBINSON, Nancy Elizabeth, pen names LYON, Eliza; BENNETT, Elizabeth, b. 12 Aug. 1929, Gawler, S. Australia. Writer; Broadcaster. Publs: Change on Change, 1971; Ed., Bend Down & Listen, 1972; Ed., Stagg of Tarcowie, 1973; Sweet Breathes the Breast, 1974. Contbr. to var. Aust. jrnls. & radio. Mbrships: Aust. Soc. Authors; Aust. Jrnlsts.' Assn.; S. Aust. Histl. Assn.; S. Aust. Writers' Fellowship; Adelaide Press Club; Mastectomy Assn. (Fndn. Pres., 1973-74). Address: Mannanarie Stud Farm, Box 24, Jamestown 5491, S. Australia.

ROBINSON, Noel Mary, b. 11 Mar. 1929, Melbourne, Australia. Television Playwright. Educ: B.A., Sydney Univ.; Barnard Coll., Columbia Univ., N.Y. Publs: (stage play) Glasstown, 1974. Mbr., Writers' Guild GB. Address: c/o Andrew Mann Ltd., 32 Wigmore St., London W18 9DF, UK.

ROBINSON, Norman Hamilton Galloway, b. 7 Oct. 1912, Troon, Scotland, UK. Professor of Divinity, Univ. of St. Andrews. Educ: M.A., D.Litt., Univ. of Glasgow; B.D., Univ. of Edinburgh; Oxford Univ. Publs: Faith & Duty, 1950; The Claim of Morality, 1952; Christ & Conscience, 1956; The Groundwork of Christian Ethics, 1971. Contbr. to: Theologians of Our Time, 1966; Dict. of Christian Theol., 1969; Talk of God, 1969; Preface to Christian Studies, 1971; Scottish Jrnl. Theol.; Jrnl. Theol. Studies; Relig. Studies. Mbrships: Soc. for Study of Theol.; Royal Inst. Philos.; Societas Ethica. Recip.. Hon. D.D., Univ. of Edinburgh, 1964. Address: Arcan, Tay St., Newport-on-Tay, Fife DD6 8AQ, UK.

ROBINSON, Reginald Hesslewood, b. 3 June 1891, Sheffield, UK. Chartered Electrical Engineer. Educ: B.Eng., Sheffield Univ. Publs: The Inside of Electrical Machines, 1948. Contbr. to: The Electrician (series of 28 articles), 1947. Fellow, Instn. of Elec. Engrs. Address: 8 Solent Dr., Barton-on-Sea, New Milton, Hants. BH25 7AW, UK.

ROBINSON, Richard Dunlop, b. 11 Feb. 1921, Yakima, Wash., USA. Professor of International Management. Educ: B.A., Univ. of Wash.; M.B.A., Harvard Univ.; Ph.D., MIT. Publs: Investment in Turkey, 1956; Cases in International Business, 1962; The First Turkish Republic, 1963; International Business Policy, 1964; Highlevel Manpower Development, the Turkish Case, 1965; International Management, 1967; International Business Management, A Guide to Decision Making, 1973. Contbr. to num. profl. jrnls. Mbrships: Fellow, Int. Acad. of Mgmt., 1972; Past Pres., Acad. of Int. Bus.; Past Chmn., Inst. of Current World Affairs. Address: 89 Ash St., Weston, MA, USA.

ROBINSON, Robert, b. 17 Dec. 1927, Liverpool, UK. Writer; Broadcaster. Educ: M.A., Exeter Coll., Oxford. Publs: Landscape with Dead Dons, 1956; Inside Robert Robinson, 1965; The Conspiracy, 1968. Contbr. to: Times; Sunday Times; Observer; New Statesman; Punch. Address: 16 Cheyne Row, London SW3, UK.

ROBINSON, Thomas Rufer Barnard, b. 10 Apr. 1905, London, UK. Technical Journalist (Ret'd). Educ: Northampton Polytech., London. Publs: Modern Clocks, 1934-55, 4th ed. in preparation; Modern Watch Repairing (co-author); Battery Clocks, 1975. Contbr. to: Ency. Britannica; Retail Jeweller & Horol. Review; Horol. Jrnl.; Am. Jeweler & Horol.; BBC radio & TV; ITV. Mbrships: Fellow, Brit. Horol. Inst.; Coun. for Places of Worship (Clocks Sub-Comm.). Address: 8 Malmesbury Close, Redland, Bristol BS6 7TR, UK.

ROBINSON, Timothy Michael, b. 1934, Croydon, Surrey, UK. Employed by Church Commissioner. Educ: M.A., Magdalen Coll., Oxford Univ. Publ: When Scholars Fall, 1961. Contbr. to: Listener; Workshop New Poetry;

Teaching Juniors; Adventurers; Key Notes; Pilgrim. Mbr., Crime Writers' Assn. Address: 42 Foxley Lane, Purley, Surrey, UK.

ROBINSON, William Albert, b. 13 Aug. 1902, Kenosha, Wis., USA. Writer; Shipbuilder; Circumnavigator; Medical Researcher. Publs: Ten Thousand Leagues over the Sea, 1932; Deep Water & Shoal, 1932; Voyage to Galapagos, 1936; To the Great Southern Sea, 1956; Return to the Sea, 1972. Contbr. to: Travel Mag.; Rudder Mag.; Sports Illustrated; Life Mag.; Colliers; etc. Mbrships: Pres., Assn. Antifilarienne, Tahiti & W.A. Robinson Taiaro Atoll Rsch. Sanctuary, Tahiti; VP, Assn. pour la protection de la nature, French Polynesia. Recip., Legion of Hon., 1955. Address: P.O. Box 14, Papeete, Tahiti.

ROBINSON, (Rev.) William Gordon, b. 1903, Liverpool, UK. University Lecturer in Ecclesiastical History. Educ: Univs. of Liverpool, Manchester & Oxford; M.A.; Ph.D.; B.D. Publs: William Roby, 1766-1830; New Testament Treasure; The Gospel & the Church in a Pagan World; An Introduction to the New Testament; New Testament Detection; The Literature of the New Testament. Contbr. to jrnls. inclng: Congl. Quarterly; Trans. Congl. Histl. Soc. Address: Craigneish, Highfield Rd., Grange-over-Sands, Cumbria, UK.

ROBLES, Mireya, b. 1934, Guantánamo, Oriente, Cuba. Writer; Painter; Teacher. Educ: Inst. de Guantánamo; Havana Univ.; Russell Sage Coll., N.Y., USA; SUNY at Albany; B.A.; M.A.; Ph.D. Publs: Petits Poèmes. Contbr. to: Revista de Occidente; Azor; Caracola; Mod. Langs.; El Escritor; Latina; Esquirla; Thesaurus; El Dia; etc. Mbrships: AAUP; Rensselaer Histl. Soc.; Am. Assn. Tchrs. of Spanish & Portuguese. Address: Birch Brook Manor, 87 S. Highland Ave., Apt. B-25, Ossining, NY 10562, USA.

ROBOTTOM, John Carlisle, b. 1934, Birmingham, UK. Education Officer, BBC. Educ: B.A., Dip. Sec. Ed., Univ. of Birmingham. Publs: Modern China, 1967; Modern Russia, 1969; Making the Modern World (series Ed. & co-author), 1970; Twentieth Century China, 1970; Making the 19th Century, 1974. Address: 11 Knutswood Close, Birmingham B13 0EN, UK.

ROBSON, Jeremy Michael, b. 1929, Llandudno, N. Wales, UK. Managing Director, Robson Books; Chief Editor, Vallentine Mitchell Publishers, 1969-73. Educ: Haberdashers' Aske's Hampstead Schl.; Regent St. Polytechnic Schl. of Jrnlsm.; Alliance Française. Publs: (poetry) Thirty-Three Poems, 1964; In Focus, 1970; Ed., Poems from Poetry & Jazz in Concert, 1969; The Young British Poets, 1971; Modern Poets in Focus, Vols. 2 & 4, 1972; Poetry Dimension, 1973. Contbr. to: Tribune; Outposts; Poetry Review; London Mag.; Encounter. New Statesman; etc. Address: 37 Briardale Gdns., London NW3 7PN, UK.

ROBSON, Robert, b. 1929, Haltwhistle, Northumberland, UK. Fellow & Assistant Tutor, Trinity College, Cambridge. Educ: M.A., Ph.D., Trinity Coll., Cambridge Univ. Publs: The Attorney in Eighteenth Century England, 1959; Ed., Ideas & Institutions of Victorian Britain, 1967. Address: Trinity College, Cambridge, UK.

ROCHE, Paul, b. 1928, Musoorie, India. Poet; Author; former Poet-in-Residence, Fontbonne College, 1970. Educ: Ph.B., Lic. Phil., Univ. Gregoriana, Rome. Publs: The Rat & the Convent Dove, 1952; O Pale Galilean, 1954; The Rank Obstinacy of Things, 1962; Vessel of Dishonor, 1964; The Oedipus Plays of Sophocles, 1958; The Orestes Plays of Aeschylus, 1962; Prometheus Bound, 1962; The Love Songs of Sappho, 1966; Three Plays by Plautus, 1968; All Things Considered, 1966; To Tell the Truth, 1967; Three Plays of Euripides (Alcestis, Medea, The Bacchae), 1974; Enigma Variations, 1975. Mbrships: Soc. Authors; Poetry Soc. Address: The Stables, The Street, Aldermaston, Berks., UK.

RODAHL, Kaare, b. 17 Aug. 1917, Brønnøysund, Norway. Physician; Physiologist; Author. Educ: M.D., 1948, D.Sc., 1950, Oslo Univ. Publs: Tre år som fallskjermhopper, 1945; The Ice Capped Island, 1946; Nytt land under vingene, 1947; North, 1953; The Last of the Few, 1963; Be Fit for Life, 1966; Stress, 1972; Akiviak, 1974. Contbr. to: Symposia: Bone as a Tissue, 1960; Muscle as a Tissue, 1962; Fat as a Tissue, 1964; Nerve as a Tissue, 1966. Address: Maaltrostveien 40, Holmenkollen, Oslo 3, Norway.

RODD, John, b. 12 Mar. 1905, Greenhithe, Kent, UK. Cabinetmaker. Publs: The Repair & Restoration of Furniture, 1954, revised & enlarged ed. forthcoming. Address: 1830 McMicken Rd., Sydney, B.C., Can.

RODDA, Percival Charles, pen names HOLT, Gavin; LOW, Gardner, b. 9 June 1891, Port Augusta, S. Australia. Journalist; Novelist. Publs. incl: Tango, 1928; Providence Hall, 1943; Golden Corn, 1945; The House Upstairs, 1949; (as Gavin Holt) Eyes in the Night, 1927; Dark Lady, 1933; Green for Danger, 1929; Ladies in Ermine, 1947; No Curtain for Cora, 1950; To-night is for Death, 1952; Take Away the Lady, 1954; Dusk at Penarder, 1956; Garlands for Sylvia, 1958; Pattern of Guilt, 1959; Irina, 1965; Sole Survivor, 1969; & 29 other books, also num. short stories, plays, TV scripts, libretti. Contbr. to var. Am. mags. Mbrships: Aust. Jrnlsts.' Assn. Address: 36 Meadow Flats, St. Ives, Cornwall, UK.

RODGER, Ian Graham, b. 14 June 1926, London, UK. Writer. Educ: B.A., Durham Univ. Publs. incl: The Sun is Dead, 1960; Nine Flowers, 1961; A Hitch in Time, 1967; Seven Beds to Christmas, 1968; (plays) Cromwell at Drogheda, 1961; Blake, 1962; Death of Hampden, 1963; A Voice Like Thunder, 1964; Loyal Servant, 1965; The Decline of Conroy Wilkin, 1965; The Warriors, 1968; The Open Boat, 1968; Wycliffe, 1969; The Great Society, 1969; The True Sir John, 1969; A Short Visit to Cockaigne, 1970; (TV plays) Sweet England's Pride (Elizabeth R. No. 6); The Red Arrows, 1972; Going South, 1974; & var. transls. from Norwegian & Swedish. Contbr. to: Listener (radio drama critic, 1958-63); etc. Mbr., Soc. Authors. Address: 17 The Green, Brill, Aylesbury, Bucks., UK.

RODGERS, (Sir) John (Charles), b. 5 Oct. 1906, York, UK. Company Director; Member of Parliament; Author. Educ: M.A., Keble Coll., Oxford. Publs. incl: Mary Ward Settlement — A History, 1930; The Old Public Schools of England, 1938; The English Woodland, 1941; English Rivers, 1948; One Nation (co-author), 1950; York, 1951; Ed., Thomas Gray's Poems, 1953; Change is our Ally (co-author), 1954; & num. pol. pamphlets. Contbr. to: Spectator; Adelphi; Criterion; Hist. Today; etc. Mbrships: F.R.S.A.; Soc. of Authors (former Exec. Comm. Mbr.); Chmn., New Engl. Lib. Ltd.; Dir., Hist. Today Ltd. Hons. incl: Kt. Grand Cross, Order of Civil Merit, Spain. Address: 72, Berkeley House, Hay Hill, London W1, UK.

RODRIGO, Robert, pen name RODNEY, Bob, b. 11 Apr. 1928, Newmarket, UK. Manager, Daily Mirror Punters Club; Former Golf Writer. Publs: The Racing Game, 1958; Search & Rescue, 1958; Peter May, 1960; Berlin Airlift, 1960; The Braddocks (w. J. & B. Braddock), 1963; The Paddock Book, 1967; The Birdie Book, 1967; Master Golfer (w. J. Hitchcock), 1967; Golf with Gregson, 1968. Contbr. to: Golf Illustrated; Golf World Newswkly. Mbrships: Assn. of Golf Writers; Nat. Union of Jrnlsts. Address: 14 Oaklands Rd., Groombridge, Tunbridge Wells TN3 9SB, UK.

RODRIGUEZ, Cirilo, b. 31 Dec. 1927, Segovia, Spain. Journalist; Radio-TV Foreign Correspondent. Publs: The World of Mrs. Dibble, 1967; Cronicas de America, 1967; Adios Mister Nixon, 1974. Mbrships: Assn. de la Prensa, Madrid; For. Press Assn., N.Y., USA. Hons: Ondas Award, for The World of Mrs. Dibble, 1967; Nat. Radio & TV Award for political coverage, 1969; Antena de Oro Award, for best int. reporting, 1971. Address: 225 E. 36 St., N.Y., NY 10016, USA.

RODRIGUEZ-ALCALA, Hugo Rosendo, b. 25 Nov. 1917, Asuncion, Paraguay. Professor of Spanish & Comparative Literature. Educ: J.D., 1943; Ph.D., 1953. Publs: Estampas de la Guerra, 1939; Horas Liricas, 1939; Korn, Romero, Guiraldes, 1958; Mision y Pensamiento de Francisco Romero, 1959; Ensayos de Norte a Sur, 1960; El Arte de Juan Rulfo, 1965; Sugestion y Ilusion, 1967; La Dicha Apenas Dicha, 1967; Historia de la Literatura Paraguaya, 1970; Palabras de los Dias, 1972; El Canto de Aljibe, 1972; Literatura Hispanoamericana, 1973. Contbr. to num. profl. jrnls. Mbrships: Int. Assn. Hispanistas; Int. Inst. Ibero-Am. Lit.; Paraguaran Acad. Spanish Lang. Address: Univ. of Calif.; Dept. of Spanish & Portuguese, Riverside, CA 92502, USA.

RODRIGUEZ MONEGAL, Emir, b. 28 July 1921. Writer. Educ: Montevideo Univ. Publs: El juicio de los parricidas, 1956; Obras completas de José Enrique Rodó (Ed.), 1957; Las raíces de Horacio Quiroga, 1960; Literatura uruguaya del medio siglo, 1966; El viajero immovil: Introduction a Pablo Neruda, 1966; Vinculo de Sangre, 1969. Contbr. to Mundo Nuevo, Paris (Ed.). Address: Mundo Nuevo, 97 rue St. Lazare, Paris 9e, France.

RODRÍGUEZ SOLÍS, Eduardo, b. 13 Oct. 1938, Mexico City, Mexico. Playwright; Novelist. Educ. incl: B.A., Nat. High Schl.; Drama Schl., Nat. Inst. Fine Arts. Publs. incl: (short stories) La puerta de los clavos, 1966; (novel) No es la Soledad, 1969; (ballet) Entrar y entrar en la galeria, 1972; (plays) Helicóptero de miercoles, 1973; Una relación cercana al éxtasis, 1974. Mbr., Nat. Union of Authors. Hons. incl: for Doncella vestida de blanco: Hon. Mention, Nat. Contest, Mexican Inst. of Social Security, 1974. Address: Edificio 57, Entrada B, Dept. 403, Conjunto Lomas de Sotelo, Mexico 10, D.F., Mexico.

RODWAY, Allan Edwin, b. 25 Oct. 1919, Hayfield, Derbys., UK. University Teacher. Educ: M.A., Univ. of Cambridge; Ph.D., Univ. of Nottingham. Publs: Godwin & the Age of Transition, 1952; The Common Muse, 1957, 1965; The Romantic Conflict, 1963; Science & Modern Writing, 1964; Two Poets (poems w. Malcolm Bradbury), 1967; Poetry of the 1930s, 1967; Ed., Midsummer Night's Dream, 1969; The Truths of Fiction, 1970; English Comedy, Its Role & Nature from Chaucer to the Present Day, 1975. Contbr. to num. lit. jrnls. Mbr., AUT. Address: The White House, 63 Radford Bridge Rd., Nottingham, UK.

RODWAY, Cecil George Reedon, b. 10 May 1911, Cheltenham, Glos., UK. Public Relations Officer; Freelance Journalist; Artist. Educ: Studies at Cheltenham Coll. of Art. Publs: num. handbooks for N. Rhodesia Govt. Info. Dept. Contbr. to: Rhodesia Farmer; Agricl. Supplement, The Herald, Salisbury, Rhodesia; Chronicle, Bulawayo; Ctrl. Africa Post; Farming in Zambia; Archt. & Bldr., S. Africa; Rand Daily Mail; Personality; Veld & Vlei; Field, UK; Bldr.; Field & Stream, USA; etc. Mbrships: Inst. of P.R., UK; Inst. of Jrnlsts., UK; Guild of Agricl. Jrnlsts., UK; F.R.S.A., 1953; F.R.G.S., 1954-68. Address: P.O. Sedgefield, 6573, Repub. of S. Africa.

ROE, Frederic Gordon, b. 1894, London, UK. Former Editor Connoisseur Magazine. Publs: David Cox, 1924; The Nettlefold Catalogue (co-author), 1937-38; Etty & the Nude (co-author), 1943; The Nude, From Cranach to Etty & Beyond, 1944; English Period Furniture, 1946; English Cottage Furniture, 1949, revised ed., 1961; Victorian Furniture, 1952; Windsor Chairs, 1953; The Victorian Child, 1959; Victorian Corners, 1968; Women in Profile, 1970. Mbrships: F.S.A.; F.R.S.A.; F.R.Hist.Soc. Address: 19 Vallance Rd., Alexandra Pk., London N22 4UD, UK.

ROE, Ivan, pen name SAVAGE, Richard, b. 12 Nov. 1917, London, UK. Author. Publs: The Breath of Corruption, 1946; Murder Goes to School, 1947; Murder for Fun, 1948; The Horrible Hat, 1949; The Poison & the Root, 1950; Set Free Barabbas, 1950; The Green Tree & the Dry, 1950; The Salamander Touch, 1952; Shelley: The Last Phase, 1953; When the Moon Died, 1955; The Jester of God, 1956; Strangers' Meeting, 1957; The Lightning's Eye, 1957; The Innocents, 1958; A Style of Your Own, 1972. Mbr., Soc. of Authors. Address: 5 The Chestnuts, 3 Bolton Rd., London W4 3TE, UK.

ROEBUCK, Derek, b. 22 Jan. 1935, Stalybridge, UK. University Professor of Law; Author. Educ: M.A., Oxford; M.Com., NZ. Publs. incl: The Law of Contract: Text & Materials for Students of Business, Vol. I, 1966, Vol. II, 1968; Law of Commerce (co-author), 1968; Credit & Security in Japan (co-author), 1973; Credit & Security in the Philippines (co-author), 1973; Credit & Security in Korea (co-author), 1973; Credit & Security in the Republic of China in Taiwan (co-author), 1973; Law of Contract: Text & Materials, 1974. Mbrships: Law Soc., UK; Law Soc. & Bar Assn., Tas. Address: 10 Lord St., Sandy Bay, Hobart, Tas., Australia 7005.

ROEBUCK, John Athey, b. 1920, Grimethorpe, Yorks., UK. Group Staff Personnel Officer. Educ: Ph.D., Taylor Univ., Colo. Springs, USA. Publs: The Life Mind Man, 1948; E Tenebris Lux, 1951; The Roebuck Story (w. Senator The Hon. A. W. Roebuck, Q.C.), 1963. Contbr. to var. profl. dicts., etc. Mbrships: F.R.S.A.; M.I.P.M.; A.M.B.I.M.; Exec. Comm., Brit. Poetry-Drama Guild, 1948; Lecture Panel; Rsch. Panel Mass-Observation, 1949; Assoc. Fac. Mbr., Taylor Univ., 1952; UK Agt. & Corres., 1953—. Recip., Award of Hon. & Life Mbrship., Int. Coun. of Ldrs. & Schlrs., Congress of Drs., 1969. Address: Inglenook, Stockingate, South Kirkby, Pontefract, West Yorks. WF9 3RA, UK.

ROESCH, Roberta, b. Hackettstown, N.J., USA. Writer; Newspaper Columnist. Educ: N.Y. Univ. Publs. incl: World's Fairs, 1962; Money, Jobs, Futures, 1964; Women in Action, 1965. Contbr. to: Reader's Digest; Good Housekeeping; Pageant; Weight Watchers; Family Wkly.; Girl Talk; Parents; Am. Home; Together; Home Life; Better Homes & Gdns.; Extension; Writer; Toronto Star Wkly.; Success Unlimited; Today's Family Digest; Women's World; Hillman Publs.; Fawcett Publs.; news servs.; etc. Mbrships: Soc. Mag. Writers; Authors' Guild; N.J. Press Women. Address: 131 Prospect Ave., Westwood, NJ 07675, USA.

ROFE, (Fevzi) Husein, b. 1922, Manchester, UK. Teacher; Translator; Author; Lecturer; Orientalist. Educ: Univ. of London. Publs: The Path of Subud, 1959; Reflections on Subud, 1961; Advanced English Conversations, 1970. Contbr. to: The Changing Orient, 1974; Lookeast; Eastern Horizon; Orientations; Far Eastern Econ. Review; Forum World Features; Pet Ind.; Tropical Fish Hobbyist. Mbrships: Fellow, Royal Asiatic Soc. Address: Asian Development Bank, P.O. Box 789, Manila, Philippines.

ROGALSKI, Aleksander, b. 23 Oct. 1912, Niszczewice, Inowroclaw, Poland. Critic; Essayist. Educ: M.A., 1936, Ph.D., 1945, Univ. of Poznan. Publs. incl: "The Bridge over the Abyss". On Thomas Mann, 1963, 2nd ed., 1968; "American Studies": on the Transcendental Current in the Literature of USA, 1971; "New Constellation", Essays on the contemporary Situation of Mankind, 1973; "Authors, Works, Attitudes", Selected Literary Essays, 1974. Contbr. to var. jrnls. Recip., lit. awards. Address: ul. Noskowskiego 24, 61 — 705 Poznan, Poland.

ROGERS, Alan, b. 1933, Wallington, Surrey, UK. Senior Lecturer in Medieval & Local History. Educ: M.A., Ph.D., Nottingham Univ. Publs: The Making of Stamford, 1965; The Medieval Buildings of Stamford, 1970; History of Lincolnshire, 1970; This Was Their World, 1972. Contbr. to: Bulletin of Local History (Ed.); etc. Mbrships: F.R.Hist.S.; F.S.A. Address: Dept. of Adult Educ., Univ. Park, Nottingham Univ., Nottingham, UK.

ROGERS, Cyril Harold, b. 21 Nov. 1907, Cambridge, UK. Writer. Publs: Budgerigars, 1957; Canaries, 1957; Foreign Birds, 1958; Parrots, 1958; Parrot Guide, 1969; Budgerigars, 1969; Pet Birds, 1970; Budgerigars, 1970; Seed Eating Birds, 1974; Budgerigars, Foreign Birds, Budgerigars & their Care, & Parrakeets, all 1975. Contbr. to: Cage & Aviary Birds. Address: Midda Beck, Mill Lane, Aldringham, Leiston, Suffolk IP16 4PZ, UK.

ROGERS, Franklin R(obert), b. 25 July 1921, NYC, USA. Professor of American Literature. Educ: B.A., Fresno State Coll., Calif., 1950; M.A., 1952; Ph.D., Univ. of Calif., Berkeley, 1958. Publs: Mark Twain's Burlesque Patterns, 1960; The Pattern for Mark Twain's Roughing It, 1961; (Ed., works by Mark Twain) Simon Wheeler Detective, 1963; Satires & Burlesques, 1967; Roughing It, 1972. Contbr. to: Jrnl. of Engl. Germanic Philol.; Bull. of N.Y. Pub. Lib.; Comparative Lit.; Am. Lit.; 19th Century Fiction. Mbrships: MLA; AAUP. Address: Dept. of Engl., San Jose State Univ., San Jose, CA 95192, USA.

ROGERS, George William, b. 15 Apr. 1917, San Fran., Calif., USA. Research Economist. Educ: B.A., 1942, M.A., 1943, Univ. of Calif., Berkeley; M.P.A., 1948, Ph.D., 1950, Harvard Univ. Publs: Alaska in Transition: The Southeast Region, 1960, 2nd ed., 1967; The Future of Alaska: the Economic Consequences of Statehood, 1962, 2nd ed., 1970; Change in Alaska: People, Petroleum, Politics, 1971. Contbr. to: Alaska Review of Bus. & Econ. Conditions; The Polar Record; Inter-Nord; Arctic. Mbr., profl. orgs. Recip. acad. hons. Address: 1790 Evergreen Ave., Juneau, AK 99801, USA.

ROGERS (Col.), Hugh Cuthbert Basset, b. 11 June 1905, Wylam-on-Tyne, UK. Army Officer, Retired. Educ: R.M.C., Sandhurst. Publs. incl: The Pageant of Heraldry, 1955; Weapons of the British Soldier, 1960; Troopships & Their History, 1963; Battles & Generals of the Civil War, 1642-1651, 1968; Artillery through the Ages, 1970; Chapelon: Genius of French Steam, 1972; Napoleon's Army, 1974. Contbr. to profl. jrnls. Mbr., Soc. of Authors. Hons: O.B.E., 1940. Address: Wingate, 209 Reading Rd., Wokingham, Berks., RG11 1LJ, UK.

ROGERS, Neville William, b. 1908, Margate, Kent, UK. Professor of English. Educ: B.A., D.Lit., Birkbeck Coll., London. Publs: Keats Shelley & Rome, 1949; Shelley at

Work, 1956; Italian Regional Tales of the 19th Century (transl. & ed. w. Archibald Colquhoun), 1961; The Esdaile Poems of Shelley, 1966; Shelley, Selected Poetry, annotated, 1968; Poetical Works of Shelley, OET, Vol. 1, 1972, Vol. 2, 1975. Contbr. to: Times Lit. Supplement; Review Engl. Studies; Mod. Lang. Review; Times; Listener; Ency. Britannica; London Mag.; etc. Mbrships: F.R.S.L.; Nat. Liberal Club; Authors' Soc. Address: 22 Clavering Ave., Barnes, London SW13, UK.

ROGERS, Thomas Percy, pen name ROGERS, John, b. 12 Feb. 1897, Peterborough, UK. Former Secretary, Director & Managing Director, Rio de Janeiro Flour Mills & other companies. Publs: The Secretary's Manual (w. L. M. Cohen); (2 correspondence courses for members of the Forces) Secretarial Practice, 1941. Contbr. to: The Secretary; Country Fair. Mbrships. incl: Coun., Chartered Inst. of Secs., 1945-68, Treas., 1952. Address: Hartfield, 47 The Green, Eltisley, Huntingdon, Cambs. PE19 4TG, UK.

ROGERSON, Alan Thomas, b. 17 Jan. 1943, Birkenhead, Cheshire, UK. Research Director, School Mathematics Project. Educ: B.Sc. 1965, M.Sc. 1969, London Univ.; Cert. Ed., 1966, Dip.Ed., 1970, Cambridge Univ.; D.Phil., Balliol Coll., Oxford, 1972. Publs: Millions Now Living Will Never Die: A Study of Jehovah's Witnesses, 1969, Dutch & German Transls., 1971; The School Mathematics Project Further Mathematics, 1969; Vectors & Mechanics (co-author), 1971; Differential Equations & Circuits (co-author), 1971; Revised Advanced Mathematics (Ed. & co-author), vols. 1 & 2, 1973. Contbr. to: Math. Gazette; Maths. in Schl. Mbrships: Univ. Assn. for Sociol. of Relig.; var. math. assns. Address: c/o Wolfson Coll., Oxford, UK.

ROGERSON, Fred, pen name FORDE, Rogerson, b. 29 Oct. 1927, Stockport, UK. Author. Publs: (plays) Christmas Presents, 1973; Almost a Fairy-Tale, 1973; Weird is the Night, 1973. Contbr. to num. jrnls., ranging from Mayfair to Brownie Annual. Address: 17 Brinnington Rd., Stockport, Cheshire SK1 2AA, UK.

ROGOZ, Adrian, b. 19 Apr. 1921, Bucharest, Romania. Writer. Educ: Ph.B., Bucharest Univ. Publs: Omul şi Năluca, 1965; Genetic Epistemology of Jean Piaget, 1973; Preţul Secant al Genunii, 1974; Riddles & Roots of the Graphematical Invariances, 1975. Contbr. to: Secolul XX; Viaţa Românească. Mbrships: Writers' Union, Socialist Repub. of Romania; Cyberarts Romanian Investigators' Club; Sec., (Sci. Fiction) Lit. Circle of Romanian Writers. Hons: State Prize, 1954; Prize, 1st Nat. Sci. Fiction Contest, 1956; Eurocon I Prize, 1st European Sci. Fiction Congress, Trieste, 1972. Address: Intrarea Antrenorilor 1, Bucharest I, Romania.

ROHAN, Dorine Virginia (Mrs.), b. 27 Nov. 1942, Cork, Repub. of Ireland. Writer. Educ: Pvte.; & Sorbonne Univ., Paris, France. Publs: Marriage — Irish Style (non-fiction), 1969; Barriers Within (fiction), 1974. Contbr. to: Irish Times; Irish Press; Cork Examiner; Woman's Choice; Dublin Mag.; Irish Woman's Jrnl.; Irish Independent; Radio Telefis Eireann. Mbrships. incl: Lit. Club of Ireland (Comm.); PEN, Ireland (Comm.). Address: Badger Hill, Kilcroney, Bray, Co. Wicklow, Repub. of Ireland.

ROLAND, Betty, b. 22 July 1903, Kaniva, Vic., Australia. Author. Educ: Private. Publs: The Touch of Silk, 1942; The Forbidden Bridge, 1961; Lesbos, the Pagan Island, 1963; The Bush Bandits, 1966; The Other Side of Sunset, 1972; No Ordinary Man, 1974. Contbr. to: Harper's Bazaar; Theatre Arts Monthly; Overland (Aust.). Mbrships: Soc. Authors, London; Aust. Soc. Authors; PEN; Soc. Women Writers; Aust. Jrnlsts. Assn. Hons: 3 Act Play in W. Aust. Drama Competition, 1937. Address: Montsalvat, Hillcrest Ave., Eltham, Vic. 3095, Australia.

ROLAND-HOLST, Adrianus, b. 23 May 1888, Amsterdam, Netherlands. Author. Educ: Univ. of Oxford, UK. Publs: Vodzbij de Wegen (verse), 1920; De Afspraak, 1925; De Wilde Kim (verse), 1925; Een Winter aan Zee (verse), 1937; Vuur in Sneeuw (verse), 1968; Contbr. to: De Gids; Tirade. Mbrships: Maatschappij der Nederlandse Letterkunde; Vereeniging der Nederlandse Letterkunde. Recip., P.C. Hooftprijs, 1955. Address: Frankenstate, Bergen N.-H., Netherlands.

ROLBIECKI (Rev.), John J., b. 1 Apr. 1889, Winona, Minn., USA. Clergyman; Educator; Teacher. Educ: A.M., 1919, Ph.D., 1921, Cath. Univ. of Am. Publs: The Political Philosophy of Dante Alighieri, 1921; The Prospects of

Philosophy, 1939. Contbr. to dictionaries & encys., inclng. The Books of Popular Science (15 vols.) & Dictionary of Philosophy; Asst. Ed., The Catholic World (jrnl). Address: 1347 W. Broadway, Winona, MN 55987, USA.

ROLFE, Sheila Constance, b. 4 Jan. 1935, London, UK. Writer. Educ: B.A., Univ. of B.C., Can. Publs: Amulets & Arrowheads, 1967; Sasquatch Adventure, 1975. Contbr. to: Racquets Can.; radio (book reviews). Mbr., Vancouver Lawn Tennis & Badminton Club. Address: 3269 W. 49th Ave., Vancouver, B.C., V6N 3T5, Can.

ROLIN, Dominique, b. 22 May 1913, Brussels, Belgium. Writer. Publs. incl: Les Marais, 1942; Moi qui ne suis qu'amour, 1948; Le Lit, 1950; Le Souffle, 1952; Le Gardien, 1955; Le Maison La Forêt, 1965; Maintenant, 1967; Le Corps, 1969; Les Eclairs, 1971; Lettre au vieil homme, 1973; Deux, 1975. Contbr. to Le Point. Mbr., Jury Fémina, 1958-65. Recip., Fémina Prize, 1952. Address: 36 rue de Verneuil, 75007 Paris, France.

ROLL, (Sir) Eric, b. 1907, Former Professor of Economics & Commerce, University of Hull. Educ: B.Com. & Ph.D., Univ. of Birmingham. Publs: An Early Experiment in Industrial Organisation, 1930; Spotlight on Germany, 1933; About Money, 1934; Elements of Economic Theory, 1935; The Combined Food Board, 1957; The World After Keynes, 1968; A History of Economic Thought, 1973. Contbr. to: Econ. Jrnl.; Economica; Am. Econ. Review. Hons: K.C.M.G.; C.B. Address: D2 Albany, Piccadilly, London W1, UK.

ROLLE, Andrew Frank, b. 12 Apr. 1922, Providence, R.I., USA. Professor of History; Author. Educ: M.A., Ph.D., Univ. Calif., L.A. Publs. incl: The Golden State, 1965; California: A History, 1969; The Lost Cause: Confederate Exiles in Mexico, 1965; The Immigrant Unpraised: Italian Adventurers & Colonists in an Expanding America, 1968, Italian version Gli Emigrati Vittoriosi, 1972; The American Italians: Their History & Culture, 1973. Contbr. to: Encys. Americana & Britannica; & var. acad. & histl. jrnls. Mbrships. incl: Southern Calif. Psychoanalytic Soc. (Clinical Assoc.). Hons. incl: C'wlth Club Award for non-fiction, 1969; Rsch. Schlr. Rockefeller Fndn. Rsch. Ctr., Bellagio, Italy, 1970-71; Cavaliere al Ordine di Merito, Italy, 1975. Address: Hist. Dept., Occidental Coll., L.A., CA 90041, USA.

ROLLINS, Cyril Bernard, b. 19 May 1914, Birmingham, UK. Electrical Sales Engineer. Publs: The D'Oyly Carte Opera Company, A Record of Productions (w. R. John Whitts), 1962; Victor Saville (w. Robert J. Wareing), 1972. Address: 16 Cotysmore Rd., Sutton Coldfield, Warwicks., UK.

ROLLINSON, William, b. 1937, Barrow, Cumbria, UK. University Lecturer. Educ: B.A., M.A., Manchester Univ. Publs: A History of Man in the Lake District, 1967; A Tour in the Lakes Made in 1797, 1968; Lakeland Walls, 1969; A Tour Through the Isle of Man, 1794, 1970; Life & Tradition in the Lake District, 1974. Contbr. to: John Soulby, Printer, Ulverston. Mbrships: Fellow, Royal Geog. Soc.; Inst. of Brit. Geogs. Address: Dept. of Ext. Studies, The Univ., Liverpool 3, UK.

ROLO, Paul Jacques Victor, b. 6 Nov. 1917, Alexandria, Egypt. University Professor of History. Educ: M.A., Balliol Coll., Oxford Univ. Publs: George Canning, 1965; Entente Cordiale, 1969. Contbr. to: Hist.; Engl. Histl. Review. Fellow, Royal Histl. Soc. Address: Barlaston Lea, Barlaston, Staffs., UK.

ROLPH, John Alexander, b. 11 Jan. 1926, Harrow, Middlesex, UK. Rare Book Dealer. Publs: Dylan Thomas: A Bibliography, 1956. Fndr. & Partner, Scorpion Press. Address: Manor House, Pakefield St., Lowestoft, Suffolk NR33 0JT, UK.

ROLT, Lionel Thomas Caswall, b. 11 Feb. 1910, Chester, UK. Author. Educ: Hon. M.A.; Hon. M.Sc.; F.R.S.L.; C.I.Mech.E. Publs: Narrow Boat; Worcestershire; Green & Silver; Inland Waterways of England; Horseless Carriage; Railway Adventure; Winterstoke; Isambard Kingdom Brunel; Thomas Telford; The Stephensons; The Aeronauts, A History of Ballooning; Landscape with Machines (autobiog.); Victorian Engineering, 1970; From Sea to Sea, The Canal du Midi; Navigable Waterways. Contbr. to num. jrnls. Mbrships. incl: Co-Fndr., Inland Waterways Assn.; Fndr., Talyllyn Railway Preservation Soc.; Soc. of Authors; Soc. for Hist. of Technol. Address: The Cottage, Stanley Pontlarge, Winchcombe, Glos., UK.

ROMANO, Deane Louis, occasional pen name CAIRO, Jon, b. 4 Jan. 1927, El Paso, Tex., USA. Author; Screenwriter; Novelist. Educ: Art Inst. of Chgo., 1 yr.; var. courses, N.Y. Univ., UCLA, Univ. of Calif., Berkeley. Publs: Posh, 1968; The Town That Took a Trip, 1968; Flight From Time One, 1972. Mbrships: Writers Guild of Am. (W.); Sci. Fiction Writers of Am. Address: 4612 Fern Pl., L.A., CA 90032, USA.

ROMBOLA, John,b. 9 Apr. 1940, Bklyn., N.Y., USA. Painter-Artist. Educ: Bklyn. Mus.; Pratt Inst. Art Schl. Publs: Rombola, by Rombola, 1965; Rombola's People, 1970. Contbr. to: Vogue; Town & Country; Harper's Bazaar; Look; Horizon; Holiday; Travel & Leisure; participant in var. solo exhibs. & grp. shows. Address: 3804 Farragut Rd., Bklyn., NY 11210, USA.

ROMERO, Luis, b. 24 May, 1916, Barcelona, Spain. Educ: Bus. studies. Publs. incl: (poetry) Cuerda Tensa, 1950; (novels) La Noria, 1952; Carta de Ayer, 1953; Las Viejas Voces, 1955; Los Otros, 1956; La noche buena, 1957; La Corriente, 1961; El cacique, 1963; (histl.) Tres días de Julio, 1967; also books in Catalan, short stories, travel, histl., etc. Contbr. to: La Vanguardia; Historia y Vida; & num. others. Mbr. Hispanic Soc. of N.Y. Hons: Nadal Novel Prize, 1952; Planeta Novel Prize, 1963. Address: Calle Calabria 152, Barcelona, Spain.

ROMMEL, Mimi Dayton, pen name ROMMEL, Dayton, b. Dubuque, Iowa, USA. Writer. Educ: Rosary Coll., River Forest, Ill.; Univ. of Chgo.; B.A., Ctr. Coll., Danville, Ky.; Univ. of Ky. Publs: Our Bright Summer Days are Gone, 1960; Cry of Peacocks, 1963; Run for the Roses, 1964. Contbr. to: Chgo. Daily News Panorama; Louisville Courier Jrnl.; Filson Club Jrnl; Story Ed., Hallmark Hall of Fame, 1969-73. Mbrships: Nat. Acad. of TV Arts & Scis.; Authors' Guild; Arts Club Chgo.; Arts Club Wash. D.C.; Chgo. Unlimited; Filson Club; DAR. Hons. incl: Clio Award for What a Day commercial for Hallmark, 1971; Hermes Award for same; Chgo. Ad Woman of Yr., 1972. Address: 260 E. Chestnut, Chgo., IL 60611, USA.

RÓNAI, Mihály András, b. 14 Mar. 1913, Budapest, Hungary. Journalist; Essayist; Poet. Educ: Bach. degree, Szeged Univ., Hungary. Publs. incl: Két háború Közt (Between Two Wars, poems), 1937; Parisi rege (Paris Tale, war memoirs), 1947; Ujvilági utazás (New World Journey, travels), 1957; Itália Virágoskertje (Flower Garden of Italy, hist. of mediaeval & renaissance lit. w. transls.), 1964; Hirtelen ébredés (Sudden Awakening, select. of poems), 1967; Magyar Muzsa (Hungarian Muse, essays), forthcoming. Contbr. to num. newspapers, jrnls., reviews, encys., anthols., etc., also to Hungarian Broadcasting Corp. Mbr., num. lit. & profl. orgs. Recip., sev. awards. Address: Gorkij fasor 40, 1068 Budapest, Hungary.

RONALDS, Mary Teresa, b. 30 May 1946, Forest Hill, London, UK. Author. Educ: Coloma Teacher Training Coll., W. Wickham. Publs: The Eyewitness, 1965; Myself My Sepulchre, 1969; The Lion at Midnight, 1971; Prince's Masque, 1973; Gateway to the Gods, 1973; A Victorian Masque, 1975. Recip., PEN Silver Award (Authors under 25 category), for Myself My Sepulchre. Agent: Curtis Brown Ltd. Address: 205 Grangehill Rd., London SE9 1SR, UK.

RONAN, Colin Alistair, b. Chiswick, London, UK. Freelance Writer; Editor. Educ: Imperial Coll.; Univ. Coll., London; M.Sc. Publs: The Universe, 1966; Their Majesties Astronomers, 1967; Invisible Astronomy, 1969; Edmond Halley: Genius in Eclipse, 1970; Lost Discoveries, 1973; Galileo, 1974. Ed., Jrnl. Brit. Astronomical Assn., 1965-. Contbr. to: Ency. Britannica; Sunday Times; Hist. of 20th Century; Weekend Telegraph; Geog. Mag. Mbrships: Assn. Brit. Sci. Writers; Fellow, Royal Astronomical Soc.; Brit. Soc. Hist. of Sci. Address: 39 New Rd., Barton, Cambridge CB3 7AY, UK.

RÓNASZEGI, Miklós, b. 5 June 1930, Budapest, Hungary. Novelist. Educ: B.A. Publs: (novels) A nagy játszma (The Big Game), 1955; Hináros tenger (Tangled Ocean), 1957; A királynő kalóza (The Pirate of the Queen), 1961; Szinház az egész világ (All the World's a Stage, 1963; Keserü Komédia (Bitter Comedy), 1965; An indián hercegnő (The Indian Princess), 1966; Indián halál (Indian Death), 1968; Az indián királyfi (The Indian Prince), 1969; A rovarok lázadása (The Rebellion of Insects), 1970; Az ördögi liquor (Diabolical liquor), 1972; A rettenetes Kartal (Dreaded Kartal), 1974. Contbr. to: Móra Ferenc Publs. (Ed.); etc. Mbrships. incl: PEN; Assn. Hungarian Writers. Address: 1074 Budapest, VII Rákóczi ut. 68, Hungary.

RONILD, Peter, b. 25 Sept. 1928, Copenhagen, Denmark. Author; Actor. Publs: (short stories) Tomorrow the Mushroom Cloud, 1959; Feeding of Snakes in Dead Grass, 1966; The Air Piano, 1972; The Great Dancer, 1974; (novels) The Bodies, 1964; Speak Low, the Moon is Asleep, 1968; var. transls. of TV plays, film, radio play, essays into German, Engl., French, Dutch. Mbrships: Danish Authors' Soc.; Danish Press Assn.; Danish Writers' Club; Danish Playwriters' Assn. Hons: Prize Winner, Danish Radio Short Story Competition, 1960; Schlrship., 1966-69, Travel Schlrship, 1972, Danish Min. of Cultural Affairs. Address: Fredericiagade 12, 1310 Copenhagen K, Denmark.

RONNIE, Arthur William, b. 12 Aug. 1931, L.A., Calif., USA. Television & Motion Picture Publicist. Educ: Assoc. in Arts Degree, L.A. City Coll., 1952. Publs: Locklear: The Man Who Walked on Wings, 1973. Contbr. to: Air Classics; Aloft; Am. Aviation Histl. Soc. Jrnl.; Am. Heritage; Am.-Scandinavia Review; Arch. W.; Cross & Cockade Jrnl.; Jrnl. Broadcasting; Detroit News; Sunday Mag.; Long Beach Indep. Press-Telegram Sunday Mag.; L.A. Mag.; Metrop. Opera News; Page One; Relics; San Fran. Mag.; Sea Classics; Sound Stage; etc. Mbrships: Cath. Press Coun.; Sherlock Holmes Soc. L.A.; PEN. Address: 13041 Roscoe Blvd., Sun Valley, CA 91352, USA.

RÖNNQVIST, Anna Edine, b. 18 Jan. 1899, Påläng, Kalix, Sweden. Author. Publs: Hon. Maria, short stories, 1957; Solvåren (novel), 1961; Stenstrand (novel), 1971; Barnbok, Ett år med Agnes (radio series), 1974. Contbr. to: Norrländsk Tidskrift; Lions Tidning; Fäbodminnen. Mbrships: Swedish Authors' Union; Norlandic Authors' Soc.; Authors' Ctr. Hons: Author's Grant, Swedish Landsbygden, 1962; Author's Grant, Lions, 1962; Norrbottens Läns Cultural Award, 1974. Address: PL 594, 952 00 Kalix, Sweden.

ROOFF, Madeline, b. 1900, London, UK. Writer; University Lecturer in Social Administration. Educ: Bedford Coll. & London Schl. of Econs.; Univ. of London; B.A. Publs: Youth & Leisure, 1935; The Cambridge Evacuation Survey (contbr.), 1941; Voluntary Societies & Social Policy, 1957; A Hundred Years of Family Welfare, 1972. Mbrships. incl: J.P.; Survey Organiser, Carnegie United Kingdom Trust; Educ. & Dev. Organiser, Nat. Coun. of Girls' Clubs. Address: 40 Richmond House, Park Village E., London NW1 3SX, UK.

ROOK, William Alan, b. 31 Oct. 1909, Ruddington, Notts., UK. Company Director; Author. Educ: B.A.(Engl. Lit.), Oxford Univ. Publs: Songs From a Cherry Tree, 1938; Soldiers, This Solitude, 1942; These Are My Comrades, 1943; We Who Are Fortunate, 1945; Not As a Refuge, 1948; Diary of an English Vineyard, 1970. Contbr. to: John o' London's Weekly; Life & Letters Today; Poetry (London); Poetry Quarterly; Times Lit. Supplement; Bugle Blast; Kingdom Come; Listener; Mod. Reading; New Engl. Weekly; Now; Tribune; Wartime Harvest; Poetry (Chgo.); Poetry Review. Address: Stragglethorpe Hall, Lincoln, Lincs., UK.

ROOKE, Daphne Marie, pen name POINTON, Robert, b. 6 Mar. 1914, Boksburg., S. Africa. Novelist. Publs: A Grove of Fever Trees, 1950; Mittee, 1951; Ratoons, 1953; Wizards' Country, 1957; Beti, 1959; A Lover for Estelle, 1961; The Greyling, 1962; Diamond Jo, 1965; Boy on the Mountain, 1969; Margaretha de la Porte, 1974; Apples in the Hold. Mbr., PEN. Recip., Afrikaanse Pers Bpk Novel Prize, 1946. Address: P.O. Bardouroka, N.S.W., Australia 2315.

ROOT, Waverley Lewis, b. 15 Apr. 1903, Providence, R.I., USA. Author. Educ: A.B., Tufts Univ., Medford, Mass. Publs: The Truth About Wagner (co-author), 1929; The Secret History of the War, 3 vols., 1945; Winter Sports in Europe, 1956; The Food of France, 1958; Contemporary French Cooking (co-author), 1962; The Cooking of Italy, 1968; Paris Dining Guide, 1969; The Food of Italy, 1971. Contbr. to: New Yorker; Liberty; Rdr.'s Digest; Encounter; Am. Schlr.; Esquire; Gourmet; Travel & Leisure; McCall's; Town & Country; etc. Mbrships: Pres., Anglo-Am. Press Assn. of Paris; VP, Overseas Press Club, N.Y., USA. Address: 124 rue du Cherche-Midi, 75006 Paris, France.

ROOTHAM, Jasper St. John, b. 21 Nov. 1910, Cambridge, UK. Managing Director, Lazard Brothers & Co. Ltd.; Assistant to Governor, Bank of England, 1965-67; Adviser to Governor, 1946-62. Educ: M.A., St. John's Coll., Cambridge Univ. Publs: Miss-Fire, 1946; Demi-Paradise, 1960; Verses 1928-72, 1973. Contbr. to: Sunday Times;

Tablet; Old Lady. Mbrships: Nat. Farmers' Union; Performing Rights Soc.; Northern Counties Club; Overseas Bankers' Club. Address: Crag House, Wall, Hexham, Northumberland, UK.

ROOTS, Ivan Alan, b. 3 Mar. 1921, Maidstone, UK. Professor of Modern History. Educ: B.A., 1941, M.A., 1945, Balliol Coll., Oxford. Publs: The Committee at Stafford 1643-5 (w. D. H. Pennington), 1957; The Great Rebellion 1642-60, 1966; Cromwell, a Profile, 1973. Contbr. to: Observer; Time & Tide; Listener; Engl. Histl. Review; Hist.; Co-Fndr., The Rota. Mbrships: Fellow, Royal Histl. Soc.; Soc. of Authors; PEN; Radio Writers' Assn.; Econ. Hist. Soc.; Ecclesiastical Hist. Soc.; Histl. Assn. Address: Dept. of Hist., Univ. of Exeter, Exeter, UK.

ROPER, Neil Campbell Ommanney, b. 9 June 1941, Gourock, Scotland, UK. Freelance Translator/Interpreter. Educ: Perugia Univ., Italy; Schl. of Interpreters, Geneva Univ., Switz. Publs: Tides of Destiny (poetry), 1971; (transls.) Catalogie to Mostra Biennale dell' Antiquariato, Florence, 1965; Firmament of Seas/Monde Mers, 1971; The Most Beautiful Horses, 1971. Contbr. to: (anthols.): Gardens of Within; Alba d'Oro, Bouquets of Poems, 1971; Gems of Modern British Poetry. Mbrships: Assoc., Inst. of Linguistis; Fndr Fellow, Int. Poetry Soc., Derbys., UK. Hons. incl: Dip di Benemerenza, Rome (for poem, Stranger), 1971; Grand Prix d'edition, Belgium, 1971; Cert. of Merit, The Writer, 1972. Address: Glebe House, East Meon, Petersfield, Hants., UK.

ROSA, Joseph George, b. 20 Nov. 1932, Chiswick, London, UK. Communications Executive; Freelance Journalist. Publs: They Called Him Wild Bill, 1964, revised & enlarged ed., 1974; Alias Jack McCall, 1967; The Gunfighter: Man or Myth? , 1969; The Pleasure of Guns (w. Robin May), 1974. Contbr. to: Guns Mag.; Guns Review; True West; Old West; Lloyd's Log; Heritage; etc. Mbrships: Arms & Armour Soc., London; Engl. Westerners' Soc.; Western Writers Am. Inc.; Kan. State Histl. Soc.; Mont. Histl. Soc.; Westerners Int.; Westerners of Chicago, Kan. & Kan. City; Brit. Film Inst. Address: 17 Woodville Gdns., Ruislip, Middx. HA4 7NB, UK.

ROSASPINA, Vico Ferdinando, b. 11 Feb. 1917, Marseilles, France. Test Pilot; General Aviation Commercial & Promotional Manager. Publs: Moderno Pilotaggio Razionale. Contbr. to books & jrnls. in field inclng: ALATA; Esquire (Italian ed.); Jane's all the World (Italian sect.); Il Giornale; Aviation Week; Flight. Mbrships. incl: Ordine Nazionale die Giornalisti. Hons. incl: 1st class, Premio Giornalistico Massai, 1964. Address: Via Aurelio Saffi, 31, Milan, Italy.

ROSE, Brian Waldron, b. 1915, London, UK. College Departmental Head. Educ: Trinity Coll., Dublin; Univ. of Witwatersrand, S. Africa; B.A. (Soc. Scis.); B.Ed.; M.A.; Ph.D. Publs: No Mean City; Modern Narrative Poetry, 1953; Modern Lyrical Verse, 1958; Lines of Action, 1961; Bible Plays, 1961; Commonwealth Short Stories, 1962; Education in Southern Africa, 1970; Modern Trends in Education; The Outsiders. Contbr. to: Rand Daily Mail; Folklore; Engl. Studies in Africa. Mbrships: Royal C'wlth. Soc.; Int. Soc. for Study of Communication. Address: 81 Greenside Rd., Greenside, Johannesburg, Repub. of S. Africa.

ROSELAAR, Greta, pen name TREVES, Luisa, b. 15 Nov. 1919, Amsterdam, Netherlands. Dramatist; Literary Advisor for Theatre; Translator. Educ: B.A. Publs: The Ring & the Kelim, 1949; Winterwake, 1950; Don Juan's Letter, 1951; The Minotaur, 1952; The House of the Mountebanks, 1953; Beatrice's Choice, 1954; Arabesque, 1955; Crisis in Egypt, 1955; The Vegetarian Shoemaker, 1956; Rachel, 1959; Content, 1969; Bright New Day, 1974. Contbr. to sev. jrnls. Mbrships: Chmn., Soc. of Dutch Theatre, Radio & TV Dramatists; PEN; Netherlands Lit. Soc. Hons: City of Amsterdam Prize, 1949 & 1951; Prize, Netherlands Lit. Soc., 1949. Address: Schubertstraat 40, Amsterdam 09, Netherlands.

ROSELLE, Daniel, b. 11 Aug. 1920, Bklyn., N.Y., USA. Editor; Director of Publications; Author. Educ: B.S.S., CCNY, 1940; M.A., 1947, Ph.D., 1950, Columbia Univ. Publs. incl: A World History, 1966; Our Western Heritage: A Cultural & Analytic Approach (co-author), 1972; Transformations: Understanding World History Through Science Fiction, 1973, vol. II, 1974; A Parent's Guide to Social Studies, 1974. Contbr. to: Social Educ.; Social Studies; Univ. Review; Nat. Jewish Monthly; etc. Mbrships.

incl: Am. Histl. Assn.; Soc. for French Histl. Studies. Hons. incl: Ed. Writing Awards, Educl. Press Assn. of Am., 1972, 1973; Eleanor Fishburn Award, 1972. Address: c/o Nat. Coun. for the Social Studies, 1201 16th St. NW., Wash. DC 20036, USA.

ROSEMONT, Henry Jr., b. 20 Dec. 1934, Chicago, Ill., USA. Associate Professor of Philosophy. Educ: A.B., Univ. Ill., 1962; Ph.D., Univ. Wash., 1967; MIT. Publs: Work, Technology & Education (w. Walter Feinberg), 1974. Contbr. to: Philos. W. & E.; Choice; Studies in Philos. & Educ.; Monumenta Serica; Jrnl. Aesthetic Educ.; Educl. Theory; Mod. Lang. Jrnl.; Can. Forum; etc. Mbrships: Soc. for Asian & Comp. Philos. (Mbr. Exec. Comm.); Am. Philosl. Assn.; Am. Acad. Relig.; Profl. Staff Congress. Hons. incl: Nat. Sci. Fndn., Sci. Fac. Fellow, 1969-70; MIT Fellow, 1971-72. Address: 183 Waltham St., Lexington, MA 02173, USA.

ROSEN, Dan, b. 31 Aug. 1935, Phila., Pa., USA. Freelance Writer. Educ: Temple Univ., Phila., Pa. Contbr. to: Nation; Saturday Review/World; Nat. Observer; Argosy; True; Dun's Review; Fin. World; Boston Globe; Newsday; New Times; Flying; Columbia Jrnl. of World Bus.; Air Progress; Fin.; etc. Mbrships: Authors' Guild; Authors' League of Am.; Soc. of Mag. Writers. Recip., Russell Sage Fndn. Fellowship, 1973. Address: 10 West 74th St., N.Y., NY 10023, USA.

ROSEN, Sidney, b. 5 June 1916, Boston, Mass., USA. University Professor, Physical Science & Education. Educ: A.B., Univ. of Mass.; M.A., Ph.D., Harvard Univ. Publs: Galileo & the Magic Numbers, 1958; Doctor Paracelsus, 1959; The Harmonious World of Johann Kepler, 1961; Concepts in Physical Science (w. Siegfried & Dennison), 1965; Wizard of the Dome, 1969. Contbr. to num. profl. jrnls. Mbrships. incl: Fellow, AAAS; Am. Assn. of Physics Tchrs.; Authors' Guild. Hons: Fulbright Fellowship, 1963; Clara Ingram Judson Mem. Award, 1970. Address: 1417 Mayfair Rd., Champaign, IL 61820, USA.

ROSENBERG, Bruce Alan, b. 27 July 1934, NYC, USA. University Professor. Educ: B.A., Hofstra Univ., 1955; M.A., Pa. State Univ., 1960; Ph.D., Ohio State Univ., 1965. Publs: Medieval Literature & Folklore Studies, 1970; The Art of the American Folk Preacher, 1970; Custer & the Epic of Defeat, 1974. Contbr. to: Publs. of Mod. Lang. Assn.; Philol. Quarterly; Neuphilologische Mitteilungen; Jrnl. Am. Folklore; Chaucer Review; etc. Mbrships. incl: M.L.A.; Medieval Acad. Am.; Am. Folklore Soc. Hons: James Russell Lowell Prize, 1970; 2nd Prize, Chicago Folklore Competition, 1970; Fellow, Am. Coun. Learned Socs., 1967; Fellow, Nat. Endowment for Humanities, 1972. Address: 223 Burrowes, Univ. Park, PA 16802, USA.

ROSENBERG, Morris, b. 6 May 1922, Brooklyn, N.Y., USA. Professor of Sociology. Educ: B.A., Brooklyn Coll., 1946; M.A., 1950, Ph.D., 1953, Columbia Univ., N.Y. Publs: Co-Ed., The Language of Social Research, 1955; Occupations & Values, 1957; What College Students Think (co-author), 1960; Society & the Adolescent Self-Image, 1965; The Logic of Survey Analysis, 1968; Black & White Self-Esteem (co-author), 1972; Continuities in the Language of Social Research (co-Ed.), 1972. Contbr. to: Am. Jrnl. of Sociol.; Am. Sociol. Review; Soc. Forces; Pub. Opinion Quarterly; Human Rels.; Am. Behavioral Sci. Mbrships. incl: Am. Sociol. Assn.; Past Pres., D.C. Sociol. Assn. Address: Dept. of Sociol., 4224 Ridge Lea Rd., SUNY at Buffalo, Amherst, NY 14226, USA.

ROSENBERGER, Francis Coleman, b. 22 Mar. 1915, Manassas, Va., USA. Attorney at Law. Educ: Univ. of Va.; Geo. Wash. Univ.; LL.B. converted to J.D. Publs: The Virginia Poems, 1943; XII Poems, 1946; Poems 1943-1946, 1947; Ed., anthols., inclng. Virginia Reader: A Treasury of Writings from the First Voyages to the Present, 1948, 2nd ed., 1972; American Sampler: A Selection of New Poetry, 1951; Records of the Columbia Hist. Society, 7 vols., 1960-74. Contbr. to num. anthols. & poetry jrnls.; Book Reviewer, var. newspapers inclng. Washington Post, N.Y., Herald Tribune, Washington Star, N.Y. Times. Address: 6809 Melrose Dr., McLean, VA 22101, USA.

ROSENBERGER, Homer Tope, b. 23 Mar. 1908, Lansdale, Pa., USA. Researcher; Writer; Historical, Museum Commissioner. Educ: B.Sc., Albright Coll., 1929; M.A., 1930, Ph.D., 1932, Cornell Univ.; LL.D., Albright Coll., 1955. Publs. incl: Testing Occupational Training & Experience, 1948; What Should We Expect of Education?, 1956; Letters from Africa, 1965; Adventures & Philosophy of a Pennysylvania Dutchman: An Autobiography in a Broad Setting, 1971; Man and Modern Society, Philosophical Essays, 1972; Mountain Folks: Fragments of Central Pennsylvania Lore, 1974. Contbr. to histol. & educl. jrnls. Address: 2121 Mass. Ave., N.W., Wash DC 20008, USA.

ROSENBLITH, Judy Francis, b. 20 Mar. 1921, Salt Lake City, Utah, USA. Professor of Psychology. Educ: A.B., Univ. of Calif., LA; M.A., Ph.D., Harvard Univ. Publs: Readings in Child Development: Causes of Behavior, 1973; Readings in Educational Psychology: Causes of Behavior, 1973; Ed., The Causes of Behavior: Readings in Child Development & Educational Psychology (w. W. Allinsmith), 1962, 3rd ed., Causes of Behavior (w. W. Allinsmith & J. P. Williams), 1972. Contbr. to: Child Dev.; Biol. of the Neonate; Jrnl. of Abnormal & Soc. Psychol.; Psychol. Reports & Monographs; Am. Jrnl. of Psychol.; etc. Mbrships. incl: Fellow, Am. Psychol. Assn.; Sec., Soc. for Rsch. in Child Dev., 1965-69. Address: 164 Mason Ter., Brookline, MA, USA.

ROSENFELD, Friedrich, pen name FELD, b. 5 Dec. 1902, Vienna, Austria. Journalist; Film & Drama Critic; Fiction Editor. Educ: Univ. of Vienna. Publs: Tirilin's Travels Around the World, 1931; 1414 Goes on Holiday, 1948; The Musical Umbrella, 1950; The Runaway Echo, 1950; The Raven Yuan, 1962; The Cabinboy of the Santa Maria, 1966; The Master of Mainz, 1967; The King's Comedians, 1967; about 60 children's books, written in German & transl'd into num. langs.; num. radio plays. Contbr. to sev. German & Swiss jrnls. Mbrships: Ctr. of German-speaking Writers Abroad, PEN; Belgian Soc. of Writers, Composers & Eds.; Assn. of German Writers. Recip., sev. prizes for children's books. Address: 7 First Ave., Bexhill-on-Sea, Sussex, UK.

ROSENGREN, Bernt, b. 17 June 1937, Stockholm, Sweden. Author; Literary Critic. Publs. incl: Ror i läl (novel), 1963; Nytorgaren (poetry), 1966; En dröm om styrka (novel), 1968; Den sprängda ligan (novel), 1969; Beväpningar (poetry), 1970; Svampe och Busen (children's book), 1972; Du är inte ofarlig (TV drama), 1974. Contbr. to: Aftonbladet, 1965—; Bonniers Litterära Magasin, 1965-69. Mbrships. incl: Swedish Union of Writers. Recip., TUC Cultural Prize, 1971. Address: Glanshammarsgatan 49, 124 46 Bandhagen, Stockholm, Sweden.

ROSENSAFT, Menachem Z., b. 1948, Bergen Belsen, Germany. Author. Educ: Johns Hopkins Univ., Balt., USA. Publs: Moshe Sharett, Statesman of Israel, 1966; Fragments Past & Future (verse), 1970; Not Backward to Belligerency: Israel & the Arab States, 1970; Ed., Bergen Belson Youth Mag., 1965. Contbr. to: Jerusalem Post; Jewish Chronicle; Jewish Quarterly; etc. Address: 179 E. 70th St., N.Y., NY 10021, USA.

ROSENTHAL, Eric, b. 10 July 1905, Cape Town, S. Africa. Author; Broadcaster. Educ: Univ. of Witwatersrand, Johannesburg. Publs: over 40 books on Southern Africa incing: From Drury Lane to Mecca, 1931; Other Men's Millions, 1953; River of Diamonds, 1957; Encyclopedia of Southern Africa, 1961, 6th ed., 1973; Southern African Dictionary of National Biography, 1966; General De Wet, 3rd ed., 1968; Stars & Stripes in Africa, 2nd ed., 1968; They Walk By Night, 3rd ed., 1968; Runner & Mail Coach, 1969; Meet Me at the Carlton, 1972; You Have Been Listening, 1974; The Rand Rush, 1974. Contbr. to Ency. Britannica. Mbrships: PEN; Inst. of Jrnlsts.; Soc. of Authors. Address: P.O. Box 3800, Cape Town, Repub. of S. Africa.

ROSENTHAL, Harold David, b. 30 Sept. 1917, London, UK. Magazine Editor; Lecturer; Broadcaster. Educ: B.A., Univ. of London, 1940; Dip.Ed., Inst. of Educ., 1946. Publs: Sopranos of Today, 1956; Two Centuries of Opera at Covent Garden, 1958; A Concise Oxford Dictionary of Opera (w. John Warrack), 1964; Opera Bedside Book, 1965; Mapleson Memoires (Ed. & annotator), 1966; Covent Garden — A Short History, 1967. Contbr. to var. jrnls., UK & abroad. Mbrships: Coun. & Mgmt. Comm., Friends of Covent Garden; Music Sect., Critics' Circle. Address: 6 Woodland Rise, London N10 3UH, UK.

ROSEVEARE, Ursula Stella Catherine, b. 26 Oct. 1914, London, UK. Teacher; Lecturer; Broadcaster. Educ: B.A., King's Coll., London, 1934; Pensionnat Français, Nijwegen, Holland, 1935. Publs: Selected Stories from the Ballet, 1954. Contbr. to sev. jrnls.; radio; TV. Mbrships: Univ.

Women's Club; Press Club; PEN; Critics' Circle, London; Imperial Soc. of Tchrs. of Dancing. Address: 4 Abbey's, 15 Abbey Hill, Kenilworth, Warwicks., UK.

ROSHWALB, Irving, b. 24 Jan. 1924, NYC, USA. Statistician. Educ: B.S., CCNY, 1943; M.A., Columbia Univ., 1947. Publs: How to Conduct Surveys, 1970; Nomograms for Marketing Research, 1971; Games Your Father Played, 1972; Dictionary for Marketing Research, 1974. Contbr. to: Jrnl. Advt. Rsch.; Jrnl. Mktng. Rsch.; Jrnl. Am. Statistical Assn.; Sci. Mbrships: Am. Assn. for Pub. Opinion Rsch.; World Assn. for Pub. Opinion Rsch.; Int. Assn. Survey Statns.; Mkt. Rsch. Coun. Address: 9 Sycamore Dr., Great Neck, NY 11021, USA.

ROSKAM, Karel Lodewijk, pen names KALAMU; DUTCHMAN, b. 7 Mar. 1931, Amsterdam, Netherlands. Radio Commentator; Former Teacher. Educ: Doct. in Law, Free Univ., Amsterdam. Publs: Apartheid & Discrimination, 1960; Alleen voor Blanken, 1961; Dekolonisatie van Afrika, 1973. Contbr. to jrnls. incing: Kroniek von Afrika (ed., 1966-71); African Soc. Rsch. Documents (ed., 1970 & 1971); Orbis Terrarum (ed.); Vrÿ Nederland (columnist, 1963-66). Mbr., civic & pol. orgs. Address: Meidoornstraat 14, Bussum, Netherlands.

ROSKILL, Mark Wentworth, b. 10 Nov. 1933, London, UK. Art Historian & Critic. Educ: B.A., 1956, M.A., 1961, Univ. of Cambridge; M.A., Harvard Univ., USA, 1957; M.F.A., Ph.D., Princeton Univ., N.J., 1961. Publs: English Painting from 1500 to 1865, 1959; Dolce's "Aretino" & Venetian Art-Theory of the Sixteenth Century, 1968; Van Gogh, Gauguin & the Impressionist Circle, 1970; How Art History Works, 1975; Ed., The Letters of Vincent van Gogh, 1963. Contbr. to: Art News; Arts Mag.; Art Int.; Listener; Burlington Mag.; Oud Holland; Victorian Studies; Paris Review; Counter/Measures. Mbr., Coll. Art Assn. of Am. Recip., Fellowships, Am. Coun. of Learned Socs., 1965-66 & 1974-75. Address: Dept. of Art, Univ. of Mass., Amherst, MA 01002, USA.

ROSOCHA, Stephen, b. 27 May 1908, Drahovo, Carpatho-Ukraine. Editor, Probojem Mag., 1933-44, Nastup Weekly, 1938-44, Prague, Czechoslovakia; New Pathway, Winnipeg, Canada, 1952-53; Vilne Slovo, Toronto, 1960—. Educ: Grad., Charles Univ., Prague, 1934; B.A., Ukrainian Free Univ., Prague, 1936; LL.D. Publs: Parliament of Carpatho-Ukraine, 1949; 21 Days in Europe, 1974. Contbr. to: "Slovo" Almanachs, 1961-75; num. newspapers & mags., Europe & Can. Mbrships. incl: Carpatho-Ukrainian Parliament & Staabs (HQ) Officer, Carpatho-Ukrainian Army Karpatsha Sich; Ukrainian Cultural & Educl. Ctr., Winnipeg, Can.; Ukrainian Jrnlsts.' Assn., Toronto; Can. Br., Shevchenko Soc. of Scis.; Free Ukrainian Acad. of Sci., Winnipeg. Address: 196 Bathurst St., Toronto, Ont. M5T 2R8, Can.

ROSS, Alan, b. 6 May 1922, Calcutta, India. Editor. Educ: St. John's Coll., Oxford Univ. Publs. incl: The Derelict Day, 1947; The Forties, 1950; Poetry 1945-50, 1951; The Bandit on the Billiard Table, 1954 (revised as South to Sardinia, 1960); Australia 55, 1956; To Whom It May Concern, 1958; Ed., The Cricketer's Companion, 1960; African Negatives, 1962; North from Sicily, 1965; Poems 1942-67, 1968; Tropical Ice, 1972; The Taj Express, 1973; Ed., London Mag. Stories 1—8, 1964-73. Contbr. to: London Mag. (Ed.); Observer (staff, 1950-71); var. jrnls. Mbrships: F.R.S.L. Recip., Atlantic Award for Lit., 1946. Address: 5 Pelham Cres., London SW7, UK.

ROSS, Ian Simpson, b. 9 Aug. 1930, Dundee, UK. Professor of English, University of British Columbia. Educ: M.A., St. Andrews Univ.; B.Litt., Oxon.; Ph.D., Tex. Publs: Lord Kames & the Scotland of His Day, 1972; Correspondence of Adam Smith (w. Ernest C. Mossner), forthcoming. Contbr. to: Philol. Quarterly; Review of Engl. Lit.; Tex. Studies in Lit. & Lang.; Huntingdon Lib. Quarterly; Studies in Scottish Lit. Mbr., sev. profl. & lit. orgs. Recip., sev. acad. grants. Address: 5788 Angus Dr., Vancouver, B.C. V6M 3N8, Can.

ROSS, Isaac, pen name ROSS, George, b. 29 July 1907, Johannesburg, S. Africa. Accountant. Educ: Bach. of Commerce, Witwatersrand Univ., Johannesburg. Publs: plays all w. Campbell Singer: Any Other Business, 1959 (as Calculated Risk, adapted by Joseph Hayes for Broadway, USA 1963); Guilty Party, 1962; Difference of Opinion, 1964; Those in Favour, 1973. Mbrships: Soc. of Authors, UK; League of Dramatists, USA. Address: 26 St. Stephens Ave., London W13 8ES, UK.

ROSS, Sam, b. 10 Mar. 1912, Narodich, Russia. Writer. Educ: B.S., Northwestern Univ. Publs: He Ran All the Way, 1947; Someday Boy, 1948; The Side-Walks are Free, 1950; Port Unknown, 1951; This Too, Is Love, 1953; You Belong to Me, 1955; The Tight Corner, 1956; The Hustlers, 1956; Ready for the Tiger, 1964; Day of the Shark, 1967; Hang-Up, 1968; The Fortune Machine, 1970; The Golden Box, 1971; Solomon's Palace, 1973. Mbr., Writers' Guild Am. W. Address: 2923 Grayson Ave., Venice, CA 90291, USA.

ROSS, Sinclair, b. 22 Jan. 1908, Shellbrook, Sask., Can. Retired Bank Official. Publs: (novels) As for Me & My House, USA 1941; The Well, Can. 1958; Whir of Gold, Can. 1970; (short stories) The Lamp at Noon & Other Stories, 1968. Contbr. to: Queen's Quarterly, Kingston, Ont. Address: Apartado 5362. Barcelona, Spain.

ROSS, William Edward Daniel, pen names ROSS, Marilyn; ROSS, Clarissa; ROSS, W. E. D.; RANDOLPH, Ellen; STEEL, Tex, b. 16 Nov. 1912, St. John, N.B., Can. Author. Educ: Univs. of Okla., Chgo. & Mich., USA. Publs: 239 books inclng. Dark Shadows, 1968; Our Share of Love, 1969; Shadows over the Garden, 1971; China Shadow, 1974; 600 short stories. Contbr. to: London Evening News; N.Y. Daily News; Saint Mystery Mag.; Mike Shayne Mystery Mag; etc. Mbrships. incl: Can. Authors' Assn. (Nat. Exec. & Pres., N.B. Br.); Soc. of Authors, UK; Authors' League of Am. Hons: Dominion Drama Festival Prize for Playwriting, 1934; Collection of Works in Boston Univ., 1968-. Address: P.O. Box 190, Rothesay, N.B. EOG 2WO, Can.

RÖSSEL, James, b. 15 May 1912, Stockholm, Sweden. Writer; Translator. Educ: Fil.kand., Univ. of Stockholm, 1936. Publs: Mark Twain, 1945; Kvinnorna och kvinnororelsen, 1950; Inter Alia (essays), 1951; Amerikanska skämttecknare, 1955; . . .et cetera (essays), 1963; Diverser (humorous verse), 1967. Mbr., Swedish Writers' Guild. Address: Kungsstensgatan 61 I, 113 29 Stockholm, Sweden.

ROSSI, Marianna, b. N.Y., USA. Copywriter; Author; Artist. Educ: Adelphi Univ., Garden City, L.I.; Rutgers Univ., Paterson, N.J. Publs: The Mustard Seed, 1964; Beyond A Shadow of Doubt, 1971. Contbr. to: McCall's Mag.; Fate Mag.; Beyond Reality Mag.; Brooklyn Eagle; Poets of Am., 1941; Caligraph Anthols., 1947-48; Terror & Fantasy Anthol. of 1974; var. Am. pol. jrnls. Ed., Engl. Sect., Italian Chronicle newspaper. Mbrships: Int. Acad. of Poets, 1964; Am.-Vatican Artists & Writers. Hons. incl: Citation as Most Important N. Am. Woman Writer against Communism, Journalistica Roma, Italy, 1968; Authors Award, Newark Coll. of Engrng., 1974; Writers Award, Steuben Police Org. of N.J.; 1st Prize for war poem, Prisoner of War, Anton Romatka Poetry Classes, Greenwich Village, NYC. Address: 15 Highfield Ct., Wayne, NJ 07470, USA.

ROSSITER, Percival Stuart Bryce, b. 1923, Leyton, Essex, UK. Editor, Blue Guides, 1963—. Educ: King's Coll., Cambridge; M.A. Publ: The London Quiz Book, 1957. Contbr. to: Varsity; Observer; Daily Telegraph; Guardian; Swimming Times; etc. Address: 27 Hillside Gdns., Walthamstow, London E17, UK.

ROSS-MACDONALD, Malcolm John, future pen name MACDONALD, Malcolm, b. 29 Feb. 1932, Chipping Sodbury, Glos., UK. Writer. Educ: Nat. Dip. in Design (Painting), 1954; Slade Dip. (Painting), 1958. Publs: The Big Waves, 1962; Spare Part Surgery (w. D. Longmore), 1968; Machines in Medicine (w. D. Longmore), 1969; The Heart (w. D. Longmore), 1971; The World Wildlife Guide (author/ed.), 1971; Beyond the Horizon, 1971; Kristina's Winter (radio play), 1972; Conditional People (radio play), 1973; Every Living Thing, 1974; Doors Doors Doors, 1974; Life in the Future, 1975; World From Rough Stones (under pen name), 1974. Mbrships: Soc. of Authors; Radio Writers Assn. Address: c/o Agent, David Higham Assocs., 5-8 Lower John St., London W1R 4HA, UK.

ROSS WILLIAMSON, Hugh, b. 2 Jan. 1901, Romsey, Hants., UK. Author. Publs. incl: The Poetry of T. S. Eliot, 1932; The Arrow & the Sword, 1947; The Silver Bowl, 1948; The Gunpowder Plot, 1951; The Great Prayer, 1955; The Day They Killed the King, 1957; A Wicked Pack of Cards, 1961; The Marriage Made in Blood, 1968; The Great Betrayal, 1971; (plays) In a Glass Darkly, 1931; Heart of Bruce, 1959; Pavane for a Dead Infanta, 1968; (autobiography) The Walled Garden, 1953. Former Contbr.

to: Strand Mag.; Bookmen. Mbr., R.S.L. Address: 11a St. Barnabas Rd., Cambridge, UK.

ROSTAND, Jean, b. 30 Oct. 1894. Writer; Biologist. Publs. incl: La loi des riches; Igance ou l'Écrivain; Les Chromosomes; L'Aventure humaine; La Vie des Vers à soie; La Vie & ses problèmes; L'Homme; Pensées d'un biologiste; Les Idées nouvelles de la génétique; L'Evolution des espèces; La genèse de la Vie; L'Avenir de la Biologie; Science & Génération; Esquisse d'une histoire de la biologie; Ce que je Crois. Mbr., French Acad. Recip., Kalinga Prize, 1959. Address: 29 rue Pradier, 92 Ville d'Avray (Seine-et-Oise), France.

ROSTEN, Leo (Calvin), pen name ROSS, Leonard Q., b. 11 Apr. 1908, Lodz, Poland. University Lecturer; Consultant. Educ: Ph.B., 1930, Ph.D., 1937, Chgo. Univ. Publs. incl: (novels) The Education of Hyman Kaplan, USA & UK 1937; The Return of Hyman Kaplan, USA & UK 1959; Captain Newman, M.D., UK 1961, USA 1962; A Most Private Intrigue, USA & UK 1967; (non-fiction) The Washington Correspondents, 1937; The Many Worlds of Leo Rosten, 1964 (as The Leo Rosten Bedside Book, UK 1965); The Joys of Yiddish, USA 1968, UK 1970; Rome Wasn't Burned in a Day, 1972; var. screenplays. Mbrships: Authors' League of Am. (Nat. Bd.); NEA. Recip., num. grants & awards. Address: c/o Doubleday & Co. Inc., 277 Park Ave., N.Y., NY 10017, USA.

ROTH, Christian, pen name (as newspaper columnist) BRDLBRMPFT, b. 27 June 1945, Zurich, Switz. Typographer. Educ: Schl. of Applied Art, Zurich. Publs: Die Fuenf Unbekannten, 1970; Christopher Rotta, 1975. Contbr. to Echo vom Maiengrün. Mbr., Soc. of German-speaking Authors. Address: Eggental 71, CH-5607 Hägglingen, Aargau, Switz.

ROTH, Gerhard Jurgen, b. 24 June 1942, Graz, Austria. Writer. Publs: Die Autobiographie des Albert Einstein, 1972; Der Ausbruch des ersten Weltkriegs, 1972; Der Wille zur Krankheit, 1973; Herr Mantel und Herr Hemd, 1974; Der grosse Horizont, 1974. Contbr. to Protokolle. Mbrships: Forum-Stadrpark Graz; Grazer Autorenversamm-lung. Hons: Lit. Grants, 1972, 1973; Forderungspreis für Lit., Graz, 1974. Address: Brucknerstrasse 6, A-8010 Graz, Austria.

ROTH, Henry, b. 8 Feb. 1906, Tysmenica, Austria-Hungary. Waterfowl Farmer. Educ: B.S., CCNY, 1928. Publs: Call It Sleep (novel), 1934, republd. 1960, UK 1963; var. short stories. Hons: Grant, Nat. Inst. Arts & Letters, 1965; Townsend Harris Medal, CCNY, 1965; D. H. Lawrence Fellowship, Univ. of N.M., 1968. Address: 741 Chavez Rd., Albuquerque, NM 87107, USA.

ROTH, June Doris Spiewak, b. 16 Feb. 1926, Haverstraw, N.Y., USA. Author. Educ: Pa. State Univ., 1942-44. Publs: Freeze & Please Home Freezer Cookbook, 1963; Rich & Delicious Low Calorie Cookbook, 1964; Thousand Calorie Cookbook, 1967; Fast & Fancy Cookbook, 1969; How to Use Sugar to Lose Weight, 1969; How to Cook Like a Jewish Mother, 1969; Take Good Care of my Son, Cookbook for Brides, 1969; The Indoor/Outdoor Barbecue Book, 1970; Pick of the Pantry Cookbook, 1970; Let's Have a Brunch Cookbook, 1971; The On-Your-Own Cookbook, 1972; Edith Bunker's All in the Family Cookbook, 1972; Healthier Jewish Cookery, The Unsaturated Fat Way, 1972; Elegant Desserts, 1973; Old-Fashioned Candymaking, 1974. Mbrships: Authors' League of Am.; Soc. of Mag. Writers. Address: 1057 Oakland Court, Teaneck, NJ 07666, USA.

ROTH, Philip, b. 19 Mar. 1933, Newark, N.J., USA. Writer. Educ: A.B., Bucknell Univ., Lewisburg, Pa., 1954; M.A., Univ. of Chgo., Ill., 1955. Publs: Goodbye, Columbus, 1959; Letting Go, 1962; When She Was Good, 1967; Portnoy's Complaint, 1969; Our Gang, 1971; The Breast, 1972; The Great American Novel, 1973; My Life as a Man, 1974; Reading Myself & Others, 1975. Contbr. to: Esquire; Am. Review; N.Y. Review of Books; Paris Review; Partisan Review; Atlantic; Harper's. Mbrships: Nat. Inst. of Arts & Letters; Am. Acad. of Arts & Scis. Hons. incl: Daroff Award, Jewish Book Coun. of Am., 1959; Nat. Book Award for Fiction, 1960; Rockefeller Fndn. Grant, 1965. Address: Farrar, Straus, & Giroux, 19 Union Sq., N.Y., USA.

ROTHA, Paul, b. 3 June 1907, London, UK. Film Producer; Journalist; Writer. Educ: Slade Schl. of Art. Publs. incl: The Film Today, 1931; Television in the

Making, 1956; Documentary Diary, a History of the British Documentary Film, 1973; (films) The World is Rich; A City Speaks; Cover to Cover; Cradle of Genius, 1959; The Life of Adolf Hitler, 1961; De Overval (Silent Raid), 1962. Contbr. to Connoisseur, 1927-28. Mbrships: Coun. Brit. Film Acad., (Chmn., 1951); Critics' Circle, London. Hons. incl: Brit. Film Acad. Award, 1948. Address: c/o John Farquarson, 13 Red Lion Sq., London WC1, UK.

ROTHENSTEIN, (Sir) John Knewstub Maurice, b. 11 July 1901, Director of The Tate (1938-64) & Other Art Galleries; University Professor. Educ: M.A., Worcester Coll., Oxford Univ., 1927; Ph.D., Univ. Coll., London, 1931. Publs. incl: An Introduction to English Painting, 1934; Augustus John, 1944; Modern English Painters, 3 vols., 1952-74; Turner, 1960; Sickert, 1961; Paul Nash, 1961; Francis Bacon, 1967; (autobiog. in 3 parts) Summer's Lease, 1965; Brave Day, Hideous Night, 1966; Time's Thievish Progress, 1970; Edward Burra, 1972. Mbrships. incl: Athenaeum Club. Hons. incl: Kt., 1952; C.B.E., 1948; Kt.-Cmdr., Order Aztec Eagle Mexico, 1953. Address: Beauforest Ho., Newington, Dorchester-on-Thames, Oxford OX9 8AG, UK.

ROTHSCHILD, Joseph, b. 5 Apr. 1931, Fulda, Germany. Professor of Political Science. Educ: A.B., 1951, A.M., 1952, Columbia Univ., USA; D.Phil., Oxford Univ., UK 1955. Publs: The Communist Party of Bulgaria: Origins & Development; 1883-1936, 1959; Communist Eastern Europe, 1964; Pilsudski's Coup d'Etat, 1966; East Central Europe Between the Two World Wars, 1974. Contbr. to var. pol. jrnls.; etc. Mbrships: Phi Beta Kappa; Acad. of Pol. Sci.; Am. Assn. for the Advancement of Slavic Studies; Am. Pol. Sci. Assn. Hons: Henryk Gruber Prize, Pilsudski Soc. of Am., 1968; J. S. Guggenheim Fellow, 1967-68. Address: 445 Riverside Drive, N.Y., NY 10027, USA.

ROTHSCHILD, Richard Charles, b. 24 Mar. 1895, Chgo., Ill., USA. Writer. Educ: B.A., Yale Univ., 1916. Publs: Paradoxy, The Destiny of Modern Thought, 1931; Reality & Illusion, A New Framework of Values, 1934; Three Gods Give an Evening to Politics, 1936. Address: 1165 Park Ave., N.Y., NY 10028, USA.

ROTHWELL, Talbot, b. 12 Nov. 1916, Bromley, UK. Screenwriter. Educ: Brighton Art Coll. Publs: (stage plays) Queen Elizabeth Slept Here; Meet the Wives; Once Upon a Crime; Anything for Baby; (films) The "Carry On" series. Mbr., Screenwriters' Guild. Address: The Paddock, Fulking, Henfield, Sussex, UK.

ROUBAIX, Paul, b. 13 June 1920, near Cape Town, S. Africa. Teacher; Writer. Educ: M.A., York; B.A., Cape Town; B.Ed., Toronto. Publs. incl: Storm en onder Eenbedrywe, 1951; Nuwe Apostoliese Gesangboek (transl.), 1968; California Would Be Heaven & Other Plays, 1975; Let My Jesus Live, 1975; (plays) Spanish Flames, 1948; Storm, 1948; Here Endeth, 1948; Though I Speak, 1948; Dream Without Blossoms, 1951; Bitter Road, 1951; Hour of Glory, 1956; Cry, Mr. Zero, 1967. Contbr. to newspapers & mags. Mbrships: Past Pres., S. African Arts Union; Fndn. Exec. Mbr., Southern African Lawn Tennis Union; Artists' Workshop, Toronto. Hons. incl: Prizewinner, Scopus Club Drama Festival, 1956. Address: 184 Woodsworth Rd., Willowdale, Ont., Can.

ROUCEK, Joseph S., b. 30 Sept. 1902, Slany, Czech. Professor of Sociology & Political Science (Ret'd). Educ: B.A., Occidental Coll., USA, 1925; Ph.D., 1928, M.A., 1937, N.Y. Univ. Publs. incl: Politics of the Balkans, 1939; Balkan Politics, 1948; The Development of Educational Sociology: School, Society & Sociology, 1956; Behind the Iron Curtain (w. Kenneth V. Lottich), 1964; The Czechs & Slovaks in America, 1967. Contbr. to num. Am. & for. jrnls. Mbrships: Am. Sociol. Assn.; Am. Pol. Sci. Assn. Hons: Cmdr., Kt. of the Crown of Romania; Cmdr., Kt. of the Crown of Yugoslavia. Address: 395 Lakeside Drive, Bridgeport, CT 06606, USA.

ROUD, Richard, b. 6 July 1929, Boston, Mass., USA. Film Festival Director; Journalist; Film Critic, The Guardian, 1963-70; Roving Arts Critic, The Guardian, 1970—. Educ: B.A., Univ. Wis., USA, 1950; Univ. Montpellier, France, 1950-51; Univ. Birmingham, UK, 1951-53. Publs: Godard, 1967, revised ed., 1970, latest ed., 1971; Sträub, 1971, latest ed., 1972. Contbr. to: Sight & Sound; Film Comment. Mbr., Critics' Circle. Address: 107 Park St., London W1Y 3FB, UK.

ROUDY, Pierre, b. 1927, Angoulême, France. Director, National Drama School, Paris; Editor, Plays for Children,

Magnard (Publisher); Professor, National School of Journalism. Educ: Bordeaux Univ.; Sorbonne, Paris; Lic. ès Lettres; D. ès Lettres. Publs: L'espoir au clou, 1957; La Florisane, 1958; Promenades dans Pary (radio series), 1970; Promenades Artistiques (TV series), 1971; La Chasse est Finie (play), 1972; Méthodologie de la Langue Anglaise, 1972; The Four Seasons by Wesker (transl.), 1972; La Princesse du Portugal by T. Dery (transl.), 1972; sev. plays in French & Engl. Contbr. to: Les Temps Modernes; Europe; Preuves; Education; etc. Mbrships: Pres., Arts et Education; Ministerial Commn. on Theatre & Educ.; Int. Commn. on Theatre & Educ. Agent: Bureau Littéraire International. Address: 21 rue Blanche, Paris 9, France.

ROUECHÉ, Berton, b. 16 Apr. 1911, Kan. City, Mo., USA. Writer. Educ: B.A., Univ. of Mo. Publs: Black Weather (novel), 1945; 11 Blue Men (Engl. title, Annals of Medical Detection), 1955; The Incurable Wound, 1956; The Delectable Mountains, 1958; What's Left, 1968; The Orange Man, 1972; Feral (novel), 1974; Desert & Plain, the Mountains & the River, 1975. Contbr. to: New Yorker. Hons: Albert Lasker Med. Jrnlsm. Awards, 1950, 1960; Mystery Writers of Am. Special Award, 1955; Am. Med. Assn. Med. Jrnlsm. Award, 1970. Address: Stony Hill Rd., Amagansett, L.I., N.Y., USA.

ROUNTREE, Thomas J., b. 22 July 1927, Pinckard, Ala., USA. University Professor of English. Educ: B.A., Troy State Univ., Ala., 1950; M.A., Univ. of Ala., 1952; Ph.D., Tulane Univ., 1962. Publs: This Mighty Sum of Things, 1965; The Last of the Mohicans: Notes, 1965; Emma: Notes, 1967; Critics on Hawthorne, 1972; Critics on Melville, 1972; Critics on Emerson, 1973. Contbr. to: Publs. of MLA; Jrnl. of Am. Folklore; & other lit. jrnls. Mbrships. incl: MLA; The Wordsworth Circle. Hons. incl: Prewitt Semmes Creative Writing Awards, 1951, 1953; 1st Prize Short Story Award, Birmingham Fest. of Arts, Ala., 1963. Address: Box U-342, Univ. of S. Alabama, Mobile, AL 36688, USA.

ROUQUETTE, Max, b. 8 Dec. 1908, Argelliers, Languedoc, France. Doctor of Medicine; Writer. Educ: B.A., M.D. Publs: (poetry) Somnis dau Matin, 1957; Somnis de la Nuoch, 1942; La Pietat dau Matin, 1963; (novels) Verd Paradis (I), 1961; Verd Paradis (II), 1974; (plays) Le Médecin de Cucugnan, 1955; La Comedie du Miroir, 1957. Contbr. to var. theatrical prods. Mbrships: PEN (Pres. Langue d'oc); L'Institut d'Etudes Occitanes (Pres., 1946-50). Recip., Grand Prix Dramatic Art Casino d'Enghien, 1958. Address: 2 rue de l'Ançien, Courrier 34000, Montpellier, France.

ROUSE, Michael Henry, b. 12 Mar. 1940, Ely, UK. Teacher. Educ: Kesteven Coll. of Educ. Publs: Spinney Abbey & Wicken, 1972; Ely Cathedral City & Market Town (w. Reg. Holmes), 1972; A View into Cambridgeshire, 1974; A City Celebrates, 1974. Contbr. to: Cambs. Huntingdon & Peterborough Life; Tomorrow, Nat. Young Conservative Newspaper (Ed., 1971-75). Mbrships: E. Cambs. Dist. Coun.; City of Ely Coun. Address: 5 Lynton Dr., Ely, Cambs., UK.

ROUSSEAUX, André, b. 23 Mar. 1896. Author; Critic. Publs. incl: Littérature du XX Siècle, 6 vols., 1938-58; Le Monde Classique, 7 vols., 1942-56; Le Prophète Péguy, 2 vols., 1946; & num. works of criticism. Contbr. to Figaro. Mbr., PEN. Recip., Legion of Honour. Address: 5 rue d'Assas, Paris 6e, France.

ROUSSIN, André Jean Paul, b. 22 Jan. 1911. Playwright. Educ: Inst. Mélizan, Marseilles. Publs. incl: Une grande fille toute simple; Le Tombeau d'Achille; La Sainte Famille; La Petite Hutte; Nina; Bobosse; La main de César; Le Mari; la Femme & la Mort; L'Amour Fou; La Mamma; L'Ecole des Autres; Un amour qui ne finit pas; La Voyante; La Locomotive; On ne sais jamais; Patience & Impatience; Un contentement raisonnable. Mbr., French Acad. Hons: Officier de Mérite Nat.; Legion of Honour; Commander, Arts & Letters. Address: 12 Place de Victoires, Paris 2e, France.

ROUTLEY, Erik Reginald, b. 31 Oct. 1917, Brighton, UK. Minister, United Reformed Church; Professor of Church Music. Educ: M.A., 1943, B.D., 1946, D.Phil., 1952, Oxon.; F.R.S.C.M., 1965; Fellow, Westminster Choir Coll., USA, 1971. Publs: Hymns & Human Life, 1952; Hymns & the Faith, 1955; The Gift of Conversion, 1957; The English Carol, 1958; The English Free Churches, 1960; Into a Far Country, 1962; 20th-Century Church Music, 1964; The Man for Others, 1964; Words, Music & the

Church, 1968; The Musical Wesleys, 1969; The Puritan Pleasures of the Detective Story, 1972. Contbr. to var. relig. jrnls. Mbr., Ch. Socs. Address: Westminster Choir Coll., Princeton, NJ 08540, USA.

ROWAT, Donald C., b. 1921, Somerset, Man., Can. University Professor, Educ: B.A., Toronto Univ., 1943; M.A., Columbia Univ., USA, 1946; Ph.D., 1950. Publs. incl: The Reorganisation of Provincial-Municipal Relations in Nova Scotia, 1949; Your Local Government, 1955, paperback ed., 1962, 1965, 1968; The Ombudsman: Citizens' Defender, 1965; The Canadian Municipal System: Essays on the Improvement of Local Government, 1969; The University Society & Government, 1970; Provincial Government & Politics: Comparative Essays, 1972, 1973; The Ombudsman Plan: Essays on the Worldwide Spread of an Idea, 1973; The Government of Federal Capitals, 1973. Address: Dept. of Pol. Sci., Carleton Univ., Ottawa 1, Can.

ROWE, Alick Edward, b. 18 Sept. 1938, Kingston, UK. Playwright; Former Teacher. Educ: M.A., Cambridge Univ. Publs: (TV Plays) The Master & the Mask, 1970; Up School, 1970; Refuge for a Hero, 1972; Harriet's Back in Town (4 episodes in series), 1973; Intimate Strangers (3 episodes in series), 1974; Just Fine, 1974. Radio Plays: The Great Balloon Debate, 1970; Fawcettı Fawcettı, 1970; A Passing of Power, 1970; Accomplices, 1971; Exposure, 1971; Apples & Tea, 1972; Observations on a Jesting Man, 1972; No Frontiers for the Captain, 1974; var. adaptations. Contbr. to: 19; Reveille; Esquire; Good Housekeeping; Introduction 5, 1974. Mbr., Writers' Guild of GB. Address: Pwll Fforest, Pengenffordd, Talgarth, Powys LD3 OET, UK.

ROWEN, Herbert Harvey, b. 22 Oct. 1916, NYC, USA. Historian. Educ: B.S. (Social Sci.), CCNY, 1936; M.A., 1948; Ph.D., 1951, Columbia Univ. Publs. incl: A History of Early Modern Europe 1500-1815, 1961; Ed. & transl., America: A Dutch Historian's Vision from Afar & Near, by J. Huizinga, 1962; Ed., The Low Countries in Early Modern Times: A Documentary History, 1972. Contbr. to: Reviews in European Hist. (Ed.); French Histl. Studies; etc. Mbrships. incl: Am. Histl. Assn.; Nederlands Historisch Genootschap. Address: 3 Lemore Circle, Rocky Hill, NJ 08553, USA.

ROWEN, Ruth Halle, b. 1918, NYC, USA. University Teacher; Professor, CUNY. Educ: Barnard Coll.; Columbia Univ.; M.A.; Ph.D. Publs: Early Chamber Music; Hearing — Gateway to Music (co-author). Contbr. to: Music Quarterly; Piano Quarterly. Mbrships: Am. Musicol. Soc.; Nat. Fedn. Music Clubs. Address: 115 Central Park W., Apt. 25D, N.Y., NY 10023, USA.

ROWLAND, Arthur Ray, b. 6 Jan. 1930, Hampton, Ga., USA. Librarian. Educ: A.B., Mercer Univ., Macon, Ga., 1951; Master of Librarianship, Emory Univ., Atlanta, Ga., 1952. Publs: Reference Services, 1964; A Bibliography of the Writings on Georgia History, 1966; Historical Markers of Richmond County, Georgia, 1966, rev. ed., 1971; A Guide to the Study of Augusta and Richmond County, Georgia, 1967; The Catalog & Cataloging, 1969. Contbr. to: Lib. Resources & Tech. Servs.; R.Q.; Nat. Genealogical Soc. Quarterly; Richmond Co. Hist. Fndr., Richmond Co. Histl., official jrnl. of Richmond Co. Histl. Soc., 1969—. Address: 1339 Winter St., Augusta, GA 30904, USA.

ROWLAND-ENTWISTLE, Theodore, pen name BRIQUEBEC, John, b. 30 July 1925, Lancs., UK. Director, Features Agency. Publs: Teach Yourself the Violin, 1967; Winston Churchill, 1972; Napoleon, 1973; Famous Composers (w. Jean Cooke), 1974; Famous Explorers (w. Jean Cooke), 1974; Animal World (w. Jean Cooke), 1975. Contbr. to: New Jr. World Ency.; Mind Alive; Ency. of Africa; Rules of the Game; etc. Mbrship: F.R.G.S. Address: West Dene, Stonestile Lane, Hastings, Sussex TN35 4PE, UK.

ROWLEY, Brian Alan, b. 3 June 1923, Horwich, Lancs., UK. University Teacher. Educ: M.A., Ph.D., Corpus Christi Coll., Cambridge. Publs: Ed., Novalis, Three Works, 1955; Keller: Kleider machen Leute, 1960; The Fundamentals of German Grammar on one card (w. G. A. Wells), 1963; Rudolf Steiner, The Tension between East & West (transl.), 1963. Contbr. to: Outposts; German Life & Letters; Mod. Lang. Quarterly; Now; Prospect; Oasis; Cambridge Review; etc. Mbrships: Comm., Mod. Humanities Rsch. Assn., 1966—; Jt. Sec., Engl. Goethe Soc., 1962—; Jt. Sec., Conf. of Univ. Tchrs. of German in GB & Ireland, 1959-67. Address: 13 Brettingham Ave., Cringleford, Norwich NR4 6XG, UK.

ROWSE, Alfred Leslie, pen name A. L. ROWSE, b. 4 Dec. 1903, Cornwall, UK. Historian. Educ: D.Litt., Christ Church, Oxford. Publs. incl: Tudor Cornwall, 1949, 1969; The Spirit of English History, 1943; The England of Elizabeth, 1950; The Early Churchills, 1956; Poems Partly American, 1959; William Shakespeare: A Biography, 1963; The Elzabethan Renaissance, Vol. I, 1971, Vol. II, 1972; Shakespeare, the Man, 1973; Sex & Society in Shakespeare's Age, 1974; Peter, the White Cat of Trenarran, 1974. Mbrships: Brit. Acad.; F.R.S.L. Address: All Souls Coll., Oxford, UK.

ROY, Claude, b. 28 Aug. 1915. Writer. Educ: Paris Univ. Publs. incl: L'Enfance de L'Art, 1941; Clefs pour l'Amerique; Clefs pour la Chine; Descriptions Critiques; La Nauit est le manteau des pauvres; Le Soleil sur la Terre; Le Malheur d'Aimer; Le Journal des voyages; L'Homme en Question; La Sagesse des Nations; Léone & les Siens; L'Amour du Théâtre; La Dérobée; Jean Vilar; Defense de littérature, 1968; Le Verbe Aimer, 1969; Le Soleil des Romantiques, 1974; Enfantasques, 1974. Contbr. to: Paesie; Fonatine; etc. Hons: Croix de Guerre; Prix Femina-Vacaresco, 1970. Address: Eds. Gallimard, 5 rue Sebastien-Bottin, Paris 7e, France.

ROY, Gregor Andrew, b. 7 Mar. 1929, Bonnybridge, Stirlingshire, Scotland, UK. Writer & Scholar. Educ: M.A., Univ. of Glasgow. Publs: Goldsmith's Vicar of Wakefield, 1965; Alexander Pope's Rape of the Lock, 1965; Kafka's The Trial & the Castle, 1966; Greene's The Power & the Glory, 1966; Cervantes' Don Quixote, 1965; Beat Literature, 1966; The Politics of the Gospel by Jean-Marie Paupert (transl.), 1969. Contbr. to: The Nation; Cross Currents Quarterly; Cath. World; Commonweal; Columbia; Jubilee; Mademoiselle; America; Cath. Ency.; etc. Mbrships. incl: Authors' Guild; Screen Actors' Guild. Hons: Relig. Arts. Fest. Poetry Award, Rochester, N.Y., 1962; Am. Heritage Award, J. F. K. Lib., 1974. Address: 1654 3rd Ave., Apt. 11, N.Y., NY, USA.

ROY, Kuldip Kumar, pen name KULDIP, R. K., b. 28 Feb. 1935, Lahore, India (now Pakistan). Editor; Literary Critic; Poet-Translator. Educ: B.A.(Hons.), Punjab Univ.; D.Litt., Canberra, Aust. Publs: The Marketing of Tea, 1959; Mirza Ghalib, 1960; Waris Shah, 1971; Stray Thoughts & Other Poems, 1972; The Swami & The Comrade — A Hindu/Marxist Dialogue, 1973; Subramanya Bharati, 1974; Living My Own Death, 1974. Contbr. to: Hist. of Argic.; Lib. Hist. Review; Rsch. in Tourism; Legal Hist.; Asian Jrnl. of European Studies; etc. Hons: Valor Award, NYC, USA, 1966; Bruce Hartmann Trophy, Sydney, Aust., 1971; Edward Hatton Award, London, UK, 1971. Address: 55 Gariahat Rd., Calcutta 700019, India.

ROZEWICZ, Tadeusz, b. 9 Oct. 1921, Radomsko, Poland. Poet; Playwright. Educ: Univ. of Cracow. Publs. incl: (poetry) Niepokój; Czerwona rekawiczka; Czas Ktory idzie; Rownina; Srebrny klos; Rozmowa z ksieciem; Zielona róza; Nic w plaszczu Prospera; Twarz; (plays) Kartoteka; Grupa Laokoona; Akt przerywany; Smieszny Staruszek; Wyszedt z domu; Spaghetti i miecz; Stara kobirta wysiaduje. Hons: State Prize for Poetry, 1955, 1956; Lit. Prize, Cracow, 1959; Prize, Minister of Culture & Art, 1962. Address: Gliniana 53/1, Wroclaw, Poland.

RUBENS, Bernice, b. 26 July 1927, Cardiff, UK. Documentary Film Writer & Director. Educ: B.A., Univ. Coll., S. Wales & Monmouthchire, 1947. Publs: (novels) Set on Edge, 1960; Madame Sousatzka, 1962; Mate in Three, 1965; The Elected Member, UK 1969 (as Chosen People, USA 1969); Sunday Best, 1971. Hons: Am. Blue Ribbon Award (for film-making), 1968; Booker Prize, 1970. Address: 16 Frognal Gdns., London NW3, UK.

RUBERT Y CANDAU, José María, b. 5 Feb. 1901, Villarreal, Castellón, Spain. Lecturer & Researcher in Philosophy. Educ: Theol. studies; Ph.D., Central Univ. of Madrid. Publs: ¿ Qué es filosofía? , 1947; Ser y Vida, 1950; La Filosofía del siglo XIV a través de Guillermo Rubió, 1952; Fundamento constitutivo de la Moral, 1956; El sentido último de la vida, 1958; Fenomenología de la acción del hombre, 1961; La realidad de la Filosofía, 2 vols., 1970. Contbr. to: Arbor; Revista Española de Filosofía; etc. Tech. Ed., Diccionario Enciclopédico Labor, 8 vols. Mbr., Bd. of Dirs., Spanish Soc. of Philos., 1956-. Hons: Menéndez Pelayo Prize, 1949, 1952; Raimundo Lulio Prize, 1956, 1964; CSIC; Grant, March Fdn., 1957. Address: Calle Esteban Mora 32, Madrid 27, Spain.

RUBINSTEIN, Alvin Zachary, b. 23 Apr. 1927, NYC, USA. University Professor. Educ: B.B.A., CCNY, 1949; M.A., 1950, Ph.D., 1954, Univ. of Pa. Publs: The Soviets in International Organizations, 1964; Yugoslavia & the Nonaligned World, 1970; The Foreign Policy of the Soviet Union, 3rd ed., 1972; Soviet & Chinese Influence in the Third World (Ed.), 1975. Contbr. to: Problems of Communism; Am. Pol. Sci. Review; Orbis; Current Hist.; Studies in Comp. Communism; Int. Org.; etc. Mbrships: Am. Pol. Sci. Assn.; Am. Assn. for the Advancement of Slavic Studies; Int. Studies Assn. Address: Dept. of Pol. Sci., Univ. of Pa., Phila., PA 19174, USA.

RUCK, Berta (Mrs. Oliver Onions), b. 1878. Novelist. Educ: Slade Schl., London; Caloressi's, Paris, France. Publs. incl: His Official Fiancée; Sir or Madam; Tomboy in Lace; Hopeful Journey; Song of the Lark; Fantastic Holiday; The Men in Her Life; A Wish a Day; Romantic Afterthought; Love & a Rich Girl; Sherry & Ghosts; Runaway Lovers; Rendezvous at Zagarelli's; Shopping for a Husband; A Trickle of Welsh Blood; Asset to Wales; Ancestral Voices; (memoirs) A Smile for the Past; num. others; appeared in TV prog., Yesterday's Witness, 1970. Address: Bryntegwel, Aberdovey, Merioneth, Wales, UK.

RUDEBECK, Lars E. A., b. 10 Oct. 1936, Lund, Sweden. Associate Professor of Political Science. Educ: Ph.D., Uppsala Univ., 1967. Publs: Party & People: A Study of Political Change in Tunisia, 1967, 1969; Ideologies of the Third World, 1969 (in Swedish); Development & Politics, 1970 (in Swedish); Guinea-Bissau: A Study of Political Mobilization, 1974. Contbr. to: Jrnl. of Mod. African Studies; Scandinavian Pol. Studies; Swedish Pol. Sci. Review; Tiden; etc. Mbrships: Swedish Pol. Sci. Assn.; Swedish Assn. of Lit. Authors. Address: Prästgårdsgatan 13 C, 752 30 Uppsala, Sweden.

RUDHYAR, Dane, b. 23 Mar. 1895, Paris, France. Writer; Composer; Painter. Educ: B.Phil., Sorbonne Univ., Paris. Num. publs. incl: Art as Release of Power, 1920; The Astrology of Personality 1936; New Mansions for New Men, 1938; Triptych, 1966; The Planetarization of Consciousness, 1970; Rania, 1973; An Astrological Mandala, 1973; The Astrology of America's Destiny, 1974; Occult Preparations for a New Age, 1975. Contbr., num. articles to Am. mags. Mbrships. incl: Authors' Guild; Am. Fedn. of Astrologers; World Univ. Address: P.O. Box 174, Escondido, CA 92025, USA.

RUDNICKI, Adolf, b. 19 Feb. 1912, Warsaw, Poland. Writer. Publs: (in Polish) Rats; Soldiers; The Unloved One; Summer; Flight From Yasna Polyana; Living & Dead Seas; The Baton, or To Each What He Least Cares For; Blue Pages, 8 vols. of short stories & essays; The Cow; Golden Windows; The Young Sufferings; Manfred; Fifty Stories. Contbr. to Kuznica, (co-Ed., 1945-49). Recip., State Prize, 1955, 1966. Address: Ul. Kanonia 18, Warsaw, Poland.

RUE, Leonard Lee III, b. 20 Feb. 1926, Paterson, N.J., USA. Naturalist; Nature Photographer; Author; Lecturer. Publs: Animals in Motion, 1957; Tracks & Tracking, 1958; The World of the White Tailed Deer, 1960, of the Beaver, 1961, of the Racoon, 1962, of the Red Fox, 1967, of the Ruffed Grouse, 1969; Cottontail Rabbit, 1963; New Jersey Out-of-Doors, 1964; Pictorial Guide to the Mammals of North America, 1965, to the Birds of North America, 1968; The Sportsman's Guide to Game Animals of North America, 1966; Game Birds of North America, 1972. Contbr. to jrnls. Mbr., var. orgs. Recip., num. awards. Address: R.D. No. 2, Box 88, Blairstown, NJ 07825, USA.

RUHEN, Olaf, b. 24 Aug. 1911, Dunedin, NZ. Author. Publs. incl: Land of Dahori, 1957; Naked under Capricorn, 1957; White Man's Shoes . . . ; 1960; Tangaroa's Godchild, 1962; The Flockmaster, 1963; Mountains in the Clouds, 1963; Minerva Reef, 1963; Lively Ghosts, 1964; The Broken Wing, 1965; Harpoon in my Hand, 1966; Corcoran's the Name, 1968; Scan the Dark Coast, 1969. Contbr. to: The Age, Melbourne (Lit. critic); The Australian, Sydney; Ency. Britannica; Nat. Geographic Socs. Special Publs., Saturday Evening Post (until 1965); Argosy; Today. Mbr., Aust. Soc. of Authors (Fndn. Comm. mbr.). Address: 9 Cross St., Mosman, N.S.W. 2088, Australia

RUHLE, Günther, b. 3 June 1924, Giessen, Germany. Journalist. Dr.Phil., Univ. of Frankfurt. Publs: Theater für die Republik, 1917-33, 1967; Zeit und Theater (Vom Kaisserreich zur Republik; Von der Republik zur Diktatur; Diktatur und Exil), 3 vols., 1972-74; Ed., Marieluise

Fleisser: Gesammelte Werke, 1972. Contbr. to: Theater heute. Mbr., PEN. Recip., Theodor Wolf Prize, 1963. Address: 6 Frankfurt/Main, Altheimstr. 5, W. Germany.

RUIZ HARRELL, Rafael, b. 6 Oct. 1933, Mexico City, Mexico. University Teacher. Educ: Ph.D., Univ. of Mexico; M.Philos. of Sci. Publs: (poetry) Ocho cosas de papel, 1952; Te cantaron la muerte, 1961; Y, en vano, primavera, 1965; (novel) Las aporias del pirot o sae la enganosa crueldad de las hormigas, 1975. Contbr. to: Poesia de Am.; Bellas Artes; Artes y Letras de Mexico; Revista Mexicana de Literaturea, Eduador 000; etc. Recip., Schlrship, Ctr. Mexicano de Excritoses 1955, 1957. Address: Mimosa 48, Mexico 20, D.F., Mexico.

RULE, Leonard Guy, pen name LEONARD, Guy, b. 19 July 1905, London, UK. Author; Freelance Journalist. Publs: Space, 1966; Flame of the Lamp (Scientific Glassware), 1967; Our Contributor (Freelance Journalism), 1968; Fire, 1973. Contbr. to: Times; Observer; Doctor. Med. World; Fin. Times; Press Assn.; Jewish Chronicle; Sunday Express; Ctrl. Off Info.; BBC radio; etc. Mbrships: Nat. Union Jrnlsts. (Fndr. Chmn., London Freelance Br.); Press Club, London (Life Mbr.). Recip., M.B.E., 1945. Address: 55 Ridgmount Gdns., Bloomsbury, London WC1E 7AU, UK.

RULER, John, pen name ALEXANDER, John, b. 5 June 1936, Bromley, Kent, UK. Journalist. Author of chapts. on riding holidays abroad in "The Horseman's Companion" & "The Horse & Pony Gift Book", 1975. Contbr. to: Croydon Advertiser (travel Ed.); Riding Mag. (travel corres.); Riding Annual; The Scotsman. Address: 24 Hilldown Rd., Hayes, Bromley, Kent, UK.

RUNCIMAN, Steven (James Cochran Stevenson), b. 7 July 1903, West Denton, UK. Historian. Educ: B.A., M.A., Trinity Coll., Cambridge. Publs. incl: The Emperor Romanus Lecapenus, 1929; Byzantine Civilisation, 1933; The Medieval Manichee, 1947; History of the Crusades, 3 vols.,1951-54; The Eastern Schism, 1955; The Sicilian Vespers, 1958; The White Rajahs, 1960; The Fall of Constantinople, 1965; The Great Church in Captivity, 1968; The Last Byzantine Renaissance, 1970; The Orthodox Church & the Secular State, 1972. Mbrships. incl: Fellow, Brit. Acad.; Fellow, Royal Histl. Soc.; F.R.S.L. Hons. incl: 10 hon. degrees; Kt., 1958; Silver Pen Award, PEN, 1969. Address: Elshieshields, Lockerbie, Dumfriesshire DG11 1LY, UK.

RUNDBERG, Arvid, b. 30 Aug. 1932, Väddö, Stockholm, Sweden. Author. Publs. incl: sev. TV & radio plays & film scripts; De sista, 1962; Mr. Bilks död, 1963; Mannen från Amerika, 1964; Mannen i mitten, 1965; Luna, 1966, Hajgraven, 1967; Kvinnorna i Valerosa, 1968; Byggnadsarbetare, 1969; Den stora kappseglingen, 1969; Nittonhundradsextionio, 1970; Personakt A 4420, 1972; En svensk arbetares memoarer, 1973; Barnsonaten, 1973. Hons. incl: Kungafonden, City of Stockholm. Address: Drakenbergsgatan 19, 117 41 Stockholm, Sweden.

RUNYON, Charles, W., pen name WEST, Mark, b. 9 June 1928, Sheridan, Mo., USA. Writer. Educ: Univ. of Mo., Schl. of Jrnlsm., Columbia, Mo.; Univ. of Ind., Indpls., Ind.; Munich Univ., Germany. Publs: Death Cycle, 1965; Black Moth, 1969; No Place to Hide, 1970; Ames Holbrook, 1972; Power Kill, 1972; Pigworld, 1972; Soulmate, 1974; I, Weapon, 1974; Prettiest Girl I Ever Killed; Color Him Dead; Bloody Hills. Mbrships: Mystery Writers of Am.; Sci. Fiction Writers of Am.; Mo. Writers Guild; St. Francis Writers Soc., Farmington, Mo. Hons: Edgar Allen Poe Scroll, 1973; Gold Medal, Mo. Writers Guild, 1973. Address: Route 1, Box 220, Farmington, MO 63640, USA.

RUSH, Myron, b. 1 Jan. 1922, Chgo., Ill., USA. Professor. Educ: A.B., 1942, Ph.D., 1951, Univ. of Chgo. Publs: The Rise of Khrushchev, 1958; Political Succession in the USSR, 1965, 2nd ed., 1968; Strategic Power & Soviet Foreign Policy (co-author), 1966; How Communist States Change Their Rulers, 1974. Contbr. to: Commentary; World Pol.; Current Hist. Recip., 3 fellowships. Address: 312 E. Upland Rd., Ithaca, NY 14850, USA.

RUSH, Philip, b. 24 Feb. 1908, London, UK. Historical Novelist. Educ: London Univ. Publs. incl: Rogue's Lute, 1944; Mary Read, Buccaneer, 1945; Freedom is the Man, 1946; Crispin's Apprentice, 1948; He Sailed with Dampier, 1948; A Cage of Falcons, 1954; Great Men of Sussex, 1956;

Strange People, 1957; More Strange People, 1958; Strange Stuarts, 1959; He Went With Franklin, 1960; How Roads Have Grown, 1960; Apprentice-at-Arms, 1960; The Young Shelley, 1961; Weights & Measures (co-author), 1962; The Castle & the Harp, 1963; The Book of Duels, 1964; Frost Fair, 1965; That Fool of a Priest, 1970; A Face of Stone, 1973. Address: 45 Castle St., Canterbury, Kent, UK.

RUSINEK, Michał, b. 29 Sept. 1904, Cracow, Poland. Writer; Novelist. Educ: Jagiellonian Univ., Cracow. Publs: An Azure Parade (poetry), 1930; (novels) Storm Over Pavement, 1933, 7th ed., 1970; The Man from the Gate, 1934, 7th ed., 1970; The Wild Meadow Platoon, 1937, 8th ed., 1974; Land of Milk & Honey, 1938, 8th ed., 1974; The Law of Autumn, 1947, 7th ed., 1969; The Spring of the Admiral, 9th ed., 1974; Tales-Memories (non-fiction), 3rd ed., 1974; Plays, reportages, short stories. Contbr. to: Ed., Polish Lit. Mbrships: Dir., Polish Acad. of Lit., 1933-39; Gen. Sec., Polish PEN, 1945—. Recip., Cracow Lit. Prize, 1933. Address: 02562 Warszawa, Odolanska-St. 30, Poland.

RUSS, Joanna, b. 22 Feb. 1937, Bronx, N.Y., USA. Writer. Educ: B.A., Cornell Univ., 1957; M.F.A., Yale Schl. of Drama, 1960. Publs: Picnic on Paradise, 1968; And Chaos Died, 1970; The Female Man, 1975. Contbr. to: Fantasy & Sci. Fiction; Village Voice; Coll. Engl.; Red Clay Reader; Extrapolation; Orbit; New Dimensions; Quark; Manhattan Review; Cimarron Review; Again Dangerous Visions; Little Mag.; Monmouth Review; Arlington Quarterly; Discourse; etc. Mbrships: Sci. Fiction Writers of Am.; MLA. Recip., Nebula Award, Sci. Fiction Writers of Am., 1972. Address: Dept. of English, Univ. of Colorado, Boulder, CO 80302, USA.

RUSSELL, (Baron) Edward Frederick Langley, of Liverpool, b. 10 Apr. 1895, Liverpool, UK. Author. Educ: St. John's Coll., Oxford. Publs. incl: The Scourge of the Swastika, 1954; The Knights of Bushido, 1958; If I Forget Thee, 1960; The Trial of Adolf Eichmann, 1962; The Tragedy of the Congo, 1962; South Africa, Today & Tomorrow, 1963; Was Hanratty Guilty?, 1965; Caroline the Unhappy Queen, 1967; The Return of the Swastika, 1968; Henry of Navarre, 1969; The French Corsairs, 1970. Hons: C.B.E.; M.C. (2 bars). Address: 15 Wansford Rd., Woodford Green, Essex, UK.

RUSSELL, Francis, b. 12 Jan. 1910, Boston, Mass., USA. Writer. Educ: Univ. of Breslau; A.B., Bowdoin Coll.; A.M., Harvard Univ. Publs: Three Studies in 20th Century Obscurity, 1954; Tragedy in Dedham, 1962; The Great Interlude, 1964; The Shadow of Blooming Grove, 1968; The Making of the Nation, 1968; The Confident Years, 1969; Forty Years On, 1971; The Concise History of Germany, 1973; A City in Terror, 1975; President Makers from Mark Hanna to Joseph Kennedy, 1976. Contbr. to: Am. Heritage; Ency. Americana; Horizon; Christian Sci. Monitor; New England Quarterly; etc. Mbrships. incl: Dir., Goethe Soc. of New England; Fellow, Soc. of Am. Histns.; Authors' Guild. Hons. incl: Mystery Writers of Am. Award, 1962. Address: The Lindens, Sandwich, MA, USA.

RUSSELL, Jeffrey Burton, b. 1 Aug. 1934, Fresno, Calif., USA. Professor of History. Educ: B.A., 1955, M.A., 1957, Univ. of Calif., Berkeley; Ph.D., Emory Univ.; Jr. Fellow, Soc. of Fellows, Harvard Univ., 1961. Publs: Dissent & Reform in the Early Middle Ages, 1965; Medieval Civilization, 1968; A History of Medieval Christianity, 1968; Religious Dissent in the Middle Ages, 1971; Witchcraft in the Middle Ages, 1972. Contbr. to histl., relig. jrnls. Address: Dept. of Hist., Univ. of Calif., Riverside, CA 92507, USA.

RUSSELL, Josiah Cox, b. 3 Sept. 1900, Richmond, Ind., USA. Professor Emeritus of History. Educ: Univ. of Rome, 1920-21; A.B., Earlham Coll., 1922; M.A. 1923, Ph.D. 1926, Harvard Univ. Publs: The Shorter Latin of Master Henry of Avranches Relating to England (w. J. P. Heironimus), 1935; Dictionary of Writers of Thirteenth Century England, 1936; British Medieval Population, 1948; Late Ancient & Medieval Population, 1958; Medieval Regions & their Cities, 1972. Contbr. to: Am. Histl. Review; Speculum; Engl. Histl. Review; Annales; Annales du Midi; Demography; other profl. jrnls. Mbr., var. profl. orgs. Hons. incl: Guggenheim Fellowship, 1930-31; Fulbright Professor, Univ. of Wales, UK, 1952-53. Address: 16 South Wind Circle, St. Augustine, FL 32084, USA.

RUSSELL, Lao, b. Ivinghoe, Bucks., UK. Author; Artist; Sculptor; Natural Scientist. Publs. incl: God Will

Work With You But Not For You, 1955; An Eternal Message of Light & Love, 1964; Love: A Scientific & Living Philosophy of Love & Sex, 1966; My Love I Extend to You, 1966; Why You Cannot Die! — The Continuity of Life: Reincarnation Explained, 1972; also sev. books w. husband, Dr. Walter Russell, inclng. The One-World Purpose: A Plan to Dissolve War by a Power More Mighty than War, 1960. Hons: One of 6 best books, N.Y. Herald Tribune, 1955. Address: Swannanoa Palace, Waynesboro, VA 22980, USA.

RUSSELL, Martin, b. 25 Sept. 1934, Bromley, UK. Author. Publs: No Through Road, 1965; No Return Ticket, 1966; Danger Money, 1968; Hunt to a Kill, 1969; Deadline, 1971; Advisory Service, 1971; Concrete Evidence, 1972; Double Hit, 1973; Crime Wave, 1974; Phantom Holiday, 1974. Mbr., Crime Writers' Assn. Address: 1 Rosehill Cottages, Perrymans Lane, Burwash, Etchingham, Sussex, UK.

RUSSELL, Ray (Robert), b. 4 Sept. 1924, Chgo., Ill., USA. Author; Editor. Educ: Chgo. Conservatory of Music; Kenneth Sawyer Goodman Mem. Theatre (Div. of Art Inst. of Chgo.). Publs: Sardonicus, 1961; The Case against Satan, 1972; The Little Lexicon of Love, 1966; Unholy Trinity, 1967; The Colony, 1969; Sagittarius, 1971; & articles in 60 anthols. & textbooks. Contbr. to: The Paris Review; Playboy (Assoc. Ed., 1954-55; Exec. Ed., 1955-60; Contbrng. Ed., 1968—); Ed., The Permanent Playboy; also film screenplays. Mbr., Writers' Guild of Am., West, Inc. Address Calif., USA.

RUSSELL, Roy, b. 7 Aug. 1918, Blackpool, Lancs, UK. Author & Dramatist. Publs. incl: (for TV) No Hiding Place; Fothergale; The Saint; The Troubleshooters; A Man of Our Times; Champion House; Sexton Blake; Dixon of Dock Green; Doomwatch; Crime of Passion; Crown Court; A Family at War; The Onedin Line; Intimate Strangers; A House in Regent Place (four plays); The Lonely Sea & Sky (documentary). Mbrships: Coun. Mbr., Writers' Guild of GB, 1963-; Soc. of Authors; League of Dramatists; Guild of Drama Adjudicators. Contbr. of articles on drama to var. mags. Address: c/o Dalzell Durbridge Authors Ltd., 14 Clifford St., London W1, UK.

RUSSO, Albert, pen name ROVIN, Alex, b. 26 Feb. 1943, Kamina, Zaire. Writer; Language Teacher. Educ: B.Sc., N.Y. Univ., USA; Degree, Collegium Palatinum, Heidelberg, W. Germany. Publs: .Incandescences, 1970; Eclats de Malachite, 1971; La Pointe du Diable, 1973; Mosaïque Newyorkaise, 1975; transls. into French of two contemporary English plays. Contbr. to: Anthologie de la Poésie Française Contemporaine; Tribune Poétique. Mbrships. incl: PEN; Soc. of French-Speaking Writers. Hons. incl: Regain Prize, for Eclats de Malachite, 1971; Colette Prize, for La Pointe du Diable, 1974. Address: 247 Avenue Winston Churchill, 1180 Brussels, Belgium.

RUSSO, John Paul, b. 31 May 1944, Boston, Mass., USA. Professor of English Literature. Educ: A.B., Harvard Coll., 1965; M.A., 1966, Ph.D., 1969, Harvard Univ. Publs: Alexander Pope: Tradition & Identity, 1972; Bibliography of I. A. Richards in I. A. Richards Essays in his Honor (R. A. Brower et al.). Hons: Bowdoin Prize, Harvard Univ., 1969; Mellon Fellowship, 1974. Address: Dept. of Engl., Univ. of Chgo., Chgo., IL 60637, USA.

RUUTH, Alpo Armas, b. 17 Mar. 1943, Helsinki, Finland. Writer. Publs: Naimisiin, 1967; Kämppä, 1969; Korpraali Julin, 1971; Kotimaa, 1974. Contbr. to: Parnasso. Mbrships: Finnish Writers' Union; Finnish Playwrights' Union; Eino Leino Soc.; Kiila. Recip., State Prize, 1969. Address: Louhikkotie 20 b G 126, 00770 Helsinki 77, Finland.

RUUTH, Marianne, b. Kumla, Sweden. Writer. Publs: Drömmen om Hollywood, 1970; Look to the Blue Horse, 1973; Game of Shadows, 1974; A Question of Love, 1975; Tapestry of Terror, 1975. Mbrships: Mensa; Hollywood For. Press Assn. Address: 3128 Waverly Dr., Los Angeles, CA 90027, USA.

RYALLS, Alan, b. 22 Feb. 1919, Sheffield, UK. Editor; Writer. Publs: Enjoy Camping Holidays, 1963; Your Guide to Hungary, 1967; Your Guide to Cyprus, 1969; Camping with B.P., 1970; Bulgaria for Tourists, 1972; Better Camping (w. Roger Marchant), 1973. Contbr. to: Ency. Britannica; Observer 'Time Off'; Guardian; Sun; Jewish Chronicle; News of the World; Scotsman; Camping & Caravanning; Camping & Caravan Monthly. Mbrships: Guild of Travel Writers of GB; Nat. Union of Jrnlsts. Recip., Award for Best Travel Article on Bulgaria, 1969. Address: 22 Dulwich Wood Ave., London SE19 1HD, UK.

RYAN, Cornelius John, b. 5 June 1920, Dublin, Repub. of Ireland. Author; Editor. Publs: Star Spangled Mikado, 1948; MacArthur, 1951; Across the Space Frontier (co-author), 1952; Conquest of the Moon, 1953; One Minute to Ditch, 1957; The Longest Day, 1959; The Last Battle, 1965; A Bridge Too Far, 1974. Contbr. & Roving Ed., Reader's Digest. Mbrships: Authors' League of Am.; Writers' Guild of Am.; Nat. Press Club; Overseas Press Club of Am. Hons. incl: Most Disting. Mag. Writing Award, Univ. of Ill., 1956; Benjamin Franklin Award; Bancarelia Prize for Lit., Italy, 1962; Gold Medal for Lit., Eire Soc., Boston, 1966. Address: 135 Old Branchville Rd., Ridgefield, CT 06877, USA.

RYAN, Paul Ryder, b. 5 Jan. 1932, Mineola, N.Y., USA. Writer; Editor. Educ: B.A., Boston Univ.; M.A., Sorbonne, Paris, France; Ph.D., N.Y. Univ., USA. Contbr. to: Drama Review (Exec. Ed.); Partisan Review; Plays & Players; Theater Heute; Sipario; N.Y. Times; Travail Theatral. Mbrships: Am. Soc. of Mag. Eds.; Am. Soc. of Mag. Writers; Authors' Guild. Address: 51 W. 4th St., N.Y., NY 10012, USA.

RYAN, Peter Charles, b. 18 Nov. 1939, Harrogate, Yorks., UK. Writer. Educ: Ampleforth Coll., Yorks.; B.A. Trinity Coll., Dublin, Repub. of Ireland. Publs: Invasion of the Moon, 1969, 1971; Journey to the Planets, 1972, 1973; Planet Earth, 1972; The Ocean World, 1973; UFO's & Other Worlds, 1975. Contbr. to: Ed., Facts of Life Series, Sunday Times Mag., 1974; Radio & TV. Mbrships: F.G.S.; London; Fellow, Brit. Interplanetary Soc.; Assn., Brit. Sci. Writers; AAAS.; Nat. Union of Jrnlsts. Address: 11 Moore Park Rd., London SW6 2JB, UK.

RYAN, T. Antoinette, b. 1 May 1924, Mont., USA. Research Psychologist. Educ: A.B., Sacramento State Univ./Stanford Univ.; M.A., Sacramento State Univ.; Ph.D., Stanford Univ. Publs: Guidance for Emerging Adolescents, 1970; Organization & Administration of Guidance, 1972. Contbr. to: Jrnl. of Counseling Psychol.; Counseling Psychol.; Educl. Technol.; Voc. Guidance Quarterly; etc. Mbrships: Fellow, Am. Psychol. Assn.; VP., Am. Educl. Rsch. Assn., 1970-72; Chmn., Special Interest Grp. on Systems Rsch., 1970—. Hons. incl: Nat. Award for Outstanding Rsch., Am. Personnel & Guidance Assn., 1966. Address: 4956 Waa St., Honolulu, HI 96821, USA.

RYDÉN, Håkan, b. 4 Apr. 1928, Uppsala, Sweden. Editor-in-Chief of Land Magazine; Director of Publishing Department. Educ: Agricl. Coll. Publs: FAO Study, 1968; Agricultural Credit Through Cooperatives & Other Institutions; The Population Explosion & World Resources (Befolkningsexplosionen och världens resurser) co-author. Contbr. to Land Mag. Mbr., Swedish Soc. Profl. Jrnlsts. (Chmn.). Recip., Swedish Jrnlst. Prize, 1971. Address: Herrhagsvägen 5, 19030 Sigtuna, Sweden.

RYDENFELT, Sven, b. 23 Jan. 1911, Hjärnarp, Sweden. University Lecturer. Educ: D.Econ. Publs: De bostadslösa och samhället, 1952; Kommunismn i Sverige, 1954; Vårt dynamiska näringlsiv, 1965; Förändringars vindar över svensk industri, 1968; Vår paradoxala bostadspolitik, 1973. Contbr. to jrnls. & newspapers. Mbrships: Swedish Union of Authors; Chmn., Econ. Soc. of Scania; Econ. Soc. of Stockholm. Recip., Author's Premium, Fndn. of Swedish Authors, 1970. Address: Kastanjegatan 6B, 22359 Lund, Sweden.

RYDER, John, b. 6 Oct. 1917, London, UK. Publisher. Typographic Artist. Publs: Printing for Pleasure, 1955; A Suite of Fleurons, 1956; Artists of a Certain Line, 1960; Six on the Black Art, 1962; Lines of the Alphabet, 1965; The Officina Bodoni, 1972; Flowers & Flourishes, 1975. Contbr. to: Scholarly Publng.; Graphis; Librarium; Pvte. Libs.; Book Collector. Mbrships. incl: Fellow, Soc. of Indl. Artists. Address: The Bodley Head Ltd., 9 Bow St., London WC2E 7AL, UK.

RYDSTEDT, Anna Viola Magdalena, b. 22 Apr. 1928, Ventlinge, Sweden. Author; People's High School Teacher. Educ: B.A. Publs: (collects. of poems) Bannlyst prästinna, 1953; Lökvår, 1957; Min punkt, 1960; Presensbarn, 1964; Jag var ett barn, 1970. Contbr. to: Kvällsposten; Sydsvenska Dagbladet. Mbrships: Swedish Union of Authors; PEN. Hons: Culture Prize, City of Lund; Samfundet De Nios Prize; Culture Prize, City of Stockholm. Address: Nytorgsgatan 11B, 11645 Stockholm, Sweden.

RYE, Sven, b. 26 Feb. 1906, Randers, Denmark. Writer; Newspaper Correspondent. Educ: Study of jrnlsm., Denmark; Studies in Budapest, Vienna, Sorbonne, Paris. Publs: Skyerne Traekker Sammen (Clouds Are Gathering), 1941; Man Skal Jo Gå På Jorden (We Have to Walk This Earth), 1942; num. short stories & 400 songs; Filmscript, The Silent Witness. Contbr. to num. newspapers: Corres., 30 Scandinavian newspapers & mags.; Sunday Times (London). Mbrships: Grt. L.A. Press Club; USA; Songwriters Hall of Fame, ASCAP; VP, Hollywood For. Press Assn. Hons: Schlrships., Jrnlsts. Assn., Odense; Freedom Medal, King Christian X of Denmark; Medal, Danish Tourist Coun.; D.Litt., Trinity S. Bible Coll. & Sem., Mullins, S.C., USA. Address: 3906 Franklin Ave., Hollywood, CA 90027, USA.

RYGA, George, b. 27 July 1932, Richmond Pk., Alta., Can. Poet; Lyricist; Novelist; Short Story Writer; Dramatist. Publs: Song of My Hands, 1956; Hungry Hills, 1963; Ballad of a Stonepicker, 1965; The Ecstasy of Rita Joe, 1970; The Ecstasy of Rita Joe & Other Plays, 1971; Captives of the Faceless Drummer, 1971; Sunrise on Sarah, 1973; Paracelsus, 1974; (lyrics for record albums) Grass & Wild Strawberries, 1969; The Ecstasy of Rita Joe, 1973; (lyrics for chorale-symphs.) A Feast of Thunder, by M. Surdin, 1971; Twelve Ravens For The Sun, by M. Theodorakis, 1974. Contbr. to: McLean's Mag.; The Atlantic Advocate; Tamarack Review; Can. Theatre Review. Mbrships: Writers Union of Can.; Assn. of Can. Radio & TV Artists. Recip., Can. Coun. Sr. Arts Grant, 1972. Address: R.R.2, Summerland, B.C. VOH 120, Can.

RYING, Matts, b. 14 Sept. 1919, Husby-Oppunda, Sweden. Radio Producer. Educ: B.A., 1946. Publs: Söndagsskola, 1947; Blindskrift, 1948; Blodskontur, 1952; Midnattsmässa, 1962; Intryck i Sverige, 1965; Diktare idag, 1971; Kritiker idag, 1972; Galleri, 1972; Nattliga ackord, 1974; Resa och rast, 1975. Contbr. to jrnls. inclng: Horisont; Lyrikvännen. Mbr., PEN Club. Address: Mittelvägen 6, 122 32 Enskede, Sweden.

RYTKHEU, Yuri Sergeevich, b. 8 Mar. 1930, Uellen, Magadan Region, USSR. Writer. Educ: Leningrad Univ. Publs: (short stories) Friends & Comrades; People of Our Coast, 1953; Farewell to the Gods, 1961; Nunivak, 1963; The Walrus of Dissent, 1964; Blue Peppers, 1964; (novels) When the Snow Melts, 1960; The Sorceress of Konerga, 1960; The Saga of Chukotka, 1960; The Magic Gauntlet, 1963; In the Vale of the Little Sunbeams, 1963; Wings Are Becoming Stronger in Flight, 1964; (verses) Bear Stew, 1965. Recip., Badge of Honour. Address: Union of Writers, Ul. Vorovskogo 52, Moscow, USSR.

RYTON, Royce Thomas Carlisle, b. 1924, Worthing, UK. Actor; Writer. Educ: Lancing Coll.; Webber Douglas Schl. of Dramatic Art. Plays publd: Make Believe, 1952; The Painted Face, 1964; Penguins Can't Fly (w. Robert Sloman), 1969; Holiday in Spala, 1969; Singular Grace, 1971; Crown Matrimonial, 1972; The Prince & the 45', 1973. Agent: Dr. Jan Van Loewen. Address: 64 Kingfisher Dr., Ham, Richmond, Surrey, UK.

S

SAARTO-HAGERT, Tuula Kaarina, b. 14 Feb. 1942, Helsinki, Finland. Writer. Publs: Yön jälkeen, 1968; Omat ympyrät, 1970; Suljetut ovet, 1972; Jussi, 1972; Punaisten kukkien maa, 1973; Kohtaus Venetsiassa, 1974. Contbr. to: Eeva; Me Naiset. Mbrships: PEN; Finnish Soc. of Writers; Soc. of Writers for the Young; Press-klub. Hons: State Prize, 1973; Prize Soc. of Writers for the Young, 1973. Address: Jakomäentie 6b I 202, 00770 Helsinki 77, Finland.

SABATIER, Pierre, b. Paris, France. Author; Playwright, Broadcaster; Composer. Educ: Lic. & Dr. ès lettres, Lic. & Dr. en droit, Paris. Publs. incl: L'Esthétique des Goncourt, 1920, 1970; La Morale de Stendhal, 1920, 1973; Vie de Sainte Roseline, 1929, 1974; Vices, 1932; Vertus, 1933; Essai sur Germinie Lacerteux, 1945; (plays & adaptations) Le démon de la chair, 1927; Le Souper de Venise, 1938; J'ai régné cette nuit, 1953; Le Manteur, 1969; Médée, 1972; L'Homme, la Bête & la Vertu, 1975; num. transls., & other radio, TV & stage plays. Dir., Radio-TV Française progs., sev. yrs. Contbr. to radio & jrnls. Mbr., num. acad. & profl. orgs. Recip., num. hons. & lit. awards. Address: 79 quai d'Orsay, 75007 Paris, France.

SABATIER, Robert, b. 17 Aug. 1928. Writer. Publs: Alain & le nègre, 1953; Le Marchand de sable, 1954; Boulevard, 1956; Canard au sang, 1958; La Sainte-Farce, 1960; La Mort d'un figuir, 1962; Dessin sur un trottoir, 1964; Une Chinoise d'Afrique, 1966; Le Allumettes Suédoises, 1969. Mbr., Acad. Goncourt. Hons: Lauréat, Soc. des gens de lettres; Grand Prix de Poésie, French Acad., 1969; Antonin Artaud Prize; Prix Appollinaire. Address: 23 rue Fantin Latour, Paris 16ᵉ, France.

SABATO, Ernesto, b. 24 June 1911, Rojas, Argentina. Writer. Publs: Uno y el Universo, 1945; Hombres y Engranajes, 1951; Heterodoxia, 1953; El Escritor y sus Fantasmas, 1963; Tres Aproximaciones a la Literatura de Nuestro Tiempo, 1969; (novels) El Tunel, 1948; Heroes y Tumbas, 1961; Abaddon, 1974. Contbr. to: Il Giornale (Milan, Italy); etc. Mbrships: Club of Rome; Jerusalem Comm.; Comite pour l'Universalité de l'Unesco, 1975. Hons: Ribbon Hon., Argentine Soc. Letters, 1946; Inst. For. Rels. Prize, 1973; Argentine Writers' Soc. Grand Prize, 1974. Address: Langeri 3135, Santos Lugares, Argentina.

SABINE, Ellen S., b. 23 Feb. 1908, NYC, USA. Artist; Author; Teacher; Researcher. Educ: N.Y. Schl. of Fine & Applied Arts, 1924; Pratt Inst., N.Y., 1925-27. Publs: American Antique Decoration, 1956, 2nd ed., 1973; American Folk Art, 1958, 2nd ed., 1973; Early American Decorative Patterns, 1962, 2nd ed., 1973. Mbr., Esther Stevens Brazer Guild of Histl. Soc. of Early Am. Decoration, Inc. Address: 21-A Yorkshire Court, Lakehurst, NJ 08733, USA.

SACHS, Bernard, b. 18 Mar. 1908, Kamaai, Lithuania (now USSR). Writer; Editor, South African Opinion. Educ: B.A., Univ. of Witwatersrand, Johannesburg, S. Africa. Publs: Multitude of Dreams, 1949; The Utmost Sail, 1956; Personalities & Places (Series I), 1960; The Road from Sharpeville, 1961; Personalities & Places (Series 2), 1965; Herman Charles Bosman, 1973; Mist of Memory, 1974. Contbr. to Commentary, N.Y., USA. Address: 53 Royal Crescent, Hillbrow, Johannesburg, Repub. of S. Africa.

SACHS, Murray, b. 10 Apr. 1924, Toronto, Ont., Can. Professor of French Literature. Educ: B.A., Univ. of Toronto, 1946; A.M., 1947, Ph.D., 1953, Columbia Univ., USA. Publs: The Career of Alphonse Daudet, 1965; The French Short Story in the 19th Century, 1969; Anatole France: The Short Stories, 1974. Contbr. to: Publs. of MLA; French Review; Mod. Lang. Review. Mbrships. incl: MLA; Modern Humanities Rsch. Assn. Recip., Chevalier, Ordre des Palmes Académiques, France, 1971. Address: 280 Highland Ave., West Newton, MA 02165, USA.

SACKETT, Harold B. (Hal), pen name OLD PIONEER, b. 1 Aug. 1897, Frisco, Utah, USA. Outdoorsman; Columnist; Trailer Insurance Specialist. Educ: N.W. Univ. of Law, Long Beach, Calif.; 6 months, Citrus Coll., Univ. of Calif. Publs: Steelhead (w. Claude M. Kreider). Contbr. to: Western Mobile Home News (outdoor column, 18 yrs.; Ed., subsidiary N.W. paper); Ed., News-sheet, Fishing News & Views. Mbrships. incl: Outdoor Writers' Assn. of Am.; Outdoor Writers of West. Hons. Mbr., Fishing House of Fame, 1954; var. athletic awards. Address: P.O. Box 607, Bend, OR 97701, USA.

SAENZ DE SANTA MARIA, Carmelo, b. 14 July 1913, Vitoria, Spain. Professor. Educ: Ph.D., Georgetown Univ., USA; Dr. Fil. y Letras, Univ. of Madrid. Publs: Diccionario Cakchiquel-Español, 1940; El Licenciado Don Francisco Marroquín, Primer Obispo de Guatemala, 1964; Introducciòn Crítica a la Historia Verdadera de Bernal Díaz del Castillo, 1967; Obras Completas de Cronistas e Historiadores de Indias. Contbr. to: Revista de Indias; Revista de Historia de América, México; Anuario de Estudios Americanos; Anales de la Sociedad de Geografía e Historia de Guatemala. Mbrships. incl: Inst. Vizcaino de Cultura Hispánica (exec. comm.); Inst. de Cultura Hispánica de Madrid. Address: Universidad de Deusto, Ap. 1, Bilbao, Spain.

SÄFVESTAD, Vikar A., b. 15 July 1918, Enköping, Sweden. Head, County of Jonkoping Agricultural Board. Educ: M.Sc., 1949, Ph.D., 1965, Royal Agricl. Coll. of Sweden, Uppsala. Publs: Simplified Programming at Individual Farms (w. Johnsson & Renborg), 1959; The Stenungsund Project, An Analysis of Differences between Farmers Engaged & not Engaged in Course Activity, 1966; Part-Time Farming — Problems & Possibilities, 1964. Mbrships: Int. Assn. of Agricl. Economists; Swedish Bd., Assn. of Scandinavian Agricl. Scis. Address: Lantbruksnämnden, 55102 Jönköping, Sweden.

SAGAN, Carl Edward, b. 9 Nov. 1934, NYC, USA. Astronomer. Educ: A.B., 1954, S.B., 1955, S.M., 1956, Ph.D., 1960, Univ. of Chgo. Publs. incl: The Atmospheres of Mars & Venus, 1961; Planets, 1966; Planetary Exploration, 1970; Planetary Atmospheres, 1971; The Air War in Indochina, 1971; UFOs: A Scientific Debate, 1972; The Cosmic Connection: An Extraterrestrial Perpsective, 1973; Mars & the Mind of Man, 1973; Communication with Extraterrestrial Intelligence, 1973; Life Beyond Earth & the Mind of Man, 1973. Contbr. to encys. & num. popular & scientific jrnls. Hons. incl: John W. Campbell Jr. Mem. Award, 1974; D. Klumpke-Roberts Prize, Astron. Soc. of Pacific, 1974. Address: 302 Space Sciences Bldg., Cornell Univ., Ithaca, NY 14850, USA.

SAGAN, Françoise, pen name of QUOIREZ, Françoise, b. 21 June 1935. Writer. Publs: (novels) Bonjour Tristesse; Un Certain Sourire; Dans un Mois, dans un An; Aimez-Vous Brahms . . . ? ; Les Merveilleux Nuages; La Chamade; Le Garde du Coeur, 1968; Un peu de soleil dans l'eau froide, 1969; Deux Bleus à l'Ame; (plays) Un Château en Suède; Les Violons; Parfois . . . ; La Robe Mauve de Valentine; L'Echarde; Le Cheval Evanoui; Un piano dans l'herbe, 1970; Zaphorie, 1973; (autobiographical) Toxique. Recip., Prix des Critiques, 1954. Address: Eds. Flammarion, 26 rue Racine, Paris 6ᵉ, France.

SAGARDIA SAGARDIA, Angel, b. 11 Oct. 1901, Zaragoza, Spain. Musicologist; Pianist; Lecturer. Educ: Zaragoza Conserv. of Music. Publs. incl: Manuel de Falla, 1946; La Zarzuela y sus compositores, 1958; Índice de la Revista 'Ateneo', 1960. Pablo Sarasate y su posición de la Música, 1961; El mar y la música, 1961; Cuatro músicos vascos, Padre San Sebastián, Usandizaga, Telleria y Arambarri, 1965; Vida y Obra de Manuel de Falla, 1967; Gaztambide y Arrieta, 1969; Amadeo Vives, Vida y Obra, 1971; Diccionario de Músicos Vascos, 3 vols., 1972. Contbr. to: Hoja del Lunes; El Noticiero; Vida Vasca; Gran Diccionario Enciclopédico de Selecciones de Readers Digest. Recip., Nat. Prize of Musicol. Address: Calle General Pardiñas 87, Madrid 6, Spain.

SAHA, Marcus Marion, b. 17 Dec. 1937, Rosenberg, Tex., USA. Television & Motion Picture Writer. Educ: B.A., Notre Dame Univ., 1962; Univ. Calif., L.A. TV Credits for Peyton Place, 20th Century Fox, 1968; Mod. Squad, Paramount, 1969; Courtship of Eddie's Father, MGM, 1970; Nakia, Columbia, 1974; Sunshine, Universal, 1974; Emergency!, Universal, 1975; & num. unproduced screenplays. Contbr. to: Strategy & Tactics; Moves; General; (Ed. Staff): Games & Puzzles. Mbrships: Writers' Guild Am. W.; Writers' Guild Open Door Prog. (Instr., 1969-71). Hons. incl: Samuel Goldwyn Creative Writing Award, 1964. Address: 2129 Ocean Ave., Apt. 5, Santa Monica, CA 90405, USA.

SAHGAL, Nayantara (Pandit), b. 10 May 1927, Allahabad, India. Writer. Educ: B.A., Wellesley Coll., Mass., USA, 1947. Publs: (novels) A Time to Be Happy, USA & UK, 1958; This Time of Morning, USA & UK, 1965; Storm in Chandigarh, USA & UK, 1969; The Day in Shadow, India, 1971, USA, 1972; (autobiog.) Prison & Chocolate Cake, USA & UK, 1954; From Fear Set Free, USA & UK,

1963; (non-fiction) History of the Freedom Movement, India, 1970. Contbr. to: Illustrated Wkly. of India; Regularly to Indian mags. & newspapers, 1965—. Address: 25—C Sujan Singh Pk., New Delhi 3, India.

SAHL, Hans, b. 20 May 1902, Dresden, Germany. Poet; Critic; Translator; Novelist. Educ: Univs. of Munich, Leipzig, Breslau, Berlin; Ph.D. Publs: Jemand. Passion eines Menschen (poetry), 1938; Die hellen Nächte, 1941; Furlough from Death (radio play), 1942; The Few & the Many (novel), 1959; George Grosz., 1966; transls. of Am. & Brit. plays into German, i.e. Thornton Wilder, Tennessee Williams; Arthur Miller, John Osborne, etc. Contbr. to: Süddeutsche Zeitung; Die Welt; Der Monat; etc. Mbrships: German Acad.; PEN; For. Press Assn. Recip., W. German Officer's Cross of Merit, 1959. Address: 800 West End Ave., N.Y., NY 10025, USA.

SAINT, Dora Jessie, pen name READ, Miss, b. 17 Apr. 1913, Norwood, UK. Writer; Teacher. Publs: Village School, 1955; Village Diary, 1957; Thrush Green, 1959; The Market Square, 1966; News from Thrush Green, 1970; Tyler's Row, 1972; The Christmas Mouse, 1973. Contbr. to: Punch; Times Educl. Supplement; BBC Radio. Address: c/o Michael Joseph, 52 Bedford Square, London WC1B 3EF, UK.

ST. JOHN, John, b. 7 Feb. 1917, Gillingham, UK. Publisher; Director, William Heinemann Ltd. Publs: Roast Beef & Pickles, 1955; A Trick of the Sun, 1956; The Small Hours, (co-author), 1957, Surgeon At Arms (co-author), 1958, 2nd ed. 1975; Probation — The Second Chance, 1961; Alphabets & Reading, (co-author), 1969; To the War with Waugh, 1973, 2nd ed. 1974. Jt. Ed., Science Survey; Ed., sev. other books. Contbr. to sev. newspapers & mags. Mbrships. incl: PEN; Authors' Soc. Address: 40 Arkwright Rd., London NW3 6BH, UK.

ST. JOHN, Patricia Mary, b. 5 Apr. 1919, St. Leonards, Sussex, UK. Missionary & Teacher; Author. Publs: Tanglewood Secret, 1948; Treasures of the Snow, 1950; Star of Light, 1953; Rainbow Garden, 1960; Biography of Harold St. John, 1961; Twice Freed, 1969; Breath of Life, 1970. Contbr. to: The Witness. Hons: Eisteddfod Poetry Prize, 1937; Best Children's Relig. Fiction Prize, CSSM; Award for Book of the Month for Schls., Swiss Educl. Prog., 1954. Address: Hope House, 8 Marshan, Tangier, Morocco, N. Africa.

ST. JOHN, Robert, b. 9 Mar. 1902, Chgo., Ill., USA. Writer; Lecturer. Publs: From the Land of Silent People, 1942; It's Always Tomorrow, 1944; Shalom Means Peace, 1949; Tongue of the Prophets, 1952; Through Malon's Africa, 1954; Foreign Correspondent, 1957; Ben-Gurion, 1959; The Boss, 1960; The Man Who Played God, 1963; Roll Jordan Roll, 1965; Jews, Justice & Judaism, 1969; Eban, 1973. Recip., D.Litt. Address: Box 116, Route 2, Waldorf, MD 20601, USA.

ST. JOHN, Wylly Folk, b. 20 Oct. 1908, Bamberg Co., S.C., USA. Author; Journalist. Educ: A.B., Jrnlsm., Univ. of Ga., 1930. Publs. incl: The Secrets of the Hidden Creek, 1966; The Mystery of the Gingerbread House, 1969; The Ghost Next Door, 1971; The Mystery of the Other Girl, 1971; Uncle Robert's Secret, 1972; The Secret of the Seven Crows, 1973; The Mystery Book Mystery, 1975. Contbr. to num. mags.; Staff Writer, Atlanta Jrnl. & Constitution Sunday Mag., 1941—. Mbrships: Authors' League; Mystery Writers of Am.; Nat. Soc. for Lit. & the Arts; Authors' Guild; Atlanta Press Club. Hons: Ga. Author of the Year, 1968; Ga. Author of Year for Fiction, 1973; Theta Sigma Phi Award for Jrnlsm., 1970; Mystery Writers of Am. Special Award, Nominee for 'Edgar' in Jvnle. Category, 1973, 1974. Address: 198 Dogwood Ave., Social Circle, GA 30279, USA.

SAINT-MARTIN, Fernande, b. 28 Mar. 1927, Montreal, P.Q., Can. Writer; Journalist; Art Critic. Educ: M.A., McGill Univ., Montreal; Ph.D., Univ. de Montreal. Publs: La litterature et le non-verbal, 1958; Structures de l'espace pictural, 1968. Contbr. to: Vie des Arts; Liberte; etc. Mbrships. incl: Int. Assn. of Art Critics; Int. Assn. of Experimental Aesthetics; Soc. of Can. Writers. Recip., 1st Prize, Essay Sect. on Contemp. Arts, Centenary Commn., 1967. Address: 3516 Northcliffe, Montreal, P.Q., Can.

ST. OMER, Garth, b. Castries, St. Lucia, W. Indies. Writer. Educ: Grad. in French, Univ. of W. Indies, Jamaica. Publs: (novels) A Room on the Hill, 1968; Shades of Grey, 1968; Nor Any Country, 1969; J, Black Bam & the

Masqueraders, 1972. Contbr. to: Introduction 2, 1968. Address: c/o Faber & Faber Ltd., 3 Queen Square, London WC1, UK.

SAINZ, Gustavo, b. 13 July 1940, Mexico City, Mexico. Novelist. Publs: Gazapo, Mexico 1965, Argentina 1969, transls. publd. N.Y. 1968, 1969, France 1968, Italy 1969; Autobiografía, 1966, Italian transl. 1969; Autorretrato con Amigos (Revista de Bellas Artes Sept.-Oct. 1966); Obsesivos dĺas Circulares, 1969; La Princesa del Palacio de Hierro, 1974. Contbr. to: Plural; Bellas Artes; TriQuarterly; Revista Mexicana de Ciencia Politíca. Address: Rio Nazas 77-6, México 5, D.F., Mexico.

SAKAI, Sadao, pen name, MIZUTA, Akira, b. 20 May 1936, Tokyo, Japan. News Correspondent on Military & Middle East Affairs. Educ: Grad., Tokyo Metrop. Univ. Publs: Natural Calamity in Japan, 1965; Nuclear War, 1969. Contbr. to: Kyodo News Serv. (Wire News Agcy.) Address: c/o Kyodo News Serv., Akasaka Aoi-Cho, Minatoku, Tokyo, Japan.

SAKAJIAN, Rosemary, b. 2 Mar. 1912, Franklin, Mass., USA. Freelance Writer. Contbr. of stories, articles & poems to var. mags. in USA & Can. Mbrships: Nat. League of Am. Pen Women; Nat. Writers' Club. Address: 261 Christopher Drive, San Fran., CA 94131, USA.

SAKS, Edgar Walter, pen name SKS, b. 25 Jan. 1910, Tartu, Estonia. Industrial Manager. Educ: LL.B., Univ. of Tartu, 1933. Publs. incl: Kodutu, 1929; Aestii, 1960; Esto-Europa, 1966; Commentaries on the Liber Census Daniae, 1974. Mbrships: Min. of Educ., Gov. of Estonian Repub. in Exile, 1971—; Official Deleg., Can. PEN, Int. PEN Congress, Menton, 1969; Official Deleg., Estonian PEN Ctr., Int. PEN Congress, Dublin, 1971; Dir., Can. PEN Ctr., 1967-72; Dir., Estonian PEN Ctr., 1971—; R.S.L., UK; Estonian Learned Soc., N.Y., USA. Recip., Lit. Prize for "Kodutu", Estonia, 1929. Address: 5438 Coolbrook Ave., Montreal, P.Q. H3X 2L4, Can.

SAKSA, Sulo Josef, pen name SARKKA, Juuso, b. 28 June 1909, Kangasniemi, Finland. Farmer; Author. Publs: Satu-Tyttö ja Ville Vekkuli, 1947; Virta Päättyy Suvantoon, 1953. Contbr. to: Savon Sanomat; Seura; Yhteishyvä; Kangasniemen Kunnallislehti; Länsi-Savo; Maaseudun Tulevaisuus; Kotiliesi. Mbrships: Kangasniemen Verolautakunta; Nuoriso ja Raittiuslautakunta; Terveydenhoitolautkunta; Vaimosniemen Kansakoulun Johtokunta; Sec., Maatalousyhdistys, Kangasniemi; Chmn., Nuorisoseura, Kangasniemi. Recip., sev. schlrships. & prizes. Address: Vaimosniemi, 51200 Kangasniemi, Finland.

SALACROU, Armand Camille, b. 9 Aug. 1899. Playwright. Educ: Faculties of Med., Law & Letters, Univ. of Paris. Publs. incl: (plays) Le Pont l'Europe, 1927; Atlas-Hotel, 1931; Une femme libre, 1934; La Terre est ronde, 1938; Histoire de Rire, 1939; Les Fiancés du Havre, 1944; Les Nuits de la colère, 1946; L'Archipel Lenoir, 1947; Les Invités du Bon Dieu; Sans Interdit, 1953; Le Miroir; Une Femme trop honnête, 1956; Boulevard Durand, 1960; Comme les Chardons, 1964. Mbrships: Soc. of Dramatic Authors; Int. Theatre Inst. Recip., Legion of Honour. Address: 1 bis avenue Foch, Paris 16e, France.

SALCEDO-BASTARDO, José Luis, b. 1926, Carúpano, Venezuela. Diplomat; University Professor. Educ: Univs. of Paris & Venezuela Central; London Schl. of Econ. Publs. incl: En Fuga hacia la Gloria, 1947; Visión y Revision de Bolívar, 1957; Biografia de Don Egidio Montesinos, 1957; Tesis para la Unión, 1963; Bases de una Acción Cultural, 1965; Historia Fundamental de Venezuela, 1970; La Concienciadel Presente, 1971; Caraboбo: Nacionalidad e Historia, 1972; Bolivar: Un Continente y un Destino, 1972; Mbrships: Pres., Nat. Inst. of Culture & Fine Arts, 1965-67; VP, Supreme Electoral Coun. Address: Apartado Postal 2777, Caracas, Venezuela.

SALINGER, Herman, b. 23 Dec. 1905, St. Louis, Mo., USA. University Professor. Educ: A.B., Princeton Univ., 1927; M.A., Stanford Univ., 1929; Ph.D., Yale Univ., 1937. Publs. incl: (poetry) Angel of our Thirst, 1950-51; A Sign is the Sword, 1963; (transls.) Twentieth-Century German Verse: A Selection, 1962; Rudolf Hagelstange: Ballad of the Buried Life, 1962; Karl Krolow: Poems Against Death, 1969. Contbr. to var. lit. pubis. Mbrships: MLA, 1932—; Sec.-Treas., Int. Arthur Schnitzler Rsch. Assn., 1961-72. Hons: Badge of Hon. Poetry Prize, 1942; Roanoke-Chowan Award (poetry), 1963. Address: 3444 Rugby Rd., Durham, NC 27707, USA.

SALINGER, J(erome) D(avid), b. 1 Jan. 1919, NYC, USA. Writer. Educ: Valley Forge Mil. Acad., Pa.; N.Y. Univ.; Columbia Univ. Publs: The Catcher in The Rye (novel), USA & UK, 1951; Nine Stories, 1953 (as For Esmé — With Love & Squalor, & Other Stories, UK, 1953); Franny, & Zooey, USA, 1961, UK, 1962; Raise High the Roof Beam, Carpenters, & Seymour: An Introduction, USA & UK, 1963. Address: c/o Harold Ober Assocs., 40 E. 49th St., N.Y., NY 10017, USA.

SALISBURY, Harrison Evans, b. 14 Nov. 1908, Mpls., Minn., USA. Writer. Educ: B.A., Univ. of Minn. Publs: An American in Russia, 1955; Moscow Diary, 1959; The Shook-Up Generation, 1959; The Northern Palmyra Affair, 1962; Orbit of China, 1967; Behind the Lines — Hanoi, 1967; The 900 Days — Siege of Leningrad, 1969; To Peking — And Beyond, 1972. Mbrships: Century Assn.; Nat. Press Club; Pres., Inst. of Arts & Letters. Recip., Pulitzer Prize, 1955. Address: Box 70, Taconic, CT 06079, USA.

SALISBURY-JONES, (Sir) Guy, b. 4 July 1896, London, UK. Army Major-General (ret'd.); Former Marshal of the Diplomatic Corps. Educ: Royal Mil. Coll., Sandhurst; Ecole Speciale Militaire, St. Cyr, France. Publs: So Full a Glory, 1954. Hons: G.C.V.O.; C.M.G.; C.B.E.; M.C.; Grand Officier, Légion d'honneur, France. Address: Mill Down, Hambledon, Portsmouth, Hants. PO7 6RY, UK.

SALJE, Sven Edwin, b. 15 Feb. 1914, Jämshög, Sweden. Author. Publs: Dimmorna lyfter, 1940; På dessa skuldror, 1942; Människors rike, 1944; Du tysta källa, 1946; Vingslag i natten, 1948; De flyendes eldar, 1950; Den söker icke sitt, 1953; Livets gäster, 1955; Man ur huse, 1958; Kustridaren, 1960; Dessa dina bröder, 1964; Längs livets stränder, 1967; Natten och brödet, 1968; Lågan i kvällen, 1971; Hem till havet, 1973. Mbr., Swedish Union of Authors. Hons. incl: Prize, Swedish Authors' Fund, 1964; Kt. Cmdr., Vasa Order, 1974. Address: Box 2065, Jämshög, 293 02 Olofström 2, Sweden.

SALKEY, (Felix) Andrew (Alexander), b. 30 Jan. 1928, Colon, Panama. Writer; Broadcaster. Educ: B.A., London Univ., UK, 1955. Publs. incl: (novels) A Quality of Violence, 1959; Escape to an Autumn Pavement, 1960; The Late Emancipation of Jerry Stover, 1968; The Adventures of Catullus Kelly, 1969; Come Home, Malcolm Heartland, 1972; (juvenile) Hurricane, 1964; Earthquake, 1965; Drought, 1966; Riot, 1967; Ed., var. collects. Caribbean stories, prose & verse. Contbr. to BBC Radio. Hons: Helmore Poetry Prize, London Univ., 1955; Guggenheim Fellowship, 1960; Deutscher Kinderbuchpreis, 1967. Address: Flat 8, Windsor Ct., Moscow Rd., Queensway, London W2, UK.

SALKOWITZ, Sy, b. 21 Apr. 1926, Phila., Pa., USA. Television Writer. Educ: B.A., Yale Univ., 1950; Grad. Schl., Univ. of Calif., L.A., 1971. Mbrships: Writers' Guild of Am., West (Bd. of Dirs., 1966-70); Writers' Guild Fndn. (Bd. of Dirs., 1966—); Acad. TV Arts & Sci. (Gov. Hollywood Chapt., 1970—, Trustee Nat. Acad., 1974—); Dirs.' Guild of Am. Hons: C.I.N.E. Golden Eagle, 1969; Nominee, Writers' Guild Award, 1970; Edgar Allen Poe Award, Mystery Writers of Am., 1974. Address: Malibu, Calif., USA.

SALMINEN, Ester Valborg Sahlin, b. 2 May 1905, Lerbäck, Sweden. Author; Former Teacher. Educ: Preparatory Schl. Tchrs. Exam., 1927. Publs: Sagoskogen, 1938; Hjältar och trol, 1940; Den underbara trädgarden (God's first children), 1944; Den nye konungen, 1946; Lillebror Sotare, 1952; Sanger om blommor och fjärilar, 1956; Den stora floden, 1956; Växter i liv och legend, 1967; Asarnas äventyr, 1968; jt. author of sev. textbooks. Mbrships. incl: Swedish Union of Authors. Recip., Award for lit. servs., Swedish Authors Fndn., 1960. Address: Thulehem 55, 223 67 Lund, Sweden.

SALO, Arvo Jaakko Henrik, b. 2 May 1932, Merikarvia, Finland. Writer. Educ: studied Pol. & Soc. Sci., Univ. of Helsinki. Publs: Lapualaisooppera, 1966; Tilauksia, 1966; 1960-Luku (w. Bo Ahlfors), 1970. Contbr. to: Suomen Sosialidemokraatti. Mbrships: Finnish Writers' Union; Finnish Playwrights' Union. Recip., Eino Leino Prize, 1964. Address: Saariniemenkatu 1844, 00530 Helsinki 53, Finland.

SALOLA, Eeero, pen names LAURI; LAURI, Pikku; DIOGENES, b. 1 June 1902, Mathildedahl, Pernio. Education Counsellor; University Instructor; Author & Editor. Educ: Pub. Schls. Tchng. studies at univ. level.

Publs. incl: Ilman fritsaria, 1929; Kevaista kylvoa, 1939; Holmolan kyla, 1960; Robinson Crusoe lapsille, 1962; The History of the Art of Recitation in Finland & Literature in Finland, 1968; var. schl. textbooks. Contbr. to: Kansakoulum Lehti; Opettajain Lehit. Chief Ed., Valistuksen Lastenlehti; 1931-51, Joulupukki, 1936-65. Mbr. & Hon. Mbr., lit. & other orgs. Recip., Ponkalan Saatio Prize, 1968. Address: Pohjois-Hesperiankatu 9 A, 00260 Helsinki 26, Finland.

SALOM, Jaime, b. 25 Dec. 1925, Barcelona, Spain. Playwright. Educ: M.D., Univ. of Barcelona. Publs. incl: El baúl de los disfraces, 1965, 3rd ed., 1973; Parchis Party, 1966; Espejo para dos mujeres, 1966; Falta da pruebas, 1968; La casa de la Chivas, 1969, 1973; Los delfines, 1969; La playa vacia, 1971; Viaje en un trapecio, 1971; Teatro Representativo Español, 1972; La noche de los cien pájaros, 1973; Tiempo de Espadas, 1973. Hons: Premio de la Crítica de Madrid, 1969, 1973; Premio Nacional de Literatura, 1969; Premio Alvarez Quintero de la Real Academia Española, Madrid, 1972; Premio "Bravo", 1974. Address: Mallorca 279, Barcelona 9, Spain.

SALOMONE, A. William, b. 18 Aug. 1915, Guardiagrele, Italy. Wilson Professor of European History; Historian. Educ: B.A., La Salle Coll., USA, 1938; M.A., 1940, Ph.D., 1943, Univ. of Pa. Publs: Italian Democracy in the Making, 1945; L'Età Giolittiana, 1949; Readings in 20th Century European History, 1950; Italy in the Giolittian Era, 1960; Italy from the Risorgimento to Fascism, 1970, 1971. Contbr. to: Am. Histl. Review; Jrnl. of Mod. Hist.; Revista Storica Italiana; other profl. jrnls. Mbr., var. histl. assns. Hons. incl: Adams Prize, Am. Histl. Assn., 1946; Order of Merit, Italian Repub., 1960; Centennial Award, La Salle Coll., 1963; Citation, Soc. for Italian Histl. Studies, 1976; Nat. Endowment of Humanities; & var. fellowships. Address: 320 Chelmsford Rd., Rochester, NY 14618, USA.

SALOMONSON, Kurt, b. 18 July 1929, Hjoggböle, Skellefteå, Sweden. Author. Publs: Grottorna, 1956; Mannen utanför, 1958; Sveket, 1959; Skiljevägen, 1962; Sista skiftet, 1967. Contbr. to: Dagens Nyheter; Vi; SIA (trade jrnl.). Mbrships: Swedish Authors' Assn.; PEN. Hons: Lit. Prize, Svenska Dagbladet, 1962; Swedish State Prize for Authors of High Lit. Merit., 1962. Address: Frihetsvägen 51, III, 175 33 Järfälla, Sweden.

SALT, Colin McBride, b. 4 June 1939, Auckland, NZ. Photographer. Publs: My Cobber, 1967; Born to Obey, 1972. Contbr. to: NZ Herald; Sunday Herald; Auckland Star; Jrnl. of Agric.; Weekly News Annual. Address: 17 Summer St., Stanley Bay, Devonport, Auckland, NZ.

SALT, Valerie Rose (née Guy), b. 22 Jan. 1938, Rotrua, NZ. Journalist. Publs: My Cobber, 1967; Born to Obey, 1972. Contbr. to: NZ Herald; Sunday Herald. Address: 17 Summer St., Stanley Bay, Devonport, Auckland, NZ.

SALTER, Elizabeth Fulton, b. Angaston, Australia. Writer. Educ: Univ. Adelaide. Publs: Death in a Mist, 1957. Will to Survive, 1958; There Was a Witness, 1961; The Voice of the Peacock, 1963; Once Upon a Tombstone, 1965; The Last Years of a Rebel, 1967; Daisy Bates, 1971; The Lost Impressionist, 1975. Mbrships: Crime Writers' Assn.; PEN; Soc. Authors (Aust.). Address: 9 Regina Ct., 40 Fitzjohn's Ave., London NW3, UK.

SALTER, James, b. 10 June 1926, Passaic, N.J., USA. Writer. Publs: The Hunters, 1957; The Arm of Flesh, 1961; A Sport & a Pastime, 1967; Light Years, 1975. Contbr. to: Paris Review. Hons: 3 Stories in O. Henry Prize Story Collections of 1970, 1972 & 1974 respectively. Address: Box 2738, Aspen, CO 81611, USA.

SALVADORI, Max William (Massimo), b. 16 June 1908, London, UK. Teacher. Educ: Licencle es Sciences Sociales, Geneva, 1929; Dott.Sc. (Pol.), Rome, 1930. Publs: NATO: A Twentieth Century Community of Nations, 1957; Liberal Democracy, 1957; The Economics of Freedom: American Capitalism Today, 1959; Locke & Liberty, 1959; Cavour & the Unification of Italy, 1961; La Resistenza nell' Anconetano e nel Piceno, 1962; The American Economic System, 1963; Da Roosevelt a Kennedy, 1964; Italy, 1965; Modern Socialism, 1968; European Liberalism, 1972; A Pictorial History of the Italian People, 1972; Breve Storia della Resistenza Italiana, 1974; The Rise of Modern Communism, 1974. Contbr. to var. histl. jrnls. Recip., D.Litt., 1959. Address: 36 Ward Ave., Northampton, MA 01060, USA.

SAMARAKIS, Antonis, pen name KYPRIANOS, Iossif, b. 16 Aug. 1919, Athens, Greece. Author. Educ: Dip., Fac. of Law, Athens Univ. Publs. incl: (short stories) Zititai Elpis (Wanted: Hope), 1954, 9th ed. 1975; Arnoumai (I Refuse), 1961, 8th ed. 1974; To Diavatirio (The Passport), 1973, 5th ed. 1975; (novels) Sima Kyndinou (Danger Signal), 1959, 9th ed. 1975; To Lathos (The Flaw), 1965, 15th ed. 1975; (as Kyprianos) an anthol. of children's poems, 1947; works transld. into 22 langs.; many filmed. Contbr. to num. mags. & jrnls. Mbrships incl: PEN; Nat. Soc. Greek Authors. Hons. incl: Greek Nat. Book Award, 1962; Prize of the 12, 1966; Grand Prix de Lit. Policière, France, 1970. Address: 53 Taygetou & Ippolytou Sts., Athens 806, Greece.

SAMAYOA CHINCHILLA, Carlos, b. 10 Dec. 1898, Guatemala City. Writer. Educ: Nat. Inst. of Varones. Publs: Madre Milpa, 1934; Cuatro Suertes, 1936; La Casa de la Muerta, 1941; El Dictador y Yo, 1950; Estampas de la Costa Grande, 1954; El Quetzal no es Rojo, 1956; Chapines de Ayer, 1957; The Art of the Ancient Maya, 1959; Aproximacion al Arte Maya, 1964. Contbr. to Diario de Centro América, 1922-28. Mbrships: Gen. Directorate of Fine Arts (Co-Fndr.); Dir., Guatemala Inst. of Anthropol. & History. Num. medals & awards. Address: 4a Calle 14-22, Zona 13, Guatemala City, Guatemala.

SAMCHUK, Ulas, b. 20 Feb. 1905, Derman, Rowno, Ukraine. Writer. Educ: Univ. of Breslau, Germany; Ukrainian Univ. of Prague, Czech., 1928-32. Publs. incl: (novels) Volynia, 3 vols., 1932, 1935, 1937; What Fire Doesn't Heal, 1959; On Solid Land, 1967; (tril.) Ost, 1948, The Farm of Moros, 1948, Darkness, 1957; Paradise Regained (short stories), 1936. Contbr. to var. lit. jrnls. Mbrships: PEN; Ukrainian Writers' Assn. in Exile. Hons: Lit. Prize, Assn. of Writers & Jrnlsts. of Lvov, 1934; Hon. Medal, Shevchenko Sci. Soc., Toronto, 1965; Hon. Award, Ukrainian Can. Comm. for Cultural Activity, 1974. Address: 429 Glenlake Ave., Toronto, Ont. M6P 1G5, Can.

SAMPEDRO, Jose Luis, b. 1 Feb. 1917, Barcelona, Spain. University Professor of Economics. Educ: Licenciado, Econ. Scis., 1947; Dr. Econ. Scis., 1950. Publs. incl: (sci.) The European Future of Spain, 1960; Economic Structure, 1969; Conscience of Underdevelopment, 1973; (in Engl.) Regional Profiles of Spain, 1964; Decisive Forces in World Economics, 1967; (fiction) Congreso en Estocolmo, 1952; El Rio que nos lleva, 1962; El Caballo Desnudo, 1970; (plays) La Paloma de Carton, 1950; Un Sitio para vivir, 1956. Mbrships: Colegio Nacional de Economistas; Assn. Española de Ciencia Reg. Recip., Premio Nacional de Teatro Calderon de la Barca, 1950. Address: Marqués de Urquijo 11, Madrid 8, Spain.

SAMPSON, R. Neil, b. 29 Nov. 1938, Spokane, Wash., USA. Soil Conservationist. Educ: B.S. (Agric.), Univ. of Idaho, 1960; M.P.A., Harvard Univ., 1974. Contbr. to: Scouting; All Outdoors; Incredible Idaho; Idaho Farmer; Soil Conserv.; Jrnl. Am. Inst. of Planners; Snowmobiling; Boise Business. Mbrships: Soil Conserv. Soc. of Am. (Sect. Pres., Southwest Idaho, 1973); Outdoor Writers' Assn. of Am.; Conserv. Educ. Assn. Hons: Fed. Civil Servant of 1972, Boise, Idaho. Address: 5209 York Road, Alexandria, VA 22310, USA.

SAMPSON, Ronald Victor, b. 12 Nov. 1918, Lancs., UK. University Lecturer. Educ: M.A., Keble Coll., Oxford; D.Phil., Nuffield Coll., Oxford. Publs: Progress in the Age of Reason, 1957; Equality & Power, 1965; Tolstoy: the Discovery of Peace, 1973. Contbr. to: The Nation (N.Y., USA). Address: Beechcroft, Hinton Charterhouse, Bath, Somerset, UK.

SAMUEL, (Viscount) Edwin Herbert, b. 1898, London, UK. Writer; University Lecturer. Educ: Balliol Coll., Oxford; Columbia Univ., N.Y. Publs. incl: A Primer of Palestine, 1932; The Theory of Administration, 1947; Problems of Government in the State of Israel, 1956; The Structure of Society in Israel, 1969; A Lifetime in Jerusalem: Memoirs, 1969; (short stories) My Friend Musa, 1963; The Cucumber King, 1965; His Celestial Highness, 1968; The Man Who Liked Cats, 1970; (for children) Capt. Noah & His Ark. Recip., C.M.G. Address: 15 Rashba Rd., Jerusalem, Israel.

SAMUEL, Richard Herbert, b. 23 Mar. 1900, Elberfeld, Germany. Professor of Germanic Studies (retired). Educ: Dr.Phil., Berlin; Ph.D., Cantab.; M.A., Melbourne. Publs. incl: Education & Society in Modern Germany (w. R.H. Thomas), 1949; Chief Ed., Works & Correspondence of Friedrich von Hardenberg (Novalis), 4 vols., 1960-75; "Urfaust." Goethe's Faust in its Original Version, 1958; H.v. Kleist: Prinz Friedrich von Homburg, 1967; H.v. Kleist: Der Zerbrochene Krug, 1964, 2nd ed., 1969. Contbr. to: Mod. Lang. Review; Euphorion; & num. other lit. jrnls. Mbrships. incl: Fellow, Aust. Acad. of the Humanities; Patron, Aust. Goethe Soc.; Hon. Mbr., MLA of Am.; etc. Recip., Gold Medal, Goethe Inst., Munich, 1967. Address: 65 Bay St., Brighton, Vic., Australia 3186.

SANCHEZ, Eduardo R., b. 22 Feb. 1942, Pasay City, Philippines. Journalist. Educ: B.Sc. (For. Serv.), Univ. of Philippines. Contbr. to: Data for Decision (designer & producer); all major dailies & wklies in Philippines before imposition of martial law. Mbrships: estab. & developed Reg. Ref. Serv. of the Press Fndn. of Asia; Philippine Press Inst. (Dir.). Address: 8 Alpine St., Merville Park, Paranaque, Rizal, Philippines.

SANCHEZ ESPESO, German, b. 22 Jan. 1940, Pamplona, Navarra, Spain. Film Producer. Educ: Grad. (Philos. & Cinematography), Univ. of Valladolid: TV Prods. Cert., Prado del Rey Studios, Madrid. Publs: "Pentateuch" Penthalogy: Experimento en Genesis, 1967; Sintomas de Exodo, 1969; Laberinto Levitico, 1972; De Entre Los Numeros (banned in Spain, to appear soon in S. Am.). Mbr., Ed. Coun., Ediciones del Centro. Address: Somontin 104-6°-D, Madrid 33, Spain.

SÁNCHEZ PAREDES, Pedro, b. 11 June 1926, Mataró, Spain. Translator; Literary Critic. Educ: Lic. Law. Publs: (novels) Dios ha pasado sobre los bosques, 1963; La Ley Viva, 1964; La Gran Apostasía, 1968; Sphairos, 1969; Teluria, un pais de tinieblas, 1972; also collect. of plays, Siete Apocalipsis, 1965; (biog.) El Marqués de Sade, un profeta de infierno, 1974. Contbr. to: Jano, Barcelona; Futuro presente, Madrid. Recip., Temas de Madrid Prize, 1966. Address: Calle Gen. Ramírez de Madrid 18, 1°-C, Madrid 20, Spain.

SANDAUER, Arthur, b. 14 Dec. 1913, Sambor, USSR (formerly Poland). Writer; University Professor. Educ: Dr., Cracow Univ.; Prof., Warsaw Univ. Publs: Death of the Liberal (stories), 1947; Poets of Three Generations (essays), 1955; Lyrics & Logics (essays), 1967; Transls. of Euripides, Aristophanes, Theocritus. Mbrships: Union of Polish Writers; PEN. Recip., Prize for "Lyrics & Logics", Zycic Literackie, 1969. Address: Warsaw, Karlowicra 20/1, Poland.

SANDBERG, (Jonkheer) Henri Willem, b. 17 Aug. 1898, Batavia (now Djakarta Raya). Indonesia. Journalist. Educ: 2 yrs. at Univ. Publs: Transl., B. Llañes, Alphonse XIII, 1922; Transl., L. Bruun, Van Zanten's Eiland van Gelukzaligheid, 1924; Schaduw (poems), 1931; Andrée, (novel) 1940; Transl., Dostoievsky, Een Onaangename Geschiedenis, 1948; Transl., Sartre, De Lichtekooi, 1949. Contbr. to: Het Vaderland (Art Corres.); Kampioen. Recip., Chevalier, Légion d'Honneur, France. Address: 45 Bushmead Ave., Bedford, Beds., UK.

SANDBERG, Lucille, b. 4 July 1906, Greenback Mines, Ore., USA. Public Health Nurse; Author. Educ: R.N., L.A. Gen. Hosp.; post-grad. work, N.Y. Polyclin. & Chgo. Lying-In Hosps.; PHN & B.S., UCLA, 1946. Publs: Six Islands, poems of the Hawaiian Islands, 1953; In Bamboo Stalks, haiku & tanka, 1963; Roundup, traditional poems of the West, 1966; Lotus Mood, haiku & tanka, 1967. Contbr. of poems to num. newspapers, mags. & anthols. inclng: Caxton Poetry Review; Anthol. of Desert Poetry. Mbr., var. lit. orgs. Recip., sev. awards. Address: 2130 N. Baker St., Bakersfield, CA 93305, USA.

SANDBLAD-HANESON, (Emelie Cecilia Sofia), Sonja, pen name TORPARE, Tord, b. 21 Dec. 1889, Gothenburg, Sweden. High School Teacher; Former Journalist. Educ: B.A. Publs: Salig Prostens Trälkvinna, 1916; Hemmets Ekonomiska Organisation, 1924; Prästaskräcken och den Bottenlösa Prästasäcken, 1924; Tonen från Himlen, 1952; Mbrships: Swedish Authors' Union; Tanums Härads Lottakår (Chief 1936-46). Hons: Silver Medal, Riksförbundet Sveriges Lottakårers; Gold Medal, Bohuslän-Dals. Address: Box 111, 450 81 Grebbestad, Sweden.

SANDERLIN, George, b. 5 Feb. 1915, Balt., Md., USA. Professor of English. Educ: B.A., Am. Univ., 1935; Ph.D., Johns Hopkins Univ., 1938. Publs. incl: Across the Ocean Sea: A Journal of Columbus's Voyage, 1966; 1776: Journals of American Independence, 1968; Benjamin

Franklin: As Others Saw Him, 1971; Bartolome de Las Casas: A Selection of His Writings (transl. & ed.), 1971; The Settlement of California, 1972; A Hoop to the Barrel: The Making of the American Constitution, 1974. Contbr. to acad. jrnls. & encys. Recip., sev. acad. hons. Address: San Diego State Univ., San Diego, CA, USA.

SANDERS, Frederick William Thomas, pen names WEALDEN WANDERER; HOBO DIARIST, b. 9 Aug. 1908, Pluckley, Kent, UK. Retired from Shipbuilding, Salvage. Publs. incl: Kentish (Wealden) Dialect, 1935; Natural History of Mundy Bois, 1937; Psychical Research in Haunted Kent, 1946; Pluckley Was My Playground, 1956; A Business History of Chatham High Street, 1838-1961, 4 vols., 1961. The Chatham Dockyard Diary, 1898-1936, 1964; Lawrence of Arabia: A Psychological Study, 1938; num. short stories. Contbr. to local & county press, mags. Hons: Outstanding Cartophilic Writer of Year Shield, 1954. Address: 42 Sydney Rd., Chatham, ME4 5PP, Kent, UK.

SANDERS, James Edward, b. 4 Mar. 1911, Dargaville, NZ. Journalist; Author. Educ: Massey Univ., Palmerston N., NZ. Publs: The Time of My Life, 1967; The Green Paradise, 1971; The Shores of Wrath, 1972; Kindred of the Winds, 1973; High Hills of Gold, 1973; Our Explorers, 1974; New Zealand VC Winners, 1974; Fire in the Forest, forthcoming; The Lamps of Maine, forthcoming; Where Lies the Land, forthcoming. Contbr. as columnist, Sunday Herald, Auckland. Address: "Landfall", 42 Roberta Ave., Glendowie, Auckland 5, NZ.

SANDERS, Lawrence, b. 1920, Brooklyn, N.Y., USA. Author; Editor. Educ: Grad., Wabash Coll., Ind., 1940. Publs. incl: The Anderson Tapes; The Pleasures of Helen; Love Songs; The First Deadly Sin, 1973. Contbr. to: num. mags. (over 100 short stories & articles); Mechanix Illustrated (staff, 9 yrs.); Sci. & Mechs. (Ed., 4 yrs.). Hons. incl: The First Deadly Sin, Book-of-the-Month Selection, Oct., 1973. Address: c/o G. P. Putnam's Sons, 200 Madison Ave., N.Y., NY 10016, USA.

SANDERS, Norman Joseph, b. 22 Apr. 1929, Birkenhead, UK. Professor of English Literature. Educ: B.A.(Engl. lang. & lit); Postgrad. dip. in educ.; Ph.D., Birmingham Univ. Publs: Shakespearian Essays, 1964; William Shakespeare: Comedian, 1965; Robert Greene's: James the Fourth, 1970; Ed., 4 Shakespeare plays. Contbr. to: Mod. Lang. Review; Review of Engl. Lit.; Renaissance Quarterly; Shakespeare Studies; etc. Mbrships. incl: Marlowe Soc.; Mod. Lang. Assn., Am.; Int. Assn., Univ. Profs. of Engl. Hons. incl: Univ. of Tenn. Disting. Tchng. prof., 1968. Address: Avenue Hse., Bishopton, Stratford-upon-Avon, Warwicks., UK.

SANDERS, Ronald, b. 7 July 1932, Union City, N.J., USA. Writer; Editor. Educ: B.A., Kenyon Coll., Gambier, Ohio, 1954; M.A., Columbia Univ., N.Y., 1957; Sorbonne, Paris, France, 1960-61. Publs: Socialist Thought: A Documentary History (co-author), 1964; Israel: The View from Masada, 1966; The Downtown Jews, 1969; Reflections on a Teapot, 1972. Contbr. to: N.Y. Times; New Republic; Nation; Commentary; Commonweal; Ed., Midstream. Recip., B'nai B'rith Book Award, 1970. Address: 515 Park Ave., N.Y., NY 10022, USA.

SANDERSON, Nora Brocas, b. 14 Feb. 1905, Opotiki, NZ. Author; former Nurse. Publs: Hospital in New Zealand, 1962; The Ordeal of Nurse Thompson, 1963; The Two Faces of Nurse Roberts, 1963; Shadows in the Ward, 1964; A Partner for Doctor Philip, 1964; The Taming of Nurse Conway, 1964; The Case for Nurse Sheridan, 1965; The Mysterious Nurse Savenley, 1965; Nurse without Portfolio, 1965; Nurse Meredith, 1966; Nurse Joanne's Final Choice, 1966; Junior Nurse on Ward 7, 1967; Urgent Case for Doctor Belmont, 1967; No Welcome for Nurse Jane, 1968; No Bells Were Ringing, 1968; Stranger to the Truth, 1969; A Place in the Sun, 1969; Heart of Stone, 1970; Come in from the Cold, 1971; num. transls. into Dutch, Danish, Swedish & Portuguese. Mbrships: British Romantic Novelists' Assn.; NZ Women Writers' Soc.; S. Island Writers' Soc.; Friends of the Museum Soc., Canterbury; Life Mbr., St. John Ambulance Soc. Address: 746 Main South Rd., Christchurch 4, NZ.

SANDERSON, William Henry, occasional pen name ALEXANDER, Hank, b. 27 Sept. 1923, Helper, Utah, USA. Library Assistant; Range Conservationist (ret'd.). Educ: B.S., Utah State Univ.; Ph.D., Nazarene Coll., London; Cert. Grapho-analyst. Contbr. to var. metaphys.

mags., poetry anthols., jrnls., etc. Mbrships. incl: Avalon Poetry Group; World Poetry Soc. Intercontinental. Recip., Award, World Univ. Address: 515 East First South, Salt Lake City, UT 84102, USA.

SANDFORD, Jeremy, b. 5 Dec. 1934. Writer. Educ: Oxford Univ. Publs: Synthetic Fun, 1967; Cathy Come Home, 1967; Whelks & Chromium, 1968; Edna the Inebriate Woman, 1971; Down & Out in Britain, 1971; In Search of the Magic Mushrooms, 1972; Gypsies, 1973. Contbr. to: Romano Drom (Ed.). Mbrships: Cyrenians (Dir.); Gypsy Coun. (Exec.). Hons: Screen Writers Guild of GB Award, 1967, 1971; Prix Italia for TV drama, 1968; Critics' Award for TV Drama, 1971. Address: 10 Bell Lane, Twickenham, Middx., UK.

SANDFORD, Kenneth Leslie, b. 14 Aug. 1915, Auckland, NZ. Commission Chairman. Educ: LL.B. Publs: Dead Reckoning, 1955; Dead Secret, 1957; Mark of the Lion, 1962. Mbrships: PEN; NZ Law Soc. Hons: C.M.G., 1974. Address: Box 27300, Wellington, New Zealand.

SANDLES, Arthur, b. 11 Nov. 1935, Durham, UK. Journalist. Contbr. to: Financial Times (Leisure Ed.); var. mags.; radio & TV. Recip., Thomson Travel Writer, 1971. Address: Yew Park Cottage, Beckley, Rye, Sussex, UK.

SANDMAN LILIUS, Irmelin, b. 14 June 1936. Author. Publs: Bonadea, 1967; Fru Sola Trilogy — Gullkrona gränd, 1969, Gripanderska gården, 1970, Gångande Grå, 1971; Kung Tulle, 1972; Kapten Grunnstedt, 1974. Mbr., Soc. of Swedish Lang. Authors in Finland. Hons: Lit. Prizes of Finnish State, 1965, 1970; Nils Holgerson Plaque, 1972; IBBY Hon. List, 1974. Address: Vårdberget, Hangö, Finland.

SANDON, Eric Charles Rothwell, b. 4 May 1912, Bickley, Kent, UK. Architect. Educ: Archtl. Assn., London; A.R.I.B.A., 1940; F.R.I.B.A., 1970. Publs: A View into the Village: A Study of Suffolk Building, 1969. Contbr. to East Anglian Daily Times (book reviews). Mbrships. incl: F.R.S.A. Address: Outlands, California, Woodbridge, Suffolk, UK.

SÁNDOR, András, b. 11 July 1923, Vienna, Austria. Writer; Translator. Educ: Classical & Romance Philol. Publs: (in Hungarian) Övék a Föld (They Have the Earth), 1948; Hiradás a Pusztáról (Report on the Farmstead), 1950; Huszonnégyen kezdték (Twenty-four Were Beginning), 1951; A Nyugtalan Ember (The Fidgety Man), 1954; Transls. novels Miguel Angel Asturias & Jose Eustasio Ribera into Hungarian, 1967-74. Contbr. to: Uj Irás (New Writing); Vezetőkepzés (Mgmt. Rsch.); World Tobacco. Mbrships: Hungarian Assn. Writers; Sci. Assn. Food Ind.; State Mgmt. Rsch. Centre. Recip., József Attila Prize, 1951. Address: Bethlen-u. 8, 3300 Eger, Hungary.

SÁNDOR, László, b. 20 Mar. 1909, Budapest, Hungary. Translator; Art Historian; Critic. Educ: Art Hist. dip., Repin Inst. Publs: transls. of poems & lit. works by: Karel Čapek, F. X. Šalda, Milo Urban, Panas Mirny, Ivan Franko, Oles Khonchar, Maxim Gorky, Mikhail Sholokhov, etc. Contbr. to: Kortárs, Nagyvilág, Napjaink, Magyar Könyvszemle; etc. Mbrships: PEN; Hungarian Writers' Union; Hungarian Soc. of Lit. Hist. Hons: Medal for Socialist Culture, 1966; Golden Degree, Order of Labour, 1969; Hon. Dip., Union of Soviet Writers, 1970. Address: 1098 Budapest IX, Táviró u. 23/II.1. Hungary.

SANDVIK, Kjell, b. 4 July 1929, Trondheim, Norway. Journalist. Educ: Arhaus Univ., Denmark; Norwegian Corres. Schl.; Uppsala Univ. Publs. incl: expo (poems), 1968; Dikt ved breen, 1969; Makene (novel), 1970; Visa i graset (poems), 1972; Vestbagoya Meieri (historic study of life of peasants in the North), 1974; Isbilders lys (poems), 1974. Contbr. to jrnls. & mags. Mbrships: Norwegian Soc. of Authors; Norsk Forfattersentrum. Chmn., Union of North-Norwegian Authors. Hons: Stipend, City of Tromso, 1969. Address: 8370 Leknes i Lofoten, Norway.

SANGUINETI, Edoardo, b. 9 Dec. 1930, Genoa, Italy. Professor of Italian Literature, University of Genoa. Educ: B.A., Univ. of Turin. Publs. incl: Laborintus, 1956; Opus metricum, 1960; Interpretazione di Malebolge, 1961; Tra liberty e crepuscolarismo, 1961; Tre studi danteschi, 1961; Alberto Moravia, 1962; K. e altre cose, 1962; Capriccio italiano, 1963; Triperuno, 1964; Ideologiae linguaggio, 1965; Guido Gozzano, 1966; Il realismo di Dante, 1966; Il Giuoco dell'Oca, 1967; Teatro, 1969; Il Giuoco del Satyricon, 1970; Storie naturali, 1971; Wirrwarr, 1972;

Catamerone, 1974. Address: via Cabella, 11/8 — 16122 Genoa, Italy.

SANNE, Sven Torkel, b. 25 July 1930, Uddevalla, Sweden. Dairy Nutritionist. Educ: Agronomist, Agr.lic., Agric. Coll., Uppsala; M.S., Cornell Univ., USA. Publs., co-author of sev. textbooks on animal feeding & foodstuffs, inclng: Animalieproduktion; Fodermedlen; Kvigornas uppfödning och inkalvning. Contbr. to jrnls. inclng: Lantmännen: Land. Mbrships: Sec. & Cashier, Assn. of Swedish Agricl. & Forestry Jrnlsts. Address: Lantmännen, Box 12238, S — 10226 Stockholm, Sweden.

SANNIE, James Dauphin, b. 8 Aug. 1906, Accra, Ghana. Author; Journalist; Proprietor-Principal, Enisan Rapid Commercial School. Educ: Hdmaster. Tchrs. Cert. "A". Publs: Ga & Dangme Customs, Part I, Kofi & Akua Series 1-3 (Ella Griffin, ed.); New Methodist Ga Hymn Book; Your Teeth Are Precious (co-author). Contbr. to Mansralo-Ghanaian Bi-Weekly Newspaper (Publs. Off.). Mbr., num. orgs. Address: P.O. Box 3380, Accra, Ghana.

SANSOM, William, b. 18 Jan. 1912, London, UK. Writer. Publs. incl: (short stories) Fireman Flower, UK, 1944, USA, 1945; Something Terrible, Something Lovely, UK, 1948, USA, 1954; A' Touch of the Sun, UK, 1952, USA, 1958; The Stories of William Sansom, UK & USA, 1963; The Ulcerated Milkman, 1966; The Vertical Ladder, 1969; (novels) The Face of Innocence, UK & USA, 1951; The Cautious Heart, UK & USA, 1958; Goodbye, UK, 1966, USA, 1967; Hans Feet in Love, 1971; (non-fiction) Marcel Proust & his World, 1972; var. juvenile & travel books. Mbrship: F.R.S.L. Recip., Schlrship. 1946, Bursary, 1947, Soc. of Authors. Address: c/o Elaine Greene Agcy., 31 Newington Green, London NW6, UK.

SÁNTA, Ferenc, b. 4 Sept. 1927, Brassó, Rumania. Research Worker, Hungarian Academy of Sciences. Publs: Winter Blooming (short stories), 1956; Wolves on the Threshold (short stories), 1961; Fifth Stamp, 1963; Twenty Hours, 1964; Traitor, 1965; Night (drama), 1969; God on the Cart (short stories), 1972. Mbrships: PEN, Budapest, Hungary; Mbr., Praesidium, Assn. of Hungarian Writers. Hons: József Attila Prize, Budapest, 1956 & 1965; Kossuth Prize, Budapest, 1973; Gold Nymph Prize, Monte Carlo Film Festival. Address: Budapest 1025, Áldás-u. 11, Hungary.

SANTEN, Sal(omon), b. 3 Aug. 1915, Amsterdam, Netherlands. Author. Publs: Jullie is Jodenvolk, 1969; Sneevliet, rebel, 1971; Deze Vijandige Wereld, 1972; Adiós Compañeros, 1974; Een Geintje, 1975. Contbr. to: Maatstaf; Vrij Nederland; Hon. Ed., Propria Cures (lit. student paper). Mbr., Vereniging van Letterkundigen. Address: Drakenstein 36, Amsterdam, Netherlands.

SANTOS-RUIZ, Angel, b. 19 July 1912, Reinosa (Santander), Spain. Professor of Biochemistry; Author. Educ: M.D., Salamanca Univ.; Pharm.D., Madrid Univ. Publs: Las Hormonas en Medicina, 1947; Bioquimica de los Lipidos, 1950; Tratado de Bioquimica, 2 vols., 1970-71. Contbr. to: Nature; Plant Sci. Letters; Physiol. Chem. & Phys.; Annales pharmaceutiques françaises; Revista Espanola de Fisiologia; Nuestro Tiempo; Anales de la Real Academia de Farmacia, etc. Address: Ministro Ibañez-Martin No. 2, Madrid (15), Spain.

SANTSCHI, Madeleine, b. 6 Dec. 1916, Vevey, Switz. Writer; Journalist. Educ: Univ. studies. Publs: La Pièce se joue à l'intérieur, 1959; Sonate, 1965; (transls. from Italian) Les Amoureux, Metaponto, La Terre du Souvenir, by A. Pierro, 1972; Pagelle, by A. Pizzuto, 2 vols., 1973-74. Contbr. to: Gazette de Lausanne; Le Monde; 24 Heures Lausanne; Tribune de Lausanne. Mbr., Gruppe Olten (Swiss Writers' Grp.). Address: La Cerisaie, 1008 Jouxtens-Lausanne, Switz.

SANYAL, Probodh Kumar, b. 7 July 1905, Calcutta, India. Writer. Educ: City Coll., Calcutta. Publs: Jajabar, 1928; Kalarab, Nishipadma, 1932; Priyabandhabi, Mahaprasthaner Pathe, 1933; Anka-Banka, 1939; Nad-O-Nadi, 1940; Jalakallol, 1944; Hasubanu, 1952; Devatatma Himilaya, 1955; Russian Diary, Bibagi Bhramar, 1960; Uttar Himalaya Charit, 1965. Contbr. to: Kallol; Kali-Kalam; Desh; Bijali; Amrita; Bazar Patrika; Jugantar; etc. Mbrships. incl: Rabindra Sadan; Nat. Lib.; Writers' Club; Himalayan Assn. (Pres.); Himalayan Fedn. Calcutta (Fndr.-Pres.). Hons: M.A. for creative lit. from Calcutta Univ.; Gold Medal Calcutta Univ. Address: 6 Ballygunge Terrace, Golpark, Calcutta 19, India.

SAPINSLEY, Alvin, b. 23 Nov. 1921, Providence, R.I., USA. Television & Screen Playwright. Educ: B.A., Bard Coll., Annandale-on-Hudson, N.Y. Mbr., Writers' Guild of Am., West, Inc. Hons: Annual Award, Mystery Writers of Am. (for Sting of Death), 1955; Nomination for Writing Achievement. TV-Radio Writers' Annual Award (for Gannon); Hon. Mention, Harcourt Brace Awards for Best TV Plays (for Lee at Gettysburg), 1957. Address: 15029 Greenleaf St., Sherman Oaks, CA 91403, USA.

SAPORTA, Marc, b. 20 Mar. 1923, Constantinople, Turkey. Journalist. Educ: B.A., M.A., Sorbonne Univ.; Dr. Law., Madrid Univ., Spain. Publs: (novels) Le Furet, 1959; La Quête, 1961; La Distribution, 1961; Composition No. 1, 1962; Les Invités, 1964; (essays) Le Grand Défi USA-URSS (w. Georges Soria) Vol. 1, 1967, Vol. 2, 1968; Histoire du Roman Américain, 1970; La Vie Quotidienne aux USA, 1972. Contbr. to: Informations & Documents (Ed. in Chief, 1954—); L'Express; Quinzaine Littéraire; etc. Address: 9 Rue Saint Didier, Paris, France.

SAPPINGTON, Dorothy E., pen name MARSHALL, Dorothy, b. 29 Nov. 1912, St. Louis, Mo., USA. Copy Writer; Artist; Librarian. Educ: Schl. of Fine Arts, Wash. Univ., St. Louis; B.F.A., Boston Mus. Schl. Publs: Winky Pig (children's book), 1935. Contbr. to: Antique Mag.; Aust. Christian; Sunday Schl. & youth publs; book jacket notes; advt. brochures. Mbrships. incl: Past Pres., St. Louis Writers' Guild; St. Louis & Mo. Writers Guilds. Address: 224 Arbor Lane, Webster Groves, MO 36119, USA.

SARABHAI. Bharatidevi, b. 31 July 1912, London, UK. Writer; Educator. Educ: Grad., Bombay Univ., India, 1933; Grad., Oxford, UK, 1936. Publs: (plays) The Wall of the People, 1942; Two Women, 1952; Be Nari; Ghar Lakhoti, 1956. Contbr. to: London Mercury; India; Art & Culture; Our India; Behar Herald; New Horizon; Mod. Review; Hindusthan; Trikal (Bengali); Mod. Engl. Poetry; Poet; Partisan Review. Mbrships: PEN; Gujarat Vernacular Soc.; Gujarat Sahitya Sabha; Pres., Theatre Ctr., India, Affiliated to ITI of UNESCO, 1960. Recip., 2nd Bombay State Prize for Gujarati Plays, 1956. Address: The Retreat, Shahibag, Ahmedabad 380 004, Gujarat, India.

SARGESON, Frank, b. 23 Mar. 1903, Hamilton, NZ. Solicitor of New Zealand Supreme Court; Writer. Publs: I Saw in my Dream, 1949; Memoirs of a Peon, 1965; The Hangover, 1967; Joy of the Worm, 1969; Man of England Now, 1972; Once Is Enough, 1973; The Stories of Frank Sargeson, 1973. Contbr. to: Landfall; Islands. Mbrships: Pres. of Hon., NZ PEN, 1974. Recip., Litt.D., Univ. of Auckland, 1974. Address: 14 Esmond Rd., Takabuna, Auckland 9, NZ.

SARNAT, Marshall, b. 1 Aug. 1929, Chgo., Ill., USA. Professor of Finance. Educ: B.A., Hebrew Univ.; M.B.A., Ph.D., Northwestern Univ. Publs: Saving & Investment through Retirement Funds in Israel, 1966; The Development of the Securities Market in Israel, 1966; Investment & Portfolio Analysis, 1972. Contbr. to: Am. Economic Review; Jrnl. of Finance; other profl. jrnls. Address: Nayot 34, Jerusalem, Israel.

SARNO (Rev.), Ronald Anthony, S. J., b. 26 Sept. 1941, Jersey City, N.J., USA. Catholic Priest. Educ: A.B., 1965, M.A., 1966, Boston Coll.; M. Divinity, Woodstock Coll., 1972. Publs: Achieving Sexual Maturity, 1969; Let Us Proclaim the Mystery of Faith, 1970; The Story of Hope, 1972; Prayers for Modern, Urban, Uptight Man, 1974. Contbr. to: Classical Bulletin; Classical Folio; Chgo. Studies; Review for Religious; Bible Today; Sacred Heart Messenger; Cath. News; Annals of Science; L.I. Catholic; other relig. jrnls. Mbr., Int. Platform Assn. Address: St. Ignatius Retreat House, Searingtown Rd., Manhasset, NY 11030, USA.

SAROYAN, William, b. 31 Aug. 1908, Fresno, Calif., USA. Writer. Publs. incl: (short stories) The Daring Young Man on the Flying Trapeze, USA, 1934, UK, 1935; The Trouble with Tigers, USA, 1938, UK, 1939; My Name is Aram, USA, 1940, UK, 1941; The Assyrian, USA, 1950, UK, 1951; Best Stories, UK, 1964; (plays) My Heart's in the Highlands, 1939; The Time of Your Life, 1939; Hello, Out There, 1949; Don't Go Away Mad, 1949; The Cave Dwellers, 1958; Sam, The Highest Jumper of Them All, UK, 1961; 10 novels; num. vols. autobiog. & essays. Mbr., Nat. Inst. Arts & Letters. Hons. incl: N.Y. Drama Critics' Circle Award, 1940; Pulitzer Prize (refused), 1940. Address: 2729 W. Griffin Way, Fresno, CA 93705, USA.

SARRAUTE, Nathalie, b. 18 July 1902, Ivanowo, USSR. Writer. Educ: Sorbonne; Paris Schl. of Law; Oxford Univ., UK. Publs. incl: Tropismes, 1939 (Tropisms, UK, 1964); Portrait d'un Inconnu, 1948 (Portrait of a Man Unknown, UK, 1959); Martereau, 1953, UK, 1964; Le Planétarium, 1959 (The Planetarium, UK, 1962); Les Fruits d'Or, 1963 (The Golden Fruits, UK, 1965); Entre la Vie & la Mort, 1968 (Between Life & Death, UK, 1969); (plays) Le Silence, Le Mensonge, 1967 (Silence, & The Lie, UK, 1969); Isma, 1970; Vous les Entendez? , 1972 (Do You Hear Them? , UK, 1973). Recip., Prix. Int. de Lit., 1964. Address: 12 Ave. Pierre 1 de Serbie, Paris 16^e, France.

SARRI, I. Margareta, b. 10 Dec. 1944, Stockholm, Sweden. Author. Publs: Då Simon Fjällborg med Flera Kom till Insikt (When Simon Fjällborg, Among with Others, Arrived at the Truth), (novel), 1971; Man Borde Hänga sig i en Tall (Hang Myself Now), (novel), 1972. Contbr. to var. mags. Mbr., Swedish Union of Authors. Address: Nikkaluokta no. 11, 981 01 Kiruna, Sweden.

SARRÜF, Füad, b. 20 Dec. 1900. Author; University Official. Educ: B.A.; LL.D.; Am. Univ. of Beirut. Publs. incl: Conquests of Modern Science; Pillars of Modern Science, 1935; Horizons of Modern Science, 1939; The Conquest Goes on, 1944; Horizons Without End, 1958; Man & the Universe, 1961; Modern Science in Modern Society, 1966; The Eternal Fire. Contbr. to: Al-Muqtataf; Ed., Al-Mukhtar; Al-Ahram; Al-Abhath. Mbrships. incl: Lebanese Nat. Rsch. Coun.; Chmn., Exec. Bd., UNESCO; Egyptian Assn. for Adv. of Sci., 1930-52. Num. Hons. Address: 55 rue du Caire, Hamra, Beirut, Lebanon.

SARTON, May, b. 3 May 1912, Wondelgem, Belgium. Writer; Lecturer. Publs. incl: (verse) Inner Landscape, USA & UK, 1939; The Land of Silence, 1953; A Private Mythology, 1966; A Grain of Mustard Seed, 1971; A Durable Fire, 1972; (novels) The Bridge of Years, 1946; A Shower of Summer Days, USA, 1952, UK, 1954; Faithful Are the Wounds, USA & UK, 1955; The Small Room, USA, 1961, UK, 1962; Mrs. Stevens Hears the Mermaids Singing, USA, 1965, UK, 1966; Kinds of Love, 1970; (autobiog.) Plant Dreaming Deep, 1968. Mbrship: Fellow, Am. Acad. Arts & Scis. Recip., num. poetry prizes, awards, fellowships & hon. docts. Address: Nelson Village, Munsonville, NH 03457, USA.

SARTRE, Jean-Paul, b. 5 June 1905, Paris, France. Author. Educ: Degree in Philos., 1930. Publs. incl: La Nausée (Nausea), 1937; Huis-Clos, 1943; Les Chemins de la Liberté (The Paths of Liberty), 1944-45; The Age of Reason, 1947; Iron in the Soul, 1950; The Psychology of Imagination, 1951; Oeuvres Complètes (Complete works), 1952; Les Sequestrés d'Altona, 1959; Critique de la Raison Dialectique, 1961; Words (memoirs), 1964; Literary & Philosophical Essays, 1968; The Communists & Peace, 1969; Politics & Literature, 1973. Contbr. to: Les Temps Modernes (Fndg. Ed.). Refused all official hons., inclng. Nobel Prize for Lit., 1964. Address: c/o Hamish Hamilton Ltd., 90 Gt. Russell St., London WC1, UK.

SARVIG, Ole, b. 27 Nov. 1921, Copenhagen, Denmark. Writer. Publs: Cycle of Poetry in 6 books; other poems; sev. novels, essays on contemporary art & cultural hist. inclng: The Graphic Work of Edvard Munch; Krisens Billedbog (The Picture Book of Crisis — gen. essay on modernism), 1952/62. transl. into Danish of William Shakespeare. Contbr. to: Information (art Ed. 1950-52); Danish TV (art Ed. 1952-53); Scandinavian Art Mag. Mbrships: Danish Acad.; PEN; Exec., Danish Authors' Soc. Hons: Critics' Prize, 1960; Danish Acad. Prize, 1967; Lyric Prize, 1969. Address: Klostergaarden, DK-4171 Glumsø, Denmark.

SÁSDI, Sándor, (Alexander), b. 3 Sept. 1898, Varga, Hungary. Writer. Publs. incl: Aratástól Hohullásig (From Harvest to Snowfall), 1940; Fehér kenyér (White Bread), 1946; Ruzsinka (Rosie), 1954; Bosszu (Revenge), 1955; Boldog hajlék (Happy Home), 1957; Árnyék (The Shadow), 1958; Elhagyott szeretö (The Forlorn Lover), 1960; A sárga bohóc (The Yellow Baiazzo), 1970; A rigó sirja (The Tomb of the Blackbird), 1972. Mbrships: Hungarian PEN; Soc. of Hungarian Writers; Hungarian Repub. Fund for Arts. Hons: Laureate of József Attila, highest degree, 1955; Golden Medals of Merit, 1968 & 1973. Address: Mátyásföld, László ucca 9/a, Budapest 1165, Hungary.

SATA, Ineko, b. 1 June 1904, Nagasaki, Japan. Writer. Publs: Kyarameru Koba kara (From a caramel factory); Kurenai (Scarlet); Onna no Yado (The Women's Inn); Juei (The Shadow of Trees). Contbr. to: Kodansha; Shinchosha.

Mbr., Japan Writers' Assn. Hons: Prize for Woman Writers, 1963; Prize of Mr. Noma, 1972. Address: 12 – 12 – 3 chome, Kita Shinjuku, Shinjuku – ku, Tokyo, Japan.

SATTLEY, Helen R. b. 8 Jan., Saint Paul, Minn., USA. Retired Director School Libraries, N.Y.; Associate Professor Western Reserve University, 1950-53; Assistant Professor, Columbia University, 1947-50; Member of the Board of Education, N.Y., 1953-72. Educ: B.A., M.A., Northwestern Univ., Evanston, Ill.; B.S. in Lib. S., Western Reserve Univ., Cleveland, Ohio. Publs: Young Barbarians, 1947; Shadow Across the Campus, 1957; Day the Empire State Went Visiting, 1958; Annie, 1961; Cons. Ed. for var. publs. Contbr. to var. acad. jrnls. Mbrships. incl: ALA; Am. Assn. Schl. Libs.; L.I. Hist. Soc.; Authors' Guild. Hons: Dodd Mead Libns. Award, 1957 & Child Study Award, 1958 for Shadow Across the Campus. Address: 433 W. 21st St., N.Y., NY 10011, USA.

SAUKILA, Walters Simeon, b. 1905, Zede, near Blantyre, Malawi. Retired Schoolmaster & Civil Servant. Publs: Mankhwala Opezera Chuma, 1970, & ed. in Engl. lang. under title of Money. Contbr. to: Bantu Mirror, Rhodesia; Nkhani Za, Nyasaland; Kuunika mag. Mbrships: Nat. Tchrs'. Assn.; Civil Servants' Assn. Recip., 1st Class Prizes in Engl. & Chichewa langs., Annual Agricl. Show Essay Competition, Limbe, 1940. Address: P.A. Ntambanyama, P.O. Thyolo, Malawi.

SAUL, George Brandon, b. 1 Nov. 1901, Shoemakersville, Pa., USA. Emeritus Professor of English. A.B., 1923, A.M., 1930, Univ. of Pa.; Ph.D., 1932. Publs. incl: The Wild Queen, 1967; Hound & Unicorn: Coll. Verse – Lyrical, Narrative & Dramatic, 1969; Withdrawn in Gold (essays), 1970; Traditional Irish Literature & Its Background, 1970; In Mountain Shadow (novel), 1970; Liadain & Curithir (novella & short stories), 1971; The Stroke of Light (collect. of poems), 1974; var. books on Yeats. Contbr. to: The Lyric; Ariz. Quarterly; Jrnl. of Irish Lit. (contbrng. ed.); Contemporary Verse; New Republic; Queen's Quarterly; Dublin Mag.; etc. Mbrships. incl: Am. Comm. for Irish Studies. Recip., sev. lit. awards. Address: Owls' Watch, 136 Moulton Rd., Storrs, CT, USA.

SAUNDERS, Marion, b. 24 Jan. 1922, Blackburn, Lancs., UK. Teacher. Educ: Saffron Walden Trng. Coll., Essex. Publs: Take a Word, Books 1-3 (educl.); Fen Blow, 1972; The Chimney Has Eyes, 1973. Address: 30 Egremont St., Ely, Cambs., UK.

SAVAGE, John Brian, b. 5 Feb. 1931, Cambridge, Mass., USA. Cartoonist. Educ: B.A., Fordham Univ., 1953. Publs: The Savage Eye, 1971; So This Is Love, 1971; Play Me Or Trade Me, 1972; Sex 'n Violence, 1973. Contbr. to: NY Times; Saturday Review; Harpers; Playboy; Esquire; Saturday Evening Post; Look; New Yorker; True. Mbrships: Charter, Exec. Comm., Chmn. of Mbrship. Comm., Cartoonist's Guild. Address: 119 E. 89th St., N.Y., NY 10028, USA.

SAVERY, Constance Winifred, pen names CLOBERRY, Elizabeth; RYCON, b. 31 Oct. 1897, Froxfield, Wilts., UK. Author. Educ: M.A., Somerville Coll., Oxford, 1920. Publs. incl: Forbidden Doors, 1929; Pippin's House, 1931; Moonshine in Candle Street, 1937; Green Emeralds for the King, 1938; The Good Ship Red Lily, 1944; Dark House on the Moss, 1948; Scarlet Plume, 1953; Magic in My Shoes, 1958; The Reb & the Redcoats, 1961; God's Arctic Adventurer, 1973; & num. others. Contbr. to: Times; Times Educl. Supplement; Scottish Educl. Jrnl.; Child Life. Mbr., Soc. of Authors. Recip., Jr. Gold Seal, 1944. Address: Trevalfry, Halesworth Rd., Reydon, Southwold, Suffolk IP18 6NH, UK.

SAVILLE, Eugenia Curtis, b. 7 July 1913, Pa., USA. Associate Professor of Musicology & Music Literature. Educ. incl: B.M., N.J. State Tchrs'. Coll.; M.A. (Musicol.), Columbia Univ. Publs: Italian Vocal Duets from the Early Eighteenth Century, 1969; Giovanni Carlo Maria Clari: Eighteenth Century Musician of Pisa, forthcoming. Contbr. to var. music jrnls. Mbrships. incl: Int. Musicol. Soc.; AAUP; Mus. Lib. Assn. Hons: Duke Rsch Coun. Grants, 1954-55, 1959-60, 1970, 1973; rsch fellowship, Chapelbrook Fndn., Boston, 1965-1966. Address: Music Dept., Duke Univ., Box 6695 Coll. Station, Durham, NC 27708, USA.

SAVILLE, Leonard Malcolm, pen name SAVILLE, Malcolm, b. 21 Feb. 1901, Hastings, Sussex, UK. Author. Publs. incl: (series) Lone Pine Adventures; Marston Baines

Thrillers; Susan & Bill Books; Fabulous Buckinghams: Michael & Mary Stories; Nettleford Novels; (others) Come to London; King of Kings; Strange Story; Malcolm Saville's Country Book; Malcolm Saville's Seaside Book; Adventure of Lifeboat Service; See How It Grows; Jane's Country Year. Mbrships: Soc. of Authors; Writers' Action Grp. Address: Chelsea Cottage, Winchelsea, Sussex TN36 4HU, UK.

SAVORY, Alan Forsyth, b. 11 Jan. 1905, Blickling, UK. Author; Naturalist. Publs: Norfolk Fowler, 1953, 2nd ed. 1973; Lazy Rivers, 1956; Thunder in the Air, 1960. Contbr. to: Shooting Times & Country Mag.; Country Life; The Field; E. Anglian Mag.; Angling Mag. Mbrships. incl: Norfolk Club; Norwich Angling Club. Address: Riverdale, 20 Strumpshaw Rd., Brundall, Norwich, Norfolk, UK.

SAVORY, Robert, b. 22 Sept. 1938, Nairobi, Kenya. Pasture Agronomist. Educ: B.Sc., M.Sc., London Univ. Publs: Pasture Handbook for Malawi (w. Derrick Thomas), 1971. Mbrships: Aust. Inst. of Agricl. Sci.; Tropical Grasslands Soc. of Aust.; Aust. Soil Sci. Soc. Address: UNDP/FAO Livestock Proj., Box 613, Lilongwe, Malawi.

SAXTON, Carolyn Naught, b. 7 Nov. 1920, Elizabeth, N.J., USA. Poetess; Writer. Educ: B.A., Syracuse Univ. Publs: Sonnets on Identity, 1944; The Pine & the Power, 1973; A Guide to the Writing of Poetry (in preparation). Contbr. to: Ideals; Poetry; Scholastic Press. Mbrships. incl: N.J. Poetry Soc.; Instr., Poetry Workshop. Recip., N.J. Authors' Award, 1974. Address: 128 Mountain Ave., Warren, NJ 07060, USA.

SAYE, Albert B., b 29 Nov. 1912, Rutledge, Ga., USA. Professor; Author. Educ: A.B., 1934, M.A., 1935, LL.B., 1957, Univ. of Ga.; Dip., Univ. of Dijon, France, 1938; Postgrad. study, Cambridge Univ.; Ph.D., Harvard Univ. 1941. Publs. incl: New Viewpoints in Georgia History, 1943; Constitutional History of Georgia 1970; Principles of American Government, 7th ed., 1974; Georgia History & Government, 1973. Contbr. to profl. jrnls. Mbr., Desmosthenian Lit. Soc. Address: Dept. of Pol. Sci., Univ. of Ga., Athens, GA 30602, USA.

SAYLES, George Osborne, b. 20 Apr. 1901, Chesterfield, Yorks., UK. Academic. Educ: M.A., 1923, D.Litt., 1932, Glasgow Univ.; Univ. Coll., London. Publs. incl: Ed., Select Cases in the Court of King's Bench, 7 vols., 1936-71; Medieval Foundations of England, 1948; The Governance of Medieval England from the Conquest to Magna Carta (w. H. G. Richardson), 1963, 2nd ed., 1974; The King's Parliament of England, 1974. Contbr. to var. jrnls. Mbrships: Fellow, Brit. Acad.; Royal Irish Acad.; Fellow, Royal Histl. Soc. Hons: James Barr Ames Medal, 'aw Fac., Harvard Univ., 1958; Hon. D.Litt., Trinity Coll., Dublin, 1965. Address: Warren Hill, Crowborough, Sussex, UK.

SAYYAD, Imdad Ali Shah, pen name HUSSAINI, Imdad, b. 10 Mar. 1941, Tikhur, Hyderabad, Sind, Pakistan. Subject Specialist on Sind Text Book Board; Cataloguer; Writer. Educ: M.A.(Sindhi). Publs: Compiler, Catalogue of Religious Books in Sindhi, 1971. Contbr. to: Mehran; Rooh-Rehau; Soohni; Naeiu Zindagi; Maroara; Soojhero; Barsat. Mbrships: Sindhi Adabi Sangat; Bazm-e-Talbul Mola. Recip., Tulu Competition Prize, 1970. Address: F 45/580 Khokhar Para, Hyderabad, Sind, Pakistan.

SCALAPINO, Robert Anthony, b. 19 Oct. 1919, Kan., USA. Professor of Political Science. Educ: A.B., Santa Barbara Coll., 1940; M.A., 1943, Ph.D., 1948, Harvard Univ. Publs. incl: Communism in Korea (w. Chong-Sik Lee) 2 vols., 1972; Elites in the People's Republic of China (Ed. & Contbr.), 1972; Asia & the Major Powers, 1972. Contbr. to: Survey: China & the Road Ahead, 1973; Foreign Affairs: China & the Balance of Power, 1973; num. other mags. Mbrships. incl: Nat. Comm. on US-China Rels., 1966—. Recip., num. acad. hons. Address: Pol. Sci. Dept., Univ. of Calif., Berkeley, CA 94720, USA.

SCANNELL, Johannes Petrus, pen name SCANNELL, Jan, b. 26 Jan. 1916, Utrecht, S. Africa. Publisher. Educ: B.A.; U.E.D. Publs: Die Dwaling van Frederik Oppel, 1953; Keeromstraat (Ed.), 1965; Afrikaanse Kernensiklopedie (Ed.), 1965; Uit die Skemerland (Ed.), 1966; Uit die Volk Geboie, 1968; Die Berg van die Jong Mannej, 1970; Vlugteling op Puntjiesbaai, 1971. Contbr. to: Die Huisgenoot; Sarie Marais. Assoc. Mbr., S. African Acad. of Arts & Scis. Address: 29 Broadway, Bellville 7530, Repub. of S. Africa.

SCANNELL, Vernon, b. 23 Jan. 1922, Spilsby, UK. Writer. Educ: Leeds Univ. Publs: The Fight, 1953; The Face of the Enemy, 1960; The Dividing Night, 1962; The Tiger & the Rose, 1972; Selected Poems, 1972; The Winter Man, 1974. Contbr. to jrnls. inclng: The New Statesman; The Listener; Encounter; Times Lit. Supplement; London Mag. Hons: Hinemann Award for Lit. & Fellow, Royal Soc. of Lit., 1960; Cholmondeley Poetry Award, 1974. Address: Folly Cottage, Nether Compton, Sherborne, Dorset DT9 4QG, UK.

SCANTLAN, Samuel William, b. 24 Feb. 1901, Cuba, Mo., USA. Minister of the Gospel. Educ: A.B., 1936, D.D., 1957, Okla. Bapt. Univ., Shawnee. Publs: Manual for Baptist Associational Missions, 1951; Andrew Potter — Baptist Builder, 1955; Through God's Revolving Doors (poetry), 1964; T. B. Lackey — The Man & an Epoch, 1971. Contbr. to: Progressive Farmer, Ga.; Home Life. Bapt. Messenger, Okla.; Bapt. Program, Nashville, Tenn.; Okla. Farmer & Stockman; Orbit Mag., Okla.; weekly columns in Davis News, Okla. & Crawford Mirror, Steelville, Mo. Mbrships. incl: Poetry Soc. of Okla.; Okla Writers Soc.; State Histl. Soc., Okla.; Southern Bapt. Coven. Hist. Soc. Hons. incl: 2nd Place, Poetry Soc. of Okla. State Contest, 1970. Address: 402 S. 6th St., Davis, OK 73030, USA.

SCARBROUGH, George Addison, b. 20 Oct. 1915, Benton, Tenn., USA. College English Professor. Educ: B.A., Lincoln Mem. Univ., Harrogate, Tenn.; M.A., Univ. of Tenn., Knoxville. Publs: Tellico Blue, 1949; The Course Is Upward, 1951; Summer So-Called, 1956. Contbr. to: N.Y. Times; Saturday Review of Lit.; Poetry; Southern Poetry Review; Harper's; etc.; also var. anthols. Mbrships: Poetry Soc. of Am.; Pres., Sopherim (lit. soc.), Univ. of the S., Sewannee, Tenn. Hons. incl: Borestone Mtn. Award, 1961; Mary Rugeley Ferguson Poetry Award, 1964. Address: 100 Darwin Lane, Oak Ridge, TN 37830, USA.

SCARFE, Allan John, b. 30 Mar. 1931, Melbourne, Australia. School Teacher; Author. Educ: B.A., Dip.Ed., Melbourne Univ.; Trained Primary Tchrs. Cert., Bendigo Tchrs. Coll. Publs: (w. Wemdy Scarfe): A Mouthful of Petals, 1967, 1972; Tiger on a Rein, Report on the Bihar Famine, 1969; People of India, 1972; The Black Australians, Aboriginals — the Past & the Future, 1974; Victims or Bludgers?, 1974; J. P. His Biography, 1974-75. Mbrships: Pres., Warrnambool Br., Vic. Second. Tchrs. Assn.; Past Comm. Mbr., Warrnambool Br., Community Aid Abroad. Address: 8 Bostock St., Warrnambool, Vic. 3280, Australia.

SCARFE, Wendy Elizabeth, b. 21 Nov. 1933, Adelaide, S.A., Australia. Teacher. Educ: B.A., Melbourne Univ.; Assoc. Tchrs. Trng. Cert., Mercer House, Melbourne. Publs: Shadow & Flowers (poems), 1965; (w. Allan Scarfe) A Mouthful of Petals, 1967, 1972; Tiger on a Rein, Report on the Bihar Famine, 1969; People of India, 1972; The Black Australians, Aboriginals — the Past & the Future, 1974; Victims or Bludgers?, 1974; J. P. His Biography, 1974-75. Comm. Mbr., & Past Pres., Warrnambool Br., Community Aid Abroad. Address: 8 Bostock St., Warrnambool, Vic. 3280, Australia.

SCARLYN WILSON, Norman, b. 24 Mar. 1901, St. Leonards-on-Sea, Sussex, UK. University Administrative Officer; Extra-Mural Lecturer. Educ: Pembroke Coll., Cambridge Univ.; B.A., 1922, M.A., 1926. Publs: "Mr. Pendlebury", 9 detective novels under pen name Anthony Webb, w. Alex McLachlan; Under own name — Everyday French; European Drama; Ed., Notes & Introduction to texts by Corneille, Mme. de Sevigné, & others. Contbr., short stories & articles to mags. & newspapers. Address: 87 Gough Way, Cambridge CB3 9LN, UK.

SCARNE, John, b. Steubenville, Ohio, USA. Game Consultant; Author. Publs: Scarne on Dice, 1945, 1974; Scarne on Cards, 1950, 1974; Scarne on Card Tricks, 1950; Scarne on Magic Tricks, 1952; Scarne's Complete Guide to Gambling, 1962, 1974; The Odds Against Me, 1967; Scarne's Encyclopedia of Games, 1973. Contbr. to: Ency. Britannica; World Book Ency. Address: 4319 Meadowview Ave., North Bergen, NJ 07047, USA.

SCARPITTI, Frank R., b. 12 Nov. 1936, Butler, Pa., USA. Professor of Sociology. Educ: B.A., Cleveland State Univ., 1958; M.A., 1959, Ph.D., 1962, Ohio State Univ. Publs: Schizophrenics in the Community: An Experimental Study in the Prevention of Hospitalization (w. Simon Dinitz & Benjamin Pasamanick), 1967; Combating Social Problems: Techniques of Intervention (w. Harry Gold),

1967; Youth & Drugs (w. John H. McGrath), 1970; Group Interaction as Therapy (w. Richard Stephenson), 1974. Social Problems, 1974; Deviance: Action, Reaction, Interaction, 1975. Contbr. to num. jrnls. Mbrships. incl: Am. Sociol. Assn.; Am. Soc. Criminol. Hons. incl: Hofheimer Prize for Rsch., Am. Psych. Assn., 1967. Address: 104 Radcliffe Dr., Nottingham Green, Newark, DE 19711, USA.

SCHACHTER, Gustav, b. 27 May 1927, Botosani, Romania. Professor of Economics. Educ: B.S., CCNY, 1954; M.B.A., 1956, Ph.D., 1962, N.Y. Univ. Publs: The Italian South, Economic Development in Mediterranean Europe, 1965; The Yugoslav System "Socialism of the Future", 1967; The Chinese System "Asian Communism", 1968; The Economist Looks at Society (w. E. Dale), 1973. Contbr. to: Economic Development & Cultural Change, 1967; econ. jrnls. Mbrships. incl: Am. Econ. Assn.; Italian Hist. Assn.; Peace Sci. Soc. (Int.). Hons. incl: N.Y. Univ. Fndrs. Day Award, 1963. Address: 26 Egmont St., Boston, MA 02146, USA.

SCHAEFFER, Pierre, b. 14 Aug. 1910. Engineer; Writer; Composer. Educ: Ecole Polytechnique, France. Publs: Amérique, nous t'ignorons, 1946; Les Enfants de coeur, 1949; A la Recherche d'une Musique concrète, 1952; Traité des Objets musicaux, 1966; La Musique Concrète, 1967; Solfège de l'objet sonore, 1967; Le Gardien de Volcan, 1969; L'Avenir à reculons, 1970; Machines à communiquer, vol. I, 1970, vol. II, 1972. Mbr., Nat. Centre for Sci. Rsch. Hons: Legion of Honour; Chevalier des Palmes Académiques. Address: 13 rue des Petits-Champs, 75001 Paris, France.

SCHAFER, Walter Erich, b. 16 Mar. 1901, Hemmingen, Wurttemberg, Germany. Theatrical Manager; Writer. Educ: Ph.D.; Univ. Tubingen; Agricl. Univ. Stuttgart-Hohenheim. Publs. incl: (books) Gunther Rennert — Regisseur in unserer Zeit, 1962; Wieland Wagner, 1970; Die Stuttgarter Staatsoper, 1972; John Cranko — Uber den Tanz, 1974; (plays) Richter Feuerbach; Leutnant Vary; Die Reise nach Paris; Die Verschworung; Hora mortis; (radio plays) Malmgren; Spiel der Gedanken; Die Himmelfahrt des Physikers M.N. Hons. incl: Kleist-Preis, 1930; Cross of Merit, Bundesrepublik Deutschland; Civic Medal, Stuttgart. Address: Feuerreiterweg 32, 7 Stuttgart-Sonnenberg, W. Germany.

SCHALEKAMP, Jean-A., b. 26 June 1926, Rotterdam, Netherlands. Writer; Literary Translator. Educ: Univ. of Paris, France. Publs: De Dolle Trams, 1964; Bedankt voor Alles, 1966; Alles onder Handbereik, 1970; Kroniek van een Langzame Ondergang, 1975. Contbr. to: Literair Paspoort; Insula, Spain; El Urogallo, Spain. Mbrships: PEN; Vereniging van Letterkundigen. Address: Apartado 777, Palma de Mallorca, Spain.

SCHARNDORFF, Werner, b. 24 July 1925, Vienna, Austria. International Special Correspondent, Researcher & Analyst; Lecturer. Educ: D.Phil., Univ. of Vienna, 1949. Publs: History of the Communist Party of the USSR, 1960; International Communism, 1961; Moskaus permanente Säuberung, 1964; Nikita Sergeyevich Khrushchov, 1971. Contbr. to: Politiker des XX. Jahrhunderts, vol. II, 1971-72; Studies of the USSR; Politische Studien; Politische Meinung; Ostprobleme; Österreichische militärische Zeitschrift; etc. Mbrships: Union of For. Corres.'s in Vienna; Austrian Writers' Union. Recip., Hon. Mbrship., Inst. for Constitutional Law, Philos. of State & Pol. Scis., Salzburg Univ., 1970. Address: Hellbrunnerstr. 7A/IV/21, A-5020 Salzburg, Austria.

SCHARY, Dore, b. 31 Aug. 1903, Newark, N.J., USA. Writer. Director; Producer. Publs: Case History of a Movie, 1950; For Special Occasions, 1962; The Storm in the West (w. Sinclair Lewis), 1963. Contbr. to reviews & newspapers. Mbrships. incl: Treas., Dramatists Guild. Pres., Dramatist Guild Fund; Authors League; Screenwriters Guild. Num. hons. incl: Acad. Award, Best Story, "Boys Town", 1939; Antoinette Perry Award, Best Play, "Sunrise at Campobello", 1959; num. mag. awards. Address: 50 Sutton Place S., N.Y., NY 10022, USA.

SCHAUPP, Joan Pomprowitz, b. 29 Sept. 1932. Housewife. Educ: B.S., Univ. Wis., 1954. Publs: Jesus Was a Teenager, 1972. Contbr. to: Green Bay Press Gazette (formerly Women's Ed.); Spirit; Milwaukee Jrnl.; Milwaukee Sentinel; Marriage; Columbia; Parent Educator; Franciscan Message; Franciscan Herald; Transp. Topics; etc. Mbrships. incl: Nat. Press Club; Nat. Press Women; Wis.

Coun. Writers; Wis. Reg. Writers; Communications Advsry Bd., Diocese Green Bay; UWGB Fndr's. Assn. (Bd. Govs.). Hons. incl: 1st Place Wis. Press Women Contest, 1973; 2nd place mag. feature & interview, Wis. Press Women, 1973. Address: 940 Urbandale Ave., De Pere, WI 54115, USA.

SCHECHTER, Ruth Lisa, b. Boston, Mass., USA. Poet. Educ: N.Y. Univ. Publs: Near the Wall of Lion Shadows, 1969, 2nd ed., 1970; Movable Parts, 1971; Suddenly Thunder, 1972; Offshore, 1974. Contbr. to: N.Y. Quarterly; Southwest Review; Beloit Poetry Jrnl.; Prairie Schooner; Up from Under; The 19th Moon; Wagner Lit. Review; Red Clay Reader; Forum; Cornell Dialogue; Manhattan Review; & sev. anthols. Mbrships: Poetry Soc. of Am.; Am. Poetry Therapist; Poetry Forum; Vt. Writers League. Hons: Fellowships, The MacDowell Colony, 1963, 1970; Poet-in-Residence, Mundelein Coll., Chgo., Ill.; Cons. in Poetry Therapy, Odyssey House, N.Y. Address: 9 Van Cortlandt Place, Croton-on-Hudson, NY 10520, USA.

SCHEIBE, Fred Karl, b. 2 Dec. 1911, Germany. University Professor; Editor; Artist. Educ: B.A., Clark Univ., USA, 1938; M.A., Univ. of Pa., 1941; Ph.D., Univ. of Cinn., 1954. Publs: Dem Licht entgegen, 1941; Life & Poetry, 1942; Isle of Tears, 1942; Wiskonsin Erlebnis, 1942; Lost Souls, 1944; Rubinrot, 1944; Reflections, 1948; All, Erde und Mensch, 1950; Walther von der Vogelweide — Troubadour of the Middle Ages, 1969. Contbr. to: Fndr.-Ed., Hartwick Review, 1965-70; Lit. Ed., Christian Educator; Nat. Poetry Anthol., 1957; Vienna World Anthol. of Poetry, 1964—; Assoc. Ed. & contbr., Emory & Henry Review; Contbr., German-Am. Studies; etc. Mbrships. incl: MLA; Int. Inst. Arts & Letters; Nat. Soc. of Lit. & the Arts. Recip., var. acad. & cultural awards. Address: 379 Harbor Drive, Cape Canaveral, FL 32920, USA.

SCHENK, Magdalena Geertruida, pen names SCHENK, Lenie, & V. D. DRIFT, L., b. 16 Jan. 1907, Rotterdam, Netherlands. Writer. Educ: Ph.D., Utrecht Univ. Publs: Vorstenhuizen in onze Tijd (Royalty in our Time) (w. J. Spaan), 1962; Avontuur met het Woord (Adventure with the Word) (w. J. Spaan), 1964; Prins Claus, 1972; var. books about Dutch royal family. Contbr. to: Nieuwe Rotterdamse Courant/Handelsblad; Ed., Vakbond van Schrijvers; Ed., De Bejaarden (for care of elderly); De Nederlandse Post, Cape Town. Mbrships: PEN; Bd., Authors' Assn. Recip., Kt., Order of Orange-Nassau, 1959. Address: NZ Voorburgwal 171, Amsterdam, Netherlands.

SCHENKMANIS, Ulf, b. 6 July 1934, Göteborg, Sweden. TV Director & Producer. Publs: about 25 children's books. Contbr. to: Värmlands Folkblad; Biblioteksbladet; Sågverken; etc. Mbrships: Swedish Authors' Soc.; Swedish TV Prods. Soc.; Children's Film Comm. Address: Sjöängsgatan 24, Karlstad, Sweden.

SCHICK, George Baldwin Powell, pen name BALDWIN, George (occasionally), b. 20 July 1903, Aurora, Ill., USA. University Professor of Literature & Reading Improvement. Educ: Ph.D., M.A., Ph.D., Univ. of Chgo., Ill. Publs: Handbook for Instructors in Developmental Reading (co-author), 1958; Design for Good Reading, 1962, 1969; Guidebook for Teachers of Reading, 1966; Reading at Efficient Rates, 1970; Developing Reading Proficiency, 1971; A Guide to the Teaching of Reading, 1973. Ed., Nat. Reading Assn. Yearbooks, 1966-70. Contbr. to: Jrnl. Developmental Reading (Fndg. Ed.); Jrnl. of Reading (Ed.); Notes & Queries; other profl. publs. Mbr., var. profl. assns. Recip., var. hons. for servs. to reading improvement. Address: 5042 McKenzie Dr., Placentia, CA 92670, USA.

SCHIFFMAN, Joseph, b. 13 June 1914, NYC, USA. College Professor. Educ: B.A., L.I. Univ., Bklyn., N.Y., 1937; M.A., Columbia Univ., N.Y., 1947; Ph.D., N.Y. Univ., 1951. Publs: (Ed.) Selected Writings on Religion & Society, by E. Bellamy, 1955; Looking Backward, by E. Bellamy, 1959; Brook Farm, by L. Swift, 1961; Three Shorter Novels, by H. Melville, 1962; The Duke of Stockbridge, by E. Bellamy, 1962; American Literature: A Survey (co-author). Contbr. to: PMLA; Am. Lit.; Mod. Lang. Quarterly; Review of Relig.; Cassel's Ency. of World Lit., 1973; etc. Mbrships. incl: Hd., Am. Lit., Int. Bibliog. Comm., MLA of Am., 1961-64. Pres., Metrop. N.Y. Chapt., Am. Studies Assn., 1958-59. Recip., Fulbright-Hays Awards to India and France, 1964 & 1965-66. Address: 551 S. Hanover St., Carlisle, PA 17013, USA.

SCHILDT, Gustaf Ernst Göran, b. 11 Mar. 1917, Helsinki, Finland. Author; Art Critic. Educ: Doct. Philos.,

Helsinki Univ. Publs: (novels) Önskeleken, 1943; Ön som förtärdes, 1970; (art criticism) Gide et l'homme (French), 1946; Cézanne, 1947; Kontrakurs, 1963; Finnish Sculpture, 1970; (travel books) In the Wake of Odysseus, 1953; In the Wake of a Wish, 1954; The Sun Boat, 1957; The Sea of Icarus, 1959; Det Gyllene Skinnet, 1964. Contbr. to: Svenska Dagbladet (Art Critic), Stockholm; etc. Mbrships: PEN; Mod. Art Soc. Finland (Pres.). Address: Villa Skeppet, Ekenäs, Finland.

SCHILLER, Fred, b. 6 Jan. 1920, Vienna, Austria. Playwright; Screen & Television Author. Educ: B.A., (Jrnlsm.), Columbia Univ., USA. Publs: (plays) Come On Up, Anything Can Happen (co-author); Demandez Vicky (co-author); Finder Please Return; (films) Something to Shout About; Flying Deuces; Grand Slam; They Met on Skis; Pistol Packin' Mama; Heat's On; TV: Adaptor, G. B. Shaw, The Inca of Perusalem, for NBC, 1958; 82 shows on major networks. Contbr. to: McCall's Mag. Mbrships: Writers' Guild of Am., West; Dramatists' Guild of Am., N.Y.; Soc. des Auteurs & Compositeurs Dramatiques, Paris, France. Recip., Lit. Prize, for story, Ten Men & a Prayer, Bur. for Intercultural Educ., 1947. Address: 149 S. Wetherly Dr., L.A., CA 90048, USA.

SCHILPP. Paul Arthur, b. 6 Feb. 1897, Dillenburg, Germany. Educ: A.B., Baldwin-Wallace Coll., USA, 1916; M.A., Northwestern Univ., 1922; B.D., Garrett Theol. Sem., 1922; Ph.D., Stanford Univ., 1936. Num. publs. incl: Do We Need a New Religion? 1929; Kant's Pre-Critical Ethics, 1938; Lamentations on Christmas, 1945; Human Nature & Progress, 1954; The Crisis in Science & Education, 1963; Fndr., Ed. & Pres., Lib. of Living Philosophers, 15 vols. from John Dewey, 1939 to Karl Popper, 2 vols., 1974. Contbr. to num. books, encys., jrbls.; Ed., Coll. of the Pacific Publs. in Philosophy, 3 vols., 1932-34; Cons. in Philos., Ency. Britannica. Hons. incl: Special Lectr., var. univs.; US State Dept. Rep., Pakistan Philos. Contress, 1956. Mbr., Kany workshop, Univ. of Cologne. Address: 9 Hillcrest Dr., Carbondale, IL 62901, USA.

SCHIRMER, Joseph Earl, b. 16 Feb. 1916, Balt., Md., USA. Professional Philatelist; Freelance Writer; Retired Naval Officer & Tool Engineer. Educ: Engrng. Coll., 1 yr.; num. USN engrng. courses; Tchr. Trng. course. Publs: Rewrote standard textbook for Boilermen used by USN, early 1950s. Contbr. to: Stamps; Western Stamp Collector; Linn's Stamp Weekly; Jrnl. of Sports Philately (Assoc. Ed.); Jrnl., Assn. Int. des Journalistes Philateliques; Topical Times; Our Navy; The Rosary; World Coins; Coin World. Mbr., num. sporting, social & philatelic orgs., inclng. Assn. Int. des Journalistes Philateliques & Am. Philatelic Soc. (Writers Unit). Address: Apt. 2B Hudson Towers, 7300 Blvd. East, N. Bergen, NJ 07047, USA.

SCHIRMER, Walter F., b. 18 Dec. 1888, Düsseldorf, Germany. University Professor (Emeritus). Educ: Doct. Philos.; Univs. München, Berlin, Bonn, Oxford, Freiberg. Publs: Antike, Renaissance und Puritanismus, 1924, 2nd ed., 1932; Der englische Frühumanismus, 1931, 2nd ed., 1963; Geschichte der englischen Literatur, 1939, 5th ed., Geschichte der englischen und amerikanischen Literatur, 1968; John Lydgate, 1952; Engl. ed., 1961. Mbrships: Deutsche Akademie der Wissenschaften Berlin, 1943; Rheinisch Westfälisch Akademie Düsseldorf, 1948. Hons: Mod. Lang. Assn. Am. (Hon. Mbr.); Mod. Humanities Rsch. Assn. (Hon. Mbr.). Address: 53 Bonn, Joachimstr. 16, W. Germany.

SCHLAPP, Manfred, b. 30 Aug. 1943, Innsbruck, Austria. Professor. Educ: Dipl. Psych.; Mag.lit. (B.A.) Ph.D. Publs: Steckbrief der Hinterwelt, 1971; Das Grosse Unbehagen, 1973. Contbr. to: Horizont; ORF. Mbrships. incl: PEN. Address: Postfach 34647, Vaduz, Liechtenstein.

SCHLEBECKER, John Thomas, b. 8 Feb. 1923, Ft. Wayne, Ind., USA. Museum Curator. Educ: B.A., Hiram Coll., 1949; M.A., Harvard Univ., 1951; Ph.D., Univ. of Wis., 1954. Publs: Cattle Raising on the Plains, 1900-1961, 1963; A Bibliography of Books & Pamphlets on the History of American Agriculture, 1969; Living Historical Farms Handbook, 1972; The Use of the Land: Essays on American Agricultural History, 1973. Contbr. to hist. jrnls.; Ed., Living Historical Farms Bulletin. Hons: Agricl. Hist. Soc. Award, 1954; Neb. State Histl. Soc. Award, 1969. Address: 11220 Mitscher St., Kensington, MD 20795, USA.

SCHLEIER, Gertrude, b. 23 June, 1934, NYC, USA. Author. Educ: Univ. Wash.; N.Y. Univ. Publs: A Time for Living, 1961. Contbr. to: Good Housekeeping Mag.; etc.

Mbrships: Educl. Alliance (Pres. Lit. Soc. & Integration Comm.). Recip., Short Story Contest Award from N.Y. Univ., 1970. Address: 212 E. Broadway, Apt. G1605, N.Y., NY 10002, USA.

SCHLESINGER, Arthur, Jr., b. 15 Oct. 1917. Educator. Educ: B.A.; Harvard Univ.; Peterhouse Coll., Cambridge. Publs. incl: The Age of Jackson, 1945; Kennedy or Nixon, 1960; The Politics of Hope, 1963; A Thousand Days: John F. Kennedy in the White House, 1965; The Crisis of Confidence: Ideas, Power & Violence in America, 1969; The Imperial Presidency, 1973. Contbr. to num. jrnls. Mbrships. incl: Am. Histl. Assn.; Nat. Inst. of Arts & Letters. Hons. incl: Pulitzer Prize for Hist., 1946, for Biography, 1966; Nat. Book Award, 1966; Gold Medal, Nat. Inst. of Arts & Letters, 1967. Address: City Univ. of NY, 33 W. 42nd St., N.Y., NY 10036, USA.

SCHLESINGER, Hugo, b. 5 May 1920, Biala, Poland. Author; Journalist; Economist. Educ: Econ. & Admin. Schl., Cracow, Poland; Univ. Florence, Italy; Cath. Univ. Sao Paulo, Brazil. Publs. incl: Quid est veritas?, 1943; L'Arte Polacca, 1944; English Proverbs & Sayings, 1945; Querra e pace, 1945; Paderewski e l'Italia, 1945; Zyd Polski-Zolnierz Polski, 1945; Polonica Brasileira, 1947; Shalom Jerusalem (co-author), 1969; Pingos de Verade, 1970; Dialética de um re-encontro, 1970; Um quarto de seculo de arte-cenica, 1971; Moderna Enciclopédia de Aministração de Empresas (6 vols.), 1972; Os papas e os judeus (co-author), 1973; Contribuição Judaica a Literatura Universal, 1973; Pela nossa e vossa liberdade, 1975; Anatomia do Antisemitismo, 1975. Contbr. to: Encontro; etc. Mbrships. incl: Brazilian Authors' Assn.: etc. Recip. of over 40 acad., mil., civ. & cultural hons. Address: Caixa Postal 5026, Sao Paulo, Brazil.

SCHLÜTER, Herbert, b. 16 May 1906, Berlin, Germany. Writer; Translator. Publs: Das Späte Fest, 1927; Die Rückkehr der Verlorenen Tochter, 1932; Nach Fünf Jahren, 1947; Im Schatten der Liebe, 1948; Nacht Uber Italien, 1960; transls. from Engl., French & Italian into German. Contbr. to poetry anthols., 1927 & 1928. Mbrships: Tukankreis, Munich; PEN. Address: Steinhauser Str. 31, D8 Munich 80, W. Germany.

SCHMANDT, Raymond Henry, b. 20 Sept. 1925, Ind., USA. Educator. Educ: B.A., 1947, M.A., 1949, St. Louis Univ.; M.A., 1952, Ph.D., 1952, Univ. of Mich. Publs: History of the Catholic Church (w. Thomas P. Neill), 1957, 2nd ed., 1965; Europe & Asia (w. Sr. M. Marguerite & others), 1961; Leo XIII & the Modern World (w. Edward T. Gargan), 1961; Ed., The Popes Through History series, 1961-68. Contbr. to num. prof. jrnls. Mbrships. incl: Am. Histl. Assn. AAUP. Recip., Christian R. & Mary F. Lindback award, 1969. Address: 2216 George's Lane, Phila., PA 19131, USA.

SCHMEISER, Douglas A., b. 22 May 1934, Bruno, Sask., Can. Professor & Dean of Law. Educ: B.A.; LL.B.; LL.M.; S.J.D. Publs: Civil Liberties in Canada, 1964; Cases & Comments on Criminal Law, 1966; Cases on Canadian Civil Liberties, 1971; Crimal Law: Cases & Comments, 2nd ed., 1973. Mbrships: Past Pres., Can. Assn. of Law Tchrs.; Sask. Coun., Can. Bar Assn.; Law Soc. of Sask. Address: Coll. of Law, Univ. of Sask., Saskatoon, Sask., Can.

SCHMICK, Bruce David, pen names GRANT, Madison Andrew; O'HARA, Sterling Elsworth, b. 20 Feb. 1949, Elmira, N.Y., USA. Assistant to the Auditor, Tompkins County Trust Company, Ithaca, N.Y. Educ: A.A.S., Corning Community Coll., N.Y. Publs: The Whispering Winds, 1971; Brainchildren, 1972; The Hidden Place, 1972; Poems, 1973; More Poems, 1973; Verse & Worse, 1974. Contbr. to: Poetry of the Year; Elmira Sunday Telegram; New World Mag.; New Dawn Publs: Spafaswap Mag.; Best Poets 20th Century. Mbrships. incl: Clover Int. Poetry Assn.; Ithaca Writers' Assn.; Ithaca Poetry Assn. Hons. incl: 6th Prize Award, Clover Int. Poetry Competition, 1974. Address: 55 South St., Trumansburg, NY 14886, USA.

SCHMIDHAUSER, John R., b. 3 Jan. 1922, USA. Professor of Political Science. Educ: B.A., Univ. of Dela., 1949; M.A., 1952, Ph.D., 1954, Univ. of Va. Publs: The Supreme Court as Arbiter in Federal State Relations, 1789-1957, 1958; The Supreme Court: Its Politics, Personalities & Procedures, 1960; Constitutional Law in the Political Process, 1963; The Supreme Court & Congress (w. Larry L. Berg), 1972; Political Corruption in America (w. Larry L. Berg & Harlan Hahn). Contbr. to: num. profl. jrnls.; 5 anthols. Mbrships. incl: Am., Western & Midwest

Pol. Sci. Assns.; AAUP. Hons. incl: Sesquicentennial Award for Pub. Serv., Univ. of Va., 1969. Address: Dept. of Pol. Sci., Univ. of Southern Calif., LA, CA 90007, USA.

SCHMIDT, Alfred Paul, b. 31 Mar. 1941, Vienna, Austria. Writer. Publs: Bester Jagt Spengler (prose), 1971; Als Die Sprache Noch Stumm War (prose), 1974; Das Kommen Des Jonnie Ray (novel), 1975. Contbr. to Manuskripte, Graz. Mbr., Forum Stadtpark, Graz. Address: Hüttenbrennergasse 52/14, 8010 Graz, Austria.

SCHMIDT, Arno Otto, b. 18 Jan. 1914, Hamburg, Germany. Novelist. Educ: Univ. of Breslau. Publs. incl: Leviathan, 1949; Brands Haide, 1951; Das steinerne herz, 1956; Dya na sore, 1958; Rosen & Porree, 1959; Kaff, 1960; Belphegor, 1961; Trommler beim Zaren, 1966; Der Triton mit dem Sonnenschirm, 1969; Zettels Traum, 1970; Die Schule der Atheisten, 1972; & num. transls. from Engl. incl. Faulkner; Joyce; Cooper; Collins; etc. Hons. incl: Grand Prize for Lit., Lit. Acad., Mainz.; Fonatnepreis, 1964; Goethe Prize, 1973. Address: 3101 Bargfeld Krs. Celle Nr. 37, W. Germany.

SCHMIDT, Eberhard, b. 7 Oct. 1937, Dranske/Rügen, Germany. Author. Publs: Durch die Wildnis, 1973; Inselleben, 1973; Zwanzigmal Lyrik, 1973; Maske und Spiegel, 1974; Absichten, 1974; Texte durch drei (co-author), 1974. Contbr. to: Unio; Der Literat; Zikade (Ed.); etc. Mbrships: Verband Deutscher Schriftsteller; Literarische Union, Saarbrucken. Address: Schaumbergstrasse 14, 6695 Tholey, Germany.

SCHMIDT, Gerhard Johann, b. 25 June 1902, Berlin, Germany. Professor. Educ: Univs. of Berlin, Munich, Freiburg, N.Y.; Dr. rer. polit., Univ. of Berlin. Publs: Der konstante Geldwert von Oresmius bis Knapp, 1925; An Introduction into the History, Theory & Administration of Money, 1970. Contbr. to num. jrnls.; US & Europe. Address: Rm. 1511 Hotel Greystone, Broadway at 91st St., N.Y., NY 10024, USA.

SCHMIDT, Joël Paul Armand, b. 31 Jan. 1937, Paris, France. Literary Adviser & Critic. Educ: B.A., Sorbonne, Paris. Publs: Dictionnaire de la Mythologie grecque & romaine, 1965; Les Antonins, 1969; Le Christ des Profondeurs, chrétiens des premiers siècles, 1970; Vie & mort des esclaves dans la Rome antique, 1973; Trésors de la Grece ancienne, 1973. Contbr. to: La Quinzaine Littéraire; Hebdo T.C.; Réforme; Encyclopédie Alpha; Encyclopaedia Universalis; Prefaces to var. books. Mbrships: Soc. of Men of Letters of France; Union of Lit. Critics; Int. Assn. of Lit. Critics. Hons: Broquette-Gonin Prize, French Acad., 1973; Chevalier of Arts & Letters, 1974. Address: 38 Rue de Vaugirard, 75006 Paris, France.

SCHMITT, Willi, pen names SMIT, Will; SMITH, Gordon, b. 21 July 1929, Roden, Saarlouis, Germany. Businessman. Educ: Business & Philology. Publs: 7 novels in press; 70 short stories, thrillers & real-life stories in var. newspapers & mags. Contbr. to: Sonntagsgruss; Schalt ein; Der Wegweiser; Saarzeitung; Saarbrücker Zeitung; etc.; also TV & radio series, Ereignisses des Lebens. Mbrships: Verband deutscher Schriftsteller; Interessengemeinschaft deutschsprachiger Autoren. Recip., Book Prize of Styria, Austria, 1969; & other hons. Agent: Axel Poldner, 8800 München 21, Rauheckstr. 11, W. Germany. Address: 663 SLS-Steinrausch, Kurt Schumacher Allee, 137, W. Germany.

SCHMULLER, Aaron, b. 27 May 1910, Lakowitz-Minsk, Russia. Owner-Director of Publishing Company. Publs: Man in the Mirror, 1944; Moments of Meditation, 1953; Treblinka Grass, 1957; Crossing the Borderland, 1959; Legend of His Lyre, 1960; Tokens of Devotion, 1966; While Man Exists, 1970; Triumphalis, 1973; 65 at 65: Poems & Translations, 1975. Contbr. to: Poet Lore; Phylon of Atlanta Univ.; Green World of La. Univ.; Humanist; Literary Review of Fairleigh Dickinson Univ.; Human Voice Quarterly; Wis. Poetry Mag.; etc. Mbrships: Poetry Soc. of Am.; Am. Poetry League. Address: 9227 Kaufman Pl., Bklyn., NY 11236, USA.

SCHNEEWEISS, Heinrich (Gebhard Franz), b. 21 Feb. 1930, Bregenz, Austria. Librarian; Translator. Publs. incl: (poetry) Auf meiner Zunge der Kobold, 1964; Memorandum eines Antipoden, 1964; So und nicht anders, 1974; (transls.) Zwischen augen und atem, 1964; Organon, 1964; Lied zwischen den Zähnen, 1972; Ohne Namen, 1972; Reptilien wieder erhaltlich, 1973; Kees der Junge (play), 1974. Mbr., Vereniging Van Letterkundigen,

Amsterdam, 1964—. Recip., Grants from art fndns., Rotterdam & Amsterdam. Address: Toulonselaan 22-24, Dordrecht, Netherlands.

SCHNEIDER, Herman, b. 31 May, 1905, Kreschov, Poland. Writer. Educ: B.S. & M.S., CUNY. Publs. incl: (all w. wife, Nina Schneider) Let's Find Out, 1946; How Your Body Works, 1949; Your Telephone & How It Works, 1952; Science Fund with Milk Cartons, 1953; Let's Find Out About Electricity, 1956; Heath Science Series, Grades 1–6, revised, 1973; Science Fun with a Flashlight, 1975; Got a Minute?, 1975. Mbrships. incl: Nat. Sci. Tchrs. Assn.; NEA; Fellow, AAAS; Nat. Assn. of Sci. Writers. Recip., Hon. Litt.D., Fairleigh Dickinson Univ., 1967. Address: 21 W. 11th St., N.Y., NY 10011, USA.

SCHNEIDER, Karl-Hermann, b. 3 Mar. 1948, Kassel, W. Germany. Finance Official. Publs. incl: Kluge Kopf für Kluge Kopf, 1973; Freud und Leid, 1974; & 8 other books. Contbr. to var. newspapers. Mbr., German Writers' Union. Address: D-3500 Kassel 1, Blücherstrasse 3, W. Germany.

SCHNEITER, Erwin, b. 19 Nov. 1917; Basle, Switzerland. Central President, Swiss organisation, Schule & Elternhaus. Educ: Studied at Univs. of Berne & Zurich. Publs: Aus meinen Stunden; Ich suche Dich; An stillen Ufern; Aufklang & Uebergang (all poems). Contbr. to: Erziehungsschriften—Reihe, Schule & Elterhaus (Ed.); Var. articles in jrnls. & newspapers. Mbrships: Schweizerischer Schriftsteller Verein; Bernischer Schriftsteller Verein; PEN Club, Basle. Hons: Lit. Prize, Berne, 1943; Prize of hon., Stiftung für Schweizerisches Schrifttum, 1943; Prize, Schweizerische Schillerstiftung, 1944; Lit. Prize, Berne, 1957. Address: Buchholzstr. 22, CH-3066 Stettlen/BE, Switzerland.

SCHNURRE, Wolfdietrich, b. 22 Aug. 1920, Frankfurt, Germany. Writer. Educ: Humanistisches Gymnasium. Publs. incl: (poems) Kassiber, 1956; Abendlander, 1957; (short stories) Man Sollte Dagegen Sein, 1960; Funke im Reisig, 1963; Scnuree heiter, 1970; (for children) Die Zwengel, 1967; Gocko, 1970; Die Sache mit den Meerschweinchen, 1970; Immer merhr Meerschweinchen, 1971; Wie der Koalabar wieder lachen lernte, 1971; (satire) Der wahre Noah, 1974. Mbrships. incl: PEN; Acad. for Speech. Hons. incl: Immermann Prize, Dusseldorf, 1959; Mackensen Lit. Prize, 1962. Address: Goethestr. 29, Berlin 37, W. Germany.

SCHOCHET, J. Immanuel, pen names SCHEALTIEL, Nochumm J.; ORYAH, Yehudith, b. 27 Aug. 1935, Basle, Switz. Professor; Author; Rabbi. Educ: B.A., M.A., Ph.D., D.D.; Windsor, Toronto, Waterloo Univs.; & McMaster Univ., Hamilton, Ont., Can.; Lubavitch Yeshiva Coll., Brooklyn, N.Y., USA. Publs. incl: Igereth Hakodesh, 2 vols., 1968, 3rd ed., 1974; Mystical Concepts in Chassidism, 2nd ed., 1974; The Great Maggid, Vol. I, 1974; He'aroth Vetziyunim, 1974. Contbr. to: Tradition; Judaism; Yiddishe Heim; Can. Jewish News; Toronto Hebrew Herald; etc. Mbrships. incl: Philos. Soc.; Can. Soc. Biblical Studies. Hons. incl: Can. Coun. Fellowships, 1969-70, 1970-71; Can. Fndn. Jewish Culture Award, 1972. Address: 55 Charleswood Drive, Downsview, Ontario M3H 1X5, Canada.

SCHOFIELD, Michael, b. 24 June 1919, Leeds, UK. Social Psychologist. Educ: Cambridge Univ.; Harvard Grad. Schl. of Bus. Admin., USA. Publs: The Sexual Behaviour of Young People, 1965; Social Research, 1969; The Strange Case of Pot, 1971; The Sexual Behaviour of Young Adults, 1973. Contbr. to: New Soc.; Spectator; Guardian; Sunday Times. Mbr., Soc. of Authors. Address: 28 Lyndhurst Gdns., London NW3, UK.

SCHOLES, Olive, b. Oldham, Lancs., UK. Educ: London; Paris. Publs: Poems for & about Children, 1912. Contbr. to: Nash's; Chambers's Jrnl.; The Queen; Home Chat; Woman's Friend; Woman's Own; Woman's Companion; The Empire Review; The Lady; The Field; Country Life; Christian Science Monitor; Sentinel; The Golden Hour Book of Verse; Coventry Evening Telegraph; Royal Leamington Spa Courier; & num. others. Former mrbships: Quill Club, 1908; Poetry Soc., London, 1918; Oldham Poetry Soc. (Sec. to 1927). Address: Treblok, St. Mawes, Truro, Cornwall TR2 5BH, UK.

SCHOLL, John, b. 7 Aug. 1922, Maquoketa, Iowa, USA. Novelist. Publs: The Changing of the Guard; The Lemmings of Euphoria; The Country Boy & other stories; Novella, The Box. Contbr. to: Lyrical Iowa 20th Annual;

Copy Ed., Telegram, Salt Lake City, Utah, 1949, Sentinel, Milwaukee, Wis., 1952, Commercial Appeal, Memphis, Tenn., 1958-59, Times, Detroit, Mich., 1960; etc. Mbr., Authors' Guild, Authors' League of Am. Hons: Silver Battle Star, Presidential Citation, World War II Victory Medals, 1945; MacDowell Mem. Lit. Fellowship, 1961. Agent: Joan Foley, N.Y. Address: 5911 Pierce 303, Arvada, CO 80003, USA.

SCHONBERG, Harold C., b. 29 Nov. 1915. Music Critic. Educ: N.Y. Univ. Publs: The Guide to Long-Playing Records: Chamber & Solo Instrument Music, 1955; The Collector's Chopin & Schumann, 1959; The Great Pianists, 1963; The Great Conductors, 1967; Lives of the Great Composers, 1970; Grandmasters of Chess, 1973. Contbr. to: Int. Ency. of Music & Musicians (Ed.); Am. Music Lover; Musical Courier; N.Y. Times; Gramophone, London. Recip., Pulitzer Prize for Criticism, 1971. Address: c/o N.Y. Times, Times Sq., N.Y., USA.

SCHONFIELD, Hugh Joseph, b. 17 May 1901, London, UK. Historian. Educ: Univ. of Glasgow. Publs: some 40 books, inclng: Secrets of the Dead Sea Scrolls, 1955; The Authentic New Testament, 1955; The Passover Plot, 1965; The Politics of God, 1970; The Pentecost Revolution (US title, The Jesus Party), 1974. Mbrships: Chmn., H. G. Wells Soc.; Soc. of Authors; PEN. Hons: Dr. of Sacred Lit., 1955; Fellow, Int. Inst. of Arts & Letters, 1958; nominated for Nobel Peace Prize, 1959. Address: 35 Hyde Pk. Sq., London W2 2NW, UK.

SCHORER, Mark, b. 17 May 1908, Sauk City, Wis., USA. Professor of English. Educ: A.B. 1929, Ph.D. 1936, Univ. of Wis.; M.A., Harvard Univ., 1930. Publs. incl: (novels) A House Too Old, 1935; The Wars of Love, USA & UK, 1954; (short stories) The State of Mind: 32 Stories, 1947; The State of Mind: 22 Stories, UK, 1956; (non-fiction) William Blake, 1946; Sinclair Lewis: An American Life, USA, 1961, UK, 1963; The World We Imagine, USA, 1968, UK, 1969; D. H. Lawrence, 1968; Ed., num. lit. & critical anthols. Mbrships. incl: Am. Acad. Arts & Scis.; Authors' Guild. Hons. incl: D.Litt., Univ. of Wis., 1962; num. fellowships. Address: 68 Tamalpais Rd., Berkeley, CA 94708, USA.

SCHORSCH (Sister), M. Dolores, O.B.S., b. 16 June 1896, Morris, Ill., USA. Author; Educator; Administrator. Educ: B.A.; M.A.; B.S.; Ed.D. Publs: Jesu-Maria Course in Religion, 5th ed. (co-author); Our Lord & Our Lady; Life of Our Lord in Art (film script); Early History of the Church (8 film scripts). Contbr. to: Relig. Educn. Jrnl.; Family Life; Cath. Educr.; Cath. Audio-Visual Educrs. Mbrships. incl: Am. Assn. of Higher Educ.; Am. Psychol. Assn.; Am. Cath. Philos. Assn.; Nat. Cath. Educ. Assn.; Am. Benedictine Acad. Recip., sev. acad. hons. Address: 7416-30 N. Ridge Ave., Chgo., IL 60645, USA.

SCHOTMAN, Johann Wilhelm, b. 10 Mar. 1892, Hoogeveen, Netherlands. Physician; Psychiatrist; Philosopher; Writer; Painter. Educ: M.D., Univ. of Leyden. Publs: (poetry) Van de Wankele Morgen, 1919; Der Geesten Gemoeting, 1927; Cloisonné, 1931; Hellevaart, 1946; (prose) Het vermolmde Boeddhabeeld, 3 vols., 1927-31; Wind in Bamboestengels, 1946; Asfalt en Arcadie, 1953; (philos. & psychol.) Naar Open Water, 1936; De Macht tot Vrijheid, 1941. Contbr. to: De Gids; De Nieuwe Gids; Ned. Bibliografie. Mbrships: PEN; Koninkl. Mij der Letterkunde; Oudheidkundig Genootschap Ver. v. Letterkundigen. Address: Willemskade 11, Zwolle, Netherlands.

SCHOULGIN, Eugene, b. 19 Apr. 1941, Oslo, Norway. Author. Educ: studied classical archaeol. & langs. & hist. of arts, Uppsala & Stockholm Univs. Publs: The Rabbit Cages (novel), 1970; The Powderhouse (short stories), 1971; The Day the Snow Came (novel), 1974. Contbr. to E. German anthol., Norwegische Erkundungen, 1975. Mbrships: Norwegian Soc. of Authors; Swedish Union of Authors. Address: Wittstocksgatan 11n.b., 115 25, Stockholm, Sweden.

SCHRANK, Joseph, b. 10 July 1900, NYC, USA. Playwright; Author of Children's Books. Publs: Seldom & the Golden Cheese; The Plain Princess & the Lazy Prince; The Cello in the Belly of the Plane; The Puppy in the Pet Shop Window; Wall Street, Anyone? ; 5 screenplays inclng: A Slight Case of Murder & The Magnificent Pepe; 4 stageplays, inclng. Page Miss Glory & Good Hunting. Contbr. to: NY Times Book Review; Esquire. Mbrships: Dramatists' Guild; Authors' League of Am. Address: 263 West End Ave., N.Y., NY 10023, USA.

SCHROEDER, Paul Walter, b. 23 Feb. 1927, Ohio USA. Historian. Educ: Ph.D., Univ. of Texas, 1958. Publs: The Axis Alliance & Japanese-American Relations, 1958; Metternich's Diplomacy at Its Zenith 1820-1823, 1962; Austria, Great Britain & the Crimean War, 1972. Contbr. to: A. Histl. Review; Jrnl. of Mod. Hist.; Central European Hist.; Can. Jrnl. of Hist.; Can. Histl. Review; etc. Mbrships. incl: Rsch. Comm., Am. Histl. Assn., 1975-77; Am. Assn. Adv'ment of Slavic Studies. Hons: Beveridge Prize, 1956; Walter P. Webb Mem. Prize, 1962. Address: Dept. of Hist., Univ. of Ill., Urbana, IL 61801, USA.

SCHROEVERS, Marinus, b. 30 Apr. 1927. Oude Niedorp, Netherlands. Journalist & Essayist. Publs: Het oudste Frankrijk, 1970; De Auto (w. Francesca Hart), 1974; Cinema en Theater (w. Francesca Hart), 1975; Van Gogh achterna (w. photographer Dirk de Herder), 1975; Reiswerk (w. Dirk de Herder), forthcoming. Contbr. to Dutch radio; etc. Mbr., Writers' Union, Amsterdam. Recip., Jaarprijs Genootschap voor Reclame. Address: 21 Sarphatikade, Amsterdam, Netherlands.

SCHUBERT, Elspeth Nora, pen name SCHUBERT, Elspeth Harley, b. 21 Feb. 1907, Edinburgh, UK. Translator. Publs: has transl. num. works from Swedish to Engl. inclng. Stringberg's The People of Hemsö, 1959; Frans G. Benglsson's A Walk to an Ant Hill, 1950; Harry Martinson's Aniasa, 1961; Runa Lindstrom's The Play of Heaven, 1955; Eyvind Johnson's The Days of His Grace, 1968. Mbr., Swedish Union of Authors. Recip., Award, Swedish Acad. of Letters, 1961. Address: La Garde Freinet, 83310 Cogolin, France.

SCHUCHART, Max, b. 16 Aug. 1920, Rotterdam, Netherlands. Information Attaché. Publs: The Netherlands, 1972; Poetry; (transl.) Lord of the Rings, by J. R. Tolkien; In the Skin Trade & A Prospect of the Sea, by Dylan Thomas; The Once & Future King, by T. H. White; Watership Down, by Richard Adams. Contbr. to: New Engl. Review; Dutch lit. mags. & newspapers. Hons: UNESCO Fellowship for Jrnlsm., 1947; Nijhoff Prize, 1958. Address: Burg. Patijnlaan 134, The Hague, Netherlands.

SCHULBERG, Budd (Wilson), b. 27 Mar. 1914, NYC, USA. Writer; Production Company President. Educ: A.B., Dartmouth Coll., 1936. Publs. incl: (novels) What Makes Sammy Run? , USA & UK, 1941 (co-author, play, prod. 1964); The Harder They Fall, USA & UK, 1947; Waterfront, USA, 1955, UK, 1956; Sanctuary V, USA, 1970, UK, 1971; (short stories) Some Faces in the Crowd, USA, 1953, UK, 1954; (non-fiction) The Four Seasons of Success, 1972; var. screenplays. Mbr., Authors' Guild. Hons. incl: Num. awards for screenplays On the Waterfront, 1954, & A Face in the Crowd, 1958; D.Litt., Dartmouth Coll., 1960. Address: c/o Ad Schulberg, 300 E. 57th St., N.Y., USA.

SCHUMANN, Maurice, pen name SIDOBRE, André, b. 10 Apr. 1911, Paris, France. Politician; Writer & Broadcaster. Educ: Lic.-ès-lettres, Univ. of Paris. Publs. incl: Le Germanisme en Marche, 1938; Mussolini, 1939; Honneur & Patrie, 1945; Le Vrai Malaise des Intellectuels de Gauche, 1957; (novels) Le Rendezvous avec quelqu'un, 1962; La Voix du Couvrefeu, 1964. Contbr. to: L'Aube; Le Temps Présent; La Vie Catholique; etc.; BBC French serv., 1940-44. Mbrships. incl: Int. Movement for Atlantic Union (Pres., 1966—). Hons. incl: Chevalier de la Légion d'honneur; Compagnon de la libération; Croix de Guerre; LL.D., Cambridge Univ., 1972. Address: 53 Ave. du Maréchal-Lyautey, Paris 16e, France.

SCHWANFELDER, Werner, pen name ANFELD, Wes, b. 6 Apr. 1951, Nuremberg, German Fed. Repub. Student of Economics. Educ: Univ. level. Contbr. to: Spontan; Further Nachrichten. Mbrships: Young Jrnlsts. Union; Soc. of German Speaking Authors. Address: Waldstrasse 9, 8501 Obermichelbach, W. Germany.

SCHWARTZ, Lita Linzer, b. 14 Jan. 1930, NYC, USA. Psychologist. Educ: A.B., Vassar Coll., 1950; Ed.M., Temple Univ., Phila., 1956; Ph.D., Bryn Mawr Coll., 1964. Publs: Ed., Current Concerns in Educational Psychology, 1968, rev. ed., 1970; American Education: A Problem-Centered Approach, 1969, 2nd ed., 1974; Educational Psychology: Focus on the Learner, 1972; The Exceptional Child: A Primer, at press. Contbr. to: Jrnl. of Personality Assessment. Address: 411 Lodges Lane, Elkins Park, PA 19117, USA.

SCHWARTZ, Rhoda (Josephson), b. 28 Dec. 1923, Atlantic City, N.J., USA. Editor, American Poetry Review. Contbr. to: (anthols.) About Women, 1973; Jewish American Literature, 1974; Speaking for Ourselves, 1975; Doing the Unknown, forthcoming; Red War Sticks; (jrnls.) The Nation; Books, UK; Am. Poetry Review; Out of Sight Press. Address: Kennedy House — Apt. 1520, 1901 J. F. K. Blvd., Phila., PA 19103, USA.

SCHWARTZMAN, Sylvan David, b. 8 Dec. 1913, Baltimore, Md., USA. Professor; Rabbi. Educ: B.A., 1937; M.B.A., 1970, Univ. of Cinn.; B.H.L., 1937; M.A., Rabbi, 1941, Hebrew Union Coll.; Ph.D., Vanderbilt Univ., 1952. Publs. incl: Rocket to Mars, 1953, 2nd ed., 1969; Meeting Your Life Problems (co-author), 1959; Reform Judaism Then & Now, 1971; Personal Record Book, 1974. Contbr. to: Relig. Educ.; CCAR Jrnl.; etc. Mbrships. incl: Ctrl. Conf. of Am. Rabbis (Exec. Bd., Comm. on Continuing Educ. etc.). Hons. incl: Emanuel Gamoran Curriculum Award, 1963. Address: 2561 Erie Ave., Cinn., OH 45208, USA.

SCHWARZ, David, b. 9 Dec. 1928, Piotrków Tryb., Poland. Writer; Researcher; Lecturer. Educ: Fil.lic., 1971. Publs: Swedish Immigration & Minority Policy 1945-68, 1971; Can Immigrants Be Swedish?, 1973; Immigration & Ethnic Minority Research. A Bibliography, 1973. Ed., Swedish Minorities, 1966; Identity & Minority, 1971. Contbr. of articles on ethnic minorities & immigration problems to var. newspapers & jrnls. Mbrships: Swedish Union of Authors; Swedish Psychol. Assn. Address: Dept. of Sociology, University of Stockholm, Fack, S—104 05 Stockholm 50, Sweden.

SCHWARZ, Helmut, b. 31 May 1928, Vienna, Austria. University Professor. Educ: Dr. Phil., Univ. of Vienna. Publs: (plays) Arbeiterpriester, 1955; Die Beförderung, 1961; Das Fehlurteil, 1965; Die Enthüllung, 1967; (books) Regie — Idee und Praxis moderner Theaterarbeit, 1965; Max Reinhardt und das Wiener Seminar, 1973. Contbr. to: Neue Zürcher Zeitung; Austrian Radio. Mbrships: Int. Theatre Inst.; IMDT; Genossenschaft dram. Schriftsteller. Hons: Dramatists Award, Upper Austria, 1955; City of Vienna Award, 1956. Address: Mariannengasse 32, Vienna 1090, Austria.

SCHWARZ-BART, André, b. 1928, Metz, Lorraine, France. Writer. Educ: Sorbonne, Paris. Publs: Le Dernier des Justes, 1959 (The Last of the Just, UK, 1960); Un Plat de Porc aux Bananes Vertes (A Plate of Pork with Green Bananas) w. Simone Schwarz-Bart, 1967; A Woman Named Solitude, 1973. Hons: Prix Goncourt, 1959; Jerusalem Prize, 1967. Address: c/o Editions du Seuil, 27 rue Jacob, Paris VIe, France.

SCHWEDHELM, Karl, b. 14 Aug. 1915, Berlin, Germany. Director of Dept. of Literature, S. German Radio, Writer. Educ: Berlin Univ. Publs: Dichtungen der Marceline Desbordes-Valmore, 1947; Fährte der Fische, 1955; E. Glissant: Carthago, 1959; Nelly Sachs, 1968; Propheten des Nationalismus, 1969; Hagia Sophia, 1973. Contbr. to: German TV; Der Weisse Turm. Mbrships: Acad. Scis. & Lit., Mainz; PEN. Address: Bachstrasse 10, D-7057 Winnenden, W. Germany.

SCHWENCK, Julius Rae, b. 10 Aug. 1900, Evanston, Wyo., USA. Science Educator; Consultant Chemical Engineer. Educ: A.B., Univ. Utah, 1921; Ch.E., Stanford Univ., Calif., 1923; Univ. Calif. Publs. incl: A Textbook of Chemistry (w. Stella Goostray), 9th ed., 1966; Experiments in Applied Chemistry (w. Stella Goostray), 4th ed., 1966; Basic Organic Chemistry (w. Raymond M. Martin), 1951; Basic Principles of Chemistry (w. Raymond M. Martin), 1958; Basic Principles of Experimental Chemistry (w. Raymond M. Martin), 1958; Science Curriculum Development in the Secondary Schools, 1965. Mbr., Calif. Writers' Club. Hons. incl: US Bur. Mines Fellowship, 1921; Nat. Sci. Fndn. Fellowship, 1962. Address: 8735 Fallbrook Way, Sacramento, CA 95826, USA.

SCHWIEBERT, Ernest George, b. 17 Oct. 1895, Deshler, Ohio, USA. Professor. Educ: B.A., Capital Univ.; M.A., Ohio State Univ.; Univ. of Chgo.; Ph.D., Cornell Univ.; Rsch., Wittenberg, Germany, Halle, Jena, Heidelberg. Publs. incl: Reformation Lectures, 1937; Luther & His Times, 1950; A History of U.S. Air Force Ballistic Missiles, 1965. Contbr. of chapts. to books, encys. & US & European jrnls. Hons. incl: Martha Kinney Cooper Ohioana Lib. Award, for biog., 1951. Address: 104 Library Place, Princeton, NJ 08540, USA.

SCICLUNA, (Sir) Hannibal Publius, b. 15 Feb. 1880. Solicitor; Museum Director; Librarian; Writer. Educ: Royal Malta Univ. Publs: The Archives of the SM Order of Malta, 1912; The French Occupation of Malta 1798-1900, 1923; The Order of St. John of Jerusalem, 1929; The Book of Deliberations of the Venerable Tongue of England, 1949; The Church of St. John in Valletta, 1955; The Order of St. John of Jerusalem & Places of Interest in Malta & Gozo, 1969; num. histl. & documentary works. Hons: Kt., 1955; M.B.E., 1935; M.A.(Oxon), 1938; LL.D., Malta, 1966; FSA, London 1946, Scotland, 1959; Légion d'honneur, 1950; Grand Cross, Order St. Maurice, & St. Lazarus, 1973; many others. Address: Samuelston, E. Saltoun, Pencaitland, E. Lothian, Scotland, UK.

SCLASCIA, Leonardo, b. 8 Jan. 1921. Writer. Educ: Inst. Magistrale Caltanissette. Publs: Le parrocchie di Regalpetra, 1956; Gli zii di Sicilia, 1958; Il giorno della civetta, 1961; Pirandello e la Sicilia, 1961; Il consiglio d'Egitto, 1963; A ciascuno il suo, 1963; Morte dell'inquisitore, 1964; Feste religiose in Sicilia, 1965; Recitazione della controversia liparitana, 1969; Il contesto, 1971; Il mare colore del vino, 1973. Hons. incl: Premio Crotone; Premio Prato. Address: Via Redentore 131, Caltanissetta, Italy.

SCOBEY, Joan, b. 19 May 1927, NYC, USA. Writer. Educ: B.A., Smith Coll. Publs: Creative Careers for Women, 1968; What is a Mother, 1968; What is a Father, 1969; What is a Brother, 1970; What is a Sister, 1970; What is a Grandmother, 1971; What is a Grandfather, 1971; What is a Friend, 1971; What is a Pet, 1971; Do-It-All-Yourself Needlepoint, 1971; Celebrity Needlepoint, 1972; Needlepoint From Start to Finish, 1972; Rugmaking From Start to Finish, 1972; Gifts From The Kitchen, 1973; Rugs & Wall Hangings, 1974. Contbr. to: Family Cir.; Woman's Day; McCall's; Good Housekeeping. Mbr., Soc. of Mag. Writers. Address: 9 Lenox Pl., Scarsdale, NY 10583, USA.

SCOTT, A. C., b. 3 Dec. 1909, Leeds, Yorks., UK. Professor of Theatre. Publs: Kabuki Theatre of Japan, 1955; Classical Theatre of China, 1957; Traditional Chinese Plays, Vol. I, 1967, Vol. II, 1969, Vol. III, 1974; The Theatre in Asia, 1972. Contbr. to: World Theatre; Groves Dictionary of Music. Mbrships: Soc. of Authors, London; Assn. for Asian Studies; Am. Theatre Assn. Recip., Guggenheim Fellowship, 1970. Address: Department of Theatre & Drama, University of Wisconsin, Madison, WI 53706, USA.

SCOTT, Arthur Finley, b. 30 Nov. 1907, Kroonstad, South Africa. Lecturer; Author. Educ: M.A., Emmanuel Coll., Cambridge; Oxford Univ. Publs. incl: Meaning & Style, 1938; Poetry & Appreciation, 1939; The Craft of Prose, 1963; Poems for Pleasure, 1955; The Poet's Craft, 1957; Close Readings, 1968; Who's Who in Chaucer, 1975; The Georgian Age, 1970; The Stuart Age, 1974; Witch Spirit Devil, 1975; The Plantagenet Age, 1975. Contbr. to: Teaching of Written Eng.; The Can. Teacher's Guide. Mbrships. incl: Soc. of Authors; R.S.L.; Nat. Book League; Chmn., Higher Educ. Comm., Kettering, 1945-48. Address: 59 Syon Park Gdns., Osterley, Isleworth, Middx., UK.

SCOTT, Franklin Daniel, b. 4 July 1901, Cambridge, Mass., USA. Emeritus Professor of History; Library Curator. Educ: Ph.B., M.A., Univ. of Chgo., Ill.; Univ. of Stockholm, Sweden; M.A., Ph.D., Harvard Univ., USA. Publs: Bernadotte & the Fall of Napoleon, 1935; The United States & Scandinavia, 1950; American Experience of Swedish Students, 1956; Peopling of America, 1972; Scandinavia, 1975; Ed., World Migration in Modern Times, 1968. Mbrships. incl: Chmn., sev. comms., Am. Histl. Assn.; Pres., Ed., & Chmn., Ed. Bd., Swedish Pioneer Histl. Soc.; Historiska Föreningen. Hons: LL.D., Ill. Coll., Jacksonville, 1958; LL.D., Doane Coll., Crete, Neb., 1964; Fil. Dr., Uppsala Univ., Sweden, 1970. Address: 624 W. 10th St., Claremont, CA 91711, USA.

SCOTT, J(ames) M(aurice), b. 13 Dec. 1906. Author; Explorer. Educ: M.A., Clare Coll., Cambridge Univ. Publs. incl: Gino Watkins, 1935; Land of Seals, 1949; Bright Eyes of Danger, 1950; Hudson of Hudson's Bay, 1950; Vineyards of France, 1950; Captain Smith & Pocahontas, 1953; Sea-wyf & Biscuit, 1955; Choice of Heaven, 1959; The Tea Story, 1964; The Book of Pall Mall, 1965; Dingo, 1966; The Devil You Don't, 1967; In a Beautiful Pea-Green Boat, 1968; The White Poppy, 1968, From Sea to Ocean, 1969; A Walk Along the Appenines, 1973. Recip., O.B.E., 1945. Address: Thatched Cottage, Yelling, Cambs., UK.

SCOTT, John, b. 26 Mar. 1912, Phila., Pa., USA. Writer. Educ: Univ. of Wis.; Magnitogorsk Metall. Inst., USSR; Sorbonne, Paris. Publs: Behind the Urals, 1942; Europe in Revolution, 1942; Democracy Is Not Enough, 1944; Duel for Europe, 1942; Political Warfare; China, The Hungry Dragon, 1967; Hunger, 1969; Divided They Stand, 1972. Publs: Time; Life; Reader's Digest. Mbrships: Overseas Press Club; Coun. on For. Rels.; Acad. of Pol. Scis.; Author's Guild. Address: Peaceable Ridge, Box 71, Ridgefield, CT 06877, USA.

SCOTT, J(ohn) D(ick), b. 26 Feb. 1917, Lanarkshire, UK. Editor. Educ: M.A., Edinburgh Univ. Publs: (novels) The Cellar, 1947 (as Buy It for a Song, USA, 1948); The Margin, UK, 1949, USA, 1950; The Way to Glory, UK & USA, 1952; The End of an Old Song, UK, 1953, USA, 1954; The Pretty Penny, UK, 1963, USA, 1964; (non-fiction) The Administration of War Production (w. R. Hughes), 1956; Life in Britain, UK & USA, 1956; The Siemens Brothers, 1858-1958, 1958; Vickers: A History, UK, 1963, USA, 1964; Ed., Finance & Dev., 1963—. Contbr. to Spectator (Lit. Ed., 1953-56). Address: 1517 30th St. N.W., Wash., DC 20007, USA.

SCOTT, John Sherman, pen name DOCTOR J, b. 20 July 1937, Bellaire, Ohio, USA. Playwright. Educ: B.A., S.C. State Coll., Orangeburg, 1961; M.A., 1966, Ph.D., 1972, Bowling Green State Univ., Ohio. Publs: (plays) Ride a Black Horse, 1971; The Alligator Man, 1972; Karma's Kall, 1974. Contbr. to: Black Lines; Players; Ohio Speech Jrnl.; Dramatics. Mbr., N.Y. Dramatists' League. Recip., Nat. Playwrights Conf. Selection (for Ride a Black Horse), Eugene O'Neill Mem. Theatre Ctr., 1970. Address: 1801 Brownstone Rd., Toledo, OH 43614, USA.

SCOTT, Nathan A. Jr., b. 24 Apr. 1925, Cleveland, Ohio, USA. Educator. Educ: A.B., Univ. of Mich., 1944; B.D., Union Theol. Sem., 1946; Ph.D., Columnia Univ., 1949. Publs. incl: Negative Capability: Studies in the New Literature & the Religious Situation, 1969; The Unquiet Vision: Mirrors of Man in Existentialism, 1969; Nathanael West, 1971; The Wild Prayer of Longing: Poetry & the Sacred, 1971; Three American Moralists — Mailer, Bellow, Trilling, 1973. Contbr. to num. relig. & lit. publs. Mbrships: Kent Fellow, Soc. of Relig. in Higher Educ.; Am. Philos. Assn.; MLA; Am. Acad. of Relig. Address: 5517 S. Kimbark Ave., Chgo., IL 60637, USA.

SCOTT, Otto J., b. 26 May 1918, NYC, USA. Author. Publs: The Exception, 1968; The Creative Ordeal, 1974; Robespierre: VOice of Virtue, 1974. Mbr., Overseas Press Club, NYC. Address: 3843 Southview Dr., San Diego, CA, USA.

SCOTT, Paul (Mark), b. 25 Mar. 1920, London, UK. Writer. Publs. incl: (novels) Johnnie Sahib, 1952; The Alien Sky, 1953 (as Six Days in Marapore, USA, 1953); The Mark of the Warrior, UK & USA, 1958; The Chinese Love Pavilion, 1960 (as The Love Pavilion, USA, 1960); The Bender, UK & USA, 1963; The Corrida at San Feliu, UK & USA, 1964; The Jewel in the Crown, UK & USA, 1966; The Day of the Scorpion, UK & USA, 1968; The Towers of Silence, UK & USA, 1972. Mbrship: F.R.S.L. Hons: Lit. Fellowship, Eyre & Spottiswoode, 1951; Grant, Arts Coun., 1969. Address: c/o David Higham Assocs., 5-8 Lower John St., Golden Sq., London W1R 4HA, UK.

SCOTT, Sheila, b. Worcester, UK. Lecturer; Writer; Actress; Aviator. Publs: I Must Fly, 1968; On Top of the World, 1973; Barefoot in the Sky, 1974. Mbrships: Liveryman, Guild Air Pilots & Navigators, London; Inst. Jrnlsts.; Actors' Equity; Zonta; United Servs. & Royal Aero Club; Ninety-Nines (Fndr.-Mbr., Brit. Sect.); Brit. Airships & Balloon Club (Co-Fndr.); Fellow, Royal Geogl. Soc. Hons: O.B.E., 1968; Dip. Academia Romana vel Sodalitia Quirinale, 1966; Harmon Trophy (USA), 1967; Britannia Trophy (UK), 1968; Gold Medal, Royal Aero Club (UK), 1971; & over 100 World Class Records incl. 1st solo pilot in light aircraft over True North Pole. Address: 593 Park West, London W2 2RB, UK.

SCOTT, Virgil Joseph, b. 1 Aug. 1914, Vancouver, Wash., USA. Professor of Creative Writing & Modern Literature; Author. Educ: A.B., 1936, M.A., 1937, Ohio State Univ.; Ph.D., 1945. Publs: The Dead Tree Gives No Shelter, 1947; The Hickory Stick, 1948; Studies in the Short Story, 1949, 4th ed., 1971; The Savage Affair, 1958; I, John Mordaunt, 1964; The Kreutzman Formula, 1974. Contbr. to: Argosy; Good Housekeeping; Esquire. Mbrships. incl: MLA; Am. Authors' League. Hons: Ohioana

Lib. Award for The Hickory Stick, 1948; Mich. Writers' Citation, for the Savage Affair, 1958. Address: 62 W. Sherwood Rd., Williamston, MI 48895. USA.

SCOVEL, Myra, b. 11 Aug. 1905, Mechanicville, N.Y., USA. Writer; Poet; Former Medical Missionary Worker. Educ: Syracuse Univ. Schl. of Nursing; Columbia Univ. Publs. incl: The Chinese Ginger Jars, 1962; Richer by India, 1964; To Lay a Hearth, 1968; The Weight of a Leaf, (poems), 1970; The Happiest Summer, 1971; The Gift of Christmas, 1972; Juveniles, plays. Contbr. to var. anthols., periodicals, etc. Mbrships: Former Pres., NYC Br., Nat. League of Am. Pen Women; Poetry Soc. of Am.; Women Poets of N.Y. Hons. incl: Prizes for poems, books, plays. Address: 37 Farley Drive, Stony Point, NY 10980, USA.

SCRUTON, Roger Vernon, b. 27 Feb. 1944, Buslingthorpe, Lincs., UK. University Lecturer. Educ: B.A., M.A., Ph.D., Jesus Coll., Cambridge Univ. Publ: Art & Imagination, 1974. Contbr. to: Proceedings Aristotelian Soc.; Mind; Philos.; Brit. Jrnl. Aesthetics; Spectator; Encounter. Mbrships: Aristotelian Soc.; Athenaeum. Address: 118 Harley St., London W1, UK.

SCULL, Florence Doughty, b. 16 June 1905, Somers Point, N.J., USA. Public School Administrator; Author. Educ: B.S., 1931, M.A., 1934, Tchr.'s Coll., Columbia Univ. Publs: Bear Teeth for Courage, 1964; John Dickinson Sounds the Alarm, 1972. Mbrships. incl: Atlantic City Art Ctr.; Pres., Somers Point Pub. Lib. Assn. Address: 41 E. Meyran Ave., Somers Point, NJ 08244, USA.

SCULLARD, Howard Hayes, b. 9 Feb. 1903, Bedford, UK. Emeritus Professor of Ancient History, University of London. Educ: M.A., Ph.D., St. John's Coll., Cambridge. Publs: Scipio Africanus, 1930; A History of the Roman World, 753-146 B.C., 1935; Oxford Classical Dictionary (jt. Ed.), 1949; Roman Politics, 220-150 B.C., 1951; From the Gracchi to Nero, 1959; The Etruscan Cities & Rome, 1967; Scipio Africanus: Soldier & Politician, 1970; The Elephant in the Greek & Roman World, 1974; Ed., Aspects of Greek & Roman Life, of which some 25 vols. are publd. Mbrships. incl: F.B.A.; F.S.A.; VP, Roman Soc. Address: 6 Foscote Rd., Hendon, London NW4, UK.

SCULLY, Kenrick, pen name, DAWES, John, b. 11 Sept. 1921, Tamworth, N.S.W., Australia. Journalist. Publs: Tale of Tickery Too, 1950; Every Man for Himself, 1954, 3rd ed., 1968; Fire on the Earth, 1958; This Crowd Beats Them All (Ed.), 1960, 2nd ed., 1961; Two Chancellors of England (Ed.), 1964; They Passed This Way (w. W. Delaney), 1969. Contbr. to num. Cath. jrnls., also to Prism. Mbrships. incl: Aust. Jrnlsts. Assn.; Jrnlst.'s Club, Sydney. Recip., sev. awards from Poetry Soc. of Aust. Address: 112 Campsie St., Campsie, N.S.W., Australia 2194.

SEALEY, Leonard George William, b. 7 May 1923, London, UK. Educational Author & Consultant. Educ: Tchrs. Cert., Peterborough Trng. Coll.; Dip. Ed., M.Ed., Univ. of Leicester. Publs: The Creative Use of Mathematics, 1961; Communication & Learning (co-auth.), 1962; Exploring Language, 1968; Introducing Mathematics, 1969; Basic Skills in Learning, 1970; Let's Think About Mathematics, 1971; Lively Reading, 1973; Ed., Our World Ency., 1974. Mbrships: F.R.S.A. Address: 11 Chilton St., Plymouth, MA 02360, USA.

SEAMAN, Barbara Ann, b. 11 Sept. 1935, NYC, USA. Writer; Lecturer. Educ: B.A., Oberlin Coll., 1956; Advanced Sci. Writing Cert., Schl. Jrnlsm., Columbia Univ., N.Y. Publs: The Doctors' Case Against the Pill, 1969 & German, Dutch & Engl. eds.; Free & Female, 1972, 2nd ed., 1973 & S. Am., Engl., Spanish, Turkish, Dutch, Japanese & Israeli eds. Contbr. to: N.Y.; MS; N.Y. Times; Look; Ladies Home Jrnl.; Family Circle; Cosmopolitan; Village Voice; Saturday Review; Wash. Post Outlook; TV and radio. Mbrships. incl: Women's Med. Ctr. (VP 1970-72); Am. Cancer Soc. (Motivation Comm.); Jewish Women for Affirmative Action (Advsry. Coun.). Address: c/o Shirley Fisher, McIntosh & Otis, 18 E. 41st St., N.Y., NY 10017, USA.

SEARLE, Humphrey, b. 26 Aug. 1915, Oxford, UK. Composer. Educ: M.A., New Coll., Oxford, 1937; Royal Coll. of Music; Vienna Conservatorium. Publs: The Music of Liszt, 1954, revised 1966; 20th Century Counterpoint, 1954, 1955; Ballet Music — an Introduction, 1958, revised 1973; 20th Century Composers 3 — Britain & Holland, 1972. Contbr. to: Ency. Brit.; Grove's Dictionary of Music; Music Times; The Listener; etc. Mbrships. incl: Coun.,

Composers' Guild, GB; Liszt Soc. (Patron); Royal Musical Assn. Hons. incl: Italia Prize, 1965; C.B.E., 1968. Address: 44 Ordnance Hill, London NW8 6PU, UK.

SEAVER, Paul Siddall, b. 19 Mar. 1932, Phila., Pa., USA. Historian. Educ: B.A., Haverford Coll.; M.A., Ph.D., Harvard Univ. Publs: The Puritan Lectureships. The Politics of Religious Dissent, 1560-1662, 1970. Contbr. to: Am. Histl. Review; Jrnl. of Mod. Hist.; Ch. Hist.; Archive for Reformation Hist. Mbrships: Am. Histl. Soc.; Histl. Assn.; Am. Soc. of Ch. Hist.; Conference on Brit. Studies; Econ. Hist. Soc. Address: Dept. of Hist., Stanford Univ., Stanford, CA, USA.

SEBAI, Youssef Mohamed., b. 1917, Egypt. Writer. Educ: Mil. Acad.; Cairo Univ. Publs: (novels) Land of Hypocrisy; I am Going Away; Among the Ruins; Death of a Water Carrier; The Return; Nadia; (short stories) A Nation That Laughed; A Night of Wine; Sheikh Zo'orob; (plays) Om Ratiba; Behind the Curtain; Stronger Than Time. Contbr. to Arissala al Gadida, (Ed., 1953-56). Mbr., High Coun. of Arts, Letters & Social Sci. Num. Prizes & decorations. Address: Villa Sebai, Mokatam City, Cairo, United Arab Repub.

SEBEOK, Thomas A., b. 1920, Budapest, Hungary. Professor of Linguistics, of Anthropology, & of Uralic & Altaic Studies. Educ: B.A., Univ. of Chgo., USA, 1941; M.A., 1943, Ph.D., 1945, Princeton Univ. Num. publs. incl: Spoken Hungarian, 1945; Spoken Finnish, 1947; Studies in Cheremis, 9 vols., 1953-61; Psycholinguistics: A Survey of Theory & Research Problems, 1954; 2nd ed. 1965; Ed., Style in Language, 1960; Ed., Current Trends in Linguistics, 14 vols., 1963-75; Portraits of Linguists, 2 vols., 1966. Contbr. to num. books & profl. jrnls. Num. mbrships. incl: Pres., Linguistic Soc. of Am. 1975; Sev. ed. bds. of profl. publs. Address: 1104 Covenanter Dr., Bloomington, IN 47401, USA.

SEDGWICK, Michael Carl, b. 20 Mar. 1926, Maidenhead, UK. Automobile Historian & Writer. Educ: Corpus Christi Coll., Oxford. Publs: Early Cars, 1962; Cars in Colour, 1968; Cars of the 1930's, 1970; Veteran & Vintage Cars in Colour, 1971; FIAT: A History, 1974; Cavalcade of Cars, 1974. Contbr. to: Asst. Ed., Veteran & Vintage Mag.; Classic Car; Complete Ency. of Cars; L'Album du Fanatique de l'Automobile; Automobil Chronik; Old Cars; Restored Cars; UK Rsch. Assoc., Automobile Quarterly; etc. Mbrships. incl: Dating Comm., Veteran Car Club of Gr. Brit.; Advsry. Bd., Nat. Motor Mus., Beaulieu. Recip., Veteran & Vintage Trophy, 1971. Address: Pippbrook, Chichester Rd., Midhurst, Sussex GU29 9PF, UK.

SEDURO, Vladimir Ilyich, pen name HLYBINNY, Vladimir, b. 24 Dec. 1910, Minsk, Russia. Educ: B.A., State Univ., Minsk, 1933; M.A., State Univ., Leningrad, 1939; Ph.D., Acad. of Scis., Minsk, 1941; Postdoctoral study, Columbia Univ., USA. Publs. incl: Dostoevsky Study in the USSR, 1955; The Byelorussuan Theater & Drama 1955; Dostoevsky in Russian Literary Criticism, 1846-1956, 1957; Smolensk Land, 1963; On the Shores beneath the Sun, 1964; In the Holy Land, 1972; Dostoevsky's Image in Russia Today, 1975; also books in French & German. Contbr. to num. jrnls. in US, Europe & USSR. Mbrships. incl: N.Am. Dostoevsky Soc.; Pres., Byelorussian-Am. Scientific & Lit. Club, Troy, N.Y.; Am. Rep., Int. Dostoevsky Soc. Address: 29 Mellon Ave., Troy, NY 12180, USA.

SEEBACHER-MESARITSCH, Alfred, b. 23 Aug. 1925, Grosslobming, Styria, Austria. Journalist. Publs: Das neunte Gebot, 1956; Hexen-Report, 1972; Gold in steirischen Bergen, 1974; (play) Requiem für Anna, 1974; (play) Der Bürgermeister, 1974. Mbrships: PEN; Styrian Authors' League, Graz. Hons: Polen Prize, Warsaw, Poland, 1963; Playwrights' Award, Arnfelser Castle Dramas, 1974. Address: A-8010 Graz, Brucknerstr. 6/22, Austria.

SEGAL, Erich, b. 16 June 1937, Bklyn., N.Y., USA. Professor of Classical Literature. Educ: A.B., 1958, M.A., 1959, Ph.D., 1964, Harvard Univ. Publs: Roman Laughter: The Comedy of Plautus, 1968; Euripides: A Collection of Critical Essays, 1968; Transl., Plautus: Three Comedies, 1969; Love Story (novel), 1970; Fairytale, 1973. Contbr. to N.Y. Times Book Review. Mbrships: ASCAP; Authors' League; Dramatists' Guild; Screen Writers' Guild; PEN. Hons: Guggenheim Fellowship, 1968; Acad. Award Nomination for Screenplay of Love Story, 1970; Humboldt Stiftung, W. Germany, 1973. Address: c/o Lazarow (rm 1106), 119 W. 57th St., N.Y., NY 10019, USA.

SEGAL, Helen Gertrude, b. 5 Sept. 1929, Johannesburg, S. Africa. Teacher. Educ: B.A., Univ. of Witswatersrand. Publs: Lacking a Label, forthcoming. Contbr. to: New Coin; New Nation; Contrast; Wurm. Ophir; de Arte; Unisa Engl. Studies; Jewish Affairs; Purple Renoster. Address: 7 Dunbar St., Yeoville, Johannesburg, S. Africa.

SEGAL, Lore, b. 8 Mar. 1928, Vienna, Austria. Writer. Educ: B.A., Univ. of London, UK. Publs: Other People's Houses, 1964, paperback ed., 1973; Gallows Songs (transl. from Christian Morgenstern, w. W. D. Snodgrass), 1967; (children's books) Tell Me a Mitzi, 1970; All the Way Home, 1973; The Juniper Tree & Other Tales from Grimm (transl.), 1973. Contbr. to: New Yorker; Saturday Evening Post; Commentary; Quarterly Review; Epoch; N.Y. Times; New Repub.; Mademoiselle; Atlantic; Hudson Review; etc. Mbr., PEN. Hons: Guggenheim Fellowship, 1965-66; Nat. Coun. on Arts & Humanities, 1967-68; CAPS Grant, 1972-73. Address: 280 Riverside Drive, N.Y., NY 10025, USA.

SEGAL, Martin, b. 5 Feb. 1921, Warsaw, Poland. Economist. Educ: B.A., Queens Coll., 1948; M.A., 1950, Ph.D., 1953, Harvard Univ. Publs: Wages in the Metropolis, 1960; The Rise of the United Association, 1971. Contbr. to: Quarterly Jrnl. of Econs.; Review of Econs. & Stats.; Indl. & Labor Rels. Review. Mbrships: Am. Econ. Assn.; Indl. Rels. Rsch. Assn. Recip., Alumnus of the Yr., Queens Coll., 1962. Address: Dept. of Econs., Dartmouth Univ., Hanover, NH 03755, USA.

SEGAL, Muriel, b. 6 Oct. 1913, London, UK. Writer. Educ: USA; Australia; France. Publs: Marriage is My Business (w. Heather Jenner); Men & Marriage, 1970, 2nd ed., 1971; Painted Ladies, 1972; Dolly on the Dais, 1972; Virgins of Various Sorts (forthcoming). Contbr. to num. Brit. newspapers; wkly column for Aust. Press; BBC TV; etc. Mbr., Women's Press Club (Fndr.-Mbr.). Address: 9 Cicely House, Cochrane St., St. John's Wood, London NW8, UK.

SEGAL, Ronald Michael, b. 14 July 1932, Cape Town, S. Africa. Author. Educ: B.A.; Univ. of Cape Town; Trinity Coll., Cambridge. Publs: The Tokolosh, 1960; African Profiles, 1962; Into Exile, 1963; The Crisis of India, 1965; The Race War, 1966; America's Receding Future, 1968; The Struggle Against History, 1971; Whose Jerusalem? The Conflicts of Israel, 1973; The Decline & Fall of the American Dollar, 1974; (Ed.) Sanctions Against South Africa, 1964; South West Africa: Travesty of Trust, 1967. Mbr., S. African Freedom Assn. Address: Old Manor House, Manor Rd., Walton-on-Thames, Surrey, UK.

SEGHERS, Anna, b. 19 Nov. 1900. Writer. Publs. incl: Der Aufstand der Fischer von Sankt Barbara, 1928; Die Gefährten, 1932; Das siebte Kreuz, 1942; Transit, 1948; Die Toten bleiben jung, 1949; Der Mann & sein Name, 1952; Der Bienenstock, 1953; Brot & Salz, 1958; Die Entscheidung, 1959; Das Licht auf dem Galgen, 1961; Karibische Geschichten, 1962; Uber Tolstoi— Über Dostojewski, 1963; Die Kraft der Schwachen, 1965; Das wirkliche Blau, 1967; Das Vertraune, 1968; Sonderbare Begegnungen. Mbrships: German Acad. of Arts; Pres., German Writers' Assn. Hons. incl: Lenin Peace Prize. Address: Aufbau Verlag, Französischestr. 32, Berlin W8, Germany.

SEIBEL, Werner, pen name LEBIÉS, René, b. 8 Nov. 1946, Waldeck, Hessen, German Federal Repub. Teacher. Author of Der Himmel ist rot wie ein Regenbogen (poems), 1973. Mbrships: Literarischer Union, Saarbrücken; Arbeitsgemeinschaft junger publizisten, arjupust; Interessengemeinschaft deutschsprachiger Autoren. Recip., silver pen award Interessengemeinschaft deutschsprachiger Autoren, 1973. Address: Waldstr. 7, 3501 Niestetal 1, W. Germany.

SEID, Ruth, pen name SINCLAIR, Jo, b. 1 July 1913, Bklyn., N.Y., USA. Writer. Publs: Wasteland, 1946; Sing At My Wake, 1951; The Changelings, 1955; Anna Teller, 1960; The Long Moment (play), 1951. Contbr. to: Am. Judaism; Esquire; Coronet; Ken; Harper's; Saturday Evening Post; Cosmopolitan; Reader's Digest; Glamour, Epoch; num. anthols. Mbrships: Authors Guild of Am.; PEN; Elected Daughter of Mark Twain, 1969. Hons. incl: Annual Fiction Award, Jewish Book Coun. of Am., 1956; Lit. Award, Cleveland Arts Prize, 1961; Wolpaw Playwriting Grantee, Jewish Community Ctrs., Cleveland, 1970. Address: 1021 Wellington Rd., Jenkintown, PA 19046, USA.

SEIDENFADEN, Erik, b. 24 Apr. 1910, Hasle, Denmark. Writer; College Warden. Publs: Civil War in Spain, 1936; Hitler Protects Denmark, 1943; Spidser, 1948; Den hellige krig om det hellige land, 1956; Nuclear Arms & Foreign Policy, 1960; Disengagement, 1961; Disarmament, 1962; Nato & Denmark, 1968; The Roads Towards Europe, 1970. Contbr. to: Berlingske Tidende; Nationaltidende; Information; Fremtiden; Times. Mbrships: Coun. of Inst. of Strategic Studies, London; Coun. of Admin., Univ. of Paris. Recip., M.B.E. Address: La Fondation Danoise, 9 blvd. Jourdan, Paris 14e, France.

SELBOURNE, David Maurice, b. 4 June 1937, London, UK. Writer. Publs: The Play of William Cooper & Edmund Dew-Nevett, 1968; The Two-Backed Beast, 1969; Dorabella, 1970; The Damned, 1971; Samson, 1971; Class Play, 1972; Class Plays, 1975; An Eye to China, 1975. Address: c/o Unna & Durbridge Ltd., 14 Beaumont Mews, London W1, UK.

SELBY, Hubert Jr., b. 23 July 1928, Brooklyn, NYC, USA. Writer. Publs: Last Exit to Brooklyn, 1964; The Room, 1971. Address: 635 Westbourne Drive, Hollywood, CA 90069, USA.

SELÇUK, Füruzan, pen name FÜRUZAN, b. 29 Oct. 1935, Istanbul, Turkey. Author. Publs: Parasíz Yatílí,1971, 5th ed. 1975; Kuşatma, 1972, 3rd. ed. 1974; Benim Sinemalarím, 2nd ed., 1973; 47'liler, 1975. Contbr. to num. jrnls. Recip., Sait Faik Short Story Prize, 1971. Address: Ölçek Sokak. No. 99/10, Orkide Ap., Harbiye, Istanbul, Turkey.

SELDON TRUSS, Leslie, b. 1892. Author. Publs. incl: Gallows Bait, 1928; The Hunterstone Outrage, 1931; Rooksmiths, 1936; Foreign Bodies, 1938; The Disappearance of Julie Hints, 1940; Where's Mr. Chumley, 1949; Never Fight a Lady, 1951; Death of No Lady, 1952; Put out the Light, 1954; The Long Night, 1956; In Secret Places, 1958; One Man's Death, 1960; A Time to Hate, 1962; Walk a Crooked Mile, 1964; Eyes at the Window, 1966; The Bride that Got Away, 1967; The Hands of the Shadow, 1968; The Corpse that Got Away, 1969; var. short stories & serials. Address: Dale Hill House, Ticehurst, Sussex, UK.

SELF, Margaret Cabell, b. 12 Feb. 1902, Cincinnati, Ohio, USA. Author. Publs: approx. 37 books, inclng: The Horseman's Encyclopedia, 1945; Horseman's Companion, 1949; The How & Why of Horses, 1961; Horses of the World, 1961; Complete Book of Horses & Ponies; The Horseman's Almanac, 1966; The Young Rider & His First Pony, 1969; The Hunter in Pictures, 1971; How to Buy the Right Horse, 1972; The Nature of the Horse, 1973. Contbr. to: Ed., Block Island Times, R.I. Mbrships. incl: Fndr., Commandant, New Canaan Mounted Troop, Jr. Cavalry. Address: Block Is., RI 02087, USA.

SELIGSON, Esther, b. 25 Oct. 1941, Mexico City, Mexico. Teacher. Educ: M.A. Publs: Tras la Ventana un Árbol, 1969; Otros son los Sueños, 1973. Contbr. to: Plural; Revista de la Universidad de México; Diálogos. Mbr., PEN. Hons: Fellowship, Centro Mexicana de Escritores, 1969-70; Xavier Villaurrutia Prize, 1973. Address: Fuente de Jupiter 48, Mexico, 10, D.F., Mexico.

SELIMOVIĆ, Mehmed-Meša, b. 26 Apr. 1910, Tuzla, Yugoslavia. Writer. Educ: Grad., Fac. of Philos. Publs: Uvrijedjeni Čovjek (Insulted Man), 1947; Prva Četa (First Company), 1950; Tišine (Silences), 1961; Tudja Zémlja (Foreign Land), 1963; Magla I Mjesećine (Mist & Moonlight), 1965; Dervis I Smrt (Dervish & Death), 1966; Eseji I Ogledi (Essays & Reviews), 1966; Za I Protiv Vuka (Pro & Con Vuk), 1967; Tvrdjava (Fortress), 1970; Sabrana Djela (Collected Works), 1970-72; Sjećanja (Memories), 1972; Ostrvo (Island), 1974. Contbr. to sev. Yugoslav Mags. Mbrships. incl: PEN; Yugoslav Writers' Union; Serbian Acad. of Scis. & Arts. Hons. incl: Hon. Doctorate, Univ, of Sarajevo; Sev. lit prizes. Address: 11000 Belgrade, Jovanova 39, Yugoslavia.

SELIN, Elis Alban Immanuel, b. 26 Mar. 1891, Helsinki, Finland. Clergyman. Educ: Degree in theol., Helsinki Univ., 1918. Publs: Utskärs, 1931; Utskärsbor I, 1934; Det Gamla utskärssläktet, 1937; Hitis utskär, 1941; Strand-Henriks väg, 1948; Herodias dotter, 1948; Midsommarlek, 1950; Utskärsprästen, 1953; Präestens andra hustru, 1954; Du är prästens dotter, 1956; Inga utskärsbor, 1956; Änglafröjd, 1960; Luthers pslamer, 1935; Stormfåglarna, 1964; Pastor Eva, 1967. Contbr. to: Hufudstadsbladet & other Swedish newspapers & mags. in Finland. Mbr., Finnish-Swedish Writers Assn. Recip., Writer Schlrships, 1948, 1952. Address: Artturi Kannistjovägen 10 C 19, 11320 Helsinki, Finland.

SELLIN, Eric, b. 7 Nov. 1933, Phila., Pa., USA. Professor. Educ: A.B., 1955, M.A., 1958, Ph.D., 1965, Univ. of Pa. Publs: Night Voyage, 1964; The Dramatic Concepts of Antonin Artaud, 1968; Trees at First Light, 1973; Borne Kilométrique, 1973; Tanker Poems, 1973. Contbr. to: Books Abroad; N.Y. Times; New Directions; L'Esprit Créateur; Jrnl. of Mod. Lit.; Yale Review; Jrnl. des Poètes; etc. Mbrships: Phi Beta Kappa; MLA; AAUP; Am. Assn. of Tchrs. of French; VP, Am. Assn. for the Study of Dada & Surrealism. Hons. incl: Cape Rock Quarterly Prize Poet, 1971; Nat. Endowment for the Humanities Sr. Fellowship, 1973-74. Address: 312 Kent Rd., Bala-Cynwyd, PA 19004, USA.

SELMAN, Elsie E., pen name SELMAN, Taylor, b. 5 June 1919, London, UK. Bookshop Manageress. Publs: The Marshmead Murders, 1969; Murder Grows Roots, 1970. Contbr. to: She mag. Mbr., W. Country Writers' Assn. Address: 1 Bayham Road, Knowle, Bristol BS4 2EA, UK.

SELSAM, Millicent Ellis, b. 30 May 1912, Bklyn, USA. Author. Educ: B.A., Bklyn. Coll., 1932; M.A., Columbia, 1934. Publs. incl: Vegetables from Stems & Leaves, 1972; More Potatoes, 1972; How Puppies Grow, 1972; Is This a Baby Dinosaur, 1971: A First Look at Leaves, 1972; A First Look at Fish, 1972; A First Look at Mammals, 1973; The Apple & Other Fruits, 1973; Questions & Answers about Horses, 1973; A First Look at Birds, 1974; Bulbs, Corms & Such, 1974. Mbrships: Am. Nature Study Soc.; Authors Guild; AAAS. Hons: Eva L. Gordon Award, Am. Nature Study Soc., 1964; Four-Leaf Clover Award, Lucky Book Club, 1973. Address: 100 West 94th St., NYC, NY 10025, USA.

SELVON, Samuel (Dickson), b 20 May 1923, Trinidad. Writer. Publs: (novels) A Brighter Sun, UK, 1952, USA, 1953; An Island is a World, 1955; The Lonèly Londoners, UK, 1956, USA, 1957; Turn Again, Tiger, UK, 1958, USA, 1959; I Hear Thunder, UK & USA, 1963; The Housing Lark, 1965; The Plains of Caroni, 1969; Those Who Eat the Cascadura, 1972; (short stories) Ways of Sunlight, UK & USA, 1958. Hons: Guggenheim Fellowship, 1954, 1968; Travelling Schlrship., Soc. of Authors, 1958; Schlrship., Trinidad Govt., 1962; Grant, Arts Coun., 1967, 1968; Humming Bird Medal, Trinidad, 1969. Address: 36 Woodside Ave., London SE25, UK.

SELYE, Hans, b. 26 Jan. 1907, Vienna, Austria. Professor; Director. Educ: M.D., Ph.D., German Univ. of Prague, Czech.; D.Sc., McGill Univ., Montreal, Can. Publs. incl: The Stress of Life, 1956; From Dream to Discovery, 1964; In Vivo. The Case for Supramolecular Biology, 1967; Anaphylactoid Edema, 1968; Experimental Cardiovascular Diseases, 1970; Hormones & Resistance 1971; Stress Without Distress, 1974. Contbr. to var. jrnls. Mbrships: Fndr.-Mbr., Sci. Coun., Am. Heart Assn.; Pres., Sect. on Endocrinol., Pan Am. Med. Assn., 1973. Hons: Medal, Med. Soc., WHO, 1971; Starr Medal, Can. Med. Assn., 1972; Companion of Order of Can. Address: 659 Milton St., Montreal, P.Q., Can.

SEMBENE, Ousmane, b. 8 Jan. 1923, Ziguinchor, Senegal. Writer; Film Director. Publs: Docker Noir, 1956; O Pays Mon Beau Peuple, 1957; Voltaique; L'Harmattan; Le Mandat, Vehi-Ciosane, 1966; Xala, 1973. Mbrships: Pres., Les Cinéastes Sénégalais Associés; Fédération Pan Africaine des Cineastes. Hons. incl: Grand Prix Littéraire, Festival des Arts Nègres, Dakar, 1966; Prix Lotus des Ecrivains Afro-asiatique, 1971; var. film awards, inclng. 2nd Prize Silver Medal, Moscow, 1st Prize Afro-Asiatique, 1971, & 1st Prize, Phila. Black Film Festival, 1973, for "Emitai". Address: B.P. 8087 Yoff, Dakar, Senegal.

SEMMLER, Clement William, b. 23 Dec. 1914, Mercunda, S. Australia. Deputy General Manager, Australian Broadcasting Commission; Writer. Educ: B.A., 1936, M.A., 1939, Univ. Adelaide. Publs. incl: (essays) For the Uncanny Man, 1963; Ed., Literary Australia, 1965; Barcroft Booke, 1965; A.B. "Banjo" Paterson, 1965; Ed., Stories of the Riverina, 1965; Kenneth Slessor, 1966, 2nd ed., 1969; (short stories) Coast to Coast 1965-1966, 1966; The Banjo of the Bush, 1966, 2nd ed., 1967; The World of Banjo Paterson, Great Australian, 1967; Douglas Stewart, 1974. Contbr. to var. Aust. jrnls. & newspapers. Mbrships.

incl: Univ. Club, Sydney. Recip., O.B.E., 1972. Address: 15 Cowper St., Longueville, N.S.W. 2066, Australia.

SENDER, Ramón José, b. 3 Feb. 1901. Author; Educator. Educ: Inst. de Teruel; Madrid Univ. Publs. incl: Pro Patria, 1934; Counter-attack in Spain, 1938; A Man's Place, 1940; Dark Wedding, 1943; Chronicle of Dawn, 1944; The King & the Queen, 1948; The Affable Hangman, 1954; Exemplary Novels of Cibola, 1963; Aventura equinoccial de Lope de Aguirre, 1970; Nocturno de los, 1970; Tanit, 1970; Las criaturas saturnianas, 1971; La antesala, 1973; El fugitivo, 1973. Contbr. to El Sol (Ed., 1924-31). Hons. incl: Spanish Mil. Cross of Merit; Planeta Prize. Address: Am. Lit. Agency, 11 Riverside Dr., N.Y. NY, USA.

SEPEHRI, Sohrab, b. 25 Dec. 1928, Kashan, Iran. Painter. Educ: Grad., Fac. of Fine Arts, Univ. of Teheran. Publs: (poems) The Death of Colour, 1951; The Life of Dreams, 1953; The Collapse of the Sun, 1961; The Green Volume, 1967. Recip., First Prize, Min. of Culture & Art, Teheran Biennial. Address: 26, 24th St., Guisha Ave., Teheran, Iran.

SERAFIMOV, Serafim Nikolaev, pen name, SEVERNYAK, Serafim, b. 10 July 1930, Gorna Lipnitsa, Bulgaria. Writer. Publs: (in Bulgarian) A Sandal-Wood Fan, 1966; Wings, 1967; Between the Rose & the Lion, 1969; Ballad of Ohrid, 1971; White Cares, 1972. Contbr. to: Savremennik; September; Plamuk. Mbr. Union of Bulgarian Writers; Hons: Dimitrov Prize, 1971; Honoured Worker in Culture, 1974. Address: Sofia, kv. Geo Milev bl. 1o6-v, Bulgaria.

SERISAWA, Kojiro, b. 5 May 1897. Author. Educ: Univs. of Tokyo & Paris. Publs: Death in Paris, 1940; One World, 1954; Mrs. Aida, 1957; Under the Shadow of Love & Death, 1953; House on the Hill, 1959; Parting, 1961; Love, Intelligence & Sadness, 1962; Fate of Man, 14 vols., 1962-71. Mbrships: PEN; Japanese Acad. Hons: Prix des Amitiés Françaises, 1959; Prize of Japanese Govt., 1970; Japanese Acad. Prize, 1972. Address: 5-8-3 Higashinakano, Nagano-ku, Tokyo, Japan.

SERLE, Alan Geoffrey, b. 10 Mar. 1922, Melbourne, Australia. University Lecturer. Educ: B.A., Melbourne Univ., 1947; D.Phil., Oxon., 1950. Publs: The Golden Age, 1963; The Rush to be Rich, 1971; From Deserts the Prophets Come, 1973. Contbr. to jrnls. inclng: Histl. Studies; Meanjin Quarterly. Address: 31 Lisson Grove, Hawthorn, Vic., Australia.

SERVADIO, Gaia Cecilia Metella, pen names GAIO; G. S., b. 13 Sept. 1938, Padua, Italy. Writer. Publs: Melinda, 1968; Don Juan — Salome, 1969; Il Metodo, 1970; Angelo La Barbera — a profile of a Mafia Boss, 1974. Contbr. to: Sunday Times; Daily Telegraph; Observer; Partisan Review; Evening Standard; La Stampa; L'Ora; BBC broadcasts; etc. Mbr., Cultural Comm., For. Press Assn., London. Address: 31 Bloomfield Terrace, London SW1, UK.

SERVAIS, Jean M. A. E. A., b. 27 Sept. 1902, Liège, Belgium. Professor of Literature. Educ: D.Litt., Univ. of Liège. Publs. incl: (poems) D'Exil & de Tristesse, 1946; Rediviva Vita, 1974; (novels & short stories) Horoscope, 1955; Itinéraires, 1966; Roycourt, 1974; (plays) Iphigénie, 1956; Alceste, 1958; Médée, 1965; (radio plays) Monsieur Tic Tac, 1947; Un Pauvre Homme Tout Ordinaire, 1952; Le Roi aux Yeux Crevés, 1960; (essay) Jean Rogister, un Musicien du Coeur, 1972. Ed., La Vie Wallonne, 1950—. Mbrships. incl: Assn. of Belgian Writers; Writers of the Ardennes Soc. Hons. incl: Radio Play Prize, Radio Geneva Int. Competition, 1948; Grand Prize for Dramatic Lit., Exposition 1958. Address: Rue Wiertz 13, B4000 Liège, Belgium.

SERVAN-SCHREIBER, Jean-Jacques, b. 13 Feb. 1924, Paris, France. Politician; Author & Journalist. Educ: Ecole Polytechnique. Publs: Lieutenant en Algérie. Lieutenant in Algeria, UK), 1957; Le Défi Americain, 1967 (The American Challenge, UK, 1968); Le Réveil de la France (The Spirit of May, UK), 1968; Le Manifeste (The Radical Alternative, UK), 1970. Contbr. to: Le Monde (Diplomatic Ed., 1948-53); l'Express (Fndg. Dir., 1953-69; Pres., Groupe-Express Pubng. Co.). Mbrships. incl: Fédn. Nat. des Anciens d'Algérie (Fndg. Pres.). Recip., Mil. Cross. Address: 25 rue de Berri, Paris 8e, France.

SERVIEN, Louis-Marc, b. 8 Jan. 1934. Company President & Managing Director. Educ: Lic. Law, Econs. & Commercial Sci., Univ. of Lausanne, Switz.; Univ. of London, UK; Univ. of Cologne, Germany; Dr. Acc., Rome, Italy. Publs. incl: Les Fonds de Placement Collectif en Suisse, 1964; I Fondi Communi di Investimento: Una Nuova Forma di Risparmio, 1967; Investment Trusts: Moderne Kapitalanlage, 1968; Mutual Funds, Why Not?, 1968; Quelques Réflexions à Propos du Nouveau Statut Juridique des Fonds de Placement Suisses, 1969; Fondos de Inversion, Une Nueva Formula de Ahorro, 1970; Fondi d'Investimento in Svizzera, 1972. Mbrships. incl: Int. Real Estate Fed.; Int. Assn. of Fin. & Fiscal Law. Recip., Commn. of the Concordia Order, Sao Paulo, Brazil. Address: 23 ch. du Levant, 1005 Lausanne, Switz.

SETHNA, Minocher Jehangirji, b. 1 Nov. 1911, Bombay, India. Professor. Educ: Ph.D., Bombay Univ.; Barrister-at-Law, Middle Temple, London, UK. Publs: Indian Company Law, 7th ed., 1967; Photography, 1970; Society & the Criminal, 3rd ed., 1971; Art of Living, 1972; Jurisprudence, 3rd ed., 1973; Mercantile Law, 7th ed., 1975; Health & Happiness, 1975. Contbr. to: Bombay Law Reporter; Indian Advocate; Maharashtra State Bar Coun. Jrnl. Mbrships: Past Pres., Indian Schl. of Synthetic Jurisprudence; Fellow, Royal Econ. Soc. Address: Sethna House, 251 Tardeo Rd., Bombay-7, India.

SETH-SMITH, Michael, b. 11 June 1928, Cobham, Surrey, UK. Author. Educ: Charterhouse. Publs: History of Steeplechasing, 1966; Bred for the Purple, 1967; Lord Paramount of the Turf, 1969; History of Richard Johnson & Nephew, 1973; Steve — Life & Times of Steve Donoghue, 1974; History of British Commercial Vehicle Industry, 1975; International Stallions & Studs, 1974. Contbr. to: Tatler; Brit. Race Horse; Stud & Stable; Racing info. Bur.; The Horse (Ed.). Address: Sylvans, Tilford Rd., Farnham, Surrey, UK.

SETON, Anya (Anya Seton Chase), b. NYC, USA (as Brit. subject). Author. Publs: (USA, UK & 8 other countries) My Theodosia, 1941; Dragonwyck, 1944; The Turquoise, 1946; The Hearth & the Eagle, 1948; Foxfire, 1951; Katherine, 1954; The Winthrop Woman, 1958; Devil Water, 1962; Avalon, 1966; Green Darkness, 1972; (juvenile) The Mistletoe & Sword, 1956; Washington Irving, 1960. Mbrships: Pen & Brush (Hon.), N.Y.; PEN. Address: Binney Lane, Old Greenwich, CT 06870, USA.

SETTERLIND, Bo Alf Ingemar, b. 24 Aug. 1923, Vaxjo, Sweden. Poet. Publs. incl: Moon Cradle, 1948; The Heaven of Poets, 1950; Halleluja, 1951; Alexandrine, 1952; Hamlet in Strangnas, 1953; A Strange Company, 1955; Hovering Over the Panic, 1956; The Box of Pandora, 1957; The Transfigured Flower, 1959; The Boy Who Believed in the Devil, 1962; Stranger on the Beach, 1964; Madagaskar, 1966; From Night to Nightingale, Love Poems, 1967; Mary & the Child, 1970; Eyes of Ash, 1970; Heaven Has Landed, 1971; Poet in Peru, 1973; Poems 1948-72, 1973; On this Speck of Dust, 1974. Contbr. to sev. jrnls. Mbr., Swedish Union of Authors. Recip., sev. hons. Address: Ekegarden, S—15200 Strängnäs, Sweden.

SETZEKORN, William David, b. 12 Mar. 1935, Mt. Vernon, Ill., USA. Architect. Educ: Kan. State Univ.; Harvard Grad. Schl. of Design. Publs: Origin & History of the Family Setzekorn, 1970; Looking Forward to a Career in Architecture, 1973; Heraldry: The Ancient Art of Designing Coats of Arms, 1974; Formerly British Honduras: A Profile of the New Nation of Belize. Contbr. to num. nat. mags. Mbrships. incl: Authors Guild; Nat. Writers Club; Heraldry Soc., London. Address: 5374 Granville Ct., Fremont, CA 94536, USA.

SEUFERT, Karl Rolf, b. 1 Dec. 1923, Frankfurt am Main, Germany. Teacher; Author. Publs: Die Karawane der weissen Männer, 1961; Die Türme von Mekka, 1963; Die Vergessenen Buddhas, 1965; Das Jahr in der Steppe, 1969; Abenteuer Afrika, 1971; Einmal China und zurück, 1972; 3000 Jahre Afrika, 1973; Durch den schwarzen Kontinent, 1973. Mbr., German Writers Union. Hons. incl: Jr. Book Award, Boys' Clubs of Am., 1964; Deutscher Jugendbuch Preis, 1969 & 1972; Kurt-Lütgen Sachbuch Preis, 1973. Address: Adam-von-Itzsteinstr. 22, 6229 Hallgarten, E. Germany.

SEXTON, Anne, b. 9 Nov. 1928, Newton, Mass., USA. Poet. Publs: To Bedlam & Bart Way Back, 1960; All My Pretty Ones, 1962; Live or Die, 1966; Love Poems, 1969; Transformations, 1971; The Book of Folly, 1972; The

Death Notebooks, 1974; The Awful Rowing Toward God, 1975. Contbr. to: New Yorker; Harper's; Hudson, Yale, Partisan, Saturday, & Am. Poetry Reviews; Nation; Poetry; etc. Mbrships: F.R.S.L. Hons. incl: Pulitzer Prize for Poetry, 1967; D.Lit., Tufts Univ., 1970, Regis Coll., 1971, Fairfield Univ., 1971. Address: 14 Black Oak Rd., Weston, MA 02193, USA.

SEXTON, Virginia Staudt, b. 30 Aug. 1916, NYC, USA. Professor of Psychology. Educ: B.A., Hunter Coll., 1936; M.A., Fordham Univ., 1941; Ph.D., 1946. Publs: Catholics in Psychology: A Historical Survey (w. H. Misiak), 1954, Spanish ed., 1955; History of Psychology: An Overview (w. H. Misiak), 1966; Historical Perspectives in Psychology: Readings (w. H. Misiak), 1971; Phenomenological Existential & Humanistic Psychologies: A Historical Survey (w. H. Misiak), 1973. Contbr. to: Jrnl. of Psychol.; Am. Psychol.; Psychol. Bull.; Jrnl. of Genetic Psychol.; Educ.; Jrnl. of Gen. Psychol.; etc. Fellowships: Am. Psychol. Assn.; AAAS; Int. Coun. of Psychols.; N.Y. Acad. Scis. Address: 188 Ascan Ave., Forest Hills, NY 11375, USA.

SEYMOUR, Arabella Charlotte Henrietta (married name MUNRO), b. 8 Dec. 1949, London, UK. Writer. Publs: Maid of Destiny, 1971; The Bitter Chalice, 1972; Flesh & the Devil; The Man Who Collected Women (w. A. K. Munro); The Blood Countess; The History of Jealousy (in preparation). Contbr. to: Hist. of Essex Jrnl., 1965; Look Now Mag., 1972. Mbrships: Soc. of Authors; Soc. Women Writers & Jrnlsts. Agent: David Higham Assocs. Address: 4 St. Margaret's Rd., Wanstead, London E12 5DP, UK.

SEYMOUR, William Kean, b. 1887. Writer. Publs. incl: (verse) The Street of Dreams, 1914; Swords & Flutes, 1919; Caesar Remembers, 1929; Chinese Crackers, 1938; Collected Poems, 1946; The First Childermas (verse play), 1959; The Cats of Rome, 1970; (fiction) The Little Cages, 1944; Names & Faces, 1956; (biog.) Jonathan Swift, 1967; Ed., var. anthols. Contbr. to: Poetry Review; Contemporary Review; etc. Mbrships: Poetry Soc. (VP, 1947—); Charles Lamb Soc. (VP); W. Country Writers' Assn. (VP & Chmn.); PEN. Hons: D.Litt., Free Univ., Asia, 1968; Presidential Gold Medal for Poetry, Philippines, 1968. Address: White Cottage, Old Alresford, Alresford, Hants., UK.

SGARLATO, Nico, pen name CASTELLANO, Franco, b. 16 Nov. 1944, Albenga, Italy. Journalist; Author. Publs: Veteran & Vintage Aircraft in Italy, 1971; Italian Air Force, 1972; Electronic Warfare, 1972; Helicopters, 1973. Contbr. to: Italian ed., Air Int.; Ala rotante; Rivista Aeronautica; Sr. Ed. & Publr., Periodical Mag. Dept., Ermanno Albertelli Editore. Mbr., Italian Aerospace Jrnlsts.' Union. Address: Via Genova 21—1B, 17031 Albenga (Savona), Italy.

SHACKLE, George Lennox Sharman, b. 14 July 1903, Cambridge, UK. Emeritus Professor of Economics. Educ: B.A., London Univ., 1931; Ph.D., London Schl. of Econs., 1937; D.Phil., New Coll., Oxford Univ. 1940. Publs: Expectations, Investment & Income, 1938, 1968; Expectation in Economics, 1949, 1952; Decision, Order & Time in Human Affairs, 1961, 1969; A Scheme of Economic Theory, 1965; The Years of High Theory, 1967; Expectation, Enterprise & Profit, 1970; Epistemics & Economics, 1972; An Economic Querist, 1973; Keynesian Kaleidics, 1974. Mbrships: Fellow, Brit. Acad., 1967—. Address: c/o Dept. of Economic History, Univ. of Liverpool, P.O. Box 147, Liverpool L69 3BX, UK.

SHACKLETON, (Lord) Edward Arthur Alexander, b. 15 July 1911, London, UK. Businessman. Educ: M.A., Magdalen Coll., Oxford. Publs: Arctic Journeys; Nansen, The Explorer (biog.); Borneo Jungle (co-author). Mbrships: Royal Geog. Soc. (Pres., 1971-74; former VP); ASLIB (Pres., 1963-65); Arctic Club (Pres., 1960); Brit. Assn. of Indl. Eds. (Pres., 1960-64); Parly. & Sci. Comm. (VP). Address: Long Coppice, Canford Magna, Nr. Wimborne, Dorset, UK.

SHADBOLT, Maurice Francis Richard, b. 4 June 1932, Auckland, NZ. Author. Publs. incl: (short stories) The New Zealanders, 1959, 3rd ed., 1975; Summer Fires & Winter Country, 1963, 2nd ed., 1966; (novellas) The Presence of Music, 1967; (non-fiction) New Zealand: Gift of the Sea, 1963, revised ed., 1974; The Shell Guide to New Zealand, 1968; (novels) Among the Cinders, 1965; This Summer's Dolphin, 1969; An Ear of the Dragon, 1971; Strangers & Journeys, 1972, 2nd ed., 1973; A Touch of Clay, 1974; Danger Zone, 1975. Mbr., PEN (Chmn. Auckland Br. 1973-75). Hons. incl: State Lit. Schlr., 1960 & 1970;

Katherine Mansfield NZ Short Story Award, 1963 & 1967; Pacific Area Travel Assn. Award Jrnlsm., 1971; Sir James Wattie Book Yr. Award, 1973. Address: 35 Arapito Rd., Titirangi, Auckland 7, NZ.

SHAFFER, Olive Charlotte, b. 13 July 1896, Masonville, W.Va., USA. Elementary School Teacher. Educ: A.B., Shepherd Coll.; M.A., W.Va. Univ. Publs: (Contbr. to anthols.) Poetry Digest, 1945; Book of Modern Poetry, 1941; Poets of America, 1941; Of America We Sing, 1944; Yearbook of Modern Poetry, 1971; From Sea to Sea in Song, 1971. Contbr. to: Poetry Broadcast, 1946. Mbrships: W.Va. 4H All Stars (VP); Int. Platform Assn.; Bus. & Profl. Women's Clubs (Pres. & VP). Hons. incl: Cert. Merit Am. Poets' Fellowship Soc. disting. contbn. poetry, 1973. Address: 127 Mt. View St., Petersburg, W.Va., USA.

SHAFFER, Peter Levin, b. 15 May 1926. Playwright. Educ: Trinity Coll., Cambridge. Publs: (plays) Five Finger Exercise, 1958; The Private Ear & The Public Eye, 1962; The Royal Hunt of the Sun, 1964; Black Comedy, 1965; White Liars, 1967; The Battle of Shrivings, 1970; Equus, 1973; & var. TV plays. Hons: N.Y. Drama Critics' Circle Award, 1959-60; Evening Standard Drama Award, 1958. Address: 18 Earls Terrace, Kensington High St., London W8, UK.

SHAGINYAN, Marietta Sergeevna, b. 21 Mar. 1888. Writer. Educ: D.Philos. Publs. incl: Your Own Destiny, 1916; Adventures of a Society Lady, 1923; The Five-Year Plans, 1947; Goethe, 1950; Nizami Studies, 1955; The Ulyanov Family, 1957; Sergei Rachmaninoff, 1964; Travels Through Europe: Holland, Great Britain, France, 1966; Three Days on the Fiat, 1967. Mbr., Acad. of Sci., Armenia. Hons. incl: State Prize, 1951; Order of Lenin, 1967; Red Banner of Labour; Order of the Red Star. Address: Arbat 45, Flat 9, Moscow, USSR.

SHAH, Idries, b. 16 June 1924, Simla, India. Author; University Professor. Publs. incl: Oriental Magic, 1956; Destination, Mecca, 1957; The Secret Lore of Magic, 1957; Tales of the Dervishes, 1967, 4th impression, 1973; The Sufis, 1968, 3rd ed., 1974; Reflections, 1968, 3rd ed., 1971; Book of the Book, 1969, 3rd ed., 1973; The Dermis Probe, 1970; The Magic Monastery, 1972; Subtleties of the Inimitable Mulla Nasrudin, 1973; The Elephant in the Dark, 1974. Mbrships. incl: F.R.S.A.; PEN; Soc. of Authors; Authors' Club. Hons. incl: Outstanding Book of Yr. Award, for Reflections, BBC Critics Prog.; 6 1st Prizes, UNESCO Int. Book Yr., 1972. Address: c/o C. Hoare & Co., 37 Fleet Street, London EC4P 4DQ, UK.

SHAH, Narottam, b. 26 June 1926, Karachi, Pakistan. Economist; Journalist. Educ: M.A., Ph.D., Bombay Univ., India. Publs: incl: Biography of Lenin, History of the World in 4 parts. Contbr. to: Commerce; Jrnl., Indian Inst. of Bankers; Granth; Vyapar. Mbr., Sec., Indian Assn. for Rsch. in Natl. Income & Wealth. Recip., Nehru Award for Biography of Lenin, 1972. Address: 38/3 Patrakar Housing Soc., Patrakar Nagar, Bandra East, Bombay 400 051, India.

SHAHANE, Vasant Anant, b. 18 Dec. 1923, Parbhani, India. Professor; Principal, University College. Educ: B.A., 1944, LL.B., 1946, M.A., 1947, Univ. of Bombay; Ph.D., Univ. of Leeds, UK, 1958. Publs: E. M. Forster A Reassessment, 1962; Perspectives in E. M. Forster's A Passage to India, 1968; Khishwant Singh, 1972; Notes on Walt Whitman's Leaves of Grass, 1972; Rudyard Kipling Activist & Artist, 1972. Contbr. to num. profl. jrnls.; Ed. Bd. Mbr., Indian Jrnl. of Am. Studies. Mbr., Indian PEN, & Poetry Soc., London. Address: English Dept., Univ. Coll. of Arts, Osmania Univ., Hyderabad, Andhra Pradesh, India 500007.

SHAHIED, Ishak I., b. 22 Apr. 1936, Kom Baddar, Egypt. Senior Research Chemist, US Air Force. Educ: B.A., Eastern N. Coll., Quincy, Mass., USA, 1959; M.S., Univ. of Tenn., 1964; Ph.D., Colo. State Univ., 1973; Univ. of Ga.; Univ. of Mo. Publs: The Physiology & Biochemistry of Hormones, forthcoming; The Biochemistry of Foods, Vitamins & Minerals, forthcoming; var. papers on hormones. Mbr., AAAS. Recip., var. Rsch. Assistantships, 1966-73. Address: 643 Patterson St., Fairborn, OH 45324, USA.

SHAKDANY, Yehuda, b. 1 May 1904, Stryj, Austria-Hungary. Government Official (retired). Educ studies in Philos. & Sociol. Publs: Das Demokratische Totalitäts-System, 1945, reprinted as Totale Demokratie, 1968; Insane Life, 1958, reprint 1972; Chajej Taatuim,

1972; Haitztrubal, 1973; Das Weisse Licht, 1973. Contbr. to: Aufbau (N.Y., USA); etc. Mbrships. incl: PEN; World Cultural Coun., Berlin, Germany, 1961; Assn. Int. des Decores d'Ordres Chevaleresques, Palermo, Italy, 1970; Verband deutscher Schriftsteller; Accad. Teatina per le Scienze, Italy, 1971. Address: P.O. Box 569, 11 Alcalay St., Jerusalem, Israel.

SHALLCRASS, John James, b. 11 Sept. 1922, Auckland, NZ. Teacher. Educ: M.A. & Dip. in Educ., Victoria Univ. of Wellington. Publs: Educating New Zealanders, 1967; Maori Education (w. J. L. Ewing), 1970; Secondary Schools in Change, 1973; Spirit of an Age (Ed. w. J. L. Robson), 1975. Contbr. to: NZ Listener; Post Primary Jrnl.; Nat. Educ.; Educ.; Lanfall; Charisma; Comment; W.E.A. Review; Jrnl. of Educl. Psychol.; Act. Mbrships: Past Pres., Assn. for the Study of Childhood; NZ Educl. Inst.; Post Primary Tchrs. Assn. Address: 11 Pembroke Rd., Wellington 5, NZ.

SHAMBROOK, Rona, pen name RANDALL, Rona, b. Birkenhead, Cheshire, UK. Actress; Journalist; Fiction Writer. Publs: 36 novels since 1940 inclng: I Married a Doctor; The Cedar Tree; Leap in the Dark; The Merry Andrews; Hotel de Luxe; Walk into my Parlour; books transld. into 7 langs. Contbr. to women's mags., UK, C'wlth., USA, Scandinavia & Europe (short stories & serials). Mbrships. Women's Press Club, London; PEN; Soc. Women Writers & Jrnlsts. Address: 10 Browning Mews, New Cavendish St., London W1, UK

SHAMBURGER, (Alice) Page, b. Aberdeen, N.C., USA. Writer. Educ: Marjorie Webster Coll. Publs: Tracks Across the Sky, 1964; Classic Monoplanes, 1966; Aces & Planes of World War I, 1968; Command the Horizon, 1968; Summon the Stars, 1970; The Curtiss Hawks, 1972. Contbr. to var. mags. Mbrships. incl: Aviation Writers Assn.; Curator, Int. Women's Air & Space Mus.; num. flying orgs. Hons. incl: Best Non-Fiction Book of Yr. in aviation, for Summon the Stars, 1970. Address: 500 Carolina St., Aberdeen, NC 28315, USA.

SHANKMAN, Florence V., b. 16 July 1912, Norwalk, Conn., USA. College Professor; Reading Consultant; Author. Educ: B.S., 1934, M.A., 1936, Tchrs. Coll., Columbia Univ., N.Y.; M.A., 1955, Ed.D., 1959, N.Y. Univ. Publs. incl: How to Teach Study Skills (w. R. Kranyik), 1963; Successful Practices in Remedial Reading, 1963; Research Studies in Reading, 2 vols., 1969; Readings in the Language Arts, 3 vols., 1969; Reading Success with Young Children, 1970; Teaching Techniques With Phonis, Linguistics & Games, 1971; Games & Activities to Reinforce Reading Skills, 1972; Activities & Games to Reinforce Phonics & Linguistics, 1973. Contbr. to profl. jrnls. Mbrships. incl: Int. Reading Assn.; Assn. for Childhood Educ. Int.; AAUP. Address: 32 West Ave., S.Norwalk, CT 06854, USA.

SHANKS, Michael James, b. 12 Apr. 1927, London, UK. Economist; Journalist; Director-General, Social Affairs Commission, of the European Communities. Educ: M.A., Balliol Coll., Oxford, 1950. Publs: The Stagnant Society, 1961 (revised 1972); Britain & the New Europe (w. John Lambert), 1962; The Lessons of Public Enterprise (Ed), 1963; The Innovators, 1967; The Quest for Growth, 1973. Contbr. to: Encounter; Fin. Times; The Listener; etc. Fellow, Brit. Inst. of Mgmt. Address: Enderley, Stony Lane, Little Kingshill, Great Missenden, Bucks, UK.

SHANNON, William Vincent, b. 24 Aug. 1927, Worcester, Mass., USA. Member of the Editorial Board, The New York Times. Educ: B.A., Clark Univ., Worcester, 1947; M.A., Harvard Univ., 1948. Publs: The Truman Merry-Go-Round (w. Robert S. Allen); 1950; The American Irish, 1964; The Heir Apparent, 1967; They Could not Trust the King, 1974. Contbr. to: Harper's; N.Y. Times Mag.; Worldview. Mbrships: Nat. Press Club; Cosmos Club; Century Club; Authors' Guild; etc. Hons. incl: NY Newspaper Guild Page One Award, 1951; Litt.D., Clark Univ., 1964 & Coll. New Rochelle, 1971; Alicia Patterson Fellowship, 1969-70; Gold Medal, Eire Soc. of Boston, 1975. Address: NY Times, 1920 L St., N.W., Wash. DC 20036, USA.

SHARELL, Richard, b. 6 Oct. 1893, Graz, Austria. Retired Teacher of Natural Sciences & Art. Educ: Coll.; Tchrs. Acad., for 4 yrs.; 2 yr. Advanced Exam. Publs: The Tuatara, Lizards & Frogs of New Zealand, 1966; New Zealand Insects & their Story, 1971. Contbr. to sci. & educl. mags. Mbrships; incl: Former Pres., Aquarian &

Terrarian Soc., Graz. Austria; Entomol. Soc. of NZ. Address: 21 Karamu St., Eastbourne nr. Wellington, NZ.

SHARIPOV, Adiy, b. 1912. Politician; Writer. Educ: M.Sc., Kazakh Pedagogical Inst. Publs. incl: (novel) Guerilla's Daughter, 1961; Creative Activity of Jumgali Sain, 1963. Mbrships. incl: Bd., Kazakh S.S.R. Union of Writers; Supreme Soviet, USSR, 1966-70. Address: Kazakh Union of Writers, Alma-Ata, USSR.

SHARKANSKY, Ira, b. 25 Nov. 1938, Fall River, Mass., USA. Professor of Political Science. Educ: B.A., Wesleyan Univ., 1960; M.S., 1961, Ph.D., 1964, Univ. of Wis.-Madison. Publs. incl: Spending in the American States, 1968; Regionalism in American Politics, 1970; The Routines of Politics, 1970; Public Administration: Policy-Making in Government Agencies, 1970, 3rd ed., 1975; The Maligned States: Policy Accomplishments, Problems, & Opportunities, 1972; Politics & Policy-Making in American Governments (w. D. S. Van Meter), 1975. Contbr. to: (Ed. bd.) Jrnl. of Pols.; Social Sci. Quarterly; Am. Pols. Quarterly; etc. Address: Dept. of Pol. Sci., Univ. of Wis.-Madison, Madison, WI 53706, USA.

SHARMAT, Marjorie Weinman, b. 12 Nov. 1928, Portland, Me., USA. Writer. Educ: Grad., Westbrook Jr. Coll., 1948. Publs. incl: Rex, 1967; 51 Sycamore Lane, 1971; A Visit with Rosalind, 1972; Nate the Great, 1972; Sophie & Gussie, 1973; Morris Brookside, a Dog, 1973; Morris Brookside is Missing, 1974; Nate the Great Goes Undercover, 1974; I Want Mama, 1974; I'm Not Oscar's Friend Any More, 1975; Walter the Wolf, 1975; Nate the Great & the Lost List, 1975. Contbr. to var. mags. Mbrships. incl: Authors' Guild. Hons. incl: Sequoia List, best children's books of Okla., 1973-74, 1974-75. Address: 51 Sycamore Lane, Irvington-on-Hudson, NY 10533, USA.

SHARP, Doreen Maud, b. 21 Feb. 1920, Upper Norwood, London, UK. Senior Lecturer. Educ: Tchrs. Certs. in Shorthand, Typewriting & Off. Practice. Publs: Secretarial Typing, Secretarial Dictation, Teacher's Handbook & Solutions (all w. H. M. Crozier), 1965, 2nd ed., 1972; Typing Mailable Copy, 1973; Through Practice to Production, 1974; The Secretary in Europe (w. G. R. Sharp), 1975. Contbr. to: Memo; Office Skills; English Counties Periodicals; Camping & Outdoor Life. Mbrships. incl: Fellow, Royal Soc. of Arts (Moderator & a Chief Examiner); Soc. of Authors. Address: 4 Seabrook Dr., West Wickham, Kent BR4 9AJ, UK.

SHARP, Harold Spencer, pen name H.S.S., b. 23 Dec. 1909, Alameda, Calif., USA. Librarian; University Professor (Retired). Educ: B.S., 1954, M.A., 1957, Ind. Univ., Bloomington. Publs. incl: Index to Characters in the Performing Arts (w. Marjorie Z. Sharp), Part I — Non-Musical Plays, 1966, Part II — Operas & Musical Productions, 1969, Part III — Ballets, 1972, Part IV — Radio & Television, 1973; Handbook of Pseudonyms & Personal Nicknames, 1972. Contbr. to var. profl. jrnls. etc. Mbrships: Pres., Wis. Chapt., Special Libs. Assn., 1959-63; Prog. Chmn., Sec., VP. Recip., 1st Prize, Nat. Lib. Week Publicity Award, 1962; Address: 2110 Springfield Ave., Fort Wayne, IN 46805, USA.

SHARP, Ilsa Marie, occasional pen name NG, Ai Sha; SMITH, Virginia. b. 11 Oct. 1945, Glos., UK. Journalist; Editor, magazines. Educ: B.A. (Chinese Studies), Leeds Univ.; Dip. d'Etudes Françaises, Univ. de Poitiers, France. Publs: Solid as a Rock (co-author), 1972; This Singapore, 1975. Contbr. to: Financial Times (Singapore corres.); Daily Express; Euromoney; Far Eastern Econ. Review; Singapore Trade & Ind. mag.; New Directions (Ed. Advisor); etc. Mbrships. incl: Nat. Union of Jrnlsts.; Soc. for Anglo-Chinese Understanding; Singapore Film Soc. (VP), etc. Address: Times Publng. Sdn. Bhd., 422 Thomson Rd., Singapore 11.

SHARP, Keith Haberfield, b. 18 Dec. 1938, Chelsfield, Kent, UK. Freelance Writer. Publs: The House of Mammon, 1971. Contbr. to: Christian Sci. Monitor; Bulletin (Sydney); BBC. Mbr., Aust. Soc. of Authors. Address: Denefield, Main Rd., Knockholt, Sevenoaks, Kent, UK.

SHARP, Margery, b. 1905, UK. Writer. Educ: B.A., Bedford Coll., Univ. of London. Publs. incl: (novels) Rhododendron Pie, UK & USA, 1930; The Flowering Thorn, UK, 1933, USA, 1934; The Nutmeg Tree, UK & USA, 1937; Cluny Brown, UK & USA, 1944; Britannia Mews, UK & USA, 1946; The Foolish Gentlewoman, UK & USA, 1948; The Gypsy in the Parlour, UK & USA, 1954;

Martha in Paris, UK, 1962, USA, 1963; The Sun in Scorpio, UK & USA, 1965; In Pious Memory, USA, 1967, UK, 1968; Rosa, UK, 1969, USA, 1970; The Innocents, 1971; var. plays & juvenile books. Address: c/o Westminster Bank Ltd., St. James's Sq., London SW1, UK.

SHARP, Pauline S., b. 25 Sept. 1915, Liberty, Mo., USA. Author; Educator; Retired Funeral Director; Homemaker. Educ: B.A., Wm. Jewell Coll., Liberty, 1937; postgrad. work, Adams State Coll., Alamosa, Colo. Contbr. of articles & photos. to San Luis Valley Historian, & var. publs. of San Luis Valley Pubing. Co. Mbrships. incl: San Luis Valley Histl. Soc. (Co-Ed. of The Historian); Western Hist. Assn.; Mo., Kan. & N.M. State Histl. Socs. Address: 405 Second Ave., Monte Vista, CO, USA.

SHARPE, Myron E., b. 10 Sept. 1928, Chester, Pa., USA. President of Publishing Company. Educ: B.A., Swarthmore Coll., 1950; M.A., Univ. of Mich., 1951. Publs: Ed., Planning, Profit & Incentives in the USSR, 1966; John Kenneth Galbraith & the Lower Economics, 1973, 2nd ed., 1974. Contbr. to: Challenge, The Mag. of Econ. Affairs (Publr. & Ed., 1973—); Social Policy; Soc., Sci. & Soc. Mbrships: Am. Econ. Assn.; Nat. Assn. of Bus. Economists. Address: 901 N. Broadway, White Plains, NY 10603, USA.

SHARROCK, Roger Ian, b. 23 Aug. 1919, Robin Hood's Bay, Yorks., UK. University Professor; Editor; Author. Educ: M.A., B.Litt., St. John's Coll., Oxford. Publs: John Bunyan, 1954; Ed., Bunyan, The Pilgrim's Progress, 1960; Ed., Bunyan, Grace Abounding, 1962; Ed., Oxford Standard Authors, Bunyan, 1966; Ed., Pelican Book of English Prose, 1970; Gen. Ed., Oxford ed. of Bunyan's Miscellaneous Works. Contbr. to: Blackfriars; Durham Univ. Jrnl.; Essays in Criticism; Mod. Lang. Review; Notes & Queries; Reviews of Engl. Lit., Engl. Studies; Tablet; Times Lit. Supplement. Mbrships: Chmn., Engl. Assn., & Mgmt. Comm., World Ctr. for Shakespeare Studies. Address: 12 Plough Lane, Purley, Surrey, UK.

SHATTUCK, Roger W(hitney), b. 20 Aug. 1923, NYC, USA. Professor of French & English Literature. Educ: B.A., Yale Univ., 1947; Soc. of Fellows, Harvard Univ., 1950-53. Publs: The Banquet Years, 1958; Half Tame, 1964; Proust's Binoculars, 1965; Proust, 1974; Transl. & Ed., Selected Writings of Apollinaire, 1949; Co-Ed: The Craft & Context of Translation, 1962; Works of Alfred Jarry, 1969. Contbr. to: N.Y. Review of Books; N.Y. Times Book Review. Mbr.; Collège de Pataphysique. Hons: Guggenheim Grant, 1963; Rsch. Fellowship, Am. Coun. of Learned Socs., 1969. Address: Dept. of French Lit., Univ. of Va., Charlottesville, VA 22903, USA.

SHAW, Alan George Lewers, b. 3 Feb. 1916, Melbourne, Australia. Professor of History. Educ: B.A., Univ. of Melbourne; M.A., Christ Church, Oxford Univ., UK. Publs: Economic Development of Aust., 1944, rev., 1966; The Story of Aust., 1955, rev., 1972; Modern World History, 1959; Convicts & the Colonies, 1966; Great Britain & the Colonies, 1970; Ed., J. West, The History of Tasmania, 1971. Contbr. to: Aust. Ency., 1956; Histl. Studies; Aust. Economic Hist. Review; Jrnl. of Brit. Studies; Jrnl. of Royal Aust. Histl. Soc.; other profl. publs. Mbr., var. profl. assns. Hons. incl: Fellow, Aust. Acad. of the Humanities. Address: Dept. of History, Monash Univ., Clayton, Vic., Australia 3168.

SHAW, Charles Thurstan, b. 27 June 1914, Plymouth, UK. Archaeologist. Educ: B.A., M.A., Ph.D., Sidney Sussex Coll., Cambridge; Tchr.'s Postgrad. Dip., London Univ. Inst. of Educ. Publs: Excavation at Dawu. 1961; Archaeology & Nigeria, 1964; Igbo-Ukwu: an account of archaeological discoveries in eastern Nigeria, 1970; Africa & the Origins of Man, 1973. Contbr. to var. scholarly jrnls. Mbrships: F.S.A.; VP, Panafrican Congress on Prehist.; Permanent Coun., Union Int. des Scis. Pré- et Proto-Historiques. Recip., Amaury Talbot Prize, Royal Anthropol. Inst., 1970. Address: 37 Hawthorne Rd., Stapleford, Cambridge CB2 5DU, UK.

SHAW, Helen, b. 20 Feb. 1913, Timaru, NZ. Short Story Writer; Poet; Editor. Educ: B.A., Univ. of Canterbury. Publs. incl: The Puritan & the Waif — Symposium of Essays on Frank Sargeson (Ed.), 1954; The Orange Tree and other stories, 1957; Out of Dark, 1968; The Letters of D'Arcy Cresswell (Ed.), 1971; The Girl of the Gods, 1973; The Word & Flower, scheduled 1975. Contbr. to: World's Classics Anthologies of New Zealand Short Stories (1st & 2nd Series); Summer's Tales 2; Arena; Aryan Review (India); Aylesford Review; Expression;

Meanjin; Ocarina; Voices Int.; etc. Mbrships. incl: PEN; Int. Poetry Soc. Hons. incl: Disting. Serv. Citation, 1968 & 1971, World Poet Award, 1972, World Poetry Soc. Intercontinental. Address: 42 Bassett Rd., Auckland 5, NZ.

SHAW, Irwin, b. 27 Feb. 1913, N.Y., USA. Author. Educ: Bklyn. Coll. Publs. incl: (plays) Bury The Dead, 1939; The Gentle People, 1939; Sons & Soldiers, 1943; The Assassin, 1945; Children From Their Games, 1963; (novels) The Young Lions, 1948; Lucy Crown, 1955; Voices of a Summer Day, 1964; Rich Man, Poor Man, 1970; Evening in Byzantium, 1973; Nightwork, 1975; (short stories) Sailor Off The Bremen; Welcome to the City; Mixed Company; Whispers in Bedlam; (travel) In the Company of Dolphins. Contbr. to var. mags. Recip., O. Henry Mem. Award. Address: Klosters, Switz.

SHAW, Robert (Archibald), b. 9 Aug. 1927, Westhoughton, Lancs., UK. Stage & Film Actor. Educ: Royal Acad. Dramatic Art, London. Publs: (novels) The Hiding Place, UK & USA, 1959; The Sun Doctor, UK & USA, 1961; The Cure of Souls: I. The Flag, UK & USA, 1965; The Man in the Glass Booth, UK & USA, 1967; A Card from Morocco, UK & USA, 1969; (plays) Off the Mainland, prod. 1956; The Man in the Glass Booth, prod. & publd. UK, 1967, USA, 1968; Cato Street, prod. 1971, publd. 1972, UK; (screenplay) Figures in a Landscape, 1970; var. TV plays. Recip., Hawthornden Prize, 1962. Address: c/o Richard Hatton Ltd., 17a Curzon St., London W1, UK.

SHAY, Violet Brown, pen names SHAY, Jack; GAYTON-VERNE, David, b. 11 July 1911, New Orleans, La., USA. Writer; Poet; Artist; Secretary. Educ: Bus. Coll.; Avalon World Arts Acad. Contbr. of prose & poetry to: Avalon: This Shall Endure; American Sonnets & Lyrics; Caligraphs; Coronet; The Press Women; PEN Women; Seventeen. Mbrships: Nat. League of Am. Pen Women; State Pres., Nat. Poetry Day Assn., 1949-56; United Amateur Press Assn. of Am.; Fndr., Fellow, Int. Poetry Soc., UK. Hons. incl: 1st place, Journalism, Nat. League of Am. Pen Women; Award, Tech. Articles, Nat. Fed. of Press Women, 1958; etc. Address: 1231 Congress St., New Orleans, LA 70117, USA.

SHEARMAN, John Kinder Gowran, b. 24 June 1931, Aldershot, UK. Professor of History of Art. Educ: B.A., 1955, Ph.D., 1957, Courtauld Inst., London Univ. Publs: Andrea del Sarto, 1965; Mannerism, 1967; Raphael's Cartoons, 1972. Contbr. to: Burlington Mag.; Art Bulletin; Times Lit. Supplement; French, German & Italian periodicals. Recip., Fellowship, Inst. for Adv. Study, Princeton, USA, 1964. Address: Courtauld Inst. of Art, 20 Portman Sq., London W1, UK.

SHEEAN, (James) Vincent, b. 5 Dec. 1899, Pana, Ill., USA. Writer. Educ: Univ. of Chgo. Publs. incl: The Tide, 1933; A Day of Battle, 1938; The Eleventh Hour (as Not Peace But a Sword, USA), 1939; Bird of the Wilderness, 1941; This House Against This House, 1946; Lead Kindly Light, 1950; Rage of the Soul, 1952; Lily, 1955; The Amazing Oscar Hammerstein, 1956; First & Last Love (autobiog.), 1957; Orpheus at Eighty, 1959; Nehru: The Years of Power, USA, 1959, UK, 1960; Dorothy & Red, USA, 1963, UK, 1964. Contbr. to num. mags. & reviews, USA & UK. Address: c/o Curtis Brown Ltd., 60 E. 56th St., N.Y., NY 10022, USA.

SHEED, Wilfrid (John Joseph), b. 27 Dec. 1930, London, UK. (US citizen). Critic; Columnist. Educ: B.A., 1954, M.A., 1957, Lincoln Coll., Oxford Univ., UK. Publs. incl: Joseph, 1958; (novels) A Middle Class Education, USA, 1960, UK, 1961; The Hack, USA & UK, 1963; Square's Progress, USA & UK, 1965; Office Politics, USA, 1966, UK, 1967; Max Jamison, USA, 1970 (as The Critic, UK, 1970); (short stories) The Blacking Factory, & Pennsylvania Gothic, USA, 1968, UK, 1969; (essays) The Morning After, 1971. Contbr. to: Jubilee (Assoc. Ed., 1959-66); Commonweal; Esquire; N.Y. Times Book Review (columnist, 1971—). Address: c/o Lantz-Donadio, 111 W. 57th St., N.Y., NY 10019, USA.

SHEKERJIAN, Haig, b. 3 Nov. 1922, Chgo., Ill., USA. University Art Director. Educ: Rochester Inst. of Technol.; Univ. of N.M.; Univ. of Guadalajara, Mexico. Publs: A Book of Christmas Carols, 1963; A Book of Ballads, Songs & Snatches, 1966; Illustrator & Designer of num. books. Contbr. to: Am. Heritage; Natural Hist.; Design; Mademoiselle; Indep. Woman; etc.; Co-creator & Participator, multi-media prod., Expo '67 & State Univ.,

New Paltz; Participator, jazz-poetry prog., Carnegie Hall. Address: 4 Sparkling Ridge, New Paltz, NY 12561, USA.

SHEKERJIAN, Regina deCormier, pen name TOR, Regina, b. USA. Author; Illustrator. Publs: First 5 books of Getting to Know series, 1953-59; Discovering Israel, 1960; Growing Toward Peace (w. Eleanor Roosevelt), 1960; A Book of Christmas Carols, 1963; A Book of Ballads, Songs & Snatches, 1966; lyrics for songs; Illustrator, num. books by other authors. Contbr. to: Opinion; Am. Heritage; Natural Hist.; Indep. Woman; Mademoiselle; Design; This Day; Decade; Gale; Experiment; Glass Hill; Story; etc. Mbrships: Authors' Guild; Graphics Soc. Recip., Jewish Nat. Book Award for best jvnle. (Discovering Israel) of the Yr., 1960. Address: 4 Sparkling Ridge, New Paltz, NY 12561, USA.

SHELTON, William, b. 9 Apr. 1919, Rutherfordton, N.C., USA. Writer; Motion Picture Executive. Educ: A.B., Rollins Coll., Winter Park, Fla. Publs: Countdown, 1960; Flights of the Astronauts, 1963; American Space Exploration: The First Decade, 1967; Soviet Space Exploration: The First Decade, 1968; Man's Conquest of Space, 1968; Winning the Moon, 1970; Stowaway to the Moon (novel), 1973. Contbr. to: Sat. Review-World; Atlantic; Fortune; Time; Life; Russian Review; Bull. of Atomic Scis.; Sat. Evening Post. Mbrships: Soc. of Mag. Writers; Authors Guild; Writers Guild of Am., West. Hons. incl: Atlantic-MGM 1st Prize; Aviation/Space Writers Assn., Book of the Yr., 1968. Address: 17 Legend Lane, Houston, TX 77024, USA.

SHEPARD, Leslie Alan, b. 1917, West Ham, London, UK. London Representative, Gale Research Co., Detroit, USA; Former Film Producer, Editor, Scriptwriter. Publs: The Broadside Ballad: A Study in Origins & Meaning, UK & USA, 1962; John Pitts, Ballad Printer of Seven Dials, London 1765-1844, UK & USA, 1970; The History of Street Literature,UK & USA, 1973. Contbr. to: Film & TV Technician; New Society; Mountain Life & Work; Folk Scene; etc. Mbrships. incl: Int. Folk Music Coun.; Assn. Cinematograph, TV & Allied Techns.; Engl. Folk Dance & Song Soc.; Pvte. Libs. Assn. Address: 9 Victoria Terrace, Dundrum, Dublin 14, Repub. of Ireland.

SHEPHERD, Nan, b. 11 Feb. 1893, Cults, Aberdeen, UK. Lecturer in English Literature. Educ: M.A., Aberdeen Univ. Publs: The Quarry Wood; The Weatherhouse; A Pass in the Grampians; In the Cairngorms. Contbr. to: Ed., Aberdeen Univ. Review; Co-Compiler, The Fusion of 1860, Aberdeen Univ. Studies. Recip., Hon. LL.D., Aberdeen Univ. Address: 503 N. Deeside Rd., Cults, Aberdeen, UK.

SHEPHERD, Stella, (Mrs. Dennis H. Shepherd) (née Jardine), b. 1919, Barrow-in-Furness, UK. Head Teacher. Educ: Hull Municipal Training Coll. Publ: Like a Mantle the Sea (autobiog.), UK 1971, USA 1973. Address: The School House, Fair Isle, Shetland, UK.

SHEPPARD, Dorothy Mary, b. 13 July 1917, London, UK. Secretary; Writer; Journalist. Publs. incl: The Adventures of Wallace the Worm, 1943; The Magic Alphabet Book, 1954; Lyric the Skippety Horse, serialised in S. Africa & televised in Aust.; The Adventures of Susan & Peter; Danny the Dimpled Snowman. Contbr. to: The Cape Times; Calendar; Femina; radio: poetry & short stories; etc. Mbrships. incl: PEN; Engl. Assn., Cape Town; Cape Town Writers' Club; The Nine Club. Address: 21 Blue Waters, Beach Rd., Sea Point, C. P. 8001, Repub. of S. Africa.

SHEPPARD, Harold L., b. 1 Apr. 1922, Balt., Md., USA. Social Scientist. Educ: M.A., Univ. of Chgo., 1945; Ph.D., Univ. of Wis., 1948. Publs: When Labor Votes: A Study of Auto Workers, 1956; Poverty & Wealth in America, 1970; Where Have All the Robots Gone? , 1972. Contbr. to: Am. Sociol. Review; Am. Jrnl. of Sociol.; Soc. Sci. Quarterly; Proceedings of the Indl. Rels. Rsch. Assn. Mbrships: Am. Sociol. Assn.; Indl. Rels. Rsch. Assn.; The Gerontol. Soc. Recip., Sr. Fulbright Rsch. Professorship, France, 1957-58. Address: c/o W. E. Upjohn Inst. for Employment Research, 1101 17th St. N.W., Wash. DC 20036, USA.

SHEPPARD-JONES, Elizabeth, b. 9 May 1920, Penarth, Wales, UK. Author. Publs: I Walk on Wheels, 1958; Welsh Legendary Tales, 1959; The Search for Mary, 1960; Scottish Legendary Tales, 1962; The Empty House, The Reluctant Nurse, 1965; The Byrds' Nest, 1968; Emma & the Awful Eight, 1968; Cousin Charlie, 1973. Contbr. to:

(BBC progs.) Woman's Hour; Listen With Mother. Address: Draenen Wen, Meadow Lane, Penarth, Glam., UK.

SHERAR, Mariam Ghose, b. 1 May 1924, NYC, USA. Sociologist. Educ: M.A., Mich. State Univ. Publs: Shipping Out, 1973. Mbrships: Am. Sociol. Assn.; AAUP. Address: 299 Henry St., Bklyn., NY 11201, USA.

SHERGOLD, Norman David, b. 14 Oct. 1925, London, UK. Professor of Hispanic Studies. Educ: B.A., 1950, M.A., 1952, Ph.D., 1954, Cambridge Univ. Publs. incl: A History of the Spanish Stage from Medieval Times until the end of the Seventeenth Century, 1967; (all w. John E. Varey) El Burlador de Sevilla, 1954; Los celos hacen estrellas, 1970; Teatros y comedias en Madrid: 1600-1650, 1971; Teatros y comedias en Madrid: 1651-1665, 1973; Teatros y comedias en Madrid, 1666-1687, 1975; Contbr. to: Bulletin Hispanic Studies; Hispanic Review; Bulletin Hispanique; Mod. Lang. Review; etc. Mbrships: Mod. Humanities Rsch. Assn.; Assn. Hispanists. Address: Dept. Hispanic Studies, Univ. Coll., P.O. Box 78, Cardiff CF1 1XA, UK.

SHERMAN, Ingrid, b. 25 June 1919, Cologne, Germany. Author; Counsellor; Educator; Naturopath. Educ. incl: N.D. & D.O., Anglo-Am. Inst. of Drugless Therapy, UK, 1961; Pss.D., Sci. of Truth Inst., Cinn., Ohio, 1962. Publs. incl: Thoughts for You, 1963; For Your Reading Pleasure, 1966; Face to Face with Nature, 1966; Let Thy Heart Sing, 1967; Natural Remedies for Better Health, 1970; The Spiritual Life & Works of Dr. Ingrid Sherman, 1970. Contbr. to: Let's Live; Jrnl. of Naturopathic Med.; etc. Mbrships. incl: Co-Fndr., Acad. of Am. Poets; Poetry Cons., Armed Forces Writers League. Recip., Baronetcy, Chancery of Miensk & Byelorussia. Address: 102 Courter Ave., Yonkers, NY 10705, USA.

SHERRIFF, Robert Cedric, b. 6 June 1896. Novelist; Playwright. Educ: New Coll., Oxford. Publs. incl: (novels) The Fortnight in September, 1931; Greengates, 1936; The Hopkins Manuscript, 1938; Chedworth, 1944; Another Year, 1946; King John's Treasure, 1955; The Wells of St. Mary's, 1961; (plays) Journey's End; The Long Sunset, 1955; The Telescope, 1957; Shred of Evidence, 1960; (autobiography) No Leading Lady, 1968; & num. film adaptations. Address: Rosebriars, Esher, Surrey, UK.

SHERRIN, Ned (Edward George), b. 18 Feb. 1931, Low Ham, Somerset, UK. Film Producer. Educ: M.A., Exeter Coll., Oxford; Gray's Inn. Publs: (w. Caryl Brahms) Cindy-Ella or I Gotta Shoe; Rappel 1910; Benbow Was His Name; Paying the Piper (transl. Feydeau's Le Dindon); Ooh La La! (short stories from Feydeau); After You, Mr. Feydeau (short stories); That Was the Week That Was (Ed. w. David Frost). Address: 19 Wellington Sq., London SW3 4NJ, UK.

SHERROD, Robert Lee, b. 8 Feb. 1909. Editor; Writer. Educ: B.A., Univ. of Georgia. Publs: Tarawa, the Story of a Battle, 1944; On to Westward, 1945; 'Life's' Picture History of World War II, 1950; History of Marine Corps Aviation, 1952; Kobunsha's History of the Pacific War, 1950. Contbr. to: Time; Life; Saturday Evening Post, (Ed.). Recip., Benjamin Franklin Award, 1955. Address: c/o Curtis Publs. Co., 641 Lexington Ave., N.Y., NY 10022, USA.

SHERWIN, Judith Johnson, b. 3 Oct. 1936, NYC, USA. Poet; Playwright; Novelist. Educ: B.A., Barnard Coll., 1958; Columbia Univ. Grad. Schl., 1958-59. Publs: Uranium Poems, 1969; The Life of Riot (short stories), 1970; Impossible Buildings (poems), 1973. Contbr. to: Antioch Review; Atlantic Monthly; The Fiddlehead; The Nation; N.Y. Quarterly; etc. Mbrships: PEN; Authors' Guild; Exec. Bd., Poetry Soc. of Am. Hons. incl: Acad. of Am. Poets Prize, 1968; Rose Fellowship in Fiction, 1967; Yale Series of Younger Poets Prize, 1968. Agent: Carl Brandt, Brandt & Brandt. Address: 27 W. 86 St., N.Y., NY 10024, USA.

SHERWIN, Oscar, b. 6 July 1902, NYC, USA. Writer; Scholar; Teacher. Educ: A.B., Columbia Coll., 1922; M.A., Columbia Univ., 1928; Ph.D., N.Y. Univ., 1940. Publs. incl: Mr. Gay, 1929; Benedict Arnold: Patriot & Traitor, 1931; Prophet of Liberty: The Life & Times of Wendell Phillips, 1958; Uncorking Old Sherry: The Life & Times of Richard Brinsley Sheridan, 1960; Goldy: The Life & Times of Oliver Goldsmith, 1961; John Wesley: Friend of the People, 1961; A Man of Wit & Fashion: The Extraordinary Life & Times of George Selwyn, 1963. Contbr. to num. jrnls. & anthols.; Contbng. Ed., Phylon, 1948-52. Hons: Book Club Guild Selection, 1958; Pulpit Book Club Selection, 1961. Address: 207 W. 106th St., N.Y., NY 10025, USA.

SHERWOOD, Hugh Clements, b. 9 Feb. 1928, Boston, Mass., USA. Journalist. Educ: B.A., Yale Univ., 1948; M.S., Schl. of Jrnlsm., Columbia Univ., N.Y., 1950. Publs: The Journalistic Interview, 1969, revised ed., 1972; How to Invest in Bonds, 1974. Contbr. to: Harper's Bazaar; Nation's Bus.; Ind. Wk.; Town & Country; etc. Mbr., Soc. of Mag. Writers. Hons: Geo. Wash. Hon. Medal, Freedom Fndn., 1953; Nat. Media Award, Family Serv. Assn. of Am., 1965. Address: Apt. L 6, 109 N. Broadway, White Plains, NY 10603, USA.

SHERWOOD, Martin Anthony b. 10 Jan. 1942, Thetford, UK. Science Journalist. Educ: B.Sc., Ph.D. Publs: Ivan Pavlov (w. Elizabeth Sherwood), 1970; New Worlds in Chemistry, 1974, & in USA as The New Chemistry; Survival (fiction), 1975. Contbr. to: New Sci.; var. sci. & med. jrnls., mags., etc. Address: c/o New Scientist, 128 Long Acre, London WC2E 9QH, UK.

SHEWELL-COOPER, Wilfred Edward, b. Waltham Abbey, Essex, UK. Horticultural Advisor. Educ: Horticultural Dip. & Nat. Dip. in Horticulture, Wye Coll., London Univ. Publs. incl: The Complete Gardner, 1950; The Complete Vegetable Gardener, 1962; The Basic Book on Vegetables, 1973; The Basic Book on Flowers, 1973; The Basic Book on Rock Gardens, 1973; The Compost Flower Grower, 1973; The Complete Greenhouse Gardener, 1974; Compost Gardening, 1974; The Compost Fruit Grower, 1975. Contbr. to num. gen. & hort. mags. Mbrships. incl: F.R.S.L.; Fellow, Linnean Soc. & Lectrs. Assn.; Royal Soc. of Tchrs. Hons. incl: M.B.E.; Cmdr. du Mérite Agric., France; Kt. of Merit, Italy; Fellow & Dr., Vienna Univ.; D.Litt., Diocesan Coll., S. Africa. Address: Arkley Manor, Arkley near Barnet, Herts., UK.

SHIBLES, Warren, b. 7 July 1933, Hartford, Conn., USA. Assistant Professor of Philosophy; Manager of The Language Press. Educ: B.A., Univ. of Conn., 1958; M.A., Univ. of Colo., 1963; Ph.D.Cand., Ind. Univ., 1963-66. Publs: Philosophical Pictures, 1969, rev. ed., 1971, German ed., 1973; Wittgenstein, Language & Philosophy, 1969, rev. ed., 1971, German, Spanish & Portuguese eds., 1973; Models of Ancient Greek Philosophy, 1971; An Analysis of Metaphor, 1971; Metaphor: An Annotated Bibliography, 1971, Spanish ed., 1974; Essays on Metaphor, 1971; Emotions, 1974; Death: An Interdisciplinary Analysis, 1974. Contbr. to num. jrnls. Address: Box 342, Whitewater, WI 53190, USA.

SHILLINGFORD, John Parsons, b. 15 Apr. 1914, London, UK. Professor of Cardiology. Educ: M.B., B.S., M.D., London Univ. & London Hosp.; M.D., Harvard Med. Schl., USA; F.R.C.P., London., F.A.C.C., USA; F.A.C.P., Corres. USA. Contbr. num. sci. papers on heart disease, esp. coronary thrombosis, to med. jrnls. Mbrships. incl: Royal Soc. of Med.; Brit. Cardiac Soc.; Assn. of Physns.; Med. Soc. of London; B.M.A. Address: 6 Hurlingham Ct., Ranelagh Gdns., London SW6 3SH, UK.

SHILTON, Launcelot Rupert, b. 30 Dec. 1921, Melbourne, Australia. Minister of Religion; Dean of Sydney. Educ: B.A., Univ. of Melbourne; B.D., Univ. of London; Th.L., Aust. Coll. of Theol. Publs: 52 Thoughts for Better Living, 1961; The Word Made Flesh, 1963; 52 More Thoughts for Better Living, 1966; Speaking from the Holy Land, 1970; No No Calcutta (Ed.), 1971; New Obedience (Ed.), 1971; Guidelines for 101 Problems, forthcoming. Address: The Deanery, 2 Wallace Pde., Lindfield, N.S.W., Australia 2070.

SHINAGEL, Michael, b. 21 Apr. 1934, Vienna, Austria. Professor of English. Educ: A.B., Oberlin Coll., Ohio, 1957; M.A., 1959, Ph.D., 1964, Harvard Univ. Publs: Daniel Defoe & Middle-Class Gentility, 1968; A Concordance to the Poems of Jonathan Swift, 1972; Norton Critical Edition of Robinson Crusoe, forthcoming. Contbr. to: Philol. Quarterly; Modern Philol.; Cornell Lib. Jrnl.; Citheria. Mbr., MLA. Hons. incl: Nat. Endowment for Humanities Grant, 1966; Ford Humanities Fac. Dev. Grants, 1972, 1974. Address: 4 Payson Ter., Belmont, MA 02178, USA.

SHIPLEY, Joseph Twadell, b. 19 Aug. 1893, NYC, USA. Drama Critic. Educ: B.A., CCNY, 1912; M.A., 1914, Ph.D., 1931, Columbia Univ. Publs. incl: The Quest for Literature, 1931; Trends in Literature, 1939; Dictionary of Word Origins, 1945; Dictionary of World Literary Terms, 1943; Dictionary of Early English, 1955; Guide to Great Plays, 1956; Five Major Plays of Ibsen, 1962; Word Play, 1972. Contbr. to: Ency. Britannica; N.Y. Times Book Review; Herald-Tribune Books; Saturday Review; Nation;

etc. Mbrships: Pres., 1952-54, Sec., 1968—, N.Y. Drama Critics' Circle; PEN; etc. Address: 29 W. 46 St., N.Y., NY 10036, USA.

SHIPPEN, Katherine Binney, b. 1 Apr. 1892, Hoboken, N.J., USA. Writer. Educ: B.A., Bryn Mawr Coll.; M.A., Columbia Univ. Publs. incl: New Found World, 1945; Viking, 1947; Passage to America, 1950; Leif Eriksson, 1951; How the United Nations Share Their Skill, 1954, revised ed., 1965; Mr. Bell Invents the Telephone, 1955; This Union Cause: The Growth of Organized Labor in America, 1958; Milton S. Hershey, 1959; Portals to the Past; The Story of Archaeology (w. Anca Seidlova), 1963; The Heritage of Music, 1963; Men of Archaeology, 1964. Mbr., Authors' Guild. Address: 89 g Pomona Rd., Duffern, NY 10901, USA.

SHIR, Miriam, pen names WOLMAN-SIERACZOWA, Miriam; MARMOR, Jehudit, b. 15 May 1903, Radom, Poland. Journalist. Educ: Warsaw Univ. Publs: Hebrew-Polish Pocket Dictionary; Polish-Hebrew Pocket Dictionary, 1930; Hebrew-Yiddish Pocket Dictionary; Hebrew-Polish Dictionary, 1958; Great Polish-Hebrew Dictionary (Ed. w. David Shir), 1975; Sipurej Jeladim (Tales for Children). Contbr. to var. newspapers, mags. & Israel radio. Mbrships: Nat. Fedn. Israel Jrnlsts. (Tel Aviv); Int. Fedn. Jrnlsts. (Brussels); Assn. Acad. Women. Address: Disengoffst. 184, Tel-Aviv, Israel.

SHIRER, William Lawrence, b. 23 Feb. 1904, Chgo., Ill., USA. Broadcaster; Journalist; Author. Educ: Coe Coll. Publs: Berlin Diary, 1941; End of a Berlin Diary, 1947; The Traitor, 1950; Mid-Century Journey, 1953; Stranger Come Home, 1954; The Challenge of Scandinavia, 1955; The Consul's Wife, 1956; The Rise & Fall of the Third Reich, 1960; The Rise & Fall of Adolf Hitler, 1961; The Sinking of the Bismarck, 1962; The Collapse of the Third Republic, 1970. Hons: D.Litt.; Légion d'Honneur. Address: RFD 1, Torrington, CT, USA.

SHIRREFFS, Gordon Donald, pen names GORDON, Steward; DONALDS, Gordon, b. 15 Jan. 1914, Chgo., Ill., USA. Novelist. Educ: B.A., 1967, M.A., 1973, Calif. State Univ. Publs: about 70 novels, inclng: Showdown in Sonora, 1969; Jack of Spades, 1970; The Manhunter, 1970; Brasada, 1972; Bowman's Kid, 1973; Renegade's Trail, 1974; Shootout, 1974; The Apache Hunter, forthcoming. Sev. have been made into films. Mbrships. incl: Authors Guild; Western Writers of Am. Recip., Silver Medal, C'wlth. Club of Calif., best juvenile, 1961. Address: 17427 San Jose St., Granada Hills, CA 91344, USA.

SHOBEN, (Edward) Joseph Jr., b. 3 Oct. 1918, Ohio, USA. University Administrator & Professor. Educ: A.B., 1939, M.A., 1945, Ph.D., 1947, Univ. of S. Calif. Publs: The Psychology of Adjustment, 1956; Perspectives in Psychology, 1963; Students, Stress, & the College Experience, 1965; Learning & the Professors, 1968. Contbr. to: Liberal Educ.; Change Mag.; Jrnl. of Counseling Psychol.; Western Humanities Review; Harvard Educl. Review; Daedalus; etc. Mbrships. incl: Am. Psychol. Assn.; Am. Sociol. Assn.; Bd. Dirs., Am. Assn. of Univ. Administrs. Address: 4383 Schenley Farms Terrace, Pitts., PA 15213, USA.

SHOESMITH, Kathleen Anne, b. Keighley, UK. Teacher. Publs: Playtime Stories, 1968; Jack O'Lantern, 1969; Cloud Over Calderwood, 1969; The Tides of Tremannion, 1970; Mallory's Luck, 1971; Return of the Royalist, 1971; Do You Know? series, (12 books), 1971-73; Reluctant Puritan, 1972; The Highwayman's Daughter, 1973; Belltower, 1973; Use Your Senses series, 1973; The Black Domino, 1975. Address: 351 Fell Lane, Keighley, Yorks. BD22 6DB, UK.

SHOLOKHOV, Mikhail Aleksandrovich, b. 24 May 1905, USSR. Novelist; Soviety Deputy. Publs. incl: The Don Stories, 1926; And Quiet Flows the Don, 4 vols., 1928-40; Virgin Soil Upturned, 2 vols., 1932-59; They Fought for Their Country, 1954; The Destiny of Man, 1957; Collected Works, Vols. I-VIII, 1959-62. Mbrships. incl: Acad. of Scis., USSR; Union of Soviet Writers (Praesidium, 1954); Communist Party (Ctrl. Comm., 1962—). Hons: State Prize, 1940; Lenin Prize, 1960; Nobel Prize for Lit., 1965; LL.D., St. Andrews Univ., UK. Address: Union of Soviet Writers, ul. Vorovskogo 52, Moscow, USSR.

SHORES, Louis, b. 14 Sept. 1904. Librarian; Editor; Author. Educ: A.B.; M.S.; B.S. in Lib. Sci.; Ph.D. Publs.

incl: Basic Reference Books, 1937, 1939; Highways in the Sky, 1947; Basic Reference Sources, 1954; Instructional Materials, 1960; Mark Hopkins Log, 1966; Library-College USA, 1970; Quiet World, 1975. Contbr. to: Saturday Review; Am. Libs.; Lib. Jrnl.; Lib. Record, UK. Mbrships: ALA; Southeastern Lib. Assn. (Pres., 1951-52); Fla. Lib. Assn. (Pres. 1953). Hons: D.H.L.; Legion of Merit, USAAF, 1946; I.C. Mudge Citation, 1967; Int. Beta Phi Mu Lib. Educ. Award, 1967. Address: 2013 W. Randolph Circle, Tallahassee, FL 32303, USA.

SHOREY, Kenneth Paul, b. 19 June 1937, Toronto, Can., Movie & Theatre Critic. Educ: Can. Theatre Schl.; Stratford Shakespearean Festival Schl. of Drama. Publs: The Death of Theatre, 1975. Contbr. to: Univ. Bookman; Nat. Review; Birmingham News; Mod. Age; Cath. Messenger; Phila. Inquirer; Individualist; Intercollegiate Review; Sat. Night; New Guard. Hons: 3rd Place, Best Original Column., Ala. Press Assn., & Big '''N'' Award, Birmingham News, both 1974. Address: c/o Birmingham News, Box 2553, Birmingham, AL 35202, USA.

SHORO, Mushtaq Ahmad, b. 10 May, 1952, Darri, Sujawal, Thatta Sind, Pakistan. Editor of Digest Indalath (Rainbow); Translator for the Pakistan Broadcasting Corporation. Educ: Sind Univ. Contbr. to: Roh-Rehan; Sohani; Charan; Choudas; Tand Tanwar; Nain Zindagi; Agti-Qudam; Sojhro; Indalath; Dharti. Address: c/o Sindhi News Sect., Ctrl. News Org., Pakistan Broadcasting Corp., 25-A Satellite Town, Rawalpindi, Pakistan.

SHORT, Lucille Doughton, b. 23 July 1903, Bryan, Ohio, USA. Educator; Writer-Speaker. Educ: A.B., Ohio Wesleyan Univ.; S.B. Ed., Defiance Coll.; A.M., Boston Univ.; special courses, var. other Univs. Publs: Browning's Theory of Life; Guidelines for Teaching Foreign Languages (Latin, Spanish, French); Première. Contbr. to: Poet, Madras, India; Greenhouse; Teachers & Libns. Anthol. Mbrships. incl: Browning Soc.; World Poetry; Int. Poetry; Poetry Soc. of Tenn.; Acad. of Am. Poets; Tenn. Woman's Press & Authors Club; Chickasaw Br., Nat. League of Am. Pen Women. Recip., var. lit. hons. Address: 207 S. Marne St., Memphis, TN 38111, USA.

SHOUP, Carl Sumner, b. 26 Oct. 1902, San Jose, Calif., USA. Economist. Educ: A.B., Stanford Univ., 1924; Ph.D., Columbia Univ., 1930. Publs: The Sales Tax in France, 1930; Principles of National Income Analysis, 1947; Ricardo on Taxation, 1960; Federal Estate & Gift Taxes, 1966; Public Finance, 1969, Jap. transl., 1974, Spanish transl., 1974; Test Your Bible Knowledge (w. C. Scott), 1971, German transl., 1972. Contbr. to US & for. profl. jrnls. Address: Sandwich, NH 03270, USA.

SHRAND, David, b. 13 Nov. 1913, Cape Town, S. Africa. Income Tax Consultant & Financial Adviser. Educ: M.Com., Univ. of Cape Town; F.C.A.; C.A. (S.A.). Publs. incl: Income Tax in South Africa; The Financial & Statistical Digest of South Africa; What Every Salaried Person Should Know About Income Tax; How to re-organise your affairs so as to pay the least amount of tax; Real Estate in South Africa; The Sectional Titles Act; Today & Yesterday; Company Formalities & Precedents; Tales of Michalowsky. Contbr. to num. newspapers. Mbrships. incl: Hon. Treas., S. African PEN Ctre., (Cape). Address: P.O. Box 3461, Cape Town, S. Africa.

SHRIVER, Harry C., b. 2 Oct. 1904, Gettysburg, Pa., USA. Lawyer; Judge. Educ: Gettysburg Coll.; Dickinson Coll.; J.D., Geo. Wash. Univ. Law Schl. Publs: Justice Oliver Wendel Holmes: His Book Notices & Uncollected Letters & Papers, 1936; Judicial Opinions of Oliver Wendell Holmes, 1940; History of the Shriver Family, 1962; The Government Lawyer, 1974. Contbr. to: Am. Bar Assn. Jrnl.; Georgetown Law Jrnl.; Geo. Wash. Law Review; Harvard Law Review. Address: 8409 Fox Run, Potomac, MD 20854, USA.

SHUBIN, Seymour, pen name RICHARDS, Al, b. 14 Sept. 1921, Phila., Pa., USA. Writer. Educ: B.S., Temple Univ. Publs: Anyone's My Name, 1953; Manta, 1958; Wellville, USA, 1961. Contbr. to num. jrnls. incing. Reader's Digest; Redbook; Family Circle; Argosy; Cavalier; Stag; Emergency Medicine; Sci. Digest; STORY Mag.; Nat. Observer. Mbrships. incl: Soc. of Mag. Writers. Address: 122 Harrogate Rd., Phila., PA 19151, USA.

SHULEVITZ, Uri, b. 27 Feb. 1935, Warsaw, Poland. Author; Illustrator. Educ: T.T.D., Israel; Tel Aviv Art Inst.; Brooklyn Mus. Art Schl., USA. Publs: The Moon in my

Room, 1963; One Monday Morning, 1967; Rain Rain Rivers, 1969; Oh What a Noise, 1971; The Magician, 1973; Dawn, 1974; Illustrations: The Fool of the World & the Flying Ship, 1968; Soldier & Tsar in the Forest, 1972; The Fools of Chelm, by I. B. Singer, 1973. Contbr. to: Horn Book Mag. Mbrships. incl: Authors' Guild. Soc. of Children's Book Writers. Hons. incl: Caldecott Medal, 1969; Address: 133 W. 3rd St., N.Y., NY 10012, USA.

SHULL, Charles W., b. 26 May 1904, Kouts, Ind., USA. Political Scientist; College Professor. Educ: B.A., Ohio Welseyan Univ., 1926; M.A., 1927, Ph.D., 1929, Ohio State Univ. Publs: American Experience with Unicameralism, 1937; Introduction to Political Science (co-author), 1950; Your Government (co-author), 1951, 2nd ed., 1954; American State Legislatures (co-author), 1954; State Constitutional Revision (co-author), 1962. Contbr. to var. jrnls. Mbr., acad. & profl. orgs. Recip., sev. hons. Address: 8900 E. Jefferson, Apt. 304, Detroit, MI 48214, USA.

SHULMAN, Marshall Darrow, b. 8 Apr. 1916, Jersey City, N.J., USA. Professor of International Relations, Columbia University; Director of Russian Institute, Columbia University, 1967-74. Educ: A.B., Univ. Mich., 1937; M.A., 1948, Cert. Russian Inst., 1948, Ph.D., 1959, Columbia Univ. Publs: Stalin's Foreign Policy Reappraised, 1963; Beyond the Cold War, 1966. Contbr. to: Foreign Affairs; N.Y. Times; Survival; Europa Archiv.; Slavic Review. Mbrships. incl: Fellow, Am. Acad. Arts & Sci.; Bd., Coun. For. Rels., N.Y.; Int. Inst. Strategic Studies, London (Mbr. Coun.). Hons. incl: Whitney Sheppardson Senior Vis. Fellow at Coun. For. Rels., 1974-75; Writer in Res., Aspen Inst. Humanistic Studies, 1973. Address: 450 Riverside Dr., N.Y., NY 10027, USA.

SHULMAN, Milton, b. 1 Sept. 1913, Toronto, Can. Writer; Journalist; Critic. Educ: B.A., Univ. of Toronto; Osgoode Hall, Toronto. Publs: Defeat in the West, 1948; How to be a Celebrity, 1950; The Ravenous Eye, 1973; The Least Worst Television in the World, 1973; (juvenile) Preep, 1964; Preep in Paris, 1967; Preep & the Queen, 1970; (novels) Kill Three, 1967; Every Home Should Have One (w. H. Kretzmer, also film story), 1970. Contbr. to: Evening Standard (critic, 1948–); Sunday Express (critic, 1948-58); Daily Express (columnist, 1973–). Recip., Critic of the Yr. Award, IPC, 1966. Address: 51 Eaton Square, London SW1, UK.

SHUMAN, R(obert) Baird, b. 20 June 1934, Paterson, N.J., USA. Professor of Education. Educ: A.B., Lehigh Univ., 1951; Ed.M., Temple Univ., 1953; Cert. in Philol., Univ. of Vienna, 1954; Ph.D., Univ. of Pa., 1961. Publs: Clifford Odets, 1962; Robert E. Sherwood, 1964; William Inge, 1965; Nine Black Poets (ed.), 1968; An Eye for an Eye (ed.), 1969; A Galaxy of Black Writing (ed.), 1970; Creative Approaches to the Teaching of English-Secondary (ed.), 1974. Contbr. to: PMLA; Southern Poetry Review; Am. Lit.; Mod. Philol.; Walt Whitman Review; num. learned & profl. jrnls.; etc. Mbr., MLA; NCTE; IAUPE. Address: Box 6696, Coll. Stn., Durham, NC 27708, USA.

SHUMAN, Samuel Irving, b. 7 Aug. 1925, Fall River, Mass., USA. Professor of Law & Psychiatry. Educ: A.B., A.M., Ph.D., Univ. of Pa.; J.D., Univ. of Mich.; J.S.D., Harvard Univ. Publs: Legal Positivism, 1963; American Law (w. West), 1971; Law & Disorder, 1971. Contbr. to num. legal jrnls. Mbrships. incl: Pres.-Elect, Am. Sect., Int. Assn. for Legal & Soc. Philos.; Am. Law Inst.; Mich. Bar. Assn. Hons. incl: Probus Club Award, 1963. Address: Law Schl., Wayne State Univ., Detroit, MI 48202, USA.

SHURTER, Robert LeFevre, b. 22 Oct. 1907, Ellenville, N.Y., USA. University Professor; Writer. Educ: B.A., Amherst Coll.; M.A., Columbia Univ.; Ph.D., Western Reserve Univ. Publs: Argument, 1939; Effective Letters, 1945; Written Communication, 1954, 3rd ed., 1972; Effective Writing, 1965; Critical Thinking, 1965; The Utopian Novel in America: 1865-1900, 1973. Contbr. to: South Atlantic Quarterly; Am. Literature; other profl. jrnls. Mbr., MLA. Address: 5424 Azure Way, Sarasota, FL 33581, USA.

SHUSTER, Alvin, b. 25 Jan. 1930, Wash. DC., USA. Journalist; London Bureau Chief, New York Times. Educ: B.A., Geo. Wash. Univ. Publs: The Kennedy Years (co-author), 1964; The Road to the White House (co-author), 1964; Ed., The New York Times Guide to the Nation's Capital, 1967. Contbr. to: N.Y. Times Mag.; N.Y. Times Book Review. Mbr., Assn. Am. Corres. in London (Pres., 1974). Recip., Nieman Fellowship, Harvard Univ.,

1966-67. Address: N.Y. Times, New Printing Ho. Sq., Gray's Inn Rd., London WC1X 8EZ, UK.

SHUTTLE, Penelope Diane, b. 12 May 1947, Staines, Middx., UK. Author. Publs. incl: (novels) An Excusable Vengeance, 1967; All the Usual Hours of Sleeping, 1969; Wailing Monkey Embracing a Tree, 1974; The Terrors of Dr. Treviles (co-author), 1974; Rainsplitter in the Zodiac Garden, 1975; (poetry) Nostalgia Neurosis, 1968; Jesusa, 1972; The Hermaphrodite Album (co-author), 1973; Midwinter Mandala, 1974; Autumn Piano, 1974; Songbook of the Snow, 1974. Contbr. to: Poetry Review; Strand Mag.; Scotsman; Gall.; Matrix; Poet; etc. Hons. incl: Arts Coun. Awards, 1969, 1972; Greenwood Poetry Prize, 1972; Eric Gregory Poetry Award, 1974. Address: c/o 20 Glebe Road, Staines, Middx., UK.

SIBLEY, Mulford Quickert, b. 14 June 1912, Marston, Mo., USA. Professor of Political Science & American Studies. Educ: B.A., Central State Coll., 1933; M.A. Univ. Okla., 1934; Ph.D., Univ. Minn., 1938. Publs: Conscription of Conscience: The American Conscientious Objector in World War II (w. P. E. Jacob), 1952; (co-author, Ed.) The Quiet Battle: Writings in the Theory & Practice of Non-Violent Resistance, 1963; The Obligation to Disobey: Conscience & the Law, 1970; Political Ideas & Ideologies: A History of Political Thought, 1970. Contbr. to: Am. Pol. Sci. Review; Am. Jrnl. Pol. Sci.; Natural Law Form; etc. Mbrships. incl: Int. Pol. Sci. Assn.; Am. Pol. Sci. Assn. (Mbr. Nat. Exec. Coun., 1975—). Hons. incl: Rockefeller Fellow Pol. Philos, 1959-60. Address: 2018 Fairmount Ave., St. Paul, MN 55105, USA.

SIBLY, John, b. 30 Apr. 1920, Glos., UK. Lecturer. Educ: M.A., Cambridge Univ., 1945. Publs. (poems) Death of William Rufus, 1948; The Wonders of Astronomy, Sinfonia Elizabethana; Winter Doomset, 1965; (novels) Love in a Hut, 1957; Girl on the Run, 1959; You'll Walk to Mandalay, 1961. Contbr. to: Windmill; Christian Sci. Monitor; New Statesman; Argosy; Review of Engl. Lit.; Engl. Lit. Hist. Mbrships: PEN (1957-65); Writer's Guild of GB. Address: 62 Halesowen Rd., Halesowen B62 9BA, UK.

SID, Ulla Elisabet, b. 4 Apr. 1920, Helsingfors, Finland. Teacher of Retarded Children. Publs: Dansen (novel), 1965; Ika, 5 år får ett hem, 1970; Jagförstar mig inte på Lulu (novel), 1974. Contbr. book reviews to newspapers. Mbr., Finlands svenska författareförening. Hons: Prize for Short Story (Själen), Hufudstadsbladets Competition, 1964; Best Book for children aged 5-9, Bonniers' Competition, 1970. Address: Skarpskyttegatan 8.A. 12, 00150, Helsingfors 15, Finland.

SIDDIQI, Abulais, b. 15 June 1916, Agra, Bharat, India. University Professor & Administrator; Author. Educ: B.A., M.A., Ph.D.; Postdoctoral Rsch. in Linguistics; specialised trng. in applied linguistics. Publs. incl: Lucknow School of Urdu Poetry; Nazeer, His Age & Poetry; Lyrical Poets & Their Poetry; Mushafi — His Life & Works; Jurat — His Age & His Poetry; Contemporary Urdu Literature; Linguistics & Literature; Historical Grammar of Urdu. Contbr. to num. acad. jrnls. Mbrships: Fndr., Linguistic Rsch. Grp. of Pakistan; off., var. lang. & lit. orgs. Recip., var. hons. Address: A/5, University of Karachi, Pakistan.

SIDDIQI, Abul Fazl, b. 4 Sept. 1912, Arifpur Nawadah, Badaun, India. Agriculturist Landlord. Publs: Ahram (short stories), 1943; Tazeer (novel), 1946; Romooz-e-Baghbani (on agric.), 1950; Sarwar (novel), 1956; Char Novlet (short stories), 1966; Din Dhaley; Shakanja. Contbr. to: Naya Daut; Adabi Duniya; Noqoosh Adeb-E-Lateef; Shahkar; Nairang-E-Khyal; & other jrnls. Mbrships: Sec., Halq-E-Arbab-e-Zauq; Pakistan Writers' Guild. Hons. incl: Prize for Best Urdu Short Story, 1952-57, PEN, 1957. Address: "Baitul Qudsi", 4-FIV/7 Nazimabad, Karachi-18, Pakistan.

SIDDIQI, Shaukat, b. 20 Mar. 1923, Licknow, India. Journalist; Newspaper Editor. Educ: M.A., Pol. Sci. Publs: Khuda Ki Basti (God's Own Land), Engl. & num. other transls., 1958; Koka Beli (The Lotus), 1962; Kameengah (Hideout), 1957; num. short stories. Contbr. to Pakistani press. Mbr. & Sec. Gen., Pakistan Writers Guild. Hons: Adamjee Prize for Literature, Nat. Lit. Prize of Pakistan, for Khuda Ki Basti, 1960. Address: 24/a Block L, N. Nazimabad, Karachi, Pakistan.

SIDDIQUI, Ashraf, b. 1 Mar. 1927, Nagbari, Tangail, Bangladesh. Professor; Poet; Writer. Educ: B.A., 1948, M.A., 1950, Dacca Univ.; M.A., 1959, Ph.D., 1966, Ind.

Univ., USA. Publs. incl: Bhombal Dass (jvnle.), 1959; Bengali Riddles, 1961; Toontoony & Other Tales (jvnle.), 1961; Bengali Folklore, 1963; Folkloric Bangladesh; Our Folklore: Our Heritage, forthcoming; (in Bengali) Rabea Apa (short story), 1955; Taleb Master O Onyanya Kavita (1950); Biskanya (1955); Sat Bhai Champa (1955); Kagajer Naoka (1962); Uttar Akasher Tara (all poetry), 1958; Rabindranather Santiniketon (Memoirs), 1974; ed. & transl. num. books. Contbr. to: Asian Folklore (USA); Folklore (India); Morning News (Dacca); Observer (Dacca); Asiatic Soc. Jrnl. (Dacca); etc. Mbrships. incl: VP, Bangladesh Folklore Soc. Hons. incl: Bengali Acad., 1964; Dawood Prize (1964); UNESCO Prize, 1966. Address: 551 Dhanmondi R/A, Road 14, Dacca 5, Bangladesh.

SIEBRASSE, Glen, b. 5 Nov. 1929, Edmonton, Alta., Can. Editor. Publs: The Regeneration of an Athlete, 1965; Man: unman, 1968; Jersualem, 1971. Ed., Can. issue, Vanderbilt Poetry Review, 1972. Mbr., & Reg. Chmn., League of Can. Poets. Hons: Concours Littéraires, 1965; Pres. Medal, 1970. Address: 351 Gerald St., Lasalle, PQ H8P 2A4, Can.

SIEROSZEWSKA, Barbara-Zofia, b. 19 Aug. 1904, Zagórze near Będzin, Poland. Translator of Italian Literature. Educ: Univ. of Warsaw. Publs. incl: Bassani — Il giardino dei Finzi-Contini, 1964; Calvino — Nostri antenati, 1965, Cosmicomiche, 1968; Venturi — Bandiera bianca a Cefalonia, 1968; Signorelli — Eleonora Duse, 1972; Soldati — L'Attore, 1972; Biocca — Yanoama, 1974; Jovine — Signora Ava. Contbr. to var. jrnls. Mbrships: Union of Polish Writers; PEN; Soc. of Authors. Hons. incl: Prize for Eminent Transls., PEN, 1972; Cross of the Order of Polonia Restituta, 1972. Address: Górnośląska 16-6, 00-432 Warsaw, Poland.

SIGAL, Clancy, b. 6 Sept. 1926, Chgo., Ill., USA. Writer. Educ: B.A., Univ. of Calif., LA, 1950. Publs: (novels) Weekend in Dinlock, USA & UK, 1960; Going Away: A Report, A Memoir, USA, 1962, UK, 1963. Mbr., var. pol. orgs. Recip., Houghton Mifflin Lit. Fellowship, 1962. Address: c/o Jonathan Cape, 30 Bedford Sq., London WC1, UK.

SIGBAND, Norman Bruce, b. 27 June 1920, Chgo., Ill., USA. Professor; Consultant to Industry. Educ: B.A., 1940, M.A., 1941, Univ. of Chgo., Ill.; Ph.D., 1954. Publs: Effective Report Writing for Business, Industry & Government, 1960; Communication For Management, 1969; Management Communications for Decision Making, 1972; Communicacion Para Directivos, 1973. Contbr. to: Am. Bus. & Commercial Jrnl.; Jrnl. of Marketing; Jrnl. of Acad. of Mgt.; & others. Mbrships: Past Pres. & V.P., Am. Bus. Communication Assn.; Int. Communication Assn.; Soc. of Gen. Semantics. Address: 3109 Dona Susana Drive, Studio City, CA 91604, USA.

SIGFÚSDÓTTIR, Lára Margrét, pen name SIGFÚSDÓTTIR, Gréta, b. 20 Feb. 1910, Reykjavík, Iceland. Writer. Educ: Studied art w. Rikhardur Jónsson, 1925-28. Commercial Schl., Norway. Publs: Bak við Byrgða Glugga (Behind the Blinds), 1966; Í Skugga Jarðar (In the Shadow of Earth), 1969; Fyrir Opnum Tjöldum (The Curtain Goes Up), 1972. Contbr. to: Morgunbladid; Tíminn; Thjódviljinn. Mbr., Writer's Assn. of Iceland. Recip., Annual Grant from Icelandic Govt., 1970—. Address: Kárastíg 9, Reykjavík, Iceland.

SIGOGO, Ndabezinhle S., b. 2 June 1932, Filabusi, Rhodesia. Journalist. Publs: Usethi Ebukhweni Bakhe, 1962; Gudlindlu Mntanami, 1967; Akulazulu Emhlabeni, 1971. Contbr. to: Decal; Moto; Chirimo. Mbr., Ndebele & Shona Writers' Assn. (Chmn.). Hons: 1st Prize, Ndebele Lang. Sect., Rhodesia Lit. Bur., 1960, 1962, 1964; 3rd Prize, 1970. Address: 7574/1, Tshabalala Township, Bulawayo, Rhodesia.

SIIRALA, Aarne Johannes, b. 8 July 1919, Liperi, Finland. Professor of Systematic Theology & Religion. Educ: Cand. Theol., 1943, Dr. Theol., 1956, Univ. of Helsinki; Lic. Theol., Univ. of Lund, 1950. Publs: Gottes Gebot bei Martin Luther, 1956; Elaman Ykseys (The Oneness of Life, w. M. Siirala), 1960; The Voice of Illness, 1963; Divine Humanness, 1970. Contbr. to: Studies in Relig.; Jrnl. of Relig. & Hlth.; Dialog. Mbrships: Am. Acad. of Relig.; Can. Theol. Soc. Address: Wilfrid Laurier Univ., Waterloo Luth. Sem., Waterloo, Ont., Can.

SIKKENS, Jakob, b. 1 Nov. 1934, Groningen, Netherlands. Scientific Assistant. Educ: Dr., Soc. Geog.

Publs: Glas (experimental novel); Veilig in de Kelder (Safe in the Cellar, play). Mbr., Assn. of Authors in Holland. Address: Tiggellaan 74, Egmond a/d Hoef, Netherlands.

SILBERSCHLAG, Eisig, pen name STRONG, Eric, b. 8 Jan. 1903, Stryj, Austria. Author; Translator; Professor of Hebrew Literature. Educ: Ph.D., Univ. of Vienna. Publs: Saul Tschernichowsky, Poet of Revolt, 1968; Letters to Other Generations (poems in Hebrew), Israel 1971; From Renaissance to Renaissance, 1973. Contbr. to: Commentary; Judaism; Jewish Quarterly Review; Hadassah Mag. Mbrships. incl: Fellow, Am. Acad. for Jewish Rsch., Fellow, Middle East Studies Assn.; Nat. Assn. Profs. of Hebrew in Am. Instns. of Higher Learning (VP); AAUP. Hons: Lamed Prize for Hebrew Lit., 1946; S. Tschernichowsky Prize, Municipality of Tel Aviv, 1951; Florence Kovner Mem. Award, 1972. Address: Univ. of Texas, 2601 University Ave., Austin, TX 78712, USA.

SILLAH, Momodou Baikoro, b. 1935, Basse Santasu, Gambia. Journalist. Contbr. to: Gambia News Bulletin; W. Africa Mag. Mbrships: Assoc. of Inst. of Brit. PR; Gambian Jrnlst. Assn. Recip., Composition Prizes, Armitage Secondary Grammar Schl., 1952, Tchr. Trng. Coll., 1954. Address: c/o Information Services, Basse Santasu, Upper River Division, Gambia, W. Africa.

SILLITOE, Alan, b. 4 Mar. 1928, Nottingham, UK. Author. Publs: Saturday Night & Sunday Morning, 1958; The Loneliness of the Long Distance Runner, 1959; The General, 1960; Key to the Door, 1961; The Ragman's Daughter, 1963; The Death of William Posters, 1965; A Tree on Fire, 1967; Guzman, Go Home, 1968; A Start in Life, 1970; Travels in Nihilon, 1971; Raw Material, 1972; Men, Women & Children, 1973; The Flame of Life, 1974; Storm & Other Poems, 1974. Contbr. to: Times; Transatlantic Review; Outposts; etc. Mbrships: Soc. of Authors; Writers Action Grp.; London Library. Recip., Hawthornden Prize for Lit., 1960. Address: c/o W. H. Allen Publrs., 44 Hill St., London W1, UK.

SILONE, Ignazio, b. 1 May 1900, Pescina dei Marsi, Abruzzi, Italy. Writer; Politician. Publs. incl: (novels) Fontamara, 1933; Bread & Wine, 1937; The Seed beneath the Snow, 1941; A Handful of Blackberries, 1953; The Secret of Luca, 1959; The Fox & the Camellias, 1961; (short stories) Mr. Aristotle, 1935; (plays) And He did Hide Himself, 1944; The Story of a Humble Christian, 1969; (non-fiction) Fascism, 1934; The School for Dictators, 1938; Mazzini, 1939; Emergency Exit, 1965. Contbr. to: Tempo Presente (Co-Ed.). Mbrships: PEN (Pres., Italian Ctr., 1945–59); Italian Comm. for Cultural Freedom (Pres.). Address: Via di Villa Ricotti 36, Rome, Italy.

SILVER, Daniel Jeremy, b. 26 Mar. 1928, Cleveland, Ohio, USA. Rabbi. Educ: A.B., Harvard Coll., 1948; M.H.L. & Rabbi, Hebrew Union Coll., 1952; Ph.D., Univ. of Chgo., 1962. Publs: Ed., In the Time of Harvest, 1961; Maimonidean Criticism & the Maimonidean Controversy (1180-1240), 1965; Ed., Judaism & Ethics, 1969; A History of Judaism (w. B. Martin), 1974. Contbr. to: Jrnl. of Ctrl. Conf. of Am. Rabbis (Senior Ed., 1964-72); Judaism; Jewish Quarterly Review; Jrnl. of Biblical Lit.; Ency. Judaica; Reconstructionist. Address: c/o The Temple, University Circle & Silver Park, Cleveland, OH 44104, USA.

SILVERMAN, Hirsch Lazaar, b. 19 June 1915, NYC, USA. Psychologist; Former Professor of Psychology. Educ: B.Sc., 1936, M.Sc., 1938, CUNY; M.A., N.Y. Univ., 1948; Ph.D., Yeshiva Univ., N.Y., 1951; M.A., Seton Hall Univ., S. Orange, N.J., 1957. Publs. incl: Education Through Psychology: A Volume in Educational Psychology, 1954; Psychiatry & Psychology: Relationships, Intra-Relationships, & Inter-Relationships, 1963; Out of Yesterday & Into Tomorrow, 1970; Marital Therapy: Moral, Sociological, & Psychological Factors, 1972. Contbr. to num. books & profl. jrnls. Mbr., num. psychol., educl., philosl., & med. socs. Hons. incl. 3 hon. doctorates. Address: 123 Gregory Ave., W. Orange, NJ 07052, USA.

SILVERSTEIN, Alvin, b. 30 Dec. 1933, NYC, USA. Professor of Biology. Educ: B.A., Bklyn. Coll., 1955; M.S., Univ. of Pa., 1959; Ph.D., N.Y. Univ., 1962. Publs: The Biological Sciences, 1974; 39 jvnle. sci. books (w. Virginia Silverstein, q.v.), 1967–, inclng. Life in the Universe, 1967; The Respiratory System, 1969; The Digestive System, 1970; Mammals of the Sea, 1971; The Code of Life, 1972; Guinea Pigs: All About Them, 1972; Cancer, 1972; The Chemicals We Eat & Drink, 1973; Animal Invaders, 1974; Epilepsy, 1975. Contbr. to: Ranger Rick Nature Mag.;

Cricket Mag. Mbrships: Authors' Guild; AAAS; Am. Chem. Soc.; other (Sci.) assns. Address: R.D. 2, Lebanon, NJ 08833, USA.

SILVERSTEIN, Virginia Barbara Opshelor, b. 3 Apr. 1937, Phila., Pa., USA. Translator of Russian Scientific Literature. Educ: A.B., Univ. of Pa., 1958. Publs: 39 jvnle. sci. books w. husband Alvin Silverstein (q.v.), inclng: Life in the Universe, 1967; The Origin of Life, 1968; The Respiratory System, 1969; The Digestive System, 1970; Bionics, 1970; Mammals of the Sea, 1971; The Code of Life, 1972; Guinea Pigs: All About Them, 1972; Cancer, 1972; The Skin, 1972; Exploring the Brain, 1973; The Chemicals We Eat & Drink, 1973; Animal Invaders, 1974; Epilepsy, 1975. Contbr. to: Ranger Rick Nature Mag.; Cricket Mag. Mbr., Authors' Guild. Address: R.D.2, Lebanon, NJ 08833, USA.

SILVERWOOD, Roger, b. 23 Feb. 1932, Wakefield, Yorks., UK. Writer. Publs: Deadly Daffodils, 1969; Dying for a Drink, 1970; The Illegitimate Spy, 1972. Mbrships: Writers' Guild; Soc. of Authors; Crime Writers Assn. Address: The Lodge, Keresforth Hall Drive, Barnsley, South Yorks. S70 6NH, UK.

SIMANGO, Joyce, b. 18 Dec. 1948, Chipinga, Rhodesia. Writer. Educ: STD 6, Rhodesia Min. of Educ. Publs: Zviuya Zviri Mberi, 1974. Mbrships: Womens Club; United Bapt. Ch.; Radio Home Craft. Address: Hode Schl., P.O. Rusitu, Rhodesia, Africa.

SIMENON, Georges, b. 13 Feb. 1903, Liège, Belgium. Novelist. Publs: 212 novels, inclng. 80 books about detective Maigret; When I Was Old, 1972; works transl'd. into 47 langs., & publd. in 32 countries. Address: 155 Ave. de Cour, Lausanne, Switz.

SIMHOFFER, Kees, b. 8 Apr. 1934, The Hague, Netherlands. High School Teacher. Publs: (poems) Woorden Van Aarde, 1965; (stories) Een Been Onder Het Zand, 1967; Vermond Als Treurwilg, 1975; (novels) De Knijpkat, 1971; Een Geile Gifkikker, 1973; sev. theatre plays. Contbr. to: De Gids; Podium; De Vlaamse Gids; Nieuw Vlaams Tijdschrift; Kentering; etc. Mbrships: PEN, Netherlands; V.V.L. (Dutch Writers' Club). Recip., Vijverbergprijs (prose prize), The Hague, 1973. Address: Vezeldonk 13, Maastricht, Netherlands.

SIMION, Eugen, b. 25 May 1933, Chiojdeanca, Rumania. University Professor of Modern Rumanian Literature. Publs: Proza lui Eminescu (Eminescu's Prose), 1964; Orientări in literatura contemporană (Directions in Contemporary Literature), 1965; E. Lovinescu scepticul mîntuit (E. Lovinescu, the Absolved Sceptic), 1971; Scriitori români de azi (Rumanian Writers of Today), 1974. Contbr. to sev. lit. jrnls. Mbrships: Rumanian Writers' Union; Int. Assn. of Lit. Critics. Recip. Prize for Lit. Criticism & Hist. of Lit., Writers' Union, 1965. Address: L. Rebreanu 6, Bl. B. 1., sc. 8 et. 2, ap. 319, Bucharest, Rumania.

SIMIONESCU, Mircea Horia, b. 23 Jan. 1928, Tirgoviste, Romania. Writer. Educ: B.A. (Lit.), Bucharest Univ., 1964. Publs: The Well Tempered Jugenuous I, 1969; The Well Tempered Nyenirael II, 1970 (from a 4 vol. work of Lit.); After 1900, Around Noon, 1974; Ganymede's Kidnapping, 1975. Contbr. to most major mags. & newspapers, Romania. Mbrships: Writers' Union, Romania; Jrnlsts' Union, Romania. Address: 3 Belgrade St., Bucharest, 63, Romania.

SIMMEL, Johannes Mario, b. 1924, Vienna, Austria. Chemist; Journalist; Screenplay Writer; Author. Educ: Univ. of Vienna. Publs. incl: Begegnung im Nebel, 1946; Das Geheime Brot, 1950; Ich Gestehe Alles, 1952; Gott Schutzt die Liebenden, 1956; Affare Nina B, 1958; Es Muss Nicht Immer Kaviar Sein, 1960; Der Schulfreund (play), 1960; Bis Zur Bitteren Neige, 1961; Liebe ist nur ein Wort, 1963; Lieb Vaterland magst Ruhig Sein, 1965; Alle Menschen werden Bruder, 1967; Und Jimmy Ging zum Regenbogen, 1970; Der Stoff aus dem die Träume Sind, 1972; num. screenplays. Contbr. to var. newspapers & jrnls. Address: Chateau Perigord II, Bloc E, 27e Etage, 6 Lacets St. Leon, Monte Carlo, Monaco.

SIMMONS, Ozzie Gordon, b. 9 Oct. 1919, Winnipeg, Man., Can. Sociologist. Educ: B.S., Northwestern Univ., 1941; M.A., 1948, Ph.D., 1952, Harvard Univ. Publs: The Mental Patient Comes Home (w. Howard E. Freeman), 1963; Work & Mental Illness, 1965; Anglo Americans &

Mexican Americans in South Texas, 1974. Contbr. to: Am. Sociol. Review; Am. Anthropol.; Daedalus; Am. Jrnl. of Sociol.; Am. Jrnl. of Pub. Hlth.; etc. Mbrships. incl: Fellow, Am. Sociol. Assn., AAAS, Am. Anthropol. Assn., Soc. for Applied Anthropol.; Population Assn. of Am. Recip., Hofheimer Prize, Am. Psych. Assn., 1963. Address: Ford Fndn., 320 E. 43rd St., N.Y., NY 10017, USA.

SIMON, Alfred (Edward), b. 6 Sept. 1907, NYC, USA. Theatre Music Historian; Pianist. Educ: Columbia Preparatory H.S., 1926; piano w. Frederick V. Sittig & Albert von Doenhoff. Publs: Encyclopedia of Theater Music (co-author), 1961; Songs of the American Theater 1900-1971 (co-author), 1973; The Gershwins (co-author), 1973, UK ed., 1974. Contbr. to: N.Y. Times Guide to Listening Pleasure, 1968; Grove's Ency. of Music & Musicians; Stereo Review; etc. Mbrships: Bd. Dirs., The Players; Dutch Treat Club; Charter Mbr., N.Y. Chapt., Gilbert & Sullivan Soc. Address: 400 E. 59th Street, N.Y., NY 10022, USA.

SIMON, Claude, b. 10 Oct. 1913, Tananarive, Madagascar. Writer. Publs: Le Tricheur, 1945; La Corde Raide, 1947; Le Vent, 1957; L'Herbe, 1958; La Route des Flandres, 1960; La Palace, 1962; Histoire 1967; La Bataille de Pharsale, 1969; Les Corps Conducteurs, 1971. Hons: Prix de l'Express, 1960; Prix Médicis, 1967. Address: 3 Place Monge, Paris 5e, France.

SIMON, Lorena, b. 1897, Sherman, Tex., USA. Author; Music Teacher; Composer. Educ: Kidd Key Coll. & Conservatory; Am. Conservatory; Juilliard Music Schl.; Sherwood Music Schl.; Litt.L.D.; H.L.D.; R.P.L.; H.P.L. Publs: The Golden Key, 1958; From My Heart, 1959; Children's Story Hour, 1960; Golden Memories. Contbr. to: Today's Poets; Anthols. of Am. Poetry; N.Y. Times; Laurel Leaves; etc. Mbrships. incl: Nat. & Tex. Press Women's Assn.; Am. Poetry League; Poets Soc. of Tex. Recip., num. awards for achievements in lit. & music. Address: 411 Fifth Ave., Port Arthur, TX 77640, USA.

SIMON, Neil Marvin, b. 4 July 1927, NYC, USA. Playwright. Educ: N.Y. Univ. Publs. incl: Come Blow Your Horn, 1963; Barefoot in the Park, 1964; The Odd Couple, 1965; Sweet Charity (co-author), 1966; The Star Spangled Girl, 1966; Plaza Suite, 1969; The Sunshine Boys, 1972 (many filmed); (screenplays) After the Fox, prod. 1966; The Heartbreak Kid, 1973. Address: 225 E. 57th St., N.Y., NY 10022, USA.

SIMÓN DÍAZ, José, b. 17 July 1920, Madrid, Spain. Professor of Bibliography. Educ: Ph.D. Publs. incl: Índices de Publicaciones Periódicas, 8 vols., 1946-48; Historia del Colegio Imperial de Madrid, 2 vols., 1952-59; Bibliografía de la Literatura Hispánica, I-X, 1950-; Manual de Bibliografía de la Literatura Española, 1963, 3rd ed., 1971; Impresos del siglo XVII, 1972. Contbr. to: Revista de Literatura; Anales del Instituto de Estudios Madrileños; Revista de Filología Española; Ed., Cuadernos Bibliográficos; etc. Mbrships. incl: Advsr., Exec. Coun., Sec., Inst. of Philol., CSIC; Pres., Inst. of Madrid Studies. Address: Calle Amado Nervo 13, Madrid 7, Spain.

SIMONOV, Konstantin Mikhailovich, b. 28 Nov. 1915, Kalinin, USSR. Journalist; Author. Educ: M. Gorky Lit. Inst., Moscow. Publs. incl: (poetry) Real Men, 1938; Friends & Enemies, 1948; Selected Poems, 1960, 1964; (plays) A Story of Love, 1940; The Russians, 1942; Under the Chestnut Trees, 1945; Alien Shadow, 1949; The Fourth, 1962; (novels) Comrades in Arms, 1953; Soldiers are not Born, 1964; From Lopatin's Notes, 1965; Collected Works, 1966. Contbr. to: Pravda; Red Star; Lit. gazeta; Novy Mir. Hons. incl: Order of Lenin; Red Banner of Labour. Address: Union of Writers, Ulitsa Vorovskogo 52, Moscow, USSR.

SIMONS, Eric Norman, b. 12 Jan. 1896, Birmingham, UK. Author. Publs: 52 books inclng. The Queen & the Rebel, 1964; The Reign of Edward IV, 1966; Henry VII, 1968; Dictionary of Alloys; Dictionary of Ferrous Metals. Contbr. to: Strand Mag.; Morning Telegraph; Engineering The Engineer; Blackwood's Mag.; The Great War; Ency. Britannica; BBC Radio & TV; etc. Mbrships. incl: Soc. of Authors; Assn. of Special Libs. & Info. Bureaux. Address: Flat 3, 3 St. John's Rd., Eastbourne, Sussex BN20 7JA, UK.

SIMONS, John Donald, b. 5 Oct. 1935, Lone Oak, Tex., USA. Teacher. Educ: B.A., 1959, M.A., 1961, Univ. of Tex.; Ph.D., Rice Univ., 1966. Publs: Hermann Hesse's

Steppenwolf, 1972; Günter Grass' The Tin Drum, 1973; Thomas Mann's Death in Venice & other Stories, 1974; Dostoevsky's Crime & Punishment, 1975; Dostoevsky's Brothers Karamazov. Contbr. to: Comp. Lit.; MLN; German Quarterly; Slavic & E. European Jrnl.; Mod. Lang. Jrnl.; Can. Slavic Studies; Germanic Notes; Explicator. Mbrships: MLA; Am. Assn. of Tchrs. of German; Comp. Lit. Assn.; Int. Dostoevsky Soc. Address: 2106 Monticello Drive, Tallahassee, FL 32303, USA.

SIMPSON, Alan, b. 27 Nov. 1929, UK. Author; Scriptwriter. Publs. incl: (all w. Ray Galton) Hancock, 1961; Steptoe & Son, 1963; The Reunion & Other Plays, 1966; (TV) Hancock's Half Hour, 1954-61; Comedy Playhouse, 1962-63; Steptoe & Son, 1962-; Galton-Simpson Comedy, 1969; Clochemerle, 1971; (films) The Rebel, 1960; The Spy with a Cold Nose, 1966; Loot, 1969; Steptoe & Son, 1971; (plays) Way Out in Piccadilly, 1966; The Wind in the Sassafras Trees, 1968. Hons. incl: Scriptwriters of the Yr., 1959; Best TV Comedy Series, Screenwriters Guild, 1962, 1963, 1964, 1965; John Logie Baird Award, 1964; Best Comedy Screenplay, 1972. Address: c/o ALS Mgmt. Ltd., 67 Brook St., London W1, UK.

SIMPSON, Colin, b. 4 Nov. 1908, Sydney, NSW, Australia. Author; Former Journalist. Publs. incl: Adam in Ochre, 1951; Adam with Arrows, 1953, Adam in Plumes, 1953, combined ed. as Plumes & Arrows, 1962; Islands of Men, 1955; The Country Upstairs, 1956; Wake Up in Europe, 1959; Show Me a Mountain, 1961; Asia's Bright Balconies, 1962; Take Me to Spain, 1963; Take Me to Russia, 1964; The Viking Circle, 1966; Katmandu, 1967; Greece, The Unclouded Eye, 1968; The New Australia, 1971; Bali & Beyond, 1972; Off to Asia, 1973. Contbr. to: Trio (poems). VP, Aust. Soc. of Authors. Address: 27 Glenview Street, Gordon, NSW, Australia 2072.

SIMPSON, David Penistan, b. 3 Oct. 1917, Canterbury, Kent, UK. Schoolmaster & Former Administrator, Eton College; Author. Educ: B.A., 1940, M.A., 1943, Christ Ch., Oxford. Publs: Cassell's New Latin Dictionary, 1959; Cassell's New Compact Latin Dictionary, 1963; First Principles of Latin Prose, 1965; Writing in Latin (w. P. H. Vellacott), 1970. Address: Saddocks Farm, Eton Wick, Windsor, Berks., UK.

SIMPSON, Edith Eva, pen name FELTON, Eve, b. 17 Feb. 1902, Solon, Ohio, USA. Accounting Clerk (retired); Poet. Contbr. to: Penman Publs. (anthol.), 1966, 1967 & 1968; Poetry Parade, 1966 & 1968; Shore Publng. Co. (anthol.), 1971; Notable American Poets, 1973; Best poems of the Twentieth Century, 1973; Echoes of the Unlocked Odyssey, 1974; Yesterday's Magazette; S.W. Breeze Mag.; etc. Mbrships: Life Mbr., Int. Clover Poetry Assn., Wash. D.C.; San Diego Poets Assn. Hons. incl: var. awards, San Diego Poets Assn. Contest, 1970 & 1971; Cert. of Merit, Int. Jesse Stewart Contest, 1973. Address: 630 F St., San Diego, CA 92101, USA.

SIMPSON, Harold Brown, b. 3 Apr. 1917, Hindsboro, Ill., USA. Teacher. Educ: B.S., M.A., M.S., Univ. of Ill.; Ph.D., Tex. Christian Univ. Publs: Gaines Mill to Appomattox, 1963; Touched with Valor, 1965; Texas in the War, 1861-1865, 1966; Hood's Texas Brigade: Lee's Grenadier Guard, 1970; Hood's Texas Brigade in Reunion & Memory, 1974. Contbr. to histl. jrnls. Hons. incl: Fellow, Co. of Mil. Histns., 1963; Fellow, Tex. State Histl. Assn., 1973; Award of Merit, Am. Assn. for State & Local Hist., 1963. Address: 4913 Westhaven Dr., Ft. Worth, TX 76132, USA.

SIMPSON, Howard Russell, b. 27 Apr. 1925, Alameda, Calif., USA. Diplomat. Educ: San Fran. City Coll.; Acad. Julian, Paris; Calif. Schl. of Fine Art; Naval War Coll., Newport, R.I. Publs: To a Silent Valley, 1961; Assignment for a Mercenary, 1965; Three Day Alliance, 1971; Rendezvous Off Newport, 1973.Contbr. to: Harper's Mag.; Commonweal; Nat. Review; Naval Inst. Proceedings; Wash. Star; San Fran. Chronicle. Address: Am. Consulate Gen., 9 rue Armeny, Marseilles, France.

SIMPSON, Jacqueline Mary, b. 25 Nov. 1930, Worthing, UK. Author. Educ: B.A., Bedford Coll., Univ. of London, 1952; M.A., King's Coll., London, 1955. Publs: The Northmen Talk, 1965; The Penguin English Dictionary (co-compiler), 1965; Everyday Life in the Viking Age, 1967, revised ed., 1969; Beowulf & Its Analogues, 1968; Icelandic Folktales & Legends, 1972; The Folklore of Sussex, 1973. Contbr. to: Folklore; The Saga Book of the

Viking Soc. Mbrships: Comm., Folklore Soc.; Viking Soc. Address: 9 Christchurch Rd., Worthing, Sussex BN11 1JH, UK.

SIMPSON, Norman Frederick, b. 29 Jan. 1919, London, UK. Writer. Educ: B.A., Univ. London. Publs. incl: (Plays) A Resounding Tinkle, 1958, 3rd ed., 1968; One Way Pendulum, 1960; The Hole & Other Plays & Sketches, 1964; The Cresta Run, 1966; Some Tall Tinkles, 1968; Was He Anyone?, 1973. Contbr. to: Vogue; Transatlantic Review; etc. Mbr., Soc. Authors (League Dramatists). Address: c/o Robin Dalton Assocs., 11-12 Hanover St., London W1, UK.

SIMPSON, Robert Smith, pen name SIMPSON, Smith, b. 9 Nov. 1906, Arlington, Va., USA. Writer; retired Diplomat. Educ: B.S., 1927, M.S., 1928, Univ. Va.; LL.B., 1931, Cornell Univ. Publs: El Movimiento Obrero de los Estados Unidos de Norteamérica, 1951; Anatomy of the State Department, 1967; (Ed. & Contbr.) Needs & Resources of American Diplomacy, 1968; Instruction in Diplomacy: The Liberal Arts Approach, 1972. Contbr. to: Nation (N.Y.); For. Serv. Jrnl. (Wash. DC.); Annals (Am. Acad. Pol. & Social Serv.). Mbrships. incl: Raven Soc., Univ. Va. Lib. Assocs. Address: 4124 Downing St., Annandale, VA 22003, USA.

SINCLAIR, Andrew (Annandale), b. 21 Jan. 1935, Oxford, UK. Writer; Publisher; Film Director. Educ: B.A. 1958, Ph.D. 1962, Trinity Coll., Cambridge Univ. Publs. incl: (novels) The Breaking of Bumbo, 1959; My Friend Judas, 1959; The Project, 1960; The Hallelujah Bum (as The Paradise Bum, USA), 1963; The Raker, 1964; Gog, 1967; Magog, 1972; (non-fiction) Prohibition, 1962; A Concise History of the United States, 1967; Guevara, 1970 (all foregoing publd. also in USA); (screenplays) The Breaking of Bumbo, 1970; Under Milk Wood, 1971; Byron's Evil, 1972; var. plays & transls. Recip., Maugham Award, 1967. Address: 47 Dean St., London W1, UK.

SINCLAIR, Jo, pen name of SEID, Ruth, b. 1 July 1913, Brooklyn, N.Y., USA. Educ: Night Classes, Western Reserve Univ., Cleveland. Publs: (novels) Wasteland, USA, 1946, UK, 1948; Sing at my Wake, 1951; The Changelings, 1955; Anna Teller, USA, 1960, UK, 1961; (play) The Long Moment, prod. 1951. Contbr. to: Theme & Variation in the Short Story, 1938; America in Literature, 1944; Social Insight Through Short Stories, 1946; Cross Section, 1947. Hons. incl: Harper Prize, 1946; Daroff Mem. Award, 1956; Fund for the Repub. Prize, 1956; Wolpaw Playwriting Grant, 1969. Address: 2389 Queenston Rd., Cleveland Heights, OH 44118, USA.

SINCLAIR, Keith, b. 5 Dec. 1922, Auckland, NZ. University Teacher. Educ: M.A., Ph.D.; D.Litt. Publs. incl: The Maori Land League, 1950; Songs for a Summer (verse), 1952; Strangers or Beasts (verse), 1954; The Origins of the Maori Wars, 1957; A History of New Zealand, 1959; ed., Distance Looks our Way, 1961; A Time to Embrace (verse), 1963; William Pember Reeves: New Zealand Fabian, 1965; The Firewheel Tree (verse), 1973. Hons. incl: Hubert Church Award for Prose, PEN, 1965; F. P. Wilson Prize in NZ History, Vic. Univ., 1967. Address: 13 Mambora Cresc., Birkenhead, Auckland 10, NZ.

SINCLAIR, Olga Ellen, b. 23 Jan. 1923, Watton, Norfolk, UK. Writer; Housewife. Publs: Gypsies, 1967; The Man at the Manor, 1967; Man of the River, 1968; Knight of the Black Tower; Bitter Sweet Summer, 1970; Dancing in Britain, 1970; Children's Games 1972; Wild Dreams, 1973; Toys, 1974. Contbr. to children's comics, etc. Mbrships: Soc. Authors; Romantic Novelists' Assn.; Soc. Women Writers & Jrnlsts. Address: The Beeches, Coltishall, Norwich NR12 7JL, UK.

SINGER, Armand Edwards, b. 30 Nov. 1914, Detroit, Mich., USA. Professor of French, Spanish & Humanities. Educ: B.A., Amherst Coll., 1935; Dip., Univ. of Paris, France, 1939; M.A., 1939, Ph.D., 1944, Duke Univ.; Postgrad. study, Ind. Univ., 1964. Publs: The Don Juan Theme, Versions & Criticism: A Bibliography, 1965 (revised version of: Bibliography of the Don Juan Theme: Versions & Criticism, 1954); Humanities I & II: Anthology of Readings (co-author), 1966-67; Paul Bourget (in progress). Contbr. to: PMLA; Hispanic Review; Mod. Lang. Jrnl.; other profl. jrnls. Ed.-in-Chief, W.Va. Univ. Philol. Papers, 1950-52, 1954—. Address: 248 Grandview Ave., Morgantown, WV 26505, USA.

SINGER, Irving, b. 24 Dec. 1925, NYC, USA. Professor of Philosophy. Educ: A.B., Harvard Coll., 1948; M.A., 1949; Ph.D., 1952. Publs: Santayana's Aesthetics: A Critical Introduction, 1957, 1973; Ed., Essays in Literary Criticism of George Santayana, 1956; The Nature of Love; Plato to Luther, 1966; The Goals of Human Sexuality, 1973. Contbr. to: Hudson Review; N.Y. Review of Books; Philos. Review; Jrnl. of Sex Rsch.; Mod. Lang. Notes; Jrnl. of Philos.; Jrnl. of Aesthetics & Art Criticism; etc. Mbr., Am. Philos. Assn. Hons. incl: Bollingen Fndn. Fellowship, 1965-67; Rockefeller Fndn. Grant, 1970-72. Address: Dept. of Philos., Room 14 N 427, MIT, Cambridge, MA 02139, USA.

SINGER, Isaac Bashevis, b. 14 July 1904, Radzymin, Poland. Writer. Educ: Tachkemoni Rabbinical Sem., Warsaw. Publs. incl: (novels) The Family Moskat, 1950; The Magician of Lublin, 1960; The Manor, 1967; The Estate, 1970; (short stories) Gimpel the Fool, 1957; Short Friday, 1964; The Seance, 1968; Friend of Kafka, 1970; (autobiog.) In My Father's Court, 1966 (many transld. from Yiddish; all also publd. in UK); 9 juvenile. Contbr. to: Jewish Daily Forward (staff, 1935—). Mbrships. incl: Nat. Inst. Arts & Letters; Am. Acad. Arts & Scis. Hons. incl: Daroff Mem. Award, 1963; D.H.L., Hebrew Union Coll., L.A., 1963; Nat. Book Award, 1970. Address: 209 W. 86th St., N.Y., NY 10024, USA.

SINGH, Arjan, b. 17 Aug. 1917, Gorakhpur, India. Farmer. Educ: B.A. Author, Tiger Haven, 1973. Contbr. to: Wild Life Preservation Soc. of India; Illustrated Weekly of India. Mbr., Indian Bd. for Wild Life. Address: Tigerhaven, P.O. Pallia, Dist. Kheri, Uttar Pradesh, India.

SINGH, Khushwant, b. 2 Feb. 1915, Hadali, India (now Pakistan). Lawyer; Editor. Educ: B.A., Govt. Coll., Lahore, 1934; LL.B., King's Coll., London, UK, 1938. Publs. incl: (novels) Train to Pakistan, USA, 1955, UK, 1956 (also publd. as Mano Majra, USA, 1956); (short stories) The Mark of Vishnu, 1950; Black Jasmine, 1971; (non-fiction) The Sikhs Today, 1959, revised ed. 1964; A History of the Sikhs, 1469-1964, USA & UK, 2 vols., 1963, 1966; Ghadar, 1919 (w. S. Singh), 1966; Hymns of Nanak the Guru, 1969. Contbr. to Illustrated Wkly. of India (Ed., 1969—). Address: Illustrated Weekly of India, Dr. Dadabhoy Naoroji Rd., Bombay 1, India.

SINGH, L. P., b. 5 Mar. 1936, Ghazipur, India. Teacher. Educ: Ph.D., Delhi, 1962; Ph.D., Aust. Nat. Univ., 1965. Publs: The Politics of Economic Co-operation in Asia: A Study in Asian International Organizations, 1966. Contbr. to: Asian Survey; Pacific Affairs; Jrnl. of C'wlth. Pol. Studies. Address: Dept. of Pol. Sci., Sir George Williams Univ., Montreal, P.Q., Can.

SINGHAL, Damodar Prasad, b. 24 Sept. 1925, Bikaner, India. University Professor. Educ: M.A.; Ph.D. Publs: The Annexation of Upper Burma, 1960; India & Afghanistan: A Study in Diplomatic Relation, 1963; Nationalism in India & Other Historical Essays, 1967; India & World Civilization, 2 vols., 1969 & 1972; Pakistan, 1972. Contbr. to var. jrnls. Mbrships. incl: Fellow, Royal Histl. Soc. & Royal Asiatic Soc. Address: Univ. of Qld., Brisbane, Australia.

SINGLETON, Ralph Herbert, b. 25 May 1900, Cleveland, Ohio, USA. Professor of English. Educ: B.A., 1923, M.A., 1930, Oberlin Coll.; Ph.D. Western Reserve Univ., 1939. Publs: Two & Twenty: A Collection of Short Stories, 1962; Reviewing the Years, A Biography of John Young-Hunter (ed.), 1963; Style, 1966; Introduction to Literature (w. Stanton Millet), 1966; The Art of Prose Fiction, 1967; The Lively Rhetoric (w. Alexander Scharbach), 1968, rev. ed., 1972; The New Lively Rhetoric (w. Alexander Scharbach), 1970. Contbr. to: Publs. of MLA; Coll. Engl.; & num. others. Mbr., MLA. Address: 2280 W. Seymour Dr., Portland, OR 97201, USA.

SINKANKAS, John, b. 15 May 1915, Paterson, N.J., USA. Retired Naval Officer; Writer. Educ: B.S., Paterson State Coll., N.J. Publs: Gem Cutting, A Lapidary's Manual, 1955, 2nd ed., 1962; Gemstones of North America, 1959; Gemstones & Minerals — How & Where to Find Them, 1961; Mineralogy for the Amateur, 1964; Minerology: A First Course, 1966; Van Nostrand's Standard Catalog of Gems, 1968; Prospecting for Gemstones & Minerals, 1970; Gemstone & Mineral Data Book, 1972. Contbr. to num. mineralogical & gemmol. jrnls. Mbrships. incl: Fellow, Mineralogical Soc. of Am.; Authors' Guild; N.Y. Mineralogical Club; Gemmol. Assn. of All-Japan; Mineralogical Assn. of Can. Address: 5372 Van Nuys Court, San Diego, CA 92109, USA.

SINOR, (Prof.) Denis, b. 17 Apr. 1916, Kolozsvar, Hungary. Educator. Educ: B.A., Univ. of Budapest, 1938; M.A., Cambridge Univ., UK, 1948. Publs. incl: Orientalism & History (Ed. & Contbr.), 1954, 2nd ed. 1970; History of Hungary, 1959; Introduction a l'etude de l'Eurasie Centrale, 1963; Inner Asia: History, Civilization, Languages. A Syllabus, 1969, 2nd ed. 1971. Contbr. to: Jrnl. of Asian Hist. (Ed.). Morships. incl: Permanent Int. Altaistic Conf. (Sec-Gen.); Assn. for Asian Studies (Chmn., Dev. Comm. on Inner Asian Studies, 1973—); Pres., Am. Oriental Soc. Hons. incl: num. acad. hons. Address: Dept. of Uralic & Altaic Studies, Ind. Univ., Bloomington, IN 47401, USA.

SINTIMBREANU, Mircea-Ioan, b. 7 Jan. 1926, Baita, Romania. Professor. Educ: Univ. of Bucharest. Publs: Cu şi fără ghiozdan, 1956; Sub lupă, 1958; Extemporale, 1959; Recreaţia mare, 1961; Elefanţi cu rochiţe, 1963; Lîngă groapa cu furnici, 1964; Să stăm de vorbă fără catalog, 1966; Stafeta fanteziei, 1968; Melcul mincinos, 1971; Peripeţiile lui Hai-Hui, 1974. Contbr. to radio, TV, etc. Mbrships: Bucharest Writers' Union; Bucharest Writers' Assn. Hons. incl: Prize, Bucharest Writers' Assn., 1974. Address: Bucuresti, Str. Hristo Botev 8, et. III, ap. 7, Romania.

SIREBORN, (Karl) Axel (Malte), pen name SIR, A., b. 22 June 1915, Helsingborg, Sweden. Author. Publs: Förbjudna lekar, 1951; Möte med flicka, 1952; Men nu lyser solen, 1954, 2nd ed. as Stupad soldat, 1956; Marodörer, 1958. Contbr. to: All varldens Berattare. Mbr., Swedish Authors' Union. Recip., Grant, Swedish Authors' Union, 1955. Address: Postiljonsgatan 2B, 12 15, 222 36 Lund, Sweden.

SISLEY, Harris D. (Nick), Jr., b. 6 June 1937, McKeesport, Pa., USA. Writer. Educ: B.A., Univ. of Pitts. Publs: Hunting the Ruffed Grouse, 1970; Deer Hunting Across North America, 1975. Contbr. to: Sports Afield; Field & Stream; Am. Rifleman; Am. Hunter; Pa. Game News; Pa. Angler; Bassmaster; Am. Bass Fisherman; Fishing World; Gun Digest; etc.; syndicated weekly hunting & fishing column in Ohio & Pa. newspapers. Mbrships: Outdoor Writers Assn. of Am.; VP, Pa. Outdoor Writers Assn. Address: Alder Acres, Apollo, PA 15613, USA.

SITO, Jerzy Stanislaw, b. 8 Nov. 1934, Pinsk, Poland. Writer. Educ: Structural Engrng., London, UK. Publs: (poetry) Wiozę Swój Czas Na Ośle, 1958; Zdięcie Z Koła, 1960; Ucieczka Do Egiptu, 1964; Wiersze, Dawne I Nowe, 1974; Pasja I Potępienie Doktora Fausta (drama), 1973; (essays) W Pierwszej i Trzeiej Osobie, 1967; Szekspir Na Dzisiaj, 1971; Transls. from Shakespeare, Marlowe, Metaphysical Poets, 9 vols.; Co-Ed., Poeci języka angielskiego, 3 vols., 1969-74. Contbr. to: sev. jrnls. Mbrships: Polish Writers Union; PEN; VP, Polish Drama Writers Club. Hons: Poznan Poetry Award, 1958; Marian Kister Award for Transls., 1968. Address: Czeska 16, Warsaw 03-902, Poland.

SITWELL, (Sir) Sacheverell, b. 15 Nov. 1897, Scarborough, Yorks., UK. Writer. Publs. incl: Southern Baroque Art, 1924; The Gothic North, 1929; Conversation Pieces, 1936; Poltergeists, 1940; Primitive Scenes & Festivals, 1942; British Architects & Craftsmen, 1945; Selected Poems, 1948; Cupid & the Jacaranda, 1952; Arabesque & Honeycomb, 1957; Journey to the Ends of Time, Vol. I, 1959; Golden Wall & Mirador, 1961; Monks, Nuns & Monasteries, 1965; Southern Baroque Revisited, 1968; Gothic Europe, 1969; For Want of the Golden City, 1973; num. books of verse, 1918—. Contbr. to: Poetry Review. Recip., Freedom of Lima, Peru, 1960. Address: Weston Hall, Towcester, Horthants., UK.

SIVRIEV, Stanislav, b. 16 Sept. 1924, Zlatograd, Bulgaria. Writer. Publs: With the Single Truth, 1958; The People are Everywhere, 1963; Return After Flight, 1967; The World is Old, 1968; Coming Back, 1969; And the Earth Stopped Swaying, 1971; When I was an Officer, 1974. Contbr. to: September; PlamAk; Literatouren Front. Mbrships: Fijet; Union of Bulgarian Writers. Recip., Gold Sword, Defence Min., 1971, 1970. Address: Sofia-cntr., ul. Slavyanska, 20, Bulgaria.

SIWUNDHLA, Alice Princess Msumba, b. 7 Jan. 1928, Johannesburg, S. Africa. Author; Lecturer; Professional Model; Fashion Co-ordinator; Diplomat. Educ: B.A.; M.A.; Ph.D. cand., Spring 1975. Publs: (autobiog.) Alice Princess, 1965; My Two Worlds, 1971; third book in progress. Contbr. to study guides for LA Co. Schls. TV series,

Spotlight on Africa, 1964. Mbr., int. Platform Assn. Hons: Featured on Ralph Edwards' TV prog., This is Your Life. Address: 3920 Leland St., San Diego, CA 92106, USA.

SJÖGREN, Gunnar, b. 28 Jan. 1897, Stockholm, Sweden. Retired Businessman. Educ: B.Econ.Sci., Stockholm Schl. of Econ. Publs: Var Othello neger? och andra Shakespeareproblem (Was Othello a Negro? & other Shakespeare problems), 1959; Strövtåg i Shakespeares värld (Ventures into Shakespeare's world), 1962; Shakespeare, dramatiker, människor och myt (Shakespeare, Playwright, Man & Myth), 1967; Shakespeares samtida och deras dramatik (Shakespear's Contemporaries & their Drama), 1969; Helena Snakenborg, en svenska vid Elisabet I:s hov (Helena Snakesborg, a Swedish Lady at the Court of Elizabeth I), 1973. Contbr. to var. Shakesp. jrnls. Mbr., Swedish Authors Assn. Recip., Ph.D.,L.C., Lund Univ. Address: Dag Hammarskjöldsväg 6A, 223 64 Lund, Sweden.

SJÖMAN, Vilgot, b. 2 Dec. 1924, Stockholm, Sweden. Writer; Film Director. Publs. incl: Lektorn (The Professor), 1948; In Hollywood, 1961; Diary With Ingmar Bergman, 1963; I Was Curious, Diary With Myself, 1969; 3 plays inclng. Bodil Eller Hattasken (The Hat Box), 1964; filmscripts incl: I Am Curious Yellow. Address: Banérgatan 53, 115 22 Stockholm, Sweden.

SJÖSTRAND, Bengt Håkan Wilhelm, b. 19 Aug. 1909, Barnarp, Jonkopings län, Sweden. Professor of Education & Educational Psychology. Educ: B.D., 1932; B.A., 1935; Ph.D., 1937; D.Litt., 1941. Publs. incl: History of Education, 4 vols., 1954-65; School & Democracy, 1966; Education as an Academic Discipline, 1967; Freedom & Equality. Two Basic Principles in Swedish Education in the 1960s, 1970; Freedom & Equality as fundamental Educational Principles in Western Democracy. From John Locke to Edmund Burke, 1973. Contbr. to var. educl. jrnls. Mbrships. incl: Chmn., Swedish Psychol. Soc., 1952-54; Royal Swedish Acad. of Humanities. Address: Götavägen 5, 75236 Uppsala, Sweden.

SJÖSTRAND, Levi Valdemar, b. 22 July 1920, Jakobstad, Finland. Author. Publs: Arvet, 1958; Oro, 1960; Hård kust, 1965; Brytningstid, 1968; Kustbor, 1971; Utlämnad, 1973. Contbr. to: Kuriren. Mbrships: Finlands Svenska Författareförening; Svenska Osterbottens Litteraturförening. Recip., var. stipendiary awards. Address: Box 205, 68800 Källby, Finland.

SJÖVALL, Björn Yngve Yngvesson, b. 16 Feb. 1916, Kristianstad, Sweden. Professor of Psychology. Educ: Ph.D., Univ. of Uppsala, 1967. Publs. incl: Symbolernas bok (poems), 1950; Höjdpsykologi (Height Psychology), 1959; Psykologist praktikum, 1969; Ledarpraktikum, 1971; Kreativ livssyn (Creative View of Life), 1972; Konfrontationspraktikum, 1973. Contbr. to jrnls. Mbrships. incl: Swedish Union of Authors. Address: Värtavägen 72, 115 38 Stockholm, Sweden.

SKELTON, Robin, b. 12 Oct. 1925, Easington, Yorks., UK. Teacher; Writer. Educ: B.A., 1950; M.A., 1951. Publs: Herbert Read: A Memorial Symposium, 1970; The Hunting Dark, 1971; Two Hundred Poems from the Greek Anthology, 1971; Remembering Synge, 1971; A Different Mountain, 1971; A Private Speech, 1971; The Writings of J. M. Synge, 1971; The Practice of Poetry, 1971; J. M. Synge & His World, 1971; Synge/Petrarch, 1971; The Collected Plays of Jack B. Yeats, 1971; Three For Herself, 1972; Musebook, 1972; A Christmas Poem, 1972; The Limners, 1972; Timelight Poems, 1974; The Poet's Calling, 1974. Contbr. to num. lit. jrnls.; Ed., Malabat Review, 1972—. Mbr., PEN. Recip., F.R.S.L., 1966. Address: 1255 Victoria Ave., Victoria, B.C., Can.

SKINNER, Cornelia Otis (Mrs. A. S. Blodget). Actress; Authoress. Educ: Bryn Mawr Coll., Pa.; Sorbonne, Paris, France. Publs. incl: Tiny Garments, 1931; Dithers & Jitters, 1937; Soap Behind the Ears (as Popcorn, UK), 1941; Our Hearts were Young & Gay (w. E. Kimbrough), 1942; Family Circle, 1948; Thats Me All Over (omnibus), 1948; Nuts in May, 1950; Happy Family, 1950; Bottoms Up! , 1955; The Ape in Me, 1959; Elegant Wits & Grand Horizontals, 1962; Madame Sarah, 1967; (radio series) William & Mary; (plays) The Pleasure of His Company (w. S. Taylor); The Wives of Henry VIII; Mansion on the Hudson. Recip., Off. de l'Académie, 1953. Address: 22 E 60th St., N.Y., NY 10022, USA.

SKÖLD, Bo Sture, b. 1 Nov. 1924, Lund, Sweden. Author. Educ: B.A. Publs. incl: (plays for stage, radio & TV) Der är kallt, det är redan i Augusti (It's Cold, It's Already August), 1960; Min kära är en ros (My Love is a Rose), 1962. Ed., Nordisk Kulturtidskrift. Mbrships: Swedish Soc. of Writers (Bd.); PEN. Address: Södra Esplanaden 2, 223 54 Lund, Sweden.

SKÖRDEMAN, Bengt Olof Ingemar, b. 12 Aug. 1936, St. Levene, Sweden. People's High School Teacher. Educ: Fil.kand. Publs: Samkväm, 1970; Konferensen, 1972; Gunnar Karlsson, 1973. Mbrships: Swedish Union of Authors; Swedish Authors' Ctr.; Authors' Assn. of Norrland. Address: Idrottsvägen 4 B, S-95200 Kalix, Sweden.

SKULIMA, Loni, b. 28 Aug. 1912, Zell, Rhine Palatinate, Germany. Travel Writer. Educ: Studies in Econs., Lit. & Art at Univs. of Heidelberg & Munich. Publs: Ich strahle in dich (poems), 1956; Unvergessliche Reise, 1956; Auf silbernem Bande, 1957; Schönes Badnerland (Picture-book w. introd. essay), 1957. Contbr. to: Frankfurter Allgemeine; Westermanns Monatshefte; Merian. Mbr., Vereinigung Deutscher Reisejournalisten (German Travel Jrnlsts. Union). Address: 6900 Heidelberg, Werrgasse 9, W. Germany.

SLAATTE, Howard Alexander, b. 18 Oct. 1919, Evanston, Ill., USA. Professor of Philosophy; Clergyman. Educ: A.A., Kendall Coll., 1940; B.A., Univ. of N.D., 1942; B.D., 1945, Ph.D., 1956, Drew Univ.; Mansfield Coll., Oxford, 1949-50. Publs: Time & Its End, 1962; Fire In The Brand, 1963; The Pertinence of the Paradox, 1968; The Paradox of Existentialist Theology, 1971; Modern Science & the Human Condition, 1974. Contbr. to jrnls. Mbr., relig. & philos. socs. Recip., acad. hons. Address: 407 Grand Blvd., Huntington, WV 25705, USA.

SLANEY, George Wilson, pen name WODEN, George, b. 1 Sept. 1884, Wednesbury, Staffs., UK. Novelist. Educ: London Univ. Publs. incl: Sowing Clover, 1913; Little Houses, 1919; The Wrenfield Mystery, 1923; This Way to Fortune, 1929; Love & Let Love, 1933; Tannenbrae, 1935; The Bailie's Tale, 1937; Voyage through Life, 1940; The Golden Lion, 1944; The Lover's Tale, 1948; Helen Enchanted, 1950; Mystery of the Amorous Music Master, 1951; Simonetta, 1952; (plays) They Money's the Thing, 1921; Thistledown, 1923. Mbr., PEN (Pres., Scotland, 1944-47). Address: 91 Marlborough Ave., Glasgow W1, UK.

SLATER, Leonard, b. 1920, NY, USA. Editor, Lecturer & Consultant on writing & publishing projects. Educ: B.A., Michigan. Publs: Aly; The Pledge, 1970. Contbr. to: McCall's Mag., NY (Sr. Ed. & Columnist); Reader's Digest; Cosmopolitan; Pageant; Coronet; etc. Mbr., Overseas Press Club, NY. Address: 4370 Arista Drive, San Diego, CA 92103, USA.

SLATER, Mary, b. 5 Apr. 1909, London, UK. Travel Writer; Designer. Educ: Dip., Slade Schl., Univ. of London; Royal Acad. Schls. Schlrship. Publs: Simple Clothes for Children; More Clothes for Children; Clothes for Teens to Twenties; The Caribbean Islands; Cooking the Caribbean Way; Caribbean Cooking for Pleasure. Contbr. to: var. mags. & newspapers, UK & USA. Mbrships: Guild of Travel Writers; W. India Comm.; Sartorial Sub-comm., W. India Comm. Address: 66/105 Hallam St., London W1N 5LU, UK.

SLATTER, Gordon, b. 25 Aug. 1922, Christchurch, NZ. Schoolmaster. Educ: M.A.(Hons.), Canterbury Univ. Publs: A Gun in my Hand, 1959; The Pagan Game, 1969; On the Ball, 1970; Football is Fifteen, 1972; Great Days at Lancaster Park, 1974. Mbr., Canterbury Officers' Club. Address: 116 Scarborough Road, Christchurch 8, New Zealand.

SLATZER, Robert Franklin, b. 4 Apr. 1927, Marion, Ohio, USA. Writer; Director; Producer; Author. Educ: B.A., Ohio State Univ., Columbus; UCLA. Publs: The Hellcats, 1967; A Cowhand for the Heiress, 1969; Campaign Girl, 1971; The Punishment Pawn, 1972; The Life & Curious Death of Marilyn Monroe, 1974; The Curious Death of Marilyn Monroe, 1975; The Duke of Thieves, 1975; Many Western novels. Contbr. to num. mags. & newspapers. Mbrships: Dir., Dirs. Guild of Am.; Writers Guild of Am., W.; Nat. Acad. of TV Arts & Scis. Recip., Meritorious Achievement, Nat. Assn. of Am. TV & Broadcasters, 1966. Address: 1680 Vine St., Suite 1000, Hollywood, CA 90028, USA.

SLAUGHTER, Frank Gill, b. 25 Feb. 1908, Wash. DC, USA. Novelist; Retired Physician & Surgeon. Educ: A.B., Duke Univ.; M.D., Johns Hopkins Univ., Balt., Md. Publs. incl: That None Should Die, 1941; A Tough of Glory, 1945; The New Science of Surgery, 1946; The Stubborn Heart, 1950; Apalachee Gold, 1954; 1962; Spring in the Seaside Home, 1973. Contbr. to: September; PlamAk; Nasha Rodina; Prostori; Lit. Warrior, 1967; Doctor's Wives, 1967; The Sins of Herod, 1968; Surgeon's Choice, 1969; Countdown, 1970; Code Five, 1971; Convention, MD, 1972. Address: 5051 Yacht Club Rd., Jacksonville, FL 32210, USA.

SLAVIC, Rosalind Welcher, pen name WELCHER, Rosalind, b. 21 Oct. 1922, NYC, USA. Artist. Educ: B.A., Hunter Coll., N.Y. Publs: The Runaway Angel, 1963; The Split Level Child, 1963; The Magic Top, 1965; It's Wonderful to be in Love, 1966; Somebody's Thinking of You, 1966; Do You Ever Feel Lonely?. 1967; Please Don't Feel Blue, 1967; It Must Be Hard to Be a Mother, 1968; There Is Nothing Like a Cat, 1968; Squeeking By, 1969; Do You Believe in Magic?, 1969; Moonlight, Cobwebs & Shadows, 1970; Wouldn't You Like to Run Away?. 1971; When You're Away, 1971; I Wish You a Merry Christmas, 1971. Address: Rhododendron Rd., Fitzwilliam, NH 03447, USA.

SLAVINSKI, Petur, b. 19 Mar. 1909, Sofia, Bulgaria. Writer. Publs: The Last Assault, 1951; Invincible Life, 1950; Birds Come Flying to Us, 1957; Transformed Land, 1959; Conquered Horizons, 1962; Spring in the Seaside Home, 1973. Contbr. to: September; PlamAk; Nasha Rodina; Prostori; Lit. Front; Rabotnichesko Delo. Mbrships: PEN; Union of Bulgarian Writers; Union of Cultural Workers. Hons: Dimitrov Prize, 1952; Prize, Union of Bulgarian Writers; Dimitrov Young Communist League Prize, 1957; Honoured Worker in Culture, 1957; Award, Bulgarian Lit. Inst. Address: Sofia-13, kv. Iztok, bl.54, Bulgaria.

SLAVITT, David Rytman, pen name SUTTON, Henry, b. 23 Mar. 1935, White Plains, N.Y., USA. Writer. Educ: B.A., Yale Univ., 1956; M.A., Columbia Univ., 1957. Publs: (poetry) Suits for the Dead, 1961; The Carnivore, 1965; Day Sailing, 1969; Child's Play, 1972; Vital Signs, 1975; (novels) Rochelle, 1966; The Exhibitionist, 1967; Feel Free, 1968; The Voyeur, 1969; Anagrams, 1970; Vector, 1970; ABCD, 1972; The Liberated, 1973; The Outer Mongolian, 1973; The Killing of the King, 1974; Trans., The Eclogues & Georgics of Virgil, 1972. Contbr. to: Kenyon Review; Esquire; Yale Review; Partisan Review; Southern Review; Ga. Review. Address: Box 325, Harwich, MA 02645, USA.

SLAVOV, George, b. 15 Aug. 1932, Svishtov, Bulgaria. Journalist. Educ: Grad., Engl. Philol., Sofia State Univ., 1956. Publs: (all transls. into Bulgarian) Langston Hughes, I Am America, Too, 1962; Sherwood Anderson, Winesburg, Ohio, & Other Tales, 1963; Walt Whitman, Leaves of Grass, 1964; Stephen Crane, The Red Badge of Courage, 1965; Modern English Short Stories, 1965; E. A. Poe, Tales of Mystery & Imagination, 1966; Short Stories from All Over the World, 1967; Modern American Short Stories, 1969. Contbr. to: Radio Sofia; num. Bulgarian jrnls. Mbrships. incl: Am. br., Writers in Exile, PEN. Hons: Best Poetry & Best Prose Transl. Awards, 1965. Address: 8 Munich 40, Osterwaldstr. 73/W.81, W. Germany.

SLAVSON, Samuel R., b. 25 Dec. 1890, The Ukraine, Russia. Group Psychotherapist. Educ: B.S., Cooper Union; Columbia Coll. & Schl. of Educ., Columbia Univ., N.Y. Publs. incl: Recreation & the Total Personality, 1946; The Practice of Group Therapy, 1947; Child-Centered Group Guidance of Parents, 1958; A Textbook of Analytic Group Psychotherapy, 1964; Reclaiming the Delinquent, 1965; Group Psychotherapy for Children: A Textbook, 1974. Contbr. to psychol. jrnls. Mbr., profl. orgs. Recip., num. acad. hons. Address: 321 E. 18th St., N.Y., NY 10003, USA.

SLAVUTYCH, Yar, b. 11 Jan. 1918, Blahodatne, Ukraine. Author; Educator. Educ: B.Ed., Pedagogic Inst. of Zaporizhja, 1940; M.A., Univ. of Pa., USA, 1954; Ph.D., 1955. Publs: Moderna ukrajins'ka poezija, 1950; The Muse in Prison, 1956; Conversational Ukrainian, 1959, 4th ed., 1973; Shevchenkova poetyke, 1964; L'Ukrainian Parlé, 1968, 1969; (verse) Oasis, 1959; Trofeji 1938-1963, 1963; Mudroshchi mandriv, 1972; The Conquerors of the Prairies, 1974; (compiler & ed.) Pivnichne siajvo, 5 vols., 1964-1971; Zakhidnokanads'kyj zbirnyk, 2 vols., 1973, 1975.

Mbrships. incl: Slavic Bibliographer, MLA; VP, Can. Inst. of Onomastic Scis. Hons. incl: Lit. Prize for Poetry, 1951; Shevchenko Medal, 1974. Address: 72 Westbrook Dr., Edmonton, Alta. T6J 2E1, Can.

SLEIGH, Barbara de Riemer, b. 9 Jan. 1906, Birmingham, UK. Writer. Educ: W. Bromwich Art Schl., Staffs.; Art Tchr's. Trng. Coll. Publs. incl: (juvenile) Carbonel, 1955; The Patchwork Quilt, 1956; The Singing Wreath, 1957; The Seven Days, 1958; The Kingdom of Carbonel, 1959; No One Must Know, 1962; North of Nowhere, 1964; Jessamy, 1967; Pen, Penny, Tuppence, 1968; The Snowball, 1969; West of Widdershins, 1971; Ninety Nine Dragons, 1974; Funny Peculiar, 1975; (adult) The Smell of Privet; & num. radio plays, stories etc. Mbrships: PEN; Nat. Book League; Soc. Authors. Address: 18 Mount Ave., London W5 2RG, UK.

SLOAN, Patrick Alan, pen name SLOAN, Pat, b. 19 May 1908, Gosforth, UK. Lecturer. Educ: B.A., Univ. of Cambridge. Publs: Soviet Democracy, 1937; Russia Without Illusions, 1938; How the Soviet State is Run, 1941; Russia Friend or Foe? , 1939; Russia in Peace & in War, 1941; Russia Resists, 1941; Guide to Economics, 1970; Marx & the Orthodox Economists, 1972; Ed., John Cornford — A Memoir, 1938. Contbr. to: Quarterly Review; Contemporary Review. Mbrships: Gen. Sec., Brit. Soviet Friendship Soc., 1951-59, VP, 1960—; Chmn., Educ. Comm., S. Suburban Coop Soc., 1974—. Address: 1 Bucks Cross Cottages, Chelsfield Village, Orpington, Kent BR6 7RN, UK.

SŁOBODNIK, Włodzimierz, b. 19 Sept. 1900, Nouwoukrainka, USSR. Poet; Translator of World Poetry; Satirist; Writer for Children. Educ: Univ. of Warsaw, Poland. Publs. incl: Evening's Unquietude, 1937; House in Fergana, 1946; Collected Poetry, 1948; New Poetry, 1952; Imaginary Travels, 1957; The Weight of Earth, 1959; Letters from Paris, 1964; Song for Goodnight, 1965; Roses of the Light, 1968; Colours Collecting, 1973. Contbr. to var. lit. jrnls. Mbrships: Polish Writer's Union; PEN. Hons: Kt.'s Cross, 1953, Off.'s Cross, 1967, Polonia Restituta Order; Lodź City Award, 1956. Address: 00-355 Warsaw, ul.Tamka 34a m.lo, Poland.

SLONIMSKI, Antoni, b. 15 Oct. 1895, Warsaw, Poland. Writer. Educ: Acad. of Fine Arts, Warsaw & Munich. Publs. incl: (poetry) Harmonja; Sonety; Parada; Godzina Poezji; Alarm Liryki; Popiol i wiatr; (plays) Rodzina; Murzyn Warszawski; Wieza Babel; (other publs.) Heretyk na ambonie; Jedna strona medalu; Kroniki tygodniowe 1927-39; Artykuly pieraszej potrzeby; Zalatwione odmownie; Torpeda czasu; Alfabet wspomnien, 1974. Mbr., Polish Writers' Union, (Chmn., 1956-59). Hons: State Prize, 1955; Lit. Prize, Warsaw, 1956. Address: Aleja Roz 6 m. 13, Warsaw, Poland.

SLOSSON, Preston William, b. 2 Sept. 1892, Laramie, Wyo., USA. Professor of History. Educ: B.S., 1912, M.A., 1913, Ph.D., 1916, Columbia Univ. Publs: The Decline of the Chartist Movement, 1916; Twentieth Century Europe, 1927; The Great Crusade & After, 1930; Europe Since 1870, 1935; The Growth of European Civilization (w. others), 1942; History of the English-speaking Peoples (w. R. Mowat), 1943; From Washington to Roosevelt (w. L. Slosson), 1950; Europe Since 1815, 1954; The History of Our World (w. others), 1959; Shorter works, pamphlets, etc. Contbr. to profl. jrnls. Address: 2101 Devonshire Rd., Ann Arbor, MI 48104, USA.

SLUNG, Louis Sheaffer, pen name, SHEAFFER, Louis, b. 18 Oct. 1912, Louisville, Ky., USA. Writer. Educ: Univ. of N.C., 1930-31. Publs: O'Neill, Son & Playwright, 1968; O'Neill, Son & Artist, 1973. Mbr., Authors League of Am. Hons: Pulitzer Prize for Biog., 1974; Geo. Freeley Award of Theatre Lib. Assn., 1969; Guggenheim Fellowships, 1959, 1961 & 1969; Grants-in-aid, Am. Coun. of Learned Socs., 1960 & 1961; Grant, Nat. Endowment for Humanities, 1971. Address: c/o Little, Brown & Co., 34 Beacon St., Boston, MA 02106, USA.

SMART, John Jamieson Carswell, b. 16 Sept. 1920, Cambridge, UK. Reader in Philosophy. Educ: M.A., Glasgow Univ.; B.Phil., Queen's Coll., Oxford. Publs: Philosophy & Scientific Realism, 1963; Between Science & Philosophy, 1968; Utilitarianism for & Against (w. Bernard Williams), 1973; Ed., Problems of Space & Time, 1964. Contbr. to: Ency. of Philos.; Ency. Britannica, 1974; var. philos. jrnls. & vols. of essays. Mbrships: Fellow, Aust. Acad. of Humanities. Address: 64 Sunnyside Crescent, Wattle Glen, Vic., Australia 3096.

SMART, Roderick Ninian, b. 6 May 1927, Cambridge, UK. Professor of Religious Studies. Educ: B.A., 1952, B.Phil., 1954, Oxford Univ. Publs. incl: Reasons & Faiths, 1958; Doctrine & Argument in Indian Philosophy, 1964; Secular Education & the Logic of Religion, 1968; The Yogi & the Devotee, 1968; The Philosophy of Religion, 1970; The Concept of Worship, 1972; The Phenomenon of Religion, 1973; The Science of Religion & the Sociology of Knowledge, 1973; Mao, 1974. Contbr. to: Mind; Philos.; Monist; Relig.; Relig. Studies; etc. Mbr., num. relig. & philos. socs. Recip., Hon. D.H.L., Loyola Univ., Chgo. Address: Dept. of Relig. Studies, Univ. of Lancaster, Cartmel Coll., Bailrigg, Lancaster, UK.

SMELIK, Klaas, b. 10 Sept. 1897, Den Helder, Netherlands. Chief Mercantile Marine Engineer; Author; Playwright. Publs. incl: Always the Sea is Calling, 1938; Dutchmen Fishing in the Polar Sea; Woman in Front of the Bow; A Fleet Surrenders, 1940; Tempest over the Oceans; Hudson Nocturne, 1946; Behind the Bow; (radio plays) People along the Flood-line; Tempest Weather; Rotten Boiler; Lost Tide; (stage & TV plays) The Wreck of the Eppie Reina; M.S. Two Brethren; Sailors Ashore; Bound Home. Contbr. to sev. jrnls. Mbrships: V.V.L. (Dutch Writers' Soc.); Soc. of Stage, Radio & TV Writers. Address: Vondelstraat 180, Amsterdam, Netherlands.

SMELIK-KIGGEN, Josephine Maria Antonette, b. 18 Nov. 1913, The Hague, Netherlands. Writer. Publs: Maarten Kwak; Billy de Bever; Robby de zeehond. Contbr. to sev. jrnls. Mbrships: Soc. of Writers; Soc. of Stage, Radio & TV Writers. Recip., big Italian prize for radio work, 1936. Address: Vondelstraat 180, Amsterdam, Netherlands.

SMIDT, Kristian, b. 20 Nov. 1916, Sandefjord, Norway. Professor of English Literature; Author. Educ: Cand.philol., 1939, Dr.philos, 1949, Univ. of Oslo. Publs. incl: Poetry & Belief in the Work of T. S. Eliot, 1949, 2nd ed., 1961; James Joyce & the Cultic Use of Fiction, 1955, 2nd ed., 1959; The Tragedy of King Richard III: Parallel Texts, 1969; Memorial Transmission & Quarto Copy in Richard III, 1970; Konstfuglen og Nattergalan (essays), 1972; The Importance of Recognition, 1973. Contbr. to: Engl. Studies. Mbrships. incl: Norwegian Acad. of Arts & Scis.; Norwegian Authors' Soc.; Societas Johnsoniana, Oslo. Recip., Folger Shakespeare Lib. Fellowship, 1960-61. Address: Severin Ytrebergsgate 4, 9000 Tromsø, Norway.

SMILJANIĆ, Radomir, b. 20 Apr. 1934, Svetozarevo, Yugoslavia. Writer; Sociologist; Simultaneous Interpreter. Educ: Dip., Belgrade Philos. Univ. Publs: Alkarski dan (stories), 1964; Martinov izlazak (novel), 1965; Vojnikov put (novel), 1967; Mirno doba (novel), 1969; Neko je oklevetao Hegela (novel), 1973; Isidor, Where Are You? (play); The Case of a Champion (play), 1974; U Andima Hegelovo telo (novel), 1975. Contbr. to jrnls. Mbr., profl. orgs. Recip. sev. lit. awards. Address: Bogdana Zerajića 24/1, 11090 Belgrade, Yugoslavia.

SMIT, Gabriel, b. 25 Feb. 1910, Utrecht, Netherlands. Journalist. Publs: 12 volumes of poetry, 1931-74; Psalmen (complete version of the 150 Psalms in poetry), 1952; transls. of sev. books by Romano Guardini; Gedichten (collected poems), 1975; Dichterlyk Grensverreer (transls. of Engl., French, German, Italian & Spanish poetry), 1975. Contbr. to Dutch Radio. Hons: Amsterdam Poetry Prize, 1961; Hilversum Cultural Prize, 1962; Marianne Philips Prize for Elder Authors, 1971. Address: Gooiergracht 161, Laren N.H., Netherlands.

SMITH, Anthony Charles, pen name SMITH, A. C. H., b. 31 Oct. 1935, Kew, UK. Writer. Educ: M.A., Cambridge Univ. Publs: The Crowd, 1965; Zero Summer, 1971; Orghast at Persepolis, 1972; Paper Voices, 1975. Contbr. to: New Soc.; Transatlantic Review; Listener; Times; Daily Telegraph; Sunday Times; Observer; BBC; HTV. Mbrships: Writers' Guild; Lit. Advsry. Panel, S.W. Arts. Recip., Arts Coun. Writing Awards, 1970-71 & 1974-75. Address: 21 W. Shrubbery, Bristol BS6 6TA, UK.

SMITH, Anthony John Francis, b. 30 Mar. 1926, Cookham, Berks., UK. Writer. Educ: M.A.(Oxon.). Publs: Blind White Fish in Persia, 1953; High Street Africa, 1961; Throw Out Two Hands, 1963; The Body, 1968; The Seasons, 1970; The Dangerous Sort, 1970; Beside The Seaside, 1972; The Human Pedigree, 1975. Mbr. & Pres., Brit. Balloon & Airship Club. Address: 9 Steele's Rd., London NW3, UK.

SMITH, Bernard William, b. 3 Oct. 1916, Sydney, Australia. Art Historian. Educ: Warburg Inst., Univ. of London, UK, 1949-50; B.S., Univ. of Sydney, Aust., 1953; Ph.D., Aust. Nat. Univ. Publs: Place, Taste & Tradition, 1945; Ed., Education Through Art in Australia, 1958; European Vision & the South Pacific, 1960; Australian Painting, 1962; Architectural Character of Glebe, Sydney (co-author), 1972; Ed., Concerning Contemporary Art, 1973. Mbrships: Fellow, Aust. Acad. of Humanities; Pres., Glebe Soc., Sydney, 1969-70, 1974-75. Recip., Ernest Scott Prize for Aust. Hist., 1962. Address: 23 Avenue Rd., Glebe, NSW, Australia 2037.

SMITH, Clifford Neal, b. 30 May 1923, Wakita, Okla., USA. Writer; University Professor. Educ: B.S., M.A. Publs: Federal Land Series, vol. I, 1972, vol. II, 1973; Handbook of German-American Genealogical Research, 2 vols., forthcoming. Contbr. to: Nat. Geogl. Soc. Quarterly (Ed.); III. State Geneal. Soc. Quarterly; Friends Jrnl.; Bus. Hist.; etc. Mbrships. incl: Sons Revolution; Sons Am. Revolution; Soc. Descendants Col. Clergy; Nat. Geneal. Soc.; III. State Geneal. Soc. (Fndr. Mbr.). Hons: Gold Medal Extraordinary contbn. geneal. awarded by III. State Geneal. Soc., 1974; Cert. recognition servs. geneal. as a sci. by Am. Soc. Geneals., 1973. Address: 594 W. Lincoln Highway, DeKalb, IL 60115, USA.

SMITH, C. U., pen name CROWBATE, Ophelia Mae, b. 29 July 1901, Seattle, Wash., USA. Writer. Publs: If the Shoe Fits Wear It, 1962; Through Hell in a Hand Basket, 1963; Hello! Hello! Party Line, 1965; The Morning & the Evening, 1967; Ram Rod, 1970; Smittys Shorts, 1972; From an Owls Nest; The Facts of Life (monthly sheet of poetry). Contbr. to: K.T.W. Radio, Seattle, Wash.; num. mags. & newspapers. Mbrships: Am. Soc. of Composers, Authors & Publrs.; Poetry Soc. of S.C.; United Amateur Press; Wash. Poets Assn. Hons: Outstanding Achievement Award, Jrnl. Fiction Writing, 1974; 1st Pl., United Amateur Press Assn., 1974. Address: P.O. Box 636, Winslow, Bainbridge Island, WA 98110, USA.

SMITH, David Elvin, b. 7 Feb. 1939, Bakersfield, Calif., USA. Physician. Publs. incl: Drug Abuse Papers, 1969; The New Social Drug: Medical, Legal & Cultural Perspectives on Marijuana, 1970; The Free Clinic: Community Approaches to Health Care & Drug Abuse (co-author), 1972; It's So Good, Don't Even Try It Once: Heroin in Perspective (co-author), 1972; Drugs in the Classroom (co-author), 1973; Uppers & Downers (co-author), 1973. Contbr. to profl. jrnls.; Fnd. Ed., Jrnl. of Psychedelic Drugs. Mbr., profl. & civic orgs. Address: Youth Projects Inc., Haight Ashbury Free Medical Clinic, 1698 Haight St., San Fran., CA 94117, USA.

SMITH, Delphia Frazier, b. 24 Apr. 1921, Mammoth Spring, Ark., USA. Poet; Artist; Musician; Speaker. Publs. incl: Along Life's Way, 1961; Profiles & Footprints, 1972; Winged Thoughts, 1972; Daffodils in the Snow, 1973; Patches & Ruffles, 1973; To Catch a Dream, 1973; Brocade & Denim, 1974; Out of the Mist, 1974; Song of the Wind, 1974; Bright Remnants, 1974; Voice of the Dove, 1974; Finger of Life, 1974; Splintered Prisms, 1974; Ribbons of Thought, 1974. Contbr. to: Poet; Japan Forum; sev. anthols. Mbrships. incl: Int. Poetry Soc.; Poets' Congress; Poets Hall; Japan Forum; Citizens for Decent Lit.; World Poetry Soc. Hons. incl: Silver Medal & Dip. of Hon., Cultural Club, SS Crose, Italy, 1972; Disting. Serv. Citation, World Poetry Soc., 1972; num. certs. of achievement. Address: 202 9th St., Mammoth Spring, AR 72554, USA.

SMITH, Denison Langley, b. 2 Feb. 1924, Cheltenham, UK. Librarian, Oxford Polytechnic. Educ: M.A. (mod. langs.), Cambridge Univ., 1948. Publs: College Library Administration (w. E. G. Baxter), 1965; How to Find Out in Architecture, 1967; trans: Detail 5 (architecture), 1972. Contbr. to var. educl. & lib. jrnls. Mbr., Coun., Lib. Assn., 1971-73. Address: 40 Sunderland Ave., Oxford, UK.

SMITH, Dodie, pen name till 1935 ANTHONY, C. L., Dramatist; Novelist. Educ: Royal Acad. Dramatic Art. Publs. incl: (plays) Autumn Crocus, prod. 1931; Call It a Day, prod. 1935; Bonnet Over the Windmill, prod. 1937; Dear Octopus, prod. 1938; Lovers & Friends, prod. USA, 1943; Letter from Paris, prod. 1952; Amateur Means Lover, prod. 1961; var. collects. of plays publd.; (novels) I Capture the Castle, USA, 1948, UK, 1949; The Town in Bloom, UK & USA, 1965; It Ends with Revelations, UK & USA, 1967; A Tale of Two Families, UK & USA, 1970; (juvenile) The 101 Dalmations, UK, 1956, USA, 1957. Address: The Barretts, Finchingfield, Essex, UK.

SMITH, Dorothy Cameron, pen name GORDON, Cameo, b. St. Catharines, Ont., Can. Journalist. Educ: Writing Courses, Shaw Schls., Toronto & McMaster Univ., Hamilton, Ont. Contbr. to: Can. Children's Annual; A New Can. Anthol.; N. Am. Book of Verse; Music Unheard; Edmonton, & Montreal Yr. Books; Woman's Weekly; Woman & Home; Chatelaine, Toronto; Saturday Night, Toronto; Toronto Star; Toronto Globe & Mail; Spectator; Buffalo Evening News; St. Catharines Standard; Stoney Creek News; Artifact, Hamilton; Good Housekeeping, N.Y.; Weight Watchers, N.Y.; Ideals, USA; United Ch. Publs., Toronto; etc. Address: 52 Mountain Ave. N, Stoney Creek, Ont. L8G 3N9, Can.

SMITH, Dwight Moody, Jr., b. 20 Nov. 1931, Murfreesboro, Tenn., USA. University Professor. Educ: B.A., Davidson Coll., 1954; B.D., Duke Univ., 1957; M.A., 1958, Ph.D., 1961, Yale Univ. Publs: The Composition & Order of the New Testament, 1965; Anatomy of the New Testament, 1969, revised 1974. Contbr. to: The Use of the Old Testament in the New & Other Essays, 1972; New Testament Studies; Jrnl. of Biblical Lit.; Interpretation; Jrnl. of Relig. Mbrships. incl: Soc. of Bible Lit.; Soc. for Relig. in Higher Educ.; Studiorum Novi Testamenti Societas. Address: 2728 Spencer St., Durham, NC 27705, USA.

SMITH, Edward Ernest, pen name LINDALL, Edward, b. 30 July 1915, Adelaide, Australia. Novelist. Publs: Stranger Among Friends, 1956; No Place To Hide, 1959; The Killers of Karawala, 1961; Springs of Violence, 1963; A Kind of Justice, 1964; Northward the Coast, 1966; A Time Too Soon, 1967; The Fires of Kiwai, 1968; Roar of the Lion, 1969; A Gathering of Eagles, 1970; Mission to Lalavandi, 1970; The Last Refuge, 1972; A Lively Form of Death, 1972; Death & the Maiden, 1973; Search for Tomorrow, 1974; A Day for Angels, 1975. Contbr. to: Saturday Evening Post; Argosy; Esquire; Cosmopolitan; John Bull. Address: 6 Rutland Ave., Brighton, S. Australia 5048.

SMITH, Elizabeth Mary Hunter, pen names LORING, Lucinda; HUNTER, Mary, b. 25 Nov. 1907, Edinburgh, UK. Donkey Breeder; Writer. Educ: Edinburgh Univ.; Dip., Edinburgh Coll. Domestic Sci. Publs: The Jack Russell or Working Terrier, 1964; Delinquent Dogs (forthcoming). Contbr. to: Farmer's Wkly.; Dog Press; etc. Mbr., Soc. Authors. Address: Little Bollingham, Kington, Hereford HR5 3LE, UK.

SMITH, Elton Edward, b. 9 Nov. 1915, NYC, USA. University Professor; Pastor. Educ: B.S., N.Y. Univ., 1937; B.D., Andover Newton Theol. Schl., 1939; S.T.M., Harvard Divinity Schl., 1940; D.D., Linfield Coll., 1955; M.A., 1959, Ph.D., 1961, Syracuse Univ. Publs: The Two Voices: A Tennyson Study, 1964; William Godwin (w. E. G. Smith), 1965; Louis MacNeice, 1970. Contbr. to: Publs. of MLA; Watchman Examiner; The Student; Victorian Newsletter; Oracle; Clio; Victorian Poetry; Newsletter, Conf. on Christianity & Lit. Mbrships. incl: MLA; South Atlantic Mod. Lang. Assn. Recip., var. acad. hons. Address: 402 W. Oak Dr., Lakeland, FL 33803, USA.

SMITH, Emma, b. 21 Aug. 1923, Newquay, Cornwall, UK. Writer. Publs: Maiden's Trip; The Far Cry; Emily; Out of Hand; Emily's Voyage; No Way of Telling. Hons: Atlantic Award; John Llewellyn Rhys Mem. Prize; James Tait Black Mem. Prize. Address: c/o Peter Janson-Smith, 31 Newington Green, London N16 9PU, UK.

SMITH, Frederick E(screet), b. 4 Apr. 1922, Hull, Yorks., UK. Author; Playwright. Publs: Of Masks & Minds, 1954; Laws Be Their Enemy, 1955; 633 Squadron, 1956; Lydia Tredennis, 1957; The Sin & the Sinners, 1958; The Grotto of Tiberius, 1961; The Devil Behind Me, 1962; The Storm Knight, 1967; A Killing for the Hawks, 1967; The Wider Sea of Love, 1969; Waterloo, 1970; The Tomented, 1974; over 80 short stories. Contbr. to leading mags. Mbrships: Writers' Guild of GB; Pathfinders, London. Recip., Mark Twain Lit. Award, 1967. Address: 3 Hathaway Rd., Southbourne, Bournemouth, Dorset, UK.

SMITH, G. E. Kidder, b. 1 Oct. 1913, Birmingham, Ala., USA. Architect; Author. Educ: A.B., 1935, M.F.A., 1938, Princeton Univ. Publs: Brazil Builds (co-author), 1943; Switzerland Builds, 1950; Sweden Builds, 1950, revised ed., 1957; Italy Builds, 1955; The New Architecture of Europe, 1961; The New Churches of Europe, 1964. Contbr. to: Ency. Britannica; profl. jrnls. Mbr., Soc. of Archtl. Histns. Hons: Order of Southern Cross, Brazil, for Brazil Builds, &

exhib., 1943; Gold Medal (ENIT), Italian Govt., for Italy Builds, 1956; Conover Award for New Churches of Europe, 1965. Address: 163 E. 81st St., N.Y., NY 10028, USA.

SMITH, George Winston, b. 10 June 1911, Dixon, Ill., USA. Teacher. Educ: A.B., 1934, M.A., 1935, Univ. of Ill.; Ph.D., Univ. of Wis., 1939. Publs: Henry C. Carey & American Sectional Conflict, 1951; The Unchosen (co-author), 1962; Medicines for the Union Army: The U.S. Laboratories during the Civil War, 1962; Life in the North during the Civil War (co-author), 1966; Chronicles of the Gringos: The U.S. Army in the Mexican War, 1946-48, 1968; num. histl. articles. Address: 506 Tulane NE, Albuquerque, NM 87106, USA.

SMITH, Godfrey, b. 1926, London, UK. Associate Editor, Sunday Times. Educ: M.A., Worcester Coll., Oxford Univ. Publs: The Flaw in the Crystal, 1954; The Friends, 1957; The Business of Loving, 1961; The Network, 1965. Mbrships: Pres., Oxford Writers Club; Oxford Union. Agent: Curtis Brown. Address: 6 Abbey Gdns., London NW8, UK.

SMITH, Helen C., b. 7 June 1903, Chgo., Ill., USA. Instructor; Author. Educ: B.A., Cal. State Coll., 1926; M.S., 1962, Ph.D., 1965, Christian Coll.; Ed.D. & D.D., 1968-69; Ordained, 1968. Publs. incl: Laughing Child, 3 vols.; Off the Record; From the Countryside; Stars in My Eyes; Chiaroscura; Mirrors of Faith; But Not Yet! Contbr. of poetry to num. anthols., & articles & stories to US & for. mags. Mbrships. incl: Life Mbr. & Hon. Life Mbr., Bd. of Dirs., Wis. Reg. Writers' Assn.; Life Mbr., Coun. for Wis. Writers; Wis. Acad. of Scis., Arts & Letters; Life Mbr., Am. Lit. Assn. Hons. incl: 1st Award, jvnle. fiction, AAUW Nat. Writing Proj., 1967; Elected Poet Laureate (Am.-Visayan), 1967; 1st Award, Fleetwood Music & Arts Fest., UK, 1972; Silver Platter Award, Wis. Reg. Writers' Assn., 1973. Address: 409 Lincoln St., Evansville, WI 53536, USA.

SMITH, Iain Crichton, b. 1 Jan. 1928, Glasgow, Scotland, UK. Teacher. Educ: M.A., Aberdeen Univ. Publs: Thistles & Roses, 1961; The Law & the Grace, 1965; Consider the Lilies, 1968; The Last Summer, 1969; Survival Without Error, 1970; My Last Duchess, 1971; Selected Poems, 1970; Love Poems & Elegies, 1972; The Black & the Red, 1973. Contbr. to: Times Lit. Supplement; Listener; Spectator; etc. Hons: PEN Award; Var. Scottish Arts Coun. Awards. Address: 42 Combie St., Oban, Argyll, UK.

SMITH, Ivan Harford, b. 1 Sept. 1931, Perth, Australia. Writer. Educ: B.A., Univ. of W. Aust. Publs: The Death of a Wombat, 1972; Dingo-King, in preparation 1975; The Die-hard (w. Jocelyn Smith), in preparation 1975. Contbr. to: Aust. Broadcasting Commn. Mbrships: Aust. Soc. of Authors; Aust. Actors' Equity. Hons: Italia Prize, 1959; Ohio State Award, 1960; Aust. Nat. Film Inst. Award, 1969; Aust. Writers' Guild Award, 1970. Address: 65 Fairlawn Ave., Turramurra, NSW, Australia 2074.

SMITH, Kathleen Joan, b. 25 June 1929, Luton, UK. Writer; Broadcaster; Lecturer. Publs: Twelve Months, Mrs. Brown, 1964 (BBC radio play, 1968); A Cure for Crime, 1965; The Young & the Pity, 1966 (BBC radio play 1970); Devils' Delight, 1968; The Company of God, 1975; 3 TV plays, A Regular Friend, 1973; The Slap, 1974; The Prison Cat, 1975. Contbr. to: Thames TV; London Weekend TV; BBC; Daily Telegraph; etc. Address: Felin Faesog, Clynnog, Caernarvon, Gwynedd LL54 5DD, UK.

SMITH, Leslie Allan, b. 1922, Walthamstow, Essex, UK. Educational Consultant. Educ: Waltham Forest Tech. Coll.; Forest Trng. Coll.; B.Sc., London Schl. Econs. Publs: The British People 1902-1968, (co-author), 1970; The British Government & International Affairs (co-author), 1973; Towards a Freer Curriculum (co-author), 1974; Tradition & Change in Contemporary Education, (Ed.) 1975. Contbr. to: IDEAS; Pilot Courses for Tchrs. Mbrships: Soc. of Authors; var. educl. comms. & advsry. bodies. Address: 1 Fernhill Ct., Forest Rd., Walthamstow, London E17 3RP, UK.

SMITH, Leslie Wilfred, pen names WATKINS-SMITH, Leslie; MANDEVILLE, Wm.; BELLSMITH, Wm.; ARROWSMITH, Wm., b. 18 Apr. 1914, Chatham, Kent, UK. Clergyman. Educ: B.Sc., & M.A., Drury Coll., Southwestern Mo. State Univ. Publs: Crusader of the Airways (biog.), 1955; High Adventure in Tibet (ghost-writer for David Plymire), 1956-57. Contbr. to: Christianity Today; The Pentecostal Evangel; Christian Sci. Monitor; etc. also to sev. poetry anthols. Mbrships. incl:

Int. Clover Poetry Assn.; Mo. Writer's Guild. Recip., sev. poetry awards. Address: 921 N.Weller Ave., Springfield, MO 65802, USA.

SMITH (Mrs.), Mary J. P., pen name DREWERY, Mary, b. 9 May 1918, Malpas, Monmouths., UK. Housewife. Educ: Westfield Coll., Univ. of London, 1936-39. Publs: For children: Rebellion in the West, 1962; Devil in Print, 1963; The Silvester Wish, 1966; A Donkey Called Haryat, 1967; A Candle for St. Georgios, 1969; Where Four Winds Meet, 1971; Biography: Window on my Heart, 1973; Richard Wurmbrand: The Man Who Came Back, 1974. Mbrships. Soc. of Authors; Croydon Writers' Circle (Vice-Chmn.). Address: 20 Furze Lane, Purley, Surrey CR2 3EG, UK.

SMITH, Nila Banton, b. Altona, Mich., USA. Author; College Professor. Educ: B.A., Univ. of Chgo.; M.A., Ph.D., Columbia Univ. Publs: Learning to Read Series, 7 books, 1955-59; The Best in Children's Literature (co-author), 8 books, 1959-61; Read Faster & Get More from Your Reading (for adults), 1962; Reading Instruction for Today's Children, 1965, revised ed., 1974; American Reading Instructions, 1965; Be a Better Reader, 9 books, 1969-74 also sev. monographs. Contbr. of over 200 articles to profl. jrnls. Address: 800 W. 1st St., Apt. 1403, L.A., CA 90012, USA.

SMITH, Ophia Delilah, b. 19 Feb. 1891, Walnut Grove, Mo., USA. Writer; Lecturer; Piano Teacher. Educ: Drury Coll.; Oxford Coll. for Women, Ohio; Miami Univ., Ohio; Kan. City Conserv. of Music. Publs. incl: Southwestern Ohio: The Miami Valleys (w. W. E. Smith), 2 vols.; Buckeye Titan; Fair Oxford; Old Oxford Houses; Giles Richards & His Times; Johnny Appleseed (co-author); Contributions of the Puritans. Contbr. to num. profl. jrnls. Mbrships. incl: Nat. League of Am. Pen Women; Martha Kinney Cooper Lib. Assn. Hons. incl: 1st Prize, Histl. Writing, Nat. League of Am. Pen Women; Ohioana Lib. Fellowship, w. husband, W. E. Smith; Award, Gen. Conven., Ch. of New Jerusalem, for histl. articles. Address: 235 Lyell St., Los Altos, CA 94022, USA.

SMITH, Richard C., b. 10 Dec. 1948, Anthony, Kan., USA. Farmer. Author. Something From Inside Me, 1971. Contbr. to: Lincoln Log; Prairie Poet; Mod. Images; Reach Out; World Poet; Am. Poet; Creative Review; Poetry Prevue; United Poet; (anthols.) Southwest Poetry, 1971; Best in Poetry; The Prairie Poet Collect.; The Birth of Day; APFS Anthol., 1972; Poetry of the Yr., 1972. Mbrships: Am. Poetry Fellowship Soc.; Kan. Authors Club; Fellowship of Profl. Poets; Ill. State Poetry Soc. Recip., Cert. of Merit, Am. Poetry Fellowship Soc., 1973. Address: RR 1, Amorita, OK 73719, USA.

SMITH, (The Rev.) Robert Dickie, b. 13 Aug. 1928, Framingham, Mass., USA. Catholic Priest. Educ: A.B., Harvard Univ., 1949. Publs: The Mark of Holiness, 1961; Comparative Miracles, 1965; The Elegance of Catholic Faith, 1975. Address: 43 Sycamore Rd., S. Weymouth, MA 02190, USA.

SMITH, Robert Wayne, b. 3 Jan. 1926, Kokomo, Ind., USA. College Professor. Educ: Ind. State Univ.; A.B., 1950, M.A., 1951, Univ. Southern Calif.; Ph.D., Univ. Wis., 1957; Univ. Mich. Publs: Gen. Ed., Christ & the Modern Mind, 1972; Art of Rhetoric in Alexandria, 1974; & over 200 biogl. entries to Ancient Greek & Roman Rhetoricians, 1968. Contbr. to: Quarterly Jrnl. Speech; Anglican Theol. Review; Speech Monographs; Western Speech. Am. Speech; Christianity Today; Parly. Jrnl.; Jrnlsm. Quarterly; Ctrl. States Speech Jrnl.; etc. Mbrships: Speech Communication Assn., Southern Speech Assn.; Ctrl. States Speech Assn. Recip., Rsch. Grant, Old Dominion Fund, Univ. Va., 1961. Address: 632 Wright Ave., Alma, MI 48801, USA.

SMITH, Turk (Talbot), b. 17 June 1917, Detroit, Mich., USA. Journalist; Automotive Columnist. Contbr. to: Newsweek, 1954-64; USIA, 1953—; Arizona Highways, 1970—. Mbrships. incl: Phoenix Press Club; Ariz. Press Club; Ariz. Acad. of Sci. Address: 4825 E. Piccadilly, Phoenix, Ariz., USA.

SMITH, Valerie Winifred, b. 6 Aug. 1930, Napier, NZ. Registered Nurse. Educ: Registered Nurse; Registered Maternity Nurse. Contbr. to NZ mags. & newspapers & NZ Broadcasting Corp.; Book Reviewer. Mbr., NZ Women Writers' Soc. Address: 22 Sunset St., Taupo, NZ.

SMITH, Warren Sylvester, b. 11 Mar. 1912, Bangor, Pa., USA. University Administrator. Educ: B.A., Muhlenberg Coll., Allentown, Pa., 1933; M.A., State Univ. of Iowa, 1937. Publs: Ed., The Religious Speeches of Bernard Shaw, 1963; The London Heretics, 1967; Ed., Shaw on Religion, 1967; Ed., Bernard Shaw's Plays, 1970. Contbr. to: The Christian Century; The Shaw Review (Mbr., Bd. of Eds.); The Nation. Recip., Grant-in-Aid, Am. Coun. of Learned Socs., 1965. Address: Box 66, Lemont, PA 16851, USA.

SMITH, Wilfred Cantwell, b. 21 July 1916, Toronto, Can. University Professor. Educ: B.A., Univ. of Toronto; Rsch.; St. John's Coll., Cambridge, UK, 1938-40; M.A., 1947, Ph.D., 1948, Princeton Univ., N.J., USA. Publs: Modern Islam in India, 1943, 4th ed., 1972; Islam in Modern History, 1957, 3rd ed., 1959; The Faith of Other Men, 1962, 4th ed., 1972; The Meaning & End of Religion, 1963, 2nd ed., 1965; Modernization of a Traditional Society, 1966; Questions of Religious Truth, 1967. Ed. Bd., The Muslim World. Contbr. to: The Middle E. Jrnl.; Religious Studies; Studies in Relig./Sciences religieuses. Recip., Chauveau Medal, Royal Soc. of Can. "Humanities in Can.") 1974. Address: 6010 Inglis St., Halifax, N.S., Can.

SMITH, William, b. 10 Sept. 1910, Colne, Lancs., UK. Registered Osteopath; Male Nurse; Consulting Medical Herbalist & Naturopath. Educ: Dips. in Osteopathy, Naturopathy & Bot. Med.; State Enrolled Nursing Cert.; Fellow, Nat. Inst. of Med. Herbalists. Publs: Herbs to Ease Bronchitis, 1973; Wonders in Weeds, 1975; Herbal Tissanes Etc.; Herbs for Constipation. Contbr. to: Hlth. from Herbs; Healthy Living; H.E.A.L. Mag.; World Forum; Here's Hlth.; The Brit. Herbal Pharmacopoea; etc. Mbrships: Royal Inst. of Pub. Hlth. & Hygiene; Brit. Naturopathic & Osteopathic Assn.; Nursing Soc.; Nat. Inst. Med. Herbalists. Address: Bryn Mor, off Long Lane, Scorton, Preston PR3 1DB, UK.

SMITH, William J. T., pen name FERRAR, Gul, b. 1920, Croydon, Surrey, UK. Clergyman. Educ: Chichester Theol. Coll. Publs: The King's Men, 1958; Church Furniture, 1963; Verses, 1966; Brasses— Thurrock & District, 1970; Some Papers of the Overseer, 1971; Graffiti, 1973; The Sussex Tomb, 1973; New Poets '70, 1969; Editor's Choice, 1971; The Golden Realm of Poetry, 1973. Contbr. to: New Poets '70; Stifford Witness; Essex Jrnl. Mbrships: Monumental Brass Soc.; Essex Archaeol. Soc.; Friends of Historic Essex. Address: Boreham Vicarage, Chelmsford, Essex CM3 3EG, UK.

SMITHIES, Muriel, pen names HOWE, Muriel; REDMAYNE, Barbara, b. Castleblayney, Co. Monaghan, Repub. of Ireland. Writer. Publs: 20 novels inclng. Pendragon, 1974; First Affections, 1974; Private Road to Beyond, 1975; Heatherling, 1975. Contbr. to Cumbria Mag. Mbrships: Cumbrian Lit. Grp.; Sec. Ambleside Art Soc. Address: Middle Brig How, Skelwith Bridge, Ambleside, Cumbria, UK.

SMITHSON, Norman, b. 6 Sept. 1931, Leeds, UK. Writer & Journalist. Educ: Pitman's Coll., Leeds. Publs: The World of Little Foxy, 1969; also poetry, radio plays. Contbr. to: Own Mag. N.; Dalesman; Today; Sport & Recreation; Educ. Today; Guardian; BBC radio & TV; etc. Mbrships: Nat. Union Jrnlsts.; Yorks. Poets' Assn.; Writers' Action Grp. Hons: Writers' Guild, Zita Plaque Award, 1967 for best Brit. radio drama The Three Lodgers; & Arts Coun. Awards for drama & mag. publng. Address: 55 Woodsley Rd., Leeds LS6 1SB, Yorks., UK.

SMOLAR, Boris (Ber), b. 27 May 1897, Rovno, Ukraine. Journalist. Educ: Lewis Inst., Chgo., USA; Northwestern Univ. Medill Schl. of Jrnlsm., Chgo. Publs. incl: Soviet Jewry Today & Tomorrow, 1971. Contbr. to: Jewish Telegraphic Agcy. (Ed. in-Chief Emeritus). Hons: Doct., Balt. Hebrew Coll., 1973; Alumna Pax Medal, awarded by Pope Paul VI, 1965; Silver Medal, Israel Govt.; Bronze Peace Medal & other Israel awards; establishment of Smolar Award for Excellence in Am. Jewish Jrnlsm., Coun. of Jewish Fedns. & Welfare Funds, N.Y. Address: 147 W. 79th Street, N.Y., NY 10024, USA.

SMOLLER, Sanford Jerome, b. 13 Feb. 1937, Pittsburgh, Pa., USA. Teacher of Literature. Educ: B.A., Univ. of Calif., L.A., 1962; M.A., Columbia Univ., N.Y., 1964; Ph.D., Univ. of Wis., Madison, 1972. Author, Adrift Among Geniuses: Robert McAlmon, Writer & Publisher of the Twenties, 1975. Contbr. to Modern Fiction Studies, 1969. Address: 322 Glenway St., Madison, WI 53705, USA.

SMYTH, (Brig. Rt. Hon. Sir) John George, b. 24 Oct. 1893. Military Commander (ret'd); Member of Parliament; Journalist; Author. Educ: Sandhurst. Num. publs. incl: Lawn Tennis, 1953; The Only Enemy (autobiog.), 1959; Sandhurst: A History of the Military Cadet Colleges, 1961; The Story of the Victoria Cross, 1962; Beloved Cats, 1963; Ming, 1966; The Rebellious Rani, 1966; Bolo Whistler (biog.), 1967; The Story of the George Cross, 1968; Will to Live: The Story of Dame Margot Turner, 1970; Percival & the Tragedy of Singapore, 1971; Leadership in War (1939-45), 1974; Leadership in Battle (1914-20), 1975. Contbr. to var. newspapers as mil. corres., 1943-46. Mbrships. incl: Dir., Creative Jrnls. Ltd., 1957-63; Victoria Cross Assn. (1st Chmn., 1956-71, Pres., 1966—). Hons. incl: Hon. Brig., 1943; 1st Baronet, 1955. Address: 807 Nelson House, Dolphin Sq., London SW1V 3PA, UK.

SNAITH, Stanley, b. 16 Dec. 1903, Kendal, Westmorland, UK. Author; Librarian. Educ: FLA. Publs. incl: April Morning, 1926; London Pageant, 1935; Modern Poetry (bibliog.), 1937; Stormy Harvest, 1944; Bygone Bethnal Green (w. G. F. Vale), 1948; The Common Festival, 1950; The Siege of the Matterhorn, 1956; The Special Shelf, 1958; The Lost Road, 1968; (verse) Nanga Parbat, 1949; Homage to Rilke, & The Hawthorn in the Bombed Church, 1964; BBC scripts. Contbr. to: Oxford Jr. Ency.; Ency. Britannica; num. anthols. & jrnls. Hons: S.C. Greenwood Prize, 1949; 1st Prize, Nat. Shakespearian Sonnets Competition, 1964. Address: 17 Newton Rise, Swanage, Dorset, UK.

SNEIDER, Vern, b. 6 Oct. 1916, Monroe, Mich., USA. Writer. Educ: A.B., Univ. of Notre Dame, 1940. Publs: Teahouse of the August Moon, 1951; A Pail of Oysters, 1953; A Long Way from Home, 1956; The King From Ashtabula, 1960; West of the North Star, 1972. Contbr. to: Saturday Evening Post; Holiday; Argosy; Antioch Review; Am. Sportsman; Ford Times; NY Times Book Review; NY Herald Tribune Book Review; Chgo. Tribune Book Review. Mbrships: Authors League of Am.; Detroit Press Club. Recip., Friends of Am. Writers Award, 1952. Address: 426 N. Macomb St., Monroe, MI 48161, USA.

SNELLGROVE, Laurence Ernest, b. 2 Feb. 1928, Woolwich, London, UK. Schoolteacher; Author. Educ: Tchr.'s Dip., Culham Coll., Oxford; Assoc., Coll. of Preceptors, 1953. Publs: Suffragettes & Votes for Women, 1964; Franco & Spanish Civil War, 1965; Modern World Since 1870, 1968; The Ancient World (w. R. J. Cootes), 1971; Early Modern Age, 1972; Mainstream English (w. J. R. C. Yglesias), 1974. Address: 23 Harvest Hill, E. Grinstead, Sussex RH19 4BU, UK.

SNOW, C(harles) P(ercy), (Baron Snow of Leicester), b. 15 Oct. 1905, Leicester, UK. Writer. Educ: B.Sc., 1927, M.C., 1928, Univ. Coll., Leicester; Ph.D., Cambridge Univ., 1930. Publs. incl: (novels) Strangers & Brothers, 1940; The Light & the Dark, 1947; Time of Hope, 1949; The Masters, 1951; The New Men, 1954; Homecomings, 1956; The Conscience of the Rich, 1958; The Affair, 1960; Corridors of Power, 1964; The Sleep of Reason, 1968; Last Things, 1970 (series of 11, also publd. in USA); The Malcontents, UK & USA, 1972; (non-fiction) Variety of Men, UK & USA, 1967; Public Affairs, UK & USA, 1971; 8 plays. Mbrships. incl: F.R.S.L. Hons. incl: Black Mem. Prize, 1955; Kt., 1957; Life Peer, 1964; num. docts. & Fellowships. Address: 85 Eaton Terrace, London SW1, UK.

SNOW, Dorothy Mary Barter (Miss), b. 30 July 1897, London, UK. Teacher; Writer. Educ: B.D., King's Coll., Univ. of London; B.Litt., St. Anne's Coll., Oxford Univ.; A.K.C.; B.Sc. Publs: The Long Pursuit; Into a Far Country; David, Tony & the Bees; Fiddlers Three; The Joyous Servant (co-author). Contbr. to var. jrnls. Mbr., Soc. of Women Writers & Jrnlsts. Address: Forge House, Privett, Nr. Alton, Hants., UK.

SNOW, Helen Foster (Mrs.), pen name WALES, Nym, b. Cedar, Utah, USA. Author; Researcher. Educ: Univ. of Utah; Yenching Univ., China; Tsinghua Univ., Peking; Dip., Certified Geneal. Publs. incl: Inside Red China, 1939, 1974; Song of Ariran, 1941, 1973; China Builds for Democracy, 1941; The Chinese Labor Movement, 1945, 1970; Red Dust, 1952, revised ed., as The Chinese Communists, 1972; Historical Notes on China, 6 vols., 1961; The Land Beyond the Kuttawoo, the Madison Story, 1974; The Guilford Story, 1974. Contbr. to num. US & for. jrnls.; Book Reviewer, Peking Corres., China Wkly. Review, Shanghai, 1931-40; Book Reviewer, Sat. Review of Lit., N.Y., 1941-49. Address: 148 Mungertown Rd., Madison, CT 06443, USA.

SNOW, Lois Wheeler, b. 12 July 1920, Stockton, Calif., USA. Writer/Lecturer. Educ: B.A., Univ. of the Pacific, Calif.; Neighbourhood Playhouse of Dramatic Art, N.Y. Publs: China on Stage, 1972; A Death with Dignity, 1975. Contbr. to: Le Monde. Saturday Review of Lit.; The Nation; New Republic; Vogue Mag. Mbrships: Actors Studio, N.Y.; Actors' Equity Assn. Address: 1262 Eysins, Vaud, Switz.

SNOW, Philip Albert, b. 7 Aug. 1915, Leicester, UK. Administrator. Educ: B.A., 1937, M.A., 1940, Univ. of Cambridge. Publs: Cricket in the Fiji Islands, 1948; Visit to Schools & Universities in USA & Canada, 1964; Best Stories of the South Seas, 1967; Bibliography of Fiji, Tonga & Rotuma, 1969. Contbr. to: Dictionary of Nat. Biog.; Colonial Hist. Series; Times Lit. Supplement; Discovery; Jrnl. of Polynesian Soc.; Wisden Cricketers' Almanack; Geogl. Jrnl.; Jrnl. de la Société des Océanistes; Am. Anthropol.; The Far E. & Australasia; Transactions of Fiji Soc.; Daily Telegraph; Sunday Times. Mbrships. incl: Fellow, Royal Anthropol. Inst.; VP, Fiji Soc. Hons. incl: J.P., 1967. Address: Horton House, 6 Hillmorton Rd., Rugby, Warwickshire, UK.

SNOWDEN, Frank Martin Jr., b. 17 July 1911, York Co., Va., USA. Educator. Educ: A.B., Harvard Coll. 1932; A.M., 1933, Ph.D., 1944, Harvard Univ.; Am. Acad. in Rome, summer 1938. Publs: Blacks in Antiquity: Ethiopians in the Greco-Roman Experience, 1970, paperback ed., 1971. Contbr. to classical & educl. jrnls. Mbrships: Am. Philol. Assn.; Archaeol. Inst. of Am. Recip., Charles J. Goodwin Award of Merit, Am. Philol. Assn., 1973. Address: 4200 Mass. Ave. N.W., Apt. 415, Wash. 20018, USA.

SNYDER, Louis L., b. 4 July 1907, Annapolis, Md., USA. Educator; Historian. Educ: B.A., St. John's Coll., Annapolis, 1928; Ph.D., Univ. of Frankfurt-am-Main, Germany, 1931. Publs. incl: Race: A History of Modern Ethnic Theories, 1939; A Survey of European Civilisation, 2 vols., 1941-42; The Meaning of Nationalism, 1954; Documents of German History, 1958; The Blood & Iron Chancellor, 1967; Frederick the Great, 1970; The Making of Modern Man, 1972; The Dreyfus Case, 1973; Wendepunkte der Weltgeschichte, 1974. Gen. Ed., 116 vols. in the Van Nostrand Anvil history paperbacks. Contbr. to profl. jrnls. Hons. incl: Anisfield-Wolf Award in Race Rels., 1974; Citation, 7th Annual N.J. Writers' Conf., 1974. Address: 21 Dogwood Lane, Princeton, NJ 08540, USA.

SÖDERBERG, Sten V., b. 26 Aug. 1908, Stockholm, Sweden. Author; Journalist. Educ: Stockholm & London Univs. Publs. incl: collects. of poems & essays; Mannen som ingekände (about Alfred Nobel), 1946; Störst i Landet (novel), 1950; Vär att veta (popular sci.), 1961; Hammarskjold (biog.), 1962; Vetandets aventyr (popular sci.), 1968; History of Technology (for children), 1974. Contbr. to jrnls. Mbrships: Bd., Swedish Union of Authors; PEN. Hons. incl: Unique Prize, outstanding writer of popular sci., Acad. of Engrng. Sci., 1961. Address: Atterbomsvägen 32, 112 58 Stockholm, Sweden.

SÖDERBERG, Tom, b. 1 Dec. 1900, Stockholm, Sweden. Economic & Social Historian. Educ: Dr.phil., Univ. of Stockholm, 1932. Publs. incl: Hantverkarna i brytningstid 1820-1870, 1956; Ett hundraårigt grosshandelshus. Bendix, Josephson & Co AB, 1956; Den namnlösa medelklassen, 1956; Hantverkarna i genombrott sskedet 1870-1920; Två sekel svensk medelklass från gustaviansk tid till nutid, 1972. Contbr. to var. jrnls. Mbrships: Minerva (Swedish Union of Writers in Sci. & Arts, Pres., 1967-70); FLYCO (Authors' Unions Ctrl. Org., Pres., 1960-65). Recip., Kt. of Northern Star, 1962. Address: Karlaväg 27, 17237 Sundbyberg, Sweden.

SÖDERHJELM, Kai, pen name BERGMAN, Jonas, b. 13 Aug. 1918, Helsinki, Finland. Author. Educ: B.A., 1943; Lib. Schl. Dip., 1951. Publs: Rid mot nordväst, 1948; Nu går vi till Paris, 1949; Full belåtenhet garanteras, 1953; Mikko i kungens tjänst, 1959; Aldrig kom den sommarn, 1961; Fribiljett till äventyret, 1962, Am. ed., Free Ticket to Adventure, 1964; Hemligt uppdrag i Östersjön, 1963; Kärlek och krig, 1965; Solbacken, 1969; etc. Contbr. to Bibioteksbladet (Swedish Lib. Jrnl.); etc. Recip., Nils Holgersson Plaketten, 1960. Address: Tyghusgatan 2, S-302 32 Halmstad, Sweden.

SÖDERHOLM, Margit Charlotta, b. 17 Mar. 1905, Stockholm, Sweden. Teacher; Writer. Educ: M.A., Stockholm Univ. Publs. incl: Driver dagg faller regn (Vanish

Dew Come Rain), 1943, also filmed; Grevinna (The Countess), 1945; Where Thou Goest (Dil dugar), 1946; All jordens fröjd (All the Happiness in the World), 1948; Bröderna (The Brothers), 1950; Möte in Wien (Meeting in Vienna), 1951; Bärgad Skörd (The Harvest is In), 1952; Livets krona (The Crown of Life), 1953; Jul på Hellesta (Christmas at Hellesta), 1954; Moln över Hellesta (Clouds above Hellesta), 1955, also filmed; Resa till Delphi (Voyage to Delphi), 1956; Sommar på Hellesta (Summer at Hellesta), 1957. Recip., 1st Prize, Gt. Scandinavian Novel Competition, 1943. Address: Vartavag 37^l 11529 Stockholm, Sweden.

SOHN, Sohee, b. 12 Sept. 1917, Kyung Sung, N. Korea. Author. Educ: B.A. (Engl.), Hankook Coll. of Foreign Studies. Publs: (novels) The Valley of the Sun, 1959; The Season of Original Colours, 1962; The South Wind, 1963; Along the Valley of the Eden, 1965; Poem of the Sun, 1965; (short stories) The Story of Era, 1949; The Season of Iris Flower, 1957; Crossing the Bridge, 1965; The Sounds of Jackdaw, 1970. Contbr. to: The Han Kook Moon Hak (Korean lit.). Mbr., Korean Women Writers' Assn. (Chmn.). Hons: Lit. Prize, City of Seoul, 1961; May Lit. Prize, 1964. Address: 155 Hung-In-Dong, Sung-dong-ku, Seoul, S. Korea.

SOKOL, Anthony E., b. 28 Mar. 1897, Vienna, Austria. University Professor. Educ: Austro-Hungarian Naval Offs. Schl.; B.S., Miss. State Tchrs. Coll., USA; M.A., Ph.D., Stanford Univ.; Univ. of Vienna; Coll. of Technol., Vienna, Austria. Publs: Berühmte Forscher & Ihre Beiträge, 1938; Seapower in the Nuclear Age, 1961, Japanese transl., 1965; The Imperial & Royal Austro-Hungarian Navy; Seemacht Österreich, 1972. Contbr. to: U.S. Naval Inst. Proceedings; Brassey's Annual; Mil. Review; Mil. Affairs; Marine-Rundschau. Hons: Fulbright Professorship, Univ. of Vienna; var. grants. Address: 1641 Portola Ave., Palo Alto, CA 94306, USA.

SOKORSKI, Wlodzimierz, b. 2 July 1908, Lomza, Poland. Writer; Journalist. Educ: Warsaw Univ. Publs: (plays) Curves, 1959; Escapes, 1961; The Meeting; Silence; (other publs.) The Torn Pavement, 1936; Problems of Cultural Policy, 1947; Arts for Socialism, 1950; The Journey Diary, 1954; Drawing Thick Lines, 1958; Crumbs, 1961; The Present Day & Youth, 1963; The Modern Mass Culture, 1967; Poles of Lenino, 1971. Contbr. to Lit. Monthly, (Chief Ed.). Mbr., Polish UNESCO Comm. Hons. incl: Virtuti Militari; Order of Lenin; Banner of Labour. Address: Aleja Róz 6/5, Warsaw, Poland.

SOLÀ I DACHS, Lluís, b. 17 Jan. 1932, Barcelona, Spain. Industrialist; Writer in the Catalan Language. Educ: Textile Engr. Publs: L'Atletisme, 1965; El Be Negre, 1967; Cu-Cut!, 1967; En Patufet, 1968; Papitu, 1968; L'Esquella de la Torratxa, 1970; Xut!, 1971; Un Segle d'Humor Català, 1972. Address: Buenos Aires 15–17, 1–2, Barcelona 11, Spain.

SOLDATI, Mario, b. 17 Nov. 1906. Writer; Film Director; Actor. Educ: D.Litt.; Univs. of Turin & Columbia, USA. Publs. incl: America Primo Amore; Racconti; A Cena col Commendatore; Lettere da Capri; La Messa dei Villeggianti; Il Vero Silvestri; La Confessione; Storie di Spettri; La Busta Arancione; Le due Città, 1964; L'Attore, 1970; The Malacca Cane, 1971. Contbr. to: Il Lavoro; Il Giorno; etc. also num. films. Address: Via Cappucio 14, 20123 Milan, Italy.

SOLDEVILA ZUBIBURU, Ferran, b. 24 Oct. 1894, Barcelona, Spain. Former Professor of History; Writer. Educ: Univs. of Madrid & Barcelona. Publs. incl: La Reina Maria; Muller del Magnanim, 1928; Pere el Gran, 4 vols., 1949–; L'almirall Ramon Marquet, 1953; Historia de España, 8 vols., 1952-57, 2nd ed., 1961-64; Vida de Pere el Gran i Alfons el Liberal, 1963; Qué Cal Saber de Catalunya, 1968; Mbrships. incl: Inst. of Catalan Studies; Acad. of Letters; Int. Centre for Sardi Studies. Hons. incl: Ptaxot Prize; Prize of the Catalan Schl. of Dramatic Art. Address: Teodora Lamadrid 34, Barcelona, Spain.

SOLEV, Dimitar, b. 24 May 1930, Skopje, Yugoslavia. Journalist; Editor, Razgledi Literary Review. Educ: Fac. of Arts. Publs: Melted Snows, 1956; Whiteheath, 1957; Along the River & on the Opposite Side, 1960; The Short Spring of Mono Samonikov, 1964; Freedom's Winter, 1968; Quo Vadis Scriptor; 1971; Snails, 1974. Mbrships: Macedonian Writers' Assn.; Union of Yugoslav Writers; PEN. Hons: 11 Oct. Prize of the Repub., 1964 & 1968. Address: Dramska no. 2, 91000 Skopje, Yugoslavia.

SOLIS LLORENTE, Ramon, b. 1 Mar. 1923, Cadiz, Spain. Writer. Educ: Dr.Pol.Scis. Novels incl: La bella sirena, 1953; Los que no tienen paz, 1957; Ajena crece la yerba, 1962; Un siglo llama a la puerta, 1963; El canto de la gallina, 1965; La Eliminatoria, 1970; El dueno del miedo, 1971; Monica corazon dormido, 1974. Dir., La Estafeta Literaria, Madrid. Hons. incl: Fastenrath Award, Spanish Royal Acad. of Lang.; Nat. Lit. Prize, for Miguel de Cervantes. Address: Jorge Juan 51, 7° Izquierda, Madrid 1, Spain.

SOLMON, Lewis C., b. 17 July 1942, Toronto, Can. Economist. Educ: B.Comm., Univ. of Toronto, 1964; A.M., 1967, Ph.D., 1968, Univ. of Chgo. Publs: Economics (A Principles Text), 1972; Does College Matter? Some Evidence on the Impacts of Higher Education (Ed. w. Paul Taubman), 1973; Capital Formation by Education in 1880 & 1890, forthcoming. Contbr. to profl. jrnls. inclng: Rsch. in Higher Educ.; Sociol. of Educ.; Jrnl. of Econ. Hist.; Am. Econ. Review. Mbr., profl. orgs. Address: 1279 Casiano Rd., Los Angeles, CA 90049, USA.

SOLOMON, Goody L., b. 1 June 1929, Brooklyn, N.Y., USA. Author. Educ: B.A., Brooklyn Coll., N.Y., 1950; M.A., N.Y. Univ., 1955. Author, The Radical Consumer's Handbook, 1972. Contbr. to: Washington Star-News; Money; Woman's World; Changing Times; Barron's Weekly; Ladies' Home Jrnl.; Redbook; Stores; Modern Textiles; U.S. Consumer; Commentary Mag.; Jewish Examiner. Mbrships: Am. Newspaper Women's Club; Capitol Press Women. Address: 1712 Taylor St. N.W., DC 20011, USA.

SOLOMON, Maynard Elliott, b. 5 Jan. 1930, NYC, USA. Phonograph Record Company Proprietor & Chief Executive Officer. Educ: A.B., Brooklyn Coll., 1950. Publs: Marxism & Art, 1973; Beethoven's Immortal Beloved: Solution of a Biographical Riddle, forthcoming; The Life & Works of Beethoven, forthcoming. Contbr. to: Music & Letters; Musical Quarterly; Music Review; Am. Imago; Telos; Notes. Mbrships: Am. Musicol. Soc.; Record Ind. Assn. of Am. Address: 1 W. 72nd St., New York, NY 10023, USA.

SOLOMON, Ruth Freeman, b. 21 Apr. 1908, Kiev, Russia. Novelist. Educ: A.B., Syracuse Univ., USA, 1929; Postgrad. study, Univ. of Vienna, 1930. Publs: The Candlesticks & the Cross, 1967, 5 for. lang. eds.; The Eagle & the Dove, 1971, German ed., 1971; The Ultimate Triumph, 1974. Mbr., Authors' League of Am. Address: 34 25th Ave., San Fran., CA 94121, USA.

SOLOUKHIN, Vladimir Alexeyevich, b. 14 June 1924, Alepino Stavrovsky, USSR. Writer; Educ: M. Gorky Inst. of Lit. Publs. incl: (poetry) Rain in the Steppe, 1953; Streamlets on the Asphalt, 1959; Tale of the Steppes, 1960; How to Drink the Sun, 1961; Post-cards from Viet-Nam, 1962; (novels) The Goldmine, 1956; Beyond the Blue Seas, 1957; Country Roads of Vladimir, 1958; The Drop of Dew, 1963; A Lyrical Story, 1964; (short stories) The Loaf of Bread, 1965; White Grass, 1971. Hons: Red Banner of Labour; Badge of Honour. Address: Union of Writers, 52 Ulitsa Vorovskogo, Moscow, USSR.

SOLUNSKI, Kotce, b. 30 Mar. 1922, Macedonia, Yugoslavia. Retired Colonel. Educ: Fac. of Philosophy. Publs: Traces are not swept away (novel), 1960; Mirche Atcev (monograph), 1968; Short story about the second Macedonian Brigade, 1968; Uprising & Youth (portraits), 1970; Traces are sweeping away (novel), 1972; Prilep in the Revolution, 1972; Kuzman, (monograph) 1973; co-author, National heroes in Macedonia, 1973. Contbr. to: Striving, Contemporary; Herald (Inst. of Nat. Hist.); Macedonian Review. Mbrships: PEN; Author Assn. (VP). Hons: Yugoslav Prize, 1971; Repub. Prize, 1969, 1973. Address: Gancho Hadhipanzov St. 24, 91000 Skopje, Yugoslavia.

SOLYMÁR, József, b. 19 Mar. 1929, Tállya, Hungary. Writer; Journalist. Educ: 4 yrs. post-second. study of Hungarian lang. & lit. & philos. Publs. incl: A Girl Was Killed, 1962; From Nightfall Till Daybreak, 1962; The World Should be Inherited by Good Men, 1963; The Third Symbol, 1964; Consolation for Myself, 1964; Greetings to the Confessor (short stories), 1965; God's Lover, 1966; Worship for Every, 1969; The Two Life of Madonna, 1970; The Days of Aranka, 1974. Mbrships: Hungarian Writer's & Jrnlst.'s Assns. Address: Solymár u. 8, 1032 Budapest III, Hungary.

SOLYMOS, Ida, b. 8 Dec. 1922, Pécs, Hungary. Poetess; Literary Translator; Essayist. Publs: (poetry) The Moon

Looks Around, 1943; Waiting for Guests, 1964; Unpersonal Poems, 1969; Oath Forms — Collected Poems, 1974. Contbr. to: Sorsunk; Vigilia; Életünk; Jelenkor; Kortárs; Alföld; Tiszatáj; Élet és Irodalom; Palócföld; Napjaink; Forrás. Mbrships: Assn. of Hungarian Writers; PEN. Address: Batthyány St. 48, 1015 Budapest, Hungary.

SÓLYOM, Laszlo, b. 24 Oct. 1919, Budapest, Hungary. Author; Playwright; Journalist. Publs: Homecoming, 1952; We Will Find Out Tomorrow, 1954; A House of Sighs, 1962; Divorce on Second Instance, 1968; Sparing My Nerves, 1966; sev. Radio & TV Plays. Contbr. to: Ludas Matyi (comic weekly). Mbrships: PEN; Int. Org. Jrnlsts.; Fedn. Hungarian Writers; Fedn. Hungarian Jrnlsts. Address: Pasareti Ut 34 (1026), Budapest II, Hungary.

SOLZHENITSYN, Alexander Isayevitch, b. 11 Dec. 1918, USSR. Author. Educ: Degree, Univ. of Rostov; Moscow Inst. of Hist., Philos., & Lit. Publs. incl: One Day in the Life of Ivan Denisovich, 1962 (filmed 1971); For the Good of the Cause, USA, 1964; The First Circle & Cancer Ward, USA & UK, 1968; The Love Girl & the Innocent (play), 1969; In the Interests of the Cause, 1970; The Victor's Feast (play), 1971; Stories & Prose Poems, 1971; August 1914, 1971; Candle in the Wind (play), 1973; Gulag Archipelago, 1974. Mbr., Am. Acad. Arts & Scis. Hons: Prix du Meilleur Livre Etranger, France, 1968; Nobel Prize for Lit., 1970.

SOMAN, Shirley Camper, pen name BENTHAM, Grace, b. 7 Mar. 1922, Boston, Mass., USA. Writer; Lecturer; Social Worker; Communications Specialist. Educ: B.A., Univ. of Wis.; M.S.S., Schl. for Soc. Work, Smith Coll., Northampton, Mass. Publs: How To Get Along With Your Child, 1962, Brazil, 1974; Let's Stop Destroying Our Children, 1974. Contbr. to: Rdr.'s Digest; Cath. Digest; Good Housekeeping; Cosmopolitan; Redbook; McCalls; Parade; Soc. Serv. Outlook, Congressional Record; Assoc. Ed., My Baby Mag., & Shaw's Market News. Mbrships. incl: Nat. Acad. Arts & Scis. (Forum Comm.); Acad. of Cert. Soc. Workers; Soc. of Mag. Writers; Writers' Guild E.; Authors' League of Am.; Nat. Assn. of Sci. Writers; Am. Med. Writers' Assn.; & num. others. Address: 40 W. 75th St., N.Y., NY 10024, USA.

SOMERVILLE, James Hugh Miller, pen name SOMERVILLE, Hugh, b. 10 Nov. 1922, Singapore. Yachting Writer. Educ: R.N. Coll., Dartmouth. Publs: Yacht Racing Rules Simplified, 1954; Yacht & Dinghy Racing, 1957; Sceptre, 1958; Short History of the Royal Northern Yacht Club, 1974; Leisureguide — Sailing, 1974; Nautical Inn Signs, 1974. Contbr. to: Sunday Times (yachting corres.); Times; Scotsman; Yachting, USA (Brit. corres.). Mbr., Inst. of Jrnlsts. Address: Beeches Farm, Crowborough, Sussex, UK.

SOMLYÓ, György, b. 28 Nov. 1920, Balatonboglár, Hungary. Editor, Arion Poetry Almanack. Educ: Budapest Univ., Sorbonne Univ., Paris, France. Publs: Tó Fölött, Ég Alatt, 1963; A Költészet Évadai, 4 vols., 1963-74; Hármastükör, 3 vols., 1970; A Mesék Könyve, 1974; (transls. into French) Souvenir du Présent, 1965; Contrefables, 1974. Contbr. to: Nyugat; Szép Szó; Kortárs; Uj Irás; Élet és Irodalom; Nagyvilág; Europe; Action Poétique; Arion. Recip., 4 József Attila Prizes, 1951, 1952, 1954 & 1967. Address: Kutvölgyi ut 33, 1125 Budapest, Hungary.

SONO, Ayako, b. 17 Sep. 1931, Tokyo, Japan. Novelist. Educ: Univ. of the Sacred Heart. Publs: The Monument Without Epitaph, 1969; The Human Trap, 1972. Contbr. to: Sankei Newspaper; Shincho Weekly; Cath. Jrnl. Mbrships: Dir., Japan Writers Assn., PEN. Address: 3-5-13 Denenchofu, Ohtaku, Tokyo, Japan.

SONTAG, Susan, b. 16 Jan. 1933, NYC, USA. Writer; Film Director. Educ: B.A., Univ. of Chgo., 1951; M.A., Harvard Univ., 1955; St. Anne's Coll., Oxford Univ., UK, 1957. Publs: The Benefactor (novel), USA, 1963, UK, 1964; Against Interpretation (essays), USA, 1966, UK, 1967; Death Kit (novel), USA, 1967, UK, 1968; Trip to Hanoi, 1969; Styles of Radical Will (essays), 1969; (screenplays) Duet for Cannibals, 1969; Brother Karl, 1971. Contbr. to: Partisan Review; Harper's. Hons: Fellowship, AAUW, 1957; Rockefeller Fellowship, 1965; Guggenheim Fellowship, 1966. Address: c/o Farrar, Straus & Giroux, 19 Union Square W., N.Y., NY 10003, USA.

SONU, Hwi, b. 3 Jan. 1922, Pyongyang Bukdo, Korea. Journalist. Educ: Seoul Normal Coll., 1944. Publs:

(collective works of short stories) Sparks; Rebel; Nostalgia; & sev. novels. Contbr. to: Shin-Tong-A; Saedae; Joongang; etc. Recip., Tong-In Lit. Prize, 1957. Address: 692-15, Jungnung No. 3 Dong, Songbuk-ku, Seoul, Korea.

SOOMRO, Ibrahim Munshi, b. 1 Mar. 1934, Tando Mohammad Khan, Sind, Pakistan. Farmer. Publs: Paigam-e-Mazloom (Cry of the Oppressed); Vegeh-ja-Viryam (Lords of Vigah). Contbr. to: Taherik; Paigam; Agte Qadam; Mehran Sohni. Recip., Cash Prize, Fed. Min. for Educ. Address: P.O. Jinhan Soomro Vir Tando Mohammad Khan, Hyderabad, Sind, Pakistan.

SOPER, Eileen Louise, b. 14 Dec. 1900, Sydney, Australia. Journalist. Educ: B.A., Univ. of Otago. Publs: The Otago of Our Mothers, 1948; Young Jane, 1955; The Green Years, 1969; The Month of the Brittle Star, 1971; The Leaves Turn, 1973. Contbr. to: NZ Listener. Mbrships: Otago Bus. & Profl. Women's Club; Otago Girl Guides Assn.; Otago Univ. Staff Wives Assn.; Victoria League, Otago. Address: 6 Howard St., Macandrew Bay, Dunedin, NZ.

SOREIL, (Joseph) Arsène, pen name DELAISNE, Jean, b. 5 Feb. 1893, Rendeux-Bas, Belgium. Teacher. Educ: Studied Greek & Latin, philos. & letters (novel); Doct. & Special Doct.; Dip., Higher studies, Univ. of Paris. Publs: Introduction à l'histoire de l'Esthétique française, 3rd ed., 1966; Dure Ardenne, tales, 4th ed., 1947; Entretiens sur l'Art d'écrire, 2nd ed., 1964; Plaisir aux lettres, 1950; Art et Poésie, 1969; Fugitives, poems, 2nd ed., 1964. Contbr. to: Le Soir; La Vie Wallonne; Forces Nouvelles; Les Cahiers Mosans. Fndr. mbr., Luxembourgeoise Acad. Recip., Lit. Prize, consecration of Province of Liège, 1956. Address: 316 rue d'Yser, B 4300 Ans, Belgium.

SORENSEN, Thomas Chaikin, b. 31 Mar. 1926, Lincoln, Neb., USA. Financial Executive. Educ: B.A., 1947, Grad. Grad. studies, Univ. of Neb. & For. Serv. Inst., U.S. Dept. of State, Wash. D.C. Publs: The World War: The Story of American Propaganda, 1968. Contbr. to: Sorensen Report; Parade. Address: 250 Beverly Rd., Scarsdale, NY 10583, USA.

SORIA MARCO, Bonifacio, b. 12 Oct. 1908. Civil Servant; Writer; Painter; Inventor, "Bâiros" game. Educ: Studies in histl. & artistic rsch. Publs. incl: Sinfonía en azul, 1936; El Observatorio Astronómico Geofísico de la Cartuja granadina, 1942; Sinfonía sublime, (biog. novel on Beethoven), 1942; La Cartuja de Granada, 1942, 2nd ed., 1957; La melodía de Bâiros, 1944; La verdad de un mal, 1944; Al través de Marruecos, 1945; Bajo el sol de Guinea Ecuatorial, 1945; Madrid antiguo y moderno, 1959; En Aragón y en el Pirineo Central, 1967; En cuidades y pueblos de España, 1969. Contbr. to: Cisneros; Guadalupe; El Diario (Barcelona); Solidaridad Nacional; etc. Recip., num. prizes. Address: Calle de Embajadores 141, 7°-B, Madrid-5, Spain.

SORIANO JARA, Elena, b. 4 Feb. 1917, Fuentidueña del Tajo, Spain. Educ: Tchng. Dip.; Dip., French Inst., Madrid; courses in Pedagogy. Publs: Caza menor, 1951; La playa de los locos, 1955; Espejismos, 1955; Medea, 1955; Defensa de la Literatura, publd. as serial in El Urogallo. Contbr. to: Indice de Artes y Letras; Revista de Literatura; El español; Fndr. & Ed., El Urogallo. Mbrships: Hon. Mbr., French Inst., Madrid; Assoc. Mbr., Assn. of Spanish Univ. Women; Soc. of Authors of Spain. Address: Calle Matías Montero 24, Madrid 6, Spain.

SORLEY WALKER, Kathrine, b. Aberdeen, UK. Author; Journalist. Educ: King's Coll., Univ. of London; Besançon Univ.; Trinity Coll. of Music, London. Publs. incl: Robert Helpmann, 1958; Eyes on the Ballet, 1963, 1965 USA; Eyes on Mime, 1969 USA; Saladin, Sultan of the Holy Sword, 1971; Dance & Its Creators, 1972 USA. Contbr. to: Daily Telegraph (Ballet Critic 1962−); The Stage; Dancing Times; Hemisphere, Aust.; Ency. Brit., 1975; Enciclopedia dello Spettacolo, Italy; Review of Engl. Lit.; etc. Mbrships: Critics' Circle, London, UK; Soc. of Authors. Address: 60 Eaton Mews West, London SW1, UK.

SÖTEMANN, August L. (Guus), b. 11 Aug. 1920, Warmenhuizen, Netherlands. Professor of Dutch Literature. Educ: D.Litt. Publs: A. Roland Holst en de mythe van Ierland, 1950; Over het lezen van Kafka, 1957; Vyfenveertig seizoenen, 1960; De structuur van Max Havelaar, 1966; Over de dichter J. C. Bloem, 1974. Contbr. to: De nieuwe taalgids (Co-Ed.). Mbrships: Maatschappyder Nederlandse Letterkunde; Zuid-nederlandse Maatschappij

voor taal- en letterkunde en geschiedenis; Vereniging van Letterkundigen. Address: P. Saenredamstraat 5, Utrecht, Netherlands.

SÖTÉR, István, b. 1 June 1913, Szeged, Hungary. University Professor; Literary Historian; Novelist. Educ: Univ. of Budapest; La Sorbonne & Ecole Normale Supérieure, Univ. of Paris, France. Publs. incl: (novels & short stories) The Ghost, 1945; The Fall, 1947; The Broken Bridge, 1948; The Eden, 1961; The Lost Lamb, 1974; (essays & monographs) Jókai Mór, 1940; Play & Reality, 1946; Világtájak, 1957; Nation & Progress, 1963; Tisztuló tukrok, 1966; The Dilemma of Literary Science, 1973. Contbr. to: Hungarian & int. comparatist reviews. Mbrships: Hungarian Acad.; Int. Comp. Lit. Assn.; PEN. Hons: Kossuth Prize; Officier de l'Ordre des Arts et Lettres, France; Dr.h.c., Univ. of Paris. Address: Institute of Literary Studies, Hungarian Academy of Sciences, Menesi ut 11-13, 1118 Budapest, Hungary.

SOTO, Juan B., b. 24 Feb. 1882, Aguada, Puerto Rico. Attorney-at-Law; Author. Educ: LL.D., Ph.D., Univ. of Madrid, Spain. Publs: Philosophical Interpretations, 1915; Diplomatic Backgrounds of the Spanish-American War, 1922; Political & Juridical Studies, 1923; Puerto Rico in International Law, 1928; The Mechanistic Laws of Learning & the New German Psychology (Gestalt), 1934; The Tragedy of Thought, 1937; The University & the School in the Drama of Life, 1942. Contbr. to: Fndr. & Dir., Puerto Rico Review; Nuestro Tiempo, Madrid; La Esfera, Madrid; El Mundo, San Juan. Address: Box 21655 UPR Station, San Juan, PR 00931, USA.

SOURIAN, Peter, b. 7 Apr. 1933, Boston, Mass., USA. Writer; Teacher. Educ: B.A., Harvard Univ. Publs: Miri, 1957, UK ed. as Three Windows on Summer; The Best & the Worst of Times, 1961; The Gate, 1965. Contbr. to: N.Y. Times Book Review; The Nation; etc. Address: 30 E. 70th St., N.Y., NY 10021, USA.

SOUTHERN, Terry, b. 1 May 1924, Alvarado, Tex., USA. Writer. Educ: Southern Meth. Univ., Tex.; Univ. of Chgo.; B.A., Northwestern Univ., 1948; Sorbonne, Paris, France, 1948-50. Publs. incl: (novels) Flash & Filigree, UK & USA, 1958; Candy (w. M. Hoffenberg, as Maxwell Kenton), France, 1958 (as T. Southern & M. Hoffenberg), USA, 1964, UK, 1968; The Magic Christian, UK, 1959, USA, 1960; Blue Movie, 1970; (short stories) Red-Dirt Marijuana & Other Tastes, USA, 1967, UK, 1971; (screenplays) Dr. Strangelove, 1964; The Cincinnati Kid, 1966; Easy Rider, 1968. Recip., Brit. Screen Writers Award, 1964. Address: R.F.D., E. Canaan. CT, USA.

SOUTHWORTH, John Van Duyn, b. 5 June 1904, Syracuse, N.Y., USA. Writer; Teacher; Publisher. Educ: A.B., Harvard Univ., 1926; M.A., Columbia Univ., 1936. Publs. incl: Our Own United States, 1948; The Story of the World, 1954; War at Sea Series — The Ancient Fleets, 1968, The Age of Sails, 1968, The Age of Steam, Part I, 1970, Part II, 1972; Monarch & Conspirators; (co-author) What the Old World Gave the New, 1924; The Story of the Middle Ages, 1934; Heroes of Our America, 1952. Contbr. to profl. jrnls.; Regular feature, Hist. in Verse, in Grit Mag., 1960-62; articles in encys. Address: 815 123rd Ave., Isle of Capri, Treasure Island, FL 33706, USA.

SOYINKA, Wole, b. 13 July 1934, Abeokuta, Nigeria. Playwright; University Lecturer. Educ: B.A.; Univ. of Ibadan; Univ. of Leeds. Publs. incl: (plays) The Lion & the Jewel, 1959; The Swamp Dwellers, 1959; A Dance of the Forests, 1960; The Trials of Brother Jero, 1961; The Strong Breed, 1962; The Road, 1964; Madmen & Specialists, 1971; Jero's Metamorphosis, 1973; (novels) The Interpreters, 1964; The Forest of a Thousand Demons; A Shuffle in the Crypt, 1972; (non-fiction) The Man Died, 1972. Recip., Prisoner of Conscience Award; New Statesman Lit. Award, 1969. Address: Dept. of Engl., Univ. of Ife, Ile-Ife, Nigeria.

SPAIN, James William, b. 22 July 1926, Chicago, Ill., USA. Diplomat; Diplomat-in-Residence & Visiting Professor of History & Government at Florida State University; former Charge d'Affaires, American Embassy, Islamabad, Pakistan, 1970-72; Consul General of the United States in Istanbul, Turkey, 1972-74. Educ: M.A., Univ. Chicago, 1949; Ph.D., Columbia Univ., 1959. Publs: The Way of the Pathans, 1962, latest ed., 1973; The Pathan Borderland, 1963. Contbr. to: Middle E. Jrnl.; Am.; For. Serv. Jrnl.; For. Affairs. Mbrships: Coun. For. Affairs; Middle E. Inst.; Royal Central Asian Soc.; Cosmos (Wash. DC.); Am. For. Serv. Assn. Recip., Ford Fndn. Fellowship. Address: 707 Lothian Dr., Tallahassee, FL 32303, USA.

SPALDING, Henry Daniel, pen name SPING, Dan, b. 2 Feb. 1915, NYC, USA. Writer. Publs: The Yellow Press, 1957; Encyclopedia of Jewish Humor, 1969; Encyclopedia of Black Folklore & Humor, 1972; The Nixon Nobody Knows, 1972; The Ninth Note, forthcoming 1975; Make a Joyful Noise — 200 Years of Jewish American Humor, 1975; Encyclopedia of Irish Humor, scheduled 1976. Contbr. to num. major mags. Mbrships: Authors Guild, Inc.; Authors League of Am., Inc.; Co-Fndr., Hollywood Press Club. Address: 1615 Vista Del Mar, Hollywood, CA 90028, USA.

SPARK, Muriel Sarah, b. Edinburgh, UK. Author. Publs. incl: (fiction) The Comforters, 1957; The Go-AwayBird, 1958; Memento Mori, 1959; The Ballad of Peckham Rye, 1960; Voices at Play, 1961; The Prime of Miss Jean Brodie, 1961; The Mandelbaum Gate, 1965; The Public Image, 1968; The Driver's Seat, 1970; Not to Disturb, 1971; The Hot House by the East River, 1972; The Abbess of Crewe, 1974; (poems) The Fanfarlo & Other Verse, 1952; Collected Poems I, 1967; (for children) The Very Fine Clock, 1969; & num. critical & biographical works. Contbr. to Poetry Review (Ed., 1947-49). Mbrships: Poetry Soc.; F.R.S.L. Hons incl: C.B.E.; D.Litt. Address: c/o Macmillan, Little Essex St., London WC2, UK.

SPARROW, Louise Winslow Kidder, b. 1 Jan. 1884, Maplewood, Mass., USA. Sculptress; Writer. Educ: Univs. of Poitiers & Bordeaux, France. Publs: Lyrics & Translations, 1907; The Last Cruise, 1924; Transl., Tankas, 1924; Transl., Air Temples, 1972; Narrative Poems, 1970. Contbr. to: Rosicrucian Digest; Planetary Citizens Newsletter; Fellowship in Prayer; Understanding; var. anthols. & poetry jrnls. Mbrships: Am. Poetry League; World Poetry Soc. Intercontinental; F.R.S.A. (Life); Nat. Soc. of Lit. & the Arts. Recip., 2 awards & sev. hon. mentions for poetry. Address: 6200 Oregon Ave., N.W., Wash. DC 20015, USA.

SPEAIGHT, Robert William, b. 14 Jan. 1904. Actor; Author. Educ: M.A., Lincoln Coll., Oxford Univ. Publs. incl: Mutinous Wind, 1932; Thomas Becket, 1939; Acting, 1939; Acting Since 1939, 1948; George Eliot, 1954; Hilaire Belloc, 1957; The Christian Theatre, 1960; William Rothenstein, 1962; Ronald Knox the Writer, 1966; Teilhard de Chardin, 1967; The Property Basket, 1970; Vanier, 1970; A Bridges-Adams Letter Book, 1972; George Bernanos, 1973; Shakespeare on the Stage, 1973. Contbr. to wkly. press. Mbr., Sir Walter Scott Club (Pres., 1971-72); F.R.S.L. Hons: CBE, 1958; Off., Legion of Hon., 1969. Address: Campion House, Benenden, Kent, UK.

SPECTOR, Ivar, b. 13 Oct. 1898, Kiev, Russia. Emeritus Professor of Russian & Near Eastern History. Educ: U. & G. Cert., Tchrs. Sem., Ekaterinoslav, 1919; A.M., Northwestern Univ., USA, 1926; Ph.D., Univ. of Chgo., 1928. Publs: The Golden Age of Russian Literature, 5th ed., 1952; The First Russian Revolution (1905): Its Impact on Asia, 1962; The Soviet Union & the Muslim World, latest ed., 1967; Readings in Russian History & Culture (w. Marion Spector), 1968; An Introduction to Russian History & Culture, 5th ed., 1969. Contbr. to profl. jrnls. Mbrships. incl: R.S.A., London, 1931-38; Am. Hist. Assn.; Am. Hist. Assn. for Adv. of Slavic Studies; AAUP. Address: 8012 20th Ave., N.E., Seattle, WA 98115, USA.

SPEED, (Brigadier) Frank Warren, b. 16 Feb. 1911, Ballarat, Vic., Australia. Writer. Educ: Army Staff Coll., Queenscliff. Publs: South East Asian Peninsula Today, 1970; Indonesia Today, 1971; Malaysia & Singapore, 1973; (contbr.) Pacific Polities (Ed., Nicholson, Hughes), 1972. Contbr. to: Army Quarterly & Defence Jrnl. (London); Hemisphers (Canberra). Hons: O.B.E.; E.D. Address: Vanwall Rd., Moggill Q 4069, Australia.

SPEIGHT, Kathleen, b. 3 June 1903, Standish, Lancs., UK. University Lecturer. Educ: M.A., Manchester Univ.; D.Lett., Univ. of Florence, Italy; M.Litt., Univ. of Cambridge, UK. Publs: Teach Yourself Italian, 1943, latest ed., 1973; Ed., Il cappello del prete, by E. de Marchi, 1963. Contbr. to: Mod. Langs.; Mod. Lang. Review; Studies in Philol. Mbrships: Manchester Dante Soc. & Brit. Italian League, (Hon. Sec., 1945-70, Hon. Pres., 1970—); Soc. for Italian Studies. Address: 1 Carr Lane, Birkdale, Southport, Merseyside PR8 3EE, UK.

SPEIRS, John Hastie, b. 28 Apr. 1906, Aberdeen, UK. Retired University Reader; Author. Educ: M.A., Aberdeen Univ.; B.A., Emmanuel Coll., Cambridge. Publs: The Scots Literary Tradition, 1940, enlarged ed., 1962; Chaucer the Maker, 1951; Medieval English Poetry, 1957; Poetry

Towards Novel, 1971. Contbr. to: Scrutiny; Penguin Guide to Engl. Lit., 1954—; var. anthols. Address: 25 Grove Terrace, Highgate Rd., London NW5 1PL, UK.

SPELIOS, Thomas John, b. 1930, NYC, USA. Historian; Chemist; Writer; Lecturer in History. Educ: Columbia Univ.; Cambridge Univ.; St. Johns Univ.; B.Sci., M.A. Publs: Balkan Odyssey, 1960; Poetica, Poems & Photographs, 1961; Nile Odyssey, 1962; Voyage Into Chaos, 1965; Pictorial History of Greece, 1967; Legacy of Byzantium; In Search of Alexander's Tomb, 1972; The Eastern Question, 1973; Retreat of Hellenism, 1974. Contbr. to var. jrnls. Mbrships: Am. Writers Club; Cosmetic Chems. Soc.; Andean Explorers; Fellow, Am. Archaeol. Soc. Recip., Author Award in Hist., N.J. Tchrs. of Engl. Assn., 1967. Address: 8 Pine Ridge Rd., Port Chester, NY 10573, USA.

SPENCE, William John Duncan, pen names SPENCE, Duncan; BOWDEN, Jim; ROGERS, Floyd; FORD, Kirk, b. 20 Apr. 1923, Middlesbrough, UK. Stores Manager. Educ: St. Mary's Tchrs. Trng. Coll., Middx. Publs. incl: Valley of Revenge, 1971; Trail to Texas, 1973; Montana Justice, 1973; Hangman's Gulch, 1974; Feud Riders, 1974; Show-down in Salt Fork, 1975; A History of Whaling. Contbr. to: Northern Echo & Yorks. Gazette & Herald (regular book reviewer); Country Life; Yorks. Post; etc. Mbrships: Soc. of Authors; Soc. Nautical Rsch; Whitby Lit. & Philosophical Soc. Address: Post Office, Ampleforth College, York, UK.

SPENCER, Elizabeth, b. 19 July 1921, Carrollton, Miss., USA. Writer. Educ: B.A., Belhaven Coll., Jackson Miss.; M.A., Vanderbilt Univ., Nashville, Tenn. Publs: (Novels) Fire in the Morning, 1948, 2nd ed., 1968; The Crooked Way, 1952, Engl. ed., 1952, 2nd US ed., 1968; The Voice at the Back Door, 1956, Engl. ed., 1957; The Light in the Piazza, 1960, Engl. ed., 1961; Knights & Dragons, 1965, Engl. ed., 1966; No Place for an Angel, 1967, Engl. ed., 1968; The Snare, 1972; (stories Ship Island & Other Stories, 1968, Engl. ed., 1969. Contbr. to: New Yorker; Southern Review; Va. Quarterly; etc. Mbrships: PEN (Prog. Chmn. Can. Ctr., 1974); Authors' Guild; Alliance Française. Hons. incl: LL.D. Southwestern Univ., 1969; Bellaman Award, 1969. Address: Apt. 610, 2300 St. Matthew, Montreal, P.Q., Can.

SPENCER, Jeffry Burress, b. 2 Jan. 1927, San Fran., Calif., USA. College Professor. Educ: A.B., Univ. of Calif., Berkeley; M.A., DePaul Univ.; Ph.D., Northwestern Univ. Publs: Heroic Nature; Ideal Landscape in English Poetry from Marvell to Thomson, 1973. Mbrships: MLA; Int. Soc. for Eighteenth-Century Studies; Am. Soc. for Eighteenth-Century Studies. Hons: Henry E. Huntington Lib. Fellowship, 1973; Am. Philos. Soc. Grant, 1974; Nat. Endowment for the Humanities Summer Stipend, 1974. Address: Dept. of English, Calif. State Coll., Bakersfield, CA 93309, USA.

SPENCER, John (Walter), b. 24 Sept. 1922, Bury St. Edmunds, UK. University Teacher. Educ: B.A., 1949, M.A., 1956, Oxford Univ. Publs: Workers for Humanity, 1963; Ed. & Contbr., Language in Africa, 1963; Linguistics & Style (co-author), 1964; Co-Ed., Modern Poems for the Commonwealth, 1966; Ed. & Contbr., The English Language in West Africa, 1971; Ed., Jrnl. W. African Langs., 1964-72; Ed., W. African Lang. Monograph Series, 1964—. Contbr. to: Lingua; Phonetica; Current Trends in Linguistics; etc. Mbrships: Philol. Soc.; African Studies Assn.; Linguistics Assn. Assoc. Mbr: Inst. of Modern English Language Studies, Leeds University, UK.

SPENCER, William, b. 1 June 1922, Erie, Pa., USA. Professor of History. Educ: A.B., Princeton Univ., 1948; A.M., Duke Univ., 1950; Ph.D., Am. Univ., 1965. Publs: The Land & People of Turkey, 1958, 2nd ed., 1972; Political Evolution in the Middle East, 1962; The Land & People of Morocco, 1965, revised ed., 1973; The Land & People of Tunisia, 1967, revised ed., 1972; The Land & People of Algeria, 1969. Contbr. to: Middle East Jrnl.; Am. Hist. Review; Can. Review; Studies in Nationalism; Landscape; The Annals. Mbrships. incl: Fla. Heritage Fndn. (Sec.). Hons. incl: Carnegie Lit. Award, 1958; Fulbright-Hays Award, 1967; African Award, Soc. Rsch. Coun., 1973. Address: 1037 Betton Rd., Tallahassee, FL 32303, USA.

SPENDER, Stephen (Harold), b. 28 Feb. 1909. Poet; Critic; Professor of English. Educ: Univ. Coll., Oxford Univ. Publs. incl: 20 Poems, 1934; Poems for Spain, 1939; Ruins & Visions, 1941; Poems of Dedication, 1946; World Within

World (autobiog.), 1951; Collected Poems, 1954; The Making of a Poem, 1955; Engaged in Writing (stories), 1958; The Struggle of the Modern, 1963; The Year of the Young Rebels, 1969; The Generous Days, 1971; English & American Sensibilities (essays), 1972; Ed., D. H. Lawrence, 1973. Contbr. to: Horizon mag. (Co-Ed., 1939-41); Encounter (Co-Ed., 1953-67). Mbrships. incl: Am. Acad. Arts & Letters (Hon.). Hons. incl: C.B.E., 1962; Queen's Gold Medal for Poetry, 1971; D.Litt., Montpellier & Loyola Univs. Address: 15 Loudoun Rd., London NW8, UK.

SPERLING, Jan Bodo, b. 7 Jan. 1928, Brunswick, Germany. International Civil Servant. Educ: Master's Degree, Marburg Univ.; Ph.D., Aachen Univ. Publs: Rourkela, 1963; Die Rourkela-Deutschen, 1965; The Human Dimension of Technical Assistance, 1970. Contbr. to var. publs. & mags. on int. rels., human resources dev., mgmt. Mbrships: Soc. for Int. Dev.; Deutsche Ges. für Int. Wissenschaft; Sozialwissenschaftlicher Studienkreis für Int. Probleme. Address: D 8211 Schleching, Mühlbergweg 10, W. Germany.

SPICER, Marcella (Marcy), b. 31 Oct. 1920, Beaver Dam, Wis., USA. Educ: Univ. ext. courses in creative writing & art. Author, There Is a Voice (poetry), 1974. Contbr. to: Milwaukee Jrnl.; Wis. State Jrnl.; Portage Daily Register; The Spirit; Appleton-Post Cres.; Dinver Post; Jean's Jrnl.; Am. Poet; Prairie Poet; Midwest Chaparral; Haiku Highlights; Modern Haiku; Outstanding Contemporary Poets & var. other anthols. Recip., var. poetry prizes. Address: Shore Acres, Pardeeville, WI 53954, USA.

SPIEGEL, Henry William, b. 13 Oct. 1911, Berlin, Germany. Professor of Economics; Author. Educ: J.U.D., Univ. of Berlin, 1933; Ph.D., Univ. of Wis., USA, 1939. Publs. incl: The Economics of Total War, 1942; The Brazilian Economy, 1949; Introduction to Economics, 1951; The Rise of American Economic Thought, 1960; The Growth of Economic Thought, 1971. Contbr. to: Ency. Britannica; Int. Ency. of Social Scis.; World Book Ency.; Am. Econ. Review. Mbrships. incl: Ed. Bd., Handbook of Latin Am. Studies, 1946-60, Social Sci., 1953—; Hist. of Pol. Economy. Address: Dept. of Economics, Catholic University of America, Washington, DC 20064, USA.

SPIER, Elvire, b. 31 Mar. 1920, Buitenzorg, Netherlands E. Indies (now Indonesia). Writer. Publs. incl: (musical comedy) Santa Claus & the United Nations, 1952; Sev. radio plays inclng: Maria Dolores, 1958; Epidaurus, 1961; (TV play) The New Adam, 1973; (short stories) Checkmate, 1970; Song texts for var. choirs, 1960-70. Contbr., about 40 short stories to var. jrnls. Mbrships. incl: Dutch Writers' Guild; Assn. of Dutch Playwrights; Die Kogge European Authors Assn. Hons. incl: Dame of Order of the House of Orange; Visser-Neerlandia Prize, for TV play, The New Adam, 1973. Address: P.O. Box 9, CH-1622 Les Paccots, Switz.

SPINGARN, Lawrence Perreira, b. 11 July 1917, Jersey City, N.J., USA. Professor of English; Publisher. Educ: B.S., Bowdoin Coll.; M.A., Univ. of Mich. Publs: Rococo Summer & other Poems, 1947; The Lost River: Poems, 1951; Letters from Exile: Poems, 1961; Madame Bidet & other Fixtures: Poems, 1968; Freeway Problems & others: Poems, 1970. Contbr. to: Harper's Mag.; Kenyon Review; New England Quarterly; New Yorker; N.Y. Times; Paris Review; other lit. jrnls. Mbrships: Int. Inst. of Arts & Letters; Poetry Soc. of Am.; Poetry Soc. (London); Authors Club (London); Authors League; PEN. Recip., Huntington Hartford Award, 1950. Address: 13830 Erwin St., Va. Nuys, CA 91401, USA.

SPINRAD, Norman, b. 15 Sept. 1940, NYC, USA. Novelist. Educ: B.S., Coll. City N.Y., 1961. Publs: The Solarians, 1966; Agent of Chaos, 1967; The Men in the Jungle, 1967; Bug Back Barron, 1969; Fragments of America, 1970; The New Tomorrows, 1971; The Last Hurrah of the Golden Horde, 1971; The Iron Dream, 1973; Modern Science Fiction, 1974; Passing Through the Flame, 1975. Contbr. to: Playboy; Oui; West; Analog; L.A. Free Press; Knight; Orbit; New Worlds; etc. Mbrships: Writers' Guild Am.; Sci. Fiction Writers Am. (VP). Hons. incl: Prix Apollo, 1974. Address: c/o Lurton Blassingame, 60 E. 42nd St., N.Y., NY 10017, USA.

SPITZ, David, b. 13 Dec. 1916, NYC, USA. Professor of Political Science. Educ: B.S.S., CCNY, 1937; A.M., 1939; Ph.D., 1948, Columbia Univ. Publs: incl: Patterns of Anti-Democratic Thought, 1949, 1965; The Liberal Idea of

Freedom, 1964; Ed., Politics & Society, by R. M. MacIver, 1969; Ed., On Liberty, by J. S. Mill, 1975. Contbr. to: Am. Pol. Sci. Review; Antioch Review; Dissent; Nation; New Republic; etc. Mbrships. incl: Conf., Study of Pol. Thought (Sec.-Treas., 1971-72, 1974-75); Am. Soc. for Pol. & Legal Philos.; Am. Pol. Sci. Assn. Recip., 4 acad. hons. Address: 6 Beaver Drive, Locust Valley, NY 11560, USA.

SPITZING, Günther, b. 19 May 1931, Bamberg, Germany. Freelance Author. Publs. incl: Porträtfotos — gewusst ¡wie! (The Photoguide to Portraits), 1968, 3rd ed., 1974; Günter Spitzing's Blitzbuch (The Photoguide to Flash), 1968, 3rd ed., 1974; Vergrössern — schwarzweiss + farbig (The Photoguide to Enlarging), 1969, 6th ed., 1974; Foto-Experimente (The Photoguide to Effects & Tricks), 1970, 1974; Pette mit der Kamera: Photobook for Children, 1968, 2nd ed., 1969; Grenzbereiche der Fotographie, 1968; Kupferätzen nach Fotos, 1973; Schulfotographie Didaktik + Methodik, 1975. Contbr. to var. photog. jrnls. Mbrships: German Photog. Soc.; German Jrnlsts. Soc. Address: D-2 Hamburg 65, Stadtbahnstr.86, W. Germany.

SPRAGENS, William Clark, b. 1 Oct. 1925, Lebanon, Ky., USA. Professor of Political Science. Educ: A.B. in Jrnlsm., 1947, M.A., 1953, Univ. of Ky.; Ph.D., Mich. State Univ., 1966. Publs: Conflict & Crisis in American Politics, 1970. Contbr. to: Midwest Jrnl. of Pol. Sci.; Western Pol. Quarterly; Pol. Sci. Quarterly; Int. Behavioural Sci.; Jrnl. of Negro Hist. Mbrships: Am. Pol. Sci. Assn.; Publicity Chmn., Midwest Pol. Sci. Assn., 1974-75; Southern Pol. Sci. Assn. Hons: Falk Fellow, Mich. State Univ., 1960-61; Ford Legis. Intern, Mich. Legislature, 1961; Life Fellow, Inst. for Int. Sociol. Rsch., 1972. Address: 607 Lafayette Blvd., Bowling Green, OH 43402, USA.

SPREADBURY, Frank George, b. 1904, London, UK. Lecturer. Educ: Sen. M.I.E.E.E.; M.Inst.B.E.; A.Mus.L.C.M. Publs. incl: Fractional H.P. Electric Motors, 1951; Electrical Ignition Equipment, 1954; Electronic Measurements & Measuring Instruments, 1956; Aircraft Electrical Engineering, 1958; Electronic Rectification, 1962; Non-mechanical Energy Conversion, 1968; Principles & Characteristics of Electron Devices, 1973. Recip., Silver Medal, LCM, 1925. Address: 15 Melrose Ave., Cricklewood, London NW2 4LH, UK.

SPRIGGE, Elizabeth Miriam Squire, b. 19 June 1900. Writer; Translator; Producer. Educ: Havergal Coll., Toronto, Can.; Bedford Coll., London Univ., UK. Publs. incl: (novels) A Shadowy Third, 1929; Castle in Andalusia, 1935; The Raven's Wing, 1940; (play) Elizabeth of Austria (w. K. Sprigge), prod. 1939; (juvenile) Children Alone, 1935; The Dolphin Bottle (w. E. Muntz), 1965; (biogs.) The Strange Life of August Strindberg, 1949; Gertrude Stein, 1957; The Life of Ivy Compton-Burnett, 1973; num. transls. from Scandinavian authors, esp. Strindberg. Address: 75 Ladbroke Grove, London W11 2PD, UK.

SPRINGER, Otto, b. 18 Mar. 1905, Württemberg, Germany. Professor of Germanics. Educ: incl: Univs. of Tübingen; Uppsala, Sweden. Publs. incl: Die Nordische Renaissance in Skandinavien, 1936; Langenscheidt's Ency. Dict., Engl. & German Part I, 1962-63, Part II, 1974-75; Studien zur germanischen Philologie u. zur Literatur des Mittelalters, 1975. Contbr. to lang. jrnls. Mbrships. incl: Linguistic Soc. of Am., (VP, 1954); Fellow, Medieval Acad. of Am.; Mod. Lang. Assn. of Am. Recip.; Prize, Philos. Fac., Univ. of Tübingen, 1927. Address: 737 Williams Hall, Dept. of Germanics, Univ. of Penn., Phila., PA 19174, USA.

SPULBER, Nicolas, b. 1 Jan. 1915, Brasov, Romania. Professor of Economics. Educ: M.A., 1950, Ph.D., 1952, New Schl. for Soc. Rsch., NYC. Publs: The Economics of Communist Eastern Europe, 1957; The Soviet Economy: Structure, Principles, Problems, 1962, revised 1969; Soviet Strategy for Economic Growth, 1964; The State & Economic Development in Eastern Europe, 1966; Socialist Management & Planning, 1971. Contbr. to: Jrnl. of Econ. Lit.; Kyklos; Review of Econs. & Stats.; Weltwirtschaftliches Archiv; Challenge; etc. Mbrships: Am. Econ. Assn.; Royal Econ. Soc. Recip., title of Disting. Prof. of Econs., 1974. Address: Dept. of Econs., Ind. Univ., Bloomington, IN 47401, USA.

SPURLING, John Antony, b. 17 July 1936, Kisumu, Kenya. Playwright. Educ: Marlborough Coll.; B.A., St. John's Coll., Oxford Univ. Publs: (plays) MacRune's Guevara, 1969; In the Heart of the British Museum, 1972; (non-fiction) Beckett: A Study of His Plays (w. John

Fletcher); & unpublished produced stage & TV plays incl. (stage) Romance; Peace in Our Time; McGonagall & the Murderer; On a Clear Day You Can See Marlowe; (TV) Hope; Faith; Death of Captain Doughty, 1973; Silver, 1973. Contbr. to: Spectator; Fin. Times; Times; New Statesman; Encounter; To the Point Int.; Europa. Address: c/o Patricia Macnaughton, PLR Ltd., 33 Sloane St., London SW1, UK.

SPURR, Rita, b. Manchester, UK. Writer; Poet; Lecturer. Educ: B.A., Univ. of Manchester. Pubis: Footprint in Snow, 1954; Slide into Poetry (Ed.), 1973; I Read the Wind (Ed.), 1975. Contbr. to: Without Adam; Pattern of Poetry; John O'London's; Slide into Poetry; BBC; Country Life; Manchester Guardian; Poetry Review; etc. Mbrships: Chmn., Camden Poetry Grp., London, 1970—; Poetry Advsr. & Metropolitan Sec., Writers' Guild; Fndr. Fellow, Int. Poetry Soc.; Lancs. Authors' Assn.; Gen. Coun., Poetry Soc. of GB. Hons. incl: Diurna Actu, Manifold, 1966. Address: Flat 4, 7 Netherhall Gdns., Hampstead, London NW3 5RN, UK.

SQUIRE, Jason Edward, b. 3 Nov. 1948, Bklyn., N.Y., USA. Motion Picture Executive. Educ: B.S., Syracuse Univ., 1969; M.A., UCLA, 1972. Pubis: The Movie Business: American Film Industry Practice (ed. w. A. William Bluem), 1972, 2nd ed., 1973. Mbrships: Alpha Epsilon Rho; Sigma Delta Chi; Sigma Tau Rho. Address: 10966 Roebling Ave., L.A., CA 90024, USA.

SQUIRES, James Duane, b. 9 Nov. 1904, Grand Forks, N.D., USA. College Professor. Educ: A.B., Univ. of N.D.; 1925; A.M., Univ. of Minn., 1927; Ph.D., Harvard Univ., 1933; LL.D., Univ. of N.D., 1958. Pubis: British Propaganda in World War I, 1935; Western Civilization, 1944; The Northern Railroad of New Hampshire, 1948; Mirror to America, 1952; The Granite State of the U.S., 1956; The Story of New Hampshire, 1964; A Student's Guide to New Hampshire, 1966; The History of the First Baptist Church of New London, N.H., 1969. Contbr. to: Dict. of Am. Hist.; var. histl. jrnls. Hons. incl: Granite State Award, Univ. of N.H., 1970. Address: New London, NH 03257, USA.

SREENIVASAPURAM, Anantha Charlu, pen names ANANTASREE; SREENIVASAPURAM SODARULU, b. 1 June 1935, Korrapadu, Cuddpah Dist., India. Post Office Clerk; Author; Poet; Playwright. Pubis: Co-author w. brothers (as Sreenivasapuram Sodarulu), 20 vols. S. Indian histl. works on Vijayanagar Empire (1224 AD to 1336 AD) in Telugu prose, inclng: Kampilarayalu (Someswarudu), vol. 3 1963; Samrat Proudhadevarayalu, vol. 7, 1965; Rakshasi — Tangadi, vol. 16, 1962; Rajyaekhayamu, vol. 20 1968; Raghunadha vijayamu, vol. 17, 1966. Contbr. to periodicals, Madras & Bombay. Mbrships: Navyandhra Bharathi Punganuru; PEN. Al India Ctr., Bombay; Chittoor Taluk Telugh Writers Assn. Address: P & T Dept., B. Kothakota S.O. 517370, Madanapalle (Tq), Chittoor Dist. A.P., South India.

SREENIVASAPURAM, Narasimha Charlu, pen names SREENIVASAPURAM SODARULU; SIMHASREE; PARANKUSA, b. 13 Jan. 1927, Proddaturu, Cuddapah, Andhra Pradesh, India. Medical Practitioner; Poet; Critic; Author. Pubis: Co-author w. brothers, 20 vols. S. Indian histl. works in Telugu prose incl., Devagiri Durgamu, vol. 1, 1963; Rajyodayamu, vol. 5, 1965; Rajyakranthi, vol. 8, 1965; Nagaladevi, vol. 10, 1967; Criticism of Chittoor District Literary History, 1969. Contbr. to: Bharathi Monthly, Andhra Prabha; Madras Krishna Patrika Fortnightly; etc. Mbrships. incl: Geogl. Rsch. Soc. Ancient India (Fndr. Pres.); Navyandhra Bharathi (Fndr. VP). Recip., num. lit. hons. Address: Acharya Clinic, Tambalapalli Post, Madanapalle Tq., Chittoor District, Andhra Pradesh, India.

SREENIVASAPURAM, Ramacharlu, pen names RAMYSARI; SREENIVASAPURAM, Sodarulu, b. 22 Feb. 1939, Pengargunta, Palamaner, Chittoor District, Andhra Pradesh, India. Poet; Playwright; Author; Posts & Telegraphs Dept. Employee. Educ: Andhra Univ. Pubis: South Indian History of Vijayanagar Empire, 1224-1336 A.D., 20 vols. (co-author); also novels, short stories, poetry & radio plays. Hons: Sri Krishnadevaraya Centenary Celebrations Award, Penugonda, 1962; Zilla Parishad Award, Chittoor, 1964; Dict. Ctrl. Lib. Auth. Award, Chittoor, 1967. Address: Posts & Telegraphs Dept., Palamaner Post, Chittoor Dist., Andhra Pradesh, India.

SREENIVASAPURAM, Sesha Charlu, pen name SUBHASREEF, b. 1 Sept. 1921, Gudiyatham, Tamil Nadu, India. Medical Practitioner; Poet; Writer; Author. Pubis: Raja Drohi, vol. 13, 1961; Santhivadi, vol. 12, 1962; Pitch Prabuvu, vol. 15, 1962 (South Indian History of Vijayanagar Empire, w. Sreenivasapuram Sodarulu); Ed., Publr., Naveena, 1954—. Contbr. to: Andhra Praja; Jai Bharat; Chitragupta; Andhra Patrika. Mbrships: Pres., Progressive Writers Dist. Unit, Chittoor; Fndr. - Sec., Navyandhra Bharathi, Punganuru; PEN All India Ctr., Bombay. Recip., Ponna Award, Zamindar of Punganuru, 1965. Address: Jyothi Clinic, Punganuru Post, Chittoor Dt., Andhra Pradesh, India.

SREENIVASAPURAM, Vankata Lakshmi Narayanan, pen names SREENIVASAPURAM SODARULU; RAMAKANTH, b. 19 Feb. 1930, Proddatur, Andhra Pradesh, India. Locomotive Engine Mechanic; Poet; Writer. Pubis: Co-author w. brothers, 20 vols. S. Indian histl. works in Telugu prose incl., Devagiri Patanamu, vol. 2, 1963; Raaya Parabhavamu, vol. 6, 1965; Devikota, vol. 18, forthcoming. Contbr. to: Andhra Prabha; Andhra Patrika; Andhra Mahila; Navajeevan; etc. Mbrships: Navyandhra Bharathi (Fndr. Mbr.); All India Telugu Writers' Gen. Coun. Recip., num. lit. hons. Address: H.F. 32, B. Railway Quarters, Hoffieldpet, Arkonam Post, N.A. Dist., Tamil Nadu, India.

SRINIVAS, Krishna, pen name KESHRI, b. 26 July 1913, Srirangam, S. India. Editor. Educ: B.A., Madras Univ.; Litt.D., Univ. of Asia. Pubis: Dance of Dust, 1946; He Walks the Earth, 1950; Nirvana, 1960; Wheel, 1970; Everest, 1975. Contbr. to: Poet (Ed.-in-Chief); S. & W.; Voice Int.; Malta News; Laurel Leaves; 2nd Aeon; Tridente; etc. Mbrships. incl: Pres., World Poetry Soc. Intercontinental, Phoenix, USA; Culture Acad., Rome, Italy; Pres., All India Poets Meet, Madras. Hons: Int. Poet Laureate, Yonkers, N.Y., USA, 1971; World Poet Laureate, 2nd World Congress of Poets, Taipei, Formosa, 1973; Nominations for Nobel Prize in Lit. Address: 20A, Venkatesan Street, Madras 17, India.

STAAL, Cyril, pen name WILLS, Geoffrey, b. 23 Apr. 1912, London, UK. Author; Art Expert. Pubis: English & Irish Glass, 1968; Book of Copper & Brass, 1968; English Pottery & Porcelain, 1969; English Furniture, 2 vols., 1971; Jade of the East, 1972. Contbr. to: Proceedings, Wedgwood Soc. (Hon. Ed.); Apollo; Country Life; Countryman. Mbrships: Wedgwood Soc.; Royal Instn. of Cornwall (Coun.); Furniture Hist. Soc. (Coun.) Address: Cotehele House, Saltash, Cornwall PL12 6TA, UK.

STAALESEN, Gunnar, b. 19 Oct. 1947, Bergen, Norway. Author. Educ: Studies in French, English & Literature, Univ. of Bergen. Pubis: Uskyldstider (Days of Innocence), 1969; Fortellingen om Barbara (The Story of Barbara), 1971. Contbr. to: Bergens Arbeiderblad (as film reviewer). Mbrships: Den Norske Forfatterforening (Norwegian Authors' Union); Norsk Forfattersentrum (Norwegian Authors' Ctr.). Recip., Prize, Gyldendal Norst Forlag's Crime Novel Contest, 1974. Address: Proms gate 9, 5000 Bergen, Norway.

STABILE, James, b. 1 Mar. 1936, Somerville, N.J., USA. Writer-Editor. Educ: A.A., Paul Smith's Coll., N.Y. Contbr. to: Mich. Out-of-Doors Mag.; num. other periodicals. Mbrships: Outdoor Writers' Assn. of Am.; Metropol. N.Y. Rod & Gun Eds. Assn.; N.J. Outdoor Writers' Assn.; Wildlife Soc.; Fisheries Soc. Recip., Conserv. Communications Award, N.J. Fedn. Sportsmen's Clubs, Nat. Wildlife Fedn. & Sears-Roebuck Fndn., 1970. Address: 3720 W. Hiawatha, Okemos, MI 48864, USA.

STABLER, Arthur Phillips, b. 23 Apr. 1919, Sandy Spring, Md., USA. University Professor. Educ: B.A., 1941, M.A., 1947, Univ. of Pa., Phila.; Ph.D., Univ. of Va., Charlottesville, 1959; Fulbright Schlrshp. to Univ. of Grenoble, France, 1951-52. Pubis: The Histoires Tragiques of François de Belleforest..., 1958; The Legend of Marguerite de Roberval, 1972. Contbr. to jrnls. inclng: PMLA; Shakespeare Studies; Etudes rabelaisiennes; Shakespeare Newsletter (contbng. Ed.). Mbr., profl. orgs. Recip., acad. hons. Address: Dept. of For. Langs. & Lits., Wash. State Univ., Pullman, WA 99163, USA.

STACE, Francis Nigel, b. 10 Oct. 1915, Hamilton, NZ. Technical Editor. Educ: Bach.Engrng.(Elec. Mech.), 1937, Bach.Engrng.(Mech.), 1938, Canterbury Univ., Christchurch. Pubis: Learning, Service, Achievement (w. W. L. Newnham), 1971; The Engineering History of Electric

Supply in New Zealand, vols. 1-3 (w. L. B. Hulton), 1958-75. Contbr. to: NZ Engrng.; NZ Elec. Jrnl.; NZ Energy Jrnl. Mbrships: NZ Inst. of Engrs.; Jr. Chmbr. Int. Address: 118 Cecil Road, Wadestown, Wellington 1, NZ.

STACEY, Nicholas Anthony Howard, b. 1920. Company Director. Educ: Birmingham & London Univs. Publs: English Accountancy 1800-1954, 1954; The Changing Pattern of Distribution (w. A. Wilson), 1958; Problems of Export Marketing, 1962; Industrial Marketing Research; Management & Technique (w. A. Wilson), 1962; Mergers in Modern Business, 1966. Contbr. to: Financial News & Financial Times (Ed. staff, 1944-46). Address: 36 Chesham Place Belgravia, London SW1, UK.

STACEY, Tom, b. 11 Jan. 1930, Bletchingly, UK. Author. Educ: Oxford Univ. Publs: The Hostile Sun, 1953; The Brothers M, 1960; Summons to Ruwenzori, 1964; Today's World, 1968; The Living & the Dying, 1975. Contbr. to num. jrnls. Hons: Llewellyn Rhys Mem. Prize, 1954; Granada Award, 1961. Address: 128 Kensington Church St., London W8, UK.

STACHURA, Peter Desmond, b. 2 Aug. 1944, Galashiels, Scotland, UK. University Lecturer. Educ: M.A., Univ. of Glasgow, 1967; Ph.D., Univ. of East Anglia, 1971. Publs: Nazi Youth In The Weimar Republic, 1975. Contbr. to: Jrnl. of Contemporary Hist.; European Studies Review; Jrnl. of European Studies; Vierteljahrshefte für Zeitgeschichte; etc. Address: 5 Newhouse, St. Ninian's, Stirling, Scotland, UK.

STACK, Nicolete Meredith, pen names KENNY, Kathryn; HILL, Eileen; MEREDITH, Nicolete, b. 22 Feb. 1899, Des Moines, Iowa, USA. Author. Educ: B.A., Highland Park Coll., Des Moines. Publs. incl: Two to get Ready, 1953; Pierre of the Island, trans. Braille, 1954; Rainbow Tomorrow, 1955; Welcome Love, 1958; King of Kerry Fair, 1960; 8 books adapted from German, 1960-62; 12 mysteries for girls, 1962-72; Flight to Camelot, Whisht, Where did he go? forthcoming. Contbr. to: Highlights for Children; Atlantic Monthly; etc. Mbrships. incl: Authors' League of Am. Pen Women; Past Pres., St. Louis Writers' Guild. Hons. incl: Cath. Books of Yr., 1956; Best Book of Yr., Mo. Writers' Guild, 1958. Address: 8 Colonial Village, Jamestown House, Webster Groves, St. Louis, MO 63119, USA.

STAFF, Enid Burt, b. 2 Jan, 1911, Ipswich, UK. Actress (retired); Playwright; Lecturer on the Theatre. Publs: (plays) Not Like Other Men, 1968; The Red-Headed Galley Boy, 1969; A Mighty Pretty Soul, 1970; Love & Queenie Fish, 1970; The Hostage of Toledo, 1973; Gideon & the Sea Witch, 1975; & short stories. Contbr. to: BBC radio; etc. Address: 3 Heather Close, Colwyn Bay, Clwyd LL29 9DW, UK.

STAFFORD, Jean, b. 1 July 1915, Covina, Calif., USA. Writer. Educ: B.A., 1936, M.A., 1936, Univ. of Colo., Boulder; Heidelberg Univ., Germany, 1936-37. Publs. incl: (novels) Boston Adventure, USA, 1944, UK, 1946; The Mountain Lion, USA, 1947, UK, 1948; The Catherine Wheel, USA & UK, 1952; (short stories) Children are Bored on Sunday, USA, 1953, UK, 1954; Bad Characters, USA, 1964, UK, 1965; Collected Stories, USA, 1969, UK, 1970. Contbr. to: New Yorker. Mbr., Nat. Inst. Arts & Letters. Hons. incl: Nat. Press Club Award, 1948; O. Henry Award, 1955; Pulitzer Prize, 1970; num. grants & Fellowships. Address: c/o New Yorker, 25 W. 43rd St., N.Y., NY 10036, USA.

STAFFORD, William T., b. 31 Oct. 1924, Marianna, Fla., USA. Professor of English; Editor, Modern Fiction Studies; Writer. Educ: B.A., Univ. of Fla., 1948; M.A., Columbia Univ., 1950; Ph.D., Univ. of Ky., 1956. Publs: Melville's Billy Budd & the Critics, 1963, 2nd ed., 1968; James's Daisy Miller: The Story, The Play, The Critics, 1963; Twentieth Century American Writing, 1965; Perspectives on James's The Portrait of a Lady, 1967; Studies in The American, 1971; Frontiers of American Culture (jt. author). Contbr. to num. lit. jrnls. Mbr., num. profl. orgs. Recip., acad. hons. Address: Dept. of Engl., Purdue Univ., W. Lafayette, IN 47907, USA.

STAHL, Virginia Elizabeth McDaniel, b. 20 July 1914, Mpls., Minn., USA. Schoolteacher. Educ: B.S. in Educ., Kent State Univ., Ohio. Publs: The Few for the Many, 1966; Splashes from an Ohio Pump, 1971; Appalachian Apples, 1972; Fireflies in the Fog, 1972; Inspirational Poetry, 1973; To Canaan, To Canaan, To Canaan, 1974.

Contbr. to: NRTA Jrnl.; Wkly. column, Spirit of Democracy; Anthols. of Poetry. Mbrships: Pres., Monroe Co. Art & Crafts Guild, 1972; Educ. Chmn., Monroe Co., Nat. Ret'd Tchrs'. Assn.; Centro Studi E Scambi, Rome; Ohio Verse Writers' Guild; Pa. Poetry Soc.; W.Va. Poetry Soc.; Am. Poets' Fellowship. Recip., num. poetry awards. Address: Route 1, Woodsfield, OH 43793, USA.

STAINE, Lowell Fitzgerald, b. 4 Feb. 1938, Belize City, Brit. Honduras. Journalist. Educ: L.A. City Coll., Calif.; Extra Mural Dept., U.C.W.I., Brit. Honduras. Contbr. to: Poetry Today, Calif. (co-ed.); The Reporter, Belize, Brit. Honduras (permanent corres.). Mbrships: Hollywood For. Press Assn., Calif.; PR Mgr., Proj. Prevent, Parolee & Drug Addict Ctr., Calif. Recip., Humanitarian Award, Bd. of Dirs., Proj. Prevent, 1972. Address: P.O. Box 5302, Metropolitan Station, L.A., CA 90055, USA.

STÅL, Sven Artur Olof, pen name CALIBAN, b. 23 Oct. 1891, Stockholm, Sweden. Actor; Theatre Critic. Publs. incl: Shakespeare & the Theatre of the Future; Appell to the Royal Theatre, 1921; The Hangman's House, 1922; Theatre Nihilism, 1924; Living Moments, 1925; Through the Fourth Wall, 1930; Fiction: The Happy Years of Närsen, 1936; The Land without Sunday, 1943. Mbrships: Author's League; Art History Soc.; St. Barthélemy Acad. Address: Valhallavägen 126, 114 41 Stockholm, Sweden.

STALLYBRASS, Oliver George Weatherhead, b. 1925, Heswall, Cheshire, UK. Librarian; Editor. Educ: Clare Coll., Cambridge Univ.; London Univ.; B.A. Publs: The Ben-Oni Defence (co-author), 1966; Contbng. Ed., Aspects of E. M. Forster, 1969; Ed., Abinger Edition of E. M. Forster, 1972; Collab. Ed., The Fontana Dictionary of Modern Thought, 1975; num. transl. from Danish inclng: A. Jensen, Epp, 1967; K. Hamsun, Victoria, 1969; R. Døcker, Marius, 1970; C. Dreyer, Four Screenplays, 1971; S. Plovgaard (Ed.), Danish Public Library Buildings, 1971; J. Borgen, The Red Mist, 1971; Niels Jensen, When the Land Lay Waste, 1973; transl. in collab., Pierre Leprohon, The Italian Cinema, 1971. Contbr. to: Times Lit. Supplement; num. jrnls. Mbrships: Soc. Authors; Soc. Indexers; Nat. Book League. Agent: Curtis Brown Academic Ltd. Address: 106 Westwood Hill, London SE26, UK.

STAMATOV, Varban, b. 27 May 1924, Veliko Tirnovo, Bulgaria. Writer. Publs: (in Bulgarian) Out of Love, 1956; The Shore of the Poor, 1964; Islanders, 1968; Flagship, 1972; Letters from the Sea, 1973. Contbr. to: September. PlamAk; Literatouren Front. Mbr. Union of Bulgarian Writers. Address: ul. Laiosh Koshut, 36, Bulgaria.

STAMBLER, Irwin, b. 20 Nov. 1924, Brooklyn, NY, USA. Editor; Author. Educ: B.S., 1947; M.S., Coll. of Engrng., 1949; NY Univ.; Further studies, Tex. A. & M, Columbia, Geo. Wash. Univs., & UCLA. Publs. incl: The Battle for Inner Space, Undersea Warfare & Weapons, 1962; Encyclopedia of Popular Music, 1965; Great Moments in Auto Racing, 1967; Ency. of Folk, Country & Western Music, 1969; Shorelines of America, 1972; Revolutions in Light, 1972; Ency. of Pop, Rock & Soul, 1975. Contbr. to: Airline Mgmt. & Mktng. Mag., 1966-69; Indl. Rsch. Mag. (Corres., 1970—); Technol. Forecasts & Technol. Surveys (Co-publr. & Ed. Dir., 1969—). Fellow & Mbr., profl. orgs. Address: Suite 208, 205 S. Beverly Drive, Beverly Hills, CA 90212, USA.

STAMENOV, Marin, pen name, VOLEN, Iliya, b. 13 Oct. 1905, In Uglen, Bulgaria. Writer. Publs: Humble Folk, 1937; (play) The Times of Wolves, 1956; Job, 1964; (essays) The Quest for Truths, 1973. Contbr. to: September; PlamAk; Zlatorog; Literatouren Front; & 6 Newspapers. Mbrships: PEN; Union of Bulgarian Writers. Hons: Award, Bulgarian Acad. of Sci., 1937; Prizes of the Bulgarian Writers Union, 1964, 1967; Dimitrov Prize, 1966. Honoured Cultural Worker. Address: bul. Evlogi Georgiev, 124, Bulgaria.

STANDER, Siegfried, b. 26 Aug. 1935, Rietbron, S. Africa. Writer. Publs: This Desert Place, 1961; The Emptiness of the Plains, 1963; Strangers, 1965; The Journeys of Josephine, 1968; The Horse, 1968; The Fortress, 1972; Leopard in the Sun, 1973; The Unwanted (w. Prof. Christiaan Barnard), 1974. Contbr. to var. jrnls. Mbrships: PEN; Authors Guild. Recip. CNA Lit. Award, 1961 & 1968. Address: "Cliff Cottage", P.O. Box 23, Plettenberg Bay, Repub. of S. Africa.

STANEV, Luben, b. 4 Dec. 1924, Plovdiv, Bulgaria. Film Scriptwriter. Publs: (in Bulgarian) A Cold House, 1957; A Woman does not Sleep, 1961; View from the Hill, 1968; The Ice-Bound Bridge, 1972, 1974; The Lovely Foreign Shores, 1972; This Lovely Mature Age, 1973; A Sofia Story, 1974. Contbr. to: September; SAvremennik; PlamAk; Literatouren Front. Mbrships: Fijet; Union of Bulgarian Writers; Union of Bulgarian Film Workers. Hons: Award, Bulgarian Trade Unions, 1972; Award, Bulgarian Tourist Union, 1973. Address: Sofia, bul. Evlogi Georgiev, 104, Bulgaria.

STANEV, Nikola Stoyanov, pen name STANEV, Emillian, b. 28 Feb. 1907, Veliko Tirnovo, Bulgaria. Writer. Publs: (in Bulgarian) Wolves' Nights, 1940; The Peach Thief, 1948, Engl. ed., 1967; On a Quiet Evening, 1949; Ivan Kondarev, 1964; The Legend of Sybin, 1968; Antichrist, 1970; sev. short stories & 10 Books for Children. Contbr. to sev. Lit. Reviews & Newspapers. Mbrships: Union of Bulgarian Writers; Bulgarian Acad. of Sci. Hons: Dimitrov Prize, 1965; People's Cultural Worker, 1966; Hero of Socialist Labour, 1967; Ivan Vasov Prize, 1971. Address: Sofia, ul. Yuriy Venelin, 31, Bulgaria.

STANGE-FREERKS, Magdalene, b. 31 Mar. 1886, Hamburg, Germany. Teacher (ret'd 1928). Educ: Tchrs. Trng. Coll. Publs: Das Gericht der Tiere, Kleine Erzählungen, 1936; Das Haus am Sonnenberg, 1948, 1972; Admiral Karpfanger und sein Sohn, 1955, 2nd ed., 1971; Auf der Alten Salzstrasse, 1963, 1972; Sunte Maria von Hamburg, 1965. Mbrships: Verband Deutscher Schriftsteller (German Authors' Union); GEDOK, Hamburg. Address: 3149 Vastorf über Dahlenburg/ Lüneburger Heide, W. Germany.

STANKIEWICZ, Wladyslaw Jozef, b. 6 May 1922, Warsaw, Poland. Professor, Political Science. Educ: M.A., Univ. of St. Andrews, UK, 1944; Ph.D., London Schl. of Econs. & Pol. Sci., 1952. Publs: incl: Ed., Political Thought Since World War II, 1964; Relativism: Thoughts & Aphorisms, 1972; Canada-U.S. Relations & Canadian Foreign Policy, 1973; Ed. British Government in an Era of Reform, 1975. Contbr. to: Der Deutsche Hugenott; New Cath. Ency.; etc. Mbrships. incl: Int. Assn., Philos. of Law & Social Philos. Address: Dept. of Pol. Sci., Univ. of Brit. Columbia, Vancouver, B.C., V6T 1W5, Canada.

STANLEY, John Louis Michael, b. 17 July 1943, Cambridge, UK. Business Executive; Public Relations Consultant. Educ: Oxford Schl. of Art. Publs: Dick Emery — in Character; Citroen, A History, forthcoming. Contbr. to: Autosport (for 5 yrs.); Rdrs.' Digest; Drive; IPC (Ed., Music column, & regular motoring columns); most nat. newspapers (photographs & copy); over 500 TV progs. in UK, Japan & USA. Mbr., Guild of Motoring Writers. Address: 80 Tudor Rd., Hampton, Middlesex, UK.

STANSBY, Maurice Earl, b. 25 Apr. 1908, Cedar Rapids, Iowa, USA. Chemist. Educ: B.Sc., 1930, M.Sc., 1933, Univ. of Minn. Publs: Industrial Fishery Technology, 1963; Fish Oils, 1967. Contbr. to: Tech. & sci. encys.; sci. jrnls. (over 100 papers); num. books on foods. Mbrships: Am. Chem. Soc.; Am. Oil Chemists Soc.; Inst. Food Technologists; Pacific Fisheries Technols. (Pres., 1961). Hons: Disting. Serv. Award, US Dept. of Interior, 1966; Outstanding Achievement Award, Univ. of Minn., 1973. Address: 5105 N.E. 75th St., Seattle, WA 98115, USA.

STAPLES, Marjory Charlotte, pen name REDWOOD, Roasline, b. Invercargill, NZ. Journalist; Photographer; Author. Educ: Tchrs. Coll. Publs: (history) Yeoman of the South, 1940; Forgotten Isles of the South Pacific, 1950; (travel) On Copra Ships & Coral Isles, 1966; (biog.) My Wilderness Blossomed, 1964; (novels) Forgotten Heritage, 1966; Isle of the Golden Pearls, 1967; Stranger from Shanghai, 1968. Contbr. to: Nat. Geog. (USA); Travel; World Digest; Trident; Wide World; NZ Mirror; Aust. Women's Wkly.; Aust. House & Gdn.; S. African Home & Gdn.; Newsview; Walkabout; etc. Address: 115 Huntsbury Ave., Christchurch 2, NZ.

STAPLETON, David Frank, b. Portsmouth, UK. Deputy Head of Junior School. Educ: Dip.Ed., Liverpool Univ. Publs: Crosswords for the Primary School; Comprehensive English Exercises; Comprehensive Arithmetic Exercises; Everyday Problems in Arithmetic; Subject Crosswords; Lexicon Crosswords; School Music. Contbr. to: The Teacher. Mbrships: Assoc., Coll. Preceptors; Authors, London; Nat. Union Tchrs. Address: Locks Heath C. Junior School, Warsash, Hants., UK.

STAPLETON, (Katharine) Laurence, b. 20 Nov. 1911, Holyoke, Mass., USA. Teacher; Writer. Educ: B.A.(Hons.), Smith Coll., 1932; grad. study, Univ. of London, UK, 1932-33. Publs: Justice & World Society, 1944; The Design of Democracy, 1949; H. D. Thoreau: A Writer's Journal, 1959; Yushin's Log & Other Poems, 1969; The Elected Circle: Studies in the Art of Prose, 1973. Contbr. to: Univ. of Toronto, S. Atlantic, Philol. Quarterlies; Studies in Philol.; Mass. Review; etc. Mbrships: MLA; Engl. Assn. (London); Renaissance Soc., of Am.; Thoreau Soc. Hons. incl: Guggenheim Fellowship, 1947-48; Nat. Coun. for Arts Fellowship, 1972-73. Address: 229 N. Roberts Road, Bryn Mawr, PA 19010, USA.

STARES, John Edward Spencer, pen names ROWE, Stephen; SPENCER, Edward, b. 22 Apr. 1947, Reading, UK. Science Writer. Educ: B.S., Univ. of St. Andrews, 1969. Publs: Molecules of Life, 1972; Cell Form & Function, 1972; Ed., Chemical Disarmament: Some Problems of Verification, 1973; Ed., World Armaments & Disarmament, SIPRI Yearbook 1973; Ed., The Arms Trade with the Third World, 1975; Ed., Medical Protection against Chemical Warfare Agents, 1975. Contbr. to var. encys. & jrnls. Mbrships: Assn. of Brit. Sci. Writers; Participant, Pugwash Movt. Meetings. Address: 2 Virginia Way, Reading, Berks., UK.

STARK, Freya Madeline, b. 31 Jan 1893, Paris, France. Explorer & Writer. Educ: Bedford Coll., London; Schl. Oriental Studies, Univ. London. Publs. incl: The Valleys of the Assassins, 1934; Baghdad Sketches, 1937; East is West, 1945; Beyond Euphrates, 1951; Ionia: A Quest, 1954; Alexander's Path, 1958; The Journey's Echo, 1963; Rome on the Euphrates, 1966; The Zodiac Arch, 1968; Space, Time & Movement in Landscape, 1969; The Minaret of Djam, 1970; Turkey (w. F. Roiter), 1970; Letters (Vol. I), 1974, & 10 other books. Mbrships: Royal Geogl. Soc.; Royal Ctrl. Asian Soc.; Ladies Alpine Club. Hons. incl: D.B.E., 1972; LL.D., Glasgow Univ.; D.Litt., Durham Univ.; Fndr's. Medal, Royal Geogl. Soc.; Sir Percy Sykes Medal, Royal Ctrl. Asian Soc. Address: Asolo, Treviso, Italy.

STARK, Sheldon, b. 7 Sept. 1919, N.Y., USA. Writer. Educ: Lincoln Schl. of Tchr.'s Coll., Columbia; B.A., Dartmouth Coll. Publs. (plays): Time of Storm, 1954; The Fire Ants, 1964. Contbr. to am. network TV. Mbrships: Charter Mbr., Writers Guild of Am.; Coun., 1954-58; Coun., Authors League of Am., 1946-54; VP, Radio Writers Guild of ALA, 1949-51; Fndr., Palisades Community Theatre; Pres., 1964-66. Hons: 'Time of Storm' Best New Play of Yr., N.Y. Daily Wkr., 1954; 'The Roots' Nominee Best Dramatic Script, WGA TV, 1973-74; 'Assignment Southeast Asia' Peabody Award, Best Documentary of 1957-58. Address: 16401 Akron St., Pacific Palisades, CA 90272, USA.

STAROBINSKI, Jean, b. 17 Nov. 1920, Geneva, Switz. University Professor. Educ: D.Litt., Univ. of Geneva; M.D., Univ. of Lausanne. Publs: Jean-Jacques Rousseau, 1957; L'oeil vivant, 1961; L'invention de la liberté, 1964; La relation critique, 1971; Les emblèmes de la raison, 1973; Trois fureurs, 1974. Mbrships: Pres., Soc. Jean-Jacques Rousseau, Geneva, Rencontres Ints. de Genève, Mod. Humanities Rsch. Assn., 1975; Socio Straniero, Acad. Nazionale dei Lincei, Rome; For. Hon. Mbr., AAAS; Corres. Fellow, Brit. Acad. Hons: Prix Femina-Vacaresco, 1958; Grand Prix de lit. française, Acad. Royale de Belgique, 1972. Address: 12 rue de Candolle, 1205 Geneva, Switz.

STATEN, Pat, b. 6 Mar. 1945, Topeka, Kan., USA. Writer; Dramatist. Educ: B.A., Univ. of Colo., Boulder; M.F.A., Columbia Univ., N.Y. Publs: (plays) A Disturbance of Mirrors, 1972; Iphigenia Again, 1973; (production) 90-minute film adaptation of The Day My Father Tried to Kill Us. Contbr. to: Aphra. Mbrships: Dramatists' Guild; Authors' Guild of Am., Writers' Guild. Hons: Shubert Playwriting Fellow, 1970; Robert E. Sherwood Award, 1971; Eugene O'Neill Fellow, 1972; Va. Ctr. Creative Arts Fellow, 1973; Yaddo Fellow, 1974; MacDowell Colony Fellow, 1974, 1975. Address: 336 East 59th Street, N.Y., NY, USA.

STAUB, August W. b. 9 Oct. 1931, New Orleans, La., USA. Educator; Theatrical Director. Educ: B.A., 1952, M.A., 1956, Ph.D., 1960, La. State Univ. Publs: Contemporary Rhetoric, 1969; Introduction to Theatrical Arts, 1972; Creating Theatre, 1973; & essays in Exploring Literature, 1966. Contbr. to: Southern Speech Jrnl.;

Quarterly Jrnl. Speech; Southern Review; Dramatics; Playbill. Mbrships: Am. Theatre Assn. (Mbr. Bd., 1973, 1974); Univ. & Coll. Theatre Assn. (VP, 1973; Pres., 1974). Hons: Disting. Fac. Fellowship, Univ. New Orleans, 1970; Outstanding Educators Am. Address: 5551 Pratt Dr., New Orleans, LA 70122, USA.

STAUFFER, Robert, pen name RASCHLE, Otto, b. 23 June 1936, Berne, Switz. Freelance Author; Journalist; Translator of Hungarian poetry. Publs: Wien um 1900, 1964; (radio-plays) Lugensanger, 1966; Die Leichenschmausler, 1973; (Transls.) Sandor Weores (poetry); Magda Szabo (radio-play). Contbr. to "Boxercollage", Neues Forum, 1970. Mbr., PEN. Address: Wilhelminenstrasse 219, A-1160 Vienna, Austria.

STAVAUX, Michel, b. 6 May 1948, Sehaerbeek, Belgium. Assistant Financial Controller. Educ: Dr. Law, Univ. of Brussels; Post Grad. Special Lic., European Law. Publs: Cheval d'ivoire, 1964; Des Cactus que la mer rejettera demain, 1969; La Promenade rue Volière, 1970. Contbr. to: Le Jrnl. des Poètes; Le Figaro litteraire; Le Voie des Poètes; Les Lettres françaises. Recip., Polak Prize, French Royal Acad. of Lang. & Lit., Belgium, 1970. Address: 33c Av. du Paepedelle, 1160 Brussels, Belgium.

STAVIS, Barrie, b. 16 June 1906, NYC, USA. Playwright. Educ: Columbia Univ., 1924-27. Publs. incl: Lamp at Midnight, 1948; The Man Who Never Died, 1954; Harpers Ferry, 1967; Coat of Many Colours, 1968; histories incl: Notes of Joe Hill & His Times, 1964; John Brown: the Sword & the Word, 1970. Contbr. to: Sat. Evening Post; Reader's Digest; Folk Music; Drama Survey; etc. Mbrships. incl: PEN; Am. Theatre Assn.; New Stages (Bd. Dirs., 1947-50). Hons. incl: Nat. Theatre Conf. Award, 1948, 1949; 2 acad. hons. Address: 70 E. 96th St., N.Y., NY 10028, USA.

STAYNOVA, Anna, pen name KAMENOVA, Anna, b. 31 Dec. 1894, Plovdiv, Bulgaria. Writer. Publs: Haritina's Sin, 1930; The Town is the Same, 1933; Five Girls, 1940; Never to be Repeated, 1942; Near Sofia, 1957; Vladko in India, 1961; India, Which we Saw & Got to Love, 1963. Contbr. to: September; SAvremennik; Literatouren Front. Mbrships: Union of Bulgarian Writers; Gen. Comm. for Bulgarian-Soviet Friendship; Comm. of Women. Recip., Award, Honoured Worker in Culture, 1971. Address: Sofia, ul. Oborishte, 36, Bulgaria.

STEAD, Christina (Ellen), b. 17 July 1902, Rockdale, Sydney, Australia. Writer. Educ: Grad., Tchrs. Coll., Sydney Univ., 1922. Publs. incl: Seven Poor Men of Sydney, UK, 1934, USA, 1935; House of All Nations, UK & USA, 1938; The Man Who Love Children, USA, 1940, UK, 1941; For Love Alone, USA, 1944, UK, 1945; Letty Fox, USA, 1946, UK, 1947; The People with the Dogs, 1952; Dark Places of the Heart, USA, 1966 (as Cotter's England, UK, 1967); The Puzzleheaded Girl: 4 Novellas, USA, 1967, UK, 1968. Contbr. to: Southerly; Meanjin; New Yorker; etc. Hons. incl: Aga Khan Prize, Paris Review, 1966. Address: c/o Laurence Pollinger, 18 Maddox St., London W1, UK.

STEADMAN, John Marcellus, III, b. 25 Nov. 1918, Spartanburg, S.C., USA. Research Scholar; University Professor. Educ: A.B., 1940, M.A., 1941, Emory Univ.; M.A., 1948, Ph.D., 1949, Princeton Univ. Publs: Milton & the Renaissance Hero, 1967; Milton's Epic Characters, 1968; The Myth of Asia, 1969, 1970; Disembodied Laughter, 1972; The Lamb & the Elephant, 1974; Ed., Huntington Lib. Quarterly. Contbr. to: Milton Studies (Ed. Bd.); Complete Prose Works of John Milton (Ed. Bd.); Variorum Commentary on the Prose of John Milton (Ed. Bd.); MLA Publs: Renaissance Quarterly; num. other profl. jrnls. Mbrships. incl: MLA; Milton Soc. of Am. (Pres., 1973); Dante Soc. of Am. Address: c/o Athenaeum, 551 South Hill Ave., Pasadena, CA 91106, USA.

STEARNS, Monroe Mather, b. 28 Sept. 1913, NYC, USA. Writer. Educ: A.B., Harvard Univ., 1934. Publs. incl: Ring-A-Ling, 1959; The Key to Rome, 1961; Mark Twain, 1965; Goya, 1966; Michelangelo, 1968; Shays Rebellion, 1969; Queen Elizabeth I, 1969; Transl., Angelique in Barbary, Angelique & the King, 1960; Summer in the Ville Marie, 1962; Shalom Aviva, 1969. Contbr. to: N.Y. Times Book Review; Theatre Arts mag. Address: 300 Riverside Dr., N.Y. NY 10025, USA.

STECHOW, Wolfgang, b. 5 June 1896, Kiel, Germany. Art Historian. Educ: Dr.phil., Univ. of Göttingen, 1921;

Univs. of Freiburg & Berlin. Publs: Apollo und Daphne, 1932, new ed., 1965; Salomon van Ruysdael, 1938; Dutch Landscape Painting of the Seventeenth Century, 1966, 2nd ed., 1968; Rubens & the Classical Tradition, 1967; Peter Bruegel, 1969; Contbr. to: Am., Engl., German, Dutch, Belgian, French & Italian art hist. jrnls., 1922–. Mbrships. incl: V.P., Coll. Art Assn. of Am., 1945-46; Nat. Comm. on the Hist. of Art. Recip., sev. hon. degrees. Address: 21 Robin Pk., Oberlin. OH 44074, USA.

STEDING, Johan Arthur Willy, b. 29 Apr. 1900, Altona, Hamburg, Germany. Author; Artist. Educ: Kunstgewerbe-Schule, Hamburg-Lerchenfeld; Meisterschüler of Eagle Claw — Ernst Mueller; Meisterschüler of Oscar Boegel. Publs: Der Mensch ohne Furcht, 1920; Vom Gedanken zur Tat, 1921; Martin Steffens wilde Seefahrt, 1928; Whisky, 1931; Teufel zur See, 1932; Im Banne der Fischweid, 1938; Kein Tier ist gering, 1943; Silberne Beute (anthol.), 1963; Im Netz der Fische (anthol.), 1963. Mbrships: Authors' Union, Hamburg; Jrnlsts.' Ctr., Hamburg. Address: 2 Hamburg 70, Mariusweg 1 B, W. Germany.

STEEGMULLER, Francis, pen name KEITH, David, b. 3 July 1906, New Haven, Conn., USA. Writer. Educ: B.A. 1927, M.A. 1928, Columbia Univ.; Publs. incl: (novels) The Musicale, USA & UK, 1930; A Matter of Iodine (as D. Keith), USA & UK, 1940; The Christening Party, USA, 1960, UK, 1961; (short stories) Stories & True Stories, USA & UK, 1972; (non-fiction) Flaubert & Madame Bovary, USA & UK, 1939, revised eds. 1968; The Grand Mademoiselle, UK, 1955, USA, 1966; Apollinaire, USA, 1963, UK, 1964; Cocteau, USA & UK, 1970; var. eds. & transls. of Flaubert, etc. Mbr., Nat. Inst. Arts & Letters. Hons. incl: Nat. Book Award, 1971. Address: 200 E. 66th St., N.Y., NY 10021, USA.

STEELE, Harwood (Robert Elmes), b. 5 May 1897, Fort MacLeod, Alta, Can. Author; Lecturer. Educ: 1st class hons. degree, Anthropol. (extra-mural), McGill Univ. Publs. incl: Spirit of Iron, 1923; Policing the Arctic, 1934; Official Guide Book for T.M. the King & Queen on Canadian Tour of 1939 (co-author); Ghosts Returning, 1950; The Red Serge (short stories), 1961; RCMP, 1970; Centennial History of R.C.M.P., forthcoming. Contbr. to: Daily Express; Can. Mag.; Montreal Star; etc. Mbrships. incl: F.R.G.S.; Royal C'wlth. Soc.; Soc. of Authors; Can. Authors' Assn. Recip., sev. minor hons. Address: Warenne Lodge, Broomers Hill Lane, Pulborough, Sussex, UK.

STEEN, Marguerite, b. 1894. Novelist; Playwright. Publs. incl: Gilt Cage, 1927; The Reluctant Madonna, 1929; Hugh Walpole, a Study, 1933; The Spanish Trilogy: Matador, 1934, The Tavern, 1935, The One-Eyed Moon, 1935; The Sun is my Undoing, 1941; William Nicholson (biog.), 1943; Twilight on the Floods, 1949; Bulls of Parral, 1954; The Woman in the Back Seat, 1959; A Pride of Terrys (biog.), 1962; A Candle in the Sun, 1964; (autobiog.) Looking Glass I, 1966; Pier Glass, 1968; (plays) Matador (w. M. Lang), prod. 1936; French for Love (w. D. Patmore), prod. 1939. Fellow, Royal Soc. Lit. Address: Little Triton, Blewbury, Berks., UK.

STEEN, Vagn, b. 13 July 1928, Holbaek, Denmark. Poet; TV Producer; Critic. Educ: cand. mag., Scandinavian Philol. & Hist. Publs: Digte? (Poems?), 1964; Tear it out Yourself (poems), 1965; Write Yourself, 1965; Technically it is Possible (poems), 1967; -digte (-poems), 1972; k (poems), 1973; The Bird's Flight, 1974; var. juvenile & critical books. Contbr. to: Politiken (poetry criticism); Digte for en Daler. Mbrships: PEN; Authors' Soc. of Denmark (Bd.); Assn. Danish Artists (Pres.). Recip., var. prizes from Fndn. Danish Arts, 1965–. Address: Carl Bernhardsvej 15A, 1817 Copenhagen V, Denmark.

STEERE, Douglas V., b. 31 Aug. 1901, Harbor Beach, Mich., USA. Professor of Philosophy; Author. Publs. incl: Prayer & Worship, 1938; On Beginning from Within, 1943; Doors Into Life, 1948; Time to Spare, 1948; Friends Work in Africa, 1955; On Listening to Another (in UK as Where Words Come From), 1955; Work & Contemplation, 1957; Dimensions of Prayer, 1962; Spiritual Counsels & Letters of Baron Von Hügel (w. introductory essay), 1963; God's Irregular: Arthur Shearly Cripps, 1973. Contbr. to: var. theol. & relig. jrnls.; Ed. Bd. Mbr., Relig. in Life. Recip., 5 hon. degrees. Address: Haverford College, Haverford, PA 19041, USA.

STEFANESCU, Mircea, b. 11 Apr. 1898, Bucharest, Rumania. Writer. Educ: Law studies, Univ. of Bucharest,

1921. Publs. incl: (plays) The Small Inferno, 1948; The Rumanian Patriotics Association, 1955; Eminescu, 1964; In Search of Demetrian, 1970; Ion Creanga, 1972; Esculap & His Little Friend, 1973; short stories: Play in the Night, Play in the Day, 1971. Contbr. to: Vremea; La Zid! Mbr., Writer's Soc. of Rumania. Hons. incl: Nat. Theatre Prize, 1936; I. L. Caragiale Prize, 1949; State Laureate Prize, 1951, 1952. Distinction: Order of Work. Address: Bd.Al.I.Cuza 53 et 3, ap 4, sector 8, Bucharest, Rumania.

STEFANOV, Vassil, b. 15 Nov. 1933, Varna, Bulgaria. Dramatic Critic. Educ: University Level, Cand. of Study of Art. Publs: Drama & Composition, 1965; Contemporary Puppet Theatre, 1971; Theatrical Meetings, 1973. Contbr. to: Theatre; September; Lit. Thought; Lit. Front; Nat. Culture. Mbrships: Union of Bulgarian Writers; Union of Actors in Bulgaria. Address: Marin Drinov 28, Sofia, Bulgaria.

STEFÁNSSON, Hreidar, b. 3 June 1918, Akureyri, Iceland. Teacher. Educ: Degree, Icelandic Teachers' Coll. Publs: (w. Jenna Stefansson) 26 books inclng. Adda, 7 vols., for young girls, Girls in Mini, 2 vols., for teenagers, & 5 schl. primers, sev. reaching 4 eds. Mbrships: Icelandic Writers' Union; Assn. of Icelandic Writers; Icelandic Tchrs.' Union. Recip., Hon. prize for Writers of Books for Young People, City of Reykjavík, 1973. Address: Godheimar 16, Reykjavík, Iceland.

STEGLICH, Winfred George, b. 21 Sept. 1921, Giddings, Tex., USA. Professor of Sociology. Educ: B.A., Concordia Sem., St. Louis, Mo., 1942; M.A., 1945, Ph.D., 1951, Univ. of Tex., Austin; Fla. State Univ., Tallahassee, 1955-56. Publs: Student Guide to Sociology, 1969; Instructor's Manual, Society & Culture, 1966, 1969. Contbr. to Annals of Reg. Sci.; Rocky Mtn. Social Sci. Quarterly; Ariz. Review of Bus.; Tex. Outlook; Am. Jrnl. of Econs. & Sociol.; etc. Mbrships: Pres., Southwestern Social Sci. Assn., 1975; Pres., Southwestern Sociol. Assn., 1963; Fellow, Am. Sociol. Assn.; Population Assn. of Am. Address: 6625 Southwind, El Paso, TX 79912, USA.

STEGNER, Wallace (Earle), b. 18 Feb. 1909, Lake Mills, Iowa, USA. Former University Professor. Educ: A.B., Univ. of Utah, 1930; A.M. 1932, Ph.D. 1935, Univ. of Iowa. Publs. incl: (novels) On a Darkling Plain, 1940; The Big Rock Candy Mountain, USA, 1943, UK, 1950; Second Growth, USA, 1947, UK, 1948; All the Little Live Things, USA, 1967, UK, 1968; Angle of Repose, USA & UK, 1971; (non-fiction) The Gathering of Zion, USA, 1964, UK, 1966; 2 vols. short stories. Contbr. to: Esquire; Harper's; etc. Mbrships: Nat. Inst. Arts & Letters; Am. Acad. Arts & Scis. Recip., num. Awards, Docts., Grants & Fellowships. Address: 13456 S. Fork Lane, Los Altos Hills, CA 94022, USA.

STEIN, M. L., b. 20 July 1930, Escanaba, Mich., USA. University Professor; Author. Educ: B.A., Univ. of Mo.; M.A., Stanford Univ. Publs. incl: Your Career in Journalism, 1965; Freedom of the Press, 1966; Write Clearly . . . Speak Effectively, 1967. Under Fire: The Story of American War Correspondents, 1968; When Presidents Meet the Press, 1969; Reporting Today, 1971; Blacks in Communications, 1972; Shaping the News, 1974. Contbr. to: Saturday Review; N.Y. Times; Nation; World; etc. Mbrships. incl: Assn. for Educ. in Jrnlsm.; Soc. of Mag. Writers; etc. Recip., Soc. of Mag. Writers' Citation, 1974. Address: 2892 Walker Lee Drive, Los Alamitos, CA 90720, USA.

STEIN, Peter Gonville, b. 29 May 1926, Liverpool, UK. Regius Professor of Civil Law, Cambridge University. Educ: M.A., LL.B., Gonville & Caius Coll., Cambridge Univ.; Ph.D., Aberdeen Univ.; Admitted Solicitor, 1951. Publs: Fault in the Formation of Contract in Roman Law & Scots Law, 1958; Regulae Iuris — From Juristic Rules to Legal Maxims, 1966; Legal Values in Western Society (w. J. Shand), 1974. Contbr. to: Ency. Britannica; Dictionary of Hist. of Ideas. Mbrships: Fellow, Brit. Acad., 1974; Fellow Queens' Coll., Cambridge since 1968. Address: Queens' Coll., Cambridge, UK.

STEIN, Sol, b. 13 Oct. 1926, Chgo., Ill., USA. Book Publisher. Educ: B.S.S., CCNY, 1948; M.A., 1949, Ph.D. cand., 1949-51, Columbia Univ. Publs: The Husband, 1969; The Magician, 1971; The Living Room, 1974; sev. plays. Contbr. to num. jrnls. inclng: Commentary; New Repub.; Sat. Review/World; Book Digest. Mbrships: Hon. Life, Int. Brotherhood of Magicians; Writers Guild of Am., E. (screenwriter); Dramatists Guild (playwright). Hons. incl:

Dramatists Alliance award for best full-length play of 1953. Address: Linden Circle, Scarborough, NY 10510, USA.

STEINBERG, Erwin R., b. 15 Nov. 1920, New Rochelle, N.Y., USA. Professor & College Administrator; Author; Editor. Educ: B.S., M.S., SUNY, Albany; Ph.D., N.Y. Univ. Publs. incl: Communication in Business & Industry (co-author), 1960; Personal Integrity (co-ed.), 1961; Ed., The Rule of Force, 1962; Needed Research in the Teaching of English, 1963; Gen. Ed., "Insight" Series, 1968-73; English Then and Now (co-ed.), 1970; The Stream of Consciousness & Beyond in "Ulysses", 1973. Contbr. to: Lit. & Psychol.; Mod. Fiction Studies; James Joyce Review; Engl. Jrnl.; & num. others. Mbrships: Nat. Coun. of Tchrs. of Engl.; MLA. Address: Coll. of Humanities & Social Sciences, Carnegie-Mellon Univ., Pittsburgh, PA 15213, USA.

STEINCROHN, Peter J., b. 28 Nov. 1899, Hartford, Conn., USA. Physician; Author; Medical Journalist. Educ: M.D., Univ. of Md., 1923. Publs. incl: How to Stop Killing Yourself; The Doctor Looks at Life; Your Heart is Stronger than You Think; Low Blood Sugar. Contbr. to: Saturday Evening Post; Rdr.s' Digest; Cosmpolitan; Coronet; num. newspapers (nat. syndicated column). Mbr., var. med. assns. Address: 1430 Ancona Ave., Coral Gables, FL 33146, USA.

STEINER, George, b. 23 Apr. 1929, Paris, France. Scholar; University Professor. Educ: B.A.; M.A.; D.Phil.; Univs. of Paris, Chgo., & Harvard; Balliol. Coll., Oxford. Publs. incl: Tolstoy or Dostoevsky, 1959; The Death of Tragedy, 1961; Anno Domini: Three Stories, 1964; Language & Silence, 1967; Extraterritorial, 1971; In Bluebeard's Castle, 1971; White Knights in Reykjavik, 1973; Fields of Force, 1974. Contbr. to: Economist; Ed., Penguin Book of Med. Verse Transl., 1967. Fellow, Royal Soc. Lit. Hons. incl: O. Henry Award, 1958; Zabel Prize, Nat. Inst. of Arts & Letters, 1970. Address: 32 Barrow Rd., Cambridge, UK.

STEINER, Herbert, b. 3 Feb. 1923, Vienna, Austria. Historian; Head of Documentation Archives of Austrian Resistance. Educ: Ph.D., Vienna Univ.; Cand.Sc., Prague Univ., Czech. Publs. incl: History of the Austrian Labour Movement (1867-1889), 1964; Bibliography, Austrian Labour Movement, 3 vols., 1964-70; Condemned to Death, 1964; Died for Austria, 1968; Josef, Heinrich & Andreas Sche (biog.), 1968; Dr. Käthe Leichter (biog.), 1973. Contbr. to var. hist. jrnls. Mbrships. incl: PEN; Assn. of Hist., Vienna; Int. Assn. Labour Histns.; Labour Hist. Assn., London UK; AIMS, N.Y., USA. Hons: Theodor Körner Prizes, 1958, 1961. Address: Treustrasse 69/15/3, Vienna 20, Austria 1200.

STEINER, Kurt, b. 10 June 1912, Vienna, Austria. Professor of Political Science; Author. Educ: J.D., Univ. of Vienna, 1935; Ph.D., Stanford Univ., Calif., USA, 1955. Publs: Local Government in Japan, 1965; Politics in Austria, 1972; (chapts. in) Court & Constitution in Japan (Ed., J. M. Maki), 1964; Political Development in Modern Japan (Ed., R. E. Ward), 1968. Contbr. to: Jrnl. of Asian Studies; Am. Pol. Sci. Review; Jrnl. of Comp. Law; Wash. Law Review; Far Eastern Survey; Econ. Dev. & Cultural Change. Address: 832 Sonoma Ter., Stanford, CA 94305, USA.

STELMAKH, Mikhail Afanasyevich, b. 24 May 1912, Ukraine. Writer. Educ: Vinnitsa Pedagogical Inst. Publs: Bread & Salt; Blood is Thicker Than Water; The Big Family; Truth & Falsehood, 1961; Collected Works, 5 vols., 1962; Goose-swans are flying (children's story), 1964; Against Golden Gods, 1966; Family of Burunduk, 1968. Mbr., Supreme Soviet. Hons: Lenin Prize; State Prize; Order of Lenin (twice); Red Banner of Labour; Red Star, 2nd Class. Address: Union of Writers, Kiev, USSR.

STENBERG, Birgitta, b. 26 Apr. 1932, Stockholm, Sweden. Writer. Publs: Mikael och Poeten, 1956; Vit av Natten, 1958; Chans, 1961; Valdgasten, 1963; De Franvanda, 1964; Rapport, 1969; Skurkar, 1973. Mbrships: Författarförbundet; Författarcentrum, PEN; Swedish Union of Authors; Publicistklubben. Address: S-440 Astol, Sweden.

STENSLAND JUNKER, Karin Birgitta, b. 7 Oct. 1916, Lidingö, Sweden. Associate Professor of Pediatric Audiological Methodology; Scientist; Writer. Educ: M.A., 1958, Ph.D., 1968, Univ. of Stockholm; Dissertation, Med. Fac., Karolinska Inst., Stockholm, 1972. Publs. incl: Du Känner mig icke, 1944; Vad ska vi göra med Ture? , 1957;

De Ensamma, 1961; The Child in the Glass Ball, 1964; Selective Attention in Infants & Consecutive Communicative Behavior, 1972; Den Lilla Människan, 1975. Contbr. to var. profl. jrnls. Mbrships: Int. Coll. of Pediatrics, USA; Sällskapet Pro Patria, Sweden. Hons. incl: Svenska Scoutförbundets Silverhästsko, 1966; Svensk Damtidnings Kulturpris, 1974. Address: Åsögatan 211, 116 32 Stockholm, Sweden.

STEPHAN, John J., b. 8 Mar. 1941, Chgo., USA. Associate Professor of History. Educ: B.A., 1963, M.A., 1964, Harvard Univ.; Ph.D., Univ. of London, UK, 1969. Publs: Sakhalin: A History, 1971; The Kuril Islands: Russo-Japanese Frontier in the Pacific, 1974. Contbr. to: Asian Survey; Mod. Asian Studies; Jrnl. of Asian Studies; Mizan. Mbrships: Assn. for Asian Studies; Am. Assn. for the Advancement of Slavic Studies; AAUP. Hons: Choice Mag. Selection for Outstanding Acad. Book, 1971; Japan Culture Transl. Prize, 1973. Address: Dept. of History, University of Hawaii, 2550 Campus Rd., Honolulu, HI 96822, USA.

STEPHEN, David Douglas, b. 26 Mar. 1922, Perth, UK. Chartered Electrical & Mechanical Engineer. Educ: B.Sc., Glasgow Univ. Publs: Synchronous Motors & Condensers, 1958. Contbr. to: Elec. Review; Engrng.; AEI Engrng. Review; Bulletin of Elec. Engrng. Educ.; Elec. Times; Elec. Inds. Export; Elec. & Electronics; IEE Proceedings; Brit. Ind. & Engrng. Mbrships: Fellow, Instn. of Elec. Engrs.; Instn. of Mech. Engrs.; Inst. of Elec. & Electronics Engrs.; etc. Address: 14 Rainsbrook Ave., Rugby, Warwicks., UK.

STEPHENS, Michael Gregory, b. 4 Mar. 1946. Writer. Educ: M.A., CCNY; Yale School of Drama. Publs: Season at Coole, 1972; Alcohol Poems, 1973; Paragraphs, 1974; Still Life, 1975. Contbr. to: Tri Quarterly; Provincetown Review; Rolling Stone; Village Voice; Boston Phoenix; World; Mulch; Strange Faces; Works, Galley Sail Review; Cuchwlain; etc. Hons. incl: PEN Grant; Boskop Fndn. Award; Carnegie Fund for Authors Award; MacDowell Colony Award; Bread Loaf Writers' Conf. Award; Va. Ctr. for Arts Award. Address: 520 West 110th St. 4—A, N.Y., NY 10025, USA.

STEPHENS, Robert, b. 4 Sept. 1920, London, UK. Journalist; Author. Educ: Kings Coll., London. Publs: Cyprus: A Place of Arms, 1966; Nasser, A Political Biography, 1971; The Arabs New Frontier, 1973. Contbr. to: Observer (Assoc. Ed.) Mbrships: Royal Inst. of Int. Affaris; Int. Inst. for Strategic Studies; Coun., Brit. Soc. for Mid. E. Studies; Nat. Union of Jrnlsts. Address: c/o The Observer, 160 Queen Victoria St., London EC4, UK.

STEPHENS, Robert Oren, b. 2 Oct. 1928, Corpus Christi, Tex., USA. Professor of English. Educ: Del Mar Coll., 1945-47; B.A., Tex. A & I Coll., 1949; M.A., 1951, Ph.D., 1958, Univ. of Tex. Publs: Hemingway's Nonfiction: The Public Voice, 1968, paperback, 1969; Ernest Hemingway: The Critical Reception (to appear 1974-75). Contbr. to: Publs. of MLA; Am. Literature; Am. Quarterly; other lit. & profl. jrnls. Mbrships. incl: MLA; South Atlantic Mod. Lang. Assn.; Am. Studies Assn. Address: Dept. of English, Univ. of N.C. at Greensboro, Greensboro, NC 27412, USA.

STERLING, William, b. 14 Sept. 1926, Sydney, Australia. Film & TV Writer/Producer/Director. Educ: B.A., Dip. Ed., Univ. of Sydney, N.S.W. Publs: Writer/Dir., Alice's Adventures in Wonderland (film musical), 1972. Mbrships: Assn. Cinematograph, TV & Allied Techns.; Soc. of Film & TV Arts; Brit. Film Inst.; Assn. Dirs. & Prods. Address: 9 "Hillcrest", 51/57 Ladbroke Grove, London W11 3AX, UK.

STERN, Clarence A., b. McClusky, N.D., USA. Historian; Political Scientist; Educator. Educ: A.B., Eastern Mich. Univ., 1934; M.A., Wayne State Univ., 1938; LaSalle Ext. Univ., Chgo., 1947-49; Ph.D., Univ. of Neb., 1958. Publs: Republican Heyday: Republicanism Through the McKinley Years, 1962, 1969; Resurgent Republicanism: The Handiwork of Hanna, 1963, 1968; Golden Republicanism: The Crusade for Hard Money, 1964, 1970; Protectionist Republicanism: Republican Tariff Policy in the McKinley Period, 1971; Pro-Trust Republicanism, in preparation. Mbrships. incl: AAUP; Hon. Fellow, Harry S. Truman Lib. Inst. for Nat. & Int. Affairs, 1974; Am. Histl. Assn.; Org. of Am. Histns.; Am. Pol. Sci. Assn. Address: Dept. of Hist., Univ. of Wis., Oshkosh, WI 54901, USA.

STERN, James (Andrew), b. 26 Dec. 1904, Kilcairne, Co. Meath, Ireland. Writer; Freelance Journalist. Educ:

Royal Mil. Acad., Sandhurst, UK. Publs: (short stories) The Heartless Land, UK & USA, 1932; Something Wrong, 1938; The Man Who was Loved, USA, 1951, UK, 1952; The Stories of James Stern, UK, 1968, USA, 1969; Ed., Grimm's Fairy Tales, USA, 1944, UK, 1948; (autobiog.) The Hidden Damage, USA, 1947; Transl., num. works of Zweig, Kafka, Brecht & others from German (some as Andrew St. James). Hons: Grant, Nat. Inst. Arts & Letters, USA, 1949; Arts Coun. Award, UK, 1966. Address: Hatch Manor, Tisbury, Wilts., UK.

STERN, Karl, b. 8 Apr. 1906, Cham, Bavaria, Germany. Physician; Psychiatrist. Educ: M.D. Publs: The Pillar of Fire, 1951; Third Revolution, 1954; Dooms of Love, 1957; The Flight From Women, 1965; Love & Success, forthcoming. Contbr. to num. mags. Recip., Christopher Prize, 1951. Address: 3800 Grey Ave., Montreal, P.Q., Canada.

STERN, Malcolm Henry, b. 29 Jan. 1915, Phila., Pa., USA. Rabbi. Educ: B.A., Univ. of Pa.; B.H.L., M.H.L., & D.H.L., Hebrew Union Coll., Cinn., Ohio. Publs: Uriah P. Levy — The Blue Star Commodore (ed.), 1958; Union Songster (ed.), 1960; Americans of Jewish Descent, 1960; A Jewish Tourist's Guide to the Caribbean (w. Bernard Postal), 1972. Contbr. to: Am. Jewish Histl. Quarterly; Am. Jewish Archives; Jrnl. of the Crtl. Conf. of Am. Rabbis; Nat. Geneal. Soc. Quarterly; etc. Mbrships: Treas., Sec. V.P., Am. Soc. of Geneals.; Curator, V.P., Am. Jewish Histl. Soc. Recip., sev. acad. hons. Address: 300 E. 71st St., N.Y., NY 10021, USA.

STERN, Michael, b. 3 Aug. 1910, NYC, USA. Author; Journalist. Educ: B.S., Syracuse Univ. Publs: The White Ticket, 1936; Flight from Terror (w. Otto Strasser), 1942; Into the Jaws of Death, 1944; No Innocence Abroad, 1954; An American in Rome, 1964; Farouk, 1968; (films) Exec. Prod., Satyricon; The Heroes; The Rover. Contbr. to: mags. in USA & abroad; articles syndicated worldwide. Mbr., Overseas Press Club of Am. Address: Via Zandonai 95, 00191 Rome, Italy.

STERN, Richard G., b. 25 Feb. 1928, NYC, USA. Writer; Professor. Educ: B.A., Univ. of N.C.; M.A., Harvard Univ.; Ph.D., Univ. of Iowa. Publs: Golk, 1960; Europe or Upa & Down with Baggish & Schreiber, 1961; In Any Case, 1962; Teeth, Dying & Other Matters, 1964; Stitch, 1965; 1968: A Short Novel Etc., 1970; Other Men's Daughters, 1973; The Books in Fred Hampton's Apartment, 1973. Contbr. to num. jrnls. & mags., US & abroad. Recip., num. grants, awards & fellowships. Address: 1050 E. 59th St., Chgo., IL 60637, USA.

STERN, Robert, A. M., b. 23 May 1939, NYC, USA. Architect; Educator; Author. Educ: B.A., Columbia Univ.; M.Arch., Yale Univ. Publs: New Directions in American Architecture, 1969; George Howe, Toward a Modern American Architecture, 1975. Contbr. to: Progressive Arch.; Archtl. Forum. Mbr. & Trustee, Am. Fedn. of Arts, 1968—. Address: 200 W. 72nd St., N.Y., NY 10023, USA.

STERNBERGER, Dolf, b. 28 July 1907, Wiesbaden, Germany. Author; University Professor. Educ: Univs. of Heidelberg, Friedberg & Frankfurt; Ph.D., 1932. Publs. incl: Panorama oder Ansichten vom 19. Jh., 1938, 4th ed., 1974; Lebende Verfassung, 1956; Begriff des Politischen, 1961; Kriterien, 1965; Ich wünschte ein Bürger zu sein, 1967; Nicht alle Staatsgewalt geht vom Volke aus, 1971; Heinrich Heine und die Abschaffung der Sünde, 1972. Contbr. to: Ed., Die Wandlung, 1945-49; Co-Ed., Die Gegenwart, 1950-59; Heidelberger Politische Schriften, 1970—; Die Wahl der Parlamente, 1969—; etc. Mbrships. incl: Vice-Chmn., German Acad. of Lang. & Poetry; Hon. Pres., German PEN Ctr. Hons. incl: Goethe Medal, Hessen, 1967; J. H. Merck Award, Darmstadt, 1967. Address: Park Rosenhöhe, 61 Darmstadt, W. Germany.

STERNLICHT, Sanford, b. 20 Sept. 1931, NYC, USA. University Professor. Educ: B.S., State Univ. N.Y., 1953; M.A., Colgate Univ., 1955; Ph.D., Syracuse Univ., 1962. Publs: Gull's Way, 1961; Love in Pompeii, 1967; Black Devil of the Bayous (w. E. M. Jameson), 1970; John Webster's Imagery & the Webster Canon, 1972; Yankee Racehorse with Sails (w. E. M. Jameson), 1974. Contbr. to: N.Y. Times; N.Y. Herald Tribune; Christian Sci. Monitor; Poetry Review (London); Choice; etc. Mbrships. incl: Poetry Soc. Am.; Mod. Lang. Assn. Am. Hons. incl: John Masefield Award, 1966; Fellow Poetry Soc. Am., 1965; Leverhulme Visiting Fellow, Univ. York, UK, 1965-66. Address: 87 Sheldon Ave., Oswego, NY 13126, USA.

STETLER, Russell Dearnley Jr., b. 15 Jan. 1945, Phila., Pa., USA. Writer; Editor. Educ: B.A.(Hons.), Haverford Coll., 1966; Grad. Fac., New Schl. for Social Rsch., 1966-67. Publs: The Battle of Bogside, 1970; Palestine: The Arab-Israeli Conflict, 1972. Contbr. to: New Soc. (London); Les Temps Modernes (Paris); Ramparts (San Fran.); Monthly Review (N.Y.); Int. Bulletin (Berkeley). Address: Archetype Inc., 2512 Grove St., Berkeley, CA 94704, USA.

STEVENS, Gerald F., b. 7 Apr. 1909, Montreal, Can. Author & Lecturer. Educ: Sir George Williams Coll., Montreal. Publs. incl: Old Stone House, 1954; In a Canadian Attic, 1955, revised 3rd ed., 1964; The Canadian Collector, 1957; Frederick Simpson Coburn, 1958; Early Canadian Glass, 1961, 2nd ed., 1967; Canadian Glass 1825-1925, 1967; (pamphlets) The United Counties of Leeds & Grenville 3,000,000,000 B.C. Brockville Ontario. (catalogues) One Hundred Years of Canadian Glass 1825-1925, Royal Ontario Museum, Toronto, 1957. Contbr. to: Maclean's Mag. (columnist 1965-68); Chatelaine Mag.; Can. Review Music & Art; Can. Antiques Collector. Mbr., Orillia Fish & Game Conserv. Club. Recip., Award Merit by Am. Assn. for State & Local Hist., 1967. Address: 55 Decarie Circle, Islington, Ont., Can.

STEVENS, Halsey, b. 3 Dec. 1908, Scott, N.Y., USA. Composer; Author; Educator. Educ: B.Mus., Syracuse Univ., 1931; M.Mus., 1937; Univ. of Calif.; studied w. Ernest Bloch. Publs: The Life & Music of Bela Bartok, 1953, 2nd rev. ed., 1967. Contbr. to: Ency. Britannica; New Cath. Ency.; World Book; Musical Quarterly; Tempo; Musical Am.; etc. Mbrships. incl: Bd. of Govs., Am. Composers Alliance, 1960-61; Bd. of Dirs., Am. Liszt Soc., 1966—. Recip., Hon. Litt.D., Syracuse Univ., 1966. Address: 9631 Second Ave., Inglewood, CA 90305, USA.

STEVENS, Robert Warren, b. 29 June 1918, Ohio, USA. Professor of Economics; Author. Educ: B.A., Ohio Wesleyan Univ., 1940; M.A., 1942; Ph.D., 1950, Univ. of Mich. Publs: Readings in International Business (w. R. N. Farmer & H. Schollhammer), 1971; The Dollar in the World Economy, 1972; Vain Hopes, Grim Realities: The Economic Consequences of the Vietnam War. Contbr. to: Am. Econ. Review; Harvard Bus. Review; New Repub.; Nation; Bankers' Mag.; Social Rsch; etc. Mbrships: Am. Econs. Assn.; Chgo. Coun. on For. Rels.; Soc. for Int. Dev. Address: 918 Hinman, Evanston, IL 60202, USA.

STEVENS, Shane, b. 8 Oct. 1941, N.Y.C., USA. Author; Novelist. Educ: M.A., Columbia Univ. Publs: Go Down Dead, 1967; Way Uptown in Another World, 1971; Dead City, 1973; Rat Pack, 1974; num. for. & paperback eds. Contbr. to num. jrnls. inclng: N.Y. Times; Life. Mbrships: Exec. Bd., PEN; Publs. Comm., Authors Guild; Writers Guild of Am. Address: c/o Lynn Nesbit, Int. Creative Management, 1301 Ave. of Ams., N.Y., NY 10019, USA.

STEVENSON, Anne, pen name of Mrs. R. W. Avery, b. Cardiff, UK. Author. Educ: M.A., St. Anne's Coll., Oxford. Publs: Ralph Dacre, 1966; Flash of Splendour, 1968; A Relative Stranger, 1970; A Game of Statues, 1972; The French Inheritance, 1974. Address: c/o Hughes Massie Ltd., 69 Great Russell St., London WC1B 3DH, UK.

STEVENSON, D. E., b. 1892. Author. Publs. incl: Miss Buncle's Book, 1934; Mrs. Tim of the Regiment; The Four Graces, 1944; Rochester's Wife; Young Mrs. Savage, 1948; Music in the Hills, 1950; Mrs. Tim Flies Home, 1952; Amberwell, 1955; Anna & Her Daughters, 1958; Bel Lamington, 1961; The Blue Sapphire, 1963; Katherine Wentworth, 1964; Katherine's Marriage, 1965; The House on the Cliff, 1966; Sarah Morris Remembers, 1967; The English Air, 1968; Crooked Adam, 1969; Gerald & Elizabeth, 1969; The House of the Deer, 1970; var. publs. in USA; works transl'd. into Dutch, Danish, German & Spanish. Address: North Park, Moffat, Dumfriesshire, Scotland, UK.

STEVENSON, Lois Wellman, b. 10 Jan. 1927, Mpls., Minn., USA. Newspaper Columnist; Freelance Writer. Educ: B.A., 1949, B.S., 1960, Univ. Calif. Weekly Column written since 1968 in The Courier-News, Somerville, N.J. Weekly Column written since 1971 in The Star-Ledger, Newark, N.J. Contbr. to: Animal Cavalcade; Prevention; Emphasis. Mbrships: Women in Communications, Inc.; Outdoor Writers' Assn. Am.; Dog Writers' Assn. Am.; Quill & Scroll. Hons: Best Essay, Lena B. Kier Award, 1943; Best Essay, 20th Century Club Award, 1944; Best Feature Article, Dog

Writers' Assn. Am., 1971, 1972, 1974. Address: 49 Rock Rd. W., Green Brook, NJ 08812, USA.

STEVENSON, Richard, b. 11 Dec. 1931, Windsor, Ont., Can. Scientist. Educ: B.A.Sc., Toronto Univ., 1953; M.S.E., 1954, Mech. E., MIT, 1956, Sc.D., 1957, Mich. Univ., USA. Publs: Multiplet Structure of Atoms & Molecules, 1965; Theory of Physics, 1967; Physique — Matiere et Energie, 1971. Contbr. to: Physical Review; Cryogenics. Address: Physics Dept., McGill Univ., Montreal, P.Q., Can.

STEWART, Angus, b. 22 Nov. 1936, Adelaide, S. Australia. Author. Educ: M.A.(Oxon), Christ Ch., Oxford, UK. Publs. incl: Sandel, 1968; Snow in Harvest, 1969; Sense & Inconsequence, 1972; Tangier, 1975. Contbr. to: London Mag.; Transatlantic Review; New Statesman; var. anthols. Also writer, BBC. Mbr., Soc. of Authors. Hons: Transatlantic Review Prize, 1961; Richard Hillary Award, 1963. Address: c/o A.P. Watt & Son, 26—28 Bedford Row, London WC1R 4HL, UK.

STEWART, Desmond Stirling, b. 20 Apr. 1924. Author. Educ: M.A., B.Litt., Trinity Coll., Oxford Univ. Publs. incl: (fiction) Leopard in the Grass, 1951; The Unsuitable Englishman, 1955; The Men of Friday, 1961; The Sequence of Roles trilogy: The Round Mosaic, 1965; The Pyramid Inch, 1966, The Mamelukes, 1968; (non-fiction) Young Egypt, 1958; The Arab World (w. Eds. of Life), 1962; Early Islam (w. Eds. of Life), 1967; Orphan with a Hoop, 1967; Great Cairo, Mother of the World, 1968; The Middle East: Temple of Janus, 1972; var. transls. from Arabic. Address: Ilex House, Wells-next-the-Sea, Norfolk, UK.

STEWART, Hal D., b. 7 Mar. 1899, Glasgow, UK. Writer. Educ: Kelvinside Acad., Glasgow; Loretto. Publs. incl: Stagecraft from the State Director's Point of View, 1949; Stage Managemenet, 1957; The First Victoria (Embassy Theatre, London), 1950; Lacking a Title (Q Theatre, London), 1951; A Month of Sundays, 1933; The Beannachy Bomb, 1937; & num. one act plays inclng: Rizzio's B?ots; Mrs. Watson's Window; Trade Union; The Nineteenth Hole; Henry Hereafter. Contbr. to: Theatre & Stage. Mbrships: PEN, Green Room; Stagemanagement Assn. (Dpty. Chmn.); Players' Theatre Club. Address: 12 Goodwin's Court, London WC2N 4LL, UK.

STEWART, Harold Frederick, b. 14 Dec. 1916, Drummoyne, Sydney, Australia. Poet; Essayist; Translator. Educ: Univ. of Sydney. Publs: Phoenix Wings (poems), 1948; Orpheus & other Poems, 1956; A Net of Fireflies (Haiku transls. & Essay), 1960; A Chime of Windbells (Haiku transls. & Essay), 1969. Contbr. to: Meanjin; Quadrant; Southerly; Hemisphere; etc. Mbr., Aust. Soc. of Authors. Recip., Sydney Morning Herald Prize, for Orpheus. Address: Hotel Shirakuso, Higashi Senouchi-Cho 29, Kitashirakawa, Sakyo-Ku, Kyoto, Japan 606.

STEWART, James Stuart, b. 21 July 1896, Dundee, UK. Minister, Church of Scotland; Retired Professor of New Testament. Educ: Univs. of Edinburgh, St. Andrews, & Bonn, Germany; M.A.; B.D. Publs: The Life & Teaching of Jesus Christ, 1932; A Man in Christ: St. Paul's Theology, 1935; The Gates of New Life, 1937; The Strong Name, 1941; Heralds of God, 1945; A Faith to Proclaim, 1953; Thine Is The Kingdom, 1956; The Wind of the Spirit, 1968; River of Life, 1972; King For Ever, 1975. Hons: D.D.; Chap. to H.M. The Queen in Scotland, 1952—; Moderator, Gen. Assembly, Ch. of Scotland, 1963. Address: 6 Crawford Rd., Edinburgh, UK.

STEWART, J(ohn) I(nnes) M(ackintosh), pen name INNES, Michael, b. 30 Sept. 1906, Edinburgh, UK. Reader in English Literature. Educ: B.A., Oxford Univ., 1928. Publs. incl: (novels) Mark Lambert's Supper, 1954; A Use of Riches, UK & USA, 1957; The Last Tresilians, UK & USA, 1963; Vanderlyn's Kingdom, UK & USA, 1967; A Palace of Art, UK & USA, 1972; 34 detective novels as Michael Innes, inclng. Hamlet, Revenge! , 1937, The Weight of the Evidence, 1943, Operation Pax, 1951, Hare Sitting Up, 1959; The Open House, 1972; var. books of short stories & lit. criticism. Recip., D.Litt., Univ. of New Brunswick, Can., 1962. Address: Fawler Copse, Kingston Lisle, Wantage, Berks., UK.

STEWART, Mary Florence Elinor, b. 17 Sept. 1916, Sunderland, UK. Author. Educ: B.A., 1938, M.A., 1941, Durham Univ. Publs: Madam, Will You Talk?, 1954; Wildfire at Midnight, 1956; Thunder on the Right, 1957; Nine Coaches Waiting, 1958; My Brother Michael, 1959; The Ivy Tree, 1961; The Moon-Spinners, 1962; This Rough

Magic, 1964; Airs Above the Ground, 1965; The Gabriel Hounds, 1967; The Wind Off the Small Isles, 1968; The Crystal Cave, 1970; The Little Broomstick, 1971; The Hollow Hills, 1973; Ludo & the Star Horse, 1974. Mbrships. incl: PEN. Hons. incl: Scottish Arts Coun. Award, 1974. Address: c/o Hodder & Stoughton Ltd., St. Paul's Ho., Warwick Lane, London EC4P 4AH, UK.

STEWART, Ora Pate, b. 23 Aug. 1910, Bates, Idaho, USA. Author; Composer; Lecturer; Poet. Educ: Brigham Young Univ.; Univ. of Utah Ext. Courses. Publs: 24 books, inclng. Pages from the Book of Eve, 1946; Branches Over the Wall, 1950; Treasures Unearthed, 1953; A Letter to My Daughter, 1956; From Where I Stood, 1960; Buttermilk & Bran, 1964; Tender Apples, 1965. Contbr. to num. US & for. jrnls. & mags. Mbrships. incl: Nat. Bd. Mbr., Nat. League of Am. Pen Women; Poetry Soc. of Am.; League of Utah Writers & Pres., Utah Valley Chapt. Hons. incl: Gold Medal, Int. Poetry Shrine, 1969; Magna Cum Laude, World Poetry, 1970; Laureate of Perf. Arts, Int. Poets Laureate, 1972. Address: 383 E., 1980 N., Provo, UT 84601, USA.

STEYERMARK, Julian Alfred, b. 27 Jan. 1909, St. Louis, Mo., USA. Botanist. Educ: A.B., 1929, M.S., 1930, Wash. Univ., St. Louis; M.A., Harvard Univ., 1931; Ph.D., Wash. Univ., 1933. Publs. incl: Spring Flora of Missouri, 1940; Flora of Guatemala (w. P. C. Standley), 8 vols., 1945-58; Flora of Missouri, 1963; Flora of Auyan-tepui, 1967; Rubiaceae (Flora of Venezuela), 3 vols., 1974. Contbr. to: Flora of Venezuela, 1951-57, 1962; & num. botan. jrnls. Mbr., var. botan. assns. Hons. incl: Order of Quetzal, Guatemalan Govt.; Order of Andres Bello, Venezuelan Govt.; Citation & Award, Eugene Field Soc., 1950; num. awards for botan. work. Address: Instituto Botanico, Apartado 2156, Caracas, Venezuela.

STIFF, Dorothy Aileen, pen name KENDAL, June, b. 1921, Newport, Mon., UK. Publs: Children's & Women's stories. Contbr. to: Amalgamated Press Juvenile Prods. Mbrships: Soc. of Authors; Dorset Naturalists Trust. Address: White Gate, 8 Firs Glen Rd., West Moors, Dorset BH22 0EB, UK.

STIFTER, Herbert Josef Gustav, b. 25 Oct. 1897, Vienna, Austria. Author Educ: Ph.D., Univ. of Graz, Austria, 1922. Publs: (novels) Menschenland; Grenzenlos; Der unzähmbare Vogel; Iffinger; (essay) Licht aus Assisi; (biog.) W. N. Prachensky, ein Malerleben.; sev. transls. from Dutch & French into German; co-author of monographies & Contbr. to anthols. Contbr. to: Tyrol Jrnl. (Ed., 1924); Bergland monthly, 1926; Steyrermühlverlag, 1937; Lectr., German Lang. & Lit., 1947. Mbrships: Internationaler Schutzverband deutschsprachinger Schriftsteller, Zurich; PEN; Ctr. German-speaking Writers Abroad, London, UK. Hons. incl: Novellenpreis der Neuen Linie, Berlin; Karl-Truppen Kreuz, WWI; Silver Medal for Bravery, & other awards, WWI; Gold & Grand Badges of Hon., Austria; Hon. Consul for Austria in Netherlands. Address: Goorstraat 1, Eindhoven, Netherlands.

STIGLER, George J., b. 17 Jan. 1911, Renton, Wash., USA. Educator; Economist. Educ: B.B.A., Univ. of Wash., 1931; M.B.A., Northwestern Univ., 1932; Ph.D., Univ. of Chgo., 1938. Publs., 11 books inclng: Supply & Demand for Scientific Personnel (w. D. Blank), 1957; The Intellectual & the Market Place, 1964; Essays in the History of Economics, 1965; The Organization of Industry, 1968; The Behavior of Industrial Prices (w. J. K. Kindahl), 1970. Contbr. to jrnls. inclng: Jrnl. of Pol. Econ. (Ed.). Mbr. or Fellow, profl. orgs. Recip., acad. hons. Address: 2621 Brassie Ave., Flossmoor, IL 60422, USA.

STILES, Lindley Joseph, b. 1 July 1913, Tatum, N.M., USA. Professor of Education. Educ: A.B., 1935, M.A., 1939, Ed.D., 1945, Univ. of Colo. Publs. incl: Supervision as Guidance (co-author), 1946; Moods & Moments (poetry), 1955; Ed., The Teacher's Role in American Society, 1957; The Scholar Teacher, 1966; The Present State of Neglect, 1967; Introduction to College: Education, 1969; Policy & Perspective at the Growing Edge of Education, 1972; Theories in Teaching (author-Ed.), 1974. Contbr. to: Educ.; Jrnls. Educl. Rsch.; Gen. Educ.; Higher Educ.; etc. Mbr., var. profl. orgs. Hons. incl: Recognition Medal, Univ. of Colo., 1958; D.Litt., Rider Coll., 1967; LL.D., McKendree Coll., 1969. Address: 1211 Pleasant Road, Glenview, IL 60025, USA.

STILL, James, b. 16 July 1906, Lafayette, Ala., USA Writer; Educator. Educ: A.B., L.H.D., Lincoln Mem. Univ.; M.A., Vanderbilt Univ.; B.S., Univ. of Ill.; Litt.D., Berea

Coll. Publs: Hounds on the Mountain, 1937; River of Earth, 1940; On Troublesome Creek, 1941; Way Down Yonder on Troublesome Creek (jvnle.), 1974; The Wolfpen Rusties, 1975. Contbr. to: Atlantic Monthly; Yale Review; Esquire; Saturday Evening Post; The Nation; The New Repub.; Poetry. Mbrships: Audubon Soc.; Defenders of Wildlife. Hons: O. Henry Mem. Prize, 1939; Guggenheim Fndn. Fellow, 1941, 1946; Award, Am. Acad. Arts & Letters, 1947; "James Still Room" estab. Johnson-Camden Lib., Morehead State Univ., Ky., 1961. Address: Hindman Settlement, Hindman, KY 41822, USA.

STIRLING, Monica, b. 1916. Writer. Publs: (novels) Lovers Aren't Company, UK & USA, 1949; Dress Rehearsal, UK, 1951, USA, 1952; Ladies with a Unicorn, UK, 1953, USA, 1954; Boy in Blue, UK & USA, 1955; Some Darling Folly, UK & USA, 1956; Sigh for a Strange Land, UK, 1958; USA, 1959; A Sniper in the Heart, UK, 1960; The Summer of a Dormouse, UK & USA, 1967; (short stories) Adventurers Please Abstain, 1952; Journeys We Shall Never Make, 1957; var. biogl. & juvenile works. Contbr. to: Atlantic Monthly (War corres., 1944). Recip., Metro-Goldwyn Award, 1946. Address: c/o Harcourt, Brace & Jovanovich, 757 Third Ave., N.Y., NY 10017, USA.

STIVENS, Dal(las George), b. 31 Dec. 1911, Blayney, NSW, Australia. Writer. Publs. incl: (novels) Jimmy Brockett, 1951; The Wide Arch, 1958; Three Persons Make a Tiger, 1968; A Horse of Air, 1970; (short stories) The Tramp, 1936; The Courtship of Uncle Henry, 1946; Ed., Coast to Coast: Australian Stories 1957-58, 1959; Selected Stories, 1936-68, 1970; (non-fiction) A Guide to Book Contracts (w. B. Jefferis), 1957. Mbrships: Aust. Soc. Authors (Pres., 1967-72). Hons: C'wlth. Lit. Fund Fellowship, 1951, 1962, 1970; Miles Franklin Award, 1970. Address: 5 Middle Harbour Rd., Lindfield, NSW 2070, Australia.

STOBBS, John Louis Newcombe, b. 1921, Potters Bar, Middx., UK. Freelance Writer. Educ: M.A., Pembroke Coll., Oxford Univ. Publs: The World of Scouts, 1957; Golf (w. J. Jacob), 1963; The A.B.C. of Golf, 1964; At Random through the Green, 1966; The Search for the Perfect Swing (w. A. Cochran), 1968. Contbr. to: Leader (staff writer, 1950); Picture Post (staff writer, 1952); Golfing (Ed., 1957-60); Observer (Golf Corres., 1956-66). Address: Cherry Bounce, Potten End, Herts., UK.

STOBERSKI, Zygmunt Julian, pen names STEBELSKI, Julian; BORONIECKI, Mirosław, b. 22 Dec. 1916, Petropawłowsk, USSR. Writer; Translator. Educ: M.A., Warsaw Univ., Poland. Publs. incl: Tam gdzie malwy lśnią czerwono, 1973; Historia literatury litewskiej, 1974; Guidelines for Adoption of New Scientific & Technical Terms (prepared for UNESCO/UNISIST); Strindberg och Polen (co-author); transls. of sev. Yugoslav writers. Contbr. to var. lit. jrnls. in Poland, Yugoslavia & USSR. Mbrships: Polish Writers' Union; Polish Jrnlsts. Assn.; Polish PEN. Recip., Zasłużony działacz kultury Badge, 1967. Address: 02 626 Warszawa, Al.Niepodległości 67 m 69, Poland.

STOCKING, Marion Kingston, b. 4 June 1922, Bethlehem, PA., USA. Professor of English. Educ: A.B., Mt. Holyoke Coll., 1943; Ph.D., Duke Univ., 1952. Publs: Ed., The Journals of Claire Clairmont, 1968; Contributing Ed., Shelley & His Circle, vols. V & VI. Contbr. to: Colo. Quarterly; Keats-Shelley Mem. Bulletin; Keats-Shelley Jrnl.; Beloit Poetry Jrnl. Mbrships: MLA of Am.; Keats-Shelley Assn. Address: Beloit Coll., Beloit, WI 53511, USA.

STOCKS, John Bryan, pen name STOCKS, Bryan, b. 17 July 1917, Baildon, Yorks., UK. Freelance Writer; Playwright; Poet; Broadcaster. Educ: Univ. of Leeds. Publs: (plays) Trouble on Helicon (Best One-Act Plays of 1963/4), new ed., 1972; After You've Gone, 1969, 1972. Contbr. to: More Poems from the Forces; Northern Aspect; Poems from Hospital; I Burn for England; Sunday Times; Yorks. Life; Yorks. Post; Stage & TV Today; radio progs. Life Mbr., Arts Theatre Club, London. Co-recip., 1st Prize, Wharfedale Festival, 1962. Address: Bradda, Menston, Ilkley, W. Yorks. LS29 6NT, UK.

STOESSL, Franz, b. 2 May 1910, Vienna, Austria. Professor of Antiquities. Educ: Ph.D., Vienna Univ., 1933. Publs. incl: Die Trilogie des Aischylos, 1937; Tod des Herakles, 1945; Antike Erzähler, 1947; Euripides, Tragödien und Fragmente Vol.I, 1958, Vol.II, 1968; Personenwechsel in Menanders Dyskolos, 1960; Manander Dyskolos: Kommentar Paderborn, 1965. Contbr. to: Jrnl. of Classical Antiquity (co-Ed.) Mbr., PEN (Pres., Steir

PEN). Hons: Theodor Körnerpreis, 1954, 1958; Stadtpreis, Vienna, 1957. Address: A-8010 Graz, Wilhelm Raabegasse 17, Austria.

STOEV, Gencho Dinev, b. 5 Feb. 1925, Harmanli, Bulgaria. Writer. Publs: (in Bulgarian) A Bad Day, 1965; The Price of Gold, 1965; Like Swallows, 1970; The Cyclops, 1974. Contbr. to sev. mags. & Newspapers. Mbr. Union of Bulgarian Writers. Recip., Prize of the Union of Bulgarian Writers, 1965; Honoured Worker of Culture, 1974. Address: Sofia, kompl. Lenin bl. 68, Bulgaria.

STOJOWSKI JORDAN, Andrzej, b. 29 Mar. 1933, Lwów, USSR. Novelist; Editor. Publs: Podróż do Nieczajny (novel), 1968; Romans polski (novel), 1970; Chłopiec na kucu (novel), 1971; Kareta (novel), 1972; Zamek w Karpatach (short stories), 1973; Carskie wrota (novel), forthcoming. Mbrships: Związek Literatów Polskich; PEN. Address: Al. Rewolucji Październikowej 93 m. 57, 01-242 Warsaw, Poland.

STOKER, Alan, pen name EVANS, Alan, b. 2 Oct. 1930, Sunderland, Co. Durham, UK. Civil Servant. Publs: The End of the Running, 1966; Mantrap, 1967; Bannon, 1968; Vicious Circle, 1970; The Big Deal, 1971; Running Scared, 1975. Mbr., Crime Writers' Assn. Address: 9 Dale Road, Walton-on-Thames, Surrey KT12 2PY, UK.

STOKER, Hendrik Gerhardus, b. 4 Apr. 1899, Johannesburg, S. Africa. Emeritus Professor. Educ: B.A., 1919, M.A., 1921, Second. Schl. Tchr.'s Cert., 1921, Univ. of S. Africa; Dr.Ph., Univ. of Cologne, Germany, 1924. Publs. incl: Des Gewissen, 1925; Die Stryd om die Ordes, 1942; Beginsels en Metodes in die Wetenskap, 2nd ed., 1961; Oorsprong en Rigting, Vol. I, 1967, Vol. II, 1970. Contbr. to var. scholarly jrnls. Mbrships: Hon. Mbr., Suid-Afrikaanse Akademie vir Wetenskap en Kuns, 1971; De Vereniging voor Calvinistiese Wysbegeerte, Netherlands; Hon. Mbr., Philos. Soc. of S. Africa, 1974. Hons. incl: Stals Award, Suid-Afrikaanse Akademie vir Wetenskap en Kuns, 1964. Address: Venter Street 6, Potchefstroom 2520, Repub. of S. Africa.

STOKES, Stanley, b. 8 Sept. 1890, Exeter, Devon, UK. Publs: (verse) Black Ink; A Star in December; Painted Meadows; Where Oxen Lay; Chime of Fancy. Contbr. to: Western Morning News; Western Weekly News; Chamber's Jrnl.; The Lady; Poetry of Today; Country Life; The Field; Empire Review. Mbrships: Authors' Soc.; Authors' Club, UK. Hons: 3rd Prize, The Bookman Short Story Competition, 1927; 1st Prize, Western Morning News Christmas Carol Competition, 1932. Address: c/o National Westminster Bank, 65 High St., Exeter, UK.

STOKKELIEN, Vigdis, b. 11 Mar. 1934, Kristiansand S., Norway. Author; Playwright. Educ: Oslo Sjomannsskole (Radio-Officer), 1952; Norwegian Jrnlst. Acad., 1961. Publs: Dragsug, 1967; Den Siste Prøven, 1968; Granaten, 1969; Sommeran På Heden, 1970; Lille Gibralter, 1972; J Speilet, 1973; (plays) For Sjøforklaringen, 1970; Granaten, 1974; Sømann Savnes, 1974. Contbr. to: Moderne Erzähler der Welt; var. anthols.; Mag. for Alle; var. mags., newspapers, etc. Mbrships: Norske Dramatikeres forbund (Norwegian Dramatists' Assn.); Den norske forfatterening (Norwegian Union of Authors). Recip., M.W. Nygaards Legat, 1970. Address: Post boks 121, 3474 Åres, Norway.

STOLTZFUS, Ben Frank, b. 15 Sept. 1927, Sofia, Bulgaria. University Professor; Writer. Educ. B.A., Amherst Coll., 1949; M.A., Middlebury Coll., 1954; Ph.D., Univ. of Wis., 1959. Publs: Alain Robbe-Crillet & the New French Novel (criticism), 1964; Georges Chennevière et l'Unanimisme (criticism), 1965; The Eye of the Needle (novel), 1967; Gides Eagles (criticism); Black Lazarus (novel), 1972. Contbr. to: Comparative Literature; Mod. Lang. Notes; Mod. Fiction Studies; PMLA; Romance Notes; Etudes Cinématographiques; Revue des Lettres Modernes; etc. Hons. incl: Creative Arts Inst. Award, Univ. of Calif., 1968 & 1972; Hon. D.Litt., Amherst Coll., 1974. Address: 5128 Queen St., Riverside, CA 92506, USA.

STONE, Alan Abraham, 15 Aug. 1929, Boston, Mass., USA. Psychiatrist; Professor of Law & Psychiatry. Educ: A.B., Harvard Univ., 1950; M.D., Yale Univ., 1955; Grad., Boston Psychanal. Soc. & Inst. Inc., 1960. Publs: Longitudinal Studies of Child Personality (w. G. Onque), 1959; The Abnormal Personality Through Literature (w. Sue Stone), 1966; Mental Health & Law: A System in Transition, forthcoming. Contbr. to: Am. Jrnl. Psych.;

Harvard Law Review; Am. Jrnl. of Orthopsych.; Jrnl. of Law & Psych. Mbrships: Am. Psych. Assn.; Trustee, Fellow, Chmn., Comm. of Judicial Action, Grp. for Adv. of Psych.; Mass. Med. Soc. Address: Harvard Law Schl., Cambridge, MA 02138, USA.

STONE, Donald Adelbert Jr., b. 29 June 1937, Hackensack, N.J., USA. University Professor. Educ: A.B., Haverford Coll., 1959; Ph.D., Yale Univ., 1963. Publs: Ronsard's Sonnet Cycles, 1966; France in the Sixteenth Century, 1969; From Tales to Truths: Essays on French Fiction in the Sixteenth Century, 1973; French Humanist Tragedy: A Reassessment, 1974. Mbrships: Renaissance Soc. Am.; AATF; NEMLA. Recip., Guggenheim Fellowship, 1967-68. Address: 201 Boylston Hall, Harvard Univ., Cambridge, MA 02138, USA.

STONE, Ena Margaret, (Mrs. George Harry Stone), (née Wilson), pen names SANDOWN, Margaret; O'RANDA, Jack; b. 10 Feb. 1911, Potchefstroom, S. Africa. Private Secretary; Principal/Owner, School of Speech & Drama. Educ: B.A., Univ. of Cape Town; Licentiate, Trinity Coll., London, UK; secretarial, Underwoods, Cape Town. Publs: Author & Producer of pageant play, Floreat Rhodesia; radio play, Fate Rides the Mail, 1943; radio play, Shielding Light, 1950. Contbr. to: (two anthols.) South African Poetry, 1948 & Poetry in Rhodesia 75 Years, 1968; The Rhodesia Herald; The Bulawayo Chronicle; The Sunday Mail; Rhodesian Woman & Home; Rhodesian Poetry; The African Observer; Johannesburg Sunday Times; etc. Mbrships: PEN Club, Rhodesia; Rhodesia Inst. Allied Arts. Hons: Rhodes Trustees' Prize for Engl., 1926, 1928; var. certs., Rhodesia Inst. Allied Arts Lit. Fests.; Poems read, Rhodesia TV & C'wlth. Fest. of Poetry, London, UK. Address: 9 Lawson Ave., Milton Park, Salisbury, Rhodesia.

STONE, Irving, b. 14 July 1903, San Fran., Calif., USA. Writer. Educ: A.B., Univ. of Calif., Berkeley, 1923; M.A., Univ. of Southern Calif., L.A., 1924. Publs. incl: (novels) Pageant of Youth, 1933; Immortal Wife, USA, 1944, UK, 1950; The Passionate Journey, USA, 1949, UK, 1950; The Agony & the Ecstasy, USA & UK, 1961; The Passions of the Mind, USA & UK, 1971; (non-fiction) Men to Match My Mountains, USA, 1956, UK, 1967; The Great Adventure of Michelangelo, 1965. Mbrships. incl: Calif. Writers Guild; Acad. Am. Poets (Fndr., 1962). Hons. incl: Christopher Award, 1957; var. docts. Address: c/o Doubleday & Co., 501 Franklin Ave., Garden City, NY 11530, USA.

STONE, Peter H., b. 27 Feb. 1930, L.A., Calif., USA. Playwright; Film Scenarist. Educ: B.A., Bard Coll., N.Y., 1951; M.F.A., Yale Univ., 1953. Publs: (plays) Friend of the Family, 1958; Full Circle, 1973; (musical comedies) Kean, 1961; Skyscraper, 1965; "1776", 1969; Two By Two, 1970; Sugar, 1972; (films) Charade; Mirage; Father Goose; Arabesque; Sweet Charity; 1776; Skin Game; Taking of Pelham 1-2-3; etc. (television) Defenders; Studio One; (musical) Androcles & the Lion; (series) Adam's Rib; (novel) Charade, 1963. Mbrships. incl: Dramatists' Guild (Exec. Coun.); VP, Authors League, Hons. incl: D.Litt., Bard Coll., 1971; Emmy Award, 1963; Academy Award, 1964; Tony Award & N.Y. Drama Critics Award, 1970. Address: 160 E. 71 St., N.Y., NY 10021, USA.

STONIER, George Walter, b. 1903, Sydney, Australia. Author; Critic; Journalist. Educ: M.A., Christ Church, Oxford Univ., UK. Publs: Gog Magog, 1933; The Shadow Across the Page, 1937; Shaving through the Blitz, 1943; My Dear Bunny, 1946; The Memoirs of a Ghost, 1947; Round London with the Unicorn, 1951; Pictures on the Pavement, 1954; English Countryside in Colour, 1956; Off the Rails, 1967; Rhodesian Spring, 1968; Ed., Int. Film Annual, vols. 2 & 3; var. plays for BBC. Contbr. to: New Statesman & Nation (Asst. Lit. Ed., 1928-45); Observer; Punch; Sunday Telegraph; etc. Address: 1 Riebeeck, Acton Rd., Rondebosch, Cape Town, Repub. of S. Africa.

STOODLEY, Bartlett Hicks, b. 15 July 1907, Somerville, Mass., USA. Professor of Sociology. Educ: B.A., Dartmouth Coll., 1929; LL.B., Harvard Law Schl., 1932; M.A., Ph.D., 1948, Harvard Univ. Publs: The Concepts of Sigmund Freud, 1956; Ed., Society & Self, 1962. Contbr. to: Am. Jrnl. Sociol.; Am. Sociol. Review; Am. Anthropologist; Jrnl. Marriage & Family Living. Mbrships: Am. Sociol. Soc.; Can. Sociol. Soc.; Eastern US Sociol. Soc. Hons: Visiting Professorship Chinese Univ., Hong Kong, 1962-63 & Queen's Univ., Kingston, Ont. Address: RFD 2 Box 420, Westport Island, Wiscasset, ME 04578, USA.

STOOVÉ-BAUER, Maria Hillegonde, pen name VERPOOTEN, Maria, b. 16 July 1904, Delft, Netherlands. Writer. Publs. incl: De man die terugkwam, 1947; Henk richt een club op, 1949; Van een blauw Klompje en een Roodschoentje, 1950; Koen, 1951; Best viert toch Kerstfeest, 1955; De Stokkertjes gaantoch uit, 1962; Op bergen en in dalen (transl. into German); many stories. Contbr. to jrnls. Mbr., De Vereniging van Nederlandse Letterkundigen. Recip., 2nd prize for short story. Address: Grameystraat 9, Nÿmegen, Netherlands.

STOPPARD, Tom, b. 3 July 1937. Playwright; Novelist. Publs. incl: (plays) Rosencrantz & Guildenstern are Dead, 1967; The Real Inspector Hound, 1968; After Magritte, prod. 1970, publd. 1971; Jumpers, 1972; (radio) If You're Glad I'll be Frank, 1965; Albert's Bridge, 1967, publd. 1968; Where Are They Now?, 1970, & Artist Descending a Staircase, 1972, both publd. 1973; (TV) Teeth, 1967; Neutral Ground, 1968. Contbr. to var. Bristol newspapers (staff mbr.), 1954-60. Hons: J. Whiting Award, Arts Coun., 1967; Evening Standard Award, 1968; Prix Italia, 1968; Tony Award, USA, 1968; N.Y. Drama Critics' Circle Award, 1968. Address: Fernleigh, Wood Lane, Iver Heath, Bucks., UK.

STOPPLE, Elizabeth Carrie, pen name STOPPLE, Libby, b. Dallas, Tex., USA. Registered Nurse; Poet; Songwriter. Publs: Red Metal, 1952; Never Touch a Lilac, 1959; Singer in the Side, 1970; Peppermints, 1971; Box of Peppermints, in press. Contbr. to: Parents' Mag.; Mod. Maturity; num. anthols. Mbrships. incl: Recording Sec., Poetry Soc. of Tex., 1954-56; Poetry Soc. of Am. Hons. incl: S.W. Writers Naylor Award, 1959. Address: 2512 Welborn, Dallas, TX 75219, USA.

STOREY, David (Malcolm), b. 13 July 1933, Wakefield, Yorks., UK. Writer. Educ: Slade Schl. of Fine Art, London. Publs: (novels) This Sporting Life, UK & USA., 1960; Flight into Camden, UK & USA, 1961; Radcliffe, UK, 1963, USA, 1964; A Temporary Life, 1972; (plays) The Restoration of Arnold Middleton, 1967; In Celebration, 1969; The Contractor, UK, 1970, USA, 1971; The Changing Room, 1972; (Screenplay) This Sporting Life, 1963. Hons: Macmillan Award, 1960; Rhys Mem. Award, 1961; Maugham Award, 1963; Drama Award, Evening Standard, 1967, 1970, 1971, Writer of Yr. Award, Variety Club of GB, 1971. Address: 2 Lyndhurst Gdns., London NW3, UK.

STORM, Lesley, pen name of CLARK, Margaret. Playwright. Educ: M.A., Aberdeen Univ. Publs: Tony Draws a Horse, 1939; Great Day, 1942; Black Chiffon, 1949; The Day's Mischief, 1952; The Long Echo, 1956; Roar Like a Dove, 1957; The Paper Hat, 1965; Three Goose-quills & a Knife, 1967; Look, No Hands, 1971. Address: 3 St. Simon's Ave., London SW15, UK.

STÖVLING, Britta Maria, b. 11 June 1923, Stockholm, Sweden. Author. Educ: M.A. Publs: Job, 1971; Political Words, 1971; Chapt. on Sweden, Women in All Countries, 1974; The Earth is Ours (w. Irene Götefelt), 1974. Contbr. to: Ny Dag; Kvinnobulletinen. Mbrships: Swedish Authors' Assn.; Group 8 (Socialist Org. of Women). Hons: Authors' Fund Awards, 1972, 1974, 1975; Fredrik Ströms Mem. Fund Award, 1972. Address: Birkagatan 31, S-113 39 Stockholm, Sweden.

STOW, (Julian) Randolph, b. 28 Nov. 1935, Geraldton, Australia. Writer. Educ: B.A., Univ. of Western Aust., Nedlands. Publs: (poems) Act One, 1957; Outrider, 1962; A Counterfeit Silence, 1969; (novels) A Haunted Land 1956; The Bystander, 1957; To The Islands, 1958; Tourmaline, 1963; The Merry-go-round in the Sea, 1965; (for children) Midnite, 1967; (music theatre, w. P. Maxwell Davies) Eight Songs For a Mad King, 1969; Miss Donnithorne's Maggot, 1974. Address: c/o Richard Scott Simon Ltd., 32 College Cross, London N1 1PR, UK.

STRACHAN, Françoise, b. 1 Apr. 1940, Ewell, Surrey. Writer; Natural Therapist. Publs: The Aquarian Guide to Occult, Mystical, Religious, Magical London & Around, 1970; Casting Out the Devils, 1972; Natural Magic, 1974; Psychic Health & Exorcism, 1975. Contbr. to var. mags. inclng: Prediction; Women Speaking; Quest. Mbrships: Rsch. into Lost Knowledge Org.; Guild of Pastoral Psychol. Address: B/M Spiritos, London WC1V 6XX, UK.

STRACHAN, Winona Peacock, b. 26 June 1918, Pembroke, Mass., USA. Librarian. Educ: State Coll., Bridgewater, Mass., 1964-67. Publs: Christopher Jarrett of New Plymouth, 1957; Johnny Codliner: A Story of the American Revolution, 1961. Address: 161 High St., Duxbury, MA 02332, USA.

STRAHLER, Violet Ruth, b. 30 Sept. 1918, Dayton, Ohio, USA. Educator. Educ: B.A., Wittenberg Univ., Ohio, 1944; M.A., Miami Univ., Ohio, 1959; Ed.D., Ind. Univ., 1972. Publs. incl: You & Your World, 1960; World of Living Things, 1964; Exploring the Sciences, 1964; Teacher's Manual for Matter: Its Forms & Changes, 1969, 1972; The Earth: Its Changing Form, 1970; Teacher's Manual for the Earth: Its Changing Form, 1971; Teacher's Manual for Energy: Its Forms & Changes, 1972; Teacher's Manual for Matter: An Earth Science, 1975; Teacher's Manual for Energy: A Physical Science, 1975; A Searchbook for Matter: An Earth Science, 1975. Contbr. to profl. jrnls.; Ed., Ohio Jr. Acad. of Sci. Newsletter. Recip., Ford Fndn. Schlrship., 1952. Address: 5340 Brendonwood Lane. Dayton, OH 45415, USA.

STRAIGHT, Michael (Whitney), b. 1 Sept. 1916, Southampton, L.I., N.Y., USA. Deputy Chairman, National Endowment for the Arts. Educ: London Schl. Econs., UK; M.A., Cambridge Univ. Publs: Make this the Last War: The Future of the United States, USA & UK, 1943; Trial by Television, 1954; Carrington: A Novel of the West, USA, 1960, UK, 1961; A Very Small Remnant (novel), USA & UK, 1963; Three West (co-author), 1970. Contbr. to: New Repub. (Contbng. Ed., 1941-43, Publr., 1946-48, Ed., 1948-56). Mbrships: William C. Whitney Fndn. (Pres.). Address: c/o Alfred A. Knopf, 501 Madison Ave., N.Y., NY 10022, USA.

STRAITON, Edward Cornock, pen name BBC TV VET., b. 27 Mar. 1917, Clydebank, Scotland, UK. Veterinary Surgeon. Educ: M.R.C.V.S., Glasgow Vet. Coll. Publs: (TV Vet Books) No. 1 For Stock Farmers, 1964; No. 2 Calving the Cow & Care of the Calf, 1965; No. 3 For Pig Farmers, 1967; No. 4 Horse Book, 1971; No. 5 Sheep Book, 1972; No. 6 Dog Book, 1974. Contbr. to: Horse & Pony; Vet. Drug. Address: Veterinary Hospital, Cannock Rd., Penkridge, Stafford ST19 5RY, UK.

STRAKER, John Foster, pen name ROSSE, Ian, b. 26 Mar. 1904, Farnborough, UK. Schoolmaster. Publs: Postman's Knock, 1954; Pick up the Pieces, 1955; The Ginger Horse, 1956; A Gun to Play With, 1956; Goodbye Aunt Charlotte, 1958; Hell is Empty, 1958; Death of a Good Woman, 1961; Murder for Missemily, 1961; A Coil of Rope, 1962; Final Witness, 1963; The Shape of Murder, 1964; Ricochet, 1965; Miscarriage of Murder, 1967; Sin & Johnny Inch, 1968; A Man who cannot Kill, 1969; Tight Circle, 1970; A Letter for Obi, 1971; The Goat, 1972; The Droop, 1972. Address: Lincoln Cottage, Horsted Keynes, Haywards Heath, Sussex, UK.

STRALEY, George Henry, b. 25 Apr. 1907, Maytown, Pa., USA. Journalist; Editor. Educ: Johns Hopkins Univ. Publs: Inferno at Petersburg (w. Henry Pleasants, Jr.), 1961. Contbr. to USA & for. jrnls. & syndicates, inclng: The Luth. Mag.; The Reader's Digest; Cornoet; Illustrated London News; Stage. Address: 209 Prospect Dr., Blue Rock Manor, Wilminaton, DE 19803, USA.

STRAND, Kenneth A(lbert), b. 18 Sept. 1927, Tacoma, Wash., USA. University Professor of Church History. Educ: B.A., Emmanuel Missionary Coll., 1952; M.A., 1955, Ph.D., Hist., 1958, Univ. of Mich. Publs: over 20 books inclng. Reformation Bibles in the Crossfire, 1961; German Bibles Before Luther, 1966; Ed., Essays on the Northern Renaissance, 1968; Compiler, Woodcuts to the Apocalypse in Dürer's Time, 1968; Brief Introduction to the Ancient Near East, 1969; Open Gates of Heaven, 1970, 1972. Contbr. to profl. jrnls.; Assoc. Ed., 1968-74, Ed., 1974—, Andrews Univ. (Mich.) Sem. Studies. Address: Andrews Univ., Berrien Springs, MI 49104, USA.

STRANDZHEV, Kosta, b. 12 Jan. 1929, Plovdiv, Bulgaria. Writer. Publs: (in Bulgarian) The Third Along the Road, 1964; How Much is a Man Worth, 1967; Battering-Ram, 1968; (play) The Pines Do Not Bend, 1971; Marked People, 1971; Courage to Live, 1972; Whirlpools, 1972. Contbr. to: September, PlamAk; Trakiya; Literatouren Front. Mbr. Union of Bulgarian Writers. Recip., Prize of the Union of Bulgarian Writers, 1972. Address: Plovdiv, ul. Eddison, 1, Bulgaria.

STRATIEV, Stanislav, b. 1941, Sofia, Bulgaria. Writer. Publs: (in Bulgarian) The Lonely Windmills, 1969; Wild Duck Among the Trees, 1972; (play) A Roman Bath, 1974.

Contbr. to: September; PlamAk. Mbr., Union of Bulgarian Writers. Address: Sofia, ul. Konstantin Velichkov, 91, Bulgaria.

STREATFEILD, Noel. Novelist. Publs. incl: The Whicharts; Parson's Nine; It Pays to be Good; The Winter is Past; Grass in Piccadilly; Mothering Sunday; Aunt Clara; Judith; The Silent Speaker; (biog.) Magic & the Magician; (autobiog.) A Vicarage Family; Away from the Vicarage; Beyond the Vicarage; (juvenile) Ballet Shoes; The Circus is Coming; The Children of Primrose Lane; Party Frock; White Boots; The Bell Family; Wintle's Wonders; The Royal Ballet School; New Town; Apple Bough; The Children on the Top Floor; The Growing Summer; Caldicott Place; Thursday's Child; The Boy Pharaoh; Ballet Shoes for Anna. Address: 51 Elizabeth St., Eaton Sq., London SW1, UK.

STREET, Lucie (Mrs. Penn), b. Sussex, UK. Author; Educationist. Educ: M.A., Manchester Univ.; John Bright Fellowship; postgrad. study Comp. Lit., Sorbonne, Univ. of Paris, France. Publs: Penn of Pennsylvania: A Play, 1945; H. E. William Penn, 1947; Tomorrow's Continent (w. husband, Lt.-Col. P. Penn), 1950; Ed., I Married a Russian, Czech & Danish transls.; Spoil the Child, 1961; The Tent Pegs of Heaven; (novels) The Wind on the Morfa; Good Morning, Mirand; (poems) Autumn Phoenix. Contbr. to: Bell, A Choice of Modern Prose, 1967. Mbrships. incl: Soc. of Authors; PEN. Address: Warminghurst, High Hurstwood, Uckfield, Sussex, UK.

STRICKLAND, Stephen Parks, b. 25 Nov. 1933, Birmingham, Ala., USA. Political Scientist; Health Policy Analyst. Educ: B.A., Emory Univ., 1952; M.A., 1966, Ph.D., 1971, Johns Hopkins Univ. Publs: Hugo Black & the Supreme Court, 1967; U.S. Health Care: What's Wrong & What's Right, 1972; Politics, Science, & Dread Disease: A Short History of Medical Research Policy, 1972; Television & the Child: The Surgeon General's Quest (w. Douglass Cater), forthcoming. Contbr. to: Sci.; Sat. Review/Sci. Mbr., profl. orgs. Recip., acad. hons. Address: 3010 32nd St. N.W., Wash. DC 20008, USA.

STROBRIDGE, Truman Russell, b. 15 Oct. 1927, Sault Ste. Marie, Mich., USA. Historian. Publs: Annotated Bibliography of US Marines in American Fiction, 1962; Operation Helping Hand: The Army & the Alaskan Earthquake, 1964; US Coast Guard Annotated Bibliography, 1972; Western Pacific Operations: History of US Marine Corps Operations in World War II, 1972. Contbr. to num. profl. jrnls. Hons: Merit Award for article (co-author), Marine Corps Gazette, 1962. Address: 4721 Koester Dr., Woodbridge, VA 22193, USA.

STRÖM, Carsten Christian, b. 13 Nov. 1913, Malmö. Sweden. Artist. Educ: Schule Reimann, Berlin, 1935; Royal Acad. of Art, Copenhagen, 1947-48. Publs: Gummiguttas nya hus, 1954; Gummigutta och blåbärsmaskinen, 1955; Gummiguttas sällsamma resa, 1956; Gummigutta och svarta hatten, 1959; Tio Gammaldags sagor, 1960. Mbrships. incl: Swedish Union of Authors; Nat. Artists Org.; Lukasgillet, Lund. Address: Claesgatan 10A, 214 26 Malmö, Sweden.

STROUD, Ellen Florence, pen name HOLT, Ellen, b. 11 Nov. 1904, Merstham, Surrey, UK. Former School Principal. Educ: LL.A., St. Andrews Univ. Publs: The Farmer (E.S.A. Info. Books). Contbr. to: Farmers' Wkly; Nursery World; Evening News; The Lady. Address: 31 Ridgeway Ct., Redhill, Surrey, UK.

STROYNOWSKI, Julius, b. 26 May 1919, Czestochowa, Poland. Historian; Sociologist. Educ: M.A., Acad. of Pol. Scis., Warsaw; M.A., H.S. of Jrnlsm. Acad. of Pol. Scis., Warsaw; Ph.D., Univ. of Warsaw. Publs: Pieskie histoire, 1939; Olimpijskie Fanfary, 1956; Systemy Polityczne Współczesnego Kapitalizmu, 1962; Palmy i daktyle, 1963; Polen und Deutsche, 1972. Contbr. to: Dokumente, Cologne; Münchner Merkur; Kultura, Paris. Mbrships: PEN; Deutsche Gesellschaft für Symbolforschung. Address: D—5 Köln 41, Mommsenstr. 97, W. Germany.

STRUMPH-WOJTKIEWICZ, Stanislaw, b. 21 June 1898, Warsaw, Poland. Journalist; Novelist. Educ: B.A., Warsaw Univ. Publs. incl: The General May, 1925; The Stepsons of Europe, 1938; The Stone Bridge, 1939; Sierakowski, 1954; Traugutt, 1957; Agent No. 1, 1959; Tiergarten, 1966; The Night on Omylna River, 1967; Nigerian Holidays, 1971; Gibraltar, 1971; 5th Column in the Bristol Hotel, 1971; The Kriegsspiele, 1969; Warning to Gdynia, 1975. Contbr. to: Kurier Warszawski, 1923-37. Mbrships. incl: Union of Polish Writers, 1921—; Friends of

Book Assn.; Friends of Old Warsaw Assn. Hons. incl: Prize Kurier Polski, 1957; Prize, Min. of Defence, 1963; M.C.; Cmdr., Cross Polonia Restituta, 1971. Address: ul. Slowackiego 4, m.8, 01-627 Warsaw, Poland.

STRUNG, Norman M., b. 21 Oct. 1941, NYC, USA. Freelance Writer. Educ: B.S., Mont. State Univ., Bozeman; postgrad. studies, Univ. of Mont., Missoula. Publs: The Fisherman's Almanac (w. Dan Morris), 1970; Family Fun Around the Water, 1970; The Hunter's Almanac, 1971; Camping In Comfort (w. Sil Strung), 1971; Deer Hunting, 1972; Spinfishing (w. Milt Rosko), 1973; Misty Mornings & Moonless Nights, 1974. Contbr. to: Field & Stream; Outdoor Life; Sports Afield; Argosy; Ency. Americana; Outdoor Cookbook; Experts Book of Fishing; etc. Mbrships: Bd. of Dirs., Outdoor Writers' Assn. of Am.; Soc. of Mag. Writers; Authors' League. Address: Box 189, Rte. 3. Bozeman, MT 59715, USA.

STRUNK, Orlo, b. 14 Apr. 1925, PenArgyl, Pa., USA. University Professor. Educ: A.B., W.Va. Wesleyan Coll., 1955; S.T.B., 1957, Ph.D., 1959, Schl. of Theol., Boston Univ. Publs: Readings in the Psychology of Religion, 1959; Religion: A Psychological Interpretation, 1962; Mature Religion: A Psychological Study, 1965; The Choice Called Atheism, 1968; The Psychology of Religion; Historical & Interpretive Readings, 1971; Dynamic Interpersonalism for Ministry, 1973. Contbr. to theol., relig. & psychol. jrnls. Mbrships. incl: Am. Psychol. Assn.; Acad. of Relig. & Hlth. Address: 15 Stearns Rd., Scituate, MA 02066, USA.

STRUTTON, William Harold, b. 23 Feb. 1918, Moonta, S. Australia. Author. Educ: Adelaide Univ. Publs: A Jury of Angels, 1957; The Secret Invaders (co-author), 1958; Island of Terrible Friends, 1961; Dr. Who & the Zarbi, 1965; A Glut of Virgins (USA title The Carpaccio Caper), 1973. Contbr. to var. Brit. TV series. Mbrships: Crime Writers Assn.; Writers' Guild of GB; Critics Circle. Address: Osbrooks, Capel, Surrey RH5 5JN, UK.

STRYKOWSKI, Joe, b. 12 Mar. 1935, Chgo., Ill., USA. Writer; TV Producer; Cinematographer. Publs: Scuba, 1959; Underwater Yearbook, 1962; Scuba II, 1962; Diving for Fun, 1969; Divers & Cameras, 1974. Mbrships: Bd. Mbr., Gt. Lakes Sect., Marine Technol. Soc.; Bd. Mbr., Nat. Scuba Comm., YMCA; Bd. Mbr. & VP, Gillette Scuba Safety Assn.; Outdoor Writers Assn. of Am. Hons: Mbr. of Yr., Ill. Coun. of Divers, 1962; Diver of Yr., Metropol. YMCA Coun., 1968. Address: P.O. Box 96, Hazel Hurst, WI 54531, USA.

STUART, Alice Vandockum, b. 16 Dec. 1899, Rangoon, Burma. Poet. Educ: M.A., Somerville Coll., Oxford, UK. Publs: (verse) The Far Calling, 1944; The Dark Tarn, 1953; The Door Between, 1963; The Unquiet Tide, 1971; (prose) David Gray: The Poet of the Luggia, 1961; Co-Ed., Voice & Verse (anthol.), 1974. Contbr. to: Contemp. Review; Burns Chronicle. Mbrships. incl: Soc. of Authors; PEN, Scottish Ctr.; Scottish Assn. for the Speaking of Verse; Hon. Soc. of Tchrs. of Speech & Drama; Fellow, Int. Inst. of Arts & Letters. Hons: Lilian Bowes Lyon Award, Poetry Soc., 1955; Premium Award, Poetry Soc., 1966. Address: 57 Newington Rd., Edinburgh EH9 1QW, UK.

STUART, Francis, b. 1902, Qld., Australia. Writer. Publs. incl: (novels) Women & God, 1930; Pigeon Irish, 1932; The Coloured Dome, 1933; Glory, 1934; The Pillar of Cloud, 1948; Redemption, 1949; The Flowering Cross, 1950; Good Friday's Daughter, 1951; The Chariot, 1953; The Pilgrimage, 1955; Victors & vanquished, 1958; Angels of Providence, 1959; Black List, Section H, 1971; Memorial, 1973; (verse) We Have Kept the Faith; (autobiog.) Things to Live for, 1936. Recip., awards for verse from Royal Irish Acad., & in USA. Address: 2 Highfield Pk., Dublin 14, Repub. of Ireland.

STUART, Jesse (Hilton), b. 8 Aug. 1907, Riverton, Ky., USA. Writer. Educ: A.B., Lincoln Mem. Univ., Tenn., 1929; Vanderbilt Univ., 1931-32. Publs. incl: (verse) Man with a Bull-Tongue Plow, 1934, revised ed. 1959; Hold April, 1962; (short stories) Head o' W-Hollow, 1936; Men of the Mountains, 1941; Clearing in the Sky, 1950; Come Gentle Spring, 1969; (novels) Taps for Private Tussie, 1943 (as He'll Be Coming Down the Mountain, UK, 1947); Foretaste of Glory, 1946; Mr. Gallion's School, 1967; (autobiog.) The Thread that Runs so True, 1949; The Year of My Rebirth, USA 1956, UK 1958; var. juvenile. Recip., num. awards, grants & hon. docts. Address: W-Hollow, Greenup, KY 4144, USA.

STUART, Miranda, b. Gwelo, Rhodesia. Writer; Broadcaster. Educ: B.A., Univ. of Cape Town, S. Africa. Publs: Dead Men Sing No Songs, 1939. Contbr. to prose & poetry anthols. Mbrships: PEN; Comm. Mbr., Engl. Assn. Address: 11 Dealtry Rd., London SW15, UK.

STUART, Vivian, pen names STUART, V. A.; STUART, Alex, b. 2 Jan. 1914, Rangoon, Burma. Author. Educ: Pvte.; Univ. of London; Inst. of Pathol., Univ. of Budapest, Hungary. Publs. incl: The Captain's Table, 1953; Gay Cavalier, 1955; Dr. Lucy, 1956; The Gay Gordons, 1961; The Sheridan Series (5 novels, Indian Mutiny), UK & USA, 1960-74; The Hazard Series (6 novels, Crimean War), 1964-74; The Beloved Little Admiral (biog.), 1968; Young Dr. Mason, 1970; A Sunset Touch, 1972. Mbrships. incl: Soc. of Authors; Navy Records Soc.; Soc. for Nautical Rsch.; Mil. Hist. Soc.; Writers' Summer Schl. (Vice-Chmn., past Chmn.). Address: 461 Malton Rd., York YO3 9TH, UK.

STUART-VERNON, Charles Roy, pen names DONALD, Vivian; MONTROSE, Graham; STUART, Charles, CONTE, Charles; MacKINNON, Charles; b. Scotland, UK. Novelist. Publs., over 65 novels & 5 non-fiction works, inclng: The Clan MacKinnon, 1958; The Highlands in History, 1961; Tartans & Highland Dress, 1961; Scotland's Heraldry, 1962; Observer's Book of Heraldry, 1966; (as Charles MacKinnon): Castlemore; Merefore Tapestry; The Matriarch; (as Graham Montrose): Angel Brown Crime Series. Address: Belmont, 6 Victoria Walk, Cotham, Bristol BS6, UK.

STUBBS, Jean, b. 23 Oct. 1926, Denton, UK. Novelist. Educ: Manchester Schl. of Art. Publs: The Rose Grower, 1962; The Travellers, 1963; Hanrahan's Colony, 1964; The Straw Crown, 1966; My Grand Enemy, 1967; The Passing Star, 1970; The Case of Kitty Ogilvie, 1970; An Unknown Welshman, 1972; Dear Laura, 1973; The Painted Face, 1974. Contbr. to: Books & Bookmen. Mbrships. incl: Comm., Crime Writers' Assn.; Soc. of Authors; PEN; Detection Club. Hons: Tom Gallon Trust Award for Short Story Writing, 1964; Alternative Choice, Book of the Month Club, 1973. Address: 1 Ryfold Rd., Wimbledon Pk., London SW19 8DF, UK.

STUBER, Stanley Irving, b. 24 Aug. 1903, Gardiner, Maine, USA. Religious Executive Director; Author; Editor. Educ: A.B., Bates Coll., 1926; B.D., Rochester Theol. Sem., 1928; Th.M., Colgate-Rochester Divinity Schl., 1929; D.D., Keuka Coll. Publs. incl: How We Got Our Denominations, 1928; Treasury of the Christian Faith, 1949; Public Relations Manual, 1951; The Christian Reader, 1952; Primer on Catholicism for Protestants, 1953; Implementing Vatican II, 1967; Human Rights & Fundamental Freedoms, 1968. Contbr. to relig. jrnls. Address: 74 Burma Rd., Wyckoff, NJ 07481, USA.

STUCKI, Margaret Elizabeth, b. 9 Jan. 1928, West New York, N.J., USA. Portrait Painter. Educ: B.A., Barnard Coll., 1949; Art Students League of NYC, 1949-51; M.A., Columbia Tchrs. Coll., 1959; Ph.D., Freedom Univ., 1975. Publs: The Revolutionary Mission of Modern Art: or CRUD & other Essays on Art, 1973; War on Light: The Destruction of the Image of God in Man, 1975. Contbr. to: Nat. Anthols. Coll. Verse, Nat. Poetry Assn., 1946, 1947; Modern Am. Verse, 1949; Proceedings VIIth Int. Rorschach Congress, 1969; Hartwick Review (assoc. Ed.); For Real; Christian Educator (art Ed.). Mbrships. incl: Am. Artists Profl. League; AAUW; Brevard Poetry Club. Recip., var. awards for painting & photography. Address: 379 Harbor Dr., Cape Canaveral, FL 32920, USA.

STUPAK, Ronald Joseph, b. 28 Nov. 1934, Allentown, Pa., USA. Professor. Educ: A.B., Moravian Coll., 1961; M.A., 1964, Ph.D., 1967, Ohio State Univ. Publ: The Shaping of Foreign Policy: The Role of the Secretary of State as seen by Dean Acheson, 1969. Contbr. to: Orbis; Am. Psychologist; Worldview; Social Science; Studies on the Soviet Union; Jrnl. of Human Rels.; other profl. jrnls. Recip., num. Fellowships & grants. Address: Dept. of Political Science, Miami Univ., Oxford, OH 45056, USA.

STURMER, Wava (Regina), b. 2 Oct. 1929, Boma, Zaire, Angola. Author. Publs: Bevingad vardag, 1955; Därför att ljuset, 1967; Det är ett helvete att måla himlar, 1970; Stadens ofullmäkti ge, 1972; Möta en människa, 1973. Mbrships: Finlands Dramatikerförbund rf (Finnish Dramatists' Soc.); Finlands svenska Forfattareförening (Soc. of Swedish Authors in Finland). Recip., Svenska Litteratursällskapet, 1974. Address: Pedersespl. 12, 68 620 Jakobstad 2, Finland.

STURMTHAL, Adolf F(ox), b. 10 Sept. 1903, Vienna, Austria. University Professor. Educ: Dr.rer.pol., Univ. of Vienna, 1925. Publs. incl: The Tragedy of European Labor, 1918-1939, 1943, 1951; Unity & Diversity in European Labor, 1953; Workers Councils: A Study of Workplace Organizations on Both Sides of the Iron Curtain, 1964; Current Manpower Problems, 1964; Ed., Contemporary Collective Bargaining, 1957; White-Collar Trade Unions, 1966; Comparative Labor Movements: Ideological Roots & Institutional Development, 1972; The International Labor Movement in Transition: Essays on Africa Asia Europe & South America (co-ed.), 1973. Mbrships: Ind. Rels. Rsch. Assn.; Am. Pol. Sci. Assn.; Am. Econ. Assn. Address: 61 Greencroft, Champaign, IL, USA.

STYAN, John Louis, b. 6 July, 1923, London, UK. University Professor; Author. Educ: B.A., 1947, M.A., 1948, Cambridge Univ., UK. Publs: The Elements of Drama, 1960; The Dark Comedy, 1962, 2nd ed., 1968; The Dramatic Experience, 1965; Shakespeare's Stagecraft, 1967; Chekhov in Performance, 1971; The Challenge of the Theatre, 1972. Address: 540 Glen Arden Drive, Pitts., PA, USA.

STYLE, Colin Thomas Elliot, b. 3 Aug. 1937, Salisbury, Rhodesia. Marketing Manager with TV. Educ: Rhodes Univ., S. Africa. Contbr. to: Christian Sci. Monitor; Sewanee Review; Cornhill; Outposts; Stand; Contemporary Review (UK); Wascana Review; Dalhousie Review (Can.); Poetry Australia; New Coin; Contrast; & BBC radio (African serv.). Mbrships: Poetry Soc. Rhodesia (Chmn., 1972, 1974); PEN; Chirimo Lit. Jrnl. (former Ed.). Recip.. Rhodesian Poetry Prize, 1958. Address: P.O. Box A294, Avondale, Salisbury, Rhodesia.

STYLE, Karen O-lan, b. 23 Sept. 1943, Salisbury, Rhodesia. Compiler of the Southern Africa Section of the Annual Bibliography of The Journal of Commonwealth Literature; former Co-Editor Chirimo Magazine. Educ: B.A.; P.C.E. Contbr. to: Jrnl. C'wlth. Lit. (Leeds); Co-Prod. long-playing gramophone record of Rhodesian Poets. Mbrships: PEN; Poetry Soc. Rhodesia (Sec., 1974.) Address: P.O. Box A294, Avondale, Salisbury, Rhodesia.

STYRON, William, b. 11 June 1925, Newport News, Va., USA. College Fellow. Educ: A.B., Duke Univ., N.C., 1947. Publs: (novels) Lie Down in Darkness, USA, 1951, UK, 1952; The Long March, USA, 1956, UK, 1961; Set This House on Fire, USA, 1960, UK, 1961; The Confessions of Nat Turner, USA, 1967, UK, 1968; (stories) Ed., Best Short Stories from "Paris Review", 1959. Contbr. to: Paris Review (Advsry Ed., 1952—); Am. Scholar (Ed. Bd., 1970—). Mbrships: Nat. Inst. Arts & Letters; Am. Acad. Arts & Scis. Hons. incl: Pulitzer Prize, 1968; Howells Medal, 1970; num. docts. Address: R.F.D., Roxbury, CT 06783, USA.

SUBBIAH, Bommireddi, b. 13 Jan. 1917, Dornipadu, India. Professor. Educ: B.A., 1936, Madras Univ., India; M.P.A., 1960, Ph.D., 1965, N.Y. Univ., USA. Publs: The Tragedy of a Papal Decree, 1970; The World Population Crisis, 1971. Mbrships. incl: AAUP; Am. Soc. of Pub. Admin.; Am. Mgmt. Assn.; Am. Pol. Servs. Assn. Recip. Disting. Merit Cert., N.Y. Univ., 1965. Address: 417 Circle Dr., Hurricane, WV 25526, USA.

SUBILIA, Vittorio, b. 5 Aug. 1911, Turin, Italy. Professor of Systematic Theology. Educ: Lic. teol., Univs. of Rome & Basle. Publs. incl: Il Movimento Ecumenico, 1948; Il Problema del Male, 1959; Il Problema del Cattolicesimo, 1962; La Nuova Cattolicità del Cattolicesimo, 1967; L'Evangelo della Contestazione, 1971; I Tempi di Dio, 1971; Sola Scriptura, 1975; La Giustificazione per Fede, 1975; Parola e Silenzio di Dio, 1975; num. for. eds. of works. Contbr. to: Protestantesimo, Rome (Ed.); Revue d'Hist. & de Philos. Relig., Stradburg; etc. Mbrships: Soc. di Studi Valdesi; Soc. di Storia delle Religioni. Hons: Doct. Theol., Univ. of Paris, 1956. Address: Via Pietro Cossa 42, 00193 Rome, Italy.

SÜCHTING-KOENEMANN, Ellen Irmgard Annemarie, b. 8 July 1895, Charlottenburg, Germany. Writer; Lyric Poet; Painter. Publs: Die Schalen des Dschingis Khan (novel); Meine lieben Tiere (children's book); Fröhliche Geschichten (fairy tales). Contbr. to: Hamburger Anthologie; das Treppenhaus; num. radio progs.; num. poems. Mbr., German Writers' Union; GEMA. Address: 2000 Hamburg, 55 Blankenese, Falkensteiner Ufer 76, W. Germany.

SUHL, Yuri, b. 30 July 1908, Podhajce, Poland. Writer. Educ: Brooklyn Coll., CUNY, 1928-29; N.Y. Univ., 1929-30, 1949-53. Publs. incl: One Foot in America, 1950; Cowboy on a Wooden Horse, 1953; Ed., Transl., & Author of 6 chapts., They Fought Back: The Story of Jewish Resistance in Nazi Europe (documentary anthol.), 1967; Eloquent Crusader: Ernestine Rose (juvenile biog.), 1970; Simon Boom Gives a Wedding, 1972; An Album of Jews in America, 1972; The Man Who Made Everyone Late, 1974; On the Other Side of the Gate, 1975; The Merrymaker, 1975; also books of poetry & prose in Yiddish. Mbr., Authors Guild of Am. Hons. incl: Nat. Jewish Book Award, 1974. Address: 232 E. 6th St., N.Y., NY 10003, USA.

SÜKÖSD, Mihály, b. 4 Oct. 1933, Budapest, Hungary. Writer; Editor. Educ: B.A., Philol. Dept., Eötvös Loránd Univ., Budapest. Publs: The Outsider (novel), 1968; Variations on the Novel (essay), 1971; In Struggle with Epics (essay), 1972; Pre-trial Detention (novel), 1973. Contbr. to: Reality; New Writing; etc. Mbrships: Hungarian Writers' Assn.; PEN. Address: 1111 Egry József u. 36, Budapest, Hungary.

SULLIVAN, George Edward, b. 11 Aug. 1927, Lowell, Mass., USA. Author. Educ: B.Sc. Publs. incl: Understanding Architecture, 1971; The Rise of the Robots, 1971; How Do They Build It?, 1972; By Chance a Winner: The History of Lotteries, 1972; Sports for Your Child, 1973; The Backpacker's Handbook, 1973; How Does It Get There?, 1974; Queens of the Court, 1974; Roger Staubach, A Special Kind of Quarterback, 1974; Hank Aaron, 1974. Mbr., Authors Guild. Address: 330 E. 33rd St., N.Y., NY 10016, USA.

SULLIVAN, John Patrick, b. 13 July 1930, Liverpool, UK. Classicist; University Provost. Educ: B.A., 1953, M.A., 1957, St. John's Coll., Cambridge; B.A., 1954, M.A., 1957, Oxford. Publs. incl: Critical Essays on Roman Literature: Satire, 1963; Ezra Pound & Sextus Propertius: A Study in Creative Translation, 1964; Transl., Petronius: The Satyricon & the Fragments, 1965; The Satyricon of Petronius: A Literary Study, 1968; Penguin Critical Anthologies: Ezra Pound, 1970; Propertius: A Critical Introduction, 1975. Contbr. to: Arion (Ed., 1961-68); Arethusa (Ed., 1970-74); etc. Mbr., Am. Philol. Assn. (Dir., 1971-73). Hons. incl: Greg Bury Burney Prizes in Philos. of Relig., 1953 & 1954; Redditt Award, 1965. Address: 470 Linwood Ave., Buffalo, NY 14209, USA.

SULLIVAN, Michael, b. 8 Jan. 1942, Chicago, Ill., USA. Mathematician. Educ: B.S., De Paul Univ., 1962; M.S., 1963, Ph.D., 1967, Ill. Inst. Technol. Publs: Finite Mathematics with Applications for Business & Social Sciences (w. Abe Mizrahi), 1973; Topics in Elementary Mathematics (w. Abe Mizrahi), 1971. Mbrships. incl: Am. Maths. Soc.; Maths. Assn. Am. Hons: Lib. Sci. Book Club, alternate selection Jan. 1973 for Finite Maths. w. Applications for Bus. & Social Scis. Address: 9529 Tripp, Oak Lawn, IL 60453, USA.

SULLIVAN, Walter Seager, b. 12 Jan. 1918, NYC, USA. Journalist; Author. Educ: Yale Univ. Publs: Quest for a Continent, 1957; White Land of Adventure, 1957; Assault on the Unknown, 1961; We Are Not Alone, 1964; Continents in Motion, 1974. Contbr. to: N.Y. Times. Mbrships: US Antarctic Expeds.; Govt. Arctic Inst. of N. Am.; Am. Geographical Soc. Num. hons. incl: George Polk Mem. Award, 1959; Inst. Non-Fiction Book Prize, Frankfurt, 1965; Grady Award, 1969; Washburn Medal, 1972; Daly Medal, 1973. Address: 66 Indian Head Rd., Riverside, Conn., USA.

SULZBERGER, Cyrus Leo, b. 27 Oct. 1912. Journalist. Educ: B.S., Harvard Univ. Publs. incl: The Big Thaw, 1956; What's Wrong With US Foreign Policy, 1959; My Brother Death, 1961; The Test: De Gaulle & Algeria, 1962; Unfinished Revolution, 1965; History of World War II, 1966; A Long Row of Candles, Memoirs & Diaries, 1934-54, 1969; The Last of the Giants, 1970; The Tooth Merchant, 1973; The Age of Mediocrity, 1973; The Coldest War — Russia's Game in China, 1974. Contbr. to N.Y. Times. Address: c/o NY Times, 3 rue Scribe, Paris 9e, France.

SUMMERS, Hollis (Spurgeon Jr.), b. 21 June 1916, Eminence, Ky., USA. Distinguished Professor of English, Ohio University, Athens, 1959—. Educ: A.B., Georgetown Coll., Ky., 1937; M.A., Middlebury Coll., Vt., 1943; Ph.D., Univ. of Iowa, 1949. Publs. (novels): City Limit, 1948; Brighten the Corner, 1952; Teach You a Lesson (as Jim

Hollis, w. James Rourke), 1955; The Weather of February, 1957; The Day after Sunday, 1968; (verse): The Walks near Athens, 1959; The Peddler & Other Domestic Matters, 1967; Sit Opposite Each Other, 1970; num. uncollected short stories. Hons. incl: Saturday Review Poetry Award, 1957; Colls. of Arts & Scis. Award, 1958; LL.D., Georgetown Coll., 1965. Address: 181 North Congress St., Athens, OH 45701, USA.

SUMMERS, Joseph Holmes, b. 8 Feb. 1920, Louisville, Ky., USA. University Professor. Educ: A.B., 1941, M.A., 1948, Ph.D., 1950, Harvard Univ. Publs: George Herbert: His Religion & Art, 1954; The Muse's Method: An Introduction to Paradise Lost, 1962. Andrew Marvell: Selected Poems (ed.), 1961; The Lyric & Dramatic Milton (ed.), 1965; George Herbert: Selected Poetry (ed.), 1967; The Heirs of Donne & Jonson, 1970. Contbr. to: Yale Review; Univ. of Toronto Quarterly; Mich. Quarterly Review; PMLA; etc. Mbr., MLA. Recip., var. acad. hons. Address: 179 Crosman Terrace, Rochester, NY 14620, USA.

SUMMERSELL, Charles Grayson, b. 25 Feb. 1908, Mobile, Ala., USA. Professor of History. Educ: A.B., 1929, M.A., 1930, Univ. of Ala.; Ph.D., Vanderbilt Univ., 1940. Publs. incl: Historical Foundations of Mobile, 1949; Mobile: History of a Seaport Town, 1949; Alabama History for Schools, 1957, rev. 1960, 1965 & 1970; The Cruise of the CSS Sumter, 1965; Ed., The Journal of George Townley Fulham: Boarding Officer of the Confederate Sea Raider Alabama, 1973. Contbr. to: Ency. Britannica; Britannica Jr.; Ency. Americana; World Book Ency.; Grolier's Ency.; Jrnl. of Southern Hist.; Jrnl. of Am. Hist.; etc. Mbr., var. histl. orgs. Address: 1411 Caplewood Dr., Tuscaloosa, AL 35401, USA.

SUN, Yi, pen name LIN TING, b. 28 Jan. 1927, Kiangsu, Soochow, China. Writer. Educ: B.A., Social Educ. Dept., Provisional Educ. Acad. Publs: Eight Years in Red China, 1958; Pajama Story, 1959; First "Good Morning", 1966; Revelation (fiction), 1974. Contbr. to many mags. & newspapers, Shanghai & Hong Kong. Mbr., PEN. Address: 1046 King's Rd., 1/F, A 17, Yick Cheong Bldg., North Point, Hong Kong.

SUNDÉN, Karl Hjalmar Daniel, b. 27 Jan. 1942, Gävle, Sweden. Author. Educ: Fil. mag. Vols. of poetry; Tilltal, 1966; Älska-ettporträtt, 1968; Denandra natten, 1970; Mamele, 1973. Author, April God Morgon (novel), 1971. Contbr. to: Expressen; Var Losen. Mbr., Sveriges Författarförbund. Hons: Albert Bonniers stipendium föryngre ochnyare författare, 1971; Svenska kyrkans kulturstiftelses författarstipendium, 1971. Address: Åkerbyrägen 236, 183 35 Täby, Sweden.

SUNESSON, Lambert, pen name FRYKBERG, August, b. 9 Feb. 1918, Blötberget, Sweden. Civil Servant. Educ: Socialinstitutet, Stockholm, 1945. Publs: Vargarna, 1951; Inka Indian, 1952; Tie man till Långsyna, 1958; Tillbaka till Moria, 1958. Contbr. to: Dagens Nyheter; Morgontidningen; Aftontidningen; Veckotidningen Vi. Mbr., Swedish Union of Authors. Hons: Rabén & Sjögren Short Novel Prize, 1958; Veckotidningen Vi Prize, 1958. Address: Dalvägen 70, 141 71 Huddinge, Sweden.

SUPANGKAT, Hidayat, pen name LE BOC, b. 31 Aug. 1928, Bandung, Indonesia. Journalist (UN Permanent Correspondent). Educ: Christian Higher Schl. for Teachers. Contbr. to: Korean Herald Daily. Mbr., UN Corres.'s Assn., N.Y. Address: 94-10, 59th Ave., Apt. 1c, N.Y., NY 11373, USA.

SUR, Atul K., b. 1904, India. Author. Educ: D.Sc. Publs. incl: Sex & Marriage in India; Dynamics of Synthesis in Hindu Culture; Folk Elements in Bengali Culture; History & Culture of Bengal; Challenge of Rural Poverty; Dictionary of Company Law. Address: 11 Kalicharan Ghosh Rd., Calcutta 700 050, India.

SUTCLIFFE, Joseph Robert, pen name PLOWMAN, Giles, b. 8 Sept. 1911, Brighouse, UK. Schoolmaster. Educ: Univ. London; Goldsmiths' Coll. Contbr. to: Teacher; Remedial Educ.; & BBC radio talks. Mbrships: Lancs. Authors Assn. (Hon. Gen. Sec.); Over Wyre Probus Club (Fndr. Mbr.). Recip., 1st Prize, Article Writing Preston Writers Circle, May 1969. Address: Sea Winds, 22 Lune View, Knott End on Sea, Fylde Coast, Lancs. FY6 0AG, UK.

SUTCLIFFE, Pavella Dolores, pen name PLOUGHMAN, Nina, b. Harrogate, Yorks., UK. Secretary & Freelance

Writer. Educ: Paris, France; Medical Studies, UK. Contbr. to: Reflections, 1972; 'Twixt Thee & Me, 1973; Preston Poets' Soc. Publs.; BBC; Sunday Companion; My Wkly.; Homes & Gdns.; Shore Poets (Cleveleys); Cath. Times; etc. Mbrships: Lancs. Authors' Assn.; Preston Poets' Soc. (Hon. Sec., 1960-71); Ladies Forum; Preesall U.R. Church (Hon. Sec.). Hons: 4 Awards, Preston Poets' Soc. Annual Competition, 1965-73; 1st Prize poetry, 1968, 1st prize short story & 2nd prize poetry, 1969, Preston Writers' Circle. Address: Sea Winds, 22 Lune View, Knott End on Sea, Fylde Coast, Lancs. FY6 0AG, UK.

SUTHERLAND, Margaret, b. 16 Sept. 1941. Author. Publs: The Fledgling (novel), 1974; Hello, I'm Karen (children's fiction), 1974. Contbr. to: Landfall; Islands; Short Stories by New Zealanders, 1973, 1974; NZ Short Stories, vol. 3, 1974. Recip., Katherine Mansfield Mem. Short Story Award, 1973. Address: 16 Manuka Rd., Titirangi, Auckland, NZ.

SUTHERLAND, William Temple Gairdner, b. 24 Mar. 1906, Dundee, UK. Writer. Publs: The Golden Bush, 1953; Green Kiwi, 1956; The Silver Fern, 1959; Maui & Me, 1963; The Sixty Million Muster, 1966; Span of the Wheel, 1973. Address: 137 Moana Ave., Tahunanui, Nelson, NZ.

SVEINSSON, Guðjón, b. 25 May 1937, Breiðalur, Iceland. Teacher. Educ: Icelandic Seamans Schl. Publs: (for children & young people) Njósnir að naeturþeli (Spying in the Night), 1967; Ógnir Einidals (The Threat of Einidalur), 1968; Leyndardómur Lundeyja I & II (The Mystery of Lundeyjar), 1969-70; Svarti Skugginn (The Black Shadow), 1971; Órt Rennur Aeskublóð (Restless Young People), 1973; Hljóðin á Heidinni (The Sounds of the Hill), 1973. Contbr. to reviews inclng. Heima er Bezt. Mbr., Soc. of Icelandic Authors. Address: Mánaberg, Breiðalur, Iceland.

SWADOS, Harvey, b. 28 Oct. 1920, Buffalo, NY, USA. Professor, University of Massachusetts. Educ: B.A., Univ. of Mich., Ann Arbor. Publs. incl: Our Went the Candle (novel), 1955; On the Line (short stories), USA 1957, UK 1958; False Coin (novel), 1959; Nights in the Gardens of Brooklyn, USA 1961, UK 1962; A Radical's American (essays), 1962; The Will (novel), USA 1963, UK 1965; A Story for Teddy – And Others, USA 1965, UK 1966; A Radical at Large: American Essays, UK 1968; Standing Fast (novel), 1970; Standing up for the People: The Life & Work of Estes Kefauver, 1972. Hons. incl: Guggenheim Fellowship, 1960; National Inst. of Arts & Letters Grant, 1965; Nat. Endowment for the Arts grant, 1968. Address: Dept. of English, Bartlett Hall, Univ. of Mass., Amerst, MA 01002, USA.

SWALE, Rose, (Mrs. Colin Swale née Griffin), b. 1947, Davos, Switzerland. Traveller. Publs: Rosie Darling, 1973; Children of Cape Horn, 1974. Contbr. to: Daily Mail; Daily Express; Sunday Express; Sunday People; Reveille. Agent: Colin Swale. Address: c/o Colin Swale Coutts & Co., Fleet St. Branch, London EC4, UK.

SWANN, Peter Charles, b. 20 Dec. 1921, London, UK. Museum Director; Foundation Director. Educ. incls: B.A. & M.A., Oxford Univ., 1949. Publs: Yun Kang, 15 vols. (transl. from Japanese), 1950-58; An Introduction to the Arts of Japan, 1958; Chinese Painting, 1958; 2,000 Years of Japanese Art (w. Yukio Yashiro), 1958; Hokusai, 1960; Chinese Monumental Art, 1963; Japan, 1966. Contbr. to jrnls. Mbr., num. profl. orgs. inclng: Publs. Comm., Univ. of Toronto Press; F.R.S.A. Recip., 2 hon. degrees. Address: Samuel & Saidye Bronfman Family Fndn., 1916 Tupper St., Montreal, P.Q. H3H 1N5, Can.

SWARTHOUT, Glendon, (Fred), b. 8 Apr. 1918, Pinckney, Mich., USA. Educ: A.B., 1939, A.M., 1946, Univ. of Mich., Ann Arbor; Ph.D., Mich. State Univ., East Lansing, 1955. Publs. (novels): Willow Run, 1943; They Came to Cordura, USA & UK 1958; Where the Boys Are USA & UK, 1960; Welcome to Thebes, USA & UK 1962; The Cadillac Cowboys, 1964; The Eagle & the Iron Cross, USA & UK 1966; Loveland, 1968; Bless the Beasts & Children, USA & UK 1970; The Tin Lizzie Troop, 1972; (juveniles w. Kathryn Swarthout): The Ghost & the Magic Saber, 1963; Whichaway, USA 1966, UK 1971; TV Thompson, 1972; sev. uncollected short stories. Hons: Theatre Guild Award in playwriting, 1947; Hopwood Award, 1948; O. Henry Award, 1960. Address: 5045 Tamanar Way, Scottsdale, AZ 85253, USA.

SWARUP, Shanti, b. 19 Dec. 1916, Azamgarh, Uttar Pradesh, India. Teacher. Educ: M.A. Publs: Arts & Crafts of India & Pakistan; 5000 Years of Arts & Crafts in India & Pakistan. Contbr. to: Mod. Review, Calcutta; Hindustan Times, New Delhi; Times of India, Bombay; Singhalese Ency., Ceylon. Address: Chandra Bhawan, Civil Lines, Azamgarh, Utter Pradesh, India.

SWEARINGEN, Annette Wildman, b. 21 May 1897, St. Paul, Mo., USA. Teacher; Minister of Religion. Educ: Kansas City Univ.; Unity Schl. of Christianity, Unity Village, Mo., 1944; Licensed Tchr., 1947. Publs: Poetry Mosaic of Living, 1951; Sonnettones, 1951; Moments of Mood, 1952; Of Heart & Home, 1956; Ed., Kansas City Westport News, 1957-60. Contbr. to: Children's Activities; Kansas City Poetry Mag.; Ideals Mag.; Kansas City Star; & other books, mags. & newspapers. Mbrships: Nat. League Am. Pen Women (Mo. State Pres., 1958-60); Hemet Pen Women; Mark Twain Soc. Recip., Hon. Award, Kansas City Westport Br., Nat. League of Am. Pen Women, 1961-64. Address: 25124 Yale St., Hemet, CA 92343, USA.

SWEET, George Elliott, b. 26 Sept. 1904, Denver, Colo., USA. Geophysicist. Educ: B.S., 1927, M.S., 1928, Univ. of Okla.; Grad. studies, Harvard Univ., 1940-41. Publs: Shake-speare, The Mystery, 1956, enlarged ed., 1963; Gentleman in Oil, 1966; The History of Geophysical Prospecting, vol. I, 1966, vol. II, 1969; The Petroleum Saga, 1971; Dramas From Six Centuries (13th to 18th), forthcoming. Mbrships: Soc. pf Exploration Geophysicists; Am. Assn. Petroleum Geologists; AAAS; Phi Beta Kappa; var. hon. socs.; Santa Monica Pony League (Pres., 1959-60). Address: 502 Georgina Ave., Santa Monica, CA 90402, USA.

SWERDLOFF, Arthur Leroy, b. 13 July 1921, Balt., Md., USA. Writer/Director, Motion Pictures. Educ: A.B., Johns Hopkins Univ., 1942; M.A. Cinema, Univ. of Southern Calif., 1950. Publs. incl: (writing credits) The Brain & Behavior (TV), 1962; The Story of a Matador (TV); To Sleep . . . Perchance to Dream (TV series), 1966; The Biosatellite (film), 1966; Meeting in Progress (film), 1971; The Big Dig (film), 1973; Board Action (film), 1974. Mbrships: Writers' Guild of Am., West; Dirs'. Guild of Am. Hons. incl: Venice, & Edinburgh Film Festival Awards, 1951; Robert Flaherty Award, 1955; Art Dirs'. Guild Award, 1958; Documentary Emmy, 1959; Cine Golden Eagle, 1964, 1965, 1966, 1972, 1974. Address: 4224 Ellenita Ave., Tarzana, CA 91356, USA.

SWIGGETT, Hal, b. 22 July 1921, Moline, Kan., USA. Editor; Writer. Publs: Gun Talk (contbng. author), 1973; North American Big Game Hunting (contbng. author), 1974. Contbr. to: Ed., GUNsport & Gun Collector; Shooter's Bible; Gun Digest; Southern Outdoors; Fishing & Hunting Guide; All Outdoors; Muzzleloader; Outdoor Times; Fisherman; Shooting Times; Guns & Ammo. Mbrships: Bd. of Dirs., Outdoor Writers' Assn. of Am., 3 yrs.; Sec.-Treas., Tex. Outdoor Writers' Assn., 6 yrs., Pres., 2 yrs.; Life, Nat. Rifle Assn. Recip., Best Article in a Breed Mag., Dog Writers' Assn. of Am., 1968. Address: 200 New Moore Bldg., San Antonio, TX 78205, USA.

SWINFEN, (The Lady) Averil (née Humphreys), b. 1918. Former Social Worker; Owner Ireland's largest Donkey Stud, 1964—. Publ: The Irish Donkey, 1967. Ed., Assile Mag., Irish Donkey Soc. Contbr. to: Pony Mag.; Ezel Revue, Germany. Pres., Irish Donkey Soc. Address: Medina House, Spanish Point Donkey Stud, Co. Clare, Repub. of Ireland.

SWINNERTON, Frank (Arthur), b. 12 Aug. 1884, Wood Green, Middlesex, UK. Writer; Critic. Publs. incl: (novels) The Merry Heart, UK, 1909, USA, 1929; Nocturne, 1917; Summer Storm, UK & USA, 1926; Harvest Comedy, UK, 1937,USA, 1938; English Maiden, 1946; The Woman from Sicily, UK & USA, 1957; Quadrille, UK & USA, 1965; Nor All Thy Tears, UK & USA, 1972; (non-fiction) George Gissing, UK, 1912, USA, 1913; The Georgian Scene, USA, 1934 (as The Georgian Literary Scene, UK, 1934) revised eds. UK, 1969, USA, 1971; Swinnerton (autobiog.), USA, 1936, UK, 1937; Reflections from a Village, UK & USA, 1969. Contbr. to var. mags. & newspapers. Address: Old Tokefield, Cranleigh, Surrey, UK.

SWINTON, William Elgin, b. 1900, Kirkcaldy, Fife, UK. University Professor; Museum Keeper. Educ: B.Sc., Ph.D., Glasgow Univ. Publs: The Dinosaurs; Corridor of Life; Life Before Adam; Fossils; Fossil Reptiles & Amphibians; Fossil Birds; Wonderful World of Prehistoric Animals, 1961; Animals Before Adam, 1962; Digging for Dinosaurs, 1962. Contbr. to: Nature; New Sci.; Discovery; Illustrated

London News; Natural Hist., NY; Museums Jrnls.; Ency. Americana; etc. Mbrships. incl: Fellow, Royal Soc. Edinburgh; Arts & Letters Club, Toronto (Pres.); Brit. Assn. (Hon. Gen. Sec.). Address: 276 St. George St., Apt. 604, Toronto MR5 2P6, Can.

SYKES, Christopher Hugh, b. 17 Nov. 1907, Menethorpe, Nr. Malton, Yorks., UK. Writer. Educ: Christ Ch., Oxford; Sorbonne Univ., Paris, France. Publs: Wassmuss, 1936; Innocence & Design (w. Robert Byron), 1936; Stranger Wonders, 1937; High Minded Murder, 1943; Four Studies in Loyalty, 1946; The Answer to Question 33, 1948; Character & Situation, 1949; Two Studies in Virtue, 1953; A Song of A Shirt, 1953; Dates & Parties, 1955; Orde Wingate, 1959; Cross Roads to Israel, 1965; Nancy Aston, 1972. Contbr. to: Observer; Listener; Books & Bookmen; Encounter. Mbr., London Lib. Comm., 1959-74. Address: Swyre House, Swyre, Dorchester, Dorset, UK.

SYME, Neville Rowland, pen name SYME, Ronald, b. 13 Mar. 1913, Co. Galway, Ireland. Author. Publs. incl: The Travels of Captain Cook, 1970; Isles of the Frigate Bird, or Rarotonga Remembered, 1975. Contbr. to var. mags., USA & UK. Address: Box 95, Rarotonga, Cook Islands, S. Pacific Ocean.

SYMONDS, Richard, b. 2 Oct. 1918, Oxford, UK. United Nations Official, Resident Representative, UN Development Programme, Athens. Educ: M.A., Oxford Univ. Publs: The Making of Pakistan, 1950, 4th ed., 1966; The British & their Successors, 1966; Ed., International Targets for Development, 1970; The UN & the Population Question (w. M. Carder), 1973. Contbr. to: Jrnl. C'wlth. Pol. Studies; Int. Dev. Review; Times; Guardian. Mbrships: Royal Inst. Int. Affairs; Int. Union for Sci. Study Population; Soc. for Int. Dev. Address: UN Dev. Prog., 36 Amalias Ave., Athens, Greece.

SYMONS, Julian (Gustave), b. 30 May 1912, London, UK. Writer. Publs. incl: (novels) The 31st of February, 1950; The Narrowing Circle, 1954; The Colour of Murder, 1957; The Progress of a Crime, 1960; The Belting Inheritance, 1965; The Players & the Game, 1972 (all also Publd. USA); (non-fiction) A.J.A. Symons, 1950; A Reasonable Doubt, 1960; Crime & Detection (as a Pictorial History of Crime, USA), 1966; Between the Wars, 1972. Contbr. to: Sunday Times (reviews, 1958—). Mbrships: Crime Writers Assn. (Chmn., 1958—59); Soc. of Authors. Hons: Award, Brit. Crime Writers Assn., 1957, 1966; E. A. Poe Award, 1961, 1966. Address: 37 Albert Bridge Rd., London SW11, UK.

SYMONS, Leslie John, b. 8 Nov. 1926, Reading, UK. University Reader in Geography. Educ: B.Sc., London Schl. of Econs., 1953; Ph.D., Queens Univ., Belfast, 1958. Publs: Ed. & Contbr., Land Use in Northern Ireland, 1963; Agricultural Geography, 1967; Northern Ireland: A Geographical Introduction (co-author), 1967; Russian Agriculture, 1972; Russian Transport (co-Ed.), 1975. Contbr. to: Geog.; NZ Geog.; Irish Geog.; Scottish Geogl. Mag.; NZ Jrnl. of Geog.; Soviet Studies. Mbrships: Inst. Brit. Geogs.; Nat Assn. Soviet & E. European Studies. Address: "Squirrel's Jump", 17 Wychwood Close, Langland, Swansea SA3 4PH, UK.

SYMONS, Robert David, b. 7 Apr. 1898, d. 1 Feb. 1973, Mayfield, UK. Naturalist; Writer; Artist; Rancher. Publs: Many Trails, 1964; Hours & the Birds, 1967; The Broken Snare, 1970; Still the Wind Blows, 1971; Where the Wagon Led, 1973; North By West, 1975; Silton Seasons, 1975; Companions of the Peace, 1975. Contbr. to: The Field; Blue Jay; Can. Cattleman; etc. Hons: Sask. Conservation Award, Sask. Nat. Hist. Soc., 1965; Hon. LL.D., Univ. of Sask., 1970.

SYMONS, Scott, b. 13 July 1933, Toronto, Ont., Can. Museum Curator; Assistant Professor of Fine Art; Consultant. Educ: B.A., Trinity Coll., Univ. of Toronto, 1955; M.A., King's Coll., Cambridge Univ., UK; Dip. d'Etudes Superieures, Sorbonne, Paris, France. Publs: Place d'Armes (novel), 1967; Civic Square (novel), 1969; Heritage: A Romantic Look at Early Canadian Furniture, 1971. Contbr. to: (as Ed. Writer & Reporter) Toronto Telegram; Quebec Chronicle Telegram; Montreal Presse; Montreal Nouveau Journal. Recip., Beta Sigma Phi Award, 1968. Address: c/o McClelland & Stewart Ltd., 25 Hollinger Rd., Toronto 16, Ont., Can.

SYPHER, Wylie, b. 12 Dec. 1905, Mt. Kisco, N.Y., USA. College Teacher. Educ: A.B., Amherst Coll., 1927;

M.A., Tufts Univ., 1929; A.M., 1932, Ph.D., 1937, Harvard Univ. Publs: Guinea's Captive Kings, 1942; Enlightened England, 1947; Four Stages of Renaissance Style, 1955; The Meaning of Comedy (in Comedy), 1956; Rococo to Cubism in Art & Literature, 1960; Loss of the Self, 1962; Art History (ed.), 1963; Literature & Technology, 1968. Contbr. to: N.Y. Review of Books; Studies in Philology; Am. Scholar; etc. Mbrships: PEN; Dante Soc. Recip., var. acad. hons. Address: Dept. of Engl., Simmons Coll., Boston, MA 02115, USA.

SZABÓ, György (George), b. 10 Jan. 1932, Kapuvár, Hungary. Playwright; Essayist; Editor. Educ: degree in Italian lit. & lib. scis., Eötvös Lorand Univ., Budapest. Publs: A futurizmus (Futurism), 1962; Képek és lagunák (Pictures & Lagoons, an aesthetic "travel diary"), 1964; Játék és igazság (comedy), 1964; Pirandello, 1965; Szekrénybe zárt szerelem (Love Closed in a Cupboard, play), 1969; Napoleon és (&) Napoleon (play), 1970. Contbr. to var. jrnls. & to TV. Mbr., var. lit. orgs. Recip., sev. prizes for TV scripts. Address: Naphegy u. 39, 1016, Budapest, Hungary.

SZABÓ, Magda, b. 5 Oct. 1917, Debrecen, Hungary. Authoress. Educ: Degree, Latin Phil., Debrecen Univ., 1940. Publs: (novels) Fresco, 1958; The Fawn, 1959; Pilate, 1963; The Danaid, 1964; Genesis I.22, 1967; Kathleen Street, 1969; Old Well, 1970; The Onlookers, 1973; (children's books) Island Blue, 1959; Lala the Fairy, 1965; Abigail, 1973; poetry; plays; essays; transls. Mbr., PEN. Recip., Attila József Prize, 1960, 1972. Address: 1026 Budapest, Julia utca 3, Hungary.

SZABOLCSI, Miklós, b. 3 Mar. 1921, Budapest, Hungary. University Professor. Educ: Univ. of Budapest. Publs. incl: Monograph: József Attila, 1963; Precursors & Contemporaries, 1964; Changing World Socialist Literature, 1973; Sign & Outcry, 1971; The Clown as a Self-Portrait of the Artist, 1974; (Ed.) History of Hungarian Literature, Vols. 5 & 6. Contbr. to: Latohatar (Ed.); Neohelicon (Co-Ed.). Mbrships. incl: Hungarian Acad. of Sci.; Int. Assn. of Lit. Criticism; Int. Comp. Lit. Assn., Comité Int. d'Esthétique; etc. Recip: József Attila Prize 1962, 1964. Address: Inst. of Lit. Studies, 1118 Budapest, Menesi ut 11-13, Hungary.

SZACSVAY-FEHÉR, Tibor, pen name FEHÉR, Tibor, b. 13 Jan. 1907, Budapest, Hungary. Former Teacher of Hungarian Language & History. Educ: Tchrs. Trng. Coll. Publs. incl: The Golden Cock, 1959; The Moon Above The Tisza, 1961; The Captain of Hajdus, 1965; The Aquincum Horseman, 1968; Coloman Beauclerc, 1971; In the Shadow of the Turkish Crescent, 1973; The Iron Mace, 1974. Contbr. to var. mags. Mbrships: Authors' Assn. of Hungarian Writers; Assn. of Art. Address: Ajtosi Durer sor 13, 1146 Budapest XIV, Hungary.

SZAKONYI, Károly, b. 26 Oct. 1931, Budapest, Hungary. Writer; Dramatist. Publs: (play & novel) Férfiak (Men), 1965; (novel) Tul a városon (Beyond the Town), 1964; (short story) Francia tanya (French Farm), 1969; (plays, radio plays) Harmincnégy ember (Thirty-four Men), 1971; (plays) Ördöghegy (Devil's Hill), 1968; (radio play) Sublease & Philodendron, 1969; Adáshiba (Error in the Transmission), 1970; Hongkongi paróka (Wig of Hong Kong), 1973. Contbr. to: Uj Irás; Kortárs; radio, TV, theatre. Mbrships: Writers' Assn.; Inst. Theatre Int. Hons: SZOT Lit. Prize, 1963; József Attila Lit. Prize, 1970; Gábor Andor Lit. Prize, 1974. Address: 2000 Szentendre, Hegyalja u. 1, Hungary.

SZANCER, Henryk, pen name SZACH, Wiktor, b. 29 Nov. 1904, Tarnow, Poland. Pharmaceutical Chemist. Educ: M.Pharm., Cracow, 1926; D.Pharm., Paris, France, 1929. Publs: Dangerous Drugs — Laws, Rules & Regulations, 1930, 2nd ed., 1934; (transls.) Anleitung zum Nachweis der Gifte, by T. Sabalitschka, 1929; Incompatibilités pharmaceutiques, by A. Goris & A. Liot (w. M. Proner), 1936; Walafridi Strabi Hortulus, 1938. Contbr. to profl. jrnls. in Dutch, Engl., French, German, Italian & Polish; Polish lit. jrnls.; Am. philat. mags. Mbrships: Pharm. Soc. of GB; PEN; Am. Br., Ctr. for Writers in Exile. Address: 146-26 61st Rd., Flushing, NY 11367, USA.

SZANTO, George H., b. 4 June 1940, Londonderry, N. Ireland. Professor of Comparative Literature. Educ: B.A. (German, French), Dartmouth Coll., USA, 1962; Ph.D (Comp. Lit.), Harvard Univ., 1967. Publs: Narrative Consciousness: Structure & Perception in the Fiction of

Franz Kafka, Samuel Beckett & Alain Robbe-Grillet, 1972. Contbr. to: Texas Quarterly; Critique; Bucknell Review; Mass. Review. Mbrships: Int. Comp. Lit. Assn.; Can. Comp. Lit. Assn.; Mod. Lang. Assn. Hons. incl: Outstanding Educator of Am. Award, 1972-73. Address: 3495 Peel St., Room 304, McGill Univ., Montreal, Quebec, Can.

SZÁRAZ, György, b. 3 Nov. 1930, Budapest, Hungary. Playwright; Literary Translator. Publs: The Incorruptible, 1968; The Chief of Staff, 1969; King's Gambit, 1969; Bela III., 1970; The Tree of Wisdom, 1971; The Water Mirror, 1972; The Splendid Death, 1973; The Flight, 1974; The Water of Life, 1974; The Bells of Saint Roch, 1974. Contbr. to: Tiszatáj (lit. jrnl.). Mbr., Alliance of Hungarian Writers. Recip., Batsányi Lit. Prize, 1973. Address: Munkácsy Mihály u. 70, 2045 Törökbálint, Hungary.

SZASZ, Imre, b. 19 Mar. 1927, Budapest, Hungary. Writer. Educ: Degree in Hungarian & Engl. Lit., Budapest Univ. Publs: The Bugle Calls, 1953; Basa, 1957; Waterside Meditations, 1958; High Header, 1967; Come at Nine, 1969; Dry Martini, 1973. Contbr. to Hungarian mags. & jrnls. Mbrships: Hungarian Writers' Union; PEN. Recip., József Attila Prize, 1954. Address: Gaal Jozsef utca 1-5, 1122 Budapest, Hungary.

SZCZYGIEK, Jerzy, b. 14 Mar. 1932, Pulawy, Poland. Novelist. Educ: Master of Polish Studies. Publs: Tarnina, 1960; Milczenie, 1962; Drogi Rezygnacji, 1963; Depalające się drzewa, 1964; Sen o brzozowych bucikach, 1966; Szare rękawiczki, 1967; Ziemia bez stonca, 1968; Powódź, 1970; Nigdy cię nie opuszczę, 1972. Contbr. to: Nasz swiat (Ed.-in-Chief), Niewidomy spoldzielca (Ed.-in-Chief), both mags. for blind people. Mbrships: Polish Writers' Assn.; Polish Jrnlst. Assn.; PEN; Zaiks. Hons. incl: Polish Cross of Merit; Most Disting. Book Award, Polish Youth Orgs., 1973. Address: Nowy Swiat 35 m 6, 00029 Warsaw, Poland.

SZEBERÉNYI, Lehel, b. 19 June 1921, Losonc, Czech. Editor. Publs: (novels) Hét nap, 1953; Szalmácska, 1956; Lépcsők a felhőbe, 1957; Jeromos a kőfejű, 1966; Tibike Tartaroszban, 1969; (short stories) Kárhozat küszöbén, 1963; Költő és őrangyalai, 1965; Családi körben, 1973. Contbr. to: Kortárs; Uj Irás; Élet és Irodalom. Mbrships: Org. of Hungarian Writers; Org. of Hungarian Jrnlsts. Recip., József Attila Prize, 1951, 1953. Address: 2016 Leányfalu, Móricz Zsigmond u. 48, Hungary.

SZEKELY-MOLNAR, Imre, b. 13 Dec. 1902, Budapest, Hungary. Writer. Publs: Conversation of Two Hearts; 1000 Years Old Hungary; On the Shores of the Tisza; Aldozás pogány oltárokon; Broken Life; Erdély; hantok Heaven & Hell; Listen Sophie; Az apostol es a paradicsommadár; Főltisztulazeg. Contbr. to: Hungarian World in Am.; Liberty; Hungarian Herald; Can. Hungarian News; Nemzoetör. Mbr., PEN. Recip., Jrnlsts'. Award, Toronto, 1972. Address: 33 Ledbury St., Toronto 12, Ont., Can.

SZEL, Elisabeth, b. 26 Nov. 1926, Budapest, Hungary. Writer. Educ: Hungarian Acad. of Films. Publs: Operacion Noche y Niebla, 1962; La mujer del armino, 1965; No apta para menores, 1968; Prohibido nacer, 1969; La Casa de las Chivas, 1972; Greco asszonya, 1973; Balada de Carceles y Rameras, 1974. Mbrships: Syndicate of Film Technicians, Madrid; Sociedad Gen. de autores, Madrid. Address: Reyes Magos 14, Madrid, Spain.

SZENTKUTHY, Miklós, family name PFISTERER, b. 2 June 1908, Budapest, Hungary. Writer; Teacher. Educ: M.A. Publs. incl: (novels) Divertimento (Változatok W. A. Mozart Életéről); Doktor Haydn; Handel; Burgundi Krónika; Hitvita és Naszindulo; Arc És Alarc (Goethe); Saturnus Fia (Dürer); Angyali Gigli; Szent Orpheus Breviárivma (Három kötet, Bővitett Kiadás); (books of essays) Meghátarozások És Szerepek (Maupassant Egy Mai Iró Szemével). Contbr. to var. lit. publs. Mbrships: PEN Club; Hungarian Writers' Assn. Recip., Baumgarten Prize, 1948. Address: H—1125, Budapest XII, Szilágyi Erzsébet, Fasor 28, Hungary.

SZILVÁSI, Lajos, b. 13 Jan. 1932, Szolnok, Hungary. Writer. Publs: Grammar-School Boys, 1953; Star-Shower, 1960; Appassionata, 1961, 5 eds.; Furnished Room in the Whistle Lane, 1963, 3 eds.; And Yet Unprotected, 1964; Top of the Hill, 1965; Black Windows, 1966; Fog-Light, 1967; Cushioned Stock, 1968; Birthday in June, 1969; Air-Thirst, 1970; Watershed, 1972; Talk of the Devil . . ., 1973. Contbr. to: Indl. Law Review (Ed.). Mbrships: Union

of Hungarian Writers; Hungarian PEN; Union of Hungarian Jrnlsts. Address: 1118 Budapest, Csukló utca 8, Hungary.

SZMAGLEWSKA, Seweryna, b. 11 Feb. 1916, Pryzglow, Poland. Writer. Educ: Univs. of Warsaw, Cracow, & Lodz, 1937-39 & 1945-47. Publs: Dymy nad Birkenau (Smoke over Birkenau), 1945, 12 eds.; Prosta droga Lukasza (Luke's Straight Path), 1955, 2 eds.; Zapowiada się piękny dzień (It's Going to be a Fine Day), 1960, 5 eds.; Chleb i nadzieja (Bread & Hope), 1958, 2 eds.; Krzyk waitru (The Call of the Wind), 1965, 4 eds.; Odcienie miłości (Shades of Love), 1969, 3 eds.; Niewinni w Norymberdze (The Innocent at Nuremberg), 1972; (children's books) Czarne Stopy (Black Feet), 1960, 10 eds.; Nowy ślad Czarnych Stóp (New Trail of Black Feet), 1973. Contbr. to sev. lit. jrnls. Recip., 1st class Prize, for whole lit. output, Min. of Culture & Art, 1973. Address: Bajonska 5, 03-946 Warsaw, Poland.

SZOMBATHY, Viktor, b. 8 Apr. 1902, Rimaszombat, Hungary. Editor; Museum Director; Head Librarian. Educ: Univ. of Budapest. Publs: Ezüstantenna (poems), 1928; (novelss) Én kedves népem, 1932; Zöld negyek balladája, 1936; Elesni nem szabad, 1938; És mindenki visszatér, 1939; Különös olasz nyár, 1942; Fabriczy Félix, 1943; Der Kreis schliesst sich, 1943; A félhold vándora, 1968; A pénzhamisitó, 1969; Holló Csete, 1972; Cirok Peti, 1974; var. monographs. Contbr. to: Turista Mag.; Hungarian Szemle; Élet és tudomány. Mbrships. incl: PEN; Lit. Union of Hungary. Recip., Hungarian Gold Medal of Labour. Address: 11 Magyar Jakobinusok tere 1, 1122 Budapest, Hungary.

SZŐNYI, Sándor, b. 5 Mar. 1910, Budapest, Hungary. Journalist; Writer. Publs: Széthulló világ, 1947; Megújhodás, 1956; Rosszlányok utcájában, 1958; Álarcos istenek I-II, 1960; Farsang októberben, 1963; Ködös reggelek, 1968; Betontető, 1970; Kakas a villamoson, 1975. Contbr. to: New Hungarian Ency. (Uj Magyar Lexikon); Hungarian Lit. Ency. Mbrships: PEN; Hungarian Writer's Assn.; Recip., József Attila Prize, 1957. Address: Baranyai utca 19, 1117 Budapest, Hungary.

SZULC, Tad, b. 25 July 1926, Warsaw, Poland. Author; Journalist. Educ: Univ. of Brazil. Publs. incl: The Cuban Invasion, 1962; Latin America, 1966; Ed., US & the Caribbean, 1971; Portrait of Spain, 1972; Compulsive Spy, 1974; The Czechoslovak Invasion, 1974; Innocent at Home, 1974; The Energy Crisis, 1974. Contbr. to: New Yorker; N.Y. Mag.; N.Y. Times Sunday Mag. & Book Review; New Repub.; Esquire; etc. Mbrships. incl: Overseas Writers, Wash. DC.; Authors League & Guild, NYC. Hons. incl: Maria Moors Cabot Gold Medal, Columbia Univ., 1958; Bronze Medallion Disting. Serv. Award, Sigma Delta Chi, 1969. Address: 4515 29th St N.W., Washington DC 20008, USA.

SZUMANSKA-SZMORLIŃSKA, Ewa Maria, b. 20 May 1927, Warsaw, Poland. Writer; Journalist. Educ: Univ. of Krakow; Lotz H.S. of Dramatic Art. Publs: Traces on the Sea, 1963; Adventure in Lagos, 1964; The Scar, 1969; Waiting for a Pilot, 1966; Santa Maria, 1971; Quick, 1972; The Balance, 1972; A Different Rhythm, 1974. Contbr. to Polish Radio & TV. Mbrships: Assn. of Polish Writers; Soc. of Polish Jrnlsts.; PEN; Soc. of Authors; Zaiks; Int. Inst. Maritime Culture. Hons: Partisan Cross, 1955; Cultural Award of Merit, 1970; Cross of Polonia Restituta, 1972; Radio & TV Award of Merit, 1974. Address: Podwale 51 m 7, 50-039 Wroclaw, Poland.

SZWEJ, (Rev.) Mieczysław Kazimierz, pen name ORLOWSKI, Alex, b. 25 June 1930, Torun, Poland. Catholic Priest; Editor. Educ: M. Classical Lit., Cath. Univ. Lublin. Publs: Fajka Pokoju (The Peace Pipe), 1970; Przekwitanie (The Pastblossoms), 1972; Życie na Preriach (The Peoples on the Prairies), 1974. Contbr. to: Polish weekly CZAS, Winnipeg, Man., Can. (Ed.); Tygodnik Powszechny. Krakow, Poland; Nasza Rodzina, Paris, France; Duszpasterz na Emigracji, Rome, Italy; Związkowiec, Toronto. Mbr., Soc. of Christ for Polish Immigrants. Address: 202-597 Jefferson Ave., Winnipeg R2X 0R4, Man., Can.

T

TAAR, Ferenc Francis, b. 24 Nov. 1921, Érmihályfalva, Romania. Teacher; Film Studio Director. Educ: Debrecen Univ., Hungary. Publs. incl: (in Hungarian) A Golden Ring, 1954; Battle in Veréb Street, 1961; An Everlasting Anger, 1967; Sun over the City, 1969; Tombstone with a Ribbon, 1972; Flame & Thorn, 1973 (all plays). Contbr. to: Alföld; Palócföld. Mbr., Hungarian Writers Assn. Recip., 3rd Prize, Prague Int. Radioplay Festival, 1962. Address: 4 Holloó János, Debrecen, 4024, Hungary.

TABÁK, András, b. 15 Dec. 1938, Budapest, Hungary. Writer. Educ: B.A. Publs: The Siren Sounds (short stories), 1960; Hamstrung (novel), 1961; A Cock for Aesculap (short stories), 1963; The Sargasso Sea (novel), 1965; Seven Towers, forthcoming. Mbrships: Assn. of Hungarian Writers; Artists' Fndn. of Hungarian People's Repub. Recip., SZOT Lit. Prize, 1961. Address: Elek utca 4, 1113 Budapest, Hungary.

TABORI, George, b. 24 May 1914, Budapest, Hungary. Playwright; Novelist. Publs: Beneath The Stone (novel), 1944; The Companions of the Left Hand (novel), 1946; Original Sin (novel), 1947; The Caravan Passes (novel), 1950; Flight Into Egypt (play), 1952; The Emperor's Clothes (play), 1953; Brouhaha (play), 1958; Brecht on Brecht (play), 1961; The Cannibals (play), 1968; Pinkville (play), 1970; Clowns (play), 1971; The 25th Hour (play), 1973; sev. filmscripts. Recip., sev. awards for films. Address: c/o Kiepenhauer Verlag, Schweinfurt Str. 60, 1 Berlin 33, W. Germany.

TABORI, Paul, pen names STAFFORD, Peter; STEVENS, Christopher, b. 1908, Budapest, Hungary. Author; Consultant. Educ: Kaiser Freidrich Wilhelm Univ., Berlin, Germany; Peter Pazmany Univ., Budapest; Ph.D.; Doct. Pol. Sci. & Econs. Publs. incl: The Natural Science of Stupidity & the Art of Folly; Spider & Moonlight; Alexander Korda; Harry Price; Pictorial History of Love; Lighter than Vanity; The Green Rain; The Cleft; Song of the Scorpions; Hazard Island; num. others. Contbr. to: Penthouse; Chgo. Sun-Times; New Ldr.; etc. Mbrships: PEN (Exec. Coun., Engl. Ctr.); Crime Writers' Assn.; Critics Circle; Soc. of Authors. Agent: Carl Routledge. Address: 14 Stafford Terrace, London W8, UK.

TABRAH, Ruth M., b. 28 Feb. 1921, Buffalo, N.Y., USA. Writer; Editor. Educ: B.A.(cum laude), Univ. of Buffalo. Publs: Pulaski Place (novel), 1949; The Voices of Others (novel), 1959, paperback ed. as Town for Scandal, 1960; Hawaiian Heart (juvenile book), 1964; Hawaii Nei (non-fiction), 1967, 3rd ed., 1975; The Red Shark (jr. novel), 1970, French ed. as Le Plage des Requins, 1972; L'Amitie de Rageot, 1972; Buddhism: A Modern Way of Life & Thought (non-fiction), 1970; Ed. & Text Adaptor, Island Heritage Folktale & Legend (book series), 1973, 1974, 1975. Contbr. to: Odyssey Mag.; Cricket (children's lit. mag.); var. newspapers, USA. Mbr., Authors' Guild, Inc. Address: 108 Puako Beach Drive, Kamuela, HI 96743, USA.

TACHIHARA, Masaaki, b. 6 Jan. 1926, Daegu, S. Korea. Novelist. Educ: Waseda Univ., Tokyo, Japan. Publs: Takigi No (Nō by Bonfirelight), 1964; Shiroi keshi (White Poppies), 1966; Mai no ie (House of Nō Players), 1971; Kinuta, 1973. Contbr. to: Shincho; Bungakukai; Geijutsu Shincho; Chuokoron; Bungeishunju; Nipponkkeizaisshin-bun; Yomiurisshinbun. Mbrships: PEN; Japan Lit. Guild. Hons: Contemporary Lit. Prize, 1961; Naoki Prize, 1966. Address: 2051-7 Higashigayatsu, Kajiwarayama, Yamazaki, Kamakura, Japan.

TADA, Yūkei, b. 18 Aug. 1912, Fukui City, Japan. Novelist; Haiku Poet. Educ: B.A. in French Lit., Waseda Univ. Publs. (in Japanese): (novels) The Delta of the Yangtze River, 1941; The Sand of Asia, 1956; Basho, 1963; (short story) Snake Charmer, 1949; (essays & poems) Chopin's Raindrops on the Grass, 1957; Bashō — His Life & Aesthetics, 1968; (Haiku poems) Romantic Excerpts, 1974. Contbr. to: Bungei Shunjū; Asahi newspaper; Mainichi newspaper; Remon Haiku poem mag., Ed. Mbrships: Lit. Assn. Japan; PEN; Haiku Poets' Assn. Hons: Akutagawa Prize, 1941; Taishūbungei Konwakai Prize, 1949. Address: 3-13-53 Shinjuku, Zushi City, Kanagawa Prefecture 249, Japan.

TADEMA SPORRY, Jacoba, pen name SPORRY, Bob Tadema, b. 16 Feb. 1912, Makassar, Indonesia. Author.

Publs: History of Egypt, 1964; History of China, 1967; China with a Grin & Smile, 1967; History of Thebes, 1968; De Pyramiden van Egypte, 1971; Empire of the Pharaos, 1975. Contbr. to: Elsevier; Accent; Elegance; Arts & Auto; Organorama; Schöoner Wohnen (W. Germany). Mbr., Vereniging van Letterkundigen. Hons. incl: Lit. prizes for children's novels, 1972, 1973, 1974. Address: 5 Rembrandtlaan, Heemstede, Netherlands.

TAGG, George Frank, b. 16 Feb. 1903, Brighton, UK. Chartered Electrical Engineer. Educ: B.Sc., Brighton Tech. Coll.; Ph.D., Univ. Coll., London. Publs: A.C. Power Measurement, 1928; Revising auth., Electrical Measuring Instruments by Drysdale & Jolley, 1952; Induction Type Integrating Meters (w. G. F. Shotter), 1960; Earth Resistances, 1964; Practical Measurement of Insulation Resistance, 1968; Electrical Indicating Instruments, 1974. Contbr. to: Proceedings Instn. of Elec. Engrs.; Jrnl. of Sci. Instruments; Elec. Times. Fellowships: Instn. of Elec. Engrs.; Inst. of Physics; R.S.A. Recip., engnrng. hons. Address: 52 Tennyson Ave., Twickenham, Middx. TW1 4QY, UK.

TAIT, (Lady) Viola Wilson, b. 1 Nov. 1912, Pressburg, Bratislava, Czech. Homemaker. Educ: Royal Scottish Acad. of Music, Glasgow, UK; Lic., Trinity Coll. of Music, London. Publs: Family of Brothers. Mbrships: Chmn., Royal Acad. of Dancing, Aust., 1950-68; Lyceum Club, Melbourne. Address: 106 Leopold St., S. Yarra, Melbourne 3141, Australia.

TAKÁCS, Zsuzsa, b. 23 Nov. 1938, Budapest, Hungary. University Assistant; Poet. Educ: Grad., Spanish-Italian, Fac. of Arts. Publs: Pantomime (poems), 1969; Instructions to the Scene (poems), forthcoming. Contbr. to: Uj Irás; Élet és Irodalom. Mbr., Hungarian Writer's Assn. Address: Branyiszkó u. 25, H 1026 Budapest II, Hungary.

TAKAGI, Akimitsu, b. 25 Sept. 1920, Aomori, Japan. Author. Educ: Bach. Engrng., Kyoto Imperial Univ. Publs: (in Japanese— Tattoo, 1948; The Informer, 1965, Engl. transl., 1971; Honeymoon to Nowhere, 1965, Engl. transl., 1972, Dutch transl. (Rouw voor de bruid), 1974. Mbrships: Japanese Detective Writers' Soc.; PEN; Japanese Lit. Artists Soc. Recip., Prize Japanese Detective Writers' Club. Address: 8-8 1 Chome Honmachi, Shibuya-ku, Tokyo, Japan.

TAKÁTS, Gyula, b. 4 Feb. 1911, Tab, Hungary. Director of Museums. Educ: Ph.D. Publs: (poems) Kút, 1935; Családga helyett, 1941; Se ég, se föld, 1947; Vizitükör, 1955; Mézöntö, 1958; Évek, madarak, Selected Poems, 1965; Villámok mértana, 1968; Sós forrás, 1973; (studies) Egy kertre emlékezve, 1971; (novels) Polgárjelöltek, 1945; Szinház az "Ezüst Kancsóban", 1957. Contbr. to: Nyugat; Válasz; Kelet Népe; Magyar Csillag; Kortárs; Uj Irás; Jelenkor; Élet és Irodalom. Mbrships: Soc. of Hungarian Authors & Writers; PEN. Hons: Baumgarten Prize, 1941; József Attila Prize, 1960. Address: 7400 Kaposvár, Kovács S. u. 9, Hungary.

TAKMAN, John, b. 22 Sept. 1912, Saeffle, Sweden. Chief Medical Officer; Member of Riksdagen. Educ: Karolinska Inst., Stockholm. Publs: Vår vid Sydkinesiska Sjön (Spring on South China Sea), 1959; Ungdompsykiatri (Adolescent Psychiatry), 1962; Vietnam — Ockupanterna & Folket (Vietnam: The Occupants & the People), 1965; Socialmedicinsk Vardag (Everyday Social Medicine), 1966; Ed., Napalm (Symposium in Swedish), 1967, also Norwegian, Spanish & German transls.; Sex i Tonåren (Teenage Sex), 1967, Finnish, French, German & Icelandic transls.; The Gypsies in Sweden: A Socio-Medical Study, forthcoming. Address: Box 49034, 100 28 Stockholm, Sweden.

TAMÁS, Attila, b. 17 June 1930, Budapest, Hungary. University Reader. Educ: Cand. for sci. of lit. Publs: Költöi világképek fejlödése Arany Jánostól József Attiláig (The Progress of Poetical World Concepts from J. Arany till A. Jozsef), 1964; A költöi müalkotás fö sajátságai (The Principal Characteristics of Poetical Work), 1972; Irodalom és emberi teljesség (Literature & Human Entirety), 1973; Huszadik századi líra (Poetry of 20th Century), 1975. Contbr. to: Világirodalmi Lexikon (Ency. of World Lit.). Mbrships: Soc. of Hungarian Writers; Soc. of Hungarian Lit. Histns. Address: Trombitás u. 10, Debrecen, Hungary.

TAMER, Ülkü, b. 20 Feb. 1937, Gaziantep, Turkey. Translator; Poet. Educ: B.A., Robert Coll., Istanbul. Publs: Soğuk Otlarin Altinda, 1959; Gök Onlari Yaniltmaz, 1960;

Ezra ile Gary, 1963; Virgülün Basindan Gecenler, 1965; Içime Çektiğim Hava Değil Gökyüzdür, 1966; Siragöller, 1974. Contbr. to mags. in Turkey, USA, Germany & Yugoslavia. Mbrships: Exec. Comm., Turkish Playwrights' Soc.; Turkish Writers Syndicate; PEN. Hons: Turkish Lang. Inst. Prize for Transl., 1965; Yeditepe Poetry Prize, 1967. Address: Ankara Caddesi 40, Sirkeci, Istanbul, Turkey.

TAMKÓ SIRATÓ, Károly, b. 26 Jan. 1905, Ujvidek, Hungary. Author. Educ: Univ. Publs: Homme de papier, avec des poèmes électriques, 1928; Manifeste Dimensioniste, Paris, 1936; A Vizöntö-kor hajnalán, Poèmes, 1969. Contbr. to: Uj Irás; Élet és Irodalom; Magyar Mühely; Hid; & others. Mbrships: PEN; Hungarian Writers' Soc. Address: 1033 Budapest III, Vöröskereszt u. 14. IX. 52, Hungary.

TAMULAITIS, Vitas (Victor), b. 17 Jan. 1913, Sutkiskiai, Lithuania. Writer. Educ: Studies in Law & Biol., Univ. of Vytautas the Great, Kaunas, Lithuania, 1933-36. Publs. incl: Nimblefoot the Ant: Her Adventures, 1935; The Rabbit's Memoirs, 1935; The Spring Is Coming, 1937; Vykuka's Journal, 1937; Once Upon a Time, 1942; The Return, 1948; The Adventures of a Musician Cricket, 1961; Little Peter's Flag, 1970. Contbr. to: Children Everywhere, 1970; Can., US & German jrnls. Mbr., Lithuanian-Can. Writers' Assn., V.P., 1951-53. Hons. incl: Short Story Prizes, Lithuanian lang. newspapers, German Fed. Repub., 1948, USA, 1954. Address: 53 Ostend Ave., Toronto, Ont. M6S IL5, Can.

TAN, Siong Hoon, b. 7 Oct. 1920, Singapore. Journalist; Educator. Publs: So This Is America, 1971; Saya Yang Tau, 1973. Contbr. to: Malay Mail (Columnist, 1952—); Ency. Britannica. Mbrships: Nat. Cancer Soc. of Malaysia (Publicity Dir.); Kidney Fndn. of Malaysia (Gov.); Film Appeal Bd., Malaysia. Recip., K.M.N., 1974. Address: 175 Road 5/45, Petaling Jaya, Malaysia.

TANDORI, Dezsö, b. 8 Dec. 1938, Budapest, Hungary. Poet; Translator. Educ: B.A. Publs: (poems) Fragments for Hamlet, 1968; Cleansing of an Objet Trouvé, 1973; (transls.) Virginia Woolf, Samuel Beckett, J. D. Salinger, Thomas Mann, Robert Musil, Kafka, Poe, Byron, Robert Browning, etc. Contbr. to Hungarian & Yugoslav jrnls. Mbr., PEN. Hons: Lit. Writers Fund Competition, PEN, 1966; Robert Graves Award, Budapest, 1972; Kassák Award, Paris, 1974. Address: I. Lánchíd u. 23, 1013 Budapest, Hungary.

TANER, Haldun, b. Mar. 1915, Istanbul, Turkey. Writer. Educ: Univ. of Heidelberg; Degree in German Lang. & Hist. of Art, Istanbul; Inst. of the Theatre, Vienna. Publs. incl: (plays) The Ballad of Ali of Kesham, 1964-75; Please do not touch, 1968; The Mill, 1969; I Close my Eyes & do my Duty, 1966; The Shadow of the Donkey, 1967; Shaban The Saviour, 1968; (short story vols.) It Was Still Raining on Shishane, 1954; One Minute before Twelve, 1955; Çalskur in Moonlight, 1955; Sancho's Morning Walk, 1969. Contbr. to: Milliyet; Sanat Dergisi; Merian (Hamburg). Mbrships. incl: PEN; Vienna Dramatic Soc.; Bd., Turkish U.N.E.S.C.O. Hons. incl: First Sait Faik Award, 1955; Short Story Award, Int. Humour Fest., Bordinghera, Italy, 1972; Best Playwright Prize, Art Soc., Ankara, 1974. Address: Mühürdar cad 127 Kadikoy, Istanbul, Turkey.

TANEVSKI, Stefan, b. 7 Apr. 1918, Skopje, Yugoslavia. Medical Worker in Bacterial Laboratory. Educ: Med. Second. Schl. Publs. (histl. tragedies) Ivac, 1962; Vladimir & Kosara, 1967; Rog, 1973. Contbr. to: Makedonsk Kniga; Kulturen zirot. Mbrships: Soc. of Writers, Macedonia; PEN. Address: Karpos 4, Zgrada b—10, Vlez 1/10, 91000 Skopje, Yugoslavia.

TANG, Peter Sheng-Hao, b. 11 Apr. 1919, Hofei, Anhwei, China. Professor of Political Science; Author; Researcher; Lecturer. Educ: A.B., Nat. Chengchih Univ. 1942; A.M., 1947, Ph.D., 1952, Columbia Univ. Publs. incl: Communist China: The Domestic Scene 1949-1967 (w. Joan Maloney), 1967; Sino-Soviet Disputes: Highlights of the Issues 1956-1974, 1975; Romania between Moscow & Peking, 1975. Contbr. to num. jrnls. Mbrships: Am. Pol. Sci. Assn.; Am. Assn. for the Advancement of Slavic Studies. Hons. incl: Grantee, A. Philos. Soc., 1959, 1969; Pulbright Schlr. in Romania, 1970. Address: Dept. of Political Science, Boston College, Chestnut Hill, MA 02167, USA.

TANSELLE, George Thomas, b. 29 Jan. 1934, Lebanon, Ind., USA. Professor of English; Author & Editor.

Educ: B.A., Yale Univ., 1955; M.A., 1956, Ph.D., 1959, Northwestern Univ. Publs: Royall Tyler, 1967; Guide to the Study of United States Imprints, 1971. Contbr. to: Studies in Bibliog.; Am. Lit.; New England Quarterly; 19th Century Fiction; Book Collector; Harvard Lib. Bulletin; Mod. Lang. Review, etc.; Bibliogl. Ed., The Writings of Herman Melville, 1968—. Mbrships. incl: Am. Antiquarian Soc.; Coun. Mbr., Bibliog. Soc. of Am.; Bibliog. Soc. (London); Pvte. Lib. Assn.; MLA of Am. Hons. incl: Jenkins Prize in Bibliog., 1973. Address: 410 W. Washington St., Lebanon, IN 46052, USA.

TARAPOREVALA, Russi Jal, b. 8 Sept. 1932, Bombay, India. Economist; Former Professor of Commerce, University of Bombay. Educ: B.Com., Univ. of Bombay; M.B.A., Univ. of Calif., Berkeley, USA; M.Soc., Univ. of London, UK. Publs: The American Book Industry, 1966; Competition & Its Control in the British Book Trade, 1850-1939, 1973. Contbr. to: Jrnl. of the Royal Statistical Soc.; Times of India; Econ. Times; Fin. Express; Commerce; Capital. Mbrships. incl: Fellow, Royal Statistical Soc.; Bombay Mgmt. Assn.; Nat. Book Dev. Bd. of the Govt. of India. Recip., sev. fellowships & other acad. distinctions. Address: 210 D. Naoroji Rd., Fort, Bombay 400001, India.

TARCHILA, Dan, b. 28 Nov. 1923, Rustenari-Prahova, Rumania. Doctor; Playwright. Educ: D.M.S., Bucharest Univ., 1949. Publs. incl: Io, Mircea Voievod, 1971; 3 plays: Blue Light; Ecto — Bar; Alibi for Eternity, 1972; The Bride of the World (2 stories), 1974; num. plays for TV & radio. Mbr., Writer's Union, Rumania. Recip., Vasile Alecsandri Prize, 1959. Address: Bucuresti Str. C.A. Rosetti Nr. 36 A, Sector II, Rumania.

TARDIEU, Jean, b. 1 Nov. 1903. Writer; Former TV Producer. Educ: Paris Univ. Publs. incl: Accents; Figures; Monsieur, Monsieur; Un Mot pour un autre; Une voix sans personne; Théâtre de chambre; Poèmes à jouer; De la peinture abstraite; Choix de poèmes; Histoires Obscure; Il était une fois, deux foi, trois fois (children's book); Pages d'écriture; Le fleuve caché; Les Portes de toile; La part de l'ombre; & num. transl. from German. Hons: Legion of Honour; Chevalier, Arts & Lettres. Address: 71 Blvd. Arago, Paris 13e, France.

TARKKA, Pekka, b. 4 Dec. 1934, Helsinki, Finland. Literary Critic. Educ: Ph.D. Publs: Paavo Rintalan saarna ja seurakunta, 1966, Swedish transl., En roman och dess publik, 1970; Salama, 1973. Contbr. to: Uusi Suomi (1961-67); Helsingun Sanomat (1958-61, 1969—). Mbr., Eino Leino Soc. (Vice-Chmn.). Recip., Transls. State Prize, 1973. Address: Tehtaankatu 3 F 51, Helsinki 14, Finland.

TARN, Nathaniel, b. 30 June 1928, Paris, France. Poet; Professor of Comparative Literature. Educ. incl: B.A., 1948, M.A., 1952, King's Coll., Cambridge, UK; C.F.R.E., Sorbonne & Musee de l'Homme, France, 1950; M.A., 1952, Ph.D., 1957, Univ. of Chgo., USA. Publs: Old Savage/Young City, 1964; Penguin Modern Poets, No. 7, 1965; Where Babylon Ends, 1968; The Beautiful Contradictions, 1969; October, 1969; A Nowhere for Vallejo, 1971; Section: The Artemision, 1973; Lyrics for the Bride of God, 1975; Transl., 4 books. Address: c/o New Directions, 333 Ave. of the Americas, N.Y., NY, USA.

TARNAWSKY, Ostap, b. 3 May 1917, Lviv, Ukraine. Poet; Essayist; Translator. Educ: Dip., Polytechnic, Lviv & Graz; M.A., Drexel Univ., Phila., USA. Publs. incl: Shakespeare's Hamlet on the Ukrainian Stage, 1943, 1973; Slova i Mriyi (poetry), 1948; Zhyttia (sonnets sequence), 1952; Mosty (poetry), 1956; Samotnie Derevo (poetry), 1960; Tuha za Mitom (essays), 1966; Brat Bratovi, 1971; Kaminni Stupeni (short stories), 1975. Contbr. to var. lit. jrnls. Mbrships: Hon. Sec., Ukrainian Writers' Assn. "Slovo"; PEN, Writers in Exile; ALA. Recip., var. hons. Address: 6509 Lawnton Ave., Phila., PA, USA.

TATAY, Sándor, b. 6 May 1910, Bakonytamasi, Hungary. Writer. Publs: Thunderstorm, 1941; The Simeon Family, 5 vols., 1955-59; White Carriage, 1960; (film) The House Under the Rocks, 1958; 7 children's books. Contbr. to Kelet Népe, 1937—. Address: Gyongyosi u. 53, H-1131, Budapest XIII, Hungary.

TATE, Allen, b. 19 Nov. 1899, Winchester, Ky., USA. Professor Emeritus. Educ: B.A., Vanderbilt Univ., 1922. Publs. incl: Reactionary Essays on Poetry & Ideas, 1936; On the Limits of Poetry, 1948; The Man of Letters in the Modern World, USA & UK, 1955; Essays of Four Decades,

USA 1969, UK 1970; (verse) Poems: 1928-31, 1932. Poems, 1920-45: A Selection, UK 1947; The Swimmers, UK 1970, USA 1971; (novel) The Fathers, USA 1938, UK 1939, revised eds., 1960; Ed., num. anthols. & vols. of verse. Mbrships. incl: Nat. Inst. Arts & Letters (Pres., 1968); Acad. Am. Poets. Recip., num. Fellowships, Awards & hon. degrees. Address: Running Knob Hollow Rd., Sewanee, TN 37375, USA.

TATE, Joan, b. 23 Sept. 1922, Tonbridge, UK. Writer; Publisher's Reader; Translator (Scandinavian languages). Publs. incl: (young fiction) Jenny, 1964; The Holiday, 1966; & others; Sam & Me, 1968, USA 1969; Clipper, 1969, & others; The Tree, 1970, USA 1973; Ginger Mick, 1974, & others; Night Out, 1973, & others; (children's fiction) Gremp, 1971; Wild Boy, 1972; Ben & Annie, 1972, USA 1974; The Lollipop Man, 1967, UK 1969; & others; (non-fiction) Your Town, 1972; The Living River, 1974, & others; (educl.) How Do You Do, 1974; Paderhorn, Going Up, 1969; Disco Books & others, UK 1975. Mbrships: Soc. of Authors; PEN; Translators Assn. Address: 32 Kennedy Rd., Shrewsbury SY3 7AB, UK.

TATE, Roy, b. 21 Sept. 1941, Wash. D.C., USA. Cottage Parent with Mentally Retarded Adults. Educ: Univ. of Va., Charlottesville. Publs: Designing Learning Games for Children, 1972; The Astrology of Genius: A Study of the Nobel Prizewinners, 1973. Former Mbr., Mensa. Address: P.O. Box 516, Miami, FL 33138, USA.

TATO CUMMING, Gaspar, b. 8 June 1906, Alicante, Spain. Educ: Lic., Chem.; Lic., Jrnlsm., PR, Broadcasting Programming; Dip., Jrnlsm. for Tourists, Nat. Inst. for Tourism Studies, Madrid. Publs. incl: China y Japón, un viaje alrededor del mundo; Nueva York, un español entre rascacielos; Tokio, un español entre geishas — Panorama mundial; El mundo del espionaje; Safari, un español entre turistas; Nostalgias de Alicante. Contbr. to var. lit. jrnls. Mbrships: Assn. of PR Techns.; Assn. of Tourist Writers; Assn. of Writers & Artists; Soc. of Int. Studies. Hons: Ondas Prize for Broadcasting, 1956; var. jrnlsm. prizes. Address: Calle Lagasca 76, Madrid 1, Spain.

TAUB, Harald J., b. 13 Feb. 1918, NYC, USA. Editor; Writer. Educ: Univ. of Pa. Publs: Waldorf-In-The-Catskills, 1953; The Takers, 1970; Vitamin E for Ailing & Healthy Hearts (w. W. Shute M.D.), 1971; Keeping Healthy in a Polluted World, 1974. Contbr. to: Prevention; Pageant; Coronet. Mbrships: Overseas Press Club; Soc. of Mag. Writers. Address: 129 Bay View Ave., Belvedere, CA 94920, USA.

TAUBMAN, Hyman Howard, b. 4 July 1907. Journalist; Critic. Educ: B.A., Cornell Univ. Publs: Opera Front & Back, 1938; Music as a Profession, 1939; Music on My Beat, 1943; The Maestro, The Life of Arturo Toscanini, 1951; How to Build a Record Library, 1953; How to Bring Up Your Child to Enjoy Music, 1958; The Making of the American Theatre, 1965. Contbr. to N.Y. Times. Mbr., Phila. Music Acad. Address: 41 W. 83rd St., N.Y., NY, USA.

TAUXE, Henri-Charles, b. 26 Nov. 1933, Morges, Switz. Journalist. Educ: Univ. of Lausanne; Univ. of Marburg, W. Germany; Ph.D. Publs: La Notion de Finitude dans la Philosophie de Martin Heidegger, 1971; Freud & le Besoin Religieux, 1974. Contbr. to Studia Philosophica. Mbrships: PEN; Swiss Press Assn.; Philosl. Soc. of French Switz. Address: Chemin de Mallieu, 13, 1009 Pully, Switz.

TAYLOR, Alan John Percivale, b. 25 Mar. 1906, Southport, UK. Historian. Educ: M.A., Oxford Univ. Publs: The Habsburg Monarchy, 1941; The Course of German History: The Struggle for Mastery in Europe, 1954; Bismarck, 1955; The Troublemakers, 1957; The Origins of the Second World War, 1961; The First World War: an Illustrated History, 1963; English History 1914-1945, 1965; From Sarajevo to Potsdam, 1967; War by Timetable, 1969; Beaverbrook, 1972; The Second World War: an Illustrated History, 1975. Contbr. to: Observer; Sunday Express; New Statesman; N.Y. Review of Books. Hons: Fellow, Brit. Acad.; D.C.L., Univ. of N.B., Can.; Hon. Degree, Univ. of York. Address: 13 St. Mark's Crescent, London NW1 7TS, UK.

TAYLOR, Alastair MacDonald, b. 12 Mar. 1915, Vancouver, B.C., Can. Professor of Political Studies & Geography. Publs: Indonesian Independence & the United Nations, 1960; Peacekeeping: International Challenge & Canadian Response, 1968; Evolution-Revolution: Patterns of Development in Nature, Society, Man & Knowledge, 1971; Integrative Principles of Modern Thought, 1972; The World System: Models, Norms, Applications, 1973; Civilization — Past & Present, 7th ed., 1975. Contbr. to: profl. jrnls. Mbrships. incl: Pres., Can. Ctr. for Integrative Educ.; Can. Pol. Sci. Assn. Recip., acad. awards. Address: Queen's Univ., Kingston, Ont., Can.

TAYLOR, Cecil Philip, b. 6 Nov. 1929, Glasgow, UK. Playwright; Literary Associate, University Theatre; Literary Adviser, Northumberland Association of Youth Theatres. Publs: (plays) Bread & Butter, 1968; Allergy, 1969; Thank You Very Much, 1970; Happy Days are Here Again; (non-fiction) Making a Television Play, 1970. Mbrships: Writers' Guild GB; Soc. Playwrights. Hons: Scottish TV Theatre Award, 1969; Edinburgh Festival Fringe Award, 1974. Address: 22 Wallridge Cottages, Matfen, Northumberland, UK.

TAYLOR, Don, b. 30 June 1936, London, UK. Playwright; Director. Educ: B.A.(Hons.), M.A., Oxford Univ., 1955-58. Prods: (plays) Grounds for Marriage, 1967; Sisters, 1968; Sam Foster Comes Home, 1969; The Roses of Eyam, 1970; (TV films) The Confessions of Marian Evans, 1970; Paradise Restored, 1971; Actor, I Said, 1972; The Exorcism, 1972; The Runaway, 1973; (radio plays) At Nunappleton House, 1971; Rudkin's Dream, 1973. Agent: Margaret Ramsay. Address: New Commonwealth, 4/5 Fitzroy Square, London WC1, UK.

TAYLOR, Duncan, b. 7 Oct. 1912, Edinburgh, UK. Radio Producer. Educ: M.A., Cambridge Univ.; Educ. Dip., Inst. Educ., Univ. London. Publs: Elizabethan Age, 1955; Jim Bartholomew, 1956; Ancient Greece, 1957; Bob in Local Government, 1958; Chaucer's England, 1959; Ancient Rome, 1960; On Hadrian's Wall, 1962; The World of Nations, 1963; Fielding's England, 1966; Pompeii & Vesuvius, 1969; Short History of the Post-War World, forthcoming. Mbrships: Soc. Authors; Histl. Assn.; BBC Club. Address: 103 Corringham Rd., London NW11 7DL, UK.

TAYLOR, Elizabeth, b. 3 July 1912, Reading, UK. Author. Publs: (novels) At Mrs. Lippincotes, 1946; Palladian, 1947; A View of the Harbour, 1949; A Wreath of Roses, 1950; A Game of Hide-&-Seek, 1951; The Sleeping Beauty, 1953; Angel, 1957; In a Summer Season, 1961; The Soul of Kindness, 1964; The Wedding Group, 1969; Mrs. Palfrey at the Claremont, 1972; (collected short stories) Mister Lilley, 1954; The Blush, 1958; A Dedicated Man, 1965; (juvenile) Mossy Trotter, 1967. Contbr. to: Cornhill; New Yorker; McCalls; London Mag. Mbrships: Royal Soc. Lit.; PEN; Soc. Authors. Address: Grove's Barn, Penn, Bucks., UK.

TAYLOR, Harold Boswell, b. Birmingham, UK. Writer; Quiz Compiler. Publs: They Served Mankind, 1957; George Stephenson, 1964; Picture Reference Series, 1964—; Your Child's Education, 1965; BBC TV Top of the Form Quiz Books, 1—8, 1968—; Listening Laboratories, 1974. Contbr. to: The Teacher (formerly Feature Ed.); etc. Mbrships: Nat. Book League; Nat. Exec.; Schl. Lib. Assn. Address: The White Cottage, Clifton, Deddington, Oxford OX5 4PA, UK.

TAYLOR, (Rt. Rev.) John V., b. 11 Sept. 1914, Cambridge, UK. Church of England Bishop. Educ: B.A., M.A., Trinity Coll., Univ. of Cambridge; B.A., St. Catherine's Coll., Univ. of Oxford; Dip.Ed., Inst. of Educ., Univ. of London. Publs: Christianity & Politics in Africa, 1956; The Growth of the Church in Buganda, 1958; Christians on the Copperbelt (w. D. Lehmann), 1960; The Primal Vision, 1963; The Go-Between God, 1971; Enough is Enough, 1975. Contbr. to: Frontier; Expository Times. Hons: Collins Relig. Book Award, 1974; D.D., Wycliffe Coll., Toronto, Canada, 1963. Address: Wolvesy, Winchester, UK.

TAYLOR, Kenneth Nathaniel, b. 8 May 1917, Portland, Ore., USA. Author; Publisher. Educ: B.S., Wheaton Coll., 1938; Th.M., Northern Bapt. Theol. Sem., 1944. Publs. incl: Almost Twelve, 1968; Evolution & the High School Student, 1969; Creation & the High School Student, 1969; Taylor's Bible Story Book, 1970; The Living Bible, 1971. Mbrships: Dir., Moody Lit. Mission, 1948-62; Chmn., Bd. of Evangelical Lit. Overseas, 1951-70. Hons: Litt.D., Wheaton Coll., 1965; Nelson Bible Award, Thomas Nelson, Inc., 1973; L.H.D., Huntington Coll., 1974. Address: 1515 East Forest Ave., Wheaton, IL 60187, USA.

TAYLOR, Margaret Stewart, b. 28 July 1902, Coventry, UK. Former Librarian & Museum Curator; Author. Educ: M.A., Univ. of Oxford; F.L.A. Publs: The Crawshays of Cyfarthfa Castle, 1967; St. Helena: Ocean Roadhouse, 1969; Focus on the Falkland Islands, 1971; 2 novels about modern Wales; 5 histl. novels inclng. The Wayward Jilt, 1974. Mbrships: Fellow, Lib. Assn.; Soc. of Authors; Romantic Novelists' Assn. Address: Flat 36, St. Tydfil's Court, Caedraw Rd., Merthyr Tydfil, Mid-Glam. CF47 8HP, UK.

TAYLOR, Peter (Hillsman), b. 8 Jan. 1919, Trenton, Tenn., USA. Professor of English. Educ: A.B., Kenyon Coll., Gambier, Ohio, 1940. Publs: (short stories) A Long Fourth, 1948, UK 1949; The Windows of Thornton, 1954; Happy Families Are All Alike, USA 1959, UK 1960; Miss Leonora When Last Seen, 1963; The Collected Stories of Peter Taylor, 1969; (novel) A Woman of Means, 1950; (plays) Tennessee Day in St. Louis, 1957; A Stand in the Mountains, prod. 1971. Contbr. to: Kenyon Review. Mbr., Nat. Inst. Arts & Letters. Hons. incl: O. Henry Award, 1959; var. Fellowships. Address: Dept. of English, Wilson Hall, Univ. of Va., Charlottesville, VA 22901, USA.

TAYLOR, Rebe Prestwich, b. 10 Apr. 1911, Southport, Lancs., UK. Author. Publs. incl: Pyrennean Holiday, 1952; Rochdale Retrospect, 1956; Tatham, 1966; also children's books. Mbrships. incl: Soc. Authors; Lib. Assn.; Rochdale Conservative Assn. (Exec. Comm.); Soroptimist Club Rochdale; Rochdale Coll. Adult Educ. (Mbr. Govng. Comm.); Castleton Community Assn. (elected Mbr. Coun.). Address: 1136 Manchester Rd., Castleton, Rochdale OL11 2XX, UK.

TAYLOR, Robert Lewis, b. 24 Sept. 1912, Carbondale, Ill., USA. Reporter; Writer. Educ: B.A., Univ. of Ill., Urbana, 1933. Publs. incl: (novels) Adrift in a Boneyard, 1947; The Bright Sands, USA & UK, 1954; The Travels of Jaimie McPheeters, USA 1958, UK 1959; Two Roads to Guadalupé, USA 1964, UK 1965; (biog.) Doctor, Lawyer, Merchant, Chief, 1948; Winston Churchill, 1952; Vessel of Wrath, 1966. Contbr. to: St. Louis Post-Dispatch (Reporter, 1936-39); New Yorker (Profile Writer, 1939-48). Hons. incl: Pulitzer Prize, 1959. Address: Spectacle Mountain Rd., Kent, CT 06757, USA.

TAYLOR, Sydney, b. 30 Oct. 1904, NYC, USA. Writer; Children's Camp Dance & Dramatics Counsellor. Publs: All of a Kind Family, 1951; More All of a Kind Family, 1954; All of a Kind Family Uptown, 1957; Mr. Barney's Beard, 1961; Now That You Are Eight, 1963; A Papa Like Everyone Else, 1966; The Dog Who Came To Dinner, 1966; All of a Kind Family Downtown, 1972. Contbr. to: Highlights for Children mag.; World Over mag. Mbr., Authors League. Hons: Juvenile Lit. Nat. Prize, Follett Publishing Co., 1951; Award for best juvenile book of yr., Jewish Book Coun. of Am., 1952; Jr. Book Award Cert., Boys Club of Am., 1962. Address: 250 W. 24th St., N.Y., NY 10011, USA.

TAYLOR, Walter Harold, b. 2 Dec. 1905, Melbourne, Australia. Chartered Engineer. Educ: Royal Melbourne Inst. of Technol., 1921-25; Trinity Coll., Univ. of Melbourne, 1928-31; Hemingway Robertson Inst., 1931-32; Alexander Hamilton Inst., USA, 1945-47; Dip. Civil Engrng., 1928; B.C.E., 1931; M.C.E., 1937. Publs: Concrete Technology & Practice, 1965, 4th ed., 1975. Contbr. to: Am. Concrete Inst.; Publs. of the Cement & Concrete Assn. (UK & Aust.); Nature; Arch. Today; etc. Fellowships: Instn. of Civil Engrs.; Inst. of Engrs., Aust. Recip., 1st Bldg. Sci. Forum, Aust. Book Award, 1968. Address: 19 Lawson St., Hawthorne East, Vic. 3123, Australia.

TAYLOR, William Robin, b. 11 Oct. 1938, Lower Hutt, NZ. Novelist; School Teacher; TV playwright. Educ: Christchurch Tchr's. Coll. Publs: Episode, 1970; Mask of the Clown, 1970; The Plekhov Place, 1971; Pieces in a Jigsaw, 1972; The Persimmon Tree, 1972; The Chrysalis, 1974. Commissioned to write series, NZ TV, 1975. Contbr. to: Landfall; NZ Listener; etc. Address: 502 Albert St., Palmerston N., NZ.

TEETERS, Leone Marlatt, b. 17 May 1909, Lafayette, Ind., USA. Business Writer. Educ: Willamette Univ., Ore.; Univ. of Puget Sound, Wash.; Univ. of Wash.; Univ. of Minn. Contbr. to: Writers' Digest; Exec. Housekeeper; Am. Bicyclist; Can. Motel Mag.; Mobile Park Mgmt.; Rivers & Harbours; Fate Mag.; Am. Farm Youth Mag.; Jr. Mag. for Children; Jr. Arts & Activities; etc. Mbr., Assoc. Bus. Writers of Am. Recip., Award of Merit, for Outstanding Ed.

Contbn., Pollution Engrng. Mag. Address: 26030 135th Ave. S.E., Lot 8, Kent, WA 98031, USA.

TEGNER, Bruce, b. 28 Oct. 1929, Chgo., USA. Teacher. Educ: B.A., LaVerne Coll., Calif. Publs: Self-Defence Nerve Centers & Pressure Points; Complete Book of Jukado Self-Defense; Aikido; Self-Defense for Girls & Women; Self-Defense for Boys & Men; Judo for Fun; Self-Defense You Can Teach Your Boy; Savate; Complete Book of Karate; Complete Book of Aikido; Karate & Judo Exercises; Stick Fighting; Self-Defense; Defense Tactics for Law Enforcement; Karate; Stick Fighting; Sport Forms; Kung Fu & Tai Chi: Chinese Karate & Classical Exercise; Black Belt Judo, Karate, Jukado; Self-Defense for Women; Bruce Tegner's Complete Book of Self-Defense. Address: P.O. Box 1782, Ventura, CA 93001, USA.

TEKNŐS, Péter, b. 15 May 1920, Kaposvár, Hungary. Writer. Educ: Univ. Marxismus-Leninismus. Publs: Treasure in Thousand Colours, 1950; A Happy Woman (transl.), 1956; We Have Been in the Future, 1968; Sensations of Centuries, 1970; President's Messenger, 1974; War in the Forest (A Story of the French-Indian War 1759). Contbr. to: Hungarian Radio; Lobogó; Világosság. Mbrships: Soc. of Hungarian Writers; Soc. of Hungarian Jrnlsts.; Hungarian Lit. Fndn. Recip., Order of Merit for Socialist Country. Address: 1022 Budapest, Bogár u. 12, Hungary.

TELLECHEA IDIGORAS, Jose Ignacio, b. 13 Apr. 1928, San Sebastián, Spain. University Professor of Theology. Educ: Priest, Sem. of Vitoria, Univ. Gregoriana; D.Th.; Lic., Theol. Hist., Univ. Gregoriana; Lic., Philos. & Letters, Univ. Madrid. Publs. incl: Fray Bartolomé Carranza. Documentos Historicos, 4 vols., 1962-66; El Arzobispo Carranza y su tiempo, 2 vols.; 1968; El Obispo ideal en el siglo de la Reforma, 1963; Cathechismo Christian de B. Carranza, 1972; Obras del P. Larramendi, 2 vols., 1969-73. Contbr. to num. theol. & histl. jrnls. Address: Usandizaga 27 5°, San Sebastian, Spain.

TELLER, Neville, pen name OWEN, Edmund, b. 10 June 1931, London, UK. Civil Servant. Educ: M.A., St. Edmund Hall, Oxford Univ. Publs: Bluff Your Way in Marketing, 1966; Whodunit? — 10 Tales of Crime & Detection, 1970. Contbr. to: BBC Radio (lit. script writer); London Broadcasting Co.; etc. Mbrships: Soc. of Authors; Radiowriters' Assn. of GB. Address: 15 Ewhurst Close, Cheam, Surrey, UK.

TELLER, Walter Magnes, b. 10 Oct. 1910, New Orleans, La., USA. Writer. Educ: B.S., Haverford Coll.; M.A., Ph.D., Columbia Univ. Publs: An Island Summer, 1951; The Search for Captain Slocum, 1956; The Voyages of Joshua Slocum, 1958; Five Sea Captains, 1960; Area Code 215: A Private Line in Bucks County, 1963; Cape Cod & the Offshore Islands, 1970; Twelve Works of Naive Genius, 1972; Walt Whitman's Camden Conversations, 1973. Contbr. to: N.Y. Times Book Review; Am. Schlr.; Progressive. Mbrships: Authors' League; Am. Ctr., PEN. Address: 200 Prospect Ave., Princeton, NJ 08540, USA.

TEMPLE, Philip, b. 20 Mar. 1939, Pudsey, Yorks., UK. Author. Educ: Sloane Schl., Chelsea. Publs: Nawok!, 1962; The Sea & the Snow, 1966; The World at their Feet, 1969; Mantle of the Skies, 1971; Castles in the Air, 1973; Christchurch, 1973; Patterns of Water, 1974; South Island, 1975; The Explorer, 1975; Contbr. to: NZ Listener; NZ's Heritage; Bookworld; Landfall (Assoc. Ed.). Mbrships: PEN (NZ Ctr.); NZ Alpine Club. Address: c/o Post Office, Little Akaloa, Banks Peninsula, NZ.

TEMPLETON, Edith, b. 7 Apr. 1916. Author. Educ: Prague Med. Univ., Czechoslovakia. Publs: Summer in the Country, UK 1950, USA 1951; Living on Yesterday, 1951; The Island of Desire, 1952; The Surprise of Cremona, UK 1954, USA 1957; This Charming Pastime, 1955; Three, USA 1971. Contbr. to: New Yorker; Holiday; Atlantic Monthly; Vogue; Harper's Mag. Address: 7 Compayne Gdns., London NW6, UK.

TENAGY, Sandor, b. 19 Jan. 1936, Szekszard, Hungary. Poet; Journalist. Publs: Devout Revolt, 1960; Ironbread, 1968; My Sigh, My Blood, 1972. Contbr. to: Uj Iras; Jelenkor; Elet es Irodalom; Nepszava; Nepszabadsag; Magyar Hirlap. Mbrships: Assn. of Hungarian Writers; Artistical Fndn. of Hungarian People's Repub. Address: Tahi u. 76, 1139 Budapest, Hungary.

TENDRYAKOV, Vladimir Fedorovich, b. 5 Dec. 1923, Vologda Region, USSR. Writer. Educ: M. Gorky Lit. Inst.,

Moscow. Publs. incl: (in Russian) In The Fields; The Fall of Ivan Chuprov, 1953; III Suited, 1954; The Tight Knot, 1956; Pits & Bumps, 1957; The Wonder-Worker, 1958; Miracle Worker, 1960; Short Circuit, 1961; The Trial, 1962; The Find, 1964; Meeting with Nefertiti, 1964; Wonder-Working, 1967. Contbr. to Ogonyok. Recip., Red Banner of Labour. Address: Union of Writers, Ul. Vorovskogo 52, Moscow, USSR.

TENNANT, Kylie, b. 12 Mar. 1912, Manly, N.S.W., Australia. Writer. Educ: Sydney Univ., 1931. Publs. incl: (novels) Tiburon, 1935; Foveaux, UK 1939; Ride on Stranger, USA 1943, UK 1945; The Joyful Condemned, 1953 (complete version, as Tell Morning This, Aust. & UK 1967); (short stories) Ma Jones & the Little White Cannibals, 1967; (non-fiction) Australia: Her Story, 1953, revised ed., 1971; The Man on the Headland, Aust. 1971, UK 1972; var. juvenile plays. Mbrships: Fellowship of Aust. Writers; Advsry. Bd., C'wlth. Lit. Fund. Hons. incl: S. H. Prior Mem. Prize, 1935, 1941; Gold Medal, Aust. Lit. Soc., 1941. Address: 5 Garrick Ave., Hunter's Hill, N.S.W. 2110, Australia.

ter HAAR, Jaap (Jacob Everard), b. 25 Mar. 1922, Hilversum, Netherlands. Publs: Saskia & Jeroen (series of 9 books on own twins), 1954; Eelke (series of 6 books), 1962; Lotje-series, 1965; Boris, 1966; Beer Ligthart, 1972; History of America; History of Russia; History of French Revolution; Napoleon; History of Roman Empire; History of King Arthur; History of Low Lands (4 vols.). Publs: Muiderkring; Chmn., Dutch Writers for Youth, Dutch Writers Assn. Recip., num. awards inclng: Golden Pencil for best book of yr., 1974. Address: Eikenlaan 57, Hilversum, Netherlands.

TERLECKI, Wladyslaw, b. 18 May 1933, Czestochowa, Poland. Writer. Educ: M.A. (Polish Philol.). Publs: The Journey on a Night's Top, 1958; The Fire, 1960; Full Season, 1966; The Plot, 1966; Star Wornood, 1970; Two Heads of a Bird, 1972; The Pilgrims, 1972; The Return from Carskie Siolo, 1973. The Black Romance, 1974. Contbr. to: Polish Radio monthly lit. review. Mbr., Writers' Union. Recip., Koscielskich Prize, 1973. Address: Komorów, ul. Mazurska 1, Warsaw, Poland.

TERPSTRA, Pieter, b. 29 Dec. 1919, Leeuwarden, Netherlands. Author. Publs: (Friesian novels) Fjouwer minsken yn in stêd, 1956; De wrâld is der op tsjin, 1967; De dei is forroun, 1972; (Dutch novels) Dokter Halbertsma, 1973; De dochter van dokter Halbertsma, 1974; (detective novels) Schaduw series van Havank, 1974; Eelco Drenth series. Hons: Awarded Rely Authors' Prize 4 times. Address: Postbus 9010, Leeuwarden, Netherlands.

TERRAINE, John Alfred, b. 15 Jan. 1921, London, UK. Author; Scriptwriter. Educ: War Degree (Mod. Hist.), Oxford Univ. Publs. incl: Mons, 1960; Douglas Haig, The Educated Soldier, 1963; The Great War, 1964; The Life & Times of Lord Mountbatten, 1968; Impacts of War, 1914 & 1918, 1970; The Mighty Continent, 1974; (scripts for TV series) The Great War, 1964; The Lost Peace, 1965; The Life & Times of Lord Mountbatten, 1969; The Mighty Continent, 1974. Contbr. to: Daily Telegraph; Hist. Today. Mbrships: Royal United Servs. Inst.; Soc. of Authors. Hons: Screenwriters' Guild Documentary Award, 1964; Soc. of Film & TV Arts Script Award, 1969. Address: 74 Kensington Park Rd., London W11 2PL, UK.

TERRIS, Susan, b. 6 May 1937, St. Louis, Mo., USA. Writer of Children's Books. Educ: B.A., Wellesley Coll., Mass., 1959; M.A., San Fran. State Coll., 1966. Publs: The Upstairs Witch & the Downstairs Witch, 1970; The Backwards Boots, 1971; On Fire, 1972; The Drowning Boy, 1972; Plague of Frogs, 1973; Pickle, 1973; Whirling Rainbows, 1974; Amanda, The Panda & the Redhead, 1975; The Pencil Families, 1975; No Boys Allowed, 1975. Mbr., Authors' Guild. Recip., N.Y. Times outstanding children's book award, for Plague of Frogs, 1973. Address: 11 Jordan Ave.. San Fran., CA, USA.

TERZAKIS, Anghelos, b. 16 Feb. 1907, Nauplia, Greece. Playwright; Novelist. Educ: Univ. of Athens. Publs: (plays) Emperor Michail, 1936; The Wedding March, 1937; Theophano, 1956; Thomas with two Souls, 1962; The Ancestor, 1970; (novels) The Violet City, 1937; Princess Isabeau, 1945; Without a God, 1951; Secret Life, 1957. Contbr. to To Vima (Tribune), Athens. Hons. incl: State Theatre Prize, 1939; State Novel Prize, 1958. Mbr., Acad. of Athens, 1974. Address: 23 Stratiotikou Syndesmou St., Athens 136, Greece.

TERZI di SISSA, (Count, Prince of Pandolfina) Ottobono Luigi, b. 25 Sept. 1914, Gallese, Viterbo, Italy. Farm Manager; Writer; Journalist. Educ: Grad. in Agric. Publs: Varvàrovka Alzo Zero, 1963, 3rd ed., 1970, paperback ed., 1974; Bussola Pazza, 1967. Contbr. to: Il Giornale di Brescia; Bresciaoggi; L'Idea Liberale; Rotary; Official Bulletin of Order of Malta; local newspapers. Mbrships' Accademia Tiberina, Rome; Rotary Int. Recip., var. lit. hons. Address: Villa Terzi, I — 25038 Rovato, Brescia, Italy.

TETZNER, Ruth, pen name HALLARD, Ruth, b. 25 Nov. 1917, Flensburg, Germany. Author; Secretary. Publs. incl: Blüten im Sturm, 1958; Signale aus Traumboot und Waage (poems), 1974; Greta, 1967, 3rd ed. 1974; 2 novels forthcoming. Contbr. to: publikation (1963-69); Westdeutsche Allgemeine Zeitung (1965-66); Lübecker Nachrichten (1973-74); Unio (1965-74); Epitaph (1974); Luxemburger Quartal (1974). Mbrships: German Authors' Union (V.S.); Lit. Union, Saarbrücken; GEDOK, Bonn; Deutscher Autorenverband. Recip., Travel grant, 1965. Agent: Axel Poldner, Munich. Address: 43 Essen, Pettenkoferstr. 2, W. Germany.

TEUFEL, Dolores Enid Arlene Rouse, b. 11 June 1921, Mt. Union, Pa., USA. Executive Secretary (Ret'd). Educ: Harrisburg Bus. Coll., Pa. Publs: (poetry) Collected Poems, 1963; Reflections, 1967; Soft Sound of Beauty, 1968; Star Gazer, 1969; Footprints on the Moon, 1971; Let Freedom Ring! , 1973. Contbr. to TV, etc. Mbrships: Nat. Fedn. State Poetry Soc. Inc.; Pa. Poetry Soc. Inc.; Harrisburg Poetry Soc.; Am. Poetry League. Recip., sev. poetry prizes. Address: 322 Meadow Lane, Hershey, PA 17033, USA.

THAKAZHI PILLAI, Sivasankara, pen name THAKAZHI, b. 12 Apr. 1912, Thakazhi, Alleppey, Kerala, India. Farmer; formerly Lawyer. Educ: Dip. Law. Publs: (all transl'd. into Engl.) Paramarthangal (Unchaste), 1942; Scavenger's Son, 1946; Two Measures of Rice, 1948; Chemmeen, 1956; Children of Joseph, 1959; Anubhavangal Palichakal, 1967; Enippadigal, 1968; also 40 other novels & over 1,000 short stories. Contbr. to all major mags. in Malayalam. Mbrships: Sahitya Akademi, New Delhi (Exec. Bd.); Film Awards Comm. (All India), 1972, 1973. Hons: Sahithya Akademi Award, (Delhi), 1957; Keralasathya Akademi Award, 1968. Address: Sankara Mangalom, Thakazhi, Alleppey, Kerala, India.

THATCHER, Alice Dora, b. 14 Sept. 1912, Abertillery, UK. Housewife. Publs: 23 books for children, in 2 series, Henry the Helicopter, & Tommy the Tugboat; The Coracle Builders; Island Pony. Address: Craig-y-Mor, Parrog, Newport, Pembrokeshire, UK.

THEOBALD, Geoffrey William, b. 2 July 1896, Gorleston, Norfolk, UK. Physician. Educ: M.A., M.D., Emmanuel Coll., Cambridge. Publs: Normal Midwifery for Midwives & Nurses, 1927; Obstetric Regulations, 1928; The Pregnancy Toxaemia, 1955; Referred Pain: A New Hypothesis, 1941; The Electrical Induction of Labour, 1973; Endocrince Control of Uterine Innervation, 1973. Contbr. to: Toxaemia of Pregnancy; Modern Trends in Obstetrics & Gynaecology; British Obstetric Practices; etc. Mbrships. incl: Fndn. Fellow, Royal Coll. of Obs. & Gyn.; Physiol. Soc.; Corres., Soc. Française de Gynécol. & Austrian Obs. & Gyn. Soc. Address: 3 South Cliff Court, 11 South Cliff, Eastbourne, Sussex BN20 7AF, UK.

THEROUX, Alexander Louis, b. Medford, Mass., USA. Writer; Professor. Educ: B.A., St. Francis Coll.; M.A., Ph.D., Univ. of Va. Publs: Three Wogs, 1972; The Schinocephalic Waif, 1975; The Great Wheadle Tragedy, 1975; The Wragby Cars, 1975. Contbr. to: Esquire; Harvard Advocate; Encounter; Ga. Review; Transatlantic Review; Nat. Review; N.Y. Times Travel Sect.; Boston Arts Review; London Mag.; Antaeus. Mbrships. incl: PEN. Hons. incl: Ency. Britannica Book of the Yr., 1972. Address: Adams House C—12, Harvard Univ., Cambridge, MA 02138, USA.

THEROUX, Paul, b. 10 Apr. 1941, Medford, Mass., USA. University Lecturer; Writer. Educ: B.A., Univ. of Mass., Amherst. Publs: (novels) Waldo, USA 1967, UK 1968; Fong & the Indians, 1968; Girls at Play, USA & UK 1969; Murder at Mount Holly, UK 1969; Jungle Lovers, USA & UK 1971. Contbr. to: Atlantic; Commentary; Harper's Bazaar; Playboy; etc. Address: c/o Diana Crawford Ltd., 5 King St., London WC2, UK.

THESEN, Hjalmar Peter, b. 20 June 1925, Knysna, S. Africa. Company Director. Educ: St. Andrews Coll.,

Grahamstown; Univ. of Cape Town. Publs: The Echoing Cliffs, 1960; The Castle of Giants, 1968; Master of None, 1970; Country Days, 1975. Address: Seaford, Thesen Hill, Knysna, Repub. of S. Africa.

THEURER, Hermann, pen name THEURER-SAMEK, Hermann, b. 7 July 1928, Modling, Austria. Author; Editor, Jetzt, magazine of literature. Publs: Bergfahrt, 1966; Ecce Homo — Der Mensch, 2nd ed., 1972; Der Duden sagt, 1974; Interjektionen, 1974; Widerwartigkeiten — Weider Wertigkeiten, 1974. Mbrships: Free German Soc. of Authors; Turmbund, Innsbruck. Recip., 1st Prize, Lyric Competition, Arndt Verlag Vaterstetten, 1971. Address: A—2340 Modlong, Haydngasse 20, Austria.

THIEL, Tage, b. 18 Sept. 1909, Stockholm, Sweden. Author; Teacher. Publs. incl: poetry; novels; philosophical & biographical works; transls. of Nietzsche's works into Swedish. Mbr., Swedish Union of Authors. Address: Vårdinge Folkhögskola, 150 21 Mölnbo, Sweden.

THIELE-DOHRMANN, Klaus Heinrich, pen name WEBER, Klaus, b. 10 Jan. 1936, Hamburg, Germany. Author. Educ: B.A.; studies at Univs. of Hamburg, & Zürich, Switz.; studies in psychotherapy, C.G. Jung Inst., Switz. Publ: Psychologie des Klatsch (Psychology of Gossip), 1975. Contbr. to: Der Spiegel; Die Zeit; Deutsches Allgemeines Sonntagsblatt; Tagesanzeiger, Zürich. Mbrships: Soc. of German Authors; Radio-TV-Film Union. Address: 2000 Hamburg 52, Parkstr. 9, W. Germany.

THIESS, Frank, b. 13 Mar. 1890. Author. Educ: D.Phil.; Univs. of Berlin & Tübungen. Publs. incl: Der Tod von Falern; Die Verdammetn; Abschied vom Paradies; Der Zentaur; Die Zeit ist reif; Wir werden es nie wissen; Tsushima. Katharina Winter; Der heilige Dämon; In Memoriam Wilhelm Furtwängler; Das Menschenbild bei Knut Hamsun; Die griechischen Kaiser; Sturz nach oben; Verbrannte Erde; Plädoyer für Peking; Reich der Dämonen; Jahre des Unheils. Contbr. to Berliner Tageblatt. Mbrships. incl: PEN; Mark Twain Soc., USA. Address: Park Rosenhöhe, Darmstadt, W. Germany.

THIESSEN, John, b. 14 Apr. 1931, Desalaberry, Man., Can. Professor of German; Chairman, Department of German. Educ: Mennonite Collegiate Inst., 1952-54; United Coll., 1954-56; Ph.D., Marburg Univ., 1961. Publs: Studien Zum Niederdeutschen Wortschatz Der Kanadischen Mennoniten, 1963; Yiddish in Canada: The Death of a Language?, 1974. Contbr. to Can. Lit. Mbrships: Chmn., Man. Arts Coun.; Pres., Can.-German Acad. Exchange Assn., 1971—. Address: 305 Elm St., Winnipeg, Man., Can.

THIJSSEN, Felix Maria Adeodatus, pen names LANSER, Ruard; VAN AKOOY, Philip, b. 24 Nov. 1933, Rijswijk, Netherlands. Author. Publs. incl (Sc. fiction novels) Threatening Sun; Vikings of Tau Ceti; Aries — shadows; Brain of the Crab; Day on Aldebaran; Abaddon's Night; Echo of the Trumpet; Gates of Paradise; also adventure stories; westerns; thrillers; film scripts; radio plays; transls. from French & Engl. Mbrships: Dutch Lit. Bd. (VVL); Holland SF. Address: Le Monteil, 19410 Orgnac sur Vézère, Corrèze, France.

THINÈS, Georges Louis Jean Hubert, b. 10 Feb. 1923, Liège, Belgium. Professor, University of Louvain; Writer. Educ: Doctorate, Psychol., 1955, B.Phil., 1958, Univ. of Louvain. Publs. incl: Poésies, 1959; Contribution à la théorie de la casualité perceptive, 1962; La Problématique de la Psychologie, 1968; Les Effigies, 1970; Atlas de la Vie souterraine (w. R. Tercafs), 1972; Le Tramway des Officiers, 1974; Orphée invisible, 1974; Dictionnaire général des Sciences Humaines (w. A. Lempereur), 1975. Contbr. to: Nouvelle Revue Française; Marginales. Mbrships: PEN; Belgian Writers' Assn. Hons: Emmanuel Vossaert Prize, 1968; Francqui Prize, 1971; Rossel Prize, 1973; French Min. of Culture Prize, 1974. Address: 69 Ave. Cardinal Mercier, 3030 Heverlee, Belgium.

THIRSK, Irene Joan, b. 19 June 1922, London, UK. University Teacher in Economic History. Educ: B.A., Ph.D., Westfield Coll., Univ. of London; M.A. (Oxon). Publs: English Peasant Farming, 1957; Suffolk Farming in the Nineteenth Century, 1958; Tudor Enclosures, 1959; The Agrarian History of England & Wales, vol. IV, 1500-1640, 1967; 17th Century Economic Documents, 1972. Contbr. to: Agricl. Hist. Review (Ed., 1964-72); Hist. of Lincs. series (Ed.); Past & Present; Jrnl. Mod. Hist.; Ency. Britannica; etc. Mbrships. incl: Exec. Comm., Brit. Agricl. Hist. Soc., 1953—, Chmn., 1974—; Coun. Mbr.,

Econ. Hist. Soc., 1955—. Hons: F.B.A., 1974. Address: The Kilns, Lewis Close, Headington, Oxon., UK.

THISTLE, Melville William, b. 22 Apr. 1914, St. John's, Nfld., Can. Teacher; Author. Educ: B.Sc., 1936, M.A., 1938, Mt. Allison Univ. Publs: Peter the Sea Trout, 1954; The Inner Ring, 1968; Time Touch Me Gently, 1970. Ed., Happy Journey, by Roy Fraser, 1958. Contbr. to: Communication; Revista de Occidente; Gen. Semantics Bulletin; Saturday Night; Sci. Mbrships. incl: Int. Soc. for Gen. Semantics; Inst. of Gen. Semantics; Can. Assn. Sci. Writers. Hons. incl: Centennial Award for Engl. Poetry, Centennial Commn. of Can., 1967. Address: School of Journalism, Carleton University, Ottawa K1S 5B6, Can.

THOM, Hendrik Bernardus, b. 13 Dec. 1905, Aliwal N., South Africa. Professor. Publs. incl: History of Sheepbreeding in South Africa, 1936; Life of Gert Maritz, 1965; Church of the Vow & other Studies on the Great Trek, 1949; (Ed.) sev. source documents. Contbr. to sev. South African & European mags. Mbrships. incl: Royal Netherlands Acad. of Sci.; South African Soc. of Sci. & Art; Simon van der Stel Fndn. Hons. incl: Stals Prize of the S.A. Acad., 1952; Medal for Univ. Dev., S.A. Acad., 1969; Medal for Cultural Dev., Fed. of Cultural Socs., 1970. Address: Die Kruin, Union Ave., Stellenbosch, Repub. of S. Africa.

THOMAS, Adrienne, b. 24 June 1897, St. Avold, France. Writer. Publs: Die Katrin wird Soldat, 1930, num. eds.; Dreiviertel Neugier, 1934; Andrea, 1937; Viktoria, 1938; Reisen Sie ab, Mademoiselle, 1947; Ein Fenster am East River, 1948; Wettlauf mit dem Traum, 1950; 4 other books; all books transl'd into sev. langs. Mbr., Austrian PEN. Hons: Silver Medal for servs. to lit., City of Vienna, 1969; Title, Prof., Pres. of Repub. of Austria, 1973. Address: A-1190 Vienna, Himmelstrasse 41, Austria.

THOMAS, Barry, b. 24 Mar. 1924, Barry, S. Wales. UK Television Writer (has written for BBC TV regularly since 1958). Publs. incl: (plays, serials & adaptations) A Time to Fight; Around the Corner; Mrs. Quilley's Murder Shoes; The Buskers; The World of Tim Frazer (w. Francis Durbridge); How Green Was My Valley (adapted); Script Ed. & Writer, Z Cars, Dr. Finlay's Casebook & The Onedin Line. Address: 25 Esher Ave., Walton-on-Thames, Surrey, UK.

THOMAS, Gilbert Oliver, b. 10 July 1891, Coventry, UK. Author; Literary Journalist. Publs: 25 books, poetry, essays, biog., lit. criticism, inclng: John Masefield, 1932; William Cowper & the Eighteenth Century, 1935, revised ed., 1948; Builders & Makers, 1944; Autobiography, 1946; Collected Poems, 1969. Contbr. to: Observer; Sunday Times; Manchester Guardian; Birmingham Post; Spectator; Quarterly Review; Contemporary Review; Poetry Review; Fortnightly Review, N.Y. Times; etc. Mbr., Engl. Assn. Address: Woodthorpe, Ipplepen, Newton Abbot, Devon, UK.

THOMAS, Gordon, b. 21 Feb. 1933, Capel Seion, Drefach, Carm., UK. Author. Publs. incl: The Jack Spot Story, 1962; Miracle of Surgery, 1962; The National Health Service & You, 1963; The Parents Home Doctor, 1964; The Day their World Ended (w. Max Morgan-Witts), 1966; The San Francisco Earthquake (w. same), 1968; Shipwreck: The Strange Fate of the Morro Castle (w. same), 1971; Issels: The Biography of a Doctor, 1973; Voyage of the Damned (w. Max Morgan-Witts), 1974; Guernica (w. same), 1975. Hons: Critics Prize, VII Int. Fest., Monte Carlo, 1958; Edgar Allan Poe Award, 1972. Address: High Valley, Ashford, Co. Wicklow, Repub. of Ireland.

THOMAS, Graham Stuart, b. 3 Apr. 1909, Cambridge, UK. Horticulturist. Educ: Hort. trng., Cambridge Univ. Botanic Gdns. Publs: The Old Shrub Rose, 1955; Colour in the Winter Garden, 1957; Shrub Roses of Today, 1962; Climbing Rose, Old & New, 1965; Plants for Ground Cover, 1970. Contbr. to: Royal Hort. Soc. Jrnl.; Royal Nat. Rose Soc. Annual; Hort. Press. Mbrships. incl: Coun., Royal Nat. Rose Soc.; Fellow, Judge, Royal Hort. Soc.; Comm., Garden Hist. Soc. Hons: Veitch Mem. Medal, 1966; Victoria Medal of Hon., 1968; OBE, 1975. Address: Briar Cottage, Fairfield Lane, West End, Woking. Surrey, UK.

THOMAS, Gwyn, b. 6 July 1913. Writer; Former Schoolmaster. Educ: B.A., St. Edmund Hall, Oxford Univ.; Madrid Univ. Publs. incl: (novels) The Dark Philosophers, 1946; All Things Betray Thee, 1949; The World Cannot Hear You, 1951; A Frost on My Frolic, 1953; Point of Order, 1956; The Love Man, 1958; Ring Delirium 123,

1959; A Welsh Eye, 1964; A Hatful of Humours, 1965; Leaves in the Wind, 1968; The Sky of Our Lives, 1972; (plays) The Keep, 1961; Loud Organs, 1962; Jackie the Jumper, 1962; (autobiog.) A Few Selected Exits, 1968. Address: Cherry Trees, Wyndham Pk., Peterston-super-Ely, Cardiff, UK.

THOMAS, Hugh Swynnerton. b. 21 Oct. 1931, Windsor, UK. Writer; Professor of History. Educ: B.A., 1953; M.A., 1957, Cambridge Univ. Publs: The World's Game, 1957; The Spanish Civil War, 1961; The Suez Affair, 1967; Cuba & the Pursuit of Liberty, 1971; John Strachey, 1973; Europe, the Radical Challenge, 1973. Contbr. to: The Observer; Times Lit. Supplement; Bookworld; N.Y. Times Sunday Mag. Recip., Somerset Maugham Prize, 1962. Address: 29 Ladbroke Grove, London W11, UK.

THOMAS, I. D. E., b. 30 Apr. 1921, Llandovery, UK. Minister of Religion. Educ: B.A. & B.D., Univ. of Wales; Ph.D., Calif. Grad. Schl. of Theol. Publs: On Trial, 1949; God's Harvest, 1950; God's Outsider, 1968; Astrology & the Bible, 1970; The Hidden Hand, 1975; The Golden Treasuury of Puritan Quotations, 1975. Contbr. to jrnls. inclng: Eternity mag.; Watchman Examiner; Seren Cymru. Mbr., Bapt. & soc. orgs. Hons. incl: Hon. Cert. of Freedoms Fndn. of Valley Forge for sermon preached thu'out Am., 1973. Address: 2170 Century Pk E., Apt. 1002, Century City, CA 90067, USA.

THOMAS, Kenneth Bryn, b. 30 Sept. 1915, Sutton, UK. Medical Practitioner. Educ: Kings Coll., London; Charing Cross Hosp., London; M.R.C.S.; L.P.C.P.; D.A.(Eng.); F.F.A.R.C.S.(Eng.). Publs: James Douglas of the Pouch, and his Pupil, William Hunter, 1964; Curare, Its History & Usage, 1964; The Development of Anaesthetic Apparatus, forthcoming. Contbr. to: Jrnl. of Hist. of Med.; Dictionary of Sci. Biog.; Ed. Bd., Med. Hist.; Brit. Med. Jrnl.; Anaesthesia. Mbrships. incl: Pres., Brit. Soc. of the Hist. of Med.; Past Pres., Hist. of Med. Sect., Royal Soc. of Med., London. Address: Hennerton Old House, Wargrave, Berks., UK.

THOMAS, Leslie John, b. 22 Mar. 1931. Author. Educ: S.W. Essex Tech. Coll., Walthamstow. Publs: (autobiog.) This Time Next Week, 1964; (novels) The Virgin Soldiers, 1966; Orange Wednesday, 1967; The Love Beach, 1968; Come to the War, 1969; His Lordship, 1970; Onward Virgin Soldiers, 1971; Arthur McCann & All His Women, 1972; The Man with Power, 1973; (non-fiction) Some Lovely Islands, 1968; var. TV plays & documentaries. Contbr. to: London Evening News (special writer, 1955-66); var. local newspapers, London area. Address: Nutfield, Fairmile, Henley-on-Thames, Oxon., UK.

THOMAS, Michael Wolf, pen name WOLF, Dieter, b. 16 Apr. 1945, Wuppertal, Germany. Redakteur der Film- und Medienredaktion INDR, Hamburg. Educ: Studies in Hist., Pols. & Sociol. Publs: Documentary ist in "Auf dem Schachbrett: Die DDR", 1971; Chancen für die City, 1973. Contbr. to: Radio & TV, Hamburg; SW Broadcasting Corp., Baden-Baden; Berlin Free Broadcasting Corp.; Frankfurter Rundschau; AV-Praxis, Munich; Medium, Frankfort; etc. Mbrships: Radio, TV & Film Union (RFFU); German Authors' Assn. (VS); Film Jrnlsts'. Union. Address: 2000 Hamburg 54, Hagenbeckstr. 37, W. Germany.

THOMAS, Norman Lewis, b. 24 June 1926, Aberavon, Port Talbot, Glam., UK. Schoolmaster; Educationalist; Author. Educ: Univ. of Southampton. Publs: The Story of Swansea's Districts & Villages, vol. 1, 1964, enlarged ed., 1965, vols. 1 & 2, 1969; The Story of Swansea's Markets, 1966; The Story of Swansea's Markets & Additional Historical Data, 1967; Swansea: Old & New (co-author), 1974. Contbr. of histl. features to Welsh newspapers & mags. Recip., var. hons. Address: 35 Wentworth Crescent, The Mayals, Swansea SA3 5HT, W. Glam., UK.

THOMAS, Paul, b. 18 July 1908, Meloor, Kerala, India. Writer. Publs. incl: Women & Marriage in India, 1939; Hindu Religion, Customs & Manners, 1947; Kama Kalpa: Hindu Ritual of Love, 1956; Colonists & Foreign Missionaries of Ancient India, 1963; Indian Women Through the Ages, 1964; Incredible India, 1966; March of Free India, 1968; Kama Katha, 1969; Humour, Wit & Satire from Indian Classics, 1969; Festivals & Holidays of India, 1971; Oblique Views, 1972. Contbr. to: World Book Ency.; World Digest; Illustrated Weekly of India; etc. Mbrships. incl: Sahridaya Samathi (Lit. Soc.); Kerala Hist. Assn. Address: V/202, East Fort, Trichur-5, Kerala, India.

THOMAS, William B. (Bill), pen names LOWELL, Alan; WILLIAMS, Tom; SABRE, Mark, b. 11 Nov. 1934, Elizabethtown, Ky., USA. Photojournalist. Educ: A.B., W. Ky. State Univ., Bowling Green, 1958; AUS Intelligence Schl., Ft. Holabird, Md., 1959. Publs: Outdoor Recreation in America, 1972; Tripping in America: Off the Beaten Track, 1974; Eastern Trips & Trails, 1975; Mid-America Trips & Trails, 1975. Contbr. to: Redbook; Good Housekeeping; Parent's; Better Homes & Gdns.; Outdoor Life; etc. Mbrships: Outdoor Writers of Am.; Soc. of Am. Travel Writers; Ind. Outdoor Writers; Am. Soc. of Mag. Photographers. Address: R4, Box 411B, Nashville, IN 47448, USA.

THOMPSON, Francis George, b. 29 Mar. 1931, Stornoway, Isle of Lewis, UK. Technical College Lecturer. Educ: Fellow, Instn. of Elec. Technician Engrs. Publs: Electrical Installation Technology, 3 vols., 1968, 1969 & 1972; Harris & Lewis, 1968; Harris Tweed — the Story of an Island Industry, 1969; St Kilda & Other Hebridean Outliers, 1970; The Ghosts, Spirits & Spectres of Scotland, 1973; The Uists & Barra, 1974; The Highlands & Islands, 1974. Contbr. to num. Scottish jrnls. Mbrships. incl: Scottish Brs., Soc. of Authors & PEN; Soc. of Antiquaries of Scotland. Address: 31 Braeside Pk., Balloch, Inverness IV1 2HJ, UK.

THOMPSON, Gary Richard, b. 11 Dec. 1937, Los Angeles, Calif., USA. University Professor. Educ: B.A., Calif. State Univ., 1959; M.A., 1960, Ph.D., 1967, Univ. of S. Calif. Publs: Poe's Fiction: Romantic Irony in the Gothic Tales, 1973; (Ed.) The Gothic Imagination: Essays in Dark Romanticism, 1974. Contbr. to: Am. Lit.; Engl. Lang. Notes; Am. Lit. Schlrship; Emerson Soc. Quarterly; (Ed.) Poe Stuwies; ESQ: A Jrnl. of the Am. Renaissance; etc. Mbrships: MLA of Am.; Conf. of Eds. of Learned Jrnls. Address: Dept. of English, Purdue Univ., W. Lafayette, IN 47907, USA.

THOMPSON, Harlan Howard, pen name HOLT, Stephen, b. 25 Dec. 1894, Brewster, Kan., USA. Writer; Rancher. Educ: A.B., Univ. of Southern Calif., LA. Publs. incl: Wild Palomino, 1946; Prairie Colt, 1947; Phantom Roan, 1949; Whistling Stallion, 1951; Stormy, 1955; With the California Forty Niners, 1956; With the California Rancheros, 1960; Ranch Beyond the Mountains, 1961; (under name Harlan Thompson): Star Roan, 1952; Spook the Mustang, 1956; Outcast Stallion of Hawaii, 1957. Contbr. to: Boy's Life; Open Road for Boys; etc. Mbrships: Pres., PEN, 1958-59; Calif. Writer's Guild; Western Writers of Am. Hons. incl: Jr. Lit. Guild Selections, 1949 & 1951; Silver Medal, C'wlth Club of Calif., 1956. Address: 136 Monarch Bay, S. Laguna, CA 92677, USA.

THOMPSON, Hunter Stockton, pen name DUKE, Raoul, b. 18 Apr. 1939, Louisville, Ky., USA. Writer. Educ: Dr. Jrnlsm., Columbia Univ.; D.D. (Ch. of the New Truth). Publs: Hells Angels, 1967; Fear & Loathing in Las Vegas, 1972; Fear & Loathing on the Campaign Trail '72, 1973. Contbr. to: Nat. Affairs Ed., Rolling Stone; Playboy; Esquire; N.Y. Times Mag.; Nation; Spider; etc. Mbrships: Overseas Press Club, N.Y.; Nat. Press Club, Wash.; Vincent Black Shadow Soc., L.A. Hons: Judge, Nat. Book Awards, USA, 1974; Dr. Chemo-Therapy, Univ. of Calif. (Berkeley). Address: Owl Farm, Woody Creek, CO 81656, USA.

THOMPSON, Vivian L., b. 7 Jan. 1911, Jersey City, N.J., USA. Writer; Former Teacher. Educ: B.S., M.A., Tchrs. Coll., Columbia Univ.; Maren Elwood Schl. Profl. Writing. Publs. incl: (jrnls.) Camp-in-the-Yard, 1961; Sad Day, Glad Day, 1962; Faraway Friends, 1963; George Washington, 1964; Keola's Hawaiian Donkey, 1966; Meet the Hawaiian Menehunes, 1967; Maui-full-of-tricks, 1970; Hawaiian Tales of Heroes & Champions, 1971; Aukele the Fearless, 1972. Mbrships: Authors' Guild; Int. Mark Twain Soc. Hons: Jr. Lit. Guild Selection of Camp-in-the-Yard, 1961; N.J. Assn. of Tchrs. of Engl. Citation for Sad Day, Glad Day, 1963. Address: Box 936 Kumukoa St., Hilo, Hawaii 96720 USA.

THOMSON, Alexander Robert Azan Chisti, b. 13 June 1943, Peoria, Ill., USA. Poet; Novelist. Educ: B.A., Wabash Coll., Crawfordsville, Ind.; grad. studies, Calif. State Univ., San Fran. & Univ. of Ariz., Tucson. Publs: Before Completion (poems), 1962; Great Lakes Anthology (Ed.), 1966; Breaths (poems), 1975; The Holy Biography of Moinuddin Christie (Ed.), 1975; A Shadow of Sunlight, 1975. Contbr. to: Esquire Mag.; In Person; The Message. Mbr., Sufi Order. Address: 1108 E. Tenth St., Tucson, AZ 85719, USA.

THOMSON, Daisy Hicks, pen names ROE, M. S.; THOMSON, Jon H., b. 14 June 1918, Rothesay, Scotland, UK. Novelist. Educ: M.A., Univ. of Edinburgh. Publs: Prelude to Love, 1963; To Love & Honour, 1964; Jealous Love, 1964; Portrait of My Love, 1966; Love for a Stranger, 1966; A Truce for Love, 1967; By Love Betrayed, 1967; Journey to Love, 1967; Be My Love, 1968; My Only Love, 1969; Five Days to Love, 1969; The Italian for Love, 1970; Summons to Love, 1971; Hello My Love, 1972; Woman in Love, 1973. Contbr. to: She; Good Housekeeping; etc. Mbrships. incl: Soc. of Authors; PEN; Dante Alighieri Soc. (Dundee Br.). Address: 44 Seafield Rd., Broughty Ferry, Angus, UK.

THOMSON, Francis Paul, b. 17 Dec. 1914, Corstorphine, Scotland, UK. Chartered Engineer. Educ: Schl. of Engrng., Ctrl. London Polytechnic; Acton Tech. Coll., London; Int. Coll., Elsinore, Denmark; Extramural Dept., Stockholm Univ.; etc. Publs. incl: Postal Cheques Are Your Business, 1946; Giro — Europe's Wonder Bank, 1952; Giro Credit Transfer Systems, 1964; Money in the Computer Age, 1968; Banking Automation, 1971; Ed. (w. E. S. Thomson), A History of Tapestry by W. G. Thomson, 3rd Ed., 1973; Guglielmo ('Bill') Marconi: The First Radio Engineer, forthcoming; Alan Dower Blumlein 1903-42: Engineer Extraordinary (w. Simon J. L. Blumlein), forthcoming. Contbr. to var. bus. jrnls. Mbrships incl: Writers Action Grp.; Fndr., Brit. Giro Campaign. Recip., Frederick Marten Int. Essay Prize, 1931. Address: The Cottage, 39 Church Rd., Watford WD1 3PY, UK.

THOMSON, (The Rev.) George Ian Falconer, b. 2 Sept. 1912, Canton, China. Editor, Scripture Journals. Educ: M.A., Balliol Coll., Oxford; Westcott House, Cambridge. Publs: The Rise of Modern Asia, 1958; Changing Patterns in South Asia, 1961. Contnr. to: Observer: special articles written while travelling in China at height of Cultural Revolution, 1967; Quarterly Review; Tehology; scripture Bulletin (Assoc. Ed.); Bible Reading Fellowship (Dir., Ed.-in-Chief). Mbr., Soc. for Anglo-Chinese Understanding. Recip., Ellerton Essay Prize. Address: Jackson's Farm Hse., Yarnton, Oxford, UK.

THOMSON, George Malcolm, b. 2 Aug. 1899, Leith, UK. Journalist; Author. Educ: M.A., Univ. of Edinburgh. Publs: The Twelve Days, 1964; The Crime of Mary Stuart, 1967; Sir Francis Drake, 1972; The North West Passage, 1975. Mbrships: Soc. of Authors; Garrick Club. Address: 5 The Mount Square, London NW3 6SY, UK.

THORNDIKE, Robert Ladd, b. 22 Sept. 1910, Montrose, N.Y., USA. College Professor of Psychology & Education. Educ: B.A., Wesleyan Univ., 1931; M.A., 1932, Ph.D., 1935, Columbia Univ., N.Y. Publs: Personnel Selection, 1949; Measurement & Evaluation in Psychology & Education (w. Elizabeth P. Hagen), 1955, 3rd ed., 1969; 10,000 Careers (w. Elizabeth Hagen), 1959; Concepts of Over & Under Achievements, 1964. Contbr. to var. psychol. & educl. publs. Mbrships: Am. Educ. Rsch. Assn. (Pres.); Psychometric Soc. (Pres.). Hons: Edward L. Thorndike Award, Div. Educl. Psychol., Am. Psychol. Assn.; Butler Medal, Silver, Columbia Univ. Address: Box 327, Montrose, NY 10548, USA.

THORNER, Horace Edward, b. 3 Aug. 1909, Boston, Mass., USA. Teacher of Literature; Writer; Bookseller. Publs: Iliad of Homer (transl.), 1948; Man Who Shot God, 1951; Rubaiyat of Omar Khayyam (transl.), 1955; Index to the Novel, 1956; Round World Squared, 1966. Contbr. to: St. Louis Post Dispatch; Hong Kong Tiger Standard; etc. Mbrships. incl: F.R.S.A.; Hon. Fellow, Nat. Cum Laude Soc. Recip., var. hons.; Chess assns. Address: Swift River, Cummington, MA 01026, USA.

THORNOCK, Wanda W., b. 3 Mar. 1917, Montpelier, Idaho, USA. Writer; Artist; Poet. Educ: Grad. w. hons., Washington Schl. of Art. Publs: Book of verse, illustrated by author, forthcoming. Contbr. to: Idaho Free Press Poets' Corner; Relief Soc. of Ch. of Jesus Christ of Letterday Sts.; Ch. pamphlets; Radio & TV. Mbrships: Chmn., Gem State Writers' Guild; Int. Platform Assn. Hons: 1st Prize, Eliza R. Snow Poetry Contest, 1938; 1st Prize, Idaho Egg Inc. Poetry Contest; 3rd place, Gemstate Writers' Guild Contest; Bronze Medal & Cert. of Merit for poetry. Address: 608 19th Avenue North, Nampa, ID 83651, USA.

THORP, (Margery) Ellen, pen name THORP, Ellen, b. 22 July 1906, Rangoon, Burma. Author. Educ: B.A., Lady Margaret Hall, Oxford. Publs: Quiet Skies on Salween, 1945; Swelling of Jordan, 1950; Ladder of Bones, 1956; The Gilded Buddha (as Morwenna Thorp), 1971. Mbr., Newman Assn. Address: 3 Grovelands Close, Charlton Kings, Cheltenham, Glos. GL53 8BS, UK.

THORPE, Lewis (Guy Melville), b. 5 Nov. 1913, Surrey, UK. Professor of French. Educ. incl: Ph.D., London Univ., 1948; Docteur de l'Univ., Paris Univ., France, 1957. Recent publs. incl: Guido Farina, Painter of Verona, 1896-1957 (w. Barbara Reynolds), 1967; Einhard the Frank: The Life of Charlemagne, 1970; The Bayeux Tapestry & the Norman Invasion, 1973; The History of the Franks by Gregory of Tours, 1974. Contbr. to: Ency. Brit.; Romania; Mod. Lang. Review; etc. Mbrships. incl: Int. Arthurian Soc. (Int. Soc.; Pres., British Br.); F.R.S.A.; F.R.Hist.S.; F.S.A. Address: 26 Parkside, Wollaton Vale, Nottingham NG8 2NN, UK.

THORPY, Frank Thomas, b. 23 Aug. 1919, Invercargill, NZ. Importer-Exporter. Educ: St. Bede's Coll., Christchurch. Publs: Wine in New Zealand, 1971; Australia & New Zealand Complete Book of Wine (co-author), 1973. Contbr. to: UK Wine & Food Mag.; Aust. Epicurean; NZ Accolade, Wine Review, Heritage, NBR Review, Mkt. Place, Catering Mag.; Air NZ Flight Mag.; Alex Lichine Ency. of Wines & Spirits. Mbrships: Fndr. Mbr. & Past Pres., Auckland Wine & Food Soc.; Chmn., Visual Arts Comm., Auckland Festival of Arts. Hons: Consul of Brazil in NZ, 1967–; Kt. of Brazilian Order of Southern Cross, 1973. Address: 135 Tamaki Drive, Mission Bay, Auckland, New Zealand.

THORSEN, Magne, b. 18 Oct. 1928, Oslo, Norway. Author; Editor; Playwright. Publs: The Bird in the River Plate, 1959; The Girl Friend, 1963; In Fight & Working, 1968; Harry, 1970; The Working People of Thune, 1971; In Tune with the Times, 1971; The Workman of Aker, 1972. Contbr. to: Ed., Forfatteren; Arbeiderbladet; Sosialistisk Perspektiv. Mbr., Norwegian Soc. of Authors; Norwegian Soc. of Dramatists; Norwegian Soc. of Lit. Reviewers. Hons: Nordahl Grieg Drama Prize, 1963; City of Oslo Authors Prize, 1967; City of Olso Essay & Drama Prize, 1971. Address: Bølerlia 6, Oslo 6, Norway.

THORSRUD, Olav, b. 17 Feb. 1902, Aurdal in Valdres, Norway. Novelist. Educ: Cand. mag., Univ. of Oslo, 1927. Publs: Jeg går i skyggen, 1934; Og så kom borgerkrigen, 1937; Muld og asfalt, 1939; Dagdrivere på Canary, 1941; Gitar og mantille, 1946; Fløyten, 1966. Mbrships: Norwegian Soc. of Authors; Norwegian Ctr., PEN; Kunstnerforeningen. Address: Krokoddveien 1, 3440 Royken, Norway.

THROWER, Percy John, b. 30 Jan. 1913, Winslow, Bucks., UK. Horticulturist. Educ: Nat. Dip. in Hort. Publs: In Your Garden Week by Week, 1959; Encyclopaedia of Gardening, 1962; In Your Greenhouse, 1963; Every Day Gardening, 1969; Vegetables & Herbs from Your Garden, 1974; Step by Step Gardening, 1974. Contbr. to: Amateur Gardening; Daily Express; Woman's Own; Gardeners World, BBC TV; Blue Peter, BBC TV. Mbrships: Royal Hort. Soc.; Inst. of Park Admin. Hons: Assoc. of Hon., Royal Hort. Soc.; Vic. Medal of Hon. Address: The Magnolias, Bomere Heath, Shrewsbury, UK.

THUBRON, Colin Gerald Dryden, b. 14 June 1939, London, UK. Author. Educ: Eton Coll. Publs: Mirror to Damascus, 1967; The Hills of Adonis: A Quest in Lebanon, 1968; Jerusalem, 1969; Journey into Cyprus, 1975. Contbr. to: Cornhill; Sunday Telegraph. Mbrships: PEN; F.R.S.L.; Palestine Exploration Fund. Hon: Mirror to Damascus chosen by Book Soc., 1967. Address: Pheasants Hatch, Piltdown, Sussex, UK.

THUILLIER, Jacques Raymond, b. 18 Mar. 1928, Vancouleirs, France. Professor of History of Art, Sorbonne University. Educ: Univ. degree; D.Litt. Publs. incl: La peinture française (w. A. Chatelet), 2 vols., 1963-64; Rubens: La Galerie de Médicis au Palais du Luxembourg, 1967-69; Fragonard, 1967; Nicolas Poussin, 1969; Georges de La Tour, 1973. Contbr. to: La Revue de l'Art; L'Oeil. Mbrships: Past Pres., Soc. for French Art Hist.; Sci. Sec., Int. Comm. of Art Hist.; (C.I.H.A.); Ed. Comm., La Review de l'Art. Hons: Chevalier, Order of Arts & Letters, 1964; Chevalier, Nat. Order of Merit, 1972. Address: 129 Rue de la Pompe, 75116, Paris, France.

THULSTRUP, Ake, b. 24 Dec. 1904, Södertelje, Sweden. Historian; Essayist; Editor; Translator. Educ: Fil.lic., 1929, Ph.D., 1957, Univ. of Stockholm. Publs. incl: Konsten att översätta (The Art of Translating), 1942; Det ödesigra 1930-talet (The Fateful 1930's), 1957; Med lock och pock (German Attempts to influence Public Opinion in Sweden 1933-45), 1962; Svensk politik 1905-39 (Swedish Politics 1905-39), 1968. Contbr. to: Göteborgs Handels- & Sjöfarts-Tidning; Historisk Tidskrift; Tidsspegel; Svenska Dagbladet; etc. Mbr., var. profl. orgs. Hons: Segerstedt-stipendiet, 1949; Oversättarförbundets pris (Translators' Soc. Award), 1954; Sveriges Författarfond Premium (Swedish Authors' Fund's Award), 1959. Address: Kungsholms Strand 183, 11248 Stockholm, Sweden.

THUNBERG, Lars Anders, b. 9 July 1928, Stockholm, Sweden. Theologian. Educ: B.A., 1950; Th.D., 1965. Publs. incl: Ljuvare än honung, 1957; Solbegängelse, 1960; Hos det outgrundliga, 1962; Havets odling, 1963; Kristens resa, 1965; Microcosm & Mediator. The Theological Anthropology of Maximus Confessor, 1965; Anden och stenen, 1970; Mänsklighetstanken i äldre och nyare teologi, 1974. Contbr. to: theol. & relig. jrnls. Mbrships: VP, Nathan Söderblom Soc.; Nat. Assn. of Writers. Address: P.O. Box 68, 190 30 Sigtuna, Sweden;

THURSTON, Gavin Leonard Bourdas, b. 1911, London, UK. Coroner; Lecturer in Forensic Medicine. Educ: Guy's Hosp.; F.R.C.P.; F.R.C.G.P.; Dip. Child Hlth.; D.M.J.; Barrister-at-Law, Inner Temple. Publs: Thurston's Coroner's Practice; Coroners in Atkin's Court Forms; The Great Thames Disaster; The Clerkenwell Riot; Coroners in Halsbury's Laws of England. Contbr. to: Brit. Med. Jrnl.; Lancet; Med. World; Police Jrnl.; Solicitors' Jrnl.; Contemporary Review. Mbrships: Med. Defence Union (VP); Coroners' Soc. of England & Wales (Hon. Sec.); Authors' Club. Address: 57 Belgravia Ct., Ebury St., London SW1W 0NY, UK.

THURY, Zsuzsa, b. 22 Apr. 1901, Budapest, Hungary. Writer. Educ: Sorbonne, Paris, France. Publs: Rigo Street 20-22; Two Women, 1942; Under the Same Roof, 1952; A Good Boy, 1969; Adventures of Youth, 1967; Stylus on the Record, 1969; The Highway to Vienna, 1973. Contbr. to Hungarian & for. mags. Mbrships: PEN; Assn. of Hungarian Writers. Hons: three times recip. József Attila Award; three times awarded Gold Labor Medal. Address: Szent Istvan korut 9, 1055 Budapest, Hungary.

THURZO, Gabor, b. 26 Mar. 1912, Budapest, Hungary. Writer; Scenarist. Educ: Pazmany Univ., Budapest. Publs: Nappalok es ejszakak (Days & Nights); Hamis Penz (False Money); A Szent (The Saint). Contbr. to: Elet es Irodalom; Kortars; Tukor. Mbrships: Hungarian Writers' Assn.; PEN; COMES. Recip., József Attila Prize, 1954, 1959 & 1970. Address: Vaci Utca 55, 1056 Budapest, Hungary.

THWAITE, Anthony, b. 23 June 1930, Chester, UK. Poet; Co-Editor, Encounter. Educ: M.A., Oxford Univ. Publs: Home Truths, 1957; Contemporary English Poetry, 1959; The Owl in the Tree, 1963; Penguin Book of Japanese Verse (w. Geoffrey Bownas), 1964; The Stones of Emptiness, 1967; The Deserts of Hesperides, 1969; Japan in Colour (w. Roloff Beny), 1968; Penguin Modern Poets (w. A. Alvarez & Roy Fuller), 1970; Inscriptions, 1973; New Confessions, 1974; Poetry Today, 1974; The English Poets (w. Peter Porter), 1974; In ITaly (w. Roloff Beny & Peter Porter), 1974. Contbr. to: Observer; etc. Mbrships. incl: Soc. Authors. Recip., Richard Hillary Mem. Prize, 1968 for The Stones of Emptiness. Address: The Mill House, Low Tharston, Norfolk NR15 2YN, UK.

THYSELIUS, Thorborg Elin Tryggvesdotter, earlier pen name CASTENIUS, Sigrid, b. 31 Oct. 1906, Linköping, Sweden. Author. Educ: B.A. Publs: Drömspel (Dream Play, poems), 1935; Trolltagen (Troll Bewitched, novel), 1955; Fäbodvall (Mountain Dairy-farm, documentary), 1963; Jag star i skuld till stjärnorna (I am Indebted to the Stars, poetic novel), 1969; Den namnlöse (The Nameless Man, novel), 1969; Grass-root Murmur (poems), 1975; & sev. books for children. Mbrships. incl: Swedish Union of Authors; Authors' Ctr. Address: Hästberget, 820 40 Järvsö, Sweden.

TIBAWI, Abdul Latif, b. 29 Apr. 1910, Taibeh, Palestine. University Lecturer. Educ: B.A., Am. Univ. of Beirut, Syria; Ph.D., D.Lit., Univ. of London, UK. Publs. incl: Arab Education in Mandatory Palestine 1918-48, 1956; Lectures on the History of the Arabs & Islam, 2 vols. in Arabic, 1965, 1966; A Modern History of Syria including Lebanon & Palestine, 1969; Islamic Education: Its Traditions & Modernization into the Arab National Systems, 1972; Arabic & Islamic Themes: Historical, Educational & Literary Studies, 1974. Contbr. to: Islamic

Quarterly; Int. Review of Educ.; Middle E. Jrnl.; etc. Hons: 1st Prize in Lit., 1st Munroe Prize in Hist., Am. Univ. of Beirut. Address: Sakeena, 7 Cranbrook Drive, Esher, Surrey, UK.

TIBBLE, Anne, b. 29 Jan. 1912. Writer. Educ: B.A.(Hons.), Ed.Dip., Univ. of Leeds. Publs: John Clare: a Life (co-author), 1932, 2nd ed., 1971; The Apple Reddens, 1947; The Letters of John Clare, 1951; Co-Ed., The Prose of John Clare, 1951; John Clare: his Life & Poetry, 1956; The Everyman John Clare, 1965; Helen Keller, 1967, paperback ed., 1974; The Story of English Literature, 1970; African/English Literature, 1971. Contbr. to: Ency. Britannica. Address: Clare Cottage, Guilsborough, Northants., UK.

TIELMAN, Ingeborg, pen name TIELMAN, Inge, b. 17 Mar. 1931, Tegal Java, Indonesia. Theatre Directress; Author. Educ: Acad. of Arts, Turin, Italy. Publs. incl: (poetry) Leg je oor aan, 1961; Deelbaar Licht, 1966; work in var. anthols. inclng. Dichter van morgen, 1958; Allemaal Anders I, II, III, 1959-61; Vandaag, 1962; also author of cabaret shows inclng: PSSST, 1968; Avondkleding niet gewenst, 1970; Dat kan je niet maken, 1971-72; Cartoon & Cartoon II, 1972-73. Contbr. to: cultural & lit. jrnls. & mags. inclng: De Nieuwe Stem; Maatstaf; Haagse Schouw; Proefschrift; Euratio; etc. Mbrships. incl: Dutch Soc. of Authors; Dutch Soc. of Dramatic Arts.

TIFFT, Ellen, b. 28 June 1916, Elmira, N.Y., USA. Writer. Educ: Elmira Coll. Publs: A Door in a Wall, 1966; The Kissed Cold Kite, 1968; The Live-Long Day, 1972. Contbr. to num. jrnls. inclng: New Yorker; Anglo-Welsh Review; Everywoman's; Yale Review; Poetry; Christian Sci. Monitor; Sat. Evening Post; Transatlantic Review; Abraxas 5 Anthol.; Today's Poet; Outer Circle. Mbr., Poetry Soc. of Am. Recip., Annual Award, Poetry Book Mag., 1950. Address: Crane Rd., E. Hill, Elmira, NY 14901, USA.

TIGUE, Ethel Erkkila, b. 19 Feb. 1916, Mirginia, Minn., USA. Author; Educator. Educ: Elem. Tchng. Cert., Duluth State Tchrs. Coll.; B.Ed., Univ. of Minn. Publs: Betrayal (novel), 1959; Secret of Willow Coulee (co-author), 1966; Packy (juvenile novel), 1967; Looking Forward to a Career in Writing, 1971; You & Your Private I (co-author), 1975. Contbr. to' Mpls. Tribune; Writer; Writers' Digest; St. Paul Dispatch; var. profl. educl. mags. Recip., McKnight Fndn. Humanities Award, 1962. Address: 9457 Las Vegas Blvd. South, Apt. 247, Las Vegas, NV 89119, USA.

TIJERAS, Eduardo, b. 14 Oct. 1931, Morón de la Frontera, Spain. Press Office Editor; Author. Publs: Jugador solitario, 1969; Acerca de la felicidad y la muerte, 1972; Relato Breve en Argentina, 1973; Antologia de cronistas de Indias, 1974. Contbr. to: ABC, Madrid daily; Cuadernos Hispanoamericanos mag.; Lit. Supplement, Informaciones daily; Estafeta Literaria. Mbrships: Mutualidad Laboral de Autores de Libros; Sociedad de Autores. Recip., sev. lit. prizes. Address: Maqueda 19, 4°, B, Madrid 24, Spain.

TIKHONOV, Nikolai Semyonvich, b. 4 Dec. 1896, Leningrad, USSR. Writer; Poet. Publs. incl: (poetry) The Horde, 1922; Kirov is with us, 1941; Year of Fire, 1942; Poems of Yugoslavia, 1947; Georgian Spring, Two Streams, 1951; May Morning, 1961; Poems, 1961; The Morning of Peace, 1962; (other publs.) Novels & Stories, 1948; Stories of Pakistan, 1950; Collected Works, 6 vols., 1959; Selected Lyrics, 1964; From the View of Friends, 1967; The Green Darkness, 1967. Mbrships. incl: Lenin Prize Comm.; Supreme Soviet. Num. hons. incl: Int. Lenin Peace Prize, 1958; Lenin Prize, 1970. Address: Union of Writers, ul. Vorovskogo 52, Moscow, USSR.

TILLEMA, Herbert K., b. 23 Apr. 1942, Wash. D.C., USA. Professor of Political Science. Educ: A.B., Hope Coll., 1964; Ph.D., Harvard Univ., 1969. Publs: Appeal to Force, 1973. Mbrships: Am. Pol. Sci. Assn.; Int. Studies Assn. Hons: Woodrow Wilson Fellow, 1964-65; Nat. Sci. Fndn. Fellow, 1965-68. Address: 306 Westridge Dr., Columbia, MO 65201, USA.

TIMAR, Mate, b. 21 Nov. 1922, Endrod, Hungary. Writer. Educ: Budapest Univ. Publs. incl: (in Hungarian) Adam Majoros, Chronicle, 1968; It Dawns, 1960; Charlie the Bat, 1961; Hairy Bag, 1963; Late Dawn, 1967; Tempest, 1969; Maturity in War, 1970; And on the Seventeenth Day, 1970. Contbr. to: Hungarian Radio. Mbrships: Assn. of Hungarian Writers; Hungarian People's Repub., Art Fund; PEN. Hons: Lit. Prize, Hungarian Trade

Unions, 1958; Jozsef Attila Prize, 1962. Address: 1093 Budapest, Kozraktar u. 24, Hungary.

TIMMONS, Christopher John, b. 30 June 1926, London, UK. University Teacher. Educ: B.Sc., Ph.D., Imperial Coll. Sci. & Technol. Publs: Co-Ed., DMS UV Atlas or Organic Compounds, 1966-71; Ed., Modern Reactions in Organic Synthesis, 1970, Japanese ed., 1973; Electronic Absorption Spectroscopy in Organic Chemistry (co-author), 1970, Russian ed., 1974. Contbr. to: MTP Int. Review of Sci.; Jrnl. Chem. Soc.; UV Spectrometry Grp. Bulletin. Mbrships. incl: Chem. Soc.; Royal Inst. Chem.; Am. Chem. Soc.; Soc. Chem. Ind.; Swiss Chem. Soc. Recip., Royal Schlrship. in Sci., 1945. Address: Chemistry Dept., The University, Nottingham NG7 2RD, UK.

TIMPERLEY, Rosemary, b. 20 Mar. 1920, London, UK. Writer. Educ: B.A. (Hist.). Publs. incl: Doctor Z, 1969; The Mask Shop, 1970; House of Secrets, 1970; Walk to San Michele, 1971; The Summer Visitors, 1971; The Passionate Marriage, 1972; The Long Black Dress, 1972; Shadows in the Park, 1973; Journey with Doctor Godley, 1973; The Echo-Game, 1973; Juliet, 1974; The White Zig-Zag Path, 1974. Contbr. to: Barrie & Jenkins Ghost Stories; Fontana Paperbacks of short stories. Mbrships: Soc. of Authors; Crime Writers' Assn. Address: 21 Montague Rd., Richmond, Surrey TW10 6QW, UK.

TINDALL, (Rev. Canon) Frederick Cryer, pen name JOHN MARK, b. 2 July 1900, Hove, Sussex, UK. Minister of Religion (Anglican); Theological College Principal. Educ: A.K.C., 1922, B.D., 1923, Philos. of Relig., 1927, King's Coll., London Univ.; Ely Theol. Coll. Publs. incl: Ed., Confirmation Today, 1944; England Expects, 1946; Ed., The Theology of Christian Initiation, 1948; Ed., Baptism Today, 1949; Christian Initiation, Anglican Principles & Practice, 1951; Ed., Baptism & Confirmation Today, 1955. Contbr. to: History of Christian Thought, 1937; Ency. Britannica Yr. Book, 1939; The Guardian; relig. jrnls. Fellow, King's Coll., London, 1951. Address: Bemerton House, 71 Lower Rd., Salisbury, Wilts. SP2 9NH, UK.

TINDALL, Gillian (Elizabeth), b. 1938, London, UK. Writer. Educ: M.A., Lady Margaret Hall, Oxford Univ. Publs: (novels) No Name in the Street, 1959 (as When We Had Other Names, USA, 1960); The Water & the Sound, UK & USA, 1961; The Edge of the Paper, 1963; The Youngest, UK, 1966, USA, 1967; Someone Else, UK & USA, 1969; Fly Away Home, UK & USA, 1971; (juvenile) The Israeli Twins, UK & USA, 1963; (non-fiction) A Handbook on Witchcraft, UK, 1965, USA, 1966. Contbr. to: Guardian; New Statesman; New Society; Winter's Tales 16, 1970. Recip., Mary Elgin Prize, 1970. Address: 27 Leighton Rd., London NW5, UK.

TINDALL, Kenneth Thomas, b. 26 Jan. 1937, L.A., Calif., USA. Postal Clerk. Publs: Vindharpen (Danish), 1967; Great Heads, 1969; Die Nascher (German), 1971. Contbr. to the Beloit Poetry Jrnl. Fellow, MacDowell Colony. Winner 2nd Prize for poem, A Portrait of New York, contest sponsored by NBC, 1954. Address: c/o Hans Feitzels Forlag A/S, Snaregade 4, 1205 Copenhagen K., Denmark.

TINDER, Donald George, b. 23 July 1938, Miami, Fla., USA. Associate Editor. Educ: B.A., Yale Univ., New Haven, Conn., 1960; M.Div., Fuller Theol. Sem., Pasadena, Calif., 1964; Ph.D., Yale Univ., 1969. Contbr. to: Christianity Today (Assoc. Ed.); Baker's Dict. of Christian Ethics; New Int. Dict. of the Christian Church. Mbrships. incl: Am. Acad. of Relig.; Am. Soc. of Ch. Hist.; Evangelical Theol. Soc. Address: 1014 Washington Bldg., Wash. DC 20005, USA.

TING, Simon, pen name YEH, Hsiao, b. 19 Jan. 1925, Chen-Ti, Chuanchow, Fookien, China. Professor; Minister; Guidance Counselor. Educ: A.B., Cornell Coll., Iowa, USA, 1948; M.A., Oberlin Coll., Ohio, 1950; D.Phil., Mansfield Coll., Oxford Univ., UK, 1958; M.Div., Vanderbilt Univ. Tenn., USA, 1973. Publs. incl: Children of Light, 1956; Song of Songs, 1960; The Mysticism of Chuang Tzu, 1974. Contbr. to var. lit. jrnls. Mbrships: Vice Chmn., Cultural Affairs Comm., Chinese Literary Club, Manila, 1966-68; Pres., Philos. Assn. of the Philippines, 1974. Recip., 1st Prize for acad. treatise, Chiang Kai-shek Cultural Fndn., 1967. Address: Philippine Christian Coll., P.O. Box 907, Manila, Philippines.

TINNE, Dorothea, b. 1 June 1899, Hawkhurst, UK. Animal Painter; Sculptor; Writer. Publs: Lure of Lakeland,

1946; Cheeky & Coy, 1950; Signposts to the Wild, 1956; Adventurous Holidays, 1958; Love & Laughter, 1968. Mbr., Soc. of Wildlife Artists. Address: High Wray, Lodge Hill Rd., Farnham, Surrey GU10 3RB, UK.

TINNISWOOD, Peter, b. 21 Dec. 1936. Liverpool, UK. Writer. Educ: B.A., Univ. of Manchester. Publs: A Touch of Daniel, 1968; Mog, 1970; I Didn't Know You Cared, 1973; Except You're a Bird, 1974. Contbr. to: Times; Listener; Books & Bookmen; Western Mail; Daily Post. Hons: Authors' Club First Novel Award, 1969; Winifred Holtby Mem. Prize, 1974; F.R.S.L. Address: 29 Teilo St., Llandaff Fields, Cardiff, UK.

TISCHLER, Hans, b. 18 Jan. 1915, Vienna, Austria. Musicologist. Educ: State Dip. in Piano Tchng., 1933, Master's Dips. in Composition & Conducting, Vienna State Acad., 1935, 1936; Ph.D., Univ. of Vienna, 1937; Ph.D., Yale Univ., 1942. Publs. incl: The Perceptive Music Listener, 1955; Practical Harmony, 1964; A Structural Analysis of Mozart's Piano Concertos, 1966; A Medieval Motet Book, 1973; Willi Apel's History of Keyboard Music to 1700 (transl. & Ed.), 1973; The Great Montpellier Codex: A New Transcription, 1975-76; Complete Edition of the Earliest Motets, c. 1190-1270, 1976. Contbr. to: Acta Musicologica; Chord & Discord; Int. Review of the Aesthetics & Sociol. of Music; etc. Mbrships. incl: Am. Musicol. Soc.; Int. Musicol. Soc. Address: 711 E. 1st St., Bloomington, IN 47401, USA.

TIŠMA, Aleksandar, b. 16 Jan. 1924, Horgoš, Yugoslavia. Writer. Educ: A.M., Belgrade Univ. Publs: Nasilje, 1965; Za crnom devojkom, 1969; Knjiga o Blamu, 1972. Contbr. to: Letopis Matice srpske; Književnost; Savremnik. Mbrships: Bd., PEN Serbian Ctr.; Yugoslav Assn. of Writers. Hons: Branko Radičević Prize, 1953; October Prize, 1965. Address: Modene 1, Novi Sad, Yugoslavia.

TOCH, Henry, b. 15 Aug. 1923. Polytechnic Lecturer. Educ: B.Com., Univ. of London. Publs: How to Pay Less Income Tax, 1959, 4th ed., 1973; British Political & Social Institutions, 1960; Tax Saving for the Business Man, 1960, 3rd ed., 1975; Income Tax, 1966, 7th ed., 1974; Economics for Professional Studies, 1974. Contbr. to: Jrnl. of Bus. Law; Times Higher Educ. Supplement; Labour Weekly. Mbrships: Soc. of Authors; Assn. of Tchrs. in Tech. Insts. Address: "Candida", 49 Hawkshead Lane, North Mymms, Hatfield, Herts. AL9 7TD, UK.

TODD, Vivian Edmiston, b. 18 Feb. 1912, Spokane, Wash. D.C., USA. Curriculum Specialist. Educ: B.S., Univ. of Idaho, Moscow, 1931; M.S., 1932; Ph.D., Univ. of Chgo., 1943. Publs: Ed., The American Way of Housekeeping, 1948; (w. Helen Heffernan) The Kindergarten Teacher, 1960; The Years Before School, 1964, 1970; Elementary Teacher's Guide to Working with Parents, 1969; (w. G. H. Hunter) The Aide in Early Childhood Education, 1973. Contbr. to major educl. periodicals. Designer-author, sets of transparencies & accompanying booklets for higher educ. Mbrships. incl: Am. Educ. Rsch. Assn.; Assn. for Childhood Educ. Int.; NEA; etc. Address: 1873 Stearnlee Ave., Long Beach, CA 90815, USA.

TOGHILL, Jeffery Edwin, b. 4 July 1932, Devizes, Wilts., UK. Writer; Marine Consultant. Educ: Grad., Schl. of Navigation, Univ. of Southampton, 1948. Publs: Manual of Yacht Navigation, 1965; Seek & Annihilate, 1968; The Art of Sailing, 1968; The Boat Owner's Maintenance Manual, Pacific 1970, USA 1972, UK 1974; Let's Try Sailing, 1973; Sailing for Beginners, 1974; Fishing Boats, 1974; Ed., Australian Boating. Contbr. to: Men Only, UK; Police Gazette, USA; Fishing News (Boating Ed.), Aust. & NZ; boating mags.; women's mags. Address: Suites 3 & 4, 9 Canrobert St., Mosman, Sydney, Australia 2088.

TOLEDANO, Ralph de, b. 17 Aug. 1916, Int. Zone, Tangier, Morocco. Author; Journalist. Educ: B.A., Columbia Univ. Publs. incl: Frontiers of Jazz, 1947; Seeds of Treason, 1950; Nixon, 1956; Lament for a Generation, 1960; The Greatest Plot in History, 1963; RFK, The Man Who Would Be President, 1967; America, I-Love-You, 1968; One Man Alone — Richard Nixon, 1969; Little Cesar, The Chavez Story, 1972; J. Edgar Hoover, The Man in His Time, 1973; Hit & Run, The Ralph Nader Story, 1975. Contbr. to: Rdrs.' Digest; Nat. Review; Commonweal; etc. Mbrships. incl: Nat. Press Club. Hons. incl: Philolexian Prize for Poetry, 1935, 1938. Address: 825 New Hampshire Ave. N.W., Wash. DC 20037, USA.

TOLIVER, Raymond Frederick, b. 16 Nov. 1914, Ft. Collins, Colo., USA. Aviator; Author. Educ: Colo. State Univ.; Air Command & Staff Coll., 1947; Air War Coll., 1951. Publs: Fighter Aces, 1965; Horrido: Fighter Aces of the Luftwaffe, 1967; German transl., 1972; The Blond Knight of Germany, 1970, German transl., 1971. Address: 5286 Lindley Ave., Encino, CA 91316, USA.

TOLSTOY, Alexandra, b. 1884, Yasnaya Poliana, USSR. Curator, Tolstoy Museum; President, Tolstoy Foundation. Publs: The Tragedy of Tolstoy; I Worked for the Soviets; A Life of my Father, Leo Tolstoy. Contbr. to: Pictorial Review; Russian Review; Russian mags. & newspapers. Address: c/o Tolstoy Foundation Inc., 250 W. 57th St., N.Y., NY 10019, USA.

TOME, Momirovski, b. 4 Apr. 1927, Kičevo, Macedonia, Yugoslavia. Writer. Educ: Schl. Pol. Scis., Belgrade; Fac. of Philos., Skopje. Publs. incl: (travel) Eaves & Sands, 1957; (stories) Steps, 1959; Sin Sunday, 1961; Restlessness, 1969; Years of Insomnia, 1972; (non-fiction) Josip Broz Tito; Jovan Boshkovski; Culture in the Socialist Republic of Macedonia. Contbr. to: (Macedonia) Idnina; Sovremenost; Pogledi; etc.; (Yugoslavia) Savremenik; Stvaranje; etc. Mbrships: PEN; Macedonian Educl. & Cultural Soc. (Pres.). Hons: 13th Nov. Lit. Prize, Skopje, 1961; Climent Ohridski Nat. Lit. Prize, 1974. Address: No. 6, 954 St., Skopje, Yugoslavia.

TOMISON, Maureen (Mrs. Maurice Trowbridge), b. 1941, Falkirk, UK. Political Consultant, Granada Television; Conservative Candidate, Dundee West, 1974. Educ: St. Andrews Univ. Publ: The English Sickness, 1973. Contbr. to: Sun; Daily Sketch; Daily Express; Glasgow Herald; Bristol Evening Post. Address: Oak Dene, Slines Oak Rd., Woldingham, Caterham, Surrey, UK.

TOMLIN, Eric Walter Frederick, pen name STUART, Frederick, b. 30 Jan. 1913, Purley, Surrey, UK. Author. Educ: M.A., Oxford Univ. Publs. incl: The Western Philosophers, 1949; Living & Knowing, 1954; Simone Weil, 1954; Tokyo Essays, 1967; The Last Country, 1974. Contbr. to: Criterion; Scrutiny; Times Lit. Supplement; Spectator; Economist; etc. Mbrships. incl: Fellow, Royal Soc. of Lit., Asiatic Soc.; Aristolelian Soc. Hons: O.B.E., 1959; C.B.E., 1965. Address: Tall Trees, Morwenstow, Cornwall, UK.

TOMLINSON, Jill, b. 27 Dec. 1931, Twickenham, Middlesex, UK. Disabled Housewife; Writer of Children's Books. Publs: The Bus that Went to Church, 1965; Patti Finds an Orchestra, 1966; Pyjams, 1966; Hilda the Hen, 1967; The Owl Who Was Afraid of the Dark, 1968; Lady Bee's Bonnets, 1971; The Cat Who Wanted to go Home, 1972; The Aardvark Who Wasn't Sure, 1973; Penguin's Progress, 1975. Mbrships: Soc. Authors; Disablement Income Grp. Address: Kirbygate, Ducks Hill Rd., Northwood, Middlesex HA6 2NW, UK.

TOMPKINS, Edwin Berkeley, b. 26 Jan. 1935, Phila., Pa., USA. Historian. Educ: B.A., Yale Univ., 1957; M.A., 1960, Ph.D., 1963, Univ. of Pa. Publs: Anti-Imperialism in the United States, 1970; Peaceful Change in Modern Society, 1971; The United Nations in Perspective, 1972; Historical Editing in the United States. Contbr. to var. histl. & lit. jrnls. Mbrships: Am. Histl. Assn.; Am. Acad. of Pol. & Social Sci.; Am. Studies Assn.; Nat. Press Club. Address: National Historical Publications Commission, National Archives Building, Wash. DC 20408, USA.

TONG, Raymond, b. 20 Aug. 1922, Winchester, UK. South West Regional Director, The British Council. Educ: B.Sc.(Econ.), Dip.Ed., London Univ. Publs. incl: Angry Decade, 1950; Ed., African Helicon, African Adventure, African Episodes & African Tales, 1954-57; Figures in Ebony, 1958; Fabled City, 1960. Contbr. to: The Adelphi; Contemp. Review; Review of Engl. Lit.; Poetry Review; Ariel; Time & Tide; Meanjin Quarterly; New Humanist; English; Outposts; The Dublin Mag.; Hist. Today; etc. Mbrships. incl: Royal C'wlth. Soc.; Poetry Soc. Address: c/o Personnel Records, The Brit. Coun., 10 Spring Gdns., London SW1A 2BN, UK.

TONKIN, Leo Sampson, b. 2 Apr. 1937, Suffern, N.Y., USA. Educator. Educ: A.B., 1959, Schl. of Advanced Int. Studies, 1963, Johns Hopkins Univ.; J.D., Harvard Univ. Law Schl., 1962; Ph.D., Thomas Aquinas Coll., SUNY, 1973. Publs: Youth Information Digest, 1974; The Meaningful Alternative — Youth Involvement in the Process of Democracy, 1975. Contbr. to: Potomac Mag.; Chem.

Mag.; Indl. Rsch. Mag.; Johns Hopkins Mag. Mbrships. incl: Nat. Coord. Coun. on Drug Abuse Educ. Recip. Americanism Award, Freedoms Fndn., Valley Forge, 1973. Address: 904 Watergate Apts. S., Wash. DC 20004, USA.

TONOGBANUA, Francisco G., b. 1 Dec. 1900, Binalbagan, Negros Occ., Philippines. College Professor & Dean; Author. Educ: A.A., 1924, Ph.B., 1926, B.S.E., 1928, Philippines Univ.; M.A., Wis., USA, 1930; Ph.D., Santo Tomas, 1950. Publs. incl: (verse tril.) Fallen Leaves, 1951; Green Leaves, 1954; Brown Leaves, 1965; (poetry) 41 Christmases, 1959, 1965; Sonnets 125, 1964, 1966; My God, My Mercy, 1967, 1972; (pedagogic) A Survey of American Literature, 1948; A Survey of English Literature, 2 vols., 1949; A Survey of Filipino Literature, 1956, 4th ed., 1968; (misc.) Filipino Folk Songs, 1956; Across the Pacific, 1928-30, 1965; Cupid to Psyche (essays), 1966. Mbrships: Co-Fndr., U.P. Writers' Club; VP, Philippine Writers' Assn. Hons: Poet Laureate, Cursillo Movement, 1967; Litt.D. Address: 32 Ragang, Manresa, Quezon City, Philippines.

TONSON, Albert Ernest, b. 18 June 1917, Auckland, NZ. Company Director; Editor. Educ: Druleigh Coll. Publs: Our First Hundred Years: An Historical Record of Papatoetoe (co-author & ed.), 1961; Old Manukau, 1966. Contbr. to: NZ Armorist; Horse & Field & others. Mbrships: F.R.G.S.; F.R.S.A.; Fellow, Treas., Heraldry Soc., NZ Br.; Royal Soc. Lit.; Life, NZ Hist. Places Trust; NZ Returned Servicemens Assn.; Auckland Hist. Soc.; Auckland J.P. Assn. Address: 19 Pah Rd., Papatoetoe, Auckland, NZ.

TOONDER, Marten, b. 2 May 1912, Rotterdam, Netherlands. Author; Illustrator. Educ: Acad. Arts, Rotterdam. Publs: Tom Puss Tales, 1949; Tom Puss at the Panto; Tom Puss in Nursery Rhymeland; Als je begrijpt wat ik bedoel, 1967; Geld speelt geen rol, 1968; Zoals mijn goede vader zei, 1969; Een eenvoudige doch voedzame maaltijd, 1970. Contbr. to: Dagens Nyheter (Sweden); Berlinske Tidinge (Denmark); Handelsblad & NRC (Netherlands); Het laatste Nieuws (Belgium). Mbrships: Soc. Dutch Lit.; Authors' Guild. Recip., Kt. Order of Orange-Nassau, 1964. Address: Eyrefield Lodge, Greystones, Co. Wicklow, Repub. of Ireland.

TOPHOFF, Michael, b. 14 Sept. 1939, Bremen, Germany. Author; Psychologist. Educ: Clin. Psychol. Publs: De Falende Stad, 1965; Leeg Te Aanvaarden, 1966; Vertrektijden, 1969; De Nabijheid En De Adem, 1974. Mbrships: PEN; Netherlands Profl. Assn. of Artists. Address: De Loet 272, Castricum, Netherlands.

TORBADO, Jesús, b. 4 Jan. 1943, León, Spain. Educ: Lic. Jrnlsm. Publs: Las Corrupciones, 1966; Historias de amor, 1968; La Construcción del odio, 1968; Tierra mal bautizada, 1970; Moira estuvo aquí, 1972. Contbr. to: Cuadernos Hispanoamericanos; La Estafeta Literaria; Zona Franca; Gentlemen. Hons: Alfaguara Prize, 1965; Hucha de Oro Prize, 1972. Address: Calle S. Vicente 5, Pozuelo-Estación, Madrid 23, Spain.

TORNAI, József, b. 9 Oct. 1927, Dunaharaszti, Hungary. Writer; Poet. Publs: Paradise Bird, 1959; Earth that Reaches Heaven, 1962; You Go & Cry, 1964; Golden Gate, 1967; Timeless Time, 1969; The Name of Idols, 1970; Plucking Out, 1972; Sun-dance, 1975; Transl., The Happy Visions (anthol.). Contbr. to: Contemporary; New Writing; Life & Lit.; Theis-province; New Hungarian Quarterly. Mbrships: Assn. of Hungarian Writers; Art Fndn. of Hungarian People's Repub. Address: Meredek u. 26, 1112 Budapest, Hungary.

TÖRNQVIST, Arne, b. 26 Apr. 1932, Stockholm, Sweden. Playwright. Educ: Arts.D. Publs: (plays) Carl XVI Joseph, 1969; Leo Tolstojs testamente, 1970. Contbr. to: In the New World, 1972; Branting, 1974. Mbrships: Swedish Union of Authors; Swedish Union of Playwrights. Address: Malmgårdsvägen 55, 116 38 Stockholm, Sweden.

TÖRNUDD, Margit, pen name NIININEN, Margit, b. 18 Jan. 1905, Åbo, Finland. Retired. Educ: Ph.D., Univ. of Helsinki, 1956. Publs. incl: Tora Markman (novel), 1936; Sin egen verklighet (short stories), 1949; Värnlösa barn i samhallets vård, 1956. Mbr., Assn. of Swedish Authors in Finland, 1933—. Hons: Prize, Novel Competition, 1936; Prize, Swedish Soc. for Lit. in Finland, 1937; Prizes, Essay Competitions, 1945, 1947, 1949; Prize, Short Story Competition, 1949. Address: Kummingr. 2 F, SF — 00840 Helsingfors 84, Finland.

TORRANCE, (Ellis) Paul, b. 8 Oct. 1915, Milledgeville Ga., USA. Educational Psychologist. Educ: A.A., Ga. Mil. Coll., 1936; A.B., Mercer Univ., 1940; M.A., Univ. of Minn., 1944; Ph.D., Univ. of Mich., 1951. Publs. incl: Education & Talent, 1960; Education & the Creative Potential, 1963; Mental Health & Constructive Behaviour, 1965; Mental Health & Achievement, 1965; Torrance Tests of Creative Thinking, 1966; Issues & Advances in Educational Psychology, 1969; Encouraging Creativity in the Classroom, 1970; Creative Learning & Teaching, 1970; Is Creativity Teachable?, 1973. Contbr. to num. educl. & psychol. jrnls. Recip. var. awards for rsch. Address: Dept. of Educational Psychology, Univ. of Georgia, Athens, GA 30602, USA.

TORRANCE, Thomas Forsyth, b. 30 Aug. 1913, Chengtu, China. University Professor; Author; Editor. Educ: M.A., 1934, B.D., 1937, D.Litt., 1970, Edinburgh Univ., UK; Oriel Coll., Oxford, 1939-40; D.Th., Basel Univ., Switz., 1946. Publs. incl: Conflict & Agreement in the Church, 2 vols., 1959-60; Theology in Reconstruction, 1965; Theological Science, 1969; Space, Time & Incarnation, 1969; God & Rationality, 1971; Theology in Reconciliation, 1975. Contbr. to: Scottish Jrnl. of Theol. (Ed., w. J. K. S. Reid, 1948–); var. theol. jrnls. Hons. incl: M.B.E., 1945; Collins Relig. Book Prize, for Theological Science, 1970; 5 hon. degrees. Address: 37 Braid Farm Rd., Edinburgh EH10 6LE, UK.

TORRIE, James Hirum, b. 8 Aug. 1908, Ft. Macleod, Alberta, Can. Professor of Agronomy. Educ: B.Sc., 1931, M.Sc., 1934, Univ. of Alberta; Ph.D., Univ. of Wis., USA, 1938. Publs: Principles & Procedures of Statistics (w. R. G. D. Steel), 1960; Elementary Statistics (w. R. G. D. Steel), forthcoming. Contbr. of num. papers & reviews to var. sci. jrnls. Mbrships. incl: Fellow, Am. Soc. of Agronomy; Am. Stats. Assn.; Am. Soc. of Biologists; Crop Sci.; Natural Geographic. Recip., sev. rsch. & agricl. awards. Address: 1251 Sweet Briar Road, Madison, WI 53705, USA.

TÓTH, Endre, b. 17 Nov. 1914, Debrecen, Hungary. Editor; Writer. Publs: Egyedül A Tömegben, 1936; Örökké Viharban, 1941; Se Kint, Se Bent, 1944; A Forrás Dala, 1955; Az Elszálló Ifjusághoz, 1960; Mindenért Megfizettem, 1974. Contbr. to: Alföld; Népszava. Mbr., Soc. of Hungarian Authors. Address: Tanacsköztársaság utja 54/a, H-4027 Debrecen, Hungary.

TÓTH, Eszter, b. 26 May 1920, Debrecen, Hungary. Poet. Publs: Meghatott Vitatkozás (Moved Debate), 1948; Ikermonológ (Twin Monologue), 1966; Apu (Daddy, prose), 1971; A Választott Sokaság (The Chosen Crowd), 1974. Contbr. to: Élet és Irodalom (Life & Lit.); Kortárs (Contemporary); Uj Irás (New Scripture). Mbrships: Alliance of Hungarian Writers; PEN. Recip., József Attila Lit. Prize, 1974. Address: H-1065 Budapest, Hajós Utca 14, Hungary.

TOURELL, Wayne, b. 16 May 1941, Mosgiel, Otago, NZ. Film Director. Publs: (plays) The Long Wait, 1966; The Reciprocating Triangle, 1970. Mbrships: TV Producers & Dirs. Assn. (NZ) Inc.; NZ Producers, Dirs. & Writers Inc. Recip., Feltex TV Award for writing & directing 2 part film documentary, Hello Human Being, 1970. Address: 22 Millais St., Grey Lynn, Auckland 2, NZ.

TOURNIER, Michel, b. 19 Dec. 1924, Paris, France. Euthor. Educ: L.ès L.; D.Phil.; L.en D.; Univs. of Tübingen & Sorbonne. Publs: Vendredi ou les Limbes du Pacifique, 1967; Le Roi des Aulnes, 1970. Mbr., Goncourt Acad. Hons: Grand Prix du Roman, French Acad., 1967; Prix Goncourt, 1970. Address: le presbytère, Choisel, 78460 Chevreuse, France.

TOURTELLOT, Arthur Bernon, pen name VERNON, Arthur, b. 23 July 1913, Providence, R.I., USA. Communications Executive. Educ: Harvard Coll.; Oxford, UK. Publs: Be Loved No More, 1938; The History of the Horse, 1940; The Charles, 1941; Woodrow Wilson Today, 1946; An Anatomy of American Politics, 1950; William Diamond's Drum: The Beginning of the War of the American Revolution, 1959; A Bibliography of the Battles of Concord & Lexington, 1960; The Presidents on the Presidency, 1963; Ed., Toward the Wellbeing of Mankind, 1963; Life's Picture History of World War II, 1950. Contbr. to var. publs. Recip., TV award. Address: The Marshes, 40 Compo Beach Rd., Westport, CT 06880, USA.

TOWNEND, Peter Robert Gascoigne, b. 1935, London, UK. Author; Editor. Educ: Christ's Coll., Cambridge; M.A. (Cantab.) Publs: Out of Focus, 1971; Zoom! 1972; Fisheye, 1974; Ed., Lookout on the Costa Del Sol, 1963-66. Mbr., Crime Writers Assn. Agent: Peter Janson-Smith Ltd. Address: 2 Tregunter Rd., London SW10, UK.

TOWNSEND, Elsie Doig, b. 15 Oct. 1908, Far W., Mo., USA. Teacher; Author. Educ: B.S., Ctrl. Mo. State Univ., 1934; M.A., Mont. State Univ., 1960; & studies, Univs. of Mont., Missoula, Kan. City, & Mo., Kan. City. Publs: None to Give Away, 1970; Always the Frontier, 1972; If You Would Learn, Go Teach, 1973. Contbr. to: Stepping Stones; Daily Bread; The Herald; Restoration Witness; Course of Study for Sr. H.S. Engl. for State of Mont. Address: 3141 Santa Fe Ter., Independence, MO 64055, USA.

TOWNSEND, Joan, pen name POMFRET, Joan, b. 23 May 1913, Darwen, Lancs., UK. Freelance Writer. Publs: Summat From Home, 1964; Nowt so Queer, 1969; Lancashire Evergreens, 1969; Twixt Thee & Me, 1973; Mermaid's Moon, 1975. Contbr. to: Lancs. Life; BBC; etc. Mbrships: F.R.S.A.; Lancs. Authors' Assn. (Dpty. Chmn.); Gt. Harwood Male Voice Choir (Pres.); Romantic Novelists' Assn. Hons: Lancs. Authors' Assn. Awards, 1938, 1946, 1947, 1948, 1952, 1953, 1959, 1972; Writer of the Year, 1972; I.W.W.P. Awards, 1972 & 1974. Address: Stoops Farm, Gt. Harwood, nr. Blackburn, Lancs., UK.

TOWNSEND, John Rowe, b. 10 May, 1922, Leeds, UK. Author. Educ: M.A., Emmanuel Coll., Cambridge. Publs: Gumble's Yard (USA title, Trouble in the Jungle), 1961; The Intruder, 1969; Written for Children, 1974. Contbr. to: Guardian; N.Y. Times Book Review; etc. Hons: Silver Pen Award, Engl. PEN Ctr., 1970; Hon. Book Award, Boston Globe, USA, 1970; Edgar Award, Mystery Writers of Am., 1970. Address: 19 Eltisley Ave., Cambridge CB3 9JG, UK.

TOWNSEND, Peter, b. 22 Nov. 1914, Rangoon, Burma. Author. Publs: Earth My Friend, 1960; Duel of Eagles, 1969-70; The Last Emperor, 1975. Contbr. to: Paris Match, France. Address: La Mare aux Oiseaux, 78116 Saint Léger-en-Yvelines, France.

TOWNSEND, (Sir) (Sydney) Lance, b. 17 Dec. 1912, Geelong, Vic., Australia. Professor of Obstetrics & Gynaecology. Educ: M.B., Bach.Surg., 1935, M.D., 1959, Univ of Melbourne; Fellow, Royal Coll. Surgs., Edinburgh, UK, 1947, Royal Australasian Coll. Surgs., 1948, Royal Coll. of Obstrns. & Gynaecols., 1952. Publs. incl: Gynaecology for Students, 1961, 3rd ed., 1974; Obstetrics for Students, 1964, 2nd ed., 1969. Contbr. to: Modern Trends in Obstetrics, 1963; var. med. jrnls. Mbrships. incl: Grand Lodge, Bd. of Benevolence, 1961, & var. sr. offs., ibid., 1964-72. Hons: Fellow, Royal Coll. Physns. & Surgs. of Can., 1970, Coll. Obstrns. & Gynaecols. of S. Africa, 1972, Am. Coll. Obstrns. & Gynaecols., 1974; Kt.Bach., New Yr. Hons. 1971. Address: 28 Ryeburne Ave., Hawthorn E., Victoria, Australia 3123.

TOWNSHEND, Errol Warwick Anthony, b. 2 Feb. 1942, Kingston, Jamaica. Journalist. Educ: B.A., LL.B., Univ. of Western Ont., Can. Publs: Herb McKenley, Olympic Star (w. James Carnegie), 1974. Contbr. to: Radio Jamaica (corres.); Contrast newspaper, Toronto (Ed. Cons.). Address: 80 Blake St., Apt. 1209, Toronto 6, Can.

TOYNBEE, (Theodore), Philip, b. 25 June 1916, Oxford, UK. Journalist. Educ: Christ Church, Oxford Univ., 1935-38. Publs. incl: (novels) The Savage Days, 1937; The Barricades, UK, 1943, USA, 1944; Tea with Mrs. Goodman (as Prothalamium: A Cycle of the Holy Grail, USA), 1947; The Garden to the Sea, UK, 1953, USA, 1954; The Pantaloon series (in verse), 4 vols., 1961-68; Thanatos (w. M. Richardson), 1963; (non-fiction) Friends Apart, 1954; Ed., Fearful Choice, UK, 1958, USA, 1959; Ed., Underdogs, UK, 1961, USA, 1962; Comparing Notes (w. A. Toynbee), 1963. Contbr. to: Observer (Ed. staff, 1950–). Address: The Barn House, Brockweir, Chepstow, Monmouthshire, UK.

TRAAEN, Anna Jorbjorg, b. 4 Apr. 1952, Kongsberg, Norway. Journalist. Contbr. to: Akersus Amtstidende. Address: Norsk Journalistskole, Trondheimsun 84-86, Oslo 5, Norway.

TRACY, Honor Lilbush Wingfield, b. 19 Oct. 1913, Bury St. Edmunds, Suffolk, UK. Author. Publs: Mind You,

I've Said Nothing, 1953; Straight & Narrow Path, 1956; Silk Hats & No Breakfast, 1957; A Number of Things, 1959; First Day of Friday, 1963; Spanish Leaves, 1964; The Beauty of The World, 1967; The Quiet End of Evening, 1972; A Winter in Castille, 1973; In a Year of Grace, 1975. Contbr. to: Horizon; Encounter; Fortnightly; Listener; New Statesman; New Repub.; Atlantic Monthly. Address: Four Chimneys, Achill Sound, Co. Mayo, Repub. of Ireland.

TRACY, (Pauline) Aloise, pen name GAY, Ellen, b. 20 Nov. 1914, Bridgeport, Ill., USA. Teacher; Poet; Author. Educ: B.Ed., Eastern Ill. Univ., 1937; Grad. studies, ibid. & Univ. of Mo.; Cert., Purdue Univ. Publs: His Handiwork, 1954; Memory is a Poet, 1964; The Silken Web, 1965; A Merry Heart, 1966; In Two or Three Tomorrows, 1968; All Flesh Is Grass, 1971; Beyond the Edge, 1973. Contbr. to: Ideals; Economist Newspapers; The PEN Woman. Mbrships. incl: Nat. League of Am. Pen Women; Ill. Woman's Press Assn.; Ill. PEN Women; Nat. Fedn. of Press Women; Charter Mbr., Ill. State Poetry Soc. Address: 447 Chestnut St., Bridgeport, IL 62417, USA.

TRAN, Bich Lan, pen name NGUYÊN SA, b. 1 Mar. 1932, Hanoi, Vietnam. Professor. Educ: Lic. de Philos. Publs: Poems, 1958; Literary & Philosophical Views, 1959; Fleeting Clouds (short stories), 1964; Descartes Under Oriental Eyes, 1967; The Sixties (poems), 1970; A Few Days Working in the Mortuary Company (novel), 1972. Contbr. to: Hien Dai; Sang Tao; Van Hoc. Mbrships: VP, Vietnam Ctr., PEN, 1970-74. Recip., Nat. Lit. Prize. Address: 322 Phan thanh Gian, Saigon X, Vietnam.

TRANTER, Nigel, b. 23 Nov. 1909, Glasgow, UK. Author. Publs: 55 novels, 1936-74, inclng. Robert the Bruce (tril.), 1969-71; The Young Montrose, 1972; Montrose — Captain General, 1973; The Wisest Fool, 1974; (prose) The Fortified House in Scotland, 5 vols., 1962-70; Pegasus Book of Scotland, 1964; Land of the Scots, 1968; The Queen's Scotland, 3 vols. (The Heartland, 1971, The Eastern Counties, 1972, The North & East, 1974). Contbr. to: Scots Mag.; Scottish Field; Scotland's Mag.; Country Life; etc. Mbrships. incl: Hon. Pres., Scottish Ctr., PEN, 1973; former Chmn., Soc. of Authors & Nat. Book League, Scotland. Hons: Chevalier of Order of St. Lazarus of Jerusalem, 1961; M.A., Edinburgh Univ., 1971. Address: Quarry House, Aberlady, E. Lothian, UK.

TRÂN-THI, Thu Vân, pen name NHÃ-CA, b. 20 Oct. 1939, Hué, S. Vietnam. Writer. Publs: 39 books inclng: Poems of Nhã-Ca, 1964; Nightly Thunder of Cannons, 1965; The Mourning Turban for Hué, 1969; Vi O'i, Buộc To'i, 1974, Engl. transl., The Short Timer. Ed., Tụ chủ. Contbr. to: Hiện đại; Tiếng Nói. Mbrships: PEN; Pres. & Fndr., Reader Assn. Hons: Nat. Poetry Prize, 1966; Nat. Novel Prize, 1970. Address: 155 Hoàng Hoa Thám St., Gia-Định, S. Vietnam.

TRAPP, E. Philip, b. 22 Dec. 1923, Akron, Ohio, USA. College Professor. Educ: B.S., Kent State Univ., 1947; M.A., N.M. State Univ., 1948; Ph.D., Ohio State Univ., 1951. Publs: Exceptional Child Research & Theory, 1962, revised ed., 1972. Contbr. to Am. Psychol. Assn. profl. jrnls. Mbrships: Am. Psychol. Assn.; Ark. Psychol. Assn. (Past Pres.); Exec. Comm., Southwestern Psychol. Assn. Recip., Disting. Tchr. & Rsch. Award, Univ. of Ark., 1970. Address: 235 Palmer, Fayetteville, AR 72701, USA.

TRASLER, Gordon Blair, b. 7 Mar. 1929, Bournemouth, UK. University Teacher. Educ: Univ. Coll., Exeter, 1949-55; B.Sc. (London), 1952, Ph.D. (London), 1955; M.A. (Exeter), 1960. Publs: In Place of Parents, 1960; The Explanation of Criminality, 1962; The Shaping of Social Behaviour, 1967; The Formative Years (co-author), 1968. Contbr. to: Brit. Jrnl. Criminol.; Child Care; Nature; Brit. Jrnl. of Psychol.; Howard Jrnl.; Sociol. Review; New Soc.; Handbook of Abnormal Psychol. Mbrships: Fellow, Brit. Psychol. Soc.; Brit. Soc. of Criminol.; Howard League for Penal Reform. Address: Dept. of Psychology, The University, Southampton SO9 5NH, UK.

TRAVER, Robert, pen name of VOELKER, John Donaldson, b. 29 June 1903, Ishpeming, Mich., USA. Writer; Former Prosecuting Attorney. Educ: Northern Mich. Coll. 1922-24; LL.B., Univ. of Mich., 1928. Publs: Troubleshooter, 1943; Danny & the Boys, 1951; Small Town D.A., USA, 1954, UK, 1959; Anatomy of a Murder (novel), USA & UK, 1958; Trout Madness, 1960; Hornstein's Boy (novel), USA & UK, 1962; Anatomy of a Fisherman, 1964; Laughing Whitefish, USA, 1965, UK,

1967; The Jealous Mistress, USA & UK, 1968. Contbr. to: Detroit News (columnist, 1967-69). Recip., LL.D., Northern Mich. Coll., 1958. Address: Deer Lake Rd., Ishpeming, MI 49849, USA.

TRAVERS, Ben, b. 1886. Dramatist; Novelist. Publs. incl: A Cuckoo in the Nest, 1925; Rookery Nook, 1926 (as musical, Popkiss, 1972); Thark, 1927; A Cup of Kindness, 1929; Turkey Time, 1931; Just My Luck, 1932; Hyde Side Up, 1933; Lady in Danger, 1934; Stormy Weather, 1935; Pot Luck, 1936; Dishonour Bright, 1936; Second Best Bed, 1937; Banana Ridge, 1938; Spotted Dick, 1939; She Follows Me About, 1943; Outrageous Fortune, 1947; Wild Horses, 1952; Nun's Veling, 1956; Corker's End, 1969; (TV play) Potter, 1948; (autobiog.) Vale of Laughter, 1957. Address: 29 Watchbell St., Rye, Sussex, UK.

TRAVIS, Falcon, b. Salford, Lancs., UK. Writer. Publs: Grand Howl, 1965; Tawny Talent, 1966; Tawny Trail, 1967; Camping & Hiking, 1968; The Commonwealth Cub Scout Book, 1970; Knight Puzzle Books, 1970-75; Knight Book of Pass-Time Games, 1974; Secret Codes, 1975; Spycroft, 1974. Contbr. to: Boy's Own Paper; Eagle; Scout; Puffin Post; Daily Mail; Punch; Reader's Digest, USA; etc. Address: c/o Brockhampton Press Ltd., Salisbury Rd., Leicester LE1 7QS, UK.

TREADGOLD, Donald Warren, b. 24 Nov. 1922, Silverton, Ore., USA. Professor of Russian History. Educ: B.A., Univ. of Ore., 1943; M.A., Harvard Univ., 1947; D.Phil., Oxford Univ., 1950. Publs: Lenin & His Rivals, 1955; The Great Siberian Migration, 1957; The Development of the USSR (ed.), 1964; Soviet & Chinese Communism (ed.), 1967; Twentieth Century Russia, 3rd ed., 1972; The West in Russia & China, 2 vols., 1973; Ed., Slavic Review. Contbr. to: New Ldr.; New Repub.; Nat. Review; Agricl. Hist.; Am. Histl. Review; Russian Review; etc. Mbrships. incl: Bd. of Dirs., Am. Histl. Assn. Address: 4507 52nd N.E., Seattle, WA, USA.

TREADGOLD, Mary, b. 16 Apr. 1910, London, UK. Author. Educ: St. Paul's Girls' Schl., London; B.A., M.A., Bedford Coll., London Univ. Publs. incl: We Couldn't Leave Dinah, 1941; The Winter Princess, 1962. Mbrships: Soc. Authors; PEN. Recip., Carnegie Medal, 1941. Address: 61 Swan Ct., London SW3, UK.

TREASE, Robert Geoffrey, b. 11 Aug. 1909, Nottingham, UK. Author. Educ: Queen's Coll., Oxford Univ. Publs. incl: Bows Against the Barons, 1934; Cue for Treason, 1940; Tales Out of School, 1949; Snared Nightingale, 1957; This is Your Century, 1965; (autobiogs.) A Whiff of Burnt Boats, 1971; Laughter at the Door, 1974. Mbrships: Soc. Authors (Chmn. Mgmt. Comm., 1972-73, Coun., 1974); PEN. Recip., N.Y. Herald Tribune Award, 1966 for This is Your Century. Address: The Croft, Colwall, Malvern, Worcs. WR13 6EZ, UK.

TREDGOLD, May Arderne, b. 20 Sept. 1901, Cape Town, S. Africa. Journalist. Educ: B.A., Cape Town; Higher Dip.Educ., Rhodesia. Publs: Village of the Sea, 1965; Lucy Frances Nettlefold, 1968. Ed., Bluestocking jrnl. of S. African Assn. Univ. Women. Mbrships: PEN; Histl. Soc. of Cape Town; S. African Archaeol. Soc.; Press Club, London, UK. Address: 8 Bickley Flats, Kenilworth, Cape, Repub. of S. Africa.

TREE, Michael John, b. 6 Dec. 1926, Harrow, UK. Manager. Educ: M.A., Brasenose Coll., Oxford. Publs: Contend No More, 1958; A Career in Architecture (w. Michael Pattrick), 1961; Those Weaker Glories, 1962; The Semi-Detached Affair, 1964. Contbr. to lit. & design mags. Mbrships: Archtl. Assn. (VP, 1971); Johnson Club. Address: 49 Westminster Gdns., London SW1, UK.

TREGIDGO, Philip Sillince, b. 3 Mar. 1926, Portsmouth, UK. Writer. Educ: B.A., 1949, Dip. Ed., 1950, Oxford Univ.; M.A., Reading Univ., 1971. Publs: Practical English Usage, 1959; Background to English, 1961; Practical English 1-5, 1965-66; English for Tanzanian Schools, 1966-68; Longman New Ghana English Course 1-2, 1970-71. Contbr. to: Ghana Tchrs. Jrnl.; Engl. Lang. Tchng. Jrnl. Mbr.; Soc. Authors. Address: Winneba, 11 The Ave., Petersfield, Hants., UK.

TREMAYNE, Sydney, b. 15 Mar. 1912, Ayr, UK. Journalist. Publs: (poetry) Time & the Wind, 1948; The Hardest Freedom, 1951; The Rock & the Bird, 1955; The Swans of Berwick, 1962; The Turning Sky, 1969; Selected & New Poems, 1973. Contbr. to: Listener; Spectator; New

Statesman; etc. Address: Blawan Orchard, Westerham Hill, Kent, UK.

TRENT, Ann, pen names SERNICOLI, Davide; CROSSE, Elaine; CARLTON, Ann; DESANA, Dorothy; BLYTHE, Joyce, b. Gravesend, Kent, UK. Novelist. Publs. incl: A Tangled Web, 1953; Blessed Surrender, 1954; One Love For Ever, 1955; The Road to Romance, 1955; The Unguarded Moment, 1956; My Love, 1956; Escape to Romance, 1957; Lovers' Quest, 1957; Love Under the Stars, 1958; No Other Love, 1959; Moonlight Beguiling, 1959; Jewel of Destiny, 1960; The White Squadron, 1961; The Unforeseen Hazard, 1961. Contbr. to: Melbourne Herald, Aust. Address: Crosselands, Salisbury Rd., Carshalton Beeches, Surrey SM5 3HA, UK.

TRENTO, Joseph John, b. 22 Sept. 1947, L.A., Calif., USA. Journalist; Publisher; Author. Educ: pol. sci., 4 yrs. Publs: The National Aeronautics & Space Administration, 1973, 1974; The Bitter Pill, 1974; The Death Report, 1975. Contbr. to: Parade; Signature; Penthouse; The Nation; True; Wash. Post; radio & TV; etc. Mbrships: Int. Platform Assn.; Nat. VP, Land Equality & Freedom; Exec. Ed., San Diego Confidential. Address: 5211 Chelsea St., La Jolla, CA 92037, USA.

TREVELYAN, Katharine, b. 7 May 1908, Westminster, London, UK. Author. Educ: Somerville Coll., Oxford; Girton Coll., Cambridge. Publs: Unharboured Heaths, 1935; Fool in Love, 1962. Address: Godshill, Fordingbridge, Hants., SP6 2LN, UK.

TREVING, Nils O. B., b. 5 Dec. 1938, Huaroed, Sweden. Executive Director; Author. Educ: B.S.(Jrnlsm.), 1960, B.S.(Social & Pol. Sci.), 1961, Sweden; also studies in USA, 1956-57, Paris, France, Vienna & Austria, 1958. Publs: New Media, 1970; New AV Media, 1971; Mental Pollution, 1972; Print 80, 1973. Contbr. to: Teknisk Tidskrift; Veckans Affaerer. Mbrships. incl: Int. Publrs. Audiovisual Assn.; Former Bd. Mbr., ibid; Swedish Publicists Club; Former Sec., ibid. Address: Skepparg 5, 11452 Stockholm, Sweden.

TREVOR, Elleston, pen names HALL, Adam; SMITH, Caesar; NORTH, Howard; (formerly) SCOTT, Warwick, & RATTRAY, Simon, b. 17 Feb. 1920, Bromley, Kent, UK. Publs. incl: Chorus of Echoes, 1950; The Big Pick-Up, 1955; Gale Force, 1956; The VIP, 1959; Flight of the Phoenix, 1964; Bury Him Among Kings, 1970; (as C. Smith) Heatwave, 1957; (as A. Hall) The Berlin Memorandum, 1964; The Warsaw Document, 1971; The Tango Briefing, 1973; (as H. North) Expressway, 1973 (many of foregoing filmed); (plays) Touch of Purple, 1972; Murder By All Means, 1972. Mbrships. incl: Writers' Guild, GB; Authors' Guild of Am. Hons: Am. Mystery Writers' Award, 1965; Grand Prix de Lit. Policière, France, 1965. Address: 3717 Effingham Pl., L.A., CA 90027, USA.

TREVOR, Meriol, b. 15 Apr. 1919, London, UK. Author. Educ: B.A., Univ. of Oxford. Publs: 30 books inclng. The Arnolds, 1973. Contbr. to: Times Lit. Supplement. Mbrships: F.R.S.L. Authors' Soc.; W. Country The Arnolds, 1973; Contbr. to: Times Lit. Supplement. Mbrships: F.R.S.L. Authors' Soc.; W. Country Writers' Assn. Recip., James Tait Black Mem. Prize for biog., 1962. Address: 70 Great Pulteney St., Bath, Somerset BA2 4DL, UK.

TREVOR, William, b. 24 May 1928, Mitchelstown, Co. Cork, Ireland. Author. Educ: B.A., Trinity Coll., Dublin. Publs: The Old Boys, 1964; The Boarding House, 1965; The Love Department, 1966; The Day We Got Drunk on Cake, 1967; Mrs. Eckdorf in O'Neill's Hotel, 1969; Miss Gomez & the Brethren, 1971; The Ballroom of Romance, 1972; Elizabeth Alone, 1973. Contbr. to jrnls. inclng: Nova; Encounter; London Mag. Mbr., Irish Acad. of Lit. Hons. incl: Hawthorden Prize, 1965. Address: Stentwood House, Dunkeswell Nr. Honiton, Devon, UK.

TRICKETT, Joyce, b. 21 Nov. 1915, Uralla, N.S.W., Australia. Teacher; Broadcaster; Exhibiting Artist. Publs: The 1972. Contbr. to: Aust. Jrnl.; ABC Weekly; Woman; Women's Wkly.; Poetry periodicals. Mbrships: Actors' 1972. Contbr. to: Aust. Jrnl.; ABC Weekly; Woman; Women's Wkly.; Poetry periodicals. Mbrships: Actors' Equity; Musical Assn. of N.S.W. Recip., Prize, for Musical Jenolan Adventure. Address: 23 Lavender Crescent, Lavender Bay, North Sydney, Australia 2060.

TRICKETT, (Mabel) Rachel, b. 20 Dec. 1923, Lathom, Lancs., UK. College Fellow & Tutor. Educ: B.A., 1945, M.A., 1949, Lady Margaret Hall, Oxford Univ. Publs: (novels) The Return Home, 1952; The Course of Love, 1954; Point of Honour, 1958; A Changing Place, 1962; The Elders, 1966; A Visit to Timon, 1969; (plays) Antigone, 1954 (broadcast, 1954); Silas Marner, 1960; (criticism) The Honest Muse: A Study in Augustan Verse, UK & USA, 1967. Contbr. to: Cornhill. Hons: C'wlth. Fund Fellowship, 1949; Rhys Mem. Prize, 1953. Address: St. Hugh's Coll., Oxford, UK.

TRILLING, Lionel, b. 4 July 1905, NYC, USA. Professor of English. Educ: B.A. 1925, M.A. 1926, Ph.D., 1938, Columbia Univ. Publs. incl: Matthew Arnold, 1939, revised ed., 1949; E. M. Forster, USA, 1943, revised ed., 1965, UK, 1944, revised ed., 1967; The Middle of The Journey (novel), USA, 1947, UK, 1948, 1975; The Liberal Imagination, USA, 1950, UK, 1951; A Gathering of Fugitives, USA, 1956, UK, 1957; Beyond Culture, USA, 1965, UK, 1966. Contbr. to: Partisan Review. Mbrships: Nat. Inst. Arts & Letters; Am. Acad. Arts & Scis. Hons: Creative Arts Award, Brandeis Univ., 1968; num. docts. Address: Hamilton Hall, Columbia Univ., N.Y., NY 10027, USA.

TRILLO PAYS, Dionisio Martin Enrique, b. 1909. Author; Librarian. Educ: Univ. of the Republic, Montevideo, Uruguay. Publs: (plays) Medodia, 1940; El patio de los naranjos, 1950; (other publs.) Pompeyo Amargo, 1942; Zarzas, 1944; Estas hojas no caen en otoño, 1946. Contbr. to: Asir, (Ed., 1949—). Mbrships: Nat. Comm. for Archives of Artigas; Coun. on Legal Rights of Authors; Dir., Nat. Lib. of Uruguay. Address: Biblioteca Nacional, Guayabo 1793, Montevideo, Uruguay.

TRIMBLE, Louis Preston, pen name BROCK, Stuart, b. 2 Mar. 1917, Seattle, USA. Associate Professor of Humanities. Educ: B.A. & Ed.M., Eastern Wash. State Coll., Cheney. Publs: 69 books inclng. Anthropol, 1968; The Machine, 1972; The Bodelan Way, 1974; A Reader for Scientific & Technical English, 1975. Contbr. to sev. Machine, 1972; The Bodelan Way, 1974; A Reader for Scientific & Technical English, 1975. Contbr. to sev. profl. & other jrnls. Mbrships: Tchrs. of Engl. as a Second Lang.; Int. Assn. for Tchrs. of Engl. as a For. Lang. Address: 12840 139th Ave. N.E., Kirkland, WA 98033, USA.

TRINQUIER, Roger Paul, b. 20 Mar. 1908, La Beaume, France. Retired Colonel. Educ: French Mil. Schl. Publs: La Guerre Moderne, 1961; Le Coup d'État du 13 Mai 1958, 1962; L'État Nouveau, 1963; Notre Guerre au Katanga, 1963; Modern Warfare, 1963; La Bataille pour l'Election du Président de la République, 1964; Guerre – Subversion – Revolution, 1968. Contbr. to: Le Redressement Economique. Recip., Gen. Chassin Prize for "La Guerre Moderne". Address: 36 rue des Plantes, Paris 14e, France.

TRIPODI, Tony, b. 30 Nov. 1932, Sacramento, Calif., USA. University Professor of Social Work. Educ: B.A., 1954, M.S.W., 1958, Univ. of Calif. Berkeley; D.S.W., Columbia Univ., 1963. Publs: Clinical & Social Judgment, 1966; Exemplars of Social Research, 1969; The Assessment of Social Research, 1969; Social Program Evaluation, 1971; Social Workers at Work, 1972; Uses & Abuses of Social Research in Social Work, 1974. Contbr. to num. profl. jrnls. Mbrships: Nat. Assn. of Social Wkrs.; Acad. of Cert. Social Wkrs.; Am. Psychol. Assn.; AAAS; AAUP. Address: 330 Hazelwood, Ann Arbor, MI 48103, USA.

TRIPP, John, b. 22 July 1927, Bargoed, Wales, UK. Freelance Writer. Educ: Morley Coll., London. Publs: (poetry) Diesel to Yesterday, 1966; The Loss of Ancestry, 1969; The Province of Belief, 1971; Bute Park, 1972; The Inheritance File, 1974. Contbr. to: Poetry Wales; Anglo-Welsh Review; Planet (Lit. Ed.). Mbr., Yr Academi Gymreig (Welsh Acad. of Letters). Hons: Welsh Arts Coun. Bursaries, 1969, 1972. Address: 2 Heol Penyfai, Whitchurch, Cardiff, UK.

TRIPP, Miles Barton, b. 5 May 1923, Ganwick Corner, Herts., UK. Writer. Publs: Faith Is a Windsock, 1952; Kilo Forty, 1963; The Chicken, 1966; The Eighth Passenger, 1969; Five Minutes With a Stranger, 1971. Contbr. to var. mags., etc. Mbrships: Crime Writers' Assn. (Chmn., 1968-69); Detection Club. Soc. of Authors. Address: c/o A. D. Peters & Co., 10 Buckingham St., London WC2N 6BU, UK.

TRISCO, (Rev. Dr.) Robert Frederick, b. 11 Nov. 1929, Chgo., Ill., USA. Professor of Ecclesiastical History; Priest. Educ: B.A., St. Mary of the Lake Sem., Mundelein, Ill., 1951; S.T.L., Pontifical Gregorian Univ., Rome, Italy, 1955; H.E.D., 1962. Publs: The Holy See & the Nascent Church in the Middle Western United also jrnls., encys., & vols. of collected essays. Mbrships: Sec., Am. Cath. Histl. Assn., 1961-. Recip., also jrnls., encys., & vols. of collected essays. Mbrships: Sec., Am. Cath. Histl. Assn., 1961—. Recip., Benemerenti Gold Medal, Pope Pius XII, 1957. Address: Curley Hall, The Catholic Univ. of Am., Wash. DC 20064, USA.

TROCCHI, Alexander, b. 30 July 1925, Glasgow, UK. Writer; Painter & Sculptor. Educ: M.A., Glasgow Univ., 1950. Publs. incl: (novels) The Carnal Days of Helen Seferis, France, 1954, revised ed. USA, 1967; Young Adam, France, 1955, revised ed. UK, 1961; Cain's Book, USA, 1960, UK, 1963; Thongs, USA, 1967; Sappho of Lesbos, UK, 1971; (anthol.) Ed., Writers in Revolt, 1963; (non-fiction) Drugs of the Mind, 1970; (verse) Man of Leisure, 1971; var. transls. Contbr. to: Merlin, & Paris Quarterly (Ed., 1952-55); The Moving Times (Ed.); New Saltire; Evergreen Review; New Writers 3, 1965. Address: c/o Calder & Boyars Ltd., 18 Brewer St., London W1, UK.

TROLLIET, Gilbert, b. 13 June 1910, Chiètres, Switz. Writer; Journalist. Num. publs. incl: Cadran; Vingt Poèmes de Juin; La Bonne Fortune; La Balle au Bond; Prends garde au Jour; Laconiques, 1966; Avec la Rose; Le Fleuve & L'Etre, 1968; Douze Textuels; Fabliaux; Autoscopie, 1969; L'Ancolie; Textuels; Le Calepin, 1973; Visites, 1973. Contbr. to num. jrnls. inclng: Cahiers du Sud; Mercure de France; Cahiers de l'Herne. Mbrships. incl: PEN Int.; Swiss Writers Soc.; Soc. des gens de lettres, Paris; European Community of Writers. Hons. incl: Guillaume Apollinaire Prize, 1957; Schiller Prize, 1968; Grand Broceliande Prize, 1971. Address: 29 Quai des Bergues, 1201 Geneva, Switz.

TROTT, Rosemary Clifford, b. 8 Mar. 1904, Mt. Vernon, N.Y., USA. Author; Poet; Columnist. Educ: Bates Coll., 1942; Columbia Univ., 1947. Publs: Maine Christmas, 1946; Sea Mist & Balsam, 1958; From One Bright Spark, 1959; Blue Through Tears, 1968; By Wind & Water, 1970. Contbr. to: N.Y. Herald Tribune; Nature Mag.; Good Housekeeping; etc. Mbrships: Editl. Bd., Me. Writers' Rsch. Club; Pres., Pine Tree Br., Nat. League of Am. Pen Women; New England Regional Chmn., Nat. Poetry Chmn. & Nat. Lyric Chmn., ibid; Pres., Me. Poetry Day Assn.; Floor Ldr., Third World Congress of Poets, 1976. Recip., num. poetry prizes & awards. Address: Blueberry Hill, Freeport, ME 04032, USA.

TROUNCER, Margaret, b. Paris, France. Writer. Educ: M.A., Oxford Univ., UK. Publs. incl: The Brides Tale, 1950; The Nun, 1953; Madame Elisabeth, 1955; The Reluctant Abbess, 1957; A Grain of Wheat, 1959; Miser of Souls, 1960; A Duchess of Versailles, 1962; The Gentleman Saint, 1963; The Passion of Peter Abélard, 1965; Eleanor, 1967; The Dividing Sword, 1968; Charles de Foucauld, 1969. Contbr. to var. jrnls., etc. Mbr., Engl. Speaking Union. Hons: Prize, Cath. Lit. Fndn., N.Y., 1952; Book Guild & Book Soc. Recommendations. Address: 24 Charles St., Berkeley Sq., London W1X 7HD, UK.

TROYAT, Henri, b. 1 Nov. 1911, Moscow, Russia. Writer. Educ: Lic. in Law. Publs: Faux-Jour, 1935; l'Araigne, 1938; Dostoievsky, 1940; Puchkine, 1946; Tant que la Terre durera, 3 vol., 1950; La Neige en deuil, 1952; Les Semailles & les Moissons, 5 vols., 1958; La Lumière des Justes, 5 vols., 1962; Tolstoi, 1965; Les Eygletière, 3 vol., 1966; Gogol, 1971; Les Héritiers de l'Avenir, 1970; Le Moscovite, 3 vols., 1975. Mbr., Acad. Française. Hons: Prix Goncourt, 1938; Grand Prix de Monaco, 1962. Address: Académie Française, 23 Quai de Conti, 75006 Paris, France.

TRUEBLOOD, Paul Graham, b. 21 Oct. 1905, Macksburg, Iowa, USA. Professor Emeritus of English Literature. Educ: B.A., Willamette Univ., 1928; M.A., 1930, Ph.D., 1935, Duke Univ. Publs: The Flowering of Byron's Genius: Studies in Byron's Don Juan, 1945, 1962; Lord Byron, 1969. Contbr. to: Saturday Review; Keats-Shelley Jrnl.; Mod. Lang. Quarterly; Byron Jrnl. Mbrships: MLA; Keats-Shelley Assn. of Am.; Philol. Assn. Pacific Coast (Exec. Comm., 1964-65); Byron Soc. (Fndg. mbr., Am. Comm.). Recip., num. profl. hons. Address: 2635 Bolton Terrace S., Salem, OR 97302, USA.

TRUMBO, Dalton, b. 9 Dec. 1905, Montrose, Colo., USA. Screenwriter. Educ: Var. Univs., 1924-29. Publs. incl: (novels) Eclipse, UK, 1935; Washington Jitters, USA, 1936; Johnny Got His Gun, USA, 1939; The Remarkable Andrew, USA & UK, 1941; (play) The Biggest Thief In Town, USA, 1949, UK, 1952; (screenplays) Jealousy, 1934; Road Gang, 1936; Kitty Foyle, 1940; Our Vines Have Tender Grapes, 1945; The Brave Ones (as Richard Rich), 1957; Exodus, 1960; The Sandpiper, 1965; The Horseman, 1971; Managing Ed., Hollywood Spectator; Fndg. Ed., Screenwriter. Mbr., Writers Guild of Am. (Dir., 1945). Hons. incl: Acad. Award, 1957. Address: 8710 St. Ives Dr., Los Angeles, CA 90069, USA.

TRUSSLER, Simon, b. 11 June 1942, Tenterden, Kent, UK. Author; Editor of Theatre Quarterly & Theatrefacts. Educ: B.A., 1963; M.A., 1966, Univ. Coll., London. Publs: Theatre at Work, 1967; Eighteenth Century Comedy, 1969; Burlesque Plays of the Eighteenth Century, 1969; The Plays of John Osborne, 1969; The Plays of Arnold Wesker, 1971; The Plays of John Whiting, 1972; The Plays of Harold Pinter, 1973; Ed., Oxford Companion to the Theatre, 4th ed., forthcoming. Contbr. to: Times; Listener; Tribune; Drama Review; TV Today. Mbrships: Brit. Theatre Inst. (Mbr. Coun. Mgmt.); Soc. Authors. Recip., Arts Coun. Award, 1969. Address: Great Robhurst, Woodchurch, Ashford, Kent, UK.

TRYON, Thomas (Tom), b. 14 Jan. 1926, Hartford, Conn., USA. Actor. Educ: B.A., Yale Univ., 1949. Novel: The Other, 1971. Film appearances: Moon Pilot, 1960; The Longest Day, 1962; The Cardinal, 1964; In Harm's Way, 1966; Momento Mori, 1968. Agent: Phyllis Jackson, International Famous Agency Inc. Address: 10661 Lindamere Dr., Bel-Air, CA 90024, USA.

TRYPANIS, Constantine Athanasius, b. 22 Jan. 1909, Chios, Greece. University Professor; Minister of Culture & Sciences, Greek Government. Educ: D.Phil., Univ. of Athens; Univs. of Berlin & Munich, Germany; M.A., D.Litt., Oxford Univ. UK. Publs. incl: Callimachus, 1956; Stones of Troy, 1956; Cocks of Hades, 1958; Sancti Romani Melodi Cantica, vols. I & II (w. P. Maas), 1963-70; Pompeian Dog, 1964; Fourteen Byzantine Cantica, 1968; Penguin Book of Greek Verse, 1971. Contbr. to var. lit. jrnls. Mbrships: Acad. of Athens; F.R.S.; Int. Inst. of Arts & Letters. Recip., Heinemann Award, R.S.L., 1959. Address: 3 Georgiou Nikolaou, Kefisia, Athens, Greece.

TRZECIAKOWSKA, Anna Zofia, pen name PRZEDPELSKA-TRZECIAKOWSKA, Anna, b. 5 July 1927, Warsaw, Poland. Translator of English & American Literature. Educ: Master's degree in philol., Warsaw Univ. Publs. incl: (transls.) Dickens, Nicholas Nickleby, 1953, Old Curiosity Shop, 1963; Jane Austen, Pride & Prejudice, 1956, Persuasion, 1962; George Eliot, The Mill on the Floss, 1960; T. S. Eliot, Cocktail Party, 1959; W. Faulkner, The Reivers, 1966, The Sound & the Fury, 1971; Scott, Guy Mannering; Conrad, Suspense, 1974. Contbr. to: Odra; Literatura na Swiecie. Mbrships: PEN; Polish Writers' Union (Pres., Transls. Club). Recip., Award for Transls., PEN, 1972. Address: Langiewicza 2 m.2, 02-071 Warsaw, Poland.

TSACHEV, Climent, b. 7 Aug. 1925, Obnova, Bulgaria. Writer. Publs: (in Bulgarian) (plays) From Too Much Love, 1959; The Price of Trust, 1969; (prose) A Blessed Life, 1971; Simpler Than The Truth, 1973; Six Weekdays, One Holiday, 1974. Contbr. to: September; Plamak; Literatouren Front. Mbr. Union of Bulgarian Writers. Address: Sofia-18, bul. 9th September, 128, vh.II, Bulgaria.

TSONCHEV, Doncho, b. 27 July 1933, Levski, Bulgaria. Writer. Publs: (in Bulgarian) Red Elephants, 1968; A Novel on Wheels, 1969; Dangerous Types, 1971. Mbrships: PEN; Union of Bulgarian Writers. Recip. Prize of the Bulgarian Writers' Union, 1971. Address: Sofia ul. Yazovrska, 4, Bulgaria.

TSUKAHIRA, Toshio George, b. 22 Dec. 1915, L.A., Calif., USA. Diplomat. Educ: A.A., Meiji Univ., Tokyo, 1936; B.A., 1939, M.A., 1941, UCLA; Ph.D., Harvard Univ., 1951. Publs: The Postwar Strategy of the Japanese Communist Party, 1954; Feudal Control in Tokugawa Japan — The Sankin Kotai System, 1970. Mbrships: Assn. for Asian Studies; Am. Pol. Sci. Assn.; Am. For. Serv. Assn. Address: Dept. of State, Wash. DC 20520, USA.

TUBBS, Douglas Burnell, b. 22 Mar. 1913, London, UK. Writer; Translator. Educ: B.A., Christ's Coll., Cambridge; Harvard Univ., USA. Publs: Vintage Cars, 1959; Kent Pubs,

1964; Transl., The Technique of Motor Racing (by P. Taruffi), 1960; Transl., Works Driver (autobiog. by P. Taruffi), 1962; The Age of Motoring; The Golden Age of Toys; Romantic America; Lancaster Bomber, 1972. Contbr. to: Purnell's 1st World War Hist.; Motor; Autocar; Times; Connoisseur; etc. Address: Winfield House, Crouch, Borough Green, nr. Sevenoaks, Kent, UK.

TUCCI, Niccolò, b. 1 May 1908, Lugano, Switz. (US citizen). Writer. Educ: Doct. Law & Pol. Scis., Florence, Italy, 1933. Publs. incl: (novels) Those of The Lost Continent (Gli Atlantidi; Before My Time, USA, 1962, UK, 1963; Unfinished Funeral, USA, 1964, UK, 1965; Gli Atlantidi, Italy, 1968; Il Muro del Suo Pianto, Italy, 1972; Love & Death, USA, 1973; Guenther, Italy, 1973; (essays) How to Get Away without Murder, 1973. Contbr. to: New Yorker; New Repub.; Village Voice (co-fndr.); Nation; Harper's; etc.; num. Italian papers & mags. Hons. incl: Viareggio Prize, 1956; Bagutta Prize, 1969. Address: 25 E. 67th St., N.Y., NY 10021, USA.

TUCHMAN, Barbara W., b. 30 Jan. 1912. Historian. Educ: B.A., Radcliffe Coll., Cambridge, Mass., USA. Publs: The Lost British Policy, 1938; Bible & Sword, 1956; The Zimmerman Telegram, 1958; The Guns of August, 1962; The Proud Tower, 1966; Stilwell & the American Experience in China 1911-45, 1971. Contbr. to: Nation; New Statesman; & num. mags. & jrnls. Mbrships. incl: Nat. Inst. of Arts & Letters; Pres., Am. Soc. of Histns.; Am. Acad. of Arts & Letters.Hons. incl: Pulitzer Prize, 1963, —72. Address: 875 Park Ave., N.Y., NY 10021, USA.

TUCK, George Ralph, b. 18 Apr. 1923, Burston, Diss, Norfolk, UK. Company Group Chairman & Principal. Publs: Co-author, 150 training modules on management, marketing, sales attitudes & skills training. Contbr. to: BBC (short stories during 1950s); agric. jrnls; bus. mags. Mbrships. incl: Assoc., Guild of Agric. Jrnlsts.; Insts. of Mktng. & Mgmt. Address: "Four Winds", Halesworth Rd., Reydon, Southwold, Suffolk, UK.

TUCKER, Glenn (Irving), b. 30 Nov. 1892, Tampico, Ind., USA. Author. Educ: A.B., DePauw Univ., 1914; B.Litt., Columbia Univ., 1915. Publs. incl: Poltroons & Patriots, 2 vols., 1954; Tecumseh, 1956; High Tide at Gettysburg, 1958; Hancock the Superb, 1960; Chicamauga, 1961; Dawn Like Thunder, 1963; Mad Anthony Wayne & the New Nation, 1973. Contbr. to var. jrnls., encys., etc. Mbrships: Pres., N.C. Lit. & Histl. Assn., 1965, Western N.C. Histl. Soc., 1965. Hons: Mayflower Cup, 1956, 1964, 1966; Thomas Wolfe Mem. Award, 1958, 1966; D.Litt., DePauw Univ., 1960, Univ. of N.C., 1966. Address: Filibuster Hill, Sugar Hollow Rd., Fairview, NC, USA.

TUCKER, William Joseph, pen name SCORPIO, b. 19 Nov. 1896, London, UK. Author. Educ: D.Sc. & Ph.D., Am. Inst. of Applied Psychol., 1937; D.Sc., Temple Bar Coll., 1937. Publs. incl: The 'How' of the Human Mind, 1935; Astromedical Diagnosis, 1959; Astrology & Your Family Tree, 1960; Ptolemaic Astrology, 1962; Astronomy for Students of Astrology, 1963; Astropharmacology, 1966; Genetics & Astrology, 1971. Contbr. to: Sunday Dispatch; astrol. jrnls. Mbrships. incl: Soc. of Authors; Transl. Assn. Recip., Jyothirvibhooshan, All India Jyothisha Seminar, 1966. Address: Tuckers Lodge, 38 Kermoor Ave., Sharples, Bolton, Lancs., UK.

TUCKER, Wilson, b. 23 Nov. 1914, Deer Creek, Ill., USA. Writer. Publs. incl: The City in the Sea, 1951; The Long Loud Silence, 1952; The Time Masters, 1953; The Science Fiction Subtreasury, 1954; Wild Talent, 1954; Time Bomb, 1955; The Man in My Grave, 1956; The Hired Target, 1957; The Lincoln Hunters, 1958; To the Tombaugh Station, 1960; Last Stop, 1963; A Procession of the Damned, 1965; The Warlock, 1967; The Year of the Quiet Sun, 1970; This Witch, 1971; Ice & Iron, 1974. Contbr. to var. lit. jrnls. Mbrships: Sci. Fiction Writers of Am.; Mystery Writers of Am. Address: 34 Greenbriar Drive, Jacksonville, IL 62650, USA.

TUGWELL, Rexford Guy, b. 10 July 1891, Sinclairville, N.Y., USA. Author; Political Scientist. Educ: B.S. Econs., 1915, A.M., 1916, Ph.D., 1922, Univ. of Pa.; Litt.D., Univ. of N.M., 1933. Publs. incl: The Economic Basis of Public Interest, 1922; The Industrial Discipline, 1933; Puerto Rican Public Papers, 1945; The Place of Planning in Society, 1954; The Art of Politics, 1958; The Enlargement of the Presidency, 1960; F.D.R.: Architect of an Era, 1967; The Brains Trust, 1968; Off Course: Truman to Nixon, 1970; In Search of Roosevelt, 1972; Ed., The Presidency

Reappraised, 1974; The Emerging Constitution, 1974. Hons. incl: LL.D., Univ. of Puerto Rico 1953, Univ. of Pa. 1971; Bancroft Award, 1969. Address: Box 4068, Santa Barbara, CA, USA.

TULI, Jozsef, b. 24 Nov. 1927, Döbörhegy, Hungary. Literary Editor, Publishing House of the Hungarian Trade Unions. Educ: Coll. of Theatre & Film. Publs: Bocsánatos bün, 1963; Majd háboru után, 1972. Contbr. to: Kortárs; Képes Ujság. Mbrships: Authors' Assn. of Hungary; Assn. of Hungarian Jrnlsts. Recip., József Attila Prize, 1953. Address: 1027 Budapest, Fö utca 73, Hungary.

TULLETT, James Stuart, b. 24 Apr. 1912, Birmingham, UK. Journalist. Publs: Novels: Tar White, 1961; Yellow Streak, 1962; White Pine, 1963; Red Abbott, 1964; Hunting Black, 1965; Town of Fear, 1972; Non-fiction: Aerial Topdressing in New Zealand, 1967; Nairn Bus to Baghdad, 1970. Contbr. to var. mags. (book reviews), & to NZ Broadcasting Corp. Address: 191 Tukapa St., New Plymouth, NZ.

TULLY, Andrew Frederick, Jr., b. 24 Oct. 1914, Southbridge, Mass., USA. Newspaper Columnist; Author. Publs. incl: Era of Elegance, 1948; A Race of Rebels, 1961; Supreme Court, 1962; Capitol Hill, 1962; Berlin: Story of a Battle, 1964; The FBI's Most Famous Cases, 1965; The Time of The Hawk, 1966; White Tie & Dagger, 1967; The Super Spies, 1969; The Secret War Against Dope, 1973; The Brahmin Arrangement, 1974. Mbrships. incl: Nat. Press Club; Overseas Press Club; Fed. City Club. Hons: Ernie Pyle Award & Headliners Award, 1953. Address: 2104 48th St. N.W., Washington, DC 20007, USA.

TUOHY, Frank (John Francis), b. 2 May 1925, Uckfield, Sussex, UK. Writer; University Professor. Educ: B.A., King's Coll., Cambridge Univ., 1946. Publs: (novels) The Animal Game, UK & USA, 1957; The Warm Nights of January, 1960; The Ice Saints, UK & USA, 1964; (short stories) The Admiral & the Nuns, UK & USA, 1962; Fingers in the Door, UK & USA, 1970; (non-fiction) Portugal, UK, 1969, USA, 1970. Fellow, Royal Soc. Lit. Hons: K. Mansfield Prize, 1960; Travelling Fellowship, Soc. of Authors, 1963; Black Mem. Prize, 1965; Faber Mem. Prize, 1965. Address: c/o Macmillan & Co., Little Essex St., London WC2, UK.

TURBOTT, Evan Graham, b. 27 May 1914, Auckland, NZ. Zoologist; Director, Auckland Institute & Museum. Educ: M.Sc., Univ. of NZ; Fellow, Art Galls. & Mus. Assn. of NZ. Publs: New Zealand Bird Life, 1947; A Field Guide to New Zealand Birds (co-author), 1966, 2nd ed., 1970; A History of the Birds of New Zealand (Ed. & contbr.), 1967. Contbr. papers to ornithol. & natural hist. jrnls. & articles to newspapers & mags. Mbr., Ornithol. Soc. of NZ. Address: 23 Cathedral Pl., Auckland 1, NZ.

TURCO, Lewis Putnam, b. 2 May 1934, Buffalo, N.Y., USA. Professor of English & Writing Arts. Educ: B.A., Univ. of Conn., 1959; M.A., Univ. of Iowa, 1962. Publs: First Poems, 1960; Awaken, Bells Falling, 1968; The Book of Forms, 1968; The Literature of New York, 1970; The Inhabitant, 1970; Pocoangelini: A Fantography, 1971; Poetry, 1973. Contbr. to: New Yorker; Poetry; Saturday Review; Atlantic; New Repub.; Nation; Commonweal; Sewanee Review; Paris Review; Kenyon Review; etc. Mbr., Hon. Soc. of Cymmrodorion, London. Hons. incl: Acad. of Am. Poets Prize, Univ. of Iowa, 1960. Address: 54 W. 8th St., Oswego, NY 13126, USA.

TURK, Frances Mary, b. 14 Apr. 1915, Huntingdon, UK. Novelist; Lecturer; Critic. Publs. incl: Goddess of Threads, 1966; The Rectory at Hay, 1966; Lionel's Story, 1966; Legacy of Love, 1967; The Flowering Field, 1967; The Martin Window, 1968; The Lesley Affair, 1968; Fair Recompense, 1969; For Pity, For Anger, 1970; The Absent Young Man, 1971; Whispers, 1972. Contbr. to var. lit. jrnls. Mbrships: Comm., Romantic Novelists' Assn., 1964-66; Judge, Maj. Award, 1960, 1964; Probationary Award, 1961; Vice-Chmn., Hunts. Art Grp.; Course Ldr., Writers' Summer Schl., 1972, 1974. Address: Hillrise, Buckden, Huntingdon PE18 9UH, UK.

TURKAY, Osman Mustafa, pen name OTCUOGLU, b. 16 Mar. 1927, Kazaphani, Kyrenia, Cyprus. Writer; Journalist. Educ: Schl. of Mod. Langs., Regents St. Polytechnic, London, & London Univ. Publs: 7Telli; Uyurgezer; Beethoven'De Aydinliga Uyanmak; Evrenin Dusunde Gezgin; Kiyamet GÜNÜ Gozlemcileri; Transls. of T. S. Eliot & others into Turkish. Contbr. to var. lit. jrnls.

in Turkey, UK, & USA. Mbrships: London Ctr., PEN; Ctrl. London Br., Nat. Union of Jrnlsts.; Poetry Soc., London; Int. Poetry Soc.; Fndr. Mbr., Centro Studi E Scambi Int., Rome, Italy. Address: 22 Avenue Mansions, Finchley Rd., London NW3, UK.

TURNBULL, Patrick, b. 17 Mar. 1908, Barberton, S. Africa. Author; Former Army Officer. Educ: Royal Mil. Coll., Sandhurst, UK. Publs: The Forgotten Battalion, 1948; The Last of Men, 1960; A Phantom Called Glory, 1961; The Foreign Legion, 1964; One Bullet for the General, 1969; La Porte des Indes, 1970; Napoleon's Second Empress, 1971; Provence, 1972; Eugenie of the French, 1973. Contbr. to: Opera; Brit. Hist. Illustrated; Battle; Cosmopolitan. Mbrships: Burma Star Assn.; Savage Club. Recip., Mil. Cross. Address: 2 Pond Cottages, Chilton, nr. Didcot, Oxon., OX11 0PG, UK.

TURNELL, (George) Martin, b. 23 Mar. 1908, Birmingham, UK. Retired BBC Administrator. Educ: M.A., Corpus Christi Coll., Cambridge Univ., 1927-30; Sorbonne Univ., Paris, France, 1930-31; Solicitor. Publs: The Classical Moment, 1947; The Novel in France, 1950; Baudelaire: A Study of his Poetry, 1953; Jacques Rivière, 1953; The Art of French Fiction, 1959; Modern Literature & Christian Faith, 1961; Jean Racine — Dramatist, 1972; Transl., works by Pascal, Maupassant, Valéry, Sartre, M. Jouhandeau, J-F. Revel. Contbr. to: Times Lit. Supplement; Sunday Telegraph; Encounter; Ency. Britannica; etc. Mbrships: incl: Soc. of Authors; Inst. Français du Royaume-Uni; F.R.S.L., 1973. Address: 37 Smith St., Chelsea, London SW3 4EP, UK.

TURNER, Amédée Edward, b. 26 Mar. 1929, London, UK. Barrister-at-Law. Educ: M.A., Christ Ch., Oxford. Publs: The Law of Trade Secrets, 1962, & supplement, 1968. Mbrships: Patent Bar Assn., London; N.Y. Patent Law Assn.; Carlton Club, London. Hons: Conservative Parly. Cand., Norwich N., Gen. Elections, 1964, 1966, 1970. Address: 3 Montrose Pl., London SW1, UK.

TURNER, Bessye Tobias, b. 10 Oct. 1917, Liberty, Miss., USA. Teacher; Writer. Educ: A.B., Rust Coll., 1939; M.A., Engl., 1954, M.A., Speech, 1964, Columbia Univ. Publs: La Librae: An Anthology of Poetry for Living, 1969; Peace & Love, 1972. Contbr. to: Masters of Mod. Poetry; Enterprise Jrnl.; Miss. Tchrs. Jrnl.; Alcorn Alumni Jrnl.; Quaderni Di Poesi; Poetry Parade. Mbrships: Nat. Coun. of Tchrs. of Engl.; Speech Communication Assn.; Int. Poetry Soc.; N.Y. Poetry Forum. Hons: Cert. of Achievement, Coll. Arts, 1961; Honorable Mention, N.Y. Poetry Forum, 1974. Address: 829 Wall St., McComb, MS 39648, USA.

TURNER, Ernest Sackville, b. 17 Nov. 1909, Liverpool, UK. Author. Publs: Boys Will Be Boys, 1948; Roads to Ruin, 1950; The Shocking History of Advertising, 1952; A History of Courting, 1954; The Court of St. James's, 1959; What the Butler Saw, 1962; May It Please Your Lordship, 1971. Contbr. to: Punch; Listener; Sunday Telegraph. Mbr., London Press Club. Address: 21 Woburn Ct., Stanmore Rd., Richmond, Surrey, UK.

TURNER, James Ernest, b. 16 Jan. 1909, Foots Cray, Kent, UK. Author. Educ: Queen's Coll., Oxford Univ. Publs: (poems) The Interior Diagram, 1960; The Accident, 1966; (novel) The Crimson Moth, 1962; (autobiog.) 7 Gardens for Catherine, 1968; (ghost story) Staircase to the Sea, 1974. Contbr. to: Daily Telegraph Mag.; Poetry Review; Contemporary Review; Listener; Times Lit. Supplement. Mbr., BBC Advsry. Coun. for S.W. Address: Parsonville, St. Teath, Bodmin, Cornwall, UK.

TURNER, John Frayn, b. 9 Aug. 1923, Portsmouth, UK. Writer; Civil Servant. Publs: Service Most Silent, 1955; VCs of the Royal Navy, 1956; Prisoner at Large, 1957; Hovering Angels, 1957; Periscope Patrol, 1957; Invasion '44, 1959; VCs of the Air, 1960; Battle Stations, 1960; Highly Explosive, 1961; The Blinding Flash, 1962; VCs of the Army, 1962; A Girl Called Johnnie, 1963; Famous Air Battles, 1963; special research for Fight for the Sky by Douglas Bader, 1973; Destination Berchtesgaden, 1975; British Aircraft of World War 2, 1975. Address: 9 Southbury Lawn Rd., Guildford, Surrey, UK.

TURNER, Justin George, b. 5 Nov. 1898, Chgo., Ill., USA. Investment Executive; Historian. Educ: LL.B., DePaul Univ., 1920; LL.D., Lincoln Coll., 1956; L.M.D., Univ. of Judaism, 1960. Publs: Mary Lincoln, Her Life & Letters, 1972; Noah Brooks; American History & Life. Contbr. to num. hist. jrnls. & reviews. Mbrships. incl: Chair,

Lib. Comm., Univ. of Judaism, L.A., USA; Fellow, Pierpont Morgan Lib., N.Y.; Trustee, Nat. Fndn. for Jewish Culture; MLA of Am. Hons: Lincoln Dip. Hon., Lincoln Mem. Univ., 1962; Mary Lincoln as Best Biog. of 1972, Chgo. Friends of Lit. Address: 1115 S. Elm Drive, Beverly Hills, CA 90212, USA.

TURNER, Roger Newman, b. 29 Apr. 1940, Radlett, Herts., UK. Naturopath; Osteopath; Acupuncturist. Educ: Dip. Osteopathy, Dip. Naturopathy, Brit. Coll. Naturopathy & Osteopathy; Lic. Acupuncture, Coll. Acupuncture. Publs: Naturopathic First Aid, 1969; Diets to Help Hay Fever & Sinusitis, 1970; Diets to Help Asthma & Bronchitis, 1970; Diets to Help Heart Disease, 1971; Slimmers Guide to Calories, 1974. Contbr. to: Brit. Naturopathic Jrnl.; Jrnl. Rsch. Soc. for Natural Therapeutics. Mbrships: Brit. Naturopathic & Osteopathic Assn.; Acupuncture Assn. & Register; Rsch. Soc. for Natural Therapeutics (Hon. Sec. 1966-75, VP 1974-75). Address: 111 Norton Way S., Letchworth, Herts., UK.

TURNER, Thomas Bourne, b. 28 Jan. 1902, Prince Frederick, Md., USA. Medical Educator. Educ: B.S., St. John's Coll., Annapolis, 1921; M.D., Univ. of Md. Schl. of Med., 1925. Publs: Biology of the Treponematoses (w. David H. Hollander), 1957; Fundamentals of Medical Education, 1963; Heritage of Excellence — The Johns Hopkins Medical Institutions 1914-1947, 1974. Contbr. to sci. publs. Mbr., acad. & profl. orgs. Recip., hon. Sc.D., Univ. of Md., 1966. Address: 1426 Park Ave., Baltimore, MD 21217, USA.

TURNER, William Oliver, b. Tacoma, Wash., USA. Writer. Educ: B.A., Knox Coll., Galesburg, Ill. Publs., 18 novels inclng: Mayberly's Kill (motion picture in preparation); Call the Beast Thy Brother, 1973; Medicine Creek, 1974. Mbr., former Pres., Western Writers of Am. Address: c/o Harold Matson Co., 22 E. 40th St., N.Y., NY 10016, USA.

TURNER, William Price (Bill), b. 14 Aug. 1927, York, UK. Writer. Publs: (fiction) Bound to Die, 1967; Sex Trap, 1968; Circle of Squares, 1969; Another Little Death, 1970; Soldier's Women, 1972; Hot-Foot, 1973; (poetry) The Rudiment of an Eye, 1956; The Flying Corset, 1962; Baldy Bane, 1967; The Moral Rocking-Horse, 1970. Contbr. to: Yorkshire Post; Scotsman. Hons: Gregory Fellowship in Poetry, Leeds Univ., 1960-62; Publs. Award, Scottish Arts Coun., 1970; Fellowship in Creative Writing, Glasgow Univ., 1973-75. Address: 55 Cecil St., Glasgow G12 8RW, UK.

TURNHEIM, Fred-Sergej, b. 8 Sept. 1949, Vienna, Austria. Chief Editor; Journalist; Cameraman. Educ: Studies in Communications & the Mass Media. Publs: (film scripts) Unser Schritt ins Leben, 1966; Helmut Kurz-Goldenstein, 1971; Vietnam — Dein Leben, 1972; Am Beispiel des T.aus Bonn, 1973; Bertold Brecht — Liturgie vom Hauch, 1974. Contbr. to: Ed.-in-Chief, Anstoss i Argumente (mag.), Vienna; Chief Ed., Anstoss-background Econ. Serv., Vienna. Mbrships: Union of Jrnlsts.; Viennese Press Club "Concordia"; Bd. of Curators, Austrian Press Cards. Address: A-1210 Wien, Ruthnergasse 56-60, 15/2, Austria.

TURNLEY, Jean Ethel, b. 12 Apr. 1918, Diggers Rest, Vic., Australia. Writer. Publs: The Wife Takes a Child, 1957; Much Less a Slave, 1974. Contbr. to: Colliers (USA); Engl. Womans Weekly; Womans Own; Womens Realm; Homes & Gardens; Housewife; New Strand; Scottish Chambers; Irish Model Housekeeping; Aust. Womens Weekly; Womens Day; New Idea; Pol. Mbrships: Aust. Soc. of Authors; Fellowship of Aust. Writers; Soc. of Women Writers; Dante Alighieri Soc., Melbourne Br. Address: 3 Creswick St., Hawthorne, Australia 3122.

TURP, Ralph K., b. 21 July 1911, May's Landing, N.J., USA. Educator; School Administrator. Educ: LL.B., S. Jersey Law Schl., Camden, N.J., 1937; B.S. in Educ., 1954; Ed.M., 1957; Ed.D., Rutgers State Univ., N.B., N.J., 1967; J.D., Rutgers Schl. of Law, Camden, N.J., 1970. Publs: The Newark, New Jersey Public Schools: 1850-1965, 1967; West Jersey: Under Four Flags, 1975. Mbrships: Pres., Irvington Prins.' Assn.; Radio & TV Commn., N.J. Educ. Assn. Address: 111 Starboard St., Forked River, NJ 08731, USA.

TURTON, Godfrey Edmund, b. 4 Jan. 1901, Kildale, Yorks., UK. Author. Educ: Eton Coll.; B.A., Balliol Coll., Oxford. Publs: (fiction) My Lord of Canterbury, 1967; The

Emperor Arthur, 1968; The Devil's Churchyard, 1970; The Festival of Flora, 1972; (history) The Dragon's Breed, 1969; The Syrian Princesses, 1974. Address: 2 Linton Rd., Oxford, UK.

TURZŬN-ZADDÉ, Mirzo, b. 5 Sept. 1911, Tadzhik, USSR. Writer; Poet. Educ: Tadzhik Educ. Inst. Publs: (poetry) Spring & Autumn, 1937; Indian Songs, 1948; Hissar Valley; Child of his Fatherland; Tahir & Zukhra; I am from the Free East, 1951; Hasan Arobakesh, 1954; Voice of Asia, 1957; My Dear, 1960; Selected Works, 3 vols., 1960; Path of a Sun Ray, 1964; Epoch, Life and Creative Work, 1965; The Globe, 1966; (play) The Sentence, 1934. Mbrships. incl: Lenin Prize Comm. Hons. incl: J. Nehru Prize; Order of Lenin (4 times); State Prize in Lit. Address: Tadzhik Union of Writers, Dushanbe, USSR.

TUSIANI, Joseph, b. 14 Jan. 1924, San Marco Lamis, Italy. University Professor. Educ: Ph.D., Univ. of Naples; Litt.D., Coll. of Mt. St. Vincent. Publs: The Complete Poems of Michelangelo, 1960; Rind & All (poems), 1962; The Fifth Season (poems), 1965; Tasso's Jerusalem Delivered, 1970; Italian Poets of the Renaissance, 1971; The Age of Dante, 1974; From Marino to Marinetti, 1974. Contbr. to: N.Y. Times; New Yorker; Cath. World; Sign; Poetry Review; N.Y. Herald Tribune; La Parola; Voices; Forum Italicum; etc. Hons: Greenwood Prize, 1956; Alice Fay di Castagnola Award, 1969; "Spirit" Gold Medal for Poetry, 1969; Kt., Govt. of Italy, 1973. Address: 553 E. 188th St., Bronx, NY 10458, USA.

TUTTON, Barbara Ivy Curtis, b. 6 Aug. 1914, Romford, UK. Writer. Publs: (for children) Mystery at Bracken Dale, 1960; The Riddle of the Allabones, 1964; (novels) Take Me Alive, 1961; Rich To Die, 1962; Black Widow, 1963; Plague Spot, 1965. Contbr. to John Creasey Mystery Mag. Mbr., Soc. for Psychical Rsch. Address: Wall Nooks, Belper, Derbyshire, UK.

TUTUNJIAN, Jerry Jirair, b. 23 Nov. 1945, Jerusalem, Jordan. Managing Editor. Educ: Jrnlsm.Dip.; B.A., Jrnlsm. Contbr. to: Can. Motorist Mag.; Tamarack Review. Mbr., Toronto Press Club. Hons: Graphic Arts, 1971; N.C. Tourism Award; Cert. of Merit, Travel Ind. Assn. of Can. Address: 2 Carlton St., Toronto, Ont. M5B.1K4, Canada.

TUTUOLA, Amos, b. June 1920, Abeokuta, Nigeria. Broadcasting Company Officer. Publs: (novels) The Palm-Wine Drinkard & His Dead Palm-Wine Tapster in the Dead's Town, UK, 1952, USA, 1953; My Life in the Bush of Ghosts, UK & USA, 1954; Simbi & the Satyr of the Dark Jungle, 1955; The Brave African Huntress, UK & USA, 1958; The Feather Woman of the Jungle, 1962; Abaiyi & His Inherited Poverty, 1967. Mbr., Mbari Club of Nigerian Writers (Fndr.). Address: c/o Nigerian Broadcasting Co., Broadcasting House, Ibadan, Nigeria.

TVEITEN, Hallvard, b. 21 June 1901, Agder, Norway. Author. Educ: Tchr.'s Schl.; Oslo & Oxford Univs. Publs: Folk og Sjel, vols. I-IV (in Norwegian); Fjellharpa; Tun og Hjarta; Det heilage riket; Himmel og Jord; Det skånska folks historia (in Swedish); Skånska socknars (parochial) historia, vols. 1-12 (in Swedish); Norréne (Norse) Skaldekvad, vols. I-III (transl. Norwegian); Engelsk Harpe; Klarsisk engelsk lyrik frå William Blake til Kipling. Mbrships. incl: Swedish Union of Authors. Hons: Längmanska Kulturfondens pris, 1971; Stipendium, Sveriges Kulturfond; 1973; Diplom, Sydvenska Kulturförsningen, 1970. Address: Odengatan 84, 241 00 Eslöv, Sweden.

TWAROCH, Johannes Nepomxuk, b. 12 Mar. 1942, Weleschin, Czech. Dramatist. Educ: Mag.phil., Univ. of Vienna; Art Educ., Acad. of Plastic Arts, Vienna. Publs: (poetry) 32 Gedichte, 1963; Spiegel des Mondes (Mirror of the Moon), 1963; Mitteilung vom Zwischenreich, Etcetera 3 (Messages from the Twilight Zone, Etcetera 3), 1968; Kennkarte (Identity Card), 1970; (play) 15-07, 1970; (novel) I Korinther 13 (I Corinthians 13), 1975. Contbr. to: Kleine Zeitung, Graz; Wiener Zeitung; Arbeiter-Zeitung, Vienna; Academia. Mbrships: Chmn., Union Cath. Writers of Austria; PEN. Hons: Lyric Poetry Prize, Anstoss Mag., 1968; Prize, Austrian Nat. Bank, 1973. Address: 1120 Vienna, Schwenkgasse 16, Austria.

TYLER, Anne, b. 25 Oct. 1941, Mpls., Minn., USA. Writer. Educ: B.A., Duke Univ., N C., 1961; Columbia Univ., 1961-62. Publs: (novels) If Morning Ever Comes, USA, 1964, UK, 1965; The Tin Can Tree, USA, 1965, UK, 1966; A Slipping Down Life, 1970. Contbr. to: Seventeen;

Saturday Evening Post; Antioch Review; Harper's; Reporter; New Yorker; McCall's. Address: 222 Tunbridge Rd., Balt., MD 21212, USA.

TYNAN, Kenneth Peacock, b. 2 Apr. 1927, Birmingham, UK. Writer; Critic. Educ: B.A., Magdalen Coll., Oxford. Publs: He That Plays The King, 1950; Persona Grata (w. Cecil Beaton), 1953; Alec Guinness, 1953; Bull Fever, 1955; Curtains, 1961; Tynan Right & Left, 1967; (plays) The Quest for Corbett (w. Harold Lang), 1956; Oh Calcutta, 1969; (film) Macbeth (w. Roman Polanski), 1970. Contbr. to: Spectator; Evening Standard; Daily Sketch; Observer; New Yorker. F.R.S.L. Address: 20 Thurloe Sq., London SW7, UK.

TYSDAHL, Björn Johan, b. 20 Oct. 1933, Oslo, Norway. Reader in English Literature. Educ: Cand. philol. (Oslo), 1959, Dr. Philos. (Oslo), 1968. Publs: Joyce & Ibsen, 1968; Verdens Litteraturhistorie, Vols. 11 & 12 (co-author), 1974. Contbr. to: James Joyce Quarterly; Engl. Studies; Edda (Oslo). Address: British Institute, Univ. of Oslo, Blindern, Oslo 3, Norway.

U

UGIDOS, José, b. 11 Dec. 1900, Santander, Spain. Journalist; Lecturer. Educ: Santander Nat. Inst., Comillas Univ. Publs: Sixteen One-Act Plays; Spanish Three Spanish Plays. Contbr. to: Siluetas; Adriane; Evelyn; Lotty; etc. Mbrships: PEN; Aslib; Hispanic Coun., London; Inst. of Jrnlsts., London; Critics' Circle, London; Inst. of Linguistics, London; For. Press Assn., London; Int. Inst. Arts & Letters. Address: 7 The Close, Off Pampisford Rd., Purley, Surrey, UK.

UHRMAN, Celia, b. 14 May 1927, New London, Conn., USA. Educator; Artist; Writer; Poet. Educ: B.A., 1958, M.A., 1953, Bklyn. Coll.; postgrad. studies, Tchrs. Coll., Columbia Univ., 1961, CUNY, 1966, & Bklyn. Mus. Art Schl., 1956-57. Publs: Poetic Ponderances, 1969; A Pause for Poetry, 1970; Poetic Love Fancies, 1970; A Pause for Poetry for Children, 1973; The Chimps are Coming, 1975. Contbr. to num. jrnls. & anthols. Mbrships. incl: World Poetry Soc. Intercontinental. Recip., num. hons. & awards. Address: 1655 Flatbush Ave., Studio B811, Apt. C2010, Brooklyn, NY 11210, USA.

ULČ, Otto, b. 16 Mar. 1930, Pilsen, Czech. University Teacher. Educ: Dr. Jur., Charles Univ., Prague, 1953; M.A., 1961, Ph.D., 1964, Columbia Univ., N.Y. Publs: (in Czech.) Small Confessions of a District Judge, 1974; The Judge in a Communist State, 1972; Politics in Czechoslovakia, 1974. Contbr. to: Am. Pol. Sci. Review; Am. Jrnl. Comp. Law; Problems Communism; Studies Comp. Communism; Survey, London; Soviet Studies; Jrnl. Pols.; E. European Quarterly; etc. Mbrships: Am. Assn. Advancement Slavic Studies (Mbr. Educ. Comm.); Am. Pol. Sci. Assn.; Czech. Soc. Arts & Scis. in Am. Address: 124 Martha Rd., Binghamton, NY 13903, USA.

ULLÉN, Marian Rittsel, b. 20 Jan. 1934, Skövde, Sweden. Antiquarian w. Royal Swedish Academy of Letters, History & Antiquities. Educ: Ph.D. Publs: 8 vols. in "The Churches of Sweden, an Art Historical Inventory", covering Växjö Cathedral & chs. in Harestad, Torsby, Lycke, Sjösas, Drev, Hornaryd, Eke, Dädesjö, Gramhult, Nottebäck, Åseda, Alighult & Närke, published by Royal Swedish Acad. of Letters, Hist. & Antiquities, 1967-74. Contbr. to: Allhems, Svenskt konstnarslexikon; Kulturhistoriskt lexicon för nordisk medeltid. Mbr., Swedish Authors' League. Address: Bagarfruvägen 67, S–12355 Farsta, Sweden.

ULLMANN, Stephen, b. 13 June 1914, Budapest, Hungary. Professor of Romance Languages, University of Oxford; Fellow of Trinity College, Oxford. Educ: Modern Langs., 1932-36, Ph.D., 1936, Univ. Budapest; D.Litt., Univ. Glasgow, 1949; M.A., Oxford Univ., 1968. Publs. incl: Words & Their Use, 1951; Précis de Semantique Francaise, 1952; Style in the French Novel, 1957; The

Image in the Modern French Novel, 1960; Semantics, 1962; Language & Style, 1964; Meaning & Style, 1973. Contbr. to num. acad. jrnls. Mbrships. incl: Philol. Soc. (Pres., 1970-76); Modern Lang. Assn. (Pres., 1973). Hons: Fellow & Diamond Jubilee Gold Medallist, Inst. Linguists; Sir D. Owen Evans Mem. Lectr., Univ. Coll. Wales, Aberystwyth, 1972. Address: 128 Evans Lane, Kidlington, Oxford OX5 2JB, UK.

ULLMANN, Walter, b. 1910, Pulkau, Austria. Professor of Medieval History, University of Cambridge; Fellow of Trinity College, Cambridge. Educ: Univs. of Vienna, Innsbruck, Munich; M.A., Litt.D., Cambridge Univ., UK. Publs. incl: The Medieval Idea of Law, 1946; The Growth of Papal Government in the Middle Ages, 1955, 4th ed., 1970, revised German transl., 1960; Principles of Government & Politics in the Middle Ages, 1961, 3rd ed., 1974 & for. eds.; A History of Political Ideas in the Middle Ages (paperback), 1965, 3rd ed., 1970; Individual & Society in the Middle Ages, 1967; The Carlingian Renaissance, 1969; A Short History of the Papacy in the Middle Ages, 1972, 1974. Contbr. to num. profl. jrnls. & publs., UK & Europe. Mbrships: Fellow, Brit. Acad.; Eccles. Hist. Soc. (Pres., 1969-70). Address: Trinity Coll., Cambridge CB2 1TQ, UK.

ULLRICH, Hermann Joseph, b. 15 Aug. 1888, Mödling, Austria. Writer on Music; Former 2nd President of Austrian Supreme Court of Justice. Educ: Univ. of Vienna; Acad. of Music Mozarteum, Salzburg. Publs: Salzburg, Bildnis einer Stadt, 1947; Fortschritt und Tradition. Ten Years of Music in Vienna (1945-1955), 1956; Julius Bitner, A Monography, 1968; A. J. Becher, Minstrel of the Viennese Revolution of 1848, 1974. Contbr. to: Österr. Musikzeitschrift. Mbrships: Gesellschaft der Musikfreunde, Vienna; Gesellschaft für Musikwissenschaft, Vienna; VP, Wiener Mozartgemeinde. Recip., Austrian Cross, Litteris et artibus. Address: Döblinger Hauptstrasse 32, A 1190 Vienna, Austria.

ULRICH, Betty Garton, b. 28 Oct. 1919, Indpls., Ind., USA. Writer. Educ: B.S., Univ. of Wis. Publs: A Way We Go, 1970; Every Day With God, 1972. Contbr. to: Christian Herald; The Lutheran; Jrnslm. Educator. Address: 1608 Deerwood Dr., South St. Paul, MN 55075, USA.

ULUC, Dogan, b. 18 Aug. 1935, Istanbul, Turkey. Journalist. Educ: Law Schl., Istanbul Univ. Publs. incl: Publr. & Ed., United Nations Diplomat Magazine, 1970-71, Anatavan Newspaper, 1971-73, Turkey Today, 1972, Fifty Years a Republic, Turkey Today. Contbr. to: Hurriyet daily newspaper; Parade Mag. Mbrships: UN Corres's. Assn., N.Y.; For. Press Assn., N.Y.; Istanbul Gazeteciler Cemiyeti, Istanbul; Int. Press Inst.; For. Press Assn., London, until 1970. Address: UN Press Sect., Rm. 371, United Nations, N.Y., NY 10017, USA.

ULVENSTAM, Lars, b. 28 Jan. 1921, Ulvesund, Ytterby, Sweden. TV Procucer; Author. Educ: Ph.D. Publs: Wait Till Springtime Comes (novel), 1946; Harry Martinson (biog.), 1950; The Elderly Selma Lagerlof, 1955; Gothenburg — The City & Its People, 1963; TV — Idiotbox or Alarmclock, 1967; Harlem Harlem, 1971. Mbrships. incl: Writers' Guild, V.P., 1969-72. Address: Prästgatan 46, 111 29 Stockholm, Sweden.

UNDERWOOD, Michael, b. 2 June 1916, Worthing, UK. Barrister, Government Legal Service. Educ: M.A., Univ. of Oxford. Author, 24 crime novels, 1954-75. Mbrships: Detection Club; Chmn., Crime Writers' Assn., 1966-67. Address: 1 Riverbank, Datchet, Slough SL3 9BY, UK.

UNDERWOOD, Peter, pen name ALLAN, Peter, b. 1923, Letchworth Garden City, UK. Lecturer; Psychical Researcher; Consultant & Adviser, BBC & ITV. Publs: The Ghost Club, 1958; A Gazetteer of British Ghosts; Into the Occult, 1972; Horror Man — The Life of Boris Karloff, UK 1972; Karloff, USA 1972; Gazetteer of Scottish & Irish Ghosts, 1973; A Host of Hauntings, 1973; The Ghosts of Borley, 1973; Haunted London, 1973; Gazetteer of Scottish Ghosts, 1974. Contbr. to: Everyman's Ency.; Occult Review; Psychic Rschr.; Proceedings & Jrnl., Soc. of Psychical Rsch.; Publisher; etc. Mbrships. incl: VP, Unitarian Soc. for Psychical Studies; Brit. Film Inst.; Folklore Soc.; Ghost Club (Pres. & Chmn., 1960—); Soc. of Authors; PEN. Address: c/o Savage Club, 86 St. James's St., London SW1, UK.

UNGER, Alfred Herman, b. 20 Jan. 1902, Hohensalza, Germany. Dramatist; Novelist; Essayist; Television, Radio & Film Scenario Writer; Radio Commentator. Educ: Ph.D.,

Berlin Univ. Publs. incl: Diw Geschichten um den Grossen Nazarener (novel), 1926; Disraelie, der Jüdische Lord (play), 1930; Phryne the Courtesan (play), 1948; Die Berühmte Grafin Hatzfeld (play), 1961; Kurz Wie Ein Traum (play), 1962; num. German transls. of plays by Terence Rattigan, Charles Morgan, Peter Ustinov, etc. Contbr. to: BBC London; Swiss Radio; Westdeutscher Rundfunk; Deutschlandfunk. Mbr., num. lit. orgs. Hons. incl: Schiller Prize; 1st Class Order of Merit, German Fed. Repub. Address: 27 Daleham Gdns., London NW3, UK.

UNGER, Madeline, pen name KING, M. Elizabeth, b. 6 Mar. 1934, Westchester Co., N.Y., USA. Writer. Educ: B.A.; M.A., Fordham Univ., Bronx, N.Y. Publs: Dolly Morton, 1971; Hooker, 1974. Contbr. to: Ticketron Entertainment Mag. (Dining Ed.); Spotlight Mag. (columnist); Show Mag.; Single; Cosmopolitan; & other maj. mags. Mbrships. incl: Authors' Guild; Soc. of Mag. Writers; Ed., City Record, NYC (by appointment of the Mayor), 1974. Address: 320 E. 54th St., N.Y., NY 10022, USA.

UNGER, Merrill F(rederick), b. 16 July 1909, Balt., Md., USA. Professor Emeritus of Old Testament; Writer; Lecturer. Educ: A.B.(Hons.), 1930, Ph.D., 1947, Johns Hopkins Univ.; Th.M.(magna cum laude), 1944, Th.D.(magna cum laude), 1947. Dallas Theol. Sem. Publs. incl: Introductory Guide to The Old Testament, 1952, 10th ed., 1974; Archaeology & The Old Testament, 1954, 15th ed., 1974; Unger's Bible Dictionary, 1957, 21st ed., 1975; Unger's Bible Handbook, 1967, 7th ed., 1974; Unger's Guide to The Bible, 1974; Baptism & Gifts of The Holy Spirit, 1974. Hons. incl: Theol. Author of The Quarter Century, Zondervan's 25th Anniversary Award. Address: Bird Haven Estate, Route 2, Box 196A, Severna Park, MD 21146, USA.

UNGVÁRI, Tamás, b. 25 Sept. 1930, Budapest, Hungary. Professor of Literature; Publisher. Educ: M.A. & Ph.D., Univ. of Budapest; Clare Hall & Churchill Coll., Cambridge Univ., UK. Publs: Henry Fielding (biog.), 1955; Thackeray (biog.), 1956; Poetica (handbook of aesthetics), 1968; Tibor Déry (w. Georg Lukacs, in German), 1969; The History of Counterculture, 1974. Contbr. to jrnls. incling: Jrnl. of European Studies, Univ. of E. Anglia, Norwich (on Bd. of Eds.). Mbr., Exec. Comm., Hungarian Ctr., PEN. Address: Apostol u. 9/a, 1023, Budapest, Hungary.

UNKOVIC, Charles M., b. 14 Mar. 1922, Pittsburgh, Pa., USA. University Professor & Administrator; Author. Educ: B.A., 1950, M.A., 1951, Univ. of Pitts.; Ph.D., 1961. Publs: Psychology & Sociology: An Integrated Approach (w. George Kaluger), 1968; Perspective: An Introduction to Sociology (w. Burton Wright & John Weiss), 1974. Contbr. to: Crime & Delinquency; Fed. Probation; Am. Jrnl. of Corrections; Engl. Social Work Jrnl.; Jrnl. of Mental Retardation; Can. Jrnl. of Criminology & Corrections; Police Times; Children Ltd., Aust. Address: 3015 Saratoga Drive, Orlando, FL 32806, USA.

UNSTEAD, Robert John, b. 21 Nov. 1915, Deal, UK. Author. Educ: London Univ. Publs: Looking at History, 1953; People in History, 1955; Travel by Road; Houses, 1958; Looking at Ancient History, 1959; Monasteries, 1961; Black's Children's Encyclopaedia, 1962; History of Britain, 1966; Story of Britain, 1969; Castles, 1970; History of the English Speaking World, 8 vols., 1971-74; The Twenties; The Thirties, 1974. Contbr. to Hist. Today. Mbrships: Soc. of Authors; Chmn., Educl. Writers' Grp. Address: Reedlands, Thorpeness, Suffolk, UK.

UNTERMEYER, Louis, b. 1 Oct. 1885, NYC, USA. Writer; University Lecturer. Publs. incl: Food & Drink, 1932; The Donkey of God, 1933; Rainbow in the Sky, 1935; Stars to Steer By, 1940; The Inner Sanctum, Walt Whitman, 1949; Makers of the Modern World, 1955; Labyrinth of Love, 1965; The Paths of Poetry, 1966; Men & Women: The Poetry of Love, 1970; Cat O'Nine Tales, 1971; Great Humor, 1972; Fifty Modern American & British Poets: 1920-70, 1973. Contbr. to: Liberator; Seven Arts. Address: Great Hill Rd., Newtown, Conn., USA.

UNTHANK, Luisa-Teresa Brown, pen names UNTHANK, Tessa Brown, & YORK, Barbara, b. Wakefield, UK. College Lecturer; Writer. Educ: B.A., M.A., Ph.D., Univ. of Liverpool, UK. Publs: Bibliography of Maria Edgeworth, 1972. Contbr. to: Southern Folklore Quarterly; Cats' Mag.; Mich. Quarterly Review; The Dalesman; The Vegetarian; & other jrnls. Mbrships: Soc. of Authors; Soc. of Women Writers & Jrnlsts.; Soc. of Yorks. Bookmen; Mensa; Vegetarian Soc. of UK; AAUP; Nat. Coun. of Tchrs.

of Engl. Hons: Fulbright Award, 1955-56; 2 Fellowships, AAUW, 1963-64 & 1969. Address: York Cottage, Williamsburg, KY 40769, USA.

UNWIN, David Storr, pen name SEVERN, David, b. 3 Dec. 1918. Author. Publs. incl: The Governor's Wife, 1954; A View of the Heath, 1956; (juvenile, as D. Severn) Rick Afire! , 1942; A Cabin for Crusoe, 1943; Hermit in the Hills, 1945; Ponies & Poaches, 1947; Dream Gold, 1948; Treasure for Three, 1949; Crazy Castle, 1951; Burglars & Bandicoots, 1952; Drumbeats! , 1953; The Future Took Us, 1958; The Green-eyed Gryphon, 1958; Foxy-boy, 1959; Three at Sea, 1959; Clouds over the Alberhorn, 1963; Jeff Dickson, Cowhand, 1963. Recip., Authors Club First Novel Award, 1955. Address: St. Michael's, Helions Bumpstead, Haverhill, Suffolk, UK.

UNWIN, Rayner Stephens, b. 23 Dec. 1925, London, UK. Publisher. Educ: M.A., Univ. of Oxford; M.A., Harvard Univ., Cambridge, Mass., USA. Publs: The Rural Muse, 1954; The Defeat of John Hawkins, 1960. Address: 28 Little Russell St., London WC1, UK.

UPADHYAYA, Shantilal Chhaganlal, pen name BANDOPADHYAYA, Shashi Bhusan, b. 7 Apr. 1910, Gujarat, India. Curator, Chief Librarian, Victoria & Albert Museum, Bombay. Educ: M.A., LL.B., D.L., Ph.D. Publs: Critical Introduction & Engl. Transl. of: Kamsutra, by Vatsayana; Rati Rahasya, by Kokkoka. Contbr. to jrnls. of socs. below. Mbrships: All India Oriental Conf.; All India Hist. Congress; Mus. Assn. of India; Numismatic Soc. of India; Gujarat Rsch. Soc. Address: 9 Panna Park, Navrangpura, Ahmedabad 380009, Gujarat, India.

UPDIKE, John (Hoyer), b 18 Mar. 1932, Shillington, Pa., USA. Writer. Educ: A.B., Harvard Univ., 1954; Ruskin Schl. of Drawing, Oxford, UK, 1954-55. Publs. incl: (novels) The Poorhouse Fair, USA & UK, 1959; Rabbit, Run, USA, 1960, UK, 1961; The Centaur, USA & UK, 1963; Of the Farm, 1965; Couples, USA & UK, 1968; Rabbit Redux, USA, 1971, UK 1972; (short stories) The Same Door, USA, 1959, UK, 1962; The Music School, 1966; Bech: A Book, USA & UK, 1970; (verse) 70 Poems, UK, 1972. Mbr., Nat. Inst. Arts & Letters. Hons. incl: Rosenthal Award, 1960; Nat. Book Award, 1964; O. Henry Award, 1966. Address: 26 E. St., Ipswich, MA 01938, USA.

UPWARD, Edward (Falaise), pen name CHALMERS, Allen, b. 9 Sept. 1903, Romford, Essex, UK. Retired Schoolmaster. Educ: M.A., Corpus Christi Coll., Cambridge Univ., 1924. Publs: (verse) Buddha, 1924; (novels) Journey to the Border, 1938; In the Thirties, 1962; The Rotten Elements, 1969; (short stories) The Railway Accident, 1969. Mbr., Ed. Bd., The Ploughshare. Address: c/o William Heinemann Ltd., 15—16 Queen St., London W1, UK.

URBACH, Reinhard, b. 12 Nov. 1939, Weimar, Germany. Essayist. Educ: Univs. Cologne, Bonn, Vienna. Publs: Arthur Schnitzler, 1968, 2nd ed., 1972; Die Wiener Komödie und ihr Publikum, 1973; Schnitzler-Kommentar, 1974. Contbr. to: Neue Zürcher Zeitung; Mod. Austrian Lit., (Binghamton, N.Y.); Hofmannsthal-Blätter; Literatur und Kritik (Salzburg); Protokolle (Vienna). Mbrships: Arthur Schnitzler Inst., Vienna (Sec. Gen., VP); Hugo von Hofmannsthal-Gesellschaft, (Frankfurt); Int. Arthur Schnitzler Rsch. Assn. Binghamton, N.Y.). Recip., Theodor-Körner Preis, 1973. Address: Grünetorgasse 14/11, A 1090 Vienna, Austria.

URIS, Auren, b. 18 Nov. 1913, NYC, USA. Writer. Educ: B.A., New Schl. for Soc. Rsch. Publs. incl: Improved Foremanship, 1948; How to Be a Successful Leader, 1951; Discover Your Inner Self, 1959; The Manager's Job, 1962; Mastery of People, 1964; The Executive Job Market, 1965; Keeping Young in Business, 1967; Mastery of Management, 1968; Strategy of Success, 1969; The Executive Deskbook, 1970; The Turned-On Executive, 1970; The Frustrated Titan: Emasculation of the Executive, 1972; How to Win Your Boss's Love, Approval & Job (co-author), 1973; Thank God It's Monday, 1974. Address: 277 River Rd., Grandview, Nyack, NY 10960, USA.

URIS, Leon (Marcus), b. 3 Aug. 1924, Balt., Md., USA. Writer. Publs. incl: (novels) Battle Cry, USA & UK, 1953; The Angry Hills, USA, 1955, UK, 1956; Exodus, USA, 1958, UK, 1959; Mila 18, USA & UK, 1961; Armageddon: A Novel of Berlin, USA & UK, 1964; Topaz, USA, 1967, UK, 1968; Q.B.VII, USA, 1970, UK, 1971; (play) Ari, prod. 1971; (screenplays) Battle Cry, 1955; Gunfight at the

OK Corral, 1957; (non-fiction) Exodus Revisited, 1960 (as In the Steps of Exodus, UK, 1962). Hons: Daroff Mem. Award, 1959; Grant, Nat. Inst. Arts & Letters, 1959. Address: c/o Doubleday & Co. Inc., 277 Park Ave., N.Y., NY 10017, USA.

URQUHART, Frederick Burrows, b. 12 July 1912, Edinburgh, UK. Writer. Publs: Time Will Knit, 1938; I Fell for a Sailor, 1940; The Last G.I. Bride Wore Tartan, 1948; The Ferret Was Abraham's Daughter, 1949; Jezebel's Dust, 1951; Churchill Cartoon Biography, 1955; Collected Stories: vol. I, the Dying Stallion, 1967, vol. II, The Ploughing Match, 1968. Contbr. to: London Mercury; Spectator; Time & Tide; Texas Quarterly; Times Educl. Supplement; etc. Hons: Tom Gallon Trust Award, 1951; Arts Council Grant, 1966. Address: Spring Garden Cottage, Fairwarp, Uckfield, Sussex TN22 3BG, UK.

URSILLO, Margaret Cecelia, b. 18 Feb. 1920, Providence, R.I., USA. Clerk; Poet. Contbr. to many anthols. & jrnls. inclng: American Poet, 1968; Prairie Poet, 1969; W.P.S.I. Poet, 1970; Times Review; Butcher Workman; Poets Corner. Mbrships: Am. Poetry League; World Poetry Soc. Intercontinental; Montorsorrie Soc.; Platform Soc. Address: 48 Franklin St., Haworth, N.D., USA.

USHERWOOD, Stephen, b. 14 Sept. 1907, London UK. Author; BBC Producer & Scriptwriter. Educ: M.A., Oriel Coll., Oxford Univ. Publs: Reign by Reign, 1960; The Bible, Book by Book, 1962; Shakespeare, Play by Play, 1967; History From Familiar Things (5 vols.), 1969-71; Britain, Century by Century, 1972; Europe, Century by Century, 1972; Food, Drink & History, 1972; (forthcoming) The Counter-Armada, 1596. Horses, Harness & History. Contbr. to: World Today; Oxford Jr. Ency.; Country Life; Hist. Today; PLA Monthly. Mbrships: Oriel Soc.; Soc. Authors; Oxford Union; Histl. Assn. Address: 24 St. Mary's Grove, Canonbury, London N1, UK.

USLAR-PIETRI, Arturo, b. 16 May 1906, Caracas, Venezuela. University Professor of Spanish & Spanish American Literature & Civilization & Political Economics; Lawyer; Politician. Educ: Doct. Pol. Sci. Publs. incl: (novels) Las Lanzas Coloradas (The Red Lances), 1931; El Camino del Dorado (The Road to El Dorado), 1947; El Laberinto de Fortuna (The Fortune's Labyrinth), 1964; (stories) Pasos y Pasajeros (Paces & Passengers), 1965; (essays) Las Nubes (The Clouds), 1951; Del Hacer y Deshacer de Venezuela (On the Doing & Undoing of Venezuela), 1963. Contbr. to num. Venezuelan, for. newspapers & publs. Mbrships: Acads., Hist., Langs., Pol. & Social Scis. Hons. incl: Nat. Prize Lit., Venezuela. Address: Avenida Los Pinos 49, La Florida, Caracas, Venezuela.

USTINOV, Peter Alexander, b. 16 Apr. 1921. Playwright; Dramatist; Actor. Educ: London Theatre Studio. Prods: (films, writer & dir.) School for Secrets, 1947; Vice Versa, 1948; Private Angelo, 1949; Billy Budd, 1962; Lady L, 1965. Publs: (plays) The Indifferent Shepherd, 1948; The Moment of Truth, 1951; Romanoff & Juliet, 1956; The Life in My Hands, 1963; Half Way Up a Tree, 1967; (novels) The Loser, 1960; Krumnagel, 1971. Mbrships: Brit. Film Acad.; F.R.S.A.; Rector, Dundee Univ., 1968. Recip., 3 Emmy Awards for Best TV Actor. Address: c/o Film Rights Ltd., 113 Wardour St., London W1, UK.

UTLEY, Robert Marshall, b. 31 Oct. 1929, Bauxite, Ark., USA. Historian. Educ: B.S., Purdue Univ., 1951; M.A., Ind. Univ., 1952. Publs: Custer & the Great Controversy: Origin & Development of a Legend, 1962; The Last Days of the Sioux Nation, 1963; Frontiersmen in Blue: The United States Army & the Indian 1848-1865, 1967; Frontier Regulars: The United States Army & the Indian 1866-1891, 1973. Contbr. to: Am. W.; Am. Hist. Illustrated; Am. Heritage; var. profl. jrnls. Mbrships. incl: Fndr. & former Pres., Western Hist. Assn.; Am. Histl. Assn. Hons: Buffalo Award, N.Y. Westerners, 1964; Award of Merit, Am. Assn. State & Local Hist., 1964; Litt.D., Purdue Univ., 1974. Address: 6529 Hitt Ave., McLean, VA 22101, USA.

UTTLEY, Alison. Author. Educ: B.Sc., Manchester Univ. Publs. incl: The Country Child, 1931, paperback 1963; Candlelight Tales, 1936; High Meadows, 1938, new ed., 1967; A Traveller in Time, 1939, 1973; Country Hoard, 1943; The Washerwoman's Child (play) 1947; Buckinghamshire, 1950; The Stuff of Dreams, 1953; A Year in the Country, 1957; Snug & Serena Go to Town,

1961; Lavender Shoes, 1970; (essays) Cuckoo in June, 1964; A Peck of Gold, 1966; Secret Places, 1972; Sam Pig Books, 1940—; Grey Rabbit Books; Brown Mouse Books; etc. Recip., Hon. Litt.D., Manchester Univ., 1970. Address: Thackers, Beaconsfield, Bucks., UK.

V

VA'A, Felise, b. 22 Nov. 1941, Apia, Western Samoa. Journalist. Educ: Canterbury & Massey Univs., NZ. Contbr. to: Oceania & Beyond (anthol.); Samoan Sun (Assoc. Ed., 1975—); Pacific Islands Monthly; var. NZ newspapers & acad. jrnls. Mbrships: Govt. Family Planning Advsry. Comm.; VP, Western Samoa Amateur Athletic Assn.; Rosicrucian Order; AMORC. Address: P.O. Box 1227, Apia, Western Samoa.

VACA CANGAS, Cesar, b. 29 Dec. 1908, Noreña, Spain. Priest; Doctor. Educ: Theol. studies; Lic. Med. Publs. incl: Guias de almas, 1948; Psicoanálisis y dirección espiritual, 1953; La castidad y otros temas espirirtuales, 1954; Ensayos de psicología religiosa, 1958. Contbr. to: Ya. Address: PP Agustinos, Los Negrales, Madrid, Spain.

VACHON, Brian, b. 3 Oct. 1941, Wash. D.C., USA. Editor. Contbr. to: Vt. Life; Look; Playboy; Psychol. Today; Seventeen; McCalls; N.Y. Times; N.Y. Daily News; Newsweek; Saturday Review. Address: 39 Loomis St., Montpelier, VT 05602, USA.

VACZEK, Louis Charles, pen name HARDIN, Peter, b. 26 Nov. 1913, Szeged, Hungary. Chemist; Author; Lecturer; Editor. Educ: B.Sc., McGill Univ., Montreal, Can.; Carleton Coll., Ottawa; State Univ. of Iowa, Iowa City, USA. Publs: River & Empty Sea, 1950; The Frightened Dove, 1951; The Hidden Grave, 1955; The Golden Calf, 1956; The Troubador, 1960; The Enjoyment of Cnemistry, 1964. Contbr. to: Time-Life books; Encys. Jrnls. & Reviews. Mbrships: Nat. Assn. of Sci. Writers; Pres., Midland Authors Soc. Address: 516 N. Oakdale, Chgo., IL 60657, USA.

VADASZ, Ferenc, b. 22 June 1916, Komárom, Hungary. Journalist. Educ: Univ. of Pol. Scis. Publs: Szeged Gaol, 1948; Battle with the Hungarian Hell, 1961; Young Men from the Remete Street, 1962; The Thirteenth Winter, 1966; The Great Optimist, 1967; The Wind Stops Blowing, 1968; Into the Light from Beneath the Earth, 1969; A Piece of the Sky, 1970; Others Die, 1972; The Lawyer, 1975; Without Legends, 1975; 4 other works. Ed. & Contbr. to Népszabadság. Mbrships: PEN; Hungarian Lit. Fndn. Recip., SZOT (Trade Union Art Prize), 1971. Address: 1119 Budapest, Fehérvári út 153, Hungary.

VAGTS, Miriam Beard (Mrs. Alfred Vagts), b. 19 Nov. 1901, Manchester, UK. Educ.: Vassar Coll., USA, 1917-18; Barnard Coll., 1920-21. Publs: Realism in Romantic Japan, 1930; A History of Business, 1938, rev. ed., 1963. Contbr. to: N.Y. Times. Address: Box 56, Sherman, CT 06784, USA.

VAJDA, György M(ihály), b. 4 Feb. 1914, Bártfa, Hungary (now Czechoslovakia). Professor of Comparative Literature, University of Szeged. Educ: Ph.D., Univ. of Budapest, 1937. Publs: Schiller, 1953; Lessing, 1955; Ed., Szinházi kalauz (Theatre Guide), 1960, 2 later eds.; Állandóság a változásban (Constancy in Change), 1968; Co-Ed. & Contbr., Studien zur Geschichte der deutsch-ungarischen literarischen Beziehungen, 1969. Contbr. to: Neohelicon (Co-Ed.); Acta Litteraria Academiae Scientiarum Hungaricae; Arcadia; Etudes Germaniques; Voprosy Literatury; Yearbook of Comparative & Gen. Lit. Mbrships. incl: PEN; Int. Comparative Lit. Assn.; Hungarian Writers Confedn. Recip., Gold Medal for Achievement, 1974. Address: 1082 Budapest, Üllöi út 42, Hungary.

VALEV, Dimitur, b. 4 Oct. 1929, Lessovo, Bulgaria. Writer. Publs: (in Bulgarian) Growing Up, 1961; The Outskirts, 1966; We, Our Majesties, 1969; Rage, 1969;

South Wind, 1970; Heat, 1973; The Ford, 1974. Contbr. to: PlamAk; September; Literatouren Front. Mbr., Union of Bulgarian Writers. Recip., Prize of the Union of Bulgarian Writers, 1972. Address: Sofia ul. V. Kolarov, 41, Bulgaria.

VALTIALA, Kaarle-Juhani Bertel, pen name NALLE, b. 2 Jan. 1938, Helsinki, Finland. Writer. Educ: M.A., Univ. of Helsinki, 1962. Publs: Landet Marita, 1961; Åtta Noveller, 1963; Äventyret, 1965; Varning för människan, 1968; Notvarp i Sargassohavet, 1972; Lotus, 1973; Tonga, 1974. Contbr. to: Hufvudstadsbladet, Helsinki. Mbrships: Union of Swedish Writers in Finland; Union of Finnish Playwrights. Address: Kopingsvagen 34.D.42, 02700 Grankulla, Finland.

VAN ALSTYNE, Richard W., b. 19 Aug. 1900, Sandusky, Ohio, USA. Historian. Educ: B.A., Harvard Univ., 1922; M.A., Univ. of Southern Calif., 1924; Ph.D., Stanford Univ., 1928. Publs: American Diplomacy in Action, 1944, 2nd ed., 1968; The Rising American Empire, 1966, 2nd ed., 1974; Empire & Independence: The International History of the American Revolution, 1965; Genesis of American Nationalism, 1970; The United States & East Asia, 1973. Contbr. to: Current Hist.; Jrnl. of Am. Hist.; etc. Mbrships. incl: Am. Soc. for 18th Century Studies; Conf. on Brit. Studies; Athenaeum Club, London, UK. Hons: Officier d'Académie, 1938. Address: 1214 S. Tuxedo, Stockton, CA 95204, USA.

VAN ATTA, Winfred, b. 18 Oct. 1910, Hidalgo, Ill., USA. Public Relations Executive. Publs: Shock Treatment, 1961; Hatchet Man, 1963; Nicky, 1965; A Good Place to Work & Die, 1970; The Adam Sleep, in preparation. Contbr. to: Rdrs. Digest; Cosmopolitan; Good Housekeeping; Family Circle; Coronet; Liberty; Colliers; Saturday Evening Post; etc. Recip., Edgar Allen Poe Award, Mystery Writers of Am., 1961. Address: Dogwood Lane, Skyview Acres, Pomona, NY 10970, USA.

van BEEK, Geert, b. 13 Mar. 1920, Gennep, Netherlands. Dutch Teacher. Educ: Tchrs. Sem.; Dutch lang. & lit. Publs: Buiten Schot, 1961; De gekruisigde rat, 1965; Het Mexicaanse paardje, 1966; Blazen tot honderd, 1967; De steek van een schorpioen, 1968; De 1500 meter, 1971. Contbr. to: Elseviers' Mag.; Raam. Mbrships: PEN; Maatschappij der Nederlandse Letterkunde; Vereniging van Letterkundigen. Hons: Anne Frank Prize, 1962; Lit. Prize, Province of N. Brabant, 1966; Vijverberg Prize, 1968. Address: Vijverweg 21, Veghel, Netherlands.

VANCE, Leigh, b. 18 Mar. 1922, Harrogate, UK. Screen & Television Writer & Producer. Educ: Ctr. Schl. of Dramatic Art; Santa Monica Coll. Publs: incl: (films) Heart of a Child, 1957; The Frightened City, 1962; Dr Crippen, 1964; Crossplot, 1969; The Black Windmill, 1974; Plays for BBC TV, Armchair Theatre. Contbr. to: TV Series; Spectator; Picture Post; Lilliput; Colliers. Mbrships: Pres., Int. Writers Guild, 1969; Chmn., Exec. Comm., 1970-74; Fndng. Vice-Chmn., Writers Guild of GB, 1959; Trustee, 1964—. Hons: Edgar Allen Poe Award, 1961; ZITA Award, Writers Guild of GB, 1964. Address: 1801 Bel Air Rd., L.A., CA 90024, USA.

VAN COPPENOLLE, Renée, b. 3 Apr. 1920, Arlon, Belgium. Teacher. Publs: Chansons au bond de ma Plaine, 1970; Un Cri dans le Matin, 1971; Hymnes pour l'Office Divin, 1972; Le Pelerin de l'Aube, 1973; Arlon, une Ville, une Mère, 1974. Contbr. to: Envoi. Mbrships. incl: Scriptores Catholici, Brussels; Assn. Royale des Ecrivains Francophones, Brussels. Hons. incl: Prix Renée Rodriguez, Lyon, France, 1972; Silver Medal, Ditta Dioguardi, Italy, 1972; Gold Medal, Arts, Sciences, Lettres, Paris, France, 1973; Ier Grand Prix International, Jules Sottiaux, Belgium, 1973. Address: Fichermont, Chemin de la Croix 21, B.1410 Waterloo, Belgium.

VAN DANTZIG, Albert, b. 16 Mar. 1937, Amsterdam, Netherlands. Lecturer. Educ: Cert. d'Etudes Politiques, Dip. EPHE, Doct., Univ. of Paris, France. Publs: Het Nederlandse Aandeel in de Slavenhandel, 1968; A Short History of the Forts & Castles of Ghana (w. B. Priddy), 1971; Les Hollandais & l'Essor de L'Ashanti & du Dahomey, 1680-1740, 1975. Contbr. to: Cahiers d'Etudes Africaines; Revue Française d'Histoire d'Outre-Mer; Transactions of the Histl. Soc. of Ghana; Hist. in Africa. Mbr., Histl. Soc. of Ghana (publs. mgr.). Address: History Dept., Univ. of Ghana, P.O. Box 12, Legon, Ghana.

van den BOGAERT, Piet Franciscus Martinus, pen name BREEDVELD, Walter, b. 25 July 1901, 's Hertogenbosch,

Netherlands. Writer. Publs. incl: Gerda Goppertz, 1940; Hexpoor, 1953; Sandra, 1954; Hall en Hefferly, 1955; De Kivieten, 1955; De Open Stad, 1964. Mbr., Vereniging van Letterkundigen. Hons: Kempische Cultuurdagen Prize; City of s'Hertogenbosch Prize. Address: Generaal Winckelmanstraat 239, 't Laar, Tilburg, Netherlands.

VAN den BREMT, Frans Albert, b. 1 July 1919, Meerbeke, Belgium. Publisher; Author. Educ: Dr.Phil. & Litt.; Laureat of Belgian Acad. Publs: Willem de Fesch, Nederlands componist en virtuoos, 1948; Bruxelles, 1973; Bruxelles/Grand-Place, 1974; Belgique-Villes d'art, 1974. Contbr. to: Grove's Dictionary of Music & Musicians; Die Musik in Geschichte und Gegenwart; Algemene Muziekencyclopedie; De grote Nederlandse Larousse-encyclopedie; etc.; Chief Ed., De Periscoop (lit. & art review). Mbr., Org. mondiale de la presse périodique. Address: R. Neyberghlaan 144, B-1020 Brussels, Belgium.

VANDERHEIDE, Antonie Albertus, b. 11 Mar. 1945, Zwolle, Netherlands. Editor & Publisher of The Windmill Herald, B.C. since 1969. Contbr. to var. Dutch newspapers; etc. Mbrships: Ethnic Press Assn. of B.C. (Pres., 1973—); Burnaby-Edmonds Progressive-Conservative Assn. (Pres., VP); Dist. 1, Christian Labour Assn. Can. (VP); Christian Labour Assn. Can. (Dir.). Address: P.O. Box 533, New Westminster, B.C., Can. V3L 4Y8.

van der HOEST, Pieter, b. 12 Nov. 1946, Rotterdam, Netherlands. Journalist; Editor. Educ: HBS. Contbr. to: Rotterdamsch Nieuwsblad; Haagsche Post. Ed., Chronos Mag. Mbr., Nederlandse Vereniging van Journalisten. Address: Tafelberg 67, Dordrecht, Netherlands.

VAN DER KLIS, Joke M., 6 Dec. 1947, Eindhoven, Netherlands. Correspondent. Publs: Graue Hefte I (poems), 1973; Gegendarstellungen (poems), 1974; & num. other poems & short stories. Mbrships: German Authors' Union (VS); Printing & Paper Union; Werkkreis Literatur der Arbeitswelt. Address: 2 Hamburg 20, Eppendorfer Landstr. 24, W. Germany.

van der LUGT, Arie, b. 30 Mar. 1917, Vlaardingen, Netherlands. Author. Educ: M.O.Ned., Psych., Leiden Univ. Publs. incl: The Song of the Sea, 1950, 2nd ed., 1973; The Crazy Doctor, 1950; God Shook the Sea, 1953; The Forlorn Village, 1955; The Last Colony, 1968; The Women of Arnefjord, 1970; further 30 plays, 20 juvenile books, 80 plays & some scenarios. Contbr. to: Cath. Illustrated; Revue; Panorama; var. Dutch mags. Mbrships: Dutch Writers' Guild; Vereniging van Letterkundigen, Amsterdam. Hons: Vliebergh Prizes, Louvain, Belgium, 1948, 1950; Ceres Theater Prize for play, Farmer Without Land, 1960. Address: Boscheind 34a, Luyksgestel, Netherlands.

van der POST, Laurens (Jan), b. 13 Dec. 1906, Philippolis, S. Africa. Writer; Former Farmer. Publs. incl: (novels) In a Province, UK, 1934, USA, 1935; The Face Beside the Fire, UK & USA, 1953; Flamingo Feather, UK & USA, 1955; The Seed & the Sower, UK & USA, 1963; The Hunter & the Whale, UK & USA, 1967; (non-fiction) Venture to the Interior, USA, 1951, UK, 1952; The Lost World of the Kalahari, UK & USA, 1958; A Portrait of All The Russias, UK & USA, 1967. Mbrships: F.R.S.L. Hons. incl: C.B.E., 1947; S. African Ctrl. News Agcy. Prize, 1963, 1967; Yorks. Post Prize, 1967; D.Litt., Univ. of Natal, 1965. Address: 27 Chelsea Towers, Chelsea Manor Gdns., London SW3, UK.

VAN DER VEER, Matthijs Henri Jacob Theodor, b. 14 Sept. 1940, The Hague, Netherlands. Director, Mankind Research Foundation Europa. Publs: (Dutch) Nieuwe Sporen naar het Verleden; Verborgen Wereld; Flitsende Feiten; (Engl.) Hidden Worlds, 1974. Contbr. to: Psychic Researcher; De Post; Brès; Delta. Mbr., Dutch Soc. of Lit. Address: Londenweg 297, Vlaardingen, Netherlands.

VAN DER VET, Antonie Carel Wouter, b. 3 June 1919, The Hague, Netherlands. Newspaper Editor. Educ: HBS-B. Publs: Gefluisterd Relaas (poems), 1945; Het Vluchtend Geluk (novel), 1948; Het portret (novel), 1958; Rotterdam (social econs.), 1973. Contbr. to: Algemeen Dagblad; Ignu; Elsevier. Mbrships. incl: Veren van Letterkundigen; Nederl Journalistenvereniging. Recip., Hon. Mention, City Coun. of The Hague for Huygensprys, 1947. Address: Scholderlaan 3, Renesse (Zld), Netherlands.

VAN DE WAARSENBURG, Hans, pen name BRAC, Hans, b. 21 July 1943, Helmond, Netherlands. Poet; Teacher. Publs: Poëzie '61-'69 (collected poems), 1972; De

Vergrijzing (poetry), 1972; Tussen nat mos en een begrafenis (poetry), 1973. Contbr. to: '61; Manifest; Kentering Lit. Review (Ed.); Maatstaf; Raam; Tirade; De Gids; Vlaamse Gids; Nieuw Vlaams Tijdschrift; Septentrion; Delta; Akzente; etc. Mbr., Netherlands Ctr., PEN (Gen. Sec., 1970-). Recip., Jan Campert Award for Poetry, 1973. Address: Pergamijndonk 92, Maastricht, Netherlands.

VANDIVER, Frank Everson, b. 9 Dec. 1925, Texas, USA. Educator. Educ: M.A., Univ. of Tex., 1949; Ph.D., Tulane Univ., 1951; M.A., Oxon., 1963. Publs. incl: Field of Glory: a Pictorial Narrative of American Wars, 1960; The First Public War, 1861-65, 1961; That Elusive Civil War, 1967; Their Tattered Flags: The Epic of the Confederacy, 1970; The Southwest: South or West? , 1975; Ed. War Memoirs, by Jubal A. Early, 1960. Contbr. to: Ency. Americana; Ency. Britannica; World Book; etc. Jrnl. of Southern Hist. (assoc. Ed.). Mbrships. incl: Am. Histl. Assn.; Am. Assn. for Higher Educ. Hons. incl: Outstanding Civ. Serv. Medal, 1974; num. acad. hons. inclng: Guggenheim Fellowship, 1955. Address: 6134 Chevy Chase, Houston, TX 77027, USA.

VAN DOOREN, Leonard Alfred Theophile, b. 29 Dec. 1912, Brondesbury Pk., London, UK. President, Capernwray Bible Schools; Director, Capernwray Hall Conference Centre & Latimer Publishing Company. Publs: Prayer, the Christian's Vital Breath, 1962; Come See the Place, 1962; Challenge of the Macedonian Call, 1963; Letters to Francisco, 1967; Becoming Fishers of Men, 1967; Introducing the Old Testament, 1968; Introducing the New Testament, 1972; The Life I Now Live, 1974; num. booklets. Address: Capernwray Hall, Carnforth, Lancs. LA6 1AG, UK.

VAN DOREN, Charles, b. 12 Feb. 1926, NYC, USA. Editor; Publisher. Educ: B.A., St. John's Coll., Md., 1947; M.A., 1949, Ph.D., 1959; Columbia Univ., N.Y. Publs. incl: The Idea of Progress, 1967; How to Read a Book (co-author, revised ed.), 1973; Webster's American Biographies (Ed.), 1974; Great Treasury of Western Thought (co-Ed.), 1975. Mbrships: Author's Guild; Arts Club of Chgo. Address: Encyclopaedia Britannica, 425 N. Michigan Ave., Chicago, IL 60611, USA.

VAN DOREN, Mark, b. 13 June 1894, Hope, Ill., USA. Former Professor of English. Educ: A.B., 1914, A.M., 1915, Univ. of Ill.; Ph.D., Columbia Univ., 1920. Publs. incl: The Poetry of John Dryden, 1920, revised ed., 1931 (as John Dryden, 1946, 1960); American & British Literature since 1890 (w. C. Van Doren), 1925, revised ed., 1939; Shakespeare, USA, 1939, UK, 1941; Collected Poems, 1939; Nathaniel Hawthorne, USA, 1949, UK, 1959; The Happy Critic, USA, 1961, UK, 1962; Collected Stories, 3 vols., 1962-68; Collected & New Poems, 1963; Three Plays, 1966; 3 novels. Mbr., Am. Acad. Arts & Sci. Hons. incl: Pulitzer Prize, 1940; num. awards & docts. Address: Falls Village, CT 06031, USA.

VAN HAGELAND, Albert, pen names JACOBY, John; RIETHUYZE, M.; GEERTEN, Bert; RUTGEERTS, Albert, b. 22 June 1919, Aarschot, Belgium. Literary Agent. Publs. incl: Hendrik Conscience en het Volksleven, 1953; Kamp om de Koningskroon, 1957; Ernest Claes en Wij, 1959; De Magische Zee, 1961, French ed., La Mer Magique, 1973; Moderne Magie en Hekserij, 1965, 2nd ed., 1974; Ed., num. anthols. of weird & fantasy themes. Contbr. to num. folklore, lit., histl., humorous, & other jrnls. & newspapers. Mbrships: Flemish Folklore Soc.; Cons., Antwerp Mus. Commn. on Folklore; Flemish Periodical Press Assn.; Assn. of Flemish Authors. Hons: Prof. Boon Prize, 1953; Baekelmans Prize, Belgian Acad. for Dutch Lang. & Lit., 1958. Address: Blutsdelle 10, B 1641 Alsemberg, Belgium.

VAN HOOREBEECK, Albert, b. 7 Mar. 1915, Ixelles, Belgium. Aviation Writer. Publs: L'Épopée de l'Atlantique Nord, 1967; Le Conquête de l'Air, 2 vols., 1967; Les Tours du Monde Aériens, 1969; La geste de L'Ile de Pâques; Encyclopedia de Aviacion & Astronautica, 1974. Contbr. to: Aviation & Astronautique; Forces Aériennes Françaises; Bulletin, Aviation Mus. of Belgium. Mbrships: Assn. des Ecrivains Belges; PEN; Assn. des Journalistes Profl. de l'Aeronautique & de L'Astronautique. Hons: Prix d'Histoire, Aéro-Club de France, 1967; Prix de la Presse Aeronautique Belge, 1973. Address: Ave. V. Van Gogh 15, 1140 Brussels, Belgium.

van HOUWENINGE, Joachimus Johannes, pen name VAN HOUWENINGE, Chiem, b. 20 Nov. 1940, The Hague, Netherlands. Actor; Director; Writer. Educ: Toneelschool,

Amsterdam; Univ. of Amsterdam. Publs. incl: films; TV plays; The Hero of the Revolution, 1968; The Last Train, 1968. Contbr. to: L'Avant Scene. Mbrships: Netherlands Writers Assn.; Netherlands Soc. of Theatrical Arts. Recip., Viser Neerlandia Prys, 1967. Address: Broekrade 8-9, Vlaardingen, Netherlands.

VAN KAMPEN, Anthony Cornelis, b. 28 Aug. 1911, Hellevoetsluis, Netherlands. Writer. Publs: Corsicaans avontuur, 3 vols., 1950; Jungle, 3 vols., 1952; Runamara, 1960; Het Zilveren Spoor, 1961; Het land dat God vergat, 1967; The Life of Mary Bryant — Convict, 3 vols., 1968; Geschonden Eldorado, 1971; Betty Smit — Free Lance voor God, 1973; De laatste grens, 1974. Ed., De Blauwe Wimpel (The Blue Riband), nautical monthly. Mbrships: Vereniging van Letterkundigen; Nederlandse Maatschappij van Letterkunde; Federatie van Nederlandse Journalisten. Hon. Kt., Order of St. Sylvester. Address: Kerkedijk 25, Bergen (N.H.), Netherlands.

VAN LAERHOVEN, Bob (Victor Flora), b. 8 Aug. 1953, Arendonk, Belgium. Translator; Freelance Journalist. Publs: Phobie (psychol. novel), 1972; Kip en Vel (sci. fiction & horror stories), 1973; Pluk mij, dappere (anthol. of speculative fiction), 1974. Contbr. to: New Writings in SF; Pulp; Ides ... et Autres; Sci. Fiction Times, Germany. Mbrships: Flemish Writers Soc.; SFan. Recip., SFan Award, 1974. Address: Spoorwegstraat 72, 2300 Turnhout, Belgium.

VAN LOGGEM, Manuel, b. 8 Mar. 1916, Amsterdam, Netherlands. Writer; Psychologist. Educ: Doct. Psychol., Univ. Amsterdam. Publs: (novels) Moses, 1947, 2nd ed., 1969; A Sun on Hiroshima, 1963; The Love Life of the Priargs, 1968; The Time of the Coffins, 1969; Gold & Homicide, 1969; Pair-puppets, 1974; (collected stories) Insects in Plastic, 1950, 3rd ed., 1968; Primeval Times, 1966; (play) A Mess of Mushrooms, 1974; (essay) The Psychology of Drama, 1960. Mbr., PEN. Hons: Bookweek Prize, 1955; Van der Vies Prize, 1963; Visser Neelandia Prize, 1965. Address: Nieuwe Keizersgracht 59, Amsterdam, Netherlands.

van MANEN PIETERS, Jos, b. 21 Mar. 1930, Zaandam, Netherlands. Author. Publs: Tuinfluiter, 1955; Gods Geheimschrift, 1958; Rosemarie, 1962; Er gebeurt geen wonder, 1963; Dit is myn haven, 1967; Vergeet het maar, 1968; Geef my een teken van leven, 1971; Alleen van horen zaggen, 1974. Mbrships: V.V.L.; Schryverskontakt (soc. of Christian authors). Recip., Athos Prize, 1965. Address: Emmalaan 6, Ede, Netherlands.

van MEER, Joyce, b. 28 Aug. 1926, Creston, Iowa, USA. Freelance Journalist. Educ: B.A., Univ. of Md.; Ariz. State Coll.; Am. Univ. Publs: Living with the Dutch, 1972. Contbr. to: CBS; Assoc. Press; Radio Nederland, Hilversum; Wall St. Jrnl.; Voice of Am.; N. Am. Newspaper Alliance, N.Y. Mbrships: VP, Nieuwspoort Int. Press Ctr., The Hague, 1967-73; Adj. Sec., For. Press Assn., Netherlands, 1965-74. Address: Laan van Meerdervoort 96B, The Hague, Netherlands.

van MELSEN, Andreas Gerardus Maria, b. 10 Nov. 1912, Zeist, Netherlands. Professor. Educ: D.Sc., Univ. of Utrecht. Publs: Wijsgerig verleden der atoomtheorie, 1941; From Atomos to Atom, 1952; The Philosophy of Nature, 1953; Science & Technology, 1961; Evolution & Philosophy, 1965; Physical Science & Ethics, 1967; Science & Responsibility, 1970. Mbrships: Royal Netherlands Acad. Arts & Scis.; Int. Inst. Philos.; Philosl. Assn. Thomas van Aquino; Thijmgenootschap; var. acad. & sci. assns. Hons: Acad. degree, Duquesne at Pitts., USA, 1953; Kt., Order of Netherlands Lion, 1960. Address: Adrianaweg 7, Nijmegen, Netherlands.

van NÝNATTEN DOFFEGNIES, Henrica Judith, b. 16 Feb. 1898, Diepenveen, Overýssel, Netherlands. Writer. Publs: 20 books, most have been transl'd into Scandinavian langs., titles incl: Huis van Licht en Schaduw, 1938; Moeder Geerte, 1938; Henne, 1944; Het Stenen Bakbeest, 1969; Wendela, 1970. Address: Park Boswýk, flat 655, Doorn, Netherlands.

VAN OIRSCHOT, Anton, b. 27 Oct. 1927, Helvoirt, Netherlands. Publs. incl: The Golden Head, 1960; Dutch Castles & Country Houses (co-author), 1960; Buying Antiques, 8 vols., vol. I, Furniture, 1967, II, Clocks, 1968, III, Copper & Pewter, 1968, IV, Fireplaces, 1969, V, Books, Maps & Prints, 1970, VI, Iron Works, 1971, VII,

Glass, 1971, VIII, Buying Antiques Where?, 1971, IX, Copper & Bronze, 1973, X, Pewter, 1973, XI, Cases & Chests, 1974; Antiques Omnibus, 1972; Giant-Stories (co-author), 1972; Specialities of the Netherlands, 1974; Ghosts & Castles, 1974. Recip., Gouden Hooft-Prijs, 1960. Address: Nemerlaer Castle, Haaren N.B., Netherlands.

VAN OVER, Raymond, b. 29 June 1934, Inwood, L.I., N.Y., USA. Writer. Publs: Explorer of the Mind: Biographical Study of William McDougall's Work in Psychical Research, 1967; I Ching, The Chinese Book of Changes, 1971; A Treasury of Chinese Literature, 1972; Psychology & Extrasensory Perception, 1972; Unfinished Man, 1972; The Chinese Mystics, 1973; Taoist Tales, 1973; The Psychology of Freedom, 1974; Eastern Mysticism, From Arabia to Japan, 2 vols., 1975; Sun Songs, Creation Myths from Around the World, 1975; Ecstasy, The Perilous Journey, 1976. Mbrships.: Soc. for Sci. Study of Relig.; Am. & Brit. Socs. for Psychical Rsch.; Ctr. for Integrative Educ. Address: 463 W. St., N.Y., NY 10014, USA.

VAN PRAAG, Siegfried Emanuel, b. 8 Aug. 1899, Amsterdam, Netherlands. Author. Educ: Tchrs. Trng. Coll.; Amsterdam Univ. Publs. incl: Madame de Pompadour, 1936; The Western Jews & their Literature since 1860, 1926; Sam Levita's Dance of Life, 1928; The Crazy Virgin; The Ghetto, 1930; We & the Animals, 1932; Cosmopolitans, 1933; Jerusalem of the West, 1961; The Old Darshan, 1971; (autobiog.) The Eagle & The Mole, 1973. Mbrships. incl: PEN; Soc. of Dutch Lit. (Leyden). Hons: Officier d'Academie, 1940; Kt. Order Oranje Nassau, 1969; Silver Medal Honour, City Amsterdam, 1974; Assn. Amsterdam Booksellers Prize, 1962 for Jerusalem of the West. Address: 27 Avenue Antoine Depage, 1050 Brussels, Belgium.

VAN PRAAG CHANTRAINE, Jacqueline, b. 1 June 1922, Brussels, Belgium. University Teacher. Educ: Lic., Classical Langs.; Doct., Classical Langs., specialising in Spanish & Latin Am. Publs: Gabriel Miro ou le visage du Levant, terre d'Espagne, Paris, 1959. Contbr. to: Revista Hispánica Moderna; Thesaurus; La Torre; Cuadernos Americanos; Revue des langues neo-latines. Mbr., Assn. Int. de los Hispanistas (AIH). Hons: Prix Leopold Rosy, Royal Acad. of French lang. & lit., Belgium; Prix, Province of Brabant. Address: 36 Ave. des Gaulois, Brussels, Belgium.

VAN RAVENZWAAIJ, Ger, b. 7 Mar. 1901, Amsterdam, Netherlands. Musicologist; Author; Critic. Educ: Univ. of Amsterdam. Publs: Book of Songs "Com nu met Sang", 1942-43; Muzikale Ommegang (dict.), 1948; Music in Short, 1949; Dutch Folk Songs, 1951; Henry Purcell (hist.), 1955; Muzikale luister in Nederland, 1974; sev. encys. Contbr. to: Noordhollandse Dagbladen; Utrechts Nieuwsblad; De Gelderlander. Mbrships: Soc. of Dutch Authors; Vereniging Nederlandse Muziekgeschiedenis; Theatre Critics' Circle; Sec., Jacob Obrecht Soc. Address: Van der Helstlaan 24, Hilversum, Netherlands.

VAN SCOYK, Robert, b. 13 Jan. 1928, Dayton, Ohio, USA. Television Writer; Story Editor. Educ: Columbia Univ.; N.Y. Univ. Publs: Best Short Stories of 1958 (contbng. author). Contbr. to: Ellery Queen's Mystery Mag.; Humanist; Dayton Daily News; Num. TV progs. & theatre presentations. Mbrships: Writers Guild of Am., W., Inc.; Nat. Acad. of TV Arts & Scis. Hons: Silver Gavel Award for TV Drama, Am. Bar Assn., 1960; Nosotros Award for Creation of Latin TV Image, 1972. Address: 1740 Westridge Rd., L.A., CA 90049, USA.

VAN SEIJEN, Adam, b. 29 Apr. 1922, Leeuwarden, Friesland. Writer. Publs. incl: De Simmer Fan It Lok (novelle in Frisian lang.); num. educl. books for children; num. records of plays adapted from famous books; TV play, forthcoming. (by order of Het Centrum voor Nederlandse Dramaturgie). Contbr. to: Dutch & Belgian Radio stns. Vara, Kro, Tros, Ncrv & Brt (plays for children & adults); Taptoe, Jippo, Okki (educl. mags. for Benelux); women's mags. etc.; Mbr., Vereniging van Letterkundigen (VvL). Address: Pampus 7, Kuinre (Ov.), Netherlands.

VAN SERTIMA, Ivan Gladstone, b. 26 Jan. 1935, Kitty Village, Georgetown, Guyana. University Professor. Educ: B.A. Publs: River & the Wall, 1958; Caribbean Writers, 1968; Swahili Dictionary of Legal Terms, 1973; They Came Before Columbus, 1975. Contbr. to: Inter-Am. Review. Mbrships: AAUP. Caribbean Artists Movement. Address: 238 Harrison Ave., Highland Park, NJ 08904, USA.

VANSITTART, Jane, b. Exmouth, Devon, UK. Author. Publs: So Fair a House, 1961; Prelude to Mutiny, 1962; The Devil's Wind, 1963; Surgeon James's Journal 1815, 1964; Kathrine Fry's Journal, 1966; The So Beloved, 1967; The Silver Swan, 1970; Adventurers of the Mayflower, 1971; From Minnie with Love, 1974. Mbr., Devonshire Soc. Hon: Histl. novel award, RNA, 1963, film script made by Appleby. Address: 6 Raddenstile Ct., Exmouth, Devon, UK.

VAN SLYKE, Berenice, b. 13 July 1891, Fort Wayne, Ind., USA. Writer. Educ: B.A., Wellesley Coll. Publs: The San Luca (transl. from French), 1935; Power of the Sun (novel), 1931; This Was Sandra (novel), 1938. Contbr. to anthols. & jrnls. inclng: Sat. Review; Sat. Evening Post; N.Y. Times; Contemp. Verse. Mbr., Poetry Soc. of Am. Hons. incl: 1st Prize, Annual Awards, Poetry Soc. of Am., 1958 & 1968. Address: Penglas, Valley Cottage, NY 10989, USA.

VAN TASSEL, Alfred James, b. 9 Aug. 1910, Twin Falls, Idaho, USA. University Professor. Educ: B.S., Univ. Calif., 1934; Univ. Pa.; Ph.D., Columbia Univ., 1964. Publs: Mechanization in the Lumber Industry, 1940; Environmental Side Effects of Rising Industrial Output, 1971; Our Environment: The Outlook for 1980, 1973; (forthcoming) The Environmental Price of Energy; The Cost of Living With Nature; Urban Transportation; The Outlook for the 1980's. Contbr. to: Int. Yearbook; Technol. Forecasting; Quarterly Jrnl. Econs. & Bus.; Ill. Bus. Review. Mbrships. incl: Am. Econ. Assn.; Acad. Pol. Sci.; Hofstra Univ. Club. Hons: Exec. Sec. UN Sci. Conf. on Conserv. & Utilization Resources, Lake Success, N.Y., 1949. Address: 2 Hemlock Lane, Glen Cove, N.Y., USA.

VAN TIL, William, b. 8 Jan. 1911, NYC, USA. Writer; Professor. Educ: B.A., 1933; Columbia Coll., M.A., 1935; Tchrs. Coll., Columbia Univ.; Ph.D., Ohio State Univ., 1946. Publs. incl: Education: A Beginning, 1971, 1974; Curriculum: Quest for Relevance, 1971, 1974; Education in American Life (co-author), 1972. Contbr. to num. profl. & lit. jrnls. Mbrships: Pres., Assn. for Supervision & Curric. Dev., John Dewey Soc. for the Study of Educ. & Culture, Nat. Soc. of Coll. Tchrs. of Educ. Hons: Award, N.J. Collegiate Press Assn.; Ohio State Univ. Centennial Achievement Award. Address: Lake Lure, R.R. 32, Box 316, Terre Haute, IN 47803, USA.

van TOL, Dick, pen name POINTER, Dick, b. 16 May 1925, Amsterdam, Netherlands. Psychiatrist. Educ: Med., Psych. & Neurol. Trng., Univ. of Amsterdam. Publs: Revolver met monogram, 1963; 1/2 paar schoenen, 1963; Allemaal koffie? vroeg Nina, 1970; sev. other short stories & detective novels. Contbr. to: var. profl. jrnls.; Dutch mags. & newspapers; Med. Contbr., Nieuwe Rotterdamsche courant, 1960-64. Mbr., Dutch Vereniging voor letterkundigen. Recip., Special Short Story Award, 1966. Address: Stadionweg 94, Amsterdam, Netherlands.

VAN TRICHT, Elisabeth Emmy, pen name de JONG-KEESING, Elisabeth, b. 15 July 1911, Amsterdam, Netherlands. Writer; Former Teacher. Educ: B.A., 1935, Doct. Degree, 1939, Amsterdam. Publs: De Jade Bodhisatva, 1952; Wennen aan de Wereld, 1959; De Zalenman, 1960; Van Amstel tot Jangtse, 1960; De Blinde Spinners, 1962; Men Zoekt Nog Steeds, 1966; Golven Waarom Komt de Wind, a biography of Inayat Khan, 1973, & Engl. ed. titled Inayat Khan, A Biography, 1974. Contbr. to: Het Toneel; De Gids; Levende Talen; etc. Mbrships: incl: PEN; Maatschappij der Nederlandse Letterkunde. Hons. incl: Comm. of Netherlands Collective Propaganda Book Prize, 1960. Address: Laan van Avegoor 18, Ellecom, Netherlands.

van 't SANT-van BOMMEL, Aartje Wilhelmina, pen name van 't SANT, Mien, b. 23 Feb. 1901, Gorinchem, Netherlands. Author. Publs: 63 books incl. (novels) Langs de Zelfkant, 1965; De Vrouwe van de Oldehoeve, 1968; De Aukeshof, 1969; Met lege handen, 1971; Vrouwen om Victor, 1972; Studentenhuwelijk, Slapen zonder Morgen, 1973; Hoeve De Terp, 1974; De Zonen van de Terp, 1974; (juvenile) Elsbeth, 1956; De brug komt klaar, 1958; De Lusthof, 1970; Ikkon niet anders zijn, 1973. Mbrships. incl: Union Dutch Authors. Address: Planterslaan 20, De Witte raaf, Leersum (U), Netherlands.

van VOGT, A(lfred) E(lton), b. 26 Apr. 1912, Man., Can. Author. Publs. incl: Slan, 1946; The World of Null-A, 1948; The Voyage of the Space Beagle, 1950; Destination: Universe, 1952. Empire of the Atom, 1956; Pawns of Null-A, 1956; The Violent Man, 1962; The Wizard of Linn, 1962; The Silkie, 1969; Quest For the Future, 1970; The Money Personality (non-fiction), 1973; Future Glitter, 1973; The Man With 1000 Names, 1974; The Secret Galactics, 1974. Contbr. to var. mags. Mbrships: Authors' Guild; Sci. Fiction Writers of Am.; Count Dracula Soc. Hons. incl: B.A., Golden State Coll., 1953; Mrs. Ann Radcliffe Lit. Award, Count Dracula Soc., 1968. Address: 2850 Belden Dr., Hollywood, CA 90068, USA.

VAN VELDE, Jacoba Catharina, b. 10 May 1913, The Hague, Netherlands. Writer; Translator. Publs: De grote zaal (The Big Ward), 1953; Een blad in de wind (A Leaf in the Wind), 1961. Contbr. to: Les Lettres Nouvelles; Les Lettres Françaises; etc. Mbrships: PEN; Maatschappy der Nederlandse Letterkunde; Vereniging van Letterkundigen. Recip., Lit. Award, 1954. Address: Herengracht 587, Amsterdam, Netherlands.

VANVUGT, Ewald, b. 16 Apr. 1943, 's-Hertogenbosch, Netherlands. Author. Publs: Particular Strange Thief, 1963; Darwin & Palls, 1964; My Women, 1967; Guru, 1968; La Ilaha Illala, 1971; Top Boy & Man, 1971; The Kiss of India, 1972. Mbrships: The Busy Bee Coop. Publng. House, Amsterdam; Netherlands Ctr., PEN. Address: Sarphatistraat 205, Amsterdam, Netherlands.

van ZANTEN, Ek (Ernst Arnold), b. 15 Nov. 1910, Amsterdam, Netherlands. Psychologist. Publs: (poetry) Rockanje, 1954; Inward, 1964; The Smile of a Scorpio, 1973. Mbr., Assn. of Lit. Men. Address: Stadhouderskade 96, Amsterdam, Netherlands.

VARANNAI, Aurel, b. 13 Sept. 1900, Budapest, Hungary. Author; Editor; Dramatist. Educ: LL.D., Univ. of Budapest; Lic. es Lettres, Sorbonne, Paris, France. Publs: John Bowring & the Hungarian Literature, 1963; Seven Storeys (radio play), 1964; While Tea is Boiling (one-act play), 1964; Echo from England, 1974; Alfius the Usurer (short stories), forthcoming. Contbr. to: The Economist, London (corres.), 1935-41; Reuters, London (corres.), 1945-48; N.Y. Times. Mbrships: Assn. of Hungarian Writers; Union of Hungarian Jrnlsts.; PEN; Fészek Club. Address: IX Liliom utca 33, 1094 Budapest, Hungary.

VARDA, Agnès, b. 30 May 1928. Film Writer & Director. Educ: Sorbonne Univ., Paris. Prods: (films) Le Pointe-Courte, 1954; Cleo de 5 à 7, 1961; Le Bonheur, 1964; Les Créatures, 1965; Loin du Vietnam, 1967; Lions Love, 1969; Nausicaa, 1970; (short films) O Saisons, O Châteaux, 1957; L'Opera-Mouffe, 1958; Du côté de la Côté, 1958; Salut les Cubains, 1963; Uncle Yanco, 1967; Black Panthers, 1968. Contbr. to: Realités; Marie-France; Plaisir de France. Hons. incl: Prix Méliès, 1962; Prix Louis Delluc, 1965; Bronze Lion, Venice; Silver Bear, Berlin, 1965. Address: 86 rue Daguerre, Paris 14e, France.

VARDAMAN, George T., b. 6 Aug. 1920, San Antonio, Tex., USA. Professor of Administration, College of Business Administration, University of Denver. Educ: A.B., M.A., Univ. of Denver; Ph.D., Northwestern Univ. Publs. incl: Managerial Control Through Communication, 1968; Cutting Communication Costs & Increasing Impacts, 1970; Effective Communication of Ideas, 1970; Dynamics of Managerial Leadership, 1973; Communication in Modern Organizations, 1973. Contbr. to num. profl. jrnls. Mbrships. incl: Cons. Ed., Petrocelli Books in Mgmt. & Communication, Mason & Lipscomb Publng. Co., N.Y.; Ed. Bd., Jrnl. of Bus. Rsch. Address: P.O. Box 691, Indian Hills, CO 80454, USA.

VARGA, Imre, b. 16 Dec. 1919, Bekes, Hungary. Editor. Educ: Ph.D., Debrecen, 1947. Publs. incl: Foggy Morning (novel & short stories), 1953; The Limping Prophet (novel & short stories), 1961; Entangled Offsprings (novel), 1975. Contbr. to: Kortárs; Uj Irás; Jelenkor; Alföld. Mbrships: Hungarian Writers' Assn.; Ady Soc. of Debrecen (until 1949). Hons: 1st Prize, Csillag short story competition, 1948; 3rd Prize, Szepirodalmi Konyvkiado novel competition, 1974. Address: Lorant ut 9, H—1125 Budapest, Hungary.

VARGA, Katalin, b. 26 Mar. 1928, Budapest, Hungary. Editor. Educ: Univ. Fac. of Arts. Publs: (poems) The Escaped Childhood, 1960; The Second Sky, 1963; Burning Briar, 1966; Exiled Words, 1969; (novels) My Dear Daughter, 1971; Bonca, My Friend, 1974; Barley & Kid, 1974; (books for children) Gögös gúnàr Gedeon, 1962, 10th ed., 1974; Mosó Masa mosodàja, 1965, 5th ed., 1974; ÈN, TE, Ö, 1974. Contbr. to: Hungarian TV; Kortàrs. Mbr.,

Hungarian Writers' Assn. Address: Budapest 1093, Közraktàr U 12/A, Hungary.

VARGAS LIOSA, Mario, b. 28 Mar. 1936. Writer. Educ: Univs. of San Marcos, Lima & Madrid. Publs. incl: Los Jefes, 1958; La Cuidad y los perros, 1962; La Casa Verde, 1965; Los Cachorros, 1966; Conversacíon en la Catedral, 1970. Contbr. to: La Cronica, Lima; La Industria, Piura; Radio Panamericana, Lima; TV. Hons: Leopoldo Alas Prize, 1958; Prix Biblioteca Breve, 1962; Critics Española Prize, 1963; Gallegos Prize, 1967. Address: c/o Embassy of Peru, London SW1, UK.

VÄRING, Astrid, b. 15 Dec. 1892, Umeå, Sweden. Author; Journalist. Publs. incl: Frosten, 1926; Vintermyren, 1927; Släkten, 1934; Katinka, 1942; I som här inträden, 1944 (also filmed). Contbr. to var. jrnls. Mbrships. incl: PEN Club; Swedish Assn. of Authors. Recip., Great Scandinavian Novel Prize, 1942. Address: Örnbogatan 70, 161 39 Bromma, Sweden.

VARKONYI, Mihaly, b. 25 Jan. 1931, Ujpəst, Hungary. Writer. Educ: Tech. Univ. Publs: Bread & Cross (short Stories), 1960; Role in the Small Hours (short stories), 1964; The Witness (novel), 1967; Legend on the Train (novel & short stories), 1968; Least Said . . .? (pol. pamphlet), 1969; Divorce (short stories), 1973. Contbr. to: Nèpszabadsag; Népszava; Magyar Hirlap; Magyar Ifjùsàg; Élet ès Irodalom; Uj Iràs; Kortárs. Mbrships: Hungarian Writer's Assn.; Soc. of Hungarian Jrnlsts. Hons: Prize, World Youth Festival, 1960, Hungarian Trade Union, 1961; 2nd Prize, Moscow Film Festival, 1962. Address: 1138 Budapest, Ròbert Kàroly Ktt. 20.VI.81, Hungary.

VARMA, Baidya Nath, b. 1 Jan. 1921, Bargaon, India. Professor of Sociology, City University of New York. Educ: B.A., Patna Univ., 1941; M.A., Univ. of Mo., USA, 1949; Ph.D., Columbia Univ., 1958. Publs: A New Survey of the Social Sciences, 1962; Contemporary India, 1965; Laws, 1973, The New Social Sciences, 1976; Modernization for What?, 1976. Contbr. to: The Young Indian; Trans India; Indian Jrnl. of Soc. Rsch.; Int. Jrnl. of Contemporary Sociol.; Am. Jrnl. of Sociol.; Am. Sociol. Review; Am. Sociologist; Am. Anthropologist; Jrnl. of Asian Studies. Mbrships: Fellow, Am. Sociol. Assn.; Pres., S. Asian Sociologists, 1974; Life, Indian Sociol. Soc. & Indian Acad. Hindi Schirship.; Elected, Sigma Kappa Alpha, Pi Gamma Mu & Pi Delta Epsilon; Am. Anthropol. Assn.; Assn. for Asian Studies. Hons: Chmn., Pres. or Moderator, sev. comms. & seminars. Address: Mithila, 62 Belvedere Dr., Yonkers, NY 10705, USA.

VARNER, John Grier, b. 30 Mar. 1905, Mt. Pleasant, Tex., USA. University Professor. Educ: B.A., Austin Coll., Sherman, Tex., 1926; M.A., 1932; Ph.D., 1940, Univ. of Va., Charlottesville. Publs: Edgar Allan Poe & the Philadelphia Saturday Courier, 1933; El Inca: the Life & Times of Garcilaso de la Vega, 1968; Transl. & Ed., The Florida of the Inca (w. J. J. Varner), 1951. Contbr. to: Ency. Americana; Notable Am. Women. Mbrships: Real Academia de Ciencias, Bellas Letras y Nobles Artes, Spain; Tex. Inst. of Letters; Latin Am. Studies Assn. Recip., Grants for Rsch. in Spain, Am. Philos. Soc. & Univ. of Tex. Rsch. Coun., 1954. Address: 2510 Jarratt Ave., Austin, TX 78703, USA.

VAS, István, b. 24 Sept. 1910, Budapest, Hungary. Poet; Writer. Publs. incl: Mit akar ez az egy ember? (collected poems), 1970; Nehéz szerelem (Hard love, autobiog. novel), 1972; Az ismeretlen isten (The unknown God, collected essays), 1973; Önarckép a hetvenes években (Self-portrait in the seventies, poems), 1974; Hét tenger éneke (selected poetical transls.). Contbr. to most Hungarian lit. reviews. Mbrships: Comms., Hungarian Writers Union & PEN. Recip., num. prizes & awards, inclng: Kossuth Prize, 1970; Pro Arte Medal, 1972; Kt., Order of Palmes Acad., 1972. Address: Groza Péter rakpart 17, 1013 Budapest, Hungary.

VASALLO RAMOS, Jesús, pen name DEL RIO, Xavier, b. Ciudad Rodrigo, Spain. Journalist. Educ: Grad., Jrnlsm. Publs: La Ultima Nave; Caminos de Gloria. Contbr. to: Arriba; El Alcazar; Sabado Grafico; Cadena de la Prensa del Movimiento. Num. hons. incl: Virgen del Carmen Prize; Italian Cinema Prize; Valladolid Prize; City of Valencia Theatre Prize; Malaga Prize. Address: Paseo de la Habana, 19–9° Madrid – 16, Spain.

VASSILEV, Hristo Petkov, pen name VASSILEV, Orlin, b. 4 Dec. 1904, Vranyak, Bulgaria. Writer. Publs: (in

Bulgarian) The Wild Forest, 1935; The Island of the Lepers, 1939; A Tooth for a Tooth, 1944; Alarm, 1948; Love, 1952; Happiness, 1954; The Buried Sun, 1959; A Beaming Dawn, 1972. Contbr. to: PlamAk; September. Mbrships: PEN; Union of Bulgarian Writers. Hons: Prize of the Union of Bulgarian Writers, 1948; Dimitrov Laureate Prize, 1950; Award, People's Worker in Culture, 1969; Hero of Socialist Labour, 1974. Address: Sofia, kompl. VL. Zaimov, 9-a, Bulgaria.

VAUGHAN, Hilda (Mrs. Charles Morgan), b. Builth, Breconshire, UK. Novelist. Educ: private. Publs: (novels) The Battle to the Weak; Here Are Lovers; The Invader; Her Father's House; The Soldier & the Gentlewoman; A Thing of Nought; The Curtain Rises; Harvest Home; Pardon & Peace; Iron & Gold; The Candle & the Light; (plays w. Laurier Lister) She, too, was Young; Forsaking All Others; & an Introduction to Thomas Traherne's Centuries. Mbrships: F.R.S.L. Address: c/o Roger Morgan, 30 St. Peter's Sq., London W6 9UH, UK.

VAUGHAN, Paul, b. 24 Oct. 1925, London, UK. Journalist. Educ: M.A. (Oxon.). Publs: Doctors Commons, 1959; Family Planning, 1969; The Pill on Trial, 1970. Contbr. to: Truth; Time & Tide; Spectator; Observer; Sunday Times; Listener; Med. Tribune; Med. News; Family Doctor; World Med.; BBC TV & Radio progs. inclng. Horizon, New Worlds, Kaleidoscope. Mbrships: Med. Jrnlsts. Assn. (former Chairman); Assn. of Brit. Sci. Writers (former Comm. Mbr.). Address: 17 Courthope Rd., Wimbledon SW19 7RD, UK.

VAUGHAN WILLIAMS, Ursula, b. 15 Mar. 1911, Valletta, Malta. Publs: Verse, 5 vols., 1941-58; R.V.W. A Biography of Ralph Vaughan Williams, 1964; Metamorphoses (novel), 1966; Set to Partners (novel), 1968; Ralph Vaughan Williams, a Pictorial Biography (w. John Lunn), 1972; var. opera & cantata libretti. Mbrships: Govng. Body, Royal Acad. of Music; VP, Morley Coll.; Chmn. of Trustees, Music Info. Ctr.; Exec. Comm., Musician's Benevolent Fund; Hon. F.R.A.M., 1974. Address: 69 Gloucester Cres., London NW1 7EG, UK.

VAUGHN, Ruth Wood, b. 31 Aug. 1935, Wellington, Tex., USA. College Professor; Writer. Educ: B.A., M.A., Univ. of Kan.; Ph.D.Cand., Univ. of Okla. Publs. incl: Fun for Christian Youth, 1960; Dreams Can Come True, 1964; God's Masterpiece, 1965; No Matter the Weather, 1968; Hey! Have You Heard?, 1970; Celebrate With Words, 1971; Fools Have No Miracles, 1972; Even When I Cry, 1975; Thank You For Caring, 1975; Proclaiming Christ in Central America, 1976. Contbr. to: Decision; Home & Life; War Cry; Christian Herald; Presby. Outlook; The Preacher's Mag., & num. others. Mbrships. incl: Int. Platform Assn.; Women in Communications Int.; Phi Lambda Theta. Recip., Outstanding Educator of Am. Award, 1974. Address: 2805 Windsor Blvd., Oklahoma City, OK 73127, USA.

VAZAKAS, Byron, b. NYC, USA. Poet. Vols. of Poetry: Transfigured Night, 1946; The Equal Tribunals, 1961; The Marble Manifesto, 1966; Nostaligas For A House of Cards, 1970. Contbr. of poems to some 50 mags. & anthols. inclng: Commonweal; Harpers Bazaar; Hudson Review; The Nation; New World Writing; N.Y. Times; Partisan Review; Va. Quarterly; Kenyon & Sewanee Reviews; Saturday Review; 100 Modern Poems; Modern American Poetry. Recip., var. minor lit. awards, & Amy Lowell Travelling Fellowship in Poetry. Address: 1623 Mineral Springs Road, Reading, PA 19602, USA.

VÁZQUEZ IGLESIAS, Pura, b. 31 Mar. 1918, Orense, Spain. Teacher. Educ: Tchr. Trng. Cert. Publs. incl: (in Castilian) Margenes Veladas, 1944; En torno a la Voz, 1948; Madrugada Fronda, 1951; Desde la Niebla, 1951; Tiempo mío, 1952; Columpio de Luna a Sol; Destinos, 1955; Manaña del Amor, 1956; 13 Poemas a mi Sombra, 1959; Presencia de Venezuela, 1966; Rondas de Norte a Sur, 1968; Os poetas, 1971; Los Sueños Desandados; (in Galician) Intimas, 1952; O Desacongo, 1971; Borboriños, forthcoming. Contbr. to: ABC; num. lit. jrnls. in Spain, Portugal, N. & S. Am.; Spanish Radio & TV; BBC. Hons. incl: La Región Poetry Prize, Orense, 1940; Boscán Prize, 1950; 2nd Prize, Ciudad de Barcelona, 1954, 1955. Address: Calle Centro 13, 1°A, Cerro Prieto, Móstoles, Madrid, Spain.

VEGHAZI, Steven Nicholas, b. 24 Dec. 1923, Gyöngyös, Hungary. Rabbi; University Professor. Educ: Docts. Hist. & Archeol.; Univ. Pázmány Péter, & Theol. Sem., Budapest. Publs: History of the Jewish Community of Debrecen, 1967; The Role of Jewry in the Economic Life of Hungary, 1969; 125 anos en el estudio comparado de las religiones, 1973; El antisemitismo en la Antigüedad, 1974; El siglo de oro de las religiones orientales, 1974; 17 siglos de la historia judía en Hungría, 1974; Manuel del Judaismo (forthcoming). Contbr. to num. relig. jrnls., etc. Mbrships. incl: Rabbinical Assembly, N.Y. Address: Avenida de los Incas 3518, Buenos Aires, Argentina.

VELEA, Nicolae, b. 13 Apr. 1936, Cepari, Curtea de Arges, Romania. Writer. Educ: B.A. Publs: The Gate, 1960; Eight Short Stories, 1964; Guard of Harmony, 1965; Low Flight, 1965; The Box with Crickits (for children), 1972; In the War, an Acre of Flowers, 1973; Early to Rise, in Vain, 1974; Demetrius & His Two Days (for children), 1974. Contbr. to: Romînia literara; Contemporanul; Luciefèrue; var. Romanian newspapers. Mbrships: Assn. of Writers; Assn. of Cinema Soc. Hons. incl: Prizes for Prose, Union of Writers, 1960, 1974; Acad. Prize, 1961; Cultural Merit Award of RSR, 1967; Youth Prize, for "Low Flight", 1968. Address: et.1, apt. 20, Str.Mozart Wr. 2, Sector 1, Bucharest, Romania.

VELICHKOV, Georgy, b. 1938, Slien, Bulgaria. Writer. Publs: (in Bulgarian) Simple Wonders, 1966; A Lonely Moon in the Sky, 1972. Contbr. to: September; PlamAk. Mbr., Union of Bulgarian Writers. Address: Sofia ul. Milin Kamuk 59, Bulgaria.

VENKATASUBBIAH, Hiranyappa, b. 12 Nov. 1915, Mysore, India. Journalist. Educ: B.A., Univ. of Mysore. Publs: Structural Basis of Indian Economy, 1940; Asia in the Modern World, 1947; Indian Economy Since Independence, 1961; Anatomy of Indian Planning, 1969. Contbr. to: India Quarterly, New Delhi; Asian Affairs, London; Econ. Corres.-European Corres.-Cpty. Ed., The Hindu, 1956-74. Mbrships: Past VP & Mbr., Exec. Comm., Indian Coun. of World Affairs; Fndr. Mbr., Inst. for Soc. & Econ. Change, Bangalore; Sec., Indian Jrnlsts.' Assn. of GB, 1970-72. Recip., Mitsui Award for Asian Understanding, Press Fndn. of Asia, Manila, 1973. Address: A-36 Gulmohar Park, New Delhi 110049, India.

VENNARD, Edwin, b. 4 Sept. 1902, New Orleans, La., USA. Executive & Consultant. Educ: B.S.(Mech. & Elec. Engrng.). Publs: The Electric Power Business, 1962, 2nd ed., 1970; Government in the Power Business, 1968. Contbr. to: Elec. World; Elec. Light & Power Mag.; Pub. Utility Fortnightly. Mbrships: IEEE; Greenwich Country Club. Hons: Am. Power Conf. Citation. Hon. Mbr., US Nat. Comm. of World Energy Conf. Address: Khakum Wood, Greenwich, CT 06830, USA.

VERCORS, pen name of BRULLER, Jean, b. 26 Feb. 1902, Paris, France. Graphic Artist & Engraver. Publs. incl: Le Silence de la Mer, 1941; Le Sable du Temps, 1945; Portrait d´une amitié, 1954; Divagations d´un Français en Chine, 1956; Sylva, 1961; La Bataille du Silence, 1967; Le Radeau de la Méduse, 1969; Hamlet & Oedipe, 1970; Sillages, 1972; Sept Sentiers du Désert, 1972; Questions sur la Vie, 1973; Comme un Frère, 1973; num. eds. of engravings, etc. Mbrships: PEN; Pres., Nat. Comm. of Writers. Address: Moulin des Iles, Faremoutiers, Seine-et-Marne, France.

VERGER y VENTAYON, Maria, b. 29 Sept. 1917, Alcudia, Mallorca, Spain. Librarian. Educ: Univ. of Barcelona. Publs. incl: Clarors Matinals, 1929; Tendal D'estrelles, 1930; L'estela d'or, 1934; Biografia de La Familia Jenny, 1940; Biografia de Salomon, 1940; Rutas Maravillosas, 1966; Por la Senda de Las Rosas, 1970. Contbr. to: Dir., GEMA; Subdir., Plusultra; Dir., Lit. Page, El Nacional & Woman's Sect., Mundo Catolico. Mbrships: Gen. Authors' Soc. of Spain; Spanish Soc. of Writers & Artists; Writers' Guild of Spain. Hons. incl: Prize, Provincial Archives, Barcelona. Address: Residencia Ayala, Jorge Juan 41 3⁰, Madrid 1, Spain.

VERHESEN, Fernand, b. 3 May 1913, Brussels, Belgium. Teacher. Educ: B.Phil. & B.Litt., Univ. of Brussels; Tchng. Cert. Num. publs. incl: Passage de la terre, 1940; Poésies allégres de Lope de Vega, 1952; Poètes d'Espagne & d'Amerique latine, 1960; Voix & voies de la poésie française contemporaine, 1960; Poésie hispano-amércaine, 1966; Poésie de Belgique, 1969; Franchir la nuit, 1972; Le citoyen de l'oubli — V.Huidobro, 1974; sev. transls. of Spanish poets. Contbr. to sev. lit. publs. Mbrships. incl: Royal Acad. of French Lang. & Lit.; Dir., Int. Ctr. of Poetry Studies; Dir., Int. Lib. of Poetry; Ed. Comm., Jrnl. des Poètes. Recip., Laureate, French

Acad. Address: 96 Rue de la Croix de Fer, 1000 Brussels, Belgium.

VERISSIMO, Erico Lopes, b. 17 Dec. 1905. Editor; Writer. Educ: Coll. Cruzeiro do Sul, Porto Alegre. Publs. incl: (in Brazilian) Crossroads, 1935; The Rest is Silence, 1946; Consider the Lilies of the Field, 1947; Time & the Wind, 1952; Night, 1954; His Excellency the Ambassador, 1966; (in Engl.) Brazilian Literature, 1945; Mexico, 1959. Contbr. to Revista do Globo (Chief Ed., 1931-40). Hons: D.Litt.; Graca Aranha Prize, 1935; Machado de Assis Prize, 1935. Address: Rua Felipe de Oliveira 1415, Porto Alegre, Rio Grande do Sul, Brazil.

VERRAL, Charles Spain, pen name EATON, George L., b. 7 Nov. 1904, Highfield, Ont., Can. Writer. Educ: Upper Can. Coll., Toronto, 1919-23. Publs. incl: The Wonderful World Series, 1956; The Great Locomotive Chase, 1956; Andy Burnett, 1958; The Shaggy Dog, 1959; The Winning Quarterback, 1960; The Case of the Missing Message, 1960; Jets, 1962; Story of Outer Space, 1962; Robert Goddard, Father of the Space Age, 1963. Contbr. to mags., newspapers & radio. Mbrships. incl: Mystery Writers of Am. Address: 79 Jane St., N.Y., NY 10014, USA.

VERSCHRAEGHEN, Louis Omer, b. 14 Apr. 1909, Oudenaarde, Belgium. Journalist. Educ: Doct. in Chem., Univ. of Louvain; Doct. Degree, Univ. of Montpellier. Author, Contribution a l'interpretation biologique de la Politique, 1947. Contbr. to: Le Soir, Brussels. Mbr., PEN Club français de Belgique. Address: 14 Hoogstraet, Oudenaarde, Belgium.

VERWEY-NIJLAND, Mea, b. 2 Mar. 1892, Noordwijk, Netherlands. Writer. Educ: Leiden Univ. Publs: (poetry) Golfslag; Stem van het hart, 1934; De verdolven landen, 1945; De melodie, 1946; (vols. of lit. biog.) De betekenis van Johannes van Vloten, 1928; De briefwisseling van Albert Verwey met contemporaries, 1959; Albert Verwey en Stefan George (letters 1895-1907), 1965; Karl Wolfskehl und Albert Verwey, 1969. Contbr. to: De Beweging; Groot-Nederland; De nieuwe taalgids; other lit. jrnls. Mbrships: Maatschappij der Nederlandse Letterkunde, Leiden; PEN. Recip., Hon. Doct. in Lit. Address: Vinkenbaan 33, Santpoort-Zuid, Noord-Holland, Netherlands.

VESAAS, Halldis Moren, b. 18 Nov. 1907, Trysil, Norway. Writer. Publs: Harpeog Dolk, 1929; Morgonen 1931; Strender, 1933; Lykkelege Hender, 1936; Hildegunn, 1942; Tung Tids Tale, 1945; Treet, 1949; I Ein Annan Skog, 1955; Sett og Levd, 1957; Imidtbos Bakkar, 1974; var. children's books. Contbr. to: Dagbladet; Syn og Segn. Mbrships: Norwegian Writer' Assn.; PEN. Recip., The Dobloug Prize, 1960. Address: 3890 Ytre Vinje, Norway.

VESTDYK, Simon, b. 17 Oct. 1898, Harlingen, Netherlands, d. 23 Mar. 1971. Author. Educ: H.B.S., Univ. of Amsterdam. Publs. incl: Rumeiland, 1940; Aktaion onder de sterren, 1941; De Vuuraanbidders, 1947. Mbrships: Royal Acad., Vlaanderen; Vereniging van Letterkundigen; PEN. Recip., all major Dutch lit. prizes; Dutch candidate for Nobel Prize, 1956. Address: Torenlaan 4, Doorn, Netherlands.

VESTLY, Anne-Cath, b. 15 Feb. 1920, Rena, Norway. Author of Children's Books. Publs: Ole Aleksander Series (5 vols., 1953-56); Åtte små series (5 vols., 1957-61); Knerten series (6 vols., 1962-65 & 1973-74); Aurora series (7 vols., 1966-72) & two plays produced. Contbr. to Norwegian Broadcasting Corp. since 1946. Mbrships: Norwegian Authors Assn.; Playwright's Assn.; Assn. Authors Children's Lit. Recip., 2 lit. prizes from Dept. Culture. Address: Nøklesvingen 30, Oslo 6, Norway.

VESTRE, Bernt, b. 21 Aug. 1927, Haugesund, Norway. University Lecturer. Educ: Degrees in French Lit., History & Philosophy. Publs: Sporet av en sti, 1957; Albert Camus og menneskets revolte, 1960; Sartre — Introduction to a Translation, 1967; Hume — Introduction to a Translation, 1971; En hane til Asklepios, 1972; Det er noe du ikke kan fa, 1973; Dobbeltportrett, 1974. Contbr. to: Samtiden; Vinduet. Mbrships: Norwegian PEN; Norwegian Assn. of Authors. Address: Grinibraten 64, 1300 Sandvika, Norway.

VÉSZI, Endre, b. 19 Oct. 1916, Budapest, Hungary. Writer; Poet; Playwright. Publs: Ünnepronto, 1936; Gyerekkel a karján, 1938; Csillagtérkép, 1956; Hangok és sorsok, 1965; A Piros Oroszlán, 1966; A tusz zavarbaejtö halála, 1972; Tériszonv. 1974; A teljesseg igézetében, 1974.

Contbr. to: Kortars; Uj Iras; Elet es Irodalom; New Hungarian Quarterly. Mbrships: Hungarian Writers' Union; PEN. Hons: József Attila Lit. Prize, 1966; TV Prize, Monte Carlo, 1968. Address: 1013 Budapest, Attila ut 22, Hungary.

VEVERS, Henry Gwynne, b. 13 Nov. 1916, Girvan, Scotland, UK. Assistant Director of Science, Zoological Society of London. Educ: B.A., 1938, M.A., 1947, Ph.D., 1949, Magdalen Coll., Oxford Univ. Publs: The British Seashore, 1954; The Nature of Animal Colours (w. H. M. Fox), 1960; The Underwater World, 1971; 5 Bodley Head Natural Sci. Picture Books. Contbr. to: Nature; New Scientist; Sci. American; BBC Publs. Mbr., var. profl. assns. Address: The Zoological Society of London, Regent's Park, London NW1, UK.

VIAL, Claude, b. 6 May 1928, Ghent, Belgium. Journalist; Radio & TV Scriptwriter & Editor; Playwright. Educ: B.A., Univ. of Ghent, 1950; B.A., Free Univ. of Brussels, 1952; Schaerbeek Acad., Brussels. Publs: Le Grand Pessimiste (play for children), 1965; Thyl Ulenspiegel (radio play), 1972; La Nuit des Temps (stage play), 1974; sev. radio & TV plays & film scripts, 1955—. Contbr. to: Femmes d'Aujourd'hui. Mbrships. incl: PEN; Int. Fedn. of Writers & Jrnlsts. of Tourism; Gen. Assn. of the Belgian Press. Hons. incl: Children's Play Prize, Int. Competition, 1965; Gold Medal, Leonardo da Vinci Int. Acad., 1966; Medal, Nat. Fedn. of Belgian Drama Clubs, 1972. Address: Avenue de la Renaissance 58, 1040 Brussels, Belgium.

VIALAR, Paul, b. 18 Sept. 1898. Writer. Educ: Lycée Janson-de-Sailly, Paris. Publs. (15 plays & 90 novels) incl: La rose de la mer, 1939; La mort est un commencement, 8 vols., 1948; Chronique française du XXème Siècle, 10 vols. to date; Les Invités de la chasse, 1969; Les Députés; Ceux du Cirque; Safari vérité, 1970; Mon seul amour; la Caille & le Butor, 1972. Mbrships. incl: Coun. Alliance Francaise; Pres., Int. Writers' Guild; Pres., Nat. Fed. of Authors' Socs.; Pres., Assn. of Sports Writers. Hons. incl: Legion of Honour; Croix de Guerre. Address: 34 Ave. Victor Hugo, Boulogne sue Seine, France.

VIAU, Roger, b. 11 May 1906, Montreal, Can. Retired President of Manufacturing Company. Educ: B.Litt., Univ. of Montreal; Ecole des Hautes Etudes Commerciales, Montreal. Publs: Contes en Noir & en Couleur (short stories), 1948; Au Milieu, la Montagne (novel), 1951; Cavelier de la Salle (biog.), 1960; Lord Durham (biog.), 1962; La Porte Ouverte (anthol.), 1969; Vivre au Québec (anthol.), 1972; Fleur de Lis (anthol.), 1973. Contbr. to: Amérique Française. Mbrships: Soc. des Ecrivains Canadiens (past Treas.); Montreal Mus. of Fine Arts (past VP); Numismatic & Antiquarian Soc. (past Pres.); PEN. Address: 3445 Drummond St., Apt. PH 2, Montreal, P.Q. H3G 1X9, Can.

VICKERS, Brian, b. 13 Dec. 1937, Cardiff, UK. Professor of English Literature; Author. Educ: B.A. 1962, Ph.D., 1967, Cambridge Univ. Publs: Francis Bacon & Renaissance Prose, 1968; The Artistry of Shakespeare's Prose, 1968; The World of Jonathan Swift, 1968; Classical Rhetoric in English Poetry, 1970; Towards Greek Tragedy, 1973; Shakespeare: the Critical Heritage, Vols. I-IV, 1974-75. Contbr. to: Times Lit. Supplement; Review of Engl. Studies; Neue Zürcher Zeitung; Yearbook of Engl. Studies; Mod. Lang. Review; Critical Quarterly; Engl. Lang. Notes; Shakespeare Jahrbuch (West). Address: Im Resigarten, 8357 Guntershausen, Switz.

VICTOR VILLELA, Víctor Rogelio Villela Gutiérrez, b. 6 Mar. 1937, Guerrero, Mexico. Poet. Educ: Studied jrnlsm., 2 yrs. Publs: Paisaje desde una Hora (poems), 1972; Palabras para Convencer (short stories), 1974. Contbr. to: Revista de Bellas Artes; El Heraldo Cultural. Mbr., PEN, Mexican br. Recip., Schlrship., Centro Mexicano de Escritores, 1970-71. Address: José Ibarrarán 57-4, México, 19, D.F., Mexico.

VIDAL, Gore, pen name BOX, Edgar, b. 3 Oct. 1925, W. Point, N.Y., USA. Writer. Publs. incl: (novels) Williwaw, USA, 1946, UK, 1970; The City & the Pillar, USA, 1948, revised ed., 1965, UK, 1949, revised ed., 1966; The Judgment of Paris, USA, 1952, UK, 1953; Julian, USA & UK, 1964; Washington, D.C., USA & UK, 1967; Myra Breckinridge, USA & UK, 1968; Two Sisters, USA & UK, 1970; 3 detective novels as E. Box. (plays) Visit to a Small Planet, 1957; The Best Man, 1960; Romulus. 1966; An

Evening with Richard Nixon, 1972; var. screenplays, stories, essays. Address: Casa Willi, Klosters, Switz.

VIDLER, Alexander Roper, b. 27 Dec. 1899, Rye, UK. Clerk in Holy Orders; University Lecturer. Educ: B.A., Litt.D., Selwyn Coll., Cambridge. Publs: The Modernist Movement in the Roman Church, 1934; The Orb & the Cross, 1945; Prophecy & Papacy, 1954; The Church in the Age of Revolution, 1961; F.D. Maurice & Company, 1966; A Variety of Catholic Modernists, 1970. Contbr. to: Times Lit. Supplement; Jrnl. of Theol. Studies; Jrnl. of Ecclesiastical Hist.;Theol. Hons. incl: Hon. D.D., Edinburgh Univ.; Hon. Fellow, Kings' Coll., Cambridge. Address: Friars of the Sack, Rye, Sussex TN31 7HE, UK.

VIDOR, Miklós, b. 22 May 1923, Budapest, Hungary. Novelist; Poet. Educ: Dr. of Hungarian Lang., German Lit. & Aesthetics. Publs: (poetry) On the Border, 1947; Monologue, 1957; Empty Season, 1966; (novels) Tide-race, 1954; Strangers, 1958; Pawn on the Chess-board, 1968; Hurt People, 1973; (short stories) Guests of Baucis, 1963; Voluntarily Shipwrecked Persons, 1974. Contbr. to: Élet és Irodalom; Kortárs. Mbrships: Hungarian Art Fndn.; Union of Hungarian Writers; PEN. Recip., József Attila Prize, 1955. Address: Puskin utca 17, 1088 Budapest, Hungary.

VIETH VON GOLSSENAU, Arnold, pen names RENN, Ludwig; POVEDA, Antonio, b. 22 Apr. 1889, Dresden, Germany. Writer. Educ: Univ. Publs: 20 books inclng: Krieg, 1928; Russlandfahrten, 1932; Adel im Untergang, 1944; Vom Alten & Neuen Rumanien, 1952; Im Spanischen Krieg, 1955; Meine Kindheit & Jugend, 1957; Krieg ohne Schlacht, 1957; Herniu & Armin, 1958; Auf den Trummern des Kaiserreichs, 1961; Camilo, 1963; Inflation, 1963; Zu Fuss zum Orient, 1966; Ausweg, 1967. Mbrships. incl: PEN; German Authors' Soc.; German Acad. of Arts. Hons. incl: 4 prizes for children's books, 1954-58; 2 nat. prizes; D.Phil. Address: Berlin 1138, Am Kornfeld 98, E. Germany.

VIGH, Antal, b. 14 Oct. 1933, Jánkmajtis, Hungary. Writer; Teacher. Publs: Korai szivárvány, 1963; Nyugtalan homok, 1965; Bekötöut, 1967; Ár és iszap, 1969; Egyedül a Kastelyban, 1969; Aranyolma, 1970; Északi utakon, 1972; Erdöhaton Nyiren, 1973; Miért beteg a magyar futball, 1974. Contbr. to: Valósag; Új Iràs; Kortárs; Élet és Irodalom. Mbrships: Magyar Irok Szövetsége; Magyar Nepköztarsasag Müvèszeti alap. Address: Lipótmezei u. 8/a, 1021 Budapest II, Hungary.

VIIRLAID, Arved, b. 11 Apr. 1922, Padise, Estonia. Compositor. Publs. incl: (novels) Tormiaasta, 2 vols., 1949; Ristideta hauad, 2 vols., 1952; Seitse kohtupäeva, 1957; Vaim ja ahelad, 1961; Kustuvad tuled, 1965; Sadu jõkke, 1965; Bambuskardina ees, 1970; Kes tappis Eerik Hormi? ; 1974; Seireng er loe, 1975; (verse) Hulkuri evangeelium, 1948; Uks suveöhtune naeratus, 1949; Jäätanud peegel, 1962; Hõllalaulud, 1967. Contbr. to sev. Estonian, Am., & Can. jrnls. Mbrships: Exec. Comm., Estonian PEN; Can. PEN Ctr.; Estonian Writers' Assn.; World Poets' Soc.; United Poets Laureate Int. Hons. incl: 5 lit. prizes for prose, 1950-69; Karta & Pres. Medal, United Poets Int., 1967; Estonian Lit. Prize, 1968. Address: 63 Glen Davis Cres., Toronto, Ont., M4E 1X7, Can.

VILA SEIMA, José, b. 18 Aug. 1924, Valencia, Spain. Lecturer in History & Literature. Educ: Dr. Jrnlsm. & Info. Scis.; D.Litt. Publs. incl: André Gide y Paul Claudel, frente a frente, 1952; Benavente, fin de siglo, 1952; Tres ensayos sobre la Literature y nuestra guerra, 1956; Ideario de Manuel José Quintana, 1961; Edición crítica de 'los Intereses Creados' de Benavente, 1970; Antología de la literatura maya, 1974; La espiral de Carlos Onetti, 1974; El americanismo de Vargas Llosa, 1974. Contbr. to: Arbor; Cuadernos Hispanoamericanos; Revista Española de Antropología y Etnografía; La Actualidad Española; Ya, etc. Mbr., var. insts. Address: Calle Félix Boix 6, Madrid 16, Spain.

VILLA, Jose Garcia, b. 5 Aug. 1914, Manila, Philippines. Poet; Critic. Educ: B.A., Univ. of N.M.; postgrad. studies, Columbia Univ. Publs: Footnote to Youth (fiction), 1933; Many Voices, 1939; Poems by Doveglion, 1941; Have Come, Am Here (poetry), 1942; Volume Two (poetry), 1949; Selected Poems & New, 1958; Poems Fifty-Five, 1962; Poems in Praise of Love, 1962; Selected Stories, 1962; The Portable Villa, 1963; The Essential Villa, 1965; Ed., special issues of var. jrnls., 1946-48. Contbr. to num. anthols. Hons. incl: Am. Acad. Arts & Letters Award, 1942; Shelley Mem. Award, 1959;

D.Litt., Far Eastern Univ., 1959; Phillippines Cultural Heritage Award, 1962; Nat. Artist in Lit., 1973; D.H.L., Univ. of Philippines, 1973. Address: 780 Greenwich St., N.Y., NY 10014, USA.

VILLIERS, Alan John, b. 23 Sept. 1903, Melbourne, Australia. Author; Sailor. Publs. incl: Falmouth for Orders, 1929; By Way of Cape Horn, 1930; Cruise of the Conrad, 1937; The Way of a Ship, 1950; The Quest of the Schooner Argus, 1957; The Western Ocean, 1957; Give Me a Ship to Sail, 1958; Oceans of the World, 1963; Captain Cook, the Seaman's Seaman, 1967; The War with C. Horn, 1971; The Bounty Ships of France, 1972. Mbrships. incl: Cutty Sark Soc.; Pres., Soc. for Nautical Rsch.; Trustee, Nat. Maritime Museum; F.R.G.S. Hons. incl: Camoens Prize for Lit., 1954; D.S.C. Address: 1A Lucerne Rd., Oxford OX2 7QB, UK.

VINACKE, W. Edgar, b. 26 July 1917, Denver, Colo., USA. College Teacher. A.B., Univ. Cinn., 1939; Ph.D., Columbia Univ., 1942. Publs: The Psychology of Thinking, 1952, 2nd ed., 1974; Dimensions of Social Psychology (w. W. Wilson & G. M. Meredith), 1964; Foundations of Psychology, 1968; Ed., Readings in General Psychology, 1968. Contbr. to: Jrnl. Abnormal & Social Psychol.; Child Dev.; Psychol. Bulletin; etc. Mbrships. incl: Am. Psychol. Assn.; Am. Sociol. Assn.; Soc. Expmtl. Social Psychol. (Chmn., 1967-69); Am. Assn. Advancement Sci.; Int. Coun. Psychol. Hons: Fellow, Guggenheim Fndn., 1959; Fellow, Fund Advancement Educ., 1955-56. Address: Dept. Psychol. State Univ. N.Y., Buffalo, NY 14226, USA.

VINGEDAL, Sven Erik Axel, pen name REDAX, b. 4 Dec. 1906, Stockholm, Sweden. Archivist. Educ: People's H.S.; Mus. Trng. Publs. incl: The Inheritance of the Street (poems), 1944; Porcelain Marks. A Book about Porcelain, Earthenware & Other Ceramic Marks, 1949, 5th ed., 1975; The Chronicles of Roslag I-II, 1960-64; Amor & Josephine, 1963; Saints in the Church Porch, 1971. Contbr. to var. jrnls. Mbrships; Täby Local Hist. Soc.; Swedish Writers' Union; Strindberg Soc.; Uppland's Antiquarian Soc. Hons: Täby Cultural Prize, 1967; Gold Medal, Uppland's Antiquarian Soc., 1966; Award of 10,000 kronor, Swedish Writers' Union, 1973. Address: Centralvägen 36, 183 51 Täby, Sweden.

VINING, Elizabeth Gray, pen name GRAY, Elizabeth Janet, b. 6 Oct. 1902, Germantown, Phila., USA. Writer. Educ: A.B., Bryn Mawr Coll., Pa.; B.S. in L.S., Drexel Univ. Lib. Schl. Publs: Young Walter Scott, 1935; Adam of the Road, 1942; Windows for the Crown Prince, 1952; The Virginia Exiles, 1954; Friend of Life, 1958; Return to Japan, 1960; Take Heed of Loving Me, 1964; Flora Macdonald, 1966; I, Roberta, 1967; Quiet Pilgrimage, 1970; Mr. Whittier, 1974. Mbrships: PEN Am. Chapt.; Authors' Guild. Hons: Newbery Award, 1943; Constance Lindsay Skinner Award, 1954; Litt.D., Haverford Coll., 1958. Address: Kendal at Longwood, Box 194, Kennett Square, PA 19348, USA.

VINTER, Michael, pen name GIBBARD, T. S. J., b. 26 Dec. 1927, Wembley, Middlesex, UK. Novelist. Publs: (as Michael Vinter) African Nights, 1947; Colour of Dried Blood, 1967; Die Here a Stranger; A Vintage So Evil, 1968; Place of Execution, 1969; All This Shall Perish, 1970; Rat in a Trap, 1970; Wounds of Treason, 1972; (as T. S. J. Gibbard) Vandals of Eternity. Contbr. to: Wide World; Courier; Wkly. Telegraph; Boys' Own Paper; Cage & Aviary Birds; etc. Mbrships: Crime Writers' Assn.; Parrot Soc. Address: 10 Wentworth Rd., Hertford, Herts., UK.

VINTILĂ, Petru, b. 12 June 1922, Orsova, Mehedinti, Romania. Journalist; Writer. Educ: Fac. of Letters & Philos., Bucharest. Publs: (short stories) Line of Life; The Dancer & the Cipher; Hyena & the Circus; Two Vikings & a Girl; (plays) The House Which Ran Out Through the Door; The Vikings; (poetry) 5 Sights; Poems. Contbr. to: Contemporanul; Scînteia; România Literară; etc. Mbr., Romanian Writers' Union. Recip., Romanian Writers' Union Prize for Jrnlsm., 1962. Address: 2 Crăitelor St., 6 Bucharest, Romania.

VIQAR AZIM, Syed, b. 15 Aug. 1910, Allahabad, India. Teacher; Author. Educ: M.A., Univ. of Allahabad, 1934; Degree in Tchng., Muslim Univ., Aligarh, 1937. Publs. incl: Afsananigari, 1935, 2nd ed., 1948; Naya Afsana, 1946, 2nd ed., 1957; Hamaridastanen, 1956, 2nd ed., 1966; Fan Aur Fankar, 1968; Urdu Ka Classical Drama, vols. 7–13, 1968-74; Iqbal Shair Aur Falsafi, 1969; Iqbal Muasreen Ki Nazar Men, 1973. Contbr. to num. quarterly & monthly

Urdu mags., Indo-Pakistan; var. vols., Lit. Hist. of Indo-Pakistan Lit.; Ency. of Islam (Urdu ed.). Ed., 1 vol., Lit. Hist. of Indo-Pakistan Lit.; Ajkal, Delhi; Mah-I-Nau, Karachi; Nuqoosh, Lahore. Recip., sev. lit. prizes. Address: 7E/Block C, Samanabad, Lahore, Pakistan.

VIRAG, Moricz, b. 23 Sept. 1909, Budapest, Hungary. Author. Educ: Dr.phil. Publs. incl: Apam regenye, 1953; Szerencse, 1953; Balga szüzek, 1958; Pokhalo, 1959; Moricz Zsigmond szerkeszto ur, 1963; Fasor, 1973. Contbr. to: Magyar Nemzet; Elet es Jrodalom; etc. Mbrships: Magyar Jroh Szovetsege; Magyar Notanacs; etc. Recip., Hungarian lit. awards, 1954 & 1969. Address: Mese u. 9, Budapest 1121, Hungary.

VIRTA, Nikolai Evegenievich, b. 19 Dec. 1906, Tambov Region, USSR. Writer. Publs: (all in Russian) incl: (plays) Earth, 1937; Our Daily Bread, 1947; In Summer the Sky is High, 1960; Thirst, 1961; Golgotha, 1961; Winds Blew & Blew, 1962; (novels) The Adventurer, 1937; Steep Hills, 1955; Soil Returned, 1960; Field Marshal, 1961; Akshushka, 1962; Two Days of their Life, 1962; Fast Running Days, 1965; Novels of Last Years, 1965; Cat with a Long Long Tail, 1966; The End of a Career, 1967. Recip., State Prize (4 times). Address: Union of Writers, 52 ulitsa Vorovskogo, Moscow, USSR.

VISCOTT, David, pen names FIELDING, Richard; SCOTT, Ian, b. 24 May 1938, Boston, Mass., USA. Psychiatrist; Author. Educ: A.B., Dartmouth Coll., 1959; M.D., Tufts Med. Schl., 1963. Publs: Labyrinth of Silence, 1970; Feel Free, 1971; How to Make Winning your Lifestyle, 1972; The Making of a Psychiatrist, 1973; Dorchester Boy, 1973; How to Live with Another Person, 1974; American Greetings, 1974; also 12 children's books. Contbr. to: Advt. Age; Cosmopolitan Quizzes; Today's Hlth.; Psych.; Archives of Gen. Psych.; etc. Mbrships: Authors' League; Authors' Guild; PEN; AFTRA. Address: 68 Emerson Rd., Wellesley Hills, MA, USA.

VISHER, Halene Hatcher, b. 18 June 1909, Murray, Ky., USA. Educator; Author; Consultant. Educ: A.B., Murray State Univ., 1930; M.A., George Peabody Coll., 1932; M.A., 1955, Ph.D., 1960, Ind. Univ. Publs: Better Living Through Wise Use of Resources, 1951; Conservation Principles & Concepts for Use in Secondary Schools, 1960. Conservation of Natural Resources (w. others), 1971. Contbr. to: Jrnl. of Geog.; Economic Geog.; Geographic Approaches to Soc. Educ.; Schl. Sci. & Maths.; Forest & Waters; Education; Ind. Soc. Studies Quarterly; Bloomington (Ind.) Tribune; Daily Herald Telephone; & others. Recip., Jrnl. of Geog. Prize for outstanding contributions to Jrnl. of Geog. 1953. Address: 1221 Dogwood Drive, Murray, KY 42071, USA.

VISHINSKI, Boris, b. 6 June 1929, Skopje, Yugoslavia. Writer & Journalist. Educ: Fac. of Law. Publs: Shadows & Thirst, 1958; A Girl, 1962; Frames & Echoes, 1965; The Rainbow, 1971; Macedonian Vistas, 1972; Ancient Shores, 1974; Ratsin, 1975. Gen. Ed., Macedonian Review Eds. Ed.-in-Chief, Macedonian Review, & Kulturen zhivot (Cultural Life). Mbrships: Writers' Union of Yugoslavia; Writers' Soc. of Macedonia; PEN; Fedn. of Yugoslav Jrnlsts. Recip., Kosta Ratsin Award, 1959. Address: 91000 Skopje, Njegoševa 26, Yugoslavia.

VISSER, Audrae Eugenie, b. 3 June 1919, Hurley, S.D., USA. Teacher. Educ: B.S., S.D. State Univ., Brookings, 1948; M.A., Univ. of Denver, Colo., 1954. Publs: Rustic Roads, 1961. Poems for Brother Donald, 1974; Meter for Momma, 1974. Contbr. to Prairie Poets, Eds. 1, 2 & 3, 1949, 1958, 1966. Mbrships. incl: Int. Platform Assn.; Nat. League Am. Pen Women; Nat. Fedn. State Poetry Socs.; S.D. State Poetry Soc. Hons: Hope Massie Award, 1972; Poet Laureate, S.D., 1974; Spoon River Poetry Award, 1974; Laura Van Nuys Award, 1974. Address: Elkton, SD 57026, USA.

VITORITTO, Elvira Wanza, b. 5 Aug. 1900, Trenton, N.J., USA. Educator; Retired Social Worker. Educ: Teaching Certs., Carroll Robbins Trng. Schl., N.J.; Rider Coll. Publs: Boulevard & Backstreet, 1972; Substance & Dreams, 1973; Another Dawn — Another Flowering, 1974. Contbr. to: Explorer; Prairie Poet; Am. Poetry, United Poets; Major Poets; etc. Mbrships: Int. Writer's Fellowship; Am. Poets Fellowship Soc.; N.J. Poetry Soc.; World Poetry Day Assn.; United Poets Laureate Int.; World Poetry Soc. Intercontinental; Am. Poetry League; Int. Poet's Shrine. Hons: Exhibitions of Poetry, Florence, 1971 & Rome,

1972; Num. awards & prizes for poetry. Address: P.O. Box 116, W. Trenton, NJ 08628, USA.

VOGEL, Manfred, b. 25 Jan. 1923, Berlin, Germany. Writer; Translator. Publs. incl: Feuertaufe, 1952; So ein Theater, 1960; Festspielereien, 1961; Und neues Leben blüht aus den Kulissen I/II, 1963; Traum und Tag, 1967; several plays; new German transls. & adaptations of Shakespeare, 1969-. Mbr., PEN. Address: Spittelauerlände 7, Vienna 1090, Austria.

VOGENITZ, David George, pen name GEORGE, David, b. 4 Jan. 1930, Milwaukee, Wis., USA. Writer. Educ: B.A., Univ. of Wis., Milwaukee, 1952; M.A., Univ. of Calif., Long Beach, 1961; M.A., Ball State Univ. (European Div.), Muncie, Ind., 1972; other univ. courses, USA, UK, Germany & Spain. Publs: The Gypsy with the Green Guitar, 1967, 2nd ed., 1969; The Flamenco Guitar, 1969. Mbrships: Soc. of Authors (London); Pomezia (Barcelona); Gypsy Lore Soc. (Liverpool); Instituto de Cultura Hispanica (Madrid). Agent: Harvey Hurtt. Address: c/o Harvey Hurtt, 1019 Shattuck Ave., Berkeley, CA 94707, USA.

VOGL-HUGER, Anna-Valeria, b. 20 May 1915, Neustadt Westpr., Germany. Writer. Educ: Univ. of Munich. Publs: Worte und Orte (poems), 1967; Zwischentöne (essays & short stories), 1970; Hier und auf fernen Bahnen (poetry), 1972; Anklänge und Stimmungen (essays & short stories), 1973; Die Frau ohne Tränen (play), 1974. Mbrships: Regensburger Writers Grp.; Soc. of German Lang. Authors; Kronenburger Lit. Circle, Recip., Silver Plume for Prose of J.Gd.A., 1973. Address: Unghauser-Str. 21, D-8263 Burghausen, W. Germany.

VOGT, Evon Zartman, Jr., b. 20 Aug. 1918, Gallup, N.M., USA. Professor of Anthropology. Educ: A.B., 1941, M.A., 1946, Ph.D., 1948, Univ. of Chgo. Publs. incl: Navaho Veterans, 1951; Modern Homesteaders, 1955; Ed., Reader in Comparative Religion, 1958; Water Witching USA, 1959; Ed., Desarrollo Cultural de los Mayas, 1964; Zinacantan, 1969; Ed., Handbook of Middle American Indians, vols. 7 & 8, 1969; The Zinacantecos of Mexico, 1970; Ed., Aerial Photography in Anthropological Field Research, 1974. Mbrships. incl: Am. Anthropol. Assn.; Fellow, Ctr. for Advanced Study in Behavioral Scis.; Fellow, Royal Anthropol. Soc., GB, & Am. Acad. Arts & Scis. Recip., Fray B. de Sahagún Prize, Repub. of Mexico, 1969. Address: William James Hall 430, Harvard Univ., Cambridge, MA 02138, USA.

VOGT, Johan Herman, b. 23 Sept. 1900, Oslo, Norway. University Professor. Publs: The Collapse of Dogmatism in Economics, 1937; Warfare & Neutrality, 1938; Russia & the Northern Countries, 1945; Thoughts on Politics, 1948; Apologia of Xantippe, 1954; Poetry & Police, 1957; In the School of Errors, 1960; The Lost Dream, 1974. Mbrships: Pres., Econ. Soc., 1958-63; Pres., Norwegian PEN, 1968-. Address: Institute of Economics, Oslo Univ., Oslo 3, Norway.

VOGT, Walter, b. 31 July 1927, Zürich, Switz. Writer; Psychiatrist. Educ: Dr. med.; Radiologist FMH; Psychiatrist FMH. Publs: Wüthrich (novel), 1966; Der Vogel auf dem Tisch (novel), 1968; Schizophrenie der Kunst (essays), 1971; Der Wiesbadener Kongress (novel), 1972; Mein Sinaitrip (sermon), 1972; Klartext (poems), 1973; Briefe aus Marokko (Letters), 1974; Der Irre und sein Arzt (prose), 1974. Contbr. to: Die Weltwoche, Zürich; Drehpunkt, Basel; etc. Mbr., Gruppe Olten (Swiss Authors' Club). Hons' Award, Swiss Schiller Inst., 1972; Literary Award, City of Berne, 1973. Address: Weststr. 3, CH 3074 Muri-BE, Switz.

VOITINOVICI, Alexandru, pen name VOITIN AL, b. 6 Aug. 1915, Pascani, Iassy, Romania. Magistrate. Educ: Lic. degree, Law Fac., Univ. of Iassy. Publs: Concrete (poetry), 1933; The Judgement By the Fire (verse drama), 1957; People in Fight (drama tril.), 1964; The Trial of Horia (drama), 1967; Goodbye, Your Majesty! (drama), 1967; Three Tragic Comedies, 1968; Avram Iancu, the Cavalry of the Victory (drama), 1970; Glasses Full with Smoke (poetry), 1974. Contbr. to: Adeverül Literar; Jurnalul Literar; România Literară; Contemporanul; etc. Mbr., Romanian Writers' Assn. Address: 60 Mihail Eminescu St., Bucharest I, 22 Romania.

VÖLKERT-MARTEN, Jürgen, b. 23 May 1949, Gelsenkirchen, Germany. Author. Publs: Keine Zeit für Träumer (poems), 1974; Ein Mensch wie ich ... (prose),

1974; in anthols: Wir Kinder von Marx und Coca-Cola, 1971; Gedichte aus der Bundeswehr, 1973; Assemblyline Fliessband, 1973; Ulcus Molle's Scenen Reader 73/74, 1974; bundes deutsch — Lyrik zur Sache Grammatik, 1974; Gegendarstellungen, 1974. Contbr. to: publikation; Edelgammler; Literatur/Manuskript; UNIO; ICON; Pages; Wegwarten; Oldenburger Hefte; Epitaph; Blätter für Lyrik und Kurzprosa. Mbrships: Lit. Union, Saarbrücken; Lit. Workshop, Gelsenkirchen. Address: D-465 Gelsenkirchen, Im Lindacker 17, W. Germany.

VOLLENWEIDER, Ernest François, b. 27 Jan. 1921, Zürich, Switz. Association Secretary. Publs: (novels) Der Mensch und die Lochkart, 1957; Richtung Süden, 1959; Roland fliegt nach Mexiko, 1961; Die Stadt der Gerechten, 1968; (short stories) Das Gewissen rollt mit, 1970. Contbr. to var. reviews. Sec., Swiss Writers' Assn. Recip., Prize, Competition, City of Zürich, 1969. Address: Hirzenbachstr. 52, Zürich, Switz.

VOLLEWENS-ZEYLEMAKER, Greta, pen name van ARDENNEN, Aye, b. 31 Aug. 1898, Amsterdam, Netherlands. Writer. Publs: De eeuwige vraag, 1939; Rondom een oude kerk (verhalenbundel), 1942; en vele jeugdboeken waaronder "de Zesde", 1947. Contbr. to: Het Kind; De vrouw en haar huis; Nederland; Elseviers maandblad; Morks mag.; Zonneschÿn; Okki-Taptoe; de Vuurslag. Mbrships. incl: Soc. of Authors (V.V.L.). Address: Hoornbruglaan 84, Rÿswyk 2-H, Netherlands.

VOLTES, Pedro, b. 1 July 1926, Reus, Spain. Professor of Economic History; Director, Institute of History. Educ: LL.D.; D.Litt.; M.Pol.Sci.; M.Econ.Sci.; Grad., Ind. Coll. of the Armed Forces, Wash. D.C., USA. Publs: (biogs.) Charles VI of Austria, 1953; Charles III of Spain; Economic History of Spain, 1972-74; 100 monographs & other books. Ed.-Fndr., Cuadernos de Historia Economica de Cataluña, 1968-. Mbrships: Past Sec., Commn. of Monuments of Barcelona; Bd. of Museums of Barcelona; Soc. for Gen. Systems Rsch. of Am. Hons: Kt.-Cmdr., Orders of Civic Merit, Naval Merit, Civil Merit, Isabel la Catolica & Alfonso El Sabio of Spain; Palmes Acad., France; Merit, Repub. of Italy. Address: Santa Lucia 1, Barcelona, Spain.

vom SCHEIDT, Martha, pen name SAALFELD, Martha, b. 15 Jan. 1898, Landau, Pfalz, Germany. Author. Educ: Univ. of Heidelberg (Philos. & Hist. of Art) Publs. incl: (poems) Deutsche Landschaft, 1946; Herbstmond, 1958; (play) Staub aus der Sahara, 1932; (stories) Idyll in Babensham, 1947; Das Süsse Gras, 1948; Der Wald, 1949; (novels) Pan ging vorüber, 1954; Anna Morgana, 1956; Mann im Mond, 1961; Judengasse, 1965; Isi oder die Gerechtigkeit, 1970. Contbr. to: Neue Rundschau; Merkur; etc. Mbrships: PEN; German Authors' Assn.; Deutsche Akad. für Sprache und Dichtung. Hons: Lit. Award, Rhineland Palatinate, 1949 & 1963; Award, Bavarian Acad. of Fine Arts, 1955; Lit. Award, Munich, 1973. Address: 6748 Bad Bergzabern, Zeppelinstr. 13, W. Germany.

VON BORN, Heidi Karin Helena Adelheid, b. 13 May 1936, Stockholm, Sweden. Author. Educ: B.A. Publs: Det fortrollade huset, 1956; Leken ar forbi, 1957; Molnen kommer med morgonen, 1958; Pavane, 1959; Tre, 1960; Martinas dagar, 1962; Frigangare, 1964; Insida, 1966; Sparhunden, 1968; Handen full, 1969; Dagar som de faller, 1972; Den tredje handen. Contbr. to: Horisont; Ord och Bild. Hons: Stockholm Stads meritstipendium, 1963; Boklotteriets stpiendium, 1964; Stockholm stads stipendium, 1969. Address: Lansmangarden, Lada 7012, Ro Rimbo, Sweden.

von der MEHDEN, Fred. Robert, b. 1 Dec. 1927, San Fran., USA. Professor. Educ: B.A., Univ. of Pacific; M.A., Claremont Grad. Schl.; Ph.D., Univ. of Calif. Publs: Religion & Nationalism in Southeast Asia, 1963; Politics of the Developing Nations, 1964; Issues of Political Development (w. Anderson & Young), 1967; Comparative Political Violence, 1973; Southeast Asia 1930-1970, 1974. Contbr. to: Jrnl. of Asian Studies; Social Rsch.; etc. Mbrships: Am. Pol. Sci. Assn.; Assn. of Asian Studies; Southern Pol. Sci. Assn. Address: 12530 Mossycup Dr., Houston, TX 77001, USA.

VONDRA, Josef, b. 11 June 1941, Vienna, Austria. Writer. Educ: De La Salle Coll., Malvern, Vic., Australia. Publs: Timor Journey, 1967; The Other China, 1968; Hong Kong — City Without a Country, 1969; A Guide to Australian Cheese, 1970; Paul Zwilling, 1974. Contbr. to: Reader's Digest; etc. Mbr., Aust. Jrnlsts. Assn. Recip., Aust.

Govt. Lit. grant, 1975. Address: P.O. Box 5, S. Yarra, Vic., Australia 3141.

Von MAUTNER MARKHOF, (Dkfm.) Georg. J. E., pen name MARCHET, Gian, b. 11 June 1926, Vienna, Austria. Instrialist; Journalist. Educ: Grad., Econs. Publs: Bürgertum und Unternehmer in der Defensive, 1959; Die Verschwörung der Inquisitoren, 1974. Contbr. to: Neue Ordnung, Vienna. Mbr., Concordia Press Club. Address: A-1110 Vienna, Simmeringer Hauptstr. 101, Austria.

VON MEHREN, Arthur Taylor, b. 10 Aug. 1922, Albert Lea, Minn., USA. Professor of Law. Educ: B.S., 1942, LL.B., 1945, Ph.D., 1946, Harvard Univ.; studies at Univ. of Zurich, Switz., 1947-48, & Univ. of Paris, France, 1948-49. Publs: The Civil Law System: Cases & Materials for the Comparative Study of Law, 1957; Contbng. Ed., Law in Japan, 1963; The Law of Multistate Problems: Cases & Materials on Conflict of Laws (w. Trautman), 1965. Contbr. to: Am. Jrnl. Comp. Law (Bd. of Eds.); Harvard Law Review; Jrnl. du Droit Int.; Ed. Comm., Int. Ency. Comp. Law. Mbr., num. profl. assns. Recip., Guggenheim Fellowship, 1968-69. Address: 68 Sparks St., Cambridge, MA 02138, USA.

VON MERVELDT, (Gräfin) Eka, b. 20 May 1911, Kowanowko, Oborniki, Poland. Journalist; Travel Writer. Publs: Weltreisen für Anfänger, 1963; Reisen zu neuen Weltwundern, 1968; Mexico City für Anfänger, 1968. Contbr. to: Die Zeit; Merian. Mbrships: German Press Club; Union of German Travel Jrnlsts. Recip., Theodor Wolff Prize, 1968. Address: Hallerstr. Hochhaus 5F, 2 Hamburg 13, W. Germany.

VONNEGUT, Kurt, Jr., b. 11 Nov. 1922, Indpls., Ind., USA. Writer; Teacher. Educ: Cornell Univ., 1940-42; Univ. of Chgo., 1945-47. Publs. incl: (novels) Player Piano, USA, 1952, UK, 1953; The Sirens of Titan, USA, 1959, UK, 1962; Mother Night, USA, 1961, UK, 1968; Cat's Cradle, USA & UK, 1963; Slaughterhouse-Five, USA, 1969, UK, 1970; (short stories) Canary in a Cathouse, 1961; Welcome to the Monkey House, 1968; (play) Happy Birthday, Wanda June, prod., 1970. Hons. incl: Purple Heart; Guggenheim Fellowship, 1967; Grant, Nat. Inst. Arts & Letters, 1970. Address: Scudder's Lane, W. Barnstable, MA 02668, USA.

VON NUMERS, Lorenz T. G. G., b. 25 Jan. 1913, Abo, Finland. Embassy Cultural Attaché. Educ: Helsinki Univ. Publs: (poetry) Svart harnesk, 1934; Porträtt med blomma, 1936; Havslyktan, 1942; (novels) Snäckans bröder, 1946; Spel-med fyra knektar, 1948; Basturesan, 1953; Lara, 1954; Den druckna myran, 1959; Drottningens handelsmän, 1964; (essays) Lansarna vid Jordan, 1964; Vinet som kaniken drack, 1967; (short stories) Månen är en säl, 1951; & transls. of French classics. Mbrships: Soc. of Swedish Authors in Finland; Swedish Authors' Union. Recip., Elsa Thulin Medal, Sweden. Address: 5 ave. Bosquet, 75007, Paris, France.

VON POST (Ambassador), C. Eric A. T., b. 31 Oct. 1899, Trelleborg, Sweden. Diplomat. Educ: Jur. kand., fil. kand., Univ. of Uppsala. Publs: Strövtåg i Istanbul, 1953; Ramazan (poems), 1955. Contbr. to var. mags. Mbrships: Swedish PEN; Sveriges Författarförbund (Swedish Authors' Union). Address: Ch. de la Fontanettaz 5, Pully-La Rosiaz, CH-1012 Lausanne, Switz.

VON RIMANOCZY, (Baron) Charles Adolf, pen name ELAND, Charles, b. 1906, London, UK. Works Manager, Meditek & Illumina Industries, 1965-74. Educ: Inst. Engrng. Technol., London; A.M.I.E.T. Publs: Dossier Closed, 1970; The Desperate Search, 1971; The Gold Hijack, 1972. Agent: J. C. Walls. Address: Gorleston Rd., Sea Point, Cape, Repub. of S. Africa.

VON ROSEN, Björn, b. 25 Oct. 1905, Rockelstad, Södermanland, Sweden. Painter. Educ: Etching Schl., Swedish Acad. of Arts. Publs: Gröna Kammarn, 1940; Berget & solen, 1949; Axel Fridell, 1951; Om djur & annat, 1951; Mitt Hundliv, 1959; Grå Fågel, 1960; Bestiarium (w. H. Martinson), 1964; Ekot av ett Horn, 1965; Samtal med en Nötvätcka, 1966; Om Naturtrohet & andra Funderingar om Konst, 1968; Minnen från Vidden, 1973. Contbr. to: Svenska Dagbladet (reviews of books on country topics 1941-46); Bonniers Litterära Mag.; Svensk Jakt; Hundsport. Address: Majliden, 150 10 Gnesta, Sweden.

von WILLEBRAND-HOLLMERUS, Margit, b. 2 Apr. 1894, Helsinki, Finland. Author. Publs: Hedvig och Desirée, 1941; Det borde vara glömt, 1942; Ursula Kastell porten,

1944; En man utan ära, 1945; Buden och fri, 1946; (histl. novels) Kejsabal för Juliana, 1954; Julianas hjarta, 1956; Unga arvingar, 1960; Sin egen domare, 1962; Kristall-Kulan, 1964; Det är inger som fråger oss, 1969; Ljug inte för honom, 1970; Grindrna, 1972; (short stories) Långräga ifrån; 20 other books, children's books & plays for theatre, TV, radio. Contbr. to var. newspapers & mags. in Finland & Sweden. Mbrships. incl: Soc. Swedish Authors in Finland. Hons. incl: Langman Award (Sweden), 1971; Lybeck Award for novel Hedwig och Desirée, 1942. Address: Stenbäcksgatan 4b 8, Helsinki 25, Finland.

VOSS, Carl Hermann, b. 8 Dec. 1910, Pitts., Pa., USA. Author; Educator; Clergyman; Lecturer. Educ: B.A., Univ. of Pitts., Pa., 1931; Master of Divinity, Union Theological Sem., NYC, 1935; Ph.D., Univ. of Pitts., Pa., 1942. Publs: The Universal God, 1953; The Palestine Problem Today: Israel & Its Neighbours, 1953; This is Israel, 1956; Rabbi & Minister: The Friendship of Stephen S. Wise & John Haynes Holmes, 1965: In Search of Meaning: Living Religions of the World, 1968; Stephen S. Wise: Servant of the People — Selected Letters, 1969; A Summons Unto Men: An Anthology of the Writings of John Haynes Holmes, 1971; Quotations of Courage & Vision, 1972. Contbr. to var. relig. jrnls. Address: 708 Oaks Marianna Trail E., Jackonsville, FL 32211, USA.

VOSS, E(rnst) Theodor, b. 25 Dec. 1928, Hilden. Germany. Associate Professor of German Literature. Educ: D.Phil., Bonn Univ., 1958. Publs: Erzählprobleme des Briefromans, 1960; Critical editions of: J. J. Engel, Über Handlung, Gespräch und Erzählung, 1965; J. H. Voss, Idyllen, 1968; & S. Gessner, Idyllen, 1973. Contbrns: Co-Ed. & Co-Fndr., Sammlung Metzler; Mbr., Ed. Bd., Monatshefte, 1966-67; Mbr., Ed. Bd., Germanic Review, 1970—. Mbrships: AAUP; MLA of Am.; Int. Vereinigung für Germanische Sprach- und Literaturwissenschaft. Recip., Humanities Rsch. Grant, Columbia Univ., 1971. Address: 311 Hamilton Hall, Dept. of German, Columbia Univ., N.Y., NY 10027, USA.

VRIESLAND, Victor Emanuel van, b. 1892, Netherlands. Writer. Educ: Gymnasium, The Hague; Dijon Univ. Publs. incl: (essays) Herman Hana, 1920; Grondslag van Verstandhouding, 1946; Vereenvoudigingen, 1952; Vooronderzoek, 1946; Le Vent se couche, 1949; Tegengif, 1959; (play) Havenstad, 1933; (novel) Het Afschied van de Wereld in drie Dagen, 1926; (anthologies) Poezie door alle eeuwen, 3 vols., 1939, 1953, 1954; In den Hof van Eros; De Vergetenen, 1955. Contbr. to: De Vrije Bladen; Forum; De Nieuwe Stem; etc. Mbrships. incl: PEN; Soc. of Authors. Hons. incl: Huyghens Prize. Address: Weesperzijde 25, Amsterdam, Netherlands.

VRIGNY, Roger, b. 19 May 1920. Writer; Broadcaster. Educ: L.ès L.; Paris Univ. Publs: (novels) Arban; Laurena; Barbegal; La Nuit de Mougins; Fin de Journée; Le Serment d'Amboise; La Vie brève; (other publs.) Marute; L'Enlèvement d'Arabelle; L'Impromptu du réverbère; Les Irascibles; La Dame d'onfrede. Contbr. to radio & TV. Recip., Prix Femina, 1963. Address: 4 rue Jean-Ferrandi, Paris 6e, France.

VYVYAN, John, b. 3 Oct. 1908, Hove, UK. Author. Publs: The Shakespearean Ethic, 1959; Shakespeare & the Rose of Love, 1960; Shakespeare & Platonic Beauty, 1961; A Case Against Jones, 1966; In Pity & in Anger, 1969; The Dark Face of Science, 1971; Sketch for a World-Picture, 1972. Address: c/o Hope Leresche & Steele, 11 Jubilee Place, London SW3, 3TE, UK.

W

WADE, David, b. 2 Dec. 1929, Edinburgh, UK. Writer. Educ: B.A., Queens' Coll., Cambridge Univ., 1952. Author of six plays for radio, also talks, adaptations etc. for radio & TV. Contbr. to: Times (radio critic); etc. Mbrships: Inst. for Cultural Rsch.; Critics Circle; Broadcasting Press Guild. Address: 4a Queen Anne's Gdns., London W4, UK.

WADE, (Rev.) Francis Clarence, S. J., b. 11 Nov. 1907, Whitesboro, Tex., USA. Teacher; Priest of the Society of Jesus. Educ: A.B., 1930, Xavier Univ.; M.A., 1932; S.T.L., 1939, St. Louis Univ. Publs: John of St. Thomas' Outlines of Logic, 1955; Teaching & Morality, 1963; Cajetan's Commentary on Being & Essence, 1964. Contbr. to: Review of Metaphysics; Jrnl. of Philos.; Modern Schoolman. Mbr., var. philos. assns. Address: 1404 W. Wisconsin Ave., Milwaukee, WI 53233, USA.

WADE, (Hugh) Mason, b. 3 July 1913, N.Y., USA. Historian. Educ: Harvard, 1935; For. Serv. Inst., 1943. Publs: Margaret Fuller, 1940; Selected Writings of M. Fuller, 1941; Francis Parkman, 1942; Journals of F. Parkman, 1947; The French-Canadian Outlook, 1946; The French Canadians, 1760-1967, 1968; Regionalism & the Canadian Community, 1867-1967, 1969; The International Megalopolis, 1969. Contbr. to var. jrnls. Mbrships: Pres., Can. Hist. Assn., 1965; Chmn., Am. Sect., Jt. Can.-Am. Comm., Am. Hist. Assn., 1963-65. Hons: Dr. ès Lettres, Univ. of Ottawa, 1964; Centennial Commn. Grant, 1967; Dr. Sci. Soc., Univ. Laval, 1973. Address: R.R.2, Windsor, VT 05089, USA.

WADE, Rosalind Herschel, b. 11 Sept. 1909, London, UK. Author; Journalist; Lecturer. Publs: over 32 novels inclng. The Raft; Treasure in Heaven; Come Fill the Cup; A Small Shower. Contbr. to: Contemporary Review (Ed., 1970—). Mbrships: Lit. Panel of Southern Arts; Chmn. & VP, Soc. Women Writers & Jrnlsts.; Chmn., Guildford Ctr. Poetry Soc.; Chmn., Alresford Histl. & Lit. Soc.; Nat. Book League Coun.; Coun. Mbr., Nat. Poetry Soc. Hons: Poetry Prize, Int. Poetry Who's Who, 1972; Keats $2000 Poetry Prize, 1975. Address: White Cottage, Old Alresford, Hants., UK.

WADIA, Maneck S., b. 22 Oct. 1931, Bombay, India. Management Consultant. Educ: B.A., St. Xavier's Coll., 1952; M.A., Ind. Univ., USA, 1955; Ph.D., 1957; M.B.A., 1958. Publs: The Nature & Scope of Management, 1966; Marketing Management, 1966; Management & the Behavioural Sciences, 1968; Cases in International Business, 1970. Contbr. to: Bus. Horizons; Advanced Mgmt.; Calif. Mgmt. Review; Int. Review of Int. Scis.; etc. Mbrships: Acad. of Mgmt.; Soc. of Applied Anthropol. Recip., Award, Invited Papers, Acad. of Mgmt. Address: 1660 Luneta Dr., Del Mar, CA 92014, USA.

WADIA, Sophia, b. 13 Sept. 1901, Bogota, Colombia, S.Am. Editor. Educ: Baccalaureat es Sciences, Lycee Molière, Sorbonne, Paris, France, 1920; Postgrad. Dips., Columbia Univ., NYC, USA, 1921-25, Schl. of Oriental Studies, London, UK, 1928-29. Publs: Brotherhood of Religions, 1939; Preparation for Citizenship, 1941. Contbr. to: Aryan Path (Ed., 1930—); Indian PEN (Ed., 1934—). Mbrships. incl: Fndr.-Organizer, All-India Ctr. Int. PEN, 1933—; Fndr-Mbr., Indian Inst. World Culture, Bangalore, Life Pres., 1958—; Pres., Asian Book Trust. Recip., Padmashri Award by Pres. of India, Repub. Day Awards, 1960. Address: Theosophy Hall, 40 New Marine Lines, Bombay 400 020, India.

WAGENKNECHT, Edward, b. 28 Mar. 1900, Chicago, Ill., USA. Writer; Emeritus Professor of English. Educ: Th.B., Union Theol. Coll., Chicago, 1921; Ph.B., 1923, M.A., 1924, Univ. Chicago; Ph.D., Univ. Wash., 1932. Approx. 60 publs. inclng: The Man Charles Dickens, 1929, revised ed., 1966; Longfellow: A Full-Length Portrait, 1955; Nathaniel Hawthorne: Man & Writer, 1961; William Dean Howells: The Friendly Eye, 1969; The Personality of Milton, 1969; James Russell Lowell: Portrait of a Many-Sided Man, 1971; Ambassadors for Christ, 1972; The Personality of Shakespeare, 1972; (novels as Julian Forrest) Nine Before Fotheringhay, 1966; The Glory of the Lilies, 1969. Contbr. to acad. jrnls. Address: 233 Otis St., W. Newton, MA 02165, USA.

WAGER, Walter Herman, pen name, TIGER, John, b. 4 Sept. 1924, NYC, USA. Writer. Educ: B.A., Columbia Univ., 1943; LL.B., Harvard Univ., 1946; LL.M.,

Northwestern Univ., 1949. Publs: Death Hits the Jackpot, 1954; Operation Intrigue, 1956; I Spy, 1965; Camp Century (non-fiction), 1962; Masterstroke, 1966; Superkill, 1966; The Playwrights Speak (non-fiction), 1967; Wipeout, 1967; Countertrap, 1967; Death Twist, 1968; The Girl Who Split, 1969; Sledgehammer, 1970; Viper Three, 1971; Swap, 1972; Telefon, 1975. Mbrships: Writers' Guild; Authors' League; Drama Desk. Address: c/o ASCAP, One Lincoln Plaza, N.Y., NY 10023, USA.

WAGNER, Charles Abraham, b. 10 Mar. 1910, NYC, USA. Poet; Journalist; Historian. Educ: B.A., M.A., Columbia Univ., NYC. Publs: Poems of the Soil & Sea, 1923; Nearer the Bone: New Poems, 1930; Ed., Prize Poems (w. Mark Van Doren), 1931; Harvard: Four Centuries & Freedoms, 1950. Contbr. to: Bookman; Saturday Review of Lit.; Poetry; A Mag. of Verse; N.Y. Times; etc. Mbrships: Poetry Soc. of Am.; Authors League. Hons: 1st Prize, Poetry Mag., 1931; 1st Prize, Poetry Soc. of Am. Award, 1971; 2nd Prize, Int. Who's Who in Poetry Award, 1973. Address: 106 Morningside Drive, N.Y., NY 10027, USA.

WAGNER, Francis Stephen, b. 28 Feb. 1911, Krupina, Czech. Librarian; Historian; Educator. Educ: Ph.D., Univ. Szeged, 1940. Publs. incl: Czech & Slovak Historiography, 1938; Citanka, 1939; First Period of Slovak Nationalism, 1940; Cultural Revolution in East Europe, 1955; Szechenyi & the Nationality Problem in the Hapsburg Empire, 1960; The Hungarian Revolution in Perspective, 1967; Towards a New Central Europe, 1970. Contbr. to: Am. Quarterly; Histl. Abstracts; Free World & Slavic Reviews; Dolgozatok; etc. Mbr., Am., Can. & int. profl. orgs. Hons. incl: Hist. Award, Univ. of Szeged, 1935, 1936; Univ. Students' Nat. Award in Hist., Hungarian Acad. of Scis., 1937. Address: 4610 Franklin Street, Kensington, MD 20795, USA.

WAGONER, David Russell, b. 5 June 1926, Massillon, Ohio, USA. Editor; Professor of English. Educ: B.A., Pa. State Univ.; M.A., Ind. Univ. Publs. incl: (poems) Dry Sun, Dry Wind, 1953; The Nesting Ground, 1963; Staying Alive, 1966; Riverbed, 1972; Sleeping in the Woods, 1974; (novels) The Man in the Middle, 1954; Rock, 1958; Baby, Come on Inside, 1968; Where is My Wandering Boy Tonight?, 1970; The Road to Many a Wonder, 1974; Tracker, 1975; Ed., Straw for Fire, 1973. Hons. incl: Nat. Coun. on Arts Award, 1970; Blumenthal-Leviton-Blonder Prize, Poetry, 1974. Address: 1075 Summit Ave. E., Seattle, WA, USA.

WAHLUND, Per Erik, b. 24 July 1923, Stockholm, Sweden. Author. Educ: Fil. dr., Univ. of Uppsala. Publs: Vakttjanst, 1942; Kammarmusik, 1944; Atersken, 1951; Luftspegling, 1952; Korsbarstradet, 1954; Bambuflojten, 1956; Ressallskap, 1956; Bordssamtal, 1964; Avsidesrepliker, 1966; Londonpromenader, 1967; Japansk poesi, 1968; Japansk dagbok, 1968; Ridafall, 1969; Kammarradinnans konterfej, 1970; Rostlagen, 1971; Lekverk, 1972; Sjalvstudier, 1974. Contbr. to: Uppsala Nya Tidning; Expressen; Bonniers Litteratra Mag.; Svenska Dagbladet; var. int. papers. Mbrships: Swedish Union of Authors; Swedish Soc. of Translators; Swedish Assn. of Drama Critics; PEN. Address: Tegnergatan 12, 752 27 Uppsala, Sweden.

WAIDSON, Herbert Morgan, b. 20 June 1916, Walsall, Staffs., UK. Professor of German. Educ: M.A., Univ. of Birmingham; D.Phil., Univ. of Leipzig, Germany. Publs. incl: The Modern German Novel, 1959, 2nd ed.; The Modern German Novel 1945-65, 1971; ed., German Short Stories 1945-55, 1957; German Short Stories 1900-45, 1959; German Short Stories 1955-65, 1969; Modern German Stories, 1961; Gotthelf, Sie Schwarze Spinne, 1956; Goethe, Egmont, 1960; Böll, Doktor gesammeltes Schweigen (w. G. Seidmann), 1963. Contbr. to: Times Lit. Supplement; Books Abroad; Mod. Lang. Review; etc. Mbrships. incl: MLA; Mod. Humanities Rsch. Assn. Address: 29 Myrtle Grove, Sketty, Swansea SA2 0SJ, UK.

WAIN, John Barrington, b. 14 Mar. 1925, Stoke-on-Trent, Staffs., UK. Writer. Educ: B.A., 1946, M.A., 1950, St. John's Coll., Oxford Univ. Publs. incl: (fiction) Hurry on Down, 1953; A Travelling Woman, 1959; Strike the Father Dead, 1962; The Young Visitors, 1965; The Smaller Sky, 1967; A Winter in the Hills, 1970; The Life Guard & Other Stories, 1971; (poetry) A Word Carved on a Sill, 1956; Letters to 5 Artists, 1969; The Shape of Feng, 1972; (autobiog.) Sprightly Running, 1962; (criticism) Essays on Literature & Ideas, 1963; The Living World of Shakespeare, 1964; A House for the Truth, 1972.

Hons incl: First Fellow in Creative Arts, Brasenose Coll., Oxford, 1971-72. Address: c/o Macmillan & Co., Ltd., Little Essex St., London WC2, UK.

WAINHOUSE, David Walter, b. 15 Sept. 1900, Vilna, Lithuania. Diplomat; Author. Educ: A.B., Harvard Coll.; A.M., Harvard Grad. Schl.; LL.B., J.D., Harvard Law Schl.; B.C.L., Oxford Univ., UK. Publs: History of American Foreign Policy (co-author), 1940, 2nd ed., 1944; Remnants of Empire, 1964; International Peace Observation, 1966; Arms Control Agreements: Designs for Verification & Organization, 1968; International Peacekeeping at the Crossroads, 1973. Contbr. to: Christian Sci. Monitor; New Repub.; var. law jrnls. Address: 4301 Massachusetts Ave. N.W., Wash. DC 20016, USA.

WAINWRIGHT, Gordon Ray, pen name GORDON, Ray, b. 1927, Frodingham, Lincs., UK. Head, Department Liberal Studies, Wearside College, Sunderland. Educ: Nottingham Univ.; Hull Univ.; B.A.; Cert. Ed. Publs: Efficiency in Reading, 1965; Towards Efficiency in Reading, 1968; Rapid Reading Made Simple, 1972. New Statesman; Indl. Soc.; Municipal Review; Educ. & Training: Tribune; Accountancy; Mgmt. in Action; Data Systems; Indl. & Commercial Training; Sunday Times. Mbrships: F.R.S.A.; Soc. of Authors; Brit. Inst. Mgmt.; Assn. for Liberal Educ. Address: 22 Hawes Ct., Seaburn Dene, Sunderland, SR6 8NU, UK.

WAKATAMA, Pius Musarurwa, b. 13 June 1939, Masinkana Village, Marandellas, Rhodesia. Writer. Educ: B.A. & M.A., Wheaton Coll., USA. Publs: Dandadzo Rengano (Shona Ethnol. of short stories), 1967; Musa Series (Shona fiction for children), 1967; Kufa Hakuna Memba (Christian doctrine in Shona), 1967; Mukushi nevana Vake (novel), 1968; Grades 6 & 7 Shona Reader (contbr.), 1972; Jesus Christ Lord of the Universe & Hope of the World (contbr.), 1974. Contbr. to num. mags. & newspapers. Mbr., Lambda Iota Tau. Recip., 2nd Prize, Rhodesia Lit. Bur., 1967. Address: 14 Pazarangu Ave., Harari Township, Salisbury, Rhodesia.

WAKEFORD, John, b. 29 Nov. 1936, Plymouth, UK. Lecturer. Educ: Glasgow Univ.; B.A., Nottingham Univ.; Ph.D., Brunel Univ. Publs: The Strategy of Social Enquiry, 1968; The Cloistered Elite, 1970; Ed: Power in Britain, 1974. Contbr. to: Sociology; Brit. Jrnl. of Sociol.; Times Higher Educl. Supplement; Law Soc. Gazette; New Society; etc. Mbrships: Brit. Sociol. Assn. (Hon. Gen. Sec., 1974—); Soc. for Rsch. into Higher Educ.; Am. Sociol. Assn. Address: Long Lane Cottage, Quernmore, Lancaster, UK.

WAKEHAM, (Mabel) Irene, b. 28 June 1912, Watford, Herts., UK. Educator. Educ: B.A., Andrews Univ., Berrien Springs, Mich., 1934; M.A., Univ. of Southern Calif., 1939; Ph.D., Stanford Univ., 1965. Publs: Oral English, 1952; Strictly Confidential, 1955; Though the Heavens Fall, 1970. Contbr. to: Seventh-day Adventist ch. publs. Mbrships: Nat. Coun. of Tchrs. of Engl.; Br. Treas., AAUW. Hons. incl: Andrews Univ. Hall of Fame, 1974. Address: 3922 Broadmor Rd., Huntsville, AL 35810, USA.

WALCOTT, Robert, b. 24 Jan. 1910, Boston, Mass., USA. Historian; College Professor; Author. Educ: A.B., Harvard Coll., 1931; M.A., 1932, Ph.D., 1938, Harvard Univ.; grad. seminars, Inst. Histl. Rsch., Univ. of London, UK, 1934-35, 1959-60. Publs: English Politics in the Early 18th Century, 1956; The Tudor-Stuart Period of English History: a Review of Changing Interpretations, 1965; (chapt. in) Changing Currents in British History (Ed., E. Furber), 1965. Contbr. to: Jrnls. of Mod., British Hist.; Engl. & Am. Histl. Reviews; Bulletin of Inst. of Histl. Rsch.; Annals of Acad. Pol. & Social Sci. Address: 1559 Burbank Rd., Wooster, OH 44691, USA.

WALDEN, Howard T., II, b. 3 Jan. 1897, Hackensack, N. J., USA. Writer. Publs: Upstream & Down, 1938, reprinted 1945; Big Stony, 1940, reprinted 1947; Ed., Angler's Choice (anthol.), 1947; Familiar Freshwater Fishes of America, 1964; Native Inheritance: The Story of Corn in America, 1966; Anchorage Northeast, 1971; The Last Pool, 1972. Ed. Dir., Corn Industries Rsch. Fndn., 1947-62. Contbr. to: Field & Stream; Outdoor Life; N.Y. Times Mag. Hon. Mbr., Eugene Field Soc., St. Louis, Mo., 1947. Address: Jordan Bay, R.R. 2, Shelburne, N.S., Can., and Sneden's Landing, Palisades, NY, USA.

WALDRON, Robert S., b. 1922, Southampton, UK. Accountant. Publs: Modern Trends in the Form of Published Accounts, 1961; Understanding Accounts, 1967;

Target for Careers: Accountancy, 1968; Modern Published Accounts, 1969; Dicksee's Auditing, 1969. Contbr. to: Guardian; Sunday Times; Acct.; City Press; Acct.'s Digest; Acctcy.; Certified Acct.'s Jrnl.; etc. Mbrships. incl: Fellow, Inst. Chartered Accts.; Fellow, Assn. Certified & Corporate Accts.; Brit. Inst. Mgmt. (Assoc.); Fellow, Inst Arbitrators. Address: United City Merchants (Investments) Ltd., 3/5 Swallow Place, Princes St., London W1A 1BB, UK.

WALEN, Harry L., b. 26 June 1915, Winchester, Mass., USA. Educator. Educ: B.A., 1937, M.A., 1942, Harvard Univ. Publs: Co-author, Ed., English Literature, 1964; 1970, 1975; American Literature, 1967, 1970, 1975; Types of Literature, 1964, 1970, 1974. Family Travel — Camping, 1954, 1959. Contbr. to: Studies in Adolescence, 1975; var. educl. jrnls. inclng. Engl. Jrnl.; NASSP Bulletin; Coll. Verse; Engl. Educ.; Educl. Ldrship., etc. Mbrships. incl: New England Assn. Tchrs. Engl. (Pres., 3 terms) Headmasters' Assn.; Nat. Assn. Second. Schl. Principals; Boston Authors' Club. Hons. incl: Citation, Nat. Coun. Tchrs. of Engl., 1970. Harry L. Walen annual Book Award for Creative Writing, Needham HS, 1971—; C'wlth. Fellow, Mass. State Dept. Educ., 1972. Address: 6 Floral St., Newton Highlands, MA 02161, USA.

WALES, Robert, b. 12 July 1923, Greenock, UK. Playwright; Filmscript Writer for TV drama & dramatized documentary. Publs: The Cell, 1971; 3 full-length plays produced professionally in the theatre; short stories broadcast in Aust. & on BBC, UK. Mbrships: Soc. of Authors; League of Dramatists. Hons: for 'The Searchers' (short story): 1st Prize, Lit. Comp., Univ. of New England, Aust., 1960; for 'Wings on the Morning': F.N.Q.A.T.A. Drama Comp. Award, 1961; for 'The Hobby Horse': Coff's Harbour Centenary Play Comp., 1961. Address: c/o Fraser & Dunlop Ltd., 91 Regent St., London W1, UK.

WALKER, Benjamin, b. 25 Nov. 1923, Calcutta, India. Writer. Educ: M.A. Publs: Persian Pageant, 1950; Angkor Empire, 1955; Hindu World, 2 Vols., 1968; Sex & the Supernatural, 1970; Beyond the Body, 1974; Oriental Mythology, 1975. Contbr. to: Pacific Affairs; Man, Myth & Magic; Ency. of the Unexplained. Mbr., Soc. of Authors, UK. Address: 84 Church Rd., Teddington, Middx., UK.

WALKER, David (Harry), b. 9 Feb. 1911, Dundee, UK. Writer. Educ: Royal Mil. Coll., Sandhurst, 1929-30. Publs. incl: (novels) Geordie, UK & UK, 1950; Digby, UK & USA, 1953; Harry Black, UK & USA, 1954; Where the High Winds Blow, UK & USA, 1960; Winter of Madness, UK & USA, 1964; Mallabec, UK & USA, 1965; Come Back, Geordie, UK & USA, 1966; Devil's Plunge (as CAB-Intersec, USA), 1968; The Lord's Pink Ocean, UK & USA, 1972; var. short stories & juvenile books. Mbrships. incl: F.R.S.L.; Roosevelt Campobello Int. Pk. Commn. (Chmn.). Hons: Gov.-Gen's Award, Can., 1953, 1954; D.Litt., Univ. of N.B., 1955. Address: Strathcroix, St. Andrews, N.B., Can.

WALKER, David Maxwell, b. 9 Apr. 1920, Glasgow, UK. University Professor. Educ: M.A., 1946, LL.B., 1948, Univ. of Glasgow; Ph.D., 1952, LL.D., 1960, Univ. of Edinburgh; LL.B., 1957, LL.D., 1968, Univ. of London. Publs: Law of Damages in Scotland, 1955; Law of Delict in Scotland, 1966; The Scottish Legal System, 4th ed., 1976; Principles of Scottish Private Law, 2nd ed., 1975; Law of Civil Remedies in Scotland, 1974. Contbr. to: Mod. Law Review; Jrnl. of the Soc. of Pub. Tchrs. of Law; Juridical Review; Scots Law Times. Mbrships: Fac. of Advocates, Edinburgh; Hon. Soc. of the Middle Temple,London, Fellow, Soc. of Antiquaries in Scotland. Recip., Hon. LL.D., Edinburgh Univ., 1974. Address: 1 Beaumont Gate, Glasgow G12 9EE, UK.

WALKER, Donald Smith, b. 6 Apr., 1918, Ashton-under-Lyne, Lancs., UK. Schoolmaster. Educ: M.A., St. Catharine's Coll., Cambridge. Publs: The Mediterranean Lands, 3rd ed., 1965; A Geography of Italy, 2nd ed., 1967. Contbr. to: Shackleton's Europe, 1964. Address: 66 The Rise, Ponteland, Newcastle upon Tyne NE20 9LH, UK.

WALKER, Eunice Arnaud, b. Monett, Mo., USA. Writer. Educ: A.B., Univ. of Ark.; Grad. studies, Geo. Wash. Univ., Wash D.C. Publs: Woodrow Wilson, 1967. Contbr. to: Reader's Digest; Saturday Evening Post; Space Jrnl.; Dept. of State Mag. Mbrships. incl: Nat. League of Am. Pen Women; Nat. Fedn. of Press Women; Nat. Press Club; Nat. Histl. Assn.; Nat. Archives; Smithsonian Instn.; Nat. Trust for Hist. Preservation. Hons. incl: Commendations, Dept. of

State & Exec. Off. of the Pres., USA. Address: 205 James Thurber Ct., Falls Church, VA 22046, USA.

WALKER, Kenneth Richard, b. 17 Oct. 1931, Otley, Yorks., UK. Economist; University Professor of Economics. Educ: B.A., Univ. of Leeds, 1953; D.Phil., Oxford Univ., 1956. Publs: Planning in Chinese Agriculture: Socialisation & the Private Sector 1956-1962, 1965. Contbr. to: Econ. Trends in Communist China, 1968; Scottish Jrnl. of Pol. Economy; Econ. Dev. & Cultural Change; China Quarterly. Address: 4 Harpenden Rd., St. Albans, Herts., UK.

WALKER, Margaret (Abigail), b. 7 July 1915, Birmingham, Ala., USA. Professor of English & Institute Director. Educ: B.A., Northwestern Univ., Ill., 1935; M.A., 1940, Ph.D., 1965, Univ. of Iowa; Yale Univ., 1954. Publs: (verse) For My People, 1942; Ballad of the Free, 1966; (novels) Come Down from Yonder Mountain, Can., 1962; Jubilee, 1965. Hons: Yale Series of Younger Poets Award, 1942; Rosenthal Fellowship, 1944; Houghton Mifflin Lit. Fellowship, 1966. Address: 2205 Guynes St., Jackson, MS 39213, USA.

WALKER, Marshall John, b. 23 Jan. 1912, Bath, N.Y., USA. Physicist. Educ: B.Chem., 1933, A.M., 1936, Cornell Univ.; Ph.D., Pa. State Univ., 1950. Publs: The Nature of Scientific Thought, 1963. Mbrships: Am. Phys. Soc.; Am. Optical Soc.; Am. Assn. of Phys. Tchrs.; AAUP; Conn. Acad. of Arts & Scis. Address: Star Route, Chaplin, CT 06235, USA.

WALKER, Peter Norman, pen names CORAM, Christopher; FERRIS, Tom; MANTON, Paul; DEAN, John; POPE, Adrian; b. 1936, Glaisdale, Whitby, Yorks., UK. Police Lecturer in Criminal Law. Publs: Over 25 since 1967 incl: Carnaby & the Hijackers, 1967; Carnaby & the Assassins, 1968; Espionage for a Lady, 1968; A Call to Die, 1969; Carnaby & the Conspirators, 1969; Carnaby & the Saboteurs, 1970; Fatal Accident, 1970; Panda One on Duty, 1971; Special Duty, 1971; The Courts of Law, 1971; History of Punishment, 1971. Contbr. to: Police; Police Review; Police Jrnl.; Punch; local press; etc. Mbrships. incl: Soc. of Authors; Crime Writers' Assn. Agent: Bolt & Watson. Address: Coram Cottage, Ampleforth, York, UK.

WALKER, Ralph Spence, b. 25 May 1904, Aberdeen, UK. University Professor (Emeritus), formerly Molson Professor of English Literature & Chairman of the English Department, McGill University, Montreal. Educ: M.A., Aberdeen Univ.; B.A., M.A., Cambridge Univ. Publs: John Knox's History of the Reformation, 1940; James Beattie's Diary 1773, 1947; James Beattie's Daybook, 1773-98, 1948; Ben Jonson's Discoveries, 1953; James Boswell's Correspondence with John Johnston of Grange, 1966; Letters of Thomas Twining (forthcoming). Contbr. to var. acad. jrnls. Mbrships. incl: Int. Assn. Univ. Profs. Engl. Hons. Incl: Schlr., St. Catharine's Coll., Cambridge Univ. Address: Peaveley House, 3 Church St., Haslingfield, Cambridge CB3 7JE, UK.

WALKER, Ronald R., b. 2 Sept. 1934, Newport News, Va., USA. Journalist; Educator. Educ: B.S., Pa. State Univ., 1956; Nieman Fellow, Harvard Univ., 1970-71. Mng. Ed. & Ed. Page Ed., San Juan Star, P.R. Contbr. to: N.Y. Times; Nation Mag.; Commonwealth; Wash. Post; Boston Globe. Mbrships: Nat. Conf. of Ed. Writers; Caribbean Studies Assn.; Newspaper Guild of Am. Address: Grad Schl. of Jrnlsm., Columbia Univ., N.Y., NY 10027, USA.

WALKER, Stella Archer, pen names ARCHER, S.; ARCHER-BATTEN, S., b. Leicester, UK. Writer. Publs: Horses of Renown, 1954; The Controversial Horse (w. R. S. Summerhays), 1966; Sporting Art: England 1700-1900, 1972; Compiler, In Praise of Horses (anthol.), 1953; Long Live the Horse (anthol.), 1955. Contbr. to: Horse & Hound; Country Life; The Field; Art & Antiques; British Racehorse; Light Horse; Riding; Horseman's Yr.; Pony; Chronicle of the Horse (USA); Plaisirs Equestres (France); Co-Ed., Summerhays Ency. for Horsemen. Address: Watermill Farm, Rushlake Green, Heathfield, Sussex, UK.

WALKINSHAW, Lawrence H(arvey), b. 25 Feb. 1904, nr. Battle Creek, Mich., USA. Doctor of Dental Surgery; Writer. Educ: D.D.S., Univ. of Mich. Publs: The Sandhill Cranes, 1949; Cranes of the World, 1973. Contbr. to: The Auk; Wilson Bulletin; Condor; Ibis; Ostrich; Jack-Pine Warbler (Ed., 1939-48); Ind. Audubon Quarterly; Oriole; Blue Jay; Migrant; Audubon Mag.; Am. Birds; Neb. Bird Review; Mbrships: Am. Ornithol. Union (Sec., 1961-64); Wilson Ornithol. Soc.; Mich. Audubon Soc. (VP, 1939-48); Wilson Ornithol. Soc.

(Coun., 1st & 2nd VP, Pres.); Southwestern Mich Dental Soc. (VP & Pres., 1947-48). Hons: Amateur Sci. of Yr., Mich. Acad. of Scis.; Fellow, Am. Ornithol's. Union, 1950. Address: 1145 Scenic Dr., Muskegon, MI 49445, USA.

WALKÓ, György, b. 29 Dec. 1920, Budapest, Hungary. Literary Historian; Essayist; Editor. Educ: Ph.D., Budapest. Publs: Bertolt Brecht, 1959; Igy élt Goethe, 1964; Weimar és a német klasszicizmus, 1974; Katarzis nélkül, 1975. Contbr. to jrnls. inclng: Nagyvilag. Mbrships: Exec. Comm., PEN; Hungarian Writers Assn. Address: Keleti Károly u. 16, H — 1924 Budapest, Hungary.

WALL, Joseph Frazier, b. 10 July 1920, Des Moines, Iowa, USA. Professor of History. Educ: B.A., Grinnell Coll., 1941; M.A. Harvard Univ., 1942; Ph.D., Columbia Univ., 1951. Publs: Henry Watterson: Reconstructed Rebel, 1956; Andrew Carnegie, 1970; Interpreting 20th Century America (w. Richard Lowitt), 1972. Contbr. to: Jrnl. of Am. Hist.; Am. Hist. Review; Am. Heritage. Mbrships: Soc. of Am. Histns.; Exec. Bd., Org. of Am. Histns.; Am. Histl. Assn.; Western Hist. Assn.; Am. Studies Assn. Hons. incl: Bancroft Prize in Am. Hist., 1971; Johnston-Bingham Prize in Iowa Lit., 1971. Address: 1409 Broad St., Grinnell, Iowa, 50112, USA.

WALL, Mervyn, b. 23 Aug. 1908, Dublin, Repub. of Ireland. Secretary, Irish Arts Council; Writer; Literary Critic; Radio Critic. Educ: Bonn, Germany; Univ. Coll., Dublin; B.A., Nat. Univ. Ireland. Publs: The Unfortunate Fursey, 1946; The Return of Fursey 1948; Leaves for the Burning, 1952; No Trophies Raise, 1956; Forty Foot Gentlemen Only, 1962; A Flutter of Wings, 1974. Contbr. to var. lit. mags. & jrnls. Ireland, UK, USA; etc. Mbrships: Irish Acad. Letters (Hon. Sec. & Treas., 1968-74); Royal Dublin Soc. Address: 16 Castlepark Road, Sandycove, Dun Laoghaire, County Dublin, Repub. of Ireland.

WALL, Richard, b. 2 June 1944, Abergavenny, UK. Historian. Educ: B.A., 1965, M. Philos., 1969, Univ. London. Publs: Household & Family in Past Time (w. Peter Laslett), 1972. Contbr. to: Local Population Studies (Ed.); etc. Address: 6 Metcalfe Rd., Cambridge, UK.

WALLACE, Barbara Brooks, b. Soochow, China. Writer. Educ: B.A., UCLA. Publs: Claudia, 1969; Andrew the Big Deal, 1970; The Trouble with Miss Switch, 1971; Victoria, 1972; Can Do, Missy Charlie, 1974; The Secret Summer of L.E.B., 1974. Mbrships: Corres. Sec., Wash. Children's Book Guild; Authors' Guild; Am. Penwomen. Recip. Am. Penwomen Award for Claudia, 1970. Address: 2708 George Mason Pl., Alexandria, VA 22305, USA.

WALLACE, Doreen, b. 18 June, 1897, Lorton, UK. Former Teacher; Novelist. Educ: M.A., Somerville Coll., Oxford. Publs. incl: Barnham Rectory, 1934; Going to Sea, 1936; The Time of Wild Roses, 1938; Green Acres, 1941; The Noble Savage, 1945; Willow Farm, 1948; How Little We Know, 1949; The Younger Son, 1954; The Money Field, 1957; Richard & Lucy, 1959; Woman with a Mirror, 1963; The Turtle, 1969; Elegy, 1970; An Earthly Paradise, 1971; A Thinking Reed, 1973. Address: Wortham Manor, Diss, Norfolk, UK.

WALLACE, Irving, b. 19 Mar. 1916, Chgo., Ill., USA. Author. Educ: Williams Inst., Berkeley, Calif.; Los Angeles City Coll., Calif. Publs: The Fabulous Originals, 1956; The Square Pegs, 1958; The Chapman Report, 1961; The Prize, 1963; The Three Sirens, 1964; The Man, 1965; The Seven Minutes, 1969; The Word, 1972; The Fan Club, 1974; The People's Almanac, 1975. Contbr. to: Ency. Britannica; Am. Oxford & Colliers Encys.; Playboy; Cosmopolitan; Ramparts; var. mags., UK, France, Sweden, Japan, etc. Mbrships. incl: Soc. of Authors; PEN. Hons. incl: Supreme Award of Merit, Geo. Wash. Carver Mem. Inst., 1964; Kt. of Mark Twain, 1973; Popular Culture Award of Excellance, 1974. Address: c/o Paul Gitlin, Counselor-at-Law, 7 W. 51st., N.Y., NY 10019, USA.

WALLACE-CLARKE, George, pen name JAFFA, George, b. 1916, Exeter, UK. Land Agent, Ministry of Defence. Educ: Coll. of Estate Mgmt.; A.R.I.C.S.; F.R.S.H. Publ: Your Rights as a Ratepayer, 1973. Contbr. to: Ideal Home Mag.; Books & Bookmen; The Field; Built Environment; New Middle East; Police Review. Mbrships: Soc. of Authors; Land Inst. Address: Sanston, Grasmere Rd., Chestfield, Whitstable, Kent, UK.

WALLACE-CRABBE, Christopher Keith, b. 6 May 1934, Richmond, Australia. Senior Lecturer in English.

Educ: M.A., Melbourne Univ. Publs: The Music of Division, 1959; In Light & Darkness, 1963; The Rebel General, 1967; Where the Wind Came, 1971; Selected Poems, 1973; Melbourne or the Bush, 1974. Contbr. to: Meanjin Quarterly; Poetry Aust.; Age; Westerly; New Poetry; etc. Mbrships: Australian Soc. Authors; Bluegum Poetry Club. Recip., Harkness Fellowship, Yale Univ., 1965-67. Address: 52 Glenard Dr., Heidelberg 3084, Australia.

WALLACE-HADRILL, John Michael, b. 29 Sept. 1916, Bromsgrove, Worcs., UK. Chichele Professor of Modern History & Fellow of All Souls College, Oxford University. Educ: M.A., D.Litt., Corpus Christi Coll., Oxford Univ. Publs: The Barbarian West, 1952; France, Government & Society (w. J. McManners), 1957; The Chonicle of Fredegar, 1960; The Long-Haired Kings, 1962; Early Germanic Kingship, 1971. Contbr. to: Engl. Histl. Review; Hist.; Jrnl. Roman Studies; Jrnl. Theol. Studies; Speculum; etc. Mbrships. incl: Fellow Brit. Acad.; Royal Histl. Soc. (VP). Recip., Lothian Prize, Oxford Univ., 1938. Address: All Souls Coll., Oxford, UK.

WALLACH, Ira, b. 22 Jan. 1913, NYC, USA. Author. Educ: Cornell Univ., N.Y. Publs: The Horn & the Roses, 1947; How to be Deliriously Happy, 1950; Hopalong-Freud, 1951; Hopalong-Freud Rides Again, 1952; Gutenberg's Folly, 1954; How to Pick a Wedlock, 1956; Muscle Beach, 1959; The Absence of a Cello, 1960. Mbrships: Authors' League; Writers' Guild Am.; Airplane Owners & Pilots Assn. Recip., Writers' Guild GB Award, 1968 for Best Comedy Screenplay, Hot Millions. Address: 345 W. 58th St., N.Y., NY 10019, USA.

WALLENQUIST, Åke (Anders Edvard), b. 16 Jan. 1904, Vastervik, Sweden. Professor Emeritus of Astronomy; Author. Educ: M.A., 1925, Ph.D., 1932, Univ. of Uppsala. Publs: Op weg naar het oneindige, 1934; Den moderna, astronomin och dess världsbild Astronomi, 1951, Finnish ed., 1958; Astronomi, 1958; Introduktion till Astronomin, 1961, 3rd ed., 1970; Astronomiskt Lexikon, 1962, 2nd ed., 1970, (trans., Am., Engl., Spanish, Danish); Astrofysikens grunder, 1968; Mars, den gåtfulla planeten, 1970; Våra gramar i rymden, 1975. Contbr. to: Astronomisk Tidsskrift; Svenska Dagbladet; Forskning och Framsteg; Kosmos. Recip., Swedish Prize for Popular Books, 1965. Address: Norrlandsgatan 34D, S–752 29 Uppsala, Sweden.

WALLNER, Christian Johannes, pen name WINKLER, Johannes, b. 30 Mar. 1948, Gmunden, Austria. Educ: Univ. of Salzburg, 1966-74. Publs: Fallt Gott aus allen Wolken? (essay), 1971; Deheim ist daheim (country stories), 1972; Wespennest (essay/lyrics), 1973; Literaturmagazin, 1974; Da nahm der Koch den Loffel, 1974; Kurbiskern (prose), 1975. Contbr. to: Wespennest (Vienna); Manuskripte (Graz); Collection (Salzburg); etc. Mbrships. incl: Grazer Autorenversammlung; Journalistengewerkschaft. Hons: Georg Trakl Prize, 1972; Lit. Prize of Upper Austria, 1973; Stipendium, Dramatic Ctr. of Vienna, 1973-74, & Min. Educ. & Arts, 1975. Address: Wolfsgartenweg 16, A-5020 Salzburg, Austria.

WALMSLEY, Arnold Robert, pen name ROLAND, Nicholas, b. 29 Aug. 1912, Cotta, Ceylon. Retired Diplomat. Educ: M.A., Hertford Coll., Oxford Univ. Publs: The Great One, 1967; Natural Causes, 1969; Who Came by Night, 1971. Mbr., Travellers' Club, London. Hons: M.B.E., 1946; C.M.G., 1965. Address: Manor Farm, Dunmow Rd., Bishop's Stortford, Herts., UK.

WALSER, Martin, b. 24 Mar. 1927, Wasserburg, Germany. Writer. Educ: Dr. Phil. Publs: Ein Flugzeug ueber dem Haus, 1955; Ehen in Philippsburg, 1957; Halbzeit, 1960; Das Einhorn, 1966; Die Gallistl'sche Krankheit, 1972; Der Sturt, 1973. Mbrships: J. G. Druck und Papier; Deutsche Academie fur Sprache und Dichtung; PEN. Hons: Preis der Gruppe 47, 1955; Hermann Hesse Preis, 1957; Gerhart Hauptmann Preis, 1962; Schiller-Förderpreis, 1965; Bodensee Literaturpreis, 1967. Address: 7773 Nussdorf, Zum Hecht 32, W. Germany.

WALSH, Barbara Mary, pen name (for art work) HAYCOCK, Barbara, b. 3 Sept. 1932, South Shields, Co. Durham, UK. Writer; Artist. Contbr. to: BBC; Radio Telefis Eireann. Mbrships: Irish PEN (Hon. Treas. 1969-); Dublin Sketching Club (Comm.). Address: 16 Lakelands Pk., Terenure, Dublin 6, Repub. of Ireland.

WALSH, Joseph J., b. 21 Dec. 1915, Waterford City, Repub. of Ireland. Newspaper Owner, Publisher, Editor;

Company Director. Educ: Waterpark Coll.; Colls. of Technol. & Printing, Dublin & London. Publs: Olympic Odyssey — Across the World for Sport, 1959, 1969; Waterford's Yesterdays & Tomorrows — An Outline of Waterford History, 1968. Ed. & Chief Contbr., Old Waterford Soc. Jrnl., 1970-74; Ldr. Writer & Ed., Munster Express, Waterford. Mbrships: Chmn., Old Waterford Soc., Reginald's Tower Advsry. Comm., Waterford Corp., S.E. Reg., Publicity Club of Ireland; var. offs. & Exec. Mbr., Provincial Newspaper Assn. of Ireland. Address: Cliff Grange, Tramore, Co. Waterford, Repub. of Ireland.

WALSH, William Joseph, b. 23 Feb. 1916, London, UK. Professor of Commonwealth Literature. Educ: M.A., Cambridge Univ.; M.A., London Univ. Publs: Use of Imagination, 1959; A Human Idiom, 1965; Coleridge: The Work & the Relevance, 1967; A Manifold Voice: Studies in Commonwealth Literature, 1970; R. K. Narayan, 1971; V. S. Naipaul, 1973; Ed., Commonwealth Literature, 1973; Readings in Commonwealth Literature, 1973; D. J. Enright: Poet of Humanism, 1974. Contbr. to: Encounter; Spectator; Listener; New Statesman; Lugano Review; Sewanee Review; etc. F.R.S.A., 1970. Address: 27 Moor Dr., Headingley, Leeds LS6 4BY, UK.

WALTARI, Mika, b. 19 Sept. 1908, Helsinki, Finland. Writer; Literary Critic. Educ: Helsinki Univ. Publs. incl: Michael the Finn, 1950; The Sultan's Renegade, 1951; The Dark Angel, 1953; A Nail Merchant at Nightfall, 1955; Moonscape, 1956; The Etruscan, 1956; The Tongue of Fire, 1958; The Secret of the Kingdom, 1961; The Tree of Dreams, 1965; The Roman, 1966. Contbr. to: Maaseudun Tulevaisuus; Suomen Kuvalehti. Mbr., Finnish Acad. Hons. incl: Pro Finlandia Award, 1952; Finnish Lion. Address: Tunturikatu 13, Helsinki 10, Finland.

WALTER, Nina Willis, b. 11 June 1900, Palmyra, Mo., USA. Emeritus Professor; Writer. Educ: A.B., UCAL; M.A., Univ. of Southern Calif. Publs: (poetry) Brush Strokes, 1948; People-Watching, 1966; Cameos, 1974; (textbooks) Mastering English Composition, 1961; Let Them Write Poetry, 1962; (juvenile) Teeny Weeny, 1971. Contbr. to many jvnle., denominational & nat. mags. Mbrships: MENSA; Poetry Soc. of Southern Calif.; Calif. Fed. of Chaparral Poets; Am. Poetry League; Writers Club of Whittier, Calif.; etc. Address: 9331 Cosgrove St., Pico Rivera, CA 90660, USA.

WALTER, William Grey, b. 1910, Kansas City, Mo., USA. Departmental Director, Physiological Dept., Burden Neurological Institute. Educ: M.A., Sc.D., Cambridge Univ., UK. Publs: Discussions on Child Development; Brain Mechanisms & Consciousness; The Living Brain, UK & USA; Further Outlook; The Curve of the Snowflake, USA. Contbr. to: Hill & Parr, Electro-encephalography; EEG Clin. Neurophysiol.; Jrnl. of Mental Sci.; Jrnl. Physiol.; Discovery; Sci. Am.; Nature; Macy Fndn. publs. Agent: Duckworth. Address: 20 Richmond Park Rd., Bristol BS8 3AP, UK.

WALTERS, John Beauchamp, b. 7 Nov. 1906, Hastings, Sussex, UK. Author; Journalist. Educ: King's Coll., Univ. of London. Publs: Will America Fight, 1940; Light in the Window, 1942; Mind Unshaken, 1961; The Essence of Buddhism, 1962; Splendour & Scandal, 1968; Aldershot Review, 1970; The Royal Griffin, 1972. Contbr. to var. jrnls. & newspapers in UK, USA & Aust. Mbr., Inst. of Jrnlsts. Address: Merridale, Rowledge nr. Farnham, Surrey, UK.

WALTON, Richard John, b. 24 May 1928, Saratoga Springs, N.Y., USA. Writer. Educ: B.A., Brown Univ., 1951; M.Sc., Columbia Univ., 1954. Publs: The Remnants of Power: The Tragic Last Years of Adlai Stevenson, 1968; America & the Cold War, 1969; Beyond Diplomacy, 1970; Cold War & Counter-revolution: The Foreign Policy of John F. Kennedy, 1972; Congress & American Foreign Policy, 1972; Canada & the USA, 1972; The United States & Latin America, 1972; The United States & the Far East, 1974. Contbr. to: N.Y. Times; Nation; Wash. Post; etc. Mbrships: PEN; Authors' Guild; Acad. Pol. Sci.; Am. Histl. Assn. Address: 24 Cornelia St., N.Y., NY 10014, USA.

WAMBLE, G. Hugh, b. 6 Feb. 1923, Cairo, Ga., USA. Minister; Professor of Church History. Educ: B.A., Mercer Univ., Macon, Ga., 1948; B.D., 1951, Th.D.(Ph.D.), 1956, Southern Bapt. Theol. Sem., Louisville, Ky.; postgrad. work, Duke Univ., N.C., 1958-59; M.A., Univ. of Mo., 1966. Publs: Through Trial to Triumph, 1958; The Shape of Faith, 1962; A History of Christian Thought, 1964.

Contbr. to: Review & Expositor; Foundations; Church History; Mo. Histl. Review. Mbr., var. relig. & histl. assns. Recip., James B. Duke Fellowship, Duke Univ., N.C., 1958-59. Address: 4840 N.E. Chouteau Dr., Kansas City, MO 64119, USA.

WARD, Elizabeth Honor, pen name WARD, S. Leslie, b. 12 Apr. 1926, Birmingham, UK. Teacher; Housewife; Writer. Educ: B.Sc. (Physics); Dip.Ed., Birmingham Univ. Publs: Touchdown to Adventure, 1957; Senior Physics, part 1 1965, part 2 1966; The Story of Creation, 1973; Essential Senior Physics (w. Prof. A. H. Ward), 1975. Contbr. to: Schl. Sci. Review. Mbrships: Inst. of Physics; Soc. of Authors. Recip., Scripture Union Lit. Competition, 1956. Address: Box 8085, Woodlands, Lusaka, Zambia.

WARD, Frederick E., b. 7 June 1937, Kansas City, Mo., USA. Writer. Educ: Univ. of Mo., Kan. City; Adv. Schl. of Contemporary Music, Toronto, Can. Publs: Riverlisp, 1974. Address: P.O. Box 82, Blockhouse, Lunenburg Co., N.S., Canada.

WARD, John Towers, b. 27 July 1930, Horsforth, UK. Historian. Educ: B.A., 1953, M.A., 1957, Ph.D., 1957, Magdalene Coll., Cambridge. Publs: The Factory Movement, 1962; Sir James Ciraham, 1967; Ed., Popular Movements 1970; The Factory System I, 1970, 1972; The Factory System II, 1970, 1973; Co-Ed., Land & Industry, 1971, 1974; Chartism, 1973. Contbr. to: Robert Owen, Prince of Cotton Spinners (ed., J. Butt), 1971; The Conservative Leadership (Ed., D. G. Southgate), 1974; Ency. Brit.; Engl. Hist. Review; Scottish Hist. Review; Transport Hist.; Indl. Archaeol. Mbrships. incl: Royal Histl. Soc.; Histl. Assn. Address: Dept. of Hist., Univ. of Strathclyde, Glasgow, UK.

WARD, William Arthur, b. 17 Dec. 1921, Oakdale, La., USA. College Administrator. Educ: B.Sc., McMurry Coll., Abilene, Tex., 1948; M.Sc., Okla. State Univ., 1949; Doctoral Study, Univ. of Tex. at Austin & N. Tex. State Univ., Denton. Publs: Thoughts of a Christian Optimist, 1968; For This One Hour, 1969; Prayer Is, 1969; Fountains of Faith, 1970; Allegiance to America, 1971; Positive Power for Successful Salesmen (w. others), 1972; Brighten Your Corner, 1973. Contbr. to: mags. in US & abroad; Contbng. Ed., Quote Mag. Mbrships. incl: Pres., Ft. Worth Mus. of Sci. & Hist., 1972-73. Recip., Hon. LL.D., Okla. City Univ., 1962. Address: 2141 Green Hill Circle, Ft. Worth, TX 76112, USA.

WARDEN, Lewis Christopher, b. 26 Aug. 1913, St. Clairsville, Ohio, USA. Lawyer; Author; Editor. Educ: B.A., Ohio State Univ., 1934; LL.B., 1937, J.D., 1969, Harvard Univ. Publs. incl: The Life of Blackstone, 1938; Court Rules, 1946; Torrent of the Willows, 1954; Murder on Wheels, 1964; Consumer Credit Protection, 1973; On the Uniform Probate Code, 1974. Contbr. to: Am., Ohio Jurisprudence, 2nd eds.; Fla., N.Y. Jurisprudence; Am. Law Reports, 2nd ed.; Case & Comment; etc. Mbrships incl: Harvard Law Schl., Ohio State Univ. Assns. & Century Clubs; Phi Beta Kappa; Pi Sigma Alpha. Hons. incl; Presidential Cert. of Commendation, 1946; Nat. Advsry. Bd. Mbr., Am. Security Coun., 1972–. Address: 1903 N.E. 15th Street, Gainesville, FL 32601, USA.

WARE, George Whitaker, b. 22 Dec. 1902, Belen, Miss., USA. Agriculturalist; lecturer. Educ: B.S., Univ. of Ark., 1924; M.S., Cornell Univ., 1935; Cert. in Int. Nutritional Problems, Western Reserve Univ., 1944. Publs: Southern Vegetable Crops, 1939; German & Austrian Procelain, 1952, 1966; Raising Vegetables, 1959; The New Guide to Happy Retirement, 1968; Producing Vegetable Crops, 1974. Contbr. to: Progressive Farmer; Southern Farmer; Antiques Mag.; Hobbies; var. newspapers. Hon. Mbr., Nat. Assn. Authors & Jrnlsts. 1939. Address: 4301 Columbia Pike, Apt. 506, Arlington, VA 22204, USA.

WARNER, Francis, b. 21 Oct. 1937, Bishopthorpe, Yorks., UK. University Fellow, Tutor & Lecturer. Educ: St. Catharine's Coll., Cambridge, 1956-59. Publs: (poetry) Perennia, 1962; Early Poems, 1964; Experimental Sonnets, 1965; Madrigals, 1967; The Poetry of Francis Warner, 1970; (plays) Maquettes (trilogy of one-act plays), 1972; Lying Figures, (pt. I, Requiem, a trilogy), 1972; Meeting Ends, (pt. III), 1974; Killing Time, (pt. II), 1975. Contbr. to: Antios.; & var. jrnls. Recip., Messing Int. Award for Disting. Contributions to Lit., 1972. Address: St. Peter's Coll., Oxford, UK.

WARNER, Rex (Ernest), b. 9 Mar. 1905, Birmingham, UK. Professor of English. Educ: B.A., Oxford Univ., 1928. Publs. incl: (novels) The Wild Goose Chase, 1937; The Aerodrome, 1941; Men of Stones, 1949; Imperial Caesar, 1960; The Convert, 1967; (non-fiction) The Kite, 1936, revised ed. 1963; The Cult of Power, 1946; Men & Gods, 1950; Athens at War, 1970 (all except The Kite also publd. USA); Transl., num. Greek & Latin classics. Hon. Mbr., New England Classical Assn. Hons: Black Mem. Prize, 1961; Cmdr., Royal Order of Phoenix, Greece, 1963; D.Litt., Rider Coll., N.J., 1968. Address: Horse Barn Hill Lane, Storrs, CT 06268, USA.

WARNER, Sylvia Townsend, b. 6 Dec. 1893, Harrow, Middx., UK. Writer. Publs: (novels) Lolly Willowes, 1926; Mr. Fortune's Maggot, 1927; Summer Will Show, 1936; After the Death of Don Juan, 1938; The Corner that Held Them, 1946; The Flint Anchor, 1952; (poems) The Espalier, 1925; Time Importune, 1928; Opus 7, 1931; Whether a Dove or Seagull (co-author), 1934; T. H. White (biog.), 1968; 8 vols. of short stories, 1932-70. Contbr. to: New Yorker; Spectator; Grove's Dict. of Music. F.R.S.L. Hons: Prix Menton, 1968; Hon. A.A.A.L., 1972. Address: c/o Chatto & Windus, 40 William IV St., London WC2, UK.

WARREN, James E(ward), Jr., b. 11 Dec. 1908, Atlanta, Ga., USA. Writer; Teacher. Educ: A.B., M.A.T., Emory Univ. Publs: This Side of Babylon, 1938; Against the Furious Men, 1946; Selected Poems, 1967; The Winding of Clocks, 1968; Listen, My Land, 1971; Mostly of Emily Dickinson, 1972; How to Write a Research Paper, 1972; Walking With Candles, 1973; The Teacher of English: His Materials & Opportunities, 1974. Contbr. to: N.Y. Times; N.Y. Herald Tribune; Ga. Life; Poetry Review; etc. Mbrships: Fellow, Int. Inst. of Arts & Letters; Trustee, Ga. Writers Assn.; Poetry Soc. of Ga.; Poetry Soc. of Am.; Fndr., Acad. of Am. Poets. Hons: Poetry Soc. of Am. Annual Award, 1937; Lit. Achievement Award for Poetry, Ga. Writers Assn., 1967. Address: 544 Deering Rd. N.W., Atlanta, GA, USA.

WARREN, Hans (Johannes Adrianus Menne), b. 20 Oct. 1921, Borssele, Netherlands. Author; Literary Critic; Translator. Publs: Transl., main works of De Sade into Dutch; Verzamelde Gedichten 1941–; 1971 (collected poems), 1972; De Olympos, 1973; Herakles op de Tweesprong, 1974; Een Liefdeslied, 1974; Betreffende Vogels, 1974; 't Zelve Anders, 1974. Contbr. to: Maatstaf. Mbr., Netherlands Soc. of Authors. Hons: van der Hoogt Prize, 1958; Pierre Bayle Prize, 1970; Zeeuwse Prijs, 1971. Address: Pijkesweegje 1, Kloetinge, Post Goes, Netherlands.

WARREN, Robert Penn, b. 24 Apr. 1905, Guthrie, Ky., USA. Writer; Teacher. Educ: B.A.(summa cum laude), Vanderbilt Univ., Nashville, Tenn., 1925; M.A., Univ. of Calif., Berkeley, 1927; studies at Yale Univ. Grad. Schl., 1927-28; B.Litt., Oxford Univ., UK, 1930. Publs. incl: XXXVI Poems, 1936; Night Rider (novel), 1939; All The King's Men (novel), 1946; Brother to Dragons (verse), 1953; Promises (verse), 1957; Flood (novel), 1964; Selected Poems, 1966; Audubon: A Vision (verse), 1969; Homage to Theodore Dreisser, 1971; Meet Me in the Green Glen (novel), 1971; Or Else — Poem/Poems, 1968-74, 1974. Contbr. to: Harper's; New Repub.; New Yorker; Sewanee, Southern, Yale, Kenyon Reviews; etc. Mbr. & Off., var. lit. orgs. Hons. incl: Pulitzer Prize for Fiction, 1974, & Poetry, 1958; Bollingen Prize for Poetry, 1967; Nat. Medal for Lit., 1970. Address: 2495 Redding Rd., Fairfield, CT, USA.

WARREN, (William) Preston, b. 26 Jan. 1901, New Glasgow, P.E.I., Can. Professor Emeritus of Philosophy. Educ: B.A., Acadia Univ., 1925; B.D., 1927, Ph.D., 1929, Yale Univ., USA. Publs: Transl., Masaryk, Humanistic Ideals, 1938, new ed., 1971; Masaryk's Democracy: A Philosophy of Scientific & Moral Culture, 1941; Ed., Principles of Emergent Realism: Essays by Roy Wood Sellars, 1970; Ed., Neglected Alternatives, Critical Essays by Roy Wood Sellars; Roy Wood Sellars, 1975. Contbr. to: Philos. & Phenomenol. Rsch.; Ethics; Bucknell Review. Mbr., var. profl. assns. Recip., num. schlrships. & Fellowships. Address: 41 Plymouth St., Bridgewater, MA 02324, USA.

WARREN, Winifred Darden, pen name DARDEN, Winifred, b. 1 Oct. 1906, Taylor, Tex., USA. Home Maker. Educ: B.A., Baylor Univ., Waco, Tex., 1928. Publs. (poems) A Butterfly & A Poet, 1965; Pen Wheels, Waco Chapter Poetry Society of Texas (co-author), 1967-68; Books of Poems, Waco Chapter Poetry Society of Texas (co-author), 1969-70, 1970-72. Mbrships: AAUW; Am.

Poetry League; Poetry Soc. of Tex.; Sec., Waco Chapt.; Int. Comm., Centro Studi E Scambi Int., 1966. Hons. incl: Cert. of Merit, Acad. Leonardo Da Vinci, 1968. Address: Route 2, Box 60, Waco, TX 76710, USA.

WARTH, Robert Douglas, b. 16 Dec. 1921, Houston, Tex., USA. Professor of History. Educ: B.S., Univ. of Ky., 1943; M.A., 1945; Ph.D., 1949, Univ. of Chgo. Publs: The Allies & the Russian Revolution, 1954, 2nd ed. 1973; Soviet Russia in World Politics, 1963; Joseph Stalin, 1969; Lenin, 1973. Contbr. to: Jrnl. of Mod. Hist.; Slavic Review; The Nation; Ency. Int.; etc. Mbrships: Am. Histl. Assn.; Am. Assn. Advancement of Slavic Studies; AAUP. Address: 640 W. Cooper Dr. Lexington, KY 40502, USA.

WASIOLEK, Edward, b. 27 Apr. 1924, Camden, NJ, USA. Professor of Slavic & Comparative Literature; Author. Educ: B.A., Rutgers Univ., 1949; M.A., 1950, Ph.D., 1955, Harvard Univ.; Cert., Univ. of Bordeaux, France, 1951. Publs: Nine Soviet Portraits (co-author), 1955; Dostoevsky, the Major Fiction, 1964; The Notebooks for the Major Novels of Dostoevsky, 5 vols., 1967-70; Ed., The Gambler & Polina Suslova's Diary, 1972. Contbr. to: Saturday Review; PMLA; Mod. Fiction Studies; Chgo. Review; etc. Mbrships. incl: Ed. Advsry. Bd., MLA. Recip., Laing Prize for Most Disting. Publ., Univ. of Chgo., 1972. Address: Butterfield Lane, Flossmoor, IL 60637, USA.

WASS, Albert, b. 8 Jan. 1908, Valaszut, Hungary. Writer; Professor. Educ: M.S., Univ. of Debrecen, 1930; D.Lit., Univ. of Kolosvar, 1944. Publs: Farkasverem (novel), 1937; A kastély árnyékában, 1942; Adjátok vissza a hegyeimet, 1948, (Engl. ed. as Give Me Back My Mountains, 1968); Damnation Row, 1964; The Red Star Wanes, 1966; & 22 other novels & children's stories. Contbr. of stories & articles to: Pasztortuz Lit. Review, 1935-44; Helicon, 1935-43; Hungarian Quarterly, 1937-44; Magyar Vilaghirado, 1969–; also syndicated columns in num. Hungarian wkly. papers. Mbrships. incl: Hungarian Royal Acad.; Kisfaludy Soc., Budapest; Fndr. & Pres., Am.-Hungarian Lit. Guild; Int. Platform Assn. Hons: Baumgarten Lit. Prize, 1937; Klebelsberg Lit. Prize, 1942; Zrinyi Lit. Prize, 1944. Address: Rt. 1, Box 59, Astor, FL 32002, USA.

WATEN, Judah, b. 1911, Odessa, Russia. Novelist; Book Reviewer; Literary Critic. Educ: Christian Bros. Coll., Perth, Aust.; Univ. H.S., Melbourne. Publs: Alien Son, 1952; The Unbending, 1954; Shares in Murder, 1957; Time of Conflict, 1961; Distant Land, 1964; Season of Youth, 1966; From Odessa to Odessa (travel), 1969; So Far No Further, 1971; The Dour Decade: The 1930's, 1971; Bottle-O, 1973; Co-ed., Classic Australian Short Stories, 1974. Contbr. to: Melbourne Age; Sydney Morning Herald; Meanjin; Jewish Quarterly; Labour Monthly. Mbrships: PEN; Soc. of Authors; Fellowship of Aust. Writers. Address: 1 Byron St., Box Hill, Victoria, Australia 3128.

WATERFIELD, Gordon, b. 24 May 1903, Nackington House, Canterbury, UK. Retired Journalist; Foreign Correspondent; BBC External Services 1947-1963. Educ: M.A., New Coll., Oxford Univ. Publs: (biogs.) Lucie Duff Gordon, 1937; Layard of Nineveh, 1963; Sultans of Aden, 1968; Professional Diplomat, Sir Percy Loraine of Kirkharle, 1973; Re-edited Sir Richard Burton's First Footsteps in East Africa, 1966; Re-edited Lady Duff Gordon's Letters From Egypt, 1862-1869, 1969; Egypt, 1967. Contbr. to: Times Lit. Supplement; etc. Mbrships: Soc. Authors; Travellers' Club, London. Recip., O.B.E., 1963. Address: White Gates, Wittersham, Tenterden, Kent, UK.

WATERHOUSE, Keith Spencer, b. 6 Feb. 1929, Leeds, UK. Writer. Publs: (novels) There is a Happy Land, 1957; Billy Liar, 1960; Jubb, 1963; The Bucket Shop, 1968; (collected stories) Passing of the Third Floor Buck, 1974. Contbr. to: Punch; Daily Mirror columnist (1970–). Mbr., PEN. Address: 70 St. Paul St., London N1, UK.

WATERS, Frank, b. 25 July 1902, Colo. Springs, Colo., USA. Writer. Educ: Colo. Coll., 3 yrs. Publs: incl: Fever Pitch, 1930; Midas of the Rockies, 1937; The Man Who Killed the Deer, 1942; The Colorado, 1946; Masked Gods: Navajo & Pueblo Ceremonialism, 1950; The Earp Brothers of Tombstone, 1960; Leon Gaspard, 1964; The Woman at Otowi Crossing, 1966; Pumpkin Seed Point, 1969; Pikes' Peak, 1971; To Possess the land, 1973; Mexico Mystique, 1975. Contbr. to: N.Am., Yale, Southwest, S.D. Reviews; Denver, Western Histl. Quarterlies; etc. Mbr. & Dir., N.M. Arts Commn., 1967. Hons: D.Litt., Colo. State Univ. &

Univ. of Albuquerque, N.M., 1973. Address: Box 1127, Taos, NM 87571, USA.

WATKINS, William Jon, b. 19 July 1942, Coaldale, Pa., USA. Associate Professor. Educ: B.S., Rutgers Univ., 1964; M.Ed., Rutgers Grad. Schl. of Educ., 1965. Publs: Ecodeath (w. E. V. Snyder), 1972; The God Machine, 1973; Clickwhistle, 1973; Best Science Fiction: 1973 (contbng. author), 1974; A Kind of a Hole (play), 1974; No Quarter Asked, No Quarter Given, 1975. Contbr. to: Worlds of If; Vertex; Cosmopolitan. Mbrships: Sci. Fiction Writers of Am.; World Future Soc. Recip., PER SE Award for One Act Plays, 1970. Address: 1406 Garven Ave., Wanamassa, NJ 07712, USA.

WATNEY, John Basil, b. 13 Jan. 1915, London, UK. Author. Educ: Bachelier es Lettres (Philosophie), Poitiers, France; B.A., Oxford Univ., UK. Publs: The Enemy Within, 1946; The Unexpected Angel, 1949; Common Love, 1954; Leopard with a Thin Skin, 1959; The Quarrelling Room, 1960; The Glass Facade, 1963; He Also Served, 1971; Clive of India, 1974; Beer is Best, 1974. Contbr. to num. mags. & newspapers. Agent: Hope Leresche & Steele. Address: c/o Hope Leresche & Steele, 11 Jubilee Place, London SW3, UK.

WATSON, Berry Bascom, b. 30 Apr. 1897, Lexington, Mo., USA. Editor; Journalist. Educ: Univ. of Mo., 1916-17. Contbr. to newspapers & mags: Farm Ed., Hannibal Courier-Post, 1952-64; Columnist, Uncle Bud's Hobby Shop, 1955-56; Sportsmen's Field Notes, 1956-73; Publr., The Nemo Journal of Rural Progress, 1973-74. Mbrships. incl: Newspaper Farm Eds. of Am.; Outdoor Writers Assn. of Am.; Nat. Writers Club. Address: P.O. Box 308, Palmyra, MO 63461, USA.

WATSON, Colin, b. 1 Feb. 1920, Croydon, Surrey, UK. Writer. Publs. Coffin, Scarcely Used, 1958; Bump in the Night; Hopjoy was Here; The Flaxborough Crab; Broomsticks over Flaxborough; The Naked Nuns, 1975; non fiction: Snobbery with Violence, 1971. Mbrships: Detection Club; Crime Writers' Assn. Recip., Crime Writers' Assn. Critics' Award (Silver Dagger), 1962, 1967. Address: 3 Stanhope Terrace, Horncastle, Lincs., UK.

WATSON, James, b. 8 Nov. 1936, Darwen, UK. Lecturer. Educ: B.A., Univ. of Nottingham. Publs: Sign of the Swallow, 1967; The Bull Leapers, 1970; Gilbert Makepeace Lives! (BBC radio play), 1972; Legion of the White Tiger, 1973; Liberal Studies in Further Education – an Informal Survey, 1973. Contbr. to: Times; Guardian; Studio; Arts Review. Mbr., Assn. for Liberal Educ. Address: Flat B2, Vale Towers, London Rd., Tunbridge Wells, Kent, UK.

WATSON, John Arthur Fergus, b. 24 July 1903, London, UK. Former Juvenile Court Magistrate; Past President, Royal Institution of Chartered Surveyors. Publs: incl: Meet the Prisoner, 1939; The Child & the Magistrate, 1942, 3rd ed., 1965; British Juvenile Courts, 1948; Which Is the Justice? 1969; Nothing But the Truth – Expert Evidence in Principle & Practice, 2nd ed., 1975; The Incompleat Surveyor, 1973; The Modern Juvenile Court (w. P. M. Austin), 1975. Contbr. to: Times; Sunday Times; Solicitors' Jrnl.; Magistrate; etc. Mbrships. incl: a Chmn., Inner London Juvenile Cts., 1936-68; Lands Tribunal, 1957-69. Hons: C.B.E., 1965; J.P. Address: Elmdon Old Vicarage, Nr. Saffron Walden, Essex, UK.

WATSON, Julia, pen names HAMILTON, Julia; DE VERE, Jane, b. 18 Sept. 1943. Historical Novelist, Biographer & Consultant. Educ: Huddersfield Art Coll. Publs. incl: (as Julia Watson) The Lovechild, 1967, 2nd ed., 1968; Medici Mistress, 1969; The King's Mistress, 1970; The Wolf & the Unicorn, 1971; (as Jane De Vere) The Scarlet Women, 1969; The Tudor Rose, 1972; Saffron at Court of Edward III, 1972; (as Julia Hamilton) Son of York, 1973; Katherine of Aragon, 1972; Anne of Cleves, 1972; Last of the Tudors; (biog.) The Vixen Queen: Margaret of Anjou, Wife of Henry VI; & 6 books forthcoming. Mbrships: Soc. Authors; Romantic Novelists' Assn. Address: 4 Lansdowne Grove, Hough Green, Chester, Cheshire CH4 8LD, UK.

WATSON, Nancy Dingman, b. N.J., USA. Author. Educ: A.B., Smith Coll. Publs: What Is One? , 1954; When Is Tomorrow? , 1955; Annie's Spending Spree, 1955; What Does A Begin With? , 1956; Katie's Chickens, 1965; Sugar on Snow, 1965; Tommy's Mommy's Fish, 1971; New

Under the Stars, 1972; The Birthday Goat, 1974; Muncus Agruncus, 1975; Peoples & Places of the American Revolution, 1975. Mbrships: Authors' League of Am.; Alpha Soc. Address: West Hill Farm, Putney, VT 05346, USA.

WATSON, Philip Saville, b. 15 Oct. 1909, Idle Bradford, UK. Emeritus Professor of Theology. Educ: B.A., Durham Univ., 1931; M.A., 1934; B.A., Cambridge Univ., 1934; M.A., 1939; B.D., 1950; D.D., 1960. Publs: The State as a Servant of God, 1946; Let God be God, 1947, 1970; The Concept of Grace, 1959; The Message of the Wesleys, 1964; (Trans.) A. Nygren, Agape & Eros, 1939, 1953; Essence of Christianity, 1960. 1973; Meaning & Method, 1972; (Trans. & Ed.), Luther's Commentary on Galatians, 1953; The Bondage of the Will, 1972; Collab., Luther & Erasmus, 1969. Contbr. to num. theol. publs. Mbrships: Soc. for the Study of Theol.; Am. Theol. Soc.; Am. Acad. of Relig.; AAUP. Hons: D.D., Glasgow, 1959 & Ohio Wesleyan, 1962. Address: 60 Court Ave., Old Coulsdon, Surrey, UK.

WATSON, Vera, b. 25 Oct. 1906, Atcham, Nr. Shrewsbury, UK. Author. Publs: Parisian Holiday, 1939; Mary Russell Mitford, 1949; A Queen at Home, 1952; The British Museum, an historical guide to the antiquities, 1973. Contbr. to: Times Lit. Supplement; Daily Telegraph; Engl. Mbrships: Charles Lamb Soc.; Brit. Mus. Soc.; Royal Overseas League. Address: 51 Beaufort Mansions, Beaufort St., London SW3 5AF, UK.

WATT, D.C., b. 1928, Rugby, UK. Reader in International History. Educ: M.A., Oriel Coll., Oxford Univ. Publs. incl: Britain & the Suez Canal, 1956; Britain Looks to Germany, 1965; Personalities & Policies, 1965; A History of the World in the 20th Century (co-author), 1967; Co-Ed., Studies in International History, 1968; Ed., Contemporary History in Europe, 1969; Ed., Hitler's Mein Kampf, 1969; Co-ed., Current British Foreign Policy 1970 (72), 1971 (73), 1972 (74); Too Serious a Business, 1974. Contbr. to: Times; Spectator; Financial Times; Int. Affairs; World Today; Europe Archiv; New Middle East; etc.; Ed., Survey of Int. Affairs. Mbrships. incl: Assn. Contemporary Histns.; Inst. Strategic Studies. Address: c/o London Schl. of Economics, Aldwych, London WC2, UK.

WATT, Elsie Gowans, pen name GOWANS, Elsa, b. 22 May 1902, Ste. Anne de Bellevue, P.Q., Can. Freelance Writer; Retired Foods & Nutrition Specialist. Educ: B. Household Sci., McGill Univ., 1924; Specialist Tchrs. Cert., P.Q., 1924; Cert. in Pub. Hlth., Univ. of Toronto, 1948. Contbr. to: Can. Food Jrnls.; Can. Hosp. Jrnl.; Can. Nutrition Notes; Jrnl. Can. Dietetic Assn.; Family Herald & Weekly Star; This Week; St. Ives Times & Echo, UK; var. mags. & newspapers, USA. Mbr., Can. Authors Assn.; Can. Dietetic Assn. Address: 802—450 Simcoe St., Victoria, B.C., Can. V8V I14.

WATT, William Montgomery, b. 14 Mar. 1909, Ceres, Fife, UK. Professor of Arabic & Islamic Studies, University of Edinburgh. Educ: M.A., 1930, Ph.D., 1944, Edinburgh Univ.; B.A., B.Litt., M.A., Balliol Coll., Oxford Univ. Publs: Muhammad at Mecca, 1953; Muhammad at Medina, 1956; Islam & the Integration of Society, 1961; Muhammad, Prophet & Statesman, 1961; Islamic Spain, 1965; The Influence of Islam on Medieval Europe, 1972; the Formative Period of Islamic Thought, 1973; The Majesty that was Islam, 1974. Contbr. to: Der Islam; Oriens; Times Lit. Supplement; etc. Mbr., Brit. Assn. Orientalists (Chmn. 1965). Recip., Hon. D.D. Aberdeen, 1966. Address: The Neuk, Dalkeith, Midlothian EH22 1JT, UK.

WATTS, Alan James, b. 20 Mar. 1925, Southbourne, Sussex, UK. Lecturer in Physics. Educ: B.Sc., London. Publs: Wind & Sailing Boats, 1965; Weather Forecasting Ashore & Afloat, 1968; Instant Weather Forecasting, 1968; The Wind Pilot, forthcoming, 1975. Contbr. to: Yachting World; Yachts & Yachting; Sunday Times; Weather; Essex Co. Standard; var. books; etc. Mbrships: Fellow, Royal Meterol. Soc.; Soc. of Authors; Royal Yachting Assn. Address: Ryelands, Elmstead Market, Colchester, Essex, UK.

WATTS, Anthony John, b. 3 Apr. 1942, Frome, Somerset, UK. BBC Studio Technician. Publs: Japanese Warships of World War II, 1966; The Loss of the Scharnhorst, 1970; Pictorial History of the Royal Navy, Vol. I, 1970, Vol. II, 1971, Vol. III, forthcoming; The Imperial Japanese Navy, 1971. Contbr. to: Warships & Navies Review (Ed.). Mbrships: US Naval Inst.; Licentiate, London Coll. of Music, 1964. Address: "Hunters Moon",

Hogspudding Lane, Newdigate Dorking, Surrey RH5 5DS, UK.

WATTS, Mabel, pen name LYNN, Patricia, b. 20 May 1906, London, UK. Author of children's books. Publs. incl: A Cow in the House, 1956; Everyone Waits, 1959; Henrietta & the Hat, 1962; Weeks & Weeks, 1962; The Day It Rained Watermelons, 1964; The Narrow Escapes of Solomon Smart, 1966; The Story of Zachary Zween, 1967; Yin Sun & the Lucky Dragon, 1969; While the Horses Galloped to London, 1973; Knights of the Square Table, 1974. Contbr. to: var. schl. textbooks, juvenile mags; BBC; Aust. Broadcasting Corp.; etc. Mbr., Burlingame Writers Club; Pres., ibid., 1962. Hons: Book Selections & Awards by var. lit. orgs. Address: 1520 Ralston Ave., Burlingame, CA 94010, USA.

WAUGH, Alec, b. 8 July 1898, London, UK. Novelist. Educ: Royal Mil. Coll., Sandhurst. Publs. incl: The Loom of Youth, 1917; Hot Countries, 1930; So Lovers Dream, 1931; The Balliols, 1934; Going Their Own Ways, 1938; His Second War, 1944; The Lipton Story, 1950; The Sugar Islands, 1958; In Praise of Wine, 1959; Fuel for the Flame, 1960; My Place in the Bazaar, 1961; The Early Years of Alec Waugh, 1962; A Family of Islands, 1964; The Mule on the Minaret, 1965; My Brother Evelyn & Other Profiles, 1967; A Spy in the Family, 1970; The Fatal Gift, 1973. Address: c/o Brandt-Brandt, 101 Park Ave., N.Y., NY 10017, USA.

WAUGH, Auberon Alexander, b. 17 Nov. 1939, Pixton Park, Dulverton, Somerset, UK. Writer. Educ: Christ Ch., Oxford. Publs. incl: The Foxglove Saga, 1960; Path of Dalliance, 1963; Who Are the Violets Now, 1965; Biafra: Britain's Shame (non-fiction), 1969; A Bed of Flowers, 1971; Country Topics, 1974. Contbr. to: Books & Bookmen; Private Eye; Evening Standard; New Statesman; Esquire; Spectator; Times; News of the World; Cath. Herald; Sun. Mbrships. incl: PEN; Soc. of Authors; Writers' Action Grp.; Nat. Union of Jrnlsts.; Nat. Farmers' Union. Address: Combe Florey House, Taunton, Somerset, UK.

WAY, Peter Howard, b. 4 Nov. 1936, London, UK. Author. Educ: B.A., Durham Univ. Publs: The Kretzmer Syndrome, 1967; A Perfect State of Health, 1969; Pieces of a Game, 1972. Contbr. to: Sunday Times; New Statesman; New Society; Guardian. Address: 5 Egerton Dr., Greenwich, London SE10, UK.

WAYMAN, Vivienne, b. 19 June 1926, London, UK. Author of Children's Books. Educ: Dip. in Design, St. Martin's Schl. of Art; Art Tchrs. Dip., Inst. of Educ., London. Publs: The Rose Boy at Penny Spring, 1968; Emma of Larkwater Hall, 1969; The Alabaster Princess, 1970; The Cage in the Apple Orchard, 1972; The Seventh Bull Maiden, 1974. Address: 42 Old Church Lane, Stanmore, Middx., UK.

WAŻYK, Adam, b. 17 Nov. 1905, Warsaw, Poland. Writer. Publs: (poems) Semaphores, 1924; Eyes & Mouth, 1925; Heart of the Grenade, 1943; Poem for Adulths, 1955; The Labyrinth, 1961; The Waggon, 1963; (stories) Family Myths, 1938; The Episode, 1961; (essay) Case of Taste, 1966; The Play & the Experience, 1974. Mbr., PEN. Recip., PEN Club Prize. Address: Aleja Roz 8, 0556 Warsaw, Poland.

WEALE, Anne, b. 20 June 1929, Liverpool, UK. Novelist. Publs: Winter Is Past, 1955; The Lonely Shore, 1956; The House of Seven Fountains, 1957; Sweet to Remember, 1958; Hope For Tomorrow, 1959; The House on Flamingo Bay, 1962; The Silver Dolphin, 1963; Three Weeks in Eden, 1964; The Night of the Hurricane, 1965; Terrace In the Sun, 1966; The Sea Waif, 1967; South from Sounion, 1968; Sullivan's Reef, 1970; A Treasure For Life, 1972; The Fields of Heaven, 1974. Contbr. to: Antique Collecting. Mbrships: Coun. of E. Anglian Writers; Jane Austen Soc. Address: Lingard, Tasburgh, Norfolk NR15 1NB, UK.

WEAVER, Clarence Lahr, b. 5 Nov. 1904, Delaware, Ohio, USA. Librarian. Educ: A.B., Ohio Wesleyan Univ., Delaware, Ohio, 1926; B.S., Lib. Schl., Western Reserve Univ., Cleveland, Ohio, 1934; M.S., Schl. of Lib. Sci., Univ. of Mich., Ann Arbor, 1959. Publs: With All My Love, 1936; Tech. Ed., The History of the State of Ohio, 1941-42; A Bard's Prayers, 1968. Contbr. to: Ed., The Quickening Seed, 1933-46; Ed., Bardic Echoes, 1960—; Ohio State Archaeological & Histl. Soc. Quarterly. Mbrships: World Poetry Soc. Intercontinental; Centro Studi E. Scambi Int.;

Verse Writer's Guild; Ohio Poetry Day Assn.; Bards of Grand Rapids; V.P., Poetry Soc. of Mich., 1972—. Address: 1036 Emerald Ave. N.E., Grand Rapids, MI 49503, USA.

WEAVER, Roger Keys, b. 2 Feb. 1935, Portland, Ore., USA. College Teacher of Poetry Writing. Educ: B.A., Univ. of Ore., 1957; M.A., Univ. of Wash., 1962; M.F.A., Univ. of Ore., 1965. Publs: Ed., Anthology of Commonwealth Poetry (w. Joe Bruchac), forthcoming; Second Skin (poetry), forthcoming. Contbr. to: North Am. Review; Mass. Review; Nimrod; Northwest Review; Hyperion; Friends' Jrnl.; Colo. Quarterly; Poet (India); College English; etc. Hons. incl: No. 1 Featured Poet, Writers' Conf., Linn-Benton Community, 1974. Address: 228 N.W. 28, Corvallis, OR 97330, USA.

WEBB, Charles, b. 9 June 1939, San Fran., Calif., USA. Novelist. Educ: B.A., Williams Coll., 1961. Publs: The Graduate, 1962; Marriage of a Young Stockbroker, 1968; Orphans & Other Children, 1973. Recip., Hutchinson Prize, 1960. Address: Box 182, Hastings on Hudson, NY 10706, USA.

WEBB, Ethel, occasional pen name ROCH, Dalby, b. 3 July 1925, Birmingham, UK. Writer. Educ: B.A., Univ. of W.A., Aust. Publ: Enjoy Poetry (co-author), 1969. Contbr. to: Sandgropers, A W. Aust. Anthol., 1973; Twentieth Century, Aust.; Westerly; Poetry Mag.; Poetry Aust.; Thought, India; Aust. Broadcasting Commn.; Cath. Radio & TV; Educl. Mag., Vic.; Saturday, N.S.W.; var. women's mags. Mbrships: Aust. Soc. of Authors; Assoc., Aust. Writers' Profl. Serv.; Fellowship of Aust. Writers; Soc. of Women Writers. Hons: Commendation, State of Vic. Lit. Competition, 1967; 1st Prize, Goondiwindi Poetry Prize, Qld., 1973; 3rd Prize, Sir. T. Wardle Lit. Competition, Bunbury, W.A., 1973. Address: 29 Napier St., Cottesloe, W.A., Australia 6011.

WEBB, Graham, b. 6 July 1930, Oxford, UK. Writer. Publs: The Cylinder Musical Box Handbook, 1968; The Disc Musical Box Handbook, 1971; Inside the Antique Trade (w. Ronald Pearsall), 1974; The World of Mechanical Music, 1975; The Collectors Book of Care & Repair, 1975. Contbr. to: most major antique jrnls. Address: Gunnarsgill Hall, Gunnerside, Richmond, Yorks., UK.

WEBB, Harri, b. 7 Sept. 1920, Swansea, UK. Author. Educ: M.A., Oxford Univ. Publs: The Green Desert, 1969; A Crown for Branwen, 1974. Contbr. to: Poetry Wales; Anglo-Welsh Review. Mbrships: Yr. Academi Gymreig; Cymdeithas Emrys ap Iwan. Recip., Welsh Arts Coun. Prize, 1970. Address: 2 Rose Row, Cwmback, Aberdare CF44 0BN, UK.

WEBB, Rozana, b. 31 Mar. 1908, Memphis, Tenn., USA. Writer; Lecturer. Publs: The Thirteenth Man, 1962; The Monsoon Breeds, 1965; Eternal the Flow, 1966; Coffee Break, 1967; The Way, 1969; The Ghost Walkers, 1974. Contbr. to: Voices; Voices Int.; Nimrod; Different; S. & W.; Tangent; Poetry India; Am. Bard; Wis. Poetry; Quest; Poetry Dial; Brand X; num. other jrnls. & anthols. Mbrships. incl: Nat. Writers; Calif. Fedn. of Chaparral Poets; San Joaquin Artists & Writers; Int. Platform Assn. Hons. incl: Golden Pegasus Prize, Calif. Fedn. of Chaparral Poets, 1969; Silver Trophy, S. & W., 1970. Address: P.O. Box 467, Visalia, CA 93277, USA.

WEBER, Annemarie, pen name HENNING, Katja, b. 8 June 1918, Berlin, Germany. Author. Publs: (novels) Korso, 1961; Westend, 1966; Roter Winter, 1969; Der grosse Solen von Wulkow, 1972; Die jungen Cötter, 1974. Contbr. to num. jrnls & mags. Mbrships: PEN; Deutscher Schriftstellerverband (German Authors' Soc.). Recip., Berlin Arts Award, 1962. Address: 1 Berlin 19, Heerstr. 30, W. Germany.

WÉBER, Antal, b. 9 June 1929, Vértesboglár, Hungary. University Professor. Educ: Dr.Phil., Fac. of Philos., Hungarian & Engl. Lit., Eötvös Loránd Univ., Budapest. Publs: The Origin of the Hungarian Novel, 1959; Aspects of Literary Currents & Tendencies, 1974. Contbr. to: Hist. of Lit.; Criticism; Acta Litteraria. Mbrships: Int. Assn. of Comp. Lit.; Gen. Sec. of Hungarian Lit. Histns. Address: VI Liszt Ferenc Tér 6, 1061 Budapest, Hungary.

WEBER, Eugen, b. 24 Apr. 1925, Bucharest, Rumania. Professor of History. Educ: Cambridge; Sorbonne & Inst. of Pol. Studies, Paris, France; B.A., M.A., M.Litt., Emmanuel Coll., Cambridge, UK. Publs: The Nationalist Revival in France, 1959; The Western Tradition, 1959; Paths to the

Present, 1960; Action Francaise, 1962; Satan franc-macon, 1964; Varieties of Fascism, 1964; The European Right (w. H. Rogger), 1965; A Modern History of Europe, 1971. Contbr. to: Am. Hist. Review; Jrnl. of Mod. Hist.; (Ed. Bd.), Jrnl. of Contemp. Hist.; French Hist. Studies; Reviews in European Hist. Recip., num. acad. hons. Address: 11579 Sunset Blvd., L.A., CA 10049, USA.

WEBER, Hulda, b. 6 Feb. 1909, NYC, USA. Artist (under name KATZ, Hilda); Poet. Publs. incl: (children's stories) Wizzie Stories (3); Juan & the Prize; One Small Cruise; Why is this Night Different? ; The Sabbath is a Delight; Jose & Sea Mamma; also poetry. Contbr. to: Poetry Digest; Flatbush Mag.; Christian Home; Blue River Poetry Mag.; Am. Bard; Orphic Lute; Wis. Poetry Mag.; Vespers; Bitterroot Mag.; Villager; Scimitar & Song; (anthols.) Blue River Anthol., 1959; Treasures of Parnassus — Best Poems, 1962; Golden Harvest Anthol., 1967; Int. Poetry Soc. Anthol., 1974; & num. others. Mbrships. incl: Poetry Soc. of Am.; Authors' League; Authors' Guild; Int. Poetry Soc.; Int. Poets' Shrine. Hons. incl: Ed.'s Award, Blank Verse, Orphic Lute, 1963; Bettie Payne Wells Award, Am. Bard, 1972; num. biog. listings. Address: 915 W. End Ave., Apt. 5D, N.Y., NY 10025, USA.

WEBER, Jean Paul, b. 3 Dec. 1917, Paris, France. Professor of French Literature & Philosophy. Educ: Agrégé de Philos., Dr. ès Lettres, Sorbonne Univ., Paris. Publs: Meurtre à l'Observatoire, 1959; L'Orient Extrême, 1960; Genèse de l'Oeuvre Poétique, 1961; Domaines thématiques, 1964; Néo-critique & Paléo-critique, 1966; Stendhal, 1970; La Psychologie de l'Art, 4th ed., 1972 (also Engl., Spanish & Serbo-Croat transls.). Contbr. to: Nouvelle Revue Française; Figaro Littéraire; Table Ronde; Les Lettres Nouvelles; Études Françaises (Montreal); Revue Philosophique; other profl. jrnls. Mbr., Am. Soc. Moral & Pol. Scis. Hons. incl: Prix Broquette-Gonin, Acad. Française, 1961; Chevalier, Palmes académiques, 1974. Address: 8200-8 Blvd. E, N. Bergen, NJ 07047, USA.

WEBER-FAGHERAZZI, Cläre, b. 2 Apr. 1906, Metz, Lorraine. Educ: Ph.D. Publs: Wanderung im Mond, forthcoming. Contbr. to: Unio; Prométhée, Almanach; Unsere Katze; Kinderpost Saarbrücker Zeitung. Mbrships: German Authors' Assn. (V.S.), Saarbrücken; Literarische Union/Saar. Address: Inhaberin und Leiterin der Hartnackschule, 66 Saarbrücken, Rathausplatz 3, W. Germany.

WEBSTER, Hugh Colin, b. 24 Oct. 1905, Hobart, Tas., Australia. Physicist. Educ: B.Sc., 1926, D.Sc., 1941, Univ. of Tas.; M.Sc., Univ. of Melbourne, 1928; Ph.D., Univ. of Cambridge, UK, 1932. Publs: Medical & Biological Physics, 1948, 2nd ed., 1961. Contbr. to: Proceedings of the Royal Soc.; Proceedings of the Physical Soc.; Aust. Jrnl. of Physics. Nature. Recip., C.M.C., 1959. Address: 12 Tarcoola St., St. Lucia, Brisbane, Qld., Australia 4067.

WEBSTER, Norman William, b. 21 Aug. 1920, Barrow-in-Furness, Cumbria, UK. Physicist. Educ: B.Sc., Univ. of London. Publs: Joseph Locke, Railway Revolutionary, 1970; Britain's First Trunk Line, the Grand Junction Railway, 1972; The Great North Road, 1974. Contbr. to: Cornhill; Cumbria; Herts. Countryside. Mbrships: Inst. of Phys.; Soc. of Authors. Address: Wetherlam, Ecchinswell, Newbury RG15 8UB, UK.

WEDDE, Ian Curtis, b. 17 Oct. 1946, Blenheim, NZ. Writer. M.A., Auckland Univ. Publs: (poetry) Homage to Matisse, 1971; Made Over, 1974; Pathway to the Sea, 1974; (transl. poetry) Selected Poems of Mahmoud Darwish, 1973. Contbr. to: Landfall; London Mag.; Poetry Aust.; Meanjin Quarterly; NZ Listener; Stand (Newcastle); Poetry NZ; Young NZ Poets (anthol.); etc. Mbrships: PEN; Stand Quarterly (NZ, Ed.). Hons: Robert Burns Fellow, Univ. Otago, 1972; State Writing Bursary, 1974. Address: 31 Currie St., Port Chalmers, NZ.

WEDGWOOD, (Dame) Cicely Veronica, b. 20 July 1910. Historian. Educ: M.A., Oxford Univ. Publs. incl: Strafford, 1935; The Thirty Years' War, 1938; Oliver Cromwell, 1939; William The Silent, 1944; Richelieu, 1949; English Literature in the 17th Century, 1950; Montrose, 1952; The King's War, 1958; Poetry & Politics Under the Stuarts, 1960; Thomas Wentworth: A Revaluation, 1961; The Trial of Charles I, 1964; Milton & His World, 1969. Mbrships. incl: PSN; Inst. of Adv. Study, Princeton, USA; Am. Acad.; F.R.S.L.; F.R.Hist.L. Hons. incl: Goethe Medal; D.Litt. Address: c/o Dept. of Hist., Univ. Coll., London, WC1, UK.

WEEKS, Donald, b. Detroit, Mich., USA. Writer; Editor; Former Magazine Art Director. Educ: Cranbrook Acad. of Art, Bloomfield Hills, Mich.; Wayne State Univ., Detroit. Publs: Ed., The Drawings of Heinrich Kley, USA 1968; Corvo, UK 1971; Ed., Letters to James Walsh, 1972; Ed., In His Own Image, by Fr. Rolfe/Baron Corvo, 1974; Ed., The Rule of the Order of Sanctissima Sophia & the Gazette of the Order, 1974. Contbr. to: The New Yorker; The Aylesford Review, Kent; The Antigonish Review, Nova Scotia; The Tablet; The Private Library; Notes & Queries. Recip., Gold Medal Award as Art Director, Friends Mag., Ceco Publishing Co., Detroit. Address: 156 Lambeth Rd., London SE1, UK.

WEES, Frances Shelley, b. 29 Apr. 1902, Gresham, Ore., USA. Writer; Public Relations Counsellor. Educ: Tchr.'s Cert. Publs. incl: No Pattern for Life, 1951; Someone Called Maggie Lane, 1951; Quarantine, 1956; Under the Quiet Water, 1956; Empty the Haunted Air, 1956; M'Lord, I Am Not Guilty, 1956; The Keys of My Prison, 1960; Pathways to Reading (4 books); Untravelled World; This Necessary Murder, 1960; Where Is Jenny Now, 1960; The Country of the Strangers, 1960; The Last Concubine, 1966; Faceless Enemy, 1968; num. transls. Contbr. to Ladies' Home Jrnl.; etc. Mbrships: DAR; Heliconian Club; Media Club of Can. Address: R.R. 3, Stouffville, Ont. L0H 1Lo, Can.

WEGNER, Armin T(heophil), b. 16 Oct. 1886, Wuppertal-Elberfeld, German Fed. Republic. Writer. Educ: Dr. jur., Univ. H.S. Publs: Antlitz der Stadte (poems), 1917; Der Weg ohne Heimkehr, 1919; Im Hause der Gluckseligkeit, 1920; Der Knabe Hussein, 1921; Die Strasse mit den tausent Zielen, 1924; Moni oder die Welt von unten, 1929; Funf Finger uber dir, 1930; Jagd durch das tausendjahrige Land, 1932; Fallst du, umarme auch die Erde oder der Mann der an das Wort glaubt. Contbr. to: Der Aufbau (N.Y.); etc. Mbrships. incl: PEN; Verband Deutscher Schriftsteller (Munich). Hons. incl: Literature Prize of Alexander-Schroder Fndn., 1966. Address: Via della Purificazione 77, 00187 Rome, Italy.

WEHRLI, Peter K., b. 30 July 1939, Zurich, Switz. TV-Editor; Travel Writer. Educ: Univ. of Zurich; Sorbonne, Paris, France. Publs: Arrivals, 1970; Albanien, Reise ins europäische China, 1971; Catalogue of Everything, 1974; Catalogue of the 134 most important observations during a long Railway Journey, 1974. Contbr. to: LA Free Press, Signatures, Miami Herald, USA; Il Ponte, Le Vie del Mondo, Italy; Il Polz, Malta; Premieres mondiales, France; Garuda, Switz; etc. Mbrships. incl: Swiss Authors' Assn.; Swiss Press Assn. Hons. incl: Jugendbuhne Leimback Award, 1959; Award of Govt. of Zurich, 1972. Address: Ankenweid 24, 8041 Zurich, Switz.

WEI, Rex, pen name WILLIAMS, Rex, b. 1923, Taiwan. Broadcaster; Scriptwriter; Journalist. Educ: Liang Nam Univ.; Taiwan Univ.; B.A. Publs: Terror, 1959; Nightmare, 1960; Shared Lovers, 1971; Came I, 1973. Contbr. to: Radio Taiwan (1955-57); Radio Hong Kong; Hong Kong Tiger Standard (1958-60); Images; Process; Int. Times; Dadd mag. Mbr., Brit. Actors Equity Assn.; Writers' Guild of GB. Agent: London Management & Representation Ltd. Address: 39 North End House, Fitzjames Ave., Kensington, London W14, UK.

WEIBEL, Peter, b. 5 Mar. 1944, Odessa, USSR. Poet; Author; Artist; Editor; Film-maker. Educ: Dip., Sorbonne Univ., Paris, France; Ph.D., Univ. of Vienna, Austria. Publs: Expanded Cinema, Film 11, 1969; Bild-kompendium Wiener Aktionismus und Film, 1970; Inkontinenz I (w. F. Kaltenbeck & W. Schimanovich), 1971; Undationen, 1973; Kritik der Kunst — Kunst der Kritik, 1973; Studien zur Theorie der Automaten (co-ed.), 1974; also films & video tapes. Contbr. to: Manuskripte; Neues Forum; Protokolle; Film; Heute Kunst. Fndr. mbr., Authors' Soc., Graz. Hons. incl: Austrian State Lit. Grant, 1973; Art Award, Film & TV, Berlin, 1974. Address: Nordbergstr. 16/22, A-1090 Vienna, Austria.

WEIDMAN, Jerome, b. 4 Apr. 1913, NYC, USA. Writer. Educ: CCNY, 1930-33; Washington Square Coll., N.Y., 1933-34; N.Y. Univ. Law Schl., 1934-37. Publs. incl: (novels) I Can Get It For You Wholesale, 1937; The Lights Around the Shore, 1943; The Third Angel, 1953; The Enemy Camp, 1958; Word of Mouth, 1964; Fourth Street East, 1971; (short stories) The Horse That Could Whistle Dixie, 1939; My Father Sits in the Dark, 1961 (all also Publd. UK); (plays) Fiorello!, 1960; Tenderloin, 1961 (both w. G. Abbott); Ivory Tower, 1969. Mbr., Authors League of Am. (pres., 1968–). Hons. incl: Pulitzer Prize,

1960; A. Perry Award, 1960. Address: 1035 5th Ave., N.Y., NY 10028, USA.

WEIDNER, Edward W., b. Mpls., Minn., USA. Professor of Community Sciences. Educ: B.A., 1942, M.A., 1943, Univ. of Minn.; Ph.D., 1946. Publs: American City Government (w. William Anderson), 1950; American Government (w. William Anderson), 1951; State & Local Government (w. William Anderson), 1953; The International Programs of American Universities, 1958; Government in the Fifty States (w. William Anderson & Clara Penniman), 1960; Intergovernmental Relations as Seen by Public Officials, 1960; The World Role of Universities, 1962; Technical Assistance in Public Administration Overseas, 1964; Prelude to Reorganization: The Kennedy Foreign Aid Message of March 22, 1961, 1969; Ed., Development Administration in Asia, 1970. Contbr. to num. profl. jrnls. Address: Dept. of Community Scis., Univ. of Wis., Green Bay, WI, USA.

WEIGEL, Hans, b. 29 May 1908, Vienna, Austria. Writer. Publs: O du mein Osterreich; Lern dieses volk der hirten kennen; Flucht vor der grosse; Karl Kraus (biog.). Hons: Austrian Cross of Hon. for Sci. & Art, 1st Class, 1966; City of Vienna Prize for Publishing, 1972. Address: Barmhartstalstrasse 55, A-2344 Maria Enzersdorf, Austria.

WEILHARTNER, Rudolf, b. 12 Apr. 1935, Zell an der Pram, Austria. Teacher. Educ: Tchrs. Trng. Coll. Publs. incl: (poetry) Genesismeditationen, 1967; Schneefelder, 1968; Hommage á Kaspar Hauser, 1975; (prose) Eine Existenz auf dem Lande, 1969; Die Unterstände, 1970; (radio drama) Schamscha, 1967; auerungen, 1969; Sprachgestöber, 1974; Pfauenschrei, 1975; etc. Mbrships: PEN; Autorenkreis; Innviertler Künstlergilde. Hons: 1st Lyrik-Preis der österreichischen Jugendkulturwoche, 1967; Hörspielförderungspreis des österreichischen Rundfunks, 1968; Preis des Wiener Kunstfonds, 1969; Anerkennungspreis zum Österreichischen Staatspreis, 1970; Theodor-Körner-Preis, 1972; 1st Preis der Koref-Stiftung, 1975. Address: A-4752 Riedau, Schwaben 8, Austria.

WEINBAUM, Eleanor Perlstein, b. Beaumont, Tex., USA. Writer; Real Estate Management. Educ: Ward-Belmont Coll.; L.H.D., Univ. Libre, Asia, 1972. Publs: From Croup To Nuts, 1941; The World Laughs With You, 1950; Jest For You, 1954; Shalom, America, 1970. Contbr. to: Poem; Sky Scriptures-Seydell Quarterly, 1964; The Am. Poet Mag.; Today Poets; Nat. Poetry Day Anthol. Mbrships: Tex. Poetry Soc.; United Poets Laureate Int.; World Poetry Soc. Hons: Disting. Serv. Citation, World Poetry Soc., 1970, 2nd Prize, Book Contest, Corpus Christi Writers Conf., 1966. Address: 203—a Gilbert Bldg., Beaumont, TX, USA.

WEINBAUM, Martin Albert, b. 15 July 1902, Kuestrin, Germany. Emeritus Professor of History. Educ: Univs. of Freiburg & Berlin; Ph.D. Publs: Verfassungsgeschichte Londons, 1929; London unter Eduard I und II., 2 vols., 1933; The Incorporation of Boroughs, 1937; British Borough Charters, 1307-1660, 1943; Dilthey's Philosophy of Existence (w. Wm. Kluback), 1970. Contbr. to profl. jrnls. inclng: Speculum; Engl. Histl. Review; The Histn. Mbrships. incl: Royal Histl. Soc.; Medieval Acad. of Am.; Am. Histl. Assn. Recip., Adolphus Ward Prize in Hist., Univ. of Manchester, 1937. Address: 133-33 Sanford Ave., Flushing, NY 11355, USA.

WEIR, Molly, b. Glasgow, UK. Actress; Writer. Educ: Skerry's Coll.; Glasgow Univ. Publs: Molly Weir's Recipes, 1960, Latest ed., 1971; Shoes Were For Sunday, 1970; Best Foot Forward, 1972; A Toe on the Ladder, 1973. Contbr. to: People's Jrnl.; Scots Mag.; Scotsman; Glasgow Herald; Woman's Way; Scottish Gardener; BBC Woman's Hour & 12 Noon. Mbrships: BBC Club; Actor's Equity. Address: Primrose Cottage, 26 Moss Lane, Pinner, Middx, HA5 3AX, UK.

WEISBERG, Harold, b. 8 Apr. 1913, Phila., Pa., USA. Writer. Publs: 4 books in Whitewash series, 1965, 1966, 1967, 1974; Oswald in New Orleans: Case for Conspiracy with the CIA, 1967; Frame-Up — The Martin Luther King/James Earl Ray Case, 1971. Address: Route 8, Frederick, MD 21701, USA.

WEISHEIPL, James Atharasius, b. 3 July 1923, Oshkosh, Wis., USA. Roman Catholic Priest; Professor of the History of Medieval Science. Educ: Univ. Wis.; Philos. Lic.,

Dominican House Studies, River Forest, Ill., 1946; Ph.D., Pontifical Univ. St. Thomas Aquinas, Rome, 1953; D.Ph., Univ. Oxford, 1957. Publs: Nature & Gravitation, 1955, reprinted, 1961; The Development of Physical Theory in the Middle Ages, 1959, latest ed. 1971; La teoría física en la edad media, 1967; Friar Thomas d'Aquino: His Life, Thought and Works, 1974; Ed., The Dignity of Science, 1961. Contbr. to: Thomist; Sapientia; etc. Mbrships. incl: Hist. Sci. Soc. Recip., Vis. Fellowship Corpus Christi Coll., Oxford, 1973-74. Address: Pontifical Inst. Medieval Studies, 59 Queens Park Cres., Toronto, Ont. M5S 2C4, Can.

WEISS, David, b. 12 June 1909, Phila., Pa., USA. Novelist. Educ: B.Sc., Temple Univ., 1933; Fellowship, New Schl. of Social Rsch., 1943-45. Publs. incl: The Guilt Makers, 1953; Naked Came I, 1963; The Assassination of Mozart, 1970; No Number is Greater Than One, 1972; Myself, Christopher Wren, 1973; Physician Extraordinary, 1975. Contbr. to: Dance Mag.; Books & Bookmen; hist. ed. on films for producer David O. Selznick; etc. Recip., Frieder Award, best novel on a Jewish Theme, 1953. Address: 235 West End Ave., N.Y., NY 10023, USA.

WEISS, Peter, b. 1916. Writer. Educ: Art Acad., Prague. Publs. incl: (plays) Nacht mit Gästen, 1963; Die Verfolgung & Ermordung Jean Paul Marats, 1964; Die Ermittlung, 1965; Vietnam Dialogue, 1967; Wie dem Herrn Mockinpott das Leiden ausgetrieben wird, 1968; Trotzki im Exil, 1970; (prose) Abschied von den Eltern, 1961; Fluchtpunkt, 1962; Das Gespräch der drei Gehenden, 1963; Rekonvaleszenz, 1972. Hons: Heinrich-Mann Prize, Acad. of Arts, E. Berlin, 1966; Charles Veillon Prize for Lit. Address: c/o Suhrkamp Verlag, Lindenstr. 29-35, 6 Frankfurt-am-Main, W. Germany.

WEISSTUB, David Norman, b. 26 Oct. 1944, Port Arthur, Ont. Can. Professor of Law. Educ: B.A., Columbia Univ., 1963; M.A., Univ. of Toronto, 1965; J.D. Yale Law Schl., 1970. Author, Heaven Take My Hand, 1968. Contbr. to: The Can. Forum; Can. Dimension; Can. Jrnl. of Theol.; Anthol. of Lit. Recip., hon. mention, Norma Epstein, Nat. Writing Competition, 1968. Address: Osgoode Hall Law Schl., York Univ., 4700 Keele St., Downsview, Ont. M3J 2R5, Can.

WEITZMANN, Kurt, b. 7 Mar. 1904, Almerode, Germany. Professor Emeritus of Art & Archaeology. Educ: Univs. of Munster, Wurzburg, Vienna; Ph.D., Univ. of Berlin, 1929. Publs. incl: Illustrations in Roll & Codex: A Study of the Origin & Method of Text Illustration, 1947, 2nd ed., 1970; Ancient Book Illumination, 1959; The Monastery of Saint Catherine at Mount Sinai: The Church & Fortress of Justinian (co-author), 1973. Contbr. to: Am. Jrnl. Archaeol.; Art Bulletin; Hesperia; Byzantion; etc. Mbr., profl. orgs. Hons. incl: Dr. honoris causa, Univ. of Heidelberg, 1967, Univ. of Chgo., 1968. Haskins Medal, Medieval Acad. of Am., 1974. Address: 209 McCormich Hall, Princeton University, Princeton, NJ 08540, USA.

WELBOURN, Richard Burkewood, b. 1 May 1919, Rainhill, Lancs., UK. Professor of Surgery. Educ: B.A., 1940, M.B. & B.Ch., 1942, M.A. & M.D., 1953, Univ. of Cambridge. Publs: Clinical Endocrinology for Surgeons (w. D. A. D. Montgomery), 1963; Medical & Surgical Endocrinology (w. D. A. D. Montgomery), 1974. Contbr. to var. med. & surg. jrnls. & anthols. Mbrships. incl: Med. Rsch. Coun.; Past Pres., Surg. Rsch. Soc. Recip., James Berry Prize for publd. work on surg. of the endocrine system, Royal Coll. of Surgs. of England, 1967-69. Address: 6 Broomfield Rd., Kew Gdns., Richmond, Surrey TW9 3HR, UK.

WELCH, Ann Courtenay, pen names EDMONDS, Ann; DOUGLAS, Ann, b. 20 May 1917, London, UK. Writer. Publs: Cloud Reading for Pilots, 1943; Gliding & Advanced Soaring, 1947; The Woolacombe Bird, 1964; The Story of Gliding, 1965; The New Soaring Pilot, 1970; Pilots Weather, 1973. Contbr. to: Flight Int., UK; Flying, USA; Aircraft, Aust.; Shell Aviation, UK. Mbrships: Fellow, Royal Aeronautical Soc.; Soc. of Authors; Fellow, Royal Meteorol. Soc. Hons: O.B.E.; Silver Medal, Royal Aero Club; Lilienthal & Bronze Medals, Fedn. Aeronautique Int. Address: 14 Upper Old Park Lane, Farnham. Surrey. UK.

WELCH, Mary Ross, b. 30 May 1918, Newburgh, N.Y., USA. Retired Clerk. Publs: Bury Me Deep, 1948; Trying for Purple, 1953; The Color of Loneliness, 1958; Prouder than Wine, 1965; The Cross Will Splinter, 1970. Contbr. to: Hudson Valley Mag.; Sign.; Am. Poetry League Bull.; Bag

Poetry Annual; Prairie Poet; Bay Shore Breeze; Hooriers Challenger; Am. Bard; Queen of all Hearts; Bapt. Leader; etc. Mbrships: Bd. Dirs. & Registrar, St. Davids Christian Writers Assn.; Pres., Writers Guild of the Mid-Hudson Valley. Hons: 2nd Prize, St. Davids Christian Writers Conference Contest, 1973; Hon. Mention, Bag Press Poetry Contest; Hon. Mention, Chaparral Contest. Address: P.O. Box 898, Poughkeepshie, NY 12602, USA.

WELCH, Mary Scott (Stewart), b. 14 Dec. 1919, Chgo., Ill., USA. Writer. Educ: A.B., Univ. of Ill., Champaign-Urbana, 1940. Publs: Esquire Books without By-line: Handbook for Hosts; Esquire Etiquette; The Art of Keeping Fit; Esquire Cook Book; (others) Your First Hundred Meals, 1947; Esquire's Party Book (w. Ronnie Welch), 1965; What Every Young Man Should Know (w. the Eds. of Esquire), 1970; Seventeen's Guide to Travel, 1970; The Family Wilderness Handbook, 1973; (for children): Pets; Paris. Contbr. to: Redbook; McCall's; Ladies Home Jrnl.; House Beautiful; Seventeen; Glamour; num. other women's & popular mags. Mbrships. incl: Authors' League; Soc. of Mag. Writers; Civil Liberties Unions, Am. & N.Y.; var. ecol. & feminist orgs. Address: 55 Park Ave., N.Y., NY 10016, USA.

WELD, John, b. 24 Feb. 1905, Birmingham, Ala., USA. Writer. Educ: Auburn Univ. Publs: Don't You Cry For Me, 1940; The Pardners, 1941; Sabbath Has No End, 1942; Mark Pfeiffer, Md., 1943. Mbrships: Authors League of Am.; Screen Writer's Guild; The Players, N.Y.; Kappa Sigma; Irvine Coast Country, Newport Beach, Calif. Address: 1213 Emerald Bay, Laguna Beach, CA 92651, USA.

WELLARD, James Howard, b. 12 Jan. 1909, London, UK. Freelance Writer; Former Journalist & Professor of English. Educ: B.A.(Hons.), London; Ph.D., Chgo., USA. Publs. incl: A Man & His Journey, 1962; The Great Sahara, 1963; Lost Worlds of Africa, 1966; The Sun Gazers, 1968; Desert Pilgrimage, 1970; Babylon, 1972; The French Foreign Legion, 1974; The Search for Lost Worlds, 1975. Contbr. to: Encounter; Times; New Soc.; Geogl. Mag.; Horizon; etc. Mbrships: Fellow, Royal Geogl. Soc.; Soc. of Authors. Hons: Rockefeller Fellow, 1933-35; Fulbright Fellowship, 1958-59. Address: 14 The Pryors, East Heath Rd., London NW3, UK.

WELLEK, René, b. 22 Aug. 1903, Vienna, Austria. Sterling Professor Emeritus of Comparative Literature. Educ: D.Phil., Charles Univ., Prague, Czech., 1926; Grad. Schl., Princeton Univ., USA, 1927-28. Publs. incl: Immanuel Kent in England, 1931; The Rise of English Literary History, 1941; A History of Modern Criticism 1750-1950, 4 vols. to date, 1955—; Confrontations, 1965; Discriminations, 1970. Contbr. to: Am. Schlr.; Comp. Lit.; Arcadia; Philol. Quarterly; etc. Mbrships. incl: Am. Comp. Lit. Assn.; MLA. Hons. incl: Guggenheim Fellowships, 1953, 1957, 1967; 12 Hon. Docts., inclng. Oxford, Harvard, Rome, Louvain, Munich. Address: 377 St. Ronan Street, New Haven, CT 06511, USA.

WELLER, Allen Stuart, b. 1 Feb. 1907, Chgo., Ill., USA. Teacher; Museum Director. Educ: Ph.B., 1927, Ph.D., 1942, Univ. of Chgo.; M.A., Princeton Univ., 1929. Publs: Francesco di Giorgio, 1439-1501, 1942; Abraham Rattner, 1956; Art USA Now, 2 vols., 1962; The Joys & Sorrows of Recent American Art, 1968; La Nueva Imagen: Happenings en el arte, 1970. Contbr. to var. art & lit. jrnls. Mbrships: Bd. of Dirs., Coll. Art Assn., 1953-57, 1965-69; Exec. Comm., Nat. Assn. of Schls. of Art, 1955-58; Edit. Advsry. Bd., Chmn., Humanities Comm., Field Enterprises Educl. Corp., 1964-72. Address: 412 West Iowa St., Urbana, IL 61801, USA.

WELLER, George Anthony, b. 13 July 1907, Boston, Mass., USA. Journalist. Educ: B.A., Harvard Coll., 1929; Univ. of Vienna, Austria, 1930-31; Max Reinhardt Schl. of Theatre, Vienna, 1930-31. Publs. incl: Not to Eat, Not for Love, 1933, (transl.) Fontamara by Ignazio Silone, under pen name Michael Wharf, 1934; The Crack in the Column, 1949; The Paratroops, 1958; Story of Submarines, 1962. Contbr. to: New Yorker; Sat. Evening Post; N.Y. Times (for. corres. 1932-36); Chgo. Daily News (for. corres. 1940-72); etc. Mbrships. incl: Stampa Estera, Italy. Hons. incl: Pulitzer prize for jrnlsm., 1943; George Polk Mem. Prize, 1955. Address: c/o Stampa Estera, via della Mercede 55, Rome, Italy.

WELLES, George Orson, b. 6 May 1915. Actor; Producer. Publs: Mr. Arkadin, 1957; (Ed. w. Roger Hill)

Everybody's Shakespeare, 1933; Mercury Shakespeare, 1939; (play) Chimes at Midnight, film, 1964; (films) Citizen Kane, 1940; The Lady from Shanghai, 1946; Macbeth, 1947; The Third Man, 1949; Moby Dick, 1956; Othello, 1956; Crack in the Mirror, 1960; A Man for All Seasons, 1967; The Kremlin Letter, 1969; Waterloo, 1970; Ten Days' Wonder, 1972. Mbr., Am. Acad. of Arts & Sci.; Hons. incl: Claire Senie Award, 1938; Special Acad. Award, 1971. Address: 10464 Bellago Rd., Bel Air, Calif., USA.

WELLS, Frank Charles Robert, pen name ROBERTS, Martin, b. 31 Jan. 1929, London, UK. Bank Manager. Educ: Goldsmith's Coll., Univ. London. Publs: The Parasaurians, 1969, 2nd ed., 1974; Candle in the Sun, 1971; Right-Handed Wilderness, 1973. Contbr. to: BBC; Guardian; Radio Eireann; SF Monthly; Galaxy; Worlds of If; Sci. Fantasy; Impulse; etc. Address: 151C Griffin Rd., London SE18 7PZ, UK.

WELSH, Alexander, b. 29 Apr. 1933, Albany, N.Y., USA. Professor. Educ: A.B., 1954, M.A., 1957, Ph.D., 1961, Harvard Univ. Publs: The Hero of the Waverley Novels, 1963, reprint 1968; The City of Dickens, 1971. Contbr. to var. scholarly jrnls. Recip., Guggenheim Fellowship, 1969-70. Address: Dept. of English, Univ. of Calif., L.A., CA 90024, USA.

WELTY, Eudora, b. 13 Apr. 1909, Jackson, Miss., USA. Writer. Educ: State Coll. for Women; B.A., Univ. of Wis., 1929; Schl. of Advt., Columbia Univ., 1930-31. Publs. incl: (novels) The Robber Bridegroom, USA, 1942, UK, 1944; Delta Wedding, USA, 1946, UK, 1947; The Ponder Heart, USA & UK, 1954; Losing Battles, 1970; (short stories) A Curtain of Green, 1941; The Golden Apples, USA, 1949, UK, 1950; The Bride of the Innisfallen, USA & UK, 1955; 13 Stories, 1965. Mbr., Am. Acad. Arts & Letters. Hons. incl: Howells Medal, 1955; Creative Arts Award, Brandeis Univ., 1965; D.Litt., Denison Univ., Ohio, 1971. Address: 1119 Pinehurst St., Jackson, MS, USA.

WEMMERSLAGER van SPARWOUDE, Jan Bernard, pen name LANDELL, Olaf J.de, b. 16 May 1911, Cheribon, Java, Indonesia. Author. Publs. incl: Spiegel aan de wand, 1938; Nachtfluistering, 1944; Ave Eva, 1946; De porselain-tafel, 1951; De appels bloeien, 1951; Blonde Martijn, 1968; Met hermelijn-stappen, 1969; Daar gaat een prinses voorbij, 1969; Overpeinzing, (gift-publ.) 1970; December (tales, 1970; Open dichtwoord (poetry), 1971; Maneschijn over uw hart, (tales) 1972; Kroelen met de Kroon, 1972; Het bloeien v.d. Porselein-boom, 1974. Contbr. to: De Vrouw en Haar Huis; Elsevier's Weekblad; Dutch radio progs. Mbrships: Soc. of Authors; Soc. for Music Copywrights. Hons: Dutch Bookshop Distinction Award, 1950, Major Award, 1951; Dutch Soc. of Circulating Libs. Award, 1956. Address: Javalaan 11, Hilversum, Netherlands.

WENHAM-STRUGNELL, George Kenneth, b. 18 Nov. 1899, S. Hackney, Middlesex, UK. Retired Civil Defence Officer. Educ: St. Dunstan's Coll.; King's Coll., London. Publs: Seagates to the Saxon Shore, 1973. Contbr. to var. local histl., relig. jrnls., mags. & reviews. Mbr., Naval & Mil. Club, London. Recip., T.D. Address: Haylings Lodge, Leiston, Suffolk, UK.

WENTZ, Frederick K., b. 21 Jan. 1921, Penn., USA. Professor of Church History. Educ: incl: B.D., Gettysburg Sem., 1945; Ph.D., Yale Univ., 1954; D.D., Hartwick Coll., 1972. Publs. incl: The Layman's Role Today, 1963; My Job & My Faith, 1967; Lutherans in Concert, 1968; Set Free for Others, 1969. Contbr. to: Lutheran Quarterly (Ed. 1966-70); Int. Jrnl. of Relig. Educ.; Interpretation; etc. Mbrships: Am. Soc. of Ch. Hist.; Am. Lutheran Histl. Conf. Address: 272 N. Broadmoor, Springfield, OH 45504, USA.

WEÖRES, Sandor, b. 22 June 1913, Szombathely, Hungary..Writer. Educ: Ph.D. Publs: The Tower of Silence, 1956; Evocation of the Soul, 1958; Collected Works, 1970. Contbr. to: Hungarian lit. jrnls. Mbr., PEN. Hons: Baumgarten Prize, 1935; Kossuth Prize, 1968. Address: Murakozi u. 10/a, Budapest 1025 II, Hungary.

WERNER, Victor Emile, b. 22 Sept. 1894, Bklyn., N.Y., USA. Management Consultant, US Government; Lecturer-Author; Memory Expert. Educ: Cert., Wash. Univ. Schl. Engrng.; 1942; A.A., 1958, B.B.A., 1963, Geo. Wash. Univ. Publs: Werner's 200-Year Calendar, 1936, 4th ed., 1973; Memory Methods, 1949, 3rd ed., 1965; Short-cut Memory, 1968, 2nd ed., 1971. Contbr. to: Radio; Catholic Digest; Nat. Enquirer; Fed. Times; Army, Navy & Air Force

Times; Psychic Observer; Fate; Retirement Living; Toastmaster Int.; Assoc. Ed., Kings Co. VFW Bulletin. Mbrship. incl: Am. Assn. of Trng. Dirs.; Danish Club of Wash.; Life Mbr., Veterans of For. Wars of US. Hons. incl: US GOvt. 30-Yr. Serv. Award, 1964; Army Cert. of Achievement, 1964; Army Patriotic Civ. Serv. Award, 1966. Address: 7418 Holly Ave., Tokoma Pk., MD 20012, USA.

WERNSTRÖM, Sven Gunnar, b. 3 Apr. 1925, Stockholm, Sweden. Author. Publs: Mexikanen, 1963; Befriaren, 1965; De hemligas ö, 1966; Resa på en okänd planet, 1967; Upproret, 1968; Kamrat Jesus, 1971; Mannen på tåget, 1971; Trälarna, 1973; Trälarnas söner, 1974; Trälarnas döttrar, 1974. Mbr., Swedish Union of Authors. Recip., Nils Hogersson Prize, 1974. Address: Åsvägen 3, 610 24 Vikbolandet, Sweden.

WERTHAM, Fredric, b. 1895, Bavaria, Germany. Neurologist; Psychiatrist. Educ: King's Coll., London; Univs. of Würzburg, Erlangen, Munich; Postgrad., London, Munich, Paris, Vienna. Publs. incl: Dark Legend, 1941, rev., 1967; The Show of Violence, 1949, rev., 1967; Seduction of the Innocent, 1954; The Circle of Guilt, 1956; A Sign for Cain, an Exploration of Human Violence, 1966, enlarged eds., 1967 & 1973; The World of Fanzines, 1974. Contbr. to psychomed. & lit. jrnls. Mbrships. incl: Authors Guild; Mystery Writers of Am.; Am. Neurol. & Psych. Assns. Hons. incl: Top Hon. Award, Chgo. Book Clin., 1974. Address: Bluehills, Kempton Rte. 1, PA 19529, USA.

WESTCOTT, Glenway, b. 11 Apr. 1901, Kewaskum, Wis., USA. Writer. Educ: Univ. of Chgo., 1917-19. Publs. incl: (novels) The Grandmothers, 1927; The Pilgrim Hawk, USA, 1940, UK, 1946; Apartment in Athens, 1945 (as Household in Athens, UK, 1945); (short stories) Goodbye, Wisconsin, USA, 1928, UK, 1929; (verse) Natives of Rock, 1936; (non-fiction) Fear & Trembling, 1932; 12 Fables of Aesop, Newly Narrated, 1954; Images of Truth, USA, 1962, UK, 1963. Mbrships: Nat. Inst. Arts & Letters (Pres., 1959-62); Am. Acad. Arts & Letters. Hons: Harper Prize, 1927; D.Litt., Rutgers Univ., 1963. Address: Hay-Meadows, Rosemont, NJ, USA.

WESCOTT, Roger Williams, b. 28 Apr. 1925, Phila., Pa., USA. Professor of Anthropology. Educ: B.A., M.A., Ph.D., Princeton Univ., USA; B.Litt., Oxford Univ., UK, 1952. Publs: A Comparative Grammar of the Albanian Language, 1955; Introductory Ibo, 1961; Bini Phonology, 1962; Bini Morphology, 1962; Bini Lexemics, 1963; An Outline of Anthropology, 1965; The Divine Animal: An Exploration of Human Potentiality, 1969; Ed., Language Origins, 1974; co-author of 9 other books. Contbr. to scholarly jrnls. Mbr., profl. orgs. Recip., acad. hons. Address: 11 Green Hill Rd., Madison, NJ, USA.

WESENICK, Ermine Gilmour, b. 26 June 1890, Mo., USA. Artist; Writer. Educ: Fed. Schl. of Art, Mpls., Minn. Publs: (poetry) Against the Wind, 1967; To Remember By, 1960, revised as Sage Brush, 1973. Contbr. to var. newspapers. Mbrships: Kan. Authors' Club; Chaparral Poets; United Amateur Press. Address: 908 Bridge St., Humboldt, KS 66748, USA.

WESKER, Arnold, b. 24 May 1932, Stepney, London, UK. Playwright. Publs: (plays) The Kitchen, 1957; Chicken Soup with Barley, 1958; Roots, 1959; I'm Talking About Jerusalem, 1960; Chips with Everything, 1962; Menace, 1963; Their Very own Golden City, 1964; The Four Seasons, 1965; The Friends, 1970; (other publs.) The Old Ones, 1972; The Journalists, 1972; The Wedding Feast, 1973; Love Letters on Blue Paper, 1974; Say Goodbye You may Never See Them Again, 1974. Recip., Premio Marzotte Drama Prize, 1964. Address: 27 Bishops Rd., London N6, UK.

WESLEY, George R., b. 31 July 1931, Houston, Texas, USA. Professor of Psychology. Educ: B.A., Univ. of Houston, 1957; M.A., 1959, Ph.D., 1965, Univ. of Denver. Publs. incl: The U.S. of A. & Other Writings, 1971; A Primer of Misbehaviour: an introduction to abnormal psychology, 1972; Letters to my Shrink (w. Bee Sweatt), 1973; Ed., Motivation: a book of readings, forthcoming. Contbr. to: New Voices in Am. Poetry; Test Collect. Bulletin; A Sourcebook of Mental Health Measures; etc. Mbrships. incl: N.C. Psychol. Assn.; NEA; Am. Mensa; VP local chapt., AAUP. Address: Rt. 3, Box 308, Boone, NC 28607, USA.

WEST, Albert John Frederick, b. 1925, Edgware, UK. Geographer; Educationist. Educ: Univ. Coll., London; Heriot Watt Coll., Univ. of Birmingham; Edinburgh Univ.; Loughborough Coll.; Inst. of Educ., London; B.Sc.; P.G.C.E; M.Ed. Publs. incl: Singapore Geography Series, 5 vols.; Photographic Geography; Understanding Contours & Landforms; New Secondary Atlas; Science & Nature, 5 vols.; Revision Notes in Geography, 4 vols.; Teaching of Geography, Examination Technique in Geography, 2 vols.; Revision Notes Series, 25 vols.; Student Introduction Series, 8 vols.; Examination Technique Series, 20 vols.; South-East Asia & Continent of Asia (w. J. Rose); South & Central America. Contbr. to: Link; I.A.A.M. Tchng. of Geog. Address: 10 Wilton Cresc., Alderley Edge, Cheshire, UK.

WEST, Anthony C., b. 1 July 1910, Co. Down, N. Ireland, UK. Writer. Publs: (novels) The Native Moment, USA, 1959, UK, 1961; Rebel to Judgement, USA, 1962; The Ferret Fancier, UK, 1962, USA, 1963; As Towns with Fire, UK, 1968, USA, 1970; (short stories) River's End & Other Stories, USA, 1957, UK, 1959. Recip., Atlantic Award, 1946. Address: Bryn Goleu, Llanberis, Gwynedd, Wales, UK.

WEST, Anthony (Panther), b. 4 Aug. 1914, Hunstanton, Norfolk, UK. Magazine Writer. Publs. incl: (novels) On a Dark Night, 1949 (as The Vintage, USA, 1950); Another Kind, UK, 1951, USA, 1952; The Trend is Up, USA, 1960, UK, 1961; David Rees, Among Others, USA & UK, 1970; (non-fiction) D. H. Lawrence, 1951, revised ed. 1966; The Crusades, USA, 1954 (as All About the Crusades, UK, 1967); Principles & Persuasions, USA, 1957, UK, 1958; Elizabethan England, USA & UK, 1965; Ed., The Galsworthy Reader, 1968. Contbr. to: New Yorker (Staff, 1950–). Recip., Houghton Mifflin Lit. Fellowship, 1950. Address: c/o New Yorker, 25 W. 43rd St., N.Y., NY 10036, USA.

WEST, Jessamyn, b. 1907, Ind., USA. Writer. Educ: A.B., Whittier Coll., Calif.; Univ. of Calif., Berkeley. Publs. incl: (novels) The Friendly Persuasion, USA, 1945, UK, 1946; Cress Delahanty, USA, 1953, UK, 1954; South of the Angels, USA, 1960, UK, 1961; A Matter of Time, USA, 1966, UK, 1967; Leafy Rivers, USA, 1967, UK, 1968; Crimson Ramblers of the World, Farewell, USA, 1970, UK, 1971; (short stories) Love, Death & the Ladies' Drill Team, 1955 (as Learn to Say Goodbye, UK, 1957); Ed., A Quaker Reader, 1962; var. screenplays. Hons: T. Monsen Award, 1958; num. degrees. Address: c/o Harcourt, Brace & Jovanovich, 750 Third Ave., N.Y., NY 10017, USA.

WEST, Luther Shirley, pen name (for poetry) PRAECEPTOR HUMILIS, b. 6 Sept. 1899, Utica, N.Y., USA. University Professor & Dean. Educ: B.S., N.Y. State Coll. of Agric., Cornell Univ., 1921; Ph.D., Cornell Univ., 1925; var. postdoct. & other courses. Publs. incl: Practical Malariology (co-author), 1946, Portuguese transl., 1951, 2nd ed., 1963; The Housefly: Its Natural History, Medical Importance & Control, 1951; The Free-living Protozoa of the Upper Peninsula of Michigan (w. F. C. Lundin), 1963; Annotated Bibliography of Musca Domestica Linnaeus (w. O. B. Peters), 1973. Contbr. to num. profl. & educl. jrnls. Mbrships. incl: Int. Mark Twain Soc.; Mich. Acad. Sci. Arts & Letters (Pres., 1965-66). Address: 137 W. Ridge St., Marquette, MI 49855, USA.

WEST, Morris, pen names MORRIS, Julian; EAST, Michael, b. 26 Apr. 1916, Melbourne, Australia. Writer. Educ: B.A., Melbourne Univ., 1937. Publs. incl: (novels) Moon in My Pocket (as J. Morris), 1945; The Big Story (as The Crooked Road, USA), 1957; The Devil's Advocate, UK & USA, 1959; The Shoes of the Fisherman, UK & USA, 1963; The Ambassador, UK & USA, 1965; The Tower of Babel, UK & USA, 1968; Summer of the Red Wolf, 1971; (non-fiction) Children of the Sun (as CHildren of the Shadows, USA), 1957; 2 plays. Mbrships: F.R.S.L.; Fellow, World Acad. Arts & Scis. Hons. incl: Black Mem. Prize, 1960; D.Litt., Univ. of Calif., 1968. Address: c/o Paul R. Reynolds, 599 5th Ave., N.Y., NY 10017, USA.

WEST, Paul, b. 23 Feb. 1930, Eckington, Derbys., UK. Professor of English. Educ: B.A., Birmingham Univ., 1950; M.A., Columbia Univ., USA, 1953. Publs. incl: (verse) The Snow Leopard, UK, 1964, USA, 1965; (novels) Alley Jaggers, UK & USA, 1966; I'm Expecting to Live Quite Soon, USA, 1970, UK, 1971; Bela Lugosi's White Christmas, UK & USA, 1972; Colonel Mint, USA & UK, 1972; (non-fiction) The Modern Novel, UK, 1963, USA,

1965; Words for a Deaf Daughter, UK, 1969, USA, 1970. Contbr. to: New Statesman; N.Y. Times Book Review; Book World; Penguin Mod. Stories, 8, 1971; etc. Recip., var. Fellowships. Address: 117 Burrowes Bldg., Pa. State Univ., University Park, PA 16802, USA.

WEST, Rebecca, pen name of ANDREWS, Cicily Fairfield, b. 25 Dec. 1892, London, UK. Writer. Publs. incl: (novels) The Judge, UK & USA, 1922; The Thinking Reed, UK & USA, 1936; The Fountain Overflows, USA, 1956, UK, 1957; The Birds Fall Down, UK & USA, 1966; (non-fiction) The Strange Necessity, UK & USA, 1928; Black Lamb & Grey Falcon, 2 vols., UK, 1937, USA, 1941; The Meaning of Treason, USA, 1947, revised as The New Meaning of Treason, 1964, UK, 1949, revised ed. 1965; The Court & the Castle, USA, 1957, UK, 1958. Mbrships. incl: F.R.S.L. (Companion of Lit); Am. Acad. Arts & Letters. Hons. incl: D.Litt., NY Univ.; D.B.E., 1959. Address: Ibstone House, Ibstone, High Wycombe, Bucks., UK.

WEST, Tristram Frederick, pen name PROSPERO, b. 19 Apr. 1911, Heath, Herts., UK. Scientist; Editor; Author. Educ: B.Sc., M.Sc., Ph.D. & D.Sc., Univ. of London. Publs: Synthetic Perfumes (w. D. H. R. Barton), 1949; DDT & Newer Persistent Insecticides (w. G. A. Campbell), 1950; Chemical Control of Insects (w. J. E. Hardy), 1961; Chemicals for Pest Control (w. G. E. Hartley), 1969. Ed., series of monographs on chem. ind. (w. J. Davidson Pratt). Contbr. to sci. jrnls. Mbrships. incl: F.R.I.C. Address: Wahroonga, Tylers Causeway, Nr. Newgate St., Hertford, Herts. SG13 8QN, UK.

WESTERVELT, Virginia Veeder, b. 19 Sept. 1914, Schenectady, N.Y., USA. Writer; Teacher. Educ: B.A., Wellesley Coll., Mass.; M.A., Syracuse Univ., N.Y.; further study, Columbia & N.Y. Univs., Ithaca Coll., & Ctrl. Schl. Speech & Drama, London, UK. Publs: Getting Along in the Teenage World, 1957; Choosing a Career in A Changing World, 1959; The World Was His Laboratory, the Story of Wills R. Whitney, 1964; Incredible Man of Science: Irving Langmuir, 1968. Contbr. to: N.Y. Times; Am. Girl; Luth.; Compact; Conquest; Mod. Maturity; etc. Mbrships. incl: Nat. League Am. Pen Women; Calif. Writers' Guild. Hons. incl: Nat. League Am. Pen Women Prizes, 1970, 1971. Address: 1050 Bermuda Drive, Redlands, CA 92373, USA.

WESTHEIMER, David, pen name SMITH, Z. Z., b. 11 Apr. 1917, Houston, Tex., USA. Writer. Educ: B.A., Rice Univ., 1937. Publs: Summer on the Water, 1948; The Magic Fallacy, 1950; Watching out for Dulie, 1960; Von Ryan's Express, 1963; My Sweet Charlie 1965, play, 1966; Song of the Young Sentry, 1967; Lighter than a Feather, 1971; Over the Edge, 1972; Going Public, 1973; The Olmec Head, 1974; The Avila Gold, 1974. Mbrships: Authors' Guild of Am.; Writers' Guild of Am. W.; Mystery Writers of Am. Address: 407 North Maple Drive 206, Beverly Hills, CA 90210, USA.

WESTLAKE, Donald E. (Edwin Edmund), pen names, CLARK, Curt; COE, Tucker; CULVER, Timothy J.; STARK, Richard, b. 12 July 1933. Writer. Publs. incl: The Mercenaries, 1960; Killing Time, 1961; 361, 1962; Killy, 1963; The Fugitive Pigeon, 1965; God Save the Mark, 1967; Adios, Scheherezade, 1970; I Gave At The Office, 1971; Bank Shot, 1972; Cops & Robbers, Gangway (w. Brian Garfield), 1973; Help I Am Being Held Prisoner, Jimmy The Kid, 1974; Two Much, 1975; 20 novels as Richard Stark; 5 novels as Tucker Coe; 1 novel as Curt Clark; 1 novel as Timothy J. Culver. Recip., Edgar Award, Mystery Writers of Am., 1966. Address: c/o Henry Morrison, 58 W. 10th St., N.Y., NY 10011, USA.

WESTMAN-BERG, Karin Birgitta, b. 17 June 1914, Uppsala, Sweden. Freelance Writer; Former Professor of Literary History. Educ: Ph.D. in Hist. of Lit. Publs: Studies in C.J.L. Almquist's Views on Women, 1962; Contbng. Ed., Sex Roles in Literature from Antiquity to the 1960s, 1968; Contbng. Ed., Sex Discrimination Past & Present, 1972. Contbr. to: Samlaren; Hertha; Am.-Scandinavian Review. Mbr., PEN. Hons: Award,: Fund of Swedish Authors, 1971; Award, County of Västernorrland, 1974. Address: O Slottsg. 10, 75235 Uppsala, Sweden.

WESTON, Burns H., b. 5 Nov. 1933, Cleveland, Ohio, USA. Professor of Law & Director, Center for World Order Studies, Coll. of Law, Univ. of Iowa. Educ: B.A., Oberlin Coll.; LL.B., 1961, J.S.D., 1970, Yale Law Schl. Publs: International Claims: Postwar French Practice, 1971; International Claims: Their Settlement by Lump Sum Agreements (co-author), 1975; Toward World Order &

Human Dignity: Essays in Honor of Myres S. McDougal (co-ed. & contbr.), 1975. Contbr. to: Fordham, Univ. of Chgo., Univ. of Pa. Law Reviews; Va. Jrnl. Int. Law; Ky. Law Jrnl.; etc. Mbr., var. legal & profl. orgs. Hons. incl: Rockefeller Fndn. & Sterling Fellowships, Yale Law Schl. Address: College of Law, Univ. of Iowa, Iowa City, IA 52242, USA.

WETTER, Gustav A(ndreas), b. 4 May 1911, Mödling, Austria. Professor of Marxist Philosophy. Educ: Dr. Phil., 1932, Lic. Theol., 1936, Dr. scientiarum ecclesiasticarum orientalium, 1943. Publs: Dialectical Materialism, 1952, Engl. ed., 1958, 5th ed., 1960; Soviet Ideology Today, 1962, Engl. ed., 1966. Mbrships: Am. Assn. for Advancement of Slavic Studies; Deutsche Gesellschaft für Osteuropakunde. Address: Piazza della Pilotta 4, I 00187 Rome, Italy.

WEYBRIGHT, Victor (Royer), b. 1903, Md., USA. Publisher. Educ: Univs. of Pa. & Chgo.; L.H.D.; LL.D. Publs: Spangled Banner: A Biography of Francis Scott Kay, 1935; The Americas, South & North, 1941; Buffalo Bill & the Wild West, USA & UK, 1955; The Making of a Publisher, Regnal, USA, 1967, UK, 1968. Contbr. to num. mags & reviews, USA. Mbrships. incl: Soc. of Authors, UK; Authors Guild, USA; PEN. Address: 50 E. 77th St., N.Y., NY 10021, USA.

WEYL, Nathaniel, b. 20 July 1910, NYC, USA. Writer; Social Scientist. Educ: B.Sc., Columbia Coll., 1931; postgrad., London Schl. Econs., UK, 1931-32, Columbia Univ., USA, 1932-33. Publs. incl: Treason, 1950; Red Star Over Cuba, 1961; The Creative Elite in America, 1967; The Jew in American Politics, 1968; Traitor's End, 1970; American Statesmen on Slavery & the Negro (co-author), 1971. Contbr. to: N.Y. Times Book Review; Nation; Mankind Quarterly; Cath. Digest; Esquire; Mod. Age; etc. Mbrships: Vice Chmn., Am. Mensa; Cmdr., Mil. & Hospitaller Order of St. Lazarus of Jerusalem; var. profl. socs., USA & abroad. Address: 855 Oleander St., Boca Ration, FL 33432, USA.

WEYMANN, Gert, b. 31 Mar. 1919, Berlin, Germany. Theatre Director; Playwright. Educ: Berlin Univ. Publs: (plays) Generationen; Eh' die Brücken verbrennen; Das Liebesmahl eines Wucherers; Familie; Der Anhalter; Die Übergabe. Recip., Gerhart Hauptmann Prize, 1954. Address: 1 Berlin 31, Karlsruhrstr. 7, Germany.

WEYRAUCH, Wolfgang Karl Joseph, b. 15 Oct. 1907, Königsberg, Germany. Writer; Editor. Educ: Univs. of Frankfurt & Berlin. Publs. incl: Der Main, 1934; An die Wand geschreiben, 1950; Die Minute des Negers, 1953; Anabisis, 1959; Totentanz, 1961; Das tapfere Schneiderlein, 1963; Auf der bewegten Erde, 1967; Ein Clown sagt, 1971; Mit dem Kopf durch die Wand, 1972; Das Ende von Frankfurt am Main, 1973; Wer fängt an?, 1974; Dostojevski, 1974. Contbr. to Ulenspiegel. Mbrships. incl: PEN; German Acad. Hons. incl: Andreas-Gryphius Prize, 1973. Address: Darmstadt, Alexandraweg 23, W. Germany.

WHALE, Patricia Freda, pen name, BREAM, Freda, b. 26 May 1918, Christchurch, NZ. Teacher. Educ: M.A., Univ. of NZ, 1940. Publs: Chalk Dust & Chewing Gum, 1971; Whistles for the Postie, 1972; I'm Sorry, Amanda, 1974. Contbr. articles & short stories to: NZ Broadcasting Corp. (also gives radio talks, etc.); NZ Women's Weekly; NZ Listener; Thursday Mag. Recip., acad. hons. Address: 69 Waima Cres., Titirangi, Auckland, NZ.

WHALEY, Barton Stewart, pen name BARTON, S. W., b. 1928, San Fran., Calif., USA. Historian. Educ: B.A., Chinese Studies, Univ. Calif., 1951; Schl. Oriental & African Studies, 1954-57, London Univ.; Ph.D., Pol. Sci., MIT, 1969. Publs: A Study of Word-of-Mouth Communication in China, 1961; Codeword Barbarossa, 1973; On the Prevalence of Guile, forthcoming. Contbr. to: Orbis; Slavic Review; Am. Pol. Sci. Review; Christian Sci. Monitor. Mbrships. incl: Fellow, Royal Asiatic Soc., 1955-61; Mystery Writers Am. Address: c/o Julian Bach Lit. Agcy. Inc., 18 E. 48th St., N.Y., NY 10017, USA.

WHEATLEY, Dennis Yates, b. 8 Jan 1897, London, UK. Author. Publs. incl: The Forbidden Territory, 1933; The Devil Rides Out, 1935; The Second Seal, 1950; To the Devil a Daughter, 1954; Stranger than Fiction, 1959; The Satanist, 1960; Dangerous Inheritance, 1965; White Witch of the South Seas, 1968; Gateway to Hell, 1970; The Devil & All His Works, 1971; The Strange Story of Linda Lee, 1972; The Irish Witch, 1973; Desperate Measures, 1974.

Mbrships: F.R.R.L.; F.R.S.A.; Pres., Old Comrades' Assn. Recip., Bronze Star, USA. Address: 60 Cadogan Sq., London SW1, UK.

WHEATLEY, George Prescott Brereton, b. 9 May 1909, Bangalore, India. Retired Schoolmaster (Music Specialist & Riding Instructor. Educ: L.R.A.M.; A.R.C.M.; L.G.S.M.; L.T.C.L.; M.R.S.T. Publs: Keep Your Own Pony, 1962; Stable Management for the Owner Groom, 1966; The Pony Riders' Book, 1966; Schooling a Young Horse, 1968; Let's Start Riding, 1970; The Pony Rider's Companion, 1975. Contbr. to: Riding; Pony Mag.; Horse World; Family Pets; Ency. of the Horse. Address: c/o Rupert Crew Ltd., King's Mews, London WC1N 2JA, UK.

WHEELER, Hugh Callingham, pen names QUENTIN, Patrick; PATRICK, Q.; STAGGE, Jonathan, b. London, UK. Playwright; Novelist. Educ: B.A., Univ. of London. Publs: (plays as Hugh Wheeler) Big Fish, Little Fish, 1961; Look: We've come Through, 1961; We Have Always Lived in the Castle, 1966; Irene, 1972; A Little Night Music, 1972; Candide, 1973; (as Patrick Quentin) Puzzle for Fools; Fatal Woman; and 15 others; (as Jonathan Stagge) Death; My Darling Daughters; Three Fears; & 7 others; (as Q. Patrick) Death & the Maiden; Darker Grows the Valley; & 6 others. Hons: Edgar Allen Poe Award, 1962, 1973; Drama Critics Circle Award, 1972, 1973, etc. Address: Twin Hills Farm, Monterey, MA 01245, USA.

WHEELER, Ruth Lellah, b. 11 Oct. 1899, Artesia, Calif., USA. Teacher; Writer. Educ: B.A., M.A. (Educ. & Jrnlsm.). Publs. incl: Meadow Wings, 1936; Pastor La Rue, 1937; His Messenger, 1939, 2nd ed., 1963; Little Killdeer, 1945; Out-Door Friends, 1947; On the Trail, 1950; Smoke in the Sky, 1956; Miracle of the Book, 1960; Land Beyond the Mountains, 1963; The Story of North American Birds, 1965; My Father's World, 1965; Let's Talk About Giants, 1966; Light the Paper Lantern, 1967; Night Sunset, 1973. Contbr. to: Review & Herald; Life & Hlth.; Winner. Recip., Graphic Arts Award, 1965. Address: Box 386, Angwin, CA 94508, USA.

WHEELER, Sessions Samuel, b. 27 Apr. 1911, Fernley, Nev., USA. Educator. Educ: B.Sc., 1934, M.Sc., 1935, Univ. of Nev. Publs: Paiute, 1965; The Desert Lake, 1967; The Nevada Desert, 1971; conservation textbooks. Contbr. to: Field & Stream; regional mags.; etc. Mbrships. incl: Western Hist. Assn.; Western Writers of Am. Hons. incl: Disting. Nevadan Award, Univ. of Nev., 1963; Conservation Educ. Award, Nat. Wildlife Fedn. & Sears Roebuck Fndn., 1965. Address: 25 Moore Lane, Reno, NV 89502, USA.

WHITE, Antonia, b. 31 Mar. 1899, London, UK. Writer. Educ: Acad. Dramatic Art, 1919-20. Publs. incl: (novels) Frost in May, UK, 1933, USA, 1934; The Lost Traveller, UK & USA, 1950; The Sugar House, 1952; Beyond the Glass, UK, 1954, USA, 1955; (short stories) Strangers, 1954; (Play) Three in a Room, 1947; (non-fiction) The Hound & the Falcon, 1965; num. transls. from French of works of Colette, Christine Arnothy, etc. Contbr. to: Life & Letters; Time & Tide; Daily Mirror; Sunday Pictorial (all pre-war). Mbrships: F.R.S.L. Hons: Clairouin Prize for transl., 1950; Arts Coun. Grant, 1967, 1969. Address: 42 Courtfield Gdns., London SW5, UK.

WHITE, Charles (A.C.G.), pen name GWYN, Siarl, b. 11 Feb. 1928, Carshalton, Surrey, UK. Artist. Educ: Sutton & Cheam Schl. of Art, 1943-45; Newport Coll. of Art, 1944; Kingston-upon-Thames Coll. of Art, 1946; Slade, London Univ., 1949-51; N.N.D.; D.F.A. Publs: Wales Sketch Book, 1963; Observations, 1971. Contbr. to: Art Review & continental art mags. Mbrships: Fndr. Mbr., Young Contemporaries; F.R.S.A.; Exec. Comm., S. Wales Grp.; Fellow, F.P.S.; Soc. of Graphic Artists; Fndr. Mbr., European Grp. Address: Ashgrove Studio, Llantwit Major, Glam., Wales, UK.

WHITE, Dorothy Shipley, b. 29 Jan. 1896, Phila., Pa., USA. Historian. Educ: B.A., Bryn Mawr Coll.; M.A., Columbia Univ.; B.F.A., Temple Univ.; Ph.D., Univ. of Pa. Publs: Seeds of Discord: De Gaulle Free France & the Allies, 1964, French ed., Les Origines de la Discords, 1967; French Colonization De Gaulle & Black Africa, forthcoming. Contbr. to: Orbis; Espoir; Etudes Gaulliennes. Mbrships incl: Acad. des Scis. Outre Mer; Comite Universitaire pour l'Etude des Idées Gaulliannes; Inst. de Gaulle, Paris. Recip., Prize for non-fiction, Athenaeum of Phila., 1964. Address: 717 Glengarry Rd., Phila., PA 19118, USA.

WHITE, E. B., b. 11 July 1899, Mt. Vernon, NY, USA. Writer. Educ: A.B., Cornell Univ. Publs: The Lady is Cold, 1929; Is Sex Necessary? (w. James Thurber), 1929; Every Day is Saturday, 1934; The Fox of Peapack, 1938; Quo Vadimus, 1938; A Subtreasury of American Humor (w. Katharine S. White), 1941; One Man's Meat, 1943; Stuart Little, 1945; The Wild Flag, 1946; Here Is New York, 1949; Charlotte's Web, 1952; The Second Tree from the Corner, 1954; The Points of My Compass, 1961; The Trumpet of the Swan, 1970. Contbr. to: New Yorker; Harpers; Atlantic Monthly; Holiday. Mbrships. incl: Am. Acad. of Arts & Letters. Recip., num. lit. awards. Address: North Brooklin, ME, USA.

WHITE, Florence M., b. 26 Dec. 1910, NYC, USA. Writer. Educ: B.A., Hunter Coll., NYC; LL.B., Schl. of Law, St. Johns Univ., Bklyn., N.Y. Publs: My House Is the Nicest Place, 1963; One Boy Lives In My House, 1965; Your Friend, the Insect, 1968; Your Friend, the Tree, 1969; How to Lose Your Lunch Money, 1970; How to Lose Your Best Friend, 1972; Cesar Chavez, Man of Courage, 1973; Malcolm X, 1975; (educl. films) Biography of Hidalgo, 1971; Biography of Juarez, 1971; How to Lose your Lunch Money, 1972. Mbrships: PEN; Calif. Writers Guild; S. Calif. Coun. on Lit. for Children & Young People. Address: 273 South Oakhurst Drive, Beverly Hills, CA 90212, USA.

WHITE, James, b. 7 Apr. 1928, Belfast, UK. Publicity Officer. Publs: The Secret Visitors, 1957; Hospital Station, 1962; Star Surgeon, 1962; Second Ending, 1963; Deadly Litter, 1964; Open Prison, 1965; The Watch Below, 1966; All Judgment Fled, 1968; The Aliens Among Us, 1969; Tomorrow is Too Far, 1971; Major Operation, 1971; Dark Inferno, 1972; The Dream Millennium, 1974. Contbr. to var. sci. fiction mags., UK & USA. Mbrships: Sci. Fiction Writers of Am.; Kts. of St. Fantony. Recip., Europa Special Sci. Fiction Award, 1972. Address: 10 Riverdale Gardens, Belfast BT11 9DG, UK.

WHITE, James Dillon, pen names PETO, James; KRULL, Felix, b. 8 Aug. 1913, London, UK. Professionally engaged in Life Assurance; Author. Publs. incl: The Edge of the Forest, 1951; The Spoletta Story, 1952; Genevieve, 1955; Night on the Bare Mountain, 1957; The Tall Ship, 1958; Brave Captain Kelso, 1959, & later books in series; The Hound of Heaven, 1966; Sweet Evil, 1968; Lords of Human Kind, 1971; The Running Lions, 1972; The Leipzig Affair, 1974. Contbr. to: Post Mag.; Smith's Trade News; London Evening News. Mbrships. incl: Fellow, Chartered Ins. Inst.; Army & Navy Club. Hons: Book Soc. Recommendations, 1952, 1958. Address: Watchfield, St. Mary's Rd., Leatherhead, Surrey KT 22 8EY, UK.

WHITE, Jon Manchip, b. 22 June 1924, Cardiff, Wales, UK. Author; Professor of English. Educ: M.A.(Hons.), Dip. Anthropol., St. Catharine's Coll., Cambridge. Publs. incl: (novels) Mask of Dust, 1953; No Home But Heaven, 1956; The Mercenaries, 1958; Nightclimber, 1968; The Game of Troy, 1971; The Garden Game, 1973; (verse) Dragon, 1943; The Routh of San Romano, 1952; The Mountain Lion, 1971; (non-fiction) Ancient Egypt, 1952; Anthropology, 1954; Marshal of France, 1962; The Land God Made in Anger, 1969; Diego Velazquez, 1969; Cortes & the Downfall of the Aztec Empire, 1971; Ed., Life in Ancient Egypt. Mbrships: Soc. of Authors; Egyptian Exploration Soc. Address: c/o Curtis Brown Ltd., 60 E. 56th St., N.Y., NY 10022, USA.

WHITE, Osmar Egmont Dorkin, pen name DENTRY, Robert, b. 2 Apr. 1909. Journalist. Educ: Sydney Univ. Publs. incl: (fiction as Robert Dentry) Green Armour, 1945; Parliament of a Thousand Tribes, 1965, revised ed., 1973; Time Now, Time Before, 1967; Under the Iron Rainbow, 1967; Encounter at Kharmel, 1972; (non-fiction) Guide to Australia, 1968, revised ed., 1974; A Guide & Directory to Australian Wine, 1973. Mbrships: Aust. Soc. Authors; Aust. Jrnlsts. Assn. Address: 35 John St., Lower Templestowe, Vic., Australia.

WHITE, Owen Roberts, b. 28 Apr. 1945, Boston, Mass., USA. Behavioral Researcher. Educ: B.A., Willamette Univ., Salem, Ore., 1967; M.A., 1970, Ph.D., 1971, Univ. of Ore., Eugene. Publs: Glossary of Behavioral Terminology, 1971; Exceptional Teaching for Exceptional Children: A multi-media training package for teachers (w. Norris G. Haring). Contbr. to: Teaching Special Children; Mental Retardation: Rehabilitation & Counseling; Jrnl. of Schl. Psychol. Mbrships: Am. Educl. Rsch. Assn.; Coun. for Exceptional Children; Wash. Educl. Rsch. Assn. Address: 23031 N.E. 61st, Redmond, WA 98052, USA.

WHITE, Patrick (Victor Martindale), b. 28 May 1912, London, UK. Writer. Educ: B.A., King's Coll., Cambridge Univ. 1935. Publs. incl: (novels) Happy Valley, UK, 1939, USA, 1940; The Aunt's Story, UK & USA, 1948; The Tree of Man, USA, 1955, UK, 1956; Voss, USA & UK, 1957; The Solid Mandala, USA & UK, 1966; The Vivisector, USA & UK, 1970; (short stories) The Burnt Ones, USA & UK, 1964; (plays) Four Plays, UK, 1965, USA, 1966. Hons: Gold Medal, Aust. Lit. Soc., 1956; Miles Franklin Award, 1958, 1962; Smith Lit. Award, 1959; Nat. Conf. Christians & Jews' Brotherhood Award, 1962. Address: 20 Martin Rd., Centennial Pk., Sydney, NSW 2021, Australia.

WHITE, Robin, b. 12 July 1928, Kodaikanal, India. Author. Educ: B.A., Yale Univ., USA, 1950; Creative Writing Fellow, Stanford Univ., 1956-57. Publs: House of Many Rooms, 1958; Elephant Hill, 1959; Men & Angels, 1961; Foreign Soil, 1962; All in Favor Say No, 1964; His Own Kind, 1967; Be Not Afraid, 1972. Contbr. to: Nat. Wildlife; Harper's; New Yorker; N.Y. Times; Reporter; Saturday Evening Post; Ladies' Home Jrnl; Early Years; Writer; Camping Jrnl.; Seventeen; Colo. Quarterly; etc. Mbrships: Authors Guild; Soc. of Mag. Writers. Hons. incl: Curtis Prize, 1950; Harper Prize, 1959; O. Henry Prize, 1960; Ed./Press Award, 1974. Address: Box 691, Mendocino, CA 95460, USA.

WHITE, Terence de Vere, b. 29 Apr. 1912. Literary Editor; Retired Solicitor. Educ: B.A., LL.B., Trinity Coll., Dublin. Publs. incl: The Road of Excess, 1945; Kevin O'Higgins, 1948; A Fretful Midge, 1957; An Affair with the Moon, 1959; The Remainder Man, 1963; Lucifer Falling, 1965; The Parents of Oscar Wilde, 1967; Ireland, 1968; The Lambert Mile, 1969; The March Hare, 1970; Mr. Stephen, 1971; The Anglo-Irish, 1972; The Distance & the Dark, 1973. Contbr. to: Irish Times (Lit. Ed., 1961–); 19th Century; Cambridge Review; Horizon. Mbrships. incl: Irish Acad. Letters; Royal Hibernian Acad. (Hon. Prof. of Lit.). Address: 5 Wellington Pl., Dublin 4, Repub. of Ireland.

WHITE, Theodore H., b. 6 May 1915, Boston, Mass., USA. Former Journalist; Author. Educ: B.A., Harvard Univ. Publs. incl: Stilwell Papers, 1948; Fire in the Ashes, 1953; The Mountain Road, 1958; The View from the Fortieth Floor, 1960; The Making of the President 1960, 1961; The Making of the President 1964, 1965; Caesar at the Rubicon, 1968; The Making of the President, 1968, 1969; The Making of the President 1972, 1973. Contbr. to: Time; New Republic; Reporter; Colliers. Mbrships: Bd., Ency. Britannica. Hons. incl: Ben Franklin Award; Overseas Press Club Award; Pulitzer Prize, 1962; Emmy Award, 1964, 1967. Address: 168 E. 64th St., N.Y., NY 10021, USA.

WHITE, William, b. 4 Sept. 1910, Paterson, N.J., USA. Professor; Writer; Editor. Educ: A.B., Univ. of Tenn., Chattanooga, 1933; M.A. Univ. of Southern Calif., 1937; Ph.D., Univ. of London, 1953. Publs. incl: A. E. Housman: A Centennial Momento, 1959; Whitman: The People & John Quincy Adams, 1961; The Collected Writings of Walt Whitman (jt. auth.), 1961–; Wilfred Owen: A Bibliography, 1967; By-Line: Ernest Hemingway, 1967; Guide to Ernest Hemingway, 1969; Studies in The Sun Also Rises, 1969; Checklist of Ernest Hemingway, 1970; Walt Whitman's Journalism: A Bibliography, 1969; Walt Whitman in Our Time, 1970; Edwin Arlington Robinson: A Supplementary Bibliography, 1971; Walt Whitman in Europe Today (w. Roger Asselineau), 1972; Kai Lung: Six (Ernest Bramah), 1974. Recip., var. hons. Address: 25860 W. 14 Mile Rd., Franklin, MI 48025, USA.

WHITEHEAD, Edward Anthony, b. 1933, Liverpool, UK. Dramatist. Educ: Christ's Coll., Cambridge; M.A. Publs. (plays): The Foursome, 1972; Alpha Beta, 1972; Under the Age, BBC 1972; The Punishment, BBC 1972; Juvenilia, BBC 1972; The Millenarian, BBC 1972; The Sea Anchor, 1974. Contbr. to: New Statesman. Mbr., The Dramatists. Agent: Margaret Ramsay Ltd. Address: 16 Oakley Gdns., Chelsea, London SW3 5QG, UK.

WHITEHEAD, John Simms, b. 2 Feb. 1946, Wash. D.C., USA. University Teacher. Educ: B.A., Ph.D., Yale Univ.; M.A., Univ. of Cambridge, UK. Publs: The Separation of College & State: Columbia, Dartmouth, Harvard & Yale, 1776-1876, 1973. Mbrships: Hist. Cons. & Brit. Rep., Klemen Kaalund Kirk Ltd., Copenhagen, Denmark; Brit. Assn. of Am. Studies. Address: Selwyn College, Cambridge, UK.

WHITEHOUSE, Roger, b. 23 Aug. 1939, Mansfield, UK. Architect; Photographer; Designer. Educ: Dip., Archtl. Assn. Schl. of Arch., 1963. Publs: New York: Sunshine & Shadow, 1974. Contbr. to: Interiors Mag., N.Y.; Archtl. Design, London. Mbrships: Archtl. Assn.; Assoc., Royal Inst. Brit. Archts. Address: 33A Christchurch Hill, London NW3 1LA, UK.

WHITEMORE, Hugh, b. 16 June 1936, Tunbridge Wells, UK. Playwright & Screenwriter. Educ: Royal Acad. of Dramatic Art, London. Plays incl: (BBC) The Wednesday Play; Play of the Month; Theatre 625; Elizabeth R.; Thirty Minute Theatre; Play for Today; Kafka's Am.; Cervantes' Don Quixote; David Copperfield; Moll Flanders; (ITV) Armchair Theatre; All Creatures Great & Small; The Blue Bird. Contbr. to: Drama Critic, Queen Mag.; num. TV & film jrnls. Mbrships: Writers' Guild of GB; Savage Club. Recip., Writers' Guild Award for best TV Dramatization, 1971, 1972. Address: c/o Margaret Ramsay Ltd., 14a Goodwin's Court, St. Martins Lane, London, WC2, UK.

WHITFIELD, John Humphreys, pen name PILIO, Gerone, b. 2 Oct. 1906, Wednesbury, UK. Serena Professor of Italian Language & Literature, 1946-74. Educ: B.A., 1928, M.A., 1933, Magdalen Coll., Oxford. Publs: Petrarch & the Renaissance, 1943; Machiavelli, 1947; Dante & Virgil, 1949; Giacomo Leopardi, 1954; A Short History of Italian Literature, 1960; Leopardi's Canti in English Verse, 1962; Discourses on Machiavelli, 1969; etc. Contbr. to var. scholarly jrnls. Chmn., Soc. for Italian Studies, 1962-74. Hons: Edmund Gardner Prize, London, 1959; Amedeo Maiuri Prize, Rome, 1965; Cavaliere Ufficiale, 1960, Commendatore, 1972, Ordine al Merito Repubblica Italiana. Address: 2 Woodbourne Rd., Edgbaston, Birmingham 15, UK.

WHITING SPILHAUS, Margaret, (Mrs. Ludolph Spilhaus), b. 1889, Forest Hill, London, UK. Educ: South African Coll. (out student); Newnham Coll., Cambridge. Publs: The Limber Elf, 1920; South African Nursery Rhymes, 1925; Background of Geography, 1935; First South Africans, with translation of Diary of Adam Tas, 1949; Indigenous Trees of the Cape Peninsula, 1950; Under a Bright Sky, 1959; South Africa in the Making, 1966; The Land They Left; Doorstep-Baby, 1969; The Happy Little House; Company's Men, 1973. Contbr. to: histl.-geogl. maps; general press. Mbr., PEN, UK. Address: 205 College Rd., Rondebosch, Cape, Repub. of S. Africa.

WHITLOCK, Ralph, b. 7 Feb. 1914, Salisbury, Wilts., UK. Author; Agricultural Consultant. Publs. incl. 31 books on natural hist., agriculture, children's books, topographics, etc. Contbr. to: The Field (Agricl. corres. 1946—); Western Gazette; Daily Telegraph; BBC TV & radio; etc. Mbrships: Fellow, Zool. Soc.; Brit. Ornithologists Union; Farmers' Club. Address: The Lodge, Limington, Yeovil, Somerset, UK.

WHITMAN, Alden, b. 27 Oct. 1913, New Albany, N.S., Can. Obituary Writer; Author. Educ: A.B., Harvard Univ., 1934. Publs: Portrait; Adlai E. Stevenson, 1965; The Obituary Book, 1971; The End of a Presidency (co-author), 1974. Contbr. to: N.Y. Times; L.A. Times; Newsday; Wash. Post; Ed., Harvard Mag. Address: Major's Path, Southampton, NY 11968, USA.

WHITNEY, Owen Derek, b. 30 Jan. 1931, Midhurst, Sussex, UK. Senior Lecturer in Counselling. Educ: M.A., Postgrad. Cert. in Social Work, Keble Coll., Oxford Univ. Publs: A Majority Without Education, 1961; The Family & Marriage in a Changing World (w. Kenneth Walker), 1965; The Nature of Caring (w. Elizabeth Whitney), 1969; Counselling Training (w. E. Whitney), 1972; Beyond Counselling, 1975; The Mouse & The Elephant (w. Sarah Whitney). Contbr. to: New Era; Jrnl. of Nat. Marriage Guidance Coun.; Educ. & Social Work (symposium). Mbr., Soc. of Authors. Address: Ford Cottage, Drayton St. Leonards, Oxon., UK.

WHITTICK, Arnold, b. 17 May 1898, Ilford, Essex, UK. Writer on Art, Architecture, Town & Country Planning. Educ: Dip. in Hist. of Art, London Univ.; var. art schls., London. Publs. incl: Symbols for Designers, 1935; The Small House: Today & Tomorrow (co-author), 1947, 1957; European Architecture in the 20th Century, Vol. I, 1950, Vol. II, 1953, Vol. III & combined work, 1974; Symbols, Signs & their Meanings, 1960, 1971; New Towns — The answer to Megalopolis (co-author), 1963, 1969; Ed.-in-Chief & Contbr., Ency. of Urban Planning, 1974. Contbr. to: Times; Guardian; Archt.; etc. Mbrships. incl:

F.R.S.A.; Soc. of Authors; Int. Jrnlsts. Recip., Leverhulme Rsch. Award. Address: 4 Netherwood, Gossops Green, Crawley, Sussex RH11 8PT, UK.

WHITTINGTON-EGAN, Richard, pen names BARRINGTON, Nicholas; DOUGHTY, Nigel; CURZON, Charles, b. 22 Oct. 1924, Liverpool, UK. Author; Journalist. Publs: Liverpool Colonnade, 1955; Liverpool Roundabout, 1957; The Quest of the Golden Boy, 1960; The Life & Letters of Richard Le Gallienne (w. G. T. Smerdon), 1960; Murder, Mayhem & Mystery, 1967; Liverpool Characters & Eccentrics, 1968; The Pocket Money Guide, 1968; Liverpool Soundings, 1969; The Ordeal of Philip Yale Drew, 1972; Liverpool: This is My City, 1972; The Riddle of Birdhurst Rise, 1975. Contbr. to: Chambers's Jrnl.; Books & Bookmen; The Contemporary Review; etc. Mbrships: The Medico-Legal Soc.; Crime Writers' Assn. Address: Assoc. Newspapers Ltd., Northcliffe House, London, EC4, UK.

WHYTE, Donald, pen name SENNACHIE, b. 13 Mar. 1926, Newtongrange, Midlothian, UK. Genealogist; Record Agent. Educ: Lic. in Heraldry & Geneal., Inst. of Heraldic & Geneal. Studies, England. Publs: Kirkliston: A Short History, 1956; Scottish Emigration to North America, 1969; A Dictionary of Scottish Emigrants to U.S.A., 1972; West Lothian: The Eastern District, 1969; Bathgate Hills Country Park, 1973. Contbr. to: The Scottish Geneal.; The Irish Ancestor; etc. Mbrships. incl: Fellow, Soc. of Antiquaries of Scotland; Fndr. Mbr., Scottish Geneal. Soc. Recip., var. acad. hons. Address: 4 Carmel Rd., Kirkliston, W. Lothian EH29 9DD, UK.

WHYTE, William Hollingsworth, b. 1 Oct. 1917, W. Chester, Pa., USA. Writer. Educ: Princeton Univ. Publs: Is Anybody Listening, 1952; The Organisation Man, 1956; The Exploding Metropolis, 1959; Cluster Development, 1964; The Last Landscape, 1968. Contbr. to Fortune Mag. Mbr., Am. Conservation Assn. Hons: Ben Franklin Award, 1955; LL.D. Address: 175 E. 94th St., N.Y. NY 10028, USA.

WIBBERLEY, Leonard Patrick O'Connor, pen names, O'CONNOR, Patrick; HOLTON, Leonard; WEBB, Christopher, b. 9 Apr. 1915, Dublin, Ireland. Novelist. Publs. over 90 novels & sev. plays, inclng: The Mouse That Roared; The Mouse on the Moon; The Mouse on Wall Street; The Road from Toomi; Meeting with a Great Beast; The Last Stand of Father Felix; Man of Liberty (a biography of Thomas Jefferson); The Centurion; The Testament of Theophilus. Contbr. to: Sat. Evening Post; N.Y. Times; LA Times. Mbrships: Author's Guild; Dramatist's League. Hons. incl: Authors Club of LA Special Award, 1973. Address: Box 522, Hermosa Beach, CA 90254, USA.

WIBBERLEY, Mary Cynthia, b. 30 June 1934, Manchester, Lancs., UK. Writer. Publs: Black Niall, 1973; Beloved Enemy, 1973; Master of Saramanca, 1973; Laird of Gaela, 1973; Man at La Valaise, 1973; The Benedict Man, 1974; Logan's Island, 1974; Snow on the Hills, 1974; Kyle's Kingdom, 1974; Dark Viking, 1975; Country of the Vine, 1975; The Dark Isle, 1975; That Man Bryce, 1975. Mbrships: Soc. of Authors; Romantic Novelists' Assn. Address: 8 Hackness Road, Chorlton-cum-Hardy, Manchester M21 1HB, UK.

WICK, Dodee, b. 20 Feb. 1907, Duluth, Minn., USA. Journalist. Educ: Univ. of Minn., 1928. Contbr. to: Life Mag.; Wick Newspapers, Inc. Mbr., Int. Platform Assn. Address: 135D St. S.E., Wash. DC 20003, USA.

WICKMAN, Asta, b. 26 Apr. 1895, Gothenburg, Sweden. Translator. Publs. incl: (transls.) Ryskt (anthol.), 1945; Min första kärlek, by Ivan Turgenjev, 1946; Den unge Tolstoj, by Tatiana Tolstoj-Suchotin, 1948; Ryska Berättare (anthol.), 1949; Vita nätter, by Ricarda Huch, 1957; Damen med hunden, by Anton Tjechov, 1955; Mitt liv, by Anton Tjechov, 1960; Herdepipan, by Anton Tjechov, 1960. Contbr. to var. newspapers, & lit. jrnls. Mbr., Transls. Sect.; Swedish Soc. of Authors, 1954—. Hons: Royal Swedish Acad., 1951, 1961; Samfundet De Nio, 1952; Kungastipendiet, 1954; Boklotteriet, 1957; Premium & Dip., Swedish Fund of Authors, 1962, 1973. Address: Eriksbergsgatan 14^V, 114 30 Stockholm, Sweden.

WIDDEMER, Margaret, b. 30 Sept. 1893, Doylestown, Pa., USA. Poet; Novelist. Publs. incl: (poetry) Factories, 1917; Collected Poems, 1927; Hill Garden, 1936; Dark Cavalier: Collected Poems, 1958; (other publs.) Graven

Image, 1923; Ladies Go Masked, 1939; Let Me Have Wings, 1941; Lani, 1948; Red Cloak Flying, 1950; Prince in Buckskin, 1952; Basic Principles of Fiction Writing, 1953; Golden Friends I Had (memoirs), 1964; The Red Castle Women, 1968; A Rope to Hang My Love, 1972. Hons: D.Litt.; M.A. Address: 1 W. 67th St., N.Y., NY, USA.

WIDENMANN, Wilhelm Thomas Konstantin, b. 11 Mar. 1943, Tuebingen, Germany. Teacher. Publs: Magische Zaubereien und telepathische Scherze, 1963; Ei-ei-ei-wie schön ist Zauberei: Kurioses aus dem Reich der Magie, 1970; Ed., Neue eröeffnete Geheimnisse magischer Kunststücke zum gesellschaft-ergóetzenden Zeitvertreib 1797, 1975. Contbr. to: Der literat; etc. Mbrships: E.T.A. Hoffmann-Gesellschaft; Wilhelm Busch-Gesellschaft; Schopenhauer-Gesellschaft; John Paul Gesellschaft; Hugo von Hoffmannsthal-Gesellschaft. Address: 7 Stuttgart, Seestrasse 68, W. Germany.

WIEBE, Rudy H., b. 4 Oct. 1934, Fairholme, Sask., Can. Writer; University Professor. Educ: B.A., Th.B., M.A.; Univ. of Alta., Man.; Univs. of Iowa, USA, Tuebingen, German Fed. Repub. Publs. incl: (fiction) Peace Shall Destroy Many, 1962; First & Vital Candle, 1966; The Blue Mountains of China, 1970; The Temptations of Big Bear, 1973; Where is the Voice Coming From? 1974; (collects. of stories) The Story-Makers, 1970; Ed., Stories from Western Canada, 1972; Short Stories in English, 1976. Contbr. to: Maclean's Mag.; Can. Lit.; Jrnl. Can. Fiction; etc. Mbrships: VP, Writers' Union of Can.; Can. Coun. Arts Advsry. Bd. Hons. incl: Gov. Gen.'s Award for Fiction, 1974. Address: 5315-143 Street, Edmonton, Alta., Can.

WIEGAND, Ursula, pen name SONNTAG, Uschi, b. 27 Mar. 1930, Beuthen, Germany. Writer; Secretary. Publs: Randnotizen, Verse v. 1950-60, 1972-73; Beobachtungen, 1973; Tagträume, Lyrik-Prosa 1950-60, 1973-74; Wer den Wind erhört . . . 1968-70, Prosa, 1973-74; Zwischenbemerkungen, Verse, 1974-75; Wie Perlen im Meer, Aphorismen, 1974-75; Was bleibt ist die Liebe, Lyrik-Prosa, 1974-75. Contbr. to num. lit. jrnls. Mbrships. incl: Lit. Union; Free German Writers' Assn.; Soc. of German Authors; Regensburg Writers' Grp. Address: D-58 Hagen-Helfe, Kettelerstr. 76, W. Germany.

WIENANDT, Elwyn Arthur, b. 23 July 1917, Aniwa, Wis., USA. University Administrator & Professor. Educ: B.Mus., Lawrence Coll., Wis., 1939; M.Mus., Univ. of Denver, 1948; Ph.D., State Univ. of Iowa, 1951. Publs: Choral Music of the Church, 1965; The Anthem in England & America, 1970; Opinions on Church Music, 1974; The Bicentennial Collection of American Music, vol. 1, 1974. Contbr. to: Jrnl. of Am. Musicol. Soc.; MLA Notes; Christian Century; Diapason; Western Folklore; Music Review. Mbr., profl. orgs. Recip., acad. hons. Address: 1216 Cliffview Dr., Waco, TX 76710, USA.

WIENERS, John Joseph, b. 6 Jan. 1934. Author; Poet. Educ: A.B., Boston Coll., 1954; Black Mtn. Coll., 1955-56; M.A., SUNY, Buffalo, 1973. Publs: Selected Poems, 1968; Reconnaissances in the Bay Areas, 1958; Ace of Pentacles, 1963; Nerves, 1972; Revelations of Saint Bernadette, 1973. Contbr. to: Poetry; The Boston Globe; The Paris Review; Six Pack Five Inc.; Stone Soup Periodicals; The Poetry Project Newsletter. Mbrships: Nat. Travel Club; Acad. of Am. Poets. Address: 44 Joy St., Boston, MA 02114, USA.

WIERWILLE, Victor Paul, b. 31 Dec. 1916, New Knoxville, Ohio, USA. Clergyman; Author. Educ: A.B., Lakeland Coll., 1938; B.D., Mission House Sem., Sheboygan, Wis., 1941; M.Th., Princeton Univ., 1941; Th.D., Pikes Peak Sem., Colo., 1958. Publs. incl: Victory Through Christ, 1945; Receiving the Holy Spirit Today, 1955, 6th ed., 1972; The Bible Tells Me So, 1971; The Word's Way, 1971; Power for Abundant Living, 1971; The New Dynamic Church, 1971; Jesus Christ Is Not God, 1974. Contbr. to var. jrnls. Fndr., The Way Mag., 1945, The Way Int. Fine Arts & Histl. Ctr., Sidney, Ohio, 1074. Address: R.D.I., New Knoxville, OH 45871, USA.

WIESNER, Heinrich, b. 1 July 1925, Ramlingsburg, Baselland, Switz. Primary School Teacher. Publs: Der innere Wanderer (poems), 1951; Leichte Boote (poems), 1958; Lakonische Zeilen, 1965; Lapidare Geschichten, 1967; Schauplätze. Eine Chronik, 1969; Rico. Ein Fall (story), 1970; Der Jass (one-act play), 1971; Neue Lakonische Zeilen, 1972; Notennot. Schulgeschichten, 1973. Contbr. to: Radio & TV; Neue deutsche Hefte; Schweizer Monatshefte; Spektrum; etc. Mbr., Gruppe Olten (Swiss Writers' Grp.). Hons: Lyric prize, Radio

Beromünster, 1958; Award, Swiss Schiller Inst., 1969; Story prize, Zürich, 1970; Award, Pro Helvetia Inst., 1973. Address: Im Pfeiffengarten 38, 4153 Reinach, Switz.

WIGENS, Anthony John, b. 16 July 1931, Harrow, Middlesex, UK. Writer. Publs: Successful Moviemaking, 1962; How to use 8mm at Work, 1964; A View into Hertfordshire, 1970; Ed., Hertfordshire Gardens, 1970. Mbr., Nat. Union Jrnlsts. Address: 11 Warren Way, Digswell, Welwyn, Herts. AL6 0DQ, UK.

WIGHTMAN, George Brian Hamilton, b. 5 June 1933, Dibden, Hants., UK. Company Director. Educ: M.A., Trinity Coll., Cambridge. Publs: Birds Through a Ceiling of Alabaster, 1975; The Flower Fed Buffaloes (stage prod.). Contbr. to: New Statesman; Tribune; Author; BBC Third Prog. Mbrships: Gen. Coun. of Poetry Soc.; Soc. of Authors; Royal TV Soc.; Soc. of Film & TV Arts; Aristotelian Soc.; Fndr., Nat. & London Poetry Secretariats; Poets' Workshop. Recip., Judge Guiness Poetry Prizes, Cheltenham Festival of Lit., 1968, 1969. Address: 11 Bramham Gardens, London SW5, UK.

WIGHTON, Charles Ernest, b. 21 Mar. 1913, Invergowrie, Perthshire, UK. Author; Editor. Educ: Harris Acad., Dundee. Publs: They Spied on England, 1958; Hitler's Spies & Saboteurs, 1958; Pin Stripe Saboteurs, 1959; Dope International, 1960; Eichmann, 1951; Heydrich, 1962; World's Greatest Spies, 1963; Democratic Dictator, 1964. Contbr. to: Ed., German Int., 1964—; Num. jrnls. etc. Mbrships: Brit. Nat. Union of Jrnlsts.; London Press Club. Address: Blumenstrasse 9, 4954 Barkhausen (Porta Westfalica), W. Germany.

WIJKMARK, Carl-Henning, b. 21 Nov. 1934, Stockholm, Sweden. Writer; Translator. Educ: Univs. of Munich, Lund & Stockholm; B.A., 1957; Doct. Arts, 1967. Publs: (all in Swedish) Storm Centre (anthol. of modern German prose, in transl.) (w. Stig Jonasson), 1964; German Novels from Thomas Mann to Günter Grass, 1965; The French Novel after 1945, 1968; The Hunters of Karinhall (novel), trans. Finnish, Am. trans. & Int. Film forthcoming, 1972; Running Away from my Countrymen (TV play on Brecht), 1974; var. transls. Contbr. to: Ord & Bild; BLM (Sweden). Mbr., Swedish Union of Authors. Address: Virvelvindsvägen 1, 161 40 Bromma (Stockholm), Sweden.

WIJNBERG, Lea, b. 10 July 1910, Amsterdam, Netherlands. Journalist; Author. Publs: The Art of Writing, 1956, 3rd ed., 1970; Majoor A.M. Bosshardt (biog.), 1962; Religious Experience in the Mirror of Consciousness (w. Peter Warnaar), 1974. Contbr. to: De Europese Gemeente; Haarlemsch Dagblad. Mbrships: Parl. of Netherlands Union of Jrnlsts.; & Hon. Mbr., Freelance Sect. of Union; Union of Writers. Hons: Press Prize of Yr., Info. Off. for Nutrition, 1965; Address: Prinsengracht 533, Amsterdam 1002, Netherlands.

WILBUR, Marguerite Eyer, b. 14 Oct. 1889, Evanston, Ill., USA. Writer; Translator; Editor. Educ: B.A., Stanford Univ.; M.A., Univ. of Southern Calif. Publs: The East India Company, 1945; Immortal Pirate, 1947; Rascal & Adventurer, 1949; The Unquenchable Flame, 1952; Thomas Jefferson, 1962. Mbr., Arts & Letters. Recip., hon. doct. degree. Address: 656 Park Ln., Santa Barbara, CA 93103, USA.

WILCKE, Ella Kristina, b. 14 May 1896, Stockholm, Sweden. Author. Educ: Fil. kand., Uppsala Univ. Publs. incl: En sommar på egen hand, 1940; På stormiga öar, 1964; Farofylld kust, 1964. Contbr. to sev. wkly. reviews. Mbr., Swedish Authors' Union. Hons: Prize, for En sommar på egen hand; Prize, Sveriges Författarfond, 1940; Boklotteriet, 1964. Address: Stockholmsvägen 68, 182 74 Stocksund, Sweden.

WILDER, Billy, b. 22 June 1906, Austria. Film Writer, Producer & Director. Prods. incl: Ninotchka; What a Life; The Major & the Minor; Double Indemnity; The Lost Weekend; The Emperor Waltz; A Foreign Affair; Sunset Boulevard; Stalag 17; Love in the Afternoon; Some Like it Hot; The Apartment; Irma La Douce; Kiss Me Stupid; The Fortune Cookie; The Private Life of Sherlock Holmes; Avanti; The Seven Year Itch; The Spirit of St. Louis; Witness for the Prosecution; Emil & the Detectives. Recip., 6 Acad. Awards. Address: Sam Goldwyn Studios, 1041 N. Formosa Ave., Hollywood, CA 90046, USA.

WILDER, Thornton (Niven), b. 17 Apr. 1897, Madison, Wis., USA. Writer. Educ: A.B., Yale Univ., 1920; A.M.,

Princeton Univ., 1926. Publs. incl: (novels) The Cabala, USA & UK, 1926; The Bridge of San Luis Rey, USA & UK, 1927; The Woman of Andros, USA & UK, 1930; Heaven's My Destination, UK, 1934, USA, 1935; The Ides of March, USA & UK, 1948; The Eighth Day, USA & UK, 1967; (plays) The Long Christmas Dinner, 1931; Our Town, 1938; The Skin of Our Teeth, 1942. Mbrships: Am. Acad. Arts & Letters; PEN. Hons. incl: Pulitzer Prizes, 1928, 1938, 1943; Austrian Ehrenmedaille, 1959; Nat. Book Award, 1968; Order of Merit, Peru; num. docts. Address: 50 Deepwood Dr., Hamden, CT 06517, USA.

WILDING, Michael, b. 5 Jan. 1942, Worcester, UK. Reader in English. Educ: B.A., 1963, M.A., 1968, Lincoln Coll., Oxford. Publs. incl: Australians Abroad (w. Chas. Higham), 1967; Marvell: Modern Judgements, 1969; Milton's Paradise Lost, 1969; Cultural Policy in Great Britain (w. Michael Green & Richard Hoggart), 1970; Aspects of the Dying Process, 1972; Living Together, 1974; The Short Story Embassy, 1975; The West Midland Underground, 1975. Contbr. to: Stand; Sydney Morning Herald; Mod. Lang. Review; Gen. Ed., Asian & Pacific Writing series, Univ. of Qld. Press. Mbrships. incl: Aust. Soc. of Authors; Sydney Filmmakers' Co-op. Address: Dept. of Engl., Univ. of Sydney, N.S.W. 2006, Australia.

WILES, John, b. 25 Sept. 1924, Kimberley, S. Africa. Author; Playwright; Television Scriptwriter. Publs: The Moon to Play With, 1954; The Try-Out, 1955; Scene of the Meeting, 1956; Leap to Life, 1957; The Asphalt Playground, 1958; The Everlasting Childhood, 1956; March of the Innocents, 1964; A Short Walk Abroad, 1969; & num. stage plays & TV scripts. Mbrships: PEN; Soc. Authors; Writers' Guild GB. Recip., John Llewelyn Rhys Mem. Prize, 1954; Writers' Guild Award for best TV Documentary Script (shared), 1974. Address: 13 Somerset Ave., London SW20, UK.

WILFORD, John Noble, b. 4 Oct. 1933, Murray, Ky., USA. Assistant National Editor, The New York Times. Educ: B.S., Univ. of Tenn., 1955; M.A., Syracuse Univ., N.Y., 1956; Adv. Int. Reporting Fellow, Columbia Univ., N.Y. Publs: We Reach the Moon, 1969. Mbrships: Gov., Overseas Press Club; Aviation/Space Writers' Assn. Hons: Book Award, Aviation/Space Writers' Assn., 1970; G. M. Loeb Achievement Award, Univ. of Conn., 1972; Press Award, Nat. Space Club, 1974. Address: 229 W. 43rd St., N.Y. Times, N.Y., 10036, USA.

WILGUS, A. Curtis, b. 2 Apr. 1897, Platteville, Wis., USA. Historian; Bibliographer; University Professor. Educ: M.A.; Ph.D.; Univs. of Wis. & Calif. Publs. incl: An Outline of Hispanic American History, 1927; South American Dictators, 1937,—63; The Caribbean: Peoples, Problems & Prospects, 1953; The Caribbean: The Central American Area, 1961; The Caribbean: Its Health Problems, 1965; Latin-America 1492-1942; A Guide to Historical & Cultural Development Before World War II, 1973. Contbr. to num. jrnls. Mbrships. incl: Nat. Coun., Inst. of Int. Educ: Acad. of Am. Franciscan Hist. Num. Awards. Address: 1140 N.E. 191st St., N. Miami Beach, Fla., USA.

WILKINS, Thurman, b. 29 June 1915, Malden, Mo., USA. Professor of English. Educ: B.A., UCLA, 1939; M.A., Univ. of Calif., Berkeley, 1947; Ph.D., Columbia Univ., 1957. Publs: Clarence King: A Biography, 1958; Clarence King's Mountaineering in the Sierra Nevada (ed.), 1963; Thomas Morgan: Artist of the Mountains, 1966; Cherokee Tragedy: The Story of the Ridge Family & the Decimation of a People, 1970. Contbr. to: Dictionary of Am. Biog.; Am. Oxford Ency.; Am. Scene Mag.; Ariz. & the W.; Mont., The Mag. of Western Hist.; Pacific Histl. Review; Assoc. Ed., Mil. Affairs, 1945-47; etc. Mbrships. incl: MLA; Soc. of Am. Histns.; Am. Studies Assn.; Authors Guild. Recip., Cert. of Commendation, Am. Assn. for State & Local Hist., 1971. Address: 211 W. 106th St., N.Y., NY 10025, USA.

WILKINSON, Bertie, b. 21 Jan. 1898, Bingley, UK. Professor of Medieval History (Retired). Educ: B.A., 1923, M.A., 1924, Ph.D., 1929, Univ. of Manchester. Publs: Chancery Under Edward III, 1929; Studies in the Constitutional History of the XIII & XIV Centuries, 1937; Constitutional History, 1216-1399 (3 vols.), 1948-58; Constitutional History. XV Century, 1964; The Later Middle Ages in England, 1969; The Creation of Medieval Parliaments, 1972. Contbr. to var. scholarly jrnls. Mbrships: Fellow, Royal Soc. of Can.; Medieval Acad. of Am. Hons: Chauveau Medal, Royal Soc. of Can., 1968; LL.D., Toronto Univ., 1968. Address: 66 Woodlawn Ave. W., Toronto, Ont. M4V IG7, Can.

WILKINSON, Denys Haigh, b. 5 Sept. 1922, Leeds, UK. Physicist. Educ: M.A.; Ph.D.; Sc.D., Cambridge Univ. Publs: Ionization Chambers & Counters, 1951; Isospin in Nuclear Physics, 1969. Contbr. to: Nuclear Physics; Physical Review; etc. Mbrships: F.R.S.; Fellow, Am. Physical Soc.; Fellow, Inst. of Physics. Hons. incl: Bruce Preller Prize, 1969; Tom W. Bonner Prize, 1974; num. acad. hons. Address: 82 Oxford St., Woodstock, Oxford, UK.

WILKINSON, John Burke, b. 24 Aug. 1913, NYC, USA. Author. Educ: B.A., Harvard Univ., 1935; Lionel Harvard Studentship, Cambridge Univ., UK, 1936. Publs. incl: Night of the Short Knives, 1964; The Helmet of Navarre, 1965; Cardinal in Armor, 1966; Young Louis XIV, 1969; The Adventures of Geoffrey Mildway (trilogy), 1969; Cry Spy! (anthol.), 1970; Cry Sabotage! (anthol.), 1972; Francis In All His Glory, 1972. Contbr. to var. lit. jrnls. Mbrships: VP, Nat. Lawn Tennis Hall of Fame, USA, 1962-; Hon. Mbr., Brit. Int. Lawn Tennis Club, 1948; Authors' League, USA; Mystery Writers of Am. Recip., Commendatore, Italian Order of Merit, 1958. Address: 3210 Scott Pl., NW, Wash. DC 20007, USA.

WILKINSON, Roderick, b. 31 Mar. 1917, Glasgow, UK. Director of Personnel. Publs: Murder Belongs to Me, 1963; The Big Still, 1964; Everything Goes Dead, 1966; The Network, 1967; Erfolgsrezipe für Modernen Managers, 1970; & over 30 TV & radio plays. Address: 96 Inveroran Drive, Bearsden, Glasgow G61 4HG, UK.

WILLARD, John Anderson, b. 23 Aug. 1915, Augusta, Mont., USA. Corporation Executive. Educ: B.A., Univ. of Mont., 1938. Publs: Game is Good Eating, 1954; Adventure Trails in Montana, 1964; Charles M. Russell (CMR) Book, 1970. Contbr. to: Roundup; Hoofprints; Yellowstone Corral; Westerners Int. Mbrships: Bd. of Dirs., Outdoor Writers Assn. of Am., 1950-51; Mont. Histl. Soc. Address: 3119 Country Club Circle, Billings, MT 59102, USA.

WILLATT, Stephen Thomas, b. 12 Mar. 1933, London, UK. Soil Physicist; Senior Lecturer, School of Agriculture, La Trobe University, Bundoora, Victoria, Australia since 1970; formerly Senior Research Officer, Agricultural Research Council of Malawi, Mulanje, Malawi. Educ: B.Sc., Univ. W. Aust., 1955; M.Sc., Univ. N.S.W., 1963. Publs: (contbr.) Physical Aspects of Soil Water & Salts in Ecosystems, 1973. Contbr. to: Tropical Agric.; Agricl. Meteorol.; Rhodesian Jrnl. Agric. Rsch.; Jrnl. Agricl. Engrng. Rsch. Mbrships: Aust. Soc. Soil-Sci. (VP, Victorian Br.); Aust. Inst. Agricl. Sci. Address: 22 Arden Cres., Rosanna, Vic., Australia.

WILLEE, Albert William, b. 8 Mar. 1916, Brighton, Sussex, UK. Physical Educator: B.A., Dip. Phys. Educ., Univ. of London; M.S., Ph.D., Univ. of Ore., USA; B.Ed., Univ. of Melbourne. Publs: Playground Games for Secondary Boys (w. L. C. Williams), 1954; Small Apparatus for Primary School Physical Education, 1955; Dynamic Football — A Guide to Fitness, 1967. Mbr., num. profl. & Histl. assns. Recip., V.R.D., 1962. Address: 24 Belgravia Ave., Box Hill North, Vic., Australia 3129.

WILLETT, John William Mills, b. 24 June 1917, Hampstead, London, UK. Writer. Educ: M.A., Christ Ch., Oxford. Publs: Popski, 1954; The Theatre of Bertolt Brecht, 1959; Brecht on Theatre (ed. & transl.), 1964; Art in a City, 1967; Expressionism, 1970. Contbr. to: Times Lit. Supplement; Var. other jrnls., home & abroad. Mbr., Soc. of Authors. Address: Volta House, Windmill Hill, London NW3 6SJ, UK.

WILLETTS, Ronald Frederick, b. 2 Apr. 1915, Halesowen, UK. Professor of Greek. Educ: B.A., 1937, M.A., 1938, Dip. Educ., 1939, Birmingham Univ. Publs: Aristocratic Society in Ancient Crete, 1955; The Ion of Euripides, 1958, 2nd ed., 1970; Cretan Cults & Festivals, 1962; The Plutus of Aristophanes, 1965; The Law Code of Gortyn, 1967; Everyday Life in Ancient Crete, 1969; Blind Wealth & Aristophanes, 1970; Gen. Ed. of the series, States & Cities of Ancient Greece, 1970–; (poetry) The Trobriand Islanders, 1960. Contbr. to num. acad. jrnls., etc. Mbrships. incl: Hellenic Soc. (Coun. 1967-70). Hons. incl: Brit. Coun. Special Lecturer, 1973. Address: Schl. Hellenic & Roman Studies, Univ. Birmingham, P.O. Box 363, Birmingham B15 2TT, UK.

WILLIAMS, Alan Moray, b. 17 June 1915, Petersfield, UK. Foreign Correspondent. Educ: M.A., King's Coll., Cambridge; Copenhagen Univ. Publs: The Road to the West, 1945; Children of the Century, 1947; Copenhagen —

Praise & Protest, 1965; Denmark — Praise & Protest, 1969. Contbr. to: Sunday Times; Guardian; News Chronicle. Mbrships: PEN; Soc. of Authors of G.B.; Nat. Union of Journalists; I.F.J.; Dansk Forfatterforening. Address: Scandinavian Features Service, Postbox 4, 3450 Allerod, Denmark.

WILLIAMS, (David) Gwyn, b. 24 Aug. 1904, Port Talbot, UK. Retired Professor of English Literature. Educ: B.A., Univ. Coll. Wales, Aberystwyth; M.A., Jesus Coll., Oxford Univ. Publs: Personal Landscape (co-author), 1945; The Rent that's Due to Love, 1950; An Introduction to Welsh Poetry, 1953; The Burning Tree, 1956; Presenting Welsh Poetry, 1959; This Way to Lethe, 1962; Green Mountain, 1963; Turkey, 1967; Inns of Love, 1970; The Avocet, 1970; Eastern Turkey, 1972; Welsh Poems, 1973; Foundation Stock, 1974; Two Sketches of Womanhood, 1975; Twrci a'i Phobl, 1975. Contbr. to: Welsh Review; Hudson Review; London Mag.; etc. Mbrships. incl: Soc. Authors; Acad. Gym. Address: Treweithan, Trefenter, Aberystwyth, UK.

WILLIAMS, Dorian, pen name PIED PIPER, b. 1 July 1914, Aldershot, UK. Lecturer; Commentator; Author. Publs: Clear Round, 1956; Pendley & a Pack of Hounds; The Horseman's Companion; Batsford Book of Horses; Showing Horse Sense; Lost (novel); Great Riding Schools of the World. Contbr. to: Horse & Hound; Field; Country Life. Ed., Horseman's Year, 1954. Address: Foscote Manor, Bucks., UK.

WILLIAMS, Emlyn, b. 1905, Wales, UK. Actor; Playwright. Educ: M.A., Christ Church Coll., Oxford Univ. Publs: (plays) A Murder has been Arranged; Glamour; Full Moon; Vigil; Vessels Departing; Spring, 1600; Night Must Fall; He Was Born Gay; The Corn is Green; The Light of Heart; The Morning Star; The Druid's Rest; The Wind of Heaven; Trespass; Accolade; Someone Waiting; (adaptations) A Month in the Country; The Master Builder; (autobiog.) George, 1961; Beyond Belief, 1967; (films) The Last Days of Dolwyn (author, co-director, actor), 1948; etc. Hons: C.B.E., 1962; LL.D., Univ. of Bangor. Address: c/o Agent, J. H. de Lannoy, Planned Theatre Ltd., 11 Aldwych, London WC2, UK.

WILLIAMS, Eric, b. 13 July 1911, London, UK. Publs: The Wooden Horse, 1949; The Tunnel, 1951; The Escapers, 1953; Complete and Free, 1957; Dragoman, 1959; The Borders of Barbarism, 1961; More Escapers, 1966; (for children) Great Escape Stories, 1958; Great Air Battles, 1971. Mbr., Soc. of Authors. Address: Yacht ESCAPER, c/o Union Bank of Switzerland, Bern, Switz.

WILLIAMS, Glanmor, b. 5 May 1920, Dowlais, Glamorgan, UK. Professor of History. Educ: B.A., M.A., Univ. of Wales; D.Litt. Publs: The Welsh Church, 1962; Welsh Reformation Essays, 1967; Reformation Views of Church History, 1971; Ed., Glamorgan County History, vol. III, 1971 & vol. IV, 1974. Contbr. to: History; English Historical Review; Economic History Review; Welsh History Review; Cambridge Jrnl. Mbrships: Fellow, Royal Histl. Soc.; Chmn., Bd. of Celtic Studies, ibid; Advsry. Coun. on Pub. Records; Brit. Lib. Bd. Address: 11 Grosvenor Rd., Swansea SA2 0SP, UK.

WILLIAMS, Ifor Wyn, b. 31 Aug. 1923, Bangor, UK. Headmaster. Publs: The Slim Hero, 1962; The Sweet Smoke, 1964; 412 on her Leg, 1967; Heat from the West, 1971; Knife in the Earth, 1974. Publs: num. radio scripts for BBC Schls. Broadcasts; sev. scripts for BBC TV plays. Mbrships: V.P., Union of Welsh Authors; Druidic Order of Gorsedd of Bards of Gt. Britain. Hons. incl: Adventure Novel Prize, Nat. Eisteddfod of Wales, 1966; BBC Wales TV Play Competition Prize, 1970; Prose Medal for novel, Nat. Eisteddfod of Wales, 1971; Competition Prize, Welsh Publrs. Novel of the Yr., 1973. Address: Ael-y-Bryn, Ffordd Sychnant, Conway, Gwynedd, UK.

WILLIAMS, Jay, pen name DELVING, Michael, b. 31 May 1914, Buffalo, N.Y., USA. Author. Educ: Univs. Pa. & Columbia. Publs. incl: The Good Yeoman, 1948; The Siege, 1955; Solomon & Sheba, 1959; Smiling the Boy Fell Dead, 1966; Uniad, 1968; The Devil Finds Work, 1969; Die Like a Man, 1970; A Shadow of Himself, 1972; Stage Left, 1974; (children's books) The Battle for the Atlantic, 1959; The Hawkstone, 1971; The Hero from Otherwhere, 1972; Petronella, 1973; & The Danny Dunn Books. Contbr. to: Saturday Evening Post; Story; Esquire; etc. Mbrships: Authors' League Am.; Soc. Authors (UK). Hons. incl: PNLA Young Readers Award 1961 & 1963; Lewis Carroll

Shelf Award, 1973. Address: c/o Russel & Volkening Lit. Agcy., 551 5th Ave., N.Y., NY 10017, USA.

WILLIAMS, Jeanne, pen names, ROWAN, Deirdre; CRECY, Jeanne; WILLIAMS, J.R., b. 10 Apr. 1930, Elkhart, Kan., USA. Publs., 24 books, adult, juvenile & gothic, incing: The Horsetalker, 1961; Tame the Wild Stallion, 1957; Hands of Terror (UK title, Lady Gift), 1972; Freedom Trail, 1973; The Lightning Tree, 1973; Dragons' Mount, 1973; Silver Wood, 1974; Shadow of the Volcano, 1975; The Lime Tree, 1975; The Winter Keeper, 1975; The Night Hunters, 1975; Winter Wheat, 1975; Judas Burning, forthcoming. Mbrships. incl: Western Writers of Am. (Pres., 1974-75); var. other lit. orgs. Recip., sev. awards. Address: 4330 Osage, Tucson, AZ 85718, USA.

WILLIAMS, John A., b. 1925, Jackson, Miss., USA. Author. Educ: B.A., Syracuse Univ., 1950. Publs. incl: The Angry Ones, 1960; Night Song, 1961; Sissie, 1963; The Man Who Cried I Am, 1967; Sons of Darkness, Sons of Light, 1969; The King God Didn't Save, 1970; Captain Blackman, 1972; Flashbacks, 1973; Mothersill & the Foxes, 1975. Contbr. to: Co-Ed., Amistad, Vintage, 1969-71; Ed. Bd., Audience Mag., 1970-72; num. mags. & jrnls. Mbrships: Coun., Authors Guild; Bd., Rabinowitz Fndn.; Hons: Nat. Inst. of Arts & Letters, 1962; Centennial Medal, Syracuse Univ., 1970; Dist. Prof. Engl., LaGuardia Community Coll., CUNY, 1973-75. Address: 35 W. 92nd St., N.Y., NY 10025, USA.

WILLIAMS, John Edwin Stuart, b. 13 Aug. 1920, Mountain Ash, Wales, UK. Head of Department, City of Cardiff College of Education. Educ: B.A., M.A., Univ. Coll., Cardiff. Publs: Last Fall, 1962; Green Rain, 1967; Dic Penderyn & Other Poems, 1970; Banna Strand, 1974; Ed., Poems, 1969; Ed., The Lilting House, 1969. Contbr. to: English; Transatlantic Review; Decal; Anglo-Welsh Review; Wales; Planet; Poetry Wales; BBC; etc. Mbrships: Welsh Acad.; Cardiff New Theatre Trust. Recip., Welsh Arts Coun. Lit. Prize, 1971. Address: 52 Dan-y-Coed Rd., Cyncoed, Cardiff, UK.

WILLIAMS, John Herbert, b. 16 July 1908, St. Leonards-on-Sea, UK. Educ: B.A., London Univ., 1930. Publs: Suddenly at The Priory, 1957; Heyday for Assassins, 1958; Hume: Portrait of a Double Murderer, 1960; Mutiny, 1917, 1963; The Idea of May, 1968; The Home Fronts 1914-1918, 1972; (script writing & rsch.). The Great War, BBC, 1963-64; The Lost Peace, BBC, 1965; The World at War, ITV, 1972-73. Contbr. to: Hist. of the 20th Century; Hist. Makers; Chambers's Jrnl. Mbrships: PEN; Crime Writers Assn.; Soc. of Authors. Address: Sandes House, 25 Filsham Rd., St. Leonards-on-Sea, Sussex TN38 0PA, UK.

WILLIAMS, Moyra, b. 5 Dec. 1917, London, UK. Clinical Psychologist. Educ: B.Litt., 1949, D.Phil., 1955, Oxford Univ. Publs: Horse Psychology, 1955; Adventures Unbridled, 1960; Health & Happiness in Old Age (w. Celia Westropp), 1960; Riding is my Hobby, 1961; Mental Testing in Clinical Practice, 1966; A Breed of Horses, 1971; Brain Damage & the Mind, 1971. Contbr. to: Behaviour of Domestic Animals (ed., Hafez); Amnesia (ed., Whitty & Zangwill), 1966; Perspectives of Child Psychiatry (ed., Howells), 1969; The Psychological Assessment of Handicapped (ed., Mittler), 1970; Equine Vet. Jrnl.; Neuropsychologia; most Brit. & Am. psychol. jrnls. Address: Leyland Farm, Gawcott, Buckingham, UK.

WILLIAMS, Pieter Daniel De Wet, pen name WILLIAMS, Pieter or Pedro, b. 29 July 1929, Natalspruit, Transvaal, S. Africa; Lecturer in English. Educ: B.A., Wits.; B.Ed., Stel. Contbr. to num. lit. jrnls. Mbrships: S.A. Poetry Soc.; S.A. Coun. for Engl. Educ.; Engl. Acad. of S. Africa. Hons: Prize, for German poetry transl., Goethe Inst., 1953; 1st Prize, Poetry, Cape Town Eisteddfod, 1966; 2nd Prize, State Poetry Competition, Dept. Cultural Affairs, 1967; B.A., UNISA; T.T.H.D., J.T.T.C. Address: Dept. of English, Univ. of the O.F.S.; Bloemfontein 9301, S. Africa.

WILLIAMS, Raymond Henry, b. 31 Aug. 1921, Llanfihangel Crucouney, UK. Writer; University Professor. Educ: B.A., M.A., Litt.D., Hon. D. Univ., Cantab. Publs. incl: Drama from Ibsen to Eliot, 1952, revised ed., Drama from Ibsen to Brecht., 1968; Drama in Performance, 1954, revised ed., 1968; Culture & Society, 1780-1950, 1958; Border Country (novel), 1960; The Long Revolution, 1961; Communications, 1962, revised ed., 1968; Second Generation (novel), 1964; The English Novel from Dickens to Lawrence, 1970; Orwell, 1971; The Country & the City, 1973; Television: Technological & Cultural Form, 1974.

Contbr. to jrnls. Mbr., Soc. of Authors. Address: Jesus Coll., Cambridge, UK.

WILLIAMS, Robert Coleman, b. 4 Jan. 1940, Bridgend, Glamorgan, UK. Company Director. Educ: Jesus Coll., Oxford Univ., 1958-62; M.A. (Oxon.). Publs: Ladycross (poetry), 1962; Concordance to the Collected Poems of Dylan Thomas, 1967. Mbrships. incl: Royal Soc. of Lit.; Medieval Acad. of Am.; Early Engl. Text. Soc.; MLA. Address: P.O. Box 4, Llansteffan, Carmarthen, Dyfed, UK.

WILLIAMS, Tennessee (Thomas Lanier), b. 26 Mar. 1911, Columbus, Miss., USA. Writer. Educ: A.B., Univ. of Iowa, 1938. Publs. incl: (plays) The Glass Menagerie, 1945; 27 Wagons Full of Cotton, 1946, revised ed. 1953; A Streetcar Named Desire, 1947; The Rose Tattoo, 1951; Cat on a Hot Tin Roof, 1955; Sweet Bird of Youth, 1959; The Night of the Iguana, 1962; The Milk Train Doesn't Stop Here Anymore, 1964; (novel) The Roman Spring of Mrs. Stone, 1950 (all also publd. UK); (screenplay) Baby Doll, 1956; var. short stories & verse. Mbr., Nat. Inst. Arts & Letters. Hons: Pulitzer Prizes, 1948, 1955; num. other awards & grants. Address: c/o Audrey Wood, Int. Famous Agcy., 1301 Ave of the Americas, N.Y., NY 10019, USA.

WILLIAMS, Ursula Moray, b. 19 Apr. 1911, Petersfield, Hants., UK. Writer of Children's Books. Educ: Private & Art Schl. Publs: Adventures of the Little Wooden Horse, 1938; Nine Lives of Island Mackenzie, 1959; The Three Toymakers Trilogy; The Noble Hawks; A Picnic with the Aunts, 1973; The Line, 1974; more than 60 books since 1932, many on TV & radio. Contbr. to: Puffin Post; Cricket (USA); etc. Mbrships: Nat. Book League; W. England Writers' Soc. Hons: The Three Toymakers published in Honor Book, 1972; 1st Hon. Life Mbr. Puffin Club, 1974. Address: Court Farm Ho., Beckford, nr. Tewkesbury, Glos., UK

WILLIAMS, Wirt Alfred Jr., b. 21 Aug. 1921, Goodman, Miss., USA. University Teacher; Novelist. Educ: B.A., Delta Univ., Miss.; M.A., La. State Univ.; Ph.D., Univ. of Iowa. Publs: The Enemy, 1951; Love In a Windy Space, 1957; Ada Dallas, 1959; A Passage of Hawks, 1963; The Trojans, 1966; The Far Side, 1972. Contbr. to: Miss. Quarterly; Statement; LA Times; N.Y. Times Book Review; Book World; Kenyon Review. Mbrships: Authors League of Am.; United Calif. Profs.; AAUP. Recip., 3 nominations for Pulitzer Prize in fiction. Address: 3549 Laurelvale, Studio City, CA 91604, USA.

WILLIAMS-ELLIS, (Lady) Amabel. Novelist; Writer of Children's Books. Publs. incl: An Anatomy of Poetry; The Big Firm; Men Who Found Out; Noah's Ark; How you are Made; To Tell the Truth; A History of English Life; Learn to Love First; Headlong Down the Years; Women in War Factories; The Art of Being a Woman; The Art of Being a Parent; A Food & People Geography; Changing the World; Modern Scientists at Work; Darwin's Moon, A Life of Alfred Russel Wallace; Life in England, 6 vols. Address: Plas Brondanw, Penrhyndeudraeth, Merioneth, N. Wales, UK.

WILLIAMSON, Audrey, b. 29 May 1913, Surrey, UK. Author; Journalist. Publs. incl: Old Vic Drama, 1948; Theatre of Two Decades, 1951; Wagner Opera, 1962; Bernard Shaw: Man & Writer, 1963; Thomas Paine: His Life, Work & Times, 1973; Wilkes: 'A Friend to Liberty', 1974. Contbr. to: Guardian; Scotsman; Theatre Arts; Musical Am.; Opera. Book Reviewer: Tribune. Mbrships. incl: Shaw Soc.; Labour Hist. Soc.; Keats-Shelley Mem. Assoc. Recip., 1st Prize, Crime Writers' Assn., 1970, for Mystery of Princes in the Tower, later publ'd. in Sunday Times. Address: c/o Curtis Brown Ltd., 1 Craven Hill, London W2 3EW, UK.

WILLIAMSON, Henry, b. 1 Dec. 1895, Parkstone, Dorset, UK. Writer. Publs. incl: (novels) The Flax of Dream, 5 books, UK & USA, 1921-33, revised eds., 1929-48; Tarka the Otter, UK & USA, 1927; Salar the Salmon, 1935; A Chronicle of Ancient Sunlight (series of 15 books), 1951-69; (short stories) The Village Book, UK & USA, 1930; The Labouring Life, 1932 (as As the Sun shines, USA, 1933); Tales of Moorland & Estuary, 1953; Collected Nature Stories, 1970; (autobiog.) The Story of a Norfolk Farm, 1941; A Clear Water Stream, UK, 1958, USA, 1959. Recip., Hawthornden Prize, 1928. Address: Ox's Cross, Braunton, N. Devon, UK.

WILLIAMSON, Tony (Anthony George), b. 18 Dec. 1934, Manchester, UK. Dramatist. Publs: (novels) The Connector, 1975/76; The Fabulous Assassin, 1975/76; (screenplays) Night Watch; Woman Hunt; The Fabulous Assassin; (TV plays) Victim; Ask Any Neighbour; Tears of God; /TV series) The Avengers; Department S; The Persuaders; Jason King; The Champions; Z Cars; Dr. Finlay; The Spies; Spy Trap. Mbr., Writers' Guild of GB. Recip., Writers' Guild Award, for episode of TV series, 1965. Address: c/o Robin Lowe, P.L.R. Ltd., 33 Sloane St., London SW1, UK.

WILLIAMSON, William Landram, b. 13 Aug. 1920, Ky., USA. Professor of Library Science. Educ. incl: B.A. (Am. Hist.), Univ. of Wis., 1941; B.A. (Lib. Sci.), Emory Univ., 1942; M.S. Columbia Univ., 1949; Ph.D., Univ. of Chgo., 1959. Publs: William Frederick Poole & the Modern Library Movement, 1963; Ed: The Impact of the Public Law 480 Program, 1967; Ed: Assistance to Libraries in Developing Nations, 1971. Contbr. to: Lib. Quarterly; Coll. & Rsch. Libs. Mbrships. incl: Am. Lib. Assn.; AAUP; Archons of Colophon. Address: 5105 Tomahawk Trail, Madison, WI 53705, USA.

WILLIE, Charles Vert, b. 8 Oct. 1927, Dallas, TX, USA. Professor of Education & Urban Studies, Harvard University. Educ: B.A., Morehouse Coll., Ga., 1948; M.A., Atlanta Univ., Ga., 1949; Ph.D., Syracuse Univ., NY, 1957. Publs: incl: Church Action in the World, 1969; Ed: The Family Life of Black People, 1970; Black Students at White Colleges, 1972; Race Mixing in the Public Schools, 1973; Ed. (w. others): Racism & Mental Health, 1973; Oreo, 1975. Contbr. to num. profl. jrnls. Mbrships: Eastern Sociol. Soc. (Pres., 1974-75); Fellow, Am. Sociol. Assn.; Am. Pub. Health Assn. Recip., 3 acad. hons. Address: 41 Hillcrest Rd., Concord, MA 01742, USA.

WILLINGHAM, Calder (Baynard, Jr.,), b. 23 Dec. 1922, Atlanta, Ga., USA. Writer. Educ: Univ. of Va., Charlottesville, 1941-43. Publs. incl: (novels) End as a Man, USA, 1947, UK, 1952; Geraldine Bradshaw, USA, 1950, UK, 1964; Reach to the Stars, USA, 1951, UK, 1965; Natural Child, 1952; To Eat a Peach, 1955; Eternal Fire, USA & UK, 1963; Providence Island, USA & UK, 1969; (short stories) The Gates of Hell, USA, 1951, UK, 1966; (screenplays) Paths of Glory, 1957; End as a Man, 1958; One-Eyed Jacks, 1962; The Graduate, 1967; Little Big Man, 1970. Address: c/o Vanguard Press, 424 Madison Ave., N.Y., NY 10017, USA.

WILLIS, Anthony Armstrong, pen name ARMSTRONG, Anthony, b. 2 Jan. 1897, Esquimalt, BC, Canada. Educ: Trinity Coll., Cambridge, UK. Publs. incl. (novels): Patrick Undergraduate; Patrick Engaged; Patrick Helps; No Dragon, No Damsel; The Trail of Fear; The Trail of the Black King; The Poison Trail; (vols. humorous articles): Warriors at Ease; Percival & I; How To Do It; Me & Frances; Livestock in Barracks; Britisher on Broadway; Nothing to do with the War; Prune's Progress; (other books): Laughter Omnibus; The Naughty Princess; We Like the Country; Spies in Amber; The Strange Case of Mr. Pelham; Saying Your Prayers; etc. (plays): Well Caught; Sitting on a Fence; Ten-Minute Alibi; Mile-Away Murder; sev. w. others. Contbr. to: Punch (as AA); BBC. Address: The Knapp, Grayswood Rd., Haslemere, Surrey, UK.

WILLIS, John Alvin, b. 16 Oct. 1916, Morristown, Tenn., USA. Editor; Teacher. Educ: B.A., Milligan Coll.; M.A., Univ. of Tenn.; Grad. work, Ind. Univ., Harvard Univ. Asst. Ed., Theatre World, 1945-65; Screen World, 1949-65; Opera World, 1952-54; Pictorial History of American Theatre, 1950, 1960, 1970; Pictorial History of Silent Screen, 1953; Great Stars of the American Stage, 1952; Pictorial History of Opera in America, 1954; Pictorial History of Talkies, 1958; Pictorial History of Television, 1959. Ed., Theatre World, 1965–. Screen World, 1965–; Dance World, 1966–. Mbr., N.Y. Drama Desk. Address: 190 Riverside Drive, N.Y., NY 10024, USA.

WILLIS, Ted (Lord Willis of Chislehurst), b. 13 Jan. 1918, Tottenham, UK. Author. Publs: Woman in a Dressing Gown & Other TV Plays, 1959; Whatever Happened to Tom Mix?, 1970; Death May Surprise Us, 1974; Left-Handed Sleeper, forthcoming. Mbrships: Past Pres., Writers' Guild of GB; Exec. Comm., League of Dramatists; F.R.S.A.; Press Club. Hons: Award for Outstanding TV Writing, Writers' Guild of GB; Award for Outstanding Contbn. to TV & Films, Variety Club of GB; Silver Medal, Royal Soc. of Arts. Address: 5 Shepherds Green, Chislehurst, Kent BR7 6PB, UK.

WILLKENS, William Henry Robert, b. 5 Aug. 1919, New Britain, Conn., USA. Professor of Education. Educ:

A.B., Univ. of Pitts., Pa., 1942; B.D., Colgate-Rochester Divinity Schl., 1949; M.Ed., 1954, Ph.D., 1958, Univ. of Pitts., Pa. Publs: A Christian Style of Life, 1966; The Youth Years, 1967; Man Responds to God, 1968; Ed. & Co-author, Guidebook for New Professionals in Education, 1971, 2nd ed., 1974. Contbr. to var. relig. jrnls. Address: 109 Farmington Drive, Butler, PA 16001, USA.

WILLNER, Sven Evert, b. 7 Apr. 1918, Purmo, Finland. Journalist. Educ: Swedish Social Inst., Helsinki, 1947. Publs: På flykt från världsåskådningar, 1964; Om krig, 1966; Dikt och politik, 1968; Möjligheter, 1970; Öppna dörrar, 1972; Mellan hammaren och städet, 1974. Contbr. to: Nya Argus; Horisont; Ord och Bild; Ydin. Bd. Mbr., Soc. of Finnish-Swedish Authors, 1960-. Hons: SLS, Swedish Soc. of Lit. in Finland, 1965, 1969, 1973; Lit. Prize, Finnish State, 1971. Address: 10600 Ekenäs, Finland.

WILLOUGHBY-HIGSON, Philip John, pen names HIGSON, P. J. W.; HIGSON, Philip, b. 21 Feb. 1933, Newcastle-under-Lyme, Staffs., UK. Author; Lecturer. Educ: B.A., 1956, M.A., 1959, Ph.D., 1971, Univ. of Liverpool; postgrad. Cert. Ed., Madeley Coll. of Educ., 1972. Publs: Poetry: Poems of Protest & Pilgrimage, 1967; To Make Love's Harbour, 1967; The Riposte & Other Poems, 1971; Burlando's Mistress & Other Poems, 1974; Bandelaire: Flowers of Evil & Other Authentical Poems, ed. & transl. (w. E. Elliot R. Ashe), 1974; History: The Bizarre Barons of Rivington, 1965. Chmn., Cestrian Press. Contbr. to: Chester Poets; One; The Complete Peerage; var. histl. & antiquarian books & jrnls. Mbrships. incl: Soc. of Authors; F.R.S.A. Recip., Chester Fest. Poetry Competition Award, 1973. Address: Sr. Common Room, Chester Coll., Cheyney Rd., Chester CH1 4BJ, UK.

WILMINK, Willem Andries, b. 25 Oct. 1936, Enschedé, Netherlands. University Lecturer. Educ: Doctorandus, Univ. of Amsterdam. Publs: Brief van een Verkademeisje, 1966; Goejanverwellesluis, 1971; Een vreemde tijger, 1972; Dat overkomt iedereen wel, 1973. Contbr. to: Tirade; De Revisor. Mbr., V.V.L. (Dutch Writers' Assn.). Recip., Louis Davids Prize, 1974. Address: Valeriusstraat 212, Amsterdam, Netherlands.

WILSON, Alexander (Sandy) Galbraith, b. 19 May 1924, Sale, Cheshire, UK. Writer; Composer. Educ: Oxford Univ. Publs: This is Sylvia, 1954; The Poodle From Rome, 1962; (plays & musicals) See You Later, See You Again, 1951; The Boy Friend, 1953; The Buccaneer, 1955; Valmouth, 1958; Divorce Me Darling, 1965; Sandy Wilson Thanks the Ladies, 1971. Contbr. to BBC. Address: 2 Southwell Gdns., London SW7, UK.

WILSON, Angus (Frank Johnstone), b. 11 Aug. 1913, Bexhill, Sussex, UK. Professor of English Literature. Educ: B.A., Merton Coll., Oxford Univ., 1936. Publs. incl: (novels) Hemlock & After, UK & USA, 1952; Anglo-Saxon Attitudes, UK & USA, 1956; The Old Men at the Zoo, UK & USA, 1961; Late Call, UK, 1964, USA, 1965; No Laughing Matter, UK & USA, 1967; (short stories) The Wrong Set, UK, 1949, USA, 1950; A Bit off the Map, UK & USA, 1957; (play) The Mulberry Bush, 1956. Mbrship: F.R.S.L. (Companion of Lit.); Nat. Book League (Chmn.). Hons. incl: Black Mem. Prize, 1959; C.B.E., 1968; Yorks. Post Book Award, 1971. Address: Felsham Woodside, Bradfield St. George, Bury St. Edmunds, Suffolk, UK.

WILSON, Anthony David, b. 20 May 1927, Rugby, UK. Science Correspondent, BBC Television News. Educ: M.A., Cambridge Univ. Publs: Broadcasting: Sound & Vision, 1968; The Communicators & Society, 1969; The Science of Self (also as Body & Anti-Body), 1972; Atoms of Time Past (also as The New Archaeology), 1975; Penicillin in Perspective (forthcoming). Contbr. to: Listener; Yr. Book World Affairs; etc. Recip., Glaxo Travelling Award, 1974. Address: 49 St. James's Ave., Hampton Hill, Middlesex TW12 1HL, UK.

WILSON, (Sir) (Archibald) Duncan, b. 12 Aug. 1911, Winchester, UK. University Academician; Former Diplomat. Educ: Balliol Coll., Oxford. Publs: Ed., Communist China: Policy Documents 1955-59, 1962; Life & Times of Vuk Stefanović Karadžić, 1970. Contbr. to: Int. Affairs; Encounter; London Mag. Hon. Mbr., Acad. of Pol. Scis., N.Y., USA. Address: Corpus Christi Coll., Cambridge CB2 1RH, UK.

WILSON, Barbara, b. 13 July 1932, Hoylandswaine, nr. Sheffield, Yorks., UK. Writer. Publs: Look Up the Wind,

1964; Charged to the Account, 1966; They Conquer Love, 1967; Stubborn Clay, 1969; Before You Answer, 1970; The River Within Us, 1972; The Oldest Confession, 1973. Address: 27 Wigginton Rd., Tamworth, Staffs. B79 8RH, UK.

WILSON, Colin Henry, b. 26 June 1931, Leicester, UK. Author. Publs: The Outsider, 1956; Religion & the Rebel, 1957; Ritual in the Dark, 1960; Introduction to the New Existentialism, 1967; A Casebook of Murder, 1969; The Occult, 1971; New Pathways in Psychology, 1972; The Schoolgirl Murder Case, 1974; The Book of Booze, 1974. Contbr. to: Spectator; Books & Bookmen. Mbr., Savage Club, London. Address: Gorran Haven, Cornwall, UK.

WILSON, (Daphne) Merna, pen name WILSON, Merna, b. 5 June 1930, Que Que, Rhodesia. Buyer. Publs: Explosion, 1965; Turn the Tide Gently, 1967; Reap the Whirlwind, 1969. Contbr. to: African World; Personality; Scope; Cape Argus; Fair Lady; PEN Anthols.; Bulawayo Chronicle; Sunday Mail; Rhodesia Herald; Rhodesia Calls; Rhodesian Annual; Writer; Dag; Two Tone; Rhodesian Poetry Review; Voices Int.; New Coin; Longmans Anthols. Mbrships: PEN, Rhodesia; Hon. Life Mbr., Rhodesia Writers' Club; Salisbury Writers Club. Hons: 2nd prize, Shakespeare 4th Centenary Sonnet, 1964; 2nd prizes Greenwood Poetry Prize, 1966. Address: 14 Dorchester Rd., Cotswold Hills, Salisbury, Rhodesia.

WILSON, Derek Alan, pen name PRESTON, Hugh, b. 10 Oct. 1935, Colchester, UK. Author. Educ: M.A., Peterhouse, Cambridge Univ. Publs: East Africa Through a Thousand Years, 1968; A Student's Atlas of African History, 1971; A Tudor Tapestry, 1972; A History of South & Central Africa, 1974; The A-Z of World History, 1975; Feast in the Morning, 1975. Mbrships. incl: United Oxford & Cambridge Club; Soc. Authors; Furniture Hist. Soc. Recip., Archbishop Cranmer Prize, Cambridge Univ., 1968. Address: Camborne Cottage, Drinkstone, Suffolk, UK.

WILSON, Dorothy Clarke, b. 9 May 1904, Gardiner, Me., USA. Author. Educ: A.B., Bates Coll., Lewiston, Me., 1925. Publs: Over 70 relig. plays incing. Twelve Months of Drama, 1934; (novels) The Herdsman, a Story of Amos, 1946; House of Earth, 1952; Jezebel, 1955; The Gifts, 1957; The Journey, 1957; (biogs.) Take My Hands, Story of Dr. Mary Verghese, 1963; Ten Fingers for God, Story of Dr. Paul Brand, 1965; Handicap Race, 1967; Palace of Healing, 1968; Lone Woman, Story of Elizabeth Blackwell, the first Woman Doctor, 1970; The Big-Little World of Doc. Pritham, 1971; Bright Eyes, Story of an Omaha Indian, 1974; Stranger & Traveler, Story of Dorothea Dix, 1975. Hons. incl: Litt.D., Bates Coll.; Westminster Relig. Fiction Award, for Prince of Egypt, 1949. Address: 114 Forest Ave., Orono, Maine, USA.

WILSON, Ethel, b. 20 Jan. 1888, S. Africa. Writer; Former Teacher. Publs: (novels) Hetty Dorval, USA, 1947, UK, 1948; The Innocent Traveller, Can. & UK, 1949; The Equations of Love, with Tuesday & Wednesday, & Lilly's Story, Can. & UK, 1952; Lilly's Story, USA, 1952; Swamp Angel, Can., UK & USA, 1954; Love & Salt Water, Can. & UK, 1956; (short stories) Mrs. Golightly & Other Stories, Can. & UK, 1961. Hons: D.Litt., Univ. of B.C., Can., 1955; Can. Coun. Medal, 1962; Lorne Pierce Medal, 1964; Medal of Serv., Order of Can., 1970. Address: 2890 Point Grey Rd., Apt. 308, Vancouver, B.C., Can.

WILSON, Frank, b. 1914, Mauritius. Writer. Educ: M.A., St. John's Coll., Cambridge Univ., UK. Publs: Food for the Golden Age; Art into Life; Art as Understanding. Agent: Campbell, Thomson & McLaughlin. Mbrships incl: PEN. Address: 6 Pembroke Studios, London W8, UK.

WILSON, Harriett Charlotte, b. 14 Sept. 1916, Berlin, Germany. Sociologist. Educ: B.Sc. (Econ.), L.S.E., UK., 1946; Ph.D., Univ. of Wales, 1959. Publs: Delinquency & Child Neglect, 1962, 2nd ed. 1964; Socially Deprived Families in Britain (w. Robert Holman & others), 1970, 2nd ed. w. supplement 1973. Contbr. to: Brit. Jrnl. of Criminol.; New Soc.; Social Work Today; Policy & Politics; etc. Mbrships. incl: Child Poverty Action Grp. (Fndr.-mbr., 1st Hon. Sec., now Vice Chmn); Brit. Sociol. Assn.; Howard League for Penal Reform. Address: 4 Plymouth Drive, Birmingham B45 8JB, UK.

WILSON, Helen Helga, pen (Maiden) name MAYNE, H. H., b. 25 Jan. 1902, Zeehan, Tas., Australia. Author. Educ: B.A., Univ. of Western Australia, Nedlands. Publs: The

Golden Age, 1958; Where the Winds Feet Shine, 1959; If Gold Rust, 1960; A Show of Colours, 1970; Island of Fire, 1973; Gateways to Gold; Westward Gold; The Golden Miles. Contbr. to Meanjin; Premier Lit. Quarterly of Aust.; Sydney Bulletin; Geogl. Mag.; Num. other mags.; 7 anthols. Mbrships. incl: Comm. of Mgmt., Aust. Authors Soc.; Histl. Soc., Manly, N.S.W. Recip., Num. prizes & recommendations in var. lit. competitions. Address: 40 Bower St., Manly, N.S.W., Australia, 2095.

WILSON, John Abraham Ross, b. 25 Aug. 1911, Trout Lake, B.C., Can. Professor of Education. Educ: B.A., 1932, Cert. as Tchr., 1933, M.A., 1939, Univ. of B.C.; Ed.D., Ore. State Univ., USA, 1951. Publs: Kindergarten Evaluation of Learning Potential (KELP) (w. Mildred C. Robeck), 1967; Psychological Foundations of Learning & Teaching (w. Mildred C. Robeck & William B. Michael), 1969, 2nd ed., 1974; Ed., Diagnosis of Learning Difficulties, 1971; Psychology of Reading; Foundation of Instruction (w. Mildred C. Robeck), 1974. Contbr. to var. profl. jrnls. Mbrships: Pres., Calif. Educl. Rsch. Assn., Calif. Assn. for Student Tchng. Address: 2519 Chapala St., Santa Barbara, CA 93105, USA.

WILSON, Mitchell, b. 17 July 1913, NYC, USA. Writer. Educ: B.Sc., N.Y. Univ., 1934; M.A., Columbia Univ., 1938. Publs. incl: (novels) Footsteps Behind Her, 1941; None So Blind, USA, 1945, UK, 1947; The Kimballs, USA, 1947, UK, 1950; Live With Lightning, USA, 1949, UK, 1950; My Brother, My Enemy, USA, 1952, UK, 1953; Meeting at a Far Meridian, USA & UK, 1961; The Huntress, USA & UK, 1966; Passion to Know, USA & UK, 1972 (var. novels also publd. in Russian); (non-fiction) American Science & Invention: A Pictorial History, 1954. Address: 1016 5th Ave., NY, USA.

WILSON, Pat, b. 25 Oct. 1910, Middlesbrough, Cleveland, UK. Playwright; Lecturer. Publs: (plays) Summer's Tale, 1968; Four For a Boy, 1971; Rector's Return, 1972; Jan Adamant; The Enchanted Pantomime; Snow Queen; No, My Darling Daughter; Hogmanay Hurray; Thy Kingdom Come; Get It All Together; One More Time; Hairy Christmas; Balletwho, 1974; (1-act plays) Funeral Tea; The Re-Union; The Little Miracle; New Broom; Send Us Victorias; The Tektite; A Mixed Bag; The Rummage Sale; Silver Wedding; Queen Bee; Back Door to Heaven, 1975. Fellow of Int. Poetry Soc. Hons. incl: O.Z. Whitehead Dublin Festival Theatre Award; London Playgoers Play Award; Dame Flora Robson Award. Address: 66 Marwood Drive, Great Ayton, Middlesbrough, Cleveland TS9 6PD, UK.

WILSON, Phillip (John), b. 12 May 1922, Lower Hutt, NZ. Writer. Educ: M.A.(NZ). Publs: Some Are Lucky, 1960; The Maori lander, 1961; Beneath the Thunder, 1963; Pacific Flight, 1964; The Outcasts, 1965; William Satchell, 1968; New Zealand Jack, 1973; Pacific Star, forthcoming. Contbr. to: PEN Gazette (Ed.); Am. Quarterly; NZ Listener; Landfall; Islands; NZ Heritage; Arena. Life Mbr., PEN. Hons: Fulbright Schlr., 1951-52; NZ Schlrship. in Letters, 1958. Address: 12 Bank Road, Wellington 5, NZ.

WILSON, R(obert) L(awrence), b. 24 June 1939, St. James, Minn, USA. Historian; Writer; Researcher. Educ: Carleton Coll., Northfield, Minn. Publs. incl: Samuel Colt Presents, 1961; The Arms Collection of Colonel Colt, 1963; The Rampant Colt, 1969; Colt Commemorative Firearms, 1969, 2nd ed., 1974; Theodore Roosevelt Outdoorsman, 1969; Ed., Antique Arms Annual, 1971; The Book of Colt Engraving, 1974; The Book of Winchester Engraving, 1975. Contbr. to: Am. Rifleman; Sports Afield; Arms Gazette; etc. Mbrships. incl: Am. Soc. Arms Collectors; Co. of Mil. Histns.; Am. Histl. Assn.; N.Y. Histl. Soc.; Hon. Dir., Tex Gun Collectors Assn. Address: 51 Lakewood Circle North, Manchester, CT 06040, USA.

WILSON, Rosa Loretta (Finger), b. 28 July 1909, Hoisington, Kan., USA. Teacher & Librarian. Educ: B.A., Univ. of Kan., Lawrence, 1931; M.Ed., Wichita State Univ., Kan. Publs: A Study of the Emotions in the Poetry of Rafael Alberti. Mbrships. incl: NEA; AAUW; ALA; Am. Assn. of Tchrs. of Engl.; Am. Assn. of Tchrs. of Spanish & Portuguese; Am. Assn. of Schl. Libns. Recip., sev. prizes for poetry & light verse. Address: 121 N. Fountain, Wichita, KS 67208, USA.

WILSON, Rosamond, pen name ROLLESTON, Rosamond, b. 29 Sept. 1910, Timatu, NZ. Housewife. Publs: Times Have Changed, 1963; William & Mary Rolleston, 1971. Mbr., PEN, NZ. Recip., Wattie Book of

the Year Award, 1971. Address: 6 Mariri Rd., Kelburn, Wellington 5, New Zealand.

WILSON, Sloan, b. 8 May 1920, Norwalk, Conn., USA. Writer. Educ: B.A., Harvard Univ., 1942. Publs: (novels) Voyage to Somewhere, 1947; The Man in the Gray Flannel Suit, USA, 1955, UK, 1956; A Summer Place, USA & UK, 1958; A Sense of Values, USA 1960, UK, 1961; Georgie Winthrop, USA & UK, 1963; Janus Island, USA & UK, 1967; All the Best People, USA, 1970, UK, 1971; (non-fiction) Away from It All, USA, 1969, UK, 1970. Contbr. to: Providence Jrnl.; Time; N.Y. Herald Tribune (Educ. Ed., 1956-58). Address: c/o Morton Leavy, Weissberger & Frosch, 120 E. 56th St., N.Y., NY, USA.

WILSON, Thomas, b. 23 June 1916, Belfast, UK. Adam Smith Professor of Economics. Educ: B.A., Queen's Univ., Belfast, 1938; Ph.D., London Univ., 1940; M.A., Oxford Univ., 1946. Publs: Fluctuations in Income & Employment, 1942; Oxford Studies in the Price Mechanism, 1951; Inflation, 1961; Planning & Growth, 1964. Pensions Inflation & Growth, 1974; Contbr., Economic Sovereignty & Regional Policy, 1975. Contbr. to: Econ. Jrnl.; Economica; Oxford Econ. Papers; & other jrnls. Mbrships. incl: Royal Econ. Soc.; Scottish Econ. Soc.; Am. Econ. Assn. Recip., O.B.E., 1945. Address: 8 The University, Glasgow G12 8QQ, UK.

WILSON, William E., b. 12 Feb. 1906, Evansville, Ind., USA. Writer. Educ: A.B., A.M., Harvard Univ. Publs. incl: The Wabash, 1940; Yesterday's Son, 1941; Crescent City, 1947; Abe Lincoln of Pigeon Creek, 1949; The Strangers, 1953; The Raiders, 1955; On the Sunny Side of a One-Way Street, 1958; The Angel & the Serpent, 1964; Indiana, 1966; Every Man is my Father, 1973. Contbr. to: New Yorker; Atlantic; Esquire; Am. Heritage; N.Y. Times; Balt. Sun; Tatler; Toronto Star; Am. Lit.; Colo. Quarterly. Hons. incl: Southeastern Theatre Assn. Award, 1962; Litt.D., Univ. of Evansville, 1962; Award of Merit, Am. Assn. State & Local Hist., 1964. Address: 1326 Pickwick Pl., Bloomington, IN 47401, USA.

WILTGEN, (The Rev.) Ralph Michael, b. 17 Dec. 1921, Chicago, Ill., USA. Roman Catholic Priest; Divine Word Missionary; Journalist; Historian. Educ: Doct. Mission. Sci., Pontifical Gregorian Univ., Rome; Sems., USA. Publs: Gold Coast Mission History 1471-1880, 1956; The Rhine Flows into the Tiber: The Unknown Council, 1967, French ed., 1973; The Religious Life Defined, 1970. Contbr. to: Verbum SVD (Rome); Nouvelle Revue de science missionnaire (Switz.); Worldmission (N.Y.); New Cath. Ency. Mbrships: Société des Océanistes (Paris); Intercontinental Club (Rome). Recip., Bene Merenti Medal from Pope Pius XII, 1953. Address: Collegio del Verbo Divino, Cas. Post. 5080, 00153 Rome, Italy.

WIMSATT, William K., b. 17 Nov. 1907, Wash. DC, USA. Sterling Professor of English, Yale University. Educ: A.B. (summa cum laude), 1928, M.A., 1929, Georgetown Univ.; Ph.D., Yale Univ., 1939. Publs. incl: The Prose Style of Samuel Johnson, 1941; Philosophic Words, 1948; The Verbal Icon, 1954; The Portraits of Alexander Pope, 1965; Ed., English Stage Comedy, 1955; Co-ed., Boswell for the Defense, 1959; Ed., Explication As Criticism, 1963; Ed., The Idea of Comedy, 1969; Ed., Literary Criticism, Idea & Act, 1974. Mbrships. incl: Conn. Acad. Arts & Letters; MLA; Am. Acad. Arts & Scis. Hons. incl: 5 acad. degrees; Guggenheim Fellowship, 1946-47; Ford Fndn. Fellowship, 1953-54. Address: 80 Cold Spring St., New Haven, CT 06520, USA.

WINBERG, Anna-Greta, pen name (before 1965) PERROLF, Anna-Greta, b. 7 Dec. 1920, Stockholm, Sweden. Columnist. Publs: Dessa korta timmar, 1961; I stallet for, 1963; Na, 1965; Alska nastan, 1968; Nar nagon bara sticker, 1972; Nar nagot bara hander, 1974. Contbr. to: Husmodern. Mbrships: Bd., Swedish Union of Authors, 1964–; Soroptimist Int. Recip., King's Fndn. of Swedish Culture, 1968. Address: Ynglinga-gatan 19, 113 47 Stockholm, Sweden.

WINCEK, Marianne, b. 26 July 1931, Antonienhütte, Poland. Businesswoman. Contbr. to: Lyrik und Prosa (State Univ. N.Y., Buffalo); Stimmen (Switz.); Publikation; Rheinpfalz; Neue Westfälische; etc. Mbr,, Soc. German-speaking Authors. Address: 1 Berlin 44, Teupitzer Str. 70, W. Germany.

WINCHESTER, Clarence, pen names TANNER-RUTHERFORD, C.; ORNIS; b. 17 Mar. 1895, London,

UK. Editor. Publs. incl: Sonnets & Some Others; Aerial Photography (w. F. L. Wills); The Devil Rides High; An Innocent in Hollywood; City of Lies; The Black Poppy; A Great Rushing of Wings & Other Poems; Let's Look at London; The Captain Lost His Bathroom; Earthquake in Los Angeles; Three Men in a Plane; Ed. & Designer, The Royal Philatelic Collection; Ed., World Film Ency.; Wonders of World Engrng.; Mind & Matter; etc. Contbr. to: num. Brit. & USA periodicals. Address: 60 Jireh Court, Haywards Heath, Sussex RH16 3BH, UK.

WINDELER, Robert, b. 1943, NY, USA. Biographer; Contributing Editor, People Magazine, Time Inc.; former Correspondent, New York Times. Educ: Columbia Univ., NY; Duke Univ., Durham, NC; M.S.; B.A. Publs. (biogs.): Julie Andrews, 1970; Sweetheart: The Story of Mary Pickford, 1973. Contbr. to: Sunday Observer; Time; People; Good Housekeeping; NY Times; Life; Stereo Review. Address: 64 E. 80th St., N.Y. NY 10021, USA.

WINDER, Mavis Areta, pen names WINDER, Mavis; WYNDER, Mavis Areta, b. 21 Sept. 1907, Timaru, NZ. Novelist. Publs: 29 novels, 1949-73, inclng. Smile At the Storm, 1967; Life Is for Living, 1969; Folly Is Joy, 1973; sev. transls. into Dutch, Norwegian, French & German. Contbr. to: var. mags., UK, Aust., Can., Norway, Denmark, Finland, Netherlands & Belgium. Life/Fndr.Mbr., Romantic Novelists Assn. Address: 45 Cholmondeley Ave., Christchurch 2, New Zealand.

WINDHAM, Donald, b. 2 July 1920, Atlanta, Ga., USA. Writer. Publs: (novels) The Dog Star, USA, 1950, UK, 1951; The Hero Continues, USA & UK, 1960; Two People, USA, 1965, UK, 1966; (short stories) The Hitchhiker, Italy, 1950; The Warm Country, UK, 1960, USA, 1962; (play) You Touched Me (w. Tennessee Williams), 1957; (autobiog.) Emblems of Conduct, 1964. Contbr. to: Dance Index mag. (Ed., 1943-45); Paris Review. Recip., Guggenheim Fellowship, 1960. Address: 230 Central Pk. S., N.Y., NY 10019, USA.

WINDISCH-GRAETZ, (Princess) Mathilde, b. Prague, Czechoslovakia. Freelance Writer & Translator; Photographer. Publs: The Spanish Riding School (illustrator). Contbr. to: Connoisseur; Vogue; Homes & Gardens; Everybody's; Times; Riding. Address: 46 Roland House, Roland Gdns., London SW7, UK.

WINDROW, Martin Clive, b. 1944, Woking, Surrey, UK. Editorial Director, Alban Book Services Ltd.; Series Editor, Osprey Publishing "Men-at-Arms" Series. Educ: Wellington Coll. Publs: 7 titles, Aircraft Profile Series, 1965-67; German Air Force Fighters of the Second World War, (2 vols.) 1968 & 1970; Luftwaffe Colour Schemes & Markings 1935-1945, 1971; Ed. & Contbr., The Universal Soldier, 1971; 5 titles, Men-at-Arms Series, 1971-73; Military Dress of N. America, 1665-1970, 1973; Military Dress of the Peninsular War, 1974; Military Dress of the Hundred Days, 1975; (w. F. K. Mason): Air Facts & Feats, 1970; Know Britain, 1972; Know Aviation, 1973. Contbr. to: Mayfair; History of Aviation; Airfix; Military Modelling; Battle. Address: 40 Zodiac Ct., 165 London Rd., Croydon, Surrey CRO 2RJ, UK.

WINEGARTEN, Renee, b. 23 June 1922, London, UK. Writer. Educ: M.A., Ph.D., Girton Coll., Cambridge. Publs: French Lyric Poetry in the Age of Malherbe, 1954; Writers & Revolution: the fatal lure of action, 1974. Contbr. to: French Studies; Mod. Lang. Review; Wiener Lib. Bulletin; Commentary; Midstream; etc. Mbr., Soc. of Authors. Address: 12 Heather Walk, Edgware, Middx. HA8 9TS, UK.

WINETROUT, Kenneth, b. 8 Sept. 1912, Galion, Ohio, USA. College Professor. Educ: A.B., 1935; M.A., 1939, Ph.D., 1947, Ohio State Univ. Publs: F.C.S. Schiller & the Dimensions of Pragmatism, 1967; Arnold Toynebee: The Ecumenical Vision, forthcoming. Contbr. to: Bulletin of Atomic Scis.; Christian Century; Educl. Theory; Jrnl. of Gen. Semantics; Jrnl. of Individual Psychol. Mbrships. incl: Philos. of Educ. Soc.; Int. Soc. for Gen. Semantics. Address: 10 Hickory Lane, Hampden, MA 01036, USA.

WINFREY, Dorman H., b. 4 Sept. 1924, Henderson, Tex., USA. Librarian; Author; Editor. Educ: B.A., 1950, M.A., 1951, Univ. of Tex.; Ph.D., 1962. Publs: incl: Ed., Texas Indian Papers 1825-1916, 4 vols., 1959-61; A History of Rusk County, Texas, 1961; Julien Sidney Devereux & his Monte Verdi Plantation, 1964; The Indian Papers of Texas & the Southwest 1825-1916 (Ed., w. James M. Day), 5 vols., 1966; Arturo Toscanini in Texas: The 1950 NBC

Symphony Orchestra Tour, 1967; Gen. Ed., Presidents & Governors of Texas Series, 1969—. Contbr. to var. histl. jrnls. Hons. incl: Awards of Merit, Am. Assn. State & Local Hist., 1961, 1964. Address: 6503 Willamette Dr., Austin, TX 78723, USA.

WINGATE, John Allan, b. 15 Mar. 1920, Carbis Bay, Cornwall, UK. Author; Former Naval Officer & Schoolmaster. Educ: Royal Naval Coll., Dartmouth. Publs: Submariner Sinclair, 1959; Jimmy-the-One, 1960; Sinclair in Command, 1961; Nuclear Captain, 1962; Sub-Zero, 1963; Torpedo Strike, 1964; Never So Proud, 1966; Full Fathom Five, 1967; Last Ditch, 1970; HMS Belfast, 1972; In the Blood, 1973; Below the Horizon, 1974; 63 Bulkhead, 1975. Mbrships: Authors' Soc.; Naval Records Soc. Recip., D.S.C. Address: Rêve de Mer, Chemin des Vergers, 06610 La Gaude, France.

WINGATE (Sir), Ronald Evelyn Leslie, b. 30 Sept. 1889, London, UK. Civil Servant; Company Director. Educ: Balliol Coll., Oxford. Publs: Wingate of the Sudan, 1956; Not in the Limelight, 1959; Lord Ismay, 1966. Contbr. to: Royal United Serv. Instn. Jrnl.; Times Lit. Supplement; Quarterly Mag.; Country Life. Address: Barford Manor, Barford St. Martin, Salisbury, Wilts. SP3 4AH, UK.

WINGER, Odd Thorn, pen name OWI, b. 8 Jan 1923, Trondheim, Norway. Journalist. Educ: Coll. level (examen artium). Publs: Mot Land's End, 1953; Falsk kvartett, 1962; Novemberspill (short stories), 1965; Vinteren, 1966; Seileren, 1967; Nattegjest, 1968; Reisen (short stories), 1969; Supermarked, 1971; Bilisten (short stories), 1974; also 4 children's books. Contbr. to Dagbladet. Mbrships: Norwegian Soc. of Authors; Norwegian Press Assn. Hons: Gyldendals jubileumslegat, 1967; Olaf Schous legat, 1968; Statens stipendium, 1975. Address: Anna Rogstads vei 22, Oslo 5, Norway.

WINGFIELD DIGBY, George, b. 2 Mar. Sherbourne, Dorset, UK. Author. Keeper Emeritus, Victoria & Albert Museum. Educ: Trinity Coll., Cambridge; Univs. of Paris & Grenoble. Publs: Work of the Modern Potter in England, 1952; Meaning & Symbol in Three Modern Artists, 1955; Symbol & Image in William Blake, 1957; Elizebethan Embroidery, 1963; The Devonshire Hunting Tapestries (w. W. Hefford), 1972; Tapestries Medieval & Renaissance; (co-author) History of the West Indian Peoples, 4 vols., 1951-56; The Bayeaux Tapestry, 1957. Address: 72 Palace Gdns. Terr., London W8, UK.

WINKEL, Gary H., b. 24 Mar. 1938, Alhambra, Calif., USA. Associate Professor of Environmental Psychology. Educ: B.A., Univ. of Calif., L.A., 1960; M.S., 1963, Ph.D., 1965, Univ. of Wash. Publ: An Introduction to Environmental Psychology (co-author), 1974; Ed., Environment & Behavior, 1969—. Contbr. to: Proshansky & others (Eds.), Environmental Psychology, 1970; Anderson (Ed.), On Streets, forthcoming. Mbrships: Environmental Design Rsch. Assn. (Bd of Dirs.); Assoc., AAAS; Fellow, Am. Geogl. Soc. Address: Environmental Psychology Prog., CUNY, 33 W. 42nd St., N.Y., NY 10036, USA.

WINKLER, Judith, b. 17 May 1937, Budapest, Hungary. Journalist. Contbr. to: Ed. Staff Mbr., Haaretz Daily. Mbrships: Israeli Jrnlst. Assn.; Int. Fedn. of Jrnlsts.; Int. Assn. of Women & Home Page Jrnlsts.; Israel Rep., AIP (Int. Assn. of Jrnlsts.). Address: 39 Hamayan Str., Givatayim, Israel.

WINSTON, Brian Norman, b. 7 Nov. 1941, Evesham, UK. Television Producer. Educ: B.A. & M.A., Univ. of Oxford. Publs: Dangling Conversations Volume One — The Image of the Media, 1973; Dangling Conversations Volume Two — Hardwear, Softwear, 1974. Mbrships. incl: Standing Conf. on Broadcasting. Address: Radcot Cottage, Radcot, Clanfield, Oxford, UK.

WINSTON, Sarah, pen name LORENZ, Sarah E., b. 15 Dec. 1912, NYC, USA. Writer. Educ: N.Y. Univ., 1930-31; Barnes Fndn., Merion, Pa. Publs: And Always Tomorrow, 1963; Our Son, Ken, 1969, 1970; Everything Happens for the Best, 1969, 1970. Contbr. to: The Am. Home; Today; Phila. Inquirer Sunday Supplement. Mbrships: Nat. League Am. Pen Women; League of Women Voters (PR Chmn. 1950-51); Friends of Barnes Fndn. Hons: 1st Prizes Biennial Contests, Nat. League Am. Pen Women, 1970 & 1972; Nominee, Phila. Gimbel Award, 1972, 1973. 2 books recorded as Talking Books, Lib. of Congress. Address: 1838 Rose Tree Lane, Havertown, PA 19083, USA.

WINTER, Keith, b. 22 Oct. 1906. Novelist; Dramatist. Educ: Lincoln Coll., Oxford Univ. Publs: (novels) Other Man's Saucer; The Rats of Norway (also play); Impassioned Pygmies; (plays) Ringmaster; The Shining Hour; Worse Things Happen at Sea; Old Music; Weights & Measures; We at the Cross Roads; Miss Hallelujah; The Passionate Men; Round the Corner; (musicals) Nell; Promise You the Stars; Say When! , & Pegasus (both w. A. Goland); (films) The Red Shoes; Above Suspicion; Devotion; Uncle Harry. Address: c/o Monica McCall, Int. Famous Agcy., 1301 6th Ave., N.Y., NY 10019, USA.

WINTER, Lewis Bland, b. 1898, Chatham, Kent, UK. Retired Physiologist. Educ: Royal Mil. Acad., Woolwich; Christ's Coll., Cambridge Univ.; St. Thomas's Hosp.; M.A.; M.D. Publs: We Who Adventure, 1956; Nor They Understand, Aust., 1966. Contbr. to: Yachting Monthly; Mod. Boating. Mbrships: Physiol. Soc., UK; Soc. of Authors, UK. Address: 50 Hamilton St., Lane Cove, NSW, Australia.

WINTER, Nathan H., b. 20 Mar. 1926, NYC, USA. Educator. Educ: B.A., N.Y. Univ., 1949; B.R.E., Jewish Theol. Sem. of Am., 1951; J.D., Bklyn. Law Schl., 1954; M.A., 1955, Ph.D., 1963, N.Y. Univ. Author, Jewish Education in a Pluralist Society, 1966. Contbr. to: Ency. Judaica, Jerusalem, Israel. Mbrships: Pres., Educators Assembly, Nat. Jewish Educl. Org.; V.P., Nat. Coun. for Jewish Educ.; Bd. of Consultants, United Synagogue of Am.; Bd. of Dirs., Chmn., Jt. Personnel Comm., Am. Assn. for Jewish Educ., Nat. Coun. for Jewish Educ. & Comm. on Educ. Address: 46 Burroughs Way, Maplewood, NJ 07040, USA.

WINTER, Ruth, b. 29 May 1930, Newark, N.J., USA. Writer & Columnist. Educ: B.A., Upsala Coll., E. Orange, N.J. Publs. incl: Beware of the Foods You Eat, 1971; How To Reduce Your Medical Bills, 1972; So You Have Sinus Trouble, 1973; A Consumers Dictionary of Food Additives, 1973; So You Have A Pain In the Neck, 1974; A Consumers Dictionary of Cosmetic Ingredients, 1974; Ageless Aging, 1974. Contbr. to var. consumer mags. Mbrships. incl: Soc. of Mag. Writers; Nat. Assn. of Sci. Writers; Am. Med. Writers' Assn.; N.J. Daily Newspaper Womens' Assn. Recip., N.J. Daily Newspaper Womens' Award. Address: 44 Holly Drive, Short Hills, NJ 07078, USA.

WINTERBOTTOM, John Miall, b. 26 Aug. 1903, Cape Town, S. Africa. Ornithologist. Educ: B.Sc., Ph.D., Univ. Coll., London, UK. Publs: The Bird & its Environment, 1965; The Farmer's Birds, 1967; Some Birds of the Cape, 1969; An Introduction to Animal Ecology in Southern Africa, 1971. Contbr. to: Ibis; Ostrich; Annals of S. African Mus. Mbrships: Pres., S. African Ornithol. Soc., 1971—; F.Z.S. of London; Corres. Mbr., Brit. Ornithols. Union; Corres. Fellow, Am. Ornithols'. Union; Hon. Mbr., Societé Ornithologique de France. Hons: Gill Mem. Medal, S. African Ornithol. Soc., 1960; Sr. Scott Mem. Medal, S. African Biol. Soc., 1969. Address: 9 Alexandra Avenue, Oranjezicht, Cape Town, Repub. of S. Africa.

WINTERS, Leslie John, b. 22 June 1923, London, UK. School Music Department Head; Freelance Lecturer & Adjudicator. Educ: Univ. of London, Goldsmiths' Coll.; L.R.A.M.; A.Mus. T.C.L.; Cert. in Educ., Univ. of London. Publs: Pleasure & Practice with the Recorder, 6 books, 1963; Read & Play — A Musical Recorder Course, 2 books, 1964; The School Recorder Book of Carols, 1966; Pleasure & Practice Music Cards, 3 books, 1975. Contbr. to var. profl. jrnls. Mbrships: Inc. Soc. of Musicians; Royal Musical Assn.; Brit. Fedn. of Music Festivals; Soc. of Recorder Players. Address: 23 Mount View Rd., North Chingford, London E4 7EF, UK.

WINWARD, Walter, b. 4 Dec. 1937, Liverpool, Lancs., UK. Writer. Publs: The Success, 1967; The Conscripts, 1968; A Cat With Cream, 1970; And Cry For The Moon, 1974; Fives Wild, 1975. Contbr. to: Penthouse; Books & Bookmen; London Evening News. Address: c/o London Mgt. Ltd., 235-241 Regent St., London W1A 2JT, UK.

WIPPERSBERG, Walter J. M., b. 4 July 1945, Steyr, Austria. Author; Producer (film, theatre & radio). Educ: Univ. of Vienna. Publs. incl: In den Regen (play), 1970; In die Traufe (play), 1970; Maghreb (novel) 1970; Schlafen auf dem Wind (jvnle.), 1971; Federico: Ein Beispiel (radio drama), 1972; Der Kater Konstantin (jvnle.), 1973; Fluchtversuch (novel), 1973; Francesco (radio drama), 1973; Konstantin wird berühmt (jvnle.), 1974; Goethe live:

Ifigenie (radio drama), 1974; Wer Ohren hat (radio drama), 1974. Hons. incl: Lit. Award, Upper Austria, 1969; Film Award, Vienna, 1969; Theodor Körner Prize for Lit., 1970; Austrian State Prize for Children's Books, 1971; Children's Books Prize, Vienna, 1972. Address: A-4460 Losenstein 235, Austria.

WIRTANEN, Atos Kasimir, pen names SAWYER; FINN, Huck, MUSKETÖREN, b. 27 Jan. 1906, Saltvik, Åland, Finland. Writer. Publs. incl: Den Skapande Handen, (The Creating Hand), 1931; Kaos och Kristall (aphorisms), 1935; Stoft och Öde, 1940; Amor Fati (poems), 1943; Nietzsche den Otidsenlige (Nietzsche the Unseasonable), 1945; Tekniken, Människan, Kulturen, 1959; August Strindberg, Liv. & Dikt, in German, 1962, Scandinavian & Japanese transls.; Mot Mörka Makter (Against Dark Powers), 1963; Aforistik i Urval (selected aphorisms), 1965; Lenin, Elämä & Työ (Life & work), 1970; Poliittiset Muistelmat 1972, in Swedish, 1973. Mbrships: Assn. of Swedish Authors, Finland; Swedish Lit. Soc., Finland. Recip., Ph.D., Helsinki Univ., 1973. Address: Bergmansgatan 19 A 12, Helsinki 14, Finland.

WISBESKI, Dorothy Gross, b. 24 July 1929, Elizabeth, N.J., USA. Children's Librarian; Lecturer. Educ: B.S., Newark State Tchrs. Coll., 1950; Rutgers Univ., N.B., 1951-53; Profl. Libn.'s Permanent Cert., State of N.J., 1957. Publs: Okee, the Story of an Otter in the House, 1964; The True Story of Okee the Otter, 1967; Picaro, a Pet Otter, 1971. Mbrships: Gvng. Body, S. Bound Brook, N.J.; Councilwoman; Coun. Pres., 1975; Pres., Bd. of Dirs., Bound Brook Coop. Nursery Schl., 1971—; Asst. 4-H Club Ldr.; N.J. Lib. Assn.; N.J. Histl. Soc. Recip., Author's Award, N.J. Tchrs. of Engl., 1964, 1967. Address: 201 (Box 436) High St., South Bound Brook, NJ 08880, USA.

WISE, Charles Conrad, Jr., b. 1 Apr. 1913, Wash. D.C., USA. Attorney; Federal Administrator; Author. Educ: A.B., Geo. Wash. Univ., D.C.; J.D., Law Schl., ibid.; Master Fiscal Admin., Columbia Univ. Publs: Windows on the Passion, 1967; Windows on the Master, 1968; Ruth & Naomi, 1971. Ed., Poems of Terry Wise, 1968, 2nd ed., 1970. Contbr. to: Spiritual Frontiers; What is Meditation?, 1974. Address: Solon-Lair, Cross Keys, Penn Laird, VA 22846, USA.

WISEMAN, Adele, b. 1928, Winnipeg, Man., Can. Writer. Publs: The Sacrifice (novel), USA & UK, 1956; Old Markets, New World, Can., 1964. Hons: Beta Sigma Chi Award; Gov.-Gen.'s Award; Nat. Conf. Christian & Jews Brotherhood Award; Guggenheim Fellowship, all 1957. Address: c/o Macmillan Co. Ltd., St. Martin's House, 70 Bond St., Toronto 2, Ont., Can.

WISEMAN, Donald John, b. 25 Oct. 1918, Emsworth, Hampshire, UK. Professor of Assyriology. Educ: B.A., 1936-39, A.K.C., 1939, King's Coll., London; B.A., 1948, M.A., 1952, Wadham Coll., Oxford; D.Litt., Univ. of London, 1969. Publs: The Alalakh Tablets, 1953; Chronicles of Chaldaean Kings, 1956; Cylinder Seals of Western Asia, 1958; Vassal-Treaties of Esarhaddon, 1958. Contbr. to: Anatolian Studies; Ed., Iraq; Jrnl. of Nr. Eastern Studies; Sumer; Ency. Britannica. Mbrships: Fellow, Soc. of Antiquaries; Dir., British Schl. of Archaeol., Iraq, 1961-65; Chmn., ibid., 1970—; Fellow, British Acad., 1966. Address: 16 Downs Rd., Cheam, Sutton SM2 7EQ, Surrey, UK.

WITCHELL, Nicholas Newton Henshall, b. 23 Sept. 1953, Cosford, UK. Journalist. Educ: LL.B., Leeds Univ. Publs: The Loch Ness Story, 1974. Contbr. to Mayfair Mag. Mbr., Nat. Union of Jrnlsts. Address: 10 Wallace Fields, Epsom, Surrey KT17 3AT, UK.

WITHAM, W(illiam) Tasker, b. 20 May 1914, Worcester, Mass., USA. Educator. Educ: B.A., Drew Univ., 1936; M.A., Columbia Univ., 1940; Ph.D., Univ. of Ill., 1961. Publs: Americans As They Speak & Live, 1945; Panorama of American Literature, 1947; Living American Literature, 1947; The Adolescent in the American Novel, 1920-60, 1964, rev., 1975. Contbr. to: Am. Lit.; Annual Bibliography of English Lang. & Lit. Mbrships: Modern Humanities Rsch. Assn.; MLA of Am.; Midwest MLA. Address: Dept. of English & Journalism, Ind. State Univ., Terre Haute, IN 47809, USA.

WITT, Harold (V.), b. 6 Feb. 1923, Santa Ana, Calif., USA. Writer. Educ: B.A., B.L.S., Univ. of Calif., Berkeley; M.A., Univ. of Mich. Publs: Family in the Forest, 1956; Superman Unbound, 1956; The Death of Venus, 1958;

Beasts in Clothes, 1961; Winesburg by the Sea: A Preview, 1970; Pop. by 1940: 40,000, 1971; Now, Swim, 1974; Surprised by Others at Fort Cronkhite, 1975. Contbr. to: New Yorker; Poetry; New Repub.; Nation; N.Y. Times; Kenyon, Hudson, Paris, Saturday Reviews; Poetry Northwest; etc. Mbrships: Poetry Soc. of Am.; Int. Poetry Soc. Hons. incl: Emily Dickinson Award, Poetry Soc. of Am., 1972; Poet Lore Descriptive Poetry Award, 1974. Address: 39 Claremont Ave., Orinda, CA 94563, USA.

WITTKOFSKI, Joseph Nicholas, b. 9 Sept. 1912, Findlay, Ohio, USA. Clergyman; Psychotherapist. Educ: St. Joseph's Coll., Ind.; B.A., St. Gregory's Sem., Cinn., Ohio; Maryknoll Sem., N.Y.; Univ. of Ill.; M.S., Fordham Univ., N.Y. Publs: Pittsburgh Catechism, 1945; The Secret Way, 1949; Little Book of Contemplation, 1950; Unity in Faith, 1953; The Pastoral Use of Hypnotic Technique, 1960, 2nd ed., 1971; Faith for Living, 1971. Contbr. to: The Living Ch.; The Christian Challenge; Am. Ch. News; etc. Address: 509 6th St., Charleroi, PA 15022, USA.

WITTON-DAVIES, Carlyle, b. 10 June 1913, Bangor, Caern., UK. Archdeacon of Oxford & Canon of Christ Church. Educ: B.A., Coll. of N. Wales; M.A., Exeter Coll., Oxford; Cuddesdon Coll., ibid.; Hebrew Univ., Jerusalem, Israel. Publs: Journey of a Lifetime, 1962; Trans., Martin Buber's The Prophetic Faith, 1949. Contbr. to: The Mission of Israel, 1963; Oxford Dict. of the Christian Church, 2nd ed., 1974; Theol.; Jrnl. of Theol. Studies. Mbrships: Soc. of O.T. Study; Chmn., Exec. Comm., Coun. of Christians & Jews. Address: Archdeacon's Lodging, Christ Ch., Oxford, UK.

WIT-WYROSTKIEWICZ, Boguslaw-Wladyslaw, pen name WIT, b. 9 Dec. 1946, Olkusz, Kraków, Poland. Writer. Educ: M.Phil. Publs: Podróz Do Verony (poetry), 1974; Smierc Victoria Yarry W Santiago (poetry), 1974; Spotkanie Z Melpomena (theatre essays), 1974. Contbr. to: Kierunki; Za i Przeciw; Polish Radio. Mbrships: Lit. Club, Zakopane; Polish Podhalan Men's Socs. Recip., Lit. Award, Int. Folk Festival. Address: Harenda 52, Zakopane 34-506, Poland.

WOELFEL, Ursula, b. 16 Sept. 1922, Duisburg-Hamborn, Germany. Writer. Educ: Germanic Studies & Education. Publs: Fliegender Stern, 1959; Feuerschuh und Windsandale, 1962; Mond Mond Mond, 1962; Joschis Garten, 1965; 27 Suppengeschichten, 1968; 28 Lachgeschichten, 1969; Die grauen und die grünen Felder, 1970; Du wärst der Pienek, 1973; 29 Verrückte Gechichten, 1974. Mbr., PEN. Hons: German Children's Book Award, 1962; Hans Christian Andersen Award Honour List, 1964 & 1972; Austrian Sponsorship in Children's Literature, 1972. Address: Rodensteiner Weg 10, 6101 Brandau-Neunkirchen/Odenwald, W. Germany.

WOETZEL, Robert Kurt, b. 5 Dec. 1930, Shanghai, China. University Professor & Foundation President; Author. Educ: B.A., Columbia Univ., 1952; Ph.D., Oxford Univ., UK, 1958; LL.D., Univ. of Bonn, W. Germany, 1959. Publs. incl: The Nuremberg Trials in International Law, 1960, 2nd ed., 1962; The Philosophy of Freedom, 1966, 3rd ed., 1969; Toward a Feasible International Criminal Court, 1970; The Establishment of an International Criminal Court, 1973. Contbr. to: Saturday Review of Lit.; Guardian; Economist; Criminal Law Review; Int. Rels.; World Today; Pilot; Boston Globe; San. Fran. Chronicle; etc. Address: Harlaxton House, 286 Central St., Auburndale (Newton), MA 02166, USA.

WOJTASIEWICZ, Olgierd Adrian, b. 11 Dec. 1916, Kielce, Poland. Research Worker; University Professor. Educ: LL.M., 1938, M.A., 1939, Ph.D., 1951, Warsaw Univ. Publs. incl: Introduction to Translation Theory, 1957; var. papers on linguistics; var. transls. from Chinese classical & mod. lit.; transls. from Engl. drama & lit., inclng. The Family Reunion by T. S. Eliot, This Way to the Tomb by Ronald Duncan; transls. of sci. books from Polish into Engl. Mbrships: Union of Polish Writers; PEN; Authors' Assn. ZAIKS; Polish Oriental, Linguistic, Cybernetic, Semiotic, Sociol. Socs. Address: Hoza 5/7 m. 31, 00-528 Warsaw, Poland.

WOLANIN, Sophie Mae, b. 11 June 1915, Alton, Ill., USA. Educator; Scholar; Civic Worker; Senior Secretary, Financial Company. Educ: Cert., Secl. Sci., 1946; B.S.c., Bus. Admin., 1948; Univ. of S.C. Contbr. to: Commercial Ldr. & S. Bergen Review, N.J.; Ldr.-Free Press; N. Arlington Ldr. & Bergen Sunday Ldr.; Oakland News, Pitts., Pa.; Pittsburczanin; Assoc. Ed., WCC News,

Westinghouse Credit Corp. Mbrships. incl: Univ. of S.C. Alumni Assn.; Life Mbr., AAUW; Am. Acad. Pol. & Soc. Sci.; Anglo-Am. Histl. Soc.; Int. Platform Assn.; UN Assn. of USA. Hons. incl: PhD., Bus. Admin., Colo. State Christian Coll., 1972; Woman of Yr., Bus. & Profl. Women's Club, Pitts., 1972; Nat. Register Prominent Ams. & Int. Notables, 1973; Women's Hall of Fame, Seneca Falls, N.Y.; Nat. Advsry. Bd., Am. Security Coun., Wash. D.C.; Life Mbr., Acad. Pol. Sci., Columbia Univ., N.Y.; Life Mbr., Am. Counselors' Soc.; num. biog. listings. Address: 5223 Smith-Stewart Rd., S.E., Girard, OH 44420, USA.

WOLANOWSKI, Lucjan Wilhelm, b. 26 Feb. 1920, Warsaw, Poland. Writer. Educ: Univ. of Grenoble, France; US State Dept. Schlrship., Prog. for Ldrs., 1965. Publs. incl: As Far As We Can, 1959; The Goddess's Mirror, 1961; Crown Jewels, 1963; Farther Than Beyond, 1964; Babs Over the Pole (children's book), 1964; The Never-Never Postman, 1968; Breathtaking Reports, 1969; Heat & Fever, 1973; Longing After Lapu-Lapu, 1973. Contbr. to: Swiat; Dookola Swiata; Przekroj; etc. Mbrships. incl: PEN; Union of Polish Writers; Polish Jrnlsts. Assn. Hons: Best Reporting Award, Polish Jrnlsts. Assn., 1963; Polish Book of Yr. Award, 1973. Address: ul. Odolanska 23m.9, 02-562, Warsaw, Poland.

WOLF, Edmund, b. 23 Apr. 1910, Vienna, Austria. Playwright. Educ: LL.D., Dr.Pol. Econs., Univ. of Vienna; Grad., Max Reinhardt Acad. of Dramatic Arts, Vienna. Publs: (plays) Musik im Hof, 1932; Kleines Leben, grosse Liebe, 1935; Guardian Angel, 1938; Augen der Liebe, 1947; Wisely Wanton (Zwei zu dritt, 1950); Raübergeschichte (Pas moral pour deux sous), 1953; (TV film documentary) Auserwählt in Jerusalem. Contbr. to: Suddeutsche Zeitung, Munich; Die Zeit, Hamburg; Monat, Germany. Address: 17 Gardnor Mansions, Church Row, London NW3, UK.

WOLF-CATZ, Helma, b. 31 May 1900, Nieuw-en St. Joosland, Middelburg, Netherlands. Novelist; Essayist. Publs: (novels) De Dreiging, 1946, revised ed., 1965; Diepzee, 1960 & Luchtkristal, 1967, first & last novels in 7 novel cycle; (histl. novel) De vrÿheid is een nachtegaal in zilvergrÿs, 1971; (essays) Kastelen, hun personages, hun schatten, 1965; Kleine geschiedenissen van grote Kastelen, 1975. Contbr. to: Ons Erfdeel mag.; Amersfoortse Courant; Veluws Dagblad; etc. Mbrships: PEN; Union Dutch Authors; Soc. Dutch Lit. Hons. incl: ANWB Prize, 1966. Address: In de Zwaantjes, Fortlaan 22, Bussum, near Amsterdam, Netherlands.

WOLFCATZ, Loeka, b. 16 Dec. 1930, Amsterdam, Netherlands. Author of juvenile literature; Reviewer. Publs: Carina, 1968; Helma Wolf-Catz (essay), 1969; Adventures at Berestein, 1967; Adventure with a Flemish Master, 1971. Contbr. to: Nieuwe Apeldoornse Courant. Mbr., Union of Authors. Address: Fortlaan 22, Bussum, Netherlands.

WOLFE, Bernard, b. 28 Aug. 1915, New Haven, Conn., USA. Screenwriter. Educ: B.A., Yale Univ., 1935. Publs: (non-fiction) Plastics: What Everyone Should Know, 1945; Hypnotism Comes of Age (w. R. B. Rosenthal), 1948; (novels) Really the Blues (w. M. Mezzrow), USA, 1946, UK, 1947; Limbo, USA, 1952 (as Limbo 90, UK, 1953); The Late Risers, 1954; In Deep, USA, 1957, UK 1958; The Great Prince Died, USA & UK, 1959; The Magic of their Singing, 1961; Come on Out, Daddy, 1963; Move Up, Dress Up, Drink Up, Burn Up, 1968. Address: c/o Eliot Gordon Co., 8888 Olympic Blvd., Beverly Hill, CA, USA.

WOLFE, Gene, pen name COPPERFIELD, David, b. 7 May 1931, NYC, USA. Journalist. Educ: B.S.M.E., Univ. of Houston, 1956; Tex. A & M; Miami Univ. Publs: Operation Ares, 1970; The Fifth Head of Cerberus, 1972; Peace, 1975. Contbr. to: Orbit; Universe; Analog; Galaxy; The Mag. of Fantasy & Sci. Fiction; Worlds of If. Mbr., Am. Soc. of Bus. Press Eds. Recip., Nebula Award, 1973. Address: Box 69, Barrington, IL 60010, USA.

WOLFF, Geoffrey, b. 5 Nov. 1937, L.A., Calif., USA. Novelist. Educ: A.B., Princeton Univ., N.J., 1961; Churchill Coll., Cambridge Univ., UK, 1963-64. Publs: Bad Debts, 1969; The Sightseer, 1974. Contbr. to: Lit. Ed., New Times, 1974; Books Ed., Newsweek, 1969-71; Book Ed., Wash Post, 1965-69; Atlantic Monthly; New Repub.; New Ldr.; Life; Time; N.Y. Times Book Review; Mademoiselle; Saturday Review; Book Week; Book World; L.A. Times; Am. Schlr. Mbrships: PEN; Coffee House. Hons: Woodrow Wilson Schlr., 1961-62; Fulbright Schlr., 1963-64; Guggenheim Fellow, 1972-73; Sr. Fellow, Nat. Endowment for the Humanities, 1974-75. Address: Prickly Mountain, Warren, VT 05674, USA.

WOLFF, Robert Paul, b. 27 Dec. 1933, NYC, USA. Professor of Philosophy. Educ: A.B., Harvard, 1953; A.M., 1954; Ph.D., 1957. Publs: Kant's Theory of Mental Activity, 1963; A Critique of Pure Tolerance (w. B. Moore & H. Marcuse), 1965; The Poverty of Liveralism, 1968; The Ideal of the University, 1969; In Defense of Anarchism, 1970; The Autonomy of Reason, 1973. Contbr. to Nation; New Repub.; Bull. of Atomic Scis.; N.Y. Times Book Review. Mbrships: Am. Philos. Assn.; Am. Soc. of Legal & Pol. Philos. Address: 26 Barrett Place, Northampton, MA 01060, USA.

WOLFF, Sula (Mrs. Henry Walton), b. 1 Mar. 1924, Berlin, Germany. Child Psychiatrist; Author; Translator. Educ: M.A., B.M., B.Ch., Oxford Med. Schl.; Inst. of Psych., Maudsley Hosp., London. Publs: Transl., A Short History of Psychiatry, 1959, 2nd ed., 1971; Children Under Stress, 1969, 2nd ed., 1973. Contbr. to var. profl. jrnls. on psych. & child psych. Address: 38 Blacket Place, Edinburgh EH9 1RL, UK.

WOLFF, Victoria, pen name MARTELL, Claudia, b. 10 Dec. 1909, Heilbronn, Germany. Writer. Educ: B.A., Univs. of Heidelberg & Munich. Publs. incl: The White Evening Dress; And Seven Shall Die; Fabulous City; Brainstorm. Contbr. to: Weltwoche, Zurich; Madame, Munich; Bild & Funkm ibid. Mbrships: PEN; World Affairs Club; Hollywood For. Press Assn. Address: 911 Schumacher Drive, L.A., CA 90048, USA.

WOLFF, William Deakin, pen name MARTINDALE, Spencer, b. 1902, London, UK. Writer. Publs: Lambeth Streets, 1934; Colours & Windows (poems), 1951; (as S. Martindale) The Sunlit Child, 1956; Hilda, 1958; Betty & Julia, 1961. Contbr. to: Poetry Review; Acct. Mbrship: Fellow, Inst. Chartered Accts. Address: 85 Malden Hill, New Malden, Surrey, KT3 4DS, UK.

WOLFFENBUTTEL-VAN ROOIJEN, Hendrina Johanna Maria, b. 17 Aug. 1901, Delft, Netherlands. Teacher; Author. Educ: Tchrs. Cert. Publs. incl: Biblical History, An Introduction to Bible Reading for the Family, 2 vols., 1950, revised 10th ed., 1962; (novels) Life is an Adventure; Southern Blood; Happiness is No News; The Merchant Woman (originally The Syrian), 1973; num. children's books, radio & theatre plays. Contbr. to lit. jrnls. Mbr., Union Authors. Address: Vliegerweg 7, Culemborg, Netherlands.

WOLFGANG, Marvin E., b. 14 Nov. 1924, Millersburg, Pa., USA. University Professor of Sociology & Law. Educ: A.B., Dickinson Coll., 1948; M.A., 1950, Ph.D., 1955, Univ. of Pa. Publs: Patterns in Criminal Homicide, 1958; The Measurement of Delinquency, 1964; Crime & Race, 1964; 1970; The Subculture of Violence, 1967; Crime & Culture, 1968; Delinquency in a Birth Cohort, 1972. Contbr. to var. profl. jrnls. Mbrships: Pres.. Am. Acad. of Pol. & Social Sci., Am. Soc. of Criminol. Address: Univ. of Pa., Ctr. for Studies in Criminology & Criminal Law, 3718 Locust St., Phila., PA 19174, USA.

WOLPERT, Roland Howard, b. 30 Dec. 1923, Bklyn., N.Y., USA. Television Writer; Former Journalist. Educ: B.B.A., CCNY; advanced writing course, Am. Theatre Wing Profl. Trng. Prog., Columbia Univ. Writes both comedy & drama. Teleplays shown in over 70 countries. Contbr. to: The Protectors (creator); The Bold Ones; World Premiere Movie — Deadlock; ABC Movie of the Week — But I Don't Want to Get Married; Circle Films — Thriller; num. series. Mbrships: Writers Guild of Am.; Dramatists Guild; Authors League of Am.; Am. Newspaper Guild. Address: c/o Writers Guild of Am., W., Inc., 8955 Beverly Blvd., CA 90048, USA.

WOLRIGE GORDON, Anne, b. 16 Oct. 1936, London, UK. Writer. Publs: Peter Howard, Life & Letters, 1969, German transl., 1971, French transl., 1973; Blindsight, 1970; Dame Flora, 1974. Address: Ythan Lodge, Newburgh, Aberdeenshire, AB4 0AD, UK.

WOLSAK-EIJBERGEN, Wilhelmina, pen name FREEZER, Harriet, b. 9 Nov. 1911, The Hague, Netherlands. Journalist; Writer. Educ: Acad. of Arts, The Hague. Publs: Luchtkasteel op Poten, 1952; Brieven aan een Grote Dochter, 1962; Wat doe je? O niks, 1965; Houd je nog een beetje van me? , 1971; Het Onderste uit de Man, 1972; De Vrouw in de Middenleeftijd, 1974. Contbr. to

newspapers & jrnls. Mbrships: Lit. Soc., Amsterdam; Utrecht Provincial Assn. of Arts & Scis. Recip., Prize for transl. of book by Roald Dahl. Address: Vermeerlaan 31, Bilthoven, Netherlands.

WOLSELEY, Roland Edgar, b. 9 Mar. 1904, NYC, USA. Teacher. Educ: B.S., M.A., Northwestern Univ. Publs. incl: Exploring Journalism (co-author), 1943, 3rd ed., 1957; Journalism in Modern India (Ed. & Contbr.), 1953, 2nd ed., 1964; Face to Face with India, 1954; Understanding Magazines, 1965, 2nd ed., 1969; The Low Countries, 1969; The Black Press, USA, 1971; The Changing Magazine, 1973. Contbr. to: Nation; Saturday Review; S. Atlantic Quarterly; etc. Mbrships: Pres., Assn. for Educ. in Jrnlsm.; Authors' League of Ctrl. N.Y. Hons. incl: D.Litt., Albright Coll., 1955; Frank Luther Mott Award, 1971. Address: 1307 Westmoreland Ave., Syracuse, NY 13210, USA.

WOLTERS, Oliver William, b. 8 June 1915, Reading, UK. Professor of Southeast Asian History, Cornell University. Educ: B.A., Oxford Univ., 1937; Ph.D., Univ. of London, 1962. Publs: Early Indonesian Commerce. A Study of the Origins of Srivijaya, 1967; The Fall of Srivijaya in Malay History, 1970. Contbr. to: Jrnl. of The Royal Asiatic Soc.; Bulletin of the Schl. of Oriental & African Studies. Mbrships. incl: Royal Asiatic Soc., London; Soc. Asiatique, Paris; Trustee, Breezewood Fndn., Md., USA. Recip., O.B.E., 1952. Address: 112 Comstock Rd., Ithaca, NY 14850, USA.

WONG, Lai Chuen, b. 24 Apr. 1922, Canton, China. Lecturer. educ: B.A. Publs: Sun Yat-Sen & Hong Kong, 1966; Youth Today, 1972; Shout, 1972. Contbr. to: Youth Today Mag. (Chief Ed.); The Kung Kwa Po & Wah Kiu Yat Po. Mbr. of PEN. Address: 22 Reservoir Road 3/F, Room 302 Shun Fung Lau, Aberdeen, Hong Kong.

WONNACOTT, Ronald Johnston, b. 11 Sept. 1930, London, Ont., Can. Professor of Economics. Educ: B.A., 1955; Univ. of Western Ont., A.M., 1957; Ph.D., 1959; Harvard Univ., USA. Publs. incl: Canadian American Dependence: An Interindustry Analysis of Production & Prices, 1961; Free Trade Between U.S. & Canada (w. Paul Wonnacott), 1967; Introductory Statistics (w. T. H. Wonnacott), 1969; *Econometrics (w. T. H. Wonnacott), 1970. Contbr. to: Jrnl. of Pol. Econ.; Can. Jrnl. of Econs. & Pol. Sci.; Atlantic Community Quarterly; Can. Public Policy-Analyse de Politiques; etc. Mbr., var. profl. assns. Recip., var. fellowships. Address: 171 Wychwood Park, London, Ont., Can.

WOOD, Charles Gerald, b. 6 Aug. 1932, St. Peter Port, Guernsey, UK. Dramatist; Screenwriter. Educ: Birmingham Coll. of Art. Publs. incl: (plays) Cockade, 1964; Fill the Stage with Happy Hours, 1967; Dingo, 1967; H, 1970; Veterans, 1972; Death or Glory Boy, 1975; (films) The Knack; Help; How I Won the War; Long Day's Dying; The Charge of the Light Brigade; Bed Sitting Room; The Merry Widow; Tartar Steppe. Mbrships. incl: Soc. of Authors; Radiowriters' Assn. Hons: London Mag., Evening Standard Drama Awards, 1963; Screenwriters' Guild Award, 1965; Evening Standard Drama Award, 1972. Address: "Horseshoes", Epwell, Banbury, Oxon., UK.

WOOD, Charles Tuttle, b. 29 Oct. 1933, St. Paul, Minn., USA. Professor of Medieval History. Educ: A.B., 1955, A.M., 1957, Harvard Coll.; Ph.D., 1962. Publs: The French Apanages & the Capetian Monarchy 1224-1328, 1966; Philip the Fair & Boniface VIII, 1967, 2nd ed., 1971; The Age of Chivalry, 1970, in USA as The Quest for Eternity, 1971. Contbr. to: Am. Histl. Review; Speculum; Traditio; Hist. & Theory; French Histl. Studies; Studia Gratiana. Address: 7 N. Balch St., Hanover, NH 03755, USA.

WOOD, David, b. 21 Feb. 1944, Sutton, UK. Actor; Writer; Composer. Educ: B.A., Worcester Coll., Oxford. Publs: (musical plays for children), The Owl & the Pussycat Went to See . . . (w. Sheila Ruskin), 1970; The Plotters of Cabbage Patch Corner, 1972; Flibberty & the Penguin, 1974; Hijack Over Hygenia, 1974; The Papertown Paperchase, 1974; Larry the Lamb in Toytown (w. Sheila Ruskin), 1975. Contbr. to: Drama. Mbrships: Soc. of Authors; Brit. Actors Equity Assn.; Green Room Club. Address: c/o Fraser & Dunlop Ltd., 91 Regent St., London W1, UK.

WOOD, Fergus James, b. 13 May 1917, London, Ont., Can. Research Associate (Geophysics); Scientific Writer & Editor. Educ: A.B., Univ. of Calif., Berkeley, USA, 1938; postgrad. studies, Univ. of Calif., 1938-39, Yerkes Observ.,

Univ. of Chgo., 1939-40, Univ. of Mich., 1940-42, & Calif. Inst. of Technol., 1946. Publs: Ed.-in-Chief, vols. 1 & 2A, & Sci. Coord., vols. 2B 2C & 3, The Prince William Sound, Alaska, Earthquake of 1964 & Aftershocks, 1966-69; The Strategic Role of Perigean Spring Tides in Nautical History & North American Coastal Flooding, 1635-1975, 1975; also documentary film scripts. Contbr. to num. encys. & ref. works. Hons. incl: Special Achievement Award for Sci. Writing, U.S. Dept. of Commerce, 1970. Address: 10408 Sweetbriar Pkwy., Silver Spring, MD 20903, USA.

WOOD, Lorna, b. 16 June 1913, Pex Hill, Lancs., UK. BBC Monitor. Publs. incl: The Crumb-Snatchers; Gilded Sprays; The Hopeful Travellers; (books for children) The "Hag Dowsabel" books; Holiday on Hot Bricks; The Handkerchief Man; The Golden-Haired Family; The Dogs of Pangers; Pangers Pup. Contbr. to: Sunday Times; Lady; Homes & Gardens; Woman; etc. Mbr., Soc. of Authors. Address: c/o Williams & Glyn's Bank, Market Sq., Reading, Berks., UK.

WOODALL, Stella, b. 15 Jan. 1899, Hillsboro, Tex., USA. Author; Poet; Historian; Biographer. Publs. incl: Women of the Bible; Lectures on St. John; Lectures on St. Paul; (poetry) Most Asked For Poems; Inspirational Poems; Golden Treasures; An Adventure in Friendship. Ed. & Publr., Adventure in Poetry Mag.; Tex. Ed., Poet; Ed., Anthol. of Tex. Poems; Contbr. to var. lit. jrnls. Mbrships: Nat. VP, Am. Poetry League; Pres., Stella Woodall Poetry Soc., San Antonio Br., Nat. League of Am. Pen Women. Hons: Poet Laureate of Tex. (Alt), 1973; Poet Laureate Int., 1974; Litt.D., 1974. Address: 3915 SW Military Drive, San Antonio, TX 78211, USA.

WOODBERRY, Joan Merle, b. 10 Feb. 1921, Narrabri, NSW, Australia. Author. Educ: B.A(Hons.), Dip.Ed., Sydney; B.Ed., Melbourne; M.A., Tasmania. Publs: Ash Tuesday, 1968; Little Black Swan; The Cider Duck; A Garland of Gannets; Come Back Peter; "Rafferty" series; Historic Hobart; Andrew Bent. Mbrships: Aust. Jrnlsts. Assn.; Writers Fellowship. Hons: Children's Book of Yr. Award, 1962; Players' Award, 1967; Woman of Distinction Award, 1973. Address: 657 Nelson Rd., Mt. Nelson, Tasmania, Australia 7007.

WOODCOCK, George, b. 8 May 1912, Winnipeg, Man., Can. Writer. Educ: Morley Coll., London. Publs: Anarchism, 1962; Faces of India, 1963; The Crystal Spirit, 1966; Proudhon, 1966; Canada & the Canadians, 1970; Odysseus Ever Returning, 1970; Herbert Read, 1972; The Rejection of Politics, 1972; Who Killed the British Empire? , 1974; & 30 more anthols. & books of hist., biog., travel, criticism, verse. Contbr. to: Encounter; Commentary; Sewanee Review; Nation; Canadian Lit. (Ed.); etc. Mbrships. incl: Fellow, Royal Soc. Can.; Fellow, Royal Geogl. Soc. Hons. incl: D.Litt., Universite d'Ottawa; Gov-Gen's. Award Lit., 1966; Molson Prize, 1973. Address: 6429 McCleery St., Vancouver, B.C. V6N 1G5, Can.

WOODHAM-SMITH, Cecil C., Writer. Educ: M.A., St. Hilda's Coll., Oxford. Publs: Florence Nightingale, 1950; Lonely Crusader, 1951; Lady in Chief, 1953; The Reason Why, 1954; The Great Hunger, 1962; Queen Victoria: Her Life & Times, vol. 1 (1819-61), 1972. Hons: C.B.E.; James Tait Black Mem. Prize, 1950; D.Litt.; LL.D.; A.C. Benson Medal, 1969. Address: 44 Mount St., London W1, UK.

WOOD-LEGH, Kathleen-Louise, b. 2 Sept. 1901, Ont., Can. University Teacher of History. Educ: B.A., McGill Univ.; M.A., St. Hilda's Coll., Oxford, UK; B.Litt., Ph.D., Litt.D., Newnham Coll., Cambridge. Publs: Studies in Church Life in England Under Edward III, 1934; A Small Household of the XVth Century, 1956; Perpetual Chantries in Britain, 1965. Contbr. to: Engl. Histl. Review; Cambridge Histl. Jrnl. Mbrship: Fellow, Royal Histl. Soc. Hons: Leverhulme Award, 1946; acad. hons. Address: 49 Owlstone Rd., Cambridge CB3 9JH, UK.

WOODROOF, Horace Malcolm, b. 17 Nov. 1906, Nashville, Tenn., USA. Writer. Publs: Stone Wall College, 1970. Contbr. to var. newspapers. Bd. Mbr., Nashville Chapt., 7th Step Fndn. Honored as Mbr. of Gold Star Club, formed by The Tennessean to honor three-star forum letter writers for three consecutive yrs., 1973. Address: 108 Monticello Ave., Madison, TN 37115, USA.

WOODROOF, Jasper Guy, b. 23 May 1900, Mountville, Ga., USA. Food Scientist (Distinguished Professor Emeritus); Horticulturist. Educ: B.S.A., 1922, M.S.A., 1926, Univ. of Ga.; Univ. of Calif.; Ph.D., Mich. State Univ., 1932. Publs: Peanuts: Production, Processing, Products, 1967, 2nd ed., 1974; Tree Nuts: Production, Processing, Products. Vol. I, 1967, Vol. II, 1968; Coconuts: Production, Processing, Products, 1970; Beverages: Carbonated & Non-Carbonated, 1974; Commercial Fruit Processing, 1975; over 200 Tech. Rsch. Reports. Contbr. to: World Review Nutrition & Dietetics, 1969; var. profl. jrnls. Mbrships incl: Fellow, AAAS; Ga. Writers Assn. Recip., var. Disting. Serv. Awards. Address: Route 5 Box 220, Griffin, GA 30233, USA.

WOODRUFF, Michael Francis Addison, b. 3 Apr. 1911, London, UK. Professor of Surgery. Educ: D.Sc., M.D., M.S., Queen's Coll., Melbourne Univ., Aust. Publs: Deficiency Diseases in Japanese Prison Camps (w. A. Dean Smith), 1951; Surgery for Dental Students, 1954; The Transplantation of Tissues & Organs, 1960. Contbr. to: Transplantation; Brit. Jrnl. of Cancer; Lancet; etc. Mbrships. incl: F.R.S.; F.R.C.S.; Brit. Assn. for Cancer Rsch. (Pres.); Int. Transplantation Soc. (Past Pres.); Am. Surgical Assn. Recip., Lister Medal, Royal Coll. of Surgeons, 1969. Address: The Bield, 506 Lanark Rd., Juniper Green, Midlothian EH14 5DH, UK.

WOODS, Alvin Edwin, b. 17 Mar. 1934, Murfreesboro, Tenn., USA. Biochemist. Educ: B.S., 1956, Middle Tenn. State Univ; M.S., 1958, Ph.D., 1962, N.C. State Univ. Publs: Food Chemistry, 1973. Contbr. to: Biochem.; Biochem. & Biophys. Rsch. Communications; Clin. Chem.; Diseases of the Nervous System; Atomic Absorption Newsletter; Jrnl. of Dairy Sci. Mbrships. incl: Fellow, Am. Inst. of Chems.; Am. Chem. Soc. Address: Dept. of Chem., Middle Tenn. State Univ., Murfreesboro, TN 37130, USA.

WOODS, Clee, pen names FOREST, Lee; PARK, D. U.; WARBRIDGE, C. W., b. 20 Sept. 1893, Sandstone, W. Va., USA. Writer. Educ: A.B., Univ. of Denver, 1924. Publs. incl: Buckaroo Clan of Montana, 1935; Rebels Rendezvous, 1936; Riders of the Sierra Madre, 1937; Luis Terrazas, World's Greatest Cattleman (biog.), 1975. Contbr. to num. mags. Mbr., Western Writers of Am. Hons. incl: 1st Prize, Colo. Mag. contest, 1950. Address: 1303 Quincy St. N.E., Albuquerque, NM 97110, USA.

WOODWARD, C. Vann, b. 13 Nov. 1908, Vanndale, Ark., USA. Historian. Educ: Ph.B., Emory Univ., 1930; M.A., Columbia Univ., 1932; Ph.D., Univ. of N.C., 1937. Publs: Tom Watson: Agrarian Rebel, 1938; The Battle for Leyte Gulf, 1947; Reunion & Reaction, 1951; Origins of the New South, 1951; The Strange Career of Jim Crow, 1955; The Burden of Southern History, 1960; American Counterpoint, 1971. Contbr. to var. jrnls. Mbrships: Pres., Am. Histl. Assn., 1969, Org. of Am. Histns., 1968-69. Hons: LL.D., Univ. of Mich., 1971; D.Litt., Princeton Univ., 1971; L.H.D., Columbia Univ., 1972; D.Litt., Cambridge Univ., 1975. Address: 83 Rogers Rd., Hamden, CT 06517, USA.

WOODWARD, Ian (Denzil William), b. 29 June 1941, Brecon, UK. Writer; Critic; Broadcaster. Educ: B.A., London Univ. Publs: Birds in the Garden, 1963; Caring for Cage Birds, 1964; Balletgoing, 1967, Am. ed., 1968; Ballet & the Dance, 1967, Dutch ed., 1968; Lives of the Great Composers, Books 1 & 2, 1969; Ballet, 1969; Clowns & Clowning, 1975; Lives of the Great Composers, Book 3, 1975; Teach Yourself Ballet, 1975. Contbr. to books & jrnls., incing: Viewpoints for Secondary Schools, 1975; The Guardian; The Sun; London Evening News; TV Times; Radio Times; The Christian Science Monitor. Mbrships. incl: Nat. Union Jrnlsts. Agent: Mrs. Doreen Montgomery, Rupert Crew Ltd., London. Syndication agent: Miss Hally Sorauer, 10 W. Drive Gdns., Harrow Weald, Middx. HA3 6TT, UK. Address: 19 Gallows Hill, Hunton Bridge, King's Langley, Herts. WD4 8PG, UK.

WOODWARD, Ralph Lee, Jr., b. 2 Dec. 1934, New London, Conn., USA. Historian. Educ: A.B., Ctrl. Coll., Fayette, Mo., 1955; M.A., 1959, Ph.D., 1962, Tulane Univ., New Orleans. Publs: Class Privilege & Economic Development: The Consulado de Comercio of Guatemala, 1793-1871, 1966; Robinson Crusoe's Island: A History of the Juan Fernandez Islands, 1969; Positivism in Latin Am., 1850-1900, 1971; Central America, A Nation Divided, 1975. Contbr. to: Hispanic Am. Histl. Review; Jrnl. of Inter-Am. Studies; etc. Mbrships: Gen. Comm., Conf. on Latin Am. Hist., Am. Histl. Assn. Address: Dept. of Hist., Tulane Univ., New Orleans, LA 70118, USA.

WOOLF, Dennis, b. 10 Nov. 1934, London, UK. Television Writer, Producer & Director. Educ: B.A.,

Brasenose Coll., Oxford. Publs: num. progs. for World In Action; (TV plays) Harold Was Alright, 1963, Virginia, 1964, Goodbye, That's All, 1967; Happy Days Are Here Again, 1971. Mbrships: Writers' Guild of GB; Assn. of Cinematograph TV & Allied Technicians; Soc. of Film & TV Arts. Address: 169 Didsbury Rd., Stockport, Cheshire, UK.

WOOLF, Douglas, b. 23 Mar. 1922, NYC, USA. Freelance Writer; Itinerant Worker. Educ: Harvard Univ., 1939-42; A.B., Univ. of N.M., 1950. Publs: (novels) The Hypocritic Days, 1955; Fade Out, USA, 1959, UK, 1968; Wall to Wall, 1962; John-Juan, Japan, 1967; Ya! & John-Juan, 1971; The Spring of the Lamb, 1972; (short stories) Signs of a Migrant Worrier, 1965. Address: P.O. Box 215, Tacoma, WA, USA.

WOOLF, Harry, b. 12 Aug. 1923, NYC, USA. University Provost. Educ: B.S., 1948, M.A., 1949, Univ. of Chgo.; Ph.D., Cornell Univ., 1955. Publs: The Transits of Venus, 1959; Quantification: Essays in the History of Measurement in the Natural & Social Sciences, 1961; Science as a Cultural Force, 1964. Contbr. to: ISIS; Sci.; Am. Sci.; Am. Histl. Review; Colloquia Copernicana; etc. Mbrships: incl: Deleg., Univs. Rsch. Assn., 1973—; Advsry. Coun., Schl. Adv. Int. Studies, Wash. DC, 1973—; Advsry. Bd., Smithsonian Rsch. Awards, ibid, 1975—; Am. Histl. Soc., 1971—; Fellow, Royal Astonl. Soc.; VP, AAAS, 1960, Fellow, 1960—; Hist. of Sci. Soc., 1956—. Hons. Phi Beta Kappa; Phi Alpha Theta; Sigma Xi. Address: 1904 Sulgrave Ave., Baltimore, MD 21209, USA.

WOOLLEY, Richard Van Der Reit, b. 24 Apr. 1906, Weymouth, UK. Astronomer. Educ: Sc.D., Cambridge Univ., UK. Publs: Eclipses of the Sun & Moon (w. F. W. Dyson); The Outer Layers of a Star (w. D. W. N. Stibbs). Contbr. to: Royal Observatory Bulls.; Monthly Notices of the Royal Astronomical Soc. Recip., Gold Medal, Royal Astronomical Soc. Address: S.A. Astronomical Observatory (CSIR), Observatory Cape, S. Africa.

WORBOYS, Annette Isobel, pen names EYRE, Annette; MAXWELL, Vicky, b. Auckland, NZ. Novelist. Publs: 20 romantic, 3 suspense novels, 1961-74 inclng: The Lion of Delos; The Way of the Tamarisk, 1975. Contbr. to var. popular mags. Mbrships: Crimewriters' Assn.; Soc. of Women Writers & Jrnlsts.; Romantic Novelists Assn.; Tunbridge Wells & Dist. Writers' Circle. Hons: Runner-up for Best Romantic Novel of Yr. Award, for The Magnolia Room, 1972. Address: The White House, Leigh, Nr. Tonbridge, Kent TN11 8RH, UK.

WORCESTER, Donald Emmet, b. 29 Apr. 1915, Tempe, Ariz., USA. Professor of History. Educ: B.A., Bard Coll., 1939; M.A., 1940, Ph.D., 1947, Univ. of Calif. at Berkeley. Publs: The Growth & Culture of Latin America (co-author), 1956, new ed., 1970-71; Sea power & Chilean Independence, 1962, Spanish ed., 1971; The Three Worlds of Latin America, 1963; American Civilization (co-author), 1964, new ed., 1968; The Makers of Latin America, 1966; Brazil: From Colony to World Power, 1973. Contbr. to: N.M. Histl. Review; Pacific Histl. Review; Fla. Histl. Quarterly; Ariz. & the West; other histl. & western jrnls. Mbrships. incl: Western Writers of Am. (Pres., 1973-74). Western Hist. Assn. (Pres., 1974-75). Address: Rt. 2 Box 61, Aledo, TX 76008, USA.

WORDEN, Alastair Blair, b. 12 Jan. 1945, Cambridge, UK. University Teacher. Educ: M.A., D.Phil.(Oxon), St. Edward's Schl., Oxford; M.A., Ph.D.(Cantab.), Pembroke Coll., Oxford, 1963-66. Author, The Rump Parliament 1648-1653, 1974. Mbrships: Rsch. Fellow, Pembroke Coll., Cambridge, 1969-72; Fellow of Selwyn Coll., Cambridge, 1972-74. Address: St. Edmund Hall, Oxford, UK.

WORMELL, Peter Royaon, b. 28 June 1928, Colchester, Essex, UK. Journalist; Farmer; Broadcaster; Public Relations Officer. Publs: History of West Bergholt, 1946. Contbr. to: Essex Co. Standard (Agricl. Corres. 1954—); Arable Farming (regular page); Big Farm Mgmt.; Euro Farm Bus.; Farm; Modern Farmer; Fin. Times; E. Anglian Daily Times; others. Mbrships. incl: Guild of Agricl. Jrnlsts.; Farmers' Club, London (Chmn., Jrnl. & publicity Comm.); N. Essex Engl. Speaking Union (Chmn.). Address: Langenhoe Hall, Colchester, Essex, UK.

WORMSER, Richard Edward, pen name FRIEND, Ed, b. 30 Jan. 1908, NYC, USA. Educ: Princeton Univ., N.J. Publs: Pass Through Manhattan, 1940; The Lonesome Quarter, 1950; Battalion of Saints; The Yellowlegs, 1966; &

about 60 crime stories, 1933-1973; (juvenile) Ride a Northbound Horse, 1964; The Kidnapped Circus, 1968; Gone to Texas, 1970; The Black Mustanger. Contbr. to: Saturday Evening Post; Wall St. Jrnl.; etc. Mbrships. incl: Santa Cruz Valley (Ariz.) Art Assn., 1974-75. Hons. incl: Western Heritage Award for Best Juvenile Western of Yr., 1971, for The Black Mustanger. Address: Box 1314, Tubac, AZ, USA.

WORNER, Philip Arthur Incledon, pen names INCLEDON, Philip; SYLVESTER, Philip, b. 30 Jan. 1910, Southampton, UK. Tutor. Educ: Univ. of Southampton; M.A., Oxon. Publs: Freedom is My Fame, 1942; The Cactus Hedge, 1951; The Calling of Wenceslas, 1960; Wrack, 1971. Contbr. to: Worcester Evening News; BBC broadcasts. Mbrships: Royal Soc. of Lit.; Soc. of Authors; Lib. Assn.; A.T.C.D.E.; Hon. V.P., Worcester Writers Circle. Address: The Rookery, 216 Henwick Rd., Worcester, UK.

WORNUM, Miriam, pen name DENNIS, Eve, b. 1898, San Fran., Calif., USA. Painter; Writer. Publs: Star Dust; (as E. Dennis) Death for Safety, 1948; Portrait in the Dark, USA & UK, 1950; An Embroidery & Other Poems, 1961 (also Dutch transl.). Contbr. to num. mags. & tech. books. F.R.S.A. Address: 1020 Green St., San Fran., CA 94133, USA.

WORRALL, Ralph Lyndal, b. 7 Apr. 1903, Sydney, Australia. Medical Practitioner. Educ: M.B., Ch.M., Sydney, 1926; D.P.H., UK, 1946. Publs: Footsteps of Warfare, 1936; The Outlook of Science, 2nd ed., 1946; Energy & Matter, 1948. Contbr. to: News Review, London, 1944-45; Woman's Weekly, Sydney, 1946-47. Mbrships: Fellow, Royal Soc. of Med.; Inst. of Biol.; Soc. of Authors. Address: 31 Braeside Ave., Sevenoaks, Kent, UK.

WORSLEY, Eleanor Edith Joan, b. 7 Feb. 1909, Kent, UK. Playwright. Publs: Black Feathers, 1970; The Proxy, 1972 (one-act plays). Contbr. to: (short stories) Katawakes; (poems) All People are Poets, vol. 3; Hyacinths & Biscuits, USA. Mbr., Nat. Playwrights' Assn. Hons: 2nd Prize, Drama Competition, Ifield Theatre Club, Sussex, 1969, for Black Feathers; Green Room Trophy Cup, St. Helier, Jersey, 1971. Address: 5 Vincent Rd., Dorking, Surrey, UK.

WORTHINGTON, Edgar Barton, b. 13 Jan. 1905, London, UK. Biologist. Educ: M.A., Ph.D., Cambridge Univ. Publs: Inland Waters of Africa (co-author), 1932; Science in Africa, 1937; Middle East Science, 1946; Life in Lakes & Rivers (co-author), 1951, 2nd ed., 1972; Science in the Development of Africa, 1950, French ed., 1960; The Evolution of the International Biological Programme, 1975. Contbr. to var. mags., reviews, etc. Mbrships: F.L.S.; F.Z.S.; F.R.G.S.; F.R.S.A.; F.Inst.Biol.; Athenaeum Club. Hons: Mungo Park Medal, Royal Scottish Geogl. Soc., 1939; C.B.E., 1966. Address: Colin Godmans, Furners Green, Nr. Uckfield, Sussex, UK.

WORTHY, Brian Johnson, pen name JOHNSON, Brian, b. 5 Mar. 1933, Hartlepool, UK. Education Officer. Educ: M.A., Clare Coll., Cambridge; Univ. Coll., Durham. Publs: The Long March Home, 1975. Mbr., Soc. of Educ. Offs. Address: 20 Cortland Rd., Nunthorpe, Cleveland.

WOSORNU, Lade, b. 24 Mar. 1937, Galo, Volta Region, Ghana. Surgeon; Senior Lecturer, Ghana Medical School. Educ: M.B., Ch.B., 1963, M.D. 1972, Glasgow Univ., F.R.C.S. (Edinburgh), 1966; F.R.C.S. (England), 1966. Publs: Some Common Diseases of the Human Body: Aspects of Health Education for Everyman, forthcoming. Contbr. to: Ghana Med. Jrnl.; Tropical Doctor. Mbrships: Ghana Med. Assn. (past Sec.-Gen.); other profl. assns., UK & W. Africa. Recip., Brunton Mem. Prize, 1963. Address: 40 Slater Ave., Korle Bu, Accra, Ghana.

WOUK, Herman, b. 27 May 1915, NYC, USA. Novelist; Dramatist. Educ: A.B., Columbia Univ., 1934. Publs. incl. (novels): Aurora Dawn, 1947; The City Boy, 1948; The Caine Mutiny, 1951; Young Blood Hawke, 1963; Don't Stop the Carnival, 1965; The Winds of War, 1972; (drama): The Traitor, 1949; The Caine Mutiny Court Martial, 1953; Nature's Way, 1957. Mbrships: Coun., Author's Guild, USA; Author's League; Dramatist's Guild. Hons. incl: Pulitzer Prize for Fiction, 1952; Columbia Univ. Medal for Excellence, 1952. Address: c/o Harold Matson Co. Inc., 22 E. 40th St., N.Y., NY 10016, USA.

WRANGLÉN, Karl Gustaf (Gösta), b. 19 Mar. 1923, Orebro, Sweden. University Professor. Educ: Chem. Eng., 1947, Dr. Eng., 1950, Royal Inst. of Technol., Stockholm;

Dr. Techn., 1955. Publs: Studies on the Growth Form & Structure of Electrodeposited Metals, 1955; Metallers Korrosion och Ytskydd, 1967; Korrosionslära, 1967; An Introduction to Corrosion & Protection of Metals, 1972. Mbrships: Pres., 1975-76, Int. Soc. of Electrochemistry; Advsry. Editl. Bds., Electrochimica Acta, Corrosion Sci. & Jrnl. of Applied Electrochemistry. Address: Dept. of Electrochem. & Corrosion Sci., Royal Inst. of Technol., S-100 44 Stockholm, Sweden.

WREDE, (Baroness) Renata, b. 6 Sept. 1923, Helsinki, Finland. Artist (Painter). Educ: Royal Acad. of Fine Arts, Copenhagen, Denmark. Publs: Mitt Romerska Lejon (My Roman Lion), 1971, Engl., Norwegian & Finnish transls.; Juvelskrinet (The Jewel Casket), 1973. Mbr., Soc. of Swedish Authors in Finland. Recip., Award, Svenska Litteratursällskapet i Finland, 1972. Address: Emmeholm, S 291 69 Kristianstad 12, Sweden.

WRIGHT, Celeste Turner, b. 17 Mar. 1906, St. John, N.B., Can. Professor of English; Poet. Educ: A.B., UCLA, 1925; M.A., Univ. of Calif., Berkeley, USA, 1926; Ph.D., 1928. Publs: Etruscan Princess & Other Poems, 1964; A Sense of Place, 1973. Contbr. to: Poetry; Harper's; Yale Review; PMLA; Mod. Philol.; Philol. Quarterly; Jrnl. of Engl. & Germanic Philol.; Studies in Philol.; 20th Century Fiction. Mbrships: Poetry Soc. Am.; MLA. Hons. incl: Reynolds Lyric Prize, 1963; C'wlth. Club of Calif. Silver Medal, one of four best books by Calif. authors in 1973, 1974. Address: 1001 D. St., Davis, CA 95616, USA.

WRIGHT, Charles (Stevenson), b. 4 June 1932, New Franklin, Mo., USA. Freelance Writer. Publs: (novels) The Messenger, 1963, UK, 1965; The Wig, USA, 1966, UK, 1969; Black Studies, 1972. Contbr. to: Best Negro Short Stories, 1968; Village Voice (Columnist). Address: c/o Farrar, Straus & Giroux, 19 Union Sq. W., N.Y., NY 10003, USA.

WRIGHT, Esmond, b. 5 Nov. 1915, Newcastle-on-Tyne, UK. University Professor. Educ: M.A., Univ. of Durham, UK; M.A., Univ. of Va., USA. Publs: Washington & the American Revolution, 1957; Fabric of Freedom, 1961; Benjamin Franklin & American Independence, 1966; Ed., Causes & Consequences of the American Revolution, 1966. Mbrships: Chmn., Brit. Assn. for Am. Studies, 1965-68; Fellow, Royal Histl. Soc. Address: Inst. of U.S. Studies, 31 Tavistock Sq., London WC1, UK.

WRIGHT, Frederick Richard, b. 1894, London, UK. Extension Lecturer, Surrey University, Guildford. Educ: Selwyn Coll., Cambridge; Ripon Hall, Oxford; M.A.(Cantab). Publs: Parallels of Power, 1966; Edward Heath & his Predecessors; Ed. & Contbr., Local History: Oxted & Limpsfield. Contbr. to: Oxted & Limpsfield Review; Surrey Mirror. Co-Fndr., Oxted & Dist. Histl. Soc., 1960. Recip., O.B.E. Address: Midway, 13 Gresham Rd., Limpsfield, Oxted, Surrey RH8 0BS, UK.

WRIGHT, Judith Arundell (Mrs. J. McKinney), b. 31 May 1915, Armidale, NSW, Australia. Writer. Publs: The Generations of Men (biog. novel), 1955; Preoccupations in Australian Poetry (criticism), 1964; The Nature of Love (short Stories), 1966; (verse) The Moving Image, 1946; Woman to Man, 1950; The Gateway, 1953; The Two Fires, 1955; Birds, 1960; Five Senses, 1963; The Other Half, 1966; Collected Poems, 1971; also 4 books for children, critical essays & monographs. Alive, 1972. Contbr. to: var. anthols., mags., reviews, etc. Coun. Mbr., Aust. Soc. of Authors. Hons: Grace Leven Prizes, 1951, 1972; Ency. Britannica Writers' Award, 1964. Address: Long Rd., North Tamborine, Queensland, Australia.

WRIGHT, Lionel Percy, pen name WRIGHT, Lan, b. 8 July 1923, Watford, UK. Purchasing Manager. Publs: Who Speaks of Conquest, 1958; A Man Called Destiny, 1961; Dawns Left Hand, 1962; Spaceborn, 1964; The Creeping Shroud, 1966; Assignment Luther, 1967; A Planet Called Pavanne, 1968. Contbr. to: New Worlds Mag.; Nabula Mag.; S.F. Adventure Mag.; Sci. Fantasy Mag. Mbrships: F.R.S.A.; Inst. of Purchasing & Supply. Address: 15 Park Lane, Colney Heath; St. Albans, Herts., UK.

WRIGHT, Margaret Anne, b. 2 Aug. 1925, Wellington, NZ. School Teacher. Educ: Trained Tchrs.' Cert., Wellington Tchrs.' Coll.; Vic. Univ. Contbr. to: NZ Schl. Publs. Bulletin for Primary Schls.; Ed., Women's Sect., Straight Furrow, Federated Farmers of NZ, 8 yrs.; NZ Countrywoman; NZ Home Jrnl.; Eve; NZ Weekly News; NZ Broadcasting Serv.; Te Aho. Mbrships: NZ Women Writers'

Soc.; Women's Div., Federated Farmers NZ; Country Women's Inst. of NZ. Hons. incl: 1st Pl., Catherine Mitchell Educl. & Cultural Soc. Essay, 1967; 1st Pl., Assoc. Country Women of the World Int. Essay, 1974. Address: Schoolhouse, Wainuiomata, Wellington, NZ.

WRIGHT (The Very Rev.), Ronald (William Vernon) Selby, b. 12 June 1908, Glasgow, UK. Minister; A Chaplain of HM The Queen. Educ: Melville Coll.; M.A., D.D., Edinburgh Univ. Publs: Asking Them Questions — 1, 2, 3 & Selection, 1936-53; Asking Them Questions — New Series, 1972-73; Fathers of the Kirk, 1960; A Manual of Church Doctrine (w. T. F. Torrance), 1960; Take Up God's Armour, 1967; The Kirk in the Canongate, 1956, 2nd ed., 1958; Several Volumes of Broadcast Talks, 1942-70; Our Club, 1954, 2nd ed., 1969. Contbr. to: Chambers Ency.; Oxford Dictionary of Christian Ch.; Ed., Scottish Forces Mag. Address: Manse of the Canongate, Edinburgh EH8 8BR, UK.

WULFF, Michael, b. 4 Apr. 1940, Hamburg, Germany. Writer. Educ: Univ., (thesis for Ph.D. in progress). Publs: (poetry) Dichtung, 1975; (essays) Der Umgang mit Alkoholikern. Wie Sollen sich die Mitmenschen des Alkoholikers verhalten?, 1975. Contbr. to: German, Austrian Radio & TV (ORF); Lit. & Criticism to: Die Horen; Das Pult; Podium; Neue Wege; Anthols.; also exhibs. visual poetry; etc. Mbrships: German Authors' Assn. (VS); Lit. Ctr. Inc., Hamburg; Democratic Cultural League of W. Germany (Lit. Sect.). Address: 2 Hamburg 13, Grindelhof 73, W. Germany.

WURLITZER, Rudolph G., b. 3 Jan. 1937, Cinn., Ohio, USA. Writer. Educ: Columbia Univ. Publs: (novels) Nog, 1968; Flats, 1970; Quale, 1972; (screenplays) Two Lane Blacktop, 1971; Pat Garrett & Billy The Kid, 1973. Contbr. to: Examine; Atlantic Monthly; Paris Review; Rolling Stone; News Republic. Mbr., PEN. Recip., 1st Prize, Short Story Contest, Atlantic Monthly, 1967. Address: 234 E. 23rd St., N.Y., NY 10010, USA.

WURM, Franz, b. 16 Mar. 1926, Prague, Czech. Writer. Educ: B.A., Queen's Coll., Oxford, UK. Publs: Anmeldung, 1959; Anker und Unruh, 1964; Břehy v zádech (selected poems), 1974; Elder Without Susanna/Bad ohne Susanna, 1975; transl.: Gedichte/Schriften zur bildenden Kunst by René Char, 1963; Hypnos by René Char, 1963; Die fixe Idee, by Paul Valéry, 1965; Der Aufrechte Gang, by M. Feldenkrais, 1969. Contbr. to: Neue Rundschau (Berlin); Spektrum (Zurich); Nachlese (Basle); Revue de Belles-Lettres (Geneva); num. other jrnls. throughout Europe. Mbrships: PEN; SDS, Zurich. Recip., Ehrengabe der Stadt Zurich, 1964. Address: Promenadengasse 12, 8001 Zurich, Switz.

WYATT, Rachel Evadne, b. 14 Oct. 1929, Bradford, UK. Writer. Publs: The String Box, 1970; about 14 radio plays prod. by CBC. Contbr. to: Chatelaine; Punch; The Guardian; num. other mags. & newspapers. Mbrships: Assn. of TV & Radio Artists; Can. Authors' Assn.; Writers' Union of Can. Address: Apt. 805, Mackenzie House, 3460 Simpson St., Montreal 139, P.Q., Can.

WYBOURNE, Brian Garner, b. 5 Mar. 1935, Morrinsville, NZ. Professor of Physics. Educ: M.Sc.; Ph.D. Publs: Spectroscopic Properties of Rare Earths, 1965; Symmetry Principles & Atomic Spectroscopy, 1970; Classical Groups for Physicists, 1974. Contbr. to: Jrnl. of Math. Phys.; Phys. Review; Int. Jrnl. of Quantum Chem.; etc. Mbrships: Fellow, Royal Soc. of NZ. Recip., Hector Medal, 1970. Address: Phys. Dept., Univ. of Canterbury, Christchurch, NZ.

WYKES, Alan, b. 21 May 1914, Wallington, Surrey, UK. Author; Journalist. Publs. incl: Pursuit Till Morning; The Music Sleeping; The Brabazon Story (co-author); Mariner's Tale; Snake Man; Nimrod Smith; The Royal Hampshire Regiment; A Sex By Themselves; Party Games; Gambling; The Great Yacht Race; The Nuremberg Rallies; Hitler; Himmler; Heydrich; Hitler's Bodyguard; Goebbels; Lucretia Borgia; Doctor Cardano; The Turning Point; Abroad; The Doctor & His Enemy; An Eye on the Thames; The Horse in History. Contbr. to: Assoc. Newspapers; Evening Standard; Times; Spectator; Sunday Times; British History Illustrated; etc. Address: 382 Tilehurst Rd., Reading, Berks. RG3 2NG, UK.

WYLIE, Laurence William, b. 19 Nov. 1909, Indpls., Ind., USA. University Professor. Educ: A.B., 1931, A.M., 1933, Ind. Univ.; Ecole Libre des Scis. Politiques, 1929-30;

Ph.D., Brown Univ., 1940; Publs: Saint-Marc Girardin, Bourgeois, 1947; Village in the Vaucluse, 1957; In Search of France (co-author), 1963; Chanzeaux, Village of Anjou (co-author), 1965; Deux Villages, 1970; Les Français (co-author), 1970; France: The Events of May-June 1968, A Critical Bibliography, 1973; A Repertory of French Gestures (film), 1974. Contbr. to jrnls. Mbr., profl. orgs. Recip., acad. hons. Address: 1540 William James Hall, Harvard Univ., Cambridge, MA 02138, USA.

WYMAN, Walker DeMarquis, b. 7 Dec. 1907, Danville, Ill., USA. Teacher; Author. Educ: B.Ed., Ill. State Univ.; M.A., Ph.D., Univ. of Iowa. Publs. incl: The Wild Horse of the West, 1945, 4th ed., 1972; California Emigrant Letters, 1952; Nothing But Prairie & Sky, 1954, 2nd ed., 1970; The American Adventure (w. M. Ridge), 1964; Ed., History of the Wisconsin State Universities, 1968; The Lumberjack Frontier, 1969; Frontier Woman, 1972; Charles Round Low Cloud (w. W. Clark), 1972; History of the Chippewa, forthcoming. Contbr. to histl. mags. Hons. incl: Selection of The Lumberjack Frontier by Am. Lib. Assn. & Engl. Speaking Union, 1969. Address: 415 Crescent St., River Falls, WI 54022, USA.

WYND, Oswald, pen name BLACK, Gavin, b. Tokyo, Japan. Novelist. Educ: Edinburgh Univ. Publs. incl: 14 novels as Oswald Wynd; 10 novels as Gavin Black; transl. of num. books & short stories in ten langs. Contbr. to: New Statesman; Spectator; Satevepost; Argosy; Woman's Day; Good Housekeeping; etc. Mbrships: Soc. of Authors; PEN; Crime Writers' Assn. Recip., Doubleday novel prize, 1947. Address: St. Adrian's Crail, Fife KY10 3SU, UK.

WYNDHAM, Lee, b. 16 Dec. 1912, Melitople, Russia (US citizen, 1942-). Author; Lecturer; Consultant. Publs: over 50 books inclng. On Your Toes Susie! series, 1953-61; Binkie's Billions, 1954; Gamel Bird Ranch, 1955; Candy Stripers, 1958; The Timid Dragon, 1960; The Little Wise Man (w. Robert Wyndham), 1960; Chip Nelson & the Contrary Indians, 1960; Thanksgiving, 1963; Ed., Chinese Mother Goose Rhymes (w. R. Wyndham), 1968; Writing for Children & Teenagers, 1968, revised eds., 1972, 1974; The Winter Child, 1970; Tales the People Tell in Russia, 1970; Holidays in Scandinavia, 1975. Contbr. to: Phila. Inquirer (Book Critic); N.Y. World-Telegram & Sun; Morris Co.'s Daily Record; var. nat. mags. Mbrships. incl: Soc. of Children's Book Writers; Authors' Guild. Address: Blackwell Ave., Morristown, NJ 07960, USA.

WYNN, Dale Richard, b. 20 Nov. 1918, Derry, Pa., USA. College Professor of Education. Educ: B.S., 1939, M.A., 1946, Bucknell Univ., Lewisburg, Pa.; Ed.D., Columbia Univ., N.Y., 1952. Publs. incl: Careers in Education, 1960; Organization of Public Schools, 1964; Elementary School Administration & Supervision (w. W. Elsbree & H. McNally), 3rd ed., 1967; American Education, 7th ed., 1972. Contbr. to num. educl. publs. Mbrships: Chmn., Comm. for the Advancement of Schl. Admin., Am. Assn. of Schl. Admstrs., 1970-73; Sec.-Treas., Nat. Conf. of Profs. of Educl. Admin., 1954-58. Address: 4514 Bucktail Drive, Allison Park, PA 15101, USA.

WYNN, Daniel Webster, b. 19 Mar. 1919, Wewoka, Okla., USA. Clergyman; Educator. Educ: B.A., Langston Univ., Okla., 1941; B.D., 1944, M.A., 1945, Howard Univ., Wash. D.C.; Ph.D., Boston Univ., Mass., 1954. Publs: The NAACP Versus Negro Revolutionary Protest, 1955; The Chaplain Speaks, 1956; Moral Behavior & the Christian Ideal, 1961; Timeless Issues, 1967; The Black Protest Movement, 1974; The Protestant Church Related College, 1975. Contbr. to: Ency. of Black Am., 1974; Interpreter Mag.; Jrnl. of Relig. Thought; Relig. Educ. Mag. Mbrships: Am. Educ. Assn.; Nat. Assn. of United Meth. Colls. & Univs. Recip., Hon. D.D., Eden Theol. Sem., Webster Groves, Mo., 1959. Address: 3926 Drakes Branch Rd., Nashville, TN 37218, USA.

WYNNE-TYSON, Timothy Jon Lynden, b. 1924, Brockhurst, Hants., UK. Publisher; Journalist. Publs. incl: Accommodation Wanted; Square Peg; Don't Look & You'll Find Her; The Civilised Alternative; Food for a Future. Contbr. to: Observer; Sunday Times; Times Lit. Supplement; Spectator; Time & Tide; Tribune; New Statesman; Poetry Review; Apollo; Country Life; etc. Mbr., Nat. Book League. Address: Paddocks, Fontwell, Sussex, UK.

WYTRWAL, Joseph Anthony, b. 24 Oct. 1924, Detroit, Mich., USA. High School Administrator & Principal; Editor; Columnist. Educ: Ph.B., 1949, M.Ed., 1950, Univ. of

Detroit; M.Ed., 1954, B.A., 1957, Wayne State Univ.; M.A., 1955, Ph.D., 1958, Univ. of Mich. Publs: American's Polish Heritage, 1961; Poles in American History & Tradition, 1969; Poles in America, 1969. Contbr. to: Polish Am. Studies; Congressional Record; Ga. Histl. Quarterly; etc. Mbrships: Polish Am. Histl. Assn.; Detroit Schoolmen's Club. Hons: Coe Fellowship Award, Univ. of Wyo., 1958; Am. Heritage Award, Chgo. Div., Polish Am. Congress. Address: 5695 Lumley St., Detroit, MI 48210, USA.

Y

YAFFE, James, b. 31 Mar. 1927, Chicago, Ill., USA. Writer. Educ: B.A., Yale Univ. Publs: Poor Cousin Evelyn & Other Stories, 1951; (novels) The Good-for-Nothing, 1953; What's the Big Hurry? , 1954; Nothing But the Night, 1957; Nobody Does You Any Favors, 1966; Mister Margolies, 1962; The Voyage of the Franz Joseph, 1970; (non-fiction) The American Jews, 1968; So Sue Me! , 1972; (plays) The Deadly Game, 1960; Ivory Tower (w. Jerome Weidman), 1966. Contbr. to: Atlantic Monthly; Esquire; Saturday Review. Mbrships: PEN; Writers: Guild Am.; Authors League; Am. Assn. Univ. Profs. Recip., Nat. Arts Fndn. Award, 1966. Address: 1215 N. Cascade, Colo, Springs, CO, USA.

YAGI, Kyohei, b. 3 Oct. 1922, Tokyo, Japan. Journalist. Educ: Grad., Tokyo Univ., 1950. Publs: Price Mechanism of Japan, 1964; British Way of Life, 1973. Contbr. to Yomiuri Shinbun. Address: No. 9-9, 5-Chome Shimoigusa, Suginami-Ku, Tokyo, Japan.

YAMASAKI, Takeo, pen name SHIBUKAWA, Gyô, b. 1 Mar. 1905, Honami-mura, Kaho-gun, Fukuoka-ken, Japan. Novelist; Critic; Professor. Educ: Tokyo Univ. Publs: Tarukiriko (Lake Tarukiri), 1940; Gicho Socrates (The Chairman Socrates), 1965; Kurohae (Black South Wind), 1966. Contbr. to: Shincho; Tenbo; Umi. Mbrships: Writers' Assn. Japan (Nihon Bungeika Kyokai); PEN. Address: 5-12-16 Naritahigashi, Suginami-ku, Tokyo, Japan.

YAP, Diosdado Maurillo, pen name DOC, b. 5 Dec. 1907, Baybay, Philippines. Editor & Publisher. Educ: B.S., 1930, Ill. Inst. of Technol., Chgo., USA; M.A., 1932, Geo. Wash. Univ.; M.S., 1933, Nat. Univ., Wash. DC., LL.B., 1943, Southern Univ., Wash. DC, Ph.D., 1934, Webster Univ., Atlanta, Ga. Publs: History of Higher Education in the Philippines; Secondary in the Philippines; What Now for Free China?, Filipinos in America; Author, Ed., Publr., Know Your Congress, & Our Nation's Capitol. Contbr. to: Manila Chronicle; Philippines Free Press; Jrnl. of Commerce; & other jrnls. Mbrships. incl: White House Press Assn.; Am. Acad. of Pol. & Soc. Sci. Recip., LL.D., Southeastern Univ. Address: 5306 Belt Rd. N.W., Chevy Chase, Wash. DC 20015, USA.

YARROW, Arnold, b. 17 Apr. 1920, London UK. Television Script Writer. Publs: Softly Softly Casebook, 1973; Softly Softly Murder Casebook. Mbr., Soc. of Authors. Address: 23 Craven Cottages, Hofland Rd., London W14 0LN, UK.

YARSHATER, Ehsan Ollah, pen name RAH-SEPAR, b. 3 Apr. 1920, Hamadan, Persia. Teacher; Editor; Researcher. Educ: Lic., Persian Lit., 1941, Law, 1944, Univ. of Tehran, Iran; D.Litt., 1947; M.A., Univ. of London, UK, 1951; Ph.D., 1960. Publs. incl: Persian Poetry in the 15th Century, 1955; A Grammar of Southern Tati Dialects, 1969. Ed., Theorems & Remarks (Avicenna), 1954; Iran Faces the Seventies, 1971. Contbr. to var. lit. publs. Mbrships: Am. Oriental Soc.; Royal Asiatic Soc.; Pres., Book Soc. of Persia, 1957—. Hons: Royal Prize for best book of Yr., Tehran, 1959; UNESCO Award, 1961. Address: 450 Riverside Drive, N.Y., NY 10027, USA.

YARWOOD, Doreen, b. 12 Dec. 1918, London, UK. Author; Artist. Educ: Hammersmith Schl. Arts & Crafts, London, 1934-36, Clapham Schl. of Art, 1936-39, Inst. of Educ., Univ. of London, 1939-40. Publs: English Costume,

1952, 4th ed., 1972; Outline of English Costume, 1967, 3rd ed., 1972; The English Home, 1956; English Houses, 1966; The Architecture of England, 1963, 2nd ed., 1967; Outline of English Architecture, 1965; The Architecture of Italy, 1970; Robert Adam (biog.), 1970; The Architecture of Europe, 1974; European Costume, 1975. Contbr. to: Tchrs. World. Mbrships. incl: Costume Soc.; Soc. of Authors; Assn. Art Histns. Address: 65 York Ave., East Sheen, London SW14 7LQ, UK.

YATES, Richard, b. 3 Feb. 1926, Yonkers, N.Y., USA. Assistant Professor of English. Publs: (novels) Revolutionary Road, USA, 1961, UK, 1962; A Special Providence, 1969; (short stories) Eleven Kinds of Loneliness, USA, 1962, UK, 1963; Ed., Stories for the Sixties, 1962. Hons: Guggenheim Fellowship, 1962; Grant, Nat. Inst. Arts & Letters, 1963; Creative Arts Award, Brandeis Univ., 1964; Grant, Nat. Fndn. on Arts, 1966; Rockefeller Grant, 1967. Address: 3827 E. 25th North, Wichita, KS 67221, USA.

YATES, William Edgar, b. 30 Apr. 1938, Hove, Sussex, UK. Professor of German. Educ: B.A., 1961, M.A., 1965, Ph.D., 1965, Emmanuel Coll., Cambridge Univ. Publs: Grillparzer, A Critical Introduction, 1972; Nestroy, Satire & Parody in Viennese Popular Comedy, 1972; Contbr., The Penguin Companion to Literature, vol. 2, 1969; Das Grillparzer-Bild des 20. Jahr-hunderts, 1972; Theater und Gesellschaft. Das Volksstück im 19. und 20. Jahr-hundert, 1973. Contbr. to: Mod. Lang. Review; Maske und Kothurn; Forum for Mod. Lang. Studies; etc. Mbrships. incl: Mod. Humanities Rsch. Assn. Recip., Schlrship. 1955, Cambridge Univ. Address: 7 Clifton Hill, Exeter EX1 2DL, UK.

YEGANEH, Mohammed, b. May 1923, Zandjan, Iran. Economist. Educ: B.A., Law, 1945, B.A., Econs., 1946, Tehran Univ.; M.A., Columbia Univ., N.Y., USA, 1950. Publs: Perspectives decennales des developpements economiques en Tunisie, 1960; Economics & the Middle Eastern Oil (w. Charles Issawi), 1962. Contbr. to: Middle E. Jrnl.; Econ. Rsch. Bulletin, Tehran Univ. Mbrships: UN Advsry. Comm. on Application of Sci. & Technol. to Dev.; Bd. of Trustees, Reza Shah Kabir Univ., Iran; Chmn., High Coun. of Agricl. Dev., Bank of Iran. Hons: Homayoon Medal, 1966; Dev. Medal, 1967; Homayoon Medal, 1974. Address: Central Bank of Iran (Bank Markazi Iran), Ferdowsi Ave., Tehran, Iran.

YELDHAM, Peter, b. 25 Apr. 1927, Gladstone, N.S.W., Australia. Playwright. Plays: Birds on the Wing, 1969-70; She Won't Lie Down, 1972; Fringe Benefits (co-author), 1973; Away Match (co-author), 1974. Feature Films incl: The Comedy Man, 1963; The Liquidator, 1965; Age of Consent, 1968. TV Plays incl: Reunion Day; Stella; Thunder on the Snowy; East of Christmas; The Cabbage Tree Hat Boys. Contbr. to num. Brit. TV series. Mbrships: Writers Guild of Gt. Brit. (exec. coun. 1972—); Aust. Writers Guild; Savage Club. Recip., Merit Award for Brit. TV series, 1962. Address: The Oaks, Ashtead Woods Rd., Ashtead, Surrey, UK.

YELLEN, Samuel, b. 7 July 1906, Vilna, Lithuania. Professor of English Literature. Educ: B.A., Western Reserve Univ., 1926; M.A., Oberlin Coll., 1932. Publs: American Labor Struggles, 1936; In the House & Out, & Other Poems, 1952; The Passionate Shepherd: A Book of Stories, 1957; The Wedding Band. A novel, 1961; New & Selected Poems, 1965; The Convex Mirror: Collected Poems, 1971. Contbr. poems, stories & sketches to var. periodicals. Mbrships. incl: PEN. Hons. incl: Daroff Mem. Fiction Award, 1962. Address: 922 E. Univ. St., Bloomington, IN 47401, USA.

YELLOTT, Barbara Leslie Jordan, pen name JORDAN, Barbara Leslie, b. 30 Sept. 1915, NYC, USA. Poet. Educ: Columbia Univ., 1933-34. Publs: Web of Days, 1949; Comfort the Dreamer, 1955. Contbr. to: N.Y. Times; N.Y. Herald Tribune; Fla. Mag. of Verse; Ariz. Repub.; the Diamond Anthology, Poetry Soc. of Am., 1971; The Lyric; Toledo Blade; Driftwind; Poetry Chapbook; etc. Mbrships: Poetry Soc. of Am.; N.Y. Women Poets; Histn., Valley of the Sun Br., Nat. Soc. of Arts & Letters. Address: 901 W. El Caminito, Phoenix, AZ 85021, USA.

YEO, Cedric Arnold, b. 10 Sept. 1905, Port Hill, P.E.I., Can. University Professor. Educ: B.A., Dalhousie Univ., Halifax, N.S., 1928; Ph.D., Yale Univ., 1933. Author, A History of the Roman People, 1962. Contbr. to: Transactions of Am. Philol. Assn.; Finanzarchiv (Tübingen); Am. Hist. Review. Mbrships: AAUP; Am. Hist. Soc.; Deleg.,

State Democratic Convention, Louisville, 1968; Mason. Address: Box 493, Dept. of Hist., Eastern Ky. Univ., Richmond, KY 40475, USA.

YERBY, Frank (Garvin), b. 5 Sept. 1916, Augusta, Ga., USA. Writer. Educ: A.B., Paine Coll., Augusta, 1937; M.A., Fisk Univ., Tenn., 1938. Publs. incl: (novels) The Foxes of Harrow, 1946; The Vixens, 1947; A Woman Called Fancy, 1951; Captain Rebel, 1956; The Garfield Honor, 1961; The Old Gods Laugh, 1964; An Odor of Sanctity, 1965; Goat Song, 1968; Judas, My Brother, 1968; Speak Now, 1969; The Dahomean, 1971; The Girl from Storyville, 1972 (all also publd. in UK). Contbr. to: Harper's; Common Ground; Black Am. Lit., 1969. Address: c/o Mr. Own Laster, William Morris Agcy., 1350 Ave. of the Americas, N.Y., NY 10019, USA.

YILDIZ, Bekir, b. 3 Mar. 1933, Urfa, Turkey. Writer. Publs: Reşo Aga; Kara Vagon; Kaçakçi Şahan; Sahipsizler; Evlilik Şirketi; Harran; Beyaz Türkü; Alman Ekmegi.; var. further eds. of foregoing. Contbr. to num. Turkish mags. Mbrships: FIJET (Turkish Ctr.); Turkish Writers' Syndicate. Hons: MAY Lit. Prize; Sait Faik Short Story Prize; CIDALC Prize, Int. Film Festival, Karlovy Vary. Address: Asya Matbaasi, Arif Paşa sokak, Cağaloğlu, Istanbul, Turkey.

YLIRUUSI, Tauno, b. 4 May 1927, Tampere, Finland. Playwright. Educ: M.A., Helsinki Univ., 1951. Publs: (plays) Murder for Fun, 1961; The Bottle & the Book, 1964; The Other Luther, 1968; Lucian, 1970; A Woman's Place, 1971; The Wings of an Angel, 1971; A Scoundrel by the Name of Alexander Solzhenitsyn, 1974; Le Dimanche des Criminels (TV play in 5 parts, for French TV), 1975; nine books & sev. short stories. Contbr. to: Finnish Illustrated. Mbrships: Finnish Dramatists' Soc.; Société des Auteurs et Compositeurs Dramatiques (France); Finnish Soc. Authors. Hons.: 6 prizes for play competitions. Address: Harjuviita 1.A.4., 02100 Espoo 10, Finland.

YOAKUM, Robert H., b. 8 Mar. 1922, Phoenix, Ariz., USA. Humor Columnist for the Los Angeles Times Syndicate. Educ: Northwestern Univ., 1940-42; Univ. of Chgo., 1945-47. Contbr. to: L.A. Times Syndicate; Columbia Jrnlsm. Review; New Repub.; Nieman Reports; Int. Herald Tribune; Sunday Times, London. Address: Millerton Rd., Lakeville, CT 06039, USA.

YOFFE, Abraham B., b. 14 Mar. 1924, Baltzi, Bessarabia, Romania. Writer; Journalist. Educ: Hebrew Univ., Jerusalem, 1943-44. Publs: Poetry & Reality, 1950; Charlie Chaplin, 1955; French Dialogue, 1958; Major Events in World Literature, 1960; Hemingway, 1966; A Shlonsky, 1966; Balzac, 1971; Molière, 1971; Parallel Features in the Modern Short Story, 1974. Contbr. to: (Hebrew) Moznaim; Molad; Gazith; Gylyonoth; Measef Hasofrim; Orlogin; Itim; Ofakim; Amoth; etc. (Engl.) New Outlook; Israwl Mag.; Jewish Chronicle. Mbrships: Ctrl. Comm., Hebrew Writer's Assn.; Jrnlst.'s Assn. Recip., Fichman Prize, 1974. Address: Tel-Aviv, 21 Veidat Katowitz St., Israel.

YOKOYAMA, Michiko, b. 27 July 1903, Onomichi, Hiroshima Prefecture, Japan. Novelist. Publs: Vision of Love (short stories), 1929; Light of the Class (stories for young people), 1933; Stories for Primary School Children, 6 vols., 1934; Green Horizon (novel), 1935, in Engl. transl.; Hope for Young People (essay), 1941; How to Bring Up Good Children (essay), 1968. Contbr. to jrnls. inclng: Fujin Koron; Osaka Newspaper. Mbrships. incl: PEN; Assn. of Japanese Writers; Comm. of the UN Women's Sect., Tokyo. Hons: Asahi Newspress Prize, 1935; Osaka Asahi Newspress Prize. Address: 6 — 10, OYamacho, Shibuyaku, Tokyo, Japan.

YONG-SU, O., pen name NAN-GYE (Orchid Valley), b. 11 Feb. 1914, Kyungsangnamdo, Korea. Novelist. Educ: Grad., Tokyo Inst. of Nat. Arts, Japan. Publs: (collected short stories) Wild Berry, 1950; Sea Shore Village, 1956; Brightness & Darkness, 1958; Echoes, 1960; Water-Lily, 1965; Selected Short Stories of O Yong-su, 7 vols., 1973. Mbrships: Dir., Assn. of Korean Writers; Korean PEN. Recip., Asian Liberty Lit. Prize, 1959. Address: 531-27 Sangmoondong, Dobong-ku, Seoul, Korea.

YOO, Young Hyun, pen name YOO, Grace S., b. 15 July 1927, Hongsong, S. Chungchung Province, S. Korea. Librarian. Educ: LL.B., Korea Univ., 1957; M.A.L.S., George Peabody Coll. for Tchrs., 1958; LL.M., Seoul Nat. Univ., 1960. Publs. incl: Source Materials on Korean

Economy, 1966; Two Korean Brothers, 1970; Wisdom of the Far East: A Dictionary of Proverbs, Maxims, & Classical Phrases of the Chinese, Japanese & Korean, 1972. Contbr. to: KLA Bulletin; Monthly Legis. Reports; etc. Mbrships: Councillor & Ed., KLA; ALA; Korean Legal Ctr.; Korean Soc. for Criminal Law & Criminol. Recip., Int. Coop. Admin. Grant, 1957-58. Address: 10204 Bessmer Lane, Fairfax, VA 22030, USA.

YORKE, Margaret, b. 30 Jan 1924, Surrey, UK. Novelist. Publs: 11 early novels, 1957—; Dead In the Morning, 1970; Silent Witness, 1972; Grave Matters, 1973; No Medals for the Major, 1974; Mortal Remains, 1974; The Small Hours of the Morning, 1975. Contbr. to: Var. mags.; radio. Mbrships: Comm. Mbr., Crime Writers' Assn.; Soc. of Authors. Address: Oriel Cottage, Long Crendon, Bucks., HP18 9AL, UK.

YORKE, Susan. Author; Lecturer. Educ: B.A., Vassar Coll.; Univ. of Chgo.; Univ. of Hamburg; N.Y. Schl. of Soc. Rsch. Publs: The Widow, 1952; Naked to Mine Enemies, 1954; Freighter, 1956; Poule De Luxe, 1958; The Seduction, 1960; Agency House, 1962; Captain China, 1962; Star Sapphire, 1965; The Adventuress, 1966. Contbr. to num. jrnls. in USA, Can., UK, Aust., France, Germany, Italy, Switz., Scandinavia, Mexico, Argentina & Malaysia. Mbrships: incl: PEN; Past Co-Pres. & Sec., Soc. of Women Writers, Aust. Recip., Award, Aust. Wide Short Story Contest, 1972. Address: 5/9 Laguna St., Vaucluse, N.S.W., Australia.

YOSHIMURA, Toshio, b. 30 Jan. 1934, Tokyo, Japan. Journalist; University Lecturer. Educ: Coll. Econs., Kanto Gakuin Univ., Yokohama; Grad. Schl., Cornell Univ., Ithaca, N.Y., USA. Publs: Economist's Journey to Australia, 1975; Invitation to the South Pacific, 1976. Contbr. to: Asia Pacific Forum; Nishi-Nippon Shimbun; Int. Mgmt.; etc. Mbrships: Japan Socs. for Asian Studies, For. Trade; For. Correspondents' Club of Japan. Hons: Grand Prize, Fairchild News & Reporting Contest, 1959; Grand Prize, Daily News Record News & Reporting Contest, 1962. Address: Apt. 411 Kanazawa Hakkei Mans., 4417 Mutsu-ura-machi, Kanazawa-ku, Yokohama, 236, Japan.

YOSHIOKA, Tatsuo, b. 6 June 1917, Ishinomaki, Miyagi, Japan. Novelist. Educ: Waseda Univ. Publs: Orange Canal, 1956; Blood Sunday, 1966. Contbr. to: Shinpyo; Chuókoron. Mbrships: PEN; Japanese Lit. Men's Soc. Recip., Bungakusha Prize, 1951. Address: Yawatacho 4-9-5, Musashinoshi, Tokyo, Japan.

YOUNG, Chesley Virginia Barnes, pen name BARNES, Chesley Virginia, b. 7 Sept. 1919, Hamburg, Ark., USA. Author; Civic Worker. Educ: B.A., Univ. of Ark.; M.A., Tchrs. Coll., Columbia Univ. Publs: How to Read Faster & Remember More (w. M. N. Young), 1963; Magic of a Mighty Memory, 1971. Ed: Card Tricks (by W. Jonson), 1952; Magic Tricks (by W. Jonson), 1952. Contbr. to: The Means Family of America, 1972; num. mags. Mbrships: Am. Soc. of Composers, Authors & Publrs.; Wash. Square Bus. & Profl. Women's Club. Address: c/o Morris N. Young, M.D., 170 Broadway, N.Y., NY 10038, USA.

YOUNG, Constance, (née SMEDLEY), b. Johannesburg, S. Africa. Freelance Writer. Educ: L.T.C.L. Contbr. to: Tales of South Africa, 1963; New South African Writing, vol. I, 1964; Argus; Cape Times; Personality; Milady; Playtime; Outspan; S. African Broadcasting Corp.; etc. Mbrships: PEN; Hon. Treas., Engl. Assn. (S. African Br.); Cape Town Writers' Club. Hons: Tied for 3rd place, PEN Int. Short Story Competition, 1962; num. S. African lit. awards. Address: Dennerode, 26 Kromboom Rd., Rondebosch, Cape Town, S. Africa.

YOUNG, George Kennedy, b. 8 Apr. 1911, Moffatt, UK. Banker. Educ: M.A., St. Andrews Univ.; M.A., Yale Univ., USA; Univs. Dijon, Giessen. Publs: Masters of decision, 1962; Merchant Banking, 1966; Finance & World Power, 1968; Who Goes Home?, 1969; What Are Europeans?, 1971; Who Is My Liege?, 1972. Ed., State & Economy, 1972. Contbr. to: Scotsman; Glasgow Herald. Mbrships: Royal Inst. Int. Affairs; Inst. for Strategic Studies; S. Place Ethical Soc.; Anglo-German Assn.; Anglo-Israel Assn. Hons: C.B.; C.M.G.; M.B.E. (Mil.); U.S. Medal Freedom (w. Bronze Palm). Address: 37 Abbotsbury Ho., London W14, UK.

YOUNG, Janet Randall, pen names RANDALL, Janet; YOUNG, Jan, b. 6 Mar. 1919, Lancaster, Calif., USA. Author. Educ: UCLA. Publs. incl: Across the Tracks, 1958; One Small Voice, 1961; Saddles for Breakfast, 1961; Pony Girl, 1963; Seeing Heart, 1965; Forged in Silver, 1968; Buffalo Box, 1969; Island Ghost, 1970; To Save a Tree, 1971; Chavez & the Migrant Workers, 1972. Mbrships: Western Writers of Am.; Nat. League of Am. Pen Women. Address: 460 Main St., Ferndale (Box 607), CA, USA.

YOUNG, Kenneth, b. 27 Nov. 1916, Wakefield, UK. Journalist. Educ: B.A., Univ. of Leeds, 1934. Publs: A. J. Balfour, 1963; Churchill & Beaverbrook, 1966; Rhodesia & Independence, 1967, 2nd ed., 1969; The Greek Passion, 1969; Sir Alec Douglas-Home, 1970; Diaries of Sir Bruce-Lochart, vol. I, 1973; Harry, Lord Rosebery, 1974. Contbr. to: Blackwoods Mag.; Encounter; Spectator. Mbrships. incl: F.R.S.L., 1964-; Soc. of Authors; Press Club. Address: 35 Central Parade, Herne Bay, Kent, UK.

YOUNG, Lois Horton, b. 2 Apr. 1911, Hamburg, N.Y., USA. Educator; Writer. Educ: A.B., Hunter Coll., NYC; grad. Studies, N.Y. Theol. Sem. Publs: Teaching Kindergarten Children, 1959; God's World of Wonder, 1964; The Little Church That Grew, 1965; Through Hospital Windows, 1966; No Biscuits at All, 1966; For a Child's Day, 1967; Whatever Happened on Peony Street, 1968; The Brown Shoes, 1970; Dimensions for Happening, 1971; Kindergarten Storytime, 1972. Contbr. to var. books & mags. Hons: Hymn Soc. of Am. Awards, 1959, 1966. Address: 303 Windsor Mill Rd., Ext. Baltimore, MD 21207, USA.

YOUNG, Louise Buchwalter, b. 20 July 1919, Springfield, Ohio, USA. Writer; Editor. Educ: B.A., Vassar Coll., 1940. Publs: Ed., Exploring the Universe, 1963, revised ed., 1971; Ed., Mystery of Matter, 1965; Ed., Population in Perspective, 1968; Best Foot Forward, 1968; Ed., Evolution of Man, 1970; Power over People, 1973. Contbr. to: Sci. & Pub. Affairs. Recip., Cert. of Merit, Friends of Am. Writers, 1974. Address: 755 Sheridan Rd., Winnetka, IL 60093, USA.

YOUNG, Marguerite (Vivian), b. 1909, Indpls., Ind., USA. Writer; University Teacher. Educ: Ind. Univ.; B.A., Butler Univ., Indpls., 1930; M.A., Univ. of Chgo., 1936; Univ. of Iowa. Publs: Prismatic Ground (verse), 1937; Moderate Fable (verse), 1944; Angel in the Forest, USA, 1945, UK, 1967; Miss MacIntosh, My Darling (novel), USA, 1965; UK, 1966. Hons: Grant, AAUW, 1943; Grant, Nat. Inst. Arts & Letters, 1945; Guggenheim Fellowship, 1948; Newberry Lib. Fellowship, 1951; Rockefeller Fellowship, 1954. Address: 375 Bleecker St., N.Y., NY 10014, USA.

YOUNG, (Brig.) Peter, b. 1915, Fulham, London, UK. Military Historian. Educ: M.A., Trinity Coll., Oxford Univ. Publs. incl: Bedouin Command, 1956; The Great Civil War: A Military History (w. A. H. Burne), 1959; Cromwell, 1962; World War 1939-45, 1967; The British Army 1642-1970, 1967; The Israeli Campaign, 1967, 1967; Charge, or How to Play War Games (w. J. P. Lawford), 1967; Decisive Battles of the Second World War (anthol.), 1967; Strangers in Oxford (w. Margaret Toynbee), 1973; Ed., Purnell's Hist. of The First World War. Contbr. to: Jrnl. Soc. for Army Hist. Rsch.; Chamber's Ency.; etc. Mbrships. incl: F.S.A.; F.R.G.S.; Fellow, Royal Histl. Soc.; Inst. Jrnlsts. Hons: D.S.O.; M.C. Agent: London Management. Address: Bank House, Ripple, Tewkesbury, Glos. GL20 6EP, UK.

YOUNG, Philip, b. 26 May 1918, Boston, Mass., USA. Professor; Writer. Educ: A.B., Amherst Coll., 1940; Ph.D., Univ. of Iowa, 1948. Publs: Ernest Hemingway, 1952; Ernest Hemingway: a Reconsideration, 1966; The Hemingway Manuscripts: an Inventory, 1967; Three Bags Full: Essays in American Fiction, 1970. Contbr. to: Kenyon Review; Southern Review; Sewannee Review; Atlantic Monthly; N.Y. Times Book Review; Book World; etc. Mbr., PEN. Recip., D.H.L., 1971. Address: 525 West Park Ave., State College, PA 16801, USA.

YOUNG, Rena Mary (Reed), (Mrs. Laster Young), pen name YOUNG, Rena Reed, b. 20 Aug. 1905, Lucas, Kan., USA. Writer; Poetess. Educ: Fort Hays Kan. State Coll.; Kan. Univ., Lawrence; B.A., 1971. Contbr. to: Kan. City Star; Topeka Daily Capital; Hays Daily News; Ellis Review; Lucas Indep.; Coll. Ldr.; Locomotive Engrs.' Mag.; Fireman & Enginemen's Mag.; Kan. Authors' Club Organ; KUC Student Newsletter & Anthol., 1970. Mbrships: Kan.

Authors' Club; Coll. Lit. Club. Address: 102 W. 15th St., Ellis, KA 67637, USA.

YOUNG, Roland Stansfield, b. 1906, Portage La Prairie, Man., Can. Consultant. Educ: Univ. of Alta.; Cornell Univ., USA; M.Sc.; Ph.D. Publs: Cobalt, A.C.S. Monograph 149; Industrial Inorganic Analysis; Analytical Chemistry of Cobalt; Chemical Analysis in Extractive Metallurgy; Chemical Phase Analysis; num. papers. Contbr. to chem. metall. & other tech. publs. Address: 1178 Beach Dr., Victoria, B.C., Can.

YOUNG, Stanley Preston, b. 1906, Greencastle, Ind., USA. Professor of Drama (ret'd.); Writer. Educ: Chgo. & Columbia Univs., USA; Munich Univ., Germany; Grenoble. Univ., France; Ph.B.; M.A. Publs. (verse drama): Robin Landing; (novel): Sons Without Anger; (juveniles): Young Hickory; Mayflower Boy; (drama): Mr. Pickwick; Tippicanoe & Tyler Too; Bright Rebel; Ask my Friend Sandy; Laurette; Best Short Plays, 1939, 1943, 1947, 1958; (sev. plays prod. on Broadway). Contbr. to: New Yorker; Saturday Review; Botteghe Oscure; Harper's Bazaar; etc. Agent: Brandt & Brandt Dramatic Dept. Address: 208 Wheatley Rd., Old Westbury, L.I., NY 11568, USA.

YOUNG, Vernon, pen name HALES, Norman, b. 27 Aug. 1912, London, UK. Literary & Film Critic. Educ: A.B., Univ. Calif. Publs. incl: (novel) The Spider in the Cup, 1954; Cinema Borealis: Ingmar Bergman & the Swedish Ethos, 1971; On Film: Unpopular Essays on a Popular Art, 1972. Contbr. to: Ency. of Film, vol. I, 1975; The Hudson Review; Parnassus: Poetry in Review; Art Int.; The Lugano Review; Dialogue; Arts (Ed., 1955-65); NY Times; Accent; Industria; Film Quarterly. Recip., Hudson Review Fellowship (Rockefeller Fndn.), 1957. Address: Rindögatan 18, 115 36 Stockholm, Sweden.

YOUNG-JAMES, Douglas Alexander de Singleton, b. 10 July 1914, Newport, Isle of Wight, UK. Solicitor; Estate Agent; Royal Air Force Officer. Educ: Bristol Univ. Publs: Teaching of Dramatic Art — Myfany James (Ed.), 1962; Memoirs of an Asp (autobiog.), 1962; Donald Campbell (biog.), 1968. Contbr. to ASP Mag. Mbrships: Wiseman Soc.; Royal Soc. of Lit.; RAF Club; Fellow, Dir.'s Inst., 1967; Dir., St. Hugh's Soc.; Pres., Aspian Soc.; Coun., United Servs. Cath. Assn., 1958—; Grand Prior of London Sovereign Order of St. John of Jerusalem. Address: 21 Ilchester Mansions, Abingdon Rd., London W8 6AE, UK.

YOURCENAR, Marguerite, b. 8 June 1903, Brussels, Belgium. Writer. Publs. incl: Alexis ou le Traité du vain combat, 1929; Pindare, 1932; La Mort conduit l'Attelage, 1934; Feux, 1936; Les Songes & Les Sorts, 1938; Nouvelles Orientales, 1938; Le Coup de Grâce, 1939; Mémoires d'Hadrien, 1951; Les Charités d'Alcippe, 1956; Le Mystère d'Alceste, 1963; L'Oeuvre au Noir, 1968; Entretiens Radiophoniques, 1972; num. transl. incl: Virginia Woolf; Henry James; Constantine Cavafy. Mbr., Belgian Acad. Hons. incl: Prix Femina, 1964; Prix Combat, 1963. Address: Petite Plaisance, Northeast Harbor, ME 04662, USA.

YUAN, Kichiner Ni-Cheng, b. 15 Nov. 1904, Hsing Hwa, Kingsa Province, Repub. of China. Editor; Writer. Educ: Lic. en Droit, Univ. of Paris, France. Publs. incl: A Diary on the Making of National Constitution, 1970; Stories of Events in the Hsieh Chi Villa, 1971; The Other Shore, 1972; Gentlemen of the Elder Generation, 1972; Tales of Hang Chow, 1974; Selected Essays, 1974. Contbr. to: Shih Tai Kung Lun (Time Review); Sheng Liu; Eastern Miscellany. Mbrships: Chmn., Bd. of Dirs., Chekiang Assn. on the Study of Admin.; Press Coun. of the Repub. of China. Address: 23, Lane 13, Yung Kang St., Taipei, Taiwan 106, Repub. of China.

YURICK, Sol, b. 18 Jan. 1925, NYC, USA. Writer. Educ: A.B., NY Univ., 1950; M.A., Brooklyn Coll., N.Y., 1961. Publs: (novels) The Warriors, USA, 1965, UK, 1966; Fertig, USA & UK, 1966; The Bag, USA, 1968, UK, 1970. Address: c/o Simon & Schuster Inc., 630 Fifth Ave., N.Y., NY 10020, USA.

Z

ZACIU, Mircea, b. 27 Aug. 1928, Oradea, Romania. Professor of Romanian Literature. Educ: Grad., 1952, Ph.D., 1967, Univ. Cluj, Romania. Publs: (in Romanian) The Mask of Genius, 1967; Glossis, 1970; Collages, 1972; The Order & Adventure, 1973; Bivouac, 1974. Contbr. to: Romania literară; Steaua; Tribuna; Cahiers roumains d'Etudes littéraires (Romania); Romanian Studies; Slavic Review. Mbrships: Int. Assn. Lit. Critics (Paris); Writers' Union Romania (mbr. Union Coun.); Acad. Soc. & Pol. Sci., Romania. Recip., Writers' Union Prize, 1973; Romanian Acad. Award, 1975. Address: Cluj, Strada Biserica Ortodoxă 12, Romania.

ZACK, Arnold Marshall, b. 7 Oct. 1931, Lynn, Mass., USA. Arbitrator; Attorney. Educ: A.B., Tufts Coll., Medford, Mass., 1953; LL.B., Yale Law Schl., New Haven, Conn., 1956; M.P.A., 1961, M.A., 1963, Harvard Univ., Cambridge, Mass. Publs: Labor Training in Developing Countries, 1964; Ethiopia's High Level Manpower, 1964; Factfinding & Interest Arbitration in the Public Sector, 1974; Grievance Arbitration in the Public Sector, 1974. Contbr. to profl. & other jrnls. inclng: Arbitration Jrnl.; Labor Law Jrnl.; Int. Dev. Review; Africa Report. Mbrships. incl: Treas., Nat. Acad. of Arbitrators, 1972-75; Mass. Bar Assn. Past N.E. Pres., Indl. Rels. Rsch. Assn. Address: 170 W. Canton St., Boston, MA 02118, USA.

ZÁGONI, Ferenc, b. 19 Feb. 1921, Budapest, Hungary. Author. Educ: Univ. of Scis., Budapest. Publs: Sodró hullámok (Carrying Billows), 1960; Boldog nyár (Happy Summer) 1961; Madárijesztő (Scarecrow), 1964; A megjelölt ember (The Marked Man), 1965; Kitérő (Siding), 1965; Rozsda (Rust), 1971; Emberek, utak, sorsok (People, Ways, Fates), 1974. Contbr. to Tükör (Mirror). Mbrships: Hungarian Writers' Assn.; Hungarian Jrnlsts.' Assn. Hons: Lit. Standard Prize, 1965; Silver Spear Art Prize, 1972; Order of Labour, 1974. Address: 1121. Eötvös u. 7, Hungary.

ZAGÓRSKI, Jerzy, pen names MAGISTER JURAŚ, ZAG, b. 13 Dec. 1907, Kiev, Ukraine. Poet; Essayist; Playwright; Art Critic; Translator. Educ: M.A., Stefan Batory Univ. Vilna, 1936. Publs. incl: (plays) Olympus & Earth, 1957; Serafyt's Necklace, 1962; (essays) India in the Centre of Europe, 1947; Sketches, 1958; Where the Devil Writes Letters, 1969; (poetry) Edge, 1959; Elder Tree, 1963; Stray Bullet, 1969; Verses, 1972; (transls.) Plays of Lermontov, 1963; Poetry of Rusthaweli, 1966. Contbr. to num. Polish jrnls. Mbrships. incl: Union Polish Writers (VP, 1947); PEN (VP, 1970—); Poetry Club Warsaw (Chmn., 1972—). Hons. incl: 1st Prize for underground poetry Warsaw, 1943; Polish PEN Prize for poetry transl., 1964. Address: Ul. Mickiewicza 18 m. 32, 01-517 Warsaw, Poland.

ZALKA, Miklós, b. 25 May 1928, Budapest, Hungary. Writer. Educ: degree by corres., Zrinyi Miklós Mil. Acad., 1958. Publs: Nehéz ut, 1953; Aknamező, 1959; Különös ember, 1962; A mi utcánk, 1967; A bőrzekés, 1967; Mindenkihez (histl. essay), 1969; A távolban Kánaán, 1970; A dzsungel vére (report from a Vietnamese village), 1971; Rizs és bambusz (short stories from Vietnam), 1971; És felnő az elefánt (documents & legends on fndn. of Vietnamese Peoples Army), 1973. Mbr., lit. orgs. Recip., Special Prizes, 1962 & 1969. Address: Abonyi u. 27, 1146 Budapest XIV, Hungary.

ZALOKOSTAS, Christos, b. 1896. Writer; Politician; Industrialist. Educ: Munich Polytechnic. Publs. incl: The Chronicle of Slavery, 1945; King Alexander, 1946; Poverty in the Sun, 1952; Marina, 1957; Address: Amerikis 21, Athens, Greece.

ZAMFIRESCU, Dan-Mircea, b. 21 Dec. 1933, Bucharest, Romania. Literary Historian. Educ: incl: Degree in Russian & Romanian lang. & lit., Univ. of Bucharest; Dr. in Romanian Philol. Publs. incl: Studi si Articole de Literature Romana Yeche, 1967; Spre noi Insine, 1971; Istorie si Cultura (essays), 1975. Contbr. to: Scinteia; Romania liberia; Tribuna Romania; etc. Mbrships: Writers Union, Romania; Romanian Soc. of Byzantine Studies; Soc. of Philol. Scis.; Slavistics Assn. of Romania. Hons. incl: Perpessicius Prize, 1971. Address: Sandu Aldea 73, Bucharest 1, Romania.

ZAMORE, Karl Otto, b. 22 Mar. 1904, Huddinge, Sweden. Author; Translator. Publs. incl: Selma Lagerlöf,

1958; Finnish Persons, 1956; Nobel Prize-Winners (Peace), 1957; & about 30 books transl'd. into Swedish from Engl., Danish & German. Contbr. to: Svenske Jrnl.; etc. Swedish Union Authors; Swedish Soc. Transls. (Gen. Sec., 1964-70); Swedish Geneal. Soc.; Juryman Court of Stockholm, 1954-74. Hons: Sveriges Författarfond Prizes, 1955, 1959, 1962; Swedish State Author's Pension since 1971. Address: Stamgatan 69, 125 39 Alvsjö, Stockholm, Sweden.

ZANGWILL, Oliver Louis, b. 29 Oct. 1913, E. Preston, Sussex, UK. University Teacher. Educ: M.A., Cambridge Univ., 1939. Publs: An Introduction to Modern Psychology, 1950, 1963; Current Problems in Animal Behaviour (jt. ed. & part author), 1960; Cerebral Dominance & its Relationship to Psychological Function, 1960; Amnesia (jt. ed. & part author), 1966. Contbr. to: Nature; Times Lit. Supplement; var. med. & psychol. jrnls. Mbrships: Pres., Brit. Psychol. Soc., 1974-75, Expmtl. Psychol. Soc., 1962-63; Assn. of Brit. Neurols.; Hon. Mbr., Assn. Française de Neurol. Address: King's College, Cambridge, UK.

ZAPFFE, Peter Wessel, b. 18 Dec. 1899, Tromsö, Norway. Author; Teacher. Educ: Law; Ph.D., 1941. Publs: Om det Tragiske, 1941; Vett og Uvett, 1942; (drama) Den Fortapte Sönn, 1951; Indföring i litterär Dramaturgi, 1961; Den logiske Sandkasse, 1966; Essays og Epistler, 1967; Barske Gläder, 1969; Dikt og Drama, 1970; Lyksalig Pinsefest, 1972; (play) Hos doktor Wangel (as Ib Henriksen), 1974. Contbr. to: Farmand; Edda; Minerva; Spektrum; Janus; Turistforeningens Aarbok. Mbrships: Den norske Forfatterforening; Kunstnerforeningen; Norsk Tindeklub. Hons. incl: Det akademiske Kollegiums prisbelønning for Om det Tragiske. Address: Nedre Baastadvei 6, 1370 Asker, Norway.

ZARAGOZA, Cristóbal, b. 4 Mar. 1923, Villajoyosa, Alicante, Spain. Writer. Educ: Arts degree. Publs. incl: No tuvieron la tierra prometida, 1969; Un puño llama a la puerta, 1970; El cambio de camisa, 1971; Der letzte Sonntag, 1972; Los domingos vacíos, 1974; Manú. 1974; Pájaros cantores, 1974. Contbr. to: La Estafeta Lit., Madrid; El Noticiero Universal, Barcelona; Diario de Barcelona. Mbrships: Ateneo de Barcelona; Biblioteca Ctrl. de Barcelona; Colegio Oficial de Doctores y Licenciados en Filosofía y Letras de Barcelona y Baleares. Recip., Libro Amigo de Lit. Española. Address: calle Escorial, 112-2°-2ª, Distrito 12, Barcelona, Spain.

ZAREV, Vladimir, b. 5 Oct. 1947, Sofia, Bulgaria. Writer. Publs: (in Bulgarian) Restless Feelings, 1971; The Large Queer Garden, 1972; So Lovely, Painful, Infinite, 1972; Denubian Novellas, 1974. Contbr. to: September; PlamAk; Suvremennik. Mbr., Union of Bulgarian Writers. Recip., Prize of the Gen. Coun. of Trade Unions, 1974. Address: Sofia, ul. Yakoubitsa, 2 kv. Lozenets, Bulgaria.

ZAWODNY, Janusz K., b. 11 Dec. 1921, Warsaw, Poland. University Professor of International Relations. Educ: B.S., 1950, M.A., 1951, State Univ. of Iowa; Ph.D., Stanford Univ., 1955. Publs: The Uprising of Warsaw, 1944, 1975; Death in the Forest: The Story of the Katyn Forest Massacre, 1962, 1972; Guide to the Study of International Relations, 1967; Man & International Relations: Contributions of the Social Sciences to the Study of Conflict & Integration, 2 Vols., 1967. Contbr. to: Int. Ency. Soc. Sci. Mbr., Inst. for Adv. Study, Princeton, 1971-72. Address: Dept. of Political Science, Wharton School, Univ. of Pennsylvania, Phila., PA 19174, USA.

ZAYNI, Abdul Husayn, b. 28 Aug. 1932, Kerbala, Iraq. University Professor. Educ: B.B.A., Am. Univ. of Beirut, Lebanon, 1957; Ph.D., Moscow State Univ., USSR, 1965. Publs: Elements of Statistical Methods, 1968; Demographic Statistics, 1969; Industrial Statistics, 1971; Methods & Measures of Agricultural Statistics, 1973; A Study in the National Income Statistics in Iraq, 1973; Economic Statistics in Iraq, 1975. Contbr. to var. Iraqui mags. Mbr., Iraqui Econ. Assn. Address: College of Administration & Economics, Baghdad, Iraq.

ZBINDEN, Hans, b. 26 Aug. 1893, Berne, Switz. University Professor. Educ: Ph.D.; Univs. of Berne & Zürich. Publs. incl: Zur geistigen Lage Amerikas, 1931; Der Kampf um den Frieden, 1934; Die Moralkrise des Abendlandes, 1941; Von der inneren Freiheit, 1948; Gefahren der modernen Demokratie, 1948; Der Mensch im Spannungsfeld der modernen Technik, 1970; Die geistige Situation der Jugend Heute, 1971; transl. Benjamin

Contant & A. de Tocqueville. Mbrships. incl: Swiss Authors' Assn. Address: Alleeweg 13, Berne, CH 3000, Switz.

ZEA AGUILAR, Leopoldo, b. 30 June 1912, Mexico. University Professor. Educ: Ph.D. Publs. incl: El Positivismo en México, 1943; Conciencia y posibilidad del Mexicano, 1952; Hombre de nuestros Dias, 1959; Democracias y Dictaduras en Latinoamérica, 1960; The Latin American Mind, 1963; L'Amerique dans l'Histoire, 1963; Latinamérica en la Formacion de nuestro tiempo, 1965; Latin America & the World, 1969. Contbr. to Tierra Nueva. Mbrships. incl: European Soc. for Culture. Var. hons. Address: Vizcainoco 14, Chimalistac, Villa Obregon, Mexico 20, D.F., Mexico.

ZEINER, Anna-Christina, b. 3 Jan. 1942, Vienna, Austria. Writer. Educ: Studies in Law, 1960-64, 2 State Exams., Studies in Philos. & Psychol., 1973-, Univ. of Vienna. Publs: Der Prinz auf der Untertasse, 1969. Mbr., Concordia Press Club. Recip., Dip., Die schönsten Bücher Österreichs, 1970. Address: 1030 Vienna, Reisnerstr. 41/18, Austria.

ZELAZNY, Roger Joseph, b. 13 May 1937, Euclid, Ohio, USA. Author. Educ: B.A., Western Reserve Univ., 1959; M.A., Columbia Univ., 1962. Publs. incl: This Immortal, 1966; The Dream Master, 1966; Four for Tomorrow, 1967; Lord of Light, 1967; Isle of the Dead, 1969; Nine Princes in Amber, 1970; The Doors of His Face, The Lamps of His Mouth & Other Stories, 1971; Jack of Shadows, 1971; The Guns of Avalon, 1972; Today We Choose Faces, 1973; To Die in Italbar, 1973. Contbr. to: Amazing Stories; Mag. of Fantasy & Sci. Fiction; Analog. Mbrships: Authors Guild; Authors League of Am.; etc. Recip., num. sci. fiction awards. Address: c/o Henry Morrison, 58 W. 10th St., N.Y., NY 10011, USA.

ZELK, Zoltan, b. 18 Dec. 1906, Érmihályfalva, Hungary. Poet. Publs: Witness of Creation (selected poems), 1945; Hoar-frost on the Rose-tree (selected poems), 1967; Gull (collected poems), 1973; also 20 vols. of poetry; verses & tales for children; essays. Contbr. to: New Writing; Contemporary; Life & Lit. Mbrships: Hungarian Writers' Assn.; Hungarian Lit. Fndn.; Hungarian PEN. Hons: Baumgarten Prize, 1948; Kossuth Prizes, 1949, 1954; Jozsef Attila Prizes, 1951, 1974; Graves Prize, 1971. Address: Ormezei lkt. III/A.VI.38, 1112 Budapest XI, Hungary.

ZELLNER, Arnold, b. 2 Jan. 1927, N.Y.C., USA. Professor of Economics. Educ: A.B. (Physics), Harvard Univ., 1949; Ph.D. (Econs), Univ. of Calif., 1957. Publs. incl: Estimating the Parameters of the Markov Probability Model from Aggregate Time Series Data (w. T. C. Lee & G. C. Judge), 1970; An Introduction to Bayesian Inference in Econometrics, 1971; Studies in Bayesian Econometrics & Statistics in Honor of Leonard J. Savage (Ed. w. S. E. Fienberg), 1975. Contbr. to econ. & statl. jrnls. Mbrships: Fellow, Econometric Soc.; Fellow, Am. Stats. Assn.; AAAS; Am. Econ. Assn. Address: 5628 S. Dorchester Ave., Chicago, IL 60637, USA.

ZELTNER, Gerda, b. 27 July 1915, Zurich, Switz. Literary Critic. Educ: Dr. Romanistic Letters; Univs. of Zurich, Switz., Rome, Italy, & Paris, France. Publs: Das Wagnis des französischen Gegenwartsromans, 1960; Die eigenmächtige Sprache, 1965; Das Ich und die Dinge, 1968; Beim Wort genommen, 1973; Im Augenblick der Gegenwart, 1974. Contbr. to: Neue Rundschau; Schweizer Monatshefte; Die Weltwoche; Neue Zurcher Zeitung; etc. Mbrships: PEN; Olten Grp.; Acad. of Mainz. Hons: Town of Zurich Award, 1960; Canton of Zurich Award, 1965; Award of Mainz Acad., 1968. Address: Rutistrasse 11, CH-8032 Zurich, Switz.

ZENNSTRÖM, Per-Olov, pen names DAG, Sven; ROSÉN, Georg; "Z", b. 26 July 1920, Tofte, Norway. Writer; Journalist. Publs: (monogs.) Ernst Josephson, 1946; Picasso, 1948; Linné-Sveriges Upptäckare, Naturens namngivare, 1957; Lucifer, En bok om Axel Danielsson, 1967; Linderot-Masslinjen, 1973; (essays) I Bestämt Syfte, 1972; Kommunistisk Kritik I & II, 1974. Contbr. to: Kulturfront, 1940-44; Konst och Kultur, 1945-49; Konstrevy; Paletten; Bonniers Litterära Magasin; Vår Tid; Socialistisk Debatt; Ord & Bild. Mbr., Swedish Authors' Union. Recip., sev. official lit. stipends. Address: S:t Eriksgatan 55, 11234 Stockholm, Sweden.

ZERMATTEN, Maurice, b. 22 Oct. 1910, St. Martin, Switz. Writer. Educ: Univ. of Fribourg. Publs: 50 vols., inclng: Le Coeur inutile, 1936; Le Chemin difficile; La Colère de Dieu; Le Sang des Morts; Christine; L'Esprit des Tempêtes; La Montagne sans Etoiles; La Fontaine d'Aréthuse; Le Cancer des Solitudes; Le Bouclier d'Or; Pays sans Chemins; Une Soutane aux Orties; La Porte blanche; Un Amour à Grenchen-Nord; Sev. essays & plays. Contbr. to sev. jrnls. Mbrships. incl: PEN; French Soc. of Men of Letters; Swiss Writers Soc. Hons. incl: D.Litt., Univ. of Fribourg; Gottfried Keller Prize, 1959; French Lang. Diffusion Prize, French Acad., 1974; Alpes-Jura Prize, 1974. Address: Gravelone 54, 1950 Sion, Switz.

ZIEGLER, Philip Sandeman, b. 24 Dec. 1929, Ringwood, Hants., UK. Publisher. Educ: New Coll., Oxford. Publs: The Duchess of Dino, 1962; Addington, 1965; The Black Death, 1968; King William IV, 1971; Omdurman, 1973. Contbr. to: Times; Daily Telegraph; Spectator; etc. F.R.S.L. Address: 22 Cottesmore Gdns., London W.8., UK.

ZIMMER, Paul Jerome, b. 18 Sept. 1934, Canton, Ohio, USA. Publisher. Educ: B.A., Kent State Univ. Publs: The Ribs of Death, 1967; The Republic of Many Voices, 1969. Contbr. to: Yankee; Field; Va. Quarterly; Prairie Schooner; Southern Poetry Review; Northwest Review; Poetry Northwest; etc. Hons. incl: Best Poems of 1970: Borestone Mtn. Awards; Poetry Prize, Yankee Mag., 1970; Writing Fellowship, Nat. Endowment for Arts, 1974. Address: 5515 Hobart St., Pitts., PA 15217, USA.

ZIMMERMAN, Joseph Francis, b. 29 June 1928, Keene, N.H., USA. Professor of Political Science; Author. Educ: B.A., Univ. of N.H., 1950; M.A., 1951, PhD., 1954, Syracuse Univ. Publs: State & Local Government, 1962, 2nd ed., 1970; The Massachusetts Town Meeting: A Tenacious Institution, 1967; The Federated City: Community Control in Large Cities, 1972. Contbr. to: Pub. Admin., Nat. Civic Reviews; The Annals; Admin.; Planning & Admin.; Popular Govt.; The Am. Co.; Planning; Jrnl. of Urban Law. Address: Grad. School of Public Affairs, State Univ. of N.Y. (Albany), Mohawk Tower, Albany, NY 12222, USA.

ZINCĂ, Haralamb, b. 4 July 1923, Roman, Romania. Author. Educ: Grad., M. Eminescu Lit. Schl., Bucharest. Publs: War Journal, 1954; Out of Hundreds of Masts, 1964; Death Comes on the Tape Recorder, 1967; Dr. King's Eyes, 1968; And H-Hour Came, 1971; The Black Sedan, 1973; The '01' Jet Fighter Will Take Off At Dawn, 1974. Contbr. to: Luceafărul; Romănia Literară; Viaţa Romănească; Scînteia; Viaţa Militară; Pentru Patrie; etc. Mbrships: Writers' Assn. of Bucharest; Leading Coun., Romanian Writers' Union. Recip., Prose Award, Writers' Assn. of Bucharest, 1971. Address: Str. M. Eminescu 56, Bucharest, Romania.

ZINGARELLI, Italo, b. 9 July 1891. Journalist; Writer. Educ: LL.d. Publs. incl: La marina nella guerra attuale, 1915; La marina italiana, 1915; L'invasione, 1919; Il volto di Vienna, 1925; Das Erbe von Versailles, 1930; Vienna non imperiale, 1930; Vienna, 1935; Vecchia Austria, 1937; I paesi danubiani e balcanici, 1938; Vicino e lontano Oriente, 1940; Questo è il giornalismo, 1946; I tre imperialismi, 1949; I Padrone del Mondo, 1952; Lo stivale delle mille leghe, 1962. Contbr. to: Ora; Corriere della Sera; Epoca; Secolo; Stampa; Agenzia Stefani; Il Tempo; Libera Stampa; Ed., Il Globo. Address: Piazza Stefano Jacini 5, Rome, Italy.

ZINIAK, M. Serge, pen name KHMARA, Sergey, b. 25 May 1905, Alesiau, Byelorussia. Journalist. Educ: Univ. level. Publs: Pathway of Crans (poems), 1939; We (poems), 1949; Legends of Kryvicians Gods (Byelorussian Mythol.), 1950; Legends of Byelorussian Land (novel), 1951. Contbr. to: Bayavaya Uskalos (Ed.); Byelorussian Voice (Ed.); Run Viesnachodu; Kalossie; Dakumanty i Fakty. Mbrships: Fndr. Mbr., Byelorussian Lit. Assn.; Pres., Fedn. Free Byelorussian Jrnlsts. Hons: Jrnlsm. Award, EPAO, 1969; Acad. Degree, People's of Am. Univ., NYC, USA, 1972. Address: 24 Tarlton Rd., Toronto, Ontario M5P 2M4, Canada.

ZINKL, Herbert, b. 30 Oct. 1929, Kapfenberg, Austria. Manager; Journalist. Educ: Commercial trng. Publs: Anker im Dasein (poems), 1973. Contbr. to newspapers & mags. in Germany, Switz., Austria, Yugoslavia. Mbrships: PEN; Styrian Authors' League. Hons: Lyric Poetry Prize, City of Graz, 1956; Lit. Award, Province of Styria, 1974. Address: Pesendorferweg 7, A 8010 Graz, Austria.

ZINNES, Harriet, b. Hyde Park, Mass., USA. Poet; Professor of English; Literary & Art Critic. Educ: B.A., Hunter Coll., 1939; M.A., Brooklyn Coll., 1944; Ph.D., N.Y. Univ., 1953. Publs: Waiting & other Poems, 1964; An Eye for an I, 1966; Entropisms, in New Directions 27, 1973; The Fiction of Anaïs Nin, in Casebook of Anaïs Nin, 1974. Contbr. to: (anthols.) A New Folder, 1959; Out of the War Shadow, 1967; N.Y. Times Book of Verse, 1970; (jrnls.) The Nation; Carleton Miscellany; Prairie Schooner; Poetry; other lit. jrnls. Mbrships: PEN Am. Ctr.; Poetry Soc. of Am.; Acad. of Am. Poets. Hons: Res. Fellowships, MacDowell Colony, 1971, 1972, 1973, 1974. Address: Dept. of English, Queens Coll. of CUNY, Flushing, NY 11367, USA.

ZODHIATES, Spiros, b. 13 Mar. 1922, Nicosia, Cyprus. Clergyman; President of AMG International; Editor. Educ: B.Th., Nat. Bible Inst., N.Y., USA, 1947; M.A., Schl. of Educ., N.Y. Univ., 1951. Publs: Behavior of Belief, 1959; Was Christ God? , 1966; The Pursuit of Happiness, 1966; A Christian View of War & Peace, 1966; To Love Is to Live, 1967; Conquering the Fear of Death, 1970; A Richer Life for You in Christ, 1972; The Song of the Virgin, 1973; Tongues! ? , 1974; The Perfect Gift, 1974; A Revolutionary Mystery, 1974; num. books in Greek. Ed., The Voice of the Gospel. Address: 18 Grand Ave., Ridgefield Park, NJ 07660, USA.

ZOLKIEWSKI, Stefan, pen name ZLK, b. 9 Dec. 1911, Warsaw, Poland. University Professor. Educ: Dr. Phil. Publs. incl: Stare i nowe literaturoznastwo, 1950; Spor o Mickiewicza, 1952; Kultura i polityka, 1958; Perspektywy literatury XXu., 1960; O kulturze Polski Ludowej, 1964; Kultura à semictikă, 1969; Kultura literacka 1918-32, 1974. Contbr. to: Kuźnica; Studia Sociologicsne; Pamietnik literacki; Polityka; Studia semiotycsne; Semiotica; Informations sur les sciences sociales (UNESCO); etc. Mbrships: Polish Acad. Scis.; Polish Semitics' Soc.; Soc. of Polish Men of Letters; PEN. Hons: State Prizes, 1953, 1964. Address: Aleja Róź 6-14, Warsaw 00556, Poland.

ZOLLA, Elèmire, b. 9 July 1926, Turin, Italy. Writer, Chairman, American Literature, University of Rome. Educ: Dr. Jur. Eclissi dell'intellectuale, 1959 (as The Eclipse of the Intellectual, USA, 1969); I Mistici 1963, expanded ed. 1975; Storia del fantasticare, 1964; Le potenze dell'anima, 1968; I letterati e lo sciamano, 1969 (as The Writer & the Shaman, USA, 1973); Che cos'e la tradizione, 1972; Introduzione all'alchimia, 1975. Contbr. to: Corriere della sera (Milan); La Nacion (Buenos Aires); Conoscenza Religiosa (Ed., 1969—). Address: Piazza S. Anselmo 2, Rome, Italy.

ZOLOTOW, Charlotte, b. 26 June 1915, Norfolk, Va., USA. Writer; Editor; Lecturer; Teacher. Educ: B.A., Univ. of Wis. Num. publs. incl: The Park Book, 1944; The Storm Book, 1952; Aren't You Glad, 1960; The Quarrelling Book, 1963; Rose, A Bridge & a Wild Black Horse, 1964; Big Sister & Little Sister, 1966; The New Friend, 1968; River Winding, 1970; A Father Like That, 1971; Wake Up & Goodnight, 1971; Hold My Hand, 1972; William's Doll, 1972; Summer Night, 1974; My Grandson Lew, 1974; The Unfriendly Book, 1975. Mbrships: PEN Assoc.; Author's Guild. Address: c/o Harper & Row Inc., 10 E. 53rd St., N.Y., NY 10022, USA.

ZORNOW, William Frank, b. 13 Aug. 1920, Cleveland, Ohio, USA. Professor. Educ: A.B., 1942, A.M., 1944, Ph.D., 1952, Case-Western Reserve Univ., Cleveland. Publs: Lincoln & the Party Divided, 1954, 2nd ed., 1972; Kansas: a History of the Jayhawk State, 1957; America at Mid-Century, 1959. Contbr. to books, encys. & jrnls. inclng: Kansas: the First Century, 1956; Abraham Lincoln: A New Portrait, 1959; America: History & Life. Mbr., hist. orgs. Recip., Award of Merit, Am. Assn. for State & Local Hist.. 1958. Address: Dept. of Hist., Kent State Univ., Kent, OH 44242, USA.

ZSOLDOS, Peter, b. 20 Apr. 1930, Szentes, Hungary. Musical Producer. Educ: Liszt Ferenc Musical Acad. Publs: The Viking Returns, 1963; Remote Fire, 1967; The Task, 1971; Counterpoint, 1973; Die Wiking Kehrt zurück, 1973. Mbr., Hungarian Assn. of Writers. Hons: Eurocon I, 1972. Address: Gyula utca 1, 1016 Budapest, Hungary.

ZUCKERMAN, Arthur Jacob, b. 16 Dec. 1907, NYC, USA. Professor of Jewish History & Civilization. Educ.

incl: Rabbi, Hebrew Union Coll., 1931; Ph.D., Columbia Univ., 1963. Publs. incl: The Political Uses of Theology (in Studies in Medieval Culture, ed. John R. Sommerfelt), 1970; A Jewish Princedom in Feudal France, 768-900, 1972; Unpublished Materials on the Relationship of Early Fifteenth Century Jewry to the Central Government, 1975. Mbrships. incl: Am. Histl. Assn. Recip., Award, Jewish Book Coun., Am., 1973. Address: 375 Riverside Drive, N.Y., NY 10025, USA.

ZUCKMAYER, Carl, b. 27 Dec. 1896. Playwright; Poet. Publs. incl: (plays) Schinderhannes, 1927; Katharina Knie, 1928; Der Schelm von Bergen, 1934; The Moon in the South, 1937; Second Wind, 1941; Des Teufels General, 1946; Barbara Blomberg, 1949; Ulla Winblad, 1953; Das kalte Lict, 1955; Die Uhr Schlagt Eins, 1966; (novels) Magdalena von Bozen, 1936; Herr uber Leben & Tod, 1938; (poetry) Der Baum, 1926; Collected Works, 1946, 1948, 1950, 1952; (memoirs) Als wär ein Stück von mir, 1966. Hons. incl: Büchner Prize, 1929; Goethe Prize, 1952. Address: CH-3906, Saas-Fëe, Switz.

ŻUKROWSKI, Wojciech, b. 14 Apr. 1916, Cracow, Poland. Writer. Educ: Jagiellonian & Wrocław Univs. Publs: Z kraju milczenia (stories); Piórkiem flaminga (stories); Córeczka (stories); Okruchy weselnego tortu (stories); Dni kleski (novel); Bathed in Fire (novel & film); Kamienne Tablice (novel); Szczęściarz (novel); Plaza nad Styksem (novel); Dom bez ścian (travel); Wedrówki z moim Guru (travel); India, W krainie milona słoni (travel); Niesmiały narzeczony (travel); The Last Days (film); W Głebi Zwierciadła (criticism); Łarambole (criticism). Contbr. to jrnls. Mbr., lit. orgs. Recip., num. awards & decorations. Address: Karowa 14/16 m22, Warsaw 00 324, Poland.

ZULAWSKI, Juliusz, pen name JZ, b. 7 Oct. 1910, Zakopane, Poland. Author; Translator. Publs. incl: (poems) Pole Widzenia, 1948; Wiersze z notatnika, 1957; Kartki z drogi, forthcoming; (novels) Wyprawa o zmierzchu, 1936, 2nd ed., 1957; Skrzydlo dedala, 1949; (critical biogs.) Byron nieupozowany, 1964; 2nd ed., 1966; Wielka podroz Walta Whitmana, 1971; Ed., Byron's Selected Works, 4 vols., 1954-60; Co-Ed., Polish Anthol. of English & American Poets, 3 vols., 1969-74; translator of num. poetic works, classic & mod., chiefly Engl. & Am. Mbrships: VP, Polish PEN; Polish Writers' Assn. Hons. incl: PEN Awards, Poland, 1969, USA, 1971. Address: Iwicka 8A m 8, 00-735, Warsaw, Poland.

ZURCHER, Louis Anthony, b. 13 May 1936, San Fran., Calif., USA. Social Psychologist; University Professor; Chairman, Department of Sociology. Educ: B.A., Univ. of San Fran., 1961; M.A., 1963, Ph.D., 1965, Univ. of Ariz. Publs. incl: Paroled but not Free (w. Rosemary J. Erickson, Wayman J. Crow, & Archie V. Connett), 1973; Citizens for Decency: A Study of Anti-Pornography Crusades (w. R. George Kirkpatrick), 1975. Contbr. to num. profl. jrnls.

etc. Mbrships: Am. Psychol. Assn.; Am. Sociol. Assn. Abraham Maslow Vis. Fellow, W. Behavioral Scis. Inst., 1970. Address: Dept. of Sociology, The Univ. of Texas at Austin, TX 78712, USA.

ZURHORST, Charles S., b. 3 Dec. 1913, Wash. D.C., USA. Writer. Educ: St. John's Coll., Annapolis, Md. Publs: Conservation is a Dirty Word, 1968; The Conservation Fraud, 1970; The First Cowboys, 1973; The First Cowboy, 1974. Contbr. of num. articles & short stories to mags. & anthols. Mbrships: Nat. Press Club, Wash. D.C.; O'seas Press Club, N.Y. Address: Woodruff St., Litchfield, CT 06759, USA.

ZUSPAN, Frederick Paul, b. 20 Jan. 1922, Ohio, USA. Physician Educator; Obstetrician-Gynaecologist; Clinical Neuronendocrinologist; Medical Editor. Educ. incl: M.D., Ohio State Univ. Schl. of Med., 1951. Publs. incl. num. obstetrics papers. Contbr. to: Am. Jrnl. of Obst. & Gynaecol. (Ed.); Current Concepts in Obst. & Gynaecol. (Ed., book series); Jrnl. of Reproductive Med. (Fndng. Ed.); Excerpta Medica (Cons. Ed.); Acta Cytologica (Ed. Advsry. Bd.); etc. Mbrships. incl: Barren Fndn. (Pres.); Am. Acad. of Reproductive Med. (Pres.) Hons. incl: Shirley Schneck Award, Excellence in Hypnosis, 1969. Address: 2400 Coventry, Upper Arlington, Columbus, OH 43221, USA.

ZUURVEEN, Toos Maria, b. 2 Dec. 1934, Leeuwarden, Netherlands. Author. Publs: (for young people) Vonken van Mac, 1953; Verboden Terrein, 1966; Eigen Weg, 1967; Vlinder in het Net, 1966; De sleutel is gebroken, 1970; (children's) Max, de Geleidehond, 1960; Tobias, de ekster, 1967; Lutje, de pony, 1971. Mbr., Vereniging van Letterkundigen. Recip., Decoration for "Max, de geleidehond", Royal Dutch Guide Dog Club, 1960. Address: Leeuwerikstraat 18, Vries (Dr.), Netherlands.

ZWARENSTEYN, Hendrik, b. 16 Feb. Feb. 1913, Tuban, Java. Professor of Business Law. Educ: J.Cand. & J.D., Leiden Univ., Netherlands; Ph.D., Univ. of Amsterdam. Publs: Introduction to Law, 1960, revised ed., 1968; Legal Aspects of Hotel Administration, 1961; Fundamentals of Hotel Law, 1963; Extraterritorial Reach of American Antitrust Law, 1970. Contbr. to: Am. Bus. Law Jrnl.; Nederlands Juristen Blad. Mbr., legal & acad. orgs. Recip., sev. acad. hons. Address: 1370 Jolly Rd., Okemos, MI 48864, USA.

ZWILLINGER, Frank, b. 29 Nov. 1909, Vienna, Austria. Writer. Educ: Ph.D. Publs: Wandel & Wiederkehr (Change & Comeback: poetry), 1950; Der magische Tanz (The Magic Dance: ballads), 1960; Galileo Galilei (play), 1962; Gedichte (Poetry) 3 vols., 1963; Geist und Macht (Spirit & Power) 4 plays, 1973. Mbrships: PEN; Lions Int. St. Cloud. Hons: Theodor Körner Prize, for Promotion of Sci. & Art, Vienna, 1964; TV Prize ZDF, Germany, 1966; Professor h.c. Austria, 1967; Golden Award, Vienna, 1970. Address: 38 rue de Villeneuve, 92380 Garches, France.

ADDENDUM

ALEĆKOVIĆ, Mira, b. 2 Feb. 1927, Novi Sad, Yugoslavia. Writer. Educ: Fac. of Lit., Belgrade Univ., 1952; Sorbonne, France, 1953; Publs. incl: (verse) Trois Printemps, 1949; Traces sans Pas, 1953; Clairière, 1956; Cette Nuit, la Dernière, 1960; Poésies, 1972; (novels) Pourquoi tu grondes le Fleuve, 1955; l'Aube, 1963; 3 juvenile novels & 16 books children's verse. Contbr. to: Kryizeine novine; Politica; num. other European lit. jrnls. Mbrships. incl: Union Yugoslav Writers (former Pres. & VP); Comm. Yugoslav Women; PEN. Hons. incl: Youth Poetry Prize, Serbian Repub., 1950; 1st Prize for Children's Verse, Moscow, 1966; Chevalier, French Legion of Hon., 1971; Medal of Merit, City of Belgrade, 1975; People's Order of Merit. Address: Bulevar Revolucije 17, 11000 Belgrade, Yugoslavia.

ALLEN, Maury, b. 2 May 1932, Brooklyn, N.Y., USA. Author; Newspaper Reporter. Educ: B.A., CCNY, 1953. Publs: Reprieve from Hell, 1961; Great Moments in Sports, 1963; Voices of Sport, 1964; Now Wait a Minute, Casey, 1964; The Incredible Mets, 1969; Joe Namath's Sportin' Life, 1969; Bo/Pitching & Wooing, 1973; Where Have You Gone, Joe DiMaggio?, 1975. Contbr. to: Sports Illustrated; Sport; True; Pageant; Coronet; Saturday Evening Post; Signature. Mbrships: Baseball Writers Assn. of Am. (Chmn., N.Y. Chapt.); Mag. Writers Assn. of Am.; Am. Newspaper Guild. Hons: Best Sports Stories, 1969, 1971, 1973. Address: 157 Northfield Ave., Dobbs Ferry, NY 10522, USA.

ANDERSON, (James) Norman (Dalrymple), b. 29 Sept. 1908, Aldeburgh, UK. Professor of Oriental Laws; Director, University Institute; Q.C. Educ: B.A. 1930, LL.B. 1931, M.A. 1934, LL.D. 1955, Cambridge Univ. Publs. incl: Islamic Law in Africa, 1954; Islamic Law in the Modern World, 1959; Christianity: The Witness of History, 1969; Christianity & Comparative Religion, 1970; Morality, Law & Grace, 1972; A Lawyer among the Theologians, 1973. Contbr. to: Mod. Law Review; Studia Islamica; Jrnl., Royal Ctrl. Asian Soc.; etc. Mbrships: Fellow, Brit. Assn.; Soc. Pub. Tchrs. of Law (Pres., 1968-69). Hons. incl: O.B.E., 1945; D.D., St. Andrews Univ., 1974. Address: 12 Constable Close, London NW11, UK.

ASTUDILLO ASTUDILLO, Sergio Ruben, pen name BRAGELONE, b. 22 June 1939, Cuenca, Ecuador. Lawyer; Diplomat; Journalist. Educ: Lic. Law, Univ. of Cuenca; studied Jrnlsm., Quito. Publs. incl: (verse) Del Crepúsculo, 1958; Canción para Lobos, 1963, 4 eds., Engl. & French transls.; Las Elegias de la Carne, 1964; La Larga Noche de los Lobos, 1970; Diez al Revés del Tiempo; (essays) Señal de Galápagos, 1961; Es te es el Pueblo, 1970. Contbr. to: Mercurio (former Ed.); Tiempo, Quito; etc.; Latin-Am. cultural jrnls. Mbrships. incl: Ecuadorian House of Culture; Nat. Union Jrnlsts., Ecuador. Hons. incl: 1st Prize, Univ. World Poetry Contest, Prague, Czech. Address: Embajada del Ecuador, Casilla 62124, Caracas, Venezuela.

BADDOO, Baldwiin Sempy, b. 6 Jan. 1930, Accra, Ghana. Homeopathic, Osteopathic & Naturopathic Practitioner; Author; Researcher. Educ: Dips., Insight Inst., & Modern Thought Schl. of Natural Therapeutics, London, UK, 1950-60; Dip. in Osteopathy, Ph.D., Chgo Med. Coll. of Homepathy, USA, 1961-65; Gen. Register Osteopaths, UK. Publs: Anatomy of Plane Crashes, 1962; Your Guide to 1972, 1973, 1974, 1975. Contbr. to: Ghanaian Times, & Weekly Spectator (Feature Writer 1966–); Ideal Woman (columnist). Mbrships. incl: Fellow, Fedn. Brit. Astrologers; Ghana Assn. Writers. Address: P.O. Box 7602, Accra-North, Ghana.

BAILEY, (Sir) Harold Walter, b. 16 Dec. 1899, Devizes, UK. University Professor. Educ: B.A., M.A., Univ. W. Australia; B.A., M.A., D.Phil., Oxford Univ. Publs: Zoroastrian Problems in the Ninth Century Books, 1943, 1971; Khotanese Texts, Vols. I-VI, 1945-67; Khotanese Buddhist Texts, 1951; Saka Documents, Portfolios I-IV, 1960-67; Saka Documents, Text volume, 1968. Contbr. to learned periodicals. Hons: Fellow, British Acad., 1944; Knighthood, 1960; Membre de l'Institut de France, 1968; Hon. Doctor of Letters, Univ. of West Aust., 1963 & Aust. Nat. Univ., 1970; Hon. Fellow, Queens' Coll., 1967 & Aust. Acad. of the Humanities, 1971; Triennial Gold Medal, Royal Asiatic Soc., 1972; Pres., Soc. for Mithraic Studies & Soc. for Afghan Studies, 1972. Address: Queens' Coll., Cambridge, UK.

BANK, Theodore (Ted) Paul II, pen name ADAMS, Weld, b. 31 Aug. 1923, Patterson, La., USA. Explorer; Anthropologist; Educator. Educ: Harvard Univ.; B.S. 1947, M.S. 1950, Rsch. 1950-54, Univ. of Mich. Publs: Birthplace of the Winds, USA, 1956, UK, 1957; Student Manual for Cultural Anthropology, 1966; People of the Bering Sea, 1971. Contbr. to: Sci. Am.; Nat. Hist.; Think; Kiwanis Mag.; Sci.; Am. Antiquity; etc.; Alaska Book, & other anthols. Mbrships. incl: Am. Inst. for Exploration, Inc. (Exec. Dir. & Trustee, 1960–); Explorers Club (Contbng. Ed., Explorers Jrnl., 1961–); Fellow, AAAS. Recip., var. Scholarships. Address: 1809 Nichols Rd., Kalamazoo, MI 49007, USA.

BARTLETT, Norman, b. 17 Jan. 1908, Monmouthshire, UK. Journalist & Diplomatic Attaché (ret'd). Educ: B.A., Dip.J., Univ. of Western Aust., Perth; Aust. Nat. Univ., Canberra. Publs: The Pearl Seekers, 1954; With the Australians in Korea, 1954; Island Victory, 1955; Land of the Lotus Eaters, 1959; The Gold Seekers, 1965. Contbr. to: Meanjin Quarterly; Quadrant; Aust. Quarterly; etc. Mbrships: Aust. Soc. of Authors; Aust. Fellowship of Writers; Imperial Serv. Club; The Siam Soc. Address: 31 Scott St., Narrabundah, Canberra, ACT 2604, Australia.

BARZUN, Jacques, b. 1907, Créteil, France. University Professor, 1967-75; Literary Adviser, Scribners, 1975–. Educ: Columbia Coll. Grad. Schl.; Columbia Univ.; A.B.; M.A.; Ph.D. Publs. incl: The French Race; Of Human Freedom; Darwin, Marx, Wagner; Teacher in America; Berlioz & the Romantic Century, 2 vols., 3rd ed. 1969; Selected Letters of Lord Byron; Music in American Life; The Modern Researcher, 2nd ed., 1970; The House of Intellect; Science, The Glorious Entertainment; The American University; A Catalogue of Crime; On Writing, Editing & Publishing; Evenings with the Orchestra; The Use & Abuse of Art; Clio & the Doctors. Contbr. to: The Am. Scholar; Harper's Mag.; Encounter; Science; Critical Inquiry. Address: 597 Fifth Ave., N.Y. NY 10017, USA.

BAVIERA, Silvio Riccardo, b. 8 Aug. 1944, Zurich, Switz. Writer; Publisher. Publs: Alias dankt der Leserschaft, 1967; Der Sechzehnkampf des Hans Anders, 1968; Ein Tage- & Nächtebuch des Hans Anders, 1969; Das Vermächtnis des Hans Anders, 1970. Contbr. to: Tagesanzeiger; Zürcher AZ; Nat. Zeitung; Badener Tagblatt; Luzerner Nachrichten; Annabelle; Neutralität; Zürcher Almanach I & II; GratisBuch; etc. Mbr., Olten Grp. Hons: Incentive Prize, City of Zürich, 1969; Werkjahr, City of Zurich, 1970; Recognition, Grant, Canton of Zurich & Swiss Confederation, 1972. Address: Dienerstrasse 22, 8004 Zürich, Switz.

BAXT, Robert, pen name SIR JOHN LATHAM PROFESSOR OF LAW, b. 27 June 1938, Shanghai, China. Professor of Law. Educ: B.A., 1959, LL.B., 1963, Univ. of Sydney, Aust.; LL.M., Harvard Univ., USA, 1964. Publs: Asst. Ed., Masterman & Solomon, Australian Trade Practices Law, 1967; The Concrete Pipes Case: It's Impact on Australian Business, 1972; 2nd Aust. Supplement to Gower, Modern Company Law, 3rd ed.; Cases & Materials on Corporations & Associations (w. A. B. Afterman), 1972, 2nd ed. 1975). Contbr. to: Aust. Bus. Law Review (Ed.); Aust. Law Jrnl. (Commercial Law Ed.); Chartered Acct. in Aust.; etc. Address: 88 Essex Rd., Mt. Waverley, Vic. 3149, Australia.

BERRY, (Julia) Elizabeth, b. 18 Nov. 1921, Jones, Ala., USA. Educator; Writer. Educ: A.B., Ctrl. Mo. State Univ., 1942; A.M., Univ. of Mich., 1948; Ph.D., Columbia Univ., 1955. Publs. incl: Guiding Students in the English Class, 1958; The Careers of English Majors, 1967; The Gifted Women in Our Midst, 1971. Contbr. to: Weiss, An English Teacher's Reader, 1962; Jrnl. of Coll. Student Personnel (abstracter); other profl. jrnls. Mbrships. incl: Am. Personnel & Guidance Assn. (Senate, 1964, 1966); Am. Coll. Personnel Assn.; Nat. Coun. Tchrs. of Engl. Recip., Grant, Nat. Coun. Tchrs. of Engl. Address: 606 W. Mechanic, Harrisonville, MO 64701, USA.

BIEBER, Margarete, b. 31 July 1879, Schoenau, W. Germany. Author; Art Historian. Educ: Berlin Univ., 1901-05; Ph.D., Bonn Univ., 1906. Publs. incl: The History of the Greek & Roman Theater, 1960; The Sculpture of the Hellenistic Age, 1961; Copies: A Contribution to the History of Greek & Roman Art, 1974. Contbr. to: Am. Jrnl. Archaeol.; Classical World; Jahrbuch, Deutschen

Arcaeol. Inst.; Art Bulletin; Athenische Mitteilungen, etc. Mbrships: Am. Inst. Archaeol.; German Archaeol. Inst.; Soc. for Arts & Scis., Boston, USA. Hons: Litt.D., Columbia Univ., USA, 1954; Int. Fellowship, Am. Academic Women. Address: 605 W. 113th St., Apt. 33, N.Y., NY 10025, USA.

BIRD, Michael John, pen names BANNEN, Neil; BENNETT, Jordan, b. 31 Oct. 1928, London, UK. Writer. Publs: Foreign Office – Confidential, 1961; The Town That Died, 1962; The Secret Battalion, 1964. Contbr. to: BBC TV & Radio; Independent TV. Mbrships: Writers Guild of GB; Crime Writers Assn. Address: 13 Buristead Rd., Great Shelford, Cambridge CB2 5EJ, UK.

BISWAS, Chitta Ranjan, pen name CHIRANJIB, b. 1 Sept. 1939, Khulna, now Bangladesh. Journalist (Sports Reporter). Educ: B.A. Publs: Kanoji Angre, 1971; Napethey, 1971; Jai Thekey Jai Cricketey, 1972; Khelar Mather Antoraley, 1972; Sera Sera Kheloar, 1972; Khela Dhular Adhunik Niam Kanun, 1973; Khela Dhular Nepathey, 1974. Contbr. to: Ananda Bazar Patrika; Ultorath; Cinema Jagat Prosad, Calcutta; Ittefaq, Dacca. Mbrships: Nat. Union Jrnlsts., India; Press Club, Calcutta; Sports Jrnlsts. Assn., W. Bengal. Address: 2/186F, Sree Colony, Calcutta 700047, India.

BOLSTAD, Öivind, pen names EIKAN, Theo; EDEN, Martin; KJÖLHALER, Tobias, b. 1 Feb. 1905, Vardö, Norway. Writer. Publs. incl: (novels) Gamle Winckels Testament, 1948; Spökefuglen på Toska, 1957; Familien We's Kroniken, 7 vols., 1967-75; (plays) Metamorforse; Patrioten; Tyv i Lyset; Den Röde Begonia; (TV plays) You are the Murderer, Prague; The Traitors, Berlin, 1956; num. radio plays, 1931–; about 600 short stories inclng. collect. Ut en Medalje, USSR, 1962; (non-fiction) Sagaen om Norskebygdene på Grönland (w. A. W. Brögger). Contbr. to: Magasinet; Politikens Mag.; Profil; etc. Mbrships. incl: Norwegian Writers Soc.; Dramatists Assn.; Oslo Arts Soc. Hons. incl: Life Stipend, Norwegian State, 1945–; Honour Prize, Swedish Acad., 1973; num. other awards. Address: Strömmeveien 115a, 5064 Straumsgrend, Norway.

BOTTRALL, Margaret Florence Saumarez, b. 27 June 1909, Sydney, Australia. University Teacher. Educ: Lady Margaret Hall, Oxford; Yale Grad. Schl.; M.A. Oxon; M.A. Cantab. Publs: George Herbert, 1954; Every Man a Phoenix, 1958; Macmillan Casebook Series: Blake's Songs of Innocence & Experience, 1970 & G. M. Hopkins: Poems, 1975. Contbr. to: Economist (regular reviewer of lit. criticism & biography). Mbr., PEN. Address: 72 Cavendish Ave., Cambridge CB1 4UT, UK.

BOUDREAUX, Emeline M. Broussard, pen name BROUSSARD, Emeline, b. 26 May 1908, St. Martinville, La., USA. Songwriter; Poet. Publs: Cavalcade of Poetry, 1963; Melody of the Muse, 1964; A Burst of Trumpets, 1966; Versatility in Verse, 1966; Lyric Louisiana, IV, 1967-69; The Soul & the Singer, 1968; New Voices in the Wind, 1969. Contbr. to Radio & TV, La. & Can. Mbr., La. Poetry Soc. Hons. incl: 1st Prizes for French Songs, Dairy Festival, Abbeville, La., 1964, & Rice Festival, Crowley, La., 1966; 1st Prize for French Poems, Poetry Day, New Orleans, 1968. Address: Rt. 2, Box 85, St. Martinville, LA 70582, USA.

BRAMBLETT, Agnes Cochran, b. 3 Oct. 1886, Rivoli, Ga., USA. Writer; Poet; Lecturer. Publs. incl: Legend of the Weaver of Paradise, 1928; Wind-Mad, 1935; Wolves of Troreness, 1944; Eve & the Fallen Star, 1948; My Brother, Oh My Brother, 1953; People at Work, & Other Poems; With Lifted Heart. Contbr. to: Ga. Mag.; Atlanta Jrnl.; N.Y. Sun; Balt. Sun; Versecraft; Visions; etc. Mbrships: Atlanta Writers Club; Nat. League Am. Pen Women; Ga. Writers Assn.; Dixie Coun. Jrnlsts. & Authors. Hons. incl: D.Litt., Tift Coll., 1971; A.C. Bramblett Day proclaimed by Gov. of Ga., May 17 1974. Address: 94 Country Club Dr., Forsyth, GA 31024, USA.

BROOKE-TAYLOR, Tim, b. 17 July 1940, Buxton, UK. Actor; Writer. Educ: M.A., Pembroke Coll., Cambridge Univ. Publs: The Goodies File, 1974. Address: 49 Platt's Lane, London NW3 7NL, UK.

BROWNLEE, William Hugh, b. 17 Feb. 1917, Sylvia, Kan., USA. Professor of Religion. Educ: B.A., Sterling Coll., 1939; Th.B. 1942, Th.M., 1946, Pitts.–Xenia Theol. Sem.; Ph.D., Duke Univ., 1947. Publs: The Dead Sea Scrolls of St. Mark's Monastery (co-author), 1950; The Dead Sea Manual of Discipline, 1951; The Text of Habakkuk in the

Ancient Commentary from Qumran, 1959; The Meaning of the Qumran Scrolls for the Bible, 1964. Contbr. to: Interpretation; Harvard Theol. Review; Biblica; Revue de Qumran; etc. Mbrships. incl: Am. Schls. Oriental Rsch.; Soc. Biblical Lit. (former VP). Hons. incl: D.D., Sterling Coll., 1960; var. Fellowships. Address: 1534 Wells Ave., Claremont, CA 91711, USA.

BUCKLAND, Raymond Brian, pen name EARLL, Tony, b. 31 Aug. 1934, London, UK. Writer. Educ: B.A. 1958, M.A., 1960, Kings Coll., London Univ.; Ph.D., Brantridge Coll., Sussex, 1966; D.D., Life Sci. Ch., Rolling Meadows, Ill, USA. Publs: A Pocket Guide to the Supernatural, 1969; Practical Candle-Burning, 1970; Witchcraft Ancient & Modern, 1970; Witchcraft from the Inside, 1971; Here is the Occult, 1974; The Tree, 1974; Amazing Secrets of the Psychic World, 1974; (as T. Earll) Mu Revealed, 1970. Contbr. to: Seax-Wica Voys (Ed.), N.H., USA. Mbrships. incl: Weirs Chmbr. of Comm. (Bd. of Dirs.). Address: P.O. Box 238 Weirs Beach, NH 03246, USA.

BUFFINGTON, Tiny Louise, pen names BUFF, Lou; MYHHB, Cesi, b. 6 May 1925, Wicksburg, Ala., USA. Teacher; Poet; Lecturer. Educ: B.A. in Engl. Publs: Armchair Treasures, 1971; Southern Echoes (forthcoming). Contbr. to num. mags., anthols. & newspapers. Mbrships: Charter mbr., Ala. State Poetry Soc. (Chmn. of Publs., & Local Chapt. Chmn.); Centro Studi e Scambi Int.; Pensters; Int. Poetry Soc.; Laurel Publrs. Poetry Symposium; Ala. Writers' Conclave. Recip., num. certs. & awards. Address: P.O. Box 524, Jay, FL 32565, USA.

CALLINAN, Bernard James, b. 2 Feb. 1913, Melbourne, Australia. Consulting Engineer. Educ: B.C.E., Dip. Town & Regional Planning, Melbourne Univ. Publs: Independent Company, 1953-54. Contbr. to: Jrnl., Inst. of Engrs., Aust.; Proceedings, Royal Soc. of Vic. Mbrships: Fellow, Instn. Civil Engrs., UK (Coun., 1962-65); Fellow, Instn. Engrs., Aust. (Coun., 1958–; Pres., 1971); Fellow, Royal Town Planning Inst., & Royal Aust. Town Planning Inst. Hons: M.C., 1943; D.S.O., 1945; C.B.E., 1971; P.N. Russell Mem. Medal, 1972. Address: Belulic, 111 Sackville St., Kew 3101, Australia.

CATLIN, (Sir) George (Edward Gordon), b. 29 July 1896. Former University Professor; concerned with Atlantic Community Policy, 1925–; Founder & Acting Chairman, Movement for Atlantic Union (UK). Educ: New Coll., Oxford (M.A.); Ph.D., Cornell Univ., USA. Publs. incl: The Science & Method of Politics, 1926, 1964; Study of the Principles of Politics, 1929, 1967; Anglo-Saxony & its Tradition, 1939; Anglo-American Union as Nucleus of World Federation, 1942; The Unity of Europe, 1945; Mahatma Gandhi, 1948; What Does the West Want? , 1957; Systematic Politics, 1962; The Grandeur of England & the Atlantic Community, 1966; For God's Sake, Go, (autobiog.) 1972; Atlanticism, 1973. Ed. & Special For. Corres., People & Freedom; Co-fndr., (w. H. G. Wells, Arnold Bennett & others) Realist Mag. Fellow & VP, World Acad. Arts & Scis.; F.R.S.L. Address: 5 Wilton Pl., London SW1, UK.

CLARK, Sandra, b. 24 May 1942, Bridlington, Yorks., UK. Playwright. Educ: B.A.(Hons.) Philos. Publs: (plays. prod.) Down But Not Out, 1972; A Quick Thing, 1973; Apollo 11 Through Tananarive & Other Station; Hanging On, 1974; (film) Man's Estate, or How It Is (1973). Address: Kensington House, Northgate, Cottingham, Yorks., UK.

COLLINS, David Raymond, b. 29 Feb. 1940, Marshalltown, Iowa, USA. Educator; Author; Lecturer. Educ: B.S., 1962, M.S. in Counselling 1966, Western Ill., Univ. Publs: Kim Soo & His Tortoise, 1970; Great American Nurses, 1971; Walt Disney's Surprise Christmas Present, 1972; Linda Richards, 1973; Harry S. Truman, 1974. Contbr. to: Plays: Instructor; Venture; Hearthstone; Cath. Boy; Cath. Miss; Child Life; etc. Mbrships. incl: Authors Guild; Soc. Children's Book Writers; Writers' Studio (Pres., 1967-71). Hons. incl: J. M. Thomas Award for Poetry, 1965; Bobbs-Merill Award, Ind. Univ., 1971; Quad City Writer of Yr., 1972. Address: 3724 15th Ave., Moline, IL 61265, USA.

de GRAFT-JOHNSON, John Coleman, b. 21 Mar. 1919, Accra, Ghana. Economist; Historian; Diplomat. Educ: B.Com., M.A., Ph.D., Edinburgh Univ., UK. Publs. incl: African Glory, UK, 1954, 1955, USA, 1956, transl'd. Czech 1956, Italian 1957; African Experiment, 1958; An

Introduction to the African Economy, India, 1959. Contbr. to: Ency. Britannica; Proceedings, Ghana Acad. Arts & Scis.; Transactions, Ghana Histl. Soc.; Econ. Bulletin, Ghana (Ed., 1970—); etc. Mbrships. incl: Fellow, Ghana Acad. Arts & Scis. (Hon. Sec., 1971, 1972), Histl. Soc. of Ghana (Pres., 1961-67), Ghana Econ. Soc. Recip., Grand Cross Order of Merit, Luxemburg. 1970. Address: Dept. of Economics, Univ. of Ghana, Legon, Accra, Ghana.

DIAS, Reginald Walter Michael, b. 3 Mar. 1921, Colombo, Ceylon. University Lecturer; College Fellow; Barrister-at-Law. Educ: M.A., LL.B., Trinity Hall, Cambridge Univ., UK. Publs: Wise & Winfield's Jurisprudence, 6th ed., 1947; Jurisprudence, 3rd ed., 1970; Bibliography of Jurisprudence, 2nd ed. 1970; Co-Ed., Clerk & Lindsell on Torts, 14th ed. 1975. Contbr. to: Ency. Britannica, 1964; Dictionary of Hist. of Ideas, 1973; Law Quarterly Review; Mod. Law Review; Cambridge Law Jrnl.; Tulane Law Review; Univ. of Toronto Law Jrnl.; Cambridge Review; Listener; etc. Mbrships: Inner Temple; Soc. Pub. Tchrs. of Law. Address: 5 Babraham Rd., Cambridge, UK.

DUPRAY, Sophia Maria Michelina, b. Lier, Belgium. Poet; Secretary. Educ: Studies Nursing, Ecole Ste. Berlinde, Antwerp; Ecole de Servs. Social, Brussels. Publs: Fougue Amoureuse (poems), 1956; Alice Nahon (boig. & transl. of poems), 1958; Terpsichore (poems), 1960; Le Roman des Servantes, 1964; Transl., S. Streuvels, Arbres (novel), 1960, & var. other Dutch & Persian works. Contbr. to: Voix du Nord; Arts & Sanas, Paris; Cahiers Luxembourgeois; etc. Mbrships. incl: PEN; Assn. Belgian Writers; Belgian Artistic Fedn. Hons. incl: Prize for Tales & Legends, France; French Humanities Prize for verse; Bronze Medal, UFACSI, Auvergne, France, 1963. Address: Kapucienessenstraat 13, B 2000 Antwerp, Belgium.

PSEUDONYMS OF INCLUDED AUTHORS

The following constitutes a list of pen names of all those included in the biographical section with cross-reference to the name under which the entry appears. Those who wished to be entered in the main body of the book under a pen name have not been included in this list.

Aachen, C. V. - Melcher, Gil,
    (Gilbert Wayne)
Abbasi, Najam - Abbasi, Najmuddin
Acal, Luis Jacobo - Dominguez Aragones,
    Edmundo
Adams, John - Morlan, John E.
Adams, John Paul - Kinnaird, Clark
Adams, Sam - Poindexter, Joseph B.
Adams, Weld - Bank, Theodore
Adrian, Mary - Jorgensen, Mary Venn
Adytum - Curl, James Stevens
Agard, H. E. - Evans, Hilary
Ahm, George - Möllerstedt, Gunnar
Aida - Amin, Khalidah A.
Aird, Catherine - McIntosh, Kinn Hamilton
Airlie, Catherine - MacLeod, Jean Sutherland
Akerman, Richard - Noel Hume, Ivor
Akilon - Akilandam, Perungalur V.
Albrecht, Willi - Prins, Sonja
Alexander, Hank - Sanderson, William H.
Alexander, Joan - Pepper, Joan
Alexander, John - Ruler, John
Aliki - Brandenberg, Aliki
Allan, Ann - Lilly, Isabella P.
Allan, Peter - Underwood, Peter
Allen, Edmund - Reeve-Jones, Alan E.
Allured, Lloyd - Hoffman, Donald
Alm, Monica - Olausson, Rune E.
Althea - Braithwaite, Althea
Al Van-Gar - Radwanski, Pierre A.
Ames, Felicia - Burden, Jean P.
Amis, Breton - Best, Rayleigh B. A.
Amnon III - Evans, William
Amstein, Martin - Riess, Curt
Anantasree. - Sreenivasapuram, Anantha
    Charlu
Anderson, Ella - MacLeod, Ellen Jane
Andreev, Vesselin - Andreev, Georgy
Andrews, Cicily Fairfield - West Rebecca
Anfeld, Wes - Schwanfelder, Werner
Anni, Makituvan - Honkanen, Hilja Loviisa
    Valkeapää
Anthony, C. L. - Smith, Dodie
Anwar - Anwar, Sayyed
ap Evans, Humphrey - Drummond Humphrey
Ap Robert, Alun - Hughes, Goronwy Alun
Aquarius - Allen, John E.
Archer-Batten, S. - Walker, Stella Archer
Archer, S - Walker, Stella Archer
Argos - Baquero, Arcadio
Arlandson, Lee - Arlandson, Leone R.
Armstrong, Anthony - Willis, Anthony
    Armstrong
Arrowsmith, Wm. - Smith, Leslie Wilfred
Arthur, Gladys - Osborne, Dorothy G.
Arthur, Hugh - Christie-Murray, David
ARW 493 - Foghammar, Stig S.
Ashe, Susan - Best, Carol A.
Askew, Jack - Hivnor, Robert H.
Asquith, Nan - Pattinson, Nancy E.

Assiac - Fraenkel, Heinrich
Atheling, William, Jr. - Blish, James
Attaboy - Hetherington, John Rowland
Auchterlonie - Green, Dorothy
A Vagabond Schoolmarm - Nicholson,
    Lillie M.
Avery, (Mrs) R. W. - Stevenson, Anne
Avery, Richard - Cooper, Edmund
Avon, Margaret - Keatley, Sheila Marjorie
Awi-Dafna, S. P. - Bentov, Shmuel P.
Aylmer, Felix - Jones, Felix Edward Aylmer
Babcock, G. - Livingston, Braniff I.
Balaam - Lamb, Geoffrey F.
Baldry, Enid - Citovich, Enid
Baldwin, George - Schick, George B. P.
Balfour, Patrick - Kinross, (Lord) Patrick
    Balfour
Bancroft, Robert - Kirsch, Robert
Bandopadhyaya, Shashi Bhusan - Upadhyaya,
    Shantilal Chhaganlial
Bannen, Neil - Bird, Michael John
Baraka, Imamu Amiri - Jones (Everett) LeRoi
Barber, Antonia - Anthony, Barbara
Bard, W. E. - Bard, William E.
Barkton, S. Rush - Brav, Stanley R.
Barnes, Chesley Virginia - Young, Chesley
    Virginia Barnes
Barnsley, Alan G. - Fielding, Gabriel
Barpe - Barquero Pena, Jose E.
Barrett, Paul - Booth, Rosemary F.
Barrington, Nicholas - Whittington-Egan,
    Richard
Barton, Harry - Barton, Arthur H.
Barton, S. W. - Whaley, Barton Stewart
Batchelor, Paula - Gibbs, Peter B.
Baxter, Gillian - Hirst, Gillian Jose
    Charlotte
Baxter, Shane - Norwood, Victor G. C.
Bazin, Hervé - Bazin, Jean Pierre Marie
BBC TV VET. - Straiton, Edward Cornock
Beachcomber - Morton, John Cameron Andrieu
    Bingham
Beavers, Col. H. O. - Rickell, Walter L.
Beck, Maximilian - Plaue, Ernst M.
Beebe, B. F. - Johnson, Burdetta Fay Beebe
Bell, Christopher - Mandel, Loring
Bell, Colin Kane - Bell, Colin A.
Bell, H. D. - Bradbury, Frederick P.
Bellman, Erik M. - Falkner, Annemy
Bellman, Walter - Barrett, Hugh G.
Bellsmith, Wm. - Smith, Leslie Wilfred
Belvedere, Lee - Grayland, Valerie M.
Bender, Jay - Deindorfer, Robert Greene
Bennett, Elizabeth - Robinson, Nancy E.
Bennett, Jean Frances - Dorcy (Sister) Mary
    Jean, O.P. (Frances E. Dorcy)
Benoit, Frank - Hart, Lewis Vincent
Benoit, Lew - Hart, Lewis Vincent
Ben, P. - Bentov, Shmuel P.
Benko, Nancy - Atkinson, Nancy

Bennett, Jordan - Bird, Michael
Bentham, Grace - Soman, Shirley Camper
Berg, Rilla - France, Thelma E. M.
Berglund, Sven G. - Lundberg, (Sven Gunnar) Ingemar
Bergman, Jonas - Söderhjelm, Kai
Bernd, Peter - Orthofer, Peter B.
Berne, Leo - Davies, Leslie Purnell
Berquin, Jean - Hennequin, Bernard
Berrisford, Judith M. - Lewis, Clifford & Mary
Bersogli, Bragi - Jonasson, Jakob
Beta - Boyle, Wilfred
Beti, Mongo - Biyidi-Awala, Alexandre
Betteridge, Anne/Potter, Margaret
Beulah - Kershau, Beulah Sevenney
BGr. - Gullander, Eric Gustaf Bertil
Bhatia, June - Bhatia, Jamunadevi
Biassen, Sal - Bonnekamp, Sonja M.
Biddestone, Neil - Graham, Bertie N. G. G.
Binner Ina - Binner, Ethel I.
Binter, C. - Burtis, Charles E.
Birkenhead, Edward - Birkenhead, Elijah
Bisonius - Allen, John E.
Bjornstad, Marianne - Engh, Bjorg L.
Black, Gavin - Wynd, Oswald
Blacker, Hereth - Chalke, Herbert Davis
Blacklin, Malcolm - Chambers, Aidan
Blackwell, John - Collings, Edwin Geoffrey
Blairman, Jacqueline - Pinto, Jacqueline
Blake, Monica - Muir, Marie Agnes
Blake, Robert - Davies, Leslie Purnell
Blanch Lyon Herald - Franklyn, Charles A. H.
Bland, Jennifer - Bowden, Jean
Blauth, Christopher - Blauth-Muszkowski, Peter C.
Blengh - Engh, Bjorg L.
Bliss, Carlyse - Brechin, Carlyse B.
Blue, S. G. - Farley, George M.
Blythe, Joyce - Trent, Ann
Boe, Pieter - Brocher, Tobias H.
Bohemian - Channing-Renton (Capt), Ernest Matthews
Bold, Ralph - Griffiths, Charles T. W.
Boll, Ernest - Boll, Theophilus E. M.
Bolster, Evelyn - Bolster, (Sister) M. Angela
Bonett, John - Coulson, John Hubert Arthur
Borden, Lee - Deal, Borden
Borel, Helene - Hegeler, Sten
Boroniecki, Miroslaw - Stoberski Zygmunt Julian
Bosanac, R. - Colakovic, Rodoljub
Bosquet, Alain - Bisk, Anatole
Boswell, - Gordon, Giles A. E.
Boulendov, Boris - de Bourbon, Louis Adelberth (Prince-Duke of Normandy
Bowden, Jim - Spence, William John Duncan
Bowdoin, William - Brannon, William T.
Bowie, Jim - Norwood, Victor G. C.
Box, Edgar - Vidal, Gore
Brac, Hans - Van De Waarsenburg, Hans
Bradley, Sam - Bradley, Samuel McKee
Bragelone - Astudillo Astudillo, Sergio Ruben
Brand, Bart - Faherty, William B.
Brand, J. F. - Faherty, William B.
Brand, Mona - Fox, Mona A.
Brandon, Sheila - Rayner, Claire
Brdlbrmpft - Roth, Christian
Bream, Freda - Whale, Patricia Freda
Breedveld, Walter - van den Bogaert, Piet Franciscus Martinus

Brendall, Edith - Bertin, Eddy C.
Brennan, Tim - Conroy, Jack, (John Wesley)
Brent, Calvin - Hornby, John Wilkinson
Bridgeman, Richard - Davies Leslie Purnell
Briony, Henry - Ellis, Oliver C. Jointly with Gibbons-Turner, D. M.
Briquebec, John - Rowland-Entwistle, Theodore
Brock, Stuart - Trimble, Louis Preston
Bronston, William - Brannon, William T.
Brooke, Carol - Ramskill, Valerie P.
Broussard, Emeline - Boudreaux, Emeline M. Broussard
Brown, George - Jenkins, Norman
Brown, Irwin - Murray, David Stark
Bruller, Jean - Vercors
Bryans, Robin - Bryans, Robert H.
Brysson Morrison, N. - Morrison, Nancy (Agnes) Brysson Inglis
Bubulkiewicz, Nepomucen - Nepomucka, Krystyna
Buff, Lou - Buffington, Tiny Louise
Burfield, Eva - Ebbett, Frances Eva
Burg, David - Dolberg, Alexander
Burgeon, G. A. - Barfield, Arthur Owen
Burke, Jonathan - Burke, John F.
Burt, Gill - Melcher, Gil (Gilbert Wayne)
Busby, Jonathan - Allen, Eric
Butler, Richard - Allbeury, Theo E.
Buysman, F. M. - Franse, Petrus W.
Cade, Jack - Arnot, Robin P.
Cade, Robin - Nicole, Christopher R.
Cadwr - Palsson, Herman
Cahones, Carolyn - Bowart, Walter H.
Cairo, Jon - Romano, Deane L.
Caldwell, Elinor - Breton-Smith, Clare
Caliban, - Stål, Sven Artur Olof
Callian, Selma - Kalichman, Claire
Calvin, Henry - Hanley, Clifford Leonard Clark
Calzolari, Gino - Orlando, Ruggero
Camand, Richard - Coekelberghs, Amand Joseph Richard
Cameron, Donald - Bryans, Robert H.
Campbell, Clyde Crane - Gold, Horace L.
Campbell, Francis S. - Kuehnel T-Leddihn, (Ritter von) Erik M.
Campbell, Karen - Beaty, Betty
Cameron, Ian - Payne, Donald G.
Candy, Edward - Neville, Barbara A.
Carette, Louis - Marceau, Felicien
Carfax, Catherine - Fairburn, Eleanor
Carmichael, Harry - Ognall, Leo H.
Cansfield, Paul - Norwood, Victor G. C.
Carat - Barat, Endre
Carlton, Ann - Trent, Ann
Carr, Michael - Clark, Russell John
Carr, Roberta - Roberts, Irene
Carrick, Edward - Craig, Edward Anthony
Carrick, John - Crosbie, Hugh Provan
Carstens, Netta - Laffeaty, Christina
Carter, Avis M. - Allen, Kenneth S.
Cash, Grady - Cash, Grace
Cashel, John - Booth, Harry J.
Cassells, John - Duncan, William Murdoch
Castellano, Franco - Sgarlato, Nico
Castenius, Sigrid - Thyselius, Thorburg Elin Tryggvesdotter
Castle, Frances - Blackburn, Evelyn B.
Castweazle, Eleanor - Raynes, Frederica R. R.
Catamaran - Bing, Jon
Catay - Mendoza Romero, Maria Luisa

Fletcher, Scott - Pfeiffer, C. Boyd
Flowerdew, Phyllis - Kingsbury, Phyllis May
Fonn, Belle - Ford-House, Iris E.
Ford, Kirk - Spence, William John Duncan
Ford, Langridge - Coleman-Cooke, John
Ford, Norrey - Dilcock, Noreen
Forde, Nicholas - Elliott-Cannon, Arthur
    Elliott
Forde, Rogerson - Rogerson, Fred
Forest, Lee - Woods, Clee
Forrest, Norman - Morland, Nigel
Forrester, Helen - Bhatia, Jamunadevi
Forrester, Mary - Humphries, Elsie Mary
Fortina, Martha - Laffeaty, Christina
Fosca, Francois - de Traz, Georges
Fosk, Nicholas - Higginbottom David
Foster, George - Haswell, Chetwynd John
    Drake
Fox, Petronella - Balogh, Penelope
Francis, C. D. E. - Howarth, Partick John
    Fielding
Francis, Dick - Francis, Richard S.
Franklin, Max - Deming, Richard
Franks, Lew - Hart, Lewis Vincent
Fraser, Jane - Pilcher, Rosamunde E.
Frazier, Arthur - Bulmer, Henry K.
Fredric, Keith - Rickell, Walter L.
Freeman, Thomas - Fehrenbach, T. R.
Freezer, Harriet - Wolsak-Eijbergen,
    Wilhelmina
French, Jane - Mercer, Marilyn
Frenk, Mariana - Frenk-Westheim, Mariana
Froy, Herald - Deghy, Guy
Friend, Ed - Wormser, Richard Edward
Frykberg, August - Sunesson, Lambert
Fun-Chi - Lung, Chu-Yung
Fune, Jonathan - Fletcher, John W. J.
Füruzan - Selçuk, Füruzan
Gaio, G. S. - Servadio, Gaia C. M.
Gale, John - Pilikian, Hovhanness I.
Gamma - Booth, Andrew D.
Gangolf - Jullig, Karl Hans
Gannold, John - Langdon, John F. C.
Gardiner, Jae - Lee, Polly J. G.
Garland, Bennett - Garfield, Brian F. W.
Garnett, Roger - Morland, Nigel
Garrard, Christopher - Milton, John R.
Garrison, Chuck - Garrison, Charles J.
Gay, Ellen - Tracy, (Pauline) Aloise
Gay, Francis - Gee, Herbert L.
Gayton-Verne, David - Shay, Violet B.
Gazdag, Erzsi - Gazdag, Erzsebet
Geerten, Bert - Van Hageland, Albert
George, David - Vogenitz, David George
George, Jonathan - Burke, John F.
Germany, Jo - Germany, Vera J.
G. G.-J. - Gustaf-Janson, Gosta
Gibb, Lee - Deghy, Guy
Gibbard, T. S. J. - Vinter, Michael
Gilbert, Nan - Gilbertson, Mildred G.
Gill, Hugh - Hugill, Robert
Gilles - Baert, Adriaan G. C.
Gillespie, Nan - Buranelli, Agnes W.
Glasbrenner - Fielhauer, Otto M.
Goama, Muriel - Cox, Edith Muriel
Gonzalez, Arky - Gonzalez, Arturo F. Jr.
Gordon, Cameo - Smith, Dorothy
    Cameron
Gordon, Ray - Wainwright, Gordon Ray
Gordon, Steward - Shirreffs, Gordon D.
Gowans, Elsa - Watt, Elsie Gowans
Grabb, Cesar - Benitez De Castro, Cecilio
Grace, Joseph - Hornby, John Wilkinson

Graeme, Bruce - Jeffries, Graham Montague
Graf Willibald - Durben, Wolfgang
Graham, Janet - Rance, Janet M.
Graham, Neill - Duncan, William Murdoch
Grange, Peter - Nicole, Christopher R.
Grant, C. B. S. - Haga, Enoch John
Grant, Don - Glut, Donald F.
Grant, Madison Andrew - Schmick, Bruce D.
Grashoff, Cok - Grashoff, Pieter
Gray, Betsy - Poole, Gray J.
Gray, Dulcie - Denison, Dulcie Winifred
    Catherine
Gray, Elizabeth Janet - Vining, Elizabeth Gray
Grayn, Michael - Englebert, Michel A. G. J.
Green, Janet - McCormick, Victoria
Green, O. O. - Durgnat, Raymond Eric
Greene, Robert - Deindorfer, Robert Greene
Greenfield, Bernadotte - Darby, Edith M.
Grenelle, Lisa - Munroe, Elizabeth Lee
Grey, Carol - Lowndes, Robert Augustine Ward
Greysun, Doriac - Bertin, Eddy C.
Grill, Sebastian - Groll, Gunter
Guéhenno, Marcel - Guéhenne, Jean
Guenard, C. - Kurko, Kaarlo Sakari
Guiness Bryan - Moyne, (Baron) Bryan
    Walter Guiness
Gumucio - Gómez Mesa, Luis
Gwenffrwd, Alun - Hughes, Goronwy Alun
G. W. M. - Melcher, Gil (Gilbert Wayne)
Gwyn, Siarl - White, Charles (A. C. G.)
Gyles, Sheila - Fraser, Shelagh
Habakuk - Fielhauer, Otto M.
Haddo, Oliver - Puechner, Ray
Haddon, Sarah - Green, Madge
Hadham, John - Parkes, (Rev.) James W.
Hagar, Judith - Polley, Judith A.
Hagel, Jan - Orthofer, Peter B.
Hageman, Janna G. - Grashoff, Pieter
Haggard, William - Clayton, Richard Henry
    Michael
Hagon, Priscilla - Allan, Mabel E.
Hagrizi, Natan - Gross, Natan
Hales, Joyce - Coombs, Joyce
Hales, Norman - Young, Vernon
Hall, Adam - Trevor, Elleston
Hallard, Ruth - Tetzner, Ruth
Hallgarten, S. F. - Hallgarten, Siegfried
    Solomon "Fritz"
Halliday, Dorothy - Dunnett, Dorothy
Hamilton, Julia - Watson, Julia
Ham - Mulligan, Hugh A.
Hamilton, Jack - Brannon, William T.
Hamilton, Kay - De Leeuw, Cateau Wilhelmina
Hamilton, William S. - Brannon, William T.
Hammond, Jane - Poland, Dorothy E. H.
Hamond, Sam - Hamod, Hamode Samuel
Handleman, Mark - Cullison, Alvin Edwin
Hank - Bruns, Henry P.
Hankins, Clabe - McDonald, Erwin Lawrence
Hannson, Gestur - Bjornsson, Vigfus
Haper, Matthias - Reichelt, Hans-Peter
Hara, Paul - Kurko, Kaarlo Sakari
Harbinson, Robert - Bryans, Robert H.
Harbour, Dave - Harbour, David F.
Hardin, Peter - Vaczek, Louis, Charles
Harding, George - Raubenheimer, George H.
Hardy, Adam - Bulmer, Henry K.
Hardy, Bobbie - Hardy, Marjorie Enid
Harington, Joy - Harington, Dorothy Joy
    Nora Pepys
Harland, Elizabeth M. - Pickering, Margaret F.
Harle, Elizabeth - Roberts, Irene
Harley, John - Marsh, John

Jordan, Barbara Leslie - Yellot, Barbara
   Leslie Jordan
Juan Sin Cielo - Carrion, Alejandro
Jubilate - Coppage, George, Herman
Jucker, Iwan - Isler, Ursula
Jurat, Bert - Hochheimer, Albert
Justiciar - Powell-Smith, Vincent
JZ - Zulawski, Juliusz
Kailand, Alexander - Keilson, Hans
Kajot - Kucharski, Jan Edward
Kakabiku - Kwami, Frederick Baldwin
Kalamu - Roskam, Karel L.
Kalid Rah, A. - Bowart, Walter H.
Kallio, Sinikka - Nevanlinna, Sinikka S.
Kallio-Visapää, Sinikka - Nevanlinna,
   Sinikka S.
Kalmin, Aida - Amin, Khalidah A.
Kamenova, Anna - Staynova, Anna
Kane, Francis - Robbins, Harold
Karachiwala - Aqeel, Shafi
Kare, Kaarina - Honkanen, Hilja Loviisa
   Valkeapää
Karlsson, Kari - Bjornsson, Vigfus
Karus, Ike - Bowart, Walter H.
Kaye, Barbara - Muir, Barbara Kenrick
Kaye, Barbara - Muir, Marie Agnes
Kaye, Tom - Kaye, Barrington
Keith, David - Steegmuller, Francis
Keith, Donald - Monroe, Keith
Keith, Leigh - Gold, Horace L.
Kell, Joseph - Burgess, Anthony
Kelly, Tim - Kelly, Thomas Eugene
Kendal, June - Stiff, Dorothy Aileen
Kendal, Robert - Forster, Reginald K.
Kennedy, Elliot - Godfrey, Lionel R. H.
Kenneggy, Richard - Nettell, Richard G.
Kenny, Kathryn - Stack, Nicolete Meredith
Kent, Alexander - Reeman, Douglas E.
Kent, Mallory - Lowndes, Robert Augustine
   Ward
Kent, Margaret - Kent, (Ellen Louisa) Margaret
Keshri - Srinivas, Krishna
Khmar, Sergey - Ziniak, M. Serge
Killanin, Michael - Killanin, (Lord)
Kimberley, Hugh - Morland, Nigel
King, David - Pehrson, Howard V.
King, M. Elizabeth - Unger, Madelaine
King, Paul - Drackett, Phil.
King, R. G. Jr. - King, Rufus
Kirk, Michael - Knox, William (Bill)
Kisiel. - Kisielewski, Stefan
Kisjókai, Erzsébet Mária
Kisner, Jack - Kisner, Jacob
Kjölhaler, Tobias - Bolstad, Öivind
Knark - Gjessing, Ketil
Koenig, Kirk - Davis, Frank
Koenigsgarten, H. F. - Garten, Hugo F.
Kooiker, Leonie - Kooyker-Romyn Johanna Maria
Koopman, Wanda - Prins, Sonja
Koralov, Emil - Doncev-Koralov, Emil
Kortooms, Toon - Kortooms, Antonius Johannes
Kos, Wincenty - Kossobudzki, Leszek Wincenty
   Roman
Kowsikan - Krishna Murthy, Ventatraman
Kragen, Jinx - Morgan, Judith Ann
K'Rasco - Carrasco Martinez, Castulo
Krisjonsdottir, Hanna - Kristjonsdottir,
   Johanna
Kr. Jón - Isfeld, Jón (Kristjánsson)
Krull, Felix - White, James Dillon
Kryptos, - Hidden, Norman Frederick
Kuldip, R. K. - Roy, Kuldip K.
Kuznetsov, Anatoli - Anatoli, A.

Kyprianos, Iossif - Samarakis, Antonis
Lacey, John - Alexander, Boyd
Lagos, Concha - G. de Lagos, Maria C.
Lambert, Christine - Albrand, Martha
Lambert, Francoise - Lambert, (Madame Gaillard)
Lancaster, George - Ripley, Francis J.
Landell, Olaf J. de. - Wemmerslager van
   Sparwoude, Jan Bernard
Lane, Edward - Dick, Kay
Lane, Elizabeth - Farmers, Eileen E.
Lang, Elmy - Lang-Dillenburger, Elmy
Lang, Frances - Mantle, Winifred Langford
Langland, William - Muntz, (Isabelle) Hope
Lanser, Ruard - Thijssen, Felix Maria
   Adeodatus
Latham, Sir John, Professor of Law - Baxt,
   Robert
L'Aubanelenco - Drutel, Marcelle Louise Marie
Lauri - Salola, Eeero
Lauri, Pikku - Salola, Eeero
Lawrence, David - Morris, David Henry St.
   Lawrence
Lazar, Andre - Bajomi, Lazar Endre
Lebert, Randy - Brannon, William T.
Lebiés, René - Seibel, Werner
Lebo, Deli - Lebo, Dell
Le Boc - Supangkat, Hidayat
Lechicka, Beata - Nepomucka, Krystyna
Lee, Andrew - Auchincloss, Louis S.
Lee, Gardiner - Lee, Polly J. G.
Lee, Herbert d'H - Kastle, Herbert David
Lee, Manfred B. - Dannay Frederic
Lèfevre-Géraldy, Paul - Géraldy, Paul
L'Emigrante - Baccari, Antonio
Lenormand, S. - Prins, Sonja
Leona - Button, Margaret H.
Leonard, Guy - Rule, Leonard G.
Lepel, Herrman - Gurster, Eugen
Leslie, Doris - Fergusson Hannay, (Lady)
Leslie, Robert - Roberts, Sonia L.
Lester-Rands, A. - Judd, Frederick Charles
Leszcza, Jan - Londzin, Victor
Lewis, Carson - Milton, John R.
Lewis, Paul - Gerson, Noel B.
L. I. - Imesch, Ludwig
L. I-E. - Imesch, Ludwig
Lightner, A. M. - Hopf, Alice Lightner
Lindall, Edward - Smith, Edward Ernest
Lindgren - Lindgren-Utsi, Ethel J.
Lindley, Erica - Quigley, Aileen
Lindsay, Martin - Lindsay of Dowhill, (Sir)
   Martin
Lin Ting - Sun, Yi
Llewellyn, Richard - Lloyd, Richard D. V. L.
Lloyd, Charles - Birkin, Charles L.
Locke, Lucie - Price, Lucie H. L.
Lomond, Judy - Ellmers, Judith C.
Long, Bee Bacherig - Long, Beatrice P.
Lorenz, Sarah E. - Winston, Sarah
Loring, J. M. - Crozetti, Ruth G. Warner (Lora)
Loring, Lucin da - Smith, Elizabeth Mary
   Hunter
Low, Dorothy Mackie - Low, Lois Dorothea
Low, Gardner - Rodda, Percival C.
Lowell, Alan - Thomas, William B. (Bill)
Lowing, Anne - Geach, Christine
Lowö, Hans - Lindén, Erik H. E.
Ludlow, George - Kay, Ernest
Luellen, Valentina - Polley, Judith A.
Lum, Peter - Crowe (Lady) Bettina Lum
Lynch, Grey - Dorworth, Alice Grey
Lynton, Ann - Rayner, Claire
Lyon, Eliza - Robinson, Nancy E.

Lyon, Jessica - De Leeuw, Cateau Wilhelmina
Lynn, Patricia - Watts, Mabel
Ma - Jacobson, Marcus A. I.
Mac - McGovern, Berhard Stephen Patrick
Maccall, Isobel - Boyd, Elizabeth O.
MacDonald, Angus - MacDonald Douglas, Ronald Angus
Macdonald, (John) Ross - Millar, Kenneth
Macdonald, Malcolm - Ross-MacDonald, Malcolm J.
MacGregor, Fiona - Johnston, Beryl
MacIntosh, Joan - MacIntosh, Phoebe-Joan
Mack, Evalina - McNamara, Lena Brooke
MacKinnon, Charles - Stuart-Vernon Charles Roy
Maclean, Christina - Casement, Christina
MacLeod, Robert - Knox, William (Bill)
MacNeil, Duncan - McCutchan, Philip Donald
MacNib - Mackie, Albert David
Magal, Ran - Ghilan, Maxim
Magellan - Ghilan, Maxim
Magill, Marcus - Hill, Brian
Magister Juraś, Zag - Zagórski, Jerzy
Magnus, M. C. - Rau, Chalapathi
Maicas, Victor - Maicas Borrell, Abelardo
Maicas, Victor - Maicas Borrell, Abelardo
Mair, Margaret - Crompton, (Mrs) Margaret Norah
Maj - Jacobson, Marcus, A. I.
Majorick, Bernard - Beljon, Joop
Malloch, Peter - Duncan, William Murdoch
Malm, Margaretha - Pettersson, H. Bertil N.
Mandeville, Wm. - Smith, Leslie Wilfred
Manton, Paul - Walker, Peter Norman
Mapes, Mary A. - Ellison, Virginia T. H.
Maplesden, Ray - Pearce, Raymond M.
Marceau, Felicien - Carette, Louis-Albert
March, Hilary - Adcock, Almey St. J.
Marchant, Catherine - Cookson Catherine Ann
Marchet, Gian - Von Mautner Markof, (Dkfm) George J. E.
Margerson, David - Davies, David Margerison
Margo - Boulanger, Margo
Marilue - Johnson, Marilue Carolyn
Markham, Robert - Amis, Kingsley W.
Marmor, Jehudit - Shir, Miriam
Marsh, Andrew - O'Donovan, John P.
Marshall, Dorothy - Sappington, Dorothy E.
Marshall, James Vance - Payne, Donald G.
Marshall, Lovat - Duncan, William Murdoch
Martell, Claudia - Wolff, Victoria
Martin, Ann - Best, Carol A.
Martin, C. R. - Riess, Curt
Martindale, Spencer - Wolff, William Deakin
Martinheimo, Asko - Mattson, Asko Erik Vilhelm
Martyn, John L - Losada Martin, Juan
Martyn, Myles - Elliott-Cannon, Arthur Elliott
Maruna, Annikki - Aaltonen, Annikki
Marynen, Joannes - Matthyssen, Joannes Michael
Mascall, Margery D. - Netherclift, Beryl C.
Mason, Val - Hackleman, Wauneta A.
Masters, W. W. - Masters, William Walter
Masterson, Louis - Hallbing, Kjell Kåre
Matsuno, Masako - Kobayashi, Masako
Maung Hauk - Hobbs, Cecil
Maxwell, Vicky - Worboys, Annette Isobel
May - Moore, Eva Beate
Mayne, H. H. - Wilson, Helen Helga
McBain, Ed - Hunter, Evan
McCabe, Cameron - Borneman, Ernest
McCall, Craig - Melcher, Gil, (Gilbert Wayne)
McCall, John Corey - Morland, Nigel
McCann, Philip - Felstein, Ivor

McClean, Kathleen - Hale, Kathleen
McCormick, Donald - McCormick, George Donald King
McCutcheon, James - Lundgren, Paul Arthur
McDiarmid, Hugh - Grieve, Christopher M.
McDonnell, Jinny - McDonnell, Virginia (Bleecker)
McGavin, Moyra - Crichton E(leanor) Moyra
McGlinn, Dwight - Brannon, William T.
McGrew, Jan - McGrew, Janice Weggener
McGrew, Janice W. - Mcgrew, Janice Weggener
McIntosh, J. T. - Macgregor, James Murdoch
McMullen Catherine - Cookson, Catherine Ann
McNeill, Janet - Alexander, Janet
Meabey, Leonard - Gander, Leonard M.
Mego, Al - Roberts, Arthur O.
Meilen, Bill - Meilen, Wilm-Artur
Melville, Jeannie - Butler, Gwendoline
Mendel, Jo - Gilbertson, Mildred G.
Mentor - Jones, Frank H.
Meredith, Nicolete - Stack, Nicolete Meredith
Merin, Peter - Bihalji-Merin, Oto
Merkrid De Jong Van Hage, T. P. - Rempt, Jan D.
Merlin, David - Moreau, David Merlin
Miao, Yung Yu Kwun - Lee, Ying
Michaels, Steve - Avallone, Michael, Jr.
Michaud, E. G. - Mitchell, (Sister) Elaine
Mieczyslawa - Radzymińska, Jósefa
Miller, Karl - Mandel, Loring
Miller, Margaret J. - Dale, Margaret Jessy
Miller of Diller - Miller, Dora O.
Milligan, Spike - Milligan, Terence Alan
Mirabaux, Alain - Liegeois, Fernand
Miranda, Maria - Krenz-Senior, Ethel Rosabelle
Mireya - López De Serantes, Josefina
Mirus-Kauba, Ludmilla - Mirus Ludmilla
Mitchell, Scott - Godfrey, Lionel R. H.
Mizuta, Akira - Sakai, Sadao
Mlad-Miltijad - Djuricic, Mladen
Modena, Maria - Kreis, Erna
Monro, Gavin - Monro-Higgs, Gertrude
Monroe, Grace - Bail, Grace M. S.
Monroe, Grace - Bail, Grace M. S.
Montelbaen, Maria - Kelk, Fanny
Montrose, Graham - Stuart-Vernon Charles Roy
Montross, David - Backus, Jean
Moor, Emily - Deming, Richard
Moorshead, Henry - Pine, Leslie G.
Morand, Rene - Kurko, Kaarlo Sakari
Moreno, Nick - Deming, Richard
Morgan, Jinx - Morgan, Judith Ann
Morine, Hoder - Conroy, Jack (John Wesley)
Morland, Dick - Hill, Reginald Charles
Morley, Wilfred Owen - Lowndes, Robert Augustine Ward
Morrell, John - Olson, Thomas C. M.
Morris, David - Morris, David Henry St. Lawrence
Morris, David St. L. - Morris, David Henry St. Lawrence
Morris, James - Morris, Jan
Morris, Julian - West, Morris
Morrison, Victor - Glut, Donald F.
Møy - Moy, Ragnhild Margrethe
M. Riethuyze - Van Hageland, Albert
Muir, Alan - Morrison, Thomas James
Muir, John - Morgan, Thomas Christopher
Mumpsimus - Charles-Edwards, Thomas
Muni, Narad - Anand, Mulk Raj
Munro, Ronald Eadie - Glen, Duncan M.
Muraji Uchiki - Muraji Uchiki, Tamotsu Uchiki
Murray, Frances - Booth, Rosemary F.

Poveda, Antonio - Vieth Von Golssenau, Arnold
Powell, Neil - Innes, Brian
Powell, Patsy - Long, Beatrice P.
Prado, Alberto - Laguerre, Enrique A.
Praeceptor Humilis - West, Luther Shirley
Pressley, Hilda - Nickson, Hilda
Preston, Hilary - Nickson, Hilda
Preston, Hugh - Wilson, Derek Alan
Priestwood, Gwen - Nelson, Gwendoline Ethel
Prospero - West, Tristram Frederick
Przedpelska-Trzeciakowska, Anna -
   Trzeciakowska, Anna Zofia
Przem. - Bystrzycki, Przemyslaw M.
Pullein-Thompson, Christine - Popescu,
   Christine
Queen, Ellery - Dannay, Frederic
Quentin, Patrick - Wheeler, Hugh Callingham
Quoirez, Françoise - Sagan, Françoise
Radcliffe, Jocelyn - Beardsley, Charles
Rae, Doris - Rae, Margaret D.
Ragged Staff - Coley, Rex
Rah-Separ - Yarshater, Ehsan Ollah
Raittila, Anna-Maija - Nieminen, Anna-Maija
Rakhmanny, Roman - Olynyk, Roman
Ralegh, Elizabeth - Dibley, Kathleen
Ramakanth - Sreenivasapuram, Vankata Lakshmi
   Narayanan
Ramsey, Christopher - Davis, Frank
Ramsey, Diana - Brandes, Rhoda
Ramysari - Sreenivasapuram, Ramacharlu
Rana, J. - Bhatia Jamunadevi
Rand, James S. - Attenborough, Bernard George
Randall, Janet - Young, Janet Randall
Randall, Rona - Shambrook, Rona
Randell, Beverley - Price, Beverley J.
Randolph, Ellen - Ross, William E. D.
Random, Alan - Kay, Ernest
Rankine, John - Mason, Douglas Rankine
Raphael, Ellen - Hartley, Ellen Raphael
Raschle, Otto - Stauffer, Robert
Rault, Walter - Gorham, Maurice A. C.
Rautapalo-Rapp, T. - Rautapalo, Tauno E.
Raymond, Mary - Heathcott, Mary
Read, Miss - Saint, Dora J.
Reade, Hamish - Gray, Simon J. H.
Reader, Paul - Arce Robledo, Carlos de
Redax - Vingedal, Sven Erik Axel
Redman, Joseph - Pearce, Brian L.
Redmayne, Barbara - Smithies Muriel
Redstone, Sylvia - Honnor, Sylvia Crofts
Redwood, Rosaline - Staples, Marjory
   Charlotte
Reeman, Douglas - Kent, Alexander
Reeves, Joyce - Gard, Joyce
Reid, Meta M. - Reid, Meta A. C. J.
Remerond - De Saulieu, Thierry
Renault - Laurent, Emmanuel
René, Hans Evert - Renérius, Hans-Evert
Renn, Ludwig - Vieth Von Golssenau, Arnold
Rety, Michael - Franse, Petru W.
Reynolds, Mack - Cogswell, (Brig.-Gen.)
   Theodore. R.
Rich, Barbara - Rinkoff, Barbara J.
Richards, Al - Shubin, Seymour
Richardson, C. - Munsey, Cecil Richard Jr.
Richardson, Susanne - Davies Iris
Richmond, Rod - Glut, Donald F.
Rieol, Bernarda - Brocker, Hildegard L. H.
Ristare, Bo - Lindén, Erik H. E.
Rivers, Georgia - Clark, Marjorie
Rivière, Elena - Haywood, Helen R.
Robert, Dominique - Loup, Thérèse
Roberts, John Storm - Roberts, John A. S.

Roberts, Martin - Wells, Frank Charles Robert
Robertson, Elspeth - Ellison, Joan Audrey
   Anderson
Robertson, Helen - Edmiston, Helen Jean Mary
Robin - Roberts, Eric
Roch, Dalby - Webb, Ethel
Rodney, Bob - Rodrigo, Robert
Roe, M. S. - Thomson, Daisy Hicks
Rogers, Floyd - Spence, William John Duncan
Rogers, John - Rogers, Thomas P.
Rogers, Keith - Harris, Marion Rose
Rogers, Mick - Glut, Donald F.
Rokeby, John - Collins, Peter Blumfeld
Roland, Nicholas - Walmsley, Arnold Robert
Rolleston, Rosamond - Wilson, Rosamond
Rommel, Dayton - Rommel, Mimi D.
Ron, Paul A. - Bentov, Shmuel P.
Ronald, E. B. - Barker, Ronald E.
Rooth, George - Bakker, Johan
Rosén, Georg - Zenneström, Per-Olov
Ross, Barnaby - Dannay, Frederic
Ross, Catherine - Beaty, Betty
Ross, Clarissa - Ross, William E. D.
Ross, George - Ross, Isaac
Ross, Leonard O. - Rosten, Leo C.
Ross, Marilyn - Ross, William E. D.
Rosse, Ian - Straker, John Foster
Rostron, P. R. - Hulbert, Joan Margery
Rostron, Primrose - Hulbert, Joan Margery
Rousseau, J. J. - Nienaber, Petrus J.
Rovin, Alex - Russo, Albert
Rowan, Deirdre - Williams, Jeanne
Rowe, Stephen - Stares, John Edward Spencer
Rowland, Iris - Roberts, Irene
Ruell, Patrick - Hill, Reginald Charles
Russell, Rex - Langdon, John F. C.
Russell, Shane - Norwood, Victor G. C.
Rutgeerts, Albert - Van Hageland, Albert
Ruth - Buczkowski, Marian
Rybot, Doris - Ponsonby, D. A.
Rycon - Savery, Constance W.
Ryland, Lee - Arlandson, Leone R.
Saalfeld, Martha - vom Scheidt, Martha
Sabre, Mark - Thomas, William B. (Bill)
Safari Scribe - Brooks Virginia F. W.
Saddler, Allen - Richards, Ronald C. W.
Sagar, Krishna - Merz, Natasha
Saint-Laurent, Cecil - Laurent, Jacques
Saklatvala, Beram - Marsh, Henry
Saleck, Jean Charlot - Breitbach, Joseph
Salminen, Hellevi - Matihalti, Hellevi
   Marja-Liisa Salminen
Salt, Jonathan - Neville, Derek
Sandaval, Jaime - Marlowe, Dan J.
Sanders, Robert - Meier, Henk J.
Sandown, Margaret - Stone, Ena Margaret
Sands, Martin - Burke, John F.
Santa Maria - Powell-Smith, Vincent
Sara - Blake, Sally
Sarkka, Juuso - Saksa, Sulo J.
Sarnian - Falla, Frank W.
Saunders, Patricia M. - Godsiff, Patricia M.
Savage, David - Hossent, Harry
Savage, Richard - Roe, Ivan
Saville, Malcolm - Saville, Leonard M.
Sawyer - Wirtanen, Atos Kasimir
Sayles, (Mrs) Philip L. - Hogarth Grace
   W. Allen
Scaldis, Eva - Evenhuis, Gertie
Scannell, Jan - Scannell, Johannes P.
Scarrott, Michael - Fisher, A. S. T.
Schealtiel, Nochumm J. - Schochet, J. Immanuel
Schenk, Lenie - Schenk, Magdalena G.

Taurus - Honey, Philip
Tavis, Alec - Dunnett, Alastair MacTavish
Taylor, Sam - Goodyear, Stephen F.
Tellier, Jacques - Foy, Louis A.
Tempest, Sarah - Ponsonby, D. A.
Temple, Edith - Murrells, Joseph
Thakazhi - Thakazhi, Pillai, Sivasankara
The Gordons - Gordon, Gordon & Mildred
Theurer-Samek, Hermann - Theurer, Hermann
The Valley Sportsman - Foldi, Ernest J.
Thiery, Dr. Herman - Daisne, Johan
Thoene, Peter - Bihalji-Merin, Oto
Thomas, G. K. - Davies, Leslie Purnell
Thomas, M. L. - Jeier, Thomas
Thomson, Joan - Charnock, Joan Paget
Thomson, Jon H. - Thomson, Daisy Hicks
Thorburn, John - Goldsmith, John H. T.
Thorne, Bradley D. - Glut, Donald F.
Thorp, Ellen - Thorp, (Margery) Ellen
Tibbetts, William - Brannon, William T.
Tielman, Inge - Tielman, Ingeborg
Tiger, Jack - Puechner, Ray
Tiger, John - Wager, Walter Herman
Titulescu, Jonathan - Farrell, James T.
Toba - Baccari, Antonio
Tor, Regina - Shekerjian, Regina D.
Tornata, Ben - Lo Bello, Nino
Torpare, Tord - Sandblad-Haneson, Sonja
Toussaint, Jacky - Lourens-Koop, Adriana L. K.
Tracy, David - Engerbretson, David L.
Treves, Luisa - Roselaar, Greta
Trevor, Charlotte - Roberts, Sonia L.
Trevor, Joy - Linskill, Doris Joy
Trimalcion, Fidelio - Benitez De Castro, Cecilio
Tring, Stephen - Meynell, Laurence W.
Trixie - Long, Beatrice P.
Trotter, Sallie - Crawford Sallie Wallace Brown
Tsui, Ying - Lo, Ngar Y.
Tudoran, Radu - Bogza Nicolae
Turner, Mary - Lambot, Isobel M.
Tuulipuu - Reijonén, Tuuli
Tuuri, Tauno - Rautapalo, Tauno E.
Twist, Ananias - Nunn, William C.
Tyler, Lillian - Fountain, Helen Van A.
Tyrone, Paul - Norwood, Victor G. C.
Uncle Gillis - Combs, Joseph Franklin
Underwood, Miles - Glassco, John
Unthank, Tessa Brown, - Unthank, Louis-Teresa Brown
Uroyan, Luis - Laguerre, Enrique A.
Ursula, Sanna - Honkanen, Hilja Loviisa Valkeapää
Vaivoryte, Bale - Januta, Petronele
Vale, Keith - Clegg, William Paul
Vallabh, Vali Ram - Hansrajani Kewal Ram
Van Akooy, Philip - Thijssen, Felix Maria Adeodatus
van Ardennen, Aye - Vollewens-Zeylemaker, Greta
van der Steen, Maria - Pepers, Anna E.
Van Houweninge, Chiem - Van Houweninge, Joachimus Johannes
van Renkum, Lodewyk, - de Bourbon (Prince-Duke of Normandy
van Someren, Liessje - Putland-Van Someren, Elizabeth J.
van Staphorst, Jan - Kingma, Marten Jan
van 't Sant, Mien - van 't Sant-van Bommel, Aartje Wilhelmina
Vandu Mama - Krishna Murthy, Ventatraman
Vane, Michael - Humphries, Sydney Vernon

Vardre, Leslie - Davies Leslie Purnell
Vassilev, Orlin - Vassilev, Hristo Petkov
Veits, Ulf - Lindberg, Karl S.
Vernon, Arthur - Tourtellot, Arthur Bernon
Vernon, Claire - Breton-Smith, Clare
Verpooten, Maria - Stoové-Bauer, Maris Hillegonde
Vezhinov, Paul - Gugov, Nikola Delchev
Vicarion, Count Palmiro - Logue, Christopher
Victor, Charles B. - Puechner, Ray
Vigilans - Rice, Brian K.
Viking, Ted - Louwen, Jan
Vipont, Charles - Foulds, Elfrida V.
Vipont, Elfrida - Foulds, Elfrida V.
Vitezovic, Tomislav - Kuehnel T-Leddihn, (Ritter von) Erik M.
Voelker, John Donaldson - Traver, Robert
Voitin, Al. - Voitinovici, Alexandru
Volen, Iliya - Stamenov, Marin
Voyle, Mary - Manning, Rosemary
Vrijbuiter - Fortuin, Herman B.
Waggener, Janice - McGrew, Janice Weggener
Wakefield, Elizabeth - Montgomery, Mamie Elizabeth Wakefield
Wales, Nym - Snow, Helen Foster (Mrs)
Walford, Christian - Dilcock, Noreen
Walsh, Robert - Gardner, R. Brian
Wandelganger - Faas, Henry C.
Warbridge, C. W. - Woods, Clee
Ward, S. Leslie - Ward, Elizabeth Honor
Warner-Crozetti, R. - Crozetti Ruth G. Warner (Lora)
Warriner, Geraldine - Murray, Blanche Geraldine
Watkins-Smith, Leslie - Smith, Leslie Wilfred
Wayne, Marcia - Best, Carol A.
Wealden Wanderer - Sanders, Frederick W. T.
Webb, Christopher - Wibberley, Leonard Patrick O'Connor
Webster, Noah - Knox, William (Bill)
Wede - Espy, Willard R.
Weir, John - Cross, Colin John
Welburn, Vivienne - Furlong, Vivienne C.
Welcher, Rosalind - Slavic, Rosalind Welcher
Welcome, John - Brennan, John N. H.
Wendolin - Durben, Wolfgang
Werner, Katherina - Gotz, Gerd
West, Mark - Runyon, Charles W.
Westmacott, Mary - Mallowan, (Dame) Agatha Mary Clarissa
Weston, Matt - Pehrson, Howard V.
White, G. A. - Millar, James Primrose Malcolm
Whitley, George - Chandler, Arthur Bertram
Wib - King, Ruby Thompson (Mrs)
Wictor - Gyllensten, Lars Johan Wictor
Wijnhuis, Herman - Nijhuis, Harry
Wijnstroom, Christy - Hoppen-Ram Henderika Wilhelmina Christina
Wilde, Hilary - Breton-Smith, Clare
Williams, J. R. - Williams, Jeanne
Williams, Pieter or Pedro - Williams, Pieter Daniel De Wet
Williams, Rex - Wei, Rex
Williams, Tom - Thomas, William B. (Bill)
Williams, Violet M. - Boon, Violet M.
Willis, Maud - Lottman, Eileen
Willoughby, Hugh - Harvey, Charles Nigel
Wills, Geoffrey - Staal, Cyril
Wilson, Crane - O'Brien, Cyril C.
Wilson, David - MacArthur, David Wilson
Wilson, John Burgess - Burgess, Anthony
Wilson, Merna Wilson, (Daphne) Merna
Winder, Mavis - Winder, Mavis Areta

LITERARY AGENTS

The following list of agents does not claim to be exhaustive although every effort has been made to make it as comprehensive as possible.

In all instances, authors are advised to send preliminary letters to agents before submitting manuscripts.

UNITED KINGDOM AGENTS

ACTAC (THEATRICAL AND CINEMATIC) LIMITED
16 Cadogan Lane, London SW1, UK.
Contact: Emanuel or Thelma Wax.

ADAMASTOR PRESS AND LITERARY AGENCY, LIMITED
6 Somerton Road, London NW2, UK.
Contact: Sydney Clouts or Marjorie Clouts.
Handles full-length, non-fiction books.

ALBEMARLE SCRIPTS (LONDON) LIMITED
9 Blenheim Street, New Bond Street, London W1, UK.
Contact: Norman Payne.

ALLDRIDGE AND DAVIS
40 Oulton Avenue, Sale, Cheshire 33M 2WA, UK.
Contact: John Alldridge or Wyn Davis.
Play agents.

ALPHA BOOK AGENCY
49c South End, Croydon, Surrey CR0 1BF, UK.
Contact: P. H. Hargreaves.
Educational MSS only.

A.L.S. MANAGEMENT LIMITED
67 Brook Street, London W1Y 1YD, UK.
Contact: B. Vertue.

ANGLO-GERMAN LITERARY AGENCY
87 Upper Selsdon Road, South Croydon, Surrey CR2 0DP, UK.
Contact: Gordon or Walburg Fielden.
Specializes in works written in German as well as English. Handles all types of full-length work for book publication, particularly in the fields of natural history and information books for children.

STEPHEN ASKE
39 Victoria Street, London SW1H 0EE, UK.
Contact: A. S. Knight.
Accepts full-length and short MSS. Handles theatre, films, television and sound broadcasting.

ASSOCIATED PLAYS AND PLAYERS
Suite 4, 41 Charing Cross Road, London WC2H 0AR, UK.

THE AUTHORS' ALLIANCE
Hinton Woodlands, Bramdean, Alresford, Hampshire, UK.
Contact: Mrs. Deborah Greenep.
Does not accept short stories or articles.

MICHAEL BAKEWELL AND ASSOCIATES LIMITED
118 Tottenham Court Road, London W1, UK.

ROGER BARNETT ASSOCIATES
143 Holborn, London EC1, UK.
Contact: Roger Barnett.
Accepts full-length and short MSS.

ROBERT BARTLETT SCRIPTS LIMITED
60 Braybrook Street, London W12, UK.

ALAIN BERNHEIM LIMITED
44 Chelsea Square, London SW3, UK.

B.K.M. (PERSONAL MANAGEMENT LIMITED)
27 Curzon Street, London W1, UK.
Contact: Barry Krost or David Baker.

BOLT AND WATSON LIMITED
8 Storey's Gate, London SW1, UK.
Contact: David Bolt or Sheila Watson.
Accepts full-length and short MSS. Handles translations, theatre, films, television and sound broadcasting.

CURTIS BROWN ACADEMIC
1 Craven Hill, London W2 3EP, UK.
Contact: Graham Watson, Chairman or Andrew Best, Managing Director.
Represents academic writers.

CURTIS BROWN LIMITED
1 Craven Hill, London W2 3EP, UK.
Contact: Graham Watson, Chairman or Peter Grose, Managing Director.
Represents book and short story writers throughout the world.

CHRISTOPHER BUSBY LIMITED
44 Great Russell Street, London WC1B 3PA, UK.
Contact: C. R. Busby or A. M. Busby.
Does not handle stage plays, unsolicited short stories and articles, poetry, or unsolicited television scripts.

MYLES BYRNE
Embassy Theatre, Western Road, Hove, Sussex BN3 1AE, UK.
Contact: Myles Byrne.
Specializes in plays, television and film scripts. Does not undertake to sell short stories, verse or children's books.

JOHN CADELL LIMITED
64 Highgate High Street, London N6 5HX, UK.
Contact: John Cadell.
Considers writing for the theatre, television and radio only.

CAMPBELL THOMSON AND McLAUGHLIN LIMITED
80 Chancery Lane, London WC2A 1DD, UK.
Contact: Christine Campbell Thomson, John McLaughlin, Hal Cheetham or John Parker.
Accepts full-length and short MSS.

C AND B (THEATRE)
Calder & Boyars, Limited
Publishers, 18 Brewer Street, London W1R 4AS, UK.
Contact: J. M. Calder, Marion Boyars or Michael Hayes.
Handles the sale of dramatic rights to amateur and professional theatre companies, radio, television and film.

E. J. CARNELL LITERARY AGENCY
17 Burwash Road, Plumstead, London SE18 7QY, UK.
Contact: Leslie Flood.
Specialize in science fiction.

CASSEL-GERARD LIMITED
182 Moor Lane, Chessington, Surrey KT9 2BH, UK.
Contact: Leon or Pamela Cassel-Gerard.

C.C.A. PERSONAL MANAGEMENT LIMITED
White House, 29 Dawes Road, London SW6 7DT, UK.
Contact: Howard Pays or Freddie Vale.

JONATHAN CLOWES LIMITED
19 Jeffrey's Place, London NW1 9PP, UK.
Contact: Jonathan Clowes, Ann Evans, Donald Carroll or Enyd Clowes.
Handles theatre, films, television and sound broadcasting.

ELSPETH COCHRANE AGENCY
31A Sloane Street, London SW1, UK.
Contact: Miss Elspeth Cochrane.
Handles writers of theatre, film, television and sound broadcasting scripts.

ROSICA COLIN LIMITED
4 Hereford Square, London SW7 4TU, UK.
Contact: Rosica Colin.
Specializes in general publishing, original MSS, theatre and foreign rights but handles all types of MSS except poetry and newspaper articles.

GEORGE COOPER MANAGEMENT
12 The Shrubberies, George Lane, South Woodford, London E18 1BD, UK.

DONALD COPEMAN LIMITED
52 Bloomsbury Street, London WC1B 3QT, UK.
Contact: Donald Copeman or L. G. Turney.

RUPERT CREW LIMITED
King's Mews, Gray's Inn Road, London WC1 2JA, UK.
Contact: F. R. Crew, K. A. Crew, D. Montgomery or S. Russell.
Handles authors and feature writers wanting world representation.

DALZELL DURBRIDGE AUTHORS LIMITED
14 Clifford Street, London W1, UK.
Contact: Stephen Durbridge.
Represents writers solely in the dramatic media — films, theatre, radio and television.

ALFRED DAVIS AND ASSOCIATES LIMITED
3rd Floor, Eagle House, 110 Jermyn Street, London SW1, UK.
Contact: A. Davis, Chairman and Managing Director or M. C. Philip, Deputy Managing Director.

FELIX DE WOLFE AND ASSOCIATES
1 Robert Street, Adelphi, London WC2N 6BH, UK.
Contact: Felix de Wolfe.
Represents playwrights, dramatists, non-fiction writers relating to the entertainment profession and screenwriters.

WILLIAM DORAN
3 Egerton Garden Mews, London SW3, UK.

PETER DOUGLAS LIMITED
205 Howard House, Dolphin Square, London SW1, UK.

Contact: Peter Douglas.
Specializes almost exclusively in non-fiction.

BRYAN DREW LIMITED
81 Shaftesbury Avenue, London W1, UK.

DOREEN ENGLISH AGENCY
2 Hazlebury Road, London SW6 2NB, UK.

ENGLISH THEATRE GUILD LIMITED
Ascot House, 52 Dean Street, London W1V 6CJ, UK.
Contact: Laurence Fitch or Judith Truman.

EPOQUE LIMITED
Carmelite House, London EC4Y 0JA, UK.
Contact: A. Tarbard or Stuart Martin.
Represents writers for theatre, film, television and sound broadcasting.

EVANS PLAYS
Montague House, Russell Square, London WC1B B5X, UK.
Contact: Ann Lee.

NORMA FARNES MANAGEMENT LIMITED
9 Orme Court, London W2, UK.

JOHN FARQUHARSON LIMITED
15 Red Lion Square, London WC1R 4QW, UK.
Contact: Innes Rose, George Greenfield or Vanessa Holt.
Special interest in academic writers but also handles films, television and sound broadcasting. Full-length and short MSS.

PETER FETTERMAN
27 Blandford Street, London W1, UK.

FILM RIGHTS, LIMITED
113-117 Wardour Street, London W1, UK.
Contact: John E. Hunter, D. M. Sims, Dorothy Mather, Maurice Lambert or Laurence Fitch.
Handles theatre, films, television and sound broadcasting.

LAURENCE FITCH LIMITED
113-117 Wardour Street, London W1V 4EH, UK.
Contact: Laurence Fitch.
Handles all types of MSS except poetry.

FRASER AND DUNLOP SCRIPTS LIMITED
91 Regent Street, London W1R 8RU, UK.
Contact: Kenneth Ewing, Jill Foster, Richard Wakeley or Timothy Corrie.
Represents writers in television, theatre, films, publishing (fiction, non-fiction and children's) and radio.

FREELANCE PRESENTATIONS LIMITED
117 Charterhouse Street, London EC1, UK.
Interested in television and film scripts, novels and serials.

SAMUEL FRENCH LIMITED
26 Southampton Street, Strand, London WC2E 7JE, UK.
Contact: A. W. Hogg.

NOEL GAY MUSIC CO. LIMITED
24 Denmark Street, London WC2H 8NJ, UK.
Contact: R. C. Walker.
Specializes in fiction, television and film scripts.

J. H. GIBSON'S LITERARY AGENT
4—5 Vernon House, Sicilian Avenue, London
WC1 2QH, UK.
Contact: J. F. Gibson.
Handles full-length fiction and non-fiction for
adults and children.

ERIC GLASS LIMITED
28 Berkeley Square, London W1X 6HD, UK.
Contact: Eric Glass.
Specializes in screen, stage and TV plays as well
as fiction and non-fiction books.

ERIC GOODHEAD (Management) LIMITED
8 Bolton Street, London W1, UK.

CLIVE GOODWIN ASSOCIATES
79 Cromwell Road, London SW7 5BN, UK.
Contact: Phil Kelvin.
Represents the first class writers in England for
television, film and theatre.

**GREEN AND UNDERWOOD LIMITED,
PERSONAL MANAGEMENT**
11 Garrick Street, London WC2, UK.
Contact: Peter T. Green or Geoffrey Underwood.
No restrictions.

ELAINE GREENE LIMITED
31 Newington Green, Islington, London
N16 9PU, UK.
Contact: Elaine Greene.
Does not handle plays, original film scripts or
poetry. Will handle articles and short stories
written by existing clients only.

PLUNKET GREENE LIMITED
110 Jermyn Street, St. James's Square, London
SW1, UK.
Contact: T. Plunket Greene.
Handles full-length scripts for theatre, films,
television and sound broadcasting.

GRIFFITHS AND GRIFFITHS
The Flat, East Lodge, The Green, Frant, nr.
Tunbridge Wells, Kent, UK.
Contact: Lt.-Col. W. N. Griffiths or Mrs. M.M.
Griffiths.
Short stories only.

ROGER HANCOCK LIMITED
8 Waterloo Place, Pall Mall, London SW1Y 4AW,
UK.
Contact: R. T. Hancock or B. T. Codd.

ROBERT HARBEN LITERARY AGENT
3 Church Vale, London N2 9PD, UK.
Contact: Robert Harben.
Representative of publishers for The Netherlands
and English and American agents. Interested in
placing top class German books on history,
sociology, etc., in England.

GORDON HARBORD
Flat 9, Parkside, Knightsbridge, London
SW1X 7JR, UK.
Interested in all types of MSS except poetry.

ALEC HARRISON AND ASSOCIATES
International Press Centre, Shoe Lane, London
EC4A 3JB, UK.
Contact: Alec Harrison.

Specializes in non-fiction works ranging from the
educational to the autobiographical.

HATTON AND BRADLEY, LIMITED
8 South Molton Street, London W1, UK.
Contact: Donald Bradley, Henry E. St. L. King,
or Camille Marchetta.
Interested in theatre, film, television and sound
broadcasting.

**THE MICHAEL HAYES LITERARY AGENCY
LIMITED**
9 Melbourne Court, 253 Cromwell Road, London
SW5, UK.
Contact: M. P. Hayes or M. C. Hayes.
No specialities. No new clients accepted at this
time.

FRANCIS HEAD
503 Carrington House, Hertford Street, London
W1Y 7TD, UK.
Contact: Mrs. Francis Head.
Specializes in television — plays, comedy and
dramatic series, documentaries — but also works
in the legit theatre, feature films, publishing and
radio on behalf of clients.

A. M. HEATH AND COMPANY LIMITED
40—42 William IV Street, London WC2N 4DD,
UK.
Contact: Cyrus Brooks, Chairman or Mark
Hamilton, Managing Director.
Interested in work of new and established
writers. Handles theatre, films, television and
sound broadcasting and accepts full-length and
short MSS.

SHIRLEY HECTOR AND ASSOCIATES
13 Gledhow Gardens, London SW5 0AY, UK.
Handles fiction and non-fiction including
subsidiary rights.

FAITH HENRY
12A Belsize Park Gardens, London NW3, UK.

MICHAEL HENSHAW
20 Fitzroy Square, London W16, UK.

DAVID HIGHAM ASSOCIATES, LIMITED
5—8 Lower John Street, Golden Square, London
W1R 4HA, UK.
Contact: David Higham, Bruce Hunter,
Jacqueline Korn or Anthony Crouch.
Represents every kind of writer and provides
authors with a complete service throughout the
world. Deals with all rights.

THE HOWARD AGENCY
12 Palgrave Road, London W12 9NB, UK.
Contact: H. Kaufman.

HOWES AND PRIOR LIMITED
66 Berkeley House, Hay Hill, London W1X 7LH,
UK.
Contact: E. C. P. Howes or R. M. F. Prior.
Represents the business interests of a few
screenplay writers.

HUGHES MASSIE LIMITED
69 Great Russell Street, London WC1B 3DH,
UK.
Contact: Edmund Cork, N. E. Cork, J. E. Lunn
or Joan M. Ling.

Interested in theatre, films, television, sound broadcasting and translations. Full-length and short MSS.

INTERCONTINENTAL LITERARY AGENCY
45—46 Chandos Place, London WC2N 4HX, UK.
Contact: Anthony Gornall.
Only handles translation rights on behalf of partners in London and New York.

INTERNATIONAL COPYRIGHT BUREAU LIMITED
26 Charing Cross Road, London WC2H 0DG, UK.
Specializes in radio and television plays, films and fiction books.

INTERNATIONAL FAMOUS AGENCY LIMITED
11—12 Hanover Street, London W1, UK.
Contact: Laurence Evans.

INTERPRESS
9 Mountview Road, Orpington, Kent, UK.
Contact: Jack or Jean Aitken.

PETER JANSON-SMITH LIMITED
31 Newington Green, London N16 9PU, UK.
Contact: Peter Janson-Smith.
Handles television, sound broadcasting and films. Full-length and short MSS.

JOHN JOHNSON
51/54 Goschen Buildings, 12/13 Henrietta Street, London WC2E 8LF, UK.
Contact: John Johnson.
Handles plays, television and radio scripts and poetry. Does not handle journalism nor unsolicited articles for the press. Particularly interested in educational and school textbooks and the work of new writers.

JONES BLAKEY
14 Monteith Crescent, Boston, Lincolnshire PE21 9AX, UK.
Handles book length fiction and non-fiction MSS as well as theatre, television and sound broadcasting scripts.

IRENE JOSEPHY
35 Craven Street, Strand, London WC2N 5NG, UK.

KAVANAGH ENTERTAINMENTS LIMITED
170 Piccadilly, London W1V 9DD, UK.
Contact: Sonny Zahl, Peter Pritchard, John Hayes, Jon Thurley, Alex Grahame, Henry Howard or April Young.
Interested in theatre, film, television and sound broadcasting scripts.

KENYON-DEAN LIMITED
129 St. John's Hill, London SW11, UK.
Contact: P. St. C. Assinder.

ROLF KRUGER MANAGEMENT LIMITED
2 South Audley Street, London W1, UK.
Contact: Rolf or Iris Kruger.

MARY LAMBETH ASSOCIATES
22 Acol Road, London NW6, UK.

CHARLES LAVELL LIMITED
176 Wardour Street, London W1V 3AA, UK.
Contact: Carl or Kay Routledge.
No specialities.

LE DAIN MANAGEMENT
92 North Road, Highgate, London N6 4AA, UK.
Contact: Yvonne Le Dain.
Handles plays for theatre, film, television and sound broadcasting.

ERIC L'EPINE SMITH LIMITED
Bond Street House, 14 Clifford Street, London W1, UK.
Contact: Eric L'Epine Smith, Terence Carney or Doris Matheson.

HOPE LERESCHE AND STEELE
11 Jubilee Place, Chelsea, London SW3 3TE, UK.
Contact: Hope Leresche or Tessa Sayle.
Handles full-length fiction and non-fiction MSS, plays, films, television and sound broadcasting.

E. P. S. LEWIN
1 Grosvenor Court, Sloane Street, London SW1, UK.
No new clients.

LITERARY PROPERTIES LIMITED
Cobrin, Bagshot Road, Worplesdon, Surrey, UK.

SIR EMILE LITTLER
Palace Theatre, London W1, UK.
Contact: Patrick Selby.

LLOYD-GEORGE AND COWARD
31 Theberton Street, London N1 0QY, UK.
Contact: W. Lloyd-George or B. G. Coward.
Does not handle plays, poetry, science or technical books.

LONDON INDEPENDENT BOOKS, LIMITED
1A Montagu Mews North, London W1H 1AJ, UK.
Contact: Sydney Box, Carolyn Whitaker or Patrick Whitaker.
Does not handle children's books.

LONDON MANAGEMENT
235—241 Regent Street, London W1A 2JT, UK.
Contact: Dennis or Herbert van Thal.
Handles all MSS except poetry.

LONDON PLAY COMPANY
113 Wardour Street, London W1V 4EH, UK.

GEORGE McINDOE, ROBERT BARTLETT SCRIPTS LIMITED
60 Braybrook Street, London W12, UK.

BILL McLEAN
38 Glendarvon Street, London SW15 1JS, UK.

CHRISTOPHER MANN LIMITED
140 Park Lane, London W1Y 4BU, UK.
Contact: Christopher Mann or Winifred Grogan.
Specializes in films and stage and television plays.

CAROL MARTIN
179 Wardour Street, London W1, UK.

BLANCH MARVIN
21A St. John's Wood High Street, London NW8, UK.

J. A. MAXTONE GRAHAM LITERARY AGENT
4 Pound Cottages, Streatley, Berkshire RG8 9JH, UK.
Contact: J. A. Maxtone Graham.
Represents established writers only. Specializes in articles up to 5,000 words written for the American magazine markets.

P. B. MAYER
Literary Agency Department, 37A Church Road, Wimbledon, London SW19 5DQ, UK.
Acts as a literary agent between publishers not as an independent agent for authors.

MAURICE MICHAEL
Partridge Green, Horsham, Sussex, UK.
Contact: M. A. Michael or P. K. Michael.
Scandinavian, Polish, German and French language books.

RICHARD MILNE LIMITED
28 Makepeace Avenue, Highgate, London N6, UK.
Contact: R. M. Sharples or K. N. Sharples.
Handles film scripts, television and stage plays as well as a limited amount of book MSS.

WILLIAM MORRIS AGENCY (U.K.) LIMITED
Melrose House, 4 Savile Row, London W1X 1AF, UK.
Contact: Robert W. Shapiro.
Interested in theatre, film and television scripts.

DEBORAH OWEN LIMITED
78 Narrow Street, Limehouse, London E14 8BP, UK.
Contact: Deborah Owen.
Does not handle plays.

MARK PATERSON, AUTHORS' AND PUBLISHERS' AGENT
42 Canonbury Square, Islington, London N1 2AW, UK.
Specializes in psychological and psychiatric books as well as children's books. Does not accept short stories or articles.

NORMAN PAYNE AGENCY
9 Blenheim Street, New Bond Street, London W1, UK.

THE PENMAN LITERARY SERVICE
262 London Road, Westcliff-on-Sea, Essex SS0 7JG, UK.
Contact: Leonard G. Stubbs, F.R.S.A.
Handles full-length MSS, theatre, films, television and sound broadcasting.

A. D. PETERS AND COMPANY
10 Buckingham Street, London WC2N 6BU, UK.
Contact: Michael Sissons, Anthony Jones, Pat Kavanagh or Margaret Stephens.
Represents novelists, writers for film, television and radio, all categories of general non-fiction and academic authors. No children's books or foreign language material.

PL REPRESENTATION LIMITED
33 Sloane Street, London SW1X 9NP, UK.
Contact: Robin Lowe, Patricia MacNaughton or Peter Bryant.
Confines activities to dramatists in all media. Handles film rights but not concerned with publishing rights.

LAURENCE POLLINGER LIMITED
18 Maddox Street, Mayfair, London W1R 0EU, UK.
Contact: Laurence Pollinger, Gerald J. Pollinger or Rosemary Gould.
Does not handle original film stories, poetry, freelance journalistic articles or children's books.

MURRAY POLLINGER
11 Long Acre, London WC2E 9LH, UK.
Contact: Murray Pollinger.
Does not handle poetry, plays, journalism, technical or academic books.

PROGRESSIVE MANAGEMENT
11 Blenheim Street, London W1Y 0LJ, UK.
Contact: Neil Landor or Diane Landor.

RADALA AND ASSOCIATES
17 Avenue Mansions, Finchley Road, London NW3 7AX, UK.
Contact: Richard Gollner or Istvan Siklos.
Mainly represent East European writers.

MARGARET RAMSAY LIMITED
14A Goodwin's Court, St. Martin's Lane, London WC2N 4LL, UK.
Contact: Margaret Ramsay.
Represents writers for theatre, television films and radio only.

REPRESENTATION JOYCE EDWARDS
8 Theed Street, London SE1, UK.
Contact: Joyce Edwards.

DEBORAH ROGERS LIMITED
29 Goodge Street, London W1, UK.
Contact: Deborah Rogers, Ann Warnford-Davis or Patricia White.
Accepts all types of MSS.

KAY ROUTLEDGE ASSOCIATES
176 Wardour Street, London W1V 3AA, UK.
Contact: Mrs. Kay Routledge.
Handles fiction written by professional women writers.

ST. JAMES'S MANAGEMENT
22 Groom Place, London SW1, UK.

SCOTTISH CASTING OFFICE, TELEVISION, THEATRE, SCREEN, LIMITED (S.C.O.T.T.S.)
2 Clifton Street, Glasgow G3 7LA, Scotland.
Contact: Robin Richardson.
Handles theatre, films, television and sound broadcasting.

PATRICK SEALE BOOKS LIMITED
2 Motcomb Street, Belgrave Square, London SW1X 8JU, UK.
Contact: Patrick Seale or Jane Blackstock.
Handles biography, memoirs, general non-fiction, politics, crafts, art and general fiction.

VINCENT SHAW ASSOCIATES
75 Hammersmith Road, London W14 8UZ, UK.

SHAW MACLEAN
St. John's Chambers, 2–10 St. John's Road, London SW11 1QG, UK.
Contact: Michael Shaw or Alastair Maclean.
Specializes in authors writing professional or student books for the college and university markets but also handles works of general non-fiction and school books.

ANTHONY SHEIL ASSOCIATES, LIMITED
52 Floral Street, Covent Garden, London WC2E 9DE, UK.
Contact: Anthony Sheil, Giles Gordon or Gill Coleridge.
Interested in all types of MSS.

VERONICA SILVER AND ASSOCIATES
16 Sicilian Avenue, London WC1, UK.

RICHARD SCOTT SIMON LIMITED
36 Wellington Street, London WC2E 7BD, UK.
Contact: Richard Scott Simon.
Does not handle plays, poetry, children's and technical books.

SINGLETON HOWARD MANAGEMENT LIMITED
12 Palgrave Road, London W12 9NB, UK.

ROBERT SOMMERVILLE LIMITED
176 Wardour Street, London W1V 3AA, UK.
Contact: Carl or Kay Routledge.
Specializes in crime fiction.

SOUND VISION INTERNATIONAL
75 Hammersmith Road, London W14 8UZ, UK.
Contact: Vincent Shaw.

SPOKESMEN
1 Craven Hill, London W2 3EP, UK.
Contact: Graham Watson, Chairman or R. M. D. Odgers, Managing Director.
Represents playwrights, film and television script writers and directors.

ABNER STEIN
39a Cyril Mansions, London SW11 4HP, UK.
Contact: Abner Stein.
Will consider any type of MS.

RICHARD STONE
18/20 York Buildings, Adelphi, London WC2, UK.

THE STRATHMORE LITERARY AGENCY
145 Park Road, London NW8, UK.
No specialities.

THE T.I.M. ENTERPRISES LITERARY AGENCY
23 Haymarket, London SW1, UK.
Contact: Tim Satchell or Clive Stanhope.
Specializes in novels and biographies. Does not handle short stories or plays.

TRAFALGER PERRY LIMITED
12a Goodwin's Court, St. Martin's Lane, London WC2N 4LL, UK.
Contact: John H. Perry.
Primarily represents dramatists.

UNITED WRITERS
Trevail Mill, Zennor, St. Ives, Cornwall, UK.
Contact: Sydney Sheppard.
Handles romantic novels, romantic fiction and serial stories for women's magazines.

HARVEY UNNA LIMITED
14 Beaumont Mews, Marylebone High Street, London W1, UK.
Contact: Harvey Unna, Elizabeth Unna or Nina Froud.
Specializes in dramatic works for all media but also handles book MSS.

DR. JAN VAN LOEWEN LIMITED
81–83 Shaftesbury Avenue, London W1V 8BX, UK.
Contact: Dr. Jan Van Loewen, Michael Imison, Elisabeth Van Loewen or Katherine Gould.
Handles full-length fiction and general MSS, theatre, films, television and sound broadcasting.

LORNA VESTEY
30 Rostrevor Road, London SW6, UK.
Contact: Mrs. Lorna Vestey.
Deals with full-length works of all sorts including fiction, non-fiction, children's books, drama and poetry.

JAMES VICCARS (MANAGEMENT) LIMITED
179 Wardour Street, London W1, UK.
Contact: James P. Viccars.

MARGERY VOSPER LIMITED
Suite 8, 26 Charing Cross Road, London WC2H 0DG, UK.
Specializes in plays and film scripts as well as material for sound broadcasting and television.

S. WALKER LITERARY AGENCY
199 Hampermill Lane, Oxhey, Watford, Hertfordshire WD1 4PJ, UK.
Contact: Samuel Walker or Emily Kathleen Walker.
Interested in literary works of all kinds with the exception of short topical articles, poetry and stories for juveniles.

THE J. C. WALLS LITERARY SERVICE
37 Henley Grove, Henleaze, Bristol BS9 4EQ, UK.
Contact: J. C. Walls.
Interested in all types of book length material.

CECILY WARE
19 John Spencer Square, Canonbury, London N1 2LZ, UK.

A. P. WATT AND SON
26/28 Bedford Row, London WC1R 4HL, UK.
Contact: Michael Horniman or Hilary Rubinstein.
Interested in all types of MSS except plays.

GERALD WELCH MANAGEMENT
29 Churchdale Court, Harvard Road, London W4 4EE, UK.

DAVID WHITE ASSOCIATES
34 Berkeley House, Hay Hill, London W1X 7LG, UK.

WINANT TOWERS LIMITED
14 Clifford's Inn, London EC4A 1DA, UK.
Contact: Ursula R. Winant.
Does not handle plays.

CHARLOTTE WOLFERS
3 Regent Square, London WC1, UK.

HUBERT H. WOODWARD
16 Redcliffe Square, London SW10, UK.
Plays only.

U.S.A. AGENTS

CYRILLY ABELS
119 West 57th Street, New York, NY 10010,
USA.

ACKERMAN SCI-FI AGENCY
915 South Sherbourne Drive, Los Angeles,
CA 90035, USA.
Contact: Forrest J. Ackerman.
Specializes in science fiction and mystery.

BRET ADAMS LIMITED
36 East 61st, New York, NY 10021, USA.
Contact: Mr. Charles Hunt, Head of Literary
Department.
A full service agency handling all aspects of
writing.

ADAMS, RAY AND ROSENBERG
9220 Sunset Boulevard, Los Angeles, CA 90069,
USA.
Contact: Mr. Richard A. Ray.
Represents writers, producers and directors plus
the works of a great many novelists and
playwrights in the motion picture and television
industries.

MAXWELL ALEY ASSOCIATES
145 East 35th Street, New York, NY 10016,
USA.
Contact: Mrs. Ruth Aley.

AMERICAN AUTHORS INCORPORATED
342 Madison Avenue, New York, NY 10017,
USA.

AMERICAN PLAY COMPANY,
INCORPORATED
52 Vanderbilt Avenue, New York, NY 10017,
USA.
Contact: Sheldon Abend.

AM-RUS LITERARY AGENCY
25 West 43rd Street, New York, NY 10036,
USA.
Contact: Leah Siegel.
Represents Soviet authors in the USA, including
writers of children's and adults' books, fiction,
non-fiction as well as dramatists.

BART ANDREWS
7010 Lanewood Avenue, Hollywood, CA 90028,
USA.

ATLANTIC LITERARY AGENCY
16 Drake Lane, Manhasset, NY 11030, USA.

AUTHORS AND PUBLISHERS SERVICE
146—47 29th Avenue, Flushing, NY 11354,
USA.
Contact: Miriam Gilbert, Director.
Specialize in new writers but handle all types of
scripts.

ALICE BACH BOOKS
222 East 75th Street, New York, NY 10021,
USA.
Specializes in fiction and non-fiction works for
children and young adults. Also handles
television material.

JULIAN BACH LITERARY AGENCY,
INCORPORATED
3 East 48th Street, New York, NY 10017, USA.
Contact: Miss Wendy Weil.

BALSIGER-MATTHEWS LITERARY SERVICE
257 Brentwood Street, Costa Mesa, CA 92627,
USA.
301 Santa Isabel Avenue, Costa Mesa, CA 92627,
USA.
Specializes mainly in religious books plus religious
and secular how-to-do-it books. Does not handle
poetry or fictional novels. Interested in
manuscripts of book length only.

BARBER AND MERRILL
253 West 21st Street, New York, NY 10011,
USA.

BART/LEVY ASSOCIATES, INCORPORATED
8601 Wilshire Boulevard, Beverly Hills,
CA 90211, USA.

SCOTT BARTLETT ASSOCIATES
3 East 65th Street, New York, NY 10021, USA.

WARREN BAYLESS W. B. AGENCY,
INCORPORATED
156 East 52nd Street, New York, NY 10021,
USA.
Contact: Warren Bayless or Roberta Kent.
Literary and dramatic agent.

MAXIMILIAN BECKER
115 East 82nd Street, New York, NY 10028,
USA.

BILL BERGER ASSOCIATES,
INCORPORATED
535 East 72nd Street, New York, NY 10021,
USA.

LOIS BERMAN
530 East 72nd Street, New York, NY 10021,
USA.

BETHEL AGENCY
125 West 79th Street, New York, NY 10024,
USA.
Contact: Lewis R. Chambers.
Handles fiction and non-fiction books and
articles.

LURTON BLASSINGAME
60 East 42nd Street, New York, NY 10017,
USA.

THE BLOOM/MILLER ORGANIZATION
8693 Wilshire Boulevard, Beverly Hills,

CA 90211, USA.
Contact: Mel Bloom.

GEORGES BORCHARDT, INCORPORATED
145 East 52nd Street, New York, NY 10022, USA.
Contact: Georges Borchardt.
Represent both fiction and non-fiction writers. Only take on new clients recommended by authors already represented by the agency. Unsolicited MSS not considered.

BP SINGER FEATURES, INCORPORATED
3164 Tyler Avenue, Anaheim, CA 92801, USA.
Contact: Kurt Singer.
Deal in subsidiary rights. Interested in romance titles, war, science fiction, mysteries and Gothics. Serialize and syndicate books as well as distribute jacket cover art to books.

BRANDT AND BRANDT
101 Park Avenue, New York, NY 10017, USA.

CÉLINE BRÉVANNES
28 Bauer Place, Westport, CT 06880, USA.
Contact: Céline Brévannes.
Specialize in children's books. Retiring from the field but will advise people providing they send a stamped self-addressed envelope.

ANITA HELEN BROOKS ASSOCIATES
155 East 55th Street, New York, NY 10022, USA.

CURTIS BROWN, LIMITED
60 East 56th Street, New York, NY 10022, USA.
Contact: Perry H. Knowlton, Miss Martha Winston, or Miss Emilie Jacobson.

JAMES BROWN ASSOCIATES, INCORPORATED
22 East 60th Street, New York, NY 10022, USA.
Contact: James Oliver Brown, President or David Stewart Hull, Vice-President.
Do not represent poetry, plays, screenplays, articles, short stories or juvenile books unless they are written by long standing clients with published books to their credit.

NED BROWN ASSOCIATED
407 North Maple Drive, Beverly Hills, CA 90210, USA.
Literary and dramatic agent.

BRUNNER/MAZEL
64 University Place, New York, NY 10003, USA.

KNOX BURGER ASSOCIATES LIMITED
39½ Washington Square South, New York, NY 10012, USA.
Contact: Knox Burger.

SHIRLEY BURKE, LITERARY REPRESENTATIVE
370 Easy 76th Street, Suite B-704, New York, NY 10021, USA.
Contact: Miss Shirley Burke.
Interested in fiction and non-fiction in MS only. No dramatists, writers of children's stories or new authors.

RUTH CANTOR
156 Fifth Avenue, New York, NY 10010, USA.
Contact: Ruth Cantor.
Specialize in children's books but also handles general trade books, fiction and non-fiction, on the adult level. Not interested, however, in plays, screenplays, TV scripts, poetry, magazine material, articles or short stories.

THE CASSELMAN AGENCY
141 North Beverly Glen Boulevard, Los Angeles, CA 90024, USA.
Contact: Kevin M. A. Casselman.

SHIRLEY COLLIER AGENCY
1127 Stradella Road, Los Angeles, CA 90024, USA.
Literary and dramatic agent.

THE COLLINS AGENCY
225 East 57th Street, New York, NY 10022, USA.
Contact: Thomas P. Collins.
Handles fiction and non-fiction books as well as plays, films and television material.

COLLINS-KNOWLTON-WING, INCORPORATED
60 East 56th Street, New York, NY 10022, USA.
Contact: Perry H. Knowlton or Josephine Rogers.

KINGSLEY COLTON AND ASSOCIATES, INCORPORATED
321 South Beverly Drive, Beverly Hills, CA 90212, USA.
Contact: Kingsley Colton.

CREATIVE MANAGEMENT ASSOCIATES, LIMITED
600 Madison Avenue, New York, NY 10022, USA.
8899 Beverly Boulevard, Los Angeles, CA 90048, USA.
Literary and dramatic agents.

CRITICS ASSOCIATED
R.R. Number 3, Box 248, Richmond, IN 47374, USA.
Contact: Joseph E. Longstreth.

JOHN CUSHMAN ASSOCIATES, INCORPORATED
25 West 43rd Street, New York, NY 10036, USA.
Contact: John Cushman or Jane W. Wilson.

JOAN DAVES
515 Madison Avenue, New York, NY 10022, USA.
Contact: Joan Daves or Edward Davis.
No specialities.

DELACORTE PRESS
1 Dag Hammarskjold Plaza, 245 East 47th Street, New York, NY 10017, USA.

MISS ANITA DIAMANT
51 East 42nd Street, New York, NY 10017, USA.

CANDIDA DONADIO AND ASSOCIATES,
INCORPORATED
111 West 57th Street, New York, NY 10019,
USA.
Contact: Miss Candida Donadio.

DUN AND LAPHAM
31 Harrison Avenue, New Canaan, CT 06840,
USA.
Contact: Mrs. Elizabeth Dun.
Handles fiction and non-fiction books, plays and
material for juveniles.

EDUCATIONAL RESOURCES CORPORATION
128 East 74th Street, New York, NY 10017,
USA.
Contact: Charles M. Sherover.

ANN ELMO AGENCY, INCORPORATED
52 Vanderbilt Avenue, New York, NY 10017,
USA.
Contact: Ann Elmo.
Handles all types of commercial writing for the
adult and juvenile markets, fiction and
non-fiction in all lengths. Also covers the play,
television and movie markets.

FCA AGENCY, INCORPORATED
9000 Sunset Boulevard, Los Angeles, CA 90069,
USA
Contact: Frank Cooper, President.

HANNS FISCHER, LITERARY AGENCY
2332 West Farwell Avenue, Chicago, IL 60659,
USA.

THE SY FISCHER COMPANY AGENCY,
INCORPORATED
9255 Sunset Boulevard, Suite 505, Los Angeles,
CA 90069, USA.
One East 57th Street, New York, NY 10022,
USA.
Contact: Sy Fischer, President or Joel Cohen,
Vice-President.
Represents writers, producers, directors and
production companies.

MISS FRIEDA FISHBEIN
353 West 57th Street, New York, NY 10019,
USA.
Contact: Miss Frieda Fishbein.
Handles plays, books and television scripts.

BARTHOLD FLES LITERARY AGENCY
507 Fifth Avenue, New York, NY 10017, USA.
Contact: Miss Vikki Power.
Interested in adult and juvenile fiction and
non-fiction.

THE FOLEY AGENCY
34 East 38th Street, New York, NY 10016, USA.
Contact: Joseph Foley, Joan Foley or Minnie
Foley.
Fiction and non-fiction books plus limited
magazine material.

THE FOX CHASE AGENCY, INCORPORATED
60 East 42nd Street, New York, NY 10017,
USA.
Contact: A. L. Hart or J. Hart.

HAROLD FREEDMAN BRANDT AND
BRANDT DRAMATIC DEPARTMENT,
INCORPORATED
101 Park Avenue, New York, NY 10017, USA.

SAMUEL FRENCH, INCORPORATED
25 West 45th Street, New York, NY 10036,
USA.
Sub-agent dealing with other agents and not
directly with authors. Plays only.

JAY GARON-BROOKE ASSOCIATES,
INCORPORATED
415 Central Park West, New York, NY 10025,
USA.
Contact: Jay Garon.
Literary and dramatic agency.

MAX GARTENBERG
331 Madison Avenue, New York, NY 10017,
USA.

MRS. EVELYN GENDEL
319 Avenue C, New York, NY 10009, USA.

GOLDFARB LEWIS AGENCY
8733 Sunset Boulevard, Suite 202, Los Angeles,
CA 90069, USA.
Contact: Robert Goldfarb.

LARNEY GOODKIND
30 East 60th Street, New York, NY 10022, USA.
Contact: Mrs. Karen Rose Goodkind.

GRAHAM AGENCY
317 West 45th Street, New York, NY 10036,
USA.
Contact: Earl Graham.
Represents dramatists almost exclusively.

SANFORD J. GREENBURGER ASSOCIATES,
INCORPORATED
757 Third Avenue, New York, NY 10017, USA.
Contact: Francis or Ingrid Greenburger.

BLANCHE C. GREGORY, INCORPORATED
2 Tudor City Place, New York, NY 10017, USA.

REECE HALSEY AGENCY
8733 Sunset Boulevard, Los Angeles, CA 90069,
USA.

MITCHELL J. HAMILBURG AGENCY
1105 Glendon Avenue, Los Angeles, CA 90024,
USA.

HELEN HARVEY ASSOCIATES
1697 Broadway, New York, NY 10019, USA.
Contact: Charles W. Hunt.

SHIRLEY HECTOR AND ASSOCIATES
29 West 46th Street, New York, NY 10036,
USA.
Contact: Roy Gilbert.
Handles fiction and non-fiction, including
subsidiary rights.

KURT HELLMER
52 Vanderbilt Avenue, New York, NY 10036,
USA.
Handles fiction and non-fiction books as well as
plays, film and television material.

RONALD HOBBS LITERARY AGENCY
211 East 43rd Street, New York, NY 10017,
USA.
Contact: Ronald Hobbs.
Represents screenplays along with fiction and
non-fiction book length MSS.

HOLUB AND ASSOCIATES
432 Park Avenue South, New York, NY 10016,
USA.
5 Glen Oaks Avenue, Summit, NJ 07801, USA.
Contact: William Holub.
Specialize in religious material aimed at general
and specialized (clergy and religious) audiences.
No fiction or children's books.

ILA INTERNATIONAL LITERARY AGENCY
305 East 75th Street, New York, NY 10021,
USA.
Contact: Tomas D. W. Friedmann or Miss
Ingeborg Grundmann.
Primarily works between publishers in the sale of
foreign language rights, co-productions, etc. Want
only popular and best selling works, series of
books rather than individual volumes. Prefer
non-fiction to fiction.

INTERNATIONAL FAMOUS AGENCY
9255 Sunset Boulevard, Los Angeles, CA 90069,
USA.
Contact: Ben Benjamin or Michael Medavoy.
1301 Avenue of the Americas, New York,
NY 10019, USA.
Contact: Miss Monica McCall or Miss Lynn
Nesbit.

INTERNATIONAL LITERARY AGENTS
LIMITED
535 Evelyn Place, Beverly Hills, CA 90210, USA.
Contact: Ms. Peri Winkler, President.

ALEX JACKINSON
55 West 42nd Street, New York, NY 10036,
USA.

MARGOT JOHNSON AGENCY
405 East 54th Street, New York, NY 10022,
USA.
Contact: Miss Margot Johnson.

NANNINE JOSEPH
200 West 54th Street, New York, NY 10019,
USA.
Contact: Nannine Joseph.
Handles no plays, TV or radio material. Has not
accepted new clients since 1962.

KAHN LIFFLANDER AND RHODES AGENCY
853 Seventh Avenue, New York, NY 10019,
USA.
Contact: Barbara Rhodes.
Handles dramatists, adult fiction and non-fiction,
juveniles, movie scripts and TV scripts.

VIRGINIA KIDD With James Allen and Beth
Blish LITERARY AGENTS
Box 278, Milford, PA 18337, USA.
1 Sheridan Square, New York, NY 10014, USA
Contact: Virginia Kidd, James Allen or Beth
Blish.
Specializes in speculative fiction but handles all
the popular genres as well as mainstream fiction
and non-fiction.

BERTHA KLAUSNER INTERNATIONAL
LITERARY AGENCY, INCORPORATED
71 Park Avenue, New York, NY 10016, USA.
Contact: Bertha Klausner.
Handles adult and juvenile fiction and non-fiction
books, plays, television and motion picture
scripts.

LUCY KROLL AGENCY
390 West End Avenue, New York, NY 10024,
USA.
Contact: Lucy Kroll.
Represents writers of full-length fiction,
non-fiction and drama. Does not accept
unsolicited MSS and does not handle short
stories, poetry, children's literature or other
specialized work.

ROBERT LANTZ-CANDIDA DONADIO
LITERARY AGENCY, INCORPORATED
111 West 57th Street, New York, NY 10019,
USA.
Literary and dramatic agency.

PHOEBE LARMORE
5 Milligan Place, New York, NY 10011, USA.

MICHAEL LARSEN/ELIZABETH POMADA
LITERARY AGENTS
1029 Jones Street, San Francisco, CA 94109,
USA.
Contact: Elizabeth Pomada.
Handles adult and juvenile, fiction and
non-fiction, trade books.

IRVING PAUL LAZAR
211 South Beverly Drive, Beverly Hills,
CA 90212, USA.
680 Madison Avenue, New York, NY 10021,
USA.
Contact: Irving Lazar.
Represents writers for theatre and motion
pictures.

LENNIGER LITERARY AGENCY,
INCORPORATED
437 Fifth Avenue, New York, NY 10016, USA.
Contact: August Lenniger or Grace Lenniger.
Handles teenage and juvenile fiction and
non-fiction books and magazine articles.

ROBERT LESCHER
155 East 71st Street, New York, NY 10021,
USA.
Contact: Miss Susan Corridan.

HENRY LEWIS AGENCY
9172 Sunset Boulevard, Hollywood, CA 90069,
USA.
Represents writers for the theatre, television and
motion pictures. Accepts no MSS unless
accompanied by a self-addressed, stamped return
envelope.

PATRICIA LEWIS/INGRID HALLEN
450 Seventh Avenue, New York, NY 10001,
USA.

ROBERT LEWIS
500 Fifth Avenue, New York, NY 10036, USA.

THE STERLING LORD AGENCY,
INCORPORATED

660 Madison Avenue, New York, NY 10021, USA.
Contact: Sterling Lord or Helen Brann.

DONALD MacCAMPBELL INCORPORATED
12 East 41st Street, New York, NY 10017, USA.
Contact: Donald MacCampbell, President, Kathleen MacCampbell, Vice-President or Maureen Moran, Editor.
Handles adult books only.

GERARD McCAULEY AGENCY, INCORPORATED
P.O. Box 456, Cranbury, NJ 08512, USA.
551 Fifth Avenue, New York, NY 10017, USA.
Contact: Gerard F. McCauley.
Specializes in non-fiction but does not handle juveniles.

KIRBY McCAULEY
220 East 26th Street, New York, NY 10010, USA.
Contact: Kirby McCauley.
Handles all types of commercial writing but special emphasis on genre fiction (mysteries, science fiction, fantasy) and biographies. Full length books only, unless by special arrangement.

McINTOSH AND OTIS, INCORPORATED
18 East 41st Street, New York, NY 10017, USA.
Contact: Miss Julie Fallowfield or Miss Elizabeth Otis.

McINTOSH, McKEE AND DODDS, INCORPORATED
22 East 40th Street, New York, NY 10016, USA.

BETTY MARKS
51 East 42nd Street, New York, NY 10017, USA.
Handles adult and juvenile fiction and non-fiction books as well as magazine articles.

ELAINE MARKSON
44 Greenwich Avenue, New York, NY 10011, USA.
Contact: Elaine Markson.

MISS ELISABETH MARTON
96 Fifth Avenue, New York, NY 10011, USA.
Contact: Mrs. Jo Ann Burbank.

HAROLD MATSON COMPANY, INCORPORATED
22 East 40th Street, New York, NY 10016, USA.
Contact: Harold Matson.

TONI MENDEZ, INCORPORATED
140 East 56th Street, New York, NY 10022, USA.

SCOTT MEREDITH LITERARY AGENCY, INCORPORATED
580 Fifth Avenue, New York, NY 10036, USA.
Contact: Scott Meredith, President, Sidney Meredith, Secretary-Treasurer, or Jack Scovil, Editorial Director.
Handles general fiction and non-fiction, books and magazines, juveniles, plays, TV scripts, motion picture rights and properties.

MRS. TONI MILFORD
50 East 86th Street, New York, NY 10028, USA.

ROBERT P. MILLS, LIMITED
156 East 52nd Street, New York, NY 10022, USA.
Contact: Bob Mills.
Handles a wide variety of general fiction and non-fiction but does not represent dramatists.

MOLSON-STANTON ASSOCIATES AGENCY, INCORPORATED
10889 Wilshire Boulevard, Suite 929, Los Angeles, CA 90024, USA.
Not accepting new clients.

HOWARD MOOREPARK
500 East 77th Street, New York, NY 10021, USA.

WILLIAM MORRIS AGENCY
151 El Camino, Beverly Hills, CA 90212, USA.
435 North Michigan Avenue, Chicago, IL, USA.
1350 Avenue of the Americas, New York, NY 10019, USA.

HENRY MORRISON INCORPORATED
58 West 10, New York, NY 10011, USA.
Contact: Henry Morrison.
Represents novelists and screenwriters.

MARVIN MOSS
9200 Sunset Boulevard, Suite 601, Los Angeles, CA 90069, USA.
Contact: Marvin Moss.
Mainly represents writers for the motion picture and television industries.

CHARLES NEIGHBORS, INCORPORATED
240 Waverly Place, New York, NY 10011, USA.

B. K. NELSON LITERARY AGENCY
210 East 47th Street, New York, NY 10017, USA.
Contact: Bonita K. Nelson.

ELLEN NEUWALD, INCORPORATED
905 West End Avenue, New York, NY 10025, USA.
Contact: Ellen Neuwald.
Represents playwrights as well as fiction and non-fiction writers.

NICHOLAS LITERARY AGENCY
161 Madison Avenue, New York, NY 10016, USA.
Contact: Miss Georgia C. Nicholas.

HAROLD OBER ASSOCIATES, INCORPORATED
40 East 49th Street, New York, NY 10017, USA.
Contact: Dorothy Olding.

DOROTHEA OPPENHEIMER
866 United Nations Plaza, New York, NY 10017, USA.
Contact: Dorothea Oppenheimer.
Represents writers of adult fiction and non-fiction.

MISS EVELYN OPPENHEIMER
4505 Fairway, Dallas, TX 75219, USA.
Handles fiction and non-fiction adult books.

PARK AVENUE LITERARY AGENCY
230 Park Avenue, New York, NY 10017, USA.
Contact: Miss Marie Wilkerson.

RAY PEEKNER LITERARY AGENCY
2625 North 36th Street, Milwaukee, WI 53210, USA.
Contact: Ray Puecher.
Handles booklengths, fiction and non-fiction, adult and juvenile. No poetry, plays, juvenile picture books or unsolicited MSS.

MARJORIE PETERS AND PIERRE LONG
5744 South Harper Avenue, Chicago, IL 60637, USA.
Contact: Marjorie Peters or Pierre Long.
Represents poets, short story writers, novelists, playwrights and article/essay writers.

PHOENIX LITERARY AGENCY, INCORPORATED
225 East 49th Street, New York, NY 10017, USA.
Contact: Robert Dattila.

ARTHUR PINE ASSOCIATES, INCORPORATED
1780 Broadway, New York, NY 10019, USA.
Contact: Arthur Pine.
General fiction and non-fiction books.

SIDNEY E. PORCELAIN AGENCY
Box J, Rocky Hill, NJ 08553, USA.

SUSAN ANN PROTTER
156 East 52nd Street, Penthouse — 1, New York, NY 10022, USA.
Contact: Susan Ann Protter.
Handles writers of both fiction and non-fiction for adults only.

RAINES AND RAINES AUTHORS' REPRESENTATIVES
244 Madison Avenue, New York, NY 10016, USA.
Contact: Joan or Theron Raines.
Handle all fields.

PAUL R. REYNOLDS, INCORPORATED
599 Fifth Avenue, New York, NY 10017, USA.

VIRGINIA RICE
301 East 66th Street, New York, NY 10021, USA.

FLORA ROBERTS, INCORPORATED
116 East 59th Street, New York, NY 10022, USA.

ROBINSON LITERARY AGENCY
Snyder Square North, 4511 Harlem Road, Buffalo, NY 14226, USA.
Contact: Ms. Janet Robinson.
Handles fiction, non-fiction, plays, and how-to books. Does not represent poets or short story writers.

ROBINSON-WEINTRAUB AND ASSOCIATES, INCORPORATED
8438 Melrose Place, Los Angeles, CA 90069, USA.
Contact: Stuart Robinson.
Represents writers primarily for motion picture and television.

MRS. MARIE RODELL
141 East 55th Street, New York, NY 10022, USA.
Contact: John Meyer.

JANE ROTROSEN
212 East 48th Street, New York, NY 10017, USA.
Contact: Ms. Rotrosen.
Handles fiction and non-fiction books as well as material for television and motion pictures.

RUSSELL AND VOLKENING, INCORPORATED
551 Fifth Avenue, New York, NY 10017, USA.
Contact: Diarmuid Russell or Timothy Seldes.

GLORIA SAFIER-BOB BARRY, INCORPORATED
667 Madison Avenue, New York, NY 10021, USA.

LEAH SALISBURY, INCORPORATED
790 Madison Avenue, New York, NY 10021, USA.
Contact: Leah Salisbury.
Represents authors of plays, films, TV material and fiction and non-fiction books.

JOHN SCHAFFNER LITERARY AGENT
425 East 51st Street, New York, NY 10022, USA.
Contact: John Schaffner or Victor Chapin.
Handles fiction and non-fiction books as well as magazine material. Does not deal with dramatic material.

AD SCHULBERG AGENCY
300 East 57th Street, New York, NY 10022, USA.
Contact: Ad Schulberg.

DAVID H. SCOTT
225 East 57th Street, New York, NY 10022, USA.
Handles fiction and non-fiction.

RITA SCOTT, INCORPORATED
25 Sutton Place South, New York, NY 10022, USA.
Contact: Rita Scott.
Represents fiction and non-fiction book writers as well as juveniles.

SCOTT AND SMITH ASSOCIATES
9720 Wilshire Boulevard, Beverly Hills, CA 90212, USA.
Contact: Joan Scott or Ray C. Smith.

SELIGMANN AND COLLIER
280 Madison Avenue, New York, NY 10016, USA.
Contact: James F. Seligmann or Oscar Collier.

SHAPIRO/WEST AND ASSOCIATES, INCORPORATED
141 El Camino Drive, Beverly Hills, CA 90212, USA.
Contact: George Shapiro.

H. E. SHUSTER AND COMPANY
4930 Wynnefield Avenue, Philadelphia, PA 19131, USA.

JEROME S. SIEGEL ASSOCIATES
8733 Sunset Boulevard, Los Angeles, CA 90069, USA.
Contact: Jerome Siegel.

MAX SIEGEL AND ASSOCIATES, AUTHORS' AGENTS
154 East Erie Street, Chicago, IL 60611, USA.
Handles general fiction and non-fiction books, magazines and juveniles.

EVELYN SINGER AGENCY
P.O. Box 163, Briarcliff Manor, NY 10510, USA.
Contact: Evelyn Singer.
Represents adult and juvenile fiction and non-fiction.

ELYSE SOMMER, INCORPORATED
Box E, 962 Allen Lane, Woodmere, NY 11598, USA.
Handles book and magazine material.

MAEVE SOUTHGATE, INCORPORATED
41 Fifth Avenue, New York, NY 10003, USA.
Handles fiction and non-fiction books as well as motion picture rights.

PHILIP G. SPITZER
111—25 76th Avenue, Forest Hills, NY 11375, USA.
Contact: Philip G. Spitzer.

RENEE SPODHEIM ASSOCIATES
698 West End Avenue, Forest Hills, NY 11375, USA.
No specialities.

MRS. CAROLYN WILLYOUNG STAGG
Lester Lewis Associates, Incorporated, 156 East 52nd Street, New York, NY 10022, USA.

LARRY STERNIG LITERARY AGENCY
2407 North 44th Street, Milwaukee, WI 53210, USA.
Contact: Larry Sternig.
Handles professional writers who turn out a wide variety of books, articles and short stories.

TONI STRASSMAN
130 East 18th Street, New York, NY 10003, USA.
No new clients accepted.

GUNTHER STUHLMANN
65 Irving Place, New York, NY 10003, USA.
Contact: Gunther Stuhlmann.
Handles books, both fiction and non-fiction, juveniles, as well as all subsidiary rights to same, including foreign, motion picture and television. No plays, poetry or short fiction accepted.

H. N. SWANSON, INCORPORATED
8523 Sunset Boulevard, Los Angeles, CA 90069, USA.
Contact: H. N. Swanson.
Serves the motion picture and television industries. Represents dramatists, with main thrust being fiction, and authors for the magazine and general book market.

TAMS-WITMARK MUSIC LIBRARY INCORPORATED
757 Third Avenue, New York, NY 10017, USA.

ROSLYN TARG LITERARY AGENCY, INCORPORATED
250 West 57th Street, New York, NY 10019, USA.

J. H. VAN DAELE
225 East 57th Street, New York, NY 10022, USA.
Contact: Jacqueline H. Van Daele.
Handles only psychiatrically oriented books, including all the behavioral sciences, aimed at the popular market. New clients obtained through recommendation only.

AUSTIN WAHL AGENCY
21 East Van Buren Street, Chicago, IL 60605, USA.

JAMES A. WARREN ASSOCIATES
6257 Hazeltine Number 2, Van Nuys, CA 91401, USA.
Contact: James A. Warren, Barbara Thorburn or Frank Bisignano.
Does not handle poetry.

A. WATKINS, INCORPORATED
77 Park Avenue, New York, NY 10016, USA.
Contact: Armitage Watkins, Miss Peggy Caulfield, Mrs. Marian McNamara or Mrs. Gloria C. Loomis.
Handles fiction, non-fiction and children's book properties.

LEW WEITZMAN AND ASSOCIATES
9171 Wilshire Boulevard, Suite 427, Beverly Hills, CA 90210, USA.
Contact: Lew Weitzman.
Represents writers for the motion picture and television industries.

WENDER AND ASSOCIATES, INCORPORATED
30 East 60th Street, New York, NY 10022, USA.
Contact: Phyllis B. Wender.

ALBERT WHITMAN
560 West Lake Street, Chicago, IL 60606, USA.

MAX WILKINSON ASSOCIATES
Shelter Island, NY 11964, USA.

ANNIE LAURIE WILLIAMS, INCORPORATED
18 East 41st Street, New York, NY 10017, USA.

LAMBERT WILSON ASSOCIATES
8 East Tenth Street, New York, NY 10003, USA.
Contact: Lambert Wilson, Director.
Specializes in the handling of book properties.

MARY YOST ASSOCIATES
141 East 55th Street, New York, NY 10022, USA.
Contact: Miss Mary Yost.

ZIEGLER ASSOCIATES, INCORPORATED
9255 Sunset Boulevard, Los Angeles, CA 90069, USA.
Represents authors, writers, producers and directors.

AGENTS OTHER THAN
UNITED KINGDOM OR USA

Argentina

INTERNATIONAL EDITORS COMPANY
Avenida Cabildo 1156, Buenos Aires, Argentina.

LAURENCE SMITH
Avenida de los Incas 3110, Buenos Aires, Argentina.

Australia

DOROTHY BLEWETT ASSOCIATES
50 View Hill Crescent, Eltham, Victoria 3095, Australia.

CURTIS BROWN (AUSTRALIA) PTY. LIMITED
P.O. Box 19, Paddington, NSW 2021, Australia.
Contact: Tim Curnow.
Handles book-length fiction, non-fiction and educational works, stage plays, radio, TV and film scripts and short stories.

CHARTER BOOKS PTY. LIMITED
Foveaux House, 63 Foveaux Street, Surry Hills, NSW 2101, Australia.
Contact: Bruce Semler, Malcolm Newell or Donald McLean.
Especially interested in educational books and information type books including historical, natural science, geographical and political. Documentary-fiction also welcomed.

HAMPTON PRESS FEATURES SYNDICATE
5 Dick Street, Henley, NSW 2111, Australia.

NGV AGENCIES
4a Alfred Street, Woolwich, NSW 2110, Australia.
Contact: Babette Johnson.
Specializes in full length fiction and non-fiction.

MARY WILSON AND ASSOCIATES PTY. INCORPORATED
11 Harrison Crescent, Hawthorn, Victoria 3122, Australia.
Contact: Eileen Hamilton, Manager.

YAFFA SYNDICATE PTY. LIMITED
Box 606, G.P.O. Sydney, NSW 2001, Australia.

Belgium

INTERNATIONAL LITERAIR AGENTSCHAP
Blankenbergestraat 23, 9000 Gent, Belgium.
Contact: Dr. Hugo Tomme.

A. VAN HAGELAND LITERARY AGENCY
Blutsdelle 10, B-1641 Alsemberg, Belgium.
Contact: Albert van Hageland.
Specialities include science fiction, supernatural, horror and anthologies. Features and magazine material not requested. Handles international transactions and all kinds of printed popular literature for Dutch language rights.

Brazil

DR. J. E. BLOCH
Rua Oscar Freire 416, Ap. 83, 01426 São Paulo, Brazil.
Contact: Dr. J. E. Bloch.
Interested in all Brazilian authors' works.

Bulgaria

JUSAUTOR — COPYRIGHT PROTECTION AGENCY
P.O.B. 872, Sofia, Bulgaria.
The agency promotes literary, dramatic, musical, scientific and other works by Bulgarian authors, supplies information, grants options, and in the capacity of the exclusive representative of the Bulgarian authors negotiates and makes the contracts with foreign publishers and other foreign users of their works. The agency acts as an intermediary between foreign authors, publishers and agencies and Bulgarian users of their works.

Canada

CANADIAN SPEAKERS' AND WRITERS' SERVICE
44 Douglas Crescent, Toronto, Ontario M4W 2EJ, Canada.

SCARGALL OF MARKHAM
One Talisman Crescent, Markham, Ontario L3P 2C8, Canada.
Contact: Peter O. Scargall.
Represents authors of all modes of writing.

Czechoslovakia

DILIA — THEATRICAL AND LITERARY AGENCY
P.O. Box 34, 12824 Prague 28, Czechoslovakia.
Contact: Mr. Karel Bousek.
Activity is limited to the Czech Socialist Republic. Protects the authors' rights of all dramatic and other works, of theatre, radio, film and television plays and works connected with them, including their musical and graphic parts.

LITA — SLOVENSKA LITERARNA AGENTURA
ulica Cs. Armady 31/111, Bratislava, Czechoslovakia.
Contact: Mr. Ladislav Luknar.
Represents all the authors living in Slovakia including dramatists, writers of children's books, non-fiction and fiction writers, authors of musico-dramatic works, etc.

Denmark

A/S BOOKMAN
12 Fiolstraede, DK-1171 Copenhagen K, Denmark.
Handles British, American, French and Italian authors' rights in Scandinavia.

PREBEN JÖRGENSEN
37 Haandvaerkerhaven, DK-2400 Copenhagen NV, Denmark.

EDITH KIILERICH
Fiolstraede 12, DK-1171 Copenhagen K, Denmark.

ALBRECHT LEONHARDT
Løvstraede 8, DK-1152 Copenhagen K, Denmark.

KURT E. MICHAELS
Jaegersborg Alle 19, DK-2920 Charlottenlund, Denmark.

SVEND MONDRUP INTERNATIONAL LITERARY AGENCY
Tordenskjoldsgate 32, DK-1055 Copenhagen, Denmark.

CARL STRAKOSCH AND OLAF NORDGREEN
Nyhavn 5, DK-1051 Copenhagen K, Denmark.

Finland

WERNER SODERSTROM
Bulevardi 12, Helsinki, Finland.

France

AGENCE BATAILLE
65 rue St. André-des-Arts, 75006 Paris, France.
Contact: Mme. Marie-Claude Bataille.

AGENCE HOFFMAN
77 Boulevard Saint-Michel, 75005 Paris, France.
Contact: Boris or Georges Hoffman or Madame Merrily de Douhet.
Represents American, British and German agents and publishers for French volume translation sales, television (French language) and motion picture contracts, and negotiations of worldwide translation rights for a limited number of authors represented directly by the agency.

JEAN-PIERRE BOSCQ
65 rue du Fauborg Saint-Honoré, 75008 Paris, France.

WILLIAM ASPENWALL BRADLEY
18 Quai de Béthune, Paris 4, France.
Contact: Mrs. W. A. Bradley.

BUREAU LITTÉRAIRE D. CLAIROUIN
66 rue de Miromesnil, 75008 Paris, France.
Contact: Mme. Marie Schebeko.
Handles the literary works of a limited number of writers of various nationalities. Does not accept unsolicited MSS.

BUREAU LITTÉRAIRE INTERNATIONAL MARGUERITE SCIALTIEL
14 Rue Chanoinesse, 75004 Paris, France.
Contact: Geneviève Ulmann.
Represents writers of all sorts of books as well as theatrical works.

MLLE. SABINE DELATTRE
9 rue Christine, 75006 Paris, France.

MME. FRANÇOISE GERMAIN
8 rue de la Paix, 75002 Paris, France.

MADAME MICHELLE LAPAUTRE
6 rue Jean Carries, 75007 Paris, France.
Contact: Michelle Lapautre.
Represents American, English and Israeli publishers and agents for the sale of French translation rights.

ALICE LE BAYON
113 Boulevard Saint-Germain, Paris, France.

McKEE AND MOUCHE
14 rue du Regard, Paris VI, France.
Contact: Douglas McKee or Madame Donine Mouche.
Handles only French translation rights in material published in the United States or in Great Britain.

IRMGARD MATTHIAS-PAUL ESTIENNE, AGENTS LITTÉRAIRES
27 rue du Dragon, 75006 Paris, France.

LA NOUVELLE AGENCE
7 rue Corneille, 75006 Paris, France.
Contact: Mme. Mary Kling.

SERGE OUVAROFF
17 Avenue Victor-Hugo, Paris 16, France.

JANINE QUET — BUREAU LITTÉRAIRE
20 rue de la Michodière, 75002 Paris, France.

MAURICE RENAULT
2 rue de Florence, F-75008 Paris, France.

HÉLÉNA STRASSOVA
4 rue Git-Le-Coeur, 75006 Paris, France.
Contact: Héléna Strassova.
No restrictions.

W. J. TAYLOR-WHITEHEAD
60 rue Madame, 75006 Paris, France.
French rights representative.

LE TELESCOPE, AGENCE LITTÉRAIRE
10 rue Mayet, 75006 Paris, France.

MME. ELLEN WRIGHT
20 rue Jacob, 75006 Paris, France.
French rights representative.

Germany — Federal Republic

AGENCE HOFFMAN
8 München 40, Seestrasse 6, Federal Republic of Germany.
Contact: Frau Dagmar Henne.
Handles negotiations of German translation rights.

FRITZ ALBRECHT INTERNATIONALE AGENTUR
Brahmsallee 29/1, 2000 Hamburq 13, Federal Republic of Germany.

WINFRIED BLUTH LITERARY AGENCY
5630 Remscheid, Augustinusstr. 43, Federal Republic of Germany.

BUCHAGENTUR MÜNCHEN
Maria-Eich-Str. 54b, 8032 Gräfelfing, Federal Republic of Germany.
Contact: Dr. Hanns Martin Elster.

GEISENHEYNER AND CRONE,
INTERNATIONAL LITERARY AGENTS
7 Stuttgart 1, Gymnasiumstrasse 31 B, Federal
Republic of Germany.
Handles German and foreign literary rights.

GUSTAV GREVE, LITERARISCHE AGENTUR
1000 Berlin 12, Fasanenstr. 15, Federal Republic
of Germany.

HANS HERMANN HAGEDORN
Erikastr. 142, 2000 Hamburg 20, Federal
Republic of Germany.

ILA INTERNATIONAL LITERARY AGENCY
2000 Hamburg 39, Zesenstr. 16, Federal
Republic of Germany.

INTERLITA—LITERATURAGENTUR PETER
VILIMEK GmbH
15 Postf. 150210, 1000 Berlin 31, Federal
Republic of Germany.
Contact: Peter Vilimek.

KARL LUDWIG LEONHARDT
LITERARISCHE AGENTUR
An der Alster 22, 2000 Hamburg 1, Federal
Republic of Germany.

MÜNCHNER VERLAGSBÜRO HORST
HODEMACHER-AXEL POLDNER
8 Munich 19, Barellistrasse 7, Federal Republic
of Germany.

THOMAS SCHLUCK LITERARY AGENCY
9 Zietenstrasse, 3000 Hanover, Federal Republic
of Germany.

WILFRIED TH. SIEBER
Postf. 2842, 4980 Bunde 1, Federal Republic of
Germany.
Interested in science fiction and speculative
literature.

SKANDINAVIA VERLAG
D—1 Berlin 12, Knesebeckstrasse 100, Federal
Republic of Germany.
Contact: Marianne Weno or Michael Günther.
Represents most of the modern Scandinavian
dramatists for the German speaking countries.

HERTA WEBER-STUMFOHL,
LITERARISCHES BÜRO
Waldpromenade 32, 8035 Gauting, Federal
Republic of Germany.
Contact: Herta Weber-Stumfohl.
Handles translations from Swedish into German.

Greece

ANGLO-HELLENIC AGENCY
5 Koumpari Str., Kolonaki Square, Athens 138,
Greece.
Represents Greek authors.

Hungary

ARTISJUS, AGENCY FOR LITERATURE,
THEATRE AND MUSIC
H—1364 Budapest, P.B. 67, Hungary.
Contact: Mrs. Vera Acs.

Handles translation rights for every Hungarian
author all over the world in any field of writing.

Iceland

SVEINBJÖRN JONSSON
P.O. Box 438, Reykjavik, Iceland.
Handles general fiction and non-fiction, books
and magazines, plays, radio and TV scripts.

India

KUNNUPARAMPIL P. PUNNOOSE
Sector VI-806, R.K. Puram, New Delhi 110022,
India.
Contact: Kunnuparampil P. Punnoose.

Israel

BAR-DAVID LITERARY AGENCY
P.O. Box 1104, Tel Aviv, Israel.
Contact: Abraham Mor.
Represents authors and publishers in Israel from
all over the world.

MOADIM — PLAY PUBLISHERS AND
LITERARY AGENTS
144 Hayarkon Street, 63 451 Tel Aviv, Israel.
Contact: Manfred Geis.
Represents almost all foreign plays translated
into Hebrew and produced by Israeli theatres.
Specializes in guarding the performing rights of
Israeli and foreign plays vis a vis producers and
theatres abroad and the Israeli theatres
respectively.

Italy

AGENZIA LETTERARIA INTERNAZIONALE
3 Corso Matteotti, 20121 Milan, Italy.

MARIA-PIA D'ARBORIO
Viale Tiziano 5, Rome, Italy.

URSULA CAPUTO
Via Pisacane 25, 20129 Milan, Italy.

CREATIVE MANAGEMENT ASSOCIATES
LIMITED
Via Lazio 9, 00189 Rome, Italy.

DAIS, AGENZIA LETTERARIA GIA FABIO
COËN
Via Nicotera 7, 00195 Rome, Italy.

EULAMA S.A.
Europäisch — Lateinamerikanische
Verlagsagentur, Via Magliano Sabina 68 int. 20,
I-00199 Rome, Italy.
Contact: Lic.phil. Harald Kahnemann, Director.
Primarily a publishers' agency but does handle
the rights of a few authors. Open to all fields of
literary works and handles all language areas of
the world with a particular stress in Europe and
Latin America.

WILLIAM MORRIS ORGANISATION S.P.A.
Via Nomentana 60, I-00161 Rome, Italy.

NATOLI AND STEFAN LITERARY AGENCY
Galleria Buenos Aires 14, I-20124 Milan, Italy.

RIZZOLI
Via Civitavecchia 102, Milan, Italy.

TRANSAFRICA
Via Trieste 34, 25100 Brescia, Italy.

Japan

KAIGAI HYORON SHA
P.O. Box 81, Akasaka, Tokyo 107, Japan.
Contact: Lawrence E. Kern, Jr.
Represents foreign and Japanese authors in the sale of their properties to Japanese publishers for publication in Japan.

ORION PRESS, INTERNATIONAL LITERARY AGENCY
1-55 Kanda-Jimbocho, Chiyoda-ku, Tokyo 101, Japan.
Contact: Jintaro Takano.

CHARLES E. TUTTLE COMPANY, INCORPORATED
1-2-6 Suido, Bunkyo-ku, Tokyo 112, Japan.

Kenya

AFRICA AGENCY
P.O. Box 20521, Nairobi, Kenya.

The Netherlands

GRETA BAARS-JELGERSMA, AUTEURSBUREAU
Den Heuvel 73, Velp 6200, The Netherlands.

H. J. W. BECHT'S UITGEVERSMAATSCHAPPIJ B.V.
Herengracht 172, Amsterdam 1002, The Netherlands.

ALEXANDER GANS LITERAIR AGENT
Witte De Withstraat 20, Noordwijk Aan Zee, The Netherlands.
Contact: Alexander Gans.
Represents mainly English and American literary agents as well as Belgium and Dutch rights.

INTERNATIONAL BUREAU VOOR AUTEURSRECHT B.V.
Vondelstraat 102, Amsterdam W.1, The Netherlands.
Contact: Hans Keuls.

INTERNATIONAL LITERATUUR BUREAU
Koninginneweg 2A, Hilversum, The Netherlands.
Contact: Hein or Menno Kohn.
Specializes in placing authors' rights in Holland and through the world.

PRINS AND PRINS LITERARY AGENTS
de Lairessestraat 6, P.O. Box 5400, Amsterdam 1007, The Netherlands.

THE SCHMAGER PRESS INTERNATIONAL, LITERARY AND PUBLISHING AGENCY
P.O. Box 889, Amsterdam-Centrum, The Netherlands.

Nigeria

AFRICA AGENCY
P.O. Box 3810, Lagos, Nigeria.

Norway

EMBLA LITERARY AGENCY
P.O. Box 109, 1371 Asker, Norway.
Handles fiction, non-fiction, children's books, theatre, radio and television.

MRS. CARLOTA FRAHM
P.O. Box 5385, Oslo 3, Norway.

HANNA-KIRSTI KOCH LITERARY AGENCY
P.O.B. 3043, Oslo 2, Norway.
Contact: Mr. Eilif Koch.
All round literary agent handling books, articles and short stories for weekly magazines.

KVINNER OG KLAER ALLERS
Postboks 6185, Etterstad, Oslo 6, Norway.

Poland

AGENCJA AUTORSKA sp.z. o.o.
Post Box 133, 00-950 Warsaw, Poland.
Contact: Leopold Rybarski or Andrzej Mierzejewski.

Portugal

ILIDIO DA FONSECA MATOS
Rue De S. Bernardo, 68-3, Lisbon 2, Portugal.
Handles the book rights of properties received from publishers and literary agents in USA and UK.

South Africa

THE INTERNATIONAL PRESS AGENCY (PTY.) LIMITED
P.O. Box 682, Cape Town 8000, South Africa.
Contact: Ursula A. Barnett.
Sub-agents for British and American literary agents.

Spain

A.C.E.R.
Bolonia 5, Madrid 2, Spain.
Contact: Mr. Marcel Laignoux.
Represents mainly German and French publishers for the exclusive handling of Spanish and Portuguese world rights of all books published by them in the field of documents, essays, novels, non-fiction, psychology, sociology, human sciences and theology.

AGENCIA LITERARIA CARMEN BALCELLS
Avda. Glmo. Franco 580, Barcelona 11, Spain.
Contact: Magdalena Oliver.

ANDRES DE KRAMER, AGENCIA LITERARIA
Castello 30, Madrid 1, Spain.

INTERNATIONAL EDITORS COMPANY
Rambla de Cataluna 39, Barcelona 7, Spain.

JOSÉ MOYA AND UTE KÖRNER DE MOYA —
LITERARY AGENCY
Ronda Guinardo 32 5° 5ª, Barcelona 13, Spain.
Contact: José Moya or Ute Körner de Moya.
Represents foreign publishers, agents and authors
for the Spanish speaking territory.

UNIVERSITAS-AGENCIA LITERARIA JULIO
F. YANEZ
Calle Madrazo, No. 6 2° 2ª, Barcelona 6, Spain.
Contact: Mr. or Mrs. J. F. Yanez.
Particularly devoted to fiction and non-fiction
subjects such as biographies, history, topical
features, technology, sociology, etc.

Sweden

ARLECCHINO TEATERFÖRLAG
Skeppargatan 3, 114-52 Stockholm, Sweden.

D. RICHARD BOWEN
Post Box 30037, S—200 61 Malmo 30, Sweden.
Contact: D. Richard Bowen.
Agent for translations and licenced editions of
books. Handles titles translated into European
languages in particular.

GÖSTA DAHL AND SON AB
Aladdinsvägen 14, 161 38 Bromma, Sweden.

LENA I. GEDIN
Linnegatan 38, 114 47 Stockholm, Sweden.

FOLMER HANSEN, BUREAU LITTERAIRE
INTERNATIONAL
Gerd Widestedt-Ericsson, Lundag. 4, 171 63
Solna, Sweden.
Theatre agent.

NORDISKA TEATERFÖRLAGET AB
Norrlandsgatan 16, 111 43 Stockholm, Sweden.
Stora Nygatan 15, 411 08 Göteborg, Sweden.
Play agents representing authors of plays,
children's plays, and musicals for the stage, radio
and television.

A. B. RABEN AND SJÖGREN BOKFÖRLAG
104 30 Stockholm 45, Tegnérgatan 28, Sweden.

LENNART SANE AGENCY
Box 25044, S—20047 Malmo 25, Sweden.
Contact: Lennart Sane.
Represents Scandinavian authors world wide and
a great number of American, British and French
authors, agents and publishers in Scandinavia,
Germany and Holland. Interested in fiction,
non-fiction as well as children's books.

TEATERFÖRLAG ARVID ENGLIND AB
Karlavägen 56, 102 43 Stockholm 5, Sweden.
Contact: Christer Englind.
Represents drama writers, both domestic and
foreign.

Switzerland

GESELLSCHAFT FÜR VERLAGSWERTE
GmbH
Hafenstr. 38, 8280 Kreuzlingen, Switzerland.

DR. RUTH LIEPMAN
Maienburgweg 23, 8044 Zurich, Switzerland.

LINDER AG
Postfach, 8039 Zurich, Switzerland.
Does not represent authors directly.

LITPRESS
Rudolf Streit and Company, Amtshausgasschen 3,
3011 Bern, Switzerland.

MOHRBOOKS
Klosbachstrasse 110, 8030 Zurich, Switzerland.
Contact: Rainer Heumann.
No specialities.

NEUE PRESSE AGENTUR
Haus am Herterberg, Haldenstrasse 5, CH-8500
Frauenfeld-Herten, Switzerland.
Contact: Rene Marti.
Handles novels, light entertainment and exclusive
articles including popular scientific works,
medical articles and reports.

Turkey

NURCIHAN KESIM LITERARY AGENCY
Basinköy, Ahmet Ihsan Blok 6, Istanbul, Turkey.
Contact: Mrs. Nurcihan Kesim.
Handles every subject related to copyright.
Represents some German authors but mainly
American and English authors.

ONK COPYRIGHT AGENCY
P.O.B. 983, Istanbul, Turkey.
Contact: Osman N. Karaca.
Only agency which represents Turkish writers.
Official representative of the Turkish
Playwrights' Society. Deals with cinema and
television as well as literature and theatre.

USSR

THE COPYRIGHT AGENCY OF THE
USSR/VAAP
6a Bolshaya Bronnaya, K—104 Moscow 103104,
USSR.
Contact: B. Pankin, Chairman of the Board or M.
Shisigin, Vice-Chairman.
Ensures the protection of the rights of Soviet and
foreign authors in scientific, literary and artistic
works when they are used in the territory of the
USSR, and the rights of Soviet authors in their
works when they are used abroad.

Yugoslavia

JUGOSLOVENSKA AUTORSKA AGENCIJA
Majke Jevrosime 38, Belgrade, Yugoslavia.